The CASSELL
CONCISE DICTIONARY

CASSELL

Cassell
Wellington House
125 Strand
London
WC2R 0BB

Cassell's English Dictionary first published 1891
Last complete revision 1962
Cassell's Concise English Dictionary first published 1989
Last revised edition 1994
The Cassell Concise Dictionary first published 1997
This special edition first published 1997

British Library Cataloguing in Publication Data
A catalogue entry for this book is available from the British Library

ISBN 1–85079–341–7

Printed and bound in Great Britain by Mackays of Chatham PLC, Kent

Contents

Acknowledgements

Consultant Editor	Lesley Brown
Publisher	Nigel Wilcockson
Lexicographers	Steve Curtis Jessica Feinstein Rosalind Fergusson Pandora Kerr Frost Alice Grandison John McIlwain Ruth Blackmore Martin Manser Katherine Seed George Davidson Patricia Marshall Anne Seaton David Hallworth
Database editors	Paul Blendis Rachel Coldicutt Alex Williams
Additional proof-readers	Lyn Elias Alisa Salamon Agnes Young
Database technology	Gentian I.T. Consultants
Typographic consultants	Newton Engert Partnership
Typesetting	Gem Graphics
Project management	Book Creation Services

The publishers also wish to thank John Kahn and Nicholas Jones for their assistance.

How to use *The Cassell Concise Dictionary*

The entry

Each entry in *The Cassell Concise Dictionary* begins with the headword in bold type. For most words this is immediately followed by the pronunciation, any variant spellings or forms, then the (first) relevant part of speech. Inflections (plurals of nouns, parts of verbs etc.) which are irregular or which may cause spelling difficulty follow the part-of-speech label.

Where the headword has more than one meaning, senses are numbered **1**, **2** etc. and ordered on a basis of current frequency or importance. Closely related uses may share a number, subdivided as **a**, **b** etc. Sense numbering starts afresh for second or subsequent parts of speech.

The etymology, if given, is placed at the end of the entry in square brackets. Any usage note on the headword or its nested entries follows the etymology, marked off on a separate line, though in very long entries, containing a number of nested words, usage notes are sometimes included at the appropriate point in the middle of the entry.

Other types of entry give expansions for abbreviations, or direct the user to words elsewhere in the dictionary.

Arrangement of entries

By no means all words included in the dictionary are headwords. Many words or expressions which are derived from the same root are grouped or 'nested' together, e.g. **applicable** is under **apply**. This not only demonstrates at a glance the relationship of words but also allows many more words to be included than would otherwise be the case. The majority of such words are easy to find since their positions in the dictionary are very close alphabetically to the points they would have been entered at as separate headwords. Where this is not the case cross-reference entries are generally included, e.g. **acritude** is cross-referred to **acrid**.

Organization of entries

Many headwords have more than one meaning and more than one derived or related word. The nested words and expressions are arranged in two categories – idioms/phrases and compounds/derivatives.

The idioms group consists of phrases that include the headword, e.g. **to bring about**, **again and again**, and some cross-references to compound words not beginning with the headword. Idioms are placed immediately after the last meaning of the last part of speech of the headword, and are in strict alphabetical order.

The compound and derivative group comprises single units beginning with the headword or its root, either in combination with another word or words, e.g. **airport**, **brother-in-law**, **office hours**, or with a suffix, e.g. **happily**, **strangeness**. Compounds and derivatives are placed immediately after the last meaning of the last idiom (or of the headword if no idioms are included). Those with predictable meanings are generally not defined, in order to save space. Compounds and derivatives may have their own idioms and secondary compounds/derivatives, and these follow the appropriate nested word, organized as they would be for a headword. This means some deviation from strict alphabetical order to show relationships, e.g. **simplification** follows its root verb **simplify**.

Usage notes relevant to individual idioms or compounds/derivatives may either follow the whole entry or the nested entry itself, on a new line.

Spellings

The recommended modern British spellings are given first. North American alternatives are specified where applicable.

Where a variant spelling is provided, the alternative is generally given only once, but can be assumed to be possible for any nested words or phrases in the entry.

Compounds given in only one form (solid, e.g. **eyesight**, hyphenated, e.g. **basket-maker**, as two words, e.g. **sleeping bag**) may often quite correctly be spelt in one of the other styles.

Some common misspellings are entered in alphabetical positions where users may try to look a particular word up.

Labels

Descriptive labels in brackets have been added where appropriate. They fall into three main categories – stylistic labels, e.g. (*coll.*), (*poet.*), (*offensive*), geographical labels, e.g. (*N Am.*), (*New Zeal.*), and field or subject labels, e.g. (*Law*), (*Comput.*). A list of abbreviations used appears on pp. ix–xi.

Cross-references

The word cross-referred to appears with small capitals for usual lower case, e.g. **am** BE, [shortened form of ANGLO-SAXON].

Symbols

Obsolete and archaic words, phrases and meanings are preceded by a dagger sign †
Misspellings are preceded by a cross ☒

Pronunciation

See pp. xii–xiv.

Chief Abbreviations

All are given here in roman, though some of them may also appear in italics as labels.

Other standard abbreviations used, such as those for books of the Bible, points of the compass, units of measurement etc. will be found in their alphabetical places in the main text.

a.	adjective
abbr.	abbreviation
abl.	ablative
Abor.	Aboriginal
acc.	accusative; according
adapt.	adaptation
adv.	adverb
A-F	Anglo-French
Afr.	African
alln.	allusion
alt.	altered, alteration; alternative
Am. Ind.	American Indian
Am. Sp.	American Spanish
anal.	analogous, analogy
Ang.-Ind.	Anglo-Indian
Ang.-Ir.	Anglo-Irish
appar.	apparently
Arab.	Arabic
Aram.	Aramaic
Archit.	Architecture
assim.	assimilated, assimilation
Assyr.	Assyrian
Astrol.	Astrology
Astron.	Astronomy
at. no.	atomic number
attrib.	attributive, attribute
augm.	augmentative
Austral.	Australia, Australian
aux.	auxiliary
b.	born
Biol.	Biology
Bot.	Botany
Braz.	Brazilian
Bret.	Breton
Bulg.	Bulgarian
Byz.	Byzantine
c.	circa, about
Can.	Canada, Canadian
Carib.	Caribbean
Cat.	Catalan
Celt.	Celtic
cent.	century
cents.	centuries
Chem.	Chemistry
chem.	chemical
Chin.	Chinese
cogn.	cognate
coll.	colloquial; collateral
collect.	collective
comb.	combination
comb. form	combining form
comp.	comparative
Comput.	Computing
cond.	conditional
conf.	confusion
confs.	confusions
conj.	conjunction; conjugation
conn.	connected
constr.	construction, constructed; construed
contr.	contraction
Copt.	Coptic
Corn.	Cornish
corr.	corruption; corresponding
cp.	compare
d.	died
Dan.	Danish
dat.	dative
def.	definition
deriv.	derivation, derivative
derog.	derogatory
dial.	dialect, dialectal
dim.	diminutive
Dut.	Dutch
EFris.	East Frisian
Egypt.	Egyptian
ellipt.	elliptical, elliptically
emphat.	emphatic, emphatically
Eng.	English
erron.	erroneous, erroneously
esp.	especially
etym.	etymology
euphem.	euphemistic, euphemistically
Eur.	European
exc.	except
F	French
f.	feminine
facet.	facetious, facetiously
fam.	familiar
fem.	feminine
fig.	figurative, figuratively
fl.	floruit, flourished
Flem.	Flemish
freq.	frequentative

Fris.	Frisian
fut.	future
fut.p.	future participle
G	German
Gael.	Gaelic
gen.	genitive
Geol.	Geology
Geom.	Geometry
ger.	gerund, gerundive
Goth.	Gothic
Gmc.	Germanic
Gr.	Ancient Greek
Gram.	Grammar
Heb.	Hebrew
Her.	Heraldry
Hind.	Hindustani
Hist.	History
Hung.	Hungarian
Icel.	Icelandic
ident.	identical; identified
imit.	imitative, imitatively
imper.	imperative
impers.	impersonal
incept.	inceptive
Ind.	India, Indian
ind.	indicative
Indo-Eur.	Indo-European
inf.	infinitive
influ.	influenced
instr.	instrumental
int.	interjection
intens.	intensive
interrog.	interrogative, interrogatively
intr.	intransitive
Ir.	Irish
iron.	ironical, ironically
irreg.	irregular, irregularly
It.	Italian
Jap.	Japanese
L	Latin
LG	Low German
lit.	literal, literally
Lith.	Lithuanian
loc.	locative
M	middle (period of a language)
m.	masculine
Math.	Mathematics
MDan.	Middle Danish
MDut.	Middle Dutch
ME	Middle English
Med.	Medicine
med.	medieval
Mex.	Mexican
MF	Middle French
MG	Middle German
MHG	Middle High German
Mil.	Military
Mineral.	Mineralogy
mod.	modern
Mongol.	Mongolian
Mus.	Music
n.	noun
N Am.	North America, North American
Naut.	Nautical
neg.	negative, negatively
neut.	neuter
New Zeal.	New Zealand
nom.	nominative
Norm.	Norman
North.	Northern
Norw.	Norwegian
NT	New Testament
O	Old (period of a language)
obj.	objective
OBret.	Old Breton
obs.	obsolete
ODan.	Old Danish
OE	Old English
OED	Oxford English Dictionary
OF	Old French
OFris.	Old Frisian
OHG	Old High German
OIr.	Old Irish
OIt.	Old Italian
ON	Old Norse
ONF	Old Northern French
onomat.	onomatopoeic
ONorthum.	Old Northumbrian
OPers.	Old Persian
opp.	opposed, opposition
OProv.	Old Provençal
orig.	originally, origin
ORus.	Old Russian
OS	Old Saxon
OScand.	Old Scandinavian
OSlav.	Old Slavonic
OSp.	Old Spanish
OSwed.	Old Swedish
OT	Old Testament
part.	participle, participial
pass.	passive
perf.	perfect
perh.	perhaps
Pers.	Persian
pers.	person; personal

Peruv.	Peruvian
Philos.	Philosophy
Phoen.	Phoenician
phr.	phrase
pl.	plural
poet.	poetical, poetry
Pol.	Polish
pop.	popular, popularly
Port.	Portuguese
poss.	possessive; possibly
p.p.	past participle
pred.	predicative
pref.	prefix
prep.	preposition
pres.	present
pres.p.	present participle
pret.	preterite
Print.	Printing
priv.	privative
prob.	probably
pron.	pronoun; pronounced
pronun.	pronunciation
prop.	proper, properly
Prov.	Provençal
prov.	provincial
Psych.	Psychology
redupl.	reduplication, reduplicative
ref.	reference, referring
reflex.	reflexive
rel.	related
rel. pron.	relative pronoun
Rom.	Romance
Rus.	Russian
S Afr.	South Africa, South African
Sansk.	Sanskrit
Sc.	Scottish
Scand.	Scandinavian
Semit.	Semitic
Serb.	Serbian
Shak.	Shakespeare
sing.	singular
sl.	slang
Slav.	Slavonic
Sp.	Spanish
subj.	subjunctive
suf.	suffix
superl.	superlative
Swed.	Swedish
syl.	syllable
Theol.	Theology
tr.	transitive
trans.	translation
Turk.	Turkish
ult.	ultimately
US	United States of America
usu.	usually
v.	verb
var.	variant
verb.a.	verbal adjective
verb.n.	verbal noun
v.i.	verb intransitive
voc.	vocative
v.refl.	verb reflexive
v.t.	verb transitive
W	West
WG	West German, West Germanic
W Ind.	West Indian
Zool.	Zoology

Guide to Pronunciation

Introduction

The respelling scheme used for pronunciation is designed to provide a compromise between accuracy and understanding by the majority of users. As few specialized phonetic symbols and additional accents or marks on letters are used as will fulfil this aim. A full list of symbols/letters and their equivalents follows below, with transcriptions given alongside the words used as examples.

Pronunciations are given in round brackets.

As in previous editions, the particular variety of pronunciation aimed for is that of the 'ordinary educated English speaker', which some users will recognize under the label of 'Received Pronunciation'.

Where variant spellings or nested headwords differ in pronunciation (and this includes stress) from the main headword, partial or full pronunciations are also given for these. Where partial pronunciations appear, it should be assumed that the remaining (untranscribed) part of the word concerned is pronounced as before, or with only predictable (and often unconscious) slight vowel modifications associated with the new pronunciation pattern.

In longer entries, there may be more than one variety of difference in pronunciation from the headword. In such cases, any nested word *not* given a transcription should be assumed to revert to the pronunciation pattern of the headword. The exceptions to this are variants and secondary derivatives of a nested word which closely follow it and usually have minimal difference from it in form; for example, under **drama** (drah´mə), the nested **dramatic** has the partial pronunciation (drəmat´-), and is followed immediately by **dramatical** and after its meanings by **dramatically**, in which case **dramatical** and **dramatically** follow **dramatic** in pattern and *not* **drama**.

It can also be seen from this illustration that derivatives formed by adding suffixes (e.g. **-ly**, **-ness**) or including other formative elements which are consistently pronounced, are assumed to be known by the user.

Stress

Stress (´) is shown in pronunciations immediately *after* the syllable which is stressed, e.g. (tī´gə) = **tiger**. Stress is *not* given on words of one syllable nor, usually, on compounds composed of two or more separate words.

Usage notes

A small number of usage notes comment on pronunciation: usually where an individual meaning has an idiosyncratic pronunciation or where North American practice seems particularly noteworthy.

Symbols

Vowel sounds:

ah	far	(fah)	ī	bite	(bīt)
a	fat	(fat)	o	not	(not)
ā	fate	(fāt)	ō	note	(nōt)
aw	fall	(fawl)		lower	(lō´ə)
	north	(nawth)	oo	blue	(bloo)
	paw	(paw)	ŭ	sun	(sŭn)
	soar	(saw)	u	foot	(fut)
e	bell	(bel)		bull	(bul)
ē	beef	bēf	ū	muse	(mūz)
œ	her	(hœ)	ə	again	(əgen´)
	fur	(fœ)		silent	(sī´lənt)
i	bit	(bit)		sailor	(sā´lə)
	happy	(hap´i)		amaze	(əmāz´)

Note: the natural sound of many unstressed vowels is represented, as shown above, by the symbol ə; some unstressed vowels in this dictionary are (more accurately) transcribed as (-i-), as in (ilek´trik).

Diphthongs:

(i) Vowel sounds incorporating the final unpronounced 'r' of standard British English:

eə	fair	(feə)
	mare	(meə)
	mayor	(meə)
īə	fear	(fiə)
	deer	(diə)
īə	fire	(fīə)
ūə	pure	(pūə)
uə	poor	(puə)

(ii) Others:

ow	bout	(bowt)
	cow	(kow)
oi	join	(join)

Foreign vowels not dealt with by the main system

(i) Nasalized:

ā	(vēvā´)	(bon) viv*ant*
ī	(vī´)	(coq au) v*in*
ō	(bō)	b*on* (vivant)

(ii) Rounded:

ü	(vü´)	(déjà) vu
	(ü´bə)	Übermensch

Consonants:

b	bit	(bit)	ng	sing	(sing)
ch	church	(chœch)	p	pit	(pit)
d	dance	(dahns)	r	run	(rŭn)
dh	this	(dhis)	s	sit	(sit)
f	fit	(fit)	sh	ship	(ship)
g	get	(get)	t	tin	(tin)
h	hit	(hit)	th	thin	(thin)
j	just	(jŭst)	v	van	(van)
k	kit	(kit)	w	win	(win)
kh	loch	(lokh)	y	yet	(yet)
l	lid	(lid)	z	maze	(māz)
m	man	(man)	zh	measure	(mezh´ə)
n	nut	(nŭt)			

Note: where a sound represented by two symbols, e.g. (-ng-), is followed by another syllable which begins with the second symbol, here (-g-), and where the stress mark falls elsewhere, a centred dot is used to show where the syllable break occurs, for example as in (ang·glōəmer´ikən).

Proprietary Terms

This book includes some words which are or are asserted to be proprietary names. The presence or absence of such assertions should not be regarded as affecting the legal status of any proprietary name or trade mark.

THE DICTIONARY

A[1] (ā), **a** (*pl.* **As, A's**) the first letter of the English and other versions of the Roman alphabet, corresponding to the Greek alpha (A, α), derived from the Phoenician. It has five principal sounds: (1) open as in *far, father, mikado*, marked in this dictionary ah; (2) short as in *fat, man, ample*, left unmarked, a; (3) long, as in *fate, fame*, marked ā; (4) broad as in *fall, appal*, marked aw; (5) the long sound historically modified by the letter *r*, as in *fair, bear*, marked eə. In unstressed syllables *a* is often obscured, as in *desperate, amidst*, marked ə. In conjunction with other vowels *a* also represents a variety of sounds, as in *death, hair, pea, boat* etc. ~*symbol* **1** the first in a series, the highest in a range, e.g. of marks, etc. **2** the first known quantity in an algebraic expression. **3** (*Mus.*) **a** the sixth note in the diatonic scale of C major. **b** the scale of a composition in which the keynote is A. **4** in Britain formerly, a film certified as suitable for all but requiring parental consent for children under 14. **5** a blood type in the ABO system. **from A to B** from one point or position to another. **from A to Z** from beginning to end. **A1** *a.* **1** first class. **2** (*coll.*) excellent, first-rate. **3** first class in Lloyd's Register of ships. **A3** *n.* a standard paper size, 420 x 297 mm. **A4** *n.* a standard paper size, 297 x 210 mm. **A5** *n.* a standard paper size, 210 x 148 mm. **A-bomb** *n.* an atomic bomb, as distinct from a hydrogen bomb. **A-frame** *n.* **1** a frame shaped like a capital A. **2** (*esp. N Am.*) a house constructed on a framework of this shape. ~*a.* having an A-frame. **A level** *n.* (a pass in) an examination in a subject at the Advanced level of the General Certificate of Education. **A-line** *a.* (esp. of a dress or skirt) that is wide at the bottom and close-fitting at the top. **A-road** *n.* esp. in Britain, a trunk road or a main road. **A-side** *n.* the side of a gramophone record or tape cassette that is usu. played first or that has the more important material recorded on it. **A sizes** *n.pl.* the ISO standard sizes for sheets of paper, each being double the following size in the series, as A1 841 x 594 mm, A2 594 x 420 mm etc. **A-team** *n.* **1** the first or best team in a sport. **2** a team of skilled capable people brought together for a specific task.

A[2] *abbr.* **1** academy, academician. **2** ampere. **3** answer. **4** Associate.

Å *abbr.* ångstrom(s).

a[1] (ə, ā), **an** (ən, an) *a.* a weakened form of *one*, sometimes called the indefinite article, used before singular nouns or noun phrases to denote an individual of a class. *A* is used before words beginning with a consonant, *h* aspirate, or *eu* or *u*, with the sound of *yu*, also before *one* (wŭn). *An* is used before vowels and sometimes before *h* in an unaccented syllable, e.g. *an historian*. In such phrases as *50 pence a pound, twice a week*, it has a distributive force. In such phrases as *all of a piece* it means 'the same'. Also used before collective phrases like *a hundred men, a dozen eggs, a few, a good many*, i.e. a hundred of men etc. [OE *an*, one]

a[2] *abbr.* **1** acre. **2** alto. **3** anno (in the year). **4** ante (before). **5** are (metric unit of area).

a-[1] (ə) *pref.* **1** on, in, engaged in, as in *afoot, aboard, adying*. **2** away, out, intensifying the action of verbs, as in *arise, awake*. **3** of, from, as in *akin, athirst*. [sense 1 OE *on, an*; sense 2 OE *ar-, a-* (cp. G *er-*); sense 3 OE *of, af*]

a-[2] (ə) *pref.* **1** from, as in *avert*. **2** at, to, as in *amass, ascent*. **3** out of, utterly, as in *amend, abash*. [sense 1 L *ā, ab*; sense 2 *ad-* to, sometimes through F *à* (as in *achieve*); sense 3 ME, from OF *e-* from L *ex-, e-*]

a-[3] (ā, a, ə) *pref.* not, without, as in *achromatic, amoral*. [Gr. *a-, an-*]

-a[1] (ə) *suf.* forming nouns from Greek, Latin and Romance feminine singulars esp. in ancient or Latinized names for plants and animals, as in *calendula, amoeba*; in geographical names, as in *Asia*; in names of oxides, as in *magnesia*; in ancient or Latinized feminine forenames, as in *Gloria, Claudia*.

-a[2] (ə) *suf.* forming plural nouns as in the Greek or Latin neuter plural for words ending in *-on*, as in *criteria*, or *-um*, as in *errata*, and for the names of zoological groups, as in *Carnivora, Lepidoptera*.

-a[3] (ə) *suf.* (*coll.*) representing elided forms used in colloquial speech, esp. of *of*, as in *sorta, pinta*; of *to*, as in *gotta, gonna*; of *have*, as in *musta, shoulda*.

AA *abbr.* **1** Alcoholics Anonymous. **2** anti-aircraft. **3** Automobile Association.

AAA *abbr.* **1** Amateur Athletic Association. **2** American Automobile Association. **3** Australian Automobile Association.

AAM *abbr.* air-to-air missile.

A and M *abbr.* (Hymns) Ancient and Modern.

A and R *abbr.* **1** artists and recording. **2** artists and repertoire.

aardvark (ahd´vahk) *n.* the African anteater, *Orycteropus afer*. [Dut. *aarde*, earth, *varken*, pig]

aardwolf (ahd´wulf) *n.* (*pl.* **aardwolves** (-wulvz)) a hyena-like carnivorous mammal, *Proteles cristatus*, of southern Africa. [Dut. *aarde*, earth, *wolf*, wolf]

Aaronic (eəron´ik), **Aaronical** (-əl) *a.* of or relating to Aaron, his descendants, or the Jewish priesthood. **Aaron's beard** *n.* **1** rose of Sharon or large flowered St-John's wort, *Hypericum calycinum*. **2** a Chinese herb, *Saxifraga sarmentosa*, with hanging stems bearing clusters of hairy leaves. **Aaron's rod** *n.* any of certain plants that flower on long stems, e.g. great mullein, *Verbascum thapsus*, and golden rod.

A'asia *abbr.* Australasia.

aasvogel (ahs´fōgəl) *n.* (*S Afr.*) a vulture. [Afrikaans *aas*, carrion, *vogel*, bird]

AAU *abbr.* (*US*) Amateur Athletic Union.

AB *abbr.* **1** able(-bodied) seaman; able rating. **2** (*US*) Bachelor of Arts.

Ab[1] *abbr.* antibody.

Ab[2] Av.

ab-[1] (ab, əb) *pref.* off, from, away, apart, as in *abrogate, abuse* (cp. Gr. *apo*, Eng. *of, off*, G *ab*); in L and F derivatives often assimilated to a subsequent consonant or reduced to *a*, as in *assoil, avert, abstract*. [L *ab*]

ab-[2] (əb) *pref.* to, as in *abbreviate*. [L *ad-*, to, assim. to consonant *b*]

abaca (ab´əkə) *n.* **1** Manila hemp. **2** the plant from which this is obtained, *Musa textilis*. [Sp.]

aback (əbak´) *adv.* **1** by surprise (*I was taken aback by the news*). **2** with the sails pressed against the mast. **3** †backwards. **4** †behind. [ME *abak*, OE *onbæc* (*on-*, on, *bæc*, back)]

abactinal (abəktī´nəl, abak´ti-) *a.* of or relating to that part of a radiate animal that is opposite the mouth. [L *ab-*, from, away, Gr. *aktis aktinos*, a ray]

abacus (ab´əkəs) *n.* (*pl.* **abaci** (-sī)) **1** a counting-frame; an apparatus of beads sliding on wires for facilitating arithmetical calculations. **2** a flat stone crowning the capital of a column and supporting the architrave. [L *abacus*, Gr. *abax -akos*, a tablet]

Abaddon (əbad´ən) *n.* **1** a destroyer, the angel of the Bottomless Pit, Apollyon (Rev. ix.11). **2** hell, the Bottomless Pit. [Heb. *ābad*, he perished]

abaft (əbahft´) *adv., prep.* **1** in, on or towards the rear of a ship. **2** behind. [A-[1], on; OE *beæftan*]

abalone (abəlō´ni) *n.* an edible gastropod mollusc of the genus *Haliotis*, that has an ear-shaped shell, perforated with breathing holes. [Am. Sp. *abulón*]

abandon (əban´dən) *v.t.* **1** to give up completely (*abandon hope*). **2** to desert or forsake (a person); to leave or leave behind (a ship, possessions). **3** to surrender (oneself) unreservedly, e.g. to indolence or vice. **4** to give up (something) before it is completed or ended. **5** to yield to the control of another person. *~n.* freedom from conventional restraint, careless freedom of manner. **abandoned** *a.* **1** (of a person) deserted or forsaken; left behind, left empty, left unused. **2** uninhibited, unrestrained. **3** wholly given up to wickedness, profligate. **abandonee** (-nē) *n.* (*Law*) a person to whom anything is abandoned, e.g. an underwriter to whom salvage is formally surrendered. **abandonment** *n.* [OF *abandoner*, to leave at liberty, from *à bandon*, at liberty; low L *ad-*, to, *bandum*, jurisdiction, proclamation, OHG BAN]

à bas (a ba´) *int.* down with. [F]

abase (əbās´) *v.t.* to lower, humble or degrade. **abasement** *n.* the act of abasing; a state of humiliation, degradation. [OF *abaissier* (F *abaisser*), to lower, from late L *abassāre* (AD-, *bassāre*), late L *bassus*, low]

abash (əbash´) *v.t.* to embarrass or put to shame by exciting a sense of guilt, mistake or inferiority. **abashed** *a.* **abashedly** (-shid-) *adv.* **abashment** *n.* confusion produced by shame, consternation. [OF *esbaïr* (F *ébahir*), pres.p. *esbaïssant*; OF *es-* (L *ex-*) *baïr*, to express amazement, BAH]

abask (əbahsk´) *adv., a.* (*poet.*) in the sunshine, basking.

abate (əbāt´) *v.t.* **1** to lessen, esp. to make less violent or intense. **2** to deduct or subtract (from a price or sum). **3** (*Law*) to annul (a writ); to terminate (a nuisance). *~v.i.* to lessen or diminish, esp. to become less violent or intense. **abatable** *a.* **abatement** *n.* **1** an act of abating. **2** an amount by which a price, sum etc. is reduced. **abater** *n.* [OF *abatre*, to beat down; *à* (L *ad*) *batre*; late L *batere*, L *batuere*, beat]

abatis (ab´atis, -tē), **abattis** *n.* (*pl.* **abatis, abatises, abattis, abattises**) a defence work made of felled trees with their boughs directed outwards. **abattised** (-tīzd) *a.* defended by an abatis. [F *abatis*, from OF *abatre*, to beat down]

abatjour (abazhooə´) *n.* a skylight. [F]

abattoir (ab´ətwah) *n.* a public slaughterhouse. [F]

abaxial (abak´siəl) *a.* (*Bot.*) facing away from the stem. [AB-[2], AXIS[1]]

abaya (əbā´yə) *n.* an outer garment without sleeves, as worn by Arabs. [Arab. *'abā'*]

abba (ab´ə) *n.* **1** father (in the invocation *Abba, father*). **2** an episcopal title in the Syriac and Coptic churches. [Aram. *abba*, O Father]

abbacy (ab´əsi) *n.* (*pl.* **abbacies**) the office and jurisdiction of an abbot. **abbatial** (əbā´shəl) *a.* of or relating to an abbey or abbot. [late L *abbatia*, from *abbas*, ABBOT]

Abbasid (əbas´id, ab´əsid) *n.* (*Hist.*) a caliph or other member of the dynasty that ruled in Baghdad from 750 to 1258. *~a.* of or relating to this dynasty.

abbé (ab´ā) *n.* **1** a French abbot. **2** in France, a title used in addressing any cleric; any man entitled to wear clerical dress. [F *abbé*, an abbot, L *abbas -atem*]

abbess (ab´is, -es) *n.* the lady superior of an abbey. [OF *abaesse*, L *abatissa* fem. of *abbas*, ABBOT]

Abbevillian (abvil´iən) *n.* the period or culture of the early Palaeolithic in Europe. *~a.* of or relating to this period or culture. [*Abbeville*, town in N France]

abbey (ab´i) *n.* **1** a monastic community governed by an abbot or abbess. **2** a building either now or formerly inhabited by a body of monks or nuns. **3** a church attached to an abbey. [OF *abeie, abaie*, as ABBOT]

abbot (ab´ət) *n.* **1** the superior of an abbey. **2** the superior of a monastery. **abbotship** *n.* the state or office of an abbot. [L *abbas*, Gr. *abbas abbatos*, Syriac *abba*, father]

abbr., abbrev. *abbr.* abbreviation.

abbreviate[1] (əbrē´viāt) *v.t.* to shorten (esp. a word or phrase) by omitting certain parts of it. **abbreviation** (-ā´shən) *n.* **1** the act of abridging or contracting. **2** an abridged or shortened form, esp. of a word. **3** an abridgement. **abbreviator** *n.* **1** a person who abridges or curtails. **2** an officer in the Roman Chancery who abridges the petitions granted by the Pope. [L *abbreviātus*, p.p. of *abbreviāre*, to shorten (*ab-*, *ad-*, *brevis*, short)]

abbreviate[2] (əbrē´viət) *a.* shortened, cut short.

ABC[1] *n.* (*pl.* **ABCs, ABC's**) **1** (*usu. pl. in US*) the alphabet. **2** (*pl. in US*) rudiments, first principles. **3** an alphabetical guide. [the first letters of the alphabet]

ABC[2] *abbr.* **1** American Broadcasting Company. **2** Australian Broadcasting Commission.

abdicate (ab´dikāt) *v.t.* to resign, to renounce formally, to give up. *~v.i.* to abandon or relinquish a throne, or other dignity or privilege. **abdicable** *a.* **abdicant** *a.* (*formal*) abdicating, renouncing. *~n.* a person who abdicates, an abdicator. **abdication** (-ā´shən) *n.* the act of abdicating. **abdicator** *n.* [L *abdicātus*, p.p. of *abdicāre* (*ab-*, from, and *dicāre*, to declare)]

abdomen (ab´dəmən) *n.* **1** the part of the body which lies between the thorax and the pelvis and contains the stomach, bowels etc. **2** the belly. **3** the posterior division of the body in the higher Arthropoda. **abdominal** (-dom´-) *a.* belonging to the abdomen. **abdominally** *adv.* **abdominal regions** *n.pl.* certain portions of the body near to or including the belly, arbitrarily marked off for convenience in anatomical study. **abdominous** (-dom´-) *a.* (*formal*) having a large abdomen, corpulent, pot-bellied. [L]

abducent (abdū´sənt) *a.* having the property of drawing back or away (applied to muscles, the function of which is to draw away or pull back the parts to which they belong. [L *abducent-*, *abducens*, pres.p. *abdūcere*, *ab-*, from *ducere*, to lead, draw]

abduct (əbdŭkt´) *v.t.* **1** to kidnap; to take away illegally (esp. a woman or child) by guile or force. **2** (of muscles) to draw (a limb) away from the central line of the body. **abduction** *n.* **1** the illegal taking away of a person, esp. a child or a woman, by fraud or force. **2** separation of parts of a bone after a fracture, or of sides of a wound. **3** a leading or drawing away. **abductor** *n.* **1** a person who, or something which, abducts. **2** a muscle which draws or pulls back any part of the body. [L *abductus*, p.p. *abducere* as ABDUCENT]

abeam (əbēm´) *adv.* on a line at right angles to the keel of a ship or the length of an aircraft; opposite the middle (of a ship etc.). [A-[1], BEAM]

abecedarian (ābəsədeə´riən) *n.* a person who teaches or is learning the alphabet. *~a.* alphabetical. [late L *abecedarium*, alphabet, from A B C D]

†**abed** (əbed´) *adv.* in bed, gone to bed.

abele (əbēl´, ā´bəl) *n.* the white poplar, *Populus alba*. [Dut. *abeel*, OF *abel*, *aubel*, late L *albellum*, L *albus*, white]

abelia (əbīʹliə) *n.* a shrub of the genus *Abelia*, that is evergreen and has pink or white flowers. [C. *Abel*, 1780–1826, English botanist]

abelian (əbīʹliən) *a.* (*Math.*) (of a group) whose members are commutative in binary operations.

Aberdeen (abədēnʹ) *n.* a breed of rough-haired Scotch terrier. **Aberdeen Angus** *n.* a breed of hornless, black Scottish beef cattle. **Aberdonian** (-dōʹ-) *n.* a native or inhabitant of Aberdeen. ~*a.* belonging to Aberdeen. [Scottish city]

aberdevine (abədivīnʹ) *n.* the siskin. [etym. uncertain]

aberrant (əberʹənt) *a.* **1** (*Biol.*) deviating from the normal type. **2** inconsistent with the usual or accepted standard. **3** wandering from the right course or way. **aberrance** *n.* **aberrancy** *n.* [L *aberrant-*, *aberrans* pres.p. of *aberrāre*, *ab-*, from, *errāre*, to wander]

aberration (abərāʹshən) *n.* **1** deviation from, or inconsistency with, the norm. **2** a departure from a person's normal behaviour or way of thinking, that often seems strange or inexplicable. **3** (*Biol.*) deviation from the normal type. **4** the difference between the true and observed position of a heavenly body, due to the observer's velocity caused by the earth's rotation. **5** the failure of focused rays to unite in a point due to a defect in a lens or mirror.

abet (əbetʹ) *v.t.* (*pres.p.* **abetting,** *past, p.p.* **abetted**) **1** to encourage or aid (a person) in crime or wrongdoing by word or deed. **2** to countenance, stimulate or instigate (chiefly in a bad sense). **abetment** *n.* the act of abetting, countenancing or encouraging. **abetter, abettor** *n.* **1** an accessory to a crime. **2** a person who encourages or instigates another. [OF *abeter*, to instigate, deceive; AD-, *beter*, see BAIT]

abeyance (əbāʹəns) *n.* **1** the state of being suspended or temporarily unused. **2** dormancy, quiescence. **in abeyance 1** suspended, temporarily out of use. **2** (*Law*) waiting for an occupant or owner. **abeyant** *a.* [OF *abeance* (*à*, to, *béer*, late L *badāre*, to gape)]

ABH *abbr.* actual bodily harm.

abhor (əbhawʹ, əbawʹ) *v.t.* (*pres.p.* **abhorring,** *past, p.p.* **abhorred**) **1** to hate extremely, loathe, detest. **2** †to shrink from with horror. **abhorrence** (-hoʹ-), **abhorrency** *n.* **1** extreme hatred, aversion, repugnance, loathing. **2** an abhorred thing. **abhorrent** *a.* **1** exciting repugnance, loathing or hatred. **2** opposed to, inconsistent with. **abhorrently** *adv.* **abhorrer** *n.* a person who abhors or detests – nickname of the court party in the reign of Charles II who signed the address of abhorrence against the Whigs (1679). [L *abhorrēre*, to shrink from (AB-[1], *horrēre*, to bristle, shudder)]

Abib (āʹbib) *n.* the first month of the ancient Hebrew calendar, corresponding to Nisan. [Heb. *ābīb*, a full green ear of corn]

abide (əbīdʹ) *v.t.* **1** to endure, bear, tolerate. **2** to submit to. **3** †to await, encounter, withstand. ~†*v.i.* (*past, p.p.* **abided,** (*rare*) **abode** (əbōdʹ)) **1** to dwell or live in a place. **2** to stay, wait. **3** to continue, remain firm. **to abide by 1** to comply with, act upon (terms, a decision). **2** to stay faithful to (a promise). **abidance** *n.* continuance. **abider** *n.* a person who abides or continues. **abiding** *a.* continuing, permanent, durable. ~*n.* continuance, residence. **abidingly** *adv.* **abiding-place** *n.* (*poet.*) a place of abode. [OE *abīdan* (A-[1], *bīdan*, to bide)]

†**abigail** (abʹigāl) *n.* a lady's maid. [Heb.]

ability (əbilʹiti) *n.* (*pl.* **abilities**) **1** the capacity or power (to do something). **2** physical or mental capacity or talent. **3** (*pl.*) special talents or competence. [OF *ableté*, see ABLE]

-ability -ABLE.

ab initio (ab inishʹiō) *adv.* from the beginning. [L]

abiogenesis (ābīōjenʹəsis) *n.* the theoretical process by which animate matter can be produced from something inanimate; the supposed spontaneous generation of animate matter. **abiogenetic** (-netʹ-) *a.* **abiogenetically** *adv.* **abiogenic** *a.* **abiogenist** (-ojʹ-) *n.* a person who holds the hypothesis of abiogenesis. [Gr. *a-*, priv., *bios*, life, GENESIS]

abiotic (ābīotʹik) *a.* not living, not produced by living organisms. [Gr. *a-*, priv., *biotikos*, from *bios*, life]

☒ **abismal** common misspelling of ABYSMAL (under ABYSM).

abject (abʹjekt) *a.* **1** miserable and wretched. **2** very humble and submissive (*an abject apology*). **3** servile, degraded, contemptible. **4** mean, low. **abjectly** *adv.* **abjectness, abjection** *n.* [L *abjectus*, cast away, p.p. of *abjicere* (*jacere*, to cast)]

abjure (əbjooəʹ) *v.t.* **1** (*formal*) to renounce, recant, retract or abrogate upon oath. **2** to vow to avoid or refrain from (*to abjure the company of women*). ~*v.i.* (*formal*) to take an oath of abjuration. **abjuration** (abjurāʹshən) *n.* **1** the act of forswearing, abjuring or renouncing on oath. **2** a denial or renunciation on oath. **abjuratory** (-rāʹ-) *a.* **abjurement** *n.* **abjurer** *n.* [L *ab-*, from, *jurāre*, to swear]

Usage note The verbs *abjure* and *adjure* should not be confused: *abjure* means to renounce under oath and *adjure* to urge or entreat solemnly.

Abkhazian (əbkahʹziən, -kāʹ-) *n.* **1** a native or inhabitant of Abkhazia in Georgia. **2** the Caucasian language of the Abkhazians. ~*a.* of or relating to Abkhazia or Abkhazian.

abl. *abbr.* ablative.

ablactate (əblakʹtāt) *v.t.* to wean from the breast. **ablactation** (ablaktāʹshən) *n.* **1** the weaning of a child from the breast. **2** the cessation of the secretion of milk in the breast. **3** grafting by inarching. [L *ab-*, from, away, *lactāre*, suckle (*lac, lactis*, milk)]

ablation (əblāʹshən) *n.* **1** the surgical removal of any body tissue or part. **2** the wearing away of rock, glaciers etc., esp. by the action of water. **3** the melting away of expendable parts of a spacecraft on re-entry into the earth's atmosphere. **ablate** *v.t.* to remove by ablation. [L *ab-*, from, *lātus*, p.p. of *fero*, I bear]

ablative (abʹlətiv) *a.* **1** taking away, separating, subtractive. **2** of or in the case called ablative. ~*n.* the case in Latin and other languages expressing separation, instrumentality, and other relations expressed in English by the prepositions from, by, with etc. **ablatival** (ablətīʹ-) *a.* **ablative absolute** *n.* in Latin grammar, a construction with noun and participle, noun and adjective, in the ablative case, expressing time or circumstances: corresponds to the English nominative absolute.

ablator (əblāʹtə) *n.* **1** the heat shield of a space vehicle that melts away during re-entry into the atmosphere. **2** a surgical instrument used in ablation.

ablaut (abʹlowt) *n.* a vowel change in the middle of a word indicating modification in meaning, as *sit, set, rise, raise, ring, rang, rung*. [G *ab-*, off, *Laut*, sound]

ablaze (əblāzʹ) *a., adv.* **1** on fire, in a blaze. **2** brilliant. **3** excited.

able (āʹbəl) *a.* (*comp.* **abler,** *superl.* **ablest**) **1** having sufficient physical, mental, moral or spiritual power, or acquired skill, or sufficient financial and other resources to do something indicated. **2** gifted, vigorous, active. **able-bodied** *a.* **1** having a sound, strong body. **2** experienced, skilled. **able-bodied rating, able-bodied seaman** *n.* a rating able to perform the full range of duties. **abled** *a.* having all the usual abilities or abilities of a certain kind (*differently abled*). **ableism, ablism** *n.* discrimination in favour of able-bodied people. **ableist** *a., n.* **able rating, able seaman** *n.* an able-bodied rating. **ably** (āʹbli) *adv.* **1** in an able manner. **2** with ability. [OF *hable*, *able*

(F *habile*), L *habilis*, handy (*habēre*, to have, hold)]

-able (əbəl) *suf.* 1 that may be, is fit or suitable for, as in *eatable, movable, saleable*. 2 causing or showing, as in *comfortable, reasonable*. 3 that is subject to, as in *taxable, indictable*. 4 †that may, as in *suitable*. **-ability** (əbil´iti) *suf.* forming nouns. **-ably** (əbli) *suf.* forming adverbs. [F *-able*, L *-abilis*]

ablegate (ab´ligət) *n.* a papal envoy sent with insignia to new cardinals etc. [L *ablegatus*, one sent away]

ablism ABLEISM.

abloom (əbloom´) *a., adv.* blooming, in a state of bloom.

ablush (əblŭsh´) *a., adv.* blushing, ruddy.

ablution (əbloo´shən) *n.* 1 (*often pl.*) the act of washing, cleansing or purifying by means of water or other liquids. 2 a ceremonial or symbolic washing or cleansing, esp. carried out by a priest. 3 a building containing washing facilities, as in a military camp. 4 the state of being washed. 5 the water used for washing. **ablutionary** *a.* [L *ab-*, away, *luere*, to wash, pres.p. *abluens -tis*]

ABM *abbr.* antiballistic missile.

abnegate (ab´nigāt) *v.t.* to deny oneself, to refuse, to renounce, to abjure. **abnegation** (-ā´shən) *n.* 1 denial, renunciation. 2 self-sacrifice. **abnegative** (-gā´-) *a.* implying denial, negative. **abnegator** *n.* [L *ab-*, from, away, *negāre*, to deny (p.p. *abnegātus*)]

abnormal (abnaw´məl) *a.* 1 not normal, usual or typical, anomalous, departing from the ordinary type. 2 relating to, or dealing with, abnormal phenomena. **abnormality** (-mal´-) *n.* (*pl.* **abnormalities**) 1 departure from the normal, usual or typical. 2 an abnormal thing or event. 3 irregularity, deformity. **abnormally** *adv.* **abnormal psychology** *n.* the study of behaviour that differs markedly from accepted norms. **abnormity** *n.* [F *anormal*, assim. to L *abnormis* (*ab-*, from, *norma*, rule); see NORMAL]

Abo (ab´ō) *n.* (*pl.* **Abos**) (*offensive*) an Australian Aborigine. ~*a.* Aboriginal. [ABORIGINE]

aboard (əbawd´) *adv., prep.* 1 on board, on or in (a boat, ship, train, aircraft etc.). 2 into or on to (a boat, ship, train, aircraft etc.). 3 (*Naut.*) (of a ship) alongside (another vessel). **all aboard!** a call to warn passengers to board a ship, train etc. that is about to depart. [A-[1], BOARD, and F *à bord*, on board]

abode[1] ABIDE.

abode[2] (əbōd´) *n.* 1 (*formal or facet.*) home, place of residence; a habitation. 2 †a stay, continuance for a longer or shorter period in any place. [see ABIDE]

aboil (əboil´) *a., adv.* boiling, on the boil.

abolish (əbol´ish) *v.t.* 1 to do away with, put an end to, destroy. 2 to annul, cancel or revoke (used of laws, customs, institutions or offices). **abolishable** *a.* **abolisher** *n.* **abolishment** *n.* **abolition** *n.* 1 the act of abolishing or doing away with. 2 the state of being abolished. **abolitionism** *n.* **abolitionist** *n.* a person who entertains views in favour of the abolition of a law, institution etc., esp. one who favoured the abolition of slavery during the movement against it in the 18th and 19th cents. [F *abolir* (*aboliss-*), L *abolescere*, *abolēre* (*ab-*, from, *olēre*, to grow)]

abomasum (abəmā´səm) *n.* (*pl.* **abomasa** (-sə)) the fourth stomach in a ruminating animal. [L *ab-*, from, *omāsum*, paunch]

abominate (əbom´ināt) *v.t.* to loathe, to detest, to hate exceedingly. **abominable** *a.* 1 very loathsome, physically or morally, hateful and repellent. 2 (*coll.*) very bad, awful (*abominable luck*). **abominableness** *n.* **abominable snowman** *n.* the yeti. **abominably** *adv.* **abomination** (-ā´shən) *n.* 1 extreme hatred or loathing. 2 something that is vile, hateful or repellent. 3 an object of extreme hatred, loathing or aversion. 4 the state of being greatly hated or loathed. [L *abōminātus*, p.p. of *abōminārī* (*ab-*, from, OMEN), to dislike]

aboral (abaw´rəl) *a.* away from the mouth, opposite the mouth. [AB-[1], ORAL]

aborigine (əbərij´ini), **Aborigine** *n.* 1 an indigenous or original inhabitant of a continent, country or district. 2 an aboriginal inhabitant of Australia. 3 (*pl.*) the earliest fauna and flora of an area. **aboriginal, Aboriginal** *a.* 1 original, indigenous, inhabiting a place from the earliest times. 2 of or relating to the Aboriginal inhabitants of Australia. ~*n.* 1 an original inhabitant. 2 an aboriginal inhabitant of Australia. 3 a member of the original fauna or flora. 4 any one of the languages of the Australian Aboriginals. **aboriginally** *adv.* 1 from the beginning, from the first. 2 originally. [L *aborigines* (*ab-*, from, *origine*, the beginning)]

Usage note Both *Aborigine(s)* and *Aboriginal(s)* are acceptable as nouns for the indigenous people of Australia. Use of *Aborigine* as an adjective, however, is best avoided.

aborning (əbaw´ning) *adv., a.* (*esp. NAm.*) (while) being born or produced (*die aborning*).

abort (əbawt´) *v.t.* 1 to cause (a foetus) to be expelled from the womb before it is able to survive independently; to cause (a mother) to undergo an abortion. 2 to give birth to before the proper time; to miscarry. 3 to terminate prematurely or in the early stages. 4 to abandon (a military or space mission) before it is completed, because of technical or other difficulties. 5 (*Biol.*) to cause to undergo partial or total arrest of development. ~*v.i.* 1 (of a foetus) to be expelled from the womb prematurely; (of a mother) to miscarry. 2 to end prematurely or unsuccessfully. 3 (*Biol.*) (of an organism) to undergo partial or entire arrest of development. ~*n.* 1 an undertaking, esp. a space flight, that is terminated prematurely. 2 the act of terminating an undertaking prematurely. **abortient** (-shənt) *a.* (*Bot.*) barren, sterile. **abortifacient** (-tifā´shənt) *n.* a device or drug to induce abortion. ~*a.* inducing abortion. [L *abort-*, p.p. stem of *aborīrī* (*ab-*, off, away, *orīrī*, to arise, grow)]

abortion (əbaw´shən) *n.* 1 a procedure to induce the premature expulsion of a foetus. 2 the expulsion of a foetus before the proper time. 3 the act of miscarrying. 4 an aborted foetus. 5 anything that fails or is terminated prematurely. 6 (*Biol.*) arrest in the development of an organism. 7 a monster, a misshapen creature. **abortionist** *n.* 1 a person who performs abortions. 2 a supporter of the right of women to have an abortion.

abortive (əbaw´tiv) *a.* 1 ineffectual, failing in its effect. 2 resulting in or intended to result in abortion. 3 brought forth in an immature or rudimentary state. 4 †imperfectly formed, misshapen. 5 (*Biol.*) arrested in development. **abortively** *adv.* **abortiveness** *n.*

ABO system (ābēō´) *n.* a system for typing human blood according to the presence or absence of certain antigens.

aboulia (əboo´liə), **abulia** (-oo´-, -ū´-) *n.* loss of will-power, as a symptom of mental illness. **aboulic, abulic** *a.* [Gr. *a-*, priv., *boulē*, will]

abound (əbownd´) *v.i.* 1 to be present in great quantities. 2 to be rich (in), to be copiously supplied (with). **abounding** *a.* plentiful, copious. [OF *abunder, abonder*, L *abundāre*, to overflow (*ab-*, away, *unda*, a wave)]

about (əbowt´) *prep.* 1 concerning, in connection with; in the nature or content of; so as to affect or change. 2 near in time or space. 3 surrounding, so as to surround, around the outside of. 4 in various directions from, or at various points surrounding (a central point) (*The garden lay about us in ruins*). 5 here and there within (*wandering about the house*). 6 engaged in (*be about one's business*). ~*adv.* 1 (*coll.*) approximately; nearly, almost (*felt about done in*). 2 (*coll.*) here and there, in no particular direction; in different places and, usu., having various experiences (*been about a bit*). 3 nearby or present in a particular locality. 4 all around, in every direction. 5 to face in the opposite direction. 6 in succession or rotation. 7 (*Naut.*) to or on the opposite tack. **to be about to** to be on the point of (doing something). **to be (all) about** to be essentially, to have as its main point. **to have about one** to be carrying, to have with one. **about-face, about-turn** *v.i.* to turn right round, face the opposite way. ~*n.* 1 a turn to face the opposite way. 2 a complete change in attitude etc. [OE *ābūtan, onbūtan* (*on-*, on, *be*, by, *ūtan*, outside)]

above (əbŭv´) *prep.* 1 over, at or to a higher point than. 2 in excess of, more than. 3 superior to, more important than. 4 too virtuous or noble for; untouched by because of (one's) reputation, honesty, skill etc. (*above suspicion*). 5 beyond the understanding of. 6 despite the noise or loudness of (*heard above the noise of the crowd*). 7 (*formal*) more than and in preference to (*loved his country above everything*). 8 upstream of. 9 †to a period or time before. ~*adv.* 1 overhead, in a higher place or position; upstairs, on a higher floor (*the apartment above*). 2 at a previous point. 3 on the upper side. 4 in heaven. 5 upstream. ~*n.* 1 the aforesaid. 2 an upper part or side. ~*a.* above mentioned, given at a previous point in something written. **above all** 1 principally. 2 before everything else. **above oneself** arrogant; conceited. **above one's head** HEAD[1]. **over and above** OVER. **above board, above-board** *adv., a.* (done) openly; without dishonesty or trickery. **above ground, above-ground** *adv., a.* 1 (situated, working etc.) on the surface of the earth, not buried, not underground. 2 (*facet.*) alive. **above par** *a.* 1 at a premium. 2 of superior quality. [OE *ābūfan* (*an*, on, *be*, by, *ūfan*, over)]

ab ovo (ab ō´vō) *adv.* from the beginning. [L, from the egg]

Abp. *abbr.* archbishop.

abracadabra (abrəkədab´rə) *int.* a word used as a magic word by conjurors when performing tricks. ~*n.* 1 used as a word charm, a jingle or nonsensical phrase. 2 nonsense, gibberish. [a cabbalistic word used as a charm when written in triangular form - the first line containing the whole word, the others successively omitting first and last letters, till the last consists of only the final A - it was worn as an amulet, and was considered to ward off or cure certain diseases: etym. uncertain]

abrade (əbrād´) *v.t.* to rub or wear away by friction. **abradant** *a.* abrasive. **abrader** *n.* [L *abrādere* (*ab-*, off, *rādere*, to scrape)]

Abrahamic (ābrəham´ik), **Abrahamitic** (-mit´ik), **Abrahamitical** (-mit´ikəl) *a.* of or relating to the patriarch Abraham or the dispensation under which he lived.

abranchial (əbrang´kiəl), **abranchiate** (-ət) *a.* without gills. ~*n.* an animal that at no period possesses gills. [Gr. *a-*, priv., *branchia*, gills]

abrasion (əbrā´zhən) *n.* 1 the act of rubbing away or wearing down. 2 the state of being rubbed away or worn down. 3 a superficial lesion of the skin; an area of damage caused by rubbing or wearing away. **abrasive** (-siv) *a.* 1 tending to rub or wear away; able to polish by abrading. 2 (of a person's manner) causing friction or irritation. ~*n.* a substance, such as emery, used for grinding or rubbing down. [L *abrāsio*, from *abrādere*, ABRADE]

abraxas (əbrak´səs) *n.* 1 a word used as a charm, denoting a power which presides over 365 others, and used by some Gnostics to denote their supreme god. 2 a gem with this word, or the corresponding mystical image engraved on it. [late Gr.]

abreaction (abriak´shən) *n.* the ridding oneself of a complex by reliving in feeling or action repressed fantasies or experiences. **abreact** *v.t.* to rid oneself of in this way.

abreast (əbrest´) *adv.* 1 side by side with the fronts in line. 2 up to the standard (of). 3 up to date, aware (of). [OE *a-*, on, BREAST]

☒ **abreviate** common misspelling of ABBREVIATE.

abridge (əbrij´) *v.t.* 1 to reduce the length of (a book) by excision or recasting. 2 to shorten, curtail. **abridgeable, abridgable** *a.* **abridgement, abridgment** *n.* 1 a condensed version; an abstract, a summary. 2 the act of abridging. 3 the state or process of being abridged. **abridger** *n.* [OF *abregier, abrigier*, L *abbreviāre*, to shorten]

abroach (əbrōch´) *adv.* 1 broached, pierced. 2 in a position to allow the enclosed liquor to run out freely. ~*a.* tapped or opened.

abroad (əbrawd´) *adv.* 1 in or to a foreign country. 2 widely, at large, far and wide. 3 (*formal*) (of news, rumour) circulating. 4 †outdoors, out of one's house. **from abroad** from a foreign country.

abrogate (ab´rəgāt) *v.t.* to annul by an authoritative act; to repeal, to make void. **abrogation** (-ā´shən) *n.* the act of abrogating; repeal. **abrogator** *n.* [L *abrogātus*, p.p. of *abrogāre* (*ab-*, away, *rogāre*, to ask, propose a law)]

Usage note The verbs *abrogate* and *arrogate* should not be confused: *abrogate* means to annul or repeal, and *arrogate* to claim unjustifiably.

---

abrupt (əbrŭpt´) *a.* 1 sudden, unexpected. 2 brusque, curt. 3 very steep, precipitous. 4 (*Bot.*) truncated, shaped as if cut off below or above. 5 (*Geol.*) (of strata) suddenly emerging above ground. **abruption** *n.* 1 a sudden or violent breaking off. 2 the state of being broken off. **abruptly** *adv.* **abruptness** *n.* [L *abruptus*, p.p. of *abrumpere* (*ab-*, off, *rumpere*, to break)]

ABS *abbr.* anti-lock braking system.

abs- (abs) *pref.* away, off, from, as in *abstain, absterge, abstruse*. [L AB-[1], away, from]

abscess (ab´ses) *n.* a gathering of pus in any tissue or organ, accompanied by pain and inflammation. **abscessed** *a.* [L *abscessus*, p.p. of *abscēdere* (*abs-*, away, *cēdere*, to go)]

abscise (absīz´) *v.t., v.i.* to separate from the stem of a plant by abscission. **abscisic acid** (-sī´zik) *n.* a plant hormone that inhibits germination and promotes the shedding of leaves, fruit etc. **abscission** (-sish´ən) *n.* 1 (*Bot.*) the natural process whereby leaves, fruit, branches etc. detach themselves from the stem of a plant. 2 the act of cutting off; the state of being cut off. [L *abscis-*, *abscindere*, to cut off]

abscissa (əbsis´ə) *n.* (*pl.* **abscissas, abscissae** (-ē)) (*Math.*) the x co-ordinate that shows the distance of a point from a vertical axis along a horizontal line. [L *abscissa linea*, from p.p. of *abscindere*, to cut]

abscission ABSCISE.

abscond (əbskond´) *v.i.* 1 to go away secretly or in a hurry. 2 to go out of the jurisdiction of a court, to hide oneself to avoid legal proceedings. **absconder** *n.* a person who absconds, a fugitive from justice. [L *abscondere* (*abs-*, away, *condere*, to hide, from *con-*, *cum-*, with, and *-dere*, to put)]

abseil (ab´sāl) *v.i.* to descend a vertical or steeply sloping surface, such as a rock face, using a rope attached at the top and wound round the body. ~*n.* a descent involving abseiling. [G *abseilen* (*ab-*, down, *Seil*, rope)]

absence (ab´səns) *n.* 1 the state of being absent from a place, event etc. 2 a period of being absent. 3 a lack (of); the non-existence (of). **absence of mind** *n.* inattention to what is happening.

absent[1] (ab´sənt) *a.* 1 away from or not present in a place; not in attendance. 2 lacking, missing, not present where it is expected to be found. **3** inattentive to what is happening around one. **absentee** (-tē´) *n.* **1** a person who is habitually absent from duty, work, school or home. **2** a landlord who lets an estate and lives away. *~a.* habitually absent from duty etc. or from one's estate. **absenteeism** *n.* the fact or practice of being a habitual absentee, esp. from work. **absently** *adv.* in an absent-minded way. **absent-minded** *a.* inattentive, abstracted in mind from immediate objects or business. **absent-mindedly** *adv.* **absent-mindedness** *n.* [L *absentem*, acc. of *absens*, pres.p. of *abesse*, to be away]

absent[2] (əbsent´) *v.t.* (*reflex.*) to keep oneself away. [L *absentāre* (*absens*)]

absidal APSIDAL (under APSE).

absinthe (ab´sinth, absĩt´), **absinth** *n.* **1** wormwood. **2** a liqueur flavoured with wormwood. **absinthian** (-sin´-) *a.* absinthic. **absinthic** (-sin´-) *a.* **1** of or relating to or derived from wormwood. **2** bitter. **absinthin** (-sin´thin) *n.* the bitter principle in *Artemisia absinthium* (wormwood). **absinthinate** (-sin´-) *v.t.* to impregnate with wormwood. [F, from L *absinthium*, Gr. *apsinthion*, wormwood]

absit omen (absit ō´men) *int.* may the threatened evil not take place; God forbid. [L, may the omen be absent]

absolute (ab´səloot) *a.* **1** complete, utter (*an absolute scandal*; *absolute bliss*). **2** independent, unlimited, under no restraint (*absolute power*). **3** arbitrary, despotic. **4** universally valid, not relative or conditional (*an absolute standard*). **5** not subject to doubt or uncertainty (*the absolute truth*). **6** (*Gram.*) **a** (applied to a grammatical case) not determined by any other word in a sentence. **b** (of an adjective) used as a noun as in 'the poor'. **c** (of a transitive verb) used without a direct object, as in 'if looks could kill'. **7** (*Philos.*) existing independently of any other cause. **8** (*Chem.*) free from mixture. **9** (*Physics*) measured from vacuum, as 'the absolute pressure of steam'. **10** (of a legal decree) final. *~n.* something, such as a standard or value, that is universally valid and not relative or conditional. **the Absolute** the Self-existent, the First Cause or God of theism. **the absolute** (*Philos.*) that which exists independently of any other cause. **absolute alcohol** *n.* (*Chem.*) ethanol that contains 1% or less of water or other impurities. **absolutely** *adv.* **1** totally, unconditionally. **2** used to express agreement or assent. **absolute magnitude** *n.* the magnitude of a star at a distance of 32.6 light years (10 parsecs) from the earth. **absolute majority** *n.* a number of votes polled which exceeds the combined total for all other candidates. **absolute music** *n.* music which does not endeavour to illustrate or depict, as contrasted with programme music. **absoluteness** *n.* **absolute pitch** *n.* **1** the ability to recognize the pitch of any note, or to reproduce any note, without reference to any other note. **2** a fixed standard of pitch defined by vibrations per second. **absolute temperature** *n.* temperature measured from the absolute zero. **absolute zero** *n.* the zero of the absolute scale of temperature, equal to -273.15° C. **absolutism** *n.* **1** despotic government. **2** the theological doctrine of absolute predestination. **3** the doctrine of the Absolute. **absolutist** *n.* **1** a person who is in favour of arbitrary government. **2** a metaphysician who holds the theory of the Absolute. *~a.* of or relating to absolutism or despotism. **absolutistic** (-tis´-) *a.* absolutist. [OF *absolut*, L *absolūtus*, p.p. of *absolvere*, to ABSOLVE]

absolution (absəloo´shən) *n.* **1** acquittal, remission, forgiveness. **2** the declaration of pardon of sins by a priest to a penitent or a congregation after private or general public confession. [see ABSOLVE]

absolutism, absolutist etc. ABSOLUTE.

absolve (əbzolv´) *v.t.* **1** to set free from obligation etc.; to release, pardon; acquit, pronounce not guilty. **2** to pronounce forgiveness of sins to (a penitent). **3** to pardon or pronounce forgiveness for. **absolver** *n.* a person who absolves or pardons. [L *absolvere* (*ab-*, from, *solvere*, to loosen)]

absonant (ab´sənənt) *a.* discordant, inharmonious, unreasonable. [L *ab-*, from, *sonantem*, acc. of *sonans*, pres.p. of *sonāre*, to sound]

absorb (absawb´, -zawb´) *v.t.* **1** to suck or soak up, drink in. **2** to imbibe by capillarity. **3** to incorporate. **4** to fully occupy the attention of, to engross. **5** to take in and transform (radiant energy, sound) without transmission or reflection. **6** to reduce or deaden the force of (impact, a blow). **7** to use up or consume (energy, income, resources). **absorbable** *a.* **absorbability** (-bil´-) *n.* **absorbance** *n.* capacity to absorb light. **absorbed** *a.* fully engrossed. **absorbedly** *adv.* **absorbent** *a.* absorbing, capable of or tending to absorb, absorptive. *~n.* **1** a vessel in an organism which takes nutritive matter into the system. **2** a substance which has the power of absorbing gases or liquids. **absorbency** *n.* the state or quality of being absorbent. **absorbent cotton** *n.* (*N Am.*) cotton-wool. **absorber** *n.* **1** something which absorbs. **2** the part of a caloric-engine that absorbs heat. **absorbing** *a.* occupying one's complete attention. **absorbingly** *adv.* **absorption** (-sawp´-, -z-) *n.* **1** the act of absorbing. **2** the process of being absorbed. **absorption spectrum** *n.* the spectrum produced when electromagnetic radiation passes through a selectively absorbing medium. **absorptive** (-sawp´-, -z-) *a.* having power to absorb, tending to absorb, absorbent. [F *asorber*, from L *absorbēre* (*ab-*, off, away, *sorbēre*, to suck up)]

absquatulate (əbskwot´ūlāt) *v.i.* (*N Am.*, *sl.*) to run away, make off quickly, scram.

abstain (əbstān´) *v.i.* **1** to keep oneself away, refrain (from). **2** to refrain voluntarily from intoxicating liquors. **3** to refrain from voting. **abstainer** *n.* [F *abstenir*, from L *abstinēre* (*abs-*, away, *tenēre*, to hold)]

abstemious (əbstē´miəs) *a.* sparing, not self-indulgent, esp. in the use of food and strong liquors. **abstemiously** *adv.* **abstemiousness** *n.* [L *abstemius* (*abs-*, from, *tēmum*, strong drink, a word extant only in derivatives, *tēmētum*, *tēmulentus*)]

abstention (əbsten´shən) *n.* **1** the act of abstaining or refraining, esp. from exercising one's right to vote. **2** a formally recorded instance of a person's not using their vote.

abstinence (ab´stinəns) *n.* **1** the act or practice of refraining from some indulgence. **2** continence, fasting. **abstinent** *a.* practising abstinence. *~n.* an abstainer. **abstinently** *adv.* [L *abstinens*, pres.p. of *abstinēre*; see ABSTAIN]

abstract[1] (əbstrakt´) *v.t.* **1** to draw or take away, remove. **2** (*euphem.*) to steal. **3** to separate mentally, to consider apart from other things. **4** to epitomize, summarize. **5** to separate by chemical distillation. **6** to extract. **abstracted** (-strak´-) *a.* absent-minded, inattentive, withdrawn in thought. **abstractedly** *adv.* **1** absent-mindedly. **2** in the abstract, separately. **abstractedness** *n.* [L *abstractus*, p.p. of *abstrahere* (*abs-*, from, *trahere*, to draw)]

abstract[2] (ab´strakt) *a.* **1** not related to tangible, concrete or particular instances, theoretical, ideal. **2** (of a noun) denoting an intangible. **3** abstruse. **4** (of art) non-representational, achieving its effect by geometrical design or patterns of shape and colour. *~n.* **1** an abstract term. **2** a summary, an epitome. **3** an abstract work of art. **in the abstract** without reference to individual cases, abstractly, ideally, theoretically. **abstract expressionism** *n.* a 20th-cent. artistic movement in which the artist's emotions and feelings are expressed by non-representational forms in informal compositions. **abstractly** *adv.* **abstractness** *n.* **abstract noun,**

abstract term *n.* a name of a quality, in contra-distinction to a concrete term which is a name of a thing. **abstract number** *n.* a number used without reference to a particular object. **abstract of quantities** *n.* apportionment of quantity and cost of materials in a building. **abstract of title** *n.* **1** an epitome of the evidences of ownership. **2** an extract.

abstraction (əbstrak´shən) *n.* **1** the act of abstracting or separating. **2** taking away. **3** (*euphem.*) stealing. **4** the state of being engrossed in thought; absent-mindedness. **5** the process of considering separately the quality of an object. **6** a mental conception so formed. **7** an abstract idea. **8** the faculty by which people form abstract ideas. **9** an abstract work of art. **abstractionism** *n.* **1** the theory and practice of abstract art. **2** the love of abstract ideas. **abstractionist** *n.* [as ABSTRACT[1]]

abstractive (abstrak´tiv) *a.* **1** possessing the power or quality of abstracting. **2** tending to abstraction. **abstractively** *adv.*

abstruse (əbstroos´) *a.* **1** difficult to understand, recondite, profound. **2** wilfully difficult to understand. **abstrusely** *adv.* **abstruseness** *n.* [L *abstrūsus*, p.p. of *abstrūdere* (*abs-*, away, *trūdere*, to push)]

absurd (əbsœd´) *a.* **1** incongruous, ridiculous, ludicrous. **2** contrary to or inconsistent with reason; nonsensical, logically contradictory. **the absurd** existence as regarded in absurdism. **absurdism** *n.* artistic expression of the philosophical idea of absurdity. **absurdist** *n., a.* **absurdity** *n.* (*pl.* **absurdities**) **1** the quality or state of being absurd. **2** folly, extremely inappropriate or ridiculous behaviour. **3** an absurd notion, statement or action. **4** the idea, found esp. in existentialist philosophy, that the world is an entirely unpredictable and irrational place. **absurdly** *adv.* **absurdness** *n.* [F *absurde*, from L *absurdus* (*ab-*, away, *surdus*, deaf)]

ABTA (ab´tə) *abbr.* Association of British Travel Agents.

abulia ABOULIA.

abundance (əbŭn´dəns) *n.* **1** a more than sufficient quantity or number (of). **2** wealth, affluence. **3** fullness or benevolence (of heart). **4** a call in solo whist whereby the caller undertakes to win nine tricks. **abundant** *a.* **1** plentiful, fully sufficient, more than sufficient, ample. **2** overflowing with, having a plentiful supply of (*abundant in mineral resources*). **abundantly** *adv.* **abundant number** *n.* a number, the sum of whose aliquot parts exceeds the number itself. [OF *abondance*, from L *abundantia* (*abundant-*, stem of pres.p. of *abundāre*, to ABOUND)]

abuse[1] (əbūz´) *v.t.* **1** to put to an improper use, misuse. **2** to insult, to use coarse language to. **3** to use in an illegitimate sense, to pervert the meaning of. **4** to maltreat, act cruelly to. **5** to subject to physical, esp. sexual, assault or mistreatment. **abusable** *a.* capable of being abused. **abuser** *n.* [OF *abuser*, L *abūsus*, p.p. of *abūtī* (*ab-*, from, amiss, *utī*, to use)]

abuse[2] (əbūs´) *n.* **1** improper treatment or employment, misuse. **2** a corrupt practice or custom. **3** insulting or scurrilous language. **4** perversion from the proper meaning. **5** physical maltreatment; sexual assault or mistreatment. **abusive** *a.* **1** scurrilous or insulting (language); using such language. **2** subjecting others to physical or sexual abuse. **3** improper, incorrectly used, misapplied. **abusively** *adv.*

abut (əbŭt´) *v.i.* (*pres.p.* **abutting,** *past, p.p.* **abutted**) **1** to be contiguous. **2** to border (on or upon). **3** to form a point or line of contact. **4** (of a building) to lean (on or upon). *~v.t.* to be contiguous with, to border on. **abutment** *n.* **1** the state of abutting. **2** something which abuts or borders. **3** a pier or wall, or the part of a pier or wall, against which an arch rests. **4** the junction between a supporting structure and the thing supported. **abuttal** *n.* abutment, esp. the abutting part of a piece of land. **abutter** *n.* **1** a person who or something which abuts. **2** the owner of property that abuts. [OF *abouter*, *abuter*, (*à* to, *but*, end), cp. F *abouter*, to join end to end]

abuzz (əbŭz´) *a., adv.* buzzing with activity, conversation etc.

abysm (əbiz´m) *n.* (*poet.*) an abyss. **abysmal** *a.* **1** extremely bad. **2** profound, immeasurable. **3** of or relating to an abyss. **abysmally** *adv.* [OF *abisme* (F *abîme*), late L *abyssimus*, superl. of *abyssus*]

abyss (əbis´) *n.* **1** a vast physical depth, chasm or cavity. **2** anything conceived of as immensely deep and unfathomable or difficult to get out of (*an abyss of despair*). **3** catastrophe, a catastrophic situation (*drew back from the abyss*). **4** primeval chaos; hell. **abyssal** *a.* **1** of or relating to an abyss. **2** of or relating to the lowest depths of the sea beyond 300 fathoms (about 550 m). **3** of or relating to the depths below the surface of the earth; plutonic. [L *abyssus*, Gr. *abussos* (*a-*, without, *bussos*, depth), bottomless]

Abyssinian (abəsin´iən) *a.* belonging to Abyssinia (now Ethiopia) or its inhabitants. *~n.* **1** a native or inhabitant of Abyssinia. **2** a member of its Church. **Abyssinian cat** *n.* a breed of long-eared cat, of African origin.

AC *abbr.* **1** aircraftman. **2** alternating current. **3** ante Christum (before Christ). **4** appellation contrôlée. **5** athletic club. **6** Companion of the Order of Australia.

Ac *chem. symbol* actinium.

a/c *abbr.* account.

ac- (ək) *pref.* AD-, assim. to *c*, *k*, *qu*, as in *accommodate, accord, acquire.*

-ac (ak) *suf.* of or relating to, as in *cardiac, demoniac* (adjectives so formed are often used as nouns). [Gr. *-akos*]

ACA *abbr.* Associate of the Institute of Chartered Accountants.

acacia (əkā´shə) *n.* **1** a tree of the extensive genus *Acacia*, with pinnated leaves or else phyllodes, and small flowers in balls or spikes: some species yield catechu and others gum arabic. **2** the N American locust tree or false acacia, *Robinia pseudoacacia.* **acacia tree** *n.*

academe (ak´ədēm, -dēm´) *n.* **1** academia. **2** (*poet.*) an academy. **academia** (akədē´miə) *n.* **1** the world of academics; the life of scholarship. **2** universities etc. collectively. [probably derived from a misunderstanding of Milton's 'Grove of Academe' (Academos)]

academic (akədem´ik) *a.* **1** of or relating to an academy, college or university. **2** scholarly, relating to the more advanced levels of esp. theoretical subjects. **3** impractical, unrelated to practical concerns. **4** (of art and artists) conforming to conventionally taught rules and techniques. **5** (**Academic**) of or relating to the Platonic school of philosophy. *~n.* **1** a member of the staff of an academy, college or university etc. **2** a person belonging to the academy of Plato, or adhering to the Academic philosophy. **academical** *a.* **1** academic. **2** unpractical. *~n.* (*pl.*) academical dress, cap and gown. **academically** *adv.* **academician** (əkadəmish´ən) *n.* **1** a person belonging to an academy or association for the promotion of science, literature or art. **2** (**Academician**) a Royal Academician. **academicism** (akədem´-) *n.* **1** conformity with rules and tradition in art. **2** neglect of the easily accessible in favour of the more academic or abstruse. **academic year** *n.* a period of a year or less, measured from the time of the arrival or return of students to an institution to the end of the final term or semester.

academy (əkad´əmi) *n.* (*pl.* **academies**) **1** a society or institution for promoting literature, science or art. **2** a place of higher education or training in a specialized subject (*academy of music*). **3** any school or place of study, now used mainly in the names of particular schools. **the Academy** 1 the grove or garden near Athens where Plato taught; the philosophical system of Plato; Plato's followers. 2 the Royal Academy; the French Academy. **academism** *n.* 1 academicism. 2 Platonism. **academist** *n.* an Academic philosopher, a member of an academy. **Academy Award** *n.* an award, presented annually in the United States by the Academy of Motion Picture Arts and Sciences, for outstanding achievement in the world of film, commonly called an *Oscar.* [F *académie*, L *acadēmīa*, Gr. *akadēmeia* (the gymnasium in the suburbs of Athens where Plato taught, named after the hero *Akadēmos*)]

Acadian (əkā´diən) *a.* belonging to Acadia in Nova Scotia. ~*n.* 1 a native or inhabitant of Acadia, esp. an early French settler or a descendant of one of these. 2 a descendant of French settlers in Acadia who were deported to Louisiana. [F *Acadie*, Nova Scotia]

acajou (ak´əzhoo) *n.* 1 the cashew-nut tree, *Anacardium occidentale.* 2 a gummy substance derived from this tree. 3 mahogany, or a wood resembling it. [F *acajou*, Brazil. Sp. *acaju*]

-acal (əkəl) *suf.* 1 adjectives ending in *-ac* being often used as nouns, *-al* was added to distinguish the adjective, e.g. *demoniacal, maniacal.* 2 *-al* is also added to adjectives to show a less intimate connection with the original noun, e.g. *cardiacal.* [Gr. *akos*, -AC, -AL[1]]

acanthopterygian (akanthoptərij´iən) *a.* belonging to the Acanthopterygii, a large order of fishes, having the dorsal fin or fins entirely, and the other fins partially, supported by spinous rays. ~*n.* any individual of the Acanthopterygii. **acanthopterygious** *a.* [Gr. *akantha* (see ACANTHUS), *pterux*, a wing, *pterugion*, a little wing]

acanthus (əkan´thəs) *n.* 1 any plant or shrub of the genus *Acanthus*, which is native to the Mediterranean but widely grown for its large spiny leaves and white or purple flowers. 2 a conventional ornament resembling the foliage of the acanthus, used to decorate the capitals of the Corinthian and Composite orders. **acanthaceous** (-thā´shəs) *a.* armed with spines or prickles. **acanthine** (-thīn) *a.* 1 of, relating to or resembling the acanthus. 2 prickly. 3 ornamented with the acanthus leaf. **acantho-** *comb. form* (*Bot.*) spiny, having thorns or thornlike processes. **acanthoid** (-thoid), **acanthous** *a.* prickly, spinous. [L *acanthus*, Gr. *akanthos* (*akantha*, a thorn, *akē*, a point)]

a cappella (a kəpel´ə, ah kəpel´ə), **alla cappella** (ala) *a., adv.* (of choral music) without instrumental accompaniment. [It. *a cappella*, in chapel style]

acariasis, acaricide etc. ACARUS.

acarpous (əkah´pəs) *a.* 1 producing no fruit. 2 sterile, barren. [Gr. *akarpos* (*a-*, priv., *karpos*, fruit)]

acarus (ak´ərəs) *n.* a mite of the genus *Acarus.* **acariasis** (akərī´əsis) *n.* disease caused by mites. **acaricide** (əkar´isīd) *n.* a substance that kills mites, a remedy for itching. **acarid** (ak´ərid), **acaridan** (-kar´-), **acaridean** (-rid´i-) *a.* belonging to the order Acarina, which includes mites and ticks. ~*n.* any small arachnid of the order Acarina. **acaroid** (-oid) *a.* **acarology** (-ol´-) *n.* [Gr. *akari*, a mite (*a-*, priv., *keirein*, to cut)]

ACAS (ā´kas) *abbr.* Advisory, Conciliation and Arbitration Service.

acatalectic (əkatəlek´tik) *a.* 1 having the full number of metrical feet. 2 (*formal*) not breaking off short; complete. ~*n.* a verse having the complete number of feet. [late L *acatalēcticus*, Gr. *akatalēktos* (*a-*, priv., CATALECTIC)]

acausal (ākaw´zəl) *a.* not causal. [A-[3], CAUSE]

acc. *abbr.* 1 acceptance. 2 accompanied. 3 according. 4 account. 5 accusative.

accablé (akablā´) *a.* crushed, overwhelmed. [F, p.p. of *accabler*, to overwhelm (fem. *accablée*)]

Accadian AKKADIAN.

accede (əksēd´) *v.i.* 1 to agree (to), assent (to). 2 to become a party (to a treaty, agreement). 3 to come to or attain (an office or dignity). **accedance** *n.* [L *accēdere* (*ac-*, *ad-*, to, *cēdere*, to come)]

accelerando (əchelərán´dō) *a., adv.* (*Mus.*) with increasing speed. ~*n.* (*pl.* **accelerandos, accelerandi** (-dē)) a passage to be performed in this way. [It.]

accelerate (əksel´ərāt) *v.t.* 1 to increase the speed or rate of progress. 2 to hasten, to bring nearer in point of time. ~*v.i.* to increase in velocity or rate of progress, to move faster. **acceleratedly** *adv.* **acceleration** (-ā´shən) *n.* 1 the act of accelerating, or the state of being accelerated. 2 progressive increase of speed or rate of progress. 3 the ability to gain speed rapidly. 4 rate of increase of velocity, measured by time-units. **accelerative** *a.* **accelerator** *n.* 1 (in vehicles) a device for increasing the supply of fuel into the carburettor, thus causing the engine to run at an accelerated speed. 2 any chemical or apparatus for speeding up a process or reaction, such as the development of photographic film or the setting of concrete. 3 an electrical appliance for accelerating charged particles such as electrons or protons to high velocities or energies. **accelerator board, accelerator card** *n.* a circuit board which can increase the speed of a small computer. **accelerator nerve** *n.* a nerve that accelerates the frequency of the heartbeat. **acceleratory** *a.* **accelerometer** (-om´itə) *n.* an instrument for measuring acceleration. [L *accelerāre*, to hasten (*ac-*, *ad-*, to, *celer*, swift); -ATE[3]]

accent[1] (ak´sənt) *n.* 1 a manner of speaking or pronunciation peculiar to an individual, a locality or a nation. 2 a particular prominence given to a syllable by means of stress or higher musical pitch. 3 a mark used in writing or printing to direct the stress of the voice. 4 a mark used in writing or printing certain languages, usu. placed over particular letters, to show how those letters are to be pronounced or to distinguish a word from a homograph. 5 particular prominence, emphasis or attention given to something (*with the accent on quality*). 6 musical stress; metrical or rhythmical stress. 7 (*pl.*) words, language. [F *accent*, L *accentum*, acc. of *accentus* (*ad-*, to, *cantus*, singing)]

accent[2] (əksent´) *v.t.* 1 to lay stress upon (a syllable or word, or a note or passage of music). 2 to mark with emphasis, make conspicuous. 3 to mark with a written or printed accent. **accentual** *a.* 1 of or relating to accent. 2 rhythmical. 3 of or relating to accented verse as distinguished from that governed by quantity. **accentuate** *v.t.* 1 to pronounce or mark with an accent. 2 to lay stress on, to emphasize. **accentuation** (-ā´shən) *n.* 1 the application of accent. 2 stress, emphasis. 3 a mode of pronunciation.

accentor (əksen´tə) *n.* a bird of the genus *Prunella* (formerly *Accentor*), as the hedge sparrow. [med. L *accentor* (*ad-*, to, *cantor*, singer)]

accentual, accentuate etc. ACCENT[2].

accept (əksept´) *v.t.* 1 to consent to take (something offered). 2 to give a positive response to (an invitation, recommendation). 3 to behave in a friendly or approving way towards (*accepted her as a member of the family*). 4 to admit the truth of, to receive as valid or adequate. 5 to admit, to be willing to acknowledge. 6 to be willing to submit to (a referee's decision). 7 to undertake the responsibilities or duties of. 8 to regard as suitable or valid as a means of payment (*don't accept credit cards*). **acceptable** *a.* 1 adequate, satisfactory. 2 welcome, pleasing. **acceptability** (-bil´-), **acceptableness** *n.* **acceptably** *adv.* **acceptance** *n.* 1 the act of receiving a thing offered or due. 2 a positive response. 3 agreement to terms or proposals; an act of accepting an invitation etc. 4 friendly or approving behaviour towards. 5 general approval or belief. 6 admission, acknowledgement. 7 an accepted bill of exchange. 8 the act of subscribing, or the subscription to, a bill of exchange. **acceptancy** *n.* 1 acceptance. 2 willingness to accept. **acceptant** *a.* willingly receiving. ~*n.* a person who accepts. **acceptation** (-tā´shən) *n.* 1 the act of accepting. 2 favourable reception. 3 the recognized sense or meaning of an expression. **accepted** *a.* generally recognized or approved. **acceptor** *n.* 1 a person who accepts a bill of exchange. 2 an impurity added to a semiconductor to increase the number of positively charged current carriers and hence the conductivity. 3 a molecule etc. which receives electrons when a bond is formed. 4 an electric circuit which resonates at a particular frequency. [F *accepter*, L *acceptāre*, freq. of *accipere* (*ac-*, *ad-*, to, *capere*, to take)]

access (ak´ses) *n.* 1 admission to a place or person. 2 freedom to obtain or use something. 3 approach. 4 a means of approach or entry, a passage, channel. 5 a sudden, usu. violent, attack of a disease or emotion. ~*v.t.* 1 to gain access to, esp. to retrieve (data) from computer storage. 2 to place data in (computer storage). ~*a.* designating, of or relating to radio and television programmes made by the general public. **accessible** (-ses´-) *a.* 1 capable of being approached or reached; easy to approach, reach or obtain. 2 (of a person) readily available (esp. to subordinates); approachable. 3 not difficult to understand. **accessibility** (-bil´-) *n.* **accessibly** *adv.* **access road** *n.* a road that gives access to a particular place. **access time** *n.* the time interval that occurs between requesting data and its delivery from computer storage. [L *accessus*, p.p. of *accēdere*; see ACCEDE]

accessary ACCESSORY.

accession (aksesh´ən) *n.* 1 coming to the throne; becoming the holder of an office, rank or dignity; entering upon a particular condition or status. 2 the act of acceding to a treaty, agreement etc. 3 an increase, addition, esp. a book added to the stock of a library. 4 an improvement or addition to property by growth or labour expended; the owner's right to the increased value of property so improved. ~*v.t.* to enter in an accession book; to record the acquisition of (for a library, museum etc.). **accession book** *n.* a register of additions to the stock of books in a library. **accession number** *n.* the serial number given to a volume on its arrival in a library.

accessory (akses´əri), **accessary** *n.* (*pl.* **accessories, accessaries**) 1 a supplementary thing, esp. an additional part designed to improve the appearance, performance, comfort etc. of a vehicle, appliance etc. 2 an item, e.g. a scarf, gloves, that accompanies and usu. matches a woman's dress. 3 a person who is involved in, and shares the guilt of, a crime without actually being present when it is committed. ~*a.* 1 supplementary, additional; accompanying. 2 contributive to some effect; acting in subordination to a principal. 3 assisting in the commission of a crime. **accessorial** (-aw´-) *a.* **accessorize, accessorise** *v.t.* to add accessories to (a dress). **accessory after the fact** *n.* a person who assists or conceals an offender who has committed a crime. **accessory before the fact** *n.* a person who plans a crime or encourages someone else to commit one.

acciaccatura (əchakətoo´rə) *n.* (*pl.* **acciaccaturas, acciaccature** (-rā)) a short grace note played rapidly. [It. *acciaccare*, to crush together]

accidence (ak´sidəns) *n.* that part of grammar which deals with the inflection of words. [L *accidentia*, pl. neuter n. or the same word taken as fem. sing.; see ACCIDENT]

accident (ak´sidənt) *n.* 1 an event proceeding from an unknown cause; the unforeseen effect of a known cause. 2 something that happens unexpectedly or by chance. 3 a mishap, esp. one that results in danger or injury. 4 chance. 5 (*coll.*) an instance of involuntary urination or defecation. 6 (*Geol.*) a surface irregularity in a formation. 7 (*Philos.*) a property or quality of a thing not essential to our conception of it. 8 a mere accessory, an attribute. **by accident 1** unintentionally. 2 by chance, fortuitously. **accidental** (-den´-) *a.* 1 occurring by chance or unexpectedly. 2 not according to the usual order of things. 3 adventitious, non-essential. ~*n.* 1 a non-essential property. 2 a sharp, flat or natural sign occurring in music before a particular note, and that is not in the key-signature. **accidentally** *adv.* **accident-prone** *a.* apparently more liable than other people or things to suffer mishaps. **accident-proneness** *n.* [F *accident*, L *accidens -entis*, pres.p. of *accidere* (*ac-*, *ad-*, to, *cadere*, to fall)]

accidie (ak´sidi), **acedia** (əsē´diə) *n.* an abnormal mental condition characterized by extreme apathy and listlessness. [ME, OF *accide*, med. L *accidia*, Gr. *akēdia* (*a-*, priv., *kēdos*, care)]

accipiter (əksip´itə) *n.* a raptorial bird of the genus *Accipiter*, containing the hawks. **accipitral** *a.* **accipitrine** (-trīn, -trin) *a.* 1 belonging to or resembling hawks. 2 rapacious, predatory. [L *accipiter* (*accipere*, to take, accept)]

acclaim (əklām´) *v.t.* 1 to applaud loudly; to greet or receive with great enthusiasm. 2 to announce publicly and with great enthusiasm (that someone has obtained a particular office or honour) (*acclaimed him as emperor*). ~*v.i.* to applaud or shout loudly. ~*n.* 1 enthusiastic applause, praise or approval. 2 a shout of joy. **acclaimer** *n.* **acclamation** (akləmā´shən) *n.* 1 the act of acclaiming; enthusiastic applause or approval. 2 the expression of approval (of a proposal) by shouts and applause. 3 (*usu. pl.*) a shout of approval or enthusiasm. **by acclamation** by a large majority or unanimously, without a ballot. **acclamatory** (-klam´-) *a.* [L *acclāmāre* (*ac-*, *ad-*, to, *clāmāre*, to shout)]

acclimatize (əklī´mətīz), **acclimatise** *v.t.* 1 to habituate to a new climate or environment. 2 to adapt for existence and propagation in a new climate. **acclimation** (aklimā´shən), **acclimatation** (-mətā´-) *n.* acclimatization by nature, spontaneous accommodation to new conditions as distinguished from acclimatization by humans. **acclimatization** (-zā´shən) *n.* 1 the act or process of acclimatizing. 2 the state of being acclimatized. 3 the modification of the constitution of an organic being which enables it to exist in a climate other than its own. [F *acclimater*]

acclivity (əkliv´iti) *n.* (*pl.* **acclivities**) 1 an upward slope, as distinct from *declivity*. 2 the talus of a rampart. **acclivitous** *a.* characterized by an acclivity or acclivities. **acclivous** (əklī´-) *a.* rising with a slope, ascending. [L *acclīvitātem*, acc. of *acclīvitas* (*ac-*, *ad-*, *clīvus*, a slope)]

accolade (ak´əlād) *n.* 1 an award or honour, (an expression of) praise and approval. 2 the ceremony of conferring knighthood by an embrace, putting hand on neck, or a gentle stroke with the flat of a sword. 3 a brace uniting several staves. [F *accolade*, It. *accolata*, fem. p.p. of *accolare* (L *ac-*, *ad-*, *collum*, neck), to embrace about the neck]

accommodate (əkom´ədāt) *v.t.* 1 to provide lodging for. 2 to have or provide space for. 3 to fit, adapt or adjust. 4 to bring into harmony or concord, reconcile. 5 to do a favour for, oblige. 6 to supply or furnish (with). **accommodating** *a.* obliging, complying, yielding to others' desires. **accommodatingly** *adv.* **accommodation** (-ā´shən) *n.* 1 (*usu. pl.*, *N Am.*) a place to live or stay, lodgings. 2 space, or a place, to keep or store something. 3 adjustment, adaptation; the state of being fitted or adapted. 4 a reconciliation or compromise, a mutually convenient or agreeable arrangement. 5 the act of doing someone a favour or of supplying or furnishing something. 6 (*pl., NAm.*) a seat in a vehicle. 7 a loan. 8 adjustment of the focus of the eye. **accommodation address** *n.* an address to which mail may be sent, used by a person or business unable or unwilling to give a permanent address. **accommodation bill, accommodation note** *n.* a bill or note drawn for the purpose of raising money, and not for value received. **accommodation ladder** *n.* a light ladder fixed outside a vessel for access to a small boat, jetty etc. **accommodation platform, accommodation rig** *n.* a structure built or adapted to provide accommodation at sea for workers in the offshore oil industry. **accommodation road** *n.* a road giving access to a place that is not a public road. **accommodation unit** *n.* a dwelling. **accommodative** *a.* **accommodativeness** *n.* [L *accommodāre* (*ac-*, *ad-*, *commodus*, fitting; COM-, with, *modus*, measure)]

accompany (əkŭm´pəni) *v.t.* (*3rd pers. sing. pres.* **accompanies,** *pres.p.* **accompanying,** *past, p.p.* **accompanied**) 1 to go with, escort, attend as a companion. 2 to exist along with; to be a characteristic or result of. 3 to supplement (*accompanied by a bottle of decent claret*). 4 to play the instrumental accompaniment for. ~*v.i.* to play the accompaniment. **accompanier** *n.* **accompaniment** *n.* 1 something superadded to or attendant upon another thing. 2 something which gives greater completeness to. 3 the part or parts performed by instruments accompanying the soloist. **accompanist** *n.* the performer who plays the instrumental accompaniment. [F *accompagner*]

accomplice (əkŭm´plis) *n.* a partner, esp. in crime. [F *complice*, L *complicem*, nom. *complex* (*com-*, together, *plicāre*, to fold); *ac* is either indefinite art. *a* or due to erroneous assim. to *accomplish*]

accomplish (əkŭm´plish) *v.t.* 1 to complete, to finish. 2 to carry out, fulfil, achieve. **accomplishable** *a.* **accomplished** *a.* 1 complete, finished. 2 highly skilled, consummate. 3 having the graces and social skills perfecting one for society. **accomplisher** *n.* **accomplishment** *n.* 1 the act of accomplishing or fulfilling. 2 the state of being accomplished. 3 something achieved. 4 an acquirement, attainment, esp. a social skill. [OF *acomplir* (mod. F *accomplir*, pres.p. *accomplissant*) from late L *accomplēre* (*ac-*, *ad-*, *complēre*, to fill up)]

accord (əkawd´) *v.t.* 1 to grant, to bestow. 2 to adapt, to make consistent, to adjust. ~*v.i.* to agree, to correspond or be in harmony (with). ~*n.* 1 agreement, assent. 2 harmony or harmonious correspondence; mutual adjustment or conformity. 3 a treaty. **according as** in proportion to. **according to** 1 in proportion or relation to (*according to age and experience*). 2 as stated or reported by. 3 depending on. 4 in conformity with (*went according to plan*). **according to Cocker** COCKER. **according to Hoyle** HOYLE. **of one's own accord** voluntarily. **with one accord** with the assent of all. **accordance, accordancy** *n.* agreement, harmony. **in accordance with** in conformity with, in such a way as to correspond to (*carried out in accordance with your instructions*). **accordant** *a.* agreeing, consonant, harmonious, in tune. **accordantly** *adv.* **accorder** *n.* **accordingly** *adv.* 1 suitably, in accordance. 2 therefore, consequently. [OF *acorder*, late L *accordāre* (L *cor, cordis*, heart)]

accordion (əkaw´diən) *n.* a small portable keyed instrument in which the notes are produced by bellows acting on metallic reeds. **accordionist** *n.* a player on the accordion. **accordion-pleating** *n.* pleats with very narrow folds resembling the bellows of an accordion. [It. *accordare*, to tune; -ION]

accost (əkost´) *v.t.* 1 (*formal*) to approach, to speak to, to address. 2 (*formal*) (of a prostitute) to solicit. 3 †to come side by side with, to border, to adjoin. ~†*v.i.* 1 to be contiguous. 2 to sail along the coast. ~†*n.* address, salutation, greeting. **accostable** *a.* [F *accoster*, late L *accostāre* (*ac-*, *ad-*, to, *costa*, a rib, side)]

accouchement (akooshmã´) *n.* confinement, lying-in, delivery. **accoucheur** (-shœ´) *n.* a person who assists women at childbirth. **accoucheuse** (-shœz´) *n.* a midwife. [F *accoucher* and -MENT]

account (əkownt´) *v.t.* 1 to regard as, to deem, consider. 2 †to reckon, compute, count. ~*n.* 1 a recital, description or narrative. 2 an explanation or justification of one's own conduct given usu. to someone in authority. 3 a facility at a bank etc. that enables a customer to deposit, hold and withdraw money; the amount of money in such an account. 4 a business arrangement whereby a supplier, shop etc. allows a customer to buy goods on credit (*have an account at the chemist's*). 5 (*often pl.*) a statement of monetary transactions or receipts and expenditure showing a balance. 6 a statement of goods or services supplied with a calculation of money due, a bill, an invoice. 7 on the Stock Exchange, the fortnightly period from one settlement to another. 8 a regular client or customer, or the work or business associated with that client; an area of business assigned to some other person or company. 9 (*pl.*) the practice of counting or reckoning. 10 profit, advantage (*turn to account*). 11 importance, consequence (*of little account*). 12 behalf, sake. **by all accounts** according to what most people say, in most people's opinion. **in account with** having business relations with. **of no account** valueless, negligible. **on account** 1 on credit. 2 as an interim payment. **on account of** for the sake of, because of. **on no account** by no means. **on one's own account** 1 for one's own purpose or benefit. 2 at one's own risk; on one's own responsibility. **to account for** 1 to give, or to serve as, an explanation of. 2 to render an account for (expenditure, payments made etc.). 3 to give a formal explanation or justification of. 4 to kill or destroy or defeat (an enemy, opponent). **to bring to account** to call to account. **to call to account** 1 to require an explanation from. 2 to reprimand. **to find one's account in** to find advantage, profit in. **to give a good account of** to be successful, do (oneself) credit. **to hold to account** to hold responsible. **to keep account of** to keep a record of. **to leave out of account** to disregard. **to make account of** 1 to set a value upon. 2 to consider. **to settle accounts with** to have one's revenge on. **to square accounts with** to settle accounts with. **to take account of** 1 to pay attention to, to consider. 2 to make allowance for. **to take into account** to take account of. **to turn to (good) account** to derive advantage from. **accountable** *a.* 1 liable to be called on to give an account of something. 2 responsible. **accountability** (-bil´-) *n.* **accountableness** *n.* **account-book** *n.* a register of business transactions. **account day** *n.* a day of reckoning. **account executive** *n.* a person in a business, esp. in advertising, who manages a client's account. **accounting** *n.* the practice or skill of keeping and checking accounts. **account rendered** *n.* a bill that has been sent to a client but for which payment has not been received. **accounts payable** *n.pl.* money that a company owes. **accounts receivable** *n.pl.* money that is owing to a company. [OF *aconter*, late L *acomptāre* (*ac-*, *ad-*, to, *com-*, together, *putāre*, to reckon)]

Usage note It is best not to use *as* after the verb and its object. *She accounted it to be wrong* and *She accounted it wrong* are generally acceptable, but *She accounted it as wrong* is not.

---

accountant (əkown´tənt) *n.* 1 a person whose occupation is the keeping or preparation of business accounts. 2 a public officer charged with the duty of keeping and inspecting accounts. 3 †a person who is liable to render account. **accountancy** *n.* the profession or business of an accountant. **accountant-general** *n.* the principal accountant in large mercantile houses, companies or public offices. **accountantship** *n.*

accoutre (əkoo´tə), (*N Am.*) **accouter** *v.t.* **1** to dress, to equip. **2** to array in military dress. **3** to equip for military service. **accoutrement** (-trəmənt), (*N Am.*) **accouterment** (-təmənt) *n.* **1** a soldier's equipment, excepting arms and dress. **2** (*usu. pl.*) dress, outfit, equipment. [med. F *accoustrer* (F *accoutrer*), prob. from *à* prep. and *coustre, coutre*, sew]

accredit (əkred´it) *v.t.* **1** to attribute (a saying, discovery etc.) (to a person). **2** to credit (a person) (with a saying, discovery etc.). **3** to give official recognition to, sanction. **4** to send with credentials (as an ambassador). **accreditation** (-ā´shən) *n.* **accredited** *a.* **1** recognized officially, generally accepted. **2** conforming to an official standard of quality. **accredited milk** *n.* milk that has passed bacterial-content tests and has been produced by a periodically examined herd. [F *accrediter* (*à crédit*; see CREDIT)]

accrescence (əkres´əns) *n.* **1** continued growth, increase. **2** something which grows on a thing, an accretion. **accrescent** *a.* (*Bot.*) continuing to grow after it has flowered. [L *accrescere*, to grow]

accrete (əkrēt´) *v.i.* **1** to grow together. **2** to combine round a nucleus. ~*a.* (*Bot.*) grown together by adhesion (of parts normally separate). **accretion** *n.* **1** increase by organic growth. **2** increase in growth by external additions. **3** the growing together of parts naturally separate, as the fingers. **4** the result of such growth. **5** a part added by one of these processes. **6** (*Law*) the accession or adhesion of foreign matter to something (chiefly used of land deposited from a river or the sea). **7** (*Law*) an increase in a beneficiary's share of an estate due to another beneficiary's failing to claim a share. [L *accrētus*, p.p. of *accrēscere*, to grow (*ac-, ad-*, to, *crēscere*)]

accrue (əkroo´) *v.i.* **1** to grow, to increase. **2** to arise, to fall, come (to) as a natural growth. ~*v.t.* to amass. **accrual** *n.* [OF *acreue*, growth, orig. p.p. of *acroître* (L *accrēscere*), to grow]

acct. *abbr.* **1** account. **2** accountant.

acculturate (əkŭl´chərāt) *v.i.* to adopt the values and traits of another culture. ~*v.t.* to cause to do this. **acculturation** (-ā´shən) *n.* [L *ac-, ad-*, to, CULTURE, -ATE[3]]

accumulate (əkū´mūlāt) *v.t.* **1** to heap up, pile one thing above another. **2** to bring together by degrees, to amass. **3** to take (several university degrees) at a time. ~*v.i.* to grow in size, number or quantity, by repeated additions. **accumulation** (-lā´shən) *n.* **1** the act of accumulating or amassing; the state of being accumulated. **2** something that has been accumulated. **3** a mass. **4** the increase of capital by the retention of earned interest. **5** the process of taking a number of university degrees. **accumulative** *a.* **1** cumulative, arising by accumulation. **2** organized in such a way as to accumulate. **3** acquisitive; tending to amass or to hoard. **accumulatively** *adv.* **accumulator** *n.* **1** a person who or something that accumulates. **2** an apparatus for storing hydraulic or electric energy, esp. a rechargeable electric cell or battery. **3** a bet, usu. on four or more races, in which the winnings from one race are staked on the next. **4** a location in a computer where numbers are stored or arithmetic operations are performed. **5** a person who takes university degrees by accumulation. [L *accumulātus*, p.p. of *accumulāre*, to heap up (*ac-, ad-*, to, *cumulāre*)]

accurate (ak´ūrət) *a.* **1** in precise accordance with a rule or standard or with the truth. **2** without error or defect. **3** careful, precise, exact. **accuracy** (-rəsi) *n.* (*pl.* **accuracies**) **1** exactness; correctness resulting from care; precision. **2** conformity to a standard. **3** precision of fit. **accurately** *adv.* **accurateness** *n.* [L *accūrātus*, p.p. of *accūrāre* (*ac-, ad-, cūrāre*, from *cūra*, care)]

accursed (əkœ´sid, əkœst´), **accurst** (əkœst´) *a.* **1** lying under a curse. **2** execrable, detestable. [OE *ācursod*, p.p. of *ācursian* (*a-*, intens., *cursian*, to curse)]

accusation ACCUSE.

accusative (əkū´zətiv) *a.* **1** of or belonging to the formal case of direct objects in inflected languages. **2** denoting a word representing a direct object in uninflected languages. ~*n.* **1** the accusative case. **2** a word or form in this case. **accusatival** (-tī´-) *a.* of or relating to the accusative. **accusatively** *adv.* [F *accusatif*, L *accūsātīvus* (ACCUSE), lit. trans. of Gr. *aitiatikē*, the case of accusing or of effect]

accuse (əkūz´) *v.t.* **1** to charge with a crime, offence or fault, to indict. **2** to lay the blame formally on (a person or thing). **accusable** *a.* liable to be charged with a crime or fault, blameworthy, censurable. **accusal** *n.* **accusation** (akūzā´shən) *n.* **1** the act of accusing. **2** the state of being accused. **3** a charge brought against someone. **accusatorial** (-taw´-) *a.* involving accusation or indictment in a case in which judge and prosecutor are distinct (contrasted with inquisitorial). **accusatorially** *adv.* **accusatory** *a.* containing or involving an accusation. **accused** *a.* **the accused** the defendant or defendants in a criminal case. **accuser** *n.* **accusingly** *adv.* [OF *acuser*, L *accūsāre* (*ac-, ad-*, to, *cause*, reason, cause, lawsuit)]

accustom (əkŭs´təm) *v.t.* to habituate (oneself, someone) (to), to make familiar by use. **accustomary** *a.* **accustomed** *a.* **1** used (to), inured (to) (*become accustomed to army life*). **2** in the habit of (*I'm accustomed to take wine with my dinner*). **3** often practised, usual, familiar, ordinary, habitual. **accustomedness** *n.* [CUSTOM]

AC/DC (āsēdē´sē) *a.* (*sl.*) bisexual. [*a*lternating *c*urrent, *d*irect *c*urrent]

ace (ās) *n.* **1** the single point on cards or dice. **2** a card or domino with only one mark upon it. **3** a person who is particularly skilful or successful in any activity, esp. sport. **4** a fighter-pilot who has brought down many hostile aircraft. **5** in tennis, a service or stroke which one's opponent cannot return. **6** (*N. Am*) in golf, a hole in one. ~*a.* (*sl.*) excellent, brilliant, first-rate. ~*v.t.* (in tennis) to serve an ace against (someone). **to play one's ace** to make use of the most effective thing one has available. **within an ace of** very close to, within a hair's breadth of (*came within an ace of colliding with a truck*). **ace high** *a.* in a card game, having the ace as the top-ranking card. **ace in the hole** *n.* (*N Am.*) an ace up one's sleeve. **ace up one's sleeve** *n.* an unsuspected advantage, something effective kept in reserve. [OF *as*, L *as*, a unit]

-acea (ā´shə) *suf.* used to form names of classes or orders of animals, e.g. *Cetacea, Crustacea* etc. [L suf., pl. neut. of *-āceus*, of the nature of]

-aceae (ā´shiē) *suf.* used to form names of orders or families of plants, e.g. *Rosaceae*. [L suf., fem. pl. qualifying *plantae*; see -ACEA]

-acean (ā´shən) *suf.* used to form singular nouns or adjectives corresponding to collective nouns in *-acea*, e.g. *crustacean, cetacean*. [L -ACEA, *-āceus*]

acedia ACCIDIE.

acellular (āsel´ūlə) *a.* **1** not having or consisting of cells. **2** (esp. of protozoa) consisting of a single cell.

acentric (āsen´trik) *a.* **1** without centre. **2** not about a centre. [Gr. *a-*, priv., *kentron*, centre]

-aceous (ā´shəs, ā´siəs) *suf.* of the nature of, belonging to, like: forming adjectives from nouns in natural science, e.g. *crustaceous, cretaceous, farinaceous, filaceous*. [L suf. -ACEA and -OUS]

acephal- (əsef´əl, əkef´-) *comb. form* headless: used to form various scientific terms, chiefly botanical and zoological. **acephalan** *a.*, *n.* **acephalous** (əsef´ələs, əkef´-) *a.* **1** without a head. **2** having no superior or ruler. **3** short of the beginning (as in a verse or manuscript). **4** (*Zool.*) with no distinct head, as in one division of the Mollusca. **5** (*Bot.*) with lateral instead of terminal style. [Gr. *akephalos* (*a-*, priv., *kephalē*, head)]

acer (ā´sə) *n.* a tree or shrub of the genus *Acer*, comprising over 100 species including the sycamore and maples. [L, a maple tree]

acerbic (əsœb´ik) *a.* **1** sour, astringent. **2** bitter or harsh in speech or manner. **acerbically** *adv.* [L *acerbus*, bitter]

acerbity (əsœ´biti) *n.* (*pl.* **acerbities**) **1** sourness, with roughness or astringency, as of unripe fruit. **2** harshness of speech, action or temper. **3** bitterness of suffering. [F *acerbité*, L *acerbitātem*, acc. of *acerbitas* (*acerbus*, bitter)]

acerose (as´ərōs) *a.* (*Bot.*) shaped like a needle, needle-sharp. [L *acerosus*, full of chaff, mistakenly assim. to *acer*, sharp]

☒ **acessory** common misspelling of ACCESSORY.

acet- (əsēt´, əset´), **aceto-** (-tō) *comb. form* **1** of the nature of vinegar. **2** acetic. **3** acetic acid. [L *acētum*, vinegar (*acēre*, to be sour)]

acetabulum (asətab´ūləm) *n.* (*pl.* **acetabula** (-lə)) **1** an ancient Roman vessel for holding vinegar. **2** a cavity in any bone designed to receive the protuberant head of another bone, e.g. the socket of the hip-joint in man. **3** the socket in which the leg of an insect is inserted. **4** any one of the suckers on the arms of a cuttlefish. **5** the cup-shaped fructification of many lichens. **6** the receptacle of certain fungi. [L *acētābulum*, from *acētum*, vinegar, *-abulum*, dim. of *-abrum*, a vessel or holder]

acetal (as´ital) *n.* any of a class of compounds formed by the reaction of an alcohol with an aldehyde. [G *Azetal*, from ACET-, ALCOHOL]

acetaldehyde (asətal´dəhīd) *n.* a volatile liquid aldehyde used in the manufacture of organic compounds. [ACET-, ALDEHYDE]

acetate (as´ətāt) *n.* **1** a salt of acetic acid. **2** cellulose acetate. **3** a photographic film or a textile made from cellulose acetate. **acetated** *a.* treated with acetic acid. **acetate fibre, acetate silk** *n.* a synthetic textile fibre or silk made from cellulose acetate. [ACET-]

acetic (əsē´tik, əset´-) *n.* **1** of or relating to vinegar, akin to vinegar. **2** sour. **acetic acid** *n.* the acid which imparts sourness to vinegar. [ACET-]

acetify (əset´ifī) *v.t.* (*3rd pers. sing. pres.* **acetifies,** *pres.p.* **acetifying,** *past, p.p.* **acetified**) **1** to convert into vinegar. **2** to render sour. *~v.i.* to become sour. **acetification** (əsetifikā´shən) *n.* the process of making into vinegar, or of rendering sour. [ACET-]

aceto- ACET-.

acetone (as´itōn) *n.* **1** an inflammable liquid obtained by distilling acetated or organic substances and used in the manufacture of chloroform and as a solvent. **2** a ketone. [G *Azeton*, from ACET-, ONE]

acetous (as´itəs), **acetose** (-ōs) *a.* **1** having the character of vinegar, sour. **2** causing acetification. [ACET-]

acetyl (as´itil, əsē´-) *n.* the radical of acetic acid. **acetylcholine** (-kō´lēn, -līn) *n.* a chemical released at nerve endings that transmits nerve impulses. **acetylide** (əset´ilīd) *n.* any of a class of salts formed from acetylene and a metal. **acetylsalicylic acid** (asitilsalisil´ik) *n.* the chemical name for aspirin. [ACET-, -YL]

acetylene (əset´əlēn) *n.* a gas composed of carbon and hydrogen, which burns with an intensely brilliant flame; ethyne. [ACET-, -YL, -ENE]

Achaean (əkī´ən) *a.* **1** of or relating to Achaea in ancient Greece. **2** esp. in Homer, Greek. *~n.* **1** an inhabitant of Achaea. **2** esp. in Homer, a Greek. [L *Achaeus* from Gr. *Akhaios*]

Achaemenid (əkī´mənid, əkē´-), **Achaemenian** (akimē´niən) *a.* of or relating to a dynasty of Persian kings from Cyrus I to Darius III (553–330 BC). *~n.* a member of this dynasty. [Gr. *Akhaimenēs*, the name of the dynasty's founder]

acharnement (ashah´nəmã) *n.* **1** bloodthirsty fury, ferocity. **2** gusto. [F]

ache (āk) *v.i.* **1** to suffer continuous dull pain; to be the source of an ache. **2** to long (for or to do). *~n.* **1** continuous dull pain (in contradistinction to a twinge). **2** mental distress or longing. **aching** *a.* **achingly** *adv.* with great desire or longing. **achy** *a.* suffering from or subject to an ache or aches. [OE *acan*]

☒ **acheive** common misspelling of ACHIEVE.

achene (əkēn´), **achaene** *n.* a small dry carpel, with a single seed, which does not open when ripe. **achenial** *a.* [Gr. A-[3], *chainein*, to gape]

Acheulian (əshoo´liən), **Acheulean** *a.* of or relating to the period of Lower Palaeolithic culture, typified by remains discovered in St Acheul, and placed by archaeologists between the Chellean and the Mousterian epochs. *~n.* this culture. [St *Acheul*, town in N France]

achieve (əchēv´) *v.t.* **1** to perform, accomplish, finish. **2** to attain, acquire, or bring about by an effort. **achievable** *a.* **achievement** *n.* **1** the act of accomplishing. **2** the thing achieved. **3** a heroic deed, an exploit. **4** performance in a standardized test. **5** a complete heraldic composition. **6** a funeral escutcheon. **achiever** *n.* [OF *achever*, from phrase *venir à chef*, late L *ad caput venīre*, to come to a head]

achillea (akil´iə, akilē´ə) *n.* any plant of the genus *Achillea*, such as the milfoil or yarrow, which are aromatic and have white, yellow or purple flowers. [L from Gr. *Akhilleios*, Achilles, who is supposed to have used the plant medicinally]

Achillean (akilē´ən) *a.* **1** like Achilles. **2** heroic, invincible. **3** invulnerable. **Achilles heel** (əkil´iz) *n.* a person's vulnerable point or fatal weakness (Achilles' mother Thetis having held him by the heel when she dipped him in the river Styx to make him invulnerable). **Achilles' tendon** *n.* the tendon or ligature connecting the muscles of the calf to the heel-bone. [*Achilles*, the hero of the *Iliad*]

achilous (əkī´ləs) *a.* (*Bot.*) without lips. [Gr. A-[3] *cheilos*, lip]

aching ACHE.

achiral (ākī´rəl) *a.* (of a crystal or molecule) not chiral. [A-[3], CHIRAL]

achlamydeous (akləmid´iəs) *a.* having neither calyx nor corolla, as the willows. [Gr. *a-*, priv., *chlamus -udos*, a cloak]

achondroplasia (əkondrəplā´ziə, ā-) *n.* (*Med.*) a hereditary bone disorder in which cartilage fails to ossify into long bones, resulting in very short limbs. [A-[3], Gr. *khondros*, cartilage, *plasis*, moulding]

achromatic (akrəmat´ik) *a.* **1** colourless. **2** transmitting light without decomposing it into its primary colours. **achromatically** *adv.* **achromatism** (əkrō´-), **achromaticity** (əkrōmətis´-) *n.* the quality or state of being achromatic. **achromatize** (əkrō´-), **achromatise** *v.t.* to deprive of colour. **achromatopsy** (əkrō´mətopsi) *n.* colour blindness. [Gr. *achrōmatos* (A-[3], *chrōma -atos*, colour)]

achy ACHE.

acicular (əsik´ūlə) *a.* resembling a needle in shape or sharpness. **acicularly** *adv.* **aciculate** (-lət), **aciculated** (-lātid) *a.* **1** having needle-like bristles. **2** marked with fine, irregular streaks. [L *acicula*, a small needle, -AR[1]]

acid (as´id) *a.* **1** sour, tart, sharp to the taste. **2** sharp or sour in manner or speech. **3** having the properties of an acid, reacting as an acid. **4** (of rocks) having a large proportion of silica. **5** (of colours) intensely bright. *~n.*

1 a compound of hydrogen in which the hydrogen can be replaced by a metal, or with a basic metallic oxide, to form a salt of that metal and water. 2 a sour substance. 3 (*sl.*) LSD. **to put on the acid** (*Austral.*) to scrounge, to cadge. **acid cloud** *n.* an area of mist or low cloud containing high concentrations of pollutant acids harmful to crops etc. **acid drop** *n.* a boiled sweet with a sour taste. **acid head** *n.* (*sl.*) a person who uses LSD. **acid house** *n.* 1 a youth cult concerned with highly electronically synthesized disco or pop music (and the taking of psychedelic drugs). 2 disco or pop music of this kind. **acidic** (-sid´-) *a.* acid. **acidify** (əsid´ifī) *v.t.* (*3rd pers. sing. pres.* **acidifies,** *pres.p.* **acidifying,** *past, p.p.* **acidified**) 1 to render acid or sour. 2 to convert into an acid. ~*v.i.* to become acid. **acidifiable** (-fī´-) *a.* capable of being rendered acid. **acidification** (-fikā´shən) *n.* 1 the act or process of acidifying. 2 the state of being acidified. **acidimeter** (asidim´itə) *n.* an instrument for measuring the strength of acids. **acidimetry** (-dim´itri) *n.* **acidity** (-sid´-) *n.* (*pl.* **acidities**) 1 the quality of being acid. 2 sourness, tartness, sharpness. 3 hyperacidity. **acid rain** *n.* precipitation made acidic and thus harmful to crops etc. by the release of (industrial) pollutants, esp. sulphur and nitrogen compounds, into the atmosphere. **acid rock** *n.* rock music featuring unusual amplified instrumental effects. **acid test** *n.* 1 an absolute and definite test. 2 a critical ordeal. [L *acidus,* sour (*acēre,* to be sour)]

acidosis (asidō´sis) *n.* a condition characterized by the appearance of excess acid in the urine and bloodstream. **acidotic** (-dot´-) *a.*

acidulous (əsid´ūləs) *a.* 1 a little sour or acid, moderately sharp to the taste, subacid. 2 sharp or sour in manner or speech. **acidulate** *v.t.* 1 to render slightly acid. 2 to flavour with an acid. **acidulated** *a.* 1 rendered slightly acid. 2 flavoured with acid. 3 soured, embittered in temper. [L *acidulus,* dim. of *acidus*]

acierate (as´iərāt) *v.t.* to turn into steel. **acierage** *n.* the process of electroplating a metal with iron or steel. **acieration** (-ā´shən) *n.* [F *acier,* late L *aciārium,* L *acies,* edge]

acinus (as´inəs) *n.* (*pl.* **acini** (-ī)) 1 any of the drupels that make up a compound fruit, such as the raspberry. 2 a small stone as found in a grape, berry etc. 3 a compound gland with saclike secreting ducts; the terminus of such a duct. 4 †a bunch of fleshy fruit, esp. a bunch of grapes. **aciniform** (əsin´-) *a.* clustered like grapes. [L *acinus,* a berry growing in a cluster]

-acious (ā´shəs) *suf.* 1 abounding in, characterized by, inclined to. 2 added to verbal stems to form adjectives, e.g. *loquacious, tenacious.* [L *-ax -ācis* and -OUS]

-acity (as´iti) *suf.* the quality of: forming nouns of quality from adjectives in -ACIOUS. [F *-acité,* L *ācitas -tātem*]

ack-ack (akak´) *a.* (*coll.*) anti-aircraft. ~*n.* (*coll.*) anti-aircraft guns or fire. [phonetic names for the letters AA, formerly used by British Army signallers]

ackee (ak´ē), **akee** *n.* 1 a tropical African tree, *Blighia sapida,* also cultivated in the West Indies. 2 the red, pear-shaped fruit of this tree, which is edible when cooked.

†**ack-emma** (akem´ə) *n.* (*coll.*) morning, a.m. [see ACK-ACK]

acknowledge (əknol´ij) *v.t.* 1 to admit the truth of, to recognize, accept. 2 to confess, to admit. 3 to recognize the authority of. 4 to give a receipt for, confirm receipt (of something). 5 to express appreciation or gratitude for. 6 to show awareness or recognition of, e.g. by a gesture. **acknowledgeable** *a.* **acknowledgement, acknowledgment** *n.* 1 the act of acknowledging. 2 recognition, acceptance; confession, admission. 3 a receipt for money or goods; a letter confirming receipt of a letter, invoice etc. 4 an expression of gratitude, esp. (*usu. in pl.*) an author's expression of gratitude to other people. 5 something given or done in return for a service or message. [OE *on,* KNOWLEDGE, or from obs. n. *acknowledge* (*acknowe,* OE *on, cnāwan,* to know)]

-acle (ak´əl, əkəl) *suf.* diminutive of nouns, e.g. *tabernacle, miracle.* [L *-āculum*]

aclinic (əklin´ik) *a.* not dipping, situated where the magnetic needle does not dip. **aclinic line** *n.* the magnetic equator. [Gr. *a-,* priv., *klinein,* to bend, see -IC]

acme (ak´mi) *n.* 1 the top or highest point, the culmination, peak or perfection (of achievement, excellence etc.). 2 the maturity of life. 3 the crisis or turning-point of a disease. [Gr. *akmē,* an edge]

acne (ak´ni) *n.* 1 a skin condition characterized by pimples. 2 a pimple on the skin. **acned** *a.* [prob. Gr. *aknesis,* without itch]

☒ **acolade** common misspelling of ACCOLADE.

acolyte (ak´əlīt) *n.* 1 a person assisting a priest in a service or procession. 2 an attendant, ministrant. 3 a faithful follower. [late L *acolythus, acolitus,* from Gr. *akolouthos,* a follower]

☒ **acomodate** common misspelling of ACCOMMODATE.

aconite (ak´ənīt) *n.* 1 a plant of the genus *Aconitum,* esp. *A. napellus,* the common monk's-hood or wolf's-bane. 2 a poison drug used medicinally, obtained from the root of this plant. **aconitic** (-nit´-) *a.* **aconitine** (əkon´itīn) *n.* a poisonous alkaloid substance derived from the genus *Aconitum.* [F *aconit,* L *aconītum,* Gr. *akonīton*]

acorn (ā´kawn) *n.* the fruit of the oak. **acorn barnacle, acorn shell** *n.* 1 a barnacle of the family Balanidae. 2 a multivalve cirriped, *Balanus balanoides,* allied to the barnacles. **acorned** *a.* (*Her.*) bearing acorns as a charge. [OE *æcern* (*æcer,* a field), fruit of the field, i.e. of the open country]

acotyledon (əkotilē´dən) *n.* 1 any plant of the class *Acotyledones.* 2 a plant without distinct seed-lobes. **acotyledonous** *a.* 1 having no cotyledons. 2 of or relating to a plant without visible seed-lobes. [mod. L *acotylēdones,* from Gr. *a-,* priv., COTYLEDON]

acoustic (əkoos´tik), **acoustical** (-əl) *a.* 1 of or relating to hearing, sound or acoustics. 2 of or relating to the ear, constituting part of the physical apparatus for hearing (*acoustic nerve*). 3 of or relating to musical instruments whose sound is not electronically amplified. 4 (of building materials) designed to absorb or control sound. 5 (of a mine) that can be detonated by sound waves. ~*n.* the acoustics of a room or building. **acoustically** *adv.* **acoustic coupler** *n.* a modem that enables computer data to be transmitted along a telephone line by converting it into acoustic form. **acoustician** (-tish´ən) *n.* 1 an expert in acoustics. 2 a person who investigates the phenomena of sound. **acoustics** *n.* 1 the science of sound and its phenomena, and of the phenomena of hearing. 2 (*as pl.*) the properties of a room or building that determine sound quality. [F *acoustique,* from Gr. *akoustikos* (*akouein,* to hear)]

acquaint (əkwānt´) *v.t.* to make (someone, oneself) aware of or familiar with (usu. followed by *with*). **acquaintance** *n.* 1 knowledge of any person or thing. 2 the state of knowing, or becoming known to, a person. 3 a person, or the persons collectively, whom one knows, but with whom one is not intimate. **to make one's acquaintance with** to meet or encounter (someone or something) for the first time. **to make the acquaintance of** to get to know. **acquaintanceship** *n.* 1 the state of being acquainted. 2 the relation of mutual acquaintance. **acquainted** *a.* 1 known to another or each other. 2 familiar (with). [OF *acointer,* late L *adcognitāre* (*ad-,* to, *cognitum,* p.p. of *cognoscere,* to know; *co-, cum-,* with, *gnoscere, noscere,* to know)]

acquiesce (akwies´) *v.i.* 1 to submit or remain passive. 2 to assent, to accept tacitly, to concur (in). **acquiescence** *n.* **acquiescent** *a.* 1 submissive. 2 accepting, assenting. **acquiescently** *adv.* **acquiescingly** *adv.* [F *ac-*, *ad-*, to, *quiēscere*, to rest, from *quies*, rest]

acquire (əkwīə´) *v.t.* 1 to gain, or obtain possession of, by one's own exertions or abilities. 2 to come into possession of. **acquirable** *a.* capable of being acquired. **acquirability** (-bil´-) *n.* **acquired** *a.* **acquired characteristic** *n.* a characteristic of an organism that is attained through environmental influences rather than genetically. **acquired immune deficiency syndrome** *n.* Aids. **acquired taste** *n.* something which one learns to like. **acquirement** *n.* 1 the act of acquiring. 2 the object gained. 3 a personal attainment, esp. a mental one. [OF *aquerre*, *acquerre*, from L *acquīrere* (*ac-*, *ad-*, to, *quaerere*, to seek)]

acquisition (akwizish´ən) *n.* 1 the act of acquiring. 2 the object acquired. 3 a gain, an acquirement. **acquisitive** (əkwiz´-) *a.* eager to acquire possessions; materialistic. **acquisitively** *adv.* **acquisitiveness** *n.*

acquit (əkwit´) *v.t.* (*pres.p.* **acquitting,** *past, p.p.* **acquitted**) 1 to declare not guilty. 2 to release from an obligation, suspicion or charge. 3 †to pay (a debt). ~*v.refl.* 1 to conduct (oneself) in a particular way. 2 to discharge (oneself) of (the duties of one's position). **acquittal** *n.* 1 a deliverance from a charge by legal process; being declared not guilty. 2 discharge or release from a promise, debt or other obligation. 3 performance. 4 discharge of duty. **acquittance** *n.* 1 the act of releasing from a charge or debt. 2 a receipt in full. 3 discharge of duty. **acquitter** *n.* [OF *acquiter*, late L *aquitāre* (AC-, *quiētāre*, to settle)]

acre (ā´kə) *n.* 1 a measure of land containing 4840 sq. yd. (0.4 ha). 2 (*pl.*) large areas or amounts (of). 3 a piece of tilled or enclosed land. 4 †a field (surviving in place names). **acreage** *n.* 1 the area of any piece of land in acres. 2 acres taken collectively or in the abstract. **acred** *a.* [OE *æcer*, a field (cp. OS *accar*, OHG *achar*, L *ager*, Gr. *agros*, Sansk. *ajras*)]

acrid (ak´rid) *a.* 1 sharp, pungent, biting to the taste. 2 irritating, corrosive. 3 bitterly irritating to the feelings. 4 of irritating temper and manners. **acridly** *adv.* **acridness, acridity** (əkrid´-) *n.* sharpness, pungency, bitterness of manner or speech. **acritude** *n.* [L *ācer ācris*, sharp, pungent, prob. assim. to ACID]

acridine (ak´ridēn) *n.* a colourless, crystalline solid used in the making of dyes and drugs. [ACRID, -INE]

acriflavine (akriflā´vin, -vēn) *n.* an aniline dye, solutions of which form a strong antiseptic. [L *ācer*, sharp; *flavus*, yellow]

Acrilan® (ak´rilan) *n.* a type of acrylic fibre or fabric used for clothing, carpets etc.

acrimony (ak´riməni) *n.* (*pl.* **acrimonies**) bitter, bad-tempered and accusatory feeling or speech. **acrimonious** (-mō´-) *a.* bitter, bad-tempered and recriminating and reproachful. **acrimoniously** *adv.* **acrimoniousness** *n.* [L *ācrimōnia* (*ācer ācris*, -MONY), sharpness]

acritude ACRID.

acro- (ak´rō) *comb. form* situated on the outside, beginning, termination, extremity, point or top, e.g. *acrobat, acrogenous.* [Gr. *akros*, outermost, at the top]

acrobat (ak´rəbat) *n.* 1 a performer of daring gymnastic feats, such as a tumbler or a tightrope walker. 2 a person who rapidly changes their opinions or loyalties. **acrobatic** (-bat´-) *a.* 1 of or relating to an acrobat or the performances of an acrobat. 2 involving great agility or spectacular skill. **acrobatically** *adv.* **acrobatics** *n.pl.* 1 the feats performed by an acrobat. 2 the skill required to perform these. 3 any agile performance. **acrobatism** *n.* the feats or occupation of an acrobat. [F *acrobate*, Gr. *akrobatos* (ACRO-, *batos*, verb.a. of *bainein*, to go)]

acrogen (ak´rəjən) *n.* 1 a cryptogam, a plant distinguished by growth from growing points at the extremity of the stem. 2 any one of the higher cryptogams (mosses, clubmosses and ferns). **acrogenous** (əkroj´-) *a.* 1 of the nature of an acrogen. 2 increasing at the summit. [Gr. ACRO-, *genēs*, born]

acrolith (ak´rəlith) *n.* a statue having only the head and extremities of stone. [Gr. ACRO-, *lithos*, stone]

acromegaly (akrōmeg´əli) *n.* a disease the chief feature of which is the enlargement of the face and of the extremities of the limbs. **acromegalic** (-gal´-) *a.* [Gr. *akron*, a point; *megas megalou*, great]

acronychal (əkron´ikəl), **acronycal,** (*N Am.*) **acronical** *a.* taking place in the evening or at sunset. **acronychally** *adv.* [Gr. ACRO-, *nux nuktos*, night]

acronym (ak´rənim) *n.* a word formed from initials, e.g. *NATO, laser.* **acronymic** (-nim´-) *a.* [ACRO-, Gr. *onoma*, name]

acropetal (əkrop´itəl) *a.* in the direction of the apex. **acropetally** *adv.* [Gr. *akron*, a point; L *petere*, to seek]

acrophobia (akrəfō´biə) *n.* an abnormal dread of high places. **acrophobic** *a.* [ACRO-, -PHOBIA (under -PHOBE)]

acropolis (əkrop´əlis) *n.* the citadel or elevated part of a Greek town, esp. that of Athens. [Gr. ACRO-, *polis*, city]

across (əkros´) *prep.* 1 from one side to the other of (*go across the road*). 2 on the other side of (*lives across the street*). 3 spanning, covering, extending etc. from one side of to the other (*a bridge across the river*). 4 transversely in relation to, forming a cross with. 5 so as to cross (boundaries, divisions etc.) (*across the political and religious divide*). ~*adv.* 1 to the other side. 2 on the other side. 3 from one side to the other. 4 (in a crossword puzzle) relating to the horizontal series of squares. **across the board** affecting or applying in all cases. [OE *a-*, on, CROSS]

acrostic (əkros´tik) *n.* 1 a composition in which the lines are so disposed that their initial letters taken in order constitute a word or short sentence. 2 an abecedarian poem. ~*a.* relating to or containing an acrostic. **acrostical** *a.* **acrostically** *adv.* in the manner of an acrostic composition. [Gr. *akrostichis* (ACRO-, *stichos*, a row)]

acroter (əkrō´tə, ak´rətə), **acroterium** (akrətē´riəm), **acroterion** (-tē´rion) *n.* (*pl.* **acroters, acroteria**) 1 a pedestal on a pediment, for the reception of a figure. 2 (*usu. pl.*) a pinnacle. **acroterial** *a.* of or relating to or having the character of an acroter. [Gr. *akrotērion*]

acrylic (əkril´ik) *a.* denoting or made from polymers of acrylic acid or its derivatives. ~*n.* 1 an acrylic textile fibre. 2 paint containing an acrylic resin. 3 a painting executed in acrylic paint. **acrylic acid** *n.* an acid used in the manufacture of acrylic resins. **acrylic resin** *n.* a resin consisting of a polymer of acrylic acid or one of its derivatives, used in making paints, adhesives, and for cast and moulded goods.

ACT *abbr.* Australian Capital Territory.

act (akt) *n.* 1 something that is done or being done, a deed. 2 the process of doing (*in the act of*). 3 a statute, law or edict of a legislative or judicial body. 4 any one of the principal divisions of a play, usu. subdivided into smaller portions called scenes. 5 a short entertainment, such as in a variety show, given by a particular performer or group of performers, esp. one that is particularly associated with and repeatedly given by the performer. 6 a group who give such a performance. 7 a document proving the truth of some transaction. 8 (*usu. pl.*) a record of the proceedings, decisions etc. of a committee, society etc. 9 (*pl.* **Acts**) the Acts of the Apostles, the book of the New Testament which follows the four Gospels and relates the history of the early Church. ~*v.t.* 1 to perform (a play). **2** to play the part of. **3** to impersonate or pretend. **4** to demonstrate or pretend using gestures. ~*v.i.* **1** to take action, to do something. **2** to be in action or operation. **3** to produce an effect, to exert power. **4** to behave, to conduct oneself. **5** to perform as an actor. **6** to pretend to be (*act stupid*). **in the (very) act** in the actual commission of some deed. **to act for** to be the (esp. legal) representative of. **to act on/ upon** **1** to follow, to carry out (advice, recommendation). **2** to have an effect on, to influence. **to act out** to represent (a scene, one's desires) in physical action or by performance. **to act up** (*coll.*) **1** to behave badly. **2** to function badly, to give trouble. **to get in on the act** (*coll.*) to become involved in an undertaking, esp. so as to benefit. **to get one's act together** (*coll.*) **1** to organize or prepare oneself properly. **2** to start to behave in a more responsible or more appropriate way. **to put on an act** (*coll.*) to pretend. **actable** *a.* **1** capable of being performed on the stage. **2** practically possible. **acting** *a.* **1** performing dramatically. **2** operating. **3** doing temporary duty. ~*n.* **1** performance, execution, action. **2** dramatic performance. **acting pilot officer** *n.* an RAF rank immediately below pilot officer. **Act of Attainder** *n.* (*Hist.*) BILL OF ATTAINDER (under BILL[1]). **act of God** *n.* the operation of uncontrollable natural forces in causing an event. **act of grace** *n.* a concession or privilege that cannot be claimed as of right. **actor** *n.* **1** a performer. **2** a person who represents a character on the stage. **3** a doer. **actor-manager** *n.* a person who both manages and performs with a theatre company. **actress** (-tris) *n.* a female actor. [F *acte*, or directly from L *actus*, a doing, and *actum* (pl. *acta*), a thing done, from *agere*, to do, to drive]

ACTH *abbr.* adrenocorticotrophic hormone.

actin- ACTINO-.

actinia (aktin´iə) *n.* (*pl.* **actiniae** (-ē), **actinias**) a sea anemone of the genus *Actinia*.

actinic (aktin´ik) *a.* **1** of or relating to rays, esp. the radiation from the sun. **2** (of rays) that can produce a photochemical effect. **actinic rays** *n.pl.* electro-magnetic rays capable of affecting photographic emulsions, including X-rays, ultraviolet, infrared rays etc. **actinism** (ak´-) *n.* **1** the property in rays of light by which chemical changes are produced. **2** the radiation of light or heat.

actinide (ak´tinīd), **actinoid** (-oid) *n.* any of a series of radioactive elements beginning with actinium and ending with lawrencium.

actinium (aktin´iəm) *n.* a radioactive metallic element, at. no. 89, chem. symbol Ac, found in pitchblende.

actino- (ak´tinō), **actin-** *comb. form* **1** indicating a radial shape or structure. **2** of or relating to radiation, esp. solar radiation, and radioactivity. [Gr. *aktis aktinos*, a ray]

actinograph (aktin´əgrahf) *n.* an instrument which registers the variations of chemical influence in solar rays.

actinoid ACTINIDE.

actinometer (aktinom´itə) *n.* an instrument for measuring the intensity of radiation, esp. of the sun's rays. **actinometric** (-met´-) *a.* **actinometry** *n.*

actinomorphic (aktinəmaw´fik), **actinomorphous** (-fəs) *a.* (*Bot.*) having a radial shape or structure that is symmetrical about its axis, like the buttercup.

actinomycete (aktinōmī´sēt) *n.* any of an order of filamentous bacteria, *Actinomycetales*, that includes both soil-inhabiting and disease-producing micro-organisms.

actinotherapy (aktinōther´əpi) *n.* the treatment of disease by exposure to actinic radiation.

actinozoan ANTHOZOAN.

action (ak´shən) *n.* **1** the state, condition or fact of acting or doing. **2** anything done or performed; a deed, an exploit. **3** energetic activity or forcefulness, esp. as a characteristic of a person (*a man of action*). **4** the exertion of a force, effect or influence (*the action of sunlight on the surface of the leaf*). **5** (*coll.*) exciting activity. **6** (*Mil.*) **a** combat, fighting. **b** a small-scale military engagement. **c** †a battle. **7** the way in which something operates or works; the mechanism of a machine or of a musical instrument, esp. a piano or an organ; the sensitivity to the player's touch of a keyboard instrument. **8** the events constituting the main storyline, or the main source of interest and suspense, in a play, novel etc. **9** a legal process, a lawsuit. **10** the particular style of movement of an animal, esp. a horse, or of an athlete. **11** industrial action. ~*int.* a command, given by the director of a film, to begin the shooting of a scene. ~*v.t.* **1** to implement, to put into effect. **2** to take action concerning. **3** to take legal action against. **in action** **1 a** working, operating. **b** (of artillery) firing. **2** in combat, fighting. **out of action** not working, unable to operate. **the action** (*coll.*) the principal or most lively activity. **to go into action** **1** to begin to take action, esp. energetically. **2** to go into battle. **to take action** to do something, esp. something energetic or decisive or something intended as a protest. **actionable** *a.* furnishing ground for an action at law. **actionably** *adv.* so as to be actionable. **action committee, action group** *n.* a body formed to take positive action to achieve an end. **action man** *n.* (*coll.*) **1** a man noted for physical fitness and taking part in demanding physical activities. **2** a man noted for favouring firm and decisive action. **action-packed** *a.* full of exciting events. **action painting** *n.* abstract expression using spontaneous actions of smearing, throwing etc. to apply paint. **action point** *n.* a proposal for action, esp. one that arises out of a discussion, interview etc. **action radius** *n.* the distance an aircraft can cover without running short of fuel before returning to its base or starting-point. **action replay** *n.* the repetition, often in slow motion, of a small piece of film showing an important or decisive (sporting) incident. **action research** *n.* research which is undertaken in the course of a job or activity, esp. in education, and intended to improve the methods and approach of the participants. **action stations** *n.pl.* the positions taken by military personnel in readiness for or during battle. ~*int.* a command to take up these positions. [F *action*, L *actiōnem*, acc. of *actio*, a doing, performance; see ACT]

activate (ak´tivāt) *v.t.* **1** to make active, to induce activity in. **2** to make radioactive. **3** to make (more) reactive. **activated** *a.* **activated carbon** *n.* carbon in the form of an absorbent powder used for purifying liquids and gases. **activated sludge** *n.* aerated sewage that contains anaerobic bacteria and is used to promote decomposition and purification in untreated sewage. **activation** (-ā´shən) *n.* **activator** *n.*

Usage note The meanings of the verbs *activate* and *actuate* overlap, but *activate* is more common of physical effects, and *actuate* of feelings or abstract qualities.

active (ak´tiv) *a.* **1** characterized by action, work or the performance of business; continually employed, busy (*an active life*; *like to keep active*). **2** that involves the performance of actual work or the making of an actual contribution; involved or participating in something in this way (*active assistance*; *active support*; *active member*). **3** able to move about and perform tasks (*less active since her illness*). **4** physically energetic (*very active children*). **5** communicating action or motion, initiating or furthering a process (*active ingredient*). **6** in actual operation or capable of actual operation. **7** (of a volcano) still liable to erupt. **8** radioactive. **9** (of a form of a verb) attributing the action expressed by the verb to the person or thing that performs it (as opposed to *passive*). **active birth** *n.* an approach to childbirth that encourages the mother to remain active, to move around and to adopt whatever position feels comfortable. **active carbon** *n.* ACTIVATED CARBON (under ACTIVATE). **active duty** *n.* (*N Am.*) ACTIVE SERVICE (under ACTIVE). **active list** *n.* a list of officers available for full military duty. **actively** *adv.* **1** in an active manner. **2** in such a way as to give actual effect to what one thinks or feels (*to actively dislike someone*). **active matrix** *n.* an electronic display system with individually controlled pixels. **active service** *n.* military duty in an operational area. **in/ on active service** on service. **active transport** *n.* a process, requiring the expenditure of energy, whereby ions and molecules pass across a membrane from areas of low concentration to areas of high concentration with the assistance of enzymes. **active vocabulary** *n.* the stock words which an individual is competent to use in their own speech or writing. **active voice** *n.* the form of the verb that attributes the action expressed to the subject. **activism** *n.* the policy of taking decisive or militant action. **activist** *n.* a person who takes decisive, sometimes militant, action in support of a (political or social) cause. **activity** (-tiv´-) *n.* (*pl.* **activities**) **1** the quality or state of being active. **2** exertion of energy; liveliness, vigorous action. **3** a pursuit, occupation, recreation. **4** radioactivity. [F *actif -ve*, L *activus*]

acton (ak´tən) *n.* (*Hist.*) **1** a vest or jacket of quilted cotton, worn under mail. **2** a jacket of leather or other material protected with plates or mail. [OF *auqueton* (F *hoqueton*), Sp. *alcoton* (*algodon*), Arab. *al-qūtun*, the cotton]

actor, actress ACT.

actual (ak´chuəl) *a.* **1** existing in act or reality, real, genuine. **2** present, current. **actual bodily harm** *n.* physical injury intentionally caused and giving grounds for criminal prosecution, but less serious than grievous bodily harm. **actual energy** *n.* kinetic energy. **actuality** (-al´-) *n.* (*pl.* **actualities**) **1** the state of being actual. **2** reality. **3** (*usu. pl.*) an existing condition. **actualize, actualise** *v.t.* **1** to make actual. **2** to describe realistically. **actualization** (-zā´shən) *n.* a making real or actual realization. **actually** *adv.* **1** in fact, in reality. **2** as a matter of fact. **3** at present. [F *actuel*, L *actuālis* (*actus*, verb.n. of *agere*, to act); see ACT, -AL[1]]

actuary (ak´chuəri) *n.* (*pl.* **actuaries**) an officer of a mercantile or insurance company, skilled in statistics, esp. on the expectancy of life and the average proportion of losses by fire and other accidents. **actuarial** (-eə´ri-) *a.* of or belonging to actuaries or their profession. [L *actuārius*, amanuensis, account-keeper]

actuate (ak´chuāt) *v.t.* **1** to put in action, to cause to operate. **2** to impart motion to. **3** to motivate, to induce. **actuation** (-ā´shən) *n.* **actuator** *n.* [med. L *actuātus*, p.p. of *actuāre* (*actus*)]

Usage note See note under ACTIVATE.

acuity (əkū´iti) *n.* sharpness, acuteness (of a point, an acid, disease or wit). [F *acuité*, med. L *acuitātem* (*acus*, needle, *acuere*, to sharpen)]

aculeus (əkū´liəs) *n.* (*pl.* **aculei** (-liī)) **1** (*Zool.*) a sting. **2** (*Bot.*) a prickle. **aculeate** (-ət), **aculeated** (-ātid) *a.* **1** having a sting. **2** set with prickles; prickly. **3** pointed, incisive, pungent. [L *acūleus*, a sting (dim. of *acus*, a needle)]

acumen (ak´ūmən) *n.* acuteness of mind, shrewdness, keen penetration. [L *acūmen* (*acuere*, to sharpen)]

acuminate[1] (əkū´minət) *a.* tapering to a point. [L *acuminatus*, pointed]

acuminate[2] (əkū´mināt) *v.t.* to sharpen, to point, to give keenness or poignancy to. **acuminated** *a.* **1** brought to a point. **2** sharp, stinging. **acumination** (-ā´shən) *n.* **1** the act of making sharp. **2** termination in a sharp point. **acuminose** *a.* (*Bot.*) terminating gradually in a flat, narrow end; inclined to be acuminate.

acupressure (ak´ūpreshə) *n.* massage using the fingertips applied to the points of the body used in acupuncture. [after *acupuncture*]

acupuncture (ak´ūpŭngkchə) *n.* a system of medical treatment in which the body surface is punctured by needles at specific points to relieve pain, cure disease or produce anaesthesia. **acupuncturist** (ak´-, -pŭngk´-) *n.* a practitioner in acupuncture. [L *acus*, needle, PUNCTURE]

☒ **acurate** common misspelling of ACCURATE.

acushla (əkush´lə) *n.* (*Ir.*) darling. [Ir. *a chuisle* (*moi chroi*), O pulse (of my heart)]

acut- ACUTI-.

acute (əkūt´) *a.* **1** sharp, keen, penetrating. **2** quick to perceive minute distinctions, sensitive to detail. **3** (of pain) sharp, piercing. **4** (of an illness) attended with violent symptoms, and coming speedily to a crisis. **5** (of an angle) less than a right angle. **6** (of a problem, shortage) critical, very serious, requiring urgent attention. **7** shrill, high in pitch. ~*n.* an acute accent. **acute accent** *n.* a mark (´) placed over some vowels in certain languages to indicate the quality of the vowel or the degree of stress to be given to it. **acutely** *adv.* **acuteness** *n.* **acute rheumatism** *n.* RHEUMATIC FEVER (under RHEUMATIC). [L *acūtus* (*acuere*, to sharpen)]

acuti- (əkū´ti), **acut-** *comb. form* sharp, acute, as in *acutangular, acutifoliate, acutiform.* [L *acūtus*, sharp]

ACW *abbr.* Aircraftwoman.

-acy (əsi) *suf.* forming nouns of quality, state, condition etc.; e.g. *fallacy, infancy, magistracy, piracy.* [L *-ācia, ātia*, Gr. *-ateia*]

acyclovir (āsī´kləvēə) *n.* an antiviral drug used in the treatment of Aids and herpes.

acyl (ā´sīl) *n.* the monovalent radical of a carboxylic acid. [ACID, -YL]

AD *abbr.* in the year of our Lord. [L *anno Domini*]

Usage note AD comes before dates which are cardinal numerals (*AD 91*), but may follow ordinals (*the third century AD*).

ad (ad) *n.* (*coll.*) short for ADVERTISEMENT (under ADVERTISE).

ad- (əd) *pref.* signifying motion towards, direction to, adherence etc., e.g. *adduce, adhere, adjacent, admire* (this prefix undergoes many alterations to assimilate it with the initial consonant of the root, examples of which will be found in their respective places). [L *ad*, to, at]

-ad[1] (ad) *suf.* **1** forming nouns denoting a group or unit of a specific number, as in *monad, triad.* **2** forming female patronymics, as in *naiad.* **3** (in the titles of epic or mock-epic poems) of or relating to, as in *Iliad.* [Gr. *-ad*, nom. *-as*, gen. *-ados*]

-ad[2] (əd) *suf.* forming nouns, as in *salad, ballad.* [F -ADE]

-ad[3] (ad) *suf.* forming adverbs, esp. in anatomical descriptions, indicating direction towards a specified part, as in *caudad.*

Ada (ā´də) *n.* a computer programming language developed for real-time applications, esp. in military systems. [the mathematician *Ada* Augusta King, Countess of Lovelace, 1815–52]

adage (ad´ij) *n.* a proverb; a pithy maxim handed down from old time. [F *adage*, L *adagium* (*ad-*, to, *agium*, a saying, from *aīo*, I say)]

adagio (ədah´jiō, -zhiō) *adv.* (*Mus.*) slowly, gracefully. ~*a.* slow, graceful. ~*n.* (*pl.* **adagios**) a slow movement or passage of a soft, tender, elegiac character. **adagietto** (-et´ō) *n.* (*pl.* **adagiettos**) a slow, graceful movement or passage somewhat quicker than an adagio.

adagissimo (-jis´imō) *adv.* very slowly. [It. *ad agio*, at leisure]

Adam[1] (ad´əm) *n.* 1 the first man, in the Bible and in the Koran. 2 the unregenerate state of man. **not to know someone from Adam** KNOW. **adamic** (ədam´-), **adamical** *a.* 1 of or relating to Adam, resembling Adam. 2 naked. **adamically** *adv.* **Adam's ale** *n.* water. **Adam's apple** *n.* 1 a protuberance on the forepart of the throat formed by the thyroid cartilage. 2 the lime, the orange or the shaddock (from the idea that it was the forbidden fruit). [Heb. *ā-dām*, man]

Adam[2] (ad´əm) *a.* of or relating to a decorative style of architecture and furniture designed by the Scottish brothers Robert and James Adam in the 18th cent.

adamant (ad´əmənt) *a.* 1 immovably resolved, stubbornly determined. 2 †hard, incapable of feeling. ~*n.* a legendary stone of impenetrable hardness, often taken to be the lodestone or the diamond. **adamancy** *n.* **adamantine** (-man´tīn), †**adamantean** (-man´tiən) *a.* (*poet.*) 1 made of adamant. 2 incapable of being broken. **adamantly** *adv.* [OF *adamaunt*, L *adamas -antem*, Gr. *adamas* (*a-*, priv., *damaō*, I tame)]

Adamite (ad´əmīt) *n.* 1 a descendant of Adam. 2 a member of a sect who professed to re-establish a state of innocence, and went naked. **adamitic** (-mit´-), **adamitical** *a.* of or relating to the Adamites. **adamitism** *n.* [ADAM[1]]

adapt (ədapt´) *v.t.* to fit, to adjust, to make suitable for a new purpose or conditions. ~*v.i.* to change so as to become fit or suitable for new conditions. **adaptable** *a.* 1 capable of being adapted. 2 able to adapt easily. **adaptability** (-bil´-) *n.* **adaptation** (adəptā´shən) *n.* 1 the act of adapting; the state of being adapted. 2 anything which has been adapted. 3 (*Biol.*) the process of modification that enables an organism to survive better in its environment. **adaptedness** *n.* **adaptive** *a.* 1 tending to adapt. 2 suitable. **adaptively** *adv.* **adaptive radiation** *n.* the evolutionary diversification of a group of organisms as they spread and occupy new environments. **adaptor, adapter** *a.* 1 a person or thing that adapts. 2 an accessory for connecting a plug etc. fitted with terminals of one type to a supply point fitted with terminals of another type, or for connecting several appliances to a single supply point. 3 any device for connecting differing parts or making pieces of equipment compatible with one another. [F *adapter*, L *adaptāre* (*ad-*, to, *aptare*, from *aptus*, fit)]

Adar (ā´dah) *n.* the sixth civil month, or twelfth ecclesiastical month of the Jewish year (corresponding to part of February and March). [Heb. *ādār*]

adaxial (adak´siəl) *a.* (*Bot.*) facing the stem. [AD-, AXIS[1]]

ADC *abbr.* 1 aide-de-camp. 2 analog-digital converter.

add (ad) *v.t.* 1 to put together with, join with or put into (*add a spoonful of milk*). 2 to combine (numbers) in order to make a total. 3 to say or write in addition. ~*v.i.* to perform the operation of addition. **to add in** to include. **to add on** to attach as a supplement or extension. **to add to** to increase (*You're simply adding to my difficulties*). **to add to the gaiety of nations** GAIETY. **to add up** 1 to perform the operation of addition. 2 to produce a correct total when added. 3 to make sense, to show a consistent pattern. **to add up to** to amount to. **added** *a.* **adder**[1] *n.* 1 an adding machine. 2 a circuit in a calculator or computer that adds binary numbers. **addible** *a.* capable of being added. **addibility** (-bil´-) *n.* **addition** *n.* 1 the process of combining two or more numbers or quantities into one sum. 2 a person or thing that is added. 3 †the title or designation given to a person beyond their name and surname. **in addition** as well, also. **additional** *a.* added; supplementary. **additionally** *adv.* **additive** *a.* 1 that may be or is to be added. 2 characterized by addition. ~*n.* something added, esp. a substance added to food to preserve or enhance it. **additive-free** *a.* (of food) containing no chemical additives. **additively** *adv.* **add-on** *n.* 1 something supplementary. 2 a computer peripheral. [L *addere* (*ad-*, to, *dare*, to put)]

addax (ad´aks) *n.* (*pl. in general* **addax,** *in particular* **addaxes**) a species of antelope, *Oryx nasomaculata*. [Afr.]

addendum (əden´dəm) *n.* (*pl.* **addenda** (-də)) 1 a thing to be added, an addition. 2 an appendix. [L *addendum*, ger. of *addere* (ADD)]

Usage note *Addenda* is sometimes used as a singular noun (*an addenda*), but it should always be a plural.

---

adder[1] ADD.

adder[2] (ad´ə) *n.* 1 the common viper, *Vipera berus.* 2 (with epithet) any of various other venomous snakes of the family Viperidae, as puff-adder, death-adder. **adder's tongue** *n.* a fern of the genus *Ophioglossum*. **adderwort** *n.* bistort, *Polygonum bistorta*. [OE *nædre* (*n* has disappeared through mistaken division of *a naddre* as *an addre*)]

addict[1] (ədikt´) *v.t.* to cause (someone, oneself) to become dependent on something, esp. a narcotic drug. **addicted** *a.* 1 dependent, esp. on a narcotic drug. 2 enthusiastically devoted to something. **addictedness** *n.* **addiction** *n.* 1 a condition of physical dependence on something, esp. a narcotic drug. 2 the act of addicting. 3 (*coll.*) an extreme devotion to something. **addictive** *a.* 1 that causes addiction. 2 (*coll.*) compulsively pleasurable, attractive, watchable etc. [L *addictus*, p.p. of *addicere* (*ad-*, to, *dicere*, to say)]

addict[2] (ad´ikt) *n.* 1 a person who has become addicted to some habit, esp. the taking of drugs. 2 (*coll.*) a person who is extremely devoted to something, esp. a pastime or sport (*a football addict*).

Addison's disease (ad´isənz) *n.* a disease characterized by undersecretion of steroid hormones from the adrenal cortex, causing weakness, weight loss and browning of the skin. [Thomas *Addison*, 1793–1860, British physician]

addition, additive ADD.

addle (ad´əl) *a.* 1 (of an egg) putrid, bad. 2 (*in comb.*) muddled, confused (*addle-headed*). 3 empty, vain. ~*v.t.* 1 to make addle or addled. 2 to cause to become confused or deranged. ~*v.i.* (of an egg) to become putrid. **addled** *a.* 1 (of an egg) rotten. 2 mentally confused or deranged. **addle-headed, addle-brained, addle-pated** *a.* muddled, confused, eccentric or deranged. **addlement** *n.* [OE *adela*, mire, filth]

address (ədres´) *n.* 1 the place where a person lives or a business, an organization etc. has its premises. 2 the written form of this used on letters etc. 3 a speech or discourse delivered to an audience. 4 tact, skill, adroitness. 5 a number that identifies a location in a computer memory where a particular piece of data is stored. 6 (*pl.*) a man's attentions to a woman whom he wishes to woo, courtship. 7 bearing in conversation. ~*v.t.* 1 to write the address on (a letter, envelope). 2 to speak to. 3 to deliver a speech or discourse to. 4 to direct (a message, protest etc.) to. 5 to direct one's attention to; to deal with. 6 to adopt a position facing (the ball, target), when preparing to hit, shoot etc. ~*v.i.* to present a formal address. **to address oneself to** 1 to speak to. 2 to apply oneself to; to deal with. **to pay one's addresses to** to court. **addressable** *a.* (*Comput.*) able to be accessed by means of an address. **addressee** (-ē´) *n.* a person to whom a letter, parcel or communication is addressed. **addresser** *n.* 1 ADDRESSOR (under ADDRESS). 2 a machine for addressing envelopes, wrappers etc. **Addressograph**® (-əgrahf) *n.* a machine for addressing envelopes, wrappers etc.

addressor *n.* **1** the person who addresses (a letter, envelope etc.). **2** a person who speaks to someone else. [F *adresser*, late L *addrictiare* (*ad-*, to, *drictum*, *directum*, DIRECT)]

adduce (ədūs´) *v.t.* to bring forward as a proof or illustration, to cite, to quote. **adducent** *a.* (of the adductor muscles) bringing or drawing to a given point. **adducer** *n.* **adducible** *a.* capable of being adduced. **adduct** (ədŭkt´) *v.t.* to draw (a body part) inwards or towards another part. **adduction** *n.* **1** the act of leading or drawing to or together. **2** the act of citing. **adductive** *a.* tending to lead or draw to or together. **adductor** *n.* a muscle which brings one part of the body towards or in contact with another part. [L *addūcere* (*ad*, to, *dūcere*, to lead)]

-ade (ād) *suf.* forming nouns denoting action, e.g. *cannonade, ambuscade*; a person or body involved in action, e.g. *brigade, cavalcade*; product of action, e.g. *masquerade*; sweet drink, e.g. *lemonade*. [F *-ade* (cp. *-ada* in Sp. and Prov.), L *-āta*, f. sing. p.p. of verbs in *-āre*]

aden-, adeni- ADENO-.

adenectomy (adənek´təmi) *n.* (*pl.* **adenectomies**) the surgical removal of a gland.

adenine (ad´ənēn, -nin) *n.* one of the four purine bases in DNA and RNA.

adenitis (adənī´tis) *n.* inflammation of the lymphatic glands.

adeno- (ad´ənō), **adeni-** (-i), **aden-** *comb. form* connected with a gland or glands, glandular; used in medical terms, e.g. *adenitis, adenopathy*. [Gr. *adēn*, an acorn, a gland]

adenoid (ad´ənoid) *a.* having the form of a gland, glandular. *~n.pl.* **1** adenoid tissue. **2** a spongy growth at the back of the nose and throat, impeding respiration and speech. **adenoidal** (-oi´dəl) *a.*

adenoma (adənō´mə) *n.* (*pl.* **adenomas, adenomata** (-ətə)) a benign tumour formed of glandular tissue.

adenopathy (adənop´əthi) *n.* **1** disease of a gland or glands. **2** enlargement of the lymphatic glands.

adenosine (əden´əsēn, -sin) *n.* a compound of adenine and the sugar ribose, that forms part of RNA and various compounds that provide energy in cells. **adenosine triphosphate** *n.* one of the adenosine compounds that is a major source of energy for all living cells. [*adenine* and *ribose*]

adept[1] (ədept´, ad´ept) *a.* thoroughly versed, highly skilled. **adeption** *a., n.* **adeptly** *adv.* **adeptness** *n.* [L *adeptus*, p.p. of *adipisci* (*ad-*, to, *apisci*, to attain)]

adept[2] (ad´ept) *n.* **1** a person who is completely versed in any science or art. **2** †a person who was supposed to have obtained the elixir of life and the philosopher's stone.

adequate (ad´ikwət) *a.* **1** equal to a requirement, sufficient; competent. **2** barely sufficient, just good enough. **3** proportionate, commensurate. **adequacy** *n.* **adequately** *adv.* [L *adaequātus*, p.p. of *adaequāre* (*ad-*, to, *aequāre*, to make equal, from *aequus*, equal)]

à deux (a dœ´) *a., adv.* of or between two (people). [F]

adhere (ədhiə´, ədiə´) *v.i.* **1** to stick (to). **2** to remain firmly attached (to). **3** to continue to give support to. **4** not to deviate (followed by *to*). [L *adhaerēre* (*ad-*, to, *haerēre*, to stick)]

adherence (ədhiə´rəns, ədiə´-) *n.* **1** the state or quality of adhering. **2** firm attachment. **3** continuing support or loyalty. **4** continuing and precise observance. **adherent** *a.* **1** sticking. **2** tenaciously attached. *~n.* **1** a supporter, a partisan, a follower. **2** a devotee. [F *adhérence*, L *adhaerentia*, verbal n., from *adhaerens -ntem*, pres.p. of *adhaerēre*]

Usage note The meanings of *adherence* and *adhesion* overlap, but *adherence* particularly corresponds to figurative or abstract senses of *adhere*, and *adhesion* to the more literal or physical.

---

adhesion (ədhē´zhən, ədē´-) *n.* **1** the act or state of sticking, attaching oneself to, or joining. **2** the union of structures or tissues that are normally separate. **3** the fusion of two surfaces, as the two opposing surfaces of a wound in healing. **adhesive** (-siv, -ziv) *a.* **1** having the power of adhering. **2** sticky, clinging. *~n.* a substance used for sticking things together. **adhesively** *adv.* **adhesiveness** *n.* **1** the power of sticking. **2** stickiness. **3** the propensity to form attachments with people. [ADHERE]

Usage note See note under ADHERENCE.

---

adhibit (ədhib´it) *v.t.* (*pres.p.* **adhibiting,** *past, p.p.* **adhibited**) **1** to apply, to administer (a remedy). **2** to append, to affix. **adhibition** (adhibish´ən, adi-) *n.* application, employment, use. [L *adhibit-*, stem in *adhibit-us*, p.p. of *adhibēre* (*ad-*, to, *habēre*, to hold)]

ad hoc (ad hok´, hōk´) *a., adv.* for a particular purpose only, specially. [L, to this]

ad hominem (ad hom´inem) *a., adv.* **1** directed to or against the person, not disinterested. **2** (of an argument) based on or appealing to emotion rather than reason. [L, to the man]

adiabatic (adiəbat´ik) *a.* **1** impervious, esp. to heat. **2** without loss or gain of heat. **adiabatically** *adv.* [Gr. *adiabatos* (*a-*, not, *dia*, through, *batos*, passable, from *baino*, I go); -IC]

adiaphorism (adiaf´ərizm) *n.* indifference with regard to non-essential matters, esp. those not specifically prescribed or forbidden by Scripture, in religion or ethics; latitudinarianism. **adiaphorist** *n.* **1** a person who holds that dogmas or rites are matters of indifference. **2** a moderate Lutheran. **3** a latitudinarian. *~a.* **1** of or relating to the adiaphorists. **2** theologically indifferent. [Gr. *adiaphoros*, not different (*a-*, not, *dia*, apart, *pherein*, to bear); -ISM]

☒ **adict** common misspelling of ADDICT.

adieu (ədū´, ədyœ´) *int., n.* (*pl.* **adieux** (-z)) God be with you, good-bye, farewell. [F *à*, to, *Dieu*, God]

ad infinitum (ad infinī´təm) *adv.* to infinity, without end. [L]

ad interim (ad in´tərim) *a., adv.* for the meantime. [L]

adios (adios´) *int.* goodbye. [Sp. *a*, to, *Dios*, God]

adipocere (ad´ipəsiə, -ōs-) *n.* a greyish-white fatty or soapy substance, into which the flesh of dead bodies buried in moist places is converted. **adipocerous** (-os´ərəs) *a.* of the nature of adipocere. [F *adipocire* (L *adeps -ipem*, fat, F *cire*, L *cera*, wax)]

adipose (ad´ipōs) *a.* of or relating to animal fat, fatty. *~n.* animal fat, esp. the fat on the kidneys. **adipescent** (-pes´-) *a.* growing fat. **adipic** (ədip´-) *a.* derived from fat. **adipose fin** *n.* the fatty dorsal fin of some fishes, such as the salmon family. **adipose tissue** *n.* the vesicular structure in which fat is deposited. **adiposity** (-pos´-) *n.* [L *adeps -ipem*, fat]

adit (ad´it) *n.* **1** an approach, entrance, passage. **2** a more or less horizontal entrance to a mine. [L *aditus*, approach (*ad-*, to, *īre*, to go)]

Adivasi (ahdivah´si) *n.* (*pl.* **Adivasis**) a member of any of the aboriginal tribes of India. [Hind.]

Adj., Adjt *abbr.* adjutant.

adj. *abbr.* **1** adjective. **2** adjustment.

adjacent (əjā´sənt) *a.* lying near (to); contiguous; neighbouring, bordering. **adjacency** *n.* the state of lying adjacent or near to. **adjacently** *adv.* [L *adjacentem*, pres.p. of *adjacēre* (*ad-*, to, at, *jacēre*, to lie)]

adjective (aj´iktiv) *a.* **1** added to. **2** dependent. **3** forming an adjunct to a noun substantive. *~n.* a word or phrase joined to, or grammatically linked to, a substantive to define and limit its signification. **adjectival** (-tī´-) *a.* **1**

of, relating to or being an adjective. 2 that uses many adjectives. **adjectivally** *adv.* [F *adjectif -ve*, L *adjectīvus, adjectus*, p.p. of *adjicere* (*ad-*, to, *jacere*, to throw); -IVE]

adjoin (ajoin´) *v.t.* 1 to be next to and contiguous with. 2 †to join or add, to unite. ~*v.i.* to be contiguous. **adjoining** *a.* adjacent, contiguous; neighbouring. [OF *ajoindre*, L *adjungere* (*ad-*, to, *jungere*, to join)]

adjourn (əjœn´) *v.t.* 1 to put off or defer till a later period. 2 to suspend (a meeting) in order to meet at a later period or elsewhere. 3 to postpone till a future meeting. ~*v.i.* 1 to cease proceedings till a later period. 2 to move elsewhere. **adjournment** *n.* 1 the act of adjourning. 2 the time during which or to which business or a meeting (esp. of a public body) is postponed. **adjournment debate** *n.* a brief debate in the British House of Commons before the House is adjourned, which allows members to raise matters that would not otherwise be discussed. [OF *ajorner*, late L *adjornāre*, appoint a day (*jurnus*, day, L *diurnus*)]

adjudge (əjŭj´) *v.t.* 1 to pronounce officially or formally (*adjudged to be at fault*). 2 to award by a judicial decision. 3 to adjudicate. 4 †to condemn, to sentence. **adjudgement, adjudgment** *n.* [OF *ajūger*, L *adjūdicāre*; see ADJUDICATE]

adjudicate (əjoo´dikāt) *v.t.* 1 to give a decision regarding, to judge, to determine. 2 to pronounce. ~*v.i.* 1 to sit as a judge. 2 to act as a judge in a competition. **adjudication** (-ā´shən) *n.* 1 the act of adjudicating. 2 the decision or judgement of a judge or court. **adjudicator** *n.* [L *adjūdicāre* (*ad-*, to, *jūdicāre*, to judge)]

adjunct (aj´ŭngkt) *n.* 1 any thing joined to another without being an essential part of it. 2 an associate, assistant or subordinate. 3 (*Gram.*) an extension of the subject or predicate. 4 (*Logic*) a non-essential attribute. ~*a.* 1 added to, or conjoined with, any person or thing. 2 auxiliary; subordinate. **adjunction** *n.* 1 a joining to. 2 the act of joining. 3 a thing joined. **adjunctive** (əjŭngk´-) *a.* joining, having the quality of joining. ~*n.* anything joined to another. **adjunctively, adjunctly** *adv.* by way of adjunct, in connection with. [L *adjunctus*, p.p. of *adjungere* (*ad-*, to, *jungere*, to join)]

adjure (əjooə´) *v.t.* 1 to charge upon oath, or on pain of divine displeasure. 2 to entreat with great earnestness. **adjuration** (-ā´shən) *n.* 1 the act of adjuring. 2 an appeal under penalty of a curse. 3 a solemn entreaty. **adjuratory** *a.* containing or characterized by an adjuration. [L *adjūrāre*, to swear to (*ad-*, to, *jūrāre*, to swear); late L, to put to an oath]

Usage note See note under ABJURE.

adjust (əjŭst´) *v.t.* 1 to regulate; to make slight alteration to, esp. to achieve greater accuracy. 2 to arrange; to put in the correct order or position. 3 to make suitable or correspondent (to). 4 to accommodate, settle or harmonize (differences). 5 to assess (insurance claims). ~*v.i.* to adapt or conform (to a new situation, environment etc.). **adjustable** *a.* **adjuster** *n.* 1 a person who or a thing that adjusts. 2 a person who assesses settlements in respect of insurance claims. **adjustment** *n.* 1 the act of adjusting; the state of being adjusted. 2 a device that regulates. 3 a settlement of claims, liabilities etc. [OF *ajuster*, late L *adjuxtāre*, bring together (*ad-*, to, *juxta*, near)]

adjutant (aj´ətənt) *n.* 1 an officer in each regiment who assists the commanding officer in matters of business, duty and discipline. 2 an assistant. 3 an adjutant bird. **adjutancy** *n.* the office of adjutant. **adjutant bird** *n.* either of two large wading birds of the stork family, *Leptoptilos dubius* or *L. jauanicus*, natives of SE Asia. **adjutant general** *n.* (*pl.* **adjutants general, adjutant generals**) 1 a senior officer of the general staff with administrative functions. 2 the executive officer to a general. [L *adjutans*, pres.p. of *adjūtāre*, freq. of *adjūvāre*, see ADJUVANT]

adjuvant (aj´əvənt) *a.* 1 helping. 2 (of cancer therapy) applied after the initial treatment, esp. to prevent the development of secondaries. ~*n.* 1 an assistant, helper, auxiliary. 2 an auxiliary, enhancing ingredient in a prescription. 3 a substance, injected with an antigen, to enhance the body's immune response to it. [L *adjūvāre* (*ad-*, to, *jūvāre*, to help); -ANT]

ad lib (ad lib´), **ad libitum** (lib´itum, lībē´təm) *adv.* 1 at pleasure, to any extent. 2 (*Mus.*) at the performer's discretion to change time or omit passages. **ad-lib** *v.t.* (*pres.p.* **ad-libbing,** *past, p.p.* **ad-libbed**) to say, perform, interject etc. without notes or preparation. ~*v.i.* to extemporize. ~*a.* improvised, extempore. ~*n.* an improvised speech, line etc. **ad-libber** *n.* [L]

ad litem (ad lī´təm) *a.* (of a guardian) appointed for a lawsuit. [L]

Adm. *abbr.* admiral.

adman (ad´man) *n.* (*pl.* **admen** (-men)) (*coll.*) a person who works in advertising.

admass (ad´mas) *n.* the mass viewers and listeners to whom television and radio advertising is directed. [ADVERTISEMENT (under ADVERTISE), MASS[2]]

admeasure (admezh´ə) *v.t.* 1 to ascertain the dimensions, weight etc. of (a vessel) for the purposes of official registration or rating. 2 to measure out, to apportion. **admeasurement** *n.* 1 the act of measuring; the dimensions ascertained. 2 apportionment of shares. [OF *amesurer*, late L *admensūrāre*]

admin (ad´min) *n.* (*coll.*) administration, administrative work.

adminicle (ədmin´ikəl) *n.* 1 an aid, support. 2 (*Sc. Law*) corroborative evidence, esp. of the contents of a missing document. **adminicular** (adminik´ūlə) *a.* auxiliary, corroborative. [L *adminiculum*, a prop, (*manus*, hand)]

administer (ədmin´istə) *v.t.* 1 to manage or conduct as chief agent. 2 to superintend the execution of (e.g. laws). 3 to direct the taking of (an oath). 4 to dispense, supply or perform the rites of (a sacrament). 5 to give (medicine, remedy). 6 to deliver (a rebuke). 7 to manage and dispose of (the estate of a deceased person). ~*v.i.* 1 to act as administrator. 2 to minister (to). **administrable** *a.* **administrant** *a., n.* **administration** (-trā´shən) *n.* 1 the act of administering. 2 the management of the affairs of a business, organization etc. 3 the people entrusted with this. 4 the management of public affairs, the conduct of government. 5 a government. 6 the period in office of a government, president etc. 7 (**Administration**) (in the US) a government board or agency. 8 (*Law*) the management and distribution of the estate of a deceased person, esp. an intestate. **administrative** (-trə-) *a.* 1 of or relating to administration. 2 executive. **administratively** *adv.* 1 in an administrative manner. 2 with regard to administration. **administrator** (-trā-) *n.* 1 a person who administers, manages, dispenses or furnishes. 2 (*Law*) a person who administers the estate of an intestate. 3 a person who is generally skilled in organizing and managing things. **administratorship** *n.* **administratrix** (-triks) *n.* (*pl.* **administratrices** (-sēz)) a female administrator. [OF *aministrer*, L *administrāre*]

admirable (ad´mirəbəl) *a.* 1 worthy of admiration. 2 excellent, highly satisfactory. **admirability** (-bil´-), **admirableness** *n.* **admirably** *adv.* [ADMIRE]

admiral (ad´mirəl) *n.* 1 the commander of a fleet or a division of a fleet (a rank having four grades in the Royal Navy: Admiral of the Fleet, Admiral, Vice-Admiral and Rear-Admiral). 2 either of two butterflies, *Vanessa atalanta*, the red, and *Limenitis sibylla*, the white admiral butterfly. 3 the commander of a fishing fleet. **admiralship** *n.* the office or position of an admiral. [OF *amiral*, Arab. *amir*, a prince (Latinized as *amīrālis*, and through confusion with *admirāri*, converted into *admirālis*)]

admiralty (ad´mirəlti) *n.* (*pl.* **admiralties**) **1** the office of admiral. **2** the maritime branch of the administration of justice. **the Admiralty 1** the Government department that formerly dealt with the British navy. **2** the Lords Commissioners who formerly administered naval affairs in Great Britain. **3** the building where they transacted business. **Admiralty Board** *n.* (*Hist.*) a board responsible for policy with respect to the Royal Navy within the framework of the British Ministry of Defence.

admire (ədmīə´) *v.t.* **1** to have a high opinion of, to respect. **2** to regard with pleasure and approval. **3** to express admiration of. **4** †to wonder at. *~v.i.* to feel admiration, to wonder, to be astonished. **admiration** (-mirā´shən) *n.* **1** pleasure or respect excited by anything pleasing or excellent. **2** pleased contemplation. **3** a person or thing that is admired. **4** †wonder. **admirer** *n.* **1** a person who feels admiration. **2** a suitor, lover. **admiring** *a.* **admiringly** *adv.* [F *admirer*, L *admīrāri* (*ad-*, at, *mīrāri*, to wonder)]

admissible (ədmis´ibəl) *a.* **1** fit to be considered as an opinion or as evidence. **2** (*Law*) allowable as evidence. **3** capable of being admitted. **4** qualified for entrance to an office. **admissibility** (-bil´-) *n.* the quality of being admissible. **admissibly** *adv.* **admission** (-shən) *n.* **1** permission or the right to enter. **2** a charge made or paid for entry. **3** an acknowledgement, a confession. **4** a concession made in an argument. **5** a person admitted to a hospital. **admissive** *a.* tending to admit, implying admission. [late L *admissibilis*, from *admissus*, p.p. of *admittere*, to ADMIT]

admit (ədmit´) *v.t.* (*pres.p.* **admitting**, *past*, *p.p.* **admitted**) **1** to concede, to acknowledge. **2** to accept as valid or true. **3** to allow to enter. **4** to allow to become a member or to participate or share. **5** (of a hospital) to accept (a patient) for residential treatment. **6** (of a space) to have room for, to accommodate. *~v.i.* to give access (*admits into the dining room*). **to admit of** to allow of, to be capable of. **to admit to** to acknowledge one's guilt or responsibility in respect of. **admittable** *a.* admissible. **admittance** *n.* **1** the act of admitting. **2** entrance given or permitted. **3** a measure of the ease of flow of an alternating current, the reciprocal of impedance. **admittedly** *adv.* I admit, it is true. [OF *amettre*, L *admittere* (*ad-*, to, *mittere*, to send)]

admix (admiks´) *v.t.* **1** to mix, to mingle. **2** to add as a further ingredient. **admixture** (admiks´chə, ad´-) *n.* **1** the act of mixing. **2** something added to something else; an alloy; a foreign element. [L *ad-*, to, MIX (formed like L *admiscere*, p.p. *admixtus*)]

admonish (ədmon´ish) *v.t.* **1** to reprove gently. **2** to urge, exhort. **3** to warn, caution. **admonisher** *n.* **admonishment** *n.* **1** the act of admonishing. **2** an admonition. **admonition** (admənish´ən) *n.* **1** (a) gentle reproof. **2** a friendly caution or warning. **admonitive** *a.* implying admonition. **admonitively** *adv.* **admonitor** *n.* **admonitory** *a.* [OF *amonester*, late L *admonestāre*, L *admonēre*, (*ad-*, to, *monēre*, to advise)]

adnate (ad´nāt) *a.* (*Biol.*) growing or grown closely attached to another part or organ along its whole surface. [L *adnātus* (*agnātus*) (*ad-*, to, *nātus*, *gnātus*, born)]

ad nauseam (ad naw´ziam, -si-) *adv.* to the point of producing disgust or nausea. [L]

adnominal (adnom´inəl) *a.* **1** of or relating to an adnoun. **2** attached to a noun. [L *adnōmen* (var. of *agnōmen*), added name]

adnoun (ad´nown) *n.* an adjective used as a noun. [L *ad-*, to, NOUN (formed like *adverb*)]

Adnyamathanha (ad´nyəmŭthənə) *n.* an Aboriginal language of S Australia.

ado (ədoo´) *n.* **1** activity. **2** trouble, difficulty, fuss. **without further/ more ado** straight away, without delay. [Scand. *at*, to, DO¹]

-ado (ah´dō, ā´dō) *suf.* forming nouns, e.g. *desperado*, *renegado*, *tornado* (*bravado*, *gambado*, *strappado*, and some other terms, are alterations of words in *-ade*). [Sp. and Port. *-ado*, L *-ātus*, in p.p. of verbs in *āre*]

adobe (ədō´bi) *n.* **1** a sun-dried brick. **2** a clay used in making such bricks. **3** a building made of adobe bricks. [Sp. *adobe*, from *adobar*, to daub, plaster, late L *adobāre*]

adolescent (adəles´ənt) *a.* **1** growing up; between puberty and maturity. **2** typical of people of this age. **3** immature; silly. *~n.* a person in the age of adolescence. **adolescence** *n.* the period between childhood and adulthood. [F *adolescent*, L *adolēscens -ntem*, pres.p. of *adolēscere*, to grow up]

Adonai (ədō´nī, adənī´) *n.* the Lord; a name for God in the Old Testament. [Heb. *ădōnāi*, my lord; see ADONIS]

Adonis (ədō´nis) *n.* (*pl.* **Adonises**) **1** a handsome young man; a beau, a dandy. **2** a butterfly, *Polyommatus adonis*. **adonic** (ədon´-) *a.* **1** of or relating to Adonis. **2** of a metre composed of a dactyl or a trochee and spondee. [Gr., name of a youth beloved by Venus for his beauty, Phoen. *adōn*, lord, title of a divinity]

adopt (ədopt´) *v.t.* **1** to take into any relationship, as child, heir, citizen, candidate etc. **2** to take (a child) as one's own. **3** to embrace, to espouse (a principle, cause etc.). **4** to take over (an idea, argument etc.) as if it were one's own. **5** to accept (a report, accounts) officially. **6** (of a local authority) to accept responsibility for the maintenance of (a road etc.). **adopted** *a.* taken as one's own, accepted into some intimate relation such as that of one's child. **adopter** *n.* a person who or something which adopts. **adoption** *n.* the act of adopting. **adoptional** *a.* of or relating to adoption. **adoptive** *a.* due to or by reason of adoption. **adoptive father** *n.* the man who has adopted a child. **adoptively** *adv.* **adoptive mother** *n.* the woman who has adopted a child. [F *adopter*, L *adoptāre* (*ad-*, to, *optāre*, to choose)]

adore (ədaw´) *v.t.* **1** to regard with the utmost respect and affection. **2** to worship as a god. **3** (*coll.*) to like very much. **4** (in the Roman Catholic Church) to offer reverence to. *~v.i.* to offer worship. **adorable** *a.* **1** charming, delightful, fascinating. **2** worthy of the utmost love and respect. **adorableness** *n.* **adorably** *adv.* **1** delightfully. **2** in a manner worthy of adoration. **adoration** (adərā´shən) *n.* **1** ardent love or esteem. **2** worship, veneration. **adorer** *n.* **1** a person who adores, a worshipper, a votary. **2** an admirer, lover. **adoring** *a.* **adoringly** *adv.* [OF *aörer*, *aourer* (F *adorer*), L *adōrāre* (*ad-*, to, *ōrāre*, to pray, from *os oris*, the mouth)]

adorn (ədawn´) *v.t.* **1** to decorate, ornament, embellish. **2** to add attractiveness to. **adorner** *n.* **adorning** *n.* adornment. **adorningly** *adv.* **adornment** *n.* **1** a decoration, ornament or embellishment. **2** the act of adorning. [OF *aörner* (F *adorner*), L *adornāre* (*ad-*, to, *ornāre*, to deck)]

ADP *abbr.* **1** adenosine diphosphate. **2** automated data processing.

ad personam (ad pœsō´nam) *adv.* to the person. *~a.* personal. [L]

ad rem (ad rem´) *a.*, *adv.* to the point, to the purpose. [L, to the matter]

adrenal (ədrē´nəl) *a.* near the kidneys. **adrenal gland** *n.* a small gland adjacent to each kidney that secretes adrenalin and steroid hormones. [L *ad-*, to; *renes*, kidneys]

adrenalin (ədren´əlin), **adrenaline** *n.* **1** a hormone secreted by the adrenal glands that stimulates the heart muscle and increases blood pressure. **2** a crystalline substance derived from the adrenal glands of cattle and sheep, used as a stimulant.

adrenocorticotrophic (ədrēnōkawtikōtrof´ik), **adrenocorticotropic** (-trop´ik) *a.* stimulating the adrenal cortex. **adrenocorticotrophic hormone** *n.* a hormone produced by the pituitary gland that stimulates the activity of the adrenal cortex. **adrenocorticotrophin** (-trof´in) *n.* adrenocorticotrophic hormone.

☒ **adress** common misspelling of ADDRESS.

adrift (ədrift´) *a.*, *adv.* **1** drifting; unable to steer. **2** detached from its moorings; unfastened. **3** wandering, at a loss, at the mercy of circumstances. **4** inaccurate; not keeping to a course, guideline, schedule etc. **5** (*coll.*) out of touch; not well informed. **6** (*coll.*) absent without leave.

adroit (ədroit´) *a.* dexterous, active, clever, mentally or physically resourceful. **adroitly** *adv.* **adroitness** *n.* [F *à*, to, *droit*, right, late L *drictum* (L *directum*); see DIRECT]

adscititious (adsitish´əs) *a.* assumed, adopted, derived from without, supplemental. **adscititiously** *adv.* [L *adscitus* (*as-cītus*) p.p. of *adscīscere*, adopted, received from others (*ad-* to, *scīt-*, part. stem of *scīscere*, to acknowledge, freq. of *scīre*, to know)]

adscript (ad´skript) *a.* (of feudal serfs) attached to the soil. *~n.* a person held to service, a serf. **adscription** (-skrip´shən) *n.* **1** ascription. **2** attachment, as a feudal inferior. [L *adscriptus*, p.p. of *adscrībere* (*ad-*, to, *scrībere*, to write)]

adsorb (ədsawb´, -z-) *v.t.* to take up and cause to adhere in a thin film on the surface. *~v.i.* to concentrate and adhere to the surface of a solid. **adsorbable** *a.* **adsorbate** *n.* a substance that is adsorbed. **adsorbent** *n.* a solid substance that adsorbs gases, vapours or liquids that contact it. *~a.* capable of adsorbing. **adsorption** (-sawp´-, -z-) *n.* concentration of a substance on a surface. **adsorptive** *a.* [L, *ăd-*, to, *sorbēre*, to suck in]

adsuki ADZUKI.

ADT *abbr.* Atlantic Daylight Time.

aduki ADZUKI.

adulate (ad´ūlāt) *v.t.* to fawn upon, to flatter servilely. **adulation** (-lā´shən) *n.* **1** the act of fawning or flattering servilely. **2** servile flattery. **adulator** *n.* **adulatory** *a.* [L *adūlātus*, p.p. of *adūlārī*, to flatter]

adult (ad´ŭlt, ədŭlt´) *a.* **1** grown to maturity. **2** grown up, full-grown. **3** of or for adults. **4** (*euphem.*) containing sexually explicit material, pornographic. *~n.* **1** a person, animal or plant that has grown to maturity. **2** (*Law*) a person who has reached the age of majority. **adult education** *n.* part-time, usu. non-vocational courses for people over school-leaving age. **adulthood, adultness** *n.* [L *adultus*, p.p. of *adolescere*, to grow up (*ad-*, to, *olescere*, freq. of *olēre*, to grow)]

adulterate (ədŭl´tərāt) *v.t.* to corrupt or debase (anything) by mixing it with an inferior substance. *~a.* **1** adulterated. **2** spurious, debased by admixture. **adulterant** *n.* anything which adulterates or is used to adulterate. *~a.* adulterating. **adulterately** *adv.* **adulterateness** *n.* **adulteration** (-ā´shən) *n.* **1** the act or result of adulterating. **2** the state of being adulterated. **3** an adulterated substance. **adulterator** *n.* a person who adulterates. **adulterine**[1] (-īn) *a.* **1** spurious, counterfeit. **2** illegal, unlicensed. [L *adulterātus*, p.p. of *adulterāre*, commit adultery, corrupt (*ad-*to, *alterāre*, to change, from *alter*, other), cp. *adulter*, an adulterer, a debaser of the coinage]

adulterine[1] ADULTERATE.

adulterine[2] ADULTERY.

adultery (ədŭl´təri) *n.* (*pl.* **adulteries**) **1** voluntary sexual intercourse on the part of a married person with someone other than their spouse. **2** an instance of this. **adulterer** *n.* a person who has committed adultery. **adulteress** *n.* a woman who has committed adultery. **adulterine**[2] (-rīn) *a.* conceived in adultery. **adulterous** *a.* of or relating to adultery, having committed adultery. **adulterously** *adv.* [L *adultērium* (superseding older *avoutrie*, from OF *avouterie*, L *adulter*); see ADULTERATE]

adumbrate (ad´əmbrāt) *v.t.* **1** to outline, to sketch out. **2** to indicate faintly as if by a shadow. **3** to foreshadow. **4** to overshadow. **adumbrant** *a.* **adumbration** (-brā´shən) *n.* **1** the act of adumbrating. **2** an outline; a faint, imperfect representation. **adumbrative** (ədum´brətiv) *a.* faintly representing. [L *adumbrāre*, to cast a shadow (*ad-*, to, *umbrāre*, to shadow, from *umbra*, shadow)]

adv. *abbr.* **1** adverb. **2** adverbial. **3** adversus (against). **4** advocate.

ad valorem (ad vəlaw´rem) *a.*, *adv.* (of a tax) in proportion to the value of the goods. [L, according to value]

advance (ədvahns´) *v.t.* **1** to bring or move forward or upwards. **2** to supply before or on credit. **3** to promote, to further. **4** to put forward for attention. **5** to set to an earlier time; to bring forward to an earlier date or time. **6** to raise. *~v.i.* **1** to move forward. **2** to progress. **3** (of prices) to rise. *~n.* **1** the act or process of moving forward. **2** progress; an example of progress, development or increased sophistication. **3** a payment made beforehand; a loan. **4** a rise (in price). **5** (*pl.*) amorous overtures. **6** promotion. *~a.* **1** done, supplied etc. beforehand. **2** (of position) forward. **in advance 1** beforehand. **2** in front. **to advance on** to move towards menacingly. **advanced** *a.* **1** more highly developed, sophisticated etc. than the norm. **2** situated far forward. **3** (of a person's age) far on; (of a child) precocious. **4** (of opinions) ahead of the times. **advanced gas-cooled reactor** *n.* a nuclear reactor in which the uranium fuel core is cooled by circulating carbon dioxide. **Advanced level** *n.* A LEVEL (under A[1]). **Advanced Supplementary level** *n.* AS LEVEL. **advance guard** *n.* a detachment which precedes the advance of the main body of an army. **advance man** *n.* (*pl.* **advance men**) (*N Am.*) a person who visits a place before a visit by a political or public figure in order to make suitable arrangements. **advancement** *n.* **1** the act of advancing; the state of being advanced. **2** preferment. **3** furtherance, improvement. **4** the application beforehand of property to which children are prospectively entitled; the property so applied. **advance note** *n.* a draft for payment of one month's wages given to a member of a ship's crew when signing on. **advancer** *n.* **1** a person who advances. **2** a promoter. **3** a moneylender. [OF *avancer*, pop. L *abanteāre*, from *abante* (*ab-*, away, *ante*, before)]

advantage (ədvahn´tij) *n.* **1** a favourable condition or circumstance. **2** superiority of any kind; a superior or better position. **3** profit, benefit. **4** in tennis, the next point scored after deuce. *~v.t.* **1** to benefit. **2** to further, to promote the interests of. **to advantage** so as to display the best points. **to have the advantage of 1** to be in a better position than. **2** to recognize (someone) who does not recognize you. **to take advantage of 1** to make good use of; to profit by. **2** to exploit or abuse unscrupulously or unfairly. **3** to seduce. **to turn to advantage** to derive benefit from (a thing originally seen as a handicap). **advantaged** *a.* placed at advantage. **advantageous** (advəntā´jəs) *a.* **1** conferring advantage. **2** profitable, beneficial. **advantageously** *adv.* **advantageousness** *n.* [F *avantage*]

advection (advek´shən) *n.* the transfer of heat by the horizontal movement of air. [L *advectus*, p.p. of *advehere* (*ad-*, towards, *vehere*, to carry)]

advent (ad´vent) *n.* **1** (**Advent**) the season of the

Christian year including the four Sundays before Christmas. 2 the Incarnation of Christ; the Second Coming. 3 any arrival, a coming. **Advent Calendar** *n.* a calendar for Advent, usu. with numbered doors or windows to be opened one a day. **Adventism** (-vən-) *n.* **Adventist** (-vən-) *n.* a person who believes that the Second Coming of Christ is imminent. [OF *advent, auvent,* L *adventus,* arrival (*ad-,* to, *venire,* to come)]

adventitious (advəntish´əs) *a.* 1 accidental, casual. 2 extraneous, foreign. 3 (*Biol.*) developing in an unusual position. 4 (*Law*) coming otherwise than by direct succession. **adventitiously** *adv.* **adventitiousness** *n.* [L *adventicius,* coming from abroad]

adventure (əđven´chə) *n.* 1 an enterprise in which hazard or risk is incurred and for which enterprise and daring are required. 2 any novel or unexpected event. 3 enterprise and daring. 4 a speculation. ~*v.t.* to risk, to hazard, to put in danger. ~*v.i.* 1 to venture. 2 to dare. **adventure holiday** *n.* a holiday centred round outdoor activities having an element of danger, such as rock-climbing and canoeing. **adventure playground** *n.* a children's playground containing objects that can be built with, climbed on and used in creative play. **adventurer** *n.* 1 a person who seeks adventures. 2 a person who seeks to gain social position by false pretences. **adventuresome** (-səm) *a.* adventurous. **adventuresomeness** *n.* **adventuress** *n.* a female adventurer, a woman who seeks to gain social position by false pretences. **adventurism** *n.* hasty, ill-considered, opportunistic action, esp. in politics. **adventurous** *a.* 1 fond of adventure. 2 venturesome, daring, rash. 3 involving risk; perilous, hazardous. **adventurously** *adv.* **adventurousness** *n.* [OF *aventure,* L *adventūra,* fut.p. of *advenīre*; see ADVENT]

adverb (ad´vœb) *n.* a word or phrase qualifying a verb, an adjective or another adverb. **adverbial** (-vœ´-) *a.* **adverbially** *adv.* [F *adverbe,* L *adverbium* (*ad-,* to, *verbum,* word)]

adversary (ad´vəsəri) *n.* (*pl.* **adversaries**) 1 an opponent. 2 an enemy, a foe. **adversarial** *a.* 1 involving conflict or opposition. 2 antagonistic, hostile. 3 (of a legal process) involving parties or interests that are in opposition to one another. **adversarious** (-seə´-) *a.* **adversative** (-vœ´-) *a.* denoting opposition or antithesis. ~*n.* a word or proposition expressing opposition. [OF *aversier,* L *adversarius*; see ADVERSE]

Usage note Pronunciation as (advœ´səri), with stress on the second syllable, is best avoided.

adverse (ad´vœs) *a.* 1 unpropitious, unfavourable. 2 hostile, inimical. 3 acting in a contrary direction; opposite in position. **adversely** *adv.* **adverseness** *n.* **adversity** (-vœ´-) *n.* (*pl.* **adversities**) 1 adverse circumstances, misfortune, calamity, trouble. 2 an instance of this. [OF *avers, advers,* L *adversus,* p.p. of *advertĕre* (*ad-,* towards, *vertere,* to turn)]

Usage note The adjectives *adverse* and *averse* should not be confused: *adverse* means inimical or unfavourable, and *averse* unwilling or disinclined.

advert[1] (ədvœt´) *v.i.* 1 to refer (to). 2 to direct attention to. **advertence, advertency** *n.* attention, notice, regard. **advertent** *a.* attentive, heedful. **advertently** *adv.* [F *avertir,* late L *advertĕre* (*ad-,* to, *vertĕre,* to turn)]

advert[2] (ad´vœt) *n.* (*coll.*) short for ADVERTISEMENT (under ADVERTISE).

advertise (ad´vətīz) *v.t.* 1 to publicly describe (a product, service, vacancy etc.) in order to promote awareness, increase sales, invite applications etc. 2 to give public notice of; to make publicly known. 3 to inform. ~*v.i.* 1 to issue advertisements. 2 to give public notice of a wish or need (for). **advertisement** (-vœ´tiz-) *n.* 1 a paid announcement in a newspaper or on radio, television etc. 2 the act of advertising. 3 a public notice. **advertiser** *n.* a person who or a journal which advertises. **advertising** *n.* 1 publicity. 2 advertisements. 3 the business of securing publicity. [F *avertiss-,* stem of *avertir, avertissement,* L *advertere*; see ADVERT[1]]

advertorial (advətaw´riəl) *n.* a newspaper feature which is commissioned and often supplied by an advertiser, though appearing in the form of an editorial or impartial report. [ADVERTISEMENT (under ADVERTISE), EDITORIAL (under EDIT)]

advice (ədvīs´) *n.* 1 counsel, opinion as to a course of action. 2 a formal or official notice. 3 (*usu. pl.*) information or notice. 4 news. **to take advice** 1 to seek advice, esp. from an expert. 2 to act on advice given. [OF *avis,* L *ad-,* to, *vīsum,* seen (*vidēre,* to see)]

advise (ədvīz´) *v.t.* 1 to counsel (a person). 2 to recommend (a course of action). 3 to inform, to notify. ~*v.i.* 1 to give advice. 2 (*chiefly N Am.*) to consult. 3 †to deliberate, to reflect. **advisable** *a.* 1 right, proper, to be recommended, expedient. 2 capable of being advised. **advisability** (-bil´-) *n.* **advisably** *adv.* **advised** *a.* 1 acting with deliberation. 2 well considered, deliberate. **advisedly** (-zid-) *adv.* with mature deliberation. **advisement** *n.* (*N Am.*) consideration, deliberation. **adviser, advisor** *n.* 1 a person who advises, esp. in a professional capacity. 2 a person appointed by a British education authority to give advice on current teaching methods and facilities. **advisership** *n.* **advising** *n.* advice, counsel. **advisory** *a.* 1 having the function or power to advise. 2 containing advice. [OF *aviser,* late L *advisāre*; see ADVICE]

advocaat (ad´vəkah) *n.* a sweet thick liqueur containing raw egg and brandy. [Dut.]

advocate[1] (ad´vəkət) *n.* 1 a person who defends or promotes a cause. 2 a person who pleads a cause in a civil or criminal court. 3 (*Sc.*) a barrister. 4 an intercessor. **advocacy** *n.* (*pl.* **advocacies**) 1 verbal support or argument in favour (of). 2 judicial pleading. 3 the office of advocate. **advocateship** *n.* 1 the office of an advocate or intercessor. 2 advocacy. [L *advocātus,* p.p. (used as n.) of *advocāre* (*ad-,* to, *vocāre,* to call)]

advocate[2] (ad´vəkāt) *v.t.* to plead in favour of, recommend. **advocatory** (-ā´-) *a.* of or relating to advocacy.

advowson (ədvow´zən) *n.* the right of presentation to a vacant benefice in the Church of England. [OF *avoson,* L *advocatiōnem* (ADVOCATE[1], -ION)]

advt. *abbr.* advertisement.

adynamia (adinā´miə) *n.* lack of power, nervous debility, physical prostration. **adynamic** (-nam´-) *a.* 1 of or relating to adynamia. 2 weak, asthenic; without force. [Gr. *adunamia* (*a-,* not, *dunamis,* power)]

adytum (ad´itəm) *n.* (*pl.* **adyta** (-tə)) the innermost and most sacred part of a temple. [L *adytum,* Gr. *aduton* (*a-,* not, *dutos,* verb.a. from *duein,* to enter)]

adze (adz), (*also N Am.*) **adz** *n.* a cutting tool with an arched blade at right angles to the handle. ~*v.t.* to shape by means of an adze. [OE *adesa*]

adzuki (ədzoo´ki), **adsuki** (-soo´-), **aduki** (ədoo´-) *n.* 1 a plant, *Phaseolus angularis,* grown esp. in China and Japan. 2 the small round reddish-brown edible seed of this plant. **adzuki bean** *n.* the adzuki plant or its seed.

ae (ā) *a.* (*Sc.*) one, a.

-ae (ē) *suf.* forming the plural of non-naturalized Latin words, e.g. *laminae, Rosaceae, Homeridae.* [L]

AEA *abbr.* Atomic Energy Authority.

AEC *abbr.* Atomic Energy Commission (in the US).

aedile (ē´dīl) *n.* a magistrate in ancient Rome who had charge of public works, games, roads and buildings. **aedileship** *n.* [L *aedīlis* (*aedes,* a building), -ILE]

AEEU *abbr.* Amalgamated Engineering and Electrical Union.

aegis (ē´jis) *n.* 1 in Greek myth, a shield belonging to

Zeus or Athene. 2 protection, a protective influence. **under the aegis of** under the auspices of. [L *aegis*, Gr. *aigis*]

aegrotat (īˊgrətat) *n.* 1 a note certifying that a student is sick. 2 a degree awarded to a student unable to sit the relevant examinations because of illness. [L *aegrotat*, he is sick (*aeger*, sick)]

-aemia (ēˊmiə), (*esp. N Am.*) **-emia, -haemia** (hēˊ-), (*esp. N Am.*) **-hemia** *comb. form* of, relating to or denoting blood, esp. a specified condition of the blood. [Gr. *haima*, blood]

Aeolian (ēōˊliən), (*esp. N Am.*) **Eolian** *a.* 1 of or relating to Aeolus (god of the winds in Greek myth). 2 of or relating to Aeolia, the coastal region of NW Asia Minor. 3 (**aeolian, eolian**) wind-borne. **Aeolian harp, aeolian harp** *n.* a stringed instrument played by a current of air. **Aeolian mode** *n.* (*Mus.*) the ninth of the church modes, represented by the ascending natural diatonic scale A to A. [L *Aeolius*, a. from *Aeolis* (Gr. *Aiolis*), or *Aeolus* (Gr. *Aiolos*), -AN]

Aeolic (ēolˊik) *a.* 1 of or belonging to Aeolia. 2 denoting or relating to one of the three great dialects of the Greek language. ~*n.* this dialect. [Gr. *aiolikos* (a. from Aeolis)]

aeolipile (ēˊəlipīl, ēolˊ-), **aeolipyle, eolipile, eolipyle** *n.* an apparatus for demonstrating the force of steam generated in a closed chamber and escaping through a small aperture. [F *aeolipyle*, L *Aeoli pylae*, Gr. *Aiolou pulai*, gates of Aeolus]

aeolotropy (ēəlotˊrəpi) *n.* change of physical qualities consequent on change of position, as of the refracting properties of Iceland spar. **aeolotropic** (-tropˊ-) *a.* [Gr. *aiolos*, changeful, *tropia*, turning]

aeon (ēˊən, -on), (*esp. N Am.*) **eon** *n.* 1 a period of immense duration. 2 an age of the universe. 3 a period of a thousand million years. 4 in Platonism, Neoplatonism and Gnosticism, an emanation from or phase of the Deity. **aeonian** (ēōˊ-) *a.* (*poet.*) eternal, everlasting. [L *aeon*, Gr. *aiōn*]

aepyornis (ēpiawˊnis) *n.* (*pl.* **aepyornises**) any of a genus, *Aepyornis*, of gigantic fossil birds much larger than the ostrich, found in Madagascar. [Gr. *aipus*, tall, *ornis*, bird]

aer- AERO-.

aerate (eəˊrāt) *v.t.* 1 to subject to the action of atmospheric air. 2 to charge with carbon dioxide. 3 to oxygenate (the blood) by respiration. **aerated** *a.* 1 exposed to the action of the air, charged with air. 2 charged with carbon dioxide gas. 3 effervescent. 4 (*coll.*) angry or excited. **aeration** (-rāˊshən) *n.* the act of aerating. **aerator** *n.*

AERE *abbr.* Atomic Energy Research Establishment.

aerial (eəˊriəl) *a.* 1 of or relating to the air. 2 occurring, moving, growing, operating in or inhabiting the air. 3 of, for or using aircraft, effected by or operating from or against aircraft. 4 airy, thin, gaseous. 5 atmospheric. 6 high, elevated. 7 imaginary, immaterial, refined. ~*n.* a collector or radiator of electromagnetic waves for radio, television etc. **aerialist** *n.* a trapeze artist or tightrope walker. **aeriality** (-alˊ-) *n.* airiness, unsubstantiality. **aerially** *adv.* **aerial perspective** *n.* the representation of distance and space on a plane surface. **aerial photograph** *n.* a photograph taken from an aircraft for military or surveying purposes. **aerial railway** *n.* a wire or cable stretched from point to point across rivers, valleys etc. for transporting loads. **aerial surveying** *n.* a method of surveying by the use of aerial photographs. **aerial torpedo** *n.* a torpedo launched from an aircraft. [L *aērus*, Gr. *aerios* (*āer*, air), -AL[1]]

aerie EYRIE.

aeriform (eəˊrifawm) *a.* of the form or nature of air; gaseous.

aero- (eəˊrō), **aer-** *comb. form* 1 of or relating to the air or atmosphere, e.g. *aerodynamics.* 2 of or relating to aircraft, aeronautics, e.g. *aerodrome.* [Gr. *aēr aeros*, the air]

aerobatics (eərəbatˊiks) *n.pl.* spectacular flying or stunts by an aircraft.

aerobe (eəˊrōb) *n.* an organism that requires oxygen for life. **aerobic** (-rōˊ-) *a.* 1 using or requiring oxygen, occurring in the presence of oxygen. 2 of or involving aerobes. 3 of or relating to aerobics. **aerobically** *adv.* **aerobics** *n.pl.* physical exercises designed to improve heart and lung function, esp. (*often sing. in constr.*) a system of exercises consisting of routines of rhythmic dancelike movements and stretches, usu. performed to music.

aerobiology (eərōbīolˊəji) *n.* the study of airborne microorganisms. **aerobiological** (-əlojˊikəl) *a.* **aerobiologically** *adv.* **aerobiologist** *n.*

aerodrome (eəˊrədrōm), (*N Am.*) **airdrome** (eəˊdrōm) *n.* 1 an area, with any buildings attached, for the operation of esp. light aircraft. 2 an air station. [Gr. *dromos*, race, racecourse]

aerodynamics (eərōdīnamˊiks) *n.* the science which deals with the forces exerted by gases in motion. **aerodynamic** *a.* 1 of or involving aerodynamics. 2 designed so as to minimize wind resistance. **aerodynamically** *adv.*

aerodyne (eəˊrədīn) *n.* any heavier-than-air machine, such as an aircraft.

aeroembolism (eərōemˊbəlizm) *n.* the formation of nitrogen bubbles in the blood and tissues, caused by too rapid a reduction in atmospheric pressure (see CAISSON DISEASE (under CAISSON)).

aero-engine (eəˊrōenjin) *n.* an engine used to power an aircraft.

aerofoil (eəˊrəfoil), (*N Am.*) **airfoil** (eəˊfoil) *n.* a winglike structure constructed to obtain reaction on its surfaces from the air; one of the flying surfaces of an aeroplane.

aerogram (eəˊrəgram) *n.* 1 a radiogram, a wireless message. 2 (*also* **aerogramme**) a single sheet of lightweight paper with a printed postage stamp that folds up for sending by airmail; a letter written on this.

aerography (eərogˊrəfi) *n.* the description of the properties etc. of the air.

aerolite (eəˊrəlīt), **aerolith** (-lith) *n.* 1 a stone which falls through the air to the earth. 2 a meteoric stone. **aerolitic** (-litˊ-) *a.* [Gr. *lithos*, a stone]

aerology (eərolˊəji) *n.* the department of science that deals with the atmosphere. **aerological** (-lojˊ-) *a.* **aerologist** *n.*

aerometer (eəromˊitə) *n.* an instrument for measuring the weight and density of air and gases. **aerometric** (-əmetˊrik) *a.* **aerometry** (-omˊətri) *n.* pneumatics.

aeronaut (eəˊrənawt) *n.* a person who pilots, navigates or flies in a balloon or airship. **aeronautic** (-nawˊ-), **aeronautical** *a.* of or relating to aeronautics. **aeronautics** *n.* the science or art of travel through the air. [Gr. *nautēs*, a sailor]

aeronomy (eəronˊəmi) *n.* the science of the upper atmosphere of the earth and other planets. **aeronomist** *n.*

aerophyte (eəˊrəfīt) *n.* a plant which grows entirely in the air, as distinguished from one growing on the ground.

aeroplane (eəˊrəplān) *n.* a mechanically-driven heavier-than-air flying-machine with fixed wings as lifting surfaces.

aerosol (eəˊrəsol) *n.* 1 a suspension of fine particles in air or gas, as in smoke or mist. 2 a substance dispersed as an aerosol from a pressurized metal container. 3 such a container.

aerospace (eəˊrəspās) *n.* 1 the earth's atmosphere and the space beyond. 2 the science or industry concerned with aerospace. ~*a.* of or relating to aerospace, to travel or operation in aerospace, or to vehicles used in aerospace.

aerostat (eəʹrəstat) *n.* an aircraft that is supported in the air statically, i.e. lighter-than-air. **aerostatic** (-statʹ-) *a.* of or relating to aerostatics. **aerostatics** *n.* **1** the science which deals with the equilibrium and pressure of air and gases. **2** the study of flying in lighter-than-air craft. [F *aérostat* (Gr. *statos*, verb. a., standing)]

aerostation (eəʹrōstāshən) *n.* the science of flying lighter-than-air craft.

aerotowing (eəʹrōtōwing) *n.* the towing of gliders by powered aircraft.

aerotrain (eəʹrōtrān) *n.* a train that glides above its track supported on a cushion of air.

aeruginous (irooʹjinəs) *a.* of the nature of or resembling verdigris. [L *aerūginōsus*, rusty (*aerūgo -inis*, verdigris, from *aes aeris*, copper)]

aery[1] (eəʹri) *a.* (*poet.*) **1** airy. **2** ethereal, unsubstantial, visionary. [L *āerius* (*āer*, the air)]

aery[2] EYRIE.

Aesculapian (ēskūlāʹpiən), **Esculapian** *a.* **1** of or belonging to Aesculapius, the Greek god of medicine. **2** medical; medicinal. [L]

aesthesia (esthēʹziə), **aesthesis** (-sis), (*N Am.*) **esthesia, esthesis** *n.* capacity to feel or sense, sensibility. **aesthesiometer** (-omʹitə) *n.* an instrument for testing the sensibility of the skin. [see ANAESTHESIA]

aesthete (ēsʹthēt, esʹ-), (*esp. N Am.*) **esthete** (esʹ-) *n.* a person who professes a special appreciation of the beautiful, esp. in the arts. **aesthetic** (əsthetʹ-), **aesthetical** *a.* **1** of or relating to aesthetics. **2** appreciating the beautiful in nature and art. **3** in accord with the laws of the beautiful, or with principles of taste. ~*n.* a set of principles defining beauty or good taste in art. **aesthetically** *adv.* **aesthetician** (-tishʹ-) *n.* **1** a person who studies aesthetics. **2** (*N Am.*) a beautician. **aestheticism** *n.* **1** the quality of being aesthetic. **2** devotion to the study of the beautiful. **aestheticize, aestheticise** *v.t.* **aesthetics** *n.* the theory or philosophy of the perception of the beautiful. [Gr. *aisthētēs*, one who perceives]

aestival (ēsʹtivəl, esʹ-), (*esp. N Am.*) **estival** (esʹ-) *a.* **1** of or belonging to the summer. **2** produced in the summer. **aestivate** *v.i.* **1** to remain in a place during the summer. **2** (of an animal) to fall into a summer sleep or torpor. **aestivation** (-āʹshən) *n.* **1** the internal arrangement of a flower bud, prefloration. **2** the act of remaining torpid in the summer. [L *aestīvālis*, from *aestīvus* (*aestus*, heat)]

aet., aetat. *abbr.* aetatis.

aetatis (ītahʹtis) *prep.* at the age of. [L]

aether, aethereal ETHER.

aetiology (ētiolʹəji), (*esp. N Am.*) **etiology** *n.* (*pl.* **aetiologies, etiologies**) **1** the study of causation. **2** an investigation into the cause of anything. **3** (*Med.*) the study of the cause of disease; the cause of a specific disease. **aetiologic** *a.* **1** of or relating to aetiology. **2** (*Philos.*) (of an explanation) based on causal precedents. **aetiologically** *adv.* **aetiologist** *n.* [Gr. *aitiologia*, from *aitia*, cause]

AEU *abbr.* (*Hist.*) Amalgamated Engineering Union.

AF *abbr.* audio frequency.

af- (əf) *pref.* AD-, assim. to *f*, e.g. *afford.*

afar (əfahʹ) *adv.* at or to a (great) distance. **from afar** from a great distance away.

AFC *abbr.* **1** Air Force Cross. **2** Association Football Club.

AFDCS *abbr.* Association of First Division Civil Servants.

†afeard (əfiədʹ), **afeared** *a.* afraid, frightened. [OE p.p. of *afǣran* (*a-*, intens., *fǣran*, to frighten)]

affable (afʹəbəl) *a.* good-natured, friendly, approachable. **affability** (-bilʹ-) *n.* **affableness** *n.* **affably** *adv.* [L *affābilis* (*af-*, *ad-*, to, *fāri*, to speak), -ABLE]

affair (əfeəʹ) *n.* **1** a matter, a concern, something that is to be done. **2** a sexual or romantic relationship, esp. an extramarital one. **3** an event or sequence of events, esp. one that attains public fame or notoriety. **4** (*coll.*) a thing. **5** (*pl.*) public or private business. **6** (*pl.*) finances. **7** (*pl.*) circumstances. [OF *afaire* (*à*, to, *faire*, to do, L *facere*)]

affaire (afeəʹ), **affaire de cœur** (də kœʹ), **affaire du cœur** (dü kœʹ) *n.* a love affair. [F]

affairé (afeəʹrā) *a.* busy. [F]

affect[1] (əfektʹ) *v.t.* **1** to act upon, have an effect upon, exert an influence upon. **2** (of a disease) to attack. **3** to touch or stir emotionally. **affecting** *a.* touching, moving. **affectingly** *adv.* [F *affecter*, L *affectāre*, freq. of *afficere* (*ad-*, to, *facere*, to do, act)]

Usage note The verbs *affect* and *effect* should not be confused: *affect* means to have an effect on, and *effect* to bring about.

affect[2] (əfektʹ) *v.t.* **1** to make a pretence of, to feign; to pretend (*affect unconcern*). **2** to imitate or assume (*affect an air of indifference*). **3** to pose as. **4** to make a show of liking. **5** (of plants, animals) to live or grow in. **6** to be drawn naturally to. **affectation** (afektāʹshən) *n.* **1** pretentiousness. **2** a mannerism, form of behaviour etc. adopted or contrived in order to impress. **3** assumption, adoption. **4** pretence. **affected** *a.* **1** pretentious, given to affectation. **2** artificially adopted, contrived. **3** †disposed, inclined. **affectedly** *adv.* **affectedness** *n.* [as AFFECT[1]]

affect[3] (afʹekt) *n.* (*Psych.*) an emotion or emotional state that is associated with or causes an idea or an action. [G *Affekt* from L *affectus*, disposition, from *afficere*, see AFFECT[1]]

affection (əfekʹshən) *n.* **1** fondness, love. **2** a state of the body due to any cause, malady, disease. **3** (*usu. pl.*) an emotion. **4** a psychological disposition. **5** the act of affecting; the state of being affected. **affectional** *a.* **1** of or relating to the affections. **2** having affections. **affectionate** (-nət) *a.* **1** of a loving disposition. **2** tenderly disposed. **3** indicating or expressing love. **affectionately** *adv.* **affectionateness** *n.* [F *affection*, L *affectiōnem*]

affective (əfekʹtiv) *a.* **1** of or relating to the affections, emotional. **2** (*Psych.*) of or relating to affects. **affectivity** (-tivʹ-), **affectiveness** *n.* [F *affectif, -ive* from late L *affectivus*, as AFFECT[1]]

affenpinscher (afʹənpinshə) *n.* **1** a European breed of dog, resembling the griffon, that has tufts of hair on the face. **2** a dog of this breed. [G *Affe*, monkey, *Pinscher*, terrier]

afferent (afʹərənt) *a.* bringing or conducting inwards or towards, esp. conducting nerve impulses towards the brain or spinal cord. [L *afferre* (*ad-*, to, *ferre*, to bring), -ENT]

affettuoso (afetuōʹsō) *adv.* (*Mus.*) with feeling. [It.]

affiance (əfīʹəns) *v.t.* (*formal*) to promise solemnly in marriage, to betroth. [OF *afiancer*, late L *affidare*, to trust]

affiant (əfīʹənt) *n.* (*N Am.*) a person who makes an affidavit.

affiche (əfēshʹ) *n.* a poster, placard. [F *afficher*, to fasten (L *af-*, *ad-*, to, *ficher*, L *figicāre*, from *figere*)]

affidavit (afidāʹvit) *n.* a voluntary affirmation sworn before a person qualified to administer an oath. [late L, he made oath, from *affidāre*; see AFFIANCE]

affiliate[1] (əfilʹiāt) *v.t.* **1** (*usu. pass.*) to connect with a larger organization. **2** to receive as a member or branch. ~*v.i.* to become connected or associated, combine (with). **affiliable** *a.* capable of being affiliated or assigned. **affiliation** (-āʹshən) *n.* the act of affiliating; the process of being affiliated. **affiliation order** *n.* a legal order requiring the father of an illegitimate child to make maintenance payments. [L *affīliāre*, to adopt (*ad-*, to, *fīlius*, a son)]

affiliate[2] (əfil´iət) *n.* a person, company, branch etc. that is affiliated to an organization. ~*a.* that is an affiliate. [as AFFILIATE[1]]

affined (əfīnd´) *a.* joined in affinity; related; closely connected. [F *affiné* (L *affīnis*, related to)]

affinity (əfin´iti) *n.* (*pl.* **affinities**) **1** a natural attraction or inclination to, or liking for, something. **2** relationship, esp. relationship by marriage as opposed to consanguinity or relationship by blood. **3** a close connection or structural resemblance. **4** a resemblance due to, or suggesting, common origin. **5** chemical attraction, the property by which elements unite to form new compounds. **affinity card** *n.* **1** a bank card linked with a particular charity to which the issuing bank pays a proportion of the money spent using the card. **2** a discount card issued to members of an affinity group. **affinity group** *n.* a group linked by a common purpose or interest. [F *affinité*, L *affīnitātem* (*af-*, *ad-*, to, *finis*, end, border)]

Usage note After *affinity* the prepositions *with* and *between* are preferred to *to* and *for*, which do not imply the necessary mutual relationship.

affirm (əfœm´) *v.t.* **1** to assert positively or solemnly; to allege confidently. **2** to confirm, to ratify. **3** to declare the existence or worth of something, or one's commitment to it. **4** (*Logic*) to state affirmatively. ~*v.i.* to make a solemn affirmation in lieu of oath. **affirmable** *a.* **affirmance** *n.* confirmation, ratification, assertion. **affirmant, affirmer** *n.* a person who makes an affirmation. **affirmation** (afəmā´shən) *n.* **1** the act of affirming anything; something which is affirmed. **2** a solemn declaration made under penalties, in lieu of oath. **3** a statement or declaration of the existence, truth, worth etc. of something. **affirmative** *a.* **1** containing an assertion that something is true or valid. **2** expressing agreement, approval, consent. ~*n.* **1** an affirmative statement or reply. **2** a word or phrase that indicates agreement, approval or consent. ~*int.* (*esp. N Am.*) yes. **in the affirmative** (*N Am.*) so as to indicate agreement, approval, consent; yes. **the affirmative** (*N Am.*) the proposing side in a debate. **affirmative action** *n.* (*N Am.*) a policy designed to favour and assist persons or groups who are often discriminated against, positive discrimination. **affirmatively** *adv.* [OF *afermer*, L *affirmāre* (*af-*, *ad-*, to, *firmāre*, from *firmus*, strong)]

affix[1] (əfiks´) *v.t.* **1** to fix, fasten, attach. **2** to annex, to subjoin. **3** to impress (a stamp). **affixation** (-ā´shən) *n.* **1** AFFIXTURE (under AFFIX[1]). **2** the addition of an affix. **affixture** (-chə) *n.* **1** the act of affixing. **2** attachment. [med. L *affixāre*, freq. of L *affīgere* (*af-*, *ad-*, to, FIX)]

affix[2] (af´iks) *n.* **1** an addition. **2** a word or syllable added to the beginning or the end of, or inserted in a word or root to produce a derived word or inflection, a prefix, suffix or infix.

afflatus (əflā´təs) *n.* **1** inspiration. **2** poetic impulse. [L *afflātus*, from *afflāre* (*af-*, *ad-*, *flāre*, to blow)]

afflict (əflikt´) *v.t.* to inflict bodily or mental pain on; to cast down; to trouble. **afflicted** *a.* **to be afflicted with** to suffer from. **afflictingly** *adv.* **affliction** *n.* **1** the state of being afflicted. **2** calamity, trouble, misery, distress. **3** a mental or bodily ailment. **afflictive** *a.* **1** causing affliction. **2** distressing. **afflictively** *adv.* [OF *aflit*, L *afflictus*, p.p. of *afflīgere* (*af-*, *ad-*, to, *flīgere*, dash, strike)]

Usage note The verbs *afflict* and *inflict* should not be confused: *afflict* refers to the immediate source of pain and trouble, and *inflict* to a secondary cause of the source of pain: a torturer inflicts pain *on* or *upon* their victim, who is afflicted *by* or *with* pain.

affluent (af´luənt) *a.* **1** wealthy, prosperous. **2** abundant, copious. **3** flowing freely. ~*n.* a tributary. **affluence** *n.* **1** wealth, prosperity. **2** (*formal*) the state of flowing in, influx. **3** †abundance. **affluently** *adv.* [F *affluent*, L *affluentem*, pres.p. of *affluere* (*af-*, *ad-*, to, *fluere*, flow)]

afflux (af´lŭks) *n.* a flowing towards or in. [med. L *affluxus* from *affluere*, see AFFLUENT]

afford (əfawd´) *v.t.* **1** to be able to bear the expense of, to have the money, the means etc. to. **2** to be able to ignore the disadvantages of (*We can't afford to offend them*). **3** to provide, furnish, supply. **affordable** *a.* **affordability** (-bil´-) *n.* [OE *ge-forthian* (*ge-*, intens., *forthian*, to further)]

afforest (əfor´ist) *v.t.* to plant trees on; to convert into forest. **afforestation** (-ā´shən) *n.* the act of converting waste or other land into forest. [med. L *afforestāre* (*af-*, *ad-*, to, *foresta*)]

affranchise (əfran´chīz) *v.t.* to make free; to set at liberty physically or morally. **affranchisement** (-chiz-) *n.* the act of making free, emancipation. [F *afranchiss-*, a stem of *afranchir*]

affray (əfrā´) *n.* a breach of the peace, a fight or disturbance involving two or more persons in a public place. ~†*v.t.* to frighten, to scare. [OF *effreër*, *esfreër*, late L *exfridāre* (*ex-*, intens., OHG *fridu*, cp. OE *frith*, peace)]

affreightment (əfrāt´mənt) *n.* (a contract for) the hiring of a ship for conveyance of goods by sea. [F *affrètement*, from *affréter*, to freight a ship]

affricate (af´rikət) *n.* a speech sound, such as *ch* in *church*, combining an initial plosive with a following fricative or spirant.

†**affright** (əfrīt´) *v.t.* to frighten, to terrify. ~*a.* frightened. ~*n.* **1** fright, terror. **2** a cause of fright or terror. **affrightedly** *adv.* [ME *afright*, p.p., OE *āfyrhted*, p.p. (*ā-*, intens., *fyrhtan*, to frighten)]

affrite AFREET.

affront (əfrŭnt´) *v.t.* **1** to insult openly. **2** to offend the dignity or modesty of. **3** to confront, esp. in a hostile way, to accost. ~*n.* **1** an open insult. **2** contemptuous, rude treatment. **affrontingly** *adv.* [OF *afronter*, late L *affrontāre* (*af-*, *ad-*, to, against, *frontem*, acc. of *frons*, forehead)]

affusion (əfū´zhən) *n.* **1** a pouring on of liquid. **2** baptism. [L *affundere* (*af-*, *ad-*, to, *fundere*, *fus-*, to pour)]

Afghan (af´gan) *a.* of or belonging to Afghanistan. ~*n.* **1** a native or inhabitant of Afghanistan. **2** the language of Afghanistan, Pashto. **3** an Afghan hound. **4** (**afghan**) a knitted or crocheted thick woollen blanket or shawl. **5** an Afghan coat. **Afghan coat** *n.* a type of sheepskin coat with the skin outside, often embroidered and with a shaggy border. **Afghan hound** *n.* a tall slim hunting dog with long silky hair. [Pashto *afghānī*]

aficionado (əfishənah´dō) *n.* (*pl.* **aficionados**) a keen follower or fan. **aficionada** (-də) *n.* (*pl.* **aficionadas**) a keen female follower or fan. [Sp. *aficionar*, from *afición*, affection]

afield (əfēld´) *adv.* **1** away, at a distance, abroad. **2** to or in the field.

afire (əfīə´) *adv., pred.a.* **1** on fire. **2** intensely or passionately aroused.

aflame (əflām´) *adv., pred.a.* **1** flaming. **2** feeling passionate emotion or intense excitement.

aflatoxin (af´lətoksin) *n.* a carcinogenic toxin produced in badly stored peanuts, maize etc. by the mould *Aspergillus flavus*. [*Aspergillus flavus*, TOXIN]

AFL-CIO *abbr.* American Federation of Labor and Congress of Industrial Organizations.

afloat (əflōt´) *a., adv.* **1** floating. **2** at sea, aboard ship. **3**

out of debt, solvent. **4** in circulation, current. **5** covered with liquid. **6** in full swing. **7** moving about, adrift.

☒ **afluent** common misspelling of AFFLUENT.

aflutter (əflŭt´ə) *a., adv.* in an excited or nervous state.

AFM *abbr.* Air Force Medal.

afoot (əfut´) *adv.* **1** on foot. **2** in progress, in action.

afore (əfaw´) *adv., prep.* **1** †before. **2** †in front (of). **aforementioned** *a.* mentioned earlier. **aforethought** *a.* premeditated. [OE *onforan* (ON prep., *foran*, in front)]

a fortiori (ā fawtiaw´ri, ah) *adv.* with still more reason, much more, still more conclusively.

afoul (əfowl´) *a., adv.* fouled, entangled, in collision. **to fall/ run afoul of** (*N Am.*) to fall foul of.

afraid (əfrād´) *a.* **1** filled with fear, terrified. **2** apprehensive. **3** regretfully admitting or of the opinion. [p.p. of AFFRAY]

afreet (af´rēt, əfrēt´), **affrite, afrit** *n.* a demon or monster of Muslim mythology. [Arab. *ifrīt*]

afresh (əfresh´) *adv.* again, anew, freshly.

African (af´rikən) *a.* of or relating to Africa. ~*n.* **1** a native or inhabitant of Africa. **2** a person, wherever born, who belongs ethnologically to one of the African peoples. **Africana** (-kah´nə) *n.pl.* objects typical of or relating to Africa, esp. in the form of a collection. **African-American** *n.* a black American. ~*a.* of or relating to black Americans. **African elephant** *n.* the species of elephant, *Loxodonta africana*, found in Africa, which is larger than the Indian elephant and never domesticated. **Africanism** *n.* a characteristic of Africa or of African culture or language. **Africanist** *n.* a person who specializes in the study of African culture, affairs etc. **Africanize, Africanise** *v.t.* **1** to make African. **2** to bring under black African influence or control. **Africanization** (-zā´shən) *n.* **African mahogany** *n.* **1** any of various African hardwood trees, esp. of the genus *Khaya*, that resemble mahogany. **2** the wood obtained from these trees. **African violet** *n.* a tropical African plant, *Saintpaulia ionantha*, with velvety leaves and pink, white or violet flowers. [L *Africa*]

Africander AFRIKANDER.

Afrikaans (afrikahns´) *n.* the language, descended from and similar to Dutch, spoken by Afrikaners and some people of mixed descent in South Africa (one of the official languages of the Republic of South Africa).

Afrikander (afrikan´də), **Africander** *n.* **1** a breed of longhorn, humpbacked cattle originating from southern Africa; an animal of this breed. **2** a breed of southern African fat-tailed sheep; an animal of this breed. **3** †an Afrikaner. [Afrikaans *Afrikaander*, from Dut. *Afrikaner* assim. to *Hollander* etc.]

Afrikaner (afrikah´nə) *n.* **1** a person born in South Africa of white parents whose mother tongue is Afrikaans. **2** a S African gladiolus. **Afrikanerdom** *n.* (*esp. S Afr.*) **1** the Afrikaner people collectively. **2** their nationalistic feeling or consciousness. **3** their former political ascendancy. [Dut.]

afrit AFREET.

Afro (af´rō) *a.* (of a hairstyle) characterized by thick, bushy hair. ~*n.* (*pl.* **Afros**) an Afro hairstyle.

Afro- (af´rō) *comb. form* of or relating to Africa or Africans.

Afro-American (afrōəmer´ikən) *n., a.* AFRICAN-AMERICAN (under AFRICAN).

Afro-Caribbean (afrōkaribē´ən, -kərib´iən) *n.* a person of African descent from the Caribbean. ~*a.* of or relating to Afro-Caribbeans.

Afrocentric (afrōsen´trik) *a.* **1** centred on African or Afro-American history and culture, esp. in order to promote a sense of cultural pride and identity in black Americans. **2** regarding African affairs, culture etc. as pre-eminent.

afrormosia (afrəmō´ziə) *n.* **1** any tree of the African genus *Afrormosia*, with dark hard wood used for furniture. **2** this wood. [L *Afr-*, *Afer*, Afr. *Ormosia*, genus name]

aft (ahft) *a., adv.* **1** towards or at the stern of a vessel. **2** abaft. [OE *æftan*]

after (ahf´tə) *prep.* **1** at a later time than. **2** behind. **3** in pursuit or search of. **4** in view of, considering. **5** in spite of. **6** concerning. **7** (of a name) with reference to. **8** next in rank or importance to. **9** in imitation of; from an original by. **10** according to. ~*a.* **1** later, subsequent. **2** located (further) towards the rear or stern. ~*adv.* **1** later, subsequently. **2** behind. ~*conj.* at a later time than that when. **after all** ALL. **after one's own heart** HEART. **after you** a polite formula inviting someone to go ahead. **afterbirth** *n.* the placenta, the secundine. **afterburner** *n.* **1** a device that initiates afterburning in a jet engine. **2** a device that removes or neutralizes potentially dangerous components of the exhaust gases of an internal-combustion engine. **afterburning** *n.* **1** the injection of fuel into the hot exhaust gases of a jet engine to generate extra thrust. **2** irregular burning of fuel in a rocket motor after the cessation of the main burning. **3** combustion that persists in an internal-combustion engine after the ignition has been switched off. **aftercare** *n.* **1** care or supervision following a person's discharge from hospital, prison etc. **2** after-sales service to a customer. **3** subsequent care or maintenance. **afterdamp** *n.* choke damp; carbon dioxide gas resulting from the combustion of firedamp in coal mines. **afterdeck** *n.* the deck behind the bridge of a ship. **after-effect** *n.* an effect that follows some time after the cause. **afterglow** *n.* **1** a glow in the western sky after sunset. **2** (*coll.*) a feeling of pleasure after an enjoyable experience. **after-hours** *a.* occurring after normal working, business etc. hours. **after-image** *n.* the image that remains for a moment after looking away from an object at which one has been gazing steadily. **afterlife** *n.* **1** life after death. **2** a person's life subsequent to the time in question. **aftermarket** *n.* **1** the market in components and spares. **2** (on the Stock Exchange) the market in shares subsequent to their original issue. **afterpains** *n.pl.* the contractions which follow childbirth, and by which the afterbirth is expelled. **afterpiece** *n.* a short piece acted after a more important play. **afters** *n.pl.* (*coll.*) what follows the main course at a meal. **after-school** *a.* occurring after normal school hours. **aftershave** *n.* a cosmetic, usu. astringent, lotion applied to the face after shaving. **aftershock** *a.* a tremor occurring after the main shock of an earthquake. **aftertaste** *n.* **1** a taste that persists after eating or drinking. **2** an impression or feeling that remains. **afterthought** *n.* **1** something that one thinks of or does after the original or proper occasion for it is past. **2** a belated addition. **afterward, afterwards** *adv.* **1** subsequently. **2** at a later period. [OE *æfter* (*af*, off, *ter*, comp. suf.; cp. Gr. *apo-ter-o*)]

aftermath (ahf´təmahth) *n.* **1** consequences or after-effects. **2** a second crop of grass springing up after the first has been mowed. [OE *mæth*, a mowing]

aftermost (ahf´təməst) *a.* nearest the stern. [OE *æftemæst*, superlative]

afternoon (ahf´tənoon) *n.* **1** the latter part of the day between noon or lunchtime and evening. **2** the later part of something. ~*a.* occurring during the afternoon. ~*int.* (*coll.*) good afternoon. **afternoons** *adv.* (*coll.*) during most afternoons. **afternoon tea** *n.* a light meal, usu. served in the late afternoon, typically consisting of small sandwiches, scones, cakes and biscuits etc. accompanied by cups of tea.

AG *abbr.* **1** adjutant-general. **2** attorney general. **3** Aktiengesellschaft, a German joint-stock company.

Ag *chem. symbol* silver. [L *argentum*]

ag- (ag, əg) *pref.* AD-, assim. to *g*, e.g. *aggravate, aggrieve*.

Aga® (ah´gə) *n.* a type of stove with several ovens which is permanently lit. **Aga saga** *n.* (*facet.*) a novel featuring middle-class country life.

aga (ah´gə), **agha** *n.* a Turkish civil or military officer of high rank. **Aga Khan** *n.* the nominated hereditary spiritual head of the Ismaili sect of Muslims. [Turk. *agha*, a master]

again (əgen´, əgān´) *adv.* 1 a second time, once more; afresh, anew. 2 in addition. 3 moreover, besides. 4 on the other hand. **again and again** with frequent repetition, repeatedly. [OE *ongean* (*on*, prep., on or in, *gagn, gegn*, in a direct line with, opposite)]

against (əgenst´, əgānst´) *prep.* 1 in opposition to, opposite to, in contrast to. 2 in contact with, in preparation or provision for. **against the clock** CLOCK[1]. **against the grain** GRAIN. [AGAIN]

agal (agahl´) *n.* a band worn by Bedouin Arabs that keeps the keffiyeh in place. [Arab. *ikāl*, bond, rope]

agama (ag´əmə, əgah´mə) *n.* any land lizard of the Old World genus *Agama*.

agamic (əgam´ik), **agamous** (ag´əməs) *a.* characterized by absence of sexual action, asexual, parthenogenetic. **agamically** *adv.* [Gr. *agamos* (*a-*, not, *gamos*, marriage)]

agamogenesis (agəmōjen´əsis) *n.* asexual reproduction. **agamogenetic** (-net´-) *a.* of or relating to agamogenesis, generated or reproduced asexually. **agamogenetically** *adv.* [Gr. *agamos*, GENESIS]

agamospermy (agəməspœ´mi) *n.* the formation of seeds without fertilization by division of the ovule. [Gr., as AGAMIC, *sperma*, seed]

agamous AGAMIC.

agapanthus (agəpan´thəs) *n.* an ornamental plant with bright blue flowers, of the African genus *Agapanthus* and of the order Liliaceae. [Gr. *agapē*, love, *anthos*, a flower]

agape[1] (əgāp´) *a., adv.* in an attitude or condition of wondering expectation.

agape[2] (ag´əpē) *n.* (*pl.* **agapes, agapae** (-pē)) 1 a 'love-feast', a kind of feast of fellowship held by the early Christians in connection with the Lord's Supper. 2 Christian love. [Gr. *agapē*, brotherly love]

agar-agar (āgah·ā´gah), **agar** *n.* a gelatinous substance obtained from seaweeds and used for the artificial cultivation of bacteria. [Malay]

agaric (əgar´ik) *n.* any fungus of the family *Agaricaceae*, which have a cap and a stalk and include the edible mushroom. ~*a.* fungoid. [L *agaricum*, Gr. *agarikon*]

agate (ag´ət, -āt) *n.* 1 any semi-pellucid variety of chalcedony, marked with bands or clouds, or infiltrated by other minerals, and used for seals, brooches etc. 2 a coloured toy marble that resembles this. 3 (*N Am.*) ruby or 5½ point type. [F *agathe*, It. *àgata*, L *achātes*, Gr. *achatēs*]

agave (əgā´vi) *n.* any of a genus of spiny-leaved plants, *Agave*, that includes the century plant. [L *agave*, Gr. *agauē*]

agaze (əgāz´) *adv.* (*poet.*) gazing, in a gazing attitude.

age (āj) *n.* 1 the length of time that a person or thing has existed. 2 a period or stage of life. 3 a distinct period of the past, an epoch; a period of geological time; a generation. 4 (*usu. pl., coll.*) a long time. 5 the latter portion of life. 6 (legal) maturity, majority. ~*v.i.* (*pres.p.* **ageing, aging**, *past, p.p.* **aged**) 1 to show the signs of becoming older. 2 to grow old. 3 to mature. ~*v.t.* to cause to grow old or to show signs of age. **of age** having reached the full legal age (18). **over age** OVER. **under age** UNDER. **age bracket** *n.* those people whose ages fall between two particular points, considered as a group. **aged** (ājd, ā´jid) *a.* 1 (*pred.*) of a certain age. 2 old. 3 that has been subject to ageing. 4 (of a horse) over six years old. ~*n.pl.* (**the aged**) old people. **agedness** *n.* the state of being old, the state of having attained a certain age. **age group** *n.* a group of people or things classed together by virtue of their age. **ageing, aging** *a.* 1 becoming or appearing older. 2 (esp. of an item of dress) making the wearer appear older. ~*n.* 1 growing older. 2 maturing; the process of developing or being allowed to develop its full strength, taste etc. 3 giving the appearance of greater age. 4 a change in the properties of certain metals that occurs after heat treatment or cold working. **ageism** *n.* discrimination on grounds of age. **ageist** *a.* supporting or practising ageism. ~*n.* an ageist person. **ageless** (-lis) *a.* never growing aged, never coming to an end. **age-long** *a.* lasting a very long time. **age of consent** *n.* the age at which a person's consent is legally valid, esp. a person's consent to sexual intercourse. **age of discretion** *n.* the age when one is judged able to using one's discretion (in English law, 14). **age-old** *a.* that has been in existence for a very long time. **age-range** *n.* the span of ages between two particular points. [OF *aage, edage*, late L *aetāticum* (L *aetas -atis*, from *aevitas aevum*, an age)]

-age (ij) *suf.* forming nouns, denoting actions, as in *breakage, passage*; a collection, group or set, as in *acreage, peerage*; a state or condition, as in *dotage, bondage*; a charge or fee payable, as in *postage*; the result of an action, as in *damage, wreckage*; a place or house, as in *anchorage, orphanage*. [OF *-age*, late L *-āticum*, neut. of a. in *-āticus*]

agee (əjē´) *adv.* (*Sc.*) 1 to one side. 2 awry. [*a-*, on, GEE[1], to move aside]

ageism, ageless etc. AGE.

agency AGENT.

agenda (əjen´də) *n.* 1 (*pl.* **agendas**) a list of the business to be transacted. 2 (*pl.*) things to be done, engagements to be kept. **on the agenda** requiring attention, requiring to be done. **agendum** *n.* a thing to be done, an engagement to be kept. [L, pl. of *agendum*, neut. ger. of *agere*, to do]

agent (ā´jənt) *n.* 1 a person who acts or transacts business on behalf of another. 2 a person or company that offers a specific service or acts as a broker. 3 a person who or something which exerts power; something that produces an effect; the material cause or instrument. 4 a travelling salesperson. 5 a spy. **agency** *n.* (*pl.* **agencies**) 1 a commercial organization offering a specific service. 2 a place where an agent conducts business. 3 the business, functions etc. of an agent. 4 causative action, instrumentality. 5 active working, operation. 6 immediate or intervening action. 7 (*esp. N Am.*) an administrative department of a government. 8 a place of business, office, commercial organization. **agent-general** *n.* (*pl.* **agents-general**) a representative of the Australian state or a Canadian province. **agential** (ājen´shəl) *a.* 1 of or relating to an agent. 2 agentive. **agentive** (ā´jen-) *a.* (of an affix or noun case) that signifies the agent of the verb. ~*n.* the agentive case; a word in this case. **agent noun** *n.* a noun that denotes the person or thing that performs a particular action e.g. *speaker, accelerator.* **Agent Orange** *n.* a herbicide containing dioxin as an impurity, used as a defoliant in the Vietnam war (so called from the orange marking on the container). [L *agentem*, acc. of *agens*, pres.p. of *agere*, to do]

agent provocateur (azhã provokatœ´) *n.* (*pl.* **agents provocateurs** (azhã provokatœ´)) a person employed to detect suspected political offenders by leading them on to some overt action. [F]

ageratum (ajərā´təm) *n.* a plant of the tropical genus *Ageratum*, usu. having clusters of purple flowers. [Gr. *ageraton*, an aromatic herb]

agger (aj´ə) *n.* 1 a mound. 2 the rampart of a Roman camp. [L, from *aggere* (AD-, *gerere*, to carry)]

agglomerate[1] (əglom´ərāt) *v.t.* to heap up or collect into a ball or mass. ~*v.i.* to gather in a mass.

agglomeration (-āˊshən) *n.* 1 the act of agglomerating. 2 a mass, a heap. **agglomerative** *a.* [L *agglomerāre* (*ag-*, *ad-*, to, *glomus -meris*, a ball)]

agglomerate[2] (əglomˊərət) *a.* collected into a mass; heaped up. ~*n.* 1 a mass. 2 a mass of volcanic fragments united by heat. [as AGGLOMERATE[1]]

agglutinate[1] (əglooˊtināt) *v.t.* 1 to cause to adhere; to glue together. 2 to cause (bacteria, blood cells etc.) to collect into clumps. 3 to compound (simple words or roots) with little change into more complex terms. ~*v.i.* 1 to unite, cohere. 2 to form compound words. **agglutination** (-āˊshən) *n.* 1 the act of gluing or cementing. 2 the clumping together of red blood cells, bacteria etc. 3 the formation of simple word or roots into compound terms. **agglutinative** (-nə-) *a.* [L *agglutināre* (*ag-*, *ad-*, to, *gluten -inis*, glue)]

agglutinate[2] (əglooˊtinət) *a.* 1 glued together. 2 consisting of simple words, or roots, combined into compounds. [as AGGLUTINATE[1]]

aggrandize (əgranˊdīz), **aggrandise** *v.t.* 1 to make great in power, wealth, rank or reputation. 2 to cause to appear greater than in reality; to exaggerate. 3 to exalt. **aggrandizement** (-diz-), **aggrandization** (-zāˊshən) *n.* the act of aggrandizing; the state of being aggrandized. [F *agrandir* (lengthened stem *-iss-*), to greaten (L *ad-*, to, *grandis*)]

aggravate (agˊrəvāt) *v.t.* 1 to make worse or more severe. 2 (*coll.*) to exasperate, to provoke, to irritate. **aggravating** *a.* 1 provoking. 2 rendering less excusable. **aggravatingly** *adv.* **aggravation** (-āˊshən) *n.* 1 the act of aggravating; the state of being aggravated. 2 something which aggravates. 3 an addition to a burden, wrong, crime, abuse or charge. [L *aggravātus*, p.p. of *aggravāre* (*ad-*, to, *gravāre*, to make heavy, *gravis*, heavy)]

aggregate[1] (agˊrigāt) *v.t.* 1 to collect together. 2 to bring together into a mass or whole. ~*v.i.* 1 to form an aggregate. 2 to unite. **aggregation** (-āˊshən) *n.* 1 the act of collecting together; the state of being aggregated. 2 an aggregate. **aggregative** *a.* [L *aggregātus*, p.p. of *aggregāre* (*ag-*, *ad-*, to, *grex gregis*, a flock)]

aggregate[2] (agˊrigət) *a.* 1 collected together; collected into a mass. 2 formed of separate parts combined into a mass or whole. 3 consisting of florets united together. 4 consisting of individuals united in a compound organism. 5 composed of distinct minerals. ~*n.* 1 a mass formed by the union of individual units or particles; the total, the whole. 2 material, esp. crushed particles, to be bonded together with cement to form concrete. 3 (*Geol.*) a rock that consists of a number of different minerals. **in the aggregate** collectively. **aggregate fruit** *n.* a fruit, such as a blackberry, formed from several carpels derived from the same flower. [as AGGREGATE[1]]

aggress (əgresˊ) *v.i.* to begin an attack or quarrel. ~*v.t.* to attack, to assault. **aggression** (-shən) *n.* 1 (an) unprovoked attack or injury. 2 vigour, forcefulness or self-assertiveness. 3 violation of a country's territorial integrity or sovereignty by another country. 4 a hostile attitude or outlook. **aggressive** *a.* 1 involving an act of aggression. 2 offensive, pugnacious. 3 vigorous, forceful or self-assertive. 4 making the first attack. **aggressively** *adv.* **aggressiveness** *n.* **aggressor** *n.* the person, country etc. that begins hostilities, a quarrel etc. [F *aggresser*, late L *aggressāre*, freq. of *aggredior* (*ad-*, *gradior*, I walk)]

aggrieve (əgrēvˊ) *v.t.* 1 to cause grief, annoyance or pain to. 2 to perpetrate injustice against. **aggrieved** *a.* having a grievance. **aggrievedly** *adv.* [OF *agrever*, L *ad-*, *gravāre*, to weigh down (*gravis*, heavy)]

aggro (agˊrō) *n.* (*coll.*) 1 aggressive, annoying behaviour; troublemaking. 2 trouble, problems. [short for AGGRAVATION (under AGGRAVATE)]

agha AGA.

aghast (əgahstˊ) *a.* 1 dismayed; appalled, horrified. 2 struck with terror. [p.p. of obsolete v. *agast*, to frighten; OE *gǣstan*]

agile (ajˊīl) *a.* 1 having the ability to move quickly and gracefully. 2 mentally quick, nimble, active. **agilely** *adv.* **agility** (əjilˊ-) *n.* [L *agilis*, nimble (*agere*, to do)]

agin (əgin) *prep.* (*dial. or facet.*) against. [obs. prep. *again*, against]

aging AGEING (under AGE).

agio (ajˊiō) *n.* (*pl.* **agios**) 1 the difference in value between one kind of currency and another. 2 money-changing. 3 the charge for changing notes for cash, or one kind of money for another. **agiotage** (-tij) *n.* 1 money-changing. 2 speculation in stocks. 3 stock-jobbing. [It. *agio*, ease]

agist (əjistˊ) *v.t.* 1 to provide pasture for (the cattle of others) at a certain rate. 2 to lay a public rate on (land or landowners). [OF *agister* (*à*, to, *gister*, *géter*, to lodge)]

agitate (ajˊitāt) *v.t.* 1 to shake or move briskly. 2 to excite, to disturb, to perturb. 3 to consider, discuss, debate etc., in order to bring forward for public discussion. ~*v.i.* to arouse public feeling or opinion for or against something. **agitation** (-āˊshən) *n.* 1 the act of agitating; the state of being agitated. 2 commotion, perturbation. 3 attempts to stir up public excitement or to initiate action. **agitator** *n.* 1 a person who or something which agitates. 2 a person who excites or keeps up political agitation. 3 a mechanical contrivance for shaking and mixing. [L *agitātus*, p.p. of *agitāre*, freq. of *agere*, to drive]

agitato (ajitahˊtō) *adv.*, *a.* (*Mus.*) in an agitated manner. [It.]

agitprop (ajˊitprop) *n.* the dissemination, usu. through the arts, of political, esp. pro-Communist, propaganda. [Rus. *agitatsiya*, agitation, and *propaganda*]

aglet (agˊlit), **aiglet** (āˊ-), **aiguillette** (āgwiletˊ) *n.* 1 the metal tag of a lace. 2 a taglike ornament on a uniform. 3 a spangle. [F *aiguillette*, dim. of *aiguille*, needle (late L *acūcula*, L *acicula*, dim. of *acus*, needle)]

agley (əglāˊ) *adv.* (*Sc.*) astray, awry.

aglow (əglōˊ) *a.*, *adv.* in a glow.

AGM *abbr.* annual general meeting.

agma (agˊmə) *n.* 1 the symbol (ŋ) used to represent the speech sound ng as in *sing*. 2 this speech sound.

agnail (agˊnāl) *n.* a piece of torn skin or a sore at the root of a toe- or fingernail. [OE *angnægl* (*ang*, tight, painful, *nægl*, nail)]

agnate (agˊnāt) *n.* 1 a descendant through the male line from the same male ancestor. 2 a relative on the father's side. ~*a.* 1 related by descent from a common male ancestor. 2 related on the father's side. 3 allied, akin. **agnatic** (-natˊ-) *a.* of or relating to descent on the father's side. **agnation** (-nāˊshən) *n.* 1 relationship on the father's side. 2 descent from a common male ancestor, in contradistinction to cognation or descent from the same female ancestor. [F *agnat*, L *agnātus* (*ad-*, *gnātus*, born, p.p. of (*g*)*nascī* to be born)]

agnolotti (agnəlotˊi) *n.* small pieces of pasta stuffed with meat etc. [It.]

agnomen (agnōˊmən) *n.* (*pl.* **agnomina** (agnomˊinə)) a fourth name sometimes appended to the cognomen by the ancient Romans, usu. in honour of a great exploit. [L *ad-*, to, (*g*)*nōmen*, name]

agnosia (agnōˊsiə) *n.* loss of the ability to recognize familiar things or people, esp. after brain damage. [Gr. A-[3], GNOSIS, knowledge]

agnostic (əgnosˊtik) *n.* 1 a person who believes that knowledge of the existence of God is impossible. 2 a person who denies that humans have any knowledge except of material phenomena. 3 a person who professes uncertainty about any subject; a sceptic. ~*a.* of or relating to agnostics or their teachings.

agnostically *adv.* **agnosticism** (-sizm) *n.* **1** the teachings of the agnostics. **2** the state of being agnostic. [Gr. *agnōstos*, ignorant of, unknown, unknowable (*a-*, not, *gno-*, know)]

Agnus Dei (agnūs dā´ē) *n.* **1** a figure of a lamb bearing a flag or cross. **2** a part of the Mass beginning with the words *Agnus Dei*. **3** a musical setting of this part of the Mass. **4** a cake of wax stamped with such a figure of a lamb and blessed by the Pope. [L, the Lamb of God]

ago (əgō´) *adv.* before this time. [ME *agone*, p.p. of v. *ago* (*a-*, forth, GO[1])]

Usage note It is best to avoid the use of *since* rather than *that* or *when* after *ago*, as both *since* and *ago* imply an earlier period (so *It is 3 days since it happened, but 2 days ago that I was told*).

agog (əgog´) *a.*, *adv.* in a state of eager expectation. [perh. from OF *en gogues* (*gogue*, mirth, fun)]

-agog -AGOGUE.

agogic (əgoj´ik) *a.* of or characterized by variations of stress in speech or musical rhythm produced by the lengthening of a syllable or note. **agogics** *n.* variation of stress by lengthening of duration. [Gr. *agogē*, tendency]

à gogo (ə gō´gō) *adv.* in abundance, galore. [F]

-agogue (əgog), (*N Am.*) **-agog** *comb. form* **1** indicating a person or thing that leads, as in *demagogue*, *pedagogue*. **2** indicating a substance that stimulates the secretion of something as in *galactagogue*. [Gr. *agōgos*, leading]

agoing (əgō´ing) *adv.* in a state of motion.

agon (ā´gon, -gōn) *n.* (*pl.* **agones** (əgō´nēz)) **1** (in ancient Greece) a festival or games at which prizes were competed for. **2** a conflict, struggle. [Gr., contest, from *agein*, to lead]

agonic (əgon´ik) *a.* having no dip, denoting an imaginary line on the earth's surface, drawn through the two magnetic poles. [Gr. *agōnios*, without an angle (*a-*, not, *gōnia*, angle)]

agonist (ag´ənist) *n.* **1** any muscle whose action is opposed by another muscle. **2** a substance which, when combined with a receptor, triggers a physiological response. **3** a competitor in an agon; a person engaged in a struggle. **agonistic** (-nis´-), **agonistical** *a.* **1** of or relating to a chemical agonist. **2** combative, argumentative, very competitive. **3** (of animal behaviour) relating to conflict. **agonistically** *adv.* [Gr. *agōnistēs*, contestant, from *agōn*, contest, see AGON]

agonize (ag´ənīz), **agonise** *v.t.* to subject to extreme pain; to torture. *~v.i.* **1** to suffer agony. **2** to make desperate or convulsive efforts. **3** (*coll.*) to struggle desperately to come to a decision or conclusion (over). **agonized** *a.* expressing agony. **agonizing** *a.* causing agony. **agonizingly** *adv.* [L *agonizare*]

agony (ag´əni) *n.* (*pl.* **agonies**) **1** anguish of mind. **2** extreme physical pain. **3** the death struggle. **4** the mental anguish of Christ in Gethsemane. **to pile on the agony** (*coll.*) to exaggerate, to describe in the most sensational terms. **agony aunt** *n.* **1** the person who writes the replies for an agony column. **2** a woman who gives sympathetic advice. **agony column** *n.* **1** the part of a newspaper or magazine dealing with readers' problems. **2** the column in a newspaper devoted to advertisements for missing friends and other matters of a personal kind. **agony uncle** *n.* a man who writes the replies for an agony column. [L *agōnia*, from Gr. *agōnia*, contest (from *agōn*, see AGONIST)]

agora[1] (ag´ərə) *n.* the public square, forum or market place of an ancient Greek town. [Gr.]

agora[2] (agərah´) *n.* (*pl.* **agorot** (-rot´)) a monetary unit of Israel equal to one hundredth of a shekel. [Heb. *ăgōrāh*]

agoraphobia (agərəfō´biə) *n.* abnormal dread of open spaces. **agoraphobe** *n.* a person who suffers from agoraphobia. **agoraphobic** *a.*, *n.* [AGORA[1]]

agorot AGORA[2].

agouti (əgoo´ti), **agouty, aguti** *n.* (*pl.* **agoutis, agouties, aguties**) a small W Indian and S American rodent, *Dasyprocta agouti*. [Tupi *aguti*]

AGR *abbr.* advanced gas-cooled reactor.

agraffe (əgraf´), (*N Am. also*) **agrafe** *n.* **1** a sort of hook, formerly used as a clasp or fastening. **2** a cramp used by builders to hold stones together. [F *agrafe* (*à*, *grappe*, late L *grappa*, OHG *chrapfo*, hook)]

agraphia (əgraf´iə) *n.* loss of the cerebral power of expressing one's ideas in writing. **agraphic** *a.* [Gr. *a-*, not, *graphein*, to write]

agrarian (əgreə´riən) *a.* **1** of or relating to the land and cultivation. **2** of or relating to landed property or cultivated land. **3** (of plants) growing wild in the fields. **4** the epithet of an ancient Roman law pertaining to the division of conquered territory. *~n.* a person in favour of the redistribution of landed property. **agrarianism** *n.* **1** an equitable redistribution of land. **2** political agitation concerning land or land-tenure. [L *agrārius*, pertaining to land (*ager*, land)]

☒ **agravate** common misspelling of AGGRAVATE.

agree (əgrē´) *v.i.* **1** to be of one mind, to hold the same opinion. **2** to consent, to accede (to). **3** to live in concord. **4** to reach an agreement or settlement. **5** to harmonize, to coincide (with). **6** to suit; to have a beneficial effect, be good for. **7** to be in grammatical concord (with). *~v.t.* **1** to admit, to concede. **2** to reach agreement about. **3** to give consent or approval to. **4** to concert, to reconcile, to render consistent with one another. **to agree to differ** DIFFER. **to be agreed** to have reached agreement. [OF *agréer*, late L *aggrātāre* (*ad-*, to, *grātāre*, to make agreeable, from *grātus*, pleasing)]

agreeable (əgrē´əbəl) *a.* **1** affording pleasure, pleasing, pleasant. **2** favourable, disposed to. **3** corresponding, conformable, suitable to. **agreeability** (-bil´-), **agreeableness** *n.* **agreeably** *adv.* [as AGREE]

agreement (əgrē´mənt) *n.* **1** the fact of being of one mind; concurrence in the same opinion. **2** an arrangement mutually acceptable; a contract duly executed and legally binding. **3** conformity, correspondence. **4** grammatical concord.

☒ **agression** common misspelling of AGGRESSION (under AGGRESS).

agrestic (əgres´tik) *a.* **1** rural, rustic. **2** clownish, uncouth. [L *agrestis* (*ager*, a field)]

agribusiness (ag´ribiznis) *n.* **1** agriculture conducted as a strictly commercial enterprise, esp. using advanced technology. **2** an organization engaged in this. **3** the businesses involved in producing and marketing farm produce taken as a whole. [AGRICULTURE, BUSINESS]

agriculture (ag´rikŭlchə) *n.* the science and practice of cultivating the soil, growing crops and rearing livestock. **agricultural** (-kŭl´-) *a.* of or relating to the culture of the soil. **agriculturalist** (-kŭl´-), **agriculturist** *n.* a person engaged in agriculture. **agriculturally** *adv.* [L *agricultūra* (*ager agri*, field, *cultūra*, CULTURE)]

agrimony (ag´rimәni) *n.* (*pl.* **agrimonies**) **1** any plant of the genus *Agrimonia*, one species of which (*A. eupatoria*) was formerly valued as a tonic. **2** any of various other similar plants, e.g. hemp agrimony. [late L *agrimōnia*, L *argemōnia*, Gr. *argemōnē*]

agro- (ag´rō) *comb. form* of or relating to fields, soil or agriculture. [Gr. *agros*, land]

agrobiology (agrōbīol´əji) *n.* the study of plant nutrition etc., in relation to soil management. **agrobiological** (-loj´-) *a.* **agrobiologist** *n.*

agrochemical (agrōkem´ikəl) *n.* a chemical for use on the land or in farming. *~a.* of or producing agrochemicals.

agroforestry (agrōfor´istri) *n.* farming that incorporates the cultivation of trees.

agronomy (əgron´əmi) *n.* the science of land management, cultivation and crop production. **agronomic** (-nom´-), **agronomical** *a.* of or relating to agronomy. **agronomics** *n.* the science of land management as a branch of economics. **agronomist** *n.* a person who is skilled in agronomy. [Gr. *agronomos*, an overseer (*agros*, land, *nomos*, dispensing, from *nemein*, to dispense)]

aground (əgrownd´) *a., adv.* **1** on the shallow bottom of any water. **2** on the ground. [*a*-, on, GROUND[1]]

agt. *abbr.* agent.

ague (ā´gū) *n.* **1** a malarial fever, marked by successive hot and cold paroxysms, the latter attended with shivering. **2** any fit of shivering or shaking. **agued** *a.* affected with ague. **aguish** *a.* of the nature of or subject to ague. [OF *ague*, fem.a., L *acūta*, sharp]

aguti AGOUTI.

AH *abbr.* in the year of the Hegira (AD 622), from which is dated the Muslim era. [L *anno Hegirae*]

ah (ah) *int.* used to express various emotions, according to the manner in which it is uttered, e.g. sorrow, regret, fatigue, relief, surprise, admiration, appeal, remonstrance, aversion, contempt, mockery. [OF *a*, L *ah*]

aha (əhah´) *int.* an exclamation of surprise, triumph or mockery. [*a* combined with HA[1]]

ahead (əhed´) *adv.* **1** in front, further on. **2** forward, esp. in a straight line. **3** in the future. **ahead of 1** in front of, in the line of progress of. **2** further on than, making better progress than. **3** in advance of (*ahead of his time*). **4** awaiting (someone) in the future. **to be ahead** to be in the lead, to be winning.

ahem (əhem´) *int.* an exclamation used to attract attention or merely to gain time. [HEM[2]]

ahimsa (əhim´sə) *n.* the Hindu and Buddhist doctrine of non-violence towards all living things. [Sansk. *ahimsā*, without injury]

ahistorical (āhistor´ikəl) *a.* not historical; taking no account of history. [A-[3], HISTORICAL (under HISTORIC)]

-aholic (əhol´ik), **-oholic** *comb. form* (a person) having an addiction. [after ALCOHOLIC (under ALCOHOL)]

ahoy (əhoi´) *int.* (*Naut.*) used in hailing another ship or to attract attention. [HOY[1]]

à huis clos (a wē klō´) *adv.* behind closed doors, in private; in camera. [F]

AI *abbr.* **1** artificial insemination. **2** (*Comput.*) artificial intelligence.

ai (ah´ē) *n.* (*pl.* **ais**) a three-toed sloth, *Bradypus tridactylus*, from S America. [Braz. Sp. *aï*, sound of its cry]

AID *abbr.* **1** Agency for International Development (in the US). **2** artificial insemination by donor.

aid (ād) *v.t.* to assist, to help; to give financial assistance to. ~*n.* **1** help, assistance. **2** anything, e.g. an implement, machine, book, that assists in the performance of a task. **3** financial or material assistance given by one country to another. **4** (*Hist.*) a subsidy granted by Parliament to the sovereign. **5** in medieval history, a contribution by a vassal for the ransom of his lord, on the occasion when the lord's eldest son was made a knight, or to furnish a dowry for his eldest daughter. **in aid of 1** in support of. **2** (*coll.*) intended for. [OF *aider*, L *adjutāre*, freq. of *adjuvāre* (*ad*-, to, *juvāre*, to help)]

aide (ād) *n.* an assistant, a help. **aide-de-camp** (ād·dəkamp´, kā´, ed-) *n.* (*pl.* **aides-de-camp** (-kamp´, -kā´)) an officer who receives and transmits the orders of a general or other senior officer. **aide-mémoire** (ādmemwah´) *n.* (*pl.* **aides-mémoire, aides-mémoires** (ādmemwah´)) an aid to memory, a memorandum, a memorandum-book. [F]

Aids (ādz), **AIDS** *n.* a condition in which the body's immune system is attacked by a virus, leaving the body defenceless against disease. **Aids-related complex** *n.* a condition in which a patient infected with the Aids virus suffers early, minor symptoms which may develop into Aids. [*a*cquired *i*mmune *d*eficiency *s*yndrome]

aiglet AGLET.

aigrette (ā´grit, āgret´) *n.* **1** an ornamental feather or plume, esp. from the egret. **2** a spray of gems worn on the head. **3** any light feathery tuft or spray. [F *aigrette*]

aiguille (āgwēl´, ā´-) *n.* **1** a slender, needle-shaped peak of rock. **2** an instrument used in boring holes for blasting. [F, see AGLET]

aiguillette AGLET.

AIH *abbr.* artificial insemination by husband.

aikido (īkē´dō) *n.* a Japanese martial art using throws, locks and twisting techniques to turn an opponent's own momentum against them. [Jap. *ai*, harmonize, *ki*, spirit, *dō*, way]

ail (āl) *v.i.* to be in pain, trouble or ill health. ~†*v.t.* to trouble, to cause pain or uneasiness of body or mind to. **ailing** *a.* affected with illness, sick, suffering. **ailment** *n.* a (slight) disorder or illness, sickness, indisposition. [OE *eglan* (Goth. *agljan*), from *egle*, troublesome (Goth. *aglus*, difficult, hard)]

aileron (ā´ləron) *n.* the hinged portion on the rear edge of the wing-tip of an aeroplane that controls lateral balance. [F, tip of a wing]

aim (ām) *v.t.* **1** to point at a target with (a missile or weapon), to level (a gun) at a target. **2** to direct (a blow, remark, criticism) at. ~*v.i.* **1** to point a weapon, direct a blow etc. (at). **2** to intend, to endeavour (to do). **3** to try to achieve or attain. **4** to take aim. ~*n.* **1** an intention, a purpose. **2** the fact of aiming a weapon, missile etc. **3** the point or object aimed at. **4** the direction in which a missile travels. **to take aim** to direct a gun, missile etc. (at). **aimer** *n.* **aimless** *a.* purposeless, objectless. **aimlessly** *adv.* **aimlessness** *n.* [OF *aësmer*, late L *adaestimāre* (perh. confused with OF *esmer*, L *aestimāre*, to reckon)]

ain't (ānt) *contr.* (*coll.*) **1** are not. **2** is not, am not. **3** have not, has not. [contr. of *aren't*, *are not*]

Ainu (ī´noo) *n.* (*pl.* **Ainu, Ainus**) **1** an indigenous Japanese people living in N Japan, Sakhalin, the Kuriles and adjacent parts. **2** the language of the Ainu. [Ainu, man]

aioli (īō´li), **aïoli** *n.* mayonnaise flavoured with garlic. [F. from Prov. *ai*, garlic, *oli*, oil]

air (eə) *n.* **1** the mixture of gases which envelops the eart, chiefly consisting of oxygen and nitrogen; the atmosphere. **2** open space. **3** the medium of broadcasting, airwaves. **4** (the operation of, or transportation by) aircraft. **5** a distinctive quality, an aura, atmosphere. **6** manner, appearance, mien, gesture. **7** (*usu. pl.*) affectation, haughtiness. **8** a light wind, a breeze. **9** a tune, melody, either solo or in harmony. ~*v.t.* **1** to expose to open or fresh air, to ventilate. **2** to dry or warm (as clothes) by exposing to heat. **3** to express publicly (a grievance, an opinion). **4** to show off, to parade. ~*v.i.* to become aired. **by air** in an aircraft. **in the air 1** (of an opinion, feeling) perceptible; current or becoming current. **2** (of a project, plan) as yet unsettled, in the process of being decided. **off the air** not broadcasting. **on the air** broadcasting; being broadcast. **to give oneself airs** to behave in an affected or haughty manner. **to take the air** to go for an airing. **to tread/walk on air** to feel elated. **up in the air** as yet unsettled, in the process of being decided. **air bag** *n.* a safety device in a car consisting of a bag that inflates automatically in a collision, cushioning the passengers against the impact. **air base** *n.* a place used as a base for operations by, or for the housing of, military aircraft. **air-bed**, (*N Am.*) **air mattress** *n.* a bed or mattress inflated with air. **air bladder** *n.* a vesicle containing air, esp. the swimming-bladder of fishes. **airborne** *a.* **1** (of troops etc.) carried by air. **2** (of an aircraft) in the air, in flight. **air brake** *n.* 1 a brake worked by compressed air. 2 a device, esp. a movable flap, to reduce the speed of an aircraft. **airbrick** *n.* a perforated brick or iron grating for admitting air through a wall. **air bridge** *n.* a service by air transport between two places. **airbrush** *n.* a device for spraying paint by compressed air. ~*v.t.* to paint with an airbrush. **air burst** *n.* the explosion of a bomb in the air. **Airbus®** *n.* a particular type of large passenger jet aeroplane. **Air Chief Marshal** *n.* an officer in the RAF corresponding in rank to a general in the Army. **Air Commodore** *n.* an officer in the RAF corresponding in rank to a brigadier in the Army. **air-condition** *v.t.* to equip (as a building) with an air-conditioning system. **air-conditioned** *a.* **air-conditioner** *n.* **air-conditioning** *n.* an apparatus for, or the process of, purifying the air circulating in a room or building and controlling its temperature and humidity. **air-cool** *v.t.* to cool (an engine) by circulating air. **air corridor** *n.* a path for air traffic in an area where flying is restricted. **air cover** *n.* 1 protection for ground troops or operations provided by aircraft. 2 the aircraft providing this protection. **aircraft** *n.* (*pl.* **aircraft**) a flying-machine of any type, whether heavier or lighter than air. **aircraft carrier** *n.* a ship designed for the housing and servicing of aircraft, with a deck where they can take off and land. **aircraftman, aircraftwoman** *n.* (*pl.* **aircraftmen, aircraftwomen**) (a person of) the lowest rank in the RAF. **aircrew** *n.* 1 (*pl.* **aircrews**) the crew of an aircraft. 2 (*usu. as pl.* **aircrew**) a member of such a crew. **air curtain** *n.* a down-draught of warm air across an entrance to maintain the temperature inside a building. **air cushion** *n.* 1 a cushion or pillow inflated to make it resilient. 2 the body of air supporting a hovercraft. **airdrome** AERODROME. **airdrop** *n.* a delivery of supplies or troops by parachute from an aircraft. ~*v.t.* (*pres.p.* **airdropping,** *past, p.p.* **airdropped**) to drop (supplies etc.) by parachute. **air-dry** *v.t.* (*3rd pers. sing. pres.* **air-dries,** *pres.p.* **air-drying,** *past, p.p.* **air-dried**) to dry by exposing to the air. **air-engine** *n.* any engine driven by the compression and expansion of heated air. **air-entrained concrete** *n.* concrete that has minute air bubbles dispersed through in order to improve its frost resistance. **airer** *n.* a clothes-horse. **airfield** *n.* a field specially prepared for the landing and taking-off of aircraft. **airflow** *n.* the flow of air past a moving surface or vehicle, or as created in a wind tunnel. **airfoil** AEROFOIL. **air force** *n.* the branch of a country's armed forces organized for warfare in the air. **air-force blue** *n.* a greyish blue colour as used for uniforms in the RAF. **airframe** *n.* the structure and external surfaces of an aircraft or rocket, excluding the engines. **airglow** *n.* the faint light produced by radiation from the upper atmosphere, detectable in the night sky. **airgun** *n.* a gun from which missiles are projected by compressed air. **airhead** *n.* 1 (*Mil.*) a base inside enemy territory for aircraft operations. 2 (*sl.*) a stupid person. **airhole** *n.* 1 an opening to admit air. 2 a flaw in a casting. 3 an air pocket. **air hostess** *n.* (*dated*) an air stewardess. **airing** *n.* 1 exposure to the free action of the air, or to a fire or heat. 2 a walk or ride in the open air. **airing cupboard** *n.* a heated cupboard fitted with racks for airing, esp. sheets and other household linen. **air-intake** *n.* 1 an opening or valve that allows air to be drawn into something, esp. an engine. 2 the amount of air drawn in. **air jacket** *n.* 1 a heat-retaining or heat-regulating casing filled with air. 2 a life jacket. **air lane** *n.* a path regularly used by aircraft. **airless** *a.* 1 not open to the air. 2 close, musty. 3 calm, still. **airlessness** *n.* **air letter** *n.* AEROGRAM. **airlift** *n.* the transport of supplies, goods etc. by air, esp. in an emergency. **airline** *n.* 1 a commercial organization operating regular transport by air. 2 a pipe through which air is supplied to a diver. 3 (*esp. N Am.*) a beeline. **airliner** *n.* a passenger-carrying aeroplane flying along a regular air route. **airlock** *n.* 1 a chamber that has airtight doors and allows entrance to or exit from an area where the air is under pressure. 2 an obstruction in a pipe caused by a bubble of air. **airmail** *n.* 1 mail conveyed by aircraft. 2 the postal system of conveying mail by air. **airman** *n.* (*pl.* **airmen**) 1 a pilot or a member of the crew of an aircraft. 2 a non-commissioned member of the RAF. **Air Marshal** *n.* an officer in the RAF corresponding in rank to a lieutenant-general in the Army. **air mechanic** *n.* a mechanic employed in the repair of aircraft. **air mile** *n.* 1 a nautical mile used for measuring distances flown by aircraft. 2 (*usu. pl.*) a point entitling the buyer of an airline ticket or other product to free air travel for a certain distance. **airmiss** *n.* a near-collision of aircraft. **air piracy** *n.* the hijacking of an aircraft. **airplane** *n.* (*N Am.*) an aeroplane. **air plant** *n.* an epiphyte. **air pocket** *n.* 1 an area of rarefied atmosphere where an aircraft is apt to drop unexpectedly. 2 an air-filled space, e.g. in a pipe. **airport** *n.* 1 a place where civil aircraft take off and land, often with extensive passenger facilities, customs, freight terminals etc. 2 an opening to admit air. **air power** *n.* the strength of a country in military aircraft. **air pump** *n.* a device for pumping air into or out of something. **air raid** *n.* an attack on a town, troops etc. by hostile aircraft. **air rifle** *n.* a rifle which operates by compressed air. **air sac** *n.* 1 a tiny air cell in the lungs, an alveolus. 2 an air-filled space connecting with the lungs in birds. **airs and graces** *n.pl.* would-be elegant or genteel mannerisms intended to impress. **air screw** *n.* the propeller of an aircraft. **air-sea rescue** *n.* 1 rescue from the sea by aircraft. 2 the combined use of boats and aircraft for rescue at sea. **air shaft** *n.* a vertical passage into a mine, tunnel etc. for the purpose of ventilation. **airship** *n.* a lighter-than-air flying-machine driven by an engine. **airsick** *a.* affected by airsickness. **airsickness** *n.* nausea caused by the motion of aircraft. **airside** *n.* the part of an airport complex beyond the passport control, customs etc., where the aircraft are boarded or loaded (cp. LANDSIDE (under LAND)). **airspace** *n.* the atmosphere above (a certain part of) the earth, esp. above a particular country. **air speed** *n.* the speed of an aeroplane or airship relative to the air, as distinct from its speed relative to the ground. **air station** *n.* an airfield, usu. one with facilities for aircraft maintenance. **airstream** *n.* a current of air. **air strike** *n.* an attack by aircraft. **airstrip** *n.* a strip of even ground where aircraft can take off or land. **air terminal** *n.* a building where passengers assemble to be taken to an airport. **airtight** *a.* 1 not allowing air to pass in or out. 2 unassailable. **airtime** *n.* broadcasting time, esp. on radio, allotted to a particular topic, record etc. **air-to-air** *a.* 1 between aircraft in flight. 2 launched from one aircraft at another. **air-to-surface** *a.* launched from an aircraft at a target on the earth's surface. **air-traffic control** *n.* the ground-based organization which determines the altitudes, routes etc. to be used by aircraft in a particular area. **air-traffic controller** *n.* **Air Vice-Marshal** *n.* an officer in the RAF corresponding in rank to a major-general in the Army. **airwaves** *n.pl.* (radio) broadcasting channels. **airway** *n.* 1 a passage for air into the lungs; a tubelike device inserted into the throat to enable air to reach the lungs. 2 a fully organized air route. 3 a tunnel in a mine, fitted with valvelike doors, for the passage of air in one direction. **airwoman** *n.* (*pl.* **airwomen**) 1 a female pilot or member of an aircraft crew. 2 a female non-commissioned member of the RAF. **airworthy** *a.* (of an aeroplane) examined and passed as fit for flying. **airworthiness** *n.* [OF *air*, L *āer-em*, Gr. *aēr* (*aēmi*, I blow)]

Airedale (eə´dāl) *n.* a large breed of terrier with a rough-haired, tan-coloured coat; a dog of this breed. [*Airedale* in Yorkshire]

☒ **airoplane** common misspelling of AEROPLANE.

airt (eət) *n.* (*Sc.*) a point of the compass, a direction. [Gael. *aird*]

airy (eə´ri) *a.* (*comp.* **airier**, *superl.* **airiest**) **1** well-ventilated. **2** spacious; uncluttered or unconstricted. **3** nonchalant; flippant; offhand. **4** light as air. **5** light and graceful in movement. **6** visionary; unreal. **7** situated high up in the air, lofty. **8** of or belonging to the air. **airily** *adv.* in a nonchalant or offhand way. **airiness** *n.* **airy-fairy** *a.* (*coll.*) fanciful, unrealistic.

aisle (īl) *n.* **1** a division of a church, esp. one parallel to, and separated by pillars from, the nave. **2** a passage between the seats in a church, theatre, cinema etc. **3** a passage between rows of shelving in a supermarket. **4** (*chiefly N Am.*) a corridor, gangway. **aisled** *a.* having aisles. [OF *ele*, L *āla* (*axilla*) wing]

ait (āt), **eyot** (āt, ā´ət) *n.* a small island, esp. one in a river or lake. [OE *īggath, īgeoth* (*īg*), island]

aitch (āch) *n.* the letter *h.* **to drop one's aitches** DROP. [phonetic spelling]

aitchbone (āch´bōn) *n.* **1** the rump bone. **2** the cut of beef over this bone. [OF *nache*, sing. of *naches*, the buttocks, L *naticas -icae*, dim. of *nates* (for loss of *n*, cp. ADDER[2])]

ajar[1] (əjah´) *a., adv.* (of a door) partly open. [obs. *char* (OE *on cerre*, on the turn)]

ajar[2] (əjah´) *adv.* in a jarring state, at discord. [A-[1], JAR[1]]

AK *abbr.* Alaska.

aka, AKA *abbr.* also known as.

Akela (ahkā´lə) *n.* the adult leader of a group of Cub Scouts. [the name of the leader of the wolfpack in *The Jungle Book* by Rudyard Kipling]

akimbo (əkim´bō) *adv.* with the hands resting on the hips and the elbows turned outwards. [ME *in kenebowe*, in a keen (sharp) bow]

akin (əkin´) *a.* **1** allied by blood relationship. **2** allied in properties or character. [A-[1], KIN]

Akkadian (əkā´diən), **Accadian** *n.* **1** a member of a Semitic people inhabiting the ancient Babylonian kingdom of Akkad (now central Mesopotamia) before 2000 BC. **2** the language of this people. ~*a.* of or relating to this people or their language.

☒ **aknowledge** common misspelling of ACKNOWLEDGE.

akvavit AQUAVIT.

AL *abbr.* Alabama.

Al *chem. symbol* aluminium.

al- (əl) *pref.* AD-, assim. to *l*, e.g. *alliteration.*

-al[1] (əl) *suf.* forming adjectives: *annual, equal, mortal.* [L *-ālis*]

-al[2] (əl) *suf.* forming nouns, esp. denoting the enactment of the action of a verb: *arrival, acquittal.* [OF *-aille, ail*, from L *-ālia*, neuter pl., from *-alis*]

Ala. *abbr.* Alabama.

ala (ā´lə) *n.* (*pl.* **alae** (-ē)) a wing or winglike anatomical or plant part. **alar** (ā´lə), **alary** (-əri) *a.* **1** of or relating to a wing. **2** winglike, wing-shaped. **alate** (-āt), **alated** *a.* having wings or winglike processes. [L *āla*, wing]

à la (a la´) *prep.* **1** in the fashion of, after the manner of, after. **2** (of food) prepared with or in the style of. [F]

alabaster (al´əbastə) *n.* a fine, soft, usu. white or semi-transparent form of gypsum, widely used for making ornaments. ~*a.* **1** made of alabaster. **2** white and translucent like alabaster. **alabastrine** (-bas´trin, -trīn) *a.* made of or resembling alabaster. [OF *alabastre*, L *alabaster -astrum*, Gr. *alabastros -on, alabastos*, said to be from the name of a town in Egypt]

à la carte (a la kaht´) *a., adv.* **1** (of a menu) having each dish priced separately. **2** (of a dish) priced separately, not part of a set menu. **3** with the freedom to select what you want. [F, by the bill of fare]

†**alack** (əlak´) *int.* used to express sorrow. †**alackaday** *int.* shame on the day! alas, the day! [*a*, ah, LACK, ah! lack, or ah! loss]

alacrity (əlak´riti) *n.* briskness, eagerness; vivacity, sprightliness. [L *alacritās* (*alacer*, brisk)]

Aladdin's cave (əlad´inz) *n.* a place that contains fabulous treasures or great riches. **Aladdin's lamp** *n.* an object that enables its owner to gratify any wish. [*Aladdin*, a character in *The Arabian Nights' Entertainments*]

à la mode (a la mōd´) *adv., a.* **1** fashionable. **2** (of meat) braised in wine. **3** (*N Am.*) served with ice cream. **alamode** *n.* a thin kind of black silk. [F *à la mode*, in the fashion]

alar ALA.

alarm (əlahm´) *n.* **1** warning of approaching danger. **2** a device for waking people from sleep or arousing attention. **3** terror mingled with surprise. **4** †a summons to arms. **5** in fencing, a challenge. ~*v.t.* **1** to frighten; to startle or agitate. **2** to rouse to a sense of danger. **alarm bell** *n.* a bell rung to sound an alarm. **alarm call** *n.* a telephone service that allows the subscriber to be called at a pre-arranged time, usu. early in the morning. **alarm clock** *n.* a clock that can be set to make a loud noise at a particular hour. **alarming** *a.* frightening, disturbing. **alarmingly** *adv.* **alarmism** *n.* **alarmist** *n.* **1** a person who needlessly spreads alarm, a scaremonger. **2** a person who is easily alarmed. ~*a.* that needlessly spreads alarm. †**alarum** (əlar´əm) *n.* an alarm. **alarums and excursions** (as a stage direction) a confused noise as of preparations for battle. [OF *alarme*, It. *all'arme*, to arms!]

alary ALA.

Alas. *abbr.* Alaska.

alas (əlas´) *int.* used to express sorrow, grief, pity or concern. [OF *a*, ah! *las*! wretched (L *lassus*, wearied, wretched)]

alate, alated ALA.

alb (alb) *n.* a long white surplice with close sleeves worn by priests and servers at some church services. [OF *albe*, late L *alba* (fem. a., *albus*, white)]

albacore (al´bəkaw) *n.* **1** a large long-finned species of tunny, *Thunnus alalunga.* **2** any of various allied species. [Port. *albacor* (Arab. *al*, the, *bukr*, a young camel, a heifer)]

Albanian (albā´niən) *a.* of or relating to Albania or its inhabitants. ~*n.* **1** a native or inhabitant of Albania. **2** the language of Albania.

albata (albā´tə) *n.* an alloy like silver; a variety of German silver. [L *albāta*, fem. of *albātus*, whitened, from *albus*]

albatross (al´bətros) *n.* **1** any long-winged large-bodied bird of the family *Diomedeidae*, esp. *Diomedea exulans*, the largest known seabird, the great albatross. **2** a burden or handicap from which a person cannot escape. **3** in golf, a score of three under par for a hole. [Port. *alcatraz, alcatruz*, Arab. *al*, the, *quadras*, bucket, the pelican (corrupted through assim. to L *albus*, white)]

albedo (albē´dō) *n.* (*pl.* **albedos**) the fraction of incident light reflected by a planet or other body or surface. [late L, whiteness (L *albus*, white)]

albeit (awlbē´it) *conj.* although, even though, notwithstanding. [ME *al be it*]

albert (al´bət) *n.* a short kind of watch-chain, fastened to a waistcoat buttonhole. [Prince Albert, 1819–61, consort of Queen Victoria]

albescent (albes´ənt) *a.* becoming or passing into white; whitish. **albescence** *n.* [L *albēscere*, to grow white (*albus*), -ENT]

Albigenses (albijen´sēz) *n.pl.* a sect of Catharist reformers in Languedoc, who separated from the Church of Rome in the 12th cent. **Albigensian** *a.* [L from *Albigeoi*, inhabitants of the town of Albi (L *Albiga*)]

albino (albē´nō) *n.* (*pl.* **albinos**) **1** a human being, or animal, having the colour pigment absent from the skin, the hair and the eyes, so as to be abnormally light in colour. **2** a plant in which little or no chlorophyll is developed. **albinic** (-bin´-) *a.* **albinism** (al´bi-) *n.* **albinotic** (-binot´-) *a.* [Port., an albino black (L *albus*, white)]

Albion (al´biən) *n.* (*esp. poet.*) Britain or England. **perfidious Albion** PERFIDIOUS (under PERFIDY). [L *albus*, white]

albite (al´bīt) *n.* white feldspar, soda feldspar. **albitic** (-bit´-) *a.* of, relating to or of the nature of albite. [L *albus*, white, -ITE[1]]

album (al´bəm) *n.* **1** a blank book for the insertion of photographs, poetry, drawings or the like. **2** (*N Am.*) a visitors' book. **3** a collection of pieces of recorded music issued on one or more long-playing records, cassettes, CDs etc. [L *album*, neut. of *albus*, white]

albumen (al´būmin) *n.* **1** the white of an egg. **2** albumin. **3** the substance interposed between the skin and embryo of many seeds; the endosperm or perisperm. **albumenize** (-bū´-), **albumenise** *v.t.* to coat (a photographic paper or plate) with an albuminous solution. [L *albumen -inis*, white of egg (*albus*, white)]

albumin (al´būmin) *n.* any of several water-soluble proteins existing in animals, in the white of egg, in blood serum and in plants. **albuminize** (-bū´-), **albuminise** *v.t.* **1** to albumenize. **2** to convert into albumin. **albuminoid** (-bū´minoid), **albuminoidal** (-oi´-) *a.* resembling or of the nature of albumin. ~*n.* a scleroprotein. **albuminous** (-bū´-), **albuminose** (-nōs) *a.* consisting of, resembling or containing albumin. **albuminuria** (-nū´riə) *n.* **1** the presence of albumin in the urine. **2** the diseased condition causing this. [as ALBUMEN]

alburnum (albœ´nəm), **alburn** (al´bœn) *n.* the sapwood in exogenous stems, between the inner bark and heartwood. **alburnous** *a.* of or relating to alburnum. [L *alburnum* (*albus*, white)]

alcade ALCAYDE.

alcahest ALKAHEST.

alcaic (alkā´ik) *a.* of or relating to Alcaeus, a lyric poet born in Mitylene, *c.* 600 BC, or to a kind of verse he invented. ~*n.* (*usu. in pl.*) Alcaic strophes. [L *alcaicus*, Gr. *alkaikos* (*Alkaios*, prop. name)]

alcaide ALCAYDE.

alcalde (alkal´dā) *n.* the judge or mayor of a Spanish, Portuguese or Latin American town. [Sp., from Arab. *al*, the, *qādī*, judge]

alcayde (alkād´), **alcade, alcaide** *n.* **1** the governor of a fortress in Spain, Portugal etc. **2** the warden of a prison, a gaoler. [Sp. *alcaide*, *alcayde*, Arab. *al*, the, *qāid*, leader, commander (*qāda*, lead)]

alchemy (al´kəmi) *n.* (*pl.* **alchemies**) **1** the chemistry of the Middle Ages, the search for an alkahest, the philosophers' stone, and the panacea. **2** a magic power of transmutation. **alchemic** (-kem´-), **alchemical** *a.* of or relating to alchemy. **alchemically** *adv.* **alchemist** *n.* a person who studies or practises alchemy. **alchemistic** (-mis´-) *a.* **alchemize, alchemise** *v.t.* to transmute. [OF *alchemie*, *alquimie*, med. L *alchimia*, Arab. *al*, the, *kimia* (late Gr. *chemeia*, prob. Egyptian art, confused with *chumeia*, a mingling, from *cheein*, to pour)]

alcheringa (alchəring´gə), **alchera** (al´chərə) *n.* the golden age or dreamtime in the mythology of Australian Aboriginals. [Austral. Abor.]

alcid (al´sid) *n.* a bird of the auk family. [new L *Alcidae*, family name from *alka*, see AUK]

alcohol (al´kəhol) *n.* **1** a colourless liquid produced by fermenting sugars and constituting the intoxicating agent in various drinks. **2** any of a class of compounds analogous to common alcohol that contain one or more hydroxyl groups. **3** any intoxicating drink containing alcohol. **alcohol abuse** *n.* excessive use of alcohol. **alcoholate** (-āt) *n.* a crystalline compound in which alcohol acts as water of crystallization. **alcohol-free** *a.* **1** (of a drink) containing no alcohol. **2** (of a bar etc.) serving no alcoholic drinks. **alcoholic** (-hol´-) *n.* a person who is addicted to alcohol. ~*a.* of, relating to or containing alcohol. **alcoholism** *n.* **1** addiction to or excessive use of alcohol. **2** the action of (excessive) alcohol on the human system. **alcoholize, alcoholise** *v.t.* **1** to rectify (a spirit). **2** to mix, saturate with alcohol. **alcoholization** (-zā´shən) *n.* **alcohol lamp** *n.* (*N Am.*) a spirit-lamp. **alcoholometer** (-om´itə) *n.* an instrument for measuring the proportion of pure alcohol in a liquor. **alcoholometrical** (-met´-) *a.* of or relating to the process of alcoholometry. **alcoholometry** (-om´itri) *n.* the act, art or process of ascertaining the quantity of pure alcohol in a liquor. [med. L *alcohol*, Arab. *al-koh'l* (*al*, the, *koh'l*, powder to stain the eyelids)]

alcopop (al´kōpop) *n.* an alcoholic drink tasting and packaged like a soft drink. [*alco*hol, POP[1]]

alcotot (al´kōtot) *n.* a small sachet of an alcoholic drink. [*alco*hol, TOT[1]]

alcove (al´kōv) *n.* **1** a recess in a wall. **2** a vaulted recessed area, as in a garden wall. **3** a covered or secluded spot; a summerhouse. [F *alcôve*, Sp. *alcoba*, Arab. *alqobbah*, the vault]

Ald. *abbr.* alderman.

aldehyde (al´dihīd) *n.* **1** a volatile liquid that can be obtained from alcohol by oxidation; acetaldehyde, ethanal. **2** any of an extensive class of organic compounds of the same type. **aldehydic** (-hī´-) *a.* [abbr. of L *alcohol dehydrogenatum*, alcohol deprived of hydrogen]

al dente (al den´ti, -tā) *a.* (esp. of cooked pasta) firm when bitten. [It., to the teeth]

alder (awl´də) *n.* **1** a tree, *Alnus glutinosa*, growing in moist places. **2** any of various other plants whose leaves more or less resemble those of the alder. **alder buckthorn** *n.* a shrub, *Frangula alnus*, with small black berry-like fruits. **alder fly** *n.* any neuropterous insect of the genus *Sialis*, that are found near streams. [OE *alr*, *aler*, *alor* (cp. Icel. *ôlr*, OHG *elira*, L *alnus*)]

alderman (awl´dəmən) *n.* (*pl.* **aldermen**) **1** (*Hist.*) (in England and Wales) a civic dignitary, elected from among members of a council, ranking next below the mayor. **2** (in the US, Canada, Australia etc.) a male elected member of the city council. **3** (*Hist.*) EALDORMAN. **aldermanic** (-man´-) *a.* of or relating to an alderman. **aldermanship** *n.* the office or dignity of an alderman. **alderperson** *n.* (*N Am.*) an alderman or alderwoman (non-sexist use). **alderwoman** *n.* (*pl.* **alderwomen**) (in the US, Canada, Australia etc.) a female elected member of a city council. [OE *ealdor*, *alder*, a chief (cp. OLD) MAN]

Alderney (awl´dəni) *n.* an animal of a breed of cattle originating on Alderney Island. [one of the Channel Islands]

Aldine (awl´dīn) *a.* **1** of, belonging to or printed by Aldus Manutius (a celebrated Venetian printer of the 16th cent.) or his family. **2** type modelled on that used by him. [*Aldus*, -INE]

Aldis lamp (awl´dis) *n.* a hand-held lamp for sending signals in Morse code. [A. C. W. *Aldis*, d. 1953, the inventor]

aldosterone (aldos´tərōn) *n.* a steroid hormone produced by the adrenal glands that regulates salt levels. [*al*dehyde, *ster*ol (as *cholesterol*) -ONE]

aldrin (awl´drin, al´-) *n.* an extremely poisonous chlorine-containing insecticide. [the German chemist Kurt *Alder*, 1902–58]

ale (āl) *n.* **1** an intoxicating drink made from malt by fermentation, orig. distinguished from beer in not being flavoured with hops. **2** beer. **3** (*N Am.*) a type of beer fermented rapidly at high temperature. **ale-conner** (āl´konə) *n.* (*Hist.*) an examiner or inspector of ale. **alecost** (āl´kost) *n.* the plant costmary formerly used to flavour ale. **alehouse** *n.* a tavern licensed to sell ale. **alewife**[1] *n.* (*pl.* **alewives**) a woman who keeps an alehouse (see also ALEWIFE[2]). [OE *ealu*]

aleatory (ā´liətəri), **aleatoric** (-tor´ik) *a.* **1** depending upon an uncertain event or chance. **2** (of music) allowing the performer a random choice of certain elements. [L *āleātōrius*, from *āleātor*, a dice-player (*ālea*, dice)]

alec (al´ik), **aleck** *n.* (*Austral.*, *sl.*) a stupid person. [contr. of SMART ALEC (under SMART)]

☒ **aledge** common misspelling of ALLEGE.

alee (əlē´) *a.*, *adv.* **1** on the lee side. **2** to leeward. [ON *á hlé*, a sea phrase (*á*, on, *hlé*, shelter)]

alegar (ā´ligə) *n.* **1** vinegar made from ale. **2** malt vinegar. [ALE, F *aigre*, sharp, sour]

Alemannic (aləman´ik) *n.* the group of High German dialects of Alsace, Switzerland and SW Germany. [late L *Alemanni*, Germanic people]

alembic (əlem´bik) *n.* a vessel made of glass or copper formerly used for distilling. [F *alambique*, Arab. *al-anbīq*, the still, Gr. *ambix -ikos*, a cup]

aleph (al´ef) *n.* the first letter of the Hebrew alphabet. **aleph-null** *n.* the cardinal number indicating the number of elements in the set of all positive integers; the smallest infinite cardinal number.

alert (əlœt´) *a.* **1** watchful, vigilant. **2** brisk, lively. ~*n.* **1** warning of danger. **2** a period during which a state of enhanced preparedness to defend against or respond to an attack is in force. **3** a warning by siren or otherwise of a threatened air raid. ~*v.t.* **1** to warn. **2** to put on guard. **3** to arouse. **on alert** (of troops etc.) in a state of enhanced readiness to respond to an attack, a crisis etc. **on the alert 1** on the watch. **2** on one's guard. **3** ready, prepared. **alertly** *adv.* **alertness** *n.* [F *alerte*, *allerte*, *à l'erte*, It. *all'erta*, on one's guard (*all'*, to the, *erta*, fem. p.p. of *ergere*, L *ērigere*, to erect)]

aleuron (əlū´ron), **aleurone** (-rōn) *n.* a protein found in the form of grains in ripening seeds. [Gr. *aleuron*, flour (*aleō*, I grind)]

alevin (al´ivin) *n.* a young fish, esp. a young salmon. [F, from OF *aleuer*, to rear, from L *allevare* (*ad-*, to, *levāre*, to raise)]

alewife[1] ALE.

alewife[2] (āl´wīf) *n.* (*pl.* **alewives** (-wīvz)) a N American fish, *Clupea serrata*, resembling the shad but smaller. [perh. N Am. Indian]

alexanders (aligzahn´dəz) *n.* (*pl.* **alexanders**) a European plant, *Smyrnium olusatrum*, formerly used as a vegetable. [OE *alexandre*, med. L *alexandrum*, prob. from L *holus atrum* black vegetable]

Alexander technique (aligzahn´də) *n.* a technique involving exercises, manipulation etc., designed to improve posture and movement by increasing awareness of them and thus avoid physical strain. [F. M. *Alexander*, d. 1955, Australian actor and originator of the technique]

Alexandrian (aligzahn´driən) *a.* **1** of or relating to Alexandria in Egypt. **2** of or relating to Alexander the Great. **3** belonging to or relating to the Hellenistic schools of philosophy and literature of Alexandria. **4** (of a writer, thinker) erudite and derivative rather than creative and original. ~*n.* a native or inhabitant of Alexandria.

alexandrine (aligzahn´drīn) *n.* a verse line containing twenty syllables in French, or six iambic feet in English prosody, usu. divided by a caesura. [F *alexandrin*, from *Alexandre*, a fifteenth-cent. poem written in this metre]

alexandrite (aligzahn´drīt) *n.* a dark green chrysoberyl. [the Russian tsar *Alexander* I, 1777–1825]

alexia (əlek´siə) *n.* (a brain defect resulting in) the inability to understand written or printed words, word-blindness. [Gr. *a-*, not; *lexis*, speech, but confused with L *legere*, to read]

alexin (əlek´sin) *n.* a substance present in blood serum, which, combining with an antibody or antiserum, gives protection against disease. [Gr. *alexein*, to ward off]

alexipharmic (əleksifah´mik) *a.* preserving against poison. ~*n.* an antidote. [F *alexipharmaque*, Gr. *alexipharmakon* (*alexō*, I ward off, *pharmakon*, poison)]

alfalfa (alfal´fə) *n.* a plant, *Medicago sativa*, with flowers and leaves similar to those of clover, that is widely cultivated as forage, a salad vegetable and a commercial source of chlorophyll. [Sp.]

alfresco (alfres´kō) *a.*, *adv.* in the open air, open-air. [It. *al fresco*, in the fresh]

alga (al´gə) *n.* (*pl.* **algae** (-gē)) a seaweed or other plant belonging to the Algae, a major group of simple aquatic or subaquatic plants, including the seaweeds, that lack differentiation into stems, roots and leaves. **algal** *a.* of or relating to seaweeds or other algae. **algal bloom** *n.* WATER-BLOOM (under WATER). **algicide** (-jisīd) *n.* a substance that destroys algae. **algin** (-j-) *n.* a jelly-like substance obtained from seaweed. **alginate** (-jināt) *n.* a salt of alginic acid used as a stabilizing and thickening agent in pharmaceuticals, food and plastics. **alginic** (-jin´-) *a.* of, relating to or obtained from seaweed. **alginic acid** *n.* an insoluble acid found in some algae, such as kelp. **algist** (-j-) *n.* a botanist who specializes in algae. **algoid** (-goid) *a.* of the nature of or like algae. **algology** (-gol´-) *n.* the branch of botany dealing with algae. **algological** (-gəloj´-) *a.* **algologist** (-gol´-) *n.* an algist. **algous** *a.* of or relating to, resembling or full of seaweed.

algebra (al´jibrə) *n.* **1** the branch of mathematics in which letters are used as symbols for quantities, and signs represent arithmetical processes. **2** any of a number of systems which use symbols to denote basic operations and relationships. **algebraic** (-brā´-), **algebraical** *a.* **1** of or relating to algebra. **2** involving or employing algebra. **algebraically** *adv.* **algebraist** (-brā´ist), **algebrist** *n.* a person who is skilled in algebra. **algebraize** (-brəīz), **algebraise** *v.t.* **1** to reduce to an algebraic form. **2** to solve by means of algebra. [Arab. *al-jebr*, the reunion of parts]

-algia (al´jiə) *comb. form* denoting pain (in a particular place), e.g. *neuralgia*. [Gr. *algos*, pain]

algid (al´jid) *a.* cold, esp. after feverishness. **algidity** (-jid´-) *n.* a state of coldness. [F *algide*, L *algidus* (*algēre*, to be cold)]

algin, algist etc. ALGA.

Algol (al´gol), **ALGOL** *n.* a computer language used chiefly for mathematical purposes. [*algo*rithmic *l*anguage]

algolagnia (algəlag´niə) *n.* sexual gratification derived from inflicting or suffering pain. **algolagnic** *n.*, *a.* [Gr. *algos*, pain, *lagneia*, lust]

algology, algologist ALGA.

algometer (algom´itə) *n.* an instrument for estimating degrees of sensitiveness to pain. [Gr. *algos*, pain, *metron*, measure]

Algonquian (algong´kwiən), **Algonkian** (-kiən) *n.* **1** a family of N American Indian languages. **2** a member of a people speaking an Algonquian language. ~*a.* of these languages or people.

Algonquin (algong´kwin), **Algonkin** (-kin) *n.* (*pl.* **Algonquin, Algonquins, Algonkin, Algonkins**) **1** a member of a N American Indian people formerly living in the valley of the Ottawa and around the northern tributaries of the St Lawrence. **2** their language, a dialect of Ojibwa. **3** Algonquian. ~*a.* **1** of or relating to the Algonquins or their language. 2 Algonquian. [F, from Micmac Indian *algoomaking*, at the place of spearing fish]

algorism (al´gərizm) *n.* 1 the Arabic system of counting, the decimal system. 2 computation of arithmetic using any numeration. 3 an algorithm. [med. L *algorismus*, Arab. *al-Khuwārizmi*, native of the Khwārazm (Khiva), cognomen of the ninth-cent. Persian mathematician Abu Ja´far Muhammad ben Musa]

algorithm (al´gəridhm) *n.* a rule or set procedure for solving a mathematical problem, esp. using a computer. **algorithmic** (-ridh´mik) *a.* **algorithmically** (-ridh´-) *adv.* [from ALGORISM, influenced by Gr. *arithmos*, number]

algous ALGA.

alguazil (algwəzil´) *n.* 1 a mounted official at a bullfight. 2 in Spain or other Spanish-speaking countries, an inferior officer of justice, a constable. [Sp. *alguazil* (*-cil*), Arab. *alwazir*, the vizier]

Alhambra (alham´brə) *n.* the Moorish palace and citadel at Granada in Spain. **alhambresque** (-bresk´) *a.* resembling the Alhambra or its style of architecture. [Arab. *al-hamra'*, the red house]

alias (āl´iəs) *adv.* otherwise (named or called). ~*n.* (*pl.* **aliases**) an assumed name. [L]

alibi (al´ibī) *n.* (*pl.* **alibis**) 1 the plea (of a person accused) of having been elsewhere when the offence was committed; the evidence to support such a plea. 2 (*coll.*) an excuse (for failing to do something). ~*v.t.* (*3rd pers. sing. pres.* **alibis,** *pres.p.* **alibiing,** *past, p.p.* **alibied**) to provide with an alibi. ~*v.i.* to provide an alibi. [L, elsewhere, loc. of *alius* (cp. *ibi, ubi*)]

alicyclic (alisī´klik) *a.* (of an organic compound) having aliphatic properties but containing a ring of carbon atoms. [*ali*phatic, *cyclic*]

alidad (al´idad), **alidade** (-dād) *n.* an arm or index showing degrees on a circle in an astrolabe, quadrant, theodolite etc. [F *alidade*, med. L *alhidada*, Arab. *al-'idādah* (*al*, the, *'adad*, upper arm)]

alien (ā´liən) *a.* 1 unfamiliar; strange, incongruous. 2 foreign, of foreign extraction; belonging to a foreign country. 3 unacceptable, repugnant to; not compatible or consistent. 4 estranged. 5 extraterrestrial, coming from another world. 6 (of a species) naturalized after introduction from elsewhere. ~*n.* 1 a foreigner; a foreign-born non-naturalized resident. 2 a being from another world. 3 an alien species. [OF *alien*, L *aliēnus*, a stranger, or of a stranger (*alius*, another)]

alienate (ā´liənāt) *v.t.* 1 to cause to become unfriendly or hostile, to estrange. 2 to cause to feel isolated or estranged. 3 (*formal*) to take away, divert (someone's affections). 4 to transfer to the ownership of another. **alienable** *a.* that may be alienated. **alienability** (-bil´-) *n.* **alienation** (-nā´shən) *n.* 1 the act of alienating; state of being alienated. 2 the feeling of being estranged from one's social environment. 3 a mental disorder in which the inhibition of a person's feelings results in the self and the outside world coming to seem unreal. 4 the state of critical detachment from the action and characters of a play which an audience, according to the theories of Berthold Brecht, ought to maintain. **alienator** *n.* **alienee** (-nē´) *n.* (*Law*) a person to whom the ownership of property is transferred. [OF *aliéner*]

aliform (ā´lifawm) *a.* shaped like a wing. [new L *āliformis*, from L *āla*, wing]

alight[1] (əlīt´) *v.i.* (*past, p.p.* **alighted**) 1 to get down, descend, dismount. 2 to reach the ground, to settle. 3 to come by chance, to happen (on). [OE *ālīhtan* (*a-*, intens., *līhtan*, to jump down from a horse)]

alight[2] (əlīt´) *a., adv.* 1 on fire. 2 illuminated. [p.p. of *alīhtan*, *onlīhtan*, to shine upon, light up (confused with forms like ABLAZE, AFIRE)]

align (əlīn´), **aline** *v.t.* 1 to range or place in a line. 2 to place in a position of agreement with others. ~*v.i.* to fall into line. **alignment** *n.* 1 the act of ranging in line or being ranged. 2 objects arranged in a line or lines. 3 the ground plan of a road or earthwork. 4 agreement or alliance with others. 5 the act of taking a side or associating with a party, cause, etc. [F *aligner* (*à*, to, *ligner*, from L *līneāre*, to line, from *līnea*, a line)]

alike (əlīk´) *a.* similar. ~*adv.* equally, in the same manner, similarly. [OE *onlīc* (*on-*, on, *līc*, like); also OE *gelīc* (*ge-*, together, *līc*, like); cp. OHG *gelīh* (G *gleich*) and Icel. *ālīkr*]

aliment (al´imənt) *n.* 1 nutriment, food. 2 support, sustenance. 3 (*Sc.*) alimony. 4 mental nutriment. ~*v.t.* 1 to nourish. 2 to make provision for the maintenance of. **alimental** (-men´-) *a.* 1 of or relating to aliment. 2 nutritive. **alimentally** *adv.* **alimentary** *a.* 1 of or relating to aliment or nutrition; nutritious, nourishing. 2 sustaining, supporting. **alimentary canal** *n.* the great tube or duct from mouth to anus conveying food to the stomach and carrying off solid excreta from the system. **alimentation** (-tā´shən) *n.* 1 the act or quality of affording nourishment. 2 sustenance, support. [L *alimentum* (*alere*, to nourish)]

alimony (al´iməni) *n.* (*esp. N Am.*) payment of means of support, esp. the proportional part of a person's income allowed for the support of a spouse after legal separation or divorce, or for other causes. [L *alimōnia* (*alere*, to nourish)]

aline ALIGN.

aliped (al´iped) *a.* having a winglike membrane connecting its digits. ~*n.* a wing-footed creature, e.g. a bat. [L *ala*, wing; *pes pedis*, foot]

aliphatic (alifat´ik) *a.* 1 fatty. 2 belonging or relating to a class of organic compounds containing open chains of carbon atoms in the molecular structure, not aromatic. [Gr. *aleiphar*, an unguent]

aliquot (al´ikwot) *a.* of or relating to a number that is contained an integral number of times by a given number. ~*n.* an integral factor, an aliquot part. **aliquot part** *n.* a part that is a division of the whole without remainder, as 50p of £1, 10 g of 1 kg. [F *aliquote*, late L *aliquota*, (fem. a. from *aliquot*, several, so many)]

alive (əlīv´) *adv.* 1 living, existent. 2 in force or operation; of current interest, topical. 3 lively, active, full of life. 4 sensitive, responsive (to). 5 swarming or teeming (with); full of. 6 (of an electric circuit) live. **alive and kicking** (*coll.*) in a very lively state. **alive and well** still alive (esp. despite contrary assumptions). **look alive!** look sharp, make haste. [ME *on live*, OE *on life* (*on*, prep., *līfe*, dat. of *lif*, LIFE)]

alizarin (əliz´ərin) *n.* the red colouring matter of madder. ~*a.* (of a dye) derived from this. [F *alizari* (prob. Arab.)]

alkahest (al´kəhest), **alcahest** *n.* the universal solvent of the alchemists. [imit. Arab., prob. invented by Paracelsus (early 16th cent.)]

alkali (al´kəlī) *n.* (*pl.* **alkalis, alkalies**) 1 a compound of hydrogen and oxygen with sodium, potassium or other substances, which is soluble in water, and produces caustic and corrosive solutions capable of neutralizing acids and changing the colour of litmus to blue. 2 any water-soluble chemical base. 3 alkaline products, such as caustic potash and caustic soda. 4 any soluble salt present to excess in soil. **alkali-flat, alkali-land** *n.* any one of several wide waste districts in Colorado and Nevada, covered with an alkaline efflorescence. **alkalify** (-li-) *v.t.* (*3rd pers. sing. pres.* **alkalifies,** *pres.p.* **alkalifying,** *past, p.p.* **alkalified**) to convert into an alkali. ~*v.i.* to be converted into an alkali. **alkalifiable** (-lifī´-) *a.* capable of being converted into an alkali. **alkali metal** *n.* each of the metals, the hydroxides of which are alkalis (potassium, sodium, caesium, lithium, rubidium, francium). **alkalimetry** (-lim´ətri) *n.* the measurement of the strength of alkalis. **alkalimetrical** (-met´-) *a.* **alkaline** (-līn) *a.* **1** having the properties of an alkali. **2** containing an alkali. **alkaline earth** *n.* (an oxide of) any of the alkaline earth metals. **alkaline earth metal** *n.* each of the metals calcium, strontium, magnesium, radium and beryllium. **alkaline metal** *n.* an alkali metal. **alkalinity** (-lin´iti) *n.* **1** the state of being alkaline. **2** the amount of alkali or base in a solution. **alkalize, alkalise** *v.t.* to render alkaline. **alkalization** (-zā´shən) *n.* the act of rendering alkaline. **alkaloid** (-oid) *a.* resembling an alkali in properties. ~*n.* any of a large group of natural organic nitrogenous bases derived from plants, some of which are used as medicinal drugs. **alkalosis** (-ō´sis) *n.* an abnormal increase in the alkalinity of body fluids or tissue. [F *alcali*, Arab. *al-qalī*, calcined ashes of saltwort]

alkane (al´kān) *n.* any of a series of aliphatic hydrocarbons including methane, ethane, butane and octane.

alkanet (al´kənet) *n.* **1** a red dye material obtained from *Alkanna tinctoria.* **2** the plant itself. [Sp. *alcana*, Arab. *al henna*, HENNA]

alky (al´ki), **alkie** *n.* (*pl.* **alkies**) (*sl.*) an alcoholic.

alkyd (al´kid) *n.* any of a group of synthetic resins derived from alkyls and acids, used in paints, protective coatings and adhesives. [*alky*l, aci*d*]

alkyl (al´kil) *n.* any monovalent hydrocarbon radical of the alkane series, e.g. methyl, ethyl, butyl. **alkylation** (-ā´shən) *n.* the introduction of an alkyl into a compound. [ALCOHOL, -YL]

all (awl) *a.* **1** the whole (quantity, duration, extent, amount, quality or degree) of. **2** every one of. **3** any whatever. **4** the greatest possible. ~*pron.* **1** all the persons or things concerned; everyone, everything. **2** the whole. ~*n.* **1** one's entire strength or resources. **2** the whole, the totality. ~*adv.* **1** wholly, entirely, completely. **2** (in scoring for games) each, apiece. **3** (*coll.*) very. **after all 1** when everything has been taken into account. **2** in spite of everything that was done, said etc. **3** against expectation or probability. **all aboard!** ABOARD. **all about it** the whole of the matter. **all along** throughout, all the time. **all and sundry** everyone, anyone who cares to do something. **all around** (*N Am.*) all round. **all but** almost. **all ears** EAR[1]. **all for** (*coll.*) very much in favour of. **all hands** (*Naut.*) the entire crew. **all in 1** including everything. **2** (*coll.*) exhausted. **all in all** all things considered. **all manner of** MANNER. **all of** as much, far etc. as, no less than (*all of thirty miles to Bath*). **all one** of no importance (to). **all out 1** with maximum effort. **2** at full speed. **all over 1** completely; everywhere. **2** finished (*all over with*; *it's all over*). **3** (*coll.*) typical of (*that's him all over*). **4** (*coll.*) excessively attentive to (*was all over her*). **all round 1** all things considered; in most respects. **2** for everyone (present) (*drinks all round*). **all set** (*coll.*) ready to start. **all square** SQUARE. **all the better/ more/ worse** so much the better/ more/ worse. **all the go** GO[2]. **all there** THERE. **all the same 1** nevertheless; in spite of what has been said; in spite of this. **2** a matter of indifference. **all the time** TIME. **all the way** WAY. **all the while** WHILE. **all together** in a body, altogether. **all told** TELL[1]. **all very well** used to express rejection of or scepticism about a positive or consolatory statement. **and all** (*coll.*) too, as well. **and all that** with all the rest of it. **at all 1** in any respect, to any extent, in any degree. **2** of any kind, whatever. **for all that** FOR. **in all** in total, altogether. **on all fours** FOUR. **on all hands** HAND. **to be all eyes** EYE[1]. **to be all up with** to be hopeless for. **all-American** *a.* **1** representing the whole of America or of the US. **2** typifying US ideals (*all-American boy*). **3** selected (by a panel of journalists) as one of the top amateur sportsmen in the US. ~*n.* an all-American sportsman. **All Blacks** *n.pl.* (*coll.*) the New Zealand international Rugby Union team. **all clear** *n.* a signal indicating that danger has passed or that one can proceed safely. **all comers** *n.pl.* anyone who accepts a challenge. **all-day** *a.* that lasts or is available all day. **all-embracing** *a.* comprehensive. **all-fired** *adv.* (*N Am., coll.*) infernally. **All Fools' Day** *n.* the 1st of April (from the custom of practising then on the credulity of one's neighbours). **all fours** *n.* **1** the four legs of a quadruped, the arms and legs of a human being. **2** a game of cards named from the four cards by which points are counted. **†all-hail** *int., n.* a salutation expressing respect or welcome. **All Hallows** *n.* All Saints' Day. **All Hallows' Eve** *n.* Hallowe'en. **all-important** *a.* of utmost importance. **all-in** *a.* in which everything is included. **all-in wrestling** *n.* a form of wrestling with almost no restrictions. **all-inclusive** *a.* in which everything is included. **all-in-one** *a.* combining two or more functions, items etc. in a single thing. **all-night** *a.* that lasts, is open, is available etc. throughout the night. **all-out** *a.* **1** with maximum effort. **2** at full speed. **all-over** *a.* covering the whole surface of something. **all-overish** *a.* (*coll.*) feeling generally unwell. **all-party** *a.* involving all the political parties concerned. **all-pervading, all-pervasive** *a.* that pervades or seems to pervade everything. **all-powerful** *a.* supremely or overwhelmingly powerful. **all-purpose** *a.* suitable for all purposes. **all right, alright** *a., adv.* (*coll.*) **1** correct, satisfactory, in good condition, safe etc. **2** satisfactorily. **3** yes.

Usage note The spelling *alright* for *all right* is best avoided.

all-round *a.* good in all respects. **all-rounder** *n.* **1** a person who is generally competent or versatile. **2** a person who is good at several sports or several aspects of one sport, esp. cricket. **All Saints** *n.pl.* the saints collectively. **All Saints' Day** *n.* a church festival (1 Nov.) in honour of the saints collectively. **all-seater** *a.* (of a stadium, football ground) having no standing accommodation for spectators. **all-singing-all-dancing** *a.* (*facet.*) lavishly or comprehensively equipped, accessoried etc. **All Souls** *n.pl.* the souls of the pious dead. **All Souls' Day** *n.* the day (2 Nov.) on which the Roman Catholic Church commemorates all the faithful departed. **all-star** *a.* composed of star performers. **all-ticket** *a.* (of an event) for which admission is exclusively by ticket bought in advance. **all-time** *a.* exceeding all others, as yet unsurpassed. ~*n.* a record high or low level. **all-up weight** *n.* the total weight of an aircraft with its load when in the air. **all-weather** *a.* suitable for all types of weather. **all-wheel drive** *n.* FOUR-WHEEL DRIVE (under FOUR). [OE *eal* (sing.), *ealle* (pl.), old Mercian form *alle*; (OHG *al*)]

alla breve (alə brā´vi) *n.* (*Mus.*) a time signature including two or four minims to the bar.

alla cappella A CAPPELLA.

Allah (al´ə) *n.* the name of God among Muslims. [Arab. *allah*, contr. of *al-ilāh*, the god (cp. Heb. *ĕlōah*)]

allantois (əlan´tōis) *n.* (*pl.* **allantoides** (aləntō´idēz)) a foetal membrane acting as an organ of respiration and excretion in reptiles, birds and mammals. **allantoic** (-tō´-) *a.* [Gr. *allantoeidēs*, sausage-shaped]

allay (əlā´) *v.t.* **1** to quiet, to still, to calm (fear); to diminish (suspicion). **2** to abate, to alleviate, to relieve (pain). [*a-*, intens. pref., LAY[1] (ME form *alleyen*; confused with *aleggen*, to alleviate, and also with *aleye*, allege, and *allay*, alloy)]

allegation (aligā´shən) *n.* **1** the act of alleging. **2** an assertion without proof, a statement of what one undertakes to prove. [as ALLEGE]

allege (əlej´) *v.t.* **1** to affirm positively but without or before proof. **2** to adduce as an authority, to plead as an excuse. **allegedly** (-jid-) *adv.* as has been alleged or stated. [*adlēgiāre*, Latinization of OF *esligier*, late L *exlītigāre* (L *lītigāre*, to contend at law); treated as if from *allēgāre*, to send, bring forward]

allegiance (əlē´jəns) *n.* **1** the obligation of subjects to their sovereign or citizens to their country or government. **2** loyalty, devotion. [ME *legeance*, OF *ligeance* (LIEGE); *a-* (L *ad-*) prefixed through confusion with obs. *allegance* (L *allegātio*)]

allegory (al´igəri) *n.* (*pl.* **allegories**) **1** a story, play, picture etc. in which the characters and events depicted are meant to be understood as representing other, usu. abstract spiritual or psychological, entities. **2** the genre which comprises such works. **3** the technique of symbolic representation. **4** a person or thing invested with symbolic meaning. **allegoric** (-gor´-), **allegorical** *a.* **1** of, relating to or consisting of allegory. **2** resembling an allegory. **allegorically** *adv.* **allegorist** *n.* a writer of allegories. **allegorize, allegorise** *v.t.* to convert into an allegory, to interpret allegorically. *~v.i.* to use allegory, to speak or write in a figurative manner. [L *allegōria*, Gr. *allegoria*; speaking otherwise than one seems to speak]

allegro (əleg´rō) *a.* (*Mus.*) brisk, lively. *~adv.* briskly, quickly. *~n.* (*pl.* **allegros**) a movement or passage in allegro time or manner. **allegretto** (aləgret´ō) *adv.* a little slower than allegro. *~n.* (*pl.* **allegrettos**) a movement or passage to be performed allegretto. [It.]

allele (əlēl´, al´-) *n.* an allelomorph. **allelic** *a.* [G *Allel*, short for ALLELOMORPH]

allelomorph (əlē´ləmawf, əlel´-) *n.* **1** any of two or more contrasted characteristics, inherited as alternatives, and assumed to depend on genes in homologous chromosomes. **2** any of two or more genes determining such alternative characteristics. **allelomorphic** (-maw´-) *a.* [Gr. *allelon*, of one another; *morphē*, form]

alleluia (aliloo´yə), **alleluya, hallelujah** (hal-) *int.* praise be to God. *~n.* **1** an utterance of 'alleluia', an offering of praise to God. **2** a song of praise to God. **3** the part of a Mass containing this. [Heb. *halelū jāh*, praise Jehova]

allemande (al´imand, al´mand, almād´) *n.* **1** any of various German dances of the 17th and 18th cents. **2** the music for or suitable for this (occurring as a movement in a suite). [F, fem. of *allemand*, German]

Allen screw (al´ən) *n.* a screw with a hexagonal socket in the head. **Allen key** *n.* an L-shaped tool designed to fit and unscrew an Allen screw. [name of US inventor]

allergy (al´əji) *n.* (*pl.* **allergies**) **1** an abnormal response or reaction to some food or substance innocuous to most people. **2** hypersensitiveness to certain substances inhaled or touched. **3** (*coll.*) an aversion, antipathy. **allergen** (-jən) *n.* a substance that induces allergy. **allergenic** (-jen´-) *a.* **allergic** (-lœ´-) *a.* **1** caused by allergy. **2** having an allergic response (to). **3** (*coll.*) averse (to). **allergist** *n.* a specialist in the treatment of allergy. [Gr. *allos*, other; ENERGY]

alleviate (əlē´viāt) *v.t.* to lighten, lessen, mitigate. **alleviation** (-ā´shən) *n.* **1** the act of alleviating. **2** relief, mitigation. **alleviative** *n.* that which alleviates. **alleviator** *n.* **alleviatory** *a.* [late L *alleviātus*, p.p. of *alleviāre* (*al-*, *ad-*, to, *levāre*, to lift)]

alley[1] (al´i) *n.* (*pl.* **alleys**) **1** a passage, esp. between or behind buildings. **2** a narrow street or lane. **3** a bordered walk in a garden or park. **4** a narrow enclosure for playing at skittles etc. **5** (*esp. N Am.*) the space between the tramlines of a tennis court. **alleyed** *a.* formed into alleys, laid out as an alley. [OF *alee* (*aller*, to go)]

alley[2] ALLY[3].

alliaceous (aliā´shəs) *a.* **1** of or relating to the plant genus *Allium*, which contains the onion and garlic. **2** having the taste or smell of onion or garlic. [L *allium*, garlic, -ACEOUS]

alliance (əlī´əns) *n.* **1** the act of allying; the state of being allied. **2** agreement committing two or more states, individuals etc. to act together. **3** union by such a treaty or agreement. **4** the parties allied. **5** union or connection of interests. **6** union by marriage, affinity. **7** (*Bot.*) a group of related families. [OF *aliance*]

allied ALLY[1].

alligator (al´igātə) *n.* **1** a large reptile, native to America and China, that resembles a crocodile but differs from it esp. by having a broader snout. **2** the skin of this animal used as leather, or a material resembling it. **3** (*pl.*) shoes made from this. **alligator clip** *n.* a clip with serrated edges for gripping. **alligator pear** *n.* an avocado. **alligator snapper, alligator tortoise** *n.* a large freshwater snapping turtle. [Sp. *el lagarto*, the lizard (L *lacerta*)]

alliterate (əlit´ərāt) *v.i.* **1** to commence with the same letter or sound. **2** to practise alliteration. **alliteration** (-ā´shən) *n.* commencement of two or more words or accented syllables, in close connection, with the same letter or sound. **alliterative** *a.* of or relating to alliteration. **alliteratively** *adv.* [L *ad-*, to, *litera*, a letter]

allium (al´iəm) *n.* a plant of the genus *Allium*, containing garlic, leeks, onions etc. [L]

allo- (al´ō) *comb. form* different, other, as in *allomorph*, *allopathy*. [Gr. *allos*, other]

allocate (al´əkāt) *v.t.* **1** to assign, allot, apportion. **2** to localize. **allocable** (-əkəbəl) *a.* **allocation** (-ā´shən) *n.* **1** the act of allocating. **2** an amount or thing allocated. **allocator** *n.* [late L *allocātus*, p.p. of *allocāre* (*ad-*, to, *locāre*, to place, *locus*, a place)]

allochthonous (alok´thənəs) *a.* (of rocks, deposits) formed elsewhere than where they are presently situated. [Gr. ALLO-, *khthōn -onos*, earth]

allocution (alәkū´shən) *n.* a formal address, esp. one delivered by the Pope to the bishops and clergy, or to the Church generally. [L *allocūtiōnem* (*ad-*, to, *loqui*, to speak)]

allodium (əlō´diəm), **alodium, allod** (al´od) *n.* (*pl.* **allodia, alodia, allods**) landed property held in absolute ownership. **allodial** *a.* **1** of or relating to allodium. **2** held independently, in contradistinction to feudal. **allodially** *adv.* [med. L *allodium*, from Gmc. *alod* (*al*, all or whole, *ōd*, estate, cp. OHG *ōt*)]

allogamy (əlog´əmi) *n.* (*Bot.*) cross-fertilization. **allogamous** *a.* reproducing by cross-fertilization. [Gr. ALLO-, -GAMY]

allograft (al´əgrahft) *n.* a tissue graft from a genetically unrelated donor.

allograph (al´əgrahf) *n.* a signature written by one person on behalf of another. [Gr. ALLO-, *graphē*, writing]

allomorph (al´əmawf) *n.* **1** any of the two or more forms of a morpheme. **2** any of two or more crystalline forms of a substance. **allomorphic** (-maw´-) *a.* [Gr. ALLO-, *morphē*, form]

allopathy (əlop´əthi) *n.* the treatment of disease by including effects of a different kind from those produced by the disease; ordinary medical practice, as opposed to homoeopathy. **allopathic** (aləpath´-) *a.* of, relating to or practising allopathy. **allopathically** *adv.* **allopathist** *n.* a person who practises allopathy. [Gr. ALLO-, -PATHY (under -PATH)]

allopatric (aləpat´rik) *a.* (*Biol.*) occurring in geographically separated areas. [Gr. ALLO-, *patra*, fatherland]

allophone (al´əfōn) *n.* any of the two or more forms of a phoneme. **allophonic** (-fon´-) *a.* [Gr. ALLO-, -PHONE]

allot (əlot´) *v.t.* (*pres.p.* **allotting,** *past, p.p.* **allotted**) to distribute, to grant, to bestow, to assign as one's share. **allotment** *n.* **1** the act of allotting. **2** the share assigned. **3** a small plot of land let, usu. by a local authority, for cultivation. **allottee** (-ē´) *n.* the person to whom allotment is made. [A-F *aloter* (*a-*, L *ad-*, to, LOT)]

allotropy (əlot´rəpi) *n.* variation of physical properties without change of substance (e.g. diamond, graphite and charcoal are allotropic forms of carbon). **allotrope** (al´ətrōp) *n.* any one of the forms in which a substance exhibiting allotropy exists. **allotropic** (alətrop´ik) *a.* 1 of or relating to allotropy. 2 existing in diverse states. **allotropically** *adv.* in an allotropic manner. **allotropism** *n.* allotropy. [Gr. *allotropia*, from *allotropos* (ALLO-, *tropos*, turn, manner, from *trepein*, to turn)]

allow (əlow´) *v.t.* 1 to permit. 2 to assign, set aside for a purpose. 3 to give, grant or provide (a limited quantity or sum). 4 to acknowledge, concede. 5 to take into account, give credit for. 6 †to praise, sanction, approve. **to allow for** to make allowance or deduction for. **to allow of** to accept, to admit. **allowable** *a.* **allowableness** *n.* **allowably** *adv.* **allowance** *n.* 1 a fixed quantity or sum allowed to a particular person or for a specific purpose. 2 a deduction or discount, made in consideration of something. 3 an amount of income not subject to income tax. 4 the act of allowing; tolerance. 5 (*NAm.*) pocket money. ~*v.t.* to put upon allowance. **to make allowance/ allowances for** to take (mitigating circumstances) into account. [OF *alouer*, from two verbs whose meanings were often confused: (1) L *allaudāre*, to praise, (2) low L *allocāre*, to place, to admit as proved]

alloy[1] (al´oi) *n.* 1 an inferior metal mixed with one of greater value. 2 a mixture of metals. 3 an amalgam. 4 any base admixture. 5 the standard of purity, the quality of gold and silver. [formerly *alay* or *allay*, OF *alai*, from *aleier*, to combine, L *alligāre* (*ad-*, to, *ligāre*, to bind)]

alloy[2] (əloi´) *v.t.* 1 to mix with a baser metal. 2 to mix (metals). 3 to mix with anything base or inferior. 4 to diminish, to impair.

☒ **allready** common misspelling of ALREADY.

allseed (awl´sēd) *n.* any of various many-seeded plants, esp. *Radiola linoides* of the flax family.

allspice (awl´spīs) *n.* 1 (a spice prepared from) the berry of the pimento, said to combine the flavour of cinnamon, cloves and nutmeg. 2 any of various other aromatic shrubs.

allude (əlood´, əlūd´) *v.i.* 1 to make indirect reference (to), to hint at. 2 (*loosely*) to mention, to refer (to). **allusion** (-zhən) *n.* 1 a reference to anything not directly mentioned. 2 a hint. **allusive** *a.* 1 containing an allusion. 2 hinting at an implied meaning, characterized by allusion. **allusively** *adv.* **allusiveness** *n.* [L *allūdere* (*ad-*, to, *lūdere*, to play)]

Usage note (1) *Allude* and *allusion* imply indirectness, and should not be used simply for refer, a reference. (2) *Allusion* and *illusion* should not be confused: an illusion is a deception.

allure (əlūə´) *v.t.* 1 to attract or tempt by the offer of some real or apparent good. 2 to entice. 3 to fascinate, to charm. ~*n.* charm, sex appeal. **allurement** *n.* 1 the act of alluring or enticing. 2 something which allures; a bait, an enticement. **alluring** *a.* enticing, attractive. **alluringly** *adv.* [OF *alurer*, *aleurrer* (*à*, to, *leurrer*, to lure)]

allusion ALLUDE.

alluvia, alluvial ALLUVIUM.

alluvion (əloo´viən) *n.* 1 the wash of the sea against the land. 2 (*Law*) the formation of new land by the action of flowing water. [F *alluvion*, L *alluviōnem*, acc. of *alluvio*, a washing against; see ALLUVIUM]

alluvium (əloo´viəm) *n.* (*pl.* **alluvia**) (a fine-grained fertile soil derived from) transported matter which has been washed away and later deposited by rivers, floods or similar causes. **alluvial** *a.* 1 of or relating to alluvium. 2 deposited from flowing water. [L, neut. of a. *alluvius* (*ad-*, to, *luere*, to wash)]

ally[1] (əlī´) *v.t.* (*3rd pers. sing. pres.* **allies**, *pres.p.* **allying**, *past, p.p.* **allied**) 1 to unite by treaty, confederation, marriage or friendship. 2 to connect; to combine. **Allied** *a.* of the Allies, esp. during the First and Second World Wars. **allied** *a.* 1 united, associated. 2 of the same type, related. [OF *alier*, L *alligāre* (*ad-*, to, *ligāre*, to bind)]

ally[2] (al´ī) *n.* (*pl.* **allies**) 1 a state, person, group etc. that has an alliance with another. 2 something akin to another in structure or properties. **the Allies** in World War I, the nations united against the central European powers; in World War II, the nations united against the Axis powers.

ally[3] (al´i), **alley** *n.* (*pl.* **allies, alleys**) a superior kind of playing-marble or taw. [said to be dim. from ALABASTER]

alma (al´mə), **almah** *n.* an Egyptian dancing girl. [Arab. *'almah*, learned, knowing]

almacantar (alməkan´tə), **almucantar** *n.* 1 an instrument for determining time and latitude. 2 a smaller circle of the celestial sphere parallel to the horizon, a parallel of altitude. [F *almicantarat* or *almucantarat*, med. L *almi-* or *almucontarath*, Arab. *al-muquantarāt*, pl. of *muquantarah*, sundial, from *quantarah*, a bridge]

alma mater (almə mā´tə, mah´-), **Alma Mater** *n.* the university, college or school that a person attended. [L, fostering mother]

almanac (awl´mənak), †**almanack** *n.* 1 a register of the days of the year, with astronomical data and calculations, civil and ecclesiastical festivals etc. 2 an annual directory or compendium of information. [F *almanach*, med. L *almanac* (etym. uncertain)]

almandine (al´məndīn) *n.* a precious deep red garnet. [formerly *alabandine*, L *alabandina*, from *Alabanda*, a city of Caria]

almighty (awlmī´ti) *a.* 1 omnipotent. 2 possessed of unlimited ability, strength or power. 3 (*coll.*) very great, very loud. ~*adv.* (*coll.*) exceedingly. **the Almighty** God. **almightiness** *n.* **almighty dollar** *n.* (*coll.*) 1 money. 2 feverish love of money. [OE *ealmihtig* (ALL, MIGHTY (under MIGHT[1]))]

almond (ah´mənd) *n.* 1 a small widely cultivated tree of the rose family, *Prunus dulcis.* 2 the edible kernel of the fruit of this tree. 3 anything shaped like an almond, e.g. a tonsil. **almond-eyed** *a.* having narrow, almond-shaped eyes. **almond oil** *n.* oil extracted from the kernels of almonds and used in cosmetics and for flavouring and medicinal purposes. **almond paste** *n.* marzipan. **almond tree** *n.* the tree *Prunus dulcis.* [OF *almande*, L *amygdala*, Gr. *amygdalē*]

almoner (al´mənə, ah´-) *n.* 1 (*Hist.*) an official distributor of alms or bounty. 2 (*Hist.*) a medico-social worker attached to a hospital. 3 a hospital official who assesses the amount of payments to be made by patients for their treatment. **almonry** (-ri) *n.* (*pl.* **almonries**) 1 a place where alms are distributed. 2 the residence of an almoner. [OF *aumoner*, late L *almosinarius* (see ALMS)]

almost (awl´məst) *adv.* nearly, very nearly, well-nigh. [OE *ælmǣst*, for the most part]

alms (ahmz) *n.pl.* 1 anything given out of charity to the poor. 2 charity. **almshouse** *n.* a house where poor people are lodged and provided for by charitable endowment. [OE *ælmesse*, L *eleēmosyna*, Gr. *eleēmosunē* (*eleēmōn*, a. from *eleos*, pity)]

almucantar ALMACANTAR.

alodium ALLODIUM.

aloe (al´ō) *n.* 1 a succulent plant of the genus *Aloe*, having fleshy, toothed leaves and bitter juice. 2 any of various other plants, e.g. the American aloe. 3 (*pl.*) the inspissated juice of plants of the genus *Aloe*, a purgative drug. **aloetic** (-et´ik) *a.* 1 of or relating to the aloe or aloes. 2 consisting entirely or chiefly of aloes. ~*n.* an aloetic medicine. **aloe vera** (veə´rə) *n.* a

Caribbean aloe whose juice is used in various medical and cosmetic preparations. [L *aloë*, Gr. *aloē*]

aloft (əloft´) *adv.* **1** high up, on high. **2** upwards. **3** in the rigging, at the masthead. [Icel. *a lopt*, in the air (cp. LIFT[1])]

alogical (əloj´ikəl) *a.* **1** not logical, not rational. **2** opposed to logic. [A-[3], LOGICAL (under LOGIC)]

alone (əlōn´) *a., adv.* **1** with no other present. **2** without help from others. **3** lonely. **4** only, solely (*He alone knew the truth*). **5** without others of the same opinion (*was alone in believing*). **6** without equal, unique. [ME *al one* (ALL, ONE)]

along (əlong´) *prep.* **1** from one end to the other of. **2** over or through the length, or part of the length of. **3** beside and extending over the length of. *~adv.* **1** forward, onward. **2** into a more advanced state. **3** in company with someone or oneself (*bring him along*). **4** to or at a particular place. **5** over the length of something; lengthwise. **along with** in company or together with. **alongshore** *adv.* **1** in a line with, and nearly parallel to, the shore. **2** along and on the shore. **alongshoreman** *n.* (*pl.* **alongshoremen**) a fisherman engaged in coastal fishing. **alongside** *adv.* **1** by the side of something. **2** to the side of something. *~prep.* **1** by the side of. **2** to the side of. **alongside of** side by side with. [OE *andlang* (*and*, against, *lang*, long; cp. OHG *ant-*, Gr. *anti*]

aloof (əloof´) *adv.* away, at a distance apart. *~a.* distant or unsympathetic in manner. **to stand/ keep aloof** to take no part in, to keep away; to remain by oneself, remain unsympathetic. **aloofness** *n.* the state of keeping aloof. [*a-*, on, ME *loof* (cp. Dut. *to loef*, to windward) see LUFF]

alopecia (aləpē´shə) *n.* baldness. [Gr. *alopekia*, fox-mange]

aloud (əlowd´) *adv.* **1** audibly. **2** †loudly, with a loud voice.

alow (əlō´) *adv.* in or into the lower part of a ship, opposed to aloft.

alp (alp) *n.* **1** a high mountain. **2** pasture ground on the side of a mountain. **3** a formidable obstacle. **the Alps** the chain of mountains separating France from Italy and running through Switzerland into Austria etc. **alpenstock** (al´pənstok) *n.* a long stick shod with iron, used in mountaineering. **alphorn** (alp´hawn), **alpenhorn** (alp´ən-) *n.* a very long wooden horn used by herdsmen in the Swiss Alps. **Alpine** (-pīn) *a.* of, relating to or growing on the Alps. **alpine** (al´pīn) *a.* **1** of, relating to or growing on any high mountain. **2** growing above the tree line. **3** of or relating to ski events such as slalom and downhill racing. *~n.* **1** a plant native or suited to high mountains. **2** a plant suitable for rockeries. **alpinism** (-pin-) *n.* mountain–climbing. **alpinist** (-pin-) *n.* a mountaineer, esp. one who climbs in the Alps. [L *Alpes*, pl., etym. uncertain]

alpaca (alpak´ə) *n.* **1** the domesticated llama of Peru. **2** the wool of the domesticated llama. **3** cloth made from this wool. [Sp. *alpaca* (Arab. *al-*, the, Peruv. Sp. *paco*]

alpargata (alpahgah´tə) *n.* a light, rope-soled canvas shoe, an espadrille. [Sp.]

alpenhorn, alpenstock ALP.

alpha (al´fə) *n.* **1** the first letter of the Greek alphabet (Α, α). **2** a first-class mark for a piece of work, in an examination etc. **Alpha** *n.* **1** the chief or brightest star in a constellation. **2** a codeword for the letter *a*. **alpha and omega** *n.* the beginning and the end; the essential or most important part, point etc. **alpha decay** *n.* the process of radioactive decay that results in the emission of alpha particles. **alpha particle** *n.* a positively-charged particle emitted by certain radioactive substances, e.g. radium. It has been identified as a doubly-ionized helium atom. **alpha plus** *a.* superlatively good. **alpha radiation** *n.* alpha particles emitted from a radioactive isotope. **alpha rays** *n.pl.* rays consisting of streams of alpha particles. **alpha rhythm, alpha wave** *n.* the pattern of electrical activity of the brain associated with a person awake but at rest. **alpha securities, alpha stocks** *n.pl.* the Stock Exchange stocks which are most frequently traded. **alpha test** *n.* a test of a new product, esp. in computer software, carried out by the developer before release for beta testing. *~v.t.* to put (a product) through such a test. [Gr. *alpha*, Heb. *āleph*, an ox, a leader]

alphabet (al´fəbet) *n.* **1** the letters or characters used in writing a language, arranged in order. **2** a set of signs or symbols representing letters. **3** the rudiments of a subject. *~v.t.* **1** to arrange in the order of the alphabet. **2** to designate by letters of the alphabet. **alphabetic** (-bet´-), **alphabetical** *a.* **1** of or relating to the alphabet. **2** arranged in the order of the letters of the alphabet. **alphabetically** *adv.* **alphabetize, alphabetise** *v.t.* to arrange in alphabetical order. **alphabetization** (-zā´shən) *n.* **alphabet soup** *n.* **1** a type of soup containing noodles in the shapes of letters of the alphabet. **2** a confusing mass or string of initials, acronyms, abbreviations etc., as found in some official or technical documents. [L *alphabētum*, Gr. *alpha*, *bēta*, (Heb. *bēth*, a house), the first two letters]

alphanumeric (alfənūmer´ik), **alphameric** (-mer´ik), **alphamerical** *a.* consisting of or using both letters and numbers. [ALPHABET, NUMERIC]

alpine, Alpine ALP.

already (awlred´i) *adv.* **1** beforehand, before some specified time. **2** in anticipation. [ALL, READY]

alright ALL RIGHT (under ALL).

Alsatian (alsā´shən) *a.* belonging to Alsace, a region of E France. *~n.* **1** a native or inhabitant of Alsace. **2** a breed of large, German wolflike dog, the German shepherd dog; a dog of this breed. [from *Alsatia*, L name for Alsace]

alsike (al´sīk, -sik) *n.* a species of clover, *Trifolium hybridum*. [*Alsike*, place in Sweden]

also (awl´sō) *adv., conj.* **1** in addition, as well. **2** likewise, in like manner, besides. **also-ran** *n.* **1** an unplaced horse in a race. **2** (*coll.*) an unimportant person, a failure. [ALL, SO[1]]

alstroemeria (alstrəmē´riə) *n.* a plant of the originally S American genus *Alstroemeria*, of the amaryllis family, cultivated for their brightly coloured orchid-like flowers. [Klas von *Alstroemer*, d. 1796, Swedish botanist]

alt (alt) *n.* (*Mus.*) high tone; the higher register of sounds. **in alt** in the octave commencing with G directly above the treble staff. [Prov.; L *altum*, high]

alt. *abbr.* **1** alternate. **2** altitude. **3** alto.

Alta. *abbr.* Alberta (Canada).

Altaic (altā´ik) *a.* of or relating to the peoples, and to the languages of the peoples (Turanian or Ural-Altaic), lying near the Altai mountains and the Arctic ocean.

altar (awl´tə) *n.* **1** a sacrificial block or table; a place of sacrifice, commemoration or devotion. **2** the communion table. **to lead to the altar** to marry (a woman). **altar boy** *n.* a boy who assists the priest during a service. **altar cloth** *n.* **1** the linen cloth which covers an altar. **2** an altar frontal. **altarpiece** *n.* a picture or ornamental sculpture over the altar (or communion table) in a church. **altarwise** *adv.* after the manner, or in the position of an altar. [L *altāre* (*altus*, high)]

altazimuth (altaz´iməth) *n.* an instrument for measuring altitude and azimuth. [*alt-* (for ALTITUDE), AZIMUTH]

alter (awl´tə) *v.t.* **1** to cause to vary or change in some degree. **2** to modify. **3** (*N Am., Austral., euphem.*) to castrate or spay. *~v.i.* to undergo some change. **alterable** *a.* capable of being altered. **alterability** (-bil´-) *n.* **alteration** (-ā´shən) *n.* **1** the act of altering. **2**

the change made. **alterative** *a.* tending to produce alteration. ~*n.* a medicine which alters the processes of nutrition and reduces them to a healthy state. [F *altérer*, late L *alterāre* (*alter*, other, same root as *al-ius*)]

altercate (awl´təkāt) *v.i.* **1** to dispute hotly. **2** to wrangle. **altercation** (-ā´shən) *n.* **1** wrangling. **2** a vehement dispute. [L *altercāt-*, part. stem of *altercārī*]

alter ego (awltə ē´gō, al-, eg´-) *n.* (*pl.* **alter egos**) **1** a second self. **2** a trusted friend. **3** a plenipotentiary. [L, another I]

alternate[1] (awl´tənāt) *v.t.* **1** to arrange or perform by turns. **2** to cause to succeed by turns or reciprocally. **3** to interchange. ~*v.i.* **1** to happen or succeed one another by turns. **2** to change repeatedly from one condition or state to another. **3** (of an electric current, voltage etc.) to change from positive to negative and back again by turns. **alternant** (-tœ´-) *a.* **1** alternating. **2** (*Mining*) consisting of alternating layers. **alternating** *a.* that alternate(s) or interchange(s); changing from positive to negative and back. **alternating current** *n.* an electric current that changes from positive to negative regularly and frequently. **alternation** (-ā´shən) *n.* **1** the act of alternating; the state of being alternate. **2** antiphonal reading or singing. **alternation of generations** *n.* the alternation of different forms of reproduction (sexual and parthenogenetic, haploid and diploid, etc.) in a life cycle. [L *alternatus*, p.p. of *alternāre*, to do by turns (*alternus*, every other, from *alter*, other)]

alternate[2] (awltœ´nət) *a.* **1** done or happening by turns, first one and then the other. **2** every other, every second. **3** (of a sequence) consisting of alternate things. **4** (of plant parts) placed on opposite sides of an axis at successive levels. **5** (of angles) formed at opposite ends and on opposite sides of a straight line that cuts two other lines. **alternately** *adv.*

Usage note The adjectives *alternate* and *alternative* should not be confused: *alternate* means every other, and *alternative* offering a choice of two.

---

alternative (awltœ´nətiv) *a.* **1** offering a choice of two things. **2** being the other of two things open to choice. **3** denoting or relating to a lifestyle, practice, art form etc. which functions outside, and constitutes an alternative to, conventional or institutionalized methods or systems. ~*n.* **1** the permission or opportunity to choose between two things. **2** either of two courses which may be chosen. **alternative birth, alternative birthing** *n.* any method of childbirth that differs from a standard delivery in hospital with a medical team in attendance. **alternative comedy** *n.* comedy that rejects conventional (racial and sexual) stereotypes as a source of humour. **alternative energy** *n.* energy fuelled from renewable or environment-friendly sources. **alternative fuel** *n.* a fuel to power motor vehicles other than petrol. **alternatively** *adv.* **alternative medicine** *n.* any system of medicine or medical treatment, such as homoeopathy or osteopathy, that does not use orthodox practices or substances. **Alternative Service Book** *n.* a modernized version of the liturgy of the Church of England, used as an alternative to the Book of Common Prayer. **alternative society** *n.* a group that rejects the values and forms of conventional society. **Alternative Vote** *a.* denoting a system of voting in which voters list the candidates in order of preference and in which, if no candidate obtains more than 50% of first preferences, the votes for the lowest-scoring candidate are redistributed according to second preferences. [as ALTERNATE[1]]

Usage note See note under ALTERNATE[2].

---

alternator (awl´tənātə) *n.* a dynamo for generating an alternating electric current.

althorn (alt´hawn) *n.* an instrument of the saxhorn family, esp. the E flat alto or tenor saxhorn. [G]

although (awldhō´) *conj.* though, notwithstanding, however. [ALL, *adv.*, THOUGH]

alti- (al´ti) *comb. form* high, highly, height. [L *alto-* etc., from *altus*, high]

altimeter (al´timētə, altim´itə) *n.* an instrument that indicates height above a given datum, usu. sea level. **altimetrical** (altimet´-) *a.* **altimetry** (altim´ətri) *n.* the science of measuring heights.

altissimo (altis´imō) *adv.* (*Mus.*) in the second octave above the treble stave. [It. superl. of ALTO]

altitude (al´titūd) *n.* **1** vertical height. **2** height above sea level. **3** elevation of an object above its base. **4** the elevation of a heavenly body above the horizon. [L *altitūdo* (*altus*, high)]

alto (al´tō) *n.* (*pl.* **altos**) **1** the lowest female voice, contralto. **2** the highest adult male voice, countertenor. **3** a singer possessing such a voice. **4** the part of the music sung by persons possessing the alto voice. **5** an alto instrument, esp. an alto saxophone. ~*a.* **1** to be sung by altos. **2** being the second- or third-highest in pitch of a family of instruments (*alto clarinet*). **alto clef** *n.* the clef which establishes middle C on the third line of the stave. **altoist** *n.* a person who plays the alto saxophone. [It., high (viz. *canto* singing)]

altocumulus (altōcū´mūləs) *n.* in meteorology, intermediate-altitude cloud in rounded masses with a level base. [L *altus*, high, CUMULUS]

altogether (awltəgedh´ə) *adv.* **1** wholly, completely, entirely. **2** inclusive of everything. **3** on the whole, in view of all things. **the altogether** (*coll.*) the nude. [ALL, *adv.*, TOGETHER]

Usage note In writing, it is conventional to distinguish between *altogether* and *all together*, which means 'all at one place' or 'all at one time'.

---

alto-relievo (altōrəlyā´vō) *n.* (*pl.* **alto-relievos**) **1** high relief, standing out from the background by more than half the true proportions of the figures carved. **2** a sculpture of this type. [It. *alto-rilievo*]

altostratus (altōstrah´təs) *n.* in meteorology, intermediate-altitude cloud forming a continuous level layer. [L *altus*, high, STRATUS]

altrices (al´trisēz) *n.pl.* birds whose young are very immature after hatching and depend entirely on the parents for food. **altricial** (altrish´əl) *a.* hatching immature young. ~*n.* an altricial bird. [L pl. of *atrix*, feeder, nurse]

altruism (al´trooizm) *n.* devotion to the good of others (as opposed to egoism). **altruist** *n.* a person who practises altruism. **altruistic** (-is´-) *a.* **altruistically** *adv.* [F *altruisme*, It. *altrui* (F *autrui*), L *alteri huic* (to this other)]

ALU *abbr.* (*Comput.*) arithmetic and logic unit.

alula (al´ūlə) *n.* (*pl.* **alulae** (-lē)) the bastard wing. [L, dim. of *alā*, wing]

alum (al´əm) *n.* **1** a double sulphate of aluminium and potassium. **2** any of a series of double sulphates of a monovalent metal or group. **3** a family of analogous compounds. **4** (*Mineral.*) any of various minerals, alums or pseudo-alums. [OF *alum* (F *alun*), L *alumen*]

alumina (əloo´minə) *n.* the oxide of aluminium occurring as corundum and a constituent of all clays. [L *alumen*]

aluminium (alūmin´iəm), (*N Am.*) **aluminum** (əloo´minəm) *n.* a white, ductile metallic element, at. no. 13, chem. symbol Al, with good resistance to corrosion, used as a basis for many light alloys. **aluminiferous** (-nif´ərəs) *a.* containing or yielding aluminium. **aluminium bronze** *n.* a compound of aluminium and copper. **aluminize** (-loo´-), **aluminise** *v.t.* to coat with aluminium. [see ALUMINA]

aluminosilicate (əlūminōsil´ikāt) *n.* a silicate containing a proportion of aluminium, esp. a rock-forming silicate such as feldspar.
aluminous (əloo´minəs) *a.* composed of or relating to aluminium or alumina.
aluminum ALUMINIUM.
alumnus (əlŭm´nəs) *n.* (*pl.* **alumni** (-nī)) **1** a former pupil or student (of a particular place of education). **2** (*N Am.*) a graduate. **alumna** (-nə) *n.* (*pl.* **alumnae** (-nē)) a female alumnus. [L, foster-child]
alveolus (alvē´ələs, -viō´ləs) *n.* (*pl.* **alveoli** (-lī)) **1** a little cavity. **2** an air sac in the lungs. **3** a tooth socket. **4** the cell of a honeycomb. **alveolar** *a.* **1** of, relating to or having alveoli or an alveolus. **2** of or relating to the sockets of the teeth. **3** socket-shaped. **4** (of a consonant) produced with the tip of the tongue touching the roof of the mouth behind the front teeth. **alveolate** (-lət) *a.* **1** honeycombed. **2** deeply pitted. [L *alveolus*, dim. of *alveus*, a cavity]
always (awl´wāz), †**alway** *adv.* **1** on all occasions, in all cases. **2** repeatedly, regularly. **3** in any event, whatever the circumstances. **4** forever; till the end of one's life. [OE *ealne weg*, acc. (ALL, WAY)]
alyssum (əlis´əm) *n.* **1** a plant of the cruciferous genus *Alyssum*, that includes *A. saxatile.* **2** a related plant, *Lobularia maritima*, sweet alyssum. [Gr. *alusson*]
Alzheimer's disease (alts´hīməz) *n.* a degenerative disease of the central nervous system characterized by a deterioration of mental faculties resembling premature mental senility or dementia. [Alois *Alzheimer*, 1864–1915, German physician]
AM *abbr.* **1** amplitude modulation. **2** anno mundi (in the year of the world). **3** associate member. **4** (*chiefly N Am.*) Master of Arts (L *Artium Magister*).
Am *chem. symbol* americium.
Am. *abbr.* America, American.
am BE.
a.m. *abbr.* ante meridiem (before noon).
amabile (amah´bili) *adv.* (*Mus.*) amiably, tenderly, sweetly. [It., amiable]
amadavat AVADAVAT.
amadou (am´ədoo) *n.* a tinder prepared from a dried fungus steeped in saltpetre, used as a match and a styptic. [F *amadou*, OProv. *amador*, L *amātōrem*, a lover (*amāre*, to love)]
amah (ah´mə) *n.* (in the Far East and India) a maidservant or nanny. [Port. *ama*, wet nurse]
amain (əmān´) *adv.* energetically, violently, in full force, at full speed, at once. [OE *a-*, on, *mægen*, might]
amalgam (əmal´gəm) *n.* **1** a compound of different things. **2** a mixture of any other metal with mercury. **amalgamate** *v.t.* **1** to mix, unite, combine, to compound into one mixture. **2** to combine (another metal) with mercury. ~*v.i.* to combine, to blend, to merge into one. **amalgamation** (-ā´shən) *n.* **1** the act of amalgamating. **2** the blending of different things. **3** a homogeneous union. **amalgamative** *a.* tending to combine. [F *amalgame*, med. L *amalgama*, prob. from Gr. *malagma*, an emollient, a plaster (*malassein*, to soften)]
amanuensis (əmanūen´sis) *n.* (*pl.* **amanuenses** (-sēz)) a person employed to write what another dictates or to copy manuscripts. [L *amanuensis* (viz. *servus*), a scribe (*ā mānu*, by hand, *-ensis*, suf. pertaining to)]
amaranth (am´əranth), †**amarant** (-ant) *n.* **1** an imaginary flower supposed never to fade. **2** a purple colour. **3** any of a genus of plants, *Amaranthus*, that includes love-lies-bleeding and prince's feather. **amaranthine** (-an´thīn) *a.* **1** of or relating to amaranth. **2** unfading. [L *amarantus*, Gr. *amarantos* (*a-*, not, *marainein*, to wither)]
amaryllis (əmaril´is) *n.* an autumn-flowering bulbous plant. [Gr. *Amarullis*, name of a country girl in pastoral poetry]
amass (əmas´) *v.t.* **1** to make or gather into a heap. **2** to collect together, to accumulate. **amasser** *n.* [F *amasser* (*à*, to, *masse*, mass, L *ad*, *massam*)]
amateur (am´ətə, -chə) *n.* **1** a person who practises anything as a pastime, as distinguished from one who does so professionally. **2** a person who competes in a sport for enjoyment rather than payment. **3** a person who is fond of an art, pastime etc., a devotee. **4** a person who dabbles or is unskilled in a subject. ~*a.* **1** engaging in something for enjoyment; not professional, not receiving payment. **2** involving or for amateurs. **3** amateurish. **amateur detective** *n.* a person with theories supposed to explain police problems. **amateurish** *a.* not up to the professional standard. **amateurishly** *adv.* **amateurishness** *n.* **1** the quality of being amateurish. **2** an inferior standard of execution. **amateurism** *n.* **1** the state, condition or practice of an amateur. **2** dilettantism. [F *amateur*, L *amātōrem* (*amāre*, to love)]
amative (am´ətiv) *a.* amorous. **amativeness** *n.* amorousness, erotic propensity. [L *amāre*, to love]
amatol (am´ətol) *n.* an explosive consisting of a mixture of ammonium nitrate and trinitrotoluene. [*am*monium, *tol*uene]
amatory (am´ətəri) *a.* **1** of or relating to love or sexual desire. **2** causing or designed to cause love. **amatorial** (-taw´-) *a.* of or relating to love or courtship. **amatorially** *adv.* [L *amātorius* (*amātor*, a lover)]
amaurosis (amawrō´sis) *n.* partial or total blindness from disease of the optic nerve, usu. without visible defect. **amaurotic** (-rot´-) *a.* affected with amaurosis. [Gr. *amaurōsis* (*amauroein*, to darken, from *amauros*, dark)]
amaze (əmāz´) *v.t.* to astound, to overwhelm with wonder, to bewilder. ~†*n.* extreme astonishment, wonder, bewilderment, amazement. **amazed** *a.* **amazedly** (-zid-) *adv.* **amazedness** (-zid-) *n.* **amazement** *n.* **1** overwhelming surprise. **2** the state of being amazed. **amazing** *a.* **amazingly** *adv.* [OE *āmasian* (*a-*, intens. pref.), to confound; see also MAZE]
Amazon (am´əzən) *n.* **1** any of a fabled race of Scythian female warriors. **2** a female warrior. **3** (**amazon**) a tall, strong woman; a virago. **amazon ant** *n.* an ant of the genus *Polyergus*, the neuters of which enslave the young of other species. **Amazonian** (-zō´-), **amazonian** *a.* **1** of or relating to the fabled Amazons; warlike, strong. **2** of or relating to the river Amazon (named from the female warriors recorded there by the early Spaniards). [Gr. *amazōn* (foreign word explained by Greeks as *a-*, not, *mazos*, breast, from legend that they cut away the right breast to use the bow more freely)]
ambassador (ambas´ədə) *n.* **1** a high-ranking diplomat sent by a state as its permanent representative in another country or on a particular mission abroad. **2** a representative, messenger; a promoter (e.g. of peace). **ambassador-at-large** *n.* (*pl.* **ambassadors-at-large**) a US ambassador not accredited to a particular foreign government. **ambassador extraordinary** *n.* (*pl.* **ambassadors extraordinary**) a high-ranking diplomat sent on a special mission. **ambassadorial** (-daw´-) *a.* **ambassador plenipotentiary** *n.* (*pl.* **ambassadors plenipotentiary**) an ambassador armed with full powers to sign treaties etc. **ambassadorship** *n.* **ambassadress** (-dris) *n.* **1** a female ambassador. **2** the wife of an ambassador. [F *ambassadeur*, OSp. *ambaxador*, late L *ambaxiāre*, *ambactiāre* (*ambactia*, a mission, office, from Celt. *ambactus*, a servant, from *amb-*, about, and Celt. root *ag-*, to drive, cognate with L *agere*)]
amber (am´bə) *n.* **1** a yellowish translucent fossil resin, found chiefly on the southern shores of the Baltic, used for ornaments, mouthpieces of pipes, and in the manufacture of some varnishes. **2** the colour of amber,

an orange yellow or brownish yellow. **3** a warning light of this colour, esp. a traffic light. *~a.* made of or coloured like amber. **amber gambler** *n.* (*coll.*) a person who drives at speed past an amber traffic light to avoid having to stop at red. [F *ambre*, Arab. *'anbar*, ambergris]

ambergris (am´bəgrēs) *n.* a light, fatty, inflammable substance, ashy in colour, found floating in tropical seas (a secretion from the intestines of the cachalot or sperm whale, it is used in perfumery, and was formerly used in cookery and medicine). [F *ambre gris*, grey amber]

ambiance AMBIENCE (under AMBIENT).

ambidextrous (ambidek´strəs), **ambidexterous** *a.* **1** using both hands with equal facility. **2** double-dealing. **ambidexterity** (-ster´-) *n.* **ambidextrously** *adv.* **ambidextrousness** *n.* [med. L *ambidexter* (*ambi-*, both, on both sides, *dexter*, right-handed)]

ambient (am´biənt) *a.* surrounding, encompassing on all sides; of or relating to the immediate surroundings. **ambience** (am´biəns, ãbiãs´), **ambiance** *n.* a surrounding atmosphere or influence, an environment. **ambient music** *n.* atmospheric electronic music. [L *ambiens -entis* pres.p. of *ambīre* (*amb-*, on both sides, about, *īre*, to go)]

ambiguous (əmbig´ūəs) *a.* **1** susceptible of two or more meanings. **2** of doubtful meaning, equivocal, obscure. **3** of uncertain position or classification. **ambiguity** (-bigū´-) *n.* (*pl.* **ambiguities**) **1** the state or an instance of being ambiguous; an ambiguous expression. **2** uncertainty of meaning. **ambiguously** *adv.* **ambiguousness** *n.* [L *ambiguus*, doubtful, from *ambigere* (*amb-*, both ways, *agere*, to drive)]

Usage note See note under AMBIVALENT (under AMBIVALENCE).

ambisonics (ambison´iks) *n.* a system of multi-channel high-fidelity sound reproduction which surrounds the listener with sound. [L *ambi-*, on both sides, SONICS (under SONIC)]

ambit (am´bit) *n.* **1** scope, extent. **2** boundary, limit. [L *ambitus*, a going about (see AMBIENT)]

ambition (ambish´ən) *n.* **1** a desire for power, success, superiority or excellence. **2** a strong desire to achieve anything, usu. something advantageous or creditable. **3** the object of such desire. **ambitious** *a.* **1** actuated by or indicating ambition. **2** highly desirous (of); eager and determined (to do). **3** necessitating great effort, resources, skill etc. **ambitiously** *adv.* **ambitiousness** *n.* [F *ambition*, L *ambitiōnem*, soliciting for votes, *ambīre* (*amb-*, about, *īre*, to go)]

ambivalence (ambiv´ələns), **ambivalency** (-si) *n.* the simultaneous existence in the mind of two incompatible feelings or wishes. **ambivalent** *a.* **ambivalently** *adv.* [L *ambo*, both, *valens*, being worth]

Usage note The adjectives *ambivalent* and *ambiguous* should not be confused: *ambivalent* refers to uncertainty of attitude, and *ambiguous* to different possible meanings or interpretations.

ambivert (am´bivœt) *n.* a person who fluctuates between introversion and extroversion. **ambiversion** (-vœ´shən) *n.* [L *ambi*, on both sides, *vert-* from *vertere*, to turn]

amble (am´bəl) *v.i.* **1** to walk at a leisurely relaxed pace. **2** (of a horse, mule) to move by lifting the two feet on one side alternately with the two feet on the other. **3** to ride an ambling horse. *~n.* **1** an easy relaxed pace. **2** a leisurely walk, a stroll. **3** a pace like that of an ambling horse. **ambler** *n.* **1** an ambling horse. **2** a person whose gait resembles that of an ambling horse. **ambling** *a.* [OF *ambler*, L *ambulāre*, to walk]

amblyopia (ambliō´piə) *n.* dimness of vision without any obvious defect in the eye. **amblyopic** (-op´-) *a.* affected with or relating to amblyopia. [Gr. *ambluōpos*, a. (*amblus*, dull, *ōps ōpos*, eye)]

ambo (am´bō) *n.* (*pl.* **ambos, ambones** (-bō´nēz)) a pulpit or reading desk in early medieval churches. [late L *ambo -ōnem*, Gr. *ambōn*]

amboyna (amboi´nə), **amboina** *n.* the finely variegated wood of *Pterospermum indicum*. [from name of island]

ambrosia (ambrō´ziə) *n.* **1** the fabled food of the gods. **2** anything very pleasant to the taste or the smell. **3** bee-bread. **4** a composite plant of the genus *Ambrosia*, allied to wormwood. **ambrosia beetle** *n.* any of various beetles of the family Scolytidae which bore tunnels into solid wood and feed on fungi growing in the tunnels. **ambrosial** *a.* **1** containing the qualities of ambrosia. **2** delicious, fragrant. **3** ethereal, divine. **ambrosially** *adv.* [Gr. *ambrosia*, fem. of a. *ambrosios*, from *ambrotos* (*a-*, not, *brotos*, mortal)]

ambry AUMBRY.

ambsace (amz´ās), **amesace** (āmz´-) *n.* **1** both aces, the lowest possible throw at dice. **2** bad luck, misfortune, worthlessness. [OF *ambes as*, L *ambas as*, both aces]

ambulance (am´būləns) *n.* **1** a vehicle for the transport of wounded, injured or sick people. **2** a moving hospital which follows an army in the field. **ambulance-chaser** *n.* (*coll.*) a person who tries to profit from another's tragedy, grief etc., esp. a lawyer who offers to pursue a claim for damages on behalf of accident victims. **ambulance man** *n.* a male member of an ambulance crew. **ambulance woman** *n.* a female member of an ambulance crew. [F *ambulance*, L *ambulans -ntem*, pres.p. of *ambulāre*, to walk]

ambulate (am´būlāt) *v.i.* (*formal*) to walk about. **ambulant** *a.* **1** walking or moving about. **2** (*Med.*) (of a patient) able to walk. **3** (*Med.*) (of a treatment) not confining the patient to bed. **ambulation** (-lā´shən) *n.* (*formal*) the act of walking. [L *ambulat-*, part. stem of *ambulāre*, see AMBULANCE]

ambulatory (am´būlətəri) *a.* **1** of or relating to walking. **2** fitted for walking. **3** not confined or confining to bed. **4** movable, temporary. *~n.* (*pl.* **ambulatories**) a place to walk in, esp. an aisle or a cloister in a church or a monastery. [as AMBULATE]

ambuscade (ambəskād´) *n.* **1** an ambush, a lying in wait to attack an enemy. **2** the force placed in ambush. *~v.i.* to lie in ambush. *~v.t.* **1** to ambush. **2** to place in ambush. [F *embuscade*, Sp. *emboscada* or It. *imboscata*, from late L *imboscāre* (see AMBUSH)]

ambush (am´bush) *n.* **1** a surprise attack by forces. **2** the concealment of forces for such an attack; the locality chosen; the force employed. **3** any lying in wait. *~v.t.* **1** to lie in wait for. **2** to attack from ambush. *~v.i.* to lie in wait. **ambush television** *n.* (*esp. N Am.*) television in which members of the public participating in a show are confronted with unexpected personal information. [OF *embusche*, from v. *embuscher*, late L *imboscāre*, to set in ambush (*in*, in, *boscus*, a bush, thicket)]

AMDG *abbr.* to the greater glory of God. [L *ad majorem Dei gloriam*]

ameba AMOEBA.

ameer AMIR.

ameliorate (əmē´liərāt) *v.t.* (*formal*) to make better, to improve. *~v.i.* to grow better. **amelioration** (-ā´shən) *n.* **1** the act of making better; the state of being made better. **2** improvement. **ameliorative** *a.* **ameliorator** *n.* [F *améliorer*, OF *ameillorer* (*à*, to, *meillorer*, from late L *meliōrāre*, from *melior*, better)]

amen (ahmen´, ā´men) *int.* so be it, may it be as it has been asked, said or promised (said esp. at the end of a prayer or hymn). *~n.* **1** an utterance of the word 'Amen', an expression of assent. **2** a concluding word. **amen to that!** used to express agreement or the hope that the previous speaker's wish will be fulfilled. **to say amen to** to express agreement with or approval of. [L *āmēn*,

Gr. *amēn*, Heb. *ā-mēn*, certainty, truth, certainly, verily (*āman*, to strengthen, confirm)]

amenable (əmēnˊəbəl) *a.* **1** willing to cooperate, readily persuaded, tractable, responsive. **2** (*Law*) (of a person) answerable, liable. **3** (*Law*) (of a thing) subject, liable. **amenability** (-bilˊ-) *n.* **1** the quality or state of being amenable. **2** tractableness. **amenableness** *n.* **amenably** *adv.* [F *amener* (*à*, to, *mener*, to lead, bring, from late L *mināre*, from L *minārī*, to threaten)]

amend (əmendˊ) *v.t.* **1** to alter (a person or thing) for the better, to improve. **2** to remove errors from, to correct. **3** to formally alter (a bill or resolution). *~v.i.* to abandon evil courses, grow better. **amendable** *a.* **amendment** *n.* **1** a change for the better. **2** something added to a bill or motion; an addition to the US constitution. **3** improvement in health. **4** reformation. **5** a correction of error in a writ or process. **amends** *n.* reparation, satisfaction, compensation. **to make amends** to compensate or make up (for). [OF *amender*, L *ēmendāre* (*e-*, *ex-*, out of, *menda*, fault)]

Usage note See note under EMEND.

amende honorable (əmãnd onorahˊbəl) *n.* (*pl.* **amendes honorables** (əmãndˊ onorahˊbəl)) an open or public apology, often accompanied by some form of amends.

amenity (əmēˊniti, -menˊ-) *n.* (*pl.* **amenities**) **1** the quality of being pleasant or agreeable; attractions, charms. **2** a feature or facility conducive to the usefulness or attractiveness of something. **3** (*pl.*) pleasing manners, civilities. **amenity bed** *n.* a bed in a hospital for which the patient pays a charge in order to enjoy certain amenities, e.g. privacy. [L *amoenitātem* (*amoenus*, pleasant, allied to *amāre*, to love)]

amenorrhoea (əmenərēˊə), (*esp. N Am.*) **amenorrhea** *n.* the abnormal cessation of menstruation. [Gr. *a-*, not, *men*, a month, *rhoia*, flow]

ament[1] (əmentˊ), **amentum** (-təm) *n.* (*pl.* **aments, amenta** (-tə)) a catkin. **amentaceous** (aməntāˊshəs) *a.* [L *amentum*, a thong or strap]

ament[2] AMENTIA.

amentia (əmenˊshiə) *n.* severe congenital mental deficiency. **ament**[2] (əmentˊ, āˊ-) *n.* a person with amentia. [L *a-*, *ab-*, from, *mens -tis*, mind]

amentum AMENT[1].

Amer. *abbr.* **1** America. **2** American.

Amerasian (amərāˊshən, -zhən) *a.* of mixed American and Asian parentage. *~n.* an Amerasian person, esp. someone fathered by an American serviceman in Korea or Vietnam. [*American*, *Asian*]

amerce (əmœsˊ) *v.t.* **1** to punish by fine. **2** to exact something from. **3** to punish. **amercement** *n.* **1** the infliction of an arbitrary fine. **2** the fine inflicted. **amerciable** *a.* liable to amercement. [A-F *amercier*, *à merci*, at the mercy of the court (*à*, at, *merci*, MERCY)]

American (əmerˊikən) *a.* of or relating to the continent of America, esp. to the US. *~n.* **1** a native or inhabitant of N, S or Central America. **2** a native or inhabitant of the US. **3** the English language as spoken in the United States. **Native American** NATIVE. **Americana** (-rikahˊnə) *n.pl.* objects typical of or relating to America, esp. in the form of a collection. **American aloe** *n.* the century plant. **American dream** *n.* the notion that America offers the possibility of success to any individual. **American football** *n.* a football game somewhat resembling rugby, played with an oval ball and teams of 11 players. **American Indian** *n.* a member of any of the indigenous peoples of N, S or Central America, usu. with the exception of the Inuit people. **Americanism** *n.* **1** anything characteristic of the US, esp. a word or phrase peculiar to or borrowed from the US. **2** attachment to or political sympathy with the US. **Americanize, Americanise** *v.t.* **1** to naturalize as an American. **2** to assimilate political customs or institutions to those of the US. *~v.i.* to become American in character, manners or speech. **Americanization** (-zāˊshən) *n.* **American Legion** *n.* an association of American ex-servicemen, founded in 1919. **American plaice** *n.* a N Atlantic fish, *Hippoglossoides platessoides*. **American plan** *n.* inclusive terms at a hotel etc.

Usage note The term *Native American* is now sometimes preferred to *American Indian*, though not by all the peoples to whom the names are applicable.

americium (əmerisˊiəm) *n.* an artificially-created, metallic radioactive element, at. no. 95, chem. symbol Am.

Amerind (amˊərind), **Amerindian** (-rinˊdiən) *n.* an American Indian. *~a.* of or relating to American Indians. [contr. American Indian]

amesace AMBSACE.

amethyst (amˊəthist) *n.* a violet-blue variety of crystalline quartz, supposed by the ancients to prevent intoxication. **amethystine** (-tīn) *a.* composed of, containing or resembling amethyst. [L *amethystus*, Gr. *amethustos*, a remedy against drunkenness (*a-*, not, *methuein*, to be drunken, from *methu*, strong drink)]

Amharic (amharˊik) *n.* the official language of Ethiopia. *~a.* of or relating to this language. [*Amhara*, a province of Ethiopia]

amiable (āˊmiəbəl) *a.* **1** friendly, kindly-disposed, likeable. **2** possessed of qualities fitted to evoke friendly feeling. **amiability** (-bilˊ-) *n.* **amiably** *adv.* [OF *amiable*, L *amicābilis* (AMICABLE), (confused with OF *amable*, L *amābilis*, lovable (*amāre*, to love)]

amianthus (amianˊthəs), **amiantus** (-təs), †**amiant** (amˊiənt) *n.* a variety of asbestos, a fibrous kind of chrysolite of a greenish colour. **amianthoid** (-thoid) *a.* resembling amianthus. *~n.* a kind of asbestos. [L *amiantus*, Gr. *amiantos*, undefiled (*a-*, not, *miainein*, to stain)]

amicable (amˊikəbəl) *a.* **1** friendly. **2** designed to be friendly. **3** resulting from friendliness. **amicability** (-bilˊ-) *n.* **amicableness** *n.* **amicably** *adv.* [L *amicābilis* (*amicāre*, to make friendly, *amīcus*, friend)]

amice[1] (amˊis) *n.* a piece of white linen worn on the neck and shoulders at Mass by Roman Catholic and some Anglican priests. [early form, *amyte*, OF *amit*, L *amictus*, p.p. of *amicīre* (*amb-*, around, *jacere*, to cast)]

amice[2] (amˊis) *n.* a hood, cap or cape worn by members of certain religious orders. [OF *aumuce*, Sp. *almucio* (perh. from Arab. *al-*, the, and G *Mütze*, cap)]

amicus curiae (əmēkəs kūˊriē) *n.* (*pl.* **amici curiae** (əmēkī)) a disinterested adviser in a court of law. [L, friend of the court]

amid (əmidˊ), **amidst** (əmidstˊ) *prep.* **1** in the midst or middle. **2** among. **amidships,** (*N Am. also*) **amidship** *adv.* in the middle part of a ship. [ME *amiddes*, OE *on middan*, in the middle (adverbial *s* is properly a sign of gen. case)]

amide (amˊīd) *n.* **1** any of various organic compounds constituted as if obtained from ammonia by the substitution of one or more univalent organic acid radicals for one or more atoms of hydrogen. **2** any of various compounds formed by substitution of another element or radical for an atom of hydrogen in ammonia. **amidic** (əmidˊ-) *a.* **amido-** *comb. form* containing the characteristic amide group of ammonia with one hydrogen atom replaced by an acid radical. [AMMONIA, -IDE]

Amidol® (amˊidol) *n.* a compound of phenol, chemical formula $C_6H_3(NH_2)_2(OH)_2HCl$, used in the form of a soluble crystalline powder as a photographic developer.

amidships, amidship AMID.

amigo (əmēˊgō) *n.* (*pl.* **amigos**) (*N Am., coll.*) a friend (also often used as a form of address). [Sp.]

amine (am´īn, -ēn, ā´-) *n.* any of various organic compounds derived from ammonia by the substitution of one or more univalent hydrocarbon radicals for one or more atoms of hydrogen. **aminic** (əmin´-) *a.* **amino** (əmē´nō) *a.* containing the characteristic amine group of ammonia with one hydrogen atom replaced by a hydrocarbon radical. **amino acid** *n.* an organic acid containing one or more amino groups, esp. any of those that occur as the constituents of proteins. [AMMONIA, -INE]

amir (əmiə´), **ameer** *n.* the title of several Muslim rulers, esp. formerly in India and Afghanistan. [Arab. *amīr*, nobleman, prince (*amara*, he commanded); cp. EMIR]

Amish (ā´mish, ah´-, am´-) *a.* of or belonging to a strict US Mennonite sect. *~n.pl.* the members of this sect. [G *Amisch*, from Jakob *Amman* or *Amen*, 17th-cent. Swiss Mennonite leader]

amiss (əmis´) *a.* faulty, unsatisfactory, wrong. *~adv.* wrongly, astray, in a faulty manner, unsatisfactorily. **to take amiss** to be offended by. [MISS[1]]

amitosis (amitō´sis, āmī-) *n.* cell division without mitosis. [A-[3], MITOSIS]

amitriptyline (amitrip´tilēn) *n.* a tricyclic anti-depressant drug with a mildly tranquillizing effect. [*ami*no, *trypt*amine, meth*yl*, -INE]

amity (am´iti) *n.* friendship, concord, mutual good feeling, friendly relations. [F *amitié*, late L *amīcitātem* (*amīcus*, friendly, from *amāre*, to love)]

ammeter (am´ətə) *n.* an instrument for measuring the strength of the electric current in a circuit. [AMPERE, -METER]

ammo (am´ō) *n.* (*coll.*) short for AMMUNITION.

ammonal (am´ənəl) *n.* an explosive compound containing aluminium mixed with ammonium nitrate. [*ammon*ium, *al*uminium]

ammonia (əmō´niə) *n.* **1** a pungent volatile gas, powerfully alkaline, a compound of nitrogen and hydrogen first obtained from sal ammoniac. **2** a solution of ammonia in water, containing ammonium hydroxide. **ammoniac** (amənī´ak), **ammoniacal** *a.* of, relating to or possessing the properties of ammonia. **ammoniated** (-ātid) *a.* combined with ammonia. **ammonify** *v.t.* (*3rd pers. sing. pres.* **ammonifies,** *pres.p.* **ammonifying,** *past, p.p.* **ammonified**) to treat or combine with (a compound of) ammonia. **ammonification** (-fikā´shən) *n.* **ammonium** (-əm) *n.* the ion or radical derived from ammonia by addition of a hydrogen ion or atom. **ammonium hydroxide** *n.* a solution of ammonia in water. [adopted from L *sal ammōniacus*, salt of Ammon, Gr. *ammōniakos*, of (Jupiter) Ammon; see SAL AMMONIAC (under SAL[1])]

ammonite (am´ənīt) *n.* the shell of a genus of fossil cephalopods, curved like the ram's horn on the statue of Jupiter Ammon. [med. L *cornu Ammonis*, horn of Ammon]

ammonium AMMONIA.

ammunition (amūnish´ən) *n.* **1** any projectiles, e.g. bullets, shells, rockets, that can be discharged from a weapon. **2** offensive missiles generally. **3** anything that can be used to advantage in a dispute or argument. [F *amunition* (MUNITION), formed by vulgar confusion of *la munition* with *l'amunition*]

amnesia (amnē´ziə, -zhə) *n.* loss of memory. **amnesiac** (-ziak), **amnesic** (-zik) *n.* a person suffering from amnesia. *~a.* of or relating to amnesia. [Gr. *amnēsia*]

amnesty (am´nəsti) *n.* (*pl.* **amnesties**) **1** a general pardon. **2** a period during which offences may be admitted without incurring punishment. *~v.t.* (*3rd pers. sing. pres.* **amnesties,** *pres.p.* **amnestying,** *past, p.p.* **amnestied**) to grant amnesty to. [L from Gr. *amnēstia*, from *amnēstos*, forgotten (*a*-, not, *mna-omai*, I remember)]

amniocentesis (amniōsentē´sis) *n.* the removal of a sample of amniotic fluid from the womb, by insertion of a hollow needle, in order to test for chromosomal abnormalities in the foetus. [Gr. AMNION, *kentesis*, pricking, puncture]

amnion (am´niən) *n.* (*pl.* **amnions, amnia**) the innermost membrane with which the foetus in the womb is surrounded. **amniote** (-ōt) *n.* any of the group of vertebrates (reptiles, birds and mammals) which possess an amnion in the foetal state. *~a.* of or relating to these animals. **amniotic** (-ot´-) *a.* of or relating to, characterized by, contained in or of the nature of an amnion. **amniotic fluid** *n.* the fluid contained by the amnion in which the foetus is suspended. [Gr., caul, dim. of *amnos*, a lamb]

amoeba (əmē´bə), (*N Am.*) **ameba** *n.* (*pl.* **amoebas, amoebae** (-bē), (*N Am.*) **amebas, amebae**) a microscopic organism of the simplest structure, consisting of a single protoplasmic cell, which is extensile and contractile so that its shape is continually changing. **amoebiasis** (-bī´ə-) *n.* (*pl.* **amoebiases**) infection with amoebas, esp. so as to cause dysentery. **amoebic** *a.* **1** amoeba-like. **2** caused by amoeba. **amoebic dysentery** *n.* dysentery caused by intestinal infection with certain types of amoebae. **amoeboid** *a.* resembling an amoeba. [Gr. *amoibē*, change]

amok (əmok´), **amuck** (əmŭk´) *adv.* in a frenzy, esp. as below. **to run amok** to rush about in a wild, uncontrollable rage, attacking people indiscriminately. [Malay *amoq*, engaging furiously in battle]

among (əmŭng´), **amongst** (əmŭngst´) *prep.* **1** in the midst of; surrounded by. **2** in the number of. **3** in the category or class of. **4** by sharing or dividing between a group of. **5** involving a group of. [ME *amonges*, OE *onmang, on gemange* (*on*, prep., *gemang*, crowd) in a crowd, allied to *mengan*, to mingle]

amontillado (əmontilah´dō) *n.* (*pl.* **amontillados**) a kind of medium dry sherry. [Sp. *vino amontillado*, wine of *Montilla*, a town in Spain]

amoral (āmor´əl, ə-) *a.* not concerned with morals; having no moral principles. **amoralism** *n.* **amoralist** *n.* a non-moral person. [Gr. *a*-, not, MORAL]

Usage note The adjectives *amoral* and *immoral* should not be confused: *amoral* means having no reference to morality, and *immoral* contrary to morality.

amoretto (əməret´ō) *n.* (*pl.* **amoretti** (-ti)) a cupid. [It. dim. of *amore*, love]

amorist (am´ərist) *n.* **1** a person who makes a study of or writes about love. **2** a lover, a gallant, a philanderer.

amoroso[1] (amərō´zō) *adv., a.* (*Mus.*) to be performed lovingly. [It.]

amoroso[2] (amərō´zō) *n.* (*pl.* **amorosos**) a full rich type of sherry. [Sp., amorous]

amorous (am´ərəs) *a.* **1** naturally inclined to love. **2** in love. **3** lecherous. **4** relating to, or belonging to, love. **amorously** *adv.* **amorousness** *n.* [OF *amoros*, L *amōrōsus*]

amorphous (āmaw´fəs, ə-) *a.* **1** shapeless. **2** irregularly shaped. **3** (*Biol.*) not conforming to a normal standard. **4** not crystalline, uncrystallized. **5** ill-arranged, unsystematic, unorganized. **amorphism** *n.* **1** lack of regular form. **2** absence of crystallization. **amorphousness** *n.* the quality of being amorphous. [Gr. *amorphos*, shapeless (*a*-, not, *morphē*, form)]

amortize (əmaw´tīz), **amortise** *v.t.* **1** to liquidate (a debt) by instalments or by regular transfers to a sinking fund. **2** to write off (an asset) by gradual transfers to a sinking fund. **3** to alienate in mortmain. **amortization** (-zā´shən) *n.* **1** the use of a sinking fund to liquidate a debt or write off an asset. **2** the act or right of alienating lands in mortmain. [F *amortir*, to bring to death, possibly from a late L *admortīre* (*ad*-, to, *mortem*, death)]

amount (əmownt´) *v.i.* **1** to run into an aggregate by the accumulation of particulars; to mount up (to), to add up (to). **2** to be equivalent (to). *~n.* **1** a (numerical) quantity. **2** the sum total. **3** the full effect, value, significance of something. **4** a principal sum plus the interest on it. [OF *amonter* (*a mont*, to a mountain, L *ad montem*)]

amour (əmuə´) *n.* a love affair, esp. a secret one; an amorous intrigue. **amourette** (amuret´) *n.* a petty love affair. [OF *amur, amour*, L *amōr-em*, love]

amour propre (amuə propr´rə) *n.* self-esteem. [F]

amp (amp) *n.* **1** short for AMPERE. **2** short for AMPLIFIER (under AMPLIFY).

ampelopsis (ampəlop´sis) *n.* any climbing or creeping plant of the genus *Ampelopsis*, that includes the Virginia creeper. [Gr. *ampelos*, vine; *opsis*, appearance]

ampere (am´peə) *n.* a unit by which an electric current is measured, the current sent by 1 volt through a resistance of 1 ohm. **amperage** *n.* the strength of an electric current measured in amperes. **ampere-hour** *n.* the quantity of electricity delivered in 1 hour by a 1-ampere strength current. **amperemeter** *n.* AMMETER. **ampere turn** *n.* the product of the number of turns in the coil of wire of an electromagnet and the number of amperes flowing through. [André M. *Ampère*, 1775–1836, French physicist]

ampersand (am´pəsand) *n.* the sign '&'. [a corruption of *and per se and*, 'and' by itself makes 'and']

amphetamine (amfet´əmēn, -min) *n.* (a derivative of) a synthetic drug which has a stimulant action on the brain. [*a*lpha, *m*ethyl, *ph*enyl, *et*hyl, *amine*]

amphi- (am´fi) *comb. form* **1** both. **2** of both kinds. **3** on both sides. **4** around. [Gr. *amphi*, prep., on both sides]

amphibian (amfib´iən) *n.* **1** any vertebrate animal of the class Amphibia, that have an aquatic gill-breathing larval stage followed by a terrestrial lung-breathing adult stage. **2** any animal that can live either on land or in water. **3** an aircraft, tank or other vehicle adapted for both land and water. *~a.* **1** of or relating to the Amphibia. **2** amphibious. **amphibious** *a.* **1** capable of living both on land and in water. **2** designed for operation on land and in water. **3** of, relating to or trained for the invasion of foreign shores via the sea. **4** of mixed nature. **amphibiousness** *n.* [L *amphibium*, from Gr. *amphibion*, creature living in both elements (AMPHI-, *bios*, life)]

amphibiology (amfibiol´əji) *n.* the branch of zoology which deals with the Amphibia. **amphibiological** (-loj´-) *a.*

amphibole (am´fibōl) *n.* any of a group of silicate and aluminosilicate minerals including hornblende and tremolite that usu. occur in the form of long slender dark-coloured crystals. **amphibolite** (-līt) *n.* a rock consisting essentially of amphibole. **amphibolitic** (-lit´-) *a.* [F from Gr. *amphibolos*, uncertain; so-called because of the variety in the structure of these minerals]

amphibology (amfibol´əji), **amphiboly** (-fib´əli) *n.* (*pl.* **amphibologies, amphibolies**) **1** an ambiguous expression, esp. a sentence composed of unambiguous words that is susceptible of a double meaning because of its construction. **2** the use of such expressions; ambiguity; equivocation. **amphibological** (-loj´-) *a.* **amphibologically** *adv.* **amphibolous** (-fib´-) *a.* ambiguous, doubtful. [F *amphibologie*, late L *amphibologia* (L *amphibolia*), Gr. *amphibolia* (AMPHI-, *ballein*, to throw), -LOGY]

amphibrach (am´fibrak) *n.* a metrical foot of three syllables, the middle one long and the first and third short. [Gr. *amphibrachus*, (*brachus*, short)]

amphictyon (amfik´tiən) *n.* (*pl.* **amphictyons**) a delegate to the council of an amphictyony. **amphictyonic** (-on´-) *a.* of or relating to an amphictyon or amphictyony. **amphictyony** *n.* (*pl.* **amphictyonies**) **1** a confederation of states for the maintenance of temples and their associated cults. **2** the council of amphictyons. [Gr. *amphiktuones* (AMPHI-, *ktuones*), dwellers about, neighbours]

amphimacer (amfim´əsə) *n.* CRETIC. [Gr. *amphimakros* (*makros*, long)]

amphimixis (amfimik´sis) *n.* **1** sexual reproduction. **2** the fusion of gametes. [Gr. AMPHI-, *mixis*, a mingling]

amphioxus (amfiok´səs) *n.* (*pl.* **amphioxuses, amphioxi** (-sī)) a lancelet. [Gr. AMPHI-, *oxus*, sharp]

amphipod (am´fipod) *n.* any small sessile-eyed crustacean of the order Amphipoda, having two kinds of feet, one for walking and one for swimming. *~a.* amphipodous. **amphipodous** *a.* having two kinds of feet, one for walking and one swimming. [Gr. *pous podos*, foot]

amphiprostyle (amfip´rəstīl) *n.* a temple having a portico at each end. [F from L *amphiprostylus*, Gr. *amphiprostulos* (*prostulos*, PROSTYLE)]

amphisbaena (amfisbē´nə) *n.* (*pl.* **amphisbaenas, amphisbaenae** (-nē)) **1** a fabled snake said by the ancients to have a head at each end, and to be able to move in either direction. **2** a serpentiform lizard of the genus *Amphisbaena*, having the tail short and blunt so that it resembles a second head. [Gr. *amphisbaina* (*amphis*, both ways, *bainein*, to go)]

amphitheatre (am´fithiətə), (*N Am.*) **amphitheater** *n.* **1** an oval or circular building with rows of seats rising one above another round an open space. **2** a place of public contest. **3** a semicircular gallery in a theatre. **4** a valley surrounded by hills. **amphitheatrical** (-at´-) *a.* [Gr. *amphitheatron* (see AMPHI-, THEATRE)]

amphora (am´fərə) *n.* (*pl.* **amphoras, amphorae** (-ē)) an ancient two-handled vessel for holding wine, oil etc. **amphoric** (-for´-) *a.* (*Med.*) (of breathing) resembling the sound made by blowing into an amphora. [L *amphora*, Gr. *amphoreus* (*phoreus*, a bearer, from *pherein*, to bear)]

amphoteric (amfəter´ik) *a.* able to react as both an acid and a base. [Gr. *amphoteros*, each of two]

ampicillin (ampisil´in) *n.* a semisynthetic penicillin used to treat infections esp. of the urinary and respiratory tract. [*am*ino, *penicillin*]

ample (am´pəl) *a.* (*comp.* **ampler**, *superl.* **amplest**) **1** of large dimensions, wide, great. **2** more than enough, fully sufficient, liberal. **3** (*euphem.*) (of a person) large; fat. **ampleness** *n.* **amply** *adv.* [F *ample*, L *amplus*]

amplexicaul (amplek´sikawl) *a.* (*Bot.*) embracing or clasping the stem. [L *amplexus*, p.p. of *amplector*, I embrace, *caulis*, a stem]

amplify (am´plifī) *v.t.* (*3rd pers. sing. pres.* **amplifies**, *pres.p.* **amplifying**, *past, p.p.* **amplified**) **1** to increase, make greater, esp. to increase the strength of (a signal) or the loudness of (sound). **2** to enlarge or dilate upon. *~v.i.* **1** to speak or write at greater length or in greater detail. **2** to expatiate. **amplification** (-fikā´shən) *n.* **1** enlargement or extension. **2** diffuseness. **3** increase in strength of a signal or sound. **4** an enlarged representation. **amplifier** *n.* **1** an electrical or electronic circuit or system to amplify signals, esp. in sound reproduction. **2** a complete unit which performs this function. [L *amplificare* (see AMPLE)]

amplitude (am´plitūd) *n.* **1** extent, size, bulk, greatness. **2** abundance. **3** breadth or scope. **4** the angular distance of a heavenly body, at its rising or setting, from the east or the west point of the horizon. **5** the magnitude of the variation from a main position or value of a vibration or oscillation, or of an alternating current or wave. **amplitude modulation** *n.* **1** (transmission of a signal by) modulation of the amplitude of a radio carrier wave in accordance with the characteristics of the signal carried. **2** broadcasting using this system of transmission. [L *amplitudo* (see AMPLE)]

ampoule (am´pool), (*N Am.*) **ampule** (-pūl) *n.* a sealed phial containing one dose of a drug. [F]

ampulla (ampul´ə) *n.* (*pl.* **ampullae** (-ē)) **1** a nearly globular flask with two handles, used by the ancient Romans. **2** a vessel for holding consecrated oil, wine etc. **3** (*Biol.*) the dilated end of any vessel. **4** a spongiole of a root. **ampullaceous** (-ā´shəs) *a.* **1** resembling a globular flask. **2** bottle-shaped. **3** swelling. [L]

amputate (am´pūtāt) *v.t.* to cut off (a limb or part of a limb) from an animal body by surgical operation. **amputation** (-tā´shən) *n.* the act of amputating. **amputator** *n.* **amputee** (-tē´) *n.* a person who has had a limb surgically removed. [L *amputātus*, p.p. of *amputāre* (*amb-*, about, *putāre*, to prune, lop)]

amrita (amrē´tə) *n.* the ambrosia of the gods in Hindu mythology. [Sansk.]

amt *abbr.* amount.

amtrac (am´trak), **amtrak** *n.* (*N Am.*) an amphibious tracked vehicle for landing assault troops. [*am*phibious *trac*tor]

amu *abbr.* atomic mass unit.

amuck AMOK.

amulet (am´ūlət) *n.* anything worn about the person as an imagined preservative against sickness, witchcraft etc. [F *amulette*, L *amulētum*, a talisman]

amuse (əmūz´) *v.t.* **1** to cause to laugh, smile or feel cheerful. **2** to keep pleasantly occupied, to entertain. **amusement** *n.* **1** anything which amuses; play, diversion. **2** the act of amusing, the excitement of laughter. **3** the state of being amused. **4** a mechanical device, sideshow etc. providing entertainment at a fairground, amusement arcade etc. **amusement arcade** *n.* a covered space containing coin-operated game and gambling machines. **amusement park** *n.* an outdoor area with permanent fairground rides and other amusements. **amusing** *a.* entertaining, diverting, causing laughter or smiles. **amusingly** *adv.* [OF *amuser*, to cause to muse (*à*, to, *muser*, to stare), see MUSE[2]]

amygdala (əmig´dələ) *n.* (*pl.* **amygdalae** (-lē)) an almond-shaped body part, such as a tonsil or a lobe of the cerebellum. **amygdale** (-dāl), **amygdule** (-dūl) *n.* an oval cavity in volcanic rock formed by a gas bubble and subsequently filled with a mineral. **amygdalin** (amig´dəlin) *n.* a crystalline substance extracted from bitter almonds, and found amorphous in the leaves of the cherry laurel. **amygdaloid** (əmig´dəloid) *a.* almond-shaped. *~n.* an igneous rock containing amygdales. **amygdaloid nucleus** *n.* a mass of grey matter, shaped roughly like an almond, found inside each cerebral hemisphere and associated with the sense of smell. [L *amygdala*, Gr. *amugdalē*, an almond]

amyl (am´il) *n.* (*used attrib.*) a monovalent group, C_5H_{11}, derived from pentane. **amylaceous** (-ā´shəs) *a.* of, relating to or of the nature of starch. **amylase** (-ās) *n.* any of various enzymes that break down starch and glycogen. **amylene** (-ēn) *n.* a hydrocarbon, with anaesthetic properties. **amyloid** (-oid) *a.* resembling or containing starch; starchy. *~n.* a non-nitrogenous starchy substance deposited in tissues in certain degenerative diseases. **amylopsin** (-op´sin) *n.* an enzyme in pancreatic juice that converts starch into sugar. [L *amylum*, starch]

Amytal® (am´itəl) *n.* a crystalline compound used as a sedative and hypnotic. [*amy*l, barbi*tal*]

an[1] A[1].

†**an[2]** (an) *conj.* if. [AND]

an. *abbr.* in the year. [L *anno*]

an- (an, ən) *pref.* **1** AD- assim. to *n*, as in *annex*, *announce*. **2** ANA-. **3** A-[3], not, before a vowel, as in *anaesthetic*, *anarchy*.

-an (ən) *suf.* of, belonging or relating to, e.g. *human*, *pagan*, *publican*, *Christian*, *Unitarian*, *European* etc. [L *-ānus* (sometimes through F *-ain*, retained in *captain*, *chaplain* or F *-en*, or through It., Sp. or Port. *-ano*)]

ana (ah´nə) *n.* (*pl.* **ana**) **1** (*as pl.*) literary gossip or anecdotes, usu. of a personal or local kind. **2** (*as pl.*) a collection of reminiscences, gossip or memorable sayings. **3** (*as sing.*) an item in such a collection. [-ANA]

ana- (an´ə), **an-** (an) *pref.* **1** up, as in *anadromous*. **2** back, backwards, as in *anachronism*, *anatropous*. **3** again, as in *Anabaptism*. [Gr. *ana*, upon, up, backwards]

-ana (ah´nə), **-iana** (iah´nə) *suf.* **1** objects relating to, as in *Africana*, *Americana*, *Victoriana*. **2** sayings of, anecdotes concerning, as in *Johnsoniana*, *Virgiliana*. [L *-āna*, neut. pl. of *-ānus*]

Anabaptism (anəbap´tizm) *n.* the doctrine that baptism should only be given to adults. **Anabaptist** *n.* **1** a member of a German sect which arose in the 16th cent. and advocated baptism only of adults and a form of Christian communism. **2** a person who rebaptizes. **3** (*derog.*) a Baptist. *~a.* of or relating to Anabaptism. **Anabaptistical** (-tis´-) *a.* [L *anabaptismus*, Gr. *anabaptismos* (see ANA-, BAPTISM (under BAPTIZE))]

anabas (an´əbas) *n.* a fish of the genus *Anabas* that includes the climbing perch, which can leave the water. [Gr. *anabas*, part. of *anabainein* (ANA-, *bainein*, to walk)]

anabasis (ənab´əsis) *n.* (*pl.* **anabases** (-sēz)) **1** a military advance up-country. **2** the expedition of Cyrus the Younger into Asia, narrated by Xenophon. [Gr. *anabasis*, going up (*anabainein*, see ANABAS)]

anabatic (anəbat´ik) *a.* (of wind or air currents) moving upwards. [Gr. *anabatikos*, ascending (*anabainein*, see ANABAS)]

anabiosis (anəbīō´sis) *n.* **1** a state of suspended animation or greatly reduced metabolism. **2** the ability to return to life from this state or from apparent death. **anabiotic** (-bīot´ik) *a.* [Gr. *ana-*, again, *bios*, life]

anabolism (ənab´əlizm) *n.* the building up of complex substances by assimilation of nutriment, with storage of energy. **anabolic** (anəbol´-) *a.* **anabolic steroid** *n.* any of a group of synthetic steroid hormones that cause rapid growth in body tissues, esp. skeletal muscle, and are sometimes (illegally) taken by athletes. [Gr. *anabolē*, rising up]

anabranch (an´əbrahnch) *n.* (*Austral.*) a tributary rejoining the main stream of a river and thus forming an island.

anachronism (anak´rənizm) *n.* **1** the assigning of an event, custom or circumstance to a wrong period or date. **2** anything out of date or incongruous with the present. **anachronic** (anəkron´ik) *a.* wrong in date, characterized by anachronism. **anachronically** *adv.* **anachronistic** (-nis´-) *a.* of, relating to or involving an anachronism. **anachronistically** *adv.* [F *anachronisme*, L *anachronismus*, Gr. *anachronismos* (*anachronizein*, to refer to a wrong time)]

anacoluthon (anəkəloo´thon) *n.* (*pl.* **anacolutha** (-thə)) **1** lack of grammatical sequence in a sentence. **2** a change of structure in a sentence that renders it ungrammatical. [Gr. *anakolouthon* (*an-*, not, *akolouthos*, following, from *keleuthos*, road)]

anaconda (anəkon´də) *n.* *Eunectes murinus*, a very large semiaquatic S American boa. [Sinhalese, *henakandāya*, whip snake (*hena*, lightning, *kanda*, stem)]

anacreontic (ənakrion´tik) *a.* **1** of or relating to the Greek poet Anacreon, or the metre used by him. **2** erotic, convivial. *~n.* an erotic or convivial poem. [L *Anacreonticus*, from Gr. *Anakreōn*]

anacrusis (anəkroo´sis) *n.* (*pl.* **anacruses** (-sēz)) an upward beat at the beginning of a verse, consisting of an unstressed syllable or syllables. [Gr. *anakrousis* (*krouein*, to strike)]

anadem (an´ədem) *n.* (*poet.*) **1** a garland or fillet. **2** a chaplet or crown of flowers. [L *anadēma*, Gr. *anadēma* (*ana-*, *deein*, to bind)]

anadromous (ənad´rəməs) *a.* (of fish) ascending rivers to deposit spawn. [Gr. (*dromos*, running)]

anaemia (ənē´miə), (*esp. N Am.*) **anemia** *n.* 1 lack of haemoglobin or of red corpuscles in the blood, leading to pallor and lack of energy. 2 pallor, bloodlessness. **anaemic**, (*N Am.*) **anemic** *a.* 1 of, relating to or suffering from anaemia. 2 lacking vitality. 3 pale. [Gr. *anaimia* (*an*-, not, *haima*, blood)]

anaerobe (aneə´rōb, an´ə-) *n.* an organism that thrives best, or only, in the absence of oxygen. **anaerobic** (anərō´bik) *a.* [Gr. *a*-, not, *aer*, air, *bios*, life]

anaesthesia (anəsthē´ziə), (*N Am.*) **anesthesia** *n.* 1 loss of bodily sensation due to nerve damage or other abnormality. 2 general or local loss of sensation, artificially induced for surgical purposes. **anaesthetic** (-thet´-) *a.* producing anaesthesia. ~*n.* a substance which produces anaesthesia (during surgical operations). **anaesthetically** *adv.* by way of an anaesthetic, so as to cause anaesthesia. **anaesthetics** (-thet´iks) *n.* the study of anaesthesia. **anaesthetist** (-nēs´thə-), (*N Am.*) **anesthesiologist** (-thēziol´əjist) *n.* a person who administers an anaesthetic, a person skilled in producing anaesthesia. **anaesthetize** (-nēs´thətīz), **anaesthetise** *v.t.* to administer an anaesthetic to. **anaesthetization** (-zā´shən) *n.* the process of effecting anaesthesia. [Gr. *anaisthēsia* (AN-, not, *aisthe*-, stem of *aisthanomai*, I feel)]

anaglyph (an´əglif) *n.* 1 a composite photograph in superimposed complementary colours which gives a stereoscopic image when viewed through special glasses. 2 a figure cut or embossed in low relief. **anaglyphic** (-glif´-), **anaglyptic** (-glip´-) *a.* 1 of or relating to an anaglyph. 2 wrought in low relief. **Anaglypta®** (-glip´-) *n.* a type of thick white wallpaper with a heavily embossed pattern. **anaglyptics** *n.* the art of working in low relief. [Gr. *anagluphē* (*gluphein*, to carve)]

anagnorisis (anəgnor´isis) *n.* (*pl.* **anagnorises** (-sēz)) (in Greek tragedy) a recognition that leads to the denouement. [L, from Gr. *anagnōrisis* (*gnōrizein*, to recognize)]

anagoge (an´əgōji, -gō´-), **anagogy** *n.* mystical, allegorical or spiritual interpretation. **anagogic** (-goj´-), **anagogical** *a.* 1 of or relating to anagoge. 2 mysterious, elevated, spiritual. **anagogically** *adv.* [L; Gr. *anagōgē* (*agein*, to lead)]

anagram (an´əgram) *n.* a word or sentence formed by transposing the letters of another word or sentence. **anagrammatic** (-mat´-), **anagrammatical** *a.* of, relating to or containing an anagram. **anagrammatically** *adv.* **anagrammatism** (-gram´-) *n.* the art or practice of making anagrams. **anagrammatist** *n.* a person who makes anagrams. **anagrammatize, anagrammatise** *v.t.* to transpose so as to form into an anagram. [F *anagramme*, Gr. *anagramma* (*graphein*, to write)]

anal (ā´nəl) *a.* of, relating to or situated near the anus. **anally** *adv.* **anal-retentive** *a.* (of a person or personality type) excessively fussy and concerned about tidiness (supposedly on account of conflicts over toilet training in infancy). ~*n.* an anal-retentive person.

anal. *abbr.* 1 analogous, analogy. 2 analyse, analysis.

analects (an´əlekts), **analecta** (-lek´tə) *n.pl.* literary gleanings, collected literary fragments or short extracts. **analectic** (-lek´-) *a.* [L, from Gr. *analekta*, from *analegein*, to gather up]

analeptic (anəlep´tik) *a.* restorative, increasing the strength. ~*n.* a restorative medicine. [Gr. *analēptikos* (*lambanein*, to take)]

analgesia (anəljē´ziə) *n.* loss of sensibility to pain. **analgesic** *n.* a drug that relieves pain. ~*a.* insensible to pain. [Gr., painlessness]

anally ANAL.

analog ANALOGUE.

analogous (ənal´əgəs) *a.* presenting some analogy or resemblance. **analogously** *adv.* [L *analogus*, Gr. *analogos*, according to proportion]

Usage note Pronunciation with (-j-) (after *analogy*) is best avoided.

---

analogue (an´əlog), (*Comput., N Am.*) **analog** *n.* 1 an analogous word or thing, a parallel. 2 a physical object or quantity, such as a hand on a watch or a voltage, used to measure or represent another quantity. 3 something that has a similar function to, but a different origin from, something else. 4 a chemical compound related to another one by the replacement of hydrogen atoms by alkyl groups. ~*a.* 1 (*Comput.*) (*usu.* **analog**) of or relating to information having a continuous range of values. 2 (*Comput.*) (*usu.* **analog**) measuring or displaying information on a continuous scale. 3 (of a watch) having a dial and hands. **analog computer** *n.* a computer in which directly measurable, varying physical quantities, such as current or voltage, represent the numbers on which arithmetical operations are to be performed. [F *analogue*, Gr. *analogon* (see ANALOGOUS)]

analogy (ənal´əji) *n.* (*pl.* **analogies**) 1 similitude of relations, conformity, similarity; a comparison used to demonstrate this. 2 reasoning from a parallel case. 3 the relation between anatomical parts agreeing in function but not in origin. 4 (*Math.*) proportion, or the similitude of ratios. 5 imitation of existing words or linguistic patterns in forming new words, inflectional forms etc. **analogic** (-loj´-), **analogical** *a.* of, relating to or involving analogy. **analogically** *adv.* **analogist** *n.* a person who is occupied with analogy. **analogize, analogise** *v.t.* to represent or explain by analogy. ~*v.i.* to reason from analogy. [L *analogia*, Gr. *analogia* (*logos*, word, relation, proportion, whence *logia*)]

analyse (an´əlīz), (*N Am.*) **analyze** *v.t.* 1 to take to pieces, resolve into its constituent elements. 2 to examine minutely. 3 to determine the elements of (a chemical compound). 4 to examine critically. 5 to resolve (a sentence) into its grammatical elements. 6 to psychoanalyse. **analysable** *a.* **analysand** (-and´) *n.* a person undergoing psychoanalysis. **analyser** *n.* a person who or something which analyses. [F *analyser*, v. from n. *analyse*, analysis (L, from Gr. *analusis* (*luein*, to loosen); or direct from n. *analyse*)]

analysis (ənal´isis) *n.* (*pl.* **analyses** (-sēz)) 1 the process of analysing; a report or statement of the results of this process. 2 separation into constituent elements. 3 resolution of a chemical compound into its elements to ascertain composition, purity etc. 4 resolution of mathematical problems by reducing them to equations. 5 psychoanalysis. 6 in cricket, a statement of a bowler's performance in terms of overs bowled, wickets taken, runs conceded etc. **in the final/ last/ ultimate analysis** in the end, when everything has been taken into consideration. [Gr. *analusis*]

analyst (an´əlist) *n.* 1 a person who analyses. 2 a psychoanalyst.

analytic (anəlit´ik) *a.* 1 of or relating to analysis. 2 capable of, given to or skilled in analysing. 3 resolving anything into its constituent parts. 4 (of languages) using separate words instead of inflections. 5 (*Logic*) (of a statement) true or false by definition. **analytical** *a.* analytic. **analytical chemist** *n.* a chemist who carries out the process of analysis by chemical means. **analytical geometry** *n.* geometry that uses coordinates to determine the position of a point. **analytically** *adv.* **analytics** *n.* the science of analysis.

analyze ANALYSE.

anamnesis (anəmnē´sis) *n.* (*pl.* **anamneses** (-sēz)) 1 recollection. 2 the doctrine of recollection of a previous existence. 3 (*formal*) a patient's medical history. 4 the part of the Eucharist that recalls the Passion,

Resurrection and Ascension of Christ. **anamnestic** (-nes´-) *a.* [Gr. *anamnēsis*, remembrance (*anamimnēskein*, to remember)]

anamorphosis (anəmaw´fəsis) *n.* (*pl.* **anamorphoses** (-sēz)) **1** a distorted projection of any object so contrived that if looked at from one point of view, or reflected from a suitable mirror, it will appear properly proportioned. **2** (*Bot.*) degeneration causing change of appearance. **anamorphic** *a.* [Gr. *anamorphōsis*, n. of *anamorphoein*, to transform (*morphē*, form)]

ananas (ənah´nəs, an´ənas), **anana** *n.* the pineapple plant or its fruit. [Port. *ananás*, Guarani *anānā* (*s* mistaken for pl.)]

anandrous (ənan´drəs) *a.* lacking stamens. [Gr. *anandros*, without a husband (*an-*, priv., *anēr andros*, male)]

anapaest (an´əpest, -pēst), (*esp. N Am.*) **anapest** *n.* a metrical foot consisting of three syllables, the first two short and the third long, a reversed dactyl. **anapaestic** (-pes´-) *a.* composed of anapaests. ~*n.* an anapaestic line or verse. [L *anapaestus*, Gr. *anapaistos*, reversed (*paiein*, to strike)]

anaphora (ənaf´ərə) *n.* **1** the commencement of successive sentences or clauses with the same word or words. **2** the use of a word, such as a pronoun, to refer to a preceding word or phrase without repetition. **3** the consecration and offering of the elements at the Eucharist. **anaphoric** (-anəfor´-) *a.* **1** of or relating to anaphora. **2** referring to a preceding word or phrase. **anaphorically** *adv.* [L, from Gr. *anaphorē*, a carrying back (*pherein*, to bear)]

anaphrodisiac (ənafrədiz´iak) *a.* that suppresses or decreases sexual desire. ~*n.* an anaphrodisiac drug or thing. [AN-; Gr. *aphrodisiakos*, venereal]

anaphylaxis (anəfilak´sis) *n.* a condition of increased or extreme sensitivity to a foreign substance introduced into the body following previous contact. **anaphylactic** *a.* [ANA-; Gr. *phulassein*, to guard]

anaplasty (an´əplasti) *n.* plastic surgery. **anaplastic** (-plas´-) *a.* [Gr. *anaplastos*, that can be moulded]

anaptyxis (anəptik´sis) *n.* the insertion of a short vowel between two consonants to facilitate pronunciation. [Gr. *anaptuxis* (*ana-*, back, *ptussein*, to fold)]

anarch (an´ahk) *n.* (*poet.*) a promoter of anarchy or leader of revolt. [Gr. *anarchos*, without a ruler (*an-*, without, *archos*, ruler)]

anarchy (an´əki) *n.* **1** disorder, lawlessness. **2** absence of government; lack of settled government. **3** political anarchism or the utopian society resulting from this. **anarchic** (-ah´-), **anarchical** *a.* **anarchically** *adv.* **anarchism** *n.* the doctrine that government should be abolished; a theory of government based on the free agreement of individuals rather than on submission to law and authority. **anarchist** *n.* **1** a person who aims at producing anarchy. **2** a person opposed to all forms of government, a supporter of anarchism. [Gr. *anarchia*, as ANARCH]

anarthrous (ənah´thrəs) *a.* **1** without the (Greek) article. **2** without joints. [Gr. *an-*, without, *arthron*, joint]

anasarca (anəsah´kə) *n.* dropsy in the cellular tissue. **anasarcous** *a.* puffy, affected with anasarca. [Gr. *ana*, up, *sarx sarca*, flesh]

anastigmat (anəstig´mat), **anastigmat lens** *n.* a lens free from astigmatism, which refers every point on the scene accurately to a corresponding point image. **anastigmatic** (-mat´-) *a.* free from astigmatism. [Gr. *stigmē*, a dot]

anastomose (ənas´təmōz) *v.i.* **1** to communicate by anastomosis. **2** to interosculate, to intercommunicate. ~*v.t.* to join by anastomosis. **anastomosed** *a.* joined by anastomosis. **anastomosis** (-mō´-) *n.* (*pl.* **anastomoses** (-sēz)) **1** the uniting of vessels, such as veins, arteries, sap-vessels etc., by connecting branches. **2** the surgical joining of two hollow parts. **anastomotic** (-mot´-) *a.* **1** of or relating to anastomosis. **2** (*Med.*) tending to remove obstructions from vessels. ~*n.* a medicine which removes obstructions from vessels. [F *anastomoser*, v. from mod. L *anastomōsis*, from Gr. *anastomoein*, to provide with a mouth (*stoma*)]

anastrophe (ənas´trəfi) *n.* inversion of the natural order of the words in a sentence or clause. [Gr. (*ana*, back, *strephein*, to turn)]

anathema (ənath´əmə) *n.* (*pl.* **anathemas, anathemata** (-them´ətə)) **1** an object of loathing. **2** the formal act by which a person or thing is cursed, excommunication. **3** the person or thing cursed. **4** a curse, denunciation. **anathematize, anathematise** *v.t.* to excommunicate, to curse, to put under a ban. ~*v.i.* to curse. [L, an excommunicated person, from Gr. *anathema* (*ana*, up, *tithēmi*, I put)]

Anatolian (anətō´liən) *a.* **1** of or relating to Anatolia, the Asian part of Turkey. **2** denoting or relating or belonging to an ancient family of languages, related to the Indo-European family and including Hittite. ~*n.* **1** a native or inhabitant of Anatolia. **2** the Anatolian family of languages.

anatomy (ənat´əmi) *n.* (*pl.* **anatomies**) **1** the science of the structure of organized bodies. **2** the physical structure of an animal or plant or of one of its parts. **3** a treatise on the science or art of anatomy. **4** the art of dissecting an organized body so as to discover its structure, and the make-up, arrangement and interrelation of its parts. **5** the act of dissecting. **6** (*coll.*) the human body. **7** a minute examination, reduction to parts or elements, analysis. **anatomic** (anətom´-), **anatomical** *a.* **1** of or relating to anatomy. **2** of or relating to a bodily structure. **anatomically** *adv.* **anatomist** *n.* a person who practises or is skilled in anatomy. **anatomize, anatomise** *v.t.* **1** to examine minutely, analyse. **2** to dissect, to make a dissection of. [F *anatomie*, L *anatomia*, Gr. *anatomia*, abstract n. (*anatomē*, cutting up, from *temnein*, to cut)]

anatta, anatto ANNATTO.

anbury (an´bəri) *n.* (*pl.* **anburies**) a soft wart on a horse's neck. [perh. from OE *ang-*, pain (cp. AGNAIL), BERRY]

ANC *abbr.* African National Congress.

anc. *abbr.* ancient.

-ance (əns) *suf.* forming nouns denoting a state or action, as in *distance, fragrance, parlance, riddance.* [F *-ance*, L *-antia* and *-entia*]

ancestor (an´sestə) *n.* **1** any person from whom another person is descended; a progenitor. **2** an organism of low type from which others of higher type have been developed. **3** any thing or person regarded as the forerunner of a later thing or person. **ancestral** (-ses´-) *a.* **1** of or relating to ancestors. **2** derived from or possessed by ancestors. **ancestress** (-tris) *n.* a female ancestor. **ancestry** (-tri) *n.* (*pl.* **ancestries**) **1** a line of ancestors. **2** high birth, honourable lineage. **3** ancient descent. [OF *ancestre*, L *antecessor*, one who goes before (*ante*, before, *cēdere*, go)]

anchor (ang´kə) *n.* **1** a heavy hooked iron instrument dropped from a ship to grapple the bottom and prevent drifting. **2** anything shaped like an anchor. **3** something that holds an object in place. **4** a source of security or confidence. **5** an anchorperson. ~*v.t.* **1** to secure by means of an anchor. **2** to fix firmly. ~*v.i.* **1** to come to anchor. **2** to take up a position. **3** to settle, rest, to sit down. **at anchor 1** held by an anchor. **2** at rest. **to cast anchor 1** to drop the anchor into the sea. **2** (of a person) to settle down. **to weigh anchor** to raise the anchor preparatory to sailing. **anchorage** (ang´kərij) *n.* **1** a place suitable for anchoring in; any place where a vessel is anchored. **2** the act of anchoring. **3** duty paid for permission to anchor. **4** a source of security. **5** something that offers a secure hold to something else. **6** the hold on the sea-bottom by an anchor. **anchored**

a. **1** held by an anchor. **2** firmly fixed. **3** applied to a heraldic cross, the extremities of which are bent back like the flukes of an anchor. **anchorless** *a.* **1** without an anchor or firm hold. **2** drifting. **anchorman, anchorwoman** *n.* (*pl.* **anchormen, anchorwomen**) **1** a television or radio broadcaster who introduces and links the various reports etc. making up a (news) programme. **2** in sport, the last team member to compete, esp. in a relay race. **3** in sport, the person at the back of a tug-of-war team. **anchorperson** *n.* (*pl.* **anchorpersons, anchorpeople**) an anchorman or anchorwoman. **anchor plate** *n.* [OE *ancor*, L *ancora*, Gr. *agkūra*, an anchor]

anchorite (angˊkərīt) *n.* **1** a religious recluse, a hermit; an early Christian recluse. **2** a person of solitary habits. **anchoress, ancress** (-kris) *n.* a female anchorite. **anchoret** (-ret) *n.* an anchorite. **anchoretic** (-retˊ-), **anchoretical** *a.* **anchoritic** (-ritˊ-), **anchoritical** *a.* of or relating to an anchorite, or a reclusive life. [F *anachorète*, L *anachōrēta*, Gr. *anachōrētēs* (*ana-*, *chōreein*, to withdraw, retire)]

anchovy (anˊchəvi, anchōˊvi) *n.* (*pl.* **anchovies**) any of various small fish of the herring family, esp. *Engraulis encrasicolus*, caught in the Mediterranean, pickled for exportation, and used in sauces etc. **anchoveta** (-chəvetˊə) *n.* a small Pacific anchovy, *Cetengraulis mysticetus*, used as bait. **anchovy pear** *n.* a W Indian fruit, *Grias cauliflora*, which is eaten as a pickle. **anchovy toast** *n.* toast spread with anchovy paste or anchovies. [Sp. *anchova*, perhaps Basque *anchua*, a dried fish]

anchusa (ankūˊzə, anchūˊzə) *n.* any Eurasian plant of the genus *Anchusa*, similar to borage. [L from Gr. *agkhousa*]

anchylose, anchylosis ANKYLOSE.

ancien régime (āsyā rāzhēmˊ) *n.* (*pl.* **anciens régimes**) **1** the political and social system of France before the French Revolution. **2** any superseded order. [F]

ancient[1] (ānˊshənt) *a.* **1** of or belonging to time long past. **2** past, former, esp. of the times before the Middle Ages, that is before the end of the Western Empire (AD 476). **3** very old. **4** antiquated. **the Ancient of Days** the Deity. **the ancients** those who lived in former (esp. classical) times. **ancient Greek** *n.* the Greek language as recorded until about 300 BC. **ancient history** *n.* **1** history of ancient times, esp. to the end of the Western Empire, AD 476. **2** (*coll.*) information, gossip etc. that is widely known. **ancient lights** *n.pl.* windows that have acquired by long usage (not less than 20 years) the right to light from adjoining property. **anciently** *adv.* **1** in ancient times; long ago. **2** in a very old-fashioned manner. **ancient monument** *n.* a historic building or ruin dating from the Middle Ages or earlier, preserved by government order. **ancientness** *n.* the quality or state of being ancient. **ancient world** *n.* the history of the civilizations of the Mediterranean and the Near East, up to the time of the fall of the Western Roman Empire in AD 476. [OF *ancien*, late L *antiānus*, old (*ante*, before), -AN, assim. to -ENT]

ancient[2] (ānˊshənt) *n.* (*Hist.*) **1** a flag, a standard. **2** a standard-bearer, an ensign. [corr. of ENSIGN]

ancillary (ansilˊəri) *a.* **1** auxiliary, supplementary, esp. providing support to a central service or industry. **2** subservient, subordinate. ~*n.* (*pl.* **ancillaries**) **1** a person who assists or supplements. **2** an ancillary device or thing. [L *ancillāris* (*ancilla*, a maid)]

ancipital (ansipˊitəl), **ancipitous** (-təs) *a.* (*Bot.*) flattened and having two sharp edges. [L *anceps -ipitis*, two-headed (*an-*, *ambi-*, on both sides, *caput -itis*, head)]

ancon (angˊkon) *n.* (*pl.* **ancones** (-kōˊnēz)) **1** a bracket or console supporting a cornice. **2** either of a pair of projections on a block of stone by which it can be lifted or moved. **3** the elbow. [L, from Gr. *akōn*, a bend]

ancress ANCHORITE.

-ancy (ənsi) *suf.* forming nouns expressing quality or state, e.g. *constancy, elegancy, infancy, vacancy.* [-ANCE]

and (and, ənd) *conj.* **1** the copulative which joins words and sentences: connecting words that are to be considered together or in relation to each other; implying consequence; implying a sequence in time; used to join identical words with an intensifying force; used to join identical words but implying a contrast (*fish and chips*; *Antony and Cleopatra*; *One move and I'll shoot*; *She married and started a family*; *It gets worse and worse*; *for days and days*; *There are helpers and there are helpers*). **2** plus. **3** (*coll.*) to, after *try, go* etc. **4** †if, whether, as if, though. **and/ or** indicating that either or both of two possibilities may occur, be chosen etc. [OE *and, ond, end*, cp. OHG *anti* (cognate with L *ante*, before, Gr. *anti*, against); OE *and-*, over against as in *andswarian*, answer; *and*, and if, was often shortened to *an*]

-and (and) *suf.* forming nouns meaning a person or thing that is about to undergo a specified process (*analysand, graduand, multiplicand*).

Andalusian (andəlooˊziən) *a.* of or relating to Andalusia, a region of S Spain. ~*n.* **1** a native or inhabitant of Andalusia. **2** the language or dialect of Andalusia. **andalusite** (-sīt) *n.* a variety of aluminium silicate, used as a refractory and gemstone, first found in Andalusia.

andante (andanˊti) *a., adv.* (*Mus.*) moderately slow. ~*n.* a moderately slow movement, piece or passage. **andante affettuoso** *adv.* (*Mus.*) slowly and tenderly. **andante con moto** (kon mōˊtō) *adv.* slowly but with movement. **andante grazioso** *adv.* slowly and gracefully. **andante maestoso** *adv.* slowly and majestically. **andante sostenuto** *adv.* slow, but sustained. **andantino** (-tēˊnō) *a., adv.* rather quicker than andante. ~*n.* (*pl.* **andantinos**) a movement or piece of this character. [It.]

Andean (andēˊən) *a.* of or relating to the Andes mountains. **Andean condor** *n.* a large S American vulture, *Vultur gryphus*.

Anderson shelter (anˊdəsən) *n.* an air-raid shelter formed of arched corrugated steel. [Sir J. *Anderson*, 1882–1958, British Home Secretary, 1939–40]

andesite (anˊdəsīt) *n.* a fine-grained volcanic rock. [*Andes*, S American mountain chain, -ITE[1]]

andiron (anˊdīən) *n.* a horizontal bar raised on short legs, with an ornamental upright in front, placed on each side of the hearth to support logs in a wood fire; a firedog. [OF *andier*]

andro- (anˊdrō) *comb.form* of or relating to the male sex, or to male flowers. [Gr. *anēr andros*, a man, a male]

androecium (andrēˊsiəm, -shi-) *n.* (*pl.* **androecia** (-ə)) the stamens of a flower collectively. [Gr. *aner*, a man, *oikion*, a house]

androgen (anˊdrəjən) *n.* **1** a male sex hormone. **2** any substance with male sex hormone activity. **androgenic** (-jenˊ-) *a.*

androgyne (anˊdrəjīn) *n.* **1** a hermaphrodite. **2** an androgynous plant. **androgynous** (-drojˊi-) *a.* **1** presenting the characteristics of both sexes in the same individual. **2** bearing both stamens and pistils in the same flower or on the same plant. **androgyny** (-drojˊini) *n.* hermaphroditism, the presence of male and female organs in one individual. [F *androgyne*, L *androgynus*, Gr. *androgunos*, male and female in one (*gunē*, woman)]

android (anˊdroid) *n.* a robot having human form. [Gr. ANDRO-, -OID]

andromeda (andromˊidə) *n.* a plant of a genus of heaths, *Andromeda*. [Gr. name of the daughter of Cepheus and Cassiopeia rescued by Perseus]

androsterone (andros´tərōn) *n.* a male sex hormone occurring in the testes and in urine. [Gr. ANDRO-, *sterol* (as *cholesterol*)]

-androus (an´drəs) *suf.* having male organs or stamens, e.g. *diandrous, monandrous.* **-andry** (an´dri) *suf.* forming nouns. [L *-andrus*, Gr. *-andros*, male (*anēr andros*, man)]

-ane (ān) *suf.* **1** forming adjectives, e.g. *humane, mundane, urbane.* **2** forming names of hydrocarbons, e.g. *methane, pentane, hexane.* [L *-ānus*, cp. -AN; also formed to range with -ENE, -INE and -ONE in chemical terminology for hydrocarbons]

anecdote (an´ikdōt) *n.* a brief account of an interesting or amusing fact or incident, esp. a biographical one. **anecdotage** (-dō´tij) *n.* **1** garrulous old age (as if from DOTAGE). **2** anecdotes collectively. **anecdotal** (-dō´-) *a.* of, relating to or consisting of anecdotes. **anecdotic** (-dot´-), **anecdotical** *a.* **1** of or relating to anecdotes. **2** in the habit of relating anecdotes. **anecdotist** *n.* a person given to relating anecdotes. [med. L *anecdota*, Gr. *anekdota*, things unpublished (*an-*, not, *ekdotos*, published, from *ek-*, out, *didōmi*, I give)]

anechoic (anikō´ik) *a.* free from echoes. [Gr. *an-*, not, *echoic* (ECHO)]

†anele (ənēl´) *v.t.* **1** to anoint with oil. **2** to give the sacrament of extreme unction to. [ME *anelien*, OE *o-*, on, ME *elien*, to oil (*ele*, L *oleum*, oil)]

anemia ANAEMIA.

anemo- (ənem´ō) *comb. form* wind. [Gr. *anemos*, wind]

anemograph (ənem´əgrahf) *n.* an instrument which automatically records the velocity and direction of the wind. **anemographic** (-graf´-) *a.* of or relating to an anemograph. [Gr.]

anemometer (anəmom´itə) *n.* an instrument for measuring the velocity of wind, a wind gauge. **anemometric** (-met´-) *a.* **anemometry** (-tri) *n.* [Gr.]

anemone (ənem´əni) *n.* any of a genus of plants, *Anemone*, with brilliantly-coloured flowers, esp. *Anemone nemorosa*, sometimes called the windflower, common in Britain. **sea anemone** SEA. [Gr. *anemōnē*, windflower (*anemos*, wind)]

Usage note Pronunciation as (ənen´əmi), with transposition of the *m* and second *n*, is best avoided.

anemophilous (anəmof´iləs) *a.* wind-fertilized; having the pollen carried away by the wind. [Gr. *philos*, loving]

anencephaly (anənsef´əli, -kef´-) *n.* a congenital defect in which part or all of the brain is missing. **anencephalic** (anensəfal´ik, -kə-) *a.* [Gr. *an-*, not, ENCEPHALON]

†anent (ənent´) *prep.* concerning, touching, in respect of. [OE *on-efen* (*on*, in, *efen*, even, equal), even with, on a level with]

-aneous (āniəs) *suf.* forming adjectives, e.g. *extraneous, instantaneous.* [L *-āneus*]

aneroid (an´əroid) *a.* operating without liquid. ~*n.* an aneroid barometer. **aneroid barometer** *n.* a barometer which measures the pressure of air by its action on a springy metallic box from which the air has been partially exhausted. [F *anëroide* (Gr. *a-*, priv., *nēros*, wet, -OID)]

anesthesia, anesthetic etc. ANAESTHESIA.

anestrus ANOESTRUS.

aneurin (ənūə´rin, an´ūrin), **aneurine** *n.* thiamine. [*a*nti, poly*neur*itis, vitam*in*]

aneurysm (an´ūrizm), **aneurism** *n.* an abnormal dilatation in an artery, particularly of the aorta. **aneurysmal** (-riz´-) *a.* [Gr. *aneurusma*, a widening (*an*, *ana*, up, *eurunein*, to widen, from *eurus*, wide)]

anew (ənū´) *adv.* **1** again; once again. **2** afresh; in a different way.

anfractuose (anfrak´tūōs), **anfractuous** (-əs) *a.* winding, sinuous, tortuous. **anfractuosity** (-os´-) *n.* **1** circuitousness, tortuousness. **2** a winding depression separating convolutions of the brain. **3** intricacy. [L *anfractuōsus*, winding, L *anfractus* (*an-*, *ambi-*, around, *frangere*, to break)]

angary (ang´gəri), **angaria** (-gah´riə) *n.* (*Law*) the confiscation or destruction by a belligerent of neutral property, esp. shipping, subject to claim for compensation. [F *angarie*, from late L *angaria*, enforced service, from Gr. *angareia*, duty of a mounted courier]

angel (ān´jəl) *n.* **1** a messenger from God. **2** a ministering spirit. **3** a guardian or attendant spirit. **4** a member of the lowest order of the celestial hierarchy. **5** a benign, innocent or adorable creature. **6** a conventional representation of the heavenly messenger. **7** (*coll.*) a financial backer, esp. of a theatrical production. **8** (*coll.*) an unexplained radar echo. **9** an old English gold coin, orig. the angel-noble, varying in value from 33p upwards, and bearing the figure of the archangel Michael. **angel cake,** (*esp. N Am.*) **angel food cake** *n.* a light sponge cake made with egg whites. **angel dust** *n.* the hallucinogenic drug phencyclidine. **angelfish** *n.* (*pl. in general* **angelfish**, *in particular* **angelfishes**) **1** any of several brightly-coloured tropical fishes with laterally compressed bodies. **2** a small tropical American fish with black and silver stripes, often kept in aquariums. **3** an angel shark. **angelhood** *n.* **angelic** (anjel´ik), **angelical** *a.* **1** resembling or of the nature of an angel. **2** supremely good, beautiful, innocent etc. **angelically** *adv.* **angel-noble** *n.* the coin the angel. **angelolatry** (-ol´ətri) *n.* angel-worship. **angelology** (-ol´-) *n.* the doctrine or theory of angelic beings. **angel shark** *n.* a fish of the family *Squatinidae*, allied to the rays and sharks and named from the winglike expansion of the pectoral fins (also called *monkfish*). **angels-on-horseback** *n.* oysters rolled in bacon. [OE *ængel*, *engel*, L *angelus*, Gr. *angelos*, a messenger; soft *g* due to OF *angele*]

Angeleno (anjəlē´nō) *n.* (*pl.* **Angelenos**) a native or inhabitant of Los Angeles, California. [Am. Sp.]

angelica (anjel´ikə) *n.* **1** an umbelliferous plant, *Angelica archangelica*, used in medicine, and as a preserve or sweet. **2** candied angelica root. [med. L *herba angelica*]

angelus (an´jələs) *n.* (*pl.* **angeluses**) **1** a short devotional exercise in the Roman Catholic Church in honour of the Incarnation. **2** the angelus bell. **angelus bell** *n.* a bell rung early in the morning, at noon and in the evening, as a signal to say the angelus. [first word of opening, *Angelus domini*]

anger (ang´gə) *n.* rage, fierce displeasure, passion excited by a sense of wrong. ~*v.t.* to make angry, to enrage. ~*v.i.* to become angry. **angry** (ang´gri) *a.* (*comp.* **angrier**, *superl.* **angriest**) **1** wrathful, expressing anger. **2** inflamed, painful. **3** suggesting anger, threatening. **angrily** *adv.* **angry young man** *n.* (*pl.* **angry young men**) **1** any of a group of young British writers of the 1950s, including Kingsley Amis (1922–96) and John Osborne (1929–95), who showed intense hostility towards the traditions, mores and ruling classes of Great Britain. **2** any rebellious young man. [Icel. *angr*, grief, sorrow]

Angevin (an´jəvin) *n.* **1** a native or inhabitant of Anjou in N central France. **2** a member of the Plantagenet dynasty, esp. any of the English kings from Henry II to John. ~*a.* **1** of or relating to Anjou. **2** of or relating to the Plantagenets, esp. between 1154 and 1204.

angina (anjī´nə) *n.* **1** any disease causing inflammation or constriction of the throat, esp. quinsy. **2** angina pectoris. **anginal** *a.* [L *angīna*, quinsy, from Gr. *ankhōnē*, strangling]

angina pectoris (anjīnə pek´təris) *n.* a heart condition marked by paroxysms of intense pain due to over-exertion when the heart is weak or diseased. [L *pectoris*, of or in the chest]

angio- (an´jiō), **angi-** *comb.form* vascular; of or relating to the vessels of organisms. [Gr. *angeion*, a vessel (dim. of *angos*, a chest)]

angiography (anjiog´rəfi) *n.* X-ray photography of the blood vessels. **angiograph** (an´-), **angiogram** *n.* a photograph made by angiography.

angioma (anjiō´mə) *n.* (*pl.* **angiomas, angiomata** (-tə)) a tumour composed of blood or lymph vessels. **angiomatous** *a.*

angioplasty (anjiōplas´ti) *n.* (*pl.* **angioplasties**) an operation undertaken to repair or unblock a blood vessel, e.g. by laser or by the insertion and inflation of a balloon.

angiosperm (an´jiəspœm) *n.* a plant of the class Angiospermae, that has its seed enclosed in a vessel or ovary. **angiospermous** (-spœ´-) *a.* having the seeds enclosed in an ovary. [as ANGIO-, Gr. *sperma*, seed]

Angle (ang´gəl) *n.* a member of one of the Low German tribes that settled in Northumbria, Mercia and East Anglia. **Anglian** (-gli-) *a.* of or relating to the Angles. *~n.* an Angle. [L *anglus*, OE *engle*, the people of *Angul*, district of Holstein, so-called from its shape (see ANGLE[1])]

angle[1] (ang´gəl) *n.* **1** the inclination of two lines towards each other. **2** the space between the lines or planes inclined to each other. **3** a corner. **4** an angular projection. **5** a point of view from which something is considered, an approach. **6** the direction from which something is looked at or photographed. *~v.t.* **1** to move, place, turn, direct at an angle. **2** to present (a report, news story etc.) in a particular way or from a particular point of view. *~v.i.* to proceed or turn at an angle. **angle brackets** *n.pl.* printed or written brackets in the form < >. **angled** *a.* **1** having an angle or angles. **2** biased. **angle-iron** *n.* an angular piece of iron used to strengthen a framework of any kind. **angle of attack** *n.* the angle between the chord line of an aerofoil and the relative airflow, or of a hydrofoil and the relative flow of water surrounding it. **angle of incidence** *n.* the angle made by a ray of light meeting a surface and a line perpendicular to the surface. **angle of reflection** *n.* the angle made by a ray of light reflecting from a surface and a line perpendicular to that surface. **angle of refraction** *n.* the angle at which a ray of light is turned from its direct course in passing through a given medium. **angle of repose** *n.* the slope at which a mass of loose material comes to rest if left to itself. **Anglepoise®** *n.* a desk lamp with an adjustable, jointed arm that holds its position by means of a spring. **angle-tie** *n.* a piece of timber placed across an angle in roofing. [OF *angle*, L *angulum*, from same root as ANGLE[2]]

angle[2] (ang´gəl) *v.i.* **1** to fish with rod and line. **2** (*fig.*) to fish (for), to try to elicit, as a compliment. **3** to get something by craft. *~v.t.* to fish (a stream) with rod and line. *~†n.* **1** a fish-hook. **2** a rod and line for fishing. **angler** *n.* a person who fishes with a rod. **angler fish** *n.* *Lophius piscatorius*, a small British fish which attracts its prey by filaments attached to its head. **angleworm** *n.* an earthworm used as bait by anglers. **angling** *n.* **1** the art or practice of fishing with a rod and line. **2** trying to find out by craft. [OE *angel*, *ongul*, fish-hook (cp. L *oncus*, hook, Gr. *ankōn*, a bend)]

Anglican (ang´glikən) *a.* of or belonging to the Church of England or any Church in communion with it. *~n.* a member of the Anglican Church. **Anglicanism** *n.* the teachings and practices of the Anglican Church. [med. L *Anglicānus*, from *Anglicus* (*Anglus*, ANGLE)]

anglice (ang´glisē, -si) *adv.* in English. [L]

Anglicism (ang´glisizm) *n.* **1** an English idiom. **2** an English custom or characteristic. **3** English political principles. **4** attachment to what is English. **Anglicist, Anglist** *n.* a student or specialist in English language, literature or culture. **Anglicize, Anglicise** *v.t.* **1** to make English. **2** to give an English form to. **3** to turn into English. [L *Anglicus*, English]

Anglo (ang´glō) *n.* (*pl.* **Anglos**) **1** an Anglo-American. **2** any white North American who is not of Latin extraction. **3** a Scots, Irish or Welsh player who plays for an English club in any sport. *~a.* of or relating to Anglos. [shortened form of ANGLO-SAXON]

Anglo- (ang´glō) *comb.form* **1** English; of or belonging to England or the English. **2** partially English (the meaning completed by another word). [L *Anglus*]

Anglo-American (ang·glōəme´rikən) *n.* an American of English parentage or descent. *~a.* **1** of or belonging to Anglo-American people. **2** of, relating to or between England or Britain and the US.

Anglo-Catholic (ang·glōkath´lik) *a.* Anglican, but of Catholic not Protestant tendencies. *~n.* a High Church member of the Church of England. **Anglo-Catholicism** (-thol´-) *n.* the doctrine that the English Church is a branch of the Catholic Church but not of the Roman Church.

Anglocentric (ang·glōsen´trik) *a.* considering England as the centre or English customs, practices etc. as the norm.

Anglo-French (ang·glōfrensh´) *a.* **1** of, relating to or between England or Britain and France. **2** of or relating to Anglo-French. *~n.* the French language of medieval England.

Anglo-Indian (ang·glōin´diən) *n.* **1** an English person born, or long resident, in the Indian subcontinent. **2** a person of mixed British and Indian descent. *~a.* **1** of or belonging to Anglo-Indians. **2** of, relating to or between England or Britain and India. **3** (of a word) adopted into English from an Indian language.

Anglo-Irish (ang·glōī´rish) *a.* **1** of or between Britain and Ireland, esp. the Republic of Ireland. **2** of the Anglo-Irish people. *~n.* **1** the English language as used in Ireland. **2** (*collect.*) the section of Irish people of English Protestant descent. **3** (*collect.*) the people of mixed English and Irish parentage.

Anglomania (ang·glōmā´niə) *n.* excessive fondness for English manners and customs. **Anglomaniac** (-ak) *n.*

Anglo-Norman (ang·glōnaw´mən) *a.* **1** of or relating to the Normans in England after the Norman Conquest. **2** of, relating to or between England and Normandy. **3** of or relating to the Anglo-French language. *~n.* the Anglo-French language.

Anglophile (ang´glōfīl), **Anglophil** (-fil) *n.* an admirer of England or of the English. *~a.* showing admiration of England or the English. **Anglophilia** (-fil´iə) *n.* **Anglophilic** (-fil´ik) *a.*

Anglophobe (ang´glōfōb) *n.* a hater of England or of the English. **Anglophobia** (-fō´-) *n.* fear or distrust of England.

anglophone (ang´glōfōn) *n.* a person who speaks English. *~a.* of or belonging to an English-speaking nation.

Anglo-Saxon (ang·glōsak´sən) *a.* **1** of or relating to the English people before the Norman Conquest. **2** of or relating to English people of European descent. **3** of or relating to English-speaking people generally. **4** of or relating to Old English. **5** of or belonging to the English Saxons as distinct from the Continental Saxons. *~n.* **1** a member of the Anglo-Saxon peoples. **2** Old English.

angora (ang·gaw´rə) *n.* **1** a goat with long silky hair. **2** the hair itself, or a fabric made of it. **3** a long-haired variety of the domestic cat. **4** a breed of rabbit with long, fine fur. **5** a yarn or fabric made from angora rabbit hair. [*Angora* (now Ankara, in Turkey), L *Ancyra*, Gr. *Ankura*]

angostura (ang·gəstū´rə) *n.* a febrifugal bark, used also in the preparation of bitters. **Angostura Bitters®** *n.pl.* a brand of aromatic bitters used in flavouring alcoholic drinks. [*Angustura*, a town on the Orinoco (now called Ciudad Bolivar)]

angry, angrily ANGER.

angst (angst) *n.* a nonspecific feeling of anxiety and guilt produced esp. by considering the imperfect human condition. [G *Angst*, Dan. *anqst*]

ångström unit (ang´strəm) *n.* a unit of length used to express the wavelengths of different kinds of radiations, equivalent to 1/254,000,000 in. (10^{-10} m). [A. J. *Ångström*, 1814–74, Swedish physicist]

anguine (ang´gwin) *a.* of, relating to or resembling a snake; snaky. [L *anguīnus* (*anguis*)]

anguish (ang´gwish) *n.* excessive pain or distress of body or mind. *~v.t.* to afflict with extreme pain or grief. **anguished** *a.* showing or expressing extreme pain or grief. [OF *anguisse*, *angoisse*, the sense of choking, L *angustia*, tightness, narrowness (*angustus*, narrow; *angere*, to stifle, choke)]

angular (ang´gūlə) *a.* **1** having angles or sharp corners. **2** forming an angle. **3** in an angle. **4** measured by an angle. **5** bony, lacking in plumpness or smoothness. **6** stiff, formal, unaccommodating, crotchety. **angular distance** *n.* the space included between the lines drawn from two objects to the eye. **angularity** (-lar´-) *n.* **angularly** *adv.* **angular momentum** *n.* a measure of momentum of a body rotating on an axis, the product of its mass and its angular velocity. **angular motion** *n.* motion of a body as measured by the increase of the angle made with some standard direction by a line drawn from the body to a fixed point. **angular velocity** *n.* rate of rotation about an axis, measured by the angle turned through per unit time, usu. radians per second. **angulate** (-lāt) *a.* angular, formed with angles or corners. *~v.t.* to make angular. **angulation** (-lā´shən) *n.* **1** the making of angles. **2** angular form or structure. [L *angulāris* (*angulus*, ANGLE[1])]

angwantibo (ang·gwan´tibō) *n.* (*pl.* **angwantibos**) a rare small, gold-coloured primate, *Arctocebus calabarensis*, of W central Africa, similar to the loris. [Efik]

anharmonic (anhahmon´ik) *a.* (*Math.*, *Physics*) not harmonic. [F *anharmonique* (Gr. *an-*, not, *harmonikos*, HARMONIC)]

anhedral (anhē´drəl) *n.* the downward angle between the wing of an aircraft and the horizontal. *~a.* having an anhedral.

anhinga (anhing´gə) *n.* a darter, esp. the American *Anhinga anhinga*. [Port., from Tupi *áyinga*]

anhydride (anhī´drīd) *n.* a chemical substance formed from another, esp. an acid, by removing the elements of water. [ANHYDROUS]

anhydrite (anhī´drīt) *n.* a colourless, orthorhombic mineral, calcium sulphate or anhydrous gypsum.

anhydrous (anhī´drəs) *a.* **1** having no water in the composition. **2** esp. destitute of water of crystallization. [Gr. *anudros* (*an-*, not, *hudōr*, water)]

ani (ah´ni) *n.* (*pl.* **anis**) any of various S and Central American birds of the genus *Crotophaga* of the cuckoo family, that have black plumage, a curved bill and a long tail. [Sp. from Tupi]

aniconic (anīkon´ik) *a.* **1** that symbolizes but does not resemble. **2** (of a deity) not represented in human or animal form. [Gr. *an-*, not, *eikōn*, image]

☒ **anihilate** common misspelling of ANNIHILATE.

anil (an´il) *n.* **1** the indigo plant. **2** indigo. [F, from Sp. *añil*, Arab. *an-nīl* (*al-*, the, *nīl*, from Sansk. *nīlī*, indigo, from *nīlas*, blue)]

anile (an´īl, ā´-) *a.* **1** of or resembling an old woman. **2** old-womanish. **3** feeble-minded. **anility** (-nil´-) *n.* the state of being old-womanish, dotage. [L *anīlis* (*anus*, an old woman)]

aniline (an´ilīn) *n.* a chemical base used in the production of many beautiful dyes, and orig. obtained from indigo, now chiefly from nitrobenzene. **aniline dye** *n.* any synthetic dye, esp. one made from aniline. [ANIL]

anima (an´imə) *n.* **1** (*Psych.*) a person's true inner self, as opposed to the *persona*. **2** the feminine aspect of the male personality. [L, mind, soul]

animadvert (animədvœt´) *v.i.* **1** to criticize or censure (with *on* or *upon*). **2** to direct attention to. **animadversion** (-shən) *n.* criticism, comment, censure, reproof. [L *animadvertere* (*animus*, the mind; *ad-*, to, *vertere*, to turn)]

animal (an´iməl) *n.* **1** an organized being possessing life, sensation and the power of voluntary motion. **2** any one of the lower animals as distinct from humans, esp. a mammal or quadruped. **3** a human being whose animal nature is abnormally strong, a brute. **4** (*coll.*) a person, thing or organization. *~a.* **1** of, belonging to or derived from animals, their nature or functions. **2** carnal. **3** of or relating to animals as distinguished from vegetables or minerals. **animal-free** *a.* not containing or using animal products. **animal husbandry** *n.* the breeding and care of domestic animals. **animalism** *n.* **1** behaviour or a characteristic typical of animals. **2** the theory which views mankind as merely animal. **3** sensuality. **animalist** *n.* **1** a believer in animalism. **2** a supporter of animal rights. **animality** (-mal´-) *n.* **1** animal nature. **2** the phenomena of animal life, animal life as distinct from vegetable life. **animalize, animalise** *v.t.* **1** to make into an animal. **2** to make into animal substance. **3** to brutalize. **animalization** (-zā´shən) *n.* the act or process of animalizing. **animal kingdom** *n.* animals generally, viewed as one of the three great divisions of natural objects. **animal liberation** *n.* a movement aimed at securing animal rights. **animally** *adv.* physically, as opposed to intellectually. **animal magnetism** *n.* **1** the quality of being attractive esp. to members of the opposite sex. **2** MESMERISM. **animal rights** *n.pl.* the rights of animals to live without being exploited by humans (often used *attrib.*, as in *animal rights protest*). **animal spirits** *n.pl.* **1** liveliness, cheerfulness or exuberance. **2** †the principle of sensation and volitional movement. [L, n. from neut. a. *animāle*, having breath (*anima*, breath)]

animalcule (animal´kūl), **animalculum** (-ləm) *n.* (*pl.* **animalcules, animalcula** (-lə)) an animal so small as to be invisible to the naked eye. **animalcular** *a.* of or relating to animalcules. [L *animalculum*, dim. of *animal*]

animalism, animality ANIMAL.

animate[1] (an´imāt) *v.t.* **1** to give life or spirit to; to enliven, to vivify. **2** to actuate, to inspire. **3** to stir up. **4** to give the appearance of movement to. **5** to produce as an animated cartoon. **animated** *a.* **1** possessing life. **2** full of life or spirits; vivacious, lively. **3** moving as if alive. **animated film** *n.* a film produced by photographing a series of drawings or objects, each varying slightly in position from the preceding one, to give the illusion of movement. **animated graphics** *n.pl.* computer graphics featuring moving pictures or shapes. **animatedly** *adv.* in a lively manner, vivaciously. **animating** *a.* life-giving, quickening, inspiring. **animatingly** *adv.* **animation** (-ā´shən) *n.* **1** the act of animating. **2** the state of being animated, vitality. **3** life, vivacity. **4** (the techniques used in the production of) an animated cartoon. **animator** *n.* an artist who prepares material for animated cartoons. [L *animātus*, p.p. of *animāre*, to give life to, -ATE[3]]

animate[2] (an´imət) *a.* **1** living, endowed with life. **2** lively.

animateur (animətœ´) *n.* a person who is the animating force behind something; a promoter, a sponsor. [F]

animatronics (animətron´iks) *n.* **1** the technique of making and using lifelike, esp. animal, robots. 2 the technique of editing and processing filmed images of real animals to produce particular effects, e.g. the simulation of spontaneous speech.

animé (an´imā) *n.* 1 a W Indian resin, used for varnish. 2 any of various similar resins. [F, animated, i.e. alive with insects]

animism (an´imizm) *n.* 1 the attribution of a living soul to inanimate objects and to natural phenomena. 2 a spiritual (not a materialist) theory of the universe. **animist** *n.* a believer in animism. **animistic** (-mis´-) *a.* [L *anima*]

animosity (animos´əti) *n.* (*pl.* **animosities**) hostility, enmity; extreme dislike. [F *animosité*, L *animōsitātem* (*animōsus*, spirited)]

animoso (animō´sō) *adv.* (*Mus.*) with spirit. [It.]

animus (an´iməs) *n.* 1 animosity. 2 a motive, intention or spirit actuating feeling, usu. of a hostile character. 3 the masculine part of the female personality. [L, mind, spirit, passion]

anion (an´īən) *n.* an ion that moves towards the anode, a negatively charged ion; cp. *cation.* **anionic** (anīon´ik) *a.* 1 of or relating to anions. 2 having an active anion. [Gr. *ana*, up, *iōn*, going]

anise (an´is) *n.* an umbelliferous plant, *Pimpinella anisum*, cultivated for its aromatic seeds, which are carminative, anciently confused with the dill. **aniseed** (-sēd) *n.* the seed of the anise, used as a flavouring. **anisette** (-zet´) *n.* a liqueur made from aniseed. [F, from L *anīsum*, Gr. *anison*, *anēthon*, anise, or dill]

aniso- (anī´sō) *comb.form* odd, unequal, unsymmetrical. [Gr. *anisos*, unequal, uneven (*an-*, not, *isos*, equal)]

anisomeric (anīsōme´rik) *a.* 1 not isomeric. 2 not having the same proportions. [Gr. *meros*, a part]

anisometric (anīsōmet´rik) *a.* having unsymmetrical parts or unequal measurements.

anisotropy (anīsot´rəpi) *n.* the fact of possessing different physical properties in different directions, as with wood along and across the grain. **anisotropic** (-trop´-) *a.*

ankh (angk) *n.* a cross with a loop above the crosspiece, that was in ancient Egypt the emblem of life, or male symbol of generation. [Egypt., life or soul]

ankle (ang´kəl) *n.* 1 the joint by which the foot is united to the leg. 2 the part of the leg between foot and calf. ~*v.i.* 1 to use the ankles to increase the force exerted on the pedals when cycling. 2 (*sl.*) to walk. **ankle-biter** *n.* (*Austral.*, *N Am.*, *sl.*) a child. **ankle-bone** *n.* the talus, the bone that forms the ankle joint. **ankle-deep** *a.*, *adv.* so deep as to cover the ankles. **ankle sock** *n.* a short sock that just covers the ankle. **anklet** *n.* 1 an ornamental chain or band worn round the ankle. 2 a fetter, strap or band for the ankle. 3 (*N Am.*) an ankle sock. [OE *anclēow*, perh. cogn. with Dut. *anklaauw* (cp. *klaaw*, claw); mod. *ankle* may be from OFris. *ankel*, Dut. *enkel* (cp. L *ang-*, bend, crook, root of *angulus*)]

ankus (ang´kəs) *n.* an elephant goad. [Hind.]

ankylosaur (angkī´ləsaw) *n.* a member of a suborder of dinosaurs, *Ankylosauria*, which were heavily armoured, short-legged, herbivorous quadrupeds.

ankylose (ang´kilōz), **anchylose** *v.t.* 1 to stiffen (a joint) by ankylosis. 2 to consolidate (two separate bones). ~*v.i.* 1 to become stiff. 2 to grow together. **ankylosis** (-lō´-) *n.* 1 the formation of a stiff joint by the fusion of bones or fibrous tissue. 2 the fusion of two bones. **ankylotic** (-lot´-) *a.* [Gr. *agkulōsis*, stiffening of joints, from *agkuloein*, to crook (*agkulos*, crooked)]

ann. *abbr.* 1 annals. 2 annual.

anna (an´ə) *n.* a former monetary unit and coin of India, Burma and Pakistan, equal to one-sixteenth of a rupee. [Hind. *ana*]

annals (an´əlz) *n.pl.* 1 a narrative of events arranged in years. 2 historical records. **annal** *n.* 1 the record of one year's events. 2 in a chronicle, a record of a single item. **annalist** *n.* a person who writes annals. **annalistic** (-lis´-) *a.* [L *annāles*, annual (*annus*, year)]

annates (an´āts) *n.pl.* the first year's revenue of Roman Catholic ecclesiastics on their appointment to a benefice, paid to the Pope. [F *annate*, med. L *annāta*, fruits of a year (*annus*, year)]

annatto (ənat´ō), **anatta** (ənat´ə), **anatto** (-ō) *n.* 1 an orange-red dye used to colour food, fabric etc. 2 the tropical American tree, *Bixa orellana*, from whose pulpy seeds this dye is obtained. [Carib]

anneal (ənēl´) *v.t.* 1 to temper (glass or metals) by subjecting them to intense heat, and then allowing them to cool slowly. 2 (*fig.*) to temper or toughen. 3 to recombine a nucleic acid in its duplex form. ~*v.i.* (of a nucleic acid) to undergo annealing. ~*n.* the process of annealing. **annealing** *n.* [OE *onælan* (*ælan*, to burn), whence ME *anelen*, later confused with OF *neeler*, to enamel, late L *nigellāre*, to blacken (*nigellus*, dim. of *niger*, black)]

annelid (an´əlid) *n.* any of the Annelida, a class of invertebrate animals with elongated bodies composed of annular segments that includes the earthworm. **annelidan** *a.* of or relating to the Annelida. ~*n.* an annelid. [mod. L, F *annelés*, ringed creatures, OF *annel*, ring, L *annelus*, dim. of *anulus*, ring]

annex (əneks´) *v.t.* 1 to unite to, add on to, esp. to something larger; to append to a book or document. 2 to take possession of (territory). 3 to append as a condition, qualification or consequence. 4 (*coll.*) to steal. **annexable** *a.* able to be annexed. **annexation** (aneksā´shən) *n.* 1 the act of annexing. 2 something annexed (often with the idea of unlawful acquisition). **annexe** (an´eks), (*esp. N Am.*) **annex** *n.* 1 an appendix. 2 a supplementary or subsidiary building; an extension to a main building. [F *annexer*, L *annexum*, p.p. of *annectere* (*ad-*, to, *nectere*, to bind)]

annihilate (ənī´əlāt) *v.t.* 1 to reduce to nothing, to blot out of existence, to destroy completely. 2 (*coll.*) to defeat comprehensively, to trounce, to thrash. 3 (*Physics*) to cause to undergo annihilation. ~*v.i.* (*Physics*) to undergo annihilation. **annihilation** (-ā´shən) *n.* 1 the act of annihilating; the state of being annihilated. 2 complete destruction. 3 (*coll.*) total defeat. 4 (*Physics*) the combining of an elementary particle and its antiparticle with spontaneous transformation into energy. **annihilationism** *n.* the doctrine that the wicked are annihilated after death. **annihilationist** *n.* a person who holds this doctrine. **annihilator** *n.* [L *annihilātus*, p.p. of *annihilāre* (*ad-*, to, *nihil*, nothing)]

anniversary (anivœ´səri) *n.* (*pl.* **anniversaries**) 1 the annual return of any remarkable date. 2 the celebration of such an annually recurring date. ~*a.* 1 recurring at the same date in succeeding years. 2 of or relating to an anniversary. [L *anniversārius* (*annus*, year, *versus*, p.p. of *vertere*, to turn)]

Anno Domini (anō dom´inī) *adv.* in the year of Our Lord (indicating a date reckoned from the beginning of the Christian era). ~*n.* (*coll.*) old age. [L]

annotate (an´ətāt) *v.t.* to make notes or comments upon. ~*v.i.* to write notes or comments. **annotatable** *a.* **annotation** (-ā´shən) *n.* 1 the act of annotating. 2 an explanatory note. **annotative** *a.* **annotator** *n.* [L *annotātus*, p.p. of *annotāre*, (*ad-*, to, *notāre*, to mark)]

announce (ənowns´) *v.t.* 1 to make known, to proclaim. 2 to declare officially, or with authority. 3 to make known the approach or arrival of. **announcement** *n.* **announcer** *n.* a person who announces the items of a broadcasting programme, reads news summaries etc. [OF *anoncer*, L *annuntiāre* (*ad-*, to, *nuntiāre*, to report, bear a message, *nuntius*, messenger)]

annoy (ənoi´) *v.t.* 1 to cause to feel irritated, displeased or angry. **2** to tease, to molest, to trouble, to put to inconvenience by repeated or continued acts. ~*v.i.* to cause annoyance. **annoyance** *n.* **1** the act of annoying. **2** the state of being annoyed. **3** something which annoys. **annoyed** *a.* displeased, irritated, angry. **annoyer** *n.* **annoying** *a.* **annoyingly** *adv.* [OF *anoier, anuier*, to molest, annoy, from *anoi, anui*, annoyance, vexation, L *in odio*, in hatred]

annual (an´ūəl) *a.* **1** returning or happening every year. **2** reckoned by, or done or performed in a year. **3** (*Bot.*) lasting only a single year or season. ~*n.* **1** a book published every year, a year book. **2** a plant which lives for a year only. **annual general meeting** *n.* a yearly, statutory meeting of the shareholders of a company, members of a society etc., at which reports are presented and officers elected. **annualize, annualise** *v.t.* to adjust or calculate according to a yearly rate. **annually** *adv.* year by year, yearly. **annual ring** *n.* a ring of wood seen in the cross-section of a plant stem or root, indicating one year's growth. [F *annuel*, late L *annuālis* (L *annālis*, years, from *annus*, year)]

annuity (ənū´iti) *n.* (*pl.* **annuities**) **1** a sum of money payable annually. **2** an investment insuring fixed annual payments for a specified period. **annuitant** *n.* a person who receives an annuity. [F *annuité*, med. L *annuitātem* (*annuus*, yearly)]

annul (ənŭl´) *v.t.* (*pres.p.* **annulling,** *past, p.p.* **annulled**) **1** to render void, cancel, abolish. **2** to declare the invalidity of (a marriage). **annulment** *n.* the act of annulling; revocation; abolition. [OF *anuller*, late L *annullāre* (*ad-*, to, *nullus*, none)]

annular (an´ūlə) *a.* ring-shaped. [L *annulāris* (*annulus*, ring, dim. of *ānus*, a round shape)]

annunciate (ənŭn´siāt) *v.t.* **1** to announce, to proclaim the approach or arrival of. **2** to bring tidings of. **annunciation** (-ā´shən) *n.* the act of announcing. **the Annunciation** **1** the announcement of the Incarnation made by the angel Gabriel to the Virgin Mary. **2** the church festival (Lady Day, 25 March) in honour of that event. **annunciator** *n.* **1** a person who or something that announces. **2** a visual indicator, e.g. for electric bells or telephones, to show which of several electrical circuits has been activated. **3** a visual or audible device indicating the position of a train. [ANNOUNCE]

annus mirabilis (anəs, anus mirah´bilis) *n.* (*pl.* **anni mirabiles** (anē mirah´bilēz)) a remarkable year. **annus horribilis** (horib´ilis) *n.* a year of personal or general misfortune and calamity. [L, year of wonders]

anoa (ənō´ə) *n.* a small deerlike water buffalo native to Sulawesi. [Sulawesi]

anode (an´ōd) *n.* **1** the positive electrode or pole in an electrolytic cell. **2** the negative electrode of a primary cell delivering current. **3** the positive electrode which collects electrons in an electronic valve. **anodal** (-nod´-), **anodic** *a.* **anodize, anodise** *v.t.* to give a protective surface coating of an oxide to (a metal) by making it the anode of an electrolytic cell. **anodizer** *n.* [Gr. *anodos*, a way up]

anodyne (an´ədīn) *a.* **1** assuaging pain. **2** alleviating distress of mind, soothing to the feelings. **3** bland, undemanding; uncontroversial. ~*n.* **1** a medicine which assuages pain. **2** anything which alleviates distress of mind or soothes the feelings. [late L *anōdynus*, Gr. *anōdunos* (*an-*, not, *odunē*, pain)]

anoesis (anōē´sis) *n.* (*pl.* **anoeses** (-sēz)) (*Psych.*) a state in which consciousness of sensation is not accompanied by thought. **anoetic** (-et´ik) *a.* [Gr. A-[3], *noēsis*, understanding]

anoestrus (anē´strəs), (*N Am.*) **anestrus** *n.* a state of sexual quiescence or inactivity. [AN-, OESTRUS]

anoint (ənoint´) *v.t.* **1** to smear with oil or an ointment, esp. to pour oil on as a religious ceremony. **2** to consecrate with oil. **anointed** *a.* **1** smeared with oil or unguent. **2** consecrated. ~*n.* a consecrated person. **anointer** *n.* **Anointing of the Sick** *n.* in the Roman Catholic Church, the anointing of a sick, infirm or dying person with consecrated oil. [OF *enoint*, anointed, p.p. of *enoindre* (L *in-*, *ungere*, to smear, p.p. *unctus*)]

anole (ənō´li) *n.* any small tropical American lizard of the genus *Anolis*, esp. *A. carolinensis*, the green anole. [Carib]

anomalure (ənom´əlūə) *n.* a squirrel-like rodent of the family *Anomaluridae* that have tails with rough scales on the underside. [new L *anomalurus* (Gr. *anōmalos*, abnormal, *oura*, tail)]

anomaly (ənom´əli) *n.* (*pl.* **anomalies**) **1** (an) irregularity. **2** (a) deviation from the common or established order, abnormality. **3** the angular distance of a planet or satellite from its last perihelion or perigee. **anomalistic** (-lis´-) *a.* irregular, abnormal. **anomalistic month** *n.* the time in which the moon passes from perigee to perigee. **anomalistic year** *n.* the time occupied by the earth (or other planet) in passing from perihelion to perihelion: it is slightly longer than a tropical or sidereal year. **anomalous** *a.* **1** deviating from rule. **2** irregular, abnormal. **anomalously** *adv.* **anomalousness** *n.* [L *anōmalia*, Gr. *anōmalia*, unevenness, *anōmalos* (*an-*, not, *ōmalos*, even)]

anomie (an´omi), **anomy** *n.* the breakdown or absence of moral and social standards in an individual or society. **anomic** (ənom´ik) *a.* [F *anomie*, Gr. *anomia*, lawlessness (*a-*, priv., *nomos*, law)]

anon (ənon´) *adv.* (*dated, poet. or facet.*) **1** immediately, thereupon. **2** soon after, in a little while. [OE *on ān*, in one moment]

anon. (ənon´) *abbr.* **1** anonymous. **2** an anonymous author.

anonymous (ənon´iməs) *a.* **1** nameless. **2** having no name attached. **3** of unknown or unavowed authorship or origin. **4** lacking distinctive characteristics, nondescript. **anonym** (an´ənim) *n.* **1** a person whose name is not made known. **2** a pseudonym. **anonymity** (anənim´iti) *n.* **anonymized, anonymised** *a.* made anonymous. **anonymized screening** *n.* BLIND SCREENING (under BLIND). **anonymously** *adv.* **anonymousness** *n.* [Gr. *anōnumos* (*an-*, not, *onoma*, name)]

anopheles (ənof´əlēz) *n.* any of a genus of mosquitoes, *Anopheles*, that includes the malarial mosquito *A. maculipennis*. [Gr.]

anorak (an´ərak) *n.* **1** a warm waterproof jacket, usu. with a hood. **2** (*coll.*) a person who is considered boring and socially inept, usu. for devotion to some unfashionable, solitary or very studious pursuit. [Inuit *ánorâq*]

anorexia (anərek´siə) *n.* **1** loss of appetite. **2** anorexia nervosa. **anorexia nervosa** (nœvō´sə) *n.* a psychological disorder characterized by an aversion to eating and fear of gaining weight. **anorexic, anorectic** (-rek´-) *a.* **1** suffering from anorexia (nervosa). **2** causing loss of appetite. **3** (*coll.*) extremely thin. ~*n.* **1** a person suffering from anorexia (nervosa). **2** a substance that causes loss of appetite. [Gr. *an-*, not, *orexis*, longing]

anorthosite (ənaw´thəsīt) *n.* a coarse-grained rock that consists almost entirely of plagioclase feldspar. [Gr. *an-*, not, *orthos*, right]

anosmia (ənoz´miə) *n.* absence or loss of the sense of smell. **anosmatic** (anozmat´-) *a.* lacking the sense of smell. [mod. L, from Gr. *an-*, priv., and *osmē*, smell]

another (ənŭdh´ə) *a.* **1** an additional, one more. **2** one of the same kind as (*She's another Navratilova*). **3** a different (*try another brand*). **4** any other. ~*pron.* **1** an additional one. **2** a different one. **3** some other unnamed person, esp. an additional party to a legal action. **A. N. Other** (ā en ŭd´hə) *n.* in a team list etc., a player or person who has yet to be selected or named. **another place** *n.* the other House (of Parliament).

ANOVA (an´əva) *n.* a statistical procedure to divide the variations in a set of observations into particular components. [*an*alysis *o*f *va*riance]
anovulant (anov´ūlənt) *n.*, *a.* (a drug) that inhibits ovulation. [AN-, L *ovulum*, dim. of *ovum*, egg]
anoxia (ənok´siə) *n.* deficiency of oxygen to the tissues. **anoxic** *a.* [AN-, OXYGEN]
ansate (an´sāt) *a.* having a handle. [L *ansatus*, from *ansa*, handle]
Anschluss (an´shlus) *n.* the forced union of Austria with Germany in 1938. [G, annexation]
anserine (an´sərīn) *a.* **1** of or belonging to the goose. **2** gooselike, stupid, silly. [L *anserīnus*, pertaining to a goose (*anser*)]
ANSI *abbr.* American National Standards Institution.
answer (ahn´sə) *n.* **1** a reply to a question, appeal, objection or charge. **2** a solution of a problem. **3** something done in return. **4** a practical reply. **5** (*Law*) a written reply to a bill of charges. ~*v.t.* **1** to reply or respond to. **2** to act on a signal or summons from (*answer the door*). **3** to solve; to reply correctly to. **4** to be sufficient for or suitable to. ~*v.i.* **1** to reply, to respond. **2** to be suitable or satisfactory. **to answer back** to reply rudely or cheekily. **to answer for** to be responsible or answerable for. **to answer the description** DESCRIPTION (under DESCRIBE). **to answer to 1** to correspond, to suit. **2** to be responsible or answerable to. **answerable** *a.* **1** liable to be called to account, responsible (for, to). **2** capable of being answered. **answerability** (-bil´-) *n.* **answerer** *n.* a person who answers (to a question etc.). **answering** *n.* **answering machine** *n.* a recording device that answers telephone calls and allows the caller to leave a message. **answering service** *n.* a business that receives and answers telephone calls on its clients' behalf. **answerphone** *n.* a telephone answering machine. [OE *andswaru*, a reply (*and-*, against, *swar-*, stem of *swerian*, to swear)]
ant (ant) *n.* a small, social, hymenopterous insect of the family Formicidae. **to have ants in one's pants** (*coll.*) to be extremely fidgety and restless. **ant-bear** *n.* **1** the giant anteater of S America. **2** an aardvark. **antbird** *n.* an ant thrush. **antcow** *n.* an insect, esp. an aphid, that is kept and 'milked' by ants for the sweet-tasting substance it excretes. **anteater** *n.* **1** an edentate mammal, with a long extensile tongue, which it thrusts into anthills and withdraws covered with ants. **2** an echidna. **3** an aardvark. **4** an ant thrush. **antheap, anthill** *n.* **1** the mound or hillock raised by a community of ants. **2** a very crowded or busy place. **anting** *n.* the placing by birds of live ants in their plumage. **ant-lion** *n.* a neuropterous insect, the larvae of which construct a kind of pitfall for ants and other insects. **ant's eggs, ant-eggs** *n.pl.* (*coll.*) the pupae of ants. **antsy** (ant´si) *a.* (*N Am., coll.*) excited, agitated, fidgety. **ant thrush** *n.* a tropical bird, allied to the thrush, which feeds chiefly on ants. [OE *æmette*, gradually contracted to *amte, ante, ant*]
ant- ANTI-.
-ant (ənt) *suf.* **1** forming adjectives, as *distant, elegant, trenchant*. **2** denoting an agent, a person who or thing that produces an effect, as in *accountant, merchant*. [L *-antem*, acc. sing. of pres.p. in *-ans*]
antacid (antas´id) *a.* counteracting acidity. ~*n.* a medicine that counteracts acidity of the stomach.
antagonist (antag´ənist) *n.* **1** an opponent; a person who contends or strives with another. **2** a muscle which counteracts another, and is in turn counteracted by it. **3** a drug that counteracts the action of another or of a substance occurring naturally in the body. **antagonism** *n.* **1** opposition. **2** conflict, active disagreement. **3** (an) opposing force, action or principle. **antagonistic** (-nis´-) *a.* **antagonistically** *adv.* **antagonize, antagonise** *v.t.* **1** to arouse hostility or opposition in. **2** to counteract, to make antagonistic, put in active opposition. ~*v.i.* to act in opposition. [late L *antagōnista*, Gr. *antagōnistēs*, an adversary, from *antagōnizesthai*, (*ant-, anti-*, against, *agōnizesthai*, to struggle)]
antalkali (antal´kəlī) *n.* (*pl.* **antalkalis, antalkalies**) something that neutralizes an alkali. **antalkaline** (-līn) *a.* counteracting the effect of an alkali. ~*n.* a medicine that counteracts the effect of an alkali.
Antarctic (antahk´tik) *a.* **1** of or belonging to the S Pole or the region within the Antarctic Circle. **2** opposite to the Arctic. ~*n.* the Antarctic regions. **Antarctic Circle** *n.* a parallel of the globe, 23° 28´ distant from the S Pole, which is its centre. [ME *antartik*, OF *antartique*, L *antarcticus* (ANT-, ARCTIC)]

Usage note Pronunciation as (antah´tik), without the (k) before the (t), is best avoided.

ante (an´ti) *n.* **1** the stake which a poker player puts down after being dealt a hand, but before drawing. **2** (*coll.*) amount paid, price. ~*v.t.* (*3rd pers. sing. pres.* **antes,** *pres.p.* **anteing,** *past, p.p.* **anted**) **1** to stake. **2** to pay. **to up the ante 1** to increase the (asking) price or cost. **2** to increase the risks, demands, etc. involved in something. [L, before]
ante- (an´ti) *pref.* before in time or position. [see ANTE]

Usage note The spellings of words beginning with *ante-* (before) and *anti-* (against, pronounced the same in British English) should not be confused.

ante-bellum (antibel´əm) *a.* existing before the war, esp. the American Civil War. [L *ante*, before, *bellum*, war]
antecede (antisēd´) *v.t.* to precede, to go before or in front of. **antecedence** *n.* **1** a going before in point of time. **2** precedence, anteriority. **3** (*Astron.*) an apparent motion contrary to the true motion. **antecedent** *a.* **1** going before in time, prior, anterior. **2** presumptive, a priori. ~*n.* **1** something which goes before. **2** (*Gram.*) the word phrase, clause etc. to which another word, esp. a relative pronoun, refers. **3** (*pl.*) past circumstances, background. **4** the conditional clause of a hypothetical proposition. **5** (*dated*) the first term of a mathematical ratio. **antecedently** *adv.* [L *antecēdere* (*ante-*, before, *cēdere*, to go)]
antechamber (an´tichāmbə) *n.* an anteroom. [F *antichambre*]
antechapel (an´tichapəl) *n.* the part of a chapel between the western wall and the choir screen.
antedate (an´tidāt) *n.* a date preceding the actual date. ~*v.t.* **1** to happen earlier than, precede. **2** to date before the true date. **3** to assign to an earlier date. **4** to cause to happen prematurely.
antediluvian (antidiloo´viən) *a.* **1** of or relating to the period before the biblical Flood. **2** old-fashioned, antiquated. ~*n.* **1** a person who lived before the Flood. **2** a very old or old-fashioned person. [L *dilūvium*, flood]
antelope (an´tilōp) *n.* (*pl. in general* **antelope,** *in particular* **antelopes**) **1** an animal of the genus *Antilope*, of the family Bovidae, containing ruminants akin to the deer and the goat. **2** leather made from the skin of such an animal. [OF *antelop*, late L *antalopus*, late Gr. *antholops*]
antenatal (antinā´təl) *a.* **1** happening or existing before birth. **2** dealing with pregnancy or pregnant women.
antenna (anten´ə) *n.* (*pl.* **antennae** (-nē), **antennas**) **1** (*pl.* **antennae**) a sensory organ occurring in pairs on the heads of insects and crustaceans; a palp, a feeler. **2** (*pl.* **antennas**) an aerial. **antennal, antennary** *a.* of or relating to the antennae. **antenniferous** (-nif´-) *a.* having antennae. **antenniform** (-fawm) *a.* shaped like an antenna. [L, sail-yard]
antenuptial (antinŭp´shəl, -chəl) *a.* happening before marriage. **antenuptial contract** *n.* (*S Afr.*) a contract

setting out terms and conditions that is drawn up before two people marry.

antependium (antipen´diəm) *n.* (*pl.* **antependia** (-iə)) a covering for the front of an altar, a frontal. [late L (*ante-*, *pendēre*, to hang)]

antepenult (antipənŭlt´) *n.* the last syllable but two. **antepenultimate** (-imət) *a.* last but two. ~*n.* the last but two. [L *antepaenultimus* (L *paene*, almost, *ultimus*, latest, last)]

ante-post (antipōst´) *a.* (of betting) done in advance of the event concerned, esp. before the runners' numbers are posted.

anterior (antiə´riə) *a.* **1** at the front, more to the front. **2** preceding, prior. **anteriority** (-or´-) *n.* **anteriorly** *adv.* [L, comp. of *ante*, before]

antero- (an´tərō) *comb. form* front, in front, used in the formation of technical adjectives and adverbs. [ANTERIOR]

anterograde amnesia (antərōgrād amnē´ziə) *n.* loss of memory of events subsequent to a trauma causing brain damage, while the memory of previous events remains relatively unimpaired.

anteroom (an´tirum) *n.* a room leading into or forming an entrance to another.

anthelion (anthē´liən) *n.* (*pl.* **anthelia** (-ə)) a mock sun, a luminous ring projected on a cloud or fog bank opposite the sun. [late Gr. neut. of *anthēlios*, opposite the sun (*hēlios*, sun)]

anthelix ANTIHELIX.

anthelmintic (anthəlmin´tik), **anthelminthic** (-thik) *a.* destroying or remedial against parasitic, esp. intestinal, worms. ~*n.* a remedy for intestinal worms. [Gr. ANTH-, *helmins -minthos*, a worm]

anthem (an´thəm) *n.* **1** a portion of Scripture or of the Liturgy set to music, often in an elaborate choral setting. **2** a national anthem. **3** a song that is particularly associated with a group, institution etc. **4** a song of gladness or triumph. **5** a hymn in alternate parts. [OE *antefn*, late L *antiphōna*, see ANTIPHON]

anthemion (anthē´miən) *n.* (*pl.* **anthemia** (-ə)) a palmette, honeysuckle or conventional leaf or floral design. [Gr., little flower, dim. of *anthos*, a flower]

anther (an´thə) *n.* the pollen-bearing organ of flowering plants. **antheral** *a.* of or relating to an anther or anthers. [MF *anthere*, L *anthēra*, medicine made of flowers, Gr. *anthēra*, fem. a., flowery (*anthos*, a bud)]

antheridium (anthərid´iəm) *n.* (*pl.* **antheridia** (-diə)) the male spore-bearing organ, analogous to an anther, of cryptogams. [mod. L *anthēra*, see ANTHER; Gr. *-idion*, dim. ending]

antherozoid (anthərəzō´id) *n.* a motile male gamete produced in an antheridium. [ANTHER, Gr. *zōon*, -OID]

anthocyanin (anthōsī´ənin), **anthocyan** *n.* any of a class of scarlet to blue plant pigments. [Gr. *anthos*, a flower, *kuanos*, blue]

anthology (anthol´əji) *n.* (*pl.* **anthologies**) **1** any collection of selected poems or other literary pieces. **2** a collection of songs, paintings etc. **anthological** (-loj´-) *a.* **anthologist** *n.* the compiler of an anthology. **anthologize, anthologise** *v.t.* to put into an anthology. ~*v.i.* to compile an anthology. [Gr. *anthologia*, a gathering of flowers (*anthos*, flower, *legein*, to collect)]

Anthony (an´təni) *n.* the smallest in a litter of pigs. **St Anthony's fire** SAINT. [St *Anthony*, the patron saint of swineherds]

anthozoan (anthəzō´ən), **actinozoan** (aktinō-) *n.* any of a class, Anthozoa or Actinozoa, of radiated animals containing the sea anemones and coral polyps. [Gr. *anthos*, a flower, *zōon*, animal]

anthracene (an´thrəsēn) *n.* a crystalline substance with blue fluorescence obtained from tar, used in the manufacture of chemicals. [Gr. *anthrax*, coal]

anthracite (an´thrəsīt) *n.* a non-bituminous coal, burning with intense heat, without smoke, and with little flame. **anthracite stove** *n.* a stove for domestic heating specially constructed to burn anthracite coal. **anthracitic** (-sit´-) *a.* [L *anthracītes*, Gr. *anthrakitēs*, resembling coals (*anthrax*, coal, carbon)]

anthracnose (anthrak´nōs) *n.* a fungal disease of plants that causes dark, sunken spots to appear. [Gr. *anthrax*, coal, *nosos*, disease]

anthracosis (anthrəkō´sis) *n.* a lung disease caused by the inhalation of coal dust. [Gr. *anthrax*, coal, -OSIS]

anthrax (an´thraks) *n.* **1** an infectious, often fatal bacterial disease of sheep and cattle transmissible to humans. **2** a malignant pustule in humans derived from animals suffering from this. [L from Gr., a carbuncle, also coal]

anthropic (anthrop´ik) *a.* of or relating to human beings. **anthropic principle** *n.* a principle of cosmology which maintains that theories of the origin of the universe must necessarily take into account the development of individual human existence. [Gr. *anthrōpikos*, from *anthrōpos*, man]

anthropo- (an´thrəpō), **anthrop-** *comb. form* **1** human. **2** of or relating to mankind. [Gr. *anthrōpos*, a man]

anthropocentric (anthrəpōsen´trik) *a.* **1** centring on human beings. **2** regarding mankind as the measure and aim of the universe.

anthropogeny (anthrəpoj´əni), **anthropogenesis** (-jen´əsis) *n.* the science or study of the origin of human beings. **anthropogenic, anthropogenetic** (-net´-) *a.*

anthropogeography (anthrəpōjiog´rəfi) *n.* the geography of the distribution of the races of mankind.

anthropoid (an´thrəpoid) *a.* **1** resembling human beings, of human form. **2** belonging to the suborder Anthropoidea which includes the higher apes and man. **3** (of a person) apelike. ~*n.* a creature, esp. one of the higher apes, resembling a human being in form.

anthropology (anthrəpol´əji) *n.* **1** the study of human beings, esp. in regard to the customs, societies, rituals etc. they have evolved. **2** the study of the physical and mental evolution of human beings in the widest sense. **anthropological** (-loj´-) *a.* **1** of or relating to anthropology. **2** dealing with the natural history of mankind. **anthropologically** *adv.* **anthropologist** *n.* a person who studies or is versed in anthropology.

anthropometry (anthrəpom´ətri) *n.* the scientific measurement of the human body. **anthropometric** (-met´-), **anthropometrical** *a.*

anthropomorphic (anthrəpəmaw´fik), **anthropomorphous** (-fəs) *a.* **1** possessed of a form resembling that of a human being. **2** of or relating to anthropomorphism. **anthropomorphism** *n.* the attribution of a human form or character to the Deity, or of human characteristics to the lower animals. **anthropomorphist** *n.* a person who attributes the human form or human characteristics to the Deity, or other things. **anthropomorphize, anthropomorphise** *v.t.* to give a human shape or attribute human characteristics to. [Gr. *anthrōpomorphos* (*anthrōpos*, man, *morphē*, form)]

anthropophagous (anthrəpof´əgəs) *a.* feeding on human flesh, cannibal. **anthropophagite** *n.* a cannibal. **anthropophagy** *n.* the practice of eating human flesh, cannibalism.

anthropophyte (anthrop´əfīt) *n.* a plant accidentally introduced into an area during cultivation of another species.

anthroposophy (anthrəpos´əfi) *n.* a system of esoteric philosophy enunciated by Rudolf Steiner (1861–1925), who defined it as 'the knowledge of the spiritual human being... and of everything which the spirit man can perceive in the spiritual world'. [Gr. *anthrōpos*, a man, and *sophia*, knowledge]

anti (an´ti) *prep.* opposed to. ~*n.* (*pl.* **antis**) an opponent of a policy, political party etc.

anti- (an´ti), **ant-** *pref.* forming nouns and adjectives indicating opposition to something, as in *anti-apartheid*; the prevention of something, as in *anticoagulant*; the opposite of something, as in *anti-clockwise*; a rival, as in *antipope*; something that is unlike the conventional form, as in *anti-hero*. [Gr. *anti*, against]

Usage note See note under ANTE-.

anti- (+ a– words) anti-abortion *a.* opposed to the practice or legalization of abortion. **anti-abortionist** *n.* **anti-abrasion** *a.* that prevents abrasion. **anti-ageing,** (*N Am.*) **anti-aging** *a.* intended to counter the effects of ageing. **anti-aircraft** *a.* employed against hostile aircraft. **anti-American** *a.* opposed or hostile to American policy, values etc. **anti-apartheid** *a.* opposed to the policy of apartheid. **anti-aristocratic** *a.* opposed to the notion of an aristocracy, or to the practices, values etc. of aristocrats, or to aristocrats as such.

antiar (an´tiah) *n.* **1** the upas tree. **2** the poison obtained from it. [Javanese *antjar*]

anti- (+ b–c words) antibacterial *a.* that combats the action of or destroys bacteria. **antiballistic** (antibəlis´tik) *a.* (of a missile) designed to intercept and destroy a ballistic missile in flight. **antibiblical** *a.* opposed or contrary to the Bible or its teachings. **antibiosis** (antibīō´sis) *n.* antagonistic association between two organisms or between one organism and a substance produced by the other. **antibiotic** (-ot´-) *a.* inimical to life, esp. bacteria. ~*n.* a substance produced by a microorganism or synthetically which inhibits the growth of or kills another microorganism. **antibody** (an´ti-) *n.* (*pl.* **antibodies**) a substance produced in the blood in response to the presence of an antigen and capable of counteracting toxins. **anti-Bolshevik** *a.*, *n.* (a person who is) opposed to the Bolsheviks, their actions, and their political philosophy etc. **anti-Bolshevism** *n.* **anti-Bolshevist** *a.*, *n.* **anti-British** *a.* opposed or hostile to British policy, values etc. **anticancer** *a.* used in the treatment of cancer. **anticapitalist** *a.*, *n.* (a person who is) opposed to capitalism. **anticapitalistic** *a.* **anticathode** (anti-kath´ōd) *n.* the target electrode for a stream of electrons in an X-ray tube, from which the X-rays are emitted. **anti-Catholic** *a.*, *n.* (a person who is) opposed or hostile to or prejudiced against Roman Catholics and Catholicism. **anti-Catholicism** *n.* **anticensorship** *a.* opposed to any form of censorship. **antichlor** *n.* a substance used to remove chlorine after bleaching. **antichurch** *a.* hostile to the Church. **anticlassical** *a.* opposed or contrary to classical principles in art. **anticlerical** *a.* opposed to (the political influence of) the clergy. **anticlericalism** *n.* **anticlimax** *n.* **1** the opposite of climax. **2** a descent or decrease in impressiveness; bathos. **anticlimactic** *a.* **anticlockwise** *a.*, *adv.* in the reverse direction from that taken by the hands of a clock. **anticoagulant** *a.*, *n.* (a drug) that hinders blood clotting. **anticodon** *n.* a unit of genetic code in a transfer RNA molecule, that corresponds to a particular codon in messenger RNA and consists of a sequence of three nucleotides. **anti-communist** *a.*, *n.* (a person who is) opposed to communism. **anti-constitutional** *a.* opposed to the constitution of the country, or to sound constitutional principles. **anti-convulsant** *a.*, *n.* (a drug) used in treating or controlling (epileptic) convulsions. **anticorrosive** *a.* that prevents corrosion. **anticyclone** *n.* the rotary outward flow of air from an atmospheric region of high pressure. **anti-cyclonic** (-klon´-) *a.*

antic (an´tik) *n.* **1** (*pl.*) grotesque, ridiculous or troublesome behaviour. **2** a ludicrous action. **3** †a merry-andrew, a buffoon. ~*a.* †grotesque, odd, ludicrous, whimsical. [It, *antico*, L *antīquus*, ancient]

Antichrist (an´tikrīst) *n.* **1** a personal antagonist of Christ spoken of in the New Testament. **2** an opponent of Christ. **antichristian** (-kris´-) *a.* **1** opposed to Christ or to Christianity. **2** of or relating to Antichrist. ~*n.* **1** a person opposed to Christ or to Christianity. **2** an adherent of Antichrist. **antichristianism** *n.* [OF *antecrist*, L *antechristus*, Gr. *antichristos*]

anticipate (antis´ipāt) *v.t.* **1** to foresee and act in advance of (*anticipates my every move*). **2** to expect (*I don't anticipate any problems*). **3** to forestall, to thwart by acting first. **4** to cause to happen earlier, to hasten. **5** to look forward to. ~*v.i.* to speak, write or do something before the expected or appropriate time. **anticipant** *a.* anticipating, expecting. ~*n.* a person who anticipates. **anticipation** (-ā´shən) *n.* **1** the act of anticipating. **2** expectation, presentiment, foresight. **3** the introduction of a note before the chord about to be played. **anticipative** *a.* **1** anticipating. **2** containing an anticipation. **anticipatively** *adv.* **anticipator** *n.* **anticipatory** *a.* [L *anticipātus*, p.p. of *anticipāre* (*ante-*, before, *capere*, to take)]

Usage note The use of *anticipate* to mean expect is best avoided.

anticlinal (antiklī´nəl) *a.* **1** (*Geol.*) forming a ridge so that the strata lean against each other in opposite directions. **2** (*Bot.*) perpendicular to the surface. ~*n.* (*Geol.*) an anticlinal axis, fold or line from which the strata dip in opposite directions. **anticline** (an´-) *n.* (*Geol.*) an anticlinal fold. [Gr. *klinein*, to lean]

anti- (+ d– words) antidazzle *a.* (of a mirror) designed to prevent a driver being dazzled by the headlights of a vehicle behind. **antidemocratic** *a.* opposed or contrary to democratic principles. **antidepressant** *a.*, *n.* (a drug) used in treating or preventing mental depression. **antidesiccant** *a.*, *n.* (a chemical) that inhibits the drying out of a plant. **antidevolutionist** *a.*, *n.* (a person who is) opposed to devolution. **antidiuretic** *a.*, *n.* (a substance) that decreases the flow of urine. **antidiuretic hormone** *n.* vasopressin.

antidote (an´tidōt) *n.* **1** a medicine designed to counteract poison or disease. **2** anything intended to counteract something harmful or unpleasant. **antidotal** (-dō´-) *a.* [L *antidotum*, Gr. *antidoton*, a remedy, neut. of *antidotos*, given against (ANTI, *didōmi*, I give)]

antidromic (antidrom´ik) *a.* **1** (of nerve fibres) conducting nerve fibres in the opposite direction to normal. **2** (of plants) denoting the ability to twine to the left or right within the same family.

anti- (+ e–g words) anti-ecclesiastical *a.* opposed or hostile to the Church. **anti-episcopal** *a.* opposed to bishops or to episcopacy in Churches. **anti-erosion** *a.* that inhibits or prevents erosion. **anti-establishment, anti-Establishment** *a.* opposed to the Establishment in a particular society and its practices, values etc. **antifascist** *a.*, *n.* (a person who is) opposed to fascism. **antifebrile** *a.*, *n.* (a drug) that reduces fever. **antiflash** *a.* that protects against the flash from explosions. **antifouling** *a.*, *n.* (a paint or coating) that inhibits the growth of barnacles and other organisms on the bottoms of ships. **antifreeze** (an´ti-) *n.* a substance added to the water in car radiators to lower the freezing point. **anti-friction** *a.*, *n.* (a substance) that reduces friction. **anti-friction metal** *n.* any of various alloys used for high-speed bearings. **anti-g** (antijē´) *a.* designed to counteract the gravitational forces experienced during high acceleration. **anti-government, anti-Government** *a.* opposed to or subversive of a government.

antigen (an´tijən) *n.* a substance introduced into the body which stimulates the production of antibodies. [Gr. *gennaein*, to engender]

anti- (+ h–l words) (an´ti-) **anti-hero** *n.* (*pl.* **anti-heroes**) a principal character in a play, novel etc. who lacks noble or traditional heroic qualities. **anti-heroic** (-hirō´-) *a.* **antihistamine** *n.* a drug that counteracts the effects of histamine in allergic reactions. **anti-imperialism** *n.* opposition to imperialism. **anti-imperialist** *a., n.* **anti-imperialistic** *a.* **anti-inflammatory** *a., n.* (a drug) that reduces inflammation. **anti-inflationary** *a.* intended to counteract the effects of or prevent inflation in an economy. **anti-jamming** *a., n.* (procedures or a device) intended to prevent the jamming of radar or radio signals. **antiknock** *n.* a compound which is added to petrol to prevent knocking. **anti-lock** *a.* (of a braking system) designed to prevent locking and skidding when the brakes are suddenly applied. **antilogarithm, antilog** (an´-) *n.* the number represented by a logarithm. **antilogarithmic** (-ridh´-) *a.*

antihelix (antihē´liks), **anthelix** (anthē´liks) *n.* (*pl.* **antihelices** (-sēz), **anthelices**) the curved elevation within the helix of the ear. [Gr. *anthelix* (*helix*, a spiral, the outer ear)]

antilogy (antil´əji) *n.* (*pl.* **antilogies**) contradiction in terms or in ideas. [Gr. *antilogia* (*logia*, speaking)]

anti- (+ m– words) antimacassar *n.* a covering for chairs, sofas etc. to prevent their being soiled by (macassar) oil on the hair, or as an ornament. **anti-marketeer** *n.* an opponent of Britain's membership of the European (Economic) Community. **antimasque** (an´ti-), **antimask** *n.* a grotesque interlude between the acts of a masque. **antimatter** (an´ti-) *n.* hypothetical matter composed of antiparticles. **antimetabolite** (antimitab´əlīt) *n.* any drug that disrupts the normal metabolic processes within cells, esp. one used against cancer. **antimilitarism** *n.* opposition to militarism. **antimilitarist** *a., n.* **antimilitaristic** *a.* **antimissile** *a.* intended to destroy a ballistic missile or to defend a place against attack by such missiles. **antimodernist** *a., n.* (a person who is) opposed to modernism in art. **antimonarchist** *a., n.* (a person who is) opposed to monarchy in general or to the monarchy of a particular country.

antimony (an´timəni) *n.* a bright bluish-white brittle metallic element, at. no. 51, chem. symbol Sb, occurring naturally and used esp. in the manufacture of alloys and semiconductors. **antimonial** (-mō´-) *a.* of, relating to or containing antimony. ~*n.* a medicine containing antimony. **antimonial wine** *n.* sherry in which tartar emetic has been dissolved, formerly used medicinally. **antimoniate** (-ət) *n.* a salt of antimonic acid. **antimonic** (-mon´-) *a.* of or relating to antimony, applied to compounds in which antimony combines as a pentavalent element. **antimonic acid** *n.* an acid containing two equivalents of antimony and five of oxygen. **antimonious** (-mō´-) *a.* containing or composed of antimony, applied to compounds in which antimony combines as a trivalent element. [med. L *antimōnium*, prob. from Arab.]

anti- (+ n–o words) antinational *a.* opposed to the interest of one's country, or the national party. **anti-Nazi** *a., n.* (a person) opposed to the Nazi regime or ideology or to any regime or ideology considered to be similar to the Nazi one. **antineutron** *n.* the antiparticle of a neutron. **antinode** (an´ti-) *n.* (*Physics*) a region of maximum vibration between two nodes. **antinoise** (antinoiz´) *a.* **1** that reduces or eliminates noise. **2** that acts against any nuisance produced by noise. **antinovel** (an´ti-) *n.* a novel in which the normal conventions of the genre are dispensed with or subverted. **anti-nuclear** *a.* opposed to the use of nuclear power or weapons. **antioxidant** *n.* **1** (*Chem.*) any substance that prevents deterioration due to oxidization, esp. in stored foodstuffs. **2** (*Biol.*) any substance that removes oxidizing agents from a living organism, e.g. vitamin C or E.

antinomian (antinō´miən) *a.* **1** opposed to the moral law. **2** of or relating to the Antinomians. ~*n.* **1** a person who holds that the moral law is not binding on Christians. **2** (**Antinomian**) a member of a German sect of the 16th cent. said to hold this opinion. **antinomianism** *n.* rejection of the moral law. [med. L *Antinomi*, name of sect (Gr. *anti*, against, *nomos*, law)]

antinomy (antin´əmi) *n.* (*pl.* **antinomies**) **1** a contradiction between two laws. **2** a conflict of authority. **3** intellectual contradiction, opposition between laws or principles that appear to be equally founded in reason; paradox. [L from Gr. *antinomia*]

anti- (+ p– words) antipapal *a.* opposed to the pope or the papacy. **antiparallel** *a.* (*Physics*) parallel but pointing or rotating in the opposite direction. **antiparticle** (an´tipahtikəl) *n.* an elementary particle with the same mass as but opposite charge to another particle. **antiperiodic** *a., n.* (a drug) that is effective against the periodicity of diseases. **anti-personnel** *a.* (of a weapon etc.) designed to kill or injure people. **antiperspirant** *n., a.* (a substance) used to reduce perspiration. **antiphlogistic** *a., n.* (a drug) which allays inflammation. **antipole** *n.* **1** the opposite pole. **2** the direct opposite. **antipolitical** *a.* opposed or averse to politics and politicians. **antipope** *n.* a pope elected in opposition to the one canonically chosen. **anti-Protestant** *a., n.* (a person who is) opposed or hostile to, or prejudiced against, Protestants and Protestantism. **antiproton** *n.* a particle having the same mass as a proton and an equal but negative charge. **antipruritic** *a., n.* (a drug or agent) that relieves itching. **antipyretic** *a., n.* (a medicine) that prevents or allays fever.

antipasto (antipas´tō) *n.* (*pl.* **antipastos, antipasti** (-tē)) an hors d'oeuvre. [It. *anti-*, before, *pasto*, food]

antipathic (antipath´ik) *a.* **1** of contrary character or disposition. **2** (*Med.*) exhibiting or exciting contrary symptoms, allopathic. [F *antipathique* (*antipathie*, ANTIPATHY)]

antipathy (antip´əthi) *n.* (*pl.* **antipathies**) **1** hostile feeling towards; aversion, dislike. **2** a person or thing that is the object of such feeling. **antipathetic** (-thet´-), **antipathetical** *a.* having an antipathy or contrariety to. **antipathetically** *adv.* [L, from Gr. *antipatheia* (*pathein*, to suffer)]

antiphon (an´tifon) *n.* **1** a sentence sung by one choir in response to another. **2** a series of such responsive sentences or versicles. **3** a short sentence said or sung before the psalms, canticles etc., in the Roman Catholic Church, an anthem. **4** an answer. **antiphonal** (-tif´-) *a.* **1** sung or recited alternately. **2** consisting of antiphons. ~*n.* an antiphonary. **antiphonally** *adv.* **antiphonary** (-tif´-) *n.* (*pl.* **antiphonaries**) a book containing a collection of antiphons. **antiphony** (-tif´-) *n.* (*pl.* **antiphonies**) **1** alternate chanting or singing by a choir divided into two parts. **2** any musical or sound effect that echoes or answers another. **3** an antiphon. [late L *antiphōna*, Gr. *antiphōna*, pl. of *antiphōnon*, an anthem (*anti-*, in return, *phōnē*, voice)]

antiphrasis (antif´rəsis) *n.* the use of words in a sense contrary to their ordinary meaning. **antiphrastic** (-fras´-) *a.* [late L, from Gr. *antiphrasis* (*anti-*, contrary, *phrazein*, to speak)]

antipodes (antip´ədēz) *n.pl.* **1** a place on the surface of the globe diametrically opposite to another. **2** a pair of places diametrically opposite. **3** the direct opposite of some other person or thing. **4** people who live directly opposite to each other on the globe. **the Antipodes** Australia and New Zealand. **antipodal** *a.* **1** of or relating to the antipodes. **2** situated on the opposite side of the globe. **antipode** (an´tipōd) *n.* an exact opposite. **antipodean** (-dē´-) *a.* of, relating to or from the antipodes. ~*n.* **(Antipodean)** a person from the Antipodes. [L, from Gr. *antipodes*, sing. *antipous* (*anti-*, against, *pous*, foot)]

antiquary (an´tikwəri) *n.* (*pl.* **antiquaries**) **1** a student, investigator, collector or seller of antiquities or antiques. **2** a student of ancient times. **antiquarian** (-kweə´riən) *a.* **1** of, relating to or dealing in antiques or rare and ancient books. **2** of or relating to the study of antiquities. **3** (of paper) of the size 52 ins (133.35 cm) x 30 ins (77.47 cm). ~*n.* an antiquary. **antiquarianism** *n.* **antiquarianize, antiquarianise** *v.i.* [L *antiquarius*]

antiquated (an´tikwātid) *a.* old-fashioned, out of date, obsolete. [as ANTIQUARY]

antique (antēk´) *a.* **1** ancient, old, that has been in existence for a long time. **2** old-fashioned, antiquated. ~*n.* **1** a piece of furniture, ornament etc., made in an earlier period and valued by collectors. **2** a relic of antiquity. **3** any very old thing or person. ~*v.t.* (*3rd pers. sing. pres.* **antiques,** *pres.p.* **antiquing,** *past, p.p.* **antiqued**) to give an antique appearance to. **the antique** the ancient style in art. [F *antique*, L *antīquus*, *anticus* (*ante-*, before)]

antiquity (antik´witi) *n.* (*pl.* **antiquities**) **1** the state of being ancient, great age. **2** ancient times, esp. the period of European history before the Middle Ages. **3** (*usu. pl.*) a relic of ancient times. **4** (*usu. pl.*) manners, customs, events etc. of ancient times. **5** the ancients. [as ANTIQUE]

anti- (+ r– words) anti-racism *n.* opposition to all forms of prejudice or persecution on grounds of race. **anti-racist** *a., n.* **antirational** *a.* opposed or contrary to reason or rationalism. **antirationalism** *n.* **antireligious** *a.* opposed or hostile to religion. **antirepublican** *a.* opposed to republicanism or republican principles. **antirevolutionary** *a., n.* (*pl.* **antirevolutionaries**) (a person who is) opposed to revolution in general or in principle, or opposed to the aims, methods, policies etc. of a particular revolution or revolutionary movement. **antirust** *a.* intended to prevent or treat rust.

antirrhinum (antirī´nəm) *n.* any plant of a genus, *Antirrhinum*, that includes the snapdragon. [L, from Gr. *antirrhinon* (*anti-*, instead of, *rhis, rhinos*, nose)]

anti- (+ s– words) anti-sabbatarian *a., n.* (a person who is) opposed to sabbatarian views. **antiscientific** *a.* hostile or contrary to science. **antiscorbutic** *n., a.* (a medicine or remedy) used in treating or preventing scurvy. **antiscriptural** *a.* opposed to Scripture. **anti-Semite** *n.* a person who is hostile towards or prejudiced against Jews. **anti-Semitic** *a.* **anti-Semitism** *n.* **antiseptic** *a.* **1** counteracting sepsis, or putrefaction, by inhibiting the growth of microorganisms. **2** free from contamination. **3** lacking interest, warmth or excitement, sterile. ~*n.* an antiseptic substance. **antisepsis** *n.* the principle of antiseptic treatment. **antiserum** *n.* (*pl.* **antiserums, antisera**) a serum containing antibodies. **antishock** *a.* designed or intended to resist shocks. **antiskid** *a.* intended to prevent skidding. **antislavery** *a.* opposed to slavery. **antisocial** *a.* **1** opposed to the interest of society, or to the principles on which society is constituted. **2** unsociable. **anti-Soviet** *a.* (*Hist.*) opposed or hostile to, or subversive of, the Soviet Union. **antistatic** (antistat´ik) *a., n.* (an agent) that counteracts the effects of static electricity. **anti-submarine** *a.* designed to destroy submarines or to defend against submarine attack.

antistrophe (antis´trəfi) *n.* **1** the return movement from left to right of a Greek chorus, answering the movement of a strophe. **2** the poem or choral song recited during this movement. **3** any choral response. **antistrophic** (-strof´-) *a.* [L, from Gr. *antistrophē* (*strophē*, a turning, a verse)]

anti- (+ t– words) anti-tank *a.* designed to destroy tanks or defend against tank attacks. **antiterrorism** *n.* opposition to terrorism; procedures to combat terrorism. **antiterrorist** *a.* **antitetanus** *a.* preventing tetanus. **antitetanic** *a.* **antitetanin** *n.* an antitoxin used for curing or preventing tetanus. **antitheft** *a.* intended to prevent something from being stolen. **antitheism** *n.* opposition to belief in a god. **antitheist** *n.* **antitheistic** *a.* **antitoxin** *n.* an antibody or antiserum formed in the body which neutralizes the action of toxins. **antitoxic** *a.* **antitrade** *a., n.* (a wind) blowing in an opposite direction to that of the trade winds. **antitrinitarian** *a., n.* (a person who is) opposed to the doctrine of the Trinity. **antitrinitarianism** *n.* **antitrust** *a.* (*N Am.*) opposing trusts or monopolies which adversely affect competition.

antithesis (antith´əsis) *n.* (*pl.* **antitheses** (-sēz)) **1** the direct opposite. **2** opposition, contrast. **3** sharp opposition or contrast between words, clauses, sentences or ideas. **4** a counter proposition. **antithetic** (-thet´-), **antithetical** *a.* **1** of, relating to or marked by antithesis. **2** contrasted. **3** sharply opposed. **antithetically** *adv.* [Gr. (*thesis*, a setting, from *tithēmi*, I place)]

antitype (an´titīp) *n.* **1** the thing or person that is represented by a type or symbol. **2** an opposite type. **antitypal** (-tī´-) *a.* of the nature of an antitype. **antitypical** (-tip´-) *a.* [Gr. *antitupos*, answering to, as an impression to a die (*tupos*, a blow, a stamp, cogn. with *tuptein*, to strike)]

anti- (+ v– words) antiviral *a.* effective against viruses. **antivirus** *n.* software designed to protect a computer system against a virus. **antivivisection** *a.* opposed to vivisection. **antivivisectionism** *n.* **antivivisectionist** *n., a.*

antivenin (antiven´in) *n.* serum obtained from animals immunized against snake venom, used as an antidote against snake-bite. [L *venenum*, poison]

anti- (+ w–z words) antiwar *a.* opposed to war, pacifistic. **anti-Zionism** *n.* opposition or hostility to Zionism. **anti-Zionist** *a., n.*

antler (ant´lə) *n.* **1** a branch of the horns of a stag or other deer. **2** either of the branched horns of a deer. **antlered** *a.* **1** having antlers. **2** branched like stags' horns. [OF *antoillier*, late L *antoculārem* (*ramum*), the branch (orig., the lowest or brow antler) which is in front of the eye (*ante-*, before, *oculus*, eye)]

Antonine (an´tōnīn) *a.* of or relating to the Roman emperors Antoninus Pius and Marcus Aurelius and their reigns (AD 137–80). ~*n.* either of these two emperors.

antonomasia (antənəmā´ziə) *n.* **1** the substitution of an epithet for a proper name, e.g. *the Corsican* for Napoleon. **2** the use of a proper name to describe one of a class, e.g. a *Cicero* for an orator. **antonomastic** (-mas´-) *a.* characterized by antonomasia. **antonomastically** *adv.* [L, from Gr. *antonomasia*, *antonomazein*, to name instead (*anti-*, instead, *onomazein*, to name)]

antonym (an´tənim) *n.* a term expressing the reverse of some other term, as 'good' to 'bad'. [Gr. *antōnumia* (*anti-*, instead of, *onuma*, a name)]

antre (an´tə) *n.* (*poet.*) a cavern or cave. [F from L *antrum*, cave]

antrum (antrəm) *n.* (*pl.* **antra** (-trə)) a natural anatomical cavity, particularly one in bone. [L from Gr. *antron*, a cave]

ANU *abbr.* Australian National University.

anuran (ənū´rən) *n.* any tailless amphibian vertebrate of the order Anura which includes the frogs and toads. ~*a.* of or relating to this order. [new L *Anura*, from Gr. *an-*, without, *ouros*, tail]

anuria (ənū´riə) *n.* inability to secrete urine, usu. due to kidney disorder. [Gr. *an-*, without, *ouron*, urine]

anus (ā´nəs) *n.* **1** the lower, excretory opening of the intestinal tube. **2** the inferior aperture of a monopetalous flower. [L, a rounding, a ring]

anvil (an´vil) *n.* **1** the iron block, usu. with a flat top, concave sides and a point at one end, on which smiths hammer and shape their work. **2** anything resembling a smith's anvil in shape or use, esp. a bone in the ear, the incus. [OE *onfilti* (etym. uncertain)]

anxious (angk´shəs) *a.* **1** troubled or fearful about some uncertain or future event. **2** inspiring anxiety, distressing, worrying. **3** eagerly desirous (to do something). **anxiety** (angzī´əti) *n.* (*pl.* **anxieties**) **1** the state of being anxious. **2** trouble, solicitude or mental distress. **3** eager desire. **4** a cause of anxiety. **5** (*Psych.*) a mental disorder symptomized by chronic uneasiness. **anxiolytic** (angziōlit´ik) *n.*, *a.* (a drug) that alleviates anxiety. **anxiously** *adv.* [L *anxius* (*angere*, to choke)]

any (en´i) *a.*, *pron.* **1** one, unspecified, among several (*pick any card*). **2** some or an unspecified number (*Read any good books lately?*). **3** a minimal amount (*makes hardly any difference*). **4** whichever, whatever (*any day will suit me*). *~adv.* (*usu. with a negative*) at all, to an appreciative degree (*hasn't made it any better*). **any day now** very soon, very shortly. **any longer** for any further length of time; now, from this point on. **any minute now** very soon, very shortly. **anymore** (*N Am.*) any more. **any more** for any further length of time; now, from this point on. **any old** (*coll.*) any, no matter which or what. **anytime** (*N Am.*) any time. **any time** (*coll.*) whenever, at any time. **any time now** very soon, very shortly. **not having any** (*coll.*) unwilling to tolerate or put up with something; unwilling to participate in something. **anybody** *n.*, *pron.* **1** any person; any one. **2** a person of little importance (*I'm not just anybody!*). **3** a person of some importance (*is she anybody?*). **anybody's 1** (of a game, contest) evenly balanced. **2** (*coll.*) (of a person) able to be seduced, bribed etc. by anybody. **anybody's guess** GUESS. **anyhow** *adv.* **1** anyway. **2** in a disorderly fashion, imperfectly, haphazardly. **anyone** *n.*, *pron.* any person, anybody. **anyplace** *adv.* (*N Am.*) anywhere. **any road** *adv.* (*dial.*) anyway, in any case. **anything** *pron.*, *n.* any object, thing, event, action of any kind (*be prepared for anything*). *~adv.* in any way (*if you're anything like me*). **anything but** not at all (*it's anything but easy*). **like anything** (*coll.*) very fast, vigorously, intensely etc. **anyway** *adv.* **1** nevertheless, in any case, in any event. **2** in any manner or fashion. **3** to resume. **anyways** *adv.* (*N Am.*, *coll.*) anyway. **anywhere** *adv.* in or to any place. †**anywise** *adv.* **1** in any manner, case, or degree. **2** anyhow. [OE *ænig* (*ān*, one, *-ig*, a. ending)]

Usage note In writing, it is conventional to distinguish between *anyone* and *any one*: *any one* means any individual one (as in *I could kill any one of you*), while *anyone* means anybody at all (*I couldn't kill anyone*).

Anzac (an´zak) *n.* **1** a soldier in the Australian or New Zealand forces, in the war of 1914–18. **2** any Australian or New Zealander, esp. a soldier. **Anzac Day** *n.* April 25, a public holiday in Australia and New Zealand to commemorate the Anzac landing at Gallipoli in 1915. [*A*ustralian (and) *N*ew *Z*ealand *A*rmy *C*orps]

Anzus (an´zəs), **ANZUS** *n.* a pact for the security of the Pacific, formed in 1952 by Australia, New Zealand and the US. [acronym]

AO *abbr.* Officer of the Order of Australia.

a/o *abbr.* account of.

AOB *abbr.* any other business.

AOC *abbr.* **1** Air Officer Commanding. **2** appellation d'origine contrôlée.

A-OK (āōkā´) *a.* in good or perfect working order. [*a*ll systems *OK*]

aorist (ā´ərist) *n.* a Greek tense expressing indefinite past time. *~a.* aoristic. **aoristic** (-ris´-) *a.* **1** indefinite in point of time. **2** of or relating to an aorist tense. [Gr. *aoristos*, unlimited (*a-*, not, *horizein*, to limit)]

aorta (āaw´tə) *n.* (*pl.* **aortas**) **1** the largest artery in the body. **2** the main trunk of the arterial system proceeding from the left ventricle of the heart. **aortic** *a.* of or relating to the aorta. [late L, from Gr. *aortē* (*aerein*, to lift)]

à outrance (a ootrãs´) *adv.* **1** to the end. **2** to the death. [F]

AP *abbr.* Associated Press.

ap-[1] (ap) *pref.* AD-, assim. to *p*, e.g. *appear*, *approve*.

ap-[2] APO-.

apace (əpās´) *adv.* at a quick pace, speedily, fast.

Apache (əpach´i) *n.* (*pl.* **Apache, Apaches**) **1** a member of a N American Indian people of the SW US and N Mexico. **2** the language of this people. *~a.* of or relating to this people or their language. **apache** (əpash´) *n.* (*pl.* **apaches** (əpash´)) a hooligan or street ruffian or robber, originally from Paris. **apache dance** *n.* a dance routine, originally from French vaudeville, supposedly depicting a French gangster and his moll, in which the female dancer appears to be violently thrown around. [Mex. Sp.]

☒ **apall** common misspelling of APPAL.

apanage (ap´ənij), **appanage** *n.* **1** lands or an office assigned for the maintenance of a member of a royal house, esp. a younger son. **2** a perquisite. **3** a necessary adjunct or attribute. [OF *apaner*, to nourish, med. L *apānāre* (*ap-*, *ad-*, to, *pānis*, bread)]

☒ **aparent** common misspelling of APPARENT.

apart (əpaht´) *adv.* **1** parted, at a distance from one another. **2** into two or more pieces or parts. **3** to or on one side. **4** not being taken into account. **5** independently. **6** distinct from others. **apart from 1** with the exception of, leaving out. **2** in addition to. **apartness** *n.* [F *à part*, to one side, singly, L *ad partem*]

apartheid (əpah´tāt, -tīt) *n.* (a policy of) racial segregation. [Afrikaans, APART, -HOOD]

apartment (əpaht´mənt) *n.* **1** (*pl.*) a suite of rooms, lodgings. **2** (*chiefly N Am.*) a flat. **3** a single room in a house. **apartment building, apartment house** *n.* (*N Am.*) a block of flats. **apartment hotel** *n.* (*N Am.*) a hotel that lets furnished suites of rooms on a short- or long-term basis. [F *appartement*, from It. *appartamento*, from *appartare*, to divide, from *a parte*, apart]

apatetic (apətet´ik) *a.* (of an animal's coloration) closely resembling that of another species or of its surroundings.

apathy (ap´əthi) *n.* **1** absence of feeling or passion. **2** lack of interest, indifference. **3** mental indolence. **apathetic** (-thet´-) *a.* characterized by apathy; listless, emotionless, indifferent. **apathetically** *adv.* [F *apathie*, L *apathia*, Gr. *apatheia* (*a-*, not, *pathein*, to suffer)]

apatite (ap´ətīt) *n.* a common mineral, consisting of calcium phosphate in combination with other elements, esp. fluorine, that is used in the making of fertilizers. [G *Apatit*, Gr. *apatē*, deceit, from its resemblance to other minerals]

apatosaurus (əpatəsaw´rəs) *n.* (*pl.* **apatosauruses**) a very large herbivorous dinosaur of the genus *Apatosaurus*, formerly *Brontosaurus*, having a long neck and tail, a small head and trunklike legs. [Gr. *apatē*, deceit, *sauros*, lizard]

APB *abbr.* (*N Am.*) all-points bulletin.

ape (āp) *n.* **1** a tailless primate, esp. one of the Pongidae (a gorilla, chimpanzee, orang-outan or gibbon). **2** (*loosely*) any monkey. **3** a mimic, an imitator. **4** a clumsy, coarse or brutish person. *~v.t.* to imitate or mimic. **to go ape** (*N Am.*) to go berserk; to go crazy. **apeman** *n.* (*pl.* **apemen**) any of various extinct primate species thought to have been intermediate between the higher apes and humans. **apery** (ā´pəri) *n.* (*pl.* **aperies**) mimicry, esp. if silly or pretentious. **apish** *a.* **1** of the nature of or like an ape. **2** silly, foolish. **apishly** *adv.* **apishness** *n.* [OE *apa* (cp. Dut. *aap*, Icel. *api*, OHG *affo*)]

apeak (əpēk´) *adv., pred.a.* (*Naut.*) in a vertical or nearly vertical position; pointed upwards. [F *à pic*, vertically, vertical (*à*, at, *pic*, summit)]

☒ **apear** common misspelling of APPEAR.

aperçu (apœsoo´) *n.* **1** a concise exposition, an outline, a brief summary. **2** an insight. [F, p.p. of *apercevoir*, to perceive]

aperient (əpiə´riənt) *a.* laxative, purgative, deobstruent. ~*n.* a laxative medicine. [L *aperīre*, to open]

aperiodic (āpiəriod´ik) *a.* **1** not occurring regularly. **2** (*Physics*) **a** not having a periodic motion. **b** (of an instrument) sufficiently damped to reach equilibrium without oscillation. **aperiodicity** (-dis´-) *n.*

aperitif (əperitēf´) *n.* a short drink, usu. alcoholic, taken as an appetizer. [F]

aperture (ap´əchə) *n.* **1** an opening, a hole, a gap, a passage. **2** (the diameter of) the space through which light passes in an optical instrument. **3** the diameter of a lens. [L *apertura*]

apery APE.

apetalous (əpet´ələs) *a.* without petals. [Gr. *apetalos*, leafless (*a-*, not, *petalon*, leaf)]

APEX[1] *abbr.* Association of Professional, Executive, Clerical and Computer Staff.

APEX[2] (ā´peks), **Apex** *n.* a discounted fare on some air, sea and rail journeys paid for no later than a specified number of days before departure. [acronym for *A*dvance *P*urchase *Ex*cursion]

apex (ā´peks) *n.* (*pl.* **apexes, apices** (ā´pisēz)) **1** the tip, top, vertex or summit of anything. **2** the culmination, climax. **apical** (-pikəl) *a.* **1** of or relating to an apex. **2** placed at the summit. **apically** *adv.* **1** at the apex. **2** towards the apex. [L]

apfelstrudel (ap´fəlstroodəl) *n.* a dessert of Austrian origin consisting of flaky pastry filled with a spiced apple mixture.

aphaeresis (əfiə´rəsis), **apheresis** *n.* the taking away of a letter or syllable at the beginning of a word. [L, from Gr. *aphairēsis* (*aph, apo*, away, *airein*, to take)]

aphagia (əfā´jiə) *n.* inability or unwillingness to swallow. [Gr. *a-*, not, *phagia* from *phagein*, to swallow]

aphasia (əfā´ziə) *n.* (partial) loss of the power to express or understand anything in words. **aphasic** *a.* [Gr., speechlessness]

aphelion (əfē´liən) *n.* (*pl.* **aphelia** (-ə)) the point most distant from the sun in the orbit of a planet or a comet. [L *aphēlium*, Gr. *aph' hēlion*, away from the sun]

apheliotropic (əfēliətrop´ik) *a.* bending or turning away from the sun. **apheliotropically** *adv.* **apheliotropism** (-ot´-) *n.* [Gr. *tropikos*, turning]

aphesis (af´əsis) *n.* a form of aphaeresis, in which an unaccented vowel at the beginning of a word is lost. **aphetic** (əfet´-) *a.* of or relating to aphesis. **aphetize, aphetise** *v.t.* to shorten by aphesis. [Gr., from *aphienai* (*aph-, apo-*, away, *ienai*, to let go)]

aphid (ā´fid) *n.* **1** any of a family of minute insects, Aphididae, which are very destructive to vegetation, comprising among others the greenfly, black fly, American blight etc. **2** a plant-louse. **aphidian** (ə-) *a.* of or relating to aphids or aphides. ~*n.* an aphid or plant-louse. [back formation from *aphides* (see APHIS)]

aphis (ā´fis, af´-) *n.* (*pl.* **aphides** (-dēz)) an aphid, esp. of the genus *Aphis.* [genus name coined by Linnaeus]

aphonia (əfō´niə), **aphony** (af´əni) *n.* inability to speak or loss of voice caused by disease of the vocal tract. **aphonic** (əfon´-) *a.* [Gr., from *aphōnos*, voiceless (*a-*, not, *phōnē*, voice)]

aphorism (af´ərizm) *n.* a detached, pithy sentence, containing a maxim or wise precept. **aphorismic** (-riz´-) *a.* **aphorist** *n.* a person who writes or utters aphorisms. **aphoristic** (-ris´-) *a.* **aphoristically** *adv.* **aphorize, aphorise** *v.i.* to utter or write aphorisms. [Gr. *aphorismos*, a definition, from *aphorixein* (*aph-, apo-*, off, *horizein*, to mark)]

aphrodisiac (afrədiz´iak) *a.* exciting sexual desire. ~*n.* a drug that arouses or increases sexual desire. **aphrodisian** *a.* [Gr. *aphrodisiakos*, from *aphroditios*, from *Aphroditē*, the goddess of sensual love]

aphthae (af´thē) *n.pl.* the minute specks seen in the mouth and tongue in thrush. [L, from Gr. *aphthai* (prob. cogn. with *haptein*, to set on fire, inflame)]

aphyllous (əfil´əs) *a.* without leaves. [Gr. *aphullos* (*a-*, not, *phullon*, leaf)]

apian (ā´piən) *a.* of or relating to bees. [L *apianus*, from *apis*, a bee]

apiarian (āpieə´riən) *a.* relating to bees or bee-keeping. ~*n.* an apiarist. **apiarist** (ā´-) *n.* a person who rears bees, a bee-keeper. **apiary** (ā´-) *n.* (*pl.* **apiaries**) a place where bees are kept. [L *apiārium*, neut. of *apiārius*, pertaining to bees (*apis*, bee)]

apical, apices APEX.

apiculate (əpik´ūlāt), **apiculated** *a.* (*Bot.*) terminating abruptly in a little sharp point. [mod. L *apiculus*, dim. of APEX]

apiculture (ā´pikŭlchə) *n.* bee-keeping; bee-rearing. [L *apis*, a bee]

apiece (əpēs´) *adv.* for or to each, severally. [*a piece*, for one piece]

apish APE.

APL (āpēel´) *n.* a computer programming language designed for mathematical applications. [*a pro*gramming *l*anguage]

aplanatic (aplənat´ik) *a.* (of a lens etc.) free from spherical aberration. **aplanat** (ap´lənat) *n.* an aplanatic surface or instrument. [Gr. *aplanētos* (*a-*, priv., *planaein*, to wander)]

aplasia (əplā´ziə) *n.* defective or arrested development in a body tissue or organ. **aplastic** (-plas´-) *a.* [A-[3] Gr. *plasis*, formation]

aplenty (əplen´ti) *adv.* in plenty, in abundance.

aplomb (əplom´) *n.* self-possession, coolness. [F *aplomb*, perpendicular (*à plomb*, by the plummet)]

apnoea (apnē´ə), (*N Am.*) **apnea** *n.* a breakdown or cessation of breathing. [Gr. *apnoia* (*a-*, not, *pnoia*, breath)]

apo- (ap´ō), **ap-** *pref.* away, detached, separate, as in *apology, apostrophe.* [Gr. *apo*, away, from]

Apoc. *abbr.* **1** Apocalypse. **2** Apocrypha, apocryphal.

apocalypse (əpok´əlips) *n.* **1** any revelation or prophetic disclosure, esp. relating to the end of the world. **2** a vast decisive or cataclysmic event or confrontation. **the Apocalypse 1** the revelation granted to St John the Divine. **2** the book of the New Testament in which this is recorded. **apocalyptic** (-lip´-), **apocalyptical** *a.* **1** of or relating to the revelation of St John. **2** of the nature of a revelation or apocalypse. **3** prophesying disaster or doom. **apocalyptically** *adv.* [L *apocalypsis*, Gr. *apokalupsis*, from *apokaluptein*, to uncover (*apo-*, off, *kaluptein*, to cover)]

apocarpous (apəkah´pəs) *a.* having the carpels wholly or partly distinct. [APO-, Gr. *karpos*, fruit]

apochromat (apəkrō´mat) *n.* a lens that reduces chromatic aberrations. **apochromatic** (-krəmat´ik) *a.* relatively free from chromatic or spherical aberration. [Gr. APO-, *chrōma, chrōmatos*, colour]

apocope (əpok´əpi) *n.* a cutting off or dropping of the last letter or syllable of a word. [L, from Gr. *apokopē* (*apo-*, away, *koptein*, to cut)]

apocrine (ap´əkrīn, -in) *a.* (of a gland) whose secretions include parts of the cells of the gland. [Gr. APO-, *krīnein*, to sift, to separate]

apocrypha (əpok´rifə) *n.pl.* writings or statements of doubtful authority. **the Apocrypha** a collection of 14 books in the Old Testament, included in the Septuagint and the Vulgate, but not written in Hebrew originally, nor reckoned genuine by the Jews, nor inserted in the Authorized Version of the Bible. **apocryphal** *a.* **1** of or relating to the Apocrypha. **2** spurious, fabulous. **apocryphally** *adv.* [Gr. *apokrupha*, neut. pl., things hidden, from *apokruptein* (*apo*, away, *kruptein*, to hide)]

apod (ap´əd), **apode** (ap´ōd) *n.* a footless creature, a bird, fish or reptile in which the feet or corresponding members are absent or undeveloped. **apodal** *a.* **1** footless. **2** having no ventral fin. [Gr. *apous* (*a-*, not, without, *pous podos*, foot)]

apodictic (apədik´tik), **apodeictic** (-dīk´-) *a.* **1** clearly demonstrative. **2** established on uncontrovertible evidence. **apodictically, apodeictically** *adv.* [L *apodīcticus*, Gr. *apodeiktikos* (*apodeiknunai*, to show)]

apodosis (əpod´əsis) *n.* (*pl.* **apodoses** (-sēz)) the consequent clause in a conditional sentence, answering to the protasis. [L, from Gr. *apodosis*, a giving (*apodidonai*, to give back)]

apodyterium (apəditiə´riəm) *n.* (*pl.* **apodyteria** (-riə)) the apartment in ancient baths or palaestras where clothes were taken off. [L, from Gr. *apodutērion* (*apo-*, off, *-duein*, to put, dress)]

apogamy (əpog´əmi) *n.* (*Bot.*) the absence of sexual reproductive power, the plant perpetuating itself from an unfertilized female cell. **apogamous** *a.* **apogamously** *adv.* [Gr. *apo-*, away from, *gamos*, marriage]

apogee (ap´əjē) *n.* **1** the point in the orbit of the moon or any planet or satellite which is at the greatest distance from the earth. **2** the most distant point in the orbit of a satellite from the planet round which it revolves. **3** the furthest point, the highest point, the culmination. **apogean** *a.* [F *apogée*, late L *apogæum*, Gr. *apogaion*, neut. a., away from the earth (APO-, *gaia*, earth)]

apolitical (āpəlit´ikəl) *a.* **1** uninterested in political affairs, politically neutral. **2** without political significance.

Apollinaris (əpolineə´ris) *n.* an effervescent mineral water from a spring in the Ahr valley. [Saint *Apollinaris*, Bishop of Laodicea, died *c.* AD 390]

Apollonian (apəlō´niən) *a.* **1** of or relating to Apollo, the Greek and Roman god of the sun, music and poetry. **2** rational, controlled, harmonious (esp. as opposed to *Dionysian*). [L *Apollonius*, from Gr. *Apollōnios*]

apologetic (əpoləjet´ik), **apologetical** *a.* **1** regretfully acknowledging or excusing an offence. **2** of or relating to a reasoned defence or vindication. **3** hesitant, diffident. **apologetically** *adv.* **apologetics** *n.* defensive argument, esp. the argumentative defence of Christianity. [F *apologétique*, L *apologēticus*, Gr. *apologētikos* (*apologeesthai*, to speak in defence)]

apologia (apəlō´jiə) *n.* a vindication or formal defence of one's conduct, views etc. [L, from Gr.]

apologist, apologize APOLOGY.

apologue (ap´əlog) *n.* a fable designed to impress some moral truth upon the mind, esp. a beast-fable or a fable of inanimate things. [F, from L *apologus*, from Gr. (*apo-*, off, *logos*, speech)]

apology (əpol´əji) *n.* (*pl.* **apologies**) **1** a regretful acknowledgement of offence. **2** an explanation, excuse. **3** a defence, vindication. **4** a wretched substitute for the real thing. **apologist** *n.* a person who defends or vindicates by reasoned argument. **apologize, apologise** *v.i.* to make an apology or excuse, to express regret. [L *apologia*, from Gr. (*apo-*, off, *legein*, to speak)]

apolune (ap´əloon, ap´ō-) *n.* the point in a body's lunar orbit where it is furthest from the moon. [APO-, L *luna*, moon]

apomixis (apəmik´sis) *n.* (*pl.* **apomixes** (-sēz)) reproduction without fertilization. **apomictic** *a.* **apomictically** *adv.* [Gr. APO-, *mixis*, mixing]

apophthegm (ap´əthem), (*N Am.*) **apothegm** *n.* a terse pointed saying, a maxim expressed in few but weighty words. **apophthegmatic** (-thegmat´-) *a.* **1** of, relating to or using apophthegms. **2** sententious, pithy. **apophthegmatically** *adv.* [Gr. *apophthegma* (*apo-*, off, out, *phthengesthai*, to speak)]

apoplexy (ap´əpleksi) *n.* **1** a sudden loss of sensation and of power of motion, generally caused by rupture or obstruction of a blood vessel in the brain, a stroke. **2** (*coll.*) a violent fit of anger. **apoplectic** (-plek´-) *a.* **1** of, relating to or tending to cause apoplexy. **2** predisposed to apoplexy. **3** violently angry. ~*n.* a person liable to or afflicted with apoplexy. [F *apoplexie*, late L, from Gr. *apoplēxia* (*apoplēssein*, to cripple with a blow)]

apoptosis (apəptō´sis) *n.* the death of cells as part of the normal growth and development of an organism. **apoptotic** (-tot´ik) *a.* [Gr., falling off]

aporia (əpaw´riə, əpor´iə) *n.* **1** in rhetoric, a real or affected doubt about what to do. **2** a difficulty, a puzzling thing. [Gr. *aporos*, impassable]

aport (əpawt´) *adv.* on or towards the port side of a ship.

aposematic (apəsimat´ik) *a.* (of the colouring of some animals) providing protection against predators.

aposiopesis (apəsīəpē´sis) *n.* (*pl.* **aposiopeses** (-sēz)) a stopping short for rhetorical effect. [L, from Gr., from *aposiōpaein* (*apo-*, off, away, *siōpaein*, to be silent)]

apositic (apəsit´ik) *a.* **1** causing aversion to food. **2** tending to weaken appetite. [Gr. *apositikos*, exciting distaste for food]

apostasy (əpos´təsi) *n.* (*pl.* **apostasies**) **1** (a) renunciation of religious faith, moral allegiance or political principles. **2** in the Roman Catholic Church, renunciation of religious vows. [L, from Gr. *apostasia*, previously *apostasis* (*apo-*, away, *stasis*, a standing, from *sta-*, stem of *histēmi*, I stand)]

apostate (əpos´tāt) *n.* a person who apostatizes. ~*a.* **1** unfaithful to creed or principles. **2** rebel, rebellious. **apostatic** (apəstat´-), **apostatical** *a.* **apostatize** (-tə-), **apostatise** *v.i.* to abandon one's creed, principles or party; to commit apostasy. [OF *apostate*, late L *apostata*, Gr. *apostatēs*]

a posteriori (a postiəriaw´ri, ah) *a.*, *adv.* reasoning from consequences, effects, things observed to causes; inductive, as opposed to a priori or deductive. [L]

apostil (əpos´til) *n.* a marginal note, gloss, annotation. [F *apostille* (etym. uncertain)]

apostle (əpos´əl) *n.* **1** (**Apostle**) any one of the twelve men appointed by Christ to preach the gospel. **2** a first Christian missionary to any region, or a missionary who has pre-eminent success. **3** the leader of, or an outstanding figure in, a movement, esp. of reform. **4** a member of a council of twelve appointed to preside over the Mormon Church. **apostle-bird** *n.* an Australian babbler which forms flocks of about twelve. **Apostles' Creed** *n.* a Christian creed, each clause of which is said to have been contributed by one of the Apostles. **apostleship** *n.* **apostle spoons** *n.pl.* (tea)spoons whose handles end in figures of the Apostles, formerly a frequent present of sponsors in baptism. **apostolate** (-təlāt) *n.* **1** the office of apostle. **2** leadership, esp. in the propagation of a doctrine. **apostolic** (apəstol´-), **apostolical** *a.* **1** of or relating to the Apostles. **2** derived directly from or agreeable to the doctrine or practice of the Apostles. **3** of the character or nature of an apostle. **4** of or relating to the Pope as St Peter's successor, papal. **apostolically** *adv.* **Apostolic Fathers** *n.pl.* those Christian Fathers or writers contemporaneous with the Apostles or their immediate disciples. **Apostolic See** *n.* the papacy. **apostolic succession** *n.* uninterrupted transmission of spiritual authority through bishops, from the Apostles. [OF *apostle*, *apostre*, L *apostolus*, Gr. *apostolos*, a messenger (*apo-*, away, and *stellein*, to send)]

apostrophe[1] (əpos´trəfi) *n.* the sign (') used to denote the omission of a letter or letters, and as the sign of the

English possessive case. **apostrophize**[1], **apostrophise** *v.t.* to mark an omission of a letter or letters from a word by inserting an apostrophe. [F *apostrophe*, from L *apostrophus*, from Gr. *apostrophos*, turned away]

apostrophe[2] (əpos´trəfi) *n.* a rhetorical figure in which the speaker addresses one person in particular, or turns away from those present to address the absent or dead. **apostrophic** (apəstrof´ik) *a.* **apostrophize**[2], **apostrophise** *v.t.* to address in or with apostrophe. [L, from Gr. *apostrophē*, a turning away (*apostrephein*, to turn away)]

apostrophize[1] APOSTROPHE[1].

apostrophize[2] APOSTROPHE[2].

apothecary (əpoth´ikəri) *n.* (*pl.* **apothecaries**) **1** †a person who prepares and sells medicines, a druggist or pharmaceutical chemist. **2** a licentiate of the Apothecaries' Society. **apothecaries' measure** *n.* a system of liquid capacity measure formerly used in pharmacy, based on the minim, fluid drachm and fluid ounce. **apothecaries' weight** *n.* a system of weights formerly used in pharmacy, based on the grain, scruple, drachm and troy ounce. [OF *apotecaire*, late L *apothēcārius*, from *apothēca*, a storehouse, Gr. *apothēkē* (*apo-*, away, *tithēmi*, I put)]

apothecium (apəthē´siəm, -shiəm) *n.* (*pl.* **apothecia** (-siə, -shiə)) the spore-case in lichens. [mod. L, from Gr. *apothēkē*, see APOTHECARY]

apothegm APOPHTHEGM.

apotheosis (əpothiō´sis) *n.* (*pl.* **apotheoses** (-sēz)) **1** deification, transformation into a god. **2** a sublime example of something. **3** a deified ideal. **4** enrolment among the saints. **apotheosize** (-poth´-), **apotheosise** *v.t.* to deify, to exalt, to glorify. [L, from Gr. *apotheōsis* (*apo-*, *theoō*, I deify, from *theos*, a god)]

apotropaic (apətrəpā´ik) *a.* intended or supposed to avert evil influences. [Gr. *apotropaios* (APO-, *trepō*, turn)]

app. *abbr.* **1** apparent, apparently. **2** appendix. **3** (*Comput.*) application. **4** appointed. **5** apprentice.

appal (əpawl´), (*esp. N Am.*) **appall** *v.t.* (*pres.p.* **appalling**, *past, p.p.* **appalled**) to horrify, to shock, to dismay. **appalling** *a.* **1** horrifying, shocking. **2** unsatisfactory, unpleasant. **appallingly** *adv.* [OF *apalir*, *apallir*, to grow pale, to make pale]

Appaloosa (apəloo´sə) *n.* **1** a N American breed of horse with a spotted coat. **2** a horse of this breed. [prob. from the *Palouse* Indians]

appanage APANAGE.

apparat (apərat´, ap´-) *n.* (*Hist.*) the party organization of the Communist party in the Soviet Union and similar states. **apparatchik** (-chik) *n.* **1** a member of an apparat. **2** a bureaucrat or official in any political party or other organization, esp. a zealous one. **3** a Communist agent. [Rus.]

apparatus (apərā´təs, -rah´-) *n.* (*pl.* **apparatuses**, **apparatus**) **1** equipment generally. **2** the instruments employed in scientific or other research. **3** equipment or a machine used for a specific function. **4** the administrative workings of a (political) system or organization. **5** materials for critical study. **6** the organs by which any natural process is carried on. **apparatus criticus** (krit´ikəs) *n.* the annotations, notes, variant readings etc. used in literary criticism and investigation. [L *ad-*, to, *parare*, to prepare]

apparel (əpa´rəl) *n.* **1** (*N Am. or formal*) dress, attire, clothes. **2** ornamental embroidery on ecclesiastical vestments. **3** †the outfit of a ship. ~*v.t.* (*pres.p.* **apparelling**, (*N Am.*) **appareling**, *past, p.p.* **apparelled**, (*N Am.*) **appareled**) **1** †to dress, to clothe. **2** †to equip, to fit out. **3** †to adorn, to embellish, to ornament. [OF *aparail*, n., and *apareiller*, v., to dress (*à*, L *ad-*, to, *pareiller*, to assort, make fit, from *pareil*, like, late L *pariculum*, dim. of *par*, equal)]

apparent (əpar´ənt, -peə´-) *a.* **1** to be seen, visible, in sight. **2** plain, obvious, indubitable. **3** appearing (in a certain way), seeming. **apparent horizon** *n.* SENSIBLE HORIZON (under SENSIBLE). **apparently** *adv.* **1** to external appearances. **2** seemingly, as distinguished from actually. **3** †manifestly, evidently. **apparent magnitude** *n.* the brightness of a star etc. as observed. **apparent time** *n.* SOLAR TIME (under SOLAR). [OF *aparant*, *aparent*, L *appārentem*, p.p. of *appārēre*, to come into sight]

apparition (apərish´ən) *n.* **1** the fact of appearing or becoming visible, esp. suddenly or strangely. **2** a strange appearance. **3** a spectre, phantom, ghost. **4** the reappearance of a star, planet or comet after occultation. **apparitional** *a.* [F, from L *appāritiōnem*, from *appārēre*, see APPEAR]

apparitor (əpar´itə) *n.* an officer in a civil or ecclesiastical court who summons witnesses to appear. [L, see APPEAR]

appeal (əpēl´) *v.i.* **1** to make an earnest request (for) or a formal or earnest request (to). **2** to attract or be of interest (to). **3** to refer to some person or thing for corroboration or support. **4** (*Law*) to refer one's case to a superior court for reconsideration. **5** in cricket, to ask the umpire for a decision on whether a batsman is out; to shout out something for this purpose. **6** to challenge a decision given by an umpire, referee etc. ~*v.t.* (*Law*) to refer (a case, conviction) for review to a superior court. ~*n.* **1** the act of appealing. **2** a request for aid, esp. for money for charitable purposes. **3** reference or recourse to another person or authority, esp. a higher court. **4** power of attracting or interesting. **5** entreaty. **to appeal to the country** COUNTRY. **appealable** *a.* that may be appealed against. **appealing** *a.* **1** attractive, arousing interest. **2** of the nature of an appeal, suppliant. **appealingly** *adv.* **appealingness** *n.* [OF *apeler*, to invoke, L *appellāre* (*ad-*, to, *pellere*, to drive)]

appear (əpiə´) *v.i.* **1** to become or be visible. **2** to be manifest. **3** to seem. **4** to present oneself. **5** to be published; to come before the public. **appearance** *n.* **1** the act of appearing. **2** the act of appearing formally or publicly. **3** the outward or visible form of a person or thing. **4** external show, pretence. **5** (*pl.*) the outward signs or impressions by which a person, situation etc. is assessed. **6** (*Philos.*) a phenomenon; a thing as it is perceived by the senses. **to all appearances** so far as could be ascertained, apparently. **to keep up appearances 1** to keep up an outward show of affluence, respectability etc. **2** to conceal the absence of something desirable. **to make an appearance** to put in an appearance. **to put in an appearance** to attend a function or to visit a person, usu. briefly and often. [OF *aper-*, stem of *aparoir*, to appear (pres. subj. *apere*), L *appārēre* (*ad-*, to, *pārēre*, to come into sight)]

appease (əpēz´) *v.t.* **1** to quiet, to pacify, to calm, to assuage, to allay. **2** to conciliate by acceding to demands. **3** to satisfy (an appetite, thirst etc.). **appeasable** *a.* **appeasement** *n.* **1** the act of appeasing; the state of being appeased. **2** the endeavour to preserve peace by giving way to the demands of an aggressor power. **3** the thing that appeases, satisfies or makes peace. **appeaser** *n.* [OF *apeser*, *apaisier* (*à*, to, *pais*, peace, L *ad pacem*, *pax*)]

appellant (əpel´ənt) *a.* **1** appealing, challenging. **2** relating to appeals. ~*n.* **1** a person who appeals to a higher tribunal or authority. **2** (*formal*) a person who makes an appeal. **appellate** (-ət) *a.* of, relating to or dealing with appeals. **appellation** (apəlā´shən) *n.* (*formal*) **1** a name, designation. **2** naming, nomenclature. **appellative** *a.* **1** (*Gram.*) (of a noun) common as opposed to proper; designating a class. **2** of or relating to the giving of names. ~*n.* **1** an appellation, a name. **2**

a common as opposed to a proper noun. **appellatively** *adv.* [F *appellant*, see APPEAL]

appellation contrôlée (apəlasyõ kõtrō´lā), **appellation d'origine contrôlée** (dorēzhēn) *n.* a guarantee, in the labelling of some French wines and foodstuffs, that the product conforms to statutory regulations in respect of its origin, quality, strength etc. [F]

append (əpend´) *v.t.* 1 to add or subjoin. 2 to hang on to or upon. **appendage** (-dij) *n.* 1 something added or appended. 2 a subordinate or subsidiary organ or process, such as a limb or branch. **appendant** *a.* attached, annexed, joined on. ~*n.* 1 that which is attached or annexed. 2 an appendix, a corollary. [L *appendere* (*ad-*, to, *pendere*, to hang)]

appendectomy (apəndek´təmi), **appendicectomy** (əpendisek´təmi) *n.* (*pl.* **appendectomies, appendicectomies**) the excision of the vermiform appendix.

appendices APPENDIX.

appendicitis (əpendisī´tis) *n.* inflammation of the vermiform appendix.

appendicle (əpen´dikəl) *n.* a small appendage. **appendicular** (apəndik´-) *a.* 1 of or of the nature of an appendicle. 2 of or relating to the vermiform appendix. [L *appendicula*, dim. of *appendix*]

appendix (əpen´diks) *n.* (*pl.* **appendixes, appendices** (-disēz)) 1 a supplement to a book or document containing useful material. 2 a small process arising from or prolonging any organ, esp. the vermiform appendix of the intestine. 3 something appended; an adjunct or concomitant. [L, see APPEND]

apperceive (apəsēv´) *v.t.* 1 to be conscious of perceiving. 2 to assimilate by reference to previous experience. **apperception** (-sep´shən) *n.* 1 perception of one's own mental processes. 2 consciousness of one's self. 3 understanding and assimilation of a new perception in terms of previous experiences. **apperceptive** *a.* [OF *aperceveir*, mod. L *appercipere* (*ad-*, to, *percipere*, see PERCEIVE)]

appertain (apətān´) *v.i.* 1 to relate (to). 2 to belong (as a part to a whole, as a possession, or as a right or privilege). 3 to be suitable or appropriate (to). [OF *apartenir*, late L *appertinēre* (*ad-*, to, *pertinēre*, to pertain)]

appetence (ap´itəns), **appetency** *n.* (*pl.* **appetences, appetencies**) 1 instinctive desire, craving, appetite. 2 natural propensity. 3 affinity. **appetent** *a.* 1 longing, eagerly desirous. 2 of or relating to desire and volition. [F *appétence*, L *appetentia*, from *appetent-*, *appetens*, pres.p. of *appetere* (*ad-*, to, *petere*, to seek)]

appetite (ap´ətīt) *n.* 1 desire for food. 2 the desire to satisfy a natural function. 3 inclination, disposition or desire for something. **appetitive** (əpet´i-) *a.* possessed of or characterized by appetite. **appetizer, appetiser** *n.* a stimulant to appetite, esp. food or drink served before or at the beginning of a meal. **appetizing, appetising** *a.* stimulating appetite or hunger; tasty, delicious. **appetizingly** *adv.* [OF *apetit*, L *appetitus*]

applaud (əplawd´) *v.i.* to express approbation, esp. by clapping the hands. ~*v.t.* to approve, commend or praise in an audible and significant manner. **applause** (əplawz´) *n.* 1 the act of applauding. 2 praise or approval emphatically expressed. [L *applaudere* (*ad-*, together, *plaudere*, to clap)]

apple (ap´əl) *n.* 1 the round, firm, fleshy fruit of the apple tree. 2 any similar fruit. 3 a tree, genus *Malus*, that bears apples. 4 the fruit of the forbidden tree in the Garden of Eden. 5 anything resembling an apple in shape or colour. **Big Apple** BIG. **she's apples** (*Austral., coll.*) everything is fine. **apple brandy** *n.* a spirit made from apples. **apple-cart** *n.* a cart of or for apples. **to upset the apple-cart** to disrupt plans or arrangements. **apple-cheeked** *a.* having chubby rosy cheeks. **Apple Isle** *n.* (*Austral., coll.*) Tasmania. **applejack** *n.* (*N Am.*) apple brandy. **apple of discord** *n.* 1 the golden apple contended for as prize of beauty by Juno, Minerva and Venus. 2 a cause of contention. **apple of one's eye** *n.* 1 anything very dear or precious. 2 the pupil of the eye (formerly supposed to be a solid body). **apple pie** *n.* a pie consisting of apples enclosed in a crust. **apple-pie bed** *n.* a bed prepared as a practical joke, with sheets folded short or tucked in hard so as to prevent one stretching one's full length. **apple-pie order** *n.* perfect order. **apples and pears** *n.pl.* (*sl.*) stairs. **apple sauce** *n.* 1 sauce made from apples. 2 (*N Am., coll.*) insincere praise, nonsense. [OE *æpl*, *æppel* (OHG *aphul*, G *Apfel*)]

Appleton layer (ap´əltən) *n.* an ionized layer in the upper atmosphere, above the Heaviside layer, which reflects radio waves. [Sir Edward *Appleton*, 1892–1965, British physicist]

appliance, applicant etc. APPLY.

appliqué (ap´likā) *n.* ornamental work laid on some other material. **appliquéd** *a.* treated with work of this kind. [F, p.p. of *appliquer*, to apply]

apply (əplī´) *v.t.* (*3rd pers. sing. pres.* **applies,** *pres.p.* **applying,** *past, p.p.* **applied**) 1 to put to (practical) use, to employ. 2 to bring to bear, to bring into operation (a rule, law). 3 to operate (a brake). 4 to put or rub on. ~*v.i.* 1 to offer oneself for a job, position etc. 2 to make a formal request (for). 3 to be relevant (to). 4 to have recourse (to). **to apply oneself** to work, study etc. in a concentrated and diligent fashion. **appliance** (-plī´-) *n.* 1 an apparatus, device or contrivance. 2 anything applied as a means to an end. 3 the act of applying. 4 a fire engine. **applicable** (ap´li-, əplik´-) *a.* 1 capable of being applied. 2 fit, suitable, appropriate; relevant. **applicability** (-bil´-) *n.* **applicant** (ap´li-) *n.* a person who applies, esp. for a job. **application** (aplikā´shən) *n.* 1 the act of applying, esp. an ointment; the thing applied. 2 (a) petition, request. 3 the use to which something is put. 4 relevance. 5 disciplined and sustained work or study. 6 close attention. **application program** *n.* a computer program that performs a specific task for a user. **applications package** *n.* a computer program or programs with appropriate documentation designed to perform a specific task. **applicative** (ap´likə-) *a.* 1 relevant, applicable. 2 practical. **applied** *a.* 1 practical. 2 put to practical use. **applied mathematics** *n.* the application of mathematics to branches of physical research, as mechanics, astronomy etc. **applied science** *n.* science of which the abstract principles are put to practical use in solving problems. [OF *aplier*, L *applicāre* (*ad-*, to, *plicāre*, to fold together, fasten)]

appoggiatura (əpojətoo´rə) *n.* a grace note before a significant note. [It.]

appoint (əpoint´) *v.t.* 1 to nominate, designate (to a position, office). 2 to decide on, to fix (a time, place). 3 to decree, ordain. 4 to assign, to grant (a thing to a person). 5 to declare (a person) to have an interest in a property. ~*v.i.* to issue a decree. **appointed** *a.* furnished, equipped. **appointee** (-tē´) *n.* 1 a person who receives an appointment. 2 (*Law*) a person in whose favour an appointment is executed. **appointment** *n.* 1 an arrangement to meet at a specific time. 2 the act of appointing, esp. to a position or office. 3 the job or position to which someone is appointed. 4 a person who is appointed to something. 5 (*pl.*) equipment, fixtures and fittings. 6 (*Law*) the official declaration of the destination of any specific property. 7 decree, ordinance. [OF *apointer* (*à*, to, *point*, the point)]

☒ **appology** common misspelling of APOLOGY.

apport (apawt´) *n.* 1 in spiritualistic terminology, a material object made to appear without material agency. 2 the production of such an object. [L *apportāre*, to bring]

apportion (əpaw´shən) *v.t.* to share out in just or suitable proportions. **apportionment** *n.* the act of apportioning; the state of being apportioned. [OF *apportionner*]

apposite (ap´əzit) *a.* fit, apt, appropriate. **appositely** *adv.* **appositeness** *n.* **apposition** (-zish´-) *n.* **1** the act of putting together or side by side; juxtaposition, addition. **2** (*Gram.*) the placing together of two words, esp. of two nouns, one being a complement to the other. **appositional** *a.* relating to apposition. **appositive** (əpoz´-) *a.* (*Gram.*) placed in apposition. [L *appositus*, p.p. of *appōnere* (*ad-*, to, *pōnere*, to place, put)]

appraise (əprāz´) *v.t.* **1** to estimate the worth, value or quality of. **2** to set a price on, to value. **3** to make an official assessment of the performance of (an employee). **appraisable** *a.* **appraisal** *n.* **1** an authoritative valuation. **2** an estimate of worth. **3** a formal assessment of an employee's performance. **appraisee** (-zē´) *n.* a person whose performance is appraised. **appraisement** *n.* **1** the act of appraising. **2** estimated value or worth. **appraiser** *n.* **1** a person who appraises. **2** a person authorized to fix the value of property. **appraisive** *a.* [PRAISE]

Usage note The verbs *appraise* and *apprise* should not be confused: *appraise* means to estimate or assess, and *apprise* to inform.

appreciate (əprē´shiāt, -si-) *v.t.* **1** to esteem highly. **2** to feel gratitude for. **3** to understand. **4** to be sensitive to (delicate impressions). **5** to form an estimate of the value, merit, quality or quantity of. **6** to raise in value. *~v.i.* to rise in value. **appreciable** (-shə-) *a.* capable of being appreciated; significant, considerable. **appreciably** *adv.* in a way that can be estimated, to an appreciable extent. **appreciation** (-ā´shən) *n.* **1** gratitude or grateful recognition. **2** an estimate or assessment of the worth or value of something. **3** understanding of or sensitivity to something. **4** a rise in value. **5** a critical study or review, esp. a favourable one. **appreciative** (-shə-) *a.* **1** feeling or expressing appreciation. **2** esteeming favourably. **appreciatively** *adv.* **appreciativeness** *n.* **appreciator** *n.* **appreciatory** (-shə-) *a.* [L *appretiātus*, p.p. of *appretiāre*, to fix a price on (*ad*, to, *pretium*, a price)]

apprehend (aprihend´) *v.t.* **1** to seize, grasp or lay hold of mentally. **2** to seize, to arrest. **3** to fear, to dread, to anticipate with anxiety. *~v.i.* to understand. **apprehensible** *a.* capable of being perceived. **apprehensibility** *n.* **apprehension** (-shən) *n.* **1** fear, dread of what may happen. **2** ability to perceive or grasp mentally. **3** the act of laying hold of, seizing or arresting. **4** conception, idea. **apprehensive** *a.* **1** anticipative of something unpleasant or harmful, fearful, anxious. **2** characterized by or fitted for (mental) apprehension. **3** †perceptive, sensitive, discerning. **apprehensively** *adv.* **apprehensiveness** *n.* [F *appréhender*, L *apprehendere* (*ad-*, to, *prehendere*, to seize)]

apprentice (əpren´tis) *n.* **1** a person who is bound by a formal agreement, indentures, to work for an employer for a period of time in order to learn some trade or craft which the employer agrees to teach. **2** a learner, a tyro, a novice. *~v.t.* to bind as an apprentice. *~v.i.* (*N Am.*) to work as an apprentice. **apprenticeship** *n.* **1** the state or position of an apprentice. **2** the training of an apprentice. **3** the term for which an apprentice is bound. [OF *aprentis*, from *apprendre*, to learn (L *apprehendere*, see APPREHEND)]

apprise (əprīz´) *v.t.* to inform, to make aware, to bring to the knowledge or notice of. [F *appris*, p.p. of *apprendre*, see APPREHEND]

Usage note See note under APPRAISE.

†**apprize** (əprīz´) *v.t.* **1** to put a price on. **2** to estimate the worth of. [OF *aprisier*, to appraise (*à*, to, *prisier*, to prize or praise, perhaps from *à prix*, cp. *mettre à prix*)]

appro (ap´rō) *n.* (*coll.*) short for APPROVAL (under APPROVE). **on appro** on approval.

approach (əprōch´) *v.i.* **1** to come, go or draw near or nearer. **2** (of an aircraft) to prepare to land. **3** in golf, to play an approach shot. *~v.t.* **1** to come near to. **2** to accost or communicate with (a person) with a view to making a proposal, securing something etc. **3** to begin to deal with (a task, problem). **4** to resemble; to be equal to. **5** to approximate to, to be close to. **6** to attempt to bribe or influence. **7** †to bring closer. *~n.* **1** the act of drawing near. **2** avenue, entrance, access. **3** a way of dealing with a person or thing. **4** (*often pl.*) communication with a person for a particular purpose; sexual advances. **5** an approximation. **6** the course taken by an aircraft in preparation for landing. **7** in golf, an approach shot. **approachable** *a.* **1** capable of being approached. **2** easy to deal with. **3** friendly. **approachability** (-bil´-) *n.* **approach road** *n.* a road that gives access to a motorway. **approach shot** *n.* **1** in golf, a stroke that should take the ball on to the green. **2** in tennis, a shot, usu. played deep, that is intended to enable the player to approach the net. [OF *aprochier*, late L *appropiāre* (*ad-*, to, *propius*, comp. of *prope*, near)]

approbate (ap´rəbāt) *v.t.* **1** (*chiefly N Am.*) to express approval of. **2** (*Sc. Law*) to approve formally as valid.

approbation (aprəbā´shən) *n.* **1** the act of approving. **2** approval, commendation, praise. **approbatory** (aprəbā´təri, ap´-) *a.* containing, expressing or implying approval.

appropriate[1] (əprō´priāt) *v.t.* **1** to take as one's own, esp. unlawfully or without permission. **2** to take possession of. **3** to devote to or set apart for a special purpose or use. **appropriable** *a.* **appropriation** (-ā´shən) *n.* **1** the act of appropriating; the state of being appropriated. **2** something which is appropriated, esp. a sum of money or a portion of revenue appropriated to a specific object. **appropriative** *a.* **1** appropriating. **2** involving appropriation. **3** tending to appropriate. **appropriator** *n.* a person who appropriates. [L *appropriātus*, p.p. of *appropriāre* (*ad-*, to, *proprius*, one's own)]

appropriate[2] (əprō´priət) *a.* **1** suitable, fit, becoming. **2** (*formal*) set apart for a particular person or use; particular, peculiar. **3** annexed or attached to. **appropriately** *adv.* **appropriateness** *n.* fitness, suitability.

approve (əproov´) *v.t.* **1** to commend, sanction, confirm. **2** to esteem, accept or pronounce as good. **3** †to demonstrate practically. *~v.i.* to express a favourable opinion or to feel approbation (of). **approvable** *a.* **approval** *n.* **1** favourable opinion. **2** an act or the act of sanctioning. **on approval 1** on trial to ascertain if suitable. **2** (of goods) to be returned if not suitable. **approved** *a.* **1** officially sanctioned. **2** regarded with approval. **3** tried, proved, tested. **approved school** *n.* formerly in Britain, a state boarding school for juvenile offenders (boys under 15, girls under 17). **approvement** *n.* (*Law*) the improvement of commons by enclosure for purposes of husbandry. **approver** *n.* a person who approves, sanctions or commends. **approving** *a.* **approvingly** *adv.* [OF *aprover*, L *approbāre* (*ad-*, to, *probāre*, to test, try)]

Usage note When *approve* refers to feeling or expressing approval, *approve of* is preferred to the use with a direct object (so *They approved the decision* should mean that they confirmed or sanctioned it, rather than that they thought it good).

approx. (əproks´) *abbr.* approximate, approximately.

approximate[1] (əprok´simāt) *v.t.* **1** to cause to approach (esp. in number or quantity), to make almost the same as. 2 to draw or bring near. ~*v.i.* 1 to be more or less identical or equal (to). 2 to draw near, to approach. **approximation** (-āʹshən) *n.* 1 something approximate, esp. a mathematical value that is sufficiently accurate for a purpose though not exact. 2 the act of approximating or approaching. 3 (*Math.*) a coming or getting nearer to a quantity sought, when no process exists for ascertaining it exactly. 4 an imprecise account or version. **approximative** *a.* of an approximate character. **approximatively** *adv.* [L *approximātus*, p.p. of *approximāre* (*ad*-, to, *proximus*, very near, superl. of *prope*, near)]

approximate[2] (aprokʹsimət) *a.* 1 nearly approaching accuracy. 2 rough, inexact. 3 closely resembling. 4 (*Biol.*) set very close together. 5 very close to. **approximately** *adv.* [as APPROXIMATE[1]]

appui (apwēʹ) *n.* 1 the stay (of a horse) upon the bridle-hand of its rider. 2 (*Mil.*) defensive support. [F, from *appuyer*, late L *appodiāre*, to lean upon (*ad*-, upon, *podium*, a support, from Gr. *podion*, base, *pous podos*, foot)]

appulse (əpŭlsʹ) *n.* the very close approach of two celestial bodies without the occurrence of occultation or eclipse. [L *appulsus*, approach, *appellere* (*ad*-, to, *pellere*, to drive)]

appurtenance (əpœʹtinəns) *n.* (*formal*) a thing which belongs to something else; an adjunct, an accessory, an appendage. **appurtenant** *a.* of or relating to, belonging to, pertinent. ~*n.* an appurtenance. [OF *apurtenaunce*, late L *appertinēntia*, from *appertinēre* (APPERTAIN)]

APR *abbr.* annual percentage rate (of credit etc.).

Apr. *abbr.* April.

apraxia (əprakʹsiə) *n.* (partial) loss of the ability to execute voluntary movements. [Gr., inaction (*a*-, priv., *praxis*, action)]

☒ **apreciate** common misspelling of APPRECIATE.

après-ski (apreskēʹ) *n., a.* (of or intended for) the social time following a day's skiing. [F]

apricot (āʹprikot, apʹ-) *n.* 1 a soft-fleshed, yellow to orange stone-fruit allied to the plum. 2 the tree, *Prunus armeniaca*, on which it grows. 3 the colour of the ripe fruit. [formerly *apricock*, Port. *albricoque*, Sp. *albaricoque*, Arab. *al-burqūq* (*al*, the, corr. of Gr. *praikokion*, from L *praecoqua*, apricots, neut. pl. of *praecoquum*, from *praecox*, early ripe), assim. to F *abricot*]

April (āʹprəl) *n.* the fourth month of the year. **April Fool** *n.* a victim of a practical joke on 1 April. **April Fool's day, April Fools' day** *n.* 1 April, from the custom of playing practical jokes on people on that day. **April shower** *n.* a sudden, brief shower of rain (common in the month of April). [OF *avrill*, L *Aprīlis* (prob. from *aperīre*, to open)]

a priori (ā priawʹri, -rī, ah) *adv.* from the cause to the effect; from abstract ideas to consequences; deductively. ~*a.* 1 deductive; derived by reasoning from cause to effect. 2 prior to experience. 3 abstract and unsupported by actual evidence. **apriorism** (āpriʹərizm), **apriority** (āpriorʹəti) *n.* [L, from what is before]

apron (āʹprən) *n.* 1 a garment worn in front of the body to protect the clothes, or as part of a distinctive dress, e.g. of bishops, Freemasons. 2 anything resembling an apron in shape or function, such as a leather covering for the legs in an open carriage. 3 the extension of the stage in some theatres beyond the proscenium. 4 the surfaced area on an airfield. 5 an extensive deposit of sand, gravel etc. 6 an endless conveyor belt formed of metal slats. 7 a protective plate shielding the operator on various machines. **aproned** *a.* wearing an apron. **apronful** *n.* (*pl.* **apronfuls**) as much as can be held in an apron. **apron string** *n.* the string of an apron. **tied to the apron strings** unduly controlled by a wife, mother etc. [OF *naperon*, a large cloth, dim. of *nape*, a tablecloth, L *nappa*, a cloth (cp. formation of ADDER[2])]

apropos (aprəpōʹ) *adv.* 1 opportunely, seasonably. 2 by the way. ~*a.* 1 bearing on the matter in hand; to the point. 2 appropriate. 3 opportune, seasonable. **apropos of** with regard to, concerning. [F *àpropos*, L *ad prōpositum*, to the thing proposed (*prōpōnere*, to propose)]

apse (aps) *n.* 1 a semicircular, or polygonal, and generally dome-roofed, recess in a building, esp. at the east end of a church. 2 an apsis. **apsidal**[1] (apsīʹdəl, apʹsidəl), **absidal** (ab-) *a.* of, relating to or of the shape of an apse. [see APSIS]

apsidal[1] APSE.

apsidal[2] APSIS.

apsis (apʹsis) *n.* (*pl.* **apsides** (-sidēz)) 1 either one of two points at which a planet or satellite is at its greatest or least distance from the body around which it revolves. 2 an apse. **apsidal**[2] (apsīʹdəl, apʹsidəl) *a.* [L *apsis*, *absis*, Gr. *apsis -idos*, fastening, felloe of a wheel, curve (*aptein*, to fasten, join)]

apt (apt) *a.* 1 fit, suitable, proper, relevant. 2 having a tendency (to), likely. 3 quick, ready. **aptly** *adv.* **aptness** *n.* [L *aptus*, p.p. of obs. v. *apere*, to fasten (used as p.p. of *apiscī*, to reach)]

apteral (apʹtərəl) *a.* (*Archit.*) 1 without columns at the sides. 2 (of a church) without side aisles. [Gr. *apteros* (*a*-, not, without, *pteron*, a wing)]

apterous (apʹtərəs) *a.* 1 (of insects) wingless, or having only rudimentary wings. 2 (*Bot.*) without membranous winglike expansions. [Gr. *apteros* (*a*, not, *pteron*, a wing)]

apteryx (apʹtəriks) *n.* the kiwi, a bird from New Zealand, about the size of a goose, with rudimentary wings. [Gr. *a*-, not, *pteron*, a wing]

aptitude (apʹtitūd) *n.* 1 a natural talent or ability. 2 fitness, suitability, adaptation. 3 (*formal*) aptness, a tendency towards, or proneness to something. [F, from med. L *aptitūdo*, n. of quality from *aptus*, APT]

apyretic (apiretʹik) *a.* without fever. [Gr. *apuretos* (*a*-, not, *puretos*, fever)]

apyrexy (apʹireksi) *n.* the intermission or abatement of a fever. [L, from Gr. *apurexia* (*a*-, not, *puressein*, to be feverish)]

aq. *abbr.* water. [L *aqua*]

aqua (akʹwə) *n.* 1 water, liquid, solution. 2 the colour aquamarine. ~*a.* aquamarine. [L]

aqua- (akʹwə), **aqui-** (akʹwi) *comb. form* of or relating to water. [L *aqua*]

aquaculture (akʹwəkŭlchə), **aquiculture** (akʹwi-) *n.* the cultivation of aquatic organisms for human use.

aqua fortis (akwəfawʹtis), **aquafortis** *n.* nitric acid. **aquafortist** *n.* a person who etches or engraves with aqua fortis. [L *fortis*, strong]

☒ **aquaint** common misspelling of ACQUAINT.

aqualeather (akwəledhʹə) *n.* tanned fishskin.

Aqua Libra® (akwə lēʹbrə) *n.* a drink made from mineral water and fruit juices.

aqualung (akʹwəlŭng) *n.* a portable diving apparatus, strapped on the back and feeding air to the diver as required. ~*v.i.* to dive with an aqualung.

aquamarine (akwəmərēnʹ) *n.* 1 a bluish-green variety of beryl, named from its colour. 2 this colour. ~*a.* bluish-green. [L *aquamarina*, seawater]

aquanaut (akʹwənawt) *n.* 1 a skin-diver. 2 a person who lives or explores under water. [L *aqua*, water, Gr. *nautēs*, sailor]

aquaplane (akʹwəplān) *n.* a board on which one is towed, standing, behind a motorboat. ~*v.i.* 1 to ride on an aquaplane. 2 (of a car etc.) to slide on a film of water on a road surface.

aqua regia (akwə rēʹjə) *n.* a mixture of nitric and hydrochloric acids, capable of dissolving gold and platinum. [L, royal water, from its use in dissolving gold, the royal (L *regius*) metal]

aquarelle (akwərel´) *n.* **1** a kind of painting in Chinese ink and very thin transparent watercolours. **2** the design so produced. **aquarellist** *n.* a person who paints in aquarelle. [F, from It. *acquerella*, dim. of *acqua* (L *aqua*), water]

aquarist (ak´wərist) *n.* the keeper of an aquarium.

aquarium (əkweə´riəm) *n.* (*pl.* **aquariums, aquaria** (-riə)) **1** an artificial tank, pond or vessel in which aquatic animals and plants are kept alive. **2** a place in which such tanks are exhibited.

Aquarius (əkweə´riəs) *n.* a zodiacal constellation giving its name to the 11th sign, which the sun enters on 21 Jan. [L, the water-carrier]

aquarobics (akwərō´biks) *n.* (*sing. or pl. in constr.*) exercises performed in water to music. [AQUA, AEROBICS (under AEROBE)]

aquatic (əkwat´ik) *a.* **1** living or growing in or near water. **2** played or performed on or in water. **3** of or relating to water. ~*n.* an aquatic animal or plant. **aquatics** *n.pl.* sports or athletic exercises on or in the water. [L *aquaticus*]

aquatint (ak´wətint) *n.* **1** a method of etching on copper to produce tones similar to those of watercolour. **2** a design so produced. [F *aqua-tinte*, It. *acqua tinta* (L *aqua*, water, *tincta*, dyed, from *tingere*, to dye)]

aquavit (ak´wəvēt, -vit), **akvavit** (ak´və-) *n.* an alcoholic spirit flavoured with caraway seeds. [Scand. *akvavit*, from med. L *aqua vitae*]

aqua vitae (akwə vē´tī) *n.* strong spirits, brandy etc. [L, water of life]

aqueduct (ak´widŭkt) *n.* **1** an artificial channel, esp. an artificial channel raised on pillars or arches for the conveyance of (drinking) water from place to place. **2** a bridge carrying a canal. **3** a small canal, chiefly in the heads of mammals. [L *aquaeductus* (*aquae*, of water, *ductus*, conveyance, from *ducere*, to lead)]

aqueous (ak´wiəs, ā´-) *a.* **1** consisting of, containing, formed in or deposited from water. **2** watery. **aqueous humour** *n.* the watery fluid in the eye between the cornea and the lens. **aqueous rocks** *n.pl.* **1** rocks deposited in water. **2** sedimentary rocks. [L *aqueus*]

aquiculture AQUACULTURE.

☒ **aquiesce** common misspelling of ACQUIESCE.

aquifer (ak´wifə) *n.* a water-bearing layer of rock, gravel etc. **aquiferous** (əkwif´-) *a.* conveying, bearing or yielding water.

aquiform (ak´wifawm, ā´-) *a.* **1** in the form or state of water. **2** liquid.

aquilegia (akwilē´jə) *n.* a usu. blue-flowered plant of a genus, *Aquilegia*, of acrid plants, order Ranunculaceae, commonly known as columbine. [L *aquila*, an eagle]

aquiline (ak´wilīn) *a.* **1** of or relating to an eagle; eagle-like. **2** (esp. of noses) hooked, curved, like an eagle's bill. [L *aquilinus*, eagle-like (*aquila*, an eagle)]

☒ **aquire** common misspelling of ACQUIRE.

☒ **aquit** common misspelling of ACQUIT.

aquosity (əkwos´iti) *n.* wateriness. [med. L *aquōsitas*, from *aquōsus*, watery]

AR *abbr.* **1** Arkansas. **2** Autonomous Republic.

Ar *chem. symbol* argon.

ar- (ə) *pref.* AD-, assim. to *r*, e.g. *arrest*, *arrogate*.

-ar[1] (ə) *suf.* **1** forming adjectives, as in *angular*, *linear*, *lunar*. **2** forming nouns, as in *scholar*, *exemplar*. [F *-aire*, *-ier*, from L *-aris*]

-ar[2] (ə) *suf.* forming nouns, as in *pillar*. [F *-er* or L *-ar*, *-are*, neut. of *-aris*]

-ar[3] (ə) *suf.* forming nouns, meaning the agent, e.g. *bursar*, *mortar*, *vicar*. [OF *-ier* (F *-aire*), L *-ārius*, *-ārium*]

-ar[4] (ə) *suf.* forming nouns, var. of -ER[1], -OR[1] assim. to -AR[3], e.g. *beggar*, *liar*. [-ER[1]]

ARA *abbr.* Associate of the Royal Academy.

Arab (ar´əb) *n.* **1** a member of a Semitic people orig. inhabiting Arabia and now much of the Middle East. **2** a horse of a breed originating from Arabia. ~*a.* of or relating to the Arabs, or to Arabia. **Arabian** (ərā´biən) *a.* of or relating to Arabia or to Arabs. ~*n.* **1** a native or inhabitant of Arabia. **2** (*chiefly N Am.*) an Arab. **Arabian camel** *n.* a camel with one hump, *Camelus dromedarius*, of the N African and Near Eastern deserts; also called *dromedary*. **Arabic** *a.* of or relating to Arabia, the Arabs, or to Arabic. ~*n.* the language of the Arabs. **Arabic numeral** *n.* any of the figures, 1,2,3 etc., as opposed to a Roman numeral. **arabist** *n.* a student of the Arabic language or culture. [F *Arabe*, L *Arab -em* (nom. *Arabs*), Gr. *Araps -abos*]

Arab. *abbr.* **1** Arabia, Arabian. **2** Arabic.

araba (ərah´bə) *n.* an Oriental wheeled carriage. [Arab. and Pers. *arābah*]

arabesque (arəbesk´) *a.* **1** Arabian in design. **2** in the style of arabesque. ~*n.* **1** surface decoration composed of flowing lines fancifully intermingled, usu. representing foliage in a conventional manner, without animal forms. **2** a posture in ballet dancing with one leg raised behind and the arms extended. [F]

Arabian, Arabic etc. ARAB.

arabica (ərab´ikə) *n.* **1** coffee or coffee beans from the tree *Coffea arabica*, widely grown in South America. **2** this tree. [L, fem. of *arabicus*, Arabic]

arabis (ar´əbis) *n.* a plant of the genus *Arabis* of cruciferous plants largely grown on rockwork, also called *rock cress*. [med. L *Arabis*, Arab; prob. from its liking for stony places]

arable (ar´əbəl) *a.* **1** (of land) ploughed or capable of being ploughed, fit for tillage. **2** of or relating to tillage. [L *arābilis* (*arāre*, to plough)]

Araby (ar´əbi) *n.* (*poet.*) Arabia. [OF *arabi*]

araceous AROID.

arachnid (ərak´nid) *n.* any individual of the class Arachnida, which contains the spiders, scorpions, ticks and mites. **arachnidan** *n.*, *a.* **arachnidean** (-nid´i-) *a.* of or belonging to the arachnids. ~*n.* an arachnid. **arachnoid** (-noid) *a.* **1** (*Bot.*) cobweb-like, covered with long filamentous hairs. **2** of, belonging to or resembling the Arachnida. **3** of or relating to the arachnoid membrane. ~*n.* the arachnoid membrane. **arachnoid membrane** *n.* the transparent membrane lying between the pia mater and the dura mater, that is the middle of the three membranes enveloping the brain and spinal cord. **arachnologist** *n.* a person who studies arachnology. **arachnology** (araknol´-) *n.* the scientific study of spiders or of the Arachnida generally. **arachnophobia** (əraknəfō´biə) *n.* abnormal fear of spiders. **arachnophobe** (-nəfōb´) *n.* **arachnophobic** (-nəfō´bik) *a.* [Gr. *arachnē*, a spider]

aragonite (ar´əgənīt) *n.* a grey or white mineral, composed of calcium carbonate, found in sedimentary rocks. [*Aragon*, region of Spain, where it was first discovered]

arak ARRACK.

Araldite® (ar´əldīt) *n.* an epoxy resin used as a strong adhesive. [etym. uncertain]

ARAM *abbr.* Associate of the Royal Academy of Music.

Aramaean (arəmē´ən) *a.* of or relating to ancient Aram, or Syria, or its language. ~*n.* **1** a Syrian. **2** the Syrian language. **Aramaic** (-mā´ik) *a.* **1** applied to the ancient northern branch of the Semitic family of languages, including Syriac and Chaldean. **2** of or belonging to Aram. ~*n.* the Aramaic language, still spoken in parts of Syria and Lebanon, the lingua franca of the Near East from the 6th cent. BC. [L *aramaeus*, Gr. *Aramaios*]

Aran (ar´ən) *a.* knitted in a style that originated in the Aran Islands off the W coast of Ireland, typically with a thick cream-coloured wool.

Aranda (əran´də), **Arunta** (ərŭn´tə) *n.* (*pl.* **Arandas, Aranda, Aruntas, Arunta**) **1** a member of an aboriginal tribe of central Australia. **2** the language spoken by this tribe. ~*a.* of or belonging to this tribe. [Austral. Abor.]

araneidan (arənē´dən) *a.* of or belonging to the Araneida (or Araneae), the order comprising spiders. ~*n.* a spider. **araneiform** (-ifawm) *a.* shaped like a spider. [L *arānea*, a spider]

arapaima (arəpī´mə) *n.* a very large primitive freshwater fish of S America. [Tupi]

arational (ārash´ənəl) *a.* not concerned with reason, non-rational.

araucaria (arawkeə´riə) *n.* a tree of the coniferous genus *Araucaria*, one species of which (*A. imbricata*), the monkey-puzzle, is common in Britain as an ornamental tree. **araucarian** *a.* [*Arauco*, in Chile]

arb (ahb) *n.* (*sl.*) ARBITRAGEUR (under ARBITRAGE).

arbalest (ah´bəlest), **arbalist** (-list), **arblast** (-blahst) *n.* a large, medieval crossbow for firing arrows and other missiles. [OF *arbaleste*, L *arcuballista* (*arcus*, a bow, *ballista*, a military engine for hurling missiles)]

arbiter (ah´bitə) *n.* **1** a judge. **2** a person appointed to arbitrate between contending parties. **3** an umpire. **4** a person who has power to decide according to their absolute pleasure. **arbiter elegantiarum** (eligantiah´rəm), **arbiter elegantiae** (eligan´tiī) *n.* a judge in matters of taste or etiquette. [L *arbiter* (*ar-*, *ad-*, to, *biter*, a comer, from *bītere*, to go, go to see)]

arbitrage (ah´bitrij) *n.* traffic in bills of exchange or stocks so as to take advantage of rates of exchange in different markets. **arbitrageur** (-trahzhœ´) *n.* [F, from *arbitrer*, to arbitrate]

arbitral ARBITRATE.

arbitrament (ahbit´rəmənt) *n.* **1** decision by arbitrators. **2** power or liberty of deciding. **3** the award or decision given by arbitrators. [ME, from OF *arbitrement*, from L *arbitramentum*]

arbitrary (ah´bitrəri) *a.* **1** (apparently) random, irrational. **2** determined by one's own will or caprice, capricious. **3** subject to the will or control of no other, despotic. **arbitrarily** (ah´-, -treə´rə-) *adv.* **arbitrariness** *n.* [L *arbitrarius* or F *arbitraire*, as ARBITRATE]

arbitrate (ah´bitrāt) *v.t.* **1** to hear and judge as an arbitrator. **2** to decide, to settle. ~*v.i.* to act as arbitrator or umpire. **arbitral** *a.* of or relating to arbitration. **arbitration** (-rā´shən) *n.* the hearing or determining of a dispute by means of an arbitrator. **arbitrator** *n.* **1** a person chosen or appointed to hear and settle impartially a dispute between two or more parties, esp. an industrial dispute. **2** an umpire, an arbiter. **arbitratorship** *n.* [L *arbitrari*, to give judgement]

arbitress (ah´bitris) *n.* **1** a female arbiter in a dispute etc. **2** a woman who has absolute power. [OF *arbitresse*, fem. of *arbitre*, L *arbiter*]

arblast ARBALEST.

arbor[1] (ah´bə) *n.* **1** a main shaft or axle on which something, e.g. a cutting or milling tool, rotates in a machine. **2** a rotating mandrel in a lathe on which the piece to be worked on is fitted. [F *arbre*, tree, axis, from L *arbor*, tree]

arbor[2] ARBOUR.

arboraceous (ahbərā´shəs) *a.* **1** resembling a tree. **2** woody, wooded.

Arbor Day (ah´bə) *n.* a spring holiday in the US, Australia and other countries dedicated to tree-planting. [L *arbor*, tree]

arboreal (ahbaw´riəl) *a.* **1** of or relating to trees. **2** connected with or living in trees. **arboreous** (-riəs) *a.* **1** thickly wooded. **2** arborescent.

arborescent (ahbəres´ənt) *a.* **1** having treelike characteristics. **2** branching like a tree, dendritic. **arborescence** *n.* **arborescently** *adv.* [L *arborēscens -tem*, pres.p. of *arborēscere*, to grow into a tree]

arboretum (ahbərē´təm) *n.* (*pl.* **arboretums, arboreta** (-tə)) a botanical garden for the rearing and exhibition of rare trees. [L *arbor*, tree]

arboriculture (ah´bərikŭlchə, ahbaw´-) *n.* the systematic culture of trees and shrubs. **arboricultural** (-kŭl´-) *a.* **arboriculturist** (-kŭl´-) *n.*

arborization (ahbərīzā´shən), **arborisation** *n.* **1** treelike appearance. **2** treelike formation or markings in crystalline substances. **3** a treelike appearance in distended veins caused by inflammation.

arbor vitae (ahbaw vē´tī) *n.* **1** the tree of life. **2** any of several Asian and N American evergreens of the genus *Thuja*. **3** a dendriform appearance in a vertical section of the cerebellum. [L, tree of life]

arbour (ah´bə), (*N Am.*) **arbor** *n.* **1** a bower formed by trees or shrubs planted close together or trained on lattice-work; a shady retreat. **2** †a garden, herb garden or orchard. **arborous** *a.* **1** of or belonging to trees. **2** formed by trees. **arboured** *a.* [ME *erber*, from OF *herbier*, from L *herba*, grass: influenced by L *arbor*, tree]

arbovirus (ah´bəvīrəs) *n.* (*pl.* **arboviruses**) any of a group of viruses transported by mosquitoes, ticks etc. that cause diseases such as yellow fever. [*ar*thropod-*bo*rne VIRUS]

arbutus (ah´būtəs) *n.* (*pl.* **arbutuses**) an evergreen shrub or tree of the genus *Arbutus*, of which *A. unedo*, the strawberry tree, is cultivated as an ornamental tree in Britain. [L]

ARC[1] *abbr.* Agricultural Research Council.

ARC[2] (ahk) *n.* Aids-related complex. [acronym]

arc (ahk) *n.* **1** a portion of the circumference of a circle or other curve. **2** something curved in shape. **3** the luminous arc or bridge across a gap between two electrodes when an electric current is sent through them. **4** that part of a circle which a heavenly body appears to pass through above or below the horizon. ~*v.i.* (*3rd pers. sing. pres.* **arcs**, *pres.p.* **arcing, arcking,** *past, p.p.* **arced, arcked**) to form an (electric) arc. **arc lamp, arc light** *n.* an electric lamp in which such an arc or bridge is the source of illumination. **arc weld** *v.t.* to weld (metal) by means of an electric arc. **arc welding** *n.* [OF *arc*, L *arcum arcus*, a bow]

ARCA *abbr.* Associate of the Royal College of Art.

arcade (ahkād´) *n.* **1** a walk or passage with an arched roof. **2** a covered passage with shops on each side. **3** a series of arches and their columns or piers. **4** an amusement arcade. **arcaded** *a.* furnished with or formed like an arcade. [F, from It. *arcata*, arched, fem. p.p. of *arcare*, to bend, arch (*arco*, a bow, L *arcum arcus*, a bow)]

Arcadian (ahkā´diən) *a.* **1** of or relating to Arcadia, a district of the Peloponnesus, the ideal region of rural happiness. **2** (*poet.*) ideally rustic or pastoral. ~*n.* **1** an inhabitant of Arcadia. **2** (*poet.*) an idealized peasant or country-dweller. **Arcadianism** *n.* an ideal rustic condition, pastoral simplicity. [L *Arcādius*]

Arcady (ah´kədi) *n.* (*poet.*) Arcadia, as the idealized rural paradise.

arcana[1] (ahkah´nə, -kā´-) *n.* either of the two divisions, major or minor, of the Tarot pack.

arcana[2] ARCANUM.

arcane (ahkān´) *a.* secret, esoteric. [see ARCANUM]

arcanum (ahkā´nəm) *n.* (*pl.* **arcana** (-nə)) **1** anything hidden. **2** a mystery, a secret, esp. one of the supposed secrets of the alchemists. [L, neut. of a. *arcānus*, from *arcēre*, to shut up (*arca*, a chest)]

arch[1] (ahch) *n.* **1** a curved structure arranged so that the parts support each other by mutual pressure, used as an opening or a support, e.g. for a bridge. **2** anything resembling this, a vault, a curve. **3** a curved anatomical structure, as of the bony part of the foot. **4** an archway. ~*v.t.* **1** to cover with or form into an arch or arches. **2** to overarch, to span. ~*v.i.* to assume an arched form. **arching** *a.* forming an arch, curved. ~*n.* an arched structure. **archway** *n.* an arched entrance or vaulted passage. [OF *arche*, L *arca*, chest (confused with *arc*, L *arcus*, a bow)]

arch[2] (ahch) *a.* 1 self-consciously teasing, roguish or mischievous. 2 knowing. **archly** *adv.* **archness** *n.* [ARCH-, used as a separate word]

arch- (ahch), **archi-** (-i) *pref.* 1 chief, principal, as in *archbishop, archdeacon, archdiocese.* 2 leading, pre-eminent, esp. in a bad sense, as in *arch-enemy; arch-hypocrite.* [OE *erce-, ærce-, arce-*, L *archi-*, Gr. *archi-* (*archos*, chief, *archein*, to be first, *archē*, beginning)]

Archaean (ahkē´ən), (*N Am.*) **Archean** *a.* of, relating to or belonging to the earliest geological period or the rocks formed in this time. [Gr. *archaios*, ancient]

archaeo- (ah´kiō), **archeo-** *pref.* 1 of or relating to ancient times; primitive. 2 of or relating to the study of remains from archaeological sites. [Gr. *archaios*, ancient, primitive]

archaeoastronomy (ahkiōastron´əmi), **archeoastronomy** *n.* the study of prehistoric sites with a view to establishing the astronomical beliefs and practices of ancient civilizations. **archaeoastronomer** *n.*

archaeobotany (ahkiōbot´əni), **archeobotany** *n.* the study of plant remains that are found at archaeological sites.

archaeology (ahkiol´əji), (*N Am. also*) **archeology** *n.* the science or special study of antiquities, esp. of prehistoric remains. **archaeologic** (-loj´-), **archaeological** *a.* of or relating to archaeology. **archaeologically** *adv.* **archaeologist** *n.* **archaeologize, archaeologise,** (*N Am.*) **archeologize** *v.i.* [late L *archaeologia*, from Gr. *arkhaiologia*, study of ancient things]

archaeomagnetism (ahkiōmag´nətizm), **archeomagnetism** *n.* the dating of prehistoric objects by reference to the direction and intensity of the earth's magnetic field in previous ages.

archaeopteryx (ahkiop´təriks) *n.* a bird of the fossil genus *Archaeopteryx*, containing the oldest known bird. [Gr. *pteron*, a wing, a bird]

Archaeozoic (arkiəzō´ik), (*esp. N Am.*) **Archeozoic** *a.* of or relating to the earliest geological era, the dawn of life on the earth. ~*n.* this period, the earlier division of the Precambrian era.

archaic (ahkā´ik) *a.* 1 old-fashioned, antiquated. 2 (of a word) belonging to an earlier period, no longer in general use. 3 of or belonging to a much earlier period, ancient. 4 primitive. **archaism** (ah´-) *n.* 1 an old-fashioned habit or custom. 2 an archaic word or expression. 3 affectation or imitation of ancient style or idioms. **archaist** (ah´-) *n.* 1 a person who affects old-fashioned habits, an imitator of ancient style. 2 an antiquary. **archaistic** (-is´-) *a.* 1 imitating or affecting old-fashioned habits or ancient style. 2 tending to archaism in language. [Gr. *archaikos*, primitive, ancient (*archaios*, old, *archē*, beginning)]

archaize (ah´kāīz), **archaise** *v.i.* to imitate or affect ancient manners, language or style. ~*v.t.* to make archaic. [Gr. *archaizein*, to be old-fashioned, copy the ancients]

archangel (ahk´ānjəl) *n.* 1 an angel of the highest rank. 2 an angel of the eighth order in the celestial hierarchy. 3 the plant angelica. 4 a kind of fancy pigeon. **archangelic** (-anjel´-) *a.* [OF *archangel*, L *archangelus*, Gr. *archangelos*]

archbishop (ahchbish´əp) *n.* a chief bishop; a metropolitan; the spiritual head of an archiepiscopal province. **archbishopric** *n.* 1 the office of archbishop. 2 the district under the jurisdiction of an archbishop. [L *archiepiscopus*]

archdeacon (ahchdē´kən) *n.* 1 a church dignitary next below a bishop in the care of the diocese. 2 a chief deacon. **archdeaconry** *n.* (*pl.* **archdeaconries**) 1 the portion of a diocese over which an archdeacon exercises jurisdiction. 2 the rank or office of an archdeacon. 3 an archdeacon's residence. **archdeaconship** *n.* [L *archidiāconus*, Gr. *archidiakonos*]

archdiocese (ahchdī´əsis, -sēs) *n.* the see of an archbishop.

archduke (ahch´dūk) *n.* a chief duke, esp. a son of an Emperor of Austria. **archducal** (-dū´-) *a.* of or relating to an archduke. **archduchess** *n.* 1 the wife of an archduke. 2 a daughter of an Emperor of Austria. **archduchy** (-dŭch´i) *n.* (*pl.* **archduchies**) the territory ruled over by an archduke. [OF *archeduc*]

Archean ARCHAEAN.

archegonium (ahkigō´niəm) *n.* (*pl.* **archegonia** (-iə)) the female sex organ in mosses, ferns and some conifers. [Gr. *archegonos*, originator of a race]

arch-enemy (ahchen´əmi) *n.* (*pl.* **arch-enemies**) 1 a principal enemy. 2 Satan, the Devil.

archeoastronomy ARCHAEOASTRONOMY.

archeobotany ARCHAEOBOTANY.

archeology, archeological etc. ARCHAEOLOGY.

archeomagnetism ARCHAEOMAGNETISM.

Archeozoic ARCHAEOZOIC.

archer (ah´chə) *n.* 1 a person who uses the bow and arrow, a bowman. 2 an archer fish. **the Archer** the constellation of Sagittarius. **archeress** (-ris) *n.* a female archer. **archer fish** *n.* a fish, *Toxotes jaculator*, from SE Asia, that has the power of projecting water from its mouth to a considerable distance. **archery** *n.* the act or art of shooting with bow and arrow. [A-F *archer*, OF *archier*, late L *arcārius*, archer (*arcus*, a bow)]

archetype (ah´kitīp) *n.* 1 the primitive or original type, model or pattern on which anything is formed, or assumed to be formed. 2 a typical or perfect example of something. 3 (*Psych.*) an inherited mental image, supposed by Jung to constitute part of the collective unconscious. 4 a recurrent symbol or motif in art or literature. **archetypal** (ah´-, -tī´-), **archetypical** (-tip´-) *a.* 1 of or relating to an archetype. 2 primitive, original. **archetypally, archetypically** *adv.*

arch-fiend (ahchfēnd´) *n.* 1 the chief fiend. 2 Satan, the Devil.

arch-foe (ahchfō´) *n.* (*poet.*) a principal foe.

arch-hypocrite (ahch·hip´əkrit) *n.* a person notorious for extreme hypocrisy.

archi- ARCH-.

archidiaconal (ahkidīak´ənəl) *a.* of, relating to or holding the office of an archdeacon. **archidiaconate** (-nət) *n.* the office or territory of an archdeacon. [L *archidiāconus*, an archdeacon]

archiepiscopal (ahkiəpis´kəpəl) *a.* of or relating to an archbishop or an archbishopric. **archiepiscopate** (-pət) *n.* 1 the office, dignity, or jurisdiction of an archbishop, an archbishopric. 2 an archbishop's tenure of office. [L *archiepiscopus*, Gr. *archiepiskopos*, an archbishop]

archil ORCHIL.

Archilochian (ahkilō´kiən) *a.* 1 of or relating to the Greek satiric poet Archilochus (*c.* 714–676 BC), or to the metre he reputedly introduced. 2 severe, bitter. ~*n.* a verse in the metre reputedly introduced by Archilochus.

archimage (ah´kimāj) *n.* 1 a chief magician. 2 a wizard, an enchanter.

archimandrite (ahkiman´drīt) *n.* the superior of a monastery or convent in the Greek Church, corresponding to an abbot in the Roman Catholic Church. [late L *archimandrīta*, late Gr. *archimandritēs* (*archi-*, chief, *mandra*, an enclosure, a monastery)]

Archimedean (ahkimē´diən) *a.* of, relating to or invented by Archimedes, a Greek mathematician (*c.* 287–212 BC). **Archimedean screw, Archimedes' screw** *n.* an instrument for raising water, formed by a tube wound into the form of a screw inside or around a long cylinder. **Archimedes' principle** *n.* the law that a body in fluid is subject to an upward force, and shows a loss of weight, equal to the weight of water it displaces.

archipelago (ahkipel´əgō) *n.* (*pl.* **archipelagoes, archipelagos**) **1** any area of sea or water studded with islands. **2** these islands collectively. **archipelagic** (-laj´-), **archipelagian** (-lā´ji-) *a.* of or relating to an archipelago. [It. *arcipelago* (*arci-*, Gr. *archi-*, chief, *pelago*, gulf, pool, L *pelagus*, Gr. *pelagos*, sea)]

architect (ah´kitekt) *n.* **1** a person who plans and draws the designs of buildings, and superintends their erection. **2** a naval architect. **3** a contriver or a designer of something. **architective** *a.* of or relating to architecture. **architecture** *n.* **1** the art or profession of designing buildings. **2** a style of building. **3** architectural work, buildings and structures collectively. **4** the structure or design of anything. **5** the design and structural arrangement of the hardware components of a computer or computer system. **architectural** (-tek´-) *a.* **architecturally** *adv.* **1** in an architectural style. **2** with regard to architecture. **architectural salvage** *n.* the removal of architectural features (such as fireplaces, doorframes, mouldings) from buildings about to be demolished, for reuse elsewhere. [L *architectus*, Gr. *architektōn* (ARCHI-, *tektōn*, a builder, allied to *technē*, art)]

architectonic (ahkitekton´ik), **architectonical** *a.* **1** of or relating to architecture or architects. **2** of or relating to the organization of knowledge. **architectonics** *n.* **1** the science of architecture. **2** the systematization of knowledge. **3** construction or systematic design in a literary or other artistic work. [L *architectonicus*, Gr. *architektonikos*; see ARCHITECT]

architrave (ah´kitrāv) *n.* **1** the lowest portion of the entablature of a column, immediately resting on the column itself. **2** the ornamental moulding round a door or window. **architrave cornice** *n.* an entablature comprising architrave and cornice only, without a frieze. [ARCHI-, L *trabem*, nom. *trabs*, a beam]

archive (ah´kīv) *n.* **1** (*usu. pl.*) a place in which (historical) records are kept. **2** (historical) records officially preserved. ~*v.t.* **1** to store (records) in an archive. **2** (*Comput.*) to transfer (data) to a less-used file. **archival** (-kī´-) *a.* **archivist** (-ki-) *n.* **1** a person who has charge of archives. **2** a keeper of records. [F *archive*, *archif*, late L *archīvum*, *archīum*, Gr. *archeion*, public office (*archē*, government)]

archivolt (ah´kivōlt) *n.* **1** the inner contour of an arch. **2** the mouldings and ornaments on this inner contour. [It. *archivolto*, *arcovolta* (*arco*, L *arcus*, arch, *volta*, vault, *volto*, arched)]

archlute (ahch´loot) *n.* a large bass lute with a double neck. [ARCH-, LUTE[1]]

archon (ah´kon) *n.* any one of the nine chief magistrates of ancient Athens after the time of Solon. **archonship** *n.* **1** the office of an archon. **2** the time during which he held office. [Gr. *archōn*, ruler, pres.p. of *archein*, to rule]

arch-priest (ahchprēst´) *n.* **1** a senior priest among the secular clergy of the Orthodox Church. **2** (*Hist.*) a kind of dean or vicar to a bishop who performed several of the bishop's functions when the latter was absent.

-archy (ah´ki) *comb. form* denoting government or rule of a particular type or by a particular group, as in *oligarchy*, *monarchy*.

ARCM *abbr.* Associate of the Royal College of Music.

arcology (ahkol´əji) *n.* (*pl.* **arcologies**) an ideal city where architecture and ecology are harmoniously combined. [*ar*chitecture, ec*ology*]

ARCS *abbr.* Associate of the Royal College of Science.

Arctic (ahk´tik) *a.* of or relating to the north, the North Pole, or the region within the Arctic Circle. ~*n.* **1** the North Pole. **2** Arctic regions. **arctic** *a.* **1** designed for use in very cold conditions. **2** (*coll.*) extremely cold. ~*n.* (*N Am.*) a waterproof overshoe with buckles. **Arctic Circle** *n.* a parallel of the globe, 23° 28´ distant from the North Pole, which is its centre. **arctic fox** *n.* a small species of fox, *Alopex lagopus*, with beautiful fur, found in N America within the Arctic Circle. [OF *artique*, L *articus*, from Gr. *arktikos*, belonging to the Great Bear (*arktos*, bear)]

Usage note Pronunciation as (ah´tik), without the (k) before the (t), is best avoided.

arctophile (ahk´tōfīl) *n.* a person who loves or collects teddy bears. [Gr. *arktos*, bear, -PHILE]

arcuate (ah´kūāt), **arcuated** (-tid) *a.* **1** curved like a bow. **2** arched. **arcuately** *adv.* **arcuation** (-ā´shən) *n.* arched work in building. [L *arcuātus*, p.p. of *arcuāre*, to curve like a bow (*arcus*, bow)]

arcus senilis (ahkəs senē´lis) *n.* a bow- or ring-shaped opaque area around the cornea of the eye, often seen in elderly people. [L, senile bow]

-ard (əd, ahd) *suf.* **1** denoting disposition to do something to excess, e.g. *drunkard*, *sluggard*. **2** forming other nouns, e.g. *poniard*, *Spaniard*. [OF *-ard*, *-art*, G *-hart*, *-hard*]

ardent (ah´dənt) *a.* **1** glowing, fierce, intense, eager, zealous, fervid. **2** burning, on fire. **ardency** *n.* **ardently** *adv.* **ardent spirits** *n.pl.* alcoholic spirits (orig. meaning inflammable, combustible spirits). [OF *ardant*, pres.p. of *ardoir*, to burn, L *ardēre*, to burn]

ardente (ahden´ti) *a.* (*Mus.*) ardent, fiery. [It.]

ardour (ah´də), (*N Am.*) **ardor** *n.* **1** intensity of emotion, fervour, passion. **2** zeal, enthusiasm, eagerness. **3** fierce heat. [OF *ardor*, L *ardorem*]

arduous (ah´dūəs) *a.* **1** laborious, difficult. **2** involving much labour, strenuous, energetic. **3** steep and lofty, hard to climb. **arduously** *adv.* **arduousness** *n.* [L *arduus*, steep, difficult]

are[1] (ah) *n.* a metric unit of area equal to 100 square metres (1076.44 sq. ft.). [F, from L *area*]

are[2] BE.

area (eə´riə) *n.* **1** a particular extent of surface, a region, a tract of country. **2** a section of a larger space or surface or of a building etc., esp. one designated for a particular purpose. **3** the measurable extent of a surface. **4** a geographical or administrative division. **5** a sphere of interest or study. **6** the sunken court, partly enclosed by railings, giving access to the basement of some dwelling-houses; a space left open round a basement to obviate damp. **the area** in football, the penalty area. **area code** *n.* (*N Am.*, *Austral.*) a three-digit code number dialled before the subscriber's number when making international calls. **area steps** *n.pl.* steps leading from the street down to the basement. **areaway** *n.* **1** (*N Am.*) an area giving access to a basement. **2** a passageway between buildings. [L]

areca (ar´ikə, ərē´-) *n.* a tree of a genus of palms, *Areca*, esp. *A. catechu*, which yields the betel-nut. **areca nut** *n.* the betel-nut. [Port., from Tamil *adaikāy* (*adai*, clustering, *kāy*, nut)]

areg ERG[2].

arena (ərē´nə) *n.* **1** an area enclosed by seating in which sports events or entertainments take place, an amphitheatre. **2** (*Hist.*) the floor of an amphitheatre where combats took place, originally strewn with sand to absorb the blood. **3** a field of conflict. **4** a sphere of action. **arenaceous** (arənā´shəs) *a.* **1** sandy. **2** in the form of sand. **3** composed partly or entirely of sand. **arena stage** *n.* a stage completely surrounded by seats. [L *arēna*, *harēna*, sand]

aren't (ahnt) *contr.* **1** (*coll.*) are not. **2** (in questions) am not.

areography (ariog´rəfi) *n.* the description of the

physical features of the planet Mars. [Gr. *areos*, pertaining to *Arēs*, Mars, -GRAPHY]

areola (ərē´ələ) *n.* (*pl.* **areolae** (-lē)) **1** (*Anat.*) **a** a dark circle round the human nipple. **b** a similar circle round a pustule. **2** any minute space enclosed by lines or markings. **3** any one of the interstices in organized tissue. **areolar** *a.* of, relating to or consisting of areolae. **areolar tissue** *n.* loose fibrous connective tissue, the cellular tissue underlying the skin. **areolate** (-lət) *a.* marked or marked off by intersecting lines. **areolation** (ariəlā´shən) *n.* the state of being areolate. **areole** (ar´iōl) *n.* **1** an areola. **2** a slightly depressed spot on a cactus from which a spine or spot grows. [L dim. of *area*]

arête (ərət´) *n.* a sharp ascending ridge of a mountain. [F *arête* (OF *areste*), L *arista*, an ear of corn, a spine]

argali (ah´gəli) *n.* (*pl.* **argalis, argali**) the wild sheep of Asia, *Ovis ammon.* [Mongol.]

argent (ah´jənt) *n.* **1** (*Her.*) the white colour representing silver. **2** †silver. *~a.* **1** (*poet.*) silver. **2** silvery-white. **argentiferous** (-tif´-) *a.* producing silver. [F, from L *argentum*]

Argentine (ah´jəntīn), **Argentinian** (-tin´iən) *a.* of or relating to Argentina. *~n.* a native or inhabitant of Argentina. **the Argentine** Argentina.

argentine (ah´jəntīn) *a.* **1** of or containing silver. **2** silvery. *~n.* **1** any small fish of the family Argentinidae with silvery scales. **2** silver-plated metal, imitation silver. [F *argentin*, L *argentinus*]

argie-bargie ARGY-BARGY.

argil (ah´jil) *n.* white clay, potter's earth. **argillaceous** (-ā´shəs) *a.* **1** of the nature of clay. **2** containing a large amount of clay. **argilliferous** (-lif´-) *a.* producing or yielding clay. [F *argille*, L *argilla*, Gr. *argillos*, white clay (*argēs*, white)]

arginine (ah´jinīn) *n.* one of the essential amino-acids found in plant and animal proteins. [G *Arginin*, etym. uncertain]

Argive (ah´gīv, -jīv) *a.* **1** of or relating to Argos in ancient Greece. **2** (esp. in Homer) Greek. *~n.* **1** a native of Argos. **2** (esp. in Homer) a Greek. [L *Argīvus*, Gr. *Argeios* (*Argos*, city of Argolis, in the Peloponnesus)]

argol (ah´gol) *n.* **1** an impure acid potassium tartrate deposited from wines. **2** crude cream of tartar. [ME *argoile*]

argon (ah´gon) *n.* an inert gas, at. no. 18, chem. symbol Ar, one of the gaseous constituents of the atmosphere, discovered in 1894. [Gr. *argos*, neut. *argon*, not working (*a-*, not, *ergon*, work)]

Argonaut (ah´gənawt) *n.* **1** any of the legendary heroes who accompanied Jason in the ship *Argo* to seek the Golden Fleece. **2** (**argonaut**) a cephalopod mollusc of the genus *Argonauta*, containing the paper nautilus. **argonautic** (-naw´-) *a.* of or relating to the Argonauts or their expedition. [L *argonauta*, Gr. *argonautēs*]

argosy (ah´gəsi) *n.* (*pl.* **argosies**) **1** a large vessel for carrying merchandise. **2** a carrack. **3** a richly-laden ship. [prob. It. *una Ragusea* (*nave*), a Ragusan (ship)]

argot (ah´gō) *n.* **1** the phraseology or jargon of a class or group. **2** thieves' slang. **3** slang generally. **argotic** (-got´-) *a.* slangy. [F]

argue (ah´gū) *v.t.* (*3rd pers. sing. pres.* **argues**, *pres.p.* **arguing**, *past, p.p.* **argued**) **1** to (try to) exhibit or prove by reasoning. **2** to discuss, debate. **3** to convince by logical methods. *~v.i.* **1** to quarrel, to exchange views heatedly. **2** to bring forward reasons (for or against). **to argue the toss** (*coll.*) to continue to dispute about a matter that has already been decided. **arguable** *a.* capable of being argued. **argufy** *v.i.* (*3rd pers. sing. pres.* **argufies**, *pres.p.* **argufying**, *past, p.p.* **argufied**) (*coll.*) to argue. **argufier** *n.* **1** a person who argues. **2** a contentious person. [OF *arguer*, late L *argūtāre* (freq. of *arguere*, to prove, make clear)]

argument (ah´gūmənt) *n.* **1** an exchange of views, esp. an angry or passionate one. **2** (a) debate, discussion. **3** a reason, series of reasons or demonstration put forward. **4** the process of reasoning. **5** an abstract or summary of a book. **6** the subject of a discourse. **7** a mathematical variable whose value determines that of a dependent function. **argumentation** (-mentā´shən) *n.* **1** the act or process of methodical reasoning. **2** a systematic argument. **argumentative** (-men´-) *a.* **1** having a natural tendency to argue, disputatious. **2** controversial. **3** consisting of or relating to argument or reasoning. **argumentatively** *adv.* **argumentativeness** *n.* **argument from design** *n.* (*Theol.*) the argument for the existence of God based on the structure and design of the universe.

Argus (ah´gəs) *n.* **1** a vigilant watcher or guardian. **2** an Asian pheasant, having the plumage marked with eyelike spots. **3** a butterfly of the genus *Polyommatus*, which has eyelike spots on the wings. **Argus-eyed** *a.* very observant, sharp-sighted. [L, from Gr. *Argos*, the mythic guardian of Io, fabled to have a hundred eyes]

argute (ahgūt´) *a.* **1** shrill, sharp. **2** quick, keen, shrewd. **arguteness** *n.* [L *argūtus*, shrill, p.p. of *arguere*, ARGUE]

argy-bargy (ahjibah´ji), **argie-bargie** *n.* (*pl.* **argy-bargies, argie-bargies**) (*coll.*) (a) dispute, argument. *~v.i.* (*3rd pers. sing. pres.* **argy-bargies, argie-bargies**, *pres.p.* **argy-bargying, argie-bargying**, *past, p.p.* **argy-bargied, argie-bargied**) (*coll.*) to have a noisy quarrel or fight. [Sc., Eng. dial. *argy*, to argue]

argyle (ahgīl´) *a.* knitted or woven with a diamond-shaped pattern in two or more colours. *~n.* a sock made of material with this pattern. [Campbell of *Argyle* (Argyll), whose tartan the pattern resembles]

aria (ah´riə) *n.* a song, esp. in an opera or oratorio, for one voice supported by instruments. [It.]

Arian[1] (eə´riən) *a.* of or relating to Arius or his doctrine. *~n.* a follower of Arius of Alexandria (*c.* 250–336) who denied that Christ was consubstantial with the Father. **Arianism** *n.* the system of doctrine held by Arius and his followers. [L *Arīānus* (*Arīus*, *Arius*, Gr. *areios*, *Arios*, prop. name)]

Arian[2] ARIES.

Arian[3] ARYAN.

-arian (eə´riən) *suf.* forming adjectives meaning belonging to, believing in, or nouns meaning a person who belongs to, believes in, or is associated with: e.g. *humanitarian, sabbatarian, sexagenarian, trinitarian.* [L *-ārius*]

arid (ar´id) *a.* **1** dry, parched, without moisture. **2** barren, bare. **3** dry, uninteresting. **aridity** (ərid´-), **aridness** *n.* **1** the quality or state of being dry or parched. **2** dryness, drought. **3** barrenness. **4** absence of interest or appeal. **aridly** *adv.* [L *āridus* (*ārēre*, to dry)]

ariel (eə´riəl) *n.* a Middle Eastern and African gazelle. [Arab. *aryil*, *ayyil*, stag]

Aries (eə´rēz) *n.* **1** the Ram, the first of the zodiacal constellations, which the sun enters in the month of March. **2** a person born under this sign. **Arian**[2] *a.* of or relating to Aries. *~n.* a person born under Aries. [L]

arietta (ariet´ə) *n.* a short lively air, tune or song. [It., dim. of ARIA]

ariette (ariet´) *n.* an arietta. [F, from It. *arietta*]

aright (ərīt´) *adv.* **1** right, rightly, properly, becomingly. **2** correctly, without failure or mistake. [*a-*, on, RIGHT (*rights*, from *rihtes*, gen.)]

aril (ar´il) *n.* (*Bot.*) an accessory seed-covering, more or less incomplete but often brightly coloured and fleshy, formed by a growth near the hilum. **arillate** (əril´āt), **arilled** *a.* having an aril. **arillode** (-ōd) *n.* a false aril, near the micropyle. [mod. L *arillus*, med. L *arilli*, Sp. *arillos*, raisins]

arioso (ahriō´zō) *a.*, *adv.* (*Mus.*) in a songlike style, melodious(ly). ~*n.* (*pl.* **ariosos**) a piece or passage played arioso. [It.]

-arious (eəˊriəs) *suf.* forming adjectives meaning connected with, belonging to, e.g. *gregarious, vicarious.* [L *-ārius*]

arise (ərīzˊ) *v.i.* (*past* **arose** (ərōzˊ), *p.p.* **arisen** (ərizˊən)) **1** to appear, to come into being, notoriety etc. **2** to originate (from), to occur as a result. **3** to come to notice. **4** (*poet.*) to assume an upright position after lying or sitting, to get up. **5** to rise up, to ascend. **6** to rise from the dead. **arisings** *n.pl.* materials which constitute the secondary or waste products of industrial processes. [OE *ārīsan* (*a-*, intens., *rīsan*)]

arista (ərisˊtə) *n.* (*pl.* **aristae** (-tē)) **1** an awn. **2** a bristle or bristle-like process. **3** a bristle on the antennae of various flies. **aristate** (-tāt) *a.* awned, having an arista. [L]

aristo (arˊistō) *n.* (*pl.* **aristos**) short for ARISTOCRAT (under ARISTOCRACY).

aristocracy (aristokˊrəsi) *n.* (*pl.* **aristocracies**) **1** the nobility. **2** a ruling body of nobles. **3** government by the highest class of citizens or by the nobles. **4** a state so governed. **5** the highest or best of any class or group. **aristocrat** (arˊistəkrat) *n.* **1** a noble. **2** a member of an aristocracy. **3** a person who has aristocratic tastes or style. **4** (*rare*) a person who favours aristocratic government. **aristocratic** (-kratˊ-), **aristocratical** *a.* **1** of or relating to an aristocracy or to aristocrats. **2** grand, stylish. **aristocratically** *adv.* [L *aristocratia*, Gr. *aristokratia* (*aristos*, the best, *kratein*, to rule, hence *kratia*, rule)]

Aristophanic (aristəfanˊik) *a.* **1** of or relating to Aristophanes (*c.* 450–380 BC), an Athenian comic poet and dramatist. **2** witty, broadly comic.

Aristotelian (aristətēˊliən), **Aristotelean** *a.* of or relating to Aristotle (384–322 BC), the famous Greek philosopher, or to his philosophy. ~*n.* a follower or student of the philosophy of Aristotle. **Aristotelianism** *n.* **Aristotle's lantern** (arˊistotəlz) *n.* (*Zool.*) a cone-shaped framework of muscles and calcareous plates that supports the teeth of sea urchins (compared by Aristotle to a ship's lantern).

Arita (ərēˊtə) *n.* a type of Japanese porcelain with asymmetrical decoration. [a town in Japan]

arithmetic[1] (ərithˊmətik) *n.* **1** the science of numbers. **2** computation by figures. **3** arithmetical knowledge or skill. **arithmetician** (ərithmətishˊən) *n.* a person who is skilled in arithmetic. [OF *arismetique*, late L *arismetica*, L *arithmētica*, Gr. *arithmētikē techne*, art of counting (*arithmeein*, to count, *arithmos*, number)]

arithmetic[2] (arithmetˊik), **arithmetical** (-əl) *a.* of or relating to arithmetic. **arithmetically** *adv.* **1** in an arithmetical manner. **2** according to the principles of arithmetic. **arithmetic and logic unit** *n.* (*Comput.*) the section of a central processing unit where arithmetic operations are carried out. **arithmetic mean** *n.* the average value of a set of numbers or terms, found by dividing the sum of the terms by the number. **arithmetic progression** *n.* **1** a series of numbers that increase or decrease consecutively by a constant quantity. **2** increase or decrease by a constant quantity. **arithmetic series** *n.* a series showing arithmetic progression.

-arium (eəˊriəm) *suf.* forming nouns meaning place for or connected with, as in *aquarium, herbarium, sacrarium.* [L, neut. of a. in *-ārius* (-ARY[1])]

Ariz. *abbr.* Arizona.

Ark. *abbr.* Arkansas.

ark (ahk) *n.* **1** a ship, a boat, esp. Noah's ark. **2** †a chest, a box. **3** a refuge. **4** (**Ark**) ARK OF THE COVENANT (under ARK). **out of the ark** (*coll.*) extremely old or old-fashioned. **Ark of the Covenant, Ark of the Testimony** *n.* **1** the cupboard containing the scrolls or tables of the Law in a synagogue. **2** (*Bible*) the sacred chest symbolizing the presence of God among the Hebrew people. [OE *arc* (cp. Goth. *arka*, Icel. *örka*, L *arca*)]

arm[1] (ahm) *n.* **1** the upper limb of the human body on either side, from the shoulder to the hand. **2** anything resembling the human arm. **3** a sleeve. **4** the forelimb of any of the lower mammals. **5** a flexible limb or appendage, with armlike functions, in invertebrates. **6** the part of a chair etc. on which a person's arm rests. **7** a branch of a tree; a projecting branch of the sea, a mountain, river etc.; a projecting or armlike part of a machine, instrument etc. **8** a division of a service or organization. **9** power, authority. **10** in sport, the ability to throw or pitch effectively. **11** either of the parts of a yard on each side of the mast. ~*v.t.* **1** †to put one's arms round. **2** †to take by the arm. **an arm and a leg** (*coll.*) a great amount of money. **arm in arm** with the arms interlinked. **as long as your arm** (*coll.*) extremely long. **at arm's length 1** at a distance. **2** at a sufficient distance to avoid undue familiarity. **3** (of negotiations) such that each party preserves its freedom of action. **in arms** (of a baby) needing to be carried, too young to walk. **in someone's arms** being embraced by someone. **on someone's arm** (of a person) walking arm in arm with someone or supported by someone's arm. **under one's arm** held between the arm and the body. **within arm's reach** that can be reached without moving from one's position. **armband** *n.* a band of material encircling the coat-sleeve, usu. black to indicate mourning. **armchair** *n.* a chair, usu. a comfortably upholstered one, with arms to support the elbows. ~*a.* **1** (of a critic, strategist etc.) having no practical involvement with or knowledge of something. **2** participated in from the comfort of one's own home. **armful** *n.* (*pl.* **armfuls**) as much as the arm or arms can hold. **armhole** *n.* the hole in a garment to admit the arm. **armless**[1] *a.* without arms or branches. **armlock** *n.* a wrestling hold in which part of the opponent's body is gripped tight by the arm or arms. **armpit** *n.* the hollow under the arm at the shoulder. **armrest** *n.* a support for the arm. **arms-length** *a.* **1** (of a relationship) lacking closeness or intimacy. **2** (of a business transaction) that disregards any connection between the parties concerned and is conducted purely on market terms. **arm-twisting** *n.* the use of force or psychological pressure to persuade someone to do something. **arm-wrestling** *n.* a contest in which two people sitting opposite each other with their elbows on a table and their arms vertical, clasp hands and attempt to force their opponent's arm down flat on to the table. [OE *earm* (cp. Dut. *arm*, L *armus*, shoulder, Gr. *harmos*, joint, shoulder)]

arm[2] (ahm) *n.* **1** (*usu. in pl.*) a weapon. **2** any branch of the military service. **3** (*pl.*) the military profession. **4** (*pl.*) heraldic bearings. **5** (*pl.*) armour. **6** (*pl.*) war. ~*v.t.* **1** (*also reflex.*) to furnish or equip with offensive or defensive weapons. **2** to furnish with a protective covering. **3** to equip with tools or other appliances. **4** to make ready (a bomb etc.) for explosion. ~*v.i.* **1** to take up weapons, put on armour etc. **2** to prepare for war. **to arms! 1** take your weapons. **2** prepare for battle. **to bear arms** BEAR[2]. **to lay down one's arms 1** to cease fighting. **2** to surrender. **to take (up) arms 1** to prepare to fight. **2** to begin to fight. **under arms 1** bearing arms. **2** ready for service. **3** in battle array. **up in arms 1** (*coll.*) angry, indignant, protesting. **2** in revolt. **armed** *a.* **1** equipped with weapons or armour. **2** prepared for war. **3** having claws, teeth, horns etc., or with natural armour. **4** having thorns, prickles etc. **5** equipped with anything required for action or defence. **6** (of an explosive device) ready to be detonated. **armed to the teeth** TOOTH. **armed forces** *n.pl.* the military personnel of a country; its army, navy, airforce etc. **armed struggle** *n.* the use of military action by e.g. a liberation or nationalist movement to achieve political power. **arming** *n.* **1** the act of equipping with weapons or means of defence. **2** equipment for any purpose. **3** furnishing with heraldic devices. **armless**[2] *a.* destitute of weapons of offence or defence. **arms race** *n.* rivalry between nations, esp. (formerly) between the US and USSR, in building up stocks of (nuclear) weapons. [F *armes*, L *arma*, weapons]

armada (ahmah´də) *n.* **1** an armed fleet, esp. the fleet sent by Philip II of Spain against England in 1588. **2** any large (armed) force. [Sp., fem. of *armado*, armed, p.p. of *armar* (L *armāre*)]

armadillo (ahmədil´ō) *n.* (*pl.* **armadillos**) any of several small burrowing edentate animals of the family Dasypodidae, native to S America, encased in bony armour, and capable of rolling themselves into a ball. [Sp., dim. of *armado* (see ARMADA)]

Armageddon (ahməged´ən) *n.* **1** the final battle between good and evil at the end of the world. **2** the place where this battle will be fought. **3** a great and destructive battle or conflict. [Gr. from Heb. *har megiddōn*, mountain district of Megiddo, the site of various OT battles, used as a name in Rev. xvi.16]

Armagnac (ah´mənyak) *n.* a dry brandy from SW France. [region of France]

Armalite® (ah´məlīt) *n.* a lightweight automatic high-velocity rifle.

armament (ah´məmənt) *n.* **1** the arms and munitions of war, esp. the weapons with which a warship, aircraft etc. is equipped. **2** the act of arming a fleet or army for war. **3** †an armed force. [L *armamentum*]

armamentarium (ahməmenteə´riəm) *n.* (*pl.* **armamentariums, armamentaria** (-iə)) the equipment, medicines etc. collectively, that are available to a doctor or other medical practitioner. [L, arsenal]

armature (ah´məchə) *n.* **1** the revolving part, wound with coils, of an electric motor or dynamo. **2** the moving part of an electromagnetic device. **3** a piece of soft iron placed in contact with the poles of a magnet to preserve and increase its power. **4** the protective outer covering of an animal or plant. **5** the supportive framework for a model in clay etc. **6** †weapons, armour. [L *armatura*]

Armenian (ahmē´niən) *a.* of or relating to Armenia. *~n.* **1** a native or inhabitant of Armenia. **2** the language spoken by the Armenians. **3** a member of the Armenian Church. [L, from Gr. *Armenia*, former kingdom, now region of W Asia]

armes parlantes (ahm pahlăt´) *n.pl.* (*Her.*) coats of arms which show devices that directly illustrate the name of the bearer, e.g. that represent the name Churchill by a church and a hill. [F]

armet (ah´mit) *n.* a kind of helmet consisting of a rounded iron cap, a spreading protection for the back of the neck, and visor, beaver and gorget in front, which superseded the basinet in the 15th cent. [F *armet*, OF *armette*, dim. of *arme*]

armiger (ah´mijə) *n.* **1** an esquire. **2** a person entitled to heraldic bearings. **armigerous** (-mij´-) *a.* entitled to heraldic bearings. [L (*arma*, arms, *gerere*, to bear)]

armillary (ah´miləri, -mil´-) *a.* **1** of or relating to bracelets. **2** consisting of parts resembling bracelets. **armillary sphere** *n.* (*Hist.*) a skeleton celestial globe or sphere consisting of metallic circles mechanically fixed to represent the celestial equator, the ecliptic, the colures etc. [L *armilla*, bracelet]

Arminian (ahmin´iən) *a.* of or relating to Arminius, i.e. James Harmensen, the Dutch theologian (1560–1609) who maintained the doctrine of free will against Calvin. *~n.* a follower of Arminius. **Arminianism** *n.*

armipotent (ahmip´ətənt) *a.* (*poet.*) powerful or mighty in arms (an epithet of Mars). [L *armipotens* (*arma*, arms, *potens*, powerful)]

armistice (ah´mistis) *n.* a cessation of fighting for a stipulated time during war; a truce. **Armistice Day** *n.* 11 Nov., the day on which an armistice was signed in 1918. [F *armistice* (L *arma*, arms, *-stitium*, from *sistere*, to stop)]

armless[1] ARM[1].

armless[2] ARM[2].

armlet (ahm´lit) *n.* **1** a small ornamental band worn on the arm. **2** a badge on a band around the arm. **3** a small arm of the sea, a lake etc.

armoire (ahmwah´) *n.* a chest, a cupboard. [F, from L *armārium* (see AUMBRY)]

armor ARMOUR.

Armoric (ahmor´ik) *a.* of or relating to Brittany, the ancient Armorica. *~n.* the language of Armorica. **Armorican** *a.* Armoric. *~n.* a Breton.

armory[1] (ah´məri) *n.* (*pl.* **armories**) the science of heraldry. **armorial** (-maw´-) *a.* of or relating to heraldic arms. *~n.* a book containing coats of arms. **armorist** *n.* a person who is learned in heraldry or skilled in blazoning arms. [OF *armoierie*, from *armoier*, a blazoner, *armoier*, to blazon]

armory[2] ARMOURY (under ARMOUR).

armour (ah´mə), (*N Am.*) **armor** *n.* **1** a defensive covering worn by a person in combat, esp. by a medieval warrior. **2** a defensive covering, usu. of metal plates, protecting a vehicle, warship etc. **3** tanks and other armoured vehicles collectively. **4** a protective covering enclosing an animal or plant. **5** heraldic bearings. **6** the watertight dress of a diver. *~v.t.* to equip, cover or protect with armour. **armour-bearer** *n.* a person who carried the armour and weapons of a warrior; a squire. **armoured** *a.* **1** (*Mil.*) protected by armour. **2** (*Mil.*) consisting of units using armour or armoured vehicles. **3** (of glass) strengthened. **armoured car** *n.* **1** (*Mil.*) a vehicle, similar to a small tank, with light armour and armament, used esp. for reconnaissance. **2** any car or other vehicle strengthened with armour plate. **armoured concrete** *n.* FERRO-CONCRETE. **armoured cruiser** *n.* a cruiser armed like (usu. not so heavily as) a battleship. **armourer** *n.* **1** a person who makes or repairs arms or armour. **2** an officer in charge of the arms of a regiment, ship etc. **armour plate** *n.* **1** tough, heavy steel, often surface-hardened, used as a defensive covering for tanks, warships etc. **2** a plate made of this material. **armour-plated** *a.* covered or protected with armour plate. **armour plating** *n.* (a covering made of) armour plate. **armoury,** (*N Am.*) **armory** *n.* (*pl.* **armouries,** (*N Am.*) **armories**) **1** a place for keeping arms, an arsenal. **2** a large stock or an array of weapons, defensive materials etc. **3** a stock of resources such as arguments, objections etc. on which one can draw. **4** (*N Am.*) a place where arms are manufactured. **5** (*N Am.*) a place where people are trained in the use of arms and military drill, a drill hall. **6** (*pl.*, *Can.*) a drill hall used as a headquarters by a reserve unit of the armed forces. [OF *armure*, *armeüre*, L *armātūra* (see ARMATURE)]

army (ah´mi) *n.* (*pl.* **armies**) **1** a body of people organized for land warfare. **2** a large subdivision of the land forces of a nation. **3** a multitude, a very large number. **4** any large organized body, esp. one with a military structure (e.g. the *Salvation Army*). **the army** the military profession. **army ant** *n.* any of various ants which travel in vast numbers destroying animals and plants. **Army List** *n.* an official list of the serving and reserve officers of the British army. **army worm** *n.* any of the larvae of various flies and moths, esp. in America and Africa, that move about in large swarms destroying crops. [F *armée*, fem. p.p. of *armer*, to arm (L *armāre*)]

arnica (ah´nikə) *n.* **1** a tincture prepared from *Arnica* *montana*, mountain tobacco, and used as an application for bruises, sprains etc. **2** any composite plant of the genus *Arnica*. [etym. unknown]

aroid (eə´roid), **araceous** (ərā´shəs) *a.* belonging to the family Araceae, which includes the *Arum* genus of plants. [ARUM]

†**aroint** (əroint´), **aroynt** *int.* avaunt! begone! [etym. uncertain]

aroma (ərō´mə) *n.* **1** the fragrance in a plant, spice, fruit, wine etc. **2** an agreeable odour or smell. **3** a subtle pervasive quality. **aromatherapy** *n.* the use of (massage with) essential plant oils to promote physical and mental well-being and in healing. **aromatherapeutic** *a.* **aromatherapist** *n.* [late L, from Gr. *arōma*, a spice]

aromatic (ərəmat´ik) *a.* **1** of or relating to an aroma. **2** fragrant, spicy. **3** (*Chem.*) belonging or of or relating to a class of organic compounds containing a benzene ring in the molecular structure. ~*n.* **1** a fragrant drug, a spice. **2** (*Chem.*) a benzene-type additive to motor fuel. **aromatically** *adv.* **aromaticity** (ərōmətis´-) *n.* **aromatize** (ərō´-), **aromatise** *v.t.* **1** to render aromatic or fragrant; to perfume, to scent. **2** (*Chem.*) to convert (a compound) to an aromatic structure. **aromatization** (-zā´shən) *n.* **1** the act of rendering aromatic. **2** the state of being so aromatized. [F *aromatique*, L *arōmaticus*, Gr. *arōmatikos*]

arose ARISE.

around (ərownd´) *prep.* **1** surrounding, round about. **2** on all sides of; enveloping. **3** along the circuit of. **4** at various points within or surrounding (*dotted around the arena*). **5** from place to place in. **6** passing or having passed on a curved course (*around the corner*). **7** (*esp. NAm.*) approximately at or in. ~*adv.* **1** on all sides, all round; in a circle. **2** here and there, at various points; at random. **3** (*coll.*) in existence; in circulation; available (*been around for years*). **4** (*coll.*) in the vicinity, at hand (*It's lucky you were around*). **5** approximately. **6** (*coll.*) in many different places or situations acquiring experience. **to have been around 1** (*coll.*) to have acquired a wide experience. **2** (*coll.*) to be worldly-wise and shrewd.

arouse (ərowz´) *v.t.* **1** to raise, stir up, awaken. **2** to excite, stimulate. **3** to stimulate sexually. **arousable** *a.* **arousal** *n.* **arouser** *n.*

ARP *abbr.* air raid precautions.

arpeggio (ahpej´iō) *n.* (*pl.* **arpeggios**) **1** a chord played on a keyed instrument by striking the notes in rapid succession instead of simultaneously. **2** the notes of a chord played or sung in ascending or descending progression, esp. as an exercise. [It. *arpeggiare*, to play the harp (*arpa*, a harp)]

arquebus HARQUEBUS.

arr. *abbr.* **1** arrives. **2** arranged.

arrack (ar´ək), **arak** *n.* a distilled spirit from the East, esp. one distilled from coconut or rice. [Arab. *'araq*, juice, essence, sweat (*'arqua*, he sweated)]

arraign (ərān´) *v.t.* **1** to cite before a tribunal to answer a criminal charge. **2** to accuse, to charge with wrongdoing. **3** to find fault with. **arraigner** *n.* **arraignment** *n.* **1** the act of arraigning; the fact of being arraigned. **2** accusation, charge. [OF *araisnier*, late L *arratiōnāre* (*ad-*, to, *ratio -ōnem*, reason)]

arrange (ərānj´) *v.t.* **1** to adjust, to put in proper order. **2** to plan or settle circumstances in readiness for. **3** to work out or agree the order or circumstances of. **4** to adapt (a musical composition) for other voices or instruments. **5** to adapt (a play etc.) for broadcasting. ~*v.i.* **1** to make plans or preparations (for, to). **2** to come to an agreement (with). **arrangeable** *a.* **arrangement** *n.* **1** the act of arranging, the state of being arranged. **2** the manner in which things are arranged. **3** settlement, disposition, preparation. **4** a grouping or combination of things in a particular way. **5** (*pl.*) dispositions in advance, preparations. **6** the adaptation of a musical composition for instruments or voices for which it was not written; a piece of music so adapted. **arranger** *n.* [OF *arangier* (*à*, to, *rangier*, to range, from *rang*, rank or file; cp. OHG *hring*)]

arrant (ar´ənt) *a.* **1** notorious, downright, unmitigated. **2** complete, thorough. **arrantly** *adv.* shamelessly, infamously. [var. of ERRANT (as in 'an outlawe or a theef erraunt', i.e. wandering or roving thief)]

arras (ar´əs) *n.* **1** a rich tapestry. **2** a wall-hanging made of this, esp. one concealing an alcove. [*Arras*, the town in N France, where the tapestries were formerly made]

array (ərā´) *n.* **1** an impressive display or collection. **2** an orderly arrangement or disposition, esp. of troops for battle. **3** (*poet.*) dress, attire. **4** an arrangement of numbers or mathematical symbols in rows and columns. **5** (*Comput.*) a set of storage locations etc., referenced by a single identifier. **6** (*Law*) a panel of jurors. **7** an arrangement of aerials to give specific directional characteristics. ~*v.t.* **1** to deck, to adorn, to dress up. **2** to set in order; to marshal (troops) for battle. **3** (*Law*) to draw up (a panel of jurors). **arrayal** *n.* [A-F *arayer*, OF *araier* (Prov. *aredar*, early Rom. and It. *arredare*), from *a-*, *ad-*, to, LG *rēde*, ready (cp. OE *rǣde*)]

arrears (əriəz´) *n.pl.* that which remains unpaid or undone. **in arrear/ arrears** behindhand, esp. in payment; unpaid; undone, uncompleted. **arrearage** (-rij) *n.* **1** that which is in arrears, outstanding or kept back. **2** arrears, items overdue. [from obs. *arrear*, from OF *arere* (cp. F *arrière*), backward (L *ad-*, towards, *retro*, behind)]

arrest (ərest´) *v.t.* **1** to apprehend, esp. to apprehend and take into legal custody. **2** to stop, check. **3** to seize and fix (the sight, mind etc.). **4** to seize (a ship) by legal authority. **5** to stay (legal proceedings etc.). ~*n.* **1** seizure, detention, esp. by legal authority. **2** a stoppage, stay, check. **under arrest** in legal custody. **arrestable** *a.* **1** (of an offence) making the offender liable to be arrested without a warrant. **2** liable to arrest. **arrested development** *n.* physical or psychological development arrested at some stage of its progress. **arrester** *n.* **1** a person who or something which arrests. **2** a contrivance for slowing or stopping something, esp. a wire or arrangement of wires on the deck of an aircraft carrier. **3** (*Sc. Law*) (*usu.* **arrestor**) the person who arrests a debt or property in another's hands. **4** a lightning conductor. **arrester hook** *n.* a device that enables an aircraft landing on an aircraft carrier to check speed by catching on an arrester cable. **arresting** *a.* striking, catching the attention. **arrestingly** *adv.* **arrestment** *n.* **1** (*Law*) seizure of property by legal authority. **2** (*Sc. Law*) the process by which a creditor detains the effects of a debtor, which are in the hands of third parties, till the money owing is paid. **arrest of judgement** *n.* staying of proceedings after a verdict on the grounds of possible error. **arrestor** ARRESTER (under ARREST). [OF *arester*, late L *adrestāre* (*ad-*, to, at, *restāre*, to stay, stop, from *re-*, back, *stāre*, stand)]

arrhythmia (əridh´miə, ā-) *n.* an irregularity or alteration in the rhythm of the heartbeat. **arrhythmic** *a.* [Gr. *a-*, priv., *rhuthmos*, RHYTHM]

arrière-ban (arieəbã´) *n.* **1** in French history, a summons to the king's vassals to do military service. **2** an army mobilized by this means. [F]

arrière-pensée (arieəpã´sā) *n.* **1** a mental reservation. **2** an unrevealed intention. [F]

arris (ar´is) *n.* (*pl.* **arris, arrises**) the line in which two straight or curved surfaces forming an exterior angle meet each other. [OF *areste*, ARÊTE]

arrive (ərīv´) *v.i.* **1** to come to a place, position, during a journey or movement; to reach a destination. **2** (of an object) to be brought. **3** (*coll.*) (of a baby) to be born. **4**

(of an event, time) to occur. 5 (*coll.*) to attain fame, success or recognition. **to arrive at** 1 to reach, to get to. 2 to agree upon (a decision); to attain to (a conclusion). **arrival** *n.* 1 the act of coming to a place, a journey's end or destination. 2 the coming to a position, state of mind etc. 3 a person who or thing which has arrived. 4 (*coll.*) a newborn child. [OF *ariver*, late L *arrībāre, arrīpāre* (*ad rīpam*, to shore)]

arrivederci (ərēvədœ´chi) *int.* goodbye, to our next meeting. [It.]

arriviste (arēvēst´) *n.* 1 a social climber, a parvenu. 2 a self-seeker, esp. in politics. [F]

arroba (arō´bə) *n.* 1 a unit of weight used in some Spanish-speaking countries equivalent to 25 lbs (11.35 kg). 2 a unit of weight used in some Portuguese-speaking countries equivalent to 33 lbs (15 kg). [Sp. and Port. from Arab. *ar-rub*, the quarter]

arrogance (ar´əgəns), **arrogancy** (-si) *n.* 1 the act or quality of being arrogant. 2 undue assumption. [F *arrogance*, L *arrogantia*]

arrogant (ar´əgənt) *a.* 1 insolent, assuming, overbearing, haughty. 2 claiming or assuming too much. **arrogantly** *adv.* [F *arrogant*, L *arrogantem*, pres.p. of *arrogāre* (see ARROGATE)]

arrogate (ar´əgāt) *v.t.* to make unduly exalted claims or baseless pretensions to (a thing) for oneself or for someone else. **arrogation** (-ā´shən) *n.* 1 the act of claiming or assuming unwarrantably. 2 undue pretension. [L *arrogātus*, p.p. of *arrogāre* (*ad-*, to, *rogāre*, to ask)]

Usage note See note under ABROGATE.

arrondissement (arōdēs´mā) *n.* 1 a territorial division of a French department. 2 an administrative district of some large French cities, esp. Paris. [F]

arrow (ar´ō) *n.* 1 a slender, straight, sharp-pointed missile shot from a bow. 2 anything resembling an arrow in shape or function, esp. a sign indicating direction. 3 (*pl., coll.*) darts. ~*v.t.* to indicate or mark with an arrow or arrows. ~*v.i.* to move swiftly like an arrow. **arrow-grass** *n.* 1 any plant of the genus *Triglochin*. 2 a kind of pampas grass. **arrowhead** *n.* 1 the pointed head of an arrow. 2 anything shaped like an arrowhead, esp. a decorative mark. 3 a water plant of the genus *Sagittaria*, the leaves of which resemble arrowheads. **arrow-headed** *a.* shaped like the head of an arrow; sagittate, cuneiform. **arrowroot** *n.* 1 a nutritious starch extracted from the tubers of several species of *Maranta*. 2 the food prepared from this substance. 3 a plant of the genus *Maranta*, which includes *M. arundinacea*, the tubers of which were used to absorb poison from wounds, esp. those made by poisoned arrows. **arrowwood** *n.* any of various trees or shrubs, esp. certain species of viburnum, whose long, straight stems were used by American Indians to make arrows. **arrow worm** *n.* a chaetognath. [OE *arewe, earh* (Goth. *arhwazna*; allied to L *arcus*, a bow)]

arroyo (ərō´yō) *n.* (*pl.* **arroyos**) (*N Am.*) a dried-up watercourse, a rocky ravine. [Sp.]

arse (ahs), (*esp. N Am.*) **ass** (as) *n.* 1 (*taboo*) the buttocks, the rump, the hind parts. 2 (*taboo*) the anus. 3 (*sl.*) the fag-end. **to arse about/ around** (*taboo sl.*) to act in a stupid or irritating manner. **arsehole,** (*esp. N Am.*) **asshole** *n.* 1 (*taboo*) the anus. 2 (*sl.*) a stupid or worthless person. **arselicker** *n.* (*sl.*) a sycophant, toady. **arselicking** *n., a.* [OE *ærs, ears* (Icel. and MHG *ars*; cp. Gr. *orrhos*)]

arsenal (ah´sənəl) *n.* 1 a place for the storage, or manufacture and storage, of naval and military weapons and ammunition. 2 (*fig.*) a stock or supply of things, e.g. arguments, that can be compared with weapons. [It. *arsenale, arzenà, darsena*, Arab. *dār aççinā'ah* (*dār*, house, *al*, the, *çinā'ah*, art, trade)]

arsenic[1] (ahs´nik) *n.* a brittle, semi-metallic steel-grey element, at. no. 33, chem. symbol As. [OF *arsenic*, L *arsenicum*, Gr. *arsenikon* (by assim. to *arsenikos -on*, male, masculine), Arab. *az-zernikh* (*al*, the, *zernikh*, orpiment, Pers. *zerni*, orpiment, *zar*, gold)]

arsenic[2] (ahsen´ik) *a.* of or containing arsenic, esp. applied to compounds in which arsenic combines as a pentavalent element. **arsenical** *a.* 1 of or relating to arsenic. 2 having arsenic in the composition. ~*n.* a drug or insecticide containing arsenic. **arsenious** (-sē´-) *a.* of or containing arsenic, esp. applied to compounds in which arsenic combines as a trivalent element. **arsine** (ah´sēn) *n.* arsenic trihydride, a colourless poisonous gas.

arsis (ah´sis) *n.* (*pl.* **arses** (-sēz)) the stressed syllable in metre, esp. in Greek or Latin verse. [L from Gr. *arsis*, a raising, a lifting (*airein*, to lift)]

arson (ah´sən) *n.* the wilful setting on fire of another's house or other property, or of one's own with intent to defraud the insurers. **arsonist** *n.* [OF *arson*, late L *arsio -ōnem* (*ardēre*, to burn, p.p. *arsus*)]

arsy-versy (ah´sivœsi) *adv.* (*sl.*) 1 backwards; in reverse order. 2 upside down. [ARSE, L *versus*, turned]

art[1] (aht) *n.* 1 creative activity concerned with the production of aesthetic objects or of beauty in general. 2 any of the branches of this activity, e.g. music, painting, writing. 3 the products of this collectively. 4 creative activity specifically of a visual or representational kind; visual works of art. 5 human skill or workmanship as opposed to nature. 6 skill in the production of aesthetic objects; excellent workmanship. 7 a method, technique. 8 a facility, knack. 9 (*pl.*) the academic subjects concerned with creative or critical skills rather than scientific or technical ones. 10 (*pl.*) the faculty concerned with such subjects. 11 craft, cunning. 12 (*pl.*) schemes, wiles. ~*a.* 1 of or relating to the visual arts or visual works of art. 2 intended to be decorative or artistic. 3 produced by conscious artistry in accordance with artistic criteria, not commercial, popular or traditional in origin. **Art Deco** (dek´ō) *n.* a style of decorative art of the 1920s and 1930s characterized by bold geometrical forms. **art form** *n.* 1 a medium of artistic expression. 2 an established form in music or literature. **artful** *a.* 1 crafty, cunning. 2 characterized by art or skill. 3 †artificial, unreal. **artfully** *adv.* **artfulness** *n.* **art house** *n.* a cinema that specializes in showing films characterized by artistic quality or specialist interest rather than popular appeal. **art-house** *a.* **artless** *a.* 1 guileless, simple, unaffected. 2 without art. 3 unskilful, clumsy. 4 uncultured, natural. **artlessly** *adv.* **artlessness** *n.* **Art Nouveau** (noovō´) *n.* a style of decorative art of the late 19th and early 20th cents. characterized by sinuous curving forms. **art of self-defence** *n.* boxing or fencing. **art of war** *n.* strategy and tactics. **art paper** *n.* paper coated with a composition of china clay, making it suitable for fine printing. **arts and crafts** *n.pl.* decorative design and handicraft. **art therapy** *n.* art, esp. visual art, used as a means of assisting psychological recovery, personal development etc. **art union** *n.* (*Austral., New Zeal.*) a lottery. **artwork** *n.* the illustrative material in a magazine, book etc. **arty,** (*esp. N Am.*) **artsy** *a.* (*comp.* **artier, artsier,** *superl.* **artiest, artsiest**) (*coll.*) self-consciously or pretentiously affecting the artistic. **arty-crafty** *a.* more showily artistic than functional. **arty-farty, artsy-fartsy** *a.* (*coll.*) pretentiously artistic. [OF *art*, L *ars artem* (stem *ar-*, to fit)]

†**art**[2] BE.

art. *abbr.* article.

artefact (ah´tifakt), **artifact** *n.* 1 a product of human skill or workmanship. 2 a simple object of archaeological importance or interest. 3 (*Biol.*) a feature not naturally present introduced during the preparation or examination of something. **artefactual** *a.* [L *ars artis*, art, *factus*, made]

artel (ah´tel) *n.* a cooperative organization of peasants, craftsmen etc. in the former Soviet Union or pre-revolutionary Russia. [Rus.]

artemisia (artimiz´iə) *n.* any herbaceous, perennial plant of the genus *Artemisia*, that includes wormwood, mugwort and sagebrush. [L, from Gr. *artemisia* (*Artemis*, Diana)]

artery (ah´təri) *n.* (*pl.* **arteries**) **1** any of the membranous pulsating vessels conveying blood from the heart to all parts of the body. **2** a main channel of communication or transport. **arterial** (-tiə´-) *a.* **1** of, relating to or contained in an artery or arteries. **2** of or relating to the oxygenated blood that circulates in the arteries. **3** constituting an important channel for communications or transport. **arterialize, arterialise** *v.t.* **1** to convert (venous blood) into arterial blood by exposing to the action of oxygen in the lungs. **2** to provide with arteries. **arterialization** (-zā´shən) *n.* the process of converting venous into arterial blood. **arterial road** *n.* a main road for swift, long-distance traffic between the chief industrial centres. **arteriole** (ahtiə´riōl) *n.* a small branch of an artery. **arteriosclerosis** (ahtiəriōsklərō´sis) *n.* thickening and loss of elasticity in the walls of the arteries. **arteriosclerotic** (-rot´-) *a.* **arteritis** (ahtərī´tis) *n.* inflammation occurring in the arteries. [L *artēria*, Gr. *artēria* (prob. from *aeirein*, to raise)]

artesian well (ahtē´ziən, -zhən) *n.* a well in which water is obtained by boring through an upper retentive stratum to a subjacent water-bearing stratum, the water being forced to the surface by natural pressure. [F *Artésien*, from *Artois*, an old province of France]

Artex® (ah´teks) *n.* a textured paint covering for ceilings and walls. ~*v.t.* to give a textured surface to.

arthr- ARTHRO-.

arthralgia (ahthral´jə) *n.* pain in a joint. **arthralgic** *a.*

arthritic (ahthrit´ik) *a.* of or suffering from arthritis. ~*n.* a person with arthritis. **arthritis** (-thrī´-) *n.* (painful) inflammation of one or more joints causing stiffness. [L *arthrīticus*, Gr. *arthrītikos*, from *arthron*, a joint (orig. through OF *artetique*, afterwards corrected)]

arthro- (ah´thrō), **arthr-** *comb. form* **1** of or relating to joints. **2** characterized by joints. [Gr. *arthron*, a joint]

arthromere (ah´thrəmiə) *n.* a body segment of an arthropod. [Gr. *meros*, part]

arthroplasty (ah´thrəplasti) *n.* surgical repair of a joint. [Gr. *plastos*, moulded]

arthropod (ah´thrəpod) *n.* a member of the Arthropoda, a phylum of invertebrate animals with segmented bodies and jointed limbs, including the insects, arachnids and crustaceans. **arthropodal, arthropodous** *a.* of or belonging to the Arthropoda. [Gr. *pous podos*, a foot]

Arthurian (ahthuə´riən) *a.* of or relating to King Arthur, the legendary early medieval king of Britain, or his knights.

☒ **Artic** common misspelling of ARCTIC.

artic (ah´tik) *n.* short for ARTICULATED LORRY (under ARTICULATE[1]).

artichoke (ah´tichōk) *n.* **1** a composite plant, *Cynara scolymus*, somewhat like a large thistle: the receptacle and fleshy bases of the scales are eaten as a vegetable. **2** JERUSALEM ARTICHOKE. [It. *articiocco*, *articioffo* (OSp. *alcarchofa*); Arab. *al-kharshūf*]

article (ah´tikəl) *n.* **1** an item, a piece, a distinct element. **2** a commodity, a thing, an object. **3** an item of trade, use or property. **4** a prose composition, complete in itself, in a newspaper, magazine, encyclopedia etc. **5** a point of faith or duty. **6** a distinct statement, clause or provision in an agreement, statute, indictment, code or other document. **7** each of the adjectives, *a*, *an*, *the*, or their equivalents in other languages, when these are considered to form a separate part of speech. **8** (*pl.*) a formal agreement. **9** (*pl.*) terms, conditions. ~*v.t.* **1** to bind (an apprentice), indenture. **2** †to indict. **articled** *a.* (esp. of a lawyer's clerk) bound under article of apprenticeship. **articles of association** *n.pl.* the statutes of a limited liability company. **Articles of War** *n.pl.* (*Hist.*) a code of discipline for the British Army and the Royal Navy. [F *article*, L *articulus*, dim. of *artus*, joint]

articular (ahtik´ūlə) *a.* of or relating to the joints. [L *articulāris* (see ARTICLE)]

articulate[1] (ahtik´ūlāt) *v.t.* **1** to utter (words) distinctly. **2** to express (an idea, thought) clearly and coherently. **3** to connect by means of a joint. **4** to join together in proper order. **5** to joint. ~*v.i.* **1** to speak distinctly, to utter intelligible sounds. **2** to form a joint (with). **articulated** *a.* **articulated lorry** *n.* a long lorry with separate tractor and trailer sections connected so as to allow the tractor to turn at an angle to the remainder. **articulation** (-lā´shən) *n.* **1** the act or process of speaking. **2** articulate sound, utterance, speech. **3** the process or method of jointing. **4** the state of being jointed; a jointed structure. **5** a joint. **6** (*Bot.*) the point at which a deciduous member separates from the plant. **articulator** *n.* **1** a person who pronounces words. **2** a person who articulates skeletons. **articulatory** *a.* of or relating to articulation. [as ARTICLE]

articulate[2] (ahtik´ūlət) *a.* **1** able to express oneself clearly and coherently; clearly and coherently expressed. **2** formed by the distinct and intelligent movements of the organs of speech. **3** (*Biol.*) jointed; composed of segments. **articulately** *adv.* **articulateness** *n.*

artifact ARTEFACT.

artifice (ah´tifis) *n.* **1** a clever expedient, a contrivance. **2** cunning, trickery. **3** a cunning trick. **4** skill, dexterity. **artificer** (-tif´-) *n.* **1** a maker, a contriver. **2** a craftsman. **3** a mechanic employed to make and repair military stores. [F *artifice*, L *artificium* (*ars artis*, art, *-ficium*, suf. from *facere*, to make)]

artificial (ahtifish´əl) *a.* **1** made or produced by human agency, not natural. **2** not real, factitious, fake. **3** affected in manner, insincere. **4** (*Biol.*) relating to superficial characteristics rather than to natural relationships. **artificial horizon** *n.* **1** an instrument that indicates an aircraft's position with respect to the horizontal. **2** a small trough containing mercury, the surface of which affords a reflected image of a heavenly body, used in taking altitudes etc. in places where there is no visible horizon. **artificial insemination** *n.* artificial injection of semen into a female. **artificial intelligence** *n.* **1** the ability of a computer, robot etc. to perform as an intelligent being. **2** the area of study dealing with the development of machines capable of imitating intelligent human-like mental processes. **artificiality** (-al´-) *n.* **artificialize, artificialise** *v.t.* to render artificial. **artificial kidney** *n.* a machine that performs the functions of a human kidney outside the body. **artificial language** *n.* an invented language, esp. one intended as an international means of communication or for use with computers. **artificially** *adv.* **artificialness** *n.* **artificial respiration** *n.* **1** any of various methods of manually or mechanically resuscitating a person who has stopped breathing. **2** any method of maintaining breathing by means of a machine. **artificial silk** *n.* synthetically produced filaments that resemble natural silk in appearance. **artificial system** *n.* (*Biol.*) a system of classification not based on natural affinity. [as ARTIFICE]

artillery (ahtil´əri) *n.* (*pl.* **artilleries**) **1** large-calibre guns, cannons, mortars etc., with their equipment for use in land warfare. **2** the branch of the military service in charge of these weapons. **3** the science and practice of gunnery. **4** devices for casting heavy missiles, e.g. ballistas, catapults. **artillerist** *n.* an artilleryman. **artilleryman** *n.* (*pl.* **artillerymen**) **1** an artillery soldier. **2** a person practically acquainted with the principles of gunnery. **artillery plant** *n.* a tropical American plant of the genus *Pilea*, that discharges its pollen in explosive puffs. [OF *artillerie*, *artiller*, to fortify, equip, late L *artillātor*, a maker of machines (*articula*, *ars*, art)]

artiodactyl (ahtiōdak´til) *a.* **1** having an even number of toes. **2** of or belonging to the order Artiodactyla which includes camels, pigs and ruminants. *~n.* an ungulate with an even number of toes. [Gr. *artios*, of even number, *daktulos*, finger, toe]

artisan (ah´tizan, -zan´) *n.* a skilled manual worker; a handicraftsman, a mechanic. [F, prob. from It. *artigiano* (L *artītus*, p.p. of *artīre*, to instruct in arts)]

artist (ah´tist) *n.* **1** a person who practises any of the fine arts, esp. that of painting. **2** any artistic performer, an artiste. **3** a person who works at anything with the devotion and skill associated with an artist. **4** (*sl.*) a person who frequently practises, or is proficient in, a particular, esp. dubious, activity (*piss artist*). **artistic** (-tis´-) *a.* **1** of or relating to art or artists. **2** made or done with particular skill or taste; aesthetically pleasing. **3** having a natural talent for one or other of the arts, esp. painting. **artistically** *adv.* [F *artiste*, It. *artista*, late L *artista* (*ars artis* art)]

artiste (ahtēst´) *n.* **1** a public performer, an actor, dancer, musician, acrobat etc. **2** a highly proficient cook, hairdresser etc. [F]

artsy ARTY (under ART[1]).

artsy-fartsy ARTY-FARTY (under ART[1]).

arty. *abbr.* artillery.

arugula (əroo´gūlə) *n.* (*N Am.*) rocket, a Mediterranean plant used in salads. [It. dial., ult. from L *eruca*, colewort]

arum (eə´rəm) *n.* **1** a plant of the European genus *Arum*, usu. with a white spathe and arrow-shaped leaves, e.g. the cuckoo pint. **2** any of several other plants of the family Araceae. **arum lily** *n.* an African plant of the genus *Zantedeschia*, with a large ornamental white spathe and yellow spadix (also called *calla lily*). [L, from Gr. *aron*]

arundinaceous (ərŭndinā´shəs) *a.* **1** resembling a reed. **2** reedy. [L *arundo -inis*, a reed, -ACEOUS]

Arunta ARANDA.

arvo (ah´vo) *n.* (*pl.* **arvos**) (*Austral., coll.*) afternoon.

-ary[1] (əri) *suf.* **1** forming adjectives meaning of or relating to, connected with, belonging to, engaged in, as in *elementary*, *necessary*, *voluntary*. **2** forming nouns meaning a thing connected with or used in or a place for, as in *antiquary*, *statuary*, *aviary*, *granary*. [L *-ārius -ārium*]

-ary[2] (əri) *suf.* equivalent to -AR[1] and sometimes to -ARY[1] e.g. *exemplary*, *military*, *contrary*. [L *-āris*]

Aryan (eə´riən), **Arian** *n.* **1** a member of any of the peoples speaking a language of the Indo-European family, esp. the Indo-Iranian branch. **2** the parent language of the family, Indo-European. **3** in Nazi terminology, a Caucasian, non-Jewish person, esp. of the Nordic type. *~a.* **1** of or belonging to any of the Aryan peoples. **2** of or relating to the Aryan language. **3** in Nazi terminology, Caucasian, non-Jewish. **Aryanize, Aryanise** *v.t.* to imbue with Aryan characteristics. [Sansk. *ārya*, noble, a worshipper of the gods of the Brahmins; the earlier *Arian* (from L *ariānus*) of Aria, eastern Persia (Gr. *Areia*, *Aria*, prob. from OPers. *Ariya*, a national name)]

aryl (ar´il) *n.* any monovalent aromatic hydrocarbon radical, e.g. phenyl. **arylation** (-ā´shən) *n.* the introduction of an aryl radical into a compound. [*ar*omatic, -YL]

AS *abbr.* **1** Advanced Supplementary (level). **2** Anglo-Saxon. **3** antisubmarine.

As *chem. symbol* arsenic.

as[1] (az) *adv.* in or to the same degree (followed by *conj.* governing pronoun, n. phr. or relative clause) (*as happy as we/us, as pretty as a picture, not as clever as she is*). *~conj.* **1** while; at the time that. **2** since, because. **3** expressing manner (*viewed as a mistake*). **4** (preceded by *so*) expressing result (*so small as to be invisible*). **5** expressing concession (*good as it is*). **6** in the role, position or state of (*speaking as one who knows the situation*). **7** for instance (*herbs, as thyme, parsley etc.*). *~pron.* **1** that, who, which (*I go to the same doctor as he does*). **2** a fact that (*it's not easy, as you know*). **as and when** to the degree and at the time that. **as for/ regards/ to** regarding, concerning. **as from/ of** from (the specified time or date). **as if/ though** as it would be if. **as it is** in the present state, actually. **as it were** in a certain way, to some extent, so to speak. **as long as** LONG[1]. **as much** MUCH. **as per** according to. **as per usual** USUAL. **as soon as** SOON. **as such** SUCH. **as was** (*coll.*) in a previous state. **as well** WELL[1]. [OE *eal swā*, all so, quite so (ME *alswa*, *also*, *als*, *as*)]

Usage note After the second *as* in the comparisons *as...as, so...as, the same...as*, the objective pronoun (*him, us* etc.) is the everyday choice. The subjective (*he, we* etc.), though required by strict grammatical rule, is now considered rather pedantic.

---

as[2] (as) *n.* (*pl.* **asses**) a Roman copper coin, orig. of 12 oz (340 g) but frequently reduced. [L]

as- (əs) *pref.* AD-, assim. to *s*, as *assimilate*, *assume*.

ASA *abbr.* **1** Advertising Standards Authority. **2** Amateur Swimming Association. **3** American Standards Association.

asafoetida (asəfet´idə, -fē´-), (*esp. N Am.*) **asafetida** *n.* a gum resin, with a strong unpleasant smell of garlic, obtained from some plants of the genus *Ferula*, formerly used in medicine and currently as a herbal remedy and in cookery. [med. L *asa* (Pers. *aza*, mastic), *foetida*, stinking]

asana (ah´sənə) *n.* any of the positions taught in yoga. [Sansk.]

a.s.a.p. *abbr.* as soon as possible.

☒ **asassin** common misspelling of ASSASSIN.

asbestos (asbes´təs, az-) *n.* a fibrous form of certain minerals that is practically incombustible and resistant to chemicals, formerly widely used as a heat-resistant or insulating material. *~a.* **1** made of asbestos. **2** like asbestos in nature. **asbestine** (-tīn) *a.* made of or like asbestos. **asbestosis** (-tō´sis) *n.* a lung disease caused by breathing in asbestos particles. [Gr., inextinguishable (*a-*, not, *sbestos*, from *sbenunai*, to quench)]

ascarid (as´kərid), **ascaris** (-ris) *n.* (*pl.* **ascarids, ascarides** (-dēz)) any of the genus *Ascaris* of intestinal nematode worms. [Gr. *askaris*]

ascend (əsend´) *v.i.* **1** to go or come from a lower to a higher place, position or degree, to rise, to be raised. **2** to slope upwards. **3** to proceed from a lower to a higher plane of thought, quality, degree, rank. **4** to go back in order of time. **5** (*Mus.*) to rise in pitch. **6** (of a letter) to have a part projecting upward. *~v.t.* **1** to climb or go up, to go to a higher position upon; to go to the top or summit of. **2** to follow (a river) upstream or towards its source. **3** to mount. **to ascend the throne** to become king or queen. **ascendant, ascendent** *a.* **1** moving upwards, rising. **2** predominating, ruling. **3** (*Astrol.*) just above the eastern horizon. **4** (*Astron.*) moving towards the zenith. *~n.* **1** (*Astrol.*) the point of the ecliptic which is rising in the eastern horizon at a particular moment. **2** the sign of the zodiac that contains this point. **3** superiority, supremacy. **in the ascendant 1** dominant, predominant, supreme. **2** rising. **ascendancy** *n.* **1**

controlling influence. 2 governing power. **ascender** *n.* 1 a part of a lower-case letter, e.g. *b* or *d*, that rises above the body of the letter. b a letter having this. 2 a person or thing that ascends. **ascendible, ascendable** *a.* **ascending** *a.* 1 rising; moving upwards. 2 (*Bot.*) curving upwards. **ascending axis** *n.* the stem of a plant. [L *ascendere* (*ad-*, to, *scandere*, to climb)]

ascension (əsen´shən) *n.* 1 the act of ascending. 2 (**Ascension**) the ascent of Christ to heaven. 3 (**Ascension**) Ascension Day; Ascensiontide. 4 the rising of a celestial body above the horizon. **ascensional** *a.* relating to ascension. **Ascension Day** *n.* the day on which the Ascension of Jesus Christ is commemorated – the Thursday but one before Whit Sunday, Holy Thursday. **Ascensiontide** *n.* the ten days between Ascension Day and Whit Sunday. [see ASCEND]

ascent (əsent´) *n.* 1 the act or process of ascending, upward motion. 2 a slope. 3 a way by which one may ascend. 4 advancement, rise. 5 a movement back in time or ancestry.

ascertain (asətān´) *v.t.* 1 to discover, learn or verify by investigation, examination or experiment. 2 to find out. 3 †to make sure of. **ascertainable** *a.* **ascertainment** *n.* [OF *acertainer*, *acertener* (*à*, to, CERTAIN)]

ascesis (əsē´sis) *n.* (*pl.* **asceses** (-sēz)) the practice of self-discipline. [Gr. *askēsis*, training]

ascetic (əset´ik) *a.* 1 severely abstinent, austere, practising rigorous self-discipline, esp. for spiritual or religious ends. 2 of or relating to the ascetics or their mode of life. ~*n.* 1 any person given to rigorous self-denial and mortification. 2 any of the early Christian hermits who practised rigorous self-denial and mortification. **ascetical** *a.* concerned with the attainment of spiritual perfection by means of self-discipline. **ascetically** *adv.* **asceticism** *n.* the mode of life of an ascetic. [Gr. *askētikos*, given to exercises, *askētēs*, an athlete, a monk (*askeein*, to work, exercise)]

asci ASCUS.

ascidian (əsid´iən) *n.* a tunicate of the order Ascidiacea, the adults of which are sedentary, e.g. the sea squirt. [as ASCIDIUM]

ascidium (əsid´iəm) *n.* (*pl.* **ascidia** (-iə)) a pitcher- or flask-shaped plant part, such as the leaf of the pitcher plant. [L, from Gr. *askidion*, a small leather bottle (*askos*, a wine skin)]

ASCII (as´ki) *n.* a standard system for representing alphanumeric symbols as binary numbers, used in data processing. [acronym for *A*merican *S*tandard *C*ode for *I*nformation *I*nterchange]

ascites (əsī´tēz) *n.* dropsy causing swelling of the abdomen. **ascitic** (-sit´-), **ascitical** *a.* suffering from abdominal dropsy. [Gr. *askites*]

Asclepiad (əsklē´piad) *n.* a line of verse consisting of a spondee, two (or three) choriambs and an iambus. **Asclepiadean** (-dē´ən), †**Asclepiadic** (-ad´-) *a.* of or relating to the metre called Asclepiad. [*Asclepiades*, a Greek poet of the 3rd cent. BC, who invented it]

asclepias (əsklē´piəs), **asclepiad** (-iad) *n.* a plant of the genus *Asclepias*, or order Asclepiadaceae, containing the milkweeds etc., principally from N America. [Gr. *asklēpias -ados*, *Asklēpios*, Aesculapius]

asco- (as´kō) *comb. form* indicating an ascus or bladder. [from Gr. *askos*, bladder]

ascomycete (askōmī´sēt) *n.* a fungus of the Ascomycetes, a large class of fungi, including penicillium and yeasts, having spores formed in asci. **ascomycetous** *a.* [ASCO-, Gr. *mukētes*, pl. of *mukēs*, fungus]

ascorbic acid (əskaw´bik) *n.* vitamin C, occurring in vegetables, fruits etc.

ascot (as´kot) *n.* a cravat with wide square ends. [*Ascot*, racecourse in England where it was probably first worn]

ascribe (əskrīb´) *v.t.* 1 to attribute, to impute, to assign (to). 2 to consider as belonging (to). **ascribable** *a.* [L *ascrībere* (*ad-*, to, *scrībere*, to write)]

ascription (əskrip´shən) *n.* 1 the act of ascribing; a thing which is ascribed. 2 a statement ascribing glory or praise to God at the end of a sermon. [L *ascrīptio* (*ascrīptus*, p.p. of *ascrībere*)]

ascus (as´kəs) *n.* (*pl.* **asci** (-kī)) a cell in which spores are formed in an ascomycete. [Gr. *askos*, wineskin, bladder, bag]

asdic (az´dik) *n.* an early form of apparatus for detecting the presence and position of submarines. [acronym for *A*llied *S*ubmarine *D*etection *I*nvestigation *C*ommittee]

-ase (āz) *suf.* forming nouns denoting enzymes, such as *amylase*.

ASEAN (ā´sian) *abbr.* Association of South East Asian Nations.

aseismic (āsīz´mik) *a.* 1 free of, or virtually free of, earthquakes. 2 (of buildings) proof or protected against earthquake shocks. [A-[3], SEISMIC]

aseity (āsē´iti) *n.* (*Philos.*) the fact of being self-derived, having no other source. [medieval L *aseitas* (L *ā*, from, *sē* (abl.), oneself)]

☒ **asend** common misspelling of ASCEND.

asepsis (āsep´sis) *n.* 1 the condition of being aseptic. 2 the process of making aseptic. **aseptic** *a.* 1 not liable to or free from contamination by harmful micro-organisms. 2 preventing such contamination. ~*n.* an aseptic substance. **asepticism** (-sizm) *n.* treatment by aseptic or antiseptic principles. **asepticize, asepticise** *v.t.* to treat by these methods, to render aseptic. [Gr. *a-*, not, SEPSIS]

asexual (asek´sūəl, -shəl) *a.* 1 without sex, sexual organs or sexual functions. 2 (*Biol.*) (of reproduction) without union of gametes. 3 without sexual content or interest. **asexuality** (-sūal´-, -shūal´-) *n.* **asexually** *adv.* [A-[3], SEXUAL]

ASH (ash) *abbr.* Action on Smoking and Health.

ash[1] (ash) *n.* 1 the residuum left after the burning of anything combustible. 2 powdery mineral matter ejected from volcanoes. 3 (*pl.*) the remains of anything burnt, esp. the remains of a cremated dead body preserved in an urn or coffin. 4 (*pl.*, *poet.*) a buried corpse, a dead body. **the Ashes** a cricketing trophy competed for in test match series between England and Australia consisting of a pottery urn containing a cremated cricket bail. **to be/ lie in ashes** to be utterly destroyed. **ash bin** *n.* a receptacle for ashes and other household refuse. **ash blond** *n.* 1 a very pale blond colour. 2 a person with hair of this colour. ~*a.* of or having hair of this colour. **ash blonde** *n.*, *a.* (a woman) having ash blond hair. **ashcan** *n.* (*N Am.*) a dustbin. **ash-coloured** *a.* of a colour between brown and grey. **ash heap** *n.* a collection of ashes and other refuse. **ash-pan** *n.* a pan beneath a furnace or grate for the reception of ashes. **ashtray** *n.* a small container for tobacco ash, cigarette butts etc. **Ash Wednesday** *n.* the first day of Lent, so called from the Roman Catholic practice of marking the foreheads of the people with ashes on that day. **ashy** *a.* 1 of or composed of ashes. 2 covered with ashes. 3 whitish-grey. 4 pale. **ashy-pale** *a.* very pale, ashen. [OE *æsce*, *asce*, *axe* (cp. Icel. *aska*, Goth. *azgō*)]

ash[2] (ash) *n.* 1 (*also* **ash-tree**) a forest tree, *Fraxinus excelsior*, with grey bark, pinnate leaves and tough, close-grained wood. 2 the wood of the ash-tree. 3 a runic letter in Old English (ᚨ), named from the word of which it was the first letter. 4 the ligature æ, as in Old English (the Roman equivalent of the runic letter). ~*a.* made from ash. **ash-key** *n.* the winged seed-vessel of the ash. **ashplant** *n.* an ash-tree sapling used as a walking stick. [OE *æsc* (cp. Icel. *askr*, OHG *asc*, cp. G *Esche*)]

ashamed (əshāmd´) *a.* 1 feeling shame, either abashed by consciousness of one's own error or guilt or on account of some other person or thing. 2 unwilling or hesitant. **ashamedly** (-mid-) *adv.* [p.p. of *ashame*, obs. v. (*a-*, intens., SHAME), OE *asceamod*]

ashen[1] (ash´ən) *a.* 1 ash-coloured, between brown and grey. 2 pale. 3 of or relating to ashes.

ashen[2] (ash´ən) *a.* 1 of or relating to the ash-tree. 2 †made of ash.

ashet (ash´it) *n.* (*Sc., North., New Zeal.*) a large flat plate or dish. [F *assiette*]

Ashkenazi (ashkənah´zi) *n.* (*pl.* **Ashkenazim** (-zim)) 1 an E European or German Jew. 2 a Jew of E European or German descent (cp. *Sephardi*). [Heb. *Ashkenaz* (Gen. x.3)]

ashlar (ash´lə), **ashler** *n.* 1 a square-hewn stone used in a building. 2 masonry built of these. 3 thin masonry built as a facing to rubble or brick work. **ashlared** *a.* covered with ashlar. **ashlaring** *n.* 1 upright boards that form a wall in garrets, by cutting off the angle between roof and floor. 2 ashlar masonry. [OF *aiseler*, L *axilla*, dim. of *axis*, axis, board, plank]

ashore (əshaw´) *adv.* 1 to the shore. 2 on the shore. 3 on land.

ashram (ash´rəm) *n.* 1 (in India) a hermitage for a holy man or place of retreat for a religious community. 2 any place of religious or communal life modelled on an Indian ashram.

Asian (ā´shən, -zhən) *a.* of, relating to or belonging to Asia or its people. ~*n.* 1 a native or inhabitant of Asia. 2 a person of Asian descent, esp. (in Britain) from the Indian subcontinent. **Asian flu** *n.* a severe type of influenza caused by a virus isolated during an epidemic in Asia in 1957. [L *Asiānus*, Gr. *Asiānos*, from *Asia*]

Asiatic (āshiat´ik, -zhi-) *a.* Asian. ~*n.* (*offensive*) an Asian. **Asiatic cholera** *n.* CHOLERA. [L *Asiāticus*, Gr. *Asiātikos*]

Usage note Because of a supposed association with racist ideology, the use of *Asiatic* to refer to people has come to be considered highly offensive, and is best avoided.

aside (əsīd´) *adv.* 1 at, to or towards one side. 2 away. 3 to a place that is out of hearing or more private. 4 apart, not entering into consideration. 5 as an aside. ~*n.* 1 something spoken so as to be audible only to the person addressed, esp. a speech by an actor, which others on stage are not supposed to hear. 2 a digression. **aside from** apart from. [formerly *on side*]

asinine (as´inīn) *a.* 1 stupid, ridiculous. 2 of, relating to or resembling asses. **asininity** (-nin´-) *n.* asinine behaviour, obstinate stupidity. [L *asinīnus* (*asinus*, an ass)]

-asis (əsis) *suf.* forming names of diseases, e.g. *elephantiasis*. [L *-ăsis*, Gr. *-āsis*]

ask (ahsk) *v.t.* 1 to put a question to, to enquire of; to put (a question). 2 to seek to obtain by words, to request. 3 to enquire concerning, to request to be informed about. 4 to invite. 5 to solicit or state (a price required). 6 to demand, to require. 7 †to publish (the banns of marriage). ~*v.i.* 1 to make a request, petition or demand. 2 to enquire, to request to be informed (about). **ask me another** (*coll.*) I don't know. **for the asking** (obtainable) for nothing or for very little effort. **I ask you!** 1 used to express disapproval or dismay. 2 used rhetorically to solicit the agreement of the person one is speaking to. **if you ask me** in my opinion. **to ask a blessing** BLESS. **to ask after** to request information about, esp. about (the health of) another person. **to ask for** to behave in such a way as to invite (trouble etc.). **to ask for it** (*coll.*) to act in such a way as to make trouble, unpleasant consequences etc. inevitable. **to ask the hand of** HAND. **asker** *n.* 1 a person who asks or enquires. 2 a petitioner, a suppliant, a beggar. **asking price** *n.* the price set by a seller. [OE *ascian*]

askance (əskans´), **askant** (əskant´) *adv.* 1 obliquely, sideways, askew, squintingly. 2 with mistrust, suspicion or disapproval. [etym. uncertain]

askari (askah´ri) *n.* (*pl.* **askari, askaris**) an indigenous E African soldier. [Arab. *askar*, an army]

askew (əskū´) *adv.* 1 in an oblique direction. 2 out of true, awry. ~*a.* oblique, awry, skew. [SKEW]

aslant (əslahnt´) *adv., a.* in a slanting or oblique direction. ~*prep.* across in a slanting direction.

asleep (əslēp´) *adv., pred.a.* 1 in or into a state of sleep. 2 inactive, inattentive, unresponsive. 3 numb. 4 (*euphem.*) dead.

ASLEF (az´lef) *abbr.* Associated Society of Locomotive Engineers and Firemen.

AS level (āes´) *n.* (a pass in) an examination in a subject at the Advanced Supplementary level of the General Certificate of Education, equivalent to half an A level.

aslope (əslōp´) *a.* sloping, oblique. ~*adv.* 1 with a slope. 2 aslant, obliquely, crosswise. [OE *aslopen*, p.p. of *aslūpan*, to slip away; or *a-*, on, SLOPE]

ASM *abbr.* air-to-surface missile.

☒ **asma** common misspelling of ASTHMA.

asmoulder (əsmōl´də) *a., adv.* smouldering.

asocial (āsō´shəl) *a.* 1 not social. 2 antisocial; inconsiderate or hostile towards others. 3 hostile to society as such or life in society. [A-[3], SOCIAL]

asp[1] (asp), **†aspic** (as´pik) *n.* 1 a small venomous hooded serpent, *Naja haje*, the Egyptian cobra. 2 a European viper, *Vipera aspis*. [L *aspis*, Gr. *aspis*]

†asp[2] ASPEN.

asparagine (əspar´əjīn) *n.* an amino acid occurring in proteins, found in asparagus and other vegetables. [ASPARAGUS, -INE]

asparagus (əspar´əgəs) *n.* 1 any plant of the genus *Asparagus*, esp. *A. officinalis*, a culinary plant, the tender shoots of which are eaten. 2 the edible shoots of this plant. **asparagus fern** *n.* a decorative fernlike plant, *Asparagus setaceus*. [L, from Gr. *asparagos* (etym. uncertain)]

aspartame (əspah´tām) *n.* an artificial sweetener derived from aspartic acid. [*aspart*ic acid phenyl*a*lanine *m*ethyl *e*ster]

aspartic acid (əspah´tik) *n.* a nonessential amino acid present in many proteins, that acts as a neurotransmitter. [F *aspartique*, from ASPARAGUS]

aspect (as´pekt) *n.* 1 a particular element or feature of something. 2 a way of regarding or viewing something. 3 (of a building) a position facing in a particular direction; outlook. 4 the appearance or visual effect. 5 (*formal*) a facial expression. 6 (*Gram.*) a verbal form that expresses such features as continuity, repetition etc. 7 (*Astrol.*) the situation of one planet with respect to another. **aspect ratio** *n.* 1 the ratio of the width to the height of the picture on a television or cinema screen. 2 the ratio of the span of an aerofoil to its mean chord. **aspectual** (aspek´chuəl) *a.* of or relating to a grammatical or astrological aspect. [L *aspectus*, p.p. of *aspicere*, to look at (AD-, to, at, *spicere*, to look]

aspen (as´pən), **†asp** *n.* a poplar, *Populus tremula*, remarkable for its quivering leaves; also called *trembling poplar*. ~*a.* 1 of or relating to the aspen. 2 made of the wood of the aspen. 3 †like an aspen, trembling, quaking. [OE *æspe* (cp. OHG *aspâ*, G. *Espe*)]

asper (as´pə) *n.* (*Hist.*) a small Turkish silver coin, later only a monetary unit. [F *aspre* or It. *aspero*, late Gr. *aspron*, white money (*aspros -on*, white, perh. from L *asper*, rough)]

asperate (as´pərāt) *a.* (*Bot.*) with a rough surface from being covered with short stiff hairs. [L *asperātus*, p.p. of *asperāre*, to roughen (*asper*, rough)]

asperge (əspœj´) *v.t.* to besprinkle, esp. with holy water. ~*n.* an aspergillum. **asperges** (-jēz) *n.* a short rite preceding Mass involving the sprinkling of the congregation with holy water by the celebrant. **aspergillum** (aspəjil´əm), **aspergill** *n.* (*pl.* **aspergilla** (-lə), **aspergillums, aspergills**) the brush used to sprinkle holy water. **aspergillus** (-jil´əs) *n.* (*pl.* **aspergilli** (-jil´ī)) any of a genus of fungi, *Aspergillus*, including many moulds that grow on decaying organic matter, named from their resemblance to the aspergillum. [F *asperger*, L *aspergere* (*ad-*, to, *spargere*, to sprinkle)]

asperity (əsper´iti) *n.* (*pl.* **asperities**) **1** harshness of manner, acrimony. **2** roughness of surface. **3** a rugged excrescence. **4** harshness of sound. [OF *asprete*, L *asperitātem*, nom. *asperitas* (*asper*, rough)]

aspermia (āspœ´miə, ə-) *n.* total absence of semen. [Gr. *a-*, not, *sperma*, seed]

asperse (əspœs´) *v.t.* **1** (*formal*) to spread disparaging reports about, to defame. **2** to scatter or strew upon, to besprinkle. **aspersion** (-shən) *n.* **1** calumny, slander, a false report or insinuation. **2** the act of sprinkling. **3** something which is sprinkled. **to cast aspersions on** to make disparaging or slanderous remarks about. **aspersive** *a.* **aspersively** *adv.* **aspersorium** (aspəsaw´riəm) *n.* (*pl.* **aspersoria** (-riə)) **1** a vessel containing holy water with which worshippers sprinkle themselves. **2** an aspergillum. **aspersory** *a.* [L *aspersus*, p.p. of *aspergere* (see ASPERGE)]

asphalt (as´falt) *n.* **1** a bituminous pitch that occurs naturally or as a residue from petroleum distillation. **2** a mixture of this with gravel or other material, used for roofing, road surfacing etc. ~*v.t.* to cover, surface or line with asphalt. **asphalter** *n.* a person or machine that lays asphalt. **asphaltic** (-fal´-) *a.* **1** of or relating to asphalt. **2** consisting of or containing asphalt. [late L *asphaltum*, Gr. *asphalton* (foreign in origin)]

asphodel (as´fədel) *n.* **1** a mythical undying flower, said to bloom in the Elysian fields. **2** a plant of the S European liliaceous genus *Asphodelus*, or related genera. [Gr. *asphodelos* (etym. uncertain), see also DAFFODIL]

asphyxia (əsfik´siə, ā-) *n.* **1** a lack of oxygen in the blood, leading to unconsciousness or death. **2** suffocation. **asphyxial** *a.* of or relating to asphyxia. **asphyxiant** *a.*, *n.* (something) that causes asphyxia. **asphyxiate** *v.t.* **1** to affect with asphyxia. **2** to suffocate. ~*v.i.* **1** to undergo asphyxia. **2** to suffocate. **asphyxiation** (-ā´shən) *n.* **1** the act of asphyxiating or the process of being asphyxiated. **2** suffocation. [Gr. *asphuxia* (*a-*, not, *sphuzein*, to throb, pulsate)]

aspic[1] (as´pik) *n.* **1** a savoury jelly used as a garnish or in which game, hard-boiled eggs, fish etc., may be embedded. **2** a dish of meat etc. moulded in aspic. [F, etym. uncertain, perh. from *aspic*, asp, because of the coldness or colour of the dish]

aspic[2] ASP[1].

aspidistra (aspidis´trə) *n.* a plant of the liliaceous genus *Aspidistra*, formerly often grown as a house plant. [Gr. *aspis*, a shield; *astron*, star]

aspirant ASPIRE.

aspirate[1] (as´pirāt) *v.t.* **1** to pronounce with an exhalation of breath. **2** to prefix the letter *h* or its equivalent to. **3** to draw out (gas, fluid) from a cavity by suction. **4** to supply air to (an internal-combustion engine). **aspiration**[1] (-ā´shən) *n.* **1** the act of breathing. **2** the act of aspirating. **3** an aspirated sound. **aspirator** *n.* **1** (*Med.*) an instrument for evacuating a cavity by means of an exhausted receiver. **2** an instrument for drawing air or gas through a tube. **3** a person who or something which aspirates. [L *aspīrātus*, p.p. of *aspirāre* (see ASPIRE)]

aspirate[2] (as´pirət) *a.* **1** pronounced with an exhalation of breath. **2** prefixed by or blended with the sound of *h.* ~*n.* a consonant pronounced with an exhalation or the sound of *h.*

aspiration[1] ASPIRATE[1].

aspiration[2] ASPIRE.

aspire (əspiə´) *v.i.* **1** to long, desire eagerly. **2** to seek to attain (to). **3** (*poet.*) to rise, to mount up. **aspirant** (as´pir-) *a.* aspiring, aiming at a higher position. ~*n.* **1** a person who aspires. **2** a candidate. **aspiration**[2] (aspirā´shən) *n.* **1** the act of aspiring. **2** steadfast desire or ambition. **3** a seeking for better things. **aspiring** *a.* **1** eagerly desirous of some high object, ambitious. **2** (*poet.*) tapering upwards, soaring. **aspiringly** *adv.* **aspiringness** *n.* [L *aspīrāre* (*ad-*, to, *spīrāre*, to breathe, blow)]

aspirin (as´prin) *n.* (*pl.* **aspirin, aspirins**) (*Med.*) (a tablet containing) acetylsalicylic acid, used as a painkiller.

asplenium (əsplē´niəm) *n.* any fern of the genus *Asplenium* that is found worldwide and includes several species that are grown as house plants (cp. *spleenwort*). [Gr. *asplēnon* (*a-*, not, *splēn*, spleen) from its being a reputed cure for the spleen]

asquint (əskwint´) *adv.* **1** out of the corner of the eye, obliquely. **2** with a squint. **3** with distrust, suspicion. **4** with crafty designs, furtively. [*a-*, on, and a word corresponding to Dut. *schuinte*, slope, slant]

ass[1] (as) *n.* (*pl.* **asses**) **1** either of two wild quadrupeds, *Equus africanus* (of Africa) and *E. hemionos* (of Asia), allied to the horse, but of smaller size, with long ears and a tufted tail. **2** a donkey. **3** a stupid person. **to make an ass of** to treat as an ass, to render ridiculous. **to make an ass of oneself** to make oneself appear foolish, play the fool. **asses' bridge** *n.* the fifth proposition of Euclid, Bk.I, the *pons asinorum*, so called from its being considered difficult to learn and a bar to progress for some. [OE *assa*, *esol* (cp. Dut. *ezel*, G. *Esel*, Goth. *asilus*, L *asinus*)]

ass[2] ARSE.

assagai ASSEGAI.

assai (əsī´) *adv.* (*Mus.*) very, as *largo assai*, very slow. [It., enough]

assail (əsāl´) *v.t.* **1** to attack violently by physical means. **2** to attack with argument, abuse, censure, questioning etc. **3** to approach with intent to overcome. **4** to beset, disturb. **assailable** *a.* **assailant** *a.* assailing, attacking. ~*n.* a person who attacks another physically. [OF *asailer*, *assailler*, late L *adsalīre* (*ad*, to, at, *salīre*, to leap)]

Assamese (asəmēz´) *a.* of or relating to Assam, its people or its language. ~*n.* (*pl.* **Assamese**) **1** a native or inhabitant of Assam. **2** (*as pl.*) the people of Assam. **3** the official Indic language of Assam.

assassin (əsas´in) *n.* **1** a person who kills by surprise or secret assault (generally for money or for fanatical, political etc. motives). **2** any one of a body of Muslim fanatics, in the time of the Crusades, who were sent to murder secretly the Christian leaders and others. **assassinate** *v.t.* **1** to kill by surprise or secret assault. **2** to murder (esp. a political or religious leader) by sudden violence. **3** to injure or destroy (a person's character or reputation). **assassination** (-ā´shən) *n.* **assassinator** *n.* **assassin bug** *n.* a predatory or bloodsucking insect of the family Reduviidae. [F *assassin* or It. *assassino*, med. L *assassīnus*, Arab. *hashshāshin*, hashish-eaters]

assault (əsawlt´) *n.* **1** a violent physical or verbal attack. **2** (*Law*) a threatening word or act. **3** an act of or attempt at rape. **4** the charge of an attacking body on a fortified place. **5** a determined attempt. ~*v.t.* **1** to make a violent physical or verbal attack on. **2** to attack (a fortified place) by sudden rush; to storm. **3** (*Law*) to attack with threatening words or with blows. **4** to rape or attempt to rape. ~*a.* (*Mil.*) used in or for an assault. **assaultable** *a.*

assault and battery *n.* (*Law*) an assault followed by a physical attack. **assault course** *n.* an obstacle course used for training soldiers. [OF *asaut, assaut,* L *ad-,* to, at, *saltus,* a leap (ASSAIL)]

assay (əsā´, as´ā) *n.* **1** the scientific determination of the quantity of metal in an ore, alloy, bullion or coin. **2** the chemical analysis of a substance to determine its content. **3** a metal or other substance analysed. **4** a trial, examination. **5** †an attempt, endeavour. ~*v.t.* **1** to determine the amount of metal in (an ore, alloy, bullion or coin). **2** to subject to chemical analysis. **3** to show (content) as a result of assaying. **4** to try, to test. **5** †to try to do, attempt. ~*v.i.* to attempt, to endeavour. **assayer** *n.* a person who assays metals. **assaying** *n.* the act or process of determining the amount of a particular substance in a compound. **assay office** *n.* an office which assays precious metals and awards hallmarks. [OF *assai,* L *exagium,* from *exagere, exigere,* to weigh, try (*ex-,* out, *agere,* to drive, deal)]

assegai (as´əgī), **assagai** *n.* (*pl.* **assegais, assagais**) a slender lance of hard wood, esp. that of the southern African tribes. [Arab. *azzaghayah* (*al,* the, Berber *zaghayah*); either through F *azagaye* or Port. *azagaia*]

assemble (əsem´bəl) *v.t.* **1** to call or bring together. **2** to arrange in order. **3** to fit together the component parts of. **4** (*Comput.*) to convert (a program) from assembly language to machine code. ~*v.i.* to meet or come together; to gather, to congregate. **assemblage** (-blij) *n.* **1** a gathering, assembling; a concourse. **2** a collection. **3** the act or process of putting together; something made from assembled pieces. **assembler** *n.* **1** a person who or thing which assembles. **2** (*Comput.*) **a** a computer program that automatically translates assembly language into machine code. **b** an assembly language. **assembly** *n.* (*pl.* **assemblies**) **1** the act of assembling; the state of being assembled. **2** a body of people met together for some common purpose. **3** a meeting of all or some of the members of a school. **4** a deliberative, legislative or religious body. **5** a lower house in some legislatures. **6** the conversion of assembly language into machine code. **7** (*Mil.*) a signal, esp. a drumbeat, summoning soldiers to prepare to march. **assembly language** *n.* a low-level computer language in which instructions written in mnemonics correspond directly to instructions in machine code. **assembly line** *n.* a sequential arrangement of workers and machines operating from stage to stage in assembling some product. **assemblyman** *n.* (*pl.* **assemblymen**) a member of a legislative assembly. **assembly room** *n.* a room in which public assemblies, balls, concerts etc. are held. **assembly woman** *n.* (*pl.* **assemblywomen**) a female member of a legislative assembly. [OF *assembler,* late L *assimulāre, ad-,* to, *simul,* together]

assent (əsent´) *v.i.* **1** to express agreement. **2** to agree to or sanction something proposed. **3** †to admit a statement as true. ~*n.* **1** the act of admitting, agreeing to or concurring in; agreement, acquiescence. **2** sanction. **assentation** (asentā´shən) *n.* the action of assenting, esp. with obsequiousness or servility. **assentient** (-shənt) *a.* assenting to. ~*n.* a person who assents or agrees. **assentingly** *adv.* **assentor** *n.* a person who gives assent, esp. one who signs the nomination of a Parliamentary candidate after the proposer and seconder. [OF *asenter,* L *assentīre* (*ad-,* to, *sentīre,* to feel)]

assert (əsœt´) *v.t.* **1** to affirm, to declare positively, to maintain. **2** to insist on (a claim etc.). **3** (*refl.*) to put (oneself) forward, insist on one's rights etc. **assertable** *a.* **assertion** *n.* **1** the act of asserting. **2** a positive statement, an affirmation. **assertive** *a.* **1** characterized by assertion, forthright. **2** self-assertive. **3** dogmatic. **assertively** *adv.* **assertiveness** *n.* **assertor, asserter** *n.* **1** a person who maintains or defends. **2** an advocate. **3** a person who makes an assertion. [L *assertus,* p.p. of *asserere,* to add to, take to oneself (*ad-,* to *serere,* to join, bind)]

asses[1] AS[2].

asses[2] ASS[1].

assess (əses´) *v.t.* **1** to estimate, to judge the quality or worth of; to value. **2** to value (property, income etc.) for the purpose of taxation. **3** to fix by authority the amount of (a tax, fine etc. for a person or community). **4** to tax, fine etc. (in or at a specified sum). **assessable** *a.* **1** capable of being assessed. **2** liable to be assessed. **assessably** *adv.* **assessment** *n.* **1** (an) estimation, appraisal. **2** the act of assessing. **3** the amount assessed. **4** an official valuation for taxation purposes. **assessor** *n.* **1** a person who makes an assessment, esp. of the value of property for taxation or of the performance of students. **2** a person who evaluates insurance claims. **3** a person who sits near and advises a judge or magistrate on technical points, commercial usage, navigation etc. **4** a person who shares another's rank and sits beside them. **assessorship** *n.* [OF *assesser,* late L *assessāre,* freq. of *assidēre* (*ad-,* to, *sedēre,* to sit)]

assets (as´ets) *n.pl.* **1** all the property of a person or company which may be liable for outstanding debts. **2** property in general. **3** (*Law*) **a** goods sufficient to satisfy a testator's debts and legacies. **b** property or effects that may be applied for this purpose. **asset** *n.* a useful or valuable resource. **asset-stripping** *n.* the practice of buying a company and selling off its assets to make a profit. **asset-stripper** *n.* [A-F *asetz,* OF *asez,* enough, late L *ad satis,* sufficiency (*satis,* enough)]

asseverate (əsev´ərāt) *v.t.* **1** to affirm with solemnity. **2** to assert positively. **asseveration** (-ā´shən) *n.* **1** the act of asseverating. **2** a solemn affirmation. **3** an emphatic declaration or confirmation, an oath. [L *asseverātus,* p.p. of *asseverāre* (*ad-,* to, *sevērus,* earnest, serious)]

assibilate (əsib´ilāt) *v.t.* to pronounce (a sound) with or as a sibilant. ~*v.i.* to become converted into a sibilant. **assibilation** (-ā´shən) *n.* [L *assibilāre* (*ad-,* to, *sibilāre,* to hiss)]

assiduous (əsid´ūəs) *a.* hard-working, persevering; conscientious. **assiduity** (asidū´-) *n.* **1** constant or close application to the matter in hand, perseverance, diligence. **2** (*pl.*) persistent endeavours to please, constant attentions. **assiduously** *adv.* **assiduousness** *n.* [L *assiduus,* from *assidēre* (see ASSESS)]

assign (əsīn´) *v.t.* **1** to allot, to apportion. **2** to designate for a specific purpose. **3** to name, to fix. **4** to ascribe, to attribute. **5** (*Law*) to transfer, to surrender. ~*n.* a person to whom a property or right is transferred. **assignable** *a.* capable of being transferred, designated or pointed to as a source or reason. **assignation** (asignā´shən) *n.* **1** a meeting, esp. an illicit one between lovers. **2** an appointment to meet, esp. illicitly. **3** the act of assigning. **4** attribution of origin. **5** (*Sc. Law*) a transference of property or right. **assignee** (-nē´) *n.* **1** an agent, a representative. **2** (*Law*) a person to whom a right or property is transferred. **assignment** *n.* **1** the act of assigning; allotment, allocation. **2** a specific task or mission. **3** a position or job to which one is assigned. **4** a legal transference of right or property. **5** the instrument by which such transference is effected. **6** the right or property transferred. **7** attribution. **assignor** (-naw´) *n.* a person who transfers a right or property. [OF *assigner,* L *assignāre* (*ad-,* to, *signāre,* to mark)]

assignat (as´ignat, asinyah´) *n.* paper money issued by the Revolutionary Government of France (1790–96) on the security of state lands. [F]

assimilate (əsim´ilāt) *v.t.* **1** to take as nutriment and convert into living tissue, to incorporate in the substance of an organism. **2** to take in (information) and comprehend. **3** to absorb into a population or group. **4**

to incorporate. **5** to make similar or alike. **6** to adapt (a speech sound) so as to resemble an adjacent sound. **7** to liken, to compare. ~*v.i.* **1** to become absorbed or incorporated. **2** to be incorporated in the substance of a living organism. **3** to become similar. **assimilable** *a.* capable of being assimilated. **assimilability** (-bil´-) *n.* the capability of being assimilated. **assimilation** (-ā´shən) *n.* **1** the act or process of assimilating; the state of being assimilated. **2** the process by which an organism converts nourishment into its own substance. **3** comparison. **assimilationist** *n.* a person who advocates or promotes racial or cultural integration. ~*a.* of, relating to or promoting the views of assimilationists. **assimilative** *a.* having the power of assimilating. **assimilator** *n.* a person who or something which assimilates. **assimilatory** (-lə-) *a.* tending to assimilate. [L *assimilāre* (*ad-*, *similis*, like), -ATE[3]]

assist (əsist´) *v.t.* **1** to help, to aid, to give support or succour to. **2** to act as a subordinate to. ~*v.i.* **1** to give help or aid. **2** to be present (at). ~*n.* (*N Am.*) **1** an act of assisting. **2** in sport, an action that helps a team to score, put out an opponent etc. **3** a credit awarded for this. **assistance** *n.* help, aid, support, succour, furtherance. **assistant** *n.* **1** a person who assists another. **2** an auxiliary. **3** SHOP ASSISTANT (under SHOP). ~*a.* aiding, helping, auxiliary. **assisted place** *n.* (in the UK) a place as a student at a fee-paying school, the cost of which is partly or wholly paid by the state. **assistor** *n.* (*Law*) an assistant, a person who aids or is accessory. [F *assister*, L *assistere* (*ad-*, to, *sistere*, to place, from *stāre*, to stand)]

assize (əsīz´) *n.* **1** (*pl.*) from 1815 to 1971, the sessions held periodically by the judges of the Supreme Court in each county in England and Wales for the administration of civil and criminal justice. **2** †(in the US) a formal session or sitting of a legislative or administrative body; a decree or edict made at such a sitting. **3** (*Sc. Law*) a trial by jury; a jury. [OF *asise*, orig. fem. p.p. of *asseoir*, sit at (L *assidēre*, see ASSESS)]

assoc. *abbr.* **1** associate. **2** associated. **3** association.

associate[1] (əsō´shiāt, -sō´si-) *v.t.* **1** to connect in the mind or imagination. **2** to join, to unite, to combine, to connect. **3** to connect (oneself) as a partner, supporter, friend, companion etc. (with). ~*v.i.* **1** to unite or combine for a common purpose. **2** to keep company or mix (with). **associable** *a.* **1** capable of being (mentally) associated. **2** liable to be affected by sympathy with other bodily parts. **3** †companionable. **associability** (-bil´-) *n.* **association** (-ā´shən) *n.* **1** the act of combining for a common purpose. **2** a society formed for the promotion of some common object. **3** fellowship, intimacy, cooperation, connection. **4** mental connection of ideas, memories, sensations etc. **5** a memory, thought or feeling connected with some object, place etc. and recalled to the mind in connection with it. **6** a plant community growing in a uniform habitat and forming part of a larger ecological unit. **7** the formation of loosely held aggregates of molecules, ions etc. **associational** *a.* **Association Football** *n.* football played between two teams of eleven players, with a round ball which may not be touched with the hands except by the goalkeepers. **associationism** *n.* (*Psych.*) the theory which accounts for mental and moral phenomena by association of ideas. **associationist** *n.* **associative** (-ətiv) *a.* **1** of, relating to or promoting association. **2** (*Math., Comput.*) involving the property of quantities linked by operators to yield the same result independent of their grouping so long as their order remains the same, such that $x+(y+z) = (x+y)+z$. [L *associāre* (*ad-*, to, *sociāre*, to join, from *socius*, an ally), -ATE[3]]

associate[2] (əsō´shiət, -sō´si-) *a.* **1** connected or joined in a common enterprise. **2** having equal rank or status. **3** in the same group or category. **4** having less than full status. ~*n.* **1** a partner, colleague, esp. in business. **2** a friend, ally or companion. **3** a person who has partial membership or subordinate status in an association or institution. **4** something generally found with something else. **associate professor** *n.* (*N Am.*, *Austral.*, *New Zeal.*) a university teacher ranking immediately below a professor. **associateship** *n.*

assonant (as´ənənt) *a.* **1** corresponding in sound. **2** rhyming in the accented vowels, but not in the consonants, as *keep* and *seen*. **3** corresponding in consonant sounds, but with different vowels, as *lick* and *lack*. ~*n.* an assonant word. **assonance** *n.* **1** the quality of being assonant. **2** a word or syllable that is assonant with another. **3** correspondence or resemblance in other respects. **assonate** (-āt) *v.i.* [F, from L *assonāre* (*ad-*, to, *sonāre*, to sound; *sonus*, sound)]

assort (əsawt´) *v.t.* **1** to arrange or dispose in groups of the same type, to classify. **2** to furnish with an assortment of merchandise. ~*v.i.* to suit, to agree, to match, to be in congruity or harmony (with). **assortative** *a.* tending to assort. **assortatively** *adv.* **assortative mating** *n.* (*Biol.*) non-random mating involving the selection of similar partners. **assorted** *a.* **1** of various sorts, miscellaneous. **2** arranged in groups, sorts. **3** (*usu. preceded by adv.*) matched. **assortment** *n.* **1** a collection of things of various kinds. **2** a collection of things assorted. **3** the act of assorting; the state of being assorted. [OF *assorter* (F *assortir*) (*à*, to, *sorte*, sort, manner, kind, L *sors*, *sortis*)]

ASSR *abbr.* (*Hist.*) Autonomous Soviet Socialist Republic.

asst. *abbr.* assistant.

assuage (əswāj´) *v.t.* **1** to soothe, to lessen the violence or pain of, to allay, to mitigate. **2** to appease, satisfy. **3** to calm, to pacify. **assuagement** *n.* **1** the act of assuaging; mitigation, abatement. **2** something that assuages. **assuasive** *a.* assuaging, mitigating, soothing. [OF *assouagier*, L *assuāviāre* (*suāvis*, sweet)]

assume (əsūm´) *v.t.* **1** to take for granted, to accept without proof or as a hypothesis. **2** to pretend, feign. **3** to take upon oneself, to undertake (a task, office). **4** to take on, adopt (a quality, characteristic). **5** to arrogate, appropriate, pretend to, to claim. ~*v.i.* **1** to be arrogant or pretentious. **2** to claim more than is one's due. **assumable** *a.* **assumed** *a.* **1** fictitious; feigned, false. **2** taken for granted. **3** usurped, pretended. **assumedly** (-mid-) *adv.* **assuming** *a.* arrogant, haughty. ~*n.* assumption, presumption. [L *assūmere*, to take to oneself (*ad-*, to, *sūmere*, to take)]

Usage note *Assume* usually implies greater tentativeness (and less arrogance) than *presume*.

---

assumpsit (əsŭmp´sit) *n.* (*Law, Hist.*) **1** an oral or unsealed contract, founded on a consideration. **2** an action to enforce such a contract. [L, he has taken upon him]

assumption (əsŭmp´shən) *n.* **1** the act of assuming. **2** the thing assumed; a supposition, a postulate. **3** arrogance. **4** (**Assumption**) the bodily reception of the Virgin Mary into heaven; the feast (15 Aug.) in honour of this event. **assumptive** *a.* **1** taken for granted. **2** arrogant. [L *assūmptus*, p.p. of *assūmere*, ASSUME]

assure (əshuə´) *v.t.* **1** to give confidence to, to convince. **2** to tell positively. **3** to ensure, guarantee. **4** to make safe or secure. **5** to ensure the payment of compensation in case of loss of (esp. life), to insure. **assurance** *n.* **1** the act of assuring. **2** a positive declaration. **3** certainty, security. **4** self-confidence, self-reliance, intrepidity. **5** audacity, impudence. **6** insurance, esp. a contract to pay a given sum on a person's death in return for an annual premium. **assured** *a.* **1** certain, guaranteed. **2** confident, convinced. **3** self-confident, full of assurance. 4 insured. ~*n.* 1 a person whose life is insured. 2 the beneficiary of an assurance policy. **to rest assured** to be secure in the knowledge (that). **assuredly** (-rid-) *adv.* **assuredness** (-rid-) *n.* **assurer** *n.* 1 a person who or something which gives assurance. 2 an insurer, an underwriter. 3 a person who takes out a policy of assurance. **assuring** *a.* creating assurance, inspiring confidence. **assuringly** *adv.* [OF *aseürer*, late L *adsēcūrāre* (*ad-*, to, *sēcūrus*, safe)]

assurgent (əsœ´jənt) *a.* (*Bot.*) pointing upwards; rising upwards in a curve. [L *assurgere* (*ad-*, to, against, *surgere*, to rise)]

Assyrian (əsir´iən) *a.* of or relating to the ancient kingdom of Assyria. ~*n.* 1 a native or inhabitant of Assyria. 2 the language of Assyria. **Assyriology** (-ol´-) *n.* the study of the history, language and antiquities of Assyria. **Assyriological** (-loj´-) *a.* **Assyriologist** *n.*

AST *abbr.* Atlantic Standard Time.

astable (āstā´bəl) *a.* 1 not stable. 2 (of an electrical circuit) switching spontaneously between two states. [Gr. *a-*, not, STABLE[1]]

astarboard (əstah´bəd) *adv.* on or towards the starboard side of a ship.

astatic (əstat´ik, ā-) *a.* 1 not remaining fixed; unstable, unsteady. 2 (*Physics*) not having the tendency to assume a particular direction or orientation. **astatic galvanometer** *n.* a galvanometer with two mutually compensating magnets that reduce the effect of the earth's magnetic field. [Gr. *astatos* (*a-*, not, *sta-*, stem of verb, stand)]

astatine (as´tətēn) *n.* a radioactive element, at. no. 85, chem. symbol At, formed in minute amounts by radioactive decay or made artificially. [Gr. *astatos*, unstable (see ASTATIC)]

aster (as´tə) *n.* 1 any of a genus, *Aster*, of composite plants with showy, daisy-like heads. 2 a star-shaped figure seen in a cell during mitosis. [L, from Gr. *astēr*, a star]

-aster (as´tə) *suf.* forming nouns meaning an inferior practitioner of an art, as in *criticaster*, *poetaster*. [L, diminutive and contemptuous termination]

asteriated (astiə´riātid) *a.* (of a crystal or gemstone) exhibiting asterism.

asterisk (as´tərisk) *n.* a mark (*) used in printing to call attention to a note, to mark omission etc. ~*v.t.* to mark with an asterisk. [L *asteriscus*, Gr. *asteriskos*]

asterism (as´tərizm) *n.* 1 a small cluster of stars. 2 three asterisks (⁂) to draw attention to something important. 3 the starlike figure visible in some mineral crystals, as in the asteriated sapphire. [Gr. *asterismos*]

astern (əstœn´) *adv., a.* 1 in, at or towards the stern of a ship. 2 behind a ship. 3 backwards.

asteroid (as´təroid) *n.* 1 any of the small celestial bodies that orbit the sun, esp. between the orbits of Mars and Jupiter, a planetoid, a minor planet. 2 a member of the class Asteroidea, a starfish. ~*a.* 1 having the shape or appearance of a star. 2 of, relating to or resembling a starfish. **asteroidal** (-roi´-) *a.*

asthenia (əsthē´niə) *n.* absence of strength; debility, diminution or loss of vital power. **asthenic** (-then´-) *a.* 1 of, relating to or affected with asthenia. 2 (of a person's physique) characterized by a small trunk and long limbs. ~*n.* an asthenic person. **asthenosphere** (-then´əsfiə) *n.* (*Geol.*) the semifluid upper layer of the earth's mantle that is thought to be capable of movement and to account for such phenomena of the lithosphere as continental drift. [mod. L, Gr. *astheneia*, from *asthenes*, weak (*a-*, without, *sthenos*, strength)]

asthma (as´mə) *n.* a respiratory disorder, usu. allergic in origin, characterized by wheezing, constriction of the chest, and usu. coughing. **asthmatic** (-mat´-) *a.* 1 of, relating to or affected with asthma. 2 wheezy, puffing. ~*n.* a person affected with asthma. **asthmatical** *a.* **asthmatically** *adv.* [Gr. *asthma -matos*, from *azein*, to breathe hard (*aein*, to blow)]

Asti (as´ti) *n.* (*pl.* **Astis**) an Italian white wine. **Asti spumante** *n.* a sparkling form of this wine. [town in NW Italy]

astigmatism (əstig´mətizm) *n.* a defect of the eye or of a lens as a result of which a point source of light tends to be focused as a line. **astigmatic** (astigmat´ik) *a.* of, relating to, or characterized by astigmatism. [Gr. *a-*, not, *stigma*, point]

astilbe (əstil´bi) *n.* any plant of the perennial saxifragaceous genus *Astilbe*, having spikes or plumes of tiny red or white flowers. [new L from Gr. *a-*, not, *stilbē*, fem. of *stilbos*, glittering]

astir (əstœ´) *a., adv.* 1 in motion. 2 in commotion, in excitement. 3 out of bed. [*a*, on, STIR[1]]

ASTM *abbr.* American Society for Testing and Materials.

astomatous (əstom´ətəs) *a.* 1 mouthless. 2 of or relating to the Astomata, a group of ciliate Protozoa without a determinate mouth. [Gr. *a-*, without, *stoma stomatos*, a mouth]

astonish (əston´ish) *v.t.* to strike with sudden surprise or wonder, to amaze, to surprise. **astonishing** *a.* **astonishingly** *adv.* **astonishment** *n.* 1 the act of astonishing; the state of being astonished; amazement. 2 an object causing amazement. [earlier *astony*, ME *astone*, OF *estoner* (F *étonner*), to amaze (L *ex-*, out, *tonāre*, to thunder)]

astound (əstownd´) *v.t.* to strike with amazement, to shock with alarm, wonder, or surprise. **astounding** *a.* **astoundingly** *adv.* [ME *astoned*, p.p. of *astone*]

astraddle (əstrad´əl) *adv.* 1 in a straddling position. 2 astride.

astragal (as´trəgəl) *n.* 1 (*Archit.*) a small semicircular moulding or bead, round the top or the bottom of a column. 2 a glazing bar, esp. in a bookcase. 3 the astragalus. **astragalus** (əstrag´-) *n.* 1 the talus, the bone with which the tibia articulates below. 2 any of a large genus of leguminous plants, *Astragalus*, containing the milk-vetch. [L *astragalus*, Gr. *astragalos*]

astrakhan (astrəkan´, -kahn´) *n.* 1 the tightly curled, usu. black or grey fleece obtained from lambs orig. from Astrakhan. 2 a fabric with a pile in imitation of this. [*Astrakhan*, a city and region in SE Russia]

astral (as´trəl) *a.* 1 of or relating to the stars. 2 starry. 3 star-shaped. 4 of or relating to the supposed astral body or material composing it. **astral body** *n.* (*pl.* **astral bodies**) a supposed kind of spiritual body coexisting with the physical body and surrounding it like an aura, which some occultists claim to be able to perceive, to project to a distance etc. **astral year** *n.* SIDEREAL YEAR (under SIDEREAL). [L *astrālis* (*astrum*, Gr. *astron*, a star)]

astraphobia (astrəfō´biə), **astrophobia** *n.* a morbid fear of thunder and lightning. **astraphobic** *a., n.* [Gr. *astrapē*, lightning, -PHOBIA (under -PHOBE)]

astray (əstrā´) *a., adv.* 1 in or into sin, crime or error. 2 out of or away from the right way. **to go astray** GO[1]. **to lead astray** LEAD[1]. [prob. OF *estraié*, p.p. of *estraier*, to stray (L *extra-*, out of bounds, *vagāre*, to wander)]

astride (əstrīd´) *a., adv.* 1 with a leg on either side. 2 with legs apart. ~*prep.* 1 with a leg on either side of. 2 extending across.

astringent (əstrin´jənt) *a.* 1 causing contraction of body tissues. 2 styptic. 3 stern, severe, harsh. ~*n.* an astringent substance. **astringency** *n.* 1 the quality of being astringent. 2 sternness, severity, harshness. **astringently** *adv.* [L *astringere*, as astrict]

astro- (as´trō) *comb. form* 1 of or relating to the heavenly bodies, planets or stars, as in *astrology*, *astronomy*. 2 of or relating to outer space, as in *astronaut*. [Gr. *astron*, a star]

astrobiology (astrōbīol´əji) *n.* a branch of biology concerned with the search for life beyond the earth.

astrochemistry (astrōkem´istri) *n.* the study of the chemistry of celestial bodies and particles in interstellar space.

astrodome (as´trədōm) *n.* **1** a dome window in an aircraft to enable astronomical observations to be made. **2** a large sports stadium covered by a translucent domed roof.

astrodynamics (astrōdīnam´iks) *n.* the study of the motion of bodies in outer space and of the forces acting on them.

astrogeology (astrōjēol´əji) *n.* the study of the geology of the moon, etc.

astrohatch (as´trəhach) *n.* an astrodome in an aircraft.

astroid (as´troid) *n.* (*Math.*) a hypocycloid with four cusps (resembling a square with concave sides). [ASTRO-, -OID]

astrolabe (as´trəlāb) *n.* an instrument, usu. consisting of a graduated disc with a sighting device, formerly used to measure the altitude of celestial bodies and as an aid to navigation. [OF *astrelabe*, med. L *astrolabium* (L *lab-*, stem of v. to take)]

astrology (əstrol´əji) *n.* the study of a supposed connection between the changing aspects of the heavenly bodies and the changing course of human life, with predictions of events and advice on conduct. **astrologer** *n.* a person who practises or studies astrology. **astrological** (astrəloj´-), **astrologic** *a.* **astrologically** *adv.* [F *astrologie*, L *astrologia* (Gr. *logos*, discourse)]

astrometry (astrom´ətri) *n.* the branch of astronomy concerned with measuring the position and motion of heavenly bodies.

astronautics (astrənaw´tiks) *n.* the science of travel through space. **astronaut** (as´-) *n.* a person who travels or is trained to travel into space beyond the earth's atmosphere in a spacecraft. **astronautical** *a.* [Gr. ASTRO-, *nautēs*, a sailor]

astronavigation (astrōnavigā´shən) *n.* navigation of a ship, aircraft or spaceship by observation of the stars.

astronomy (əstron´əmi) *n.* the science which studies all phenomena of the heavenly bodies, space and the physical universe. **astronomer** *n.* a person who studies or practises astronomy. **Astronomer Royal** *n.* an honorary title awarded to an eminent astronomer in Great Britain. **astronomic** (astrənom´-) *a.* **1** of or relating to astronomy. **2** enormously large or great. **astronomical** *a.* astronomic. **astronomical clock** *n.* **1** a complex clock which shows astronomical phenomena, such as the phases of the moon. **2** a clock which gives sidereal time. **astronomical day** *n.* SIDEREAL DAY (under SIDEREAL). **astronomically** *adv.* **astronomical unit** *n.* a unit of length equal to the mean distance of the earth from the sun, about 93 million miles (150 million km), used for measuring distances in the solar system. **astronomical year** *n.* a year determined by astronomical observations, as opposed to a civil year. [OF *astronomie*, L *astronomia*, Gr. from *astronomos*, star-arranging, a. (*nemein*, to distribute, arrange)]

astrophobia ASTRAPHOBIA.

astrophotometer (astrōfətom´itə) *n.* an instrument for measuring the intensity of sidereal light.

astrophysics (astrōfiz´iks) *n.* the branch of astronomy concerned with the physics and chemistry of celestial objects and their origin and evolution. **astrophysical** *a.* relating to astrophysics. **astrophysicist** *n.*

Astroturf® (as´trōtœf) *n.* an artificial grass surface, esp. for sports fields.

astute (əstūt´) *a.* **1** acute, discerning, shrewd. **2** clever, wily, cunning. **astutely** *adv.* **astuteness** *n.* [L *astūtus*, crafty, cunning (*astus*, craft, cunning)]

astylar (əstī´lə) *a.* (*Archit.*) without columns or pilasters. [*a-*, not, Gr. *stulos*, a pillar]

asunder (əsŭn´də) *adv.* (*formal*) apart, separately, in different pieces or places. [OE *on sundran*]

ASW *abbr.* antisubmarine warfare.

asylum (əsī´ləm) *n.* **1** protection from extradition given by one country to a person, esp. a political refugee, from another. **2** (a) shelter, (a) refuge. **3** an institution formerly affording relief and shelter to the afflicted, unfortunate or destitute, esp. an institution for the treatment of the mentally ill. **4** a place of refuge for criminals and debtors, a sanctuary. [L, from Gr. *asūlon*, neut. of *asūlos*, inviolable (*a-*, not, *sulē*, a right of seizure)]

asymmetry (əsim´ətri) *n.* (*pl.* **asymmetries**) **1** lack of symmetry, or of proportion; an instance of this. **2** (*Math.*) incommensurability. **asymmetric** (asimet´-, ā-), **asymmetrical** *a.* not symmetrical; out of proportion. **asymmetrically** *adv.* [Gr. *asummetria* (*a-*, not, *summetria*, SYMMETRY)]

asymptomatic (əsimptəmat´ik, ā-) *a.* (of a disease) not exhibiting symptoms. [A-[3], SYMPTOMATIC (under SYMPTOM)]

asymptote (as´imtōt) *n.* a straight mathematical line continually approaching some curve but never meeting it within a finite distance. **asymptotic** (-tot´-), **asymptotical** *a.* **asymptotically** *adv.* [Gr. *asumptōtos*, not coinciding (*a-*, not, *sum-*, *sun-*, together, *ptōtos*, falling, from *piptein*, to fall)]

asynchronous (əsing´krənəs, ā-) *a.* not coincident in point of time. **asynchronism, asynchrony** *n.* lack of coincidence in time. **asynchronously** *adv.* [A-[3], SYNCHRONOUS]

asyndeton (əsin´ditən) *n.* (*pl.* **asyndeta** (-tə)) a rhetorical figure by which the conjunction is omitted, as 'I came, I saw, I conquered'. **asyndetic** (asindet´ik) *a.* [Gr. *asundeton* (*a-*, not, *sun-*, with, *deein*, to bind)]

asynergia (asinœ´jiə), **asynergy** (əsin´əji) *n.* lack of coordination between muscles or parts, e.g. as a result of brain disease or damage. [Gr. *a-*, not, *sunergos*, SYNERGY]

asyntactic (asintak´tik, ā-) *a.* loosely organized with regard to syntax; irregular, ungrammatical. [Gr. *asuntaktos* (*a-*, not, *sun-*, together, *tassein*, to range)]

asystole (əsis´təli) *n.* the absence of heartbeat. **asystolic** (asistol´ik) *a.* [A-[3], SYSTOLE]

At *chem. symbol* astatine.

at (at) *prep.* **1** denoting nearness or precise position in time or space or on a scale. **2** denoting direction to or towards. **3** denoting engagement in (an occupation, activity) or a state of being in (a condition, relation). **4** denoting a value or rate. **5** denoting the object of an emotion. **at all** ALL. **at hand** HAND. **at home** HOME[1]. **at it** **1** at work, engaged, busy. **2** (*coll.*) engaged in a habitual (usu. disapproved of) activity. **3** (*coll.*) having sexual intercourse. **at one** in harmony. **at that** moreover. **where it's at** **1** where the really important or fashionable activity is taking place. **2** where the real significance lies. **at-home** *n.* a gathering or party held in one's own home. [OE *æt* (cp. Icel. *at*, L *ad*)]

at. *abbr.* atomic.

at- (ət) *pref.* AD-, assim. to *t*, e.g. *attain*, *attend*.

Atabrine ATEBRIN.

ataman (at´əmən) *n.* (*pl.* **atamans**) an elected leader or general of the Cossacks. [Rus. from Pol. *hetman*, from G *Hauptmann* (*Haupt*, head, *Mann*, man)]

ataraxia (atərak´siə), **ataraxy** (at´-) *n.* impassiveness, calmness, indifference, stoicism. **ataractic, ataraxic** *a.* calming, tranquillizing. ~*n.* an ataractic substance or drug.

atavism (at´əvizm) *n.* **1** recurrence of some characteristic of a more or less remote ancestor. **2** reversion to a primitive or ancestral form. **atavistic** (-vis´-) *a.*

atavistically (-vis´-) *adv.* [F *atavisme*, L *atavus*, an ancestor]

ataxia (ətak´siə), **ataxy** (ətak´si, at´-) *n.* loss of the power of coordination of the muscles, resulting in irregular, jerky movements. **ataxic, atactic** *a.* **1** of or relating to ataxy. **2** irregular. [Gr. *ataxia* (*a-*, not, *taxis*, order, from *tassein*, to arrange)]

ATC *abbr.* **1** air-traffic control. **2** Air Training Corps.

ate EAT.

-ate[1] (āt, ət) *suf.* **1** forming nouns of office or function, e.g. *curate, episcopate.* **2** forming nouns denoting a group, e.g. *electorate.* **3** forming nouns denoting the salts of acids, e.g. *acetate, carbonate.* **4** forming nouns denoting the product of a process, e.g. *condensate, filtrate.* [L *-ātus* in nouns of state or as p.p. of 1st conj. verbs ending in *-are*, through OF *-at*, *-é(e)*]

-ate[2] (āt, ət) *suf.* **1** forming participial adjectives, e.g. *desolate, separate, situate.* **2** forming other adjectives by analogy, e.g. *roseate, ovate.* [from L *-ātus*, p.p., see -ATE[1], via F *-é*]

-ate[3] (āt) *suf.* forming verbs, e.g. *desolate, separate*, corresponding to adjectives in the same form, or others produced on the same model, e.g. *fascinate, isolate.* [L *-āre* (p.p. *-ātus*), through or influ. by F *-er*]

Atebrin® (at´əbrin), (*N Am.*) **Atabrine** (-brīn) *n.* quinacrine.

atelectasis (atəlek´təsis) *n.* **1** failure of the lung to inflate at birth. **2** partial or complete collapse of the lung, usu. caused by bronchial obstruction. [new L from Gr. *atelēs*, imperfect, *ektasis*, extension]

atelier (ətel´yā, at´-) *n.* a workshop, an artist's studio. [F, OF *astelier*, from *astelle*, small plank or splint]

a tempo (a tem´pō) *adv., a.* (*Mus.*) in the original tempo or time.

Athanasian (athənā´shən, -zhən) *a.* of or relating to Athanasius, bishop of Alexandria (*c.* 296–373), or the creed attributed to him. **Athanasian creed** *n.* a creed stating the doctrine of the Trinity and the Incarnation, with damnatory clauses, formerly attributed to Athanasius.

atheism (ā´thiizm) *n.* **1** disbelief in the existence of a God or gods. **2** †godlessness, wickedness; disregard of God and God's laws. **atheist** *n.* a person who disbelieves, or denies the existence of a God. ~*a.* atheistic, godless, impious. **atheistic** (-is´-), **atheistical** *a.* **atheistically** *adv.* [F *athéisme*, from Gr. *atheos* (*a-*, not, *theos*, God)]

atheling (ath´əling) *n.* (*Hist.*) a member of an Anglo-Saxon noble family, often restricted to a prince of the royal blood or to the heir apparent. [OE *ætheling* (*æthel*, noble family, *-ing*, one belonging to)]

athematic (athimat´ik) *a.* **1** (*Mus.*) not based on themes. **2** (*Gram.*) having a suffix attached to the stem without an intervening vowel.

athenaeum (athənē´əm), (*N Am.*) **atheneum** *n.* **1** a literary or scientific club or institution. **2** a literary club-room, a public reading-room or library. [L, from Gr. *Athēnaion*, the temple of Athene in ancient Athens, where professors taught and orators and poets declaimed]

Athenian (əthē´niən) *n., a.* (a native or inhabitant) of Athens.

athermancy (athœ´mənsi) *n.* the power of stopping radiant heat or infrared radiation. **athermanous** *a.* impermeable by radiant heat. [Gr. *athermantos* (*a-*, not, *thermainein*, to heat, from *thermē*, heat)]

atheroma (athərō´mə) *n.* the deposition of fatty material on the inner coat of the arteries. **atheromatosis** (-tō´sis) *n.* **atheromatous** *a.* [L, a tumour containing gruel-like matter, from Gr. *athērōma*, from *athērā*, gruel]

atherosclerosis (athərōsklərō´sis) *n.* arteriosclerosis characterized by deposits of fatty material in the arteries. **atherosclerotic** (-rot´-) *a.* [ATHEROMA, SCLEROSIS]

athetosis (athətō´sis) *n.* a condition, caused by a cerebral lesion, that is characterized by involuntary writhing movements of the fingers and toes. **athetoid** (ath´-) *a.* [Gr. *athetos*, out of position, -OSIS]

athirst (əthœst´) *a.* (*poet.*) **1** thirsty, oppressed with thirst. **2** eager, eagerly desirous. [OE *ofthyrst, ofthyrsted*, p.p. of *ofthyrstan*, to be thirsty]

athlete (ath´lēt) *n.* **1** a person trained to compete in events, such as running, weight-throwing and jumping, requiring strength, agility, speed or stamina. **2** a healthy, vigorous person, esp. one with a natural aptitude for sports and physical activities. **athlete's foot** *n.* a fungal infection of the foot affecting the skin between the toes. **athletic** (-let´-) *a.* **1** of or for athletes or athletics. **2** physically strong, fit and active. **3** muscular, robust and well-proportioned. **athletically** *adv.* **athleticism** *n.* **1** the state of being athletic; fitness and agility. **2** the practice of athletics. **3** devotion (esp. excessive) to athletics. **athletics** *n.* **1** the type of competitive sporting events engaged in by athletes, esp. track and field events. **2** (*N Am.*) sports and games of any kind. **3** the practice of physical exercises by which muscular strength is developed. **athletic support** *n.* a jockstrap. [L *athlēta*, Gr. *athlētēs*, from *athlein*, to contend (*athlon, aethlion*, a prize)]

Atholl brose (athəl brōz´), **Athole brose** *n.* a mixture of whisky and honey, often with oatmeal. [*Atholl* in Scotland, BROSE]

-athon (əthon´) *suf.* denoting an event or contest that continues for a long time, e.g. *talkathon, danceathon.* [from *marathon*]

athwart (əthwawt´) *prep.* **1** from side to side of, across. **2** against, opposing. ~*adv.* **1** transversely, from side to side, crosswise. **2** so as to thwart. [*a-*, on, THWART]

-atic (a´tik, ətik) *suf.* forming adjectives, e.g. *aquatic, fanatic, lunatic.* [F *-atique*, L *-āticus*]

-atile (ətīl) *suf.* forming adjectives chiefly denoting possibility or quality, e.g. *fluviatile, volatile.* [F *-atile*, L *-ātilis*]

atilt (ətilt´) *a., adv.* **1** tilted up. **2** †as if thrusting at an antagonist in a joust. **to run atilt** to attack.

-ation (ā´shən) *suf.* forming abstract nouns from verbs, e.g. *agitation, appreciation, ovation.* [L *-ātio -ōnis*]

-ative (ətiv, ā-) *suf.* forming adjectives, e.g. *demonstrative, representative, talkative.* [L *-ātīvus, -a, -um*]

Atlantean (ətlan´tiən) *a.* **1** of or like the Titan Atlas; very strong. **2** of or relating to the legendary continent or civilization of Atlantis.

atlantes ATLAS.

Atlantic (ətlan´tik) *a.* **1** of or occurring in or near the Atlantic Ocean. **2** of or relating to the Atlas mountains in N Africa. **the Atlantic** the Atlantic Ocean. **Atlantic Charter** *n.* a joint declaration by Great Britain and the US in 1941 laying down 'certain principles as a basis for a better future for the world'. **Atlanticism** (-sizm) *n.* belief in close cooperation and mutual support between the countries of W Europe and N America. **Atlanticist** *a., n.* **Atlantic Ocean** *n.* the ocean between Europe and Africa in the east and America in the west. **Atlantic Standard Time, Atlantic Time** *n.* the standard time, four hours behind GMT, in a time zone that includes the eastern parts of Canada. [*Atlantis*, the legendary island in the West whose site is occupied by the Atlantic Ocean]

atlas (at´ləs) *n.* (*pl.* **atlases**) **1** a book containing a collection of maps. **2** a book containing a collection of charts or plates. **3** (*Anat.*) the first cervical vertebra, in humans, that supports the skull. **4** (*Archit.*) (*pl.* **atlantes**) a figure of a man carved in stone and used as a column supporting an entablature. **5** a large size of drawing paper, 26 x 17 in. (65 x 42 cm). [Gr. *Atlas*

-*antos*, a Titan fabled to hold up the pillars of the universe]

ATM *abbr.* automated teller machine.

atm. *abbr.* 1 atmosphere. 2 atmospheric.

atman (aht´mən) *n.* in Hinduism, the innermost self, the soul or the Universal Soul, the supreme spiritual principle. [Sansk. *ātman*, breath, soul]

atmo- (at´mō) *comb. form* of or relating to vapour or to the atmosphere. [Gr. *atmos*, vapour]

atmolysis (atmol´əsis) *n.* (*pl.* **atmolyses** (-sēz)) the separation of gases in combination based on their different rates of diffusion through a porous substance.

atmometer (atmom´itə) *n.* an instrument for measuring the moisture exhaled in a given time from any humid surface. **atmometry** *n.*

atmosphere (at´məsfiə) *n.* 1 the gaseous envelope surrounding any of the celestial bodies, esp. that surrounding the earth. 2 the air in any given place. 3 mental or moral environment. 4 a prevailing mood or tone felt to be present in a place, work of art etc. 5 (*coll.*) a feeling of tension between people. 6 a unit of pressure corresponding to the average pressure of the earth's atmosphere at sea level and equal to a pressure of about 15 lb. per square inch (101,325 N/m^2). 7 a gaseous envelope surrounding any substance. **atmospheric** (-fer´-), **atmospherical** *a.* 1 of or relating to the atmosphere. 2 existing in the atmosphere, or produced by the atmosphere. 3 having or creating a particular atmosphere. **atmospherically** *adv.* **atmospheric pressure** *n.* the pressure exerted by the atmosphere on the surface of the earth. **atmospherics** *n.pl.* 1 (audible interference in communications produced by) electromagnetic waves generated by an electric discharge between two clouds or from a cloud to earth. 2 effects deliberately intended to create a particular mood. 3 such a deliberately created atmosphere. [ATMO-, Gr. *sphaira*, a ball]

at. no. *abbr.* atomic number.

atoll (at´ol) *n.* a coral island, consisting of an annular reef surrounding a lagoon. [Maldive *atollon*, atoll]

atom (at´əm) *n.* 1 the smallest particle taking part in chemical action, the smallest particle of matter possessing the properties of an element. 2 such a particle as a source of nuclear energy. 3 the smallest conceivable portion of anything. 4 a body or particle of matter originally thought to be incapable of further division. **atom bomb** *n.* a bomb in which the explosion is due to atomic energy released when atoms of uranium, plutonium etc. undergo nuclear fission. **atomic** (ətom´-) *a.* 1 of or relating to an atom or atoms. 2 of, relating to or using atomic energy or atom bombs. 3 extremely small. **atomically** *adv.* **atomic bomb** *n.* ATOM BOMB (under ATOM). **atomic clock** *n.* an electronic apparatus which makes use of molecular or atomic resonances to generate precise intervals of time. **atomic energy** *n.* the energy liberated when the nucleus of an atom undergoes change, e.g. by fission of uranium or by fusion of hydrogen, nuclear energy. **atomicity** (-is´-) *n.* 1 the number of atoms in a molecule of an element or of a compound. 2 the fact of being made up of atoms. 3 valency. **atomic mass** *n.* the mass of an atom measured in atomic mass units. **atomic mass unit** *n.* a unit of mass used to express atomic and molecular weight that is equal to one twelfth of the mass of an atom of carbon-12. **atomic number** *n.* the number of protons in the nucleus of an atom (the atomic number determines the chemical properties of an atom). **atomic physics** *n.* the branch of physics that is concerned with atomic structure and the nature and properties of subatomic particles. **atomic pile** *n.* a nuclear reactor. **atomic power** *n.* nuclear power. **atomic spectrum** *n.* the emission or absorption spectrum characteristic of an element that arises from electron transitions within the atom. **atomic structure** *n.* the structure of the atom conceived as a central positively charged nucleus, made up of protons and neutrons, surrounded by negatively charged orbiting electrons. **atomic theory** *n.* 1 the theory that atoms are composed of subatomic particles. 2 the theory that all matter is made up of atoms, that all atoms of the same element are alike and that they combine with atoms of other elements to form compounds in a definite proportion. **atomic volume** *n.* the volume occupied by the mass of an element equal to its atomic weight. **atomic warfare** *n.* warfare with nuclear weapons. **atomic weight** *n.* RELATIVE ATOMIC MASS (under RELATIVE). **atomism** *n.* 1 (*Philos.*) the doctrine that the ultimate constituents of the universe are tiny, individual particles. 2 (*Psych.*) the theory that experiences and mental states are composed of elementary units. 3 atomic theory. **atomist** *n.* **atomistic** (-mis´tik) *a.* **atomize, atomise** *v.t.* 1 to reduce to atoms. 2 to reduce to fine particles or to a spray. **atomization** (-zā´shən) *n.* **atomizer** *n.* an instrument for reducing a liquid, such as a disinfectant or perfume, into spray. **atom smasher** *n.* (*coll.*) an accelerator for increasing the energy of charged particles. [Gr. *atomos*, indivisible]

†**atomy**[1] (at´əmi) *n.* (*pl.* **atomies**) 1 a minute particle, an atom. 2 a diminutive being. [L *atomī*, atoms, construed as if sing.]

†**atomy**[2] (at´əmi) *n.* (*pl.* **atomies**) 1 a skeleton, an anatomical preparation. 2 an emaciated person, a living skeleton. [*anatomy*, first syl. mistaken for article *an*]

atonable ATONE.

atonal (ātō´nəl) *a.* (*Mus.*) without a fixed key. **atonality** (-nal´-) *n.* [ATONIC]

atone (ətōn´) *v.i.* to make expiation or satisfaction for some crime, sin or fault. ~†*v.t.* 1 to expiate. 2 to make at one, to bring into concord. 3 to conciliate, to appease. **atonable** *a.* able to be expiated. **atonement** *n.* 1 the act of atoning. 2 reparation, expiation, amends. 3 the propitiation of God by the expiation of sin. **Day of Atonement** DAY. **the Atonement** (*Theol.*) the expiation of the sin of humankind by the suffering and death of Christ. **atoningly** *adv.* [AT, ONE]

at-oneness (ətwŭn´nəs) *n.* the condition of being at one, reconcilement, harmony. [AT, ONE, -NESS]

atonic (əton´ik) *a.* 1 without an accent, unaccented. 2 lacking physiological or muscular tone. ~*n.* an unaccented word or syllable. **atony** (at´-) *n.* 1 lack of physiological, esp. muscular, tone. 2 enervation. 3 lack of stress on a syllable or word. [med. L *atonicus*, Gr. *atonos*, without tone (*a*-, not, *tenein*, to stretch)]

atop (ətop´) *adv.* on or at the top. ~*prep.* (*also* **atop of**) on or at the top of.

atopy (at´əpi) *n.* (*pl.* **atopies**) a hereditary tendency to acute allergic reactions. **atopic** (-top´-) *a.* [Gr. *atopia*, strangeness]

-ator (ā´tə) *suf.* forming nouns denoting a person or thing performing an action e.g. *equator*, *agitator*, *commentator*. [L, cp. -OR]

-atory (ətəri, ā´təri) *suf.* forming adjectives meaning related to or involving a verbal action, e.g. *commendatory*. [L *-atorius*, cp. -ORY[1]]

ATP *abbr.* adenosine triphosphate.

atrabilious (atrəbil´iəs), **atrabiliar** (-bil´iə) *a.* 1 melancholic, hypochondriacal. 2 splenetic, bitter-tempered. **atrabiliousness** *n.* [L *ātra bīlis*, black bile]

atrazine (at´rəzīn) *n.* a white crystalline compound widely used as a weedkiller. [*amino triazine*]

atrium (at´riəm, ā´-) *n.* (*pl.* **atria, atriums**) 1 the central court in an ancient Roman house. 2 a central hall rising the whole height of a large building and usu. with a glass roof and galleries on the upper floors. 3 a central hall or glazed court with rooms opening off it. 4 a forecourt or vestibule in front of a church. 5 a body cavity esp. either of the two upper chambers of the heart into which the veins pour the blood. **atrial** *a.* [L]

atrocious (ətrō´shəs) *a.* 1 very bad, execrable. 2 savagely and wantonly cruel, characterized by heinous wickedness. 3 stern, fierce, violent. **atrociously** *adv.* **atrociousness** *n.* **atrocity** (ətros´-) *n.* (*pl.* **atrocities**) 1 an act of extreme cruelty or ruthlessness, esp. against defenceless victims. 2 excessive cruelty or other flagrant wickedness. 3 something that shows execrable taste, workmanship etc. [L *atrox -ōcis* (*āter*, black)]

atrophy (at´rəfi) *n.* (*pl.* **atrophies**) 1 a wasting of the body, or (one of) its organs, through lack of nourishment or disease. 2 mental or spiritual starvation. *~v.t.* (*3rd pers. sing. pres.* **atrophies,** *pres.p.* **atrophying,** *past, p.p.* **atrophied**) to affect with atrophy, to cause to waste away. *~v.i.* to waste away. **atrophied** *a.* [F *atrophie*, L *atrophia*, from Gr., from *atrophos*, ill-fed (*a-*, not, *trephein*, to nourish)]

atropine (at´rəpēn, -pin), **atropin** *n.* a poisonous alkaloid obtained from deadly nightshade, *Atropa belladonna*, used in the treatment of intestinal spasm and to counteract the slowing of the heart. **atropism** *n.* atropine poisoning. [Gr. *atropos*, inflexible, name of one of the Fates]

att. *abbr.* attorney.

attaboy (at´əboi) *int.* (*chiefly N Am., coll.*) used to express encouragement.

attach (ətach´) *v.t.* 1 to fasten on, connect. 2 to affix. 3 to attribute (importance, significance etc.). 4 to include or append (a condition). 5 (*reflex.*) to join, to become a member of, to take part in. 6 to appoint to an organization, military, police etc. unit, temporarily. 7 to lay hold on, arrest, indict, esp. to seize (a person or goods) by a writ of attachment. *~v.i.* 1 to adhere; to be connected. 2 to be inherent in or attributable (to). **attachable** *a.* 1 capable of being attached. 2 liable to attachment. **attached** *a.* 1 joined, fastened. 2 fond of; joined by bonds of love, friendship or sympathy. 3 incident, connected. 4 (*coll.*) married, engaged or in a long-term relationship. 5 (*Zool.*) stationary, as opposed to free. 6 (*Archit.*) joined to a wall; not standing clear. **attachment** *n.* 1 the act of attaching. 2 the means by which anything is attached. 3 a thing that is or can be attached, esp. a device that can be fitted to a machine to perform a special function. 4 fidelity, affection, devotion. 5 a temporary posting or secondment. 6 (*Law*) **a** apprehension, esp. for contempt of court. **b** the seizure of goods or estate to secure a debt or demand. **c** the writ or precept by which such apprehension or seizure is effected. [OF *atachier* (F *attacher*), from *a*, to, Genevan F *tache* (cp. Port. *tacha*, nail, Eng. *tack*, LG *takk*)]

attaché (ətash´ā) *n.* 1 a junior member of an ambassador's staff. 2 a specialist attached to an ambassador's staff. 3 (*N Am.*) an attaché case. **attaché case** *n.* a flat rectangular case for carrying papers etc. [F]

attack (ətak´) *v.t.* 1 to launch a physical or armed assault on. 2 to subject to hostile words or writings; to criticize or abuse strongly. 3 to begin (a piece of work) with determination. 4 (of a physical agent, disease etc.) to exert a destructive or harmful influence on. 5 to take the initiative in trying to score points, goals etc. against. *~v.i.* 1 to make an attack. 2 to take offensive action in a game or sport. *~n.* 1 the act of attacking; an onset, an assault. 2 violent abuse or injury. 3 a sudden fit of illness, panic etc. 4 the beginning of active work on something. 5 vigour and decisiveness in undertaking something. 6 a (crisp and decisive) manner of beginning a musical piece or passage. 7 an offensive or scoring move in a game or sport. 8 the players in a team who attack. **attackable** *a.* [F *attaquer*, It. *attaccare*, to join (battle) (see ATTACH)]

attain (ətān´) *v.i.* to arrive at some object. *~v.t.* 1 to reach, gain; to arrive at. 2 to accomplish. **attainable** *a.* **attainability** (-bil´-) *n.* **attainableness** *n.* **attainment** *n.* 1 the act of attaining. 2 something which is attained. 3 a personal achievement or accomplishment. [OF *ateign-*, pres. stem of *ataindre*, to reach, attain (L *ad-*, to, *tangere*, to touch)]

attainder (ətān´də) *n.* 1 (*Hist.*) the forfeiture of civil rights as the legal consequence of a sentence of death or outlawry for treason or felony; the act or process of attainting a criminal. 2 †taint of dishonour. [OF *ataindre*, to ATTAIN (meaning modified by confusion with *taindre*, to dye, stain)]

attaint (ətānt´) *v.t.* 1 (*Hist.*) to condemn or subject to attainder. 2 to infect. 3 to taint, stain. *~n.* 1 attainder. 2 †a stain, blot. [OF *ataint*, p.p. of *ataindre*, see ATTAIN]

attar (at´ə), **otto** (ot´ō) *n.* a fragrant essence, or essential oil, esp. of roses. [Pers. *'atar*, essence, Arab. *'uṭūr*, aroma]

attempt (ətempt´, ətemt´) *v.t.* 1 to try, endeavour (to do, achieve, effect etc.). 2 to make an effort to achieve. 3 to set out to climb (a mountain). 4 †to try to seduce. 5 †to attack. *~n.* 1 an endeavour, effort, undertaking. 2 something produced or achieved as a result of trying; something imperfect as contrasted with something perfect. 3 an assault (on life, honour etc.). **†to attempt the life of** to try to kill. **attemptable** *a.* **attemptability** (-bil´-) *n.* [OF *atempter*, to undertake, L *attemptāre*, *attentāre* (*ad-*, to, *tentāre*, strive after)]

attend (ətend´) *v.t.* 1 to be present at. 2 to go regularly to (church, a school etc.). 3 to accompany, escort. 4 to look after, wait upon. 5 (*chiefly pass.*) to result from. 6 †to apply the mind to. 7 †to wait for, to expect. *~v.i.* 1 to pay attention, apply the mind (to). 2 to apply one's efforts or energies (to). 3 to be present. 4 to be in attendance. 5 to wait upon or for a person. **attendance** *n.* 1 the act of attending. 2 presence. 3 the (number of) persons attending. 4 †a train of servants. **in attendance** waiting, attendant (on). **attendance allowance** *n.* a state benefit in the UK paid to people, esp. the disabled, who need frequent or continual care and supervision. **attendance centre** *n.* (in the UK) a place which young offenders must attend regularly as a minor penalty. **attendant** *a.* 1 following as a consequence. 2 accompanying, waiting (on), ministering. *~n.* 1 a person who attends or accompanies another; a servant. 2 a person employed to assist, guide etc. the general public. 3 (*formal*) an attender. 4 a logical or natural consequence. **attendee** (atendē´) *n.* an attender at an event. **attender** *n.* 1 a person who is present at an event. 2 a person who pays attention. [OF *atendre*, to wait, L *attendere* (*ad-*, to, *tendere*, to stretch)]

attention (əten´shən) *n.* 1 the act or state of directing the mind to, or concentrating the mind on, some object. 2 the mental faculty of attending. 3 consideration, notice (*brought to my attention*). 4 watchful care. 5 (*usu. pl.*) an act of courtesy or kindness; an act indicating love or the desire to woo. 6 (*Mil.*) a position in which the body is held rigidly erect with the feet together and hands by the sides. *~int.* 1 (*Mil.*) a command to stand at attention. 2 used as a means of attracting or commanding attention, usu. so that an announcement can be made. **attentional** *a.* relating to attention or concentration. **attention span** *n.* the length of time that a person is able or willing to direct their attention to a particular object. **attention value** *n.* the degree to which an advertisement has been noticed or remembered by readers or viewers. [see ATTEND]

attentive (əten´tiv) *a.* 1 paying attention; listening carefully. 2 polite, courteous. 3 heedful, regardful. **attentively** *adv.* **attentiveness** *n.*

attenuate[1] (əten´ūāt) *v.t.* **1** to make thin or slender. **2** to reduce the strength, intensity or force of, to weaken. **3** to dilute, diminish the density of. **4** to reduce the amplitude of (an electric current). *~v.i.* to become thin or weak. **attenuated** *a.* **attenuation** (-ā´shən) *n.* **1** the act of attenuating. **2** diminution of thickness, density, strength or force. **3** emaciation. **4** reduction in strength of radiation as it passes through the medium between the source and destination. **attenuator** *n.* a circuit to provide attenuation of the current, voltage or power of a signal. [L *attenuātus*, p.p. of *attenuāre* (*ad-*, to, *tenuis*, thin)]

attenuate[2] (əten´ūət) *a.* **1** slender. **2** tapering. **3** thin in consistency.

attest (ətest´) *v.t.* **1** to vouch for, to certify. **2** to give evidence or proof of. **3** to testify, bear witness that. **4** (*Hist.*) to recruit for the military by putting on oath to serve if called upon. *~v.i.* **1** to bear witness. **2** (*Hist.*) to declare one's readiness to serve in the military if called upon. **attestation** (atestā´shən) *n.* **1** the act of attesting. **2** evidence, proof. **3** formal confirmation. **4** formal verification. **5** the administration of an oath, esp. of the oath of allegiance. **attested** *a.* certified as being free from disease, esp. from the tuberculosis bacillus. **attestor** *n.* a person who attests or vouches for. [F *attester*, L *attestārī* (*ad-*, to, *testis*, a witness)]

Attic (at´ik) *a.* **1** of or belonging to Attica, its capital, Athens, or the Greek dialect spoken there. **2** classical, refined. *~n.* the Attic dialect, esp. of ancient Greek. **Atticism** (-sizm) *n.* **1** idiom and style characteristic of Attic Greek. **2** concise and elegant expression. **Atticize** (-sīz), **Atticise** *v.i.* **1** to conform to the idiom of Attica or Athens, or to Greek habits or modes of thought. **2** to side with the Athenians. **Attic order** *n.* an architectural order of small square pillars at the uppermost part of a building. **Attic salt, Attic wit** *n.* refined, delicate wit, for which the Athenians were famous. [L *Atticus*, Gr. *Attikos*]

attic (at´ik) *n.* **1** the top storey of a house. **2** a room in this storey. **3** a low storey placed above an entablature or cornice. [F *attique*, as ATTIC]

attire (ətīə´) *v.t.* **1** to dress, esp. in fine or formal clothing. **2** to array, adorn. *~n.* dress, clothes. **attired** *a.* dressed, decked, arrayed. **attiring** *n.* dress, apparel, trappings. [OF *atirer* (*à*, to, *tire*, a row) (see TIER)]

attitude (at´itūd) *n.* **1** a mental position or way of thinking with respect to someone or something. **2** behaviour indicating opinion and sentiment. **3** bearing or gesture, expressing action or emotion. **4** a posture or position taken by a person, animal or object. **5** the posture in which a figure is represented in painting or sculpture. **6** the position of an aircraft or spacecraft in relation to a plane of reference. **7** (*sl.*) a provocatively insolent, truculent or non-cooperative manner or mode of behaviour. **8** (*sl.*) very self-confident style, swagger. **9** a position in ballet in which the body is held upright with one leg raised and bent behind. **to strike an attitude** to assume an exaggerated or theatrical posture. **attitude of mind** *n.* habitual mode of thinking and feeling. **attitudinize** (-tū´din-), **attitudinise** *v.i.* **1** to practise or assume attitudes; to pose. **2** to behave or act affectedly. [F, from It. *attitudine*, L *aptitūdinem* (*aptus*, fitted)]

attn. *abbr.* attention, for the attention of.

atto- (at´ō) *comb. form* (*Math.*) denoting a factor of 10^{-18}. [Dan. or Norw. *atten*, eighteen]

attorn (ətœn´) *v.t.* **1** to acknowledge (a new owner) as one's landlord. **2** to assign, transfer. *~v.i.* to transfer service or fealty to a new lord. [OF *atorner* (*à*, to, *tourner*, L *tornāre*, to turn)]

attorney (ətœ´ni) *n.* (*pl.* **attorneys**) **1** a legally authorized agent or deputy. **2** (*N Am.*) a lawyer, a barrister, a solicitor, esp. one qualified to act for another in legal proceedings. **Attorney-General** *n.* (*pl.* **Attorneys-General, Attorney-Generals**) the chief law officer in England, the US and other countries, and legal adviser to the government. **Attorney-Generalship** *n.* the office or dignity of the Attorney-General. **attorneyship** *n.* **1** the office of an attorney. **2** agency, proxy. [OF *atorné*, (fem.) *atornée*, p.p. of *atorner*, assign]

attract (ətrakt´) *v.t.* **1** to draw to oneself or itself or cause to approach (physically or in an immaterial sense). **2** to cause to desire; to arouse interest or fascination in. **3** (of a magnet, gravity) to exert an influence on that causes a thing to approach. *~v.i.* to exert the power of attraction, to be attractive. **attractable** *a.* that may be attracted. **attractability** (-bil´-) *n.* capability of being attracted. **attractant** *a.* that attracts. *~n.* a substance that attracts (esp. insects). **attraction** *n.* **1** the action or power of attracting. **2** a person, thing, quality or characteristic that attracts. **3** a force causing two objects, molecules etc. to be drawn together or to resist separation. **4** (*Gram.*) an influence exerted by one linguistic element which causes a change in another, esp. to an incorrect form. **attractive** *a.* **1** pleasing to the senses, appealing, alluring. **2** that appears advantageous, profitable etc. **3** that has the ability to pull something towards itself. **attractively** *adv.* **attractiveness** *n.* **attractor** *n.* [L *attractus*, p.p. of *attrahere* (*ad-*, to, *trahere*, to draw)]

attrib. *abbr.* **1** attribute, attributed (to). **2** attributive, attributively.

attribute[1] (at´ribūt) *n.* **1** a quality ascribed or imputed to any person or thing, as an essential characteristic. **2** a characteristic, a feature. **3** a symbolic or other object recognized as appropriate to a person, office, rank etc. **4** an attributive word. **5** (*Logic*) that which may be predicated of any subject. [L *attribūtus -um*, p.p. of *attribuere*, to assign (*ad-*, to, *tribuere*, to give)]

attribute[2] (ətrib´ūt) *v.t.* (*with to*) **1** to regard as caused by. **2** to regard as having been produced or created by. **3** to regard as possessing. **4** to regard as characteristic of. **attributable** *a.* **attribution** (atribū´shən) *n.* **1** the act of attributing. **2** something which is ascribed. **attributive** (ətrib´-) *a.* **1** relating to an attribute. **2** (*Gram.*) (of an adjective) expressing an attribute of a noun and usu. immediately preceding it. **3** (*Logic*) assigning an attribute to a subject. *~n.* a word denoting an attribute, now generally restricted to adjectives. **attributively** *adv.*

attrit (ətrit´) *v.t.* (*pres.p.* **attritting,** *past, p.p.* **attritted**) (*N Am., coll.*) **1** to wear down (an enemy, opponent) by constant (small-scale) action. **2** to kill. [back-formation from ATTRITION]

attrition (ətrish´ən) *n.* **1** the act or process of wearing away, esp. by friction. **2** abrasion. **3** a constant wearing down or weakening, as of an adversary. **4** (*esp. N Am., Austral.*) reduction in the size of the workforce by natural wastage. **5** (*Theol.*) sorrow for sin on account of the punishment due to it. [ME from late L *attritio*, from *atterere* (*ad-*, to, *terere*, to rub)]

attune (ətūn´) *v.t.* **1** to accustom, acclimatize. **2** to bring (an instrument) to the right pitch; to put (instruments) in tune with one another. **3** (*poet.*) to make tuneful. *~n.* **1** tuneful accord. **2** harmony. [*at-*, AD-, TUNE]

ATV *abbr.* all-terrain vehicle.

at. wt. *abbr.* atomic weight.

atypical (ātip´ikəl) *a.* not typical, not conforming to type. **atypically** *adv.* [A-[3], TYPICAL]

AU *abbr.* **1** Ångström unit. **2** astronomical unit.

Au *chem. symbol* gold. [L *aurum*]

aubade (ōbahd´) *n.* **1** a poem or musical piece announcing or greeting dawn. **2** music performed at daybreak. [F, from Sp. *albada* (*alba*, dawn)]

auberge (ōbœzh´) *n.* an inn in France. **aubergiste** (-zhēst´) *n.* a keeper of an auberge, an inn-keeper. [F *auberge*, OF *alberge*, *helberge*, OHG *heri-berga*, army shelter (cp. G *Herberge*, inn, and Eng. HARBOUR)]

aubergine (ō´bəzhēn) *n.* **1** the eggplant, *Solanum melongena.* **2** its ovoid, characteristically dark purple fruit used as a vegetable and in stews. **3** a dark purple colour. [F, dim. of *auberge*, *alberge*, Sp. *alberchigo*, apricot]

aubrietia (awbrē´shə) *n.* a plant of a genus, *Aubretia*, of dwarf, perennial, spring-flowering rock plants of the family Cruciferae. [Claude *Aubriet*, 1668–1743, French botanist]

auburn (aw´bən) *a.* **1** reddish-brown. **2** †yellowish. ~*n.* a reddish-brown colour. [OF *auborne*, L *alburnus*, whitish (*albus*, white)]

AUC *abbr.* (in Roman dates) from the foundation of the city. [L *ab urbe condita*]

au courant (ō koorã´) *a.* fully informed, up to date with the situation. [F]

auction (awk´shən) *n.* **1** a public sale of goods, usu. one in which each bidder offers a higher price than the preceding. **2** auction bridge; the sequence of bids made in a game of auction bridge. ~*v.t.* to sell by auction. **auction bridge** *n.* a version of bridge in which the players bid for the advantage of choosing trump suit. **auctioneer** (-niə´) *n.* a person who sells goods by auction, or conducts auctions. ~*v.t.*, *v.i.* to sell by auction. [L *auctio -ōnem*, an increase, auction (*auctus*, p.p. of *augēre*, to increase)]

auctorial (awktaw´riəl) *a.* of or relating to an author or the occupation of an author. [L *auctor*, -IAL]

audacious (awdā´shəs) *a.* **1** bold, daring, spirited. **2** impudent, shameless. **audaciously** *adv.* boldly, impudently. **audaciousness** *n.* **audacity** (-das´-) *n.* **1** courage, daring, gallantry. **2** effrontery. [L *audax -acis* (*audēre*, to dare)]

☒ **audiance** common misspelling of AUDIENCE.

audible (aw´dibəl) *a.* **1** capable of being heard. **2** clear or loud enough to be heard. **audibility** (-bil´-) *n.* **audibleness** *n.* **audibly** *adv.* [med. L *audibilis* (*audīre*, to hear)]

audience (aw´diəns) *n.* **1** an assembly of hearers or spectators at a meeting, play, concert etc. **2** the people who read a book. **3** the people who regularly watch or listen to a particular television or radio programme, performer etc. **4** a formal interview granted by a superior to an inferior. **5** †the act of hearing, attention. [F *audience*, L *audientia* (*audiens -ntem*, pres.p. of *audīre*)]

audile (aw´dīl) *a.* **1** of or relating to sound or hearing. **2** characterized by awareness and retention of sounds. ~*n.* a person whose mind or memory responds to or retains sounds rather than visual images. [*aud*itory, -ILE]

audio (aw´diō) *a.* **1** of or relating to sound or its reproduction, transmission or broadcasting. **2** of, relating to or using audio frequencies. ~*n.* the (electronic) reproduction and transmission of sound. **Audio-Animatronics®** *n.* ANIMATRONICS. **audio cassette** *n.* a cassette of audiotape. **audio conference** *n.* a conference conducted using audio telecommunications. **audio frequency** *n.* a frequency in the range corresponding to that of audible sound waves. **audiotape** *n.* **1** magnetic tape for recording and reproducing sound. **2** a length or cassette of this tape. **3** a recording made on this tape. ~*v.t.* to make a recording on audiotape of. **audiotypist** *n.* a typist trained to type directly from material on a dictating machine. **audiotyping** *n.* [L *audīre*, to hear]

audio- (aw´diō) *comb. form* **1** of or relating to hearing. **2** of or relating to sound or sound reproduction.

audiology (awdiol´əji) *n.* the science of hearing. **audiological** (-loj´-) *a.* **audiologist** *n.*

audiometer (awdiom´itə) *n.* an application of the telephone for testing the sense of hearing. **audiometric** (-met´-) *a.* **audiometry** (-tri) *n.*

audiophile (aw´diōfīl) *n.* a person with an enthusiastic interest in high-fidelity sound reproduction.

audiovisual (awdiōvizh´uəl) *a.* (esp. of teaching methods or aids) directed at or involving hearing and sight.

audiphone (aw´difōn) *n.* an instrument which, when pressed against the teeth, enables people with some types of deafness to hear by conveying sound waves to the auditory nerves. [L *audīre*, to hear, Gr. *phōnē*, sound]

audit (aw´dit) *n.* **1** an official examination of accounts. **2** any formal review or examination. **3** (*N Am.*) an audited account. **4** †a hearing, an audience. ~*v.t.* **1** to examine officially and pronounce as to the accuracy of (accounts). **2** (*N Am.*) to attend (a class) without working for credits or intending to sit an examination. [L *audītus*, hearing (*audīre*, to hear)]

audition (awdish´ən) *n.* **1** a trial performance by a singer, musician, actor etc. applying for a position or role. **2** (*formal*) the act or faculty of hearing. ~*v.t.* to test by an audition. ~*v.i.* to give a trial performance. **auditive** (aw´-) *a.* of or relating to hearing. [L *auditio -ionis*, hearing, from *audīre*, to hear]

auditor (aw´ditə) *n.* **1** a person appointed to audit accounts. **2** a hearer, a member of an audience. **3** (*N Am.*) a person who audits a class. **auditorial** (-taw´-) *a.* **1** auditory. **2** of or relating to an audit of accounts. **auditorially** *adv.* **auditorship** *n.* [OF *auditeur*, from L *auditor*, hearer]

auditorium (awditaw´riəm) *n.* (*pl.* **auditoriums**, **auditoria** (-riə)) **1** the part of a building occupied by the audience. **2** (*N Am.*) a building with a large hall for public meetings, sports events etc. **3** (*N Am.*) a large room or hall, e.g. in a school. [L *auditorium*, from *auditorius*, concerning hearing]

auditory (aw´ditəri) *a.* of or relating to the organs or sense of hearing, perceived by the ear. ~*n.* **1** †an audience, people assembled to hear. **2** †a place for hearing, an auditorium. **auditory meatus** *n.* the passage of the ear. [L *auditorius*]

AUEW *abbr.* Amalgamated Union of Engineering Workers.

au fait (ō fā´) *a.* **1** having up-to-date knowledge, fully informed. **2** familiar, well acquainted (with). [F, to the point]

au fond (ō fõ´) *adv.* basically. [F, at the bottom]

auf Wiedersehen (owf vē´dəzān) *int.* farewell, goodbye. [G]

Aug. *abbr.* August.

Augean (awjē´ən) *a.* **1** of or relating to Augeas (mythical king of Elis, whose stable, containing 3,000 oxen, had not been cleaned for 30 years, till Hercules, by turning the river Alpheus through it, cleaned it in a day). **2** filthy. [L *Augeas*, Gr. *Augeias*]

auger (aw´gə) *n.* **1** a carpenter's tool, somewhat resembling a very large gimlet, worked with both hands, for boring holes in wood. **2** a similar instrument of larger size, for boring into soil or rock. [OE *nafugār* (*nafu*, the nave of a wheel, *gār*, a borer)]

†**aught**[1] (awt), **ought** *n.* **1** anything whatever. **2** a whit, a jot or tittle. ~*adv.* in any respect. [OE *āwiht* (*a*, one, *wiht*, a creature)]

aught[2] OUGHT[2].

augite (aw´gīt) *n.* a greenish, brownish-black or black variety of aluminous pyroxene found in igneous rocks. **augitic** (-git´-) *a.* [L, from Gr. *augitēs*, prob. a turquoise (*augē*, lustre)]

augment[1] (awgment´) *v.t.* **1** to increase, to make larger or greater in number, degree, intensity etc.; to extend, to enlarge. **2** (*Mus.*) to increase (an interval) by a semitone. **3** to prefix a grammatical augment to. ~*v.i.* to increase, to become greater in size, number, degree etc. **augmentation** (-tā´shən) *n.* **1** the act of augmenting. **2** the state of being augmented. **3** the thing added. **4** increase, addition. **5** the reproduction of a melody or passage in notes of greater length than those in which it was first treated. **augmentative** (-men´-) *a.* **1** having the power or quality of augmenting. **2** (of an affix) increasing the force of the original word. **3** (of a word) formed by an augmentative affix. ~*n.* an augmentative element or word. [F *augmenter*, L *augmentum*, an increase (*augēre*, to increase)]

augment[2] (awg´mənt) *n.* a grammatical prefix in the form of a vowel used in the older Indo-European languages to denote past time.

au gratin (ō grat´ī) *a.* (of a dish) with a light crust, usu. made by browning breadcrumbs and cheese. [F, from *au*, masc. form of À LA, GRATIN]

augur (aw´gə) *v.t.* **1** to foretell from signs or omens. **2** to betoken, portend. ~*v.i.* **1** to make predictions of future events from signs or omens. **2** to be a sign or foreboding. ~*n.* **1** a religious official among the Romans who professed to foretell future events from omens derived chiefly from the actions of birds, inspection of the entrails of slaughtered victims etc. **2** a soothsayer, a diviner. **augural** (-gū-) *a.* of or relating to an augur or to augury. **augurship** *n.* **augury** (-gū-) *n.* (*pl.* **auguries**) **1** the art or practice of the augur; divination. **2** an omen, prognostication, foreboding. [L (prob. *avis*, a bird, *-gur*, telling, connected with *garrīre*, to talk, *garrulus*, talkative; Sansk. *gar*, to shout)]

August (aw´gəst) *n.* the eighth month of the year, named in honour of Augustus Caesar.

august[1] (awgŭst´) *a.* **1** majestic, stately, inspiring reverence and admiration. **2** dignified, worshipful. **augustly** *adv.* **augustness** *n.* [L *augustus*, honoured, venerable]

august[2] AUGUSTE.

Augustan (awgŭs´tən) *a.* **1** of or belonging to Augustus Caesar (63 BC–AD 14), or his age in which Latin literature reached its highest development. **2** classical, refined, distinguished by correct literary taste. **3** of or relating to a period in the literature of any language, e.g. the eighteenth century in English literature, marked by a striving for classical refinement. ~*n.* a writer of the Augustan period of any literature.

auguste (owgoost´), **august** *n.* a type of circus clown who plays the role of the clumsy bungler. [G]

Augustine (awgŭs´tin, aw´gəstin) *n.* an Augustinian friar. **Augustinian** (-tin´-) *a.* **1** of or relating to St Augustine (354–430), Bishop of Hippo (396–430), or to his doctrine of grace and predestination. **2** belonging or relating to a religious order whose rule derives from the writings of St Augustine. ~*n.* **1** an adherent of the doctrines of St Augustine. **2** a member of an Augustinian order. [F *Augustin*, L *Augustīnus* (see also AUSTIN)]

auk (awk) *n.* a northern seabird of the family Alcidae, with black and white plumage, heavy body and short wings, esp. the great auk (now extinct), the little auk and the razorbill. **auklet** *n.* any of various small auks, esp. as found in the N Pacific. [Swed. *alka*, a puffin]

auld (awld) *a.* (*Sc., North.*) old. **auld lang syne** *n.* long ago, the (good) times long gone by. **Auld Reekie** *n.* Edinburgh.

aulic (aw´lik) *a.* **1** of or relating to a royal court. **2** courtly. **Aulic Council** *n.* the personal council of the sovereign in the Holy Roman Empire, functioning mainly as a judicial body. [F *aulique*, L *aulicus*, Gr. *aulikos* (*aulē*, a court)]

aumbry (awm´bri), **ambry** (am´-) *n.* (*pl.* **aumbries, ambries**) **1** a niche or cupboard in a church for books and sacred vessels. **2** †a cupboard, a locker, a chest. [OF *armarie*, late L *armāria*, chest or cupboard, L *armārium* (*arma*, arms, tools, gear)]

au naturel (ō natūrel´) *a., adv.* **1** in the natural state. **2** uncooked or plainly cooked. **3** (*coll., euphem.*) naked.

aunt (ahnt) *n.* **1** the sister of one's father or mother. **2** one's uncle's wife. **3** (*coll.*) a woman friend of a child. **my sainted aunt** (*coll.*) used to express surprise, disbelief etc. **aunthood** *n.* **auntie, aunty** *n.* (*pl.* **aunties**) **1** a familiar form of AUNT. **2** a familiar form of address by children to a woman friend. **3** (*coll.*) (**Auntie**) a nickname for the BBC. **Aunt Sally** *n.* **1** a game in which a figure, often with a pipe in its mouth, is set up, and the players endeavour to knock the figure down or break the pipe by throwing sticks or balls at it. **2** an object of ridicule. **auntship** *n.* [OF *aunte*, L *amita*; till 17th cent. *naunt* is common (*my naunt for mine aunt*; cp. F *tante*, prob. *ta ante*)]

au pair (ō peə´) *n.* a person, esp. a girl, from a foreign country who performs domestic tasks in exchange for board and lodging. ~*v.i.* to work as an au pair. [F, on equal terms]

aura (aw´rə) *n.* (*pl.* **auras, aurae** (-rē)) **1** a distinctive atmosphere or quality. **2** a subtle emanation from any body, esp. a mystic light produced by and surrounding the body of a living creature which is said to be visible to people of supernormal sensitivity. **3** a sensation (as of a current of cold air rising to the head) that precedes an attack in epilepsy, hysteria etc. **aural**[1] *a.* of or relating to an aura. [L, from Gr. *aura*, breath, breeze]

aural[1] AURA.

aural[2] (aw´rəl) *a.* **1** of or relating to the ear. **2** received by the ear. **aurally** *adv.* **auriform** (-fawm) *a.* having the form of an ear. **aurist** *n.* a specialist in ear diseases. [L *auris*, the ear]

Usage note See note under ORAL.

aureate (aw´riət) *a.* **1** golden, gold-coloured. **2** brilliant, splendid. **3** (of language or literary style) over-elaborate and embellished. [late L *aureātus*, *aureus*, golden]

aureole (aw´riōl), **aureola** (-rē´ələ) *n.* **1** the gold disc surrounding the head in early pictures of religious figures, and denoting glory, a nimbus. **2** a luminous envelope surrounding the body, a vesica piscis. **3** a glorifying halo, glory. **4** the halo round the moon in total eclipses of the sun, a corona. **5** a halo of radiating light round the sun or moon. [L *aureola*, golden, fem. of *aureolus*, from *aurum*, gold (*aureola corona*, golden crown)]

au revoir (ō rəvwah´) *int.* farewell, goodbye. [F]

auric (aw´rik) *a.* of or relating to gold, applied to compounds in which gold is trivalent. **aurous** *a.* of or relating to gold, applied to compounds in which gold is univalent. [L *aurum*, gold]

auricle (aw´rikəl) *n.* **1** an atrium of the heart. **2** an earlike sac on the surface of each atrium of the heart. **3** the external ear, that part which projects from the head. **4** any process shaped like the lobe of the ear. **auricled** *a.* having an auricle or auricles. [L *auricula*, external ear, dim. of *auris*, ear]

auricula (awrik´ūlə) *n.* a garden flower, *Primula auricula*, sometimes called bear's ear, from the shape of its leaves. [AURICLE]

auricular (awrik´ūlə) *a.* **1** of, relating to, using or known by the sense of hearing. **2** shaped like an auricle. **3** of or relating to an auricle of the heart. ~*n.* **1** an auricular organ. **2** a tuft of feathers covering the auditory orifice in birds. **auriculate** (-lət) *a.* having ears, or appendages resembling ears. [late L *auriculāris*, cp. AURICLE]

auriferous (awrif´ərəs) *a.* yielding or producing gold. [L *aurifer* (*aurum*, gold, *-fer*, producing)]

auriform AURAL[2].

Aurignacian (awrignā´shən) *a.* of or relating to the period of Upper Palaeolithic culture typified by human remains and implements etc. of stone, horn and bone found in the cave of Aurignac, Haute-Garonne. [F *Aurignacien*, from *Aurignac*, SW France]

aurist AURAL².

aurochs (aw´roks) *n.* (*pl.* **aurochs**) the extinct wild ox, *Bos primigenius.* [G *Aurochs* (*Auerochs*), OHG *ur-ohso* (cp. OE *ūr*), whence L *ūrus*]

aurora (awraw´rə) *n.* (*pl.* **auroras, aurorae** (-rē)) **1** a peculiar illumination of the night sky common within the polar circles, consisting of streams of light ascending towards the zenith. **2** (*poet.*) morning twilight, dawn. **aurora australis** (ostrah´lis) *n.* the aurora seen in the southern hemisphere. **aurora borealis** (bawriah´lis) *n.* the aurora seen in the northern hemisphere. **auroral** *a.* **1** of or relating to an aurora. **2** of or relating to the dawn or to the rise or beginning of anything. **3** rosy, roseate. [L, the goddess of the dawn]

aurous AURIC.

AUS *abbr.* Australia (IVR).

auscultation (awskəltā´shən) *n.* **1** listening with the ear or stethoscope to the sounds made by the internal organs, to judge their condition. **2** the act of listening. **auscultate** (aws´-) *v.t.* to examine by auscultation. **auscultator** (aws´-) *n.* **auscultatory** (-kŭl´-) *a.* [L *auscultātiō -nem*, from *auscultāre*, to listen (*aus auris*, the ear)]

Auslese (ows´lāzə) *n.* a usu. sweetish white wine from Germany or Austria made from selected ripe grapes. [G, choice, selection]

auspex (aws´peks) *n.* in ancient Rome, a person who took the auspices; an augur. [L (*avis*, bird, *spex*, an observer, from *specere*, to observe)]

†**auspicate** (aws´pikāt) *v.t.* to inaugurate, initiate. [L *auspicātus*, p.p. of *auspicāre*, to take omens]

auspice (aw´spis) *n.* **1** (*usu. pl.*) patronage, protection. **2** (*often pl.*) a (favourable) portent, sign or omen. **3** an omen drawn from the actions of birds. **under the auspices of** under the leadership, encouragement or patronage of. **auspicious** (-spish´-) *a.* **1** having favourable omens, auguring good fortune. **2** conducive to prosperity or success. **auspiciously** *adv.* **auspiciousness** *n.* [F *auspice*, L *auspicium*]

Aussie (oz´i), **Ozzie** *n.* (*coll.*) **1** an Australian. **2** Australia. ~*a.* Australian.

austenite (aw´stənīt) *n.* a solid solution of carbon or another element with one of the phases of iron. **austenitic** (-nit´ik) *a.* [Sir William Roberts-*Austen*, 1843–1902, English metallurgist]

Auster (aws´tə) *n.* (*poet.*) the south wind. [L]

austere (ostiə´) *a.* **1** severely simple, unadorned. **2** ascetic, abstemious. **3** severe, stern, rigorous. **austerely** *adv.* **austereness** *n.* **austerity** (-ter´-) *n.* (*pl.* **austerities**) **1** severe simplicity and lack of adornment. **2** self-denial, asceticism. **3** (*pl.*) ascetic or penitential practices. **4** sternness, severity. **5** a policy of reducing the availability of luxury goods and maintaining strict financial controls. [OF, from L *austērus*, from Gr. *austēros*, dry, harsh (*auein*, to dry, parch)]

Austin (os´tin) *a., n.* (an) Augustinian. [syncopated form of AUGUSTINE]

austral (os´trəl) *a.* **1** southern. **2** (**Austral**) of or relating to Australia or Australasia. [L *australis* (AUSTER, south wind)]

Australasian (ostrəlā´zhən) *a.* of or relating to Australasia, a general name for Australia, New Zealand, Tasmania and the surrounding islands. ~*n.* a native or inhabitant of Australasia. [F *Australasie*, L *australis*, *Asia*]

Australian (ostrāl´yən) *a.* of or belonging to Australia. ~*n.* **1** a native or inhabitant of Australia. **2** a person of Australian descent. **Australian bear** *n.* the koala. **Australianism** *n.* **1** an Australian idiom or characteristic. **2** devotion to Australia, its culture, political independence etc. **Australianize, Australianise** *v.t.*, *v.i.* to adapt to Australian circumstances or the Australian way of life. **Australian Rules (football)** *n.* a game similar to rugby football played in Australia on an oval pitch with an oval ball between teams of 18 players. **Australian salmon** *n.* a large green and silver marine fish, *Arripis trutta.* **Australian terrier** *n.* a short-legged breed of terrier, small and wire-haired. **Australoid** (os´trəl-) *a.* of, relating to or denoting a racial group including and typified by the Aborigines of Australia. ~*n.* a member of this group. [AUSTRAL]

Australopithecus (ostrələpith´ikəs) *n.* a fossil primate of the extinct genus *Australopithecus* whose remains have been found in Southern Africa. **australopithecine** (-sēn) *n., a.* (an individual) of the genus *Australopithecus* or a related genus. [L *australis*, southern, Gr. *pithēkos*, ape]

Australorp (os´trəlawp) *n.* an Australian utility type of black Orpington fowl. [*Austral*ia, *Orp*ington]

Austrian (os´triən) *n.* **1** a native or inhabitant of Austria. **2** a person of Austrian descent. ~*a.* of or relating to Austria. **Austrian blind** *n.* a window blind with several vertical lines of shirring in the fabric, that forms a series of ruches when raised.

Austro-¹ (os´trō) *comb. form* **1** southern. **2** Australian. [AUSTER]

Austro-² (os´trō) *comb. form* Austrian.

AUT *abbr.* Association of University Teachers.

aut- AUTO-.

autacoid (aw´təkoid) *n.* (*Med.*) an internal secretion, a hormone or chalone. [Gr. *autos*, self; *akos*, a drug; *eidos*, form]

autarch (aw´tahk) *n.* an absolute sovereign, an autocrat. **autarchic** (-tah´-), **autarchical** *a.* **autarchy** *n.* (*pl.* **autarchies**) **1** absolute sovereignty, autocracy. **2** despotism. **3** a country under autarchic rule. [Gr. *archein*, to rule]

autarky (aw´tahki) *n.* (*pl.* **autarkies**) **1** self-sufficiency, esp. national economic self-sufficiency. **2** a state that is economically self-sufficient. **autarkic** (-tah´-), **autarkical** *a.* **autarkist** *n.* [Gr. *autarkeia*]

autecology (awtikol´əji) *n.* (the study of) the ecology of an individual organism or species. **autecological** (-loj´-) *a.* [AUTO-, ECOLOGY]

auteur (ōtœ´, aw-) *n.* a film director who is thought of as having a more than usually dominant role in the creation of their films and a unique personal style. [F, author]

authentic (awthen´tik) *a.* **1** of undisputed origin, genuine, really proceeding from the professed source. **2** entitled to acceptance or belief, trustworthy, credible. **3** vested with all legal formalities and legally attested. **4** (*Mus.*) (of performances, recordings) played on instruments of the composer's time and in a manner appropriate to that time and to the composer's expectations. **5** (*Mus.*) (of a mode) having the notes between the final and the octave above. **authentically** *adv.* **authenticate** *v.t.* **1** to establish the genuineness, truth or credibility of. **2** to verify the authorship of. **3** to render authentic or valid. **authentication** (-ā´shən) *n.* **authenticator** *n.* **authenticity** (-tis´-) *n.* [OF *autentique*, L *authenticus*, Gr. *authentikos*, vouched for, *authentēs*, one who does things himself (AUTO-)]

author (aw´thə) *n.* **1** the composer of a literary work. **2** a person whose profession is writing, esp. books. **3** the works of an author. **4** the originator, producer or efficient cause of anything. ~*v.t.* **1** to be the author of (something written). **2** to be the originator or cause of. **authoress** (-ris) *n.* (*often felt to be derog.*) a female author. **authorial** (-thaw´-) *a.* **authoring** *n.* (*Comput.*) the writing of programs, creation of databases etc. for computer applications, esp. educational ones, and multimedia products. **authorism** *n.* **authorless** *a.* **1** without an acknowledged author. **2** anonymous.

authorship *n.* 1 the profession of a writer of books. 2 the origin of a literary work. 3 the personality of an author. [OF *autour*, L *auctor-em* (*auctus*, p.p. of *augere*, to make to grow)]

authority (awthor´əti) *n.* (*pl.* **authorities**) 1 legitimate power to command or act. 2 (*often pl.*) a person or body exercising this power. 3 delegated power or right to act. 4 power, weight or influence, derived from character, station, mental superiority and the like. 5 weight of testimony, credibility. 6 the standard book or work of reference on any subject. 7 an expert, one entitled to speak with authority on any subject. 8 the author or the source of a statement. 9 confidence resulting from the possession of skill. **authoritarian** (-teə´-) *n.* 1 a person who places obedience to authority above personal liberty. 2 a domineering or dictatorial person. ~*a.* 1 believing in, favouring or enforcing strict obedience to authority. 2 of, relating to or favouring government by a small group with wide powers. 3 domineering, dictatorial. **authoritative** *a.* 1 accepted as possessing authority, as being true, valid, reliable etc. 2 (of a person, manner) commanding, assertive, self-confident. 3 supported by authority, official. **authoritatively** *adv.* **authoritativeness** *n.* [F *autorité*, L *auctoritātem* (*auctor*)]

Usage note The adjectives *authoritarian* and *authoritative* should not be confused: *authoritarian* means favouring or enforcing obedience to authority, and *authoritative* deserving respect or obedience as an authority.

authorize (aw´thərīz), **authorise** *v.t.* 1 to give authority to, to empower. 2 to sanction. 3 to warrant legally. 4 to justify, afford just ground for. **authorizable** *a.* **authorization** (-zā´shən) *n.* 1 the act of authorizing. 2 a document etc. that authorizes something. **authorized** *a.* **Authorized Version** *n.* the English translation of the Bible published in 1611.

autism (aw´tizm) *n.* a disorder of mental development, usu. evident from childhood, marked by complete self-absorption, lack of social communication and inability to form relationships. **autistic** (-tis´-) *a.* [Gr. *autos*, self, -ISM]

auto (aw´tō) *n.* (*pl.* **autos**) (*chiefly N Am.*) short for AUTOMOBILE.

auto. *abbr.* automatic.

auto- (aw´tō), **aut-** *comb. form* 1 self. 2 one's own. 3 from within or by oneself. 4 operating independently; self-propelling, self-regulating. [Gr. *autos*, self]

autoantibody (awtōan´tibodi) *n.* (*pl.* **autoantibodies**) an antibody produced in reaction to an antigen contained within the organism itself.

autobahn (aw´təbahn) *n.* a motorway in Germany, Austria or Switzerland. [G]

autobiography (awtəbīog´rəfi) *n.* (*pl.* **autobiographies**) 1 a memoir of one's life, written by oneself. 2 the writing of one's own memoirs. **autobiographer** *n.* a person who writes an account of their own life. **autobiographic** (-graf´-), **autobiographical** *a.* **autobiographically** *adv.* [AUTO-, BIOGRAPHY]

autocar (aw´təkah) *n.* a vehicle driven by its own mechanical power, a motor vehicle.

autocephalous (awtōsef´ələs) *a.* 1 (of an eastern Church) having the power to appoint its own synod, bishop etc. 2 (of a bishop, Church) independent. **autocephaly** *n.* [Gr., having an independent head]

autochanger (aw´tōchānjə) *n.* 1 a device that allows records to be dropped one by one from a stack on to a turntable. 2 a record player with such a device.

autochthon (awtok´thən, -thōn) *n.* (*pl.* **autochthons**, **autochthones** (-thənēz)) 1 any one of the original or earliest known inhabitants. 2 an aboriginal animal or plant. **autochthonal**, **autochthonic** (-thon´ik) *a.* **autochthonism** *n.* original occupation of, or the fact of being indigenous to, a region. **autochthonous** *a.* 1 native, indigenous. 2 occurring, formed or originating in the place where found. **autochthony** *n.* the condition of being autochthonous. [Gr., sprung from the land itself]

autoclave (aw´təklāv) *n.* 1 a sealed vessel used for chemical reactions at high temperature and pressure. 2 an apparatus using superheated steam for sterilizing, cooking etc. ~*v.t.* 1 to put in an autoclave. 2 to sterilize etc. in an autoclave. [F (AUTO-, *clave* from L *clavis*, key)]

autocracy (awtok´rəsi) *n.* (*pl.* **autocracies**) 1 absolute government by a single person. 2 the power wielded by an autocrat. 3 a country under autocratic rule. [Gr. *autokrateia* (AUTO-, *krateein*, to rule)]

autocrat (aw´təkrat) *n.* 1 a sovereign with uncontrolled authority. 2 a dictatorial person. **autocratic** (-krat´-) *a.* 1 of or relating to autocracy; ruled by an autocrat. 2 absolute, despotic. **autocratically** *adv.* [F *autocrate*, Gr. *autokratēs*]

autocross (aw´tōkros) *n.* the sport of motor racing across country or on unmade roads.

Autocue® (aw´təkū) *n.* a device that displays the text to be spoken by a person on television.

autocycle (aw´tōsīkəl) *n.* a pedal cycle with motor attachment.

auto-da-fé (awtōdafā´) *n.* (*pl.* **autos-da-fé** (awtō-)) 1 a sentence pronounced by the Inquisition. 2 the execution of this judgement. 3 the burning of a heretic. [Port., action for the faith]

autodestruct (awtōdistrŭkt´) *a.* having the power to destroy itself or to initiate self-destruction. ~*v.i.* to destroy itself.

autodidact (awtōdī´dakt) *n.* a self-taught person. **autodidactic** (-didak´-) *a.* [Gr. *autodidaktos* (AUTO-, *didaskein*, to teach)]

autodyne (aw´tōdīn) *a.* (of an electrical circuit) in which the same elements and valves are used both as oscillator and detector. [*auto-*, hetero*dyne*]

auto-erotism (awtōer´ətizm), **auto-eroticism** (-irot´-) *n.* self-produced sexual pleasure or emotion, e.g. masturbation. **auto-erotic** (-irot´-) *a.*

autofocus (aw´tōfōkəs) *n.* a facility in some cameras for automatically focusing the lens.

autogamy (awtog´əmi) *n.* self-fertilization. **autogamous** *a.*

autogenous (awtoj´ənəs) *a.* 1 self-engendered, self-produced, independent. 2 (of a graft, vaccine) originating from sources within the patient's own body. 3 (of a weld) produced by melting the edges of the metal. [Gr. *autogenēs* (AUTO-, *genēs*, produced, *gen-*, stem of *gignesthai*, to be begotten)]

autogiro (aw´tōjīrō), **autogyro** *n.* (*pl.* **autogiros, autogyros**) an aircraft in which the lifting surfaces are the freely-rotating blades of a large horizontal airscrew.

autograft (aw´təgrahft) *n.* a surgical graft that moves tissue from one point to another in the same individual's body.

autograph (aw´təgrahf) *n.* 1 a signature written esp. by a celebrity for an admirer. 2 a person's own handwriting. 3 a manuscript in an author's own handwriting. ~*a.* written by the author. ~*v.t.* 1 to write one's signature on or in, esp. at the request of an admirer. 2 to write with one's own hand. **autographic** (-graf´-), **autographical** *a.* 1 written by one's own hand. 2 of or relating to autographs or autography. **autographically** *adv.* **autography** (-tog´-) *n.* 1 writing with one's own hand. 2 one's own handwriting. 3 a process of reproducing handwriting or drawing in facsimile. [L *autographus*, Gr. *autographos* (AUTO-, *graphein*, to write)]

autogyro AUTOGIRO.

Autoharp® (aw´tōhahp) *n.* a zither-like instrument

having dampers which stop selected strings from sounding and allow chords to be played.

autohypnosis (awtōhipnō´sis) *n.* 1 the process of putting oneself into a hypnotic trance. 2 a self-induced state of trance. **autohypnotic** (-not´ik) *a.* **autohypnotically** *adv.*

autoimmune (awtōimūn´) *a.* of or caused by antibodies that attack the molecules, cells etc. normally present in the organism producing them. **autoimmunity** *n.* **autoimmunization** (-īzā´shən), **autoimmunisation** *n.*

autointoxication (awtōintoksikā´shən) *n.* reabsorption of toxic matter produced by the body.

autolysis (awtol´isis) *n.* the breakdown of cells by the action of enzymes produced in the cells themselves. **autolyse** (aw´təlīz), (*esp. N Am.*) **autolyze** *v.t.* to cause autolysis in. ~*v.i.* to undergo autolysis. **autolytic** (-lit´-) *a.* [Gr. *lysis*, loosening]

automat (aw´təmat) *n.* 1 a vending machine. 2 (*N Am.*) a restaurant or room equipped with automatic machines for supplying food etc. [AUTOMATIC]

automata AUTOMATON.

automate AUTOMATION.

automatic (awtəmat´ik) *a.* 1 self-acting, self-regulating; operating without direct or continuous human intervention. 2 (of actions, behaviour) spontaneous, involuntary, reflex. 3 (*derog.*) (of actions, behaviour) habitual, merely mechanical. 4 (*Psych.*) carried on unconsciously. 5 (of a firearm) repeatedly ejecting the empty shell, introducing a new one and firing, until the trigger is released. 6 (of a vehicle) having automatic transmission. ~*n.* 1 an automatic firearm. 2 a motor vehicle with automatic transmission. **automatically** *adv.* **automaticity** (-tis´-) *n.* **automatic pilot** *n.* a device which automatically maintains an aircraft or spacecraft on a predetermined course. **automatic transmission** *n.* power transmission in a motor vehicle in which the gears change automatically. [Gr. *automatos*, acting of itself (AUTO-, *-matos*, allied to Sansk. *matas*, thought, known)]

automation (awtəmā´shən) *n.* 1 the use of self-regulating or automatically programmed machines in the manufacture of goods. 2 the introduction of such machinery to save labour. **automate** (aw´-) *v.t.* to make automatic; to bring automation to. ~*v.i.* to apply automation. [AUTOMATIC]

automatism (awtom´ətizm) *n.* 1 the quality of being automatic. 2 involuntary action. 3 (*Psych.*) the performance of actions without conscious control. 4 automatic routine. **automatist** *n.* **automatize, automatise** *v.t.* 1 to make automatic. 2 to automate. **automatization** (-zā´shən) *n.* [AUTOMATIC]

automaton (awtom´ətən) *n.* (*pl.* **automatons, automata** (-tə)) 1 a machine that is activated by a concealed mechanism and power source within itself, a robot. 2 a machine of this kind that simulates human or animal actions. 3 a person who acts mechanically or leads a life of monotonous routine. **automatous** *a.* 1 acting spontaneously. 2 of the nature of an automaton. [L, from Gr., neut. of *automatos*, see AUTOMATIC]

automobile (awtəməbēl´, aw´-) *n.* (*chiefly N Am.*) a motor car. **automobilia** (-bil´iə) *n.pl.* collectors´ items to do with cars and motoring. **automobilist** (-bē´-) *n.* [F (AUTO-, MOBILE)]

automotive (awtəmō´tiv) *a.* 1 self-propelling. 2 of or relating to motor vehicles.

autonomy (awton´əmi) *n.* (*pl.* **autonomies**) 1 the right of self-government. 2 an independent state or community. 3 freedom to act as one pleases. 4 in Kantian philosophy, freedom of the will. 5 organic independence. **autonomic** (-nom´-) *a.* 1 (*Biol.*) occurring involuntarily, spontaneous. 2 of, relating to or mediated by the autonomic nervous system. **autonomic nervous system** *n.* the part of the vertebrate nervous system that regulates the involuntary actions of the heart, glands and some muscles. **autonomist** *n.* an advocate of autonomy. **autonomous** *a.* 1 of or possessing autonomy. 2 self-governing or partially self-governing. 3 able to act or acting independently. 4 (*Biol.*) having organic independence, not dependent on other organisms or parts. **autonomously** *adv.* [Gr. *autonomia*, independence, *autonomos*, independent (AUTO-, *nomos*, law)]

autopilot (aw´tōpīlət) *n.* AUTOMATIC PILOT (under AUTOMATIC).

autopista (awtōpēs´tə) *n.* a motorway in Spain. [Sp. AUTO-, *pista*, track]

autoplasty (aw´tōplasti) *n.* repair of a lesion by healthy tissue from the same body. **autoplastic** (-plas´-) *a.*

autopsy (aw´topsi, -top'-) *n.* (*pl.* **autopsies**) 1 a post-mortem examination. 2 a critical examination. 3 a personal observation. ~*v.t.* (*3rd pers. sing. pres.* **autopsies**, *pres.p.* **autopsying**, *past, p.p.* **autopsied**) to perform a post-mortem examination on. [Gr. *autopsia* (AUTO-, *opsis*, sight)]

autoradiograph (awtōrā´diəgrahf) *n.* a photograph produced by radiation from, and showing the distribution of, radioactive particles in a body. **autoradiographic** (-graf´ik) *a.* **autoradiography** (-og´rəfi) *n.*

autorotation (awtōrōtā´shən) *n.* rotation resulting from the shape or structure of an object in an airflow, not from a power source. **autorotate** *v.i.*

autoroute (aw´tōroot) *n.* a motorway in France. [F *auto*, car, *route*, road]

autoschediasm (awtōsked´iazm) *n.* something hastily improvised. **autoschediastic** (-as´-), **autoschediastical** *a.* hastily improvised. **autoschediaze** (-āz) *v.t.* to improvise. [AUTO-, Gr. *schediasma*, from *autoschediazein*, to act or speak offhand (*autoschedios*, offhand, on the spur of the moment)]

autosome (aw´təsōm) *n.* a chromosome other than a sex chromosome. **autosomal** (-sō´-) *a.* [Gr. *autos*, self, *soma*, body]

autostrada (aw´tōstrahdə) *n.* a motorway in Italy. [It.]

autosuggestion (awtōsəjes´chən) *n.* suggestion arising from oneself, esp. the unconscious influencing of one's own beliefs, physical condition etc. **autosuggestive** *a.*

autotelic (awtōtel´ik, awtə-) *a.* that is an end in itself. [AUTO-, Gr. *telos*, end]

autotimer (aw´tōtīmə) *n.* a device that can be set to turn an appliance, e.g. a cooker, on or off at a predetermined time.

autotomy (awtot´əmi) *n.* 1 voluntary separation of a part of the body, e.g. the tail, as in certain lizards. 2 self-amputation. [Gr. *autos*, self, *tomos*, cutting]

autotoxic (awtətok´sik) *a.* self-poisoning. **autotoxication** (-ā´shən) *n.* **autotoxin** *n.* a poisonous substance produced within the organism it attacks.

autotrophic (awtətrof´ik) *a.* (of or relating to organisms) capable of manufacturing organic foods from inorganic sources, as by photosynthesis. **autotroph** (aw´tətrōf) *n.* such an organism.

autotype (aw´tōtīp) *n.* 1 a facsimile. 2 a photographic printing process for reproducing photographs in monochrome; a print made by this process. 3 a true impress. ~*v.t.* to reproduce by the autotype process. **autotypy** (-tīpi) *n.* the process of reproducing in autotype.

autowinder (aw´tōwīndə) *n.* an electrically powered device that automatically winds on the film in a camera after a photograph has been taken.

autoxidation (awtoksīdā´shən) *n.* oxidation that occurs spontaneously on exposure to atmospheric oxygen.

autumn (aw´təm) *n.* 1 the season of the year between summer and winter — astronomically, it extends from the autumnal equinox to the winter solstice; popularly, it comprises the months from September to November in the northern hemisphere and from March to May in the southern. 2 the stage of late maturity or incipient decline, e.g. in human life. **autumnal** (-tŭm´nəl) *a.* 1 relating to, characteristic of or produced in autumn. 2 of or relating to the declining period of life. ~*n.* a plant which flowers in autumn. **autumnal equinox, autumn equinox** *n.* the time when the sun crosses the equator in autumn (this happens about 22 Sept. in the northern hemisphere and about 21 March in the southern). **autumn crocus** *n.* a plant of the genus *Colchicum*, meadow saffron. [OF *automne*, L *autumnus*]

autunite (aw´tənīt) *n.* a mineral consisting of a hydrous phosphate of uranium and calcium. [*Autun*, town in France, one of the places where it was discovered]

aux. *abbr.* auxiliary.

auxiliary (awgzil´yəri) *a.* 1 helping, aiding. 2 subsidiary (to). 3 applied to verbs used in the conjugation of other verbs. ~*n.* (*pl.* **auxiliaries**) 1 a person who or something which helps or assists. 2 (*Gram.*) an auxiliary verb. 3 (*pl.*) foreign or allied troops in the service of a nation at war. 4 (*N Am.*) a group that helps or assists, esp. with charitable activities. **auxiliary verb** *n.* (*Gram.*) a verb used in the conjugation of other verbs. [L *auxiliārius*, from *auxilium*, help (*augēre*, to increase)]

auxin (awk´sin) *n.* any of a group of growth-promoting plant hormones. **auxology** (-sol´-) *n.* the study of growth, esp. in humans. **auxologist** *n.* [Gr. *auxein*, to grow]

AV *abbr.* 1 audio-visual. 2 Authorized Version (of the Bible).

Av (av), **Ab** (ab) *n.* the fifth ecclesiastical month, or 11th civil month of the Jewish year (corresponding roughly with August).

Av. *abbr.* avenue.

a.v., A/V *abbr.* ad valorem.

av. *abbr.* 1 average. 2 avoirdupois. 3 avenue.

avadavat (av´ədəvat, avədəvat´), **amadavat** (am-) *n.* an Indian and SE Asian waxbill of the genus *Amandava*. [*Ahmabad*, in India]

avail (əvāl´) *v.i.* 1 to be of value, use, profit or advantage. 2 to be helpful. 3 to be effectual or sufficient. ~*v.t.* to be of use or advantage to. ~*n.* worth, value, profit, advantage, use. **of no avail** ineffectual, in vain. **to avail oneself of** to take advantage of, make use of. **to little avail** ineffectually, with little useful result. **without avail** ineffectual, in vain. [OF *vail*, 1st pers. pres. sing. of *valoir*, L *valēre*, to be worth]

available (əvā´ləbəl) *a.* 1 capable of being employed; at one's disposal. 2 at hand, accessible. 3 (of a person) unoccupied, contactable. 4 (*coll.*) free for a sexual relationship. 5 (*N Am.*) suitable for public office etc. 6 (*Law*) valid. 7 †advantageous. **availability** (-bil´-) *n.* **availableness** *n.* **availably** *adv.*

avalanche (av´əlahnsh) *n.* 1 a mass of snow, ice and debris falling or sliding from the upper parts of a mountain. 2 a sudden overwhelming arrival or build-up. 3 the cumulative production of charged particles resulting from the collisions of a single charged particle with matter to produce further particles which in turn collide etc. ~*v.i.* to descend or arrive like an avalanche. ~*v.t.* to overwhelm as or like an avalanche. [Swiss F (F *valanche*, influ. by *avaler*, to descend to the valley)]

avant (avā´) *adv., a.* before, in front. **avant-brace** (-brās) *n.* VAMBRACE. **avant-courier** *n.* 1 a forerunner, a precursor. 2 (*pl.*) scouts, skirmishers. [F, before, now principally found in the form *van-* or *vant-*]

avant-garde (avāgahd´) *a.* 1 in advance of contemporary artistic tastes or trends; experimental, progressive. 2 radical, daring. ~*n.* the people who create or take up avant-garde or experimental ideas, esp. in the arts. **avant-gardism** *n.* **avant-gardist** *n.* [F, vanguard]

Avar (ā´vah) *n.* 1 a member of a people of the NE Caucasus. 2 the Caucasian language of the Avars. 3 (*Hist.*) a member of an E European tribe defeated by Charlemagne.

avarice (av´əris) *n.* excessive desire for wealth; greed, covetousness. **avaricious** (-rish´əs) *a.* **avariciously** *adv.* [OF, from L *avāritia*, from *avārus*, greedy (*avēre*, to wish, desire)]

avascular (əvas´kūlə, ā-) *a.* without blood vessels. [A-[3], VASCULAR]

avast (əvahst´) *int.* (*Naut.*) stay! stop! desist! [prob. from Dut. *hou' vast*, or *houd vast*, hold fast]

avatar (av´ətah) *n.* 1 in Hinduism, the descent of a god or released soul to earth. 2 the incarnation of a Hindu god; incarnation. 3 a manifestation, a phase. 4 an archetypal example of a concept or principle. [Sansk. *avatāra*, descent]

†**avaunt** (əvawnt´) *int.* be off! away with you! begone! [AVANT]

avdp. *abbr.* avoirdupois.

Ave., ave. *abbr.* avenue.

ave (ah´vā) *int.* hail! welcome! farewell! (in allusion to the classical custom of greeting the dead). ~*n.* 1 an Ave Maria. 2 any one of the small beads on a rosary on which prayers are counted. 3 a shout of welcome or adieu. **ave-bell** *n.* the bell rung when the Ave Maria should be recited. **Ave Maria, Ave Mary** *n.* 1 the Hail Mary; the angelical salutation (Luke i.28) with that of St Elisabeth (i.42), to which a prayer is added, the whole being used as a form of devotion. 2 the ave-bell. [L, hail (*avēre*, to fare well)]

avenaceous (avənā´shəs) *a.* of, relating to or resembling oats. [L *avēnāceus*, from *avēna*, oats]

avenge (əvenj´) *v.t.* 1 to execute vengeance on account of or on behalf of. 2 to take vengeance for. ~*v.i.* to execute vengeance. **to be avenged** to execute vengeance on one's own behalf. **avengeful** *a.* **avengement** *n.* **avenger** *n.* a person who avenges somebody or something. **avenger of blood** *n.* in Mosaic law, the person on whom it devolved to punish murder by death. **avenging** *a.* [OF *avengier* (*à*, to, *vengier*, L *vindicāre*, to claim, to revenge)]

Usage note *Avenge* implies greater justification and less purely personal motivation than *revenge*.

avens (av´əns) *n.* (*pl.* **avens**) 1 a rosaceous plant of the genus *Geum*, esp. the wood avens or herb bennet, *G. urbanum*, and the water avens, *G. rivale*. 2 a related alpine plant, the mountain avens, *Dryas octopetala*. [OF *avence* (etym. uncertain)]

aventail (av´əntāl), **aventayle** *n.* (*Hist.*) the movable part of a helmet in front, which may be lifted to admit fresh air. [OF *esventail* (L *ex-*, out, *ventus*, wind)]

aventurine (əven´churin), **aventurin** *n.* 1 a gold-spangled Venetian glass (made by a process which was discovered accidentally, hence the name). 2 a quartz of similar appearance spangled with scales of mica or some other mineral. [F, from It. *avventurino* (*avventura*, chance)]

avenue (av´inū) *n.* 1 a way or means of approaching an objective or gaining an end. 2 a broad street or road, typically lined with trees. 3 an approach to a country house or similar building, lined with trees; a way or path lined with trees. 4 the rows of trees bordering such a way or approach. 5 (*N Am.*) a road in a grid system running perpendicular to another. [F, fem. p.p. of *avenir*, to come to, L *advenīre* (*ad-*, to, *venīre*, to come)]

aver (əvœ´) *v.t.* (*pres.p.* **averring**, *past, p.p.* **averred**) 1 (*formal*) to assert or declare positively. 2 (*Law*) to allege. 3 (*Law*) to prove, to justify. **averment** *n.* 1 the act of averring; affirmation, positive assertion. 2 (*Law*) an affirmation alleged to be true, and followed by an offer to verify. **averrable** *a.* [F *avérer*, late L *āverāre* (*ad*, to, *verum*, truth)]

average (av´ərij) *n.* 1 the typical or prevailing number, quantity, proportion, level or degree; the general standard. 2 the value obtained by adding together a set of numbers and dividing the result by the number of members of the set. 3 (*Law*) a a loss arising from damage to a ship or cargo at sea. b appointment of such loss among the parties interested. 4 a charge payable by the owner of goods over and above the freight. ~*v.t.* 1 to calculate the average of. 2 to assess the ordinary standard of. 3 to divide proportionately to the number involved. 4 to be or consist of on average. 5 to do, have or take as a mean rate or value. ~*v.i.* to be or amount to as an average. ~*a.* 1 ascertained by taking a mean proportion between given quantities. 2 medium, ordinary, usual. 3 mediocre. **on (an) average** 1 usually, typically. 2 taking the mean calculated from a number of examples. **to average out** to attain an acceptable level in the long run. **to average out at** to come to (a certain figure) when the average is calculated. **average adjuster** *n.* an assessor who deals with claims for losses at sea. **averagely** *adv.* [F *avarie* (etym. uncertain; cp. Sp. *averia*, It. *avaria*, Dut. *avarij*, *haverij*, G *Haferei*)]

averrable AVER.

Averroist (avərō´ist) *n.* a follower of Averroës (1126–1198), an Arab physician and philosopher who taught a kind of pantheism blending Aristotelian and Islamic ideas. **Averroism** *n.*

averse (əvœs´) *a.* 1 unwilling, disinclined, reluctant (to). 2 feeling repugnance or dislike. 3 (*Bot.*) turned away from the main axis. **aversely** *adv.* **averseness** *n.* **aversion** (-shən) *n.* 1 disinclination, dislike, repugnance. 2 an object of dislike. **aversion therapy** *n.* therapy designed to stop undesirable behaviour by associating it with an unpleasant sensation (e.g. an electric shock). **aversive** *a.* [L *aversus*, p.p. of *āvertere* (*a-*, *ab-*, away, *vertere*, to turn)]

Usage note See note under ADVERSE.

avert (əvœt´) *v.t.* 1 to turn away. 2 to ward off, to prevent. **avertible** *a.* [F *avertir*, from L *āvertere*, to turn away (*avertir* seems to have represented both *advertere* and *āvertere*, the meaning being differentiated later)]

Usage note The verbs *avert* and *avoid* should not be confused: *avert* implies some definite action taken in advance, while *avoid* means simply to escape or evade.

Avesta (əves´tə) *n.* the sacred scriptures of Zoroastrianism. **Avestan** *a.* of the Avesta. ~*n.* the ancient Iranian language of the Avesta. [Pers.]

avg. *abbr.* average.

avgolemono (avgəlem´ənō) *n.* Greek chicken soup made with egg yolks and lemon. [mod. Gr.]

AVI *abbr.* Automatic Vehicle Identification.

avian (ā´viən) *a.* of or relating to birds. **aviarist** *n.* **aviary** *n.* (*pl.* **aviaries**) a large cage or building in which birds are kept. [L *avis*, a bird, -AN]

aviation (āviā´shən) *n.* 1 the subject of aircraft; the practice of operating aircraft. 2 the design and manufacture of aircraft. 3 the art or skill of flying or travelling in the air. **aviate** (ā´-) *v.i.* to fly in or pilot an aircraft. ~*v.t.* to pilot (an aircraft). **aviator** *n.* a person who flies, or is a member of the crew of, an aircraft. **aviatrix** (āviā´triks) *n.* a female aviator. [F, from L *avis*, a bird]

aviculture (ā´vikŭlchə) *n.* the breeding and rearing of birds. **aviculturist** (-kŭl´-) *n.*

avid (av´id) *a.* 1 very keen, enthusiastic. 2 ardently desirous (of); extremely eager (for). **avidity** (-vid´-) *n.* 1 great keenness, enthusiasm; eagerness. 2 the strength of the interaction between an antibody and antigen. 3 the strength of an acid or base in relation to its degree of dissociation. **avidly** *adv.* [L *avidus*, greedy (*avēre*, to crave)]

avidin (av´idin) *n.* a protein found in egg white that prevents the absorption of biotin. [AVID, BIOTIN]

avifauna (ā´vifawnə) *n.* the birds in any district taken collectively. **avifaunal** *a.*

avionics (āvion´iks) *n.* (the science concerned with) the development and use of electronic and electric equipment in aircraft and spacecraft. [*avi*ation electr*onics*]

avirulent (āvir´ūlənt) *a.* not virulent. [A-[3], VIRULENT]

avitaminosis (āvitəminō´sis) *n.* (*pl.* **avitaminoses** (-sēz)) (a) disease resulting from vitamin deficiency.

avizandum (avizan´dəm) *n.* (*Sc. Law*) 1 private consideration by a judge or court before passing judgement. 2 a period of time given to this. [med. L, gerund of *avizāre*, to consider]

AVM *abbr.* Air Vice-Marshal.

avocado (avəkah´dō) *n.* (*pl.* **avocados**) 1 (*also* **avocado pear**) the pear-shaped fruit of a Central American tree, *Persea americana*. 2 this tree. 3 a green colour, either a dull green resembling the skin or a light green resembling the flesh of the fruit. ~*a.* of the colour avocado. [Sp., 'advocate', a popular substitute for Aztec *ahuacatl*]

avocation (avəkā´shən) *n.* 1 a minor employment or occupation. 2 a person's ordinary employment, a calling, a vocation. [L *āvocātiōnem*, from *āvocāre* (*ā-*, *ab-*, away, *vocāre*, to call)]

avocet (av´əset), **avoset** *n.* a wading bird of the genus *Recurvirostra*, having a long slender bill curved upwards. [F *avocette*, It. *avosetta*]

Avogadro's constant (avəgah´drōz), **Avogadro's number** *n.* the number of molecules or atoms in one mole of substance. **Avogadro's law, Avogadro's hypothesis** *n.* the law that equal volumes of all gases contain the same number of molecules at the same temperature and pressure. [A. *Avogadro*, 1776–1856, Italian physicist]

avoid (əvoid´) *v.t.* 1 to keep at a distance from, to shun. 2 to refrain from. 3 to escape, evade. 4 (*Law*) to nullify, to invalidate, to quash. **avoidable** *a.* capable of being avoided. **avoidability** (-bil´-) *n.* **avoidably** *adv.* **avoidance** *n.* 1 the act of shunning or avoiding. 2 the act of making void or annulling. **avoider** *n.* [A-F *avoider*, OF *esvuidier* (*es-*, out, *vuidier*, to void, from *vuit*, *vuide*, empty)]

Usage note See note under AVERT.

avoirdupois (avwahdoopwah´, avədəpoiz´) *n.* 1 a system of weights based on the unit of a pound of 16 ounces, equal to 7000 grains (0.4536 kg). 2 (*chiefly N Am.*) weight, heaviness. **avoirdupois weight** *n.* weight reckoned by this system. [OF *avoir* (*aveir*) *de pois*, things of weight (*avoir*, *aveir*, goods, property, L *habēre*, to have, *de*, of, *pois*, *peis*, L *pensum*, weight)]

avoset AVOCET.

†**avouch** (əvowch´) *v.t.* 1 to affirm, vouch for, guarantee as certain. 2 to own, acknowledge, avow. 3 to maintain, to justify. ~*v.i.* to vouch, give assurance or guarantee. **avouchable** *a.* **avouchment** *n.* [OF *avochier*, L *advocāre* (*ad*, to, *vocāre*, to call)]

avow (əvow´) *v.t.* 1 to own, to acknowledge, to admit (of one's free will). 2 to state, allege, declare. **avowable** *a.* **avowal** *n.* an open declaration, a free admission. **avowed** *a.* 1 acknowledged. 2 self-acknowledged. **avowedly** (-id-) *adv.* [OF *avouer*, L *advocāre*, to call upon, to call in as patron (*ad-*, to, *vocāre*, to call), more or less identified with sense of *a*, to, and *vouer*, L *votāre*, to vow (*vōtum*, a vow)]

avulsion (əvŭl´shən) *n.* 1 the act of tearing away or violently separating. 2 a fragment or part torn off. 3 (*Law*) sudden removal of land (without change of ownership) by flood, alteration in the course of a river etc. **avulse** *v.t.* to remove by avulsion. **avulsive** *a.* [L *āvulsiōnem*, from *āvellere* (*a-*, *ab-*, from, *vellere*, to pluck)]

avuncular (əvŭng´kūlə) *a.* 1 of or relating to an uncle. 2 benevolent or friendly like an uncle. [L *avunculus*, a maternal uncle]

aw (aw) *int.* (*chiefly N Am. or Sc.*) used to express sympathy, disapproval, appeal etc. **aw-shucks** *a.* (*N Am., coll.*) self-deprecating, self-conscious, apologetic.

awa' (əwah´) *adv.* (*Sc.*) 1 away, gone. 2 forward, onward. [AWAY]

AWACS (ā´waks) *abbr.* Airborne Warning and Control System (a US defence system of aircraft equipped with radar).

await (əwāt´) *v.t.* 1 to wait for, look out for, expect. 2 to be in store for. ~*v.i.* 1 to wait, esp. expectantly. 2 to be in store. [ONorthF *awaitier* (OF *agaitier*), to lie in wait for (*à*, to, *waitier*, *gaitier*, see WAIT)]

awake (əwāk´) *v.i.* (*past* **awoke** (əwōk´), **awaked,** *p.p.* **awoken** (əwō´kən), *past, p.p.* **awaked**) 1 to wake from sleep, cease sleeping. 2 to become active or alert. 3 to become conscious of or alive to something. ~*v.t.* 1 to arouse from sleep, or from lethargy or inaction. 2 to excite to action or new life; to stir up, revive (*awoke feelings of compassion*). ~*a.* 1 not asleep; roused from sleep. 2 vigilant, aware, alive (to). **to be awake up** (*Austral., coll.*) to be aware, to be alert. **awakable** *a.* **awaken** *v.t.* 1 to arouse from sleep, awake. 2 to make aware or conscious. ~*v.i.* to awake. **awakenable** *a.* **awakening** *a.* 1 waking up, rising as if from sleep. 2 fitted to inspire activity, rousing. ~*n.* 1 the act of waking. 2 a stirring up, a rousing of interest or attention. **awakenment** *n.* an awakening. [two OE verbs were early confused, *awæcnan* (*a-*, on, WAKE[1]), *awōc*, *awacen*; and *awacian*, *awacode* (*awæcnan* gave us *awaken* and *awakened*, *awacian* gave *awake*, *awaked*). Both verbs were intr., meaning, to arise from sleep, cease sleeping; the tr. senses were supplied by *āweccan*, to rouse, which was gradually superseded by *awake*]

award (əwawd´) *v.t.* 1 to grant or confer, esp. as a prize for merit or as something needed. 2 to adjudge, to assign by judicial sentence. ~*n.* 1 a prize, sum of damages, or other thing awarded. 2 the decision of a judge, arbitrator or umpire. 3 the document embodying the terms of such a decision. **awarder** *n.* [A-F *awarder*, OF *esguarder*, from *es-*, L *ex-*, out of, OLG *wardēn* (OHG *wartēn*), watch, guard (cp. WARD)]

aware (əweə´) *a.* 1 apprised, cognizant, conscious. 2 well informed in a specified field (*environmentally aware*). 3 (*coll.*) sensitive and perceptive. **awareness** *n.* [OE *gewær* (*ge-*, intens., *wær*, aware, wary) (cp. OHG *gawar*, G *gewahr*)]

awash (əwosh´) *adv.* 1 on a level with the water. 2 afloat and at the mercy of the waves. ~*a.* covered with water; flooded. **awash with** full of, having an abundance of; having too much or too many of.

away (əwā´) *adv.* 1 from a place, person, cause or condition. 2 absent, at another place. 3 apart, at a distance. 4 in the other direction. 5 into another place; until gone or removed. 6 continuously, constantly. 7 directly, without hesitation, freely. 8 at a sporting opponent's ground. ~*a.* 1 absent. 2 distant. 3 played at a sporting opponent's ground. ~*n.* a (football) match played or won at an opponent's ground. ~*int.* begone! go away! **away back** long ago. **away from it all** in or to a place without the stresses of everyday life. **away with** 1 take away. 2 (*esp. negative*) †bear, endure, tolerate. **far and away** beyond comparison, by a large margin. **out and away** OUT. **to do away with** DO[1]. **to make away with** MAKE[1]. [OE *onweg*, on the way]

awe (aw) *n.* 1 dread mingled with veneration. 2 solemn, reverential wonder. ~*v.t.* 1 to inspire with solemn fear or reverence. 2 to restrain by profound respect or reverential fear. **to keep in awe** to restrain by fear. **awe-inspiring** *a.* 1 exciting awe or wonder. 2 (*sl.*) marvellous, impressive. **aweless** *a.* not feeling awe or dread. **awelessness** *n.* **awesome** (-səm) *a.* 1 inspiring awe. 2 full of or displaying awe. 3 (*sl.*) marvellous, impressive. **awesomely** *adv.* **awesomeness** *n.* **awe-stricken, awe-struck** *a.* overwhelmed with awe. [Icel. *agi* (cp. OE *ege*, fear, also *ōga*, terror)]

aweary (əwiə´ri) *a.* (*poet.*) tired, weary.

a-weather (əwedh´ə) *adv.* 1 to the weather side, as opposed to the lee side. 2 towards the wind. **aweather of** on the weather side of.

aweel (əwēl´) *int.* (*Sc.*) well; well then. [*ah well* (cp. F *eh bien*)]

☒ **aweful** common misspelling of AWFUL.

aweigh (əwā´) *adv.* (*Naut.*) (of an anchor) raised vertically just off the bottom.

aweto AWHETO.

awful (aw´fəl) *a.* 1 extremely disagreeable, frightful, terrible, monstrous; very bad of its kind. 2 (*coll.*) very great, excessive. 3 inspiring awe; worthy of profound reverence. 4 †filled with awe. **awfully** *adv.* 1 in an awful manner. 2 (*coll.*) exceedingly, very. **awfulness** *n.* [AWE]

awheto (əwā´tō), **aweto** *n.* (*pl.* **awhetos, awetos**) (*New Zeal.*) a caterpillar affected with a parasitic fungus, from the dried body of which a tattoo dye is obtained. [Maori]

awhile (əwīl´) *adv.* for some time; for a little. [OE *āne hwīle*]

a-wing (əwing´) *adv., a.* on the wing, flying.

awkward (awk´wəd) *a.* 1 lacking dexterity, bungling, clumsy. 2 ungraceful, ungainly. 3 unhandy, ill-adapted for use. 4 embarrassed, ill at ease. 5 embarrassing. 6 not easy to manage or deal with; requiring care and tact. 7 deliberately uncooperative or unhelpful. 8 †froward, perverse, cross-grained. **awkwardly** *adv.* **awkwardness** *n.* **awkward squad** *n.* the body of recruits not sufficiently drilled to take their place in the regimental parade. [ME *awk*, contrary, untoward (Icel. *afug*, *ofug*, turned the wrong way), -WARD]

awl (awl) *n.* a hand tool with a cylindrical tapering blade, sharpened at the end, for making holes for stitches in leather. **awlwort** *n.* a plant of the genus *Subularia*, esp. *S. aquatica*, a British species, named from the shape of the leaves. [OE *æl* (cp. OHG *ala*, G *Ahle*)]

awn (awn) *n.* any one of the bristles springing from a bract in the inflorescence of some cereals and grasses. **awned**[1] *a.* having awns. **awnless** *a.* [Icel. *ögn*, chaff, a husk (cp. OHG *agana*, G *Ahne*)]

awned[1] AWN.

awned[2] AWNING.

awning (aw´ning) *n.* 1 a covering of tarpaulin, canvas or other material used as a protection from sun or rain, as above the deck of a ship. 2 a shelter resembling an awning. **awned**[2] *a.* fitted with an awning. [etym. uncertain, perh. from F *auvent*, penthouse]

awoke, awoken AWAKE.

AWOL (ā´wol) *a., adv.* absent without authorization from one's post or position of duty. ~*n.* a member of the armed forces who is absent without authorization. [*a*bsent *w*ith*o*ut *l*eave]

awry (ərī´) *adv.* 1 obliquely, crookedly. 2 erroneously, amiss. ~*a.* 1 crooked, distorted, oblique. 2 wrong.

axe (aks), (*esp. N Am.*) **ax** *n.* (*pl.* **axes**) 1 a hand tool for cutting or chopping, consisting of an iron or steel blade with a sharp edge fitted to a handle or helve. 2 any similar tool or weapon, such as a battleaxe. 3 a stone-dressing hammer. 4 (*sl.*) **a** a guitar. **b** †a saxophone. ~*v.t.* 1 to chop or cut with an axe. 2 to dismiss (staff) for reasons of economy. 3 to make drastic reductions in (expenditure, services etc.); to abandon (an enterprise). **the axe** 1 dismissal from employment. 2 drastic reduction in expenditure, staff etc.; abandonment of an enterprise. **axe-breaker** *n.* an Australian tree, *Notelaea longifolia*, whose timber is very hard. **axeman** *n.* (*pl.* **axemen**) 1 a woodman. 2 a warrior armed with a battleaxe. 3 a psychopath who kills with an axe. 4 (*sl.*) a guitarist. **axe to grind** *n.* 1 an ulterior motive. 2 a grievance to air. [OE *æx* (cp. Icel *öx*, OHG *acchus*, G *Axt*, L *ascia*, Gr. *axinē*)]

axel (ak´səl) *n.* a jump in ice-skating incorporating one and a half turns. [*Axel* Paulsen, 1855–1938, Norwegian skater]

axenic (āzē´nik) *a.* uncontaminated by undesirable microorganisms. [A-[3], Gr. *xenos*, stranger]

axes[1] AXE.

axes[2] AXIS[1].

axil (ak´səl) *n.* the hollow where the base of a leaf joins the stem or where a branch leaves the trunk. **axilla** (-sil´ə) *n.* (*pl.* **axillae** (-lē), **axillas**) 1 the armpit. 2 an axil. **axillar, axillary** *a.* 1 of or relating to the armpit. 2 of, relating to or arising from the axil. [L *axilla*, an armpit]

axile AXIS[1].

axilla, axillar etc. AXIL.

axiology (aksiol´əji) *n.* the philosophy of values. **axiological** (-loj´-) *a.* **axiologist** *n.* [Gr. *axios*, worthy]

axiom (ak´siəm) *n.* 1 a self-evident or generally accepted truth. 2 (*Math.*) a self-evident proposition, assented to as soon as enunciated. **axiomatic** (-mat´-), **axiomatical** *a.* 1 self-evident, containing an axiom or axioms. 2 full of maxims. **axiomatically** *adv.* [F *axiome*, L *axiōma*, from Gr. (*axioō*, I esteem, from *axios*, worthy)]

axis[1] (ak´sis) *n.* (*pl.* **axes** (-sēz)) 1 a real or imaginary straight line round which a body revolves, or round which its parts are arranged, or to which they have a symmetrical relation. 2 a fixed reference line used, as on a graph, in locating a point. 3 the second cervical vertebra. 4 the central stem, core or main skeletal support of (a part of) an organism. 5 the central shaft of growth of a plant. 6 an imaginary line round which a crystal can be symmetrically built up. 7 (*Geol.*) a central ridge. 8 (*Math.*) a straight line in a plane figure about which it is conceived to revolve to generate a solid. 9 a line dividing a regular figure into two symmetrical parts. 10 a ray of light passing through the centre of or falling perpendicularly on a lens. 11 the straight line from the lens of the eye to the object seen. 12 the line on which a balance turns. 13 (*pl.*) the sloping timbers of a roof, the principals. 14 a core alliance between countries etc. to which others may become allied. **the Axis** the political collaboration (Rome–Berlin axis) between Nazi Germany and Fascist Italy from 1935–43. **axial** *a.* 1 of or relating to an axis. 2 forming an axis. 3 round an axis. **axiality** (-al´-) *n.* the quality of being axial. **axially** *adv.* in the direction of the axis. **axial pitch** *n.* in mechanics, the pitch of a screw measured in a direction parallel with the axis. **axile** (-īl) *a.* situated in the axis of anything. [L, the axle (cp. Gr. *axōn*, Sansk. *aksha*, OE *eax*)]

axis[2] (ak´sis), **axis deer** *n.* (*pl.* **axis, axises, axis deer**) a S Asian deer with a white-spotted coat, *Cervus axis*. [L, an Indian wild animal]

axle (ak´səl) *n.* 1 the pin or bar on which a wheel revolves or wheels revolve, or which revolves with a wheel. 2 a pivot or support. 3 an axle tree. **axled** *a.* provided with an axle. **axlepin** *n.* a linchpin. **axle tree** *n.* a beam or bar connecting the wheels of a vehicle, on the ends of which the wheels revolve. [Icel. *öxull* (cp. Goth. *ahsuls*, Gmc. *ahsā*, Sansk. *aksha*, L *axis*, Gr. *axōn*)]

Axminster (aks´minstə), **Axminster carpet** *n.* a variously coloured and patterned woven carpet with a tufted pile. [*Axminster*, town in Devon where a type of patterned carpet was orig. woven]

axolotl (ak´səlotəl) *n.* a salamander of the genus *Ambystoma* that retains the larval form when fully grown, esp. a small Mexican salamander, *A. mexicanum*. [Aztec *a-*, *atl*, water, *xolotl*, servant]

axon (ak´son) *n.* the projection from a nerve cell that typically conducts impulses away from the cell. [Gr. *axon*, axis]

axonometric (aksənōmet´rik) *a.* (of a drawing etc.) showing vertical and horizontal lines projected to scale but inclined to the principal axes of the object represented.

ay AYE[1].

ayah (ī´ə) *n.* a nurse for European children or a maidservant in a European household in the Indian subcontinent or in other former British territories. [Port. *aia*, nurse]

ayatollah (īətol´ə) *n.* a leader of the Shiite Muslims in Iran. [Pers. *āyatollāh*, sign of God, from Arab. (*aya*, sign, *allah*, God)]

aye[1] (ī), **ay** *adv.*, *int.* yes. ~*n.* 1 an affirmative vote in the House of Commons. 2 (*pl.*) those who vote in the affirmative. **aye, aye, sir** (*Naut. or facet.*) yes, sir; very well, sir. **the ayes have it** the motion is passed. [perh. an alt. form of YEA; or from I, expressing assent]

†**aye[2]** (ā) *adv.* 1 always, ever. 2 in all cases, on all occasions. **for (ever and) aye** for ever, to all eternity. [ME *ai*, *ei*, Icel. *ei*, *ey* (cogn. with OE *ā*, Goth. *aiw*, L *ævum*, Gr. *aei*)]

aye-aye (ī´ī) *n.* a small lemur found in Madagascar, *Daubentonia madagascariensis*. [F, from Malagasy *aiay*, from its cry]

Aylesbury (ālz´bəri) *n.* (*pl.* **Aylesburys**) a breed of large domestic duck. [town in Bucks.]

Aymara (ī´mərah) *n.* (*pl.* **Aymara, Aymaras**) 1 a member of an Indian people of Bolivia and Peru. 2 their language. ~*a.* of or relating to the Aymara or their language.

ayond (əyond´), **ayont** (əyont´) *prep.* (*Sc., North.*) beyond.

Ayrshire (eə´shə) *n.* a breed of cattle highly prized for dairy purposes. [former county in Scotland]

ayurveda (ahyəvā´də, -vē´də) *n.* an ancient Hindu system of medicine, health and healing. **ayurvedic** *a.* of or relating to the Hindu philosophy of medicine and healing. [Sansk. *āyur*, life, *veda*, knowledge]

AZ *abbr.* Arizona.

az. *abbr.* azimuth.

azalea (əzāl´yə) *n.* any of various shrubby plants of the genus *Rhododendron*, with showy and occasionally fragrant flowers. [Gr., fem. of *azaleos*, dry (either from dry wood or its liking for dry soil)]

azeotrope (ā´ziətrōp, əzē´ə-) *n.* (*Chem.*) a mixture of liquids in which the boiling point remains constant during distillation at a given pressure. **azeotropic** (-trō´pik, -trop´ik) *a.* [A-[3], Gr. *zeō*, to boil, *tropos*, turning]

Azerbaijani (azəbījah´ni) *n.* (*pl.* **Azerbaijanis**) 1 a native or inhabitant of Azerbaijan in the Caucasus. 2 the Turkic language of Azerbaijanis. ~*a.* of or relating to the Azerbaijanis or their language.

Azeri (əzeə´ri) *n.* (*pl.* **Azeris**) 1 a member of a people living in Azerbaijan, Armenia, and adjacent regions. 2 their Turkic language. ~*a.* of or relating to the Azeris or their language.

azide (ā´zīd) *n.* a salt or ester of hydrazoic acid, containing the monovalent group or ion N_3. **azidothymidine** (āzīdōthī´midēn) *n.* AZT. [F, *azote*, nitrogen]

Azilian (əzil´iən) *a.* of or relating to the period of culture typified by the remains found in the cavern of Mas-d'Azil in the French Pyrenees. ~*n.* this culture.

azimuth (az´iməth) *n.* 1 an angular distance from a point of the horizon to the intersection with the horizon of a vertical circle passing through a celestial body. **2** the horizontal angle or direction of a compass bearing. **magnetic azimuth** MAGNETIC (under MAGNET). **true azimuth** TRUE. **azimuthal** (-imū´-) *a.* of or relating to the azimuth. **azimuthally** *adv.* in a circle parallel to the horizon. **azimuthal projection** *n.* a type of map projection in which a region of the earth is projected on to a plane tangential to it. [F *azimut*, Arab. *assamūt* (*al*, the, *sumut*, ways or points, sing. *samt*)]

azine (ā´zēn) *n.* an organic compound with more than one nitrogen atom in a six-atom ring.

azo- (ā´zō) *comb. form* having two adjacent nitrogen atoms. **azo dye** *n.* a dye whose molecules have two adjacent nitrogen atoms between carbon atoms. [see AZIDE]

azoic (əzō´ik) *a.* **1** having no trace of life. **2** (*Geol.*) destitute of organic remains, in the time that antedates life. [Gr. *azōos*, lifeless (A-[3], *zoē*, life)]

AZT (āzedtē´) *n.* an antiviral drug derived from thymine used in the treatment of HIV. [*azido*t*hymidine*]

Aztec (az´tek) *a.* **1** denoting, of or relating to the leading Mexican Indian people at the time of the Spanish invasion (1519). **2** (*loosely*) of or relating to Mexico before the Spanish invasion. *~n.* **1** a member of the Aztec people. **2** their language. [Nahuatl *aztecatl*, men of the north]

azuki ADZUKI.

azure (azh´ə, ā´-) *n.* **1** the deep blue of the sky. **2** (*poet.*) the vault of heaven. **3** (*Her.*) the blue of coats of arms, represented in engraving by horizontal lines. **4** lapis lazuli. **5** a bright blue pigment or dye. *~a.* **1** resembling the deep blue of the sky. **2** (*Her.*) blue. **3** (*poet.*) clear, unclouded. **azurite** (-rīt) *n.* blue carbonate of copper. [OF *azur*, med. L *azura*, Arab. *lazward*, Pers. *lājward*, *lāzhward*, lapis lazuli]

azygous (az´igəs) *a.* (*Biol.*) unpaired, occurring singly, not as one of a pair. *~n.* a structure occurring singly. **azygously** *adv.* [Gr. *azugos*, unyoked (A-[3], *zugon*, a yoke)]

B

B[1] (bē), **b** (*pl.* **Bs, B's, Bees**) the second letter of the English and other versions of the Roman alphabet, corresponding to the Greek beta (Β, β) and the Phoenician and Hebrew beth. It is pronounced as a voiced bilabial plosive. ~*symbol* **1** the second of a series, the second highest in a range, e.g. of marks, etc. **2** the second known quantity in an algebraic expression. **3** (*Mus.*) **a** the seventh note of the diatonic scale of C major. **b** the scale of composition in which the keynote is B. **4** a blood type in the ABO system. **5** magnetic flux density. **B film** *n.* **1** a supporting film. **2** a low-budget film. **B-lymphocyte, B-cell** *n.* a lymphocyte originating in bone marrow that produces antibodies. **B movie, B picture** *n.* B FILM (under B[1]). **B road** *n.* a road of secondary importance. **B-side** *n.* the side of a gramophone record or tape cassette that is usually played second or that has the least important material recorded on it.

B[2] *abbr.* **1** Bachelor. **2** Baron. **3** bel. **4** Belgium. **5** bishop (in chess). **6** (of pencil lead) black. **7** Blessed. **8** British.

B[3] *chem. symbol* boron.

b *abbr.* **1** barn (in physics). **2** barrel. **3** billion. **4** book. **5** born. **6** bottle. **7** bowled. **8** bye.

BA *abbr.* **1** Bachelor of Arts. **2** British Academy. **3** British Airways. **4** British America. **5** British Association (for the Advancement of Science). **6** Buenos Aires.

Ba *chem. symbol* barium.

BAA *abbr.* British Airports Authority.

baa (bah) *n.* (*pl.* **baas**) the cry or bleat of a sheep. ~*v.i.* (*past* **baaed, baa'd**) to cry or bleat as a sheep. **baa-lamb** *n.* a lamb (used to or by children). [from the sound]

BAAB *abbr.* British Amateur Athletic Board.

BAAF *abbr.* British Agencies for Adoption and Fostering.

Baagandji (bah´gənji) *n.* an extinct SE Australian Aboriginal language.

Baal (bā´əl, bahl) *n.* (*pl.* **Baalim** (-lim)) **1** the chief male divinity among the Phoenicians. **2** a false god. **Baalism** *n.* **1** worship of Baal. **2** idolatry. **Baalist** *n.* **1** a worshipper of Baal. **2** an idolater. **Baalite** (-īt) *n.* [Heb. *ba'al*, lord]

BAAS *abbr.* British Association for the Advancement of Science.

baas (bahs) *n.* (*S Afr.*) boss, overseer. **baasskap** (bah´skap) *n.* domination, esp. by whites. [Afrikaans]

baba (bah´bah) *n.* (**rum baba**) a small cake soaked in rum. [F, from Pol. *baba*, old woman]

babacoote (bab´əkoot) *n.* the indri, a short-tailed woolly lemur, *Indri indri*, from Madagascar. [Malagasy *ba-bako-to*]

babassu (babəsoo´) *n.* **1** a Brazilian palm tree, *Orbignya martiana* or *O. speciosa*. **2** the nut from this tree, which yields oil. [Port. *babaçú*, prob. from Tupi]

Babbitt (bab´it) *n.* a dull, complacent businessman (or other person) with orthodox views and little interest in cultural values. **Babbittry** *n.* [character in the novel *Babbitt* (1922) by Sinclair Lewis]

babbitt (bab´it) *n.* **1** babbitt metal. **2** a bearing-lining made of this. ~*v.t.* to line (a surface) with babbitt metal or other soft alloy. **babbitt metal, babbitt's metal** *n.* an alloy of tin, antimony and copper, used in bearings to diminish friction. [Isaac *Babbitt*, 1799–1862, American inventor]

babble (bab´əl) *v.i.* **1** to talk incoherently; to make inarticulate sounds. **2** to talk childishly or inopportunely; to prattle. **3** (of streams, birds etc.) to murmur. **4** (of hounds) to give tongue without reason. ~*v.t.* to prate; to utter; to blab. ~*n.* **1** incoherent talk. **2** shallow, foolish talk; prattle. **3** confused murmur, as of a running brook. **4** background noise on a telephone line caused by conversations on other lines. **babblement** *n.* **1** idle, foolish talk. **2** senseless, indiscreet talk. **3** babble, as of streams. **babbler** *n.* **1** an unintermitting and shallow talker. **2** a gossip. **3** a person who tells secrets. **4** a long-legged thrush, of the family Timaliidae. [from *ba ba*, the earliest attempts of a child to speak, -LE[1] (cp. Dut. *babbelen*, F *babiller*, G *pappelen* etc.)]

babe (bāb) *n.* **1** a young child, a baby. **2** a foolish or childish person. **3** (*sometimes derog., sl.*) a girl, a woman. [prob. from obs. *baban*, imit. from childish speech (cp. BABBLE)]

babel (bā´bəl) *n.* **1** noisy confusion, tumult, disorder. **2** a noisy gathering. **3** a lofty structure. **4** a visionary project. [Heb., confusion, Babylon, the city and tower described in Gen. xi, the place where the confusion of tongues is said to have occurred (perh. from Assyr. *bab-ilu*, the Gate of God)]

Babi (bah´bē), **Babee** *n.* **1** a follower of the Bab (1819–50), who forbade polygamy, begging and alcohol (and was executed for heresy). **2** BABISM (under BABI). **Babism** (bah´bizm) *n.* a Persian religious movement founded by Mirza Ali Mohammed (the Bab) in 1844. **Babist** *n.*

babiche (babēsh´) *n.* (*Can.*) laces or thongs made of rawhide. [F]

babirusa (babiroo´sə), **babiroussa** *n.* the wild hog of eastern Asia, *Babyrousa babyrussa*, in the male of which the upper canines grow through the lip and turn backwards like horns. [Malay *babī rūsa*, hog like a deer (*babi*, hog, *rusa*, deer)]

baboo BABU.

baboon (bəboon´) *n.* **1** a monkey of the genera *Papio* and *Mandrillus*, with long doglike snout, great canine teeth, callosities on the buttocks, and capacious cheek-pouches. **2** an ungainly or ugly person; an unintelligent person. **baboonery** *n.* (*pl.* **babooneries**) **1** behaviour like that of a baboon. **2** a troop of baboons. [F *babuin*, mod. *babouin* (etym. unknown)]

babouche (bəboosh´), **babuche** *n.* a Turkish heel-less slipper. [Arab.]

babu (bah´boo), **baboo** *n.* (*pl.* **babus, baboos**) **1** in the Indian subcontinent, Hindu gentleman, a respectful title corresponding to English Mr. **2** (*Ang.-Ind., offensive*) an Indian clerk who writes English; a Bengali with a superficial English education. [Hind. *babu*]

babul (bah´bool) *n.* any of several trees of the genus *Acacia*, bearing small yellow flowers and yielding gum arabic and tannin. [Pers.]

babushka (bəboosh´kə) *n.* **1** a grandmother, an old woman. **2** a Russian triangular headscarf. [Rus. *babushka*, grandmother, from *baba*, old woman]

baby (bā´bi) *n.* (*pl.* **babies**) **1** an infant; a child in arms. **2** the youngest person in a family, group etc. **3** a foolish, childish person. **4** (*coll.*) a girl, a girlfriend. **5** (*sl.*) a pet project; a person or thing in which one has a special personal interest. ~*a.* **1** small or smaller than usual. **2** newly born, young. ~*v.t.* (*3rd pers. sing. pres.* **babies,** *pres.p.* **babying,** *past, p.p.* **babied**) to make a baby of, to treat like a baby. **to carry/ hold the baby 1** (*coll.*) to be left to bear the brunt of something. **2** (*coll.*) to be landed with something. **to throw away/ out the baby with the bathwater** to reject the essential along with the inessential. **baby bonus** *n.* (*Can., coll.*) family allowance. **baby boom** *n.* (*coll.*) a sharp increase in the birthrate of a population. **baby boomer** *n.* (*coll.*) a person born during a baby boom, esp. in the years following World War II. **baby-bouncer** *n.* a seat or harness on springs, in which a baby can bounce. **baby break** *n.* a period of time taken out of a woman's career to enable her to bring up her children. **baby buggy** *n.* (*pl.* **baby buggies**) **1** a light pushchair. **2** (*N Am.*) a pram. **baby carriage** *n.* (*N Am.*) a pram. **baby-face** *n.* **1** a face like a baby's. **2** a person with a face like this. **baby-faced** *a.* **baby-farmer** *n.* a person who takes in infants to nurse for payment. **baby grand** *n.* a small grand piano. **Babygro®** (-grō) *n.* (*pl.* **Babygros**) an all-in-one baby garment made of a stretch fabric. **babyhood** *n.* infancy. **babyish** *a.* **babyishly** *adv.* **babyishness** *n.* **babyism** *n.* **baby-minder** *n.* a person who looks after infants when their parents are at work etc. **baby ribbon** *n.* narrow ribbon. **baby's breath, babies' breath** *n.* **1** a tall plant, *Gypsophila paniculata*, which bears very small white or pink flowers. **2** any of several other plants bearing small fragrant flowers. **babysitter** *n.* a person who looks after a child while the parents are out. **babysit** *v.i.* (*pres.p.* **babysitting,** *past, p.p.* **babysat**). **baby-snatcher** *n.* **1** a person who abducts an infant. **2** a person who marries or goes out with someone much younger. **baby talk** *n.* **1** the speech of young children. **2** an adult's attempt to speak like this. **baby tooth** *n.* (*pl.* **baby teeth**) MILK TOOTH (under MILK). **baby walker** *n.* a frame on wheels for supporting a baby learning to walk. **baby wipe** *n.* a wet tissue or cloth used for cleaning a baby's bottom or the face, hands etc. [dim. of BABE]

Babylon (bab´ilon) *n.* **1** Rome, the papacy (regarded as corrupt by some Protestants). **2** a great and dissolute city. **3** white society (regarded as corrupt by some blacks). **Babylonian** (-lō´-) *a.* **1** of or relating to Babylon. **2** gigantic, magnificent, luxurious. **3** popish, scarlet (from the fancied identification of the Scarlet Woman (Rev. xvii.4) with Rome). **Babylonian captivity** *n.* **1** the exile of the Jews in Babylon after the capture of Jerusalem in 586 BC. **2** the exile of popes in Avignon, France from 1309–77. **Babylonic** (-lon´-) *a.* **Babylonish** *a.* [L *Babylōn*, Gr. *Babulōn*, Heb. *Bābel*: the ancient capital of the Chaldean empire]

Bacardi® (bəkah´di) *n.* (*pl.* **Bacardis**) a Caribbean rum. [the manufacturer]

bacca (bak´ə), **baccy** (-i) *n.* short for TOBACCO.

baccalaureate (bakəlaw´riət) *n.* **1** an examination qualifying successful candidates for higher education in more than one country. **2** the university degree of bachelor. [med. L *baccalaureus*, as if from *bacca lauri*, laurel berry, late L *baccalāris*, BACHELOR]

baccarat (bak´ərah), **baccara** *n.* a gambling card game between banker and punters. [F *baccara*]

baccate (bak´āt) *a.* **1** berried, bearing berries. **2** berry-like. [L *baccātus* (*bacca*, berry)]

bacchanal (bak´ənəl) *a.* **1** of or relating to Bacchus, the god of wine, or his festivities. **2** characterized by drunken revelry. ~*n.* **1** a votary of Bacchus. **2** a drunken reveller. **3** a song or dance in honour of Bacchus. **4** (*pl.*) a festival in honour of Bacchus. **5** an orgy. **bacchanalia** (-nā´liə) *n.pl.* **1** the festival of Bacchus. **2** bacchanals. **3** drunken revelry. **bacchanalian** *a.* **1** of or relating to bacchanals. **2** bacchanal. ~*n.* **1** a bacchanal. **2** a drunken reveller. **bacchanalianism** *n.* **bacchant** *n.* (*pl.* **bacchants, bacchantes** (bəkan´tēz)) **1** a votary of Bacchus. **2** a drunken reveller. ~*a.* **1** worshipping Bacchus. **2** fond of drinking. **bacchante** (-kan´ti) *n.* a priestess of Bacchus. **bacchantic** (-kan´-) *a.* **bacchic** *a.* **1** of or relating to Bacchus or his worship. **2** frenzied; riotously festive. [L *bacchānālis* (*Bacchus*, Gr. *Bakchos*, the god of wine)]

bacchius (bəkī´əs) *n.* a metrical foot of three syllables, two long and one short. [L, from Gr. *bakcheios*]

bacci- (bak´si) *comb. form* of or relating to a berry or berries. [L *bacca*, a berry]

bacciferous (baksif´ərəs) *a.* bearing berries.

bacciform (bak´sifawm) *a.* berry-shaped.

baccivorous (baksiv´ərəs) *a.* berry-eating.

baccy *n.* BACCA.

bach[1] (bach), **batch** *n.* (*Austral., New Zeal.*) a small cottage or habitable hut.

bach[2] BACHELOR.

bachelor (bach´ələ) *n.* **1** an unmarried man. **2** (*also* **bachelor girl**) an unmarried woman. **3** a holder of the first degree of a university etc., ranking below master or doctor. **4** †a young knight who followed the banner of another. **knight bachelor** KNIGHT. **bach**[2] *n.* (*coll.*) a bachelor. ~*v.i.* to live as a bachelor. **bachelorhood** *n.* **1** the state or condition of a bachelor. **2** the position of bachelor of arts. **bachelorism** *n.* a peculiarity of a bachelor. **Bachelor of Arts** *n.* (a holder of) one of the first level of degrees awarded by a university etc., esp. to students in the humanities. **bachelor's buttons** *n.pl.* **1** the double buttercup *Ranunculus acris*. **2** any of several other plants with button-like flowers. **bachelorship** *n.* [OF *bacheler*, late L *baccalāris* (cp. *baccalārius*, a farm labourer, perh. from late L *bacca*, L *vacca*, a cow)]

bacillus (bəsil´əs) *n.* (*pl.* **bacilli** (-ī)) a microscopic, rodlike (disease-causing) bacterium. **bacillar** *a.* shaped like a rod. **bacillary** *a.* **1** of, relating to or consisting of little rods. **2** of, relating to or caused by bacilli. **bacilliform** (-ifawm) *a.* rod-shaped. [late L, a little rod, dim. of *baculus*, a stick]

bacitracin (basitrā´sin) *n.* an antibiotic used esp. in treating skin infections. [L *bacillus* and Margaret *Tracy*, a child in whom the substance was found]

back[1] (bak) *n.* **1** the hinder part of the human body, from the neck to the lower extremity of the spine. **2** the corresponding portion in the lower vertebrates, and the analogous part in the invertebrates. **3** the spine (*broke her back*). **4** the surface of any object opposite to the face or front; the side or part normally facing away. **5** the outer surface of the hand, the convex part of a book, the thick edge of a knife etc. **6** the hinder part, the rear, the part away from the actor or speaker. **7** the ridge or upper surface of a hill. **8** the keel of a ship. **9** a diagonal parting in a seam of coal. **10** that side of an inclined mineral ore nearest the surface. **11** any one of the players whose duty it is to defend the goal in football and other field games; the position of such a player. ~*a.* **1** situated behind or in the rear. **2** coming back, turned back, reversed. **3** behind in time. **4** remote, distant, inferior. ~*adv.* **1** in a direction to the rear. **2** to the place from which one came. **3** to a former state, position or condition. **4** behind, not advancing, behindhand. **5** in return, in retaliation. **6** in a position behind, away from the front. **7** in a state of check. **8** in time past. **9** again. **10** in returning. ~*v.t.* **1** to furnish with a back or backing. **2** to be at the back of. **3** to support materially or morally, to second, to uphold. **4** to bet in favour of. **5** to mount or get on the back of. **6** to write on the back of, to countersign, to endorse. **7** to cause to move back. **8** to push back. **9** to reverse the action of. ~*v.i.* **1** to retreat, to recede. **2** to move in a reversed direction. **at a person's back 1** pursuing a person. **2** giving support to a person. **at the back of one's mind** not consciously thought of. **back and belly** all over, completely. **back and forth** FORTH. **back of** (*N Am.*) behind. **back of beyond** an extremely remote place. **behind someone's back** secretly, surreptitiously. **on one's back** 1 floored. 2 at the end of one's tether. 3 laid up. **on the back burner** BURNER (under BURN[1]). **on the back of** 1 weighing as a heavy burden on. 2 in addition to. **the Backs** the college grounds backing on to the River Cam in Cambridge. **to back down/ out** 1 to move backwards. 2 to retreat from a difficult situation. **to back into** 1 to knock into (someone or something) with a backward motion. 2 (of a train) to run backwards into a station or siding. **to back off** 1 to withdraw, to retreat. 2 to stop pursuing a course. **to back on to** to have its back next to. **to back the field** to bet against all the horses except one. **to back the wrong horse** to make a bad choice. **to back up** 1 to support. 2 to render support to (a team-mate) in cricket and other games. 3 to duplicate (a computer data file) as security against damage to the original. 4 (of water) to build up behind something. 5 to reverse (a vehicle) to an intended position. 6 to build up into a queue (of traffic etc.). **to back water** to reverse the motion of the oars when rowing. **to break the back of** 1 to overburden. 2 to perform the greater part of (a piece of work). **to get off someone's back** to stop harassing someone. **to go back on** to fail to abide by or honour. **to know like the back of one's hand** to know thoroughly or intimately. **to put/ get someone's back up** 1 to offer resistance. 2 to cause resentment. 3 to feel resentment and show it. **to put one's back into** to make a strenuous effort to perform (a task). **to see the back of** to get rid of. **to turn one's back** to turn away, to flee. **to turn one's back on/ upon** 1 to abandon, to forsake. 2 to ignore. **with one's back to the wall** in a critical position. **with one's back up against the wall** in a critical position. **backache** *n.* a pain in one's back. **back-band** *n.* a strap or chain put across the cart saddle of a horse to support the shafts. **backbar** *n.* a shelving unit for bottles etc. behind a bar. **backbeat** *n.* (*Mus.*) an accent on a normally unaccented beat. **backbench** *n.* the seat of a backbencher. **backbencher** *n.* a member of Parliament without portfolio. **backbite** *v.t.*, *v.i.* to slander, censure or speak ill (of). **backbiter** *n.* **backbiting** *n.*, *a.* making malicious comments. **backblocks** *n.pl.* (*Austral.*, *New Zeal.*) the interior parts of the continent or a station, esp. those far from a river. **backblocker** *n.* a person who lives there. **backboard** *n.* 1 a board strapped across the back to prevent stooping. 2 a board forming the back of anything. 3 a board behind the basket used in basketball, off which the ball can rebound. 4 a board attached to the rim of a waterwheel to prevent the water running off the floats. **back boiler** *n.* a boiler built into the back of a domestic fireplace. **back-bond** *n.* (*Sc. Law*) a deed by which a party holding a title acknowledges that it is held in trust for a certain purpose. **backbone** *n.* 1 the bony framework of the back, the spine, the spinal column. 2 a main support or axis. 3 strength of character, firmness, decision. 4 (*N Am.*) the spine of a book. **to the backbone** thoroughly. **backboned** *a.* **back-boxes** *n.pl.* the boxes on the top of the upper case in hot-metal printing, usu. appropriated to small capitals. **backbreaker** *n.* (*coll.*) an arduous task. **back-breaking** *a.* physically exhausting. **back-cast** *n.* 1 a reverse. 2 a relapse. ~*a.* thrown backwards. **backchat** *n.* (*coll.*) flippant retort, answering back. **backcloth** *n.* 1 the curtain at the back of a stage. 2 the background. **backcomb** *v.t.* to comb backwards with short, sharp strokes, making (the hair) fuzzy. **backcountry** *n.* thinly populated districts. **backcourt** *n.* the part of a tennis court near the service line. **back-crawl** *n.* the backstroke in swimming. **backcross** *v.t.* (*Biol.*) to mate (a hybrid) with one of its parents. ~*n.* 1 the product of this. 2 an instance of this. **backdate** *v.t.* 1 to apply retrospectively from a particular date (e.g. a pay rise). 2 to put an earlier date on than the real one. **back door** *n.* 1 a back or private entrance. 2 an indirect or circuitous way or means. **back-door** *a.* clandestine. **backdown** *n.* an act of backing down. **back-draught** *n.* 1 a backward draught of air. 2 a hood for producing back-draught in a fire. **backdrop** *n.* a backcloth. **backed** *a.* 1 (*chiefly in comb.*) provided with a back. 2 supported, seconded, betted on. 3 endorsed, accepted. **back-end** *n.* (*coll.*, *dial.*) late autumn. **backer** *n.* 1 a person who backs or supports, by money or credit. 2 a person who bets on a horse or an event. 3 a bookmaker, a bookie. 4 a small slate laid on the back of a large one at certain points. **backfall** *n.* a throw or fall on the back in wrestling. **backfield** *n.* 1 the area of play behind the scrimmage line in American football. 2 (the positions of) the players in this area. **backfill** *v.t.* to refill (a hole or excavation) with earth. **backfire** *n.* 1 premature combustion in the cylinder. 2 a controlled fire set to make a barrier of scorched earth against the advance of a forest fire. ~*v.i.* 1 to emit a loud noise as a result of premature combustion in the cylinder. 2 (*coll.*) to fail and have the opposite effect. **backflip** *n.* a backward somersault with straight arms and legs. **back-formation** *n.* 1 the formation of a new word as if it were formed, e.g. by contraction, from an existing one (as *burgle* from *burglar*). 2 a new word so formed. **background** *n.* 1 the ground or surface behind the chief objects of contemplation. 2 that part of a picture, stage-scene or description which represents this. 3 the setting; relevant information about preceding events etc. 4 (*fig.*) an inferior or obscure position. 5 a person's upbringing, education and history. 6 unwanted electrical noise. **background music** *n.* music intended to be played while something more important is happening or being done. **background radiation** *n.* low-level radiation present in the soil and atmosphere. **back hair** *n.* the long hair at the back of a person's head. **backhand** *n.* 1 a stroke in tennis etc. played with the hand turned backwards towards the opponent. 2 handwriting sloped backwards. ~*a.* executed with a backhand. **backhanded** *a.* 1 with the back of the hand. 2 directed backwards. 3 indirect (*a backhanded compliment*). 4 executed with a backhand. **back-hander** *n.* 1 a blow with the back of the hand. 2 a backhand stroke. 3 (*coll.*) an indirect attack. 4 (*coll.*) a bribe. 5 a drink out of one's proper turn. **backhoe** *n.* (*N Am.*) a type of mechanical excavator. **backing** *n.* 1 supporting, seconding. 2 the thing or the body of persons which forms a back or support. 3 money supplied for a project by an investor. 4 musical accompaniment, esp. for a popular song. 5 a piece forming the back or lining the back. 6 putting back. 7 backward motion, esp. of the wind in an opposite direction to that of the sun. 8 opaque varnish put on the back of a negative to obviate halation. 9 perfecting a sheet printed on one side by printing on the other. 10 putting the shoulder on a book before putting the cover on. 11 (*pl.*) refuse from wool or flax after dressing it. **backing group** *n.* a group that provides a musical backing. **backing store** *n.* a computer storage device that supplements the main memory. **backing track** *n.* a track of recorded musical backing. **backlash** *n.* 1 a strong adverse reaction. 2 a jarring reaction in a piece of mechanism. 3 excessive play between parts of a mechanism. **backless** *a.* 1 having no back. 2 (of an article of clothing) having a low-cut back. **backlight** *n.* a light projected on a subject from a source behind the camera. **backlist** *n.* a list of a publisher's books that are still in print. **backlit** *a.* illuminated from behind. **back-lock** *n.* a type of hold in wrestling. **backlog** *n.* 1 reserves or arrears of unfulfilled orders, unfinished work etc. **2** an accumulation of business. **3** (*N Am.*) a large log placed at the back of the fire. **backmarker** *n.* the competitor at the back or with the least chance in a race. **backmost** *a.* furthest back. **back number** *n.* **1** a past issue of a newspaper or magazine. **2** (*sl.*) an out-of-date person or thing. **backpack** *n.* **1** a rucksack. **2** the oxygen supply etc. carried by an astronaut. *~v.i.* to hike with a rucksack. **backpacker, backpacking** *n.* **back pages** *n.pl.* pages on the left-hand side of an open book. **back passage** *n.* (*coll.*) the rectum. **backpay** *n.* arrears of pay. **back-pedal** *v.i.* (*pres.p.* **back-pedalling,** (*N Am.*) **back-pedaling,** *past, p.p.* **back-pedalled,** (*N Am.*) **back-pedaled**) **1** to press back the pedals of a cycle. **2** to reverse a course of action. **3** to restrain one's enthusiasm. **back-pressure** *n.* resistance to the working of a piston, caused by waste steam or atmospheric pressure. **back-projection** *n.* the projection of a picture from behind a screen. **backrest** *n.* a support or rest for the back. **backroom boys** *n.pl.* (*coll.*) scientists and others who work in the background unrecognized. **backsaw** *n.* a small saw with a stiffened back. **backscatter** *n.* (*Physics*) the scattering of radiation by deflection. *~v.t.* to scatter (radiation) by deflection. **backscattering** *n.* the reverse scattering of radiation. **back-scratcher** *n.* **1** a hand-shaped appliance with out-stretched fingers for scratching the back. **2** a flatterer; a person who does favours for another in the expectation of gain. **back-scratching** *n.* **1** flattery. **2** toadyism; the doing of mutual favours. *~a.* that toadies or does favours in the expectation of gain. **back seat** *n.* **1** the seat at the back of anything, such as a car or theatre. **2** a position of less importance. **to take a back seat** **1** to accept an inferior role. **2** to withdraw from the forefront. **back-seat driver** *n.* **1** a passenger in a car who offers unwanted advice. **2** a person who offers advice on matters which do not concern them. **backset** *n.* **1** a setback, a reverse. **2** a counter current. **back settlement** *n.* **1** an outlying settlement. **2** (*pl.*) the backwoods. **back-settler** *n.* a backwoodsman. **backshift** *n.* **1** work at the end of the day, between day-shift and night-shift. **2** the group of workers undertaking such work. **backside** *n.* **1** (*coll.*) the buttocks. **2** the back or hinder portion of anything. **backsight** *n.* **1** a sight taken backwards in land surveying. **2** the sight of a rifle near the stock. **back slang** *n.* a peculiar kind of slang in which ordinary words are pronounced backwards (such as, *Cool the eslop* (or *slop*), Look, the police). **backslapping** *a.* hearty in a demonstrative or vigorous way. **backslash** *n.* a reverse solidus. **backslide** *v.i.* (*past, p.p.* **backslid,** *p.p.* **backslidden**) **1** to fall into wrongdoing or false opinions. **2** to relapse. **backslider** *n.* **backspace** *v.i.* to move a typewriter carriage or a cursor back one space using a key. *~n.* a typewriter or computer key that does this. **backspacer** *n.* a backspace. **back-speed** *n.* the second-speed gear of a lathe. **backspin** *n.* in tennis, golf etc., the spin of a ball against the direction it is moving in, imparted to dull the bounce. **backstage** *a., adv.* **1** behind the scenes. **2** out of public view. **backstairs** *n.pl.* **1** stairs at the back of a house. **2** the private stairs in a large house or palace for the use of servants etc. *~a.* clandestine, underhand, scandalous. **backstair** *a.* clandestine, backstairs. **backstay** *n.* a rope or stay extending with a slant aft from a mast-head to the side of a ship. **backstitch** *n.* a method of sewing with stitches that are made to overlap. *~v.t., v.i.* to sew in this manner. **backstop** *n.* **1** a fielder in cricket or baseball who stands behind the person batting. **2** this fielding position. **3** a screen or barrier used to stop the ball in some sports. **backstreet** *n.* **1** a street away from the centre of the town. **2** (*pl.*) the poorer streets of a town. **back-street abortion** *n.* an abortion performed by an unqualified person. **back-string** *n.* **1** a string at the back. **2** the fastener of a pinafore. **backstroke** *n.* **1** a swimming stroke performed on the back. **2** a return stroke. **back talk** *n.* (*N Am., coll.*) backchat. **back to back** *adv.* **1** with backs facing each other. **2** (*N Am.*) consecutively. **back-to-back** *a.* **1** (of a house) with its back adjoining another so that they face in opposite directions. **2** (*N Am.*) consecutive. *~n.* a back-to-back house. **back to front** *a., adv.* **1** in reverse, the wrong way round. **2** in disorder. **back-to-nature** *a.* involving enthusiasm or desire for a simpler, more natural life. **backtrack** *v.i.* **1** to retrace one's steps. **2** to reverse an opinion, attitude etc. **backup** *n.* **1** support. **2** reinforcement, reserve. **3** the act or process of duplicating a computer data file for security. **4** a duplicate copy of a computer data file. **5** a queue of traffic etc. built up. **backup light** *n.* (*N Am.*) a reversing light. **backveld** *n.* (*S Afr.*) country far removed from towns. *~a.* remote, rural, primitive. **backvelder** *n.* **backwash** *n.* **1** the wash from the oars of a boat in front. **2** the dragging motion of a receding wave. **3** a backward current. **4** eddy or swirl caused by a ship's propeller. **5** the rush of air from an aircraft engine. **6** reaction; aftermath. **backwater** *n.* **1** a remote place out of touch with mainstream or advanced thought or behaviour. **2** water dammed back or that has overflowed. **3** a piece of water without current fed by the back flow of a river. **4** a backward current of water. **5** a creek or lagoon separated from the sea by a narrow strip of land and communicating with it by barred outlets. **6** the wash thrown back by a waterwheel or the paddles or screws of a steamboat. **back-way** *n.* **1** a way leading to the back. **2** a roundabout way; a bypath. **backwoods** *n.pl.* **1** remote, uncleared forest land. **2** (*derog.*) a remote, uncultured area. **backwoodsman** *n.* (*pl.* **backwoodsmen**) **1** a settler in the backwoods. **2** an uncultivated person. **3** (*coll.*) a peer who rarely attends the House of Lords. **backyard** *n.* **1** a yard behind a house etc. **2** (*N Am.*) a back garden. **in one's own backyard** near one's own home, close by, locally. [OE *bæc*]

back² (bak) *n.* a large tub used in brewing, distilling, dyeing etc. [Dut. *bak*, trough, tub, F *bac*, ferry-boat, punt, late L *baccus*, ferry-boat]

backgammon (bak´gamən) *n.* **1** a game played by two persons on a table with pieces moved according to the throw of dice. **2** the highest win in backgammon. *~v.t.* to defeat at backgammon. [BACK¹, GAME¹]

backsheesh BAKSHEESH.

backwards (bak´wədz), **backward** *adv.* **1** with the back foremost. **2** towards the back or rear. **3** behind, towards the starting-point. **4** towards past time. **5** towards a worse state or condition. **6** in reverse order. **backward** *a.* **1** directed to the back or rear. **2** directed the way from which one has come, reversed. **3** reluctant, unwilling. **4** (esp. of the season, crops etc.) behind in time, late. **5** behind in progress; mentally handicapped. **6** towards or into past time. **7** in cricket, denoting the position of a fielder behind a line through the stumps at right angles to the wicket. **backward and forward** **1** to and fro. **2** in an uncertain or vacillating manner. **backwards and forwards** backward and forward. **to bend/ fall/ lean over backwards** to go to great pains, esp. to help. **backwardation** (-ā´shən) *n.* a consideration paid by a seller of stock for the privilege of delaying its delivery. **backwardly** *adv.* **1** in a backward direction. **2** in a reluctant or negligent manner. **backwardness** *n.* [orig. *abackward*]

baclava BAKLAVA.

bacon (bā´kən) *n.* the cured back and sides of a pig. **to bring home the bacon** **1** (*coll.*) to succeed. **2** (*coll.*) to provide a living. **to save one's bacon** (*coll.*) to escape from injury or loss. **bacon-like** *a.* in a state of fatty degeneration. **bacony** *a.* [OF, from OHG *bacho* (MHG *backe*), buttock, ham]

Baconian (bəkō´niən) *a.* 1 of or relating to Bacon or his inductive philosophy. 2 experimental, inductive. ~*n.* 1 a follower of the inductive system of natural philosophy. 2 a believer in the conceit that Bacon was really the author of Shakespeare's works. [Francis *Bacon*, 1561–1626]

bacteri- BACTERIO-.

bacteria BACTERIUM.

bactericide (baktiə´risīd) *n.* an agent that destroys bacteria. **bactericidal** *a.*

bacterio- (baktiə´riō), **bacteri-** *comb. form* of or relating to bacteria.

bacteriology (baktiəriol´əji) *n.* the scientific study of bacteria. **bacteriological** (-loj´-) *a.* **bacteriologically** *adv.* **bacteriologist** *n.*

bacteriolysis (baktiəriol´isis) *n.* the destruction of bacteria. **bacteriolytic** (-lit´-) *a.* [Gr. *lusis*, dissolution]

bacteriophage (baktiə´riəfāj) *n.* a virus which destroys bacteria. **bacteriophagic** (-faj´-) *a.* [Gr. *phagein*, to eat]

bacteriostasis (baktiəriəstā´sis) *n.* inhibition of the growth of bacterial cells. **bacteriostat** (-tiə´riōstat) *n.* any substance which stops the growth of bacteria without killing them. **bacteriostatic** (-stat´-) *a.* [Gr. *stasis*, standing]

bacterium (baktiə´riəm) *n.* (*pl.* **bacteria**) a member of a large group of microscopic unicellular organisms found in soil, water and as saprophytes or parasites in organic bodies. **bacterial** *a.* [Gr. *baktērion*, dim. of *baktron*, a stick]

Usage note *Bacteria* is commonly used as a singular noun (*a bacteria*), but it should always be a plural, with *bacterium* as the singular.

bacteroid (bak´təroid) *a.* of the nature of or resembling a bacterium.

Bactrian (bak´triən) *a.* of or relating to Bactria in central Asia. **Bactrian camel** *n.* a camel with two humps, *Camelus ferus*.

baculine (bak´ūlīn) *a.* characterized by the stick, cane or flogging. [L *baculum*, a stick]

bad (bad) *a.* (*comp.* **worse**, *superl.* **worst**) 1 not good, worthless; unsatisfactory; unpleasant. 2 defective, faulty, incorrect. 3 evil, hurtful, harmful; wicked, morally depraved, offensive. 4 noxious, painful, dangerous, pernicious. 5 in ill-health, sick. 6 injured, diseased. 7 sorry for what one has done, guiltily responsible. 8 (*Law*) invalid. 9 (*N Am., sl.*) very good. ~*n.* 1 that which is bad. 2 a bad state or condition. **bad cess to you!** CESS[2]. **bad scran to you!** SCRAN. **from bad to worse** to a worse state from an already bad one. **in a bad light** LIGHT[1]. **in a bad way** ill, seriously out of sorts. **in bad odour** ODOUR. **in bad taste** TASTE. **in someone's bad books** BOOK. **like a bad penny** PENNY. **not (so) bad** quite good. **to come to a bad end** END. **to go bad** to decay. **to go to the bad** to go to ruin, to go to the dogs. **to make bad weather** WEATHER. **too bad** TOO. **to the bad** 1 to ruin. 2 to the wrong side of an account. **with a bad grace** GRACE. **badass** (bad´as) *n.* (*esp. N Am., sl.*) 1 an aggressive person. 2 a troublemaker. ~*a.* 1 aggressive. 2 bad or worthless. 3 excellent. **bad bargain** *n.* a purchase or sale adverse to the party under consideration. **bad blood** *n.* mutual hostility or ill feeling. **bad break** *n.* (*coll.*) 1 bad luck. 2 a mistake. **bad breath** *n.* breath that smells. **bad company** *n.* 1 a person who is boring or not fun to be with. 2 a person who is not suitable as a friend, or a group of such people. **bad debt** *n.* a debt that cannot be recovered. **baddish** *a.* rather bad. **baddy, baddie** *n.* (*pl.* **baddies**) (*coll.*) a criminal or wrong-doer, esp. an evil character in fiction, cinema, television or radio. **bad egg, bad lot, bad penny** *n.* 1 a bad speculation. 2 a ne'er-do-well. **bad faith** *n.* intent to deceive. **bad form** *n.* 1 bad manners. 2 lack of breeding. **bad hair day** *n.* (*sl.*) a day on which one would rather not face the world, a day on which everything seems to go wrong for one. **bad hat** *n.* a rogue, ne'er-do-well. **bad job** *n.* (*coll.*) a sad or unfortunate turn of affairs. **badlands** *n.pl.* 1 tracts of arid country in the western states of America. 2 unsafe parts of a country. **bad language** *n.* swearing. **bad lot** *n.* a disreputable person, a person of bad character. **badly** *adv.* (*comp.* **worse**, *superl.* **worst**) 1 in a bad manner. 2 improperly, wickedly, evilly. 3 unskilfully, imperfectly. 4 defectively. 5 faultily. 6 dangerously, disastrously. 7 (*coll.*) very much, by much. **to want something badly** to want something very much. **badly off** *a.* not wealthy or fortunate. **bad mouth** *n.* (*coll.*) malicious gossip, abuse. **bad-mouth** *v.t.* (*coll.*) to abuse, to criticize. **badness** *n.* 1 the quality of being bad. 2 inferiority. 3 incorrectness, faultiness. 4 wickedness. 5 worthlessness. **bad news** *n.* (*coll.*) a person who or thing that is undesirable. **bad patch** *n.* (*coll.*) a sequence of bad experiences. **bad quarter of an hour** *n.* MAUVAIS QUART D'HEURE. **bad sailor** *n.* a person who is liable to be seasick. **bad shot** *n.* a wrong guess. **bad show** *n., int.* (something) badly done. **bad temper** *n.* an angry mood, a tendency to anger. **bad-tempered** *a.* irritable or ungracious. **bad-temperedly** *adv.* **bad turn** *n.* a disservice. **bad word** *n.* 1 criticism of someone. 2 (*coll.*) a swear-word. [etym. uncertain]

bade BID.

badge (baj) *n.* 1 a distinctive mark, sign or token. 2 an emblem sewn on clothing. 3 (*Her.*) a cognizance. 4 (*Naut.*) an ornament on the quarters of small vessels, near the stern. 5 a feature or quality that characterizes. ~*v.t.* to mark with or as with a badge. [etym. uncertain]

badger (baj´ə) *n.* 1 a nocturnal plantigrade mammal of the weasel family, with thick body and short legs and a head with two stripes, *Meles meles*, found in Britain, Europe and Asia. 2 a related mammal, *Taxidea taxus*, found in N America. 3 a painter's brush, or angler's fly, made of badgers' hair. ~*v.t.* to worry, to tease, to annoy like dogs baiting a badger. **badger-baiting, badger-drawing** *n.* the setting of dogs to draw a badger from its earth or from a barrel. **badger-dog** *n.* the dachshund (orig. used to draw badgers). [etym. uncertain (prob. in allusion to white mark on face)]

badigeon (bədij´ən) *n.* 1 a mixture of plaster and freestone used by sculptors to repair defects in stone, and by builders to present the appearance of stone. 2 a mixture of sawdust and glue, used to conceal defects in woodwork. [F, etym. unknown]

badinage (bad´inahzh, -nij) *n.* light good-humoured, playful talk, banter. [F, from *badiner*, to jest (*badin*, silly, late L *badāre*, to gape)]

badminton (bad´mintən) *n.* 1 a game resembling tennis, but played, usu. indoors, with shuttlecocks instead of balls. 2 a kind of claret-cup. [name of country seat of Duke of Beaufort]

BAe *abbr.* British Aerospace.

Baedeker (bā´dikə) *n.* 1 any of the series of guide-books published by the firm of Karl Baedeker (1801–59). 2 any similar guide-book.

baffle (baf´əl) *v.t.* 1 to bewilder, perplex, confound. 2 to thwart, defeat. 3 to frustrate, elude, escape, circumvent. 4 to regulate the volume or flow of. 5 †to scoff at. ~*v.i.* to struggle ineffectually. ~*n.* 1 a defeat. 2 a rigid appliance that regulates the distribution of sound-waves from a producer. **baffle board** *n.* a device to prevent the carrying of noise, esp. to prevent sound from spreading in different directions. **bafflement** *n.* **baffle plate** *n.* a plate used to direct the flow of fluid or to reduce noise etc. **baffler** *n.* **baffling** *a.* 1 bewildering. 2 thwarting. 3 (of winds) variable, shifting. **bafflingly** *adv.* [perh. F *beffler*, to deceive, mock, or *bafouer*, to hoodwink (OF *befel*, mockery, It. *beffa*, Prov. *bafa*, a scoff, perh. from *baf!* an imit. int.)]

baft (baft) *n.* a cheap coarse fabric. [prob. Pers., wrought, woven]

BAFTA (baf´tə) *abbr.* British Academy of Film and Television Arts.

bag (bag) *n.* **1** a pouch, small sack or other flexible receptacle. **2** a measure of quantity, varying with different commodities. **3** the contents of such a measure. **4** a game-bag, the result of a day's sport or of a hunting expedition. **5** a purse, a money-bag. **6** an item of luggage; a handbag. **7** a sac or baglike receptacle in animal bodies containing some secretion; an udder. **8** (*pl.*) folds of skin under the eyes. **9** (*pl.*) loose clothes, esp. trousers. **10** (*pl.*, *coll.*) quantities. **11** (*sl.*) a slovenly, bad-tempered or ugly woman, often in *old bag*. ~*v.t.* **1** to put into a bag. **2** to take, seize, appropriate. **3** (*coll.*) to steal. **4** (*coll.*) to claim by speaking first (*Bags I get breakfast first tomorrow*). **5** to shoot or catch for a game-bag. ~*v.i.* (*pres.p.* **bagging**, *past*, *p.p.* **bagged**) **1** to swell as a bag. **2** to hang loosely. **3** (*Naut.*) to drop away from the direct course. **bag o' moonshine** (*coll.*) nonsense. **in the bag** (*coll.*) secured or as good as secured. **to give someone the bag to hold** to slip off, leave in the lurch. **whole bag of tricks** WHOLE. **bag and baggage** *n.* **1** with all belongings. **2** entirely, completely. **bag-fox** *n.* a fox brought alive to a meet and turned out of a bag. **bagful** *n.* (*pl.* **bagfuls**) as much or as many as a bag will hold. **bagging** *n.* cloth, canvas or other material for bags. **baggy** *a.* (*comp.* **baggier**, *superl.* **baggiest**) **1** loose. **2** bulging out like a bag. **3** (of trousers etc.) stretched by wear. **baggily** *adv.* **bagginess** *n.* looseness. **bag lady** *n.* (*pl.* **bag ladies**) (*coll.*) a female vagrant. **bagman** *n.* (*pl.* **bagmen**) **1** (*coll.*) a travelling salesman. **2** a vagrant. **3** (*N Am.*, *sl.*) a person who collects and transports money for gangsters. **4** (*Can.*) a fund-raiser for a political party. **bag of bones** *n.* a living skeleton, someone very thin. **bag of nerves** *n.* (*coll.*) BUNDLE OF NERVES (under BUNDLE). **bag-swinger** *n.* (*Austral.*) a bookmaker. **bag-wash** *n.* a system of laundry-work by which a comprehensive charge is made for a bagful of garments. **bag-wig** *n.* a wig fashionable in the 18th cent. in which the back hair was enclosed in a bag. **bagworm** *n.* a caterpillar or larva of the family Psychidae, which forms a protective covering from silk, leaves etc. **bagworm moth** *n.* a moth of the bagworm family. [etym. uncertain; perh. Icel. *baggi*]

BAGA *abbr.* British Amateur Gymnastics Association.

☒ **bagage** common misspelling of BAGGAGE.

bagasse (bəgas´) *n.* **1** the refuse products in sugar-making. **2** cane-trash. [Sp. *bagazo*, residue]

bagatelle (bagətel´) *n.* **1** a game played on a nine-holed board with pins obstructing the holes, with nine balls to be struck into them. **2** a trifle, a negligible amount. **3** a light piece of music. [F, from It. *bagatelle*, a trifle (perh. dim. of *baga*, baggage)]

bagel (bā´gəl) *n.* a ring-shaped bread roll. [Yiddish *beygel*]

baggage (bag´ij) *n.* **1** luggage; belongings packed for travelling. **2** portable belongings, esp. the tents, furniture, utensils and other necessaries of an army. **3** knowledge and experience as encumbrances. **4** a woman of loose character. **5** (*facet.*) a playful arch young woman. ~*a.* used for carrying or looking after or convoying baggage. **baggage-car** *n.* (*N Am.*) a railway luggage-van. **baggage-man, baggage-master** *n.* (*N Am.*) a guard in charge of passengers' luggage. **baggage-train** *n.* the part of an army that conveys the baggage. [OF *bagage* (*baguer*, to tie up, or *bagues*, bundles; It. *baga*, a wine-skin; see also BAG)]

bagging, baggy BAG.

bagnio (ban´yō) *n.* (*pl.* **bagnios**) **1** a brothel. **2** an oriental prison for slaves. **3** a bathing-house, a bath. [It. *bagno*, L *balneum*, a bath]

bagpipe (bag´pīp) *n.* a musical instrument of great antiquity, now chiefly used in the Scottish Highlands, consisting of a windbag and several reed-pipes into which the air is pressed by the player. **bagpiper** *n.*

baguette (baget´), **baguet** *n.* **1** a narrow stick of French bread. **2** a precious stone cut into a rectangular shape. **3** a small semicircular moulding. [F, rod, from L *baculum*]

bah (bah) *int.* expressing contempt. [perh. from F *bah!*]

bahadur (bəhah´duə) *n.* a ceremonious title formerly given in India to officers and distinguished officials. [Hind., brave]

Baha'i (bəhah´i) *n.* (*pl.* **Baha'is**) a follower of a religious movement originating in Iran in the 19th cent., which stresses the validity of all world religions and the spiritual unity of all humanity. **Baha'ism** *n.* **Baha'ist** *n.* [Pers. *baha'i*, lit. of glory]

Bahamian (bəhā´miən) *n.* **1** a native or inhabitant of the Bahamas. **2** a person descended from Bahamians. ~*a.* of or relating to the Bahamas.

Bahasa Indonesia (bəhahsə indənē´ziə) *n.* the official language of Indonesia. [Indonesian *bahasa*, language, from Sansk. *bhāsā* speech]

baht (baht) *n.* (*pl.* **baht**) the standard unit of currency in Thailand.

Bahutu HUTU.

baignoire (bān´wah) *n.* a box at the theatre on the lowest tier. [F, orig. a vessel for bathing in, from *baigner*, to bathe]

bail[1] (bāl) *n.* **1** the temporary release of a prisoner from custody on security given for their due surrender when required. **2** the money security, or the person or persons giving security, for the due surrender of a prisoner temporarily released. **3** security, guarantee. ~*v.t.* **1** to procure the liberation of (a prisoner) by giving sureties. **2** to admit to or release on bail. **3** to deliver (goods) in trust on an expressed or implied contract. **to bail out 1** to procure release on bail from prison. **2** to rescue from difficulty. **to forfeit bail** to jump bail. **to go bail** to stand bail. **to jump bail** (*coll.*) to fail to appear when required after release on bail. **to stand bail** to secure freedom until trial for an accused on payment of surety. **bailable** *a.* **1** entitled to be admitted to bail. **2** admitting of bail. **bail bandit** *n.* an offender who breaks the law while on bail. **bail-bond** *n.* a bond entered into by a prisoner upon release on bail, and their sureties. **bailment** *n.* **1** delivery of goods. **2** delivery in trust. **3** the bailing of a prisoner. **bailout** *n.* financial help given to a person or company to prevent collapse. **bailsman** *n.* (*pl.* **bailsmen**) a person who gives bail. [OF *bail*, safe keeping, from *bailler*, L *bāiulāre*, to carry, to guard (*bāiulus*, a porter)]

bail[2] (bāl) *n.* **1** in cricket, either of the crosspieces laid on top of the wicket. **2** a division between the stalls of a stable. **3** (*Austral.*, *New Zeal.*) a framework for securing the head of a cow while she is being milked. **4** a bar on a typewriter that holds the paper in position. **5** †the outer line of fortifications, a palisade. **6** †the wall of the outer courtyard in a feudal castle, a bailey. ~*v.i.* to surrender by throwing up the arms. ~*v.t.* **1** to make (a person) surrender by throwing up their arms. **2** (*Austral.*, *New Zeal.*) to fasten (up) the head of (a cow) for milking. **3** to buttonhole. **bailer**[1] *n.* in cricket, a ball that hits off the bails. [OF *bail* (etym. uncertain, perh. from *baillier*, to enclose)]

bail[3] (bāl), **bale** *v.t.* **1** to throw (water) out of a boat with a shallow vessel. **2** to empty (a boat) of water. **to bail out** BALE[3]. **bailer**[2] *n.* a person or thing which bails water out of a boat etc. [obs. n. *bail*, a bucket, bailer, F *baile*, a bucket (prob. from late L *bacula*, dim. of *baca*, *bacca*, a shallow vessel)]

bail[4] (bāl) *n.* **1** a hoop or ring. **2** the arched support for an awning or hood. **3** the handle of a kettle. [ME *beyl*, Icel. *beygla*, hoop, guard of a sword-hilt]

bailee (bālē´) *n.* a person to whom goods are entrusted for a specific purpose. [BAIL[1]]

bailer[1] BAIL[2].

bailer[2] BAIL[3].

bailey (bā´li) *n.* (*pl.* **baileys**) **1** the wall enclosing the outer court of a feudal castle. **2** the outer court itself. **3** any other courts or enclosures of courts (*the outer bailey; the inner bailey*). [BAIL[2] (perh. from med. L *balium*)]

Bailey bridge (bā´li) *n.* (*Mil.*) a bridge of lattice steel construction made of standard parts for rapid erection and transport. [Sir Donald *Bailey*, 1901–85, its inventor]

bailie (bā´li) *n.* **1** a Scottish municipal magistrate corresponding to an English alderman. **2** †a Scottish magistrate with duties corresponding to those of an English sheriff. [ME *bailli*, OF *bailli* (obs. *baillis*, *baillif*), BAILIFF]

bailiff (bā´lif) *n.* **1** a sheriff's officer who executes writs and distrains. **2** an agent or steward to a landowner. **3** (*N Am.*) a courtroom official who keeps order etc. **4** an officer appointed for the administration of justice in a certain bailiwick or district. **5** a foreign magistrate of similar standing (e.g. *Bailly* or first civil officer of the Channel Isles). **6** †a king's administrative officer (still used in *High Bailiff of Westminster, Bailiff of Dover Castle*). [OF *baillif* (nom. *baillis*), late L *bāiukīvus* (see BAIL[1])]

bailiwick (bā´liwik) *n.* **1** the district within which a bailie or bailiff possesses jurisdiction. **2** (*coll.*) the range of a person's interest or authority. [BAILIE, WICK[2]]

bailor (bā´lə) *n.* (*Law*) a person who entrusts another person with goods for a specific purpose. [BAIL[1]]

Baily's beads (bā´liz) *n.pl.* the brilliant points of sunlight that appear to be strung round the moon just at the beginning and end of a solar eclipse. [Francis *Baily*, 1774–1844, English astronomer]

bain-marie (bãmərē´) *n.* (*pl.* **bains-marie** (bãmərē´)) a vessel of boiling water into which saucepans are put for slow heating; a double saucepan. [F (L *balneum Mariae*, the bath of Maria)]

Bairam (bīram´) *n.* either of two Muslim festivals following the Ramadan, the *Lesser* lasting three days, the *Greater*, which falls seventy days later, lasting four days. [Turk., from Pers. *bairām*]

bairn (beən) *n.* (*Sc. or North.*) a child. [OE *bearn* (cp. Icel. *barn*, Goth. *barn*, Gmc. *beran*, to bear)]

bait (bāt) *v.t.* **1** to furnish (a hook, gin, snare etc.) with real or sham food to entice prey. **2** to tempt, entice, allure. **3** to set dogs to worry (an animal). **4** to worry, harass, torment. **5** to give food to (a horse) on a journey, to feed. ~*v.i.* to stop on a journey for rest or refreshment. ~*n.* **1** an attractive morsel put on a hook, gin, snare etc., to attract fish or animals. **2** worms, insects, grubs, small fish etc., so used. **3** food, refreshment on a journey. **4** a halt for refreshment. **5** a temptation, allurement. **6** BATE[1]. **baiting** *n.* (*usu. in comb.*) worrying with dogs, such as *badger-baiting, bear-baiting, bull-baiting.* [Icel. *beita*, to cause to bite (*bita*, to bite)]

baize (bāz) *n.* a coarse woollen material something like felt. [F *baies*, pl. fem of a. *bai* (L *badius*), chestnut-coloured]

bajra (bahj´rə) *n.* a type of Indian millet. [Hind.]

bake (bāk) *v.t.* **1** to cook by dry conducted (as opposed to radiated) heat, to cook in an oven or on a heated surface. **2** to dry and harden by means of fire or by the sun's rays. ~*v.i.* **1** to cook food by baking. **2** to undergo the process of baking. **3** to become dry and hard by heat. **4** (of a person, weather etc.) to be very hot, be affected by the heat of the sun. **to bake blind** BLIND. **baked** *a.* that has been baked. **baked Alaska** *n.* a dessert of ice-cream covered with meringue baked in an oven. **baked beans** *n.pl.* haricot beans baked and usu. tinned in tomato sauce. **bakehouse** *n.* a house or building in which baking is carried on. †**bake-meat, baked-meat** *n.* pastry, a pie. **baker** *n.* a person whose occupation is to bake bread, biscuits etc. **baker's dozen** *n.* thirteen. **bakery** *n.* (*pl.* **bakeries**) **1** the trade or calling of a baker. **2** a bakehouse. **3** a baker's establishment. **bakestone** *n.* a stone or metal plate on which muffins and cakes are baked. **baking** *n.* **1** the action of cooking by dry heat. **2** the quantity baked at one operation. **baking powder** *n.* a powder of bicarbonate of soda and tartaric acid used as a raising agent. **baking soda** *n.* sodium bicarbonate. [OE *bacan*]

Bakelite® (bā´kəlīt) *n.* a synthetic resin made from formaldehyde and phenol, used for insulating purposes and in the manufacture of plastics, paints and varnishes. [LH *Baekeland*, 1863–1944, inventor]

Baker day (bā´kə) *n.* any one of the days during the British school year set aside for the training of teachers. [Kenneth *Baker*, b. 1934, politician]

Bakewell tart (bāk´wel) *n.* an open tart with a pastry base, containing jam and almond paste. [*Bakewell* in Derbyshire]

baking BAKE.

baklava (bəklah´və), **baclava** *n.* a cake made from layered pastry strips with nuts and honey. [Turkish]

baksheesh (bak´shēsh), **bakhshish, backsheesh** *n.* a gratuity, a tip (used without the article). [Pers., a present]

balaclava (baləklah´və), **balaclava helmet** *n.* a tight woollen covering for the head, ears, chin and neck. [*Balaclava* in Crimea]

balalaika (baləlī´kə) *n.* a three-stringed triangular-shaped musical instrument resembling a guitar. [Rus.]

balance (bal´əns) *n.* **1** (*often pl.*) a pair of scales. **2** any other instrument used for weighing. **3** equipoise, an equality of weight or power; stability. **4** the amount necessary to make two unequal amounts equal. **5** the difference between the debtor and creditor side of the account. **6** harmony of design, perfect proportion; desirable relative volume. **7** (*coll.*) the remainder, the residue. **8** a contrivance for regulating the speed of a clock or watch. **9** an impartial state of mind. **10** that which renders weight or authority equal. **11** a zodiacal constellation, Libra. **12** the seventh sign of the zodiac, which the sun enters at the autumnal equinox. ~*v.t.* **1** to weigh. **2** to compare by weighing. **3** to compare. **4** to bring to an equipoise, to equalize, to steady. **5** to adjust an account, to make two amounts equal. **6** to sway backwards and forwards. ~*v.i.* **1** to be in equipoise, to have equal weight or force. **2** to have the debtor and creditor side equal. **3** to oscillate. **4** in dancing, to move to and fro in an opposite direction to that of one's partner. **in the balance** in an uncertain or undecided state. **on balance** taking all factors into consideration. **to hang in the balance** to be unresolved. **to hold the balance** to have the power of deciding. **to keep one's balance** **1** not to tumble, to avoid falling. **2** to remain sane and sensible. **to lose one's balance** **1** to tumble. **2** to be upset mentally. **to strike a balance** to reckon up the balance on a statement of credit and indebtedness. **balanced** *a.* **1** having good balance. **2** sane, sensible (*often in comb.*, such as *well-balanced*). **balance of mind** *n.* sanity. **balance of payments** *n.* the difference over a period of time between the total payments (for goods and services) to, and total receipts from, abroad. **balance of power** *n.* **1** a condition of equilibrium among sovereign states, supposed to be a guarantee of peace. **2** a condition of having power because other greater powers are equal. **balance of trade** *n.* the difference between the imports and exports of a country. **balancer** *n.* **1** a person who or that which balances. **2** an acrobat. **3** an organ in lieu of the posterior wing on each side of the Diptera. **balancer meal** *n.* poultry meal mixed with various nutritive ingredients. **balance-reef** *n.* the closest reef, a lower fore-and-aft sail. **balance sheet** *n.* a tabular statement of accounts, showing receipts and expenditure. **balance-step** *n.* the goose-step. **balance wheel** *n.* the wheel regulating the beat in clocks, watches etc. **balancing act** *n.* the act of achieving a balance between different needs or situations (*Trying to keep all the children happy required quite a balancing act*). [F, from L *bilancem* (nom. *bilanx*), two-scaled, in *libra bilanx* (*bi-*, two, *lanx*, a flat plate)]

balas (bal´əs) *n.* a rose-red variety of the spinel ruby. [OF *balais*, low L *balascius*, Arab. *balakhsh*, Pers. *Badakhshān* (L *Balaxia*), name of district near Samarkand where found]

balata (bal´ətə) *n.* **1** any of various Central American trees which yield latex, esp. *Mankara bidentata*. **2** the dried latex of this. [Am. Sp., of Carib. origin]

balboa (balbō´ə) *n.* the unit of currency in Panama. [Vasco Nuñez de *Balboa*, *c.* 1475–1517]

Balbriggan (balbrig´ən) *n.* a knitted cotton fabric used for hose and other goods. [*Balbriggan*, in Co. Dublin, where it was orig. made]

balcony (bal´kəni) *n.* (*pl.* **balconies**) **1** a gallery or platform projecting from a house or other building. **2** in theatres, a tier of seats between the dress circle and the gallery. **3** (*N Am.*) the dress circle. **balconied** *a.* [It. *balcone*, *balco*, OHG *balcho*, a scaffold]

bald (bawld) *a.* **1** without hair upon the crown of the head. **2** (of species of birds, animals etc.) having no feathers or hair on the head. **3** bare, treeless, leafless. **4** (*coll.*) (of a tyre etc.) having a worn-away surface. **5** (of horses) streaked or marked with white. **6** trivial, meagre. **7** destitute of ornament or grace. **8** undisguised, shameless. **bald as a coot** completely bald (alluding to the broad base of the bill across the coot's forehead). **bald eagle** *n.* the American white-headed eagle, *Haliaeetus leucocephalus*, the emblem of the US. **baldhead** *n.* a person who is bald. **bald-headed** *a.* with a bald head. **to go at it bald-headed** to attack or undertake something boldly, regardless of consequences. **balding** *a.* going bald. **baldish** *a.* **baldly** *adv.* **1** in a bald manner. **2** nakedly, shamelessly, inelegantly. **3** plainly. **baldmoney** *n.* (*pl.* **baldmoneys**) SPIGNEL. **baldness** *n.* **baldpate** *n.* **1** a person who is bald. **2** a variety of duck and pigeon. ~*a.* bald. **bald-pated** *a.* having no hair on the head. **baldy, baldie** *n.* (*pl.* **baldies**) (*coll.*) a person who is bald. ~*a.* bald. [ME *balled*, etym. uncertain (perh. from Celt. *bal*, white mark on animal's face; cp. W *ceffyl bàl*, a horse with white forehead, Welsh and Gael. *bal*, spot, mark)]

baldachin (bawl´dəkin), **baldachino** (-kē´nō), **baldaquin, baudekin** (baw´dikin), **baudkin** (bawd´kin) *n.* **1** a canopy over an altar, throne or doorway, generally supported by pillars, but sometimes suspended from above, formerly of the material described below. **2** †a kind of rich brocade of silk and gold. [F and Sp. *baldaquin*, It. *baldacchino* (*Baldaco*, *Bagdad*, whence it originated)]

balderdash (bawl´dədash) *n.* **1** rubbish, nonsense. **2** confused speech or writing. **3** a jumble of words. [etym. uncertain]

baldric (bawl´drik), **baudric** (bawd´-) *n.* a richly ornamented girdle or belt, passing over one shoulder and under the opposite, to support dagger, sword, bugle etc. **baldric-wise** *adv.* worn like a baldric. [ME *baudrik*, *baudry*, OF *baudrei* (cp. MHG *balderich* and low L *baldringus*, perh. from L *balteus*, a belt)]

bale[1] (bāl) *n.* **1** a package. **2** a certain quantity of goods or merchandise, wrapped in cloth or baling-paper and corded for transportation. ~*v.t.* to pack in a bale or bales. **bale-goods** *n.pl.* goods done up in bales, as distinguished from those packed in barrels, boxes etc. **baler** *n.* a machine that makes bales of hay, straw etc. **baling** *n.* the process of putting goods into bales. **baling-paper** *n.* (*N Am.*) stout paper for packing. **baling-press** *n.* a press used to compress goods before putting them into bales. [OF *bale* (prob. from MHG *balla*, *palla*)]

†**bale**[2] (bāl) *n.* **1** evil, mischief, calamity. **2** pain, sorrow, misery. **baleful** *a.* **1** full of evil. **2** pernicious, harmful, deadly. **balefully** *adv.* **balefulness** *n.* [OE *bealo* (cp. OS and OFris. *balu*, OHG *balo*), evil]

bale[3] (bāl), **bail** *v.i.* (*followed by out*) to abandon an aeroplane in the air and descend by parachute. ~*v.t.* (*followed by out*) to help out of a difficulty. [BAIL[3]]

baleen (bəlēn´) *n.* whalebone. ~*a.* of whalebone. **baleen whale** *n.* a whale of the suborder Mysticeti having plates of whalebone in its mouth, with which it filters plankton. [OF *baleine*, L *balaena*, a whale]

☒ **balence** common misspelling of BALANCE.

Balinese (bahlinēz´) *n.* (*pl.* **Balinese**) **1** a native or inhabitant of Bali. **2** (*as pl.*) the people of Bali. **3** the language spoken by the people of Bali. ~*a.* of or relating to Bali.

balk BAULK.

Balkan (bawl´kən) *a.* of or relating to the region of SE Europe which includes the Balkan Peninsula. **the Balkans** the Balkan countries. **Balkanize** (bawl´kənīz), **Balkanise** *v.t.* to split (a region) into a number of smaller and often mutually hostile states, as occurred in the Balkan Peninsula during the 19th and early 20th cents. **Balkanization** (-zā´shən) *n.*

ball[1] (bawl) *n.* **1** a spherical body of any dimensions, a globe. **2** such a body, differing in size, make and hardness, used in games. **3** anything made, rolled or packed into a spherical shape. **4** a rounded natural object or part of the body; a planetary or celestial body (usu. with qualifying adjective). **5** (*pl.*, *sl.*) testicles. **6** (*pl.*, *sl.*) courage, nerve. **7** (*pl.*, *sl.*) a mess, a bungle. **8** a globular body of wood, ivory or other substance used for voting by ballot. **9** a throw, delivery, pass or cast of the ball in games. **10** a game with a ball. ~*v.t.* **1** to make, roll or pack into a ball. **2** to clog (as a horse's foot with a collection of snow). ~*v.i.* **1** to gather into a ball. **2** to become clogged. **3** (of bees) to cluster round the queen when they swarm. **on the ball 1** alert. **2** in control. **the ball is in your court** it is your move, it is your turn to act. **to balls up** (*sl.*) to mess up or botch (a situation). **to have the ball at one's feet** to have a chance or opportunity. **to keep/ start the ball rolling** to keep the conversation, debate, work or game from flagging. **to make a balls of** (*sl.*) to make a mess of; to botch, do badly. **to play ball** (*coll.*) to cooperate (*I've asked him, but he just won't play ball*). **ball and socket** *n.* an instrument made of brass with a universal screw, capable of being turned in any direction. **ball-and-socket joint** *n.* **1** a joint formed by a ball playing in a socket, and admitting of motion in any direction. **2** joints like those of the human hip and shoulder. **ball-bearing** *n.* **1** (*usu. pl.*) a bearing containing loose metallic balls for lessening friction. **2** an axle-bearing of this kind. **3** a metal ball used in such a bearing. **ballboy** *n.* a boy who retrieves the balls that go out of play in a game of tennis. **ball cartridge** *n.* a cartridge containing a bullet. **ballcock, balltap** *n.* a self-acting tap which is turned off or on by the rising or falling of a hollow ball on the surface of the water in a cistern, boiler etc. **balled** *a.* formed into a ball. **ballgame** *n.* **1** a game played with a ball. **2** (*N Am.*) baseball. **a different ballgame** (*coll.*) something quite different. **ballgirl** *n.* a girl who retrieves the balls that go out of play in a game of tennis. **ball lightning** *n.* floating luminous balls sometimes seen during thunderstorms. **ball of**

fire *n.* (*coll.*) a dynamic or lively individual. **ball of the eye** *n.* **1** the pupil of the eye. **2** the eye itself. **ball of the foot** *n.* the rounded part of the base of the great toe. **ball of the thumb** *n.* the corresponding part of the hand. **ballpark** *n.* **1** a park or field where ballgames are played. **2** (*NAm.*) a baseball field. **3** (*coll.*) a sphere of activity. **in the right ballpark** (*coll.*) approximately right, on the right lines. **ballpark figure** *n.* (*coll.*) an approximate amount. **ballpoint (pen)** *n.* a pen with a tiny ball in place of a nib as its writing point. **ball-proof** *a.* impenetrable by bullets. **ball-race** *n.* **1** a ball-bearing. **2** a groove in which the balls of a ball-bearing roll. **balls!** *int.* (*sl.*) nonsense. **balls-up** *n.* (*taboo sl.*) **1** a mess. **2** a botched situation. **ballsed-up** *a.* **ballsy** (bawl´zē) *a.* (*comp.* **ballsier,** *superl.* **ballsiest**) (*sl.*) manly or brave, gutsy. **ball valve** *n.* a valve opened or closed by the rising of a ball. [ME *balle*, Icel. *böllr*, Gmc. *balluz*]

ball[2] (bawl) *n.* a social assembly for dancing. **to have a ball** (*coll.*) to have a good time. **to open the ball 1** to lead off in the first dance. **2** to commence operations. **ballroom** *n.* a room used for balls. **ballroom dancing** *n.* formal social dancing to dances such as the foxtrot, tango and two-step. [F *bal*, OF *baler*, to dance, late L *ballāre* (prob. from Gr. *ballizein*, to dance)]

ballad (bal´əd) *n.* **1** a light simple song, esp. a slow sentimental one. **2** a popular song, generally of a personal or political character, formerly printed as a broadside. **3** a simple spirited poem usu. narrating some popular or patriotic story. **balladeer** (-diə´) *n.* a ballad-singer, a composer of ballads. **ballad-farce, ballad-opera** *n.* a play in which ballads are introduced into the spoken dialogue. **ballad-maker** *n.* a writer of ballads. **ballad metre** *n.* common metre. **ballad-monger** *n.* **1** a person who sells ballads. **2** a contemptuous epithet for a composer of ballads. **balladry** *n.* **1** the ballad style of composition. **2** ballads collectively. **ballad-singer** *n.* a person who sings ballads, formerly esp. in the streets. **ballad-wise** *adv.* in the form of a ballad. [OF *balade*, Prov. *balada*, a dancing song (late L *ballāre*, see BALL[2])]

ballade (bəlahd´) *n.* **1** a poem consisting of three eight-lined stanzas rhyming *a b a b b c b c*, each having the same line as a refrain, and with an envoy of four lines, an old form revived in the 19th cent. **2** a short lyrical piano piece or similar composition. **ballade royal** *n.* stanzas of seven or eight decasyllabic lines, rhyme royal. [F, see BALLAD]

ballast (bal´əst) *n.* **1** stones, iron or other heavy substances placed in the bottom of a ship or boat to lower the centre of gravity and make her steady. **2** gravel or other material laid as foundation for a railway, or for making roads. **3** a mixture containing coarse gravel for making concrete. **4** a device for stabilizing an electric current. **5** something which tends to give intellectual or moral stability. **6** (*coll.*) solid foods, food containing carbohydrate. *~v.t.* **1** to furnish with ballast; to lay or pack with ballast. **2** to steady, to give stability to. [*ballast* in most Eur. languages; oldest form prob. OSwed. and ODan. *barlast*, mere load (*bar*, bare, *last*, load)]

ballerina (balərē´nə) *n.* (*pl.* **ballerinas, ballerine** (-nā)) a female ballet dancer; a female dancer taking a leading part in a ballet.

ballet (bal´ā, -li) *n.* **1** a form of dramatic representation consisting of dancing and mime to set steps. **2** an example of this. **3** a piece or suite of music for this. **4** a company performing this. **ballet dancer** *n.* a dancer esp. in ballet. **ballet dancing** *n.* **balletic** (-et´-) *a.* **ballet-master, ballet-mistress** *n.* the director of a ballet. **balletomane** (bəlet´əmān) *n.* an enthusiast for the ballet. **balletomania** (-mā´niə) *n.* [F, dim. of *bal*, BALL[2]]

ballista (bəlis´tə) *n.* (*pl.* **ballistae** (-ē), **ballistas**) a military engine used in ancient times for hurling stones, darts and other missiles. [L, from Gr. *ballein*, to throw]

ballistic (bəlis´tik) *a.* **1** of or relating to the hurling and flight of projectiles. **2** moving by gravity alone. **to go ballistic** (*sl.*) to become explosively angry, lose one's temper. **ballistically** *adv.* **ballistic missile** *n.* (*Mil.*) a missile guided over the first part of its course but then descending according to the laws of ballistics. **ballistic pendulum** *n.* an instrument for measuring the velocity of projectiles. **ballistics** *n.* the science of the flight of projectiles. [see BALLISTA]

ballocks BOLLOCKS.

ballon d'essai (balõ desā´) *n.* (*pl.* **ballons d'essai** (balõ)) a trial balloon. [F]

balloon (bəloon´) *n.* **1** a spherical or pear-shaped bag of light material, which when filled with heated air or gas rises and floats in the air (to the larger kinds a car is attached, capable of containing several persons, and these balloons are used for scientific observations, reconnoitring etc.). **2** an inflatable rubber bag used as a child's toy or for decoration. **3** a ball or globe surmounting a pillar, cupola etc. **4** a spherical glass receiver, used in distilling; a large spherical drinking glass. **5** a frame or trellis on which trees or plants are trained. **6** the shape into which fruit trees are trained. **7** a line enclosing the words or thoughts of a cartoon character. **8** anything inflated or hollow. *~v.i.* **1** to go up in a balloon. **2** to swell out. *~v.t.* to kick high in the air in a wide arc. **when the balloon goes up** when the action begins, when the troubles start. **balloon angioplasty** *n.* a technique for treating blocked arteries, in which a tiny balloon is inserted into the blockage and inflated. **balloon barrage** *n.* a line or series of captive balloons employed as a defence against enemy aircraft. **ballooner** *n.* **1** a balloonist. **2** a balloon-like sail. **3** a dress or other object that swells out like a balloon. **balloon-fish** *n.* (*pl. in general* **balloon-fish,** *in particular* **balloon-fishes**) a fish belonging to the genus *Diodon*, members of which are able to distend their bodies with air. **ballooning** *n.* **1** the practice of making balloon ascents. **2** aeronautics. **3** (*NAm.*) the practice of running up stock above its value. **balloonist** *n.* **1** a person who makes balloon ascents. **2** an aeronaut. **balloon tyre** *n.* a low-pressure tyre, large in section. [It. *ballone*, a large ball, from *balla*]

ballot (bal´ət) *n.* **1** the method or system of secret voting. **2** the total votes recorded. **3** a ticket, paper or other instrument (orig. a ball) used to give a secret vote. **4** drawing of lots by means of balls or otherwise. *~v.t.* (*pres.p.* **balloting,** *past, p.p.* **balloted**) **1** to select by drawing lots. **2** to ask to vote secretly, to take a ballot of. *~v.i.* **1** to vote secretly, to hold a ballot. **2** to draw lots. **to ballot for** to choose by secret voting. **ballot box** *n.* a box into which ballots are put in voting, or from which balls are taken in drawing lots. **ballot paper** *n.* a voting-paper used in voting by ballot. [It. *ballotta*, dim. of *balla*]

bally (bal´i) *a.* (*sl., euphem.*) bloody. [alt.]

ballyhoo (balihoo´) *n.* **1** noisy and unprincipled propaganda. **2** a great fuss about nothing. [etym. uncertain]

ballyrag (bal´irag), **bullyrag** (bul´irag) *v.t.* (*pres.p.* **ballyragging, bullyragging,** *past, p.p.* **ballyragged, bullyragged**) (*sl.*) **1** to revile, abuse, assail with violent language. **2** to victimize with practical jokes. *~v.i.* **1** to use violent or abusive language. **2** to engage in horseplay. [etym. unknown]

balm (bahm) *n.* **1** the fragrant juice, sap or gum of certain trees or plants. **2** fragrant ointment or oil. **3** anything which soothes pain, irritation or distress. **4** perfume, fragrance. **5** a plant of the genus *Balsamodendron*, which yields balm. 6 any of several fragrant garden herbs. ~*v.t.* 1 to anoint or impregnate with balm. 2 to soothe, to assuage. **balm-cricket** *n.* the cicada. **Balm of Gilead** (gil'iad) *n.* 1 a resin formerly in use as an antiseptic and soothing ointment. 2 any tree of the genus *Commiphora*, from which such resin may be obtained. 3 the balsam fir or balsam poplar. **balmy** *a.* (*comp.* **balmier**, *superl.* **balmiest**) 1 producing balm. 2 impregnated with or having the qualities of balm. 3 soft, soothing, healing. 4 fragrant, mild. 5 (*sl.*) rather idiotic, daft, silly. **balmily** *adv.* **balminess** *n.* [OF *basme*, L *balsamum*, BALSAM (spelling gradually reassimilated to L *bal-*)]

Balmoral (balmor'əl) *n.* 1 (*also* **Balmoral bonnet**) a kind of Scottish cap. 2 (*pl.*) heavy walking boots, laced in front. 3 a kind of petticoat. [a royal residence in Scotland]

balneology (balniol'əji) *n.* the science of treating diseases by bathing and medicinal springs. **balneological** (-loj'-) *a.* **balneologist** *n.* [L *balneum*, a bath]

baloney (bəlō'ni), **boloney** *n.* (*pl.* **baloneys, boloneys**) 1 (*sl.*) idiotic talk, nonsense. 2 (*N Am.*) BOLOGNA. [thought to be from *Bologna sausage*]

BALPA *abbr.* British Air Line Pilots Association.

balsa (bawl'sə) *n.* 1 an American tropical tree, *Ochroma lagopus*. 2 balsa wood. **balsa wood** *n.* light, strong wood from this tree used for rafts, model aircraft etc. [Sp.]

balsam (bawl'səm) *n.* 1 a vegetable resin with a strong fragrant odour, balm. 2 a tree or shrub yielding a resin of this kind. 3 any plant of the genus *Impatiens*, as garden balsam, *I. balsamina*. 4 a medicinal preparation made with oil or resin for applying to wounds or soothing pain. 5 any of other various preparations of resins mixed with volatile oils. 6 anything that possesses healing or soothing qualities. 7 a preservative essence supposed by alchemists to pervade all organic bodies. ~*v.t.* 1 to impregnate or perfume with balsam. 2 to heal, soothe. 3 to embalm. **balsam apple** *n.* 1 a tropical plant of the gourd family bearing a highly coloured fruit. 2 garden balsam. **balsam fir** *n.* a N American fir, *Abies balsamea*, which yields Canada balsam. **balsamic** (-sam'-) *a.* 1 having the qualities of balsam. 2 mitigating, assuaging pain, soothing. 3 like a warm, soothing oily medicine. **balsamically** *adv.* **balsamic vinegar** *n.* a dark, sweet, Italian vinegar used esp. in salad dressings. **balsamiferous** (-mif'-) *a.* **balsamous** *a.* **balsam poplar** *n.* a N American poplar, *Populus balsamifera*, that yields balsam. **balsamy** *a.* 1 balsam-like. 2 balmy. [L *balsamum*]

Balti (bal'ti) *n.* a type of curry composed of meat and vegetables cooked in an iron pot. [etym. uncertain; perh. Hindi, bucket]

Baltic (bawl'tik) *a.* 1 denoting, of or relating to a sea in N Europe or its bordering countries. 2 of or denoting Baltic as a group of languages. ~*n.* 1 the area around the Baltic sea. 2 a branch of the Indo-European languages comprising Latvian, Lithuanian, Lettish and Old Prussian. **Baltoslav** *n.* **Baltoslavic, Baltoslavonic** *n.* a supposed subfamily of Indo-European languages containing Baltic and Slavonic. [L *Baltia*, Scandinavia]

Baltimore (bawl'timaw), **Baltimore oriole** *n.* a N American oriole, *Icterus galbula*, the male of which has a black head and orange plumage. [named after colours of Lord *Baltimore*, proprietary of Maryland]

baluster (bal'əstə) *n.* 1 a small column, usu. circular, swelling towards the bottom, and forming part of a series called a balustrade. 2 a post supporting a handrail, a banister. 3 a small pillar, swelling in the middle, in a two-light window. **balustered** *a.* **balustrade** (-strād) *n.* a range of balusters, resting on a plinth, supporting a coping or rail, and serving as a protection, barrier, ornament etc. **balustraded** *a.* [F *balustre*, It. *balausta*, *balaustra*, L *balaustium*, Gr. *balaustion*, flower of the wild pomegranate (from supposed resemblance to its calyx-tube)]

bam (bam) *v.t.* (*pres.p.* **bamming**, *past, p.p.* **bammed**) to cheat, hoax, bamboozle. ~*v.i.* to hoax. ~*n.* 1 a hoax, a mystification. 2 a cock-and-bull story. [perh. abbr. from BAMBOOZLE]

bambino (bambē'nō) *n.* (*pl.* **bambinos, bambini** (-ni)) 1 a child, a baby. 2 an image of the infant Jesus in the crib, exhibited at Christmas in Roman Catholic churches. [It., a baby]

bamboo (bamboo') *n.* (*pl.* **bamboos**) 1 any giant tropical grass of the subfamily Bambusidae. 2 the stem of such grass used as a stick, thatch, building material etc. ~*v.t.* to beat with a bamboo. **bamboo curtain** *n.* the barrier set up between Communist China and the rest of the world. **bamboo shoot** *n.* an edible shoot of young bamboo. [etym. uncertain; perh. from Canarese *bănbŭ*, *banwu*]

bamboozle (bamboo'zəl) *v.t.* 1 to mystify for purposes of fraud; to cheat, to swindle. 2 to bewilder, confuse. ~*v.i.* to practise trickery. ~*n.* bamboozlement. **bamboozlement** *n.* 1 the act or process of bamboozling. 2 a tricky deception, a hoax. **bamboozler** *n.* [etym. uncertain; cp. BAM]

ban (ban) *v.t.* (*pres.p.* **banning**, *past, p.p.* **banned**) 1 to interdict, to proscribe. 2 †to curse, anathematize. ~*v.i.* to utter curses. ~*n.* 1 a formal prohibition. 2 a public proclamation. 3 an edict of excommunication, an interdict. 4 a curse, a formal anathematization. 5 †an imprecation, execration. 6 †a proclamation of outlawry. 7 †denunciation, proscription, outlawry. [OE *bannan*, to summon, Gmc. *bannan*, to proclaim, root *ba-* (cp. L *fārī*, to speak, Gr. *phēmi*, I speak)]

banal (bənahl') *a.* commonplace, trite, petty. **banality** (-nal'-) *n.* (*pl.* **banalities**) 1 a commonplace, trite remark. 2 commonplaceness, triviality. [F *banal*, from *ban* (late L *bannum*), BAN]

banana[1] (bənah'nə) *n.* 1 a tropical and subtropical treelike plant, *Musa sapientum*, closely allied to the plantain. 2 the fruit of this, a large, elongated berry, growing in clusters. **to be/ go bananas** (*sl.*) to be or go insane. **Bananaland** *n.* (*coll.*) Queensland. **banana republic** *n.* (*derog.*) a small tropical country, politically unstable, economically dependent on the export of fruit, and dominated by foreign capital. **banana skin** *n.* 1 the skin of a banana. 2 any episode or occurrence which leads to humiliation or embarrassment, esp. in a political context. **banana split** *n.* a dessert consisting of a banana sliced length-wise and filled with ice-cream, cream etc. **banana tree** *n.* [through Sp. or Port. from name in Guinea]

banana[2] (bənah'nə) *n.* (*coll.*) an opponent of all further construction on and development of land. [acronym for *b*uild *a*bsolutely *n*othing *a*nywhere *n*ear *a*nyone]

banausic (bənaw'sik) *a.* 1 mechanical, considered merely fit for a mechanic; uncultured. 2 materialistic. **banausocracy** (banawsok'rəsi) *n.* government by the uncultured, vulgar elements of society. [Gr. *banausikos*, from *banausos*, working by fire, mechanical (*baunos*, a furnace)]

Banbury cake (ban'bəri) *n.* a kind of pastry cake filled with mincemeat, supposed to be made at Banbury in Oxfordshire.

banc (bangk), **banco** (-ō) *n.* the judicial bench. **in banc** sitting (as a Superior Court of Common Law) as a full court. **in banco** in banc. [L (*in*) *banco* (*bancus*, a bench)]

banco[1] (bang'kō) *n.* bank money of account, as distinguished from ordinary currency. [It., bank, see BANK[1]]

banco[2] BANC.

band[1] (band) *n.* **1** a flat slip or band (BAND[2]), used to bind together, encircle or confine, or as part of an article of apparel. **2** a transverse stripe. **3** a specific range of frequencies or wavelengths. **4** a classificatory range or division. **5** a simple gold ring. **6** a broad, endless strap for communicating motion. **7** a track of a record or magnetic tape. **8** a division of pupils according to ability. **9** (*pl.*) a pair of linen strips hanging down in front of the collar and forming part of clerical, legal or academical dress. **10** the collar of a shirt, a collar or ruff. **11** a bandage. **12** (*Geol.*) a bandlike stratum. **13** a space between any two ribs on the fruit of umbellifers. **14** a slip of canvas used to strengthen the parts of a sail most liable to pressure. **Band-Aid®** *n.* a small adhesive plaster with a medicated gauze pad. **band-aid** *n.* a stopgap, a thing used as a temporary solution. *~a.* (of measures etc.) temporary. **bandbox** *n.* **1** a box of cardboard or other thin material for holding collars, hats, millinery etc., originally used for bands or ruffs. **2** a flimsy affair. **like something out of a bandbox** immaculately smart. **band brake** *n.* a flexible band that grips the periphery of a drum or wheel. **band-fish** *n.* (*pl. in general* **band-fish,** *in particular* **band-fishes**) a Mediterranean fish of the genus *Cepola* (from their ribbon-like shape). **bandpass** *n.* the range of frequencies transmitted through a filter. **bandsaw** *n.* an endless steel saw, running rapidly over wheels. **band-wheel** *n.* a wheel worked by means of an endless strap. **bandwidth** *n.* **1** the range of frequencies used for a particular radio transmission. **2** the range of frequencies within which an amplifier (or other electronic device) operates most efficiently. [late ME *bande*, F *bande*, a strip, Prov. and It. *benda*, OHG *binda* (Gmc. *bindan*, see BAND[4])]

†**band**[2] (band) *n.* **1** that which binds, confines or restrains. **2** a fillet, a tie, a chain. **3** any one of the cords on which a book is sewn. **4** a bond, a tie, a uniting influence. **5** (*pl.*) fetters, manacles. [ME *band*, Icel. *band* (Gmc. *bindan*, to bind)]

band[3] (band) *n.* **1** a company of musicians playing together. **2** an organized company; a confederation. **3** an assemblage of people. **4** (*N Am.*) a herd, a flock. **big band** BIG. **when the band begins to play 1** when things get lively. **2** when trouble begins. **bandleader** *n.* the leader of a band of musicians. **bandmaster** *n.* the leader or conductor of a band of musicians. **Band of Hope** *n.* an association of children pledged to total abstinence. **bandsman** *n.* (*pl.* **bandsmen**) a member of a band of musicians. **bandstand** *n.* an elevated platform for the use of a band of musicians. **bandwagon** *n.* the musicians' wagon in a circus parade. **to climb/jump on the bandwagon** to try to be on the winning side. [F *bande* (Prov., Sp. and It. *banda*, a sash, ribbon), prob. from OHG *Bant*]

band[4] (band) *v.t.* **1** to bind or fasten with a band. **2** to mark with a band. **3** to form into a band, troop or society. *~v.i.* to unite, to assemble. [F *bander*, from *bande*; or from the nouns BAND[1] and BAND[2]]

bandage (ban´dij) *n.* **1** a strip of flexible material used to bind up wounds, fractures etc. **2** the operation of bandaging. **3** a strip of flexible material used to cover up something. **4** (*Archit.*) a tie or bond. *~v.t.* to bind up with a bandage. [BAND[1]]

bandanna (bandan´ə), **bandana** *n.* **1** a silk handkerchief of a type orig. of Indian manufacture, having white or yellow spots on a coloured ground. **2** a cotton handkerchief or neckerchief similarly printed. [Hind. *bāndhnū*, a mode of spot-dyeing]

B. & B., b. and b. *abbr.* bed and breakfast.

bandeau (ban´dō) *n.* (*pl.* **bandeaux** (-dōz)) **1** a narrow band or fillet for the head. **2** a bandage. [F, from OF *bandel*, dim. of *bande*, BAND[2]]

banderilla (bandərē´yə, -rēl´-) *n.* a little dart ornamented with ribbons, which bullfighters stick in the neck of the bull. **banderillero** *n.* (*pl.* **banderilleros**) a bullfighter who sticks banderillas into the bull. [Sp., dim. as BANNER]

banderole (ban´dərōl), **banderol** *n.* **1** a long narrow flag with a cleft end flying at a masthead. **2** any small ornamental streamer. **3** the small square of silk hanging from a trumpet. **4** a flat band with an inscription, used in the decoration of buildings of the Renaissance period. [F *banderole*, dim. of *bandière*, *bannière*, BANNER]

bandicoot (ban´dikoot) *n.* **1** (*also* **bandicoot rat**) a large Asian rat of the genus *Bandicota*. **2** a marsupial of the family Peramelidae, which has some resemblance to this. [Telegu *pandi-kokku*, pig-rat]

banding (ban´ding) *n.* **1** the action of binding or marking with a band. **2** the formation of bands; the state of being banded. **3** a banded pattern or structure.

bandit (ban´dit) *n.* (*pl.* **bandits, banditti** (-dit´ē)) **1** a person who is proscribed, an outlaw. **2** a brigand. **banditry** *n.* **banditti** *n.* a company of bandits. [It. *bandito*, p.p. of *bandire*, to proscribe, low L *bandīre*, *bannīre* (BAN)]

bandog (ban´dog) *n.* **1** an aggressive cross-breed fighting dog. **2** †a large fierce dog, kept chained, a mastiff, a bloodhound. [orig. *band-dog*, from BAND[2]]

bandolier (bandəliə´), **bandoleer** *n.* **1** a belt worn over the right shoulder and across the breast, with little leather loops to receive cartridges. **2** a similar belt used to support a musket and 12 charges of powder and shot in small wooden boxes. **3** (*usu. pl.*) the cases or boxes containing charges. [F *bandouillere*, It. *bandoliera*, or Sp. *bandolera* (*bandola*, dim. of *banda*, BAND[1])]

bandoline (ban´dəlēn) *n.* a gummy substance applied to the hair to keep it smooth and flat. [F]

bandore (bandaw´, ban´-) *n.* an old musical instrument somewhat resembling a lute. [Sp. *bandurria*, *bandola*, or Port. *bandurra*, *mandore*, L *pandūra*, Gr. *pandoura*]

bandy[1] (ban´di) *v.t.* (*pres.p.* **bandying,** *past, p.p.* **bandied**) **1** to beat or throw to and fro as at the game of tennis or bandy. **2** to toss to and fro or toss about like a ball. **3** to give and take, to exchange (esp. blows, arguments etc.). **4** to band together, make into a faction. *~v.i.* **1** to throw a ball about. **2** to contend, to wrangle. **3** to be factious, to strive, fight. *~n.* **1** the game of hockey. **2** a club, bent and rounded at the lower end, used in this game for striking the ball. **3** a return stroke at tennis. **to bandy words** to wrangle. **bandy ball** *n.* bandy or hockey. [etym. uncertain; cp. F *bander*, to bandy at tennis, perh. from *bande*, side]

bandy[2] (ban´di) *a.* (*comp.* **bandier,** *superl.* **bandiest**) **1** crooked, bent outwards. **2** bandy-legged. **bandy-legged** *a.* having legs that bend outwards. [etym. uncertain]

bane (bān) *n.* **1** a cause of ruin or mischief. **2** ruin, destruction, mischief, woe. **3** poison (*chiefly in comb.*, such as *henbane, rat's bane* etc.). **baneberry** *n.* (*pl.* **baneberries**) **1** herb Christopher, *Actaea spicata*. **2** the black berries of this, which are very poisonous. **baneful** *a.* poisonous, harmful, destructive. **banefully** *adv.* **banefulness** *n.* **banewort** *n.* **1** a poisonous plant. **2** the lesser spearwort. **3** the deadly nightshade. [OE *bana*, a murderer (cp. Icel. *bani*, death, slayer, OHG *bano*, Gr. *phonos*, murder, carnage)]

bang[1] (bang) *v.t.* **1** to slam (a door), fire (a gun), beat (a musical instrument) with a loud noise. **2** to beat with loud blows. **3** to thrash, to thump; to handle roughly, to drub. **4** to cut (the front hair) square across. **5** to beat, to surpass. **6** (*sl.*) to have sexual intercourse with. **7** (*sl.*) to inject (heroin). *~v.i.* **1** to resound with a loud noise. **2** to jump or bounce up noisily. *~n.* **1** a sudden explosive noise. **2** a resounding blow, a thump. **3** impulsive motion, a dash. **4** (*sl.*) an act of sexual intercourse. **5** (*sl.*) an injection of heroin. **6** the front hair cut straight across. ~*adv.* **1** with a violent blow or noise. **2** suddenly, abruptly, all at once. **3** (*coll.*) exactly. **bang off** (*sl.*) immediately. **bang on** (*coll.*) exactly right. **to bang away at** to do something violently or noisily. **to bang on** (*coll.*) to talk loudly or at great length. **to bang one's head against a brick wall** BRICK. **to bang up** (*sl.*) to imprison or lock up. **to go (off) with a bang** to go very well, to succeed. **banger** *n.* **1** a sausage. **2** (*coll.*) a decrepit old car. **3** a small explosive firework. **4** (*sl.*) a very fine and exceptional specimen. **5** a cudgel. **bangtail** *n.* a horse with tail cut off square. **bangtail muster** *n.* (*Austral.*) the counting of cattle in which each one has its tail docked as it is counted. **bang-up** *a.* (*sl.*) fine, first-rate. [Icel. *banga*, to beat (cp. LG *bangen*, to beat, G *bengeln*, to cudgel)]

bang[2] BHANG.

bangalay (bang´gəlā) *n.* a variety of eucalyptus tree. [Austral. Abor.]

Bangladeshi (banggləde sh´i) *n.* (*pl.* **Bangladeshi, Bangladeshis**) **1** a native or inhabitant of Bangladesh. **2** (*as pl.*) the people of Bangladesh. ~*a.* of or relating to Bangladesh.

bangle (bang´gəl) *n.* a ring-bracelet or anklet. **bangled** *a.* adorned with bangles. [Hind. *bangrī*, a wrist-ring of glass]

banian BANYAN.

banish (ban´ish) *v.t.* **1** to condemn to exile. **2** to drive out or away, to expel. **banishment** *n.* **1** the act of banishing. **2** the state of being banished. **3** exile, expatriation, expulsion. [OF *banir* (lengthened stem *baniss-*), late L *bannīre* (BAN)]

banister (ban´istə), **bannister** *n.* **1** a shaft or upright supporting a handrail at the side of a staircase. **2** (*pl.*) the whole railing protecting the outer side of a staircase. [corr. of BALUSTER]

banjo (ban´jō) *n.* (*pl.* **banjos, banjoes**) **1** a stringed musical instrument, having a head and neck like a guitar and a body like a tambourine, and played with the fingers. **2** (*Austral.*, *sl.*) a shoulder of mutton. **banjoist** *n.* [blacks' pronun. of BANDORE]

bank[1] (bangk) *n.* **1** a raised shelf or ridge of ground. **2** a mound with steeply sloping sides. **3** a shelving elevation of sand, gravel etc., in the sea or in a river. **4** the margin or shore of a river. **5** the ground near a river. **6** an embankment. **7** the sides of a road, cutting or any hollow. **8** an incline on a railway. **9** a bed of shellfish. **10** a long flat-topped mass, as of ice, snow, cloud or the like. **11** the face of the coal in a mine. **12** the surface of the ground at the top of a mine-shaft. ~*v.t.* **1** to form a bank to. **2** to confine within a bank or banks; to embank. **3** to form into a bank. **4** to cause (an aircraft) to incline inwards at a high angle in turning. **5** to bring to land. **6** to fortify with earthworks. **7** to confine (the escapement of a watch). ~*v.i.* **1** to rise into banks. **2** (of an aircraft etc.) to incline inwards at a high angle in turning. **to bank up** to make up (a fire) by putting on and pressing down fuel. **bank engine** *n.* a locomotive employed to assist trains up inclines. **banker**[1] *n.* **1** a bank smack. **2** a horse good at jumping on and off high banks. **3** (*Austral.*) a swollen river. **bank fish** *n.* (*pl. in general* **bank fish,** *in particular* **bank fishes**) fish from the Newfoundland bank. **bankless** *a.* not defined or limited by a bank. **bank martin, bank swallow** *n.* the sand martin. **bankside** *n.* the sloping side of a bank. **bank smack** *n.* a Newfoundland fishing smack. **banksman** *n.* (*pl.* **banksmen**) a workman who superintends unloading at a pit mouth. [ME *banke* (Icel. *bakki*, Gmc. *bankon*; cp. *bankiz*, a bench)]

bank[2] (bangk) *n.* **1** an establishment which deals in money, receiving it on deposit from customers and investing it. **2** a building operated by such an establishment. **3** in gaming, the money which the proprietor of the table, or player who plays against the rest, has before them. **4** any store or reserve of material or information (*blood bank*). **5** a child's box for saving money in, a piggy bank. ~*v.i.* **1** to keep a bank. **2** to act as a banker. **3** to be a depositor in a bank. **4** in gaming, to form a bank, to challenge all comers. **5** (*coll.*) to count or depend (on). ~*v.t.* **1** to deposit in a bank. **2** to realize, convert into money. **to break the bank** to win the limit set by the management of a gambling house for a particular period. **bankable** *a.* **1** capable of being banked. **2** guaranteed to produce a profit. **3** guaranteed to be trustworthy. **bank balance** *n.* the amount of money in a bank account. **bank bill** *n.* **1** (*Hist.*) a bill drawn by one bank on another, payable on demand or at some specified time. **2** (*N Am.*) a bank note. **bankbook** *n.* a passbook in which the cashier enters the debits and credits of a customer. **bank card** *n.* CHEQUE CARD (under CHEQUE). **bank credit** *n.* permission to draw on a bank to a certain amount. **banker**[2] *n.* **1** a proprietor of a bank. **2** a person involved in banking. **3** a person who keeps the bank at a gaming-table. **4** the dealer in certain card games. **5** a gambling card game. **6** an identical result forecast in several entries on a football-pool coupon. **banker's card** *n.* a card issued by a bank guaranteeing payment of cheques up to a certain limit. **banker's order** *n.* an instruction to a bank to pay money etc., signed by a representative of the bank. **bank holiday** *n.* a day on which all banks are legally closed, usu. observed as a national holiday. **banking** *n.* the business engaged in by a bank. **bank machine** *n.* a cash dispenser. **bank manager** *n.* a person who is in charge of a branch of a bank. **bank note** *n.* a note issued by a bank and payable on demand. **Bank of England** *n.* the central bank of England and Wales, established in 1694, which manages the monetary systems on behalf of the government. **bank rate** *n.* the rate at which the Bank of England is prepared to discount bills of exchange (see MINIMUM LENDING RATE (under MINIMUM)). **bankroll** *n.* (*orig. N Am.*) **1** a supply of money. **2** a sum of money used to buy or invest in something. ~*v.t.* to supply the funding for (a purchase or investment). **bank statement** *n.* a list showing the transactions carried out by the holder of a bank account. **bank stock** *n.* the capital stock of a bank. [F *banque*, It. *banca*, a bench, Gmc. *bank*, BANK[1]]

bank[3] (bangk) *n.* **1** a platform or stage. **2** a seat of justice. **3** the bench for rowers, or a tier of oars, in a galley. **4** a bench or table used in various trades. **5** (*Print.*) the table on which sheets are laid. **6** the raised floor of a glass-furnace. **7** a row of keys on an organ. [OF *banc*, Gmc. *bank*, BANK[1] (cp. BENCH)]

banker[1] BANK[1].

banker[2] BANK[2].

banker[3] (bang´kə) *n.* **1** a sculptor's revolving table. **2** a bench used by bricklayers or stonemasons. [prob. corr. of It. *banco*, a statuary's table]

banket (bang´kit, -ket´) *n.* a gold-bearing conglomerate. [Afrikaans, hardbake]

bankrupt (bangk´rŭpt) *n.* **1** a person who, becoming insolvent, is judicially required to surrender their estates to be administered for the benefit of their creditors. **2** an insolvent debtor. **3** a person lacking in some necessary or desirable quality or at the end of their resources. ~*a.* **1** judicially declared a bankrupt. **2** insolvent. **3** without credit, lacking some necessary or desirable quality; at the end of one's resources. ~*v.t.* **1** to render (a person) bankrupt. **2** to render insolvent. **3** to reduce to beggary; to discredit. **bankruptcy** (-si) *n.* (*pl.* **bankruptcies**) **1** the state of being bankrupt. **2** the act of declaring oneself bankrupt. **3** (*fig.*) utter ruin; loss of reputation. **bankruptcy laws** *n.pl.* laws requiring a bankrupt to surrender their property for the benefit of their creditors to ensure their discharge. [earlier *banqueroute*, It. *banca rotta*, bank broken (BANK[2], L *rupta*, p.p. of *rumpere*, to break), assimilated to L *rupt-*]

banksia (bangk´siə) *n.* an Australian flowering shrub or tree of the genus *Banksia* of the family Proteaceae. **banksia rose** *n.* a Chinese climbing rose, *Rosa banksiae*. [Sir Joseph Banks, 1744–1820]

banlieue (bã´lyœ) *n.* **1** the territory outside the walls but within the jurisdiction of a town or city. **2** suburbs, precincts. [F, from L *banleuca* (BAN, *leuca*, a league)]

banner (ban´ə) *n.* **1** an ensign or flag painted with some device or emblem. **2** a flag, generally square, painted or embroidered with the arms of the person in whose honour it is borne. **3** the standard of a feudal lord, used as a rallying-point in battle. **4** an ensign or symbol of principles or fellowship. **5** the vexillum of a papilionaceous flower. *~a.* (*attrib.*, *N Am.*) notable, excellent. **to fight under the banner of** to follow the cause of, be an adherent of. **to follow the banner of** to follow the cause of, be an adherent of. **to join the banner of** to begin to follow the cause of, become an adherent of. **bannered** *a.* **1** furnished with banners. **2** borne on a banner. **banner headline** *n.* a headline in heavy type running across the entire page of a newspaper. **banner screen** *n.* a fire screen suspended from a pole or mantelpiece by its upper edge. [OF *baniere* (late L *bannum*, *bandum*, standard, Goth. *bandwa*, sign, token, perh. from same root as BAND[1], BIND)]

banneret (ban´ərit) *n.* (*Hist.*) **1** a knight entitled to lead a company of vassals under his banner, ranking above other knights and next below a baron. **2** a title conferred for deeds done in the king's presence on a field of battle. [OF *baneret* (*baniere*, see BANNER, *-et*, *-ate*, L *-ātus*)]

bannerette (banəret´) *n.* a small banner. [OF *banerete*]

bannerol (ban´ərōl) *n.* a banner about a yard or metre square, borne at the funeral of eminent personages and placed over the tomb. [BANDEROLE]

bannister BANISTER.

bannock (ban´ək) *n.* a flat round cake made of pease- or barley-meal or flour, usu. unleavened. [Gael. *bannach* (perh. from L *pānicium*, from *pānis*, bread)]

banns (banz) *n.pl.* proclamation in church of an intended marriage, so that any impediment may be made known and inquired into. **to forbid the banns** to allege an impediment to an intended marriage. [BAN]

banquet (bang´kwit) *n.* a sumptuous feast, usu. of a ceremonial character and followed by speeches. *~v.t.* (*pres.p.* **banqueting**, *past*, *p.p.* **banqueted**) to entertain at a sumptuous feast. *~v.i.* to take part in a banquet, to feast luxuriously. **banqueter** *n.* **1** the giver of a banquet. **2** a person entertained at a banquet; a feaster, a carouser. [F dim. of *banc*, bench (cp. It. *banchetto*, dim. of *banco*, table)]

banquette (băket´) *n.* **1** a built-in cushioned seat along a wall. **2** a bank behind a parapet on which soldiers mount to fire. **3** the long seat behind the driver in a French diligence. [F, from It. *banchetta*, dim. of *banca*, a bench, BANK[1]]

banshee (ban´shē) *n.* a supernatural being, supposed in Ireland and the Scottish Highlands to wail round a house when one of the inmates is about to die. [Ir. *bean sidhe*, OIr. *ben sīde*, woman of the fairies]

bant BANTING.

bantam (ban´təm) *n.* **1** a small domestic fowl, of which the cocks are very aggressive. **2** a small and conceited or very pugnacious person. **bantamweight** *n.* **1** a boxer, wrestler, weightlifter etc. in the weight category intermediate between flyweight and featherweight. **2** this weight category. [*Bantam* in Java, whence they were said (prob. wrongly) to have been first brought]

banter (ban´tə) *v.t.* to ridicule good-humouredly; to rally, to chaff. *~v.i.* to indulge in good-natured raillery. *~n.* good-natured raillery, chaff. **banterer** *n.* [etym. unknown]

banting (ban´ting) *n.* the reduction of obesity by abstinence from fat, starch and sugar. **bant** *v.i.* (*coll.*) to practise the method of banting. [W. Banting, 1797–1878, inventor]

bantling (bant´ling) *n.* a little child, a brat. [prob. from G *Bänkling*, a bastard (*Bank*, a bench, whence bench-begotten)]

Bantu (ban´too) *n.* (*pl.* **Bantu, Bantus**) **1** a group of languages of S and Central Africa. **2** (*Hist.*, *or offensive*) a black S African. **3** (*offensive*) a Bantu speaker. *~a.* **1** of or relating to these languages. **2** (*offensive*) of or relating to these peoples. **Bantustan** *n.* (*S Afr.*, *coll.*, *derog.*) a S African homeland.

Usage note Because of its association with apartheid, the use of *Bantu* to refer to people has come to be considered highly offensive in South Africa, and is best avoided.

---

banxring (bangks´ring) *n.* a Javanese squirrel-like tree-shrew, *Tupaia javanica*. [Javanese, *bangsring*]

banyan (ban´yan), **banian** (-yən) *n.* **1** a Hindu merchant or shop-keeper, a Bengali broker or hawker. **2** a loose morning-gown or jacket. **3** the banyan tree. **banyan hospital** *n.* a hospital for animals (named in reference to caste reverence for animal life). **banyan tree** *n.* the Indian fig tree, *Ficus indica*, the branches of which drop shoots to the ground, which taking root support the parent branches and in turn become trunks, so that one tree covers a very large extent of ground (from a tree near Gombroon, on the Persian Gulf, under which banyans or traders had built a pagoda). [Port. *banian*, a trader, Arab. *banyan*, Gujarāti *vaniyo*, one of the trading caste, Sansk. *vanij*, a merchant]

banzai (ban´zī, -zī´) *int.* a Japanese battle-cry, patriotic salute or cheer. *~a.* reckless. [Jap. *banzai*, 10,000 years, forever]

baobab (bā´əbab) *n.* **1** an African tree, *Adansonia digitata*, bearing large pulpy fruit. **2** an Australian tree, *Adansonia gregorii*. [prob. from an Afr. language]

BAOR *abbr.* British Army of the Rhine.

bap (bap) *n.* a large soft bread roll. [etym. unknown]

Bapt. *abbr.* Baptist.

baptize (baptīz´), **baptise** *v.t.* **1** to sprinkle with or immerse in water as a sign of purification and consecration, esp. into the Christian Church. **2** to consecrate, purify, initiate. **3** to christen, to give a name or nickname to. **4** to name (a ship) at launching. **5** to initiate into or to introduce to for the first time. *~v.i.* to administer baptism. **baptism** (bap´tizm) *n.* **1** the act of baptizing. **2** the ceremony of sprinkling with or immersion in water, by which a person is admitted into the Christian Church. **3** a ceremonial naming of ships, church bells etc. **4** an initiation (ceremony). **baptismal** (-tiz´-) *a.* of or relating to baptism; conferred at baptism. **baptismally** *adv.* **baptism of blood** *n.* martyrdom before baptism. **baptism of fire** *n.* **1** the baptism of the Holy Ghost, martyrdom. **2** a soldier's first experience of actual war. **3** a difficult or frightening introduction to something. **baptist** (bap´tist) *n.* **1** a person who baptizes. **2** (**Baptist**) a special title of St John, the forerunner of Christ. **3** (**Baptist**) a member of a Christian body who hold that baptism should be administered only to adult believers, and by immersion. **baptistery** (-təri), **baptistry** (-tri) *n.* (*pl.* **baptisteries, baptistries**) **1** the place where baptism is administered, originally a building adjoining the church. **2** the tank used for baptism in Baptist churches. **3** (*poet.*) baptism. [OF *baptiser*, L *baptizāre*, Gr. *baptizein* (*baptein*, to dip)]

bar[1] (bah) *n.* **1** a piece of wood, iron or other solid material, long in proportion to breadth; a pole. **2** a transverse piece in a gate, window, door, fire-grate etc. 3 a connecting piece in various structures. 4 a straight stripe, a broad band. 5 an ingot of gold or silver cast in a mould. 6 a similar block of chocolate, soap etc. 7 any thing that constitutes a hindrance or obstruction. 8 a bank of silt, sand or gravel deposited at the mouth of a river or harbour. 9 any immaterial or moral barrier or obstacle. 10 (*Law*) a plea or objection of sufficient force to stop an action. 11 the counter in a public house, hotel or other house or place of refreshment, across which liquors etc. are sold. 12 the room containing this. 13 a rail or barrier, a space marked off by a rail or barrier. 14 a counter or place where foods, goods or services are sold or provided. 15 in a law court, the barrier at which prisoners stand during trial. 16 the railing separating ordinary barristers from Queen's (or King's) Counsel, hence the profession of a barrister. 17 barristers collectively. 18 any tribunal. 19 the barrier cutting off a space near the door in both Houses of Parliament, to which non-members are admitted. 20 (*Mus.*) a vertical line drawn across the stave to divide a composition into parts of equal duration, and to indicate periodical recurrence. 21 the portion contained between two such lines. 22 a strip of metal mounted parallel to a rail, which holds points or makes a signal when depressed by the wheels of a train. 23 two horizontal lines across a shield. 24 a metal strip attached to a medal, indicative of an additional award. 25 (*pl.*) the ridged divisions in a horse's palate. 26 the part of the wall of a horse's hoof that bends inwards. ~*v.t.* (*pres.p.* **barring,** *past, p.p.* **barred**) 1 to fasten with a bar or bars. 2 to obstruct, to exclude. 3 to take exception to. 4 to hinder, to prevent. 5 to mark with or form into bars. 6 (*Law*) to stay by objection. 7 to cancel (a claim or right). 8 in betting, to exclude. 9 (*sl.*) to object to, dislike. **behind bars** in jail. **to be called within the bar** to be made a Queen's (or King's) Counsel. **to call to the bar** to admit as a barrister. **barbell** *n.* a metal bar with heavy discs at each end used for weightlifting and exercising. **bar billiards** *n.* a game played esp. in pubs, in which balls are pushed into holes in a special table using a short cue. **bar chart, bar graph** *n.* a graph containing vertical or horizontal bars representing comparative quantities. **bar code** *n.* a compact arrangement of lines of varied lengths and thicknesses which is machine-readable, e.g. printed on supermarket goods or books, giving coded details of price, quantity etc. **barfly** *n.* (*pl.* **barflies**) (*coll.*) a person who spends time in bars. **barfly jumping** *n.* the sport of jumping up and sticking on to a special wall covered in Velcro. **bar-iron** *n.* iron wrought into malleable bars. **barkeep** *n.* (*N Am.*) 1 a bartender. 2 the owner of a bar. **barkeeper** *n.* 1 (*N Am.*) a a bartender. b the owner of a bar. 2 (*Hist.*) a toll-bar keeper. **bar line** *n.* (*Mus.*) a vertical line that divides bars. **barmaid** *n.* 1 a female bartender. 2 (*N Am.*) a drinks waitress. **barman** *n.* (*pl.* **barmen**) a male bartender. **bar-parlour** *n.* a small room adjoining or containing a bar in a public house. **bar person** *n.* (*pl.* **bar persons**) a person who works in a pub or bar. **bar-posts** *n.pl.* posts sunk in the ground to admit movable bars serving the purpose of a gate. **barred** *a.* 1 furnished or secured with a bar or bars. 2 obstructed by a bar. 3 striped, streaked. **barring**[1] *n., a.* **barring-out** *n.* a rebellion by schoolchildren who shut a teacher out of the school until certain demands are conceded. **bar room** *n.* the room in a public house in which the bar is situated. **bar shoe** *n.* a horseshoe with a bar across the hinder part, to protect the frog. **bar-shot** *n.* a bar with half a cannon-shot at each end, formerly used to injure masts and rigging. **bar sinister** *n.* BEND SINISTER (under BEND). **bar stool** *n.* a tall stool at a bar. **bartender** *n.* a person who serves at the bar of a public house, hotel etc. **bartracery** *n.* window tracery characteristic of later Gothic in which the stonework resembles a twisted bar. [OF *barre*, late L *barra* (etym. unknown)]

bar[2] (bah) *n.* a unit of atmospheric pressure which is equivalent to 10^6 dynes per square centimetre (10^5 newton per square metre). [Gr. *baros*, weight]

bar[3] (bah) *prep.* except, apart from. **bar none** without exception. **bar one** except one.

bar. *abbr.* 1 baritone. 2 barometric. 3 barrel. 4 barrister.

bar- BARO-.

barathea (barəthē´ə) *n.* a fabric made from wool mixed with silk or cotton, used esp. for coats and suits. [etym. unknown]

BARB *abbr.* Broadcasters' Audience Research Board.

barb[1] (bahb) *n.* 1 the appendages on the mouth of the barbel and other fishes. 2 part of a woman's head-dress, still worn by some nuns. 3 a recurved point, as in a fish-hook or arrow. 4 a point, a sting. 5 a biting or pointed remark or comment. 6 any of the lateral filaments from the shaft of a feather. 7 (*Bot.*) a hooked hair. ~*v.t.* to furnish (fish-hooks, arrows etc.) with barbs. **barbed** *a.* having a barb or barbs; pointed, biting, hurtful. **barbed wire,** (*N Am.*) **barbwire** *n.* wire armed with sharp points, used for fences, to protect front-line trenches or to enclose prison camps. **barbless** *a.* [F *barbe*, L *barba*, beard]

barb[2] (bahb) *n.* 1 a fine breed of horse. 2 a fancy breed of pigeons. [F *barbe* (*Barbarie*, BARBARY)]

Barbadian (bahbā´diən) *n.* a native or inhabitant of Barbados. ~*a.* of or relating to Barbados.

barbarian (bahbeə´riən) *n.* 1 a savage, a person belonging to some uncivilized people. 2 a person destitute of pity or humanity. 3 (*Hist.*) a person who is not Greek, a person who is not Greek or Roman, a person outside the Roman Empire. 4 a person outside the pale of Christian civilization. 5 †a foreigner having outlandish manners and language. ~*a.* 1 rude, uncivilized, savage. 2 cruel, inhuman. **barbaric** (-bar´-) *a.* 1 of or relating to barbarians. 2 rude, uncouth, uncivilized. 3 cruel, inhuman. **barbarism** (bah´bə-) *n.* 1 absence of civilisation. 2 lack of culture or refinement, brutality, cruelty. 3 an impropriety of speech, a solecism, a foreign idiom. 4 an act of barbarism. **barbarity** (-bar´-) *n.* (*pl.* **barbarities**) 1 brutality, inhumanity, cruelty. 2 an act of brutality or cruelty. 3 the state or quality of being barbaric. **barbarize** (bah´bə-), **barbarise** *v.t.* 1 to render barbarous. 2 to corrupt (a language). ~*v.i.* 1 to grow barbarous. 2 to utter a barbarism in speech. **barbarization** (-zā´shən) *n.* 1 the act of barbarizing. 2 the state of being barbarized. **barbarous** (bah´bə-) *a.* 1 uncivilized. 2 uncultured, unpolished; uncouth. 3 cruel. 4 foreign in speech; barbarian. 5 harsh-sounding. **barbarously** *adv.* **barbarousness** *n.* [L *barbarus*, Gr. *barbaros* (prob. a word imit. of unintelligible speech)]

Barbary (bah´bəri) *a.* of or relating to Barbary, an extensive region in the north of Africa. **Barbary ape** *n.* a tailless ape, *Macaca sylvana*, found in the north of Africa, with a colony on the rock of Gibraltar. **Barbary gum** *n.* a gum obtained from *Acacia gummifera.* **Barbary hen** *n.* a guinea fowl. †**Barbary horse** *n.* a fine breed of horse from Barbary. [Arab. *Berber*, a native of Barbary (perh. from Gr. *barbaria*, country of the barbarians)]

barbastelle (bahbəstel´) *n.* a bat of the genus *Barbastella* which roosts in trees or caves. [F from It. *barbastello*]

barbate (bah´bāt) *n.* (*Bot., Zool.*) 1 bearded. 2 having small tufts of hair. [L *barbātus*]

barbecue (bah´bikū) *n.* 1 an outdoor meal at which food is prepared over a charcoal fire. 2 food, esp. meat, so cooked. 3 a framework on which food is cooked for a barbecue or meat is smoked; a very large grill or gridiron. 4 a structure containing such a framework. 5

an animal broiled or roasted whole. 6 an open floor for drying coffee beans. ~*v.t.* (*pres.p.* **barbecuing,** *past, p.p.* **barbecued**) 1 to cook on a barbecue; to smoke or dry (meat etc.) on a framework over a fire. 2 to broil or roast whole. **barbecue sauce** *n.* a spicy or strong sauce added to barbecued food. [Sp. *barbacoa*, Haitian *barbàcoa*]

barbel (bah´bəl) *n.* 1 a European freshwater fish, *Barbus vulgaris*, allied to the carp, named from the fleshy filaments which hang below the mouth. 2 the small fleshy filament hanging from the mouth of some fishes, probably organs of touch. **barbelled,** (*esp. N Am.*) **barbeled** *a.* furnished with barbels. [OF *barbel*, late L *barbellum* (nom. *-us*), dim. of *barbus*, barbel (*barba*, beard)]

barber (bah´bə) *n.* a person who shaves and cuts beards and hair; a men's hairdresser. ~*v.t.* to shave or dress the hair of. **barber's block** *n.* 1 a round block on which wigs were made up and displayed. 2 †a fop. **barber-shop** *n., a.* (denoting) a type of close harmony singing orig. for male voices, usu. quartets. **barber's itch, barber's rash** *n.* sycosis, an inflammation of the hair follicles. **barber's pole** *n.* a pole, usu. striped spirally, exhibited as a sign in front of a barber's shop. [A-F *barbour*, OF *barbeor* (L *barbātōr -em*, from *barba*, beard)]

barberry (bah´bəri), **berberry** (bœ´-) *n.* (*pl.* **barberries, berberries**) 1 a shrub of the genus *Berberis*, esp. *B. vulgaris*. 2 the red acid berry of this tree. [late L *barbaris* or *berberis* (etym. uncertain)]

barbet (bah´bit) *n.* a tropical bird of the family Capitonidae, allied to the toucans, having tufts of hair at the base of its bill. [prob. OF *barbet*, L *barbātus*, bearded (*barba*, beard)]

barbette (bahbet´) *n.* 1 a mound of earth in a fortification on which guns are mounted to be fired over the parapet. 2 a platform for a similar purpose on a warship. [F, dim. of *barbe*, beard]

barbican (bah´bikən) *n.* an outer fortification to a city or castle, designed as a cover to the inner works, esp. over a gate or bridge and serving as a watchtower. [OF *barbacan* (etym. uncertain)]

barbie (bah´bi) *n.* (*esp. Austral., sl.*) a barbecue.

barbituric (bahbitū´rik) *a.* denoting an acid obtained from malonic and uric acids. **barbital, barbitone** (bah´bitōn) *n.* (*N Am.*) a derivative of barbituric acid used as a sedative, veronal. **barbiturate** (-bit´ūrət) *n.* any compound with hypnotic and sedative properties derived from barbituric acid. [G *Barbitursäure*]

barbola (bahbō´lə), **barbola work** *n.* 1 the attachment of small flowers etc. in paste to embellish vases etc. 2 articles decorated by this means. [etym. unknown]

Barbour® (bah´bə), **Barbour jacket** *n.* a type of green waxed jacket.

barbule (bah´būl) *n.* a hooked or serrated filament given off from the barb of a feather. [L *barbula*, dim. of *barba*, beard]

barcarole (bahkərōl´), **barcarolle** *n.* 1 a song sung by Venetian gondoliers. 2 a composition of a similar kind. [F *barcarolle*, It. *barcarola*, from *barcaruola*, a boat song (*barca*, a boat)]

barchan (bah´kən) *n.* a shifting sand dune in the shape of a crescent. [Turkic *barkhan*]

bard[1] (bahd) *n.* 1 a Celtic minstrel. 2 a member of an order whose function it was to celebrate heroic achievements, and to perpetuate historical facts and traditions in verse. 3 a poet generally. 4 a poet honoured at a Welsh eisteddfod. **the Bard (of Avon)** Shakespeare. **bardic** *a.* **bardish** *a.* **bardism** *n.* the sentiments, maxims or system of the bards. **bardling** (-ling) *n.* 1 a young bard, a tyro. 2 a poetaster. **bardolatry** (-dol´ətri) *n.* the worship of Shakespeare. [Gael. and Ir. *bàrd*]

bard[2] (bahd) *n.* a slice of bacon put on meat or game before roasting. ~*v.t.* 1 to cover with slices of bacon before roasting. 2 to caparison; to adorn with trappings. [F *barde*, armour for a horse (perh. from Sp. and Port. *albarda*, a pack-saddle, Arab. *al-barda'ah*)]

bardy (bah´di) *n.* (*pl.* **bardies**) (*Austral.*) an edible wood-boring grub. [Austral. Abor. *bardi*]

bare (beə) *a.* 1 unclothed, naked, nude. 2 with the head uncovered as a mark of respect. 3 destitute of natural covering, such as hair, fur, flesh, leaves, soil etc. 4 napless. 5 unarmoured, unarmed, defenceless. 6 unsheathed. 7 poor, indigent, ill-furnished, empty. 8 simple, mere, unsupported, undisguised, open. 9 bald, meagre. 10 unadorned. ~*v.t.* 1 to strip, to make bare. 2 to uncover, unsheathe. 3 to make manifest. **bare of** without. **with one's bare hands** without using tools or weapons. **bareback** *a., adv.* without a saddle on the horse etc. being ridden. **bare-backed** *a.* 1 with the back unclothed. 2 without a saddle, bareback. **barefaced** *a.* 1 having the face bare or uncovered. 2 unconcealed, impudent, shameless. 3 beardless, whiskerless. **barefacedly** (-sid-) *adv.* **barefacedness** *n.* **barefoot** *a., adv.* with the feet naked. **barefoot doctor** *n.* a villager, esp. in Asia, who has been trained in basic health care to meet the simple medical needs of the community. **barefooted** *a.* **bareheaded** *a.* **bare-knuckle, bare-knuckled** *a.* 1 (of boxing) without gloves. 2 making no concessions. **barely** *adv.* 1 nakedly, poorly. 2 hardly, scarcely. 3 †baldly, openly, plainly, explicitly. **bareness** *n.* 1 the quality of being bare. 2 poverty, meanness. **barish** *a.* 1 rather bare. 2 poorly covered. [OE *bær* (cp. OHG *par*, G *bar*, Dut. *baar*)]

Usage note When *barely* refers to time ('only just'), a following *when* is preferable to *than* (so *She had barely got in when the phone rang*).

barège (barezh´) *n.* a light gauzy dress fabric originally made at Barèges, Hautes-Pyrénées, France.

baresark BERSERK.

barf (bahf) *v.i.* (*sl.*) to vomit, to retch. ~*n.* an act of vomiting or retching. [etym. uncertain]

bargain (bah´gin) *n.* 1 an agreement between parties, generally concerning a sale. 2 an advantageous purchase. 3 †anything bought or sold. 4 haggling, discussions as to terms. ~*v.i.* 1 to haggle over terms. 2 to make a contract or agreement for purchase or sale. **into/ in the bargain** over and above what is stipulated. **off one's bargain** released from a purchase or engagement. **to bargain away** to exchange for something of less value. **to bargain on/ for** to count on, to expect. **to make the best of a bad bargain** to do the best one can in adverse circumstances. **to strike/ make a bargain** to come to terms. **bargain and sale** *n.* a method of conveyance. **bargain basement, bargain counter** *n.* a basement or counter in a store where goods are sold which have been marked down in price. **bargainee** (-ē´) *n.* 1 the person who accepts a conveyance of bargain and sale. 2 the purchaser. **bargainer** *n.* 1 a trafficker, a haggler. 2 †a bargainor. **bargainor** (-aw´) *n.* 1 a person who transfers real property by bargain and sale. 2 the seller. [OF *bargaigner*, to trade, to haggle]

bargan (bahg´ən), **barragan** (bar´ə-) *n.* a boomerang. [Austral. Abor.]

barge (bahj) *n.* 1 a flat-bottomed freight-boat, with or without sails, used principally on canals or rivers. 2 the second boat of a man-of-war. 3 a large ornamental state or pleasure boat, an ornamental houseboat. ~*v.i.* to lurch (into), rush (against). ~*v.t.* to transport by barge. **bargee** (-jē´) *n.* a bargeman, a person in charge of a barge. **bargeman** *n.* (*pl.* **bargemen**) a person working on a barge. **bargemaster** *n.* **bargepole** *n.* the pole with which a barge is propelled or kept clear of banks etc. **would not touch with a bargepole** would not come near or associate with on account of dirt, disease or ill temper etc.[OF *barge*, late L *barga*, var. for *barca*, BARK[3]]

barge- (bahj) *comb. form* used as below. **barge-board** *n.* a projecting horizontal board at the gable-end of a building, concealing the barge-couples and warding off the rain. **barge-couples** *n.pl.* two beams mortised and tenoned together to increase the strength of a building. **barge-course** *n.* **1** the tiling projecting beyond the principal rafters in a building. **2** a wall-coping formed of bricks set on edge. [med. L *bargus*, a kind of gallows]

barghest (bah´gest), **bargest**, **bargaist** (-gāst) *n.* a doglike goblin whose apparition is said to portend calamity or death. [G *Berggeist*, mountain demon]

baric BARIUM.

barilla (bəril´ə) *n.* **1** an impure alkali obtained from the ash of *Salsola soda* and allied species. **2** an impure alkali obtained from kelp. **3** a plant, *Salsola soda*, common on the seashore in Spain, Sicily and the Canaries. [Sp.]

barish BARE.

barite, baryte BARYTES (under BARYTA).

baritone (bar´itōn), **barytone** *n.* **1** a male voice intermediate between a bass and a tenor. **2** a singer having such a voice. **3** a part for such a voice. **4** the smaller bass saxhorn in B flat or C. **5** in Greek grammar, a word unaccented on the last syllable. ~*a.* **1** having a compass between tenor and bass. **2** of or relating to such a compass. **3** in Greek grammar, unaccented on the last syllable. **baritone clef** *n.* the F clef on the middle line of the bass stave. [F *baryton*, It. *baritono*, Gr. *barutonos* (*barus*, heavy, *tonos*, tone)]

barium (beə´riəm) *n.* **1** a metallic divalent element, at. no. 56, chem. symbol Ba, the metallic base of baryta. **2** barium sulphate as administered in a barium meal. **baric** (bar´-) *a.* containing barium. **barium meal** *n.* a mixture of barium sulphate, administered to allow X-ray examination of a patient's stomach or intestines. [BARYTA, -IUM]

bark[1] (bahk) *v.i.* **1** to utter a sharp, explosive cry, like that of a dog. **2** to speak in a peevish, explosive manner. **3** to cough. **4** (*N Am.*) to tout or advertise as a barker. ~*n.* **1** a sharp, explosive cry, orig. of dogs, hence of other animals. **2** the report of a firearm. **3** a cough. **someone's bark is worse than their bite** (said of someone who) seems angry or threatening but won't actually do anything to hurt you. **to bark up the wrong tree** **1** to be on a false scent. **2** to accuse the wrong person. **barker**[1] *n.* **1** an auction tout; a vocal advertiser for a circus, fun-fair etc. **2** a person who or animal which barks. **3** a dog. **4** a clamorous assailant. **5** (*sl.*) a pistol, a cannon. **barking** *a.* **1** that barks. **2** (*sl.*) mad, crazy. **barking deer** *n.* the muntjac. **barking mad** *a.* (*coll.*) completely mad, crazy. [OE *beorcan* (cp. Icel. *berkja*)]

bark[2] (bahk) *n.* **1** the rind or exterior covering of a tree, formed of tissues parallel to the wood. **2** spent bark, tan. **3** an outer covering. ~*v.t.* **1** to strip the bark from (a tree). **2** to cut a ring in the bark so as to kill (the tree). **3** to steep in a solution of bark, to tan. **4** to graze, to abrade (the shins, elbows etc.). **5** to cover with or as with bark, to encrust. **6** to strip or scrape off. **bark beetle** *n.* a small wood-boring beetle of the family Scolytidae, which cause great damage to trees. **bark-bound** *a.* having the bark so close as to hinder the growth. **barker**[2] *n.* a person who strips the bark from a tree. **bark pit** *n.* a pit in which hides are tanned. **bark tree** *n.* any tree or shrub of the genus *Cinchona*. **barky** *a.* (*comp.* **barkier**, *superl.* **barkiest**) **1** covered with bark. **2** of the nature of or resembling bark. [Scand. (Swed. *bark*, Icel. *bōrkr* etc.)]

bark[3] (bahk), **barque** *n.* **1** (*poet.*) a ship or boat, esp. a small sailing vessel. **2** (*usu.* **barque**) a sailing vessel with three or more masts, square-rigged on the fore and main masts, schooner rigged on the mizzen or other masts. **barkentine** *n.* BARQUENTINE. **barque-rigged** *a.* rigged like a barque. [F *barque*, Prov., Sp. or It. *barca*, a small ship or boat]

barker[1] BARK[1].

barker[2] BARK[2].

Barking bloke (bah´king) *n.* the stereotypical floating male voter; cp. WORCESTER WOMAN. [a district of London]

barley (bah´li) *n.* **1** a plant of the genus *Hordeum*, a hardy, awned cereal. **2** the grain of this used for soups, malt liquors and spirits, animal feeds etc. **barley-broth** *n.* **1** broth made with barley. **2** strong beer. **barleycorn** *n.* **1** a grain of barley. **2** a former measure, the third part of an inch (about 0.8 cm). **John Barleycorn** JOHN. **barleymow** *n.* a stack of barley. **barley sugar** *n.* a hard confection, prepared by boiling down sugar, formerly with a decoction of barley. **barley water** *n.* a soothing drink made from pearl barley. **barley wine** *n.* **1** a strong kind of ale. **2** a kind of wine prepared by the ancient Greeks from barley. [OE *bærlic*, *bær-* (cp. Icel. *barr*, Gmc. *bariz*) *-lic*, -LY[1]]

barm (bahm) *n.* **1** the frothy scum which rises to the surface of malt liquor in fermentation, used as a leaven. **2** †yeast. **barmy** *a.* (*comp.* **barmier**, *superl.* **barmiest**) **1** (*sl.*) crazy, cracked, silly (cp. BALMY (under BALM). **2** of or full of barm or yeast. **3** frothing, fermenting. **barmily** *adv.* **barminess** *n.* [OE *beorma* (cp. Dan. *bārme*, Fris. *berme*, G *Bärme*)]

barmbrack (bahm´brak), **barnbrack** (bahn´-) *n.* sweet, spicy bread containing currants, dried peel etc. [Ir. *bairin breac*, speckled cake]

Barmecide (bah´misīd) *n.* a person who gives illusory benefits. ~*a.* barmecidal. **barmecidal** (-sī´-) *a.* unreal, unsatisfying, illusory. **Barmecide feast** *n.* short commons. [name of a family who ruled at Baghdad, one of whom is said in the *Arabian Nights* to have invited a beggar to an imaginary feast]

bar mitzvah (bah mits´və) *n.* **1** a Jewish boy who has reached the age of religious responsibility, usu. on his 13th birthday. **2** the ceremony and celebration marking this event. [Heb., son of the law]

barn (bahn) *n.* **1** a covered building for the storage of grain and other agricultural produce. **2** (*derog.*) a barnlike building. **3** (*N Am.*) a stable, a cowshed. **4** (*N Am.*) a covered building for the storage of large vehicles. **5** (*Physics*) a unit of area, 10^{-28} square metres (from 'as big as a barn door'). **barn dance** *n.* **1** a dance, orig. US, somewhat like a schottische. **2** a country dance held in a barn or similar building. **barn door** *n.* **1** the large door of a barn. **2** a target too big to be easily missed. ~*a.* (of fowls) reared at the barn door. **as big as a barn door** very large, unmissable. **barn owl** *n.* an owl which frequents barns, *Tyto alba*. **barnstorm** *v.i.* **1** to tour the country giving theatrical performances. **2** (*N Am.*) to tour rural areas giving political speeches at election time. **3** (*N Am.*) to perform aerobatic tricks, give flying displays. **barnstormer** *n.* **barnstorming** *a.* characteristic of a barnstormer, showy. **barnyard** *n.* **1** the yard adjoining a barn. **2** a farmyard, a barton. [OE *bern*: *berern* (*bere*, barley, *aern*, house)]

barnacle (bah´nəkəl) *n.* **1** the barnacle goose. **2** any of various cirriped crustaceans that live attached to rocks, ship bottoms etc. **3** a constant attendant. **barnacled** *a.* **barnacle goose** *n.* (*pl.* **barnacle geese**) a species of wild goose, *Branca leucopsis*, formerly supposed to be developed from the common barnacle. [OF *bernaque* (etym. uncertain, perh. from L *Hibernicae*, *Hiberniculae*, Irish goose)]

barnacles (bah´nəkəlz) *n.pl.* **1** a kind of twitch put on the nostrils of a restive horse while being shod. **2** an instrument of torture used in a similar manner. **3** (*coll.*)

a pair of spectacles, goggles. [OF *bernac*, flat-nosed (etym. unknown)]

barnbrack BARMBRACK.

barney (bah´ni) *n.* (*pl.* **barneys**) (*coll.*) **1** a noisy argument or fight. **2** †an unfair contest, esp. a prize-fight of a disreputable kind. **3** †a lark, a spree. [etym. unknown]

baro- (bar´ō), **bar-** *comb. form* weight, pressure. [Gr. *baros*, weight]

barograph (bar´əgrahf) *n.* an aneroid barometer recording the variations of atmospheric pressure. **barogram** (-gram) *n.* the record produced by a barograph.

barogyroscope (barōjī´rəskōp) *n.* a gyrostat used for demonstrating the rotation of the earth.

barology (bərol´əji) *n.* the science of weight.

barometer (bərom´itə) *n.* **1** an instrument used for measuring the atmospheric pressure, thus indicating probable weather change, and also for measuring altitudes reached. **2** any indicator of change (e.g. in public opinion). **barometric** (barəmet´-), **barometrical** *a.* **1** of or relating to the barometer. **2** measured or indicated by a barometer. **barometrically** *adv.* **barometrography** (barōmitrog´rəfi) *n.* the branch of meteorology which deals with the measurement of atmospheric pressure. **barometry** (-om´-) *n.* the art or practice of taking barometrical observations. [Gr. *baros*, weight]

baron (bar´ən) *n.* **1** a member of the lowest rank of nobility. **2** a noble, a peer. **3** a powerful head of a business or financial organization. **4** (*Hist.*) **a** a person who held land by military service from the king. **b** a Great Baron, attending the Great Council or summoned to Parliament. **5** a title of the judges of the Court of Exchequer. **6** (*Law, Her.*) a husband. **baronage** (-nij) *n.* **1** the whole body of barons, the peerage. **2** the dignity of a baron. **3** the land from which a baron derives his title, a barony. **4** a published list of barons. **baroness** (-nis) *n.* **1** the wife or widow of a baron. **2** a lady who holds the baronial dignity in her own right. **baronial** (-rō´-) *a.* **baron of beef** *n.* a joint consisting of the two sirloins. **barony** *n.* (*pl.* **baronies**) **1** the lordship, or fee, of a baron. **2** the rank or dignity of a baron. **3** a subdivision of a county of Ireland. **4** a large manor in Scotland. [OF *barun*, *baron*, acc. of *ber*, man, husband; late L *baro*, a man (L *bāro*, a simpleton)]

baronet (bar´ənit) *n.* a hereditary titled order of commoners ranking next below barons, instituted by James I in 1611. *~v.t.* to confer a baronetcy on. **baronetage** (-netij) *n.* **1** baronets collectively. **2** the dignity of a baronet. **3** a list of the baronets. **baronetcy** *n.* (*pl.* **baronetcies**) the title or rank of a baronet. [dim. of BARON (BARON, -ET[1])]

baroque (bərōk´, -rok´) *n.* **1** a style of artistic or architectural expression prevalent esp. in 17th-cent. Europe, characterized by extravagant ornamentation. **2** a similar style in music or literature. **3** an irregularly shaped pearl. *~a.* **1** baroque in style. **2** grotesque. **3** gaudy. **4** flamboyant. [F, Port. *barroco*, Sp. *barrueco*, a rough or imperfect pearl (etym. uncertain)]

baroreceptor (bar´ōriseptə) *n.* a collection of nerve endings in the body that are sensitive to changes in pressure.

baroscope (bar´əskōp) *n.* a weather glass.

barothermograph (barōthœ´məgrahf) *n.* an instrument combining a barometer and a thermometer.

barouche (bəroosh´) *n.* a double-seated four-wheeled horse-drawn carriage, with a movable top, and a seat outside for the driver. [G *Barutsche*, It. *baroccio*, L *birotus*, two-wheeled]

barque BARK[3].

barquentine (bah´kəntēn), **barkentine** *n.* a three-masted vessel, with the foremast square-rigged, and the main and mizen fore-and-aft rigged. [BARK[3], either after BRIGANTINE or from Sp. *bergantine*, a small ship]

barracan (bar´əkən), **baracan** *n.* **1** (*Hist.*) a coarse cloth resembling camlet. **2** a thin silky material. [F, from Arab. *barrakān*, a camlet cloak (Pers. *barak*, a garment made of camel's hair)]

barrack[1] (bar´ək) *n.* **1** a temporary hut. **2** (*pl.*, *pl. or sing. in constr.*) buildings used to house troops. **3** any large building resembling or used like barracks. *~v.t.* **1** to provide with barracks. **2** to put in barracks. *~v.i.* to lodge in barracks. **barrack master** *n.* an officer in charge of barracks. **barrack-room lawyer** *n.* **1** a soldier who argues with those in authority. **2** a person who gives advice in a pompous or insistent way, esp. when not qualified to do so. **barrack square** *n.* a drill ground near a barracks. [F *baroque*, It. *baracca* or Sp. *barraca* (etym. uncertain)]

barrack[2] (bar´ək) *v.i.* **1** to jeer. **2** (*orig. Austral.*) to cheer (for). *~v.t.* **1** to shout or cheer derisively at (e.g. a sports side). **2** (*orig. Austral.*) to shout support or encouragement for (a team). [perh. Ir., to boast]

barracoon (barəkoon´) *n.* (*Hist.*) a fortified African slave house. [Sp. *barracon*, *barraca* (see BARRACK[1])]

barracouta (barəkoo´tə) *n.* (*pl. in general* **barracouta**, *in particular* **barracoutas**) **1** a large edible fish of the Pacific, *Thyrsites atun*. **2** (*New Zeal.*) a thin loaf of bread. [var. of BARRACUDA.]

barracuda (barəkū´də) *n.* (*pl. in general* **barracuda**, *in particular* **barracudas**) a predatory tropical fish of the family Sphyraenidae. [Sp. *baracuta*, etym. unknown]

barrad (bar´əd) *n.* an Irish conical cap. [Ir. *baireud*, *bairread*, F *barrette*, BARRET]

barragan BARGAN.

barrage (bar´ahzh) *n.* **1** an artificial bar or dam formed to raise the water in a river. **2** the formation of such a bar or dam. **3** (*Mil.*) a screen of artillery fire behind which troops can advance, or which can be laid down to hinder an enemy advance. **4** heavy or continuous questioning or criticism. **5** a deciding heat. **barrage balloon** *n.* (*Hist.*) an anchored balloon intended to prevent hostile aircraft making machine-gun attacks. [F, from *barre*, BAR[1], -AGE]

barramundi (barəmŭn´di), **burramundi** *n.* (*pl. in general* **barramundi**, *in particular* **barramundis**) any of various percoid fishes found in Australian rivers, esp. *Lates calcarifer*. [Austral. Abor.]

barranca (bərang´kə) *n.* (*pl.* **barrancas**) (*N Am.*) a deep gorge, with steep sides. [Sp.]

barrator (bar´ətə), **barrater** *n.* a person who out of malice or for their own purposes stirs up litigation or discord. **barratrous** *a.* **barratry** (-tri) *n.* **1** (*Law*) fraud or criminal negligence on the part of a master of a ship to the owners' detriment. **2** (*Hist.*) the offence of vexatiously exciting or maintaining lawsuits. **3** traffic in selling church or public offices. [OF *barateor*, a fraudulent dealer, trickster (*barat*, fraud, perh. of Celtic origin; cp. OIr. *mrath*, *brath*, O Bret. *brat*, Welsh *brad*, betrayal, treachery; sense influenced by Icel. *barātta*, strife)]

barre (bah) *n.* a wall-mounted horizontal rail used for ballet exercises. [F, bar]

barré (bar´ā) *n.* the laying of a finger across a particular fret of a guitar etc., to raise the pitch for the chord being played. [F]

barrel (bar´əl) *n.* **1** a cask; a cylindrical wooden vessel bulging in the middle, formed of staves held together by hoops, and with flat ends. **2** the capacity or contents of such a vessel. **3** anything resembling such a vessel, as the tube of a firearm, through which the bullet or shot is discharged. **4** the belly and loins of a horse, ox etc. **5** a measure of capacity for liquid and dry goods, varying with the commodity. **6** a revolving cylinder or drum round which a chain or rope is wound. **7** the revolving cylinder studded with pins in a musical box or barrel organ. **8** the cavity behind the drum of the ear. **9** (*N Am., sl.*) money to be used for political campaigning. ~*v.t.* (*pres.p.* **barelling,** (*N Am.*) **barreling,** *past, p.p.* **barrelled,** (*N Am.*) **barreled**) to draw off into, or put or stow in barrels. ~*v.i.* (*N Am.*) to drive fast. **to have someone over a barrel 1** to have power over someone. **2** to have someone at a disadvantage. **to scrape the barrel 1** to get the last remaining bit. **2** to obtain the last scrap. **barrel-bellied** *a.* having a protuberant belly. **barrel campaign** *n.* (*N Am.*) an election fought by means of bribery. **barrel-chested** *a.* having a rounded chest. **barrel drain** *n.* a cylindrical drain. **barrelled,** (*N Am.*) **barreled** *a.* **1** packed in barrels. **2** barrel-shaped. **3** having a barrel or barrels. **barrel of fun, barrel of laughs** *n.* a source of entertainment or amusement; a person who is a great deal of fun to be with. **barrel organ** *n.* a musical instrument in which the keys are mechanically acted on by a revolving cylinder (barrel) studded with pins. **barrel roll** *n.* a manoeuvre in aerobatics in which an aircraft rolls about its longitudinal axis. **barrel vault** *n.* (*Archit.*) a semi-cylindrical vault. **barrel-vaulted** *a.* [F *baril* (etym. uncertain)]

barren (bar´ən) *a.* **1** incapable of producing offspring. **2** not producing, unfertile; bearing no fruit or vegetation. **3** fruitless, unprofitable. **4** not productive intellectually, uninventive, dull. ~*n.* **1** a tract of barren land. **2** (*pl., esp. US*) elevated land on which small trees grow but not timber. **barren of** devoid of. **barrenly** *adv.* **barrenness** *n.* **barrenwort** *n.* any plant of the genus *Epimedium*, esp. *E. alpinum*, with purple and yellow flowers. [MG *barain, baraine*, OF *baraine* (masc.), *brahain* (etym. unknown)]

barret (bar´it) *n.* **1** a little flat cap. **2** a biretta. [F *barrette, biretta*]

barrette (bəret´) *n.* (*N Am.*) a hair-clasp. [dim. of F *barre*, bar]

barretter (bəret´ə) *n.* an appliance for keeping electric current in a circuit at constant strength. [etym. unknown]

barricade (barikād´, bar´-), **†barricado** (-kā´dō) *n.* (*pl.* **barricades, †barricados, †barricadoes**) **1** a hastily-formed rampart erected across a street or passage to obstruct an enemy or an attacking party. **2** (*Naut.*) a wooden rail across the fore-part of the quarterdeck in ships of war. **3** any bar or obstruction. ~*v.t.* **1** to block or defend with a barricade. **2** to obstruct in any way by physical obstacles. [F *barricade*, Sp. *barricada*, p.p. of *barricare* (*barrica*, a barrel)]

barrico (bərē´kō) *n.* (*pl.* **barricoes**) a small cask, a keg. [Sp. *barrica*]

barrier (bar´iə) *n.* **1** an obstacle which hinders approach or attack. **2** any material or immaterial obstruction. **3** a gate at a border where customs are collected or papers examined. **4** a bar that is raised to give access. **5** an enclosing fence. **6** a limit, a boundary. **7** the sound barrier. ~*a.* of or relating to an obstruction or separating agent, often protective, as in *barrier contraceptive*. **barrier cream** *n.* a cream used to protect the hands from dirt, oils and solvents. **barrier gate** *n.* a gate in a barrier. **barrier ice** *n.* ice-floe, ice-pack. **barrier pillar** *n.* a large pillar of coal supporting the roof of a mine. **barrier reef** *n.* a coral reef running nearly parallel to the land, with a lagoon between. [A-F *barrere*, OF, *barriere*, late L *barrāria* (*barra*, bar)]

barring[1] BAR[1].

barring[2] (bah´ring) *prep.* (*coll.*) except, omitting. **barring accidents** apart from accidents, all being well. [see BAR[1]]

barrio (bar´iō) *n.* (*pl.* **barrios**) a Spanish speaking community or district, usu. sited in the poorer areas of cities in the Southwestern US. [Sp., district]

barrister (bar´istə), **barrister-at-law** *n.* (*pl.* **barristers (-at-law)**) a member of the legal profession who has been admitted to practise as an advocate at the bar; a counsellor-at-law. **barristership** *n.* [orig. *barrester*, prob. from BAR[1] or F *barre* (the bar was orig. a division among the Benchers in the Inns of Court)]

barrow[1] (bar´ō) *n.* **1** a hill. **2** a prehistoric grave mound, a tumulus. [OE *beorg* (cp. G *Berg*, Gmc. *bergoz*)]

barrow[2] (bar´ō) *n.* **1** a shallow cart with two wheels pushed by hand. **2** a wheelbarrow. **barrow boy** *n.* a street trader in fruit, vegetables or other goods with a barrow. **barrowful** *n.* as much as a barrow will hold. **barrowload** *n.* [OE *bearwe*, from *beran*, to carry (see BEAR[1])]

Bart. *abbr.* Baronet.

barter (bah´tə) *v.t.* **1** to give (anything except money) in exchange for some other commodity. **2** to exchange. ~*v.i.* to traffic by exchanging one thing for another. ~*n.* **1** traffic by exchanging one commodity for another. **2** a trade, a truck. **3** the rule for reckoning quantities of a commodity in terms of another on the principle of exchange. **to barter away 1** to dispose of by barter. **2** to part with for a consideration (usu. an inadequate one). **barterer** *n.* [OF *bareter*, from *baret*, cheat (see BARRATOR)]

bartizan (bah´tizan, -zan´) *n.* **1** a battlement on top of a house or castle. **2** a small overhanging turret projecting from the angle on the top of a tower. **bartizaned** *a.* [a modern formation from the spelling *bertisene* (or *bretising*) (see BRATTICE)]

barton[1] (bah´tən) *n.* **1** the part of an estate which the lord of the manor kept in his own hand. **2** a farmyard. [OE *beretūn* (*bere*, barley, *tūn*, enclosure)]

barton[2] BURTON.

baryon (bar´ion) *n.* (*Physics*) any member of the heavier class of subatomic particles that have a mass equal to or greater than that of the proton. [Gr. *barus*, heavy]

barysphere (bar´isfiə) *n.* the solid, heavy core of the earth, probably consisting of iron and other metals. [Gr. *barus*, heavy]

baryta (bərī´tə) *n.* barium oxide or barium hydroxide. **barytes** (-tēz), **barite** (bā´rīt), **baryte** *n.* native sulphate of barium, heavy spar (used as white paint). **barytic** (-rit´-) *a.* [Gr. *barutēs*, weight (*barus*, heavy)]

barytone BARITONE.

basal BASE[1].

basalt (bas´awlt) *n.* **1** a dark igneous rock of a black, bluish or leaden grey colour, of a uniform and compact texture, consisting of augite, feldspar and iron intimately blended, olivine also being often present. **2** a black stoneware first used by Wedgwood. **basaltic** (-sawl´-) *a.* **1** of or of the nature of basalt. **2** columnar, like basalt. **3** resembling basalt. **basaltiform** (-sawl´tifawm) *a.* [L *basaltēs*, from Gr. *basanītēs* (*lithos*) touchstone]

basan (baz´ən), **bazan** *n.* a sheepskin for bookbinding, tanned in oak or larch bark, as distinct from roan which is tanned in sumach. [F *basane*, prob. from Prov. *bazana*, Sp. *badana*, Arab. *bitānah*, lining]

basanite (bas´ənīt) *n.* **1** a black variety of quartz. **2** touchstone. [L *basanītes*, (*lapis*), Gr. *basanos* touchstone]

bas-bleu (bahblœ´) *n.* BLUESTOCKING (under BLUE). [F]

bascinet BASINET.

bascule (bas´kūl) *n.* **1** an apparatus on the principle of the lever, in which the depression of one end raises the other. **2** a bascule bridge. **bascule bridge** *n.* a kind of drawbridge balanced by a counterpoise which falls or rises as the bridge is raised or lowered. [F, a see-saw (*battre*, to bump, or *bas*, down, *cul*, the rump)]

base[1] (bās) *n.* **1** the lowest part on which anything rests. 2 the fundamental principle, groundwork; that on which something essentially depends, a basis. 3 the part of a column between the bottom of the shaft and the top of the pedestal. 4 a plinth with its mouldings constituting the lower part of the wall of a room. 5 a pedestal. 6 the bottom of anything. 7 the extremity of a part by which it is attached to the trunk. 8 the side on which a plane figure stands or is supposed to stand. 9 (*Mil.*) the imaginary line connecting the two salient angles of adjacent bastions. 10 the middle part of a transistor. 11 (*Her.*) the width of a bar parted off from the lower part of a shield by a horizontal line. 12 a starting point of an expedition etc.; a place to which a person or group returns. 13 that line or place from which a combatant draws reinforcements of men, ammunition etc. 14 the place from which a commencement is made in some ball-games. 15 the starting-post. 16 any one of the points that must be reached in scoring a run in baseball, rounders etc. 17 (*Chem.*) **a** a substance with which an acid can combine to form a salt. **b** a substance which can accept or neutralize hydrogen ions. **c** a purine or pyrimidine group. 18 any substance used in dyeing as a mordant. 19 a substance used as a foundation for another substance or process. 20 the original stem of a word; the word from which another is formed. 21 the line from which trigonometrical measurements are calculated. 22 the number on which a system of calculations depends. 23 the datum or basis for any process of reckoning, measurement or argument. *~v.t.* 1 to found, to secure. 2 to station as a base for operations etc. 3 to make a foundation for. 4 to lay on a foundation. **to make/ get to first base** 1 (*N Am., coll.*) to complete the initial stage in a process. 2 (*N Am., coll.*) to seduce. **to touch base** to make esp. prearranged contact (with) again. **basal** *a.* 1 of or relating to, situated at or constituting the base of anything. 2 fundamental. *~n.* a basal part. **basal ganglia** *n.pl.* a group of ganglia at the base of the brain, linked to the thalamus. **basal metabolism** *n.* the amount of energy consumed by an individual in a resting state for functions such as respiration and blood circulation. **baseball** *n.* 1 the national ballgame of America, akin to English rounders. 2 the ball used in this. **baseboard** *n.* 1 (*N Am.*) a skirting board. 2 a board that functions as the base of anything. **baseburner** *n.* an iron stove fed at the top, the fire being confined to the base or lower part. **basecamp** *n.* a camp used as the base for an expedition, military operation etc. **basehead** *n.* (*N Am., sl.*) a person who takes the drugs freebase or crack. **base hospital** *n.* (*Austral.*) a hospital that serves a rural area. **baseless** *a.* 1 without a base or foundation. 2 groundless. **baselessly** *adv.* **baselessness** *n.* **baseline** *n.* 1 a line used as a base. 2 the common section of a picture and the geometrical plane. 3 the back line at each end of a tennis or volleyball court etc. **baseload** *n.* the load on an electrical power supply that is more or less constant. **baseman** *n.* (*pl.* **basemen**) in baseball, a fielder who is positioned next to a base. **basement** *n.* 1 the lowest or fundamental portion of a structure. 2 the lowest inhabited storey of a building, esp. when below the ground level. **basement membrane** *n.* (*Anat.*) a thin membrane that separates the epithelium from the tissue beneath it. **base pairing** *n.* the hydrogen bonding that occurs in a DNA molecule between complementary nitrogenous bases. **base-plate** *n.* a foundation-plate. **base rate** *n.* the rate of interest on which a bank bases its lending rates. **base unit** *n.* a basic unit in a system of measurement, such as a second, metre or kilogram. **basic** *a.* 1 of, relating to or constituting a base, fundamental. 2 without luxury, extras etc. 3 unrefined, vulgar. 4 (*Chem.*) being a base, having the base in excess. 5 (of igneous rock) with little silica present in its composition. 6 in metallurgy, prepared by the basic process. **basically** *adv.* 1 fundamentally. 2 in fact. **basic dye** *n.* a dye consisting of salts of organic bases. **Basic English** *n.* a fundamental selection of 850 English words, designed by C. K. Ogden as a common first step in English teaching and as an auxiliary language. **basic industry** *n.* an industry on which the economy depends. **basicity** (-sis´-) *n.* the combining power of an acid. **basic process** *n.* a method of making steel or homogeneous iron by means of a Bessemer converter lined with non-siliceous materials. **basics** *n.pl.* fundamental principles. **basic slag** *n.* a by-product of the manufacture of steel, used as manure. **basic wage** *n.* 1 a wage earned before overtime or other extra payments are added. 2 (*Austral., New Zeal.*) the minimum living wage. **basilar** *a.* (*Zool., Bot.*) growing from, or situated near, the base. [F *base*, L and Gr. *basis* (*bainein*, to go, step, stand)]

base² (bās) *a.* 1 low in the moral scale; unworthy, despicable. 2 menial, inferior in quality. 3 alloyed, debased, counterfeit. 4 low, of little height. 5 occupying a low position. 6 †low in the social scale. 7 †illegitimate, bastard. **basely** *adv.* in a low, selfish, unworthy or despicable manner. **base metals** *n.pl.* those which are not noble or precious metals. **baseness** *n.* [F *bas*, late L *bassus*, short, stout (a cognomen)]

base jump (bās), **BASE jump** *n.* a parachute jump from a fixed point such as a high building. **base jumper** *n.* [acronym for Building, Antenna-tower, Span, Earth]

basenji (bəsen´ji) *n.* (*pl.* **basenjis**) a small central African hunting dog which cannot bark. [Bantu]

bases BASIS.

bash¹ (bash) *v.t.* 1 to strike, so as to smash or hurt. 2 (*N Am.*) to criticize heavily. *~v.i.* to strike violently; to collide. *~adv.* 1 with force. 2 with a smash or bang. *~n.* 1 a heavy blow, a bang. 2 (*sl.*) a social entertainment. **to have a bash at** to attempt. **basher** *n.* a rough, a hooligan. [imit. like *bang*, or Scand. (cp. Swed. *basa*, Dan. *baske*, to beat)]

†**bash²** (bāsh) *v.t.* to dismay, abash. [ABASH]

†**bashaw** (bəshaw´) *n.* 1 PASHA. 2 a haughty or high-handed grandee.

bashful (bash´fəl) *a.* 1 shamefaced, shy. 2 characterized by excessive modesty. 3 †without self-possession, daunted. **bashfully** *adv.* **bashfulness** *n.* [BASH²]

bashibazouk (bashibəzook´) *n.* (*Hist.*) a Turkish irregular soldier, noted for lawlessness and atrocious brutality. [Turk., one whose head is turned]

basho (bash´ō) *n.* (*pl.* **basho, bashos**) a tournament in sumo wrestling. [Jap.]

basi- (bā´si) *comb. form* of, relating to or forming the base; or at the base of. [L *basis*, BASE¹]

BASIC (bā´sik) *n.* a computer programming language using simple English terms. [acronym for Beginners All-purpose Symbolic Instruction Code]

basic BASE¹.

basicranial (bāsikrā´niəl) *a.* of or at the base of the cranium.

basidium (bəsid´iəm) *n.* (*pl.* **basidia**) (*Bot.*) a mother cell carried on a stalk and bearing spores characteristic of various fungi. **basidiomycete** (-ōmī´sēt) *n.* any of a group of fungi (including many toadstools and mushrooms) in which the spores are borne on basidia. [BASE¹]

basifugal (bāsifū´gəl) *a.* growing away from the base.

basil (baz´əl) *n.* any herb of the genus *Ocimum*, species of which are used as culinary herbs, e.g. the sweet basil, *O. basilicum*. [OF *basile*, L *basilisca* (*basiliscus* BASILISK); the botanical name *basilicum* is from Gr. *basilikon*, royal]

basilar BASE¹.

basilateral (bāsilat´ərəl) *a.* at the side of a base.

Basilian (bəzil´iən) *a.* of or relating to the monastic order instituted by St Basil in the Greek Church. *~n.* a member of the order. [St Basil, 329–79]

basilica (bəsil´ikə) *n.* (*pl.* **basilicas**) **1** a large oblong building with double colonnades and an apse, used as a court of justice and an exchange. **2** such a building used as a Christian church. **3** a church built on the same plan. **4** any one of the seven principal churches of Rome founded by Constantine the Great (4th cent.). **5** a church having special privileges granted by the Pope. **basilican** *a.* [F *basilique*, L *basilicus*, Gr. *basilikos*, royal (*basileus*, king)]

basilisk (baz´ilisk, bas´-) *n.* **1** a fabulous reptile, said to be hatched by a serpent from a cock's egg – its look and breath were reputed fatal. **2** (*Her.*) a cockatrice. **3** a tropical American lizard of the genus *Basiliscus* (named from its inflatable crest). [L *basiliscus*, Gr. *basiliskos*, kingly]

basin (bā´sən) *n.* **1** a hollow (usu. circular) vessel for holding food being prepared or water, esp. for washing; a bowl. **2** the quantity contained by such a vessel, a basinful. **3** a washbasin. **4** a hollow. **5** a pond, a dock, a reservoir; a land-locked harbour. **6** the tract of country drained by a river and its tributaries. **7** (*Geol.*) **a** a depression in strata in which beds of later age have been deposited. **b** a circumscribed formation in which the strata dip on all sides inward. **8** the scale-dish of a balance. **9** a tool used in grinding convex lenses. **basinful** *n.* (*pl.* **basinfuls**) **1** as much as a basin will hold. **2** (*coll.*) as much work or trouble as one can cope with. [OF *bacin* (F *bassin*), late L *bacchīnus* (*bacca*, a water-vessel)]

basinet (bas´inet, -net´), **bascinet, basnet** (bas´net) *n.* a light helmet, almost round, and generally without a visor. [OF *basinet*, dim. of *bacin*, basin]

basipetal (bāsip´itəl) *a.* (*Bot.*) proceeding in the direction of the base. **basipetally** *adv.*

basis (bā´sis) *n.* (*pl.* **bases** (-sēz)) **1** the base or foundation. **2** the fundamental principle, groundwork, ingredient or support. **3** the starting point. [L, BASE[1]]

bask (bahsk) *v.i.* **1** to expose oneself to the influence of genial warmth; to sun oneself. **2** (*fig.*) to luxuriate (in love, good fortune etc.). *~v.t.* to expose to natural or artificial warmth (*chiefly refl.*). **basking shark** *n.* a large shark, *Cetorhinus maximus* (from its often lying near the surface of the sea). [prob. from OScand. *bathask* (*batha sik*, bathe oneself; cp. Icel. *bathast*)]

basket (bahs´kit) *n.* **1** a wickerwork vessel of plaited osiers, twigs or similar flexible material. **2** as much as will fill a basket; a basketful. **3** the net or hoop used as a goal in basketball. **4** a goal scored in basketball. **5** a group or range (of currencies etc.) considered together. **6** (*Archit.*) the vase of a Corinthian column with its carved foliage. **7** (*coll., derog.*) a bastard. **8** a basket hilt. *~v.t.* to put in a basket. **basketball** *n.* **1** a game consisting in dropping a large ball into suspended nets or hoops. **2** the ball used in the game. **basket case** *n.* (*coll., offensive*) **1** a person who has had their arms and legs amputated. **2** a person who is incapacitated or useless. **3** a person who is having a nervous breakdown or suffering nervous strain. **basket-chair** *n.* a wickerwork chair. **basket-fish** *n.* (*pl. in general* **basket-fish,** *in particular* **basket-fishes**) a starfish of the genus *Astrophyton*. **basketful** *n.* (*pl.* **basketfuls**) as much as would fill a basket. **basket hilt** *n.* a hilt of a sword, made something like a basket to defend the swordsman's hand. **basket-hilted** *a.* having a basket hilt. **basket-maker** *n.* a person who makes baskets. **basket-making** *n.* **basketry** *n.* **1** the making of baskets; basketwork. **2** baskets collectively. **basket weave** *n.* a form of textile weave resembling chequered basketwork. **basketwork** *n.* **1** wickerwork. **2** the making of baskets or wickerwork. [etym. uncertain]

basmati rice (basmah´ti) *n.* a type of rice with a slender grain, delicate fragrance and nutty flavour.

bas mitzvah BAT MITZVAH.

basophil (bā´səfil), **basophile** (-fīl) *n.* a white blood cell with basophilic contents. **basophilic** (-fil´-) *a.* (of cells) readily stained with basic dyes.

Basque (bahsk) *n.* **1** a member of a people occupying both slopes of the western Pyrenees. **2** the language spoken by this people. *~a.* of or relating to this people or their language. **basque** *n.* a woman's jacket, often extended below the waist to form a kind of skirt. **basqued** *a.* [F, from late L *Vasco*, dweller in Vasconia, a region of W Pyrenees]

bas-relief (bahrəlēf´, bas-) *n.* **1** low relief, a kind of sculpture in which the figures project less than one-half of their true proportions above the plane forming the background. **2** a carving in low relief. [F, from It. *basso-rilievo*]

bass[1] (bās) *n.* **1** the lowest part in harmonized musical compositions; the deepest male voice. **2** a part for such a voice. **3** the lowest tones of an instrument. **4** a person who sings the bass part, a singer with such a voice. **5** a bass string. **6** a bass instrument, esp. bass guitar or double bass. **7** the player of a bass instrument. **8** the frequency output of audio equipment corresponding to the musical bass. *~a.* **1** of or relating to the lowest part in harmonized musical composition or the lowest pitch of voice; deep. **2** (of an instrument) being the lowest in pitch in its family. *~v.t.* to utter in a bass voice. **double bass** DOUBLE[1]. **bass bar** *n.* a bar of wood fixed lengthwise in the belly of stringed instruments to enable them to resist pressure. **bass clef** *n.* (*Mus.*) the F clef on the fourth line. **bass drum** *n.* **1** a large drum with a low pitch played in an orchestra or band. **2** a bass-drum player. **bassist** *n.* **1** a double-bass player. **2** a bass-guitar player. **bass viol** *n.* **1** a viola da gamba. **2** (*N Am.*) a double bass. **3** a player of either of these instruments in a mixed group of musicians. [earlier *base* (see BASE[1])]

bass[2] (bas), **basse** *n.* (*pl. in general* **bass,** *in particular* **basses**) **1** the common European perch, *Perca fluviatilis*. **2** a sea fish resembling this, *Disentrarchus labrax*, of European waters. **3** a N American fish of the genus *Morone*. **4** SEA BASS (under SEA). **5** BLACK BASS (under BLACK). [OE *bars* (cp. Dut. *baars*, G *Bars*, *Barsch*)]

bass[3] (bas) *n.* **1** the inner bark of the lime tree or any similar vegetable fibre. **2** an article made from this fibre. **bass broom** *n.* a coarse-fibred broom made from bass. **basswood** *n.* **1** an American linden tree, *Tilia americana*. **2** the wood of this tree. [BAST]

basset[1] (bas´it), **basset hound** *n.* a short-legged breed of dog, orig. used to drive foxes and badgers from their earths. [F, dim of *bas*, *basse*, low]

basset[2] (bas´it) *n.* the outcrop of strata at the surface of the ground. *~a.* tending to crop out. *~v.i.* to crop out at the surface. [etym. uncertain]

basset-horn (bas´it) *n.* a tenor clarinet with a recurved mouth. [F *cor de bassette*, It. *corno di bassetto*]

bassi BASSO.

bassinet (basinet´) *n.* **1** an oblong wicker basket with a hood at the end, used as a cradle. **2** a pram of similar shape. [F, dim of *bassin*, BASIN]

basso (bas´ō) *n.* (*pl.* **bassos, bassi** (-si)) a bass singer. **basso continuo** (kontin´ūō) *n.* (*pl.* **basso continuos**) a thorough bass. **basso profundo** (profun´dō) *n.* (*pl.* **basso profundos, bassi profundi** (-di)) **1** the lowest bass voice. **2** a singer with such a voice. **basso ripieno** (ripyā´nō) *n.* (*pl.* **bassi ripieni** (-ni)) the bass of the grand chorus, which comes in only occasionally. [It.]

bassoon (bəsoon´) *n.* **1** a wooden double-reed instrument, the bass to the clarinet and oboe. **2** a bassoonist in an orchestra etc. **3** an organ stop of similar tone, a similar series of reeds on a harmonium etc. **bassoonist** *n.* a bassoon-player. [F *basson* (*bas, basse*, -ON, or perh. *bas son*, low sound)]

basso-rilievo (basōrilyā´vō) *n.* (*pl.* **basso-rilievos**) **1** low relief, bas-relief. **2** a sculpture in low relief. [It., low relief]

bast (bast) *n.* **1** the inner bark of the lime or linden tree. **2** any similar fibrous bark. **3** a rope, mat etc. made from this fibre. [OE *bæst* see also BASS[3]]

bastard (bahs´təd) *n.* **1** (*now often offensive*) an illegitimate child or person. **2** (*sl., often considered taboo*) an obnoxious or disagreeable person. **3** (*sl., often considered taboo*) any person in general. **4** (*sl., often considered taboo*) something annoying or unpleasant. **5** anything spurious, counterfeit or false. **6** an impure coarse brown sugar. *~a.* **1** (*now often offensive*) born out of wedlock, illegitimate. **2** spurious, not genuine. **3** having the resemblance of something of a higher quality or kind, inferior. **4** of abnormal shape or size. **bastardize, bastardise** *v.t.* **1** to declare (a person) to be illegitimate. **2** to debase. **bastardization** (-zā´shən) *n.* the action of declaring or of making illegitimate. **bastard title** *n.* a short title preceding the title-page of a book. **bastard type** *n.* (*Print.*) a font of type with a face too large or too small in proportion to its body. **bastard wing** *n.* three or four quill-like feathers placed at a small joint in the middle of a bird's wing. **bastardy** *n.* illegitimacy. [OF *bast* (F *bât*), packsaddle, late L *bastum* (cp. BANTLING)]

baste[1] (bāst) *v.t.* to moisten (a roasting joint etc.) with liquid fat, gravy etc. [etym. unknown]

baste[2] (bāst) *v.t.* to beat with a stick, to thrash, cudgel. [perh. as BASTE[1], or from Scand. (Swed. *basa*, to flog, cp. Icel. *beysta*, and see BASH[1])]

baste[3] (bāst) *v.t.* to sew slightly, to tack, to fasten together with long stitches. [OF *bastir* (F *bâtir*), to baste (perh. from OHG *bestan*, to patch, *bast*, BAST, or from late L *bastīre*, to build, construct)]

bastille (bastēl´) *n.* (*Hist.*) **1** a fortified tower. **2** (*Mil.*) a small wooden fort. **3** any one of a series of huts defended by entrenchments. **4** a prison, a workhouse. [F, the state prison in Paris, destroyed in 1789, from late L *bastīlia*, pl. of *bastīle* (*bastīre*, to build)]

bastinado (bastinā´dō) *n.* (*pl.* **bastinadoes**) **1** a method of corporal punishment or torture inflicted with a stick on the soles of the feet. **2** a rod, a stick, a cudgel. *~v.t.* (*3rd pers. sing. pres.* **bastinadoes,** *pres.p.* **bastinadoing,** *past, p.p.* **bastinadoed**) to beat with a stick, esp. on the soles of the feet. [Sp. *bastonada* (*baston*, a stick)]

bastion (bas´tyən) *n.* **1** a projecting work at the angle or in the line of a fortification, having two faces and two flanks. **2** (*fig.*) a defence. **3** a rock formation resembling the fortifying work. **bastioned** *a.* [F, from It. *bastione* (*bastia*, a building), from late L *bastire*, to build]

basuco (bəsoo´kō) *n.* an impure form of cocaine which is highly addictive. [Colombian Sp.]

BASW *abbr.* British Association of Social Workers.

bat[1] (bat) *n.* **1** a wooden instrument with a cylindrical handle and broad blade used to strike the ball at cricket or similar games. **2** a blow with a bat or club. **3** a batsman. **4** a spell of batting at cricket. **5** an object with a round flat face and a handle, used to guide taxiing or landing aircraft. **6** (*dial., sl.*) beat, rate of speed. **7** a sheet of wadding used for filling quilts. *~v.t.* (*pres.p.* **batting,** *past, p.p.* **batted**) to strike with a bat. *~v.i.* to take an innings as batsman. **off one's own bat** on one's own initiative, by one's own exertions. **right off the bat** (*N Am., coll.*) straightaway. **to bat around 1** (*sl.*) to potter. **2** to discuss (an idea). **to carry one's bat** in cricket, to be not out at the end of an innings. **bat-fowling** *n.* a method of taking birds by holding a light in front of a net, and beating their roosting-places with bats or clubs. **batlet** (-lət) *n.* **1** a small bat. **2** a flat wooden mallet used for beating linen. **batsman** *n.* (*pl.* **batsmen**) **1** a person who uses the bat at cricket and other ball games. **2** the person on an airfield or aircraft carrier who guides taxiing or landing aircraft by waving a round, plainly visible bat in each hand. [etym. uncertain; perh. from OF *batte*, a club (*battre*, to beat)]

bat[2] (bat) *n.* **1** a small nocturnal mouselike mammal of the order Chiroptera, having the digits extended to support a wing-membrane stretching from the neck to the tail, by means of which it flies. **2** (*derog.*) a woman (*the silly old bat!*). **blind as a bat** having very poor eyesight. **like a bat out of hell** (*coll.*) extremely quickly. **to have bats in the belfry** (*coll.*) to be crazy; to suffer from delusions. **bats** *a.* (*coll.*) crazy, batty. **batty** *a.* (*comp.* **battier,** *superl.* **battiest**) **1** (*coll.*) mentally unstable; crazy. **2** batlike. **batwing sleeve** *n.* a sleeve shaped like a bat's wing. [ME *bakke*, from Scand. (Dan. *aften-bakke*, evening-bat, Icel. *blaka*, to flutter, flap)]

bat[3] (bat) *n.* (*only in combs.*) a packsaddle. **batman** *n.* (*pl.* **batmen**) **1** the military servant of an officer. **2** (*Hist.*) a man in charge of an officer's packhorse and its load. **batwoman** *n.* (*pl.* **batwomen**) the female military servant of a female military officer. [F *bât*, a packsaddle, OF *bast*, late L *bastum*, perh. from Gr. *bastazein*, to carry]

bat[4] (bat) *v.t.* (*pres.p.* **batting,** *past, p.p.* **batted**) to blink. **not to bat an eyelid/ eyelash/ eye 1** not to blink. **2** to show no surprise or emotion. [BATE[4]]

☒ **batallion** common misspelling of BATTALION.

batata (bətah´tə) *n.* the sweet potato. [Sp. and Port., from Taino]

Batavian (bətā´viən) *a.* **1** of or relating to Batavia, an ancient district of the Netherlands. **2** †Dutch. *~n.* **1** a native or inhabitant of Batavia. **2** †a Dutchman. [L *Batavia*, from *Batavi*]

batch[1] BACH[1].

batch[2] (bach) *n.* **1** any quantity produced at one operation or treated together. **2** as much bread as is produced at one baking. **3** a sort, lot, set, crew. *~v.t.* **1** to collect into batches. **2** to treat as a batch or in batches. **3** to group (items) for computer processing. **batch processing** *n.* **1** an industrial process that performs on batches. **2** a system by which a number of jobs submitted by users are run through a computer as a single batch. [ME *bacche* (OE *bacan*, to bake)]

☒ **batchelor** common misspelling of BACHELOR.

bate[1] (bāt), **bait** *n.* (*sl.*) a rage.

bate[2] (bāt) †*v.t., v.i.* ABATE. **with bated breath 1** with breath held in check. **2** in suspense, anxiously. [aphetic]

bate[3] (bāt) *n.* **1** alkaline lye used in tanning. **2** the vat containing this. **3** the process of steeping. *~v.t.* to steep in bate. [from Swed. *beta*, maceration, tanning (cp. G *beizen*, to steep, tan)]

†**bate**[4] (bāt) *v.i.* **1** to beat the wings, flutter impatiently. **2** to be restless or impatient. *~n.* strife, contention. [OF *batre*, late L *batere*, L *battuere*; or abbr. of DEBATE]

bateau (bat´ō) *n.* (*pl.* **bateaux** (-z)) a long, light, flat-bottomed river-boat, tapering at both ends, used in Canada. **bateau bridge** *n.* a floating bridge supported by *bateaux*. [F (cogn. with BOAT)]

bateleur (batəlœ´), **bateleur eagle** *n.* an African eagle, *Terathopius ecaudatus*, having a short tail and a crest. [F *bateleur*, juggler]

Batesian mimicry (bāt´siən) *n.* (*Zool.*) mimicry in which a species is protected by its resemblance to one that is harmful or inedible. [H. W. *Bates*, 1825–92, British naturalist]

Bath (bahth) *n.* used as below. **Bath bun** *n.* a rich bun, generally with currants. **bath chair** *n.* an old kind of wheel chair. **Bath chap** *n.* a small cured pig's cheek. **Bath Oliver®** *n.* a special kind of savoury biscuit invented by Dr W. Oliver, 1695–1764, of Bath. **Bath stone** *n.* a white building-stone quarried from the oolite near Bath. [a city in Avon famous for its hot springs]

bath[1] (bahth) *n.* (*pl.* **baths** (bahdhz)) **1** the act of washing or immersing the body in water or other fluid. **2** a (usu. large) container for water for immersing the body for washing. **3** the water or other fluid used for bathing. **4** (*usu. pl.*) a building with baths or a swimming pool. **5** (*N Am.*) a bathroom. **6** a hydropathic establishment. **7** a town having medicinal springs used for bathing. **8** a wash, a lotion. **9** the action of immersing any substance in a solution for scientific, art or trade purposes. **10** a vessel containing such a solution. **11** a solution used in such a process. *~v.t.* to wash or put (usu. a child) in a bath. **bath cube** *n.* a cube of bath salts. **bathhouse** *n.* a building which has baths for the public to use. **bath mat** *n.* **1** a mat put next to a bath. **2** a rubber mat put in a bath to make it less slippery. **bath-oil** *n.* (perfumed) oil for use in bathwater. **bathrobe** *n.* (*esp. N Am.*) a dressing gown. **bathroom** *n.* **1** a room containing a bath or shower. **2** (*esp. N Am.*) a lavatory. **3** a set of fitments for a bathroom. **bath salts** *n.pl.* perfumed crystals used for softening bathwater. **bathtub** *n.* (*esp. N Am.*) a vessel containing water for bathing, a movable bath. **bathwater** *n.* the water in a bath. [OE *bæth* (cp. Icel. *bath*, G *Bad*, Gmc. *bathom*; cogn. with L *fovere*)]

bath[2] (bath) *n.* a liquid measure among the ancient Hebrews, containing about 6½ gallons. [Heb.]

bathe (bādh) *v.i.* **1** to swim in a body of water for pleasure. **2** (*esp. N Am.*) to take a bath. *~v.t.* **1** to cleanse or soothe (a wound etc.) by applying liquid. **2** to suffuse, to moisten, to wet copiously. **3** to immerse in or as in a bath; to plunge or dip. *~n.* the act of immersing the body to take a swim (esp. in the sea, a river etc.) or a bath. **bather** *n.* a person who bathes, esp. in the sea, a river or a swimming bath. **bathers** *n.pl.* (*Austral.*) a swimming costume or swimming trunks. **bathing** *n.* **bathing costume, bathing dress, bathing suit** *n.* a garment for swimming or sunbathing in. **bathing hut** *n.* a hut for bathers to undress and dress in. **bathing machine** *n.* (*Hist.*) a kind of covered carriage to bathe in the sea from. [OE *bathian* (from *bæth*, a bath; cp. Icel. *batha*, G *baden*)]

bath mitzvah BAT MITZVAH.

batho- (bath´ō), **bathy-** (-i) *comb. form* used in compound words employed in oceanography etc. [Gr. *bathus*, deep]

batholith (bath´əlith), **batholite** (-līt) *n.* a great mass of intrusive igneous rock, esp. granite. **batholithic** (-lith´-), **batholitic** (-lit´-) *a.* [Gr. *bathos*, depth, *lithos*, a stone]

bathometer (bəthom´itə) *n.* an instrument used to ascertain the depths reached in soundings. [Gr. *bathos*, depth]

bathos (bā´thos) *n.* **1** ridiculous descent from the sublime to the commonplace in writing or speech. **2** anticlimax. **bathetic** (bəthet´-) *a.* characterized by bathos.

bathy- BATHO-.

bathymetry (bəthim´itri) *n.* the art or method of taking deep soundings. **bathymeter** *n.* **bathymetric** (bathimet´-), **bathymetrical** *a.* of or relating to sounding, or to the depth at which life is found in the sea. **bathymetrically** *adv.*

bathyscaphe (bath´iskāf), **bathyscape** (-skāp), **bathyscaph** (-skaf) *n.* a submersible vessel for deep-sea observation and exploration. [Gr. *skaphē*, light boat]

bathysphere (bath´isfiə) *n.* a strong steel deep-sea observation chamber.

batik (bat´ik, bətēk´) *n.* **1** a method of printing designs on fabric by masking areas to be left undyed with wax. **2** fabric or a piece of cloth produced by this method. [Malay, from Javanese, painted]

batiste (bətēst´) *n.* a fine cotton or linen fabric. *~a.* made of batiste. [F, perh. after *Baptiste* of Cambray, the original maker]

batlet BAT[1].

batman BAT[3].

bat mitzvah (baht mits´və), **bas mitzvah** (bahs), **bath mitzvah** (bahth) *n.* **1** a Jewish girl who has reached the age (usu. 12 years) of religious responsibility. **2** the celebrations marking this event. [Heb., daughter of the law]

baton (bat´on, bat´ən) *n.* **1** the wand used by a conductor of an orchestra etc. in beating time. **2** a short stick transferred between successive team-mates in a relay-race. **3** a knobbed staff carried and swung into the air at the head of a parade or twirled by majorettes etc. **4** a truncheon used as a badge or symbol of authority or as an offensive weapon. **5** a staff or club. **6** a bar marking divisions on the face of a clock etc. **7** a diminutive of the bend sinister, used in English coats of arms as a badge of bastardy. *~v.t.* to strike with a policeman's baton or truncheon. **baton charge** *n.* a charge by police or troops with batons. **baton gun** *n.* a gun which fires rubber or plastic bullets to control rioters. **baton round** *n.* a rubber or plastic bullet used esp. to control rioters. **baton sinister** *n.* the baton signifying illegitimacy (pop. called the *bar sinister*, cp. BEND SINISTER (under BEND)). [F *bâton*, OF *baston*]

batoon BATON.

batrachian (bətrā´kiən) *a.* of or relating to the order Anura (formerly Batrachia), which includes frogs and toads. *~n.* any individual of this order, a frog or toad. **batrachoid** (bat´rəkoid) *a.* [mod. L, from neut. pl. of a. *batrachīos*, Gr. *batracheia*, froglike (*batrachos*, frog)]

bats BAT[2].

Batswana TSWANA.

battalion (bətal´yən) *n.* **1** a main division of an army. **2** an assemblage of companies of infantry. **3** the tactical and administrative unit of infantry, consisting of from four to eight companies, and generally about 1000 strong on a war footing. **4** a large group of people acting together. [F *bataillon*, It. *battaglione* (*battaglia*, battle)]

battels (bat´əlz) *n.pl.* **1** provisions from the buttery at an Oxford college. **2** the account for these. [etym. uncertain]

batten[1] (bat´ən) *n.* **1** a strip of sawn wood used for flooring. **2** a piece of wood for clamping together the boards of a door. **3** a scantling, ledge, clamp. **4** a thin piece of wood nailed on masts etc. to prevent chafing, or to fasten down the edges of tarpaulins over the hatches. *~v.t.* to fasten or strengthen with battens. **to batten down the hatches 1** to secure the hatches of a ship. **2** to prepare for action, trouble, danger etc. **battening** *n.* **1** the act of attaching battens to a wall for nailing up laths. **2** the battens so affixed. [BATON]

batten[2] (bat´ən) *v.i.* **1** to thrive, to prosper (on). **2** to grow fat. **3** to feed on gluttonously. **4** to revel in. [prob. from Icel. *batna*, to get better, recover (*bati*, advantage, improvement; cp. Dut. *baten*, to avail, to profit; cp. BOOT[2])]

batten[3] (bat´ən) *n.* the movable bar of a loom which strikes the weft in. [F *battant*, pres.p. of *battre*, to strike]

Battenberg (bat´ənbœg) *n.* a kind of oblong cake made with sponge of two colours. [*Battenberg* in Germany]

batter[1] (bat´ə) *v.t.* **1** to strike with successive blows so as to bruise, shake or demolish. **2** to wear or impair by beating or rough usage. **3** to subject to hard, crushing attack. **4** to attack with engines of war, formerly with a battering-ram, now with artillery. **5** to bombard. *~v.i.* to hammer (at) a door. *~n.* **1** in cooking, a mixture of several ingredients, esp. eggs, flour and milk, well beaten together. **2** adhesive paste. **3** liquid mud. **4** a blow. 5 (*Print.*) a damaged area of type. **battered** *a.* 1 (of a person) subjected to violent attack, esp. regularly. 2 (of food) covered in batter and fried. **battered baby** *n.* an infant or young child who has suffered violent injury at the hands of an adult or parent. **battered wife** *n.* (*pl.* **battered wives**) a woman who has suffered violent injury at the hands of her husband or partner. **batterer** *n.* a person who batters someone (*baby-batterer*). **battering**[1] *n.* the act of striking or beating etc. **battering charge** *n.* the heaviest charge for a siege gun. **battering engine, battering machine** *n.* an engine used for battering down walls or ramparts. **battering gun, battering piece** *n.* a siege gun. **battering ram** *n.* 1 an ancient military engine used for battering down walls, and consisting of a heavy beam shod with iron, which was originally in the form of a ram's head. 2 a similar beam used to break down doors. 3 a forcible means of getting something done. **battering train** *n.* a train of artillery for siege purposes. [OF *battre*, to beat, late L *battere*, L *battuere*]

batter[2] (bat´ə) *v.i.* to incline (as walls, parapets, embankments etc.) from the perpendicular with a receding slope. ~*n.* a receding slope (of a wall etc.); a talus. **battering**[2] *a.* sloping inwards. [etym. uncertain; perh. from F *abattre*, to beat down, depress]

batter[3] (bat´ə) *n.* a batsman; a player who is batting.

battering[1] BATTER[1].

battering[2] BATTER[2].

battery (bat´əri) *n.* (*pl.* **batteries**) 1 a connected series of electric cells, dynamos or Leyden jars, forming a source of electrical energy. 2 any apparatus for providing voltaic electricity. 3 a series of nesting-boxes in which hens are confined to increase laying. 4 (*Mil.*) a number of pieces of artillery for combined action, with men, transport and equipment. 5 the tactical unit of artillery. 6 a ship's armament. 7 the fortified work, or the part of a ship, in which artillery is mounted. 8 (*Law*) an unlawful attack by beating, or even touching in a hostile manner. 9 an assailing by blows. 10 a combined series of lenses or prisms. 11 a combination of instruments and general apparatus for use in various arts or sciences. 12 an article of metal, esp. beaten copper and brass. 13 an embankment. 14 a connected series of tests. 15 the pitcher and catcher in baseball. **cross battery** CROSS. **floating battery** FLOATING (under FLOAT). **masked battery** MASKED (under MASK). **to turn someone's battery against themselves** to use someone's own arguments to confute them. **battery piece** *n.* a siege gun. **battery wagon** *n.* a vehicle used for transporting tools and material for a battery. [F *batterie* (*battre*, see BATTER[1])]

batting (bat´ing) *n.* 1 using a bat, hitting with a bat. 2 cotton fibre prepared for quilting. **batting average** *n.* a batter's or batsman's average score of runs or hits. **batting order** *n.* the order in which batters or batsmen bat. [BAT[1]]

battle (bat´əl) *n.* 1 a fight or hostile engagement between opposing armies etc. 2 fighting, hostilities, war. 3 a persistent struggle. ~*v.i.* 1 to fight, to contend (with or against). 2 (*esp. Austral.*) to struggle for a living. ~*v.t.* (*esp. N Am.*) to assail in battle, to fight against. **to battle one's way** to make one's way fighting. **to do battle** to take part in a battle or contest. **to have the battle** to be victorious. **to join battle** to commence a general combat. **battle array** *n.* the order of troops prepared for engagement. **battleaxe,** (*N Am.*) **battleax** *n.* 1 a weapon like an axe, formerly used in battle. 2 a halberd. 3 (*coll.*) a formidable woman. **battlebus** *n.* a bus used as a mobile headquarters during an election campaign. **battlecruiser** *n.* a large, heavily-armed cruiser. **battle-cry** *n.* (*pl.* **battle-cries**) a war cry, a slogan. **battled**[1] *a.* 1 drawn up in line of battle. 2 fought, contested. **battledress** *n.* comfortable, loose-fitting uniform worn by soldiers in battle. **battle fatigue** *n.* combat fatigue. **battlefield, battleground** *n.* the scene of a battle. **battlepiece** *n.* a pictorial, rhetorical or poetical description of a battle. **battleplane** *n.* a large, fighting aircraft. **battler** *n.* **battle royal** *n.* (*pl.* **battles royal**) 1 a general engagement. 2 a free fight, a general row. 3 a cock-fight in which more than two game cocks are engaged. **battleship** *n.* 1 a warship. 2 a ship adapted by armament for line of battle, as opposed to a cruiser. [OF *batayle*, late L *battuālia*, neut. pl. of a. *battuālis*, fighting (*battuere*, to beat)]

battled[1] BATTLE.

battled[2] (bat´əld) *a.* embattled, protected with battlements. [shortened from EMBATTLED]

battledore (bat´əldaw) *n.* 1 the light racket used to strike a shuttlecock in an old racket game. 2 the game in which this is used. 3 (*Hist.*) a wooden bat used for washing. **battledore and shuttlecock** *n.* the game of battledore. [etym. uncertain; prob. from Prov. *batedor*, a washing-beetle (*batre*, to beat, *-dor*, -TOR)]

battlement (bat´əlmənt) *n.* 1 a parapet with openings or embrasures, on the top of a building, orig. for defensive purposes, afterwards used as an ornament. 2 a roof having a battlement. 3 the indented crest of mountains. 4 the heights of the heavens. **battlemented** *a.* [OF *batailles*, battlements, or temporary turrets of timber; prob. confused with OF *batillement*, a redoubt (*batiller*, to fortify)]

battue (batoo´) *n.* 1 driving game from cover by beating the bushes. 2 a shoot on this plan. 3 a wholesale slaughter. [F (fem. p.p. of *battre*, to beat)]

battuta (batoo´tə) *n.* (*pl.* **battute** (-tā)) (*Mus.*) 1 a bar. 2 the beating of time. [It., a beat]

batty BAT[2].

batwoman BAT[3].

baubee BAWBEE.

bauble (baw´bəl) *n.* 1 a gew-gaw, a showy trinket. 2 a piece of childish folly. 3 a mere toy. 4 a thing of no value. 5 a short stick or wand having a head with asses' ears carved at the end of it, carried by the fools or jesters of former times. 6 a foolish, childish person. [OF *babel, baubel*, a child's plaything; perh. confused with ME *babyll, babulle*, a stick with a thong (*bablyn*, to waver, oscillate, from *bab* or *bob*)]

baud (bawd) *n.* (*pl.* **baud, bauds**) a unit which measures the rate of telegraphic or electronic transmission, equal to one information unit or (loosely) one bit of data per second. [J. M. E. *Baudot*, 1845–1903, French inventor]

baudekin, baudkin BALDACHIN.

baudric BALDRIC.

Bauhaus (bow´hows) *n.* (the principles of) a radical German school of architecture and the arts founded in 1919 and dedicated to achieving a functional synthesis of art design and technology. [G, lit. building house]

baulk (bawlk, bawk), **balk** *n.* 1 an obstacle, a hindrance, a check; a disappointment. 2 the part of a billiard or snooker table behind a transverse line behind which the cue ball is placed at the beginning of the game. 3 a beam of timber. 4 a tie-beam of a house. 5 an illegal action of a pitcher in baseball. 6 a ridge of land left (deliberately or accidentally) unploughed. ~*v.i.* to turn aside, to swerve, to refuse to leap or to proceed; to hesitate (at). ~*v.t.* 1 to check, hinder; to disappoint. 2 to avoid, let slip. 3 to pass over intentionally; to refuse. 4 to evade, frustrate. 5 to argue contentiously against. **to make a baulk** in billiards etc., to leave one's own ball and the red inside the baulk when the opponent's is in hand. **baulked** *a.* foiled, disappointed. **baulky** *a.* (*comp.* **baulkier,** *superl.* **baulkiest**) 1 (of a horse) prone to baulk or swerve. 2 perverse, unwilling. [OE *balca*, a ridge (prob. cogn. with Icel. *bālkr*, a beam, partition)]

bauxite (bawk´sīt), **beauxite** (bō´zīt) *n.* a clay which is the principal source of aluminium. **bauxitic** (-sit´ik) *a.* [*Les Baux*, near Arles]

Bavarian (bəveə´riən) *n.* **1** a native or inhabitant of Bavaria. **2** the German dialect spoken in Bavaria. *~a.* of or relating to Bavaria or its inhabitants.

bawbee (bawbē´), **baubee** *n.* **1** an old Scots copper coin equivalent to about a halfpenny. **2** (*Sc., coll.*) a halfpenny. [prob. from Alexander Orrock of Sille*bawbe*, fl.1514, Sc. mint-master]

bawd (bawd) *n.* **1** a procuress, a brothel-keeper. **2** a prostitute. **3** a go-between, a pander. **bawdry** *n.* **1** the practice of a bawd. **2** fornication. **3** obscene talk. **bawdy** *a.* (*comp.* **bawdier**, *superl.* **bawdiest**) **1** obscene, lewd. **2** of or befitting a bawd. **3** dirty. *~n.* bawdiness. **bawdily** *adv.* **1** lasciviously. **2** obscenely. **bawdiness** *n.* obscenity, lewdness. **bawdy house** *n.* a brothel. [etym. uncertain]

bawl (bawl) *v.i.* **1** to cry loudly, howl, bellow. **2** to shout at the top of one's voice. *~v.t.* **1** to shout aloud. **2** to utter with bawling. **3** to cry for sale. *~n.* a loud, prolonged shout or cry. **to bawl out** (*coll.*) to reprove fiercely. [med. L *baulāre*, to bark; or Icel. *baula*, to low, ON *baula*, a cow]

bawley (baw´li) *n.* a small fishing smack. [etym. unknown]

bay[1] (bā) *n.* **1** an arm or inlet of the sea extending into the land, with a wide mouth. **2** a recess or cirque in a range of hills. **3** (*N Am.*) an arm of a prairie extending into woods. **bay floe, bay ice** *n.* new ice formed in bays or sheltered waters. **bay salt** *n.* coarse-grained crystals of salt obtained by slow evaporation, orig. of sea water, now of a saturated solution of chloride of sodium. **Bay State** *n.* (*N Am.*) Massachusetts (formerly the colony of Massachusetts Bay). **baywood** *n.* mahogany from a tropical American tree, *Swietenia macrophylla*, of Honduras and Campeachy Bay, Mexico. [F *baie*, low L *baia*]

bay[2] (bā) *n.* **1** an opening or recess in a wall. **2** a main compartment or division, like the interval between two pillars. **3** a division of a barn or other building. **4** an internal recess in a room formed by the outward projection of the walls. **5** a platform on a railway station with a cul-de-sac, forming the terminus of a sideline. **6** a compartment or division in a ship or in the fuselage of an aircraft. **bay window** *n.* an angular window structure forming a recess in a room. [F *baie*, OF *baée*, fem. p.p. of *baer*, to gape, late L *baddāre* (fem. p.p. *badāta*)]

bay[3] (bā) *n.* **1** barking. **2** the prolonged hoarse bark of a dog. **3** the barking of a pack that has tracked down its prey. **4** the final encounter between hounds and their prey. **5** the position of a hunted animal defending itself at close quarters. *~v.i.* to bark hoarsely, as a hound at its prey. *~v.t.* **1** to bark at. **2** to bring to bay. **3** to express by barking. **at bay** in a position of defence, in great straits, in the last extremity. **to bring/ drive to bay 1** to come to close quarters with (the animal hunted). **2** to reduce to extremities. **to hold/ keep at bay** to keep back (assailing hounds or other pursuers) from attacking. **to stand at bay** to turn to face assailing hounds or one's pursuers. [OF *abai*, barking, from *abaier* (F *aboi, aboyer*)]

bay[4] (bā) *n.* **1** the bay tree or bay laurel, *Laurus nobilis.* **2** (*N Am.*) a place covered with bay trees. **3** (*pl.*) leaves or twigs of this tree, woven into a garland as a reward for a conqueror or poet. **4** fame, renown. **bayberry** *n.* (*pl.* **bayberries**) the candleberry or its fruit. **bay cherry** *n.* the cherry laurel, *Cerasus laurocerasus.* **bay laurel** *n.* the tree *Laurus nobilis.* **bay leaf** *n.* a leaf from the bay tree, dried and used in cooking to flavour sauces, stews etc. **bay rum** *n.* an aromatic, spiritous liquid, used in medicines and cosmetics, and prepared by distilling rum in which bay leaves have been steeped. **bay tree** *n.* the tree *Laurus nobilis.* [OF *baie*, L *baca*, berry]

bay[5] (bā) *a.* reddish-brown in colour, approaching chestnut. *~n.* a horse of that colour. [F *bai*, L *badius* (cp. Gael. and Ir. *buidhe*, yellow)]

bay[6] (bā) *n.* the second branch of a stag's horn, the next to the brow antler. [abbr. of *bay-antler*, OF *besantlier* (*bes*, second, ANTLER)]

bay[7] (bā) *n.* a dam or embankment retaining water. *~v.t.* to dam, hold (back) water. [etym. uncertain]

bayadère (bayadeə´) *n.* a Hindu dancing girl. [F, from Port. *bailadeira*, a dancing girl (*bailar*, to dance)]

bayonet (bā´ənit) *n.* **1** a weapon for stabbing or thrusting, attached by a band to the muzzle of a rifle, so as to convert that into a kind of pike. **2** (*pl.*) infantry. **3** military force. **4** a type of connection used to secure light-bulbs, camera lenses etc. in which pins are engaged in slots in a cylindrical fitting. *~v.t.* (*pres.p.* **bayoneting,** (*N Am.*) **bayonetting,** *past, p.p.* **bayoneted,** (*N Am.*) **bayonetted**) **1** to stab with a bayonet. **2** to compel by military force. **bayonet catch, bayonet joint** *n.* a device for securing in place two cylindrical parts by means of a turn. [etym. uncertain, said to be from *Bayonne*, France]

bayou (bīh´yoo) *n.* (*N Am.*) **1** the outlet of a lake or river. **2** a sluggish watercourse. [F *boyau*, a gut]

bazaar (bəzah´) *n.* **1** an Eastern market-place, where goods of all descriptions are offered for sale. **2** a sale of useful or ornamental articles, often handmade or second-hand, in aid of charity. **3** a shop where a variety of (ornamental) goods are sold. [Pers. *bāzār*]

bazan BASAN.

bazooka (bəzoo´kə) *n.* an anti-tank or rocket-firing gun. [after a crude pipe instrument]

BB *abbr.* **1** Boys' Brigade. **2** (on lead pencils) double black.

BBBC *abbr.* British Boxing Board of Control.

BBC *abbr.* British Broadcasting Corporation. **BBC English** *n.* the English language supposedly spoken by BBC announcers and newsreaders.

BBFC *abbr.* British Board of Film Classification.

bbl. *abbr.* barrels.

BBQ *abbr.* barbecue.

BBSRC *abbr.* Biotechnology and Biological Sciences Research Council.

BC *abbr.* **1** before Christ. **2** British Columbia. **3** British Council.

Usage note BC follows any style of date (*91 BC; the third century BC*).

BCD *abbr.* (*Comput.*) binary-coded decimal.

BCE *abbr.* before the Common Era.

BCF *abbr.* **1** British Chess Federation. **2** British Cycling Federation.

BCG *abbr.* Bacillus Calmette-Guérin, used in anti-tuberculosis vaccine.

BCNZ *abbr.* Broadcasting Corporation of New Zealand.

BCPL *abbr.* Basic Computer Programming Language.

BD *abbr.* Bachelor of Divinity.

BDA *abbr.* **1** British Deaf Association. **2** British Dental Association. **3** British Diabetic Association.

Bde. *abbr.* Brigade.

bdellium (del´iəm) *n.* **1** a tree of any of several species of *Balsamodendron*, which produces gum resin. **2** the gum resin of these trees. [L, from Gr. *bdellion, bdella, bdolchon*, Heb. *bedōlakh*, perh. a pear]

Bdr. *abbr.* Bombardier.

BDS *abbr.* Bachelor of Dental Surgery.

BE *abbr.* **1** Bachelor of Engineering. **2** Bachelor of Education. **3** bill of exchange.

be (bē) *v., often aux.* (*pres. ind. 1st pers. sing.* **am** (am), *2nd pers. sing.* **are** (ah), †**art** (aht), *3rd pers. sing.* **is** (iz), *pl.* **are** (ah), *pres. subj.* **be,** *pres.p.* **being,** *past ind., 1st,*

3rd pers. **was** (woz), *2nd pers. sing.* **were** (wœ), †**wast** (wost), †**wert** (wœt), *pl.* **were,** *past subj.* **were,** *p.p.* **been** (bēn)) **1** to exist, to live, to have a real state of existence, physical or mental. **2** to become, remain, continue. **3** to happen, occur, come to pass. **4** to have come or gone to or to occupy a certain place. **5** to have a certain state or quality. **6** used as a copula, asserting the connection between the subject and the predicate (*They are old*; *It was a fox*; *Yesterday was my birthday*; *The tickets were £6 each*; *You are everything to your parents*). **7** (*aux. v.*) used in complex verb phrases expressing mood, aspect, or tense, such as passive, continuous, future or (*literary or dial.*) perfect (*He was killed*; *They were singing*; *You are to sit here*; *She is gone*). **been (and gone) and** (*sl.*) used to express surprise or annoyance at what someone has done. **be that as it may** even if that is true. **to be at** to occupy oneself with. **to be off** OFF. **be-all** *n.* **1** all that is to be. **2** the consummation, the finality. **be-all and end-all** *n.* the sole object or idea in view. [OE *bēon* (cp. Sansk. *bhū-*, Gr. *phuein*, L *fui*, Gmc. *beo-*); OE *am, eom, eart, earun, aron* (cp. Sansk. *asmi, asī*, Gr. *eimi, essi, eisin*, L *sum, es, sunt*, Gmc. *es*); OE *wæs, wære, wæron* (cp. Sansk. *vas-*, to remain, dwell, live, Goth. *wisan*, to remain, continue, OFris. *wesa*, Icel. *vera*)]

Usage note After the verb *to be*, the objective pronoun (*her, him, me, us, them*) is the everyday choice (*It is me, Is it them?* etc.). The subjective (*I, he, she* etc.) is now considered rather pedantic in speech, though it would be appropriate in formal written contexts.

be- (bi) *pref.* **1** about, by, e.g. *besmear*, to smear all over, *bedaub*, to daub about, *before*, about the front of, *below*, on the low side of, *besiege*, to sit around. **2** making intransitive verbs transitive or reflexive, e.g. *bemoan, bespeak, bethink.* **3** forming verbs from nouns or adjectives, e.g. *befool, befriend, benumb.* **4** having a privative force, as in *behead, bereave.* **5** compounded with nouns, signifying to call this or that, as in *bedevil, belady, bemadam.* **6** intensive, e.g. *becrowd, bedrug, bescorch.* **7** making adjectives, e.g. *bejewelled, bewigged.* [OE *be-, bī, by*]

BEA *abbr.* British Epilepsy Association.

BEAB *abbr.* British Electrical Approvals Board.

beach (bēch) *n.* **1** a sandy or pebbly seashore. **2** the strand on which the waves break. **3** shingle. *~v.t.* to haul or run (a ship or boat) on a beach. **beach ball** *n.* an inflatable ball that is used on the beach. **beach buggy** *n.* a low motor vehicle that can be driven on sand. **beachcomber** *n.* **1** a wrecker, a water-rat. **2** a long wave rolling in from the ocean. **3** a settler in the Pacific Islands, living by pearl-fishing and other means. **4** a loafer in these conditions. **beached** *a.* **1** run aground on a beach. **2** having a beach. **beachfront** *n.* (*esp. N Am.*) SEAFRONT (under SEA). **beachgrass** *n.* a coarse grass, *Arundo arenaria*, growing on the sea-shore. **beachhead** *n.* a fortification established on a beach by landing forces. **beachmaster** *n.* an officer who directs the process of disembarking troops. **beach plum** *n.* **1** a N American shrub, *Prunus maritima*, which grows in coastal regions. **2** the fruit of this. **beachside** *attrib. a.* next to the beach (*a beachside café*). **beachwear** *n.* clothes that are designed for wearing on the beach. **beachy** *a.* (*comp.* **beachier,** *superl.* **beachiest**) **1** like a beach. **2** pebbly, shingly. [etym. unknown]

Beach-la-mar (bēchləmah´) *n.* a Creole spoken in the W Pacific. [Port. *bicho do mar*, F *bêche-de-mer*, sea cucumber (from the trade in these)]

beacon (bē´kən) *n.* **1** a burning cresset fixed on a pole or on a building. **2** a signal-fire on an eminence. **3** a conspicuous hill. **4** a watchtower. **5** a lighthouse. **6** a fixed signal to give warning of a shoal or rock, or to indicate the fairway. **7** a transmitter concentrating its radiation in a narrow beam, to act as a guide to aircraft. **8** anything which gives notice of danger. **9** a Belisha beacon. *~v.t.* **1** to light up with beacon-fires. **2** to mark with beacons. **3** to lead, to guide. *~v.i.* to shine like a beacon. **beaconage** *n.* **1** money paid for the maintenance of beacons, buoys etc. **2** a system of lighting shoals etc. [OE *bēacen* (cp. OS *bōkan*, OHG *Bouhhan*)]

bead (bēd) *n.* **1** a small globular perforated body of glass, coral, metal or other material. **2** a beadlike drop threaded on a string to form a rosary. **3** the same used as an ornament. **4** a beadlike drop of a liquid, a bubble. **5** the front sight of a gun. **6** the inner edge of a tyre. **7** (*Archit.*) a narrow semicircular moulding. **8** an ornament resembling a string of beads. **9** (*pl.*) a necklace. **10** (*pl.*) a rosary. *~v.t.* **1** to ornament with beads or beading. **2** to thread beads. *~v.i.* to form beads. **to draw a bead on** to aim at. **to tell/ say one's beads** to count the rosary, to say one's prayers. **beaded** *a.* **bead frame** *n.* an abacus. **bead house** *n.* **1** a house of prayer. **2** an almshouse. **beading** *n.* **1** the formation of beads. **2** beadwork. **3** (*Archit.*) a bead (moulding). **4** a bead of a tyre. **beadroll** *n.* a list of names (orig. of benefactors) to be prayed for. **beadsman, beadswoman, bedesman, bedeswoman** *n.* (*pl.* **beadsmen, beadswomen, bedesmen, bedeswomen**) (*Hist.*) **1** a person appointed to pray for another. **2** an almsman or almswoman. **bead tree** *n.* any of various trees whose seeds are used as rosary beads. **beadwork** *n.* ornamental work in beads. **beady** *a.* (*comp.* **beadier,** *superl.* **beadiest**) **1** (of eyes) small and bright like beads. **2** covered with beads or bubbles, foaming. **beadily** *adv.* **beadiness** *n.* **beady-eyed** *a.* **1** having eyes like beads. **2** watchful, observant. [OE *bed-* (only in comb.), *gebed*, prayer (*biddan*, to pray)]

beadle (bē´dəl) *n.* **1** a messenger, crier or usher of a court. **2** a petty officer of a church, parish, college, city company etc. **beadledom** *n.* **1** beadles collectively. **2** the characteristics of beadles. **3** stupid officiousness. **beadleship** *n.* [OE *bydel*, a herald, or OF *bedel* (F *beadeau*); Gmc. *budiloz*, from *buidan*, to announce]

beadsman, beadswoman BEAD.

beagle (bē´gəl) *n.* **1** a small dog orig. bred for hunting hares by members of the hunt on foot. **2** a person who scents out or hunts down. **3** (*Hist.*) an officer of the law. **beagler** *n.* **beagling** *n.* [etym. unknown]

beak (bēk) *n.* **1** the pointed bill of a bird. **2** any beaklike process, such as the mandibles of a turtle or an octopus. **3** (*coll.*) a hooked or prominent nose. **4** the prow of an ancient war-galley, often sheathed with brass, and used as a ram. **5** a promontory of land etc. **6** a spout. **7** (*sl.*) a magistrate. **8** (*sl.*) a headmaster or headmistress. *~v.t.* to seize or strike with the beak (esp. in cockfighting). **beaked** *a.* **1** having a beak or beaklike process. **2** (*Bot.*) rostrate. **3** (*Her.*) having the beak and legs of a different tincture from the body. **beaky** *a.* (*comp.* **beakier,** *superl.* **beakiest**). [F *bec*, low L *beccus*, prob. of Celtic origin]

beaker (bē´kə) *n.* **1** a large wide-mouthed drinking vessel. **2** the contents of a beaker. **3** an open-mouthed glass vessel with a lip, used in scientific experiments. **Beaker Folk** *n.pl.* a prehistoric people inhabiting Britain and Europe during the Bronze Age (named from the beakers found in their burial sites). [Icel. *bikarr* (cp. G *Becher*, late L *bīcārium*, from Gr. *bīkos*)]

beam (bēm) *n.* **1** a large, long piece of timber squared on its sides, esp. one supporting rafters in a building. **2** a ray or collection of rays of light or radiation. **3** a series of radio or radar signals. **4** the direction indicated by such signals. **5** a broad smile. **6** the part of a balance from which the scales are suspended. **7** the pole of a carriage. **8** the part of a loom on which the warp is wound. **9** a cylinder on which cloth is wound as it is woven. **10** the main piece of a plough to which the handles are fixed. **11** the main trunk of a stag's horn. **12** the heavy iron lever which transmits motion in a beam engine. **13** a transverse piece of timber, supporting the deck and staying the sides of a ship. **14** the width of a ship or boat. **15** the shank of an anchor. *~v.t.* **1** to emit or direct in rays, to radiate. **2** to transport in a beam of energy. *~v.i.* **1** to send out rays of light. **2** to shine radiantly. **3** to smile brightly. **4** to be transported in a beam of energy. **broad across/ in the beam 1** (of a ship) wide. **2** (of a person) having wide hips, having large buttocks. **off the beam 1** off the course indicated by a radio beam. **2** off the mark. **on the beam 1** on the course indicated by a radio beam. **2** on the mark. **3** (*Naut.*) at right-angles to the keel. **beam-compass, beam-compasses** *n.* an instrument for describing large circles, consisting of a beam of wood or brass, with sliding sockets bearing steel or pencil points. **beam-ends** *n.pl.* the ends of the beams of a ship. **on one's beam-ends 1** thrown so much to one side that the beams are in the water. **2** penniless, quite destitute. **beam engine** *n.* an engine with a beam connecting piston rod and crank, in contradistinction to one in which the piston rod is applied directly to the crank. **beamer** *n.* (*coll.*) in cricket, a fast ball bowled at the batsman's head. **beaming** *a.* bright, shining. **beam transmission** *n.* a method of short-wave radio transmission in which the energy radiated is concentrated by a reflector system of wires within a limited angle for reception in a particular zone. **beam tree** *n.* the whitebeam, *Pyrus aria*, the timber of which is used for axle-trees. **beamy** *a.* (*comp.* **beamier**, *superl.* **beamiest**) **1** (of ships) massive, broad in the beam. **2** shining, radiant, brilliant. **3** antlered. [OE *bēam* (cp. OHG *boum*, G *Baum*, Dut. *boom*)]

bean (bēn) *n.* **1** the kidney-shaped seed in long pods of *Faba vulgaris* and allied plants. **2** the seeds of other plants in some way resembling those of the common bean. **3** (*sl.*) the head. **4** (*pl.*, *N Am.*, *sl.*) anything at all (*You don't know beans*). *~v.t.* (*esp. N Am.*, *sl.*) to hit on the head. **full of beans** energetic and vigorous. **not a bean** (*sl.*) no money. **to give someone beans** (*sl.*) **1** to punish. **2** to scold. **beanbag** *n.* **1** a small cloth bag filled with dried beans used in games. **2** a large cushion filled with foam or polystyrene beads, used as a seat. **bean caper** *n.* **1** a shrub, *Zygophyllum fabago*, which grows in E Mediterranean regions. **2** a flower bud of this, which can be eaten. **bean-counter** *n.* (*orig. N Am.*, *coll.*, *derog.*) **1** an accountant. **2** a miser, a penny-pincher. **bean curd** *n.* an extract of soybean in the form of jelly, custard or cake, which is used in Chinese and other Asian cooking. **beanery** *n.* (*pl.* **beaneries**) (*N Am.*, *sl.*) a cheap restaurant. **beanfeast** *n.* (*coll.*) **1** an annual dinner given by an employer to employees. **2** a celebration. **bean-fed** *a.* **1** fed on beans. **2** in good condition. **beanfly** *n.* (*pl.* **beanflies**) an insect of purple colour found on beans. **bean goose** *n.* a migratory goose, *Anser fabalis*. **beanie, beany** *n.* (*pl.* **beanies**) a small close-fitting cap like a skullcap. **beano** (-ō) *n.* (*pl.* **beanos**) (*coll.*) a treat, a spree, a beanfeast. **bean paste** *n.* a fermented paste made from soybeans and various other ingredients, used in Chinese and other Asian cooking. **beanpole** *n.* **1** a tall, thin pole used to support bean plants. **2** (*coll.*) a tall thin person. **bean sprout** *n.* a young shoot of the mung bean used as a vegetable in Chinese cooking, and in salads. **beanstalk** *n.* the stem of the bean. **beanstraw** *n.* the haulm of bean plants. **bean tree** *n.* any of various trees bearing seeds in pods, esp. the carob tree, *Ceratonia siliqua*. **bean trefoil** *n.* **1** a leguminous plant of the genus *Anagyris*. **2** the laburnum, *Cytisus laburnam*. **3** the buckbean or bogbean, *Menyanthes trifoliata*. [OE *bēan* (cp. Dut. *boon*, Icel. *baun*, OHG *pona*, G *Bohne*)]

bear[1] (beə) *n.* (*pl. in general* **bear**, *in particular* **bears**) **1** a plantigrade mammal of the family Ursidae, with a large head, long shaggy hair, hooked claws and a stumpy tail. **2** a rough unmannerly man. **3** either of the northern constellations, the Great or the Little Bear. **4** a person who sells stock for future delivery in the expectation that prices will fall, a speculator for the fall. **5** a teddy bear. **6** (*esp. N Am.*, *sl.*) a police officer, the police. *~v.i.* to speculate for a fall in stocks. *~v.t.* to produce a fall in the price of (stock etc.). **like a bear with a sore head** in a very bad mood, irritable. **the Bear** (*coll.*) Russia. **bear-baiting** *n.* (*Hist.*) the sport of baiting a chained bear with dogs. **bearberry** *n.* (*pl.* **bearberries**) **1** an evergreen trailing shrub of the genus *Arctostaphylos*. **2** the barberry. **beargarden** *n.* **1** (*Hist.*) a place in which bears were kept and baited. **2** a rude, turbulent assembly. **bear-hug** *n.* a tight hug. **bearish** *a.* **1** bearlike. **2** rough, rude, uncouth. **3** in the stock market, characterized by a fall in prices. **bear leader** *n.* (*coll.*) a travelling tutor. **bear market** *n.* on the Stock Exchange, a market with falling prices, as distinct from *bull market*. **bearpit** *n.* **1** a sunken area in a zoo for bears to live in. **2** a rowdy scene or place. **bear's breech** *n.* a plant of the genus *Acanthus*, esp. *A. mollis*. **bear's ear** *n.* the common auricula, *Primula auricula*. **bear's foot** *n.* stinking hellebore, *Helleborus fetidus*. **bearskin** *n.* **1** the skin of a bear. **2** a shaggy woollen cloth, used for overcoats. **3** the tall fur cap worn by some regiments in the British Army. [OE *bera* (cp. Dut. *beer*; Icel. *bera*, *björn*, G *Bär*)]

bear[2] (beə) *v.t.* (*past* **bore** (baw), *p.p.* **borne** (bawn)) **1** to carry, to wear, to show or display (e.g. armorial bearings). **2** to bring. **3** to sustain, to support the weight of (material or immaterial things). **4** to be responsible for, to wield. **5** to suffer, to endure, to tolerate. **6** to admit of. **7** to thrust, to press. **8** to give birth to. **9** to produce, to yield. **10** (*refl.*) to behave. *~v.i.* **1** to incline, take a certain direction (as to the point of the compass) with respect to something else. **2** to suffer, to be patient. **to bear against 1** to rest upon. **2** to be in contact with. **to bear a hand** HAND. **to bear arms 1** to be a soldier. **2** (*Her.*) to be entitled to a coat of arms. **to bear away 1** to carry off. **2** to win. **3** to change the course of a ship when close-hauled, and put her before the wind. **to bear (away) the bell** BELL[1]. **to bear comparison (with)** COMPARISON. **to bear down 1** to overwhelm, to crush, to subdue. **2** to use the abdominal muscles to assist in giving birth. **to bear down on 1** to sail in the direction of. **2** to approach purposefully. **to bear fruit** (*fig.*) to have a successful outcome. **to bear hard 1** to press, to urge. **2** to have a grudge against. **3** †to resent. **to bear hard/ heavily on** to oppress. **to bear in mind** to remember, to take into account. **to bear off 1** to carry off. **2** to win. **to bear on 1** to press against. **2** to be relevant to. **to bear out** to confirm, to justify. **to bear repeating** to be worth repeating. **to bear the brunt** BRUNT. **to bear up 1** to endure cheerfully. **2** (*Naut.*) to put the helm up so as to bring the vessel before the wind. **to bear up for** to sail before the wind towards. **to bear upon** to be relevant to. **to bear with** to put up with, to endure. **to bear witness** WITNESS. **to bring to bear** to apply, bring into operation. **bearable** *a.* **bearability** (-bil´-) *n.* **bearableness** *n.* **bearably** *adv.* **bearer** *n.* **1** a person who or thing which bears, carries or supports. **2** a person who helps to carry a corpse to the grave or to hold the pall. **3** a porter. **4** a person who holds or presents a cheque. **5** a bringer of anything. **6** the holder of any rank or office. **7** a support. **8** the pieces supporting the winders of a stair. **9** an animal or plant producing its kind. **10** (*Hist.*) in India, Africa etc., a personal or domestic servant. **bearing** *n.* **1** endurance, toleration. **2** mien, deportment, carriage, manner, behaviour. **3** relation, connection. **4** the space between the two fixed extremities of a piece of timber, or between one of the extremities and a post or wall. **5** a carrier or support for moving parts of any machine. **6** any part of a machine that bears the friction. **7** (*Her.*) a charge, a device. **8** relation, relevance, aspect. **9** the direction in which an object lies from a ship. **10** (*pl.*) relative position; one's sense of this. **to get/ find one's bearings** to re-establish one's position. **to lose one's bearings** to be uncertain of one's position. **bearing cloth** *n.* the robe in which an infant is carried to the font at baptism. **bearing-rein** *n.* a fixed rein for holding a horse's head up. [OE *beran* (cp. Goth *bairan*, OHG *beran*, L *ferre*, Gr. *pherein*)]

beard (biəd) *n.* **1** the hair on the lower part of a man's face, esp. on the chin. **2** the analogous hairy appendage in animals. **3** the hairy appendages in the mouth of some fishes, gills of some bivalves etc.; a byssus. **4** the awn of grasses. **5** the bristles of a feather. **6** hairs occurring in tufts. **7** (*Print.*) the part of a type above and below the face to allow for ascending and descending letters. **8** the barb of an arrow. *~v.t.* **1** to oppose with resolute effrontery; to defy. **2** to take hold of by the beard. **bearded** *a.* **1** furnished with a beard or similar appendage. **2** barbed, hooked, jagged. **bearded tit** *n.* a small Eurasian songbird, *Panurus biarmicus*, which is common in reed-beds (also called the *reedling*). **beardie** *n.* **1** (*coll.*) a man with a beard. **2** (*Austral.*) a variety of codfish. **beardless** *a.* **1** without a beard. **2** youthful, immature. **beardlessness** *n.* [OE]

Béarnaise sauce (bāənāz´) *n.* a rich sauce made with egg yolks, lemon juice or wine vinegar, herbs and shallots. [F, *Béarn* in SW France]

beast (bēst) *n.* **1** any of the animals other than man. **2** a quadruped esp. a large wild one. **3** an animal to ride or drive. **4** a domestic animal, esp. ox or cattle. **5** a brutal person. **6** an objectionable person. **7** an objectionable thing. **the beast 1** Antichrist (Rev. xiii). **2** man's carnal or brutal instincts. **beast fable** *n.* a story in which animals are the dramatis personae, much prevalent in the earlier forms of literature. **beastie** *n.* **1** (*Sc.*) a small animal. **2** (*coll.*) an insect. **beastlike** *a.* **beastly** *a.* (*comp.* **beastlier,** *superl.* **beastliest**) **1** like a beast in form or nature. **2** brutal, filthy, coarse. **3** disgusting, offensive. **4** disagreeable. *~adv.* **1** in a beastly manner. **2** (*coll.*) exceedingly, very. **beastliness** *n.* **beast of burden** *n.* an animal used for carrying loads, esp. a mule. **beast of prey** *n.* a carnivorous animal. [OF *beste*, L *bestia*]

beastings BEEST.

beat (bēt) *v.t.* (*past* **beat,** *p.p.* **beaten**) **1** to strike with repeated blows; to thrash. **2** to bruise or break by striking or pounding. **3** to work (metal etc.) by striking. **4** to strike (bushes etc.) in order to rouse game. **5** to mix or agitate by beating. **6** (of water, wind etc.) to strike or impinge on, to dash against. **7** to conquer, overcome, master. **8** to perplex. **9** to tread, as a path. **10** to play (an instrument or tune) by striking. **11** to indicate (time) with a baton or by gestures etc. **12** to cause to move rhythmically. *~v.i.* **1** to strike against some obstacle. **2** to pulsate, throb. **3** to knock. **4** to move rhythmically. **5** to mark time in music. **6** (*Naut.*) to make way against the wind. *~n.* **1** a strong musical accent or rhythm. **2** the rise or fall of the hand or foot in regulating time. **3** a stroke or blow. **4** a stroke upon the drum, the signal given by such a blow. **5** a pulsation, a throb. **6** a periodic variation in amplitude caused by the combination of oscillations of different frequencies. **7** a certain assigned space regularly traversed at intervals by patrols, police etc. **8** sphere, department, range. **9** a beatnik. *~a.* beaten. **to beat about** to tack. **to beat about the bush 1** to approach a matter in a roundabout way. **2** to shilly-shally. **to beat a retreat** to retire to avoid confrontation. **to beat around the bush** (*N Am.*) to beat about the bush. **to beat at the post** to pip at the post. **to beat back** to compel to retire in a confrontation. **to beat down 1** to throw or cast down. **2** to force down (a price) by haggling. **3** to force (a seller) to lower a price by haggling. **4** to come down from the sky strongly. **to beat hollow** to excel or surpass in a great degree. **to beat in** to crush. **to beat into** to knock into by dint of blows; to instil. **to beat it** (*sl.*) to go away. **to beat off** to drive away by blows. **to beat one's brains** to puzzle, to ponder laboriously. **to beat one's breast** to show grief or sorrow. **to beat out 1** to extend by beating, to hammer out. **2** to extinguish by beating. **to beat the bounds** to mark the boundary of a parish by striking it with light rods. **to beat the clock** to complete a task within the allotted time. **to beat the drum for** DRUM[1]. **to beat the hell out of** HELL. **to beat the tattoo** (*Mil.*) to beat to quarters. **to beat time** (*Mus.*) to regulate or measure the time by a motion of the hand or foot. **to beat to it** to reach somewhere or achieve something before another person. **to beat up 1** to injure seriously by beating. **2** to bring to a fluid or semi-fluid mass by beating. **3** to make way against wind or tide. **to beat up and down** to run first one way, then another, as a hunted animal. **to beat up for** to make great endeavours to procure. **to beat up for recruits** to collect recruits. **beatable** *a.* **beaten** *a.* **1** subjected to repeated blows. **2** defeated, vanquished, weary, exhausted. **3** trodden smooth, plain or bare. **4** prostrated by the wind. **beaten track** *n.* **1** the usual method. **2** the ordinary way. **off the beaten track 1** away from the places people usually go. **2** unusual. **beaten in detail** DETAIL. **beater** *n.* **1** a person who beats. **2** a person employed to rouse game, esp. grouse or pheasant. **3** an instrument for beating, pounding or mixing. **4** (*N Am., coll.*) an old vehicle. **beat generation** *n.* **1** (*orig. N Am.*) a bohemian movement of poets, writers etc. of the 1950s who rejected prevailing social and cultural values. **2** young people of the 1950s and early 1960s characterized by unconventional attitudes and self-conscious bohemianism in behaviour and dress. **beating** *n.* **1** the action of striking repeated blows. **2** a punishment or chastisement by blows. **3** pulsation, throbbing. **4** an overthrow, defeat. **5** sailing against the wind. **to take a beating** to suffer verbal or physical punishment. **to take some/ a lot of beating** to be difficult to improve upon. **beat music** *n.* popular music characterized by a pulsating rhythm. **beatnik** (-nik) *n.* (*often derog.*) a member of the beat generation. **beat-up** *a.* (*coll.*) damaged with long or rough use. [OE *bēatan* (cp. OHG *pōzan*)]

beatify (biat´ifī) *v.t.* (*3rd pers. sing. pres.* **beatifies,** *pres. p.* **beatifying,** *past, p.p.* **beatified**) **1** in the Roman Catholic Church, to declare (a deceased person) blessed in heaven. **2** to render supremely blessed or happy. **beatific** (bēətif´-) *a.* **1** making one supremely blessed or happy. **2** suggesting blessedness. **beatifically** *adv.* **beatification** *n.* **1** the Pope's declaration that a deceased person is blessed in heaven and that definite forms of public reverence should be paid to them, the first step towards canonization. **2** the act of making blessed; the state of being blessed. **beatific vision** *n.* the vision of the glories of heaven. **beatitude** (-tūd) *n.* **1** supreme felicity. **2** heavenly bliss. **3** any of the states of special blessedness announced in the Sermon on the Mount. **4** a title of the patriarchs in the Orthodox Church. [L *beātificāre*, (*beātus*, happy, *facere*, to make)]

beatnik BEAT.

beau (bō) *n.* (*pl.* **beaus** (bōz), **beaux** (bō, bōz)) **1** a suitor, lover, sweetheart. **2** a man unduly attentive to dress and social fashions and etiquette; a fop, a dandy. *~v.t.* **1** to act as beau to. **2** to escort. **beau geste** (zhest´) *n.* (*pl.* **beaux gestes** (bō zhest´)) a gracious gesture. **beau idéal** (ēdāal´) *n.* (*pl.* **beaux idéals** (bōz ēdāal´)) the highest conceivable type of excellence. **beauish** *a.* 1 after the manner of a beau; like a beau. 2 foppish. **beau monde** (mōd´) *n.* the fashionable world. [OF *beau, bel,* L *bellus,* fine, pretty (perh. *benlus,* dim. of *benus,* related to *bene,* well, *bonus,* good)]

Beaufort scale (bō´fət) *n.* a scale of wind velocity ranging from 0 = calm to 12 = hurricane. [Sir Francis *Beaufort,* 1774–1857, English admiral and hydrographer]

Beaujolais (bō´zhəlā) *n.* a usu. red, light Burgundy wine from the Beaujolais district. **Beaujolais Nouveau** (noovō´) *n.* Beaujolais wine in the first year of its vintage. [F, district in the Lyonnais, SE France]

Beaune (bōn) *n.* a usu. red Burgundy wine. [district in Côte-d'Or, France]

beauty (bū´ti) *n.* 1 that quality or assemblage of qualities which gives the eye or the other senses intense pleasure. 2 that characteristic in a material object or an abstraction which gratifies the intellect or the moral feeling. 3 a beautiful person, esp. a woman. 4 beautiful women generally. 5 a beautiful feature or characteristic. 6 embellishment, grace, charm. 7 a particular aspect that gives satisfaction or (*iron.*) the reverse. 8 a very fine example of its kind. 9 (*coll.*) a shocking or bad person; a scamp. ~*v.t.* 1 to adorn. 2 to beautify. **beaut** *n.* (*esp. Austral., sl.*) something or someone outstanding. ~*int., a.* great, excellent. **beauteous** *a.* (*poet.*) endowed with beauty; beautiful. **beauteously** *adv.* **beauteousness** *n.* **beautician** (-tish´-) *n.* a person who administers or who operates an establishment administering beauty treatment. **beautiful** *a.* 1 full of beauty; possessing the attributes that constitute beauty. 2 satisfactory, palatable, delicious. 3 (*iron.*) egregious. ~*n.* (*poet.*) a person who or thing which is beautiful. **the beautiful** the abstract notion of the qualities constituting beauty. **beautifully** *adv.* **beautifulness** *n.* **beautify** (-fī) *v.t.* (*3rd pers. sing. pres.* **beautifies,** *pres.p.* **beautifying,** *past, p.p.* **beautified**) to make beautiful. ~*v.i.* to grow beautiful. **beautification** (-fikā´shən) *n.* **beautifier** *n.* a person who or that which beautifies. **beauty parlour,** (*N Am.*) **beauty parlor** *n.* a shop specializing in beauty treatments. **beauty queen** *n.* a woman picked as the most attractive in a contest. **beauty salon** *n.* a beauty parlour. **beauty sleep** *n.* sleep before midnight. **beauty specialist** *n.* a person who makes a speciality of beauty treatment. **beauty spot** *n.* 1 a beautiful place or landscape. 2 a small mark such as a mole on the face, considered to be attractive. 3 a patch or spot placed upon the face to heighten some beauty. 4 a foil. **beauty treatment** *n.* improvement of a person's appearance by artificial means. [OF *biaute, beïtet* (late L *bellus,* see BEAU)]

beaux arts (bōz ah´) *n.pl.* fine arts. [F]

beaux esprits BEL ESPRIT.

beauxite BAUXITE.

beaver[1] (bē´və) *n.* (*pl. in general* **beaver,** *in particular* **beavers**) 1 an amphibious rodent mammal, of the genus *Castor,* with broad tail, soft fur and habits of building huts and dams. 2 the fur of this animal. 3 a hat made of such fur. 4 †beaver cloth. 5 (*sl.*) a man with a beard. 6 (**Beaver**) a six- or seven-year-old child who is a member of a group affiliated to the Scout Association. **to beaver away at** to work hard at. **beaverboard** *n.* a building board of wood-fibre material. **beaver cloth** *n.* a felted cloth for overcoats. **beaver dam** *n.* an obstruction placed across a stream by beavers. **beaver lamb** *n.* lambskin made to resemble beaver fur. **beaver-rat** *n.* the musquash or muskrat. **beaverteen** (-tēn) *n.* a twilled cotton fabric with looped filling or pile. **beaver-tree, beaver-wood** *n.* (*N Am.*) the sweet bay. [OE *beafer* (cp. Dut. *bever,* G *Biber,* L *fiber*)]

beaver[2] (bē´və) *n.* 1 the lower part of a visor. 2 the visor of a helmet. **beavered** *a.* 1 provided with a beaver. 2 wearing a beaver hat. [OF *bavière,* bib, from *baver,* to foam, slaver (*bave,* froth, slaver)]

bebop (bē´bop) *n.* a variety of jazz music which developed in the 1940s, distinguished from the earlier jazz tradition by its more complex melodies and harmonies and faster tempos (see BOP[1]). **bebopper** *n.* [imit. of the rhythm]

becalm (bikahm´) *v.t.* 1 to deprive (a ship) of wind. 2 to render calm or still. 3 to quiet, to tranquillize, to soothe.

became BECOME.

because (bikoz´) *conj.* 1 by cause of, by reason of, on account of, for. 2 for this reason, inasmuch as. [*be-,* by, CAUSE]

Usage note See note under REASON.

---

beccafico (bekəfē´kō) *n.* (*pl.* **beccaficos**) a small migratory songbird, of the genus *Sylvia,* eaten as a delicacy in continental Europe. [It., fig-pecker (*beccare,* to peck, *fico,* fig)]

béchamel (bā´shəmel) *n.* a white sauce made with cream or milk and flavoured with onions and herbs. [the Marquis de *Béchamel,* d. 1704, its French inventor]

†**bechance** (bichahns´) *v.i.* to chance, to happen. ~*v.t.* to befall.

becharm (bichahm´) *v.t.* to charm, to fascinate.

bêche-de-mer (beshdəmeə´) *n.* (*pl.* **bêche-de-mer, bêches-de-mer** (besh-)) 1 the sea-slug or trepang, *Holothuria edulis,* an echinoderm eaten by the Chinese. 2 BEACH-LA-MAR. [F, from Port. *bicho do mar,* worm of the sea]

beck[1] (bek) *n.* 1 a nod, a gesture of the finger or hand. 2 a bow or curtsy. 3 a mute signal of assent or command. 4 the slightest indication of will. ~*v.i.* 1 to make a mute signal. 2 to make obeisance, to curtsy. ~*v.t.* to call by a beck. **at someone's beck and call** 1 ready to obey someone's orders instantly. 2 subject to someone's every whim. [BECKON]

beck[2] (bek) *n.* 1 a brook, a rivulet. 2 a mountain or moorland stream. [Icel. *bekkr* (Swed. *bäck,* G *Bach*)]

becket (bek´it) *n.* (*Naut.*) anything used to confine loose ropes, tackle or spars, such as a large hook, a rope with an eye at one end; a bracket, pocket, loop etc. [etym. uncertain]

beckon (bek´ən) *v.i.* to make a signal by a gesture of the hand or a finger or by a nod. ~*v.t.* to summon or signal to by a motion of the hand, a nod etc. [OE *bēacnian, biecnian* (*beacen,* a sign, BEACON)]

becloud (biklowd´) *v.t.* 1 to cover with or as with a cloud. 2 to obscure.

become (bikŭm´) *v.i.* (*pres.p.* **becoming,** *past* **became** (-kām´), *p.p.* **become**) 1 to pass from one state or condition into another. 2 to come into existence. 3 to come to be. ~*v.t.* 1 to be suitable to, befit, be proper to or for. 2 to be in harmony with. 3 to look well upon. **to become of** to happen to, befall. **becoming** *a.* 1 befitting, suitable, proper. 2 in harmony or keeping. 3 graceful in conduct, attire etc. **becomingly** *adv.* **becomingness** *n.* [OE *becuman* (BE-, *cuman,* to come; cp. Goth. *bikwiman,* G *bekommen*)]

becquerel (bek´ərel) *n.* a unit which measures the activity of a radioactive source. [Antoine Henri *Becquerel,* 1852–1908, French physicist]

becurl (bikœl´) *v.t.* 1 to curl. 2 to deck with curls.

B.Ed. *abbr.* Bachelor of Education.

bed (bed) *n.* 1 an article of domestic furniture to sleep on. 2 the resting-place of an animal; any impromptu resting-place. 3 the use of a bed in marriage, conjugal rights, childbirth. 4 a plot of ground in a garden. 5 the flat surface on which anything rests. 6 the channel of a river. 7 the bottom of the sea. 8 a horizontal course in a wall. 9 a stratum, a layer of rock. 10 an aggregation of small animals disposed in a bedlike mass. 11 a layer of oysters. 12 the central portion of a gun-carriage. 13 the foundation of a road, street or railway. **14** the bottom layer or support on which a mechanical structure or machine is laid. *~v.t.* (*pres.p.* **bedding,** *past, p.p.* **bedded**) **1** to put in bed. **2** to plant in a bed or beds. **3** to have sexual intercourse with. **4** to fix in a stratum or course. **5** to place in a matrix of any kind, to embed. *~v.i.* **1** to form a stratum or course. **2** to go to bed. **†to be brought to bed** to be delivered of a child. **to bed out** to plant out in beds. **to get out of bed on the wrong side** to begin the day in a foul mood. **to go to bed 1** to retire at the end of the day. **2** to have sexual intercourse (with). **to keep one's bed** to remain in bed (from sickness etc.). **to lie in the bed one has made** to suffer for one's own misdeeds or mistakes. **to make a bed** to put a bed in order after it has been used. **to make up a bed** to prepare sleeping accommodation at short notice. **to put to bed 1** to settle (a child etc.) in bed for the night. **2** to complete work on (a newspaper) so that it can go to press. **to take to one's bed** to be confined to bed (from sickness etc.). **bed and board** *n.* **1** lodgings and food. **2** connubial relations. **bed and breakfast** *n.* **1** in a hotel etc., overnight accommodation with breakfast. **2** a hotel etc. providing this. **bed-and-breakfast** *v.t.* to sell (shares) and buy them back the next morning. *~a.* of or relating to a share deal of this kind. **bedbug** *n.* a bloodsucking insect of the genus *Cimex*, which infests filthy bedding. **bedchair** *n.* a chair with a movable back, to support an invalid in bed. **bedchamber** *n.* **1** a sleeping apartment. **2** a bedroom. **bedclothes** *n.pl.* sheets, blankets and coverlets for a bed. **bedcover** *n.* a bedspread. **beddable** *a.* (*coll.*) sexually attractive. **bedder** *n.* **1** a plant for bedding-out. **2** a charwoman or bedmaker in a Cambridge college. **bedding** *n.* **1** a bed with the clothes upon it. **2** bedclothes. **3** litter for domestic animals. **4** a bottom layer or foundation. **5** the stratification of rocks. **6** the line or plane of stratification. **bedding-plane** *n.* **1** a plane of stratification. **2** the top or bottom surface of a stratum. **bedding plant, bedding-out plant** *n.* a plant intended to be set in a bed. **beddy-byes** *n.* bed, sleep (used by or to children). **bedfast** *a.* confined to bed. **bedfellow** *n.* **1** a person who sleeps in the same bed with another. **2** an associate. **bedhangings** *n.pl.* hangings or curtains for a bed. **bedhead** *n.* the head end of a bed. **bed-hop** *v.i.* (*pres.p.* **bed-hopping,** *past, p.p.* **bed-hopped**) (*coll.*) to have casual sexual affairs. **bedjacket** *n.* a jacket to be worn in bed, e.g. in hospital. **bedlinen** *n.* sheets and pillow cases etc. for a bed. **bedmaker** *n.* **1** a person who makes beds. **2** a person who makes students' beds and cleans the rooms in a college. **bedmate** *n.* a bedfellow. **bed moulding** *n.* the moulding under a projection, such as the corona of a cornice. **bed of roses** *n.* a comfortable place. **bedpan** *n.* **1** a chamber utensil for urination and defecation when confined to bed. **2** a warming-pan. **bedplate** *n.* the cast-iron or steel plate used as the base plate of an engine or machine. **bedpost** *n.* any one of the upright supports of a bedstead. **bedquilt** *n.* a counterpane, a coverlet. **bedrest** *n.* (of an invalid) confinement to bed. **bedrid, bedridden** *a.* confined to bed through age or sickness. **bedrock** *n.* **1** the rock underlying superficial formations. **2** the bottom, foundation, fundamental principles. **3** the lowest possible state. **bedroll** *n.* bedding rolled up so as to be carried by a camper etc. **bedroom** *n.* **1** a sleeping apartment. **2** †room in a bed. **bedside** *n.* the space beside a bed, esp. a sickbed. *~a.* of or relating to the sick-chamber. **bedside manner** *n.* a doctor's manner in attending a patient. **bed-sitting room, bedsit, bedsitter** *n.* a bedroom and sitting room combined, usu. with cooking facilities. **bedskirt** *n.* (*N Am.*) a valance around a bed. **bedsock** *n.* a thick sock to be worn in bed. **bedsore** *n.* a sore produced by long confinement to bed. **bedspread** *n.* a counterpane, a coverlet. **bedstead** (-sted) *n.* a framework on which a mattress is placed. **bedstraw** *n.* **1** straw covered with a sheet and used as a bed or palliasse. **2** any herbaceous plant of the genus *Galium*, esp. lady's bedstraw *G. verum*. **bedswerver** *n.* a person unfaithful to marriage vows. **bedtable** *n.* a table or tray designed to be used in bed. **bedtick** *n.* a bag or oblong case into which the feathers, hair, straw, chaff etc., of a bed are put. **bedtime** *n.* the usual hour for going to bed. **bedward** *adv.* **1** in the direction of bed. **2** towards bedtime. **bed-wetting** *n.* the act of involuntarily urinating in bed. **bed-wetter** *n.* [OE *bed, bedd* (cp. Goth. *badi*, G *Bett*; perh. from Indo-Eur. *bhodh-*, whence L *fodere*, to dig, from idea of dug-out, lair)]

bedabble (bidab´əl) *v.t.* to sprinkle, to wet; to splash, to stain.

bedad (bidad´) *int.* (*Ir.*) by God. [BY, DAD]

bedaub (bidawb´) *v.t.* to daub over, to besmear, to bedizen.

bedazzle (bidaz´əl) *v.t.* to confuse by dazzling. **bedazzlement** *n.* **bedazzlingly** *adv.*

bedder, bedding BED.

bedeck (bidek´) *v.t.* to deck out, to adorn.

bedeguar (bed´igah) *n.* a mossy growth on rose briers. [F *bédeguar*, Pers. and Arab. *bādāwar*, wind-brought, some thorny plant]

bedel (bē´dəl), **bedell** *n.* an officer at an English university, esp. Oxford or Cambridge, who performs ceremonial functions. [BEADLE]

bedevil (bidev´əl) *v.t.* (*pres.p.* **bedevilling,** (*esp. N Am.*) **bedeviling,** *past, p.p.* **bedevilled,** (*esp. N Am.*) **bedeviled**) **1** to torment. **2** to confound, confuse; to obstruct. **3** to treat with diabolical violence or ribaldry. **4** to bewitch. **bedevilment** *n.* **1** a state of utter confusion or disorder. **2** bewildering trouble. **3** demoniacal possession.

bedew (bidū´) *v.t.* to moisten or sprinkle with dewlike drops.

Bedford cord (bedfəd kawd´) *n.* a tough woven fabric similar to corduroy. [an English town]

†bedight (bidīt´) *a.* adorned, decked out.

bedim (bidim´) *v.t.* (*pres.p.* **bedimming,** *past, p.p.* **bedimmed**) **1** to render dim. **2** to obscure.

bedizen (bidī´zən, -diz´ən) *v.t.* to deck out in gaudy vestments or with tinsel finery. **bedizenment** *n.* **1** bedizening. **2** gaudy attire, finery.

bedlam (bed´ləm) *n.* **1** a scene of wild uproar. **2** madness, lunacy. **3** †an asylum. *~a.* **1** of or belonging to a madhouse. **2** mad, foolish, lunatic. **†bedlamite** (-īt) *n.* **1** a licensed beggar. **2** a lunatic. *~a.* mad, lunatic. [the priory of St Mary of *Bethlehem*, incorporated as a royal foundation for lunatics, 1547]

Bedlington terrier (bed´lingtən) *n.* a breed of grey, crisp-haired terrier. [town in Northumberland]

Bedouin (bed´uin), **Beduin** *n.* (*pl.* **Bedouin, Beduin**) **1** a nomadic Arab, as distinguished from one living in a town. **2** a gypsy, a wanderer. *~a.* **1** of or relating to the nomadic Arabs. **2** nomad. [F *bédouin*, Arab. *badawīn*, pl. *badawīy*, wild, wandering (*badw*, a desert)]

bedowrie shower (bidow´ri) *n.* (*Austral.*) a red dust storm.

bedraggle (bidrag´əl) *v.t.* to soil by trailing in the wet or mire. **bedraggled** *a.*

Beds. (bedz) *abbr.* Bedfordshire.

Beduin BEDOUIN.

bee (bē) *n.* **1** a four-winged insect of the genus *Apis*, which collects nectar and pollen and is often kept in hives for the honey and wax it produces. **2** any closely allied insect of the superfamily Apoidea, e.g. *carpenter bee, bumble-bee*. **3** a busy worker. **4** (*N Am.*) a social meeting for work usu. on behalf of a neighbour. **busy bee** BUSY. **the bee's knees** (*coll.*) (someone or something) wonderful, admirable. **to have**

a bee in one's bonnet to have a crazy fancy or be cranky on some point. **beebird** *n.* **1** the spotted flycatcher, *Muscicapa grisola.* **2** (*N Am.*) the kingbird, *Tyrannus tyrannus.* **bee-bread** *n.* **1** a mixture of honey and pollen, on which bees feed their larvae. **2** any of several plants yielding nectar. **bee-cuckoo** *n.* an African bird, *Cuculus indicator*, also called the honeyguide. **bee dance** *n.* a dance that worker bees perform as a way of showing other bees where food is located. **bee-eater** *n.* a tropical Old World bird of the genus *Merops*, esp. *M. apiaster.* **bee glue** *n.* the substance with which bees fill up crevices in their hives. **beehive** *n.* **1** a receptacle (usu. of wood or straw and dome-shaped) for bees. **2** a hive of activity. **3** a hairstyle in which the hair is piled up. *~a.* shaped like a beehive. **beehive house, beehive hut** *n.* a dwelling in which a roof of drystone masonry covers a single chamber formed by stone walls, each course being set successively inward. **bee-keeping** *n.* the occupation of keeping bees. **bee-keeper** *n.* **beeline** *n.* the shortest route between two places, that which a bee is assumed to take. **to make a beeline for** to make straight for. **bee-master, bee-mistress** *n.* a person who keeps bees. **bee moth** *n.* WAX MOTH (under WAX[1]). **bee orchid, bee orchis** *n.* a British orchid, *Ophrys apifera*, the flower of which resembles a bee. **beeswax** *n.* the wax secreted by bees for their cells, used to make polishes. *~v.t.* to rub or polish with beeswax. **beeswing** *n.* **1** the second crust, a fine filmy deposit in an old port wine. **2** old port. [OE *bēo, bī* (cp. Dut. *bij*, G *Biene*)]

Beeb (bēb) *n.* (*coll.*) the BBC.

beech (bēch) *n.* **1** a forest tree of the genus *Fagus*, esp. *F. sylvatica*, the common beech, with smooth bark and yielding nuts or mast. **2** the wood of this tree. **3** (*Austral.*) any of various Australian trees resembling this. **beech-drops** *n.pl.* (*N Am.*) any of several plants parasitic on the roots of the beech. **beechen** *a.* **1** of or relating to the beech. **2** made of beechwood. **beech-fern** *n.* any of several ferns, esp. *Phegopteris connectilis.* **beech marten** *n.* a stone marten. **beechmast** *n.* (*pl.* **beechmast**) the fruit of the beech tree. **beechnut** *n.* the nut of the beech, two of which lie in the prickly capsule. **beech oil** *n.* oil expressed from beechmast. **beech tree** *n.* **beechwheat** *n.* BUCKWHEAT. **beechwood** *n.* the wood of the beech tree. **beechy** *a.* (*comp.* **beechier,** *superl.* **beechiest**) abounding in beech trees. [OE *bēce, bōece* (cp. Dut. *beuk*, G *Buche*, Gr. *phēgos*, L *fāgus*)]

beef (bēf) *n.* (*pl.* **beeves** (bēvz), **beefs**) **1** the flesh of the ox, cow or bull, used as food. **2** (*pl.* **beeves**) an ox, esp. one fatted for the market *(usu. in pl.)*. **3** flesh, muscle. **4** (*sl.*) (*pl.* **beefs**) a complaint. *~v.i.* to grumble, to grouse. **to beef up** (*coll.*) to strengthen, reinforce. **beefburger** *n.* a hamburger. **beefcake** *n.* (*sl.*) men with muscular physiques, esp. as displayed in photographs. **beefeater** *n.* **1** a person who eats beef. **2** a well-fed servant. **3** an African bird of the genus *Buphaga*, allied to the starling. **4** a warder of the Tower of London, a Yeoman of the Guard. **beefsteak** *n.* a thick slice of beef from the hindquarters. **beefsteak fungus** *n.* an edible reddish bracket fungus, *Fistulina hepatica*, that grows on oak trees. **beefsteak tomato** *n.* (*esp. N Am.*) a beef tomato. **beef tea** *n.* the nutritive juice extracted from beef by simmering. **beef tomato** *n.* a large variety of tomato. **beefwood** *n.* **1** any of various trees that produce very hard wood, esp. *Casuarina equisetifolia.* **2** the wood of these trees. **beefy** *a.* (*comp.* **beefier,** *superl.* **beefiest**) **1** like beef. **2** fleshy. **3** stolid. **4** muscular. **beefily** *adv.* **beefiness** *n.* **1** fleshiness. **2** weight, stolidity. [OF *boef*, L *bovem* (nom. *bos*, cp. Gr. *bous*, Gael. *bō*, Sansk. *go*, cp. COW[1])]

Beelzebub (biel´zibŭb) *n.* **1** the prince of evil spirits, Satan. **2** an evil spirit. [L *Beelzebūb*, Gr. *beelzeboub*, Heb. *ba'al-z'būb*, lord of flies, a god worshipped in Ekron (II Kings i.2)]

been BE.

beep (bēp) *n.* a short sound as made by a car horn or an electronic device, usu. as a warning. *~v.i.* to make such a sound. *~v.t.* **1** to cause (e.g. a car horn) to sound. **2** (*esp. N Am.*) to summon with a beeper. **beeper** *n.* **1** a device that emits a beeping sound. **2** (*N Am.*) a bleeper.

beer (biə) *n.* **1** an alcoholic drink brewed from fermented malt, hops, water and sugar. **2** any malt liquor prepared by brewing, including ale and porter. **3** any of various other fermented liquors, such as *ginger-beer*, *spruce-beer* etc. **4** a drink of any of these. **beer and skittles** *n.* enjoyment or pleasure; all one could wish. **beer barrel** *n.* a barrel used to contain beer. **beer belly** *n.* a protruding stomach, caused by much beer-drinking. **beer cellar** *n.* **1** an underground room where beer is stored. **2** a basement where beer is sold or drunk. **beer engine, beer pump** *n.* a machine for pumping up beer from the cellar to the bar. **beer garden** *n.* a garden or outdoor area with tables where beer and other refreshments may be consumed. **beer gut** *n.* (*sl.*) BEER BELLY (under BEER). **beer hall** *n.* a large room where beer is sold and drunk. **beerhouse** *n.* a public house that sells beer but not spirits. **beer mat** *n.* a small mat made of card, to be put under a glass. **beer money** *n.* **1** a money allowance in lieu of beer. **2** a tip. **beery** *a.* (*comp.* **beerier,** *superl.* **beeriest**) **1** abounding in beer. **2** like beer. **3** under the influence of beer. **4** fuddled. **beerily** *adv.* **beeriness** *n.* a condition approaching intoxication. [OE *bēor* (cp. Dut. and G *Bier*)]

beest (bēst) *n.* the first milk drawn from a cow after calving. **beestings, beastings** *n.pl.* (*also constr. as sing.*) beest. [OE *bēost* (OHG *Biost*, Dut. *biest*)]

beeswax, beeswing BEE.

beet (bēt) *n.* **1** any plant of the genus *Beta*, whose root is used as a salad and in sugar-making. **2** (*N Am.*) beetroot. **beetroot** *n.* **1** the root of the beet used as a salad. **2** the red colour of beetroot. *~a.* of this colour. **beet sugar** *n.* sugar from sugar beet. [OE *bēte*, L *beta*]

beetle[1] (bē´təl) *n.* **1** an insect of the order Coleoptera, the upper wings of which have been converted into hard wing-cases, the under ones being used for flight, if it is able to fly, the name being popularly confined to those of black colour and large size. **2** any insect resembling these, such as the cockroach. **3** a game in which the players attempt to complete a beetle-shaped drawing according to the throw of a dice. **to beetle along/ off** to hurry, scuttle along. **beetle-crusher** *n.* (*sl.*) **1** a large foot. **2** a heavy boot. **3** a policeman. **4** a soldier. [OE *bitela, bitula*, from *bitan*, to bite]

beetle[2] (bē´təl) *n.* **1** a maul; a heavy wooden mallet for driving stones, stakes or tent-pegs into the ground, hammering down paving-stones and other ramming and crushing operations. **2** a machine with rollers, used to give lustre to cloth. *~v.t.* **1** to beat with a beetle. **2** to give lustre to (cloth) with a beetle. **as deaf as a beetle** **1** very deaf. **2** stupidly deaf. **beetlebrain** *n.* (*coll.*) an idiot. **beetlebrained** *a.* [OE *bȳtel, bȳtl*, Gmc. *bautilos*, from *bautan*, to beat (cp. OE *beatan*, to *beat*)]

beetle[3] (bē´təl) *v.i.* to jut out, hang over. *~a.* projecting, overhanging, scowling. **beetle-browed** *a.* having projecting or overhanging brows. **beetling** *a.* jutting, overhanging, prominent. [etym. unknown]

beetroot BEET.

beeves BEEF.

BEF *abbr.* British Expeditionary Force.

befall (bifawl´) *v.t.* (*past* **befell** (-fel´), *p.p.* **befallen**) to happen to. *~v.i.* to happen. [OE *befealtan* (BE-, *fallan*, FALL)]

befit (bifit´) *v.t.* (*pres.p.* **befitting,** *past, p.p.* **befitted**) **1** to be suitable to or for. **2** to become, suit. **3** to be incumbent upon. **befitting** *a.* **befittingly** *adv.*

befog (bifog´) *v.t.* (*pres.p.* **befogging,** *past, p.p.* **befogged)** 1 to obscure, to confuse. 2 to involve in a fog.

befool (bifool´) *v.t.* 1 to make a fool of. 2 to dupe, delude.

before (bifaw´) *prep.* 1 in front of, in time, space, rank or degree. 2 in the presence or sight of. 3 under the cognizance of. 4 under the influence or impulsion of. 5 in preference to. *~adv.* 1 ahead, in front. 2 beforehand, already, in the past. 3 on the front. *~conj.* 1 earlier than. 2 sooner than, rather than. **before Christ** (of a date) before the birth of Christ (e.g. 1000 BC). **before God** with the knowledge or in the sight of God. **before the wind** with the wind right aft. **before-cited** *a.* cited in a preceding part. **beforehand** *adv.* in anticipation, in advance, before the time. **to be beforehand** 1 to forestall. 2 to be earlier than expected. **before-mentioned** *a.* mentioned before. [OE *beforan* (*be-, bi-*, by, *foran*, adv., before, *fore*, prep., before, above, Gmc. *fora*, for)]

befoul (bifowl´) *v.t.* 1 to make dirty, to soil. 2 to defile, to degrade.

befriend (bifrend´) *v.t.* to become a friend of, to favour, help.

befuddle (bifŭd´əl) *v.t.* 1 to confuse, baffle. 2 to stupefy with drink. **befuddlement** *n.*

beg[1] (beg) *v.i.* (*pres.p.* **begging,** *past, p.p.* **begged)** 1 to ask for alms, to live by asking alms. 2 to make an earnest request or entreaty. 3 (of a dog) to sit up on the hind quarters expectantly. *~v.t.* 1 to ask or supplicate in charity. 2 to ask earnestly, to crave, entreat. 3 to ask politely or formally for. **I beg your pardon** PARDON. **to beg off** to seek to be released from some obligation. **to beg one's bread** to live by begging. **to beg pardon** to apologize. **to beg the question** 1 to assume the thing to be proved. 2 to raise the question. 3 (*coll.*) to avoid facing the difficulty. **to go begging** 1 to be acceptable to nobody. 2 to be left after everyone has eaten etc. **beggar** *n.* 1 a person who begs. 2 a person who lives by asking alms. 3 a person in indigent circumstances. 4 (*coll.*) a fellow; a youngster. 5 †a suppliant, a petitioner. *~v.t.* 1 to reduce to want. 2 to impoverish. 3 to exhaust, to outdo. **to beggar description** to go beyond one's power of expression. **beggarly** *a.* 1 like a beggar. 2 poverty-stricken. 3 mean, contemptible. *~adv.* in the manner of a beggar. **beggarliness** *n.* **beggar-my-neighbour** *n.* 1 a game of cards in which players try to deprive other players of cards. 2 the making of profits at the expense of others. **beggary** *n.* 1 the state or condition of a habitual beggar. 2 extreme indigence. **begging** *n.* asking for alms, esp. as a living. **begging bowl** *n.* 1 a bowl held out by a beggar for money or food. 2 an appeal for help. **begging letter** *n.* a letter asking for money. [etym. uncertain; perh. from OF *begard*, a lay brother, corr. to the BEGUINE]

Usage note The use of *beg the question* to mean raise the question is commonly seen as a misunderstanding, and is best avoided.

beg[2] BEY.

†**begad** (bigad´) *int.* by God.

began BEGIN.

beggar, begging BEG[1].

Beghard (beg´əd) *n.* a lay brother, belonging to a 13th-cent. Flemish religious order like the Beguines. [med. L *Beghardus*, from F *Beguine*, or directly from *Bègue*, see BEGUINE]

begin (bigin´) *v.i.* (*pres.p.* **beginning,** *past* **began** (-gan´), *p.p.* **begun** (-gŭn´)) to come into existence, to arise, to start; to commence. *~v.t.* to be the first to do, to do the first act of, to enter on, to commence. **to begin at** to start from. **to begin on/ upon** to start work on. **to begin school** to start school. **to begin with** 1 to take first. 2 firstly. **beginner** *n.* 1 a person who originates anything. 2 a person who is the first to do anything. 3 a young learner or practitioner. 4 the actor or actors who appear first on the stage at the start of a play. **beginner's luck** *n.* good luck shown by someone new to a game etc. **beginning** *n.* 1 the first cause, the origin. 2 the first state or commencement. 3 first principles, rudiments. **the beginning of the end** the point at which the outcome becomes clear. [OE *beginnan* (cp. Dut. and G *beginnen*, to begin, OE *ginan*, to yawn, Indo-Eur. *ghī*, L *hiāre*, to gape)]

Usage note In standard English, the past tense of *begin* is *began*, not *begun*.

begird (bigœd´) *v.t.* (*past, p.p.* **begirt** (-gœt´), **begirded)** to encircle with or as with a girdle. [OE *begierden*, BE-, GIRD[1]]

begone (bigon´) *int.* get you gone, go away, depart.

begonia (bigō´niə) *n.* a plant of the genus *Begonia*, cultivated chiefly for their ornamental foliage. [Michel *Bégon*, 1638–1710, French patron of science]

begorra (bigor´ə) *int.* (*Ir.*) by God!

begrime (bigrīm´) *v.t.* to blacken or soil with grime.

begrudge (bigrŭj´) *v.t.* 1 to grudge. 2 to envy (a person) the possession of. **begrudgingly** *adv.*

beguile (bigīl´) *v.t.* 1 to deceive, cheat, deprive of or lead into by fraud. 2 to charm away the tedium or weariness of, to amuse. 3 to bewitch. **beguilement** *n.* 1 the act of beguiling. 2 a wile, temptation, deceit. **beguiler** *n.* a person who beguiles, a deceiver, a cheat. **beguiling** *a.* deceiving, charming, wiling away. **beguilingly** *adv.* so as to beguile. [BE-, *guile*, obs. v., to deceive (see GUILE)]

Beguine (bigēn´, beg´in) *n.* a member of certain sisterhoods which arose in the Netherlands in the 12th cent. (some of which still exist), whose members are not bound by perpetual vows, and may leave the community when they please. **beguinage** (bāgēnahzh´, beg´inij) *n.* a house or establishment for Beguines. [the founder Lamberthe *Bègue*, late 12th cent.]

beguine (bigēn´) *n.* music or dance in bolero rhythm, of S American or W Indian origin. [F]

begum (bā´gəm) *n.* 1 a queen, princess or lady of high rank in the Indian subcontinent. 2 (**Begum**) the title of a married Muslim woman. [Hind. *bigam*, Turk. *bigīm*, princess, fem. of *beg*, BEY]

begun BEGIN.

behalf (bihahf´) *n.* interest, lieu, stead. **in behalf of** (*N Am.*) on someone's behalf, on behalf of. **on behalf of** 1 on account of, for the sake of. 2 representing. 3 (*coll.*) on the part of. [OE *be healfe*, by the side, blended with *on healfe*, on the side of]

Usage note The use of *on behalf of* to mean *on the part of* (done by, proceeding from) is best avoided. There are two participants or sets of participants when something is done or felt on behalf of another. The distinction can be seen in *a terrific effort on the part of the team on behalf of their fans.*

behave (bihāv´) *~v.refl.* to conduct, to demean. *~v.i.* 1 to conduct oneself or itself. 2 to conduct oneself well, to display good manners. 3 to function properly. *v.t.* †to handle, to exercise, to employ. **behaviour** (-yə), (*esp. N Am.*) **behavior** *n.* 1 outward deportment, carriage. 2 manners, conduct, demeanour. 3 the manner in which a thing acts. 4 (*Psych.*) response to a stimulus. **on one's best/ good behaviour** behaving well when particularly required to do so. **behavioural** *a.* of or relating to behaviour. **behaviouralist** *n.* a behaviourist. **behavioural science** *n.* the scientific study of the behaviour of human beings and other organisms. **behaviourism** *n.* 1 the guiding principle of certain psychologists who hold that the proper basis of psychological science is the objective study of behaviour under stimuli. 2 the practice of this principle. **behaviourist** *n.* a proponent of behaviourism. **beha-**

vioristic (-ris´-) *a.* **behaviour therapy** *n.* a method of treating neurotic disorders (e.g. a phobia) by gradually conditioning the patient to react normally. [BE-, HAVE]

behead (bihed´) *v.t.* to cut the head off, to kill by decapitation. [OE *behēadian* (*be-*, by, *hēafod*, head)]

beheld BEHOLD.

behemoth (bē´əmoth, bihē´-) *n.* a huge person or thing. [Heb., the animal described in Job xl.15-24, prob. the hippopotamus, from Egypt. *p-ehe-mau*, water-ox]

behest (bihest´) *n.* (*formal*) **1** a command. **2** an injunction. [OE *behœs* (*behatan*, to promise)]

behind (bihīnd´) *prep.* **1** at the back of. **2** inferior to. **3** after, later than. **4** in support of. **5** responsible for the existence or doing of. **6** in the rear of. **7** past in relation to. *~adv.* **1** at the back, in the rear. **2** towards the rear. **3** in the past. **4** backwards, out of sight, on the further side. **5** in reserve. **6** in arrears. *~n.* **1** the back part of a person or garment. **2** the posterior. **3** in Australian Rules football, a kick etc. from which the ball crosses the behind line; a score from this. **behind someone's back** without someone's knowledge. **behind the scenes** SCENE. **behind the times** old-fashioned, out of date. **behind time** late. **to come from behind** to make a late spurt to win after lagging behind. **to put behind one 1** to get on with one's life after. **2** to refuse to think about. **behindhand** *a., adv.* **1** dilatory, tardy. **2** backward, unfinished. **3** in arrears. **behind line** *n.* in Australian Rules football, the line between an inner and outer goalpost. [OE *behindan* (BE-, *hindan*, adv., at the back)]

behold (bihōld´) *v.t.* (*past, p.p.* **beheld** (-held´)) **1** to see. **2** to look attentively at, observe with care. **3** to view. **4** to consider. *~v.i.* to look. *~int.* lo!, see. **beholden** *a.* obliged, indebted, under obligation of gratitude (with *to*). **beholder** *n.* a person who beholds; a spectator. [OE *bihaldan* (BE-, *healdan*, hold, keep)]

behoof (bihoof´) *n.* advantage, use, profit, benefit. [OE *behōf* (*behōflīc*, useful) (cp. Dut. *behoef*, G *Behuf*; *be-*, Goth. *hafjan*, OE *hebban*, to heave, cp. L *capere*, to take)]

behove (bihōv´), (*N Am.*) **behoove** (-hoov´) *v.t.* **1** to befit, to be due to, to suit. **2** to be needful to. **3** to be incumbent on. **behoveful** *a.* needful, necessary. [OE *bihōvian*, *behōfian* (see BEHOOF)]

beige (bāzh) *n.* **1** a light brownish yellow colour. **2** a fabric made of undyed and unbleached wool. *~a.* **1** of a light brownish yellow. **2** †grey. [F]

being (bē´ing) *n.* **1** the state of existing; existence. **2** lifetime. **3** nature, essence. **4** a thing or person existing. **5** a thing or person imagined as existing. **for the time being** TIME. **in being** existing. [BE]

bejabers (bijā´bəz), **bejabbers** (bijab´əz) *int.* (*Ir.*) used to express surprise. [a modification of *by Jesus!*]

bejewelled (bijoo´əld), (*N Am.*) **bejeweled** *a.* decorated with jewels.

bekah (bē´kah) *n.* a Hebrew weight of ¼ ounce (Exodus xxxviii.26). [Heb.]

bel (bel) *n.* a measure for comparing the intensity of noises, currents etc., the logarithm to the base 10 of the ratio of one to the other being the number of bels. [Alexander Graham *Bell*, 1847–1922, inventor of the telephone]

belabour (bilā´bə), (*N Am.*) **belabor** *v.t.* **1** to beat, to thrash. **2** to assault verbally. **3** to dwell unduly on. **4** to cultivate with labour, to labour at.

belar (bē´lah), **belah** *n.* a variety of casuarina tree, *Casuarina glauca.* [Austral. Abor.]

belated (bilā´tid) *a.* **1** very late; behind time. **2** too late. **3** overtaken by night, benighted. **belatedly** *adv.* **belatedness** *n.*

belay (bilā´) *v.t.* **1** to fasten (a running rope) by winding it round a cleat or belaying-pin. **2** to turn a rope round (an object). **3** to secure (a climber) to a rope. *~n.* **1** a turn of a rope round an object. **2** that around which a climber's rope is belayed. *~int.* stop; enough. **belaying-pin** *n.* **1** a stout pin to which running ropes may be belayed. **2** a projection round which a rope can be tied or hitched. [OE *belecgan*, to lay round, envelop; (nautical use perh. from Dut. *beleggan*, to cover, belay)]

bel canto (bel kan´tō) *n.* a style of operatic singing characterized by purity of tone and exact phrasing. [It., beautiful singing]

belch (belch) *v.i.* **1** to eject wind noisily by the mouth from the stomach. **2** to issue out, as by eructation. *~v.t.* **1** to expel from the mouth noisily or with violence. **2** to eject (smoke etc.), to throw out. **3** to utter in a noisy or drunken manner. *~n.* **1** the act of belching, an eructation. **2** an eruption, a burst (of smoke or fire). [OE *bealcan*]

beldam (bel´dəm), †**beldame** *n.* **1** an old woman. **2** a hag, a witch. **3** a grandmother, a remote ancestress. [F *belle, bel*, expressing relationship, DAM[2], mother]

beleaguer (bilē´gə) *v.t.* **1** to besiege. **2** to harass. **beleaguerment** *n.* siege, blockade, harassment. [Dut. *belegeren*, besiege (*be-*, around, *leger*, a bed, a camp)]

☒ **beleive** common misspelling of BELIEVE.

belemnite (bel´əmnīt) *n.* **1** a conical, sharply pointed fossil shell of a cephalopod of the order Belemnoidea, allied to the cuttlefish. **2** any such cephalopod. **belemnitic** (-nit´-) *a.* of, relating to or characterized by belemnites. [Gr. *belemnon*, a dart (*ballein*, to throw)]

bel esprit (bel esprē´) *n.* (*pl.* **beaux esprits** (bōz esprē´)) **1** a person of genius. **2** a wit. [F, fine mind]

belfry (bel´fri) *n.* (*pl.* **belfries**) **1** a bell tower attached to or separate from a church or other building. **2** the chamber for the bells in a church tower. **3** the frame on which a ship's bell is hung. [OF *berfrei, berfroi*, MHG *bercfrit* (*berc.*, protection, shelter, *fride*, OHG *fridis*, peace), a protection tower, a siege tower]

Belg. *abbr.* **1** Belgian. **2** Belgium.

belga (bel´gə) *n.* a former Belgian unit of exchange, equivalent to 5 francs. [L, *Belgicus*, Belgian]

Belgian (bel´jən) *a.* of or relating to Belgium or to the Belgians. *~n.* **1** a native or inhabitant of Belgium. **2** a kind of canary. **Belgian hare** *n.* a large breed of domestic rabbit, dark red in colouring. **Belgic** *a.* of the ancient Belgae or of Belgium. [L *Belga, Belgicus*]

Belial (bē´liəl) *n.* **1** the Devil, Satan. **2** one of the fallen angels. [Heb. *b'li-yaal*, worthlessness]

belie (bilī´) *v.t.* (*pres.p.* **belying,** *past, p.p.* **belied**) **1** to tell lies about, to slander. **2** to misrepresent. **3** to be faithless to. **4** to fail to perform or justify. **5** †to counterfeit, to imitate. **6** †to fill with lies. [OE *belēogan* (BE-, *lēogan*, to lie)]

belief (bilēf´) *n.* **1** religion, religious faith. **2** reliance, confidence. **3** the mental act or operation of accepting a fact or proposition as true. **4** a thing believed to be true. **5** an opinion firmly held, a persuasion. **beyond belief** incredible. **the Belief** the Apostles' Creed. [BE-, OE *lēafa, gelēafa* (cp. G *Glaube*)]

believe (bilēv´) *v.t.* **1** to accept as true. **2** to be of the opinion that. **3** to have confidence in or reliance on. **4** to give credence to. *~v.i.* **1** to have faith. **2** to have religious faith. **believe it or not** (*coll.*) although it may seem incredible (the statement is true). **to believe in 1** to trust in, to rely on. **2** to believe in the existence of. **to believe one's ears** (*usu. with neg.*) to accept that what one is hearing is correct. **to believe one's eyes** (*usu. with neg.*) to accept that what one is seeing is true. **to make believe** to pretend. **would you believe it?** (*coll.*) does this not seem incredible? **believable** *a.* **1** capable of being believed. **2** credible. **believability** (-bil´-) *n.* **believableness** *n.* the quality of being believable. **believably** *adv.* **believer** *n.* **1** a person who believes. **2** a convert to Christianity or any other religion.

believing *a.* exercising belief or the virtue of faith. **believingly** *adv.* 1 in a believing manner. 2 with faith. [see BELIEF]

☒ **beligerent** common misspelling of BELLIGERENT.

†**belike** (bilīk´) *adv.* likely, possibly, perhaps.

Belisha beacon (bilē´shə) *n.* a flashing orange globe on a post to indicate a street crossing for pedestrians. [Leslie Hore-*Belisha*, 1893–1957, British politician]

belittle (bilit´əl) *v.t.* 1 to depreciate or undermine verbally. 2 to make little. 3 to dwarf. **belittlement** *n.* **belittler** *n.* **belittlingly** *adv.*

bell[1] (bel) *n.* 1 a hollow body of cast metal, usu. in the shape of an inverted cup with recurved edge, so formed as to emit a clear musical sound when struck by a hammer. 2 a buzzer or ringing device that functions as a signal like a bell. 3 the sound of a bell, esp. as a signal. 4 (*Naut.*) **a** the bell struck on board ship every half-hour to indicate time. **b** a space of half an hour. 5 any object in nature and art of a form similar to that of a bell. 6 the vase, basket or cushion of a Corinthian capital. 7 a bell-shaped corolla. 8 the catkin containing the female flowers of the hop. ~*v.i.* 1 to have the shape of a bell. 2 (of hops) to be in flower. ~*v.t.* 1 to provide with a bell. 2 to give the shape of a bell to. 3 to utter loudly. **one to eight bells** (*Naut.*) a watch of four hours. **to bear away the bell** to carry off the prize. **to bear the bell** to be first. **to bell the cat** 1 to be a ringleader in a hazardous movement. 2 to grapple with a dangerous opponent (in allusion to the fable of the mice wishing to put a bell on the cat). **to curse by bell, book and candle** to excommunicate solemnly by a ceremony in which these objects were used symbolically. **to give someone a bell** to telephone someone. **to ring a bell** 1 to revive a memory. 2 to sound familiar. **bellbird** *n.* a bird with a bell-like song, as any Central or S American bird of the genus *Procnias*, an Australian flycatcher, *Oreoica gutturalis*, or a New Zealand honeyeater, *Anthornis melanura*. **bell-bottom** *n.* 1 a flare below the knee of a trouser leg. 2 (*pl.*) trousers with this type of flare. **bell-bottomed** *a.* **bellboy, bellhop** *n.* (*N Am.*) a hotel page-boy. **bell-buoy** *n.* a buoy to which a bell is attached, rung by the motion of the waves. **bellcot, bellcote** *n.* a small turret for a bell or bells. **bellcrank** *n.* a crank adapted to communicate motion from one bell wire to another at right angles to it. **bellflower** *n.* a bell-shaped flower or plant with such flowers, of the genus *Campanula*. **bell-founder** *n.* a caster of bells. **bell-founding** *n.* **bell-foundry** *n.* (*pl.* **bell-foundries**) a manufactory of bells. **bell gable** *n.* a gable in which bells are hung. **bell-glass** *n.* a bell-shaped glass for protecting plants. **bellhanger** *n.* a person who hangs or fixes bells. **bellhanging** *n.* the act or process of fixing bells. **bell jar** *n.* a bell-shaped glass cover used in laboratories to protect apparatus or contain gases in experiments etc. **bellman** *n.* (*pl.* **bellmen**) a public crier who attracts attention by ringing a bell. **bell metal** *n.* an alloy of copper and tin, usu. with a little zinc, used for bells. **bell pull** *n.* a cord or handle by which a bell is rung. **bell punch** *n.* a ticket punch in which a bell is rung each time it is used. **bell push** *n.* a button which operates an electric bell. **bell-ringer** *n.* a person whose business it is to ring a church or public bell at stated times. **bell-ringing** *n.* **bell-rope** *n.* the rope by which a bell is rung. **bells and whistles** *n.pl.* (*coll.*) showy but inessential accessories or additional features. **bell-shaped** *a.* shaped like a bell, campanulate. **bell telegraph** *n.* a telegraph instrument in which needles are replaced by two bells, signals on one of which represent dots and on the other dashes, of the Morse system. **bell tent** *n.* a conical tent. **bell turret** *n.* a turret in which bells are hung. **bell-wether** *n.* 1 the sheep that wears a bell and leads a flock. 2 (*fig.*) a leader. **bellwort** *n.* any plant of the family Campanulaceae. [OE *belle* (*bellan*, to bellow)]

bell[2] (bel) *n.* the cry of a stag at rutting time. ~*v.i.* (of a stag) to bellow. [OE *bellan*, to bark, bellow]

belladonna (belədon´ə) *n.* 1 deadly nightshade or dwale, *Atropa belladonna*. 2 a drug prepared from the leaves and root of this plant. **belladonna lily** *n.* a bulbous plant, *Amaryllis belladonna*, which grows in S Africa, and has white or pink flowers. [It., lit., a fine lady]

belle (bel) *n.* 1 a beautiful woman. 2 a reigning beauty. **belle amie** (amē´) *n.* (*pl.* **belles amies** (belz amē´)) 1 a female friend. 2 a mistress. **belle époque** (āpok´) *n.* the period of security and comfort enjoyed by the wealthy before the outbreak of World War I. **belle laide** (lād´) *n.* (*pl.* **belles laides** (bel lād´)) a woman who is attractive in spite of being ugly. **belle vue** (vū) *n.* a fine sight. [F, from L *bella*, fem. of *bellus*, fine, pretty]

belles-lettres (bellet´rə) *n.pl.* (*also constr. as sing.*) polite literature, the humanities, pure literature. **belletrism** *n.* devotion to belles-lettres. **belletrist** *n.* a person devoted to belles-lettres. **belletristic** (-letris´tik) *a.* of or relating to belles-lettres. [F, lit., fine letters]

bellicose (bel´ikōs) *a.* warlike; inclined to war or fighting. **bellicosity** (-kos´-) *n.* inclination to war. [L *bellicosus* (*bellum*, war)]

bellied BELLY.

belligerent (bilij´ərənt) *a.* 1 carrying on war. 2 of or relating to persons or nations carrying on war. 3 aggressive. ~*n.* a nation, party or individual engaged in war. **belligerence, belligerency** *n.* 1 the state of being at war. 2 aggressive or warlike behaviour. **belligerently** *adv.* [F *belligérant*, L *belligerans -ntem*, pres.p. of *belligerāre* (*bellum*, war, *gerere*, to wage)]

bellow (bel´ō) *v.i.* 1 to emit a loud hollow sound (as a bull). 2 to raise an outcry or clamour, to bawl, to vociferate. 3 to emit a loud hollow sound (as the sea, the wind, artillery etc.). ~*v.t.* to utter with a loud hollow voice. ~*n.* the roar of a bull, or any similar sound. [OE *bellan*]

bellows (bel´ōz) *n.pl.* (*also constr. as sing.*) 1 an instrument or machine for supplying a strong blast of air to a fire or a wind instrument. 2 the expansible portion of a photographic camera. 3 (*fig.*) the lungs. **pair of bellows** PAIR. **bellows fish** *n.* 1 (*dial.*) the snipe fish, *Macrorhamphosus scolopax*. 2 (*N Am.*) the frogfish. [ME *belu, belw* (pl. *belwes, belowes*), Icel. *belgr* (cp. OE *bœlig*), a bag (see BELLY)]

Bell's palsy (belz) *n.* a paralysis of the face, usu. temporary. [Sir Charles *Bell*, 1774–1842, Scottish anatomist]

belly (bel´i) *n.* (*pl.* **bellies**) 1 that part of the human body in front which extends from the breast to the insertion of the lower limbs. 2 the corresponding part of a four-legged animal. 3 the part containing the stomach and bowels. 4 the stomach, the womb. 5 that part of the body which demands food. 6 appetite, gluttony. 7 the front or lower surface of an object. 8 anything swelling out or protuberant. 9 a cavity, a hollow surface. 10 the interior. 11 the bulging part of a violin or a similar instrument. ~*v.t.* (*pres.p.* **bellying**, *past, p.p.* **bellied**) to cause to swell out, to render protuberant. ~*v.i.* to swell or bulge out, to become protuberant. **to go belly up** 1 (*esp. N Am., coll.*) to go bankrupt. 2 (*esp. N Am., coll.*) to die. **bellied** *a.* 1 having a belly (*in comb.*). 2 corpulent. 3 (*Bot.*) ventricose. **bellyache** *n.* a pain in the stomach. ~*v.i.* (*coll.*) to express discontent, to whine. **bellyacher** *n.* **bellyband** *n.* a band passing under the belly of a horse, ass or other beast of burden to keep the saddle in place. **bellybound** *a.* (*sl.*) constipated, costive. **belly button** *n.* (*coll.*) the navel. **belly dance** *n.* an erotic solo dance involving undulating movements of the abdomen. **belly dancer** *n.* **belly dancing** *n.* **bellyflop** *n.* an awkward dive into the water on to the front of the body and flat against the surface. *~v.i.* (*pres.p.* **bellyflopping,** *past, p.p.* **bellyflopped**) to perform a bellyflop. **bellyful** *n.* (*pl.* **bellyfuls**) **1** as much as fills the belly, as much food as satisfies the appetite. **2** (*coll.*) a sufficiency, more than enough. **bellying** *a.* swelling, protuberant, bulging out (of sails with wind). **belly landing** *n.* a landing of an aircraft without using the landing wheels. **belly laugh** *n.* a deep, hearty laugh. [OE *bælig, bylig,* a leather bag (Gmc. *balgiz*), *balgan,* to swell out]

belomancy (bel´ōmansi) *n.* divination by means of arrows. [Gr. *belos,* an arrow, -MANCY]

belong (bilong´) *v.i.* **1** to be the property, attribute, appendage, member, right, duty, concern or business (of) (*The book belongs to me*; *He belongs to several clubs*). **2** to be a native or resident of (*I belong to Glasgow*). **3** to be rightly placed in (*It belongs in the cupboard*; *You belong in jail*). **4** †to be appropriate, to pertain (*the things that belong to the Lord*). **belonging** *n.* **1** anything belonging to one (*usu. in pl.*). **2** a quality or endowment. **3** (*pl., coll.*) one's possessions. **belongingness** *n.* [ME *bilongen, belongen* (BE-, LONG[1])]

Belorussian (belōrŭsh´ən), **Byelorussian** (byelō-) *a.* **1** of Belarus in eastern Europe. **2** of its language or people. *~n.* **1** the Slavonic language of Belarus. **2** a native or citizen of Belarus, also called *White Russian.* [Rus. *Belorossiya, beliy,* white]

beloved (bilŭvd´, -lŭv´id) *a.* loved greatly. *~n.* a person who is greatly loved.

below (bilō´) *prep.* **1** under in place. **2** under the surface of. **3** downstream from. **4** lower on a scale than. **5** inferior to in rank, degree or excellence. **6** unworthy of, unsuitable to. *~adv.* **1** in or to a lower place, rank or station. **2** downstairs. **3** downstream. **4** lower on the same page, or on a following page. **5** on the lower side or surface. **6** on earth (as opposed to heaven). **7** in hell (as opposed to earth). **below one's breath** BREATH. **below stairs** STAIR.

Bel Paese® (bel paā´zi) *n.* a mild Italian cream cheese. [It., lit., beautiful country]

belt (belt) *n.* **1** a broad, flat strip of leather or other material worn around the waist or over the shoulder, esp. to hold clothes in place, to hold a weapon, as a safety restraint, or as a badge of rank or distinction. **2** anything resembling a belt in shape. **3** a broad strip or stripe. **4** a strait. **5** a zone or region. **6** a flat endless strap passing round two wheels and communicating motion from one to the other. **7** a strap carrying cartridges for a machine gun. **8** (*coll.*) a blow. *~v.t.* **1** to encircle with or as with a belt. **2** to fasten on with a belt. **3** to invest with a belt. **4** to deck with a zone of colour. **5** to thrash with a belt. *~v.i.* (*sl.*) to move at speed, to rush. **belt and braces** offering double security. **to belt out** to sing or emit (a sound) vigorously or with enthusiasm. **to belt up 1** (*sl.*) to stop talking (often *imper.*). **2** to fasten with a belt. **3** to put a seat belt on. **to hit below the belt** to act unfairly in a contest (from boxing). **to tighten one's belt** to make economies, to reduce expenditure. **under one's belt** secured in one's possession. **beltbag** *n.* BUMBAG (under BUM[1]). **belt drive** *n.* a transmission system using a flexible belt. **belted** *a.* **1** wearing a belt, esp. as a mark of rank or distinction. **2** furnished with a belt of any kind. **3** affixed by a belt. **4** surrounded as with a belt. **belted earl** *n.* an earl wearing (or entitled to wear) his distinctive cincture. **belted galloway** *n.* a variety of a breed of usu. black beef cattle, having a broad white band. **belter** *n.* **belting** *n.* **1** belts collectively. **2** material for belts. **3** a series of belts fixed round chimney stacks to strengthen them. **4** (*sl.*) a beating. **beltman** *n.* (*pl.* **beltmen**) (*Austral.*) the member of a beach life-saving team who swims out with a line attached to their belt. **beltway** *n.* (*N Am.*) a ring road. [OE (cp. *Balz,* L *balteus*)]

Beltane (bel´tān) *n.* **1** May Day (Old Style), one of the old Scottish quarter days. **2** a Celtic festival celebrated by bonfires on May Day. [Gael. *bealltainn* (prob. conn. with OE *bæl,* a blaze, Gr. *phalios,* bright)]

beluga (biloo´gə) *n.* **1** a large sturgeon, *Huso huso,* from the Black and Caspian Seas. **2** caviar obtained from this sturgeon. **3** the white whale, *Delphinapterus leucas.* [Rus., white]

belvedere (bel´vidiə) *n.* **1** a turret, lantern or cupola, raised above the roof of a building to command a view. **2** a summer house built on an eminence for the same purpose. [It. (*bel,* fine, *vedere,* to see)]

belying BELIE.

BEM *abbr.* British Empire Medal.

bema (bē´mə) *n.* **1** the sanctuary, presbytery or chancel of a church. **2** the platform from which Athenian orators spoke. [Gr.]

bemean (bimēn´) *v.t.* to render mean, to lower or debase.

bemire (bimīə´) *v.t.* to cover or soil with mire. **bemired** *a.* stuck or sunk in mire.

bemoan (bimōn´) *v.t.* to moan over, to deplore. *~v.i.* to moan, to lament. [OE *bimænan* (*mænan,* MOAN)]

bemuse (bimūz´) *v.t.* to make utterly confused or dazed. **bemusedly** (-zidli) *adv.* **bemusement** *n.*

ben[1] (ben) *n.* a mountain peak in Scotland etc. [Gael. *beann*]

ben[2] (ben) *prep.* (*Sc.*) in or into the inner apartment of. *~adv.* within, into or towards the inner part of a house. *~n.* an inner room (see BUT). [Sc., from ME *binne,* OE *binnan* (cp. Dut. and G *binnen*)]

bench (bench) *n.* **1** a long seat or form. **2** a carpenter's or other mechanic's work table. **3** the office of judge. **4** a seat where judges and magistrates sit in court. **5** judges or magistrates collectively, or sitting as a court. **6** other official seats and those who have a right to occupy them. **7** (*pl.*) groups of seats in the Houses of Parliament. **8** a terrace or ledge in masonry, quarrying, mining, earthwork etc. **9** (*N Am.*) a level tract between a river and neighbouring hills. **10** a tribunal. **11** a platform for exhibiting dogs. *~v.t.* **1** to exhibit (dogs) at a show. **2** (*N Am.*) to remove (a player) from a game. **3** to furnish with benches. *~v.i.* to sit on a bench (as in a court of justice). **to be raised to the bench** to be made a judge. **bencher** *n.* **1** any one of the senior members of an Inn of Court who collectively govern the Inn, and have power of 'calling to the bar'. **2** (*in comb.*) a person who sits on a particular bench in Parliament. **3** a person who sits on a bench, esp. in a tavern, a tavern-haunter. **4** †a person who sits officially on a bench. **benchmark** *n.* **1** a mark cut in some durable material in a line of survey for reference at a future time. **2** anything that serves as a standard of comparison or point of reference. *~v.t.* to test or assess using a benchmark. **benchmark test** *n.* a test using a benchmark. **Bench of Bishops** *n.* the episcopate collectively, esp. those who rank as peers. **bench show** *n.* a dog show in which the dogs are exhibited on benches or platforms. **bench table** *n.* a low seat of stone in churches and cloisters. **bench test** *n.* a test of a new component, device etc. before it is installed, to check its condition. *~v.t.* to run a bench test on. **bench warrant** *n.* a warrant issued by a judge, as distinct from a magistrate's warrant. [OE *benc* (cp. Swed. *bänk,* G *Bank,* It. *banca,* Gmc. *bankiz,* see BANK[3])]

bend (bend) *v.t.* (*past, p.p.* **bent** (bent), **bended**) **1** to bring into a curved shape (as a bow) by pulling the string. **2** to render curved or angular. **3** to deflect. **4** to direct to a certain point. **5** to apply closely. **6** to bring into operation. **7** to incline from the vertical. **8** to subdue. **9** to fasten, to make fast. **10** to tie into a knot.

~*v.i.* 1 to assume the form of a curve or angle. 2 to incline from an erect position, to bow, stoop. 3 to surrender, submit. 4 to turn in a new direction. ~*n.* 1 a bending curve or flexure. 2 incurvation. 3 a sudden turn in a road or river. 4 an inclination. 5 (*Her.*) an ordinary formed by two parallel lines drawn across from the dexter chief to the sinister base point of an escutcheon. 6 a knot. 7 (*pl.*) the crooked timbers which make the ribs or sides of a ship. 8 a shape or size in tanned leather, half a butt. **around the bend** (*N Am.*, *coll.*) round the bend. **on bended knees** 1 with the knees bent. 2 as a suppliant. **round the bend** (*coll.*) crazy, insane. **the bends** (*coll.*) caisson disease, decompression sickness. **to bend a sail** to extend or make it fast towards its proper yard or stay. **to bend over backwards** BACKWARDS. **to bend the brows** to frown. **to bend the elbow** (*coll.*) to be fond of drinking alcohol. **bendable** *a.* **bender** *n.* (*sl.*) 1 a bout of heavy drinking. 2 (*offensive*) a homosexual. 3 an old sixpence. **bend leather** *n.* the stoutest kind of leather. **bend sinister** *n.* (*Her.*) an ordinary from the sinister chief to the dexter base point, as a mark of bastardy (cp. BAR[1], BATON). **bendy** *a.* (*comp.* **bendier**, *superl.* **bendiest**). **bendiness** *n.* [OE *bendan* (Icel. *benda*, to join, strain, Gmc. *bandjan*)]

beneath (binēth´) *prep.* 1 below, under in place or position. 2 unworthy of. ~*adv.* in a lower place, below. **beneath contempt** CONTEMPT. [OE *beneothan* (*be-*, by, *neothan*, adv. below, cp. *nither*, below, Gmc. *nithar*, G *nieden*)]

benedicite (benidī´siti) *int.* bless you, good gracious. ~*n.* 1 the invocation of a blessing. 2 grace before meat. 3 the Song of the Three Holy Children, one of the canticles in the Prayer Book. 4 (*Mus.*) a setting of this. [L, bless ye! imper. of *benedīcere* (*bene*, well, *dīcere*, to speak)]

benedick (ben´idik), **benedict** (-dikt) *n.* a newly married man. [from *Benedick*, a character in *Much Ado About Nothing*]

Benedictine (benidik´tēn, -tin) *a.* of or relating to St Benedict, 480–543, or to the order of monks founded by him. ~*n.* 1 a monk or nun of the order founded (529) by St Benedict. 2 a liqueur first made by Benedictine monks (a registered name). [F *bénédictin*, L *benedictus*]

benediction (benidik´shən) *n.* 1 a blessing pronounced officially. 2 the act of blessing or invoking a blessing. 3 grace before or after meals. 4 blessedness, grace, blessing. 5 a Roman Catholic devotion including a blessing with the Host. **benedictory** *a.* of or relating to or expressing benediction. **Benedictus** (-tus) *n.* 1 the hymn of Zacharias (Luke i.68), used as a canticle in the Church of England. 2 in the Roman Catholic Church, a portion of the Mass following the Sanctus. 3 (*Mus.*) a setting of either of these. [L *benedictio -onem* (see BENEDICITE)]

benefaction (benifak´shən) *n.* 1 a gift or endowment for charitable purposes. 2 the conferring of a benefit. 3 a benefit conferred. **benefactor** (ben´ifaktə) *n.* 1 a person who gives another help or friendly service. 2 a person who gives to a religious or charitable institution. **benefactress** (-tris) *n.* a female benefactor. [L *benefactio -ōnem*, from *benefacere* (see BENEFICE)]

benefice (ben´ifis) *n.* 1 an ecclesiastical living. 2 the property attached to such a living. **beneficed** *a.* possessed of a benefice. [L *beneficium* (*bene*, well, *-ficium*, a doing, from *facere*)]

beneficent (binef´isənt) *a.* 1 kind, generous, doing good. 2 characterized by benevolence. **beneficence** *n.* 1 the habitual practice of doing good. 2 active kindness. 3 charity. **beneficently** *adv.*

beneficial (benifish´əl) *a.* 1 advantageous, helpful. 2 remedial. 3 (*Law*) a of or belonging to usufruct. b enjoying the usufruct of property. **beneficially** *adv.* [F *bénéficial*, late L *beneficialis*, from as BENEFICE]

beneficiary (benifish´əri) *n.* (*pl.* **beneficiaries**) 1 a person who receives a favour. 2 the holder of a benefice, a person who benefits under a trust. 3 a feudatory. ~*a.* holding or held by feudal tenure. [L *beneficiarius*, from as BENEFIT]

benefit (ben´ifit) *n.* 1 profit, advantage, gain. 2 an advantage, something favourable. 3 (*usu. pl.*) money or services provided under government social security or private pension schemes etc. 4 a theatrical, music-hall or other performance, the receipts from which, with certain deductions, are given to some person or charity. 5 (*Law*) the advantage of belonging to some privileged order. 6 exemption from the jurisdiction of the ordinary courts. ~*v.t.* (*pres.p.* **benefiting**, (*N Am.*) **benefitting**, *past, p.p.* **benefited**, (*N Am.*) **benefitted**) 1 to do good to. 2 to be of advantage or profit to. ~*v.i.* to derive advantage. **benefit club, benefit society** *n.* a society whose members, in return for a certain periodical payment, receive certain benefits in sickness or old age. **benefit of clergy** *n.* 1 sanction by the Church. 2 (*Hist.*) a privilege that put the clergy outside secular jurisdiction. **benefit of the doubt** *n.* the assumption of innocence in the absence of clear evidence of guilt. [OF *bienfait*, L *benefactum*, neut. p.p. of *benefacere* (see BENEFICE)]

Benelux (ben´ilŭks) *n.* 1 Belgium, the Netherlands and Luxembourg. 2 the customs union formed between these three countries in 1947. [first letters of *Be*lgium, *Ne*therlands, *Lux*embourg]

benevolent (binev´ələnt) *a.* 1 disposed to do good, kind, generous. 2 charitable. **benevolence** *n.* 1 disposition to do good. 2 charitable feeling, goodwill. 3 a forced loan formerly levied by English kings, but abolished by the Bill of Rights (1689). **benevolently** *adv.* [OF *benevolent*, L *bene volens -tem*, well wishing (*velle*, to wish)]

B.Eng. *abbr.* Bachelor of Engineering.

Bengali (bengaw´li, beng·gaw´li) *a.* of or relating to Bengal, a region coinciding with Bangladesh and the Indian state of W Bengal, formerly an Indian province, its people or language. ~*n.* (*pl.* **Bengalis**) 1 a native or inhabitant of Bengal; a person whose family came from Bengal. 2 the language of Bengalis. **Bengal light** *n.* a firework giving a vivid and sustained blue light, used as a signal. [Hind. *Bangālī*]

benighted (binī´tid) *a.* 1 involved in moral or intellectual darkness; ignorant; uncivilized. 2 overtaken by night. **benightedness** *n.*

benign (binīn´) *a.* 1 kind-hearted, gracious, mild. 2 favourable, propitious. 3 agreeable, salubrious. 4 (of a tumour etc.) not malignant. **benignant** (-nig´nənt) *a.* 1 gracious, kind, benevolent. 2 favourable, propitious. 3 (of a tumour etc.) not malignant. **benignancy** *n.* **benignantly** *adv.* **benignity** (-nig´ni-) *n.* (*pl.* **benignities**) 1 kindly feeling. 2 kindness, a favour bestowed. **benignly** *adv.* **benign neglect** *n.* neglect that is intended to benefit the subject. [OF *benigne*, L *benignus*, prob. orig. *benigenus* (*bene*, well, *-genus*, born, cp. *indigenus*)]

†**benison** (ben´izən) *n.* a blessing. [OF *beneison*, L *benedictio -ōnem*, BENEDICTION]

†**Benjamin** (ben´jəmin) *n.* 1 the youngest son. 2 the darling of a family. [alluding to Gen. xlii.4]

benjamin (ben´jəmin) *n.* benzoin. [corr. of BENZOIN]

bennet[1] (ben´it) *n.* herb bennet, *Geum urbanum*. [ME *herbe beneit*, prob. from OF *herbe beneite*, L *herba benedicta*, blessed herb, *benedictus*, p.p. of *benedīcere* (see BENEDICITE)]

bennet[2] (ben´it) *n.* a dry grass stalk.

bent[1] (bent) *n.* 1 an inclination, a bias. 2 a disposition, a propensity. 3 tension, extent, capacity. ~*a.* 1 curved. 2 intent (on), resolved (to). 3 (*sl.*) dishonest. 4 crooked. 5 (*sl.*) stolen. 6 (*sl.*, *offensive*) homosexual. **to the top of**

one's bent to one's utmost capacity, to one's full tension. **bentwood** *n.* wood steamed and curved in moulds for making furniture. ~*a.* made using bentwood.

bent[2] (bent) *n.* **1** stiff, rushlike grass, esp. of the genus *Agrostis.* **2** old grass stalks. **3** †grassy ground, unenclosed pasture. **4** †a heath. **bent-grass** *n.* any grass of the genus *Agrostis.* [OE *beonet* (cp. OHG *binuz*, G *Binse*)]

bent[3] BEND.

benthal BENTHOS.

Benthamism (ben´thəmizm) *n.* the utilitarian philosophy based on the principle of the greatest happiness of the greatest number. **Benthamite** *n.* a follower of Jeremy Bentham, a utilitarian. ~*a.* following Bentham, of or relating to utilitarianism. [Jeremy *Bentham*, 1748–1832]

benthos (ben´thos), **benthon** (-thon) *n.* the sedentary animal and plant life on the ocean bed or at the bottom of a lake. **benthal, benthic** *a.* **benthoscope** (-əskōp) *n.* a submersible sphere for studying deep-sea life, a bathysphere. [Gr. *benthos*, the depths of the sea]

bentonite (ben´tənīt) *n.* an absorbent clay used in various industries as a filler, bonding agent etc. [Fort *Benton*, Montana, where it is found]

ben trovato (ben trōvah´tō) *a.* **1** characteristic or appropriate, if not true. **2** well made up or invented. [It., lit., well found]

benumb (binŭm´) *v.t.* **1** to render torpid or numb. **2** to deaden, to paralyse. **benumbment** *n.* **1** the act of benumbing. **2** the state of being benumbed. **3** torpor. [formerly *benum*, OE *benumen*, p.p. of *beniman* (*niman*, see NUMB)]

Benzedrine® (ben´zidrēn) *n.* amphetamine.

benzene (ben´zēn) *n.* an aromatic hydrocarbon obtained from coal tar and some petroleum fractions, used in industry in the synthesis of organic chemical compounds, as a solvent and insecticide. **benzene ring** *n.* a closed chain of six carbon atoms each bound to a hydrogen atom in the benzene molecule. **benzenoid** *a.* **benzine** (-zēn), **benzin** (-zin) *n.* a mixture of liquid hydrocarbons, distilled from petroleum, used esp. as a solvent and motor fuel. **benzococaine** (-zōkōkān´) *n.* a drug used as a local anaesthetic. **benzodiazepine** (-zōdīā´zəpin, -az´-) *n.* any of a group of synthetic drugs used as sedatives and tranquillizers. **benzol** (-zol), **benzole** (-zōl) *n.* **1** unrefined benzene used as a fuel. **2** †benzene. **benzoline** (-zəlēn) *n.* **1** impure benzene. **2** benzine. **benzoquinone** (-zōkwin´ōn) *n.* a yellow compound related to benzene. **benzoyl** (-zoil) *n.* a radical derived from benzene. **benzyl** (-zil) *n.* an organic radical derived from benzene.

benzoin (ben´zoin, -zōin) *n.* **1** a resin obtained from trees of the genus *Styrax*, used in medicine and in perfumery, also called (*gum*) *benjamin.* **2** any N American lauraceous tree of the genus *Lindera*, esp. the spicebush. **3** a ketone present in the resin benzoin. **4** a camphor obtained from bitter-almond oil. **benzoic** (-zō´-) *a.* of, relating to or derived from benzoin. **benzoic acid** *n.* an acid present in benzoin and other natural resins, used in medicines, dyes, as a food preservative and in organic synthesis. [F *benjoin*, Sp. *benjui* (It. *bengivi*), Arab. *lubān jāwi*, Javanese frankincense (*lu-* mistaken for It. article *lo* and dropped)]

benzol, benzyl etc. BENZENE.

bequeath (bikwēdh´) *v.t.* **1** to leave by will or testament. **2** to transmit to future generations. **3** †to transfer, hand over. **bequeathable** *a.* **bequeathal, bequeathment** *n.* **1** the act of bequeathing. **2** a legacy. **bequeather** *n.* **bequest** (-kwest´) *n.* **1** the act of bequeathing. **2** that which is bequeathed; a legacy. [OE *becwethan* (BE-, *cwethan*, to say, cp. QUOTH)]

berate (birāt´) *v.t.* to rebuke or scold vehemently.

Berber (bœ´bə) *n.* **1** a member of the Hamitic peoples of N Africa. **2** their language. ~*a.* of or relating to this people or their language. [BARBARY]

berberis (bœ´bəris) *n.* (*pl.* **berberises**) **1** any shrub of the genus *Berberis.* **2** the berry of this shrub. **berberine** (-rēn) *n.* an alkaloid obtained from barberry roots. [see BARBERRY]

berberry BARBERRY.

berceuse (beəsœz´) *n.* (*pl.* **berceuses** (beəsœz´)) **1** a lullaby, a cradle song. **2** a piece of lulling instrumental music. [F, a cradle-rocker]

bereave (birēv´) *v.t.* (*past, p.p.* **bereaved, bereft** (-reft´)) **1** to deprive, rob or spoil of anything. **2** to render desolate (*usu. in p.p.*). **bereaved** *a.* deprived of a near relative or friend by death. **bereavement** *n.* **1** the state of being bereaved. **2** the loss of a near relative or friend by death. **bereft** *a.* deprived (esp. of something abstract, as hope, dignity etc.). [OE *berēafian* (BE-, *rēafian*, to rob; cp. G *berauben*)]

Berenice's hair (berənī´siz) *n.* a small northern constellation, near the tail of Leo. [from the myth that the hair of *Berenice*, wife of Ptolemy Euergetes, king of Egypt (3rd cent. BC), was placed in a constellation]

beret (ber´ā) *n.* a round, brimless flat cap fitting the head fairly closely. [F *béret*, Bearnais *berreto*, late L *birretum*, BIRETTA]

berg[1] (bœg) *n.* an iceberg.

berg[2] (bœg) *n.* (*S Afr.*) a mountain or hill (often used in place names). **berg wind** *n.* a hot dry wind in South Africa blowing from the north to the coast. [G *Berg*, Afrikaans *berg*, hill]

bergamot[1] (bœ´gəmot) *n.* **1** a citrus tree, *Citrus bergamia*, which yields a fragrant essential oil used in perfumery. **2** the oil itself. **3** a kind of mint, *Mentha citrata*, which yields an oil somewhat similar. [prob. from *Bergamo*, in Italy]

bergamot[2] (bœ´gəmot) *n.* a juicy kind of pear. [F *bergamotte*, It. *bergamotta*, Turk. *beg-armūdi*, prince's pear]

bergschrund (beəg´shrŭnd) *n.* a crevasse or fissure between the base of a steep slope and a glacier or névé. [G *Berg*, mountain, *Schrund*, crack, gap]

Bergsonian (bœgsō´niən) *a.* of or relating to the French philosopher Henry Bergson (1859–1941) or his theory of creative evolution and the life force. ~*n.* a follower of Bergson.

beribboned (birib´ənd) *a.* decorated with ribbons.

beriberi (beriber´i, ber´-) *n.* a degenerative disease due to a deficiency of vitamin B_1. [Sinhalese *beri*, weakness]

berk (bœk), **burk** *n.* (*sl.*) an idiot. [from *Berkeley Hunt* (in Gloucestershire), rhyming sl. for *cunt*]

Berkeleian (bahklē´ən) *a.* of or relating to Bishop George Berkeley (1685–1753) or his philosophy, which denied that the mind, being entirely subjective, could know the external world objectively. ~*n.* an adherent of the Berkeleian philosophy.

berkelium (bœkē´liəm) *n.* an artificially produced radioactive element, at. no. 97, chem. symbol Bk.

Berks. (bahks) *abbr.* Berkshire.

†**berlin** (bœlin´) *n.* a four-wheeled carriage having a hooded seat behind. **Berliner** (bœlin´ə) *n.* **1** a native or inhabitant of Berlin in Germany. **2** a lightly-fried iced bun with jam inside. [*Berlin* in Germany]

berm (bœm) *n.* **1** a narrow ledge at the foot of the exterior slope of a parapet. **2** the bank of a canal opposite the towing-path. [F *berme*, G *Berme* (Dut. *berm*)]

Bermuda shorts (bəmū´də), **Bermudas** *n.pl.* tight-fitting knee-length shorts. **Bermuda triangle** *n.* an area of the western Atlantic known for the mysterious disappearance of ships and aircraft. [the *Bermuda* Islands in the NW Atlantic]

Bernardine (bœ´nədēn) *a.* of or relating to St Bernard of

Clairvaux or the Cistercian order. ~*n.* a Cistercian monk.

berretta BIRETTA.

berry (ber´i) *n.* (*pl.* **berries**) **1** any smallish, round, fleshy fruit. **2** any one of the eggs of a fish or lobster. **3** (*Bot.*) a many-seeded, indehiscent, pulpy fruit, the seeds of which are loosely scattered through the pulp. **4** a coffee bean. ~*v.i.* (*pres.p.* **berrying,** *past, p.p.* **berried**) **1** to go berry-gathering. **2** to bear or produce berries. **3** to swell, to fill. **in berry** (of a hen lobster) bearing eggs. **berried** *a.* **1** having or bearing berries. **2** (of a hen lobster) bearing eggs. [OE *berige* (cp. Icel. *ber*, Goth. *basi*, G *Beere*)]

bersagliere (beəsalyeə´rā) *n.* (*pl.* **bersaglieri** (-rē)) **1** a sharpshooter. **2** a member of a crack corps in the Italian army. [It., from *bersaglio*, a mark]

berserk (bəsœk´), **baresark** (beə´sahk) *n.* **1** (*also* **berserker**) a Norse warrior possessed of preternatural strength and fighting with desperate fury and courage. **2** a bravo. ~*a., adv.* frenzied; filled with furious rage. **to go berserk** to lose control of one's actions in violent rage. [Icel. *berserkr* (etym. uncertain, prob. bearsark, bear-coat)]

berth (bœth) *n.* **1** a sleeping place on board ship. **2** a sleeping place in a railway carriage. **3** a place for a ship at a wharf. **4** sea room. **5** a convenient place for mooring. **6** a situation on board ship. **7** a room in a ship where any number of officers mess and reside. **8** a permanent job or situation of any kind. **9** a suitable place for keeping anything. ~*v.t.* **1** to moor in a berth. **2** to furnish with a berth. **to give a wide berth to 1** to keep away from. **2** to steer clear of. **berthage** (-ij) *n.* **1** room or accommodation for mooring ships. **2** dock dues. [etym. uncertain; perh. from OE *gebyrian*, to suit (cp. G *gebühren*), or from BEAR[2]]

bertha (bœ´thə) *n.* **1** a wide, deep collar, often of lace. **2** a small cape on a dress. [F *berthe*, from *Berthe*, Bertha (the name)]

Bertillon system (bœ´tilon) *n.* a method of recording personal measurements and other characteristics, esp. for the purpose of identifying criminals. [Alphonse *Bertillon*, 1853–1914, French anthropologist]

beryl (ber´il) *n.* **1** a gem nearly identical with the emerald, but varying in colour from pale green to yellow or white. **2** a silicate of aluminium and beryllicum, occurring usu. in hexagonal prisms. **berylline** (-īn) *a.* resembling a beryl. [OF, from L *bēryllus*, Gr. *bērullos* (Sansk. *vaidūrya*)]

beryllium (biril´iəm) *n.* a light metallic element, at. no. 4, chem. symbol Be, used as a component in nuclear reactors and to harden alloys etc.

beseech (bisēch´) *v.t.* (*past, p.p.* **besought** (-sawt´), **beseeched**) **1** to ask earnestly, implore, supplicate. **2** to ask earnestly for. **beseeching** *a.* **beseechingly** *adv.* [BE-, ME *sechen seken* (cp. Dut. *bezoeken* G *besuchen*)]

beseem (bisēm´) *v.t., v.i.* to be fit, suitable, or proper (for), to be becoming (to) (*usu. impersonal*). **beseeming** *a.* becoming, fitting. **beseemingly** *adv.* **beseemingness** *n.* **beseemly** *a.* seemly, suitable, becoming, proper.

beseen (bisēn´) *a.* **1** seen, looking, appearing. **2** dressed, furnished, accomplished. [p.p. of obs. v. *besee*, from OE *biseon*, *beseon*, to look about, to pay regard to]

beset (biset´) *v.t.* (*pres.p.* **besetting,** *past, p.p.* **beset**) **1** to set upon, to fall upon, to assail. **2** to set or surround (with). **3** †to encompass. ~*a.* set or encumbered (with difficulties, snares etc.). **besetment** *n.* **1** the state of being beset. **2** a besetting sin or weakness. **besetting sin** *n.* the sin that particularly tempts a person. [OE *bisettan*, to surround (BE-, *settan*, to SET[1])]

beside (bisīd´) *prep.* **1** by the side of, side by side with. **2** in comparison with. **3** near, hard by, close to. **4** away from, wide of. ~*adv.* besides. **beside oneself** out of one's wits with worry etc. **beside the point/ question** irrelevant. **besides** *prep.* **1** in addition to, over and above. **2** other than, except. ~*adv.* **1** moreover, further, over and above, in addition. **2** otherwise. [OE *be sīdan*, by side]

besiege (bisēj´) *v.t.* **1** to surround (a place) with intent to capture it by military force. **2** to crowd round. **3** to assail importunately. **besieger** *n.* [ME *bisegen*, *besegen* (BE-, *segen*, OF *asegier*, late L *assediāre*, from *ad-*, to, *sedium*, sitting, from *sedēre*, to sit)]

besmear (bismiə´) *v.t.* **1** to cover or daub with something unctuous or viscous. **2** to soil, to defile, to sully the reputation of.

besmirch (bismœch´) *v.t.* **1** to soil, discolour. **2** to sully the reputation of, to dishonour.

besom (bē´zəm) *n.* **1** a broom made of twigs or heath bound round a handle. **2** anything that sweeps away impurity. **3** (*North., Sc.*) a term of reproach for a woman. [OE *besma* (cp. Dut. *bezem*, G *Besen*)]

besot (bisot´) *v.t.* (*pres.p.* **besotting,** *past, p.p.* **besotted**) **1** to make sottish. **2** to stupefy, to muddle. **3** to cause to dote on. **besotted** *a.* **1** infatuated. **2** intoxicated. **3** muddled. **besottedly** *adv.* **besottedness** *n.*

besought BESEECH.

bespangle (bispang´gəl) *v.t.* to cover over with or as with spangles.

bespatter (bispat´ə) *v.t.* **1** to spatter over or about. **2** to load with abuse.

bespeak (bispēk´) *v.t.* (*past* **bespoke** (-spōk´), *p.p.* **bespoken** (-ən)) **1** to speak for, to arrange for, to order beforehand. **2** to ask. **3** to request. **4** to give evidence of. **5** to betoken, to foreshow. **6** †to speak to. ~*n.* **1** the bespeaking of a particular play. **2** an actor's benefit. **bespoke** *a.* **1** made-to-measure. **2** (of a suit etc.) made to a customer's specific requirements. **3** making or selling such articles. [OE *besprecan* (BE-, *sprecan*, SPEAK), cp. OHG *bisprācha*, detraction, G *besprechen*, to talk over]

bespectacled (bispek´təkəld) *a.* wearing spectacles.

bespoke, bespoken BESPEAK.

bespread (bispred´) *v.t.* (*past, p.p.* **bespread**) **1** to spread over. **2** to spread with. **3** to adorn. [ME *bispreden*, *bespreden* (BE-, *spreden*, to spread)]

besprinkle (bispring´kəl) *v.t.* **1** to sprinkle or scatter over. **2** to bedew. [ME *besprengil* (BE-, *sprenkel*, freq. of *sprengan*)]

Bessemer process (bes´əmə) *n.* a process invented in 1856 for the elimination of carbon and silicon etc. by forcing air into melted pig-iron. **Bessemer converter** *n.* a furnace used during this process. **Bessemerize, Bessemerise** *v.t.* [Sir Henry *Bessemer*, 1813–98, English engineer]

best (best) *a.* **1** of the highest excellence. **2** surpassing all others. **3** most desirable. ~*adv.* **1** in the highest degree. **2** to the most advantage. **3** with most ease. **4** most intimately. ~*n.* **1** the best thing. **2** the utmost. **3** (*collect.*) the best people. **4** the deciding majority (*play the best of seven games*). ~*v.t.* **1** to get the better of. **2** to cheat, outwit. **all the best** used to express goodwill on taking leave. **as best one can/ may** as successfully as one can under the circumstances. **at best** as far as can be expected. **at one's best** in prime condition, in one's prime. **at the best of times** when everything is ideal or favourable. **on one's best behaviour** BEHAVIOUR (under BEHAVE). **to be (all) for the best** to have a happy or successful outcome, though immediately unpleasant. **to do one's best** to do one's utmost. **to get the best of** to get the advantage or victory over. **to give best to** to concede defeat to, to give way to. **to give it best** (*Austral.*) to give in without trying further. **to give it one's best shot** SHOT[1]. **to have the best of** to have the advantage or victory over. **to make the best of 1** to make the most of. **2** to be content with. **to put one's best foot forward** FOOT. **to the best of** to the utmost extent of. **to the best of my belief** as far as I know. **to the best of one's ability** as well as one can. **to the best of one's knowledge** as far as one knows. **with the best of them** without having to be ashamed of one's ability etc. **best-before date** *n.* **1** the date marked on the packaging of a perishable product indicating the date before which it should be used. **2** (*coll.*) the optimum age of a person, machine etc., before decline sets in. **best bib and tucker** *n.* (*coll.*) one's best clothing, one's best outfit. **best bower** *n.* the starboard bower. **best boy** *n.* the assistant to the chief electrician of a film crew. **best buy** *n.* a recommended item, a bargain. **best end** *n.* the rib end (of a neck of lamb etc.). **best girl** *n.* (*dated coll.*) one's girlfriend, fiancée, lover etc. **best-known** *a.* most well-known or famous. **best man** *n.* a groomsman. **best part** *n.* the largest part (of), the most. **best people** *n.pl.* those considered the most select socially. **best-seller** *n.* **1** a popular book which has sold in large numbers. **2** a writer of such a book. **best-sell** *v.i.* to be or become a best-seller. **best wishes** *n.pl.* expressions of hope for the happiness, good fortune etc. of another. [OE *betst* (cp. BETTER), superl. of GOOD; adv. superl. of WELL[1]]

†**bestead**[1] (bisted´) *v.t.* **1** to help. **2** to profit. **3** to be of service to. ~*v.i.* to avail.

bestead[2] BESTED.

bested (bisted´), **bestead** *a.* situated, circumstanced (usu. with *ill, hard, hardly, sore* etc.). [ME *bistad*, p.p. of *bisteden* (BE-, *stad*, from Icel. *staddr*, p.p. of *stethja*, to stop, fix, appoint)]

bestial (bes´tiəl) *a.* **1** brutish, sensual, obscene, sexually depraved. **2** resembling a beast. **3** of or relating to the lower animals, esp. the quadrupeds. **bestiality** (-tial´-) *n.* (*pl.* **bestialities**) **1** bestial behaviour. **2** sexual relations between a person and an animal. **3** a bestial act. **bestialize, bestialise** *v.t.* **1** to make bestial. **2** to reduce to the level of a beast. **bestially** *adv.* [OF *bestial*, L *bestiālis* (*bestia*, a beast)]

bestiary (bes´tiəri) *n.* (*pl.* **bestiaries**) a moralized natural history of animals. [med. L *bestiarium* from L *bestia*, beast]

bestir (bistœ´) *v.t.* (*pres.p.* **bestirring,** *past, p.p.* **bestirred**) to rouse into activity. [OE *bestyrian* (BE-, *styrian*, STIR[1])]

bestow (bistō´) *v.t.* **1** to give as a present. **2** to stow, to lay up. **3** to stow away, to lodge, provide with quarters. **4** to expend, to lay out. **bestowal** *n.* **1** gift. **2** disposal, location. **bestower** *n.* **bestowment** *n.* bestowal.

bestrew (bistroo´) *v.t.* (*p.p.* **bestrewed, bestrewn**) **1** to strew over. **2** to lie scattered over. [OE *bestrēowian* (BE-, *strēowian*, STREW)]

bestride (bistrīd´) *v.t.* (*past* **bestrode** (-strōd´), *p.p.* **bestridden** (-strid´ən)) **1** to sit upon with the legs astride. **2** to span, overarch. [OE *bestridan* (BE-, STRIDE)]

bet (bet) *n.* **1** an act of betting, a wager. **2** a sum staked on a contingent event. ~*v.t.* (*pres.p.* **betting,** *past, p.p.* **bet, betted**) **1** to lay a wager against. **2** to stake on a contingency. ~*v.i.* to risk a sum of money or belonging against another's on a contingent event, to lay a wager. **to bet one's boots** BOOT[1]. **you bet** (*sl.*) certainly, of course, depend upon it. **better**[1], **bettor** *n.* a person who makes bets. **betting** *n.* **1** gambling by risking money on contingent events. **2** the odds on an event. **what's the betting?** I think it very likely (that). **betting shop** *n.* a bookmaker's. [perh. from ABET]

beta (bē´tə) *n.* **1** the second letter of the Greek alphabet (β). **2** a second-class mark given to a student's work. **3** (**Beta**) the second star (in brightness or position) in a constellation. **4** the second of a series of numerous compounds and other enumerations. **beta blocker** *n.* a drug that reduces the heart rate, esp. used to treat high blood pressure, but also used illegally by some sports competitors to improve their concentration and performance. **beta decay** *n.* radioactive decay accompanying the emission of an electron. **beta particle** *n.* a negatively-charged particle emitted by certain radioactive substances, identified as an electron. **beta ray** *n.* a ray consisting of a stream of beta particles or electrons. **beta rhythm, beta waves** *n.* the normal electrical activity of the brain. **beta securities, beta stocks** *n.pl.* the Stock Exchange stocks which are second most frequently traded. **beta test** *n.* a test of a new product, esp. in computer software, carried out by an external tester (typically a customer or potential customer) before final release (cp. ALPHA TEST (under ALPHA)). ~*v.t.* to put (a product) through such a test. **betatron** (-tron) *n.* (*Physics*) an electrical apparatus for accelerating electrons to high energies. [Gr.]

betake (bitāk´) *v.refl.* (*past* **betook** (-tuk´), *p.p.* **betaken**) **1** to take oneself (to). **2** to have recourse (to).

betel (bē´təl) *n.* **1** a shrubby Asian plant with evergreen leaves, *Piper betle.* **2** its leaf, used as a wrapper to enclose a few slices of the areca nut with a little shell lime, which are chewed by people in the East. **betel-nut** *n.* the nut of the betel-tree. **betel-pepper, betel-vine** *n.* the shrub betel. **betel-tree** *n.* an Asian palm, *Areca catechu* (so called because its nut is chewed with betel leaves). [Port., from Malayalam, *vettila*]

bête noire (bet nwah´) *n.* (*pl.* **bêtes noires** (bet nwah´)) a bugbear, pet aversion. [F, black beast]

beth (beth) *n.* the second letter of the Hebrew alphabet. [Heb. *bēth*, house]

bethel (beth´əl) *n.* **1** a Nonconformist chapel. **2** a mission room. **3** a seamen's church, esp. afloat. [Heb. *bēthēl*, house of God]

bethesda (bithez´də) *n.* a Nonconformist chapel. [Heb. *bethesda*, house of mercy or place of the flowing of water]

†**bethink** (bithingk´) *v.refl.* (*past, p.p.* **bethought** (-thawt´)) **1** to consider, think. **2** to collect one's thoughts. [OE *bithencan* (cp. Dut. and G *bedenken*)]

betide (bitīd´) *v.t.* (*past* **betided, betid** (-tid´), *p.p.* **betid**) **1** to happen to. **2** to betoken. ~*v.i.* to happen, to come to pass. [ME *betiden* (BE-, OE *tidan*, TIDE)]

†**betimes** (bitīmz´) *adv.* **1** at an early hour or period. **2** in good time, in time. **3** in a short time, soon.

bêtise (betēz´) *n.* **1** a foolish act or remark. **2** folly. [F, from *bête*, BEAST]

betoken (bitō´kən) *v.t.* **1** to foreshow, to be an omen of, to indicate. **2** to be a type of. [ME *bitacnen* (see BE-, TOKEN, OE *getacnian*)]

betony (bet´əni) *n.* (*pl.* **betonies**) **1** a labiate plant, *Stachys officinalis*, with purple flowers. **2** any of various similar plants. [OF *betonie*, late *betonia*, L *vettonica* (*Vettones*, a Spanish tribe)]

betook BETAKE.

betray (bitrā´) *v.t.* **1** to deliver up a person or thing treacherously. **2** to be false to. **3** to disclose treacherously. **4** to disclose against one's will or intention; to reveal incidentally. **5** to lead astray. **betrayal** *n.* **1** a treacherous giving up or violation of a trust. **2** a revelation or divulging. **betrayer** *n.* **1** a person who betrays. **2** a traitor. [ME *betraien* (BE-, *traien*, to betray), OF *traïr*, late L *trādere* (*trans-*, over, *dāre*, to give)]

betroth (bitrōdh´) *v.t.* to contract (two persons) in an engagement to marry, to engage, to affiance. **betrothal, betrothment** *n.* **1** an act of betrothing. **2** the state of being betrothed. **betrothed** *a.* engaged to be married, affianced. ~*n.* a person engaged to be married. [ME *bitreuthien* (BE-, *treuthe*, OE *trēowth*, TRUTH)]

better[1] BET.

better[2] (bet´ə) *a.* **1** superior, more excellent. **2** more desirable. **3** greater in degree. **4** improved in health. ~*adv.* **1** in a superior, more excellent or more desirable manner. **2** more correctly or fully. **3** with greater profit. **4** in a greater or higher degree. **5** more. *~n.pl.* social superiors. *~v.t.* **1** to make better. **2** to excel, to surpass, to improve on. *~v.i.* to become better, to improve. **better off** in better circumstances. **for better (or) for worse** whatever the circumstances. **for the better** in the way of improvement. **had better** would be wiser to (do), would be advised to (do). **one's better self** SELF. **to better oneself** to get on, to get a better job. **to get the better of** to defeat, to outwit. **to go one better (than)** to outdo (another person). **to think better of** to reconsider. **better days** *n.pl.* a period of prosperity. **better feelings** *n.pl.* one's moral sense; the kindlier side of one's nature. **better half** *n.* one's wife. **betterment** *n.* **1** amelioration. **2** an improvement of property. **3** improvements made on new lands. **bettermost** *a.* **1** best. **2** of the highest quality. **better part** *n.* the largest part (of), the most part (of). [OE *bet, bett*, adv., *betera*, a., comp. of good (Goth. *batiza*, Icel. *betri*, Dut. *beter*, G *besser*); adv. comp. of WELL[1]]

betting, bettor BET.

bettong (betong´) *n.* a small prehensile-tailed kangaroo. [Austral. Abor.]

between (bitwēn´) *prep.* **1** in, on, into, along or across the place, space or interval of any kind separating (two points, lines, places or objects). **2** intermediate in relation to. **3** related to both of. **4** related so as to separate. **5** related so as to connect, from one to another of. **6** among. **7** in shares among, so as to affect all. *~adv.* **1** intermediately. **2** in an intervening space or time. **3** in relation to both. **4** to and fro. **5** during or in an interval. *~n.* **1** an interval of time. **2** (*pl.*) an intermediate size and quality of sewing needle. **between ourselves** in confidence. **between you and me (and the gatepost)** in confidence. **betwixt and between** **1** (*coll.*) neither one thing nor the other. **2** (*coll.*) half and half. **3** (*coll.*) middling. **in between** intermediate(ly). **between-decks** *n.* the space between two decks. **between-maid** *n.* a tweeny. **between-whiles, betweentimes** *adv.* **1** now and then. **2** at intervals. [OE *betwēonum* (*be*, by, *twēonum*, dat. of *twēon*, twain, a. corr. to distributive numeral *twā*, two)]

†**betwixt** (bitwikst´) *prep., adv.* between. **betwixt and between** BETWEEN. [OE *betweox* (*be*, by, with either a dat. *tweoxum, tweohsum*, or an acc. pl. neut. *twiscu*, from Gmc. *twiskjo*, twofold)]

beurre manié (bœ mahnyā´) *n.* a mixture of butter and flour added to a sauce to thicken it. [F, lit., handled butter]

BeV *abbr.* billion electronvolt(s) in the US: equivalent to gigaelectronvolt(s), GeV.

bevatron (bev´ətron) *n.* an electrical apparatus for accelerating protons to high energies.

bevel (bev´əl) *n.* **1** a tool consisting of a flat rule with a movable tongue or arm for setting off angles. **2** a slope from the right angle, an inclination of two planes, except one of 90°. *~v.t.* (*pres.p.* **bevelling,** (*N Am.*) **beveling,** *past, p.p.* **bevelled,** (*N Am.*) **beveled**) to cut away to a slope, to give a bevel angle to. *~v.i.* to recede from the perpendicular, to slant. *~a.* **1** oblique, sloping, slanting. **2** at more than a right angle. **bevel edge** *n.* the oblique edge of a chisel or similar cutting tool. **bevel gear, bevel gearing** *n.* a gear or gearing for transmitting motion from one shaft to another by means of bevel wheels. **bevelling,** (*N Am.*) **beveling** *n.* **1** reducing to an oblique angle. **2** the angle so given. **3** (*Naut.*) a bevelled surface or part. *~a.* slanting, having an obtuse angle. **bevel square** *n.* a bevel (the tool). **bevel wheel** *n.* a cogged wheel, the axis of which forms an angle (usu. 90°) with the shaft. [prob. from an OF *bevel* or *buvel* (F *beveau*)]

beverage (bev´ərij) *n.* any drink other than water. **bevvy** *n.* (*pl.* **bevvies**) (*sl.*) an alcoholic drink. **bevvied** (-id) *a.* (*sl.*) drunk. [OF *beverage*, from *bevre, beivre* (cp. F *boire*), to drink, from L *bibere*, to drink, -AGE]

bevy (bev´i) *n.* (*pl.* **bevies**) **1** a flock of larks or quails. **2** a company of women. **3** a herd of roe deer. [etym. unknown]

bewail (biwāl´) *v.t.* to wail over, to lament for. *~v.i.* to express grief. **bewailer** *n.* **bewailing** *n.* loud lamentation. *~a.* that bewails or laments. **bewailingly** *adv.* mournfully, with lamentation. **bewailment** *n.* the act of bewailing.

beware (biweə´) *v.i.* **1** to be wary, to be on one's guard. **2** to take care. *~v.t.* **1** to be wary of, on guard against. **2** to look out for. [ME *be war*, be cautious, OE *wœr* wary (cp. WARE[2], v. from OE *warian*, to guard)]

bewhiskered (biwis´kəd) *a.* **1** having whiskers. **2** very old.

Bewick's swan (bū´iks) *n.* a small white swan, native to E Asia and NE Europe, a race of *Cygnus columbianus*. [T. *Bewick*, d. 1828, English engraver and naturalist]

bewig (biwig´) *v.t.* (*pres.p.* **bewigging,** *past, p.p.* **bewigged**) to adorn with a wig. **bewigged** *a.*

bewilder (biwil´də) *v.t.* to perplex, confuse, lead astray. **bewilderedly** *adv.* **bewildering** *a.* causing one to lose one's way, physically or mentally. **bewilderingly** *adv.* **bewilderment** *n.* the state of being bewildered. [BE-, *wilder, wildern*, a wilderness]

bewitch (biwich´) *v.t.* **1** to charm, to fascinate, to allure. **2** to practise witchcraft against. **bewitching** *a.* alluring, charming. **bewitchingly** *adv.* **bewitchment** *n.* fascination, charm. [ME *bewicchen* (BE-, OE *wiccian*, to practise witchcraft, from *wicca*, a wizard)]

bey (bā), **beg** (beg) *n.* (*Hist.*) a governor of a Turkish town, province or district. **beylic** (-lik) *n.* the district governed by a bey. [Turk. *bēg*]

beyond (biyond´) *prep.* **1** on, to or towards the farther side of. **2** past, later than. **3** exceeding in quantity or amount, more than. **4** surpassing in quality or degree, outside the limit of. **5** in addition to, over and above. *~adv.* **1** at a greater distance. **2** farther away. *~n.* that which lies beyond human experience or after death. **back of beyond** BACK[1]. **beyond belief** BELIEF. **beyond compare** COMPARE. **beyond comparison** COMPARISON. **beyond the pale** PALE[2]. [OE *begeondan* (BE-, *geond*, across, *-an*, from)]

bezant (bizant´, bez´-), **byzant** *n.* **1** a gold coin struck at Constantinople by the Byzantine emperors, varying greatly in value. **2** (*Her.*) a gold roundel borne as a charge. [OF *besant*, L *Byzantius nummus*, coin of Byzantium]

bezel (bez´əl) *n.* **1** a sloping edge like that of a cutting tool. **2** any one of the oblique sides of a cut gem. **3** the groove by which a watch-glass or a jewel is held. [OF *bisel* (F *bizeau*)]

bezique (bizēk´) *n.* **1** a game of cards for two players, using a double pack. **2** the combination of the jack of diamonds and queen of spades in this game. [F *besigue* (etym. uncertain)]

bezoar (bē´zaw, bez´ōə) *n.* a calculous concretion found in the stomach of certain animals and supposed to be an antidote to poisons. **bezoar goat** *n.* the Persian wild goat, the best-known example of an animal producing the bezoar. **bezoar stone** *n.* [F, through Port. or Sp. from Arab. *bāzahr, bādizahr*, Pers. *pādzahr*, counter-poison]

bf *abbr.* **1** bloody fool. **2** (*Print.*) bold face. **3** brought forward.

BFI *abbr.* British Film Institute.

BFPO *abbr.* British Forces Post Office.

BG *abbr.* Brigadier General.

bhaji (bah´ji) *n.* (*pl.* **bhajis**) **1** an Indian vegetable dish (*mushroom bhaji*). **2** a small cake or ball of vegetables mixed with gram flour and deep-fried (*onion bhaji*). [Hind. *bhājī*]

bhang (bang), **bang** *n.* **1** the dried leaves of hemp, *Cannabis sativa.* **2** an intoxicating or stupefying liquor or drug made from these. [Hind.]

bhangra (bang´grə) *n.* music based on a fusion of Asian and contemporary pop music. [Punjabi *bhangra*, a traditional folk dance]

bharal (bŭr´əl), **burhel** *n.* a wild blue-coated sheep, *Pseudois nayaur*, of the Himalayas. [Hind.]

bheesti (bēs´ti), **bheesty, bhistee, bhisti** *n.* (*pl.* **bheesties, bhistees, bhistis**) in the Indian subcontinent, a servant who supplies water to a house. [Hind.]

BHF *abbr.* British Heart Foundation.

b.h.p. *abbr.* brake horsepower.

Bi *chem. symbol* bismuth.

bi (bī) *a.* (*sl.*) bisexual. ~*n.* (*pl.* **bis** (bīz)) a bisexual.

bi- (bī), (*also before a vowel*) **bin-** (bin) *pref.* **1** double, twice. **2** doubly. **3** with two. **4** in two. **5** every two, once in every two, lasting for two. [L *bi-*, *dui-*, double (cp. *duo*, two, Gr. *di-*, *duō*, Sansk. *doi*) (used even with Eng. words, e.g. *bi-weekly*, *bi-monthly*, but chiefly with words from L, esp. scientific terms)]

biacuminate (bīəkū´minət) *a.* having two tapering points.

biangular (bīang´gūlə) *a.* having two angles.

biannual (bīan´ūəl) *a.* half-yearly, twice a year. **biannually** *adv.*

biarticulate (bīahtik´ūlət) *a.* (*Zool.*) two-jointed.

bias (bī´əs) *n.* **1** a leaning of the mind, inclination, prejudice, prepossession. **2** a distortion of a statistical result due to a factor not allowed for. **3 a** in the game of bowls, the irregular shape of a bowl, imparting oblique motion. **b** a weight formerly placed on the side of a bowl to impart oblique motion. **c** the oblique motion of a bowl. **4** a voltage applied to an electrode of a transistor or valve. **5** an edge cut slantwise across a strip of material. ~*v.t.* (*pres.p.* **biasing, biassing,** *past, p.p.* **biased, biassed**) **1** to cause to incline to one side. **2** to prejudice, to prepossess. ~*a.* slanting, oblique. ~*adv.* **1** obliquely, athwart, awry. **2** on a slant. **on the bias** (of material) cut diagonally, slanting obliquely. **bias binding** *n.* a strip of material cut slantwise, used for binding hems in sewing. **bias crime** *n.* (*N Am.*) a racially-motivated crime. **biased** *a.* not impartial, prejudiced. **bias-ply** *a.* (*N Am.*) CROSS-PLY (under CROSS). [F *biais*, oblique or obliquity (perh. from L *bifacem*, two-faced)]

biathlon (bīath´lon) *n.* an athletic event combining either cross-country skiing and rifle shooting or cycling and running. **biathlete** *n.* [BI-, Gr. *athlon*, a contest]

biaxial (bīak´siəl), **biaxal** (-səl) *a.* having two (optical) axes.

Bib. *abbr.* **1** Bible. **2** Biblical.

bib (bib) *n.* **1** a cloth or piece of shaped plastic put under a child's chin to keep the front of the clothes clean. **2** the front section of a garment (e.g. an apron, dungarees) above the waist. **3** the whiting pout, *Trisopterus luscus*, a food fish with a chin barbel. ~†*v.i.* (*pres.p.* **bibbing,** *past, p.p.* **bibbed**) **1** to drink. **2** to drink frequently; to tipple. **to poke one's bib in** (*Austral., sl.*) to interfere. **to stick one's bib in** (*Austral., sl.*) to interfere. †**bibber** *n.* a tippler. †**bibbing** *n.* tippling. **bibcock** *n.* a tap with the nozzle bent downwards. [prob. from L *bibere*, to drink]

bibelot (bib´əlō) *n.* a small article of virtu, a knick-knack. [F]

Bible (bī´bəl), **bible** *n.* **1** the sacred writings of the Christian religion, comprising the Old and New Testaments. **2** the Hebrew Scriptures. **3** a copy of these, a particular edition of these. **4** a textbook, an authority. **5** a sacred book. **Bible-basher, Bible-puncher, Bible-thumper** *n.* **1** an aggressive preacher. **2** an ardent exponent of the Bible. **Bible-bashing, Bible-punching, Bible-thumping** *n.* **Bible belt** *n.* those regions of southern and central US characterized by fervent religious fundamentalism. **Bible-Christian** *n.* a member of a sect founded (1815) by W. O. Bryan, a Cornish Wesleyan. **Bible class** *n.* a class for studying the Bible. **Bible oath** *n.* an oath administered on the Bible. **Bible paper** *n.* **1** a thin opaque paper used for Bibles, reference books etc. **2** INDIA PAPER (under INDIAN). **biblical** (bib´li-) *a.* **1** of or relating to the Bible. **2** characteristic of the Bible. **biblically** *adv.* **biblicism** (-sizm) *n.* strict adherence to the letter of the Bible. **biblicist** *n.* BIBLIST (under BIBLE). **biblism** (bib´-) *n.* adherence to the Bible as the only rule of faith. **biblist** (bib´-) *n.* **1** a person who takes the Bible as the only rule of faith. **2** a biblical scholar or student. [F, from late L *biblia* (used as fem. sing.), Gr. *biblia*, neut. pl., writings, *biblion*, dim. of *biblos*, a book (*bublos*, papyrus)]

biblio- (bib´liō) *comb. form* of or relating to books. [Gr. *biblion*, a book]

Bibliog. *abbr.* Bibliography.

bibliography (bibliog´rəfi) *n.* (*pl.* **bibliographies**) **1** the methodical study of books, authorship, printing, editions, forms etc. **2** a book dealing with this. **3** a systematic list of books of any author, printer or country, or on any subject. **4** a systematic list of works quoted or referred to in a scholarly publication. **bibliographer** *n.* **1** a person skilled in bibliography. **2** a person who writes about books. **bibliographical** (-graf´-) *a.* of or relating to bibliography. **bibliographic** *a.* **bibliographically** *adv.* **bibliographize** (-og´rəfīz), **bibliographise** *v.t.* [Gr. *bibliographia* (BIBLIO-, -GRAPHY)]

bibliolatry (bibliol´ətri) *n.* **1** excessive admiration of a book or books. **2** excessive reverence for the letter of the Bible. **bibliolater** *n.* a person addicted to bibliolatry. **bibliolatrous** *a.* addicted to bibliolatry. [BIBLIO-, -LATRY]

bibliology (bibliol´əji) *n.* **1** scientific study of books, bibliography. **2** biblical study. **bibliological** (-loj´-) *a.* of or relating to bibliology.

bibliomancy (bib´liōmansi) *n.* divination by books or verses of the Bible.

bibliomania (bibliōmā´niə) *n.* a mania for collecting and possessing books. **bibliomaniac** (-ak) *n.* a person who has such a mania. ~*a.* having or exhibiting such a mania.

bibliopegy (bibliop´əji) *n.* the art of binding books. **bibliopegic** (-əpej´-) *a.* relating to the art of book-binding. **bibliopegist** *n.* **1** a person who collects bindings. **2** a bookbinder. [Gr. *-pēgia*, from *pēgnunai*, to fix]

bibliophile (bib´liōfīl) *n.* a lover or collector of books. **bibliophilic** (-fil´ik) *a.* **bibliophilism** (-of´-) *n.* **1** love of books. **2** book-collecting. **bibliophilist** (-of´-) *n.* **bibliophily** (-of´ili) *n.* [BIBLIO-, -PHILE]

bibliophobia (bibliōfō´biə) *n.* a dread or hatred of books.

bibliopole (bib´liōpōl) *n.* a bookseller, esp. one dealing in rare books. **bibliopolic** (-pol´-), **bibliopolical** *a.* of or relating to booksellers or to bookselling. **bibliopolist** (-op´-) *n.* a bookseller. **bibliopoly** (-op´-) *n.* bookselling. [L *bibliopōla*, Gr. *bibliopōlēs* (*pōlēs*, seller)]

bibliotheca (bibliōthē´kə) *n.* (*pl.* **bibliothecas, bibliothecae** (-kē)) **1** a library. **2** a bibliography. **bibliothecal** *a.* of or relating to a library. **bibliothecary** *n.* (*pl.* **bibliothecaries**) a librarian. [L, from Gr. *bibliothēkē* (*thēkē*, a repository)]

biblism, biblist BIBLE.

bibulous (bib´ūləs) *a.* **1** addicted to alcohol. **2** readily absorbing moisture. **bibulously** *adv.* **bibulousness** *n.* [L *bibulus* (*bibere*, to drink)]

bicameral (bīkam´ərəl) *a.* having two legislative chambers or assemblies. **bicameralism** *n.* [BI-, L *camera*, CHAMBER]

bicarbonate (bīkah´bənət) *n.* a salt of carbonic acid. **bicarbonate of soda,** (*coll.*) **bicarb** (bī´-) *n.* sodium bicarbonate used as a raising agent in baking or as an antacid.

bice (bīs) *n.* **1** any of various pigments made from blue or green basic copper carbonate. **2** a pale blue or green pigment made from smalt. **3** a pale blue or green colour. [F *bis* (fem. *bise*), It. *bigio*, greyish]

bicentenary (bīsəntē´nəri) *n.* (*pl.* **bicentenaries**) a 200th anniversary. ~*a.* **1** of or relating to a bicentenary. **2** consisting of or relating to 200 years. **bicentennial** (-ten´-) *a.* **1** occurring every 200 years. **2** lasting 200 years. **3** of or relating to a bicentenary. ~*n.* a bicentenary.

bicephalous (bīsef´ələs, -kef´-) *a.* having two heads. [Gr. *kephalē*, the head]

biceps (bī´seps) *n.* (*pl.* **biceps**) **1** the large muscle in front of the upper arm. **2** the corresponding muscle of the thigh. ~*a.* having two heads, points or summits, esp. of muscles having two attachments. **bicipital** (-sip´itəl) *a.* **1** two-headed. **2** of or relating to the biceps. [BI-, L *caput*, head]

bicker (bik´ə) *v.i.* **1** to dispute, quarrel, wrangle or squabble over petty issues. **2** to quiver, glisten, flicker. **3** (*poet.*) to patter. ~*n.* a petty quarrel. **bickerer** *n.* [ME *bickere*, prob. freq. of *biken*, to thrust]

bicky (bik´i), **bikky** *n.* (*pl.* **bickies, bikkies**) (*childish and coll.*) a biscuit.

bicolour (bī´kŭlə), (*N Am.*) **bicolor** *a.* having two colours. ~*n.* a bicolour blossom or animal.

biconcave (bīkon´kāv) *a.* concave on both sides.

biconvex (bīkon´veks) *a.* convex on both sides.

bicultural (bīkŭl´chərəl) *a.* having or consisting of two cultures. **biculturalism** *n.*

bicuspid (bīkŭs´pid) *a.* having two points or cusps. ~*n.* a bicuspid tooth, one of the premolars in humans. **bicuspidate** (-dāt) *a.* two-pointed.

bicycle (bī´sikəl) *n.* a two-wheeled pedal-driven vehicle, with the wheels one behind the other and usu. with a saddle for the rider mounted on a metal frame. ~*v.i.* to ride on a bicycle. **bicycle chain** *n.* a chain that transmits power from the pedals of a bicycle to the wheels. **bicycle clip** *n.* a thin metal clip worn around the ankles by cyclists to prevent their trousers from catching on the chain. **bicycle pump** *n.* a hand pump for filling bicycle tyres with air. **bicycler, bicyclist** *n.* a person who rides a bicycle.

bicyclic (bīsī´klik, -sik´-) *a.* (*Chem.*) having two rings of atoms in the molecular structure.

bid (bid) *v.t.* (*pres.p.* **bidding,** *past* **bid, †bade** (bād), *p.p.* **bid, †bidden** (bid´ən)) **1** to offer, to make a tender of (a price), esp. at an auction or for work to be undertaken. **2** to call (a certain number of tricks) at bridge. **3** †to command. **4** †to invite, to ask. **5** †to announce, to declare. ~*v.i.* **1** to make an offer at an auction. **2** to tender. **3** to state before a game of bridge the number of tricks one intends to make. ~*n.* **1** an offer of a price, esp. at an auction or for work to be undertaken. **2** the call at bridge whereby a player contracts to make a certain number of tricks. **3** (*coll.*) an attempt to achieve or acquire something. **to bid defiance** to defy, proclaim a challenge. **to bid fair** to seem likely, to promise well. **to bid farewell/ welcome** to salute at parting or arrival. **to bid up** to raise the price of a commodity at auction by a succession of overbids. **to make a bid for** to make an attempt to gain. **biddable** *a.* obedient, willing. **biddability** (-bil´-) *n.* **bidder** *n.* **bidding** *n.* **1** a bid at an auction. **2** in cards, the act of making a bid or bids. **3** invitation, command. **bidding prayer** *n.* a prayer in which the congregation is exhorted to pray for certain objects. [two verbs blended (1) OE *beodan*, to offer, inform, command (cp. Dut. *bieden*, G *bieten*, Goth. *biudan*), (2) *biddan* to press, beg, pray (cp. Dut. *bidden*, G *bitten*, Goth. *bidjan*)]

biddy (bid´i) *n.* (*pl.* **biddies**) **1** (*derog.*) an old woman. **2** (*dial.*) a fowl. [corr. of *Bridget*]

biddy-biddy (bid´ibidi), **biddi-biddi** *n.* (*pl.* **biddy-biddies, biddi-biddies**) **1** a New Zealand grassland plant, *Acaena viridior*, related to the rose. **2** the burrs of this plant. [Maori *piripiri*]

bide (bīd) *v.t.* (*past* **bided, †bode** (bōd), *p.p.* **bided**) **1** †to abide, await. **2** †to endure, suffer. **to bide one's time 1** to await an opportunity patiently. **2** †to abide, to stay. **3** †to continue, to remain. [OE *bīdan* (cp. Dut. *beiden*, OHG *bītan*)]

bident (bī´dent) *n.* a two-pronged fork. **bidentate, bidentated** (-tātid) *a.* having two teeth or toothlike processes.

bidet (bē´dā) *n.* a low basin for bathing the genital and anal area. [F]

bidirectional (bīdirek´shənəl) *a.* functioning in two directions.

Biedermeier (bē´dəmīə) *a.* **1** (of a style of furniture) common in Germany in the first half of the 19th cent. **2** (of German painting) conventional, bourgeois. [*Biedermeier*, fictitious poet created by L. Eichrodt in 1854]

biennial (bīen´iəl) *a.* **1** happening every two years. **2** lasting two years. **3** (of a plant) taking two years to reach maturity, ripen its seeds and die. ~*n.* **1** a biennial plant. **2** a two-yearly event. **biennially** *adv.* **biennium** (-əm) *n.* (*pl.* **bienniums, biennia**) a period of two years.

bier (biə) *n.* a stand or litter on which a corpse is placed, or on which the coffin is borne to the grave. [OE *bær* (*beran*, to bear; cp. BARROW[2])]

bifacial (bīfā´shəl) *a.* having two faces.

bifarious (bīfeə´riəs) *a.* **1** double. **2** ranged in two rows.

biff (bif) *v.t.* (*coll.*) to strike, to cuff. ~*n.* a blow. [onomat.]

biffin (bif´in) *n.* a variety of deep red cooking apple. [*beefing*, from BEEF, from the colour]

bifid (bī´fid) *a.* split into two lobes by a central cleft. **bifidity** (bifid´-) *n.* **bifidly** *adv.* [L *bifidus*, from BI-, *findere*, to split]

bifocal (bīfō´kəl) *a.* **1** with two foci. **2** having bifocal lenses. ~*n.pl.* bifocal spectacles. **bifocal lenses** *n.pl.* spectacle lenses divided for near and distant vision.

bifold (bī´fōld) *a.* twofold, double.

bifoliate (bīfō´liət) *a.* having two leaves.

biform (bī´fawm), **biformed** *a.* having or partaking of two forms.

BIFU *abbr.* Banking, Insurance and Finance Union.

bifurcate[1] (bī´fəkāt) *v.i.* to divide into two branches, forks or peaks. **bifurcation** (-kā´shən) *n.* **1** division into two parts or branches. **2** the point of such division. **3** either of two forks or branches. [med. L *bifurcātus*, p.p. of *bifurcārī*, from L *bifurcus*, two-pronged (BI-, *furca*, a fork, prong)]

bifurcate[2] (bī´fəkāt, -fœ´kət) *a.* divided into two forks or branches. [as BIFURCATE[1]]

big (big) *a.* (*comp.* **bigger,** *superl.* **biggest**) **1** large or great in bulk, quantity or intensity. **2** grown up. **3** pregnant, advanced in pregnancy. **4** important. **5** (*coll.*) magnanimous. **6** (*coll.*) boastful, pompous, pretentious. **7** most important, dominant. ~*adv.* **1** in a big way. **2** (*coll.*) boastfully. **3** pretentiously. **in a big way 1** (*coll.*) to a considerable degree. **2** (*coll.*) very enthusiastically. **to come/ go over big** to impress. **too big for one's boots/ breeches** unduly self-important. **to talk big** to boast. **to think big** to have high ambitions. **Big Apple** *n.* (*N Am., sl.*) New York City. **big band** *n.* a large jazz or dance band. **big bang** *n.* **1** in cosmology, the cataclysmic explosion of superdense matter from which one theory maintains the universe evolved. **2** (**Big Bang**) the deregulation of the London Stock Exchange in 1987. **3** (*fig.*) any fundamental change in organization. **big-bellied** *a.* **1** corpulent.

2 heavily pregnant. **Big Ben** *n.* the great bell and clock in the Houses of Parliament in Westminster. **Big Board** *n.* (*N Am., coll.*) 1 the New York Stock Exchange. 2 the quotation board in the New York Stock Exchange. **big-boned** *a.* of large frame. **Big Brother** *n.* a sinister and ruthless person or organization that exercises totalitarian control (from George Orwell's novel *1984* (1949)). **big bud** *n.* a disease of plants, esp. of blackcurrants, caused by a mite. **big bug** *n.* (*sl.*) BIGWIG (under BIG). **big business** *n.* large commercial organizations, esp. when exploitative, sinister or socially harmful. **big cheese** *n.* (*sl.*) an important person. **Big Chief, Big Daddy** *n.* (*sl.*) BIGWIG (under BIG). **big deal** *int.* (*sl.*) a derisory exclamation or response. **big dipper** *n.* 1 (*orig. N Am.*) ROLLER COASTER (under ROLL). 2 (*N Am.*, **Big Dipper**) the constellation Great Bear. **big end** *n.* the crankpin end of the connecting rod in an internal-combustion engine. **Bigfoot** *n.* (*pl.* **Bigfeet**) an animal like a yeti, supposed to live in NW America (from its big footprints). **big game** *n.* large animals hunted or fished for sport. **biggie** *n.* (*coll.*) something or someone important or large. **big gun** *n.* (*sl.*) an important person. **big-head** *n.* (*coll.*) a conceited individual. **big-headed** *a.* **big-headedness** *n.* **big-hearted** *a.* generous. **big-heartedness** *n.* **bighorn** *n.* the Rocky Mountain sheep, *Ovis montana.* **big house** *n.* 1 the largest or most important house in a village or town. 2 (*sl.*) a prison. **big idea** *n.* a grand plan or scheme. **what's the big idea?** (*coll.*) what is the purpose of this? **big league** *n.* (*N Am.*) a top league in a sport, esp. baseball. **big-league** *a.* (*coll.*) major, top. **big lie** *n.* (*esp. N Am.*) an intentional distortion of facts, esp. by a politician. **big money** *n.* large amounts of money, profit or pay. **bigmouth** *n.* (*sl.*) a loud, indiscreet, boastful person. **big-mouthed** *a.* **big name** *n.* a famous person, celebrity. **bigness** *n.* the quality of being big. **big noise, big pot, big shot** *n.* (*coll.*) a person of importance. **big smoke** *n.* (*sl.*) 1 London. 2 any large town. **big stick** *n.* (*coll.*) brutal force. **big talk** *n.* boasting, bragging. **big time** *n.* (*coll.*) the highest rank in a profession, esp. in entertainment. **big-timer** *n.* **big top** *n.* a large circus tent. **big tree** *n.* (*N Am.*) the giant sequoia, *Sequoiadendron giganteum.* **big wheel** *n.* 1 a Ferris wheel. 2 (*N Am., sl.*) BIGWIG (under BIG). **bigwig** *n.* (*coll.*) a person of importance (from the large wigs formerly worn). **big words** *n.pl.* boasting, bluff, exaggeration. [etym. uncertain]

biga (bē´gə, bī´-) *n.* (*pl.* **bigae** (-gē)) a two-horse chariot. [L]

bigamy (big´əmi) *n.* (*pl.* **bigamies**) marriage with another person while a legal spouse is living. **bigamist** *n.* a person who commits bigamy. **bigamous** *a.* of, relating to or involving bigamy. **bigamously** *adv.* [F *bigamie*, from OF *bigame*, bigamist, med. L *bigamus* (*bi-*, two, Gr. *gamos*, marriage)]

biggie, biggish BIG.

bight (bīt) *n.* 1 a bending, a bend. 2 a small bay, the space between two headlands. 3 the loop of a rope. [OE *byht* (*būgan*, to bend)]

bignonia (bignō´niə) *n.* a shrub of the genus *Bignonia*, containing the trumpet flower. [Abbé Jean-Paul *Bignon*, 1662–1743, librarian to Louis XIV]

bigot (big´ət) *n.* a person unreasonably and intolerantly devoted to a particular creed, system or party. **bigoted** *a.* affected with bigotry. **bigotedly** *adv.* **bigotry** (-ri) *n.* (*pl.* **bigotries**) 1 the character, conduct or mental condition of a bigot. 2 a bigot. [etym. unknown]

bijou (bē´zhoo) *n.* (*pl.* **bijoux** (bē´zhoo)) 1 a jewel, a trinket. 2 anything that is small, pretty or valuable. ~*a.* small, pretty or valuable. **bijouterie** (-zhoo´təri) *n.* jewellery, trinkets. [F, prob. Celtic (Bret. *bizou*, from *biz*, Corn. *bis*, Welsh *bys*, finger)]

bike[1] (bīk) *n.* 1 (*coll.*) a bicycle. 2 (*coll.*) a motorcycle. 3 (*Austral., sl.*) a prostitute. ~*v.i.* to ride a bicycle. **biker** *n.* (*coll.*) 1 a motorbike enthusiast. 2 a cyclist.

bike[2] (bīk), **byke** *n.* (*Sc.*) 1 a wasps', bees' or hornets' nest. 2 a swarm, a crowd, a rabble. [Sc. and North.; etym. unknown]

bikini (bikē´ni) *n.* (*pl.* **bikinis**) a brief, two-piece swimming costume. **bikini briefs** *n.pl.* brief underpants for women. **bikini line** *n.* the area of skin at the top of the legs, as revealed by someone wearing a bikini. [atoll in the N Pacific]

bikky BICKY.

bilabial (bīlā´biəl) *a.* 1 of or denoting a consonant produced with both lips, e.g. b, p, w. 2 two-lipped. ~*n.* a bilabial consonant. **bilabiate** (-ət) *a.* (*Bot.*) having two lips.

bilateral (bīlat´ərəl) *a.* 1 having, arranged on, of or relating to two sides. 2 affecting two parties. **bilaterally** *adv.* **bilateral symmetry** *n.* symmetry if cut in only one plane. [BI-, L *laterālis* (*latus -eris*, side)]

bilberry (bil´bəri) *n.* (*pl.* **bilberries**) 1 the fruit of a dwarf moorland shrub, *Vaccinium myrtillus*, also called *whortleberry* and *blaeberry.* 2 the shrub itself. 3 any of various other shrubs of the genus *Vaccinium.* [prob. from Scand. (cp. Dan. *böllebaer*)]

†**bilbo** (bil´bō) *n.* (*pl.* **bilbos, bilboes**) 1 a rapier, a sword. 2 (*fig.*) a bully, a swashbuckler. [*Bilbao*, in Spain, where good weapons were made]

Bildungsroman (bil´dungzrōmahn) *n.* a novel dealing with the emotional and spiritual education of its central figure. [G, *Bildung*, education, *Roman*, novel]

bile (bīl) *n.* 1 a bitter yellowish fluid which is secreted by the liver and aids digestion. 2 a medical disorder caused by faulty secretion of bile. 3 anger, choler. **bile duct** *n.* the duct which conveys bile to the duodenum. **bile pigment** *n.* colouring matter existing in bile. **biliary** (bil´i-) *a.* of or relating to the bile, the ducts which convey the bile, the small intestine, or the gall bladder. **bilious** (bil´yəs) *a.* 1 biliary. 2 produced or affected by bile. 3 peevish, ill-tempered. **biliously** *adv.* **biliousness** *n.* [F, from L *bīlis*, bile, anger]

bi-level (bī´levəl) *a.* 1 having or operating on two levels. 2 arranged on two planes. 3 (*N Am.*) (of a house) having the lower storey partially below ground level. ~*n.* (*N Am.*) a bi-level house.

bilge (bilj) *n.* 1 that part on which a ship rests when aground, where the vertical sides curve in. 2 (*pl.*) the bottom of a ship's floor. 3 the dirt which collects in the bottom of the hold of a ship; bilge water. 4 (*sl.*) worthless nonsense. 5 the bulging part of a cask. ~*v.i.* 1 to spring a leak in the bilge. 2 to bulge or swell. ~*v.t.* to stave in, to cause to spring a leak in the bilge. **bilge keel** *n.* a timber fixed under the bilge to hold a vessel up when ashore and to prevent rolling. **bilge pump** *n.* a pump to carry off bilge water. **bilge water** *n.* the foul water that collects in the bilge of a ship. [corr. of BULGE]

bilharzia (bilhah´ziə), **bilharziasis** (-ī´əsis), **bilharziosis** (-iō´sis) *n.* 1 a disease caused by blood flukes, characterized by blood loss and tissue damage, which is endemic to Asia, Africa and S America (also known as *schistosomiasis*). 2 a blood fluke. [Theodor *Bilharz*, 1825–62, German parasitologist]

biliary BILE.

bilingual (bīling´gwəl) *a.* 1 knowing or speaking two languages. 2 written or composed in two languages. ~*n.* a person who knows or speaks two languages. **bilingualism** *n.* the ability to speak two languages. **bilingually** *adv.* in two languages. **bilinguist** *n.* a bilingual person. [L *bilinguis* (BI-, *lingua*, tongue)]

bilious BILE.

bilirubin (biliroo´bin) *n.* the chief pigment of bile, a derivative of haemoglobin. [L *bilis*, bile, *ruber*, red]

bilk (bilk) *v.t.* 1 to cheat, to defraud. 2 to escape from, to elude. 3 to evade payment of. 4 to spoil (an opponent's score) in cribbage. ~*n.* **1** (*sl.*) a swindler. **2** an act of spoiling an opponent's score in cribbage. **bilker** *n.* [etym. uncertain]

bill[1] (bil) *n.* **1** a statement of particulars of goods delivered or services rendered. **2** a draft of a proposed law. **3** an advertisement or public announcement printed and distributed or posted up. **4** a theatre programme. **5** (*N Am.*) a banknote. **6** (*Law*) a written statement of a case. **7** a petition to the Scottish Court of Session. **8** †a promissory note. **9** †an inventory. **10** †a document of any kind. ~*v.t.* **1** to announce by bills or placards, to cover with bills or placards. **2** to put into a programme. **3** to present an account for payment to. **to fill/ fit the bill** to prove satisfactory, to be what is required. **to foot a bill** FOOT. **to head/ top the bill 1** to have one's name at the top of a playbill. **2** to be the star attraction. **billable** *a.* **billboard** *n.* (*N Am.*) a street hoarding. **bill broker, bill discounter** *n.* a person who deals in bills of exchange and promissory notes. **bill chamber** *n.* a department of the Scottish Court of Session for summary proceedings on petition. **billed**[1] *a.* named in a programme or advertisement. **billfold** *n.* (*N Am.*) a wallet for notes. **billhead** *n.* a business form with the name and address of the firm etc. at the top. **billing** *n.* **1** sending out invoices. **2** the relative position of a performer or act in a programme or advertisement. **Bill of Attainder** *n.* a bill introduced into the British Parliament for attainting a person without judicial process. **bill of exchange** *n.* a written order from one person to another to pay a sum on a given date to a designated person. **bill of fare** *n.* **1** a list of dishes, a menu. **2** a programme. **bill of goods** *n.* (*N Am.*) a batch of goods. **to sell someone a bill of goods** to deceive someone. **bill of health** *n.* a document testifying to the state of health of a ship's company. **bill of imprest** *n.* an order entitling the bearer to have money paid in advance. **bill of indictment** *n.* an accusation in writing, submitted to a grand jury. **bill of lading** *n.* **1** a master of a ship's acknowledgment of goods received. **2** a list of goods to be shipped. **bill of privilege** *n.* a peer's petition to be tried by their peers. **Bill of Rights** *n.* a summary of rights and liberties claimed by a people and guaranteed by the state, esp. the English statute of 1689 and the first ten amendments to the US Constitution protecting the freedom of the individual. **bill of sale** *n.* a legal document for the transfer of personal property. **bill of sight** *n.* permission for a merchant to land goods for inspection of which the quantity or quality are unknown. **bill of store** *n.* **1** a licence from the customs authorities to ship dutiable goods for consumption on the voyage without payment of duties. **2** a licence to reimport goods formerly exported. **billposter** *n.* a person who sticks bills on walls etc. **billposting** *n.* **billsticker** *n.* **billsticking** *n.* [A-F and ME *bille*, late L *billa*, corr. of *bulla*, a writing, a sealed writing (formerly, a stud or seal)]

bill[2] (bil) *n.* **1** the horny beak of birds or of the platypus. **2** a beaklike projection or promontory. **3** the point of the fluke of an anchor. ~*v.i.* **1** (of doves) to lay the bills together. **2** to exhibit affection. **to bill and coo 1** to kiss and fondle. **2** to make love. **billed**[2] *a.* furnished with a beak or bill (*usu. in comb.*, as *hard-billed, tooth-billed* etc.). [OE *bile*]

bill[3] (bil) *n.* **1** an obsolete weapon resembling a halberd. **2** a billhook. **billhook** *n.* a thick, heavy knife with a hooked end, used for chopping brushwood etc. **billman** *n.* (*pl.* **billmen**) a soldier armed with a bill. [OE *bil, bill* (cp. G *Bille*)]

billabong (bil´əbong) *n.* **1** a stream flowing from a river to a dead end. **2** a creek that fills seasonally. [Austral. Abor. *billa*, river, *bong*, dead]

billed[1] BILL[1].

billed[2] BILL[2].

billet[1] (bil´it) *n.* **1** quarters assigned to a soldier or others, esp. in a civilian household. **2** a ticket requiring a householder to furnish food and lodgings for a soldier or others. **3** (*coll.*) a situation, an appointment. **4** a small paper, a note. ~*v.t.* (*pres.p.* **billeting,** *past, p.p.* **billeted**) **1** to quarter (soldiers or others), esp. on a civilian household. **2** to provide quarters for (soldiers or others) in one's household. **billetee** (-tē´) *n.* **billeter** *n.* [A-F *billette*, dim. of *bille*, BILL[1]]

billet[2] (bil´it) *n.* **1** a small log or faggot for firing. **2** a bar, wedge or ingot of gold or silver. **3** (*Archit.*) a short cylindrical piece placed lengthwise at regular intervals in a hollow moulding in Norman work. **4** (*Her.*) a rectangle set on end. [F *billete* (*billot*), dim. of *bille*, a log of wood (etym. unknown)]

billet-doux (bilādoo´) *n.* (*pl.* **billets-doux** (bilādooz´)) a love letter. [F, a sweet letter]

billiards (bil´yədz) *n.* a game with three balls, which are driven about on a cloth-lined table with a cue. **billiard ball** *n.* a ball used in billiards. **billiard cue** *n.* a tapering stick used to drive the balls. **billiard marker** *n.* **1** a person who marks the points made by players. **2** an apparatus for registering these. **billiard table** *n.* a table for playing billiards on. [F *billard*, a stick, a cue, dim. of *bille*, BILLET[2]]

billingsgate (bil´ingzgāt) *n.* scurrilous abuse, foul language. [*Billingsgate*, the former London fish market]

billion (bil´yən) *n.* (*pl.* **billions, billion**) **1** one thousand million, i.e. 1,000,000,000 or 10^9. **2** †in Britain, one million million, i.e. 1,000,000,000,000 or 10^{12}. **3** (*pl.*) any very large number. ~*a.* amounting to a billion. **billionaire** (-neə´) *n.* a person having a billion pounds, dollars etc. or more. **billionth** *a., n.* [F, coined from *million*, with pref. BI-]

billon (bil´ən) *n.* base metal, esp. silver alloyed with copper. [F, base metal, orig. mass, from *bille*, see BILLET[2]]

billow (bil´ō) *n.* **1** a great swelling wave of the sea. **2** anything sweeping onward like a mighty wave. **3** anything curved or swelling like a wave. **4** (*pl., poet.*) the sea. ~*v.i.* **1** to surge. **2** to rise in billows. **billowy** *a.* characterized by, of the nature of, or like billows. [Icel. *bylgja*, a billow (cp. OE *ballgan*, to swell)]

billy (bil´i), **billie** *n.* (*pl.* **billies**) **1** (*esp. Austral.*) a metal can or pot for boiling water etc. over a campfire. **2** (*N Am.*) a policeman's club. **billycan** *n.* (*esp. Austral.*) a billy. **billy goat** *n.* a male goat. [prob. from the personal name]

billy-o (bil´iō) *n.* used only as below. **like billy-o** (*sl.*) vigorously, strongly. [etym. unknown]

bilobed (bīlōbd´), **bilobate** (-lō´bāt) *a.* having or divided into two lobes.

bilocular (bīlok´ūlə) *a.* having two cells or compartments.

biltong (bil´tong) *n.* (*S Afr.*) strips of lean meat dried in the sun. [Afrikaans *bil*, buttock, *tong*, tongue]

BIM *abbr.* British Institute of Management.

bimanal (bim´ənəl), **bimanous** (bim´ənəs) *a.* two-handed; of or belonging to the group of animals with two hands, as in the higher primates and man. [BI-, L *manus*, a hand]

bimbo (bim´bō) *n.* (*pl.* **bimbos**) (*sl.*) **1** an attractive person, esp. a woman, who is naive or of limited intelligence. **2** a foolish or stupid person. **3** a whore. [It., a child]

bi-media (bīmē´diə) *a.* using or relating to two media, such as radio or television.

bimensal (bīmen´səl), **bimestrial** (-mes´tri-) *a.* **1** continuing for two months. **2** occurring every two months.

bimeridian (bīmərid´iən) *a.* of, relating to or recurring at midday and midnight.

bimetallism (bīmet´əlizm) *n.* the employment of two

metals (gold and silver) in the currency of a country, at a fixed ratio to each other, as standard coin and legal tender. **bimetallic** (-mital´-) *a.* 1 composed of two metals. 2 of or relating to bimetallism. **bimetallic strip** *n.* a strip of two metals bonded together which expand by different amounts when heated. **bimetallist** *n.* a supporter or advocate of bimetallism. [F *bimétallique*]

bimillenary (bīmilen´əri) *n.* (*pl.* **bimillenaries**) 1 a period of 2000 years. 2 a 2000th anniversary. ~*a.* 1 consisting of or relating to 2000 years. 2 of or relating to a bimillenary.

bimodal (bīmō´dəl) *a.* having two modes (*bimodal distribution*).

bimonthly (bīmŭnth´li) *a.* 1 occurring once in two months. 2 occurring twice a month. 3 lasting two months. ~*adv.* 1 once every two months. 2 twice a month. ~*n.* (*pl.* **bimonthlies**) a bimonthly publication.

Usage note It is often impossible to tell in a particular context whether *bimonthly*, *biweekly* and *biyearly* mean every two months, weeks etc. or twice a month etc. It is safer to use *two-monthly* and *twice-monthly* or their equivalents, or to paraphrase in some other way.

---

bin (bin) *n.* 1 a box or other receptacle for bread, corn, wine etc. 2 a container for rubbish. 3 wine from a particular bin. 4 a large canvas receptacle into which hops are picked. 5 (*sl., derog.*) a mental hospital. ~*v.t.* (*pres.p.* **binning,** *past, p.p.* **binned**) 1 to stow in a bin. 2 to throw away as rubbish. **bin-end** *n.* a bottle of wine sold off cheaply because there are so few left of the bin. **bin liner** *n.* a plastic bag used to line a rubbish bin. **binman** *n.* (*pl.* **binmen**) a refuse collector. [OE *binn* (perh. from L *benna*, of Celtic origin)]

bin- BI-.

binary (bī´nəri) *a.* 1 consisting of a pair or pairs. 2 double, dual. ~*n.* (*pl.* **binaries**) 1 something having two parts. 2 a binary number. 3 a binary star. **binary code** *n.* (*Comput.*) a system that uses the binary digits 0 and 1 to represent characters. **binary compound** *n.* a chemical compound of two elements. **binary digit** *n.* either of two digits, 0 or 1, used in a binary system of notation. **binary fission** *n.* the division of a cell into two parts. **binary form** *n.* a musical composition having two themes or sections. **binary notation** *n.* a number system using the base two (instead of base ten), numbers being represented as combinations of one and zero: because the two digits can be represented electronically as on and off, the system is used in computers. **binary number** *n.* a number expressed in binary notation. **binary star, binary system** *n.* a system of two stars revolving around a common centre of gravity. **binary tree** *n.* a diagram used for classification or decision-making, which represents choices by right- or left-branching paths. [L *bīnārius*, from *bīnī*, two each]

binaural (bīnaw´rəl) *a.* 1 relating to, having or using two ears. 2 employing two channels in recording or transmitting sound.

bind (bīnd) *v.t.* (*past, p.p.* **bound** (bownd)) 1 to tie, or fasten together, to or on something. 2 to put in bonds, confine. 3 to wrap or confine with a cover or bandage. 4 to form a border to. 5 to cover, secure or strengthen, by means of a band. 6 to sew (a book) and put into a cover. 7 to tie up. 8 to cause to cohere. 9 to make constipated. 10 to oblige to do something by contract. 11 to oblige, to engage, to compel. 12 to confirm or ratify. ~*v.i.* 1 to cohere. 2 to grow stiff and hard. 3 to tie up. 4 to be obligatory. 5 (*sl.*) to complain. ~*n.* 1 a band or tie. 2 a bine. 3 a sign which groups notes together. 4 a tie or brace. 5 indurated clay mixed with oxide of iron. 6 (*coll.*) an annoying or frustrating predicament, a bore. **to bind down** to restrain by formal stipulations. **to bind over** to place under legal obligation. **to bind up** to bandage. **binder** *n.* 1 a cover or folder for loose papers, correspondence etc. 2 something which binds or fastens. 3 a person who binds. 4 a person who binds sheaves. 5 a reaping machine that binds grain into sheaves. 6 a straw band for binding sheaves of corn. 7 a bookbinder. 8 a clip. 9 a tie-beam. 10 a bandage. 11 a cementing agent. 12 a principal part of a ship's frame, such as a keel, transom, beam etc. **bindery** *n.* (*pl.* **binderies**) a bookbinder's workshop. **binding** *a.* obligatory. ~*n.* 1 the act of binding. 2 something which binds. 3 the state of being bound. 4 the act, art or particular style of bookbinding. 5 a book cover, braid or other edging. **bindingly** *adv.* **bindingness** *n.* **bindweed** *n.* 1 a plant of the genus *Convolvulus.* 2 any of several other climbing plants, such as honeysuckle. [OE *bindan* (cp. Goth. *bindan*, G *binden*, Indo-Eur. *bhendh*)]

bindi-eye (bin´diī) *n.* a small Australian herbaceous plant, *Calotis cuneifolia*, with burlike fruits. [perh. Austral. Abor.]

bine (bīn) *n.* a flexible shoot or stem, esp. of the hop (cp. WOODBINE (under WOOD)). [BIND]

binervate (bīnœ´vət) *a.* having two nerves or leaf ribs.

Binet–Simon scale (bēnāsēmō´, -sī´mən), **Binet–Simon test** *n.* an intelligence test employing graded tasks for subjects (usu. children) according to age. [Alfred *Binet*, 1857–1911, and Theodore *Simon*, 1873–1961, French psychologists]

bing (bing) *n.* 1 (*dial.*) a heap, a pile. 2 (*Mining*) a heap of alum or of metallic ore. [Icel. *bingr* (cp. Swed. *binge*)]

binge (binj) *n.* (*coll.*) 1 a drinking spree. 2 overindulgence in anything. ~*v.i.* (*pres.p.* **bingeing, binging,** *past, p.p.* **binged**) 1 to indulge in a drinking spree. 2 to overindulge in anything. [etym. uncertain; perh. dial. *binge*, to soak]

bingo (bing´gō) *n.* 1 a game in which random numbers are called out and then marked off by players on a card with numbered squares, the winner being the first to mark off all or a predetermined sequence of numbers. 2 an exclamation made by the winner of a bingo game. 3 an exclamation expressing the suddenness of an event. [etym. uncertain]

bink (bingk) *n.* (*Sc.*) 1 a bench. 2 a shelf, a dresser. 3 a bank. [ME *benk*, BENCH]

binnacle (bin´əkəl) *n.* the case in which the ship's compass is kept. [formerly *bittacle*, Sp. *bitacula*, L *habitāculum*, a dwelling-place (*habitāre*, to dwell, freq. of *habēre*, to have, hold)]

binocular (binok´ūlə) *a.* 1 having two eyes. 2 suited for use by both eyes. ~*n.* a binocular microscope. **binoculars** *n.pl.* a field or opera glass with tubes for both eyes. **binocular vision** *n.* vision using both eyes, which gives good depth perception.

binomial (bīnō´miəl) *a.* 1 binominal. 2 of or relating to binomials. ~*n.* a mathematical expression consisting of two terms united by the signs + or -. **binomial distribution** *n.* a statistical distribution of the possible number of successful outcomes in a specified number of trials in an experiment with a constant probability of success in each. **binomially** *adv.* **binomial nomenclature** *n.* a system of classifying plants and animals using two names, the first one indicating the genus and the second the species. **binomial theorem** *n.* a formula discovered by Newton by which a binomial quantity can be raised to any power without actual multiplication. **binominal** (-nom´inəl) *a.* having two names, the first denoting the genus, the second the species. [L *nomen*, a name]

binovular (binov´ūlə) *a.* of, relating to or developed from two ova.

bint (bint) *n.* (*sl., derog.*) a girl or woman. [Arab., lit. daughter]

binturong (bin´tūrong) *n.* a SE Asian arboreal mammal,

Arctictis binturong, with a shaggy black coat and a prehensile tail.

bio- (bī´ō) *comb. form* of or relating to life or living things. [Gr. *bios*, life]

bioassay (bīōəsā´, bīōas´ā) *n.* the measuring of the strength and effect of a substance such as a drug by testing it on living cells or tissues.

bioastronautics (bīōastrənaw´tiks) *n.* the study of the effects of space travel on living organisms.

biochemistry (bīōkem´istri) *n.* the chemistry of physiological processes occurring in living organisms. **biochemical** *a.* **biochemist** *n.*

biocide (bī´ōsīd) *n.* **1** a chemical which kills living organisms. **2** the destruction of life. **biocidal** (-sī´-) *a.*

biocoenosis (bīōsēnō´sis), (*N Am.*) **biocenosis** *n.* (*pl.* **biocoenoses, biocenoses**) **1** the relationship between plants and animals that are ecologically interdependent. **2** an association of ecologically interdependent organisms. **biocoenology** (-nol´əji) *n.* **biocoenotic** (-not´ik) *a.*

biodegradable (bīōdigrā´dəbəl) *a.* capable of being broken down by bacteria. **biodegradability** (-bil´-) *n.* **biodegradation** (-degrədā´shən) *n.*

biodiversity (bīōdīvœ´sitī) *n.* the existence of a wide variety of plant and animal species.

bioenergetics (bīōenəjet´iks) *n.* the study of energy relationships in living organisms.

bioengineering (bīōenjinē´ring) *n.* **1** the provision of aids such as artificial limbs, hearts etc. to restore body functions. **2** the design, construction and maintenance of equipment used in biosynthesis. **bioengineer** *n., v.t.*

bioethics (bīōeth´iks) *n.* the study of ethical issues arising from advances in medicine and science. **bioethical** *a.* **bioethicist** (-sist) *n.*

biofeedback (bīōfēd´bak) *n.* a method of regulating involuntary body functions, e.g. heartbeat, by conscious mental control.

bioflavonoid (bīōflā´vənoid) *n.* a group of substances found in citrus fruits and blackcurrants, also called *citrin* and *vitamin P.*

biogas (bī´ōgas) *n.* gas, such as methane, that is produced by the action of bacteria on organic waste matter.

biogenesis (bīōjen´isis), **biogeny** (-oj´əni) *n.* the doctrine that living matter originates only from living matter. **biogenetic** (-jinet´-), **biogenic** (-jen´-) *a.*

biogeography (bīōjiog´rəfi) *n.* the study of the distribution of plant and animal life over the globe. **biogeographer** *n.* **biogeographical** (-jēəgraf´-) *a.*

biography (bīog´rəfi) *n.* (*pl.* **biographies**) **1** the history of the life of a person. **2** literature dealing with personal history. **biographer** *n.* a writer of biography. **biographic** (bīəgraf´-), **biographical** *a.* of, relating to or containing biography. **biographically** *adv.* [late Gr. *biographia*]

biohazard (bīōhaz´əd) *n.* a risk to human health or the environment from biological research.

Biol. *abbr.* Biology.

biology (bīol´əji) *n.* the science of physical life or living matter in all its phases. **biologic** (-loj´-) *a.* biological. **biological** *a.* of or relating to biology. **biological clock** *n.* the inherent mechanism that regulates cyclic physiological processes in living organisms. **biological control** *n.* the control of pests etc. by using other organisms that destroy them. **biological warfare** *n.* warfare involving the use of disease germs. **biologist** *n.*

bioluminescence (bīōloomines´əns) *n.* the production of light by living organisms such as insects, marine animals and fungi. **bioluminescent** *a.*

biomass (bī´ōmas) *n.* the total weight of living organisms in a unit of area.

biomathematics (bīōmathəmat´iks) *n.* the study of the application of mathematics to biology.

biome (bī´ōm) *n.* **1** a large ecological community, having flora and fauna which have adapted to the particular conditions in which they live. **2** the geographical region containing an ecological community.

biomechanics (bīōmikan´iks) *n.* the study of the mechanics of movement in living creatures.

biomedicine (bīōmed´sin, -isin) *n.* the study of the medical and biological effects of stressful environments, esp. space travel. **biomedical** (-ikəl) *a.*

biometry (bīom´itri) *n.* the statistical measurement of biological data. **biometric** (-met´-) *a.* **biometrical** *a.* **biometrician** (-trish´ən) *n.* **biometrics** *n.*

biomorph (bī´ōmawf) *n.* a decoration representing a living thing. **biomorphic** (-maw´fik) *a.*

bionics (bīon´iks) *n.* **1** the science of applying knowledge of biological systems to the development of electronic equipment. **2** the replacement of parts of the body or enhancement of physiological functions by electrical or mechanical equipment. **bionic** *a.* **1** of or relating to bionics. **2** in science fiction, having exceptional powers through the electronic augmentation of physical processes. **bionically** *adv.*

bionomics (bīōnom´iks) *n.* ecology. **bionomic** *a.*

biont (bī´ont) *n.* a living organism. **-biont** (biont) *comb. form* **-biontic** (bion´-) *comb. form* **biontic** (-on´-) *a.* forming nouns meaning belonging to a specific environment. [prob. from Gr. *biount-*, *biōn*, pres.p. of *bioun*, to live from *bios*, life]

biophysics (bīōfiz´iks) *n.* the application of physics to living things. **biophysical** *a.* **biophysicist** (-sist) *n.*

biopic (bī´ōpik) *n.* a film, often giving a glamorized and uncritical account of the life of a celebrity. [*bio*graphical *pic*ture]

bioplasm (bī´ōplazm) *n.* protoplasm. **bioplast** (-plast) *n.* a nucleus of germinal matter.

biopsy (bī´opsi) *n.* (*pl.* **biopsies**) the removal and diagnostic examination of tissue or fluids from a living body.

biorhythm (bī´ōridhm) *n.* **1** a supposed biological cycle governing physical, emotional and intellectual moods and performance. **2** any periodic change in an organism's behaviour or physiology. **biorhythmic** (-ridh´mik) *a.* **biorhythmically** *adv.*

BIOS *abbr.* (*Comput.*) basic input-output system.

bioscope (bī´ōskōp) *n.* **1** a cinematograph. **2** (*S Afr.*) a cinema.

biosensor (bī´ōsensə) *n.* an electronic chip covered with a layer of e.g. an enzyme which can sense the presence of a particular substance, used in diagnosing illness, detecting the presence of drugs etc.

-biosis (biō´sis) *comb. form* forming nouns referring to a specific mode of life. **-biotic** (biot´ik) *comb. form* forming adjectives. [Gr. *biōsis*, way of life]

biosphere (bī´ōsfiə) *n.* the portion of the earth's surface and atmosphere which is inhabited by living things.

biosynthesis (bīōsin´thəsis) *n.* the production of chemical compounds by living organisms. **biosynthetic** (-thet´-) *a.*

biota (bīō´tə) *n.* the flora and fauna of a region.

biotechnology (bīōteknol´əji) *n.* the use of microorganisms and biological processes in industry. **biotechnological** (-nəloj´ikəl) *a.* **biotechnologist** (-nol´əjist) *n.*

biotic (bīot´ik) *a.* **1** relating to life or living things. **2** (of a factor in an ecosystem) of biological origin.

biotin (bī´ōtin) *n.* a vitamin of the B complex (also known as vitamin H) found esp. in liver and egg yolk. [Gr. *biotos*, sustenance]

biotite (bī´ətīt) *n.* a black or dark-coloured micaceous mineral. [J. B. *Biot*, 1774–1862, French physicist]

bioturbation (bīōtœbā´shən) *n.* the disturbance of layers of soil by the action of living creatures.

biparous (bip´ərəs) *a.* **1** bringing forth two at a birth. **2** producing two at once. [L *parere*, to produce]

bipartisan (bīpahtizan´, -pah´-) *a.* involving or supported by two or more (political) parties. **bipartisanship** (-zan´-) *n.*

bipartite (bīpah´tīt) *a.* 1 comprising or having two parts. 2 (of an agreement etc.) affecting or corresponding to two parties. 3 (of leaves) divided into two corresponding parts from the apex almost to the base.

biped (bī´ped) *a.* having two feet. ~*n.* an animal having only two feet, such as man and birds. **bipedal** (-pē´-) *a.* **bipedalism** *n.* **bipedality** (-pidal´iti) *n.* [L *pes, pedis*, a foot]

bipetalous (bīpet´ələs) *a.* having two petals in a flower.

biphenyl (bīfē´nīl) *n.* (*Chem.*) an organic compound which contains two phenyl groups.

bipinnaria (bīpineə´riə) *n.* a starfish larva with two bands of cilia.

bipinnate (bīpin´ət), **bipinnated** (-ātid) *a.* (of a pinnate leaf) having pinnated leaflets.

biplane (bī´plān) *a.* an aircraft with two wings one above the other.

bipolar (bīpō´lə) *a.* having two poles or opposite extremities. **bipolarity** (-lar´iti) *n.*

biquadratic (bīkwodrat´ik) *a.* 1 raised to the fourth power. 2 of or relating to the fourth power. ~*n.* the fourth power, the square of a square. **biquadratic equation** *n.* an equation containing the fourth power of the unknown quantity.

birch (bœch) *n.* 1 any tree of the genus *Betula*, with slender limbs and thin, tough bark. 2 the wood of any of these trees, also called birchwood. 3 a birch-rod. 4 (*New Zeal.*) any of various similar trees. 5 (*Austral.*) a variety of beech tree. 6 (*N Am.*) a canoe made from the bark of *Betula papyracea*. ~*a.* birchen. ~*v.t.* to chastise with a birch-rod, to flog. **birch-bark** *n.* 1 the bark of *Betula papyracea*. 2 (*N Am.*) a canoe made from this. **birchen** *a.* composed of birch. **birching** *n.* a flogging. **birch-rod** *n.* a rod made from birch twigs for flogging. [OE *birce, beorc* (cp. OHG *biricha*, Sansk. *bhurja*, Icel. *björk*, Sc. *birk*)]

bird (bœd) *n.* 1 any feathered vertebrate animal of the class Aves. 2 a game bird. 3 (*sl.*) a girl, young woman. 4 (*coll.*) a person. 5 (*sl.*) a prison. 6 (*sl.*) a prison term. **like a bird** without difficulty or resistance. **(strictly) for the birds** worthless, not serious. **the bird is/ has flown** the person concerned has escaped. **the birds and the bees** reproduction; the facts of life. **to get the bird** 1 to be hissed. 2 to be fired or dismissed. **bird bath** *n.* a small usu. ornamental basin for birds to bathe in. **birdbrained** *a.* (*coll.*) stupid, silly. **birdbrain** *n.* **birdcage** *n.* a wire or wicker cage for holding birds. **bird call** *n.* 1 the cry of a bird. 2 an instrument for imitating the cry of birds. **bird-catcher** *n.* a professional trapper of birds. **bird-catching** *a.* (of plants and insects) able to trap birds. **bird cherry** *n.* a wild cherry, *Prunus padus*, which has clusters of white flowers. **birder** *n.* (*esp. N Am.*) a birdwatcher. **bird-fancier** *n.* a person who collects, breeds or rears birds. **birdie** *n.* 1 a little bird (used as a term of endearment). 2 a hole in golf made in one under par. ~*v.t.* (*3rd pers. sing. pres.* **birdies**, *pres.p.* **birdying**, *past, p.p.* **birdied**) to play (a hole) in a birdie. **birding** *n.* 1 bird-catching. 2 fowling. 3 birdwatching. ~*a.* of, relating to or used in fowling, bird-catching or birdwatching. **birding-piece** *n.* a fowling-piece. **bird in the hand** *n.* something in one's possession (alluding to the proverb a bird in the hand is worth two in the bush). **birdlime** *n.* a sticky substance used to snare birds. **bird-nesting, bird's nesting** *n.* seeking birds' nests to steal the eggs. **bird of paradise** *n.* any of the New Guinea Paradiseidae which have brilliantly coloured plumage. **bird of passage** *n.* 1 a migratory bird. 2 a person who travels frequently and rarely stays long in one place. **bird of peace** *n.* the dove. **bird of prey** *n.* a bird such as the hawk or vulture which feeds on carrion or hunts other animals for food. **bird sanctuary** *n.* an area where birds are protected. **birdseed** *n.* special seed (hemp, canary seed etc.) given to cagebirds. **bird's-eye** *a.* 1 of, belonging to or resembling a bird's eye. 2 having eye-like markings. 3 seen from above, as by the eye of a bird, esp. in *bird's-eye view*. ~*n.* 1 a kind of tobacco in which the ribs of the leaves are cut with the fibre. 2 any of several plants with small, round, bright flowers. 3 the germander speedwell. 4 a pattern used for fabric, made up of small diamond shapes with a spot in the centre of each. **bird's-eye primrose** *n.* an English wild plant, *Primula farinosa*. **bird's-foot, bird-foot** *n.* (*pl.* **bird's-foots, bird-foots**) any plant which has a part like the foot of a bird, esp. *Ornithopus perpusillus*. **bird's-foot sea-star** *n.* a British echinoderm, *Palmipes membranaceus*. **bird's-foot trefoil** *n.* a British wild flower, *Lotus corniculatus*, which has yellow flowers streaked with red. **bird's nest** *n.* 1 the nest of a bird. 2 an edible bird's nest. 3 a cask or other shelter for the lookout man at a masthead. ~*v.i.* to search for birds' nests. **bird's-nest fern** *n.* any of several exotic ferns. **bird's-nest orchid** *n.* *Neottia nidus-avis*, a British orchid. **bird's nest soup** *n.* a rich Chinese soup made from the dried coating of the nests of swifts and other birds. **birds of a feather** *n.pl.* people of similar character or interests. **bird song** *n.* the musical call of a bird or birds. **bird's-tongue** *n.* any of several plants, probably from the shape of their leaves. **bird-strike** *n.* a collision of a bird with an aircraft. **bird table** *n.* a small elevated platform for wild birds to feed from. **birdwatcher** *n.* a person who observes wild birds in their natural habitat. **birdwatching** *n.* [OE *brid*, a bird, the young of any bird (etym. uncertain)]

birefringence (bīrifrin´jəns) *n.* the formation of two unequally refracted rays of light from a single unpolarized ray. **birefringent** *a.*

bireme (bī´rēm) *n.* (*Hist.*) a Roman galley with two banks of oars. ~*a.* having two banks of oars. [L *birēmis* (BI-, *rēmus*, oar)]

biretta (biret´ə), **berretta** (biret´ə) *n.* a square cap worn by clerics of the Roman Catholic and Anglican Churches. [It. *berretta*, late L *birretum* (*birrus, byrrhus*, a mantle with a hood, prob. from Gr. *purrhos*, flame-coloured)]

biriani (biriah´ni), **biryani** *n.* an Indian dish of spiced rice mixed with meat or fish. [Urdu]

birl (bœl) *v.i.* (*Sc.*) to spin round, to rotate noisily. ~*v.t.* 1 to spin. 2 to throw, toss. ~*n.* BURL². [prob. onomat.]

Biro® (bī´rō), **biro** *n.* (*pl.* **Biros, biros**) a type of ballpoint pen. [Laszlo *Biró*, 1900–85, Hungarian inventor]

birostrate (bīros´trāt) *a.* having two beaks or beaklike processes.

birth (bœth) *n.* 1 the act of bringing forth. 2 the bearing of offspring. 3 the act of coming into life or being born. 4 that which is brought forth. 5 parentage, extraction, lineage, esp. high extraction, high lineage. 6 condition resulting from birth. 7 origin, beginning, product, creation. ~*v.t.* (*N Am., coll.*) 1 to give birth to. 2 to help (a woman) give birth. **to give birth (to)** GIVE. **birth certificate** *n.* an official document giving particulars of a person's birth. **birth control** *n.* the artificial control of reproduction, esp. by means of contraceptives. **birth control pill** *n.* a contraceptive pill. **birthday** *n.* the day on which a person was born, or its anniversary. ~*a.* of or relating to the day of a person's birth, or to its anniversary. **birthday book** *n.* a kind of diary with spaces for noting the birthdays of relatives and friends. **birthday honours** *n.pl.* knighthoods, peerages and other honours conferred on the sovereign's official birthday. **birthday present** *n.* a present given to a person on their birthday. **birthday suit** *n.* (*coll.*) one's bare skin, nudity. **birthing** *n.* the act or process of giving birth. **birthing chair** *n.* a chair in which a woman can sit while giving birth. **birthing pool** *n.* a pool in a hospital or in a woman's home in which she can give birth or experience labour. **birthmark** *n.* a mark or blemish formed on the body of a child at or before birth. **birth mother** *n.* the woman who has given birth to a child, not the adoptive mother. **birth pill** *n.* a contraceptive pill. **birthplace** *n.* the place at which someone or something was born. **birth rate** *n.* the percentage of live births to the population. **birthright** *n.* rights belonging to an eldest son, to a member of a family, order or people, or to a person as a human being. **birthstone** *n.* a gemstone associated with the month of someone's birth. **birthweight** *n.* a baby's weight at birth. [ME *byrthe*, Icel. *byrthr*, *burthr* (Gmc. *beran*, to bear)]

biryani BIRIANI.

BIS *abbr.* Bank for International Settlements.

biscuit (bis´kit) *n.* **1** a thin flour-cake baked until it is highly dried. **2** pottery moulded and baked in an oven, but not glazed. **3** a light brown colour. *~a.* light brown in colour. **to take the biscuit 1** (*coll.*) to be the best of the lot. **2** (*coll.*) to be incredible. **3** (*iron.*) to be the most foolish, unacceptable etc. **biscuity** *a.* [OF *bescoit*, F *biscuit*, L *bis coctus*, twice cooked (*coctus*, p.p. of *coquere*)]

bise (bēz) *n.* a keen, dry, northerly wind prevalent in Switzerland and adjacent countries. [F (med. L and Prov. *bisa*, OHG *bīsa*)]

bisect (bīsekt´) *v.t.* to divide into two (equal) parts. *~v.i.* to fork. **bisection** *n.* **1** division into two (generally equal) parts. **2** division into two branches. **bisector** *n.* **1** a person who bisects. **2** a bisecting line. [BI-, L *sectum*, p.p. of *secāre*, to cut]

biserial (bīsiə´riəl), **biseriate** (-ət) *a.* arranged in two rows.

bisexual (bīsek´sūəl, -shəl) *a.* **1** (*Biol.*) having both sexes combined in one individual. **2** attracted sexually to both sexes. **3** of or relating to both sexes. *~n.* a bisexual individual. **bisexuality** (-sūal´-, -sh-) *n.*

bish (bish) *n.* (*sl.*) a mistake. [etym. uncertain]

bishop (bish´əp) *n.* **1** a dignitary presiding over a diocese, ranking beneath an archbishop, and above the priests and deacons. **2** a spiritual superintendent in the early Christian Church. **3** a piece in chess, having the upper part shaped like a mitre. **4** a beverage composed of wine, oranges and sugar. **bishopric** (-rik) *n.* the diocese, jurisdiction or office of a bishop. **bishop's-cap** *n.* mitrewort. **bishop's court** *n.* an ecclesiastical court held in the cathedral of each diocese. **bishop suffragan.** *n.* a suffragan bishop. [OE *biscop*, L *episcopus*, Gr. *episkopos*, an overlooker, an inspector]

bisk BISQUE[1].

bismillah (bismil´ə) *int.* in the name of Allah. [Arab.]

bismuth (biz´məth) *n.* **1** a reddish white crystalline metallic element, at. no. 83, chem. symbol Bi, used in alloys and in medicine. **2** any compound of this element used medicinally. [G, more commonly *Wismut*]

bison (bī´sən) *n.* (*pl.* **bison**) either of two large bovine mammals of the genus *Bison*, with a shaggy coat and a large hump, the European bison, *B. bonasus*, now very rare, and the American bison, *B. bison*, commonly called buffalo, once found in great numbers in the mid-Western prairies. [L, from Gmc. *wisand* (cp. OE *wesend*, OHG *wismit*, G *Wisent*)]

bisque[1] (bisk), **bisk** *n.* a rich soup made by boiling down fish, birds or the like. [F]

bisque[2] (bisk) *n.* in tennis, golf etc., a stroke allowed at any time to the weaker party to equalize the players. [F, etym. uncertain]

bisque[3] (bisk) *n.* a kind of unglazed white porcelain used for statuettes. [BISCUIT]

bissextile (bisek´stīl) *a.* of or relating to a leap year. *~n.* a leap year. [L *bissextīlis annus*, the bissextile year (a term applied to every fourth year, because then the sixth day before the calends of March was reckoned twice)]

bistable (bīstā´bəl) *a.* (of a valve or electrical circuit) having two stable states.

bister BISTRE.

bistort (bis´tawt) *n.* a plant with a twisted root and spike of flesh-coloured flowers, *Polygonum bistorta*. [L *bistorta* (*bis*, twice, *torta tortus*, p.p. of *torquere*, to twist)]

bistoury (bis´təri) *n.* (*pl.* **bistouries**) **1** a small instrument used for making incisions. **2** a scalpel. [F *bistouri*, etym. uncertain]

bistre (bis´tə), (*esp. N Am.*) **bister** *n.* a transparent brownish yellow pigment prepared from soot. *~a.* coloured like this pigment. **bistred** *a.* coloured with or as with bistre. [F, etym. uncertain]

bistro (bēs´trō) *n.* (*pl.* **bistros**) a small bar or restaurant. [F]

bisulcate (bīsŭl´kāt) *a.* (*Zool.*) having cloven hoofs.

bisulphate (bīsŭl´fāt), (*esp. N Am.*) **bisulfate** *n.* a salt or ester of sulphuric acid.

bit[1] (bit) *n.* **1** a small portion. **2** a morsel, a fragment. **3** the smallest quantity, a whit, a jot. **4** a brief period of time. **5** a small coin (usu. with the value expressed, as a threepenny bit). **6** (*N Am., coll.*) an eighth of a dollar. **7** (*coll.*) a poor little thing. **8** somewhat or something (of). **9** BIT PART (under BIT[1]). **10** †a bite, a piece bitten off. **11** †as much as can be bitten off at once. **a bit 1** a little. **2** rather, somewhat. **bit by bit** gradually, piecemeal. **not a bit** not at all. **to bits 1** into pieces, completely apart. **2** (*coll.*) very much. **to do one's bit** to do one's share. **bit of all right** *n.* (*sl.*) a sexually attractive woman. **bit of crackling, bit of crumpet, bit of fluff, bit of skirt, bit of stuff, bit of tail** *n.* (*sl., offensive*) an attractive woman regarded as a sexual object. **bit of rough** *n.* (*sl.*) a man who is sexually attractive because of his lack of sophistication. **bit on the side** *n.* (*sl.*) **1** a sexual relationship outside one's marriage. **2** the person with whom one is having an affair. **bit part** *n.* a small role in a play. **bit player** *n.* an actor who plays small parts. **bitty** *a.* (*comp.* **bittier**, *superl.* **bittiest**) **1** scrappy, disjointed, piecemeal. **2** lacking unity. **3** (*N Am., coll.*) tiny. **bittily** *adv.* **bittiness** *n.* [OE *bita*, a bit, a morsel (cp. OFris. *bīta*, Dut. *beet*, bit, OHG *bizzo*, biting, G *Bisse*), from *bitan*, to bite]

bit[2] (bit) *n.* **1** the iron part of the bridle inserted in the mouth of a horse. **2** the cutting part of a tool. **3** the movable boring-piece in a drill. **4** the part of the key at right angles to the shank. **5** the copper head of a soldering iron. **6** the short sliding piece of tube in a cornet for modifying the tone etc. **7** a bite, the act of biting. *~v.t.* **1** to furnish with, or accustom (a horse) to, a bit. **2** to restrain. **a bit and a sup** something to eat and drink. **to champ at the bit** to be impatient. **to draw bit 1** to stop a horse by pulling the reins. **2** (*fig.*) to stop; to slacken speed. **to take the bit between one's teeth 1** to become unmanageable. **2** to act decisively. [OE *bite*, bite, biting (cp. OFris. *bit*, *biti*, Dut. *beet*, OHG *biz*, a piece bitten off, G *Bisz*, biting)]

bit[3] (bit) *n.* in binary notation, either of two digits, one or zero, a unit of information in computers and information theory representing either of two states, such as *on* and *off*. **bitmap** *n.* (*Comput.*) a method of creating a graphic image in which a bit is assigned to each dot that forms the image. *~v.t.* (*pres.p.* **bitmapping,** *past, p.p.* **bitmapped**) to represent or manipulate (data) using a bitmap. **bitmapped** *a.* using dots in this way (*bitmapped fonts*). [*b*inary dig*it*]

bit[4] BITE.

bitch (bich) *n.* **1** the female of the dog. **2** a female of allied species. **3** (*sl., derog.*) an offensive, malicious or spiteful woman. 4 (*sl.*) a complaint. 5 (*sl.*) an awkward problem or situation. ~*v.i.* (*sl.*) to moan, complain. ~*v.t.* (*sl.*) 1 to mess up, botch. 2 to be spiteful or unfair to. **bitchy** *a.* (*comp.* **bitchier**, *superl.* **bitchiest**) 1 of or like a bitch, spiteful. 2 ill-tempered. **bitchily** *adv.* **bitchiness** *n.* [OE *bicce* (etym. uncertain)]

bite (bīt) *v.t.* (*past* **bit** (bit), *p.p.* **bitten** (bit´ən)) 1 to seize, nip, rend, cut, pierce or crush with the teeth. 2 to cut, to wound. 3 to affect with severe cold. 4 to cause to smart. 5 to inflict sharp physical or mental pain on. 6 to wound with reproach or sarcasm. 7 to hold fast, as an anchor or screw. 8 to corrode. 9 to cheat, to trick. ~*v.i.* 1 to have a habit, or exercise the power, of biting. 2 to sting, to be pungent. 3 to take a bait. 4 to act upon something (of weapons, tools etc.). ~*n.* 1 the act of biting. 2 a wound made by the teeth. 3 a mouthful, a small quantity. 4 a piece seized or detached by biting. 5 pungency. 6 sharpness. 7 a hold, a grip. 8 the angle of contact between the top and bottom teeth when the mouth is closed. 9 a trickster. 10 a person who cheats. 11 †a cheat, a trick, a fraud. **to bite at** to snap at. **to bite back** to avoid saying (e.g. something hurtful). **to bite in** to corrode or eat into by means of a chemical agent, esp. to eat out (the lines of an engraving) with acid. **to bite off** to seize with the teeth and detach. **to bite off more than one can chew** to undertake more than one can manage. **to bite one's lip** LIP. **to bite (on) the bullet** BULLET. **to bite someone's head off** HEAD[1]. **to bite the dust** DUST. **to bite the hand that feeds one** HAND. **to put the bite on** (*Austral., N Am., sl.*) to borrow or extort money from. **two bites at the cherry** CHERRY. **biter** *n.* 1 a person who or thing which bites. 2 a trickster, a cheat. **biter bit** the cheater cheated; the wrongdoer paid back. **bite-size, bite-sized** *a.* 1 small enough to be eaten in one mouthful. 2 very small. **biting** *a.* 1 sharp, keen. 2 acrid, pungent. 3 stinging, caustic, sarcastic. **bitingly** *adv.* **bitten** *a.* **bitten with** infected by (a passion, mania etc.). **once bitten twice shy** after an unpleasant experience, one is more cautious. [OE *bītan* (cp. Icel. *bīta*, Gmc. *bītan*, G *beissen*, L *fid-findere*, to cut)]

bitt (bit) *n.* a strong post fixed in pairs on the deck of a ship for fastening cables, belaying ropes etc. ~*v.t.* to put around a bitt. [etym. uncertain]

bitten BITE.

bitter (bit´ə) *a.* 1 sharp or biting to the taste. 2 acrid, harsh, virulent, piercingly cold. 3 painful, distressing, mournful. ~*n.* 1 anything bitter. 2 bitterness. 3 (*coll.*) bitter beer. 4 (*pl.*) liquors flavoured with bitter herbs etc., used as appetizers or in cocktails. ~*v.t.* to make bitter. **bitter almond** *n.* a bitter variety of the almond. **bitter aloes** *n.pl.* the purgative drug aloes. **bitter-apple** *n.* COLOCYNTH. **bittercress** *n.* any of several plants of the genus *Cardamine*. **bitter cup** *n.* 1 a hard fate. 2 a heavy retribution. **bitter end** *n.* 1 the last extremity. 2 the loose end of a belayed rope. **bitterish** *a.* **bitterly** *adv.* **bitterness** *n.* **bitter orange** *n.* a Seville orange. **bitter pill** *n.* something which is unwelcome or difficult to accept. **bitter-sweet** *a.* 1 sweet with a bitter aftertaste. 2 pleasant with admixture of pain or sadness. ~*n.* 1 a mixture of sweet and bitter. 2 woody nightshade. **bitter-vetch** *n.* some species of the genus *Vicia*. [OE *biter* (prob. from *bitan*, to bite)]

bitterling (bit´əling) *n.* a small brightly coloured freshwater fish, *Rhodeus amarus*. [G]

bittern[1] (bit´ən) *n.* any of the wading birds of the heron family, esp. of the genus *Botaurus*. [ME *bitore*, OF *butor* (etym. uncertain; prob. from the bird's cry)]

bittern[2] (bit´ən) *n.* the liquid obtained when sea water is evaporated to extract the salt. [BITTER]

bittock BIT[1].

bitumen (bit´ūmin) *n.* 1 any of various solid or sticky mixtures of hydrocarbons that occur naturally or as a residue from petroleum distillation, e.g. tar, asphalt. 2 (*Austral., coll.*) a tarred road. **bitume** (-tūm´) *v.t.* to smear with bitumen. **bituminiferous** (-nif´-) *a.* yielding bitumen. **bituminize** (-tū´-), **bituminise** *v.t.* to impregnate with or convert into bitumen. **bituminization** (-zā´shən) *n.* the art, process, or state of conversion into bitumen. **bituminous** (-tū´-) *a.* of the nature of, resembling, or impregnated with bitumen. **bituminous coal** *n.* coal that flames when it burns. [L]

bivalent (bīvā´lənt, biv´ə-) *a.* 1 having a valency of two. 2 (of homologous chromosomes) associated in pairs. ~*n.* any pair of homologous chromosomes. **bivalency** *n.*

bivalve (bī´valv) *a.* having two shells or valves which open and shut. ~*n.* 1 a mollusc which has its shell in two opposite directions connected by a ligament and hinge, such as the oyster. 2 a bivalve seed-capsule. **bivalved, bivalvular** (-val´vū-) *a.* bivalve.

bivious (biv´iəs) *a.* leading two different ways. [L *via*, a way]

bivouac (biv´uak, biv´wak) *n.* 1 a temporary encampment in the field without tents etc. 2 the scene of such an encampment. ~*v.i.* (*pres.p.* **bivouacking**, *past, p.p.* **bivouacked**) to remain in the open air without tents or other covering. [F, from G *Beiwache*, a watch, keeping guard]

biweekly (bīwēk´li) *a., adv.* 1 occurring once a fortnight. 2 occurring twice a week. ~*n.* (*pl.* **biweeklies**) a periodical appearing every two weeks.

Usage note See note under BIMONTHLY.

---

biyearly (bīyiə´li) *a., adv.* 1 occurring every two years. 2 occurring twice a year.

Usage note See note under BIMONTHLY.

---

biz (biz) *n.* (*coll.*) business, work, employment. [short for BUSINESS]

bizarre (bizah´) *a.* 1 odd, whimsical, fantastic, eccentric. 2 of mixed or discordant style. 3 irregular, in bad taste. **bizarrely** *adv.* **bizarreness** *n.* **bizarrerie** (-zah´rəri) *n.* bizarreness. [F (cp. Sp. *bizarro*, handsome, gallant; It. *bizzarro*)]

Bk *chem. symbol* berkelium.

bk *abbr.* 1 bank. 2 book.

BL *abbr.* 1 Bachelor of Law. 2 Bachelor of Letters. 3 Barrister-at-Law. 4 bill of lading. 5 British Legion. 6 British Library.

bl *abbr.* 1 barrel. 2 black.

blab (blab) *v.t.* (*pres.p.* **blabbing**, *past, p.p.* **blabbed**) 1 to tell or reveal indiscreetly. 2 to betray. ~*v.i.* 1 to talk indiscreetly, to tell tales or secrets. 2 to prattle. ~*n.* 1 a chatterer, babbler. 2 a tell-tale. 3 babbling, tale-telling. **blabber** *n.* 1 a person who blabs. 2 a tell-tale, a tattler. ~*v.i.* to talk at length, often aimlessly. **blabbermouth** *n.* a blab. [ME *blobbe*]

black (blak) *a.* 1 intensely dark in colour (the opposite of white). 2 denoting total absence of colour due to absence or entire absorption of light. 3 (*also* **Black**) dark-skinned, esp. of African or Australian Aboriginal descent. 4 of or relating to black people. 5 (of the sky) heavily overcast. 6 angry. 7 implying disgrace or dishonour. 8 atrociously wicked. 9 sombre, gloomy, dirty. 10 disastrous, dismal, mournful. 11 dirty. 12 (of humour) macabre. 13 (of tea or coffee) without milk. 14 subject to a trade union ban. 15 wearing black clothes, uniform or armour. 16 destitute of light. 17 obscure. 18 dark in colour as distinguished from a lighter variety (*black bread*). ~*n.* 1 the darkest of all colours (the opposite of white). 2 a black pigment or dye. 3 (*also* **Black**) a member of a dark-skinned people, esp. of African or Australian Aboriginal descent. 4 mourning garments. 5 a minute particle of soot or dirt. 6 in a game, a black piece, ball etc. 7 the player using the black pieces. 8 the credit side of an account. ~*v.t.* 1 to blacken. **2** to soil. **3** to place under a trade union ban. **4** to polish with blacking. **black in the face** FACE. **black Africa** *n.* the part of Africa where black people predominate. †**blackamoor** *n.* a black African. **black and blue** *a.* **1** discoloured by beating. **2** livid. **Black and Tan** *n.* a member of the auxiliary police force employed in Ireland in 1919–20 (from the colour of their uniforms). **black and white** *n.* **1** printed or written matter. **2** a photograph, drawing etc., in black and white or shades of grey. **3** visual images reproduced in black and white, esp. by photography or television. *~a.* **1** monochrome as opposed to colour (of film or television). **2** recorded in writing or print. **3** divided into two extremes, not admitting of compromise. **black art** *n.* magic, necromancy. **blackball** *n.* a vote of rejection in a ballot (from the black ball sometimes used to indicate a vote against in a ballot). *~v.t.* **1** to vote against. **2** to exclude. **3** to dislike, bar. **black bass** *n.* a N American freshwater fish of the genus *Micropterus.* **black bean** *n.* **1** any of various plants of the genus *Phaseolus*, which have small black seeds. **2** the dried seed of any of these plants, used as a vegetable. **3** a fermented soya bean, used in Chinese cooking. **4** an Australian tree, *Castanospermum australe*, used to make furniture. **black beetle** *n.* a cockroach, *Blatta orientalis.* **black belt** *n.* **1** a belt awarded for highest proficiency in judo, karate etc. **2** a person entitled to wear this. **blackberry** *n.* (*pl.* **blackberries**) **1** the common bramble, *Rubus fruticosus* or *discolor.* **2** its fruit. *~v.i.* (*3rd pers. sing. pres.* **blackberries,** *pres.p.* **blackberrying,** *past, p.p.* **blackberried**) to gather blackberries. **blackberrying** *n.* gathering blackberries. **black bile** *n.* (*Hist.*) one of the four bodily humours, associated with a melancholy temperament. **blackbird** *n.* **1** a species of European thrush, *Turdus merula*, the male of which has black plumage and an orange beak. **2** any of several dark plumaged American birds. **3** (*Hist.*) a captive African or Polynesian on a slave ship. **blackbirder** *n.* **blackbirding** *n.* (*Hist.*) the kidnapping of Africans or Polynesians for slavery. **blackboard** *n.* a board painted black, used by teachers and lecturers to write and draw on. **black body** *n.* a hypothetical body which absorbs all radiation falling upon it, and reflects none. **black book** *n.* **1** a book on the black art. **2** a book recording the names of persons liable to censure or punishment. **in someone's black books** BOOK. **black bottom** *n.* a dance of the 1920s with a sinuous movement of the hips. **black box** *n.* **1** a closed unit in an electronic system whose circuitry remains hidden from the user and is irrelevant to understanding its function. **2** a flight recorder in an aircraft. **blackboy** *n.* any tree of the genus *Xanthorrhoea*, native to Australia, also called *grass tree.* **black bread** *n.* coarse, dark rye bread. **black-browed** *a.* **1** dark, gloomy. **2** threatening, forbidding. **black bryony** *n.* a climbing plant, *Tamus communis*, which has poisonous red berries and small green flowers. **blackbuck** *n.* a common Indian gazelle, *Antilope cervicapra*, also called sasin. **blackbutt** *n.* any of several Australian eucalyptus trees used as timber. **black cap** *n.* **1** (*Hist.*) a cap worn by judges in full dress, and put on when pronouncing sentence of death. **2** any English bird having the top of the head black. **blackcap warbler** *n.* a small warbler, *Sylvia atricapilla.* **black coat** *n.* a clergyman. **blackcock** *n.* the male of the black grouse. **black cod** *n.* (*New Zeal.*) a local variety of codfish. **black coffee** *n.* coffee without milk or cream. **black comedy** *n.* a play or film in which grotesque humour or farce serves to underline and expose true reality. **Black Country** *n.* the heavily industrialized Midlands of England. **blackcurrant** *n.* a garden bush, *Ribes nigrum*, or its fruit. **Black Death** *n.* a form of bubonic plague which ravaged Europe and Asia during the 14th cent. **black diamonds** *n.pl.* (*coll.*) coal. **black disc** *n.* a long-playing gramophone record, as opposed to a compact disc. **black draught** *n.* a purgative medicine. **black earth** *n.* a fertile soil covering regions in S Russia north of the Black Sea. **black economy** *n.* illegal and undeclared economic activity. **blacken** *v.t.* **1** to make black, to darken. **2** to sully, to defame. *~v.i.* to become black. **black English** *n.* the form of English spoken by some black people, esp. in the US. **black eye** *n.* **1** discoloration produced by a blow upon the parts round the eye. **2** an eye of which the iris is very dark. **black-eyed bean, black-eye bean,** (*N Am.*) **black-eyed pea** *n.* a variety of bean, *Vigna sinensis.* **black-eyed Susan** *n.* any of several flowers, esp. of the genus *Rudbeckia*, which have a dark centre and yellow petals. **blackface** *n.* **1** a black-faced sheep or other animal. **2** the make-up used by a white performer playing a black role. **blackfellow** *n.* (*derog., offensive*) an Aboriginal of Australia. **blackfish** *n.* (*pl. in general* **blackfish,** *in particular* **blackfishes**) **1** a salmon just after spawning. **2** any of several species of dark-coloured fish. **3** (*Austral.*) a small species of whale. **black flag** *n.* a flag of black cloth used as a sign that no quarter will be given or taken, as an ensign by pirates, and as the signal for an execution. **blackfly** *n.* (*pl.* **blackflies**) **1** any black aphid, esp. *Aphis fabae*, that infests beans and other plants. **2** a biting fly of the genus *Simulium* or the family Simuliidae. **Blackfoot** *n.* (*pl.* **Blackfeet**) a member of a North American Indian people (called Blackfeet from their dark moccasins). **Black Forest gateau,** (*N Am.*) **Black Forest cake** *n.* a thick chocolate cake containing whipped cream and morello cherries in layers. **Black Friar** *n.* a Dominican friar. **black frost** *n.* frost without snow or white dew. **black game** *n.* BLACK GROUSE (under BLACK). **black ginger** *n.* unscraped ginger. **black gold** *n.* (*coll.*) oil. **black grouse** *n.* a European grouse, *Tetrao tetrix.* **blackguard** (blag´ahd, blag´əd) *n.* **1** a scoundrel. **2** a low, worthless fellow. *~a.* **1** of or relating to the lowest class. **2** scurrilous, abusive. *~v.t.* to revile in scurrilous language. *~v.i.* **1** to act the part of a blackguard. **2** to behave in a riotous or indecent manner. **blackguardism** *n.* the language or actions of a blackguard. **blackguardly** (-gəd-) *a., adv.* **blackhead** *n.* **1** a pimple with a black head. **2** any of various birds with dark plumage on the head. **black-hearted** *a.* wicked, having a wicked heart. **black hole** *n.* **1** a hypothetical celestial region formed from a collapsed star, surrounded by a strong gravitational field from which no matter or energy can escape. **2** a punishment cell. **3** the guardroom. **black horehound** *n.* a labiate herb, *Ballota nigra*, with an unpleasant aroma. **black ice** *n.* a thin layer of transparent ice on roads. **blacking** *n.* **1** the action of making black. **2** a composition for giving a shining black polish to boots and shoes, harness etc. **blackish** *a.* **blackjack** *n.* **1** a large leather jug for beer. **2** (*N Am.*) a loaded stick, a bludgeon. **3** pontoon or a similar card game. **4** (*Hist.*) a pirate's flag. **blacklead** (-led) *n.* plumbago or graphite, made into pencils, also used to polish ironwork. *~v.t.* to colour or rub with blacklead. **blackleg** *n.* **1** a worker who works for an employer when other employees are on strike, a scab. **2** a gambler and cheat, a swindler, esp. on the turf. *~v.i.* (*pres.p.* **blacklegging,** *past, p.p.* **blacklegged**) to act as a blackleg. **black leopard** *n.* a leopard with black fur. **black letter** *n.* the Old English or Gothic as distinguished from the Roman character. *~a.* written or printed in this character. **black light** *n.* invisible infra-red or ultraviolet light. **blacklist** *n.* a list of persons in disgrace, or who have incurred censure or punishment. *~v.t.* to ban or prohibit (books etc.). **blackly** *adv.* **black magic** *n.* BLACK ART (under BLACK). **blackmail** *n.* **1** any payment extorted by intimidation or pressure. **2** the use of threats or pressure to influence someone's actions. **3** (*Hist.*) a tribute formerly exacted by free-booting chiefs in return for protection or immunity from plunder. *~v.t.* **1** to levy blackmail on. **2** to threaten. **blackmailer** *n.* a person who levies blackmail. **Black Maria** (mərī´ə) *n.* (*coll.*) a prison van. **black mark** *n.* a note of disgrace put against a person's name. **black market** *n.* illegal buying and selling of rationed goods. **black marketeer** *n.* **black mass** *n.* a travesty of the Mass performed by diabolists. **Black Monk** *n.* a Benedictine monk (from the colour of the habit). **black mulberry** *n.* the tree *Morus nigra*, grown for its fruit. **black Muslim** *n.* a member of a black Islamic sect in the US who want to establish a new black nation. **black nationalism** *n.* the advocacy of black self-determination and civil rights. **black nationalist** *n.* **blackness** *n.* **black nightshade** *n.* *Solanum nigrum*, with white flowers and poisonous black berries. **blackout** *n.* **1** a temporary loss of consciousness, sight or memory. **2** an electrical power failure or cut. **3** the extinguishing or concealment of lights against air attack. **4** an interruption or suppression of broadcasting, communications etc. **5** the sudden darkening of the stage in a theatre. *~v.t.* **1** to cause to blackout. **2** to censor or suppress (a broadcast etc.). **3** to obscure (windows), extinguish (lights etc.) to protect against air attack. *~v.i.* to suffer a temporary loss of consciousness, sight or memory. **Black Panther** *n.* a member of the militant black political party in the US. **black pepper** *n.* the whole or ground berries of *Piper nigrum*, the common pepper, used as a condiment. **black power** *n.* a black civil rights movement, esp. in the US and Australia. **black pudding** *n.* a kind of sausage made with blood, rice and chopped fat. **Black Rod** *n.* the chief usher of the Lord Chamberlain's department, of the House of Lords and of the Garter. **black salsify** *n.* scorzonera. **black sheep** *n.* a bad member of a group or family. **blackshirt** *n.* a member of a Fascist organization in Europe before and during World War II, esp. in Italy. **blacksmith** *n.* **1** a smith who works in iron. **2** (*N Am.*) a person who treats horses. **black snake** *n.* **1** (*N Am.*) a large non-poisonous snake, *Bascanium constrictor.* **2** any of several Old World venomous snakes, esp. *Pseudechis porphyriacus*, the Australian black snake. **black spot** *n.* **1** an area of a road where accidents are common. **2** any dangerous area. **3** any of various plant diseases that cause black blotches on the leaves, esp. of roses. **black swan** *n.* **1** an Australian swan, *Cygnus atratus*, that has black plumage and a red bill. **2** something that is very rare. **black tea** *n.* **1** tea that is fully fermented before it is dried. **2** tea without milk. **blackthorn** *n.* **1** the sloe, *Prunus spinosa* (so called from the dark colour of the bark). **2** a walking stick or cudgel of its wood. **blackthorn winter** *n.* a spell of cold weather in the spring, at the time when the blackthorn is flowering. **black tie** *n.* **1** a black bow tie worn with a dinner jacket for a formal occasion. **2** (*coll.*) formal evening dress. *~a.* denoting such an occasion. **blacktop** *n.* (*esp. N Am.*) **1** a type of bituminous material for surfacing roads. **2** a road surfaced with this. *~v.t.* to surface (a road) with blacktop. **black tracker** *n.* (*Austral.*) an Aboriginal used in tracking escaped criminals or lost travellers. **black velvet** *n.* a mixture of stout and champagne or cider. **blackwash** *n.* a lotion made from lime water and mercury. **Black Watch** *n.* the Royal Highland Regiment (from the colour of their tartan). **blackwater fever** *n.* a form of malaria in which the urine is very dark in colour. **black widow** *n.* a venomous American and Far Eastern spider, *Latrodectus mactans*, of which the female has a black body. [OE *blæc* (OHG *blah, blach*; perh. cognate with Gr. *phlegein*, L *flagrāre*, to burn)]

Usage note *Black* is now the term least likely to give offence in referring to members of a dark-skinned people.

blad (blad), **blaud** (blawd) *n.* (*Sc.*) a large specimen. [prob. onomat.]

bladder (blad´ə) *n.* **1** a membranous bag in the animal body which receives the urine. **2** any similar membranous bag (usu. with distinctive epithet, as *gall-bladder, swim-bladder* etc.). **3** the prepared (urinary) bladder of an animal. **4** an inflated pericarp. **5** a vesicle. **6** anything inflated and hollow. **7** the membrane of an animal's bladder used for airtight coverings. **8** a windbag. **bladdered** *a.* **1** put or packed in a bladder. **2** inflated, puffed up. **3** (*sl.*) very drunk. **bladder fern** *n.* a small fern, *Cystoperis fragilis*, which grows on limestone rocks and walls. **bladderkelp** *n.* BLADDER-WRACK (under BLADDER). **bladdernut** *n.* **1** BLADDER TREE (under BLADDER). **2** the fruit of the bladder tree. **bladder tree** *n.* any shrub or small tree of the genus *Staphylea*, esp. *S. pinnata.* **bladderwort** *n.* an aquatic plant of the genus *Utricularia.* **bladderwrack** *n.* a seaweed, *Fucus vesiculosus*, which has air bladders in its fronds. **bladdery** *a.* **1** of the nature of a bladder. **2** containing bladders. [OE *blǣdre* (cp. OHG *blātara*, G *Blatter*, a bladder, OE *blāwan*, L *flāre*, to blow)]

blade (blād) *n.* **1** the thin cutting part of a knife, sword etc. **2** any broad, flattened part, as of a paddle, bat, oar etc. **3** a leaf of a plant. **4** the culm and leaves of a grass or cereal. **5** the expanded part of the leaf as distinguished from the petiole. **6** the corresponding part of a petal. **7** the front part of the tongue. **8** (*poet.*) a sword. **9** (*coll.*) a dashing, reckless fellow. **10** in archaeology, a piece of hard stone used as a tool. **11** BLADE-BONE (under BLADE). *~v.i.* to put forth blades. **blade-bone** *n.* the shoulder blade in man and the lower mammals. **bladed** *a.* [OE *blæd* (OHG *plat*, G *Blatt*, Gmc. stem *blo-*, to blow, cp. L *flos*, a flower)]

blaeberry (blā´bəri), **bleaberry** *n.* (*pl.* **blaeberries, bleaberries**) (*Sc., North.*) **1** the bilberry or whortleberry. **2** any of various similar fruits or plants. [Icel. *blā, blār*, livid, dark blue (OHG *blāo*, G *blau*), whence *blāber*, bilberry]

blag (blag) *n.* (*sl.*) robbery, esp. violent robbery. *~v.t., v.i.* (*pres.p.* **blagging,** *past, p.p.* **blagged**) **1** to rob. **2** to cadge or scrounge. **blagger** *n.* [etym. uncertain]

blague (blahg) *n.* pretentiousness, humbug. **blagueur** (blahgœ´) *n.* a person given to blague. [F]

blah (blah), **blah-blah** *n.* foolish talk, chatter, exaggeration. [onomat.]

blain (blān) *n.* a pustule, a blister or sore. *~v.t.* to affect with blains. [OE *blegen* (cp. Dut. *blein*, Dan. *blegn*)]

blakey (blā´ki), **Blakey** *n.* (*pl.* **blakeys, Blakeys**) a metal toe or heel cap on a shoe or boot. [name of the manufacturer]

blame (blām) *v.t.* **1** to censure, to find fault with, to reproach. **2** to hold responsible. *~n.* **1** the act of censuring. **2** the expression of censure. **3** responsibility, accountability. **4** a fault. **blame it!** used as a mild oath. **to be to blame** to be culpable. **to have only oneself to blame** to be solely responsible for one's own problems. **blamable, blameable** *a.* deserving blame, culpable. **blamableness** *n.* **blamably** *adv.* **blameful** *a.* deserving blame. **blamefully** *adv.* **blameless** *a.* free from blame. **blamelessly** *adv.* **blamelessness** *n.* **blameworthy** *a.* deserving blame. **blameworthiness** *n.* [OF *blasmer*, L *blasphemāre*, BLASPHEME]

blanch (blahnch) *v.t.* **1** to whiten by taking out the colour. **2** to bleach, to make pale. **3** to take off the outward covering of (almonds, walnuts etc.). **4** to whiten (a plant) by the deprivation of light. **5** to plunge (vegetables, fruit, meat etc.) briefly into boiling water. **6** to palliate, whitewash. *~v.i.* **1** to lose colour. **2** to become white. ~*a.* **1** white. **2** (*Her.*) argent. **to blanch over** to try to conceal or misrepresent (e.g. a fault). [OF fem. of *blanc*, white]

blancmange (bləmonzh´) *n.* milk (usu. sweetened) thickened with cornflour or gelatine to form a jelly-like dessert. [OF *blanc-manger, -mangier* (*blanc*, as BLANCH, L *manducāre* to chew, to eat)]

blanco (blang´kō) *n.* a substance used by the armed forces to whiten or colour uniform belts, webbing etc. ~*v.t.* (*3rd pers. sing. pres.* **blancoes,** *pres.p.* **blancoing,** *past, p.p.* **blancoed**) to treat with blanco. [*Blanco*, a trademark, F *blanc*, white]

bland (bland) *a.* **1** mild, soft, gentle. **2** genial, balmy. **3** dull, insipid. **blandly** *adv.* **blandness** *n.* [L *blandus*, agreeable]

blandiloquence (blandil´əkwəns) *n.* (*coll.*) **1** smooth, ingratiating talk. **2** a flattering speech. [see BLANDISH, with L *-loquus*, speaking, from *loqui*, to speak), assim. to ELOQUENCE]

blandish (blan´dish) *v.t.* **1** to flatter gently. **2** to coax, to cajole. **blandishment** *n.* **1** flattering speech or action. **2** cajolery, charm, allurement. [OF *blandiss-*, stem of *blandir*, L *blandīrī*, to flatter (*blandus*, see BLAND)]

blank (blangk) *a.* **1** empty, void, vacant. **2** not written or printed on. **3** not filled up. **4** confused, dispirited, nonplussed. **5** pure, unmixed, downright, sheer. **6** (*euphem.*) (*also* **blankety, blanky**) used instead of an offensive adjective. ~*n.* **1** a blank space in a written or printed document. **2** a blank form. **3** a blank cartridge. **4** a vacant space, a void. **5** an uneventful space of time. **6** a piece of metal before stamping. **7** a dash written to replace an obscenity. **8** (*euphem.*) (*also* **blankety, blanky**) used instead of an offensive noun. **9** a domino with one or both halves blank. **10** a lottery ticket that draws no prize. **11** the white point in the centre of a target. **12** a level range for a firearm. **13** (*fig.*) aim, range. **14** a meaningless thing. **15** †the range of one's aim. ~*v.t.* **1** to render blank. **2** to nonplus, confuse, dumbfound. **3** to block out. **4** to cut (a metal blank). **5** (*N Am.*) to defeat without allowing (one's opponent) to score. ~*int.* a mild execration. **blank cartridge** *n.* a cartridge containing no bullet. **blank cheque** *n.* **1** a cheque with the amount left for the payee to insert. **2** complete freedom of action. **blank credit** *n.* permission to draw on a person or firm to a certain amount. **blankly** *adv.* **blankness** *n.* **blank verse** *n.* unrhymed verse, esp. the iambic pentameter or unrhymed heroic. [F *blanc*, white (It. *blanco*, L *blancus*, OHG *blanch*, Gmc. *blankoz*, shining)]

blanket (blang´kət) *n.* a a piece of woollen or other warm material, used as a bed-covering or for covering an animal, etc. ~*a.* covering all conditions or cases (*blanket medical screening*). ~*v.t.* (*pres.p.* **blanketing,** *past, p.p.* **blanketed**) **1** to cover with or as with a blanket. **2** to toss in a blanket. **3** to stifle. **4** (*Naut.*) to obstruct (a ship) by preventing wind reaching it. **5** to bring under one coverage. **6** to apply over a wide area. **born on the wrong side of the blanket** (*coll.*) illegitimate. **wet blanket** WET. **blanket bath** *n.* a wash given to a bedridden person. **blanket bog** *n.* an extensive flat peat bog found in cold wet climates. **blanketing** *n.* **1** material for blankets. **2** tossing in a blanket. **blanket stitch** *n.* a reinforcing stitch for the edge of blankets and other thick material. [OF *blankete*, *blanquette*, dim. of *blanc*, see BLANK]

blankety, blanky BLANK.

blanquette (blãket´) *n.* a stew of white meat, esp. veal, in a white sauce. [F]

blare (bleə) *v.i.* **1** to roar, bellow. **2** to sound as a trumpet. ~*v.t.* to utter with a trumpet-like sound. ~*n.* **1** sound as of a trumpet. **2** roar, noise, bellowing. [prob. imit. from the sound (cp. Dut. *blaren*, MHG *blēren*, G *plarren*)]

blarney (blah´ni) *n.* **1** smooth, flattering speech. **2** cajolery. **3** nonsense. ~*v.t.* (*3rd pers. sing. pres.* **blarneys,** *pres.p.* **blarneying,** *past, p.p.* **blarneyed**) to wheedle, to cajole. ~*v.i.* to talk in a wheedling way. [*Blarney*, near Cork, Ireland, where there is an inscribed stone in the wall of an old castle: it is said that whoever kisses it will have a cajoling tongue]

blasé (blah´zā) *a.* **1** dulled in sense or emotion. **2** worn out through over-indulgence, used up. [F, p.p. of *blaser*, to cloy]

blaspheme (blasfēm´) *v.t.* **1** to utter profane language against (God or anything sacred). **2** to abuse. ~*v.i.* to utter blasphemy, to rail. **blasphemer** *n.* **blasphemous** (blas´fə-) *a.* **1** uttering or containing blasphemy. **2** grossly irreverent or impious. **blasphemously** *adv.* **blasphemy** (blas´fəmi) *n.* (*pl.* **blasphemies**) **1** profane language towards God or about sacred things. **2** impious irreverence. **3** irreverent or abusive speaking about any person or thing held in high esteem. [OF *blasfemer*, L *blasphēmāre*, Gr. *blasphēmeein*, from *-phemos*, evil-speaking]

blast (blahst) *n.* **1** a violent gust of wind. **2** the sound of a trumpet or the like. **3** any pernicious or destructive influence on animals or plants. **4** a flatulent disease in sheep. **5** the strong current of air used in iron-smelting. **6** a blowing by gunpowder or other explosive. **7** the charge of explosive used. **8** a violent gust of air caused by the explosion of a bomb. **9** (*coll.*) a severe reprimand. ~*v.t.* **1** to blow or breathe on so as to wither. **2** to injure by some pernicious influence. **3** to blight, to ruin. **4** to blow up with gunpowder or other explosive. **5** to curse (often used as an imprecation). **6** to blow into. **7** to reprimand. **8** to shoot or shoot at. ~*v.i.* **1** to blow. **2** to use explosives. **3** to curse. **4** to emit a blast. ~*int.* used to express annoyance. **at full blast** hard at work. **to blast off** **1** (of a missile or space vehicle) to be launched. **2** (*coll.*) to start. **blasted** *a.* blighted, confounded, cursed. **blaster** *n.* **1** a person who or thing which blasts. **2** a golf club for playing from a bunker; a niblick. **blast freezing** *n.* the use of a rapid current of chilled air to freeze foods. **blast freeze** *v.t.* **blast from the past** *n.* a nostalgic song, event etc. **blast furnace** *n.* a furnace into which a current of air is introduced to assist combustion. **blast-hole** *n.* a hole containing an explosive charge for blasting. **blast-off** *n.* **1** the launch of a rocket-propelled missile or space vehicle. **2** (*coll.*) the start of something. [OE *blæst* (cp. OHG *blāst*, Goth. *-blesan*, to blow)]

-blast (blast) *comb. form* used in biological terms to indicate an embryonic cell or cell layer, as *mesoblast*, *statoblast*. [Gr. *blastos*, a bud, a germ]

blastema (blastē´mə) *n.* **1** protoplasm. **2** the initial matter from which any part is developed. **3** the thallus or frond of lichens. **4** the budding or sprouting part of a plant. [Gr., a sprout]

blasto- (blas´tō) *comb. form* of or relating to germs or buds, germinal. [see -BLAST]

blastocyst (blas´tōsist) *n.* the modified blastula in mammals.

blastoderm (blas´tōdœm) *n.* the germinal membrane enclosing the yolk of an impregnated ovum which divides into layers that develop into embryonic organs. [Gr. *derma*, skin]

blastomere (blas´tōmiə) *n.* any one of the cells formed during the primary divisions of an egg.

blastula (blas´tūlə) *n.* (*pl.* **blastulas, blastulae** (-lē)) a hollow sphere composed of a single layer of cells, produced by the cleavage of an ovum. **blastular** *a.* **blastulation** (-lā´shən) *n.*

blatant (blā´tənt) *a.* **1** very obvious, palpable. **2** loud, clamorous. **blatancy** *n.* the quality of being blatant. **blatantly** *adv.* [etym. uncertain; prob. coined by Spenser (perh. from Sc. *blaitand*, bleating)]

blather, blatherskite BLETHER.
blawort (blah´wœt, blā´-) *n.* **1** the harebell, *Campanula rotundifolia.* **2** the dark blue cornflower, *Centaurea cyanus.* [*blae* (see BLAEBERRY), WORT]
blaze[1] (blāz) *n.* **1** a bright glowing flame. **2** a glow of bright light or colour. **3** an outburst of display, glory, splendour. **4** an outburst of passion. **5** (*pl.*) the flames of hell. ~*v.i.* **1** to burn with a bright flame. **2** to shine, to glitter. **3** to be bright with colour. **4** to be eminent or conspicuous from character, talents etc. **5** to be consumed with anger. ~*v.t.* **1** to make resplendent. **2** †to pour forth (as flame). **like blazes** (*sl.*) furiously. **to blaze away 1** (of a fire) to burn brightly and strongly. **2** to fire continuously (with guns). **3** to work continuously and enthusiastically. **to blaze out 1** to cause to flare away. **2** to subside with a flare. **to blazes** to perdition, to the Devil. **to blaze up 1** (of a fire) suddenly to burst into flames. **2** to burst into anger. **what the blazes!** (*sl.*) what the hell! **blazer** *n.* **1** a flannel jacket of bright colour worn at cricket, tennis etc. **2** a jacket used in school uniform. **3** a man's plain jacket worn with non-matching trousers. **blazing** *a.* **1** emitting flame or light. **2** radiant, lustrous. **3** very angry. **blazingly** *adv.* **blazing scent** *n.* a hot scent. [OE *blæse, blase,* a blaze, a torch (cp. MHG *blas,* a torch, G *blass,* pale)]
blaze[2] (blāz) *n.* **1** a white mark on the face of a horse or other animal. **2** a white mark made on a tree by chipping off bark. **3** (*N Am.*) the path or boundary indicated by a line of such marks. ~*v.t.* **1** to mark (a tree). **2** to indicate (a path or boundary) by such marks. **to blaze a trail 1** to mark out a route. **2** to pioneer something. [Icel. *blesi* (cp. G *Blässe*)]
blaze[3] (blāz) *v.t.* **1** to proclaim. **2** to blazon. **3** to depict, emblazon. **to blaze abroad** to spread (news). [Icel. *blāsa,* to blow (cp. Dut. *blazen,* G *blasen*), from Gmc. *blœsan,* to blow (cp. L *flāre*)]
blazer, blazing BLAZE[1].
blazon (blā´zən) *n.* **1** the art of describing and explaining coats of arms. **2** renown, reputation (of virtues or good qualities). **3** armorial bearings. **4** a coat of arms. **5** a banner bearing a coat of arms. **6** proclamation, revelation. ~*v.t.* **1** to proclaim, to trumpet. **2** to describe or depict according to the rules of heraldry. **3** to decorate with heraldic devices. **4** to depict in brilliant hues. **5** to describe in fit terms. **6** to publish vauntingly. **blazonment** *n.* **1** the act of blazoning. **2** the act of diffusing abroad. **blazonry** *n.* (*pl.* **blazonries**) **1** a heraldic device. **2** the art of depicting or describing a coat of arms. **3** armorial bearings. **4** brilliant display. [F *blason,* a coat of arms (some of the later senses prob. infl. by BLAZE[3])]
bldg. *abbr.* building.
-ble (bəl) *suf.* tending to, able to, fit to (forming verbal adjectives), e.g. *conformable, durable, flexible, suitable, visible.* [-ABLE; -IBLE]
bleaberry BLAEBERRY.
bleach (blēch) *v.t.* to make white by exposure to the sun or by chemical agents. ~*v.i.* **1** to grow white. **2** to become pale or colourless. ~*n.* **1** a bleaching agent. **2** the process or act of bleaching. **bleacher** *n.* **1** a person who or something which bleaches. **2** a vessel used in bleaching. **3** (*usu. pl., esp. N Am.*) a cheap bench seat at a sports ground. **4** (*pl., esp. N Am.*) the people sitting in such seats. **bleachery** *n.* (*pl.* **bleacheries**) a place where bleaching is carried out. **bleach-field** *n.* a field in which bleaching is carried on. **bleaching** *n.* **bleaching clay** *n.* kaolin, used for sizing cotton goods. **bleaching powder** *n.* chloride of lime, a whitish powder consisting of chlorinated calcium hydroxide. [OE *blæcan* (Gmc. *blaikjan,* cp. G *bleichen,* and OE *blāc,* pale)]
bleak[1] (blēk) *a.* **1** bare of vegetation. **2** cold, chilly, desolate, cheerless. **bleakish** *a.* **bleakly** *adv.* **bleakness** *n.* [OE *blāc* (see BLEACH)]
bleak[2] (blēk) *n.* any of various small river fishes, esp. *Alburnus alburnus.* [Icel. *bleikr* (Gmc. *blaikjōn,* white, cp. BLEACH), or OE *blāc,* as BLEAK[1]]
†**blear** (bliə) *a.* dim, indistinct, misty. ~*v.t.* **1** to make (the eyes) dim. **2** to blur with or as with tears. **blearedness** (-rid-) *n.* **1** dimness, dullness. **2** haziness. **3** indistinctness. **bleary** *a.* (*comp.* **blearier,** *superl.* **bleariest**). **blearily** *adv.* **bleariness** *n.* **bleary-eyed** *a.* [etym. uncertain]
bleat (blēt) *v.i.* to cry like a sheep, goat or calf. ~*v.t.* **1** to utter in a bleating tone. **2** to say feebly and foolishly. ~*n.* **1** the cry of a sheep, goat or calf. **2** a complaint, whine. **bleater** *n.* **bleatingly** *adv.* [OE *blætan* (cp. Dut. *blaten,* OHG *plāzan,* G *blöken*)]
bleb (bleb) *n.* **1** a small blister or bladder. **2** a bubble in glass or anything similar. [cp. BLOB, BLUBBER; imit. of action of making a bubble with the lips]
bleed (blēd) *v.i.* (*past, p.p.* **bled** (bled)) **1** to emit, discharge or run with blood. **2** to emit sap, resin or juice from a cut or wound. **3** to be wounded. **4** to die from a wound. **5** to lose money. **6** to have money extorted. **7** (*coll.*) to feel acute mental pain. ~*v.t.* **1** to draw blood from. **2** (*coll.*) to extort money from. **3** in bookbinding, to cut margins too much and trench on the print. **4** to extract liquid, air or gas from (a container or closed system such as hydraulic brakes). ~*n.* an act of bleeding. **to bleed like a (stuck) pig** PIG. **to bleed white** WHITE. **to make one's heart bleed** HEART. **bled** *a.* **bled-off** *a.* (*Print.*) (of illustration pages) so arranged that the outside edges of the illustration are cut off in trimming when binding. **bleeder** *n.* **1** a person who bleeds. **2** (*coll.*) a person with haemophilia. **3** (*sl.*) a contemptible person. **bleeding** *n.* **1** haemorrhage. **2** the operation of letting blood, or of drawing sap from a tree. ~*a.* **1** running with blood. **2** (*sl.*) bloody. **3** accursed. **bleeding heart** *n.* **1** any of various plants, esp. *Dicentra spectabilis,* characterized by heart-shaped flowers. **2** (*coll.*) someone who is a do-gooder or too soft-hearted. [OE *blēdan* (cp. BLOOD)]
bleep (blēp) *n.* an intermittent, high-pitched sound from an electronic device. ~*v.i.* to emit this sound. ~*v.t.* **1** to cause to make this sound. **2** to summon with a bleeper. **to bleep out** (*coll.*) to substitute (offensive words) in recorded speech with bleeps. **bleeper** *n.* a small radio receiver emitting a bleeping sound, often carried by doctors, police officers, business people, allowing them to be contacted. [onomat.]
blemish (blem´ish) *v.t.* to impair, tarnish, sully. ~*n.* a physical or moral defect or stain, an imperfection, a flaw, a fault. [OF (*blemir, blesmir,* from *blaisme, blesme, blême,* pale (etym. uncertain))]
blench (blench) *v.t.* to flinch from. ~*v.i.* **1** to shrink back, to draw back. **2** to turn aside, to flinch. [OE *blencan,* to deceive (perh. causal to a v. *blinkan,* to BLINK)]
blend[1] (blend) *v.t.* to mix, to mingle (esp. teas, wines, spirits, tobacco etc. so as to produce a certain quality). ~*v.i.* **1** to become mingled or indistinguishably mixed. **2** to form a harmonious union or compound. **3** to pass imperceptibly into each other. ~*n.* **1** a mixture of various qualities (of teas, wines, spirits, tobacco etc.). **2** a portmanteau word. **blender** *n.* **1** a type of electric liquidizer used in the preparation of food esp. for mixing and pureéing. **2** a person or thing which blends. [OE *blendan*]
†**blend**[2] (blend) *v.t.* to blind, to make blind. [OE *blendan*]
blende (blend) *n.* a native sulphide of zinc. [G, from *blenden,* to deceive, because it yielded no lead]
Blenheim (blen´əm) *n.* **1** a breed of spaniels. **2** (*also* **Blenheim orange**) a variety of apple. [Duke of Marlborough's seat near Woodstock, Oxfordshire]
blennorrhoea (blenərē´ə), (*N Am.*) **blennorrhea** *n.*

excessive discharge of mucus, esp. from the genital and urinary organs. [Gr. *blennos*, mucus, *rheein*, to flow]

blenny (blen´i) *n.* (*pl. in general* **blenny,** *in particular* **blennies**) any of a family of small, spiny-finned sea fishes, esp. of the genus *Blennius.* [L *blennius*, Gr. *blennos*, from the mucous coating of the scales]

blent (blent) *a.* (*poet.*) mingled.

blepharitis (blefərī´tis) *n.* inflammation of the eyelids. [Gr. *blepharon*, eyelid]

blepharo- (blef´ərō) *comb. form* of or relating to the eyelids. [Gr. *blepharon*, eyelid]

blesbok (bles´bok), **blesbuck** (-bŭk) *n.* (*pl. in general* **blesbok, blesbuck,** *in particular* **blesboks, blesbucks**) (*S Afr.*) a subspecies of bontebok, a S African antelope, having a white blaze on its forehead. [Afrikaans *bles*, blaze, *bok*, buck]

bless (bles) *v.t.* **1** to consecrate, to hallow. **2** to invoke God's favour on, to render happy or prosperous, as by supernatural means. **3** to wish happiness to. **4** to extol, magnify, worship. **5** (*euphem.*) to curse. **(God) bless me!** an ejaculation of surprise etc. **(God) bless you! 1** used to express endearment, gratitude etc. **2** used to someone who has just sneezed. **to bless oneself** to make the sign of the cross (as a defence against evil spirits). **to bless one's stars** to be very thankful. **without a penny to bless oneself with** penniless (with allusion to the cross on a silver penny). **blessed** (bles´id, blest), **blest** (blest) *a.* **1** consecrated by religious rites. **2** worthy of veneration. **3** happy, fortunate, beatified, enjoying the bliss of heaven. **4** joyful, blissful. **5** (*euphem.*) cursed. *~n.* (*collect.*) the saints in heaven. **I'm blessed!** an exclamation of surprise. **blessedly** (-id-) *adv.* fortunately, happily. **blessedness** (-id-) *n.* **1** the state of being blessed, esp. by heaven. **2** happiness, bliss. **blessing** *n.* **1** consecration. **2** divine favour. **3** an invocation of divine favour or happiness. **4** a cause of happiness. **5** a gift. **6** grace before or after meat. **to ask a blessing** to say grace before meat. **blessing in disguise** *n.* something that turns out to be unexpectedly advantageous. [OE *blētsian, bledsian, blœdsian*; orig. to redden with blood, to bless (*blōd*, BLOOD)]

blet (blet), **blett** *v.i.* (*pres.p.* **bletting,** *past, p.p.* **bletted**) (of fruit) to become internally rotten, as a pear which ripens after being picked. [OF *blette*, soft, mellow]

blether (bledh´ə), **blather** (bladh´ə) *v.i.* (*coll.*) to talk nonsense volubly. *~n.* **1** voluble nonsense. **2** a person who blethers, a prattler. **bletherskate** (-skāt), **blatherskite** (-skīt) *n.* a person who talks blatant nonsense. [Icel. *blathra*, to talk nonsense (*blathr*, nonsense)]

blew BLOW[1].

blewits (bloo´its) *n.* any fungus of the genus *Tricholoma*, with edible purplish tops. [prob. from BLUE]

blight (blīt) *n.* **1** a disease caused in plants by fungoid parasites and various insects, mildew, smut, rust, aphids etc. **2** any baleful atmospheric influence affecting the growth of plants. **3** any obscure malignant influence. **4** an area of urban decay. **5** a close and overcast state of the weather. *~v.t.* **1** to affect with blight. **2** to exert a baleful influence on. **3** to mar, frustrate. **blight bird, blighty bird** *n.* (*New Zeal.*) the white-eye. **blighter** *n.* (*sl.*) a nasty fellow, a blackguard. **blightingly** *adv.* [etym. uncertain]

Blighty (blī´ti) *n.* **1** (*sl.*) (used by soldiers) Britain, home. **2** (*Mil.*) a wound that invalids one home. [Urdu *Bilati*, foreign, European]

blimey (blī´mi), **cor blimey** *int.* (*sl.*) an exclamation of astonishment. [abbr. (God) *blind me*]

blimp (blimp) *n.* **1** a small airship used for observation. **2** a soundproof covering to drown the sound of the camera mechanism in a cinema. **3** (*coll.*) someone who is narrow-minded and conservative. **4** a diehard army officer. **blimpish** *a.* [Colonel *Blimp*, cartoon character created by David Low, 1891–1963]

blind (blīnd) *a.* **1** unseeing. **2** destitute of sight either naturally or by deprivation. **3** unseen, dark, admitting no light, having no outlet. **4** of, relating to or for the use or benefit of the sightless. **5** destitute of understanding, judgement or foresight. **6** undiscerning, obtuse. **7** reckless, heedless. **8** drunk. **9** purposeless, random. **10** (of letters) imperfectly addressed. **11** (*Bot.*) having no buds, eyes or terminal flower. **12** (of a bud) abortive. *~n.* **1** a blind person. **2** (*pl.*) blind persons collectively. **3** anything which obstructs the light or sight. **4** a blinker for a horse. **5** (*coll.*) a pretence, a pretext. **6** a window-screen or shade, esp. one on rollers for coiling up, or of slats on strips of webbing. **7** (*sl.*) a drunken fit. *~v.t.* **1** to make blind, to deprive of sight (permanently or temporarily). **2** to darken, make dim. **3** (*coll.*) to deceive. **4** to darken the understanding of. *~v.i.* **1** to drive blindly and recklessly. **2** (*sl.*) to swear. **blind as a bat** BAT[2]. **blind to** incapable of appreciating. **not a blind bit of** (*sl.*) not any; not the slightest. **to bake blind** to bake (pastry intended for a pie or flan) before adding the filling. **to blind someone with science** SCIENCE. **to fly blind** to fly by the use of instruments only. **to go it blind** to act recklessly. **to swear blind** SWEAR. **to turn a blind eye to** TURN. **blindage** (-ij) *n.* a screen for troops, a mantelet. **blind alley** *n.* **1** a street, road or alley walled-up at the end. **2** a situation leading nowhere. **blind-blocking** *n.* in bookbinding, ornamentation done by impressing hot tools without gold leaf. **blind coal** *n.* a flameless anthracite. **blind corner** *n.* a corner around which one cannot see. **blind date** *n.* **1** a social engagement arranged between two people previously unknown to one another. **2** a person on a blind date. **blind ditch** *n.* a concealed ditch. **blind door, blind window** *n.* a door or window that is walled up. **blind drunk** *a.* too drunk to be able to see straight. **blinder** *n.* **1** a person who or thing which blinds. **2** (*N Am.*) a horse's blinker. **3** (*coll.*) an excellent performance, esp. in cricket, football etc. **blindfish** *n.* a fish without functional eyes found in underground streams, e.g. the *Amblyopsis speloeus* of Mammoth Cave, Kentucky. **blindfold** *v.t.* **1** to cover the eyes of, esp. with a bandage. **2** to dull or obstruct the understanding of. *~a.* **1** having the eyes bandaged. **2** devoid of foresight. **blind god** *n.* the god Cupid. **blind gut** *n.* the caecum. **blind hookey** *n.* a gambling guessing game played with cards. **blinding** *n.* **1** the process of laying sand or grit on a road to cover cracks. **2** sand or grit used in this way. *~a.* **1** causing blindness; very bright (*blinding snow*). **2** noticeable; brilliant (*a blinding show of skill*). **blindingly** *adv.* **blindly** *adv.* **blind man's buff** *n.* a game in which a player has their eyes bandaged, and has to catch and identify one of the others. **blindness** *n.* **1** sightlessness. **2** lack of intellectual or moral perception. **3** ignorance, folly, recklessness. **blind screening** *n.* the testing of unidentified samples (of blood) without the patient's knowledge. **blind side** *n.* **1** the direction in which one is most easily assailed. **2** a weakness, a foible. **blind spot** *n.* **1** a part of the retina insensitive to light, owing to the passage through it of the optic nerve. **2** a point within the service area of a radio station where signals are received very faintly. **3** a tendency to overlook faults etc. **4** a failure of understanding or judgement. **5** a weakness. **blind stamping, blind tooling** *n.* embossing a book cover without gilding. **blind stitch** *n.* sewing that does not show, or that shows at the back only. **blind-stitch** *v.t., v.i.* to sew in blind stitch. **blindstory, blindstorey** *n.* (*pl.* **blindstories, blindstoreys**) **1** a series of arches below the clerestory, admitting no light. **2** a triforium. **blind wall** *n.* a wall with no opening in it. **blindworm** *n.* an aberrant British lizard, *Anguis fragilis*, also called the slow-worm (erroneously supposed to be blind, from the small size of its eyes). [OE (also Dut. Swed., G etc.)]

blink (blingk) *v.i.* 1 to move the eyelids. 2 to open and shut the eyes. 3 to look with winking eyelids, to look unsteadily. 4 to shine fitfully. 5 to peep, to wink, to twinkle. ~*v.t.* 1 to shut the eyes to. 2 to evade, to shirk. ~*a.* blinking, twinkling. ~*n.* 1 an act of blinking. 2 a gleam, a glimmer, a twinkle (cp. ICEBLINK (under ICE)). 3 a glance, a twinkling. **on the blink** (*coll.*) (of a machine) not functioning properly. **blinked** *a.* affected with blinking. **blinker** *n.* 1 a person who blinks. 2 (*pl.*) spectacles to cure squinting, or to protect the eyes from cold, dust etc. 3 (*pl.*) screens on a bridle to prevent a horse from seeing sideways. 4 a device that blinks, esp. an indicator on a vehicle. **to wear blinkers** (*coll.*) not to see or understand what is going on around one. **blinkered** *a.* 1 wearing blinkers. 2 not understanding what is going on around one. 3 having a distorted or biased view or opinion. **blinking** *a.* (*coll.*) a euphemism for BLOODY (under BLOOD) used for emphasis. [ME *blenken* (cp. Dut. and G *blinken*; OE *blencan*, see BLENCH)]

blintz (blints), **blintze** *n.* a thin, stuffed pancake. [Yiddish *blintse*, from Rus. *blin*, pancake]

blip (blip) *n.* (*coll.*) 1 an irregularity in the linear trace on a radar screen indicating the presence of an aircraft, vessel etc. 2 an intermittent, high-pitched sound from an electronic device, a bleep. 3 a temporary movement in the performance of something, esp. in an unexpected and unwelcome direction. ~*v.i.* (*pres. p.* **blipping,** *past, p.p.* **blipped**) to make a blip. ~*v.t.* to strike or tap sharply. [imit.]

bliss (blis) *n.* 1 happiness of the highest kind. 2 the perfect joy of heaven. 3 heaven. **blissful** *a.* 1 full of bliss. 2 causing bliss. **blissfully** *adv.* in a blissful manner. **blissfully ignorant of** quite unaware of. **blissfulness** *n.* the state of being blissful. [OE *blis, bliss, blīths* (*blīthe*, happy); sense infl. by BLESS]

blister (blis´tə) *n.* 1 a pustule or thin vesicle raised on the skin by some injury, burn etc., and containing a watery fluid or serum. 2 any similar swelling on a plant, metal, a painted surface etc. 3 a blistering agent. 4 anything applied to raise a blister. 5 (*sl.*) an irritating person. ~*v.i.* 1 to rise in blisters. 2 to be covered with blisters. 3 (*Austral., coll.*) to overcharge, to demand an exorbitant sum. ~*v.t.* 1 to raise blisters on. 2 to criticize spitefully. 3 (*sl.*) to bore. 4 to damn. **blister copper** *n.* partly purified copper which has a blister-like surface. **blistered** *a.* affected with blisters. **blister fly, blister beetle** *n.* the Spanish fly, *Lytta vesicatoria*, formerly used to raise blisters. **blister gas** *n.* a poison gas which causes the skin to blister. **blister pack** *n.* a type of clear plastic and cardboard packaging for small products. **blister plaster** *n.* a plaster for raising a blister. **blister steel** *n.* steel having a blistered surface, the result of absorption of carbon in its conversion from iron. **blistery** *a.* full of blisters. [ME *blister, blester*, perh. from OF *blestre*, Icel. *blāstr*, a blowing, a swelling (*blāsa*, to blow)]

blithe (blīdh) *a.* (*poet.*) 1 gay, cheerful, joyous. 2 merry, sprightly. 3 casual, indifferent. **blithely** *adv.* **blitheness** *n.* **blithesome** (-səm) *a.* 1 blithe. 2 cheery. **blithesomeness** *n.* [OE *blīthe* (cp. OHG *blīdi*, Dut. *blijde*)]

blithering (blidh´əring) *a.* 1 (*sl.*) nonsensical, contemptible. 2 jabbering, talking senselessly. [BLETHER]

B. Litt. *abbr.* Bachelor of Letters.

blitz (blits) *n.* (*coll.*) 1 intense enemy onslaught, esp. an air raid. 2 an intensive campaign against. 3 intensive activity or action. ~*v.t.* 1 to make an enemy onslaught on. 2 to mount an intensive campaign against. 3 to subject to intensive activity. **the Blitz** the German air raids on London in 1940. **blitzkrieg** (-´krēg) *n.* an intense military attack intended to defeat the opposition quickly. [G *Blitz* lightning]

blizzard (bliz´əd) *n.* a furious storm of snow and wind. [etym. uncertain; perh. fashioned on BLOW[1], BLAST etc.]

bloat (blōt) *v.t.* 1 to cause to swell. 2 to puff up. 3 to make vain or conceited. ~*v.i.* 1 to swell. 2 to grow turgid. ~†*a.* swollen, esp. with self-indulgence. ~*n.* swollen stomachs in cattle. **bloated** *a.* 1 swollen, inflated. 2 pampered. 3 puffed up with pride. **bloatedness** *n.* [ME *bloat, blowt*, soft (prob. var. of *blote*, see BLOATER)]

bloater (blō´tə) *n.* a herring partially cured by steeping in dry salt and smoking. [ME *blote*, soft, soaked (Icel. *blautr*), whence *bloat*, to cure, *bloat*, or *bloated*, herring, bloater]

blob (blob) *n.* 1 a globular drop of liquid. 2 a spot of colour. 3 (*Naut.*) the round mass forming the base of an iron post. 4 any vague, soft form. 5 †a pustule. 6 (*sl.*) in cricket, a score of nought. ~*v.i.* (*pres.p.* **blobbing,** *past, p.p.* **blobbed**) to make a blob. ~*v.t.* to put blobs of ink, paint etc. on. **blobby** *a.* (*comp.* **blobbier,** *superl.* **blobbiest**). [BLEB]

bloc (blok) *n.* a combination of parties, or of nations. **bloc vote** *n.* BLOCK VOTE (under BLOCK). [F]

block (blok) *n.* 1 a solid mass of wood or stone; a log, a tree stump. 2 a solid unshaped mass of any material. 3 a large building, esp. one that is divided. 4 a compact or connected group of buildings, esp. when bounded by intersecting streets, regarded in the US as a method of measuring distances. 5 an obstruction, a hindrance, an impediment or its effects. 6 a pulley, or system of pulleys, mounted in a frame or shell. 7 a solid cube, used as a child's toy. 8 a piece of wood or metal on which figures are engraved for printing from. 9 a casting taken from such a block. 10 a mould on which a thing is shaped. 11 (*sl.*) the head. 12 a dull, unemotional or hard-hearted person. 13 a quantity of things treated as a unit. 14 a pad of writing or drawing paper. 15 in cricket, the position in which a batsman blocks balls. 16 a blockhole. 17 a starting block. 18 in American football, a blocking action. 19 (*Austral.*) a tract of land used for farming or settlement. 20 (*Austral.*) a building plot. 21 the piece of wood on which criminals were beheaded. 22 death by beheading. 23 in Parliament, a notice of opposition to a bill. 24 a blockhead. ~*v.t.* 1 to stop up, to obstruct. 2 to impede (progress or advance). 3 to subject to a blockade. 4 to shape (a hat) on the block. 5 in bookbinding, to emboss (a cover) by impressing a device. 6 in cricket, to stop (a ball) dead without attempting to hit it. 7 in American football, to obstruct (another player) with one's body. 8 to enclose, to shut up. 9 to stop (a train) by a block signal. 10 (*fig.*) to block up, to obstruct. 11 in Parliament, to give notice of opposition to (a bill), thus preventing its being proceeded with at certain times. **on the block** (*N Am.*) being auctioned. **to block in** to sketch roughly the broad masses of (a picture or drawing). **to block out** 1 to mark out (work) roughly. 2 to exclude (something painful) from memory. **to block up** 1 to confine. 2 to infill (a window or doorway) with bricks. **to do one's block** (*Austral., New Zeal., coll.*) to be very angry. **to put the blocks on** to prevent from going ahead. **blockage** *n.* an obstruction. **block and tackle** *n.* a system of pulleys and ropes used for lifting. **blockboard** *n.* board made from thin strips of wood with plywood veneer. **blockbuster** *n.* (*coll.*) 1 a particularly effective or successful thing or person. 2 a very heavy and effective aerial bomb. 3 a very successful and profitable film or book. **blockbusting** *a.* **block capital** *n.* BLOCK LETTER (under BLOCK). **block-chain** *n.* an endless chain on bicycles and other vehicles. **block diagram** *n.* a diagram showing interconnected parts of a process, structure etc. **blocker** *n.* **blockhead** *n.* a stupid, dull person. **blockheaded** *a.* **blockhole** *n.* in cricket, a mark in front of the wicket where the batsman rests their bat. **block-house** *n.* **1** a detached fort covering some strategical point. **2** (*Hist.*) a one-storeyed timber building, with loopholes for musketry. **3** a house of squared timber. **blockish** *a.* **1** stupid. **2** dull. **3** rough, clumsy. **4** like a block. **blockishly** *adv.* **blockishness** *n.* **block letter** *n.* **1** a wood type of large size used in printing. **2** (*pl.*) the imitation in handwriting of printed capital letters. **block machine** *n.* a machine for making tackle-blocks. **block mountain** *n.* a mountain formed by natural faults. **block plan** *n.* a sketch plan showing the outline and relative situation of buildings without detail. **block printing** *n.* printing from engraved wooden blocks. **block release** *n.* the short-term release of employees for formal study or training. **blockship** *n.* a warship used defensively, e.g. to block a channel. **block signal** *n.* a signal to stop a train when the next section of the line is not clear. **block system** *n.* a system by which a railway line is divided into sections, and no train is allowed to pass into any section till it is signalled clear. **block tin** *n.* tin cast into ingots. **block vote** *n.* a system used esp. at a trade union conference, whereby the value of a delegate's vote is based on the number of people represented. [prob. from F *bloc* (OHG *bloh*, or MHG *bloch*, G *Block*)]

blockade (blokād´) *n.* **1** the investment of a place by sea or land, so as to compel surrender by starvation or prevent communication with the outside. **2** anything that prevents access or progress. **3** imprisonment by weather or other causes. ~*v.t.* to block up, esp. by troops or ships. **to run a blockade** to pass through a blockading force. **blockade-runner** *n.* **1** a vessel that runs or attempts to run into a blockaded port. **2** the owner, captain or any of the sailors of such a vessel. [as BLOCK]

bloke (blōk) *n.* (*coll.*) a man, a fellow. [etym. unknown]

blond (blond) *a.* **1** fair or light in colour. **2** having light hair and a fair complexion. ~*n.* a person who has light hair and a fair complexion. **blonde** *a.* (of a woman or girl) blond. ~*n.* a blond woman or girl. **blonde lace** *n.* a kind of lace, orig. made of raw silk. **blondish** *a.* **blondness** *n.* [F (Sp. *blondo*, It. *biondo*, late L *blundus*), prob. of Gmc. origin]

blood (blŭd) *n.* **1** the red fluid circulating by means of veins and arteries, through the bodies of man and other vertebrates. **2** any analogous fluid in the invertebrates. **3** lineage, descent. **4** honourable or high birth, family relationship, kinship. **5** slaughter, murder, bloodshed. **6** the guilt of murder. **7** temperament, passion. **8** vitality, mettle. **9** a man of a fiery spirit, a rake, a dandy, a dissipated character. **10** the juice of anything, esp. if red. **11** sap. **12** the supposed seat of the emotions. **13** the sensual nature of man. **14** blood shed in sacrifice. **15** (*sl.*) a leader of fashion. ~*v.t.* **1** to cause blood to flow from, to bleed. **2** to inure to blood (as a hound). **3** to initiate (a person) to war or experience. **4** to stain with blood. **5** to render bloody. **6** (*fig.*) to exasperate. **in one's blood** inborn; in one's character. **one's blood is up** one is angry or ready to fight. **out for someone's blood 1** wanting revenge on someone. **2** wanting to kill someone. **the blood 1** royal blood. **2** the royal family. **to make one's blood boil** to make one furious. **to make one's blood run cold** to horrify one. **to taste blood** to want to repeat something enjoyable or successful. **blood and thunder** *n.* **1** sensational literature. **2** (*sl.*) a mixture of port wine and brandy. **blood-and-thunder** *a.* sensational, melodramatic. **blood bank** *n.* the place where blood for transfusion is stored. **bloodbath** *n.* a massacre. **blood blister** *n.* a blister containing blood, caused e.g. by a bruise. **blood-borne** *a.* carried by the blood. **blood brother** *n.* **1** a brother by both parents. **2** a man linked to another in a ceremony by the mixing of blood. **blood cell** *n.* any of the cells that circulate in the blood. **blood count** *n.* **1** a calculation of the number of red and white corpuscles in a sample of blood. **2** the number of these. **blood-curdling** *a.* horrifying. **blood-curdlingly** *adv.* **blood donor** *n.* a person from whom blood is taken for transfusion. **blooded** *a.* **1** (of horses etc.) of good pedigree. **2** having blood or disposition (*in comb.* as *warm-blooded*). **blood feud** *n.* a feud arising out of murder or homicide; a vendetta. **blood fluke** *n.* any parasitic flatworm, such as a schistosome, that lives in the blood of man and other vertebrates. **blood group** *n.* any one of the four types into which human blood has been classified for purposes of blood transfusion. **blood-guilt, blood-guiltiness** *n.* murder or homicide. **blood-guilty** *a.* guilty of murder or homicide. **blood-heat** *n.* the ordinary heat of blood in a healthy human body (about 98°F or 37°C). **blood horse** *n.* a horse of good breed or pedigree. **bloodhound** *n.* **1** a variety of hound remarkable for keenness of scent, used for tracking fugitives. **2** a person who relentlessly pursues an opponent. **3** a detective, a spy. **bloodless** *a.* **1** without blood. **2** without effusion of blood. **3** spiritless. **4** unfeeling. **bloodlessly** *adv.* **bloodlessness** *n.* **blood-letting** *n.* **1** the act, process or art of taking blood from the body, phlebotomy. **2** bloodshed. **3** excessive financial demands. **bloodline** *n.* (of animals) all the individuals in a family line regarded over generations, esp. regarding characteristics; pedigree. **bloodlust** *n.* desire for bloodshed. **blood money** *n.* **1** money paid for evidence or information leading to a conviction on a murder charge. **2** money paid to the next of kin as compensation for the murder of a relative. **3** money paid to a hired murderer. **blood orange** *n.* an orange having pulp and juice of a reddish hue. **blood plasma** *n.* blood from which all red corpuscles have been removed. **blood poisoning** *n.* a diseased condition set up by the entrance of septic matter into the blood. **blood pressure** *n.* pressure of the blood on the walls of the containing arteries. **blood rain** *n.* rain tinted reddish from contact with dust particles in the air. **blood red** *n.* a deep red colour. **blood-red** *a.* red as blood. **blood relation, blood relative** *n.* a relation by descent, not merely by marriage. **blood royal** *n.* the royal family. **blood serum** *n.* blood plasma from which the clotting factors have been removed. **bloodshed** *n.* **1** the act of shedding blood. **2** murder. **3** slaughter in war. **bloodshot** *a.* **1** red and inflamed. **2** (of the eye) suffused with blood. **blood spavin** *n.* a dilatation of the main vein inside the hock of a horse. **blood sport** *n.* a sport entailing the killing of animals, such as fox-hunting. **bloodstain** *n.* a stain produced by blood. **bloodstained** *a.* **1** stained by blood. **2** guilty of bloodshed. **bloodstock** *n.* (*collect.*) thoroughbred horses. **bloodstone** *n.* heliotrope, a variety of quartz with bloodlike spots of jasper. **bloodstream** *n.* **1** the blood circulating in the body. **2** the circulatory movement of the blood in the body. **bloodsucker** *n.* **1** any animal which sucks blood, esp. the leech. **2** an extortioner. **bloodsucking** *a.* **blood sugar** *n.* the amount of glucose circulating in the blood. **blood tax** *n.* conscription, compulsory military service. **blood test** *n.* the examination of a sample of blood for medical disorders. **bloodthirsty** *a.* (*comp.* **bloodthirstier**, *superl.* **bloodthirstiest**) **1** eager to shed blood. **2** delighting in sanguinary deeds. **bloodthirstily** *adv.* **bloodthirstiness** *n.* **blood-transfusion** *n.* transference of blood from the vein of a healthy person to the vein of a person whose blood is deficient in quantity or quality. **blood vessel** *n.* a vessel in which blood circulates in the animal body; an artery or a vein. **bloodwood, blood tree** *n.* any of several varieties of tree that exude a bright red gum esp. an Australian eucalyptus. **bloodworm** *n.* **1** the red wormlike larva of several midges, such as *Chironomus plumosus*, which live in stagnant pools and ditches. **2** a freshwater worm of the genus *Tubifex.* **3** any of several reddish worms used by anglers. **blood-wort** *n.* any of various plants, either from their red leaves or roots, or from the notion that they were efficacious in staunching blood. **bloody** *a.* (*comp.* **bloodier,** *superl.* **bloodiest**) **1** of or relating to blood. **2** stained or running with blood. **3** attended with bloodshed. **4** cruel, murderous. **5** (*sl.*) damned, devilish. **6** very, exceedingly (prob. from the bloods or hooligans of rank in the 17th or 18th cent.). **7** (*sl.*) annoying, wretched etc. *~v.t.* (*3rd pers. sing. pres.* **bloodies,** *pres.p.* **bloodying,** *past, p.p.* **bloodied**) to make bloody; to stain with blood. **to cry/ scream bloody murder** MURDER. **bloodily** *adv.* **bloodiness** *n.* **1** the state or condition of being bloody. **2** abounding with blood, as a battlefield. **bloody-bones** *n.* a bugbear, a fright. **bloody-faced** *a.* **1** having the face stained with blood. **2** sanguinary. **bloody flux** *n.* dysentery. **bloody hand** *n.* (*Her.*) the Ulster badge borne by baronets. **Bloody Mary** *n.* a drink consisting of tomato juice and vodka. **bloody-minded** *a.* **1** of a cruel disposition. **2** of an obstinate or unhelpful disposition. **bloody-mindedly** *adv.* **bloody-mindedness** *n.* **bloody murder** *n.* (*N Am.*) BLUE MURDER (under BLUE). **bloody nose** *n.* a bleeding nose. [OE *blōd* (cp. Goth. *blōth,* G *Blut,* Icel. *blōth,* Dut. *bloed*)]

bloom[1] (bloom) *n.* **1** a blossom, a flower. **2** the delicate dust on newly gathered plums, grapes etc. **3** the yellow sheen on well-tanned leather. **4** lustre, efflorescence. **5** a lens coating that increases its transparency. **6** a kind of currant. **7** flush, glow. **8** prime, perfection. **9** WATER-BLOOM (under WATER). **10** the coloured scum formed by this. *~v.i.* **1** to blossom, to come into flower. **2** to be at the highest point of perfection or beauty. *~v.t.* to coat (a lens) so as to reduce reflection from the surface. **in bloom** flowering, blossoming. **to take the bloom off** to make stale. **blooming** *a.* **1** in a state of bloom, flourishing. **2** bright, lustrous. **3** (*sl.*) euphemistic for bloody. *~adv.* (*sl.*) used as an intensifier. **bloomingly** *adv.* **bloomless** *a.* **bloomy** *a.* (*comp.* **bloomier,** *superl.* **bloomiest**) full of blooms, flowery. [Icel. *blōm,* a blossom (cp. OHG *bluomo,* G *Blume*), from the root *blō-,* to blow, to flourish (cp. L *flos, florēre*)]

bloom[2] (bloom) *n.* a mass of iron that has undergone the first hammering. *~v.t.* to hammer or squeeze (the ball, or lump of iron, from the puddling furnace) into a bloom. **bloomery** *n.* (*pl.* **bloomeries**) **1** the apparatus for making blooms out of puddled iron. **2** a furnace for making malleable iron by a direct process. [OE *blōma*]

bloomer[1] (bloo´mə) *n.* **1** (*Hist.*) a style of dress for ladies, consisting of a shorter skirt, and loose trousers gathered round the ankles. **2** (*Hist.*) a woman wearing such a dress. **3** (*pl.*) bloomer trousers. **4** (*pl.*) baggy knickers. **5** a broad-brimmed straw hat for women. [the American Mrs Amelia Jenks *Bloomer,* who advocated it in 1851]

bloomer[2] (bloo´mə) *n.* **1** a plant that blooms (*esp. in comb.,* as *early-bloomer*). **2** (*N Am.*) a person who develops in a specified way (*late bloomer*). **3** (*sl.*) a mistake, a foolish blunder.

bloomer[3] (bloo´mə) *n.* an oblong crusty loaf with rounded ends and notches on the top. [etym. uncertain]

bloomery BLOOM[2].

Bloomsbury (bloomz´bəri) *n.* (*in full* **Bloomsbury Group**) a group of writers, artists etc. associated with Bloomsbury in London in the early twentieth century. *~a.* **1** associated with or characteristic of the Bloomsbury Group. **2** intellectual; highbrow.

blooper (bloo´pə) *n.* (*esp. N Am., coll.*) a blunder; a silly mistake. [imit.]

blore (blaw) *n.* a violent gust or blast. [prob. onomat.]

blossom (blos´əm) *n.* **1** the flower of a plant, esp. considered as giving promise of fruit. **2** a flower. **3** the mass of flowers on a fruit tree. **4** promise of future excellence or development. **5** a promising person. *~v.i.* **1** to put forth flowers. **2** to bloom. **3** to flourish. **blossoming** *n.* **blossomless** *a.* **blossomy** *a.* full of blossoms. [OE *blōstma, blōstm* (prob. cognate with BLOOM[1])]

blot[1] (blot) *n.* **1** a spot or stain of ink or other discolouring matter. **2** a blotting out by way of correction. **3** a dark patch. **4** a blemish, disgrace, disfigurement, defect. **5** a fault. **6** a disgraceful action. **7** in biochemistry, a procedure for analysing molecules, esp. proteins, in which they are separated by gel electrophoresis. *~v.t.* (*pres.p.* **blotting,** *past, p.p.* **blotted**) **1** to spot or stain with ink or other discolouring matter. **2** to obliterate. **3** to dry with blotting paper, to apply blotting paper to. **4** to darken, to disfigure, to sully. **5** in biochemistry, to transfer by means of a blot. *~v.i.* to make blots, to become blotted. **to blot one's copybook 1** (*coll.*) to commit an indiscretion. **2** (*coll.*) to spoil one's good record. **to blot out** to obliterate, to efface. **blot on the escutcheon** *n.* a stain on the reputation of a person, family etc. **blotter** *n.* **1** a person or thing which blots. **2** a scribbler. **3** a paper pad or book for absorbing superfluous ink from paper after writing. **4** a blotting pad. **5** (*N Am.*) a record sheet in e.g. a police station. **blottesque** (-esk´) *a.* characterized (as a painting) by masses of colour heavily laid on. **blotting** *n., a.* **blotting book, blotting-pad** *n.* a book or pad made up of blotting paper. **blotting paper** *n.* absorbent paper for drying up ink. [etym. uncertain]

blot[2] (blot) *n.* **1** an exposed piece at backgammon. **2** a weak point, a failing. **3** a mark, a butt. [etym. uncertain (prob. conn. with Dan. *blot,* bare, naked)]

blotch (bloch) *n.* **1** a pustule, boil, botch. **2** a blot. **3** a patch. **4** a clumsy daub. *~v.t.* to blot. **blotched** *a.* marked with blotches. **blotchy** *a.* (*comp.* **blotchier,** *superl.* **blotchiest**) full of blotches. **blotchily** *adv.* **blotchiness** *n.* [prob. from BLOT[1]]

blotto (blot´ō) *a.* (*sl.*) unconscious with drink. [from BLOT[1]]

blouse (blowz) *n.* a light, loose, upper garment. *~v.t.* to make (a garment) hang in loose folds. *~v.i.* to hang in loose folds. [F (etym. unknown)]

blouson (bloo´zon) *n.* a short, loose jacket fitted or belted in at the waist. [F]

blow[1] (blō) *v.i.* (*past* **blew** (bloo), *p.p.* **blown** (blōn)) **1** to move as a current of air. **2** to send a current of air from the mouth. **3** to pant, to puff. **4** to sound, to give forth musical notes (as a horn). **5** to eject water and air from the spiracles (as cetaceans). **6** to boast, to talk big. **7** (*sl.*) to squander money, to spend. **8** (of a fuse) to melt from overloading. *~v.t.* **1** to drive a current of air upon. **2** to inflate with air. **3** to drive by a current of air. **4** to put out of breath. **5** to sound (a wind instrument or a note on it). **6** to taint by depositing eggs upon (as flies). **7** to shatter by explosives. **8** to spread (a report etc.). **9** to inflate, to puff up, to enlarge. **10** (*sl.*) (*past, p.p.* **blowed**) to curse, confound. **11** to cause (a fuse) to melt by overloading. **12** (*sl.*) to spoil (an opportunity). **13** (*sl.*) to squander. *~n.* **1** a blowing, a blast of air. **2** a breath of fresh air. **3** an egg (of a flesh-fly). **4** oviposition (of flesh-flies). **5** a single operation of a Bessemer converter. **6** a boast. **7** boastfulness. **8** (*coll.*) a spell of playing jazz. **blow it!** damn, confound it. **I'll be blowed!** (*coll.*) used to express astonishment etc. **to blow a fuse** FUSE[1]. **to blow a kiss** to kiss one's hand and blow the air towards someone. **to blow away 1** (*sl.*) to kill or destroy. **2** (*sl.*) to defeat. **3** (*sl.*) to amaze. **to blow away the cobwebs** COBWEB. **to blow hot and cold 1** to vacillate. **2** to do one thing at one time, and its opposite at another. **to blow in 1** to break inwards. **2** to make an unexpected visit. **to blow it/ something** (*coll.*) to lose a chance or advantage by committing a blunder. **to blow off 1** to escape with a blowing noise, as steam. **2** to discharge (steam, energy, anger etc.). **3** to break wind. **to blow one's lid** (*coll.*) to lose one's temper. **to blow one's mind** (*sl.*) to give one drug-induced hallucinations or a similar experience. **to blow one's own trumpet** to boast, to sing one's own praises. **to blow one's stack** (*N Am., coll.*) to lose one's temper. **to blow one's top** (*coll.*) to lose one's temper. †**to blow on/ upon** 1 to make stale or common. 2 to bring into discredit. 3 to expose. **to blow out** 1 to extinguish by blowing. 2 to clear by means of blowing. 3 (of a tyre) to burst. 4 (of a fuse) to melt. 5 (*N Am., sl.*) to defeat soundly. 6 (*N Am., sl.*) to break. **to blow over** to pass away, to subside. **to blow the gaff** GAFF². **to blow the socks off** SOCK¹. **to blow the whistle on** (*coll.*) to inform on (someone) or bring (something) to an end. **to blow up** 1 to inflate. 2 to scold, to censure severely. 3 to ruin. 4 to explode, to fly in fragments. 5 (*coll.*) to enlarge (a photograph). 6 (*coll.*) to exaggerate. 7 (*coll.*) to arise. 8 (*coll.*) to lose one's temper. **blow-ball** *n.* the downy head of the dandelion and allied plants. **blow-by-blow** *a.* (of a storyline or description) very detailed. **blow-dry** *n.* a method of styling hair while drying it with a small hairdryer. *~v.t.* (*3rd pers. sing. pres.* **blow-dries,** *pres.p.* **blow-drying,** *past, p.p.* **blow-dried**) to arrange (hair) while drying it in this way. **blow-dryer, blow-drier** *n.* **blower** *n.* 1 a person who or thing which blows. 2 a cetacean, a whale. 3 a contrivance for creating an artificial current of air. 4 an escape of gas in a mine. 5 a fissure through which gas escapes. 6 (*coll.*) a telephone, speaking-tube etc. **blowfish** *n.* (*pl. in general* **blowfish,** *in particular* **blowfishes**) any of several kinds of fish which inflate their bodies when they are frightened. **blowfly** *n.* (*pl.* **blowflies**) a fly of the family Calliphoridae, such as the bluebottle, which lays its eggs on meat. **blowgun** *n.* (*N Am.*) a tube used by American Indians for shooting darts; a blowpipe. **blowhard** *n.* a boastful person. *~a.* boastful. **blowhole** *n.* 1 an airhole. 2 a hole in the ice to which seals and whales come to breathe. 3 (*pl.*) the spiracles of a cetacean. **blowing** *n., a.* **blowing-machine** *n.* a machine for creating a current of air. **blow job** *n.* (*sl.*) an act of fellatio. **blowlamp, blowtorch** *n.* 1 a lamp used in soldering, brazing etc. 2 a burner used to remove paint. **blowline** *n.* in angling, a light line with real or artificial bait at the end, allowed to float over the surface of water with the wind. **blow moulding** *n.* a method of manufacturing plastic goods. **blow-out** *n.* (*sl.*) 1 a hearty meal. 2 a celebration. 3 an explosion of oil and gas from an oil well. 4 the puncturing of a tyre. 5 the burning out of an electrical fuse or a valve. 6 (*N Am.*) a defeat or failure. **blowpipe** *n.* 1 a tube used for increasing combustion by directing a current of air into a flame. 2 a pipe used in glass-blowing. 3 a tube used by American Indians for shooting darts by means of the breath. **blowtorch** BLOWLAMP (under BLOW¹). **blow-up** *n.* 1 the enlargement of part or whole of a photograph. 2 (*coll.*) an explosion. 3 (*coll.*) a burst of anger, a heated argument. **blowy** *a.* (*comp.* **blowier,** *superl.* **blowiest**) 1 windy. 2 exposed to the wind. [OE *blāwan* (cp. OHG *blāhan*, G *blächen*, L *flāre*)]

blow² (blō) *n.* 1 a stroke with the fist or any weapon or instrument. 2 an act of hostility. 3 a severe shock. 4 a sudden and painful calamity. **at one blow** in one action. **to strike a blow for** to show support for. [etym. uncertain]

blow³ (blō) †*v.i.* (*past* **blew** (bloo), *p.p.* **blown** (blōn)) 1 to blossom. 2 to bloom, to flourish. *~n.* 1 the state of blossoming. 2 bloom. 3 a display of blossoms. [OE *blōwan* (OHG *bluojan*, G *blühen*, cp. L *florēre*, see also BLOOM¹)]

blowze (blowz), **blowse** *n.* 1 a red-faced, bloated woman. 2 a woman with disordered hair. 3 †a wench, a beggar's wench. **blowzed** *a.* blowsy. **blowzy** *a.* (*comp.* **blowzier,** *superl.* **blowziest**) 1 having a red, bloated face. 2 untidy, sluttish. **blowzily** *adv.* **blowziness** *n.* [conn. with BLUSH]

BLT *abbr.* bacon, lettuce and tomato.

blub (blŭb) *v.i.* (*pres.p.* **blubbing,** *past, p.p.* **blubbed**) (*sl.*) to weep noisily, shed tears. [short for BLUBBER]

blubber (blŭb´ə) *n.* 1 the fat underlying the skin in whales and other cetaceans, from which train-oil is prepared. 2 (*coll.*) excess body fat. 3 noisy weeping. 4 a jellyfish. *~a.* (of the lips etc.) swollen, pouting. *~v.i.* to weep noisily. *~v.t.* 1 to wet and disfigure with weeping. 2 to utter with sobs and tears. **blubberer** *n.* **blubbery** *a.* [prob. imit. in origin (cp. BABBLE, BLEB, BUBBLE)]

blucher (bloo´khə, -chə) *n.* (*usu. in pl., Hist.*) a strong leather half-boot. [the Prussian general Gebhard von *Blücher*, 1742– 1819]

bludge (blŭj) *v.i.* (*Austral., New Zeal., sl.*) 1 to evade work. 2 to scrounge from someone. *~v.t.* to cadge, scrounge. *~n.* an easy task. **to bludge on** to impose on (someone). **bludger** *n.*

bludgeon (blŭj´ən) *n.* a short, thick stick, sometimes loaded; a blackjack. *~v.t.* 1 to strike with this. 2 to coerce verbally, or by physical force. [etym. uncertain]

blue (bloo) *a.* (*comp.* **bluer,** *superl.* **bluest**) 1 of the colour of the cloudless sky or deep sea. 2 of the similar colour of smoke, vapour, distant landscape, steel etc. 3 (*coll.*) miserable, low-spirited. 4 (*sl.*) obscene, smutty. 5 with bluish skin because of cold etc. 6 belonging to the political party which adopts blue for its colour (in Britain, usu. the Conservatives). 7 having blue as a distinguishing colour. 8 dressed in blue. 9 (of women) learned, pedantic. 10 †livid. *~n.* 1 a blue colour. 2 a blue pigment. 3 a blue substance, object or animal (as explained by context). 4 a blue jacket or cap worn as colours. 5 blue clothes. 6 a person who plays for their university in sport or athletics. 7 a supporter of a political party which has blue for its colour, such as the Conservative Party. 8 any of various small blue butterflies of the family Lycaenidae. 9 a blue powder used in laundries. 10 (*Austral., sl.*) an argument. 11 (*Austral., sl.*) (as a nickname) someone with red hair. 12 a blue ball, piece etc. in a game. 13 the sky. 14 the sea. 15 (*Austral.*) a summons. 16 a blue-coat boy. *~v.t.* (*pres.p.* **blueing, bluing,** *past, p.p.* **blued**) 1 to make blue. 2 to treat with (laundry) blue. 3 (*sl.*) to squander (money). **blue in the face** FACE. **out of the blue** unexpectedly. **the Blue** one of the three former divisions of the British Navy. **to burn blue** to burn (as candles) with a blue flame, as an omen of death, or indicating the presence of ghosts or evil spirits. **to look blue** to look frightened or depressed. **until one is blue in the face** FACE. **blue baby** *n.* a baby with a bluish discoloration of the skin due to a shortage of oxygen in the blood. **Bluebeard** *n.* 1 a man who murders his wives. 2 a person with a horrible secret. **bluebell** *n.* 1 a woodland plant, *Hyacinthoides nonscripta*, which has blue bell-shaped flowers, also called *wild hyacinth* or *wood hyacinth*. 2 (*Sc.*) the harebell, *Campanula rotundifolia*. 3 any of several other plants which have blue bell-shaped flowers. **blueberry** *n.* (*pl.* **blueberries**) 1 any of several plants of the genus *Vaccinium*, which have blue-black edible berries, also called *huckleberry*. 2 the fruit of these plants. **blue bice** *n.* a shade of blue between ultramarine and azure. **bluebird** *n.* 1 any N American songbird of the genus *Sialia*, which have blue plumage on the back or head. 2 (*fig.*) a symbol of happiness. **blue-black** *a.* of a blue colour that is almost black. *~n.* black with a tinge of blue. **blue blood** *n.* 1 aristocratic descent. 2 a person of aristocratic descent. **blue-blooded** *a.* **bluebonnet** *n.* 1 a flat Scottish cap, or bonnet, of blue wool. 2 a peasant or soldier wearing such a bonnet. 3 (*Sc.*) any species of *Centaurea* and scabious. **blue book** *n.* **1** an official report of Parliament (bound in volumes which have blue covers). **2** (*N Am.*) a list of Government officials with their salaries etc. **bluebottle** *n.* **1** the blue cornflower, *Centaurea cyanus*. **2** any of several other blue flowers. **3** the meat-fly or blowfly, *Calliphora vomitoria*. **4** †a beadle. **5** (*coll.*) a police officer. **6** (*Austral.*) a Portuguese man-of-war. **blue box** *n.* **1** (*esp. N Am.*) an electronic device used to gain illegal access to long-distance telephone lines. **2** (*esp. Can.*) a blue plastic box for storing materials to be recycled. **bluecap** *n.* **1** a bluebonnet. **2** a salmon in its first year. **3** the blue tit, *Parus caeruleus*. **blue cat** *n.* a Siberian cat, valued for its slaty-blue fur. **blue cheese** *n.* a cheese threaded by blue veins of mould induced by the insertion of copper wires during its making. **blue chip** *n.* **1** an issue of stocks or shares believed to be dependable in maintaining or increasing its value. **2** anything of worth and stability. **blue-chip** *a.* **blue coat** *n.* (*Hist.*) **1** a coat of blue, formerly the dress of the poor classes. **2** a blue coat worn by almoners and children in charity schools. **3** an individual of these classes. **blue-coat boy** *n.* a boy wearing the blue coat of a charity school, esp. a scholar of Christ's Hospital. **blue cod** *n.* (*New Zeal.*) an edible salt-water fish, *Parapercis colias*. **blue-collar** *a.* of or relating to manual work and manual workers in contrast to desk work and office employees (see WHITE-COLLAR (under WHITE)). **blue devils** *n.pl.* **1** low spirits, depression (the blues). **2** the illusions of delirium tremens. **blue ensign** *n.* a blue flag flown by the naval reserve and by some yachts and merchant vessels. **blue eye** *n.* **1** an eye with a blue iris. **2** (*Austral.*) a honeyeater with blue colouring around the eyes. **blue-eyed** *a.* having an eye with a blue iris. **blue-eyed boy, blue-eyed girl** *n.* (*coll., usu. derog.*) someone especially favoured by a person or group. **blue film, blue movie** *n.* a sexually explicit or pornographic film. **bluefish** *n.* (*pl. in general* **bluefish,** *in particular* **bluefishes**) a large voracious fish, *Pomatomus saltatrix*, which inhabits tropical and temperate waters. **blue flag** *n.* the European Union flag, allowed to be flown at beach areas which meet EU standards of cleanness of the beach and pollution-free water. **blue funk** *n.* **1** abject terror. **2** (*N Am.*) a state of despondency or depression. **blue gown** *n.* (*Hist.*) an almoner, a licensed beggar. **bluegrass** *n.* (*N Am.*) **1** the rich grass of the limestone lands of Kentucky and Tennessee (bluegrass country). **2** a kind of folk music originating from these regions. **blue-green alga** *n.* a cyanobacterium. **blue ground** *n.* KIMBERLITE. **bluegum, bluegum tree** *n.* any tree of the genus *Eucalyptus*, esp. *E. regnans*. **blueing** *n.* (*N Am.*) the blue powder used in laundries. **blueish** BLUISH (under BLUE). **bluejacket** *n.* (*sl.*) a sailor in the British Navy. **Blue John** *n.* blue fluorspar. **blue light** *n.* a composition burning with a blue flame used at sea as a night signal. **blue line** *n.* in ice hockey, either of the two lines midway between the centre of the rink and each goal. **bluely** *adv.* **Bluemantle** *n.* one of the four pursuivants in the College of Arms. **blue metal** *n.* broken blue stone used to make roads. **blue moon** *n.* **1** a very rare or unknown occurrence. **2** never. **once in a blue moon** very rarely, seldom; never. **blue mould** *n.* a blue-coloured fungus which grows on rotting food and other vegetable matter, and is induced in blue cheese. **blue movie** BLUE FILM (under BLUE). **blue murder** *n.* a loud noise; a great commotion. **to cry/scream blue murder** MURDER. **blueness** *n.* **bluenose** *n.* (*N Am.*) a native of Nova Scotia. **blue-pencil** *v.t.* (*pres.p.* **blue-pencilling,** (*N Am.*) **blue-penciling,** *past, p.p.* **blue-pencilled,** (*N Am.*) **blue-penciled**) (*coll.*) to censor, edit or mark with corrections (traditionally using a blue pencil). **Blue Peter** *n.* a small blue flag with a white square in the centre, used as a signal for sailing. **blue pill** *n.* an antibilious pill made from mercury. **blue pointer** *n.* (*Austral.*) a voracious shark with a blue back, *Isuropsis mako*. **blueprint** *n.* **1** a plan or drawing printed on specially sensitized paper: the print is composed of white lines on a blue background, and is much used for scale and working drawings of engineering designs, electrical circuits etc. **2** any original plan or guideline for future work. **3** a prototype. ~*v.t.* (*N Am.*) to work out (a plan, programme etc.). **blue ribbon** *n.* **1** the ribbon of the Garter. **2** the greatest distinction, the first prize. **3** a total abstainer's badge. **blue-ribbonism** *n.* the tenets or practice of total abstinence. **blue-ribbonite** *n.* (*esp. Hist.*) a person who wears a blue ribbon as a badge of total abstinence, a member of the Blue Ribbon Army. **blue rinse** *n.* a rinse for tinting grey hair. **blue roan** *a.* black mixed with white. ~*n.* an animal of this colour. **blue rock** *n.* ROCK DOVE (under ROCK[1]). **blue ruin** *n.* bad gin. **blues** *n.pl.* **1** (**the blues**) low spirits, depression. **2** (**the blues**) a form of melancholy, black American folk song originating in the deep south, usu. consisting of three, four-bar phrases in 4/4 time. **3** (*sing.*) a blues song. **4** (**the Blues**) the Royal Horse Guards. **5** (**the Blues**) the Conservatives. **Dark Blues** DARK. **Light Blues** LIGHT[1]. **bluesy** *a.* **blue-sky** *a.* (*coll.*) **1** purely theoretical, speculative or experimental. **2** lacking specific goals (as of a research project). **blue-sky law** *n.* (*N Am.*) a state law regulating the trading of securities, which protects investors from fraud. **bluestocking** *a.* **1** wearing blue worsted stockings, applied (contemptuously) to a literary society that met at Montagu House, London, in the latter part of the 18th cent. **2** (of women) affecting learning or literary tastes. ~*n.* a woman affecting learning or literary tastes. **bluestone** *n.* **1** any of various blue-grey building stones. **2** a dark building stone found in Australia and New Zealand. **3** any of the smaller stones used at Stonehenge, made of dolerite. **4** sulphate of copper. **bluet** *n.* a N American blue-flowered plant of the genus *Hedyotis*. **blue tit** *n.* a common tit, *Parus caeruleus*, which has a blue crown, wings and tail and yellow underparts. **blue vitriol** *n.* hydrous sulphate of copper. **blue water** *n.* the open sea. **blue whale** *n.* the largest known living mammal, *Balaenoptera musculus*, a bluish-grey rorqual. **bluey**[1] *n.* (*pl.* **blueys**) (*Austral., coll.*) **1** a bundle carried by a bushman. **2** a blanket. **to hump one's bluey** to tramp; to carry one's bundle. **bluey**[2] *a.* having a tinge of blue. **bluish, blueish** *a.* having a tinge of blue. **bluishly** *adv.* **bluishness** *n.* [ME, from OF *bleu*, from Gmc.]

bluff[1] (blŭf) *a.* **1** (of a cliff, or a ship's bows) having a broad, flattened face or front. **2** abrupt, blunt, frank, outspoken. ~*n.* a cliff or headland with a broad, precipitous front. **bluff-bowed, bluff-headed** *a.* (*Naut.*) having vertical or nearly vertical bows. **bluffly** *adv.* **bluffness** *n.* [Naut., etym. uncertain (cp. MDut. *blaf*, flat, broad)]

bluff[2] (blŭf) *n.* **1** a blinker for a horse. **2** a game of cards, called also poker. **3** (*sl.*) an excuse, a blind. **4** the action of bluffing at cards. **5** boastful language. **6** empty threats or promises. ~*v.t.* **1** to hoodwink. **2** to impose upon (one's adversary at cards) by making them believe one's hand is stronger than it is, and inducing them to throw up the game. **3** (*fig.*) to treat (rivals, political opponents, or foreign powers) in this way. ~*v.i.* to make one's adversary believe that one is strong or confident. **to call someone's bluff** to challenge someone who is bluffing; to expose someone. **bluffer** *n.* [etym. uncertain (cp. Dut. *bluffen*, to brag, boast)]

bluish BLUE.

blunder (blŭn´də) *v.i.* **1** to err grossly. **2** to act blindly or stupidly. **3** to flounder, to stumble. ~*v.t.* **1** to utter thoughtlessly. **2** to mismanage. ~*n.* a gross mistake, a stupid error. **to blunder upon** to find or discover by chance. **blunderer** *n.* a person who habitually blunders. **blunderhead** *n.* **1** a dunderhead. **2** a muddle-headed person. **blundering** *a.* **blunderingly** *adv.* [etym. uncertain]

blunderbuss (blŭn´dəbŭs) *n.* (*Hist.*) a short gun, of large bore, widening at the muzzle. [Dut. *donderbus*, thunder gun]

blunge (blŭnj) *v.t.* to mix (clay, powdered flint etc. with water) in a pug-mill. **blunger** *n.* [BLEND[1], PLUNGE]

blunt (blŭnt) *a.* **1** dull, stupid, obtuse. **2** without edge or point. **3** abrupt, unceremonious. **4** rough, unpolished. *~n.* a short, thick kind of sewing needle. *~v.t.* **1** to make less sharp, keen, or acute. **2** to deaden, to dull. *~v.i.* to become blunt. **bluntish** *a.* **bluntly** *adv.* **bluntness** *n.* **blunt-witted** *a.* dull of understanding. [etym. uncertain]

blur (blœ) *n.* **1** a smear, a blot, a stain. **2** a dim, misty effect. *~v.t.* (*pres.p.* **blurring,** *past, p.p.* **blurred**) **1** to smear, to blot. **2** to stain, to sully. **3** to render misty and indistinct. **4** to dim. *~v.i.* to become indistinct. **blurry** *a.* (*comp.* **blurrier,** *superl.* **blurriest**). **blurriness** *n.* [etym. uncertain]

blurb (blœb) *n.* a description of a book, usu. printed on the dust jacket, intended to advertise and promote it. [attrib. to Gelett Burgess, American humorist, d.1951]

blurt (blœt) *v.t.* to utter abruptly (*usu. with out*). *~v.i.* **1** to burst into tears. **2** †to puff out the lips contemptuously. *~n.* an impetuous outburst. [prob. an imit. word]

blush (blŭsh) *v.i.* **1** to become red in the face from shame or other emotion, to assume a bright red colour. **2** to be ashamed. **3** to bloom. *~n.* **1** the reddening of the face produced by shame, modesty or any similar cause. **2** a crimson or roseate hue. **3** a flush of light. **at the first blush** at the first glance; at first sight. **to put to the blush** **1** to cause to blush. **2** to make ashamed. **to spare someone's blushes** to avoid embarrassing someone by praising them too much. **blusher** *n.* **1** a person who blushes. **2** a cosmetic for reddening the cheeks. **blushful** *a.* **1** full of or suffused with blushes. **2** modest, self-conscious. **blushfully** *adv.* **blushing** *a.* **1** that blushes. **2** modest. **3** ruddy, roseate. **4** blooming. **blushingly** *adv.* **blushless** *a.* **blush rose** *n.* a white rose with pink tinge. **blush wine** *n.* (*orig. N Am.*) rosé wine. [OE *āblisian* (cp. Dut. *blozen*, to blush, Dan. *blus*, a blaze, a torch]

bluster (blŭs´tə) *v.i.* **1** to blow boisterously. **2** to be agitated (as water by wind). **3** to make a loud boisterous noise. **4** to play the bully, to swagger, to boast. *~v.t.* to disarray, to dishevel. *~n.* **1** boisterous, blowing, inflated talk, swaggering. **2** empty vaunts and threats. **blusterer** *n.* a person who or thing which blusters. **blustering** *a.* that blusters, blustery. **blusteringly** *adv.* †**blusterous** *a.* blustery. **blustery** *a.* **1** blowing boisterously. **2** tempestuous. **3** hectoring, boastful. [onomat.; cp. BLAST]

Blvd *abbr.* boulevard.

BM *abbr.* **1** Bachelor of Music. **2** British Museum. **3** bench mark in surveying.

BMA *abbr.* British Medical Association.

BMC *abbr.* British Medical Council.

BMDO *abbr.* Ballistic Missile Defence Organization.

BMEWS *abbr.* ballistic missile early warning system.

BMJ *abbr.* British Medical Journal.

BMR *abbr.* basal metabolic rate.

B. Mus. *abbr.* Bachelor of Music.

BMX *abbr.* **1** bicycle motocross, bicycle stunt riding over an obstacle course. **2** (**BMX**®) a bicycle designed for this.

Bn. *abbr.* **1** Baron. **2** battalion. **3** billion.

BO *abbr.* **1** body odour. **2** box office.

bo (bō), **boh** *int.* an exclamation intended to surprise or frighten. **bo-beep** *n.* a children's game in which a player suddenly looks out from a hiding-place and cries 'bo!' to startle their playmates. [imit.]

boa (bō´ə) *n.* **1** a genus of large S American snakes of the family Boidae, which kill their prey by crushing. **2** any such snake, e.g. a python. **3** a long fur or feather stole worn round the neck. **boa constrictor** *n.* **1** a Brazilian serpent, *Boa constrictor*, which kills its prey by crushing it. **2** any very large snake which kills its prey by constriction. [L (etym. unknown)]

boanerges (bōənœ´jēz) *n.* a loud, vociferous preacher or orator. [Gr., from Heb. *b'ney regesh*, sons of thunder (Mark iii.17)]

boar (baw) *n.* **1** the uncastrated male of the domesticated swine. **2** (**wild boar**) the male of the wild swine, *Sus scrofa*. **3** a male guinea pig. **boarish** *a.* **1** swinish, brutal. **2** sensual, cruel. **boarishly** *adv.* **boarishness** *n.* **boar's foot** *n.* the green hellebore, *Helleborus viridis*. **boar-spear** *n.* a spear used in boar-hunting. [OE *bār* (cp. Dut. *beer*, G *Bär*)]

board (bawd) *n.* **1** a piece of timber of considerable length, and of moderate breadth and thickness. **2** a flat slab of wood, used as a table, for exhibiting notices, and other purposes. **3** a table or frame on which games (such as chess, draughts etc.) are played. **4** a thick substance formed of layers of paper etc., pasted or squeezed together. **5** a piece of stout pasteboard or millboard used as one of the sides of a bound book. **6** a table, esp. for meals. **7** †a table spread for a meal. **8** food served at table. **9** daily provisions. **10** one's keep, or money in lieu of keep. **11** a council table. **12** the members of a council. **13** the persons who have the management of some public trust or business concern. **14** the side of a ship. **15** (*Mining*) a passage driven across the grain of the coal. **16** (*pl.*) the stage. **17** (*Austral.*) the floor of a shearing-shed. **18** (*Austral.*) the shearers employed in a shearing-shed. *~v.t.* **1** to furnish or cover with boards. **2** to provide with daily meals (and now usu. with lodging). **3** to board out. **4** to attack and enter (a ship) by force. **5** to go on a ship, to embark. **6** (*fig.*) to accost, to make up to. *~v.i.* to have one's meals (and usu. lodging) at another person's house. **Big Board** BIG. **board and lodging** meals and sleeping-quarters. **by the board** **1** overboard, by the ship's side. **2** ignored, rejected or disused. **on board** in or into a ship, train, bus or aeroplane. **to board out** **1** to place at board. **2** to take one's meals out. **to sweep the board** SWEEP. **boarder** *n.* **1** a person who has their food at the house of another. **2** a scholar who is boarded and lodged at a school. **3** a person who boards an enemy's ship. **board game** *n.* a game, such as chess, which is played with pieces or counters on a special board. **boarding** *n.* **1** the action of the verb to BOARD. **2** a structure of boards. **boarding house** *n.* a house in which board may be had. **boarding kennel** *n.* a place where dogs are boarded. **boarding officer** *n.* an officer who boards a ship to examine its bill of health etc. **boarding out** *n.* **1** the obtaining of stated meals at another person's house. **2** (*Hist.*) the placing of poor or destitute children in foster homes. **boarding pass** *n.* a ticket authorizing one to board an aeroplane, ship etc. **boarding school** *n.* a school in which pupils are boarded as well as taught. **Board of Green Cloth** *n.* GREEN CLOTH (under GREEN). **board of trade** *n.* **1** (*N Am.*) a chamber of commerce. **2** (**Board of Trade**) a ministry within the UK Department of Trade. **boardroom** *n.* the meeting place of a company's board of directors. **boardsailing** *n.* **1** sailing on a surf board propelled by a sail mounted with a steering bar. **2** windsurfing. **boardsailor, boardsailer** *n.* **board school** *n.* (*Hist.*) a school managed by a Board, as established by the Elementary Education Act, 1870. **board wages** *n.pl.* wages given to servants in lieu of food. **boardwalk** *n.* **1** a seaside promenade made of planks. **2** (*N Am.*) a wooden walkway over sand, marsh etc. [OE *bord*, board, plank, table (cp. Dut. *boord*,

MHG and G *Bord*, Icel. *borth*); *bord*, in the sense of border, rim, ship's side, appears to be a distinct word which was early associated; and at later periods the F *bord* (from Gmc.) influenced the development of meaning]

boart BORT.

boast (bōst) *n.* **1** proud, vainglorious assertion, a vaunt, a brag. **2** an occasion of pride. **3** laudable exultation. ~*v.i.* to brag, to praise oneself, to speak ostentatiously or vaingloriously. ~*v.t.* **1** to extol, to speak of with pride. **2** to have as worthy of pride. **boaster** *n.* a person who boasts, a bragger, a braggadocio. **boastful** *a.* **1** full of boasting. **2** vainglorious. **boastfully** *adv.* **boastfulness** *n.* **boastingly** *adv.* [etym. uncertain]

boat (bōt) *n.* **1** a small vessel, generally undecked and propelled by oars or sails. **2** a fishing vessel, mailboat or passenger ship. **3** a vessel or utensil resembling a boat, such as a sauce-boat. ~*v.t.* to transport in a boat. ~*v.i.* to sail in a boat, to row in a boat. **in the same boat** in the same circumstances or position. **to push the boat out** (*coll.*) to celebrate expensively. **to rock the boat** to disrupt existing conditions, to cause trouble. **boatable** *a.* (*N Am.*) that may be traversed by boat, navigable. **boatage** (-ij) *n.* charges for carriage by boat. **boatbill, boatbilled heron** *n.* a tropical wading bird, *Cochlearius cochlearius*, with a broad flat bill and nocturnal habits. **boat-building** *n.* the occupation of building boats. **boat-builder** *n.* **boater** *n.* **1** a person who boats. **2** a man's stiff straw hat. **boat-fly** *n.* (*pl.* **boat-flies**) a boat-shaped water-bug, *Notonecta glauca*. **boatful** *n.* (*pl.* **boatfuls**) as much or as many as a boat will hold. **boat-hook** *n.* a pole with an iron point and hook, used to push or pull a boat. **boathouse** *n.* a house by the water in which boats are kept. **boatie** *n.* (*esp. Austral., New Zeal.*) a boating enthusiast. **boating** *n.* the art, sport or practice of sailing or rowing. **boatload** *n.* **1** enough to fill a boat. **2** (*coll.*) a large number of people. **boatman** *n.* (*pl.* **boatmen**) **1** a person who lets out boats on hire. **2** a person who rows or sails a boat for hire. **boat people** *n.pl.* refugees (usu. Vietnamese) who have fled from their countries in small boats. **boat race** *n.* a race between rowing boats. **boat-train** *n.* a train conveying passengers to or from a ship. [OE *bāt*; etym. obscure, prob. from Gmc. (whence Icel. *bātr*, Dut. *boot*, and perh. F *bateau* etc.)]

boatel (bōtel´), **botel** *n.* **1** a floating hotel, a moored ship functioning as a hotel. **2** a waterfront hotel accommodating boaters. [BOAT, HOTEL]

boatswain (bō´sən), **bo's'n, bosun, bo'sun** *n.* the foreman of the crew (in the RN a warrant officer) who looks after the ship's boats, rigging, flags, cables etc. **boatswain's chair** *n.* a wooden seat suspended from ropes, used by someone working on a ship's side. **boatswain's mate** *n.* a boatswain's chief assistant. [OE *bātswegen* (boat, swain)]

bob[1] (bob) *n.* **1** a short jerking action, a curtsy. **2** a peal of courses or set of changes in bell-ringing. **3** a short hairstyle. **4** a weight or pendant at the end of a cord, chain, plumb line, pendulum etc. **5** a bobsleigh. **6** the docked tail of a horse. **7** a short line at the end of a stanza. **8** a knot or bunch of hair, a short curl, a bobwig. **9** (*Hist., sl.*) a shilling or 5 pence. **10** a shake, a jog. **11** a knot of worms used in fishing for eels. ~*v.t.* (*pres.p.* **bobbing**, *past, p.p.* **bobbed**) **1** to move with a short jerking motion. **2** to cut short (as a horse's tail). **3** to cut (hair) in a bob. **4** to rap, to strike lightly. ~*v.i.* **1** to have a short jerking motion. **2** to move to and fro or up and down. **3** to dance, to curtsy. **4** to catch with the mouth. **5** to fish for eels with a bob. **6** to ride on a bobsleigh. **to bob up** to emerge suddenly. **bobber** *n.* a person who rides on a bobsleigh. **bobbish** *a.* (*coll.*) **1** well, in good health. **2** brisk. **bobble** (bob´əl) *n.* **1** a fabric or wool ball used as decorative trimming, a pompon. **2** (*N Am.*) a mistake; a fumble. ~*v.t., v.i.* (*N Am.*) to fumble, handle ineptly or bungle. **bobble hat** *n.* a knitted hat with a bobble at the top. **bobbly** *a.* **bobcat** *n.* a N American lynx, *Felix rufus*, which has reddish-brown fur with dark spots or stripes, and a short tail. **bob-cherry** *n.* (*Hist.*) a child's game of catching in the mouth cherries suspended on a string. **bobsled** *n.* **1** a conveyance formed of two sleds or sleighs coupled together, used to transport large timber. **2** (*N Am.*) a bobsleigh. **bobsledding** *n.* **bobsleigh** *n.* a sleigh with two pairs of runners, one behind the other, often used for racing. **bobsleighing** *n.* **bobtail** *n.* **1** a tail (of a horse) cut short. **2** a horse or dog with its tail cut short. **ragtag and bobtail** RAGTAG (under RAG[1]). **bobtailed** *a.* having the tail cut short. **bobtail wig** *n.* a short wig. **bobwig** *n.* a wig having the bottom turned up in bobs or curls, in contradistinction to a full-bottomed wig. [etym. uncertain; prob. onomat.]

bob[2] (bob) *n.* a person, a fellow. **dry bob** DRY. **wet bob** WET. [prob. from *Robert*]

Bobadil (bob´ədil) *n.* a braggart. [character in Jonson's *Every Man in His Humour*]

bobber BOB[1].

bobbery (bob´əri) *n.* (*pl.* **bobberies**) **1** a row. **2** a fuss. [Hind. *bāp re!*, O father!]

bobbie pin (bob´i), **bobby pin** *n.* (*esp. N Am.*) a hairgrip.

bobbin (bob´in) *n.* **1** a spool or pin with a head on which thread for making lace, cotton, yarn, wire etc., is wound and drawn off as required. **2** a piece of wood with a string for actuating a door latch. **3** a reel, spool. **bobbinet** (-net´) *n.* machine-made cotton net, orig. imitated from bobbin lace. **bobbin lace, bobbinwork** *n.* work woven with bobbins. [F *bobine* (etym. unknown)]

bobbish BOB[1].

bobbitt (bob´it) *v.t.* to sever the penis of (one's husband or lover). [Lorena *Bobbitt*, an American who did this to her husband]

bobble BOB[1].

bobby[1] (bob´i) *n.* (*pl.* **bobbies**) (*coll.*) a policeman, a police officer. [from Sir *Robert* Peel, who introduced the new police, 1828]

bobby[2] (bob´i), **bobby calf** *n.* (*pl.* **bobbies, bobby calves**) a calf slaughtered for veal because it has been weaned. [dial.]

bobby-dazzler (bobidaz´lə) *n.* (*coll.*) an excellent striking person or thing, esp. an attractive girl. [dial., related to DAZZLE]

bobby pin BOBBIE PIN.

bobby sox (bob´i), **bobby socks** *n.* (*esp. N Am.*) ankle socks usu. worn by young girls. **bobby-soxer** *n.* an adolescent girl.

bobolink (bob´əlingk) *n.* a N American songbird, *Dolichonyx oryzivorus*. [earlier *Bob Lincoln* or *Bob o' Lincoln*, from the cry]

bobstay (bob´stā) *n.* a chain or rope for drawing a ship's bowsprit downward and keeping it steady. [etym. unknown]

bocage (bəkahzh´) *n.* woodland scenery represented in ceramics. [F BOSCAGE]

Boche (bosh) *n.* (*derog.*) a German, esp. a soldier. ~*a.* German. **the Boche** Germans, esp. German soldiers, collectively. [F sl.]

bock (bok) *n.* **1** a strong German beer. **2** a large beerglass. **3** a large glass of beer. [a mistaken sense, from F, G *Bock*, goat, used to describe a strong kind of beer, being taken for a measure]

BOD *abbr.* biochemical oxygen demand.

bod (bod) *n.* (*coll.*) **1** a person. **2** (*N Am.*) a body. [contr. BODY]

bodacious (bodā´shəs) *a.* (*sl., esp. N Am.*) excellent, wonderful. [perh. BOLD, AUDACIOUS]

bode[1] (bōd) *v.t.* **1** to foretell. **2** to presage. **3** to give promise of. 4 to forebode. ~*v.i.* to portend (well or ill). **boding** *a.* presaging, ominous. ~*n.* an omen, presentiment, prediction. **bodingly** *adv.* ominously, forebodingly. [OE *bodian* (*bod*, a message, *boda*, a messenger), cp. Icel. *botha*, to announce]

bode[2] BIDE.

bodega (bədē´gə) *n.* a shop selling wine, esp. in a Spanish-speaking country. [Sp., from L *apotheca*, Gr. *apothēkē*, a storehouse]

Bode's law (bōdz, bō´dəz) *n.* a formula for measuring the distances of the planets from the sun. [Johann Elert *Bode*, 1747–1826, German astronomer]

Bodhisattva (bodisaht´və) *n.* in Mahayana Buddhism, a person who postpones entry into nirvana in order to help suffering beings. [Sansk., one whose essence is enlightenment]

bodice (bod´is) *n.* 1 a tight-fitting outer vest for women. 2 the upper part of a woman's dress, for the body above the waist. 3 (*Hist.*) an inner vest worn by women over the corset. **bodice-ripper** *n.* (*coll.*) a romantic historical novel involving sex and violence. **bodice-ripping** *a.* [orig. *pair of bodies*]

bodiless, bodily BODY.

bodkin (bod´kin) *n.* 1 a large-eyed and blunt-pointed needle for leading a tape or cord through a hem, loop etc. 2 a pin for fastening up women's hair. 3 an instrument for piercing holes. 4 an awl-like tool for picking out letters in correcting set-up type. **to ride/ sit bodkin** to ride or sit wedged in between two others. [etym. unknown]

Bodleian (bod´liən) *a.* of or relating to Sir T. Bodley, who in 1597 restored the Library at Oxford University which now bears his name. ~*n.* the Bodleian Library. [Sir Thomas *Bodley*, 1545–1613]

body (bod´i) *n.* (*pl.* **bodies**) 1 the material frame of man or the lower animals. 2 the main trunk, excluding the head and limbs. 3 the upper part of a dress, a bodice. 4 a corpse, a dead body. 5 the main or central part of a building, ship, document, book etc. 6 the part of a car in which the driver and passengers sit. 7 a collective mass of persons, things or doctrine, precepts etc. 8 matter, substance, as opposed to spirit. 9 a human being, a person, an individual. 10 a society, a corporate body, a corporation. 11 a military force. 12 (*Philos.*) matter, substance, that which has sensible properties. 13 any substance, simple or compound. 14 (*Geom.*) a figure of three dimensions. 15 strength, substantial quality. 16 a figure-hugging woman's top resembling a swimsuit or leotard fastened beneath the crotch (and worn under a skirt or trousers). ~*v.t.* (*3rd pers. sing. pres.* **bodies,** *pres.p.* **bodying,** *past, p.p.* **bodied**) 1 to clothe with a body. 2 to embody. **body and bones** altogether. **in a body** all together. **over my dead body** (*coll.*) without my agreement, against my opposition. **to body forth** 1 to give mental shape to. 2 to exhibit, to typify. **to keep body and soul together** to survive, to maintain life. **bodied** *a.* 1 having a body. 2 embodied. **bodiless** *a.* **bodily** *a.* 1 of, relating to or affecting the body or the physical nature. 2 corporeal. ~*adv.* 1 corporeally, united with matter. 2 wholly, completely, entirely. **body bag** *n.* a strong plastic bag in which a dead body (esp. of a soldier killed in battle) is transported home. **body blow** *n.* 1 in boxing, a punch landing between the breast bone and navel. 2 a harsh disappointment or setback, a severe shock. **bodybuilder** *n.* 1 a person who develops their muscles through exercise and/or eating high protein food. 2 an exercising machine. **body-building** *n., a.* **body-check** *n.* in sports such as lacrosse or hockey, a deliberate obstruction of one player by another. ~*v.t.* to obstruct in this way. **body colour** *n.* 1 a pigment having a certain degree of consistency and tingeing power as distinct from a wash. 2 a colour rendered opaque by the addition of white. **body corporate** *n.* the nation. **body count** *n.* a calculation or estimate of the number of violent deaths, in battle or in a film etc. **body double** *n.* in films, a person who stands in for an actor during a nude scene or a stunt, where the face is not seen. **bodyguard** *n.* 1 a guard for the person of a sovereign or dignitary. 2 a retinue, following. **body language** *n.* a form of non-verbal communication by means of conscious or unconscious gestures, postures and facial expressions. **body odour** *n.* the smell of the human body, esp. the smell of sweat. **body piercing** *n.* the piercing of holes in a person's body, so that jewellery can be worn. **body politic** *n.* 1 organized society. 2 the state. **body-popping** *n.* (*orig. N Am.*) dancing with jerky, robotic movements. **body scanner** *n.* (*Med.*) an X-ray or ultrasound machine that uses a computer to produce cross-sectional pictures of the body. **body search** *n.* a search of a person's body in order to find drugs, weapons etc. **body servant** *n.* a valet. **body shop** *n.* a vehicle-body repair shop. **body snatcher** *n.* 1 (*Hist.*) a person who steals a body from a grave for the purpose of dissection; a resurrection man. 2 (*sl.*) a bailiff. 3 (*sl.*) a police officer. **body stocking** *n.* a clinging all-in-one undergarment for women, often of a sheer material. **bodysuit** *n.* 1 a top worn by girls or women which fastens beneath the crotch. 2 an undergarment worn by babies. **body warmer** *n.* a padded or quilted jacket without sleeves. **body wave** *n.* a soft light permanent wave for the hair. **body weight** *n.* the weight of a person's or animal's body. **bodywork** *n.* the metal shell of a motor vehicle. **body wrap** *n.* a beauty treatment in which the body is wrapped in hot bandages in order to cleanse the skin or improve the figure. [OE *bodig*]

Boer (buə, bō´ə, baw) *n.* a S African of Dutch birth or extraction. ~*a.* of or relating to the Boers. [Dut. *boer*, countryman, farmer (see BOOR)]

boffin (bof´in) *n.* (*coll.*) a scientist, esp. one employed by the armed services or the government. [etym. uncertain]

Bofors gun (bō´fəz) *n.* an automatic anti-aircraft gun. [*Bofors* in Sweden, where it was first made]

bog (bog) *n.* 1 a marsh, a morass. 2 wet, spongy soil, a quagmire. 3 (*sl.*) a lavatory. ~*v.t.* (*pres.p.* **bogging,** *past, p.p.* **bogged**) to sink or submerge in a bog. **to bog down** 1 to overwhelm, as with work. 2 to hinder. **to bog off** (*sl.*) to go away. **bog asphodel** *n.* a yellow-flowered marsh plant, *Narthecium ossifragum*, which has grass-like leaves. **bogbean** *n.* BUCKBEAN. **bogberry** *n.* (*pl.* **bogberries**) the cranberry. **bog butter** *n.* a fatty hydrocarbon found in peatbogs. **bog cotton** *n.* COTTON GRASS (under COTTON). **boggy** *a.* (*comp.* **boggier,** *superl.* **boggiest**) 1 of or characterized by bogs. 2 swampy. **bogginess** *n.* **bog house** *n.* (*sl.*) a lavatory, privy. **bog land** *n.* boggy soil, derogatorily applied to Ireland. **bog-lander** *n.* (*offensive*) an Irish person. **boglet** (-lit) *n.* a little bog. **bog moss** *n.* the genus *Sphagnum*. **bog myrtle** *n.* a deciduous shrub, *Myrica gale*, with catkins and grey-green leaves, also called *sweet gale*. **bog oak** *n.* oak found preserved in bogs, black from impregnation with iron. **bog spavin** *n.* distension of a horse's hock joint by effusion of synovial fluid. **bog standard** *a.* (*sl.*) basic. **bogtimber, bogwood** *n.* timber found preserved in bogs. **bogtrotter** *n.* 1 a person used to traversing boggy country. 2 (*offensive*) an Irish person. **bog violet** *n.* the butterwort, the genus *Pinguicula*. [Ir. *bogach*]

bogey[1] (bō´gi) *n.* (*pl.* **bogeys**) 1 in golf, one stroke over par on a hole. 2 (*Hist.*) a fair score or allowance for a good golfer, orig. an ideal opponent against whom a solitary player could pit themselves. ~*v.t.* (*3rd. pers. sing. pres.* **bogeys,** *pres.p.* **bogeying,** *past, p.p.* **bogeyed**) to complete (a hole) in one stroke over par. [*Bogey*, an imaginary person]

bogey[2] (bō´gi), **bogy** *n.* (*pl.* **bogeys, bogies**) 1 a spectre, a bugbear. **2** an awkward thing or circumstance. **3** (*sl.*) a piece of nasal mucus. **bogeyman** *n.* (*pl.* **bogeymen**) an evil person or spirit, used to menace children. [BOGLE]

bogey[3] (bō´gi), **bogie** *v.i.* (*3rd pers. sing. pres.* **bogeys, bogies,** *pres.p.* **bogeying, bogieing,** *past,p.p.* **bogeyed, bogied**) (*Austral.*) to bathe, to swim. ~*n.* a bathe. **bogey hole** *n.* a swimming hole. [Austral. Abor.]

boggard (bog´əd), **boggart** (-ət) *n.* (*North.*) **1** a hobgoblin. **2** a ghost. [conn. with BOGLE, BOGEY[2] etc.]

boggle (bog´əl) *v.i.* **1** to shrink back, start with fright. **2** to hesitate, make difficulties, to equivocate. **3** (*coll.*) to bungle. **4** (*coll.*) to be astounded. **5** (*coll.*) to be unable to imagine or understand. ~*v.t.* to overwhelm (mentally). [BOGLE]

bogie[1] (bō´gi), **bogy** *n.* (*pl.* **bogies**) **1** a revolving undercarriage. **2** a platelayer's truck or trolley. **3** †a long, low truck on four small wheels. **bogie-car, bogie-engine** *n.* a railway carriage or locomotive engine mounted on a bogie. [etym. uncertain]

bogie[2] BOGEY[3].

bogle (bō´gəl) *n.* **1** a hobgoblin, a spectre, a bugbear. **2** a scarecrow. [Sc., perh. from Welsh *bwg*, a goblin]

bogus (bō´gəs) *a.* **1** sham, counterfeit, spurious, fictitious. **2** (*sl., esp. N Am.*) awful, bad, disappointing. [etym. uncertain]

bogy[1] BOGEY[2].

bogy[2] BOGIE[1].

Boh. *abbr.* Bohemian.

boh BO.

bohea (bōhē´) *n.* **1** an inferior quality of black China tea. **2** (*Hist.*) the finest kind of black tea. [Chin. *Wu-i* or *Bu-i* hills, in China]

Bohemian (bəhē´miən) *a.* of or relating to Bohemia, its people or their language. ~*n.* **1** a native or inhabitant of Bohemia. **2** a Czech. **3** †the Czech language. [*Bohemia*, former kingdom in central Europe, now part of the Czech Republic]

bohemian (bəhē´miən) *n.* **1** a gypsy. **2** a person who leads a free, irregular life, despising social conventionalities. ~*a.* of or characteristic of the gypsies or of social bohemians. **bohemianism** *n.* the habits or conduct of a social bohemian. **bohemianize, bohemianise** *v.i.* to live in an unconventional way. [F *bohémien*, gypsy (because the gypsies were supposed to come from Bohemia)]

boho (bō´hō) *n.* (*pl.* **bohos**) (*coll.*) a bohemian. ~*a.* bohemian.

boiar BOYAR.

boil[1] (boil) *v.i.* **1** to be agitated by the action of heat, as water or other fluids. **2** to reach the temperature at which these are converted into gas. **3** to be subjected to the action of boiling, as meat etc., in cooking. **4** to bubble or seethe like boiling water (also of the containing vessel). **5** to be agitated with passion. ~*v.t.* **1** to cause (a liquid) to bubble with heat. **2** to bring to the boiling point. **3** to cook by heat in boiling water. **4** to prepare in a boiling liquid. ~*n.* **1** an act of boiling. **2** the state of boiling. **3** boiling point. **to boil away** to evaporate in boiling. **to boil down 1** to lessen the bulk of by boiling. **2** to condense. **to boil down to** to amount to; to mean. **to boil over 1** to bubble up, so as to run over the sides of the vessel. **2** to be effusive. **3** to lose one's temper. **boiled** *a.* **boiled shirt** *n.* (*coll.*) a dress shirt. **boiled sweet** *n.* a hard sweet made from boiled sugar. **boiler** *n.* **1** a person who boils. **2** a vessel in which anything is boiled. **3** the large vessel in a steam engine in which water is converted into steam. **4** a tank in which water is heated for domestic use. **5** (*Hist.*) a vessel for boiling clothes in a laundry, a copper. **6** a tough chicken etc. that needs to be cooked by boiling. **boilermaker** *n.* **1** a person who makes boilers. **2** a welder or plater, working in heavy industry. **3** (*sl.*) a drink consisting of draught mild beer mixed with bottled brown ale. **4** (*N Am., sl.*) a drink of whisky followed by a beer chaser. **boiler room** *n.* the room in a building that contains the boiler and other heating equipment. **boiler suit** *n.* a combined overall garment, esp. for dirty work. **boiling** *a.* **1** in a state of ebullition by heat. **2** inflamed, greatly agitated. **3** (*coll.*) (*also* **boiling hot**) very hot. ~*n.* the action of boiling. **the whole boiling (lot)** (*sl.*) the whole lot. **boiling point** *n.* **1** the temperature at which a fluid is converted into the gaseous state, esp. the boiling point of water at sea level (100°C). **2** a peak of excitement. [OF *boillir* (F *bouillir*), L *bullīre*, to bubble (*bulla*, a bubble)]

boil[2] (boil) *n.* a hard, inflamed, suppurating tumour. [OE *bȳll* (cp. Dut. *buil*, G *Beule*)]

boisterous (boi´stərəs) *a.* **1** wild, unruly, intractable. **2** stormy, roaring, noisy. **3** tumultuous, rudely violent. **boisterously** *adv.* **boisterousness** *n.* [ME *boistous*, rough]

bolas (bō´ləs) *n.* a missile, used by S American Indians, formed of balls or stones strung together and flung round the legs of the animal aimed at. [Sp. and Port., pl. of *bola*, ball]

bold (bōld) *a.* **1** courageous, daring, confident, fearless. **2** planned or executed with courage. **3** vigorous, striking. **4** audacious, forward, presumptuous. **5** steep, prominent, projecting (of a cliff or headland). **6** BOLDFACE (under BOLD). **bold as brass** wholly impudent or audacious. **to make/ be so bold** to venture, to presume. **boldface** *a.* (of type) heavy, conspicuous. **boldfaced** *a.* **1** impudent, shameless. **2** boldface. **boldly** *adv.* impudently, with effrontery. **boldness** *n.* **1** courage, enterprise, audacity. **2** effrontery, shamelessness. **bold-spirited** *a.* courageous, daring. [OE *beald*, *bald* (cp. OHG *pald*, G *bald*, quickly)]

bole[1] (bōl) *n.* the stem or trunk of a tree. [Icel. *bolr* (Dan. *bul*, log, G *Bohle*, plank, board)]

bole[2] (bōl) *n.* a brownish, yellowish or reddish, soft unctuous clay, containing more or less iron oxide. [late L *bōlus*, Gr. *bōlos*, a clod of earth]

bolection (bəlek´shən) *n.* a projecting moulding. [etym. unknown]

bolero (bəleə´rō, bol´ərō) *n.* (*pl.* **boleros**) **1** a lively Spanish dance. **2** (*Mus.*) music for or in the time of this dance. **3** a short jacket worn over a bodice. [Sp.]

Usage note The pronunciation (bol´ərō) is used only of the jacket.

---

boletus (bəlē´təs) *n.* a mushroom or toadstool of the genus *Boletus*, having the undersurface of the pileus full of pores instead of gills. **boletic** (-let´-) *a.* of or relating to the boletus. [L and Gr. *bōlites* (perh. from *bōlos*, a lump)]

bolide (bō´līd) *n.* a large meteor, usu. one that explodes and falls in the form of aerolites. [F, from L *bolidem -lis*, Gr. *bolis*, missile (*ballein*, to throw)]

bolin BOWLINE (under BOW[3]).

bolivar (bol´ivah) *n.* (*pl.* **bolivars, bolivares** (-ah´res)) the standard unit of currency in Venezuela. [Simon *Bolivar*, S American soldier and statesman, 1783–1830]

boliviano (bəliviah´nō) *n.* (*pl.* **bolivianos**) the standard unit of currency in Bolivia, equal to 100 centavos. [BOLIVAR]

boll (bōl) *n.* a rounded seed vessel or pod. **boll-weevil** *n.* a weevil, *Anthonomus grandis*, that infests the flowers and bolls of the cotton plant. [BOWL[1]]

bollard (bol´əd, -ahd) *n.* **1** (*Naut.*) a large post or bitt on a wharf, dock or on shipboard for securing ropes or cables. **2** a short post preventing motor vehicle access. [perh. from BOLE[1]]

bollocks (bol´əks), **ballocks** *n.pl.* (*sl.*) **1** testicles. **2** rubbish, nonsense, a mess. ~*v.i.* to make a mess of.

bollocking *n.* (*sl.*) a strong rebuke. [OE *beallucas*, testicles]

bologna (bəlō´nyə, bəlon´yə), **Bologna sausage** *n.* a large smoked sausage of mixed meats, also called a *polony*. [*Bologna* in Italy]

Bolognese (bolənyāz´, -nāz´) *a.* of or relating to Bologna. ~*n.* a native or inhabitant of Bologna. **spaghetti Bolognese** SPAGHETTI. **Bolognese sauce** *n.* a sauce of meat, tomatoes etc., served with pasta.

bolometer (bəlom´itə) *n.* an extremely sensitive instrument for measuring radiant heat. **bolometric** (bolәmet´-) *a.* **bolometry** *n.* [Gr. *bole*, a ray of light]

boloney BALONEY.

Bolshevik (bol´shəvik), **Bolshevist** (bol´shəvist) *n.* **1** (*Hist.*) a member of the Russian majority Socialist party which came to power under Lenin in 1917. **2** a political revolutionary. **3** (*often derog.*) a political agitator. ~*a.* that is a Bolshevik; of or relating to Bolsheviks. **Bolshevism** *n.* **bolshie** (-shi), **bolshy** *n.* (*pl.* **bolshies**) **1** (*coll.*) (*also* **Bolshie, Bolshy**) a Russian Bolshevik. **2** (*often derog.*) a political agitator. ~*a.* (*sl.*) stubborn and argumentative. **bolshiness** *n.* [Rus. *bolsheviki*, majority party]

bolster (bōl´stə) *n.* **1** a long underpillow, used to support the pillows in a bed. **2** a pad, cushion or anything resembling a pad or cushion, in an instrument, machine, ship, architecture or engineering. **3** a punching tool. **4** a short timber cap on a post to increase the bearing area. **5** a form of cold chisel used for cutting stone. ~*v.t.* **1** to support with or as with a bolster. **2** to belabour with bolsters. **3** to pad, stuff. ~*v.i.* to fight with bolsters. **to bolster up 1** to support, to prevent from falling. **2** to save from deserved chastisement, criticism or disgrace. **3** to aid, abet, countenance. **bolsterer** *n.* **bolstering** *n.* **1** prop, support. **2** padding, stuffing. **3** a fight with bolsters. [OE (OHG *polstar*, G *Polster*, Icel. *bolstr*)]

bolt[1] (bōlt) *n.* **1** a short thick arrow with a blunt or thick head. **2** a discharge of lightning. **3** the act of gulping food without chewing. **4** a measured roll of woven fabric, esp. canvas. **5** a bundle of osiers or reeds, measuring about 3 ft. (0.9 m) in circumference. **6** a sliding piece of iron for fastening a door, window etc. **7** a metal pin for holding objects together, frequently screw-headed at one end to receive a nut. **8** that portion of a lock which engages with the keeper to form a fastening. **9** a sudden start, a sudden flight. **10** the act of suddenly breaking away. **11** (*N Am.*) sudden desertion from a political party. **12** †a kind of fetter for the leg. ~*v.t.* **1** to shut or fasten by means of a bolt or iron. **2** to fasten together with a bolt or bolts. **3** to gulp, to swallow hastily and without chewing. **4** (*N Am.*) to desert (a political party). ~*v.i.* **1** to start suddenly forward or aside. **2** to run away (as a horse). **3** (*N Am.*) to break away from a political party. **4** (of a plant) to run to seed. **bolt from the blue 1** lightning from a cloudless sky. **2** an unexpected sudden event. **to bolt in** to shut in. **to bolt on 1** to fasten by bolts. **2** to add on. **to bolt out** to exclude. **bolter**[1] *n.* **1** (*N Am.*) a person that bolts or runs. **2** a horse given to bolting. **3** (*N Am.*) a person who suddenly breaks away from their party. **4** (*Hist.*) a runaway convict in Australia. **bolthead** *n.* **1** the head of a bolt. **2** a globular flask with a long, cylindrical neck, used in distilling. **bolt-hole** *n.* **1** a hole by which or into which one escapes. **2** an escape. **3** a means of escape. **bolting**[1] *n.* **1** sudden flight. **2** (*N Am.*) political desertion. **3** fastening with bolts. **4** a bundle of straw. **5** swallowing without chewing. **bolt-on** *a.* **1** able to be attached with bolts. **2** able to be added. ~*n.* a thing that can be added or bolted on. **bolt-rope** *n.* a rope sewed round the margin of a sail to prevent its being torn. **bolt upright** *a.*, *adv.* straight upright. [OE (cp. Dut. *bout*, G *Bolz*)]

bolt[2] (bōlt), **boult** *n.* a sieve for separating bran from flour. ~*v.t.* **1** to pass through a bolt or bolting cloth. **2** to examine, to try. **to bolt out** to separate by sifting. **bolter**[2] *n.* **1** a sieve. **2** a bolting cloth. **3** a sifting machine. **bolting**[2] *n.* the act or process of sifting. **bolting cloth** *n.* a fine cloth used in sifting meal. [OF *bulter, buleter* (*buletel*, a sieve), It. *burattare* (*buratto*, a sieve, late L *burra*, a coarse cloth)]

bolter[1] BOLT[1].

bolter[2] BOLT[2].

bolting[1] BOLT[1].

bolting[2] BOLT[2].

bolus (bō´ləs) *n.* (*pl.* **boluses**) **1** medicine in a round mass larger than a pill. **2** a round lump of anything. **3** anything mentally unpalatable. [late L *bōlus*, Gr. *bōlos*, a clod, lump]

bomb (bom) *n.* **1** an explosive device triggered by impact or a timer usu. dropped from the air, thrown or placed by hand. **2** (*coll.*) a great success. **3** (*coll.*) a large amount of money. **4** (*coll.*) (of a play etc.) an utter failure, a flop. **5** (*sl.*) a drugged cigarette. ~*v.t.* to attack, destroy or harm with bombs. ~*v.i.* **1** to throw, drop or detonate bombs. **2** (*coll.*) to fail utterly, to flop. **the bomb 1** the atom or hydrogen bomb. **2** nuclear arms. **bomb bay** *n.* a compartment in an aircraft for bombs. **bomb crater** *n.* a crater caused by the explosion of a bomb. **bomb disposal** *n.* the detonation or diffusing of an unexploded bomb rendering it harmless. **bombed** *a.* **1** subject to bombing. **2** (*sl.*) drunk, or under the influence of drugs. **bombed-out** *a.* **1** (of a person) made homeless by bombing. **2** (of a building etc.) destroyed by bombing. **3** (*sl.*) drunk, or under the influence of drugs. **bomber** *n.* **1** a person who throws, drops, places or triggers bombs. **2** an aircraft used for bombing. **bomber jacket** *n.* a waist-length jacket elasticated at the wrists and waist. **bombproof** *a.* (of a shelter etc.) affording safety from the explosion of a bomb. ~*n.* a bombproof structure. **bombshell** *n.* **1** a bomb thrown by artillery. **2** a total (often unpleasant) surprise. **3** (*sl.*) a very attractive woman. **bombsight** *n.* a device for aiming a bomb from an aircraft. **bomb-site** *n.* an area where buildings have been destroyed by bombing. **bomb squad** *n.* a division of a police force dealing with crimes involving bombs. [F *bombe*, Sp. *bomba*, L *bombus*, Gr. *bombos*, a humming noise]

bombard[1] (bəmbahd´, bom-) *v.t.* **1** to attack with shot and shell. **2** to assail with arguments or invective. **3** to subject (atoms) to a stream of high-speed particles. **bombardier** (bombədiə´) *n.* **1** a non-commissioned artillery officer ranking as corporal. **2** (*N Am.*) a member of a bomber crew responsible for releasing bombs. **3** †an artilleryman employed in serving mortars and howitzers. **bombardier-beetle** *n.* the genus *Brachinus*, which, when disturbed, emits fluid from the abdomen, with blue vapour and a perceptible report. **bombardment** *n.* **1** the act of bombarding. **2** an attack upon a place with shot and shell. [see BOMB]

bombard[2] (bom´bahd) *n.* (*Hist.*) the earliest form of cannon.

bombarde (bom´bahd) *n.* a medieval alto-pitched shawm. [OF *bombarde*, prob. from L *bombus*, BOMB]

bombardon (bom´bədən, -bah´-), **bombardone** *n.* **1** a brass instrument related to the tuba. **2** a bass-reed stop on the organ. [It. *bombardone*, from *bombardo*, bassoon]

bombasine (bom´bəzēn, -zēn´), **bombazine** *n.* a twilled dress fabric of silk and worsted, cotton and worsted or of worsted alone. [F *bombasin*, late L *bombācinus* (*bombax*, L *bombyx*, Gr. *bombux*, silk, cotton, orig. silkworm)]

bombast[1] (bom´bast) *n.* **1** high-sounding words. **2** inflated speech, fustian. **3** padding, stuffing. **4** †cotton-wool, esp. used as padding. ~†*a.* turgid, bombastic.

bombastic (-bas´-) *a.* **1** of the nature of bombast. **2** inflated, turgid. **3** given to inflated language. **bombastically** *adv.* in an inflated, grandiloquent style. [OF *bumbace*, cotton, late L *bombax -ācem* (L *bombyx*, see BOMBASINE)]

bombast[2] (bombast´, bom´bast) *v.t.* **1** to stuff out, to inflate. **2** to fill out with imposing language. [see BOMBAST[1]]

Bombay bowler (bomb´ā) *n.* a small, light pith helmet. [port in India]

Bombay duck (bom´bā) *n.* a small S Asian fish, *Harpodon nehereus*, when salted and dried eaten as a relish; also called *bummalo.* [Marathi *bombil*, name of the fish]

bombazine BOMBASINE.

bombe (bomb, bōb) *n.* an ice cream dessert moulded into a rounded, bomb shape. [F]

bombé (bom´bā, bō´-) *a.* protruding or round-fronted, as of furniture. [F]

bombora (bombaw´rə) *n.* (*Austral.*) dangerous broken water, usu. at the base of a cliff.

bombyx (bom´biks) *n.* any moth of the genus *Bombyx*, containing the silkworm, *B. mori.* **bombycid** (-sid) *a.* [Gr., see BOMBASINE]

bona fide (bōnə fī´di) *adv.* in good faith. *~a.* genuine. **bona fides** (-dēz) *n.* **1** good faith, sincerity. **2** (*treated as pl., coll.*) documentary evidence of acceptability. [L]

bonanza (bənan´zə) *n.* **1** a rich mine. **2** a successful enterprise. **3** a run of luck. *~a.* **1** very successful. **2** highly profitable. [N Am., from Sp., fair weather, prosperity]

Bonapartism (bō´nəpahtizm) *n.* attachment to the dynasty founded in France by Napoleon Bonaparte. **Bonapartist** *n.* an adherent of the Bonaparte dynasty. *~a.* of, relating to or supporting the Bonaparte dynasty.

bona vacantia (bōnə vəkan´tiə) *n.pl.* (*Law*) unclaimed goods. [L]

bon-bon (bon´bon, bō´bō) *n.* **1** a sweet, esp. of fondant. **2** a Christmas cracker. [F (*bon*, good, L *bonus*)]

bonce (bons) *n.* **1** (*sl.*) the head. **2** a large marble. **3** the game played with these. [etym. unknown]

bond[1] (bond) *n.* **1** a thing which binds or confines, as a cord or band. **2** (*pl.*) chains, imprisonment, captivity. **3** that which restrains or cements. **4** a binding agreement or engagement. **5** that which impedes or enslaves. **6** (*pl.*) trammels. **7** a document by which a government or a public company undertakes to repay borrowed money, a debenture. **8** adhesiveness. **9** (*Law*) a deed by which one person (the obligor) binds themselves, their heirs, executors and assigns, to pay a certain sum to another person (the obligee), their heirs etc. **10** (*Chem.*) a linkage between atoms in a chemical compound. **11** a mode of overlapping bricks in a wall so as to tie the courses together (as with English bond and Flemish bond). **12** a withe for tying a faggot. *~v.t.* **1** to put into a bonded warehouse. **2** to mortgage. **3** to bind or connect (as bricks or stones) by overlapping or by clamps. *~v.i.* to become emotionally attached. **in bond** in a bonded warehouse and liable to customs duty. **bond creditor** *n.* a creditor secured by bond. **bonded** *a.* **1** bound by a bond. **2** put in bond. **bonded debt** *n.* a debt secured by bonds issued by a corporation as distinguished from floating debts. **bonded goods** *n.pl.* goods stored, under the care of customs officers, in warehouses until the duties are paid. **bonded warehouse** *n.* a warehouse in which imported goods are stored until the duty is paid. **bonder** *n.* **1** a person who puts or holds goods in bond. **2** a stone or brick reaching a considerable distance through a wall so as to bind it together. **bondholder** *n.* a person holding a bond or bonds granted by a private person or by a government. **bonding** *n.* **1** the storing of goods in bond. **2** the act of strengthening by bonders. **3** the adherence of two surfaces glued together. **4** any union or attachment, esp. the emotional one formed between a parent and a newborn child. **bond paper** *n.* a good quality paper. **bondstone** *n.* a stone going through a wall, a bonder. **bond timber** *n.* pieces of timber built into a stone or brick wall to strengthen it. **bond-washing** *n.* dividend stripping. [var. of BAND[1]]

bond[2] (bond) *a.* in serfdom or slavery. **bondmaid** *n.* a slave girl. **bondservant** *n.* a slave. **bondservice** *n.* villeinage. **bondslave** *n.* a slave. **bondsman, bondman** *n.* (*pl.* **bondsmen, bondmen**) **1** a slave. **2** a surety. **bondswoman, bondwoman** *n.* (*pl.* **bondswomen, bondwomen**) a female slave. [OE *bōnda, bunda*, a husbandman, Icel. *bōndi* (*būa*, to till); influenced in meaning by BOND[1]]

bond[3] (bond) *n.* (*S Afr.*) a league of confederation. [Dut., from *binden*, to bind (cp. G *Bund*)]

bondage (bon´dij) *n.* **1** slavery, captivity, imprisonment. **2** subjection, restraint, obligation. **3** sadomasochistic practices involving restraints. [BOND[2]]

bone (bōn) *n.* **1** the hard material of the skeleton of mammals, birds, reptiles and some fishes. **2** any separate and distinct part of such a skeleton. **3** the substance of which the skeleton consists. **4** an article made (or formerly made) of bone or ivory, whalebone etc. **5** a stiffening material for garments. **6** a small joint of meat. **7** (*pl.*) dice. **8** a domino. **9** (*pl.*) **a** castanets made of bone. **b** the performer on these. **10** (*pl.*) the body. **11** (*pl.*) mortal remains. **12** (*pl.*) the essential part of a thing. *~a.* **1** of or relating to bone. **2** made of bone. *~v.t.* **1** to take out the bones of (for cooking). **2** (*sl.*) to steal. **3** to stiffen (a garment). **a bone to pick with someone** a cause of quarrel with or complaint against someone. **big-boned** BIG. **body and bones** BODY. **close to/ near the bone** **1** tactless. **2** indecent. **3** destitute; hard up. **to bone up** (*sl.*) to study hard, to swot. **to make no bones about** **1** to do or speak about without hesitation or scruple. **2** to present no difficulty or opposition to. **to point a/ the bone** **1** (*Austral.*) in Aboriginal magic, to will the death of an enemy. **2** (*Austral.*) to put a jinx on someone. **to the bone** **1** to the inmost part. **2** to the minimum. **to work one's fingers to the bone** FINGER. **bone ash** *n.* the mineral residue of bones burnt in the air. **bone bed** *n.* (*Geol.*) a bed largely made up of bones of animals. **boneblack** *n.* animal charcoal used as a deodorizer and as a pigment. **bonebreaker** *n.* **1** a person who or thing which breaks bones. **2** the osprey, *Pandion haliaetus.* **bone cave** *n.* a cave containing remains of prehistoric or recent animals. **bone china** *n.* porcelain made with china clay (kaolin) and bone ash (calcium phosphate). **boned** *a.* **1** possessed of bones (*in comb.*). **2** deprived of bones (for cooking). **bone dry** *a.* quite dry. **bone dust** *n.* bones ground for manure. **bone earth** *n.* BONE ASH (under BONE). **bonefish** *n.* (*pl. in general* **bonefish,** *in particular* **bonefishes**) any of several species of large game fish, esp. *Albula vulpes.* **bone grafting** *n.* introduction of a piece of bone obtained elsewhere to replace bone lost by injury or disease. **bonehead** *n.* (*sl.*) a dolt. **boneheaded** *a.* **bone idle, bone lazy** *a.* utterly idle; idle to the bone. **bone lace** *n.* a kind of thread lace orig. made with bone bobbins. **boneless** *a.* **1** without bones. **2** without backbone, having no stamina. **bonelessness** *n.* **bone marrow** *n.* a fatty substance contained in the cavities of bones. **bonemeal** *n.* bone dust used as animal feed or fertilizer. **bone of contention** *n.* a subject of dispute. **bone oil** *n.* a fetid oil obtained in the dry distillation of bones. **boner** *n.* (*N Am.*) a gross mistake, a howler. **bone-setter** *n.* a non-qualified practitioner who sets fractured and dislocated bones. **boneshaker** *n.* **1** an old-fashioned bicycle without india-rubber tyres. **2** any dilapidated or old-fashioned vehicle. **bone spavin** *n.* a bony excrescence on the inside of a horse's hock. **boning** *n.* 1 the removing of bones from poultry, fish etc. 2 the operation of levelling or judging the straightness of a surface by the eye. **bony** *a.* (*comp.* **bonier,** *superl.* **boniest**) 1 of, relating to or of the nature of bone or bones. 2 big-boned. **boniness** *n.* **bony pike** *n.* a N American fish of the genus *Lepisosteus.* [OE *bān* (cp. Dut. *been,* OHG *pein, bein,* G *Bein*)]

bonfire (bon´fīə) *n.* 1 a large fire lit in the open air on an occasion of public rejoicing. 2 a fire for burning up garden rubbish. **Bonfire Night** *n.* 5 Nov., when an effigy of Guy Fawkes is burned on a bonfire, and fireworks are let off. [BONE, FIRE]

bong (bong) *n.* a low-pitched reverberating sound. ~*v.i.* to make such a sound. [imit.]

bongo[1] (bong´gō) *n.* (*pl.* **bongos, bongoes**) a small hand drum of a type often played in pairs. **bongo drum** *n.* [S Am. Sp. *bongó*]

bongo[2] (bong´gō) *n.* (*pl. in general* **bongo,** *in particular* **bongos**) a rare antelope, *Tragelaphus euryceros,* which has spiralled horns and a red-brown coat with narrow cream stripes. [Congolese]

bonhomie (bonəmē´) *n.* good nature, geniality. **bonhomous** *a.* [F *bon,* good, *homme,* man]

boning BONE.

bonito (bonē´tō) *n.* (*pl. in general* **bonito,** *in particular* **bonitos**) 1 any of various striped tuna. 2 any of various other fish of the mackerel family. [Sp., etym. uncertain]

bonjour (bõzhuə´) *int.* good day. [F]

bonk (bongk) *v.t.* 1 (*coll.*) to hit. 2 (*sl.*) to have sexual intercourse with. ~*v.i.* 1 to bang or bump. 2 to have sexual intercourse. ~*n.* an act of bonking. [imit.]

bonkers (bong´kəz) *a.* (*sl.*) crazy, mad. [etym. uncertain]

bon mot (bõ mō´) *n.* (*pl.* **bons mots** (bõ mō´, bõ mōz´)) a witticism. [F, lit., good word]

bonne (bon) *n.* 1 a nursemaid. 2 a maid (of French nationality). [F]

bonne bouche (bon boosh´) *n.* (*pl.* **bonne bouches** (bon boosh´), **bonnes bouches**) a tasty titbit. [F, from *bonne,* good (fem.), *bouche,* mouth]

bonnet (bon´it) *n.* 1 a hat tied beneath the chin, of various shapes and materials, formerly worn by women out of doors and now usu. by babies. 2 (*esp. Sc.*) a flat cap. 3 a hat without a brim for men and boys. 4 the front part of a motor vehicle covering the engine. 5 a feathered headdress worn by American Indians. 6 a chimney cowl. 7 a protective covering to a machine etc. 8 an additional piece of canvas laced to the bottom of a sail to enlarge it. 9 a confederate, a decoy. ~*v.t.* 1 to put a bonnet on (a person). 2 to knock the hat of (a person) over their eyes. **bonneted** *a.* wearing a bonnet or cap. **bonnethead** *n.* a hammerhead shark, *Sphyrna tiburo,* with a narrow head, also called *shovelhead.* **bonnet monkey** *n.* an Indian macaque, *Macaca radiata,* with a tuft of hair like a bonnet. **bonnet rouge** (bonā roozh´) *n.* the red cap of liberty worn by revolutionaries. [OF *bonet,* stuff of which caps were made (whence *chapel de bonet,* abbr. into *bonet*), low L *bonnētus*]

bonny (bon´i) *a.* (*comp.* **bonnier,** *superl.* **bonniest**) 1 beautiful, handsome, pretty. 2 healthy-looking. 3 good, pleasant. **bonnily** *adv.* **bonniness** *n.* [F *bonne* (fem.), good]

bonsai (bon´sī) *n.* (*pl.* **bonsai**) 1 (*also* **bonsai tree**) a potted tree or shrub cultivated into a dwarf variety by skilful pruning of its roots. 2 the art or practice of cultivating trees or shrubs in this manner. [Jap., *bon,* bowl, *sai,* to grow]

bonsella (bonsel´ə) *n.* (*S Afr.*) a tip, a present.

bonspiel (bon´spēl) *n.* (*Sc.*) a curling match. [etym. unknown]

bontebok (bon´təbok), **bontbok** *n.* (*pl. in general* **bontebok, bontbok,** *in particular* **bonteboks, bontboks**) a large antelope, *Damaliscus dorcas,* which has a deep reddish-brown coat, a white tail and white patches on its head and rump. [Afrikaans, from *bont,* spotted, *bok,* buck]

bon ton (bõ tõ´) *n.* fashion, good style. [F]

bonus (bō´nəs) *n.* (*pl.* **bonuses**) 1 something over and above what is due. 2 a premium given for a privilege or in addition to interest for a loan. 3 an extra dividend. 4 a distribution of profits to policyholders in an insurance company. 5 a gratuity over and above a fixed salary or wages. **bonus share, bonus issue** *n.* a share or number of shares issued free to the holder of a paid-up share in a joint-stock company. [L *bonus,* (a) good (man)]

Usage note The phrase *added bonus* is best avoided: bonus already implies addition.

bon vivant (bõ vēvã´) *n.* (*pl.* **bon vivants** (bõ vēvã´), **bons vivants**) a person fond of good living, a gourmand. **bonne vivante** (bon vēvãt´) *n.* (*pl.* **bonne vivantes** (bon vēvãt´), **bonnes vivantes**) a female bon vivant. [F]

bon viveur (bõ vēvœ´) *n.* (*pl.* **bon viveurs** (bõ vēvœ´), **bons viveurs**) BON VIVANT. [F *bon,* good, *viveur,* a living person: not a F form]

bon voyage (bon voiahzh´, bõ vwayahzh´) *n., int.* a pleasant journey, farewell. [F]

bony BONE.

bonza (bon´zə), **bonzer** *a.* (*Austral., sl.*) excellent. [Austral. Abor.]

bonze (bonz) *n.* a Buddhist religious teacher in Japan, China and adjacent regions. [Jap. *bonzō,* Chin. *fan seng,* religious person (through F *bonze,* Port. *bonzo,* or directly)]

boo (boo) *int., n.* (*pl.* **boos**) 1 a sound used to express contempt, displeasure, aversion etc. (imitating the lowing of oxen). 2 a sound intended to surprise, esp. a child. ~*v.i.* (*3rd pers. sing. pres.* **boos,** *pres.p.* **booing,** *past, p.p.* **booed**) 1 to say or call 'boo', to jeer. 2 (of an ox) to low. ~*v.t.* to say or call 'boo' to, to jeer at. **would not say boo to a goose** would never venture to say anything, is very timid. **boohoo** (-hoo´) *int., n.* 1 the sound of noisy weeping. 2 a sound used to express contempt. ~*v.i.* (*3rd pers. sing. pres.* **boohoos,** *pres.p.* **boohooing,** *past, p.p.* **boohooed**) 1 to weep noisily. 2 to bellow, to roar. [onomat.]

boob[1] (boob) *n.* (*coll.*) 1 an error, a blunder. 2 a simpleton. ~*v.i.* to err, commit a blunder. [BOOBY]

boob[2] (boob) *n.* (*usu. in pl., sl.*) a woman's breast. **boob tube** *n.* 1 (*sl.*) a woman's elasticated, strapless top. 2 (*N Am.*) television. [etym. uncertain; earlier *bubby*]

booboo (boo´boo) *n.* (*pl.* **booboos**) (*sl.*) a mistake. [BOOB[1]]

boobook (boo´buk), **boobook owl** *n.* a brown spotted owl, *Ninox novaeseelandiae,* native to Australia and New Zealand. [from its cry]

booby (boo´bi) *n.* (*pl.* **boobies**) 1 a dull, stupid person; a dunce. 2 a gannet, esp. *Sula fusca.* **booby-hatch** *n.* 1 a small kind of companion for the half-decks of merchant ships. 2 (*N Am., sl.*) a psychiatric hospital. **boobyish** *a.* stupid, foolish, awkward. **booby prize** *n.* the prize, usu. a worthless one, given in ridicule to the player who makes the lowest score, esp. in whist drives, or the competitor who comes last. **booby trap** *n.* 1 a trap placed as a practical joke, consisting of e.g. books etc. placed on the top of a door left ajar, so that the whole tumbles on the head of the first person entering. 2 a bomb so disposed that it will explode when some object is touched. ~*v.t.* (*pres.p.* **booby-trapping,** *past, p.p.* **booby-trapped**) to set a booby trap in or on. [Sp. *bobo,* a blockhead; also, a kind of bird (prob. from L *balbus,* stammering)]

boodle (booʹdəl) *n.* (*sl.*) **1** money, capital, stock in trade. **2** a fund for bribery. **3** bribery, plunder, graft. **4** a pack, crew, lot. [etym. uncertain; perh. from Dut. *boedel*, estate, possession]

boogie (booʹgi) *v.i.* (*pres.p.* **boogieing,** *past, p.p.* **boogied**) (*sl.*) to dance to pop music. ~*n.* **1** BOOGIE-WOOGIE (under BOOGIE). **2** a dance to pop music. **boogie-woogie** (boogiwooʹgi) *n.* a jazz piano style of a rhythmic and percussive nature based on 12-bar blues. [perh. from black sl.]

boohoo BOO.

book (buk) *n.* **1** a collection of sheets printed, written on or blank, bound in a volume. **2** a literary composition of considerable extent. **3** a set of tickets, cheques, forms of receipt, stamps or the like, fastened together. **4** (*pl.*) a set of accounts. **5** a main division of a literary work. **6** a libretto, a script. **7** (*fig.*) anything that can be read or that conveys instruction. **8** a telephone directory. **9** bets on a race or at a meeting taken collectively. **10** the first six tricks gained by a side at whist etc. **11** an imaginary record or list. ~*v.t.* **1** to enter or register in a book. **2** to reserve by payment in advance (as a seat in a conveyance, theatre or the like). **3** to hand in or to receive for transmission (as a parcel, goods etc.). **4** to take the name and details of (an offender or rule-breaker), prior to making a charge. **5** to engage the services of (a performer etc.) in advance. ~*v.i.* to make a reservation. **by the book** with exact information. **in my book** according to my view of things. **in someone's bad/ black books** regarded with disfavour by someone. **in someone's good books** regarded with favour by someone. **like a book** formally, pedantically, as if one were reciting from a book. **not in the book** not allowed. **on the books** on the official list of names. **to book in** to register one's arrival. **to book up** to buy tickets in advance. **to bring to book** to convict, call to account. **to go by the book** to proceed according to the rules. **to make a book** in racing, to pay out and take winnings. **to make book** (*N Am.*) in racing, to take bets and pay out winnings. **to salt the books** SALT. **to suit one's book** to be agreeable or favourable to one. **to throw the book at 1** (*coll.*) to charge with every offence possible. **2** (*coll.*) to punish severely. **without book 1** from memory. **2** without authority. **bookable** *a.* **1** that may be reserved in advance. **2** in football, (of an offence) serious enough to be entered in the referee's notebook. **book account** *n.* an account or register of debit or credit in a book. **bookbinder** *n.* a person who binds books. **bookbindery** *n.* (*pl.* **bookbinderies**) a place for binding books. **bookbinding** *n.* **bookcase** *n.* **1** a case with shelves for books. **2** a bookcover. **book club** *n.* **1** an association of persons who buy and lend each other books. **2** a business which sells to its members a choice of books at below publishers' prices. **bookcover** *n.* **1** a pair of boards (usu. cloth- or leather-covered) for binding a book. **2** a case for periodicals, music etc. **book debt** *n.* a debt for articles supplied, entered in an account book. **booked** *a.* **1** registered. **2** entered in a book. **3** (*coll.*) caught, arrested. **booked up** *a.* with all the places reserved; full up. **bookend** *n.* a prop placed at the end of a row of books to keep them upright. **booker** *n.* a person who books, a person who makes a booking. **bookful** *n.* (*pl.* **bookfuls**) all that a book contains. ~†*a.* full of knowledge derived from books. **bookholder** *n.* in the theatre, a prompter. **bookhunter** *n.* a collector of rare books. **bookie** *n.* (*coll.*) a bookmaker who takes bets. **booking** *n.* a reservation. **booking clerk** *n.* a person who issues tickets or takes bookings. **booking hall** *n.* a room at a station where tickets are issued. **booking office** *n.* an office where tickets are issued or bookings are made. **bookish** *a.* **1** learned, studious. **2** acquainted with books only. **3** (of a word, language etc.) literary. **bookishly** *adv.* **bookishness** *n.* **bookkeeper** *n.* a person who keeps the accounts in an office etc. **bookkeeping** *n.* the art or practice of keeping accounts. **bookland** *n.* (*Hist.*) land taken from the folkland or the common land and granted to a private person. **book learning** *n.* **1** learning derived from books. **2** theory, not practical knowledge or experience. **book-learned** *a.* **booklet** *n.* a little book, a pamphlet. **book-louse** *n.* (*pl.* **book-lice**) an insect, belonging to the Psocoptera, found amongst books, papers etc. **bookmaker** *n.* **1** a person who takes bets, principally in relation to horse races, and pays out to winners as a profession. **2** a person who makes or compiles books. **bookmaking** *n.* **1** the making of a betting book; the profession of a bookmaker who takes bets. **2** the compilation of books. **bookman** *n.* (*pl.* **bookmen**) **1** a literary man. **2** a bookseller. **bookmark, bookmarker** *n.* a piece of ribbon, paper, leather etc. put in a book to mark a place. **bookmobile** *n.* (*N Am.*) a mobile library. **book of fate, book of life** *n.* the record of souls to be saved. **Book of Proverbs** *n.* a collection of maxims forming a book of the Old Testament. **Book of Psalms** *n.* a book of the Old Testament consisting of sacred songs, many of which are ascribed to David. **book of words** *n.* a libretto, script etc. **bookplate** *n.* a label with a name or device, pasted in a book to show the ownership. **bookpost** *n.* the postal system for conveying books. **bookrest, bookstand** *n.* a support for a book. **bookseller** *n.* a person whose trade it is to sell books. **bookshelf** *n.* (*pl.* **bookshelves**) a shelf for books. **bookshop** *n.* a shop where books are sold. **booksie** (-si), **booksy** *a.* (*coll.*) would-be literary. **bookstall, bookstand** *n.* a stall or stand at which books and periodicals are sold. **bookstore** *n.* (*N Am.*) a bookshop. **book token** *n.* a gift token exchangeable for books. **book value** *n.* the value of an asset, commodity or enterprise as it is recorded on paper (not always the same as its market value). **bookwork** *n.* study of textbooks, as opposed to practice and experiment. **bookworm** *n.* **1** any worm or insect which eats holes in books. **2** (*coll.*) an avid reader. **booky** *a.* (*comp.* **bookier,** *superl.* **bookiest**) (*coll.*) bookish. [OE *bōc*, a book, document, charter (cp. OHG *buoh*, G *Buch*), (possibly conn. with OE *bōece*, G *Buche*, Gr. *phages*, L *fāgus*, a beech)]

Boolean (booʹliən) *a.* being or relating to a logical system using symbols to represent relationships between entities. **Boolean algebra** *n.* a branch of symbolic logic used in computers. **Boolean logic** *n.* (*Comput.*) the use of the logical operators 'and', 'or' and 'not' in retrieving information. [George *Boole*, 1815–64, English mathematician]

boom[1] (boom) *n.* **1** a loud, deep, resonant sound. **2** a sudden demand for a thing. **3** a rapid advance in prices. **4** a burst of commercial activity and prosperity. ~*v.i.* **1** to make a loud, deep, resonant sound. **2** to rush with violence. **3** to go off with a boom. **4** to become very important, prosperous or active. ~*v.t.* to utter with a booming sound. **boom box** *n.* (*sl.*) a ghetto blaster. **boomlet** *n.* **boom town** *n.* a town undergoing rapid expansion or enjoying sudden commercial prosperity. [imit. (cp. BOMB)]

boom[2] (boom) *n.* **1** (*Naut.*) a long spar to extend the foot of a particular sail. **2** a bar, chain or line of connected spars forming an obstruction to the mouth of a harbour. **3** a line of floating timber enclosing an area of water for lumber. **4** the logs so enclosed. **5** a movable overhead pole carrying a microphone used in television, film, videotape recordings. **boomslang** (-slang) *n.* a poisonous S African tree snake, *Dispholidus typus.* [Dut. *boom*, a tree (cp. BEAM)]

boomer (booʹmə) *n.* **1** (*Austral.*) a large kangaroo. **2** a large wave. **3** (*coll.*) anything of a large size.

boomerang (booʹmərang) *n.* **1** an Aboriginal Australian missile weapon, consisting of a curved flat stick so constructed that it returns to the thrower. 2 an action, speech or argument that recoils on the person who makes it. ~*v.i.* 1 to return to the thrower. 2 (of a plan etc.) to rebound on the originator, to have the opposite of the desired effect. [Austral. Abor.]

boomslang BOOM².

boon¹ (boon) *n.* 1 a benefit, a blessing. 2 †a prayer, a petition, an entreaty. 3 †a favour, a gift. [Icel. *bōn* (cp. OE *bēn*)]

boon² (boon) *a.* 1 close, intimate. 2 jolly, convivial. **boon companion** *n.* 1 a person who is convivial or congenial. 2 a close or special friend. [F *bon*, good]

boondock (boon´dok) *n.* 1 (*usu. in pl., N Am., sl.*) remote or uncultivated country. 2 (*sl.*) a provincial area. [Tagalog *bundok*, mountain]

boondoggle (boon´dogəl) *n.* 1 work of little practical value. 2 a dishonest undertaking; a fraud. ~*v.i.* to do work of little practical value. [Scout coinage]

boong (boong) *n.* (*Austral., offensive*) an Aborigine.

boongarry (boon´gari) *n.* (*pl.* **boongarries**) the N Queensland tree kangaroo, *Dendrolagus lumholtzi.* [Austral. Abor.]

boonies (boo´niz) *n.pl.* (*N Am., sl.*) the boondocks.

boor (booə) *n.* 1 a rude, awkward or insensitive person. 2 a peasant, a rustic. **boorish** *a.* clumsy, insensitive, unmannerly. **boorishly** *adv.* **boorishness** *n.* [Dut. *boer* (G *Bauer*, from Goth. *bauan*, to till)]

boost (boost) *v.t.* 1 to push or shove upwards. 2 to advertise on a big scale. 3 to promote or encourage. 4 to enlarge or increase (e.g. the voltage in an electric circuit). 5 to elevate or raise (e.g. the pressure of an internal-combustion engine). ~*v.i.* (*N Am., sl.*) 1 to shoplift. 2 to steal. **booster** *n.* 1 a contrivance for intensifying the strength of an alternating current. 2 an auxiliary motor in a rocket that usu. breaks away when exhausted. 3 any thing or person that boosts. 4 a supplementary vaccination. [etym. uncertain]

boot¹ (boot) *n.* 1 a covering (usu. of leather) for the foot and part of the leg. 2 a luggage compartment in a car. 3 (*sl.*) a kick. 4 (*preceded by the, sl.*) summary dismissal, e.g. from employment. 5 a covering to protect the lower part of a horse's leg. 6 (*Hist.*) an instrument of torture applied to the leg and foot, formerly used in Scotland to extort confessions. 7 (*derog.*) a person. 8 a heavy sports shoe, e.g. football boot. 9 (*pl.*) a hotel servant who cleans boots, runs errands etc. ~*v.t.* 1 to kick. 2 to start (a computer program) running. 3 to equip with boots. **boot and saddle** used as a command to mount. **the boot is on the other foot/ leg** the situation is reversed. **to bet one's boots** to be absolutely certain. **to boot out** (*sl.*) to eject, dismiss, sack. **to die with one's boots on** to die fighting. **to get the boot** to be dismissed; to get the sack. **to give the boot** to dismiss; to sack. **to put/ stick the boot in** 1 to kick brutally. 2 (*sl.*) to cause further upset or harm to one already in distress. **bootblack** *n.* a person who cleans and polishes shoes. **bootboy** *n.* 1 a hooligan, a bovver boy. 2 a boy employed to clean shoes. **booted** *a.* having boots on. **booted and spurred** equipped for riding. **bootee** (-tē´) *n.* 1 a knitted boot for infants. 2 a short boot. **bootjack** *n.* a device for removing boots. **bootlace** *n.* a string for fastening boots. **bootleg** *a.* 1 illicit, smuggled (e.g. of alcohol). 2 (of a recording) pirated. ~*n.* 1 an illicit or smuggled commodity. 2 a pirated musical recording. ~*v.i.* (*pres.p.* **bootlegging,** *past, p.p.* **bootlegged**) to act as a bootlegger. **bootlegger** *n.* a person who makes, deals in or transports an illicit commodity esp. liquor. **bootlegging** *n.* **bootless¹** *a.* **bootlicker** *n.* a sycophant. **bootmaker** *n.* a person who makes boots. **bootstrap** *n.* 1 a looped strap on a boot-top enabling it to be pulled up. 2 (*Comput.*) a technique for loading the first few program instructions so that the rest of the program can be introduced from an input device. **to pull oneself up by the bootstraps** to achieve or improve one's situation by one's own efforts. **boot-top** *n.* the upper part of a boot, esp. of top-boots. **boot tree** *n.* a block inserted into a boot to stretch it or keep it in shape. [OF *bote* (F *botte*), etym. uncertain]

boot² (boot) *n.* advantage, profit (used only as below). **to boot** into the bargain, besides, in addition. **bootless²** *a.* profitless, unavailing. **bootlessly** *adv.* **bootlessness** *n.* [OE *bōt* (*bētan*, to amend, help, cp. Goth. *bōtjan*, to profit, G *Busse*, making good, atonement)]

booth (boodh, booth) *n.* 1 a stall, tent or other temporary erection at a fair, in a market, polling station etc. 2 a tent. 3 a compartment or structure containing a telephone, a table in a restaurant etc. [MDan. *bōth*, Dan. *bod* (Icel. *buth*, from *būa*, to dwell), related to Ir. and Gael. *both*, *bothan*, a hut, a bothy]

bootless¹ BOOT¹.

bootless² BOOT².

booty (boo´ti) *n.* 1 spoil taken in war. 2 property carried off by thieves. 3 (*coll.*) a gain, a prize. **to play booty** 1 to join with confederates so as to victimize another player. 2 to play to lose. [prob. from Icel. *bȳti*, barter, through F *butin* or MDut. *būte* (Dut. *buit*, booty, spoil), with influence from *bot*, BOOT²]

booze (booz), **boose, bouse** *n.* 1 (*coll.*) an alcoholic drink. 2 a drinking bout. ~*v.i.* to drink to excess, to tipple. **boozer** *n.* (*coll.*) 1 a heavy drinker. 2 a public house. **booze-up** *n.* (*sl.*) a drinking session. **boozy** *a.* (*comp.* **boozier,** *superl.* **booziest**) 1 drunk, tipsy. 2 addicted to boozing. **boozily** *adv.* **booziness** *n.* [ME *bousen*, to drink deeply; perh. from MDut. *būsen* (*buize*, a drinking-cup, cp. Dut. *buis*, OF *buse*, *buise*, a conduit)]

bop¹ (bop) *n.* 1 an innovative style of jazz music dating from the 1940s. 2 a spell of dancing, esp. to pop music. 3 a dance. ~*v.i.* (*pres.p.* **bopping,** *past, p.p.* **bopped**) to dance to bop or pop music. **bopper** *n.* 1 a fan of bop. 2 any follower of popular music. 3 a person who dances to it. [contr. of BEBOP]

bop² *v.t.* (*pres.p.* **bopping,** *past, p.p.* **bopped**) to hit, to strike. ~*n.* a hit, a blow.

bo-peep BO.

☒ **boquet** common misspelling of BOUQUET.

bor. *abbr.* borough.

bora¹ (baw´rə) *n.* a keen dry, NE wind in the upper Adriatic. [It. *borea*, L *boreas*, the north wind]

bora² (baw´rə) *n.* (*Austral.*) 1 a ritual initiation rite. 2 the sacred ground where such rites are performed. [Austral. Abor.]

boracic BORAX.

boracite (baw´rəsīt) *n.* native borate of magnesia.

borage (bŭr´ij, bor´-) *n.* a hairy, blue-flowered plant of the genus *Borago*, esp. *B. officinalis*, formerly esteemed as a cordial, and used to flavour claret cup etc. [F *bourrache* (OF *borrace*), or late L *borrāgo*]

borak (baw´rak) *n.* (*Austral., New Zeal., sl.*) chaff, banter. **to poke borak at** to ridicule, to pull someone's leg. [Austral. Abor.]

borane BORON.

borax (baw´raks) *n.* 1 the mineral salt sodium borate. 2 the purified form of this, used as an antiseptic, and in the manufacture of glass and china. **boracic** (-ras´ik), **boric** *a.* of, relating to or derived from borax or boron. **boracic acid, boric acid** *n.* an acid obtained from borax. **borate** (-rāt) *n.* a salt of boracic acid. [low L (OF *boras*), from Arab. *būrāq*]

Borazon® BORON.

borborygmus (bawbərig´məs) *n.* (*pl.* **borborygmi** (-mī)) rumbling of the stomach. **borborygmic** *a.* [Gr. *borborygmos*]

bordar (baw´də) *n.* (*Hist.*) a villein of the lowest rank, doing manual service for a cottage which he held at his lord's will. [med. L *bordārius*, cottager, from *borda*, a hut (prob. from Gmc. *bord*)]

Bordeaux (bawdō´) *n.* (*pl.* **Bordeaux** (-dōz)) a red, white or rosé wine from Bordeaux. **Bordeaux mixture** *n.* a preparation of sulphate of copper and lime for destroying fungi and other garden pests. [*Bordeaux*, in SW France]

bordello (bawdel´ō) *n.* (*pl.* **bordellos**) a brothel. [It., from OF *bordel*, cabin]

border (baw´də) *n.* **1** a brim, edge, margin. **2** a boundary line or region. **3** a frontier or frontier region. **4** (*N Am.*) the frontier of civilization. **5** an edging designed as an ornament. **6** an edging to a plot or flower bed. ~*v.t.* **1** to put a border or edging to. **2** to form a boundary to. ~*v.i.* **1** to lie on the border. **2** to be contiguous. **3** to approximate, resemble. **bordering upon 1** adjoining. **2** resembling. **the Border** the boundary between England and Scotland with the contiguous regions or between Northern Ireland and the Republic of Ireland. **Border collie** *n.* a breed of collie commonly used as a sheepdog. **bordered** *a.* **borderer** *n.* a person who dwells on a border or frontier, esp. on that between England and Scotland. **bordering** *n.* an ornamental border. **borderland** *n.* **1** land near the border between two countries or districts. **2** an indeterminate region. **3** an area for debate. **borderless** *a.* without a border, limitless. **borderline** *n.* a line of demarcation. ~*a.* on the borderline (*a borderline case*). **border plant** *n.* a decorative plant for flower borders. **Border terrier** *n.* a type of small rough-haired terrier. [OF *bordure*, low L *bordātūra* from *bordāre*, to edge, from *bordus* (Gmc. *bord*)]

bordure (baw´dūə) *n.* (*Her.*) the border of an escutcheon, occupying one-fifth of the shield. [F (see BORDER)]

bore[1] (baw) *v.t.* **1** to perforate or make a hole through. **2** to hollow out. ~*v.i.* **1** to make a hole. **2** to drill a well. **3** to push forward persistently. **4** to thrust the head straight forward (of a horse). **5** to push a horse, boat or other competitor out of the course. **6** to drive a boxing adversary on to the ropes by sheer weight. ~*n.* **1** a hole made by boring. **2** the diameter of a tube. **3** the cavity of a gun barrel. **bore hole** *n.* a shaft or pit cut by means of a special tool, esp. one made to find water, oil etc. **borer** *n.* **1** a person, tool or machine that bores or pierces. **2** a horse that bores. **3** any of various insects, insect larvae, molluscs or crustaceans that bore into rock, wood etc. **boring**[1] *n.* **1** the action of making a hole etc. **2** a hole made by boring. **3** (*pl.*) chips or fragments made by boring. [OE *borian* (*bor*, Icel, *borr*, gimlet, *bora*, Dut. *boren*, to bore, cp. L *forāre*, to bore, Gr. *pharanx*, a chasm)]

bore[2] (baw) *n.* a tidal wave of great height and velocity, caused by the meeting of two tides or the rush of the tide up a narrowing estuary. [prob. from Icel. *bāra*, a billow]

bore[3] (baw) *n.* a tiresome person, a wearisome twaddler. ~*v.t.* to weary with twaddle or dullness. **to bore the pants off someone** PANTS. **to bore to tears** to weary greatly. **boredom** *n.* **1** the characteristic behaviour of bores. **2** the condition of being bored. **3** bores collectively. **boring**[2] *a.* **boringly** *adv.* **boringness** *n.* [etym. uncertain]

bore[4] BEAR[2].

boreal (baw´riəl) *a.* **1** of or relating to the north or the north wind. **2** northern. **3** living near the north. **4** subarctic. **Boreas** (-as) *n.* **1** the god of the north wind. **2** (*poet.*) the north wind. [L, from Gr. *Boreas*, *Borras*]

borecole (baw´kōl) *n.* a curled variety of winter cabbage, kale. [Dut. *boerenkool*, peasant's cabbage (BOER)]

boree (baw´rē) *n.* any of several species of *Acacia* affording firewood. [Austral. Abor.]

boreen (bawrēn´) *n.* (*Ir.*) a lane, a bridle path. [Ir. *bothar*, pron. bō´ər, *-een*, dim. suf.]

borer BORE[1].

boric BORAX.

boric acid BORAX.

boring[1] BORE[1].

boring[2] BORE[3].

born (bawn) *a.* **1** brought into the world. **2** brought forth, produced. **3** having certain characteristics from birth. **born again** regenerate. **born and bred** by birth and upbringing. **born in/ out of wedlock** WEDLOCK. **born in the purple** PURPLE. **born on the wrong side of the blanket** BLANKET. **born to** destined to. **born with a silver spoon in one's mouth** born in luxury. **in all one's born days** (*coll.*) in all one's life so far. **not born yesterday** (*coll.*) not inexperienced, not gullible. **born-again** *a.* [orig. p.p. of BEAR[2]]

borne (bawn) *a.* carried by (*waterborne*). **borne in upon one 1** having become one's firm conviction. **2** realized by one. [BEAR[2]]

borné (baw´nā) *a.* narrow-minded, limited. [F, p.p. of *borner*, to limit]

Bornholm disease (bawn´hōm) *n.* a rare viral disease, epidemic pleurodynia. [*Bornholm*, Denmark]

bornite (baw´nīt) *n.* a valuable copper ore found in Cornwall and elsewhere. [I. von *Born*, 1742–91, Austrian mineralogist]

boro- (baw´rō) *comb. form* indicating salts containing boron.

boron (baw´ron) *n.* the element, at. no. 5, chem. symbol B, present in borax and boracic acid. **Borazon®** (-əzon) *n.* a substance compounded of boron and nitrogen that for industrial use is harder than a diamond. **boride** *n.* a compound containing boron. **borosilicate** *n.* any of several substances containing boron, silicon and oxygen. [BORAX, -ON from *carbon*]

boronia (bərō´niə) *n.* (*Austral.*) any shrub of the genus *Boronia*. [F. *Borone*, 1769–94, Italian botanist]

borough (bŭr´ə) *n.* **1** a town possessing a municipal corporation. **2** (*Hist.*) a town which sends a representative to Parliament. **3** an administrative division of London or New York. **4** a municipal corporation of a US state. **5** a county in Alaska. **borough-English** *n.* a custom existent in some parts of England by which the youngest son inherits all lands and tenements. [OE *burgh*, *burg*, Gmc. *bergan*, to shelter (OE *beorgan*); cp. G *Burg*, castle, Sc. *burgh*]

borrow (bor´ō) *v.t.* **1** to obtain and make temporary use of. **2** to obtain under a promise or understanding to return. **3** to adopt, to assume, to derive from other people. **4** to copy, imitate, feign. ~*v.i.* **1** to obtain money temporarily. **2** in golf, to play a ball uphill in order that it may roll back. **borrowed** *a.* **1** obtained on loan. **2** not genuine. **3** hypocritical. **borrowed plumes** *n.pl.* decorations or honours to which one is not entitled. **borrowed time** *n.* time that one did not expect to have, esp. additional days to live. **borrower** *n.* **borrow-pit** *n.* an excavation dug to provide material elsewhere. [OE *borgian*, from *borg*, *borh*, a pledge; Gmc. *bergan*, to protect (cp. G *borgen*, to borrow, also BOROUGH)]

borsch (bawsh), **borscht, bortsch** (bawch) *n.* Russian beetroot soup. [Rus. *borshch*]

Borstal (baw´stəl) *n.* (*Hist.*) a place of detention and corrective training for juvenile offenders, now called *youth custody centre*. **Borstal system** *n.* a system of treating juvenile offenders by education and technical instruction. [the institute in *Borstal*, near Rochester in Kent]

borstall (baw´stəl) *n.* a steep track on a hillside. [OE *beorh*, a hill, *steall*, place, stead, or *stigol*, stile]

bort (bawt), **boart** *n.* **1** small fragments split from diamonds in roughly reducing them to shape, used to make diamond powder. **2** an inferior diamond, used for cutting. [etym. uncertain (perh. OF *bort*, bastard)]

bortsch BORSCH.

borzoi (baw´zoi) *n.* (*pl.* **borzois**) **1** a Russian wolfhound of a breed with a long silky coat. **2** this breed. [Rus.]

boscage (bos´kij), **boskage** *n.* **1** wood, woodland. **2** underwood or ground covered with it. **3** thick foliage. **4** wooded landscape. [OF *boscage*, late L *boscum*, a bush]

bosh (bosh) *n.* empty talk, nonsense, folly. ~*int.* stuff! rubbish! humbug! ~*v.t.* (*sl.*) to spoil, to humbug, make a fool of. [Turk.]

bosk (bosk) *n.* a bush, a thicket, a small forest. **bosky** *a.* (*comp.* **boskier,** *superl.* **boskiest**) **1** bushy, woody. **2** covered with boscage. [ME *boske*, var. of *busk*, BUSH[1] (mod. poet. *bosk*, prob. from BOSKY (under BOSK))]

bosket (bos´kit), **bosquet** *n.* **1** a grove. **2** a plantation of small trees and underwood in a garden or park. [F *bosquet*, It. *boschetto*, dim. of *bosco*, a wood]

bos'n, bo's'n BOATSWAIN.

Bosnian (boz´niən) *a.* of or relating to Bosnia in SE Europe. ~*n.* **1** a native or inhabitant of Bosnia. **2** a person of Bosnian descent.

bosom (buz´m) *n.* **1** the breast of a human being, esp. of a woman. **2** that part of the dress which covers this. **3** the breast as the seat of emotions or the repository of secrets. **4** secret counsel or intention. **5** embrace. **6** intimate relations. **7** affection. **8** the surface of water or of ground. **9** a hollow, a cavity, the interior of anything. ~*v.t.* **1** to put into or hide in the bosom. **2** to embosom. **3** to receive into intimate companionship. **in one's bosom 1** clasped in one's embrace. **2** in one's inmost feelings. **the bosom of one's family** the midst of one's family. **bosom friend** *n.* a dearest and most intimate friend. **bosomy** *a.* (of a woman) having large breasts. [OE *bōsm* (cp. OHG *puosam*, G *Busen*, etym. unknown)]

boson (bō´son, -zon) *n.* a particle, or member of a class of particles, with an integral or zero spin, which behaves in accordance with the statistical relations laid down by Bose and Einstein. [S. N. *Bose*, 1894–1974, Indian physicist]

BOSS *abbr.* (*S Afr.*) Bureau of State Security.

boss[1] (bos) *n.* **1** a protuberant part. **2** an ornamental stud. **3** the knob in the centre of a shield. **4** (*Archit.*) an ornamental projection at the intersection of the ribs in vaulting. **5** (*Geol.*) a large mass of igneous rock. ~*v.t.* **1** to press out, emboss. **2** to furnish with bosses. **bossed** *a.* embossed, ornamented with bosses. **bossy**[1] *a.* having a boss or bosses, studded with bosses. [OF *boce* (F *bosse*), It. *bozza*, a swelling; perh. from OHG *bōzan*, to strike]

boss[2] (bos) *n.* **1** a foreman, manager. **2** a chief, leader or master. **3** the manager or dictator of a party machine. ~*a.* **1** chief, best, most highly esteemed. **2** first-rate, excellent. ~*v.t.* to manage, to direct, to control. **bossy**[2] *a.* (*comp.* **bossier,** *superl.* **bossiest**) **1** managing. **2** domineering. **bossily** *adv.* **bossiness** *n.* **bossy-boots** *n.* (*coll.*) a domineering person. [Dut. *baas*, master, orig. uncle]

boss[3] (bos) *n.* **1** a miss, a bad shot, a bungle. **2** a short-sighted person. **3** a person who squints. ~*v.t.* to miss, to bungle. ~*v.i.* to make a miss. **bosser** *n.* **boss-eyed** *a.* (*coll.*) **1** having only one eye. **2** having one eye injured. **3** squinting. **boss-shot** *n.* (*sl.*) **1** a miss. **2** an unsuccessful attempt. [dial.]

bossa nova (bosə nō´və) *n.* **1** a Brazilian dance resembling the samba. **2** the music for such a dance. [Port. *bossa*, trend, *nova*, new]

bossy[1] BOSS[1].

bossy[2] BOSS[2].

boston (bos´tən) *n.* **1** a game of cards somewhat resembling whist. **2** a slow waltz. [*Boston*, Mass., USA]

bosun, bo'sun BOATSWAIN.

Boswell (boz´wəl) *n.* **1** a biographer. **2** a minute and rather slavish biographer. **Boswellian** (-wel´-) *a.* resembling Boswell in style. **Boswellism** *n.* Boswell's style of biography. **Boswellize, Boswellise** *v.i.* to write biography in Boswell's style. [James *Boswell*, 1740–95, biographer of Samuel Johnson]

BOT, BoT *abbr.* Board of Trade.

Bot. *abbr.* Botany.

bot (bot), **bott** *n.* **1** a parasitic worm, the larva of the genus *Oestrus*. **2** (*in pl.*) a disease caused by these in horses. **3** (*in pl.*) an analogous disease in cattle and in sheep. **botfly** *n.* (*pl.* **botflies**) **1** a fly of the genus *Oestrus*. **2** a gadfly. [etym. unknown]

bot. *abbr.* **1** botany, botanical, botanist. **2** bottle. **3** bought.

botany (bot´əni) *n.* the science which treats of plants and plant life. **botanic** (bətan´-), **botanical** *a.* of or relating to botany. **botanically** *adv.* **botanic garden** *n.* (*often in pl.*) a garden laid out for the scientific culture and study of plants. **botanist** *n.* **botanize, botanise** *v.i.* **1** to collect plants for scientific study. **2** to study plants. ~*v.t.* to explore botanically. **Botany Bay** *n.* transportation (from a convict settlement in Botany Bay, New South Wales named by Captain Cook after the abundance of botanical specimens found there). **Botany wool** *n.* merino wool from Botany Bay. [F *botanique*, late L *botanicus*, Gr. *botanikos*, relating to plants, from *botanē*, a plant, *boskein*, to feed]

botargo (bətah´gō) *n.* (*pl.* **botargos, botargoes**) a relish made of the roes of the mullet and tuna. [It., from Arab. *butarkhah*, Copt. *outarakhon* (*ou-*, a, Gr. *tarichion*, dim. of *tarichos*, dried fish)]

botch[1] (boch) *n.* **1** a clumsy patch. **2** a bungled piece of work. ~*v.t.* **1** to mend or patch clumsily. **2** to put together in an unsuitable or unskilful manner. **3** to ruin. **botcher**[1] *n.* a mender, a patcher, a bungler. **botchery** *n.* **1** the results of botching. **2** clumsy workmanship. **botchy**[1] *a.* (*comp.* **botchier,** *superl.* **botchiest**) characterized by botching or bungling. **botchily** *adv.* **botchiness** *n.* [etym. uncertain (cp. PATCH)]

botch[2] (boch) *n.* an ulcerous swelling. **botchy**[2] *a.* (*comp.* **botchier,** *superl.* **botchiest**) marked with botches or excrescences. [OF *boce* (see BOSS[1])]

botcher[1] BOTCH[1].

botcher[2] (boch´ə) *n.* a young salmon, a grilse. [local; etym. uncertain]

botchy[1] BOTCH[1].

botchy[2] BOTCH[2].

botel BOATEL.

botfly BOT.

both (bōth) *a., pron.* the one and also the other, the two. ~*adv.* **1** as well the one thing as the other. **2** equally in the two cases. **to have it both ways** WAY. **to make both ends meet** END. [Icel. *bāthir, bāthi* (*bā-thir*, both they or the); OE *ba* gave the earlier *bo*]

bother (bodh´ə) *v.t.* **1** to tease, to vex. **2** to annoy, to pester. ~*v.i.* **1** to make a fuss, to be troublesome. **2** to worry oneself. **3** to take trouble. ~*int.* used to express annoyance. ~*n.* worry, disturbance, fuss. **cannot be bothered** will not make an effort. **botheration** (-ā´shən) *n.* **1** the act of bothering. **2** bother. ~*int.* bother. **bothersome** (-səm) *a.* troublesome, annoying. [etym. uncertain]

bothy (both´i), **bothie** *n.* (*pl.* **bothies**) (*esp. Sc.*) **1** a rough kind of cottage. **2** a hut, a hovel, esp. a lodging place for unmarried labourers on a Scottish farm. [etym. uncertain; cp. BOOTH]

bo tree (bō), **bodhi tree** (bō´di) *n.* the peepul or pipla tree, a fig tree, *Ficus religiosa*, held sacred by the Buddhists and planted beside their temples. [Sinhalese *bo*, Pali *bodhi*, perfect knowledge, from Gautama having received enlightenment under such a tree]

botryoid (bot´rioid), **botryoidal** (-oi´-) *a.* resembling a bunch of grapes in form. [Gr. *botruoeides* (*botrus*, a bunch of grapes, -OID)]

bott BOT.

bottine (botēn´) *n.* **1** a buskin. **2** a light kind of boot for women and children. [F, dim. of *botte*, boot]

bottle[1] (bot´əl) *n.* **1** a vessel with a narrow neck for holding liquids (usu. of glass). **2** the quantity in a bottle. **3** a baby's feeding bottle. **4** a hot-water bottle. **5** a metal cylinder for liquefied gas. **6** (*sl.*) temerity, courage, strength of will. ~*v.t.* **1** to put into bottles. **2** to preserve (fruit etc.) in jars or bottles. **on the bottle** drinking (alcohol) heavily. **the bottle** drinking. **to bottle out** (*sl.*) to fail to do something because of fear. **to bottle up 1** to conceal. **2** to restrain, repress (one's emotions). **to hit the bottle** (*sl.*) to drink a great deal of alcoholic drink. **bottle bank** *n.* a public repository for empty glass jars and bottles which are to be recycled. **bottle-brush** *n.* **1** a brush for cleaning bottles. **2** any of various plants with a flower shaped like this, such as the genus *Equisetum* or *Hipparis vulgaris.* **3** (*Austral.*) a genus of trees bearing brushlike flowers. **bottled** *a.* **1** stored in jars or bottles. **2** bottle-shaped. **3** (*sl.*) drunk. **bottle-feed** *v.t.*, *v.i.* to feed (a baby) from a bottle instead of the breast. **bottle gas** *n.* butane gas in liquid form supplied in containers for use in heating, cooking etc. **bottle-glass** *n.* coarse green glass for making bottles. **bottle green** *n.* dark green, like bottle-glass. **bottle-green** *a.* of this colour. **bottle-head** *n.* a species of whale (see BOTTLENOSE (under BOTTLE[1])). **bottleholder** *n.* **1** a person who attends a boxer in a boxing match. **2** a supporter, a second, a backer. **bottle imp** *n.* an imp supposed to be sealed up in a bottle. **bottleneck** *n.* **1** a constricted outlet. **2** an obstruction; something that holds up progress. **3** in guitar playing, a device that produces sliding effects on the strings. **4** the style of playing that uses this. **5** (*in full* **bottleneck guitar**) a guitar played like this. **bottlenose** *n.* **1** a large thick or swollen nose. **2** a whale of the genus *Hyperodon.* ~*a.* bottlenosed. **bottlenosed** *a.* having a large thick or swollen nose. **bottlenose dolphin, bottlenosed dolphin** *n.* a dolphin, *Tursiops truncatus,* which has a bottle-shaped snout. **bottle party** *n.* a drinking party to which each person brings their own alcoholic drink. **bottler** *n.* **1** a person who or machine which bottles. **2** (*Austral., New Zeal., sl.*) an excellent person or thing. **bottle tree** *n.* any of various Australian trees of the genus *Brachychiton* with a bulbous trunk resembling the shape of a bottle. **bottle-washer** *n.* **1** a person or machine that washes bottles. **2** a general factotum, an understrapper. [OF *boteile, botele,* late L *buticula,* dim. of *butis, buttis,* a cask, a BUTT[2]]

bottle[2] (bot´əl) *n.* a bundle of hay or straw. [OF *botel,* dim. of *botte*]

bottom (bot´əm) *n.* **1** the lowest part of anything, the part on which anything rests. **2** the buttocks, the posterior. **3** the seat of a chair. **4** the bed or channel of any body of water. **5** an alluvial hollow. **6** low-lying land. **7** the lowest point. **8** a deep cavity, an abyss. **9** the inmost part, the furthest point of a recess, gulf or inland sea. **10** the end of a table remote from a host, chairperson etc. **11** the lowest rank. **12** the keel of a ship, the part near and including the keel, the hull. **13** a ship as receptacle for cargo. **14** (*pl.*) dregs of liquor, sediment. **15** foundation, base. **16** source, basis. **17** †stamina, power of endurance. ~*v.t.* **1** to put a bottom to. **2** to examine exhaustively, to sound, to fathom. **3** to base or ground. **4** to touch the bottom or the lowest point of. ~*v.i.* **1** (of a ship) to touch the bottom. **2** to be based or founded (on). ~*a.* **1** of or relating to the bottom. **2** lowest. **3** fundamental. **at bottom 1** in reality. **2** at heart. **from the bottom of one's heart** HEART. **the bottom has fallen out of the market** demand has dropped suddenly. **to be at the bottom of** to be the cause of. **to bottom out** to drop to, and level out at, the lowest point (as of prices). **to get to the bottom of** to investigate and discover the real truth about. **to knock the bottom out of 1** to refute (an argument). **2** to destroy the usefulness of. **to touch bottom 1** to reach the bed of a river, bottom of a swimming pool, etc. with one's feet. **2** to reach one's farthest point of decline. **bottom dog** *n.* UNDERDOG (under UNDER- (+ A – S WORDS)). **bottom dollar** *n.* one's last coin. **to bet one's bottom dollar** to predict with the utmost confidence. **bottom drawer** *n.* a drawer in which a woman keeps her new clothes etc. before marriage. **bottomed** *a.* **1** (*usu. in comb.*) having a bottom, as *flat-bottomed.* **2** based. **3** well-grounded. **bottom gear** *n.* FIRST GEAR (under FIRST). **bottom heat** *n.* heat supplied beneath the surface by decomposing manure or by means of a greenhouse furnace. **bottomlands** *n.pl.* (*NAm.*) rich flat lands on the banks of rivers in the western states. **bottomless** *a.* **1** without a bottom. **2** having no seat. **3** fathomless, unfathomable. **bottomless pit** *n.* **1** hell. **2** (*coll.*) a very hungry or greedy person. **bottom line** *n.* **1** the concluding line in a statement of accounts, giving net profit or loss figures. **2** the final word (on). **3** the crux of a matter. **bottommost** *a.* lowest of all. **bottomry** (-ri) *n.* borrowing money on the security of a ship. ~*v.t.* (*3rd pers. sing. pres.* **bottomries,** *pres.p.* **bottomrying,** *past, p.p.* **bottomried**) to pledge (a ship) in this manner. **bottoms up!** *int.* (*coll.*) a drinking toast. **bottom-up** *a., adv.* upside-down. [OE *botm* (cp. Icel. *botn,* OHG *podam,* G *Boden,* L *fundus,* Gr. *puthmēn,* Sansk. *budhnā*)]

botulism (bot´ūlizm) *n.* a form of food poisoning caused by eating preserved food infected by *Clostridium botulinum.* [L *botulus,* a sausage]

bouclé (boo´klā) *n.* **1** a looped yarn. **2** the thick, curly material woven from such yarn. ~*a.* woven from looped yarn. [F, curly]

boudoir (boo´dwah) *n.* a small, elegantly furnished room, used as a lady's private apartment. [F, from *bouder,* to sulk]

bouffant (boo´fã) *a.* full, puffed out, as a hairstyle. [F]

bouffe OPERA BOUFFE (under OPERA[1]).

bougainvillaea (boogənvil´iə), **bougainvillea, bougainvilia** *n.* any tropical plant of the genus *Bougainvillaea,* the red or purple bracts of which almost conceal the flowers. [Louis Antoine de *Bougainville,* French navigator, 1729–1811]

bough (bow) *n.* a large arm or branch of a tree. [OE *bōg, bōh* (cp. Icel. *bōgr,* Dan. *boug,* OHG *buog,* G *Bog,* Dut. *boeg,* all meaning shoulder of man or quadruped; Gr. *pēchos,* forearm)]

bought BUY.

boughten (baw´tən) *a.* (*dial. or poet.*) bought. [irreg. p.p. from BOUGHT]

bougie (boo´zhi) *n.* **1** a wax candle. **2** a smooth, flexible, slender cylinder used for exploring or dilating passages in the human body. [F, from *Bougie,* Arab. *Bijiyah,* town in Algeria with trade in wax candles]

bouillabaisse (booyəbes´) *n.* a rich fish stew or chowder, popular in the south of France. [F]

bouilli (booyē´) *n.* meat gently simmered. [F, p.p. of *bouillir,* to boil]

bouillon (booyõ´) *n.* **1** broth, soup. **2** a fleshy excrescence on a horse's foot. **3** a puffed flounce. [as BOUILLI]

boulder (bōl´də) *n.* **1** a water-worn, rounded stone, a cobble. **2** a large rounded block of stone transported to a lesser or greater distance from its parent rock. **3** an erratic block. **4** a large detached piece of ore. **boulder clay, boulder drift** *n.* a clayey deposit of the glacial period. **boulder formation** *n.* a formation of mud, sand and clay containing boulders. **boulder period** *n.* an Ice Age, a glacial period. **bouldery** *a.* [ME (*bulderston,* Swed. dial. *bullersten,* from *bullra,* to make a noise (cp. Dan. *buldre,* to roar, rattle))]

boule[1] (bool), **boules** *n.pl.* a French game resembling bowls, played with metal balls. [F, ball]

boule[2] BUHL.
boule[3] (booʹli) *n.* a Greek legislative body. [Gr. *boulē*, senate]
boulevard (booʹləvahd) *n.* **1** a public walk on the rampart of a demolished fortification. **2** a broad street planted with trees. **3** (*esp. N Am.*) an arterial road, trunk road. **boulevardier** (booləvahʹdyā), **boulevardist** *n.* **1** a person who haunts the boulevards (of Paris). **2** a man about town. [F, perh. from G *Bollwerk*, BULWARK]
boulle BUHL.
boult BOLT[2].
boulter (bōlʹtə) *n.* a fishing line with a number of hooks attached. [etym. unknown]
bounce (bowns) *v.i.* **1** to rebound. **2** to bound like a ball. **3** to come or go unceremoniously. **4** to exaggerate, to brag. **5** (of a cheque) to be returned to the drawer. *~v.t.* **1** to slam, to bang. **2** to bully. **3** (*N Am.*) to discharge suddenly from employment. **4** (*sl.*) to throw or turn out. *~n.* **1** a heavy, noisy blow. **2** rebound. **3** a leap, a spring. **4** swagger, self-assertion. **5** impudence. **6** a boastful lie. **7** (*N Am.*) dismissal from employment. **to bounce back** to recover quickly or easily. **bouncer** *n.* **1** anything large and bouncing. **2** a boaster, a swaggerer. **3** a big lie. **4** a fine specimen of anything. **5** someone employed to eject (undesirable) people from a public place. **6** in cricket, a short, fast ball that rises sharply off the ground. **bouncing** *a.* **1** big, heavy. **2** stout, strong. **3** bustling, noisy. **bouncingly** *adv.* with a bounce. **bouncy** *a.* (*comp.* **bouncier,** *superl.* **bounciest**) **1** (of a ball) that bounces well. **2** vivacious. **3** resilient, springy. **bouncily** *adv.* **bounciness** *n.* **bouncy castle** *n.* a children's play area consisting of an inflatable base (for bouncing on) and high inflatable sides decorated to look like (usu.) a castle. [prob. imit.]
bound[1] (bownd) *n.* a leap, a spring, a rebound. *~v.i.* **1** to leap, to spring. **2** to rebound, to bounce. **by leaps and bounds** with astonishing speed. **bounder** *n.* **1** a person who or something which leaps. **2** (*sl.*) an ill-bred person. **3** (*dated*) a scoundrel. [F *bondir*, to bound, orig., to resound, L *bombitāre*, to hum, buzz (*bombus*, see BOMB)]
bound[2] (bownd) *n.* **1** a limit, a boundary. **2** limitation, restriction. **3** territory. *~v.t.* **1** to set bounds to. **2** to confine. **3** to form the boundary of. **out of bounds** (of an area, topic or person) forbidden, prohibited. **boundary** *n.* (*pl.* **boundaries**) **1** a mark indicating limit. **2** the limit thus marked. **3** in cricket, a hit that crosses the limits of the field. **boundary layer** *n.* the layer of fluid that immediately surrounds a solid object immersed in fluid. **boundary rider** *n.* (*Austral., New Zeal.*) a person who keeps the boundary fences of a station in repair. **boundary umpire** *n.* in Australian Rules, an umpire who signals when the ball is out. **bounded** *a.* having bounds. **boundless** *a.* **1** without bounds. **2** limitless. **boundlessly** *adv.* **boundlessness** *n.* [OF *bonde*, *bodne*, late L *bodena* (etym. uncertain)]
bound[3] (bownd) *a.* **1** under obligation, compelled, obliged. **2** certain (to). **3** in a cover, esp. in a cover of leather or other permanent material as distinguished from paper covers. **bound up with** **1** intimately associated with. **2** having identical aims or interests with. †**bounden** *a.* **1** bound. **2** enslaved. **3** obliged, under obligation. **bounden duty** *n.* obligatory duty. [past, p.p. of BIND]
bound[4] (bownd) *a.* **1** prepared, ready. **2** starting, destined. **3** directing one's course. [ME *boun*, Icel. *būinn*, p.p. of *būa*, to till, to get ready; *-d* added in assim. to other participles]
bounty (bownʹti) *n.* (*pl.* **bounties**) **1** goodness, gracious liberality. **2** an act of generosity, a gift. **3** a premium for joining the army or navy, or to encourage commerce or industry. **bounteous** (-tiəs) *a.* **1** full of bounty. **2** liberal, beneficent. **3** generously given. **bounteously** *adv.* **bounteousness** *n.* **bountiful** *a.* **1** full of bounty. **2** liberal, munificent. **3** plenteous, abundant. **Lady Bountiful** LADY. **bountifully** *adv.* **bounty hunter** *n.* a person who does something, esp. catches a criminal, for the reward. [OF *bonté*, *bontet*, L *bonitātem -as*, goodness, from *bonus*, good]
bouquet (bukāʹ, bukʹā, bō-) *n.* **1** a nosegay, a bunch of flowers. **2** the perfume exhaled by wine. **3** a compliment. **bouquet garni** (bukā gahʹnē) *n.* (*pl.* **bouquets garnis** (bukāz gahʹnē)) a bunch (traditionally five sprigs) of herbs for flavouring meat dishes and soups. [F, OF *bosquet*, It. *boschetto*, BOSKET]
bouquetin (booʹkətin) *n.* the Alpine ibex. [F *bouquetin*, prob. for *bouc-estain* (G *Steinbock*)]
Bourbon (buəʹbən) *n.* **1** a member of the royal family that formerly ruled France. **2** (*N Am.*) an obsolete and unteachable Democrat, a reactionary. **Bourbon biscuit** *n.* a biscuit consisting of two chocolate-flavoured pieces with chocolate cream between. **Bourbonism** *n.* adherence to the Bourbon dynasty. **Bourbonist** *n.* [French town]
bourbon (bœʹbən, buəʹbən) *n.* an American whisky made of wheat or Indian corn. [*Bourbon* County, Kentucky]
bourdon (buəʹdən) *n.* **1** a bass stop on an organ. **2** a bass reed in a harmonium. **3** the drone of a bagpipe. **4** the lowest bell in a peal of bells. **5** a low undersong or accompaniment. [F, prob. imit.]
bourg (buəg) *n.* **1** a town built under the shadow of a castle. **2** a market town. [F, from late L *burgus*, WG *burg* (cp. OE *burh*, Eng. BOROUGH)]
bourgeois[1] (buəʹzhwah) *n.* (*pl.* **bourgeois**) **1** (*sometimes derog.*) a person of the mercantile, shopkeeping or middle class. **2** a French citizen. *~a.* **1** of or relating to the bourgeoisie, middle-class or capitalist as distinguished from working-class. **2** commonplace, humdrum, unintellectual. **3** materialistic, middle-class in outlook. **bourgeoisie** (-zēʹ) *n.* **1** (*sometimes derog.*) the mercantile or shopkeeping class. **2** the middle class as opposed to the proletariat. [as BOURG]
bourgeois[2] (bəjoisʹ), **burgeois** *n.* (*Hist.*) a size of type around 9 point. [prob. from a French printer]
bourgeon BURGEON.
bourguignon (buəʹgēnyō) *a.* (of meat dishes) stewed with (Burgundy) wine. [F, Burgundian]
bourn[1] (bawn) *n.* a small stream, esp. a stream that runs periodically from springs in chalk. [var. of BURN[2]]
bourn[2] BOURNE.
†**bourne** (bawn), **bourn** *n.* a bound, a limit, a goal. [F *borne*, OF *bodne*, BOUND[2]]
bourree (booʹrā), **bourrée** *n.* **1** a folk dance from the Auvergne and Basque provinces. **2** a musical composition in this rhythm. [F]
bourse (buəs) *n.* a (French) foreign exchange for the transaction of commercial business. **the Bourse** the Paris equivalent of the Stock Market. [F, lit., purse]
boustrophedon (boostrəfēʹdən, bow-) *a., adv.* written alternately from left to right and from right to left. [Gr., as an ox turns in ploughing (*bous*, ox, *strophē*, a turning, *-don*, adv. suf.)]
bout (bowt) *n.* **1** a turn, a round, a set-to. **2** trial, essay, attempt. **3** a spell of work. **4** a fit of drunkenness or of illness. [earlier *bought*, prob. doublet of BIGHT]
boutique (bootēkʹ) *n.* **1** a fashionable clothes shop. **2** any small specialist shop. **3** a shop within a department store, hotel, airport lounge etc. [F, shop]
bouton (booʹtõ) *n.* **1** a pimple, pustule, boil. **2** the hollow at the end of the tongue of the honey bee. [F, button]
boutonnière (bootonyeəʹ) *n.* a flower or flowers worn in the buttonhole.

bouts rimés (boo rē´mā) *n.pl.* a game in which a list of rhymed endings is handed to each player to fill in and complete the verse. [F, rhymed endings]

☒ **bouyant** common misspelling of BUOYANT (under BUOY).

bouzouki (buzoo´ki) *n.* a Greek stringed instrument similar to the mandolin. [mod. Gr. *mpouzouki*]

bovate (bō´vāt) *n.* (*Hist.*) the amount of land that an ox could plough in a season, approx. 13 acres. [late L *bovāta*, *bos bovis*, an ox]

bovine (bō´vīn) *a.* **1** of or resembling oxen. **2** sluggish. **3** dull, stupid. **bovinely** *adv.* **bovine somatotrophin** *n.* a growth hormone that cows produce naturally, introduced into their feed to increase milk production. **bovine spongiform encephalopathy** *n.* a disease of the central nervous system in cattle, usu. fatal, also called *mad cow disease*. [L *bovīnus* (*bos bovis*, ox)]

Bovril® (bov´ril) *n.* a concentrated beef extract used for flavouring stews etc.

bovver (bov´ə) *n.* (*sl.*) a boisterous or violent commotion, a street fight. **bovver boot** *n.* (*sl.*) a heavy workboot worn esp. by teenage thugs. **bovver boy** *n.* (*sl.*) a member of a violent teenage gang, a hooligan. [from BOTHER]

bow[1] (bō) *n.* **1** the doubling of a string in a slip-knot. **2** a single-looped knot. **3** an ornamental knot in which neckties, ribbons etc. are tied. **4** a necktie, ribbon or the like, tied in such a knot. **5** a stringed weapon for discharging arrows. **6** a curve, a rainbow. **7** the appliance with which instruments of the violin family are played. **8** a single stroke of such an appliance. **9** any of various simple contrivances in shape like a bow. **10** a saddle bow, an oxbow. **11** (*N Am.*) the side piece of a pair of spectacles. **12** in archery, a bowman. *~v.t.* to play with or use the bow on (a violin etc.). **to draw the long bow** DRAW. **two strings to one's bow** more resources, plans or opportunities than one. **bow-bent** *a.* bent like a bow. **bow-compasses, bow-compass** *n.* compasses with the legs jointed, so that the points can be turned inwards. **bowfin** *n.* an American freshwater bony fish, *Amia calva*. **bow-hand** *n.* the hand that holds the bow in archery or in playing a stringed instrument. **bowhead** *n.* an Arctic whale, *Balaena mysticetus*. **bow-legged** *a.* having the legs bowed or bent. **bow-legs** *n.pl.* **bowman**[1] *n.* (*pl.* **bowmen**) a person who shoots with the bow, an archer. **bow net** *n.* **1** a cylinder of wickerwork with one narrow entrance, for catching lobsters. **2** a net attached to a bow or arch of metal. **bowsaw** *n.* a saw fitted in a frame like a bowstring in a bow. **bowshot** *n.* the distance to which an arrow can be shot. **bowstring** *n.* **1** the string by which a bow is stretched. **2** (*Hist.*) the string with which persons were executed in Turkey. *~v.t.* to strangle with a bowstring. **bow tie** *n.* a necktie in the form of a bow. **bow window** *n.* a bay window segmentally curved. **bowyer** (bō´yə) *n.* **1** a bowmaker. **2** a seller of bows. [OE *boga* (cp. OHG *bogo*, G *Bogen*, Gmc. *beugan*, to bend (see BOW[2]))]

bow[2] (bow) *v.i.* **1** to bend forward as a sign of assent, submission or salutation. **2** to incline the head. **3** to kneel. **4** to bend under a yoke. **5** to submit, to yield. *~v.t.* **1** to cause to bend. **2** to incline, to influence. **3** to crush. **4** to express by bowing. **5** to usher (in or out). *~n.* an inclination of the body or head, as a salute or token of respect. **to bow and scrape** to be obsequious. **to bow down 1** to bend or kneel in submission or reverence. **2** to crush, to make stoop. **to bow out 1** to make one's exit. **2** to retire, to retreat. **to make one's bow** to exit or enter formally. **to take a bow** to acknowledge applause. **bowed** *a.* **1** bent, crooked. **2** bent down. [OE *būgan*, Gmc. *beugan*, to bend, stem *bug-* (cp. L *fugere*, Gr. *pheugein*, Sansk. *bhuj*)]

bow[3] (bow) *n.* **1** (*often in pl.*) the rounded fore-end of a ship or boat. **2** the rower nearest this. **on the bow** (*Naut.*) within 45° of the point right ahead. **bowcap** *n.* a metal plate fitted on the nose of a submarine or an aeroplane. **bow-chaser** *n.* a gun in the bow of a vessel pointing forward. **bow-grace** *n.* a kind of fender round the bows and sides of a ship to prevent injury from floating ice or timber. **bowline** (bō´lin, -līn), **bolin** *n.* a rope fastened to the middle part of the weather side of a sail to make it stand close to the wind. **on a bowline** close-hauled, sailing close to the wind. **bowline knot** *n.* a kind of non-slipping knot. **bowman**[2] *n.* (*pl.* **bowmen**) the rower nearest the bow. **bow-oar** *n.* **1** the rower nearest the bow. **2** their oar. **bowsprit** (bō´sprit) *n.* (*Naut.*) a spar running out from the bows of a vessel to support sails and stays. **bow wave** *n.* a wave set up at the bows of a ship, or in front of a body moving through a fluid. [cogn. with BOUGH]

bowdlerize (bowd´lərīz), **bowdlerise** *v.t.* to expurgate (a book). **bowdlerism, bowdlerization** (-zā´shən) *n.* the act or practice of expurgating. [Thomas *Bowdler*, 1754–1825, who in 1818 published an expurgated Shakespeare]

bowel (bow´əl) *n.* **1** each of the intestines, a gut. **2** (*pl.*) the entrails, the intestines. **3** (*fig.*) the seat of tender emotions. **4** the interior, the centre. *~v.t.* (*pres.p.* **bowelling,** (*N Am.*) **boweling,** *past, p.p.* **bowelled,** (*N Am.*) **boweled**) to disembowel. **bowel movement** *n.* **1** defecation. **2** the faeces discharged. [OF *boel* (It. *budello*), late L *botellus*, dim. of *botulus*, a sausage]

bower[1] (bow´ə) *n.* **1** an arbour, a shady retreat, a summer house. **2** (*poet.*) a dwelling. **3** (*poet.*) an inner room, a boudoir. **4** the run of a bowerbird. **bowerbird** *n.* **1** any of various Australian birds of the family Ptilonorhynchidae, which build bowers or runs, adorning them with feathers, shells etc. **2** (*Austral., sl.*) a person who collects odds and ends. **bowery** *a.* **1** of the nature of a bower. **2** leafy. *~n.* (*also* **Bowery**) (*pl.* **boweries, Boweries**) a district notorious for its numerous bars, shops and cheap hotels (from the street in New York of that name). [OE *būr*, a chamber, a college (*būan*, to dwell); cp. Dan. *buur*, and G *Bauer*, a cage]

bower[2] (bow´ə) *n.* either of the two knaves in euchre. **left bower** LEFT[1]. **right bower** RIGHT. [G *Bauer*, a peasant, the knave (cp. BOER)]

bower[3] (bow´ə) *n.* **1** either of the two anchors carried in the bows. **2** the cable attached to either. **bower anchor** *n.* **bower-cable** *n.* the cable attached to a bower.

bowie knife (bō´i, boo´i) *n.* a long knife with the blade double-edged towards the point, used as a weapon in the south and south-west of US. [Col. James *Bowie*, d.1836, American soldier]

Usage note The pronunciation (boo´i) is used in the US.

bowl[1] (bōl) *n.* **1** a hollow (usu. hemispherical) vessel for holding liquids, a basin. **2** the contents of such a vessel. **3** a drinking-vessel. **4** a basin-shaped part or concavity. **5** in geography, a natural basin. **6** (*esp. N Am.*) a stadium. **7** (*N Am.*) (*in full* **bowl game**) an American football game played after the main season. **bowlful** *n.* (*pl.* **bowlfuls**). [OE *bolla*, Gmc. stem *bul-*, to swell]

bowl[2] (bōl) *n.* **1** a solid ball, generally made of wood, slightly biased or one-sided, used to play various games with. **2** (*pl.*) a game with bowls. **3** (*pl., dial.*) skittles. **4** (*pl., N Am.*) tenpin bowls. *~v.i.* **1** to play at bowls. **2** to roll a bowl along the ground. **3** to deliver the ball at cricket. **4** to move rapidly and smoothly (usu. with *along*). *~v.t.* **1** to cause to roll or run along the ground. **2** to deliver (as a ball at cricket). **3** to strike the wicket and put (a player) out. **to bowl out 1** to put (a player) out at cricket by bowling the bails off. **2** (*sl.*) to find out. **3** to convict. **to bowl over 1** to knock over. **2** to throw into a helpless condition. **3** (*coll.*) to impress. **bowler**[1] *n.* **1** a person who plays at bowls. **2** the player who delivers the ball at cricket. **bowling** *n.* **1** playing at bowls. **2** the act of delivering a ball at cricket. **bowling alley** *n.* a covered space for playing skittles or tenpin bowls. **bowling average** *n.* in cricket, a bowler's conceded runs per wicket taken. **bowling crease** *n.* the line from behind which the bowler delivers the ball at cricket. **bowling green** *n.* a level green on which bowls are played. [F *boule*, L *bulla*, a bubble]

bowler[1] BOWL[2].

bowler[2] (bō´lə), **bowler hat** *n.* an almost-hemispherical stiff felt hat. **bowler-hat** *v.t.* (*pres.p.* **bowler-hatting,** *past, p.p.* **bowler-hatted**) (*sl.*) to retire, discharge, dismiss. [*Bowler*, a hatter who made it in 1851]

bowman[1] BOW[1].

bowman[2] BOW[3].

bowser (bow´zə) *n.* **1** a tanker used for refuelling aircraft on an airfield, or for supplying water. **2** (*Austral., New Zeal.*) a petrol pump. [orig. trade name]

Bow Street officer (bō), **Bow Street runner** *n.* (*Hist.*) a police officer. [*Bow Street* in London, site of the magistrates' court]

bow-wow (bowwow´, bow´ow) *int.* used to represent the bark of a dog. ~*n.* **1** the bark of a dog. **2** a dog (used by or to children). [imit.]

Usage note The pronunciation with stress on the first syllable applies to the sense 'a dog'.

bowyang (bō´yang) *n.* (*Austral., New Zeal.*) a strap or string below the knee to prevent trousers from dragging.

bowyer BOW[1].

box[1] (boks) *n.* **1** a case or receptacle usu. with a lid and rectangular or cylindrical, adapted for holding solids, not liquids. **2** the contents of such a case. **3** a Christmas box. **4** a compartment partitioned off in a theatre, tavern, coffee house, or for animals in a stable, railway truck etc. **5** an enclosure, e.g. *telephone box, sentry box.* **6** a facility at a newspaper office where replies to advertisements may be sent. **7** a hut, a small house. **8** a rectangle enclosing print on a page. **9** a case for the protection of some piece of mechanism from injury. **10** a protective pad for the genitals worn by cricketers. **11** the penalty area in football. **12** the place where the batter or pitcher stands in baseball. **13** the driver's seat on a coach. **14** each of the compartments into which a type-case is divided. ~*v.t.* **1** to enclose in or furnish with a box. **2** to deposit (a document) in court. **3** (*Austral., New Zeal.*) to allow (sheep that should be kept separate) to run together. **in the box seat** in the most advantageous position, best placed. **in the wrong box** mistaken, out of place. **the box 1** television. **2** a television set. **to box off 1** to box-haul. **2** to partition off. **to box the compass 1** to name the points of the compass in proper order. **2** to go right round (in direction, political views etc.) and end at the starting point. **to box up 1** to shut in. **2** to squeeze together. **box bed** *n.* **1** a bedstead with sides, roof and sliding panels of wood. **2** a bedstead that folds up like a box. **box camera** *n.* a simple box-shaped camera with an elementary lens, shutter and viewfinder. **boxcar** *n.* (*N Am.*) a goods van. **boxcloth** *n.* a tough, closely woven cloth. **box coat** *n.* a heavy overcoat worn by coachmen. **box day** *n.* (*Sc. Law*) a day in vacation appointed for the lodgement of papers. **box drain** *n.* a square drain. **boxer**[1] *n.* a person who puts or packs things up in boxes. **boxful** *n.* (*pl.* **boxfuls**) the quantity of things that a box will hold. **box girder** *n.* a rectangular or square hollow girder. **box hat** *n.* a silk hat. **box-haul** *v.t.* (*Naut.*) to veer (a ship) in a particular manner when near the shore. **Boxing Day** *n.* the first weekday after Christmas, when Christmas boxes, i.e. presents in acknowledgement of services rendered throughout the year, are given. **box iron** *n.* a smoothing iron with a cavity for a heater. **box junction** *n.* a road junction with a box-shaped area painted with criss-crossed yellow lines into which traffic is prohibited from entering until there is a clear exit. **box key** *n.* a T-shaped implement for turning a water cock. **box kite** *n.* a box-shaped kite composed of open-ended connected cubes. **boxlike** *a.* **box mattress, box spring mattress** *n.* a mattress consisting of spiral springs contained in a wooden frame and covered with ticking. **box number** *n.* a number in a newspaper office to which replies to advertisements may be sent. **box office** *n.* **1** an office in a theatre or concert hall for booking seats. **2** the commercial appeal of an actor, production etc. **box pleat** *n.* a double fold or pleat. **boxroom** *n.* a room for storing boxes etc. **box spanner** *n.* a tubular spanner with the ends shaped to fit the nuts and turned by a tommy bar inserted into a transverse hole. **boxy** *a.* (*comp.* **boxier,** *superl.* **boxiest**) **1** shaped like a box. **2** (of clothes) having a square cut. **3** (of reproduced music) lacking the high and low tones. **boxiness** *n.* [see BOX[2]]

box[2] (boks) *n.* **1** a genus of small evergreen shrubs, *Buxus*, esp. the common box tree, *Buxus sempervirens.* **2** boxwood. **box elder** *n.* an American maple, *Acer negundo.* **boxen** *a.* of, made of or resembling box. **box gum** *n.* (*Austral.*) a variety of eucalyptus tree. **box tree** *n.* the common box, *Buxus sempervirens.* **boxwood** *n.* the wood of the box tree. [OE *box*, L *buxus*, Gr. *puxos*]

box[3] (boks) *n.* a blow with the open hand on the ear or side of the head. ~*v.t.* to strike (on the ear etc.) with the open hand. ~*v.i.* to fight or spar with fists or with gloves. **to box clever** (*coll.*) to act in a clever or cunning way. **boxer**[2] *n.* **1** a person who boxes, a pugilist. **2** (*Hist.*) (**Boxer**) a member of a secret society in China, ostensibly devoted to athletics, which took the leading part in the movement for the expulsion of foreigners, which came to a head in the rising of 1900. **3** a large, smooth-haired mastiff of a breed derived from the German bulldog. **4** this breed. **5** (*Austral.*) a person who organizes a game of two-up. **boxer shorts** *n.pl.* men's baggy underpants resembling the shorts worn by boxers. **boxing** *n.* the sport of fist fighting with gloves. **boxing glove** *n.* either of a pair of protective leather mittens worn by boxers. **boxing weight** *n.* each of a series of weight ranges at which boxers fight. [etym. uncertain (perh. imit.)]

Box and Cox (boks ənd koks´) *n.* two people who share a job or a room but never meet. ~*a., adv.* alternating. ~*v.i.* to share accommodation or work in this manner. [*Cox and Box*, a play by J. M. Morton]

boxer[1] BOX[1].

boxer[2] BOX[3].

boy (boi) *n.* **1** a male child. **2** a lad, a son. **3** a slave. **4** (*offensive*) a black man in a country colonized by Europeans, a black male servant or labourer. **5** (*offensive*) any male servant. **6** (*pl.*) grown-up sons. **7** (*pl., coll.*) a group of male friends. ~*int.* used to express surprise, appreciation etc. **oh boy!** used to express surprise, appreciation, delight or derision. **boyfriend** *n.* (*coll.*) a male friend, esp. a regular partner or lover. **boyhood** *n.* **1** the state of being a boy. **2** the time of life at which a male is a boy. **boyish** *a.* **1** characteristic of or suitable to a boy. **2** puerile. **boyishly** *adv.* **boyishness** *n.* **boyo** (boi´ō) *n.* (*pl.* **boyos**) (*Welsh, Ir., coll.*) boy, fellow. **Boys' Brigade** *n.* an organization founded in Britain in 1883 for the training and welfare of boys. **Boy Scout** *n.* a member of the Scout Association. **boys in blue** *n.pl.* policemen; the police. **boy's love** *n.* SOUTHERNWOOD (under SOUTH). **boy's play** *n.* **1** play such as boys engage in. **2** trifling. [etym. uncertain; perh. from EFris.

boi, young gentleman (cp. Dut. *boef*, knave, MHG *buobe*, G *Bube*)]

boyar (boi´ah, boyah´), **boiar, boyard** (boi´əd) *n.* (*Hist.*) a member of the old Russian nobility. [Rus. *boyāre*, pl. of *boyārin* (from OSlav. *bol* great, or Rus. *boi*, war)]

boycott (boi´kot) *v.t.* **1** to combine to ostracize (a person) on account of their political opinions. **2** to refuse to have dealings with. ~*n.* the action of boycotting. **boycottee** (-tē´) *n.* a person boycotted. **boycotter** *n.* **boycottism** *n.* [first used in 1880 to describe the action of the Land League towards Capt. *Boycott*, an Irish landlord]

boyla (boi´lə) *n.* a sorcerer. [Austral. Abor.]

Boyle's law (boilz) *n.* the principle that the pressure of a gas varies inversely with its volume at constant temperature. [Robert *Boyle*, 1627–91, Irish scientist]

boyo BOY.

boysenberry (boi´zənberi) *n.* (*pl.* **boysenberries**) an edible hybrid fruit related to the loganberry and the raspberry. [Rudolph *Boysen*, d. 1950, American horticulturalist]

BP *abbr.* **1** before the present (era). **2** British Petroleum. **3** British Pharmacopoeia.

bp *abbr.* **1** baptized. **2** (of alcoholic density) below proof. **3** bills payable. **4** birthplace. **5** (*also* **Bp.**) bishop. **6** boiling point. **7** blood pressure.

BPC *abbr.* British Pharmaceutical Codex.

B.Phil. *abbr.* Bachelor of Philosophy.

bpi *abbr.* bits per inch (of computer tape).

bps *abbr.* (*Comput.*) bits per second.

Bq *abbr.* becquerel.

BR *abbr.* **1** Brazil (IVR). **2** British Rail.

Br *chem. symbol* bromine.

Br. *abbr.* **1** British. **2** Brother.

bra (brah) *n.* (*pl.* **bras**) a women's undergarment that supports the breasts. **bra-burning** *a.* exceptionally feministic (from the practice of burning brassières as a token of women's independence). **braless** *a.* not wearing a bra. [abbr. of BRASSIÈRE]

brace (brās) *n.* **1** that which clasps, tightens, connects or supports. **2** a timber or scantling to strengthen the framework of a building. **3** (*pl.*) straps to support the trousers. **4** a wire dental appliance for straightening crooked teeth. **5** two taken together, a couple, a pair. **6** a rope attached to a yard for trimming the sail. **7** a sign in writing, printing or music uniting two or more words, lines, staves etc. **8** a strap connecting the body of a coach to the springs. **9** a leather thong on the cord of a drum regulating the tension of the skin. **10** a cord of a drum. ~*v.t.* **1** to encompass. **2** to gird. **3** to bind or tie close. **4** to tighten or make tense. **5** to strengthen, to fill with energy or firmness. **6** to trim (sails) by means of braces. **brace and bit** *n.* a tool used by carpenters for boring, consisting of a kind of crank in which a bit or drill is fixed. **bracer** *n.* **1** something which braces. **2** (*coll.*) a stiff drink or tonic. **3** a defence for the arm, used in archery, fencing etc. **bracing** *a.* imparting tone or strength. **bracingly** *adv.* **bracingness** *n.* [OF *brace*, *brasse*, L *brāchia*, the arms, Gr. *brachiōn*, the arm]

bracelet (brās´lit) *n.* **1** an ornamental ring or band for the wrist or arm. **2** (*pl.*, *sl.*) handcuffs. [OF *bracel*]

brach (brach) *n.* a bitch hound. [OF *brachet*, *braquet*, dim. of *brac*, OHG *bracco* (G *Bracke*), a dog that hunts by scent]

brachial (brā´kiəl, brak´-) *a.* **1** of or belonging to the arm. **2** resembling an arm. **brachiate**[1] (-ət) *a.* **1** having branches in pairs, nearly at right angles to a stem and crossing each other alternately. **2** having arms. **brachiate**[2] (-āt) *v.i.* (of various arboreal mammals) to move along by swinging from each arm alternately. **brachiation** (-ā´shən) *n.* **brachiator** *n.* [L *brāchiālis* (*brāchium*, arm)]

brachio- (brak´iō) *comb. form* having arms or armlike processes. [Gr. *brachiōn*, an arm]

brachiopod (brak´iəpod) *n.* (*pl.* **brachiopods, brachiopoda** (-op´ədə)) a bivalve mollusc of the phylum Brachiopoda, with tentacles on each side of the mouth. **brachiopodous** (-op´-) *a.* of or resembling the Brachiopoda. [Gr. *pous podos* foot]

brachiosaurus (brakiəsaw´rəs) *n.* (*pl.* **brachiosauruses**) a herbivorous dinosaur of the genus *Brachiosaurus*, characterized by the length of its front legs and its huge size.

brachistochrone (brəkis´təkrōn) *n.* the curve between two points through which a body moves in a shorter time than any other curve. [Gr. *brakhistos*, shortest, *khronos*, time]

brachy- (brak´i) *comb. form* short. [Gr. *brachus*, short]

brachycephalic (brakisifal´ik, -kefal´ik) *a.* **1** short-headed. **2** having a skull in which the breadth is at least four-fifths of the length. **3** belonging to a branch of humankind having skulls of that proportion. **brachycephalous** (-sef´ələs, -kef´-) *a.* **brachycephaly** (-sef´-), **brachycephalism** *n.* the state of being brachycephalic. [Gr. *kephalē*, head]

brachylogy (brəkil´əji) *n.* (*pl.* **brachylogies**) **1** concision of speech. **2** abridged or condensed expression. **3** inaccuracy caused by excess of brevity.

brack[1] (brak) *n.* a flaw or tear in a cloth or dress. [BREAK[1]]

brack[2] (brak) *n.* (*Ir.*) cake or bread containing dried fruit. [abbr. of BARMBRACK]

bracken (brak´ən) *n.* **1** a fern, esp. *Pteridium aquilinum*. **2** a mass of such ferns. [Swed. *bräken*, fern]

bracket (brak´it) *n.* **1** a projection with a horizontal top fixed to a wall. **2** a shelf with a stay underneath for hanging against a wall. **3** an angular support. **4** the cheek of a gun carriage, holding the trunnion. **5** a gas pipe projecting from a wall. **6** a mark used in printing to enclose words or mathematical symbols. **7** the distance between two artillery shots fired either side of the target. ~*v.t.* (*pres.p.* **bracketing,** *past, p.p.* **bracketed**) **1** to furnish with a bracket or brackets. **2** to place within brackets. **3** to connect (names of equal merit) in an honours list. **4** to associate, categorize or group (like things) together. **5** to find the range of (a target) by dropping shots alternately short of and over it. **bracket fungus** *n.* a fungus of the family Polyporaceae, which grow as shelflike projections on tree trunks. **bracketing** *n.* a skeleton support for mouldings. [formerly *bragget*, Sp. *bragueta*, dim. of *braga*, L *brāca*, sing. of *bracae*, *braccae*, breeches (the sense affected by confusion with L *brāchium*, arm)]

brackish (brak´ish) *a.* **1** partly fresh, partly salt. **2** of a saline taste. **brackishness** *n.* [formerly *brack*, Dut. *brak*]

bract (brakt) *n.* a small modified leaf or scale on the flower stalk. **bracteal** (-tiəl) *a.* of the nature of a bract. **bracteate** (-tiət) *a.* **1** formed of metal beaten thin. **2** furnished with bracts. **bracteole** (-tiōl) *n.* a small bract. **bracteolate** (-tiəlāt) *a.* furnished with bracteoles. **bractless** *a.* [L *bractea*, a thin plate]

brad (brad) *n.* a thin, flattish nail, with a small lip or projection on one side instead of a head. [ME *brad*, Icel. *broddr*, a spike (cp. OE *brord*)]

bradawl (brad´awl) *n.* a small boring-tool. [AWL]

brady- (brad´i) *comb. form* slow. [Gr. *bradus*, slow]

bradycardia (bradikah´diə) *n.* a slow heartbeat.

bradypeptic (bradipep´tik) *a.* of slow digestion.

bradypod (brad´ipod) *n.* one of the sloth family. [Gr. *pous podos*, foot]

brae (brā) *n.* (*Sc.*) **1** a slope bounding a river valley. **2** a hill. [Icel. *brā*, eyelid, brow (cp. OE *bræw*)]

brag (brag) *v.i.* (*pres.p.* **bragging,** *past, p.p.* **bragged**) to boast. ~*v.t.* **1** to boast about. **2** to challenge. **3** to bully.

~*n.* **1** a boast. **2** boasting. **3** a game of cards. ~*adv.* proudly, conceitedly. **bragger** *n.* **bragging** *n., a.* **braggingly** *adv.* [etym. uncertain]

braggadocio (bragədō´chiō) *n.* **1** an empty boaster. **2** empty boasting. [*Braggadochio* in Spenser's *Faerie Queene*]

braggart (brag´ət) *n.* a boastful person. ~*a.* given to bragging; boastful. [F *bragard*, from *braguer*, to brag]

bragging BRAG.

Brahma (brah´mə) *n.* the chief Hindu divinity, the Creator God.

brahma (brah´mə), **brahmaputra** (-poo´trə) *n.* **1** any bird of an Asian breed of domestic fowl. **2** this breed. [*Brahmaputra*, river in India]

Brahmin (brah´min), **Brahman** (-mən) *n.* **1** a member of the highest Hindu caste, the priestly order. **2** (*N Am.*) a person of superior intellectual or social status, a highbrow. **3** a breed of Indian cattle. **Brahminee**[1] (-nē´) *n.* a female Brahmin. **Brahminee**[2] (brah´minē) *a.* of or relating to the Brahmin caste. **Brahminic** (-min´-), **Brahminical** *a.* of or relating to Brahmins or to Brahminism. **Brahminism** *n.* [Sansk. *brāhmana*, from *brahman*, worship]

braid[1] (brād) *n.* **1** anything plaited or interwoven. **2** a narrow band. **3** a woven fabric for trimming or binding. ~*v.t.* **1** to intertwine, to plait. **2** to dress (the hair) in plaits or bands. **3** to tie (ribbon or bands) into the hair. **4** to trim or bind with braid. **braided** *a.* **braiding** *n.* **1** the action of plaiting or interweaving. **2** embroidery. [OE *brægd, bræd*, trick, deceit, from *bregdan, bredan*, to move to and fro, weave (cp. Icel. *bregtha*, OHG *brettan*)]

braid[2] (brād) *a.* (*Sc.*) broad.

braidism (brā´dizm) *n.* hypnotism, mesmerism. [Dr James *Braid*, 1795–1860, who applied and explained the system in 1842]

brail (brāl) *n.* **1** a piece of leather with which to bind up a hawk's wing. **2** (*pl.*) ropes used to gather up the foot and leeches of a sail before furling. ~*v.t.* **1** to fasten up (the wing of a hawk) with a brail. **2** to haul up by means of the brails. [OF *brail, braiel*, L *brācāle*, breech-girdle (*bracae*, breeches)]

Braille (brāl) *n.* a system of writing or printing for the blind, by means of combinations of points stamped in relief. ~*v.t.* to print or transcribe in Braille. **Braille music, Braille type** *n.* music or symbols designed on this system. **Braille writer** *n.* an instrument for stamping paper with these. [Louis *Braille*, 1809–52, inventor]

brain (brān) *n.* **1** the soft, whitish, convoluted mass of nervous substance contained in the skull of vertebrates. **2** any analogous organ in the invertebrates (*sing.* the organ, *pl.* the substance). **3** the seat of intellect, thought etc. **4** the centre of sensation. **5** intellectual power. **6** (*coll.*) an intelligent person. **7** (*usu. in pl., coll.*) the cleverest person in a group. **8** (*usu. in pl.*) the person who thinks up a plan. ~*v.t.*, to dash out the brains of, to kill in this way. **something on the brain** an obsession. **brainbox** *n.* (*coll.*) a clever person. **brainchild** *n.* (*pl.* **brainchildren**) a plan or project which is the product of creative thought. **brain coral** *n.* coral resembling the convolutions of the brain. **brain damage** *n.* injury to the brain, temporary or permanent. **brain-damaged** *a.* **brain death** *n.* the cessation of brain function, taken as an indication of death. **brain-dead** *a.* **1** having suffered brain death. **2** (*coll.*) lacking intelligence. **brain drain** *n.* (*coll.*) the emigration of academics or scientists looking for better pay or conditions. **brain fever** *n.* **1** inflammation of the brain. **2** fever with brain complications. **brainless** *a.* **1** destitute of brain. **2** silly, witless. **brainpan** *n.* (*coll.*) the skull. **brain power** *n.* intelligence, mental ability. **brainsick** *a.* **1** of diseased brain or mind. **2** flighty, one-sided, injudicious. **3** produced by a diseased brain. **brainstem** *n.* the stalk-shaped part of the brain which connects it to the spinal cord. **brainstorm** *n.* a sudden, violent mental disturbance. **brainstorming** *n.* intensive discussion, e.g. to generate ideas. **brains trust** *n.* a bench of persons before the microphone answering impromptu selected questions from an audience. **brain-teaser, brain-twister** *n.* (*coll.*) a perplexing problem or puzzle. **brainwashing** *n.* the subjection of a victim to sustained mental pressure, or to indoctrination, in order to extort a confession or to induce them to change their views. **brainwash** *v.t.* **brainwave** *n.* (*coll.*) a (sudden) brilliant idea. **brainy** *a.* (*comp.* **brainier**, *superl.* **brainiest**) **1** having brains. **2** acute, clever. **brainily** *adv.* **braininess** *n.* cleverness, intelligence. [OE *brægen* (Dut. *brein*, perh. conn. with Gr. *brechmos*, forehead)]

braird (breəd) *n.* the first shoots of corn or grain. ~*v.i.* to sprout. [OE *brerd*, brim, border, edge, point]

braise (brāz) *v.t.* to cook slowly in little liquid in a tightly closed pan. [F *braiser*, from *braise*, hot charcoal]

brake[1] (brāk) *n.* **1** an appliance to a wheel to check or stop motion. **2** anything that stops or hinders something. **3** a brakevan. **4** the handle of a pump. ~*v.t.* to retard by means of a brake. ~*v.i.* to apply a brake. **brake block** *n.* **1** a block applied to a wheel as a brake. **2** a block used to hold a brake shoe. **brake disc** *n.* a disc attached to a wheel, on which the brake pad presses. **brake drum** *n.* a drum attached to the hub of a wheel of a motor vehicle which has drum brakes. **brake fluid** *n.* an oily liquid used in a hydraulic brake or clutch system. **brake horsepower** *n.* the measurement of an engine's power calculated from its resistance to a brake. **brakeless** *a.* without a brake. **brake light** *n.* the red light on the rear of a vehicle which indicates braking. **brake lining** *n.* a thin strip of fabric attached to a brake shoe to increase its friction. **brakeman,** (*N Am.*) **brakesman** *n.* (*pl.* **brakemen, brakesmen**) a person in charge of a brake, a railway guard. **brake pad** *n.* a flat metal block which presses on the brake disc. **brake shoe** *n.* the curved metal block which presses on the brake drum. **brakevan** *n.* **1** a railway carriage containing a brake. **2** a guard's van. [etym. uncertain; perh. from BRAKE[2] or from OF *brac*, an arm, lever]

brake[2] (brāk) *n.* **1** an instrument for breaking flax or hemp. **2** an implement like scissors for peeling the bark off withes for baskets. **3** (*in full* **brake harrow**) a heavy harrow for breaking up clods. **4** a framework in which restive horses are confined during shoeing. **5** (*also* **break**) a light carriage in which horses are broken to harness. **6** (*also* **break**) a large wagonette. **7** (*also* **break**) a large estate car. ~*v.t.* to crush (flax or hemp). [MLG *brake* or ODut. *bracke* (Dut. *braak*), a flax-brake, Dut. *breken*, to break]

brake[3] (brāk) *n.* a mass of brushwood, a thicket. **braky** *a.* (*comp.* **brakier**, *superl.* **brakiest**) **1** full of bracken or brake. **2** rough, thorny. [etym. uncertain; perh. from MLG *brake*, tree-stumps, or conn. with BREAK[1]]

brake[4] (brāk) *n.* bracken. [BRACKEN]

†**brake**[5] BREAK[1].

bramble (bram´bəl) *n.* **1** the blackberry bush, *Rubus fructicosus*, or any allied thorny shrub. **2** the edible berry of these. **3** any of various other shrubs of the rose family, esp. the dog rose, *Rosa canina*. **brambled** *a.* overgrown with brambles. **bramble finch, brambling** (-bling) *n.* the mountain finch, *Fringilla montifringilla*. **bramble-net** *n.* a net to catch birds. **brambly** *a.* (*comp.* **bramblier**, *superl.* **brambliest**) full of brambles. [OE *brembel, brēmel*, dim. of Gmc. word corr. to OE *brom*, broom (cp. Dut. *braam*, blackberry, OHG *Brāma*, bramble, G *Brombeere*, blackberry)]

Bramley (bram´li) *n.* (*pl.* **Bramleys**) (*in full* **Bramley's seedling**) a large green variety of cooking apple which has firm flesh. [Matthew *Bramley*, an English butcher who grew it in the 19th cent.]

bran (bran) *n.* the husks of ground corn separated from the flour by bolting. **bran mash** *n.* bran soaked in water. **bran tub** *n.* a lucky dip with presents hidden in a container full of bran. [OF, etym. uncertain]

brancard (brang´kəd) *n.* a horse litter. [F, a litter, from *branche*, BRANCH]

branch (brahnch) *n.* **1** a shoot or limb of a tree or shrub, esp. one from a bough. **2** anything considered as a subdivision or extension of a main trunk, as of a mountain range, river, road, railway, family, genus, system of knowledge, legislature, commercial organization etc. **3** any offshoot, member, part or subdivision of an analogous kind. **4** a child, a scion. **5** a rib in a Gothic vault. ~*v.i.* **1** to shoot out into branches or subdivisions. **2** to diverge from a main direction. **3** to divide, to ramify. ~*v.t.* **1** to divide into branches. **2** to subdivide. **3** †to embroider with flowers or foliage. **to branch out** to broaden one's interests or activities. **branched** *a.* having branches. **brancher** *n.* **1** something which shoots out into branches. **2** a young hawk or other bird when it leaves the nest and takes to the branches. **branchless** *a.* **branchlet** *n.* a small branch, a twig. **branchlike** *a.* **branch-work** *n.* sculptured foliage. **branchy** *a.* (*comp.* **branchier,** *superl.* **branchiest**) full of branches, ramifying. [F *branche*, late L *branca*, a paw]

branchia (brang´kiə), **branchiae** (-ē) *n.pl.* the gills of fishes and some amphibia. **branchial** *a.* of, relating to or of the nature of gills. **branchiate** (-ət) *a.* characterized by gills. **branchiform** (-fawm) *a.* shaped like gills. [L *branchia, -iae*, Gr. *branchia*, pl. of *branchion*]

branchio- (brang´kiō) *comb. form* of or relating to gills.

branchiopod (brang´kiəpod) *n.* (*pl.* **branchiopoda** (-op´ədə)) an individual of a group of molluscoid animals with gills on the feet. **branchiopodous** (-op´ədəs) *a.* [Gr. *pous podos*, foot]

brand (brand) *n.* **1** a trade mark, a particular kind of manufactured article. **2** class, quality. **3** a mark made by or with a hot iron; an instrument for stamping a mark. **4** a piece of burning wood. **5** a piece of wood partially burnt. **6** (*poet.*) a torch. **7** a stigma. **8** (*poet.*) a sword. **9** a kind of blight. ~*v.t.* **1** to mark with a brand. **2** to imprint on the memory. **3** to stigmatize. **branded** *a.* **brander** *n.* a branding iron, a gridiron. ~*v.t.* to cook on a gridiron, to broil or grill. **brand from the burning** *n.* a person rescued or converted from sin or irreligion. **branding iron** *n.* an iron to brand with. **brandiron** *n.* **1** a gridiron. **2** an andiron. **3** a trivet. **brand leader** *n.* the best-selling product within its category. **brand name** *n.* a trade name for the commodities of a particular manufacturer. **brand new, bran new** *a.* as if just from the furnace, totally new. [OE (cp. Gmc. *brandoz*, from *bran-*, pret. stem of *brinnan*, to burn, OHG *brant*, brand, sword)]

brandish (bran´dish) *v.t.* to wave or flourish about (a weapon etc.). ~*n.* **1** a flourish. **2** waving. **brandisher** *n.* [F *brandir* (pres.p. *brandissant*), from Gmc. *brandoz*, see BRAND]

brandling (brand´ling) *n.* **1** a small red worm with vivid rings, used as bait in angling. **2** a salmon parr. [BRAND, -LING[1]]

brandreth (brand´rəth) *n.* **1** a wooden stand for a barrel, a rick etc. **2** a fence round a well. [Icel. *brand-reith*, a grate (*brandr*, BRAND, *reith*, a vehicle)]

brandy (bran´di) *n.* (*pl.* **brandies**) a spirit distilled from wine. ~*v.t.* (*3rd pers. sing. pres.* **brandies,** *pres.p.* **brandying,** *past, p.p.* **brandied**) **1** to mix with brandy. **2** to supply or refresh with brandy. **brandy ball** *n.* a kind of sweet. **brandy butter** *n.* a sweet sauce made with brandy, butter and sugar. **brandy glass** *n.* a balloon-shaped glass with a short stem. **brandy-pawnee** (-paw´nē) *n.* brandy and water. **brandy snap** *n.* a thin, crisp, waferlike gingerbread, usu. scroll-shaped. [formerly *brandwine*, Dut. *bran-dewijn*, burnt or distilled wine (*brandt*, p.p. of *branden*, to burn)]

brank (brangk) *n.* buckwheat, *Fagopyrum esculentum.* [etym. unknown]

brank-ursine (brangkœ´sin) *n.* the acanthus or bear's-breech. [med. L *branca ursīna*, bear's paw]

bran new BRAND NEW (under BRAND).

brant BRENT[1].

brash[1] (brash) *a.* **1** impertinent, cheeky. **2** vulgarly assertive or pushy. **3** rash. **brashly** *adv.* **brashness** *n.* [etym. unknown]

brash[2] (brash) *n.* loose, disintegrated rock or rubble. ~*a.* (*N Am.*) tender, brittle. **brash-ice** *n.* broken ice. **brashy** *a.* (*comp.* **brashier,** *superl.* **brashiest**) crumbly, rubbly. **brashiness** *n.* [etym. uncertain]

brash[3] (brash) *n.* a slight indisposition arising from disorder of the alimentary canal. [onomat.]

brass (brahs) *n.* **1** a yellow alloy of copper and zinc. **2** anything made of this alloy. **3** a brazen vessel. **4** an engraved sepulchral tablet of this metal. **5** musical wind instruments of brass. **6** (*also pl.*) the section in an orchestra composed of brass instruments. **7** (*sl.*) money. **8** effrontery, impudence. **9** HORSE BRASS (under HORSE). **10** (*coll.*) those in authority or of high military rank, TOP BRASS (under TOP[1]). **11** a brass block or die used in bookbinding. ~*a.* made of brass. **brassed off** (*sl.*) fed up. **not a brass razoo** RAZOO. **brass band** *n.* a band performing chiefly on brass instruments. **brassbounder** *n.* (*sl.*) **1** a midshipman. **2** a ship's officer in the mercantile marine. **brass farthing** *n.* (*coll.*) the lowest measure of value. **not a brass farthing** (*coll.*) no money at all. **brass hat** *n.* (*coll.*) a staff officer. **brass monkey** *n.* (*Hist.*) a brass rack in which cannon balls were stored. **cold enough to freeze the balls off a brass monkey** very cold. **brass neck** *n.* (*coll.*) impudence, audacity. **brass plate** *n.* a plate of brass engraved with name, trade or profession etc. fixed at doors etc. **brass rubbing** *n.* **1** the transfer of an image from a brass tablet to paper by placing the paper over the original and rubbing it with crayon or chalk. **2** the image copied by this method. **brass tacks** *n.pl.* (*coll.*) **1** details. **2** (*coll.*) the essential facts of the matter. **brassy** *a.* (*comp.* **brassier,** *superl.* **brassiest**) **1** resembling brass. **2** unfeeling, impudent, shameless. **3** debased, cheap, pretentious. ~*n.* (*also* **brassie**) (*pl.* **brassies**) a wooden golf club faced with brass. **brassily** *adv.* **brassiness** *n.* [OE *brœs*]

brassard (bras´ahd) *n.* **1** a badge worn on the arm. **2** an armband, armlet. [F *bras*, arm]

brasserie (bras´əri) *n.* a (usu. small) restaurant, orig. one serving beer as well as wine etc. with the food. [F, from *brasser*, OF *bracer* to brew, from *brace*, malt]

brassica (bras´ikə) *n.* any plant belonging to the genus *Brassica* of the Cruciferae family (turnip, cabbage etc.). [L, cabbage]

brassière (braz´iə, bras´-) *n.* a women's undergarment for supporting the breasts. [F]

brat (brat) *n.* a child, an infant, usu. one who is badly behaved or ragged and dirty. **brat pack** *n.* (*sl.*) a group of young celebrities, such as film stars or writers. **brat packer** *n.* **bratty** *a.* [etym. uncertain]

brattice (brat´is) *n.* **1** a partition for ventilation in a mine. **2** a partition. **3** a lining of timber. **bratticework** *n.* **bratticing** *n.* **1** bratticework. **2** (*Archit.*) open carved work. [ME *bretasce, brutaske*, OF *bretesce, breteske*, prob. from G *Brett*, board]

bratty BRAT.

bratwurst (brat´vœst) *n.* a kind of German sausage. [G *brat-*, roasted, grilled, fried, *Wurst*, sausage]

bravado (brəvah´dō) *n.* (*pl.* **bravadoes**) **1** ostentatious defiance. **2** swaggering behaviour. **3** an insolent menace. [Sp. *bravada*]

brave (brāv) *a.* **1** daring, courageous. **2** gallant, noble. **3**

showy, merry. 4 excellent, fine. ~*n.* a N American Indian warrior. ~*v.t.* 1 to defy, to challenge. 2 to meet with courage. ~*v.i.* to swagger, to show off. **to brave it out** to bear oneself defiantly in the face of blame or suspicion. **bravely** *adv.* **braveness** *n.* **bravery** (-vəri) *n.* 1 courage. 2 display, splendour. 3 finery. [F *bravo*, It. *bravo*, gallant, fine (etym. unknown)]

bravo[1] (brahvō´, brah´vō) *int.* (*fem.* **brava,** *superl.* **bravissimo** (-vis´imō), **bravissima** (-mə)) capital! well done! ~*n.* (*pl.* **bravoes, bravos**) 1 a cry of approval. 2 a cheer. [It.]

bravo[2] (brah´vō) *n.* (*pl.* **bravoes, bravos**) 1 a hired assassin. 2 a bandit, a desperado. [It.]

bravura (brəvūə´rə) *n.* 1 (*Mus.*) brilliance of execution. 2 a display of daring and skill in artistic execution. 3 a piece of music that calls out all the powers of an executant. ~*a.* requiring or showing bravura. [It., bravery]

braw (braw) *a.* (*Sc.*) fine. [BRAVE]

brawl[1] (brawl) *v.i.* 1 to quarrel noisily. 2 to babble (as running water). 3 (*Law*) to create a disturbance in a consecrated place or building. ~*v.t.* to utter loudly. ~*n.* a noisy quarrel, disturbance, a tumult. **brawler** *n.* **brawling** *a.* **brawlingly** *adv.* [etym. uncertain; prob. imit.]

brawl[2] (brawl) *n.* a French dance like a cotillion. [F *branle* (*branler*, brangle)]

brawn (brawn) *n.* 1 muscle, flesh. 2 the flesh of a boar. 3 a potted meat dish usu. made from pig's head. 4 strength, muscularity. **brawned** *a.* brawny, muscular. **brawny** *a.* (*comp.* **brawnier,** *superl.* **brawniest**) muscular, strong, hardy. **brawnily** *adv.* **brawniness** *n.* [OF *braon*, flesh for roasting, WG *brâdo*, from *brâdan*, to roast (cp. OE *brædan*, OHG *prātan*, G *Braten*)]

braxy (brak´si) *n.* 1 splenic apoplexy in sheep. 2 the flesh of a sheep which has died of this disorder. ~*a.* 1 affected by this disease. 2 belonging to a sheep that has died through disease or accident. **braxied** *a.* [etym. uncertain]

bray[1] (brā) *v.i.* to make a harsh, discordant noise, like an ass. ~*v.t.* to utter harshly or loudly (often with *out*). ~*n.* 1 a loud cry. 2 the cry of the ass. 3 a harsh, grating sound. [OF *braire*, low L *bragīre* (cogn. with L *fragor*, a crashing noise)]

†**bray**[2] (brā) *v.t.* 1 to pound or grind small, esp. with pestle and mortar. 2 to beat fine. **brayer** *n.* a wooden muller used to temper printing ink. [OF *breier* (F *broyer*), perh. conn. with BREAK[1]]

Braz. *abbr.* Brazilian.

braze[1] (brāz) *v.t.* to solder with an alloy of brass and zinc. ~*n.* 1 a brazed joint. 2 the alloy used for brazing. [OF *braser*, Icel. *brasa*, to harden by fire]

braze[2] BRAZEN.

brazen (brā´zən) *a.* 1 made of brass. 2 resembling brass. 3 shameless, impudent. ~*v.t.* 1 to face impudently (often with *out*). 2 to harden, make shameless. **braze**[2] (brāz) *v.t.* 1 to make, cover or ornament with brass. 2 to colour like brass. 3 to make hard like brass. **brazen age** *n.* the third of the mythological ages, the age of violence. **brazen-face** *n.* an impudent person. **brazen-faced** *a.* impudent, shameless. **brazenly** *adv.* **brazenness, brazenry** *n.* **brazier**[1] (-ziə) *n.* a worker in brass. **braziery** *n.* brasswork. [OE *brœsen*, from *brœs*, brass]

brazier[1] BRAZEN.

brazier[2] (brā´ziə), **brasier** (brā´zhə) *n.* 1 a large pan to hold lighted charcoal. 2 (*N Am.*) a charcoal grill. [F *brasier*, from *braise*, live coals]

brazil (brəzil´), **brazil wood** *n.* a red dyewood produced by the genus *Caesalpinia*, which gave its name to the country in S America. **brazil nut** *n.* the triangular, edible seed of the S American tree *Bertholletia excelsa*. [etym. unknown]

BRCS *abbr.* British Red Cross Society.

breach (brēch) *n.* 1 the act of breaking. 2 a break, a gap. 3 violation, whether by a definite act or by omission, of a law, duty, right, contract or engagement. 4 a rupture of friendship or alliance. 5 alienation, a quarrel. 6 a gap, esp. one made by guns in a fortification. 7 the breaking of waves. 8 a whale's leap from the water. ~*v.t.* 1 to make a breach or gap in. 2 to break (a law, contract etc.). ~*v.i.* to leap from the water (as a whale). †**to stand in the breach** to bear the brunt of an attack. **to step into the breach** to help out, esp. by replacing someone. **breach of faith** *n.* violation of trust. **breach of privilege** *n.* infringement of rights belonging to Parliament. **breach of promise** *n.* failure to keep a promise, esp. a promise to marry. **breach of the peace** *n.* 1 violation of the public peace. 2 a riot, an affray. [OE *brice*, *bryce* (*brecan*, to BREAK[1])]

bread (bred) *n.* 1 a food, made of flour or other meal kneaded into dough, generally with yeast, made into loaves and baked. 2 food. 3 livelihood. 4 (*sl.*) money. ~*v.t.* to dress with breadcrumbs before cooking. **to cast one's bread upon the waters** WATER. **to take the bread out of someone's mouth** to take away someone's means of living. **bread and butter** *n.* 1 a slice of buttered bread. 2 livelihood. ~*a.* 1 plain, practical. 2 routine, basic. 3 giving thanks for hospitality (of a letter). **bread-and-butter pudding** *n.* a pudding made with buttered bread, eggs, milk or cream, sultanas etc., baked in the oven. **bread and circuses** *n.* free food and entertainment, esp. to placate the population. **bread and wine** *n.* 1 the Lord's Supper, Holy Communion. 2 the eucharistic elements. **breadbasket** *n.* 1 a basket for holding bread. 2 (*sl.*) the stomach. 3 rich grain lands. **breadbin** *n.* a container for storing bread in. **breadboard** *n.* 1 a board on which bread is sliced. 2 an experimental arrangement of electronic circuits. **bread buttered on both sides** *n.* 1 fortunate circumstances. 2 ease and prosperity. **breadcorn** *n.* corn for making bread. **breadcrumb** *n.* 1 a fragment of the soft part of bread. 2 (*pl.*) bread crumbled for culinary purposes. **breaded** *a.* dressed with breadcrumbs. **breadfruit** *n.* 1 (*also* **breadfruit tree**) a S Sea tree, *Artocarpus altilis*. 2 the farinaceous fruit of this tree. **breadless** *a.* without bread, without food. **breadline** *n.* 1 subsistence level. 2 (*N Am.*) a queue of people waiting to be given free food. **bread pudding** *n.* a heavy cake or pudding made with bread and dried fruit. **breadroom** *n.* a place for keeping bread, esp. on board ship. **breadroot** *n.* a N American plant with an edible carrot-like root, *Psoralea esculenta*. **bread sauce** *n.* a sauce made with breadcrumbs, milk and onions. **breadstick** *n.* a long thin stick of bread dough which has been baked until crisp, sometimes with flavouring such as sesame seeds or garlic added. **breadwinner** *n.* 1 the member of a family who supports it with their earnings. 2 a trade, art, tool or machine that supports a family. [OE *brēad*, piece of a loaf (cp. OHG *prōt*, G *Brot*)]

breadth (bredth) *n.* 1 measure from side to side. 2 a piece of material of full breadth. 3 width, extent, largeness. 4 broad effect. 5 liberality, catholicity, tolerance. 6 in art, harmony of the whole. **breadthways, breadthwise** *adv.* by way of the breadth, across. [OE *brædu*, later *brede*, assim. to LENGTH etc.]

break[1] (brāk) *v.t.* (*past* **broke** (brōk), †**brake** (brāk), *p.p.* **broken** (brō´kən), **broke**) 1 to part by violence. 2 to rend apart, to shatter, to rupture, to disperse to, to impair. 3 to destroy the completeness or continuity of. 4 to subdue, to tame, to train. 5 to ruin financially. 6 to cashier, to reduce to the ranks. 7 to disable, to wear out, to exhaust the strength or resources of. 8 to disconnect, to interrupt. 9 to intercept, to lessen the force of. 10 to infringe, to transgress, to violate. 11 to fail to rejoin (one's ship) after an absence on leave. 12 to disprove (an alibi). ~*v.i.* 1 to separate into two or more portions. 2 to burst, to burst forth. 3 to appear with suddenness.

4 to become bankrupt. 5 to decline in health. 6 to change direction. 7 to twist, as a ball at cricket. 8 to make the first stroke at billiards or snooker. 9 to alter the pace (as a horse). 10 to alter (as a boy's voice at the age of puberty). 11 in boxing, (of two fighters) to come out of a clinch. 12 (of prices) to fall sharply. *~n.* 1 the act of breaking. 2 an opening, gap, breach. 3 interruption of continuity in time or space. 4 a line in writing or printing, noting suspension of the sense. 5 irregularity. 6 the twist of a ball at cricket. 7 the vertical face of the forecastle head or poop of a ship. 8 a number of points scored continuously in billiards etc. 9 the point where one voice register changes to another, as bass to tenor. 10 the corresponding point in musical instruments. 11 (*coll.*) a lucky opportunity. 12 a social blunder. 13 a short unaccompanied passage played by a soloist, often improvised. 14 a discontinuity in an electric circuit. **break a leg** (*sl.*) used to wish a person good luck. **to break a head** to injure someone. **to break a way** to make a way by forcing obstacles apart. **to break away** 1 to remove by breaking. 2 to start away. 3 to revolt. **to break bread** 1 to take a meal (with). 2 to take Communion (with). **to break camp** to take down one's tent in preparation for leaving. **to break cover** to dart out from a hiding place. **to break down** 1 to destroy, to overcome. 2 to collapse, to fail. 3 to analyse costs etc. into component parts. **to break even** to emerge without gaining or losing. **to break free/ loose** 1 to escape from captivity. 2 to shake off restraint. **to break fresh/ new ground** 1 to do something not previously done. 2 to make a start. 3 to cut the first sod. **to break ground** 1 to plough, to dig (esp. uncultivated or fallow ground). 2 to open trenches. 3 to commence operations. 4 (*Naut.*) to begin to weigh anchor. **to break in** 1 to tame, to train to something. 2 to wear in (e.g. shoes). 3 (*Austral., New Zeal.*) to bring (land) into cultivation. **to break in on** to disturb or interrupt. **to break into** 1 to enter by force. 2 to interrupt. 3 to suddenly burst out with. 4 to suddenly change to (a faster pace). **to break news** to tell something that has just happened. **to break off** 1 to detach from. 2 to cease, to desist. **to break one's duck** DUCK[1]. **to break one's word** WORD. **to break open** 1 to force a door or cover. 2 to penetrate by violence. **to break out** 1 to burst loose, to escape. 2 to burst forth (as a war). 3 to appear (as an eruption on the skin). 4 to exclaim. 5 to release (a flag). 6 to open (a container) and remove the contents. **to break rank/ ranks** RANK[1]. **to break service** to win a game of tennis in which the opposing player served. **to break someone's heart** HEART. **to break someone's serve** to win a game of tennis in which the opposing player served. **to break step** STEP. **to break the back** 1 to break the keel of a ship. 2 to get through the greater part of. **to break the ice** 1 to prepare the way. 2 to take the first steps, esp. towards overcoming formality or shyness at a gathering. **to break the mould** 1 to make unique. 2 to effect a fundamental change. **to break to pieces** PIECE. **to break up** 1 to disintegrate. 2 to lay open (as ground). 3 to dissolve into laughter. 4 to disband, to separate. 5 to start school holidays. 6 (*esp. N Am.*) to be upset or excited. **to break upon the wheel** to torture or execute by stretching upon a wheel, and breaking the limbs with an iron bar. **to break wind** WIND[1]. **to break with** 1 to cease to be friends with. 2 to quarrel with. **breakable** *a.* capable of being broken. **breakage** (-ij) *n.* 1 the act of breaking. 2 the state of being broken. 3 loss or damage from breaking. 4 an interruption. 5 change in quality of voice from one register to another. **breakaway** *n.* 1 (*Austral.*) a stampede of cattle or sheep. 2 an animal that breaks away from the herd. 3 any person, thing or group which breaks away from a main body. 4 a false start in a race. 5 in rugby, each of the two flank forwards on the outsides of the second row of a scrum. *~a.* that is or involves a breakaway. **break crop** *n.* a crop grown as a change from cereal crops. **break-dancing** *n.* an energetic type of modern dancing characterized by spinning on various parts of the body (the hands, back etc.). **break-dance** *v.i.* to dance in this manner. **breakdown** *n.* 1 downfall, collapse. 2 total failure resulting in stoppage. 3 an analysis. **breaker**[1] *n.* 1 a person who or something which breaks. 2 a person who breaks in a horse. 3 a heavy wave breaking against the rocks or shore. **breakhead** *n.* the reinforced head of a ship fitted for breaking its way through ice. **break-in** *n.* an illegal forced entry into premises, esp. for criminal purposes. **breaking** *n., a.* **breaking and entering** *n.* illegal forced entry into premises for criminal purposes. **breaking point** *n.* the limit of endurance. **breakjoint** *n.* a disposition of stones or bricks so that the joints do not fall immediately over each other. **break-line** *n.* (*Print.*) the last line of a paragraph, usu. one of less than full length. **breakneck** *a.* 1 endangering the neck, hazardous. 2 (of speed) very fast. **break of day** *n.* dawn. **breakout** *n.* an escape, esp. from prison. **break point** *n.* 1 a place or time of a break. 2 (*Comput.*) a an instruction to interrupt a sequence of instructions. b the point in a program at which this happens. 3 in tennis, a point which would allow the player receiving service to win the game. 4 the situation when this happens. 5 breaking point. **breakthrough** *n.* 1 an outcrop. 2 penetration of enemy lines. 3 an advance, a discovery. **break-up** *n.* 1 disruption, dispersal into parts or elements. 2 disintegration, decay, dissolution. 3 dispersal. **breakwater** *n.* a pier, mole or anything similar, to break the force of the waves and protect shipping. [OE *brecan* (cp. Goth. *brican*, OHG *prechan*, G *brechen*, from Gmc., stem *brek-*, cp. L *frangere*)]

break[2] BRAKE[2].

breaker[1] BREAK[1].

breaker[2] (brā´kə) *n.* a keg, a water-cask. [Sp. *barrica*]

breakfast (brek´fəst) *n.* the first meal of the day. *~v.i.* to have breakfast. *~v.t.* to provide with or entertain at breakfast. **to have someone for breakfast** to crush or destroy someone. **breakfaster** *n.* **breakfast television** *n.* early-morning television. [BREAK[1], FAST[2]]

bream[1] (brēm) *n.* 1 a freshwater fish of the genus *Abramis*, esp. *A. brama.* 2 a marine fish of the family Sparidae, a sea bream. [OF *bresme* (F *brême*), (cp. MHG *brahsem*, G *Brassen*; perh. from stem *breh-*, to glitter)]

bream[2] (brēm) *v.t.* (*Hist.*) to clear (a ship's bottom) of ooze, seaweed, shellfish etc. by burning. [etym. uncertain]

breast (brest) *n.* 1 either of the organs for the secretion of milk in women. 2 the rudimentary part corresponding to this in men. 3 the forepart of the human body between the neck and the abdomen. 4 the analogous part in the lower animals. 5 the upper forepart of a coat or other article of dress. 6 the working coalface. 7 (*fig.*) a source of nourishment. 8 the seat of the affections. 9 the affections. 10 the front, the forepart. *~v.t.* 1 to apply or oppose the breast to. 2 to stem, to oppose, to face. 3 to reach the top of (a hill). **to breast the tape** TAPE. **to breast up a hedge** to cut the face of a hedge so as to lay bare the stems. **to make a clean breast** to confess all that one knows. **breastbone** *n.* the flat bone in front of the chest to which certain ribs are attached; the sternum. **breast-deep** *a., adv.* as deep as the breast is high. **breasted** *a.* 1 having a breast. 2 decorated on the breast. **breastfeed** *v.t., v.i.* to feed (a baby) from the breast instead of the bottle. **breast-harness** *n.* a harness attached to a breastband instead of a collar. **breast-high** *a., adv.* 1 as high as the breast. 2 in hunting, (of scent) so high that the hounds race with heads erect. **breast-knot** *n.* a knot of ribbons worn on the breast. **breast-pin** *n.* 1 a pin worn on the breast or in a scarf.

2 a brooch. **breastplate** *n.* 1 armour worn upon the breast. 2 a piece of embroidered linen, adorned with precious stones, worn on the breast of the Jewish high priest. 3 the upper part of the shell of a turtle or tortoise. 4 an inscribed plate on a coffin. **breastplough** *n.* a kind of small handplough used in paring turf. **breast pocket** *n.* the inside pocket of a jacket. **breast-rail** *n.* the upper rail on a balcony. **breaststroke** *n.* a swimming stroke involving wide circling motions of the arms and legs while facing forward on one's breast. **breastsummer** (bres´əmə), **bressummer** *n.* a beam supporting the front of a building after the manner of a lintel. **breast-wall** *n.* a retaining wall. **breast-wheel** *n.* a waterwheel which receives the water at the level of its axis. **breastwork** *n.* 1 a hastily constructed parapet thrown up breast-high for defence. 2 the parapet of a building. 3 a railing or balustrade across a ship. [OE *brēost*, Gmc. *breustom* (G *Brust*, Dut. *borst*)]

breath (breth) *n.* 1 the air drawn in and expelled by the lungs in respiration. 2 the act or power of breathing. 3 a single respiration. 4 in phonetics, the expulsion of air without vibrating the vocal cords. 5 a very slight breeze. 6 (*fig.*) the time of a single respiration. 7 respite. 8 an instant. 9 a whiff, an exhalation. 10 a rumour, a whisper, a murmur. **in the same breath** done or said at the same time. **out of breath** gasping for air after exercise. **to catch one's breath** 1 to cease breathing momentarily. 2 to regain even breathing after exertion or a shock. **to hold one's breath** to stop breathing for a short time. **to save one's breath** (*coll.*) to avoid talking to someone on purpose. **to take breath** to pause. **to take one's breath away** to astonish, delight. **to waste one's breath** to talk to no avail. **breathalyse** (-əlīz), (*N Am.*) **breathalyze** *v.t.* to test for the level of alcohol in the breath of (a driver) with a breathalyser. **breathalyser, Breathalyzer®** *n.* an instrument containing crystals for measuring the level of alcohol in the breath. **breathful** *a.* 1 full of breath or wind. 2 alive. 3 odorous. **breathless** *a.* 1 out of breath. 2 dead, lifeless. 3 panting. 4 without a movement of the air. 5 excited, eager. **breathlessly** *adv.* **breathlessness** *n.* **breath of fresh air** *n.* 1 a small amount of fresh air. 2 a refreshing change. **breath of life** *n.* a necessity. **breathtaking** *a.* astonishing, marvellous. **breathtakingly** *adv.* **breath test** *n.* a test to determine the amount of alcohol in the breath. **breathy** *a.* (*comp.* **breathier,** *superl.* **breathiest**) 1 aspirated. 2 giving the sound of breathing. **breathily** *adv.* **breathiness** *n.* [OE *brǣth*, Gmc. *braethoz*, steam, or from stem *brae-* (Indo-Eur. *bhrē-*), to heat, burn]

breathe (brēdh) *v.i.* 1 to inhale or exhale air, to respire. 2 to live. 3 to take breath. 4 to move or sound like breath. 5 to be exposed to air. 6 (of fabric) to let air or moisture through. ~*v.t.* 1 to inhale or exhale (as air). 2 to emit, to send out, by means of the lungs. 3 to utter. 4 to utter softly. 5 to express, to manifest. 6 to allow breathing space to. 7 to make breathe by means of exercise. 8 to blow into (as a wind instrument). **not to breathe a word** to keep silent, keep a secret. **to breathe again/ freely/ easily** to be relieved from fear or anxiety. **to breathe down someone's neck** to cause someone discomfort with one's close supervision or constant attention. **to breathe in** to inhale. **to breathe one's last** to die. **to breathe out** to exhale. **breathable** *a.* 1 that may be breathed. 2 (of fabric) that can breathe. **breathableness** *n.* **breather** *n.* 1 a person who or thing which breathes. 2 an exercise to try the lungs. 3 (*coll.*) a rest in order to gain breath. 4 a vent in an airtight container. **breathing** *a.* 1 living. 2 lifelike. ~*n.* 1 the action of breathing. 2 a respite. 3 an aspirate. 4 either of the two signs in Greek grammar, (ʽ) or (ʼ) placed over the first vowel of a word to mark the presence or absence of the aspirate. **breathing-place, breathing-space** *n.* a pause, place or opening for breathing. **breathing-time** *n.* 1 time for recovering one's breath. 2 a pause. [from BREATH]

breccia (brech´iə) *n.* a rock composed of angular, as distinguished from rounded, fragments cemented together in a matrix. **brecciated** (-ātid) *a.* formed into breccia. **brecciation** (-ā´shən) *n.* [It., gravel, rubble (cp. F *brèche*, OHG *brecha*, breaking, *brechan*, to BREAK[1])]

bred *a.* BREED.

⊠ **bredth** common misspelling of BREADTH.

breech (brēch) *n.* (*pl.* **breeches** (brē´chiz, brich´iz)) 1 the portion of a gun behind the bore. 2 the hinder part of anything. 3 †the buttocks, the posterior. 4 (*pl.*) a garment worn by men, covering the loins and thighs, and reaching just below the knees. 5 (*pl., coll.*) any trousers. ~*v.t.* 1 to clothe or cover with or as with breeches. 2 to whip upon the buttocks. **to wear the breeches** to rule, to head the household. **breech birth, breech delivery** *n.* a birth in which the baby's buttocks or feet emerge first. **breech-block** *n.* a movable piece to close the breech of a gun. **Breeches Bible** *n.* the Geneva Bible of 1560 in which the word *breeches* was used for *aprons* in Gen. iii.7. **breeches-buoy** (brē-) *n.* a life-saving device run on a rope stretched from a wrecked vessel to a place of safety. **breeching** *n.* 1 a strong leather strap passing round the haunches of a shaft-horse. 2 a stout rope securing a gun to a ship's side. **breechless** *a.* without breeches. **breech-loader** *n.* a firearm loaded at the breech. **breech-loading** *a.* loaded at the breech. [OE *brēc*, pl. of *brōc* (MHG *Bruoch*, breeches)]

Usage note The plural pronunciation (brē´chiz) is used where there is a corresponding singular, (brich´iz) where the plural is the fixed form.

---

breed (brēd) *v.t.* (*past, p.p.* **bred** (bred)) 1 to bring forth. 2 to give birth to. 3 to raise (cattle etc.), to rear. 4 to give rise to, to yield, to produce. 5 to engender, to cause to develop. 6 to train up, to educate, to bring up. 7 (*Physics*) to create (fissile material) by nuclear reaction. ~*v.i.* 1 to be pregnant. 2 to produce offspring. 3 to come into being, to arise, to spread. 4 to be produced or engendered. ~*n.* 1 a line of descendants from the same parents or stock. 2 family, race, offspring. 3 a sort, kind. **born and bred** BORN. **bred in the bone** hereditary. **to breed in and in** to breed always with or from near relatives. **to breed true** always to produce young in harmony with the parental type. **breeder** *n.* a person who breeds, esp. one who breeds cattle and other animals. **breeder reactor** *n.* a nuclear reactor which produces more plutonium than it consumes. **breeding** *n.* 1 the act of giving birth to. 2 the raising of a breed. 3 bringing-up, nurture, rearing. 4 education, deportment, good manners. **breeding ground** *n.* a favourable environment or atmosphere for generating or nurturing ideas, bacteria etc. [OE *brēdan* (cp. G *Bruten*, OE *brōd*, BROOD)]

breeks (brēks) *n.pl.* (*Sc.*) breeches.

breeze[1] (brēz) *n.* 1 a gentle gale, a light wind. 2 a wind of force 2 to 6 on the Beaufort scale (4–31 m.p.h.) (7–50 k.p.h.). 3 a wind blowing from land at night or sea during the day. 4 a disturbance, a row. 5 a whisper, rumour. 6 (*coll.*) something which can be done or got with ease. ~*v.i.* 1 to blow gently or moderately. 2 to move in a lively way. 3 (*coll.*) to do or achieve something easily. **to breeze up** 1 to begin to blow freshly. 2 to sound louder on the breeze. 3 to approach in a carefree or lively manner. **breezeless** *a.* 1 undisturbed by any breeze. 2 still, calm. **breezy** *a.* (*comp.* **breezier,** *superl.* **breeziest**) 1 open, exposed to breezes, windy. 2 lively, brisk, jovial. **breezily** *adv.* **breeziness** *n.* [Sp. *brisa*, the NE wind, prob. from F BISE]

breeze[2] (brēz), **brize** *n.* a gadfly. [OE *briosa* (etym. uncertain)]

breeze[3] (brēz) *n.* 1 small cinders and cinder dust. 2 small coke, siftings of coke. **breeze-block, breeze-brick** *n.* a brick or block made of breeze and cement. [F *braise*, live coals (see BRAZIER)]

bregma (breg´mə) *n.* (*pl.* **bregmata** (-mətə)) the point on the skull where the coronal and sagittal sutures meet. [Gr. *brechein*, to moisten]

brehon (brē´hən) *n.* an ancient hereditary Irish judge. **Brehon law** *n.* the native Irish code of laws, abolished in the reign of James I. [OIr. *breitheamh*, a judge (*brieth*, judgement)]

breloque (brəlōk´) *n.* an ornament attached to a watch-chain. [F (etym. unknown)]

bremsstrahlung (bremz´shtrahlung) *n.* the electromagnetic radiation caused by an electron colliding with or slowed down by the electric field of a positively charged nucleus. [G *bremsen*, to brake, *Strahlung*, radiation]

Bren (bren), **Bren gun** *n.* a type of light machine-gun. [first letters of *Br*no (Czech Republic) and *En*field]

brent[1] (brent), (*N Am.*) **brant** (brant) *n.* the smallest of the wild geese, *Branta bernicla*, which visits Britain in the winter. **brent-goose** *n.* (*pl.* **brent-geese**). [etym. uncertain; cp. Swed. *brandgås*, G *Brandgans*]

brent[2] (brent) *a.* 1 steep, precipitous, lofty. 2 smooth, without wrinkles. [OE *brant*]

brer (breə) *n.* brother. [black Am. contr. of BROTHER]

bressummer BREASTSUMMER (under BREAST).

Bret. *abbr.* Breton.

brethren BROTHER.

Breton (bret´ən) *n.* 1 a native of Brittany. 2 the Celtic language of Brittany. ~*a.* of or relating to Brittany or its language.

breve (brēv) *n.* 1 a sign (˘) used in printing to mark a short vowel. 2 a note of time equal to two semibreves. 3 (*Hist.*) a papal letter. [BRIEF]

brevet (brev´it) *n.* 1 an official document conferring certain privileges. 2 a warrant conferring nominal rank of an officer without the pay. 3 the wing-badge a flying member of the RAF may put on his uniform. ~*a.* 1 conferred by brevet. 2 honorary, nominal. ~*v.t.* (*pres.p.* **breveting, brevetting,** *past, p.p.* **breveted, brevetted**) to confer (a certain rank) by brevet. [F, dim. of *bref*, a letter (cp. BRIEF)]

breveté (brevtā´) *a.* patented. [F]

brevi- (brev´i) *comb. form* short. [L *brevis*]

breviary (brē´viəri) *n.* (*pl.* **breviaries**) in the Roman Catholic Church, a book containing the divine office. [L *breviārium* (*brevis*, short)]

breviate (brē´viət) *a.* abbreviated, short. ~*n.* 1 a short summary, an abridgement. 2 a note. 3 a lawyer's brief. [L *breviātus*, p.p. of *breviāre*, to shorten, from *brevis*, short]

brevier (brəviə´) *n.* (*Hist.*) a size of type around 7 point between bourgeois and minion, in which breviaries were formerly printed. [BREVIARY]

breviped (brev´iped) *a.* short-footed, short-legged. [L *pes, pedis*, foot]

brevipennate (brevipen´ət) *a.* having short wings. [L *penna*, wing]

brevirostrate (breviros´trāt) *a.* having a short bill or beak. [L *rōstrum*, a beak]

brevity (brev´iti) *n.* 1 briefness, shortness. 2 conciseness. [L *brevitas -tātem*]

brew (broo) *v.t.* 1 to make (beer, ale etc.) by boiling, steeping and fermenting. 2 to convert into (beer, ale etc.) by such processes. 3 to prepare (other beverages) by mixing or infusion. 4 to prepare. 5 to concoct. 6 to contrive, to plot. 7 to bring about. ~*v.i.* 1 to make beer etc. by boiling, fermenting etc. 2 to undergo these or similar processes. 3 to be in preparation. ~*n.* 1 the action, process or product of brewing. 2 the quantity brewed at one process. 3 the quality of the thing brewed. **to brew up** (*coll.*) to make tea. **brewage** (-ij) *n.* 1 a mixture. 2 a concocted beverage. 3 the process of brewing. **brewer** *n.* a person whose trade is to brew malt liquors. **brewer's droop** *n.* (*sl.*) temporary sexual impotence in men due to overindulgence in alcohol. **brewer's yeast** *n.* a yeast, *Saccharomyces cerevisiae*, used in brewing and as a source of vitamin B. **brewery** (-əri) *n.* (*pl.* **breweries**) a place where beer is brewed. **brewhouse** *n.* a brewery. **brew-up** *n.* (*coll.*) an instance of making tea. [OE (*brēowan* (cp. OHG *briuwan*, G *brauen*; cp. L *dēfrutum*, new wine boiled down)]

brewis (broo´is) *n.* (*dial.*) 1 broth. 2 liquor in which meat and vegetables have been boiled. 3 bread soaked in gravy, broth etc. [OF *brouetz*, dim. of *bro*, OHG *brod*]

briar[1] BRIER[1].

briar[2] BRIER[2].

Briareus (brīā´riəs) *n.* a many-handed person. **Briarean** *a.* 1 of or relating to Briareus (a giant of Greek mythology, said to have had a hundred hands). 2 many-handed.

bribe (brīb) *n.* 1 a gift or consideration of any kind offered to anyone to influence their judgement or conduct. 2 an inducement. 3 a seduction. ~*v.t.* to influence in action or opinion by means of a gift or other inducement. ~*v.i.* to practise bribery. **bribable** *a.* **bribability** (-bil´-) *n.* **bribee** (-ē´) *n.* a person who receives a bribe. **bribeless** *a.* incapable of being bribed. **briber** *n.* a person who offers or gives bribes. **bribery** (-əri) *n.* (*pl.* **briberies**) the act of giving or receiving bribes. [OF *bribe*, a piece of bread given to a beggar]

bric-a-brac (brik´əbrak), **bric-à-brac, bricabrac** *n.* fancy ware, curiosities, knick-knacks. [F phrase *de bric et de broc*, by hook or by crook]

brick (brik) *n.* 1 a block of clay and sand, usu. oblong, moulded and baked, used in building. 2 a brick-shaped block of any material. 3 a child's block for toy building. 4 a brick-shaped loaf. 5 (*sl.*) a good person. ~*a.* 1 made of brick. 2 of a dull red colour. ~*v.t.* 1 to lay or construct with bricks. 2 to imitate brickwork (in plaster). **like a ton of bricks** (*coll.*) with great force. **to bang/ knock/ run one's head against a brick wall** to have one's efforts come to nothing. **to brick up** to block up with brickwork. **to drop a brick** to say the wrong thing, to commit a blunder. **to make bricks without straw** to perform the impossible. **to see through a brick wall** to be unusually discerning; to have extraordinary insight. **brickbat** *n.* 1 a broken piece of brick, esp. for use as a missile. 2 (*coll.*) a critical remark. **brick-built** *a.* built of bricks. **brickclay, brickearth** *n.* 1 clay used for making brick. 2 a clayey earth in the London basin. **brickdust** *n.* powdered brick. ~*a.* 1 tinged with this. 2 coloured like this. **brick-field** *n.* a field in which brickmaking is carried on. **brickfielder** *n.* (*Austral.*) a hot wind from the interior laden with dust. **brickie** *n.* (*coll.*) a bricklayer. **bricking** *n.* brickwork. **brick kiln** *n.* a kiln for baking bricks. **bricklayer** *n.* a person who lays or sets bricks. **bricklaying** *n.* **brick-nogging** *n.* brickwork built into a timber framework. **brick red** *n.* the colour of a red brick. **brick-red** *a.* of this colour. **brickwork** *n.* 1 builder's work in brick. 2 bricklaying. 3 a brickyard. **bricky** *a.* 1 full of or composed of bricks. 2 resembling bricks. **brickyard** *n.* a place where bricks are made, stored or sold. [F *brique*, a fragment (cp. MDut. *brick, bricke*), from the Gmc. root *brek-*, BREAK[1]]

brickle (brik´əl) *a.* (*Sc., North.*) 1 fragile, frail. 2 ticklish, troublesome. [parallel form to BRITTLE]

bricole (brik´əl, -kōl´) *n.* 1 in billiards, the rebound of a ball from a wall or cushion. 2 in tennis or billiards, an indirect stroke. [F *bricole*, late L *briccola* (etym. uncertain)]

bride (brīd) *n.* a woman newly married or on the point of being married. **bridal** *a.* of or relating to a bride or a wedding. ~*n.* 1 the nuptial ceremony or festival. 2 a wedding. 3 marriage. **bridally** *adv.* **bride-cake** *n.* the cake distributed to the guests at a wedding, wedding cake. **bride-cup, bride-bowl** *n.* 1 a cup or bowl handed round at a wedding. 2 a cup of spiced wine or ale prepared for a newly married couple. **bridegroom** *n.* a man about to be married or recently married. **brideman, bridesman** *n.* (*pl.* **bridemen, bridesmen**) an unmarried man who attends the groom at his wedding; a best man. **bride price** *n.* (in some societies) money or goods given to a bride's family by the bridegroom's family. **bridesmaid, bridemaid** *n.* an unmarried girl or woman who attends the bride at her wedding. **bridewort** *n.* meadowsweet. [OE *brȳd* (cp. OHG *prut*, G *Braut*, from Gmc. *brūdiz*)]

bridewell (brīd´wel) *n.* a house of correction, a prison. [a prison near St Bride's (Bridget's) Well, near Fleet Street, London]

bridge[1] (brij) *n.* 1 a structure thrown over a body of water, a ravine, another road etc. to carry a road or path across. 2 anything more or less resembling a bridge in form or function. 3 the upper bony part of the nose. 4 the thin wooden bar over which the strings are stretched in a violin or similar instrument. 5 a support for a billiard cue in an awkward stroke. 6 a partial deck extending from side to side of a steam vessel amidships. 7 an electrical circuit used for the accurate measurement of electrical quantities, e.g. resistance. 8 a partial denture. ~*v.t.* to span or cross with or as with a bridge. **to burn one's bridges** BURN[1]. **to cross a bridge when one comes to it** to cope with a difficulty only when it occurs, not to anticipate difficulties unnecessarily. **bridgeable** *a.* **bridge-building** *n.* 1 the activity of building bridges. 2 the use of diplomacy to restore friendly relations. **bridge-builder** *n.* **bridgehead** *n.* a fortification protecting the end of a bridge nearest the enemy. **bridgeless** *a.* without a bridge. **bridge of asses** *n.* ASSES' BRIDGE (under ASS[1]). **bridge of boats** *n.* a bridge supported on a number of boats moored abreast. **bridge passage** *n.* a linking passage in a piece of music or literary or dramatic work. **bridgework** *n.* 1 a partial denture. 2 the technique of making such dentures. **bridging** *n.* 1 the structure of a bridge. 2 the act of making or forming a bridge. **bridging loan** *n.* a short-term loan with a high interest rate which covers a financial transaction until a long-term loan is arranged. [OE *brycg* (cp. OHG *Brucca*, G *Brücke*, from Gmc. *brugj-*)]

bridge[2] (brij) *n.* a card game descended from whist, played by partners one of whose hand is exposed at a particular point in the game. **auction bridge** AUCTION. **bridge-marker** *n.* a device for registering the points made at bridge. **bridge roll** *n.* a long thin soft bread roll. **bridge-scorer** *n.* a person who keeps the score at bridge. [etym. uncertain]

bridle (brī´dəl) *n.* 1 a headstall, bit and bearing or riding rein, forming the headgear of a horse or other beast of burden. 2 a curb, a check, a restraint. 3 a rope by which the bowline of a ship is fastened to the leech of a sail. 4 a mooring cable. ~*v.t.* 1 to put a bridle on. 2 to control with a bridle. 3 to hold in, to check, to control. ~*v.i.* to hold up the head and draw in the chest in pride, scorn or resentment (with *up*). **bridled** *a.* wearing a bridle. **bridle-hand** *n.* 1 the hand that holds the bridle. 2 the left hand. **bridle path, bridle road, bridleway** *n.* a horse track, a path for horseriders. [OE *brīdel*, cogn. with *bregdan* (see BRAID[1])]

Brie (brē) *n.* a soft white cheese orig. produced in France. [a region in NE France]

brief (brēf) *a.* 1 short in duration. 2 expeditious. 3 short, concise. 4 curt. ~*n.* 1 a papal letter of a less solemn character than a bull. 2 instructions. 3 a short statement. 4 a writ, a summons. 5 a summary of facts and points of law given to counsel in charge of a case. 6 (*N Am.*) pleadings. 7 (*pl.*) close-fitting pants, underpants or knickers without legs. ~*v.t.* 1 to reduce to the form of a counsel's brief. 2 to instruct or retain (a barrister) by brief. 3 to give detailed instructions to. **in brief** briefly. **to be brief** to use few words. **to hold a brief for** 1 to argue in support of. 2 to be retained as counsel for. **briefcase** *n.* a flat hand-held bag for carrying papers. **briefing** *n.* the imparting of instructions or information. **briefless** *a.* 1 having no briefs. 2 without clients. **briefly** *adv.* **briefness** *n.* [OF *bref*, L *breve, brevis* (cp. Gr. *brachus*)]

brier[1] (brī´ə), **briar** *n.* 1 a thorny or prickly shrub, esp. a wild rose. 2 the stem of a wild rose on which a garden rose is grafted. **brier rose** *n.* the dog rose or other wild rose. **briery** *a.* 1 full of briers. 2 thorny. [OE *brēr, brær* (etym. uncertain)]

brier[2] (brī´ə), **briar** *n.* 1 the white or tree heath, *Erica arborea*. 2 a tobacco pipe made from the root of this. **brier-root** *n.* the root of the white heath. [F *bruyère*, heath]

Brig. *abbr.* 1 Brigade. 2 Brigadier.

brig[1] (brig) *n.* (*Sc., North.*) BRIDGE[1].

brig[2] (brig) *n.* 1 a square-rigged vessel with two masts. 2 a US Navy prison. 3 (*sl.*) any prison. [BRIGANTINE]

brigade (brigād´) *n.* 1 a subdivision of an army, varying in composition in different countries and at different dates. 2 an organized body of workers, often wearing a uniform. 3 (*coll.*) a group of people who share some characteristic, belief etc. ~*v.t.* 1 to form into one or more brigades. 2 to combine into a brigade, to bring into association as a brigade. **brigade major** *n.* a staff officer attached to a brigade. **brigadier** (-ədiə´) *n.* 1 the officer in command of a brigade. 2 the rank below that of major general. **brigadier general** *n.* (*pl.* **brigadier generals**) an officer ranking above colonel in the US army, air force and marine corps. [F, from It. *brigata*, a troop, *brigare*, to quarrel, late L *briga*, strife]

brigalow (brig´əlō) *n.* any acacia tree, esp. *Acacia harpophylla*. [Austral. Abor.]

brigand (brig´ənd) *n.* a robber, a bandit, an outlaw. **brigandage, brigandry** *n.* 1 the practices of brigands. 2 highway robbery. **brigandine** (-dēn) *n.* a coat of mail designed for easy movement (suitable as a brigand's armour). **brigandish** *a.* **brigandism** *n.* [F, prob. from It. *brigante*, pres.p. of *brigare*, see BRIGADE]

brigantine (brig´əntēn) *n.* a two-masted vessel square-rigged on both masts but with a fore-and-aft mainsail, and mainmast much longer than the foremast. [F *brigantin, brigandin*, It. *brigantino*, a pirate ship, *brigante*, BRIGAND]

bright (brīt) *a.* 1 lighted up, full of light. 2 emitting or reflecting abundance of light. 3 shining. 4 unclouded. 5 cheerful, happy, sanguine. 6 witty, clever. ~*adv.* brightly. ~*n.* 1 (*pl.*) bright colours. 2 (*pl., N Am.*) headlights on full beam. **bright and early** very early in the morning. **to look on the bright side** to be optimistic. **brighten** *v.t.* 1 to make bright. 2 to make happy, hopeful etc. ~*v.i.* 1 to become bright. 2 (of the weather) to clear up. **bright-eyed and bushy-tailed** *a.* (*coll.*) radiant with health and vigour. **brightish** *a.* **bright lights** *n.pl.* 1 the area of a city where places of entertainment are concentrated. 2 the city. **brightly** *adv.* **brightness** *n.* **bright spark** *n.* (*coll.*) a witty or lively person. [OE *beorht*, Gmc. *berhtoz*, shining]

Bright's disease (brīts) *n.* inflammation of the kidneys, nephritis. [Dr R. *Bright*, 1789–1858]

brigue (brēg) *n.* strife, intrigue. ~*v.i.* (*3rd pers. sing. pres.* **brigues**, *pres.p.* **briguing**, *past, p.p.* **brigued**) to intrigue. [F, from med. L *briga*]

brill[1] (bril) *n.* a flat sea fish, *Scophthalmus rhombus*, allied to the turbot. [etym. unknown]

brill[2] (bril) *a.* (*coll.*) excellent, very pleasing. [short for BRILLIANT]

brilliant (bril´yənt) *a.* 1 shining, sparkling. 2 lustrous. 3 illustrious, distinguished. 4 extremely clever and successful. 5 (*coll.*) excellent. ~*n.* 1 a diamond or other gem of the finest cut, consisting of lozenge-shaped facets alternating with triangles. 2 the smallest type used in English printing. **brilliance, brilliancy** *n.* **brilliantine** *n.* 1 a cosmetic for making the hair glossy. 2 (*N Am.*) a glossy fabric. **brilliantly** *adv.* [F *brillant*, pres.p. of *briller*, to shine; perh. from late L *beryllāre*, to sparkle (*berillus*, a gem)]

brim (brim) *n.* 1 the upper edge, margin or brink of a vessel, hollow or body of water. 2 the rim of a hat. ~*v.t.* (*pres.p.* **brimming,** *past, p.p.* **brimmed**) to fill to the brim. ~*v.i.* to be full to the brim. **to brim over** to overflow. **brim-full, brimful** *a.* full to the brim. **brimless** *a.* without a brim. **brimmed** *a.* 1 having a brim. 2 brim-full. **brimmer** *n.* 1 a bumper. 2 †a vessel filled to the brim. **brimming** *a.* [etym. uncertain (cp. G *Gebräme*, border, *Bräme*, brim, edge) (OE *brim*, the sea, water, is prob. not the same word)]

brimstone (brim´stōn) *n.* 1 †sulphur, esp. in the biblical context of the lake of brimstone. 2 the butterfly *Gonepteryx rhamni*, or moth *Opisthograptis luteolata*, which have yellow wings. 3 a spitfire, a termagant. [ME *bren, brennen*, to burn, STONE]

brindle (brin´dəl), **brindled** *a.* 1 tawny, with bars of darker hue. 2 streaked, spotted. [Shak. *brinded*, prob. variant of BRANDED (under BRAND)]

brine (brīn) *n.* 1 water strongly impregnated with salt. 2 the sea. 3 tears. ~*v.t.* to treat with brine, to pickle. **brine pan** *n.* a shallow vessel or pit in which brine is evaporated in the manufacture of salt. **brine pit** *n.* a pit or well of salt water. **brine shrimp** *n.* a small crustacean of the genus *Artemia*. **brinish** *a.* **briny** *a.* (*comp.* **brinier,** *superl.* **briniest**) 1 full of brine. 2 very salty. ~*n.* (*coll.*) the sea. **brininess** *n.* [OE *brȳne* (cp. Dut. *brijn*, brine, pickle)]

bring (bring) *v.t.* (*past, p.p.* **brought** (brawt)) 1 to cause to come along with oneself. 2 to bear, to carry, to conduct, to lead. 3 to induce, to prevail upon, to influence, to persuade. 4 to produce, yield, result in. **to bring about** 1 to cause, to bring to pass. 2 to reverse (the ship.) **to bring around** (*N Am.*) to bring round. **to bring back** to recall to memory. **to bring down** 1 to humble, to abase. 2 to shoot, to kill. 3 to lower (a price). 4 to carry on (a history) to a certain date. 5 to depose, to overthrow. 6 (*sl.*) to make unhappy. 7 (*coll.*) to demean. **to bring (down) about one's ears** EAR[1]. **to bring forth** 1 to bear, to produce, to give birth to. 2 to cause. **to bring forward** 1 to produce, to adduce. 2 to carry on (a sum) from the bottom of one page to the top of the next (in bookkeeping). 3 to move to an earlier date or time. **to bring home to** 1 to cause to realize. 2 to prove conclusively to, to convince. **to bring in** 1 to produce, to yield. 2 to introduce (as an action or bill). 3 to return (as a verdict). **to bring into play** to cause to operate. **to bring into the world** WORLD. **to bring low** 1 to overcome. 2 to humiliate. 3 to depress. **to bring off** 1 to bring away (from a ship, the shore etc.). 2 to procure the acquittal of. 3 to accomplish. **to bring on** 1 to cause to begin. 2 to introduce for discussion. 3 to cause to develop (more quickly). **to bring out** 1 to express, to exhibit, to illustrate. 2 to introduce to society. 3 to launch (as a company). 4 to produce upon the stage. 5 to publish. 6 to expose. **to bring over** 1 to convert. 2 to cause to change sides. **to bring round** 1 to revive. 2 to convert. **to bring someone to their senses** SENSE. **to bring the house down** to create tumultuous applause. **to bring through** to help (someone) through a crisis, illness etc. **to bring to** 1 to restore to health or consciousness. 2 to check the course of (a ship). **to bring to bear** BEAR[2]. **to bring to book** BOOK. **to bring to light** LIGHT[1]. **to bring to mind** MIND. **to bring to pass** to cause to happen. **to bring under** to subdue. **to bring up** 1 to educate, to rear. 2 to lay before a meeting. 3 to vomit. 4 to come to a stop. 5 to continue a further stage. 6 to cast anchor. **to bring upon oneself** to be responsible for (one's own problems). **to bring up the rear** REAR[1]. **bring-and-buy sale** *n.* a sale, usu. for charity, at which people bring items to sell and buy those that other people have brought. **bringer** *n.* [OE *bringan* (cp. Goth. *briggan*, OHG *pringan*, G *bringen*)]

brinish BRINE.

brinjal (brin´jəl), **brinjall** *n.* esp. in the Indian subcontinent, an aubergine. [Sansk. *vātingan*, Port. *bringella, beringela*, from Arab. *bādhinjān*, from Pers. *bādingān*]

brink (bringk) *n.* 1 the edge or border of a precipice, pit, chasm or the like. 2 the margin of water. 3 the verge. **on the brink of** on the point of; in danger of. **brinkmanship** *n.* the art of maintaining one's position on the brink of a decision or crisis. [Scand. (Icel. *brekka*, ON *brenka*)]

briny BRINE.

brio (brē´ō) *n.* spirit, liveliness. **brioso** (-ō´sō) *adv.* with spirit, vigorously. [It., vivacity]

brioche (briosh´, brē´-) *n.* 1 a kind of light sweet bread. 2 a sponge cake. [F]

briolet (brē´ōlet) *n.* a pear- or drop-shaped diamond cut with long triangular facets. [F *briller*, to sparkle]

briony BRYONY.

briquette (briket´), **briquet** *n.* 1 a block of compressed coal dust. 2 a slab of artificial stone. ~*v.t.* (*pres.p.* **briquetting, briqueting,** *past, p.p.* **briquetted, briqueted**) to compress (mineral matter etc.) into bricks by heat. [F]

brisk (brisk) *a.* 1 lively, animated, active. 2 keen, stimulating, bracing. 3 sharp-witted, fast, brief. ~*v.t.* to make brisk. ~*v.i.* to move briskly. **brisken** *v.t., v.i.* **briskly** *adv.* **briskness** *n.* [etym. uncertain (Welsh *brisg*, quick-footed, and F *brusque* have been suggested)]

brisket (bris´kit) *n.* 1 that part of the breast of an animal which lies next to the ribs. 2 this joint of meat. **brisket-bone** *n.* the breastbone. [etym. uncertain]

brisling (briz´ling, bris´-), **bristling** (bris´-) *n.* (*pl. in general* **brisling, bristling,** *in particular* **brislings, bristlings**) a small herring, a sprat. [Norw. *brisling*, from LG *Bretling*, from *bret*, broad, like OE *brād*, broad]

bristle (bris´əl) *n.* 1 a short, stiff, coarse hair, esp. on the back and sides of swine, in a beard or on a plant. 2 a similar hair in a brush etc. ~*v.t.* 1 to cause to stand up (as hair). 2 to cover with bristles. ~*v.i.* 1 to stand erect (as hair). 2 to show indignation or defiance (with *up*). 3 to be thickly beset (with difficulties, dangers etc.). **bristlecone pine** *n.* a shrubby pine, *Pinus aristata*, which is the longest-lived known tree. **bristled** *a.* having bristles. **bristletail** *n.* any small primitive wingless insect of the order Thysanura or Diplura, such as a silverfish. **bristling** *a.* **bristling with** full of, with many of. **bristly** *a.* 1 thickly covered with or as with bristles. 2 (*coll.*) quick to anger, touchy. **bristliness** *n.* [ME *bristle, brustel, brustle*, OE *byrst*, Gmc. root *bors-*]

Bristol board (bris´təl) *n.* a thick smooth white cardboard. **Bristol fashion** *a.* (*in full* **shipshape and Bristol fashion**) in good order. **Bristol milk** *n.* cream sherry. [*Bristol*, England]

bristols (bris´təlz) *n.pl.* (*sl.*) a woman's breasts. [*Bristol City*, in pl. rhyming sl. for *titties*]

Brit (brit) *n.* (*coll., sometimes derog.*) a Briton, a British subject.

Brit. *abbr.* 1 Britain. 2 British.

brit (brit) *n.* the spawn and young of the herring and the sprat. [local dial.; etym. unknown]

Britannia (britan´yə) *n.* Britain personified, esp. as a female figure in a helmet with a shield and trident. **Britannia metal** *n.* a white alloy of tin, copper and antimony. **Britannia silver** *n.* silver that is at least 95.8 per cent pure. **Britannic** *a.* British (*Her Britannic Majesty*). [L *Britannia*, OE *Breten*, *Breoten*, *Brytten*, *Breoten-land*].

British (brit´ish) *a.* 1 of or relating to Great Britain or the United Kingdom or its inhabitants. 2 of or relating to the British Commonwealth or (earlier) the British Empire. 3 of or relating to ancient Britain. ~*n.* (*as pl.*) the people of Britain. **British Commonwealth** *n.* COMMONWEALTH OF NATIONS (under COMMONWEALTH). **British Empire** *n.* (*Hist.*) the United Kingdom and the countries governed by it. **British English** *n.* English employed in Britain and not in the US or elsewhere. **Britisher** *n.* a Briton, a British subject. **Britishism, Briticism** (-sizm), *n.* an idiom employed in Britain and not in the US or elsewhere. **British Legion, Royal British Legion** *n.* an association of ex-servicemen and (now) ex-servicewomen founded in 1921 after World War I. **Britishness** *n.* **British Summer Time** *n.* the official time of one hour in advance of Greenwich Mean Time that comes into force between March and October. **British thermal unit** *n.* the quantity of heat required to raise the temperature of 1 lb (0.45 kg) of water by 1°F, equivalent to 1055.06 joules. **British warm** *n.* a short military overcoat.

Britpop (brit´pop) *n.* a type of pop music giving prominence to melody and often imitating 1960s British songs.

brittle (brit´əl) *a.* 1 liable to break or be broken, fragile. 2 not malleable. ~*n.* a brittle sweet (e.g. *peanut brittle*). **brittle-bone disease** *n.* 1 a disease which causes the bones to break easily. 2 OSTEOPOROSIS. **brittlely** *adv.* **brittleness** *n.* **brittle-star** *n.* a type of starfish of the class Ophiuroidea, with long flexible arms. [OE *brēotan*, to break]

Brittonic BRYTHONIC (under BRYTHON).

britzka (brits´kə), **britska** *n.* an open carriage with a calash top. [Pol. *bryczka*, dim. of *bryka*, a wagon]

BRN *abbr.* Bahrain (IVR).

bro. *abbr.* brother.

broach (brōch) *v.t.* 1 to open, to moot, to make public. 2 to pierce (as a cask), so as to allow liquor to flow. 3 to tap. 4 (to cause a ship) to turn suddenly to windward. ~*v.i.* (of a ship) to veer suddenly to windward. ~*n.* 1 a mason's chisel, a boring-bit. 2 a roasting-spit. 3 a tapering iron instrument. 4 an awl. 5 a first horn on the head of a young stag. 6 (*also* **broach spire**) a spire rising from a tower without a parapet. **to broach to** to veer to windward so as to present a ship's broadside to the sea. [F *broche*, a spit, late L *brocca*, a sharp stick (L *broccus*, projecting like teeth)]

broad (brawd) *a.* 1 wide, large, extended across. 2 extensive, expansive. 3 of wide range, general. 4 expanded, open, clear. 5 tolerant, liberal. 6 rough, strong, rustic. 7 coarse, obscene. 8 bold, vigorous, free in style or effect. 9 (of speech) markedly regional. ~*n.* 1 (*esp.* **the Broads**) large, freshwater lakes formed by the broadening of a river. 2 the broad portion of a thing. 3 (*N Am.*, *sl.*) a woman. 4 (*sl.*) a prostitute. ~*adv.* 1 in breadth. 2 broadly, widely. **broad across/ in the beam** BEAM. **broad as long** 1 equal upon the whole. 2 the same either way. **broad arrow** *n.* a mark resembling an arrowhead cut or stamped on British Government property. **broadaxe,** (*N Am.*) **broadax** *n.* 1 a battleaxe. 2 an axe for hewing timber. **broadband** *a.* receiving, transmitting or involving a wide range of frequencies. **broad bean** *n.* 1 a leguminous plant, *Vicia faba*, with edible seeds in a pod. 2 one of these seeds. **broad brush** *a.* (*attrib.*) general; not worked in detail. **broadcast** *a.* 1 transmitted by radio or television. 2 widely disseminated. 3 scattered by the hand (as seed). ~*n.* 1 anything transmitted to the public by radio or television. 2 broadcast sowing. ~*adv.* by scattering widely. ~*v.t.* (*past* **broadcast,** *p.p.* **broadcast, broadcasted**) 1 to sow by scattering with the hand. 2 to transmit by radio or television. 3 to disseminate widely. **broadcaster** *n.* **broadcasting** *n.* **Broad Church** *n.* 1 a party in the Church of England interpreting formularies and dogmas in a liberal sense. 2 any group that is similarly broad-minded or liberal. ~*a.* of or relating to the Broad Church. **broadcloth** *n.* 1 a fine, wide, dressed black cloth, used for men's coats etc. 2 poplin. **broaden** *v.i.* to become broader, to spread. ~*v.t.* to make broader. **broad gauge** *n.* a railway track that has a greater distance between the lines than the standard gauge. **broadleaf** *n.* 1 a non-coniferous tree. 2 (*New Zeal.*) the papauma. ~*a.* having a (relatively) broad leaf, non-coniferous. **broadleafed** *a.* **broadleaved** *a.* **broadloom** *n.* carpet woven on a wide loom. ~*a.* woven on a wide loom. **broadly** *adv.* **broadly speaking** speaking in a general way. **broad-minded** *a.* tolerant, having an open mind. **broad-mindedly** *adv.* **broad-mindedness** *n.* **broadness** *n.* coarseness, indelicacy. **broad pennant** *n.* a short swallow-tailed pennant flown on a commodore's ship. **broadsheet** *n.* 1 a large sheet printed on one side only. 2 a large format newspaper. **broadside** *n.* 1 the side of a ship above the water. 2 a volley from all the guns on one side of a ship of war. 3 a broadsheet. 4 a political attack on a person or policy. ~*v.t.* (*N Am.*) to collide with the side of (a vehicle etc.). **broadside on** sideways on. **broadsilk** *n.* silk in the piece as distinguished from ribbons. **broad spectrum** *a.* (of antibiotics etc.) wide-ranging. **broad-spoken** *a.* 1 speaking in dialect. 2 plain spoken. 3 using coarse language. **broadsword** *n.* 1 a sword with a broad blade. 2 a soldier armed with this. **broadtail** *n.* 1 the karakul sheep. 2 the black wavy fur from karakul lambs. **broadway** *n.* 1 a wide road, a main thoroughfare. 2 (**Broadway**) New York's theatre and restaurant district. **broadways, broadwise** *adv.* in the direction of the breadth. [OE *brād*, Gmc. *braid-* (cp. G *breit*)]

Brobdingnagian (brobdingnag´iən) *a.* gigantic, huge. ~*n.* a giant. [*Brobdingnag*, a country of giants in Swift's *Gulliver's Travels*]

brocade (brəkād´) *n.* silken material with raised figures. ~*v.t.* 1 to weave or work with raised patterns. 2 to decorate with brocade. **brocaded** *a.* [Sp. *brocado*, It. *broccato*, p.p. of *broccare* (*brocca*; see BROACH)]

brocard (brō´kəd) *n.* 1 an elementary principle of law. 2 a sarcastic jest. [F, low L *brocarda*, *Brocard* or *Burchard*, Bishop of Worms, compiler of *Regulae ecclesiasticae*]

broccoli (brok´əli) *n.* 1 a variety of cabbage which has greenish flower heads. 2 the stalk and head of this eaten as a vegetable. [It. pl. of *broccolo*, a sprout, dim. of *brocco*, a skewer, BROACH]

broch (brokh, brok) *n.* a prehistoric circular tower, common in Scotland. [ON *borg*, OE *burh*; cp. BOROUGH]

broché (broshā´) *a.* brocaded, woven with a raised design. [F, stitched]

brochette (broshet´) *n.* 1 a skewer. 2 small pieces of food grilled together on a skewer (like a kebab).

brochure (brō´shə) *n.* a small pamphlet. [F, from *brocher*, to stitch]

brock (brok) *n.* a badger. [OE *broc* (Welsh, Corn. and Bret. *broch*, Ir. *broc*; prob. from *brac*, spotted, cp. Gr. *phorkos*, grey)]

Brocken spectre (brok´ən) *n.* the shadow of an observer, often enlarged and surrounded by coloured lights, thrown on to a bank of cloud in a high mountain area. [*Brocken* in the Harz mountains in Germany]

brocket[1] (brok´it) *n.* a stag in its second year with its first horns, which are straight and unbranched. [F *brocard*, from *broche* BROACH]

brocket[2] (brok´it) *n.* any small deer of the genus *Mazama*, of Central and S America, which have short, straight antlers. [ME, from A-F *broque*, var. of *broche*, BROACH]

☒ **brocoli** common misspelling of BROCCOLI.

broderie anglaise (brōdəri ãglez´) *n.* open embroidery on cambric or linen. [F]

brogue (brōg) *n.* **1** a sturdy shoe. **2** (*Hist.*) a coarse, rough shoe, usu. of untanned leather. **3** a dialectal pronunciation, esp. Irish. ~*v.t.* to utter in a brogue. [Gael. and Ir. *brōg*, shoe, sandal, OIr. *broce* (prob. from OCelt. *brācca*, whence L *braccae*, BREECH]

broider (broi´də) *v.t.*, *v.i.* EMBROIDER.

broil[1] (broil) *n.* a tumult, disturbance, contention. [F *brouiller*, to tumble, trouble, confound (It. *brogliare*, to disturb, *broglio*, confusion)]

broil[2] (broil) *v.t.* **1** to cook on a gridiron; to grill. **2** to scorch. ~*v.i.* **1** to be very hot. **2** to grow hot. **3** to be in the heat; to be subjected to heat. **4** to burn, to be inflamed. ~*n.* broiled meat. **broiler** *n.* **1** a person who or thing which broils. **2** a gridiron. **3** a chicken 8–10 weeks old for broiling or roasting. **4** (*coll.*) a very hot day. [etym. uncertain]

broke[1] (brōk) *a.* (*coll.*) ruined, penniless. **to go for broke** (*sl.*) to risk everything in a venture. [p.p. of BREAK[1]]

broke[2] BREAK[1].

broken[1] (brō´kən) *a.* **1** in pieces. **2** not whole or continuous. **3** weakened, infirm. **4** crushed, humbled. **5** transgressed, violated. **6** interrupted, incoherent, ejaculatory. **7** shattered, bankrupt, ruined. **8** in painting, reduced by the addition of some other colour. **broken-backed** *a.* **1** having the back broken. **2** drooping at stem and stern from injury to the keel. **broken chord** *n.* (*Mus.*) a chord in which the notes are played successively. **broken-down** *a.* **1** decayed. **2** worn-out. **3** ruined in health, in character or financially. **broken English** *n.* halting or defective English as spoken by a foreigner. **broken-hearted** *a.* crushed in spirit by grief or anxiety. **broken-heartedness** *n.* **broken home** *n.* the home of children with separated or divorced parents. **brokenly** *adv.* with breaks, jerkily, spasmodically. **brokenness** *n.* **broken reed** *n.* an unreliable or weak person. **broken water** *n.* choppy water. **broken wind** *n.* a chronic respiratory disease of horses. **broken-winded** *a.* **1** having defective respiratory organs. **2** habitually short of breath. [p.p. of BREAK[1]]

broken[2] BREAK[1].

broker (brō´kə) *n.* **1** an agent, a factor, a middleman. **2** a person who buys and sells for others. **3** a dealer in second-hand furniture. **4** †a petty dealer, a pawnbroker. **brokerage** (-rij) *n.* **1** the business of a broker. **2** a broker's commission on sales etc. **broker-dealer** *n.* a person who works as a broker and jobber on the Stock Exchange. **broking** *n.* the trade of broker. [ME and A-F *brocour*, late L *broccātor*, from *broccāre*, to BROACH]

brolga (brol´gə) *n.* a large Australian crane, *Grus rubicunda*, which has a red-and-green head and a trumpeting call. [Austral. Abor. *burralga*]

brolly (brol´i) *n.* (*pl.* **brollies**) **1** (*coll.*) an umbrella. **2** (*sl.*) a parachute. [corr. of UMBRELLA]

bromal, bromate BROMINE.

brome grass (brōm) *n.* any grass of the genus *Bromus*, esp. *B. inermis*, a cultivated fodder-grass. [Gr. *bromos*, a kind of oats]

bromelia (brəmēl´yə), **bromeliad** (-liad) *n.* any plant of the family Bromeliaceae, esp. of the genus *Bromelia*, which have short stems and stiff spiny leaves, such as the pineapple.

bromine (brō´mēn, -min) *n.* a non-metallic, dark red, liquid element, at. no. 35, chem. symbol Br, with a strong, irritating odour. **bromal** *n.* a liquid like chloral produced by the action of bromine upon alcohol. **bromate** (-māt) *n.* a salt or ester of bromic acid. **bromic** *a.* **1** of or relating to bromine. **2** having bromine in its composition. **bromic acid** *n.* a strong acid used as an oxidizing agent. **bromide** (-mīd) *n.* **1** a combination of bromine with a metal or a radical, esp. bromide of potassium, which is used as a sedative. **2** (*coll.*) a commonplace remark, a platitude. **3** a reproduction or proof on bromide paper. **bromide paper** *n.* a sensitized paper used in printing a photograph from a negative. **bromide process** *n.* in photography, printing from negatives or enlarging on paper coated with silver bromide emulsion. **bromidic** (-mid´-) *a.* (*coll.*) dull, commonplace. **bromism** *n.* the condition produced by long treatment with bromide of potassium. **bromize, bromise** *v.t.* to treat with bromine, to prepare (a photographic plate) with a bromide. [Gr. *brōmos*, a stench]

bromo- (brō´mō) *comb.form* of or relating to bromine.

bronc (brongk) *n.* (*N Am., coll.*) a bronco.

bronchi, bronchial BRONCHUS.

bronchiectasis (brongkiek´təsis) *n.* abnormal dilation of the bronchial tubes.

bronchiole (brong´kiōl) *n.* any of the tiny branches of the bronchi. **bronchiolar** (-ō´lə) *a.*

bronchitis (brongkī´tis) *n.* inflammation of the bronchial tubes. **bronchitic** (-kit´-) *a.*

bronchocele (brong´kōsēl) *n.* abnormal swelling of the thyroid gland, goitre.

bronchodilator (brongkodīlā´tə) *n.* a substance which causes widening of the bronchi, used by people with asthma.

bronchopneumonia (brongkōnūmō´niə) *n.* pneumonia originating in the bronchial tubes.

bronchoscope (brong´kəskōp) *n.* an instrument which is inserted in the bronchial tubes for the purpose of examination or extraction. **bronchoscopic** (-skop´-) *a.* **bronchoscopically** *adv.* **bronchoscopy** (-kos´kəpi) *n.*

bronchotomy (brongkot´əmi) *n.* (*pl.* **bronchotomies**) the operation of opening the windpipe, tracheotomy.

bronchus (brong´kəs) *n.* (*pl.* **bronchi** (-kī)) **1** any of the main divisions of the windpipe. **2** any of the ramifications into which these divide within the lungs. **bronchia** (-kiə) *n.pl.* the bronchial tubes. **bronchial** *a.* of or relating to the bronchi. **bronchial tree** *n.* the branching system of the bronchial tubes. **bronchial tubes** *n.pl.* the bronchi and bronchioles. [L, from Gr. *bronchos, bronchia*]

bronco (brong´kō) *n.* (*pl.* **broncos**) a wild or half-tamed horse of California or New Mexico. **broncobuster** *n.* (*N Am., sl.*) a breaker-in of broncos. [Sp., rough, rude]

brontosaurus (brontəsaw´rəs), **brontosaur** (bron´-) *n.* (*pl.* **brontosauruses, brontosaurs**) APATOSAURUS. [Gr. *brontē*, thunder; *sauros*, a lizard]

bronze (bronz) *n.* **1** a brown alloy of copper and tin, sometimes with a little zinc or lead. **2** a brown colour, like that of bronze. **3** a work of art in bronze. **4** a bronze medal. ~*a.* made or of the colour of bronze. ~*v.t.* **1** to give a bronzelike appearance to (wood, metal, plaster etc.). **2** to brown, to tan. ~*v.i.* to become brown or tanned. **Bronze Age, Bronze Period** *n.* a period after the Stone and before the Iron Age when weapons and implements were made of bronze. **bronzed** *a.* **1** overlaid with bronze. **2** coloured like bronze, suntanned. **bronzelike** *a.* **bronze medal** *n.* a medal made of bronze, or bronze-coloured, awarded for third place in a contest. **bronze-powder** *n.* a metallic powder used in printing, painting etc. for imparting a metallic colour and lustre. **bronzewing** *n.* an Australian pigeon, *Phaps chalcoptera*. **bronzing** *n.* the process of imparting a bronzelike appearance or of becoming bronzed. **bronzite** (-zīt) *n.* a bronzelike variety of diallage. **bronzy** *a.* (*comp.* **bronzier**, *superl.* **bronziest**) **1** like bronze. **2** tinged with bronze. [F, from It. *bronzo*, bronze, *bronzino*, made of bronze, L *Brundusīnium*, made at *Brundusium*, Brindisi]

brooch (brōch) *n.* an ornamental clasp with a pin, worn on or to fasten clothing. [BROACH]

brood (brood) *n.* **1** a family of birds hatched at once. **2** offspring, progeny. **3** (*coll.*) the children in a family. **4** bee or wasp larvae. **5** a race, a species. **6** a swarm, a crowd. ~*v.i.* **1** to sit on eggs. **2** to hover with outspread wings. **3** to hang close overhead (as clouds). **4** to meditate moodily. ~*v.t.* **1** to sit upon (eggs) to hatch them. **2** to cherish under the wings. **3** to prepare by long meditation, to hatch. **4** to cherish moodily. **brooder** *n.* **1** a cover for sheltering young chickens. **2** a person who broods. **brood hen, brood mare** *n.* a hen or a mare kept for breeding. **broodingly** *adv.* **broody** *a.* (*comp.* **broodier,** *superl.* **broodiest**) **1** inclined to sit on eggs. **2** sullen, morose. **3** inclined to brood over matters. **4** (*coll.*) wanting to have a baby. **broodily** *adv.* **broodiness** *n.* [OE *brōd*, from Gmc. root *bro-*, to warm]

brook[1] (bruk) *n.* a small stream, a rivulet. **brooklet** *n.* a little brook, a streamlet. **brooklime** *n.* a kind of speedwell, *Veronica beccabunga*, growing in watery places. **brookweed** *n.* a small white-flowered plant, *Samolus valerandi*, growing in wet ground. **brooky** *a.* abounding in brooks. [OE *brōc* (etym. uncertain, cp. Dut. *broek*, a marsh, a pool, G *Bruch*, a bog)]

brook[2] (bruk) *v.t.* to endure, to support, to put up with. [OE *brūcan*, from Gmc. root *bruk-*, to use, to enjoy (cp. L *fruī*, to enjoy)]

broom (broom) *n.* **1** a shrub with yellow flowers belonging to the genus *Sarothamnus* or *Cytisus*, esp. *Cytisus scoparius.* **2** the allied genus *Genista.* **3** a besom for sweeping, orig. made of broom. **4** a long-handled brush. ~*v.t.* to sweep with a broom. **broomcorn** *n.* a variety of sorghum, *Sorghum vulgare technicum*, from the tufts of which brooms are made. **broomlike** *a.* **broomrape** *n.* a plant of the parasitic genus *Orobanche.* **broomstick, broomstaff** *n.* the handle of a broom. **broomy** *a.* **1** broomlike. **2** abounding in broom. [OE *brōm, broom*, Gmc. *braemoz* (cp. BRAMBLE)]

Bros. (bros) *abbr.* Brothers.

brose (brōz) *n.* (*esp. Sc.*) a kind of porridge made by pouring water on oatmeal or oatcake, with seasoning (see also ATHOLL BROSE). [BREWIS]

broth (broth) *n.* **1** the liquor in which anything, esp. meat, has been boiled. **2** thin soup. **3** a medium for growing cultures (e.g. of bacteria). **broth of a boy** a high-spirited fellow. [OE from Gmc. root *bru-*, to boil (cp. OE *brēowan*, to brew)]

brothel (broth´əl) *n.* premises where prostitutes sell their services. **brothel creepers** *n.pl.* (*sl.*) soft-soled suede shoes. [OE *brothen*, p.p. of *brēothan*, to go to ruin (confused with BORDELLO)]

brother (brŭdh´ə) *n.* (*pl.* **brothers, brethren** (bredh´rən)) **1** a son of the same parents or parent. **2** a person closely connected with another. **3** an associate. **4** a person of the same community, country, city, church, order, profession or society. **5** a fellow countryman, fellow citizen etc. **6** a fellow man, a fellow creature. **7** (*Bible*) a kinsman, cousin. **brother german** *n.* a brother on both sides. **brotherhood** *n.* **1** the relationship of a brother. **2** a fraternity, an association for mutual service. **3** (*N Am.*) a trade union. **4** brotherly affection or feeling. **brother-in-arms** *n.* (*pl.* **brothers-in-arms**) a fellow-soldier. **brother-in-law** *n.* (*pl.* **brothers-in-law**) **1** the brother of one's husband or wife. **2** one's sister's husband. **3** one's sister-in-law's husband. **brotherless** *a.* **brotherlike** *a.* **brotherly** *a.* **1** becoming to a brother. **2** fraternal. ~*adv.* fraternally. **brotherliness** *n.* **brother uterine** *n.* a brother born of the same mother but not the same father. [OE *brōthor* (cp. G *Bruder*, L *frāter*, Gr. *phratēr*, Sansk. *bhrātr*, Welsh *brawd*)]

Usage note *Brethren* is used in more solemn senses.

brougham (broom, broo´əm, brō´əm) *n.* (*Hist.*) **1** a close, four-wheeled carriage drawn by one horse. **2** an early motor vehicle with an open driver's seat. [Lord *Brougham*, 1778–1868]

brought BRING.

brouhaha (broo´hahhah) *n.* a tumult, a row. [F]

brow (brow) *n.* **1** the ridge over the eye. **2** the forehead. **3** the countenance generally. **4** (*fig.*) aspect, appearance. **5** the projecting edge of a cliff or hill. **6** the top of a hill. **7** a ship's gangway. **8** (*N Am.*) an inclined roadway for drawing up logs to a lumber-mill. ~*v.t.* **1** to be at the edge of. **2** to form a brow to. **to knit one's brows** to frown. **brow antler** *n.* the lowest tine of a deer's horn. **browbeat** *v.t.* (*past* **browbeat,** *p.p.* **browbeaten**) to intimidate arrogantly, to bully. **browbeaten** *a.* intimidated. **browbeater** *n.* **browed** *a.* (*in comb.*, as *beetle-browed*). [OE *brū* (cp. Icel. *brūn*, Lith. *bruwis*, Rus. *brove*, Gr. *ophrus*, Sansk. *bhrū*)]

brown (brown) *a.* **1** of the colour of dark wood, scorched paper or dark soil; of the compound colour produced by a mixture of red, black and yellow. **2** dusky, dark, suntanned. **3** (of bread) made from wholemeal or wheatmeal flour. **4** (of species) having brown coloration. ~*n.* **1** a brown colour; a compound colour produced by a mixture of red, black and yellow. **2** a pigment of this colour. **3** a brown butterfly. **4** brown clothes. **5** (in a game) a brown piece etc. ~*v.t.* **1** to make brown. **2** to give a brown lustre to (gun barrels etc.). ~*v.i.* **1** to become brown. **2** to get sunburnt. **to do brown** (*sl.*) to take in, to deceive. **brown ale** *n.* a dark, mild bottled beer. **brown bag** *n.* (*N Am.*) a brown paper bag. **brown-bagger** *n.* a person who carries their lunch in this. **brown bear** *n.* a brown bear, *Ursus arctos*, common to Europe, Asia and N America. **brown Bess** *n.* the old flintlock musket of the British Army. **brown bomber** *n.* (*coll.*) a member of the New South Wales parking police. **brown coal** *n.* lignite. **browned** *a.* **browned off** *a.* (*sl.*) **1** disappointed. **2** bored, fed up. **brown fat** *n.* a dark fatty tissue which generates body heat. **brown goods** *n.pl.* household appliances, usu. brownish in colour, such as TV sets, record players etc. as opposed to *white goods.* **brown holland** *n.* unbleached holland linen. **Brownie, Brownie Guide** *n.* a junior Guide from 8 to 11 years of age. **Brownie Guider** *n.* the adult leader of a Brownie pack. **Brownie point** *n.* (*sometimes derog.*) a supposed mark to one's credit for some achievement. **brownie** (-ni) *n.* **1** (*orig. N Am.*) a kind of nutty, dark chocolate cake cut into flat squares. **2** (*Austral.*) a kind of currant loaf. **3** a kindly domestic elf. **browning** *n.* colouring material for gravy. **brownish** *a.* **brownness** *n.* **brown-nose** *n.* (*N Am., sl.*) (*also* **brown-noser**) a sycophant. ~*v.i.* to curry favour. ~*v.t.* to curry favour with. **brown owl** *n.* **1** any of various owls, esp. the tawny owl *Strix aluco.* **2** (*coll.*) (**Brown Owl**) a Brownie Guider. **brown paper** *n.* coarse, unbleached paper for packing parcels etc. **brown rice** *n.* husked rice left unpolished. **Brownshirt** *n.* (*Hist.*) a uniformed member of the Nazi party in Germany. **brownstone** *n.* (*N Am.*) **1** a dark-brown sandstone. **2** a building of this material. **brown study** *n.* a reverie, daydream. **brown sugar** *n.* coarse, half-refined sugar. **brown trout** *n.* a common European trout, *Salmo trutta*, with a dark spotted back. **brownware** *n.* a coarse, cheap kind of pottery. **browny** *a.* [OE *brūn* (cp. Icel. *brunn*, G *braun*, Gr. *phrūnos*, a toad; F *brun* and It. *bruno* are from Gmc.)]

Brownian movement (brow´niən), **Brownian motion** *n.* random agitation of particles suspended in a fluid caused by bombardment of the particles by molecules of the fluid. [British botanist Robert *Brown*, 1773–1858]

Brownism (brow´nizm) *n.* the Congregationalist scheme of Church government adopted in a modified form by the Independents. **Brownist** *n.* [Robert *Browne*, *c.* 1550–*c.* 1633]

browse (browz) *v.t.* 1 to nibble and eat off (twigs, young shoots etc.). 2 (*Comput.*) to read or survey (data files etc.). 3 to read in a desultory way, to leaf through. ~*v.i.* 1 to feed on twigs, young shoots etc. 2 to graze. 3 to look or read, among articles in an idle manner. 4 (*Comput.*) to read through data files etc. ~*n.* 1 the tender shoots of trees and shrubs fit for cattle to feed on. 2 an act of browsing. **browser** *n.* [F *brouster, brouter* (MHG *Broz*, a bud, OS *brustian*, to bud, cp. OE *brēotan*, to break)]

BRS *abbr.* British Road Services.

BRU *abbr.* Brunei (IVR).

brucellosis (broosəlō´sis) *n.* an infectious bacterial disease in animals, caused by bacteria of the genus *Brucella*, which is also contagious to humans (also called *contagious abortion*, *Malta* or *undulant fever*). [Sir David *Bruce*, bacteriologist, 1855–1931]

brucine (broo´sēn) *n.* a poisonous alkaloid found in the seed and bark of *Nux vomica* and other species of *Strychnos*. [James *Bruce*, Scottish explorer in Africa, 1730–94]

brucite (broo´sīt) *n.* a mineral form of magnesium hydroxide. [A. *Bruce*, US mineralogist, d.1818]

bruckle (brŭk´əl) *a.* fragile, brittle, precarious, ticklish. [OE *brucol* (in *scipbrucol*, shipwreck), from *bruc*-, stem of *brekan*, to break]

Bruin (broo´in) *n.* (a personal name for) the brown bear. [Dut., lit. brown]

bruise (brooz) *v.t.* 1 to crush, indent or discolour, by a blow from something blunt and heavy. 2 to injure without breaking skin or bone, usu. with discoloration. 3 to batter, pound, grind up. 4 to hurt, disable. ~*v.i.* 1 to be susceptible to bruising. 2 to display the effects of a blow. ~*n.* 1 an injury caused by something blunt and heavy. 2 a discoloured area of the skin caused by rupture of underlying blood vessels. 3 a damaged area on a fruit. **bruiser** *n.* 1 a person who or thing which bruises. 2 (*coll.*) a large strong man, a prizefighter or boxer. [OE *brȳsan*, to bruise (combined later with OF *bruiser, brisier* (etym. uncertain), to break)]

bruit (broot) *v.t.* to rumour, to noise abroad. ~*n.* 1 an abnormal sound heard in auscultation. 2 †noise, tumult, rumour, report. [F, noise, from *bruire*, to roar]

brûlé (broo´lā) *a.* cooked with caramelized brown sugar. [F, burnt]

Brum (brŭm) *n.* Birmingham, England. **Brummie** (-i), **Brummy** *n.* (*pl.* **Brummies**) (*coll.*) a person from Birmingham. ~*a.* (*coll.*) of or relating to Birmingham. [BRUMMAGEM]

brumby (brŭm´bi) *n.* (*pl.* **brumbies**) (*Austral.*) a wild horse.

brume (broom) *n.* mist, fog, vapour. **brumal** *a.* 1 of or relating to winter. 2 wintry. **brumous** *a.* wintry, foggy. [F *brume*, fog, L *brūma*, winter (contr. of *brevima*, *brevissima*, shortest)]

Brummagem (brŭm´əjəm), **brummagem** *a.* 1 cheap and ostentatious. 2 sham, spurious. ~*n.* 1 (*dial.*) Birmingham, England. 2 an article manufactured there. 3 a counterfeit coin etc.

Brummie BRUM.

brunch (brŭnch) *n.* (*coll.*) a meal which combines a late breakfast with an early lunch. ~*v.i.* to eat brunch. [BREAKFAST, LUNCH]

brunette (brunet´), (*N Am.*) **brunet** *n.* a girl or woman with dark hair and a dark complexion. ~*a.* 1 brown-haired. 2 of dark complexion. [F, fem. dim. of *brun*, brown]

brunt (brŭnt) *n.* the shock, impetus or stress of an attack, danger or crisis. **to bear the brunt** to take the main force (e.g. of an attack). [etym. uncertain; perh. conn. with Icel. *bruna*, to advance like fire]

bruscamente (brooskəmen´ti) *adv.* (*Mus.*) 1 strongly accented. 2 roughly. [It.]

bruschetta (brusket´ə) *n.* (*pl.* **bruschettas, bruschette** (-tā)) a type of Italian open toasted sandwich, eaten as an appetizer or snack. [It.]

brush[1] (brŭsh) *n.* 1 an instrument for sweeping or scrubbing, generally made of bristles, twigs or feathers. 2 an instrument consisting of hair or bristle attached to a handle, for colouring, whitewashing, painting etc. 3 a hair pencil. 4 a brushing. 5 an attack, a skirmish. 6 a bushy tail, as of a fox. 7 a piece of metal or carbon or bundle of wires or plates, forming a good electrical conductor. 8 a brushlike discharge of electric sparks. 9 a painter, a style in painting. 10 a brushlike appearance produced by polarized light. 11 brushwood, underwood, a thicket of small trees. 12 loppings, faggots of brushwood. 13 (*Austral.*) dense forest. ~*v.t.* 1 to sweep or scrub with a brush. 2 to remove by brushing. 3 to touch lightly, as in passing. ~*v.i.* 1 to move with a sweeping motion. 2 to pass lightly. **the brush** (*fig.*) the art of painting. **to brush aside** to dismiss curtly. **to brush off** to dismiss curtly. **to brush over** to paint lightly. **to brush up** 1 to clean by brushing. 2 to revive, to tidy one's appearance. 3 to refresh one's memory. **brush discharge** *n.* a broad electrical discharge between points of high charge density when the density is insufficient to cause a spark. **brushed** *a.* 1 cleaned or smoothed with a brush. 2 (of a fabric) having a raised nap. **brushed aluminium** *n.* aluminium that has been treated so that the surface is matt. **brusher** *n.* **brush fire** *n.* a fast spreading fire which consumes dry brush and scrub. **brush kangaroo** *n.* the wallaby. **brushless** *a.* not needing a brush. **brushlike** *a.* **brush-off** *n.* (*coll.*) a brusque rebuff. **brush pencil** *n.* an artist's brush. **brush turkey** *n.* (*Austral.*) any of several birds of New Guinea and Australia, esp. *Alectura lathami*. **brush-up** *n.* an act of brushing up; a tidying of one's appearance. **brushwheel** *n.* a circular revolving brush. **brushwood** *n.* 1 a thicket, underwood. 2 low scrubby thicket. 3 loppings. **brushwork** *n.* 1 a painter's manipulation of the brush. 2 style of manipulation of the brush. **brushy** *a.* (*comp.* **brushier**, *superl.* **brushiest**) 1 resembling a brush. 2 rough, shaggy. 3 covered with brushwood. [OF *broce, brosse*, brushwood, late L *bruscia*, a thicket (prob. from OHG *bursta*, bristle); and OF *brosse, broisse*, a brush, broom (perh. of similar origin)]

brush[2] (brŭsh) *n.* (*Austral.*, *New Zeal.*, *sl.*) a young woman, a girl.

brusque (brŭsk, broosk) *a.* rough or blunt in manner, unceremonious. **brusquely** *adv.* **brusqueness** *n.* **brusquerie** (-kəri) *n.* [F, from It. *brusco*, sharp, sour; etym. uncertain]

Brussels (brŭs´əlz) *a.* made at or derived from Brussels. ~*n.* a Brussels carpet. **Brussels carpet** *n.* a kind of carpet with a backing of linen and a wool face. **Brussels lace** *n.* a kind of pillow lace. **Brussels sprout** *n.* a small sprout springing from the stalk of a variety of cabbage, and used as a vegetable. [*Brussels*, Belgium]

brut (broot) *a.* (of wine) dry, unsweetened. [F]

brute (broot) *n.* 1 an animal as opposed to a human being; a beast. 2 a person resembling a brute in lack of intelligence etc.; a violent person or animal. 3 the animal nature in humans. ~*a.* 1 stupid, irrational. 2 beastlike, sensual. 3 unconscious, material. **brutal** *a.* 1 resembling a brute. 2 savage, cruel. 3 coarse, unrefined, sensual. **brutalism** *n.* brutality. **brutalist** *n.* **brutality** (-tal´-) *n.* (*pl.* **brutalities**) 1 the quality of being brutal. 2 a brutal action. **brutalize, brutalise** *v.t.* 1 to make brutal. 2 to treat brutally. ~*v.i.* to become brutal. **brutalization** (-zā´shən) *n.* **brutally** *adv.* **brutehood** *n.* the condition of brutes. **brutify** (-fī) *v.t.* (*3rd pers. sing. pres.* **brutifies**, *pres.p.* **brutifying**, *past*, *p.p.* **brutified**) to brutalize, to render brutal. **brutification** (-fikā´shən) *n.* **brutish** *a.* **1** like a brute. **2** animal, bestial. **brutishly** *adv.* **brutishness** *n.* [F *brut, brute,* L *brūtus,* stupid]

bruxism (brŭk´sizm) *n.* the unconscious habit of grinding the teeth. [Gr. *brychein,* to gnash]

Brylcreem® (bril´krēm) *n.* a cream that is smoothed into the hair to make it shiny.

bryology (brīol´əji) *n.* **1** the science of mosses. **2** mosses collectively. **bryological** (-əloj´-) *a.* **bryologist** *n.* a student of mosses. [Gr. *bruun,* a mossy seaweed]

bryony (brī´əni), **briony** *n.* **1** a climbing plant of the genus *Bryonia,* esp. *B. dioica,* with whitish flowers. **2** BLACK BRYONY (under BLACK). [L *bryōnia,* Gr. *bruōnia* (*bruein,* to teem, swell)]

bryophyte (brī´ōfīt) *n.* a cryptogamous plant of the division Bryophyta, consisting of the liverworts and mosses. **bryophitic** (-fit´ik) *a.* of the phylum Bryozoa. [Gr. *bruon,* moss, *phuton,* a plant]

bryozoan (brīōzō´ən) *n.* any one of the lowest class of the mollusca, of the phylum Bryozoa, also called *polyzoan.* **bryozoology** (-zōol´əji, -zoo·o´-) *n.* [Gr. *bruon,* moss, *zōon, zōa,* animal, animals]

Brython (brith´ən) *n.* a member of the Celtic people occupying S Britain at the time of the Roman invasion, as distinguished from the Goidels. **Brythonic** (-thon´-), **Brittonic** (briton´ik) *n.* the southern Celtic languages, Welsh, Cornish and Breton. *~a.* of or relating to Brythonic. [Welsh *Brython,* BRITISH]

BS *abbr.* **1** (*N Am.*) Bachelor of Science. **2** Bachelor of Surgery. **3** Bahamas (IVR). **4** Blessed Sacrament. **5** British Standard(s). **6** building society.

b.s. *abbr.* **1** balance sheet. **2** bill of sale.

BSC *abbr.* Broadcasting Standards Council.

B.Sc. *abbr.* Bachelor of Science.

BSE *abbr.* bovine spongiform encephalopathy.

BSI *abbr.* British Standards Institution.

BST *abbr.* **1** bovine somatotrophin. **2** (*Hist.*) British Standard Time. **3** British Summer Time.

BT *abbr.* British Telecom.

Bt. *abbr.* **1** Baronet. **2** bought.

btu, BTU, B.th.U *abbr.* British thermal unit.

bu. *abbr.* bushel.

bub[1] (bŭb) *n.* (*N Am., coll.*) (as a form of address) boy. [cp. G *Bube,* boy]

bub[2] (bŭb) *n.* (*sl.*) **1** drink. **2** beer. [prob. imit.]

bubal (bū´bəl) *n.* the hartebeest. [L *bubalus,* from Gr. *boubalos,* oxlike antelope]

bubble (bŭb´əl) *n.* **1** a vesicle of water or other liquid filled with air or other gas. **2** a cavity in a solidified material, such as ice, amber, glass etc. **3** anything unsubstantial or unreal. **4** a cheat. **5** a fraud, a swindling project. *~a.* **1** visionary, unreal. **2** fraudulent, fictitious. *~v.i.* **1** to rise up in or as in bubbles. **2** to make a noise like bubbling water. *~v.t.* to cheat, to delude. **to bubble over** to boil over with laughter, anger, etc. **bubble and squeak** *n.* meat and vegetables fried together. **bubble bath** *n.* **1** a foaming bath preparation. **2** a bath containing this. **bubble beat** *n.* a form of techno music toned down for a mass audience, with a slower beat and fewer electronic effects. **bubble car** *n.* a midget motor car with rounded line and transparent top. **bubble chamber** *n.* an apparatus for tracking the path of a charged particle by the stream of bubbles left in its wake. **bubblegum** *n.* a kind of chewing gum that can be blown up into a bubble. **bubble memory** *n.* a data storage system in computers composed of tiny areas of bubbles of magnetism. **bubble pack** *n.* BLISTER PACK (under BLISTER). **bubbler** *n.* **1** a cheat. **2** a fish found in the Ohio (named from the peculiar noise it makes). **bubble wrap** *n.* plastic packaging material made up of air-filled pockets. **bubbly** *a.* (*comp.* **bubblier,** *superl.* **bubbliest**) **1** full of bubbles. **2** excited, vivacious. *~n.* (*coll.*) champagne. **bubbly-jock** (-jok) *n.* (*coll., esp. Sc.*) a turkey cock. [imit.; cp. BLEB, BLUBBER]

bubo (bū´bō) *n.* (*pl.* **buboes**) an inflamed swelling of the lymphatic glands, esp. in the groin or armpit. **bubonic** (-bon´-) *a.* **bubonic plague** *n.* a type of plague characterized by buboes. **bubonocele** (-bon´əsēl) *n.* hernia of the groin. [late L, from Gr. *boubōn,* the groin, a swelling in the groin]

buccal (bŭk´əl) *a.* of or relating to the cheek or the mouth. [L *bucca,* cheek]

buccaneer (bŭkəniə´) *n.* **1** a piratical rover, orig. on the Spanish Main. **2** a brazen adventurer. *~v.i.* to act the part of a buccaneer. **buccaneering** *a.* **buccaneerish** *a.* [F *boucanier,* orig. a hunter of wild oxen, from *boucan* (from a Tupi word), a gridiron or frame on which flesh was barbecued]

buccinator (bŭk´sinātə) *n.* the flat, thin muscle forming the wall of the cheek, used in blowing. [L *buccināre,* to blow the trumpet (*buccina,* trumpet)]

Buchmanism (bŭk´mənizm, buk´-) *n.* a non-denominational evangelical religious movement of American origin, also known as the Oxford Group, now more usually Moral Rearmament. **Buchmanite** (-nīt) *n.* a member of this group. [Frank *Buchman,* 1878–1961]

buck[1] (bŭk) *n.* **1** the male of the fallow deer, reindeer, goat, hare and rabbit. **2** †a dashing young fellow. **3** (*offensive*) a male N American Indian or black. **4** (*N Am., Austral., sl.*) a dollar. **5** (*sl.*) cheek. **6** (*sl.*) a marker in poker which indicates the next dealer. **7** an object used as a reminder. *~a.* (*attrib., sl.*) **1** male (*a buck antelope*). **2** (*N Am.*) of the lowest rank (*a buck private*). *~v.i.* to buckjump. *~v.t.* **1** to throw (a rider) by buckjumping. **2** (*esp. N Am.*) to oppose, resist. **to buck up 1** to hurry. **2** to improve. **3** to become cheerful or lively. **to pass the buck** (*sl.*) to shift responsibility to someone else. **bucked** *a.* (*coll.*) **1** invigorated. **2** pleased. **bucker** *n.* a buckjumper. **buckeye** *n.* **1** the horse chestnut of the US, of the genus *Aesculus.* **2** the shiny brown fruit of this. **3** (*offensive*) a native of Ohio. **buck fever** *n.* (*N Am.*) nervousness, such as that felt by inexperienced hunters. **buck-horn** *n.* **1** the horn of a buck. **2** the material of a buck's horn used for knife handles etc. **buck-hound** *n.* a small variety of the staghound. **buckish** *a.* **1** lively, frisky. **2** foppish. **buckishly** *adv.* **buckjump** *n.* a jump by a vicious or unbroken horse, with the feet drawn together and the back arched to unseat the rider. *~v.i.* to jump in this way. **buckjumper** *n.* a horse given to buckjumping. **buck-passing** *n.* shifting of responsibility to someone else. **buck rarebit** *n.* Welsh rarebit with a poached egg on top. **buckshot** *n.* a kind of coarse lead shot. **buckskin** *n.* **1** the skin of a buck. **2** a soft yellowish deerskin or sheepskin. **3** (*pl.*) buckskin breeches. *~a.* made of buckskin. **buckthorn** *n.* any thorny shrub of the genus *Rhamnus,* esp. *R. cathartica,* berries of which yield sap green. **buck-tooth** *n.* a large, protruding tooth. **buck-toothed** *a.* [Oe *bucc,* a buck, *bucca,* a he-goat (distinction between the two words doubtful) (cp. Dut. *bok,* G *Bock,* F *bouc,* a he-goat, Welsh *bwch,* a buck, all from Gmc.)]

buck[2] (bŭk) *n.* the body of a wagon or cart. **buckboard** *n.* **1** a projecting board or ledge over the wheels of a cart. **2** (*N Am.*) a light four-wheeled vehicle. **buck-cart, buck-wagon** *n.* a vehicle fitted with buckboards. [perh. OE *būc,* belly, body, trunk]

buck[3] (bŭk) *n.* **1** (*N Am.*) a sawhorse. **2** a vaulting horse.

buckbean (bŭk´bēn) *n.* a water plant having pinkish-white flowers, of the genus *Menyanthes,* esp. *M. trifoliata,* also called the *bogbean.* [etym. uncertain]

bucket (bŭk´it) *n.* **1** a vessel with a handle, for drawing or carrying water. **2** a scoop or receptacle for lifting mud, gravel, coal, grain etc. in a dredger or elevator. **3** as much as a bucket will hold. **4** the piston of a pump.

5 a whip socket. 6 a holder attached to a saddle for a carbine, rifle etc. 7 (*in pl.*) large quantities of liquid (*raining buckets*). ~*v.t.* (*pres.p.* **bucketing**, *past*, *p.p.* **bucketed**) 1 to lift or draw in buckets. 2 (*sl.*) to cheat. 3 to ride (a horse) hard. 4 to hurry or jerk while rowing. ~*v.i.* 1 to hurry the forward swing of an oar. 2 (*coll.*) to rain heavily. **to kick the bucket** (*sl.*) to die (perhaps from OF *buquet*, a beam). **bucketful** *n.* (*pl.* **bucketfuls**) as much as will fill a bucket. **bucket seat** *n.* a round-backed seat for one person in a vehicle or aeroplane. **bucket shop** *n.* 1 the office of unofficial brokers who deal in trashy stock. 2 (*coll.*) a place where cheap airline tickets are sold. [etym. uncertain (perh. OE *būc*, pitcher, or OF *buket*, *buquet*, tub, pail)]

buckie (bŭk´i) *n.* 1 a spiral shell, e.g. the whelk. 2 an obstinate, perverse person. [etym. uncertain]

buckle (bŭk´əl) *n.* 1 a link of metal etc., with a tongue or catch, for fastening straps etc. 2 a bow, a curl, a twist. 3 the state of being crisped, curled or twisted. ~*v.t.* 1 to fasten with or as with a buckle. 2 to bend, to twist. 3 to equip with a buckle. 4 to join in matrimony. 5 to prepare (oneself) resolutely. ~*v.i.* 1 to bend, to be put out of shape. 2 to be married. **to buckle down** to make a determined effort. **to buckle to** to set to work, to set about energetically. **to buckle under** to give way under stress. **buckler** *n.* 1 (*Hist.*) a small round shield. 2 a protection, a protector. 3 (*Biol.*) a hard protective covering, a carapace. 4 the interior segment of a trilobite. ~*v.t.* to defend with or as with a buckler. **buckler fern** *n.* any of the shield ferns of the genus *Dryopteris*. [OF *bocle* (F *boucle*, L *buccula*, cheek-strap of helmet, buckle (*bucca*, cheek))]

Buckley's (bŭk´liz), **Buckley's chance** *n.* (*Austral.*, *New Zeal.*, *coll.*) no chance at all. [etym. uncertain]

buckling (bŭk´ling) *n.* a smoked herring. [G *Bückling*, bloater]

buckminsterfullerene (bŭkminstəfŭl´ərēn) *n.* a form of carbon with 60 atoms arranged at the vertices of a polyhedron with hexagonal and pentagonal faces. [Richard *Buckminster Fuller*, 1895–1983, US architect and engineer]

bucko (bŭk´ō) *n.* (*pl.* **buckoes**) (*sl.*) a swaggering or bullying person. ~*a.* swaggering, bullying. [BUCK[1]]

buckram (bŭk´rəm) *n.* 1 a strong coarse kind of linen cloth, stiffened with gum. 2 †a stiff, precise manner. 3 an appearance of strength. ~*a.* 1 made of buckram. 2 †starched, stiff, precise. ~*v.i.* to stiffen with or as with buckram. **men in buckram** MAN. [OF *boucaran*, *boquerant* (It. *bucherane*, *buchirano*); etym. unknown]

Bucks. (bŭks) *abbr.* Buckinghamshire.

Buck's Fizz (bŭks) *n.* a cocktail of champagne or sparkling wine mixed with orange juice. [*Buck's* Club in London, FIZZ]

buckshee (bŭkshē´) *n.* (*sl.*) 1 something for nothing, a windfall. 2 something in addition to the agreed allowance. ~*a.* free, gratuitous. [BAKSHEESH]

buckthorn BUCK[1].

buckwheat (bŭk´wēt) *n.* a cereal plant of the genus *Fagopyrum*, esp. *F. esculentum*, the three-cornered seeds of which are given to horses and poultry, and in the US are used for cakes. [*beechwheat*, from the shape of its seeds (OE *boc*, beech)]

bucolic (būkol´ik) *a.* (*often derog.*) pastoral, rustic. ~*n.* 1 a pastoral poem. 2 a pastoral poet. 3 a peasant. **bucolically** *adv.* [L *būcolicus*, Gr. *boukolikos*, from *boukolos*, a herdsman (*bous*, ox, *kol-*, stem of v. to drive)]

bud[1] (bŭd) *n.* 1 the germ of a branch, cluster of leaves or flower, usu. arising from the axil of a leaf. 2 an unexpanded leaf or flower. 3 a gemmule which develops into a complete animal. 4 something undeveloped. ~*v.i.* (*pres.p.* **budding**, *past*, *p.p.* **budded**) 1 to put out buds. 2 to begin to grow. 3 to develop. ~*v.t.* 1 to graft (on) by inserting a bud under the bark. 2 to produce by germination. **in bud** about to flower or grow leaves. **to nip in the bud** to put a stop to at the outset. **budded** *a.* in bud. **budding** *n.* 1 grafting with a bud. 2 asexual reproduction from a parent cell, as in yeast. 3 (*Zool.*) gemmation. ~*a.* 1 having buds. 2 beginning to develop. 3 promising. 4 aspiring. **budless** *a.* **budlet** *n.* a little bud. [etym. uncertain]

bud[2] (bŭd) *n.* (*N Am.*, *coll.*) buddy; pal. [BUDDY]

Buddha (bud´ə) *n.* 1 the title given to Gautama, the founder of Buddhism, by his disciples. 2 a statue or picture of the Buddha. **Buddhism** *n.* the religious system founded in India in the 5th cent. BC by Sakyamuni, Gautama or Siddartha, teaching the existence of suffering and the way to release from suffering. **Buddhist** *n.* a follower of Buddha. ~*a.* of or connected with Buddhism. **Buddhistic** (-is´-), **Buddhistical** *a.* [Sansk. *buddha*, enlightened (p.p. of *budh*, to awake, to know)]

buddle (bŭd´əl) *n.* an oblong inclined vat in which ore is washed. ~*v.t.* to wash (ore) by means of a buddle. [etym. unknown]

buddleia (bŭd´liə) *n.* any shrub of the genus *Buddleia*, which have fragrant lilac, orange or white flowers. [Adam *Buddle*, English botanist, d. 1715]

buddy (bŭd´i) *n.* (*pl.* **buddies**) 1 (*coll.*) a close friend, pal. 2 a person who visits and counsels (in a voluntary capacity) someone suffering from Aids. ~*a.* (of a film or story) dealing with the adventures of and relationship between usu. two male partners. ~*v.i.* (*3rd pers. sing. pres.* **buddies**, *pres.p.* **buddying**, *past*, *p.p.* **buddied**) to act as a buddy to a someone suffering from Aids. **to buddy up** to become friendly. [prob. from *brother*, or var. of BUTTY[1]]

budge[1] (bŭj) *v.i.* 1 to move from one's place. 2 to change one's opinion. ~*v.t.* to cause one's opinion to budge. **to budge over/ up** to move along to make room for someone. [F *bouger*, to stir (cp. Prov. *bolegar*, to disturb oneself, It. *bulicare*, to bubble up, L *bullīre*, to boil)]

budge[2] (bŭj) *n.* a kind of fur made of lambskin with the wool outwards. ~*a.* 1 wearing budge. 2 pedantic, stiff, formal. [etym. uncertain]

budgeree (bŭj´əri), **budgery** *a.* (*Austral.*, *coll.*) good, excellent. [Austral. Abor.]

budgerigar (bŭj´ərigah) *n.* 1 an Australian green parakeet, *Melopsittacus undulatus*. 2 a coloured variety of this, bred as a cage bird. [Austral. Abor.]

budget (bŭj´it) *n.* 1 an estimate of receipts and expenditure, esp. the annual financial statement of the Chancellor of the Exchequer in the House of Commons. 2 the amount of money allowed (for a specific item etc.). 3 †a bundle, a collection of news. 4 a small leather bag. 5 the contents of such a bag. ~*v.i.* (*pres.p.* **budgeting**, *past*, *p.p.* **budgeted**) to prepare a budget or estimate (for). ~*v.t.* to make provision for in a budget. ~*a.* (*attrib.*) inexpensive. **on a budget** with a restricted amount of money to spend. **budget account, budget plan** *n.* an account which allows one to regularize payments as prescribed in a budget. **budgetary** *a.* [F *bougette*, dim. of *bouge*, a wallet, L *bulga*, of Gaulish origin (cp. OIr. *bolg*, *bolc*, a bag)]

budgie (bŭj´i) *n.* (*coll.*) a budgerigar.

buff[1] (bŭf) *n.* 1 the colour of buff leather, light yellow. 2 (*coll.*) an expert on or devotee of a subject. 3 soft, stout leather prepared from the skin of the buffalo. 4 the skins of other animals similarly prepared. 5 a soldier's coat of buff. 6 (*coll.*) the bare skin. 7 an instrument for polishing with. ~*v.t.* 1 to polish with a buff. 2 to give a velvety surface to (leather). **in the buff** (*coll.*) naked. **the Buffs** the former East Kent Regiment (from the colour of their facings). **buff coat, buff jerkin** *n.* a stout garment of buff leather orig. worn as a defence against sword-cuts. **buff-stick, buff-wheel** *n.* a stick or wheel covered with buff leather or a similar material, used for polishing metals. **buffy** *a.* coloured like buff. [contr. of *buffe* or *buffle*, F *buffle*, buffalo]

buff[2] (bŭf) *n.* a blow, a buffet. [OF *bufe, buffe*, a blow]

buffalo (bŭf´əlō) *n.* (*pl. in general* **buffalo,** *in particular* **buffaloes**) **1** an Asiatic ox of the genus *Babulus*, esp. *B. arnee*, the water buffalo. **2** a wild ox, *Syncerus caffer*, the Cape buffalo. **3** a N American bison, *Bison bison*. ~*v.t.* (*3rd pers. sing. pres.* **buffaloes,** *pres.p.* **buffaloing,** *past, p.p.* **buffaloed**) (*N Am., sl.*) to overcome or outwit. **buffalo grass** *n.* prairie grass such as *Buchloe dactyloides* of N America, or *Stenotaphrum secundatum* of Australia and New Zealand. **buffalo-robe** *n.* the skin of the American bison dressed with the hair on. [Port. *bufalo* or It. *buffalo*, L *būfalus, būbalus*, Gr. *boubalos*]

buffer (bŭf´ə) *n.* **1** a mechanical apparatus for deadening or sustaining the force of a concussion. **2** an apparatus fixed to railway carriages for this purpose. **3** the fender of a ship. **4** a fellow. **5** a chemical compound which maintains the balance of acidity/alkalinity in a solution. **6** a short-term storage unit in a computer. ~*v.t.* **1** to add or treat with a buffer. **2** to protect with a buffer. **buffered** *a.* **buffer state** *n.* a small neutral state separating two larger rival states and tending to prevent hostilities. **buffer stock** *n.* a reserve of a commodity held to minimize the effect of fluctuations in price. **buffer zone** *n.* a neutral zone separating two others. [BUFF[2]]

buffet[1] (bŭf´it) *n.* **1** a blow with the hand or fist, a cuff. **2** a blow of fate, a disaster, a misfortune. ~*v.t.* (*pres.p.* **buffeting,** *past, p.p.* **buffeted**) **1** to strike with the hand. **2** to thump, to cuff. **3** to beat back, to contend with. ~*v.i.* to struggle, to contend. **buffeting** *n.* **1** repeated blows; a beating. **2** air turbulence affecting an aircraft. **3** something difficult to contend with. [OF *bufet*, dim. of *bufe*, BUFF[2]]

buffet[2] (buf´ā) *n.* **1** a cupboard or sideboard for the display of plate, china etc. **2** (*dial.*) a low stool, footstool or hassock. **3** a refreshment bar. **4** dishes of food set out on a table from which diners help themselves. **buffet car** *n.* a coach in a train where refreshments are served. [F, etym. unknown]

buffi BUFFO.

bufflehead (bŭf´əlhed) *n.* a black and white duck, *Bucephala albeola*, also called *butterball*. [BUFFALO, HEAD[1]]

buffo (buf´ō) *n.* (*pl.* **buffi** (-ē), **buffos**) a singer in a comic opera. ~*a.* burlesque, comic. [It., comic, burlesque]

buffoon (bəfoon´) *n.* **1** a person who indulges in jests and antics. **2** a vulgar, clowning fool. **buffoonery** *n.* **buffoonish** *a.* [F *bouffon*, It. *buffone*, from *buffa*, a jest (*buffare*, orig. to puff out the cheeks)]

bug[1] (bŭg) *n.* **1** any insect of the order Hemiptera, esp. the blood-sucking, evil-smelling insect, *Cimex lectularius*, found in bedsteads etc. **2** any small insect. **3** (*sl.*) a virus. **4** (*sl.*) a viral infection. **5** a secreted radio receiver. **6** a technical hitch, a flaw, esp. in a computer program. **7** (*coll.*) an obsession, a temporary craze or fashion. **8** a self-important person, a swell. ~*v.t.* (*pres.p.* **bugging,** *past, p.p.* **bugged**) **1** to plant a hidden microphone in or on. **2** (*sl.*) to pester or irritate. **big bug** BIG. **to bug off** (*esp. N Am., sl.*) to go away. **to bug out 1** (*esp. N Am., sl.*) (of eyes) to protrude. **2** (*esp. N Am., sl.*) to depart hurriedly. **bugbane** *n.* a herb of the ranunculaceous genus *Cimifuga*, formerly used as a specific against insect pests. **bug-eyed** *a.* with bulging eyes. **bugged** *a.* **buggy**[1] *a.* (*comp.* **buggier,** *superl.* **buggiest**) infested with bugs. **bughouse** *n.* (*sl.*) an asylum. ~*a.* mad, crazy. [etym. uncertain (perh. OE *budda*, beetle, influ. by BUG[2])]

bug[2] (bŭg) *n.* †a hobgoblin, a bugbear. **bugaboo** (-əboo) *n.* **1** a bugbear, a bogey. **2** a source of worry. **bugbear** (bŭg´beə) *n.* **1** an imaginary object of terror. **2** a nuisance. **3** †a hobgoblin invoked to frighten naughty children. [perh. from Welsh *bwg*, ghost]

bugger (bŭg´ə) *n.* **1** a sodomite. **2** (*sl.*) an unpleasant, difficult or brutish person. **3** (*sl.*) something difficult, disliked, unwanted etc., a nuisance. **4** (*esp. N Am.*) used as a term of affection to a child etc. ~*int.* (*often considered taboo*) used to express annoyance, frustration etc. ~*v.t.* **1** to have anal intercourse with. **2** (*sl.*) to exhaust. **3** (*sl.*) to destroy or spoil. **bugger all** (*sl.*) nothing. **to bugger about** (*sl.*) to muddle about, to interfere with a thing. **to bugger around** (*sl.*) to muddle about, to interfere with a thing. **to bugger off** (*sl.*) to leave. **buggery** *n.* sodomy, anal intercourse. [F *bougre*, L *Bulgarus*, one of a sect of Bulgarian heretics, 11th cent., to whom homosexual practices were attributed]

buggy[1] BUG[1].

buggy[2] (bŭg´i) *n.* (*pl.* **buggies**) **1** a light, four-wheeled or two-wheeled vehicle, having a single seat. **2** a pushchair, a baby buggy. **3** any such light vehicle or carriage (e.g. beach buggy). [etym. uncertain]

bugle[1] (bū´gəl) *n.* **1** (*also* **bugle-horn**) a hunting-horn, orig. made from the horn of a wild ox. **2** a small military trumpet used to sound signals for the infantry. ~*v.t.* **1** to sound by bugle. **2** to call by bugle. ~*v.i.* to sound a bugle. **bugler** *n.* **1** a person who plays a bugle. **2** a soldier who transmits signals on a bugle. **buglet** (-glit) *n.* a small bugle. [OF *bugle*, a wild ox L *būculus*, dim. of *bos bovis*, ox]

bugle[2] (bū´gəl) *n.* a long, slender glass bead, usu. black, for trimming dresses. [etym. unknown]

bugle[3] (bū´gəl) *n.* a creeping plant of the genus *Ajuga*, esp. *A. reptans*. **bugleweed** *n.* an American plant, *Lycopus virginicus*, used as a remedy for blood-spitting. [F, from late L *būgula*]

bugloss (bū´glos) *n.* **1** any of various plants of the borage family, esp. of the genus *Anchusa*, with rough, hairy leaves. **2** viper's bugloss, *Echium vulgare*. [F *buglosse*, L *būglōssa*, Gr. *buglōssos* (*bous*, ox, *glōssa*, tongue)]

buhl (bool), **boule, boulle** *n.* **1** brass, tortoiseshell etc. cut into ornamental patterns for inlaying. **2** work so inlaid. ~*a.* (*attrib.*) inlaid with buhl. [André *Buhl*, or *Boule*, French woodcarver, 1642–1732]

build (bild) *v.t.* (*past, p.p.* **built** (bilt)) **1** to construct, to erect, to make by putting together parts and materials. **2** to have constructed or erected. **3** to establish, to develop. ~*v.i.* **1** to erect a building or buildings. **2** to make a nest. ~*n.* **1** form, style or mode of construction. **2** shape, proportions, figure. **to build in** to incorporate (into a structure etc.). **to build on 1** to found or rely on (as a basis). **2** to add (to a building). **to build up 1** to establish or strengthen by degrees. **2** to block up. **3** to erect many buildings in an area. **4** to praise. **to build upon** to found or rely on. **builder** *n.* **1** a person who builds. **2** a master builder or contractor who erects buildings under the direction of the architect. **builder's merchant** *n.* a tradesperson who supplies building materials to builders. **building** *n.* **1** the act of constructing or erecting. **2** a structure erected to form an enclosure, an edifice. **building line** *n.* a boundary between a house and a street, beyond which the owner may not build. **building site** *n.* an area where building is taking place. **building society** *n.* an organization lending money to contributors enabling them to purchase dwelling houses. **build-up** *n.* **1** a creation of favourable publicity. **2** the leading to the climax in a speech etc. **3** an increase. **built** *a.* constructed, erected, fashioned, formed (*in comb.*, as *well-built*). **built-in** *a.* **1** part of the main structure, e.g. cupboards, wardrobe. **2** fixed, included. **built-in obsolescence** *n.* the prearranged demise of a commodity through deterioration or supersedence by a newer model. **built-up** *a.* **1** having many buildings (of an urban area). **2** increased in height etc. (*built-up heels*). 3 composed of separately prepared parts. [OE *bold*, a house (whence ME *bulden*, *bilden*, to build), from Gmc. *bu-*, to dwell]

bulb (bŭlb) *n.* 1 a subterranean stem or bud sending off roots below and leaves above, as in the onion or lily. 2 a bulbil. 3 a spherical dilatation of a glass tube, as in the thermometer. 4 a light bulb. 5 a spherical swelling of any cylindrical organ or structure. *~v.i.* to take or grow into the form of a bulb. **bulbar, bulbed** *a.* having the form of a bulb. **bulbiferous** (-bif´-) *a.* producing bulbs. **bulbiform** (-bifawm) *a.* **bulbil** (-bil) *n.* a small bulb developed at the side of a larger one, or in an axil. **bulbo-** (bŭl´bō) *comb.form* 1 bulblike. 2 of or relating to the bulb, as *bulbo-tuber*. **bulbo-medullary** *a.* of or relating to the bulb of the spinal marrow. **bulbo-tuber** *n.* a corm. **bulbose** (-bōs) *a.* **bulbous** *a.* 1 of or relating to a bulb. 2 having a bulb or bulbs. 3 bulb-shaped. [F *bulbe*, L *bulbus*, Gr. *bolbos*, onion]

bulbul (bul´bul) *n.* 1 an Eastern bird of the family Pycnonotidae. 2 a singer, a poet. [Pers.]

☒ **bulettin** common misspelling of BULLETIN.

Bulg. *abbr.* Bulgarian.

bulgar (bŭl´gə), **bulgur** *n.* wheat that has been boiled and then dried.

Bulgarian (bŭlgeə´riən) *n.* 1 a native or inhabitant of Bulgaria. 2 the language of Bulgaria. *~a.* of or relating to Bulgaria, its people or language.

bulge (bŭlj) *n.* 1 a swelling on a flat or flattish surface. 2 (*coll.*) a temporary increase in volume or numbers. 3 the bilge of a ship. 4 a projection in a line of military attack or defence. 5 the protuberant part of a cask. *~v.i.* 1 to swell irregularly. 2 to be protuberant. 3 to be full. *~v.t.* 1 to swell out (a bag). 2 to push out of shape. **to get the bulge on** (*sl.*) to get an advantage over (someone). **to have the bulge on** (*sl.*) to have an advantage over (someone). **bulger** *n.* in golf, a brass or driver with a convex face. **bulging** *a.* protuberant. **bulgingly** *adv.* **bulgy** *a.* swollen so as to be clumsy. **bulginess** *n.* [OF *boulge*, *bouge*, L *bulga*; see BUDGET]

bulgur BULGAR.

bulimia (būlim´iə, bul´-), **bulimy** (bū´limi) *n.* 1 a medical condition characterized by overeating. 2 bulimia nervosa. **bulimarexia** (-ərek´siə) *n.* (*esp. N Am.*) bulimia nervosa. **bulimarexic** *a.*, *n.* **bulimia nervosa** (nœvō´sə) *n.* an emotional disorder in which the sufferer alternately overeats and induces vomiting or purging. **bulimic** *a.*, *n.* [Gr. *boulimia* (*bous*, ox, *limos*, hunger)]

bulk[1] (bŭlk) *n.* 1 magnitude of three dimensions. 2 size, great size, mass. 3 the greater portion, the main mass. 4 cargo. 5 a ship's hold or hull. 6 anything of great size. 7 the trunk of the body, esp. if large. *~v.i.* 1 to appear relatively big or important. 2 to amount. *~v.t.* 1 to pile in heaps. 2 to pack in bulk. 3 to measure the bulk of. 4 to make thicker or larger. **in bulk** 1 (of cargo) loose in the hold. 2 in large quantities. **bulk buying** *n.* 1 the purchase of goods in large quantities in order to obtain cheaper prices. 2 the purchase by one customer of the whole of a producer's output. **bulk-buy** *v.t.* **bulk carrier** *n.* a vessel or vehicle which carries a large, undivided cargo. **bulky** *a.* (*comp.* **bulkier,** *superl.* **bulkiest**) 1 of great bulk or dimensions. 2 large. **bulkily** *adv.* **bulkiness** *n.* [prob. from Icel. *būlki*, a heap, a cargo, confused with *bouk*, OE *būc*, belly]

bulk[2] (bŭlk) *n.* a framework projecting in front of a shop for displaying goods. [etym. uncertain]

bulkhead (bŭlk´hed) *n.* an upright partition dividing a ship, aircraft etc. into compartments.

bull[1] (bul) *n.* 1 the uncastrated male of any bovine mammal, esp. of the domestic species, *Bos taurus*. 2 the male of some other large animals, such as the elk, the elephant, the whale. 3 a person who speculates for a rise in stocks (see also BEAR[1]). 4 (**the Bull**) the constellation and sign Taurus. 5 a bull's-eye, a hit in the bull's-eye. 6 (*sl.*) rubbish, nonsense. *~a.* 1 of large size. 2 thickset. 3 coarse. 4 male. *~v.i.* 1 to speculate for a rise (in stocks). 2 (of a cow) to low when in season. *~v.t.* to produce a rise in (stocks etc.). **John Bull** JOHN. **to take the bull by the horns** to grapple with a difficulty boldly. **bull ant** *n.* BULLDOG ANT (under BULL[1]). **bull artist** *n.* (*Austral.*) a swanker, a blowhard. **bull at a gate** *n.* a person who does something in a clumsy way. **bull-baiting** *n.* the baiting of a bull with dogs. **bullboard** *n.* a game like quoits played on board ship with a disc thrown on to numbered squares. **bull calf** (*pl.* **bull calves**) *n.* 1 a male calf. 2 a stupid fellow. **bulldog** *n.* 1 a powerful breed of dogs formerly used to bait bulls. 2 a person who possesses obstinate courage. 3 any of the proctor's attendants at Oxford and Cambridge. 4 a gun or pistol of a certain pattern. **bulldog ant** *n.* (*Austral.*) a large red or black Australian ant with a poisonous bite. **Bulldog clip**® *n.* a metal spring clip for fastening papers together or on to a board. **bull-fiddle** *n.* (*N Am., coll.*) a double bass. **bullfight** *n.* a Spanish sport in which a bull is baited and then killed. **bullfighter** *n.* **bullfighting** *n.* **bullfinch** *n.* 1 a European songbird of the genus *Pyrrhula*, with handsome plumage. 2 a high, quickset hedge with a ditch on one side. **bullfrog** *n.* a large American frog, *Rana catesbiana*, with a deep voice. **bullhead** *n.* 1 the miller's thumb, a small river fish *Cottus gobio*, with a big head. 2 a small shark. 3 an edible freshwater fish. **bull-headed** *a.* 1 with a massive head. 2 stupid. 3 obstinate, impetuous. **bull-headedly** *adv.* **bull-headedness** *n.* **bullhorn** *n.* a loudspeaker. **bull in a china shop** *n.* an indelicate or tactless person, a blunderer. **bullish** *a.* 1 resembling a bull. 2 obstinate. 3 on the Stock Exchange, optimistic. **bullishly** *adv.* **bullishness** *n.* **bull market** *n.* on the Stock Exchange, a market with rising prices, as distinct from *bear market*. **bull-nose, bull-nosed** *a.* (*attrib.*) having a rounded end. **bullock** (-ək) *n.* 1 a castrated bull. 2 an ox. 3 a bovine animal. *~v.i.* (*Austral., New Zeal., coll.*) to work very hard. **bullocky** *n.* (*pl.* **bullockies**) (*Austral., New Zeal., coll.*) the driver of a team of bullocks. **bullpuncher** *n.* (*Austral.*) a cattle-driver. **bull pup** *n.* a young bulldog. **bullring** *n.* 1 an arena for a bullfight. 2 (*Hist.*) a place where bulls used to be baited. **bullroarer** *n.* a thin slat of wood that produces a formidable noise when swung rapidly with a string, now a plaything (orig. used in religious rites of e.g. Australian Aborigines, N American Indians). **bull session** *n.* (*N Am.*) an informal discussion, esp. between men. **bull's-eye** *n.* 1 the centre of a target. 2 something that achieves its aim. 3 a hard, peppermint-flavoured sweet. 4 a hemispherical disc of glass in the side or deck of a ship to give light below. 5 a small round window. 6 a hemispherical lens in a lantern. 7 a lantern with such a lens. 8 a boss of glass in the middle of a blown sheet. **bullshit** *n.* (*sl.*) rubbish, deceptive nonsense. *~v.i.* (*pres.p.* **bullshitting,** *past, p.p.* **bulshitted**) to talk rubbish, to attempt to deceive with nonsense. *~v.t.* to talk nonsense to. **bullshitter** *n.* **bull terrier** *n.* a breed of dog that is a cross between a bulldog and a terrier. **bulltrout** *n.* a variety of sea trout, *Salmo trutta*. [OE *bule* in *bule-hide* (see also BULLOCK (under BULL[1]), from *bulluc*), from *bellan*, to bellow]

bull[2] (bul) *n.* 1 a papal edict. 2 a leaden seal appended to a papal edict. [L *bulla*, a knob, a seal]

bull[3] (bul) *n.* 1 a ludicrous contradiction in terms, supposed to be characteristic of the Irish, an Irish bull. 2 (*sl.*) rubbish, deceptive nonsense. 3 (*N Am., sl.*) a bad blunder. [etym. unknown (cp. OF *boul*, fraud, trickery)]

bull[4] (bul) *n.* drink made by putting water into an empty spirit cask to acquire the flavour of the liquor. [etym. unknown]

bulla (bul´ə) *n.* (*pl.* **bullae** (-ē)) **1** (*Hist.*) a round pendant worn by Roman children. **2** a watery vesicle, a blister. **bullate** (-ət) *a.* blistered, puckered. [L]

bullace (bul´əs) *n.* a wild plum, *Prunus insititia*, having two varieties, one with white, the other with dark fruit. [OF *beloce*, late L *pilota*, L *pila*, a ball]

bulldoze (bul´dōz) *v.t.* **1** to level or clear (ground) using a bulldozer. **2** to force or bully. **to bulldoze one's way** to make one's way by force. **bulldozer** *n.* **1** a power-operated machine with a large blade, employed for removing obstacles, levelling ground and spreading material. **2** a person who bulldozes, a bully. [eytm. uncertain]

bullet (bul´it) *n.* **1** a metal ball or cone used in firearms of small calibre. **2** a small circle used at the start of a printed line, for emphasis. **3** a round missile. **4** a fisherman's sinker. **to bite (on) the bullet 1** to submit to an unpleasant situation. **2** to face up to something. **to get the bullet** (*sl.*) to be dismissed, get the sack. **bullet-head** *n.* **1** a round-shaped head. **2** (*esp. N Am.*) an obstinate person. **bullet-headed** *a.* **bullet-proof** *a.* impenetrable to bullets. **bullet train** *n.* a high-speed passenger train. [F *boulette*, dim. of *boule*, ball, L *bulla*, a round object]

bulletin (bul´ətin) *n.* **1** an official report of some matter of public interest, e.g. of the condition of an invalid. **2** a brief news item on radio or television, a news bulletin. **3** a periodical publication of an organization, society etc. *~v.t.* (*pres.p.* **bulletining**, *past, p.p.* **bulletined**) to announce by bulletin. **bulletin board** *n.* **1** a noticeboard. **2** a system which allows computer users to leave messages and access information. **bulletinist** *n.* [F, from It. *bulletino*, dim. of *bulletta*, a passport, a lottery ticket, dim. of *bulla*; see BULL²]

bullion (bul´yən) *n.* **1** uncoined gold and silver in the mass. **2** solid gold or silver. **3** fringe made of gold or silver wire. *~a.* made of solid gold or silver. **bullionist** *n.* an advocate for a metallic currency. [perh. from F *bouillon*, boiling, soup, med. L *bulliōnem*, acc. of *bullio* (*bullīre*, to boil); or from F *billon*, an ingot, influ. by this]

bully¹ (bul´i) *n.* (*pl.* **bullies**) **1** a blustering, overbearing person. **2** a cowardly tyrant; a person who intimidates or hurts those who don't stand up for themselves. *~a.* jolly, first-rate, capital. *~v.t.* (*3rd pers. sing. pres.* **bullies**, *pres.p.* **bullying**, *past, p.p.* **bullied**) **1** to treat in a tyrannical manner. **2** to tease, oppress, terrorize. *~v.i.* to act as a bully. **bully for you!** (*sometimes iron.*) well done! bravo! **bully boy** *n.* a thug, a hired ruffian. [etym. uncertain; perh. from Dut. *boel*, a lover (cp. MHG *Buole*, G *Buhle*)]

bully² (bul´i), **bully beef** *n.* tinned beef. [BULL¹ or BOUILLI]

bully³ (bul´i) *n.* (*pl.* **bullies**) (*also* **bully off**) in hockey, the starting of a game by striking sticks on the ground and then above the ball three times and then attempting to hit the ball. *~v.i.* (*3rd pers. sing. pres.* **bullies**, *pres.p.* **bullying**, *past, p.p.* **bullied**) to start a game of hockey.

bullyrag BALLYRAG.

bully tree (bul´i) *n.* BALATA. [corr.]

bulrush (bul´rŭsh) *n.* **1** either of two tall rushes growing in water, *Scirpus lacustris* and *Typha latifolia*, the reedmace or cat's-tail. **2** (*Bible*) the papyrus. **bulrushy** *a.* [etym. uncertain; perh. BOLE¹, implying 'strong-stemmed', or BULL¹, big (cp. BULLFROG (under BULL¹) etc.)]

bulwark (bul´wək) *n.* **1** a rampart or fortification. **2** a mole, a breakwater. **3** any shelter, protection, screen. **4** that part of the sides of a ship which rises above the upper deck. *~v.t.* to furnish with or protect as with bulwarks. [formed like Dut. *bolwerk* and G *Bollwerk*, from words represented by BOLE¹, or the MHG v. *boln*, to throw, and WORK]

bum¹ (bŭm) *n.* (*sl.*) **1** the buttocks. **2** (*Hist.*) a bum-bailiff. **bumbag** *n.* (*coll.*) a pouch, usu. fastened with a zip, for holding money and other small personal belongings, worn on a belt round the waist or hips. **bum-bailiff** *n.* (*Hist.*) a bailiff who collected debts or arrested people for non-payment. **bumboy** *n.* (*sl.*) a young male homosexual, esp. a prostitute. **bum fluff** *n.* (*sl.*) a young man's first beard growth. **bum-sucker** *n.* (*sl.*) a toady. **bum-sucking** *n.* [etym. uncertain; cp. BUMP¹; cp. F *pousse-cul*]

bum² (bŭm) *n.* (*esp. N Am., coll.*) **1** a tramp. **2** an idler, a loafer. **3** a scrounger. **4** a rascal, a blackleg. **5** a devotee of a particular form of recreation. **6** (*Hist.*) an irregular forager in the American Civil War. *~a.* **1** useless, broken. **2** worthless. *~v.i.* (*pres.p.* **bumming**, *past, p.p.* **bummed**) **1** to live like a tramp. **2** to idle. **3** to scrounge. *~v.t.* to acquire by scrounging. **on the bum** scrounging, begging. **bummer** *n.* (*esp. N Am., sl.*) **1** a person who or thing which bums. **2** an unpleasant experience. **bum rap** *n.* (*N Am., sl.*) a false charge. **bum's rush** *n.* (*N Am., sl.*) **1** (*preceded by the*) forcible ejection, as from a gathering. **2** (*preceded by the*) dismissal (of an idea or person). **bum steer** *n.* misleading information. [G *Bummler*, a loafer]

bum³ (bŭm) *v.i.* (*pres.p.* **bumming**, *past, p.p.* **bummed**) **1** to make a humming noise. **2** to boom. [onomat.; cp. BOOM¹]

bumalo (bŭm´əlō), **bummalo** *n.* (*pl.* **bumalo, bummalo**) Bombay duck; a small Asian fish, dried and used as a relish. [Marathi *bombīl*, *bombīla*]

Bumble (bŭm´bəl) *n.* **1** a beadle. **2** a self-important official. **bumbledom** *n.* **1** fussy officialism, esp. of parochial officers. **2** parish officers collectively. [*Bumble*, the beadle in Dickens' *Oliver Twist*]

bumble (bŭm´bəl) *v.i.* to buzz, to boom. *~v.t.* **1** to bustle and blunder. **2** to grumble at. *~n.* **1** a jumble, a confused heap. **2** a blunderer, an idler. **bumble-bee** *n.* a large bee of the genus *Bombus*. **bumble-puppy** *n.* **1** a child's game with marbles. **2** a game in which a ball on a string is hit so that it winds around a post to which it is attached. **3** whist or bridge played unscientifically. [imit.; cp. BOOM¹]

bumboat (bŭm´bōt) *n.* a boat used to carry provisions to vessels.

bumf (bŭmf), **bumph** *n.* (*sl.*) **1** toilet paper. **2** (*derog.*) official documents. **3** any unwanted paperwork. [BUM¹, FODDER]

bumiputra (boomipoot´rə) *n.* (*pl.* **bumiputra, bumiputras**) a Malaysian of indigenous Malay origin. *~a.* of or relating to the bumiputra. [Malay from Sansk., son of the soil]

bumkin (bŭm´kin) *n.* **1** a small boom projecting from each bow to extend the foresail. **2** a similar boom for the mainsail or the mizzen.

bummer BUM².

bump¹ (bŭmp) *n.* **1** a thump, a dull, heavy blow, an impact or collision. **2** a swelling. **3** (*Hist.*) a protuberance on the skull, said by phrenologists to indicate distinct faculties or affections. **4** a touch in a bumping race. **5** a sudden movement of an aircraft caused by currents. *~v.t.* **1** to cause to strike forcibly against anything hard or solid. **2** to hurt by striking against something. **3** to hit (against). **4** in boat racing, to strike the boat in front with the prow of one's own boat. **5** (*N Am.*) to displace (esp. a passenger on a flight). *~v.i.* **1** to strike heavily. **2** to collide. **3** to move along with a bump or succession of bumps. *~adv.* **1** with a bump. **2** with a sudden shock. **the bumps** the act of lifting someone up by the arms and legs and dropping them down to the ground. **to bump into** to meet unexpectedly, to encounter accidentally. **to bump off**

(*coll.*) to murder. **to bump up** 1 to increase (prices). 2 to raise. **bumper** *n.* 1 a person who or thing which bumps. 2 a glass filled to the brim, esp. for drinking a toast. 3 the fender of a motor vehicle. 4 a buffer. 5 (*coll.*) anything very large or wonderful or full. 6 a crowded house at the theatre. 7 in whist, a score of two games to nothing. 8 (*Austral.*) a cigarette butt. 9 in cricket, a bouncer. ~*a.* (*coll.*) 1 extraordinary, startling, fine. 2 full to the brim. **bumper car** *n.* a dodgem. **bump-start** *v.t.* 1 to start (a motor vehicle) by pushing it while engaging the gears. 2 to jump-start. ~*n.* 1 a push-start. 2 a jump-start. **bumpy** *a.* (*comp.* **bumpier**, *superl.* **bumpiest**) full of bumps, uneven, jolty. **bumpily** *adv.* **bumpiness** *n.* [onomat.]

bump[2] (bŭmp) *n.* the cry of the bittern. ~*v.i.* to cry like a bittern. [onomat.]

bumph BUMF.

bumpkin (bŭmp´kin) *n.* 1 a country lout. 2 a clumsy, thickheaded person. 3 a bashful person. [prob. Dut. *boomken*, a log]

bumptious (bŭmp´shəs) *a.* disagreeably self-assertive or self-opinionated. **bumptiously** *adv.* **bumptiousness** *n.* [facetious, from BUMP[1]]

bun[1] (bŭn) *n.* 1 a small sweet roll or cake. 2 a compact ball of hair worn at the back of the head. 3 (*pl.*, *N Am.*, *sl.*) the buttocks. **to have a bun in the oven** (*sl.*) to be pregnant. **to take the bun** 1 (*coll.*) to be the best of the lot. 2 (*coll.*) to be incredible. **bun fight** *n.* 1 a crowded tea-party. 2 a disturbance at an assembly. [perh. OF (prov.) *bugne*, fritters]

bun[2] (bŭn) *n.* (*coll.*) 1 a squirrel. 2 a rabbit. [etym. unknown]

Buna® (boo´nə, bū´-) *n.* a type of artificial rubber.

bunce (bŭns) *n.* (*sl.*) extra profit. [etym. unknown]

bunch (bŭnch) *n.* 1 a cluster of several things of the same kind growing or tied together. 2 a tuft, a knot, a bow. 3 a lot, a collection, a pack, a herd. ~*v.t.* 1 to tie up or form into a bunch. 2 to gather into folds. ~*v.i.* to come or grow into a cluster or bunch. **bunch grass** *n.* (*N Am.*) a clumped grass, esp. of the genus *Poa* or *Festuca*. **bunch of fives** *n.* a fist. **bunchy** *a.* (*comp.* **bunchier**, *superl.* **bunchiest**) 1 forming a bunch. 2 growing in bunches. **bunchiness** *n.* [prob. onomat.]

bunco BUNKO.

buncombe BUNKUM.

bund (bŭnd) *n.* an embankment, a dam or causeway. [Hind.]

Bundesrat (bun´dəzraht) *n.* 1 the Upper House of Parliament in Germany or Austria. 2 the federal council of Switzerland. [G *Bund*, confederation, *Rat*, council]

Bundestag (bun´dəztahg) *n.* the Lower House of Parliament in Germany. [G *Bund*, confederation, *tagen*, to confer]

bundle (bŭn´dəl) *n.* 1 a number of things or a quantity of anything bound together loosely. 2 a package, a parcel. 3 a set of rods, wires, fibres, nerves etc., bound together. 4 20 hanks of linen thread. 5 a group of characteristics. 6 (*sl.*) a large amount of money, a bundle of bank notes. ~*v.t.* 1 to tie up in a bundle. 2 to throw hurriedly together. 3 to hustle. 4 to sell as a package. ~*v.i.* 1 to prepare for departure, to pack up, to start hurriedly (in, off, away or out). 2 to sleep (with a person of the opposite sex) without undressing, an old custom in parts of Britain and N America. **to bundle off** 1 to send away hurriedly or unceremoniously. 2 to dismiss. **to bundle up** 1 to gather into a bundle. 2 to clothe warmly. **to go a bundle on** 1 (*sl.*) to like enormously. 2 (*sl.*) to be enthusiastic for. **bundle of nerves** *n.* (*coll.*) a timid, anxious person. **bundler** *n.* [*bund-*, p.p. stem of Gmc. *bindan*, to BIND (cp. MDut. *bondel*, G *Bündel*)]

bundook (bŭn´duk) *n.* a musket or rifle, a gun. [Hind.]

bundu (bun´doo) *n.* (*S Afr.*) the back of beyond, the far interior. [Bantu]

bung[1] (bŭng) *n.* a large cork stopper for a bung-hole. ~*v.t.* 1 to stop with a bung. 2 to close, to shut up. 3 (*sl.*) to throw, to sling. **bunged up** *a.* closed, blocked. **bung-hole** *n.* the hole in the bulge of a cask through which it is filled. [cp. MDut. *bonghe*, *bonde*, *bonne* (Dut. *bon*), L *puncta*, an orifice (fem. p.p. of *pungere*, to prick)]

bung[2] (bŭng) *a.* (*Austral.*, *coll.*) 1 dead. 2 destroyed. 3 useless. **to go bung** 1 to die. 2 to go bankrupt. [Austral. Abor.]

bungalow (bŭng´gəlō) *n.* a one-storeyed house. [Hind. *bāṅglā*, of Bengal]

bungee (bŭn´ji), **bungee cord**, **bungee rope** *n.* an elasticated cord. **bungee jumping** *n.* the sport of jumping off high places with a rubber rope tied round one's ankles or attached to a body harness, the rope stretching to break one's fall only a few feet above the ground. **bungee jump** *n.* **bungee jumper** *n.* [etym. uncertain]

bungle (bŭng´gəl) *v.t.* 1 to botch. 2 to manage clumsily or awkwardly. ~*v.i.* 1 to act clumsily or awkwardly. 2 to fail in a task. ~*n.* 1 botching. 2 mismanagement. **bungler** *n.* **bungling** *a.* clumsy, awkward, unskilful. **bunglingly** *adv.* [prob. imit., cp. BOGGLE, BUMBLE]

bunion (bŭn´yən) *n.* a swelling on the foot, esp. of the joint of the big toe. [perh. from It. *bugnone*, *bugno*, a boil or blain (cp. OF *bugne*, see BUN[1])]

bunk[1] (bŭngk) *n.* 1 a box or recess serving for a bed. 2 a sleeping berth. 3 (*N Am.*) a piece of timber on a sled to support heavy timber. ~*v.i.* to sleep in a bunk. **bunk bed** *n.* either of a pair of narrow beds built one above the other. **bunker** *n.* 1 a container or bin usu. for coal or fuel, e.g. on a ship. 2 an underground bombproof shelter. 3 a sandy hollow or other obstruction on a golf course. ~*v.t.* 1 to fill with fuel. 2 to play into a bunker. **bunkered** *a.* in golf, having hit one's ball into a bunker. **bunkhouse** *n.* a building for labourers to sleep in. [etym. uncertain]

bunk[2] (bŭngk) *v.i.* (*sl.*) to make off, to bolt. ~*n.* a bolt, a making off, an escape. **to bunk off** to play truant. **to do a bunk** to run away. [etym. unknown]

bunk[3] (bŭngk) *n.* BUNKUM.

bunko (bŭng´kō), **bunco** *n.* (*pl.* **bunkos, buncos**) (*N Am.*, *sl.*) a swindling game or confidence trick. ~*v.t.* (*3rd pers. sing. pres.* **bunkos, buncos**, *pres.p.* **bunkoing, buncoing**, *past*, *p.p.* **bunkoed, buncoed**) to swindle.

bunkum (bŭng´kəm), **buncombe** *n.* 1 political claptrap. 2 tall talk, humbug. [*Buncombe* County, N Carolina, the representative of which made a speech in Congress, 1820, merely to please his constituents]

bunny (bŭn´i) *n.* (*pl.* **bunnies**) 1 a rabbit (used by or to children). 2 (*Austral.*, *sl.*) a dupe. **bunny girl** *n.* a waitress in a nightclub who wears a sexually provocative costume including rabbit ears and tail. **bunny-hug**, **bunny-hugging** *n.* a romping kind of dance in which the partners closely embrace each other. [BUN[2], -Y[3]]

Bunsen burner (bŭn´sən), **Bunsen lamp** *n.* a burner or lamp in which air is mingled with gas to produce an intense flame. [Robert Wilhelm *Bunsen*, German chemist, 1811–99]

bunt[1] (bŭnt) *n.* 1 the middle part of a sail, formed into a cavity to hold the wind. 2 the baggy part of a fishing net. **buntline** *n.* a rope passing from the foot-rope of a square sail and in front of the canvas to prevent bellying. [etym. uncertain]

bunt[2] (bŭnt) *n.* a fungus, *Tilletia caries*, which attacks wheat. **bunted, bunty** *a.* [etym. uncertain]

bunt[3] (bŭnt) *v.t.* 1 (of an animal) to butt. 2 to cause (an aircraft) to fly in part of an inverted loop. 3 (*N Am.*) in baseball, to hit (a ball) very gently. ~*v.i.* 1 (*N Am.*) in baseball, to hit a ball very gently. 2 (of an aircraft) to fly in an inverted loop. ~*n.* an instance of bunting. [cp. BUTT[4], BOUNCE]

buntal (bŭn´təl) *n.* straw obtained from the leaves of the talipot palm. [Tagalog]

bunter (bun´tər) *n.* (*Geol.*) new red sandstone. [G *bunter Sandstein*]

bunting[1] (bŭn´ting) *n.* a bird of the family Emberizidae, related to the finches. [etym. uncertain]

bunting[2] (bŭn´ting) *n.* **1** a thin woollen material of which flags are made. **2** a flag. **3** flags collectively (e.g. strung up as decoration). [etym. uncertain]

bunya bunya (bŭnyə bŭn´yə), **bunya** *n.* (*Austral.*) a large conifer, *Araucaria bidwilli*, with edible seeds. [Austral. Abor.]

bunyip (bŭn´yip) *n.* (*Austral.*) **1** the fabulous rainbow serpent that lives in pools. **2** an impostor. [Austral. Abor.]

buoy (boi) *n.* **1** an anchored float indicating a fairway, reef, shoal etc. **2** a lifebuoy. *~v.t.* to place a buoy upon, to mark with a buoy. **to buoy up 1** to keep afloat. **2** to bear up. **3** to bring to the surface. **buoyage** (-ij) *n.* the act of providing with buoys. **buoyancy** (-ənsi) *n.* **1** the ability to float. **2** loss of weight due to immersion in a liquid. **3** power of resisting or recovering from depression, elasticity. **4** lightheartedness. **5** tendency to rise (of stocks, prices etc.). **buoyancy aid** *n.* a sleeveless jacket lined with buoyant material. **buoyant** *a.* **1** tending to float. **2** tending to keep up. **3** elastic, light. **4** easily recovering from depression. **5** light-hearted. **buoyantly** *adv.* [OF *boie* or Dut. *boei*, L *boia*, a fetter]

BUPA (boo´pə) *abbr.* British United Provident Association.

BUR *abbr.* Burma (Myanmar) (IVR).

bur[1] (bœ), **burr** *n.* **1** any prickly or spinous fruit, calyx or involucre. **2** the involucre of the burdock. **3** the catkin or cone of the hop. **4** a knot of excrescence on a tree. **5** the series of markings left in the timber, which are valuable for the effect in polished veneer etc. **6** the husk of the chestnut. **7** a person or thing hard to get rid of. **8** a lump in the throat. **9** a small drill used by dentists and surgeons. **burdock** (-dək) *n.* a coarse plant with prickly flower heads, of the genus *Arctium*, esp. *A. lappa*. **bur oak** *n.* a N American oak, *Quercus macrocarpa*. **bur walnut** *n.* walnut wood containing knots, used as veneer. [cp. Dan. *borre*, burdock]

bur[2] BURR[1].

burb (bœb) *n.* (*usu. in pl., N Am., coll.*) a suburb. [suburb]

Burberry® (bœ´bəri) *n.* (*pl.* **Burberries**) **1** a type of weatherproof cloth or clothing. **2** a raincoat.

burble (bœ´bəl) *v.i.* **1** to talk inconsequentially or excitedly. **2** (of the airflow around a body) to become turbulent. **3** to simmer, to bubble with mirth or other emotion. **4** (*Sc.*) to bubble, gurgle; to flow with a gurgling noise. *~n.* **1** a murmuring noise. **2** excited speech. **burbler** *n.* [imit., cp. BUBBLE]

burbot (bœ´bət) *n.* an eel-like flat-headed freshwater fish, *Lota lota*. [F *bourbotte* (*bourbe*, late L *borba*, Gr. *borboros*, mud)]

burden (bœ´dən), †**burthen** (-dhən) *n.* **1** something borne or carried; a load. **2** a load of labour, sin, sorrow, care, obligation, duty, taxation, expense, fate etc. **3** the principal theme, the gist of a composition of any kind. **4** the carrying capacity of a vessel, tonnage. **5** a refrain, a chorus. *~v.t.* **1** to load. **2** to lay a burden on. **3** to oppress, to encumber. **burden of proof** *n.* the obligation of proving a contention or assertion. **burdenous** *a.* **1** heavy. **2** onerous, oppressive. **burdensome** *a.* **1** hard to bear. **2** grievous, oppressive. **burdensomely** *adv.* **burdensomeness** *n.* [OE *byrthen*, OS *burthinnia*, from Gmc. stem *bur-*, of *beran*, to BEAR[2]]

burdock BUR[1].

bureau (bū´rō) *n.* (*pl.* **bureaux** (-rōz), **bureaus**) **1** a writing table with drawers for papers. **2** (*N Am.*) a chest of drawers. **3** an office. **4** a public office. **5** a government department. **bureau de change** (də shāzh´) *n.* (*pl.* **bureaux de change**) an office or kiosk (e.g. in an airport, railway station) for exchanging currencies. [F, an office, a desk, orig. baize, OF *burel*, dim. of *bure*, drugget, L *burra*, a coarse red cloth, fem. of *burrus* (perh. from Gr. *purrhos*, red)]

bureaucracy (būrok´rəsi) *n.* (*pl.* **bureaucracies**) **1** government by departments of state. **2** centralization of government. **3** officials as a body. **4** rigid adherence to procedure, inflexible government. **bureaucrat** (bū´rəkrat) *n.* **1** a government official. **2** a bureaucratist. **bureaucratic** (-krat´-) *a.* **1** of, relating to or constituting a bureaucracy. **2** tending towards bureaucracy. **bureaucratically** *adv.* **bureaucratism** (-rok´rə-) *n.* advocacy of or adherence to bureaucracy. **bureaucratist** *n.* **bureaucratize** (-rok´rə-), **bureaucratise** *v.t.* to make into a bureaucracy. **bureaucratization** (-zā´shən) *n.* [see BUREAU]

burette (būret´), (*N Am.*) **buret** *n.* a graduated glass tube for measuring small quantities of liquid. [F, dim. of *buire*, a vase (cp. *boire*, to drink)]

burg (bœg) *n.* **1** (*Hist.*) a fortress. **2** (*Hist.*) a walled town. **3** (*N Am., coll.*) a town. [G (cp. BOROUGH)]

burgage (bœ´gij) *n.* (*Hist.*) **1** a tenure by which lands or tenements in towns or cities were held for a small yearly rent. **2** property so held. [med. L *burgāgium*, from *burgus*, G *Burg*]

burganet (bœ´gənet), **burgonet** *n.* (*Hist.*) **1** a light helmet for foot soldiers. **2** a helmet with a visor. [OF *bourguignotte*, from *Bourgogne*, Burgundy]

burgee (bœ´jē) *n.* **1** a kind of small coal suitable for furnaces. **2** a triangular or swallow-tailed flag. [etym. and connection of the two senses doubtful]

burgeois BOURGEOIS[2].

burgeon (bœ´jən), **bourgeon** *v.t.* **1** to sprout, to bud. **2** to begin to grow or develop. *~n.* (*poet.*) a bud, a shoot. [OF *borjon*, prob. from Gmc. stem *bur-* (*beran*, to BEAR[2])]

burger (bœ´gə) *n.* **1** a flat round cake of minced meat or vegetables which is grilled or fried, e.g. *hamburger, beefburger*. **2** a burger served in a bread roll or bun often with a topping, e.g. *cheeseburger, chilliburger*. [ham*burger*]

burgess (bœ´jis) *n.* **1** an inhabitant of a borough possessing full municipal rights, a citizen. **2** a freeman of a borough. **3** (*Hist.*) a Member of Parliament for a borough or a university. **4** (*N Am.*) a borough magistrate or governor. **burgess-ship** *n.* the status of a burgess. [OF *burgeis*, see BOURGEOIS[1]]

burgh (bŭr´ə) *n.* **1** a Scottish town holding a charter. **2** (*Hist.*) a borough. **burghal** (bœ´gəl) *a.* of or relating to a burgh. **burgher** (bœ´gə) *n.* **1** a citizen or inhabitant of a burgh, borough or corporate town, esp. of a Continental town. **2** (*Hist., S Afr.*) a citizen of a Boer republic. **3** a descendant of a Dutch or Portuguese colonist in Sri Lanka. **burghership** *n.* the position and privileges of a burgher. [Sc. (see BOROUGH)]

burglar (bœ´glə) *n.* a person who breaks into premises with intent to commit a felony, esp. theft. **burglarious** (-gleə´ri-) *a.* **burglariously** *adv.* **burglarize, burglarise** *v.t.* (*N Am.*) to enter or rob burglariously. **burglary** *n.* (*pl.* **burglaries**). **burgle** (-gəl) *v.i.* to commit burglary. *~v.t.* to commit burglary on. [Ang.-Lat. *burglātor*, *burgātor*, perh. from ME *burgh-breche*, breach of a borough]

burgomaster (bœ´gəmahstə) *n.* the chief magistrate of a municipal town in Austria, Germany, the Netherlands or Belgium. [Dut. *burgemeester*, see BURG]

burgonet BURGANET.

burgoo (bœgoo´) *n.* (*pl.* **burgoos**) **1** a kind of oatmeal porridge or thick gruel eaten by sailors. **2** (*N Am.*) a thick soup or stew. [etym. uncertain]

burgrave (bœ´grāv) *n.* (*Hist.*) **1** the commandant of a castle or fortified town. **2** a hereditary noble ruling such a town and the adjacent domain. [G (BURG, *Graf*, count)]

burgundy (bœ´gəndi) *n.* (*pl.* **burgundies**) **1** red or white wine made in Burgundy, France. **2** a similar wine from another place. **3** the red colour of burgundy wine. *~a.* of this colour. **Burgundy mixture** *n.* a preparation of soda and copper sulphate used for spraying potatoes in order to destroy disease germs.

burhel BHARAL.

burial (ber´iəl) *n.* **1** the act of burying, esp. of a dead body in the earth; interment. **2** a funeral with burying of the body. **burial ground, burial place** *n.* a place for burying the dead. **burial mound** *n.* a tumulus. **burial service** *n.* a religious service for the burial of the dead. [OE *byrgels*, a tomb, a burying-place (*byrgan*, to bury)]

burin (bū´rin, byaw´-) *n.* **1** the cutting tool of an engraver on copper. **2** a triangular steel tool used by marble-workers. **3** an early Stone Age flint tool. [F, prob. from OHG *Bora*, a borer, through It. *borino*]

burk BERK.

burka (bœ´kə) *n.* the long veil or veiled, loose overgarment worn by Muslim women. [Urdu]

burke (bœk) *v.t.* **1** to kill secretly by suffocation. **2** to smother, to hush up. **3** to shirk (publicity) by suppressing. [*Burke*, an Irishman who (1828) killed many persons by smothering, to sell their bodies for dissection]

Burkitt's lymphoma (bœ´kits) *n.* a malignant tumour of the white blood cells, associated with infection by the Epstein-Barr virus. [Dennis *Burkitt*, British surgeon, 1911–93]

burl[1] (bœl) *n.* **1** a knot or lump in wool or cloth. **2** a knot in wood. *~v.t.* to dress (cloth) by removing knots or lumps. [OF *bourle* (prob. dim. of *bourre*, from late L *burra*, a woollen pad)]

burl[2] (bœl) *n.* (*Sc.*, *New Zeal.*, *Austral.*) **1** a spin (in a motor vehicle). **2** an attempt, a try. [BIRL]

burlap (bœ´lap) *n.* **1** a coarse kind of canvas used for sacking, upholstering etc. **2** a similar, lighter material used for dressmaking and wall-coverings. [etym. uncertain]

burlesque (bœlesk´) *a.* **1** drolly or absurdly imitative. **2** mock-serious or mock-heroic. *~n.* **1** mockery, grotesque imitation. **2** literary or dramatic representation caricaturing other work. **3** (*N Am.*) a form of theatrical variety show characterized by lewd humour, singing and dancing and striptease. *~v.t.* (*pres.p.* **burlesquing,** *past, p.p.* **burlesqued**) **1** to produce a grotesque imitation of. **2** to travesty. **burlesquely** *adv.* **burlesquer** *n.* [F, from It. *burlesco* (*burla*, a trick, banter)]

burletta (bœlet´ə) *n.* **1** a comic opera. **2** a musical farce. [It., dim. of *burla*, see BURLESQUE]

burly (bœ´li) *a.* (*comp.* **burlier,** *superl.* **burliest**) **1** stout, lusty, corpulent. **2** bluff, domineering. **burliness** *n.* [ME *burliche*, prob. from an OE *būrlīc*, suitable for a lady's BOWER[1]]

Burmese (bœmēz´) *n.* (*pl.* **Burmese**) **1** a native or inhabitant of Burma (Myanmar). **2** (*as pl.*) the people of Burma (Myanmar). **3** the language spoken by the people of Burma (Myanmar). *~a.* of or relating to Burma (Myanmar). **Burman** (bœ´mən) *n., a.* **Burmese cat** *n.* a breed of short-coated domestic cat, often dark-brown or blue-grey in colour.

burn[1] (bœn) *v.t.* (*past, p.p.* **burnt** (-t), **burned** (-d)) **1** to consume, destroy, scorch or injure by fire. **2** to subject to the action of fire. **3** to produce an effect on (anything) similar to the action of fire. **4** to treat with heat for some purpose of manufacture etc. **5** to corrode, eat into. **6** to combine with oxygen. **7** to make use of the nuclear energy of (uranium etc.). **8** to cauterize. **9** (*N Am., sl.*) to anger. *~v.i.* **1** to be on fire. **2** to be or become intensely hot. **3** to emit light, to shine. **4** to act with destructive effect. **5** to be bright, to glow with light or colour. **6** to rage, to be inflamed. *~n.* **1** the effect of burning. **2** a burnt place. **3** a firing of a space rocket engine to obtain thrust. **4** (*N Am., Austral., New Zeal.*) the clearing of vegetation by burning; an area cleared in this way. **5** (*sl.*) a cigarette. **6** (*sl.*) a car race. **to burn a hole in one's pocket** (of money) to cause one to want to spend it immediately. **to burn away** to consume entirely by fire. **to burn down** to reduce to ashes. **to burn in** to render indelible by or as by burning. **to burn in effigy** EFFIGY. **to burn low** (of fire) to be nearly out. **to burn off** to remove paint by means of softening with a blowlamp or hot iron. **to burn one's boats/ bridges** to commit oneself to something without possibility of retreat. **to burn one's fingers** FINGER. **to burn out 1** to consume the inside or contents of. **2** (*coll.*) to exhaust or render inoperative through overwork or overheating. **3** to eradicate or expel by burning. **to burn the candle at both ends** CANDLE. **to burn the midnight oil** OIL. **to burn to a cinder** CINDER. **to burn to a crisp** CRISP. **to burn up 1** to destroy, to get rid of, by fire. **2** to blaze, to flash into a blaze. **3** (*coll.*) to drive fast. **4** (*N Am., sl.*) to be furious or make furious. **to go for the burn** (*coll.*) to try to achieve the burning sensation in the muscles produced by strenuous exercise, to exercise hard. **burnable** *a.* **burned up** *a.* (*N Am., sl.*) angry. **burner** *n.* that part of a lamp or gas-jet from which the flame issues. **on the back burner** having low priority. **on the front burner** having high priority. **burning** *a.* **1** in a state of heat. **2** ardent, glowing. **3** vehement, exciting. **4** flagrant. **burning bush** *n.* *Dictamnus albus*, various species of *Euonymus*, and other shrubs with vivid foliage, fruit etc. (from the bush that burned and was not consumed in Exod. iii.2). **burning-glass** *n.* a convex lens used for causing intense heat by concentrating the sun's rays. **burningly** *adv.* **burning-point** *n.* the temperature at which volatile oils ignite, FLASHPOINT (under FLASH). **burning question, burning issue** *n.* one that excites heated discussion or that demands immediate solution. **burning shame** *n.* a flagrant shame. **burn-out** *n.* **1** exhaustion. **2** depression or disillusionment. **burnt-out** *a.* physically or emotionally exhausted. **burnt offering, burnt sacrifice** *n.* an offering or sacrifice to a deity by fire, esp. one offered to God by the Jews. **burnt sienna** *n.* the reddish-brown colour of roasted sienna. **burnt umber** *n.* **1** umber heated so as to produce a much redder brown. **2** the colour of this. **burn up** *n.* **1** (*coll.*) a fast drive in a motor vehicle. **2** the consumption of nuclear fuel in a reactor. [OE *bærnan*, tr., and *biernan*, intr., from Gmc. *brennan* (cp. G *brennen*)]

burn[2] (bœn) *n.* (*chiefly Sc.*) a small stream, a brook. [OE *burna* (cp. Dut. *born*, Goth. *brunna*, G *Brunnen*, Eng. BOURN[1])]

burnet (bœ´nit) *n.* a plant of the genus *Sanguisorba*, with pinkish flower heads. **burnet fly, burnet moth** *n.* a crimson-spotted, greenish-black moth of the family Zygaenidae. **burnet-rose** *n.* the Scottish wild rose. **burnet saxifrage** *n.* a plant, *Pimpinella saxifraga*, with leaves like burnet. [OF *burnete*, BRUNETTE]

burnish (bœ´nish) *v.t.* to polish, esp. by rubbing. *~v.i.* to become bright or glossy. *~n.* polish, gloss, lacquer. **burnisher** *n.* **1** a person who burnishes. **2** a tool for burnishing. [OF *burnir*, *brunir*, to brown, to polish]

burnous (bənoos´), **burnouse** (-ooz´) *n.* a mantle or cloak with a hood, worn by Arabs. [F, from Arab. *burnus*]

burnt BURN[1].

burp (bœp) *n.* a belch. *~v.i.* to belch. *~v.t.* to make (a baby) burp by massaging or patting on the back. **burp gun** *n.* (*N Am., sl.*) an automatic pistol or sub-machine gun. [onomat.]

burpee (bœ´pē) *n.* an exercise that consists of a squat thrust from standing position, and back to this position. [Royal H. *Burpee*, American psychologist, b. 1897]

burr[1] (bœ), **bur** *n.* **1** a whirring noise. **2** a rough sounding of the letter *r*. **3** a rough ridge or edge left on metal or other substance after cutting, punching etc. **4** an electric rotary filing tool. **5** siliceous rock occurring in bands or masses among softer formations. **6** a burrstone, a whetstone. **7** the round, knobby base of a deer's horn. **8** the roughness made by the graver on a copper plate. **9** a triangular hollow chisel. **10** a clinker, a mass of semi-vitrified brick. **11** a washer on a rivet. **12** a nebulous disc or halo surrounding the moon. *~v.t.* to pronounce with a rough sounding of the *r*. *~v.i.* **1** to speak with a burr. **2** to speak indistinctly. **3** to make a whirring noise. **burrstone** *n.* a coarse siliceous rock used for millstones.[etym. uncertain]

burr[2] BUR[1].

burrawang (bŭr´əwang) *n.* (*Austral.*) **1** any of several palmlike trees of the genus *Macrozamia*. **2** a nut from these trees. [Mount *Budawang*, New South Wales]

burrito (bərē´tō) *n.* (*pl.* **burritos**) a tortilla with a filling of beef, cheese, chicken or beans. [Mex. Sp., from *burro*, young donkey]

burro (bŭr´ō) *n.* (*pl.* **burros**) (*esp. N Am.*) a donkey. [Sp.]

burrow (bŭr´ō) *n.* a hole in the ground made by rabbits, foxes etc., for a dwelling-place. *~v.i.* **1** to excavate a burrow for shelter or concealment. **2** to live in a burrow. **3** to hide oneself. **4** to bore or excavate. **5** to investigate (into). **6** to nestle (into). **7** to dig deep while searching (e.g. in a pocket). *~v.t.* to make by means of excavating. **burrow-duck** *n.* the shelduck. **burrower** *n.* **burrowing owl** *n.* an American owl, *Speotyto cunicularia*, which nests in burrows. [prob. var. of BOROUGH]

burry (bœ´ri) *a.* (*comp.* **burrier**, *superl.* **burriest**) **1** characterized by burrs. **2** rough, prickly. [BURR[1], BURR[2]]

bursa (bœ´sə) *n.* (*pl.* **bursas, bursae** (-sē)) a synovial sac found among tendons in the body and serving to reduce friction. **bursal** *a.* **bursar** *n.* **1** a treasurer, esp. of a college. **2** a person who holds a bursary. **bursarial** (-seə´riəl) *a.* **bursarship** *n.* **bursary** *n.* (*pl.* **bursaries**) **1** the treasury of a college or a monastery. **2** an exhibition in a Scottish university. **3** a scholarship. **burse** *n.* **1** a receptacle for the cloth used to cover the sacred Elements. **2** an exhibition, a bursary or the fund for maintaining such. **bursiculate** (-sik´ūlət) *a.* **bursiform** (-sifawm) *a.* **bursitis** (-sī´tis) *n.* inflammation of a bursa. [med. L, bag, purse, from Gr. wineskin]

burst (bœst) *v.t.* (*past, p.p.* **burst**) to break, split or rend asunder with suddenness and violence. *~v.i.* **1** to be broken suddenly from within. **2** to fly open. **3** to issue or rush forth with suddenness and energy or force. *~n.* **1** a sudden and violent breaking forth. **2** a sudden explosion. **3** an outbreak. **4** a spurt, a vigorous fit of activity. **5** a drinking-bout, a spree. **6** a volley of bullets. **bursting at the seams** being too full for comfort. **to burst in 1** to enter suddenly. **2** to interrupt. **to burst out 1** to break out. **2** to exclaim. **to burst up 1** (*coll.*) to go bankrupt. **2** to collapse. **burster** *n.* **1** a person who goes bankrupt or collapses. **2** a machine which separates continuous stationery into single sheets. **burstproof** *a.* (of a door lock) able to withstand an impact. [OE *berstan*, Gmc. *brestan* (cp. Dut. *bersten*, MHG *bresten*, G *bersten*)]

burthen BURDEN.

Burton (bœ´tən) *n.* a beer from a brewery in Burton-on-Trent. **gone for a burton 1** (*sl.*) dead. **2** (*sl.*) absent, missing. [Burton-on-Trent]

burton (bœ´tən), **barton** (bah´-), **burton-tackle** *n.* a small tackle consisting of two or three pulleys. [etym. uncertain]

bury (ber´i) *v.t.* (*3rd. pers. sing. pres.* **buries**, *pres.p.* **burying**, *past, p.p.* **buried**) **1** to place (a corpse) under ground, to inter, to consign to the grave (whether earth or sea). **2** to perform funeral rites for. **3** to put under ground. **4** to consign to obscurity, oblivion etc. **5** to hide, to cover up, to embed. **to bury one's head in the sand** to ignore the facts. **to bury the hatchet** HATCHET. **buried** *a.* **1** that has been buried. **2** occupied deeply, engrossed, absorbed. **burying** *n.* burial. **burying beetle** *n.* a sexton beetle. **burying ground, burying place** *n.* BURIAL GROUND (under BURIAL). [OE *byrgan* (cp. BURIAL)]

bus (bŭs), **'bus** *n.* (*pl.* **buses,** (*N Am.*) **busses**) **1** a large passenger vehicle for transporting members of the public, hotel guests, employees etc., usu. on a set route. **2** (*coll.*) an aeroplane, car etc. **3** a series of conductors in a computer which carry information or power. *~v.i.* (*3rd pers. sing. pres.* **buses,** (*N Am.*) **busses,** *pres.p.* **bussing,** *past, p.p.* **bussed**) to go by bus. *~v.t.* **1** to transport by bus. **2** (*N Am.*) to carry or clear away (dishes) in a café or restaurant. **to miss the bus** (*coll.*) to miss an opportunity, to be too late. **busbar** *n.* **1** in an electric system, a conductor or series of conductors connecting several circuits. **2** (*Comput.*) a bus. **busboy, busgirl** *n.* (*N Am.*) a restaurant employee who clears tables etc. **bus fare** *n.* the payment for a bus journey made by a passenger. **busing, bussing** *n.* (*N Am.*) the practice of transporting children by bus to schools outside their areas to achieve evenly balanced racial numbers in classrooms. **bus lane** *n.* a traffic lane restricted to the use of buses (i.e. the lane closest to the verge or pavement). **busman** (-mən) *n.* (*pl.* **busmen**) the conductor or driver of a bus. **busman's holiday** *n.* (*coll.*) a holiday spent doing one's everyday work. **bus shelter** *n.* a shelter erected at a bus stop to protect waiting passengers against the weather. **bus station** *n.* the place in a town where buses or coaches arrive and leave from. **bus stop** *n.* a place marked by a sign at which buses stop to pick up or let off passengers. [OMNIBUS]

bus. *abbr.* business.

busby (bŭz´bi) *n.* (*pl.* **busbies**) **1** the tall fur cap worn by hussars. **2** a bearskin hat worn by the Guards. [etym. uncertain]

bush[1] (bush) *n.* **1** a thick shrub. **2** a clump of shrubs. **3** a thicket. **4** (*Hist.*) a bunch of ivy used as a tavern sign. **5** uncleared land, more or less covered with wood, esp. in Australasia. **6** anything resembling a bush. **7** the hinterland, the interior, the wild. **8** a thick growth of hair. *~v.t.* **1** to set with bushes in order to prevent poaching. **2** to cover or decorate with bushes. *~v.i.* to grow bushy. **to beat about the bush** BEAT. **to go bush** (*Austral.*) to go into the bush; to leave civilization. **to take to the bush 1** to take refuge in the backwoods. **2** to become a bushranger. **bushbaby** *n.* (*pl.* **bushbabies**) a small nocturnal African primate of the family Lorisidae; a galago. **bush basil** *n.* a herb, *Ocimum minimum*, used in cooking. **bushbuck** *n.* a small bush-dwelling African antelope, *Tragelaphus scriptus*. **bushcat** *n.* the serval. **bushcraft** *n.* a working knowledge of the ways of the bush. **bushed** *a.* **1** (*Austral.*, *New Zeal.*) lost in the bush. **2** (*sl.*) confused. **3** (*sl.*) exhausted. **bushfire** *n.* a usu. fast-spreading fire in the bush. **bush jacket, bush shirt** *n.* a belted upper garment of a lightweight material equipped with large pockets. **bush lawyer** *n.* **1** (*Austral.*, *New Zeal.*) an irregular legal practitioner. **2** (*New Zeal.*) a bramble. **bush league** *n.* (*N Am.*) a minor league. *~a.* (*attrib.*, *coll.*) inferior, unsophisticated. **bush-leaguer** *n.* **bushman** *n.* (*pl.* **bushmen**) **1** a person who lives in the Australian bush. **2** (**Bushman**) a member of a disappearing nomadic people in S Africa. **3** the language of the Bushmen. **bushmanship** *n.* **bushmaster** *n.* a large venomous snake of tropical America, *Lachesis muta*. **bushranger** *n.* (*Hist.*) a person who has taken to the Australian bush and lives by robbing travellers etc. **bushrope** *n.* a wild, vinelike plant in tropical forests. **bush sickness** *n.* a disease of animals caused by a mineral deficiency in old bush country.

bush telegraph *n.* the rapid dissemination of rumours, information etc. **bushveld, bosveld, boschveld** *n.* wooded S African grasslands. **bushwhack** *v.i.* **1** (*N Am., Austral., New Zeal.*) to clear bush. **2** to live or travel in the bush. ~*v.t.* (*N Am.*) to ambush. **bushwhacker** *n.* **1** (*N Am.*) a backwoodsman. **2** a person who clears woods and bush country. **3** an implement for cutting brushwood. **4** (*Austral.*) an inhabitant of the outback, a country bumpkin. **5** (*N Am.*) a guerrilla fighter. **bushwhacking** *n.* **1** clearing a way in the bush. **2** ambushing. **3** living in the manner of a bushwhacker. **bushy** *a.* (*comp.* **bushier,** *superl.* **bushiest**) **1** abounding with bushes. **2** shrubby, thick. **3** growing like a bush. ~*n.* (*pl.* **bushies**) (*Austral., New Zeal., coll.*) a person who lives in the bush. **bushily** *adv.* **bushiness** *n.* [ME *bush, busk,* Icel. *buskr* (cp. Dan. *busk,* OHG *Busc,* G *Busch*), late L *boscus*]

bush[2] (bush) *n.* (*also* **bushing**) the metal lining of an axle-hole or similar orifice. ~*v.t.* **1** to furnish with a bush. **2** to line with metal. **bush metal** *n.* **1** an alloy of copper and tin used for bearings etc. **2** gunmetal. [prob. from MDut. *busse* (Dut. *bus*), late L *buxis,* a box (cp. BOX[1])]

bushel[1] (bush´əl) *n.* **1** a dry measure of 8 gal. (36.37 litres). **2** (*N Am.*) a measure of 64 US pints (35.24 litres) used for dry goods. **to hide one's light under a bushel** to conceal one's skills or talents. **bushelful** *n.* (*pl.* **bushelfuls**). **bushelman, bushelwomen** *n.* (*pl.* **bushelmen, bushelwomen**). [OF *boissel* (F *boisseau*), late L *boisselus, buscellus,* dim. of *busta* (*buxida, buxis,* BOX[1])]

bushel[2] (bush´əl), *v.t.* (*pres.p.* **bushelling,** (*N Am.*) **busheling,** *past, p.p.* **bushelled,** (*N Am.*) **busheled**) to mend or alter. ~*v.i.* to mend or alter clothes. **busheller, busheler** *n.* [N Am. (cp. G *bosseln*)]

bushido (bushē´dō) *n.* the code of honour of the Japanese samurai. [Jap.]

bushing BUSH[2].

busily BUSY.

business (biz´nis) *n.* **1** employment, occupation, trade, profession. **2** serious occupation, work. **3** duty, concern, province. **4** a particular matter demanding attention. **5** (*coll.*) an affair, a matter, a concern, a contrivance. **6** commercial, industrial or professional affairs. **7** commercial activity. **8** buying and selling, bargaining. **9** a commercial establishment. **10** a shop, with stock, fixtures etc. **11** in the theatre, action, as distinct from speech. **big business** BIG. **on business** with a particular (esp. work-related) purpose. **the business** (*coll.*) exactly what is needed. **to have no business to** to have no right to. **to make it one's business** to undertake to do something. **to mean business** to be in earnest. **to mind one's own business** **1** to attend to one's own affairs. **2** to refrain from meddling. **to send someone about their business** to send someone off brusquely or summarily. **business card** *n.* a card printed with a company's name, address and phone number, and the identity of the employee or executive who carries it. **business end** *n.* (*coll.*) the point (of a tool or weapon). **business hours** *n.* fixed hours of work or for transaction of business in a shop, office etc. (esp. 9 a.m. to 5 p.m.). **businesslike** *a.* **1** suitable for or befitting business. **2** methodical, practical. **3** prompt, punctual. **4** energetic. **businessman** (-mən), **businesswoman** *n.* (*pl.* **businessmen, businesswomen**) a person who deals with matters of commerce etc., a person who runs a business. **business park** *n.* an area where businesses and light industry are accommodated. **business person** *n.* a businessman or businesswoman. **business studies** *n.pl.* a college or university course comprising courses relating to business. **business suit** *n.* a lounge suit. [OE *bisigness* (BUSY, -NESS)]

busk[1] (bŭsk) *v.i.* to perform in the street or in a public place, esp. beside a queue in order to collect money. **busker** *n.* an itinerant singer or actor, a street performer. **busking** *n.* [prob. Sp. *buscar,* to seek]

busk[2] (bŭsk) *n.* **1** a stiffening bone or plate in a corset. **2** a corset. **busked** *a.* [MF *busque* (F *busc*), etym. uncertain]

†**busk**[3] (bŭsk) *v.t.* to prepare, to dress. ~*v.i.* to get ready, to dress oneself. [prob. from Icel. *būask* (*būa -sk,* refl. of *būa,* to get ready), to get oneself ready]

buskin (bŭs´kin) *n.* **1** (*Hist.*) a kind of high boot reaching to the calf or knee. **2** the thick-soled boot worn by actors in Athenian tragedy. **3** the tragic vein. **4** tragedy. **buskined** *a.* **1** wearing buskins. **2** tragic, lofty, sublime. [cp. Sp. *borcegui,* It. *borzacchino,* F *brodequin,* OF *bousequin* (etym. uncertain)]

buss[1] (bŭs) *n.* (*esp. N Am., coll.*) a loud kiss. ~*v.t.* to kiss. [onomat. (ME *bass,* cp. F *baiser,* L *bāsiāre,* to kiss, from *bāsium,* a kiss)]

buss[2] (bŭs) *n.* a herring boat with two or three masts. [OF *busse* (cp. Dut. *buis,* med. L *bussa,* MHG *Buze,* G *Büse*)]

bust[1] (bŭst) *n.* **1** a sculptured representation of the head, shoulders and breast of a person. **2** the upper front part of the body, the breast, the bosom, esp. of a woman. **busted**[1] *a.* having breasts. **busty** *a.* (*comp.* **bustier,** *superl.* **bustiest**) (*coll.*) having large breasts. **bustiness** *n.* [F *buste,* It. *busto,* late L *bustum,* etym. unknown]

bust[2] (bŭst) *v.i.* (*past, p.p.* **busted, bust**) (*coll.*) to break or burst. ~*v.t.* **1** (*sl.*) to raid or arrest, esp. for a drug offence. **2** (*esp. N Am.*) to reduce to a lower rank; to dismiss. ~*n.* **1** (*sl.*) a drinking spree. **2** a police raid. **3** a bankruptcy. **4** (*esp. N Am.*) a punch or hit. **5** a worthless thing. **6** a bad hand in a card game. ~*a.* **1** broken, burst. **2** (*also* **busted**) bankrupt. **to bust up** **1** to quarrel and separate. **2** to bring or come to collapse. **to go bust** to go bankrupt. **busted**[2] *a.* bust. **buster** *n.* **1** something big, something astonishing. **2** a spree. **3** a dashing person. **4** (*Austral.*) a gale. **5** (*sometimes derog., coll.*) a form of address to a boy or man. **6** (*sl.*) a person who or thing which breaks or destroys. **bust-up** *n.* **1** a quarrel. **2** a collapse. [dial., var. of BURST]

bustard (bŭs´təd) *n.* any large bird of the family Otididae, allied to the plovers and the cranes. [prob. from OF *bistarde,* confused with *oustarde,* both from L *avis tarda,* slow bird (perh. due to perversion of Gr. *ōtis*)]

busted[1] BUST[1].

busted[2] BUST[2].

bustee (bŭs´tē) *n.* in the Indian subcontinent, a settlement or a collection of huts. [Hind. *bastī,* dwelling]

bustier (bŭs´tiā, bus´-) *n.* a strapless bodice. [F]

bustle[1] (bŭs´əl) *n.* **1** activity with noise and excitement. **2** stir, agitation, fuss. ~*v.i.* **1** to be active, esp. with excessive fuss and noise. **2** to make a show of activity. ~*v.t.* to make hurry; to hustle, to cause to move quickly or work hard. **bustler** *n.* [prob. onomat., or var. of *buskle,* from BUSK[1]]

bustle[2] (bŭs´əl) *n.* (*Hist.*) a pad, cushion or framework, worn under a woman's dress to expand the skirts behind. [etym. uncertain; perh. from BUSTLE[1]]

busy (biz´i) *a.* (*comp.* **busier,** *superl.* **busiest**) **1** fully occupied. **2** actively employed. **3** closely engaged, diligent. **4** characterized by activity, unresting, always at work. **5** fussy, officious, meddlesome. **6** (of a phone line) engaged. ~*v.i.* (*3rd pers. sing. pres.* **busies,** *pres.p.* **busying,** *past, p.p.* **busied**) to occupy oneself (about, in etc.). ~*v.t.* to make or keep busy. ~*n.* (*pl.* **busies**) (*sl.*) a detective; a police officer. **busily** *adv.* **busy bee** *n.* a busy worker. **busybody** *n.* (*pl.* **busybodies**) **1** an officious person. **2** a meddler. **3** a mischief-maker. **busy Lizzie** (liz´i) *n.* a popular flowering house plant, *Impatiens walleriana,* with red, pink or white flowers.

busyness *n.* the state of being busy. [OE *bysig* (*bisgian*, to occupy, to worry)]

but (bŭt) *prep.* **1** except, barring. **2** (*Sc.*) apart from, outside of. *~conj.* **1** yet still. **2** notwithstanding which. **3** except that. **4** otherwise than, not that. **5** on the contrary, nevertheless, however. *~n.* **1** a verbal objection. **2** (*Sc.*) an outer room. *~adv.* **1** only. **2** (*Sc.*) outwards. **3** (*Austral., New Zeal., Sc.*) though, however. *~v.t.* to raise an objection. **but for** were it not for. **but me no buts** bring forward no objections. **but that** were it not that. **but yet** however, on the other hand. **but and ben** *n.* (*Sc.*) a two-roomed cottage. [OE *būtan*, *būte* (BE-, *utan*, OUT), outside, beyond, except]

butadiene (būtədī´ēn) *n.* the gas used in making synthetic rubber. [L *butyrum*, butter]

butane (bū´tān) *n.* an inflammable gaseous compound; a hydrocarbon of the paraffin series found in petroleum.

butch (buch) *a.* (*sl.*) masculine in manner or appearance. *~n.* (*derog.*) **1** a lesbian with masculine manners or appearance. **2** the more dominant or masculine partner in a lesbian relationship. **3** a tough, aggressive man. [prob. a contr. of BUTCHER]

butcher (buch´ə) *n.* **1** a person whose trade it is to slaughter domestic animals for food. **2** a person who sells the flesh of such animals. **3** a person who delights in killing. **4** a salmon fly. **5** (*used possessively, sl.*) a look (rhyming slang, *butcher's hook*). *~v.t.* **1** to slaughter (animals) for food. **2** to put to death in a wanton or sanguinary fashion. **3** to spoil by bad playing, acting, reading, editing etc. **4** to criticize savagely. **the butcher, the baker, the candlestick maker** all and sundry. **butcher-bird** *n.* **1** a shrike (family Laniidae). **2** a similar bird of the Australasian family Cracticidae. **butcherly** *adv.* **butcher meat, butcher's meat** *n.* the flesh of animals killed for food, sold fresh by butchers. **butcher's broom** *n.* a prickly, evergreen British shrub, *Ruscus aculeatus.* **butcher's knife** *n.* a carving-knife. **butchery** *n.* (*pl.* **butcheries**) **1** the business of a butcher. **2** a slaughterhouse. **3** cruel and remorseless slaughter, carnage. [OF *bochier*, orig. a purveyor of goat's flesh (F *bouchier*), *boc*, a he-goat]

butene (bū´tēn) *n.* BUTYLENE (under BUTYL).

butler (bŭt´lə) *n.* **1** a servant in charge of the wine, plate etc. **2** a head servant. **butlership** *n.* **butlery** *n.* (*pl.* **butleries**) **1** a butler's pantry. **2** a buttery. **buttle** (bŭt´əl), **butle** *v.i.* to work as a butler. [OE *butuiller*, (OF *bouteillier*), med. L *buticulārius*, from *buticula*, BOTTLE[1]]

butt[1] (bŭt) *n.* **1** the hinder, larger or blunter end of anything, esp. of a tool, weapon and the like. **2** the stout part of tanned ox-hides. **3** the square end of a piece of timber coming against another piece. **4** the joint so formed. **5** the bole of a tree. **6** the base of a leaf-stalk. **7** (*N Am., sl.*) the buttocks. *~v.i.* **1** (of timber, planks etc.) to abut, to meet with the end (against). **2** to meet end to end. **butt-end** *n.* **1** the thick and heavy end. **2** the remnant. **butt hinge** *n.* a kind of hinge screwed to the edge of the door and the abutting edge of the casing. **butt joint** *n.* a joint in which the pieces come square against each other. **butt weld** *n.* a weld formed by forcing together flat iron or steel bars. [prob. Eng. (cp. Icel. *buttr*, short, *būtr*, a log, Dan. *but*, Swed. *butt*, Dut. *bot*, stumpy)]

butt[2] (bŭt) *n.* **1** a large cask. **2** a measure of 126 gall. (572.8 litres) of wine, or 108 gall. (490.98 litres) of beer. [OF *boute* (F *botte*), late L *butis*, *buttis*, a cask]

butt[3] (bŭt) *n.* **1** a goal. **2** a target, a mark for shooting. **3** the mound behind targets, the shelter for the marker. **4** (*pl.*) the distance between the targets, the shooting-range. **5** aim, object. **6** a target for ridicule, criticism or abuse. [F *but*, a goal]

butt[4] (bŭt) *v.i.* to strike, thrust or push with the head or as with the head. *~v.t.* to strike or drive away with or as with the head or horns. *~n.* a push with the head. **to butt in** to interfere, interrupt. **to butt out 1** (*esp. N Am., sl.*) to stop interfering. **2** (*N Am., sl.*) to stop doing something. **butter**[1] *n.* an animal which butts. [OF *boter* (F *bouter*), to push, thrust; senses modified by BUTT[1] in verbal sense and by ABUT]

butt[5] (bŭt) *n.* a flatfish of various kinds. [cp. Swed. *butta*, turbot, Dut. *bot*, G *Butt*, flounder]

butte (būt) *n.* (*N Am.*) an abrupt, isolated hill or peak. [prob. from F *butte*, OF *bute*, fem. form of *but*, see BUTT[3]]

butter[1] BUTT[4].

butter[2] (bŭt´ə) *n.* **1** the fatty portion of milk or cream solidified by churning. **2** a substance of the consistency or appearance of butter. **3** gross flattery. *~v.t.* **1** to spread or cook with butter. **2** to flatter grossly. **to butter up** (*coll.*) to flatter. **to look as if butter wouldn't melt in one's mouth** to look innocent. **butter-and-eggs** *n.* any of several plants with two shades of yellow in the flower, esp. yellow toadflax. **butterball** *n.* **1** a piece of butter shaped into a ball. **2** (*N Am.*) BUFFLEHEAD. **3** (*N Am., sl.*) a chubby or fat person. **butter-bean** *n.* **1** a variety of lima bean. **2** a yellow-podded bean. **butter-bird** *n.* in Jamaica, the bobolink. **butter boat** *n.* a vessel for sauce. **butter bur, butter burdock** *n.* a plant of the genus *Petasites*, which has large soft leaves. **butter-cream** *n.* a mixture of butter and sugar used as icing or cake-filling. **buttercup** *n.* a plant of the genus *Ranunculus*, esp. those species with yellow cup-shaped flowers. **buttered** *a.* **butterfat** *n.* the fat in milk from which butter is made. **butter-fingered** *a.* apt to let things fall, as if the hands were greasy. **butter-fingers** *n.* (*coll.*) a person who is butter-fingered. **butterfish** *n.* (*pl. in general* **butterfish**, *in particular* **butterfishes**) GUNNEL[1]. **butterfly** *n.* (*pl.* **butterflies**) **1** an insect with erect wings and knobbed antennae belonging to the diurnal Lepidoptera. **2** a showily dressed, vain, giddy or fickle person. **3** (*in full* **butterfly stroke**) a swimming stroke performed on the front and characterized by simultaneous wide, upward strokes of the arms. **4** (*pl., coll.*) nervous tremors. **butterflies in the stomach** (*coll.*) nervous tremors in the stomach. **butterfly bush** *n.* a buddleia, esp. *Buddleia davidii.* **butterfly fish** *n.* a fish resembling a butterfly, esp. *Blennius ocellatus*, or any brightly coloured fish of the family Chaetodontidae. **butterfly net** *n.* a fine net attached to a pole, used for catching butterflies. **butterfly nut, butterfly screw** *n.* a screw with a thumb-piece, a wing nut. **butterfly valve** *n.* a valve with two hinged pieces. **butter-icing** *n.* butter-cream. **butter knife** *n.* a small knife with a rounded blade for cutting butter. **buttermilk** *n.* that part of the milk which remains when the butter is extracted. **butter muslin** *n.* a fine loosely woven, cotton material used for protecting food from insects. **butternut** *n.* **1** the N American white walnut tree, *Juglans cinerea*, and its fruit. **2** the S American genus *Caryocar.* **butter-print, butter-stamp** *n.* a piece of carved wood to mark butter. **butterscotch** *n.* a kind of toffee made with butter. **butter tree** *n.* any of several Asian and African trees, esp. *Bassia butyracea*, and *B. parkii*, which yield a sweet buttery substance. **butterwort** *n.* a British bog plant belonging to the genus *Pinguicula*, esp. *P. vulgaris.* **buttery**[1] *a.* having the qualities or appearance of butter. **butteriness** *n.* [OE *butere*, L *būtyrum*, Gr. *bouturon* (*bous*, an ox, *turos*, cheese)]

buttery[1] BUTTER[2].

buttery[2] (bŭt´əri) *n.* (*pl.* **butteries**) **1** a room in which liquor and provisions are kept. **2** the room in which ale, bread, butter etc. are kept, esp. in a university. **buttery hatch** *n.* the half-door over which provisions are served out from the buttery. [OF *boterie*, *bouterillerie*; see BOTTLE[1]]

buttie BUTTY[2].
buttle BUTLER.
buttock (bŭt´ək) *n.* (*usu. in pl.*) **1** either of the protuberant parts of the rump, the posterior. **2** a manoeuvre in wrestling. *~v.t.* in wrestling, to throw by means of the buttock or hip. [BUTT[1], -OCK]
button (bŭt´ən) *n.* **1** a knob or disc used for fastening or ornamenting garments. **2** a small bud. **3** a small handle, knob, fastener, catch etc. for securing doors, actuating electrical apparatus etc. **4** the knob on a foil. **5** a small disc-shaped object. *~a.* (of mushrooms, blooms etc.) having a small round shape. *~v.t.* **1** to fasten or furnish with buttons. **2** to secure by means of buttons or a buttoned garment. *~v.i.* to fasten up the clothes with buttons. **not to care a button** to be quite indifferent about something. **not worth a button** of no value. **on the button** (*esp. N Am., sl.*) precisely. **the button** a button which, when pushed, puts the apparatus for nuclear war into operation. **to button one's lip** (*sl.*) to stay silent. **button-back** *n.* a chair or sofa with a quilted back set with buttons. **buttonball tree** *n.* the N American plane tree, *Platanus occidentalis.* **button chrysanthemum** *n.* a variety of chrysanthemum which has small flowers. **button-down** *a.* (of a collar) with points buttoned to the shirt. **buttoned** *a.* **buttoned up 1** (*coll.*) formal and inhibited. **2** (*coll.*) silent. **buttonhole** *n.* **1** a hole, slit or loop to admit a button. **2** a small bouquet for the buttonhole of a coat. *~v.t.* **1** to hold by the buttonhole. **2** to detain in conversation. **3** to make buttonholes in. **buttonholer** *n.* (*coll.*) a person who detains in conversation. **buttonhole stitch** *n.* a looped stitch used on buttonholes. **buttonhook** *n.* a hook for drawing buttons through buttonholes. **buttonless** *a.* **buttonlessness** *n.* **button-mould** *n.* a disc of metal or other substance to be covered with cloth, so as to form a button. **buttons** *n.* (*coll.*) a page in buttoned livery. **button-through** *a.* (of a garment) having button fastenings from top to bottom. **buttonwood tree** *n.* BUTTONBALL TREE (under BUTTON). **buttony** *a.* **1** like a button. **2** having many buttons. [OF *boton* (F *bouton*), perh. from late L *botto -ōnem*, from *bottare* or *buttare*, to thrust, sprout]
buttress (bŭt´ris) *n.* **1** a structure built against a wall to strengthen it. **2** a prop, support. **3** a spur or supporting ridge of a hill. *~v.t.* to support by or as by a buttress. [prob. from OF *bouterez*, pl. of *bouteret*, a prop (*bouter*, to push against)]
butty[1] (bŭt´i) *n.* (*pl.* **butties**) (*dial.*) **1** a partner, companion, a mate. **2** (*Hist.*) a middleman in the mining districts. **3** a barge towed by another. **butty-gang** *n.* a body of workers who undertake a job and are paid in a lump sum. **butty-system** *n.* the letting of work to a body of workers who divide the proceeds. [etym. uncertain; perh. a corr. of BOOTY]
butty[2] (bŭt´i), **buttie** *n.* (*pl.* **butties**) (*dial.*) a sandwich, a snack. [from BUTTERY or BUTTERED (under BUTTER[2])]
butyl (bū´tīl, -til) *n.* any of four isomeric forms of the chemical group C_4H_9. **butylene** (bū´tilēn) *n.* a colourless gas, formula C_4H_8. **butyl rubber** *n.* a synthetic rubber used in tyres and as a waterproofing material.
butyraceous (būtirā´shəs) *a.* of the nature or consistency of butter. **butyrate** (bū´tirət) *n.* a salt of butyric acid. **butyric** (-tir´-) *a.* of or relating to butter. **butyric acid** *n.* a colourless acid occurring in butter and other fats. **butyrine** (bū´tirīn) *n.* an oily liquid, obtained by the action of butyric acid on glycerine. **butyro-** (bū´tirō) *comb. form* butter. **butyro-acetic** *a.* applied to a combination of butyric and acetic acid. [L *būtyrum*]
buxom (bŭk´səm) *a.* **1** (of women) plump and comely. **2** blithe, jolly, full of health and spirits. **3** (of women) full-bosomed. **4** †obedient, submissive. **5** †pliant, flexible. **buxomly** *adv.* **buxomness** *n.* [ME *buhsum*, from OE *būgan*, to bow, to bend]
buy (bī) *v.t.* (*past, p.p.* **bought** (bawt)) **1** to purchase, to procure by means of money or something paid as a price. **2** to gain by bribery. **3** to redeem. **4** (*sl.*) to believe. *~n.* (*coll.*) a purchase. **to buy in 1** to buy back for the owner (at an auction). **2** to obtain a stock of (anything) by purchase. **3** to purchase (stock) and charge the extra cost to the person who had undertaken to deliver it. **to buy into** to purchase a share of or interest in (e.g. a company). **to buy it** (*sl.*) to be killed. **to buy off 1** to pay a price to for release or non-opposition. **2** to get rid of by a payment. **to buy out 1** to purchase the release of (a member of the forces) from service. **2** to buy a majority share in or complete control over (e.g. a property, a company), thereby dispossessing the original owner(s). **3** to buy off. **to buy over** to bribe. **to buy time** to delay something. **to buy up** to purchase all the available stock of. **buyable** *a.* **buy-back** *n.* the buying back of something by agreement. **buyer** *n.* a person who buys, esp. one who buys stock for a mercantile house. **buyer's market, buyers' market** *n.* a market favourable to buyers, i.e. when supply exceeds demand. **buy-in** *n.* an act of buying something in. **buyout** *n.* an act of buying somebody or something out. [OE *bycgan* (cp. Goth. *bugjan*, OS *buggean*)]
buzz (bŭz) *n.* **1** a sibilant hum, like that of a bee. **2** a confused, mingled noise. **3** stir, bustle, movement. **4** report, rumour. **5** (*sl.*) a telephone call. **6** (*sl.*) a euphoric feeling, a boost. *~v.i.* **1** to make a noise like humming or whirring. **2** to whisper, to circulate a rumour. **3** to signal by electric buzzer. *~v.t.* **1** to tell in a low whisper. **2** to spread abroad secretly. **3** (*coll.*) in aviation, to interfere with by flying very near to. **4** to make a telephone call to. **5** to signal with a buzzer. **6** (*coll.*) to throw with some violence. **to buzz about** to hover or bustle about in an annoying manner. **buzz-bomb** *n.* a flying bomb. **buzzer** *n.* **1** a buzzing insect. **2** a whisper. **3** a steam or electric apparatus for making a loud humming noise. **4** an electric warning apparatus that makes a buzzing sound. **5** a morse transmitter. **buzzing** *a.* **buzzingly** *adv.* **buzz off** *int.* (*sl.*) go away! **buzz-saw** *n.* (*N Am.*) a circular saw. **buzzword** *n.* (*sl.*) a vogue word adopted from the jargon of a particular subject or discipline. [onomat.]
buzzard[1] (bŭz´əd) *n.* **1** a bird of prey, esp. of the genus *Buteo.* **2** (*N Am.*) a vulture, esp. the turkey buzzard *Cathartes aura.* **3** a blockhead, a dunce. [OF *busard*, L *buteo*]
buzzard[2] (bŭz´əd) *n.* **1** any large nocturnal insect. **2** a stupid blunderer. [BUZZ, -ARD]
BVM *abbr. Beata Virgo Maria*, Blessed Virgin Mary. [L]
b/w *abbr.* black and white.
bwana (bwah´nə) *n.* (in Africa) sir, master. [Swahili, from Arab. *abūna*, our father]
BWI *abbr.* (*Hist.*) British West Indies.
BWR *abbr.* boiling water reactor.
by (bī) *prep.* **1** near, at, in the neighbourhood of, beside, along, through, via. **2** with, through (as author, maker, means, cause). **3** according to, by direction, authority or example of. **4** in the ratio of. **5** to the amount of. **6** during, not later than, as soon as. **7** concerning, with regard to. **8** sired by. *~adv.* **1** near at hand. **2** in the same place. **3** aside, in reserve. **4** past. *~a.* **1** side, subordinate, secondary, of minor importance. **2** private, secret, clandestine, sly. *~n.* (*pl.* **byes**) BYE[1]. **by and by 1** soon, presently. **2** later on. **3** (*N. Am.*) the future, time to come. **by and large** on the whole. **by oneself 1** alone, without help. **2** of one's own initiative. **by the by/ bye** by the way. **by the way** casually, apart from the main subject. **by-** *pref.* **1** (*also* **bye-**) subordinate, secondary. **2** near. **by-bidder** *n.* a person who bids at an auction with the view of running up the price. **by-blow** *n.* **1** a side blow. **2** the illegitimate child of a man.

by-election *n.* an election caused by the death or resignation of a member. **bygone** *a.* past. *~n.* 1 a past event. 2 (*pl.*) the past. 3 (*pl.*) past injuries. **let bygones be bygones** let us think no more of past injuries. **by-lane** *n.* a lane leading off the main road. **byline** *n.* 1 a sideline. 2 the name of the author of a newspaper or magazine article printed beside it. 3 in football, a touchline. **byname** *n.* a nickname. **bypass** *n.* 1 a road for the purpose of diverting traffic from crowded areas. 2 a pipe passing round a tap or valve, so as to leave a gas burner etc. alight. 3 a passage that allows blood to avoid blocked or damaged arteries. 4 a cutting-out of undesirable radio frequencies. *~v.t.* 1 to avoid, evade. 2 to go around. 3 to cause to use a bypass. 4 to supply a bypass. **bypass surgery** *n.* a coronary bypass. **bypath** *n.* 1 a private or unfrequented path. 2 an obscure branch of a subject. **byplay** *n.* action carried on aside while the main action is proceeding. **by-product** *n.* 1 a secondary product. 2 a secondary result. **by-purpose** *n.* an incidental purpose, esp. in manufacture. **byroad** *n.* a road little frequented. **bystander** *n.* 1 a person standing near. 2 an onlooker, an eyewitness. **bystreet** *n.* an out-of-the-way or little frequented street. **byway** *n.* 1 a bypath. 2 a secret or obscure way. 3 a short cut. 4 an out-of-the-way side of a subject. **byword** *n.* 1 a person or thing noted for a particular characteristic. 2 a common saying. 3 a proverb. 4 an object of general contempt. 5 a nickname. **bywork** *n.* work done apart from one's regular occupation. [OE *be, bi* (cp. OHG *bī, pī*, G *bei*, Goth. *bi*, L *ambi*, Gr. *amphi*)]

bye[1] (bī) *n.* 1 a subsidiary object. 2 something of an incidental or secondary kind. 3 in cricket, a run scored when the ball passes the batsman and wicket-keeper. 4 in golf, holes left over after the end of contest and played as a new game. 5 a goal at lacrosse. 6 an individual left without a competitor when the rest have been drawn in pairs, an odd man. 7 the case of being odd man. 8 an event not in the list of sports. **by the bye** BY. [BY]

bye[2] (bī), **bye-bye** (-bī´) *int.* (*coll.*) goodbye.

bye- BY- (under BY).

bye-byes (bī´bīz) *n.* sleep, bedtime, bed (used by or to children).

Byelorussian BELORUSSIAN.

byke BIKE[1].

by-law (bī´law), **bye-law** *n.* 1 a private statute made by the members of a corporation or local authority. 2 a rule adopted by an incorporated or other society. [formerly *birlaw, burlaw*, from Icel. *baer, byr*, village (cp. *baejar-lög*, a town-law, Dan. *bylov*, municipal law)]

BYOB *abbr.* bring your own bottle.

byre (bīə) *n.* a cowshed. [OE *byre*, a hut; prob. var. of *būr*, BOWER[1]]

Byronic (bīron´ik) *a.* 1 like Lord Byron or his poetry. 2 theatrical, moody. 3 affecting volcanic passion, gloom or remorse. 4 (of a man) handsomely dark, dangerously attractive to women. **Byronically** *adv.* **Byronism** (bī´-) *n.* [Lord *Byron*, British Romantic poet, 1788–1824]

byssus (bis´əs) *n.* (*pl.* **byssuses, byssi** (-ī)) 1 a textile fabric of various substances. 2 the fine linen of the Scriptures. 3 the tuft of fibres by which molluscs of the genus *Pinna* attach themselves to other bodies. 4 the threadlike stipe of some fungi. **byssaceous** (-ā´shəs), **byssoid** (-oid) *a.* consisting of fine threads. **byssal** *a.* relating to a mollusc's byssus. **byssiferous** (-sif´-) *a.* producing a byssus. **byssine** (-īn) *a.* 1 made of fine flax. 2 like byssus. **byssinosis** (-inō´sis) *n.* a lung disease contracted by cotton workers. [L, from Gr. *bussos*, a fine flax]

byte (bīt) *n.* (*Comput.*) a series of usu. eight binary digits treated as a unit. [BIT[3]]

Byz. *abbr.* Byzantine.

byzant BEZANT.

Byzantine (bīzan´tīn, biz´əntīn, -tēn) *a.* 1 of or relating to Byzantium or Istanbul (formerly Constantinople). 2 hierarchical, inflexible. 3 convoluted, complex. 4 belonging to the style of architecture developed in the Eastern Empire, characterized by the round arch, the circle, the dome and ornamentation in mosaic. *~n.* 1 an inhabitant of Byzantium. 2 a bezant. **Byzantine Church** *n.* the Greek or Eastern Orthodox Church. **Byzantine Empire** *n.* the Eastern Empire (AD 395–1453). **Byzantinesque** (-esk´) *a.* **Byzantinism** *n.* **Byzantinist** *n.* a specialist in Byzantine history, arts etc. [L *Byzantīnus*]

bz., bz *abbr.* benzene.

C

C[1] (sē), **c** (*pl.* **Cs, C's**) the third letter of the English and other versions of the Roman alphabet. Before *a, o, u, l* and *r* it is pronounced as a voiceless velar plosive like *k*, and before *e, i* and *y* like the voiceless dental fricative or soft sibilant *s* (when it has this sound before other letters it is marked *ç* in some other European alphabets). ~*symbol* **1** the third in a range of series, the third highest in the range, e.g. of marks, etc. **2** the third known quantity in an algebraic expression. **3** the first note of a diatonic scale in a composition where the keynote is C; the natural major mode. **4** 100 in Roman numerals. **5** a particular computer programming language. **6** the speed of lightning in a vacuum. **C3** *n.* (*Mil.*) the lowest category of a medical board. ~*a.* (of a person) of poor physique. **C clef** *n.* the soprano, alto or tenor clef.

C[2] *abbr.* **1** capacitance. **2** Cape. **3** Catholic. **4** Celsius, Centigrade. **5** century. **6** Conservative. **7** (*also* ©) copyright. **8** coulomb.

C[3] *chem. symbol* carbon.

c *abbr.* **1** caught. **2** cent. **3** centi-. **4** century. **5** chapter. **6** cold. **7** colt. **8** cubic.

c., ca. *abbr.* about. [L *circa*]

c/- *abbr.* (*Austral., New Zeal.*) care of.

CA *abbr.* **1** California. **2** (*Sc., Can.*) chartered accountant. **3** Consumers' Association.

Ca *chem. symbol* calcium.

ca. C.

CAA *abbr.* Civil Aviation Authority.

Caaba KAABA.

CAB *abbr.* **1** Citizens' Advice Bureau. **2** (*N Am.*) Civil Aeronautics Board.

cab[1] (kab) *n.* **1** a taxi. **2** the driver's compartment in a lorry, crane or locomotive. **3** a public, covered, horse-drawn carriage with two or four wheels. **to call a cab** to hail a taxi. **cabbie, cabby** *n.* (*pl.* **cabbies**) (*coll.*) a cab-driver. **cabman** *n.* (*pl.* **cabmen**) the driver of a horse-drawn cab. [short for CABRIOLET]

cab[2] (kab) *n.* an ancient Jewish measure of capacity equal to 4 pints (2.3l). [Heb. *qab*, a hollow vessel]

cabal (kəbal´) *n.* **1** a small body of persons closely united for some secret purpose; a junta, a clique. **2** a plot, a conspiracy. **3** the five ministers of Charles II who signed the Treaty of Alliance in 1672, the initials of whose names (Clifford, Ashley, Buckingham, Arlington and Lauderdale) happened to form the word *cabal*. ~*v.i.* (*pres. p.* **caballing**, *past, p.p.* **caballed**) to intrigue secretly with others for some private end. **caballer** *n.* [F *cabale*, from med. L CABBALA]

cabala CABBALA.

caballer CABAL.

caballero (kabəlyeə´rō) *n.* (*pl.* **caballeros**) a Spanish gentleman. [Sp., from L *caballārius* (*caballus*, horse)]

cabana (kəbah´nə) *n.* (*esp. N Am.*) a small hut, cabin or tent on the beach or at a swimming-pool, used for changing by bathers. [Sp. *cabaña*, CABIN]

cabaret (kab´ərā) *n.* **1** an entertainment or floor show consisting of singing, dancing etc. **2** a restaurant or nightclub where such entertainment is provided. [F, a tavern]

cabbage (kab´ij) *n.* **1** any of the plain-leaved, hearted varieties of *Brassica oleracea*. **2** the terminal bud of some palm trees. **3** (*coll.*) an inert or apathetic person. **cabbage butterfly** *n.* either of two species of butterfly, *Pieris brassicae* or *P. rapae*, the larvae of which cause injury to cabbages. **cabbage lettuce** *n.* a variety of lettuce with a firm heart like a cabbage. **cabbage moth** *n.* a nocturnal moth, *Mamestra brassicae*, whose larvae feed on cabbages. **cabbage palm** *n.* the cabbage tree. **cabbage-root fly** *n.* a fly, *Erioischia brassicae*, whose larvae damage the roots of cabbages. **cabbage rose** *n.* a double red rose, *Rosa centifolia*, with large, compact flowers. **cabbagetown** *n.* (*Can.*) a city slum (from the name of such an area in Toronto, the inhabitants of which were believed to live on a diet of cabbage). **cabbage tree** *n.* a palm tree with an edible terminal bud. **cabbage white** *n.* the cabbage butterfly. **cabbage worm** *n.* the larva of the cabbage butterfly, cabbage moth and other insects. **cabbagy** *a.* [F *caboche*, great head, L *caput*, head (F *choux cabus*, cabbage cole)]

cabbala (kəbah´lə), **cabala, kabala, kabbala** *n.* **1** a traditional exposition of the Pentateuch attributed to Moses. **2** mystic or esoteric doctrine. **cabbalism** (kab´ə-) *n.* **1** the system of the cabbala. **2** occult doctrine. **cabbalist** (kab´ə-) *n.* a person skilled in the Jewish cabbala, or in mystic learning. **cabbalistic** (kabəlist´-), **cabbalistical** *a.* **1** of or relating to the Jewish cabbala. **2** mysterious, occult. **cabbalistically** *adv.* [med. L, from Heb. *qabbālāh*, tradition, received doctrine (*qābal*, to receive)]

caber (kā´bə) *n.* a pole, the roughly-trimmed stem of a young tree, used in the Highland sport of tossing the caber. [Gael. *cabar*]

Cabernet (kab´ənā) *n.* **1** a variety of black grape used to make a dry red wine. **2** wine made from these grapes. [F]

cabin (kab´in) *n.* **1** a small hut or house. **2** a temporary shelter. **3** a room or compartment in a ship or aircraft for officers or passengers. **4** a driver's cab. ~*v.i.* (*pres. p.* **cabining**, *past, p.p.* **cabined**) to live in a cabin. ~*v.t.* to shelter or confine in or as in a cabin. **cabin boy** *n.* a boy who waits on the officers or passengers of a ship. **cabin class** *n.* in a passenger ship, a class of accommodation between tourist class and first class. **cabin crew** *n.* the crew in an aircraft responsible for looking after passengers. **cabin cruiser** *n.* a motor-boat with living accommodation. **cabin fever** *n.* (*Can.*) a state of depression caused by living in cramped accommodation in an isolated place for long periods of time. **cabin passenger** *n.* a person who pays for cabin accommodation in a ship. [F *cabane*, late L *capanna*, a hut]

cabinet (kab´init) *n.* **1** a piece of furniture with drawers, shelves etc., in which to keep or display curiosities or articles of value. **2** an outer case for a television set etc. **3** (*also* **Cabinet**) a deliberative committee of the principal members of government. **4** a meeting of such a committee. **5** the advisory council of a sovereign, president etc. **6** a council room. **7** †a small, private room. **8** a cabinet photograph. **cabinetmaker** *n.* a person who makes household furniture of fine quality. **cabinetmaking** *n.* **cabinet minister, Cabinet minister** *n.* a member of a cabinet. **cabinet photograph** *n.* a photographic print measuring about 4 × 6 in. (about 10 × 15 cm). **cabinet pudding** *n.* a steamed pudding, with dried fruit. **cabinetry** *n.* **cabinetwork** *n.* **1**

cabinetmaking. **2** a piece of such furniture. [dim. of CABIN, or from F *cabinet*]

cable (kā´bəl) *n.* **1** a strong, thick rope of hemp or wire. **2** the rope or chain to which an anchor is fastened. **3** a nautical unit of length, about 202 yds. (185 m) or one-tenth of a nautical mile. **4** a wire or bundle of wires insulated and in a sheath, used to conduct electricity. **5** (*Archit.*) a cable-like moulding. **6** a cablegram. **7** cable television. **8** cable stitch. ~*v.t.* **1** to send (a message) by cable. **2** to inform by cablegram. **3** to fasten with a cable. **4** to fill (the lower part of the flutings in a column) with convex mouldings. **cable car** *n.* **1** a passenger cabin suspended from an overhead cable and moved by it, esp. up and down a mountain. **2** a carriage on a funicular railway. **cablegram** *n.* a telegraphic message by submarine cable, communications satellite etc. **cable-laid** *a.* (of a rope) having three strands twisted like a cable. **cable moulding** *n.* **1** (*Archit.*) a cable-like bead or moulding. **2** in goldsmithing etc., a cable-like ornament. **cable railway** *n.* a funicular railway. **cable release** *n.* in photography, a cable that can be used to operate the shutter of a camera, to avoid the risk of camera movement while the shutter is open. **cable stitch** *n.* a series of stitches in knitting that produces a pattern resembling twisted rope. **cablet** (-lit) *n.* a small cable, less than 10 in. (25.4 cm) round. **cable television** *n.* a television service transmitted by an underground cable connected to subscribers' television sets. **cableway** *n.* a transport system for freight or passengers using containers or cable cars suspended from overhead cables. **cabling** *n.* decoration of columns by means of convex mouldings in the fluting. [ult. from L *caplum*, *capulum*, from *capere*, to take hold of (cp. OF *cable*, It. *cappio*, Dut. *kabel*)]

cabob KEBAB.

caboched (kəbosht´), **caboshed, cabossed** (-bost´) *a.* (*Her.*) borne full-faced and showing no other feature, as the heads of some animals. [from obs. v. *caboche*, F *cabocher* (L *caput*, head; cp. CABBAGE)]

cabochon (kab´əshon) *n.* a precious stone polished, and having the rough parts removed, but without facets. [F *caboche*, as CABOCHED]

caboodle (kəboo´dəl) *n.* (*coll.*) crowd, lot. **the whole caboodle** the whole lot. [BOODLE]

caboose (kəboos´) *n.* **1** the cook's house or galley on a ship. **2** (*N Am.*) the guard's van in a goods train. **3** (*N Am.*) a car on a train for the use of workmen or crew. [prob. from MDut. *kabuys* (etym. uncertain; perh. from a form *kabanhuys*, cabin-house)]

cabotage (kab´ətij) *n.* **1** coastal navigation or shipping. **2** trade between the ports of the same country. **3** the restriction of a country's internal air traffic to carriers belonging to that country. [F, from *caboter*, to coast (etym. uncertain)]

cabretta (kəbret´ə) *n.* a type of soft leather made from the skin of a S American sheep. [Sp. *cabra*, female goat]

cabriole (kab´riōl) *a.* (of table and chair legs) shaped in a reflex curve. ~*n.* in ballet, a leap in which one leg is stretched out and the other is struck against it. [F, a caper]

cabriolet (kabriōlā´, kab´-) *n.* **1** a covered, horse-drawn carriage with two wheels. **2** a type of motor-car with a folding top. [F, dim. of *cabriole*, a caper (see CAPRIOLE)]

ca'canny (kawkan´i) *n.* **1** proceeding with caution or wariness. **2** a worker's policy of going slowly. [Sc. *ca' canny*, to go gently or warily, from CALL, CANNY]

cacao (kəkah´ō, -kā´ō), *n.* a tropical American tree, *Theobroma cacao*, from the seeds of which chocolate and cocoa are prepared. **cacao bean** *n.* COCOA BEAN (under COCOA[1]). **cacao butter** *n.* COCOA BUTTER (under COCOA[1]). [Sp., from Nahuatl *cacauatl*]

cacciatore (kachətaw'ri), **cacciatora** (-rə) *a.* (of meat dishes, esp. chicken) cooked with tomatoes, onions, mushrooms, herbs etc. [It., hunter]

cachalot (kash´əlot, -lō) *n.* a member of a genus of whales having teeth in the lower jaw, esp. the sperm whale. [F, from Port. *cachalote*]

cache (kash) *n.* **1** a place in which provisions, arms, treasure etc. are hidden. **2** the hidden provisions, arms, treasure etc. ~*v.t.* to hide or conceal in a cache. **cache memory** *n.* (*Comput.*) a memory store from which data can be retrieved at very high speed. **cachepot** (kash´pō) *n.* an ornamental holder for a plant-pot. [F, from *cacher*, to hide]

cachectic CACHEXIA.

cachet (kash´ā) *n.* **1** a seal. **2** a stamp, a characteristic mark. **3** a sign of authenticity. **4** a mark of excellence. **5** prestige. **6** a flat capsule in which unpleasant-tasting drugs can be administered. [F, from *cacher*, to conceal]

cachexia (kəkek´siə), **cachexy** (-si) *n.* a loss of weight from and weakness of the body resulting from chronic disease. **cachectic** (-kek´tik) *a.* [L, from Gr. *kakhexia* (*kakos*, bad, *hexis*, habit)]

cachinnate (kak´ināt) *v.i.* (*formal*) to laugh immoderately. **cachinnation** (-ā´shən) *n.* loud or immoderate laughter. **cachinnatory** (-ā´təri) *a.* [L *cachinnāre* (onomat.)]

cacholong (kach´əlong) *n.* a white or opaque variety of opal or quartz. [Kalmuck *kaschtschilon*, beautiful stone]

cachou (kash´oo, -shoo´) *n.* **1** a small pill-like sweet for perfuming the breath. **2** catechu. [F, from Malay *kāchu* (see CATECHU)]

Usage note The spellings of the sweet *cachou* and the nut *cashew* (pronounced the same) should not be confused.

cachucha (kəchoo´chə) *n.* a lively Spanish dance in triple time. [Sp.]

cacique (kəsēk´), **cazique** *n.* **1** a chief of the indigenous inhabitants of the W Indies or the neighbouring parts of America. **2** a local political leader in this area. **caciquism** *n.* [Sp., from Haitian]

cack (kak) *n.* (*dial.*) excrement. **cack-handed** *a.* (*sl.*) **1** left-handed. **2** clumsy. **cack-handedly** *adv.* **cack-handedness** *n.* [L *cacāre*, to defecate]

cackle (kak´əl) *n.* **1** the cackling of a hen. **2** silly chatter. ~*v.i.* **1** (of a hen) to make a squawking or clucking noise. **2** to make a similar noise. **3** to chatter in a silly manner. **4** to giggle. **to cut the cackle** to get down to business. **cackler** *n.* **cackling** *n.* [ME *kakelen* (onomat.) (cp. Dut. *kakelen*, G *gackeln*)]

caco- (kak´ō) *comb. form* bad, incorrect, unpleasant. [Gr. *kako-*, *kakos*, evil, bad]

cacodemon (kakədē´mən), **cacodaemon** *n.* **1** an evil spirit. **2** a nightmare. **3** an evil person.

cacodyl (kak´ədil) *n.* a toxic organic compound of arsenic and methyl with an unpleasant smell. **cacodylic** (-dil´-) *a.* [Gr. *kakōdēs*, stinking (CACO-, *od-*, root of *ozein*, to smell), -YL]

cacoepy (kəkō´əpi) *n.* incorrect pronunciation of words. [Gr. *epos*, a word]

cacoethes (kakōē´thēz) *n.* **1** a bad habit. **2** an irresistible urge. **cacoethes scribendi** (skriben´dī, -dē) *n.* an itch for writing. [L from Gr. *kakoēthes* evil habit, neut. of a. *kakoēthēs*, ill-disposed (CACO- *ēthos*, disposition, character)]

cacography (kəkog´rəfi) *n.* **1** bad spelling. **2** bad handwriting. **cacographer** *n.* **cacographic** (kakōgraf´-), **cacographical** *a.*

cacology (kəkol´əji) *n.* **1** bad choice of words. **2** incorrect pronunciation. [Gr. *kakologia*, from *kakologos*, speaking evil (CACO-, *logos*, from *legein*, to speak)]

cacomistle (kak'əmisəl), **cacomixle** (-miksəl) *n.* a ring-tailed American mammal, *Bassariscus astutus*, related to the raccoon. [Mex. Sp., from Nahuatl *tlacomiztli*, half cougar]

cacomorphia (kakəmaw´fiə) *n.* malformation, deformity.

cacophony (kəkof´əni) *n.* (*pl.* **cacophonies**) **1** a rough, discordant sound or mixture of sounds. **2** (*Mus.*) a discord. **cacophonous** *a.* harsh-sounding, discordant. [F *cacophonie*, Gr. *kakophōnia*, from *kakophōnos*, harsh-sounding]

cactus (kak´təs) *n.* (*pl.* **cacti** (kak'tī), **cactuses**) any succulent spiny plant of the family *Cactaceae*. **cactaceous** (-tā´shəs) *a.* **cactoid** *a.* **cactus dahlia** *n.* a variety of dahlia with double flowers resembling those of a cactus. [L, from Gr. *kaktos*, a prickly Sicilian plant]

cacuminal (kəkū´minəl) *a.* (of a vowel or consonant) retroflected. ~*n.* a retroflected sound. [L *cacūmen*, point, tip, top]

CAD *abbr.* **1** computer-aided design. **2** compact audio disc.

cad (kad) *n.* (*dated*) an ill-mannered person, a person guilty of ungentlemanly conduct. **caddish** *a.* **caddishly** *adv.* [prob. short for Sc. *cadie*, *caddie*, Eng. CADET]

cadastre (kədas´tə) *n.* an official register of the ownership of land as a basis of taxation. **cadastral** *a.* [F, from late Gr. *katastikhon*, list, register]

cadaver (kədav´ə, -dahv´ə, -dā´və) *n.* a corpse, a dead body. **cadaveric** *a.* (*Med.*) cadaverous. **cadaverous** *a.* **1** corpselike. **2** deathly pale. **cadaverously** *adv.* **cadaverousness** *n.* [L]

CADCAM *abbr.* computer-aided design and computer-aided manufacture.

caddice CADDIS[2].

caddie (kad´i), **caddy** *n.* (*pl.* **caddies**) a person who assists a golfer, esp. by carrying clubs. ~*v.i.* (*3rd pers. sing. pres.* **caddies**, *pres. p.* **caddying**, *past, p.p.* **caddied**) to act as a caddie. **caddie car, caddie cart** *n.* a two-wheeled cart for carrying golf clubs. [Sc. *cadie*, *caddie*, a messenger or errand-boy, from F *cadet* (see CADET)]

caddis[1] (kad´is) *n.* the larva of the caddis fly, which lives in water in a protective case of sand, stones, sticks, leaves etc. **caddis fly** *n.* (*pl.* **caddis flies**) any insect of the order *Trichoptera*, resembling a small moth. **caddis worm** *n.* a caddis larva. [etym. uncertain]

caddis[2] (kad´is), **caddice** *n.* **1** a type of worsted yarn. **2** caddis ribbon. **caddis ribbon** *n.* a tape of worsted yarn used for garters etc. [A-F *cadace*, OF *cadaz*, the coarsest part of silk; OF *cadis*, a kind of woollen serge]

caddish CAD.

caddy[1] (kad´i) *n.* (*pl.* **caddies**) a small box in which tea is kept. [Malay *kātī*, a weight of 1½ lb (0.68 kg)]

caddy[2] CADDIE.

cade (kād) *a.* (of a young animal) brought up by hand; domesticated. ~*n.* a young animal brought up by hand, esp. a pet lamb. [etym. uncertain]

-cade (kād) *comb. form* a procession, as *motorcade*. [CAVALCADE]

cadelle (kədel´) *n.* a small beetle, *Tenebroides mauritanicus*, that feeds on stored grain, etc. [F, from Prov. *cadello*, L *catellus*, a little dog]

cadence (kā´dəns) *n.* **1** the sinking of the voice, esp. at the end of a sentence. **2** modulation of the voice, intonation. **3** local modulation or accent. **4** rhythmical beat or movement. **5** poetical rhythm or measure. **6** (*Mus.*) the close of a movement or phrase. **7** (*Mus.*) a cadenza. ~*v.t.* to put into rhythmical measure. **cadenced** *a.* **cadency** *n.* (*pl.* **cadencies**) **1** cadence. **2** (*Her.*) **a** the state of being a younger son. **b** descent from a younger branch. **cadent** *a.* **1** (*Astron.*) going down. **2** having rhythmical cadence. **3** †falling. **cadential** (kəden´shəl) *a.* of or relating to a cadence or a cadenza. [F, from It. *cadenza*, late L *cadentia* (*cadere*, to fall)]

cadenza (kəden´zə) *n.* (*pl.* **cadenzas**) (*Mus.*) a vocal or instrumental flourish of indefinite form at the close of a movement. [It., as CADENCE]

cadet (kədet´) *n.* **1** a young trainee in the army, navy, air force or police. **2** a young volunteer who receives military training while at school. **3** a younger son. **4** the younger branch of a family. **5** (*Hist.*) a young man, esp. a younger son, who served in the army as a volunteer in the hope of gaining a commission. **6** (*New Zeal.*) a sheep-farming apprentice or trainee. **cadetship** *n.* [F, from Prov. *capdet*, late L *capitellum*, dim. of L *caput*, head]

cadge (kaj) *v.t.* to get by begging. ~*v.i.* to beg. **cadger** *n.* a person who cadges. [perh. a var. of CATCH]

cadi (kah´di, kā´-), **kadi, qadi** *n.* (*pl.* **cadis, kadis, qadis**) the judge of a Muslim town or village. [Arab. *qādī* (cp. ALCAYDE)]

Cadmean (kadmē´ən), **Cadmian** (kad´-) *a.* **1** of or belonging to Cadmus, the mythical founder of Thebes. **2** Theban. **Cadmean victory** *n.* (*pl.* **Cadmean victories**) **1** a Pyrrhic victory. **2** a moral victory.

cadmium (kad´miəm) *n.* a bluish-white metallic element, at. no. 51, chem. symbol Cd. **cadmic** *a.* **cadmiferous** (-mif´-) *a.* **cadmium cell** *n.* **1** a type of photocell with a cadmium electrode. **2** a primary electrical cell used as a standard. **cadmium yellow** *n.* a yellow or orange pigment prepared from cadmium sulphide. [obs. *cadmia*, CALAMINE, L, from Gr. *kadmia*, *-meia*, Cadmean (earth)]

cadre (kah´də, kah´dri) *n.* **1** the permanent establishment or nucleus of a regiment; the skeleton of a regiment. **2** any similar nucleus or basic structure, esp. of key personnel. **3** a group of revolutionary activists. **4** a member of such a group. [F, from It. *quadro*, L *quadrum*, square]

caduceus (kədū´siəs) *n.* (*pl.* **caducei** (-siī)) the winged staff of Mercury, borne by him as messenger of the gods. **caducean** *a.* [L *cādūceus*, Doric Gr. *karukion* (*kērux*, a herald)]

caducous (kədū´kəs) *a.* (*Biol.*) falling off quickly or prematurely. **caducity** (-siti) *n.* [L *cadūcus*, easily falling (*cadere*, to fall)]

CAE *abbr.* **1** computer-aided engineering. **2** (*Austral.*) College of Advanced Education.

caecilian (sēsil´iən), **coecilian** *n.* any wormlike legless amphibian of the order Apoda (or Gymnophiona) which burrows in moist soil. [L *caecilia*, a type of lizard (*caecus*, blind)]

caecum (sē´kəm), (*N Am.*) **cecum** *n.* (*pl.* **caeca** (-kə), (*N Am.*) **ceca**) **1** the first part of the large intestine, which is prolonged into a blind pouch. **2** any similar structure in animals or plants that ends in a blind pouch. **caecal** *a.* **1** of or relating to the caecum. **2** having a blind end. **caeciform** (-si-) *a.* **caecitis** (-sī´-) *n.* inflammation of the caecum. [L *caecus*, blind]

caenogenesis (sēnōjen´isis), **cainogenesis** (kīnō-), (*N Am.*) **cenogenesis** *n.* the development in an embryo, larva etc., of adaptations that disappear at the adult stage, when they are no longer needed. **caenogenetic** (-net´-) *a.* [Gr. *kainos*, recent, GENESIS]

Caenozoic CENOZOIC.

Caen stone (kā´ən) *n.* a soft, yellowish, oolitic building-stone from Caen. [*Caen*, town in Normandy]

Caerphilly (keəfil'i), *n.* a mild-flavoured white cheese. [town in SE Wales]

caesalpiniaceous (sezalpiniā´shəs, sēz-) *a.* of, relating to or belonging to the Caesalpiniaceae, a family of chiefly tropical plants that includes brazil, carob, cassia and senna. [Andreas *Caesalpino*, 1519–1603, Italian botanist]

Caesar (sē´zə) *n.* **1** (*Hist.*) the title of the Roman emperors down to Hadrian, and of the heirs presumptive of later emperors. **2** (*Hist.*) the Emperor, the

Holy Roman Emperor; the German Kaiser. **3** an autocrat. **4** the temporal (as distinguished from the spiritual) power. **5** (*coll.*) a Caesarean section. **Caesarean** (sizeə´-), **Caesarian** *a.* **1** of or belonging to Caesar. **2** imperial. ~*n.* **1** a follower of Caesar. **2** a supporter of autocratic government. **3** (*N Am.* **Cesarian, Cesarean**) a Caesarean section. **Caesarean section** *n.* the delivery of a child through the walls of the abdomen (as Julius Caesar is said to have been brought into the world). **Caesarism** *n.* **1** absolute government. **2** imperialism. **Caesarist** *n.* **Caesar salad** *n.* a salad of cos lettuce and croutons with a dressing made from olive oil, raw egg, lemon juice and Worcester sauce (from Caesar Cardini, Mexican restaurateur). **Caesar's wife** *n.* a woman of spotless reputation. [L, cognomen of Gaius Julius *Caesar*]

caesious (sē´ziəs) *a.* bluish or greenish grey. [L *caesius*]

caesium (sē´ziəm), (*N Am.*) **cesium** *n.* a highly-reactive, silvery-white metallic element, at. no. 55, chem. symbol Cs, similar to sodium in many properties. **caesium clock** *n.* an atomic clock that makes use of the resonance frequency produced by electric activity in caesium atoms. [as CAESIOUS, from the bluish-green lines of its spectrum]

caespitose (ses´pitōs), (*N Am.*) **cespitose** *a.* **1** growing in tufts. **2** matted. **3** turfy. [mod. L *caespitōsus*, from L *caespes -item*, turf]

caesura (sizūə´rə), (*N Am.*) **cesura** *n.* (*pl.* **caesuras, caesurae** (-rē), (*N Am.*) **cesuras, cesurae**) **1** in classical prosody, the division of a metrical foot between two words, esp. in the middle of a line. **2** in modern prosody, a pause about the middle of a line. **caesural** *a.* [L, from *caesus*, p.p. of *caedere*, to cut]

CAF *abbr.* (*esp. N Am.*) cost and freight.

cafard (kafah´, kaf´ah) *n.* depression, low spirits. [F]

café (kaf´ā), **cafe** (kāf, kaf) *n.* **1** a small restaurant serving coffee, tea etc. and light inexpensive meals or snacks. **2** a coffee house or coffee bar. **3** coffee. **café au lait** (ō lā´) *n.* coffee with milk. **café bar** *n.* a café which also sells alcoholic drinks. **café noir** (nwah´) *n.* black coffee. **café society** *n.* fashionable society; people who frequent fashionable restaurants, nightclubs, etc. [F]

cafeteria (kafitiə´riə) *n.* (*pl.* **cafeterias**) a restaurant in which customers fetch their own food and drinks from the counter. [Am. Sp. *cafeteria*, a coffee shop]

cafetière (kafətyeə´, -tiə´), **cafetiere** *n.* a type of coffee-pot fitted with a plunger that forces the grounds to the bottom and holds them there while the coffee is poured. [F]

caff (kaf) *n.* (*sl.*) a café or cafeteria.

caffeic (kafē´ik) *a.* derived from coffee.

caffeine (kaf´ēn), **caffein** *n.* a vegetable alkaloid derived from the coffee and tea plants.

CAFOD (kaf´od), **Cafod** *abbr.* Catholic Fund for Overseas Development.

caftan KAFTAN.

cage (kāj) *n.* **1** a box or enclosure wholly or partly of wire or iron bars, in which animals or birds are kept. **2** any framework or structure resembling this. **3** the cabin of a lift. **4** (*Mining*) an iron structure used as a lift in a shaft. **5** a prison, prison cell or prison camp. ~*v.t.* **1** to shut up in a cage. **2** to confine. **cagebird** *n.* **1** a bird kept in a cage. **2** a type of bird normally kept in a cage. **caged** *a.* **cageling** *n.* a bird kept in a cage. [OF, from L *cavea* (*cavus*, hollow)]

cagey (kā´ji), **cagy** *a.* (*comp.* **cagier,** *superl.* **cagiest**) (*coll.*) **1** uncommunicative, secretive. **2** wary, cautious. **3** sly. **cagily** *adv.* **caginess, cageyness** *n.* [etym. unknown]

cagoule (kəgool´), **kagoule** *n.* a lightweight weatherproof jacket, usu. hooded. [F, a monk's hood]

cagy CAGEY.

cahier (ka´yā) *n.* **1** a notebook. **2** the report of a committee, esp. concerning policy. [F (OF *quayer*, see QUIRE[1])]

cahoots (kəhoots´) *n.pl.* (*sl.*) partnership, collusion (*in cahoots*).

CAI *abbr.* computer-aided instruction, computer-assisted instruction.

caiman CAYMAN.

Cain (kān) *n.* a murderer, a fratricide. **to raise Cain** (*sl.*) to make a disturbance, to make trouble. [brother of Abel, Gen. iv]

†**cain** (kān), **kain** *n.* (*Hist., Sc. and Ir.*) rent paid in kind, esp. farm produce. [Celt. *cáin*, law, tribute]

cainogenesis CAENOGENESIS.

Cainozoic CENOZOIC.

caïque (kah´ik, kī´-), **caique** *n.* **1** a light rowing boat used on the Bosporus. **2** a small sailing vessel of the eastern Mediterranean. [Turk. *qāiq*]

cairn (keən) *n.* **1** a pyramidal heap of stones, esp. one raised over a grave or to mark a summit, track or boundary. **2** a cairn terrier. **cairn terrier** *n.* a small rough-haired terrier orig. from Scotland. [Gael., Ir., Welsh *carn*]

cairngorm (keəngawm´, keən´-) *n.* a yellow or brown variety of rock crystal (found in the Cairngorm mountains in NE Scotland). [Gael., lit. blue stone]

caisson (kā´sən, kəsoon´) *n.* **1** a large, watertight case or chamber used in laying foundations under water. **2** a similar apparatus used for raising sunken vessels. **3** a floating vessel used as a dock gate. **4** an ammunition chest or wagon. **5** a sunken panel in ceilings etc. **caisson disease** *n.* symptoms resulting from a sudden return from high air pressure to normal pressure conditions; decompression sickness. [F *caisse*, L *capsa*, see CASE[2]]

†**caitiff** (kā´tif) *n.* a despicable wretch or cowardly person. ~*a.* cowardly, base, despicable. [OF *caitif*, L *captīvus*, CAPTIVE]

cajeput CAJUPUT.

cajole (kəjōl´) *v.t.* **1** to persuade by flattery or fair speech (*He cajoled me into staying*). **2** to wheedle, to coax. **3** to beguile or deceive. ~*v.i.* to use artful flattery. **cajolement** *n.* **cajoler** *n.* **cajolery** *n.* **cajolingly** *adv.* [F *cajoler*, etym. uncertain]

Cajun (kā´jən) *n.* a descendant of the French-speaking Acadians deported to Louisiana in the 18th cent. ~*a.* of or relating to the Cajuns or their music, cookery etc. [corr. of ACADIAN]

cajuput (kaj´əpŭt), **cajeput** *n.* a small tree, *Melaleuca leucadendron*, which yields a volatile oil. [Malay *kāyu pūtih*, white wood]

cake (kāk) *n.* **1** a mixture of flour, butter, eggs, sugar and other ingredients, baked usu. in a tin. **2** a small mass of baked dough. **3** a flat mass of food or any solidified or compressed substance. ~*v.t.* (*usu. pass.*) to make into a solidified or compressed mass. ~*v.i.* to assume a solidified or compressed form. **to go/ sell like hot cakes** to be sold very quickly. **to have one's cake and eat it** to take advantage of two alternatives, one of which excludes the other (*You can't have your cake and eat it*). **to take the cake** (*iron., sl.*) to be the most foolish, unacceptable etc. **cake-hole** *n.* (*sl.*) the mouth. **cakes and ale** *n.pl.* a good time. **cakewalk,** *n.* **1** a dance with high marching steps, which originated among American blacks (formerly performed for the prize of a cake). **2** (*sl.*) something easily accomplished. **3** a moving promenade at a fairground. [ON *kaka* (cp. Dan. *káge*, Dut. *koek*, G *Kuchen*)]

CAL *abbr.* computer-aided learning, computer-assisted learning.

Cal. *abbr.* **1** California. **2** Calorie (kilocalorie).

cal. *abbr.* **1** calendar. **2** calibre. **3** (small) calorie.

Calabar bean (kal´əbah) *n.* the highly poisonous seed of the climbing plant *Physostigma venenosum* of W

Africa, a source of physostigmine. [*Calabar*, port in Nigeria]

calabash (kal´əbash) *n.* **1** a kind of gourd, esp. the fruit of the calabash tree. **2** the calabash tree. **3** the shell enclosing the fruit of this tree, used for drinking vessels and other domestic utensils, and tobacco pipes. **calabash tree** *n.* a tropical American tree, *Crescentia cujete*. [F *calebasse*, Sp. *calabaza* (Cat. Sp. *carabassa*, Sic. It. *caravazza*); perh. from Pers. *kharbuz*, a melon]

calaboose (kaləboos´, kal´-) *n.* (*N Am., coll.*) a prison. [Am. F *calabouse*, Sp. *calabozo*]

calabrese (kaləbrā´zi) *n.* a type of green broccoli. [It., of Calabria in S Italy]

caladium (kəlā´diəm) *n.* any of a genus of plants belonging to the arum family, with starchy tuberous roots used in the tropics for food. [Malay *kélādy*]

calamanco (kaləmang´kō) *n.* (*pl.* **calamancoes**) **1** a Flemish woollen cloth with a fine gloss, and chequered on one side, much in use in the 18th cent. **2** (*usu. pl.*) a garment of this cloth. [etym. uncertain; cp. Dut. *kalamink*, F *calmande*, Sp. *calamaco*]

calamander (kaləman´də) *n.* a hard wood, marked with black and brown stripes, from India and Sri Lanka. [etym. uncertain]

calamari (kaləmah´ri), *n.pl.* squid, esp. in Mediterranean cookery. [It., pl. of *calamaro*, mod. Gr. *kalamari* (cp. CALAMARY)]

†**calamary** (kal´əməri) *n.* (*pl.* **calamaries**) a squid, esp. of the genus *Loligo*. [L *calamārius* (*calamus*, a pen, referring either to its pen-shaped skull or its inky fluid)]

calamine (kal´əmīn) *n.* **1** a pinkish powder of zinc carbonate and ferric oxide used in a lotion to soothe the skin. **2** (*Hist.*) zinc carbonate. [F, from med. L *calamīna* (prob. corr. of L *cadmīa*, see CADMIUM)]

calamint (kal´əmint) *n.* an aromatic herb of the genus *Clinopodium* (formerly *Calamintha*) of the mint family. [MF *calament*, med. L *calamentum*, Gr. *kalaminthē*]

calamite (kal´əmīt) *n.* a fossil plant of the Carboniferous period, related to the horsetails. [mod. L *calamītes*, from L *calamus*, a reed]

calamity (kəlam´iti) *n.* (*pl.* **calamities**) **1** extreme misfortune or adversity; disaster. **2** great distress or misery. **calamitous** *a.* causing or characterized by disaster or great or widespread distress. **calamitously** *adv.* **calamitousness** *n.* **calamity Jane** *n.* (*coll.*) a person who heralds or brings disaster. [F *calamité*, L *calamitas -atem* (cp. *incolumis*, safe)]

calamus (kal´əməs) *n.* (*pl.* **calami** (-mī)) **1** the sweet flag, *Acorus calamus*. **2** the aromatic root of this plant. **3** any palm tree of the genus *Calamus*, producing extremely long canes. **4** the quill of a feather. [L, from Gr. *kalamos*, a reed]

calando (kəlan´dō) *a., adv.* (*Mus.*) gradually becoming softer and slower. [It.]

calandria (kəlan´driə) *n.* (*pl.* **calandrias**) a sealed cylindrical vessel with tubes passing through it, used as a heat exchanger, e.g. in nuclear reactors. [Sp., lark]

calash (kəlash´) *n.* **1** a light horse-drawn carriage, with low wheels and removable top. **2** (*Can.*) a two-wheeled horse-drawn vehicle for two, with seat for the driver on the splashboard. **3** a woman's silk hood supported by a framework of whalebone. [F *calèche*, G *Kalesche*, from Slav. (Czech *kolesa*, wheels)]

calathea (kaləthē´ə) *n.* (*pl.* **calatheas**) any plant of the genus *Calathea* of S America, many of which are grown as house plants, such as the zebra plant. [L, Gr. *kalathos*, a basket]

calathus (kal´əthəs) *n.* (*pl.* **calathi** (-thī)) in classical art, a wide-topped fruit basket used as a symbol of fruitfulness. [L, Gr. *kalathos*, a basket]

calc- (kalk) *comb. form* lime, calcium. **calc-sinter** *n.* travertine. **calc-spar** *n.* calcite. **calc-tuff, calc-tufa** *n.* a porous deposit of calcium carbonate. [G *Kalk*, as CALCI-]

calcaneum (kalkā´niəm), **calcaneus** (-niəs) *n.* (*pl.* **calcanea** (-niə), **calcanei** (-niī)) the bone of the heel. **calcaneal** *a.* [L, as CALCAR[2]]

calcar[1] (kal´kah) *n.* the reverberatory furnace in which the first calcination is made in glass-making. [L *calcāria*, lime-kiln]

calcar[2] (kal´kah) *n.* (*Bot., Zool.*) a spurlike process on a petal or on a bird's leg. **calcarate** *a.* [L, from *calx -cem*, heel]

calcareous (kalkeə´riəs), **calcarious** *a.* of or containing calcium carbonate; chalky or limy. **calcareous-tufa** *n.* a porous deposit of calcium carbonate; calc-tuff. [L *calcārius*, see CALC-]

calcedony CHALCEDONY.

calceolaria (kalsiəleə´riə) *n.* (*pl.* **calceolarias**) any plant of the genus *Calceolaria*, with slipper-like flowers; slipperwort. [L *calceolus*, dim. of *calceus*, a shoe (*calx -cem*, the heel)]

calceolate (kal´siəlāt) *a.* (*Bot.*) shaped like a slipper. [L *calceolus*, dim. of *calceus*, a shoe (*calx -cem*, the heel)]

calces CALX.

calci- (kal´si) *comb. form* lime, calcium. [L *calx -cis*]

calcic (kal´sik) *a.* of, relating to or containing calcium or lime.

calcicole (kal´sikōl) *a.* (of a plant) thriving in chalk or limy soil. *~n.* a calcicole plant. **calcicolous** (-sik´ələs) *a.* [L *colere*, to inhabit]

calciferol (kalsif´ərol) *n.* a compound found in dairy products, vitamin D_2. [*calci*ferous, ergost*erol*]

calciferous (kalsif´ərəs) *a.* (*Chem.*) yielding or containing calcium salts.

calcifuge (kal´sifūj) *a.* (of a plant) not suited to chalky or limy soil. *~n.* a calcifuge plant.

calcify (kal´sifī) *v.t.* (*3rd pers. sing. pres.* **calcifies**, *pres. p.* **calcifying**, *past, p.p.* **calcified**) **1** to convert into lime. **2** to harden by the deposition of calcium salts. *~v.i.* to become calcified. **calcific** (-sif´ik) *a.* **calcification** (-ikā´shən) *n.*

calcine (kal´sin, -sīn) *v.t.* **1** to reduce to calcium oxide by heat. **2** to expel water and other volatile matter from, to desiccate by heat. **3** to purify or refine. **4** to burn to ashes. *~v.i.* to undergo calcination. **calcination** (-sinā´shən) *n.* [med. L *calcināre*]

calcite (kal´sīt) *n.* natural crystallized calcium carbonate. **calcitic** (-sit´-) *a.*

calcitonin (kalsitō´nin) *n.* a hormone produced and secreted by the thyroid gland, which inhibits the loss of calcium from the skeleton and controls the amount of calcium in the blood. [Gr. *tonos*, tone]

calcium (kal´siəm) *n.* a silver-white metallic element, at. no. 20, chem. symbol Ca. **calcium carbide** *n.* a grey compound used to produce acetylene. **calcium carbonate** *n.* a white crystalline compound occurring in limestone, chalk, marble etc. **calcium chloride** *n.* chloride of lime, bleaching powder. **calcium hydroxide** *n.* a white powder used in the production of cement, plaster etc.; slaked lime. **calcium light** *n.* limelight. **calcium oxide** *n.* lime, quicklime. **calcium phosphate** *n.* a compound that occurs in bones and is used in fertilizers.

calcrete (kal´krēt) *n.* (*Geol.*) a rock made up of particles of sand and gravel held together with calcium carbonate. [CALC-, con*crete*]

calculate (kal´kūlāt) *v.t.* **1** to compute, to determine by mathematical process, to estimate. **2** to ascertain beforehand. **3** to plan beforehand. **4** to adjust, to arrange. *~v.i.* **1** to reckon, to form an estimate. **2** to rely (on). **3** (*N Am.*) to think, to suppose. **calculable** *a.* that may be calculated. **calculability** (-bil´-) *n.* **calculably** *adv.* **calculated** *a.* **1** prearranged, intended. **2** premeditated, cold-blooded. **3** suitable, designed (to).

calculatedly *adv.* **calculating** *a.* **1** that calculates. **2** shrewd, acting with forethought. **3** scheming. **calculatingly** *adv.* **calculation** (-lā´shən) *n.* **1** the act of computing or calculating. **2** the result of this. **3** reckoning, a forecast or projection, an estimation. **4** careful planning, esp. selfish. **calculative** *a.* of or relating to calculation. **calculator** *n.* **1** an electronic device, usu. small and portable, which can carry out mathematical calculations. **2** a person who calculates. **3** a series of tables for use in calculating. [L *calculāre* (CALCULUS)]

calculus (kal´kūləs) *n.* (*pl.* **calculuses, calculi** (-lī)) **1** (*Med.*) a stony concretion formed in various organs of the body, such as the kidney. **2** (*Math.*) a method of calculation. **differential calculus** DIFFERENTIAL. **integral calculus** INTEGRAL. **calculous** *a.* (*Med.*) affected with or of the nature of a calculus. [L, a pebble, dim. of CALX]

caldarium (kaldeə´riəm) *n.* (*pl.* **caldaria** (-riə)) a Roman hot bath or room where such baths were taken. [L, from *calidus*, hot]

caldera (kaldeə´rə) *n.* (*pl.* **calderas**) a large, deep volcanic crater. [Sp., cauldron]

caldron CAULDRON.

Caledonian (kalidō´niən) *a.* **1** of or relating to Scotland; Scottish. **2** denoting a mountain building period in the Palaeozoic era. *~n.* (*poet.*) a Scotsman or Scotswoman. [L *Calēdonia*, N Britain]

calefacient (kalifā´shənt) *a.* (*Med.*) causing heat or warmth. *~n.* a medicine or other substance for increasing the heat of the body. **calefaction** (-fak´shən) *n.* **calefactive** *a.* **calefactor** *n.* a small cooking-stove. **calefactory** *a.* producing or communicating heat. *~n.* (*pl.* **calefactories**) a room in which monks used to warm themselves. [L *calefaciens -ntem*, pres.p. of *calefacere*, to warm (*calēre*, to be warm, *facere*, to make)]

calendar (kal´ində) *n.* **1** a list of the months, weeks and days of the year, with the civil and ecclesiastical holidays, festivals and other dates. **2** the system by which the beginning, length and subdivisions of the year are defined, esp. the Gregorian calendar adopted in England in 1752. **3** a table giving the times of sunrise and sunset, with other astronomical phenomena; an almanac. **4** a list or schedule of forthcoming events, appointments etc. **5** any list or register, e.g. of saints, cases awaiting trial etc. **6** a catalogue of documents in chronological order with digests of the contents. *~v.t.* **1** to register or enter in a list or calendar. **2** to arrange, digest and catalogue (documents). **calendar day** *n.* a civil day. **calendar line** *n.* DATE-LINE (under DATE[1]). **calendar month** *n.* a month according to the calendar, as distinct from *lunar month* etc. **calendar year** *n.* the period of 365 days, from 1 Jan. to 31 Dec., divided into 12 months and adopted as the legal year, with one day being added every fourth year to form a bissextile or leap year. **calendric** (-len´-), **calendrical** *a.* [OF *calendier*, L *calendārium*, an account-book]

calender[1] (kal´ində) *n.* a press or machine in which cloth or paper is passed between rollers to make it glossy. *~v.t.* to glaze by passing between rollers. †**calenderer, calendrer** *n.* **calendry** *n.* (*pl.* **calendries**) a place where cloth or paper is calendered. [F *calandre*, med. L *celendra*, L *cylindrus*, Gr. *kulindros*, a roller]

calender[2] (kal´ində) *n.* a member of an order of mendicant dervishes. [Pers. *galandar*]

calendrer CALENDER[1].

calendric CALENDAR.

calendry CALENDER[1].

calends (kal´əndz), **kalends** *n.pl.* the first day of any month in the ancient Roman calendar. **at the Greek calends** never (the Greeks had no calends). [L *calendae*, name of first day of month (old v. *calāre*, to proclaim, cp. Gr. *kalein*)]

calendula (kəlen´dūlə) *n.* a marigold, or any other plant of the genus *Calendula*. [L, dim. of *calendae*, CALENDS]

calenture (kal´əntūə) *n.* **1** a fever or delirium caused by heat, esp. suffered by sailors in the tropics. **2** fever, ardour, fury. [F, from Sp. *calentura* (L *calens -ntis*, pres.p. of *calēre*, to be hot)]

calescence (kəles´əns) *n.* increasing warmth or heat. [L *calescere*, to grow hot]

calf[1] (kahf) *n.* (*pl.* **calves** (kahvz)) **1** the young of any bovine animal, esp. of the domestic cow. **2** leather made from the skin of a calf; calfskin. **3** the young of some large animals, as of the elephant, rhinoceros, whale etc. **4** a stupid, childish person. **5** a small island near a larger one. **6** a small iceberg detached from a larger one. **in calf** (of cow, elephant, rhinoceros etc.) pregnant. **to kill the fatted calf** to have a lavish or extravagant celebration, esp. as a welcome (from the prodigal son's reception (Luke xv.23). **with calf** in calf. **calfbound** *a.* bound in calfskin. **calfhood** *n.* **calfish** *a.* **1** like a calf. **2** raw, inexperienced. **calf love** *n.* romantic attachment between a boy and a girl. **calf's-foot jelly** *n.* a jelly made by boiling a calf's foot. **calfskin** *n.* leather made from the skin of a calf, used in bookbinding and for boots and shoes. [OE *cealf* (cp. Icel. *kālfr*, Goth. *kalbō*, G *Kalb*)]

calf[2] (kahf) *n.* (*pl.* **calves** (kahvz)) the thick fleshy part of the back of the leg below the knee. **calf-length** *a.* (of a skirt, coat etc.) reaching down to the middle of the calves. **-calved** *a.* (*in comb.*, as *thick-calved*). [Icel. *kālfli*, prob. conn. with CALF[1]]

Caliban (kal´iban) *n.* a brutish man; a savage, a boor. [character in Shakespeare's *The Tempest*]

calibre (kal´ibə), (*N Am.*) **caliber** *n.* **1** the internal diameter of the bore of a gun or any tube. **2** the diameter of a bullet, shell etc. **3** quality, ability, character, standing. **calibrate** *v.t.* **1** to ascertain the calibre of. **2** to test the accuracy of (an instrument) against a standard. **3** to graduate (a gauge etc.). **calibration** (-rā´shən) *n.* **1** the act of calibrating. **2** the testing by experiment of the accuracy of a graduated scale. **3** any of the marks on a graduated scale. **calibrator** *n.* **calibred** *a.* (*also in comb.*). [F *calibre*, It. *calibro* (etym. uncertain; perh. from *qālib*, a mould)]

calices CALIX.

caliche (kalē´chi) *n.* **1** a deposit of sand, gravel or clay containing minerals (esp. Chile saltpetre), found in very dry regions. **2** a crust of sand cemented with calcium carbonate on the surface of soil in very dry regions. [Am. Sp.]

caliciform CALYCIFORM.

calicle CALYCLE.

calico (kal´ikō) *n.* (*pl.* **calicoes, calicos**) **1** cotton cloth formerly imported from the East. **2** white or unbleached cotton cloth. **3** (*esp. N Am.*) printed cotton cloth. *~a.* **1** made of calico. **2** (*N Am.*) brightly coloured, multicoloured. **calico-printing** *n.* the business or process of printing patterns on calico. [*Calicut* (now Kozhikode), town in India on the Malabar coast]

calid (kal´id) *a.* warm, tepid, hot. **calidity** (-lid´-) *n.* [L *calidus*, warm]

Calif. *abbr.* California.

calif, califate CALIPH.

Californian (kalifaw´niən) *a.* of or relating to the N American state of California. *~n.* a native or inhabitant of California. **California condor** (kalifaw´niə) *n.* a rare vulture of California, *Cymnogyos californianus*. **California poppy** *n.* a plant of the genus *Eschscholtzia*, with bright yellow or orange flowers. [name of N American state]

californium (kalifaw´niəm) *n.* an artificially-produced radioactive element, at. no. 98, chem. symbol Cf. [University of *California*, where discovered]

†**caliginous** (kəlij´inəs) *a.* **1** misty, murky. **2** dark,

obscure, gloomy. **caliginosity** (-os´iti) *n.* [L *cālīginōsus*, misty (*cāligo -inem*, mist, obscurity)]

calipash (kal´ipash) *n.* that part of a turtle next to the upper shell, containing a dull green gelatinous substance. [perh. var. of CARAPACE]

calipee (kal´ipē) *n.* that part of a turtle next to the lower shell, containing a light yellow substance. [perh. var. of CARAPACE]

caliper CALLIPER.

caliph (kā´lif, kal´-), **calif, kalif, khalif** *n.* the chief ruler in certain Muslim countries, who is regarded as the successor of Muhammad. **caliphate** (-fāt) *n.* **1** the office or dignity of a caliph. **2** his term of office. **3** his dominion. [F *calife*, med. L *calīpha*, Arab. *khalīfah*, successor]

calisaya (kalisā´ə) *n.* bark from a tree of the genus *Cinchona*, esp. *Cinchona calisaya*; a type of Peruvian bark. [Sp., from the name of a Bolivian Indian]

calisthenic, calisthenics CALLISTHENICS.

calix (kā´liks) *n.* (*pl.* **calices** (-lisēz)) a cup or chalice. [L, cp. CALYX]

calk[1] CAULK.

calk[2] (kawk) *v.t.* to copy (a drawing etc.) by rubbing the back with colouring matter and tracing the lines with a pointed instrument onto paper beneath. [F *calquer*, It. *calcare*, L *calcāre*, to tread (*calx -cem*, heel)]

calk[3] (kawk) *n.* a calkin. ~*v.t.* **1** to furnish with a calkin. **2** to rough-shoe. **3** to knock down the edges of (an iron plate or the head or point of a rivet) so as to make them fit closely. **calking-iron** *n.* an instrument used for this purpose. [as CALKIN]

calkin (kaw´kin, kal´-) *n.* **1** a sharp projection on a horseshoe to prevent slipping. **2** a set of spikes nailed on shoes or boots. [OF *calcain*, L *calcāneum*, the heel (*calx*)]

call (kawl) *v.t.* **1** to name, to designate. **2** to describe as. **3** to regard or consider as. **4** to summon, esp. in a loud voice. **5** to communicate with or summon by telephone or radio. **6** to invite. **7** to command. **8** to announce or cause to happen (*to call a strike*). **9** to appeal to. **10** to rouse from sleep. **11** to nominate, invite or summon (to a profession etc.). **12** to lure (birds etc.) by imitating their cry. **13** (*Comput.*) to transfer control to (a subroutine) by means of a calling sequence. **14** to call over (a list of names) to ascertain that all are present (*to call the roll*). ~*v.i.* **1** to speak in a loud voice; to cry aloud, to shout. **2** (of a bird etc.) to make a characteristic sound or cry. **3** to pay a short visit. **4** to make a telephone call. **5** in bridge, to make a bid. **6** in poker, to ask an opponent to show their cards. **7** in whist, to show by special play that trumps are wanted. ~*n.* **1** a loud cry. **2** a vocal address or supplication. **3** a communication by telephone or radio. **4** the cry of a bird or animal. **5** a whistle to imitate the cry of a bird or animal. **6** a short visit. **7** a summons, an invitation. **8** an invitation to become minister to a congregation. **9** a summons or signal on a bugle, whistle etc. **10** a requirement or demand. **11** duty, necessity, justification, occasion. **12** a demand for payment of instalments due (of shares etc.). **13** a call option. **at call** on call. **on call** **1** (of a doctor etc.) available to be summoned if required. **2** (of a loan etc.) to be repaid on demand. **to call a halt (to)** HALT[1]. **to call a spade a spade** SPADE[1]. **to call away** to summon away, to divert. **to call back** **1** to revoke, to withdraw. **2** to visit again. **3** to call later by telephone. **to call down** to invoke. **to call for** **1** to desire the attendance of. **2** to appeal for, to demand. **3** to require, necessitate. **4** to visit a place to bring (a person or thing) away. **5** to signal for (trumps). **to call forth** **1** to elicit. **2** to summon to action. **to call in** **1** to summon to one's aid. **2** to withdraw (money) from circulation. **3** to order the return of. **4** to pay a short visit (on, at etc.). **to call in/into question** QUESTION. **to call into being** to give existence to, to create. **to call into play** PLAY. **to call it a day** DAY. **to call names** NAME. **to call off** **1** to summon away, to order (an animal or person) to stop attacking etc. **2** to cancel. **to call on** **1** to invoke, to appeal to. **2** to pay a short visit to. **to call one's own** to regard as one's possession, to own. **to call out** **1** to say loudly, to shout. **2** to summon (troops etc.) to service. **3** to order (workers) to strike. **4** to elicit. **5** to challenge to a duel or fight. **to call over** to read aloud. **to call someone's bluff** BLUFF[2]. **to call the shots** SHOT[1]. **to call the tune** TUNE. **to call to account** ACCOUNT. **to call to mind** MIND. **to call to the bar** BAR[1]. **to call to witness** WITNESS. **to call up** **1** (*Mil.*) to mobilize. **2** to make a telephone call to. **3** to rouse from sleep. **4** to cause to remember or imagine. **5** to summon to appear. **6** to require payment of. **to pay a call** (*coll.*) to urinate or defecate. **within call** within hearing. **callable** *a.* **call alarm** *n.* a small transmitter that sends out a radio signal to summon help, used esp. by frail or elderly people living alone. **call-bird** *n.* a bird that decoys others by its call. **call-box** *n.* a public telephone box. **call-boy** *n.* **1** a person who calls actors when they are wanted on the stage. **2** a male prostitute who makes appointments by telephone. **caller**[1] *n.* a person who calls, esp. one who telephones or visits. **call-girl** *n.* a female prostitute who makes appointments by telephone. **calling** *n.* **1** an occupation, trade or profession. **2** a vocation. **3** a solemn summons to duty, faith etc. **4** the body of people employed in a particular occupation, business or vocation. **calling card** *n.* (*N Am.*) a visiting card. **calling sequence** *n.* (*Comput.*) a code used in transferring control to a subroutine. **call-loan, call-money** *n.* money lent on condition that repayment may be demanded without notice. **call-note** *n.* the call of an animal, esp. a bird, to its mate or young. **call number** *n.* a set of numbers and/or letters identifying the position of a book in a library. **call of nature** *n.* a need to urinate or defecate. **call option** *n.* on the Stock Exchange, the option of claiming stock at a certain time at a price agreed on. **call-out** *n.* an instance of summoning someone to do repairs, provide emergency services, etc. **call-over** *n.* **1** a roll-call. **2** a recital of betting prices. **call sign, call signal** *n.* a set of numbers and/or letters identifying a radio transmitter or station. **call-up** *n.* (*Mil.*) mobilization. [Icel. *kalla* (cp. Dut. *kallen*, OE *ceallian*, OHG *challōn*)]

calla (kal´ə), **calla lily** *n.* **1** the arum lily, *Zantedeschia aethiopica*. **2** a marsh plant, *Calla palustris*.

caller[1] CALL.

caller[2] (kal´ə) *a.* (*Sc.*) **1** cool, refreshing. **2** of fish, freshly caught. [perh. var. of *calver* (see CALVERED)]

calligraphy (kəlig´rəfi) *n.* **1** the art of beautiful handwriting. **2** handwriting. **calligrapher, calligraphist** *n.* **calligraphic** (-graf´-) *a.* [Gr. *kalligraphia*]

calliope (kəlī´əpi) *n.* (*N Am.*) a series of steam-whistles that produce musical notes when played by a keyboard. [Gr. *Kalliope*, Calliope, the ninth Muse, of eloquence and heroic poetry]

calliper (kal´ipə), **caliper** *n.* **1** (*pl.*) compasses with bow legs for measuring convex bodies, or with points turned out for measuring calibres. **2** a calliper rule. **3** a calliper splint. ~*v.t.* to measure by means of callipers. **calliper rule** *n.* a rule for measuring internal or external diameters etc. **calliper splint** *n.* a form of splint for the leg which takes pressure off the foot when walking. [short for *calibre-compasses*]

callipygous (kalipī´gəs), **callipygean** (-pij´iən) *a.* having beautiful buttocks. [Gr. *kallipugos*, epithet of Aphrodite (*kallos*, beauty, *pugē*, buttock)]

callisthenics (kalisthen´iks), (*esp. N Am.*) **calisthenics** *n.pl.* gymnastics promoting fitness and grace. **callisthenic** *a.* [Gr. *kallos*, beauty, *sthenos*, strength (anal. with *kallisthenes*, adorned with strength)]

callop (kal´əp) *n.* an Australian freshwater fish, *Plectroplites ambiguus*, used as food. [Austral. Abor.]

callous (kal´əs) *a.* **1** unfeeling, insensitive, unsympathetic. **2** (of skin) hardened. **callosity** (-los´-) *n.* (*pl.* **callosities**) **1** hardened or thickened skin, caused by friction, pressure, disease, injury etc. **2** a callus. **3** insensitivity, lack of feeling. **callously** *adv.* **callousness** *n.* [L *callōsus*, hard or thick-skinned]

callow (kal´ō) *a.* **1** youthful, immature, inexperienced. **2** unfledged, downy. **callowly** *adv.* **callowness** *n.* [OE *calu*, Gmc. *kalwoz*, L *calvus*, bald]

calluna (kəloo´nə) *n.* the heather, *Calluna vulgaris*. [Gr. *kallunein*, to beautify, to sweep (*kalos*, beautiful)]

callus (kal´əs) *n.* (*pl.* **calluses**) **1** an area of hard or thick skin caused by friction, pressure etc. **2** (*Med.*) a bony formation serving to unite a fracture. **3** (*Bot.*) a hard formation. ~*v.i.* (*pres. p.* **callusing,** *past, p.p.* **callused**) to form a callus. ~*v.t.* to cause to form a callus. [L]

calm (kahm) *a.* **1** still, quiet. **2** tranquil, undisturbed. ~*n.* **1** the state of being calm. **2** (*Naut.*) complete absence of wind. ~*v.t.* to make calm. ~*v.i.* to become calm. **to calm down** to make or become calm. **calmative** *a.* tending to calm. ~*n.* (*Med.*) a sedative medicine. **calmed** *a.* **calmly** *adv.* **calmness** *n.* [F *calme*, Sp. and It. *calma*, prob. from late L *cauma*, Gr. *kauma*, heat (*kaiein*, to burn)]

calmodulin (kalmod´ūlin) *n.* a protein found in most plant and animal cells, where it controls various processes involving calcium. [*cal*cium, *modul*ate, -IN[1]]

calomel (kal´əmel) *n.* mercurous chloride, an active purgative. [F, perh. from Gr. *kalos*, beautiful, *melas*, black]

Calor gas® (kal´ə) *n.* a type of bottled gas used for cooking etc.

caloric (kəlor´ik) *a.* of or relating to heat or calories. ~†*n.* the supposed fluid cause of heat. **caloricity** (-ris´-) *n.* [F *calorique*, L *calor*, heat]

calorie (kal´əri), **calory** *n.* **1** a unit of heat, equalling 4.1868 joules; the quantity of heat required to raise the temperature of 1 gram of water by 1°C, a small calorie. **2** (**Calorie**) a unit of heat equalling 1000 (small) calories, used in measuring the energy content of food. **calorifacient** (-fā´shənt) *a.* (esp. of foods) heat-producing. **calorific** (-rif´-) *a.* of, relating to or producing heat. **calorifically** *adv.* **calorific value** *n.* the amount of heat produced by the complete combustion of a given amount (usu. 1 kg) of fuel. **calorimeter** (-rim´itə) *n.* an instrument for measuring actual quantities of heat, or the specific heat of a body. **calorimetric** (-met´-) *a.* **calorimetry** (-rim´-) *n.* [F *calorique*, L *calor*, heat]

calotte (kəlot´) *n.* **1** a small skullcap worn by Roman Catholic ecclesiastics. **2** a caplike crest on a bird's head. **3** anything cap-shaped. **4** a recess hollowed out in the upper part of a room, chapel etc. to reduce the apparent height. [F, perh. dim. of *cale*, CAUL]

calotype (kal´ətīp) *n.* an early photographic process invented by W. H. Fox Talbot; a talbotype. [Gr. *kalos*, beautiful, TYPE]

caloyer (kal´əyə) *n.* a Greek Orthodox monk, esp. of the order of St Basil. [F, from It. *caloiero*, mod. Gr. *kalogēros* (*kalos*, beautiful, *-gēros*, aged)]

calpac (kal´pak), **calpack, kalpack** *n.* a high, triangular felt cap worn in the East. [Turk. *qalpaq*]

calque (kalk) *n.* a loan translation, a literal translation of a foreign expression. [F, tracing, from L *calcāre*, to tread]

Caltech (kal´tek) *n.* the California Institute of Technology.

caltrop (kal´trəp), **calthrop** (-thrəp), **caltrap** (-trap) *n.* **1** an instrument formed of four iron spikes joined at the bases, thrown on the ground to impede the advance of cavalry. **2** any of several trailing plants of the genus *Tribulus* etc., with spiny fruit, that entangle the feet. **3** the star thistle, *Centaurea calcitrapa*. **4** a water weed, such as *Potamogeton densus*, *P. crispus* or *Trapa natans*; water caltrop. [OE *calcatrippe*, *calcetreppe*, a thistle (cp. OF *kauketrape*, *cauchetrepe*), prob. from late L (L *calx -cem*, heel, late L *trappa*, OHG *trapo*, TRAP[1])]

calumet (kal´ūmet) *n.* the tobacco-pipe of the N American Indians, used as a symbol of peace and friendship; the peace pipe. [Norm. F (preserved in Canadian French); parallel to OF *chalemel* (F *chalumeau*), from L *calamellus*, dim. of CALAMUS]

calumniate (kəlŭm´niāt) *v.t.* (*formal*) **1** to slander. **2** to charge falsely with something criminal or disreputable. ~*v.i.* to utter calumnies. **calumniation** (-ā´shən) *n.* **calumniator** *n.* **calumniatory** *a.* **calumnious** *a.* **calumniously** *adv.* **calumniousness** *n.* **calumny** (kal´-) *n.* (*pl.* **calumnies**) **1** a malicious misrepresentation of the words or actions of another. **2** slander. **3** a false charge. ~*v.t.* (*3rd pers. sing. pres.* **calumnies,** *pres.p.* **calumnying,** *past, p.p.* **calumnied**) to utter calumnies about, to slander. [L *calumniātus*, p.p. of *calumniāri* (*calvī*, to deceive)]

calutron (kal´ūtron) *n.* a mass spectrometer that is used in the separation of isotopes. [*Cal*ifornia *U*niversity, -TRON]

calvados (kal´vədos) *n.* apple brandy made in Normandy. [*Calvados*, French department]

calvaria (kalveə´riə, -vah´-) *n.* the upper part of the skull of a vertebrate animal. [L, a skull (*calvus*, bald)]

Calvary (kal´vəri) *n.* (*pl.* **Calvaries**) **1** the place where Christ was crucified. **2** a life-size representation of Christ's crucifixion, usu. in the open air. **3** a representation of the successive scenes of Christ's passion. **4** (*also* **calvary**) an experience of great suffering. **Calvary cross** *n.* a cross mounted on three steps. [L *calvāria*, a skull (*calvus*, bald); trans. of Gr. *Golgotha*, Heb. *gogolthā*, the skull]

calve (kahv) *v.i.* **1** to give birth to a calf. **2** to bring forth young. **3** (of icebergs) to detach and cast off a mass of ice. ~*v.t.* to bear, bring forth. [OE *cealfian* (*cealf*, CALF[1])]

-calved CALF[2].

calvered (kal´vəd) *a.* (of salmon etc.) prepared in a particular way when fresh. [from obs. v. *calver*, etym. unknown]

calves[1] CALF[1].

calves[2] CALF[2].

Calvinism (kal´vinizm) *n.* the tenets of John Calvin, esp. his doctrine of predestination and election. **Calvinist** *n.* **Calvinistic, Calvinistical** (-nist´-) *a.* [John *Calvin*, 1509–64, Swiss theologian]

calvity (kal´viti), **calvities** (-vish´iēz) *n.* baldness. [L *calvities*, baldness (*calvus*, bald)]

calx (kalks) *n.* (*pl.* **calxes, calces** (kal´sēz)) **1** ashes or fine powder remaining from metals, minerals etc. after they have undergone calcination. **2** calcium oxide. [L *calx -cis*, lime]

calyc- CALYCI-.

calycanthus (kalikan´thəs) *n.* a N American shrub of the genus *Calycanthus*.

calyces CALYX.

calyci- (kalis´i), **calyc-** (kalis´, -lik´) *comb. form* calyx. [CALYX]

calyciform (kalis´ifawm), **caliciform** *a.* having the form of a calyx.

calycine (kal´isīn), **calycinal** (kəlis´inəl) *a.* of, belonging to, or in the form of a calyx.

calycle (kal´ikəl), **calicle, calyculus** (kalik´ūləs) *n.* **1** a small calyx. **2** a row of small leaflets at the base of the calyx on the outside. **3** the outer covering of a seed. **calycled** *a.* having a calycle. **calycular** (-lik´-), **calyculate** (-lik´ūlət) *a.* [L *calyculus*, dim. of CALYX]

calypso (kəlip´sō) *n.* (*pl.* **calypsos**) a W Indian narrative song, usu. performed to a syncopated accompaniment and made up as the singer goes along. [etym. uncertain]

calyptra (kəlip´trə) *n.* (*pl.* **calyptras**) (*Bot.*) a hood or cover, such as a root-cap. **calyptrate** (-trāt) *a.* **calyptriform** *a.* **calyptrogen** (-trəjən) *n.* (*Bot.*) a layer of cells at the tip of a root, which gives rise to the root-cap. [Gr. *kaluptra*, a veil (*kaluptein*, to cover, conceal)]

calyx (kā´liks, kal´-) *n.* (*pl.* **calyces** (-sēz), **calyxes**) **1** the whorl of leaves or sepals (usu. green) forming the outer integument of a flower. **2** a cuplike body cavity or organ. [L, from Gr. *kalux* (cp. *kaluptein*, L *cēlāre*, to cover, conceal)]

calzone (kaltsō´nā), *n.* (*pl.* **calzones, calzoni** (-ni)) a folded pizza containing a filling. [It.]

CAM *abbr.* **1** computer-aided manufacture, computer-assisted manufacturing. **2** content-addressable memory.

cam (kam) *n.* an eccentric projection attached to a revolving shaft for the purpose of giving linear motion to another part. **camshaft** *n.* a shaft bearing cams which operate the valves of internal-combustion engines. [var. of COMB]

camaraderie (kamərah´dəri) *n.* **1** comradeship. **2** good fellowship and loyalty among intimate friends. [F, from *camarade*, COMRADE]

camarilla (kamərilʹə) *n.* (*pl.* **camarillas**) a cabal. [Sp. dim. of *camara*, CHAMBER]

camass (kam´as), **camas, quamash** (kwom´ash, -mash´) *n.* any liliaceous plant, of the genus *Camassia*, esp. *Camassia quamash* or *Camassia esculenta*, the bulb of which is eaten by various N American peoples. [N Am. Ind.]

Camb. *abbr.* Cambridge.

camber (kam´bə) *n.* **1** the curvature given to a road surface to make water run off it. **2** any similar slight convexity, as on a ship's deck, the wing of an aircraft, etc. **3** a slight upward slope towards the outside of a bend in a road, racetrack, etc. **4** a piece of timber bent with an arching curve. *~v.t., v.i.* to bend, to arch. **cambered** *a.* having a camber. [F *cambre*, from *cambrer*, L *camerāre*, to vault (*camera*, chamber)]

Camberwell beauty (kam´bəwel) *n.* a butterfly, *Nymphalis antiopa*, having deep purple wings with yellow or cream borders. [*Camberwell*, in SE London]

cambist (kam´bist) *n.* **1** an expert in the science of financial exchange. **2** a money-changer. **3** a manual or other list of currency exchange rates etc. **cambism, cambistry** *n.* [F *cambiste*, late L *cambium*, exchange]

cambium (kam´biəm) *n.* (*pl.* **cambiums, cambia** (-biə)) the cellular tissue which annually increases the girth of exogenous trees and other plants. **cambial** *a.* [late L, exchange]

Cambodian (kambō´diən) *a.* of or relating to Cambodia (Kampuchea) in SE Asia. *~n.* a native or inhabitant of Cambodia.

cambrel (kam´brəl) *n.* a bent piece of wood used by butchers for hanging up carcasses. [etym. uncertain]

Cambrian (kam´briən) *a.* **1** of or belonging to Wales. **2** of or relating to the first period of the Palaeozoic era, or the geological system formed in this period. *~n.* **1** a Welshman or Welshwoman. **2** the Cambrian period or system. [L *Cambria*, *Cumbria*, Celt. *Cymry*, Welsh, *Cymru*, Wales]

cambric (kam´brik) *n.* a type of very fine white linen or cotton. [orig. made at *Cambrai*, N France]

Cambridge blue (kām´brij) *n.*, *a.* pale blue. [*Cambridge* University in E England]

Cambs. *abbr.* Cambridgeshire.

camcorder (kam´kawdə) *n.* a video camera and recorder combined in one unit.

came[1] COME.

came[2] (kām) *n.* a strip of lead used in framing glass in lattice windows. [Sc., earlier *calm*]

camel (kam´əl) *n.* **1** a large, hornless, humpbacked ruminant with long neck and padded feet, used in Africa and the East as a beast of burden. There are two species, the Arabian camel, *Camelus dromedarius*, with one hump, and the Bactrian camel, *C. bactrianus*, with two humps. **2** a watertight float attached to a boat to raise it in the water. **3** a pale brownish-yellow colour. *~a.* **1** of this colour. **2** made of camel-hair fabric. **cameleer** (-liə´) *n.* a camel-driver. **camel-hair, camel's hair** *n.* **1** the hair of a camel used to make various fabrics. **2** an artist's paintbrush made of hairs from squirrels' tails. **cameline** (-līn) *n.* a fabric made of camel-hair. *~a.* like a camel. **camelish** *a.* obstinate. **camelry** *n.* (*pl.* **camelries**) troops mounted on camels. [OE, from L *camēlus*, Gr. *kamēlos*, from Semitic (Heb. *gāmāl*, Arab. *jāmāl*)]

cameleon CHAMELEON.

camellia (kəmē´liə) *n.* an evergreen shrub, of the genus *Camellia*, with beautiful flowers. [Georg Josef *Kamel*, 1661–1706, Moravian Jesuit and traveller in the East]

†**camelopard** (kəmel´əpahd) *n.* the giraffe. [L *camēlopardus -pardālis*, Gr. *kamēlopardis* (CAMEL, PARD[2])]

Camembert (kam´əmbeə) *n.* a soft rich cheese from Normandy. [village in N France]

cameo (kam´iō) *n.* (*pl.* **cameos**) **1** a precious stone with two layers of colours, the upper being carved in relief, the lower serving as background. **2** a similar carving using other materials. **3** a piece of jewellery using such carving. **4** a short literary piece. **5** a small part in a play or film, esp. one played by a famous actor. *~a.* **1** of a cameo or cameos. **2** small and perfect. **cameo ware** *n.* pottery decorated with relief motifs on a background of a different colour. [It. *cammeo*, late L *cammaeus*; etym. unknown]

camera (kam´ərə) *n.* (*pl.* **cameras**) **1** an apparatus for taking photographs, which records an image (or a series of images in a cinecamera) on a light-sensitive surface. **2** an apparatus which records (moving) images and converts them to electrical signals for TV transmission. **3** (*pl.* **camerae** (-rē)) the private chamber of a judge. **in camera 1** in private. **2** in a judge's chamber, or with the public excluded from the court. **off camera** not being filmed. **on camera** being recorded on film. **camera crew** *n.* a group of people, including cameraman, sound recordist etc., needed to make a film or television programme. **cameral** *a.* of or relating to a judge's chamber or a legislative chamber. **camera lucida** (loo´sidə) *n.* (*pl.* **camera lucidas**) an instrument (often attached to a microscope) by which the rays of light from an object are reflected to produce an image of the object on a piece of paper or other drawing surface. **cameraman** *n.* (*pl.* **cameramen**) a person who operates a film or television camera. **camera obscura** (əbskū´rə) *n.* (*pl.* **camera obscuras**) a dark box, or small room, admitting light through a pinhole or a double-convex lens which projects an image of external objects on an internal screen. **camera-ready copy** *n.* (*Print.*) textual and/or illustrative material that is ready to be photographed for the production of printing plates. **camera-shy** *a.* unwilling to be photographed or filmed. **camerated** *a.* **1** arched. **2** (*Zool.*) divided into chambers. **camera tube** *n.* the device in a television or video camera that converts optical images to electrical signals. **camerawork** *n.* the technique or process of using a camera, esp. a film or television camera. [L, vault, from Indo-Eur. *kam-*, to cover over (cp. Gr. *kamara*, anything with a vaulted roof)]

camerlengo (kaməleng´gō), **camerlingo** (-ling´-) *n.* (*pl.* **camerlengos, camerlingos**) a papal treasurer. [It., chamberlain]

camiknickers CAMISOLE.

camion (kam´iõ) *n.* **1** a heavy lorry. **2** a dray. [F, a lorry]

camisade (kamisād´), **camisado** (-sah´dō) *n.* (*pl.* **camisades, camisados**) (*Hist.*) a night assault or surprise attack, in which the soldiers wore their shirts over their armour as a means of recognition. [F *camisade*, Sp. *camisada, camiçada*, from *camisa*, a shirt]

camisole (kam´isōl) *n.* an underbodice. **camiknickers** *n.pl.* an undergarment comprising a camisole and knickers in one piece. [F, from Sp. *camisola*, dim. of *camisa*, a shirt, see CHEMISE]

camlet (kam´lit), **chamlet** (cham´-) *n.* **1** a fabric, orig. of camel's hair, now a mixture of silk, wool and hair. **2** a strong waterproof fabric. **3** a garment of camlet. [F *camelot*, Arab. *khamlat, khaml*, an Eastern fabric]

camomile (kam´əmīl), **chamomile** *n.* an aromatic creeping plant belonging to the genera *Anthemis* or *Matricaria*, esp. *A. nobilis* or *M. chamomilla.* **camomile tea** *n.* a medicinal drink made from dried flowers of these plants. [F *camomille*, late L *camomilla*, Gr. *chamaimēlon*, lit. earth-apple]

Camorra (kəmor´ə) *n.* **1** a lawless secret society in S Italy, dating from the old kingdom of Naples. **2** any similar group. **Camorrist** *n.* [It.]

camouflage (kam´əflahzh) *n.* **1** disguise, esp. the concealment of guns, camps, buildings, vehicles etc., from the enemy by means of deceptive painting, a covering of boughs etc. **2** the natural colouring or markings of some animals, which resemble their surroundings and thus conceal them from predators. **3** concealment of one's actions. ~*v.t.* to disguise. [F *camoufler*, to disguise]

camp[1] (kamp) *n.* **1** the place where an army is lodged in tents or other temporary structures. **2** a station for training troops. **3** a body of troops in tents; an army on campaign. **4** military life. **5** the temporary quarters of gypsies, holidaymakers, Scouts or Guides, explorers, refugees etc., usu. in tents, caravans or similar structures. **6** the occupants of such quarters. **7** a body of adherents; a side. **8** a ruined prehistoric fort. **9** (*Austral.*) a halting-place for cattle. ~*v.t.* to encamp (troops). ~*v.i.* to encamp; to lodge temporarily in a tent etc., to camp out. **a foot in both camps** FOOT. **to camp out 1** to lodge in a tent etc. in the open. **2** to sleep outdoors. **3** to place (troops) in camp. **camp-bed** *n.* a light folding bed. **camp-chair** *n.* a folding chair. **camper** *n.* **1** a person who camps, esp. a holidaymaker. **2** a vehicle having living accommodation in the back. **campfire** *n.* an open fire at the centre of a camp. **camp follower** *n.* **1** a civilian who follows an army in the field. **2** a hanger-on. **camp meeting** *n.* a religious meeting in the open air or in a tent, often prolonged for days. **campsite, campground** *n.* a place set aside, or suitable, for camping. [F *camp* (cp. *champ*), It. or Sp. *campo*, L *campus*, a field]

camp[2] (kamp) *a.* **1** affectedly homosexual. **2** effeminate. **3** exaggerated, theatrical, artificial. ~*v.i.* to behave in a camp manner. ~*n.* camp behaviour. **to camp it up** to act in an exaggeratedly camp manner; to overact. **campy** *a.* **campily** *adv.* [etym. unknown]

campaign (kampān´) *n.* **1** a series of military operations aimed at a single objective. **2** military service in the field. **3** a series of operations aimed at raising public awareness, achieving reform etc., as in politics or advertising. ~*v.i.* to organize or take part in a campaign. **campaigner** *n.* [F *campagne*, the open country, It. *campagna*, L *campania*, a plain, *campus*, a field (cp. CHAMPAGNE, CHAMPAIGN)]

campanile (kampənē´li) *n.* (*pl.* **campaniles, campanili** (-li)) **1** a bell-tower, esp. a detached one. **2** a steeple. [It., from *campana*, bell]

campanology (kampənol´əji) *n.* **1** the art of bell-ringing. **2** the study of bells. **campanologer, campanologist** *n.* **campanological** (-loj´-) *a.* [L *campana*, bell]

campanula (kampan´ūlə) *n.* any plant of the genus *Campanula* with bell-shaped flowers, such as the bluebell of Scotland, the Canterbury bell etc. **campanulaceous** (-lā´-) *a.* **campanular, campanulate** (-lət) *a.* (*Bot., Zool.*) bell-shaped. [L *campana*, bell]

Campeachy wood (kampē´chi) *n.* logwood. [*Campeche*, on W coast of Mexico]

campestral (kampes´trəl) *a.* of, relating to or growing in the fields or open country. [L *campester-tris*, pertaining to a field (*campus*, a field)]

camphene (kam´fēn), **camphine** (-fēn, -fīn) *n.* **1** a terpene found in many essential oils. **2** †an oil derived from serpentine. [see CAMPHOR]

camphor (kam´fə) *n.* a whitish, translucent, volatile, crystalline substance with a pungent odour, obtained from *Camphora officinarum, Dryobalanops aromatica* and other trees, used as an insect repellent, in liniment and in the manufacture of celluloid. **camphoraceous** (-fərā´shəs) *a.* **camphorate**[1] (-rət) *n.* **camphoric** (kamfor´ik) *a.* of, relating to or containing camphor. **camphor laurel, camphor tree** *n.* the tree *Cinnamomum camphora* of E Asia, a source of camphor. **camphor wood** *n.* the wood of the camphor laurel or of an Australian tree, *Callitris robusta.* [OF *camphre*, med. L *camphora*, Arab. *kāfūr*]

camphorate[1] CAMPHOR.

camphorate[2] (kam´fərāt) *v.t.* to wash or impregnate with camphor. **camphorated oil** *n.* liniment containing camphor.

campion (kam´piən) *n.* any flowering plant of the genera *Lychnis* or *Silene.* [etym. uncertain; perh. *campion*, obs. var. of CHAMPION, from the use of such plants in champions' garlands]

campo *n.* (*pl.* **campos**) an area of level or undulating grassland, esp. in Brazil. [Am. Sp., L *campus*, a field]

campshed (kamp´shed) *v.t.* (*pres.p.* **campshedding,** *past, p.p.* **campshedded**) to line (a river bank) with piles and planks to prevent it from being worn away. **campshedding** *n.* piles and planks of this kind. **campsheet** (-shēt) *v.t.* (*pres.p.* **campsheeting,** *past, p.p.* **campsheeted**). **campsheeting** *n.* [etym. unknown]

campus (kam´pəs) *n.* (*pl.* **campuses**) **1** the buildings and grounds of a university or college. **2** a geographically separate part of a university or college. **3** the academic world in general. [L, a field]

campylobacter (kampilōbak´tə, kam´-) *n.* a bacterium that can cause gastroenteritis and other disorders. [Gr. *kampulos*, bent, BACTERIUM]

CAMRA (kam´rə) *abbr.* Campaign for Real Ale.

camshaft CAM.

camwood (kam´wud) *n.* barwood; a hard red wood from a W African tree, *Baphia nitida.* [perh. from Afr. name *kambi*]

Can. *abbr.* **1** Canada. **2** Canadian.

can[1] (kan) *v.aux.* (*pres.* **can,** †**canst** (kanst), *neg.* **cannot** (kan´ət, -not´), **can't** (kahnt), *past* **could** (kud)) **1** to be able to (*I can't swim*). **2** to be allowed to (*Can I go now?*). **3** to be possible to (*It can't be done*). **4** (*in past, coll.*) to want to (*I could murder a drink*). **could use** USE[1]. **can-do** *a.* (of an attitude, approach etc.) positive and determined. [OE *cunnan*, to know, pl. *cunnon* (cp. Dut. *kunnen*, OHG *chunnan*, G *können*, KEN, KNOW, L *gnoscere*, Gr. *gignōskein*)]

Usage note See note under MAY[1].

can[2] (kan) *n.* **1** a metal vessel for holding liquid. **2** a metal vessel in which meat, fruit, vegetables, fish etc. are hermetically sealed up for preservation; a tin. **3** a canful. **4** a shallow metal container for film. **5** (*sl.*) prison. **6** (*sl.*) a lavatory. **7** (*pl., sl.*) headphones. ~*v.t.* (*pres. p.* **canning,** *past, p.p.* **canned**) to put in cans for preservation. **can it!** (*sl.*) stop doing that! **in the can 1** filmed or recorded, processed and ready for release. **2** (*fig.*) arranged. **to carry the can** (*coll.*) to take responsibility, to accept blame. **can-buoy** *n.* a cylindrical buoy used in navigation. **canful** *n.* **canned** *a.* **1**

preserved in a can. **2** (*sl.*) drunk. **3** (of music or laughter) recorded in advance. **canner** *n.* **cannery** *n.* (*pl.* **canneries**) a place where food is canned. **can of worms** *n.* (*coll.*) a complicated and potentially problematic issue or situation. **can-opener** *n.* a tin-opener. [OE *canne* (cp. Dut. *kan*, OHG *chann*, G *Kanne*)]

Canaan (kā´nən) *n.* **1** (*fig.*) a land of promise. **2** heaven. **Canaanite** *n.* **1** an inhabitant of the land of Canaan. **2** a descendant of Canaan, the son of Ham. **Canaanitic** (-nit´-) *a.* [Heb. *k'naan*, the Promised Land of the Israelites]

Canadian (kənā´diən) *a.* of or relating to Canada. ~*n.* a native or inhabitant of Canada. **Canada Day** *n.* 1 July, a public holiday in Canada, commemorating the granting of dominion status to Canada in 1876. **Canada goose** *n.* a large N American wild goose, *Branta canadensis*, grey and brown in colour. **Canada lily** *n.* a N American lily, *Lilium canadense*, with small orange flowers. **Canadian French** *n.* the form of the French language used in French-speaking parts of Canada. ~*a.* of or relating to this language. **Canadian pondweed** *n.* a N American aquatic plant, *Elodea canadensis* or *Anacharis canadensis*, used in ponds and aquariums.

canaigre (kənā´gə) *n.* a dock plant, *Rumex hymenosepalus* of the southern states of America (esp. Texas), the root of which is used in tanning. [Mex. Sp.]

canaille (kanī´) *n.* the rabble, the mob. [F, from It. *canaglia*, *cane*, L *canis*, a dog]

canakin CANNIKIN.

canal (kənal´) *n.* **1** an artificial watercourse, esp. one used for navigation. **2** (*Anat.*, *Bot.*) a duct or tubular passage. **3** (*Zool.*) a siphonal groove. **4** (*Archit.*) a fluting, a groove. ~*v.t.* (*pres. p.* **canalling,** (*N Am.*) **canaling,** *past, p.p.* **canalled,** (*N Am.*) **canaled**) **1** to make a canal across. **2** to provide with canals. **canal boat** *n.* a long narrow boat used on canals. **canalize** (kan´-), **canalise** *v.t.* **1** to make a canal across or through. **2** to convert (a river) into a navigable waterway. **3** to provide with canals. **4** to give a desired direction to; to channel. **canalization** (-zā´shən) *n.* the construction of canals. **canal rays** *n.pl.* a steady flow of positively electrified particles which take part in the electrical discharge in a rarefied gas. **canals of Mars** *n.pl.* apparent linear markings on the surface of the planet Mars, formerly supposed by some astronomers to be waterways or zones of vegetation. [F, from L *canālis*]

canaliculus (kanəlik´ūləs) *n.* (*pl.* **canaliculi** (-lī)) (*Anat.*, *Bot.*) a small channel or groove. **caniculate, canaliculated** (-lātid) *a.* [L, dim. of *canālis*, see CANAL]

canapé (kan´əpā), **canape** *n.* **1** a small thin piece of bread or toast topped with cheese, fish etc. **2** a sofa. [F]

canard (kanahd´) *n.* **1** an absurd story, a hoax, a false report. **2** an aircraft having a tailplane mounted in front of the wings. [F, lit. a duck]

Canarese KANARESE.

canary (kəneə´ri) *n.* (*pl.* **canaries**) **1** a small yellow cagebird, *Serinus canaria*, from the Canary Islands. **2** †a light sweet wine made in the Canary Islands. ~*a.* bright yellow. **canary-coloured, canary yellow** *a.* bright yellow. **canary creeper** *n.* a climbing plant, *Tropaeolium peregrinum*, with bright yellow flowers. **canary grass** *n.* a grass of the genus *Phalaris*, esp. *Phalaris canariensis*, the source of canary seed. **canary seed** *n.* the seed of the canary grass, used as food for canaries and other cagebirds. [*Canary* Islands, a group of islands off the W coast of Africa, F *Canarie*, Sp. *Canaria*, L *Canāria Insula*, Isle of Dogs (*canis*, a dog)]

canasta (kənas´tə) *n.* a card game similar to rummy, played by two to six players, using two packs of playing cards. [Sp., a basket (see CANASTER)]

canaster (kənas´tə) *n.* **1** a coarse kind of tobacco (so named from the rush baskets in which it was orig. brought from America). **2** such a rush basket. [Sp. *canasta*, *canastro*, through L, from Gr. *kanastron*, a basket (cp. CANISTER)]

canc. *abbr.* **1** cancellation. **2** cancelled.

cancan (kan´kan) *n.* a stage dance of French origin performed by female dancers, involving high kicking of the legs. [F, etym. uncertain]

cancel (kan´səl) *v.t.* (*pres.p.* **cancelling,** (*N Am.*) **canceling,** *past, p.p.* **cancelled,** (*N Am.*) **canceled**) **1** to annul, countermand, revoke. **2** to withdraw or discontinue. **3** to obliterate by drawing lines across. **4** (*Math.*) to strike out common factors. **5** to mark (a stamp, ticket) to prevent reuse. ~*n.* **1** a cancellation or countermand. **2** the deletion and reprinting of a part of a book. **3** a page or sheet substituted for a cancelled one. **to cancel out** to neutralize, counterbalance or compensate for (one another). **cancellate** (-lət), **cancellated** (-lātid), **cancellous** *a.* **1** (*Zool.*, *Bot.*) cross-barred; reticulated. **2** (*Anat.*) (of bones) spongy, formed of cancelli. **cancellation** (-ā´shən) *n.* **1** the act of cancelling. **2** something cancelled, such as a reservation. **canceller,** (*N Am.*) **canceler** *n.* **cancelli** (-sel´ī) *n.pl.* **1** a rail of lattice-work between the choir and the body of a church. **2** (*Anat.*) the reticulation in the spongy part of bones. [F *canceller*, L *cancellāre* (*cancellus*, a grating, *cancelli*, crossbars, lattice)]

Cancer (kan´sə) *n.* **1** the fourth of the 12 signs of the zodiac, the Crab. **2** a person born under this sign. **tropic of Cancer** TROPIC[1]. **Cancerian** (-siə´riən, -seə´-) *n.*, *a.* [L *cancer* (cp. Gr. *karkinos*), a crab]

cancer (kan´sə) *n.* **1** a malignant spreading growth affecting parts of the body. **2** the disease that results from this. **3** any evil that spreads uncontrollably. **canceration** *n.* **cancered, cancerous** *a.* **cancer stick** *n.* (*sl.*) a cigarette. **cancriform** (kang´krifawm) *a.* **1** crab-like. **2** of the form of a cancer. **cancroid** *a.* **1** crablike. **2** resembling cancer. ~*n.* **1** a crustacean belonging to the crab family. **2** a type of skin cancer. [L *cancer* (cp. Gr. *karkinos*), a crab]

c and b *abbr.* in cricket, caught and bowled (by).

candela (kandel´ə, -dē´-) *n.* a unit of luminous intensity. [L *candēla*, candle]

candelabrum (kandəlah´brəm), **candelabra** (-brə) *n.* (*pl.* **candelabrums, candelabra, candelabras**) a high, ornamental candlestick or lampstand, usually branched. **candelabrum tree** *n.* an African tree, *Euphorbia candelabrum*, with branches arranged in the form of a candelabrum. [L (*candēla*, CANDLE)]

Usage note *Candelabra* is quite commonly used as a singular noun (*a candelabra*), but it should always be a plural, with *candelabrum* as the singular.

candescent (kandes´ənt) *a.* glowing with or as with white heat. **candescence** *n.* [L *candescens -entem*, pres.p. of *candescere*, to glow, to become white (*candēre*, to glow)]

c and f *abbr.* cost and freight.

C and G *abbr.* City and Guilds.

candid (kan´did) *a.* **1** frank, sincere, open. **2** outspoken, freely critical. **3** unbiased. **4** †pure, innocent. **candid camera** *n.* a small camera used to take photographs of people unposed or without their knowledge. **candidly** *adv.* **candidness** *n.* [L *candidus*, white]

candida (kan´didə) *n.* a yeastlike fungus of the genus *Candida*, esp. *C. albicans*, which causes thrush. **candidiasis** (kandidī´əsis) *n.* thrush. [L, fem. of *candidus*, white]

candidate (kan´didət, -dāt) *n.* **1** a person who seeks or is proposed for some office or appointment (so named because such persons in ancient Rome wore white togas). **2** a person or thing considered likely for a particular end (*a candidate for redundancy*). **3** a person taking an examination. **candidacy** *n.* **candidature** (-chə), **candidateship** *n.* [L *candidātus*, white-robed (see CANDIDA]

candidiasis CANDIDA.

candied, candies CANDY.

candle (kan´dəl) *n.* **1** a cylindrical body of tallow, wax etc. with a wick in the middle, used for lighting or ornament. **2** a candela. ~*v.t.* to test (eggs) by holding before a candle. **not fit to hold a candle to** not to be comparable with; to be greatly inferior to. **not worth the candle** not worth the trouble, expense etc. **Roman candle** ROMAN. **to burn the candle at both ends** to expend one's energies or exhaust oneself, esp. by staying up late and getting up early. **candleberry** *n.* (*pl.* **candleberries**) **1** a N American shrub, *Myrica cerifera*, yielding wax used for candle-making; the wax myrtle or bayberry. **2** its fruit; a bayberry or waxberry. **candle-bomb** *n.* a small bubble of glass filled with water, which bursts by the expansion of the steam when placed in the flame of a candle. **candlefish** *n.* (*pl. in general* **candlefish,** *in particular* **candlefishes**) a fish of the N Pacific, *Thaleichthys pacificus*, with oily flesh. **candleholder** *n.* a candlestick. **candlelight** *n.* **1** the light of a candle. **2** dusk; evening. **Candlemas** (-məs) *n.* the feast of the Purification of the Virgin (2 Feb.), when candles are blessed and carried in procession. **candle-nut** *n.* the fruit of the tropical tree *Aleurites mollucana*, which yields a kind of wax. **candlepower** *n.* the intensity of light emitted, expressed in candelas. **candler** *n.* **candlestick** *n.* a utensil for holding a candle. **candle tree** *n.* any tree producing nuts or fruit that yield wax for candles. **candlewick** *n.* a cotton fabric with a pattern of raised tufts, used to make bedspreads, dressing gowns etc. **candlewood** *n.* the resinous wood of any of a number of trees. [OE *candel*, L *candēla* (*candēre*, to glow, shine)]

candour (kan´də), (*N Am.*) **candor** *n.* **1** candidness, frankness, sincerity, openness. **2** freedom from malice or bias. [L *candor*]

C. and W. *abbr.* Country and Western.

candy (kan´di) *n.* (*pl.* **candies**) **1** sugar crystallized by boiling and evaporation. **2** (*N Am.*) a sweet or sweets; confectionery. ~*v.t.* (*3rd pers. sing. pres.* **candies,** *pres.p.* **candying,** *past, p.p.* **candied**) **1** to preserve with sugar, to coat with crystallized sugar. **2** to crystallize. ~*v.i.* to become candied. **candied** *a.* **1** preserved in or coated with sugar. **2** crystalline, glistening. **3** flattering, honeyed. **candy apple** *n.* (*N Am.*) a toffee apple. **candyfloss** *n.* coloured spun sugar on a stick. **candy store** *n.* (*N Am.*) a sweet shop. **candy-stripe** *n.* a pattern of alternate narrow stripes of white and a colour. **candy-striped** *a.* [orig. *sugar-candy*, F *sucre candi*, Arab. and Pers. *qand*, sugar, *qandi*, candied]

candytuft (kan´ditŭft) *n.* **1** a herbaceous plant, *Iberis umbellata*. **2** any other plant of the genus *Iberis*, esp. *I. sempervivum*, the perennial candytuft. [*Candy*, obs. var. of *Candia*, Crete, TUFT]

cane (kān) *n.* **1** a slender, hollow, jointed stem of the bamboo, sugar cane or other reeds or grasses. **2** the thin stem of the rattan or other palms. **3** such a stem used as a walking stick or an instrument of punishment. **4** any (slender) walking stick. **5** the stem of a raspberry and other plants. ~*v.t.* **1** to beat with a cane. **2** to fit or repair (a chair etc.) with interwoven strips of cane. **cane-brake** *n.* (*N Am.*) a thicket of canes. **cane chair** *n.* a chair with a seat of interwoven strips of cane. **cane grass** *n.* (*Austral.*) a type of grass (esp. *Eragrostis australasica*) with long, hard stems, growing in swamps and marshes. **cane-mill** *n.* a mill for grinding sugar cane. **caner** *n.* **cane sugar** *n.* **1** sugar made from sugar cane, as distinguished from beet sugar. **2** sucrose. **cane toad** *n.* a large toad, *Bufo marinus*, found in America and Australia. **cane-trash** *n.* the refuse of sugar cane. **caning** *n.* **1** a beating with a cane. **2** a thorough defeat. **cany** *a.* [OF *cane* (F *canne*), L *canna*, Gr. *kanna*, prob. Semit. (cp. Arab. *qanāh*, Heb. *qāneh*)]

canella (kənel´ə) *n.* **1** a W Indian tree of the genus *Canella* with aromatic bark, esp. *C. winterana*. **2** this bark. [med. L, dim. of *canna*, cane]

canephorus (kənē´fərəs) *n.* (*pl.* **canephori** (-rī)) a sculptured figure of a young woman or young man carrying a basket on their head. [Gr. *kanēphoros* (*kaneon*, basket, *-phoros*, bearing, *pherein*, to carry)]

canescent (kənes´ənt) *a.* hoary, greyish-white. **canescence** *n.* [L *cānēscere*, to grow grey (*cānus*, white)]

canfield (kan´fēld) *n.* a gambling card game similar to patience. [R. A. *Canfield*, 1855–1914, US gambler]

cangue (kang), **cang** *n.* a heavy wooden collar or yoke, formerly fixed round the neck of criminals in China. [F *cangue*, Port. *cango* (conn. with *canga*, yoke)]

canicular (kənik´ūlə) *a.* **1** of or relating to Sirius, the dog-star. **2** excessively hot, as in the dog-days. [L *canīculāris* (*canīcula*, a little dog, the dog-star, dim. of *canis*)]

canikin CANNIKIN.

canine (kā´nīn) *a.* **1** of or relating to dogs or the family Canidae. **2** doglike. ~*n.* **1** a canine tooth. **2** a dog or other mammal of the family Canidae. **canine tooth** *n.* (*pl.* **canine teeth**) either of two pointed teeth in each jaw, one on each side, between the incisors and the premolars. [L *canīnus* (*canis*, dog)]

canister (kan´istə) *n.* **1** a metal case or box for holding tea, coffee etc. **2** canister shot, or the metal case in which it is packed. **canister shot** *n.* bullets packed in metal cases which burst when fired; case-shot. [L *canistrum*, Gr. *kanastron*, a basket (*canna*, a reed)]

canker (kang´kə) *n.* **1** an ulceration in the human mouth. **2** an ulcerative ear disease of animals, esp. the dog or cat. **3** a fungous excrescence in a horse's foot. **4** a fungus growing on and injuring fruit trees and other plants. ~*v.t.* **1** to infect or rot with canker, to eat into like a canker. **2** to corrupt. ~*v.i.* to become cankered or corrupt. **cankered** *a.* **1** infected by canker. **2** crabbed, peevish. **cankerous** *a.* corrupting, destroying. **canker-worm** *n.* **1** a caterpillar that feeds on buds and leaves. **2** the larva of the geometer moths. [OE *cancer*, ONF *cancre* (F *chancre*), L *cancrum*, acc. of CANCER]

canna (kan´ə) *n.* any of a genus of ornamental plants with brightly coloured flowers. [L *canna*, CANE]

cannabis (kan´əbis) *n.* **1** any plant of the genus *Cannabis*, esp. the Indian hemp. **2** a narcotic drug obtained from the leaves and flowers of plants of this genus, esp. *C. sativa* and *C. indica*. **cannabic** *a.* **cannabin** *n.* cannabis resin. **cannabinol** *n.* a phenol, a crystalline constituent of the drug cannabis. **cannabis resin** *n.* a sticky resin, the active principle of the drug cannabis. [Gr. *kannabis*]

canned CAN².

cannel (kan´əl), **cannel-coal** *n.* a hard, bituminous coal, burning with a bright flame. [var. of CANDLE]

cannelloni (kanəlō´ni) *n.pl.* rolls of sheet pasta filled with meat etc. and baked. [It., augm. pl. of *cannello*, stalk, from *canna*, cane]

cannelure (kan´əlūə) *n.* **1** (*Archit.*) a flute, a channel. **2** a groove round a projectile. [F, a groove]

canner, cannery CAN².

cannibal (kan´ibəl) *n.* **1** a human being who feeds on human flesh. **2** any animal that feeds on its own kind. ~*a.* **1** of or relating to cannibalism. **2** like a cannibal; ravenous, bloodthirsty. **cannibalism** *n.* **1** the act or practice of feeding on one's own kind. **2** barbarity, atrocity. **cannibalistic** (-lis´-) *a.* **cannibalistically** *adv.* **cannibalize, cannibalise** *v.t.* to dismantle (a machine etc.) for its spare parts, usu. to repair a similar machine. [Sp. *Canibales*, var. of *Caribes*, Caribbeans]

cannikin (kan´ikin), **canikin, canakin** (-əkin) *n.* a small can or cup. [MDut. *kanneken* (CAN², -KIN)]
cannily, canniness CANNY.
canning CAN².
cannon¹ (kan´ən) *n.* **1** a heavy mounted gun. **2** an automatic aircraft gun. **3** artillery, ordnance. **4** a hollow sleeve or cylinder revolving independently on a shaft. **5** the ring or loop by which a bell is suspended. **cannonade** (-nād´) *n.* a continued attack with artillery against a town, fortress etc. *~v.t.* to attack or bombard with cannon. *~v.i.* to discharge heavy artillery. **cannonball** *n.* a solid shot fired from a cannon. **cannon bit** *n.* a smooth round bit for a horse. **cannon-bone** *n.* the metacarpal or metatarsal bone of a horse, ox etc. **cannoneer** (-niə´), †**cannonier** *n.* a gunner, an artilleryman. **cannon fodder** *n.* (*facet.*) soldiers, esp. infantrymen, regarded as expendable. **cannon-proof** *a.* **cannonry** *n.* (*pl.* **cannonries**) **1** cannon collectively. **2** a cannonade. **cannon-shot** *n.* **1** a cannonball. **2** the range of a cannon. [F *canon*, a law, a decree, a great gun, It. *cannone*, a great tube (*canna*, a pipe, a cane, L *canna*, CANE)]
cannon² (kan´ən) *n.* a billiards stroke by which two balls are hit successively. *~v.i.* **1** to make a cannon. **2** to come into violent contact; to collide (*He cannoned into a tree*). [corr. of *carom*, short for *carambole*, F, from Sp. *carambola* (etym. uncertain)]
cannot CAN¹.
cannula (kan´ūlə), **canula** *n.* (*pl.* **cannulas, cannulae** (-lē), **canulas, canulae**) a small tube introduced into a body cavity to withdraw a fluid. **cannular** *a.* **cannulate** (-lāt) *v.t.* to insert a cannula into. [L, dim. of *canna*, CANE]
canny (kan´i) *a.* (*comp.* **cannier**, *superl.* **canniest**) **1** knowing, shrewd, wise. **2** artful, crafty. **3** prudent, cautious. **4** frugal, thrifty. **5** (*Sc., North.*) nice, good. **6** (*Sc., North.*) attractive, good looking. **7** (*Sc., North.*) lucky, fortunate, prosperous. **cannily** *adv.* **canniness** *n.* [CAN¹]
canoe (kənoo´) *n.* a light narrow boat (orig. made from a hollowed-out tree trunk) propelled by paddles. *~v.i.* (*pres.p.* **canoeing**, *past, p.p.* **canoed**) to go in a canoe. **in the same canoe** (*New Zeal.*) belonging to the same tribe. **to paddle one's own canoe** to be independent. **canoeist** *n.* [Sp. *canoa*, from Haitian]
canon (kan´ən) *n.* **1** a rule, a regulation, a general law or principle. **2** a standard, test or criterion. **3** a decree of the Church. **4** the catalogue of canonized saints. **5** the portion of the Roman Catholic Mass in which the words of consecration are spoken. **6** a list of the books of sacred writings officially accepted as genuine; the books themselves. **7** a list of literary works, esp. an author's recognized works; the works themselves. **8** a resident member of a cathedral chapter. **9** a member of a religious body (from the fact that some cathedral canons lived in community). **10** a musical composition in which the several parts take up the same theme in succession. **11** the largest size of type, equivalent to 48 pt. **canoness** *n.* a member of a female religious community living by rule but not bound by vows. **canonical** (-non´-), **canonic** *a.* **1** of, relating to or according to canon law. **2** included in the canon of sacred writings. **3** authoritative, accepted, approved. **4** of, relating to or belonging to a cathedral chapter. **5** (*Mus.*) in canon form. **Canonical Epistles** *n.pl.* the Epistles of Peter, James, John and Jude. **canonical hours** *n.pl.* **1** the time from 8 a.m. to 6 p.m. during which marriages may legally be celebrated. **2 a** the times of the day set for prayer, according to canon law. **b** the services set for these times. **canonically** *adv.* **canonicals** *n.pl.* the full robes of an officiating clergyman as appointed by the canons. **canonicate** (-non´ikət) *n.* the dignity or office of a canon. **canonicity** (-nis´-) *n.* the quality of being canonical, esp. the authority of a canonical book. **canonist** *n.* a person versed in canon law. **canonistic** *a.* **canonize, canonise** *v.t.* **1** to enrol in the canon or list of saints. **2** to recognize officially as a saint. **3** to recognize as canonical. **4** to sanction as conforming to the canons of the Church. **canonization** (-zā´shən) *n.* **canon law** *n.* ecclesiastical law as laid down by popes and councils. **canon regular** *n.* a member of the Augustinian or Premonstratensian orders, who live as monks but also perform the duties of the clergy. **canonry** *n.* (*pl.* **canonries**) **1** the dignity or office of a canon. **2** a canon's benefice. [OE, from L, from Gr. *kanōn*, a rule (*kanē, kanna*, CANE)]
cañon CANYON.
canoodle (kənoo´dəl) *v.i.* (*coll.*) to kiss and cuddle amorously. [etym. unknown]
Canopus (kənō´pəs) *n.* **1** the bright star in the constellation Argo. **2** a Canopic vase. **Canopic** *a.* **Canopic vase, Canopic jar** *n.* an Egyptian vase with a lid shaped like a god's head, for holding the viscera of embalmed bodies. [L, name of an ancient Egyptian city, from Gr. *Kanōpos*]
canopy (kan´əpi) *n.* (*pl.* **canopies**) **1** a rich covering suspended over an altar, throne, bed, person etc. **2** any similar covering, esp. providing shelter. **3** the sky. **4** an ornamental projection over a niche or doorway. **5** the transparent roof of an aircraft cockpit. **6** the fabric portion of a parachute. **7** the topmost layer of branches and leaves in a forest. *~v.t.* (*3rd pers. sing. pres.* **canopies**, *pres.p.* **canopying**, *past, p.p.* **canopied**) to cover with or as with a canopy. **canopied** *a.* [F *canapé*, a tent or pavilion (now, a sofa), med. L *canōpeum*, L *cōnōpēum*, Gr. *kōnōpeion*, a bed with mosquito-curtains (*kōnōps*, a gnat)]
canorous (kənaw´rəs) *a.* (*formal*) tuneful, melodious, resonant. **canorously** *adv.* **canorousness** *n.* [L *canōrus* (*canere*, to sing)]
canst CAN¹.
Cant. *abbr.* **1** Canterbury. **2** (*Bible*) Canticles.
cant¹ (kant) *n.* **1** hypocritical talk; hypocritical sanctimoniousness. **2** slang or jargon. **3** (*often derog.*) a method of speech or phraseology peculiar to any sect or group. **4** the peculiar dialect of beggars, thieves etc. **5** †a monotonous whining, esp. as used by beggars. *~a.* of, relating to or of the nature of cant. *~v.i.* **1** to speak whiningly or insincerely. **2** to use cant. **canter**¹ *n.* **canting** *n.* cant. *~a.* whining, hypocritical. **canting arms** *n.* (*Her.*) armorial bearings containing a punning device or other allusion to the name of the family. **cantingly** *adv.* **cantish** *a.* [L *cantāre*, to sing, freq. of *canere*]
cant² (kant) *n.* **1** a slope, a slant, an inclination. **2** a jerk producing a slant or inclination. **3** an external angle. **4** a bevel. **5** a sloping or slanting position. *~v.t.* **1** to tip, tilt or throw, esp. with a jerk. **2** to bevel, to give a bevel to. *~v.i.* (*Naut.*) to swing round. **cant-board** *n.* a sloping board. **cant-dog, cant-hook** *n.* a metal hook on a pole, used esp. for handling logs. **canted** *a.* **cantrail** *n.* a bevelled plank placed along the top of the uprights in a railway carriage to support the roof. [Dut. *kant* (cp. OF *cant*, It. *canto*, med. L *cantus*, a corner, and perh. L *canthus*, Gr. *kanthos*, the corner of the eye, a hoop round a wheel; course of derivation uncertain)]
cant³ (kant) *a.* (*Sc., North.*) **1** strong, lusty. **2** keen, lively, brisk. **canty** *a.* (*comp.* **cantier**, *superl.* **cantiest**) lively, cheerful. **cantily** *adv.* **cantiness** *n.* [etym. uncertain; perh. from CANT², edge, angle, corner (cp. Dut. *kant*, great, clever)]
can't CAN¹.
Cantab. (kan´tab) *a.* of Cambridge (University). [abbr. of L *Cantabrigiensis*]
cantabile (kantah´bilā) *a.*, *adv.* (*Mus.*) in an easy,

flowing style. ~*n.* a piece or passage in cantabile style. [It., able to be sung (L *cantare*, to sing, freq. of *canere*)]

Cantabrigian (kantəbrij´iən) *a.* of or relating to the town or University of Cambridge, England or of Massachusetts. ~*n.* **1** a member of Cambridge or Harvard Universities. **2** a native of inhabitant of Cambridge. [L *Cantabrigia*, Cambridge]

Cantal (kan´tal), **cantal** *n.* a hard strong-flavoured French cheese. [a department in the Auvergne]

cantala (kantah´lə) *n.* **1** a tropical American plant, *Agave cantala*, from which a coarse tough fibre is obtained. **2** this fibre, used to make twine. [etym. unknown]

cantaloupe (kan´təloop), **cantaloup** *n.* a small, round, ribbed musk-melon. [F *cantaloup* (from *Cantalupo*, near Rome, where it was first raised)]

cantankerous (kantang´kərəs) *a.* disagreeable, bad-tempered; quarrelsome, crotchety. **cantankerously** *adv.* **cantankerousness** *n.* [etym. uncertain; perh. from ME *contak*, contention]

cantar KANTAR.

cantata (kantah´tə) *n.* (*pl.* **cantatas**) a poem, a short lyrical drama or (usu.) a biblical text, set to music, with solos and choruses. [It.]

cantatore (kantətaw´ri) *n.* a male professional singer. **cantatrice** (kantətrē´chā, kātatrēs´) *n.* a female professional singer. [It.]

canteen (kantēn´) *n.* **1** a restaurant or cafeteria in a factory or office where meals and light refreshments are sold at low prices to the employees. **2** a place where school meals are served. **3** a small shop or cafeteria for soldiers at a military camp or barracks. **4** a bottle or flask for carrying liquid refreshments. **5** a chest for cutlery. **6** a soldier's mess tin. **7** a chest or box in which a soldier's mess utensils, cutlery etc., are carried. [F *cantine*, It. *cantina*, cellar (perh. from *canto*, a side, a corner)]

canter[1] CANT[1].

canter[2] (kan´tə) *n.* an easy gallop. ~*v.t.* to cause (a horse) to go at this pace. ~*v.i.* to ride or move at this pace. **in/at a canter** easily. [short for *Canterbury gallop* (or *pace*), the easy, ambling pace at which pilgrims rode to the shrine of St Thomas à Beckett at Canterbury]

canterbury (kan´təbəri) *n.* (*pl.* **canterburies**) a light stand with divisions for music portfolios etc. **Canterbury bell** *n.* a plant of the genus *Campanula*, esp. *C. medium*, with bell-shaped flowers. **Canterbury lamb** *n.* frozen or chilled lamb exported from New Zealand to Britain. [a city in Kent, OE *Cantwaraburh* (*Cantware*, people of Kent); also a place in New Zealand]

cantharis (kan´tharis) *n.* (*pl.* **cantharides** (-thar´idēz)) **1** Spanish fly, a coleopterous insect having vesicatory properties. **2** any similar beetle. **cantharides** *n.pl.* Spanish flies dried and used to raise blisters or internally, also used as an aphrodisiac. **cantharidin** (-din), **cantharidine** *n.* the active principle of cantharides. [L, from Gr. *kantharis*, blistering-fly]

canthus (kan´thəs) *n.* (*pl.* **canthi** (-thī)) the angle made at the corner of the eye where the eyelids meet. [L, from Gr. *kanthos*]

canticle (kan´tikəl) *n.* a brief song, a chant, esp. one of certain portions of Scripture said or sung in churches. **Canticles, Canticle of Canticles** *n.* (*Bible*) the Song of Solomon. [L *canticulum*, dim. of *canticum*, song (*cantus*, song, *canere*, to sing)]

cantilena (kantilā´nə) *n.* (*pl.* **cantilenas**) **1** a ballad. **2** plainsong. **3** a simple flowing melody or style. [It., L *cantilēna*, a song (*cantillāre*, CANTILLATE)]

cantilever (kan´tilēvə) *n.* **1** a projecting beam, girder or bracket for supporting a balcony or other structure. **2** a beam, girder etc. that is fixed at one end only. ~*v.i.* to project as or like a cantilever. ~*v.t.* **1** to support by a cantilever. **2** to fix as a cantilever. **cantilever bridge** *n.* a bridge formed with cantilevers, resting in pairs on piers of masonry or ironwork, the ends meeting or connected by girders. [perh. CANT[2] (or from CANTLE), LEVER]

cantillate (kan´tilāt) *v.t.* to chant or intone as in synagogues. **cantillation** (-ā´shən) *n.* [L *cantillāre*, to sing low (*cantare*, freq. of *canere*, to sing)]

cantina (kantē´nə) *n.* (*pl.* **cantinas**) a bar or wine shop, esp. in Spanish-speaking countries. [Sp.]

cantle (kan´təl) *n.* **1** a fragment, a piece. **2** the projection at the rear of a saddle. ~*v.t.* to cut into pieces, to divide. **cantlet** (-lit) *n.* a morsel, a fragment. [ONF *cantel* (med. L *cantellus*, dim. of *cantus* CANT[2])]

canto (kan´tō) *n.* (*pl.* **cantos**) **1** any one of the principal divisions of a poem. **2** the upper voice part in choral music. **3** †a song. **canto fermo** (fœ´mō) *n.* **1** plainsong. **2** the main theme or melody, to which contrapuntal parts are added. [It., from L *cantus*, CANT[1]]

canton[1] (kan´ton, -ton´, kan´tən) *n.* **1** a division of a country, a small district. **2** a political division of Switzerland. **3** (*Her.*) a small division in the corner of a shield. **cantonal** (kan´-) *a.* **cantoned** (kan´-) *a.* having projecting corners. [OF, a corner, a district, It. *cantone*, from *canto*, CANT[2]]

Usage note (kan´tən) is the usual pronunciation in heraldry.

canton[2] (kanton´, -toon´) *v.t.* **1** to divide into troops or cantons. **2** to billet (troops); to provide with quarters. **cantonment** *n.* **1** temporary or winter quarters for troops. **2** (*Hist.*) a permanent military station in British India. [partly from CANTON[1], partly from F *cantonner*]

Usage note (kanton´) is the usual pronunciation for dividing into cantons, (kantoon´) for providing with quarters.

Cantonese (kantənēz´) *a.* **1** of the city of Canton in S China, or its inhabitants. **2** of the dialect of Chinese spoken there. **3** of or relating to a highly-spiced style of cookery originating there. ~*n.* (*pl.* **Cantonese**) **1** a native or inhabitant of Canton. **2** the Cantonese dialect.

cantor (kan´taw) *n.* **1** a precentor; a person who leads the singing in church. **2** the Jewish religious official who sings the liturgy. **cantorial** (-taw´-) *a.* **1** of or relating to a precentor. **2** of or relating to the north side of the choir, where the precentor has his seat, as distinct from *decanal*. **cantoris** (-taw´ris) *a.* sung by the cantorial side of the choir, as distinct from *decani*. [L, precentor (*cant-*, freq. stem of *canere*, to sing)]

cantrip (kan´trip) *n.* (*Sc.*) **1** a spell, an incantation, a charm. **2** a trick, a piece of mischief. [etym. uncertain]

Cantuarian (kantūeə´riən) *a.* of or relating to Canterbury or its archiepiscopal see. **Cantuar.** *abbr.* Cantuarensis (the official signature of the Archbishop of Canterbury). [late L *Cantuarius* (OE *Cantware*, see CANTERBURY)]

cantus (kan´təs) *n.* (*pl.* **cantus**) **1** a chant or style of singing used in the medieval church. **2** the upper voice part in choral music; canto. **cantus firmus** (fœ´məs) *n.* CANTO FERMO (under CANTO). [L, a song]

canty CANT[3].

Canuck (kənŭk´) *n.* **1** (*N Am., coll.*) a Canadian. **2** (*Can. coll.*) a French Canadian. **3** a small rough Canadian horse. ~*a.* Canadian. [prob. from *Canada*]

canula CANNULA.

canvas (kan´vəs) *n.* **1** a coarse unbleached cloth, made of hemp or flax, used for sails, tents, paintings, embroidery etc. **2** the sails of a ship or boat. **3** a sheet of canvas for oil-painting etc. **4** a painting. **5** a covered part at the ends of a racing-boat. **6** the floor of a boxing or wrestling ring. ~*a.* made of canvas. ~*v.t.* (*pres.p.* **canvassing**, (*N Am.*) **canvasing**, *past, p.p.* **canvassed**,

(*N Am.*) **canvased**) to cover with canvas. **to win by a canvas** in boat-racing, to win by a small margin. **under canvas 1** in a tent or tents. **2** with sails set. **canvasback** *n.* a N American duck, *Aythya valisineria.* [ONF *canevas,* late L *canabācius* (L *cannabis,* Gr. *kannabis,* hemp)]

canvass (kan´vəs) *v.t.* **1** to solicit votes, interest, support, orders etc. from. **2** to ascertain the opinions and feelings of. **3** to examine thoroughly, to discuss. *~v.i.* to solicit votes etc. *~n.* **1** the act of soliciting votes. **2** close examination, discussion. **canvasser** *n.* [from CANVAS, orig. to sift through canvas]

cany CANE.

canyon (kan´yən), **cañon** *n.* a deep gorge or ravine with precipitous sides, esp. of the type formed by erosion in the western plateaus of the US. [Sp. *cañon,* a tube, a conduit, a cannon, from *caña,* L *canna,* CANE]

canzone (kantsō´nā), **canzona** (-nə) *n.* (*pl.* **canzoni** (-ni), **canzonas**) **1** a Provençal or Italian song. **2** a song resembling a madrigal. **3** a type of instrumental music. **canzonet** (kanzənet´), **canzonetta** (-tə) *n.* (*pl.* **canzonets, canzonettas, canzonette** (-tā)) **1** a short air or song. **2** a light air in an opera. [It., from L *cantio -ōnem,* singing (*cant-,* freq. stem of *canere,* to sing)]

caoutchouc (kow´chook) *n.* raw rubber, the coagulated juice of certain tropical trees, which is elastic and waterproof. [F, Carib *cahuchu*]

CAP *abbr.* Common Agricultural Policy (of the EU).

cap (kap) *n.* **1** a covering for the head, usu. soft and close-fitting, with or without a peak at the front. **2** a natural or artificial covering resembling this in form or function. **3** a special form of head-covering distinguishing the holder of an office, a member of a sports team etc. **4** the lid of a bottle, covering for the point of a pen etc. **5** the top part of anything. **6** a coping. **7** (*Archit.*) a capital. **8** a porcelain crown set on the stump of a tooth. **9** a Dutch cap, a form of contraceptive device. **10** cap-paper. **11** a block pierced to hold a mast or spar above another. *~v.t.* (*pres.p.* **capping,** *past. p.p.* **capped**) **1** to cover the top of with a cap. **2** to put a cap on. **3** to protect or cover with or as with a cap. **4** (*Sc., New Zeal.*) to confer a university degree upon. **5** to select (a player) for a sports team, esp. a national team. **6** to put a limit on (spending, charges etc.). **7** to be on the top of. **8** to complete, to surpass or outdo (*to cap a story*). **9** to put a percussion cap on (a gun). **cap in hand** in a humble or servile manner. **if the cap fits, wear it** if the general remark applies to you, take it to yourself. **to cap it all** (*coll.*) as a finishing touch. **to pass/ send the cap round** to make a collection of money. **to set one's cap at** to try to attract or win (a particular person, esp. a man) for love or marriage. **cap and bells** *n.* the insignia of a jester. **cap and gown** *n.* full academic dress, comprising a mortarboard or soft hat worn with an academic gown. **cap of liberty** *n.* a soft conical cap, usu. red, given to freed Roman slaves and subsequently adopted as a symbol of freedom or republicanism, esp. during the French Revolution; a Phrygian cap. **cap of maintenance** *n.* a cap or other head-covering worn as a symbol of office or carried before the sovereign at the coronation. **capper** *n.* **capping** *a.* that caps or forms the cap (of). *~n.* something which covers or protects anything. **cap rock** *n.* a hard impervious layer of rock which overlies a gas or oil deposit. **cap screw** *n.* a threaded bolt having a cylindrical head with a hexagonal recess for turning it. **cap sleeve** *n.* a short sleeve just covering the shoulder. **capstone** *n.* **1** the top stone. **2** a coping-stone. **3** a coping. **4** the horizontal stone of a cromlech or dolmen. [OE *cæppe,* late L *cappa,* later *cāpa* (cp. OF *capel, chapel,* F *chapeau,* and CAPE[1], COPE[2])]

cap. (kap) *abbr.* **1** capacity. **2** capital (letter). **3** chapter.

capable (kā´pəbəl) *a.* **1** competent, able, skilful, qualified, fitted. **2** susceptible (of). **capability** (-bil´-) *n.* (*pl.* **capabilities**) **1** the quality of being capable. **2** capacity. **3** (*pl.*) resources, abilities, intellectual attainments. **capableness** *n.* **capably** *adv.* [F, from late L *capābilis* (formed from *capere,* to hold, on anal. of *capax -ācis,* see CAPACIOUS)]

capacious (kəpā´shəs) *a.* **1** able to hold or contain much. **2** wide, large, extensive. **3** comprehensive, liberal. **capaciously** *adv.* **capaciousness** *n.* [L *capax -ācis* (*capere,* to hold, contain), -ACIOUS]

capacitate (kəpas´itāt) *v.t.* **1** to make capable. **2** to qualify. **3** to render competent. [as CAPACIOUS]

capacity (kəpas´iti) *n.* (*pl.* **capacities**) **1** the power of containing, receiving, absorbing, producing etc. **2** room, cubic extent, volume. **3** the amount that can be contained etc. **4** capability, ability. **5** opportunity, scope. **6** relative position, character or office. **7** legal qualification or competence. **8** a measure of the output of a piece of electrical apparatus. **9** (*Hist.*) capacitance. *~a.* (*attrib.*) being the maximum number or amount that can be contained etc. (*a capacity crowd*). **to capacity** fully; to the limit. **capacitance** *n.* **1** the ability of a conductor, system etc. to store electric charge. **2** the amount stored, measured in farads. **capacitative** *a.* **capacitive** *a.* **capacitor** *n.* a device for storing electric charge in a circuit. [L *capax -ācis* (*capere,* to hold, contain), -ITY]

cap-à-pie (kap´əpē´) *adv.* (*poet. or facet.*) from head to foot (armed or dressed). [OF *cap a pie,* head to foot (L *caput,* head, *pes pedis,* foot)]

caparison (kəpar´isən) *n.* **1** (*often pl.*) ornamental coverings or trappings for a horse or other beast of burden. **2** outfit, equipment. **3** rich clothing, finery. *~v.t.* (*pres.p.* **caparisoning,** *past, p.p.* **caparisoned**) **1** to furnish with caparisons. **2** to deck out; to adorn. [MF *caparasson,* Sp. *caparazon,* med. L *caparo,* a cowl (late L *cāpa,* CAPE[1])]

cape[1] (kāp) *n.* **1** a sleeveless cloak. **2** a covering for the shoulders, sometimes attached to another garment. **caped** *a.* [F (through Sp. *capa* or It. *cappa*), from late L *cappa,* CAP]

cape[2] (kāp) *n.* a headland projecting into the sea. **the Cape 1** the Cape of Good Hope. **2** the province of South Africa containing it. **Cape buffalo** *n.* a type of ox, *Syncercus caffer,* of southern and eastern Africa. **Cape cart** *n.* (*S Afr.*) a hooded, two-wheeled vehicle. **Cape Coloured** *n.* in the Cape Province of S Africa, a person of mixed white and non-white descent. *~a.* of or relating to such a person. **Cape doctor** *n.* (*S Afr.*) a south easterly wind in the Cape. **Cape Dutch** *n.* **1** an architectural style characterized by high ornamental front gables, typical of early buildings of the Cape. **2** †Afrikaans. **Cape gooseberry** *n.* **1** a tropical plant, *Physalis peruviana,* with a small yellow edible fruit. **2** this fruit. **Cape pigeon** *n.* a species of petrel, *Daption capensis,* a winter visitor to the Cape. **capeskin** *n.* a soft leather made from the skins of S African sheep or lambs. **Cape sparrow** *n.* a species of sparrow, *Passer melanurus,* common in S Africa. [F *cap,* It. *capo,* L *caput,* head]

capelin (kap´əlin), **caplin** (kap´lin) *n.* a small Newfoundland fish, *Mallotus villosus,* of the smelt family, used as food or as bait for cod. [F and Sp. *capelan*]

capellmeister KAPELLMEISTER.

caper[1] (kā´pə) *n.* **1** a frolicsome leap, a playful or frisky movement. **2** a prank; a light-hearted or high-spirited escapade. **3** (*sl.*) any activity, esp. of questionable legality. *~v.i.* **1** to leap. **2** to skip about, to frolic. **to cut a caper** to cut capers. **to cut capers 1** to caper. **2** to act in an ostentatious manner. **caperer** *n.* [short for CAPRIOLE]

caper[2] (kā´pə) *n.* **1** a prickly shrub, *Capparis spinosa,* of S Europe. **2** (*pl.*) the flower-buds of this, usu. pickled and used for flavouring. [L *capparis*, Gr. *kapparis* (cp. PEA, L *pisum*, for loss of the *s*)]

capercaillie (kapəkā´li), **capercailzie** (-kāl´zi, -kā´li) *n.* the woodgrouse, *Tetrao urogallus*, also called the cock of the wood. [Gael. *capull coille*, horse of the wood (*capull*, L *caballus*, horse, Gael. *coille*, wood)]

capias (kā´pias, kap´-) *n.* a judicial writ ordering an officer to arrest the person named. [L, take thou, or thou mayst take]

capibara CAPYBARA.

capillaceous (kapilā´shəs) *a.* **1** resembling a hair, hair-like. **2** having many hairlike filaments. [L *capillāceus*, hairy (*capillus*, hair)]

capillary (kəpil´əri) *a.* **1** resembling a hair, esp. in fineness. **2** (of a tube etc.) having a minute bore. **3** of or relating to the hair. **4** of or relating to the capillaries, capillary action etc. ~*n.* (*pl.* **capillaries**) **1** any of the minute blood vessels in which the arterial circulation ends and the venous circulation begins. **2** a capillary tube. **capillarity** (kapilar´-) *n.* **1** the state of being capillary. **2** capillary action. **capillary action** *n.* the tendency of a fluid to ascend or descend in a capillary tube, absorbent material etc., caused by surface tension. [L *capillāris*, relating to hair (*capillus*, hair)]

capita CAPUT.

capital[1] (kap´itəl) *a.* **1** principal, chief, most important. **2** (*coll.*) excellent, first-rate. **3** involving or affecting the head. **4** punishable by death. **5** very serious or fatal. **6** (of letters) of the large size and shape used for initials, the first letter of a proper name etc. **7** relating to the main fund or stock of a corporation or business firm. ~*n.* **1** the most important city or town of a country, state etc. **2** a capital letter. **3** money used to start a business or industry. **4** money employed in earning interest or profits. **5** the main fund or stock of a corporation or business firm. ~*int.* (*coll.*) used to express great satisfaction or approval. **to make capital out of** to make profit from, to turn to one's advantage. **with a capital A etc.** used for emphasis (*This is sexism with a capital S!*). **capital account** *n.* a financial statement that shows the net value of a company, by subtracting its liabilities from its assets. **capital assets** *n.pl.* buildings, machinery, tools etc. used in business or industry; fixed assets. **capital crime** *n.* a crime punishable by death. **capital expenditure** *n.* expenditure on buildings, equipment etc. **capital gain** *n.* profit made from the sale of shares or other property. **capital gains tax** *n.* a tax levied on capital gain. **capital goods** *n.pl.* raw materials and tools used in the production of consumer goods. **capitalism** *n.* the economic system under which individuals use capital and employees to produce wealth. **capitalist** *n.* **1** a person who possesses capital. **2** a person who uses capital and employees to produce wealth. **3** a person who advocates capitalism. **capitalistic** (-lis´tik) *a.* **capitalistically** (-lis´-) *adv.* **capitalize, capitalise** *v.t.* **1** to convert into capital. **2** to use as capital. **3** to calculate or realize the present value of (periodical payments). **4** to write or print with a capital letter. **to capitalize on** to use to one's advantage. **capitalization** (-zā´shən) *n.* **capitalization issue** *n.* on the Stock Exchange, a rights issue. **capital levy** *n.* a levy on capital. **capital punishment** *n.* the death penalty. **capital ship** *n.* a warship of the most powerful kind. **capital sum** *n.* a lump sum of money, esp. payable on an insurance policy. **capital territory** *n.* the area of a country, state etc. where the capital is situated. **capital transfer tax** *n.* (*Hist.*) a tax levied on the transfer of capital, either by gift or inheritance; replaced in 1986 by inheritance tax. [F, from L *capitālis*, *capitāle*, relating to the head, chief (*caput -itis*, head)]

capital[2] (kap´itəl) *n.* the head of a pillar. [prob. from ONF *capitel* (F *chapiteau*), late L *capitellum*, dim. of L *caput -itis*, head]

capitate (kap´itāt), **capitated** (-tātid) *a.* **1** having a head. **2** shaped like a head. **3** having the inflorescence in a headlike cluster. [L *capitātus*, headed (*caput*, head)]

capitation (kapitā´shən) *n.* **1** a tax, fee or grant per person. **2** †enumeration by the head or individual. **capitation grant, capitation allowance** *n.* a subsidy or allowance calculated on the number of persons fulfilling specified conditions. [F, from late L *capitātio -ōnem* (*caput -itis*, head)]

Capitol (kap´itol) *n.* **1** the national temple of ancient Rome, situated on the Capitoline Hill, dedicated to Jupiter. **2** the building in which the US Congress meets. **3** (*NAm.*) the senate house of a state. **Capitolian** (-tō´-), **Capitoline** (-pit´əlīn) *a.* of or relating to the Roman Capitol. [L *Capitōlium*]

capitula CAPITULUM.

capitular (kəpit´ūlə) *a.* **1** of or relating to a cathedral chapter. **2** of or relating to a capitulum. **3** of or relating to the protuberant head of a bone. ~*n.* **1** a member of a chapter. **2** a statute passed by a chapter. **capitularly** *adv.* in the form of a cathedral chapter. [med. L *capitulāris*, relating to a *capitulum*, or chapter]

capitulary (kəpit´ūləri) *n.* (*pl.* **capitularies**) a collection of ordinances, esp. those of the Frankish kings. [med. L *capitulārium*, a book of decrees, from *capitulāre*, a writing divided into chapters]

capitulate (kəpit´ūlāt) *v.i.* to surrender, esp. on stipulated terms. **capitulation** (-lā´shən) *n.* **1** the act of capitulating. **2** the document containing the terms of surrender. **3** a summary of the main divisions of a subject. **capitulator** *n.* **capitulatory** *a.* [med. L *capitulāre*, to divide into chapters, to propose terms]

capitulum (kəpit´ūləm) *n.* (*pl.* **capitula** (-lə)) **1** a close cluster or head of sessile flowers. **2** a head-shaped anatomical part. [L, dim. of *caput*, head]

capiz (kap´iz) *n.* **1** a bivalve mollusc, *Placuna placenta*, found in the Philippines. **2** the shell of this mollusc, having a translucent lining which is used in lamp-shades etc. [Tagalog]

caplin CAPELIN.

cap'n (kap´ən) *n.* (*coll.*) captain. [contr.]

capo (kap´ō) *n.* (*pl.* **capos**) **1** the head of a branch of the Mafia. **2** a capo tasto. [It., head]

capon (kā´pən) *n.* a castrated cock, esp. fattened for cooking. ~*v.t.* to caponize. **caponize, caponise** *v.t.* to castrate. [OE *capun*, L *capo -ōnem*]

caponier (kapəniə´), **caponiere** *n.* a covered passage across the ditch of a fortified place. [F *caponnière*, Sp. *caponera*, orig. a capon-coop; see CAPON]

caporal (kapərahl´) *n.* a coarse kind of French tobacco. [F, a corporal]

capot (kəpot´) *n.* the winning of all the tricks at piquet by one player. ~*v.t.* (*pres. p.* **capotting**, *past, p.p.* **capotted**) to win all the tricks from. [F]

capo tasto (kapō tas´tō) *n.* (*pl.* **capo tastos**) a bar fitted across the fingerboard of a guitar or similar instrument, to alter the pitch of all the strings simultaneously. [It. *capo tasto*, head stop]

capote (kəpōt´) *n.* a long cloak or overcoat, usu. with a hood. [F, dim. of CAPE[1]]

capparidaceous (kapəridā´shəs) *a.* of or relating to the Capparidaceae, a plant family that includes the caper. [L *capparis*, caper]

capper, capping CAP.

cappuccino (kapuchē´nō) *n.* (*pl.* **cappuccinos**) **1** white coffee, esp. from an espresso machine, often topped with whipped cream or powdered chocolate. **2** a drink of this. [It., see CAPUCHIN]

capreolate (kap´riəlāt, kəprē´əlāt) *a.* having or resembling tendrils. [L *capreolus*, a tendril]

capric (kap´rik) *a.* of or relating to a goat. **capric acid** *n.* an acid, having a goatlike smell, contained in butter, coconut oil, and other compounds; decanoic acid. [L *caper -pri*, a goat]

capriccio (kəprē´chō, -chiō) *n.* (*pl.* **capriccios, capricci** (-chē)) **1** (*Mus.*) a lively composition, more or less free in form. **2** a fanciful work of art. **capriccioso** (-chō´sō, -chiō´sō) *adv.* (*Mus.*) in a free, fanciful style. [It., from *capro*, a goat]

caprice (kəprēs´) *n.* **1** a sudden impulsive change of opinion, mood or behaviour. **2** a whim, a fancy. **3** a disposition to this kind of behaviour. **4** a capriccio. **capricious** (-rish´əs) *a.* **1** influenced by caprice. **2** whimsical, uncertain, fickle, given to unexpected and unpredictable changes. **capriciously** *adv.* **capriciousness** *n.* [F, It., from *capro*, a goat]

Capricorn (kap´rikawn) *n.* **1** the zodiacal constellation of the Goat. **2** the tenth sign of the zodiac. **3** a person born under this sign. **tropic of Capricorn** TROPIC[1]. **Capricornian** (-kawn´-) *n., a.* [L *capricornus*, goat-horned (*caper*, a goat, *cornu*, a horn)]

caprification (kaprifikā´shən) *n.* the practice of suspending branches of the caprifig on the cultivated fig, so that the (female) flowers of the latter may be pollinated by wasps parasitic on the flowers of the former. [L *caprificātio -nem*, from *caprificāre*, to ripen figs, *caprificus*, the wild fig (*caper*, goat, *ficus*, fig)]

caprifig (kap´rifig) *n.* the wild fig of S Europe and SW Asia Minor, *Ficus carica*, used in caprification. [L *caprificus*; see CAPRIFICATION]

capriform (kap´rifawm) *a.* having the form of a goat. [L *caper*, a goat, -FORM]

caprine (kap´rīn) *a.* like a goat. [L *caprinus* (*caper*, a goat)]

capriole (kap´riōl) *n.* **1** a leap made by a horse without advancing. **2** in ballet, a leap made from bent knees. *~v.i.* to perform a capriole. [F *capriole* (now *cabriole*), a caper, It. *capriola* (dim. of *capra*, she-goat)]

Capri pants (kaprē´), **Capris** *n.pl.* women's tight-fitting trousers, tapering towards and ending above the ankle. [*Capri*, island off SW Italy]

caproic (kəprō´ik) *a.* of or relating to a goat. **caproic acid** *n.* an acid, having a goatlike smell, contained in butter etc.; hexanoic acid. [L *caper*, a goat, -IC (specially differentiated from CAPRIC)]

caps. *abbr.* capital letters.

capsaicin CAPSICUM.

Capsian (kap´siən) *n.* a culture of the late palaeolithic period in N Africa and S Europe. *~a.* of or relating to this culture. [L *Capsa*, Gafsa, Tunisia]

capsicum (kap´sikəm) *n.* (*pl.* **capsicums**) **1** a plant of the genus *Capsicum*, with mild or pungent fruit and seeds. **2** the fruit of a capsicum used as a vegetable or ground to produce the condiments chilli, cayenne etc. **capsaicin** *n.* the active principle of capsicums. [prob. formed irregularly from L *capsa*, a case]

capsid[1] (kap´sid) *n.* any bug of the family Miridae, feeding on plants. [Gr. *kapsis*, gulp, from *kaptein*, to gulp down]

capsid[2] (kap´sid) *n.* the outer casing of some viruses, made of protein. [L *capsa*, case]

capsize (kapsīz´) *v.t.* to upset, to overturn. *~v.i.* to be upset, to overturn. *~n.* an instance of capsizing. **capsizal** *n.* [etym. unknown; perh. from Sp. *capuzar*, to sink by the head]

capstan (kap´stən, -stan) *n.* **1** a revolving pulley or drum, either power- or lever-driven, used to wind in a rope or cable. **2** a revolving shaft in a tape recorder, which draws the tape past the head. **capstan lathe** *n.* a lathe with a revolving turret, so that several different tools can be used in rotation. [F, from Prov. *cabestan*, L *capistrāre*, to fasten (*capistrum*, a halter, from *capere*, to hold)]

capsule (kap´sūl) *n.* **1** a small envelope of gelatin containing medicine. **2** (*Anat.*) a sac or enveloping membrane. **3** (*Bot.*) a dry dehiscent seed-vessel. **4** a metallic cover for a bottle. **5** a part of a spacecraft, aircraft etc., usu. housing the instruments and crew, that can be detached or ejected. **capsular** *a.* **capsulate** (-lət), **capsulated** (-lātid) *a.* **capsuliform** *a.* **capsulize, capsulise** *v.t.* **1** to put (information) into a very condensed form. **2** to enclose in a capsule. [F, from L *capsula*, dim. of *capsa*, a case]

Capt. *abbr.* Captain.

captain (kap´tin) *n.* **1** a leader, a commander. **2** in the army, a rank between major and lieutenant; a similar rank in the air force in N America. **3** in the navy, a rank between commodore or rear admiral and commander. **4** the master of a merchant ship. **5** the pilot of a civil aircraft. **6** (*N Am.*) a police officer in charge of a precinct. **7** the leader of a side or team. **8** (*N Am.*) a head waiter or the supervisor of bell boys in a hotel. **9** the chief boy or girl in a school. **10** a general, a strategist, a great soldier, a veteran commander. **11** (*coll.*) a Guide Guider. *~v.t.* **1** to act as captain of. **2** to lead, to head. **Captain Cooker** *n.* (*New Zeal., coll.*) a wild boar (descended from swine landed there by Capt. Cook). **captaincy** *n.* (*pl.* **captaincies**). **captain-general** *n.* an honorary officer. **captainless** *a.* **captain of industry** *n.* a powerful or influential person in industry; the head of a large industry. **Captain of the Fleet** *n.* a naval staff officer. **captain's biscuit** *n.* a type of hard biscuit. **captain's chair** *n.* a wooden chair with back and arms in one semicircular piece, supported on wooden shafts. **captainship** *n.* [OF *capitain*, late L *capitaneus*, chief, *capitānus*, a chief (L *caput -itis*, head)]

caption (kap´shən) *n.* **1** the wording under an illustration, cartoon etc. **2** a subtitle or other printed or graphic material in a television broadcast or cinematograph film. **3** the heading of a chapter, section or newspaper article. **4** the heading or descriptive preamble of a legal document. *~v.t.* to provide with a caption. [L *captio -onem* (*capere*, to take)]

captious (kap´shəs) *a.* **1** fault-finding, carping, cavilling. **2** sophistical, quibbling. **captiously** *adv.* **captiousness** *n.* [L *captiōsus*, from CAPTION]

captivate (kap´tivāt) *v.t.* to fascinate, to charm. **captivating** *a.* **captivatingly** *adv.* **captivation** (-ā´shən) *n.* [L *captīvātus*, p.p. of *captīvāre* (*captīvus*, CAPTIVE)]

captive (kap´tiv) *n.* a person or animal taken prisoner or held in confinement. *~a.* **1** taken prisoner. **2** held in confinement, restraint or control. **3** unable to move away, refuse, exercise choice etc. (*a captive audience, a captive market*). **4** of or relating to captivity. **5** captivated, fascinated. **captive balloon** *n.* a balloon held by a rope from the ground. **captive time** *n.* time during which a person is not working but must be available if needed. **captivity** (-tiv´-) *n.* (*pl.* **captivities**) **1** the state of being captive. **2** a period of being captive. **the Captivity** that of the Jews in Babylon. **captor** *n.* [F *captif*, fem. *captive*, L *captīvus* (*captus*, p.p. of *capere*, to take)]

capture (kap´chə) *v.t.* **1** to take as a captive. **2** to take control of; to seize as a prize. **3** to succeed in describing in words or by drawing (a likeness etc.). **4** (*Physics*) (of an atom, molecule etc.) to acquire or absorb (an additional particle). **5** (*Comput.*) to cause (data) to be stored. *~n.* **1** the act of capturing. **2** the person or thing captured. **capturer** *n.* [F, from L *captura* (*capere*, to take)]

capuche (kəpoosh´) *n.* a hood, esp. the long pointed hood of the Capuchins. [F, from It. *capuccio*, a cowl (*cappa*, CAP)]

capuchin (kap´əchin, -ū-) *n.* **1** (**Capuchin**) a Franciscan friar of the reform of the 1520s. **2** a hooded cloak, like the habit of the Capuchins, worn by women. **3** a capuchin monkey or pigeon. **capuchin monkey** *n.* an

American monkey, *Cebus capucinus*, with thick hair like a cowl on the head. **capuchin pigeon** *n.* a variety of pigeon with cowl-like feathers in the head and neck. [It. *cappuccino*, dim. of *capuccio*, a cowl, see CAPUCHE]

caput (kap´ət) *n.* (*pl.* **capita** (-itə)) the head, the top part. [L]

capybara (kapibah´rə), **capibara** *n.* (*pl.* **capybaras, capibaras**) a S American mammal, *Hydrochoerus hydrochaeris*, the largest living rodent, allied to the guinea pig. [Tupi]

CAR *abbr.* Central African Republic.

Car. *abbr.* **1** Carolina. **2** Charles (L *Carolus*).

car (kah) *n.* **1** a small road vehicle propelled by an internal-combustion engine, usu. having four wheels and seats for two to five passengers; a motor-car. **2** a wheeled vehicle (*esp. in comb.*, as *tramcar*). **3** (*Ir.*) a jaunting-car. **4** a railway carriage (*esp. in comb.* as *dining car*). **5** (*N Am.*) any railway coach or wagon. **6** the passenger carriage below an airship, balloon, cable railway etc. **7** (*esp. N Am.*) a lift cage. **8** (*poet.*) a chariot. **car bomb** *n.* an explosive device hidden in or below a parked car, which destroys the car and usu. kills any occupants. **car boot sale** *n.* a sale of second-hand goods, from the boots of cars or from tables. **car-coat** *n.* a short coat which can be worn comfortably in a car. **carfare** *n.* (*N Am.*) a bus etc. fare. **car ferry** *n.* (*pl.* **car ferries**) a ferry that transports motor vehicles. **carful** *n.* (*pl.* **carfuls**) as many people as a car will hold. **carhop** *n.* (*coll., N Am.*) a waiter or waitress at a drive-in restaurant. **carjack** *v.t.* to hijack (a car). **carjacker** *n.* **carjacking** *n.* **carload** *n.* as much as a car will hold. **car park** *n.* a place where cars may be left for a limited period. **carphone** *n.* a cellular telephone suitable for operating in a car. **carport** *n.* an open-sided shelter for a car beside a house. **carsick** *a.* suffering from nausea or vomiting brought on by the motion of a car. **carsickness** *n.* **car-wash** *n.* an establishment with equipment for the automatic washing of cars. [ONF *carre*, late L *carra* (L *carrus*, Bret. *carr*, cp. Welsh *car*, Ir. *carr*)]

carabao (kahrəbā´ō) *n.* (*pl.* **carabaos**) the water buffalo. [Visayan *karabáw*]

carabid (kar´əbid) *n.* any beetle of the family Carabidae, the ground beetles. ~*a.* of or relating to this family. [L *cārabus*, Gr. *kārabos*]

carabine, carabineer CARBINE.

carabiniere (karəbinyeə´rā) *n.* (*pl.* **carabinieri** (-ri)) a member of the national police force in Italy. [It.]

caracal (kar´əkal) *n.* a lynx, *Felis caracal*, of N Africa and S Asia, having black-tufted ears. [Turk. *qarah qalaq*, lit. black ear]

caracara (karəkah´rə) *n.* (*pl.* **caracaras**) any of various American birds of prey that feed on carrion. [Sp. or Port., of imit. origin]

carack CARRACK.

caracol (kar´əkol), **caracole** (-kōl) *n.* **1** a half turn or wheel made by a horse or its rider. **2** a winding staircase. ~*v.i.* (*pres.p.* **caracoling**, *past, p.p.* **caracoled**) **1** to perform a caracol. **2** to caper. ~*v.t.* to make (a horse) caracol. [F *caracole*, It. *caracollo*, wheeling of a horse, Sp. *caracol*, a spiral shell, a snail (etym. uncertain; cp. Gael. *carach*, circling, winding)]

caracul KARAKUL.

carafe (kəraf´, -rahf´, kar´əf) *n.* **1** a wide-mouthed glass container for wine or water at table. **2** as much wine or water as a carafe will hold. [F, It., *caraffa* (cp. Sp. and Port. *garrafa*), Arab. *gharafa*, to draw water]

carambola (karəmbō´lə) *n.* (*pl.* **carambolas**) **1** the star fruit. **2** the SE Asian tree, *Averrhoa carambola*, that bears this fruit. [Port.]

carambole (kar´əmbōl) *n.* in billiards, a cannon. ~*v.i.* to make a cannon. [F, from Sp. *carambola*, the red ball and a certain stroke at billiards]

caramel (kar´əmel, -məl) *n.* **1** burnt sugar used for flavouring and colouring food and drink. **2** a kind of toffee. **3** the colour of caramel, a pale brown. **caramelize, caramelise** *v.t., v.i.* to turn into caramel. **caramelization** (-zā´shən) *n.* [F, from Sp. *caramello*]

carangid (kəran´jid, -rang´gid), **carangoid** (-rang´goid) *n.* any fish of the family Carangidae, including the scads, pilot fishes etc. ~*a.* of or relating to this family. [etym. uncertain]

carapace (kar´əpās) *n.* **1** the upper shell of an animal of the tortoise family. **2** any analogous covering in other animals, such as the crab. [F, from Sp. *carapacho*; etym. uncertain]

carat (kar´ət) *n.* **1** a weight (standardized as the International Carat of 0.200 g) used for precious stones, esp. diamonds. **2** (*N Am.* **karat**) a proportional measure of gold content, 24-carat gold being pure gold. [F, from It. *carato*, Arab. *qīrāt*, prob. from Gr. *keration*, fruit of the carob (dim. of *keras -atos*, a horn)]

caravan (kar´əvan) *n.* **1** a mobile home, a vehicle for living in that can be towed by a car or (esp. formerly) by a horse. **2** a covered wagon used by gypsies, showmen etc. **3** a company of merchants or pilgrims, travelling together (esp. in desert regions) for mutual security. ~*v.i.* (*pres.p.* **caravanning**, *past, p.p.* **caravanned**) to travel or live in a caravan, esp. temporarily while on holiday. **caravaneer** (-niə´) *n.* the leader of a caravan of merchants or pilgrims. **caravanette** (-et´) *n.* a large motor vehicle having living accommodation at the back. **caravanner** *n.* **caravanning** *n.* **caravan site, caravan park** *n.* a place where holidaymakers etc. can live temporarily in caravans. [F *caravane*, or directly from Pers. *karwān*]

caravanserai (karəvan´sərī), **caravansary** (-ri), **caravansera** (-rə) *n.* (*pl.* **caravanserais, caravansaries, caravanseras**) an Oriental inn with a large courtyard for the accommodation of caravans of merchants or pilgrims. [Pers. *karwān*, *-sarāy*]

caravel (kar´əvel) *n.* any of various small light ships, such as a swift Spanish or Portuguese merchant vessel of the 15th–17th cent. [F *caravelle*, It. *caravella*, late L *carabus*, Gr. *karabos*]

caraway (kar´əwā), **carraway** *n.* a European umbelliferous plant, *Carum carvi*. **caraway seed** *n.* the small dried fruit of this plant used as a flavouring. [Arab. *karawiyā* (perh. through med. L *carvi*)]

carb (kahb) *n.* (*coll.*) a carburettor. [abbr.]

carb- CARBO-.

carbamate (kah´bəmāt) *n.* a salt or ester of carbamic acid, esp. carbaryl. **carbamic acid** (-bam´ik) *n.* an amide of carbonic acid. **carbamide** (-mīd) *n.* urea. **carbaryl** (-ril) *n.* a carbamate used as an insecticide.

carbanion (kahban´īən) *n.* (*Chem.*) a negatively charged ion at the carbon position.

carbaryl CARBAMATE.

carbazole (kah´bəzōl) *n.* a substance obtained from coal tar, used to make dyes.

carbide (kah´bīd) *n.* a compound of carbon with a metal, esp. calcium carbide.

carbine (kah´bīn), **carabine** (kar´əbīn) *n.* a short rifle used by cavalry. **carbineer** (-biniə´), **carabineer, carabinier** *n.* a soldier armed with a carbine. [F *carabin* (now *carabine*); perh. from OF *calabrin*, late L. *Calabrīnus*, a Calabrian]

carbo- (kah´bō), **carb-** *comb. form* of, with, containing, or relating to carbon. [CARBON]

carbocyclic (kahbōsī´klik) *a.* denoting a compound which includes a closed ring of carbon atoms.

carbohydrate (kahbəhī´drāt) *n.* an organic compound of carbon, hydrogen and oxygen, usu. having two atoms of hydrogen to every one of oxygen, as in starch, glucose etc.

carbolic (kahbol´ik) *a.* derived from coal or coal tar. ~*n.* carbolic acid. **carbolic acid** *n.* an antiseptic and disinfectant acid; phenol. **carbolic soap** *n.* soap containing carbolic acid. **carbolize** (kah´-), **carbolise** *v.t.* to impregnate with carbolic acid.

carbon (kah´bən) *n.* **1** a non-metallic element, at. no. 6, chem. symbol C, found in nearly all organic substances, in carbon dioxide and the carbonates, and occurring naturally as diamond, graphite and charcoal. **2** carbon paper. **3** a carbon copy. **4** a rod of fine charcoal used in arc-lamps. **carbon-12** *n.* an isotope of carbon used as the standard for atomic weight. **carbon-14** *n.* a radioactive isotope of carbon used in carbon dating. **carbonaceous** (-nā´-) *a.* **1** like coal or charcoal. **2** containing carbon. **carbon arc** *n.* an arc produced between two carbon electrodes, used for lighting, or between a carbon electrode and some other material, used for welding. **carbonate**[1] (-nət) *n.* a salt of carbonic acid. **carbonate**[2] (-āt) *v.t.* **1** to impregnate with carbonic acid. **2** to aerate (water etc.). **3** to form into a carbonate. **carbonation** (-nā´shən) *n.* **carbon black** *n.* a fine black carbon powder, used in the production of rubber, ink etc. **carbon copy** *n.* **1** a duplicate of something typed, written or drawn, made by placing carbon paper between two or more sheets of paper before typing etc. **2** a person, thing or event etc. that is identical or very similar to something else. **carbon cycle** *n.* the biological cycle in which carbon compounds are circulated between living organisms and their environment. **carbon dating** *n.* a method of calculating the age of organic material (wood, bones etc.) by measuring the decay of the isotope carbon-14. **carbon dioxide** *n.* a gaseous combination of one atom of carbon with two of oxygen, a normal constituent of the atmosphere and a product of respiration. **carbon dioxide snow** *n.* dry ice. **carbon disulphide** *n.* a colourless liquid with an unpleasant smell, used as a solvent and in the production of artificial fibres. **carbon fibre,** (*N Am.*) **carbon fiber** *n.* a very strong thread of pure carbon, used for reinforcing plastics, metals etc. **carbonic** (-bon´-) *a.* of, relating to or containing carbon. **carbonic acid** *n.* a weak acid; the compound formed by carbon dioxide and water. **carbonic-acid gas** *n.* (*Hist.*) carbon dioxide. **carboniferous** (-nif´-) *a.* producing coal or carbon. **Carboniferous** *a.* of or relating to the Carboniferous period or system. **Carboniferous period** *n.* (*Geol.*) the fifth period of the Palaeozoic era, between the Devonian and the Permian. **Carboniferous system** *n.* (*Geol.*) the layer of rocks formed during the Carboniferous period, including the coal measures. **carbonize, carbonise** *v.t.* **1** to convert into carbon by the action of heat or acid. **2** to cover with carbon, charcoal, lamp-black, or the like. **carbonization** (-zā´shən) *n.* **carbon monoxide** *n.* a poisonous gas containing one atom of oxygen for each atom of carbon; a constituent of motor vehicle exhaust gases. **carbon paper** *n.* a dark-coated paper used for making carbon copies by transferring an impression of what is typed, written or drawn on the top sheet to a lower sheet. **carbon printing, carbon process** *n.* a permanent black-and-white photographic process, using paper coated with gelatin and lamp-black. **carbon steel** *n.* any of several types of steel containing carbon in varying amounts. **carbon tax** *n.* a suggested tax on fossil fuels, esp. petrol, aimed at reducing their use and so protecting the environment. **carbon tetrachloride** *n.* a colourless toxic liquid, used as a dry-cleaning solvent. **carbonyl** (-īl, -il) *a.* (*attrib.*) of or containing the divalent radical: C=O. [F *carbone*, L *carbo -ōnem*, a coal]

carbonade (kahbənād´, -nahd´), **carbonnade** *n.* a beef stew made with beer. **carbonado**[1] (-nādō, -nah´-) *n.* (*pl.* **carbonadoes, carbonados**) **1** a carbonade. **2** meat or fish scored across and grilled on coals. [F *carbonade*, Sp. *carbonada*, from Sp. *carbon*, coal]

carbonado[1] CARBONADE.

carbonado[2] (kahbənā´dō, -nah´-) *n.* (*pl.* **carbonados, carbonadoes**) a black, opaque diamond of poor quality, used industrially in drills etc. [Port., carbonated]

Carbonari (kahbənah´ri) *n.pl.* **1** members of a secret republican society in Italy and France in the early part of the 19th cent. **2** any republican revolutionists. **carbonarism** *n.* [It., charcoal burners]

carbonate, carbonic etc. CARBON.

Carborundum® (kahbərŭn´dəm) *n.* an abrasive material, esp. a silicon carbide used for grinding-wheels etc.

carboxyl (kahbok´sīl, -sil) *a.* (*attrib.*) of or containing the monovalent radical -COOH. **carboxylate** (-silāt) *n.* a salt or ester of carbolic acid. **carboxylic acid** (-sil´ik) *n.* an organic acid containing the carboxyl group.

carboy (kah´boi) *n.* a large globular bottle of green or blue glass, protected with wickerwork, used for holding corrosive liquids. [Pers. *qarāba*]

carbuncle (kah´bŭngkəl) *n.* **1** a hard, painful boil without a core, caused by bacterial infection. **2** a precious stone of a bright red colour. **3** a garnet cut in a concave cabochon. **4** (*Her.*) a carbuncle borne as a charge. **5** (*coll.*) an ugly building etc. which defaces its surroundings. **carbuncled** *a.* **carbuncular** (-bŭng´kū-) *a.* [ME *charbucle*, *carbuncle*, OF *charboucle* (ONF *carbuncle*), L *carbunculus*, a small coal, a gem]

carburation (kahbūrā´shən), **carburetion** (-resh´ən) *n.* the process of mixing the correct proportions of hydrocarbon fuel and air in an internal-combustion engine etc. [as CARBURET]

carburet (kah´būret, -ret´) *v.t.* (*pres.p.* **carburetting,** (*N Am.*) **carbureting,** *past, p.p.* **carburetted,** (*N Am.*) **carbureted**) to combine (another element) with carbon. **carburettor, carburetter,** (*N Am.*) **carburetor** *n.* an apparatus designed to atomize a liquid, esp. petrol in an internal-combustion engine, and to mix it with air in the correct proportions to ensure ready ignition and complete combustion. **carburize, carburise** *v.t.* **1** to carburet. **2** to add carbon to (wrought iron). **carburization** (-zā´shən) *n.* [F *carbure*, L *carbo* (see CARBON)]

carby (kah´bi) *n.* (*pl.* **carbies**) (*Austral., coll.*) a carburettor. [abbr.]

carcajou (kah´kəzhoo) *n.* the glutton or wolverine. [N Am. F (prob. from Algonquian)]

carcass (kah´kəs), **carcase** *n.* **1** the dead body of an animal. **2** the trunk of a slaughtered animal without the head and offal. **3** (*derog. or facet.*) the human body, dead or alive. **4** the framework or skeleton of a building, ship etc. **5** a mere shell or husk. **carcass meat** *n.* raw meat as sold in a butcher's shop. [A-F *carcois*, med. L *carcosium*, afterwards modified by MF *carquasse* (F *carcasse*), It. *carcassa*, a shell or bomb (etym. uncertain)]

carcinogen (kahsin´əjən) *n.* a substance that can give rise to cancer. **carcinogenic** (-jen´-) *a.* **carcinogenicity** (-is´iti) *n.* [CARCINOMA, -GEN]

carcinology (kahsinol´əji) *n.* the branch of zoology which deals with the Crustacea. **carcinological** (-loj´-) *a.* **carcinologist** *n.* [Gr. *karkinos*, a crab]

carcinoma (kahsinō´mə) *n.* (*pl.* **carcinomas, carcinomata** (-tə)) **1** a malignant tumour. **2** the disease cancer. **carcinomatous** *a.* **carcinosis, carcinomatosis** (-ō´sis) *n.* the spread of carcinomas or cancer through the body. [L, from Gr. *karkinōma*, cancer (*karkinos*, a crab)]

Card. *abbr.* Cardinal.

card[1] (kahd) *n.* **1** stiff paper or thin cardboard. **2** a flat, rectangular piece of this for writing or drawing on etc. **3** a small piece of card, usu. printed, such as a visiting card, a business card, a membership card, an identity card etc. **4** a folded piece of card with a picture on the front, used to send greetings (*a birthday card*; *a Christmas card*). **5** a postcard. **6** any one of a pack of oblong pieces of card, marked with symbols and pictures, used in playing games of chance or skill; a playing-card. **7** (*pl.*) a game or games played with cards; card-playing. **8** a programme, a menu, a list of events at races, regattas etc. **9** (*pl., coll.*) a worker's employment documents. **10** (*Comput.*) a punchcard. **11** a small oblong piece of plastic used for financial transactions etc., often bearing personal details that can be read electronically (*a cheque card*; *a credit card*). **12** a similar piece of plastic used for other purposes, such as a phonecard. **13** the piece of card on which the points are marked in the mariner's compass; a compass card. **14** (*sl.*) a character, an eccentric. **a card up one's sleeve** a plan or resource held secretly in reserve or in readiness; an undisclosed advantage. **in the cards** (*N Am.*) on the cards. **on the cards** possible; not improbable. **to get one's cards** to be dismissed or made redundant. **to lay one's cards on the table** to put one's cards on the table. **to play one's cards close to one's chest** to be secretive about one's intentions, resources etc. **to play one's cards well/ right etc.** to be a good strategist; to take the appropriate action to gain an advantage. **to put one's cards on the table** to disclose one's situation, plans etc. **to show one's cards** to reveal one's plans or secrets. **to stack the cards 1** to interfere with a deck of playing-cards secretly for the purpose of cheating. **2** to arrange matters to the disadvantage or advantage of someone (*The cards are stacked against us*). **to throw up the cards** to give up. **cardboard** *n.* fine pasteboard used for making light boxes and other articles. ~*a.* **1** made of cardboard. **2** without substance or reality. **cardboard city** *n.* an area of a city where homeless people set up makeshift shelters constructed from cardboard boxes etc. **card-carrying** *a.* (*attrib.*) being a full member of (a political party etc.). **card catalogue** *n.* a catalogue in which each item is entered on a separate card. **card game** *n.* a game played with cards. **cardholder** *n.* a person who has a credit card, membership card etc. **card index** *n.* an index in which each item is entered on a separate card. **card-index** *v.t.* to make a card index of. **cardphone** *n.* a public telephone where a phonecard is inserted rather than coins. **card-playing** *n.* the playing of card games. **card punch** *n.* (*Comput.*) a device which can take data from a store or processor and transfer it to punched cards. **card reader** *n.* (*Comput.*) a device which can read the data on punched cards and convert it to a form in which it can be stored or processed. **card-sharp, card-sharper** *n.* a person who swindles by means of card games or tricks with cards. **card table** *n.* a table to play cards on. **card vote** *n.* a ballot where the vote of each delegate counts for the number of their constituents. [F *carte*, It. *carta*, late L *carta*, L. *charta*, Gr. *chartē*, *chartēs*, a leaf of papyrus]

card[2] (kahd) *n.* a toothed instrument for combing wool, flax etc. or raising a nap. ~*v.t.* **1** to comb (wool, flax or hemp) with a card. **2** to raise a nap on. **carder** *n.* a person who cards wool. **carding** *a.* **carding-machine** *n.* a machine for combing out and cleaning wool, cotton etc. **carding-wool** *n.* short-stapled wool. [F *carde*, a teazel, a wool-card, It. *card*, late L *cardus*, L *carduus*, a thistle]

cardamine (kahdam´inē, kah´dəmīn) *n.* any of a genus of cruciferous plants comprising the cuckoo-flower or lady's-smock. [Gr. *kardaminē*]

cardamom (kah´dəməm), **cardamum, cardamon** (-ən) *n.* **1** an aromatic plant of SE Asia, *Elettaria cardamomum*. **2** a spice obtained from the seed capsules of this plant or of various species of *Amomum* and other genera. [L *cardamōmum*, Gr. *kardamōmon* (*kardamon*, cress, *amōmon*, an Indian spice-plant)]

cardan joint (kah´dən) *n.* in engineering, a type of universal joint which can rotate when out of alignment. **cardan shaft** *n.* a shaft with a universal joint at either end. [Geronimo *Cardano*, 1501–76, Italian mathematician]

cardboard CARD[1].

cardi- CARDIO-.

cardiac (kah´diak) *a.* **1** of or relating to the heart. **2** of or relating to the upper part of the stomach. ~*n.* **1** a stimulant for the heart. **2** a person suffering from heart disease. **cardiac arrest** *n.* cessation of the heartbeat. **cardiac tamponade** *n.* abnormal pressure on the heart caused by excessive fluid in the pericardial sac. **cardial** *a.* **cardialgia** (-al´jiə), **cardialgy** (-al´ji) *n.* **1** pain in the heart. **2** heartburn. **cardialgic** (-al´-) *a.* [F *cardiaque*, L *cardiacus*, Gr. *kardiakos* (*kardia*, the heart)]

cardie (kah´di), **cardy, cardi** *n.* (*pl.* **cardies**) (*coll.*) a cardigan. [abbr.]

cardigan (kah´digən) *n.* a knitted jacket buttoned up the front. [7th Earl of *Cardigan*, 1797–1868, whose soldiers wore such garments in the Crimea]

cardinal (kah´dinəl) *a.* **1** fundamental, chief, principal. **2** of the colour of a cardinal's cassock, deep scarlet. **3** of or relating to a hinge. ~*n.* **1** any of the ecclesiastical dignitaries of the Roman Catholic Church who elect a new pope, usu. from among their own number. **2** a cardinal number. **3** a cardinal-bird. **4** a butterfly of S Europe, *Pandorina pandora*. **5** (*Hist.*) a short cloak (orig. of scarlet) for women. **cardinalate** (-āt), **cardinalship** *n.* the office or dignity of a cardinal. **cardinal beetle** *n.* any large, scarlet beetle of the family Pyrichoidae. **cardinal-bird** *n.* a N American songbird, *Cardinalis cardinalis*, with scarlet plumage in the male. **cardinal flower** *n.* the scarlet lobelia, *Lobelia cardinalis*. **cardinal humour** *n.* any of the four bodily humours. **cardinally** *adv.* **cardinal number** *n.* any of the numbers 1, 2, 3, etc., as distinguished from the *ordinal numbers* 1st, 2nd, 3rd etc. **cardinal point** *n.* any of the four points of the compass: north, south, east and west. **cardinal's hat** *n.* the official emblem of the cardinalate, a flat red hat with fifteen tassels on each side. **cardinal signs** *n.pl.* **1** the zodiacal signs Aries, Libra, Cancer and Capricorn. **2** the two solstitial and the two equinoctial points of the ecliptic. **cardinal virtues** *n.pl.* **1** (*Philos.*) prudence, temperance, justice and fortitude. **2** (*Theol.*) faith, hope and charity. [F, from L *cardinālis* (*cardo -inis*, a hinge)]

cardio- (kah´diō), **cardi-** *comb. form* of or relating to the heart. [Gr. *kardia*, heart]

cardiogram (kah´diəgram) *n.* a reading from a cardiograph.

cardiograph (kah´diəgrahf) *n.* an instrument for registering the activity of the heart. **cardiographer** (-og´-) *n.* **cardiographic** (-graf´-), **cardiographical** *a.* **cardiography** (-og´-) *n.*

cardioid (kah´dioid) *n.* (*Math.*) a heart-shaped curve. ~*a.* heart-shaped. [Gr. *kardioeides* (*kardia*, heart, -OID)]

cardiology (kahdiol´əji) *n.* the branch of medicine concerned with the heart. **cardiological** (-əloj´-) *a.* **cardiologist** *n.*

cardiomyopathy (kahdiōmīop´əthi) *n.* a disease of the heart muscle.

cardiopulmonary (kahdiōpŭl´mənəri) *a.* of or relating to the heart and lungs.

cardiovascular (kahdiōvas´kūlə) *a.* of or relating to the heart and blood-vessels.

carditis (kahdī´tis) *n.* inflammation of the heart.

cardoon (kahdoon´) *n.* a thistle-like plant, *Cynara cardunculus*, allied to the artichoke, the leaf stalks of which are eaten as a vegetable. [F *cardon* (It. *cardone*, or Sp. *cardon*), late L *cardus*, L *carduus*, thistle]

cardy CARDIE.

CARE (keə) *abbr.* Cooperative for American Relief Everywhere.

care (keə) *n.* **1** anxiety, concern. **2** a cause of these. **3** caution, serious attention, heed. **4** supervision, protection. **5** attention or services provided for the sick etc. **6** †sorrow, grief, trouble. ~*v.i.* **1** to be concerned, interested, emotionally affected etc. **2** to be anxious or troubled. **3** to have affection, respect or liking (for). **4** to be desirous, willing or inclined (to). **care of** at or to the address of. **for all someone cares** (*coll.*) referring to someone's lack of concern or interest (*For all you care she could be dead*). **in care** (of a child) in the guardianship of the local authority. **not to care a button** BUTTON. **not to care a fig** FIG[1]. **not to care a pin** PIN. **(someone) couldn't care less** (*coll.*) used to express (someone's) complete indifference. **to care for** to provide for; to look after. **to have a care** to take care. **to take care 1** to be careful, cautious or vigilant. **2** (*coll.*) to look after oneself. **to take care of 1** to look after (*takes care of his elderly mother*). **2** to provide or pay for (*put money aside in order to take care of the bills*). **3** to deal with. **who cares?** (*coll.*) I don't care. **care assistant, care attendant** *n.* a person employed to look after the sick, disabled, elderly etc. **carefree** *a.* free from responsibility, light-hearted. **careful** *a.* **1** cautious, watchful, circumspect. **2** painstaking, attentive, exact. **3** done with care. **4** solicitous, concerned. **5** not neglecting, omitting, failing etc. (*He was careful to spell her name right*). **carefully** *adv.* **carefulness** *n.* **caregiver** *n.* a carer. **care label** *n.* a label bearing washing or cleaning instructions, attached to a garment etc. **care-laden** *a.* **careless** *a.* **1** not taking care. **2** heedless, thoughtless, unconcerned. **3** inattentive, negligent (of). **4** done without care; inaccurate. **5** casual. **carelessly** *adv.* **carelessness** *n.* **carer** *n.* a person who looks after someone, e.g. an invalid, dependent relative etc. **caretaker** *n.* a person in charge of an unoccupied house, a public building etc. ~*a.* (*attrib.*) interim. **care-worn** *a.* **caring** *a.* **1** showing care or concern. **2** providing medical care or social services (*the caring professions*). [OE *caru* (cp. OS and Goth. *kara*, sorrow, OHG *charōn*, to lament), from Gmc. *karā*-]

☒ **carecter** common misspelling of CHARACTER.

careen (kərēn´) *v.t.* to turn (a ship) on one side in order to clean, caulk or repair it. ~*v.i.* (of a ship) to heel over. **careenage** *n.* the act of, a place for, or the cost of careening. [F *cariner* (now *caréner*), ult. from L *carīna*, a keel]

career (kəriə´) *n.* **1** a course or progress through life, esp. a person's working life. **2** a person's chosen profession, business or other occupation. **3** the progress and development of a nation, party etc. **4** a running, a swift course. ~*a.* (*attrib.*) having a specified career; professional (*a career diplomat*). ~*v.i.* **1** to move in a swift, headlong course. **2** to gallop at full speed. **career break** *n.* an extended period away from one's profession or occupation, e.g. to raise a family, for study etc. **career girl, career woman** *n.* a woman who pursues a full-time career. **careerism** *n.* making personal advancement one's main objective. **careerist** *n., a.* **careers** *a.* (*attrib.*) giving advice on careers (*a careers teacher, the careers department*). **career structure** *n.* a pattern or system of advancement within a profession or organization. [F *carrière*, late L *carrāria via*, a road for cars (L *carrus*, CAR)]

caress (kəres´) *n.* **1** a gentle touch, an embrace, a kiss. **2** an act of endearment. ~*v.t.* **1** to fondle, to pet, to stroke affectionately. **2** to touch gently. **caressing** *a.* **caressingly** *adv.* [F *caresse*, It. *carezza*, late L *cāritia* (L *carus*, dear)]

caret (kar´ət) *n.* in writing or printing, a mark (^) used to show that something, which may be read above or in the margin, is to be inserted. [L, is wanting (*carēre*, to need)]

carfuffle KERFUFFLE.

cargo (kah´gō) *n.* (*pl.* **cargoes, cargos**) **1** freight carried by ship or aircraft. **2** a load of such freight. **cargo boat** *n.* a boat designed to carry freight. **cargo cult** *n.* a religion of some S Pacific islands, according to which ancestral spirits will come back in cargo boats or aeroplanes, bringing wealth for the islanders. [Sp., a load, a loading, med. L *carricum*, late L *carricāre*, to load (*carrus*, CAR)]

cariama SERIEMA.

Carib (kar´ib) *n.* **1** a member of the aboriginal people of the southern islands of the W Indies. **2** the language spoken by these people. ~*a.* of or relating to these people or their language. **Caribbean** (-bē´ən) *a.* denoting, of or relating to the Caribbean Sea, its islands or their inhabitants. ~*n.* a West Indian or Carib. [Sp. *caribe* (see CANNIBAL)]

Caribbee bark (kar´ibē) *n.* the bark of any of several W Indian trees of the genus *Exostema*, used for medicinal purposes.

caribou (kar´iboo) *n.* (*pl.* **caribou**) the N American reindeer. [Can. F, prob. from an Am. Ind. language]

caricature (kar´ikəchə, -tūə) *n.* **1** a representation of a person or thing exaggerating characteristic traits in a ludicrous way. **2** a burlesque, a parody. **3** a laughably inadequate person or thing. ~*v.t.* **1** to represent in this way. **2** to burlesque, to parody. **caricatural** *a.* **caricaturist** (-tūə´rist) *n.* [It. *caricatura* (assim. to F *caricature*), from *caricare*, late L *carricāre* (see CARGO)]

caries (keə´riēz) *n.* (*pl.* **caries**) **1** decay of the bones or teeth. **2** decay of vegetable tissue. **cariogenic** (-ōjen´-) *a.* producing caries. **carious** *a.* [L]

CARIFTA (karif´tə) *abbr.* Caribbean Free Trade Area.

carillon (kəril´yən, kar´ilən) *n.* **1** a set of bells played by the hand or by machinery. **2** a tune played on such bells. **3** a musical instrument (or part of one) imitating such bells. ~*v.i.* (*pres.p.* **carillonning**, *past, p.p.* **carillonned**) to play a carillon. **carillonneur** (-nœ´) *n.* [F, from med. L *quadrilo -ōnem*, a quaternion (of four bells)]

carina (kərē´nə, -rī´-) *n.* (*pl.* **carinas, carinae** (-nē)) (*Bot., Zool.*) a ridgelike or keel-shaped structure. **carinal** *a.* **carinate** (kar´ənāt), **carinated** *a.* [L, a keel]

caring CARE.

carioca (kariō´kə) *n.* **1** a S American dance like the samba. **2** music for this dance. **3** (*coll.*) (**Carioca**) a native or inhabitant of Rio de Janeiro. [Port.]

cariogenic CARIES.

cariole CARRIOLE.

carious CARIES.

☒ **carisma** common misspelling of CHARISMA.

†**cark**[1] (kahk) *v.t.* to burden, to harass, to worry. ~*v.i.* to be anxious, to fret, to worry. ~*n.* care, distress, anxiety. **carking** *a.* burdensome, distressing, worrying. [ONF *carkier* (cp. OF *chargier*), late L *carcāre*, *carricāre* (see CARGO)]

cark[2] (kahk) *v.i.* (*Austral., sl.*) **1** to break down. **2** to die. [etym. uncertain]

carl (kahl), **carle** *n.* (*Sc.*) **1** a countryman. **2** a man of low birth. **3** a man; a fellow. [Icel. *karl* (cp. OE *hūscarl* and CHURL)]

carline (kah´lin) *n.* any plant of the genus *Carlina*, allied to the thistle, esp. *C. vulgaris*. [F, from late L *Carlīna*, *Carolīna*, fem. of *Carolīnus*, Charlemagne (cp. L *carduus*, a thistle)]

carling (kah´ling) *n.* (*Naut.*) a strong fore-and-aft beam that supports the deck of a vessel. [Icel. *kerling*]

Carlism (kah´lizm) *n.* adherence to Don Carlos (1788–1855), second son of Charles IV, and his heirs as the legitimate sovereigns of Spain. **Carlist** *n., a.* [*Carlos*, -ISM]

Carlovingian CAROLINGIAN.

carmagnole (kahmənyōl´) *n.* a lively song and dance popular during the French Revolution. [F, an upper garment worn during the Revolution, prob. from *Carmagnola* in Piedmont]

Carmelite (kah´məlīt) *n.* **1** a member of an order of mendicant friars, founded in the 12th cent. on Mount Carmel; a White Friar. **2** a nun of a corresponding order. **3** (**carmelite**) a fine woollen fabric, usu. grey. *~a.* of or relating to the Carmelites.

carminative (kah´minətiv, -min´-) *a.* relieving flatulence. *~n.* a carminative drug or medicine. [L *carminātus*, p.p. of *carmināre*, to card wool]

carmine (kah´mīn, -min) *n.* **1** a vivid red or crimson pigment obtained from cochineal. **2** this colour. *~a.* of this colour. [F or Sp. *carmin* (med. L *carmīnus*, *carmesīnus*), Sp. *carmesi*, Arab. *qirmazī*, CRIMSON]

carnage (kah´nij) *n.* butchery, slaughter, esp. of human beings. [F, from It. *carnaggio*, late L *carnāticum* (L *caro carnis*, flesh)]

carnal (kah´nəl) *a.* **1** fleshly, bodily, sensual, sexual. **2** temporal, secular. **3** worldly, unspiritual. **carnalism** *n.* **carnalist** *n.* **carnality** (-nal´-) *n.* **carnal knowledge** *n.* sexual intercourse. **carnally** *adv.* [L *carnālis* (*caro carnis*, flesh)]

carnallite (kah´nəlīt) *n.* a white or reddish hydrous chloride of magnesium and potassium found in German and Iranian salt-mines. [Rudolf von *Carnall*, 1804–74, German mineralogist]

carnassial (kahnas´iəl) *n.* in carnivores, a large tooth adapted for tearing flesh, the first lower molar or the last upper premolar. *~a.* relating to such a tooth. [F *carnassier*, carnivorous (L *caro carnis*, flesh)]

carnation[1] (kahnā´shən) *n.* the cultivated clove pink, *Dianthus caryophyllus*, with sweet-scented double flowers of various colours. [perh. a corr. of INCARNATION (under INCARNATE[2]) or CORONATION]

carnation[2] (kahnā´shən) *n.* **1** a light rose-pink colour. **2** a flesh tint. **3** a part of a painting representing human flesh. *~a.* of this colour. [F, from L *carnātio -ōnem* (*caro*, see CARNAL)]

carnauba (kahnow´bə) *n.* **1** a Brazilian palm, *Copernicia cerifera*. **2** (*also* **carnauba wax**) a yellow wax obtained from its leaves, used in polishes. [Port.]

carnelian CORNELIAN.

carnet (kah´nā) *n.* **1** a document allowing the transport of vehicles or goods across a frontier. **2** a book of vouchers, tickets etc. [F, notebook]

carnify (kah´nifī) *v.t.* (*3rd pers. sing. pres.* **carnifies**, *pres.p.* **carnifying**, *past, p.p.* **carnified**) **1** to convert to flesh. **2** to convert (bone or tissue) into fleshy substance. *~v.i.* to alter in this way. **carnification** (-fikā´shən) *n.*

carnival (kah´nivəl) *n.* **1** a festival, esp. annual, usu. marked by processions and revelry. **2** the season immediately before Lent, in many Roman Catholic countries devoted to pageantry and riotous amusement. **3** riotous amusement, revelry. **4** a travelling funfair. [It. *carnevale*, the eve of Ash Wednesday, late L *carnelevāmen* (*caro carnis*, flesh, *levāre*, to remove), altered into It. *carne vale*, flesh, farewell]

carnivore (kah´nivaw) *n.* **1** any animal of the order Carnivora, a large order of mammals subsisting on flesh. **2** a carnivorous animal or plant. **carnivorous** (-niv´ərəs) *a.* **1** feeding on flesh. **2** (of plants) feeding on insects. **carnivorously** *adv.* **carnivorousness** *n.*

Carnot cycle (kah´nō) *n.* an ideal heat-engine cycle that gives maximum thermal efficiency and is reversible. [Nicolas *Carnot*, 1796–1832, French physicist]

carnotite (kah´nətīt) *n.* a yellow mineral, a vanadate of uranium and potassium, noted as an important source of radium. [Adolphe *Carnot*, d. 1920, French mine inspector]

carny[1] (kah´ni), **carney** *v.i.* (*3rd pers. sing. pres.* **carnies, carneys**, *pres.p.* **carnying, carneying**, *past, p.p.* **carnied, carneyed**) (*dial., coll.*) to act in a wheedling manner. *~v.t.* to wheedle, to coax. [etym. unknown]

carny[2] (kah´ni), **carney** *n.* (*pl.* **carnies, carneys**) (*N Am., sl.*) **1** a carnival. **2** a carnival worker. [abbr.]

carob (kar´əb) *n.* **1** the Mediterranean locust tree, *Ceratonia siliqua*. **2** its fruit, with an edible pulp, used as a substitute for chocolate. [F *carobe*, Arab. *kharrūbah*]

carol (kar´əl) *n.* **1** a joyous song or hymn, esp. sung at Christmas. **2** joyous warbling of birds. *~v.i.* (*pres.p.* **carolling,** (*N Am.*) **caroling**, *past, p.p.* **carolled,** (*N Am.*) **caroled**) **1** to sing carols. **2** to warble. *~v.t.* to celebrate with songs. **caroller,** (*N Am.*) **caroler** *n.* **carol-singer** *n.* a person who sings carols at Christmas, esp. for money outside private houses or in public places. **carol-singing** *n.* [OF *carole*, perh. from L *choraula*, a dance, L and Gr. *choraulēs*, a flute-player (Gr. *choros*, dance, *aulos*, a flute)]

caroli CAROLUS.

Carolina duck (karəlī´nə) *n.* a duck, *Aix sponsa*, found in the woodlands of N America. [name of two states of the USA]

Caroline (kar´əlīn), **Carolean** (-lē´ən), **Carolinian** (-lin´iən) *a.* **1** of or relating to the reigns of Charles I and II of Britain. **2** of or relating to any king called Charles. **3** Carolingian. **Caroline minuscule** *n.* a type of script developed during the reign of Charlemagne. [L *Carolus*, Charles]

Carolingian (karəlin´jiən), **Carlovingian** (kahləvin´jiən) *a.* **1** of or belonging to the dynasty of French kings founded by Charlemagne. **2** of or relating to Carolingian minuscule. *~n.* **1** a member of the Carolingian dynasty. **2** Carolingian minuscule. **Carolingian minuscule** *n.* CAROLINE MINUSCULE (under CAROLINE). [L *Carolus*, Charles]

Carolinian[1] CAROLINE.

Carolinian[2] (karəlin´iən) *a.* of or relating to either of the US states of North Carolina and South Carolina. *~n.* a native or inhabitant of either of these states.

carolus (kar´ələs) *n.* (*pl.* **caroluses, caroli** (-lī)) any of various coins of the reigns of kings called Charles, esp. a gold coin of the time of Charles I of Britain. [L *Carolus*, Charles]

carom (kar´əm) *n.* (*N Am.*) in billiards, a cannon. *~v.i.* **1** to make a cannon. **2** to rebound after striking. [short for CARAMBOLE]

carotene (kar´ətēn), **carotin** (-tin) *n.* an orange-red pigment found in plants, e.g. carrots, a source of vitamin A. **carotenoid** (kərot´inoid), **carotinoid** *n.* any of a group of pigments, including carotene, found in plants and some animals. *~a.* of, relating to or resembling a carotenoid or carotene. [L *carōta*, CARROT]

carotid (kərot´id) *a.* of or related to either of the arteries (one on each side of the neck) supplying blood to the head. *~n.* a carotid artery. [F *carotide*, Gr. *karōtides*, the two neck arteries (*karoein*, to stupefy, from *karos*, sleep, torpor)]

carouse (kərowz´) *n.* a carousal. *~v.i.* **1** to have a carousal. **2** to drink freely. **carousal** *n.* **1** a merry drinking party. **2** a drinking bout. **carouser** *n.* **carousingly** *adv.* [G *gar aus*, completely (referring to emptying a glass)]

carousel (karəsel´), (*esp. N Am.*) **carrousel** *n.* **1** (*N Am.*) a merry-go-round. **2** a rotating conveyor belt for luggage at an airport. **3** a rotating container which delivers slides to a projector. [F *carrousel*, tournament, merry-go-round]

carp[1] (kahp) *n.* any freshwater fish of the genus *Cyprinus*, esp. *C. cyprio*, the common carp. [OF *carpe*, late L *carpa*, from Gmc. (cp. Dut. *karper*, OHG *charpo*, G *Karpfen*)]

carp[2] (kahp) *v.i.* **1** to talk querulously, to complain. **2** to find fault, to cavil. **carper** *n.* **carping** *a.* **carpingly** *adv.* [Icel. *karpa*, to boast (confused with L *carpere*, to pluck at, to slander)]

-carp (kahp) *comb. form* (*Bot.*) a fruit, or a structure that develops into part of a fruit, as *pericarp*. [Gr. *karpos*, fruit]

carpaccio (kahpach´iō) *n.* an Italian hors d'oeuvre comprising thin slices of raw meat or fish, sometimes served with a dressing. [It.]

carpal CARPUS.

carpel (kah´pəl) *n.* the female reproductive organ of a flower, comprising ovary, style and stigma. **carpellary** *a.* [cp. F *carpelle*, mod. dim. of Gr. *karpos*, fruit]

carpenter (kah´pintə) *n.* **1** a person who prepares and fixes the woodwork of houses, ships etc.; a skilled woodworker. **2** (*chiefly N Am.*) a joiner. ~*v.i.* to do carpentry. ~*v.t.* to make by carpentry. **carpenter ant** *n.* any ant of the genus *Campanotus*, which bores into wood to make its nest. **carpenter bee** *n.* any bee that bores into wood or plant stems, e.g. the genus *Xylocopa*. **carpenter moth** *n.* any of several moths of the family *Cossidae*, which bore into tree bark. **carpentry** *n.* **1** the trade of a carpenter. **2** carpenter's work, esp. the kind of woodwork prepared at the carpenter's bench. [ONF *carpentier* (F *charpentier*), late L *carpentārius*, from *carpentāre*, to work in timber (*carpentum*, a wagon, from Celt., cp. OIr. *carpat*, OBret. *cerpit*)]

carpet (kah´pit) *n.* **1** a woollen or other thick fabric, usu. with a pile, for covering floors and stairs (*fitted carpet*). **2** a large piece of this, used to cover all or part of the floor of a room. **3** any similar covering, e.g. of snow, leaves etc. ~*v.t.* (*pres.p.* **carpeting**, *past, p.p.* **carpeted**) **1** to cover with or as with a carpet. **2** (*coll.*) to reprimand. **on the carpet** **1** under consideration. **2** (*coll.*) being reprimanded. **to sweep under the carpet** to conceal or ignore deliberately (a problem etc.). **carpet-bag** *n.* a travelling-bag orig. made with sides of carpet. **carpet-bagger** *n.* **1** (*chiefly N Am.*) a person who seeks political office in a place where the person has no local connections. **2** an unscrupulous opportunist or profiteer. **carpet-baggery** *n.* **carpet-beater** *n.* a racket-shaped cane utensil for beating carpets. **carpet-bedding** *n.* the formal arrangement of dwarf foliage plants. **carpet beetle**, (*N Am.*) **carpet bug** *n.* any of several beetles of the genus *Anthrenus*, whose larvae feed on carpets and other fabrics. **carpet bombing** *n.* bombing of a whole area, rather than of selected targets. **carpeting** *n.* **1** the material of which carpets are made. **2** carpets in general. **3** the action of covering with or as with carpet. **4** (*coll.*) a severe reprimand. **carpet knight** *n.* **1** a knight who has seen no military service. **2** a stay-at-home soldier. **carpetless** *a.* **carpet moth** *n.* any of various geometrid moths with mottled carpet-like patterns on their wings. **carpet plot** *n.* (*Math.*) a graph representing the values of a function of more than one variable (from its resemblance to a flying carpet). **carpet-rod** *n.* a stair-rod. **carpet shark** *n.* a shark of the genus *Orectolobus*, with two dorsal fins and the back patterned like a carpet. **carpet slippers** *n.pl.* comfortable slippers orig. made of carpet-like fabric. **carpet snake** *n.* an Australian snake, *Morelia variegata*. **carpet-sweeper** *n.* an apparatus equipped with revolving brushes and a dustpan, used for sweeping carpets. **carpet tack** *n.* a small nail for fastening down a carpet. **carpet tile** *n.* a small square of carpeting which can be laid with others to cover a floor. [OF *carpite*, late L *carpita*, *carpeta*, a thick cloth, from L *carpere*, to pluck (cp. F *charpie*, late L *carpia*, lint, made by plucking rags)]

carpi CARPUS.

carpo-[1] (kah´pō) *comb. form* of or relating to the wrist. [Gr. *karpos*, the wrist]

carpo-[2] (kah´pō) *comb. form* of or relating to fruit. [Gr. *karpos*, fruit]

carpogonium (kahpəgō´niəm) *n.* (*pl.* **carpogonia** (-niə)) the female reproductive organ of red algae. [Gr. *gonos*, seed]

carpology (kahpol´əji) *n.* the branch of botany which deals with fruits and seeds.

carpometacarpus (kahpōmetəkah´pəs) *n.* (*pl.* **carpometacarpi** (-pī)) in birds, a wing bone formed by fusion of the metacarpal bones with some of the carpal bones.

carpophagous (kahpof´əgəs) *a.* fruit-eating.

carpophore (kah´pōfaw) *n.* in some flowers, an elongated part bearing the carpels and stamens.

carpospore (kah´pōspaw) *n.* a spore produced after fertilization of the carpogonium in red algae.

carpus (kah´pəs) *n.* (*pl.* **carpi** (-pī)) **1** the wrist, the part of the human skeleton joining the hand to the forearm, comprising eight small bones. **2** the corresponding part in other animals. **carpal** *a.* of the wrist. ~*n.* a wrist bone. [L, from Gr. *karpos*, the wrist]

carr (kah) *n.* **1** an area of marshy ground or fen where willow, alder or similar trees or shrubs are found. **2** a copse of such trees or shrubs in marshy ground. [Icel. *kjarr*]

carrack (kar´ək), **carack** *n.* (*Hist.*) a large merchant ship; a galleon. [OF *caraque*, late L *carraca*, *carrica* (prob. conn. with *carricāre*, see CARGO)]

carrageen (kar´əgēn), **carragheen** *n.* **1** an edible seaweed, *Chondrus crispus*, found on N Atlantic shores; Irish moss. **2** carrageenan. **carrageenan, carrageenin, carragheenin** *n.* an extract of carrageen used in food processing. [*Carragheen*, Co. Waterford, Ireland, where it is particularly plentiful]

carraway CARAWAY.

carrel (kar´əl), **carrell** *n.* a cubicle for private study in a library. [var. of CAROL]

☒ **carress** common misspelling of CARESS.

carriage (kar´ij) *n.* **1** a passenger vehicle in a train. **2** a wheeled vehicle, esp. a horse-drawn vehicle for carrying passengers. **3** carrying, transporting, conveyance, esp. of merchandise. **4** the cost of conveying. **5** the manner or means of carrying. **6** mien, bearing, deportment. **7** the moving part of a machine which carries another part (*a typewriter carriage*). **8** the wheeled support of a cannon. **9** the wheeled framework of a vehicle as distinguished from the body. **10** the bed of a printing press on which a form is laid. **carriage forward** with the cost of carriage to be paid by the receiver. **carriage free** carried without charge to the purchaser. **carriage paid** with the cost of carriage prepaid. **carriage and four** *n.* a carriage drawn by four horses. **carriage and pair** *n.* a four-wheeled private vehicle drawn by two horses. **carriage bolt** *n.* (*esp. N Am.*) a coach bolt. **carriage clock** *n.* a portable clock in an oblong metal case with a handle on top. **carriage dog** *n.* (*dated*) a Dalmatian (from its former use as a guard dog running behind a carriage). **carriageless** *a.* **carriage line** *n.* a coach line. **carriage return key** *n.* a key that returns the carriage of a typewriter to its original position. **carriage trade** *n.* trade from well-off customers. **carriageway** *n.* the part of a road used for vehicular traffic. [ONF *cariage* (F *charriage*), from *carier*, to CARRY]

☒ **Carribean** common misspelling of CARIBBEAN (under CARIB).

carrick bend (kar´ik) *n.* a knot for joining two ropes together. **carrick bitt** *n.* (*Naut.*) either of two posts supporting a windlass. [CARRACK]

carrier (kar´iə) *n.* **1** a person, thing or organization conveying goods or passengers for payment. **2** any person or thing that carries. **3** a person or animal that transmits a disease, esp. without suffering from it. **4** a carrier bag. **5** a framework on a bicycle for holding luggage. **6** an aircraft carrier. **7** (*Physics*) an electron or hole that carries charge in a semiconductor. **8** a substance that supports a catalyst, conveys radioactive material etc. **9** any of various parts of machines or instruments which act as transmitters or bearers. **carrier bag** *n.* a strong plastic or paper bag with handles. **carrier pigeon** *n.* a pigeon of a breed trained to carry communications. **carrier rocket** *n.* a rocket that carries e.g. a satellite into orbit. **carrier wave** *n.* an electromagnetic wave which is modulated for the radio transmission etc. of a signal.

carriole (kar´iōl), **cariole** *n.* **1** a small open carriage. **2** a light covered cart. **3** (*Can.*) an ornamental sledge. [F, from It. *carriola* (*carro*, a car, L *carrus*, CAR)]

carrion (kar´iən) *n.* **1** dead, putrefying flesh. **2** garbage, filth. *~a.* **1** feeding on carrion. **2** putrid. **3** loathsome. **carrion beetle** *n.* any beetle of the family Silphidae, such as the sexton beetle, feeding on carrion. **carrion crow** *n.* a species of crow, *Corvus corone*, that feeds on small animals and carrion. **carrion flower** *n.* **1** a N American climbing plant, *Smilax herbacea*, with small green flowers that smell like carrion. **2** the stapelia. [ME and OF *caroigne*, late L *carōnia*, a carcass (*caro carnis*, flesh)]

carronade (karənād´) *n.* (*Hist.*) a short naval cannon of large bore. [*Carron*, near Falkirk, Scotland, where orig. made]

carron oil (kar´ən) *n.* a mixture of linseed oil and lime water, formerly used for scalds and burns. [as CARRONADE, from its use at the Carron ironworks]

carrot (kar´ət) *n.* **1** a plant, *Daucus carota*, with an orange-coloured tapering root, used as a vegetable. **2** this vegetable. **3** an incentive. **4** (*pl., coll.*) a person with red hair. **carrot and stick** *n.* reward and punishment, esp. as alternative means of persuasion. **carrot fly** *n.* (*pl.* **carrot flies**) an insect, *Psila rosae*, whose larvae burrow into carrot roots. **carroty** *a.* **1** of the colour of a carrot. **2** red-haired. [F *carotte*, L *carōta*, Gr. *karōton* (prob. from *kara*, head)]

carrousel CAROUSEL.

carry (kar´i) *v.t.* (*3rd pers. sing. pres.* **carries,** *pres.p.* **carrying,** *past, p.p.* **carried**) **1** to bear, transport or convey from one place to another by supporting and moving with the thing conveyed. **2** to convey or take with one. **3** to conduct or transmit. **4** to bring, to enable to go or come. **5** to transfer, as from one book, page or column to another. **6** to bear or support. **7** to have in or on. **8** to imply or involve. **9** to bear or hold (oneself) in a particular way. **10** to extend or cause to move in any direction in time or space. **11** to effect, to accomplish. **12** to win, to capture. **13** to wear (clothes). *~v.i.* **1** to act as bearer. **2** to extend or travel a distance. **3** to bear the head in a particular manner, as a horse. **4** (of a hare etc.) to run on ground that sticks to the feet. *~n.* (*pl.* **carries**) **1** the act of carrying. **2** the distance travelled by a golf ball between being struck and touching the ground. **3** the range of a firearm. **4** (*N Am.*) a portage. **to carry all before one 1** to bear off all the honours. **2** to win or gain complete success, unanimous support etc. **to carry away 1** to remove. **2** (*usu. pass.*) to excite, to inspire, to deprive of self-control. **3** (*Naut.*) to break or lose (a rope, mast etc.). **to carry back 1** to take back. **2** in accounting, to apply (a loss etc.) to the income of the previous year for tax purposes. **to carry coals to Newcastle** COAL. **to carry conviction** CONVICTION (under CONVICT[1]). **to carry forward** to transfer to another page or column. **to carry it off** to succeed, esp. under difficult circumstances. **to carry off 1** to remove. **2** to win. **3** to do or handle successfully. **4** to cause to die. **to carry on 1** to conduct or engage in (a business, a conversation etc.). **2** to continue. **3** to behave in a particular way, esp. to flirt outrageously. **4** to make a fuss. **to carry one's bat** BAT[1]. **to carry oneself** to behave (in a particular way). **to carry one's point** POINT. **to carry out 1** to perform. **2** to accomplish. **to carry over 1** to carry forward. **2** to postpone to a future occasion. **to carry the baby** BABY. **to carry the can** CAN[2]. **to carry the day** DAY. **to carry the world before one** WORLD. **to carry through 1** to accomplish. **2** to bring to a conclusion in spite of obstacles. **to carry weight** WEIGHT. **to carry with one 1** to bear in mind. **2** to convince. **carry-all** *n.* **1** (*N Am.*) a holdall. **2** (*N Am.*) a type of car with seats facing sideways. **3** a four-wheeled carriage for several persons. **carry-back** *n.* in accounting, the carrying back of a loss etc., or the amount carried back. **carrycot** *n.* a light portable cot for a baby. **carrying** *a., n.* **carrying capacity** *n.* **1** the amount or number that can be carried in a vehicle, container etc. **2** the number of people, animals or plants that an area of land can support. **carrying charge** *n.* in accounting, the cost of unproductive assets. **carryings-on** *n.pl.* behaviour (usu. of a questionable kind). **carrying trade** *n.* the transport of goods, esp. by water or air. **carry-on** *n.* **1** a fuss. **2** an instance of questionable behaviour or flirtation. **carry-out** *n., a.* (*Sc., N Am.*) (a) takeaway. **carry-over** *n.* **1** the act of carrying over. **2** something carried over. [ONF *carier*, late L *carricāre carrus*, CAR]

carse (kahs) *n.* (*Sc.*) low fertile land, usu. near a river. [prob. pl. of CARR]

carsey CARZEY.

cart (kaht) *n.* **1** a strong two-wheeled vehicle for heavy goods etc., usu. drawn by a horse. **2** a light two-wheeled vehicle (*usu. with attrib.*, as *dog cart*). **3** a light vehicle pulled or pushed by hand. **4** (*N Am.*) a supermarket trolley. *~v.t.* **1** to carry or convey in a cart. **2** (*coll.*) to carry or pull with difficulty. *~v.i.* to carry or convey goods in a cart. **in the cart** (*sl.*) in a predicament, in trouble. **to cart off** (*coll.*) to remove by force. **to put the cart before the horse** to reverse the natural or proper order. **cartage** *n.* **1** the act of carting. **2** the price paid for this. **carter** *n.* **cartful** *n.* (*pl.* **cartfuls**) the number or amount that a cart will hold. **carthorse** *n.* any of a breed of horses used for drawing carts and other heavy work. **cartload** *n.* **1** a cartful. **2** a large number or amount. **cart road, cart track** *n.* a rough road on a farm etc. **cartwheel** *n.* **1** the wheel of a cart. **2** a sideways somersault made with the arms and legs outstretched. **3** a large coin. **cartwright** *n.* a person whose trade is to make carts. [Icel. *kartr* (OE *cræt* may be cogn.)]

carte[1] (kaht) *n.* **1** a card. **2** a menu. **carte blanche** (blăsh´) *n.* (*pl.* **cartes blanches** (kaht blăsh´)) unlimited power to act (*The new manager was given carte blanche*). **carte du jour** (dü zhooə´) *n.* (*pl.* **cartes du jour** (kaht)) the menu for a particular day. [F *carte*, see CARD[1]]

carte[2] QUARTE.

cartel (kahtel´) *n.* **1** an agreement (often international) among manufacturers to keep prices high, to control production etc. **2** in politics, an alliance between two parties to further common policies. **cartelize** (kah´təlīz), **cartelise** *v.t., v.i.* to form into a cartel. **cartelization** (-zā´shən) *n.* [F, G *Kartell*, from It. *cartello*, dim. of *carta*, CARD[1]]

Cartesian (kahtē´ziən, -zhən) *a.* of or relating to the French philosopher and mathematician René Descartes (1596–1650), or his philosophy or mathematical methods. *~n.* an adherent of his philosophy or methods. **Cartesian coordinates** *n.pl.* a system for locating a point in space by specifying its distance from two lines or three planes intersecting at right angles. **Cartesianism** *n.* [mod. L *Cartesius*]

Carthusian (kahthū´ziən) *a.* of or belonging to an order of monks founded by St Bruno in 1084. *~n.* **1** a scholar of Charterhouse School. **2** a Carthusian monk. [med. L *Cartusiānūs*, L *Cartusia*, Chartreuse, in Dauphiné]

cartilage (kah´tilij) *n.* **1** an elastic, pearly-white animal tissue; gristle. 2 a cartilaginous structure. **cartilaginoid** (-laj´in-) *a.* of, relating to or resembling cartilage. **cartilaginous** (-laj´in-) *a.* **cartilaginous fish** *n.* any fish with a cartilaginous skeleton, such as the shark or ray. [F, from L *cartilāgo -āginem*; etym. unknown]

cartogram (kah´təgram) *n.* a map showing statistical information in diagrammatic form. [F *carte*, CARD[1]]

cartography (kahtog´rəfi), **chartography** (chah-) *n.* the art or practice of making maps and charts. **cartographer** *n.* **cartographic** (-graf´-), **cartographical** *a.* [F *carte*, CARD[1]]

cartomancy (kah´təmansi) *n.* fortune-telling from a selection of playing cards. [F *carte*, CARD[1], -MANCY]

carton (kah´tən) *n.* 1 a cardboard box. 2 a box made of waxed paper for holding liquids. 3 a white disc within the bull's eye of a target. 4 a shot which hits this. ~*v.t.* (*pres.p.* **cartoning**, *past*, *p.p.* **cartoned**) to put into a carton. [F, pasteboard, cardboard; It. *cartone* (*carta*, CARD[1])]

cartoon (kahtoon´) *n.* 1 an illustration, esp. comic, usu. dealing with a topical or political subject. 2 a comic strip. 3 an animated film, esp. one produced from a series of drawings. 4 a preliminary design on strong paper for a painting, tapestry, mosaic etc. **cartoonish** *a.* **cartoonist** *n.* **cartoon strip** *n.* a comic strip. **cartoony** *a.* [F *carton*, It. *cartone* (see CARTON)]

cartophily (kahtof´ili) *n.* the hobby of collecting cigarette cards. **cartophilist** *n.* [F *carte*, CARD[1], -PHILY]

cartouche (kahtoosh´), **cartouch** *n.* 1 a scroll on the cornice of a column. 2 an ornamental tablet in the form of a scroll, for inscriptions etc. 3 an elliptical figure containing the hieroglyphics of Egyptian royal or divine names or titles. [F, from It. *cartoccio* (*carta*, CARD[1])]

cartridge (kah´trij) *n.* 1 a case, esp. of metal, holding the explosive charge of a gun etc., with or without a bullet (*a blank cartridge*; *a ball cartridge*). 2 a removable, sealed container holding film for a camera, magnetic tape for a tape recorder, ribbon for a typewriter or printer etc. 3 a removable part of the pick-up arm of a record player, containing the stylus etc. 4 a replaceable container holding ink for a pen etc. **cartridge belt** *n.* a belt with pockets for cartridges. **cartridge clip** *n.* a removable container for cartridges in an automatic firearm. **cartridge paper** *n.* a type of stout, rough-surfaced paper, orig. used for cartridge-making, now used for drawing, making strong envelopes etc. [corr. of CARTOUCHE]

cartulary (kah´tūləri), **chartulary** (chah´-) *n.* (*pl.* **cartularies, chartularies**) 1 the register or collection of documents relating to a monastery or church. 2 the place where this is kept. [late L *chartulārium*, *cartulārium* (L *cartula*, dim. of *carta*, CARD[1])]

caruncle (kar´ŭngkəl, kərŭng´-) *n.* 1 a small, fleshy excrescence. 2 (*Zool.*) a wattle, comb or similar outgrowth. 3 (*Bot.*) a protuberance round or near the hilum. **caruncular** (-rŭng´-) *a.* **carunculate** (-rŭng´-), **carunculated** *a.* [obs. F *caruncule*, L *caruncula*, dim. of *caro carnem*, flesh]

carve (kahv) *v.t.* 1 to cut (solid material) into the shape of a person, thing etc. 2 to make or shape by cutting. 3 to decorate or inscribe by cutting. 4 to cut (letters, patterns etc.) into the surface of hard material. 5 to cut (esp. meat) into slices. ~*v.i.* 1 to carve wood, stone etc. as an art or profession. 2 to carve meat. **to carve out** 1 to take (a piece) from something larger. 2 to create or establish by one's own effort (*to carve out a career*). **to carve up** 1 to divide into pieces or portions, to subdivide (esp. land). 2 to drive into the path of (another vehicle), esp. in an aggressive or dangerous manner after overtaking. **carven** *a.* (*poet.*) carved. **carver** *n.* 1 a person who carves. 2 a carving knife. 3 (*pl.*) a carving knife and fork. 4 a dining chair with arms. **carvery** *n.* (*pl.* **carveries**) a restaurant providing a type of buffet service, where roast meat is carved to the customers' requirements. **carve-up** *n.* (*sl.*) the act of sharing out or distributing booty etc. **carving** *n.* 1 the act of carving. 2 a carved object or ornament. **carving knife** *n.* a large knife for carving meat. [OE *ceorfan*, from Gmc. *kerf-* (cp. Dut. *kerven*, G *kerben*), cogn. with Gr. *graphein*, to write]

carvel (kah´vəl) *n.* CARAVEL. **carvel-built** *a.* (*Naut.*) having the planks flush at the edges, as distinct from *clinker-built*.

carven CARVE.

Carver (kah´və) *n.* (*N Am.*) a chair with a rush seat and vertical and horizontal spindles in the back. [John *Carver*, *c.* 1575–1621, first governor of the colony at Plymouth, Massachusetts]

carver, carvery etc. CARVE.

caryatid (kariat´id) *n.* (*pl.* **caryatids, caryatides** (-dēz)) (*Archit.*) a figure of a woman in long robes, serving to support an entablature. **caryatic, caryatidal, caryatidean** (-tid´iən), **caryatidic** (-tid´-) *a.* [L *Caryātis*, Gr. *Karuatis -idos*, a priestess of Artemis at Caryae, in Laconia]

caryo- KARYO-.

caryophyllaceous (kariōfilā´shəs) *a.* belonging to, relating to or characteristic of the Caryophyllaceae, a family of plants that includes the pink and the carnation. [Gr. *karuophullon* (*karuon*, a nut, *phullon*, a leaf)]

caryopsis (kariop´sis) *n.* (*pl.* **caryopses** (-sēz), **caryopsides** (-sidēz)) a fruit with a single seed, to which the pericarp adheres throughout, as in grasses. [Gr. *karuon*, a nut, *opsis*, appearance]

carzey (kah´zi), **carsey, karsey, karzy, kazi** *n.* (*sl.*) a lavatory. [It. *casa*, house]

Casanova (kasənō´və) *n.* a man notorious for his amorous or sexual adventures. [Giovanni Jacopo *Casanova* de Seingalt, 1725–98, Italian adventurer and seducer of women]

casbah KASBAH.

cascabel (kas´kəbel) *n.* 1 the rear part of a type of cannon. 2 a knoblike protrusion on this part. [Sp., a small bell]

cascade (kaskād´) *n.* 1 a small waterfall, esp. one of a series of waterfalls. 2 anything resembling this, such as a loose, wavy fall of lace or hair. 3 a series of actions or processes, each triggered or fuelled by the previous one. ~*v.i.* to fall in or like a cascade. **cascade amplifier** *n.* a series of electrical amplifiers so connected that the output of each stage is amplified by the succeeding stage. [F, from It. *cascata*, p.p. of *cascare*, to fall]

cascara (kaskah´rə) *n.* 1 (*also* **cascara sagrada** (səgrah´də)) the bark of a N American buckthorn, *Rhamnus purshiana*, used as a laxative. 2 (*also* **cascara buckthorn**) this shrub or tree. [Sp.]

cascarilla (kaskəril´ə) *n.* 1 the aromatic bark of the W Indian shrub *Croton eluteria*. 2 this shrub. [Sp., dim. of CASCARA]

case[1] (kās) *n.* 1 an instance, an occurrence. 2 a state of affairs, situation, position, circumstances. 3 a set of arguments for or against a particular action or cause. 4 a question at issue. 5 a particular instance of any disease etc. 6 the patient suffering from the disease etc. 7 a solicitor's or social worker's client. 8 a matter for police investigation. 9 a cause or suit in a court of law. 10 a statement of facts or evidence for submission to a court. 11 the evidence and arguments considered collectively. 12 a cause that has been decided and may be quoted as a precedent. 13 (*Gram.*) a the form of a declinable word used to express relation to some other word in the sentence. b the system of changes in termination involved. 14 (*sl.*) an eccentric or difficult character. **as the case may be** according to the circumstances, depending on the situation. **in any case** in any event, whatever may happen. **in case 1** if, supposing that. **2** lest (*Take a map in case you get lost*). **in case of** in the event of. **in no case** under no circumstances. **in that case** if that should happen, if that is true. **in the case of** regarding. **to be the case** to be so. **to rest one's case** REST[1]. **casebook** *n.* a book describing (medical or legal) cases for record or for instruction. **case history** *n.* a record of a person's background, history etc., esp. used for clinical purposes. **case in point** *n.* an apt or relevant instance. **case law** *n.* law as settled by precedent. **caseload** *n.* the number of cases assigned to a doctor or social worker. **case of conscience** *n.* a matter in which conscience must make the decision between two principles. **case study** *n.* **1** a study or analysis of the background, history etc. of a particular person or institution. **2** the written record of such a study. **casework** *n.* medical or social work concentrating on individual cases. **caseworker** *n.* [OF *cas*, L *cāsus*, p.p. of *cadere*, to fall]

case[2] (kās) *n.* **1** a box, chest or other container. **2** a covering or sheath; that which contains or encloses something else. **3** a protective outer shell or cover. **4** a suitcase. **5** a glass box for exhibits. **6** a container and its contents (*a case of wine*). **7** (*Print.*) an oblong frame, with divisions, for type (*lower case*; *upper case*). ~*v.t.* **1** to cover with or put into a case. **2** (*sl.*) to reconnoitre (a building etc.) with a view to burglary (*to case the joint*). **case bottle** *n.* a bottle shaped to fit into a case. **case-bound** *a.* (of a book) hardbacked. **case-harden** *v.t.* **1** to harden the outside surface of (esp. iron, by converting into steel). **2** to make callous. **case knife** *n.* a knife carried in a sheath. **case-shot** *n.* CANISTER SHOT (under CANISTER). **caseworm** *n.* a caddis worm. **casing** *n.* **1** an outer shell or skin; a protective case or covering. **2** material used to make this. [ONF *casse* (F *châsse*), L *capsa* (*capere*, to receive, to hold)]

caseation (kāsiā´shən) *n.* the formation of cheese from casein when milk coagulates. [L *caseus*, cheese]

casein (kā´siin, -sēn) *n.* the protein in milk, forming the basis of cheese. **vegetable casein** VEGETABLE. **caseous** (-siəs) *a.* of or like cheese. [L *caseus*, cheese, -IN[1]]

casemate (kās´māt) *n.* an armoured vault or chamber in a fortress or ship, containing an embrasure. **casemated** *a.* [F, from It. *casamatta* (etym. uncertain)]

casement (kās´mənt) *n.* **1** a window or part of a window opening on hinges. **2** (*poet.*) a window. **3** a hollow moulding. **casemented** *a.* [from CASE[2] or from It. *casamento*, a building or frame of a building, med. L *casamentum*]

casern (kəzœn´), **caserne** *n.* (*Hist.*) any of a series of temporary buildings for soldiers between the ramparts and the houses of a fortified town; a barrack. [F *caserne*, Sp. *caserna* (*casa*, a house, L *casa*, cottage)]

cash[1] (kash) *n.* **1** coins and banknotes, as opposed to cheques etc. **2** immediate payment, as opposed to credit. **3** (*coll.*) money, wealth. ~*a.* involving cash, paid for or paying in cash (*a cash deposit*). ~*v.t.* to turn into or exchange for cash. **cash down** with money paid on the spot. **to cash in** to exchange for money. **to cash in on** (*coll.*) to profit from. **to cash in one's checks** (*sl.*) to die. **to cash up** to add up the money taken (in a shop etc.) at the end of the day. **cashable** *a.* **cash account** *n.* an account of cash paid, received, or in hand. **cash-and-carry** *a.*, *adv.* sold for cash, without a delivery service. ~*n.* (*also* **cash and carry**) a shop which trades in this way, usu. selling goods in large quantities at wholesale prices. **cash book** *n.* a book in which money transactions are entered. **cash box** *n.* a box in which money is kept. **cash card** *n.* a plastic card used to obtain money from a cash dispenser. **cash crop** *n.* a crop grown for sale, not for consumption. **cash desk** *n.* the desk in a shop where payments are made by customers. **cash dispenser** *n.* an electronic machine operated by a bank, which dispenses cash on insertion of a special card. **cash flow** *n.* the flow of money into and out of a business in the course of trading. **cashless** *a.* **1** moneyless. **2** without ready money. **3** (of financial transactions) made without using cash, e.g. by credit card, computer transfer etc. **cash limit** *n.* a limit on expenditure. **cash on delivery** *n.* a system by which goods are paid for on delivery. **cashpoint** *n.* a cash dispenser. **cash price** *n.* the price for payment in cash. **cash register** *n.* a calculating machine used in a shop etc., which has a drawer for money and displays or records the amount received. [F *casse*, box (see CASE[2])]

cash[2] (kash) *n.* (*pl.* **cash**) (*Hist.*) any of various Eastern (esp. Chinese) coins of low value. [Tamil *kasu*, a small coin (confused with CASH[1])]

cashew (kash´oo, -shoo´) *n.* **1** (*also* **cashew nut**) the kidney-shaped nut of a tropical tree, *Anacardium occidentale*. **2** (*also* **cashew tree**) this tree. **cashew apple** *n.* the fleshy fruit of the cashew tree, to which the cashew nut is attached. [F *acajou*, Tupi *acaju* (see also ACAJOU)]

Usage note See note under CACHOU.

cashier[1] (kashiə´) *n.* a person who has charge of the cash or of financial transactions in a bank, shop etc. [F *caissier*]

cashier[2] (kashiə´) *v.t.* **1** to dismiss from service, esp. from the armed forces, in disgrace. **2** to get rid of, to discard. [Dut. *casseren* (cp. F *casser*, L *quassāre*, to shatter, later blended with senses of *cassāre*, to annul)]

cashmere (kash´miə), **kashmir** *n.* **1** a fine soft wool from the hair of the Himalayan goat. **2** a soft material made from this or similar fine wool. [*Kashmir*, state to the north of the Indian subcontinent]

casimere CASSIMERE.

casing CASE[2].

casino[1] (kəsē´nō) *n.* (*pl.* **casinos**) a public establishment, or part of one, used for gambling. [It., dim. of *casa*, house, L *casa*, cottage]

casino[2] CASSINO.

cask (kahsk) *n.* **1** a barrel. **2** the quantity contained in a cask. **3** a container for transporting nuclear waste, a flask. [perh. from Sp. *casco*, a cask, a skull, a potsherd]

casket (kahs´kit) *n.* **1** a small case for jewels etc. **2** (*chiefly N Am.*) a coffin. [etym. uncertain; perh. dim. of CASK]

casque (kask) *n.* **1** a helmet. **2** a horny cap or protuberance on the head or beak of some birds. [F, from Sp. *casco*, CASK]

Cassandra (kəsan´drə) *n.* a person who prophesies evil or takes a gloomy view of the future, esp. one who is not listened to. [daughter of Priam, King of Troy, who had the gift of prophecy but was not believed]

cassareep (kas´ərēp) *n.* the boiled-down juice of the bitter cassava root, used as a condiment. [Carib]

cassata (kəsah´tə) *n.* a type of ice cream containing nuts and candied fruit. [It.]

cassation[1] (kəsā´shən) *n.* **1** annulment, abrogation. **2** reversal of a judicial sentence. [late L *cassātiō -ōnem* (*cassāre*, to make void)]

cassation[2] (kəsā´shən) *n.* (*Mus.*) an 18th-cent. instrumental composition similar to a divertimento. [G *Kassation*, a serenade, It. *cassazione*]

cassava (kəsah´və) *n.* **1** a W Indian plant, the manioc, of the genus *Manihot*, esp. *M. esculenta*, the bitter cassava, or *M. dulcis*, the sweet cassava. **2** a nutritious flour obtained from its roots. [Haitian *caçábi*]

Cassegrain telescope (kas´igrān), **Cassegrainian telescope** (-grā´niən) *n.* a type of reflecting telescope. [N. *Cassegrain*, fl. 17th cent., French scientist]

casserole (kas´ərōl) *n.* **1** an earthenware, glass etc. cooking pot with a lid. **2** the food cooked in such a pot, esp. a meat dish cooked slowly in the oven. *~v.t.* to cook in such a pot. [F (*casse*, a ladle, a pan)]

cassette (kəset´) *n.* **1** a small plastic case containing a length of audiotape, to be inserted into a cassette deck or cassette recorder; an audio cassette. **2** a similar container of videotape; a video cassette. **3** a similar container of photographic film, to be inserted into a camera. **cassette deck** *n.* a tape deck on which audio cassettes can be played or recorded. **cassette player** *n.* a machine used to play back a recorded audio cassette. **cassette recorder** *n.* a tape recorder on which audio cassettes can be played or recorded. **cassette tape** *n.* a cassette, esp. a prerecorded audio cassette. [F, casket]

cassia (kas´iə, kash´ə) *n.* **1** any plant of the genus *Cassia*, including the senna. **2** (*also* **cassia bark**) the cinnamon-like bark of *Cinnamomum cassia*. [L, from Gr. *kasia*, Heb. *qetsī´āh*, cassia bark (*qātssa'*, to bark or peel)]

cassimere (kas´imiə), **casimere** *n.* a fine twilled woollen cloth used esp. for suits. [CASHMERE]

cassingle (kasing´gəl) *n.* (*coll.*) a prerecorded audio cassette containing a single item of music, esp. pop or rock music, on each side. [CASSETTE, SINGLE]

cassino (kas´ēnō), **casino** *n.* a card game for two to four players. [CASINO[1]]

cassis (kas´ēs) *n.* a usu. alcoholic cordial made from blackcurrants. [F, blackcurrant]

cassiterite (kəsit´ərīt) *n.* a black or brown mineral, stannic dioxide, a source of tin. [Gr. *kassiteros*, tin, -ITE[1]]

cassock (kas´ək) *n.* a long, close-fitting garment worn by clerics, choristers, vergers etc. **cassocked** *a.* wearing a cassock. [F *casaque*, It. *casacca* (etym. uncertain; perh. from *casa*, house, L *casa*, cottage)]

cassoulet (kas´əlā) *n.* a dish consisting of haricot beans stewed with bacon, pork etc. [F]

cassowary (kas´əwəri) *n.* (*pl.* **cassowaries**) a large flightless bird of the Australasian genus *Casuarius*. [Malay *kasuwāri*]

cast (kahst) *v.t.* (*past, p.p.* **cast**) **1** to throw, to fling, to hurl. **2** to emit or throw by reflection. **3** to cause to fall, to direct (*to cast a glance*). **4** to throw off, to shed. **5** to dismiss, to reject. **6** to throw (a fishing line). **7** to assign the parts in (a play, film etc.). **8** to assign a particular role to (an actor) (*She was cast as Ophelia*). **9** to found, to mould. **10** to add up, compute, calculate. **11** to record or register (a vote etc.). *~v.i.* **1** to throw a fishing line. **2** to reckon accounts, to add up figures. **3** to warp. *~a.* **1** thrown. **2** made by founding or casting. *~n.* **1** the act of casting or throwing. **2** a throw. **3** the thing thrown. **4** the distance thrown. **5** the set of actors allocated roles in a play, film etc. **6** a mould. **7** the thing or shape moulded. **8** a plaster cast. **9** a throw of dice, or the number thrown. **10** chance, fortune. **11** a motion or turn of the eye. **12** a squint. **13** a twist. **14** feathers, fur etc. ejected from the stomach by a bird of prey. **15** the end portion of a fishing line, carrying hooks etc. **16** a tinge, a characteristic quality or form. **17** an adding up, a calculation. **to cast about** to make an extensive mental, visual or physical search (*to cast about for inspiration*). **to cast adrift** to cause or leave to drift. **to cast anchor** ANCHOR. **to cast around** to cast about. **to cast ashore** (of the sea, waves etc.) to throw or deposit on the shores. **to cast aside 1** to reject. **2** to give up. **to cast away 1** to reject. **2** to shipwreck. **to cast back** to turn (one's mind) back to the past. **to cast down 1** to throw down. **2** to deject, to depress. **to cast in one's lot with** LOT. **to cast loose** to set loose, to detach. **to cast lots** LOTS (under LOT). **to cast off 1** to discard. **2** to untie (a rope), to unmoor (a boat). **3** in knitting, to finish by looping together the last row of stitches. **4** (*Print.*) to estimate the amount of space a piece of copy will occupy. **to cast on** in knitting, to make the first row of loops or stitches. **to cast one's bread upon the waters** WATER. **to cast out** to expel. **to cast pearls before swine** PEARL[1]. **to cast up 1** to reckon, to add. **2** to vomit. **3** to cast ashore. **castaway** *a.* shipwrecked. *~n.* a shipwrecked person. **caster**[1] *n.* a person or thing that casts. **caster sugar** *n.* finely ground white sugar. **casting** *n.* **1** the act of allotting parts in a play, film etc. **2** anything formed by casting or founding, esp. a metal object as distinguished from a plaster cast. **casting couch** *n.* (*sl.*) a couch on which actresses are allegedly seduced by their casting director, in return for a role in his film, play etc. **casting net, cast net** *n.* a fishing net thrown into the water and immediately drawn in again. **casting vote** *n.* the deciding vote of a chairperson etc. when the votes are equal. **cast iron** *n.* an alloy of iron, cast in a mould. **cast-iron** *a.* **1** made of cast iron. **2** hard, rigid, unyielding, unchangeable. **3** incontestable, unchallengeable (*a cast-iron alibi*). **cast-off** *a.* discarded, rejected. *~n.* a person or thing cast off, esp. a discarded garment. [Icel. *kasta*, to throw]

castanet (kastənet´) *n.* (*usu. pl.*) a small spoon-shaped concave instrument of ivory or hard wood, a pair of which is fastened to each thumb and rattled or clicked as an accompaniment to music. [Sp. *castañeta*, dim. of *castaña*, L *castanea*, chestnut]

caste (kahst) *n.* **1** any one of the hereditary classes of society in India. **2** any hereditary, exclusive class. **3** the caste or class system. **4** dignity or social influence due to position. **5** a type of specialized individual among social insects, such as the worker bee. **to lose caste 1** to descend in the social scale. **2** to lose favour or consideration. **casteism** *n.* **casteless** *a.* **caste mark** *n.* a red mark on the forehead showing one's caste. [Port. *casta*, fem. of *casto*, lineage, L *castus*, pure, unmixed (cp. CHASTE)]

castellan (kas´tələn) *n.* (*Hist.*) the governor of a castle. **castellany** *n.* (*pl.* **castellanies**) the office or jurisdiction of a castellan. [ONF *castellain* (F *châtelain*), late L *castellānus* (see CASTLE)]

castellated (kas´təlātid) *a.* **1** having turrets and battlements. **2** having castles. **3** resembling a castle. **castellation** (-lā´shən) *n.* [med. L *castellātus*, p.p. *castellāre*, to build a castle (see CASTLE)]

caster[1] CAST.

caster[2] CASTOR[1].

castigate (kas´tigāt) *v.t.* (*formal*) **1** to chastise, to punish. **2** to rebuke or criticize severely. **castigation** (-ā´shən) *n.* **castigator** *n.* **castigatory** (-ā´təri) *a.* [L *castigātus*, p.p. of *castigāre*, to chasten (*castus*, CHASTE)]

Castile soap (kastēl´) *n.* a fine, hard soap, whose main constituents are olive oil and soda. [*Castile*, in Spain]

Castilian (kastil´iən) *n.* **1** a native or inhabitant of Castile in Spain. **2** the language of Castile, standard European Spanish. *~a.* **1** of or relating to Castile or its inhabitants. **2** of or relating to Castilian or standard European Spanish.

castle (kah´səl) *n.* **1** a fortified building, a fortress. **2** a mansion that was formerly a fortress. **3** the mansion of a monarch or noble. **4** a chess piece in the shape of a tower, a rook. *~v.i.* in chess, to move the king two squares to the right or left and bring up the castle to the square the king has passed over. *~v.t.* to move (the king) thus. **castled** *a.* **1** having a castle. **2** having many castles. **3** castellated. **castle nut** *n.* a nut with notched extension for a locking-pin. **castles in Spain** *n.pl.* castles in the air. **castles in the air** *n.pl.* visionary or unrealizable projects, daydreams. [ONF *castel* (OF *chastel*, *château*), L *castellum*, dim. of *castrum*, a fort]

castor[1], **caster** (kahs´tə) *n.* **1** a small swivelled wheel attached to the leg of a table, sofa, chair etc. **2** a small container with a perforated top for sprinkling the contents, esp. at table. **castor action** *n.* the tendency of a vehicle to swivel into its plane of rotation to ensure stability. **castor sugar** *n.* CASTER SUGAR (under CAST). [var. of CASTER]

castor[2] (kahs´tə) *n.* **1** an oily compound secreted by the beaver, used in medicine and perfumery. **2** the beaver. **3** a beaver hat. [F, from L, from Gr. *kastōr*, beaver, prob. Eastern in origin (cp. Sansk. *kastūrī*, musk)]

castor[3] (kahs´tə) *a.* (*Austral., sl.*) good, excellent. [etym. unknown]

castor oil (kahstəroil´) *n.* **1** an oil, used as a cathartic and lubricant, obtained from the seeds of the plant *Ricinus communis*. **2** (*also* **castor oil plant**) this plant, also grown as a house plant. **castor bean** *n.* **1** the seed of the castor oil plant. **2** (*N Am.*) the castor oil plant. **castor oil bean** *n.* the seed of the castor oil plant. [etym. uncertain; perh. from CASTOR[2]]

castrate (kastrāt´) *v.t.* **1** to remove the testicles of, to geld. **2** to deprive of reproductive power. **3** to deprive of force or vigour. **4** to expurgate unduly. **castration** *n.* **castrator** *n.* [L *castrātus*, p.p. of *castrāre*]

castrato (kastrah´tō) *n.* (*pl.* **castrati** (-tē)) (*Hist.*) a male soprano castrated before puberty to retain the pitch of his voice. [It., p.p. of *castrare* (L *castrāre*)]

casual (kazh´ūəl, kaz´ūəl) *a.* **1** happening by chance; accidental. **2** offhand (*a casual remark*). **3** occasional, temporary. **4** careless, unmethodical. **5** unconcerned, apathetic. **6** informal (*casual clothes*). ~*n.* **1** an occasional or temporary worker. **2** (*pl.*) flat-heeled shoes that slip on without lacing. **3** (*pl.*) informal clothes. **4** (*coll.*) a (football) hooligan. **casualism** *n.* the doctrine that all things exist or happen by chance. **casualist** *n.* **casualization** (-zā´shən), **casualisation** *n.* the re-employment of regular workers on a casual basis. **casual labour** *n.* workers employed irregularly. **casually** *adv.* **casualness** *n.* [F *casuel*, L *cāsuālis* (*cāsus*, CASE[1])]

casualty (kazh´ūəlti, kaz´ūəlti) *n.* (*pl.* **casualties**) **1** a person who is killed or injured in a war or in an accident. **2** anything lost or destroyed in a similar situation. **3** a casualty department (*She was taken to casualty*). **4** an accident, esp. one involving personal injury or loss of life. **casualty department, casualty ward** *n.* the department in a hospital for receiving the victims of accidents. [see CASUAL]

casuarina (kasūərī´nə) *n.* (*pl.* **casuarinas**) any tree of the genus *Casuarina*, of Australia and SE Asia, with jointed leafless branches. [mod. L, from Malay *kasuwāri*, cassowary, from a supposed resemblance of the branches to cassowary plumage]

casuist (kaz´ūist, kazh´-) *n.* **1** a person who studies or resolves moral problems, esp. one who uses plausible but false reasoning. **2** a sophist, a hair-splitter. **casuistic** (-is´-), **casuistical** *a.* **casuistically** (-is´-) *adv.* **casuistry** *n.* **1** the branch of ethics or theology which deals with cases of conscience. **2** the reasoning of a casuist. [F *casuiste* (L *cāsus*, CASE[1])]

casus belli (kahsus bel´ē, kāsəs bel´ī) *n.* (*pl.* **casus belli**) an act that provokes or justifies war. [L]

CAT *abbr.* **1** College of Advanced Technology. **2** computer-assisted testing, computer-aided testing. **3** (*Med.*) computerized axial tomography. **CAT scanner** *n.* CT SCANNER.

cat[1] (kat) *n.* **1** any mammal of the genus *Felis*, comprising the lion, tiger, leopard etc., esp. *F. catus*, the domestic cat. **2** any catlike animal. **3** (*coll.*) a spiteful woman. **4** (*sl.*) a man. **5** (*sl.*) a jazz enthusiast. **6** a cat-o'-nine-tails. **7** (*Naut.*) **a** the cathead. **b** a strong tackle used to hoist the anchor to the cathead. **8** the game of tipcat. **9** the tapered stick used in this game. **10** a type of double tripod (which always falls on its feet, as a cat is said to do). ~*v.t.* (*pres. p.* **catting**, *past*, *p.p.* **catted**) **1** (*Naut.*) to hoist to the cathead. **2** (*coll.*) to vomit. ~*v.i.* (*coll.*) to vomit. **like a cat on a hot tin roof/ on hot bricks** in a state of agitation. **like a scalded cat** SCALD[1]. **like something the cat brought/ dragged in** (*coll.*) very bedraggled or dishevelled. **no room to swing a cat** very little or not enough space. **not to have a cat in hell's chance** (*sl.*) to have no chance at all. **the cat's whiskers/ pyjamas** (*sl.*) the best or greatest person or thing (*He thinks he's the cat's whiskers*). **to fight like Kilkenny cats** to fight so violently that both parties are destroyed. **to let the cat out of the bag** to give away a secret, esp. unintentionally. **to play cat and mouse with** to tease or toy with an opponent or victim, esp. before defeating or destroying them. **to put/ set the cat among the pigeons** to stir up trouble. **to rain cats and dogs** to rain very heavily. **to see which way the cat jumps 1** to wait until others have made up their mind. **2** to sit on the fence, to remain uncommitted. **cat-and-dog** *a.* quarrelsome. **catbird** *n.* **1** a N American bird, *Dumetalla carolinesis*, with a call like the mewing of a cat. **2** any other bird with a catlike call. **catblock** *n.* (*Naut.*) a block used to hoist the anchor. **cat burglar** *n.* a thief who enters a house by climbing up the outside. **catcall** *n.* a whistle or cry of disapproval at a public meeting, show etc. ~*v.i.* to make a catcall. ~*v.t.* to deride with a catcall. **cat-eyed** *a.* able to see in the dark. **catfish** *n.* (*pl. in general* **catfish**, *in particular* **catfishes**) any of various esp. freshwater fish with barbels resembling a cat's whiskers around the mouth. **cat flap, cat door** *n.* a small flap set into a door to allow a cat to pass through. **catgut** *n.* a cord made from the intestines of animals, used for the strings of musical instruments and for surgical sutures. **cathead** *n.* (*Naut.*) a beam projecting from a ship's bows to which the anchor is secured. **cat hole** *n.* (*Naut.*) either of two holes at the stern of a ship for a cable or hawser. **cathood** *n.* **cathouse** *n.* (*N Am., sl.*) a brothel. **cat-ice** *n.* thin white ice over shallow places where the water has receded. **catlick** *n.* (*coll.*) a perfunctory wash. **catlike** *a.* **cat litter** *n.* an absorbent material spread on a tray for a cat to urinate or defecate on. **catmint** *n.* a European labiate plant, *Nepeta cataria*, with scented leaves attractive to cats. **catnap** *n.* a short sleep. ~*v.i.* (*pres.p.* **catnapping**, *past*, *p.p.* **catnapped**) to have a catnap. **catnip** *n.* catmint. **cat-o'-mountain** *n.* CATAMOUNTAIN. **cat-o'-nine-tails** *n.* a whip or scourge with nine lashes, formerly used as an instrument of punishment. **cat's cradle** *n.* a children's game played with a loop of string held between the fingers. **cat's-ear** *n.* any European plant of the genus *Hypochoeris*, esp. *H. radicata*, with yellow flowers. **Catseye®** *n.* a reflector stud on a road. **cat's-eye** *n.* a precious stone from Sri Lanka, Malabar etc., a vitreous variety of quartz. **cat's-foot** *n.* (*pl.* **cat's-feet**) **1** a European plant, *Antennaria dioica*, with woolly leaves. **2** the ground ivy. **cat's meat** *n.* horseflesh, used as food for cats. **cat's paw** *n.* **1** a dupe used as a tool (from the fable of the monkey who used the cat's paw to pick chestnuts out of the fire). **2** a light wind which just ripples the surface of the water. **3** (*Naut.*) a turn in the bight of a rope to hook a tackle on. **cat's-tail** *n.* **1** the reed mace. **2** a catkin. **catsuit** *n.* a one-piece trouser suit. **cat's whisker** *n.* a very fine wire in contact with a crystal receiver to rectify current and cause audibility. **cattery** *n.* (*pl.* **catteries**) a place where cats are bred or boarded. **cattish** *a.* catty. **cattishly** *a.* **cattishness** *n.* **catty**[1] (kat´i) *a.* (*comp.* **cattier**, *superl.* **cattiest**) **1** spiteful, malicious. **2** catlike. **cattily** *adv.* **cattiness** *n.* **catwalk** *n.* **1** a narrow walkway high above the ground, as above the stage in a theatre. **2** a narrow walkway used by the models in a fashion show. [OE *catte* (cp. Dut. *kat*, Icel, *köttr*, G *Kater*, *Katze*, Ir. and Gael. *cat*, late L *cattus*)]

cat[2] (kat) *n.* a coal and timber vessel formerly used on the NE coast of England. **catboat** *n.* a sailing-boat with one mast, towards the bows, and one large fore-and-aft sail. **cat-rigged** *a.* having the rig of a catboat. [from CAT[1]]

cat[3] (kat) *n.* **1** a catalytic converter. **2** a catamaran. [abbr.]
cat. *abbr.* **1** catalogue. **2** catechism.
cata- (kat´ə), **kata-**, **cat-**, **cath-** *pref.* **1** down; downwards. **2** against. **3** away. **4** wrongly; badly. **5** entirely; thoroughly. **6** according to. [Gr. *kata*, down, downwards]
catabasis (kətab´əsis) *n.* (*pl.* **catabases** (-sēz)) **1** a downward movement. **2** the decline of a disease. **catabatic** (katəbat´ik) *a.*
catabolism (kətab´əlizm), **katabolism** *n.* the process of change by which complex organic compounds break down into simpler compounds, destructive metabolism. **catabolic** (katəbol´ik) *a.* **catabolically** *adv.* [Gr. *katabolē*, from *kataballein* (CATA-, *ballein*, to throw)]
catacaustic (katəkaws´tik, -kos´-) *a.* (*Physics, Math.*) formed by reflected rays. ~*n.* a caustic curve formed by reflection.
catachresis (katəkrē´sis) *n.* (*pl.* **catachreses** (-sēz)) **1** the wrong use of one word for another. **2** the misuse of a trope or metaphor. **catachrestic** (-kres´-, -krē´-), **catachrestical** *a.* **catachrestically** *adv.* [L, from Gr. *katachrēsis* (*chrēsthai*, to be used)]
cataclasis (katəklā´sis) *n.* (*pl.* **cataclases** (-sēz)) (*Geol.*) the crushing of rocks by pressure. **cataclastic** (-klas´-) *a.* [Gr. *klasis*, a breaking]
cataclasm (kat´əklazm) *n.* a violent break or disruption. [Gr. *kataklasma*, from *kataklân* (*klân*, to break)]
cataclysm (kat´əklizm) *n.* **1** a violent upheaval or disaster. **2** a vast and sudden social or political change. **3** a deluge, esp. the Flood. **4** a geological catastrophe. **cataclysmal** (-kliz´-), **cataclysmic** *a.* **cataclysmically** *adv.* [F *cataclysme*, Gr. *kataklusmos*, from *katakluzein* (*kluzein*, to wash)]
catacomb (kat´əkoom) *n.* **1** (*often pl.*) a subterranean burial place, with niches for the dead, esp. the subterranean galleries at Rome. **2** any similar excavation or subterranean construction. **3** a cellar, esp. a wine-cellar. [F *catacombe*, It. *catacomba*, late L *catacumbas* (etym. uncertain; prob. a place name, but not applied to the Roman catacombs when in use)]
catadromous (kətad´rəməs) *a.* (of fish) descending periodically to spawn (in the sea or the lower waters of a river). [Gr. *katadromos* (-*dromos*, running, from *dramein*, to run)]
catafalque (kat´əfalk) *n.* a temporary stage or tomblike structure for the coffin during a state funeral service. [F *catafalque*, It. *catafalco* (etym. unknown)]
Catalan (kat´əlan) *a.* of or relating to Catalonia, its people or their language. ~*n.* **1** a native or inhabitant of Catalonia. **2** the language of Catalonia.
catalase (kat´əlāz) *n.* an enzyme involved in the decomposition of hydrogen peroxide. [CATALYSIS]
catalectic (katəlek´tik) *a.* having an incomplete metrical foot at the end of a line. ~*n.* a catalectic line. [late L *catalēcticus*, Gr. *katalēktikos*, from *katalēgein* (*lēgein*, to leave, cease)]
catalepsy (kat´əlepsi) *n.* a state of trance or suspension of voluntary sensation. **cataleptic** (-lep´tik) *a.* affected by or subject to catalepsy. ~*n.* a person subject to attacks of catalepsy. [med. L *catalēpsia*, Gr. *katalēpsis* (*lambanein*, to seize)]
catalo CATTALO.
catalogue (kat´əlog), (*N Am.*) **catalog** *n.* **1** a methodical list, arranged alphabetically or under class headings, e.g. of items for sale, books in a library etc. **2** (*N Am.*) a university calendar or list of courses. ~*v.t.* (*pres.p.* **cataloguing**, (*N Am.*) **cataloging**, *past*, *p.p.* **catalogued**, (*N Am.*) **cataloged**) **1** to enter in a catalogue. **2** to make a catalogue of. **cataloguer**, (*N Am.*) **cataloger** *n.* **catalogue raisonné** (rāzon´ā) *n.* (*pl.* **catalogues raisonnés** (kat´əlog rāzon´ā)) a catalogue in which a description of the items is given. [F, from late L *catalogus*, Gr. *katalogos*, from *katalegein* (*legein*, to choose, state)]
catalpa (kətal´pə) *n.* (*pl.* **catalpas**) any tree of the chiefly N American genus *Catalpa*, with long, thin pods. [N Am. Ind.]
catalysis (kətal´isis) *n.* (*pl.* **catalyses** (-sēz)) the acceleration of a chemical reaction by a catalyst. **catalyse** (kat´əlīz), (*N Am.*) **catalyze** *v.t.* to subject to catalysis. **catalyser** *n.* a catalytic converter. **catalyst** (kat´əlist) *n.* **1** any substance that changes the speed of a chemical reaction without itself being permanently changed. **2** any person or thing that causes change. **catalytic** (katəlit´-) *a.* relating to or involving catalysis. **catalytically** *adv.* **catalytic converter** *n.* a device fitted to the exhaust pipe of a motor vehicle to remove toxic impurities from the exhaust gases. **catalytic cracker** *n.* an industrial apparatus used to break down the heavy hydrocarbons of crude oil and yield petrol, paraffins etc. [Gr. *katalusis*, from *kataluein* (*luein*, to loosen)]
catamaran (kat´əməran) *n.* **1** a double-hulled boat. **2** a raft made by lashing two boats together. **3** a raft made by lashing logs together. **4** (*coll.*) a vixenish woman. [Tamil *katta-maram* (*katta*, tie, *maram*, wood)]
catamenia (katəmē´niə) *n.pl.* the menses. **catamenial** *a.* [Gr. *katamēnia*]
catamite (kat´əmīt) *n.* a boy kept for homosexual purposes. [L *catamītus*, corr. from Gr. *Ganymēdes*, Jove's cupbearer]
catamountain (katəmown´tən), **catamount** (kat´əmownt) *n.* **1** the leopard, panther, puma, lynx etc. **2** †a fierce, savage person. [from *cat of the mountain*]
catananche (katənang´ki) *n.* any plant of the genus *Catananche*, of the daisy family. [L *catanancē*, a plant used in love potions, Gr. *katanangkē*, a spell]
cataphoresis (katəfərē´sis) *n.* electrophoresis. **cataphoretic** (-ret´ik) *a.*
cataphyll (kat´əfil) *n.* a simplified or rudimentary leaf. **cataphyllary** (-fil´-) *a.* [Gr. *phullon*, leaf]
cataplasm (kat´əplazm) *n.* a poultice, a plaster. [Gr. *kataplasma* (*plassein*, to shape)]
cataplexy (kat´əpleksi) *n.* **1** temporary paralysis brought on suddenly by shock. **2** a condition of immobility adopted by animals shamming death. **cataplectic** (-plek´-) *a.* [Gr. *kataplēxis*, stupefaction (*plēssein*, to strike)]
catapult (kat´əpŭlt) *n.* **1** a device for propelling small stones, made from a forked stick with elastic between the prongs. **2** (*Hist.*) a military machine for hurling darts or stones. **3** a device or machine used to launch aircraft from a ship. ~*v.t.* to throw or launch with or as with a catapult. ~*v.i.* to shoot from or as from a catapult. [L *catapulta*, Gr. *katapeltēs* (*pallein*, to hurl)]
cataract (kat´ərakt) *n.* **1** a large, rushing waterfall. **2** a deluge of rain. **3** any violent rush of water. **4** (*Med.*) a disease of the eye in which the crystalline lens or its envelope becomes opaque and vision is impaired or destroyed. [F *cataracte*, L *cataracta*, Gr. *katarrhaktēs* (from *katarassein*, to dash down)]
catarrh (kətah´) *n.* **1** inflammation of a mucous membrane, esp. of the nose, causing a watery discharge. **2** this discharge. **3** a cold in the head or chest. **catarrhal**, **catarrhous** *a.* [F *catarrhe*, late L *catarrhus*, Gr. *katarrhos*, from *katarrheein* (*rheein*, to flow)]
catarrhine (kat´ərīn) *a.* (of Old World monkeys) having the nostrils in a close, oblique position. ~*n.* such a monkey. [Gr. *rhin rhinos*, the nose]
catastrophe (kətas´trəfi) *n.* **1** a great misfortune or disaster. **2** a change that brings about the conclusion of a drama; the denouement. **3** a final event, esp. one that brings disaster or ruin. **4** (*Geol.*) a violent convulsion of the earth's surface, producing changes in the relative extent of land or water. **catastrophe theory** *n.* a branch of mathematics dealing with discontinuous change in a system. **catastrophic** (katəstrof´-) *a.* **catastrophically** *adv.* **catastrophism** *a.* (*Geol.*) the theory that geological

changes have been produced by the action of catastrophes. **catastrophist** *n.* [Gr. *katastrophē* (*strephein*, to turn)]

catatonia (katətō´niə) *n.* **1** a syndrome often associated with schizophrenia, marked by periods of catalepsy. **2** (*loosely*) catalepsy, or a state of apathy or stupor. **catatonic** (-ton´-) *a.* [Gr. *tonos*, a stretching, tension]

catawba (kətaw´bə) *n.* **1** a N American variety of grape, *Vitis abrusca*. **2** wine made from this grape. [*Catawba*, a S Carolina river named after a N American Indian people]

catch (kach) *v.t.* (*past, p.p.* **caught** (kawt)) **1** to grasp, to take hold of. **2** to seize, esp. in pursuit. **3** to take in a snare, to entrap. **4** to take by angling or in a net. **5** to intercept and hold (a ball or other moving object). **6** in cricket, to dismiss (a batsman) by catching the ball. **7** to come upon suddenly, to surprise, to detect. **8** to receive by infection or contagion. **9** to be in time for (*to catch a train*). **10** to check, to interrupt. **11** to cause to become fastened or entangled. **12** to grasp, to perceive, to apprehend (*I didn't catch your name*). **13** to attract, to gain, to win. *~v.i.* **1** to become fastened or entangled. **2** to ignite. **3** to take hold. **4** to spread epidemically. **5** to communicate. *~n.* **1** the act of catching. **2** a thing or amount caught. **3** the act of catching the ball at cricket. **4** a fastening device. **5** a contrivance for checking motion. **6** an acquisition. **7** an opportunity. **8** (*coll.*) a person worth catching, esp. in marriage. **9** a trap, a snare. **10** an unexpected or concealed difficulty or drawback. **11** a game in which a ball is thrown and caught. **12** (*Mus.*) a type of round, esp. humorous. **to be caught with one's pants down** PANTS. **to catch a cold** COLD. **to catch at** to attempt to seize. **to catch a Tartar** TARTAR. **to catch at straws/ a straw** STRAW. **to catch fire** FIRE. **to catch it** (*sl.*) to get a scolding. **to catch napping** NAP[1]. **to catch on 1** (*coll.*) to become popular. **2** to understand. **to catch one's breath** BREATH. **to catch one's death of cold** DEATH. **to catch one's eye** EYE[1]. **to catch on the hop** HOP[1]. **to catch on the wrong foot** FOOT. **to catch out 1** to discover (someone) in error or wrongdoing. **2** in cricket, to dismiss (a batsman) by catching the ball. **to catch sight of** SIGHT. **to catch the sun** SUN. **to catch up 1** to reach (a person, vehicle etc. that is ahead). **2** to make up arrears. **3** (*often pass.*) to involve (*He was caught up in a plot to assassinate the president*). **4** to raise and hold. **you wouldn't catch me** (*coll.*) I would never do the thing mentioned (*You wouldn't catch me wearing a hat like that!*). **catch-22** *n.* a situation from which escape is impossible because rules or circumstances frustrate effort in any direction (from such a situation in a novel of this title by J. Heller). **catchable** *a.* **catch-all** *a.* (of a rule etc.) which covers all situations, or any not previously covered. **catch-as-catch-can** *n.* a style of wrestling in which most holds are allowed. *~a.* (*esp. N Am.*) using whatever comes to hand. **catch basin** *n.* (*N Am.*) a catch pit. **catch crop** *n.* a quick-growing green crop sown between main crops. **catch drain** *n.* an open drain along the side of a hill or canal to catch the surplus water. **catcher** *n.* **catchfly** *n.* (*pl.* **catchflies**) any plant of the genera *Lychnis* or *Silene*, from their glutinous stems which often retain small insects. **catching** *a.* **1** infectious. **2** attractive. **catchline** *n.* (*Print.*) a short line of type, esp. as a headline. **catchment** *n.* **1** the act of collecting water. **2** a surface on which water may be caught and collected. **catchment area** *n.* **1** (*also* **catchment basin**) an area from which water, esp. rainfall, drains into a river system. **2** the area from which a particular school, hospital etc. officially takes its pupils, patients etc. **catchpenny** *a.* worthless, but superficially attractive, in order to be quickly sold. **catchphrase** *n.* a phrase which comes into fashion and is much used, esp. one associated with a particular person or group. **catch pit** *n.* a pit in a drain, to catch sediment and prevent clogging. **catch points** *n.pl.* railway points placed so as to derail any vehicle accidentally running the wrong way. **catchweed** *n.* goosegrass or cleavers. **catchweight** *a.* in wrestling etc., unrestricted with regard to weight. *~n.* unrestricted weight. **catchword** *n.* **1** a word or phrase in frequent or popular use, esp. temporarily; a slogan. **2** an actor's cue. **3** a word printed under the last line of a page, being the first word of the next page. **4** the first word in a dictionary entry. **catchy** *a.* (*comp.* **catchier**, *superl.* **catchiest**) **1** (of a tune etc.) easy to pick up or remember; pleasant or attractive. **2** tricky, deceptive. **3** irregular, fitful. **4** catching. **catchily** *adv.* **catchiness** *n.* [ONF *cachier* (cp. OF *chacier*, CHASE[1], prob. from late L *captiāre* (L *captāre*, to chase, freq. of *capere*, to take)]

catchpole (kach´pōl) *n.* (*Hist.*) **1** a constable. **2** a bumbailiff. [med. L *chassipullus*, chase-fowl (CHASE[1], *pullus*, fowl)]

catchup KETCHUP.

†cate CATES.

catechetic (katəket´ik), **catechetical** (-əl) *a.* consisting of questions and answers; of or relating to catechism. **catechetically** *adv.* **catechetics** *n.* that part of Christian theology which deals with oral instruction. [CATECHIZE]

catechism (kat´əkizm) *n.* **1** a form of instruction by means of question and answer, esp. the authorized manuals of doctrine of a Christian Church. **2** any series of interrogations. **catechismal** (-kiz´-) *a.* **catechist** *n.* **1** a person who teaches by catechizing. **2** a person who imparts elementary instruction, esp. in the principles of religion. **catechistic** (-kis´-), **catechistical** *a.* **catechistically** *adv.* [as CATECHIZE]

catechize (kat´əkīz), **catechise** *v.t.* **1** to instruct by means of questions and answers. **2** to instruct in the Church catechism. **3** to question closely. **catechizer** *n.* [L *catēchizāre*, Gr. *katēchizein*, *katēcheein*, to din into the ears (*ēchein*, to sound, *ēcho*, ECHO)]

catechol (kat´ichol, -kol) *n.* a crystalline phenol found in catechu and other resins. **catecholamine** (katikō´ləmēn, -kol´ə-) *n.* any of a group of compounds derived from catechol, including adrenalin and dopamine. [CATECHU, -OL]

catechu (kat´əchoo) *n.* a brown astringent gum, obtained chiefly from the Asian tree *Acacia catechu*, used in tanning. **catechuic** (-choo´-) *a.* [Malay *kāchu*]

catechumen (katikū´mən) *n.* a person who is under Christian instruction preparatory to receiving baptism. **catechumenate** *n.* **catechumenical** (-men´-) *a.* **catechumenism** *n.* [F *catéchumène*, L *catēchūmenus*, Gr. *katēchoumenos* (*katēcheein*, see CATECHIZE)]

category (kat´igəri) *n.* (*pl.* **categories**) **1** an order, a class, a division. **2** (*Philos.*) **a** any of the ten predicaments or classes of Aristotle, to which all objects of thought or knowledge can be reduced. **b** any of Kant's twelve primitive forms of thought, contributed by the understanding, apart from experience. **categorial** (-gaw´riəl) *a.* **categorical** (-gor´ikəl), **categoric** *a.* **1** of or relating to a category or categories. **2** absolute, unconditional. **3** explicit, direct. **categorical imperative** *n.* in Kantian ethics, the absolute command of the reason as interpreter of the moral law. **categorically** *adv.* **categorize**, **categorise** *v.t.* to place in a category or categories. **categorization** (-zā´shən) *n.* [L *catēgoria*, Gr. *katēgoria*, a statement, from *katēgoros*, an accuser (CATA-, AGORA[1], the assembly)]

catena (kətē´nə) *n.* (*pl.* **catenas**, **catenae** (-nē)) **1** a chain. **2** a connected series. **catena patrum** (pah´trəm) *n.* a series of extracts from the writings of the Fathers on the Bible or on theological doctrine. **catenate** (kat´ənāt) *v.t.* to link together. **catenation** (-ā´shən) *n.* [L]

catenane (kat´ənān) *n.* a chemical compound in which

the molecules are linked together like a chain. [CATENA, -ANE]

catenary (kətē´nəri, kat´ə-) *n.* (*pl.* **catenaries**) a curve formed by a chain or rope of uniform density hanging from two points of suspension not in the same vertical line. ~*a.* of, resembling or relating to a chain, a catena or a catenary. **catenarian** (katəneə´riən) *a.* catenary. **catenary bridge** *n.* a suspension bridge hung from catenary chains. [L *catēnārius* (*catēna*, a chain)]

catenate, catenation CATENA.

cater[1] (kā´tə) *v.i.* **1** to supply food, entertainment etc. (for). **2** to provide what is needed (for). **3** to pander (to). ~*v.t.* (*N Am.*) to provide food etc. for (a party etc.). **caterer** *n.* a person who provides food etc. for social functions, esp. as a trade. **catering** *n.* **1** the trade of a caterer. **2** the food etc. for a social function. [ME *catour*, a caterer, earlier *acatour*, OF *acateor* (*acat*, *achat*, a purchasing, late L *accaptāre*, to purchase, freq. of *accipere*, to receive)]

cater[2] (kā´tə) *adv.* (*dial.*) diagonally. **cater-cornered, catty-cornered** (kat´i-), **kitty-cornered** (kit´i-) *a.* (*N Am.*) placed diagonally; diagonal; not square. ~*adv.* diagonally. [F *quatre*, L *quatuor*, four]

cateran (kat´ərən) *n.* (*Hist.*, *Sc.*) a Highland freebooter or irregular soldier. [Gael. *ceathairne*, peasantry]

caterpillar (kat´əpilə) *n.* **1** the larva of a butterfly or other lepidopterous insect. **2** (**Caterpillar®**) a Caterpillar track, tractor or tank. **Caterpillar track®** *n.* an articulated belt revolving round two or more wheels, used to propel a motor vehicle over soft or rough ground. **Caterpillar tractor®**, **Caterpillar tank®** *n.* a tractor or tank fitted with a Caterpillar track. [etym. uncertain; perh. a corr. of ONF *catepelose* (OF *chatepelose*), hairy cat (*chate*, fem. of *chat*, cat, *pelose*, L *pilōsus*, hairy)]

caterwaul (kat´əwawl) *v.i.* to make the loud howling noise of a cat on heat. ~*n.* such a noise. [CAT[1], WAUL]

†cates (kāts) *n.pl.* (*sometimes sing.*) **1** provisions. **2** dainties, delicacies. [earlier *acates*, OF *acat*, a purchase (see CATER[1])]

Cath. *abbr.* **1** Cathedral. **2** Catholic.

cath- CATA-.

Cathar (kath´ə) *n.* (*pl.* **Cathars, Cathari** (-ri)) a member of a medieval Manichaean sect in S France. **Catharism** *n.* **Catharist** *n.* [med. L *catharistae*, Gr. *katharistai*, from *katharizein* (*katharos*, clean)]

catharsis (kəthah´sis) *n.* (*pl.* **catharses** (-sez)) **1** the purging of the emotions by tragedy; emotional release achieved through dramatic art. **2** (*Psych.*) the bringing out of repressed ideas and emotions. **3** purgation of the body. **cathartic** *a.* **1** purgative. **2** causing or resulting in catharsis. ~*n.* a purgative medicine. **cathartical** *a.* **cathartically** *adv.* [Gr. *katharsis* from *kathairein* (*katharos*, clean)]

Cathay (kathā´) *n.* (*poet.*) China. [med. L *Cataya*]

cathectic CATHEXIS.

cathedra (kəthē´drə) *n.* **1** the bishop's throne in a cathedral. **2** a professorial chair. [L, from Gr. (CATH-, *hedra*, a seat)]

cathedral (kəthē´drəl) *n.* the principal church in a diocese, containing the bishop's throne. **cathedral church** *n.* a cathedral. **cathedral city** *n.* a city where there is a cathedral. [as CATHEDRA]

Catherine wheel (kath´ərin) *n.* **1** a firework that rotates like a wheel. **2** an ornamental circular window with spokelike mullions or shafts. [referring to the martyrdom of St Catherine]

catheter (kath´itə) *n.* (*Med.*) a tube used to introduce fluids to, or withdraw them from, the body, esp. to withdraw urine from the bladder. **catheterize, catheterise** *v.t.* to insert a catheter into. **catheterization** (-zā´shən) *n.* [L, from Gr. *kathetēr*, from *cathienai*, to let down (*hienai*, to send)]

cathetometer (kathitom´itə) *n.* an instrument consisting of a telescope mounted on a vertical graduated support, used for measuring small vertical distances. [L *cathetus*, a straight line perpendicular to another]

cathexis (kəthek´sis) *n.* (*pl.* **cathexes** (-sēz)) concentration of mental or emotional energy on a single object. **cathectic** *a.* [Gr. *kathexis*, retention]

cathode (kath´ōd), **kathode** *n.* **1** the negative electrode in an electrolytic cell. **2** the source of electrons in an electronic valve. **3** the positive terminal of a primary cell. **cathode ray** *n.* a stream of electrons emitted from the surface of a cathode during an electrical discharge. **cathode ray tube** *n.* a vacuum tube in which a beam of electrons, which can be controlled in direction and intensity, is projected on to a fluorescent screen thus producing a point of light. **cathodic** (-thod´-), **cathodal** *a.* **cathodic protection** *n.* the protection from corrosion of a metal structure, esp. underwater, by making the structure act as the cathode in an electrolytic cell. [Gr. *kathodos*, descent]

catholic (kath´əlik) *a.* **1** universal, general, comprehensive. **2** liberal, large-hearted, tolerant. **3** (**Catholic**) of or relating to the Church of Rome; Roman Catholic. **4** (**Catholic**) of or relating to the whole Christian Church. **5** (**Catholic**) in the Middle Ages, of or relating to the Western or Latin Church. **6** (**Catholic**) of or relating to the Anglican Church, as claiming continuity from the old, undivided Christian Church. **7** (**Catholic**) not heretical. ~*n.* **1** (**Catholic**) a Roman Catholic. **2** (**Catholic**) an Anglo-Catholic. **catholically** (-thol´-), **catholicly** *adv.* **Catholic Epistles** *n.pl.* certain epistles addressed to the Church at large, including those of Peter, James and Jude and the first epistle of John (sometimes also the second and third). **Catholicism** (-thol´-) *n.* Roman Catholic Christianity. **catholicity** (-lis´-) *n.* the quality of being catholic (in all senses). **catholicize** (-thol´-), **catholicise** *v.t.* to make catholic or Catholic. ~*v.i.* to become catholic or Catholic. **catholicization** (-zā´shən) *n.* **catholico-** (-thol´-) *comb. form* catholic and. [F *catholique*, L *catholicus*, Gr. *katholikos*, from *kath'holou*, on the whole, universally (CATH-, *holou*, gen. of *holos*, the whole)]

catholicon (kəthol´ikon) *n.* a universal medicine; a panacea. [F, from Gr. *katholikon*, neut. of *katholikos*, see CATHOLIC]

cation (kat´īən), **kation** *n.* the positive ion which in electrolysis is attracted towards the cathode. **cationic** (-on´-) *a.* [CATA-, ION]

catkin (kat´kin) *n.* the pendulous inflorescence of the willow, birch, poplar etc. [prob. from Dut. *katteken*, kitten, dim. of *katte* (CAT[1], -KIN)]

catling (kat´ling) *n.* **1** a double-edged knife used in surgical amputations. **2** a kind of catgut. **3** a string made from this. **4** †a little cat. [CAT[1], -LING[1]]

catoptric (kətop´trik) *a.* of or relating to a mirror or reflector, or to reflection. **catoptrics** *n.* the science of reflected light. [Gr. *katoptrikos*, from *katoptron*, a mirror]

catsup KETCHUP.

cattalo (kat´əlō), **catalo** *n.* (*pl.* **cattaloes, cattalos, cataloes, catalos**) a hardy cross between domestic cattle and American bison. [*catt*le, buff*alo*]

cattery, cattish CAT[1].

cattle (kat´əl) *n.pl.* **1** domesticated animals, esp. bovine mammals such as cows, bulls, oxen and bison. **2** †livestock, including horses, sheep, pigs etc. **cattle cake** *n.* a concentrated processed food for cattle. **cattle grid** *n.* a grid covering a trench in a road which prevents cattle etc. from crossing but allows vehicles to pass over. **cattle guard** *n.* (*N Am.*) a cattle grid. **cattleman** *n.* (*pl.* **cattlemen**) **1** a person who looks after cattle. **2** (*N Am.*) a person who breeds and rears cattle, a ranch owner. **cattle-plague** *n.* any of several diseases to which cattle are subject, esp. rinderpest. **cattle rustler** *n.* (*N Am.*) a cattle stealer. **cattle show** *n.* an exhibition of cattle at which prizes are given. **cattle stop** *n.* (*New Zeal.*) a cattle grid. **cattle truck** *n.* **1** a railway van for conveying cattle. **2** very crowded, uncomfortable living or travelling conditions. [ONF *catel* (OF *chatel*), late L *captāle*, L *capitāle*, neut. of *capitālis*, CAPITAL[1] (cp. CHATTEL)]

cattleya (kat´liə) *n.* any epiphytic orchid of the genus *Cattleya*, with brightly coloured flowers. [William *Cattley*, d. 1832, English horticulturalist]

catty[1] CAT[1].

catty[2] (kat´i) *n.* (*pl.* **catties**) a unit of weight used in SE Asia, equal to about 1½ lb. (0.68 kg). [Malay (cp. CADDY[1])]

catty-cornered CATER-CORNERED (under CATER[2]).

Caucasian (kawkā´zhən) *a.* **1** (*also* **Caucasoid**) of or belonging to one of the main ethnological divisions of humankind, native to Europe, W Asia, and N Africa, with pale skin. **2** of or relating to the Caucasus Mountains or the district adjoining. ~*n.* a Caucasian person.

caucus (kaw´kəs) *n.* (*pl.* **caucuses**) **1** (*N Am.*) a preparatory meeting of representatives of a political party to decide upon a course of action, party policy etc. **2** (*N Am.*) a party committee controlling electoral organization. **3** (*N Am.*) the system of organizing a political party as a machine. **4** a small group within a larger organization, esp. a political party. **5** a meeting of such a group, esp. in secret. ~*v.i.* (*pres.p.* **caucusing,** *past, p.p.* **caucused**) to hold a caucus. [etym. uncertain; perh. Algonquian *kaw-kaw-asu*, a counsellor]

caudal (kaw´dəl) *a.* of or relating to the tail or the posterior part of the body. **caudad** (-dad) *a.* towards the tail or the posterior part of the body. **caudally** *adv.* **caudate** (-dāt), **caudated** *a.* having a tail or tail-like process. [L *caudālis* (*cauda*, tail)]

caudex (kaw´deks) *n.* (*pl.* **caudexes, caudices** (-disēz)) the thickened stem and root of a plant, esp. of a palm or tree fern. [L, trunk or stem]

caudillo (kowdē´lyō, kaw-) *n.* (*pl.* **caudillos**) in Spanish-speaking countries, a military leader or head of state. [Sp., from late L *capitellum*, little head, from L *caput*, head]

caudle (kaw´dəl) *n.* a warm drink of wine and eggs formerly given to invalids. [ONF *caudel*, med. L *caldellium*, dim. of *caldum* (L *calidum*, neut. of *calidus*, warm)]

caught CATCH.

caul (kawl) *n.* **1** a part of the amnion, sometimes enclosing the head of a child when born. **2** a membrane enveloping the intestines, the omentum. **3** (*Hist.*) a net or other covering for the hair. **4** (*Hist.*) the rear part of a woman's cap. [OF *cale*, a little cap; etym. uncertain]

cauld (kawld) *a., n.* (*Sc.*) cold. **cauldrife** (kawl´drif) *a.* **1** apt to feel the cold; chilly. **2** lifeless. [COLD]

cauldron (kawl´drən), **caldron** *n.* a large, deep, bowl-shaped vessel with handles, for boiling. [ONF *caudron* (F *chaudron*), L *caldārium*]

caulescent (kawles´ənt) *a.* having a stem or stalk visible above the ground. [L *caulis*, stalk, -ESCENT (under -ESCENCE)]

caulicle, cauliferous etc. CAULIS.

cauliflower (kol´iflowə) *n.* **1** a variety of cabbage with an edible white flowering head. **2** this head eaten as a vegetable. **cauliflower cheese** *n.* a dish of cauliflower with cheese sauce. **cauliflower ear** *n.* a permanently swollen or misshapen ear, usu. caused by boxing injuries. [earlier *cole-*, *colie-florie*, from ONF *col* (cp. OF *chol*, F *chou*, *chou-fleur*), from L *caulis*, stem]

caulis (kaw´lis) *n.* (*pl.* **caules** (-lēz)) **1** (*Bot.*) the main stem or stalk of a plant. **2** (*Archit.*) any of the four principal stalks from which spring the volutes in a Corinthian capital. **caulicle** *n.* a small or rudimentary stem or stalk. **cauliferous** (-lif´-) *a.* having a stem or stalk. **cauliflory** (-flawri) *n.* (*Bot.*) the production of flowers on the stem or trunk of a plant. **cauline** (-līn) *a.* of, relating to or growing from the stem. [L, a stalk]

caulk (kawk), **calk** *v.t.* **1** to fill or seal with waterproof material. **2** (*Naut.*) **a** to stuff (the seams of a ship) with oakum. **b** to make (a ship) watertight by caulking the seams. ~*n.* waterproof material used to fill or seal. **caulker** *n.* **caulking-iron** *n.* a blunt chisel used by caulkers. [OF *cauquer* (L *calcāre*, to tread, from *calx*, the heel)]

cause (kawz) *n.* **1** that which produces or contributes to an effect. **2** (*Philos.*) the condition or aggregate of circumstances and conditions that is invariably accompanied or immediately followed by a certain effect. **3** the person or other agent bringing about something. **4** the reason, motive or ground that justifies some act or state. **5** a side or party. **6** a movement, set of principles or ideals etc. (*the feminist cause*). **7** a matter in dispute. **8** (*Law*) **a** the grounds for an action. **b** a suit, an action. ~*v.t.* **1** to produce; to be the cause of. **2** to act as an agent in producing. **3** to effect. **4** to make or induce to (*What caused you to change your mind?*). **in the cause of** in order to defend or support. **to make common cause** to unite for a specific purpose. **causable** *a.* **causal** *a.* **1** of, being or expressing a cause. **2** of or relating to cause and effect. **causality** (-zal´-) *n.* **1** the operation of a cause. **2** the relation of cause and effect. **3** (*Philos.*) the theory of causation. **causally** *adv.* **causation** (-zā´shən) *n.* **1** the act of causing. **2** the connection between cause and effect. **3** (*Philos.*) the theory that there is a cause for everything. **causative** (kaw´zə-) *a.* **1** that causes. **2** effective as a cause. **3** (*Gram.*) expressing cause. **causatively** *adv.* **cause and effect** *n.* **1** the relationship between a cause and its effect. **2** the doctrine of causation. **cause célèbre** (kōz sāleb´rə) *n.* (*pl.* **causes célèbres** (kōz sāleb´rə)) a famous or notorious lawsuit or controversy. **causeless** *a.* **causelessly** *adv.* **cause list** *n.* a list of cases due to come up for trial. **causer** *n.* [F, from L *causa*]

'cause (koz, kəz) *conj.* (*coll.*) because.

causerie (kōzərē´) *n.* **1** an essay or article in a conversational style. **2** an informal talk. [F *causer*, to chat]

causeway (kawz´wā), (*dial.*) **causey** (kaw´zi) *n.* **1** a raised road across marshy ground or shallow water. **2** a raised footway beside a road. **3** a paved road or path. ~*v.t.* to make a causeway for or across. [ONF *caucié* (OF *chaucié*, F *chaussée*), late L *calciāta via* (L *calcāre*, to tread, from *calx -cis*, heel), WAY]

caustic (kaws´tik, kos´-) *a.* **1** burning, hot, corrosive. **2** bitter, sarcastic. **3** (*Physics*) of or relating to rays of light reflected or refracted by a curved surface. ~*n.* **1** a substance that burns or corrodes organic matter. **2** (*Physics*) a caustic surface. **caustically** *adv.* **caustic curve** *n.* (*Math.*) a curve to which the rays of light reflected or refracted by another curve are tangents. **causticity** (-tis´-) *n.* **caustic potash** *n.* potassium hydroxide, an alkaline solid used in the manufacture of soap, detergents etc. **caustic soda** *n.* sodium hydroxide, an alkaline solid used in the manufacture of rayon, paper, soap etc. [L *causticus*, Gr. *kaustikos* (*kaiein*, to burn, fut. *kaus-*)]

cauterize (kaw´tərīz), **cauterise** *v.t.* **1** to burn or sear (a wound etc.) with a hot iron or a caustic substance. **2** (*fig.*) to sear. **cauterant** *a.* that cauterizes. ~*n.* a cauterizing substance or instrument. **cauterization** (-zā´shən) *n.* **cautery, cauter** *n.* (*pl.* **cauteries, cauters**) **1** the act or operation of cauterizing. **2** an instrument for cauterizing. **3** a caustic substance. [F *cautériser*, late L *cautērizāre*]

caution (kaw´shən) *n.* **1** wariness, prudence; care to avoid injury or misfortune. **2** a warning. **3** a reprimand

and injunction. 4 a formal warning to a person under arrest that what is said may be taken down and used in evidence. 5 (*Sc. Law*) bail, security, pledge. 6 (*coll.*) something extraordinary, a strange or amusing person. ~*v.t.* 1 to warn. 2 to administer a caution to. **cautionary** *a.* 1 containing, or serving as, a warning. 2 given as security. **cautioner** *n.* 1 a person who cautions. 2 (*Sc. Law*) a person who is bound as security for another. **caution money** *n.* money lodged by way of security or guarantee. **cautious** *a.* heedful, careful, wary. **cautiously** *adv.* **cautiousness** *n.* [F, from L *cautio -ōnem* (*cautus*, p.p. of *cavēre*, to take heed)]

cavalcade (kavəlkād´) *n.* 1 a company or procession of riders on horseback. 2 a procession of motor vehicles. 3 any procession. [F, from It. *cavalcata*, fem. of *cavalcato*, p.p. of *cavalcare* (late L *caballicāre*, from L *caballus*, a horse)]

cavalier (kavəliə´) *n.* 1 (**Cavalier**) a supporter of Charles I during the Civil War; a Royalist. 2 a lady's escort; a gallant or lover. 3 †a horseman, a knight. ~*a.* offhand, haughty, supercilious. **cavalier King Charles spaniel** *n.* a breed of spaniel that is slightly larger than a King Charles spaniel. [F, from It. *cavaliere* (L *caballārius*, from *caballus* horse)]

cavalla (kəval´ə), **cavally** (-i) *n.* (*pl.* **cavalla, cavallas, cavallies**) any of various tropical fish, such as the *Gnathanodon speciosus*. [Sp. and Port. *cavalla*, mackerel (It. *cavallo*, L *caballus*, horse)]

cavalry (kav´əlri) *n.* (*pl.* **cavalries**) 1 (*esp. Hist.*) a body of soldiers on horseback, part of an army. 2 a body of soldiers in armoured vehicles, part of the armed forces. **cavalryman** *n.* (*pl.* **cavalrymen**) a member of the cavalry. **cavalry twill** *n.* a strong woollen twill fabric, used esp. for trousers. [F *cavallerie*, It. *cavalleria* (*cavaliere*, CAVALIER)]

cavatina (kavətē´nə) *n.* (*pl.* **cavatinas**) 1 a short, simple song. 2 a similar instrumental composition. [It.]

cave[1] (kāv) *n.* 1 a hollow place in a rock or underground. 2 a den. 3 (*Hist.*) **a** the secession of a discontented faction from a political party. **b** such a dissident group; a body of Adullamites. ~*v.t.* 1 to hollow out. 2 to cause to cave in. ~*v.i.* 1 to give way, to cave in. 2 to explore caves as a sport or pastime. **to cave in** 1 to fall in, to collapse. 2 to give in, to yield. **cave bear** *n.* an extinct species of bear, *Ursus spelaeus*. **cave dweller** *n.* a prehistoric caveman or cavewoman. **cave-in** *n.* the act or instance of caving in. **cavelike** *a.* **caveman** *n.* (*pl.* **cavemen**) 1 a prehistoric man who dwelt in caves. 2 (*facet.*) a man of primitive instincts. **cave painting** *n.* a prehistoric picture on the wall of a cave. **caver** *n.* **cavewoman** *n.* (*pl.* **cavewomen**) a prehistoric woman who dwelt in caves. **caving** *n.* the sport or pastime of exploring caves. [F, from L *cava*, neut. pl. of *cavus*, hollow (cp. Gr. *kuar*, a cavity)]

cave[2] (kā´vi) *int.* look out! **to keep cave** to keep watch, to act as lookout. [L, beware]

caveat (kav´iat) *n.* 1 a warning, a caution. 2 (*Law*) a process to stop or suspend proceedings. **caveat emptor** (emp´taw) let the buyer beware; the purchaser is responsible for the quality of the purchase. **caveator** (-ātə) *n.* a person who enters a caveat. [L, let him beware]

cavendish (kav´əndish) *n.* a kind of tobacco softened and pressed into cakes. [perh. from the maker's name]

cavern (kav´ən) *n.* 1 a large cave or underground chamber. 2 a place resembling this, such as a large dark room. ~*v.t.* 1 to shut or enclose in a cavern. 2 to hollow out. **caverned** *a.* **cavernous** *a.* 1 hollow or huge, like a cavern. 2 full of caverns. **cavernously** *adv.* [F *caverne*, L *caverna* (*cavus*, see CAVE[1])]

caviar (kav´iah, -ah´), **caviare** *n.* the salted roes of various fish, esp. the sturgeon, eaten as a delicacy. **caviare to the general** something too refined to be generally appreciated. [cp. It. *caviale*, Turk. *havyār*]

cavicorn (kav´ikawn) *a.* having hollow horns. ~*n.* a hollow-horned ruminant. [L *cavus*, hollow, *cornu*, horn]

cavil (kav´il) *n.* (*formal*) a petty or frivolous objection. ~*v.i.* (*pres.p.* **cavilling,** (*N Am.*) **caviling,** *past, p.p.* **cavilled,** (*N Am.*) **caviled**) to argue captiously; to make trivial objections (*to cavil at the price*). **caviller** *n.* **cavilling** *a.* **cavillingly** *adv.* [OF *caviller*, L *cavillāri* (*cavilla*, jeer, mockery)]

caving CAVE[1].

cavitation (kavitā´shən) *n.* 1 the formation of a cavity or cavities. 2 the formation of a cavity or partial vacuum between a solid and a liquid in rapid relative motion, e.g. on a propeller. [as CAVITY]

cavity (kav´iti) *n.* (*pl.* **cavities**) 1 a hollow space or part. 2 a decayed hole in a tooth. **cavity wall** *n.* a wall consisting of two layers of bricks with a space between. [F *cavité* (L *cavus*, CAVE[1])]

cavo-rilievo (kahvōrəlyā´vō) *n.* (*pl.* **cavo-rilievos, cavo-rilievi** (-vē)) a sculpture made by hollowing out a flat surface and leaving the figures standing out to the original level. [It., hollow relief]

cavort (kəvawt´) *v.i.* to prance about; to caper or frolic. [perh. corr. of CURVET]

cavy (kā´vi) *n.* (*pl.* **cavies**) a S American rodent of the family Cavidae, esp. any of the genus *Cavia*, including *C. cobaya*, the guinea pig. [Galibi *cabiai*]

caw (kaw) *v.i.* to cry like a rook, crow or raven. ~*n.* this cry. [imit.]

Caxton (kaks´tən) *n.* 1 a book printed by William Caxton. 2 printing type of the same pattern as Caxton's. [William *Caxton*, *c.* 1422–91, English printer]

cay (kā, kē) *n.* a reef or bank of sand, coral etc. [Sp. *cayo*, med. L *caium*, prob. from Celt (cp. Welsh *cae*, a hedge, a field, Bret. *kaé*, an enclosure, an embankment)]

cayenne (kāen´), **cayenne pepper** *n.* the powdered fruit of various species of capsicum, a very hot, red condiment. [Tupi *kýonha*, assim. to *Cayenne*, in French Guiana]

cayman (kā´mən), **caiman** *n.* (*pl.* **caymans, caimans**) a tropical American reptile similar to an alligator, esp. any of the genus *Caiman*. [Sp. *caimán*, Carib *acáyuman*]

cayuse (kīūs´) *n.* (*N Am.*) a small American Indian horse. [N Am. Ind.]

cazique CACIQUE.

CB *abbr.* 1 citizen's band. 2 Companion of the Order of the Bath. 3 confined to barracks. 4 County Borough.

Cb *chem. symbol* columbium.

CBC *abbr.* Canadian Broadcasting Corporation.

CBD *abbr.* cash before delivery.

CBE *abbr.* Commander of the Order of the British Empire.

CBI *abbr.* Confederation of British Industry.

CBS *abbr.* Columbia Broadcasting System.

CC *abbr.* 1 Chamber of Commerce. 2 City Council. 3 closed circuit. 4 Companion of the Order of Canada. 5 County Council. 6 County Councillor. 7 Cricket Club.

cc, c.c. *abbr.* 1 carbon copy. 2 cubic centimetre.

CCD *abbr.* charge-coupled device.

CCF *abbr.* Combined Cadet Force.

CCTV *abbr.* closed-circuit television.

CD *abbr.* 1 Civil Defence. 2 compact disc. 3 Corps Diplomatique. **CD video** *n.* a system that produces high-quality stereo sound and video pictures from a compact disc.

Cd *chem. symbol* cadmium.

Cd. *abbr.* Command Paper.

cd *abbr.* 1 candela. 2 cash discount.

c.d. *abbr.* carried down.

CDC *abbr.* (*N Am.*) Centers for Disease Control.

CD-I *abbr.* compact disc interactive (a compact disc that

allows the user to interact with the images on the screen).
CDN *abbr.* Canada (IVR).
Cdn *abbr.* Canadian.
Cdr *abbr.* Commander.
Cdre *abbr.* Commodore.
CD-ROM (sēdērom´) *n.* a compact disc used with a computer system. [compact disc read-only memory]
CDT *abbr.* 1 (*N Am.*) Central Daylight Time. 2 craft, design and technology.
CDU *abbr.* Christlich-Demokratische Union (a German political party).
CE *abbr.* 1 chief engineer. 2 Church of England. 3 civil engineer. 4 Common (or Christian) Era. 5 Council of Europe.
Ce *chem. symbol* cerium.
ceanothus (seənō´thəs) *n.* (*pl.* **ceanothuses**) any N American shrub of the genus *Ceanothus*, with small ornamental flowers. [Gr. *keanothos*, a kind of thistle]
cease (sēs) *v.i.* 1 to come to an end, to stop. 2 to desist (from). ~*v.t.* 1 to put a stop to. 2 to discontinue. ~*n.* 1 a stopping, an end. 2 cessation. **without cease** without pausing or stopping. **ceasefire** *n.* 1 a command to stop firing. 2 an agreement to stop fighting, a period of truce. **cease fire!** stop firing! **ceaseless** *a.* incessant, unceasing. **ceaselessly** *adv.* **ceaselessness** *n.* [F *cesser*, L *cessāre*, freq. of *cēdere* (p.p. *cessus*), to go, to yield]
cecity (sē´siti) *n.* blindness (physical or mental). [L *caecitas*, from *caecus*, blind]
cecropia moth (sikrō´piə) *n.* a large N American moth, *Hyalophora* (or *Samia*) *cecropia*, with brightly coloured wings. [L *Cecropius*, of Cecrops, mythical king of Attica]
cecum CAECUM.
cedar (sē´də) *n.* 1 any evergreen coniferous tree of the genus *Cedrus*, with durable and fragrant wood, including the cedar of Lebanon. 2 (*also* **cedarwood**) the wood of any of these trees. **cedared** *a.* covered with cedars. **cedarn** (-dən) *a.* (*poet.*) 1 made of cedarwood. 2 consisting of cedars. **cedar of Lebanon** *n.* the tree *Cedrus libani*, of SW Asia. [OF *cedre*, L *cedrus*, Gr. *kedros*]
cede (sēd) *v.t.* 1 to give up, to surrender. 2 to yield, to grant. [L *cēdere*, to yield]
cedi (sē´di, sā´-) *n.* (*pl.* **cedi, cedis**) the standard unit of currency in Ghana. [Ghanaian]
cedilla (sədil´ə) *n.* 1 a mark (¸) placed under a *c* in French, Spanish etc., to show that it has the sound of *s*. 2 a similar mark used in other languages, such as Turkish, to denote other sounds. [Sp. *çedilla*, It. *zediglia*, dim. of Gr. *zēta*, Z]
cee (sē) *n.* 1 the third letter of the alphabet, C, c. 2 anything shaped like this letter.
Ceefax® (sē´faks) *n.* a teletext service operated by the BBC.
CEGB *abbr.* Central Electricity Generating Board.
ceil (sēl) *v.t.* 1 to line (a ceiling), esp. with plaster. 2 to provide (a room) with a ceiling. [CEILING]
ceilidh (kā´li) *n.* an informal gathering, esp. in Scotland or Ireland, for music, dancing etc. [Gael.]
ceiling (sē´ling) *n.* 1 the inner, upper surface of a room. 2 the plaster or other lining of this. 3 the upper limit of prices, wages etc. 4 the maximum height to which an aircraft can climb. 5 the base of the cloud layer or its height above the ground. **ceilinged** *a.* having a ceiling. [prob. from F *ciel*, heaven, L *caelum* (influenced by L *caelāre*, to emboss; cp. late L *caelātūra*, a vaulted roof)]
cel (sel), **cell** *n.* a celluloid for an animated film. [CELLULOID]
celadon (sel´ədon) *n.* 1 a pale grey-green colour. 2 a glaze of this colour on pottery. 3 pottery with such a glaze. ~*a.* of this colour. [F, perh. after the character of that name in D'Urfé's *Astrée*]
celandine (sel´əndīn) *n.* 1 a yellow-flowered plant related to the poppy, *Chelidonium majus*, the greater celandine. 2 a yellow-flowered plant related to the buttercup, *Ranunculus ficaria*, the lesser celandine also called *pilewort*. [OF *celindoine*, L *chelidonia*, Gr. *chelidonion*, swallow-wort, neut. of *chelidonios* (*chelidōn*, swallow)]
-cele (sēl), **-coele** *comb. form* a tumour or hernia. [Gr. *kēlē*, a tumour]
celeb (sileb´) *n.* (*coll.*) a celebrity. [abbr.]
celebrate (sel´ibrāt) *v.t.* 1 to observe, to mark (a festival, special occasion etc.) with festivities or ceremonies. 2 to perform (a religious service or ceremony), to say or sing (Mass), to administer (Communion). 3 to praise, to extol. 4 to make famous. 5 to commemorate. ~*v.i.* 1 to mark an occasion with festivities. 2 to officiate at the Eucharist. **celebrant** *n.* a priest who officiates, esp. at the Eucharist. **celebrated** *a.* famous, renowned. **celebration** (-rā´shən) *n.* **celebrator** *n.* **celebratory** *a.* **celebrity** (-leb´-) *n.* (*pl.* **celebrities**) 1 a famous person. 2 fame, renown. [L *celebrātus*, p.p. of *celebrāre* (*celeber -bris*, frequented, populous)]
celeriac (səler´iak) *n.* a variety of celery with a turnip-like root eaten as a vegetable.
celerity (səler´iti) *n.* (*formal or poet.*) speed, swiftness, promptness. [F *célérité*, L *celeritas -tātem* (*celer*, swift, cp. Gr. *kelēs*, a runner)]
celery (sel´əri) *n.* a plant, *Apium graveolens*, the blanched leaf-stalks of which are eaten cooked or raw. **celery pine** *n.* a tree of Australia and New Zealand, *Phyllocladus trichomanoides*, with shoots resembling celery. [F *céleri*, prov. It. *seleri*, *seleni*, from L, from Gr. *selinon*, parsley]
celesta (səles´tə) *n.* (*pl.* **celestas**) (*Mus.*) a keyboard instrument in which steel plates are struck by hammers. **celeste** (-est´) *n.* 1 a celesta. 2 a voix céleste. [F *céleste*, CELESTIAL]
celestial (səles´tiəl) *a.* 1 of or relating to heaven; spiritual, angelic, divine. 2 of or relating to the sky or outer space (*a celestial body*). **celestial equator** *n.* the great circle on the celestial sphere, the plane of which is perpendicular to the earth's axis. **celestial globe** *n.* a sphere representing celestial bodies and their relative positions. **celestial horizon** *n.* the great circle parallel to the sensible horizon, the centre of which is the centre of the earth. **celestially** *adv.* **celestial mechanics** *n.* the study of the motion of celestial bodies in gravitational fields. **celestial navigation** *n.* navigation by the stars etc. **celestial pole** *n.* either of the points where a projection of the earth's axis would intersect the celestial sphere. **celestial sphere** *n.* an imaginary sphere with the observer at its centre and all celestial objects on its surface. [OF, from L *caelestis*; -AL[1]]
celestine (sel´əstīn), **celestite** (-tīt) *n.* a blue, red or white mineral, strontium sulphate. [G *Zölestin*, L *caelestis*, CELESTIAL]
celiac COELIAC.
celibate (sel´ibət) *a.* 1 unmarried. 2 devoted or committed to a single life, esp. by religious vows. 3 abstaining from sexual activity. ~*n.* a celibate person. **celibacy** *n.* 1 single life; the unmarried state. 2 abstention from sexual activity. [orig. the unmarried state, from F *célibat*, L *caelibātus* celibacy (*caelebs -libem*, unmarried)]
cell[1] (sel) *n.* 1 a small room, esp. one in a prison or monastery. 2 (*Hist.*) a small religious house dependent on a larger one. 3 a subsidiary unit of a political organization, esp. a proscribed or revolutionary one. 4 (*Biol.*) the smallest unit of living matter in animals or plants. 5 a small cavity or compartment. 6 a cavity in the brain, formerly supposed to be the seat of a particular faculty. 7 a compartment in a honeycomb. 8 the cuplike cavity containing an individual zoophyte in

a compound organism. 9 a device for producing electrical energy, usually containing two electrodes in an electrolyte. 10 a small area covered by a cellular radio transmitting station. **cell block** *n.* a block of cells in a prison. **cell cycle** *n.* (*Biol.*) the growth cycle of a cell, culminating in cell division. **cell division** *n.* (*Biol.*) the division of a cell to form two new cells, e.g. in the process of reproduction. **celled** *a.* **cell-like** *a.* **cell membrane** *n.* (*Biol.*) a thin membrane surrounding a cell. **Cellnet®** *n.* a cellular radio system for mobile telecommunications. **cellphone** *n.* a portable telephone suitable for use with the cellular radio system. **cell wall** *n.* (*Biol.*) the surface layer of a cell. [OF *celle*, L *cella* (cp. *cēlāre*, to hide)]

cell² CEL.

cella (sel´ə) *n.* (*pl.* **cellae** (sel´ē)) the central chamber in a temple. [L, CELL¹]

cellar (sel´ə) *n.* 1 an underground room or vault beneath a house used for storage (*a coal cellar*). 2 a place for storing wine. 3 a stock of wine. ~*v.t.* 1 to put in a cellar. 2 to store in a cellar. **cellarage** *n.* 1 cellars collectively. 2 space for storage in a cellar. 3 a charge for cellar storage. **cellarer** *n.* 1 a monk in charge of the stores. 2 an officer of a chapter in charge of the provisions. **cellaret** (-ret´), (*NAm.*) **cellarette** *n.* 1 a small case with compartments for holding bottles. 2 a sideboard for storing wine. **cellarman** *n.* (*pl.* **cellarmen**) a person employed in a wine or beer cellar. [OF *celier* (F *cellier*), L *cellārium*]

cello (chel´ō) *n.* (*pl.* **cellos**) a four-stringed bass instrument of the violin family rested on the ground between the legs. **cellist** *n.* [abbr. of VIOLONCELLO]

cellobiose (selōbī´ōz), **cellose** (sel´ōz) *n.* a disaccharide obtained from cellulose. [CELLULOSE, BI-, -OSE²]

Cellophane® (sel´əfān) *n.* a transparent paper-like material made of viscose, chiefly used for wrapping.

cellose CELLOBIOSE.

cellular (sel´ūlə) *a.* 1 of, relating to or resembling a cell or cells. 2 (*Biol.*) composed of cells. 3 (of textiles) woven with a very open texture. **cellular blanket** *n.* a blanket with a very open texture. **cellularity** (-lar´iti) *n.* **cellular plant** *n.* a plant having no distinct stem or leaves. **cellular radio** *n.* a type of radio communication, used esp. for mobile telephones, which connects directly to the public telephone network and uses a series of transmitting stations, each covering a small area or cell. **cellular telephone** *n.* a cellphone. **cellulase** *n.* an enzyme involved in the conversion of cellulose to cellobiose. **cellulate** (-lət), **cellulated** (-lātid) *a.* formed of cells. **cellulation** (-lā´shən) *n.* **cellule** *n.* a little cell or cavity. **celluliferous** (-lif´-) *a.* **cellulite** (-līt) *n.* subcutaneous fat which gives the skin a dimpled appearance. **cellulitis** (-lī´tis) *n.* inflammation of subcutaneous tissue, caused by bacterial infection. **cellulous** *a.* [L *cellularis* (*cellula*, dim. of *cella*, CELL¹)]

celluloid (sel´ūloid) *n.* 1 a transparent flammable thermoplastic made from cellulose nitrate, camphor and alcohol, used e.g. in cinema film. 2 cinema film. 3 any of the sheets of celluloid on which the drawings etc. for an animated film are prepared.

cellulose (sel´ūlōs) *n.* 1 a carbohydrate of a starchy nature that forms the cell walls of all plants. 2 a solution of cellulose acetate or cellulose nitrate. ~*a.* containing or consisting of cells. **cellulose acetate** *n.* a chemical compound formed by the action of acetic acid on cellulose, used in the manufacture of photographic film, varnish, some textile fibres etc. **cellulose nitrate** *n.* cellulose treated with nitric acid, used in making plastics, explosives etc. **cellulosic** (-lōs´-) *a.* **cellulosity** (-los´-) *n.*

celom COELOM.

Celsius (sel´siəs) *a.* of or denoting a temperature scale in which the freezing point of water is designated 0° and the boiling point 100°. **Celsius scale** *n.* this temperature scale. [Anders *Celsius*, 1701–44, Swedish astronomer, who invented it]

Celt (kelt, selt), **Kelt** (k-) *n.* a member or descendant of an ancient people comprising the Welsh, Cornish, Manx, Irish, Gaels and Bretons, inhabiting parts of England, Scotland, Ireland, Wales and northern France. **Celtic** *a.* of or relating to the Celts or their language. ~*n.* the language of the Celts; a group of languages including Gaelic, Welsh, Cornish and Breton. **Celtically** *adv.* **Celtic cross** *n.* a Latin cross with a circle round the intersection of the arms. **Celtic fringe** *n.* 1 the inhabitants of the Scottish Highlands, Ireland, Wales and Cornwall, as opposed to the rest of the British people. 2 the Scottish Highlands, Ireland, Wales and Cornwall. **Celticism** (-sizm) *n.* a custom peculiar to the Celts. **Celticist** *n.* an expert in Celtic language or culture. [F *Celte*, L *Celtae*, pl., Gr. *Keltoi*, *Keltai*]

celt (selt) *n.* a prehistoric cutting or cleaving implement of stone or bronze. [late L *celtes*, a chisel, a hypothetical word from a reading *celte* (perh. *certe*) in the Vulgate book of Job]

cembalo (chem´balō) *n.* (*pl.* **cembalos, cembali** (-li)) a harpsichord. [abbr. of CLAVICEMBALO]

cement (siment´) *n.* 1 a powdery substance, esp. used in building to make mortar or concrete and hardening like stone. 2 any analogous material, paste, gum etc. for sticking things together. 3 a substance for filling teeth. 4 cementum. 5 anything that unites, binds or joins. ~*v.t.* 1 to unite with or as with cement. 2 to line or coat with cement. 3 to unite firmly or closely (*to cement a relationship*). ~*v.i.* to cohere. **cementation** (sēmentā´shən) *n.* 1 the act of cementing. 2 the conversion of iron into steel by heating the former in a mass of charcoal. **cementer** *n.* **cementite** *n.* a compound of iron and carbon found in carbon steel, cast iron etc. **cement mixer** *n.* a machine in which cement is mixed with water. **cementum** (-təm) *n.* the bony substance forming the outer layer of the root of a tooth. [OF *ciment*, L *caementum* (prob. short for *caedimentum*, from *caedere*, to cut)]

cemetery (sem´ətri) *n.* (*pl.* **cemeteries**) a public burial ground, esp. one that is not a churchyard. [L *caemētērium*, Gr. *koimētērion*, orig. a dormitory (*koimaein*, to put to sleep)]

cen. *abbr.* central.

cen- COENO-.

cenacle (sen´əkəl) *n.* 1 the room, or a representation of it, in which the Last Supper took place. 2 a former French literary coterie. [L *cenaculum*, a dining-room]

-cene (sēn) *comb. form* denoting a recent period of geological time, as *Miocene*, *Eocene*. [Gr. *kainos*, new]

CENELEC (sen´əlek) *n.* the electrical standards organization of the EU. [acronym for *C*ommission *E*uropéene de *N*ormalisation *Elec*trique]

cenesthesia, cenesthesis COENAESTHESIS.

C. Eng. *abbr.* chartered engineer.

ceno- COENO-.

cenobite COENOBITE.

cenogenesis CAENOGENESIS.

cenospecies (sē´nōspēshēz) *n.* (*pl.* **cenospecies**) a species whose members are related to those of another species by the ability to interbreed.

cenotaph (sen´ətahf) *n.* a sepulchral monument raised to a person buried elsewhere. **the Cenotaph** the monument in Whitehall, London, commemorating those in the British armed forces who died in the wars of 1914–18 and 1939–45. [F *cénotaphe*, L *cenotaphium*, Gr. *kenotaphion* (*kenos*, empty, *taphos*, tomb)]

Cenozoic (sēnəzō´ik), **Caenozoic, Cainozoic** (kīn-) *a.* of or relating to the third and most recent geological era. ~*n.* the Cenozoic era. [Gr. *kainos*, recent, -ZOIC]

cense (sens) *v.t.* to burn incense near or in front of. **censer** *n.* a vessel for burning incense, esp. at religious ceremonies; a thurible. [from obs. n. *cense*, incense, or short for v. INCENSE[1]]

censor (sen´sə) *n.* **1** a public officer appointed to examine books, films etc., before they are published or released, to see that they contain nothing obscene, seditious etc. **2** a person whose duty it is in wartime to see that nothing is published, or passes through the post, that might give information to the enemy. **3** (*Hist.*) a Roman officer who registered the property of the citizens, imposed the taxes, and watched over manners and morals. **4** any person given to reproof or censure of other people. **5** (*Psych.*) the superego, an unconscious mechanism in the mind that excludes disturbing factors from the conscious. ~*v.t.* **1** to act as a censor of. **2** to expurgate or delete objectionable matter from. **censorial** (-saw´-), †**censorian** (-saw´-) *a.* **censorious** (-saw´-) *a.* expressing or given to criticism or censure. **censoriously** *adv.* **censoriousness** *n.* **censorship** *n.* [L, from *censēre*, to assess]

Usage note The verbs *censor* and *censure* should not be confused: *censoring* involves suppression or removal, and *censuring* simply criticizing a work or rebuking an author severely.

censure (sen´shə) *n.* **1** blame, reproach. **2** disapproval, condemnation. **3** an expression of this. ~*v.t.* to blame; to criticize harshly; to find fault with. **censurable** *a.* **censurableness** *n.* **censurably** *adv.* [F, from L *censūra* (*censēre*, see CENSOR)]

census (sen´səs) *n.* (*pl.* **censuses**) **1** an official enumeration of the inhabitants of a country. **2** the statistical result of such enumeration. **3** any similar official enumeration (*a traffic census*). [L, from *censēre* (see CENSOR)]

cent (sent) *n.* **1** a hundredth part of the basic unit of many currencies, e.g. of the US dollar. **2** a coin of this value. **3** an insignificant coin. **4** (*coll.*) a very small sum of money (*I haven't got a cent*). **cental** *n.* a weight of 100 lb. (45.4 kg), formerly used for grain. [L *centum*, a hundred]

cent. *abbr.* **1** central. **2** century.

cent- CENTI-.

centare CENTIARE.

centaur (sen´taw) *n.* a Greek mythological figure, half man, half horse. [L *centauros*, Gr. *kentauros*; etym. uncertain]

centaurea (sentaw´riə, -rē´ə) *n.* any plant of the genus *Centaurea*, including the cornflower, knapweed etc. [as CENTAURY]

centaury (sen´tawri) *n.* (*pl.* **centauries**) any of various plants once used medicinally, esp. those of the genus *Centaurium*, such as *C. erythraea*. [L *centaurēa*, *centaurēum*, Gr. *kentaureion* (nom. *kentaureios* after the centaur Chiron)]

centavo (sentah´vō) *n.* (*pl.* **centavos**) **1** a hundredth part of the basic unit of currency of Portugal and some Latin American countries. **2** a coin of this value. [Sp.]

centenarian (sentəneə´riən) *n.* a person who has reached the age of 100 years. ~*a.* being at least 100 years old. **centenary** (səntē´nəri, -ten´əri) *n.* (*pl.* **centenaries**) the hundredth anniversary of any event, or the celebration of this. ~*a.* **1** of or relating to a centenary. **2** recurring once in 100 years. **centennial** (-ten´-) *a.* **1** lasting for or completing 100 years. **2** centenary. ~*n.* a centenary. [L *centēnārius*, from *centēni*, a hundred each (*centum*, CENT)]

center CENTRE.

centesimal (sentes´iməl) *a.* **1** hundredth. **2** by hundredth parts. ~*n.* **1** a hundredth part. **2** (*coll.*) a tiny part. **centesimally** *adv.* [L *centēsimus*, -AL[1]]

centesimo (sentes´imō, chentez´-) *n.* (*pl.* **centesimos**) **1** a hundredth part of the basic unit of currency of Italy, Panama, Uruguay etc. **2** a coin of this value. [It., Sp. as CENTI-]

centi- (sen´ti-), **cent-** *comb. form* **1** a hundred. **2** a hundredth part, esp. of a metric unit, as *centigram*, *centilitre*, *centimetre*. [L *centum*, a hundred]

centiare (sen´tieə, -tiah), **centare** (-teə, -tah) *n.* a metric unit of area equal to one square metre (10.76 sq. ft.), a hundredth part of an are.

centigrade (sen´tigrād) *a.* **1** Celsius. **2** divided into 100 degrees. [L *gradus*, a step]

centigram (sen´tigram), **centigramme** *n.* a metric unit of weight, a hundredth part of a gram.

centilitre (sen´tilētə), (*N Am.*) **centiliter** *n.* a metric unit of capacity, a hundredth part of a litre.

centillion (sentil´iən) *n.* **1** in Britain and Germany, one million raised to the 100th power, 10^{600}. **2** in N America and France, one thousand raised to the 101st power, 10^{303}. [CENTI-, MILLION]

centime (sã´tēm) *n.* **1** a hundredth part of the basic unit of many currencies, e.g. the French franc. **2** a coin of this value. [F]

centimetre (sen´timētə), (*N Am.*) **centimeter** *n.* a metric unit of length, a hundredth part of a metre. **centimetre-gram-second** *a.* of or denoting a metric system of measurement based on the centimetre, gram and second, now superseded by the SI system in science and technology.

centimo (sen´timō, then´-) *n.* (*pl.* **centimos**) **1** a hundredth part of the basic unit of currency in Spain, Paraguay, Venezuela etc. **2** a coin of this value. [Sp.]

centipede (sen´tipēd) *n.* an arthropod of the class Chilopoda with many segments, each bearing a pair of legs. [L *centipeda* (*pes pedis*, foot)]

centner (sent´nə) *n.* **1** a unit of weight equal to 100 lb. (45.4 kg). **2** in Germany and some other European countries, a unit of weight equal to 110¼ lb. (50 kg). **3** a unit of weight equal to 220½ lb. (100 kg). [G, from L *centēnārius*, CENTENARY (under CENTENARIAN)]

CENTO (sen´tō) *abbr.* Central Treaty Organization.

cento (sen´tō) *n.* (*pl.* **centos**) **1** a composition of verses from different authors. **2** a string of quotations etc. [L, a patchwork]

centr- CENTRO-.

central (sen´trəl) *a.* **1** relating to, containing, proceeding from, or situated in the centre. **2** principal, of chief importance. **Central American** *a.* of or relating to Central America, the isthmus that joins N America and S America. **central angle** *n.* (*Math.*) an angle formed by two radii at the centre of a circle. **central bank** *n.* a national bank that regulates the money supply, carries out government policy etc. **Central European Time** *n.* the standard time of W European countries, one hour ahead of Greenwich Mean Time. **central forces** *n.pl.* the centrifugal and centripetal forces. **central heating** *n.* a system of warming a whole building from a single source of heat by means of pipes, ducts etc. **centralism** *n.* a system or policy of centralization. **centralist** *n.* **centrality** (-tral´-) *n.* **centralize, centralise** *v.t.* **1** to bring to a centre; to concentrate. **2** to bring under central control. ~*v.i.* to come to a centre. **centralization** (-zā´shən) *n.* **1** the act of centralizing. **2** the system or policy of running the government or any administrative organization from a single centre. **central locking** *n.* a system whereby all the doors of a motor vehicle can be locked simultaneously. **centrally** *adv.* **central nervous system** *n.* the nerve tissue that controls the activities of the body, esp. that part of the nervous system of vertebrates consisting of the brain and spinal cord. **centralness** *n.* **central processing unit, central processor** *n.* the part of a computer which performs arithmetical and logical operations on data. **central reservation** *n.* the strip of ground that separates the carriageways of a motorway or other major road. **Central Standard Time, Central Time** *n.* the standard time of parts of N America, six hours behind Greenwich Mean Time. [L *centrālis* (*centrum*, CENTRE)]

centre (sen´tə), (*NAm.*) **center** *n.* **1** the middle point or part. **2** the middle or central object. **3** the point round which something revolves, the pivot or axis. **4** the principal point; the most important point. **5** the nucleus, the source from which anything radiates or emanates. **6** the main area for a specified activity (*the shopping centre*). **7** a political party or group occupying a place between two extremes. **8** a player in the middle position in some sports. **9** the head or leader of an organization. *~v.t.* **1** to place in the centre. **2** to collect to a point. **3** to find the centre of. *~v.i.* **1** to be fixed on a centre. **2** to be collected at one point. **3** to have as a centre, central theme etc. (*The report centred on the incompetence of the management*). *~a.* at or of the centre. **the Centre** (*Austral.*) Central Australia. **centre back** *n.* in sport, a player or position in the middle of the back line. **centre bit** *n.* a carpenter's tool consisting of a bit fixed in a brace, for boring large round holes. **centreboard** *n.* a sliding keel which can be raised or lowered. **centred** *a.* **centrefold** *n.* **1** the two facing pages at the centre of a newspaper or magazine. **2** an illustration or article occupying these pages, esp. a photograph of a nude or scantily clad person. **centre forward** *n.* in sport, a player or position in the middle of the front line. **centre half** *n.* in sport, a player or position in the middle of the defence. **centre line** *n.* a real or imaginary line that divides something into two equal halves. **centremost** *a.* **centre of attention, centre of attraction** *n.* **1** a person who draws general attention. **2** (*Physics*) the point towards which bodies gravitate. **centre of buoyancy** *n.* the centre of gravity of the liquid displaced by a floating body. **centre of flotation** *n.* the geometrical centre of gravity of the area inside the waterline of a floating body. **centre of gravity** *n.* the point about which all the parts of a body exactly balance each other. **centre of inertia, centre of mass** *n.* a point through which a body's inertial force acts coincident with the centre of gravity. **centre of pressure** *n.* the point in an immersed body where the resultant pressure acts. **centrepiece** *n.* an ornament for the middle of a table, ceiling etc. **centre punch** *n.* a tool used to mark the centre of a hole to be drilled. **centre spread** *n.* a centrefold. **centre stage** *n.* **1** the centre of the stage in a theatre, show etc. **2** the centre of attention. *~adv.* in or to this position. **centric, centrical** *a.* central. **centrically** *adv.* **centricity** (-tris´-) *n.* **centring, centreing** *n.* the woodwork or framing that supports an arch or vault during construction. **centrism** *n.* the holding of moderate political opinions. **centrist** *n.* [F *centre*, L *centrum*, Gr. *kentron*, a spike (*kentein*, to prick)]

Usage note The use of *centre about, centre around* (rather than *centre in, centre on*) is sometimes disapproved of, on the grounds that a centre is a definite point but 'about' and 'around' are vague and indefinite.

centri- CENTRO-.

centric CENTRE.

-centric (sen´trik) *comb. form* having a specified centre, as *heliocentric*. [Gr. *kentrikos*]

centrical, centricity CENTRE.

centrifugal (sentrif´ūgəl, sen´-, -fū´-) *a.* **1** tending to move away from the centre. **2** (*Bot.*) (of an inflorescence) expanding first at the summit, and last at the base. **centrifugal force** *n.* an apparent force that acts outwards on a revolving body. **centrifugally** *adv.* **centrifugal machine** *n.* a machine utilizing this force for drying or separating purposes. **centrifuge** (sen´trifūj) *n.* a centrifugal machine for separating liquids of different density, such as cream and milk. *~v.t.* to subject to centrifugal force or the action of a centrifuge. **centrifugation** (-fūgā´shən) *n.* [L *fugere*, to flee]

centriole (sen´triōl) *n.* (*Biol.*) a small rodlike part of an animal cell, which forms one of the poles of the spindle during cell division. [med. L *centriolum*, dim. of L *centrum*, CENTRE]

centripetal (sentrip´ətəl, sen´tripētəl, -pē´-) *a.* **1** tending to move towards the centre. **2** (*Bot.*) (of an inflorescence) expanding first at the base, and then at the end or centre. **centripetal force** *n.* the force that draws a revolving body towards the centre. **centripetally** *adv.* [L *petere*, to seek]

centrism, centrist CENTRE.

centro- (sen´trō), **centri-**, **centr-** *comb. form* central, centrally. [L *centrum*, centre]

centrobaric (sentrōbar´ik) *a.* of or relating to the centre of gravity. [Gr. *baros*, weight]

centroclinal (sentrōklī´nəl) *a.* (*Geol.*) (of a rock formation) with strata sloping downwards and inwards to a central point. [Gr. *klinein*, to slope]

centroid (sen´troid) *n.* the centre of mass, esp. of a geometrical figure.

centromere (sen´trəmiə) *n.* (*Biol.*) the part of a chromosome by which it is attached to the spindle during cell division.

centrosome (sen´trəsōm) *n.* a small body of protoplasm near a cell nucleus, containing the centriole. [Gr. *sōma*, body]

centrosphere (sen´trəsfiə) *n.* the part of the earth below the crust.

centrum (sen´trum) *n.* (*pl.* **centrums, centra** (-trə)) the main part of a vertebra. [L]

centum (sen´təm) *a.* denoting the group of Indo-European languages in which the original velar stops were not palatalized, as distinct from *satem*. [L, a hundred (from the sound of the letter *c* in *centum*)]

centuple (sen´tūpəl) *n.* a hundredfold. *~a.* multiplied a hundredfold. *~v.t.* to multiply a hundredfold. **centuplicate**[1] (-tū´plikāt) *v.t.* to multiply a hundredfold. **centuplicate**[2] (-ət) *n.* a centuple. *~a.* centuple. **centuplication** (-kā´shən) *n.* [F, from late L *centuplum*, nom. *-us*, L *centuplex* (*centum*, a hundred)]

centurial CENTURY.

centurion (sentū´riən, sen´-) *n.* a Roman military officer commanding a company of a hundred men. [L *centurio*]

century (sen´chəri) *n.* (*pl.* **centuries**) **1** a period of a hundred years. **2** a score of a hundred, esp. a hundred runs in cricket. **3** a group of a hundred things. **4** a division of the Roman people for the election of magistrates etc. **5** a division of a Roman legion, consisting originally of a hundred men. **centurial** (-tū´-) *a.* **century plant** *n.* the American aloe, *Agave americanus*, formerly thought to flower only once in 100 years. [F *centurie*, L *centuria* (*centum*, a hundred)]

Usage note The first century AD was 1–100, so centuries in the traditionally Christian world properly start in a year 01. Popularly, however, a century has come to be identified with all the years beginning with the same number, so that the 19th century is 1800–99 and not 1801–1900.

ceorl (chœl) *n.* in feudal times, an English freeman, below the thane and above the serf. [CHURL]

cep (sep) *n.* a type of edible mushroom, *Boletus edulis*, with a brown shiny cap. [F *cèpe*, from L *cippus*, a stake, post]

cepaceous (sipā´shəs) *a.* (*Bot.*) smelling or tasting of onion. [L *caepa*, onion]

cephal- CEPHALO-.

cephalalgia (sefəlal´jiə, kef-), **cephalalgy** (sef´əlalji, kef-) *n.* (*formal*) headache. [Gr. *algia*, pain]

cephalic (sifal´ik, kef-), **kephalic** (kef-) *a.* of or relating to the head. **cephalic index** *n.* the ratio of the greatest transverse to the greatest longitudinal diameter of the skull. [Gr. *kephalē*, the head]

-cephalic (sifal´ik, kef-), **-cephalous** (sef´ələs, kef´-) *comb. form* -headed, as *brachycephalic*, *microcephalous*. [Gr. *kephalē*, the head]

cephalin (sef´əlin, kef´-), **kephalin** (kef´-) *n.* a compound of phosphorus occurring in the brain and in nerve tissue.

cephalitis (sefəlī´tis, kef-) *n.* inflammation of the brain.

cephalization (sefəlīzā´shən, kef-), **cephalisation** *n.* in animal evolution, the development of a head at the anterior end of the body.

cephalo- (sef´əlō, kef´-), **cephal-** *comb. form* of or relating to the head. [Gr. *kephalē*, the head]

cephalochordate (sefəlōkaw´dāt, kef-) *n.* any fishlike animal of the subphylum Cephalochordata, including the lancelet.

cephalometry (sefəlom´itri, kef-) *n.* **1** the measurement of the human head by radiography, esp. in orthodontics. **2** the measurement of the head of an unborn foetus, by ultrasound or radiography.

cephalopod (sef´əlopod, kef´-) *n.* a mollusc of the class Cephalopoda, having a distinct head with prehensile and locomotive organs attached.

cephalosporin (sefəlōspaw´rin, kef-) *n.* any of a group of antibiotics derived from fungi of the genus *Cephalosporium*.

cephalothorax (sefəlōthaw´raks, kef-) *n.* (*pl.* **cephalothoraxes, cephalothoraces** (-rəsēz)) the anterior division of the body, consisting of the coalescence of head and thorax in spiders, crabs and other arthropods.

cephalotomy (sefəlot´əmi, kef-) *n.* (*pl.* **cephalotomies**) the dissection of the head.

cephalous (sef´ələs, kef´-) *a.* having a head.

-cephalous -CEPHALIC.

cepheid (sē´fiid, sef´-), **cepheid variable** *n.* (*Astron.*) a variable star with a regular cycle of variations in brightness, which allows its distance to be estimated. [Delta *Cephei*, a star of this class]

ceraceous (sirā´shəs) *a.* waxlike; waxy. [L *cēra*, wax]

ceramal (sərā´məl) *n.* a cermet. [*ceram*ic, *al*loy]

ceramic (səram´ik), **keramic** (kər-) *a.* **1** of or relating to pottery. **2** of or relating to any substance made by applying great heat to clay or another non-metallic mineral. ~*n.* **1** such a substance. **2** an article made from this. **ceramic hob** *n.* a flat cooking surface made of ceramic material, with electric heating elements underneath. **ceramic oxide** *n.* a compound of oxygen and an inorganic material that acts as a high-temperature superconductor. **ceramics** *n.pl.* **1** (*usu. sing. in constr.*) the art of pottery. **2** ceramic articles. **ceramist** (ser´-), **ceramicist** *n.* [Gr. *keramikos* (*keramos*, potter's earth, pottery)]

cerargyrite (sirah´jirīt) *n.* a soft mineral that is a source of silver, consisting of silver chloride in crystalline form; horn silver. [Gr. *keras*, a horn, *argyros*, silver]

cerasin (ser´əsin) *n.* the insoluble part of the gum of the cherry and plum trees. [L *cerasus*, cherry]

cerastes (siras´tēz) *n.* (*pl.* **cerastes**) any snake of the genus *Cerastes*, esp. the horned viper. [L, from Gr. *kerastēs* (*keras*, horn)]

cerastium (siras´tiəm) *n.* any plant of the genus *Cerastium*, with horn-shaped capsules. [as CERASTES]

cerat- CERATO-.

cerate (siə´rāt) *n.* a hard ointment or stiff medicated paste containing wax. [L *cērātum* (*cēra*, wax)]

cerated (siə´rātid) *a.* **1** waxed; covered with wax. **2** (of a bird) having a cere. [L *cērātus*, p.p. of *cērāre*, to cover with wax (*cēra*, wax)]

cerato- (ser´ətō), **kerato-** (ker´-), **cerat-**, **kerat-** *comb. form* **1** horned. **2** horny. **3** having processes like horns. **4** (*Anat.*) of or relating to the cornea. [Gr. *keras keratos*, a horn]

ceratodus (sirat´ədəs) *n.* (*pl.* **ceratoduses**) **1** any extinct lungfish of the genus *Ceratodus*, of the Mesozoic era. **2** a fossil of this fish. [Gr. *odous*, a tooth]

ceratoid (ser´ətoid) *a.* horny; hornlike.

Cerberus (sœ´bərəs) *n.* **1** a three-headed dog, fabled to guard the entrance of Hades. **2** a grim or watchful guardian. **sop to Cerberus** SOP. **Cerberean** (-biə´-) *a.* [L, from Gr. *Kerberos*]

cercal CERCUS.

cercaria (sœkeə´riə) *n.* (*pl.* **cercariae** (-riē)) a trematode worm or fluke in its second larval stage. **cercarial** *a.* **cercarian** *a.*, *n.* [mod. L, from Gr. *kerkos*, a tail]

cerci CERCUS.

cercopithecoid (sœkōpith´əkoid, -pithē´-) *n.* any primate of the superfamily Cercopithecoidea, an Old World monkey. ~*a.* of, relating to or belonging to this superfamily. **cercopithecid** (-sid) *n.* a cercopithecoid. [L *cercopithēcus*, Gr. *kerkopithēkos* (*kerkos*, a tail, *pithēkos*, an ape)]

cercus (sœ´kəs) *n.* (*pl.* **cerci** (-kī)) either of a pair of tail-like sensory appendages at the tip of the abdomen in some arthropods. **cercal** *a.* **1** of or relating to a tail. **2** of or relating to the cerci. [mod. L, from Gr. *kerkos*, a tail]

cere (siə) *n.* the patch of waxlike skin at the base of the upper beak in many birds. ~*v.t.* **1** to cover with wax. **2** to wrap in cerecloth. **cerecloth** *n.* a cloth dipped in melted wax, used to wrap dead bodies in. **cerement** *n.* **1** a cerecloth. **2** (*usu. pl.*) any burial clothes. **cereous** *a.* waxen, waxy, waxlike. **ceresin** (se´risin) *n.* a type of hard, whitish wax. [F *cire*, L *cēra* (cp. *cērāre*, to wax)]

cereal (siə´riəl) *a.* of or relating to wheat or other grain. ~*n.* **1** any edible grain. **2** a breakfast food made from a cereal. [L *cereālis* (*Ceres*, the goddess of corn)]

cerebellum (serəbel´əm) *n.* (*pl.* **cerebellums, cerebella** (-lə)) a portion of the brain situated beneath the posterior lobes of the cerebrum, responsible for balance and muscular coordination. **cerebellar, cerebellous** *a.* [L, dim. of *cerebrum*, the brain)]

cerebr- CEREBRO-.

cerebral CEREBRUM.

cerebro- (ser´əbrō), **cerebr-** *comb. form* of or relating to the brain. [L *cerebrum*, the brain]

cerebroside (ser´əbrōsīd) *n.* a lipid occurring in the myelin sheaths of nerves.

cerebrospinal (serəbrōspī´nəl) *a.* of or relating to the brain and to the spinal cord. **cerebrospinal fluid** *n.* the clear fluid that fills the spaces around the brain and spinal cord. **cerebrospinal meningitis** *n.* a form of meningitis characterized by high fever and spots on the skin.

cerebrovascular (serəbrōvas´kūlə) *a.* of or relating to the brain and its blood vessels. **cerebrovascular accident** *n.* a sudden interruption of the blood supply to the brain; a paralytic stroke.

cerebrum (ser´əbrəm) *n.* (*pl.* **cerebrums, cerebra** (-rə)) the main part of the brain, filling the upper cavity of the skull. **cerebral** *a.* **1** of or relating to the brain or the intellect. **2** intellectual rather than emotional. **3** (of sounds) made by touching the roof of the mouth with the tip of the tongue. **cerebral cortex** *n.* the mass of grey matter forming the outer layer of the cerebrum and responsible for intelligent behaviour. **cerebral dominance** *n.* the tendency for one side of the brain to have more control over certain functions, e.g. the dominance of the left cerebral hemisphere in right-handedness. **cerebral haemorrhage** *n.* bleeding into brain tissue from a cerebral artery. **cerebral hemisphere** *n.* either of the two halves of the cerebrum. **cerebralism** *n.* the theory that mental operations arise from activity of the brain. **cerebrally** *adv.* **cerebral palsy** *n.* a disability caused by brain damage before or during birth, characterized by lack of balance and muscular coordination, often with speech impairment. **cerebrate** *v.i.* to think. **cerebration** (-rā´shən) *n.* the action of the brain, whether conscious or unconscious. **cerebric** *a.* cerebral. **cerebritis** (-rī´tis) *n.* inflammation of the cerebrum. [L, the brain]

cerement CERE.

ceremonial (serəmō´niəl) *a.* of, relating to or performed with ceremonies or rites. ~*n.* **1** the prescribed order for a ceremony or function. **2** a polite usage or formality. **3** observance of etiquette. **4** in the Roman Catholic Church, the rules for rites and ceremonies. **5** the book containing these. **ceremonialism** *n.* fondness for or adherence to ceremony. **ceremonialist** *n.* **ceremonially** *adv.* [as CEREMONY]

ceremony (ser´əməni) *n.* (*pl.* **ceremonies**) **1** a prescribed rite or formality, esp. in accordance with religion or tradition. **2** an occasion when such rites or formalities are performed. **3** a usage of politeness. **4** formality (*with ceremony*). **to stand on ceremony** to be rigidly punctilious, to insist on observing formalities. **without ceremony** informally. **ceremonious** (-mō´-) *a.* **1** punctiliously observant of ceremony according to prescribed form. **2** of or involving ceremony; ceremonial. **ceremoniously** *adv.* **ceremoniousness** *n.* [OF *ceremonie*, L *caerimōnia* (cp. Sansk. *karman*, an action, a rite)]

Cerenkov radiation (chəreng´kof), **Cherenkov radiation** *n.* the electromagnetic radiation produced by particles moving faster than the speed of light in the same medium. [Pavel Alekseyevich *Cherenkov*, 1904–90, Russian physicist]

cereous, ceresin etc. CERE.

cereus (siə´riəs) *n.* (*pl.* **cereuses**) any cactus of the genus *Cereus*, esp. *C. jamacaru* of Brazil, which can grow to a height of 40 ft. (13 m). [L, a wax taper (*cēra*, wax)]

ceria, ceric CERIUM.

ceriph SERIF.

cerise (sərēs´, -rēz´) *n.* a red colour, cherry red. ~*a.* of this colour. [F, cherry, L *cerasus*, Gr. *kerasos*]

cerium (siə´riəm) *n.* a malleable grey metallic element of the rare earth group, at. no. 58, chem. symbol Ce. **ceria** *n.* ceric oxide. **ceric** *a.* of or containing tetravalent cerium. **ceric oxide** *n.* a substance used in ceramics, enamels etc. **cerite** (-rīt) *n.* a siliceous oxide of cerium. **cerium metals** *n.pl.* a group of metals including cerium, lanthanum, neodymium, praseodymium, promethium and samarium. **cerous** *a.* of or containing trivalent cerium. [after the planet *Ceres*]

cermet (sœ´mit) *n.* an alloy of a heat-resistant ceramic and a metal. [*cer*amic, *met*al]

CERN (sœn) *n.* the European Laboratory for Particle Physics, a European organization for nuclear research. [acronym for *C*onseil *E*uropéen pour la *R*echerche *N*ucléaire, its former title]

cero- (siə´rō) *comb. form* of, relating to or composed of wax. [L *cēra* or Gr. *kēros*, wax]

ceroc (serok´) *n.* a jive dance for two people, originating in France. [F *c'est le roc*, it is rock (and roll)]

cerography (siərog´rəfi) *n.* **1** the art or technique of writing, engraving etc. on or with wax. **2** printing from an engraved wax plate. **3** encaustic painting. **cerographic** (-graf´-), **cerographical** *a.* **cerographist** *n.*

ceroplastic (siərəplas´tik) *a.* **1** modelled in wax. **2** of or relating to modelling in wax. **ceroplastics** *n.* the art of modelling in wax.

cerotype (siə´rōtīp) *n.* **1** an engraving on a wax-coated copper plate, used to prepare an electrotype printing plate. **2** this process.

cerous CERIUM.

cert (sœt) *n.* (*sl.*) a certainty (*a dead cert*). [abbr.]

cert. *abbr.* **1** certificate. **2** certification. **3** certified.

certain (sœ´tən) *a.* **1** sure, convinced, assured, confident. **2** established beyond a doubt, undoubtedly true. **3** absolutely determined or fixed. **4** bound, destined, inevitable (*It is certain to go wrong*). **5** unfailing, reliable, unerring. **6** not particularized (*on a certain day*). **7** some (*a certain amount*). ~*pron.* (*as pl.*) an indefinite number or quantity (*Certain of the books were missing*). **for certain** definitely. **to make certain** to ensure, to secure. **certainly** *adv.* **1** assuredly. **2** without doubt. **3** without fail. **4** yes. **certainty** *n.* (*pl.* **certainties**) **1** that which is certain. **2** absolute assurance. **for a certainty** without doubt. †**certes** (-tiz) *adv.* certainly, assuredly. [OF *certein*, L *certus*, -AN]

Usage note See note on *certainty* under CERTITUDE.

Cert. Ed. *abbr.* Certificate in Education.

certes CERTAIN.

certifiable CERTIFY.

certificate[1] (sətif´ikət) *n.* a written testimony or document, esp. of status or ability (*a birth certificate; an examination certificate*). **Certificate of Secondary Education** *n.* **1** a former examination for secondary-school students, replaced by the GCSE. **2** the certificate or qualification thus obtained. [CERTIFY]

certificate[2] (sətif´ikāt) *v.t.* **1** to give a certificate to. **2** to license by certificate. **certificated** *a.* possessing a certificate from some examining body. **certification** (-kā´shən) *n.*

certify (sœ´tifī) *v.t.* (*3rd pers. sing. pres.* **certifies,** *pres.p.* **certifying,** *past, p.p.* **certified**) **1** to attest or testify to, esp. in writing. **2** to give a certificate to (*She is certified as a first aider*). **3** to declare legally or officially insane. **certifiable** *a.* **1** able to be certified. **2** (*coll.*) insane. **certifiably** *adv.* **certified** *a.* **certified cheque** *n.* a cheque guaranteed valid by a bank. **certified mail** *n.* (*N Am.*) recorded delivery. **certified milk** *n.* milk guaranteed free from the tuberculosis bacillus. **certifier** *n.* [F *certifier*, L *certificāre* (*certus*, certain, *facere*, to make)]

certiorari (sœtiərea´rī, -rah´rē) *n.* (*Law*) a writ issuing from a superior court calling for the records of or removing a case from a court below. [L, to be certified]

certitude (sœ´titūd) *n.* the state of being certain; certainty, conviction. [late L *certitudo* (L *certus*, certain)]

Usage note The meanings of the nouns *certitude* and *certainty* overlap, but in general *certitude* refers to subjective feeling or conviction, and *certainty* to objective fact.

cerulean (səroo´liən), **caerulean** *n.* **1** a deep blue colour. **2** sky blue. ~*a.* of this colour. [L *caeruleus* (prob. for *caelulus*, from *caelum*, the sky), -AN]

cerumen (səroo´men) *n.* the waxlike secretion of the ear. **ceruminous** *a.* [L *cēra*, wax]

ceruse (siə´roos, siroos´) *n.* **1** white lead. **2** an ointment or cosmetic made from this. **cerusite** (-sīt), **cerussite** *n.* a naturally-occurring carbonate of lead. [F *céruse*, or directly from L *cērussa* (cp. *cēra*, wax), prob. from Gr. *kēroussa* (cp. *kērous*, waxy, from *kēros*, wax)]

cervelat (sœ´vəlat, -lah) *n.* a kind of smoked sausage made from pork or beef. [F, from It. *cervellata*]

cervical (sœ´vikəl, -vī´-) *a.* **1** of or relating to the neck (*the cervical vertebrae*). **2** of or relating to the cervix of the uterus (*cervical cancer*). **cervical screening** *n.* the routine examination of women for the early signs of cervical cancer. **cervical smear** *n.* a specimen of cells taken from the cervix of the uterus to test for the presence of cancer. **cervico-** *comb. form* of, relating to or connected with the neck or cervix. [CERVIX]

cervices, cervicitis CERVIX.

cervico- CERVICAL.

cervid (sœ´vid) *n.* any mammal of the family Cervidae, including the deer. ~*a.* of, relating to or belonging to this family. [L *cervus*, a deer, -ID]

cervine (sœ´vīn) *a.* **1** of or relating to the deer family. **2** of or like a deer. [L *cervīnus* (*cervus*, a deer)]
cervix (sœ´viks) *n.* (*pl.* **cervixes, cervices** (-sēz)) a necklike part of the body, esp. the passage between the uterus and the vagina. **cervicitis** (-sī´tis) *n.* inflammation of the cervix of the uterus. [L *cervix -icis*, a neck]
Cesarean, Cesarian CAESAREAN (under CAESAR).
cesium CAESIUM.
cespitose CAESPITOSE.
cess[1] (ses) *n.* (*Sc., Ir.*) a tax. ~*v.t.* to tax, to assess. [prob. short for ASSESS]
cess[2] (ses), **sess** *n.* (*Ir., sl.*) luck. **bad cess to you** may ill luck befall you. [perh. short for SUCCESS]
cessation (səsā´shən) *n.* **1** the act of ceasing. **2** a pause. [L *cessātio* (*cessāre*, CEASE)]
cesser (ses´ə) *n.* (*Law*) cessation, coming to an end. [F, from L *cessāre*, CEASE]
cession (sesh´ən) *n.* **1** a yielding, a surrender; a ceding of territory, rights or property. **2** something that is ceded. **cessionary** *n.* (*pl.* **cessionaries**) a person who is the recipient of an assignment; an assign or assignee. [F, from L *cessio -ōnem* (*cess-*, part. stem of *cēdere*, CEDE)]
cesspit (ses´pit) *n.* **1** a cesspool. **2** a pit for refuse. [from CESSPOOL]
cesspool (ses´pool) *n.* **1** an underground container or a hole in the ground for sewage to drain into. **2** any corrupt or filthy place. [etym. uncertain]
cestode (ses´tōd) *a.* ribbon-like. ~*n.* any intestinal worm of the class Cestoda, including the tapeworms. **cestoid** (-toid) *n.* a cestode. [L *cestus*, Gr. *kestos*, a girdle]
cesura CAESURA.
CET *abbr.* Central European Time.
cetacean (sitā´shən) *a.* of, relating to or belonging to the Cetacea, an order of marine mammals including whales, dolphins etc. ~*n.* any mammal of this order. [L *cētus*, Gr. *kētos*, a whale]
cetane (sē´tān) *n.* an oily, colourless hydrocarbon found in petroleum. **cetane number** *n.* a measure of the ignition quality of diesel fuel. [sperma*ceti*, the source of a related compound, -ANE]
ceteris paribus (kātəris par´ibus) *adv.* other things being equal. [L]
cetology (sitol´əji) *n.* the study of whales. [L *cētus*, a whale]
cet. par. *abbr.* ceteris paribus.
Ceylon moss (silon´) *n.* a red seaweed, *Gracilaria lichenoides*, of the E Indian Ocean, from which agar is obtained. **Ceylon satinwood** *n.* **1** a tree, *Chloroxylon swietenia*, of India and Sri Lanka. **2** the wood of this tree. [*Ceylon*, former name of Sri Lanka]
CF *abbr.* Chaplain to the Forces.
Cf *chem. symbol* californium.
c.f. *abbr.* **1** carried forward. **2** cost and freight.
cf. *abbr.* compare. [L *confer*]
CFC *abbr.* chlorofluorocarbon.
CFD *abbr.* computational fluid dynamics.
CFE *abbr.* **1** College of Further Education. **2** Conventional Forces in Europe.
c.f.i. *abbr.* cost, freight and insurance.
CG *abbr.* **1** captain general. **2** Captain of the Guard. **3** coastguard. **4** Coldstream Guards. **5** consul general.
cg *abbr.* **1** centigram. **2** centre of gravity.
CGBR *abbr.* central government borrowing requirement.
CGM *abbr.* Conspicuous Gallantry Medal.
CGS *abbr.* Chief of General Staff.
cgs *abbr.* centimetre-gram-second.
CGT *abbr.* capital gains tax.
CH *abbr.* **1** Companion of Honour. **2** Confederatio Helvetica, i.e. Switzerland (IVR). **3** courthouse. **4** custom house.
ch. *abbr.* **1** chain. **2** champion (of dogs). **3** chapter. **4** check (in chess). **5** chestnut (of horses). **6** chief. **7** child. **8** choir organ. **9** church.
cha (chah), **char** *n.* (*coll.*) tea. [Chin.]
chabazite (kab´əzīt) *n.* a white or colourless mineral, a hydrated silicate of calcium, sodium, potassium and aluminium. [F *chabazie*, from Gr. *chabazios*, erron. for *chalazios* (*chalaza*, a hailstone)]
Chablis (shab´lē) *n.* a dry white wine made at Chablis, in central France.
cha-cha (chah´chah), **cha-cha-cha** (chahchahchah´) *n.* (*pl.* **cha-chas, cha-cha-chas**) **1** a ballroom dance of Latin American origin. **2** music for this dance. ~*v.i.* (*pres.p.* **cha-chaing**, *past, p.p.* **cha-chaed, cha-cha'd**) to dance the cha-cha. [Am. Sp.]
chacma (chak´mə) *n.* (*pl.* **chacmas**) a S African baboon, *Papio ursinus*. [Nama]
chaco SHAKO.
chaconne (shəkon´) *n.* **1** (*Mus.*) a set of variations over a continuously repeated ground bass. **2** (*Hist.*) a Spanish dance in triple time; music for this dance. [F, from Sp. *chacona*, prob. from Basque *chucun*, pretty]
chad (chad) *n.* the small pieces of paper removed when holes are punched in a computer card, paper tape etc. [etym. uncertain]
chador (chŭd´ə), **chadar, chuddar** *n.* a large veil, worn over the head and body by Muslim women. [Pers. *chaddar*]
chaet- CHAETO-.
chaeta (kē´tə) *n.* (*pl.* **chaetae** (-tē)) a bristle on the body of the earthworm and other annelids, used in locomotion. **chaetiferous** (-tif´-) *a.* (*Zool.*) having bristles. [as CHAETO-]
chaeto- (kē´tō), **chaet-** *comb. form* characterized by bristles or a mane. [Gr. *chaite*, hair, mane]
chaetodon (kē´tədon) *n.* any fish of the genus *Chaetodon*, with bristly teeth and brilliant colouring. [Gr. *odous odontos*, tooth]
chaetognath (kē´tənath, -tәgnath) *n.* any marine worm of the phylum Chaetognatha, such as the arrow worm, with a ring of bristles around the mouth. [Gr. *gnathos*, the jaw]
chaetopod (kē´təpod) *n.* an oligochaete or polychaete. [Gr. *pous podos*, foot]
chafe (chāf) *v.t.* **1** to rub so as to make sore or worn. **2** to make warm by rubbing. **3** to irritate. ~*v.i.* **1** to be made sore or worn by rubbing. **2** to fret. ~*n.* **1** a sore caused by rubbing. **2** irritation, a fit of rage. **chafer**[1] *n.* **1** a person who chafes. **2** a chafing dish. **chafery** (-fəri) *n.* (*pl.* **chaferies**) a forge in which iron is heated and welded into bars. **chafing** *a.* **chafing dish** *n.* **1** a vessel for keeping food warm or cooking at the table. **2** any vessel for heating. [OF *chaufer*, to warm (F *chauffer*), L *calefacere* (*calēre*, to glow, *facere*, to make)]
chafer[1] CHAFE.
chafer[2] (chāf´ə) *n.* a beetle of the family Scarabaeidae, such as the cockchafer. [OE *ceafor*, prob. from Gmc. *kaf-*, to gnaw (cp. Dut. *kever*, G *Käfer*)]
chaff[1] (chaf, chahf) *n.* **1** the husks of grain. **2** hay or straw cut fine for fodder. **3** the scales and bracts of grass and other flowers. **4** anything worthless. **5** thin strips of metal foil thrown from an aeroplane to confuse enemy radar. **chaff-cutter** *n.* a machine for cutting straw and hay for fodder. **chaffy** *a.* **1** like or full of chaff. **2** light, worthless. [OE *ceaf* (cp. Dut. *kaf*, OHG *cheva*)]
chaff[2] (chaf) *n.* **1** banter. **2** teasing. ~*v.t.* **1** to banter. **2** to tease. ~*v.i.* to indulge in banter or teasing. [CHAFF[1], or from CHAFE]
chaffer (chaf´ə) *v.i.* **1** to dispute about price; to haggle; to bargain. **2** to chatter. ~*n.* the act of haggling or bargaining. **chafferer** *n.* [ME *chaffare*, *chapfare* (OE *cēap*, bargain, *far*, a journey)]
chaffinch (chaf´inch) *n.* a common European bird,

Fringilla coelebs. [CHAFF[1] (from its frequenting barns), FINCH]

Chagas' disease (chah´gəs, shah´-) *n.* a tropical disease caused by the protozoan *Trypanosoma cruzi*, characterized by high fever and inflammation of the heart muscles. [Carlos *Chagas*, 1879–1934, Brazilian physician]

chagrin (shəgrin´) *n.* vexation, disappointment, mortification. ~*v.t.* (*pres.p.* **chagrining,** *past, p.p.* **chagrined**) to vex, to disappoint, to mortify. [F, from Turk. *saghrī*, SHAGREEN (from the sense of rubbing or chafing)]

chain (chān) *n.* **1** a series of links or rings fitted into or connected with each other, for binding, joining, holding, hauling etc. or for decoration, esp. as jewellery. **2** anything resembling this in form or function. **3** (*pl.*) bonds, fetters; bondage, restraint. **4** a connected series, a sequence, a range. **5** a group of shops, hotels etc. under the same ownership and run in a similar style. **6** a series of atoms linked together in a molecule. **7** a measure of 100 links, or 66 ft. (20.12 m), used in land surveying. **8** (*pl.*) strong plates of iron bolted to a ship's sides and used to secure the shrouds. **9** (*Hist.*) chain-shot. ~*v.t.* **1** to fasten or bind with a chain or chains (*The dogs were chained up*). **2** to fasten or restrict as if with a chain or chains (*She was chained to her desk*). **chain armour** *n.* chain mail. **chain belt** *n.* a chain used as a belt to transmit power. **chain bridge** *n.* a suspension bridge. **chain drive** *n.* an endless chain used as a system of transmission. **chain gang** *n.* a gang of convicts working in chains, esp. chained together. **chain gear** *n.* a gear that transmits motion by means of an endless chain, usu. passing over sprocket-wheels. **chain grate** *n.* a machine for stoking a furnace in which a rotating endless chain draws fuel into the furnace. **chainless** *a.* **chainlet** *n.* a small chain. **chain letter** *n.* a circular letter each recipient of which forwards a copy to a number of other people. **chain lightning** *n.* forked lightning. **chain link** *a.* (of fencing etc.) made of wire twisted into a diamond-shaped mesh. **chain mail** *n.* armour of interwoven links. **chain moulding** *n.* an ornamental band carved like a chain. **chain-plate** *n.* a flat iron bar bolted to a ship's side to secure the shrouds, also called channel plates. **chain printer** *n.* a type of computer printer in which the type is mounted on an endless chain. **chain pump** *n.* a machine for raising water, consisting of an endless chain fitted with buckets or discs which return upwards through a tube. **chain reaction** *n.* **1** a self-perpetuating chemical or nuclear reaction, producing energy etc., which initiates another, identical reaction. **2** any analogous series of events. **chain rule** *n.* (*Math.*) a theorem used in differentiation. **chainsaw** *n.* a power saw whose teeth are in a continuous revolving chain. **chain-shot** *n.* (*Hist.*) two cannon-balls connected by a chain to destroy spars and rigging. **chain-smoke** *v.i., v.t.* (*coll.*) to smoke continuously, lighting one cigarette from another. **chain-smoker** *n.* **chain stitch** *n.* **1** an ornamental stitch resembling a chain. **2** a looped stitch made by a sewing machine. **chain store** *n.* one of a series of retail stores under the same ownership and selling the same kind of goods. **chain-wale** *n.* CHANNEL[2]. **chain wheel** *n.* a toothed wheel which receives or transmits power by means of an endless chain. **chainwork** *n.* **1** needlework with open spaces like the links of a chain. **2** sewing with chain stitches. [OF *chaine*, L *catēna*]

chair (cheə) *n.* **1** a movable seat with a back and usu. four legs for one person. **2** a seat of authority or office. **3** a professorship. **4** a chairmanship or mayoralty. **5** the person presiding at a meeting; a chairperson. **6** this person's seat. **7** a sedan chair, a wheelchair, the electric chair etc. **8** an iron socket to support and secure the rails in a railway. ~*v.t.* **1** to act as chairperson of. **2** to carry publicly in a chair in triumph. **3** to install in a seat of authority or office. **to take a chair** to sit down. **to take the chair** to preside at a meeting. **chair-bed** *n.* a bed that folds up and becomes a chair. **chair-borne** *a.* (*coll.*) working at a desk, rather than having a more active job. **chairbound** *a.* confined to a wheelchair. **chair-car** *n.* a railway carriage with individual chairs rather than long seats. **chairlift** *n.* a series of seats suspended from an endless cable, used to carry people up and down a mountain etc. **chairman** *n.* (*pl.* **chairmen**) **1** a chairperson. **2** (*Hist.*) a person who carried a sedan chair, wheeled a bath chair etc. **chairmanship** *n.* **chairperson** *n.* the president of a meeting or the permanent president of a society, committee, board of directors etc. **chairwoman, chairlady** *n.* (*pl.* **chairwomen, chairladies**) a female chairperson. [OF *chaēre*, L *cathedra*, Gr. *kathedra* (see CATHEDRA)]

chaise (shāz) *n.* **1** a light horse-drawn carriage for travelling or pleasure. **2** a post-chaise. **3** a chaise longue. **chaise longue** (lõg) *n.* (*pl.* **chaise longues, chaises longues** (shāz lõg)) **1** a type of sofa for reclining on, with a back and armrest at one end only. **2** a chair with support for the legs. **chaise lounge** *n.* (*N Am.*) a chaise longue. [F, corr. of *chaire*, CHAIR]

chakra (chŭk´rə, chak´-) *n.* (*pl.* **chakras**) in yoga, a centre of spiritual power in the human body. [Sansk. *cakra*, a wheel]

chalaza (kəlā´zə) *n.* (*pl.* **chalazas, chalazae** (-zē)) **1** either of the two twisted albuminous threads holding the yolk in position in an egg. **2** an analogous part of a plant ovule. [Gr., hailstone]

chalazion (kəlā´ziən) *n.* (*Med.*) a small cyst on the eyelid, a meibomian cyst. [as CHALAZA]

chalc- CHALCO-.

chalcanthite (kalkan´thīt) *n.* a blue mineral, a crystalline form of hydrated copper sulphate. [L *chalcanthum*, copper sulphate solution, Gr. *chalkanthon* (CHALC-, *anthos*, flower)]

chalcedony (kalsed´əni), **calcedony** *n.* (*pl.* **chalcedonies, calcedonies**) a cryptocrystalline variety of quartz. **chalcedonic** (-don´-) *a.* **chalcedonyx** (-niks) *n.* a variety of agate. [L *chalcēdonius*, Gr. *chalkēdōn*, etym. uncertain]

chalcid (kal´sid), **chalcid fly** *n.* any tiny parasitic insect of the family Chalcididae, which lays its eggs inside another insect. [Gr. *chalkos*, copper]

chalco- (kal´kō), **chalc-** *comb. form* of or relating to copper or brass. [Gr. *chalkos*]

chalcocite (kal´kəsīt) *n.* a grey or black mineral, copper sulphide.

chalcography (kalkog´rəfi) *n.* the act or process of engraving on brass or copper. **chalcographer, chalcographist** *n.* **chalcographic** (-graf´-), **chalcographical** *a.*

chalcolithic (kalkəlith´ik) *a.* of or relating to a prehistoric period when both stone and copper or bronze implements were in use.

chalcopyrite (kalkōpī´rīt) *n.* a yellow mineral, a sulphide of copper and iron; copper pyrites, a copper ore.

Chaldean (kaldē´ən) *a.* of or belonging to ancient Chaldea or its language. ~*n.* **1** the language of Chaldea. **2** a native or inhabitant of Chaldea. **3** an astrologer. **Chaldaic** (-dā´-) *a., n.* **Chaldee** (-dē´) *n.* **1** the Chaldean language. **2** a Chaldean. **3** the Aramaic language used in the Bible. [L *Chaldeus*, Gr. *Chaldaios*, -AN]

chalet (shal´ā) *n.* **1** a small house or hut on a mountainside, esp. in Switzerland. **2** a small low house with projecting eaves. **3** a small dwelling, usu. of wood, used esp. for holiday accommodation. [Swiss F, prob. dim. of *casella*, dim. of It. or L *casa*, cottage]

chalice (chal´is) *n.* **1** (*poet.*) a cup, goblet or other drinking vessel. **2** the cup used in the Eucharist. **3** a cup-shaped flower. [OF, from L, CALIX]

chalicothere (kal´ikōthiə) *n.* any of a group of large

extinct mammals of the Tertiary period. [Gr. *chalix*, gravel, *thērion*, a small animal]

chalk (chawk) *n.* **1** soft white limestone or calcium carbonate, chiefly composed of the remains of marine organisms. **2** a piece of this or a coloured substance prepared from it, used for writing and drawing. **3** any similar substance, such as French chalk. ~*v.t.* **1** to rub, mark or write with chalk. **2** to spread with chalk as a fertilizer. **as different/ alike/ like as chalk and cheese** completely or fundamentally different. **by a long chalk** by a great deal, by far. **to chalk out** to sketch out, to plan. **to chalk up 1** to record or register (*to chalk up a high score*). **2** to charge to an account, to give or take credit for (*Chalk it up!*). **chalk and talk** *n.* formal or traditional teaching methods, using a blackboard and oral instruction from the front of the class. **chalk bed** *n.* a stratum of chalk. **chalkboard** *n.* (*N Am.*) a blackboard. **chalkface** *n.* (*coll.*) the classroom or classroom work, as opposed to the other activities or responsibilities of a teacher (*at the chalkface*). **chalk pit** *n.* a chalk quarry. **chalk-stone** *n.* a chalky concretion in the joints, occurring in chronic gout. **chalk-stripe** *n.* a pattern of narrow white stripes on a dark-coloured background. **chalk-striped** *a.* **chalk talk** *n.* (*N Am.*) an informal lecture using notes, diagrams etc. chalked on a blackboard. **chalky** *a.* (*comp.* **chalkier,** *superl.* **chalkiest**) **1** containing chalk (*chalky soil*). **2** as white as chalk. **3** containing or resembling chalk-stones. [OE *cealc* (cp. Dut., Dan., Swed., and G *kalk*), from L *calx -cis*, lime]

challah (khahlah´, hah´lə), **hallah** *n.* (*pl.* **challah, challoth** (-lot´), **hallahs, halloth**) a loaf of white bread, usu. plaited, eaten by Jews on the Sabbath. [Heb. *hallah*]

challenge (chal´inj) *n.* **1** a summons or invitation to fight a duel. **2** an invitation to take part in a contest of any kind. **3** a difficult task which stretches one's abilities. **4** a calling in question, a demand for proof or justification. **5** exception taken to a juror or voter. **6** the call of a sentry in demanding a password etc. **7** the cry of hounds on finding scent. **8** (*Med.*) a test of immunity after immunization. ~*v.t.* **1** to summon or invite to a duel. **2** to invite to take part in a contest of any kind. **3** to call on to answer or to prove or justify something. **4** to call into question. **5** to object to, to dispute, to contest. **6** to stimulate, to stretch. **challengeable** *a.* **challenged** *a.* handicapped (*usu. in comb.*, as *visually challenged*). **challenger** *n.* **challenging** *a.* demanding, stimulating. **challengingly** *adv.* [OF *chalenge*, L *calumnia*, CALUMNY (under CALUMNIATE)]

challis (shal´is, shal´i, chal´is), **challie** (shal´i) *n.* a light fabric of wool or cotton, used for clothing. [perh. a pers. name]

chalutz (hahluts´, khah-), **halutz** *n.* (*pl.* **chalutzim** (-lootsēm´, -loot´sim), **halutzim**) a member of a group of immigrants to Israel who established the first agricultural settlements (kibbutzim). [Heb. *halutz*, a pioneer]

chalybeate (kəlib´iət) *a.* impregnated with iron. ~*n.* a mineral water or spring so impregnated. **chalybite** (kal´ibīt) *n.* siderite. [L *chalybs*, Gr. *khalups -ubos*, steel, -ATE[1]]

chamade (shəmahd´) *n.* (*Mil., Hist.*) the beat of a drum or sound of a trumpet demanding or announcing a surrender or parley. [F, from Port. *chamada* (*chamar*, to summon, L *clāmāre*, to call)]

chamaephyte (kam´ifīt) *n.* a plant with buds close to the ground. [Gr. *chamai*, on the ground, -PHYTE]

chamber (chām´bə) *n.* **1** the place where a legislative assembly meets. **2** the assembly itself. **3** any similar meeting place, such as a hall of justice. **4** an association of persons for the promotion of some common object (*the Chamber of Agriculture*). **5** (*pl.*) the office or rooms of a barrister in an Inn of Court. **6** (*pl.*) a judge's private room in court. **7** (*poet.*) a room, esp. a bedroom. **8** a cave or underground cavity. **9** a hollow cavity or enclosed space. **10** the space between the gates of a canal lock. **11** that part of the bore of a gun or other firearm where the charge lies. **12** a chamber pot. **chamber counsel** *n.* a lawyer who gives opinions etc. but does not plead in court. **chambered** *a.* **1** enclosed. **2** divided into compartments or sections. **chambered nautilus** *n.* the pearly nautilus. **chambermaid** *n.* **1** a woman who cleans the bedrooms at a hotel. **2** (*N Am.*) a housemaid. **chamber music** *n.* music adapted for performance by a small group of instruments (orig. for performance in a room, as distinguished from that intended for theatres, churches etc.). **Chamber of Commerce** *n.* a board or committee appointed to promote the interests of business in a district. **Chamber of Deputies** *n.* the lower legislative assembly in the parliament of some countries, such as France. **Chamber of Horrors** *n.* a place full of horrifying objects (from a room at Madame Tussaud's waxwork exhibition devoted to famous criminals). **chamber orchestra** *n.* a small orchestra suitable for playing chamber music. **chamber organ** *n.* a small organ used esp. for preclassical music. **chamber pot** *n.* a bedroom receptacle for urine etc. **chamber practice** *n.* the practice of a chamber counsel. [OF, from L *camera*, from Indo-Eur. *kam-*, to cover (cp. Gr. *kamara*, a vault, Icel. *hamr*, a covering)]

chamberlain (chām´bəlin) *n.* **1** an officer in charge of the household of a sovereign or nobleman. **2** the treasurer of a city or corporation. **chamberlainship** *n.* [OF, from OHG *chamberling* (L *camera*, CHAMBER, -LING[1])]

Chambertin (shã´bətī) *n.* a dry red Burgundy wine. [Gevrey *Chambertin* in E France]

chambray (shom´brā) *n.* a light cotton or linen fabric with a white weft and coloured warp. [*Cambrai*, see CAMBRIC]

chambré (shom´brā) *a.* (of wine) warmed to room temperature. [F, p.p. of *chambrer*, to keep in a room]

chameleon (kəmēl´yən), **cameleon** *n.* **1** a small African lizard having the power of changing colour. **2** a changeable person. **chameleonic** (-lion´-) *a.* [L *chamaeleon*, Gr. *chamaileōn* (*chamai*, on the ground, *leōn*, a lion)]

chamfer (cham´fə) *n.* **1** in carpentry, an angle slightly pared off. **2** a bevel, a groove, a fluting. ~*v.t.* **1** to groove. **2** to bevel off. [OF *chanfrein* (*chant*, CANT[2], L *frangere*, to break)]

chamlet CAMLET.

chamois (sham´wah) *n.* (*pl.* **chamois** (-wah, -wahz)) **1** a goatlike European antelope, *Rupicapra rupicapra*. **2** CHAMOIS LEATHER (under CHAMOIS). **chamois leather** (sham´i, sham´wah) *n.* **1** soft, pliable leather, orig. prepared from the skin of the chamois. **2** a piece of this, used for polishing etc. [F, prob. from Swiss Romance dial. (cp. It. *camozza*, G *Gemse*); prob. Gmc. but etym. uncertain]

chamomile CAMOMILE.

champ[1] (champ), **chomp** (chomp) *v.t., v.i.* to bite with a crunching or grinding noise; to chew or munch noisily. ~*n.* **1** champing. **2** the noise of champing. **to champ at the bit** BIT[2]. [earlier *cham*; prob. imit.]

champ[2] (champ) *n.* (*coll.*) a champion. [abbr.]

champac (cham´pak, chŭm´pŭk), **champak** *n.* a kind of magnolia, *Michelia champaca*, much venerated in India. [Hind. *champak*]

champagne (shampān´) *n.* **1** a white sparkling wine made in the province of Champagne, France. **2** a pale yellow colour. **champagne socialist** *n.* (*derog.*) a person who claims to be a socialist but enjoys an extravagant lifestyle.

champaign (shampān´, sham´-) *n.* (*chiefly poet.*) **1** flat, open country. **2** an expanse of this. ~*a.* **1** flat, level. **2** open, unenclosed. [OF *champaigne* (see CAMPAIGN)]

champak CHAMPAC.
champers (sham´pəz) *n.* (*coll.*) champagne.
champerty (cham´pəti) *n.* (*pl.* **champerties**) (*Law*) an illegal agreement to finance a party in a suit on condition of sharing the property at issue if recovered. **champertous** *a.* [earlier *champarty*, ONF *campart*, L *campi pars*, part of the field (assim. to PARTY[1])]
champignon (shã´pinyõ) *n.* an edible mushroom, esp. the fairy-ring champignon, *Marasmius oreades*. [F, prob. from late L *campinio -ōnem* (*campus*, field)]
champion (cham´piən) *n.* **1** a person, animal or exhibit that defeats all competitors. **2** a person who argues on behalf of or defends a person or a cause. **3** (*Hist.*) a person who engaged in single combat on behalf of another. **4** †a warrior. ~*v.t.* **1** to defend as a champion. **2** to support (a cause). ~*a.* **1** superior to all rivals. **2** (*dial.*) first class, splendid, excellent. ~*adv.* (*dial.*) very well, splendidly, excellently. **championless** *a.* **Champion of England** *n.* a hereditary officer at British coronations. **championship** *n.* **1** a contest to find a champion. **2** the fact or status of being a champion. **3** the act of championing or defending. [OF, from late L *campio -ōnem*, a fighter in a duel (L *campus*, field)]
champlevé (shã´ləvā) *n.* **1** enamelling by the process of inlaying vitreous powders into channels cut in the metal base. **2** an object so enamelled. ~*a.* of or relating to this process. [F *champ*, a field, *levé*, raised]
Chanc. *abbr.* **1** Chancellor. **2** Chancery.
chance (chahns) *n.* **1** a risk, a possibility, an opportunity. **2** (*usu. pl.*) likelihood, probability (*What are the chances?*). **3** an accident, an unplanned result or occurrence. **4** fortune, luck. **5** fate, the indeterminable course of events, fortuity. ~*v.t.* (*coll.*) to risk. ~*v.i.* to happen, to come to pass (*He chanced to notice it*). ~*a.* fortuitous, accidental, unforeseen. **by any chance 1** as it happens. **2** perhaps. **by chance** accidentally; undesignedly. **on the chance 1** on the possibility. **2** in case. **the main chance 1** the most important issue. **2** an opportunity for personal gain. **3** self-interest. **to chance it** to take the risk. **to chance one's arm** to make a speculative attempt, to try something not very likely to succeed. **to chance on/ upon** to come upon accidentally. **to stand a chance** to have a prospect of success (*She doesn't stand a chance!*). **to stand a good chance** to have a reasonable prospect of success. **to take a chance** to take a risk, to risk failure. **to take chances** to behave in a risky manner. **to take one's chances** to trust to luck. **chanceful** *a.* **1** fortuitous, accidental. **2** full of opportunities. **chancer** *n.* (*sl.*) a person who takes risks in order to make a profit. **chancy, chancey** *a.* (*comp.* **chancier,** *superl.* **chanciest**) risky, doubtful. **chancily** *adv.* **chanciness** *n.* [OF *cheance*, late L *cadentia* (*cadens -tis*, pres.p. of *cadere*, to fall)]
chancel (chahn´səl) *n.* the eastern part of a church, usu. separated from the nave by a screen or by steps. [OF (see CANCEL)]
chancellery (chahn´sələri), **chancellory** *n.* (*pl.* **chancelleries, chancellories**) **1** a chancellor's court or council and official establishment. **2** the building or room occupied by a chancellor's office. **3** the position or rank of chancellor. [OF *chancelerie*, late L *cancellāria* (see CHANCELLOR)]
chancellor (chahn´sələ) *n.* **1** the president of a court, public department, or university. **2** an officer who seals the commissions etc. of an order of knighthood. **3** a bishop's law officer or a vicar-general. **Chancellor of the Duchy of Lancaster** *n.* the representative of the Crown as holder of the Duchy of Lancaster. **Chancellor of the Exchequer** *n.* the principal finance minister of the British Government. **chancellorship** *n.* **chancellory** CHANCELLERY. [OF *chancelier, cancelier*, late L *cancellārius* (L *cancellus*, a grating, see CANCEL)]
chance-medley (chahnsmed´li) *n.* **1** (*Law*) homicide by misadventure, as in repelling an unprovoked attack. **2** inadvertency. **3** pure chance or luck. [A-F *chance medlée*, CHANCE, *medler*, var. of *mesler*, to mix; cp. MEDDLE)]
chancery (chahn´səri) *n.* (*pl.* **chanceries**) **1** the court of the Lord Chancellor, the highest English court of justice next to the House of Lords, comprising a court of common law and a court of equity, now a division of the High Court of Justice. **2** (*N Am.*) a court of equity. **3** a court or office for the deposit of records. **4** an office or department attached to an embassy or consulate. **5** a chancellery. **in chancery 1** in a hopeless predicament. **2** in boxing, having one's head under an opponent's arm. **3** (*Law*) in litigation. [OF *cancellerie*, CHANCELLERY]
Chanc. Ex. *abbr.* Chancellor of the Exchequer.
chancey CHANCE.
chancre (shang´kə) *n.* (*Med.*) a hard syphilitic lesion. **chancroid** *n.* a soft ulcer caused by venereal infection. **chancroidal** *a.* **chancrous** *a.* [F, cp. CANCER, CANKER]
chancy CHANCE.
chandelier (shandəliə´) *n.* a hanging branched frame for a number of lights. [OF *chandelier*, candlemaker, candlestick (see CHANDLER)]
chandelle (shandel´) *n.* an abrupt upward turn of an aircraft, using its momentum to increase the rate of climb. ~*v.i.* to carry out this manoeuvre. [F, candle]
chandler (chahnd´lə) *n.* **1** a person who makes or sells candles. **2** a retail dealer in oil, soap, groceries etc. **3** a dealer in a specified commodity (*a ship's chandler*). **chandlery** *n.* (*pl.* **chandleries**) the establishment or the merchandise of a chandler. [OF *chandelier*, L *candēlārius* (*candēla*, CANDLE)]
change (chānj) *v.t.* **1** to make different, to alter. **2** to give up or substitute for something else (*to change one's clothes*). **3** to give or take an equivalent for in other coins or currency. **4** to exchange (*to change places*). ~*v.i.* **1** to become different. **2** to be altered in appearance. **3** to put on different clothes (*to change for dinner, to change into a dress*). **4** to pass from one state or phase to another. **5** to get off one train etc. and board another (*change at Manchester for Bolton*). **6** to become tainted, to deteriorate. ~*n.* **1** alteration, variation. **2** an instance of this. **3** shifting, transition. **4** the substitution of one thing for another; exchange. **5** an exchange; something substituted for another. **6** small coins or foreign currency given in return for other money. **7** the balance of money paid beyond the value of goods purchased. **8** novelty, variety (*for a change*). **9** (*coll.*) the change of life. **10** alteration in order, esp. of a peal of bells in bell-ringing. **11** the passing of the moon from one phase to another. **12** (*Hist.*) (*also* **'change**) a place where merchants met or transacted business. **to change colour** COLOUR. **to change countenance** COUNTENANCE. **to change down** in driving etc., to engage a lower gear. **to change gear** GEAR. **to change hands** HAND. **to change one's mind** MIND. **to change one's spots** SPOT. **to change one's tune** TUNE. **to change over** to change from one state, position, situation, system etc. to another. **to change sides** SIDE. **to change step** STEP. **to change the subject** SUBJECT[1]. **to change up** in driving etc., to engage a higher gear. **to get no change out of 1** (*coll.*) to fail to gain information from. **2** (*coll.*) not to be able to take any advantage of. **to ring the changes** to vary the ways of doing something. **changeable** *a.* **1** liable to change, variable. **2** inconstant, fickle. **changeability** (-bil´-) *n.* **changeableness** *n.* **changeably** *adv.* **changeful** *a.* **1** full of change. **2** changeable. **changefully** *adv.* **changefulness** *n.* **changeless** *a.* **1** free from change. **2** unchanging. **changelessly** *adv.* **changelessness** *n.* **changeling** (-ling) *n.* **1** a child substituted for another, esp. by fairies. **2** anything substituted for another. **3** †a waverer,

a fickle person. **change of air** *n.* **1** a different climate. **2** variety. **change of front** *n.* **1** (*Mil.*) a wheeling movement. **2** a change of attitude, a reversal of policy. **change of heart** *n.* a change of attitude, opinion etc., which often results in the reversal of a decision. **change of life** *n.* (*coll.*) the menopause. **change of scene, change of scenery** *n.* change of surroundings by travel. **change of venue** *n.* alteration of the place of trial etc., to avoid riot etc. **changeover** *n.* **1** an alteration or reversal from one state to another. **2** in a relay race, the passing of the baton from one runner to the next. **changer** *n.* **1** a person who changes anything. **2** a money changer. **change-ringing** *n.* a form of bell-ringing in which a set of bells is rung repeatedly but in slightly varying order. **change-ringer** *n.* **changing** *a.* [OF *changer*, late L *cambiāre* (*cambium*, exchange, L *cambire*; etym. uncertain)]

channel[1] (chan´əl) *n.* **1** the bed of a stream or an artificial watercourse. **2** the deep or navigable part of an estuary, river etc.; a fairway. **3** a narrow piece of water joining two seas. **4** a tube or duct, natural or artificial, for the passage of liquids or gases. **5** any means of passing, conveying or transmitting. **6** a course, line or direction. **7** a band of frequencies on which radio and television signals can be transmitted without interference from other such bands. **8** a path for an electrical signal. **9** in a computer, a route along which data can be transmitted. **10** a furrow, a groove, a fluting. **11** a gutter. ~*v.t.* (*pres.p.* **channelling,** (*N Am.*) **channeling,** *past, p.p.* **channelled,** (*N Am.*) **channeled**) **1** to guide or direct (*to channel information*). **2** to cut a channel or channels in. **3** to groove. **the Channel** the English Channel. **channelize, channelise** *v.t.* to channel. **channelization** (-zā´shən) *n.* **channel surfing** *n.* (*coll.*) moving swiftly from one television channel to another, using a remote control device. [OF *chanel*, var. of CANAL]

channel[2] (chan´əl) *n.* a plank fastened horizontally to the side of a ship to spread the lower rigging. **channel plate** *n.* a chain-plate. [CHAIN, WALE]

chanson (shã´sõ) *n.* a song. **chanson de geste** (də zhest´) *n.* (*pl.* **chansons de geste** (shãsõ də zhest´)) an Old French epic poem, usu. celebrating heroic exploits. **chansonette** (-sonet´) *n.* a little song. [F, from L *cantio -ōnis* (*cant-*, part. stem of *canere*, to sing)]

chant (chahnt) *v.t.* **1** to speak or sing rhythmically or repetitively (*to chant a slogan*). **2** to recite to music or musically, to intone. ~*v.i.* **1** to sing in an intoning fashion. **2** to perform a chant. ~*n.* **1** a song, a melody. **2** a composition consisting of a long reciting note and a melodic phrase. **3** a psalm, canticle or other piece sung in this manner. **4** a monotonous song. **5** a rhythmic or repetitive phrase, usu. spoken or sung in unison by a crowd (*a football chant*). **chanter** *n.* **1** a person who chants. **2** the pipe on a bagpipe that plays the tune. **3** a chantry priest, a chorister. **4** a precentor. [F *chanter*, L *cantāre*, freq. of *canere*, to sing]

chanterelle (shahntərel´) *n.* an edible fungus, *Cantharellus cibarius.* [F, from mod. L *cantharellus*, dim. of *cantharus*, cup]

chanteuse (shãtœz´) *n.* a female nightclub singer. [F (fem.), singer]

chantey SHANTY[2].

chanticleer (chan´tikliə, chahn´-) *n.* (*poet.*) a name for a cock, esp. as the herald of day. [OF *chantecler* (F *chanteclair*), *chanter*, CHANT, *cler*, CLEAR]

Chantilly (shantil´i) *n.* **1** (*also* **Chantilly lace**) a delicate type of lace. **2** (*also* **Chantilly cream**) whipped cream, usu. sweetened or flavoured. [a town near Paris]

chantry (chahn´tri) *n.* (*pl.* **chantries**) **1** an endowment for a priest or priests to say mass daily for some person or persons deceased. **2** the chapel or the part of a church used for this purpose. **3** the body of priests who perform this duty. **chantry priest** *n.* any one of these priests. [OF *chanterie* (*chanter*, CHANT, -ERY)]

chanty SHANTY[2].

Chanukah, Chanukkah HANUKKAH.

chaos (kā´os) *n.* **1** confusion, disorder. **2** the void, the confusion of matter said to have existed before the creation of the universe. **chaos theory** *n.* the theory that apparently random or unpredictable phenomena observed in the universe or in various branches of science are based on complex underlying principles. **chaotic** (-ot´-) *a.* **chaotically** *adv.* [L, from Gr. *chaos* (*chaskein*, to gape)]

chap[1] (chap) *v.t.* (*pres.p.* **chapping,** *past, p.p.* **chapped**) **1** to cause to crack or open in long slits. **2** (*Sc.*) to strike, to beat. ~*v.i.* to crack or open in long slits. ~*n.* (*usu. pl.*) a longitudinal crack, cleft or seam on the surface of the skin, the ground etc. **chapped** *a.* **chappy** *a.* **chapstick** *n.* a small stick of a substance used to prevent or soothe chapped lips. [ME *chappen* (MDut. *cappen*, Dut. *kappen*, Dan. *kappe*), relations of these obscure]

chap[2] (chap), **chappie** (chap´i) *n.* (*coll.*) a man, a fellow. **chapess** *n.* (*coll., facet.*) a woman. [CHAPMAN]

chap[3] (chap) *n.* **1** (*pl.*) the jaws (usu. of animals), the mouth and cheeks; the chops. **2** the lower part of the cheek. **chap-fallen** *a.* **1** having the lower jaw depressed. **2** downcast, dejected, dispirited. [var. of CHOP[3]; etym. uncertain]

chap. *abbr.* **1** chaplain. **2** chapter.

chaparajos (chaparā´khōs, sha-), **chaparejos, chaps** (chaps) *n.pl.* leather leggings worn by cowboys. [Sp.]

chaparral (shap´əral) *n.* (*N Am.*) a thicket of low evergreen oaks, or of thick undergrowth and thorny shrubs. **chaparral cock** *n.* the roadrunner. [Sp., from *chaparra*, evergreen oak]

chapati (chəpat´i), **chapatti, chupatty** *n.* (*pl.* **chapatis, chapattis, chupatties**) in Indian cookery, a round, thin loaf of unleavened bread. [Hind. *capati*]

chapbook (chap´buk) *n.* a small book, usually of tales, ballads or the like, formerly hawked by chapmen. [formed on analogy of CHAPMAN]

chape (chāp) *n.* **1** the catch or piece by which an object is attached, such as the tongue of a buckle. **2** the transverse guard of a sword. **3** the hook or tip of a scabbard. [F, from late L *cāpa*, CAP]

chapeau (shap´ō) *n.* (*pl.* **chapeaux** (-ōz)) a hat. **chapeau-bras** (-brah´) *n.* (*pl.* **chapeaux-bras** (shapōbrah´)) a small, three-cornered, flat silk hat carried under the arm. [F, from OF *chapel*, L *cappellum*, dim. of *cappa*, CAP]

chapel (chap´əl) *n.* **1** a place of worship connected with and subsidiary to a church. **2** a part containing an altar in a church. **3** a place of worship other than a church or cathedral, esp. one in a palace, mansion or public institution. **4** a Nonconformist place of worship. **5** a service, or the sort of service, at a chapel. **6** a printing office (from the legend that Caxton set up his printing press in Westminster Abbey). **7** a printers' or journalists' trade union, or a branch of it. **8** a meeting of such a trade union or branch. ~*a.* belonging to a Nonconformist church. **father of (the) chapel** FATHER. **mother of (the) chapel** MOTHER[1]. **chapel of ease** *n.* a subordinate church in a parish. **chapel of rest** *n.* an undertaker's mortuary. **chapel royal** *n.* the chapel of a royal palace. **chapelry** *n.* (*pl.* **chapelries**) the district or jurisdiction of a chapel. [OF *chapele* (F *chapelle*), from late L *cappella*, dim. of *cappa*, *cāpa*, CAP (after the *cāpa* or cloak of St Martin, which was preserved in the first chapel)]

chaperone (shap´ərōn), **chaperon** *n.* **1** a married or elderly woman who accompanies a young unmarried woman on social occasions or in public places. **2** any person who accompanies or supervises young people in public places. ~*v.t.* to act as chaperone to. **chaperonage** *n.* the duties or position of a chaperone. [F, a hood, dim. of *chape*, a cope (see CAP)]

chapiter (chap´itə) *n.* (*Archit.*) the upper part of the capital of a column. [OF *chapitre*, L *capitulum*, dim. of *caput -itis*, head]

chaplain (chap´lin) *n.* a clergyman who officiates in a private chapel, in the armed forces, or in some other establishment or institution (*a prison chaplain*). **chaplaincy** *n.* (*pl.* **chaplaincies**). **chaplainship** *n.* [OF *chapelain*, late L *cappellānus*]

chaplet (chap´lit) *n.* **1** a wreath or garland for the head. **2** a string of beads, esp. one-third of a rosary. **3** a necklace. **4** a round moulding carved into beads, olives etc. [OF *chapelet*, dim. of CHAPE]

†**chapman** (chap´mən) *n.* (*pl.* **chapmen**) **1** a person who buys and sells. **2** an itinerant merchant, a pedlar, a hawker. [OE *cēapmann* (*cēap*, CHEAP, *mann*, MAN), cp. Dut. *koopman*, G *Kaufmann*]

chappal (chap´əl, chŭp´-) *n.* a leather sandal worn in India. [Hind.]

chapped CHAP[1].

chappie CHAP[2].

chappy CHAP[1].

chaps CHAPARAJOS.

chaptalize (chap´təlīz), **chaptalise** *v.t.* to add sugar to (wine) during fermentation in order to increase the alcohol content. **chaptalization** (-zā´shən) *n.* [J. A. *Chaptal*, 1756–1832, French chemist]

chapter (chap´tə) *n.* **1** a division of a book. **2** a part of a subject. **3** a piece of narrative, an episode. **4** a period of time (*another chapter in the nation's history*). **5** a series or sequence of events. **6** a numbered division of the Acts of Parliament arranged in chronological order for reference. **7** the council of a bishop, consisting of the clergy attached to a cathedral or collegiate church. **8** a meeting of the members of a religious order. **9** a branch or meeting of certain other orders and societies. **10** a chapter house. ~*v.t.* to divide into chapters. **chapter and verse** a full and precise reference in order to verify a fact or quotation. **chapter house** *n.* **1** the place in which a chapter is held, esp. part of a cathedral or collegiate church. **2** (*N Am.*) the meeting place of a college fraternity or sorority. **chapter of accidents** *n.* **1** a series of accidents. **2** an unfortunate coincidence. [CHAPITER]

char[1] (chah) *v.t.* (*pres.p.* **charring,** *past., p.p.* **charred**) **1** to burn slightly, to blacken with fire. **2** to reduce to charcoal. ~*v.i.* to become blackened with fire. [back-formation from CHARCOAL]

char[2] (chah), **charr** *n.* (*pl. in general* **char, charr,** *in particular* **chars, charrs**) any small fish of the genus *Salvelinus*, of the salmon family, esp. *S. alpinus*. [perh. Celtic; cp. Ir. *cear*, red]

char[3] (chah) *n.* a charwoman. ~*v.i.* (*pres.p.* **charring,** *past, p.p.* **charred**) **1** to work as a charwoman. **2** to do small jobs. **charwoman, charlady** *n.* (*pl.* **charwomen, charladies**) a woman employed to do cleaning in houses, offices etc. [OE *cierr*, *cyrr*, a turn, from *cierran*, to turn (cp. CHORE)]

char[4] CHA.

charabanc (shar´əbang) *n.* (*dated*) a coach for day trippers. [F, carriage with benches]

characin (kar´əsin), **characid** (-sid) *n.* any freshwater fish of the family Characidae, including the piranha. [Gr. *charax*, a kind of fish]

character (kar´iktə) *n.* **1** the distinctive qualities or traits peculiar to a person or thing. **2** the sum of a person's mental and moral qualities. **3** moral excellence, moral strength. **4** reputation or standing, esp. good reputation. **5** a certificate of a person's capacity, moral qualities and conduct; a testimonial. **6** position, rank, capacity. **7** a person, a personage. **8** (*coll.*) an eccentric person (*She's quite a character*). **9** a personality created by a novelist, poet or dramatist. **10** a part in a play, an actor's role. **11** a letter, symbol or other mark made by writing, printing, engraving etc. **12** (*Comput.*) a symbol, e.g. a letter, punctuation mark etc., that can be used in representing data. **13** (*pl.*) letters distinctive of a particular language. **14** style of handwriting. **15** a characteristic (of a species etc.) (*generic characters*). **16** an inherited characteristic. ~†*v.t.* **1** to inscribe; to engrave. **2** to characterize. **in character** typical of a person, consistent with a person's character. **out of character** not in character. **character actor** *n.* an actor who specializes in portraying eccentric or unusual characters. **character assassination** *n.* the destruction of a person's good reputation, e.g. by spreading malicious rumours. **characterful** *a.* **characterfully** *adv.* **characteristic** (-ris´-) *n.* **1** a typical or distinctive quality or feature. **2** (*Math.*) the whole number or integral part of a logarithm. ~*a.* constituting or exhibiting a characteristic. **characteristically** *adv.* **characteristic curve** *n.* a graph that shows the relationship between two interdependent quantities, such as the density of a photographic material and the logarithm of the exposure producing it. **characteristic radiation** *n.* (*Physics*) radiation with wavelengths characteristic of the substance emitting them. **characterize, characterise** *v.t.* **1** to give character to, to stamp, to distinguish. **2** to describe as. **3** to be characteristic of. **characterization** (-zā´shən) *n.* **characterless** *a.* **characterlessness** *n.* **character recognition** *n.* (*Comput.*) a process that involves recognition of individual characters in print or writing. **character sketch** *n.* a brief description of a person's character. †**charactery** *n.* (*pl.* **characteries**) **1** characterization. **2** a mark, an impression. **3** the use of symbols to express thoughts. [F *caractère* (or OF *characte*), L *charactēr*, Gr. *charactēr* (*charassein*, to furrow, engrave)]

charade (shərahd´) *n.* **1** (*pl., usu. sing. in constr.*) a game in which a word is guessed from actions or utterances representing each syllable and the whole word. **2** any of the clues in this game. **3** a ridiculous pretence. **4** a type of riddle. [F, from Prov. *charrada* (*charra*, to chatter)]

charas (chah´rəs) *n.* hashish, cannabis resin. [Hind.]

charbroil (chah´broil) *v.t.* to grill (meat etc.) over charcoal. [CHARCOAL, BROIL[2]]

charcoal (chah´kōl) *n.* **1** an impure form of carbon prepared from vegetable or animal substances, esp. wood partially burnt under turf. **2** a stick of this used for drawing. **3** a drawing made with such a stick. **4** charcoal grey. ~*a.* charcoal grey. **charcoal biscuit** *n.* a biscuit containing wood charcoal. **charcoal burner** *n.* (*Hist.*) a person whose job was to make charcoal by partially burning wood. **charcoal grey** *n.* a dark grey colour. ~*a.* of this colour. [etym. uncertain]

charcuterie (shahkoo´təri) *n.* **1** a shop selling cold cooked meats and similar products. **2** these products. [F]

chard (chahd) *n.* a variety of beet, *Beta vulgaris*, with stalks and leaves eaten as a vegetable, also called *Swiss chard*. [F *carde*, L *carduus*, a thistle]

Chardonnay (shah´dənā) *n.* **1** a white grape grown in the Burgundy region of France and elsewhere, used to make wine. **2** a white wine made from these grapes. [F]

charge (chahj) *v.t.* **1** to ask as a price. **2** to debit (to). **3** to accuse. **4** to enjoin, to command, to exhort. **5** to give directions to, as a judge to a jury or a bishop to his clergy. **6** to entrust. **7** to rush on and attack. **8** to put (weapons) in an attacking position. **9** to put the proper load or quantity of material into; to load (a gun), to accumulate electricity in (a battery) etc. **10** to give an electric charge to. **11** to load, to fill. **12** to saturate, to pervade. ~*v.i.* **1** to make an attack or onrush. **2** (*coll.*) to demand high prices or payments. ~*n.* **1** a price demanded, a cost. **2** a financial liability, a tax. **3** an entry on the debit side of an account. **4** an accusation, esp. a formal accusation of crime. **5** an office, duty or obligation. **6** a command, a commission. **7** care, custody (*in your charge*). **8** a thing or person under one's care; a minister's congregation. **9** attack, onrush. **10** the quantity with which any apparatus, esp. a firearm, is loaded. **11** the electrical property of matter, negative or positive. **12** the amount or accumulation of electricity, e.g. in a battery. **13** instructions, directions, esp. those of a judge to a jury or of a bishop to clergy. **14** (*Her.*) anything borne on an escutcheon. **15** a load, a burden. **16** (*sl.*) a thrill. **free of charge** free, without charge. **in charge 1** on duty. **2** in command. **in charge of** responsible for. **on a charge** having been charged with a crime. **to give in charge 1** to commit to the care of another. **2** to hand over to the custody of a police officer. **to lay to the charge of** to accuse of. **to return to the charge** to begin again. **to reverse the charges** REVERSE. **to take charge** to assume control, command, responsibility etc. **to take in charge** to arrest, to take into custody. **chargeable** *a.* **1** liable to be charged or accused. **2** liable to result in a charge or accusation. **3** liable to a monetary charge. **4** liable to be demanded as a monetary charge. **5** able to be charged (to an account etc.). **6** capable of receiving an electric charge. **chargeability** (-bil´-) *n.* **charge account** *n.* a credit account at a shop. **charge card** *n.* a credit card issued by a shop or retail chain for use in its own outlets. **charge-coupled device** *n.* (*Comput.*) a storage device built into a chip which can be used only so long as it has an electric charge. **chargehand** *n.* a worker in charge of several others. **chargeless** *a.* **charge nurse** *n.* a nurse in charge of a ward. **charger** *n.* **1** a person who charges. **2** a horse, esp. a cavalry horse. **3** a device for charging a battery. **4** †a large dish. **charge sheet** *n.* a list of offenders taken into custody, with their offences, for the use of a magistrate. [F *charger*, L *carricāre* (*carrus*, CAR)]

chargé d'affaires (shahzhā dafeə´), **chargé** (shah´zhā) *n.* (*pl.* **chargés d'affaires** (shah´zhā), **chargés**) **1** a diplomatic agent acting as deputy to an ambassador. **2** an ambassador to a country of minor importance. [F, charged with affairs]

charily, chariness CHARY.

chariot (char´iət) *n.* **1** (*Hist.*) a carriage used in war, public triumphs and racing. **2** (*Hist.*) a light, four-wheeled carriage used for pleasure and on ceremonial. **3** (*chiefly poet.*) any vehicle, esp. a stately kind of vehicle. ~*v.t.* (*pres.p.* **charioting**, *past, p.p.* **charioted**) (*poet.*) to convey in a chariot. ~*v.i.* (*poet.*) to ride in a chariot. **charioteer** (-tiə´) *n.* a chariot driver. **charioteering** (-tiə´-) *n.* the art or practice of driving a chariot. **chariot race** *n.* a race in chariots. [OF *chariot*, augm. of *char*, CAR]

charisma (kəriz´mə), **charism** (kar´izm) *n.* (*pl.* **charismata** (-mətə), **charisms**) **1** personal magnetism or charm enabling one to inspire or influence other people. **2** a quality which inspires admiration or devotion. **3** a divinely given power or talent. **charismatic** (karizmat´-) *a.* **1** having charisma. **2** of or relating to the charismatic movement. **charismatically** *adv.* **charismatic movement** *n.* a Christian movement characterized by speaking in tongues, spontaneity, communal prayer, healing etc. [Gr. *charis*, grace]

charity (char´iti) *n.* (*pl.* **charities**) **1** generosity to those in need, alms-giving. **2** the money etc. so given. **3** a foundation or institution for assisting those in need. **4** kindness, goodwill. **5** an act of kindness. **6** leniency, tolerance of faults and offences, liberality of judgement. **7** love of one's fellow human beings, one of the theological virtues. **charitable** *a.* **1** of, relating to or supported by charity (*a charitable organization*). **2** generous to those in need. **3** benevolent, kindly, lenient, large-hearted. **4** dictated by kindness. **charitableness** *n.* **charitably** *adv.* **Charity Commission** *n.* a board instituted in 1853 for the control of charitable foundations. [OF *charité*, *charitet*, L *caritas -tātis* (*carus*, dear)]

charivari (shahrivah´ri), (*esp. N Am.*) **shivaree** *n.* (*pl.* **charivaris, shivarees**) **1** a mock serenade of discordant music. **2** a confusion of sounds, a hubbub. [F, from late L *caribaria*, headache]

charka (chah´kə), **charkha** *n.* (*pl.* **charkas, charkhas**) an Indian spinning wheel, used esp. for spinning cotton. [Hind.]

charlady CHAR[3].

charlatan (shah´lətən) *n.* a person who pretends to have skill or knowledge; a quack; an impostor. **charlatanic** (-tan´-), **charlatanical** *a.* **charlatanism, charlatanry** *n.* [F, from It. *ciarlatano* (*ciarlare*, to prattle)]

Usage note Pronunciation with (ch-) rather than (sh-) is best avoided.

Charles' law (chahlz), **Charles's law** (chahl´ziz) *n.* (*Chem.*) the principle that all gases at constant pressure have the same coefficient of expansion. [J. A. C. *Charles*, 1746–1823, French scientist]

Charles's wain (chahl´ziz) *n.* seven stars in the constellation the Great Bear; the Plough. [OE *Carles wægn*, the wain of *Carl* (Charlemagne); perh. from confusion of *Arcturus* (the neighbouring constellation) with *Arturus* and association of King Arthur and Charlemagne]

charleston (chahl´stən), **Charleston** *n.* a strenuous dance in 4/4 time with characteristic kicking outwards of the lower part of the legs. [*Charleston*, city in S Carolina]

charley horse (chah´li) *n.* (*N Am., sl.*) muscle stiffness or cramp, esp. in the arm or leg after exercise. [etym. uncertain]

charlie (chah´li) *n.* (*sl.*) **1** an utterly foolish person (*a proper charlie*). **2** (*pl.*) a woman's breasts. **3** (**Charlie**) cocaine. [var. of *Charles*]

charlock (chah´lok) *n.* a type of wild mustard, *Sinapis arvensis*; the field mustard. [OE *cerlic*]

charlotte (shah´lət) *n.* a kind of pudding made with fruit and thin slices of bread or layers of breadcrumbs etc. **charlotte russe** (roos) *n.* custard or whipped cream enclosed in sponge cake or sponge fingers. [F perh. from the fem. name; *russe*, Russian]

charm[1] (chahm) *n.* **1** a power or gift of alluring, pleasing, fascinating etc. **2** a pleasing or attractive feature. **3** a spell, an enchantment. **4** a thing, act or formula having magical power. **5** an article worn to avert evil or ensure good luck, an amulet. **6** a small trinket worn on a bracelet. **7** (*Physics*) a property of some elementary particles. ~*v.t.* **1** to attract, to delight, to please. **2** to enchant, to fascinate, to bewitch. **3** (*usu. pass.*) to protect with occult power (*a charmed life*). **4** to gain or influence by charm. ~*v.i.* to use charm or charms. **like a charm** perfectly. **charm bracelet** *n.* a bracelet hung with charms. **charmer** *n.* **charming** *a.* highly pleasing; delightful. ~*int.* (*iron.*) used to express disapproval. **charmingly** *adv.* **charmingness** *n.* **charmless** *a.* **charmlessly** *adv.* **charmlessness** *n.* **charm offensive** *n.* the excessive use of charm to get what one wants, achieve a goal etc. [OF *charme*, L *carmen*, a song]

charm[2] (chahm) *n.* a blended noise or confusion of voices, as of birds or children. [from obs. v. *chirm*, OE *cirman*, to shout]

Charmeuse® (shahmœz´) *n.* a soft silky fabric with a smooth finish.

charnel (chah´nəl) *a.* deathlike; sepulchral. **charnel house** *n.* a place where dead bodies or the bones of the dead are deposited. [OF *charnel*, carnal, a cemetery, late L *carnāle*, a graveyard, neut. of *carnālis*, CARNAL]

Charolais (shar´əlā, -ō-), **Charollais** *n.* (*pl.* **Charolais,**

Charollais) 1 a breed of large white beef cattle. 2 an animal of this breed. [Monts du *Charollais*, E France]

charpoy (chah´poi) *n.* (*Ang.-Ind.*) a light Indian bedstead. [Urdu *chārpāi*, Pers. *chahārpāi*, four-footed]

charqui (chah´ki) *n.* beef cut into strips and dried in the sun, jerked beef. [Quechua]

charr CHAR².

chart (chaht) *n.* 1 a map of some part of the sea, with coasts, islands, rocks, shoals etc., for the use of sailors. 2 a statement of facts in tabular form. 3 a projection of relative facts, statistics or observations in the form of a graph. 4 a skeleton map for special purposes (*a heliographic chart*). 5 (*often pl.*) a weekly list of best-selling records. ~*v.t.* 1 to make a chart of. 2 to map. **chartaceous** (-tā´-) *a.* resembling paper. **chartbuster** *n.* (*coll.*) a best-selling record. **chartist** *n.* a person who uses charts of past performance to predict future trends, esp. in the stock market. **chartless** *a.* 1 without a chart. 2 uncharted. **chart-topper** *n.* a chart-topping record. **chart-topping** *a.* being at the top of the record charts. [F *charte*, L *charta*, *carta*, Gr. *chartē*, a sheet of papyrus (cp. CARD¹)]

charter (chah´tə) *n.* 1 an instrument in writing granted by the sovereign or parliament, incorporating a borough, company or institution, or conferring certain rights and privileges. 2 a deed, an instrument. 3 a special privilege or exemption. 4 a contract for the hire of a ship, aircraft or other means of transportation. 5 a charter party. ~*a.* 1 (of an aircraft) hired by charter. 2 (of a flight) made in a charter aircraft. ~*v.t.* 1 to establish by charter. 2 to license by charter. 3 to hire (a ship, aircraft etc.) esp. by charter. 4 to hire or let by charter party. **chartered** *a.* (of an accountant, engineer etc.) qualified to the standards set by a professional body that has a royal charter. **chartered libertine** *n.* a person who is allowed to do as they please. **charterer** *n.* **Charter Mark** *n.* an award granted to an organization or institution providing a high standard of public service under the Citizen's Charter. **charter member** *n.* an original member of a society or organization. [OF *chartre*, late L *chartula*, dim. of CHART]

Charterhouse (chah´təhows) *n.* 1 a Carthusian monastery. 2 a hospital and school founded in London on the site of a Carthusian monastery, now removed. [A-F *chart rouse* (see CHARTREUSE)]

charter party (chah´tə) *n.* (*pl.* **charter parties**) an agreement in writing concerning the hire and freight of a vessel. [F *charte partie*, divided document]

Chartism (chah´tizm) *n.* the principles of an English reform movement of 1838–48, including universal suffrage, vote by ballot, annual parliaments, payment of members, equal electoral districts and the abolition of property qualifications for members. **Chartist** *n.* [L *charta*, -ISM]

chartography CARTOGRAPHY.

chartreuse (shahtrœz´) *n.* 1 a pale green or yellow liqueur made with aromatic herbs. 2 the colour of this. 3 a dish of fruit in jelly. ~*a.* of the colour of chartreuse. [La Grande *Chartreuse*, monastery near Grenoble, France, where the liqueur is made]

chartulary CARTULARY.

charwoman CHAR³.

chary (cheə´ri) *a.* (*comp.* **charier**, *superl.* **chariest**) 1 wary, prudent, cautious. 2 frugal, sparing. **charily** *adv.* **chariness** *n.* [OE *cearig* (*cearu*, *caru*, care, sorrow, Gmc. *Carā*) cp. OHG *charag*, G *karg*, sparing]

Charybdis (kərib´dis) *n.* one of a pair of alternative risks (*between Scylla and Charybdis*). **Charybdian** *a.* [L, a dangerous whirlpool off the coast of Sicily, opposite Scylla, a rock on the Italian shore; from Gr. *Charubdis*]

Chas. *abbr.* Charles.

chase¹ (chās) *v.t.* 1 to pursue, esp. at speed. 2 to hunt. 3 to drive away. 4 to put to flight. 5 (*coll.*) to try to achieve or obtain. ~*v.i.* to move rapidly, esp. in pursuit. ~*n.* 1 the act of chasing (*a car chase*). 2 the hunting of wild animals (*the thrill of the chase*). 3 an animal etc. that is chased. 4 an open hunting ground or preserve for game. 5 in real tennis, the second bounce of an unreturned ball. 6 a steeplechase. **go and chase yourself** (*coll.*) go away! **to chase the dragon** DRAGON. **to chase up** (*coll.*) to pursue or investigate in order to obtain information etc. **to give chase to** GIVE. **chase-gun** *n.* a gun mounted at the bow or stern of a ship, used for attack or defence. **chaser¹** *n.* 1 a person or thing that chases. 2 a horse used for steeplechasing. 3 (*coll.*) a drink taken after one of another kind, esp. spirits after beer. 4 a chase-gun (*bow-chaser*; *stern-chaser*). [OF *chacier*, late L *captiāre* (see CATCH)]

chase² (chās) *v.t.* 1 to engrave, to emboss. 2 to cut the thread of (a screw). **chaser²** *n.* 1 an enchaser. 2 a tool used in screw cutting. **chasing** *n.* 1 the art of embossing metals. 2 the pattern embossed. [earlier *enchase*, F *enchâsser* (*en*, L *in*, *châsse*, L *capsa*, CASE²)]

chase³ (chās) *n.* a rectangular iron frame in which type is locked for printing. [F *châsse*, L *capsa*, CASE²]

chase⁴ (chās) *n.* 1 a wide groove. 2 the part of a gun in front of the trunnions. [F *chas*, late L *capsum*, an enclosure (cp. *capsa*, CASE²), from *capere*, to hold]

chaser¹ CHASE¹.

chaser² CHASE².

chasm (kaz´m) *n.* 1 a deep cleft or fissure in the ground; a yawning gulf. 2 a breach or division between persons or parties. 3 a gap or void. 4 †a break of continuity. **chasmic** *a.* [L, Gr. *chasma*, from *chainein*, to gape]

chasmogamic (kazmōgam´ik) *a.* (*Bot.*) having flowers that open to allow cross-pollination. [Gr. *khasma*, CHASM, *gamos*, marriage]

chasse (shas) *n.* a liqueur drunk after coffee. [F *chasse-café*, chase-coffee (*chasser*, to chase)]

chassé (shas´ā) *n.* a gliding step in dancing. ~*v.i.* (*pres.p.* **chasséing**, *past*, *p.p.* **chasséd**) to perform this step. [F, chasing, gliding (*chasser*, to chase)]

chassepot (shas´pō) *n.* a breech-loading rifle used in France, 1866–74. [Antoine *Chassepot*, 1833–1905, French gunsmith]

chasseur (shasœ´) *n.* 1 a huntsman. 2 a light-armed French soldier. 3 a uniformed attendant. ~*a.* cooked in a sauce of white wine and mushrooms (*chicken chasseur*). [F, from *chasser*, to chase, hunt]

chassis (shas´i) *n.* (*pl.* **chassis** (-iz)) 1 the framework of a motor vehicle, aeroplane etc. 2 a framework supporting a piece of electronic equipment. 3 the base-frame of a cannon or gun carriage. [F, *châssis*, late L *capsum* (cp. CHASE⁴)]

chaste (chāst) *a.* 1 abstaining from all sexual intercourse, or from sex outside marriage. 2 modest, innocent, virginal. 3 free from obscenity. 4 pure in style. 5 simple, unadorned, unaffected. **chastely** *adv.* **chasteness** *n.* **chaste tree** *n.* an ornamental flowering shrub, *Vitex agnus-castus*. **chastity** (chas´-) *n.* 1 the state of being chaste. 2 virginity. 3 celibacy. 4 purity of taste and style. **chastity belt** *n.* a beltlike garment designed to prevent a woman from having sexual intercourse. [OF, from L *castus*, pure]

chasten (chā´sən) *v.t.* 1 to punish with a view to reformation; to correct; to discipline. 2 to subdue; to moderate; to restrain. 3 to purify, to refine. **chastened** *a.* **chastener** *n.* [from obs. v. *chasty*, OF *chastier*, L *castīgāre* (*castus*, chaste), or from CHASTE, -EN¹]

chastise (chastīz´) *v.t.* 1 to punish, esp. physically. 2 to reprimand severely. 3 to chasten. **chastisable** *a.* **chastisement** (chas´tiz-, -tīz´-) *n.* **chastiser** *n.* [ME *chastien*, chasten, later *chasty* (see CHASTEN), -IZE (formation obscure)]

chastity CHASTE.

chasuble (chaz´ūbəl) *n.* a sleeveless vestment worn by a priest over the alb while celebrating Mass. [F, from med. L *casubla*, *casubula*, dim. of *casa*, a little house]

chat[1] (chat) *v.i.* (*pres.p.* **chatting**, *past, p.p.* **chatted**) **1** to talk easily and familiarly. **2** to gossip. ~*n.* **1** easy, familiar talk. **2** an informal conversation. **3** gossip. **to chat up** (*sl.*) to chat to in order to establish a (sexual) relationship. **chatline** *n.* a telephone service that enables a number of callers to engage in conversation together. **chat show** *n.* a television show or radio programme in which invited celebrities are interviewed informally. **chatty**[1] *a.* (*comp.* **chattier**, *superl.* **chattiest**) **1** talkative. **2** informal (*a chatty letter*). **chattily** *adv.* **chattiness** *n.* **chat-up** *n.* (*coll.*) an instance of chatting someone up. ~*a.* used in chatting someone up (*a chat-up line*). [short for CHATTER]

chat[2] (chat) *n.* any of various birds, mostly songbirds or warblers, such as the stonechat or the whinchat. [from CHAT[1]]

chateau (shat´ō), **château** *n.* (*pl.* **chateaux** (-tōz), **châteaux**) a castle or country house in French-speaking countries. **chateau bottled** *a.* (of wine) bottled on the estate where it was produced. [F, from OF *castel*, CASTLE]

chateaubriand (shatōbrē´ā) *n.* a thick steak of beef cut from the fillet. [Vicomte de *Chateaubriand*, 1768–1848, French writer]

chatelain (shat´əlān) *n.* the lord of a castle. **chatelaine** *n.* **1** a female chatelain. **2** a chain worn on a woman's belt, to which may be attached a watch, keys, trinkets, etc. [F, master of a chateau]

chatoyant (shətoi´ənt, shatwayā´) *a.* having a changeable lustre or colour, like that of a cat's eye in the dark. ~*n.* a stone with changing lustre, such as the cat's-eye. [F, pres.p. of *chatoyer* (*chat*, cat)]

chattel (chat´əl) *n.* (*usu. pl.*) **1** (*Law*) moveable property. **2** (*Law*) any property except freehold land. **3** any personal possession (*goods and chattels*). **chattel mortgage** *n.* (*N Am.*) a mortgage on moveable property. [OF *chatel*, CATTLE]

chatter (chat´ə) *v.i.* **1** to talk idly and thoughtlessly. **2** to jabber, to prattle. **3** (of a bird etc.) to utter rapid, inharmonious sounds. **4** (of the teeth) to make a noise by rattling together. **5** to make a noise resembling this. ~*n.* **1** the sound of chattering. **2** idle talk. **3** the vibration of a tool. **the chattering classes** (*derog. or facet.*) intellectuals etc. considered as a social group enjoying political, social or cultural discussion. **chatterbox** *n.* an incessant talker. **chatterer** *n.* **1** a person who chatters. **2** any of various birds, such as the cotinga. **chattery** *a.* [onomat.]

chatty[1] CHAT[1].

chatty[2] (chat´i) *n.* an Indian earthen pitcher or water-pot. [Hind. *chāṭī*]

Chaucerian (chawsiə´riən) *a.* **1** of or relating to the poet Chaucer. **2** resembling his style. ~*n.* a student of Chaucer. **Chaucerism** (-sər-) *n.* a characteristic of Chaucer or imitated from Chaucer. [Geoffrey *Chaucer*, 1340–1400, English poet]

chaud-froid (shōfrwah´) *n.* a dish of cold meat in an aspic sauce. [F, lit. hot-cold]

chauffeur (shō´fə, -fœ´) *n.* a person employed to drive a motor car. ~*v.t.* to drive (a car or a person) as a chauffeur. ~*v.i.* to act as a chauffeur. **chauffeuse** (shōfœz´) *n.* a female chauffeur. [F *chauffer*, to heat]

chaulmoogra (chawlmoo´grə) *n.* **1** any of various trees of the family Flacourtiaceae, of tropical Asia, esp. *Hydnocarpus kurzii*. **2** oil from the seeds of this tree, used in the treatment of leprosy and other skin diseases. [Bengali]

chautauqua (chawtawk´wə, shə-) *n.* (*Hist.*, *N Am.*) an institution providing adult education, entertainment etc., esp. at outdoor meetings in the summer. [*Chautauqua*, New York State]

chauvinism (shō´vinizm) *n.* **1** exaggerated patriotism of an aggressive kind; jingoism. **2** an exaggerated and excessive attachment to any cause, such as sexism (*male chauvinism*). **chauvinist** *n.* **1** a person who believes their own ethnic group, sex etc. to be superior and despises all others. **2** a male chauvinist. **chauvinistic** (-nis´-) *a.* **chauvinistically** *adv.* [F *chauvinisme*, from Nicolas *Chauvin*, an old soldier of Napoleon]

chaw (chaw) *v.t.* to chew (esp. tobacco). ~*n.* a piece of tobacco for chewing. [CHEW]

chay (shā), **shay** *n.* (*coll.*) a chaise. [corr. of CHAISE (taken as a pl.)]

chayote (chahyō´tā, chīō´ti) *n.* **1** a tropical American climbing plant, *Sechium edule*. **2** the pear-shaped fruit of this plant, eaten as a vegetable. [Sp., Nahuatl *chayotli*]

chay root (chā, chī), **chaya root** (-ə) *n.* the root of an Indian plant, *Oldenlandia umbellata*, which yields a red dye. [Tamil *saya*]

ChB *abbr.* Bachelor of Surgery. [L *Chirurgiae Baccalaureus*]

ChE *abbr.* Chemical Engineer.

cheap (chēp) *a.* **1** low in price. **2** worth more than its price or cost. **3** charging low prices. **4** of poor quality. **5** easy to get; requiring little effort. **6** despicable (*a cheap trick*). ~*adv.* at a low price or cost. **on the cheap 1** cheaply. **2** in a miserly way. **to feel cheap** to feel ashamed or embarrassed. **to hold cheap** to despise. **to make oneself cheap** to behave with undignified familiarity. **cheap and cheerful** *a.* low in price but not unattractive. **cheap and nasty** *a.* low in price and quality. **cheapen** *v.t.* **1** to reduce the price or value of. **2** to depreciate. ~*v.i.* **1** to become cheap. **2** to depreciate. **cheapie** *n.* (*N Am.*, *sl.*) a cheap product. ~*a.* cheap. **cheapish** *a.* **cheapjack** *n.* a person who sells cheap goods of inferior quality. ~*a.* **1** cheap. **2** inferior. **cheaply** *adv.* **cheapness** *n.* **cheapo** *a.* (*sl.*) low in price and usu. of poor quality (*cheapo trainers*). **cheapskate** *n.* (*coll.*) a miserly person. [ME phrase *good cheap* (cp. F *bon marché*), OE *ceap*, price, barter (cp. Goth. *kaupōn*, to trade, G *kaufen*, to buy, *Kauf*, a purchase)]

cheat (chēt) *v.t.* **1** to defraud, to deprive. **2** to deceive, to trick. **3** to avoid or escape, esp. by luck or skill (*to cheat death*). ~*v.i.* to gain unfair advantage in a game, examination etc. by using trickery or deception or by breaking rules. ~*n.* **1** a person who cheats. **2** a trick or deception. **3** a fraud, a swindle. **cheater** *n.* **1** a person who cheats or defrauds. **2** (*pl.*, *N Am.*, *sl.*) spectacles. **to cheat on** (*coll.*) to be unfaithful to (one's wife, husband, lover etc.). [short for ESCHEAT]

Chechen (chech´en) *n.* (*pl.* **Chechens**, **Chechen**) a member of a people inhabiting the autonomous republic of Chechnya in SE Russia. ~*a.* of or relating to this people.

check[1] (chek) *n.* **1** a test for accuracy, quality etc. **2** a sudden stoppage or restraint of motion. **3** a person or thing that stops or restrains motion. **4** a reverse, a repulse, a rebuff. **5** a pause, a halt. **6** restraint, repression. **7** in chess, the situation of a king exposed to direct attack, from which it must be moved or protected. **8** a mark put against names or items in going over a list. **9** a token by which the correctness or authenticity of a document etc. may be ascertained. **10** a token serving for identification. **11** a pass entitling to readmission to a theatre. **12** (*N Am.*) a bill at a restaurant etc. **13** (*N Am.*) a token at cards. **14** (*N Am.*) a left-luggage ticket. ~*v.t.* **1** to test the accuracy, quality etc. of. **2** to confirm, to verify (*Check that the lid is shut*). **3** to cause to stop or slow down. **4** to restrain, to curb. **5** to rebuke. **6** in chess, to put an opponent's king in check. **7** to ease off (a rope etc.). **8** (*N Am.*) to mark with a tick etc. **9** (*N Am.*) to deposit (left-luggage etc.). *~v.i.* **1** to pause, to halt. **2** to agree, to correspond (with). **3** to make sure. *~int.* **1** used in chess when an opponent's king is in check. **2** used to express agreement or correspondence. **in check 1** under control or restraint. **2** (of a king in chess) exposed to direct attack. **to check in** to register on arrival at a hotel, at work etc. **to check off** to mark or tick (an item on a list etc.). **to check on 1** to keep watch on. **2** to check up on. **to check out 1** to leave a hotel, place of work etc. **2** to test for accuracy, quality etc. **3** to investigate. **4** (*N Am., sl.*) to die. **to check over** to examine for faults, errors etc. **to check through** to examine carefully (a series of items) (*to check through the records*). **to check up 1** to investigate. **2** to make sure. **to check up on** to investigate. **checkable** *a.* **check action** *n.* a device for preventing the hammer in a piano from striking twice. **check bit, check digit** *n.* (*Comput.*) a bit or digit used to detect error. **checker**[1] *n.* **check-in** *n.* **1** the act of checking in. **2** a place where one's arrival is registered. **checklist** *n.* **1** a list used in checking for accuracy, completeness etc. **2** an inventory. **checkout** *n.* **1** the act of checking out. **2** a cash desk at a supermarket. **checkpoint** *n.* a place (as at a frontier) where documents etc. are checked. **check-rein** *n.* **1** a bearing-rein. **2** a branch rein coupling horses in a team. **checkroom** *n.* **1** (*N Am.*) **a** a cloakroom. **b** a left-luggage office. **check sum** *n.* a digit that represents the sum of the digits in a digital signal, used as a check against errors. **check-up** *n.* a general examination (esp. medical). **check valve** *n.* a valve that allows a flow in only one direction. [OF *eschec*, Arab. *shāg*, Pers. *shāh*, a king]

check[2] (chek) *n.* **1** a chequered pattern, a cross-lined pattern. **2** a fabric having such a pattern. *~a.* having such a pattern (*a check shirt*). **checked** *a.* **checky** *a.* [short for *checker*, CHEQUER]

check[3] CHEQUE. **checking account** (chek´ing) *n.* (*N Am.*) a current account. [CHECK[1]]

checker[1] CHECK[1].

checker[2] CHEQUER.

checkerberry (chek´əberi) *n.* (*pl.* **checkerberries**) **1** a N American shrub, *Gaultheria procumbens*, with white flowers and edible red fruit. **2** the fruit of this plant. [*checkers*, CHEQUER]

checkerman, checkers CHEQUER.

checkmate (chek´māt) *n.* **1** in chess, the winning move or situation when one king is in check and cannot escape from that position. **2** a complete defeat. **3** a position from which there is no escape. *~int.* used in chess when an opponent's king is put into this position. *~v.t.* **1** to give checkmate to. **2** to defeat utterly, to frustrate. [OF *eschec mat*, Pers. *shāh māt*, the king is dead; see CHECK[1]]

Cheddar (ched´ə) *n.* a hard, strong-flavoured yellow cheese. [village in Somerset, near the Mendip Hills]

cheddite (ched´īt) *n.* an explosive made from a chlorate or perchlorate mixed with castor oil. [*Chedde*, town in France where first made]

cheek (chēk) *n.* **1** the side of the face below the eye. **2** impudent speech. **3** (*coll.*) impudence, sauciness. **4** effrontery, assurance (*He had the cheek to excuse me of lying*). **5** a side-post of a door, the side of a pulley. **6** either of two corresponding sides of a frame, machine, or implement. **7** (*sl.*) a buttock. *~v.t.* to be impudent to. **cheek by jowl 1** side by side. **2** in the closest proximity. **to turn the other cheek** to accept a physical or verbal attack without retaliation. **cheekbone** *n.* the prominence of the malar bone. **cheekpouch** *n.* a pouch in the mouth of some mammals, esp. rodents, used to hold food. **cheeky** *a.* (*comp.* **cheekier**, *superl.* **cheekiest**) impudent, saucy. **cheekily** *adv.* **cheekiness** *n.* [OE *cēace*, from Gmc. (cp. Dut. *kaak*, Swed. *kāk*)]

cheep (chēp) *v.i.* to chirp feebly. *~n.* the feeble cry of a young bird. **cheeper** *n.* a young bird. [onomat.]

cheer (chiə) *n.* **1** a shout of joy, encouragement or applause. **2** disposition, frame of mind, mood (*of good cheer*). **3** a state of gladness or joy. *~v.t.* **1** to make glad or cheerful. **2** to applaud or encourage with cheers. *~v.i.* **1** to grow cheerful. **2** to utter a cheer or cheers. **to cheer up 1** to make more cheerful. **2** to become more cheerful. **cheerful** *a.* **1** contented. **2** full of good spirits. **3** lively, animated. **4** willing. **5** hopeful. **cheerfully** *adv.* **cheerfulness** *n.* **cheering** *a.* **cheeringly** *adv.* **cheerio** (-riō´), **cheer-ho** (-hō´) *int.* **1** goodbye. **2** †a drinking toast. **cheerleader** *n.* (*N Am.*) a person who leads organized cheering at a rally, football game etc. **cheerless** *a.* dull, gloomy, dispiriting. **cheerlessly** *adv.* **cheerlessness** *n.* **cheerly** *adv.* (*Naut.*) cheerfully, heartily. *~a.* †cheerful. **cheers** *int.* (*coll.*) **1** a drinking toast. **2** thank you. **3** goodbye. **cheery** *a.* (*comp.* **cheerier**, *superl.* **cheeriest**) lively, sprightly, full of good spirits, genial. **cheerily** *adv.* **cheeriness** *n.* [ME and OF *chere*, the face, look, late L *cara*, face, perh. from Gr. *kara*, head]

cheese[1] (chēz) *n.* **1** the curd of milk pressed into a solid mass and ripened by keeping. **2** a cylindrical or spherical block of this. **3** anything of cheeselike form or consistency. **hard cheese** HARD. **say cheese!** used by photographers to encourage people to smile. **cheeseboard** *n.* **1** a board on which cheese is served at table. **2** the variety of cheeses on such a board. **cheeseburger** *n.* a hamburger with a slice of cheese on top. **cheesecake** *n.* **1** a kind of tart made of pastry or biscuit crumbs with a filling of cream cheese, sugar etc. **2** (*sl.*) young and attractive women, esp. scantily clad or nude. **3** pictures of such women. **cheesecloth** *n.* **1** thin cotton cloth loosely woven. **2** butter muslin. **cheese-cutter** *n.* **1** a knife with broad curved blade. **2** a device for cutting cheese, comprising a board with a wire that is pulled through the cheese. **cheese-fly** *n.* (*pl.* **cheese-flies**) a fly, *Piophila casei*, bred in cheese. **cheese-head** *a.* (of a screw or bolt) having a slotted head shaped like a short thick cylinder. **cheese-hopper** *n.* the larva of the cheese-fly. **cheesemaker** *n.* a maker of cheese. **cheesemaking** *n.* **cheese-mite** *n.* any mite of the genus *Tyroglyphus*, infesting old cheese and other foodstuffs. **cheesemonger** *n.* a person who deals in cheese, butter etc. **cheese-paring** *a.* niggardly, mean, miserly. *~n.* **1** meanness, stinginess. **2** (*pl.*) scraps of cheese. **3** (*pl.*) odds and ends. **cheese plant** *n.* SWISS CHEESE PLANT (under SWISS). **cheesepress** *n.* a device in which curds are pressed in making cheese. **cheese-skipper** *n.* the cheese-fly. **cheese straw** *n.* a long thin strip of cheese-flavoured pastry. **cheesewood** *n.* **1** an Australian tree of the genus *Pittosporum* with a hard wood of a yellowish colour. **2** the wood of this tree. **cheesy** *a.* (*comp.* **cheesier**, *superl.* **cheesiest**) **1** resembling or tasting like cheese. **2** (*coll.*) (of a smile or grin) broad but usu. insincere. **3** (*sl.*) corny. **cheesiness** *n.* [OE *cēse* (cp. Dut *kaas*, G *Käse*, L *cāseus*)]

cheese[2] (chēz) *n.* (*sl.*) **1** an important person. **2** †the real thing, the correct thing. **big cheese** BIG. [etym. uncertain]

cheese[3] (chēz) *v.t.* (*sl.*) **1** to stop. **2** to annoy or exasperate. **cheesed off** (*coll.*) bored, annoyed. **to cheese it 1** (*sl.*) †to desist. **2** (*N Am., sl.*) to run away. [etym. unknown]

cheetah (chē´tə), **chetah** *n.* a leopard-like mammal, *Acinonyx jubatus*, the swiftest land animal. [Hind. *chītā* (Sansk. *chitraka*, spotted)]

chef (shef) *n.* a professional cook, esp. the head cook of a restaurant etc. **chef de cuisine** (də kwēzēn´) *n.* a head cook. [F, CHIEF]

chef-d'oeuvre (shādœv´rə) *n.* (*pl.* **chefs-d'oeuvre** (shādœv´rə)) a masterpiece. [as CHEF, F *oeuvre*, work]

☒ **cheif** common misspelling of CHIEF.

cheil-, cheilo- CHILO-.
cheir-, cheiro- CHIRO-.
Cheka (chek´ə) *n.* (*Hist.*) the secret police in Russia (1917–22). [names of initial letters of Rus. *Chrezvichainaya Kommissiya*, extraordinary commission]
Chekhovian (chekō´viən) *a.* of, resembling or relating to the style or works of the dramatist Chekhov. [Anton *Chekhov*, 1860–1904, Russian dramatist]
chela[1] (kē´lə) *n.* (*pl.* **chelae** (-lē)) a claw (as of a lobster or crab), a modified thoracic limb. **chelate** (-lāt) *n.* (*Chem.*) a compound with molecules that contain a closed ring of atoms, including one metal atom. ~*a.* **1** (*Zool.*) of, relating to or having chelae. **2** (*Chem.*) of, relating to or forming a chelate. ~*v.i.* (*Chem.*) to form a chelate. **chelation** (-lā´-) *n.* [Gr. *chēlē*]
chela[2] (chā´lə) *n.* (*pl.* **chelas**) a student or novice in esoteric Buddhism. [Hind. *chēlā*, servant, pupil]
chelate, chelae etc. CHELA[1].
cheli- (kel´i) *comb. form* of or relating to a claw or claws. [Gr. *chēlē*, a claw]
chelicer (kilis´ərə) *n.* (*pl.* **chelicerae** (-rē)) either of the clawlike appendages on the head of scorpions and spiders. **cheliceral** *a.* **chelicerate** (-rāt, -rət) *a.* of or relating to the Chelicerata, a subphylum of arthropods with chelicerae. ~*n.* any of these arthropods. [F *chélicère*, mod. L *chelicera* (Gr. *chēlē*, a claw, *keras*, a horn)]
cheliferous (kelif´ərəs) *a.* (*Zool.*) having a chela or chelae.
cheliform (kel´ifawm) *a.* like a claw in form or shape.
cheliped (kel´iped) *n.* (*Zool.*) either of the pair of legs carrying chelae.
Chellean (shel´iən) *a.* of or relating to the period of Lower Palaeolithic culture typified by the remains found at Chelles in the valley of the Marne; Abbevillian. [*Chelles*, 13 km E of Paris, -AN]
chelone (kilō´ni) *n.* any plant of the genus *Chelone*, cultivated for its white, pink or purple flowers. [as CHELONIAN]
chelonian (kilō´niən) *n.* any reptile of the order Chelonia, containing the turtles and tortoises. ~*a.* of or relating to this order. [L, from Gr. *chelōnē*, tortoise]
Chelsea bun (chel´si) *n.* a bun made of a roll of sweet dough with raisins. **Chelsea pensioner** *n.* an old or disabled ex-soldier, an inmate of the Chelsea Royal Hospital. **Chelsea ware** *n.* a type of 18th-cent. china. [*Chelsea*, district in London]
chem. *abbr.* **1** chemical. **2** chemistry.
chem-, chemi- CHEMO-.
chemical (kem´ikəl) *a.* **1** of or relating to chemistry, its laws or phenomena. **2** of or produced by chemical process. ~*n.* a substance or agent produced by or used in chemistry or chemical processes. **chemical bond** *n.* a mutual attraction that holds atoms together in a molecule etc. **chemical change** *n.* a change involving the formation of a new substance. **chemical engineer** *n.* a specialist in chemical engineering. **chemical engineering** *n.* the branch of engineering concerned with the design and building of industrial chemical plants. **chemically** *adv.* **chemical reaction** *n.* the process of changing one substance into another. **chemical symbol** *n.* a letter or letters used to represent an atom of a chemical element. **chemical warfare** *n.* war waged using poisonous chemicals (gases, sprays, etc.). **chemical weapon** *n.* a weapon used in chemical warfare. [F *chimique*, or mod. L *chymicus* (see ALCHEMY)]
chemico- (kem´ikō) *comb. form* chemical. **chemicoelectric** *a.* of, relating to or produced by chemistry in conjunction with electricity.
chemiluminescence (kemiloomines´əns) *n.* luminescence occurring as a result of a chemical reaction, without production of heat. **chemiluminescent** *a.*
chemin de fer (shəmĩ də feə´) *n.* a variety of baccarat. [F, railway]
chemise (shəmēz´) *n.* **1** an undergarment of linen or cotton worn by women. **2** a straight, loose-fitting dress. **chemisette** (shemizet´) *n.* **1** a woman's light bodice. **2** a piece of lace worn in the opening of a dress below the throat. [F, from late L *camisia* (cp. OE *ham*, Goth. *af-hamōn*, to unclothe)]
chemisorption (kemisawp´shən) *n.* a process of adsorption involving chemical bonds. [CHEM-, ADSORPTION (under ADSORB)]
chemist (kem´ist) *n.* **1** a scientist specializing in chemistry. **2** a person qualified to dispense drugs, a pharmacist. **3** a shop where drugs, toiletries etc. are sold. [F *chimiste*, mod. L *chimista*, *chymista*, *alchimista*, ALCHEMIST (under ALCHEMY)]
chemistry (kem´istri) *n.* (*pl.* **chemistries**) **1** the science which investigates the elements of which bodies are composed, the combination of these elements, and the reaction of these chemical compounds on each other (*organic chemistry*; *inorganic chemistry*). **2** the practical application of this science. **3** the chemical composition, properties etc. of a substance. **4** any process or change conceived as analogous to chemical action, esp. emotional attraction. **inorganic chemistry** INORGANIC. **organic chemistry** ORGANIC. **physical chemistry** PHYSICAL. [as CHEMIST]
chemmy (shem´i) *n.* chemin de fer. [abbr.]
chemo- (kē´mō), **chemi-** (kem´i), **chem-** *comb. form* chemical.
chemoreceptor (kēmōrisep´tə, kem-) *n.* a sensory nerve ending which responds to a chemical stimulus.
chemosynthesis (kēmōsin´thəsis, kem-) *n.* the production of organic material by some bacteria, using chemical reactions.
chemotaxis (kēmōtak´sis, kem-) *n.* the property possessed by some cells or microorganisms of being drawn towards or repelled by certain chemical substances. **chemotactic** *a.*
chemotherapy (kēmōthe´rəpi, kem-) *n.* the treatment of disease, esp. cancer, by drugs. **chemotherapist** *n.*
chemurgy (kem´əji) *n.* the branch of chemistry which is devoted to the industrial utilization of organic raw material, esp. farm products. **chemurgic** (-œ´jik) *a.* [Gr. *ergos*, working]
chenille (shənēl´) *n.* **1** a round tufted or fluffy cord of silk or worsted. **2** a pile fabric made with similar yarn. [F, hairy caterpillar, L *canicula*, little dog, dim. of *canis*, dog]
cheongsam (chongsam´, chiong-) *n.* a Chinese woman's long, tight-fitting dress with slit sides. [Chin.]
cheque (chek), (*N Am.*) **check** *n.* **1** a draft on a bank for money payable to the bearer. **2** the printed form bearing such an order. **chequebook** *n.* a book containing cheques. **chequebook journalism** *n.* sensational journalism using stories bought at high prices. **cheque card** *n.* a card issued by a bank, guaranteeing payment of cheques up to a specified limit. [CHECK[1]]
chequer (chek´ə), (*N Am.*) **checker** *n.* **1** (*usu. pl.*) a pattern made of squares in alternating colours, like a chessboard. **2** (*pl., usu. sing. in constr.*) the game of draughts. **3** any of the pieces used in the game of Chinese chequers. ~*v.t.* **1** to form into a pattern of small squares. **2** to variegate. **3** to diversify, to fill with vicissitudes (*a chequered career*). **checkerman** *n.* (*pl.* **checkermen**) (*N Am.*) any of the pieces used in the game of draughts. **checkers** *n.pl.* (*N Am., usu. sing. in constr.*) the game of draughts. **chequer-board** *n.* **1** a chess-board. **2** a pattern resembling this. **chequered flag** *n.* a flag with black and white squares used to signal the finish in a motor race. **chequerwork** *n.* any work having a pattern of small squares. [OF *eschekier*, chessboard, late L *scaccarium*, EXCHEQUER]
Cherenkov radiation CERENKOV RADIATION.
cherish (cher´ish) *v.t.* **1** to hold dear, to treat with

affection, to protect lovingly. **2** to hold closely to, to cling to (*to cherish hopes of success*). **cherishable** *a.* **cherishingly** *adv.* [OF *cherir* (pres.p. *cherissant*), from *cher*, L *cārus*, dear]

chernozem (chœ´nəzem), **tschernosem** *n.* a dark-coloured, very fertile soil found in temperate climates. [Rus., black earth]

Cherokee (cherəkē´) *n.* (*pl.* **Cherokees, Cherokee**) **1** a member of a N American Indian people now chiefly living in Oklahoma. **2** the language of this people. ~*a.* of or relating to this people or their language. **Cherokee rose** *n.* a climbing rose, *Rosa laevigata*, with white flowers, which grows wild in the southern US.

cheroot (shəroot´) *n.* a cigar with both ends cut square off. [F *cheroute*, Tamil *shuruttu*, a roll of tobacco]

cherry (cher´i) *n.* (*pl.* **cherries**) **1** a small stonefruit of the plum family. **2** any tree of the genus *Prunus* on which this fruit grows. **3** the wood of this tree. **4** the colour of a red cherry. **5** (*sl.*) virginity. ~*a.* of the colour of a red cherry. **two bites at the cherry** a second chance (*You can't have two bites at the cherry*). **cherry brandy** *n.* a red liqueur made from brandy in which cherries have been steeped. **cherry laurel** *n.* an evergreen shrub, *Prunus laurocerasus*, with white flowers and small fruits resembling cherries. **cherry-pick** *v.i.* to select or take the best people, items etc. from a group. **cherry picker** *n.* a hydraulic crane with a platform at the end, used to raise and lower people working on overhead cables, high buildings etc. **cherry pie** *n.* **1** a pie made with cherries. **2** the garden heliotrope. **cherry plum** *n.* **1** a small Asian tree, *Prunus cerasifera*, with white flowers and cherry-like fruits. **2** the fruit of this tree. **cherry red** *n.* the colour of a red cherry. ~*a.* of this colour. **cherry stone** *n.* the endocarp of the cherry. **cherry tomato** *n.* (*pl.* **cherry tomatoes**) a strong-flavoured miniature tomato. **cherry tree** *n.* the tree on which the cherry grows. **cherrywood** *n.* the wood of the cherry tree. [ME *chery*, ONF *cherise* (OF *cerise*), L *cerasus*, Gr. *kerasos*; (for loss of *s*, cp. PEA)]

chersonese (kœsənēs´, -nēz´, kœ´-) *n.* a peninsula, esp. the Thracian peninsula. [L *chersonesus*, Gr. *chersonēsos* (*chersos*, dry, *nēsos*, an island)]

chert (chœt) *n.* a flinty type of quartz; hornstone. **cherty** *a.* resembling or containing chert. [orig. unknown]

cherub (cher´əb) *n.* (*pl.* **cherubs, cherubim** (-im)) **1** a celestial spirit next in order to the seraphim. **2** a beautiful child. **3** in art, the winged head of a child. **cherubic** (-roo´-) *a.* **1** of or relating to cherubs. **2** angelic. **3** full-cheeked and ruddy. **cherubically** *adv.* [Heb. *k'rūb*, *k'rūv*, pl. *k'rūvīm*]

chervil (chœ´vil) *n.* a garden herb, *Anthriscus cerefolium*, used in soups, salads etc. [OE *caerfille*, L *chaerephylla*, pl., Gr. *chairephullon* (*chairein*, to rejoice, *phullon*, leaf)]

Cheshire (chesh´ə), **Cheshire cheese** *n.* a mild-flavoured white or red cheese with a firm but crumbly texture, originally made in Cheshire. **to grin like a Cheshire cat** to grin broadly. [county in England]

chess[1] (ches) *n.* a game played by two persons with 16 pieces each on a board divided into 64 squares. **chessboard** *n.* the board on which chess is played. **chessman** *n.* (*pl.* **chessmen**) any of the pieces used in chess. **chess set** *n.* a set comprising 32 chessmen and a chessboard. [OF *esches*, pl. of *eschec*, CHECK[1]]

chess[2] (ches) *n.* (*usu. pl.*) any of the parallel baulks of timber used in laying a pontoon bridge. [etym. uncertain; perh. from CHESS[1]]

chessel (ches´əl) *n.* a cheese mould. [CHEESE[1]]

chest (chest) *n.* **1** a large strong box. **2** a case for holding particular commodities (*a tea chest*). **3** the quantity such a case holds. **4** a small cabinet (*a medicine chest*). **5** the fore part of the human body from the neck to the waist. **6** the treasury or funds of an institution. **to get off one's chest 1** (*coll.*) to unburden oneself of (a secret etc.). **2** (*coll.*) to admit, to declare. **to play one's cards close to one's chest** CARD[1]. **-chested** *comb.form* having a chest of a specified kind. **chest freezer** *n.* a large freezer, opening at the top. **chest of drawers** *n.* a movable wooden frame containing drawers. **chest voice** *n.* the lowest singing or speaking register of the voice. **chesty** *a.* (*comp.* **chestier**, *superl.* **chestiest**) (*coll.*) **1** suffering from, or subject to, bronchitis etc. **2** having a large chest or large breasts. **3** (*N Am.*) arrogant, self-important. **chestily** *adv.* **chestiness** *n.* [OE *cest*, L *cista*, Gr. *kistē*]

chesterfield (ches´təfēld) *n.* **1** a deeply upholstered sofa with curved arms and back of the same height. **2** a loose kind of overcoat. [Earl of *Chesterfield*]

chestnut (ches´nŭt) *n.* **1** any tree of the genus *Castanea*, esp. the Spanish or sweet chestnut, *C. sativa*. **2** the edible fruit of this tree. **3** the reddish-brown colour of this fruit. **4** a horse of this colour. **5** the horse chestnut tree or its fruit. **6** (*coll.*) a stale joke or anecdote. **7** in horses, a knob on the inside of the forelegs. ~*a.* reddish-brown. [formerly *chesten*, *chesteine*, OF *chastaigne* (F *châtaigne*), L *castanea*, Gr. *kastanea* (prob. a place-name), NUT]

chetah CHEETAH.

chetnik (chet´nik) *n.* (*Hist.*) a member of a Serbian nationalist guerrilla force active before and during the two World Wars. [Serb. *četnik*, (*četa*, a troop)]

cheval-de-frise (shəvaldəfrēz´) *n.* (*pl.* **chevaux-de-frise** (-vō-)) a portable fence, consisting of a bar armed with two rows of long spikes, for checking attacks by cavalry etc. [F, a Friesland horse]

cheval glass (shəval´) *n.* a large swinging mirror mounted on a frame. [F *cheval*, a horse, a support, GLASS]

chevalier (shevəliə´) *n.* **1** a member of some foreign orders of knighthood or of the French Legion of Honour. **2** †a knight. **3** a chivalrous man. [F (*cheval*, L *caballus*, horse)]

chevet (shəvā´) *n.* an apse. [F, pillow]

cheviot (chē´viət, chev´-) *n.* **1** (**Cheviot**) a breed of sheep with short thick wool. **2** rough cloth made from the wool of such sheep. [*Cheviot* Hills on the border between England and Scotland, where the sheep were bred]

chèvre (shev´rə) *n.* a type of cheese made from goats' milk. [F, a goat, L *capra*]

chevrette (shəvret´) *n.* a thin goatskin leather used for gloves. [F, dim. of *chèvre*, L *capra*, a goat]

chevron (shev´rən) *n.* **1** a V-shaped badge on the sleeve of a uniform, esp. of a non-commissioned officer in the armed forces. **2** one of a series of horizontal V-shaped marks on a road sign, usu. indicating a bend. **3** (*Her.*) an inverted V shape, an honourable ordinary representing two rafters meeting at the top. **4** (*Archit.*) a zigzag moulding. **5** any V-shaped stripe or pattern. [F, rafter, from L *capreoli*, used of a pair of rafters]

chevrotain (shev´rətān), **chevrotin** (-tin) *n.* a small animal of the family Tragulidae, resembling a deer. [F, dim. of OF *chevrot*, dim. of *chèvre*, a goat, L *capra*]

chevy CHIVVY.

chew (choo) *v.t.* **1** to masticate, to grind with the teeth. **2** to ruminate on, to digest mentally. ~*v.i.* **1** to masticate food. **2** to chew tobacco or gum. **3** to meditate. ~*n.* **1** the act of chewing. **2** something to be chewed, esp. a sweet. **3** a quid of tobacco. **to chew on 1** to grind continuously with the teeth. **2** to ruminate on. **to chew out** (*N Am.*, *coll.*) to reprimand. **to chew over 1** to discuss. **2** to think about. **to chew the cud** CUD. **to chew the fat 1** (*sl.*) to chat. **2** (*sl.*) to grumble, to complain. **to chew the rag** (*sl.*) to chew the fat. **to chew up 1** to damage or destroy by chewing or by a similar grinding action. **2** (*usu. pass.*, *coll.*) to make nervous or worried.

chewable *a.* **chewie** *n.* (*sl.*) chewing gum. **chewing gum** *n.* a preparation of flavoured insoluble gum for chewing. **chewy** *a.* (*comp.* **chewier,** *superl.* **chewiest**) firm-textured, suitable for or requiring much chewing. **chewiness** *n.* [OE *cēowan,* from Gmc. (cp. Dut. *kaauwen,* OHG *kiuwan,* G *kauen*)]

Cheyenne (shīan´) *n.* (*pl.* **Cheyennes, Cheyenne**) **1** a member of a N American Indian people now chiefly living in Montana and Oklahoma. **2** this people. **3** the language of this people. ~*a.* of or relating to this people or their language. [Can. F., Sioux *Sahiyena*]

Cheyne–Stokes (chānstōks´) *a.* of or denoting a cycle of respiration, esp. in comatose patients, in which breathing gradually becomes shallower, stops, then gradually increases again. [J. *Cheyne,* Sc. physician d. 1836, and W. *Stokes,* Ir. physician, d. 1878]

chez (shā) *prep.* at the house of. [F]

chg. *abbr.* charge.

chi (kī) *n.* the 22nd letter of the Greek alphabet (χ, X). [Gr.]

chiack (chī´ak), **chyack** *v.t.* (*Austral., coll.*) to tease, to poke fun at. ~*n.* teasing, banter. [*chi-hike,* a shout or greeting]

Chian (kī´ən) *a.* of or relating to Chios. ~*n.* a native or inhabitant of Chios.

Chianti (kian´ti) *n.* (*pl.* **Chiantis**) a dry red wine from Tuscany. [region of Italy]

chiaroscuro (kiahrəskoo´rō, -skuə´-) *n.* (*pl.* **chiaroscuros**) **1** the treatment or effects of light and shade in drawing, painting etc. **2** a drawing in black and white. **3** variety or contrast in a literary work etc. ~*a.* **1** obscure. **2** half-revealed. [It. (*chiaro,* L *clārus,* clear, bright, *oscuro,* L *obscūrus,* dark)]

chiasma (kīaz´mə), **chiasm** (kī´azm) *n.* (*pl.* **chiasmas, chiasmata** (-mətə), **chiasms**) **1** the connection or point of contact between paired chromosomes after crossing over during meiosis. **2** the crossing or decussation of the optic nerves. [Gr. *chiasma* (*chiazein,* to mark with a χ)]

chiasmus (kīaz´məs) *n.* (*pl.* **chiasmi** (-mī)) the inversion of order in parallel phrases, as in *you came late, to go early would be unreasonable.* **chiastic** (-as´tik) *a.* [Gr. *chiasmos,* crossing (as CHIASMA)]

chibouk (chibook´), **chibouque** *n.* a long Turkish pipe for smoking. [Turk. *çubuk*]

chic (shēk) *n.* **1** smartness, style. **2** the best fashion or taste. ~*a.* (*comp.* **chic-er,** *superl.* **chic-est**) stylish, elegant, fashionable. **chicly** *adv.* [F, etym. unknown]

Chicana CHICANO.

chicane (shikān´) *n.* **1** an artificial obstacle on a motor-racing track. **2** in bridge or whist, a hand of cards containing no trumps. **3** chicanery. ~*v.i.* †to use chicanery. ~*v.t.* †to cheat, to deceive. **chicanery** (-nəri) *n.* (*pl.* **chicaneries**) **1** artifice, deception or subterfuge, esp. legal trickery. **2** quibbling, pettifogging. [F, etym. uncertain (perh. from med. Gr. *tzukanion,* Pers. *chaugān,* a polo club)]

Chicano (chikah´nō, -kā´nō) *n.* (*pl.* **Chicanos**) a person of Mexican origin living in the US. **Chicana** *n.* (*pl.* **Chicanas**) a female Chicano. [from Sp. *mejicano,* Mexican]

chiccory CHICORY.

chichi (shē´shē) *a.* **1** showy, affectedly pretty or fashionable. **2** (of a person) fussy; pretentious; affected. ~*n.* **1** the quality of being chichi. **2** something that is chichi. [F]

chick[1] (chik) *n.* **1** a young bird about to be hatched or newly hatched. **2** (*coll.*) a young child. **3** (*sl.*) a young woman. **chickabiddy** (-əbidi) *n.* (*pl.* **chickabiddies**) a term of endearment for a child. **chickweed** *n.* **1** a garden weed, *Stellaria media,* with small white flowers. **2** any of various similar plants. [CHICKEN]

chick[2] (chik) *n.* (*Ang.-Ind.*) a door screen or blind made from strips of bamboo fastened together with twine. [Hind. *chik*]

chickadee (chik´ədē) *n.* any of various N American songbirds of the tit family, such as *Parus atricapillus.* [imit.]

chicken (chik´ən) *n.* **1** the young of the domestic fowl. **2** a domestic fowl prepared for the table. **3** the flesh of this. **4** a young or inexperienced person. **5** (*coll.*) a coward. **6** (*coll.*) a game involving a test of courage or recklessness. ~*a.* (*coll.*) cowardly. **no chicken** no longer young; older than he or she appears. **to chicken out** (*coll.*) to lose one's nerve. **to count one's chickens (before they are hatched)** to make plans which depend on something uncertain. **chicken-and-egg** *a.* of or denoting a situation in which it is impossible to distinguish between cause and effect. **chicken-breast** *n.* pigeon-breast. **chicken-breasted** *a.* pigeon-breasted. **chicken brick** *n.* an earthenware cooking vessel in two halves, in which a chicken can be roasted in its own fat. **chicken cholera** *n.* a disease affecting the domestic fowl. **chicken feed** *n.* **1** food for poultry. **2** (*coll.*) an insignificant sum of money. **3** (*coll.*) a trifling amount or matter. **chicken-hearted, chicken-livered** *a.* timid, cowardly. **chickenpox** *n.* an infectious disease, usually occurring in childhood, characterized by fever and a rash of small blisters. **chicken wire** *n.* wire netting with a small hexagonal mesh. [OE *cīcen,* pl. *cīcenu* (cp. Dut. *kieken,* G *Küchlein,* Eng. COCK[1])]

chickling (chik´ling), **chickling vetch** *n.* the cultivated vetch. [formerly *chicheling,* dim. of *chiche,* OF *chiche,* L *cicer*]

chickpea (chik´pē) *n.* **1** a dwarf species of pea, *Cicer arietinum.* **2** the edible seed of this plant. [earlier *chich,* later *chich-pease,* see CHICKLING and PEA]

chickweed CHICK[1].

chicle (chik´əl) *n.* the juice of the sapodilla, used in the making of chewing gum. [Nahuatl *tzictli*]

chicory (chik´əri), **chiccory** *n.* (*pl.* **chicories, chiccories**) **1** a blue-flowered plant, *Cichorium intybus,* the succory. **2** the root of this plant, roasted and ground for use as a coffee additive. **3** the endive. [F *chichorée, cichorée,* L *cichorium,* Gr. *kichōrion, kichōrē,* succory]

chide (chīd) *v.t.* (*past* **chided** (chid), **chid,** *p.p.* **chided, chid, chidden**) **1** to find fault with, to reprove. **2** to drive by scolding. ~*v.i.* **1** to scold. **2** to make a complaining sound. **chider** *n.* **chidingly** *adv.* [OE *cīdan*]

chief (chēf) *a.* **1** principal, first. **2** highest in authority. **3** most important, leading, main. ~*n.* **1** a leader or commander, esp. the leader of a tribe or clan. **2** the head of a department. **3** the principal thing. **4** the largest part. **5** (*Her.*) the upper third of a shield. **Chief Constable** *n.* the officer in charge of the police force of a county or other area. **chiefdom** *n.* **chiefess** (-es´) *n.* a female chief. **chief justice** *n.* in several countries, the judge presiding over the highest court. **chiefless** *a.* without a chief or leader. **chiefly** *adv.* **1** principally, especially. **2** for the most part. **Chief of Staff** *n.* the senior officer of a division of the armed forces. **Chief Rabbi** *n.* the religious head of a Jewish community. **chiefship** *n.* **chief technician** *n.* a non-commissioned officer in the Royal Air Force ranking between sergeant and flight sergeant. [OF *chef,* L *caput,* head]

chieftain (chēf´tən) *n.* **1** a general, a leader. **2** the head of a tribe or a Highland clan. **chieftaincy** *n.* (*pl.* **chieftaincies**). **chieftainess** *n.* a female chieftain. **chieftainry, chieftanship** *n.* [OF *chevetain,* late L *capitānus,* CAPTAIN]

chiffchaff (chif´chaf) *n.* a European warbler, *Phylloscopus collybita.* [onomat.]

chiffon (shif´on) *n.* **1** a gauzy semi-transparent fabric. **2** (*pl.*) trimmings, esp. of dresses. ~*a.* **1** made of chiffon. **2** (of puddings) having a fine, light consistency. **chiffonier** (-niə´), **chiffonnier** *n.* **1** a movable piece of furniture serving as a cupboard and sideboard. 2 (*esp. NAm.*) a tall chest of drawers. [F (*chiffe*, a rag)]

chigger (chig´ə) 1 a small W Indian and S American flea, *Tunga penetrans*. 2 (*NAm.*) a harvest mite or its larva. [CHIGOE]

chignon (shēn´yō) *n.* a coil or knot of long hair at the back of the head. [F, earlier *chaignon* (*chaignon du col*, nape of the neck), var. of *chaînon*, ring or link (*chaîne*, CHAIN)]

chigoe (chig´ō) *n.* the flea *Tunga penetrans*, a chigger. [W Indian form of Sp. *chico*, small]

chihuahua (chiwah´wah) *n.* (*pl.* **chihuahuas**) 1 a very small dog with big eyes and pointed ears. 2 this breed of dog. [*Chihuahua*, state and city in Mexico]

chil- CHILO-.

chilblain (chil´blān) *n.* an inflamed swelling of the hands or feet caused by bad circulation and cold. **chilblained** *a.* **chilblainy** *a.* [CHILL, BLAIN]

child (chīld) *n.* (*pl.* **children** (chil´drən)) 1 a boy or girl. 2 a son or daughter. 3 an infant, a baby. 4 an unborn baby. 5 a young person. 6 an inexperienced or childish person. 7 (*pl.*) descendants. 8 (*pl.*) the inhabitants of a country. 9 (*pl.*) disciples. 10 a person whose character is the result (of a specified environment etc.) (*a child of nature*). **child abuse** *n.* ill-treatment or neglect of a child, esp. physical or sexual abuse. **child allowance** *n.* 1 child benefit. 2 (*Hist.*) a tax allowance granted to parents of children. **childbearing** *n.* the act of carrying and giving birth to children. ~*a.* of or relating to this (*of childbearing age*). †**childbed** *n.* the state of a woman in labour; childbirth. **child benefit** *n.* a sum of money paid regularly by the state to the parent of a child. **childbirth** *n.* the time or act of giving birth to a child. **childcare** *n.* 1 daytime care and supervision provided for children while their parents are working. 2 residential care provided for children whose parents are unable to look after them. **child-centred** *a.* centred on the needs, interests etc. of the child (*child-centred education*). **child endowment** *n.* (*Austral.*) child benefit. **child guidance** *n.* professional counselling of children who are emotionally disturbed, disruptive etc. **childhood** *n.* 1 the state of being a child. 2 the period from birth to puberty. **childish** *a.* 1 of or befitting a child. 2 silly, puerile. **childishly** *adv.* **childishness** *n.* **child labour** *n.* the full-time employment of children below the legal minimum age. **childless** *a.* without offspring. **childlessness** *n.* **childlike** *a.* 1 resembling or befitting a child. 2 docile, simple, innocent, frank. **childminder** *n.* a person who looks after other people's children for payment. **child molester** *n.* a person who sexually abuses a child. **childproof** *a.* designed to be impossible for a child to operate or damage (*a childproof lock*). **child's play** *n.* easy work. [OE *cild*, from Gmc. (cp. Goth. *kilthei*, the womb, Dan. *kuld*, Swed. *kull*, a litter)]

†**Childermas** (chil´dəməs) *n.* the festival of Holy Innocents (28 Dec.). [OE *cildru*, *mæsse*, MASS]

children CHILD.

chile CHILLI.

Chilean (chil´iən) *n.* a native or inhabitant of Chile in S America. ~*a.* of or relating to Chile.

Chile pine (chil´i) *n.* the monkey-puzzle tree. **Chile saltpetre, Chile nitre** *n.* a form of sodium nitrate that occurs naturally, esp. in Chile and Peru. [*Chile*, republic in S America]

chili CHILLI.

chiliad (kil´iad) *n.* 1 a thousand. 2 a thousand years. [Gr. *chilias -ados* (*chilioi*, a thousand)]

chiliasm (kil´iazm) *n.* the doctrine of the millennium. **chiliast** *n.* **chiliastic** (-as´-) *a.* [Gr. *chiliasmos*, from *chilias*]

chill (chil) *n.* 1 coldness, a fall in bodily temperature. 2 a cold (*to catch a chill*). 3 a cold, shivering sensation preceding fever. 4 coldness of the air etc. 5 coldness of manner etc. 6 a check, a discouragement. 7 disappointment, depression. ~*v.t.* 1 to make cold. 2 to preserve (meat etc.) by cold. 3 to cool (wine etc.). 4 to cool (metal) suddenly so as to harden. 5 to depress, to dispirit, to discourage. 6 to frighten. ~*v.i.* 1 to become cold. 2 (*esp. NAm., coll.*) to hang around. ~*a.* chilly. **to chill out** (*esp. NAm., coll.*) to relax. **to take the chill off** to warm slightly. **chiller** *n.* 1 a chilled container for food or drink. 2 (*coll.*) a frightening novel, film etc., a spine-chiller. **chill factor** *n.* the lowering of the perceived air temperature, esp. by the wind. **chilling** *a.* 1 making cold. 2 depressing. 3 frightening, spine-chilling. **chillingly** *adv.* **chillness** *n.* **chillsome** *a.* (*poet.*) chilly. **chilly** *a.* (*comp.* **chillier**, *superl.* **chilliest**) 1 rather cold. 2 sensitive to the cold. 3 cold or distant in manner; unfriendly; unemotional. **chilliness** *n.* [OE *ciele*, *cele*, from Gmc. (cp. Icel. *kala*, to freeze, Dut. *kil*, chilly, L *gelu*, frost)]

chilli (chil´i), **chili, chile** *n.* (*pl.* **chillies, chilies, chiles**) the hot-tasting ripe pod of a species of capsicum, esp. *Capsicum anuum*, used to flavour, sauces, pickles etc. **chilli con carne** (kon kah´ni) *n.* a Mexican dish of minced meat with beans in a chilli sauce. **chilli powder** *n.* ground dried chillies, sometimes mixed with other spices. **chilli sauce** *n.* a hot-tasting sauce made from tomatoes, chillies etc. [Nahuatl]

chilo- (kī´lō), **cheilo-, chil-, cheil-** *comb. form* lip-shaped, labiate. [Gr. *cheilos*, a lip]

chilopod (kī´ləpod) *n.* any arthropod of the class Chilopoda, including the centipedes. [Gr. *pous podos*, foot]

Chiltern Hundreds (chil´tən) *n.pl.* certain Crown lands in Buckinghamshire and Oxfordshire, the nominal stewardship of which is granted to a Member of Parliament who wishes to vacate their seat. **to apply for the Chiltern Hundreds** to resign membership of the House of Commons.

chimaera CHIMERA.

chimb CHIME².

chime¹ (chīm) *n.* 1 the harmonic or consonant sounds of musical instruments or bells. 2 a number of bells tuned in diatonic succession. 3 the sounds so produced. 4 tune, rhythm. 5 harmony, accord. 6 agreement, correspondence. ~*v.i.* 1 to sound in harmony or accord. 2 (of bells) to ring, to strike the hour etc. 3 to accord, to agree. 4 to be in rhyme. ~*v.t.* 1 to ring (a series of bells). 2 to ring (a chime) on bells. 3 to sound (the hour etc.) by chiming. 4 to cause to sound in harmony. 5 to recite musically or rhythmically. **to chime in** 1 to join in. 2 to express agreement. **chimer** *n.* [ME *chimbe*, OF *chimble*, L *cymbalum*, Gr. *kumbalon*, CYMBAL]

chime² (chīm), **chimb** *n.* the edge of a cask or tub formed by the ends of the staves. [ME *chimb* (cp. Dut. *kim*, G *Kimme*, OE *cimb-īren*)]

chimer (chim´ə), **chimere** (-iə) *n.* a bishop's outer robe. [OF *chamarre* (etym. unknown)]

chimera (kimiə´rə, kī-), **chimaera** *n.* 1 a fabulous fire-eating monster, with a lion's head, a serpent's tail, and the body of a goat. 2 any incongruous conception of the imagination. 3 an imaginary terror. 4 any cartilaginous fish of the family Chimaeridae. 5 (*Biol.*) a hybrid of genetically dissimilar tissues. **chimeric** (-mer´-), **chimerical** *a.* purely imaginary. **chimerically** *adv.* [L *chimaera*, Gr. *chimaira*, she-goat, a monster, fem. of *chimaros*, goat]

chimichanga (chimichang´gə) *n.* a deep-fried rolled tortilla with a savoury filling. [Mex. Sp., a trinket]

chimney (chim´ni) *n.* (*pl.* **chimneys**) 1 the flue, vent or passage through which smoke etc. escapes from a fire into the open air. 2 the top part of this, projecting above a roof. 3 a glass tube placed over the flame of a lamp to intensify combustion. 4 a vent from a volcano. 5 a vertical or nearly vertical fissure in rock. 6 †a fireplace, a hearth. **chimney breast** *n.* the projecting part of the wall of a room containing the fireplace. **chimney corner** *n.* a nook or seat beside the fire, esp. inside a wide, old-fashioned fireplace. **chimney piece** *n.* a mantelpiece. **chimney pot** *n.* a tube of pottery or sheet metal above the shaft of a chimney to increase the updraught. **chimney stack** *n.* **1** a series of chimneys united in a block of masonry or brickwork. **2** a tall factory chimney. **3** a chimney top. **chimney swallow** *n.* the common swallow. **chimney sweep** *n.* a person whose business is to sweep chimneys. **chimney top** *n.* the part of a chimney projecting above a roof. [OF *cheminée*, late L *camīnāta* (L *camīnus*, hearth, stove, flue)]

chimp (chimp) *n.* (*coll.*) a chimpanzee. [abbr.]

chimpanzee (chimpanzē´) *n.* **1** a large intelligent African anthropoid ape, *Pan troglodytes.* **2** the pygmy chimpanzee. [Kongo dial.]

chin (chin) *n.* the front part of the lower jaw. **chin up!** (*coll.*) cheer up! **to keep one's chin up** (*coll.*) to remain cheerful in adversity. **to take it on the chin** to face up to (misfortune, defeat etc.) courageously. **chinless** *a.* (*coll.*) **1** having a receding chin. **2** weak-spirited, ineffectual. **chinless wonder** *n.* (*coll.*) an ineffectual person, esp. of the upper class. **-chinned** *comb. form* **chinstrap** *n.* a strap passing under the chin. **chin-up** *n.* (*esp. N Am.*) an exercise in which the body is raised by the arms, a pull-up. **chinwag** *n.* (*coll.*) a chat, a talk. *~v.i.* (*pres.p.* **chinwagging**, *past, p.p.* **chinwagged**) to chat, to gossip. [OE *cin* (cp. Dut. *kin*, G *Kinn*, Gr. *geneion*, chin, L *gena*, cheek]

china (chī´nə) *n.* **1** fine porcelain, first brought from China. **2** porcelain or ceramic ware. **3** household tableware, esp. made of china. **4** (*sl.*) one's husband or wife, a friend (from *china plate*, mate). *~a.* made of china. **china clay** (chī´nə) *n.* kaolin. **Chinagraph®** *n.* a coloured pencil used to write on china, glass etc. **china stone** *n.* a type of granite rock. **chinaware** *n.* articles made of china. [*China*, country in E Asia]

China aster (chī´nə) *n.* a Chinese garden plant, *Callistephus chinensis*, with showy aster-like flowers. **China grass** (chī´nə) *n.* the fibre of the ramie plant, *Bohmeria nivea*, used for making ropes and cordage. **China ink** (chī´nə) *n.* Indian ink. **Chinaman** (chī´nə) *n.* (*pl.* **Chinamen**) **1** (*derog., usu. offensive*) a native of China, or a person of Chinese descent. **2** in cricket, a ball bowled by a left-handed bowler, spinning from off to leg. **china-root** (chī´nə) *n.* the root of a Chinese plant, *Smilax china*, used medicinally. **China rose** (chī´nə) *n.* any of several varieties of the rose, such as *Rosa chinensis.* **China syndrome** (chī´nə) *n.* a hypothetical series of events following the meltdown of a nuclear reactor. **China tea** (chī´nə) *n.* a smoky-flavoured tea from China. **Chinatown** (chī´nə) *n.* the Chinese quarter of a town. [as CHINA]

chinch (chinch), **chinch bug** *n.* **1** a N American insect, *Blissus leucopterus*, destructive to cereal crops. **2** (*N Am.*) the bedbug. [Sp. *chinche*, L *cimex -icis*]

chincherinchee (chinchərinchē´) *n.* a S African plant of the lily family, *Ornithogalum thyrsoides*, with white flowers. [prob. imit. of the sound made when its stalks rub together]

chinchilla (chinchil´ə) *n.* (*pl.* **chinchillas**) **1** any S American rodent of the genus *Chinchilla.* **2** its soft silver-grey fur. **3** a breed of rabbit or cat. [Sp., dim. of *chinche*, see CHINCH]

chin-chin (chinchin´) *int.* (*coll.*) a familiar form of salutation or drinking toast. [Chin. *ts'ing ts'ing*]

Chindit (chin´dit) *n.* a member of the Allied commando force in Burma (now Myanmar) during World War II. [Burmese *chinthé*, a griffin]

chine[1] (chīn) *n.* **1** the backbone or spine of any animal. **2** part of the back of an animal cut for cooking. **3** a ridge. *~v.t.* **1** to cut or break the backbone of. **2** to cut (meat) along or across the backbone. **chined** *a.* (*usu. in comb.*) having a backbone; backboned. [OF *eschine* (F *échine*), perh. from OHG *skina*, a needle]

chine[2] (chīn) *n.* (*dial.*) a deep and narrow ravine. [OE *cinu*, a chink, cleft (cp. Dut. *keen*)]

chine[3] (chīn) *n.* the join between the side and bottom of a ship or boat. [var. of CHIME[2]]

chiné (shēnā´, shē´-) *a.* (of fabric) having a mottled pattern. [F, made in the Chinese fashion (*Chiné*, China)]

Chinese (chīnēz´) *n.* (*pl.* **Chinese**) **1** a native or inhabitant of China, or a person of Chinese descent. **2** (*as pl.*) the people of China. **3** the language of the Chinese. *~a.* of or relating to China. **Chinese burn** *n.* (*coll.*) a burning sensation, produced by placing both hands on a person's arm and twisting the skin in the opposite direction. **Chinese cabbage** *n.* a cabbage-like vegetable, *Brassica chinensis*, with crisp leaves. **Chinese chequers**, (*N Am.*) **Chinese checkers** *n.pl.* (*usu. sing. in constr.*) a board game played with marbles on a star-shaped board. **Chinese gooseberry** *n.* (*pl.* **Chinese gooseberries**) the kiwi, or the plant on which it grows. **Chinese lantern** *n.* **1** a collapsible lantern made of thin paper. **2** a plant, *Physalis alkekengi*, with round orange fruits in a papery calyx. **Chinese leaf, Chinese leaves** *n.* Chinese cabbage. **Chinese puzzle** *n.* a complicated or intricate puzzle or problem. **Chinese restaurant syndrome** *n.* a group of symptoms including headache, chest pain, dizziness and flushing, attributed to the excessive consumption of monosodium glutamate, as used in Chinese cookery. **Chinese wall** *n.* an agreement among different departments of a large (esp. financial) institution not to exchange sensitive information in order to avoid conflicts of interest or malpractice by members of staff. **Chinese water chestnut** *n.* a variety of sedge, *Eleocharis tuberosa*, or its edible corm. **Chinese white** *n.* an opaque white paint.

Chink (chingk) *a., n.* (*offensive*) (a) Chinese. [abbr.]

chink[1] (chingk) *n.* **1** a narrow cleft or crevice. **2** a small longitudinal opening. **3** a slit. *~v.t.* to stuff up chinks. *~v.i.* to split, to crack. **a chink in someone's armour** a weak or vulnerable point in someone's character etc. [etym. uncertain; perh. from CHINE[2]]

chink[2] (chingk) *n.* a jingling sound as of coins or glasses. *~v.t.* to cause to make this sound. *~v.i.* to make this sound. [onomat.]

Chinky (ching´ki) *n.* (*pl.* **Chinkies**) **1** (*offensive*) a Chinese person. **2** (*sl.*) a Chinese restaurant. *~a.* (*offensive*) Chinese. [abbr.]

Chino- (chī´nō) *comb. form* Chinese; of or relating to China.

chino (chē´nō) *n.* (*pl.* **chinos**) **1** a tough, twilled cotton fabric. **2** (*pl.*) trousers, often off-white, made of this fabric. [Am. Sp.]

chinoiserie (shinwah´zəri, shē-, -rē´) *n.* **1** a style of Western art and architecture using Chinese motifs. **2** an object or objects in this style. [F (*chinois*, Chinese)]

Chinook (chinook´) *n.* (*pl.* **Chinooks, Chinook**) **1** a member of a N American Indian people who formerly lived along the Columbia river. **2** the language of this people. **Chinook jargon** *n.* a jargon of N American Indian and European words formerly used in between traders and N American Indians in the region of the Columbia River. [N Amer. Ind., name of the people]

chinook (chinook´) *n.* **1** a warm dry wind blowing east of the Rocky Mountains. **2** a warm wet wind blowing west of the Rocky Mountains. **chinook salmon** *n.* a large Pacific salmon, *Oncorhynchus tshawytscha.* [as CHINOOK]

chintz (chints) *n.* a printed cotton cloth with floral devices etc., usu. glazed. **chintzy** *a.* (*comp.* **chintzier**, *superl.* **chintziest**) **1** of or resembling chintz. **2** cheap, tawdry, gaudy. **3** typical of the decor associated with chintz soft furnishings. **chintzily** *adv.* **chintziness** *n.* [formerly *chints*, pl., Hind. *chīnt* (Sansk. *chitra*, variegated)]

chip (chip) *n.* **1** a small piece of wood, stone etc. detached or chopped off. **2** the place from which such a piece has been removed. **3** (*usu. pl.*) a deep-fried strip of potato. **4** (*pl., N Am.*) thin slices of potato, potato crisps. **5** a counter used in gambling games. **6** a very small piece of semiconducting material, esp. silicon, with an integrated circuit printed on it; a microchip. **7** a thin strip of wood for making hats or baskets. **8** a basket made from such strips. **9** any thin fragment. **10** a chip shot. ~*v.t.* (*pres.p.* **chipping,** *past, p.p.* **chipped**) **1** to cut into chips. **2** to cut or break a chip or chips off. **3** to hit or kick (the ball) with a chip shot. ~*v.i.* **1** to break or fly off in chips. **2** to play a chip shot. **to chip in 1** (*coll.*) to cut into a conversation. **2** (*coll.*) to contribute (money). **to have had one's chips 1** (*coll.*) to be defeated. **2** (*coll.*) to be unable to avoid death. **when the chips are down** (*coll.*) at a moment of crisis; when it comes to the point. **chip-based** *a.* (of electronic equipment etc.) using microchips. **chip basket** *n.* **1** a wire basket in which potato chips are deep-fried. **2** a basket made from strips of thin wood. **chipboard** *n.* a thin board made of compressed wood fragments. **chip heater** *n.* (*Austral., New Zeal.*) a water heater fuelled by burning wood chips. **chip off the old block** *n.* a person resembling one of their parents, esp. in character or in behaviour. **chip on one's shoulder** *n.* a grievance, a disposition to feel badly treated. **chip pan** *n.* a pan for deep-frying potato chips etc. **chippie** *n.* (*coll.*) a chippy. **chipping** *n.* **1** a chip of wood, stone etc. **2** (*pl.*) such chips used to surface roads, roofs etc. **chippy** *a.* (*comp.* **chippier,** *superl.* **chippiest**) **1** (*sl.*) irritable. **2** (*sl.*) seedy or unwell, esp. after a bout of drinking. **3** (*N Am.*) belligerent. ~*n.* (*pl.* **chippies**) (*coll.*) **1** a chip shop. **2** a carpenter. **chippiness** *n.* **chips** *n.* (*sl.*) a ship's carpenter. **chip shop** *n.* a shop selling fish and chips and similar prepared meals to take away. **chip shot** *n.* in football or golf, a short high shot. [dim. of CHOP[1] (cp. *click, clack; clink, clank; drip, drop*)]

chipmunk (chip´mŭngk) *n.* a N American rodent of the genus *Tamias lysteri*, resembling a squirrel. [Algonquian]

chipolata (chipəlah´tə) *n.* (*pl.* **chipolatas**) a small sausage. [F, from It. *cipolla*, onion]

Chippendale (chip´əndāl) *a.* (of furniture) designed or made by Chippendale about the middle of the 18th cent., or in a similarly ornately elegant style. [Thomas *Chippendale*, English cabinetmaker, 1718–79]

chipper (chip´ə) *a.* (*esp. N Am., coll.*) **1** energetic and cheerful. **2** smart. [etym. uncertain]

chippie, chipping etc. CHIP.

chir- CHIRO-.

chiral (kīə´rəl) *a.* (of an optically active chemical compound) asymmetric, having a left-handed or right-handed structure. **chirality** (-ral´-) *n.* [Gr. *cheir*, a hand]

chi-rho (kīrō´) *n.* a monogram of the Greek letters chi and rho, the first two letters of the Greek word for Christ.

chiro- (kī´rō), **cheiro-, chir-, cheir-** *comb. form* **1** manual. **2** having hands or handlike organs. [Gr. *cheir*, a hand]

chirograph (kī´rəgrahf) *n.* a written or signed document. **chirographer** (-rog´-) *n.* a person skilled in handwriting. **chirographic** (-graf´-), **chirographical** *a.* of, relating to or in handwriting. **chirography** (-rog´-) *n.* **1** the art of writing; calligraphy. **2** character and style in handwriting. [F *chirographe*, L *chirographum*, Gr. *cheirographon*]

chiromancy (kī´rəmansi) *n.* divination by means of the hand; palmistry. **chiromancer** *n.* **chiromantic** (-man´-) *a.* [-MANCY]

chiropodist (kirop´ədist, shi-) *n.* a person skilled in the care of the feet, esp. in the removal of corns etc. **chiropody** *n.* [Gr. *pous podos*, foot]

Usage note The pronunciation (sh-) is sometimes disapproved of, though it is quite common. Historically *ch* here represents the Greek letter chi, which was pronounced hard, as (k).

chiropractic (kīrəprak´tik) *n.* spinal manipulation as a method of curing disease, disorders of the joints etc. **chiropractor** (kī´-) *n.* [Gr. *praktikos*, practical, effective]

chiropteran (kīrop´tərən) *n.* any mammal of the order Chiroptera, with membranes connecting their fingers and used as wings, consisting of the bats. **chiropterous** *a.* [Gr. *pteron*, wing, *ptera*, wings]

chirp (chœp) *v.i.* **1** (of a bird, insect etc.) to make a quick, sharp sound. **2** to talk cheerfully. ~*v.t.* to utter or sing with a sharp, quick sound. ~*n.* **1** a sharp, quick sound of a bird. **2** a sound resembling this. **chirper** *n.* **chirpy** *a.* (*comp.* **chirpily,** *superl.* **chirpiest**) **1** cheerful. **2** vivacious. **chirpily** *adv.* **chirpiness** *n.* [imit.]

chirr (chœ), **churr** *v.i.* to make a trilling monotonous sound like that of the grasshopper. ~*n.* this sound. [imit.]

chirrup (chi´rəp) *v.i.* (*pres.p.* **chirruping,** *past, p.p.* **chirruped**) to chirp, to make a twittering sound. **chirruper** *n.* **chirrupy** *a.* [CHIRP]

chisel (chiz´əl) *n.* an edged tool for cutting wood, iron or stone, operated by pressure or striking. ~*v.t.* (*pres.p.* **chiselling,** (*N Am.*) **chiseling,** *past, p.p.* **chiselled,** (*N Am.*) **chiseled**) **1** to cut, shape or engrave with a chisel. **2** (*sl.*) to take advantage of, to cheat. ~*v.i.* to cheat. **chiselled** *a.* **1** cut with or as with a chisel. **2** clear-cut (*finely chiselled features*). **chiseller** *n.* [ONF (OF *cisel*, F *ciseau*), late L *cīsellus*, forceps (L *-cisum*, from *caedere*, to cut)]

chi-square test (kī´skweə) *n.* a test used in statistics to compare data, esp. observed and theoretical values.

chit[1] (chit) *n.* **1** a child. **2** (*derog.*) a young girl. [cp. KIT[1]]

chit[2] (chit), **chitty** (chit´i) *n.* (*pl.* **chits, chitties**) **1** a voucher for money owed. **2** a requisition. **3** a receipt. **4** a memorandum. [Hind. *chitthī* (Sansk. *chitra*, mark)]

chital (chē´təl) *n.* the axis deer. [Hind. *cītal*]

chit-chat (chit´chat) *n.* chat, gossip, trifling talk. ~*v.i.* (*pres.p.* **chit-chatting,** *past, p.p.* **chit-chatted**) to chat, to gossip. [CHAT[1]]

chitin (kī´tin) *n.* the horny substance that gives firmness to the exoskeleton of arthropods and to the cell wall of fungi. **chitinous** *a.* [F *chitine*, Gr. *chitōn*, a tunic]

chitlings CHITTERLINGS.

chiton (kī´tən, -ton) *n.* **1** an ancient Greek tunic. **2** a woman's dress in this style. **3** a mollusc of the genus *Chiton*, having a shell made up of overlapping plates. [Gr. *chitōn*, a tunic]

chitter (chit´ə) *v.i.* **1** to shiver, to tremble. **2** (of the teeth) to chatter. **3** (of birds) to twitter. [CHATTER (cp. CHIP, CHOP[1] etc.)]

chitterlings (chit´əlingz), **chitlings** (chit´lingz) *n.pl.* the smaller intestines of animals, esp. as prepared for food. [etym. uncertain, cp. G *Kutteln*, entrails]

chitty CHIT[2].

chivalry (shiv´əlri) *n.* **1** the knightly system of the Middle Ages. **2** the ideal qualities which inspired it, nobleness and gallantry of spirit, courtesy, respect for and defence of the weak. **3** gallantry, devotion to the service of women. **4** †knights collectively. **5** †horsemen, cavalry. **chivalric** *a.* **1** of or relating to chivalry. **2** gallant. **chivalrous** *a.* **1** gallant, noble. **2** courteous. **chivalrously** *adv.* [OF *chevalerie*, from L *caballārius*, CHEVALIER]

chive (chīv), **cive** (sīv) *n.* a small onion-like herb, *Allium schoenoprasum.* [F *cive* or ONF *chive,* L *cepa,* onion]

chivvy (chiv´i), **chivy, chevy** (chev´i) *v.t.* (*3rd pers. sing. pres.* **chivvies, chivies, chevies,** *pres.p.* **chivvying, chivying, chevying,** *past, p.p.* **chivvied, chivied, chevied**) **1** to hurry; to pester or nag. **2** to hunt, to chase. ~*v.i.* to scamper about. [prob. from the ballad of *Chevy Chase*]

chlamydate, chlamydes CHLAMYS.

chlamydia (klǝmid´iǝ) *n.* (*pl.* **chlamydiae** (-mid´iē)) **1** any disease-causing microorganism of the genus *Chlamydia,* resembling both bacteria and viruses. **2** a sexually transmitted disease caused by such a microorganism.

chlamys (klam´is) *n.* (*pl.* **chlamydes** (-dēz)) **1** a Greek cloak or mantle. **2** the mantle of a mollusc. **3** the floral envelope of a plant. **chlamydate** *a.* (*Bot., Zool.*) having a mantle or envelope. [Gr. *chlamus -udos,* a cloak]

chloasma (klōaz´mǝ) *n.* (*pl.* **chloasmata** (-mǝtǝ)) (*Med.*) a condition in which dark patches appear on a person's skin, usu. at a time of hormonal change. [Gr. *chloasma,* greenness]

chlor- CHLORO-.

chloracne (klawrak´ni) *n.* (*Med.*) a skin disease that results from exposure to chlorinated chemicals. [CHLOR-, ACNE]

chloral (klaw´rǝl) *n.* **1** a liquid made from chlorine and alcohol. **2** chloral hydrate. **chloral hydrate** *n.* a white crystalline substance obtained from chloral, used as a hypnotic and anaesthetic. [CHLOR-, al*cohol*]

chloramphenicol (klawramfen´ikol) *n.* an antibiotic used to treat typhoid etc. [*chlor-, am*ide, *phen*o-, *ni*tro-, gly*col*]

chlorate (klaw´rāt) *n.* a salt of chloric acid.

chlorella (klǝrel´ǝ) *n.* any green freshwater alga of the genus *Chlorella.*

chloric (klaw´rik) *a.* of, relating to or containing pentavalent chlorine. **chloric acid** *n.* an acid containing hydrogen, chlorine and oxygen.

chloride (klaw´rīd) *n.* **1** a compound of chlorine with another element. **2** chloride of lime, or a similar substance. **chloride of lime** *n.* a compound of chlorine with lime, used as a disinfectant and for bleaching. **chloridize, chloridise, chloridate** *v.t.* to treat or prepare (a photographic plate etc.) with a chloride.

chlorine (klaw´rēn) *n.* a yellow-green, poisonous, gaseous element, at. no. 17, chem. symbol Cl, obtained from common salt, used as a disinfectant and for bleaching. **chlorinate** (-rin-) *v.t.* to combine or treat with chlorine. **chlorination** (-rinā´shǝn) *n.* **1** the sterilization of water with chlorine. **2** the extraction of gold by exposure of ore to chlorine gas.

chlorite[1] (klaw´rīt) *n.* a green silicate mineral. **chloritic** (-rit´-) *a.*

chlorite[2] (klaw´rīt) *n.* a salt of chlorous acid.

chloro- (klaw´rō), **chlor-** *comb. form* **1** of a green colour. **2** denoting a chemical compound in which chlorine has replaced some other element. [Gr. *chlōros,* green]

chlorofluorocarbon (klawrōfluǝrōkah´bǝn) *n.* any of various compounds of carbon, hydrogen, chlorine and fluorine, used in refrigerators, aerosols etc., some of which are harmful to the ozone layer; a CFC.

chloroform (klor´ǝfawm) *n.* a volatile fluid formerly used as an anaesthetic. ~*v.t.* **1** to administer chloroform to. **2** to render unconscious with chloroform. [F *chloroforme* (CHLORO-, *form*(*yl*), see FORMIC)]

Chloromycetin® (klawrōmī´sitin, -sē´tin) *n.* a brand of chloramphenicol.

chlorophyll (klor´ǝfil, klaw´-), (*esp. N Am.*) **chlorophyl** *n.* the green colouring matter of plants which absorbs the energy from sunlight, used in producing carbohydrates from water and carbon dioxide. **chlorophyllous** (klawrǝfil´ǝs) *a.* [Gr. *phullon,* a leaf]

chloroplast (klaw´rǝplast) *n.* a plastid containing chlorophyll.

chloroquine (klor´ǝkwēn, klaw´-) *n.* a drug used in the treatment of malaria. [CHLORO-, QUININE]

chlorosis (klawrō´sis) *n.* **1** (*Med.*) a disease affecting young people due to deficiency of iron in the blood. **2** (*Bot.*) etiolation, a blanching of plants through the non-development of chlorophyll. **chlorotic** (-rot´-) *a.*

chlorous (klaw´rǝs) *a.* of, relating to or containing trivalent chlorine. **chlorous acid** *n.* an acid containing hydrogen, chlorine and oxygen.

chlorpromazine (klawprō´mǝzēn) *n.* a tranquillizing drug. [CHLOR-, PROMETHAZINE]

ChM *abbr.* Master of Surgery. [L *Chirurgiae Magister*]

chm *abbr.* **1** (*also* **chmn**) chairman. **2** checkmate.

choc (chok) *n.* (*coll.*) a chocolate (*a box of chocs*). **choc ice** *n.* a bar of (vanilla) ice cream coated with chocolate.

chocaholic CHOCOHOLIC.

chocho (chō´chō) *n.* (*pl.* **chochos**) (*W Ind.*) a choko. [Am. Sp.]

chock (chok) *n.* a wood block, esp. a wedge-shaped block used to prevent a cask, wheel, boat etc. from shifting. ~*v.t.* **1** to wedge, support or make fast, with a chock or chocks. **2** to cram full. ~*adv.* **1** as close as possible. **2** tightly, fully. **chock-a-block,** (*coll.*) **chocka** *a., adv.* chock-full. **chocker** *a.* **1** (*coll.*) full up, crammed. **2** (*sl.*) annoyed, fed up. **chock-full** *a., adv.* **1** crammed full. **2** full to overflowing. **chockstone** *n.* in mountaineering, a stone wedged in a chimney or crack. [prob. from ONF *choque,* a log (prob. influenced by CHOKE)]

chocoholic (chokǝhol´ik), **chocaholic** *n.* a person who is very fond of or addicted to chocolate. ~*a.* of or relating to such people. [*choco*late, alco*holic*]

chocolate (chok´lit) *n.* **1** a usu. sweet food made from the roasted and ground seeds of the cacao tree (*milk chocolate; plain chocolate*). **2** a sweetmeat made of or coated with this. **3** a drink made with chocolate, usu. dissolved in hot water or milk. **4** chocolate brown. ~*a.* **1** made of or flavoured with chocolate. **2** chocolate brown. **chocolate-box** *a.* sentimentally pretty. **chocolate brown** *n.* a dark brown colour. ~*a.* dark brown. **chocolatey, chocolaty** *a.* [F *chocolat,* Sp. *chocolate,* Nahuatl *chocolatl* (*choco,* cacao, *latl,* water)]

Choctaw (chok´taw) *n.* (*pl.* **Choctaw, Choctaws**) **1** a member of a N American Indian people of Alabama. **2** the language of this people. **3** (**choctaw,** *pl.* **choctaws**) in ice skating, a change of foot and from one edge to the other. ~*a.* of or relating to the Choctaws or their language.

choice (chois) *n.* **1** the power or act of choosing. **2** the person or thing chosen. **3** the range to choose from. **4** selection, preference. **5** an alternative; the opportunity to choose (*I had no choice but to go*). **6** the best part. ~*a.* **1** selected, picked, chosen with care. **2** of great value or superior quality. **for/ from choice** by preference. **choicely** *adv.* **choiceness** *n.* [OF *chois,* from *choisir,* to choose]

choir (kwīǝ) *n.* **1** an organized body of singers. **2** a band of singers, in a church or chapel. **3** the part of the church or chapel allotted to the singers. **4** the chancel of a cathedral or large church. **5** a group of musical instruments of the same family playing together. **6** a group of birds, angels etc. singing together. **choirboy** *n.* a boy singer in a church choir. **choirgirl** *n.* a girl singer in a church choir. **choir loft** *n.* a gallery used by the choir in a cathedral or large church. **choirman** *n.* (*pl.* **choirmen**) a male singer in a choir. **choirmaster** *n.* a person who trains or conducts a choir. **choir organ** *n.* the least powerful section of a compound organ, used chiefly for accompaniments. **choir screen** *n.* a screen of lattice work separating the choir from the nave. **choir stall** *n.* a seat in the choir of a large church. [ME *queir, quere,* OF *cuer,* L *chorum -us,* Gr. *choros,* a band of dancers and singers]

choke (chōk) *v.t.* **1** to block or compress the windpipe (of), so as to prevent breathing. **2** to suffocate (as by gas, water etc.). **3** to smother, to stifle. **4** to repress, to silence. **5** to stop up, to block, to obstruct, to clog. **6** to reduce the intake of air to (a carburettor, engine etc.) and thereby enrich the fuel mixture. *~v.i.* **1** to have the windpipe blocked or compressed. **2** to be wholly or partially suffocated; to be unable to breathe. **3** to be blocked up. **4** (*sl.*) to die. *~n.* **1** the act of choking. **2** a sound of choking. **3** a device to reduce the air supply to a carburettor and thereby enrich the fuel mixture. **4** an inductance coil constructed to prevent high-frequency currents from passing. **5** the constriction of a chokebore. **6** the centre of an artichoke. **to choke back** to suppress (*He choked back his anger*). **to choke down** **1** to swallow with difficulty. **2** to choke back. **to choke off** to discourage, to suppress. **to choke up** to fill up until blocked. **chokeberry** *n.* (*pl.* **chokeberries**) **1** any of various shrubs of the genus *Aronia,* of the rose family. **2** its red or purple berry-like fruit. **chokebore** *n.* a gun barrel the bore of which narrows towards the muzzle. **choke chain** *n.* a collar-like chain attached to a dog's lead, designed to tighten around the dog's neck if it pulls on the lead. **choke cherry** *n.* (*pl.* **choke cherries**) **1** any of various N American cherry trees, esp. *Prunus virginiana.* **2** its astringent dark-coloured fruit. **choked** *a.* (*coll.*) **1** disappointed. **2** angry. **choke-damp** *n.* **1** carbon dioxide generated in mines, wells etc. **2** any similar suffocating vapour. **choke-full** *a., adv.* CHOCK-FULL (under CHOCK). **choker** *n.* **1** a necklace that fits closely round the neck. **2** a clerical collar. **3** a person or thing that chokes. **choky**[1] *a.* (*comp.* **chokier,** *superl.* **chokiest**) **1** that causes choking. **2** having a sensation of choking. [OE *ā-cēocian* (etym. uncertain)]

chokey CHOKY[2].

choko (chō´kō) *n.* (*pl.* **chokos**) (*Austral., New Zeal.*) a succulent vegetable like a cucumber. [Am. Sp. *chocho*]

choky[1] CHOKE.

choky[2] (chō´ki), **chokey** *n.* (*pl.* **chokies, chokeys**) (*sl.*) a prison. [Hind. *chaukī*]

chol- CHOLE-.

cholagogue (kol´əgog) *n.* a medicine which promotes the flow of bile. **cholagogic** (-gog´ik, -goj´-) *a.* [F, from mod. L *cholagōgum,* Gr. *cholagōgon* (*agōgos,* leading, from *agein,* to lead)]

cholangiography (kolanjiog´rəfi) *n.* X-ray photography of the bile ducts.

chole- (kol´i), **chol-** *comb. form* of or relating to bile. [Gr. *cholē,* gall, bile]

cholecalciferol (kolikalsif´ərol) *n.* a compound that occurs in fish-liver oils; vitamin D_3.

cholecyst (kol´isist) *n.* the gall bladder. **cholecystectomy** (-tek´-) *n.* (*pl.* **cholecystectomies**) surgical removal of the gall bladder. **cholecystitis** (-tī´tis) *n.* inflammation of the gall bladder. **cholecystography** (-tog´-) *n.* X-ray photography of the gall bladder.

choler (kol´ə) *n.* **1** (*Hist.*) yellow bile, the humour supposed to cause irascibility. **2** †anger; tendency to anger. **choleric** *a.* **1** irascible, angry. **2** full of choler. **cholerically** *adv.* [ME and OF *colere,* L, Gr. *cholera* (Gr. *cholē,* bile)]

cholera (kol´ərə) *n.* an acute, often fatal, bacterial infection, spread by contaminated water supplies, in which severe vomiting and diarrhoea cause dehydration. **choleraic** (-rā´-) *a.* **choleroid** *a.* [L, see CHOLER]

choleric, cholerically CHOLER.

cholesterol (kəles´tərol), †**cholesterin** (-in) *n.* a steroid alcohol occurring in body tissues, including blood and bile (high levels of cholestrol in the blood are thought to be a cause of arteriosclerosis and heart disease). **cholesteric** (koləster´ik) *a.* [Gr. *stereos,* stiff, solid]

choli (chō´li) *n.* (*pl.* **cholis**) an Indian woman's garment, a short tight-fitting bodice worn under a sari. [Hind. *colī*]

choliamb (kō´liamb) *n.* a scazon. **choliambic** (-am´-) *a.* [L *chōliambus,* Gr. *chōliambos* (*cholos,* lame, IAMBUS)]

cholic (kol´ik) *a.* of, relating to or obtained from bile. **cholic acid** *n.* an acid obtained from bile, used as an emulsifying agent.

choline (kō´lēn, -lin) *n.* a substance occurring naturally in the body, important for the synthesis of lecithin etc.

cholla (cho´lə) *n.* any of various cacti of the genus *Opuntia,* of Mexico and the south-west US. [Mex. Sp., skull, head]

chomp CHAMP[1].

Chomskian (chom´skiən) *a.* of or relating to the linguist Chomsky or his work. [Noam *Chomsky,* b. 1928, US linguist]

chondr-, chondri- CHONDRO-.

chondrify (kon´drifī) *v.i.* (*3rd pers. sing. pres.* **chondrifies,** *pres.p.* **chondrifying,** *past, p.p.* **chondrified**) to be converted into cartilage. *~v.t.* to convert into cartilage. **chondrification** (-fikā´shən) *n.*

chondrin (kon´drin) *n.* gelatin from the cartilage of the ribs, joints etc.

chondrite (kon´drīt) *n.* a meteorite containing stony granules. **chondritic** (-drit´ik) *a.*

chondritis (kondrī´tis) *n.* inflammation of cartilage.

chondro- (kon´drō), **chondr-, chondri-** (-dri) *comb. form* composed of or relating to cartilage. [Gr. *chondros,* cartilage, a granule]

chondrocranium (kondrōkrā´niəm) *n.* a skull composed of cartilage, esp. that of the human embryo.

chondroid (kon´droid) *a.* like cartilage.

chondrule (kon´drool) *n.* any of the stony granules found in a chondrite.

choo-choo (choo´choo), **choo-choo train** *n.* (*coll.*) a railway train or steam engine (used by or to children). [imit.]

chook (chuk), **chookie** (chuk´i) *n.* (*Austral., New Zeal.*) **1** (*coll.*) a chicken or other domestic fowl. **2** (*sl.*) an older woman. [Eng. dial. *chuck,* chicken]

choose (chooz) *v.t.* (*past* **chose** (chōz), *p.p.* **chosen** (chō´zən)) **1** to take by preference, to select from a number. **2** to feel inclined, to prefer (to do something rather than something else). **3** to decide willingly (to do). *~v.i.* **1** to make one's choice. **2** to have the power of choice. †**cannot choose but** have no alternative but. **there's nothing/ little to choose between them** they are almost equal, esp. equally good or bad. **to choose sides** SIDE. **to pick and choose** PICK[1]. **chooser** *n.* **choosy** *adv.* (*comp.* **choosier,** *superl.* **choosiest**) (*coll.*) hard to please, particular. **choosily** *adv.* **choosiness** *n.* **chosen** *a.* **1** selected, esp. for some special quality (*the chosen few*). **2** (*Theol.*) destined to be saved (*the chosen people*). [OE *cēosan,* from Gmc. (cp. Dut. *kiezen,* G *kiesen,* Icel. *kjōsa*)]

chop[1] (chop) *v.t.* (*pres.p.* **chopping,** *past, p.p.* **chopped**) **1** to cut with a sharp blow. **2** to cut or strike off. **3** to cut (meat, vegetables etc.) into parts or small pieces. **4** to strike (a ball) with backspin. **5** (*coll.*) to reduce or abolish. *~v.i.* to do anything with a quick motion like that of a sharp blow. *~n.* **1** the act of chopping. **2** a cutting stroke or blow. **3** a piece chopped off. **4** a thick slice of meat, esp. pork or lamb, usu. including a rib or other bone. **5** (*pl.*) broken waves of the sea. **the chop 1** (*sl.*) dismissal (from a job etc.). **2** (*sl.*) killing or being killed. **3** (*sl.*) (of a project etc.) cancellation. **to chop up** to cut into small pieces, to mince. **chophouse**[1] *n.* a restaurant specializing in chops and steaks. **chopper** *n.* **1** a person or thing that chops. **2** a butcher's cleaver. **3**

an axe. **4** (*coll.*) a helicopter. **5** (*coll.*) a motorcycle or bicycle with very high handlebars. **6** a device that periodically interrupts an electric current, light beam etc. **7** (*pl.*, *sl.*) teeth. **choppy** *a.* (*comp.* **choppier,** *superl.* **choppiest**) (of the sea) rough, with short quick waves. **choppily** *adv.* **choppiness** *n.* [var. of CHAP[1]]

chop[2] (chop) *v.i.* (*pres.p.* **chopping,** *past, p.p.* **chopped**) (of the wind etc.) to change direction suddenly. ~†*v.t.* to exchange, to barter. **to chop and change 1** to vary continuously; to fluctuate. **2** to vacillate. **to chop logic** to wrangle pedantically. [etym. uncertain (perh. from CHOP[1] or from CHAPMAN)]

chop[3] (chop) *n.* (*usu. pl.*) the jaw of an animal. **to lick one's chops** LICK. [var. of CHAP[3]]

chop[4] (chop) *n.* **1** in the Indian subcontinent and China, a seal or official stamp. **2** †brand, quality. **not much chop** (*Austral., New Zeal.*) not very good. **chophouse**[2] *n.* (*Hist.*) in China, a custom house. [Hind. *chāp*, print, stamp]

chop-chop (chopchop´) *adv., int.* at once, quickly. [Pidgin Eng. *chop*, fast]

chophouse[1] CHOP[1].

chophouse[2] CHOP[4].

choppy CHOP[1].

chopstick (chop´stik) *n.* either of two small sticks of wood or ivory used by the Chinese to eat with. [rendering of Chinese *k'wâi-tsze*, quick ones; see CHOP-CHOP]

chop suey (chop soo´i) *n.* (*pl.* **chop sueys**) a Chinese dish of shredded meat and vegetables served with rice. [Chin. *chap sui*, odds and ends]

choragus (kərā´gəs) *n.* (*pl.* **choraguses, choragi** (-jī)) **1** the leader or director of the chorus in the ancient Greek theatrical performances. **2** the leader of a band or chorus. **choragic** (-raj´-) *a.* [L *chorāgus*, Gr. *chorēgos* (*choros*, chorus, *agein*, to lead)]

choral[1] (kaw´rəl) *a.* of, for or sung by a choir or chorus. **chorally** *adv.* **choral ode** *n.* in Greek drama, a song of the chorus. **choral society** *n.* a group of people who meet to sing choral music together. [med. L *chorālis* (L *chorus*, Gr. *choros*)]

choral[2] CHORALE.

chorale (kərahl´), **choral** *n.* **1** a simple choral hymn or song, usually of slow rhythm. **2** (*esp. N Am.*) a choir. [G *Choral* (in *Choralgesang*, choral song)]

chord[1] (kawd) *n.* (*Mus.*) the simultaneous and harmonious sounding of notes of different pitch. ~*v.i.* to play, sing or arrange chords. **chordal**[1] *a.* **chording** *n.* [ACCORD]

chord[2] (kawd) *n.* **1** a straight line joining the extremities of an arc or two points in a curve. **2** (*Anat.*) a cord. **3** in engineering, one of the principle members of a truss. **4** †the string of a musical instrument. **to strike a chord 1** to cause someone to recall something. **2** to elicit an emotional response, esp. sympathy. **to touch the right chord** to elicit an appropriate emotional response. **chordal**[2] *a.* **chordate** (-dāt) *n.* any member of the Chordata, a phylum of animals with a backbone or notochord. ~*a.* of or relating to this phylum. [L *chorda*, Gr. *chordē* (CORD, before 16th cent.)]

chordal[1] CHORD[1].

chordal[2] CHORD[2].

chordate CHORD[2].

chore (chaw) *n.* **1** a small regular task, esp. a household job. **2** a boring task. [CHAR[1]]

chorea (kərē´ə) *n.* a nervous disorder characterized by irregular convulsive movements of an involuntary kind. [L, from Gr. *choreia* (*choros*, dance)]

choreograph (kor´iəgrahf) *v.t.* to compose or arrange the steps of (a stage dance or ballet). **choreographer** (-og´-) *n.* **choreographic** (-graf´-) *a.* **choreographically** *adv.* **choreography** (-og´-) *n.* [Gr. *choreia* (*choros*, dance)]

choreology (koriol´əji) *n.* the study of the movements of dancing. **choreologist** *n.* [as CHOREOGRAPH]

choriamb (kor´iamb), **choriambus** (-am´bəs) *n.* (*pl.* **choriambs, choriambi** (-bī)) a metrical foot of four syllables, of which the first and fourth are long, and the second and third short. [L, from Gr. *choriambos*]

choric CHORUS.

chorine (kaw´rēn) *n.* a chorus girl. [CHORUS, -INE]

chorion (kaw´riən) *n.* the outer membrane which envelops the embryo of a reptile, bird or mammal. **chorionic** (-on´-) *a.* **chorionic villus sampling** *n.* a diagnostic test for detecting abnormalities in a foetus, whereby small pieces of the chorion are removed and examined. **choroid** *a.* resembling the chorion. ~*n.* the vascular portion of the retina. **choroid coat, choroid membrane** *n.* the choroid. [Gr.]

chorister (kor´istə), †**chorist** (kaw´rist) *n.* **1** a person who sings in a choir, esp. a choirboy or choirgirl. **2** a member of a band of singers. **3** (*N Am.*) the leader of a choir or congregation, a precentor. [med. L *chorista*, from *chorus*, CHOIR]

chorizo (chawrē´zō) *n.* (*pl.* **chorizos**) a highly seasoned pork sausage made in Spain or Mexico. [Sp.]

chorography (kərog´rəfi) *n.* the art or practice of describing and making maps of particular regions or districts. **chorographer** *n.* **chorographic** (-graf´-), **chorographical** *a.* **chorographically** *adv.* [F *chorographie*, Gr. *chōrographia*, *chōra*, a land, a region]

choroid CHORION.

chorology (kərol´əji) *n.* the science of the geographical distribution of plants and animals. **chorological** (-loj´-) *a.* **chorologist** *n.* [Gr. *chōra*, a district]

chortle (chaw´təl) *v.i.* to make a loud chuckle. ~*v.t.* to utter with a loud chuckle. ~*n.* a loud chuckle. [coined by Lewis Carroll (cp. CHUCKLE and SNORT)]

chorus (kaw´rəs) *n.* (*pl.* **choruses**) **1** a large choir. **2** a piece of music for a large choir. **3** a group of people singing or dancing in concert in a musical comedy, opera etc. **4** the refrain of a song in which the company joins the singer. **5** a group of people or animals producing a simultaneous utterance. **6** this utterance. **7** a band of dancers and singers in ancient Greek drama. **8** the song or recitative between the acts of a Greek tragedy. **9** (the speaker of) the prologue and epilogue in an Elizabethan play. ~*v.t.* (*pres.p.* **chorusing,** *past, p.p.* **chorused**) to utter simultaneously. ~*v.i.* to speak simultaneously. **in chorus** in unison; together. **choric** (kor´-) *a.* **1** of or relating to a chorus. **2** like the chorus in a Greek play. **chorus girl** *n.* a young woman who sings or dances in the chorus in a musical comedy etc. [L, from Gr. *khoros*]

chose, chosen CHOOSE.

chough (chŭf) *n.* a large black bird of the crow family, *Pyrrhocorax pyrrhocorax*, with red legs and bill. [imit. (cp. Dut. *kaauw*, Dan. *kaa*, OF *choue*)]

choux pastry (shoo pā´stri) *n.* a rich light pastry made with eggs. [F, pl. of *chou*, cabbage]

chow (chow) *n.* **1** (*coll.*) food. **2** a chow-chow (dog). **3** (*Austral., dated, derog.*) a Chinese. [Chin.]

chow-chow (chow´chow) *n.* **1** a dog of an orig. Chinese breed with thick coat and curled tail. **2** a kind of mixed vegetable pickle. **3** preserved fruit and ginger in syrup. [Chin.]

chowder (chow´də) *n.* (*esp. N Am.*) **1** a thick soup or stew made of fish, bacon etc. **2** a picnic where chowder is eaten. ~*v.t.* to make a chowder of. [F *chaudière*, pot, L *caldāria* (see CALDARIUM)]

chowkidar (chō´kidah) *n.* (*Ang.-Ind.*) a watchman. [Urdu *chaukīdār*]

chow mein (chow mān´) *n.* a Chinese dish of meat and vegetables served with fried noodles. [Chin., fried noodles]

chowry (chow´ri) *n.* (*pl.* **chowries**) a flapper for driving away flies. [Hind. *chaunri*]

Chr. *abbr.* **1** Christ. **2** Christian. **3** Chronicles.

chrematistic (krēmətis´tik) *a.* concerning money-making. **chrematistics** *n.* political economy as it relates to the production of wealth. [Gr. *chrēmatistikos*, from *chrēmatizein*, to traffic, to make money (*chrēmatos*, money)]

chrestomathy (krestom´əthi) *n.* (*pl.* **chrestomathies**) a selection of passages with notes etc., to be used in learning a language. **chrestomathic** (-math´-) *a.* learning or teaching good and useful things. [Gr. *chrēstomatheia* (*chrēstos*, good, *matheia*, learning, from *manthanein*, to learn)]

chrism (kriz´m) *n.* consecrated oil, used in the Roman Catholic and Greek Orthodox Churches in administering baptism, confirmation, ordination and extreme unction. **chrismal** *a.* **chrismatory** *n.* (*pl.* **chrismatories**) a vessel for holding chrism. **chrisom** (-zəm) *n.* **1** chrism. **2** a chrisom-cloth. **3** (*Hist.*) a child just baptized. **4** a chrisom-child. **chrisom-cloth** *n.* a white cloth, anointed with chrism, formerly placed over the face of a child after baptism. [OE *crisma*, L and Gr. *khrisma* (Gr. *khriein*, to anoint)]

Christ (krīst) *n.* **1** a title given to Jesus of Nazareth, and synonymous with the Hebrew Messiah. **2** a picture or other image of Jesus. *~int.* (*taboo*) used to express anger, annoyance etc. **for Christ's sake** SAKE[1]. **Christhood** *n.* **Christless** *a.* without faith in or without the spirit of Christ. **Christlessness** *n.* **Christlike** *a.* **Christlikeness** *n.* **Christly** *a.* **Christ's-thorn** *n.* any of several shrubs identified with that from which Christ's crown of thorns was made. [OE *Crist*, L *Christus*, Gr. *christos*, anointed one (*chrein*, to anoint)]

Christadelphian (kristədel´fiən) *n.* a member of a millenarian Christian sect claiming apostolic origin. *~a.* of, relating to or belonging to this sect. [Gr. *christos*, *adelphoi*, brethren]

christen (kris´ən) *v.t.* **1** to receive into the Christian Church by baptism; to baptize. **2** to give a Christian name to at baptism. **3** to name. **4** to nickname. **5** (*coll.*) to use for the first time. *~v.i.* to administer baptism. **christener** *n.* **christening** *n.* [OE *cristnian*, from *cristen*]

Christendom (kris´əndəm) *n.* **1** Christians collectively. **2** that portion of the world in which Christianity is the prevailing religion. [OE *cristen* (see CHRISTEN)]

Christian (kris´chən) *n.* **1** a person who believes in or professes the religion of Christ. **2** a person whose character is consistent with the teaching of Christ. *~a.* **1** of or relating to Christ or Christianity. **2** professing the religion of Christ. **3** Christlike; having qualities consistent with Christ's teaching. **4** (*coll.*) kind, charitable. **Christian era** *n.* the chronological period since the birth of Christ. **Christianity** (-tian´-) *n.* **1** the doctrines and precepts taught by Christ. **2** the religion based on these. **3** faith in Christ and his teaching. **4** Christian character and conduct. **5** the state of being a Christian. **6** Christians collectively. **Christianize, Christianise** *v.t.* to convert to Christianity. *~v.i.* to be converted to Christianity. **Christianization** (-zā´shən) *n.* **Christianlike** *a.* **Christianly** *a.*, *adv.* **Christian name** *n.* a forename, esp. one given in baptism. **Christian Science** *n.* the religious system of the Church of Christ Scientist, including the belief that diseases can be healed without medical treatment. **Christian Scientist** *n.* [L *Christiānus*]

Christie (kris´ti), **Christy** *n.* (*pl.* **Christies**) in skiing, a turn in which the skis are kept parallel, used esp. for stopping or turning sharply. [abbr. of *Christiania*, former name of Oslo, Norway]

Christingle (kris´ting·gəl) *n.* a lighted candle held by children at Advent services etc., representing Christ as the light of the world. [perh. from G *Christkindl*, dim. of *Christkind*, Christ child]

Christmas (kris´məs) *n.* **1** the festival of the nativity of Jesus Christ celebrated on 25 Dec. **2** Christmastide. *~a.* of, relating to or appropriate to Christmas or its festivities. *~int.* (*sl.*) used to express surprise, dismay etc. **Christmas box** *n.* a present or tip given at Christmas, esp. to tradesmen. **Christmas cactus** *n.* a S American branching cactus, *Schlumbergera truncatus*, which produces red flowers in winter. **Christmas cake** *n.* a rich fruit cake, usu. iced, eaten at Christmas. **Christmas card** *n.* an ornamental card sent as a Christmas greeting. **Christmas carol** *n.* a song of praise sung at Christmas. **Christmas Day** *n.* the day of the festival of Christmas, 25 Dec. **Christmas Eve** *n.* **1** the day before Christmas Day. **2** the evening of this day. **Christmas pudding** *n.* a rich pudding eaten at Christmas. **Christmas rose** *n.* a white-flowered plant, *Helleborus niger*, flowering in winter. **Christmas stocking** *n.* a stocking that children hang up on Christmas Eve for Father Christmas to fill with presents. **Christmassy, Christmasy** *a.* **Christmastide, Christmastime** *n.* the season of Christmas. **Christmas tree** *n.* an evergreen or artificial tree kept indoors and decorated at Christmas. [OE *cristes mæsse*]

Christo- (kris´tō) *comb. form* of or relating to Christ. [L *Christus*, Gr. *christos*]

Christolatry (kristol´ətri) *n.* the worship of Christ regarded as a form of idolatry.

Christology (kristol´əji) *n.* the branch of theology concerned with Christ. **Christological** (-loj´-) *a.* **Christologist** *n.*

Christophany (kristof´əni) *n.* (*pl.* **Christophanies**) an appearance of Christ to mankind.

Christy CHRISTIE.

chrom- CHROMO-.

chroma (krō´mə) *n.* **1** purity or intensity of colour. **2** in colour television, the colour component of a signal. [Gr. *khrōma*, colour]

chromat- CHROMATO-.

chromate (krō´māt) *n.* a salt of chromic acid.

chromatic (krəmat´ik) *a.* **1** of or relating to colour. **2** coloured. **3** (*Mus.*) including notes not belonging to the diatonic scale. **chromatic aberration** *n.* the failure of different wavelengths of refracted light to focus at the same distance, causing a blurred image. **chromatically** *adv.* **chromaticism** *n.* **chromaticity** (-tis´-) *n.* the purity and dominant wavelength of colour or light. **chromatics** *n.* the science of colour. **chromatic scale** *n.* (*Mus.*) a succession of notes a semitone apart. **chromatic semitone** *n.* (*Mus.*) the interval between a note and its flat or sharp. [Gr. *chrōmatikos*]

chromatid (krō´mətid) *n.* (*Biol.*) either of the two strands into which a chromosome divides during cell division.

chromatin (krō´mətin) *n.* the portion of the nucleus of a cell, consisting of nucleic acids and protein, which readily takes up a basic stain.

chromato- (krō´mətō), **chromat-** *comb. form* of or relating to colour. [Gr. *chrōma chrōmatos*, colour]

chromatography (krōmətog´rəfi) *n.* a technique for separating or analysing the components of a mixture which relies on the differing capacity for adsorption of the components in a column of powder, strip of paper etc. **chromatogram** (krōmat´əgram) *n.* the visual record produced by separating the components of a mixture by chromatography. **chromatograph** (-mat´əgrahf) *n.* **chromatographic** (-graf´ik) *a.*

chromatophore (krōmat´əfaw) *n.* a cell in some animals that can concentrate or disperse pigment, causing the animal to change colour.

chromatopsia (krōmətop´siə) *n.* abnormal coloured vision. [Gr. *-opsia*, seeing]

chrome (krōm) *n.* **1** chromium, esp. chromium-plating. **2** anything plated with chromium. **3** a pigment containing chromium. ~*v.t.* **1** to plate with chromium. **2** to treat with a chromium compound. **chrome colour** *n.* a colour prepared from a chromium salt. **chrome dioxide** *n.* chromium dioxide. **chrome green** *n.* a dark green pigment obtained from chromic oxide. **chrome leather** *n.* leather prepared by tanning with chromium salts. **chrome steel** *n.* a hard steel containing chromium. **chrome tape** *n.* magnetic tape coated with chromium dioxide, esp. in an audio cassette. **chrome yellow** *n.* a brilliant yellow pigment containing lead chromate. [F, from Gr. *chrōma*, colour]

chromic (krō´mik) *a.* of, relating to or containing trivalent chromium. **chromic acid** *n.* an acid containing hydrogen, chromium and oxygen.

chrominance (krō´minəns) *n.* **1** the colour quality of light. **2** in television, the difference between a given colour and a reference colour of equal luminance. [CHROM-, lum*inance*]

chromite (krō´mīt) *n.* **1** a mineral consisting of chromium and iron oxide. **2** a salt of divalent chromium.

chromium (krō´miəm) *n.* a bright grey metallic element, at. no. 24, chem. symbol Cr, remarkable for the brilliance of colour of its compounds, used as a protective or decorative plating. **chromium dioxide** *n.* a chemical compound used to coat magnetic tape. **chromium-plate** *v.t.* to electroplate with chromium to give a shiny decorative or protective coating. ~*n.* such a coating. **chromium-plated** *a.* **1** electroplated with chromium. **2** showy. **chromium steel** *n.* chrome steel.

chromo (krō´mō) *n.* (*pl.* **chromos**) a chromolithograph.

chromo- (krō´mō), **chrom-** *comb.form* **1** of or relating to colour. **2** of or relating to chromium. [Gr. *chrōma*, colour]

chromodynamics (krōmōdīnam´iks) *n.* QUANTUM CHROMODYNAMICS (under QUANTUM).

chromogen (krō´məjən) *n.* **1** an organic colouring matter. **2** an animal or vegetable matter which alters in colour under certain conditions.

chromolithograph (krōmōlith´əgrahf) *n.* a picture printed in colours by lithography. ~*v.t.* to print in this way. **chromolithographer** (-og´-) *n.* **chromolithographic** (-graf´-) *a.* **chromolithography** (-og´-) *n.*

chromophore (krō´məfaw) *n.* a group of atoms that are responsible for the colour of a chemical compound.

chromosome (krō´məsōm) *n.* any of the rod-shaped structures in a cell nucleus that carry the genes which transmit hereditary characteristics. **chromosomal** (-sō´-) *a.* **chromosome map** *n.* a plan of the relative positions of genes on a chromosome. [Gr. *sōma*, body]

chromosphere (krō´məsfiə) *n.* the gaseous envelope of the sun through which light passes from the photosphere. **chromospheric** (-fe´rik) *a.*

chromotypography (krōmōtīpog´rəfi) *n.* colour printing.

Chron. *abbr.* Chronicles.

chron- CHRONO-.

chronic (kron´ik) *a.* **1** (of a disease, social problem etc.) of long duration, or apt to recur. **2** (*coll.*) habitual (*a chronic smoker*). **3** (*coll.*) very bad, severe. **chronically** *adv.* **chronic fatigue syndrome** *n.* myalgic encephalomyelitis, ME. **chronicity** (-nis´-) *n.* [F *chronique*, L, late L *chronicus*, Gr. *chronikos* (*chronos*, time)]

chronicle (kron´ikəl) *n.* **1** a register or history of events in order of time. **2** a history, a record. **3** a narrative account. ~*v.t.* to record in or as if in a chronicle. **chronicler** *n.* **Chronicles** *n.pl.* the two books of the Old Testament immediately following I and II Kings. [ME and OF *cronique*, late L *chronica*, sing., from Gr. *chronika*, neut. pl. (see CHRONIC)]

chrono- (kron´ō), **chron-** *comb. form* of or relating to time or dates. [Gr. *chronos*, time]

chronogram (kron´əgram) *n.* **1** a date given by taking the letters of an inscription which coincide with Roman numerals and printing them larger than the rest. **2** the record produced by a chronograph. **chronogrammatic** (-mat´-) *a.*

chronograph (kron´əgrahf) *n.* **1** an instrument for measuring and registering very small intervals of time with great precision. **2** a stopwatch. **chronographer** (-nog´-) *n.* **1** a chronicler. **2** a chronologist. **chronographic** (-graf´-) *a.* of or relating to a chronograph. **chronography** *n.* (*pl.* **chronographies**) a description of past events.

chronology (krənol´əji) *n.* (*pl.* **chronologies**) **1** the study of historical records etc. in order to determine the sequence of past events. **2** an arrangement of dates of historical events. **3** a tabular list of dates. **chronological** (kronəloj´-) *a.* **1** in order of occurrence in time (*in chronological order*). **2** of or relating to chronology. **chronological age** *n.* age in years, as opposed to mental etc. age. **chronologically** *adv.* **chronologist, chronologer** *n.* **chronologize, chronologise** *v.t.* to arrange in order of occurrence in time.

chronometer (krənom´itə) *n.* **1** an instrument that measures time with great precision, esp. one used in navigation at sea. **2** any instrument that measures time, such as a sundial, clock or watch. **chronometric** (kronōmet´-), **chronometrical** *a.* **chronometrically** *adv.* **chronometry** *n.*

chronoscope (kron´əskōp) *n.* an instrument registering small intervals of time, used esp. for measuring the velocity of projectiles.

chrys- CHRYSO-.

chrysalis (kris´əlis), **chrysalid** (-əlid) *n.* (*pl.* **chrysalises, chrysalides** (-dēz), **chrysalids**) **1** the last stage through which a lepidopterous insect passes before becoming a perfect insect. **2** the pupa, the shell or case containing the imago. **3** an undeveloped or transitional state. [L *chrysalis, chrysallis*, Gr. *chrusallis* (*chrusos*, gold)]

chrysanth (krisanth´, -zanth´) *n.* (*coll.*) a cultivated chrysanthemum. [abbr.]

chrysanthemum (krisan´thəməm, -zan´-) *n.* **1** any cultivated plant of the genera *Chrysanthemum* or *Dendranthema*, with brightly coloured flowers. **2** any plant of the genus *Chrysanthemum*. [L *chrȳsanthemum*, Gr. *chrusanthemon*, marigold (CHRYS-, *anthemon*, flower)]

chryselephantine (kriseləfan´tin) *a.* **1** made partly of gold and partly of ivory. **2** overlaid with gold and ivory. [Gr. *chryselephantinos*]

chryso- (kris´ō), **chrys-** *comb. form* **1** of gold. **2** of a bright yellow colour. [Gr. *chrusos*, gold]

chrysoberyl (kris´əberəl, -ber´-) *n.* a gem of a yellowish-green colour, composed of beryllium aluminate. [L *chrysobērylIus*, Gr. *chrusobērullos*]

chrysolite (kris´əlīt) *n.* a yellowish-green or brown translucent orthorhombic mineral, a variety of olivine. [OF *crisolit*, L *chrysolithus*, Gr. *chrusolithos* (*lithos*, stone)]

chrysoprase (kris´əprāz) *n.* **1** an apple-green variety of chalcedony. **2** in the New Testament, a variety of beryl. [ME and OF *crisopace*, L *chrysoprasus*, Gr. *chrusoprasos* (*prason*, a leek)]

chrysotile (kris´ətīl) *n.* a fibrous mineral, a source of asbestos. [Gr. *tilos*, fibre]

chthonian (thō´niən), **chthonic** (thon´-) *a.* of or relating to the underworld. [Gr. *chthōnios* (*chthōn chthonos*, earth)]

chub (chŭb) *n.* (*pl. in general* **chub**, *in particular* **chubs**) **1** a coarse river fish, *Leuciscus cephalus*. **2** any of various N American fishes. **chub-faced** *a.* having a plump face. [etym. unknown]

Chubb® (chŭb), **Chubb lock** *n.* a type of lock that cannot be picked.

chubby (chŭb´i) *a.* (*comp.* **chubbier,** *superl.* **chubbiest**) fat, plump, rounded (*a chubby child; chubby cheeks*). **chubbily** *adv.* **chubbiness** *n.* [CHUB]

chuck[1] (chŭk) *v.t.* **1** (*coll.*) to fling, to throw. **2** (*coll.*) to reject, to give up (*He chucked his girlfriend*). **3** to strike gently under the chin. ~*n.* **1** a slight tap or blow under the chin. **2** a toss or throw. **the chuck** (*sl.*) dismissal (from a job etc.). **to chuck away 1** (*coll.*) to discard. **2** (*coll.*) to waste. **to chuck in** (*coll.*) to abandon, to give up. **to chuck it** (*sl.*) to stop, to desist. **to chuck out 1** (*coll.*) to eject forcibly from a meeting, building etc. **2** (*coll.*) to throw away. **to chuck up 1** (*coll.*) to chuck in. **2** (*esp. N Am., sl.*) to vomit. **chucker-out** *n.* (*coll.*) a bouncer, a person employed to eject undesirable people. [earlier *chock*; prob. imit. (cp. F *choquer*, Dut. *schokken*)]

chuck[2] (chŭk) *n.* **1** a device for holding the work to be turned on a lathe, or for holding the bit in a drill. **2** a cut of beef from the neck and shoulder. **3** (*esp. N Am., dial.*) food. ~*v.t.* to fix on a lathe or drill by means of a chuck. **chuck key** *n.* an instrument for tightening or loosening a chuck. **chuck steak** *n.* beef steak from the neck and shoulder. **chuckwagon** *n.* (*N Am.*) **1** a wagon carrying food, cooking utensils etc. **2** a roadside eating place. [CHOCK]

chuck[3] (chŭk) *n.* the call of a hen to her chickens. ~*v.i.* to make such a noise. ~*v.t.* to call, as a hen does her chickens. [onomat.]

chuck[4] (chŭk) *n.* **1** (*dial.*) darling, dear. **2** (*Sc., North.*) a chick, a fowl. [var. of CHICK[1]]

chuckle (chŭk´əl) *v.i.* **1** to laugh to oneself. **2** to make a half-suppressed sound of laughter. **3** (of a hen etc.) to make a clucking noise. ~*n.* such a laugh or noise. [CHUCK[3]]

chucklehead (chŭk´əlhed) *n.* (*coll.*) a stupid person. **chuckleheaded** *a.* [prob. var. of CHUCK[2]]

chuddar CHADOR.

chuddy (chŭd´i) *n.* (*Austral., New Zeal., sl.*) chewing gum.

chuff (chŭf) *v.i.* **1** (of a steam locomotive etc.) to make a short puffing sound. **2** to move while making such sounds. ~*n.* such a sound. **chuff-chuff** *n.* a steam engine or train (used by or to children). [onomat.]

chuffed (chŭft) *a.* (*sl.*) pleased, happy. [dial. *chuff*]

chug (chŭg) *n.* a short dull explosive sound, as of an engine. ~*v.i.* (*pres.p.* **chugging,** *past, p.p.* **chugged**) **1** to make such a noise. **2** to move while making such a noise. [onomat.]

chukar (chuk´ah) *n.* an Indian partridge, *Alectoris chukar*, with red legs and bill. [Hind. *cakor*]

chukka (chŭk´ə), **chukker** *n.* any of the periods into which a polo game is divided. **chukka boot** *n.* an ankle-high boot worn esp. for playing polo. [Hind.]

chum[1] (chŭm) *n.* (*coll.*) a close friend. ~*v.i.* (*pres.p.* **chumming,** *past, p.p.* **chummed**) to share rooms with another. **to chum up** to become friendly (with). **chummy** *a.* (*comp.* **chummier,** *superl.* **chummiest**) (*coll.*) friendly. **chummily** *adv.* **chumminess** *n.* [orig. a person sharing a room, perh. from *chamber-fellow*]

chum[2] (chŭm) *n.* (*N Am.*) **1** chopped fish used by anglers as bait. **2** refuse from fish. [etym. uncertain]

chump (chŭmp) *n.* **1** (*sl.*) a silly person. **2** a cut of meat from the loin and hind leg. **3** a short, thick piece of wood. **4** (*sl.*) the head. **off one's chump** (*sl.*) crazy. **chump chop** *n.* a thick meat chop from the chump. [parallel to CHUNK (perh. influenced by CHOP[1] and LUMP[1])]

chunder (chŭn´də) *v.i.* (*Austral., sl.*) to vomit. ~*n.* vomit. **chunderous** *a.* nauseating. [etym. unknown]

chunk (chŭngk) *n.* **1** a short, thick lump of anything. **2** a large portion. **chunky** *a.* (*comp.* **chunkier,** *superl.* **chunkiest**) **1** containing or consisting of chunks. **2** short and thick. **3** small and sturdy. **4** (of clothes etc.) made of thick material (*a chunky sweater*). **chunkiness** *n.* [prob. var. of CHUCK[2]]

Chunnel (chŭn´əl) *n.* (*coll.*) a tunnel connecting England and France under the English Channel. [*Ch*annel t*unnel*]

chunter (chŭn´tə) *v.i.* (*coll.*) **1** to talk at length and meaninglessly. **2** to mutter or grumble. [onomat.]

chupatty CHAPATI.

church (chœch) *n.* **1** a building set apart and consecrated for public worship, esp. Christian worship. **2** a body of Christian believers worshipping in one place, with the same ritual and doctrines. **3** (*usu.* **Church**) Christians collectively. **4** (*usu.* **Church**) a section of Christians organized for worship under a certain form (*the Roman Catholic Church*). **5** (*usu.* **Church**) the whole organization of a religious body or association. **6** (*usu.* **Church**) the clergy as distinct from the laity. **7** (*usu.* **Church**) ecclesiastical authority or influence (*the conflict between Church and State*). **8** (*N Am.*) the communicants of a congregation. **9** a meeting for Christian worship in a church (*to go to church; after church on Sunday*). ~*v.t.* **1** †to say the thanksgiving service for (esp. a woman after childbirth). **2** (*Sc.*) to take or escort to church (esp. a bride on her first attendance after marriage). ~*a.* **1** of or relating to a church. **2** ecclesiastical. **to go into the Church** to take holy orders. **Church Army** *n.* an organization in the Church of England resembling the Salvation Army. **Church Commissioners** *n.pl.* a body of administrators who manage the finances and property of the Church of England. **churchgoer** *n.* a person who goes regularly to church. **churchgoing** *n.* the practice of regularly going to church. ~*a.* habitually going to church. **churchism** *n.* preference for and adherence to the principles of a Church, esp. of the established Church. **churchless** *a.* **1** without a church. **2** not belonging to a Church. **churchlike** *a.* befitting the Church or clerics. **churchly** *a.* appropriate to or concerned with the Church. **churchman** *n.* (*pl.* **churchmen**) **1** a cleric, an ecclesiastic. **2** a member of the Church of England. **3** a member of any Church. **4** a supporter of the Church. **churchmanly** *a.* **churchmanship** *n.* **Church Militant** *n.* Christians on earth, regarded as warring against evil, as distinct from the *Church Triumphant.* **church mouse** *n.* a very poor person (from the simile *as poor as a church mouse*). **church music** *n.* sacred music, such as that used in church services. **Church of England** *n.* the English established Church, the Anglican Church. **Church of Rome** *n.* the Roman Catholic Church. **Church of Scotland** *n.* the Scottish established Church. **church parade** *n.* a parade by Scouts, Guides etc. or by members of the armed forces in conjunction with attendance at a church service. **church school** *n.* a school controlled or supported by a particular Church, esp. the Church of England. **church service** *n.* **1** service in a church. **2** the Book of Common Prayer with the daily lessons added. **church text** *n.* a Gothic or black-letter typeface used in monumental inscriptions. **Church Triumphant** *n.* Christians in heaven, as distinct from the *Church Militant.* **churchward, churchwards** *adv.* towards the church. **churchwarden** *n.* **1** in an Anglican parish either of two officers who protect church property, superintend the performance of divine worship etc. and act as the legal representatives of the parish generally. **2** a long clay pipe with a large bowl. **churchwoman** *n.* (*pl.* **churchwomen**) **1** a female member of the clergy. **2** a female member of Church, esp. the Church of England. **3** a female supporter of the Church. **churchy** *a.* (*comp.* **churchier,** *superl.* **churchiest**) **1** making a hobby of church work and church matters. **2** aggressively devoted to the Church and intolerant of dissenters. **3** like a church. **churchi-**

ness *n.* **churchyard** *n.* the ground adjoining a church consecrated for the burial of the dead. [OE *circe, cirice,* WG *kīrika,* Gr. *kuriakon,* neut. of a. *kuriakos* (*kurios,* lord)]

churidars (choo´ridahz) *n.pl.* tight-fitting trousers worn by Indian men and women. [Hind.]

churinga (chəring´gə) *n.* (*pl.* **churinga, churingas**) (*Austral.*) a sacred amulet. [Austral. Abor.]

churl (chœl) *n.* **1** a surly, rude or ill-bred person. **2** †a person of low birth. **3** †a peasant. **4** †a serf or villein. **5** †a niggard. **churlish** *a.* **1** surly, rude, ill-bred. **2** mean, miserly. **churlishly** *adv.* **churlishness** *n.* [OE *ceorl,* from Gmc. (cp. Icel. *karl,* OHG *charal,* G *Kerl*)]

churn (chœn) *n.* **1** a large can for carrying milk long distances. **2** a vessel in which milk or cream is agitated or beaten in order to produce butter. **3** any similar device that mixes or turns. *~v.t.* **1** to agitate (milk or cream) in a churn for the purpose of making butter. **2** to make (butter) in this way. **3** to agitate with violence or continued motion (often with *up*). **4** to upset (often with *up*). *~v.i.* **1** to perform the operation of churning butter. **2** (of waves etc.) to foam, to swirl about. **3** to move or turn out in an agitated way. **to churn out** to produce rapidly and prolifically, usu. without concern for quality. **churning** *n.* **1** the action of churning or being churned. **2** the butter made at one operation. [OE *cyrin,* from Gmc. (cp. Icel. *kirna,* Dut. *karn*)]

churr CHIRR.

churrasco (churas´kō) *n.* a meat dish of S America, consisting of steak barbecued over wood or charcoal. **churrascaria** (-kəriə´) *n.* a restaurant specializing in this. [Sp., prob. from dial. *churrascar,* to burn]

chute[1] (shoot) *n.* **1** an inclined trough for conveying water, timber, grain etc. to a lower level. **2** an inclined watercourse. **3** a slide into a swimming pool. **4** a toboggan slide. [F *chute* (late L *caduta,* fem. of *cadūtus,* p.p., from L *cadere,* to fall), influenced by SHOOT]

chute[2] (shoot) *n.* (*coll.*) a parachute. **chutist** *n.* [abbr.]

chutney (chŭt´ni) *n.* (*pl.* **chutneys**) a hot seasoned condiment or pickle. [Hind. *chatnī*]

chutzpah (khuts´pə, huts´-) *n.* (*sl.*) barefaced audacity. [Yiddish]

chyack CHIACK.

chyle (kīl) *n.* the milky fluid separated from the chyme by the action of the pancreatic juice and the bile, absorbed by the lacteal vessels, and assimilated with the blood. **chylaceous** (-lā´-) *a.* **chylo-** *comb. form* chyle. **chylomicron** (-mī´kron) *n.* a tiny droplet of fat, the form in which dietary fat is carried in the blood and chyle. **chylous** *a.* [F, from L *chylus,* Gr. *chulos* (stem *chu-, cheu-, cheein,* to pour)]

chyme (kīm) *n.* the pulpy mass of digested food before the chyle is separated from it. **chymo-** *comb. form* chyme. **chymous** *a.* [L *chȳmus,* Gr. *khumos* (as CHYLE)]

chypre (shē´prə) *n.* a strong sandalwood perfume. [F, Cyprus]

CI *abbr.* **1** Channel Islands. **2** Ivory Coast (IVR). **3** (*Hist.*) Order of the Crown of India.

Ci *abbr.* curie.

CIA *abbr.* Central Intelligence Agency.

ciabatta (chəbat´ə) *n.* (*pl.* **ciabattas**) **1** a moist type of Italian bread made with olive oil. **2** a loaf of this bread. [It. dial., a slipper, from its shape]

ciao (chow) *int.* (*coll.*) used to express greeting or leave-taking. [It.]

CIB *abbr.* Criminal Investigation Branch (of the New Zealand police).

ciborium (sibaw´riəm) *n.* (*pl.* **ciboria** (-riə)) **1** a vessel with an arched cover for the Eucharist. **2** a shrine or tabernacle to receive this. **3** a baldachin canopy or shrine. [med. L, from Gr. *kibōrion,* cup-shaped seed vessel of the Egyptian water lily]

cicada (sikah´də), **cicala** (-lə), **cigala** (-gah´lə) *n.* (*pl.* **cicadas, cicadae** (-dē), **cicalas, cicale** (-lā), **cigalas**) any homopterous insect of the family Cicadidae, with stridulating organs. [L, It. and Prov. (cp. F *cigale*]

cicatrice (sik´ətris), **cicatrix** (-triks) *n.* (*pl.* **cicatrices** (-trī´sēz)) **1** the mark or scar left after a wound or ulcer has healed. **2** a mark on a stem or branch of a plant where a leaf was attached. **cicatricial** (-trish´-) *a.* **cicatricose** (-kat´rikōs) *a.* **cicatrize, cicatrise** *v.t.* to heal a wound or ulcer by scar formation. *~v.i.* (of a wound or ulcer) to heal in this way. **cicatrization** (-zā´shən) *n.* [OF *cicatrice,* L *cicatrix*]

cicatricle (sik´ətrikəl), **cicatricule** (-kūl) *n.* the germinating point in the yolk of an egg, or the vesicle of a seed. [L *cicātrīcula,* dim. of *cicatrix,* CICATRICE]

cicatrix, cicatrize etc. CICATRICE.

cicely (sis´əli) *n.* (*pl.* **cicelies**) any of several umbelliferous plants, esp. sweet cicely. [L *seselis,* Gr. *seseli, seselis* (perh. confused with *Cicely, Cecilia*)]

cicerone (chichərō´ni, sisə-) *n.* (*pl.* **cicerones, ciceroni** (-rō´ni)) a guide who explains the curiosities and interesting features of a place to strangers. [It., from *Cicero -ōnem,* the Roman orator, 106–43 BC]

Ciceronian (sisərō´niən) *a.* resembling the style of Cicero; easy, flowing. *~n.* an admirer or imitator of the style of Cicero. **Ciceronianism** *n.* [L, *Ciceroniānus* (see CICERONE)]

cichlid (sik´lid) *n.* any tropical freshwater fish of the family Cichlidae, often kept in aquaria. *~a.* of or relating to this family. **cichloid** *a.* [Gr. *kikhlē,* a sea fish]

cicisbeo (chichizbā´ō) *n.* (*pl.* **cicisbei** (-bā´ē)) the recognized lover of a married woman. **cicisbeism** *n.* the system in 18th-cent. Italy that recognized this. [It. (etym. uncertain)]

cicuta (sikū´tə) *n.* any umbelliferous plant of the genus *Cicuta,* including the water hemlock. [L]

CID *abbr.* Criminal Investigation Department.

-cide (sīd) *comb. form* **1** a person or substance that kills, as *fratricide, insecticide.* **2** a killing, as *homicide.* [F, from L *-cidium* (*caedere,* to kill)]

cider (sī´də), **cyder** *n.* **1** an alcoholic drink made from the fermented juice of apples. **2** (*N Am.*) an unfermented apple-juice drink. **cider press** *n.* a press for squeezing the juice from crushed apples. [OF *sidre* (F *cidre*), late L *sicera,* Gr. *sikera,* Heb. *shēkār,* strong drink (*shākar,* to drink to intoxication)]

ci-devant (sēdəvã´) *a.* former, of a past time. *~adv.* formerly. *~n.* a French aristocrat during the Revolution. [F]

CIE *abbr.* (*Hist.*) Companion (of the Order) of the Indian Empire.

Cie. *abbr.* Company. [F *Compagnie*]

☒ **cieling** common misspelling of CEILING.

c.i.f. *abbr.* cost, insurance, freight.

cig (sig), **ciggy** (sig´i) *n.* (*pl.* **cigs, ciggies**) (*coll.*) a cigarette.

cigala CICADA.

cigar (sigah´) *n.* a roll of tobacco leaves for smoking. **cigarette** (sigəret´), (*N Am.*) **cigaret** *n.* a cylinder of cut tobacco or aromatic herbs rolled in paper for smoking. **cigarette card** *n.* a picture card enclosed in cigarette packets. **cigarette end** *n.* the unsmoked part of a cigarette. **cigarette holder** *n.* a mouthpiece for holding a cigarette. **cigarette lighter** *n.* a device for lighting cigarettes etc. **cigarette machine** *n.* **1** a machine for making cigarettes. **2** a vending machine for cigarettes. **cigarette paper** *n.* a piece of thin paper for wrapping the tobacco in a cigarette. **cigar holder** *n.* a mouthpiece for a cigar. **cigarillo** (sigəril´ō) *n.* (*pl.* **cigarillos**) a very small cigar. **cigar-shaped** *a.* cylindrical, with tapering ends. **cigar store** *n.* (*N Am.*) a tobacconist's shop. [Sp. *cigarro* (perh. from *cigarra,* cicada)]

ciggy CIG.

ci-gît (sēzhē´) here lies (inscribed on gravestones). [F]

CIGS *abbr.* (*Hist.*) Chief of the Imperial General Staff.

cilia, ciliary etc. CILIUM.

cilice (sil´is) *n.* **1** haircloth. **2** a hair shirt. **cilicious** (-lish´-) *a.* [OE *cilic*, Gr. *kilikion*, of Cilician goats' hair]

cilium (sil´iəm) *n.* (*pl.* **cilia** (-iə)) **1** an eyelash. **2** a flagellum in a unicellular organism. **ciliary** *a.* **ciliary body** *n.* the part of the eye that connects the iris to the choroid, containing the muscle that controls the shape of the lens. **ciliate** (-ət) *a.* having cilia. ~*n.* a ciliate protozoan of the phylum Ciliophora. **ciliated** (-ātid) *a.* **ciliation** (-ā´shən) *n.* **ciliolate** (-lit, -lāt) *a.* covered with tiny hairs. [L, eyelash]

cill SILL.

CIM *abbr.* **1** computer input on microfilm. **2** computer integrated manufacture.

cimbalom (sim´bələm) *n.* a Hungarian type of dulcimer. [Hung., It. *cembalo*]

cimetidine (sīmet´idēn) *n.* a drug used in the treatment of gastric and duodenal ulcers.

cimex (sī´meks) *n.* (*pl.* **cimices** (sim´isēz)) any insect of the genus *Cimex*, containing the bedbug.

Cimmerian (simiə´riən) *a.* profoundly dark. [L *Cimmerius*, Gr. *Kimmerios*, a member of the Cimmerii, whose country was fabled to be in a state of perpetual darkness]

C.-in-C. *abbr.* Commander-in-Chief.

cinch (sinch) *n.* **1** (*coll.*) a certainty. **2** (*coll.*) an easy task. **3** a firm grip or hold. **4** (*N Am.*) a broad kind of saddle girth. ~*v.t.* **1** to furnish, fasten or tighten with or as if with a cinch. **2** to hold firmly. **3** (*sl.*) to make certain of. **to cinch up** to fasten or tighten a cinch around. [Sp. *cincha*, L *cingula*, from *cingere*, to gird]

cinchona (singkō´nə) *n.* (*pl.* **cinchonas**) **1** any S American tree of the genus *Cinchona*, whose bark yields quinine. **2** the bark of such a tree. **3** a medicinal substance derived from this bark. **cinchonaceous** (-nā´-) *a.* **cinchonic** (-kon-´) *a.* **cinchonine** (sing´kōnēn) *n.* an organic alkaloid contained in cinchona bark. **cinchonism** (sing´-) *n.* a disturbed condition of the body caused by overdoses of cinchona or quinine. **cinchonize** (sing´-), **cinchonise** *v.t.* to treat with cinchona or quinine. **cinchonization** (-zā´shən) *n.* [Countess of *Chinchón*, 1576–1639, vicereine of Peru]

cincture (singk´chə) *n.* **1** (*poet.*) a belt, a girdle. **2** an enclosure. **3** (*Archit.*) the fillet at the top and bottom of a column. [L *cinctūra* (*cinctus*, p.p. of *cingere*, to gird)]

cinder (sin´də) *n.* **1** a piece of coal that has ceased to burn but retains heat. **2** a piece of partly burnt coal or other combustible. **3** light slag. **4** (*pl.*) the refuse of burnt coal or wood; the remains of anything that has been subject to combustion. **5** (*pl.*) scoriae ejected from a volcano. **to burn to a cinder** to burn thoroughly; to render useless, inedible etc. by burning. **cinder block** *n.* (*N Am.*) BREEZE-BLOCK (under BREEZE[3]). **cinder path, cinder track** *n.* a footpath or racecourse covered with cinders. **cindery** *a.* [OE *sinder* (cp. Icel. *sindr*, G *Sinter*, slag or dross)]

Cinderella (sindərel´ə) *n.* **1** a person whose merits are unrecognized. **2** a despised or neglected person or thing. **Cinderella dance** *n.* a dance ending at midnight. [heroine of a fairy tale]

cine- (sin´i), **ciné-** (sin´ā) *comb. form* **1** cinema. **2** cinematographic, as *cine-projector*. **cine-camera** *n.* a camera for taking motion pictures. **cine-film** *n.* film suitable for use in a cine-camera.

cineaste (sin´iast), **cineast** *n.* **1** a cinema enthusiast. **2** a person who makes films. [F]

cinema (sin´əmə) *n.* (*pl.* **cinemas**) **1** a theatre where cinematographic films are shown. **2** films collectively. **3** the making of films as an art form or industry. **cinema-goer** *n.* a person who goes regularly to the cinema. **cinema organ** *n.* an organ with special effects etc. **Cinemascope®** *n.* a method of film projection on a wide screen. **cinematheque** *n.* **1** a film archive or library. **2** a small, intimate cinema. **cinematic** (-mat´-) *a.* **cinematically** *adv.* [see CINEMATOGRAPH]

cinematograph (sinəmat´əgrahf), **kinematograph** (kin-) *n.* an apparatus for projecting very rapidly onto a screen a series of photographs, so as to create the illusion of continuous motion. **cinematographer** (-tog´rəfə) *n.* **cinematographic** (-graf´-) *a.* **cinematographically** *adv.* **cinematography** (-tog´-) *n.* [F *cinématographe*, from Gr. *kinēma -atos*, movement, -GRAPH]

cinéma-vérité (sēnāmə vā´rētā), **ciné-vérité** (sēnā-) *n.* cinema which approaches a documentary style by using realistic settings, characters etc. [F, lit. cinema truth]

cinephile (sin´ifīl) *n.* a person who likes the cinema.

Cinerama® (sinərah´mə) *n.* a method of film projection on a wide screen to give a three-dimensional effect.

cineraria[1] (sinəreə´riə) *n.* (*pl.* **cinerarias**) a garden or hothouse plant, *Pericallis cruenta*, cultivated for its brightly coloured daisy-like flowers. [L *cinerārius*, ash-coloured (*cinis -eris*, ashes)]

cineraria[2] CINERARIUM (under CINERARY).

cinerary (sin´ərəri) *a.* of or relating to ashes. **cinerarium** (-reə´riəm) *n.* (*pl.* **cinerariums, cineraria** (-riə)) a place for the deposit of human ashes after cremation. **cinerary urn** *n.* an urn used to hold the ashes of the dead. **cineration** (-ā´shən) *n.* reduction to ashes, cremation. **cinerator** *n.* a furnace for cremating corpses. **cinereous** (-niə´-) *a.* ash-coloured, ash-grey. [see CINERARIA[1]]

ciné-vérité CINÉMA-VÉRITÉ.

Cingalese SINHALESE.

cingulum (sing´gūləm) *n.* (*pl.* **cingula** (-lə)) (*Anat., Zool.*) a girdle-like part or structure, such as the ridge that surrounds the base of a tooth. [L, from *cingere*, to gird]

cinnabar (sin´əbah) *n.* **1** a bright red form of mercuric sulphide. **2** vermilion. **3** a large moth, *Tyria jacobaeae*, with red and black markings. ~*a.* bright red in colour. **cinnabaric** (-bar´-) *a.* [late L *cinnabaris*, Gr. *kinnabari* (Oriental in orig.)]

cinnamon (sin´əmən) *n.* **1** a spice obtained from the aromatic inner bark of a SE Asian tree, *Cinnamomum zeylanicum*. **2** this or any other tree of the genus *Cinnamomum*. **3** the bark of any of these trees. **4** a light brownish-yellow colour. ~*a.* of this colour. **cinnamic** (-nam´-) *a.* **cinnamic acid** *n.* a weak acid used in perfumery. **cinnamon stone** *n.* a cinnamon-coloured variety of garnet, hessonite. [F *cinnamome*, L *cinnamōmum*, Gr. *kinamōmon*, Heb. *qinnāmōn*]

cinque (singk), **cinq** *n.* five, esp. the five at cards or dice. **Cinque Ports** *n.pl.* a group of five English ports: Dover, Sandwich, Hastings, Hythe and Romney (to which Winchelsea and Rye were afterwards added), which enjoyed special privileges because they offered a defence against invasion. [OF *cink* (F *cinq*), L *quinque*]

cinquecento (chingkwichen´tō) *n.* the revived classical style of art and literature that characterized the 16th cent., esp. in Italy. **cinquecentist** *n.* [It. (short for *mil cinque cento*, 1500)]

cinquefoil (singk´foil) *n.* **1** a plant of the genus *Potentilla*, with five-lobed leaves. **2** (*Archit.*) an ornamental foliation in five compartments, used in tracery etc. **3** (*Her.*) a device representing a five-petalled flower. **cinquefoiled** *a.* [OF (cp. F *quintefeuille*), L *quinquefolium* (*quinque*, five, *folium*, leaf)]

Cinzano® (chinzah´nō) *n.* an Italian vermouth.

CIO *abbr.* Congress of Industrial Organizations.

cion SCION.

cipher (sī´fə), **cypher** *n.* **1** a code or alphabet used to carry on secret correspondence, designed to be intelligible only to the persons concerned. **2** anything written in this. 3 a key to it. 4 the arithmetical symbol 0. 5 a person or thing of no importance. 6 a monogram, a device. 7 a character of any kind used in writing or printing. 8 an Arabic numeral. 9 the continued sounding of an organ pipe through a defective valve. ~*v.i.* 1 †to do arithmetic. 2 (of an organ) to continue sounding when the key is not pressed. ~*v.t.* 1 to express in cipher. 2 to work out by means of arithmetic. **cipher key** *n.* a key for reading writing in cipher. [OF *cifre* (F *chiffre*), Arab. *çifr*, empty]

cipolin (sip´əlin), **cipollino** (chipəlē´nō) *n.* (*pl.* **cipolins, cipollinos**) a green Italian marble with white zones like the section of an onion. [F *cipolin*, It. *cipollino* (*cipolla*, onion)]

cir., circ. *abbr.* circa.

circa (sœ´kə) *prep.* about, around (often used with dates) (*circa 1830*). ~*adv.* about, nearly. [L]

circadian (sœkā´diən) *a.* (of biological cycles etc.) recurring or repeated (approximately) every 24 hours. [CIRCA, and L *diēs*, day]

Circassian (sœkas´iən) *a.* of or relating to Circassia, its inhabitants or their language. ~*n.* 1 a native or inhabitant of Circassia. 2 a language of Circassia. 3 (**circassian**) a type of light cashmere of silk and mohair. [*Circassia*, a region in the Caucasus]

Circe (sœ´si) *n.* 1 an enchantress. 2 a woman who seduces men. **Circean** (-sē´ən) *a.* [L, from Gr. *Kirkē*, mythic enchantress, fabled to have turned the companions of Ulysses into swine]

circinate (sœ´sināt) *a.* (*Bot.*) rolled up (like the leaves of ferns). [L *circinātus*, p.p. of *circināre* (*circinus*, pair of compasses)]

circle (sœ´kəl) *n.* 1 a plane figure bounded by a curved line, called the circumference, in which every point is equidistant from the centre. 2 a ring, a round figure or object. 3 a round enclosure. 4 the arena of a circus. 5 a tier of seats at a theatre (*the dress circle*). 6 a number of people or things gathered or arranged in a ring (*standing in a circle*; *a circle of stones*). 7 a number of people with a common interest or bond (*the family circle*). 8 a class, a set, a coterie. 9 a sphere of action or influence. 10 a circular route. 11 any series ending as it begins and perpetually repeated (*a vicious circle*). 12 a period, a cycle. 13 a complete series. 14 an inconclusive argument in which two or more statements are brought forward to prove each other. 15 a parallel of latitude (*a great circle*). 16 in hockey, a striking-circle. 17 (*N Am.*) a circle of buildings or circular open space at the intersection of streets; a circus. 18 a territorial division (esp. in Germany). 19 (*loosely*) a round body, a sphere. ~*v.t.* 1 to move round. 2 to surround. ~*v.i.* 1 to revolve; to move in a circle. 2 to form a circle. 3 to be passed round. **to circle back** to go back to the starting point following a circular or indirect route. **to come full circle** to come round to where one started. **to go round in circles** to make no progress in spite of one's efforts. **to run round in circles** (*coll.*) to be very active without achieving much. **to square the circle** SQUARE. **circled** *a.* 1 encircled. 2 marked with a circle or circles. 3 having the form of a circle. **circler** *n.* **circlet** (-lit) *n.* 1 a small circle. 2 a ring or circular band worn on the finger, head etc. [OE *circul* (ME and OF *cercle*), L *circulus*, dim. of *circus*, ring]

circlip (sœ´klip) *n.* a split metal ring fitted into a slot or groove on a bar, shaft etc. to hold something in place. [CIRCLE, CLIP[2]]

circs (sœks) *n.pl.* (*coll.*) circumstances. [abbr.]

circuit (sœ´kit) *n.* 1 the line enclosing a space, the distance round about. 2 the space enclosed in a circle or within certain limits. 3 the act of revolving or moving round, a revolution. 4 the periodical visitation of judges for holding assizes. 5 the district thus visited. 6 the barristers making the circuit. 7 a continuous electrical communication between the poles of a battery. 8 a series of conductors, including the lamps, motors etc., through which a current passes. 9 a motor-racing track. 10 a series of sporting tournaments visited regularly by competitors. 11 a group of theatres or cinemas under the same ownership, putting on the same entertainment in turn. 12 a circular route or itinerary followed by a salesman, politician etc. (*the election circuit*). 13 a series of athletic exercises. 14 a group of Methodist churches associated together for purposes of government and organization of the ministry. **circuit board** *n.* a board on which an electronic circuit is built, with a connector to plug into a piece of equipment. **circuit-breaker** *n.* a device which stops the electric current in the event of a short circuit etc. **circuit judge** *n.* a judge who presides over a county court or crown court. **circuitous** (-kū´i-) *a.* indirect, roundabout. **circuitously** *adv.* **circuitousness** *n.* **circuitry** *n.* (*pl.* **circuitries**) 1 electric or electronic circuits collectively. 2 the design of an electric or electronic circuit. **circuit training** *n.* a form of athletic training consisting of repeated cycles of exercises. **circuity** (-kū´i-) *n.* (*pl.* **circuities**) indirect procedure. [F, from L *circuitus*, a going round, from *circumīre* (*circum*, round, *īre*, to go)]

circulable CIRCULATE.

circular (sœ´kūlə) *a.* 1 in the shape of a circle, round. 2 of or relating to a circle. 3 forming part of a circle. 4 moving in a circle. 5 cyclic. 6 (of a letter etc.) addressed in identical terms to a number of people. 7 (of an argument) inconclusive, consisting of two or more statements brought forward to prove each other. ~*n.* a letter or printed notice of which a copy is sent to many people. **circular breathing** *n.* a breathing technique used in playing a wind instrument, in which the player breathes in through the nose while forcing air out through the mouth. **circularity** (-lar´-) *n.* **circularize, circularise** *v.t.* 1 to send circulars to. 2 (*N Am.*) to canvass by means of questionnaires. **circularization** (-zā´shən) *n.* **circularly** *adv.* **circular saw** *n.* a power tool with a rotating disc notched with teeth for cutting timber etc. [ME and A-F *circuler*, OF *circulier*, L *circulāris* (*circulus*, CIRCLE)]

circulate (sœ´kūlāt) *v.i.* 1 to pass from place to place or person to person. 2 (of blood in the body etc.) to pass through certain channels and return to the starting point. 3 to move round. 4 to be diffused. 5 to move from person to person at a social gathering; to be sociable. ~*v.t.* 1 to cause to pass from place to place or person to person. 2 to spread, to diffuse. **circulable** *a.* **circulating** *a.* 1 that circulates. 2 current. 3 (*Math.*) recurring. **circulating capital** *n.* raw materials, money, goods etc. which are constantly changing hands in business or industry. **circulating decimal** *n.* a decimal which cannot be expressed with perfect exactness, and in which one or more figures recur continually in the same order; a recurring decimal. **circulating library** *n.* (*Hist.*) a small lending library, esp. one for which subscribers paid a small fee. **circulating medium** *n.* the currency of a country. **circulation** (-lā´shən) *n.* 1 the act of circulating. 2 the state of being circulated. 3 the motion of the blood in a living animal, by which it is propelled by the heart through the arteries to all parts of the body, and returned to the heart through the veins. 4 the analogous motion of sap in plants. 5 the free movement of water, air etc. 6 distribution of books, newspapers, news etc. 7 the amount of distribution, the number of copies sold. 8 a medium of exchange, currency. 9 the movement of this. **in circulation** 1 (of money) serving as currency. 2 in general use. 3 participating in social or business activities. **out of circulation** not in circulation. **circulative** *a.* 1 tending to circulate. 2 promoting circulation. **circulator** *n.* 1 a person or thing that circulates. 2 a circulating decimal.

circulatory (sœ´kūlətəri, -lā´-) *a.* of or relating to circulation, esp. of blood or sap (*the circulatory system*). [L *circulāre*]

circum- (sœ´kəm) *pref.* **1** round, about. **2** surrounding. **3** indirectly. **4** of or relating to the circumference. [L, round about, surrounding]

circumambient (sœkəmam´biənt) *a.* **1** going round. **2** surrounding. **circumambiencey, circumambience** *n.* [L *ambiēns -entem*, pres.p. of *ambīre*, to go round (*ambi-*, about, *īre*, to go)]

circumambulate (sœkəmam´būlāt) *v.t.* (*formal*) to walk or go round. *~v.i.* **1** to walk about. **2** to beat about the bush. **circumambulation** (-lā´shən) *n.* **circumambulatory** *a.* [L *ambulāre*, to walk]

circumbendibus (sœkəmben´dibəs) *n.* (*pl.* **circumbendibuses**) (*facet.*) **1** a roundabout or indirect way. **2** a circumlocution.

circumcircle (sœ´kəmsœkəl) *n.* (*Geom.*) a circle that surrounds a triangle or other polygon, touching all the vertices.

circumcise (sœ´kəmsīz) *v.t.* **1** to remove surgically or by ritual the prepuce or foreskin of (a male), or the clitoris of (a female). **2** to render spiritual and holy. **3** to purify. **circumcision** (-sizh´ən) *n.* **1** the operation of circumcising. **2** this operation as a Jewish and Muslim rite for males. **3** this operation as a traditional practice for females among some peoples. **4** spiritual purification. **5** the festival of the Circumcision of Christ, on 1 Jan. [OF *circonciser*, L *circumcīdere* (*cœdere*, to cut)]

circumference (səkŭm´fərəns) *n.* **1** the line that bounds a circle. **2** a periphery. **3** the distance round a space or a body. **4** a circuit. **circumferential** (-ren´-) *a.* **circumferentially** *adv.* [L *circumferentia* (*ferre*, to bear)]

circumflex (sœ´kəmfleks) *n.* (*also* **circumflex accent**) a mark (ˆ or ˜ in Greek) placed above a vowel to indicate accent, quality, length or contraction. *~a.* **1** marked with such accent. **2** (*Anat.*) bent, turning, or curving round something. *~v.t.* (*also* **circumflect**) to mark or pronounce with a circumflex. **circumflexion** (-flek´-), **circumflection** *n.* [L *circumflexus* (*flexus*, p.p. of *flectere*, to bend)]

circumfluent (sœkŭm´fluənt) *a.* flowing round on all sides. **circumfluence** *n.* **circumfluous** *a.* **1** flowing round. **2** surrounded by something that flows round. [L *circumfluens -entem*, pres.p. of *circumfluere* (*fluere*, to flow)]

circumfuse (sœkəmfūz´) *v.t.* **1** to pour (a fluid etc.) round. **2** to surround, to bathe in or with. **circumfusion** *n.* [L *circumfūsus*, p.p. of *circumfundere* (*fundere*, to pour)]

circumjacent (sœkəmjā´sənt) *a.* **1** lying round. **2** bordering on all sides. [L *circumjacēns -entem*, pres.p. of *circumjacēre* (*jacēre*, to lie)]

circumlocution (sœkəmləkū´shən) *n.* **1** a roundabout phrase or expression. **2** the use of roundabout, indirect or evasive language. **3** the use of many words where few would suffice. **circumlocutional, circumlocutionary** *a.* **circumlocutionist** *n.* **circumlocutory** (-lok´ū-) *a.* [L *circumlocūtio -ōnem*]

circumlunar (sœkəmloo´nə) *a.* situated or moving around the moon.

circumnavigate (sœkəmnav´igāt) *v.t.* to sail or fly completely round. **circumnavigable** *a.* **circumnavigation** (-ā´shən) *n.* **circumnavigator** *n.* [L *circumnāvigāre*]

circumnutate (sœkəmnū´tāt) *v.i.* (of the tips of growing plants etc.) to nod or turn successively to all points of the compass. **circumnutation** (-tā´shən) *n.* [L *nūtāre*, to nod]

circumpolar (sœkəmpō´lə) *a.* **1** situated round or near one of the earth's poles. **2** (*Astron.*) revolving about the pole, not setting.

circumscribe (sœ´kəmskrīb) *v.t.* **1** to draw a line around. **2** to limit, to define by bounds, to restrict. **3** to define. **4** (*Geom.*) to surround with a figure that touches at every possible point. **circumscribable** (-skrī´bəbəl) *a.* **circumscriber** *n.* **circumscription** (-skrip´-) *n.* **1** the act of circumscribing. **2** the imposing of limitations. **3** a boundary line. **4** a circular inscription. **5** a definition. **6** a geometrical figure that encloses and touches at every possible point. **circumscriptive** (-skrip´-) *a.* **circumscriptively** *adv.* [L *circumscrībere* (*scrībere*, to write)]

circumsolar (sœkəmsō´lə) *a.* revolving round or situated near the sun.

circumspect (sœ´kəmspekt) *a.* **1** cautious, wary. **2** taking everything into account. **circumspection** (-spek´-), **circumspectness** *n.* **circumspective** (-spek´-) *a.* **circumspectly** *adv.* [L *circumspectus*, prudent, p.p. of *circumspicere* (*specere*, to look)]

circumstance (sœ´kəmstəns) *n.* **1** an incident, an occurrence. **2** something relative to a fact or case. **3** a concomitant. **4** (*pl.*) the facts, relations, influences and other conditions that affect an act or an event. **5** (*pl.*) the facts, conditions etc. that affect one's way of life. **6** ceremony, pomp, fuss. **7** abundance of detail (in a narrative), circumstantiality. *~v.t.* to place in a particular situation. **in/ under no circumstances** not at all, never, in no case. **in/ under the circumstances** in the particular situation for which allowance should be made (*He did very well under the circumstances*). **circumstanced** *a.* [OF, from L *circumstantia*, from *-stāns -ntem*, pres.p. of *circumstāre* (*stāre*, to stand)]

circumstantial (sœkəmstan´shəl) *a.* **1** depending on circumstances. **2** incidental, not essential. **3** detailed, minute. **circumstantial evidence** *n.* indirect evidence inferred from circumstances. **circumstantiality** (-shial´-) *n.* **circumstantially** *adv.* **circumstantiate** (-shiāt) *v.t.* **1** to provide evidence for. **2** to describe in detail. [CIRCUMSTANCE]

circumterrestrial (sœkəmtəres´triəl) *a.* situated or moving around the earth.

circumvallate (sœkəmval´āt) *v.t.* to surround or enclose with a rampart. **circumvallation** (-ā´shən) *n.* [L *circumvallāre* (*vallāre*, from *vallum*, a rampart)]

circumvent (sœkəmvent´, sœ´-) *v.t.* **1** to go round, to avoid or evade. **2** to deceive, to outwit, to cheat. **circumvention** (-ven´-) *n.* **circumventive** (-ven´-) *a.* [L *circumventus*, p.p. of *circumvenīre* (*venīre*, to come)]

circumvolution (sœkəmvəloo´shən) *n.* **1** the act of rolling round. **2** a coil, a convolution. **3** a revolution. **4** a winding or tortuous movement. **5** (*Archit.*) the spiral in a volute. [L *circumvolvere* (*volvere*, to roll)]

circus (sœ´kəs) *n.* (*pl.* **circuses**) **1** a travelling company of clowns, acrobats, trained animals etc. **2** the place, usu. a circular tent, where they perform. **3** such a performance. **4** a set of people who travel together and put on displays, engage in sporting activities etc. **5** a circle of buildings or circular open space at the intersection of streets. **6** an amphitheatre in ancient Rome, such as the Circus Maximus, for sports and games. **7** a performance given there. **8** (*coll.*) a scene of noisy, disorganized activity. **9** a circular hollow with hills on all sides. **the Circus** (*sl.*) the British secret service. [L, a ring]

ciré (sē´rā) *n.* satin or other fabric with a waxed surface. *~a.* having such a surface. [F, waxed]

cire perdue (siə pœdū´) *n.* a method of casting bronze, using wax which is subsequently melted and replaced by the metal. [F, lost wax]

cirque (sœk) *n.* **1** (*Geol.*) a semicircular basin in a hillside or valley, caused by erosion. **2** (*poet.*) a circus or arena. **3** (*poet.*) a ring. [F]

cirrate CIRRUS.

cirrhosis (sirō´sis) *n.* a disease of the liver in which it becomes yellowish and nodular because of the death of liver cells and the growth of fibrous tissue. **cirrhotic** (-rot´-) *a.* [Gr. *kirrhos*, yellow]

cirri CIRRUS.

cirri- (sir´i) *comb. form* having fringelike appendages. [L *cirrus*, a curl]

cirriferous CIRRUS.

cirriped (sir´iped), **cirripede** (-pēd) *n.* any member of the Cirripedia, a class of marine animals related to the Crustacea, having cirriform feet and including the barnacles.

cirro- (sir´ō) *comb. form* 1 denoting cloud formed at high altitudes. 2 having fringelike appendages. [L *cirrus*, a curl]

cirrocumulus (sirōkū´mūləs) *n.* a cloud at high altitude broken up into small fleecy masses.

cirrose CIRRUS.

cirrostratus (sirōstrah´təs) *n.* a horizontal or slightly inclined sheet of cloud more or less broken into fleecy masses.

cirrus (sir´əs) *n.* (*pl.* **cirri** (-rī)) 1 a lofty feathery cloud. 2 (*Bot.*) a tendril. 3 (*Zool.*) a slender locomotive filament. 4 a barbule. **cirrate** (-rāt), **cirrose** (-rōs), **cirrous** *a.* **cirriferous** *a.* (*Bot.*) producing tendrils. **cirriform** (sir´ifawm) *a.* [L, a curl]

CIS *abbr.* Commonwealth of Independent States.

cis- (sis) *pref.* 1 on this side of. 2 (*Hist.*) on the Roman side of. 3 closer to the present time than. 4 (*Chem.*) having two groups of atoms on the same side of a given plane or double bond. [L]

cisalpine (sisal´pīn) *a.* 1 on the Roman side of the Alps. 2 south of the Alps.

cisatlantic (sisətlan´tik) *a.* on the speaker's side of the Atlantic, as distinct from *transatlantic*.

cisco (sis´kō) *n.* (*pl.* **ciscoes, ciscos**) any of several freshwater whitefish of the genus *Coregonus* of N America. [etym. unknown]

cislunar (sisloo´nə) *a.* between the moon and the earth.

cismontane (sismon´tān) *a.* on the speaker's side of the mountains, esp. on the south side of the Alps.

cispadane (sis´pədān) *a.* on this side of the river Po, esp. south of the Po. [L *Padus*, the river Po]

†**cispontine** (sispon´tin) *a.* on the north side of the Thames in London. [L *pons -tem*, bridge]

cissoid (sis´oid) *a.* (*Geom.*) contained within two intersecting curves. ~*n.* a curve with two infinite branches meeting in a cusp. [Gr. *kissoeides*, like ivy]

cissus (sis´əs) *n.* (*pl.* **cissuses**) any plant of the genus *Cissus*, such as *C. antarcticus*, the kangaroo vine. [Gr. *kissos*, ivy]

cissy SISSY (under SIS).

cist[1] (sist), **kist** (kist) *n.* a tomb consisting of a kind of stone chest or a hollowed tree trunk. [Welsh, chest (L *cista*, Gr. *kistē*)]

cist[2] (sist) *n.* a casket or chest, esp. one used for carrying the sacred utensils in Greek antiquity. [L *cista*, Gr. *kistē*, chest]

Cistercian (sistœ´shən) *n.* a member of a monastic order founded in 1098. ~*a.* of or relating to the Cistercians. [med. L *Cistercium*, Cîteaux, the first convent in France]

cistern (sis´tən) *n.* 1 a tank for storing water, esp. a water tank for a lavatory. 2 an underground reservoir. [OF *cisterne*, L *cisterna* (*cista*, a chest)]

cisterna (sistœ´nə) *n.* (*pl.* **cisternae**) (*Anat.*) a sac or space containing fluid, such as cerebrospinal fluid. [L, see CISTERN]

cistron (sis´trən) *n.* a functional gene, a section of a chromosome controlling a single function. [*cis-trans* test, a test used in genetics (CIS-, TRANS-)]

cistus (sis´təs) *n.* (*pl.* **cistuses**) any plant of the genus *Cistus*, a rock rose. [L, from Gr. *kistos*]

cit. *abbr.* 1 citation. 2 cited. 3 citizen.

citable CITE.

citadel (sit´ədəl) *n.* 1 a castle or fortified place in a city. 2 a stronghold. 3 a final retreat or refuge. 4 a Salvation Army hall. [F *citadelle*, It. *cittadella*, dim. of *cittade*, L *cīvitās -tātem*, CITY]

cite (sīt) *v.t.* 1 to quote, to allege as an authority. 2 to quote as an instance. 3 to refer to. 4 to mention in dispatches etc. 5 to summon to appear in court. **citable** *a.* **citation** (-tā´shən) *n.* 1 a quotation. 2 a mention in dispatches etc. 3 an official commendation, for bravery etc. 4 a summons. **citatory** *a.* [F *citer*, L *citāre*, freq. of *ciēre*, to rouse]

CITES (sī´tēz) *abbr.* Convention on International Trade in Endangered Species.

cithara (sith´ərə) *n.* (*pl.* **citharas**) an instrument resembling a lyre. **citharist** *n.* **citharistic** (-ris´tik) *a.* [L, from Gr. *kithara*]

cither, cithern CITTERN.

citified CITY.

citizen (sit´izən) *n.* 1 a member of a state having political rights (*a French citizen*). 2 a dweller in a town or city. 3 a freeman of a city or town. 4 (*esp. N Am.*) a civilian. **citizenhood** *n.* **citizen of the world** *n.* a cosmopolitan. **citizenry** *n.* citizens collectively. **Citizen's Advice Bureau** *n.* an office providing free advice and information to members of the public. **citizen's arrest** *n.* an arrest made by a member of the public. **citizens' band** *n.* a band of radio frequencies designated for use by private citizens for communication between individuals. **Citizen's Charter** *n.* a document setting out the rights of citizens with regard to public services. **citizenship** *n.* the state of being a citizen. [ME *citesein*, A-F *citeseyn*, OF *citeain* (*cité*, CITY, -AN)]

citole (sit´ōl, -ōl´) *n.* (*Hist.*) a stringed musical instrument. [OF, prob. from L CITHARA]

citr- CITRO-.

citrate (sit´rāt, sī´-) *n.* a salt of citric acid. **citric** (sit´-) *a.* derived from citrus fruits. **citric acid** *n.* the acid found in lemons, citrons, limes, oranges etc. [CITRON]

citrin (sit´rin) *n.* bioflavonoid, vitamin P.

citrine (sit´rin) *a.* 1 like a citron. 2 greenish-yellow. ~*n.* (*Mineral.*) a yellow, pellucid variety of quartz, false topaz. **citrinous** *a.* lemon-coloured.

citro- (sit´rō), **citr-** *comb. form* citric. [L *citrus*, CITRON]

citron (sit´rən) *n.* 1 a tree, *Citrus medica*, bearing large lemon-like fruit. 2 this fruit. [F, from late L *citro -ōnem*, L *citrus*]

citronella (sitrənel´ə) *n.* 1 any S Asian grass of the genus *Cymbopogon*. 2 a fragrant oil derived from this, used to drive away insects and in perfumery.

citrus (sit´rəs) *n.* (*pl.* **citruses**) 1 any tree of the genus *Citrus*, including the orange, lemon, citron etc. 2 (*also* **citrus fruit**) the fruit of any of these trees; an orange, lemon, lime, citron, grapefruit etc. **citrous** *a.*

cittern (sit´ən), **cither** (sith´ə), **cithern** (sith´ən) *n.* a medieval instrument resembling a lute, with wire strings. [from CITHARA]

city (sit´i) *n.* (*pl.* **cities**) 1 a town incorporated by a charter. 2 a large and important town. 3 a cathedral town. 4 the inhabitants of a city. ~*a.* 1 of or relating to a city. 2 characteristic of a city. **the City** 1 the part of London governed by the Lord Mayor and Corporation. 2 the banks and financial institutions located there. **citified, cityfied** *a.* 1 townish. 2 having the characteristics of city-dwellers. **City Company** *n.* a London livery company representing one of the medieval guilds. **city desk** *n.* 1 the editorial department of a newspaper dealing with financial news. 2 (*N Am.*) the department of a newspaper dealing with local news. **city editor** *n.* an editor in charge of a city desk. **city fathers** *n.pl.* people in charge of the administration of a city. **city hall** *n.* 1 a town hall. 2 (*N Am.*) a municipal offices. b municipal officers. c municipal government.

cityless *a.* **city manager** *n.* (*N Am.*) an official in charge of the administration of a city. **city of refuge** *n.* each of the six cities in the Holy Land appointed as places of refuge to a person who had unintentionally committed manslaughter. **city page** *n.* the part of a newspaper containing financial news. **City Remembrancer** *n.* an officer of the City of London representing the City Corporation before parliamentary committees etc. **cityscape** *n.* an urban landscape. **city slicker** *n.* (*usu. derog.*) **1** a sophisticated city dweller. **2** a smooth, plausible rogue. **city-state** *n.* (*esp. Hist.*) an independent state comprising a city and its surrounding territory. **City Technology College** *n.* a type of senior secondary school, partly funded by industry, specializing in science and technology. **cityward, citywards** *adv.* [OF *cité*, L *cīvitātem*, acc. of *cīvitās* (*cīvis*, a citizen)]

civ. *abbr.* **1** civil. **2** civilian.

cive CHIVE.

civet (siv´it) *n.* **1** a civet cat. **2** a resinous musky substance obtained from the anal pouch of this animal, used as a perfume. **3** the fur of this animal. **civet cat** *n.* a carnivorous quadruped of the family Viverridae from Asia and Africa, esp. *Viverra civetta.* [F *civette*, Arab. *zabād*]

civic (siv´ik) *a.* **1** of or relating to a city or citizens. **2** urban. **3** municipal. **4** civil. **civically** *adv.* **civic centre** *n.* a group of buildings including the town hall and local administrative offices. **civics** *n.* the study of citizenship and municipal government. [L *cīvicus* (*cīvis*, a citizen)]

civil (siv´əl) *a.* **1** of or relating to citizens. **2** domestic, not foreign. **3** municipal, commercial, legislative. **4** of or relating to social, commercial and administrative affairs, not military or naval. **5** (*Law*) of or relating to private matters, not criminal (*a civil action*; *a civil process*). **6** civilized, polite, courteous. **to keep a civil tongue in one's head** TONGUE. **civil aviation** *n.* civilian, non-military airlines and their operations, esp. commercial aviation. **civil commotion** *n.* a riot or similar disturbance. **civil day** *n.* a day reckoned from midnight to midnight (used in ordinary affairs). **civil death** *n.* (*Law, Hist.*) extinction of one's civil rights and privileges. **civil defence** *n.* a civilian service for the protection of lives and property in the event of enemy attack. **civil disobedience** *n.* a political campaign taking the form of refusal to pay taxes or perform civil duties. **civil engineer** *n.* an engineer dealing with the design, construction and maintenance of roads, railways, bridges, harbours etc. **civil engineering** *n.* **civilian** (-vil´yən) *n.* a person engaged in civil life, not belonging to the armed forces. *~a.* of or relating to civilians. **civilianize, civilianise** *v.t.* to make civilian. **civilianization** (-zā´shən) *n.* **civility** (-vil´-) *n.* (*pl.* **civilities**) **1** the quality of being civil. **2** politeness, courtesy. **3** an act of politeness or courtesy. **civil law** *n.* **1** the law dealing with private rights, as distinct from *criminal law.* **2** Roman law, non-ecclesiastical law. **civil liberty** *n.* (*pl.* **civil liberties**) (a) personal freedom, e.g. freedom of speech, within the framework of the state. **civil libertarian** *n.* **civil list** *n.* the yearly sum granted for the support of a sovereign or ruler. **civilly** *adv.* **civil marriage** *n.* a marriage performed by a civil official, not by a member of the clergy. **civil parish** *n.* a civil district for the purposes of local government etc. **civil rights** *n.pl.* the rights of an individual or group within a state to certain freedoms, e.g. from discrimination. **civil servant** *n.* a member of the civil service. **civil service** *n.* the non-military branch of the public service, dealing with public administration. **civil state** *n.* marital status. **civil suit** *n.* (*Law*) a suit for a private claim or injury. **civil war** *n.* a war between citizens of the same country. **civil year** *n.* the calendar or legal year, as distinct from an *astronomical year.* [F, from L *cīvīlis* (*cīvis*, citizen)]

civilize (siv´əlīz), **civilise** *v.t.* **1** to bring out of barbarism, to bring to a state of civilization. **2** to instruct in the arts and refinements of civilized society. **civilizable** *a.* **civilization** (-zā´shən) *n.* **1** an advanced stage of social and cultural development. **2** societies or peoples at such a stage of development. **3** a civilized society or people of the past (*the Inca civilization*). **4** the act or process of civilizing. **5** the state of being civilized. **civilized** *a.* **1** not primitive or savage; socially and culturally developed. **2** cultured, refined, sophisticated. **civilizer** *n.* [F *civiliser* (CIVIL, -IZE)]

civvy (siv´i) *n.* (*pl.* **civvies** (-iz) **1** (*pl.*) civilian clothes, as opposed to uniform (*in civvies*). **2** a civilian. *~a.* civilian. **Civvy Street** *n.* (*sl.*) civilian life.

CJ *abbr.* Chief Justice.

CJD *abbr.* Creutzfeldt-Jakob disease.

CL *abbr.* Ceylon (IVR).

Cl *chem. symbol* chlorine.

cl. *abbr.* **1** centilitre. **2** class.

clachan (klakh´ən) *n.* a small village or hamlet in the Highlands of Scotland. [Gael., orig. a circle of stones (*clach*, a stone)]

clack (klak) *v.i.* **1** to make a sharp, sudden noise like a clap or crack. **2** to chatter rapidly and noisily. *~v.t.* **1** to cause to emit a sudden, sharp noise. **2** to knock together. *~n.* **1** a sudden, sharp sound. **2** a device making such a sound. **3** rapid and noisy chattering. **4** a chatterbox. **5** a clack valve. **clacker** *n.* **1** a person or thing that clacks. **2** a clack valve. **clackety** (-əti) *a.* **clack valve** *n.* a non-return valve with a hinged flap or ball. [prob. imit. (cp. Icel. *klaka*, to twitter, F *claquer*)]

clad[1] (klad) *v.t.* (*pres.p.* **cladding,** *past, p.p.* **cladded, clad**) to provide with cladding. **cladding** *n.* a protective coating, e.g. of stone on a building or insulating material on a hot-water pipe. [as CLAD[2]]

clad[2] CLOTHE.

clad- CLADO-.

cladding CLAD[1].

clade (klād) *n.* (*Biol.*) a group of organisms sharing a unique characteristic because of evolution from a common ancestor. **cladism** (klad´-) *n.* **cladistic** *a.* **cladistics** (klədis´tiks) *n.* a method of classifying organisms based on clades. [Gr. *klados*, a twig, a shoot]

clado- (klad´o, klā´do), **clad-** *comb. form* (*Bot., Zool.*) **1** branching. **2** of or relating to branches or branchlets. [Gr. *klados*, a twig, a shoot]

cladode (klā´dōd, klad´-) *n.* (*Bot.*) a flattened stem that resembles a leaf. [Gr. *kladōdēs*, having many shoots (*klados*, a shoot)]

cladogram (klā´dōgram) *n.* (*Biol.*) a diagram illustrating the cladistic relationship between species.

claim (klām) *v.t.* **1** to demand, or challenge, as a right. **2** to assert that one has or is (something) or has done (something). **3** to affirm, to maintain. **4** to be deserving of. **5** to take or have as a consequence (*The floods claimed many lives*). *~v.i.* to make a claim on an insurance policy (*to claim for a broken windscreen*). *~n.* **1** a demand for something due. **2** a request for payment under the terms of an insurance policy. **3** an assertion. **4** a real or supposed right. **5** a title. **6** something claimed. **7** a piece of land allotted to one. **8** a piece of land marked out by a settler or miner with the intention of buying it when it is offered for sale. **to jump a claim** JUMP. **to lay claim to** to assert that one owns or has a right to. **to stake one's claim** STAKE[1]. **claimable** *a.* **claimant** *n.* a person who makes a claim. **claimer** *n.* [OF *claim-*, stem of *clamer*, L *clāmāre*, to call out]

clairaudience (kleəraw´diəns) *n.* the (supposed) faculty of hearing voices and other sounds not perceptible to the senses. **clairaudient** *n., a.* [F *clair*, clear, L *clārus*; AUDIENCE]

clairvoyance (kleəvoi´əns) *n.* **1** the (supposed) power of perceiving future events or objects not present to the senses. **2** unusual sensitivity or insight. **clairvoyant** *n.* a person having the power of clairvoyance. *~a.* of, relating to or having the power of clairvoyance. **clairvoyante** *n.* a female clairvoyant. **clairvoyantly** *adv.* [F *clair*, L *clārus*, clear, *voir*, L *vidēre*, to see]

clam (klam) *n.* **1** any of several edible bivalve molluscs, esp. *Venus mercenaria*, the hard clam, and *Mya arenaria*, the soft clam. **2** (*coll.*) a taciturn person. *~v.i.* (*pres.p.* **clamming,** *past, p.p.* **clammed**) to gather clams. **to clam up** to become silent. **clambake** *n.* (*N Am.*) **1** a beach party at which clams are cooked and eaten. **2** any noisy gathering. **clamshell** *n.* **1** the shell of a clam. **2** something resembling this, such as a hinged dredging bucket, aircraft cockpit canopy, takeaway food container etc. [prob. from OE *clamm*, bond, fetter]

clamant (klā´mənt) *a.* (*poet.*) **1** crying or begging earnestly. **2** clamorous. **clamantly** *adv.* [L *clāmans -ntem*, pres.p. of *clāmāre*, to cry out]

clamber (klam´bə) *v.i.* to climb with hands and feet, to climb with difficulty. *~v.t.* to climb with difficulty. *~n.* a climb of this nature. [prob. formed from OE *climban*, to climb (cp., however, Icel. *clambra*, to pinch together, clamp, and G *klammern*, to clamp)]

clammy (klam´i) *a.* (*comp.* **clammier,** *superl.* **clammiest**) **1** moist, damp. **2** sticky. **3** (of weather) humid. **clammily** *adv.* **clamminess** *n.* [prob. from ME *clammen*, to smear]

clamour (klam´ə), (*N Am.*) **clamor** *n.* **1** a loud and continuous shouting or calling out. **2** a continued and loud expression of complaint, demand or appeal. **3** popular outcry. *~v.t.* **1** to shout. **2** to utter or express with loud noise. *~v.i.* **1** to cry out loudly and earnestly. **2** to demand or complain noisily (*The crowd clamoured for his release*). **3** to make a loud noise. **clamorous** *a.* **clamorously** *adv.* **clamorousness** *n.* [OF, from L *clāmor* (*clāmāre*, to cry out)]

clamp[1] (klamp) *n.* **1** a frame with two tightening screws to hold pieces of wood etc. together. **2** a piece of timber or iron used to fasten things together. **3** anything rigid which strengthens, fastens or binds. **4** a back batten fastened crosswise to several boards to prevent them from warping. **5** (*Naut.*) the internal planking under the shelf on which the deck beams rest. **6** a wheel clamp. *~v.t.* **1** to unite, fasten or strengthen with a clamp or clamps. **2** to put or hold firmly. **3** to immobilize with a wheel clamp. **to clamp down (on)** to impose (heavier) restrictions (on); to attempt to suppress. **clampdown** *n.* an act of clamping down (on something). **clamper**[1] *n.* [not in early use; etym. uncertain (cp. Dut. *klampe* (now *klamp*), G *Klampe*, OE *clam*)]

clamp[2] (klamp) *n.* **1** a heap, mound or stack of turf, rubbish, potatoes etc. **2** a pile of bricks for firing. *~v.t.* **1** to pile into a heap. **2** to store in a clamp. [perh. from CLAMP[1] (cp. Dut. *klamp*)]

clamp[3] (klamp) *n.* a heavy footstep or tread. *~v.i.* to tread heavily and noisily. **clamper**[2] *n.* [imit., cp. CLUMP]

clamper[1] CLAMP[1].

clamper[2] CLAMP[3].

clan (klan) *n.* **1** a tribe or number of families bearing the same name, descended from a common ancestor, and united under a chieftain representing that ancestor (*the Highland clans*). **2** a large extended family. **3** a clique, a set. **4** a genus or species. **5** a group of animals. **clannish** *a.* **1** (of a family etc.) united closely together. **2** cliquish. **3** of or relating to a clan. **clannishly** *adv.* **clannishness** *n.* **clanship** *n.* **1** the system of clans. **2** loyalty to a clan. **clansman, clanswoman** *n.* (*pl.* **clansmen, clanswomen**) a member of a clan. [Gael. *clann* (perh. from L *planta*)]

clandestine (klandes´tin, klan´-) *a.* secret, surreptitious, underhand. **clandestinely** *adv.* **clandestineness** *n.* [F *clandestin*, L *clandestīnus* (*clam*, in secret)]

clang (klang) *v.t.* to strike together, so as to cause a sharp, ringing sound. *~v.i.* **1** to emit a sharp, ringing sound. **2** to resound. *~n.* a sharp, ringing sound, as of two pieces of metal struck together. **clanger** *n.* (*sl.*) **1** a foolish mistake. **2** a social blunder. **to drop a clanger** to make a conspicuous mistake or blunder. **clangour** (-gə), (*N Am.*) **clangor** *n.* **1** a sharp, ringing sound or series of sounds. **2** an uproar. **clangorous** *a.* **clangorously** *adv.* [L *clangere* (cp. Gr. *klangē*, a clang)]

clank (klangk) *n.* a sound as of solid metallic bodies struck together (usu. a deeper sound than *clink*, and a less resounding one than *clang*). *~v.t.* to strike together so as to make such a sound. *~v.i.* to make such a sound. **clankingly** *adv.* [onomat., or perh. from Dut. *klank*]

clannish CLAN.

clap[1] (klap) *v.t.* (*pres.p.* **clapping,** *past, p.p.* **clapped**) **1** to strike together noisily (*to clap one's hands*). **2** to applaud, by striking the hands together. **3** to strike quickly or slap with something flat. **4** to shut hastily. **5** to put or place suddenly, hastily or firmly. **6** (of a bird) to flap (the wings) noisily. *~v.i.* **1** to strike the hands together, esp. in applause. **2** to shut with a bang. *~n.* **1** the noise made by the collision of flat surfaces. **2** a sudden loud noise. **3** a peal of thunder. **4** applause shown by clapping. **5** a heavy slap. **a clap on the back** congratulations. **to clap eyes on** EYE[1]. **to clap on** to add hastily. **to clap up** to make hastily. **clapped out,** (*attrib.*) **clapped-out** *a.* (*sl.*) **1** worn out; of no more use. **2** finished, exhausted. **clapper** *n.* **1** a person or thing that claps. **2** the tongue of a bell. **3** a noisy rattle for scaring birds. **like the clappers** (*sl.*) extremely fast. **clapperboard** *n.* a pair of hinged boards clapped together at the start of a take during film shooting to help in synchronizing sound and vision. **claptrap** *n.* **1** pretentious or insincere talk. **2** showy words or deeds designed to win applause or public favour. [ME *clappen* (perh. from OE), cp. Dut. and G *klappen*, Icel. *klappa*]

clap[2] (klap) *n.* (*sl.*) gonorrhoea. [F *clapoir*, a venereal sore]

clapboard (klap´bawd) *n.* (*N Am.*) a feather-edged board used to cover the roofs and sides of houses. *~v.t.* (*N Am.*) to cover with clapboards. **clapboarding** *n.* [formed from obs. *clapholt*, LG *klappholt*]

clapper, clapperboard CLAP[1].

claptrap CLAP[1].

claque (klak) *n.* **1** a body of hired applauders. **2** the system of engaging applauders. **claquer, claqueur** (-kœ´) *n.* a hired applauder. [F, from *claquer*, to clap]

clarabella (klarəbel´ə) *n.* (*pl.* **clarabellas**) an organ stop giving a powerful fluty tone. [L *clārus*, clear, *bellus*, pretty]

clarence (klar´əns) *n.* (*Hist.*) a closed four-wheeled carriage for four passengers, with a seat for the driver. [Duke of *Clarence*, later William IV]

Clarenceux (klar´ənsū) *n.* (*Her.*) the second King of Arms. [dukedom of *Clarence*]

clarendon (klar´əndən) *n.* (*Print.*) a condensed type with heavy face. *~a.* of or relating to this type. [*Clarendon* Press, Oxford]

claret (klar´it) *n.* **1** a light red Bordeaux wine. **2** any light red wine resembling Bordeaux. **3** a reddish-violet colour. **4** (*sl.*) †blood. *~a.* claret-coloured. **claret-coloured** *a.* reddish-violet. **claret cup** *n.* a drink made of iced claret, brandy, lemon, sugar etc. [OF *clairet*, dim. of *clair*, L *clārus*, CLEAR]

clarify (klar´ifī) *v.t.* (*3rd pers. sing. pres.* **clarifies,** *pres.p.* **clarifying,** *past, p.p.* **clarified**) **1** to make clearer or easier to understand. **2** to clear from visible impurities (*to clarify butter*). **3** to make transparent. *~v.i.* to become transparent. **clarification** (-fikā´shən) *n.* **clarificatory** (-fikā´-) *a.* **clarifier** *n.* [OF *clarifier*, L *clārificāre* (*clārus*, clear, *facere*, to make)]

clarinet (klarinet´) *n.* **1** a keyed woodwind instrument with a single reed. **2** a clarinet player, esp. in an orchestra. **3** an organ stop giving a clarinet-like sound. **clarinettist,** (*esp. N Am.*) **clarinetist** *n.* [F *clarinette*, dim. of *clarine* (L *clārus*, clear)]

clarion (klar´iən) *n.* **1** (*Hist.*) a kind of trumpet, with a narrow tube, producing a loud and clear note. **2** a sound of or resembling that of a clarion. **3** an organ stop giving a similar tone. *~a.* loud and clear. *~v.t.* (*pres.p.* **clarioning,** *past, p.p.* **clarioned**) **1** to announce loudly and clearly. **2** to trumpet. [OF *claron*, med. L *clārio -ōnem* (L *clārus*, clear)]

clarity (klar´əti) *n.* clearness. [ME and OF *clarté*, L *clāritas -tātem* (L *clārus*)]

clarkia (klah´kiə) *n.* any plant of the genus *Clarkia* of herbaceous annuals with showy purple, pink or white flowers. [William *Clark*, 1770–1838, US explorer]

clary (kleə´ri) *n.* (*pl.* **claries**) any of several labiate plants of the genus *Salvia*, esp. *S. sclarea*, an aromatic herb. [OE *slaridge*, med. L *sclarea*]

clash (klash) *v.i.* **1** to make a loud noise by striking together. **2** to come into collision. **3** to disagree; to conflict. **4** (of colours) to be in disharmony. **5** (of dates etc.) to coincide, esp. inconveniently. *~v.t.* to cause one thing to strike against another so as to produce a loud noise. *~n.* **1** the noise produced by the violent collision of two bodies. **2** opposition, disagreement, conflict. **3** a collision. **4** disharmony of colours. **clasher** *n.* [imit., cp. CLACK, CRASH[1] and CRACK]

clasp (klahsp) *n.* **1** a catch, hook or interlocking device for fastening. **2** a buckle or brooch. **3** any fastening. **4** a close embrace. **5** a grasp. **6** a metal bar attached to a ribbon carrying a medal commemorating a battle or other exploit. *~v.t.* **1** to fasten or shut with or as if with a clasp or buckle. **2** to fasten (a clasp). **3** to embrace. **4** to grasp. **5** to cling to by twining or encircling. **to clasp hands** to hold or shake hands firmly or fervently. **to clasp one's hands** to put one's hands together with the fingers interlaced. **clasper** *n.* **1** a person or thing that clasps. **2** (*pl.*) a pair of organs in some insects and fishes by which the male holds the female. **clasp-knife** *n.* (*pl.* **clasp-knives**) a pocket knife in which the blade shuts into the hollow part of the handle. [ME *claspen*, *clapsen* (cp. OE *clyppan*, to grasp, embrace)]

class (klahs) *n.* **1** a number of persons or things ranked together. **2** a social rank (*the middle classes*). **3** the system of social caste or social ranking. **4** a number of pupils or students taught together. **5** an occasion when they are taught (*an evening class*; *a tap-dancing class*). **6** (*N Am.*) the students taken collectively who expect to graduate at the same time (*the class of 1988*). **7** a division according to quality. **8** (*sl.*) high quality or merit. **9** a number of individuals having the same essential qualities. **10** a division of animals or plants next above an order. *~v.t.* to assign to a class or classes. *~a.* (*sl.*) of good quality. **in a class of one's/ its own** of matchless excellence. **no class** (*coll.*) a lack of quality. †**the classes** the wealthy as opposed to the masses. **-class** *a.* (*in comb.*) of the specified quality or social rank, as *first-class*, *middle-class*. **classable** *a.* capable of being classed. **class-conscious** *a.* over-sensitive to social differences. **class-consciousness** *n.* **classism** *n.* discrimination on the ground of social class. **classist** *a.*, *n.* **classless** *a.* **1** not divided into classes. **2** not belonging to any class. **classlessness** *n.* **class-list** *n.* a classified list of candidates issued by examiners. **classmate** *n.* a person who is or has been in the same class, esp. at school. **classroom** *n.* a room in a school etc. in which classes are taught. **class war, class warfare** *n.* conflict between the social classes in a community. **classy** *a.* (*comp.* **classier**, *superl.* **classiest**) (*coll.*) **1** genteel. **2** of superior quality. **3** stylish, elegant. **classily** *adv.* **classiness** *n.* [F *classe*, L *classis* (*calāre*, to call, summon)]

class. *abbr.* **1** classic. **2** classical. **3** classification. **4** classified.

classic (klas´ik) *n.* **1** an author, artist etc. of the first rank. **2** a Greek or Latin writer of the first rank. **3** a literary or artistic work by any of these. **4** any recognized masterpiece. **5** (*pl.*) ancient Greek and Latin literature. **6** (*pl.*, *sing. in constr.*) the study of these. **7** anything in classic style. **8** a follower of classic models as opposed to romantic. **9** †a person versed in Greek and Latin literature. *~a.* **1** of the first rank, esp. in literature or art. **2** outstandingly typical (*a classic example*). **3** of or relating to the art or literature of the ancient Greeks and Romans. **4** in the style of these. **5** harmonious, well-proportioned. **6** pure, refined, restrained. **7** of standard authority. **classic ground** *n.* a place having illustrious associations. **classic orders** *n.pl.* (*Archit.*) the Doric, Ionic, Corinthian, Tuscan and Composite orders. **classic races** *n.pl.* the five principal horse races of the British season, being the 2000 Guineas, 1000 Guineas, Derby, Oaks and St Leger. [L *classicus* (*classis*, see CLASS)]

classical (klas´ikəl) *a.* **1** belonging to or characteristic of the ancient Greeks and Romans or their civilization or literature. **2** (of education) based on a study of Latin and Greek. **3** (of any of the arts) influenced by Roman or Greek models, restrained, simple and pure in form. **4** (of music) serious or traditional in style or composition, esp. of orchestral music, opera etc. rather than pop, jazz etc. **5** of or relating to music composed esp. in the 18th and 19th cents., simple and restrained in style. **6** outstanding; exemplary; of lasting merit. **7** (of physics) not involving relativity or quantum mechanics. **classicalism** *n.* **classicalist** *n.* **classicality** (-kal´-) *n.* **classical Latin** *n.* Latin of the golden age of Latin literature (*c.* 75 BC to AD 175). **classically** *adv.* **classicism** (-sizm) *n.* **1** a classic style or idiom. **2** devotion to or imitation of the classics. **3** classical scholarship. **4** advocacy of classical education. **classicist** *n.* **classicize, classicise** *v.t.* to make classic. *~v.i.* to affect or imitate a classic or classical style. **classico-** *comb. form*

classify (klas´ifī) *v.t.* (*3rd pers. sing. pres.* **classifies,** *pres.p.* **classifying,** *past, p.p.* **classified**) **1** to distribute into classes or divisions. **2** to assign to a class. **3** to restrict the availability of (information), esp. for security reasons. **classifiable** *a.* **classification** (-fikā´shən) *n.* **classificatory** (-kā´-) *a.* **classified** *a.* **1** arranged in classes. **2** (of information) of restricted availability, esp. for security reasons. **3** (of printed advertisements) arranged according to the type of goods or services offered or required. **4** (of a road) belonging to one of the categories of the national road system. *~n.* (*pl.*) classified advertisements. **classifier** *n.*

clastic (klas´tik) *a.* (*Geol.*) fragmentary; composed of materials derived from the waste of various rocks. [Gr. *klastos*, broken (*klaein*, to break)]

clathrate (klath´rāt) *n.* (*Chem.*) a solid compound in which the molecules of one component are trapped within the structure of another. [L *clāthrāre*, to provide with a lattice]

clatter (klat´ə) *v.i.* **1** to make a sharp rattling noise. **2** to fall or move with such a noise. **3** to talk idly and noisily. *~v.t.* to cause to make a rattling sound. *~n.* **1** a sharp rattling noise. **2** loud, tumultuous noise. **3** noisy, empty talk. **clatterer** *n.* **clatteringly** *adv.* **clattery** *a.* [OE *clatrian* (cp. Dut. *klateren*, LG *klätern*)]

claudication (klawdikā´shən) *n.* (*Med.*) **1** limping. **2** pain and cramp, esp. in the leg muscles, caused by an insufficient blood supply. [L *claudicare*, to limp (*claudus*, lame)]

clause (klawz) *n.* **1** a complete grammatical unit, usu. including a subject and predicate. **2** a subdivision of a compound or complex sentence (*a subordinate clause*; *a main clause*). **3** a separate and distinct portion of a document. **4** a particular stipulation. **clausal** *a.* [OF, from L *clausa*, fem. p.p. of *claudere*, to close, to enclose]

claustral (klaws´trəl) *a.* **1** of or relating to a cloister or monastic foundation. **2** cloister-like, secluded. **3** narrow-minded. **claustration** (-trā´shən) *n.* the act of shutting up in a cloister. [late L *claustrālis* (*claustrum*, an enclosed space)]

claustrophobia (klawstrəfō´biə) *n.* an abnormal fear of being in a confined space. **claustrophobe** (klaws´-) *n.* a person who suffers from claustrophobia. **claustrophobic** *a.* **1** suffering from claustrophobia. **2** causing claustrophobia. ~*n.* a claustrophobe. **claustrophobically** *adv.* [L *claustrum*, an enclosed space, Gr. *phobos*, fear]

clavate (klā´vāt) *a.* (*Biol.*) club-shaped. **claviform** (klav´ifawm) *a.* club-shaped. [L *clāvātus*, p.p. of *clāvāre*; or formed from *clāva*, a club]

clave[1] (klāv, klahv) *n.* (*Mus.*) either of a pair of hardwood sticks that make a hollow sound when struck together. [Am. Sp., L *clāvis*, a key]

clave[2] CLEAVE[2].

clavicembalo (klavichem´bəlō) *n.* (*pl.* **clavicembalos**) a harpsichord. [It.]

clavichord (klav´ikawd) *n.* a soft-toned musical instrument, one of the first stringed instruments with a keyboard, a predecessor of the pianoforte. [L *clāvis*, key, *chorda*, string]

clavicle (klav´ikəl) *n.* the collarbone. **clavicular** (-vik´ū-) *a.* [L *clāvicula*, dim. of *clāvis*, key (med. L, collarbone)]

clavicorn (klav´ikawn) *n.* any of a group of beetles, the Clavicornia, with club-shaped antennae. ~*a.* of, relating to or belonging to this group. [L *clāva*, club; *cornu*, horn]

clavier (klav´iə, kləviə´) *n.* **1** the keyboard of an organ, pianoforte etc. **2** a keyboard instrument. [F (L *clāvis*, a key)]

claviform CLAVATE.

claw (klaw) *n.* **1** the sharp hooked nail of a bird or animal. **2** the foot of any bird or animal armed with such nails. **3** the pincer of a crab, lobster or crayfish. **4** anything resembling a claw. **5** an implement for grappling or holding. **6** the hand. **7** a grasp, a clutch. ~*v.t.* **1** to tear or scratch with the claws. **2** to clutch or drag with or as with claws. **3** (*Sc.*) to scratch gently. ~*v.i.* **1** to scratch with the claws. **2** (*Sc.*) to scratch gently. **to claw away/ off** (*Naut.*) to beat to windward off a lee shore. **to claw back 1** to get back by clawing or with difficulty. **2** to take back (part of a benefit or allowance etc.) by extra taxation etc. **clawback** *n.* **1** the act of clawing back. **2** money etc. clawed back. **clawed** *a.* **1** having claws. **2** damaged by clawing. **claw hammer** *n.* **1** a hammer with claws at the back of the head to extract nails. **2** (*sl.*) a dress coat (from its shape). **clawless** *a.* [OE *clawu* (cp. Dut. *klaauw*, G *Klaue*)]

clay (klā) *n.* **1** heavy, sticky earth. **2** a hydrated silicate of aluminium, with a mixture of other substances, used to make bricks, pottery etc. **3** (*poet.*) the human body. **4** (*coll.*) a clay pipe. ~*v.t.* **1** to cover or mix with clay. **2** to purify and whiten (sugar etc.) with clay. **3** to puddle with clay. **feet of clay** FOOT. **clay court** *n.* a tennis court with a hard surface covered with crushed shale or stone. **clayey** *a.* **clayish** *a.* **claylike** *a.* **clay-pan** *n.* (*Austral.*) a hollow (often dry in summer) where water collects after rain. **clay pigeon** *n.* a clay disc thrown into the air as a target for shooting. **clay pipe** *n.* a tobacco pipe made of baked clay, usu. long. **clay-pit** *n.* a pit from which clay is dug. **claystone** *n.* a compact fine-grained rock. [OE *clǣg*, Gmc. (cp. Dut. and G *klei*, OE *clam*, Gr. *gloios*, L *gluten*)]

claymore (klā´maw) *n.* **1** a two-edged sword used by the Scottish Highlanders. **2** a basket-hilted broadsword. **3** a type of explosive mine. [Gael. *claidheamh mor*, great sword (cp. Welsh *cleddyf*, OIr. *claideb*, sword, L *clādes*, slaughter, Welsh *mawr*, Ir. *mor*, Corn. *maur*, great)]

Clayton's (klā´tənz) *a.* (*Austral.*) sham; ersatz. [trade name of a soft drink marketed as a substitute for alcohol]

-cle (kəl) *suf.* diminutive, as *cubicle*, *particle*. [-CULE]

clean (klēn) *a.* **1** free from dirt, stain, contamination, disease etc. **2** clear, unobstructed, unused (*a clean page*). **3** free from errors, defects etc. **4** pure, holy, free from ceremonial defilement. **5** attentive to personal cleanliness. **6** free from evidence of criminal activity. **7** (of a driving licence) free from endorsements or penalty points. **8** (*sl.*) not carrying or containing a gun, drugs, illegal or incriminating articles etc. **9** free from sexual references, innuendo etc. **10** producing relatively little radioactive fallout. **11** smooth, streamlined, shapely (*clean lines*). **12** adroit, dexterous, unerring. **13** complete. **14** empty, having no fish. ~*v.t.* **1** to make clean. **2** to cleanse, to purify. **3** to gut (fish, poultry etc.). **4** to remove (marks etc.). ~*v.i.* **1** to become clean. **2** to make oneself clean. ~*adv.* **1** quite, completely. **2** without qualification, absolutely. **3** in a clean manner, cleanly. **4** dexterously, cleverly. ~*n.* **1** an act of cleaning (*This carpet needs a clean*). **2** in weightlifting, the raising of a weight from the floor to shoulder level in a single movement (*clean and jerk*). **clean as a whistle** WHISTLE. **to clean down** to brush or wipe down. **to clean one's plate** to eat all the food on one's plate. **to clean out 1** to clean thoroughly. **2** to strip. **3** (*sl.*) to deprive of all money. **to clean up 1** to clear away a mess. **2** to put tidy. **3** to make oneself clean. **4** to collect all the money, profits etc. **to come clean** (*coll.*) to confess. **to make a clean breast** BREAST. **to make a clean job of** (*coll.*) to do thoroughly. **to make a clean sweep** SWEEP. **to show a clean pair of heels** HEEL[1]. **with clean hands** without blame or guilt, without being implicated. **cleanable** *a.* **clean bill of health** *n.* **1** a document certifying the health of a ship's company. **2** a statement that a person is in good health or a thing in good condition. **clean break** *n.* a quick and complete separation. **clean copy** *n.* a fair copy. **clean-cut** *a.* **1** sharply defined; clear-cut. **2** clean, neat. **cleaner** *n.* **1** a person who cleans, esp. one paid to clean the interior of a house, office, factory etc. **2** a device or substance that cleans. **3** (*pl.*) a dry-cleaners' shop. **to take to the cleaners 1** (*sl.*) to deprive of all one's money, goods etc. **2** (*sl.*) to criticize severely. **clean fish** *n.* a fish not unfit for food, as at or about spawning time. **clean-handed** *a.* free from blame in any matter. **cleanish** *a.* **clean-limbed** *a.* having well-proportioned limbs. **clean-living** *a.* upright, decent, respectable. **cleanly**[1] *adv.* in a clean manner. **cleanness** *n.* **clean-shaven** *a.* without beard or moustache. **clean sheet, clean slate** *n.* a new start, all debts etc. written off. **cleanskin** *n.* (*Austral.*) **1** an unbranded animal. **2** (*sl.*) a person without a criminal record. **clean-up** *n.* an act of cleaning up. [OE *clǣne*, Gmc. (cp. Dut. and G *klein*, small)]

cleanly[1] CLEAN.

cleanly[2] (klen´li) *a.* (*comp.* **cleanlier**, *superl.* **cleanliest**) clean in person and habits. **cleanlily** *adv.* **cleanliness** *n.* [OE *clǣnlic*, a.]

cleanse (klenz) *v.t.* **1** to make clean. **2** to purge, to purify. **3** (*Bible*) to cure. **cleanser** *n.* **cleansing** *n.* **cleansing cream** *n.* a cream used to remove dirt, make-up etc. from the face or hands. **cleansing department** *n.* the department of a local authority that deals with refuse collection, street cleaning etc. [OE *clǣnsian*]

clear (kliə) *a.* 1 free from darkness, dullness or opacity. 2 luminous, bright. 3 transparent, translucent. 4 (of the sky etc.) free from clouds or mist (*on a clear day*). 5 distinctly audible. 6 evident, easy to see. 7 lucid, easy to understand. 8 indisputable, unambiguous. 9 brightly intelligent. 10 certain, unmistaken (*I'm not clear about this*). 11 irreproachable, guiltless. 12 unobstructed (*a clear road*). 13 free, unshackled, unentangled. 14 free from commitments etc. 15 free from deduction; net, not curtailed. 16 complete (*two clear days*). ~*adv.* 1 clearly. 2 completely, quite, entirely. 3 apart, free from risk of contact (*to stand clear*). ~*v.t.* 1 to make clear; to free from darkness, opacity, obstruction etc. 2 to empty. 3 to remove trees, buildings etc. from (land), esp. in order to cultivate it. 4 to liberate, to disengage. 5 to acquit, to exonerate. 6 to obtain authorization for. 7 to pass through (customs etc.). 8 to pass or leap over without touching. 9 to gain, to realize as profit. 10 to pass (a cheque etc.) through a clearing house. 11 in football, to send (the ball) out of the defence area. ~*v.i.* 1 to become clear, bright or unclouded. 2 to become free from obstruction. 3 to dissipate, disappear etc. (*The fog gradually cleared*). **clear as a bell** perfectly sound or clear, free from any flaw. **clear as mud** (*coll.*) not clear at all. **in clear** not in code. **in the clear** free from suspicion. **out of a clear sky** as a complete surprise. **to clear away** 1 to remove. 2 to remove plates etc. after a meal. 3 to disappear. 4 to melt away. **to clear off** 1 to remove. 2 (*coll.*) to depart. **to clear one's throat** to make one's voice clear with a slight cough. **to clear out** 1 to empty. 2 to eject. 3 (*coll.*) to depart. **to clear the air** 1 to make the air cooler, fresher etc. 2 to remove misunderstandings or suspicion. **to clear the decks** DECK. **to clear the way** 1 to remove obstacles (*to clear the way for negotiations*). 2 to stand aside, to get out of the way. **to clear up** 1 to become bright and clear. 2 to elucidate. 3 to tidy up. 4 to disappear. **to get clear** GET[1]. **clearable** *a.* **clearcut** *a.* 1 regular, finely outlined, sharply defined. 2 obvious, evident. ~*v.t.* (*pres.p.* **clear-cutting,** *past, p.p.* **clear-cut**) to clear-fell (an area). **clearer** *n.* 1 a person or thing that clears. 2 a clearing bank. **clear-fell** *v.t.* to remove all trees from (an area). **clear-headed** *a.* 1 acute, sharp, intelligent. 2 sensible (*a clear-headed decision*). **clear-headedness** *n.* **clearly** *adv.* 1 in a clear manner. 2 distinctly, audibly. 3 plainly, evidently. 4 certainly, undoubtedly. **clearness** *n.* **clear-out** *n.* an act of clearing out. **clear-seeing** *a.* clear-sighted. **clear-sighted** *a.* 1 acute, discerning, far-seeing. 2 seeing clearly. **clear-sightedness** *n.* **clearstory** CLERESTORY. **clear-up** *n.* an act of clearing up, tidying or solving. **clearway** *n.* a road on which stopping or parking is forbidden. **clearwing** *n.* a moth of the family Sesiidae, with translucent wings, which flies by day. [OF *cler* (F *clair*), L *clārus*]

clearance (kliə´rəns) *n.* 1 the act of clearing. 2 the state of being cleared. 3 the removal of people, buildings etc. from an area. 4 authorization. 5 the clearing of cheques etc. 6 clear profit. 7 a certificate that a ship etc. has been cleared at the custom house. 8 the distance between the moving and the stationary part of a machine. 9 any similar clear space allowed between parts. **clearance order** *n.* a demolition order. **clearance sale** *n.* a sale of stock at reduced prices to make room for new stock.

clearcole (kliə´kōl) *n.* a preparation of size and whiting, used as a primer. ~*v.t.* to treat with this. [F, *claire colle*, clear glue or size]

clearing (kliə´ring) *n.* 1 the act of making clear, free from obstruction etc. 2 a tract of land cleared for cultivation. 3 the passing of cheques etc. through a clearing house. **clearing bank** *n.* a bank which is a member of a clearing house. **clearing house** *n.* 1 a financial establishment where cheques, transfers, bills etc. are exchanged between member banks, so that only outstanding balances have to be paid. 2 a person or agency acting as a centre for the exchange of information etc.

cleat (klēt) *n.* 1 a strip of wood secured to another one to strengthen it. 2 a strip fastened on steps etc. to prevent slipping. 3 (*Naut.*) a piece of wood or iron for fastening ropes on. 4 a wedge. ~*v.t.* to fasten or strengthen with a cleat. [ME *clete*, a wedge (cp. Dut. *kloot*, G *Klosz*, a ball or clod)]

cleave[1] (klēv) *v.t.* (*past* **clove** (klōv), **cleft** (kleft), **cleaved,** *p.p.* **cloven** (klō´vən), **cleft, cleaved**) (*poet.*) 1 to split apart, esp. with violence, to cut through, to divide forcibly. 2 to make one's way through. ~*v.i.* 1 to come apart. 2 to split, to crack. **cleavable** *a.* **cleavage** *n.* 1 the hollow between a woman's breasts, esp. as revealed by a low-cut dress or top. 2 an act of cleaving. 3 (*Biol.*) cell division. 4 the particular manner in which a mineral with a regular structure may be cleft or split. 5 the way in which a party etc. splits up. **line of cleavage** LINE[1]. **plane of cleavage** PLANE[1]. **cleaver** *n.* 1 a person or thing that cleaves. 2 a butcher's instrument for cutting meat into joints. [OE *clēofan*, Gmc. *kleuth-* (cp. Dut. *klieven*, G *klieben*, Gr. *gluphein*, to hollow out, carve)]

cleave[2] (klēv) *v.i.* (*past* **cleaved, †clave** (klāv)) (*poet.*) 1 to stick, to adhere. 2 to be attached closely. 3 to be faithful (to). [OE *clifian*, from Gmc. *kli-* (cp. G *kleben*, Dut. *kleven*, Swed. *klibba*)]

cleavers (klē´vəz), **clivers** (kliv´-) *n.* a loose-growing plant, *Galium aparine*, with hooked prickles that catch in clothes. [prob. from CLEAVE[2]]

clef (klef) *n.* (*Mus.*) a symbol at the beginning of a stave denoting the pitch and determining the names of the notes according to their position on the stave. [F, from L *clāvis*, key]

cleft[1] (kleft) *a.* divided, split. **cleft lip** *n.* a congenital fissure of the upper lip. **cleft palate** *n.* a congenital fissure of the hard palate. **cleft stick** *n.* a stick split at the end. **in a cleft stick** in a difficult situation, esp. one where going forward or back is impossible. [p.p. of CLEAVE[1]]

cleft[2] (kleft) *n.* a split, a crack, a fissure. [earlier *clift*, cogn. with CLEAVE[1] (cp. Icel., Dut. and G *kluft*)]

cleg (kleg) *n.* a gadfly, a horsefly. [Icel. *kleggi*]

cleisto- (klī´stō) *comb. form* (*Bot.*) closed. [Gr. *kleistos* (*kleiein*, to close)]

cleistogamic (klīstōgam´ik) *a.* (*Bot.*) having flowers that never open and are self-fertilized. [Gr. *gamos*, marriage]

clematis (klem´ətis, kləmā´-) *n.* any ranunculaceous plant of the genus *Clematis*, including the traveller's joy, *C. vitalba*. [late L, from Gr. *klēmatis*]

clement (klem´ənt) *a.* 1 (of weather) mild. 2 merciful. 3 gentle. **clemency** *n.* **clemently** *adv.* [L *clēmēns -entis*]

clementine (klem´əntīn, -tēn) *n.* a small, bright orange citrus fruit with a sweet flavour. [F]

clench (klench) *v.t.* 1 to close (the hands, teeth etc.) firmly. 2 to grasp firmly. 3 to fasten (a nail etc.) firmly by bending the point; to clinch. 4 to rivet. ~*n.* 1 the act or action of clenching. 2 the state of being clenched. **clencher** *n.* a person or thing that clenches or clinches. [ME *clenchen*, from OE *clencan*, extant only in *be-clencan* (cp. OHG *klenkan*, also CLING, CLINCH)]

clepsydra (klep´sidrə) *n.* (*pl.* **clepsydras, clepsydrae** (-drē)) an ancient instrument used to measure time by the dropping of water from a graduated vessel through a small opening. [L, from Gr. *klepsudra* (*kleptein*, to steal, *hudōr*, water)]

clerestory (kliə´stawri), (*esp. N Am.*) **clearstory** *n.* (*pl.* **clerestories, clearstories**) 1 the upper part of the nave, choir or transept of a large church containing windows above the roofs of the aisles. 2 (*N Am.*) a raised part of the roof of a railway carriage, containing windows or other means of ventilation. [CLEAR, STOREY]

clergy (klœ´ji) *n.* (*pl.* **clergies**) **1** the body of people set apart by ordination for the service of the Christian Church. **2** ecclesiastics collectively. **3** the clergy of a church, district or country. **benefit of clergy** BENEFIT. **clergyman** *n.* (*pl.* **clergymen**) a member of the clergy, esp. of the Church of England. **clergywoman** *n.* (*pl.* **clergywomen**) a female member of the clergy. [OF *clergie* (*clerc*, late L *clēricus*, Gr. *klērikos*, pertaining to the clergy), from *klērikos*, a lot or inheritance, with reference to Deut. xviii.2 and Acts i.17]

cleric (kler´ik) *a.* clerical. ~*n.* **1** a member of the clergy. **2** a person subject to canon law. **clerico-** *comb. form* [late L *clēricus*, see CLERGY]

clerical (kle´rikəl) *a.* **1** of or relating to the clergy. **2** of or relating to a clerk or office worker. **clerical collar** *n.* a stiff, white collar fastening at the back, as worn by clergymen. **clerical error** *n.* an error in copying. **clericalism** *n.* undue influence of the clergy. **clericalist** *n.* **clerically** *adv.* **clericals** *n.pl.* clerical dress. [late L *clēricālis*, from CLERIC]

clerihew (kler´ihū) *n.* a satirical or humorous poem, usu. biographical, consisting of four rhymed lines of uneven length. [E. *Clerihew* Bentley, 1875–1956, English writer]

clerk (klahk) *n.* **1** a person employed in an office, bank, shop etc. to assist in correspondence, bookkeeping etc. **2** a person who keeps the records, accounts etc. of a court, council etc. **3** a person who has charge of an office or department, subject to a higher authority, such as a board. **4** the lay officer of a parish church. **5** (*N Am.*) a shop assistant. **6** (*N Am.*) a hotel receptionist. **7** †a scholar, a person able to read and write. **8** †a cleric, a clergyman. ~*v.i.* to be a clerk. **clerkdom** *n.* **clerkess** *n.* a female clerk. **clerk in holy orders** *n.* (*formal*) an ordained clergyman. **clerkish** *a.* **clerkly** *a.* **Clerk of the Closet** *n.* the principal chaplain to the sovereign. **clerk of the course** *n.* an official in charge of administration of a motor- or horse-racing course. **clerk of (the) works** *n.* a surveyor appointed to supervise building work and test the quality of materials etc. **clerkship** *n.* [OE *clerc*, from OF *clerc* or late L *clēricus* (see CLERGY)]

clever (klev´ə) *a.* **1** intelligent. **2** dexterous, skilful. **3** talented. **4** ingenious. **5** cunning. **clever-clever** *a.* clever in a superficial or showy way. **clever clogs, clever Dick** *n.* (*coll.*) a person who shows off their own cleverness. **cleverish** *a.* **cleverly** *adv.* **cleverness** *n.* [etym. uncertain; conn. with OE *clifer*, a claw, *clifian*, to seize (cp. EFris. *klüfer*)]

clevis (klev´is) *n.* a forked iron at the end of a shaft or beam, or an iron loop, for fastening tackle to. [etym. uncertain; prob. conn. with CLEAVE²]

clew (kloo) *n.* **1** the lower corner of a square sail. **2** the aftermost corner of a triangular sail. **3** the cords by which a hammock is suspended. **4** †a clue. ~*v.t.* to clew up or down. **to clew down** to unfurl (a sail) by letting down the clews. **to clew up** to truss (a sail) by drawing the clews up to the yard or mast. **clew lines** *n.pl.* ropes used to clew up the smaller square sails. [OE *clīwen* (cp. Dut. *kluwen*, G *Knäuel*); see also CLUE]

clianthus (klian´thəs) *n.* (*pl.* **clianthuses**) any plant of the Australian genus *Clianthus*, with clusters of red flowers. [Gr. *kleos*, glory, *anthos*, flower]

cliché (klē´shā), **cliche** *n.* **1** a hackneyed phrase. **2** anything hackneyed or overused. **3** (*Print.*) a stereotype, esp. a stereotype or electrotype from a block. **4** a photographic negative. **clichéd, cliché'd, cliched** *a.* [F, p.p. of *clicher*, to stereotype (var. of *cliquer*)]

click (klik) *v.i.* **1** to make a slight, sharp noise, as of small hard objects knocking together. **2** (*coll.*) to fall into place, to make sense (*It didn't click until I read her note*). **3** (*coll.*) to be successful. **4** (*coll.*) to become friendly with someone, esp. of the opposite sex (*We clicked the first time we met*). **5** (of horses) to strike shoes together. ~*v.t.* **1** to cause to click (*to click one's fingers*). **2** to press (one of the buttons of a computer mouse). **3** to click on. ~*n.* **1** a slight, sharp sound. **2** a sharp clicking sound used in some languages, esp. of southern Africa. **3** the act or action of clicking. **4** the detent of a ratchet-wheel. **5** a catch for a lock or bolt. **6** a latch. **to click on** to select (an item on a computer screen) by pressing one of the buttons of a computer mouse. **click beetle** *n.* any beetle of the family Elateridae, which can right itself with a click when turned on its back. **click-clack** *n.* a repeated clicking sound. ~*v.i.* to make this sound. **clicker** *n.* [imit., cp. CLACK, Dut. *klikken*, F *cliquer*]

client (klī´ənt) *n.* **1** a person who entrusts any business to a lawyer, accountant, architect etc. **2** a customer. **3** a person who is receiving help from a social worker or charitable agency. **4** in ancient Rome, a plebeian under the protection of a noble patron. **5** †a dependant. **clientage** *n.* **1** clientele. **2** the system of patron and client in ancient Rome. **cliental** *a.* **client-centred therapy** *n.* a form of psychotherapy in which patients are encouraged to develop their own solutions to their problems. **clientless** *a.* **client-server** *a.* denoting a computer system in which networked workstations receive data from a central server. **clientship** *n.* [L *cliēns -ntis* (*cluere*, to hear, to obey)]

clientele (klēontel´) *n.* **1** clients collectively. **2** customers, patients, the patrons of a theatre or restaurant. **3** followers or adherents. **4** clientship. [L *clientēla* (more recently readopted from F *clientèle*)]

cliff (klif) *n.* **1** a high, steep rock face, esp. on the coast. **2** a precipice. **cliffhanger** *n.* **1** a story, film etc. that has one in suspense till the end. **2** a highly dramatic, unresolved ending to an instalment of a serial. **3** any similarly suspenseful or exciting situation, such as a sporting contest. **cliffhanging** *a.* **clifflike** *a.* **cliffy** *a.* **1** having cliffs. **2** craggy. [OE *clif* (cp. Dut. and Icel. *klif*, G *Klippe*)]

climacteric (klīmak´tərik, -ter´-) *n.* **1** a critical period in human life. **2** the menopause in women, or a corresponding period in men. **3** a period in which some great change is supposed to take place in the human constitution, or in the fortune of an individual, esp. in the 21st, 35th, 49th and 63rd years. ~*a.* **1** of or relating to a climacteric. **2** critical. **3** (*Med.*) occurring late in life. **climacterical** (-ter´-) *a.* climacteric. [L *clīmactēricus*, Gr. *klimaktērikos* (*klimaktēr*, the step of a ladder, a critical period in life; cp. *klimax*, CLIMAX)]

climactic CLIMAX.

climate (klī´mət) *n.* **1** the temperature of a place, and its meteorological conditions generally, with regard to their influence on animal and plant life. **2** a region considered with reference to its weather. **3** a prevailing character (*the current economic climate*). **climate of opinion** *n.* the prevailing trend of opinion. **climatic** (-mat´-) *a.* **climatical** (-mat´-) *a.* **climatically** *adv.* **climatology** (-tol´-) *n.* **1** the science of climate. **2** an investigation of climatic phenomena and their causes. **climatological** (-loj´-) *a.* **climatologist** (-tol´-) *n.* [F *climat*, late L *clima -atos*, Gr. *klima- atos*, a slope, a region (*klinein*, to slope)]

Usage note See note on *climatic* under CLIMAX.

---

climax (klī´maks) *n.* **1** the highest point, culmination. **2** an orgasm. **3** a rhetorical figure in which the sense rises gradually in a series of images, each exceeding its predecessor in force or dignity. **4** a stable final stage in the development of a plant or animal community. ~*v.i.* to reach a climax. ~*v.t.* to bring to a climax. **climactic** (-mak´-) *a.* **climactically** *adv.* [L, from Gr.

klimax, a ladder (*klinein*, to slope)]

Usage note The adjectives *climactic* and *climatic* should not be confused: the first is related to *climax*, and the second to *climate*.

climb (klīm) *v.t.* (*past, p.p.* **climbed, †clomb** (klōm)) **1** to ascend, esp. by means of the hands and feet. **2** (of a plant) to ascend, esp. by means of tendrils. *~v.i.* **1** to ascend. **2** to move in any direction by grasping or with effort (*He climbed along the ledge*). **3** (of a plant) to grow up a wall, trellis etc., esp. by means of tendrils. **4** to slope upwards. **5** to rise (*The temperature continued to climb*). **6** to rise in rank or prosperity. *~n.* **1** an ascent. **2** the act of climbing or ascending. **3** a place climbed. **to climb down 1** to descend, esp. using hands and feet. **2** to abandon one's claims, to withdraw from a position, opinion etc. **to climb into 1** to enter, esp. with effort or by climbing (*They climbed into the truck*). **2** to put on (clothes). **climbable** *a.* **climbdown** *n.* a withdrawal from a position, opinion etc. **climber** *n.* **1** a person or thing that climbs, esp. a mountaineer. **2** a creeper or climbing plant. **3** a social climber. **climbing** *n.* mountaineering. *~a.* that climbs (*a climbing plant*). **climbing frame** *n.* a framework of bars for children to climb on. **climbing irons** *n.pl.* a set of spikes fastened to the legs to assist in climbing. **climbing perch** *n.* the anabas, a freshwater fish (*Anabas testudinens*) that climbs river banks and trees. **climbing wall** *n.* a wall for mountaineering practice, specially constructed with holds for the hands and feet. [OE *climban* (cp. *clifian*, CLEAVE², Dut. and G *klimmen*)]

clime (klīm) *n.* (*poet.*) **1** a region, a country. **2** a climate. [late L *clima*, CLIMATE]

clin- CLINO-.

clinal CLINE.

clinch (klinch) *v.t.* **1** to drive home or settle (an argument, deal etc.). **2** to secure (a nail etc.) by hammering down the point. **3** (*Naut.*) to make (a rope) fast with a clinch. *~v.i.* **1** to hold an opponent by the arms in boxing etc. **2** (*coll.*) to embrace. *~n.* **1** the act of clinching. **2** (*Naut.*) a method of fastening large ropes by a half-hitch. **3** a grip or hold, esp. in boxing etc. **4** (*coll.*) an embrace. **clincher** *n.* **1** a person or thing that clinches. **2** (*coll.*) a conclusive argument or statement. **clincher-built** *a.* CLINKER-BUILT (under CLINKER²). **clinch nail** *n.* a nail with a malleable end adapted for clinching. [var. of CLENCH]

cline (klīn) *n.* **1** a gradation of forms seen in a single species over a given area. **2** a series of gradations forming a continuum. **clinal** (klī´nəl) *a.* [Gr. *klinein*, to bend]

cling (kling) *v.i.* (*past, p.p.* **clung** (klŭng)) **1** to adhere closely and tenaciously, esp. by twining, grasping or embracing. **2** to be stubbornly or tenaciously faithful (to). *~n.* a clingstone. **to cling together 1** to form one mass. **2** to resist separation. **clinger** *n.* **cling film** *n.* a kind of thin polythene film which clings to itself or anything else, used for airtight wrapping. **clingingly** *adv.* **clingstone** *n.* a kind of peach in which the pulp adheres closely to the stone. **clingy** *a.* (*comp.* **clingier**, *superl.* **clingiest**) **1** clinging. **2** showing great emotional dependence. **clinginess** *n.* [OE *clingan* (cp. Dan. *klynge*, to cluster, Swed. *klänge*, to climb)]

clinic (klin´ik) *n.* **1** a private hospital, or one specializing in one type of ailment or treatment. **2** a specialist department in a general hospital, esp. for outpatients. **3** medical and surgical instruction, esp. in hospitals. **4** a session in which advice and instruction are given on any topic. **clinical** *a.* **1** of or relating to a patient in bed, or to instruction given to students in a hospital ward. **2** detached, unemotional. **3** (of a room etc.) bare or plainly furnished; simple and functional. **clinical baptism** *n.* baptism administered to a sick or dying person. **clinical death** *n.* death judged by observing the condition of the patient. **clinically** *adv.* **clinical medicine** *n.* the branch of medicine which deals with the treatment of patients. **clinical psychology** *n.* the branch of psychology that deals with the treatment of mental illness and retardation. **clinical thermometer** *n.* a thermometer for taking the temperature of a patient. **clinician** (-nish´ən) *n.* a doctor who works with patients, as opposed to a teacher or researcher. [F *clinique*, L *clinicus*, Gr. *klinikos* (*klinē*, a bed, *klinein*, to slope, recline)]

clink¹ (klingk) *n.* a sharp, ringing sound, as when glasses or metallic bodies are struck lightly together. *~v.i.* to make this sound. *~v.t.* to cause to clink. **clinkstone** *n.* a feldspathic rock that clinks when struck. [imit.; cp. CLANK, Dut. *klinken*]

clink² (klingk) *n.* (*sl.*) a prison (*in clink*). [prob. from the name of a Southwark prison (perh. from CLINCH)]

clinker¹ (kling´kə) *n.* **1** vitrified slag. **2** fused cinders. **3** bricks run together in a mass by heat. **4** a hard type of brick. **5** (*sl.*) a resounding blow, a thumping lie etc. **6** (*sl.*) anything outstanding or remarkable. **7** (*N Am., coll.*) a mistake. [MDut. *klinckaert* (*klinken*, to CLINK¹)]

clinker² (kling´kə) *n.* (*North.*) a clinch nail. **clinker-built** *a.* (*Naut.*) built with overlapping planks fastened with clinched nails, as distinct from *carvel-built*. [from obs. v. *clink*, CLINCH]

clino- (klī´nō), **clin-** *comb. form* sloping, oblique. [Gr. *klinein*, to slope]

clinometer (klīnom´itə, klin-) *n.* an instrument for measuring angles of inclination. **clinometric** (-met´-), **clinometrical** *a.*

clint (klint) *n.* (*Geol.*) any of the blocks that make up a limestone pavement. [Dan. and Swed. *klint*]

cliometrics (klīōmet´riks) *n.* the use of statistics and statistical methods in historical research, esp. in the study of economic history. [*Clio*, the Muse of history, econo*metrics*]

clip¹ (klip) *v.t.* (*pres.p.* **clipping**, *past, p.p.* **clipped**) **1** to cut with shears or scissors. **2** to trim. **3** to cut away, to cut out (*to clip a coupon from a magazine*). **4** to pare the edges of (a coin etc.). **5** to cut (a word) short by omitting letters, syllables etc. **6** to cancel (a ticket) by snipping a piece out. **7** (*coll.*) to hit sharply. **8** (*sl.*) to swindle. *~v.i.* to run or go swiftly. *~n.* **1** an act of clipping, a shearing or trimming. **2** an extract from a film. **3** (*coll.*) a sharp blow. **4** all the wool clipped from a sheep or flock in a season. **5** (*sl.*) a fast rate. **to clip the wings of** to put a check on the ambitions of. **clip joint** *n.* (*sl.*) a nightclub etc. which overcharges. **clippable** *a.* **clipper** *n.* **1** a person or thing that clips. **2** (*pl.*) a tool for clipping hair, nails etc. **3** a fast sailing vessel with a long sharp bow and raking masts. **4** anything that moves quickly, such as a fast horse. **clipper-built** *a.* (*Naut.*) built like a clipper. **clippie** *n.* (*coll., dated*) a bus conductress. **clipping** *n.* **1** a piece clipped off. **2** (*esp. N Am.*) a press cutting. [Icel. *klippa*]

clip² (klip) *n.* **1** an appliance for gripping, holding or attaching (*a paper clip*). **2** a cartridge clip. *~v.t.* (*pres.p.* **clipping**, *past, p.p.* **clipped**) **1** to fasten with a clip. **2** to clasp, to embrace. **3** to encircle, to surround closely. **clipboard** *n.* a flat board with a spring clip at one end, to hold paper for writing. **clip-fed** *a.* (of a firearm) loaded automatically from a cartridge clip. **clip-on** *a.* that can be attached by a clip (*clip-on sunglasses*). [OE *clyppan*]

clip-clop CLOP.

clippable, clipper etc. CLIP¹.

clique (klēk) *n.* **1** an exclusive set. **2** a coterie of snobs. **cliquey, cliquy** *a.* (*comp.* **cliquier**, *superl.* **cliquiest**). **cliquish** *a.* **cliquishness** *n.* **cliquism** *n.* [F, from *cliquer*, to CLICK]

C.Lit. *abbr.* Companion of Literature.

clitellum (klitel´əm) *n.* (*pl.* **clitella** (-tel´ə)) the thick central part of the body of an earthworm. **clitellar** *a.* [mod. L, from L *clitellae*, a packsaddle]

clitic (klit´ik) *n.* (*Gram.*) an enclitic or a proclitic. ~*a.* (of a word) unable to be stressed; pronounced as part of the preceding or following word. **cliticization** (-sīzā´shən), **cliticisation** *n.* [ENCLITIC, PROCLITIC]

clitoris (klit´əris) *n.* (*pl.* **clitorises, clitorides** (-dēz)) a small erectile body situated at the apex of the vulva and corresponding to the penis in the male. **clitoridectomy** (-dek´təmi) *n.* (*pl.* **clitoridectomies**) surgical removal of the clitoris. **clitoral** *a.* [Gr. *kleitoris* (*kleiein*, to shut)]

clivers CLEAVERS.

Cllr *abbr.* Councillor.

cloaca (klōā´kə) *n.* (*pl.* **cloacae** (-sē, -kē)) **1** the excretory cavity in certain animals, birds, insects etc. **2** a sewer. **cloacal** *a.* [L]

cloak (klōk), †**cloke** *n.* **1** a loose, wide, outer garment, usu. sleeveless. **2** a covering. **3** a disguise, a blind, a pretext. **4** (*pl.*) a cloakroom. ~*v.t.* **1** to cover with or as with a cloak. **2** to disguise. **3** to hide. **under the cloak of** hidden by; using as a disguise or pretext. **cloak-and-dagger** *a.* involving mystery and intrigue. **cloakroom** *n.* **1** a room where coats, parcels etc. can be deposited. **2** a lavatory. [ME and OF *cloke*, med. L *cloca*, a bell, a horseman's cape (cp. CLOCK[1])]

clobber (klob´ə) *n.* (*sl.*) clothes. ~*v.t.* **1** to beat, to batter. **2** to defeat overwhelmingly. **3** to criticize harshly. **clobberer** *n.* [etym. uncertain; perh. from Gael. *clabar*]

cloche (klosh) *n.* **1** a glass cover, orig. bell-shaped, put over young or tender plants to preserve them from frost. **2** a close-fitting bell-shaped hat. [F, a bell]

clock[1] (klok) *n.* **1** an instrument for measuring and indicating time (*an alarm clock; a digital clock*). **2** (*coll.*) a taximeter or speedometer. **3** the seed-head of a dandelion or similar flower. **4** (*sl.*) a person's face. ~*v.t.* **1** to time using a clock or stopwatch. **2** (*sl.*) to hit. **3** (*sl.*) to see, notice. **against the clock 1** (of a task etc.) to be finished by a certain time. **2** (of a race etc.) timed by a stopwatch or similar device. **to beat the clock** BEAT. **to clock in/ on** to register on a specially constructed clock the time of arrival at work. **to clock out/ off** to register on a specially constructed clock the time of departure from work. **to clock up** to register (a specified time, speed etc.). **to put the clock back** to regress to an earlier state. **to watch the clock** to clock-watch. **clock golf** *n.* a putting game played on a lawn marked out like the dial of a clock. **clockmaker** *n.* a person who makes or repairs clocks. **clockmaking** *n.* **clock radio** *n.* an alarm clock combined with a radio, which uses the radio instead of a bell. **clock tower** *n.* a tower with a large clock at the top, esp. as part of a church or a public building. **clock-watch** *v.i.* to look at the time frequently while working, esp. so as not to work any longer than necessary. **clock-watcher** *n.* **clock-watching** *n.* **clockwise** *adv.* in the direction of the hands of a clock. **clockwork** *n.* **1** the mechanism of a clock. **2** a train of wheels producing motion in a similar fashion. **like clockwork** with unfailing regularity; mechanically, automatically; very smoothly (*to go like clockwork*). [ONF *cloque*, med. L *clocca*, *cloca*, a bell; or MDut. *clocke* (Dut. *klok*, cp. G *Glocke*, a bell, a clock); prob. orig. from Celt. (cp. OIr. *cloc*, Welsh and Corn. *cloch*, Gael. *clag*)]

clock[2] (klok) *n.* an ornamental pattern on the side of the leg of a stocking. **clocked** *a.* [etym. uncertain]

clocking (klok´ing) *n.* (*Sc.*) brooding, hatching. ~*a.* brooding, sitting. [dial. v. *clock*, var. of CLUCK]

clod (klod) *n.* **1** a lump of earth or clay. **2** a mass of earth and turf. **3** any concreted mass. **4** the shoulder part of the neck of beef. **5** lifeless matter. **6** (*coll.*) a foolish person. **cloddish** *a.* loutish, coarse, clumsy, foolish. **cloddishly** *adv.* **cloddishness** *n.* **clodhopper** *n.* (*coll.*) **1** an awkward rustic, a bumpkin. **2** a foolish or clumsy person. **3** (*usu. pl.*) a large, heavy shoe. **clodhopping** *a.* **clodpate, clodpoll** *n.* (*sl.*) **1** a stupid, thick-headed person. **2** a boor. **clod-pated** *a.* [var. of CLOT]

clog (klog) *n.* **1** a kind of shoe with a wooden sole. **2** a boot with a metal rim. **3** a block of wood attached to a person or animal to hinder free movement. **4** †anything that impedes motion or freedom. ~*v.t.* (*pres.p.* **clogging,** *past, p.p.* **clogged**) **1** to obstruct. **2** to choke up. **3** to hinder. **4** to encumber or hamper with a weight. ~*v.i.* to be obstructed or encumbered with anything heavy or adhesive. **clever clogs** CLEVER. **clog dance** *n.* a dance in which the performer wears clogs in order to produce a loud accompaniment to the music. **cloggy** *a.* (*comp.* **cloggier,** *superl.* **cloggiest**) **1** clogging. **2** adhesive, sticky. **clogginess** *n.* [etym. unknown (perh. Scand., cp. Norw. *klugu*, a knotty log)]

cloisonné (klwazənā´, klwah´-, klwahzon´-) *a.* partitioned, divided into compartments. ~*n.* cloisonné enamel. **cloisonné enamel** *n.* enamelwork in which the coloured parts are separated by metallic partitions. [F, partitioned, from *cloison*, a partition (ult. from L *clausus*, p.p. of *claudere*, to close)]

cloister (klois´tə) *n.* **1** a series of covered passages usu. arranged along the sides of a quadrangle in monastic, cathedral or collegiate buildings. **2** a place of religious seclusion. **3** a religious house or convent. ~*v.t.* to shut up in or as in a cloister or convent. **cloistered** *a.* **1** secluded. **2** sheltered from the world, reality etc. **3** monastic. **4** having a cloister or cloisters. **cloister-garth** *n.* a yard or grass plot surrounded with cloisters, often used as a burial ground. **cloistral** *a.* [OF *cloistre* (F *cloître*), L *claustrum* (*claudere*, to shut, p.p. *clausus*)]

clomp (klomp) *v.i.* to walk or tread in a heavy and clumsy fashion. [CLUMP]

clone (klōn) *n.* **1** a number of organisms produced asexually from a single progenitor. **2** any such organism. **3** (*coll.*) an exact copy. ~*v.t.* to produce a clone of. **clonal** *a.* **clonally** *adv.* [Gr. *klōn*, a shoot]

clonic, clonicity CLONUS.

clonk (klongk) *v.i.* to make a short dull sound, as of two solid objects striking each other. ~*v.t.* (*coll.*) to hit. ~*n.* a short dull sound. [onomat.]

clonus (klō´nəs) *n.* a muscular spasm with alternate contraction and relaxation, as opposed to *tonic spasm*. **clonic** (klon´-) *a.* **clonicity** (klonis´-) *n.* [Gr. *klonos*, violent commotion]

clop (klop), **clip-clop** (klip-) *n.* the sound of a horse's hoof striking the ground. ~*v.i.* (*pres.p.* **clopping, clip-clopping,** *past, p.p.* **clopped, clip-clopped**) to make such a sound. [onomat.]

cloqué (klō´kā, klok´-) *n.* a type of fabric with an embossed surface. [F, blistered]

close[1] (klōs) *a.* **1** near in time or space. **2** intimate, familiar (*a close friend*). **3** nearly alike. **4** almost equal (*a close contest*). **5** solid, dense, compact. **6** concise, compressed. **7** attentive, concentrated (*a close examination*). **8** following the original closely. **9** accurate, precise, minute. **10** without ventilation, oppressive, stifling. **11** (of the weather) warm and damp. **12** closed, shut fast. **13** pronounced with the lips or mouth partly shut (*a close vowel*). **14** confined, shut in. **15** restricted, limited, reserved. **16** retired, secret, reticent. **17** difficult to obtain, scarce. **18** parsimonious, miserly. ~*adv.* **1** near. **2** closely, tightly, thickly or compactly. ~*n.* **1** an enclosure or enclosed place. **2** a road that is closed at one end. **3** a narrow passage or street. **4** the precincts of a cathedral or abbey. **5** a small enclosed field or yard. **6** (*Sc.*) an entry from the street to building or courtyard. **close by** within a short distance; very near. **close on/ upon** nearly (*We lived there close on twenty years*). **close to** near. **close to one's heart**

HEART. **close to the bone** BONE. **to go close** (of a racehorse) to (almost) win. **to run someone close** RUN. **to sail close to the wind** WIND[1]. **close borough** BOROUGH. **close breeding** *n.* breeding between animals closely related. **close call** *n.* (*esp. N Am.*) a close shave. **close corporation** *n.* a corporation which fills up its own vacancies. **close-coupled** *a.* **1** attached close together. **2** (of a lavatory) having the cistern directly connected to the pan. **close-cropped** *a.* cut very short (*close-cropped hair*). **close-fisted, †close-handed** *a.* niggardly, miserly. **close-fistedness** *n.* **close-fitting** *a.* (of clothes) fitting tightly to the outline of the body. **close-grained** *a.* (of wood etc.) with fibres or particles densely packed. **close harmony** *n.* a kind of singing in which all the parts lie close together. **close-hauled** *a.* (*Naut.*) kept as near as possible to the point from which the wind blows. **close-in** *a.* **1** at short range. **2** close to the centre. **close-knit** *a.* closely united (*a close-knit family*). **close-lipped, close-mouthed, close-tongued** *a.* reticent, silent. **closely** *adv.* **closeness** *n.* **close quarters** *n.pl.* **1** direct contact. **2** proximity. **at close quarters 1** in direct contact, esp. with an enemy. **2** very near. **to come to close quarters** to come into direct contact, esp. with an enemy. **close-range** *a.* **1** at a short distance. **2** from a short distance. **close-run** *a.* won by a narrow margin (*a close-run election*). **close season** *n.* the breeding season, during which it is illegal to kill certain fish or game. **close-set** *a.* close together. **close shave** *n.* a narrow escape. **close-up** *n.* **1** a view taken with the camera at very close range. **2** any intimate view or examination. **closish** *a.* [as CLOSE[2]]

close[2] (klōz) *v.t.* **1** to shut. **2** to fill (up) an opening. **3** to enclose, to shut in. **4** to bring or unite together. **5** to be the end of, to conclude. **6** to complete, to settle (*to close a deal*). *~v.i.* **1** to shut. **2** to come to an end, to cease. **3** to stop doing business, esp. at the end of the working day (*The bank closes at five*). **4** to agree, to come to terms. **5** to grapple, to come to hand-to-hand fighting. **6** to coalesce. *~n.* **1** the act of closing. **2** an end, a conclusion. **3** (*Mus.*) a cadence. **to close down 1** (of a factory, shop etc.) to cease work or business, esp. permanently. **2** (of a radio or television station) to go off the air. **to close in 1** to shut in, to enclose. **2** to come nearer. **3** to get shorter (*The days are closing in*). **to close on 1** to shut over. **2** to grasp. **3** to catch up with. **to close one's eyes** to die. **to close one's eyes to** EYE[1]. **to close one's mind** MIND. **to close out** to terminate (a business, an account etc.). **to close ranks** RANK[1]. **to close the door to** DOOR. **to close up 1** to block up, to fill in. **2** to come together. **to close with 1** to agree or consent to. **2** to unite with. **3** to grapple with (*to close with the enemy*). **closable** *a.* **closed** *a.* **1** shut. **2** not doing business, esp. temporarily (*Most of the shops were closed*). **3** restricted, exclusive (*a closed society*). **4** self-contained. **behind closed doors** in private. **closed book** *n.* **1** a subject one knows nothing about. **2** a matter that has been concluded. **closed circuit** *n.* an electrical circuit with a complete, unbroken path for the current to flow through. **closed-circuit television** *n.* a television system for a restricted number of viewers in which the signal is transmitted to the receiver by cable. **closed community** *n.* a plant community in which there is no room for further colonization. **closed-door** *a.* private, not open to the public. **closed-end** *a.* limited, finite; not open-ended. **closed-in** *a.* **1** enclosed. **2** restricted. **closed season** *n.* CLOSE SEASON (under CLOSE[1]). **closed shop** *n.* a workplace where all employees must be union members. **closed syllable** *n.* a syllable that ends in a consonant. **close-down** *n.* the act of closing down. **closing time** *n.* the hour at which a shop, public house or other establishment is declared closed for business. [ME *closen*, OF *clos*, p.p. of *clore*, L *claudere*, to shut (p.p. *clausus*)]

closet (kloz´it) *n.* **1** a small room for privacy and retirement. **2** a water closet. **3** (*chiefly N Am.*) a cupboard. *~a.* **1** secret. **2** private. *~v.t.* (*pres.p.* **closeting,** *past, p.p.* **closeted**) to shut away in a private room for consultation etc. **to be closeted with** to hold a confidential conversation with. **to come out of the closet** to declare or make public one's inclinations, intentions etc., esp. to declare one's homosexuality. **closet drama, closet play** *n.* a play suitable for reading, not acting. **closet queen** *n.* (*sl.*) a man who has not declared his homosexuality. [dim. of OF *clos*, as CLOSE[1]]

closish CLOSE[1].

clostridial (klostrid´iəl) *a.* of or relating to a rod-shaped bacterium of the genus *Clostridium*, esp. one that causes disease. [Gr. *klōstēr*, a spindle]

closure (klō´zhə) *n.* **1** the act of closing. **2** the state of being closed. **3** something that closes or seals a container etc. **4** the power of terminating debate in a legislative or deliberative assembly. *~v.t.* to apply this power to (a debate, speaker or motion). [OF, from L *clausūra* (*clausus*, p.p. of *claudere*, to close)]

clot (klot) *n.* **1** a small coagulated mass of soft or fluid matter, esp. of blood. **2** a clod, a lump, a ball. **3** (*sl.*) a silly person. *~v.t.* (*pres.p.* **clotting,** *past, p.p.* **clotted**) to cause to form clots. *~v.i.* to form into clots. **clotted cream** *n.* cream produced in clots on new milk when it is simmered, orig. made in Devon. **clotty** *a.* [OE *clott*, *clot* (cp. G *Klotz*, CLEAT, CLOD)]

cloth (kloth) *n.* (*pl.* **cloths** (kloths, klodhz)) **1** a woven fabric of wool, cotton, silk etc. used for garments or other coverings. **2** any textile fabric, material. **3** a piece of this. **4** a tablecloth. **5** woven woollen fabric. **6** the dress of a profession, esp. the clergy (from their usu. wearing black cloth). **7** this profession, the clergy. **8** in the theatre, a coloured or painted curtain let up and down between stage and auditorium. **clothbound** *a.* (of a book) bound with boards covered in linen or cloth. **cloth cap** *n.* a flat cap with a peak. **cloth-cap** *a.* (*sometimes derog.*) belonging to or characteristic of the working class. **cloth-eared** *a.* (*coll.*) **1** deaf. **2** inattentive. **cloth of gold, cloth of silver** *n.* a fabric of gold or silver threads interwoven with silk or wool. [OE *clāth* (cp. G *Kleid*)]

clothe (klōdh) *v.t.* (*past, p.p.* **clothed,** (*poet.*) **clad** (klad)) **1** to provide or cover with or as with clothes. **2** to invest (with a quality). **clothes** (klōdhz, klōz) *n.pl.* **1** garments, dress. **2** bedclothes. **clothes basket** *n.* a basket for clothes to be washed. **clothes brush** *n.* a brush for removing dust etc. from clothes. **clothes horse** *n.* **1** a frame for drying clothes on. **2** (*coll.*) a fashionably dressed person. **clothes line** *n.* a line for drying clothes on. **clothes-peg,** (*N Am.*) **clothes-pin** *n.* a wooden or plastic clip used to fasten clothes on a line. **clothes-press** *n.* a cupboard for storing clothes. **clothes prop** *n.* a pole for supporting a clothes line. **clothing** *n.* clothes, dress. [OE *clāthian* (CLAD[1] is from ONorthum. *clǣthan*)]

clothier (klō´dhiə) *n.* **1** a manufacturer of cloth. **2** a person who deals in cloth or clothing. [orig. *clother*]

clothing CLOTHE.

cloture (klō´chə) *n.* (*N Am.*) closure of debate in a legislative body. *~v.t.* to closure. [F]

clou (kloo) *n.* **1** the centre of interest or attraction. **2** the principal idea. [F, a nail]

cloud (klowd) *n.* **1** a mass of visible vapour condensed into minute drops and floating in the upper regions of the atmosphere. **2** a volume of smoke or dust resembling a cloud. **3** a great number of birds, insects, snowflakes, arrows etc., moving in a body. **4** a dimness or patchiness in liquid. **5** the dusky veins or markings in marble, precious stones etc. **6** a veil which obscures or darkens. **7** obscurity, bewilderment, confusion of ideas. **8** suspicion, trouble. **9** any temporary depression.

~*v.t.* 1 to cover with clouds, to darken. 2 to mark with cloudlike spots or patches. 3 to make gloomy or sullen. 4 to sully, to stain. 5 to impair. ~*v.i.* to grow cloudy (*The sky clouded over*). **in the clouds** 1 mystical, unreal. 2 absent-minded. **on cloud nine** (*coll.*) very happy, elated. **under a cloud** in temporary disgrace or misfortune; under suspicion. **cloud base** *n.* the lowest layer of cloud or clouds. **cloudberry** *n.* (*pl.* **cloudberries**) a low mountain and moorland shrub, *Rubus chamaemorus*, with orange-coloured fruit. **cloudburst** *n.* a sudden and heavy fall of rain. **cloud-capped** *a.* 1 (of mountains etc.) having the summit or summits veiled with clouds. 2 very lofty. **cloud-castle** *n.* a daydream, a visionary scheme. **cloud chamber** *n.* an apparatus in which high-energy particles are tracked as they pass through a vapour. **cloud cover** *n.* 1 a mass of unbroken cloud or clouds. 2 the extent of this. **cloud-cuckoo-land, cloud-land** *n.* 1 a utopia. 2 a fantastic scheme for social, political or economic reform. **clouded leopard** *n.* a leopard-like arboreal mammal, *Neofelis nebulosa*. **cloud-hopping** *n.* (of an aircraft) movement from one cloud to another. **cloudless** *a.* 1 unclouded. 2 clear, bright. **cloudlessly** *adv.* **cloudlessness** *n.* **cloudlet** (-lit) *n.* a little cloud. **cloudlike** *a.* **cloud on the horizon** *n.* a matter for concern; something unpleasant which is threatening. **cloud rack** *n.* moving broken cloud or clouds. **cloudscape** *n.* 1 a view or picture of clouds. 2 picturesque cloud effects. **cloudwards** *adv.* **cloudy** *a.* (*comp.* **cloudier,** *superl.* **cloudiest**) 1 consisting of or covered with clouds. 2 not transparent (*a cloudy liquid*). 3 marked with veins or spots. 4 obscure, confused. 5 dull, gloomy, sullen. **cloudiness** *n.* [prob. from OE *clūd*, a rounded mass, conn. with CLOD]

clough (klŭf) *n.* (*dial.*) 1 a ravine. 2 a narrow valley. [OE *clōh*]

clout (klowt) *n.* 1 a blow, esp. on the head. 2 (*coll.*) power, influence. 3 (*dial.*) a piece of cloth, rag etc. 4 (*dial.*) a piece of clothing. 5 (*Hist.*) a mark for archers. 6 a clout-nail. 7 an iron plate on an axle-tree to keep it from being rubbed. ~*v.t.* 1 to strike, esp. heavily. 2 to patch, to mend roughly. 3 to cover with a piece of cloth etc. 4 to tip or plate with iron. 5 to stud or fasten with clout-nails. **clout-nail** *n.* a short nail with a large flat head for fastening metal to wood, or to stud the soles of heavy boots and shoes. [OE *clūt* (cogn. with CLOT)]

clove[1] (klōv) *n.* 1 a dried, unexpanded flower bud of the tree *Eugenia aromatica*, used as a spice. 2 this tree. 3 (*pl.*) a spirituous cordial flavoured with the spice. **clove gillyflower, clove pink** *n.* any sweet-scented double variety of *Dianthus caryophyllus*. [F *clou*, L *clavus*, a nail (*clou de girofle*, a clove), prob. assim. in sound to CLOVE[2]]

clove[2] (klōv) *n.* a small bulb forming one part of a compound bulb, as in garlic, the shallot etc. [OE *clufu* (from *cluf-*, cogn. with *clēofan*, to CLEAVE[1])]

clove[3] CLEAVE[1].

clove hitch (klōv hich´) *n.* a knot used to fasten a rope round a spar or another rope. [obs. p.p. of CLEAVE[1]]

cloven[1] (klō´vən) *a.* 1 divided into two parts. 2 cleft, split. **cloven hoof, cloven foot** *n.* 1 a hoof divided in the centre, as those of the ruminants. 2 an emblem of the god Pan or the Devil. 3 an indication of guile or evil (*to show the cloven hoof*). **cloven-hoofed, cloven-footed** *a.* [p.p. of CLEAVE[1]]

cloven[2] CLEAVE[1].

clover (klō´və) *n.* any plant of the genus *Trifolium*, with dense flower heads and usu. trifoliate leaves, used for fodder. **in clover** 1 in enjoyable circumstances. 2 in luxury. **cloverleaf** *n.* (*pl.* **cloverleaves**) a road junction in which one road passes over the other, and the connecting carriageways, having no abrupt turns, make the shape of a four-leaved clover. [OE *clāfre* (cp. Dut. *klaver*, Dan. *klōver*, G *Klee*)]

clown (klown) *n.* 1 a comic entertainer, usu. with traditional make-up and costume, in a circus or pantomime. 2 a buffoon. 3 a clumsy or foolish person. 4 a rough, ill-bred person. 5 †a rustic, a bumpkin. ~*v.i.* to play silly jokes, to act the buffoon. ~*v.t.* to perform in the manner of a clown. **clownery** *n.* **clownish** *a.* **clownishly** *adv.* **clownishness** *n.* [cp. Icel. *klunni*, CLUMP or CLOT]

cloy (kloi) *v.t.* 1 to satiate, to glut. 2 to tire with sweetness, richness or excess. **cloyingly** *adv.* [etym. uncertain; perh. from OF *cloyer* (F *clouer*), to nail]

cloze test (klōz) *n.* a test of readability or comprehension in which words omitted from the text must be supplied by the reader. [CLOSURE]

club[1] (klŭb) *n.* 1 a piece of wood with one end thicker and heavier than the other, used as a weapon. 2 a stick bent and usu. weighted at the end for driving a ball, esp. in golf. 3 (*pl.*) one of the four suits at cards denoted by a black trefoil. 4 a card of this suit. 5 a club-shaped structure or organ. ~*v.t.* (*pres.p.* **clubbing,** *past, p.p.* **clubbed**) 1 to beat with a club. 2 to seize (a weapon) by the barrel and use it as a club. **clubbed** *a.* club-shaped. **club foot** *n.* a short deformed foot. **club-footed** *a.* **club-headed** *a.* having a club-shaped head or top. **clubmoss** *n.* a species of moss of the family Lycopodiaceae, with seed vessels pointing straight upwards. **clubroot** *n.* a disease of plants of the *Brassica* (cabbage) genus in which the lower part of the stem becomes swollen and misshapen owing to the attacks of larvae. **club sandwich** *n.* a sandwich made with three slices of bread and two different fillings. **club-shaped** *a.* thicker at one end than the other. [ME *clubbe, clobbe*, prob. from Icel. *klubba, klumba*, a club, a cudgel]

club[2] (klŭb) *n.* 1 an association of persons combined for some common object, such as social intercourse, politics, sport etc., governed by self-imposed regulations. 2 the building in which such an association meets; a clubhouse. 3 the body of members collectively. 4 a commercial organization that offers discounts etc. to subscribers (*a book club*). 5 a nightclub. ~*v.t.* (*pres.p.* **clubbing,** *past, p.p.* **clubbed**) 1 to contribute for a common object or to a common stock. 2 to gather into a clump. ~*v.i.* 1 to join (together) for a common object (*We clubbed together to buy him a present*). 2 (*coll.*) to go to nightclubs. **in the club** (*sl.*) pregnant. **clubbable** *a.* 1 having the qualities necessary for club membership. 2 sociable. **clubbability** (-bil´-), **clubbableness** *n.* **clubber** *n.* 1 a member of a club. 2 a person who uses a club, esp. a frequenter of nightclubs. **clubby** *a.* (*comp.* **clubbier,** *superl.* **clubbiest**) (*esp. N Am.*) sociable. **club car** *n.* (*N Am.*) a railway coach designed like a lounge, usu. with a bar. **club class** *n.* a class of air travel designed for business people. **clubhouse** *n.* 1 the building occupied by a club, or in which it holds its meetings. 2 the establishment maintained by the members of a social or sports club, at which they meet, drink, dine or lodge temporarily. **clubland** *n.* the district round St James's and Pall Mall in London where the principal clubs are situated. **clubman, clubwoman** *n.* (*pl.* **clubmen, clubwomen**) a member of a club. **clubmate** *n.* a fellow member of a club, esp. a sports club. **clubroom** *n.* a room in which a club or society meets. **club soda** *n.* (*N Am.*) soda water. [CLUB[1]]

cluck (klŭk) *n.* 1 the guttural call of a hen. 2 any similar sound. 3 (*sl.*) a foolish person. ~*v.i.* to utter a cluck. ~*v.t.* to call or express with a cluck. **clucky** *a.* broody. [OE *cloccian*, imit.]

clue (kloo) *n.* 1 anything that serves as a guide, direction or hint for the solution of a problem or mystery, or as evidence in the detection of crime. 2 the thread of a story. ~*v.t.* (*pres.p.* **cluing, clueing,** *past, p.p.* **clued**) to provide with a clue. **not to have a clue** 1 (*coll.*) to have no idea whatever. **2** (*coll.*) to be utterly incompetent. **to clue in/ up** (*sl.*) to inform. **clued-up** *a.* (*coll.*) well informed. **clueless** *a.* (*coll.*) **1** ignorant. **2** stupid. **cluelessly** *adv.* **cluelessness** *n.* [CLEW]

clumber (klŭm´bə) *n.* a variety of spaniel with a broad head. [*Clumber*, Duke of Newcastle's seat in Nottinghamshire, where orig. bred]

clump (klŭmp) *n.* **1** a thick cluster of trees, shrubs or flowers. **2** a thick mass of small objects, organisms, cells etc. **3** a thick piece of leather fastened onto the sole of a boot. **4** a heavy blow. ~*v.i.* **1** to walk or tread in a heavy and clumsy fashion. **2** to form or gather into a clump or clumps. ~*v.t.* **1** to make a clump of. **2** (*sl.*) to beat. **clumpy** *a.* (*comp.* **clumpier**, *superl.* **clumpiest**). [cp. CLUB[1] (Icel. *klubba*, *klumba*), also G *Klumpen*, Dut. *klomp*]

clumsy (klŭm´zi) *a.* (*comp.* **clumsier**, *superl.* **clumsiest**) **1** awkward, ungainly. **2** ill-constructed, difficult to use. **3** rough, rude, tactless. **clumsily** *adv.* **clumsiness** *n.* [ME *clumsed*, p.p. of *clumsen*, to benumb (cp. CLAMMY)]

clung CLING.

Cluniac (kloo´niak) *n.* a member of a religious order, a reformed branch of the Benedictines, founded at Cluny, Saône-et-Loire, France, in the 10th cent. ~*a.* of or relating to this order. [med. L *Cluniacus*, from *Cluny*]

clunk (klŭngk) *v.i.* to make a short, dull sound, as of metal striking a hard surface. ~*n.* such a sound. **clunker** *n.* (*N Am., coll.*) **1** a useless or dilapidated machine. **2** a failure. **clunky** *a.* (*comp.* **clunkier**, *superl.* **clunkiest**) **1** clunking. **2** (*N Am.*) heavy, unwieldy. [onomat.]

clupeid (kloo´pēid) *n.* any fish belonging to the family Clupeidae, the herring family. ~*a.* of or relating to this family. **clupeiform** (kloo´pifawm) *a.* **clupeoid** (-pioid) *n.* any fish belonging to the order *Isospondyli*, including the clupeids. ~*a.* of or relating to this order. **clupeoidean** (-oi´-) *a.*, *n.* [L *clupea*, a small river-fish]

cluster (klŭs´tə) *n.* **1** a number of things of the same kind growing or joined together. **2** a bunch. **3** a number of persons or things gathered or situated close together. **4** a group, a crowd. ~*v.i.* to come or to grow into a cluster or clusters. ~*v.t.* to bring or cause to come into a cluster or clusters. **cluster bomb** *n.* a bomb which explodes to scatter a number of smaller bombs. **clustered column, clustered pillar** *n.* a pier consisting of several columns or shafts clustered together. **cluster fly** *n.* a dipterous fly, *Pollenia rudis*, that gathers in large numbers in the autumn. **cluster pine** *n.* the pinaster. [OE *clyster* (prob. from the same root as CLOT)]

clutch[1] (klŭch) *n.* **1** a snatch, a grip, a grasp. **2** the paw or talon of a rapacious animal. **3** (*pl.*) claws, grasping hands, tyrannical power. **4** a device for connecting and disconnecting two revolving shafts in an engine. **5** the pedal that operates this device in a motor vehicle. **6** a gripping device. **7** the throat of an anchor. ~*v.t.* **1** to seize, clasp or grip with the hand. **2** to snatch. **to clutch at** to try to seize or grasp. **to clutch at straws/ a straw** STRAW. **clutch bag** *n.* a woman's handbag, without a handle, carried in the hand. **clutch shaft** *n.* a shaft which engages or disengages a clutch. [ME *cloche*, *cloke*, a claw (OE *clyccan*, to bring together, clench)]

clutch[2] (klŭch) *n.* **1** a set of eggs to be hatched. **2** a brood of chickens. **3** a group of people or things. [var. of obs. *cletch*, from *cleck*, to hatch]

clutter (klŭt´ə) *v.i.* **1** to make a confused noise. **2** to bustle. ~*v.t.* to fill or strew with clutter. ~*n.* **1** a mess, a disorderly collection of things. **2** a confused noise. **3** bustle, confusion. **4** irrelevant echoes on a radar screen from sources other than the target. **to clutter up** to fill untidily. [var. of *clotter*, freq. of CLOT]

Clydesdale (klīdz´dāl) *n.* **1** a heavy, powerful breed of horse. **2** a draught horse of this breed. **3** a kind of small terrier. [*Clyde*, river in Scotland, DALE]

clypeus (klip´iəs) *n.* (*pl.* **clypei** (-iī)) the shieldlike part of an insect's head, which joins the labrum. **clypeal, clypeate** (-ət), **clypeiform** (klip´ifawm) *a.* **clypeo-** *comb. form* [L, a shield]

†**clyster** (klis´tə) *n.* an enema. ~*v.t.* to administer an enema to. [L, from Gr. *klustēr* (*kluzein*, to wash out)]

CM *abbr.* Member of the Order of Canada.

Cm *chem. symbol* curium.

Cm. *abbr.* Command paper (since 1986).

cm *abbr.* centimetre(s).

Cmd. *abbr.* Command paper (before 1956).

Cmdr. *abbr.* Commander.

Cmdre. *abbr.* Commodore.

CMEA *abbr.* Council for Mutual Economic Assistance.

CMG *abbr.* Companion of (the Order of) St Michael and St George.

Cmnd. *abbr.* Command paper (1956–86).

CMOS (sē´mos) *abbr.* (*Comput.*) complementary metal oxide silicon (*CMOS memory*).

CMV *abbr.* cytomegalovirus.

c/n, cn *abbr.* credit note.

CNAA *abbr.* Council for National Academic Awards.

CNAR *abbr.* compound net annual rate.

CND *abbr.* Campaign for Nuclear Disarmament.

cnida (nī´də, knī´-) *n.* (*pl.* **cnidae** (-dē)) the stinging-cell of the jellyfish and other coelenterates. **cnidarian** (-deə´riən) *n.* any coelenterate of the subphylum *Cnidaria*. ~*a.* of or relating to this subphylum. **cnido-** *comb. form* [Gr. *knidē*, a nettle]

cnr. *abbr.* corner.

CNS *abbr.* central nervous system.

CO *abbr.* **1** Colombia (IVR). **2** Colonial Office (before 1966). **3** Colorado. **4** Commanding Officer. **5** Commonwealth Office (since 1966). **6** conscientious objector.

Co *chem. symbol* cobalt.

Co. *abbr.* **1** company. **2** county.

co. (kō) *n.* (*coll.*) the others, similar or related people or things; only in *and co.* (*I've invited Rachel and co*). [CO.] **c/o** *abbr.* care of.

co- (kō) *pref.* **1** with, together, jointly, mutually, as in *coalesce*, *cooperate*. **2** joint, mutual, as in *co-author*, *co-heir*. **3** (*Math.*) of the complement of an angle, as in *cosecant*, *cosine*. [L, the form of *cum*, together, used before vowels etc.]

coach (kōch) *n.* **1** a long-distance bus. **2** a railway carriage. **3** a large, closed, four-wheeled, horse-drawn vehicle, used for purposes of state, or formerly for travelling. **4** a person who trains sports players. **5** a tutor who prepares students for examinations. **6** any specialized instructor (*a drama coach*). **7** a room near the stern in a large ship. **8** (*N Am.*) the economy class area of an aircraft. **9** (*Austral.*) a decoy. ~*v.t.* **1** to train. **2** to prepare for an examination. **3** to instruct or advise in preparation for any event. ~*v.i.* **1** to travel in a coach. **2** to work as a coach. **3** to study with a tutor. **to drive a coach and horses through** DRIVE. **coach bolt** *n.* a large bolt with a round head, used to secure wood to masonry. **coach box** *n.* the seat on which the driver of a horse-drawn coach sits. **coachbuilder** *n.* a person who builds or repairs the bodywork of road or rail vehicles. **coach-built** *a.* (of vehicles) built individually by craftsmen. **coach driver** *n.* the driver of a long-distance bus. **coachful** *n.* as many as a coach will hold. **coach house** *n.* an outhouse to keep a horse-drawn coach or carriage in. **coaching** *n.* **coach line** *n.* a decorative line on a motor vehicle. **coachload** *n.* a coachful (*a coachload of tourists*). **coachman** *n.* (*pl.* **coachmen**) **1** the driver of a horse-drawn coach. **2** a livery servant who drives a carriage. **3** a kind of artificial fly used in angling. **coachmanship** *n.* **coach station** *n.* a terminus or stopping place for long-distance buses. **coachwood** *n.* an Australian tree, *Ceratopetalum apetalum*, with light, close-grained wood used to make furniture. **coachwork** *n.* the bodywork of a road or rail vehicle. [F *coche*, Hung. *kocsi*, belonging to *Kocz*, village in Hungary]

coact (kōakt´) *v.i.* to act together or in concert. **coaction** *n.* **coactive** *a.* **coactively** *adv.* [L *coactus*, p.p. of *coagere*, *cōgere*, to compel (CO-, *agere*, to drive)]

coadjutor (kōaj´ətə) *n.* **1** an assistant, a helper, esp. to a bishop. **2** a colleague. **coadjutorship** *n.* **coadjutrix** (-triks) *n.* a female coadjutor. [L *coadjūtor* (*juvāre*, to help)]

co-agent (kōā´jənt) *n.* a person or thing that acts with another. ~*a.* acting with. **co-agency** *n.*

coagulate (kōag´ūlāt) *v.t.*, *v.i.* **1** to curdle, to clot. **2** to change from a fluid into a semi-solid mass. **3** to solidify. **coagulable** *a.* **coagulant** *n.* a substance which causes coagulation. **coagulation** (-lā´shən) *n.* **coagulative** *a.* **coagulator** *n.* **coagulum** (-ləm) *n.* (*pl.* **coagula** (-lə)) **1** a coagulated mass. **2** a blood clot. **3** a coagulant. [from obs. a. *coagulate*, coagulated, or directly from L *coāgulātus*, p.p. of *coāgulāre*, from *coāgulum*, dim. n. of *coagere* (CO-, *agere*, to drive, impel)]

coal (kōl) *n.* **1** a black, solid, opaque carbonaceous substance of vegetable origin, obtained from the strata usu. underground, and used for fuel. **2** a piece of this. **3** a piece of wood or other combustible substance, ignited, burning or charred. **4** a cinder. ~*v.t.* to supply with coal. ~*v.i.* to take in a supply of coal. **to carry coals to Newcastle** to bring things to a place where they abound; to do anything superfluous or unnecessary. **to haul over the coals 1** to call to account. **2** to reprimand. **to heap coals of fire on someone's head** to return good for evil, causing remorse or repentance. **coal-black** *a.* as black as coal. **coal bunker** *n.* a large receptacle for coal. **coal cellar** *n.* a basement for storing coal. **coal dust** *n.* powdered coal. **coaler** *n.* a ship that transports coal. **coalface** *n.* the exposed surface of a coal-seam. **coalfield** *n.* an area where coal abounds. **coal-fired** *a.* (of a furnace, heating system etc.) fuelled by coal. **coalfish** *n.* (*pl. in general* **coalfish,** *in particular* **coalfishes**) the saithe or coley, *Pollachius virens*, an edible fish resembling the cod. **coal gas** *n.* a mixture of gases obtained from coal and used for lighting and heating. **coal heaver** *n.* a person employed in carrying, loading or discharging coals. **coal-hole** *n.* a small cellar for storing coal. **coalhouse** *n.* a building where coal is stored. **coaling station** *n.* a port where steamships may obtain coal, esp. one established by a government for the supply of coal to warships. **coalless** *a.* **coal measures** *n.pl.* the upper division of the Carboniferous system. **coal merchant** *n.* a retail seller of coal. **coal mine** *n.* a mine from which coal is obtained. **coal miner** *n.* **coal mining** *n.* **coal oil** *n.* (*N Am.*) petroleum. **coal sack** *n.* **1** a sack for coal. **2** (*also* **Coal Sack**) a dark nebula in the Milky Way. **coal-screen** *n.* a large screen or sifting-frame for separating large and small coals. **coal scuttle** *n.* a fireside utensil for holding coal. **coal-seam** *n.* a stratum of or containing coal. **coal tar** *n.* tar produced in the destructive distillation of bituminous coal. **coal tit** *n.* COALMOUSE. **coaly** *a.* [OE *col* (cp. Dut. *kool*, Icel. and Swed. *kol*, G *Kohle*)]

coalesce (kōəles´) *v.i.* **1** to fuse into one. **2** to combine, to grow together. **3** to unite into masses or groups spontaneously. **4** to form a coalition. **coalescence** *n.* **coalescent** *a.* [L *coalescere* (CO-, *alescere*, incept. of *alere*, to nourish)]

coalition (kōəlish´ən) *n.* **1** a combination of persons, parties or states, having different interests. **2** a union of separate bodies into one body or mass. **coalition government** *n.* a government in which two or more parties of varying politics unite for a common policy. **coalitionist** *n.* [med. L *coalitio*, see COALESCE]

coalmouse (kōl´mows), **colemouse** *n.* (*pl.* **coalmice** (-mīs), **colemice**) a small dark bird, *Parus ater*, also called *coal tit* or *cole tit*. [OE *colmāse* (*col*, coal, *māse*; cp. OHG *meisa*, WG *maisa*, a bird)]

coaming (kō´ming) *n.* (*Naut.*) a raised border round a hatch etc. for keeping water out of the hold. [etym. uncertain]

coarctate (kōahk´tāt) *a.* **1** pressed together. **2** (of an insect pupa) enclosed in a hard case. **coarctation** (-tā´shən) *n.* **1** compression, constriction. **2** (*Med.*) narrowing of the aorta. [L *coarctātus*, p.p. of *coarctāre* (*artāre*, from *artus*, confined)]

coarse (kaws) *a.* **1** large in size or rough in texture. **2** rude, rough, vulgar. **3** unpolished, unrefined. **4** indecent, obscene. **5** common, of average or inferior quality. **coarse fish** *n.* any freshwater fish not of the salmon family. **coarse fishing** *n.* **coarse-grained** *a.* **1** having a coarse grain. **2** unrefined, vulgar. **coarsely** *adv.* **coarsen** *v.t.* to make coarse. ~*v.i.* to become coarse. **coarseness** *n.* **coarsish** *a.* [prob. from *in course*, ordinary (cp. MEAN[3], PLAIN[1])]

coast (kōst) *n.* **1** that part of the border of a country where the land meets the sea. **2** the seashore. **3** the seaside. **4** a swift rush downhill on a bicycle or in a car, without using motive power or applying brakes. **5** (*N Am.*) a toboggan slide. ~*v.t.* **1** to sail by or near to. **2** to keep close to. ~*v.i.* **1** to descend an incline on a bicycle or in a motor vehicle without applying motive power or brakes. **2** to proceed without any positive effort. **3** (*N Am.*) to slide down snow or ice on a toboggan. **4** to sail near or in sight of the shore. **5** to sail from port to port in the same country. **the Coast** (*N Am.*) the Pacific coast of the US. **the coast is clear 1** the road is free. **2** the danger is over. **coastal** *a.* of, relating to or bordering on a coastline. **coaster** *n.* **1** a ship that sails from port to port in the same country. **2** a small tray for a bottle or decanter on a table. **3** a small mat under a glass. **4** (*N Am.*) a toboggan. **5** (*N Am.*) a roller coaster. **coastguard** *n.* **1** a member of a body of people who watch the coast to save those in danger, give warning of wrecks, and prevent the illegal landing of persons and goods. **2** this body of people. **coasting** *a.* keeping near or in sight of the shore, as opposed to seagoing. **coastland** *n.* (*usu. pl.*) land near the sea. **coastline** *n.* the line or outline of a coast. **coast to coast** *a.*, *adv.* from coast to coast, across a whole continent. **coastward, coastwards** *adv.* **coastwise** *a.*, *adv.* along the coast. [OF *coste* (F *côte*), L *costa*, a rib, a side]

coat (kōt) *n.* **1** an outer garment with sleeves; an overcoat or jacket. **2** the hair, fur or natural external covering of an animal. **3** any integument, tunic or covering. **4** a layer of any substance covering and protecting another (*a coat of paint*). ~*v.t.* **1** to cover. **2** to spread with a layer of anything. **to trail one's coat** to invite attack. **coat armour** *n.* **1** a loose vestment embroidered with armorial bearings, worn by knights over their armour. **2** heraldic bearings. **coat check** *n.* (*N Am.*) a cloakroom with an attendant. **coat checker** *n.* (*N Am.*) a cloakroom attendant. **coat dress** *n.* a woman's dress styled like a coat. **coated** *a.* **coatee** (-tē´) *n.* a short coat for a woman or esp. a baby. **coat-hanger** *n.* a piece of shaped wood, wire, plastic etc. for hanging up clothes. **coating** *n.* **1** a covering, layer or integument. **2** the act of covering. **3** a substance spread over as a cover or for protection. **4** cloth for coats. **coatless** *a.* **coat of arms** *n.* **1** the armorial bearings of a family, corporation etc. **2** an escutcheon or shield of arms. **3** a herald's tabard. **coat of mail** *n.* armour worn on the upper part of the body, consisting of iron rings or scales fastened on a stout linen or leather jacket. **coatroom** *n.* (*N Am.*) a cloakroom. **coat-stand** *n.* a stand with hooks or pegs for hanging coats etc. on. **coat-tail** *n.* either of the long, tapering flaps at the back of a tailcoat. **on someone's coat-tails** gaining an undeserved benefit from the success of another. **to trail one's coat-tails** to trail one's coat. [OF *cote* (F *cotte*), med. L *cota, cotta*, OHG *chozza*, fem. *choz, chozzo*, a coarse, shaggy stuff or a garment of this]

coati (kōah´ti), **coatimundi** (-mŭn´di) *n.* (*pl.* **coatis, coatimundis**) a raccoon-like carnivorous mammal of the genera *Nasua* or *Nasuella*, with a long flexible snout, from Central or S America. [Tupi (*coa*, a belt, *tim*, a nose)]

co-author (kōaw´thə) *n.* a person who writes a book together with someone else. ~*v.t.* to be a co-author of.

coax[1] (kōks) *v.t.* **1** to persuade by tenderness or flattery. **2** to wheedle, to cajole. **3** to obtain by coaxing (*They coaxed the truth out of her*). **4** to handle or manipulate with care and patience (*to coax a machine to work*). **5** to handle or manipulate. ~*v.i.* to practise cajolery in order to persuade. **coaxer** *n.* **coaxingly** *adv.* [formerly *cokes*, from *cokes*, a fool]

coax[2] (kō´aks) *n.* (*coll.*) coaxial cable. [abbr.]

coaxial (kōak´siəl), **coaxal** (-səl) *a.* having a common axis. **coaxial cable** *n.* a cable having a central conductor within an outer tubular conductor. **coaxially** *adv.*

cob (kob) *n.* **1** a lump or ball of anything, esp. coal. **2** a small round loaf. **3** a spike of maize; a corn cob. **4** a cobnut. **5** a short stout horse for riding. **6** a male swan. **7** a mixture of clay and straw used for building walls. ~*v.t.* (*pres.p.* **cobbing,** *past, p.p.* **cobbed**) to punish by flogging on the buttocks with a belt or flat piece of wood. **cobby** *a.* **cob loaf** *n.* a small round loaf. **cobnut** *n.* a variety of the cultivated hazel. **cobstone** *n.* a cobblestone. [etym. uncertain]

cobalt (kō´bawlt) *n.* **1** a greyish-white, brittle, hard metallic element, at. no. 27, chem. symbol Co. **2** cobalt blue. ~*a.* deep blue. **cobalt-60** *n.* a radioactive isotope of cobalt, used in radiotherapy. **cobalt bloom** *n.* erythrite, hydrated cobalt arsenate. **cobalt blue** *n.* **1** a deep blue pigment containing cobalt aluminate. **2** the colour of this pigment. **cobalt bomb** *n.* **1** a device used in radiotherapy. **2** a hydrogen bomb encased in cobalt. **cobaltic** (-bawl´-) *a.* **cobaltous** (-bawl´-) *a.* [G *Kobold*, a mine demon, because the mineral was at first troublesome to the miners]

cobber (kob´ə) *n.* (*Austral., New Zeal., coll.*) a friend, a mate. [dial. *cob*, to take a liking to]

cobble[1] (kob´əl) *n.* **1** (*also* **cobblestone**) a rounded stone or pebble used for paving. **2** (*usu. pl.*) a roundish lump of coal. ~*v.t.* to pave with cobbles. [COB]

cobble[2] (kob´əl) *v.t.* **1** to mend or patch (esp. shoes). **2** to make or do clumsily (*to cobble together a meal*). **cobbler** *n.* **1** a person who mends shoes. **2** a mender or patcher. **3** a clumsy worker. **4** a type of pie with a topping of scones or a thick, crunchy crust. **5** a cooling drink of wine, sugar, lemon and ice. **6** (*pl., sl.*) nonsense. **7** (*Austral., New Zeal., sl.*) a difficult sheep at shearing time; the last sheep to be shorn. **cobbler's wax** *n.* a resinous substance used for waxing thread. [etym. unknown]

cobby COB.

co-belligerent (kōbəlij´ərənt) *a.* waging war jointly with another. ~*n.* a nation that joins another in waging war. **co-belligerence, co-belligerency** *n.*

coble (kō´bəl) *n.* a flat, square-sterned fishing boat with a lugsail and six oars. [Welsh *ceubal* (*ceuo*, to hollow or excavate)]

COBOL (kō´bol), **Cobol** *n.* a high-level computer language for commercial use. [acronym for *co*mmon *b*usiness *o*rientated *l*anguage]

cobra (kō´brə, kob´-) *n.* (*pl.* **cobras**) any venomous snake of the genus *Naja*, from tropical Africa and Asia, which distends the skin of the neck into a kind of hood when excited. **cobra de capello** (dē kəpel´ō) *n.* (*pl.* **cobras de capello**) an Asian cobra, *Naja tripudians*, with ringlike markings. [Port., L *colubra*, a snake]

coburg (kō´bœg) *n.* a loaf of bread with one or more cuts on top that spread out during baking. [town in Germany]

cobweb (kob´web) *n.* **1** the web or net spun by a spider for its prey. **2** the material or a thread of this. **3** anything flimsy and worthless. **4** a trap. **5** a fine-spun argument. **6** (*pl.*) old musty rubbish. **to blow away the cobwebs** to refresh oneself in the open air. **cobwebbed** *a.* **cobwebby** *a.* [COB (OE *-coppe*, found in *attorcoppe*, poison-spider), WEB]

coca (kō´kə) *n.* **1** the dried leaves of a S American plant, *Erythroxylum coca* chewed as a narcotic stimulant. **2** the plant itself. [Sp., from Quechua *cuca*]

Coca-Cola® (kōkəkō´lə) *n.* a brown-coloured soft drink flavoured with coca leaves, cola nuts etc.

cocaine (kōkān´) *n.* a drug prepared from coca leaves or synthetically, used as a narcotic stimulant and medicinally as a local anaesthetic. **cocainism** *n.* **1** addiction to cocaine. **2** physical and mental symptoms resulting from this. **cocainize** *v.t.* to anaesthetize with cocaine. **cocainization** (-zā´shən) *n.* [COCA]

coccal, cocci COCCUS.

coccidiosis (koksidiō´sis) *n.* a parasitic disease of the intestines, liver etc., found in domestic birds and mammals. [COCCUS, -OSIS]

coccoid COCCUS.

coccolith (kok´əlith) *n.* a small round body found in chalk formations, prob. extinct plankton. [Gr. *kokkos*, grain, berry]

coccus (kok´əs) *n.* (*pl.* **cocci** (kok´sī)) **1** a spherical bacterium. **2** any of the dry one-seeded carpels into which a fruit breaks up. **3** any hemipterous insect of the genus *Coccus*, including many forms harmful to plants. **4** a spore mother-cell in cryptogams. **coccal** *a.* **coccoid** *a.* [mod. L, from Gr. *kokkos*, grain]

coccyx (kok´siks) *n.* (*pl.* **coccyxes, coccyges** (-sijēz)) the lower solid portion of the vertebral column, the homologue in human of the tail of the lower vertebrates. **coccygeal** (koksij´iəl) *a.* [L, from Gr. *kokkux -ugos*, the cuckoo (from the resemblance to a cuckoo's bill)]

Cochin (koch´in), **Cochin China** (chī´nə) *n.* **1** a breed of domestic fowl with feathered legs. **2** a fowl of this breed. [*Cochin China* in Vietnam]

cochineal (kochinēl´) *n.* a red substance obtained from the dried bodies of the female cochineal insect, used in dyeing, as a food colouring and in the manufacture of scarlet and carmine pigments. **cochineal insect** *n.* the insect, *Dactylopius coccus*, from which cochineal is obtained. [F *cochenille*, Sp. *cochinilla*, L *coccineus, coccinus* (*coccum*, a berry, scarlet)]

cochlea (kok´liə) *n.* (*pl.* **cochleae** (-liē)) the anterior spiral division of the internal ear. **cochlean** *a.* **cochlear** *a.* **cochleariform** (-ar´-) *a.* spoon-shaped. **cochleate** (-ət), **cochleated** (-ātid) *a.* **1** circular, spiral. **2** (*Biol.*) twisted like a snail shell. [L, from Gr. *kokhlias*, a snail, a screw, *kokhlon*, a shellfish]

cock[1] (kok) *n.* **1** the male of birds, particularly of the domestic fowl. **2** a male salmon, lobster or crab. **3** a vane in the form of a cock, a weathercock. **4** (*sl.*) a friend, a good fellow. **5** (*sl.*) the penis. **6** (*sl.*) nonsense. **7** the hammer of a gun or pistol, which strikes against a piece of flint or a percussion cap to produce a spark and explode the charge. **8** the position of this when ready to fire. **9** a tap or valve for regulating the flow through a spout or pipe. **10** †a leader, a chief. ~*v.t.* to raise the cock of (a firearm). **by cock and pie** PIE[3]. **cock-a-doodle-doo** (-ədoodəldoo´) *n., int.* the crow of the domestic cock. **cock-a-hoop** *a.* triumphant, exultant; strutting or crowing. ~*adv.* exultantly, with crowing and boastfulness. **cock and bull story** *n.* a silly, exaggerated story. **cockcrow, cockcrowing** *n.* **1** the crow of a cock. **2** early dawn. **cock-eye** *n.* (*coll.*) an eye that squints. **cock-eyed** *a.* (*coll.*) **1** having squinting eyes. **2** irregular, ill-arranged. **3** askew. **4** eccentric, absurd (*a cock-eyed scheme*). **cockfight** *n.* a battle or match of gamecocks as a sport. **cockfighting** *n.* **cock-horse** *n.* a stick with a horse's head at the end, on which children ride; a hobby horse. **cockloft** *n.* a small loft, a garret. **cock-of-the-rock** *n.* a bird of S America, *Rupicola rupicola* or *R. peruviana*, with bright red or orange plumage and am erectile crest. **cock-of-the-walk** *n.* **1** a masterful person. **2** a leader, a chief. **cock-of-the-wood** *n.* **1** the capercaillie. **2** (*N Am.*) a type of woodpecker. **cockpit** *n.* **1** the part of the fuselage of an aircraft where the pilot and crew are accommodated. **2** the driver's compartment of a racing car. **3** a sheltered space in a sailing yacht or other small boat, where the helm is situated. **4** a part of the lower deck of a man-of-war, used as a hospital in action. **5** an area where many battles take place (*Belgium, the cockpit of Europe*). **6** a pit or area where gamecocks fight. **cockscomb** *n.* **1** the comb or crest of a cock. **2** a garden plant, *Celosia cristata*, with a plume of tiny flowers. **3** the yellow rattle, *Rhinanthus minor*. **4** a coxcomb. **cocksfoot** *n.* any pasture grass of the genus *Dactylis*, esp *D. glomerata*. **cockshy, cockshot** *n.* (*pl.* **cockshies, cockshots**) **1** a rough-and-ready target for sticks or stones. **2** a throw at this. **3** a butt of ridicule, criticism etc. **cock sparrow** *n.* **1** a male sparrow. **2** a pert or quarrelsome person. **cockspur** *n.* **1** the spur of a cock. **2** any of various plants, esp. the grass *Echinochloa crus-galli* or the N American shrub, *Crataegus crushgalli*. **3** a kind of caddis used in angling. **cock-sure** *a.* **1** self-confident, arrogantly certain. **2** perfectly sure, absolutely certain. **cocksurely** *adv.* **cocksureness** *n.* [OE *cocc* (cp. F *coq*), low L *coccum*, acc. of *coccus*, onomat. (cp. Gr. *kokku*, cuckoo)]

cock[2] (kok) *n.* **1** the act of turning or sticking anything upward, such as a hat, the ears etc. **2** the turn so given. ~*v.t.* **1** to set erect. **2** to cause to stick up. **3** to set (the hat) jauntily on one side. **4** to turn up (the nose). **5** to turn (the eye) in an impudent or knowing fashion. **6** to raise (the ears) or tilt (the head) in an attentive manner. ~*v.i.* **1** to stick or stand up, to project. **2** to strut, to swagger, to bluster. **to cock a snook** SNOOK[1]. **to cock up** (*sl.*) to ruin by incompetence; to bungle. **cocked hat** *n.* **1** a pointed triangular hat. **2** (*Hist.*) a hat with the brim turned up. **to knock into a cocked hat 1** to defeat utterly. **2** to amaze or confound. **cock-up** *n.* **1** (*sl.*) a bungled failure. **2** a turn-up of the tip of the nose. [from COCK[1]]

cock[3] (kok) *n.* a small conical pile of hay. ~*v.t.* to put into cocks. [cp. Dan. *kok*, a heap, Icel. *kokkr*, a lump, a ball]

cockabully (kok´əbuli) *n.* a small freshwater fish of New Zealand, esp. one of the genus Gobiomorphus. [Maori *kopapu*]

cockade (kəkād´) *n.* **1** a knot of ribbons worn in the hat as a badge. **2** a rosette worn in the hat by the male servants of naval and military officers etc. **cockaded** *a.* [F *coquarde*, saucy, from *coq* (cp. COCK[1])]

cock-a-leekie (kokəlē´ki), **cocky-leeky** (koki-), **cockie-leckie** (-lek´i) *n.* soup made from a fowl boiled with leeks. [Sc., COCK[1], LEEK]

cockalorum (kokəlaw´rəm) *n.* a self-important little man. [COCK[1]]

cockatiel (kokətēl´), **cockateel** *n.* a small crested parrot, *Nymphicus hollandicus*, of Australia. [Dut. *kaketielje*]

cockatoo (kokətoo´) *n.* **1** a large crested parrot of the Cacatuidae, usu. white, from Australasia. **2** (*Austral., New Zeal., coll.*) a small farmer. [Malay *kakatūa*]

cockatrice (kok´ətris, -trīs) *n.* **1** the basilisk, a deadly mythical reptile. **2** (*Her.*) a cock with a serpent's tail. **3** †anything deadly. [OF *cocatrice*, late L *caucātrix*, the treader (trans. of Gr. *ikhneumōn*, from *ikhneuein*, to track)]

cockboat (kok´bōt) *n.* a small ship's boat. [obs. *cock*, a small boat, ME *cog, cogge*, OF *coque, cogue*]

cockchafer (kok´chāfə) *n.* a large brown beetle, *Melolontha melolontha*, whose larvae feed on the roots of crops.

Cocker (kok´ə) *n.* used only as below. **according to Cocker** properly, correctly. [Edward *Cocker*, 1631–75, English teacher and arithmetician]

cocker COCKER SPANIEL.

cockerel (kok´ərəl) *n.* a young cock. [ME *cokerelle*]

cocker spaniel (kok´ə), **cocker** *n.* **1** a small spaniel of a breed used in shooting snipe etc. **2** this breed. [COCK[1], SPANIEL]

cockie-leckie COCK-A-LEEKIE.

cockily, cockiness COCKY[1].

cockle[1] (kok´əl) *n.* **1** a bivalve mollusc of the genus *Cardium*, esp. *C. edule*. **2** its ribbed shell. **3** a cockle-boat. **cockleboat** *n.* a small shallow boat. **cockleshell** *n.* **1** a cockleboat. **2** the shell of a cockle or scallop worn as the badge of a pilgrim. **cockles of the heart** *n.* the inmost feelings (*to warm the cockles of one's heart*). [F *coquille*, a shell, L *conchylia*, Gr. *konchulion*, dim. of *konchē*, a mussel]

cockle[2] (kok´əl) *n.* **1** the corncockle. **2** any of various other weeds. **3** a disease of wheat. **cocklebur** *n.* a weed of the genus *Xanthium*, having bristly burs. [OE *coccel*]

cockle[3] (kok´əl) *v.i.* to pucker up. ~*v.t.* to curl, pucker up, crease or cause to bulge. ~*n.* a pucker, crease or wrinkle in paper, cloth, glass etc. [F *coquiller*, to blister, to pucker]

cockle[4] (kok´əl) *n.* **1** (*also* **cockle stove**) a heating-stove with a kind of radiator. **2** (**cockle oast**) the furnace of an oast-house. [etym. uncertain; perh. from Dut. *kākel*, G *Kachel*, a stove-tile]

cockney (kok´ni) *n.* (*pl.* **cockneys**) **1** a native of London (traditionally, a person born within sound of the bells of St-Mary-le-Bow, Cheapside). **2** the London accent or dialect. **3** a person who speaks with it. **4** (*Austral.*) a young snapper fish, *Chrysophrys auratus*. ~*a.* of or relating to cockney, their accents or their dialect. **cockneydom** *n.* **cockneyese** (-ēz´) *n.* **cockneyfy** *v.t.* (*3rd pers. sing. pres.* **cockneyfies**, *pres.p.* **cockneyfying**, *past, p.p.* **cockneyfied**) to make cockney. **cockneyfication** (-fikā´shən) *n.* **cockneyish** *a.* **cockneyism** *n.* [ME *cokeney* (*coken*, gen. pl., *ey*, OE *aeg*), a cock's egg, a term applied to small yolkless eggs, occasionally laid by fowls; hence applied to a foolish or effeminate person, a townsman]

cockpit COCK[1].

cockroach (kok´rōch) *n.* an orthopterous insect, *Blatta orientalis* or *Periplaneta americana*, resembling a beetle, and a pest in kitchens. [Sp. *cucaracha* (assim. to COCK[1], ROACH[2])]

cockswain COXSWAIN.

cocktail (kok´tāl) *n.* **1** a drink taken esp. before a meal, usu. spirit mixed with fruit juice, bitters, other alcoholic liquor etc. **2** a dish consisting of a mixture of cold foods (*a prawn cocktail*). **3** any mixture of assorted ingredients, e.g. drinks, drugs. **4** a horse with the tail docked very short, usu. a half-bred horse. **5** an animal of mixed breeding. **6** †an ill-bred person. ~*a.* of or relating to cocktails (*a cocktail bar; a cocktail party*). **cocktail dress** *n.* a short dress suitable for wearing at cocktail parties and other semi-formal occasions. **cocktail stick** *n.* a thin pointed stick for serving snack foods. [COCK[2], TAIL[1] (a tail that cocks up, or like a cock's)]

cock-up COCK[2].

cocky[1] (kok´i) *a.* (*comp.* **cockier**, *superl.* **cockiest**) **1**

arrogant, self-important, conceited. 2 †impudent, pert, saucy. **cockily** *adv.* **cockiness** *n.* [COCK[1]]
cocky[2] (kok'i) *n.* (*pl.* **cockies**) (*Austral., New Zeal., coll.*) a small farmer. [COCKATOO]
cocky-leeky COCK-A-LEEKIE.
coco (kō'kō), **cocoa, coker** (kō'kə) *n.* (*pl.* **cocos, cocoas, cokers**) a tropical palm tree, *Cocos nucifera*, the coconut palm. **coconut** *n.* 1 the fruit of this tree, a large, rough, hard-shelled nut with a white edible lining and containing a sweet white liquid. 2 the tree itself. 3 the lining of the coconut, used in cakes, sweets etc. (*desiccated coconut*). 4 (*sl.*) the human head. **coconut butter** *n.* the solid oil obtained from the lining of the coconut. **coconut ice** *n.* a sweet made from desiccated coconut and sugar. **coconut matting** *n.* coarse matting made from the fibrous husk of the coconut. **coconut milk** *n.* the sweet white liquid found inside the coconut. **coconut palm, coconut tree** *n.* the coco. **coconut shy** *n.* a fairground game in which the aim is to knock coconuts off sticks. [Port. and Sp. *coco*, a bugbear, a grimace (*coker* is the commercial term given to distinguish it from COCOA[1])]
cocoa[1] (kō'kō) *n.* 1 a preparation from the seeds of the cacao tree, *Theobroma cacao*. 2 a drink made from this. **cocoa bean** *n.* the seed of the cacao. **cocoa butter** *n.* a buttery substance extracted from the cacao nut in the manufacture of cocoa. [corr. of CACAO]
cocoa[2] COCO.
coco-de-mer (kōkōdəmœ') *n.* 1 a palm tree of the Seychelles, *Lodoicea maldivica*. 2 the fruit of this tree, a double coconut. [F, coco of the sea]
coconut COCO.
cocoon (kəkoon') *n.* 1 a silky covering spun by the larvae of certain insects in the chrysalis state. 2 any analogous case made by other animals. 3 any protective covering. 4 a preservative coating sprayed onto machinery etc. ~*v.t.* 1 to wrap in, or as if in, a cocoon. 2 to spray with a preservative coating. ~*v.i.* to make a cocoon. **cocooned** *a.* **cocoonery** *n.* (*pl.* **cocooneries**) a place for silkworms when feeding and forming cocoons. [F *cocon*, dim. of *coque*, a shell, L *concha*, Gr. *konchē*]
cocopan (kō'kōpan) *n.* (*S Afr.*) a small wagon used in mines, running on a narrow-gauge railway track. [Zulu *'ngkumbana*]
cocotte (kəkot') *n.* 1 a small dish in which food is cooked and served. 2 (*dated*) a prostitute, a woman from the demi-monde. [F]
co-counselling (kōkown'səling), (*N Am.*) **co-counseling** *n.* a form of amateur counselling in which people feeling the need for help listen to and advise each other.
COD *abbr.* 1 cash on delivery. 2 (*N Am.*) collect on delivery.
Cod. *abbr.* codex.
cod[1] (kod) *n.* (*pl. in general* **cod,** *in particular* **cods**) any large deep-sea food fish, of the family Gadidae, esp. *Gadus morrhua*. **codder** *n.* 1 a cod fisherman. 2 a boat used in cod fishing. **codfish** *n.* (*pl. in general* **codfish,** *in particular* **codfishes**) the cod. **codling**[1] (-ling) *n.* a young cod. **cod liver oil** *n.* oil from the liver of the cod, rich in vitamins A and D. [etym. uncertain]
cod[2] (kod) *n.* 1 (*dial.*) a husk or pod. 2 (*taboo*) †the scrotum. 3 (*taboo*) †a testicle. **codpiece** *n.* (*Hist.*) a baggy appendage in the front of breeches or the tight hose worn in the 15th and 16th cents. to cover male genitals. [OE *cod, codd*, a bag]
cod[3] (kod) *n.* 1 (*sl.*) a parody. 2 (*sl.*) a hoax. ~*a.* (*sl.*) intended to deceive or burlesque; mock (*cod Latin*). ~*v.t.* (*pres.p.* **codding,** *past, p.p.* **codded**) (*sl. or dial.*) 1 to hoax. 2 to parody. ~*v.i.* to perform a hoax. [etym. unknown]
cod[4] (kod) *n.* (*sl.*) nonsense. [CODSWALLOP]
coda (kō'də) *n.* (*pl.* **codas**) 1 (*Mus.*) an adjunct to the close of a composition to enforce the final character of the movement. 2 in ballet, the concluding part of a dance. 3 any concluding part, event etc. **codetta** *n.* (*pl.* **codettas**) (*Mus.*) a short coda. [It., from L *cauda*, tail]
codder COD[1].
coddle (kod'əl) *v.t.* 1 to treat as an invalid or baby, to pamper. 2 to cook (esp. eggs) gently in water. **coddler** *n.* [prob. short for CAUDLE]
code (kōd) *n.* 1 a series of symbols, characters, letters or words used for the sake of brevity or secrecy. 2 a system of signals used for similar reasons. 3 (*Comput.*) a piece of program text. 4 a collection of statutes, a body of laws or regulations systematically arranged. 5 a collection of rules or canons. 6 the principles accepted in any sphere of art, taste, conduct etc. (*a code of practice*; *a code of conduct*). ~*v.t.* to put into a code. ~*v.i.* to be the genetic code (for). **code book** *n.* a book that lists the symbols, letters etc. used in a code. **code-breaker** *n.* a person who solves or interprets a code. **code-breaking** *n.* **code name, code number** *n.* a short name or number used for convenience or secrecy. **code-named** *a.* **coder** *n.* **codify** *v.t.* (*3rd pers. sing. pres.* **codifies,** *pres.p.* **codifying,** *past, p.p.* **codified**) 1 to collect or arrange (laws etc.) as a systematic body. 2 to put into a code. **codification** (-fikā'shən) *n.* **codifier** *n.* [F, from L *cōdex -icem*, see CODEX]
codeclination (kōdeklinā'shən) *n.* (*Astron.*) the polar distance of anything, the complement of its declination.
codeine (kō'dēn) *n.* an alkaloid obtained from morphine and used as a narcotic and analgesic. [Gr. *kōdeia*, head, poppy-head]
codependency (kōdipen'dənsi) *n.* mutual dependency for the fulfilment of emotional needs within a relationship. **codependant** *n.* **codependent** *a., n.*
co-determination (kōditœminā'shən) *n.* cooperation between management and employees, or their trade union representatives, in decision-making.
codetta CODA.
codex (kō'deks) *n.* (*pl.* **codexes, codices** (kō'disēz, kod'-)) 1 a manuscript volume, esp. of the Bible or of texts of classics. 2 (*Med.*) a list of prescriptions. [L *cōdex, caudex*, a tree-trunk, a wooden tablet, a book]
codger (koj'ə) *n.* (*coll.*) an odd old person. [prob. var. of CADGER (under CADGE)]
codices CODEX.
codicil (kod'isil, kō'-) *n.* an appendix to a will, treaty etc. **codicillary** (-sil'-) *a.* [MF *codicile* (now *codicille*), L *cōdicillus*, dim. of CODEX]
codicology (kōdikol'əji) *n.* the study of manuscripts. **codicological** *a.* **codicologically** *adv.* [F *codicologie*, L *cōdex -icis*; see CODEX]
codify CODE.
codling[1] COD[1].
codling[2] (kod'ling), **codlin** *n.* 1 a long, tapering kind of apple, used for cooking. 2 a codling moth. **codling moth** *n.* the moth *Carpocapsa pomonella*, whose larvae feed on apples and cause them to fall prematurely. **codlings-and-cream** *n.* the hairy willowherb, *Epilobium hirsutum*. [ME *querdling* (perh. Ir. *queirt*, apple-tree, -LING[1])]
codomain (kō'dəmān) *n.* (*Math.*) the set of values that a function can take in all possible expressions.
codon (kō'don) *n.* a set of three nucleotides in DNA or RNA that specifies a particular amino acid. [CODE, -ON]
codpiece COD[2].
co-driver (kō'drīvə) *n.* a person who shares the driving of a motor vehicle, esp. a rally car, with another.
codswallop (kodz'woləp) *n.* (*sl.*) nonsense. [etym. uncertain]

coed (kō´ed, -ed´), **co-ed** *n.* (*coll.*) **1** a co-educational school. **2** (*N Am.*) a girl being educated in a co-educational establishment. *~a.* co-educational. [abbr.]

co-education (kōedūkā´shən) *n.* education of the two sexes together. **co-educational** *a.*

coefficient (kōifish´ənt) *n.* **1** the numerical or constant factor of an algebraical number, as *4* in *4ab*. **2** (*Physics*) a number denoting the degree of a quality (*the coefficient of expansion*).

coel- COELO-.

coelacanth (sē´ləkanth) *n.* a large bony sea fish, *Latimeria chalumnae*, the only known living representative of the primitive subclass Crossopterygii thought to be extinct until 1938. [Gr. *koilos*, hollow, *akantha*, spine]

-coele -CELE.

coelenterate (sēlen´tərāt, -rət) *n.* any invertebrate of the phylum Coelenterata, containing the jellyfish, corals, sea anemones etc. *~a.* of or belonging to the Coelenterata. [Gr. *koilos*, hollow, *enteron*, an intestine]

coeliac (sē´liak), (*N Am.*) **celiac** *a.* **1** of or relating to the abdomen. **2** of, relating to or suffering from coeliac disease. **coeliac disease** *n.* (*Med.*) a condition involving defective digestion caused by sensitivity to gluten. [L *coeliacus*, Gr. *koiliakos* (*koilia*, bowels, *koilos*, hollow)]

coelo- (sē´lō), **coel-**, (*N Am.*) **celo-**, **cel-** *comb. form* (*Biol.*) denoting a hollow part or cavity. [Gr. *koilos*, hollow]

coelom (sē´ləm), (*N Am.*) **celom** *n.* (*pl.* **coeloms, coelomata** (-lō´mətə), (*N Am.*) **celoms, celomata**) a body cavity, esp. the space between the body wall and the intestines. **coelomate** *a.*, *n.* **coelomic** (-lom´-) *a.* [Gr. *koilōma*, cavity]

coelostat (sē´ləstat) *n.* an astronomical instrument with a mirror that rotates to continuously reflect the light from a celestial object. [L *caelum*, the sky, -STAT]

coemption (kōemp´shən) *n.* concerted action among buyers for forestalling the market by purchasing the whole quantity of any commodity.

coen- COENO-.

coenaesthesis (sēnəsthē´sis), (*esp. N Am.*) **coenesthesis, coenaesthesia** (-ziə), (*esp. N Am.*) **coenesthesia** *n.* (*Psych.*) the collective consciousness of the body, as distinguished from the impressions of the separate senses. [COEN-, Gr. *aisthesis*, sensation, from *aisthanomai*, I perceive]

coeno- (sē´nō), **ceno-, coen-, cen-** *comb. form* common. [Gr. *koinos*, common]

coenobite (sē´nəbīt), **cenobite** *n.* a monk living in a monastic community. **coenobitic** (-bit´-), **coenobitical** *a.* **coenobitism** *n.* [late L *coenobīta*, from Gr. *koinobion*, a convent (COENO-, *bios*, life)]

coenocyte (sē´nōsīt) *n.* (*Bot.*) a mass of protoplasm that contains many nuclei within a cell wall, occurring in fungi and algae.

coenosteum (sinos´tiəm) *n.* the calcareous skeleton of a coral colony. [Gr. *osteon*, bone]

coenzyme (kōen´zīm, kō´-) *n.* in biochemistry, a non-protein organic molecule that is necessary for the activity of certain enzymes. **coenzyme A** *n.* a coenzyme that plays an important part in biochemical reactions such as respiration.

co-equal (kōē´kwəl) *a.* (*poet. or formal*) **1** equal with another. **2** of the same rank, dignity etc. *~n.* a person of the same rank, as an equal. **co-equality** (-ikwol´-) *n.* **co-equally** *adv.*

coerce (kōœs´) *v.t.* **1** to restrain by force. **2** to compel to obey. **3** to enforce by compulsion. **coercible** *a.* **coercibleness** *n.* **coercion** (-œ´shən) *n.* **1** the act of coercing. **2** government by force. **coercionary** *a.* **coercionist** *n.* **coercive** *a.* **1** having power or authority to coerce. **2** compulsory. **coercively** *adv.* **coerciveness** *n.* **coercivity** (-siv´ti) *n.* (*Physics*) the force required to demagnetize a fully magnetized material, a measure of the resistance of the material to changes in magnetization. [L *coercēre* (CO-, *arcēre*, to enclose, cp. *arca*, a chest)]

coessential (kōisen´shəl) *a.* of the same essence. **coessentiality** (-shial´-) *n.* **coessentially** *adv.*

coetaneous (kōitā´niəs) *a.* **1** of the same age or period. **2** beginning to exist at the same time. [L *coaetāneus* (CO-, *aetās -ātis*, age)]

coeternal (kōitœ´nəl) *a.* equally or jointly eternal with another. **coeternally** *adv.* **coeternity** *n.*

coeval (kōē´vəl) *a.* **1** of the same age. **2** having the same date of birth or origin. **3** existing at or for the same period. *~n.* a contemporary. **coevality** (-val´-) *n.* **coevally** *adv.* [L *coaevus* (CO-, *aevum*, an age)]

coexist (kōigzist´) *v.i.* **1** to exist together at the same time or in the same place. **2** (of nations, regimes etc.) to be in a state of peaceful coexistence. **coexistence** *n.* mutual toleration by nations or regimes with differing ideologies or systems of government. **coexistent** *a.*

coextend (kōikstend´) *v.i.* to extend equally in time or space. **coextension** (-sten´shən) *n.* **coextensive** *a.* **coextensively** *adv.*

C of C *abbr.* Chamber of Commerce.

C of E *abbr.* Church of England.

coffee (kof´i) *n.* **1** a beverage made from the ground roasted seeds of a tropical Asiatic and African shrub, of the genus *Coffea*, esp. *C. arabica*. **2** a cup of this beverage. **3** the seeds of the shrub. **4** the shrub itself. **5** a pale brown colour, like milky coffee. *~a.* pale brown. **coffee bag** *n.* a small perforated bag containing ground coffee. **coffee bar** *n.* a café where coffee, snacks etc. are served. **coffee bean** *n.* a coffee seed. **coffee berry** *n.* a coffee seed. **coffee cup** *n.* a small cup from which coffee is drunk. **coffee essence** *n.* a concentrated coffee extract, often containing chicory. **coffee grinder** *n.* a coffee mill. **coffee grounds** *n.pl.* the sediment or lees of coffee after infusion. **coffee house** *n.* a house where coffee and other refreshments are sold, esp. one that was popular in 18th-cent. London. **coffee-maker** *n.* a machine for making coffee from ground coffee beans, esp. a percolator. **coffee mill** *n.* a machine for grinding roasted coffee beans. **coffee morning** *n.* a social gatherings held at mid-morning, where coffee is served. **coffee nibs** *n.pl.* shelled coffee beans. **coffeepot** *n.* a vessel in which coffee is made. **coffee room** *n.* a refreshment room in a hotel. **coffee shop** *n.* a coffee bar, esp. in a department store. **coffee stall** *n.* a street stall where non-alcoholic beverages and snacks are sold throughout the night. **coffee table** *n.* a low table in a sitting room. *~a.* suitable for display on a coffee table. **coffee-table book** *n.* a large and expensively produced illustrated book. [Turk. *qahveh*, Arab. *qahweh*]

coffer (kof´ə) *n.* **1** a chest or box for holding valuables. **2** (*pl.*) a treasury, funds, financial resources. **3** a sunken panel in a ceiling etc. *~v.t.* to enclose or store in a coffer. **coffer-dam** *n.* a watertight enclosure pumped dry to expose a river bed etc., used in laying foundations of piers, bridges etc. **coffered** *a.* **1** enclosed in a coffer. **2** ornamented with coffers. [OF *cofre*, L *cophinus*, Gr. *kophinos* (doublet of COFFIN)]

coffin (kof´in) *n.* **1** the box in which a corpse is enclosed for burial or cremation. **2** the hoof of a horse below the coronet. **3** (*Print.*) a frame for the imposing stone of a handpress or the carriage of a machine. *~v.t.* (*pres.p.* **coffining,** *past, p.p.* **coffined**) **1** to put into a coffin. **2** to put out of sight. **coffin-bone** *n.* the spongy bone in a horse's hoof around which the horn grows. **coffin corner** *n.* in American football, the corner between the goal line and the sideline. **coffin-joint** *n.* the joint above the coffin-bone. **coffin-nail** *n.* (*sl.*) a cigarette. [OF *cofin*, L *cophinus*, as COFFER]

coffle (kof´əl) *n.* a travelling gang, esp. of slaves fastened together in a line. [Arab. *qāfilah*, caravan]

C of I *abbr.* Church of Ireland.
C of S *abbr.* 1 Chief of Staff. 2 Church of Scotland.
cog (kog) *n.* 1 a tooth or projection in the rim of a wheel or other gear for transmitting motion to another part. 2 a person playing a small and unimportant part in any enterprise. ~*v.t.* (*pres.p.* **cogging,** *past, p.p.* **cogged**) 1 to furnish with cogs. 2 (*North. dial.*) to stop the revolutions of a wheel by means of a block or wedge. **cogged** *a.* **cogwheel** *n.* a wheel furnished with cogs. [from Scand. (cp. Swed. *kugge,* Norw. *kug*)]
cog. *abbr.* cognate.
cogent (kō´jənt) *a.* powerful, constraining, convincing (*a cogent argument*). **cogency** *n.* **cogently** *adv.* [L *cōgentum,* acc. pres.p. of *cōgere,* to compel (CO-, *agere,* to drive)]
cogitate (koj´ităt) *v.i.* to think, to reflect, to meditate. ~*v.t.* 1 to meditate, to devise. 2 (*Philos.*) to form an idea or conception of. **cogitable** *a.* 1 capable of being thought. 2 conceivable by the reason. **cogitation** (-tā´shən) *n.* **cogitative** (-tətiv) *a.* meditative. **cogitatively** *adv.* **cogitativeness** *n.* **cogitator** *n.* [L *cōgitātus,* p.p. of *cōgitāre,* to think (CO-, *agitāre,* freq. of *agere,* to drive)]
cogito (kō´gitō, -jitō) *n.* (*Philos.*) the principle that a being exists because it thinks or has awareness. [L, I think (from *cogito, ergo sum,* I think, therefore I am, the basic tenet of Descartes's philosophy)]
cognac (kon´yak) *n.* French brandy of fine quality, esp. that distilled in the neighbourhood of Cognac, in SW France.
cognate (kog´nāt) *a.* 1 akin, related. 2 of common origin. 3 of the same kind or nature. 4 derived from the same linguistic family or from the same word or root. ~*n.* 1 a blood relation. 2 (*Sc. Law*) a relative on the mother's side. 3 a cognate word. **cognately** *adv.* **cognateness** *n.* **cognate object** *n.* (*Gram.*) an object governed by an etymologically related verb, as *song* as in *to sing a song.* **cognation** (-nā´shən) *n.* [L *cognātus* (CO-, *gnātus, nātus,* p.p. of *gnasci, nasci,* to be born)]
cognition (kognish´ən) *n.* 1 the act of apprehending. 2 the faculty of perceiving, conceiving, and knowing, as distinguished from the feelings and the will. 3 a sensation, perception, intuition, or conception. 4 (*Law*) cognizance. **cognitional** *a.* **cognitive** (kog´-) *a.* **cognitive dissonance** *n.* psychological conflict arising from incompatible cognitions. **cognitively** *adv.* **cognitive science** *n.* the scientific study of cognition. **cognitivism** *n.* a tendency to emphasize the similarities between linguistic knowledge and non-linguistic knowledge. **cognitivist** *a.* [L *cognitio -ōnem,* from *cognoscere,* to learn (CO-, *gnoscere,* cognate with KNOW)]
cognizable COGNIZE.
cognizance (kog´nizəns), **cognisance** *n.* 1 knowledge, notice, recognition. 2 acknowledgement. 3 the range of one's perception or concern. 4 jurisdiction. 5 (*Law*) **a** judicial notice. **b** knowledge not requiring proof. **c** the right of a court to deal with a cause. 6 (*Her.*) a badge, a coat, a crest. **to have cognizance of** to know. **to take cognizance of** to take into consideration. **cognizant** *a.* 1 having cognizance or knowledge (of). 2 (*Law*) competent to take judicial notice (of). [OF *conoissance* (L *cognoscere,* see COGNITION), assim. to L *cog-*]
cognize (kognīz´), **cognise** *v.t.* (*Philos.*) to have knowledge or perception of. **cognizable** (kog´niz-) *a.* 1 knowable, perceptible. 2 (*Law*) liable to be tried and determined. **cognizably** *adv.* **cognizer** *n.* [formed from COGNIZANCE]
cognomen (kognō´mən) *n.* (*pl.* **cognomens, cognomina** (-nom´inə)) 1 a surname. 2 the last of the three names of an ancient Roman citizen. 3 a title, a name. 4 a nickname. **cognominal** (-nom´in-) *a.* **cognominally** *adv.* [L (CO-, *gnōmen, nōmen,* name, from *gno-,* stem of *gnoscere*)]
cognoscente (konyəshen´ti) *n.* (*pl.* **cognoscenti** (-ti)) a connoisseur. [It., from L *cognoscens -tem,* pres.p. of *cognoscere,* see COGNITION]
cohabit (kōhab´it) *v.i.* (*pres.p.* **cohabiting,** *past, p.p.* **cohabited**) to live together, esp. as husband and wife without being legally married. **cohabitant** *n.* **cohabitation** (-ā´shən) *n.* **cohabitee** (-tē´-) *n.* **cohabiter** *n.* [F *cohabiter,* L *cohabitāre* (CO-, *habitāre,* to dwell, freq. of *habēre,* to hold)]
co-heir (kōeə´) *n.* a joint heir. **co-heiress** *n.* a female co-heir.
cohere (kəhiə´) *v.i.* 1 to stick together. 2 to hold together, remain united. 3 to be logically consistent. **coherence, coherency** *n.* **coherent** *a.* 1 that coheres. 2 articulate, intelligible. 3 logically connected, consistent. 4 (of electromagnetic waves) having the same frequency or phase. **coherently** *adv.* **coherer** *n.* a device formerly used for detecting electromagnetic waves. [L *cohaerēre* (CO-, *haerēre,* to stick)]
coheritor (kōher´itə) *n.* a co-heir.
cohesion (kəhē´zhən) *n.* 1 coherence. 2 the act or state of sticking or holding together. 3 a tendency to stick or hold together. 4 (*Physics*) the force uniting molecules of the same nature. 5 (*Bot.*) union of organs usu. separated. **cohesive** (-siv) *a.* **cohesively** *adv.* **cohesiveness** *n.* [F *cohēsion* (L *cohaes,* port. stem. of *cohaerare,* COHERE)]
coho (kō´hō), **cohoe** *n.* (*pl.* **cohos, cohoes**) a Pacific salmon, *Oncorhynchus kisutch.* [etym. unknown]
cohort (kō´hawt) *n.* 1 a tenth part of a Roman legion, containing three maniples or six centuries. 2 a body of soldiers. 3 any band of associates. 4 a set of people in a population sharing a common attribute, e.g. age or class. 5 (*coll.*) a colleague or accomplice. [F *cohorte,* L *cohors -tem,* orig. an enclosure (CO-, *hort-,* cp. *hortus,* garden, Gr. *khortos,* GARTH, GARDEN)]

Usage note The use of *cohort* of an individual, in the sense 'colleague, accomplice', is sometimes disapproved of, though it is quite common, especially in North America.

COHSE (kō´zi) *abbr.* (*Hist.*) Confederation of Health Service Employees.
COI *abbr.* Central Office of Information.
coif (koif) *n.* 1 a close-fitting cap, esp. worn by nuns under a veil. 2 (*Hist.*) **a** the cap worn by serjeants-at-law. **b** a protective cap worn under chain mail. 3 (*N Am.*) coiffure. ~*v.t.* (*pres.p.* **coiffing,** (*N Am.*) **coifing,** *past, p.p.* **coiffed,** (*N Am.*) **coifed**) 1 to cover with a coif. 2 to arrange (the hair). 3 to arrange the hair of. **coiffed** *a.* [OF *coife,* low L *cofia,* a cap, prob. from MHG *kupfe* (*kopf,* the head)]
coiffeur (kwafœ´) *n.* a hairdresser. **coiffeuse** (-fœz´) *n.* a female hairdresser. **coiffure** (-füə´) *n.* 1 a method of dressing the hair, a hairstyle. 2 †a head-dress. **coiffured** *a.* [F, from *coiffer,* to dress the hair (*coiffe,* OF *coife,* COIF)]
coign (koin) *n.* 1 a quoin. 2 †a corner. **coign of vantage** *n.* a projecting corner affording a good view; an advantageous position. [COIN]
coil[1] (koil) *v.t.* 1 to wind (a rope etc.) into rings. 2 to twist into a spiral shape. ~*v.i.* (of a snake, a climbing plant etc.) to wind itself. ~*n.* 1 a series of concentric rings into which anything is coiled up. 2 a length of anything coiled up. 3 a single turn of anything coiled up. 4 a coiled lock of hair. 5 a wire wound round a bobbin to form a resistance or an inductance. 6 a transformer in an internal-combustion engine. 7 a metal or plastic coil inserted in the uterus as a contraceptive device. 8 a roll of postage stamps. **to coil up** 1 to twist into rings or a spiral shape. 2 to be twisted into such a shape. [OF *coillir* (F *cueillir*), L *colligere* (COL-[1], *legere,* to gather)]
†**coil**[2] (koil) *n.* 1 noise, turmoil, confusion, bustle. 2 a

fuss. **this mortal coil** the bustle or troubles of earthly life. [etym. unknown]

coin (koin) *n.* **1** a piece of metal stamped and current as money. **2** money, esp. coins. **3** a quoin. ~*v.t.* **1** to mint or stamp (money). **2** to invent, to fabricate (*to coin a new word*). **the other side of the coin** the opposite point of view. **to coin a phrase** (*iron.*) said before or after using a cliché. **to coin it in** (*sl.*) to make money rapidly. **to coin money** (*sl.*) to make money rapidly. **to pay someone back in their own coin** to give someone the same treatment that they have given others; to give tit for tat. **coin box** *n.* **1** a coin-operated telephone or other machine. **2** the receptacle for coins in such a machine. **coiner** *n.* **1** a person who coins money, esp. one who makes counterfeit coin. **2** a person who coins a word, phrase etc. **coin-op** *n.* a launderette etc. with coin-operated machines. **coin-operated** *a.* (of a machine) operated by inserting a coin. [OF, a wedge, hence a stamp on a coin, from L *cuneus*, a wedge]

coinage (koi´nij) *n.* **1** the act of coining. **2** the pieces coined, coins collectively. **3** the monetary system in use (*decimal coinage*). **4** invention, fabrication. **5** something invented, esp. a new word or expression. [OF *coignaige* (COIN, -AGE)]

coincide (kōinsid´) *v.i.* **1** to correspond in time, place, nature etc. **2** to happen at the same time. **3** to occupy the same position in space. **4** to agree, to concur. **coincidence** (-in´sidəns) *n.* **1** the act, fact, or condition of coinciding. **2** an instance of this. **3** a remarkable instance of apparently fortuitous concurrence. **4** (*Physics*) the simultaneous presence of two or more signals in a circuit etc. **coincident** (-in´sidənt) *a.* that coincides. **coincidental** (-siden´təl) *a.* **1** coincident. **2** characterized by, of the nature of or resulting from coincidence. **coincidentally** *adv.* **coincidently** *adv.* [F *coincider*, med. L *coincidere* (CO-, IN, *cadere*, to fall)]

coinheritance (kōinher´itəns) *n.* a joint inheritance. **coinheritor** *n.* a co-heir.

coinsurance (kōinshuə´rəns) *n.* joint insurance, esp. when part of the risk is borne by the owner of the insured property.

Cointreau® (kwan´trō, kwon´-) *n.* a colourless orange-flavoured liqueur.

coir (koiə) *n.* **1** coconut fibre. **2** ropes or matting manufactured from this. [Malay *kāyar*, cord]

coit (koit) *n.* (*Austral., sl.*) the buttocks. [perh. from QUOIT]

coition (kōish´ən) *n.* copulation. **coital** *a.* **coitus** (kō´itəs) *n.* the act of copulation. **coitus interruptus** (intərŭp´təs) *n.* coitus deliberately interrupted before ejaculation into the vagina. [L *coitio -ōnem*, from *coīre* (CO-, *īre*, to come)]

Coke® (kōk) *n.* Coca-Cola.

coke[1] (kōk) *n.* **1** coal from which gas has been extracted. **2** a residue in a car engine etc. formed by the incomplete combustion of petrol or other fuel. ~*v.t.* to convert into coke. [prob. the same as ME *colke*, the core of an apple; etym. uncertain]

coke[2] (kōk) *n.* (*sl.*) cocaine. [abbr.]

Col. *abbr.* **1** Colonel. **2** Colorado. **3** Colossians.

col (kol) *n.* **1** a depression in a mountain ridge; a saddle or elevated pass. **2** an area of low pressure between two anticyclones. [F, from L *collum*, neck]

col. *abbr.* column.

col-[1] (kol) *pref.* var. of COM- used before *l*.

col-[2] COLO-.

cola (kō´lə), **kola** *n.* **1** a tropical African tree of the genus *Cola*, bearing a nut which contains caffeine. **2** a soft drink flavoured with cola-nuts. **cola nut** *n.* the fruit of the cola tree. [Temne (a W Afr. language)]

☒ **colaborate** common misspelling of COLLABORATE.

colander (kol´əndə, kŭl´-), **cullender** (kŭl´-) *n.* a culinary strainer having the bottom perforated with small holes. [ult. from med. L *cōlātōrium* (*cōlāre*, to strain)]

co-latitude (kōlat´itūd) *n.* the complement of the latitude; the difference between the latitude and 90°.

colcannon (kolkan´ən) *n.* an Irish dish consisting of potatoes and green vegetables stewed together and mashed. [Ir. *cál ceannann*, white-headed cabbage]

colchicum (kol´chikəm, -ki-) *n.* **1** any plant of the genus *Colchicum*, esp. the meadow saffron, the corm and seeds of which are used in medicine. **2** the corm or seeds of the meadow saffron. **colchicine** (-sēn) *n.* an alkaloid obtained from meadow saffron, used to treat gout. [L, from Gr. *Kolchikon* (*Kolchis*, on the Black Sea)]

colcothar (kol´kəthah) *n.* a red form of ferric peroxide used as a pigment and as a polishing powder. [Arab. *qolqotār*, perh. corr. of Gr. *chalkhanthos* (*chalkos*, copper, *anthos*, a flower)]

cold (kōld) *a.* **1** low in temperature, esp. in relation to normal or bodily temperature. **2** lacking heat or warmth. **3** causing a sensation of loss of heat. **4** suffering from a sensation of lack of heat. **5** without ardour or intensity, indifferent, unconcerned. **6** lacking friendliness, unwelcoming. **7** sad, dispiriting, depressing. **8** not hasty or violent, spiritless. **9 a** (of a scent in hunting) weak. **b** not affecting the scent strongly. **c** unaffected by the scent. **10** in children's games etc., far from guessing or finding something. **11** (of a colour) bluish in tone, as opposed to warm tones such as red, yellow etc. **12** frigid, sexually unresponsive. **13** dead. **14** (*coll.*) unconscious. **15** (*coll.*) at one's mercy. **16** unrehearsed. ~*adv.* **1** without rehearsal or preparation. **2** (*esp. N Am.*) absolutely. ~*n.* **1** absence of warmth. **2** the sensation produced by absence of warmth. **3** a viral infection of the mucous membranes of the respiratory tract, accompanied by sneezing and coughing. **4** cold weather. **cold as charity** CHARITY. **in cold blood 1** without feeling, callously or ruthlessly. **2** without passion or excitement, deliberately. **out in the cold** ignored or neglected (*I was left out in the cold*). **to catch a cold 1** to contract a cold. **2** (*coll.*) to run into difficulties. **to leave cold** (*coll.*) to fail to excite or interest. **to throw/ pour cold water on** to discourage. **cold-blooded** *a.* **1** having a body temperature which varies with that of the environment. **2** unfeeling, callous. **cold-bloodedly** *adv.* **cold-bloodedness** *n.* **cold calling** *n.* the practice of making unsolicited telephone calls or visits to potential customers in order to sell products or services. **cold cathode** *n.* a cathode which emits electrons at normal temperatures. **cold chisel** *n.* a chisel for cutting cold metals. **cold comfort** *n.* poor consolation, depressing reassurance. **cold cream** *n.* a creamy ointment for cooling, cleansing or softening the skin. **cold cuts** *n.pl.* cold sliced meat. **cold-drawn** *a.* (of wire etc.) drawn in a cold state. **cold feet** *n.pl.* (*coll.*) loss of courage or confidence (*to get cold feet*). **cold fish** *n.* (*coll.*) an unemotional person. **cold frame** *n.* an unheated glass frame to protect seedlings etc. **cold front** *n.* in meteorology, the front edge of an advancing mass of cold air. **cold-hearted** *a.* unfeeling, indifferent. **cold-heartedly** *adv.* **cold-heartedness** *n.* **coldish** *a.* **coldly** *adv.* **coldness** *n.* **cold-rolled** *a.* (of metal) rolled without heating. **cold rubber** *n.* a strong synthetic rubber made at low temperatures, used for car tyres etc. **cold shoulder** *n.* **1** a rebuff (*to give someone the cold shoulder*). **2** studied indifference. **cold-shoulder** *v.t.* to treat with studied coolness or neglect, to rebuff. **cold snap** *n.* a sudden short spell of cold weather. **cold sore** *n.* a blister or cluster of blisters around the lips, caused by *herpes simplex*. **cold start** *n.* **1** the starting of an engine etc. at the ambient temperature. **2** the starting of any process without preparation. **3** (*Comput.*) the reloading of a program. **cold-start** *v.t.* to start (an engine, process etc.) in this way. **cold steel** *n.* cutting weapons, such as sword and bayonet, as opposed to firearms. **cold storage** *n.* **1** the preservation of perishable foodstuffs by refrigeration. **2** abeyance (*to put a project into cold storage*). **cold store** *n.* a large room used for cold storage. **cold sweat** *n.* sweating accompanied by chill, caused esp. by fear. **cold table** *n.* a selection of cold dishes. **cold turkey** *n.* (*sl.*) **1** the physical and psychological symptoms caused by sudden and complete withdrawal of drugs from an addict. **2** (*N Am.*) blunt treatment. **cold war** *n.* a state of psychological tension between two countries without actual fighting. **cold wave** *n.* **1** a sudden spell of cold weather over a wide area, esp. after the passage of a cold front. **2** in hairdressing, a type of permanent wave using chemicals. [OE *ceald*, from Gmc. *kal-* (cp. Icel. *kaldr*, Dut. *koud*, G *kalt*)]

cold-short (kōld´shawt) *a.* (of a metal) brittle when cold. [prob. from Swed. *kallskör* (Norw. and Dan. *koldskjör*), from *kall* or *kold* COLD, and *skor*, brittle]

cole (kōl) *n.* **1** the cabbage. **2** any of various other edible plants of the genus *Brassica*, esp. the rape. **coleseed** *n.* rapeseed. **coleslaw** *n.* a salad made of shredded raw cabbage, carrot, etc. **colewort** *n.* the cabbage. [L *caulis*, a stalk, a cabbage]

colectomy (kəlek´təmi) *n.* (*pl.* **colectomies**) surgical removal of the colon or part of it.

colemouse COALMOUSE.

coleopteran (koliop´tərən) *n.* any insect of the order Coleoptera, including the beetles and weevils, having the forewings converted into sheaths for the hind wings. **coleopterist** *n.* **coleopterous** *a.* [Gr. *koleon*, a sheath, *pteron*, a wing]

coleoptile (koliop´tīl) *n.* (*Bot.*) a protective sheath around the shoot tip in grasses. [Gr. *koleon*, a sheath, *ptilon*, a feather]

coleorhiza (koliərī´zə) *n.* (*pl.* **coleorhizae** (-zē)) the root sheath in the embryo of grasses. [Gr. *koleos*, sheath, *rhiza*, root]

cole tit (kōl´ tit) *n.* COALMOUSE.

coleus (kō´liəs) *n.* (*pl.* **coleuses**) any plant of the genus *Solenostemon*, cultivated for their variegated coloured leaves. [Gr. *koleon*, a sheath]

coley (kō´li) *n.* (*pl.* **coleys**) the coalfish.

colibri (kol´ibri) *n.* (*pl.* **colibris**) a hummingbird of the genus *Colibri*. [F, from Carib.]

colic (kol´ik) *n.* acute spasmodic pain in the intestines. **colicky** *a.* [F *colique*, L *colicus*, Gr. *kolikos* (see COLON[2])]

coliseum COLOSSEUM.

colitis (kəlī´tis) *n.* inflammation of the colon.

Coll. *abbr.* College.

coll. *abbr.* **1** colleague. **2** collection. **3** collective. **4** collector. **5** college. **6** colloquial.

collaborate (kəlab´ərāt) *v.i.* **1** to work jointly with another, esp. in literary, artistic or scientific work. **2** to cooperate with an enemy in occupation of one's own country. **collaboration** (-ā´shən) *n.* **collaborationist** *n.*, *a.* **collaborative** *a.* **collaboratively** *adv.* **collaborator** *n.* [COL-[1], L *labōrāre*, LABOUR (modelled on L *collabōrātor*)]

collage (kolahzh´) *n.* **1** a picture made of pieces of paper, fabric etc., glued on to a surface. **2** the art form in which such pictures are made. **3** any collection of diverse things or ideas. **collagist** *n.* [F, from Gr. *kolla*, glue]

collagen (kol´əjən) *n.* a fibrous protein that yields gelatin when boiled. [Gr. *kolla*, glue, -GEN]

collapsar (kəlap´sah) *n.* (*Astron.*) **1** a black hole. **2** a star that has collapsed to form a white dwarf or black hole.

collapse (kəlaps´) *v.i.* **1** to fall in, to give way, to fall down. **2** to fold together, to be collapsible. **3** to break down, to suffer from physical or nervous prostration. **4** to come to nothing. ~*v.t.* to cause to collapse. ~*n.* **1** the act or an instance of collapsing. **2** complete failure. **3** general prostration. †**collapsed** *a.* **collapsible** *a.* **1** liable to collapse. **2** made so as to fold together easily for compact storage etc. (*a collapsible table*). **collapsibility** (-bil´-) *n.* [L *collapsus*, p.p. of *collābī* (COL-[1], *lābī*, to glide down, to lapse)]

collar (kol´ə) *n.* **1** something worn round the neck, esp. the part of a garment that goes round the neck. **2** a band of leather etc. for a dog's neck. **3** a leather loop round a horse's neck to which the traces are attached. **4** a ring or round flange. **5** anything shaped like a collar or ring. **6** a marking resembling a collar round the neck of a bird etc. **7** the chain or other ornament for the neck worn by the knights of an order. **8** a cut of meat, esp. bacon, from the neck. **9** a piece of meat rolled and tied. **10** an astragal, a cincture. **11** (*Naut.*) **a** an eye in the end of a shroud or stay. **b** a rope in the form of a wreath to which a stay is confined. **12** in angling, a cast with flies attached. ~*v.t.* **1** to seize by the collar. **2** to put a collar on. **3** to capture. **4** (*coll.*) to seize. **5** (*coll.*) to accost. **6** (*sl.*) to steal. **collar-beam** *n.* a tie-beam. **collarbone** *n.* either of the bones that join the shoulder blades to the breastbone; the clavicle. **collared** *a.* **1** having or wearing a collar. **2** (of meat) rolled and tied. **3** (*coll.*) seized, arrested. **collared dove** *n.* a dove, *Streptopelia decaocto*, with a collar-like marking at the back of the neck. **collarless** *a.* **collar stud** *n.* a stud used to hold a collar to a shirt etc. [OF *colier*, L *collāre*, a band for the neck (*collum*, neck)]

collard (kol´əd), **collards** (-ədz), **collard greens** *n.* (*dial.*) a kind of cabbage that does not grow into a head. [COLEWORT (under COLE)]

collarette (koləret´) *n.* a small collar worn by women. [F *collerette*, dim. of *collier*, see COLLAR]

collate (kəlāt´) *v.t.* **1** to bring together in order to compare. **2** to examine critically in order to ascertain by comparison points of agreement and difference. **3** to place in order (printed sheets for binding etc.). **4** to assemble or merge (information etc. from different sources). **5** to appoint (a clergyman) to a benefice. **collation** *n.* **1** the act of collating. **2** a light meal (from treatises being read in monasteries at meal-times). **3** a light meal permitted on fast days in the Roman Catholic Church. **collator** *n.* **1** a person who collates manuscripts, books or sheets for binding. **2** a person who compares. **3** a bishop who appoints a clergyman to a benefice. [L *collātus*, p.p. of *conferre*, to bring together (COL-[1], *latus*, orig. *tlatus*, conn. with *tollere*, to bear, Gr. *tlētos*, borne)]

collateral (kəlat´ərəl) *a.* **1** having the same common ancestor but not lineally related. **2** side by side, parallel. **3** being by the side. **4** subsidiary, subordinate. ~*n.* **1** collateral security. **2** a collateral relation. **collateral damage** *n.* damage over and above that intended, esp. in military operations. **collaterality** (-ral´iti) *n.* **collateralize, collateralise** *v.t.* to secure (a loan etc.) with collateral security. **collaterally** *adv.* **collateral security** *n.* security for the performance of any contract, esp. the repayment of a loan, over and above the main security. [late L *collaterālis* (COL-[1], *laterālis*, from *latus -eris*, side)]

collation COLLATE.

colleague (kol´ēg) *n.* a person associated with another in any office or employment; a fellow worker. **colleagueship** *n.* [F *collègue*, L *collēga* (COL-[1], *legere*, to choose)]

collect[1] (kəlekt´) *v.t.* **1** to gather together into one body, mass or place. **2** to gather (money, taxes, subscriptions, books, works of art, curiosities etc.) from a number of sources. **3** to call for, to fetch. **4** to concentrate, to bring under control. **5** to gather from observation, to infer. ~*v.i.* **1** to come together. **2** to meet together. **3** (*coll.*) to receive money, esp. a large amount of money. ~*a.*, *adv.*

(*N Am.*) (of a telephone call etc.) paid for by the recipient. **to collect on** (*coll.*) to make money out of. **to collect oneself** to recover one's self-possession. **collectable, collectible** *a.* 1 worth collecting (*collectable works of art*). 2 that can be collected. ~*n.* a collectable item. **collectability** (-bil´-) *n.* **collected** *a.* 1 gathered, brought together. 2 cool, self-possessed, composed. **collectedly** *adv.* **collectedness** *n.* **collect on delivery** *n.* (*N Am.*) cash on delivery. **collector** *n.* 1 a person who collects money etc. (*a tax collector*). 2 a person who collects works of art, curiosities etc. (*a stamp collector*). 3 any person or thing that collects. 4 the terminal of a transistor. **collectorate** (-rət), **collectorship** *n.* **collector's item, collector's piece** *n.* an item of interest to a collector, esp. because of its value or rarity. [F *collecter*, med. L *collectare*, L *collectus*, p.p. of *colligere*, (COL-[1], *legere*, to gather)]

collect[2] (kol´ekt) *n.* a brief comprehensive form of prayer, adapted for a particular day or occasion. [F *collecte*, late L *collecta*, a summing-up, fem. p.p. of *colligere*, see COLLECT[1]]

collectanea (kolektā´niə) *n.pl.* a collection of passages from various authors, a miscellany or anthology. [L, neut. pl. of *collectāneus*, gathered together (see COLLECT[1])]

collection (kəlek´shən) *n.* 1 the act of collecting. 2 that which is collected. 3 an assemblage of books, works of art etc. 4 money contributed for religious, charitable or other purposes. 5 an accumulation. 6 the act of removing mail from a postbox, refuse for disposal etc. 7 (*pl.*) college examinations at the end of term at Oxford University etc. [OF, from L *collectio -ōnem* (see COLLECT[1])]

collective (kəlek´tiv) *a.* 1 tending to collect, forming a collection. 2 collected, aggregated, formed by gathering a number of things or persons together. 3 joint or common; cooperative (*collective action*). ~*n.* 1 a cooperative or collectivized organization or enterprise. 2 a collective noun. **collective bargaining** *n.* a method whereby employer and employees (or their representatives) determine the conditions of employment. **collective farm** *n.* a group of smallholdings, usu. state-owned or state-controlled, operated on a cooperative basis. **collective fruit** *n.* a multiple fruit. **collectively** *adv.* **collective memory** *n.* the memory of a group of people. **collectiveness** *n.* **collective noun** *n.* a noun in the singular that denotes a group of individuals, such as *family*, *herd*. **collective ownership** *n.* ownership of land, capital, and other means of production by those engaged in the production. **collective security** *n.* a policy of mutual aid against aggression. **collective unconscious** *n.* in Jungian theory, the part of the unconscious mind which is inherited and contains universal thought patterns and memories. **collectivism** *n.* an economic theory based on collective ownership. **collectivist** *n.* **collectivistic** (-is´tik) *a.* **collectivity** (kolektiv´-) *n.* **collectivize, collectivise** *v.t.* to organize on the lines of collectivism. **collectivization** (-zā´shən) *n.* [COLLECT[1], -IVE]

colleen (kolēn´) *n.* (*Ir.*) a girl, a lass. [Ir. *cailīn*, dim. of *caile*, a country-woman]

college (kol´ij) *n.* 1 an institution for further or higher education. 2 an institution providing specialized education, professional training etc. 3 an independent corporation of scholars, teachers, and fellows forming one of the constituent bodies of a university. 4 a similar foundation independent of a university. 5 a large and important secondary school, esp. a private school. 6 a body or community of persons, having certain rights and privileges, and devoted to common pursuits. **College of Arms** *n.* a corporation presided over by the Earl Marshal, and including the Kings-of-Arms, the heralds, and pursuivants, for granting armorial bearings etc. **College of Cardinals** *n.* in the Roman Catholic Church, the papal council of cardinals. **college of education** *n.* a training college for teachers. **College of Justice** *n.* (*Sc.*) the supreme civil courts. **college pudding** *n.* a small baked or steamed pudding containing dried fruit. **collegial** (-lē´jiəl) *a.* 1 of or relating to a college. 2 constituted as a college. 3 of or involving shared responsibility, as among colleagues. **collegiality** (-al´-) *n.* **collegian** (-lē´jən) *n.* 1 a member of a college. 2 a student at a university. [MF *college*, L *collēgium* (*collēga*, COLLEAGUE)]

collegia COLLEGIUM.

collegial, collegian COLLEGE.

collegiate (kəlē´jət) *a.* 1 of or relating to a college. 2 (of a town) containing a college. 3 instituted or regulated as a college. 4 (of a university) made up of various colleges. 5 of or for college students. **collegiate church** *n.* 1 a church which, though not a cathedral, has an endowed chapter of canons. 2 (*Sc.*, *N Am.*) a Presbyterian church or group of churches under a joint pastorate. **collegiately** *adv.* [L (collēgiātus, member of a college (*collēgium*, COLLEGE)]

collegium (kəlē´jiəm) *n.* (*pl.* **collegiums, collegia** (-jiə)) 1 a college of cardinals. 2 an administrative board. [L, see COLLEGIATE]

collenchyma (kəleng´kimə) *n.* plant tissue composed of elongated cells with thickened walls, occurring immediately under the epidermis in leaf-stalks, stems etc. **collenchymatous** (kolengkim´-) *a.* [Gr. *kolla*, glue, *enchuma*, infusion (EN-, *cheein*, to pour)]

Colles' fracture (kol´is) *n.* a fracture of the radius close to the wrist, with backward displacement of the hand. [Abraham Colles, 1773–1843, Irish surgeon]

collet (kol´ət) *n.* 1 a band or ring. 2 a flange or socket. 3 the part of a ring in which a stone is set. 4 in engineering, a sleeve that can be tightened round a shaft to grip it. 5 a small collar in a clock that supports the inner end of a balance spring. [F, dim. of *col*, L *collum*, the neck]

collide (kəlīd´) *v.i.* to come into collision or conflict. **collider** *n.* (*Physics*) a particle accelerator in which two beams of particles are caused to collide. [L *collīdere* (COL-[1], *lædere*, to strike, to hurt)]

collie (kol´i) *n.* 1 a sheepdog with long silky hair and a pointed nose. 2 this breed of sheepdog, originating in Scotland. [perh. COALY (under COAL), black]

collier (kol´yə) *n.* 1 a person who works in a coal mine. 2 a ship employed in the coal trade. 3 a member of its crew. **colliery** *n.* (*pl.* **collieries**) a coal mine. [ME *col*, COAL, -IER]

colligate (kol´igāt) *v.t.* 1 to bind together. 2 to bring into connection. **colligation** (-ā´shən) *n.* 1 alliance, union. 2 the mental process by which isolated facts are brought together into one concept. **colligative** (kəlig´ətiv) *a.* (*Chem.*) (of a physical property) dependent on the concentration of particles present rather than their nature. [L *colligātus*, p.p. of *colligāre* (COL-[1], *ligāre*, to bind)]

collimate (kol´imāt) *v.t.* 1 to adjust the line of sight of (a telescope). 2 to make the axes of (lenses or telescopes) collinear. 3 to make parallel. **collimation** (-ā´shən) *n.* adjustment to the line of sight. **collimator** *n.* 1 a small telescope used to adjust the line of sight of a larger optical instrument. 2 a tube attached to a spectroscope for making parallel the rays falling on the prism. [L *collīmāre*, a misreading for *collīneāre*, to aim (COL-[1], *līneāre*, from *līnea*, a line)]

collinear (kəlin´iə) *a.* (*Geom.*) in the same straight line. **collinearity** (-ar´-) *n.*

Collins (kol´inz), **collins** *n.* a drink made of spirits mixed with soda water, fruit juice, ice etc.

collision (kəlizh´ən) *n.* 1 the act of striking violently together. 2 the state of being struck violently together.

3 opposition, antagonism, conflict. 4 the clashing of interests. 5 a harsh combination of sounds etc. 6 (*Physics*) the striking or coming together of particles. **collision course** *n.* a course which will result inevitably in a collision. [L *collisio -ōnem*; see COLLIDE]

collocate (kol´əkāt) *v.t.* 1 to place together. 2 to arrange. 3 to set in a particular place. 4 to juxtapose or associate (a particular word) with another, esp. habitually. **collocation** (-ā´shən) *n.* [L *collocātus*, p.p. of *collocāre*]

collocutor (kəlok´ūtə, kol´ə-) *n.* a person who takes part in a conversation or conference. [late L, from *colloquī*, to confer (*loquī*, to talk)]

collodion (kəlō´diən) *n.* a syrupy solution of pyroxylin in ether and spirit, used in photography and medicine. **collodionize, collodionise** *v.t.* [Gr. *kollōdēs* (*kolla*, glue)]

collogue (kəlōg´) *v.i.* (*pres.p.* **colloguing,** *past, p.p.* **collogued**) to talk confidentially or plot together. [perh. from F *colloque*, a conference, or from L *colloquī* (see COLLOQUY), influenced by COLLEAGUE]

colloid (kol´oid) *n.* 1 an uncrystallizable, semi-solid substance, capable of only very slow diffusion or penetration. 2 (*Med.*) a gelatinous substance of homogeneous consistency. ~*a.* 1 gluelike, jelly-like. 2 of or relating to a colloid. 3 of or relating to the gluelike or jelly-like matter resulting from degeneration of the albuminous substance of cells. **colloidal** (kəloi´dəl) *a.* [Gr. *kolla*, glue, -OID]

collop (kol´əp) *n.* 1 a slice of meat. 2 a small piece or slice of anything. [of Scand. orig.]

colloq. *abbr.* colloquial.

colloquia COLLOQUIUM.

colloquial (kəlō´kwiəl) *a.* of, relating to or used in common or familiar conversation, not used in formal writing or in literature. **colloquialism** *n.* 1 a colloquial word or expression. 2 the use of such words or expressions. **colloquially** *adv.* [COLLOQUIUM]

colloquist COLLOQUY.

colloquium (kəlō´kwiəm) *n.* (*pl.* **colloquiums, colloquia** (-kwiə)) 1 an academic conference. 2 a seminar. [L, from *colloquī* (COL-[1], *loquī*, to talk)]

colloquy (kol´əkwi) *n.* (*pl.* **colloquies**) (*formal*) 1 a conference, conversation or dialogue between two or more persons. 2 a gathering to discuss religious or theological matters. **colloquist** *n.* a collocutor. [COLLOQUIUM]

collotype (kol´ətīp) *n.* 1 a method of lithographic printing in which the film of gelatin that constitutes the negative is used to produce prints. 2 a print obtained in this way. [Gr. *kolla*, glue]

collude (kəlood´) *v.i.* to act in concert, to conspire. **colluder** *n.* [L *collūdere* (COL-[1], *lūdere*, to play)]

collusion (kəloo´zhən) *n.* 1 secret agreement for a fraudulent or deceitful purpose. 2 such agreement between opponents in a lawsuit. **collusive** *a.* **collusively** *adv.* [F, from L *collūsio -ōnem* (*collūdere*, see COLLUDE)]

collyrium (kəlir´iəm) *n.* (*pl.* **collyriums, collyria** (-riə)) an eye-salve, a medicated eyewash. [L, from Gr. *kollurion*, a poultice (*kollura*, a roll of coarse bread)]

collywobbles (kol´iwobəlz) *n.pl.* (*coll.*) 1 a stomach-ache, an upset stomach. 2 extreme nervousness (*to have the collywobbles*). [poss. COLIC, WOBBLE]

Colo. *abbr.* Colorado.

colo- (kol´ō), **col-** *comb. form* colon. [Gr. *kolon*]

colobus (kol´əbəs) *n.* (*pl.* **colobuses**) a leaf-eating African monkey of the genus *Colobus*, with short or absent thumbs. [Gr. *kolobos*, docked]

colocynth (kol´əsinth), **coloquintida** (-kwin´tidə) *n.* 1 the climbing plant, *Citrullus colocynthis*, the bitter-apple, or its fruit. 2 an extract obtained from the pulp of this fruit and used as a purgative. [L *colocynthis*, Gr *kolokunthis*]

cologarithm (kōlog´əridhm) *n.* the logarithm of the reciprocal of a number.

cologne (kəlōn´) *n.* eau de Cologne. **Cologne water** *n.* eau-de-Cologne. [*Cologne*, city in Germany]

colon[1] (kō´lon) *n.* a punctuation mark (:) used to mark the start of a list, a long quotation etc.; also used in expressing an arithmetical ratio. [Gr. *kōlon*, a member, a limb, a clause]

colon[2] (kō´lon) *n.* the largest division of the intestinal canal, extending from the caecum to the rectum. **colonic** (kəlon´ik) *a.* of or relating to the colon. ~*n.* colonic irrigation. **colonic irrigation** *n.* cleansing of the colon by injecting a large amount of fluid into it. **colonitis** (-ī´tis) *n.* colitis, inflammation of the colon. **colonoscope** (kəlon´əskōp) *n.* a flexible lighted tube used to examine the colon. **colonoscopy** (kolənos´kəpi) *n.* (*pl.* **colonoscopies**) an examination of the colon using a colonoscope. [L, from Gr. *kolon*]

colonel (kœ´nəl) *n.* 1 the commander of a regiment; an army officer ranking below a brigadier and above a lieutenant colonel. 2 an officer of similar rank in other armed forces, such as the US Air Force. **Colonel Blimp** *n.* a blimp. **colonelcy** *n.* (*pl.* **colonelcies**). **colonelship** *n.* [F, from It. *colonello*, dim. of *colonna*, column (formerly *coronel*, also from F, due to confusion with *corona*, crown)]

colonial (kəlō´niəl) *a.* 1 of or relating to a colony, esp. to those of the British Empire or to those in America that became the US in 1776. 2 of or relating to colonialism. 3 (of architecture etc.) in a style characteristic of the British colonies in America before 1776. ~*n.* 1 a native or inhabitant of a colony. 2 a house in colonial style. **colonial goose** *n.* (*Austral., New Zeal.*) roast leg of mutton boned and stuffed. **colonialism** *n.* 1 a policy of tight control over, or exploitation of, colonies. 2 an idiom or habit peculiar to colonials. **colonialist** *n.* **colonially** *adv.*

colonist (kol´ənist) *n.* 1 a settler in or inhabitant of a colony. 2 a colonizer.

colonize (kol´ənīz), **colonise** *v.t.* 1 to found a colony in. 2 to settle in. 3 to people with colonists. 4 (of animals and plants) to become established in (a new environment). ~*v.i.* to found a colony or colonies. **colonization** (-zā´shən) *n.* **colonizer** *n.* [L *colōnus*, orig. a farmer]

colonnade (kolənād´) *n.* a series or range of columns at regular intervals. **colonnaded** *a.* [F, from It. *colonnata* (*colonna*, L *columna*, COLUMN)]

colony (kol´əni) *n.* (*pl.* **colonies**) 1 a settlement founded by emigrants in a foreign country, and remaining subject to the jurisdiction of the parent state. 2 a group of people of the same nationality in a foreign town. 3 a group of people following the same occupation in a town, esp. when they live in the same quarter. 4 a body of organisms living or growing together. **the Colonies** 1 (*Hist.*) the colonies constituting the British Empire. 2 (*Hist.*) the colonies in America which became the United States. [F, *colonie*, L *colōnia* (*colōnus*, a farmer, from *colere*, to till)]

colophon (kol´əfon) *n.* 1 a publisher's identifying symbol. 2 a device or inscription formerly at the end of a book, giving the printer's name, place, date of publication etc. [late L, from Gr. *kolophōn*, a summit]

colophony (kəlof´əni) *n.* a dark-coloured resin obtained from turpentine, rosin. [L *colophōnia* (*rēsīna*), from *Colophōn* in Asia Minor, where first obtained]

coloquintida COLOCYNTH.

color COLOUR.

Colorado beetle (kolərah´dō) *n.* a small yellow and black striped beetle, *Leptinotarsa decemlineata*, very destructive to the potato plant. [*Colorado*, state of the US]

colorant (kŭl´ərənt), **colourant** *n.* a substance used to impart colour, a pigment etc.

coloration (kŭlərā´shən), **colouration** *n.* 1 colouring, marking, arrangement of colours. 2 a method of putting on or arranging colours. **3** the act of colouring. [F, from L *colōrāre*, to colour]

coloratura (kolərətoo´rə) *n.* (*Mus.*) **1** the ornamental use of variation, trills etc. in vocal music. **2** a singer, esp. a soprano, capable of singing such ornamented music. [It. *coloratura*, L *colōrātura*, from *colōrāre*, see COLORATION]

colorific (kŭlərif´ik) *a.* **1** producing colour, having the power of imparting colour to other bodies. **2** highly coloured. [F *colorifique* (L *color -ōrem*, -FIC)]

colorimeter (kŭlərim´itə) *n.* an instrument for measuring the hue, brightness, and purity of colours. **colorimetric** (-met´rik) *a.* **colorimetry** *n.* [L *color*, colour]

colossal, colossally COLOSSUS.

colosseum (koləsē´əm), **coliseum** (koli-) *n.* **1** the amphitheatre in ancient Rome. **2** any large amphitheatre, stadium or other place of entertainment. [L, neut. a. from COLOSSUS]

colossus (kəlos´əs) *n.* (*pl.* **colossuses, colossi** (-sī)) **1** a statue of gigantic size. **2** any gigantic person, animal or thing. **3** a person of great power or genius. **colossal** *a.* **1** of, relating to or resembling a colossus. **2** huge. **3** (*coll.*) remarkable. **4** (of sculpture) twice life-size. **5** (*Archit.*) of or relating to an order having more than one storey of columns. **colossally** *adv.* [L, from Gr. *kolossos*]

colostomy (kəlos´təmi) *n.* (*pl.* **colostomies**) the surgical formation of an artificial anus by an incision made into the colon. [Gr. *stoma*, mouth]

colostrum (kəlos´trəm) *n.* **1** the first secretion from the mammary glands after parturition. **2** beestings. [L]

colotomy (kəlot´əmi) *n.* (*pl.* **colotomies**) surgical incision into the colon.

colour (kŭl´ə), (*N Am.*) **color** *n.* **1** the sensation produced by waves of resolved light upon the optic nerve. **2** that property of bodies by which rays of light are resolved so as to produce certain effects upon the eye. **3** any one of the hues into which light can be resolved, or a mixture of these. **4** any of these as distinguished from black or white. **5** that which is used for colouring, a pigment, a paint. **6** colouring; the use or effect of colour, and of light and shade in drawings, photography etc. **7** the complexion or hue of the face, esp. a healthy hue, ruddiness. **8** pigmentation of the skin, esp. dark pigmentation. **9** (*often pl.*) semblance, appearance, esp. false appearance. **10** (*pl.*) coloured ribbons etc. worn as a badge of membership of a team, party, society, club etc. **11** (*pl.*) a flag, standard, or ensign borne in an army or fleet. **12** pretence, excuse, pretext. **13** timbre, quality of tone. **14** general character, quality. **15** mood, temper, emotional quality. **16** vividness, animation. **17** (*Physics*) any of three characteristics of quarks. ~*v.t.* **1** to give or apply colour to. **2** to paint, to dye. **3** to give a new colour to. **4** to put in a false light, to misrepresent. **5** to exaggerate. **6** to influence. ~*v.i.* **1** to become coloured. **2** to turn red, to blush. **off colour** OFF. **to change colour** CHANGE. **to nail one's colours to the mast** NAIL. **to show one's true colours** **1** to reveal one's opinions, feelings or designs. **2** to throw off disguise. **trooping the colour** TROOP. **under false colours** falsely. **with flying colours** brilliantly, successfully, with credit or distinction. **colourable** *a.* **1** specious, plausible. **2** apparent, not real. **3** feigned, counterfeit. **colourableness** *n.* **colourably** *adv.* **colourant** COLORANT. **colouration** COLORATION. **colour bar** *n.* a social, political, or other discrimination against non-white people. **colour-blind** *a.* totally or partially unable to distinguish different colours, esp. the primary colours. **colour-blindness** *n.* **colour code** *n.* a system of marking different things, e.g. electric wires, in different colours for ease of identification. **colour-code** *v.t.* **Coloured** *a.* (*sometimes derog. or offensive*) **1** of other than Caucasian descent. **2** in S Africa, of mixed blood. ~*n.* a Coloured person. **coloured** *a.* **1** having a colour or colours, esp. marked by any colour except black or white. **2** Coloured. **3** having a specious appearance. **4** (*Bot.*) of any colour except green. ~*n.* **1** a Coloured. **2** (*pl.*) coloured items of laundry. **colour fast** *a.* dyed with colours that will not run, fade etc. **colour fastness** *n.* **colour filter** *n.* in photography, a layer of coloured glass etc. that transmits or absorbs light of different colours or wavelengths. **colourful** *a.* **1** having bright colour or colours. **2** interesting. **3** exotic. **colourfully** *adv.* **colourfulness** *n.* **colouring** *n.* **1** the act of giving a colour to. **2** the colour applied. **3** the art or style of using colour. **4** a false appearance. **5** the colour of a person's skin, hair etc. **colourist** *n.* a person who colours, esp. a painter. **colouristic** (-ris´-) *a.* **colourize, colourise** *v.t.* to put (e.g. a black-and-white film) into colour, esp. using computers. **colourization** (-zā´shən) *n.* **colourless** *a.* **1** without colour. **2** pale, neutral-tinted, subdued in tone. **3** dull, lacking in life and vigour. **4** neutral, impartial. **colourlessly** *adv.* **colourlessness** *n.* **colour line** *n.* a social distinction between white and non-white people in a community. **colourman** *n.* (*pl.* **colourmen**) a person who deals in paints, brushes etc. **colour printing** *n.* reproduction in two or more colours. **colour scheme** *n.* a set of colours used together in decorating. **colour-sergeant** *n.* a non-commissioned officer in the infantry ranking above an ordinary sergeant. **colour supplement** *n.* a (usu. weekly) supplement to a newspaper printed in colour and containing articles on lifestyle, entertainment etc. **colour temperature** *n.* (*Physics, Astron.*) the temperature of a black body at which it would emit radiation of the same chromaticity as a given source. **colourway** *n.* a particular colour scheme in a fabric etc., esp. one of a number of different combinations of colours. **coloury** *a.* having a good colour. [OF *color*, L *colōrem*, acc. of *color*]

Usage note The term *Coloured* is often associated with discrimination, segregation or apartheid, and can give offence. It is better to use black, Aboriginal, Asian or some other suitable alternative when referring to non-white people.

-colous (kələs) *comb. form* (*Biol.*) inhabiting (a certain environment). [L *colere*, to inhabit]

colporteur (kōl´pawtə) *n.* a person who travels about selling religious books, tracts etc. **colportage** (-tahzh, -tahzh´) *n.* [F, from *colporter* (*col*, neck, *porter*, to carry)]

colposcope (kol´pəskōp) *n.* an instrument for examining the cervix and upper vagina. **colposcopy** (-pos´kəpi) *n.* (*pl.* **colposcopies**). [Gr. *kolpos*, womb]

Colt® (kōlt) *n.* an early type of American revolver. [Samuel *Colt*, 1814–62, US inventor]

colt (kōlt) *n.* **1** a young horse, esp. a young male from its weaning until the age of four. **2** a young, inexperienced person. **3** in sport, a member of a junior team. **colthood** *n.* **coltish** *a.* **coltishly** *adv.* **coltishness** *n.* **coltsfoot** *n.* (*pl.* **coltsfoots**) a coarse-leaved, yellow-flowered plant, *Tussilago farfara*, formerly much used in medicine. [OE; etym. unknown]

colter COULTER.

colubrid (kol´ūbrid) *n.* any snake of the family Colubridae, most of which are harmless. ~*a.* of or relating to this family. **colubrine** (-brīn) *a.* **1** of, relating to, or resembling a snake. **2** of or relating to the Colubrinae, a subfamily of colubrid snakes. [L *coluber*, a snake, -ID]

colugo (kəloo´gō) *n.* (*pl.* **colugos**) a flying lemur. [etym. uncertain]

columbarium (koləmbeə´riəm) *n.* (*pl.* **columbaria** (-riə)) **1** a pigeon house; a dovecote. **2** a place of interment, esp. among the ancient Romans, fitted with niches like pigeon-holes to receive the cinerary urns. **3** a hole left in a wall to receive the end of a timber. [L, neut. of *columbārius* (*columba*, dove)]

Columbian (kəlŭmʹbiən) *a.* of or relating to the United States of America. [Christopher *Columbus*, 1451–1506, discoverer of America]

Columbine (kolʹəmbīn) *n.* the female dancer in a pantomime, the sweetheart of Harlequin. [It. *Colombina*, a comedy character]

columbine (kolʹəmbīn) *a.* of, relating to or resembling a dove or pigeon. *~n.* any plant of the genus *Aquilegia*, with five-spurred flowers, supposed to resemble five doves clustered together, esp. *A. vulgaris*. [OF *columbin*, late L *columbīna* (*columba*, a dove)]

columbite (kəlŭmʹbīt) *n.* an ore of niobium and tantalum, containing manganese and iron. [*Columbia*, the US, -ITE[1]]

columbium (kəlŭmʹbiəm) *n.* (*esp. N Am.*) niobium. [*Columbia*, the US, -IUM]

columella (kolūmelʹə) *n.* (*pl.* **columellae** (-lē)) **1** the central pillar of a univalve shell, or of corals. **2** the central axis of a fruit. **3** the central column in the capsule of mosses. **4** (*also* **columella auris**) a small bone in the middle ear of frogs, reptiles and birds. [L, dim. of *columna*, see COLUMN]

column (kolʹəm) *n.* **1** a pillar or solid body of wood or stone, of considerably greater length than thickness, usu. consisting of a base, a shaft and a capital, used to support or adorn a building, or as a solitary monument. **2** anything resembling this, such as the mercury in a thermometer, a cylindrical mass of water or other liquid, a vertical mass of smoke etc. **3** a perpendicular line of figures. **4** a perpendicular section of a page. **5** a regular article in a newspaper or magazine. **6** (*pl.*) the contents of a newspaper. **7** a support. **8** a solid body into which the filaments in some plants are combined. **9** (*Mil.*) a body of troops in deep files. **10** (*Naut.*) a line of ships behind each other. **to dodge the column** (*coll.*) to avoid work, duty, responsibility etc. **columnar** (-kəlŭmʹnə) *a.* **columned** *a.* **columniation** (kəlŭmniāʹshən) *n.* **1** the use or grouping of columns in a building. **2** arrangement in columns. **column-inch** *n.* a print measure, 1 in. (2.54 cm) deep and one column wide. **columnist** (-nist) *n.* a regular writer esp. on general subjects in a newspaper. [earlier *colompne*, OF *colompne*, *colombe*, L *columna* (cogn. with *collis*, hill, *celsus*, high)]

colure (kəlūəʹ, kolʹ-) *n.* (*Astron.*) either of two great circles passing through the equinoctial points, and cutting each other at right angles at the poles. [L *colūrus*, Gr. *kolouros* (*kolos*, docked, *ouros*, tail)]

colza (kolʹzə) *n.* **1** the rape plant. **2** rapeseed. **colza oil** *n.* oil expressed from this, and used to make lubricants, synthetic rubber etc. [F *colza*, *colzat*, LG *Kôlsôt* (Dut. *koolsaad*)]

COM (kom) *abbr.* computer output on microfilm.

Com. *abbr.* **1** Commander. **2** Commission(er). **3** Committee. **4** Commodore. **5** Commonwealth. **6** Communist.

com. *abbr.* **1** comedy. **2** commerce. **3** commercial. **4** committee. **5** common. **6** commune.

com- (kom) *pref.* **1** with. **2** together. **3** in combination. **4** completely. [L, the combining form *cum-* (chiefly before *b*, *f*, *m*, *p*)]

coma[1] (kōʹmə) *n.* (*pl.* **comas**) a state of absolute unconsciousness, characterized by the absence of any response to external stimuli or inner need. **comatose** (-tōs, -tōz) *a.* **1** in a coma. **2** sleepy, sluggish. [late L, from Gr. *kōma -atos* (cp. *koimaein*, to put to sleep)]

coma[2] (kōʹmə) *n.* (*pl.* **comae** (-mē)) **1** (*Astron.*) the nebulous covering of the nucleus of a comet. **2** (*Bot.*) the assemblage of branches constituting the head of a forest tree. **3** (*Bot.*) the tuft of hairs terminating certain seeds. [L, from Gr. *komē*, the hair]

comate (kōʹmāt), **comose** (-mōs) *a.* (*Bot.*) bearing a tuft of hair at the end. [COMA[2]]

comatose COMA[1].

comb (kōm) *n.* **1** a toothed instrument for separating, tidying and arranging the hair. **2** an ornamental toothed device for fastening the hair when arranged. **3** a rake-shaped instrument with a short handle for cleaning wool or flax. **4** anything resembling a comb. **5** the red, fleshy tuft on the head of a fowl, esp. the cock. **6** the crest of a bird. **7** the cellular substance in which bees deposit their honey, a honeycomb. **8** the crest of a wave. **9** a ridge. **10** a row of points for collecting electricity. *~v.t.* **1** to separate, tidy or arrange with a comb. **2** to curry (a horse). **3** to dress (flax, hemp, wool etc.). **4** to make a thorough search of. *~v.i.* (of a wave) to form a crest and roll over. **to comb out 1** to tidy or arrange with a comb. **2** to remove with a comb. **3** to find and remove. **4** to search thoroughly. **combed** *a.* **comber**[1] *n.* **1** a person or thing that combs. **2** a machine for combing cotton or wool. **3** a wave that forms a long crest and rolls over. **combing** *n.* **1** a tidying or dressing with a comb. **2** (*pl.*) hair removed by a comb. **combing wool** *n.* wool suitable for combing, used to make worsted. **comb-jelly** *n.* a ctenophore. **comb-out** *n.* a thorough search. [OE *camb*, from Gmc. *kambo-* (cp. Dut. *kam*, Icel. *kambr*, G *Kamm*; Gr. *gomphos*, a peg, Sansk. *gambhas*, a tooth)]

comb. *abbr.* **1** combination. **2** combined. **3** combining.

combat (komʹbat) *v.i.* (*pres.p.* **combating**, *past, p.p.* **combated**) to contend, to fight, to struggle. *~v.t.* to oppose, to strive against, to fight. *~n.* a fight, a battle. **combatable** *a.* **combatant** (-bə-) *a.* **1** engaged in combat. **2** bearing arms. **3** antagonistic. **4** (*Her.*) borne in the attitude of fighting. *~n.* a person who engages in combat. **combat dress** *n.* the uniform worn by soldiers in combat and field training. **combat fatigue** *n.* **1** nervous disturbance occurring in a very stressful situation, such as on the battlefield. **2** (*pl.*, *N Am.*) clothing worn in battle. **combative** (-bə-) *a.* **1** inclined to combat. **2** pugnacious. **combatively** *adv.* **combativeness** *n.* [OF *combatre* (COM-, *battre*, L *batuere*, to fight)]

combe (koom), **coomb** *n.* **1** a valley on the side of a hill or mountain. **2** a valley running up from the sea (often used in place names, as *Ilfracombe*). [OE *cumb* (etym. uncertain; perh. from Welsh *cwm*, *cumb*; or an application of OE *cumb*, a hollow vessel, of Gmc. origin)]

comber[1] COMB.

comber[2] (komʹbə) *n.* a British fish, *Serranus cabrilla*, of the perch family. [etym. uncertain]

combi (komʹbi) *n.* a machine or device that has a combined function. *~a.* having a combined function (*a combi oven*). [COMBINATION]

combination (kombināʹshən) *n.* **1** the act or process of combining. **2** the state of being combined. **3** a combined body or mass. **4** a group of things. **5** a union, an association. **6** the sequence of numbers that will open a combination lock. **7** combined action. **8** chemical union. **9** a motorcycle and sidecar. **10** (*pl.*) a long-sleeved undergarment covering the body and legs. **11** a sequence of chess moves. **12** (*pl.*, *Math.*) the different collections which may be made of certain given quantities in groups of a given number. **13** (*Law*) a group of people assembled or united for a common purpose, formerly of an illegal nature. **combinational** *a.* **combination lock** *n.* a lock which opens only when a set of dials is turned to show a particular combination of numbers. **combination oven** *n.* an oven with the combined function of a microwave and conventional oven. **combination room** *n.* the room in which the fellows of the colleges at Cambridge University meet after dinner; the senior common room. **combinative** (komʹbinətiv) *a.* **combinatorial** (kombinətawʹriəl) *a.* (*Math.*) of or relating to combinations of quantities. **combinatory** (komʹbinətəri) *a.* [OF, from L *combīnātio -ōnem* (*combīnāre*, to COMBINE[1])]

combine[1] (kəmbīnʹ) *v.t.* **1** to cause to unite or coalesce.

2 to bring together. 3 to have at the same time (properties or attributes usu. separate). ~*v.i.* 1 to unite, to coalesce. 2 to be joined or united in friendship or plans. 3 (*Chem.*) to unite by chemical affinity. **combinable** *a.* **combined operations** *n.* operations in which sea, air and land forces work together under a single command. **combining form** *n.* (*Gram.*) an element that occurs only in combination with another, as *micro-* in *microscope.* [L *combīnāre* (COM-, *bini*, two by two)]

combine[2] (kom´bīn) *n.* 1 a combination, esp. of persons or companies to further their own commercial interests. 2 a combine harvester. **combine harvester** *n.* a combined reaping and threshing machine. ~*v.t.* to harvest (crops) with a combine harvester.

combo (kom´bō) *n.* (*pl.* **combos**) (*coll.*) 1 a small band in jazz and popular music. 2 any combination. 3 (*Austral.*) a white man living with an Aboriginal woman. [COMBINATION]

combs (komz) *n.pl.* (*coll.*) combinations (the undergarment).

combust (kəmbŭst´) *v.t.* to burn, to consume with fire. ~*a.* (*Astron.*) situated so near to the sun as to be obscured or eclipsed by its light. **combustible** *a.* 1 capable of being set on fire, flammable. 2 irascible, hot-tempered. ~*n.* a combustible material or thing. **combustibility** (-bil´-) *n.* **combustibleness** *n.* **combustion** (-bŭs´chən) *n.* 1 the act of burning, the state of being on fire or destroyed by fire. 2 (*Chem.*) the combination of a substance with oxygen or another element, accompanied by light and heat. 3 oxidation of the tissue of organisms or of decomposing organic matter. **combustion chamber** *n.* a space in which combustion takes place, as in an internal-combustion engine. **combustive** *a.* [OF, from L *combustus*, p.p. of *combūrere* (COM-, *ūrere*, to burn)]

Comdr *abbr.* Commander.

Comdt *abbr.* Commandant.

come (kŭm) *v.i.* (*past* **came** (kām), *p.p.* **come**) 1 to move from a distance to a place nearer to the speaker or hearer. 2 to approach. 3 to be brought to or towards. 4 to move towards. 5 to travel (a certain distance) towards (*Have you come far?*). 6 to reach, to extend. 7 to arrive. 8 to arrive at some state or condition. 9 to appear. 10 to happen, to befall. 11 to be in a specified position (*B comes before C*). 12 to be available (*The skirt comes in four colours*). 13 to become, to get to be. 14 to be (*It doesn't come easy*). 15 (*in subj.*) when (a specified time or event) arrives (*come February; come the revolution*). 16 to result, to arise, to originate (from). 17 to be descended (from). 18 to bud, to shoot. 19 (*sl.*) to experience orgasm. ~*v.t.* (*sl.*) to act the part of, to produce. ~*n.* (*sl.*) semen ejaculated at orgasm. ~*int.* used to excite attention or rouse to action (when repeated it expresses remonstrance or reserve). **as... as they come** being the most typical or supreme example (*She's as lazy as they come*). **as it comes** without additions or alterations. **come again** say that again. **come along** make haste. **come hell or high water** HELL. **come off it** (*coll.*) stop behaving or talking so stupidly or pretentiously. **come on** 1 hurry up. 2 proceed. 3 used to express encouragement. **come rain or come shine** RAIN. **come to that** (*coll.*) in fact. **come what may** whatever happens. **how come?** (*coll.*) how does this happen? **if it comes to that** in that case. **to come** in the future (*in days to come*). **to come about** 1 to result, to come to pass. 2 (*Naut.*) to change direction, esp. by tacking. 3 to recover. 4 to be perceived (as). **to come across** 1 to meet with accidentally. 2 (*coll.*) to be perceived (as). **to come across with** (*sl.*) to provide or hand over. **to come along** to make progress. **to come and go** 1 to appear and disappear (as the colour in the cheeks). 2 to pass to and fro. 3 to pay a short call. **to come apart** to separate or break into parts or pieces. **to come around** (*N Am.*) to come round. **to come at** 1 to reach, to attain, to gain access to. 2 to attack. **to come away** 1 to move away, to leave. 2 to become parted or separated. **to come back** 1 to return. 2 to recur to memory. 3 to retort. 4 to become popular or fashionable again. **to come back/ down to earth** EARTH. **to come before** to be dealt with by (*to come before an industrial tribunal*). **to come between** 1 to damage a relationship between (two people). 2 to separate. **to come by** 1 to pass near. 2 to call, to visit. 3 to obtain, to gain. **to come down** 1 to descend, to fall. 2 to be humbled. 3 to decide. 4 to be handed down. **to come down on** 1 to reprimand. 2 to chastise. **to come down to** 1 to amount to. 2 to have as result. **to come down with** to contract (an ailment). **to come for** 1 to come to fetch or receive. 2 to attack. **to come forward** 1 to make oneself known, to identify oneself. 2 to offer oneself. 3 to move forwards. **to come from behind** BEHIND. **to come full circle** CIRCLE. **to come good** GOOD. **to come home** 1 to return home. 2 to affect closely. 3 to be fully comprehended. **to come home to nothing** NOTHING. **to come home to roost** to have undesirable consequences for the doer or initiator. **to come in** 1 to enter. 2 to advance or approach, to arrive at a destination. 3 to become fashionable. 4 to be received. 5 to prove to be (*to come in useful*). 6 to play a role, to have a function (*This is where the torch comes in*). 7 to accrue. 8 to assume power. 9 (*coll.*) to secure an advantage or chance of benefit. **to come in for** 1 to arrive in time for. 2 to obtain, to receive. **to come into** 1 to join with. 2 to comply with. 3 to acquire, to inherit. **to come into contact with** CONTACT. **to come into one's head** HEAD[1]. **to come into someone's mind** MIND. **to come into the world** to be born. **to come it strong** (*coll.*) to exaggerate. **to come near** 1 to approach. 2 nearly to succeed. **to come of** 1 to be descended from. 2 to proceed or result from. **to come of age** to reach the age of 18, to become an adult. **to come off** 1 to part from. 2 to be detachable. 3 to fall off. 4 to take place. 5 (*coll.*) to be accomplished. 6 to fare (*to come off best*). 7 (*sl.*) to experience orgasm. **to come on** 1 to advance. 2 to prosper. 3 to appear. 4 to begin to perform, speak, play, be broadcast etc. 5 to happen, to arise. 6 to come upon. **to come out** 1 to emerge. 2 to be revealed, to become public. 3 to be introduced into society. 4 to be published. 5 to declare something openly, esp. one's homosexuality. 6 to go on strike. 7 to turn out. 8 to be covered (in) (*She came out in a rash*). 9 (*N Am.*) to make profession of religion. 10 to be removed or solved. **to come out of** to issue forth, to proceed from. **to come out of the closet** CLOSET. **to come out with** to utter, to disclose. **to come over** 1 to cross over. 2 to change sides. 3 to affect. 4 (*coll.*) to become (*I came over dizzy*). 5 to make a casual visit. 6 to be perceived (as). **to come round** 1 to change one's opinion. 2 to recover consciousness. 3 to make a casual visit. 4 to recur. **to come short** SHORT. **to come someone's way** WAY. **to come through** 1 to survive. 2 to be successful. 3 to be received. **to come to** 1 to amount to. 2 to recover consciousness. 3 (*Naut.*) to cease moving. 4 to reach. 5 to consent. **to come to a bad end** END. **to come to a head** HEAD[1]. **to come to an end** END. **to come to a point** to taper. **to come to blows** to begin fighting. **to come to grief** GRIEF. **to come to harm** to be injured or damaged. **to come to heel** HEEL[1]. **to come to light** LIGHT[1]. **to come to mind** MIND. **to come to nothing** NOTHING. **to come to oneself** to recover one's senses. **to come to one's senses** 1 to recover consciousness. 2 to become sensible. **to come to pass** to happen. **to come to rest** to stop, to cease moving. **to come to stay** 1 to remain. 2 to have qualities of a permanent nature. **to come true** TRUE. **to come under** 1 to be classed as. 2 to be subject to (authority, influence etc.). **to come up 1** to ascend. **2** to arise. **3** to be introduced as a topic. **4** to happen. **to come up against** to encounter or confront (a difficulty etc.). **to come upon 1** to attack. **2** to befall. **3** to find, to discover. **4** to meet with unexpectedly. **to come up smiling** SMILE. **to come up to 1** to approach. **2** to be equal to. **3** to amount to. **to come up with 1** to produce. **2** to overtake. **to have it coming** COMING. **where one came in** back at the beginning. **comeback** *n.* **1** a return to popular favour. **2** (*sl.*) a retort. **3** (*Austral.*) **a** a sheep bred from pure-bred and cross-bred parents. **b** the fleece of such a sheep. **comedown** *n.* **1** a fall or decline. **2** a disappointment. **come-hither** *a.* (*coll.*) sexually alluring (*a come-hither look*). **come-on** *n.* (*sl.*) an invitation, encouragement, esp. sexual. [OE *cuman* (cp. Dut. *komen*, Icel. *koma*, G *kommen*; Sansk. *gam*, Gr. *bainein*, L *venīre*)]

come-at-able (kŭmat´əbəl) *a.* easy to reach, accessible. [COME, AT, -ABLE]

Comecon (kom´ikon) *n.* (*Hist.*) an economic organization of E European states, founded in 1949. [*Co*uncil for *M*utual *Econ*omic Aid]

comedian (kəmē´diən) *n.* **1** an entertainer who tells jokes, humorous anecdotes etc. **2** an actor or writer of comedy. [F *comédien*]

comedic COMEDY.

comedienne (kəmēdien´) *n.* a female comedian. [F]

comedist COMEDY.

comedo (kom´idō) *n.* (*pl.* **comedos, comedones** (-dō´nēz)) a blackhead. [L, glutton, from *comedere*, to eat]

comedy (kom´ədi) *n.* (*pl.* **comedies**) **1** a dramatic composition of a light and entertaining character depicting and often satirizing the incidents of ordinary life, and having a happy ending. **2** an entertaining drama of ordinary life more serious and more realistic than farce. **3** such compositions as a dramatic genre. **4** life or any incident or situation regarded as an amusing spectacle. **5** humour. **comedic** (-mē´-) *a.* **comedist** *n.* a writer of comedies. **comedy of manners** *n.* a dramatic composition satirizing social behaviour. [OF *comedie*, L *cōmaedia*, Gr. *kōmōidia*, from *kōmōidos*, a comic actor (*kōmos*, a revel, *aoidos*, a singer)]

comely (kŭm´li) *a.* (*comp.* **comelier**, *superl.* **comeliest**) **1** pleasing in appearance or behaviour. **2** becoming, decent. **comeliness** *n.* [OE *cymlic* (*cyme*, fine, beautiful, *lic*, like, -LY[1])]

☒ **comemorate** common misspelling of COMMEMORATE.

comer (kŭm´ə) *n.* **1** a person who comes or arrives. **2** a visitor. **3** (*coll.*) a potential success. **all comers** ALL.

comestible (kəmes´tibəl) *n.* (*usu. pl.*, *formal or facet.*) food. [F, from late L *comestibilis*, from *comest-*, stem of *comestus*, *comēsus*, p.p of *comedere* (COM-, *edere*, to eat)]

comet (kom´it) *n.* a luminous heavenly body, consisting of a nucleus or head, a coma, and a train or tail, revolving round the sun in a very eccentric orbit. **cometary** *a.* **cometic** (-met´-) *a.* [L *comēta*, *comētēs*, Gr. *komētēs* (*komē*, the hair)]

come-uppance (kŭmŭp´əns) *n.* (*coll.*) retribution for past misdeeds (*to get one's come-uppance*). [COME, UP, -ANCE]

†**comfit** (kŭm´fit) *n.* a sweet, esp. a nut or seed coated with sugar. [OF *confit*, L *confectum*, neut. p.p. of *conficere* (CON- *facere*, to make)]

comfort (kŭm´fət) *v.t.* **1** to console. **2** to cheer, to encourage. **3** to make comfortable. ~*n.* **1** consolation. **2** support or assistance in time of weakness. **3** encouragement. **4** a person or thing that provides consolation or encouragement. **5** ease, general well-being, absence of trouble or anxiety. **6** (*pl.*) the material things that contribute to this. **7** (*N Am.*, *dial.*) a quilted coverlet. **cold comfort** COLD. **comfortable** *a.* **1** providing comfort or security. **2** at ease, in good circumstances, free from want, hardship, trouble or pain. **3** happy, contented. **4** with a wide margin (*a comfortable lead*). **comfortableness** *n.* **comfortably** *adv.* **comforter** *n.* **1** a person or thing that comforts. **2** †a long, narrow, woollen scarf. **3** (*N Am.*) a quilted coverlet. **4** a baby's dummy. **comforting** *a.* **comfortingly** *adv.* **comfortless** *a.* **1** without comfort. **2** cheerless. **comfortlessly** *adv.* **comfortlessness** *n.* **comfort station** *n.* (*N Am.*) a public convenience. [OF *conforter*, L *confortāre*, (CON-, *fortis*, strong)]

comfrey (kŭm´fri) *n.* (*pl.* **comfreys**) a tall wild plant of the genus *Symphytum*, esp. *S. officinale*, with rough leaves and white or purplish flowers, formerly used for healing wounds. [OF *confirie*, med. L *cumfiria* (etym. uncertain)]

comfy (kŭm´fi) *a.* (*comp.* **comfier**, *superl.* **comfiest**) (*coll.*) comfortable (*a comfy chair*). **comfily** *adv.* **comfiness** *n.* [abbr.]

comic (kom´ik) *a.* **1** of or relating to comedy; laughable, absurd. **2** facetious, burlesque, intended to provoke laughter. ~*n.* **1** a comedian. **2** a droll or amusing person, a buffoon. **3** a magazine containing comic strips, esp. for children. **4** (*N Am.*) comic strips. **5** the comic aspect of things. **comical** *a.* **1** ludicrous, laughable. **2** funny, provoking mirth. **comicality** (-kal´-) *n.* **comically** *adv.* **comic opera** *n.* **1** a type of opera with humorous episodes, a light, sentimental plot and usu. some spoken dialogue. **2** a musical burlesque. **comic relief** *n.* dialogue, incidents or scenes of a comic nature alleviating the tension in a tragic play or story. **comic strip** *n.* a usu. comic narrative told in a series of pictures. [L *cōmicus*, Gr. *kōmikos* (*kōmos*, a revel)]

Usage note The meanings of the adjectives *comic* and *comical* overlap, but in general *comic* is more usual where the humour is deliberate or where comedy is the main purpose, and *comical* where the humour is unintentional or unexpected.

Cominform (kom´infawm) *n.* the Information Bureau of the Communist Parties, founded in 1947, orig. including Yugoslavia. [Rus.]

coming (kŭm´ing) *a.* **1** approaching. **2** future, to come. **3** of potential or future importance. ~*n.* the act of approaching or arriving. **not to know whether one is coming or going** to be totally confused, esp. because very busy. **to have it coming** (*coll.*) to deserve what (unpleasant thing) is about to happen. **coming and going, comings and goings** *n.* activity, movement.

Comintern (kom´intœn) *n.* the Third Communist International, founded in Moscow in 1919, dissolved in June 1943. [Rus.]

comitadji (komitaj´i), **komitadji, komitaji** *n.* a member of a band of Balkan guerrillas. [Turk. *qomitaji* member of the committee]

☒ **comitee** common misspelling of COMMITTEE.

comity (kom´iti) *n.* (*pl.* **comities**) **1** affability, friendliness, courtesy, civility. **2** an association of nations. **3** comity of nations. **comity of nations** *n.* the courtesy by which a nation allows another's laws to be recognized within its territory, so far as is practicable. [L *cōmitās -tātem* (*cōmis*, courteous)]

Comm. *abbr.* Commodore.

comm. *abbr.* **1** commentary. **2** commerce. **3** commercial. **4** commonwealth. **5** communication.

comma (kom´ə) *n.* **1** a punctuation mark (,), denoting the shortest pause in reading. **2** (*Mus.*) a minute difference of tone. **3** (*also* **comma butterfly**) a butterfly, *Polygonia c-album*, with a white comma-shaped mark beneath the hindwing. **inverted comma** INVERT[1]. **comma bacillus** *n.* a comma-shaped bacterium, *Vibrio comma*, which causes cholera. [L, from Gr. *komma*, a stamp, a clause (*koptein*, to strike, cut)]

command (kəmahnd´) *v.t.* 1 to order, to call for, to enforce. 2 to govern, to hold in subjection, to exercise authority over. 3 to control, to have at one's disposal. 4 to master, to subjugate. 5 to dominate, to overlook. *~v.i.* 1 to give orders. 2 to exercise supreme authority. *~n.* 1 an order, a bidding, a mandate. 2 power, authority (*to be in command*). 3 control, mastery. 4 a naval or military force under the command of a particular officer. 5 (*Comput.*) an instruction. 6 a working knowledge (of). **at command** 1 ready for orders. 2 at one's disposal. **at someone's command** in accordance with someone's instructions. **in command of** having control over. **under command of** commanded by. **commandant** (komənd ant´) *n.* the governor or commanding officer of a place, force etc. **Commandant-in-Chief** *n.* the supreme commandant of a place, force etc. **commandantship** *n.* **command economy** *n.* an economy in which prices, incomes and industrial activity are determined by central government rather than by market forces. **command-in-chief** *n.* the supreme command (of an army etc.). *~v.t.* to be commander-in-chief of (an army etc.). **commanding** *a.* 1 giving or entitled to give commands (*a commanding officer*). 2 dignified. 3 impressive. 4 dominating, overlooking. **commandingly** *adv.* **command language** *n.* (*Comput.*) the language used to communicate with a computer operating system. **command module** *n.* the compartment of a spacecraft from which operations are controlled. **Command Paper** *n.* a government report presented to Parliament. **command performance** *n.* a theatrical or film performance given by royal command. **command post** *n.* a place used as temporary headquarters by a military commander. **command sequence** *n.* (*Comput.*) a series of commands for a specific task. [OF *comander*, late L *commandāre* (COM-, *mandāre*, to entrust)]

commandeer (komandiə´) *v.t.* 1 to seize or make use of for military purposes. 2 to seize or make use of without permission or authority. [Dut. *kommanderen*, from F *commander*, to command]

commander (kəmahn´də) *n.* 1 a person who commands or is in authority. 2 a general or leader of a body of troops etc. 3 a naval officer between a lieutenant and a captain. 4 a police officer in London in charge of a district. 5 a knight commander. 6 a large wooden mallet. **commander-in-chief** *n.* (*pl.* **commanders-in-chief**) 1 the officer in supreme command of military forces, of a foreign expedition etc. 2 the officer in supreme command of all the naval ships in a certain district. **commander-in-chiefship** *n.* **Commander of the Faithful** *n.* a title of the caliphs. **commandership** *n.*

commandment (kəmahnd´mənt) *n.* 1 an order, a command, esp. a divine command. 2 a precept or law, esp. of the Decalogue.

commando (kəmahn´dō) *n.* (*pl.* **commandos**) 1 a body of men called out for military service; a body of troops. 2 a body of troops selected and trained to undertake a specially hazardous raid on or behind the enemy lines. 3 a member of such a body. 4 a mobile amphibious force. 5 (*Hist.*) an armed force of Boers in S Africa. *~a.* of or relating to a commando (*a commando raid*). [Port., from *commandar*, to command]

commeasure (kəmezh´ə) *v.t.* to be equal in extent, degree etc. to, to coincide with.

comme ci comme ça (kom sē kom sa´) *a.* middling, indifferent, so-so. *~adv.* indifferently. [F, like this, like that]

commedia dell'arte (kəmādiə delah´ti) *n.* Italian comedy of the 16th–18th cents., using improvisation and stock characters. [It., comedy of art]

comme il faut (kom ēl fō´) *a.* as it should be, correct, genteel. [F]

commemorate (kəmem´ərāt) *v.t.* 1 to keep in remembrance by some solemn act. 2 to celebrate the memory of. 3 to be a memorial of. **commemorable** *a.* **commemoration** (-ā´shən) *n.* 1 the act of commemorating. 2 a service, ceremony or festival in memory of some person, deed or event. 3 the annual festival commemorating benefactors to Oxford University. **commemorative** *a.* **commemoratively** *adv.* **commemorator** *n.* [L *commemorātus*, p.p. of *commemorāre* (COM-, *memorāre*, to mention, from *memor*, mindful)]

commence (kəmens´) *v.i.* (*formal*) 1 to start, to begin. 2 to originate. *~v.t.* to start, to begin. **commencement** *n.* 1 a beginning, an origin. 2 the first instance or first existence. 3 the day when the degrees of Master and Doctor are conferred, at Cambridge, Dublin and N American universities. 4 in N American schools, speech day. [OF *comencer* (cp. It. *cominciare*), from L COM-, *initiāre*, to begin (*initium*, a beginning, from IN-[1], *īre*, to go)]

commend (kəmend´) *v.t.* 1 to commit to the charge of, to entrust. 2 to recommend as worthy of notice, regard or favour. 3 to praise, to approve. †**commend me to** remember me to. **highly commended** almost as good as the top prizewinner(s). **commendable** *a.* 1 worthy of commendation. 2 †bestowing commendation. **commendableness** *n.* **commendably** *adv.* **commendation** (komendā´shən) *n.* 1 the act of commending. 2 recommendation of a person to the consideration or favour of another. 3 praise. 4 an award. **commendatory** *a.* 1 that commends. 2 holding a commendam. 3 held as a commendam. [L *commendāre* (COM-, *mandāre*, to entrust)]

commendam (kəmen´dam) *n.* 1 (*Hist.*) the holding of a vacant ecclesiastical benefice in trust until an incumbent was appointed. 2 the holding of a benefice in the absence of the regular incumbent. 3 a benefice so held. [L *in commendam*, in trust]

commensal (kəmen´səl) *a.* 1 (of an organism) living in intimate association with, on the surface of or in the substance of another, without being parasitic. 2 eating at the same table, sharing the same food. *~n.* 1 a commensal organism. 2 a person who eats at the same table or shares the same food as another. **commensalism** *n.* **commensality** (komənsal´-) *n.* [F, from med. L *commensālis* (COM-, *mensa*, table)]

commensurable (kəmen´shərəbəl) *a.* 1 measurable by a common unit. 2 proportionate (to). 3 (*Math.*) having a common factor. **commensurability** (-bil´-), **commensurableness** *n.* **commensurably** *adv.* [L *commensūrābilis* (COM-, *mensūrābilis*, from *mensūrāre*, see COMMENSURATE)]

commensurate (kəmen´shərət) *a.* 1 having the same measure or extent. 2 proportionate. **commensurately** *adv.* **commensurateness** *n.* [L *commensūrātus* (COM-, *mensūrātus*, p.p. of *mensūrāre*, to measure, from *mensūra*, a measure)]

comment (kom´ent) *n.* 1 a remark, an opinion. 2 criticism. 3 commenting (*I let it pass without comment*). 4 a note interpreting or illustrating a work or portion of a work. *~v.i.* 1 to make a comment or comments. 2 to make explanatory or critical remarks or notes (on a book or writing). 3 to criticize or make remarks (on) unfavourably. *~v.t.* to remark. **no comment** (*coll.*) I refuse to answer or comment. **commentary** *n.* (*pl.* **commentaries**) 1 a series of explanatory notes on a whole work. 2 a broadcast description of an event as it takes place. 3 a comment. 4 (*pl.*) a historical narrative. **commentate** *v.i.* to act as commentator (on). **commentation** (-tā´shən) *n.* annotation, exposition. **commentator** *n.* 1 the broadcaster of a commentary. 2 the author of a commentary. 3 an annotator, an expositor. 4 a person who comments on current affairs (*a political commentator*). **commenter** *n.* [OF *comment*, L *commentum*, an invention, a comment, neut. p.p. of *comminisci* (COM-, *minisci*, from the root *men-*, cp. *mens*, mind, *memini*, I remember)]

commerce (kom´œs) *n.* 1 trade, financial transactions. 2 the interchange of commodities between nations or individuals, buying and selling. 3 social intercourse. 4 †sexual intercourse. [F, from L *commercium* (COM-, *merx -cis*, wares, merchandise)]

commercial (kəmœ´shəl) *a.* 1 of or relating to commerce. 2 done for profit. 3 (of chemicals) of poor quality and produced in bulk for industry. ~*n.* 1 an advertisement broadcast on radio or television. 2 †a commercial traveller. **commercial art** *n.* graphic art used in advertising etc. **commercial break** *n.* a break for advertisements in a television or radio programme. **commercial broadcasting** *n.* broadcasting paid for by advertising or sponsorship. **commercialism** *n.* 1 commercial practices. 2 a trading spirit. 3 excessive emphasis on profit. **commercialist** *n.* **commerciality** (-shiăl´-) *n.* **commercialize, commercialise** *v.t.* 1 to make commercial. 2 to exploit or spoil for the sake of profit. **commercialization** (-zā´shən) *n.* **commercially** *adv.* **commercial space** *n.* an area sold or rented as business premises. **commercial traveller** *n.* an agent sent out by a company to solicit orders from retailers, a travelling sales representative. **commercial vehicle** *n.* a vehicle used for the transport of goods or passengers.

commère (kom´eə), **commere** *n.* a female compère. [F]

commie (kom´i) *n., a.* (*coll., often derog.*) (a) communist. [abbr.]

comminate (kom´ināt) *v.t.* to threaten, to denounce. **commination** (-ā´shən) *n.* 1 a threat, a denunciation. 2 in the Church of England, a service including a list of God's judgements on sinners, used on Ash Wednesday. **comminatory** (-ət-) *a.* threatening, denunciatory. [L *comminātus*, p.p. of *comminārī* (*minārī*, to threaten)]

commingle (kəming´gəl) *v.t., v.i.* (*poet.*) to mingle or mix together, to blend.

comminute (kom´inūt) *v.t.* 1 to make smaller. 2 to reduce to minute particles or to powder. 3 to divide into small portions. **comminuted fracture** *n.* a fracture in which the bone is broken into small pieces. **comminution** (-nū´-) *n.* [L *comminutus*, p.p. of *comminuere* (*minuere*, to make smaller)]

commis (kom´i) *n.* (*pl.* **commis** (kom´i, kom´iz)) 1 an agent. 2 an apprentice or assistant waiter or chef. [F, p.p. of *commettre*, COMMIT]

commiserate (kəmiz´ərāt) *v.i.* to feel or express sympathy (with). ~†*v.t.* 1 to pity. 2 to express pity or compassion for. **commiseration** (-ā´shən) *n.* **commiserative** (-ətiv) *a.* **commiseratively** *adv.* [L *commiserātus*, p.p. of *commiserārī* (*miserārī*, to pity)]

commissar (kom´isah) *n.* (*Hist.*) 1 the head of a department of government in the USSR. 2 a party official responsible for political education in the USSR. [Rus., a commissioner]

commissariat (komiseə´riət) *n.* 1 the department of the army charged with supplying provisions and stores. 2 (*Sc. Law*) the jurisidiction of a commissary. 3 (*Hist.*) a government department in the USSR. [F, as COMMISSARY]

commissary (kom´isəri) *n.* (*pl.* **commissaries**) 1 a commissioner. 2 a deputy. 3 the deputy who supplies a bishop's place in the remote parts of his diocese. 4 (*Mil.*) an officer in charge of the commissariat. 5 (*N Am.*) a restaurant or snack bar in a film studio. 6 (*N Am.*) a shop for the supply of food, equipment etc. in a military camp. **commissarial** (-seə´-) *a.* **commissary-general** *n.* (*Mil.*) the head of the commissariat. **commissaryship** *n.* [late L *commissārius*, from *commissus*, p.p. of *committere* (*mittere*, to send)]

commission (kəmish´ən) *n.* 1 the entrusting of a task or duty to another. 2 the task or duty entrusted. 3 an order, command or instruction to do or produce something. 4 the delegation of authority. 5 a number of persons entrusted with authority. 6 a document conferring rank or authority, esp. that of military and naval officers. 7 the authority to act as a factor or agent. 8 a percentage paid to a factor or agent. 9 the act of committing. 10 a body of commissioners. 11 the office of a commissioner. ~*v.t.* 1 to authorize, to empower, to appoint to an office. 2 to put (a ship, a machine etc.) into service or operation. 3 to order (the painting of a picture, writing of a book etc.). 4 to give (an artist, a writer etc.) a commission. **in commission** 1 (of a naval ship) prepared for active service. 2 entrusted with authority. 3 in operation, in working order. 4 entrusted to a commission instead of the constitutional officer. **on commission** a percentage of the proceeds of goods sold being paid to the agent or retailer. **out of commission** (of a ship, machine etc.) not in service or operation, not in working order. **commission agent** *n.* 1 (*also* **commission merchant**) a person who acts as agent for others, and is paid by a percentage. 2 a bookmaker. **commissionaire** (-neə´) *n.* a uniformed doorman at a hotel, theatre etc. **commissional** *a.* **commissioned** *a.* holding a commission, esp. in the armed forces. **commissioner** *n.* 1 a person empowered to act by a commission or warrant. 2 a member of a commission or government board. 3 the head of some department of the public service. **Commissioner for Oaths** *n.* (*Law*) a person authorized to receive affidavits and other sworn declarations. **commissionership** *n.* **commission of the peace** *n.* 1 a warrant empowering persons to serve as Justices of the Peace. 2 Justices of the Peace. [F, from L *commissio -ōnem* (see COMMISSARY)]

commissure (kom´isūə) *n.* 1 a joint, a seam. 2 the point of junction of two sides of anything separated, or of two similar organs, such as the hemispheres of the brain. 3 a suture. 4 a line of closure, as of the eyelids, lips, mandibles etc. 5 (*Archit.*) the joint of two stones. 6 the application of one surface to another. 7 (*Bot.*) the line of junction of two parts of a plant. **commissural** (-sūə´-) *a.* [L *commissūra*, from *commissus*, p.p. of *committere* (see COMMIT)]

commit (kəmit´) *v.t.* (*pres.p.* **committing,** *past, p.p.* **committed**) 1 to entrust, to deposit, to consign. 2 to perpetrate (*to commit a crime*). 3 to refer (a bill etc.) to a committee. 4 (*Law*) to send for trial or to prison. 5 to assign, to pledge. **to commit oneself** 1 to pledge or bind oneself. 2 to involve or compromise oneself. **to commit to memory** to learn by heart. **commitment** *n.* 1 the act of committing. 2 the state of being committed. 3 the delivery of a prisoner to the charge of the prison authorities. 4 an engagement to carry out certain duties or meet certain expenses. **commitment ring** *n.* a ring worn to show a committed relationship to a person to whom one is not married. **committable** *a.* **committal** *n.* 1 a sending for trial, to prison, to a mental hospital etc. 2 the burial or cremation of a corpse. **committed** *a.* 1 morally or politically dedicated. 2 obliged. **committer** *n.* [L *committere* (COM-, *mittere*, to send)]

committee[1] (kəmit´i) *n.* a board elected or deputed to examine, consider, and report on any business referred to them. **committee man, committee woman** *n.* (*pl.* **committee men, committee women**) a member of a committee. **Committee of the Whole House** *n.* the House of Commons sitting informally as a committee to discuss a bill. **Committee of Ways and Means** *n.* a committee of the House of Commons for considering proposed taxes etc. **committee stage** *n.* in Parliament, the stage at which a bill is examined in detail and may be amended. [late A-F (F *commis*), p.p. of *commettre*, L *committere*, as COMMIT]

committee[2] (komitē´) *n.* (*Law*) a person to whom the care of another person or their property is committed.

committer COMMIT.

commix (kəmiks´) *v.t., v.i.* (*poet.*) to mix together, to blend. **commixtion** (-chən) *n.* **commixture** (-chə) *n.*

commode (kəmōd´) *n.* **1** a night commode. **2** a chest of drawers. **3** a chiffonier. **4** (*N Am.*) a lavatory. **5** a headdress worn by women in the 17th cent. [F, from L *commodus*, convenient (*modus*, measure)]

commodify (kəmod´ifī) *v.t.* (*3rd pers. sing. pres.* **commodifies,** *pres.p.* **commodifying,** *past, p.p.* **commodified**) to turn into or treat as a commodity. **commodification** (-fikā´shən) *n.* [COMMODITY, -FY]

commodious (kəmō´diəs) *a.* **1** roomy. **2** †convenient, suited to its purpose. **commodiously** *adv.* **commodiousness** *n.* [OF *commodieux*, late L *commodiōsus*, for L *commodus*, as COMMODE]

commodity (kəmod´iti) *n.* (*pl.* **commodities**) **1** an article of commerce, a product or raw material that can be bought and sold. **2** something that is useful or convenient. **3** advantage, profit. **4** †convenience, expediency. **commoditization** (-īzā´shən), **commoditisation** *n.* the mass production of previously scarce or expensive consumer goods. [F *commodité*, L *commoditās* (*commodus*, see COMMODE)]

commodore (kom´ədaw) *n.* **1** an officer ranking above captain and below rear-admiral. **2** by courtesy, the senior captain when two or more warships are in company. **3** the president of a yacht club. **4** a captain of pilots. **5** the leading ship or the senior captain of a fleet of merchantmen. **Commodore-in-Chief** *n.* the supreme officer of the Royal Air Force. [formerly *commandore* (etym. obscure, from L *commandāre*, COMMAND)]

common (kom´ən) *a.* (*comp.* **commoner,** *superl.* **commonest**) **1** belonging equally to more than one. **2** open or free to all. **3** of, relating to or affecting the public. **4** often met with, ordinary, usual, familiar. **5** of low rank, position or birth. **6** vulgar. **7** inferior, mean. **8** (*Math.*) belonging to several quantities. **9** (*Gram.*) applicable to a whole class. **10** (of a syllable) variable in quantity. **11** (*Law*) of lesser importance. ~*n.* **1** a tract of open ground, the common property of all members of a community. **2** (*Law*) **a** conjoint possession. **b** right of common. **3** (*sl.*) common sense. **4** a religious service used on various occasions. **in common** shared with another or others (*They have nothing in common*). **in common with** the same way as, like. **out of the common** extraordinary, unusual. **to make common cause** CAUSE. **commonable** *a.* **1** (of land) held in common. **2** (of sheep, cattle etc.) that may be pastured on common land. **commonage** *n.* **1** the right of using anything in common. **2** the right of pasturing cattle etc. on a common. **3** common property in land. **4** anything held in common. **5** the common people. **common carrier** *n.* a person or company transporting goods or people for hire. **common chord** *n.* a note accompanied by its third and fifth. **common cold** *n.* a viral infection of the mucous membranes of the respiratory tract, accompanied by sneezing and coughing. **common crier** *n.* the public or town crier. **common denominator** *n.* **1** (*Math.*) a number that can be divided by the denominators of each of a group of fractions without remainder. **2** a feature shared by all members of a group. **commoner** *n.* **1** any one of the common people. **2** a person having a joint right in common ground. **3** a student at certain universities or schools who does not have a scholarship. **Common Era** *n.* the Christian era. **common factor** *n.* (*Math.*) a number that is a factor of two or more given quantities. **common ground** *n.* matter in a discussion accepted by both sides. **common hamster** *n.* the hamster *Cricetus cricetus.* **commonhold** *n.* the freehold tenure of one of a block of flats, the occupants of which have joint responsibility for certain services. **commonholder** *n.* **commonish** *a.* **common jury** *n.* (*pl.* **common juries**) (*Law*) a petty jury to try all cases. **common knowledge** *n.* something widely known. **common law** *n.* law based on usage or precedent rather than statutes. **common-law husband, common-law wife** *n.* a person recognized as a husband or wife after long cohabitation. **common logarithm** *n.* a logarithm to the base ten. **commonly** *adv.* **1** usually, frequently. **2** in an ordinary manner. **3** in a vulgar manner. **Common Market** *n.* the European Community. **common measure** *n.* **1** (*Mus.*) common time, two or four beats to the bar, esp. four crotchets to the bar. **2** the usual form of a ballad stanza, having four iambic lines. **3** (*Math.*) a common factor. **common metre** *n.* a metre for hymns, four lines of 8, 6, 8, 6 syllables. **common multiple** *n.* any number containing two or more numbers an exact number of times without a remainder. **commonness** *n.* **common noun, common name** *n.* the name of any one of a class of objects or concepts, as distinct from a *proper noun* or *proper name.* **common or garden** *a.* (*coll.*) ordinary. **common people** *n.pl.* ordinary people, as opposed to the nobility or aristocracy. **Common Prayer** *n.* the liturgy of the Church of England. **common property** *n.* something generally known. **common room** *n.* **1** a room in a college or school used by teachers or students for social purposes. **2** the people who use such a room. **common salt** *n.* sodium chloride. **common seal**[1] *n.* a seal of northern oceans, *Phoca vitulina.* **common seal**[2] *n.* the official seal of a corporate body. **common sense** *n.* sound practical judgement. **common-sense, commonsensical** *a.* marked by common sense. **Common Serjeant** *n.* the judge of the City of London ranking next to the Recorder. **common soldier** *n.* a private or non-commissioned officer. **common stock** *n.* (*N Am.*) ordinary shares. **common time** *n.* (*Mus.*) time with two or four beats, esp. four crotchets. **common valerian** *n.* the plant *Valeriana officianalis.* **common weal** *n.* the welfare or prosperity of the community. **†commonweal** *n.* **1** the common weal. **2** a commonwealth. **common year** *n.* a period of 365 days. [OF *comun*, L *commūnis* (*-mūnis*, bound, earlier *moenis*, obliging, ready to serve)]

commonality (komənal´iti) *n.* (*pl.* **commonalities**) **1** commonness; being shared by a number of individuals. **2** a common occurrence. **3** commonalty. [COMMONALTY]

commonalty (kom´ənəlti) *n.* (*pl.* **commonalties**) **1** the common people. **2** mankind in general. **3** a commonwealth. **4** a corporation. [OF *comunalté*, from *comunal*, L *communālis*]

commonplace (kom´ənplās) *a.* common, trivial, trite, unoriginal. ~*n.* **1** a trite remark, a platitude. **2** a general idea or topic. **3** anything occurring frequently or habitually. **4** a passage entered in a commonplace book. **commonplace book** *n.* a book in which thoughts, extracts from books etc. are entered for future use. **commonplaceness** *n.* [cp. L *locus communis*, a common topic]

commons (kom´ənz) *n.pl.* **1** the common people, esp. as part of a political system. **2** (**Commons**) the House of Commons. **3** food, esp. shared in common. **4** a ration or allowance of food.

commonweal COMMON.

commonwealth (kom´ənwelth) *n.* **1** the whole body of citizens, the body politic. **2** a free or independent state. **3** a republic. **4** (*fig.*) a body of persons having common interests. **5** (**Commonwealth**) the Commonwealth of Nations. **6** (*Hist.*) (**Commonwealth**) the form or period of republican government in England from 1649 to 1660. **7** (**Commonwealth**) the federation of Australian states. **8** †the common weal. **Commonwealth Day** *n.* a day formerly celebrated as a holiday throughout the British Commonwealth (orig. 24 May, Queen Victoria's birthday). **Commonwealth of Nations** *n.* a loose association of states that have been, or are, ruled by Britain. [cp. L *res publica*]

commotion (kəmō´shən) *n.* **1** violent motion. **2** agitation, excitement. **3** a noisy disturbance. **4** a popular tumult or insurrection. [OF *comocion*, L *commōtio -ōnem* (*motio*, from *movēre*, to move)]
commove (kəmoov´) *v.t.* to disturb, to agitate, to excite. [F *commovoir*, L *commovēre*, as COMMOTION]
commune[1] (kom´ūn) *n.* **1** a group of people, not related, living together and sharing property and responsibilities. **2** the house used by such a group. **3** a small territorial district, esp. in France or Belgium, governed by a mayor and council. **4** the inhabitants or members of the council of such a district. **communal** (kom´ūnəl, kəmū´nəl) *a.* **1** for common use or benefit; shared. **2** of or relating to a commune. **3** of or relating to the Paris Commune. **4** of or relating to the community. **5** between different communities. **communalism** *n.* **1** the theory of government by communes of towns and districts. **2** the theory or practice of living in communes. **communalist** *n.* **communalistic** (-lis´-) *a.* **communality** (-nal´-) *n.* **communalize, communalise** *v.t.* **communalization** (-zā´shən) *n.* **communally** *adv.* **communard** (-nahd) *n.* **1** a person who lives in a commune. **2** (*Hist.*) an adherent of the Paris Commune. [F, from late L *commūnia*, neut. pl. of *commūnis*, COMMON]
commune[2] (kəmūn´) *v.i.* **1** to converse together familiarly or intimately. **2** to be or feel spiritually close to (*to commune with nature*). **3** (*N Am.*) to receive Holy Communion. **communer** *n.* [OF *comunier*, L *commūnicāre* (*commūnis*, COMMON)]
commune[3] (kom´ūn) *n.* **1** intimate conversation. **2** communion. [COMMUNE[2]]
communicate (kəmū´nikāt) *v.t.* **1** to pass on, to transmit. **2** to convey (information etc.) by speech, writing, signals etc. **3** to impart, to reveal. **4** to give Holy Communion to. *~v.i.* **1** to convey information, esp. by speech or writing. **2** to share feelings etc. **3** to establish mutual understanding (with someone). **4** to be connected (with), esp. by a common door. **5** to receive Holy Communion. **communicable** *a.* capable of being transmitted or passed on (*a communicable disease*). **communicability** (-bil´-), **communicableness** *n.* **communicably** *adv.* **communicant** *a.* communicating. *~n.* **1** a person who receives Holy Communion. **2** a person who communicates information etc. **communicating door** *n.* a common door that connects two rooms. **communication** (-ā´shən) *n.* **1** the act of communicating. **2** that which is communicated. **3** news, information. **4** conversation or correspondence. **5** a means of passing from one place to another. **6** a connecting link. **7** (*pl.*) the means of communicating considered collectively (e.g. telecommunications, the press etc.). **8** the science of this. **9** (*pl., Mil.*) a system of routes and vehicles for transport. **communication cord** *n.* a device whereby a passenger can stop a train in an emergency. **communications satellite, communication satellite** *n.* an artificial satellite orbiting the earth and relaying television, telephone etc. signals. **communication theory** *n.* the study of methods of transmitting information. **communicative** *a.* **1** inclined or ready to communicate. **2** talkative, not reserved. **communicatively** *adv.* **communicativeness** *n.* **communicator** *n.* **communicatory** *a.* [L *commūnicāre* (*commūnis*, COMMON)]
communion (kəmūn´yən) *n.* **1** the act of communicating or communing. **2** participation, sharing. **3** fellowship, social intercourse. **4** (**Communion**) **a** Holy Communion. **b** the act of participating in the Eucharist. **5** union in religious faith. **6** a religious body. *~a.* (**Communion**) of or relating to Holy Communion or the Eucharist (*Communion rail*; *Communion cup*). **communion of saints** *n.* the fellowship of all Christians, living or dead. **Communion service** *n.* the service used at the celebration of the Eucharist. **Communion table** *n.* the table or altar used in the celebration of the Eucharist. [F, from L *commūnio -ōnem* (*commūnis*, COMMON)]
communiqué (komū´nikā) *n.* an official announcement. [F]
communism (kom´ūnizm) *n.* **1** a theory of government based on common ownership of all property and means of production. **2** (*usu.* **Communism**) the system of government, based on Marxist socialism, formerly practised in the USSR etc. **3** communalism. **communist** *n.* **1** an adherent or advocate of communism. **2** (*usu.* **Communist**) a member of a Communist Party. *~a.* (*also* **Communist**) of or relating to communism. **communistic** (-nis´-) *a.* **communize, communise** *v.t.* to make communal or communistic. **communization** (-zā´shən) *n.* [L *commūnis*, common]
communitarian (kəmūniteə´riən) *n.* a member of a community, esp. a communist community. *~a.* of or relating to such a community.
community (kəmū´niti) *n.* (*pl.* **communities**) **1** a body of people living in a particular place. **2** a body of individuals having common interests, occupation, religion, nationality etc. **3** society at large, the public. **4** an organized body, municipal, national, social or political. **5** a body of individuals living in a common home. **6** (*also* **Community**) a body of nations (*the European Community*). **7** common possession or liability. **8** fellowship. **9** similarity of nature or character. **10** a set of interdependent plants and animals inhabiting an area. **community architect** *n.* an architect who designs housing etc. in consultation with the local community. **community architecture** *n.* **community care** *n.* the provision of care or assistance for the sick, the elderly etc. in their own homes, rather than in residential institutions. **community centre** *n.* a building open to all residents in the locality for social, recreational and educational activities. **community charge** *n.* (*Hist.*) a flat-rate tax levied on all adults to raise money for local government, a type of poll tax. **community chest** *n.* (*esp. N Am.*) a fund for welfare work in a community raised by voluntary contributions. **community college** *n.* a centre providing educational facilities for all members of the community. **community home** *n.* a residential centre for young offenders. **community policing** *n.* the policy of assigning police officers to an area where they are known or with which they are familiar. **community policeman, community policewoman** *n.* **community radio** *n.* radio broadcasting to a smaller audience than local radio, to a town or part of a city. **community service** *n.* work for the benefit of the community, esp. as stipulated under a community service order. **community service order** *n.* a form of sentence ordering a convicted person to work for a specified time for the benefit of the community. **community singing** *n.* organized singing by the audience at a social gathering etc. **community spirit** *n.* a sense of fellowship within a community. **community worker** *n.* a person who works for the welfare of a community. [OF *communeté*, L *commūnitātem*, acc. of *commūnitās* (*commūnis*, COMMON)]
communize, communization COMMUNISM.
commute (kəmūt´) *v.t.* **1** to exchange or interchange. **2** to substitute (one payment, punishment etc.) for another. **3** to reduce the severity of (a punishment). **4** to commutate. *~v.i.* **1** to travel some distance daily to and from one's place of work. **2** (*Math.*) to have a commutative relationship. **commutable** *a.* **1** that can be commuted. **2** within commuting distance. **commutability** (-bil´-) *n.* **commutate** (kom´ūtāt) *v.t.* **1** to reverse the direction of (an electric current). **2** to convert (an alternating current) to a direct current. **commutation** (-tā´shən) *n.* **1** the act of commuting or commutating. **2** change, exchange. **3** a payment made in

commuting. 4 (*Law*) the substitution of a lesser penalty for a greater. 5 (*Math.*) the act of reversing the order of two quantities. **commutative** (kəmū´-, kom´ū-) *a.* 1 of or relating to commutation. 2 (*Math.*) giving the same result when the order of quantities is reversed. **commutatively** *adv.* **commutator** (kom´-) *n.* **commutator transformer** *n.* a device for converting direct current from low to high voltage and vice versa. **commuter** *n.* a person who commutes to and from work. ~*a.* of or relating to commuters (*commuter traffic; the commuter belt*). [L *commūtāre, mūtāre*, to change)]

comose COMATE.

comp (komp) *n.* (*coll.*) 1 a competition. 2 (*Print.*) a compositor. 3 (*Mus.*) an accompaniment. ~*v.i.* 1 (*Print.*) to work as a compositor. 2 (*Mus.*) to play an accompaniment. ~*v.t.* 1 (*Print.*) to work as a compositor on. 2 (*Mus.*) to accompany. [abbr.]

comp. *abbr.* 1 company. 2 comparative. 3 compare. 4 comparison. 5 compiler. 6 composer. 7 compound. 8 comprehensive.

compact[1] (kəmpakt´) *a.* 1 closely packed or fitted together. 2 small and practical (*a compact camera*). 3 (of a person) small and well-proportioned. 4 solid. 5 succinct. ~*v.t.* 1 to consolidate. 2 to join or pack closely and firmly together. 3 to condense. 4 to compose. **compact disc** (kom´pakt) *n.* a small disc, read by laser beam, on which sound or information is stored digitally. **compact disc player** *n.* a machine for playing compact discs. **compacted** *a.* **compaction** *n.* **compactly** *adv.* **compactness** *n.* **compacture** (-chə) *n.* 1 compact structure. 2 close union of parts. **compact video disc** *n.* a compact disc on which both pictures and sound are stored. [L *compactus*, p.p. of *compingere* (*pangere*, to fasten)]

compact[2] (kom´pakt) *n.* 1 a small flat case containing face powder, puff and mirror. 2 (*N Am.*) a middle-sized motor car. 3 a compact mass of powder. [COMPACT[1]]

compact[3] (kom´pakt) *n.* an agreement, a bargain, a covenant. [L *compactus*, p.p. of *compacīsci* (*pacīsci*, to covenant)]

compadre (kompah´dri) *n.* (*N Am., coll.*) a friend. [Sp., godfather]

compages (kəmpā´jēz) *n.* (*pl.* **compages**) a structure or system of many parts united. [L, joining together (*pag-*, root of *pangere*, as COMPACT[1])]

☒ **compair** common misspelling of COMPARE.

companion[1] (kəmpan´yən) *n.* 1 a person who associates with or accompanies another (*a travelling companion*). 2 a comrade. 3 a partner. 4 a person employed to live with another. 5 (**Companion**) a member of the lowest grade in some orders of knighthood. 6 a handbook. 7 a thing that matches or goes with another; one of a pair. 8 a piece of equipment with several uses. 9 (*Astron.*) a star that accompanies another; the fainter component of a double star. ~*a.* 1 accompanying. 2 matching. ~*v.t.* to accompany. ~*v.i.* to associate or keep company (with). **companionable** *a.* 1 fit to be a companion. 2 sociable. **companionableness** *n.* **companionably** *adv.* †**companionage** *n.* **companionate** *a.* 1 of, like or acting as a companion. 2 well-suited; well-matched. **companion-in-arms** *n.* a fellow soldier. **companionless** *a.* **Companion of Honour** *n.* a member of an order instituted in 1917. **Companion of Literature** *n.* a member of an order instituted in 1961. **companion set** *n.* a set of fire-irons on a stand. **companionship** *n.* fellowship, association, company. [OF *compaignon*, late L *compānio -ōnem* (*pānis*, bread)]

companion[2] (kəmpan´yən) *n.* (*Naut.*) 1 the raised window frame on the quarterdeck through which light passes to the cabins and decks below. 2 a companionway. **companion hatch** *n.* a covering over the entrance to a cabin. **companion hatchway** *n.* an opening leading to a cabin. **companion ladder** *n.* a ladder leading from a cabin to the quarterdeck. **companionway** *n.* a staircase between a cabin and the quarterdeck. [ult. from L *compānāticum*, provisions (cp. Dut. *kompanje*, OF *compagne*, It. *compagna, camera della compagna*, provision room or pantry)]

company (kŭm´pəni) *n.* (*pl.* **companies**) 1 society, companionship, fellowship. 2 a number of people associated together for carrying on a business. 3 a corporation. 4 a number of people assembled; an audience. 5 guests, visitors. 6 a body of actors etc. 7 a subdivision of an infantry regiment under the command of a captain. ~†*v.t.* (*3rd pers. sing. pres.* **companies,** *pres.p.* **companying,** *past, p.p.* **companied**) to accompany. ~*v.i.* (*poet.*) to associate (with), to be a companion. **in company** with others, not alone. **in company with** together with. **to be in good company** to discover that others have done the same as oneself. **to keep company (with)** 1 to associate (with). 2 to court. **to keep someone company** to go or be with someone. **to part company** PART. **company car** *n.* a car provided for the use of an employee on company business (and often also for private use). **company doctor** *n.* 1 a consultant who improves the profitability of ailing companies. 2 a medical practitioner employed by a company to provide healthcare for the staff. **company officer** *n.* a captain or a commissioned officer of lower rank. **Company of Jesus** *n.* the Jesuits. **company promoter** *n.* a person who promotes a joint-stock company. **company secretary** *n.* the chief administrative officer of a company. **company sergeant major** *n.* (*Mil.*) the highest-ranking non-commissioned officer of a company. [OF *compaignie*, from *compaignon*, see COMPANION[1]]

comparable COMPARE.

comparative (kəmpar´ətiv) *a.* 1 of or involving comparison. 2 estimated by comparison. 3 grounded on comparison. 4 (*Gram.*) expressing comparison, expressing a higher or lower degree of a quality (*a comparative adjective*). ~*n.* (*Gram.*) the comparative degree or the word or inflection expressing it. **comparatively** *adv.* **comparator** *n.* an apparatus for comparing something with a standard. [as COMPARE]

compare (kəmpeə´) *v.t.* 1 to liken (one thing to another) (*He has been compared to Nureyev*). 2 to see how (one thing) agrees with or resembles another (*Compare her essay with mine*). 3 to see how (two things) resemble each other or are related. 4 (*Gram.*) to inflect according to degrees of comparison. ~*v.i.* to bear comparison (with). ~*n.* (*poet.*) 1 comparison. 2 an equal. **beyond compare** peerless, unequalled. **to compare notes** to exchange information or opinions. **comparable** (kom´pə-) *a.* 1 capable of being compared (with). 2 worthy of being compared (to). **comparability** (kompərəbil´-, kəmparəbil´-), **comparableness** *n.* **comparably** *adv.* [OF *comparer*, L *comparāre* (COM-, *par*, equal)]

Usage note The pronunciation of *comparable* as (-par´-), with stress on the second syllable, is best avoided.

---

comparison (kəmpar´isən) *n.* 1 the act of comparing. 2 a comparative estimate. 3 a simile, contrast or illustration. 4 similarity. 5 (*Gram.*) the degrees of comparison. **beyond comparison** 1 totally different. 2 beyond compare. **degree of comparison** DEGREE. **in/ by comparison with** compared with. **to bear/ stand comparison (with)** to be as good (as) or better (than). [OF *comparaison*, L *comparātio -ōnem*, as COMPARE]

compartment (kəmpaht´mənt) *n.* 1 a division. 2 a portion of a railway carriage, room etc., separated from the other parts. 3 a portion of the hold of a ship shut off by a bulkhead and capable of being made watertight. 4 any part separated or kept separate from other parts, as in a desk, the mind etc. **compartmental** (kompahtmen´-) *a.* **compartmentalize, compartmentalise** *v.t.* to divide into separate units or categories. **compartmentalization** (-zā´shən) *n.* **compartmentally** *adv.* [F *compartiment*, It. *compartimento*, from late L *compartīre*, (COM-, *partire*, from *pars*, *-tis*, part)]

compass (kŭm´pəs) *n.* **1** an instrument indicating magnetic north, used to ascertain direction, to determine the course of a ship or aeroplane etc. **2** a mariner's compass. **3** (*usu. pl.*) a pair of compasses. **4** a circle, a circumference. **5** area, extent. **6** reach, capacity. **7** the range or power of the voice or a musical instrument. **8** a circuit, a roundabout course. ~*v.t.* **1** to go round. **2** to besiege, to surround, to hem in. **3** to comprehend. **4** to accomplish, to contrive. **pair of compasses** PAIR. **to set compass** SET[1]. **compassable** *a.* **compass card** *n.* the card or dial of a magnetic compass on which the points are drawn. **compass needle** *n.* the needle of a magnetic compass. **compass rose** *n.* a circle showing the points of the compass marked or printed on a map or chart. **compass saw** *n.* a saw for cutting curves. **compass window** *n.* a semicircular bay window. [F *compas*, a circle, a round, a pair of compasses, late L *compassus*, a circle, a circuit; later, a pair of compasses (cp. *compassāre*, to pace round, encompass; relation to *compassus* obscure)]

compassion (kəmpash´ən) *n.* pity, sympathy for the sufferings and sorrows of others. **compassionable** *a.* **compassionate** (-ət) *a.* merciful, inclined to pity, sympathetic. **compassionate leave** *n.* leave granted on account of bereavement, domestic difficulties etc. **compassionately** *adv.* **compassionateness** *n.* **compassion fatigue** *n.* the state of being unwilling or no longer willing to contribute to charities because of the sheer number or frequency of charitable appeals. [OF, from L *compassio -ōnem*, from *compatī* (COM-, *patī*, to suffer)]

compatible (kəmpat´ibəl) *a.* **1** able to co-exist, well-matched or well-suited. **2** congruous, consistent, harmonious. **3** (of electronic machinery of different types or by different manufacturers) able to work together without modification. ~*n.* a compatible piece of electronic machinery. **compatibility** (-bil´-) *n.* **compatibly** *adv.* [F, from late L *compatibilis*, from *compatī*, see COMPASSION]

compatriot (kəmpat´riət) *n.* a fellow countryman. **compatriotic** (-ot´-) *a.* **compatriotism** *n.* [F *compatriote*]

compeer (kom´piə, kəmpiə´) *n.* **1** an equal, a peer. **2** a comrade, a companion. [prob. from an OF *comper*, L *compar*]

compel (kəmpel´) *v.t.* (*pres.p.* **compelling**, *past, p.p.* **compelled**) **1** to force, to oblige (*We were compelled to agree*). **2** to cause or exact by force (*to compel obedience*). **3** †to drive with force. **compellable** *a.* (*Law*) (of a witness) who may be forced to give evidence. **compelling** *a.* arousing strong interest or admiration. **compellingly** *adv.* [OF *compeller*, L *compellere* (*pellere*, to drive)]

compendium (kəmpen´diəm) *n.* (*pl.* **compendiums, compendia** (-diə)) **1** a handbook or reference book. **2** an abridgement. **3** an epitome, a summary. **4** a brief compilation. **5** a collection of board or card games in one box. **6** any similar collection or package. **compendious** *a.* **1** summed up concisely, succinct. **2** abridged. **3** summary. **4** comprehensive but brief. **compendiously** *adv.* **compendiousness** *n.* [L, from *compendere* (*pendere*, to hang, weigh)]

compensate (kom´pənsāt) *v.t.* **1** to recompense. **2** to make amends for. **3** to counterbalance. **4** in mechanics, to provide with an equivalent weight or other device forming a compensation. ~*v.i.* **1** to make amends (for). **2** (*Psych.*) to make up for a perceived or imagined deficiency by developing another aspect of the personality. **compensation** (-sā´shən) *n.* **1** the act of compensating. **2** payment, recompense, amends. **3** that which balances or is an equivalent for something else. **4** (*Psych.*) the act or result of compensating. **5** (*N Am.*) salary, wages. **compensational** *a.* **compensation balance, compensation pendulum** *n.* a balance wheel or pendulum constructed so as to make equal time beats despite changes of temperature. **compensative** (kom´pənsətiv, kəmpen´-) *a.* compensating. ~*n.* an equivalent. **compensator** *n.* **compensatory** (kəmpen´sətəri, kompənsā´-) *a.* [L *compensātus*, p.p. of *compensāre* (*pensāre*, freq. of *pendere*, to weigh)]

compère (kom´peə), **compere** *n.* a person who introduces the items in a stage or broadcast entertainment. ~*v.t.* to act as compère of. ~*v.i.* to act as compère. [F]

compete (kəmpēt´) *v.i.* **1** to contend as a rival (with). **2** to strive in emulation. **3** to take part (in a race, contest etc.) (*to compete in marathon*). [F *compéter*, L *competere* (*petere*, to fall upon, to aim at)]

competent (kom´pitənt) *a.* **1** qualified, capable, suitable. **2** sufficient, adequate. **3** (*Law*) legally qualified (*a competent witness*). **competence, competency** *n.* **1** the state of being competent. **2** ability, skill. **3** adequate income or financial support. **4** the innate ability to acquire and understand language. **5** legal capacity or qualification. **6** admissibility (of evidence). **competently** *adv.* [F from L *competens -entem*, pres.p. of *competere*, COMPETE]

competition (kompətish´ən) *n.* **1** the act of competing. **2** a competitive game, contest etc. **3** rivalry. **4** the struggle for existence or superiority in industry or commerce. **5** the people or organizations competing against one. **6** (*Biol.*) the struggle between organisms sharing restricted or inadequate resources. **competitive** (-pet´-) *a.* **1** of, relating to or involving competition. **2** liking competition, keen to compete. **3** (of prices etc.) giving one an advantage over rivals. **competitively** *adv.* **competitiveness** *n.* **competitor** (-pet´-) *n.* **1** a person who competes. **2** a rival. [L *competitio*, from *competere*, COMPETE]

compile (kəmpīl´) *v.t.* **1** to compose using material from various authors or sources (*to compile an anthology*). **2** to assemble (various items) as in a list or dictionary. **3** to gather such items into (*to compile an index*). **4** to accumulate. **5** (*Comput.*) to put (a program or instruction written in a high-level language) into machine code. **compilation** (kompilā´shən) *n.* **1** the act of compiling. **2** that which is compiled. **3** a book for which the material has been drawn from various authors or sources. **compiler** *n.* **1** a person who compiles. **2** (*Comput.*) a program that compiles. [OF *compiler*, L *compīlāre*, to plunder, to pillage (COM-, *pīlāre*, to thrust, from *pīlum*, a javelin)]

complacent (kəmplā´sənt) *a.* **1** smug, self-satisfied. **2** satisfied, gratified. **complacency, complacence** *n.* **1** smugness. **2** a feeling of inward satisfaction. **complacently** *adv.* [L *complacens -ntem*, pres.p. of *complacēre* (COM-, *placēre*, to please)]

Usage note See note under COMPLAISANT.

complain (kəmplān´) *v.i.* **1** to express dissatisfaction or objection. **2** to state a grievance. **3** to make a charge. **4** to murmur, to find fault. **5** to express pain or suffering (*He complained of backache*). **6** to express grief, to moan or wail. ~*v.t.* to state as a complaint. **complainant** *n.* **1** a person who complains or makes a complaint. **2** (*Law*) a plaintiff. **complainer** *n.* **complaining** *a.*, *n.* **complainingly** *adv.* **complaint** *n.* **1** an expression of grievance or dissatisfaction (*to make a complaint*). **2** the subject or ground of such expression. **3** an ailment. **4** an accusation. **5** (*Law*) a formal allegation or charge. [OF *complaign-*, stem of *complaindre*, late L *complangere* (COM-, *plangere*, to bewail)]

complaisant (kəmplā´zənt) *a.* **1** courteous, deferential. **2** acquiescent, obliging. **complaisance** *n.* **complaisantly** *adv.* [F from *complais-*, stem of *complaire*, from L *complacēre* (see COMPLACENT)]

Usage note The adjectives *complaisant* and *complacent* should not be confused: a complacent person is pleased with themselves, but a complaisant person is agreeable to others.

compleat (kəmplēt´) *a.* **1** †complete. **2** skilled, accomplished (from Izaak Walton's *The Compleat Angler*).

complement[1] (kom´pliment) *n.* **1** that which is necessary to make something complete. **2** either of a pair of things that go together. **3** the full number required to man a vessel. **4** full quantity. **5** (*Gram.*) a word or phrase required to complete the predicate. **6** (*Mus.*) the interval necessary to complete an octave. **7** (*Math.*) the difference between a given angle or arc and 90°. **8** (*Math.*) the difference between a number and the next higher power of ten. **9** the class of things that do not belong to a given set. **10** in immunology, a group of proteins in the blood that combine with antibodies to destroy bacteria etc. **complemental** (-men´-) *a.* **complementally** *adv.* **complementary** (-men´-) *a.* that forms a complement. **complementarity** (-tar´iti) *n.* (*pl.* **complementarities**) **1** a state or relationship involving complementary elements. **2** (*Physics*) the principle that more than one theory may be required to describe or explain a phenomenon. **complementary angle** *n.* either of two angles that together make 90°. **complementary colour** *n.* either of two colours that produce white when mixed together. **complementary medicine** *n.* alternative medicine. [L *complēmentum*, from *complēre* (*plēre*, to fill)]

Usage note The spellings of *complement* and *compliment* (and their derivatives) should not be confused. The meanings related to *complete* are spelt *complEment* with an *e* like *complete*; the expression of praise or approval is a *complIment*.

complement[2] (kom´pliment) *v.t.* **1** to be a complement to. **2** to complete. **complementation** (-tā´shən) *n.*

complete (kəmplēt´) *a.* **1** finished (*The work is complete*). **2** entire, free from deficiency (*a complete set*). **3** absolute (*complete confidence*). **4** skilled, highly accomplished. ~*v.t.* **1** to finish. **2** to bring to a state of perfection. **3** to make whole, to make up the deficiencies of. **4** to fill in the required information on (a questionnaire, a form etc.). **5** (*Law*) to conclude (a sale of land, property etc.). **complete with** having (an important or desirable accessory). **completely** *adv.* **completeness** *n.* **completion** *n.* **completist** *n.* a person who collects things obsessively or without discrimination. ~*a.* of or relating to such a person. **completive** *a.* [L *complētus*, p.p. of *complēre*, as COMPLEMENT[1]]

complex (kom´pleks) *a.* **1** composed of several parts, composite. **2** complicated. ~*n.* **1** a set of interconnected buildings for related purposes, forming a whole. **2** any complicated whole. **3** a complicated system or network of parts. **4** a collection. **5** a group of emotions, ideas etc., partly or wholly repressed, which can influence personality or behaviour (*an inferiority complex*). **6** an obsession. **7** (*Chem.*) a compound in which molecules, ions etc. are linked or attached by co-ordinate bonds. **complexity** (-plek´siti) *n.* (*pl.* **complexities**). **complexly** *adv.* **complexness** *n.* **complex number** *n.* a number consisting of real and imaginary components. **complex sentence** *n.* a sentence consisting of a main clause and at least one subordinate clause. **complexus** (-plek´səs) *n.* **1** a complex. **2** (*Anat.*) a long, broad muscle lying along the back and side of the neck. [L *complexus*, p.p. of *complectere*, to entwine]

complexion (kəmplek´shən) *n.* **1** the colour and appearance of the skin, esp. of the face. **2** nature, character, aspect. **3** †the temperament or constitution. **complexioned** *a.* (*usu. in comb.*). **complexionless** *a.* [F, from L *complexio -ōnem*, a comprehending; later, a bodily habit or combination of qualities (*complectere*, as COMPLEX)]

complexity, complexus COMPLEX.

compliable COMPLY.

compliance (kəmplī´əns) *n.* **1** the act of complying. **2** submission, agreement, consent. **3** the capacity of a mechanical system to yield to an applied force. **in compliance with** in accordance with. **compliant** *a.* **1** yielding. **2** tending to comply. **compliantly** *adv.* [COMPLY]

complicate (kom´plikāt) *v.t.* **1** to make complex or intricate. **2** to involve. **complicacy** *n.* the state of being complicated. **complicated** *a.* **complicatedly** *adv.* **complicatedness** *n.* **complication** (-ā´shən) *n.* **1** the act of complicating. **2** the state of being complicated. **3** a complicated or complicating matter or circumstance. **4** a disease or condition arising in the course of another. [L *complicātus*, p.p. of *complicāre* (*plicāre*, to fold)]

complicity (kəmplis´əti) *n.* participation, partnership, esp. in wrongdoing. **complicit** *a.* [F *complicité*, from *complice*, from L *complex -icem*, confederate]

complier COMPLY.

compliment[1] (kom´pliment) *n.* **1** an expression or act of praise, courtesy, respect or regard. **2** (*pl.*) ceremonious greetings, courtesies, respects. **3** (*pl.*) praise. **4** †a favour, a gift, a gratuity. **to pay a compliment** to utter or perform a compliment. **to return the compliment** **1** to pay a compliment in return for one received. **2** to retaliate in kind. **complimental** (-men´-) *a.* **complimentary** (-men´-) *a.* **1** expressing praise. **2** given free of charge. **complimentarily** *adv.* **complimentary ticket** *n.* a free ticket. **compliments of the season** *n.pl.* greetings appropriate to the season, esp. Christmas. **compliments slip** *n.* a printed slip accompanying a gift etc. sent by a business company. [F, from It. *complimento*, from L *complēmentum*, COMPLEMENT[1] (perh. through Sp. *complimiento*, fulfilment of courtesies)]

Usage note See note under COMPLEMENT[1].

compliment[2] (kom´pliment) *v.t.* **1** to pay compliments to. **2** to congratulate, to praise, to flatter courteously.

compline (kom´plin, -plīn) *n.* in the Roman Catholic Church, the last part of the divine office of the breviary, sung after vespers. [ME and OF *complie*, L *complēta* (*hōra*), fem. of *complētus*, COMPLETE, because it completed the hours of daily service]

comply (kəmplī´) *v.i.* (*3rd pers. sing. pres.* **complies,** *pres.p.* **complying,** *past, p.p.* **complied**) **1** to act or be in accordance (with rules, wishes etc.) (*The design does not comply with our specifications*). **2** to assent, to agree. **compliable** *a.* compliant. **complier** *n.* [It. *complire*, from Sp. *complir* (now *cumplir*), to complete (cp. COMPLIMENT[1])]

compo[1] (kom´pō) *n.* (*pl.* **compos**) any of various compounds, such as a kind of stucco. **compo rations** *n.pl.* (*Mil.*) rations for several days for use in the field. [COMPOSITION]

compo[2] (kom´pō) *n.* (*pl.* **compos**) (*Austral., New Zeal., sl.*) compensation for injury etc. [abbr.]

component (kəmpō´nənt) *a.* serving to make up a compound or a larger whole, constituent. ~*n.* **1** a constituent part. **2** (*Math.*) any of a set of vectors equivalent to a given vector. **componental** (kompənen´-) *a.* **componential** *a.* [L *compōnens -ntem*, pres.p. of *compōnere* (*pōnere*, to put)]

comport (kəmpawt´) *v.t.* (*usu. reflex.*) to conduct (oneself), to behave. **to comport with** to suit, to agree with. **comportment** *n.* behaviour, conduct, bearing. [F *comporter*, late L *comportāre* (*portāre*, to carry)]

compos COMPOS MENTIS.

compose (kəmpōz´) *v.t.* **1** to make, arrange or construct, esp. by putting together several parts to form one whole. **2** to constitute, to make up by combination. **3** to write, construct or produce (a literary or musical work etc.). **4** to arrange or design artistically (*to compose a picture*). **5** to calm, to soothe (*to compose oneself*). **6** to settle, to adjust. **7** to arrange (type for printing) in proper order. ~*v.i.* to compose music. **composed** *a.* calm, tranquil, settled. **composed of** made up of, comprising. **composedly** (-zid-) *adv.* **composedness** (-zid-) *n.* **composer** *n.* a person who composes, esp. the author of a musical work. **composing** *a.*, *n.* **composing room** *n.* the room in a printing works where type is set. **composing stick** *n.* (*Print.*) an instrument in which a compositor sets the type from the cases, and adjusts the lines to the proper length. [F *composer* (*com-*, with, and *poser*, from L *compōnere*, see COMPOSITE[1])]

Usage note See note under COMPRISE.

composite[1] (kom´pəzit) *a.* **1** made up of distinct parts or elements. **2** compound. **3** (*Bot.*) of or relating to the Compositae, a large family of plants, so called because the heads are made up of many small flowers. ~*n.* **1** a composite substance or thing. **2** a compound. **3** a composite term. **4** (*Bot.*) a composite plant. **compositely** *adv.* **compositeness** *n.* **composite number** *n.* (*Math.*) a number which is the product of two other numbers greater than unity. **Composite order** *n.* (*Archit.*) the last of the five orders, which combines elements of the Corinthian and Ionic. **composite photograph** *n.* a photograph produced by superimposing two or more images. **composite resolution** (kom´pəzīt) *n.* a resolution made up from related resolutions from local branches (of a trade union etc.) and containing the main points of each of them. **compositive** (-poz´-) *a.* [L *compositus*, p.p. of *compōnere* (COM-, *pōnere*, to put)]

composite[2] (kom´pəzīt) *v.t.* to merge (related motions from different branches of a trade union, political party etc.) for presentation to a national conference. ~*n.* a composited motion.

composition (kompəzish´ən) *n.* **1** the act of composing or putting together to form a whole. **2** the thing composed, esp. a literary or musical work. **3** an essay, a piece written for the sake of practice in literary expression. **4** orderly disposition of parts, structural arrangement, style. **5** the arrangement of different figures in a picture. **6** a combination of several parts or ingredients, a compound. **7** constitution. **8** character, nature. **9** (*Print.*) the process of setting type. **10** the act of forming sentences. **11** the formation of compound words. **12** an agreement to terms or conditions for putting an end to hostilities or any contest or disagreement. **13** settlement by compromise. **14** compensation in lieu of that demanded. **15** the amount so accepted. **16** the arrangement of columns, piers, doors etc. in a building. **17** (*Math.*) the combination of functions in a series. **compositional** *a.* **compositionally** *adv.* **composition of forces** *n.* the combining of several forces or motions into a single (resultant) force. [F, from L *compositio*, *-ōnem*, as COMPOSITE[1]]

compositor (kəmpoz´itə) *n.* (*Print.*) a person who sets type.

compos mentis (kompos men´tis), (*coll.*) **compos** (kom´pos) *a.* in one's right mind. [L, master of or controlling the mind]

compossible (kəmpos´ibəl) *a.* capable of coexisting. [OF, from med. L *compossibilis*]

compost (kom´post) *n.* **1** a fertilizing mixture of vegetable matter etc. **2** a mixture containing this, in which plants are grown (*potting compost*). **3** any mixture. ~*v.t.* **1** to make into compost. **2** to manure with compost. **compost heap, compost pile** *n.* a heap of waste plant material decomposing into compost. [OF *composte*, L *compositus*]

composure (kəmpō´zhə) *n.* calmness, tranquillity, esp. of the mind. [COMPOSE, -URE]

compote (kom´pōt) *n.* fruit stewed or preserved in syrup. [F *compote*, OF *composte*, L *composta*, *composita*, fem. of *compositus*]

compound[1] (kom´pownd) *a.* **1** composed of two or more ingredients or elements. **2** composed of two or more parts. **3** collective, combined, composite. **4** (*Biol., Zool.*) formed by a combination of parts or of several individual organisms. ~*n.* **1** a combination, a mixture. **2** a compound word. **3** a combination of two or more elements by chemical action. **compound engine** *n.* **1** a steam engine with one or more additional cylinders of larger diameter into which the steam passes and does further work after leaving the first cylinder. **2** a piston engine with a supercharger powered by a turbine in which the exhaust gases are expanded. **compound eye** *n.* an eye made up of many separate light sensitive units, as in insects. **compound flower** *n.* **1** an inflorescence consisting of numerous florets surrounded by an involucre. **2** one of the flower heads of any of the Compositae. **compound fracture** *n.* a fracture in which the surrounding skin is injured, usually by the protrusion of the bone. **compound fruit** *n.* a fruit formed from several carpels of the same flower, or the carpels of several flowers. **compound interest** *n.* **1** interest payable on both the principal and its accumulated interest. **2** the method of calculating such interest. **compound interval** *n.* (*Mus.*) an interval greater than one octave. **compound leaf** *n.* a leaf composed of leaflets on a branched leaf-stalk. **compound microscope** *n.* a microscope with a combination of lenses. **compound number** *n.* a quantity expressed in two or more different units, as *2 hours 10 minutes*. **compound sentence** *n.* a sentence consisting of two or more clauses. **compound time** *n.* (*Mus.*) a time in which each bar contains two or more groups of main simple time units. **compound word** *n.* a word formed from two or more existing words, as *toothbrush*. [ME *compounen*, OF *componre*, *compondre*, L *compōnere* (*pōnere*, to put)]

compound[2] (kəmpownd´) *v.t.* **1** to make into one mass or whole by the combination of several constituent parts. **2** to mix, to combine. **3** to make up or form (a composite). **4** to intensify or complicate (*The drought compounded the shortage of food*). **5** to settle amicably. **6** to adjust by agreement. **7** to compromise. **8** (*Law*) to forbear to prosecute (a crime etc.) for some valuable consideration (*to compound a felony*). **9** to pay a lump sum instead of a periodical subscription. ~*v.i.* to settle with creditors by agreement. **compoundable** *a.* **compounder** *n.* **1** a person who compounds or mixes. **2** a person who effects a compromise. **3** a person who compounds a debt or a crime.

compound[3] (kom´pownd) *n.* **1** an open enclosure where workers are housed, esp. in S African mines. **2** the yard or space surrounding a house or factory in India, China etc. **3** any similar walled or fenced space, as in a prison. **4** an enclosure for animals, a pound. [Malayalam KAMPONG]

comprador (kom´prədaw), **compradore** *n.* **1** (*Hist.*) in China and Japan, a Chinese or Japanese person employed by a European business house as an agent or intermediary with native customers. **2** an agent of a foreign power. [Port., from late L *comparātor-tōrem*, from *comparāre*, to provide, to purchase]

comprehend (komprihend´) *v.t.* **1** to grasp mentally, to understand. **2** to comprise, to include. **comprehensible**

a. **1** that may be comprehended. **2** clear, intelligible. **3** that may be comprised or included. **comprehensibility** (-bil´-) *n.* **comprehensibly** *adv.* [L *comprehendere* (*prae-*, beforehand, *hendere*, obs., to seize]

comprehension (komprihen´shən) *n.* **1** the act or power of comprehending or understanding. **2** the faculty by which ideas are comprehended by the intellect. **3** (*also* **comprehension test**) an exercise to test a student's understanding of a given passage. **4** the act of comprising or including. **5** (*Hist.*) the inclusion of all Christians in the Church of England. **6** (*Logic*) †the sum of the attributes which a term implies. **comprehensive** *a.* **1** including all or most things; thorough. **2** extending widely. **3** having the power of grasping many things at once with the intellect. **4** of or relating to understanding. **5** of or relating to a comprehensive school (*comprehensive education*). **6** (of motor vehicle insurance) providing protection against all or most risks. ~*n.* a comprehensive school. **comprehensively** *adv.* **comprehensiveness** *n.* **comprehensive school** *n.* a secondary school serving all children of all abilities in an area. [L *comprehensio -ōnem*, as COMPREHEND]

compress[1] (kəmpres´) *v.t.* **1** to squeeze or press together. **2** to bring into narrower limits. **3** to condense. **compressed air** *n.* air at a higher pressure than atmospheric pressure. **compressible** *a.* **compressibility** (-bil´-) *n.* **compression** *n.* **1** the act of compressing. **2** the state of being compressed. **3** condensation. **4** a reduction in volume of fuel, air etc. causing an increase in pressure, as in an engine. **compression ratio** *n.* the ratio of the maximum volume in the cylinder of an internal-combustion engine to the minimum volume (at the end of the compression stroke). **compressive** *a.* **compressor** *n.* a device for compressing esp. air or other gases. [OF *compresser*, L *compressāre*]

compress[2] (kom´pres) *n.* (*Med.*) **1** a soft pad used to maintain pressure on an artery to stop bleeding. **2** a wet cloth for reducing inflammation.

comprise (kəmprīz´) *v.t.* **1** to contain, to include, to consist of. **2** to make up, to constitute. **3** to bring (within certain limits). **comprisable** *a.* [F *compris*, p.p. of *comprendre*, L *comprehendere*, COMPREHEND]

Usage note The meanings of *compose*, *comprise*, *consist* and *constitute* overlap, but the generally accepted uses are as follows: a whole comprises or consists of parts or material (so *The whole army comprised only two divisions, The whole army consisted of only two divisions*); parts compose or constitute a whole (so *Only two divisions composed/ constituted the whole army*); a whole is composed of or constituted of parts or material (so *The whole army was composed of/ constituted of only two divisions*). It is best to avoid the use of *comprise* instead of *compose* in expressions such as *Only two divisions comprised the whole army* and *The whole army was comprised of only two divisions*, and the use of *comprise* instead of *include* where not all the parts are specified, as in *The army comprised a Scottish division.*

compromise (kom´prəmīz) *n.* **1** a settlement by mutual concession. **2** adjustment of opposing opinions, principles or purposes by a partial surrender. **3** a medium between conflicting purposes or courses of action. ~*v.t.* **1** to place in a position of difficulty or danger. **2** to expose to risk of disgrace. **3** †to settle by mutual concession. ~*v.i.* to make a compromise. **compromiser** *n.* **compromisingly** *adv.* [F *compromis*, p.p. of *compromettre*, L *comprōmittere* (COM-, *prōmittere*, PROMISE)]

compte rendu (kōt rādü´) *n.* (*pl.* **comptes rendus** (kōt rādü´)) a statement, report or review. [F, account rendered]

Comptometer® (komptom´itə) *n.* a type of calculating machine.

comptroller (kəntrō´lə, komp-) *n.* a controller, a financial officer or executive. [CONTROLLER (under CONTROL)]

compulsion (kəmpŭl´shən) *n.* **1** the act of compelling by moral or physical force. **2** constraint of the will. **3** (*Psych.*) an irresistible impulse to perform actions against one's will. **compulsive** (-siv) *a.* **1** involving or resulting from compulsion. **2** tending to compel. **3** irresistible. **compulsively** *adv.* **compulsiveness** *n.* **compulsory** (-səri) *a.* **1** obligatory, required by law, rules, regulations etc. **2** necessary, essential. **compulsorily** *adv.* **compulsoriness** *n.* **compulsory purchase** *n.* the purchase of land or property against the owner's wishes, for a public development. [L *compulsio -ōnem* (*compellere*, COMPEL)]

compunction (kəmpŭngk´shən) *n.* **1** pricking or reproach of conscience. **2** remorse, contrition. **3** regret. **compunctionless** *a.* **compunctious** *a.* **compunctiously** *adv.* [OF from L *compunctio -ōnem*, from *compungere* (*pungere*, to prick)]

compurgation (kompəgā´shən) *n.* (*Hist.*) a trial in which a number of persons declared the accused's innocence on oath. **compurgator** (kom´-) *n.* **compurgatory** (-pœ´-) *a.* [L *compurgātio -ōnem*, from *compurgāre* (*purgāre*, to purify)]

compute (kəmpūt´) *v.t.* **1** to determine by calculation. **2** to estimate. **3** to calculate using a computer. ~*v.i.* **1** to calculate. **2** to use a computer. **computable** *a.* **computability** (-bil´-) *n.* **computation** (kompūtā´shən) *n.* **computational** *a.* **computationally** *adv.* **computative** *a.* [F *computer*, L *computāre* (*putāre*, to think)]

computer (kəmpū´tə) *n.* **1** an electronic device which does complex calculations or processes data according to the instructions contained in a program. **2** a person who computes. **computerate** *a.* computer-literate. **computer conferencing** *n.* the use of computer-based communications to enable individuals in different locations to conduct a meeting. **computer dating** *n.* the use of a computer to match the personal details of men or women seeking a compatible partner. **computer game** *n.* a game of skill in which the player uses a computer keyboard, joystick or mouse to respond to graphics on the screen. **computer graphics** *n.pl.* **1** visual images produced by a computer program on a screen, which can be manipulated and developed very rapidly, used in computer games and for simulators, etc. **2** (*sing. in constr.*) the design of programs to generate such images. **computerize, computerise** *v.t.* **1** to perform or control by means of computer. **2** to install computers in (a business, etc.). **3** to store in a computer. ~*v.i.* to install computers. **computerization** (-zā´shən) *n.* **computer language** *n.* a programming language. **computer literacy** *n.* the ability to understand and operate computers. **computer-literate** *a.* **computer programmer** *n.* a person who writes programs for computers. **computer science** *n.* the sciences connected with the construction and operation of computers. **computer system** *n.* a self-contained unit consisting of items of hardware and the necessary software to carry out a particular range of tasks. **computer virus** *n.* a self-replicating computer program which damages or destroys the memory or other programs of the host computer.

Comr. *abbr.* Commissioner.

comrade (kom´rād) *n.* **1** a friend, a companion. **2** an intimate associate. **3** a fellow soldier. **4** a fellow socialist or communist. **comrade-in-arms** *n.* (*pl.* **comrades-in-arms**) a companion or workmate. **comradely** *a.* **comradeship** *n.* [F *camarade*, Sp. *camarada*, a room-mate]

Comsat® (kom´sat) *n.* a communications satellite.

comstockery (kŭm´stokəri, kom´-) *n.* (*esp. N Am.*)

excessive censorship of literary or artistic material on the grounds of immorality. [Anthony *Comstock*, 1844–1915, US moral crusader]

☒ **comunicate** common misspelling of COMMUNICATE.

☒ **comunity** common misspelling of COMMUNITY.

Con. *abbr.* **1** Conformist. **2** Conservative. **3** Consul.

con[1] (kon) *n.* (*sl.*) a fraud, a swindle. ~*v.t.* (*pres.p.* **conning,** *past, p.p.* **conned**) **1** to deceive. **2** to swindle. **conman** *n.* (*pl.* **conmen**) a confidence man, a swindler. **con-trick** *n.* a confidence trick. [short for CONFIDENCE (under CONFIDE).]

con[2] (kon) *n.* (*usu. pl.*) a reason against (*the pros and cons*). ~*prep., adv.* against. [L *contra*, against]

con[3] (kon) *n.* (*sl.*) a convict. [abbr.]

con[4] (kon), (*N Am.*) **conn** *v.t.* (*pres.p.* **conning,** *past, p.p.* **conned**) to direct the steering of (a ship). **conner** *n.* **conning tower** *n.* the armoured shelter in a warship or submarine from which the vessel is steered. [prob. a form of *cond*, earlier *condue*, OF *conduire*, L *condūcere*, CONDUCT[1]]

†**con**[5] (kon) *v.t.* (*pres.p.* **conning,** *past, p.p.* **conned**) **1** to peruse carefully. **2** to study, to learn. **3** to know. [OE *cunnian*, see CAN[1]]

con. *abbr.* **1** conclusion. **2** contra.

con- (kon) *pref.* with; together. [COM-]

conacre (kon´ākə) *n.* (*Ir.*) the practice of subletting land already prepared for cropping. [corr. of *cornacre*]

con amore (kon amaw´rā) *adv.* **1** with devotion. **2** (*Mus.*) lovingly, tenderly. [It., with love]

conation (kənā´shən) *n.* (*Philos.*) the faculty of desiring or willing. **conational** *a.* **conative** (kon´-) *a.* of or relating to conation. **conatus** (-nā´təs) *n.* **1** an effort. **2** a natural impulse. **3** an impulse in plants and animals analogous to human effort. [L *cōnātio -ōnem*, from *cōnārī*, to endeavour]

con brio (kon brē´ō) *adv.* (*Mus.*) with vigour or spirit. [It.]

conc. *abbr.* **1** concentrated. **2** concentration.

concatenate (kənkat´ənāt) *v.t.* to join or link together in a successive series. ~*a.* joined, linked. **concatenation** (-ā´shən) *n.* [late L *concatēnātus*, p.p. of *concatēnāre* (*catēna*, a chain)]

concave (kon´kāv) *a.* having a curve or surface hollow like the inner side of a circle or sphere, as distinct from *convex*. ~*v.t.* (*poet.*) to make concave or hollow. **concavely** *adv.* **concavity** (-kav´-) *n.* (*pl.* **concavities**) **1** the state of being concave. **2** a concave surface. [F, from L *concavus* (*cavus*, hollow)]

concavo- (konkā´vō) *comb.form* **1** concave. **2** concavely. **concavo-concave** *a.* concave on both sides. **concavo-convex** *a.* **1** concave on one side and convex on the other. **2** (of a lens) having greater curvature on the concave side than on the convex side.

conceal (kənsēl´) *v.t.* **1** to hide or cover from sight or observation. **2** to keep secret. **3** to keep back from publicity or utterance. **concealable** *a.* **concealer** *n.* **concealment** *n.* **1** the act of concealing. **2** the state of being concealed. **3** a hiding place. **4** (*Law*) a suppression of material matters. [OF *conceler*, L *concēlāre* (*cēlāre*, to hide)]

concede (kənsēd´) *v.t.* **1** to yield, to give up, to surrender. **2** to admit, to grant. **3** to allow to pass unchallenged. **4** to allow an opponent to win (*to concede a goal*). ~*v.i.* **1** to yield. **2** to make concessions. **3** to admit defeat. **conceder** *n.* [L *concēdere* (*cēdere*, to yield)]

conceit (kənsēt´) *n.* **1** a vain opinion of oneself, overweening self-esteem. **2** a whim, a fanciful idea. **3** in literature, an elaborate or far-fetched image. **conceited** *a.* full of conceit, inordinately vain. **conceitedly** *adv.* **conceitedness** *n.* [L *concepta*, fem. p.p. of *concipere*, CONCEIVE (on anal. of DECEIT)]

conceive (kənsēv´) *v.t.* **1** to become pregnant with. **2** to form, as an idea or concept, in the mind. **3** to imagine or suppose as possible. **4** to think. **5** to formulate. ~*v.i.* **1** to become pregnant. **2** to form an idea or concept (of). **conceivable** *a.* capable of being conceived in the mind, imaginable, possible. **conceivability** (-bil´-) *n.* **conceivableness** *n.* **conceivably** *adv.* [OF *conceiv-*, stem of *concever*, L *concipere* (*capere*, to take)]

concelebrate (kənsel´ibrāt) *v.t.* to celebrate (Mass or the Eucharist) along with another priest. ~*v.i.* to concelebrate Mass or the Eucharist. **concelebrant** *n.* **concelebration** (-rā´shən) *n.* [L *concelebrātus* p.p. of *concelebrāre*]

☒ **concensus** common misspelling of CONSENSUS.

concenter CONCENTRE.

concentrate (kon´səntrāt) *v.t.* **1** to bring to a common focus, centre or point. **2** to reduce to a greater density or strength by removing water etc. ~*v.i.* **1** to come to a common focus or centre. **2** to direct all one's thoughts or efforts to one end (*to concentrate on one's work; I can't concentrate*). ~*a.* concentrated. ~*n.* **1** a product of concentration. **2** any concentrated substance, esp. a concentrated solution of a foodstuff. **concentrated** *a.* **1** intense. **2** having had water etc. removed (*concentrated acid*). **concentratedly** *adv.* **concentration** (-trā´shən) *n.* **1** the act or process of concentrating. **2** mental application. **3** the degree of concentration, esp. of a solution. **concentration camp** *n.* a camp for housing political prisoners and interned persons. **concentrative** *a.* **concentrativeness** *n.* the faculty of fixing the attention or thoughts on any one subject or point. [alt. of CONCENTRE as if from a L p.p. *concentrātus* (*concentrāre*)]

concentre (kənsen´tə), (*N Am.*) **concenter** *v.t.* to draw or direct to a common centre. ~*v.i.* **1** to have or come to a common centre. **2** to combine for a common object. [F *concentrer*]

concentric (kənsen´trik) *a.* **1** having a common centre (*concentric circles*). **2** (*Mil.*) concentrated (*concentric fire*). **concentrically** *adv.* **concentricity** (konsəntris´-) *n.* [OF *concentrique* or med. L *concentricus*]

concept (kon´sept) *n.* **1** a general notion, an abstract idea. **2** (*Philos.*) a general notion or idea comprising all the attributes common to a class of things. **3** (*coll.*) an idea, invention or innovation. **conception** (-sep´shən) *n.* **1** the act of conceiving. **2** the impregnation of the ovum followed by implantation in the womb. **3** origin, beginning. **4** a concept. **5** (*Philos.*) the cognition of classes, as distinct from individuals. **to have no conception of** to be unable to imagine. **conceptional** *a.* **conceptive** (-sep´-) *a.* [L *conceptum*, neut. p.p. of *concipere*, CONCEIVE]

conceptacle (kənsep´təkəl) *n.* **1** that in which anything is contained. **2** (*Bot.*) a surface cavity in fungi and algae in which reproductive bodies are produced. **3** an analogous organ in some animals. [L *conceptāculum*, dim. of *conceptum*, as CONCEPT]

conception CONCEPT.

conceptual (kənsep´tūəl) *a.* of or relating to mental concepts or conception. **conceptualism** *n.* (*Philos.*) the doctrine that universals exist only in the mind of the thinking subject (a doctrine intermediate between nominalism and realism). **conceptualist** *n.* **conceptualize, conceptualise** *v.t.* to form a concept of. ~*v.i.* to form a concept. **conceptualization** (-zā´shən) *n.* **conceptually** *adv.* [med. L *conceptuālis*, from L *conceptus*, CONCEPT]

conceptus (kənsep´təs) *n.* (*pl.* **conceptuses**) the fertilized ovum or developing embryo and surrounding tissue in the womb. [L, conception, embryo]

concern (kənsœn´) *v.t.* **1** to relate or belong to. **2** to affect. **3** to be of importance to. **4** to interest. **5** to disturb, to worry. **6** (*usu. reflex*) to involve (oneself) (*She doesn't concern herself with the financial side of the* *business*). ~*n.* **1** that which affects or is of interest or importance to a person. **2** interest, regard. **3** anxiety, solicitude. **4** a business, a firm, an establishment. **5** a matter of personal importance. **6** (*pl.*) affairs. **7** (*coll.*) an affair, a thing. **to have a concern in** to have an interest in. **to have no concern with** to have nothing to do with. **to whom it may concern** to whomever has an interest in this matter (used to address the reader of a letter of reference etc.). **concerned** *a.* **1** interested, involved, engaged (with) (*the people concerned*; *I was concerned with finding out what had happened*). **2** anxious, solicitous (about). **as far as I am concerned** in my opinion, as regards my interests. **concernedly** (-nid-) *adv.* **concernedness** *n.* **concerning** *prep.* with respect to. **concernment** *n.* (*formal*) **1** that which interests or concerns. **2** an affair, a matter, business. **3** importance. **4** anxiety. [F *concerner*, L *concernere* (*cernere*, to separate, sift), in med. L, to refer to, regard]

concert[1] (kon´sət) *n.* **1** a public musical entertainment. **2** harmony, accordance of plans or ideas. **3** concord, harmonious union of sounds. **in concert 1** acting together. **2** (of musicians) performing live on stage. **concert-goer** *n.* a person who attends concerts. **concert grand** *n.* a powerful grand piano for use at concerts. **concert hall** *n.* a hall where concerts are performed. **concert master** *n.* (*esp. N Am.*) the leader of an orchestra. **concert overture** *n.* a single-movement orchestral piece resembling an overture. **concert party** *n.* **1** a group of entertainers. **2** a group of companies or individuals who buy shares separately for subsequent amalgamation into a single holding. **concert performance** *n.* a performance of an opera etc. without costumes or scenery and without action. **concert pianist** *n.* a pianist who performs solos at concerts. **concert pitch** *n.* **1** (*Mus.*) the standard pitch, in which the A above middle C has a frequency of 440 hertz. **2** a high degree of readiness. [It. *concerto*, as CONCERT[2]]

concert[2] (kənsœt´) *v.t.* **1** to plan, to arrange mutually. **2** to contrive, to adjust. **concerted** *a.* **1** mutually planned or devised; combined (*a concerted effort*). **2** (*Mus.*) arranged in parts. [F *concerter*, It. *concertare*, to accord together (cp. Sp. *concertar*, to bargain), L *concertāre*, to dispute, to contend (CON-, *certāre*, to vie)]

concertante (konchətan´ti) *n.* (*pl.* **concertanti** (konchətan´ti)) **1** a piece of music containing a number of solo passages. **2** (*Hist.*) instrumental parts that are present throughout a musical composition. [It.]

concerti CONCERTO.

concertina (konsətē´nə) *n.* (*pl.* **concertinas**) a portable instrument having a keyboard at each end with bellows between. ~*v.i.* (*3rd pers. sing. pres.* **concertinas**, *pres.p.* **concertinaing**, *past, p.p.* **concertinaed**) to collapse or fold up like a concertina. [as CONCERT[2]]

concertino (konchətē´nō) *n.* (*pl.* **concertinos**) **1** a short concerto. **2** the soloist or soloists playing in a concert. [It., dim. of CONCERTO]

concerto (kənshœ´tō) *n.* (*pl.* **concertos, concerti** (-ti)) a composition for a solo instrument or solo instruments with orchestral accompaniment. **concerto grosso** (gros´ō) *n.* (*pl.* **concerti grossi** (gros´i)) a composition for an orchestra and a group of soloists playing together. [It.]

concession (kənsesh´ən) *n.* **1** the act of conceding. **2** the thing conceded. **3** a reduction in price granted to a particular group of people (*no concessions for senior citizens*). **4** a privilege or right granted by a government, esp. for the use of land or property. **5** the (exclusive) right to market a particular product or service in a particular area. **6** a subdivision of a township in Canada. **concessionaire** (-neə´), **concessionnaire** *n.* a person who holds a concession, esp. from the government. **concessional** *a.* **concessionary** *a.* **concessive** (-siv) *a.* **1** conceding. **2** implying concession. **3** (*Gram.*) **a** (of a phrase or clause) giving a reason why something might not have been so (in English introduced by a preposition or conjunction such as *although* or *in spite of*). **b** (of a preposition or conjunction) introducing such a phrase or clause. [F, from L *concessio -ōnem*, from *concēdere*, to CONCEDE]

conch (kongk, konch) *n.* (*pl.* **conchs, conches**) **1** a shellfish of the family Strombidae. **2** its large spiral shell. **3** a shell of this kind used as a trumpet. **4** (*Archit.*) the domed roof of an apse, or the apse itself. **concha** (kong´kə) *n.* (*pl.* **conchae** (-kē)) **1** (*Anat.*) the largest and deepest concavity in the external ear. **2** the concave ribless surface of a vault. **3** the dome of an apse. **4** an apse. **conchiferous** (kongkif´-) *a.* **1** having or producing a shell. **2** (of rocks) containing shells. [L *concha*, Gr. *konche*, mussel, cockle]

conch- CONCHO-.

concha CONCH.

conchie (kon´shi), **conchy** *n.* (*pl.* **conchies**) (*coll., derog.*) a conscientious objector. [abbr.]

conchiferous CONCH.

concho- (kong´kō), **conch-** *comb. form* shell. [L *concha*]

conchoid (kong´koid) *n.* (*Geom.*) a shell-like curve. **conchoidal** (-koi´-) *a.* **1** of or relating to a conchoid. **2** (of the fracture of a mineral etc.) shell-like, shell-shaped.

conchology (kongkol´əji) *n.* the branch of zoology that deals with shells and the animals inhabiting them. **conchological** (-loj´-) *a.* **conchologist** *n.*

conchy CONCHIE.

concierge (konsiœzh´) *n.* **1** a doorkeeper, a porter, a janitor. **2** a hotel employee who assists guests by booking tours etc. [F]

☒ **concieve** common misspelling of CONCEIVE.

conciliar (kənsil´iə) *a.* of or relating to a council, esp. an ecclesiastical council. [L *concilium*, COUNCIL]

conciliate (kənsil´iāt) *v.t.* **1** to win the regard or goodwill of, to win over. **2** to gain or win (regard, goodwill, favour etc.). **3** to pacify. **4** †to reconcile (conflicting views or conflicting parties). **conciliation** (-ā´shən) *n.* **1** the act of conciliating. **2** reconciliation of disputes etc. **conciliative** *a.* **conciliator** *n.* **conciliatory** *a.* **conciliatoriness** *n.* [L *conciliātus*, p.p. of *conciliāre* (*concilium*, COUNCIL)]

concinnous (kənsin´əs) *a.* **1** harmonious. **2** elegant. **concinnity** *n.* elegance or neatness, esp. of literary style. [L *concinnus*, well-adjusted]

concise (kənsīs´) *a.* condensed, brief, terse. **concisely** *adv.* **conciseness** *n.* **concision** (-sizh´ən) *n.* conciseness. [L *concīsus*, p.p. of *concīdere* (*caedere*, to cut)]

conclave (kon´klāv) *n.* **1** a secret assembly or private meeting. **2** the assembly of cardinals for the election of a pope. **3** the apartment where they meet. [F, from L *conclāve*, a room that may be locked (*clāvis*, key)]

conclude (kənklood´) *v.t.* **1** to bring to an end, to finish. **2** to determine, to settle. **3** to gather as a consequence from reasoning, to infer. ~*v.i.* **1** to come to an end. **2** to come to a decision. **3** to draw an inference. **to conclude** in short, finally. **concluding** *a.* **1** that concludes. **2** final. **concludingly** *adv.* **conclusion** (-zhən) *n.* **1** an end, a finish, a termination. **2** a result. **3** an inference. **4** a final decision or judgement. **5** the final part, a summing-up. **6** settlement (of terms etc.). **7** the inferential proposition of a syllogism. **in conclusion** to conclude. **to try conclusions** to engage in competition with. **conclusive** (-siv) *a.* that puts an end to argument, decisive, final. **conclusively** *adv.* **conclusiveness** *n.* **conclusory** (-səri) *a.* [L *conclūdere* (*claudere*, to shut)]

concoct (kənkokt´) *v.t.* **1** to prepare by mixing together. **2** to invent, to devise (*to concoct a lie*). **concocter** *n.* **concoction** *n.* **1** the act of concocting. **2** the thing concocted. **concoctive** *a.* **concoctor** *n.* [L *concoctus,* p.p. of *concoquere* (*coquere,* to cook)]

concomitant (kənkom´itənt) *a.* **1** accompanying. **2** existing in conjunction with. *~n.* a concomitant person or thing. **concomitance, concomitancy** *n.* **1** the state of being concomitant. **2** the doctrine of the presence in each element of the Eucharist of both the body and the blood of Christ. **concomitantly** *adv.* [L *concomitans -ntem,* pres.p. of *concomitārī* (*comitārī,* to accompany)]

concord (kong´kawd, kon´-) *n.* **1** agreement. **2** union in opinions, feelings, or interests. **3** (*Gram.*) the agreement of one word with another in number, gender etc. **4** (*Mus.*) a combination of notes satisfactory to the ear. **5** a treaty. **concordance** (kənkaw´-) *n.* **1** the state of being concordant. **2** agreement. **3** a list of the words in a book (esp. in the Bible), with exact references to the places where they occur. **concordant** (kənkaw´-) *a.* **1** in concord or harmony. **2** agreeing, correspondent. **concordantly** *adv.* [F *concorde,* L *concordia* (*cor cordis,* heart)]

concordat (kənkaw´dat) *n.* a convention or treaty, esp. between a pope and a secular government. [F, from late L *concordātum,* p.p. of *concordāre,* to agree]

concours (kōkuə´, kō´-) *n.* (*pl.* **concours** (kōkuə´, kō´kuəz)) **1** a competition. **2** a concours d'élégance. **concours d'élégance** (dālāgās´) *n.* a competition for the best car etc. judged on appearance rather than performance. [F]

concourse (kong´kaws, kon´-) *n.* **1** a confluence, a gathering together. **2** an assembly. **3** a main hall or open space at an airport, railway station etc. [OF *concours,* L *concursus* (*concurrere,* see CONCUR)]

concrescence (kəngkres´əns, kən-) *n.* **1** a growing together, coalescence. **2** union of parts, organs or organisms. [L *concrēscentia,* from *concrēscere* (see CONCRETE[1])]

concrete[1] (kong´krēt, kon´-) *a.* **1** existing, real, not abstract. **2** (*Gram.*) denoting a thing as distinct from a quality, a state, or an action. **3** specific, definite. **4** individual, not general. **5** formed by the union of many particles in one mass. **6** made of concrete. *~n.* **1** cement, coarse gravel and sand mixed with water. **2** a mass formed by concretion. *~v.t.* **1** to treat or cover with concrete. **2** to construct or embed in concrete. *~v.i.* to apply concrete. **in the concrete** in the sphere of reality, not of abstractions or generalities. **concretely** *adv.* **concrete mixer** *n.* a machine for mixing concrete, usu. in a revolving drum. **concrete music** *n.* music consisting of pieces of pre-recorded music or other sound put together and electronically modified. **concreteness** *n.* **concrete poetry** *n.* poetry which uses the visual shape of the poem to help convey meaning. **concretize** (-krə-), **concretise** *v.t.* to render concrete, solid, or specific. **concretization** (-zā´shən) *n.* [L *concrētus,* p.p. of *concrēscere* (*crēscere,* to grow)]

concrete[2] (kəngkrēt´, kən-) *v.i.* **1** to coalesce. **2** to grow together. *~v.t.* **1** to form into a solid mass. **2** to make concrete rather than abstract.

concretion (kəngkrē´shən, kən-) *n.* **1** the act of coalescing into a solid mass. **2** the mass thus formed. **3** (*Geol.*) an aggregation of particles into a ball. **4** (*Med.*) a growth of solid matter in the body, a stone. **concretionary** *a.* [L *concrētio -ōnem* (see CONCRETE[2])]

concubine (kong´kūbīn) *n.* **1** a woman who cohabits with a man without being married to him. **2** a mistress. **3** (in polygamous societies) a lawful wife of inferior rank. **concubinage** (konkū´bi-) *n.* **1** the act or state of living with a member of the opposite sex without being legally married. **2** the state of being or having a concubine. **concubinary** (konkū´bi-) *a.* **1** living in concubinage. **2** of or relating to concubinage. *~n.* (*pl.* **concubinaries**) a person living in concubinage. [F, from L *concubīna* (CON-, *cubāre,* to lie)]

concupiscence (kənkū´pisəns) *n.* (*formal*) unlawful or excessive sexual desire. **concupiscent** *a.* [L *concupiscentia,* desire, from *concupiscere,* incept. of *concupere* (*cupere,* to desire)]

concur (kənkœ´) *v.i.* (*pres.p.* **concurring,** *past, p.p.* **concurred**) **1** to coincide. **2** to agree. **3** to act in conjunction (with). **concurrent** (-kŭr´-) *a.* **1** that concurs. **2** happening or existing at the same time. **3** acting in union or conjunction. **4** consistent, harmonious. **5** contributing to the same effect or result. **6** (*Geom.*) meeting at one point, converging. *~n.* **1** a concurrent person or thing. **2** a concurrent circumstance. **concurrence** (-kŭr´-) *n.* **concurrently** *adv.* [L *concurrere* (*currere,* to run)]

concuss (kənkŭs´) *v.t.* **1** to cause concussion in. **2** to shake or agitate violently. **3** †to force or intimidate. **concussion** (-kŭsh´ən) *n.* **1** a state of unconsciousness produced by a blow to the skull, usu. followed by amnesia. **2** shaking by sudden impact. **3** a shock. **concussive** *a.* [L *concussus,* p.p. of *concutere* (CON-, *quatere,* to shake)]

condemn (kəndem´) *v.t.* **1** to censure, to blame. **2** to pronounce guilty, to give judgement against. **3** to pass sentence on (*He was condemned to death*). **4** to pronounce incurable or unfit for use. **5** to adjudge to be forfeited. **6** to doom (to), to force into a particular state. **condemnable** (-dem´ə-, -dem´nə-) *a.* **condemnation** (kondemnā´shən) *n.* **1** the act of condemning. **2** the state of being condemned. **condemnatory** (-dem´nə-) *a.* involving or expressing condemnation. **condemned cell** *n.* the cell in which prisoners condemned to death are confined before execution. [OF *condemner,* L *condemnāre* (*damnāre,* to condemn)]

condense (kəndens´) *v.t.* **1** to make more dense or compact. **2** to compress. **3** to concentrate. **4** to reduce into a denser form, esp. from a gas into a liquid. *~v.i.* **1** to become dense or compact. **2** to be reduced into a denser form. **condensable** *a.* **condensability** (-bil´-) *n.* **condensate** (-den´sāt) *v.t., v.i.* to condense. *~n.* something made by condensation. **condensation** (-sā´shən) *n.* **1** the act of condensing. **2** the state of being condensed. **3** a condensed mass or substance, esp. water on glass etc. **4** conciseness, brevity. **5** an abridgement. **6** (*Chem.*) a reaction in which molecules combine and eliminate water. **condensation trail** *n.* a vapour trail. **condensed milk** *n.* a thickened and usu. sweetened form of preserved milk. **condenser** *n.* **1** an apparatus for reducing steam to a liquid form. **2** a lens for concentrating light on an object. **3** a contrivance for accumulating or concentrating electricity, a capacitor. **4** a person or thing that condenses. [F *condenser,* L *condensāre* (*densāre,* to thicken, from *densus,* thick)]

condescend (kondisend´) *v.i.* **1** to stoop, to yield. **2** to stoop or lower oneself voluntarily to an inferior position. **3** to deign (to) (*She condescended to join us for a drink*). **4** to behave patronizingly. **condescending** *a.* **1** marked by condescension. **2** patronizing. **condescendingly** *adv.* **condescension** *n.* **1** the act of condescending. **2** gracious behaviour to imagined inferiors. **3** patronizing behaviour. [F *condescendre,* late L *condēscendere* (*dēscendere,* DESCEND)]

condign (kəndīn´) *a.* **1** worthy, adequate. **2** (of a punishment) well-deserved. **condignly** *adv.* [F *condigne,* L *condignus* (*dignus,* worthy)]

condiment (kon´dimənt) *n.* **1** a seasoning or sauce. **2** anything used to give a relish to food. **condimental** (-men´-) *a.* [F, from L *condimentum,* from *condīre,* to pickle, to spice, from *condere,* to put together, to store up (*-dere, -dāre,* to put)]

condition (kəndish´ən) *n.* **1** a stipulation, an agreement, a requirement. **2** a term of a contract. **3** that on which anything depends. **4** (*Gram.*) a clause expressing this. **5** (*pl.*) circumstances or external characteristics. **6** a state or mode of existence. 7 a (good) state of health or fitness. 8 a (long-standing) ailment (*a heart condition*). 9 high social position. 10 †rank or position in life. ~*v.t.* 1 to put in a good or healthy condition. 2 to make fit. 3 to accustom. 4 to establish a conditioned reflex in (a person or animal). 5 to put in a certain condition. 6 to test, to examine. 7 to impose conditions on. 8 to stipulate, to agree on. **in condition** in good condition, in a good state of health or fitness. **in no condition to** not fit to. **on condition that** provided that, with the stipulation that. **out of condition** in bad condition, in a bad state of health or fitness. **conditional** *a.* 1 containing, implying, or depending on certain conditions. 2 made with limitations or reservations. 3 not absolute. 4 (*Gram.*) expressing a condition. ~*n.* 1 (*Gram.*) a a conditional word, phrase or clause. b the conditional mood. 2 (*Logic*) a conditional proposition. 3 a limitation or reservation. **conditional discharge** *n.* the discharge of an offender without sentence on condition that no further offence is committed within a specified period. **conditionality** (-nal´-) *n.* **conditionally** *adv.* **conditioned** *a.* 1 of or denoting a conditioned reflex or response. 2 limited by certain conditions. 3 (*usu. in comb.*) having a certain disposition, as *ill-conditioned, well-conditioned.* **conditioned by** 1 depending on. 2 limited by. **conditioned reflex, conditioned response** *n.* (*Psych.*) a natural response to a stimulus which, by much repetition, becomes attached to a different stimulus. **conditioner** *n.* 1 a substance used to improve the condition of something (*a hair conditioner*; *fabric conditioner*). 2 any person or thing that conditions. **conditioning** *n.* 1 the establishing of conditioned reflexes etc. 2 the act of improving the condition of something. [OF *condicion*, L *condicio -ōnem*, from *condīcere*, to talk over (*dīcere*, to speak)]

condo (kon´dō) *n.* (*pl.* **condos**) (*N Am., coll.*) a condominium. [abbr.]

condole (kəndōl´) *v.i.* 1 to sorrow, to mourn, to lament. 2 to sympathize (with). **condolatory** *a.* expressing condolence. **condolement** *n.* condolence. **condolence** *n.* 1 (*often pl.*) an expression of sympathy (*to offer one's condolences*). 2 sympathy. [L *condolēre* (CON-, *dolēre*, to grieve)]

Usage note *Condoling with* a person and *consoling* them should not be confused: *condole* refers only to the expression of sympathy and not its result, whereas *console* refers to the beneficial and cheering effect of the sympathy offered.

---

condom (kon´dom) *n.* a contraceptive device, a rubber sheath worn over the penis during sexual intercourse. **female condom** FEMALE. [etym. unknown]

condominium (kondəmin´iəm) *n.* 1 joint sovereignty over a state. 2 (*N Am.*) a group of dwellings (e.g. a block of flats) of which each unit is separately owned. 3 any such dwelling. [CON-, L *dominium*, ownership]

condone (kəndōn´) *v.t.* 1 to forgive, excuse or overlook (an offence etc.). 2 to approve, esp. with reluctance. **condonable** *a.* **condonation** (kondənā´shən) *n.* **condoner** *n.* [L *condōnāre* (*dōnāre*, to give)]

condor (kon´daw) *n.* either of two vultures, *Vultur gryphus*, the Andean condor, and *Cymnagyos californianus*, the California condor. [Sp., from Quechua *cuntur*]

condottiere (kondotyeə´ri) *n.* (*pl.* **condottieri** (kondotyeə´ri)) (*Hist.*) 1 a leader of a troop of mercenaries, esp. in Italy. 2 a member of such a troop. [It.]

conduce (kəndūs´) *v.i.* 1 to contribute (to a result). 2 to tend (to). **conducive** *a.* contributing, leading, favourable (*The atmosphere was not conducive to study*). **conduciveness** *n.* [L *condūcere* (CON-, *dūcere*, to lead)]

conduct[1] (kon´dŭkt) *n.* 1 the way in which anyone acts or lives, behaviour. 2 management, direction, control. 3 the act of leading or guiding. 4 in painting, the manner of treatment. **conduct sheet** *n.* a written record of a person's offences etc. [partly directly from L *conductus*, p.p. of *condūcere* (CON-, *dūcere*, to lead), partly through OF *conduit* (L *conductus*) or OF *conduite* (cp. Sp. *conducta*, It. *condotta*), defence, escort]

conduct[2] (kəndŭkt´) *v.t.* 1 to lead, to guide. 2 to manage, to direct (*to conduct a business*). 3 (*Physics*) to transmit (heat, electricity etc.). 4 to direct the performance of an orchestra, choir etc. 5 (*reflex.*) to behave (*to conduct oneself badly*). ~*v.i.* to act as a conductor. **conductance** *n.* the ability of a substance or system to conduct electricity, the reciprocal of electrical resistance. **conducted tour** *n.* a tour lead by a guide. **conductible** *a.* capable of conducting or of being conducted. **conductibility** (-bil´-) *n.* **conduction** *n.* 1 the transmission of heat, electricity etc. by a conductor. 2 the conveyance of liquids, etc., as through a pipe or duct. **conductive** *a.* 1 able to conduct heat, electricity etc. 2 of or relating to conduction. **conductive education** *n.* an educational system in which children and adults with motor disorders are guided to attain their own goals. **conductively** *adv.* **conductivity** (kondŭktiv´-) *n.* 1 the state of being conductive. 2 the ease with which a substance transmits electricity, the reciprocal of resistivity. **conductor** *n.* 1 the director of an orchestra or choir. 2 the person in charge of collecting fares on a bus. 3 (*N Am.*) the guard of a train. 4 a body capable of transmitting heat, electricity, etc. 5 a lightning conductor. 6 a leader, a guide. 7 a director, a manager. **conductor rail** *n.* a rail that transmits electricity to an electric train. **conductorship** *n.* **conductress** *n.* a female conductor on a bus or train.

conductus (kəndŭk´təs) *n.* (*pl.* **conducti** (-tī)) a Latin vocal composition of the 12th and 13th cents. [med. L]

conduit (kon´dit, -dūit) *n.* 1 a channel, canal, or pipe, usu. underground, to convey water. 2 a tube or duct for protecting electric wires or cables. 3 a channel, a passage. [as CONDUCT[1]]

conduplicate (kəndū´plikət) *a.* (*Bot.*) having the sides folded in face to face. **conduplication** (-ā´shən) *n.* [L *conduplicātus*, p.p. of *conduplicāre*]

condyle (kon´dil) *n.* an eminence with a flattened articular surface on a bone. **condylar** *a.* **condyloid** *a.* [L *condylus*, Gr. *kondulos*, a knuckle]

cone (kōn) *n.* 1 a solid figure described by the revolution of a right-angled triangle about the side containing the right angle. 2 a solid pointed figure with straight sides and a circular or otherwise curved base. 3 anything cone-shaped, such as a wafer holder for ice cream, a temporary marker for traffic on roads etc. 4 a strobilus or dry multiple fruit, such as that of the pine tree. 5 (*also* **cone-shell**) a marine mollusc of the family Conidae. 6 a cone-shaped cell in the retina of the eye. 7 a volcanic hill. ~*v.i.* to bear cones. ~*v.t.* 1 to shape like a cone. 2 to mark (off) with traffic cones. **conoid** *n.* a cone-shaped object. ~*a.* cone-shaped. **conoidal** (-noi´) *a.* conoid. [F *cône*, L *cōnus*, Gr. *kōnos*]

☒ **conect** common misspelling of CONNECT.

coney CONY.

conf. *abbr.* compare. [L *confer*]

confab (kon´fab) *n.* (*coll.*) a chat, a conversation, a confabulation. ~*v.i.* (*pres.p.* **confabbing**, *past, p.p.* **confabbed**) to confabulate. [abbr.]

confabulate (kənfab´ūlāt) *v.i.* 1 to talk familiarly, to chat, to gossip. 2 (*Psych.*) to compensate for loss of memory by inventing imaginary experiences. **confabulation** (-lā´shən) *n.* **confabulatory** *a.* [L *confābulātus*, p.p. of *confābulāri* (CON- *fābulāri*, to converse, from *fābula*, a discourse)]

confect (kənfekt´) *v.t.* (*formal*) 1 to make by combining ingredients. 2 to construct, esp. in the imagination. **confection** *n.* 1 the act or result of mixing or compounding. 2 a sweet dish or delicacy, a sweet, a preserve. 3 a drug made palatable by compounding with a sweetening agent. 4 a ready-made dress or article of dress. **confectionary** *a.* of or relating to confections. ~*n.* (*pl.* **confectionaries**) 1 a confection. 2 a place where confections are made or stored. **confectioner** *n.* 1 a person whose trade it is to prepare or sell confections, sweets etc. 2 a pastrycook. **confectioner's custard** *n.* a type of thick sweet custard used in cakes and pastries. **confectioner's sugar** *n.* (*N Am.*) icing sugar. **confectionery** *n.* (*pl.* **confectioneries**) 1 sweets and other confections generally. 2 the art or work of making these. 3 a confectioner's shop. [L *confectus*, p.p. of *conficere* (*facere*, to make)]

confederate[1] (kənfed´ərət) *a.* 1 united in a league. 2 allied by treaty. 3 (**Confederate**) of, relating to or supporting the Confederate States. ~*n.* 1 a member of a confederation or confederacy. 2 an ally, esp. an accomplice. 3 (**Confederate**) a supporter of the Confederate States in the American Civil War (1861–65). **confederacy** *n.* (*pl.* **confederacies**) 1 a number of persons, parties, or states united for mutual aid and support; a confederation. 2 a league or compact by which several persons engage to support each other. 3 conspiracy, unlawful cooperation, collusion. **the Confederacy** the Confederate States. **confederal** *a.* **Confederate States** *n.pl.* the southern states of North America that seceded from the US in 1861 and were reincorporated after the American Civil War. **confederation** (-ā´shən) *n.* 1 the act of confederating. 2 the state of being confederated. 3 a league or alliance of states, parties etc. **confederative** *a.* [L *confoederātus*, p.p. of *confoederāre* (*foedus -eris*, a league)]

confederate[2] (kənfed´ərāt) *v.t.*, *v.i.* to unite in a league or alliance.

confer (kənfœ´) *v.t.* (*pres.p.* **conferring**, *past, p.p.* **conferred**) to bestow, to grant. ~*v.i.* 1 to consult together. 2 to compare views. **conferee** (-rē´) *n.* 1 a person who takes part in a conference. 2 a person on whom something is conferred. **conference** (kon´fə-) *n.* 1 the act of conferring; consultation, discussion. 2 a meeting for consultation or discussion. 3 a meeting of the representatives of various countries for deliberation. 4 a meeting of two branches of a legislature to adjust differences. 5 the annual meeting of the Methodist Church to transact church business. 6 (*esp. N Am.*) a league or association in sport, commerce etc. 7 the linking of a number of computers, telephones etc. for simultaneous communication. **in conference** at a meeting; engaged in consultation or discussion. **conference call** *n.* a telephone call in which a number of telephones are linked for simultaneous communication. **conferencing** *n.* participation in a conference. **conferential** (konfəren´-) *a.* **conferment**, (*esp. N Am.*) **conferral** *n.* the act or an instance of conferring a degree, honour etc. **conferrable** *a.* **conferrer** *n.* [L *conferre* (*ferre*, to bring)]

confess (kənfes´) *v.t.* 1 to own, to acknowledge, to admit (*to confess a crime*). 2 to admit reluctantly, to grant, to concede (*He confessed that he hadn't read the book*). 3 to hear the confession of. 4 (*poet.*) to reveal, to make manifest. ~*v.i.* 1 to make confession, esp. to a priest. 2 to admit (to) (*She confessed to having forgotten*). **confessant** *n.* a person who confesses to a priest. **confessedly** (-sid-) *adv.* admittedly, avowedly. **confession** (-shən) *n.* 1 the act or an instance of confessing. 2 something confessed. 3 avowal, declaration. 4 formal acknowledgement of sins to a priest in order to receive absolution. **confessional** *n.* 1 the place where a priest sits to hear confessions. 2 the practice of confession. ~*a.* of or relating to confession. **confessionary** *a.* **confession of faith** *n.* 1 a declaration of one's religious beliefs. 2 a formulary containing the creed of a Church. **confessor** *n.* 1 a person who confesses. 2 a priest who hears confessions. 3 a person who suffers religious persecution but not martyrdom. [OF *confesser*, late L *confessāre*, freq. of *confitērī* (p.p. *confessus*), *fatēri*, to acknowledge, cogn. with *fāri*, to speak, *fāma*, FAME]

confetti (kənfet´i) *n.* 1 bits of coloured paper thrown at weddings etc. 2 sweets thrown at carnivals in Italy. [It., pl. of *confetto*, a sweet, from L *confectum*, COMFIT]

confidant (konfidant´, kon´-) *n.* 1 a person entrusted with secrets, esp. with love affairs. 2 a bosom friend. **confidante** *n.* a female confidant. [F *confident, -e* (see CONFIDE)]

confide (kənfīd´) *v.i.* 1 to have trust or confidence (in). 2 to talk confidentially to (*He confided in his friend*). ~*v.t.* 1 to entrust (to). 2 to reveal in confidence (to). **confidence** (kon´fi-) *n.* 1 trust, faith. 2 self-reliance, boldness, assurance. 3 the revelation of a private matter to a friend etc. 4 the matter revealed. 5 assuredness, certainty. **in confidence** as a secret. **in someone's confidence** entrusted with someone's secrets. **to take into one's confidence** to reveal one's secrets to, to talk confidentially to. **confidence game** *n.* (*N Am.*) a confidence trick. **confidence level** *n.* in statistics, the probability that a result is reliable. **confidence man** *n.* a person who practises confidence tricks. **confidence trick** *n.* a swindle in which someone is induced to trust the swindler and usu. part with valuable property for something worthless. **confidence trickster** *n.* **confident** (kon´fi-) *a.* 1 full of confidence. 2 assured, certain. 3 self-reliant, bold. ~†*n.* a confidant. **confidential** (konfiden´-) *a.* 1 told or given in confidence. 2 entrusted with the private concerns of another. 3 private, intimate. **confidentiality** (-shial´-) *n.* **confidentially** *adv.* **confidentialness** *n.* **confider** *n.* **confiding** *a.* trusting. **confidingly** *adv.* [L *confīdere* (*fīdere*, to trust; cp. *fides*, faith)]

configure (kənfig´yə, -fig´ə) *v.t.* 1 to give shape or form to. 2 to arrange. 3 (*Comput.*) to lay out or interconnect the elements of a computer system. **configuration** (-ā´shən) *n.* 1 shape, form. 2 structural arrangement. 3 a contour or outline. 4 (*Astron., Astrol.*) the relative position of the planets at any given time. 5 (*Psych.*) a gestalt. 6 (*Comput.*) **a** the layout or interconnection of the several items of hardware making up a computer system. **b** these items of hardware. 7 (*Physics*) the arrangement of the electrons or nucleons in an atom or nucleus. 8 (*Chem.*) the spatial relationship of the atoms in a molecule. [L *configūrāre* (*figūrāre*, from *figūra*, form)]

confine[1] (kənfīn´) *v.t.* 1 to shut up, to imprison. 2 to keep within bounds. 3 to limit in application. **to be confined** 1 to be in labour or childbirth. 2 to give birth to a child. **confinement** *n.* 1 the act of confining. 2 the state of being confined. 3 labour, childbirth. 4 restraint, restriction, seclusion. **confiner** *n.* [see CONFINE[2]]

confine[2] (kon´fīn) *n.* 1 (*usu. pl.*) a boundary, a limit. 2 (*usu. pl.*) a borderland of thought or opinion. [OF *confines* (pl.), L *confines* (pl. a.), bordering upon (*fīnis*, a boundary)]

confirm (kənfœm´) *v.t.* 1 to establish or support the truth or correctness of. 2 to ratify, to make valid. 3 to strengthen. 4 to give firmness to. 5 to administer confirmation to. **confirmand** (kon´fœmand) *n.* a person being prepared for the rite of confirmation. **confirmation** (konfəmā´shən) *n.* 1 the act of confirming. 2 corroborative testimony. 3 the rite of admitting a baptized person into full membership of a Christian Church. **confirmative** *a.* **confirmatively** *adv.* **confirmatory** *a.* **confirmed** *a.* 1 established, settled. 2 beyond hope of recovery or help. 3 having received confirmation. **confirmedly** (-mid-) *adv.* **confirmedness**

(-mid-, -fœmd´-) *n.* [OF *confermer*, L *confirmāre* (*firmāre*, to make firm, from *firmus*, firm)]

confiscate[1] (kon´fiskāt) *v.t.* **1** to take or seize, esp. as a penalty. **2** to adjudge to be forfeited, or to seize as forfeited, to the public treasury. **confiscable** (kənfis´kə-), **confiscatable** (-kā´-) *a.* **confiscation** (-kā´shən) *n.* **confiscator** *n.* **confiscatory** (kənfis´kə-) *a.* [L *confiscātus*, p.p. of *confiscāre* (*fiscus*, the treasury)]

confiscate[2] (kon´fiskət) *a.* confiscated.

confiteor (kənfit´iaw), **Confiteor** *n.* a Roman Catholic formula of confession. [L, I confess]

conflagration (konflәgrā´shən) *n.* **1** a large and destructive fire. **2** a general burning. **conflagrate** (kon´-) *v.t., v.i.* [L *conflagrātio*, from *conflagrāre* (*flagrāre*, to burn)]

conflate (kənflāt´) *v.t.* **1** to fuse together. **2** to blend (two variant readings) into one. **conflation** *n.* [L *conflāre* (*flāre*, to blow)]

conflict[1] (kon´flikt) *n.* **1** a fight, a struggle, a contest. **2** a clash or the opposition of interests, opinions, or purposes. **3** (*Psych.*) the opposition of incompatible needs, desires etc. **4** mental strife. **in conflict** in opposition. [L *conflictus*, from *conflīgere* (*flīgere*, to strike)]

conflict[2] (kənflikt´) *v.i.* **1** to come into collision, to clash. **2** to strive or struggle. **3** to differ, to disagree. **4** to be incompatible. **conflicting** *a.* contradictory, irreconcilable. **confliction** *n.* **conflictive** *a.* **conflictual** *a.*

confluent (kon´fluənt) *a.* **1** flowing or running together. **2** uniting in a single stream. *~n.* **1** a stream which unites with another. **2** a tributary stream. **confluence** *n.* **1** the point of junction of two or more streams or rivers. **2** a flowing together. **3** a multitude, an assembly. [L *confluens -ntem*, pres.p. of *confluere* (*fluere*, to flow)]

conflux (kon´flŭks) *n.* confluence. [L *confluxus*, as CONFLUENT]

confocal (konfō´kəl) *a.* having common focus or foci.

conform (kənfawm´) *v.t.* **1** to make like in form, to make similar (to). **2** to accommodate, to adapt. *~v.i.* **1** to comply, to assent. **2** to comply with rules, accepted standards etc. **3** to be in harmony, agreement or accordance (with). **conformable** *a.* **1** having the same shape or form. **2** corresponding, similar. **3** compliant, conforming. **4** consistent. **5** (*Geol.*) (of strata) arranged in parallel planes. **conformability** (-bil´-) *n.* **conformably** *adv.* **conformal** *a.* (of maps) showing small areas in their true shape. **conformally** *adv.* **conformance** *n.* conformity. **conformation** (-mā´shən) *n.* **1** the manner in which a thing is formed; form, shape, structure. **2** adaptation. **3** (*Chem.*) any of the configurations of a molecule that can change its shape. **conformer** *n.* **conformist** *n.* **1** a person who accepts the prevailing orthodoxy in matters of dress, opinion etc. **2** a person who conforms to the practices of the Church of England. *~a.* orthodox, conventional. **conformism** *n.* **conformity** *n.* **1** resemblance, likeness. **2** agreement, congruity. **3** compliance with orthodoxy or convention. **4** the act of conforming to the practices of the Church of England. [F *conformer*, L *conformāre* (*formāre*, to form, fashion)]

confound (kənfownd´) *v.t.* **1** to throw into confusion. **2** to perplex, to bewilder. **3** to mix up, to confuse. **4** †to put to shame. **5** †to defeat, to overthrow. *~int.* used as a mild curse (*Confound it!*). **confounded** *a.* **1** confused. **2** (*coll.*) damned (*this confounded weather*). **confoundedly** *adv.* exceedingly, greatly (with strong disapprobation). [OF *confondre*, L *confundere* (*fundere*, to pour)]

confraternity (konfrətœ´niti) *n.* (*pl.* **confraternities**) **1** a brotherhood associated esp. for religious or charitable purposes. **2** brotherhood.

confrère (kō´freə) *n.* a fellow-member of a profession, religion, association etc. [F]

confront (kənfrŭnt´) *v.t.* **1** to face. **2** to face defiantly. **3** to oppose, to meet in hostility. **4** to face up to. **5** to bring face to face (with). **6** to stand facing. **7** to be opposite to. **8** to compare (with). **confrontation** (konfrŭntā´shən) *n.* **confrontational** *a.* [F *confronter*, late L *confrontāre*, L *confrontāri* (*frons -ntis*, forehead)]

Confucian (kənfū´shən) *a.* of or relating to Confucius or his philosophical system. *~n.* a follower of Confucius. **Confucianism** *n.* **Confucianist** *n., a.* [*Confucius*, 551–479 BC, Chinese philosopher]

confuse (kənfūz´) *v.t.* **1** to confound, to perplex. **2** to jumble up. **3** to mix or mingle so as to render indistinguishable. **4** to disconcert. **5** to mistake, to fail to distinguish between (*She confused me with my brother*). **confusable** *a.* **confusability** (-bil´-) *n.* **confused** *a.* **1** muddled, disordered. **2** perplexed, bewildered. **3** senile, suffering from confusion. **confusedly** (-zid-, -zd-) *adv.* **confusedness** (-zid-, -zd-) *n.* **confusion** *n.* **1** the act of confusing. **2** the state of being confused. **3** disorder. **4** perplexity. **5** embarrassment. **6** disturbance of consciousness characterized by impaired capacity to think or to respond in any way to current stimuli. **7** commotion. [L *confūsus*, p.p. of *confundere*, to CONFOUND]

confute (kənfūt´) *v.t.* **1** to overcome in argument. **2** to prove to be false. **confutable** *a.* **confutation** (konfūtā´shən) *n.* **1** the act or process of confuting. **2** refutation, disproof. **confuter** *n.* [L *confūtāre* (*fūt-*, stem of *fūtis*, a water-vessel, cogn. with *fundere*, to pour)]

Cong. *abbr.* **1** Congregational. **2** Congregationalist. **3** Congress. **4** Congressional.

cong. *abbr.* congregation.

conga (kong´gə) *n.* **1** a Latin American dance performed by several people in single file. **2** the music for this dance. **3** a conga drum. *~v.i.* (*3rd. pers. sing. pres.* **congas**, *pres.p.* **congaing**, *past, p.p.* **congaed** (-gəd)) to perform this dance. **conga drum** *n.* a narrow bass drum beaten by the hand. [Am. Sp.]

congé (kō´zhā) *n.* **1** leave-taking, departure, farewell. **2** dismissal. **3** permission to depart; leave. **4** (*Archit.*) a type of concave moulding. [OF *congiez*, late L *comiātus*, corr. of L *commeātus*, from *commeāre* (*meāre*, to go)]

congeal (kənjēl´) *v.t.* **1** to convert from the liquid to the solid state by cold; to freeze. **2** to coagulate. *~v.i.* **1** to become hard with cold. **2** to coagulate. **congealable** *a.* **congealment** *n.* [OF *congeler*, L *congelāre* (*gelāre*, from *gelu*, frost)]

congelation (konjəlā´shən) *n.* **1** the act or process of congealing. **2** the state of being congealed. **3** a congealed mass or substance. [CONGEAL]

congener (kon´jənə, -jē´-) *n.* **1** a person or thing of the same kind or class. **2** an organism of the same stock or family. **3** a by-product that gives a distinctive flavour, colour etc. to an alcoholic drink. **congeneric** (-er´-) *a.* **1** of the same race or genus. **2** akin, closely allied. **congenerous** (-jen´-) *a.* congeneric. [L *congener* (*genus -eris*, kind)]

congenial (kənjē´nyəl, -niəl) *a.* **1** pleasant, agreeable. **2** sympathetic, having similar tastes, character etc. **3** suitable. **congeniality** (-al´-) *n.* **congenially** *adv.*

congenital (kənjen´itəl) *a.* **1** existing from birth (*congenital disease*). **2** constitutional. **3** as if from birth (*a congenital liar*). **congenitally** *adv.* [L *congenitus* (*genitus*, p.p. of *gignere*, to produce)]

Usage note The adjectives *congenital* and *genetic* should not be confused: *congenital* has no reference to genes and heredity, and means simply existing since birth.

---

conger (kong´gə), **conger eel** *n.* any marine eel of the family Congridae, esp. *Conger conger.* [OF *congre*, L *conger*, Gr. *gongros*]

congeries (kənjiə´rēz, -jer´iēz) *n.* (*pl.* **congeries**) a collection or heap of particles, things, ideas etc. [L]

congest (kənjest´) *v.t.* **1** to crowd, to obstruct, to block. **2** to overcharge (with blood). ~*v.i.* to become congested. **congested** *a.* **1** closely crowded, obstructed, blocked. **2** affected with congestion. **congestion** (-chən) *n.* **1** an abnormal accumulation of blood in the capillaries, mucus in the respiratory system etc. **2** any abnormal accumulation (of people, traffic etc.). **congestive** *a.* inducing or caused by congestion. [L *congestus*, p.p. of *congerere* (*gerere*, to carry, bring)]

conglobate (kon´glōbāt) *v.t.* to form into a ball. ~*v.i.* to assume a globular form. ~*a.* formed into a ball. **conglobation** (-bā´shən) *n.* **conglobe** (-glōb´) *v.t.*, *v.i.* to conglobate. [L *conglobātus*, p.p. of *conglobāre* (*globus*, GLOBE)]

conglomerate[1] (kənglom´ərət) *a.* **1** gathered into a round body. **2** (of rock) composed of small pieces of rock cemented together. ~*n.* **1** a mass or thing formed from heterogeneous elements. **2** a conglomerate rock. **3** a large firm formed by the merger of several smaller firms with diverse interests. [L *conglomerātus*, p.p. of *conglomerāre* (*glomus -eris*, a ball)]

conglomerate[2] (kənglom´ərāt) *v.t.*, *v.i.* **1** to gather into a ball. **2** to collect into a mass. **conglomeration** (-ā´shən) *n.* **1** a gathering into a ball or heap. **2** a miscellaneous collection.

conglutinate (kəngloo´tināt) *v.t.* **1** to glue together. **2** to cause (the edges of a wound) to unite during healing. ~*v.i.* to stick together, to adhere. **conglutination** (-ā´shən) *n.* [L *conglūtinātus*, p.p. of *conglūtināre* (*glūten -inis*, glue)]

congo CONGOU.

Congolese (kong·gəlēz´) *a.* of or relating to the Congo or Zaire. ~*n.* (*pl.* **Congolese**) **1** a native or inhabitant of the Congo or Zaire. **2** any of the languages of the Congolese.

congou (kong´goo), **congo** (-gō) *n.* a kind of Chinese black tea. [Chin. *kong hu*, labour]

congrats (kəngrats´) *n.pl.*, *int.* (*coll.*) congratulations. [abbr.]

congratulate (kəngrach´əlāt) *v.t.* **1** to express pleasure or praise to, on account of some event or achievement. **2** to compliment, to felicitate. **3** (*reflex.*) to consider (oneself) clever, fortunate etc. ~*v.i.* to express congratulations. **congratulant** *a.*, *n.* **congratulation** (-lā´shən) *n.* **congratulations** *n.pl.* an expression of pleasure or praise (*We offered them our congratulations*). ~*int.* used to express pleasure or praise. **congratulative** *a.* **congratulator** *n.* **congratulatory** *a.* expressing congratulations. [L *congrātulātus*, p.p. of *congrātulārī*, to wish joy, from *grātus*, pleasing]

congregate (kong´grigāt) *v.t.* to gather or collect together into a crowd. ~*v.i.* to come together, to assemble. **congregant** *n.* **1** a person who congregates (with). **2** a member of a congregation, esp. of a particular place of worship. **congregation** (-gā´shən) *n.* **1** the act of gathering together. **2** the body gathered together. **3** an assembly of persons for religious worship. **4** such an assembly habitually meeting in the same place. **5** a board of ecclesiastics meeting as commissioners at Rome. **6** the assembly of qualified members of a university. **congregational** *a.* **1** of or relating to a congregation. **2** (**Congregational**) of or relating to Congregationalism. **Congregationalize, Congregationalise** *v.t.* **Congregationalism** *n.* a system of church government in which each church is self-governed, and independent of any other authority. **Congregationalist** *n.*, *a.* [L *congregātus*, p.p. of *congregare* (*gregāre*, to collect, from *grex gregis*, flock)]

congress (kong´gres) *n.* **1** a discussion, a conference. **2** a formal meeting of delegates or of envoys for the settlement of international affairs. **3** (**Congress**) **a** the legislature of the US, consisting of a Senate and a House of Representatives. **b** the body of senators and representatives during the two years for which the latter have been elected. **c** any similar legislative body or assembly. **4** a society, association or organization. **congressional** (-gresh´-) *a.* **Congressman, Congresswoman** *n.* (*pl.* **Congressmen, Congresswoman**) a member of the US Congress. [L *congressus*, p.p. of *congredī*, to meet together (CON-, *gradī*, to walk, from *gradus*, step)]

congruent (kon´gruənt) *a.* **1** agreeing, suitable, correspondent. **2** (of geometrical figures) having the same shape. **congruence, congruency** *n.* **congruently** *adv.* **congruity** (-groo´-) *n.* **congruous** *a.* suitable, conformable, appropriate, fitting. **congruously** *adv.* [L *congruere*, to agree (CON-, *-gruere*, cp. *ingruere*)]

conic (kon´ik) *a.* of, relating to or having the form of a cone. ~*n.* a conic section. **conical** *a.* **conically** *adv.* **conicalness** *n.* **conical projection, conic projection** *n.* a type of map projection in which the surface of the earth is projected onto a cone, usu. with one of the poles at the apex. **conics** *n.sing.* the branch of mathematics dealing with conic sections. **conic section** *n.* any of the curves formed by the intersection of a cone and a plane; a parabola, a hyperbola, an ellipse or a circle. [as CONE]

conidium (kənid´iəm) *n.* (*pl.* **conidia** (-nid´iə)) an asexual reproductive cell or spore in certain fungi. **conidial, conidian** *a.* **conidiophore** (-əfaw) *n.* a branch of the mycelium bearing conidia. **conidiophorous** (-of´-) *a.* [mod. L, from Gr. *konis*, dust]

conifer (kon´ifə, kō´nifə) *n.* **1** any tree or shrub of the Coniferae, an order of resinous trees, such as the fir, pine and cedar, bearing a cone-shaped fruit. **2** any cone-bearing plant or tree. **coniferous** (-nif´-) *a.* **coniform** (kō´nifawm) *a.* cone-shaped. [L]

coniine (kō´niēn), **conin** (-nin), **conine** (-nēn) *n.* an alkaloid constituting the poisonous principle in hemlock. **conium** (kō´niəm, kənī´-) *n.* **1** any plant of the umbelliferous genus *Conium*, containing the hemlock. **2** the fruit of the hemlock or the drug extracted from it. [L *conīum*, Gr. *kōneion*, hemlock]

conj. *abbr.* **1** conjugation. **2** conjunction.

conjecture (kənjek´chə) *n.* **1** guessing, surmise. **2** an opinion based on inadequate evidence. **3** in textual criticism, a proposed reading involving conjecture. ~*v.t.*, *v.i.* to guess, to surmise. **conjecturable** *a.* **conjecturably** *adv.* **conjectural** *a.* based on, involving or inclined to conjecture. **conjecturally** *adv.* [F, from L *conjectūra*]

conjoin (kənjoin´) *v.t.* to cause to unite, to join. ~*v.i.* to unite, to come together. **conjoint** *a.* united, associated, cooperating. **conjointly** *adv.* [OF *conjoign-*, stem of *conjoindre*, L *conjungere* (*jungere*, to join)]

conjugal (kon´jəgəl) *a.* of or relating to matrimony or to married life. **conjugality** (-gal´-) *n.* **conjugally** *adv.* **conjugal rights** *n.pl.* the rights of a husband or wife, esp. to sexual relations. [L *conjugālis*, from *conjugem*, acc. of *conjunx*, spouse (*jug-*, root of *jungere*, to join, *jugum*, a yoke)]

conjugate[1] (kon´jəgāt) *v.t.* **1** to inflect (a verb) by going through the voices, moods, tenses etc. **2** to combine, to join. ~*v.i.* **1** (of a verb) to be inflected. **2** (*Biol.*) to unite sexually. **3** (*Biol.*) to become fused. **4** (*Chem.*) to combine. **conjugation** (-ā´shən) *n.* **1** the act or process of conjugating. **2** the inflection of a verb. **3** a class of verbs conjugated alike. **4** (*Biol.*) the fusion of two or more cells or distinct organisms into a single mass. **conjugational** *a.* **conjugative** *a.* [L *conjugātus*, p.p. of *conjugāre* (*jug-*, as CONJUGAL)]

conjugate[2] (kon´jəgət) *a.* **1** joined in pairs, coupled. **2** agreeing in grammatical derivation. **3** (*Math.*) reciprocally related so as to be interchangeable. **4** (*Bot.*) paired. **5** (*Biol.*) united, fused. **6** (*Chem.*) (of an acid or base) related by the loss or gain of a proton. ~*n.* a conjugate thing, substance, quantity etc.

conjunct (kənjŭngkt´) *a.* **1** joined. **2** closely connected. **3** in union. **4** conjoint. ~*n.* a person or thing joined with another. **conjunction** *n.* **1** union, association, connection. **2** combination. **3** a word connecting sentences or clauses or coordinating words in the same clause. **4** (of two heavenly bodies) the state of being in apparent proximity or alignment. **in conjunction with** together with. **conjunctional** *a.* **conjunctionally** *adv.* **conjunctive** *a.* **1** serving to unite or join. **2** (*Gram.*) **a** connective, conjunctional, copulative. **b** connective in sense as well as in construction, as opposed to *disjunctive.* **3** closely united. ~*n.* a conjunctive word. **conjunctively** *adv.* **conjunctly** *adv.* **conjuncture** (-chə) *n.* **1** a combination of circumstances or events. **2** a crisis. [L *conjunctus,* p.p. of *conjungere,* see CONJOIN]

conjunctiva (konjŭngktī´və, kənjŭngk´tivə) *n.* (*pl.* **conjunctivas, conjunctivae** (-vē)) the mucous membrane lining the inner surface of the eyelids and the front of the eyeball. **conjunctival** *a.* **conjunctivitis** (kənjŭngktivī´tis) *n.* inflammation of the conjunctiva. [see CONJUNCT]

conjuration[1] CONJURE[1].

conjuration[2] CONJURE[2].

conjure[1] (kŭn´jə) *v.t.* **1** to effect by or as if by magical influence. **2** to cause to appear, disappear etc. by or as if by magic. **3** to effect by jugglery or sleight of hand. ~*v.i.* **1** to perform tricks by sleight of hand. **2** to invoke spirits, supernatural forces etc. **a name to conjure with** a person of great influence. **to conjure up 1** to cause to appear by or as if by magic. **2** to bring to the mind, to evoke (*to conjure up an image*). **conjuration**[1] (-ā´shən) *n.* **1** the act of conjuring. **2** a magic spell, a charm. **conjuring** *n.* the performance of tricks by sleight of hand; magic. **conjuror, conjurer** *n.* **1** a person who performs tricks by sleight of hand. **2** a juggler. [as CONJURE[2]]

conjure[2] (kənjuə´) *v.t.* to appeal to by a sacred name, or in a solemn manner. **conjuration**[2] (konjuərā´shən) *n.* **1** the act of conjuring. **2** †a solemn adjuration. **3** †a conspiracy. **conjurement** *n.* a solemn adjuration. [OF *conjurer,* L *conjūrāre* (*jūrāre,* to swear)]

conjuror CONJURE[1].

conk (kongk) *n.* (*coll.*) **1** the head. **2** the nose. **3** a punch on the head or nose. ~*v.t.* **1** (*sl.*) to hit (someone) on the head or nose. **2** (*coll.*) to conk out. **to conk out 1** (*coll.*) to break down, to fail. **2** (*coll.*) to die. **3** (*coll.*) to collapse from exhaustion. [perh. from CONCH]

conker (kong´kə) *n.* **1** the fruit of a horse chestnut. **2** (*pl.*) a game played with conkers threaded on strings. [E dial. *conker,* a snail shell]

con moto (kon mō´tō) *adv.* (*Mus.*) briskly, with movement. [It.]

Conn. *abbr.* Connecticut.

conn CON[4].

connate (kon´āt) *a.* **1** innate, inborn, congenital. **2** allied. **3** originating at the same time. **4** (*Biol.*) united, though originally distinct. [L *connātus,* p.p. of *connāscī* (*nāscī,* to be born)]

connatural (kənach´ərəl) *a.* **1** inborn. **2** naturally belonging (to). **3** of the same nature. **connaturally** *adv.*

connect (kənekt´) *v.t.* **1** to join, link, or fasten together. **2** to conjoin, to unite, to correlate. **3** to associate in one's mind. **4** to associate (with) as a cause or a result. **5** to establish telephone communication between. ~*v.i.* **1** to be or become connected. **2** (*coll.*) to manage to hit something (with a punch, kick etc.). **3** (of a train etc.) to have its arrival and departure times synchronized with those of other trains etc. **4** (*sl.*) to find a source of illegal drugs. **connectable** *a.* **connected** *a.* **1** united, esp. by marriage. **2** closely related. **3** coherent. **4** associated (with). **5** joined or linked together. **connectedly** *adv.* **connectedness** *n.* **connecter** *n.* **connectible** *a.* **connecting rod** *n.* a rod that transmits power from one part of a machine to another, esp. from the piston to the crankshaft in an internal-combustion engine. **connective** *a.* connecting or able to connect. ~*n.* **1** a connecting word. **2** (*Bot.*) the part between the lobes of an anther, which holds them together. **3** anything that connects. **connectively** *adv.* **connective tissue** *n.* the fibrous tissue supporting and connecting the various parts throughout the body. **connectivity** (konektiv´-) *n.* **1** the state of being connected or interconnected. **2** the capacity for connection or interconnection. **connector** *n.* [L *connectere* (*nectere,* to bind)]

connection (kənek´shən), **connexion** *n.* **1** the act of connecting. **2** the state of being connected. **3** the place where two parts or things are connected. **4** a person or thing that connects, a link. **5** a telephone link. **6** the apparatus used in linking up electric current by contact. **7** the synchronization of the departure and arrival of trains, aeroplanes etc. **8** a train, aeroplane etc., whose timetable is so synchronized (*I missed my connection*). **9** relationship (esp. by marriage). **10** a person so connected. **11** acquaintanceship. **12** a party, a religious body. **13** a body of customers or clients. **14** a business associate or contact, esp. one with influence. **15** (*sl.*) a supplier of illegal drugs. **in connection with** connected with. **in this connection** in relation to this matter. **connectional** *a.*

conner CON[4].

connexion CONNECTION.

conning tower CON[4].

conniption (kənip´shən) *n.* (*N Am., sl.*) a fit of rage or hysteria. [etym. unknown]

connive (kənīv´) *v.i.* to conspire (with). **to connive at** to disregard or tacitly encourage (a wrong or fault). **connivance** *n.* **1** passive cooperation in a fault or crime. **2** tacit consent. **connivent** *a.* (*Biol.*) convergent. **conniver** *n.* [L *connīvēre* (and a form conn. with *nicere,* to make a sign, *nictāre,* to wink)]

connoisseur (konəsœ´) *n.* **1** a person skilled in judging, esp. in the fine arts. **2** a critic, a person of taste. **3** a person with expert knowledge or appreciation (of). **connoisseurship** *n.* [F]

connote (kənōt´) *v.t.* **1** to imply, to betoken indirectly. **2** to signify, to mean. **3** to include in the meaning (said of a term denoting a subject and implying attributes). **connotation** (konətā´-) *n.* **1** the act of connoting. **2** something implied in addition to the primary meaning. **connotative** (kon´-, nō´-) *a.* **connotatively** *adv.* [late L *connotāre* (L *notāre,* to mark, from *nota,* a mark)]

connubial (kənū´biəl) *a.* of or relating to marriage. **connubiality** (-al´-) *n.* (*pl.* **connubialities**) matrimony. **connubially** *adv.* [L *connūbiālis* (*nūbere,* to veil, to marry)]

conoid, conoidal CONE.

conquer (kong´kə) *v.t.* **1** to win or gain, esp. by military force. **2** to vanquish, to overcome. **3** to gain dominion, sovereignty, or mastery over. **4** to subdue, to surmount (*to conquer a fear*). **5** to climb (a mountain), esp. for the first time. ~*v.i.* to be victorious. **conquerable** *a.* **conquering** *a.* **conqueror** *n.* **1** a person who conquers. **2** a victor. **3** a conker. [OF *conquerre,* L *conquīrere* (*quaerere,* to seek)]

conquest (kong´kwest) *n.* **1** the act of conquering. **2** a thing, person etc. that is conquered. **3** a person whose affection or compliance has been gained. **4** the acquisition of sovereignty by force of arms. **5** victory, subjugation. **to make a conquest of** to win the love or admiration of. [OF *conquest* (F *conquêt*), anything acquired by conquest, *conqueste* (F *conquête*), the act of conquering, late L *conquīsīta,* fem. p.p. of *conquīrere,* as CONQUER]

conquistador (konkwis´tədaw, -kēstədaw´) *n.* (*pl.* **conquistadors, conquistadores** (-daw´rāz)) any of the Spanish conquerors of America in the 16th cent. [Sp.]

con-rod (kon´rod) *n.* (*coll.*) a connecting rod. [abbr.]

Cons. *abbr.* 1 Conservative. 2 Constitution. 3 Consul.

cons. *abbr.* 1 consecrated. 2 consigned. 3 consignment. 4 consolidated. 5 consonant. 6 constitution. 7 construction. 8 consultant. 9 consulting.

consanguine (kənsang´gwin), **consanguineous** (-gwin´iəs) *a.* 1 of the same blood. 2 related by birth. **consanguinity** (-gwin´-) *n.* [F *consanguin -e*, L *consanguineus* (*sanguis -inis*, blood)]

conscience (kon´shəns) *n.* 1 moral sense. 2 the sense of right and wrong. 3 an inner feeling of guilt or otherwise (*a guilty conscience; to have a clear conscience*). 4 conscientiousness. **for conscience' sake** SAKE[1]. **in all conscience** (*coll.*) in all reason or fairness. **in conscience** 1 in truth. 2 assuredly. **on one's conscience** causing one to feel guilt or remorse. **conscience clause** *n.* a clause in a law etc. to relieve persons with conscientious scruples from certain requirements. **conscienceless** *a.* **conscience money** *n.* money paid voluntarily (and often anonymously), as compensation for evasion of commitments, esp. evaded tax. **conscience-stricken, conscience-struck, conscience-smitten** *a.* stung by conscience on account of some misdeed. [F, from L *conscientia*, from *conscīre* (*scīre*, to know)]

conscientious (konshien´shəs) *a.* 1 scrupulous, diligent. 2 actuated by strict regard to the dictates of conscience. **conscientiously** *adv.* **conscientiousness** *n.* **conscientious objector** *n.* 1 a person who refuses on principle to take part in war or in activities connected with it. 2 a person who takes advantage of the conscience clause. [CONSCIENCE]

conscious (kon´shəs) *a.* 1 aware of one's own existence. 2 fully aware of one's surroundings etc.; not asleep or comatose. 3 having knowledge, cognizant, aware (*conscious of her failings*). 4 intentional (*a conscious effort*). 5 self-conscious. 6 present to consciousness, felt. ~*n.* the conscious mind. **-conscious** *comb. form* very aware of, attaching importance to (*fashion-conscious*). **consciously** *adv.* **consciousness** *n.* 1 the state of being conscious. 2 knowledge, awareness, sense, perception. 3 (*Psych.*) the faculty by which one knows one's own existence, acts, feelings etc. 4 the intellectual faculties collectively or any class of them. **consciousness raising** *n.* the act or process of developing the social or political awareness of a person or group. [L *conscius*, aware, from *conscīre* (see CONSCIENCE)]

conscribe (kənskrīb´) *v.t.* to conscript. [L *conscrībere* (*scrībere*, to write)]

conscript[1] (kon´skript) *a.* enrolled, registered, enlisted compulsorily in the armed forces. ~*n.* a person compelled to serve in the armed forces. **conscript fathers** *n.pl.* 1 the senators of ancient Rome. 2 (*coll.*) the members of a town council. [L *conscriptus*, p.p. of *conscrībere* (as CONSCRIBE)]

conscript[2] (kənskript´) *v.t.* to enlist compulsorily. **conscription** *n.* compulsory enrolment for military, naval or air service.

consecrate (kon´sikrāt) *v.t.* 1 to make sacred, to hallow. 2 to dedicate to a religious purpose. 3 to devote to a particular purpose. 4 to sanctify (the bread and wine of the Eucharist). 5 to ordain (a bishop etc.). **consecration** (-rā´shən) *n.* 1 the act of consecrating. 2 the state of being consecrated. 3 the benediction of the elements of the Eucharist. 4 dedication to a sacred office, esp. that of bishop. **consecrator** *n.* **consecratory** (-rā´-) *a.* [L *consecrātus*, p.p. of *consecrāre* (*sacrāre*, to consecrate, from *sacer*, holy)]

consecution (konsikū´shən) *n.* 1 the state of being consecutive. 2 a succession or series. 3 logical or grammatical sequence. [L *consecutio*, from *consequī* (CON-, *sequī*, to follow)]

consecutive (konsek´ūtiv) *a.* 1 following without interval or break. 2 expressing logical or grammatical consequence. **consecutive intervals** *n.pl.* (*Mus.*) a succession of similar intervals in harmony, esp. consecutive fifths and octaves. **consecutively** *adv.* **consecutiveness** *n.* [F *consécutif -ive*, med. L *consecutivus* (as CONSECUTION)]

consensus (kənsen´səs) *n.* 1 general agreement, unanimity. 2 an instance of this. **consensual** *a.* (*Law*) existing or happening by consent. [L p.p. of *consentīre*, as CONSENT]

consent (kənsent´) *v.i.* to assent, to agree, to give permission. ~*n.* 1 agreement. 2 permission. 3 compliance. 4 acquiescence in feeling, thought, or action. **with one consent** unanimously. **consenter** *n.* **consenting** *a.* **consenting adult** *n.* a person over the age of consent, esp. legally able to enter into a homosexual relationship. **consentingly** *adv.* [OF *consentir*, L *consentīre* (*sentīre*, to feel)]

consentaneous (konsəntā´niəs) *a.* 1 mutually consenting, unanimous. 2 accordant. 3 simultaneous, concurrent. **consentaneity** (-sentənē´i-) *n.* **consentaneously** *adv.* **consentaneousness** *n.* [L *consentāneus* (as CONSENT)]

consentient (kənsen´shənt) *a.* 1 of one mind, unanimous. 2 consenting. **consentience** *n.* [L *consentiens -ntem*, pres.p. of *consentīre*, CONSENT]

consequent (kon´sikwənt) *a.* 1 following as a natural or logical result. 2 consistent. ~*n.* 1 that which follows as a natural and logical result. 2 the correlative to an antecedent. **consequence** *n.* 1 a result or effect. 2 importance (*of no consequence*). 3 social importance, distinction, note (*a person of consequence*). 4 a conclusion or inference. 5 (*pl., usu. sing. in constr.*) a game in which stories are made up from lines contributed by individual players unaware of what has gone before. **in consequence** as a result. **to take the consequences** to accept the (usu. unpleasant) results. **consequential** (-kwen´shəl) *a.* 1 following as a result or a necessary deduction. 2 resulting indirectly (*consequential loss*). 3 important. 4 self-important, pompous, conceited. **consequentialism** *n.* (*Philos.*) the doctrine that an action is morally right if its consequences are good and morally wrong if they are bad. **consequentialist** *a., n.* **consequentiality** (-shial´-) *n.* **consequentially** *adv.* **consequently** *adv.* 1 as a consequence. 2 accordingly, therefore. [F *conséquent*, L *consequens -ntem*, pres.p. of *consequī* (*sequī*, to follow)]

☒ **consern** common misspelling of CONCERN.

conservancy (kənsœ´vənsi) *n.* (*pl.* **conservancies**) 1 the official preservation of forests and other natural resources. 2 a body concerned with this. 3 a commission or court with jurisdiction over a particular river, port etc. [L *conservans -ntem*, pres.p. of *conservāre*]

conservation (konsəvā´shən) *n.* 1 the act of conserving. 2 preservation from waste or decay. 3 protection of natural resources and the environment, esp. from destruction by human activity. **conservational** *a.* **conservation area** *n.* an area of architectural or historical interest protected by law against undesirable environmental changes. **conservationist** *n.* a person who supports or promotes environmental conservation. **conservation of energy** *n.* (*Physics*) the theory that no energy is destroyed, but that the sum of energy in the universe remains the same although particular forces are continually being transformed. **conservation of mass** *n.* (*Physics*) the theory that the total mass in an isolated system is constant. **conservation of momentum** *n.* (*Physics*) the theory that the total momentum in an isolated system is constant. [L *conservātio* (as CONSERVE)]

conservative (kənsœ´vətiv) *a.* 1 tending or inclined to conserve what is established. 2 disposed to maintain existing institutions. 3 (**Conservative**) of or relating to the Conservative Party. 4 moderate, not extreme (*a* *conservative estimate*). **5** of or relating to conservatism. **6** conventional. ~*n.* **1** a person inclined to preserve established things. **2** a conventional person. **3** (**Conservative**) a member or supporter of the Conservative Party. **conservatism** *n.* **1** conservative character. **2** dislike of change. **3** (**Conservatism**) the political principles of the Conservative Party. **Conservative Judaism** *n.* a form of Judaism that allows moderate changes to tradition. **conservatively** *adv.* **conservativeness** *n.* **Conservative Party** *n.* a political party that supports private ownership and free enterprise. **conservative surgery** *n.* surgery in which destruction of tissues is kept to a minimum. [F *conservatif -ve*, L *conservātīvus* (as CONSERVE)]

conservatoire (kənsœ´vətwah) *n.* a public school of music or other fine art. [F, from L *conservātōrium*, see CONSERVATORY]

conservator (kon´səvātə, kənsœ´və-) *n.* **1** a person who preserves something from damage or injury. **2** a member of a conservancy. **3** a custodian, a keeper, a curator. [F *conservateur*, L *conservātor -em*, as CONSERVE]

conservatorium (kənsœvətaw´riəm) *n.* (*Austral.*) a conservatoire.

conservatory (kənsœ´vətri) *n.* (*pl.* **conservatories**) **1** a greenhouse for exotic plants. **2** a glasshouse attached to a house, used for growing plants or as a sun lounge. **3** a conservatoire. [L *conservātōrius*, a., from *conservāre*, CONSERVE]

conserve (kənsœv´) *v.t.* **1** to preserve from injury, decay, or loss. **2** to preserve (fruit etc.), esp. with sugar. ~*n.* **1** a preserve. **2** a confection. **3** preserved or candied fruit. **conserver** *n.* [F *conserver*, L *conservāre* (CON-, *servāre*, to keep, to serve)]

☒ **consession** common misspelling of CONCESSION.

consider (kənsid´ə) *v.t.* **1** to think about, to contemplate, to ponder. **2** to observe and examine. **3** to look upon as of importance. **4** to bear in mind. **5** to estimate, to regard. **6** to have or show regard for. **7** to discuss. ~*v.i.* to reflect, to deliberate. **all things considered** taking everything into account. **considerable** *a.* **1** large or great (*considerable difficulty*). **2** important, notable, worth consideration or regard. **considerably** *adv.* **considerate** (-rət) *a.* **1** characterized by regard for others. **2** †careful, deliberate, prudent. **considerately** *adv.* **considerateness** *n.* **consideration** (-ā´shən) *n.* **1** the act of considering. **2** reflection, thought. **3** regard for others, thoughtfulness. **4** a motive or ground for action. **5** something to be taken into account. **6** a recompense, a reward. **7** (*Law*) the material equivalent given in exchange for something and forming the basis of a contract. **8** †importance, worth. **in consideration of 1** as a payment for, in return for. **2** because of. **to take into consideration** to bear in mind, to take into account. **under consideration 1** being considered. **2** under discussion. **considered** *a.* carefully thought out. **considering** *prep.*, *conj.* taking into consideration, in view of. ~*adv.* (*coll.*) all in all (*She did quite well, considering*). [F *considérer*, L *consīderāre* (*sīdus -eris*, a star), orig. to examine the stars]

Usage note It is best to avoid the use of *consider as* (as in *His parents consider her as unsuitable*). The preferred constructions are with *to be* or a simple adjective (as in *His parents consider her to be unsuitable*, or *His parents consider her unsuitable*).

consign (kənsīn´) *v.t.* **1** to commit to the care, keeping or trust of another. **2** to send (goods etc.). **3** to relegate, to commit permanently. **4** to devote, to set apart. **consignable** *a.* **consignation** (konsignā´shən) *n.* the act of consigning. **consignee** (-nē´) *n.* **1** a person to whom goods are consigned. **2** an agent, a factor. **consignment** *n.* **1** the act of consigning. **2** a batch of goods consigned. **3** the document by which anything is consigned. **consignor** *n.* a person who consigns goods to another. [F *consigner*, L *consignāre* (*signāre*, to mark, to sign, from *signum*, a mark)]

consist (kənsist´) *v.i.* **1** to be composed (of). **2** to be founded or lie (in). **3** to be compatible or consistent (with). **consistency, consistence** *n.* (*pl.* **consistencies, consistences**) **1** degree of density, firmness or solidity. **2** cohesion, coherence. **3** the state of being consistent. **4** agreement, accordance. **5** harmony, compatibility. **consistent** *a.* **1** congruous, harmonious. **2** uniform in opinion or conduct, not self-contradictory. **3** compatible. **consistently** *adv.* [L *consistere* (*sistere*, to make to stand, causal of *stāre*, to stand)]

Usage note See note under COMPRISE.

consistory (kənsis´təri, kon´-) *n.* (*pl.* **consistories**) **1** the court of a bishop for dealing with ecclesiastical causes arising in his diocese. **2** the college of cardinals at Rome. **3** an assembly of ministers and elders in certain Reformed Churches. **consistorial** (-taw´-) *a.* [ONF *consistorie* (F *consistoire*), late L *consistōrium* (see CONSIST)]

consociate[1] (kənsō´shiət) *a.* associated together. ~*n.* **1** an associate. **2** a confederate, an accomplice. [L *consociātus*, p.p. of *consociāre* (*socius*, a partner, a fellow)]

consociate[2] (kənsō´shiāt) *v.t.* **1** to unite. **2** (*N Am.*) to unite in a Congregational convention. ~*v.i.* **1** to associate. **2** (*N Am.*) to meet in a Congregational convention. **consociation** (-shiā´shən) *n.* **1** association, fellowship. **2** (*Hist.*) a union of N American Congregational churches by means of pastors and delegates. **3** a subgroup of plants with one dominant species.

consocies (kənsō´shiēz) *n.* (*pl.* **consocies**) a natural community with one dominant species.

console[1] (kənsōl´) *v.t.* to comfort or cheer in trouble or distress. **consolable** *a.* **consolation** (konsəlā´shən) *n.* **1** the act of consoling. **2** the state of being consoled. **3** a fact, thing or person that consoles. **consolation prize** *n.* a prize awarded to a runner-up. **consolatory** (-sol´-, -sō´-) *a.* **consolatorily** *adv.* **consoler** *n.* **consolingly** *adv.* [F *consoler*, L *consōlārī* (*sōlārī*, to solace)]

Usage note See note under CONDOLE.

console[2] (kon´sōl) *n.* **1** the control panel of an electric or electronic system. **2** the desk or cabinet holding this. **3** a free-standing cabinet for a television set etc. **4** the frame enclosing the keyboards, stops etc. of an organ when separate from the instrument. **5** an ornamental bracket to support a shelf, cornice etc. **console table** *n.* a table supported by a console or consoles. [F, etym. uncertain]

consolidate (kənsol´idāt) *v.t.* **1** to form into a solid and compact mass. **2** to strengthen, to reinforce. **3** to combine, to unite in one whole. ~*v.i.* to become solid. **consolidated** *a.* **consolidated annuities** *n.pl.* British Government securities, consolidated into a single stock in 1751, with fixed annual interest and without a redemption date. **consolidated fund** *n.* a national fund for the payment of certain public charges. **consolidation** (-ā´shən) *n.* **consolidator** *n.* **consolidatory** *a.* [L *consolidātus*, from *consolidāre* (*solidāre*, to make solid)]

consols (kon´səlz) *n.pl.* consolidated annuities. [abbr.]

consommé (kənsom´ā) *n.* a clear soup made by boiling meat and vegetables to form a concentrated stock. [F]

consonant (kon´sənənt) *a.* **1** agreeing or according, esp. in sound. **2** congruous, in harmony. **3** (*Mus.*) producing harmony. ~*n.* **1** a letter of the alphabet which cannot be sounded by itself, as *b* or *p*. **2** a sound that is combined with a vowel sound in order to make a syllable. **consonance, consonancy** *n.* (*pl.* **consonances, con-**

sonancies) 1 accord or agreement of sound. 2 agreement, harmony. 3 recurrence of sounds. 4 assonance. 5 pleasing agreement of sounds, concord. **consonantal** (-nan´-) *a.* **consonantly** *adv.* [F, from L, pres.p. of *consonāre* (*sonāre*, to sound)]

con sordino (kon sawdē´nō) *adv.* (*Mus.*) with a mute. [It.]

consort[1] (kon´sawt) *n.* 1 a companion, an associate. 2 a mate, a partner. 3 a husband or wife, esp. of royalty. 4 a vessel accompanying another. [F *consort*, *-e*, L *consors -rtem*, sharer (*sors*, lot)]

consort[2] (kənsawt´) *v.i.* 1 to associate, to keep company (with). 2 to agree, to be in harmony (with). *~v.t.* 1 to associate. 2 to unite in harmony. 3 to attend, to escort.

consort[3] (kon´sawt) *n.* a group of musical instruments of the same type playing together. [F *concert*]

consortium (kənsaw´tiəm) *n.* (*pl.* **consortia** (-tiə), **consortiums)** 1 an association of companies, financial interests etc. 2 fellowship, coalition, union. 3 (*Law*) the right of a husband or wife to association with the other. [L, fellowship]

conspecific (konspisif´ik) *a.* of or relating to the same species.

conspectus (kənspek´təs) *n.* (*pl.* **conspectuses)** 1 a general sketch or survey. 2 a synopsis. [L, from *conspicere* (*specere*, to look)]

conspicuous (kənspik´ūəs) *a.* 1 obvious, clearly visible. 2 attracting or striking the eye. 3 remarkable, extraordinary. **conspicuous consumption** *n.* lavish spending as a display of wealth. **conspicuously** *adv.* **conspicuousness** *n.* [L *conspicuus* (*conspicere*, as CONSPECTUS)]

conspire (kənspīə´) *v.i.* 1 to combine secretly to do any unlawful act, esp. to commit treason, sedition, murder, or fraud. 2 to concur, to unite, to act together (*Circumstances conspired against us*). *~v.t.* to plot. **conspiracy** (-spir´-) *n.* (*pl.* **conspiracies)** 1 the act of conspiring. 2 a secret agreement or plan between two or more persons to commit an unlawful act that may prejudice any third person; a plot. **conspiracy of silence** *n.* an agreement not to talk about a particular subject. **conspiracy theory** *n.* a theory that some unexplained event is the result of covert action by powerful organizations. **conspirator** (-spir´-) *n.* a person who conspires. **conspiratorial** (-spirətaw´-) *a.* **conspiringly** *adv.* [F *conspirer*, L *conspirāre* (*spīrāre*, to breathe)]

con spirito (kon spir´itō) *adv.* (*Mus.*) in a lively manner, with spirit. [It.]

const. *abbr.* 1 constant. 2 constitution.

constable (kon´stəbəl, kŭn´-) *n.* 1 a police constable. 2 an officer charged with the preservation of the peace. 3 a warden, a governor. 4 (*Hist.*) a high officer of state in the Roman Empire, in France, and in England. 5 (*Hist.*) the chief officer of a royal household. **constableship** *n.* **constabulary** (-stab´ū-) *n.* (*pl.* **constabularies)** a body of police under one authority. *~a.* of or relating to the police. [OF *conestable* (F *connétable*), L *comes stabulī*, count of the stable]

constant (kon´stənt) *a.* 1 continuous, unceasing. 2 continual, occurring frequently. 3 unchanging, steadfast. 4 (*Math.*) unvarying. 5 firm, unshaken. 6 unmoved in purpose or opinion. 7 faithful in love or friendship. *~n.* 1 anything unchanging or unvarying. 2 (*Physics*) any property or relation, expressed by a number, that remains unchanged under the same conditions. 3 (*Math.*) a quantity not varying or assumed not to vary in value throughout a series of calculations. **constancy** *n.* 1 fixedness. 2 firmness of mind. 3 faithfulness, steadfastness. 4 permanence. **constantly** *adv.* 1 in a constant manner. 2 invariably, regularly. 3 continually, continuously, always. [F, from L *constans -ntem*, pres.p. of *constāre* (*stāre*, to stand)]

constantan (kon´stəntan, -tən) *n.* an alloy of copper and nickel used for electrical components because of its high electrical resistance at any temperature. [CONSTANT]

Constantia (kənstan´shiə) *n.* a S African wine from Constantia, near Cape Town.

constellate (kon´stəlāt) *v.i.* to shine with combined radiance. *~v.t.* 1 to set or adorn with or as with stars. 2 to combine into a constellation. **constellation** (-ā´shən) *n.* 1 a number of fixed stars grouped within the outlines of an imaginary figure in the sky. 2 an assemblage of splendid or brilliant people or things. 3 a grouping of related ideas etc. **constellatory** (-stel´ə-) *a.* [L *stellātus*, p.p. of *stellāre*, to set with stars (*stella*, a star)]

consternate (kon´stənāt) *v.t.* (*usu. pass.*) to frighten, to dismay. **consternation** (-ā´shən) *n.* anxiety, dismay. [L *consternātus*, p.p. of *consternāre*, to frighten, collateral with *consternere* (*sternere*, to strew)]

constipate (kon´stipāt) *v.t.* 1 to affect with constipation. 2 to confine, to restrict. **constipated** *a.* suffering from constipation. **constipation** (-ā´shən) *n.* 1 an undue retention or difficult evacuation of the faeces. 2 a restricted state. [L *constīpātus*, p.p. of *constīpāre* (*stīpāre*, to cram, to pack)]

constituent (kənstit´ūənt) *a.* 1 constituting, composing. 2 forming part of a whole. 3 having power to elect or appoint, or to construct or modify a political constitution. *~n.* 1 a person or thing that constitutes. 2 a component part. 3 a member of a body which elects a representative. 4 a person who appoints another as their agent, a client. **constituency** *n.* (*pl.* **constituencies)** 1 the whole body of constituents. 2 a body of electors. 3 the place or body of persons represented by a Member of Parliament. 4 a body of clients, customers, supporters etc. [L *constituens -ntem*, pres.p. of *constituere*, as CONSTITUTE]

constitute (kon´stitūt) *v.t.* 1 to make up or compose. 2 to form, to be (*This constitutes a major setback*). 3 to establish. 4 to enact. 5 to give legal form to. 6 to give a definite nature or character to. 7 to elect or appoint to an office or employment. **constitutor** *n.* [L *constitūtus*, p.p. of *constituere* (CON-, *statuere*, to place, to set)]

Usage note See note under COMPRISE.

---

constitution (konstitū´shən) *n.* 1 the act of constituting. 2 the nature, form, composition or structure of a system or body. 3 the physical health or strength of the body. 4 a person's mental qualities. 5 the established form of government in a state or other organization. 6 a system of fundamental rules or principles for the government of a state or other organization. 7 (*Hist.*) a law or ordinance made by civil or ecclesiastical authority. **constitutional** *a.* 1 inherent in the physical or mental constitution. 2 of, relating to or in accordance with a political constitution. 3 legal. *~n.* a walk or other exercise for the benefit of one's health. **constitutionalism** *n.* 1 government based on a constitution. 2 adherence to constitutional government. **constitutionalist** *n.* 1 an upholder of constitutional government. 2 a writer or authority on the political constitution. **constitutionality** (-nal´-) *n.* **constitutionalize, constitionalise** *v.t.* to render constitutional. **constitutionally** *adv.* **constitutional monarchy** *n.* a monarchy in which the head of the state is, in their sovereign capacity, subject to a written or unwritten constitution. [F, from L *constitūtio -ōnem*, as CONSTITUTE]

constitutive (kon´stitūtiv) *a.* 1 that constitutes or composes; component, essential. 2 that can constitute, establish or appoint. **constitutively** *adv.*

constitutor CONSTITUTE.

constr. *abbr.* construction.

constrain (kənstrān´) *v.t.* 1 to compel, to oblige (to do or not to do). 2 to restrain, to keep down by force. 3 to confine, to repress. 4 to force. **constrained** *a.* 1 acting under compulsion. 2 forced. 3 embarrassed.

constrainedly (-nid-) *adv.* **constraint** *n.* 1 the act of constraining. 2 restraint, restriction. 3 compulsion, necessity. 4 something that constrains. 5 a constrained manner. 6 reserve, self-control. [OF *constreign-*, stem of *constreindre*, L *constringere* (*stringere*, to draw tight)]

constrict (kənstrikt´) *v.t.* 1 to make smaller, narrower or tighter. 2 to compress. 3 to cause to contract. 4 to keep within limits, to restrain. **constriction** *n.* **constrictive** *a.* **constrictor** *n.* 1 anything that constricts. 2 a muscle which serves to contract or draw together. 3 a surgical instrument for constricting, a compressor. 4 a snake that kills its prey by coiling round it and squeezing it, esp. a boa constrictor. [L *constrictus*, p.p. of *constringere*, as CONSTRAIN]

construct[1] (kənstrŭkt´) *v.t.* 1 to build, to make by putting parts together. 2 to put together, to assemble. 3 to combine words to form (a clause or sentence). 4 to form by drawing (*to construct a triangle*). 5 to form mentally. **constructor** *n.* **constructorship** *n.* [L *constructus*, p.p. of *construere* (CON-, *struere*, to pile, to build)]

construct[2] (kon´strŭkt) *n.* 1 something constructed. 2 (*Psych.*) a concept or idea built up from sense impressions etc. 3 a group of words that form a phrase.

construction (kənstrŭk´shən) *n.* 1 the act or process of constructing. 2 the thing constructed. 3 a style, mode, or form of structure. 4 the syntactical arrangement and connection of words in a clause or sentence. 5 explanation, interpretation (of words, conduct etc.) (*to put a different construction on it*). 6 the act of construing. **constructional** *a.* 1 of or relating to construction. 2 structural. 3 of or relating to interpretation of language. **constructionally** *adv.* **constructionism** *n.* 1 (*esp. N Am.*) putting a certain kind of construction upon the law, legal documents etc. 2 constructivism. **constructionist** *n.* **construction site** *n.* a building site. **constructive** *a.* 1 having the ability or power to construct, tending to construct. 2 positive, tending to improve or be helpful, as opposed to *destructive* (*constructive criticism*). 3 structural, of or relating to construction. 4 inferential, virtual, implied by construction or interpretation. **constructive dismissal** *n.* action taken by an employer, such as the changing of duties, conditions etc., that forces an employee to resign. **constructively** *adv.* **constructive metabolism** *n.* the process by which nutritive material is built up into complex and unstable living matter. **constructiveness** *n.* **constructive treason** *n.* an act that may be legally interpreted as treason, though not intended or realized as such. **constructivism** *n.* an abstract style of art using geometric shapes, man-made materials, mechanical objects etc. **constructivist** *n.* [L *constructio -ōnem* (see CONSTRUCT[1])]

construe (kənstroo´) *v.t.* 1 to explain, to interpret. 2 to combine syntactically. 3 to analyse the syntactical structure of. 4 to translate. ~*v.i.* 1 to apply the rules of syntax. 2 to translate. **construable** *a.* **construal** *n.* [as CONSTRUCT[1]]

consubstantial (konsəbstan´shəl) *a.* (esp. of the three persons of the Trinity) having the same substance or essence. **consubstantiality** (-shial´-) *n.* [L *consubstāntiālis* (CON-, SUBSTANTIAL)]

consubstantiate (konsəbstan´shiāt) *v.t.*, *v.i.* to unite in one substance. **consubstantiation** (-shiā´shən) *n.* the doctrine that the body and blood of Christ are present along with the elements of the Eucharist after consecration, as distinct from *transubstantiation*. [L *consubstāntiāre*, as CONSUBSTANTIAL]

consuetude (kon´switūd) *n.* 1 custom, usage, habit. 2 familiarity. **consuetudinary** (-tū´din-) *a.* customary. [OF, from L *consuētūdo -inem*, from *consuētus*, accustomed, p.p. of *consuēscere* (*suēscere*, to become used, accustomed)]

consul (kon´səl) *n.* 1 an official appointed by a state to reside in a foreign country to protect its mercantile interests and citizens there. 2 (*Hist.*) either of the two supreme magistrates of ancient Rome, invested with regal authority for one year. 3 (*Hist.*) each of the three supreme magistrates of the French Republic, 1799–1804. **consular** (-sū-) *a.* of or relating to a consul. **consulate** (-sūlət) *n.* 1 the official residence, jurisdiction, office, or term of office, of a consul. 2 (*Hist.*) government by consuls. 3 (**Consulate**) in France, the period of consular government 1799–1804. **consul general** *n.* (*pl.* **consuls general**) the chief consul of a state, having jurisdiction over ordinary consuls. **consulship** *n.* [L]

consult (kənsŭlt´) *v.i.* 1 to take counsel together, to confer (with). 2 to deliberate. ~*v.t.* 1 to ask for advice, approval, an opinion etc. (*to consult a doctor*). 2 to refer to for information (*to consult a dictionary*). 3 to have regard for, to take into account. **consultable** *a.* **consultancy** *n.* (*pl.* **consultancies**) 1 an agency providing professional advice. 2 the position of a consultant. **consultant** *n.* 1 a person who is consulted, esp. an expert who is called on for advice and information. 2 a specialist holding the most senior appointment in a branch of medicine in a hospital. 3 a person who consults. **consultation** (konsəltā´shən) *n.* 1 the act or an instance of consulting. 2 deliberation of two or more persons. 3 a meeting of or with experts to consider a point or case. **consultative, consultatory, consultive** *a.* **consultee** (konsəltē´) *n.* a person consulted. **consulter** *n.* a person who consults. **consulting** *a.* 1 giving advice, esp. professional advice. 2 called in for consultation. 3 used for consultation (*a consulting room*). **consultor** *n.* a member of a consultative body. [L *consultāre*, freq. of *consulere*, to consult, consider (prob. as CONSUL)]

consume (kənsūm´) *v.t.* 1 to eat or drink. 2 to use up. 3 to destroy by fire, decomposition etc. 4 to dissipate, to waste, to squander. 5 (*often pass.*) to engross, to dominate, to obsess. ~*v.i.* 1 to waste away. 2 to be destroyed. **consumable** *a.* that may be consumed. ~*n.* (*usu. pl.*) a commodity that may be consumed, used up or worn out. **consumer** *n.* 1 a person who purchases goods and services for their own use. 2 a person or thing that consumes. **consumer durable** *n.* a manufactured product that lasts for a relatively long time, such as a domestic appliance. **consumer goods** *n.pl.* manufactured goods destined for purchase by consumers, as opposed to those used to produce other goods. **consumerism** *n.* 1 protection of the interests of consumers. 2 the economic theory that increased consumption of goods and services is desirable. **consumerist** *n.*, *a.* **consumer research** *n.* research into the opinions, requirements etc. of consumers. **consumer society** *n.* a society in which the consumption of goods and services is of social and economic importance. **consumingly** *adv.* [L *consūmere* (*sūmere*, to take)]

consummate[1] (kon´səmət, kənsŭm´ət) *a.* 1 complete, perfect. 2 of the highest quality or degree. **consummately** *adv.* [L *consummātus*, p.p. of *consummāre* (*summa*, a sum)]

consummate[2] (kon´səmāt) *v.t.* 1 to bring to completion, to perfect, to finish. 2 to complete (a marriage) by sexual intercourse. **consummation** (-ā´shən) *n.* 1 the act of consummating. 2 the end or completion of something already begun. 3 perfection, perfect development. **consummative** *a.* †**consummator** *n.*

consumption (kənsŭmp´shən) *n.* 1 the act of consuming. 2 the state or process of being consumed. 3 the purchase and use by individuals of goods and services. 4 a wasting disease, esp. pulmonary tuberculosis. 5 an amount consumed. **consumptive** (-tiv) *a.* 1 consuming, destructive. 2 disposed to or affected with tuberculosis. ~*n.* a person suffering from tuberculosis. **consumptively** *adv.* **consumptiveness** *n.* [L *consumptio* (see CONSUME)]

cont. *abbr.* **1** contents. **2** continent. **3** continental. **4** continued.

contact (kon´takt) *n.* **1** touch, the state of touching. **2** the act or state of meeting or communicating. **3** a business or other acquaintance who can provide one with introductions etc. **4** a person who has been exposed to an illness and is likely to carry contagion. **5** the touching of two lines or surfaces. **6** the touching of conductors, allowing electric current to flow. **7** the part of the conductor that touches the other. **8** (*usu. pl., coll.*) a contact lens. ~*v.t.* to establish contact or communication with. **to be in contact with 1** to be touching. **2** to be in communication with. **3** to be in close proximity or association with. **to come into contact with** to meet, to come across. **to make contact 1** to complete an electric circuit. **2** to touch. **3** to establish communication. **contactable** (-tak´-) *a.* **contact lens** *n.* a lens worn in contact with the eyeball in place of spectacles. **contact man** *n.* (*pl.* **contact men**) an intermediary. **contact print** *n.* a photographic print made by placing a negative directly on to photographic paper. **contact sheet** *n.* a sheet of contact prints. **contact sport** *n.* a sport in which players come into physical contact. **contactual** (-tak´-) *a.* [L *contactus*, p.p. of *contingere* (*tangere*, to touch)]

Usage note The verb is also pronounced (kəntakt´)

contagion (kəntā´jən) *n.* **1** communication of disease by contact with a person suffering from it. **2** contagious disease. **3** the transmission of social or moral qualities, emotions etc. **4** deleterious influence. **contagious** *a.* **1** communicable by contact, communicating disease by contact. **2** (*loosely*) infectious. **3** (of an emotion etc.) likely or tending to spread to others (*contagious laughter*). **contagious abortion** *n.* a contagious or infectious disease, esp. brucellosis, which causes abortion in some farm animals. **contagiously** *adv.* **contagiousness** *n.* **contagium** (-jiəm) *n.* (*pl.* **contagia** (-jiə)) the organism or substance that carries disease. [F, from L *contāgio -ōnem* (*tāg-*, root of *tangere*, to touch)]

contain (kəntān´) *v.t.* **1** to hold within fixed limits. **2** to be capable of holding. **3** to comprise, to include. **4** (*Geom.*) to enclose. **5** (*Math.*) to be exactly divisible by. **6** (*Mil.*) to hem in. **7** to prevent (a problem etc.) from extending. **8** (*also reflex.*) to restrain. **containable** *a.* **container** *n.* **1** that which contains or encloses. **2** something designed or used to contain or hold, a vessel or receptacle. **3** a large rigid box of standard size and shape used for bulk transport and storage of goods. **container-grown** *a.* (of a plant) grown in a container rather than planted in the ground. **containerize, containerise** *v.t.* **1** to put into or transport in containers. **2** to convert (a transportation system etc.) to the use of containers. **containerization** (-zā´shən) *n.* **container port** *n.* a port that specializes in handling containers. **container ship** *n.* a ship designed for the transport of containers. **containment** *n.* the act of containing or restraining, esp. hostilities to a small area, or radioactive emission to a permitted zone in a nuclear reactor. [OF *contenir*, L *continēre* (*tenēre*, to hold)]

contaminate (kəntam´ināt) *v.t.* **1** to pollute, esp. with radioactivity. **2** to corrupt, to infect. **3** to defile, to sully. **contaminable** *a.* **contaminant** *n.* a substance that contaminates. **contamination** (-ā´shən) *n.* **contaminative** *a.* **contaminator** *n.* [L *contaminātus*, p.p. of *contāmināre*]

contango (kəntang´gō) *n.* (*pl.* **contangos**) **1** the postponement of a transaction on the Stock Exchange. **2** the commission paid by a buyer for this. **contango day** *n.* the day on which a contango is fixed, the eighth day before settling day. [etym. unknown]

contd. *abbr.* continued.

Conté (kon´tā), **conté** *a.* (*attrib.*) denoting a type of hard crayon or pencil used by artists etc. (*a Conté crayon*). [N.J. *Conté*, d. 1805, French chemist]

conte (kõt) *n.* a tale, esp. a short story in prose. [F]

contemn (kəntem´) *v.t.* (*formal or poet.*) **1** to despise, to scorn. **2** to slight, to neglect. **contemner** (-tem´ə, -tem´nə) *n.* [OF *contemner*, L *contemnere* (*temnere*, to despise)]

contemplate (kon´təmplāt) *v.t.* **1** to look at, to study. **2** to meditate and reflect on. **3** to purpose, to intend. **4** to regard as possible or likely. ~*v.i.* to meditate. **contemplation** (-plā´shən) *n.* **contemplative** (-tem´plətiv) *a.* **1** given to contemplation. **2** thoughtful, studious. ~*n.* a member of a contemplative order. **contemplative life** *n.* a life passed in prayer and meditation. **contemplatively** *adv.* **contemplativeness** *n.* **contemplative order** *n.* a religious order whose members are engaged wholly in worship and meditation. **contemplator** *n.* [L *contemplātus*, p.p. of *contemplāre*, to observe (*templum*, a space of the sky for observation)]

contemporaneous (kəntempərā´niəs) *a.* **1** existing, living or happening at the same time. **2** lasting, or of, the same period. **contemporaneity** (-nē´iti) *n.* **contemporaneously** *adv.* **contemporaneousness** *n.* [L *contemporāneus* (*tempus*, *-poris*, time)]

contemporary (kəntem´pərəri) *a.* **1** living at the same time. **2** of the same age. **3** belonging to the same period. **4** up-to-date, modern. ~*n.* (*pl.* **contemporaries**) **1** a person living at the same time as another (*Shakespeare and his contemporaries*). **2** any contemporary person or thing. **contemporarily** *adv.* **contemporariness** *n.* **contemporize, contemporise** *v.t.* to make contemporary. **contemporization** (-zā´shən) *n.* [as CONTEMPORANEOUS]

contempt (kəntempt´) *n.* **1** scorn, disdain. **2** the state of being scorned. **3** shame, disgrace. **4** disregard of or disobedience to the rules, orders or regulations of a court, legislative body etc. **beneath contempt** utterly contemptible. **to hold in contempt** to scorn, to despise. **contemptible** *a.* worthy of contempt, despicable, mean. **contemptibility** (-bil´-) *n.* **contemptibleness** *n.* **contemptibly** *adv.* **contempt of court** *n.* (*Law*) disobedience or resistance to the orders or proceedings of a court of justice. **contemptuous** (-tū-) *a.* **1** expressive of contempt. **2** disdainful, scornful. **contemptuously** *adv.* **contemptuousness** *n.* [L *contemptus*, scorn]

contend (kəntend´) *v.i.* **1** to strive in opposition. **2** to strive to obtain or keep. **3** to compete. **4** to exert oneself in defence or support of anything. **5** to dispute. ~*v.t.* to maintain by argument (that). **contender** *n.* **1** a person who contends. **2** a competitor, a contestant. **3** an opponent. [OF *contendre*, L *contendere* (*tendere*, to stretch, strive)]

content[1] (kəntent´) *a.* **1** satisfied, pleased. **2** willing. ~*int.* used to express an affirmative vote in the House of Lords. ~*v.t.* to satisfy, to make content. ~*n.* **1** satisfaction, ease of mind, contentment, contentedness. **2** (*usu. pl.*) a member of the House of Lords who votes in the affirmative. **to one's heart's content** HEART. **contented** *a.* satisfied with what one has. **contentedly** *adv.* **contentedness** *n.* **contentment** *n.* **1** the state of being contented or satisfied. **2** gratification, satisfaction. [F, from L *contentus*, p.p. of *continēre*, CONTAIN]

content[2] (kon´tent) *n.* **1** capacity or power of containing; volume. **2** (*usu. pl.*) that which is contained in a vessel, bag, book, house etc. **3** the amount (of one substance) contained in a mixture, alloy etc. (*the fat content*). **4** (*pl.*) TABLE OF CONTENTS (under TABLE). **5** the meaning (of an utterance etc.) as opposed to the form. **6** (*pl., Math.*) the area or quantity contained within certain limits.

contention (kənten´shən) *n.* 1 the act of contending. 2 quarrel, strife, controversy. 3 emulation, rivalry. 4 a point contended for. **in contention** competing. **contentious** *a.* 1 disposed to or characterized by contention. 2 quarrelsome, argumentative. 3 controversial, disputed. **contentiously** *adv.* **contentiousness** *n.* [F, from L *contentio -ōnem*, from *contendere*, CONTEND]

conterminous (contœ´minəs), **coterminous** *a.* 1 having a common boundary (with). 2 having the same limits, coextensive (in range, time or meaning). **conterminal** *a.* bordering, neighbouring, contiguous. **conterminously** *adv.* [L *terminus*, a boundary]

contessa (kontes´ə) *n.* (*pl.* **contessas**) an Italian countess. [It.]

contest[1] (kəntest´) *v.t.* 1 to contend or compete for, to strive earnestly for. 2 to dispute, to call in question, to oppose. 3 to debate. ~*v.i.* to strive, to contend, to vie. **contestable** *a.* **contestant** *n.* a person who contests, a competitor. **contestation** (kontestā´shən) *n.* 1 the act of contesting. 2 disputation, controversy. 3 something contended for, a contention. **contester** *n.* [F *contester*, L *contestārī* (*testārī*, to bear witness, from *testis*, a witness)]

contest[2] (kon´test) *n.* 1 a struggle for victory or superiority, a competition. 2 a dispute, a controversy. 3 competition, rivalry.

context (kon´tekst) *n.* 1 the parts of a piece of speech or writing immediately connected with a sentence or passage quoted. 2 setting, surroundings. 3 the relevant circumstances. **in context** with the connected words, circumstances etc. **out of context** without the connected words, circumstances etc. (*Her remarks were quoted out of context*). **contextual** (-teks´tū-) *a.* **contextualism** *n.* (*Philos.*) a doctrine stressing the importance of the context of a question. **contextualist** *n.* **contextualize, contextualise** *v.t.* to put into context. **contextualization** (-zā´shən) *n.* **contextually** *adv.* [L *contextus*, p.p. of *contexere* (*texere*, to weave)]

contexture (kənteks´chə) *n.* 1 the act or manner of weaving together. 2 the disposition and relation of parts in a compound body or a literary composition. 3 structure.

contiguous (kəntig´ūəs) *a.* 1 touching, in contact. 2 adjoining, neighbouring. **contiguity** (kontigū´-) *n.* 1 contact. 2 proximity in time or space. 3 (*Psych.*) the immediate relation of two impressions, a principle of association. **contiguously** *adv.* [L *contiguus*, from *contingere* (*tangere*, to touch)]

continence, continency CONTINENT[2].

continent[1] (kon´tinənt) *n.* 1 a large continuous tract of land. 2 any of the main geographical divisions of land (Europe, Asia, Africa, Australia, the Americas and Antarctica). 3 a mainland. **the Continent** the mainland of Europe, as distinct from the British Isles. **continental** (-nen´-) *a.* 1 of or relating to a continent. 2 (*also* **Continental**) of or relating to the Continent. 3 (*Hist.*) (**Continental**) belonging to the rebel forces in the War of American Independence. ~*n.* 1 (*also* **Continental**) a native or inhabitant of the Continent. 2 (*Hist.*) (**Continental**) a Continental soldier. **continental breakfast** *n.* a light breakfast of rolls and coffee. **continental climate** *n.* a climate characteristic of the interior of a continent, with hot summers, cold winters and low rainfall. **continental day** *n.* a school day beginning early in the morning and ending early in the afternoon. **continental drift** *n.* the theory that the continents were orig. one landmass and have drifted apart slowly to their present positions. **continentalism** *n.* **continentalist** *n.* **continentalize, continentalise** *v.t.* **continentally** *adv.* **continental quilt** *n.* a duvet. **continental shelf** *n.* an area of shallow water round a landmass before the water begins to slope sharply down to the ocean depths. [L *terra continens*, continuous land]

continent[2] (kon´tinənt) *a.* 1 able to control one's bladder and bowel movements. 2 abstaining from indulgence or overindulgence in sexual and other pleasures; self-restrained. 3 chaste, temperate. **continence, continency** *n.* **continently** *adv.* [OF, from L *continēre*, CONTAIN]

contingent (kəntin´jənt) *a.* 1 dependent on an uncertain issue, conditional. 2 of doubtful occurrence. 3 accidental. 4 that may or may not be true. 5 associated. ~*n.* 1 a group of people representing or forming part of a larger body. 2 a naval or military force provided by a state for a joint enterprise. 3 a share or quota. 4 a fortuitous event. **contingency** *n.* (*pl.* **contingencies**) 1 the state of being contingent. 2 a chance or possible occurrence. 3 an accident. 4 something dependent on an uncertain issue. 5 (*pl.*) a incidental expenses. b money provided for these in an estimate. **contingency fund** *n.* a sum of money kept in reserve for incidental or unforeseen expenses. **contingency plan** *n.* a plan of action kept in reserve in case some situation should arise. **contingent liability** *n.* a liability that will arise only in a certain event. **contingently** *adv.* [L *contingens -ntem*, pres.p. of *contingere* (*tangere*, to touch)]

continua CONTINUUM.

continuable CONTINUE.

continual (kəntin´ūəl) *a.* 1 frequently recurring (*continual complaints*). 2 unbroken, incessant. **continually** *adv.* [OF *continuel*, L *continuālis*]

Usage note The adjectives *continual* and *continuous* should not be confused: *continual* implies a series of frequent repetitions, and *continuous* absence of interruption.

continuance (kəntin´ūəns) *n.* 1 the act or state of continuing. 2 duration. 3 stay (*his continuance in office*). 4 (*Law, N Am.*) an adjournment or postponement. **continuant** *a.* 1 continuing. 2 prolonged. 3 of or relating to a continuant. ~*n.* a consonant whose sound can be prolonged, such as *f, v, s, r.* [OF, from *continuer*, CONTINUE]

continuation (kəntinūā´shən) *n.* 1 the act or an instance of continuing. 2 that by which anything is continued or carried on. 3 extension or prolongation. 4 in the Stock Exchange, the carrying over of accounts, contango. **continuation day** *n.* CONTANGO DAY (under CONTANGO). **continuative** (-tin´ūətiv) *a.* 1 causing continuation, tending to continue. 2 (*Gram.*) expressing continuation. **continuator** (-tin´-) *n.* a person who continues a (literary) work begun by another. [as CONTINUE]

continue (kəntin´ū) *v.t.* 1 to carry on without interruption. 2 to keep up. 3 to take up again, to resume. 4 to extend, to complete. 5 (*Law, N Am.*) to adjourn, to postpone. ~*v.i.* 1 to remain, to stay. 2 to last, to remain in existence. 3 to resume, to recommence. 4 to persevere. **continuable** *a.* **continued** *a.* **continued fraction** *n.* a fraction in which the denominator is a whole number plus a fraction, the denominator of which is a whole number plus a fraction etc. **continuer** *n.* **continuing education** *n.* adult education, esp. part-time courses. [F *continuer*, L *continuāre* (*continuus*, CONTINUOUS)]

continuity (kontinū´iti) *n.* (*pl.* **continuities**) 1 the state of being continuous. 2 an uninterrupted succession. 3 a logical sequence. 4 the detailed description of a film in accordance with which the production is carried out. 5 the linking of television or radio programmes with broadcast announcements etc. **continuity announcer** *n.* a person who links or fills the gaps between broadcast programmes. **continuity girl, continuity man** *n.* the person responsible for seeing that there are no discrepancies or inconsistencies between the scenes of a film.

continuo (kəntin´ūō) *n.* (*pl.* **continuos**) (*Mus.*) a bass part with harmony indicated by shorthand marks; thorough bass. [It. *basso continuo*, continuous bass]

continuous (kəntin´ūəs) *a.* 1 connected without a break in space or time. 2 uninterrupted, unceasing. 3 (*Gram.*) (of a verb form) progressive. **continuous assessment** *n.* assessment of the progress of a pupil by means of checks carried out at intervals throughout the course of study. **continuous creation** *n.* the theory that the creation of the universe is a continuous process, as opposed to the *big bang* theory. **continuously** *adv.* **continuousness** *n.* **continuous stationery** *n.* (*Comput.*) paper in a long strip with regular perforations, which can be fed through a printer. [L *continuus*, from *continuāre* (*tenēre*, to hold)]

Usage note See note under CONTINUAL.

continuum (kəntin´ūəm) *n.* (*pl.* **continua** (-ūə), **continuums**) 1 (*Physics*) an unbroken mass, series or course of events. 2 a continuous series of component parts that pass into each other. [as CONTINUOUS]

conto (kon´tō) *n.* (*pl.* **contos**) a Portuguese or Brazilian monetary unit, equal to 1000 escudos or cruzeiros. [Port., from late L *computum*, COUNT[1]]

contort (kəntawt´) *v.t.* 1 to twist with violence, to wrench. 2 to distort, to twist out of shape. **contorted** *a.* twisted out of shape. **contortion** *n.* 1 the act of twisting. 2 a writhing movement. 3 a twisted shape. 4 partial dislocation of a part of the body. **contortional** *a.* **contortionist** *n.* 1 an acrobat who bends their body into various shapes. 2 a person who twists the sense of words. **contortive** *a.* [L *contortus*, p.p. of *contorquēre* (*torquēre*, to turn, to twist)]

contour (kon´tuə) *n.* 1 the defining line of any figure or body, an outline. 2 the outline of a coast or other geographical feature. 3 a contour line. 4 a line that separates parts of different colour in a design etc. ~*v.t.* 1 to make an outline of. 2 to mark with contour lines. 3 to carry (a road or railway) round a valley or hill. **contour feather** *n.* any of the feathers that determine the shape of a bird's body, forming the outline of its plumage. **contour line** *n.* a line on a map joining points at the same height or depth. **contour map** *n.* a map showing the elevations and depressions of the earth's surface by means of contour lines. **contour ploughing** *n.* ploughing round sloping ground following contour lines instead of up and down. [F, from *contourner*, to turn]

contr. *abbr.* 1 contracted. 2 contraction.

contra (kon´trə) *n.* (*pl.* **contras**) a counter-revolutionary guerrilla fighter in Nicaragua. [Sp. *contrarevolucionario*, counter-revolutionary]

contra- (kon´trə) *pref.* 1 against, opposite, contrary. 2 denoting resistance or opposition. 3 (*Mus.*) pitched below, as *contrabassoon*. [L *contra*, against]

contraband (kon´trəband) *a.* 1 prohibited, unlawful. 2 forbidden to be exported or imported. 3 of or relating to contraband. 4 smuggled. ~*n.* 1 articles forbidden to be exported or imported. 2 smuggled articles. 3 prohibited trade. 4 (*also* **contraband of war**) goods not allowed to be supplied to a belligerent nation by a neutral one. **contrabandist** *n.* 1 a dealer in contraband goods. 2 a smuggler. [Sp. *contrabanda*, It. *contrabbando*]

contrabass (kon´trəbās) *n.* a double bass.

contrabassoon (kon´trəbəsoon) *n.* a double-reeded woodwind instrument with a range an octave lower than a bassoon.

contraception (kontrəsep´shən) *n.* birth control, the taking of measures to prevent conception. **contraceptive** *n.* a device or drug for preventing conception. ~*a.* preventing conception. [CONTRA-, CONCEPTION (under CONCEPT)]

contract[1] (kəntrakt´) *v.t.* 1 to draw together. 2 to make smaller. 3 (*Gram.*) to abbreviate, to shorten. 4 to acquire, to develop. 5 to incur, to become liable for. 6 to catch (a disease) (*He contracted pneumonia*). 7 to agree to or settle by covenant. 8 to settle, to establish by contract. 9 to arrange or enter into (a marriage). ~*v.i.* 1 to become smaller or narrower. 2 to agree (to do or supply something). 3 to make or undertake a contract. **to contract in** to agree to participate in some scheme, esp. a pension scheme. **to contract out** to agree not to participate in a scheme. **contractable** *a.* (of a disease) capable of being contracted. **contractible** *a.* capable of being drawn together. **contractibility** (-bil´-) *n.* **contractile** (-tīl) *a.* 1 causing contraction. 2 having the power to shorten itself. **contractility** (-til´-) *n.* **contraction** *n.* 1 the act of contracting. 2 the state of being drawn together or shortened. 3 (*Gram.*) **a** the shortening of a word by the omission of a letter or syllable. **b** a word so shortened. 4 the shortening of a muscle, esp. during childbirth. **contractive** *a.* tending or serving to contract. [L *contractus*, p.p. of *contrahere* (CON-, *trahere*, to draw)]

Usage note In *to contract in* and *to contract out* the verb is pronounced (kon´trakt).

contract[2] (kon´trakt) *n.* 1 a formal agreement, esp. one recognized as a legal obligation. 2 the writing by which such an agreement is entered into. 3 an undertaking to do certain work or supply certain articles for a specified sum. 4 an offer or promise which has been formally accepted. 5 a formal betrothal. 6 in bridge etc., an undertaking to win a certain number of tricks. 7 (*sl.*) an agreement to kill a certain person for money. **contract bridge** *n.* a form of bridge in which points are gained only for tricks made as well as bid. **contractual** (-trak´chuəl) *a.* of or relating to a contract. **contractually** *adv.*

Usage note The form *contractural* for *contractual* is best avoided.

contractor (kəntrak´tə) *n.* 1 a person who undertakes a contract, esp. to do or supply something for a specified sum. 2 an employer of labour who contracts to do building work, usu. on a large scale. 3 a muscle that serves to contract an organ or other part of the body.

contradance CONTREDANSE.

contradict (kontrədikt´) *v.t.* 1 to deny the truth of (a statement etc.). 2 to assert the opposite of (a statement etc.). 3 to contradict a statement made by (a person). 4 to oppose, to be inconsistent with. ~*v.i.* to deny the truth of a statement. **contradictable** *a.* **contradiction** *n.* 1 the act or an instance of contradicting. 2 denial. 3 a contrary statement. 4 inconsistency. 5 that which is inconsistent with itself. **contradiction in terms** *n.* a statement that is obviously self-contradictory or inconsistent. **contradictive** *a.* contradictory. **contradictively** *adv.* **contradictiveness** *n.* [L *contrādictus*, p.p. of *contrādīcere* (*dīcere*, to speak)]

contradictory *a.* 1 affirming the contrary. 2 inconsistent. 3 mutually opposed, logically incompatible. 4 disputatious. ~*n.* (*pl.* **contradictories**) 1 a contradictory proposition. 2 the contrary. **contradictor** *n.* **contradictorily** *adv.* **contradictoriness** *n.*

contradistinguish (kontrədisting´gwish) *v.t.* to distinguish by contrasting opposite qualities. **contradistinction** (-tingk´-) *n.*

contraflow (kon´trəflō) *n.* a form of motorway traffic regulation, two-way traffic being instituted on one carriageway so that the other may be closed.

contrail (kon´trāl) *n.* a condensation trail. [abbr.]

contraindicate (kontrəin´dikāt) *v.t.* (*Med.*) to indicate the unsuitability of (a particular treatment or drug). **contraindicant** *n.* **contraindication** (-ā´shən) *n.*

contralto (kəntral´tō) *n.* (*pl.* **contraltos, contralti** (-tē)) 1 the lowest of the three principal varieties of the

female voice, the part next above the alto in choral music. 2 a person who sings this part. 3 music written for this part. ~*a.* singing or arranged for contralto. [It.]
contraposition (kontrəpəzish´ən) *n.* 1 the act of placing opposite or in contrast to. 2 (*Logic*) a kind of conversion by means of negation. **contrapositive** (-poz´-) *a., n.*
contraption (kəntrap´shən) *n.* a contrivance, a strange or improvised device. [etym. uncertain; perh. CONTRIVANCE (under CONTRIVE), TRAP[1], INVENTION (under INVENT)]
contrapuntal (kontrəpŭn´təl) *a.* (*Mus.*) of, relating to or in counterpoint. **contrapuntally** *adv.* **contrapuntist** *n.* a person skilled in counterpoint. [It. *contrapunto* (now *contrappunto*), see COUNTERPOINT]
contrarily[1] CONTRARY[1].
contrarily[2] CONTRARY[2].
contrariness[1] CONTRARY[1].
contrariness[2] CONTRARY[2].
contrariwise[1] CONTRARY[1].
contrariwise[2] CONTRARY[2].
contrary[1] (kon´trəri) *a.* 1 opposite. 2 opposed, diametrically different. 3 contradictory. 4 (*Logic*) opposed as regards affirmation and negation. 5 (of wind etc.) unfavourable, adverse. ~*n.* (*pl.* **contraries**) 1 the opposite. 2 a thing that contradicts. 3 a thing of opposite qualities. ~*adv.* 1 in an opposite manner or direction (*contrary to popular opinion*). 2 contrarily. 3 adversely. **contrary to nature** NATURE. **on the contrary** 1 on the other hand. 2 quite the reverse. **to the contrary** to the opposite effect. **contrariety** (-ī´ə-) *n.* 1 the state of being contrary. 2 opposition. 3 disagreement. 4 inconsistency. **contrarily**[1] *adv.* **contrariness**[1] *n.* **contrariwise**[1] *adv.* on the other hand, conversely. [OF *contrarie*, L *contrārius*]
contrary[2] (kəntreə´ri) *a.* (*coll.*) wayward, perverse. **contrarily**[2] *adv.* **contrariness**[2] *n.* **contrariwise**[2] *adv.* perversely.
contrast[1] (kəntrahst´) *v.t.* to set in opposition, so as to show the difference between, or the superiority or inferiority of (*Contrast the copy with the original*). ~*v.i.* to stand in contrast or opposition. **contrastingly** *adv.* **contrastive** *a.* [OF *contraster*, late L *contrāstāre* (CONTRA-, L *stāre*, to stand)]
contrast[2] (kon´trahst) *n.* 1 opposition or unlikeness of things or qualities. 2 the presentation of opposite or unlike things with a view to comparison. 3 the degree of difference in tone between the light and dark parts of a photograph or television picture. 4 a person or thing that is notably unlike another. **contrast medium** *n.* a substance used in radiography to increase the contrast of the image. **contrasty** *a.* showing great contrast between light and dark tones.
contra-suggestible (kontrəsəjes´tibəl) *a.* reacting to a suggestion by doing the opposite.
contrate (kon´trāt) *a.* (of a wheel) having teeth or cogs at right angles to the plane of the wheel. [med. L *contrata*, lying opposite]
contravallation (kontrəvəlā´shən) *n.* a chain of fortifications constructed by besiegers around the besieged place. [F *contrevallation* (L *vallatio -ōnem*; cp. CIRCUMVALLATION (under CIRCUMVALLATE))]
contravene (kontrəvēn´) *v.t.* 1 to violate, to infringe (*to contravene the rules*). 2 to be in conflict with, to obstruct. 3 to oppose, to be inconsistent with. **contravention** (-ven´shən) *n.* 1 violation, infringement. 2 an instance of this. **in contravention of** violating, infringing. [F *contrevenir*, L *contrāvenīre* (*venīre*, to come)]
☒ **contraversy** common misspelling of CONTROVERSY.
contredanse (kon´trədahns), **contradance** *n.* a French version of the English country dance. [F, from Eng. *country dance*]
contretemps (kõ´trətã) *n.* (*pl.* **contretemps** (-tãz)) 1 an unexpected event which throws everything into confusion. 2 an awkward or embarrassing occurrence or situation. 3 a disagreement, a confrontation. [F, bad or adverse time]
contrib. *abbr.* 1 contribution. 2 contributor.
contribute (kəntrib´ūt, kon´-) *v.t.* 1 to give for a common purpose. 2 to pay as one's share. 3 to write (an article or chapter) for a publication. ~*v.i.* 1 to give a part. 2 to have a share in any act or effect (*These remarks contributed to her downfall*). 3 to write for a newspaper etc. **contributable** *a.* liable to be contributed. **contribution** (kontribū´shən) *n.* 1 the act of contributing. 2 that which is contributed. 3 a subscription. 4 a levy or tax. **contributive** *a.* contributing, assisting, promoting. **contributively** *adv.* **contributiveness** *n.* **contributor** *n.* a person who contributes, esp. to a publication. **contributory** *a.* 1 contributing to the same fund, stock or result. 2 promoting the same end. 3 of or involving a contribution or contributions (*a contributory pension scheme*). ~*n.* (*pl.* **contributories**) a person liable to contribute to the assets of a company if it is wound up. **contributory negligence** *n.* partial responsibility for injury etc. by reason of failure to take adequate precautions. [L *contribūtus*, p.p. of *contribuere* (*tribuere*, to pay)]

Usage note The pronunciation (kon´-), with the stress on the first syllable, is sometimes disapproved of.

contrite (kəntrīt´, kon´-) *a.* 1 deeply sorry for wrongdoing, full of remorse. 2 thoroughly penitent. 3 showing or characterized by penitence. **contritely** *adv.* **contriteness** *n.* **contrition** (-trish´-) *n.* 1 heartfelt sorrow for wrongdoing. 2 thorough penitence. [F *contrit*, L *contrītus*, p.p. of *conterere* (*terere*, to rub, to grind)]
contrive (kəntrīv´) *v.t.* 1 to devise, to invent. 2 to bring about, to effect, to manage. ~*v.i.* to plot or scheme (against). **contrivable** *a.* **contrivance** *n.* 1 the act of contriving. 2 the thing contrived. 3 a mechanical device or apparatus. 4 a plan; a plot. 5 a trick, an artifice. 6 inventiveness. **contrived** *a.* forced, artificial. **contriver** *n.* [ME *contreve, controve*, OF *controver* (*trover*, to find, from late L *tropāre*)]
control (kəntrōl´) *n.* 1 check, restraint. 2 restraining, directing and regulating power. 3 authority, command. 4 a person who controls. 5 a means of controlling. 6 a standard of comparison for checking the results of an experiment. 7 (*pl.*) the mechanisms which govern the operation of a vehicle or machine. 8 a place where something is controlled or checked. ~*v.t.* (*pres.p.* **controlling**, *past, p.p.* **controlled**) 1 to exercise power over, to govern, to command. 2 to restrain, to regulate, to hold in check. 3 to verify or check. 4 to operate or direct (a vehicle, machine etc.). **in control** controlling. **out of control** not or no longer controlled. **under control** being controlled. **control board** *n.* a control panel. **control character** *n.* (*Comput.*) a character that functions as a signal to control some operation, e.g. start, print etc. **control column** *n.* the lever by which the elevators and ailerons of an aircraft are operated, the joystick. **control experiment** *n.* an experiment carried out on two objects so as to have a means of checking and confirming the inferences deduced. **control freak** *n.* (*coll.*) a person who wants to be fully in control of every aspect of their life and environment. **control group** *n.* a group used as a standard of comparison in an experiment. **control key** *n.* (*Comput.*) a key on a computer keyboard that is used in conjunction with other keys to perform specific functions. **controllable** *a.* **controllability** (-bil´-) *n.* **controllably** *adv.* **controller** *n.* 1 a person or thing that controls. 2 a ruler, a director. 3 a person in charge of financial planning, expenditure etc. 4 an officer appointed to verify the accounts of other officers by means of a duplicate register. 5 (*N Am.*) a person

who keeps the public accounts. **controllership** *n.* **controlling interest** *n.* a shareholding sufficiently large to ensure some control over the running of a company. **control panel** *n.* a panel containing the switches etc. for operating an electrical or mechanical system. **control rod** *n.* a rod containing a neutron-absorbing substance, used to control the power produced by a nuclear reactor. **control room** *n.* a room from which a large installation, operation etc. is controlled. **control surface** *n.* a movable surface, e.g. the elevators, rudder etc., by which the movements of an aeroplane are controlled. **control tower** *n.* a tower at an airport from which air traffic in and out is controlled. **control unit** *n.* (*Comput.*) the part of a central processor which controls the execution of a program. [OF *contre-rolle*, a duplicate roll or register]

controversy (kon´trəvœsi, kəntrov´əsi) *n.* (*pl.* **controversies**) **1** a dispute or debate, esp. one carried on in public over a long period of time. **2** disputation, disagreement. **controversial** (kontrəvœ´shəl) *a.* **1** of, relating to or arousing controversy (*a controversial decision*). **2** inclined to argue or dispute. **controversialism** *n.* **controversialist** *n.* **controversially** *adv.* [L *contrōversia*, a quarrel, from *contrōversus*, opposed (*versus*, p.p. of *vertere*, to turn)]

Usage note The pronunciation (-trov´-), with stress on the second syllable, is sometimes disapproved of.

controvert (kon´trəvœt, -vœt´) *v.t.* **1** to dispute. **2** to call in question. **3** to oppose or refute by argument. **controverter** (kon´-) *n.* **controvertible** (-vœ´-) *a.* **controvertibility** (-bil´-) *n.* **controvertibly** *adv.* **controvertist** (kon´-) *n.* [see CONTROVERSY]

contumacious (kontūmā´shəs) *a.* **1** perverse, obstinate, stubborn. **2** stubbornly opposing lawful authority. **3** (*Law*) wilfully disobedient to the orders of a court. **contumaciously** *adv.* **contumaciousness** *n.* **contumacy** (kon´tūməsi) *n.* [L *contumāx -ācis* (*tumēre*, to swell with pride)]

contumely (kon´tūmli) *n.* **1** rude, scornful abuse or reproach. **2** insolence, contempt. **3** disgrace, ignominy. **contumelious** (-mē´liəs) *a.* contemptuous, insolent, abusive. **contumeliously** *adv.* **contumeliousness** *n.* [OF *contumelie*, L *contumēlia* (cogn. with *contumāx*, see CONTUMACIOUS)]

contuse (kəntūz´) *v.t.* to bruise without breaking the skin. **contusion** (-tū´zhən) *n.* **1** the act of contusing. **2** the state of being contused. **3** a bruise. [L *contūsus*, p.p. of *contundere* (CON-, *tundere*, to beat)]

conundrum (kənŭn´drəm) *n.* (*pl.* **conundrums**) **1** a riddle. **2** a puzzling question. [etym. uncertain]

conurbation (konəbā´shən) *n.* a cluster of towns and urban districts that merge to form a densely populated area. [L *urbs*, a city]

conure (kon´ūə) *n.* any parrot of the genus *Pyrrhura*, with a long tail. [mod. L *conurus*, from Gr. *konos*, cone, *oura*, tail]

convalesce (konvəles´) *v.i.* to recover health after illness, surgery etc. **convalescence** *n.* **convalescent** *a.* recovering health. ~*n.* a person who is recovering health. **convalescent hospital, convalescent home** *n.* a hospital for convalescent patients. [L *convalēscere* (*valēscere*, incept. of *valēre*, to grow)]

convection (kənvek´shən) *n.* **1** the propagation of heat or electricity through liquids and gases by the movement of the heated particles. **2** in meteorology, the upward movement of warm air and downward movement of cool air. **convectional** *a.* **convection current** *n.* circulation resulting from convection. **convective** *a.* **convector** *n.* a heater which works by the circulation of currents of heated air. [L *convectio*, from *convehere* (*vehere*, to carry)]

convenable CONVENE.

convenance (kon´vənahns, kõvnās´) *n.* (*usu. pl.*) conventional usage or propriety. [F]

convene (kənvēn´) *v.t.* **1** to call together. **2** to convoke. **3** to summon to appear. **4** to arrange (a meeting). ~*v.i.* to meet together, to assemble. **convenable** *a.* **convener, convenor** *n.* **1** a person who calls a committee etc. together. **2** a senior trade union official. **3** (*Sc.*) the chairman of a public body or committee. [F *convenir*, L *convenīre* (*venīre*, to come)]

convenient (kənvēn´yənt) *a.* **1** suitable, opportune (*a convenient moment*). **2** useful, handy. **3** at hand, close by. **convenience** *n.* **1** the quality or state of being convenient. **2** comfort, ease. **3** a cause or source of comfort or ease. **4** advantage. **5** a thing that is useful. **6** (*pl.*) things or arrangements that promote ease and comfort or save trouble. **7** a lavatory, esp. a public lavatory. **at one's convenience** at a time that is suitable to one. **at one's earliest convenience** as soon as possible. **to make a convenience of** to take advantage of or impose on (a person). **convenience food** *n.* food bought already prepared so as to need very little further work before cooking or eating. **convenience store** *n.* a shop which sells a wide range of useful articles as well as food, and is open at times convenient to the public. **conveniently** *adv.* [L *conveniens -ntem*, pres.p. of *convenīre* (as CONVENE)]

convenor CONVENE.

convent (kon´vənt) *n.* **1** a community of religious persons, now usu. nuns. **2** the building occupied by such a community. **3** (*also* **convent school**) a school run by the members of a convent. **conventual** (-ven´tū-) *a.* belonging to a convent. ~*n.* **1** a member of a convent. **2** a member of a branch of the Franciscans who follow a mitigated rule. **conventually** *adv.* [ME and A-F *covent*, OF *convent*, L *conventus*, p.p. of *convenīre*, as CONVENE]

conventicle (kənven´tikəl) *n.* **1** a clandestine gathering, esp. for worship. **2** a meeting or place of worship of dissenters in the 16th and 17th cents. [L *conventiculum*, dim. of *conventus*, as CONVENT]

convention (kənven´shən) *n.* **1** an agreement, a treaty. **2** an accepted usage, code of conduct etc. **3** the act of convening. **4** a meeting, a conference. **5** the persons assembled. **6** (*esp. N Am.*) an assembly of representatives. **conventional** *a.* **1** of, relating to or in accordance with convention. **2** founded on custom or use. **3** observing the customs of society. **4** (of painting) following traditional and accepted models. **5** (of energy sources, warfare etc.) not nuclear. **6** agreed on by convention. **conventionalism** *n.* **conventionalist** *n.* **conventionality** (-al´-) *n.* (*pl.* **conventionalities**) **1** the state of being conventional. **2** (*often pl.*) a convention or propriety. **conventionalize, conventionalise** *v.t.* **conventionally** *adv.* **conventioneer** *n.* (*N Am.*) a person who attends a convention. [F, from L *conventio -ōnem* (*convenīre*, CONVENE)]

conventual CONVENT.

converge (kənvœj´) *v.i.* **1** to tend towards one point. **2** to meet at one point. **3** (*Math.*) to approach a definite limit by an indefinite number of steps. **4** (of opinions, ideas etc.) to tend towards the same conclusion. ~*v.t.* to cause to converge. **to converge on** to approach and meet at (a place) from different directions (*The police and emergency services converged on the scene*). **convergent** *a.* **1** tending to converge. **2** (of rays of light) that being continued will meet in a focus. **3** (of a lens) that will cause rays to meet in a focus. **4** (*Biol.*) developing similar characteristics in a similar environment. **5** (*Psych.*) (of thought) producing a logical or conventional result. **convergence, convergency** *n.* [L *convergere* (*vergere*, to turn, incline)]

conversable CONVERSE[1].

conversant (kənvœ´sənt) *a.* **1** having knowledge

acquired by study, use or familiarity. 2 well acquainted, familiar (with). 3 experienced. **conversance, conversancy** *n.* [CONVERSE[1]]

conversation (konvəsā´shən) *n.* 1 the act of conversing, informal talk. 2 an instance of this (*to have a conversation*). **to make conversation** MAKE[1]. **conversational** *a.* 1 of or used in conversation. 2 conversable. **conversationalist** *n.* a person inclined to or skilled in conversation. **conversationally** *adv.* **conversation piece** *n.* 1 a representation of figures in familiar groupings. 2 something that provides a topic of conversation. **conversation stopper** *n.* (*coll.*) a remark to which there is no ready reply. [CONVERSE[1]]

conversazione (konvəsatsiō´ni) *n.* (*pl.* **conversaziones, conversazioni** (-ni)) a social meeting devoted to literary, artistic or scientific subjects. [It., from L *conversātio -ōnem*, conversation]

converse[1] (kənvœs´) *v.i.* to talk easily and informally (with). **conversable** *a.* 1 inclined to conversation. 2 sociable, agreeable. **conversableness** *n.* **conversably** *adv.* **converser** *n.* [F *converser*, L *conversārī*, to be conversant or keep company with, pass. of *convertere*, CONVERT[1]]

converse[2] (kon´vœs) *n.* 1 something opposite or contrary. 2 a counterpart or complement. 3 (*Math.*) an inverted proposition. 4 (*Logic*) a converted proposition. 5 †conversation. ~*a.* 1 opposite, reversed, contrary. 2 reciprocal, complemental. **conversely** (kon´-, -vœs´-) *adv.* [see CONVERSE[1]]

conversion (kənvœ´shən) *n.* 1 the act or an instance of converting. 2 change from one state to another. 3 change to a new mode of life, religion, morals or politics. 4 the changing of one kind of unit, security etc. into another kind. 5 a change in the structure or use of a building. 6 a building so changed. 7 (*Logic*) transposition of the terms of a proposition. 8 (*Theol.*) the act of turning from sin to godliness. 9 (*Math.*) the clearing of an equation of fractions. 10 the transformation of fertile to fissile material in a nuclear reactor. 11 in rugby or American football, the scoring of a goal from the kick taken after a try etc. has been scored. 12 (*Psych.*) the changing of a mental conflict into a physical disorder. [F, from L *conversio -ōnem*, from *convertere*, to CONVERT[1]]

convert[1] (kənvœt´) *v.t.* 1 to change from one physical state to another, to transmute. 2 to cause to turn from one religion or party to another. 3 to change (one kind of securities.) into another kind. 4 to change the structure or use of (a building or part of a building) (*We converted the garage into a bedroom*; *They live in a converted oast house*). 5 in rugby, to complete (a try) by kicking a goal. 6 (*Logic*) to transpose the terms of (a proposition). ~*v.i.* 1 to be converted or convertible. 2 in American football, to make a conversion. **to convert to one's own use** to appropriate or make use of (another's property) wrongfully. **converter, convertor** *n.* 1 a person or thing that converts. 2 a device for changing alternating current to direct current or vice versa. 3 a device for changing a signal from one frequency to another. 4 (*Comput.*) a device that converts data from one format to another. 5 (*also* **converter reactor**) a reactor that converts fertile to fissile nuclear material. 6 a vessel used in refining molten metal, esp. in making steel. **convertible** *a.* 1 that may be converted or changed. 2 transmutable. 3 (of currency etc.) exchangeable for another kind. 4 (of a car) having a roof that can be folded back or removed. ~*n.* a convertible car. **convertibility** (-bil´-) *n.* **convertibly** *adv.* [L *convertere* (CON-, *vertere*, to turn)]

convert[2] (kon´vœt) *n.* a person who is converted from one religion, party, belief or opinion to another, esp. one who is converted to Christianity.

convex (kon´veks) *a.* having a curve or surface rounded like the outer side of a circle or sphere, as distinct from *concave*. **convexity** (-veks´-) *n.* **convexly** *adv.* **convexo-** (konvek´sō) *comb. form* convex. **convexo-concave** *a.* 1 convex on one side and concave on the other. 2 (of a lens) having greater curvature on the convex side than on the concave side. **convexo-convex** *a.* convex on both sides. **convexo-plane** *a.* convex on one side and plane on the other. [L *convexus*, arched]

convey (kənvā´) *v.t.* 1 to carry, to transport, to transmit. 2 to impart, to communicate. 3 (*Law*) to transfer (property). **conveyable** *a.* **conveyance** *n.* 1 the act or process of conveying. 2 a means of conveying, a vehicle. 3 (*Law*) a the act of transferring real property from one person to another. b the document by which it is transferred. 4 communication of ideas, meaning etc. **conveyancer** *n.* (*Law*) a person who draws up conveyances. **conveyancing** *n.* (*Law*) the drawing up of conveyances. **conveyor, conveyer** *n.* 1 a person or thing that conveys. 2 (*also* **conveyor belt**) an endless mechanical belt or moving platform which carries goods, materials etc., esp. along a production line in a factory. [OF *conveier*, *convoier*, late L *conviāre* (CON-, *via*, way)]

convict[1] (kənvikt´) *v.t.* 1 to prove guilty. 2 to return a verdict of guilty against. ~†*a.* convicted. **conviction** *n.* 1 the act of convicting. 2 the state of being convicted. 3 an instance of being convicted. 4 the state of being convinced. 5 strong belief, persuasion. 6 the act of convincing. **to carry conviction** to be convincing. **convictive** *a.* serving to convict or convince. [L *convictus*, p.p. of *convincere* (CON-, *vincere*, to conquer)]

convict[2] (kon´vikt) *n.* a criminal sentenced to a term in prison.

convince (kənvins´) *v.t.* 1 to satisfy the mind of. 2 to persuade, to cause to believe or realize. **convinced** *a.* persuaded, certain (*I'm convinced he was lying*). **convincement** *n.* conviction. **convincer** *n.* **convincible** *a.* **convincing** *a.* 1 persuasive, dispelling doubt (*a convincing explanation*). 2 positive, decisive (*a convincing victory*). **convincingly** *adv.* **convincingness** *n.* [L *convincere*, as CONVICT[1]]

convivial (kənviv´iəl) *a.* festive, social, jovial. **convivialist** *n.* **conviviality** (-al´-) *n.* **convivially** *adv.* [L *convivialis*, from *convivium*, a feast (as CON-, *vivere*, to live)]

convocation (konvəkā´shən) *n.* 1 the act of calling together. 2 an assembly, a meeting, a gathering. 3 an assembly of qualified graduates of certain universities. 4 an assembly of the clergy of a province. 5 (*esp. N Am.*) a ceremony for the conferment of degrees etc. **convocational** *a.* [as CONVOKE]

convoke (kənvōk´) *v.t.* (*formal*) 1 to call or summon together. 2 to convene. [F *convoquer*, L *convocāre* (CON-, *vocāre*, to call)]

convolute (kon´vəloot) *a.* 1 rolled or coiled together. 2 (of petals, leaves etc.) rolled up in another of the same kind. 3 convoluted. **convoluted** (-loo´tid) *a.* 1 intricate, complex. 2 convolute. **convolutedly** *adv.* **convolution** (-loo´shən) *n.* 1 the act of convolving. 2 the state of being convolved. 3 a fold, esp. in the surface of the brain. 4 a coil. 5 a winding motion. 6 intricacy, complexity. **convolutional** *a.* **convolve** (kənvolv´) *v.t.* 1 to roll or wind together. 2 to wind (one part) over another. **convolved** *a.* **convolvulus** (-vol´vūləs) *n.* (*pl.* **convolvuluses, convolvuli** (-lī)) any climbing plant of the genus *Convolvulus*, containing the bindweed. [L *convolūtus*, p.p. of *convolvere* (CON-, *volvere*, to roll)]

convoy (kon´voi) *v.t.* to accompany in transit by land or sea, for the sake of protection, esp. with a warship. ~*n.* 1 the act of convoying or escorting. 2 a protecting force accompanying persons, goods, ships etc. 3 an escort, a guard. 4 a company of merchant ships, goods vehicles etc. being convoyed or travelling together. 5 goods etc.

being convoyed. **in convoy** travelling together, with or without an escort. [F *convoier*, CONVEY]

convulse (kənvŭls´) *v.t.* **1** to agitate violently. **2** to affect with convulsions. **3** (*coll.*) to excite uncontrollable laughter in. **convulsant** *a.* inducing convulsions. ~*n.* a drug that induces convulsions. **convulsion** (-vŭl´shən) *n.* **1** (*usu. pl.*) an involuntary action of the muscular tissues of the body characterized by violent contractions and alternate relaxations. **2** a violent agitation, disturbance or commotion. **3** (*pl., coll.*) uncontrollable laughter. **convulsionary** *a.* **convulsive** *a.* **1** characterized by convulsions. **2** producing convulsions. **3** affected with convulsions. **convulsively** *adv.* **convulsiveness** *n.* [L *convulsus*, p.p. of *convellere* (*vellere*, to pluck)]

cony (kō´ni), **coney** *n.* (*pl.* **conies, coneys**) **1** a rabbit. **2** rabbit fur. **3** (*Bible*) a small animal that lives in holes among rocks, a hyrax. [OF *conil, connil*; the sing. *cony* from the pl. *conys* or *conies*, from the OF pl. *coniz*, L *cuniculus*, a rabbit (etym. uncertain)]

coo (koo) *v.i.* (*3rd pers. sing. pres.* **coos,** *pres.p.* **cooing,** *past, p.p.* **cooed**) **1** to make a soft low sound, like a dove or pigeon. **2** to speak lovingly. ~*v.t.* to say in cooing fashion. ~*n.* the characteristic sound of a dove or pigeon. ~*int.* used to express astonishment. **to bill and coo** BILL[2]. [imit.]

co-occur (kōəkœ´) *v.i.* (*pres.p.* **co-occurring,** *past, p.p.* **co-occurred**) to occur at the same time or in the same place. **co-occurrence** (-kŭr´əns) *n.*

cooee (koo´ē) *n.* a call used to attract attention. ~*int.* used to attract attention. ~*v.i.* (*3rd pers. sing. pres.* **cooees,** *pres.p.* **cooeeing,** *past, p.p.* **cooeed**) to make this call. **within (a) cooee** (*Austral., New Zeal., coll.*) within calling distance (of). [Austral. Abor.]

cook (kuk) *n.* a person who prepares food for the table with the use of heat. ~*v.t.* **1** to prepare (food) for the table by boiling, roasting etc. **2** (*coll.*) to garble, to falsify. **3** (*sl.*) to ruin. **4** (*N Am., coll.*) to do successfully. ~*v.i.* **1** to act as a cook. **2** to undergo the process of cooking. **3** (*N Am., coll.*) to proceed successfully. **to be cooking** (*coll.*) to be happening (*What's cooking?*). **to cook someone's goose 1** (*coll.*) to ruin someone's chances. **2** (*coll.*) to spoil someone's plans. **to cook the books** (*coll.*) to falsify the accounts. **to cook up** (*coll.*) to concoct (an excuse, a story etc.). **cookable** *a.* **cookbook** *n.* a book containing recipes and advice on preparing food. **cook-chill** *a.* denoting convenience food that has been cooked and chilled by the manufacturer for subsequent reheating and serving (*a cook-chill meal*). **cooker** *n.* **1** a stove or other apparatus for cooking. **2** (*coll.*) a cooking apple or similar item. **cookery** *n.* (*pl.* **cookeries**) **1** the act or art of cooking. **2** the occupation of a cook. **3** (*N Am.*) a place for cooking. **cookery book** *n.* a cookbook. **cookhouse** *n.* **1** (*Naut.*) a galley. **2** a detached kitchen in warm countries. **3** a camp kitchen. **cooking** *a.* **1** used in cooking. **2** suitable for cooking rather than eating raw (*a cooking apple; cooking chocolate*). ~*n.* cookery. **cookout** *n.* (*N Am.*) a party at which food is cooked out of doors. **cook shop** *n.* **1** a shop selling cookware. **2** (*N Am.*) an eating house. **cookware** *n.* utensils used for cooking. **cooky**[1] *n.* (*pl.* **cookies**) (*coll.*) a cook. [OE *cōc*, L *coquus*, a cook (*coquere*, to cook; cogn. with Gr. *pessein*, Sansk. *pach*)]

cookie (kuk´i) *n.* **1** (*N Am.*) (*also* **cooky,** *pl.* **cookies**) a sweet biscuit. **2** (*coll.*) a person (of a particular character) (*a smart cookie*). **3** (*Sc.*) a bun, usu. plain, sometimes with a jam filling, icing etc. **the way the cookie crumbles** the way things are or happen, an unalterable state of affairs. [prob. from Dut. *koekje*]

Cook's tour (kuks tuə´) *n.* (*coll.*) **1** an extensive but very rapid tour. **2** an extensive but very rapid and superficial survey, inspection or overview. [Thomas *Cook*, British travel agent, 1808–92]

cooky[1] COOK.

cooky[2] COOKIE.

cool (kool) *a.* **1** slightly or moderately cold. **2** not retaining or causing heat. **3** (of colours) greenish or bluish, creating a feeling of coolness. **4** aloof, unfriendly. **5** apathetic, unenthusiastic, indifferent. **6** calm, dispassionate, not showing emotion. **7** calmly impudent or audacious. **8** (*coll.*) amounting to without exaggeration, as much as. **9** (*coll.*) very good, excellent. **10** (*coll.*) sophisticated, fashionable, smart, trendy. **11** (*coll.*) acceptable. **12** (*coll.*) relaxed. **13** (of jazz) controlled and restrained. ~*n.* **1** coolness, moderate temperature. **2** a cool place. ~*v.t.* **1** to cause to lose heat, to make cool or cooler. **2** to quiet, to calm, to allay. ~*v.i.* **1** to lose heat, to become cool or cooler. **2** (of excitement, enthusiasm etc.) to become less. **3** to become less angry. **cool as a cucumber** COOL. **to cool it** (*sl.*) to calm down. **to cool one's heels** (*coll.*) to be kept waiting. **to keep one's cool** (*coll.*) to remain calm. **to lose one's cool** (*coll.*) to become upset, flustered or angry. **to play it cool** PLAY. **coolant** *n.* a fluid used for cooling or lubricating. **cool bag, cool box** *n.* an insulated bag or box in which food is kept cold. **cool cupboard** *n.* a refrigerated storage cupboard for food or drink, esp. in a shop. **cooler** *n.* **1** that which cools. **2** an apparatus or container for cooling things. **3** (*N Am.*) something for keeping things cool, such as a refrigerator or cool bag. **4** a drink consisting of wine, soda water and fruit juice. **5** (*sl.*) prison. **cool-headed** *a.* remaining, or able to remain, calm in tense, dangerous etc. situations. **cooling-off period** *n.* a period of time during which one may reconsider a decision, arrangement etc. **cooling tower** *n.* a tower in which water is cooled by trickling over wooden slats, for industrial reuse. **coolish** *a.* **coolly** *adv.* **coolness** *n.* **cool tankard** *n.* an old-fashioned drink, usu. made of wine and water mixed with lemon juice etc. **coolth** *n.* (*dial. or facet.*) coolness. [OE *cōl*, from Gmc. *kōl-, kal-* (cp. G *kühl*, L *gelu*)]

coolabah (koo´ləbah), **coolibah** (-libah) *n.* (*Austral.*) any of several species of eucalyptus trees, esp. *Eucalyptus microtheca*. [Austral. Abor.]

coolie (koo´li), **cooly** *n.* (*pl.* **coolies**) **1** an unskilled hired labourer in or from the East, esp. India and China. **2** (*offensive*) a person of Indian extraction living in South Africa. **coolie hat** *n.* a type of broad, round, conical straw hat, as formerly worn by Chinese coolies. [Hind. *qūlī*]

coom (koom), **coomb** *n.* refuse matter, such as soot, coal-dust or mould. [CULM[2]]

coomb[1] COOM.

coomb[2], **coombe** COMBE.

coon (koon) *n.* **1** (*coll.*) a raccoon. **2** (*offensive*) a black. **gone coon** GO[1]. **coonskin** *n.* **1** the fur of a raccoon. **2** a hat made of the skin and tail of a raccoon. [short for RACCOON]

coon-can (koon´kan) *n.* a card game like rummy. [Sp. *con quién*, with whom]

coop[1] (koop) *n.* **1** a cage or small enclosure for poultry or small animals. **2** a confined space, esp. a prison or prison cell. **3** a wickerwork trap for catching eels etc. ~*v.t.* to confine in or as if in a coop (often with *up, in*). [ME *cupe*, a basket, perh. from L *cupa*, a lute, a cask]

coop[2] CO-OP.

co-op (kō´op), **coop** *n.* a cooperative society, business venture, or shop. ~*a.* (of a business venture etc.) cooperative.

cooper (koo´pə) *n.* **1** a person whose trade is to make barrels, tubs etc. **2** a person who mends casks etc. on a ship. **3** a mixture of stout and porter (orig. prepared for the coopers in breweries). ~*v.t.* to make or repair (casks etc.). ~*v.i.* to work as a cooper. **cooperage** *n.* **1** the trade or workshop of a cooper. **2** the price paid for a cooper's work. **coopery** *n.* (*pl.* **cooperies**) the trade or workshop of a cooper. [prob. from WG (cp. MDut. *cuper*, MLG *küper*), med. L *cupārius*, from *cupa*, a cask]

cooperate (kōop´ərāt), **co-operate** *v.i.* **1** to work or act with another or others for a common end. **2** to be helpful, obliging or accommodating. **3** to form a cooperative business association. **4** to contribute to an effect. **cooperant** *a.* **cooperation** (-ā´shən) *n.* **1** the act of cooperating. **2** helpfulness, willingness to oblige another. **3** a form of partnership or association for the production or distribution of goods, or the formation of such partnerships or associations. **4** (*Biol.*) interaction between two species which, although not necessary for the survival of either, is of benefit to both. **cooperative** *a.* **1** working, or willing to work, with others for a common end or the common good. **2** helpful, obliging, accommodating. **3** (of a business venture etc.) owned jointly by the workers etc., for the economic benefit of them all. ~*n.* a cooperative business, shop etc. **cooperatively** *adv.* **cooperativeness** *n.* **cooperative shop, cooperative store** *n.* the shop of a cooperative society. **cooperative society** *n.* an association for the production or distribution of goods and the division of profits among the members (i.e. the customers and/or workers). **cooperator** *n.* **1** a person who cooperates. **2** a member of a cooperative society. [late L *coöperātus*, p.p. of *coöperārī* (CO-, *operārī*, to work, from *opus operis*, work)]

co-opt (kōopt´) *v.t.* **1** to elect onto a committee etc. by the votes of the members of that committee etc., as opposed to by the votes of a larger body of voters. **2** to adopt or use for one's own ends. **3** to take into or cause to join another, esp. larger, group, such as a political party. **co-optation, co-option** *n.* [L *cooptāre* (CO-, *optāre*, to choose)]

coordinate[1] (kōaw´dinət) *a.* **1** of the same order, rank, importance, power etc. **2** coordinated, involving coordination. **3** (*Chem.*) denoting a covalent bond in which the two shared electrons are provided by one of the atoms involved. **4** (*Math.*) involving or using coordinates. ~*n.* **1** (*Math.*) any of two or more numbers used as elements of reference to determine the position of any point, line or plane. **2** (*pl.*) clothes in harmonizing colours and patterns, designed to be worn together. **3** any of two or more people or things of equal rank or status. **coordinate clause** *n.* (*Gram.*) a clause having the same status as another or others in a sentence. **coordinately** *adv.* [L *ordinātus*, p.p. of *ordināre*, to arrange (*ordo -dinis*, ORDER)]

coordinate[2] (kōaw´dināt) *v.t.* **1** to make coordinate. **2** to correlate, to bring into orderly relation of parts and whole. ~*v.i.* to work well together, to produce a good effect. **Coordinated Universal Time** *n.* Greenwich Mean Time. **coordination** (-ā´shən) *n.* **1** the act of coordinating or state of being coordinated. **2** effectively coordinated activity. **3** well-balanced, dexterous, skilful etc. actions, or the ability to perform such. **coordinative** *a.* **coordinator** *n.*

coot (koot) *n.* **1** a small black British aquatic bird, *Fulica atra*, or any other bird of the same genus. **2** a stupid person. [Dut. *koet*]

cootie (koo´ti) *n.* (*N Am., New Zeal., sl.*) a body louse. [etym. uncertain; perh. from Malay *kutu*, a louse]

co-own (kō·ōn´) *v.t.* to own jointly. **co-owner** *n.* **co-ownership** *n.*

cop[1] (kop) *v.t.* (*pres.p.* **copping**, *past, p.p.* **copped**) **1** (*sl.*) to seize. **2** to arrest. **3** to catch or get (something unpleasant). **4** to obtain (drugs). ~*n.* **1** (*coll.*) a policeman. **2** (*sl.*) an arrest. **fair cop** FAIR[1]. **no cop** (*sl.*) worthless. **not much cop** (*sl.*) worthless. **to cop a plea** (*N Am., sl.*) to plea-bargain. **to cop it 1** (*sl.*) to be caught or punished. **2** (*sl.*) to be killed. **to cop out 1** (*sl.*) to refuse or avoid responsibility or a task. **2** (*sl.*) to give up, stop. **3** (*sl.*) to break a promise. **cop-out** *n.* **copper**[1] (kop´ə) *n.* (*coll.*) **1** a policeman. **2** a person who cops or seizes. **cop-shop** *n.* (*sl.*) a police station. [perh. F *caper*, to seize, from L *capere*, to take]

cop[2] (kop) *n.* **1** a conical roll or thread on the spindle of a spinning-machine. **2** (*esp. dial.*) a hill. **3** the top. [OE]

copacetic (kōpəset´ik, -sē´-), **copasetic, copesetic, copesettic** (-set´-) *a.* (*N Am., sl.*) excellent, very satisfactory. [etym. unknown]

copaiba (kōpā´bə, -pī´-), **copaiva** (-və) *n.* **1** the balsam or gum-resin obtained from the plant *Copaifera officinalis* or allied species. **2** the plant itself. [Sp., from Tupi *cupauba*]

copal (kō´pəl) *n.* **1** a resin obtained from any of a number of tropical trees. **2** a varnish made from this. [Sp., from Nahuatl *copalli*, resin, incense]

coparcener (kōpah´sənə) *n.* a coheir or coheiress. **coparcenary, coparceny** *n.* **1** joint heirship. **2** joint ownership. ~*a.* relating to coparceners.

copartner (kōpaht´nə) *n.* **1** a partner, an associate. **2** a partaker. **copartnership, copartnery** *n.*

cope[1] (kōp) *v.i.* **1** to encounter, to contend successfully (with). **2** to deal (with), manage successfully. [OF *couper*, to strike (see COUP[1])]

cope[2] (kōp) *n.* **1** an ecclesiastical sleeveless vestment worn in processions and at solemn ceremonies. **2** (*poet.*) anything spread overhead, such as a cloud or the sky. ~*v.t.* to cover with or as if with a cope or coping. ~*v.i.* to form an overhang. **copestone** *n.* **1** a coping-stone. **2** a finishing touch. **coping** *n.* the course projecting horizontally on the top of a wall. **coping-stone** *n.* **1** the topmost stone of a building. **2** a stone forming part of the coping. **3** the sloping course on a wall or buttress to throw off the water. [late L *cāpa*]

cope[3] (kōp) *v.t.* **1** to buy. **2** to barter. ~*v.i.* to make a bargain, to deal. **coper** *n.* a dealer, esp. in horses. [from LG (cp. Dut. *koopen*, cogn. with OE *cēapian*, *cēap*, see CHEAP)]

copeck (kō´pek, kop´-), **kopeck, kopek** *n.* a Russian monetary unit and coin, the hundredth part of a rouble. [Rus. *kopeika*]

copepod (kō´pipod) *n.* any of the many, usu. tiny, saltwater and freshwater crustaceans of the subclass Copepoda, some parasitic, others found in plankton. [Gr. *kōpē*, an oar, *pous podos*, foot]

coper COPE[3].

Copernican (kəpœ´nikən) *a.* of or relating to the astronomical system of the Polish astronomer Copernicus, 1473–1543, which has the sun as its centre. [*Copernicus*, L form of Pol. *Kopernik*]

copiable COPY.

copier COPY.

co-pilot (kō´pīlət) *n.* a second or assistant pilot of an aircraft.

coping COPE[2].

coping saw (kō´ping saw) *n.* a saw consisting of a blade in a U-shaped frame, used for cutting curves in wood etc. too large for a fretsaw. [OF *coper*, to cut]

copious (kō´piəs) *a.* **1** plentiful, abundant, ample. **2** producing a plentiful supply. **3** profuse, prolific, rich in vocabulary. **4** providing a lot of information. **copiously** *adv.* **copiousness** *n.* [L *cōpiōsus*, from *cōpia*, plenty]

copita (kəpē´tə) *n.* (*pl.* **copitas**) a tulip-shaped sherry glass. [Sp., dim. of *copa*, cup]

coplanar (kōplā´nə) *a.* (*Geom.*) lying on the same plane. **coplanarity** (-plənar´-) *n.*

copolymer (kōpol´imə) *n.* (*Chem.*) a polymer consisting of random or repeated sequences of more than one type of molecule. **copolymerize, copolymerise** *v.t., v.i.* **copolymerization** (-zā´shən) *n.*

copper[1] COP[1].

copper[2] (kop´ə) *n.* **1** a reddish-brown malleable, ductile metallic element, at. no. 29, chem. symbol Cu. **2** (*usu.*

pl.) a copper or bronze coin. **3** the colour of copper. **4** a large cooking pot, laundry boiler etc. (formerly made of copper). **5** any of various species of butterfly of the genus *Lycaena* or related genera, with copper-coloured wings. *~a.* made of or like copper. *~v.t.* to cover, coat etc. with copper. **copper beech** *n.* a variety of beech with copper-coloured leaves. **Copper Belt** *n.* a region of central Africa, comprising parts of Zambia and Zaire, in which there are rich deposits of copper. **copper bit** *n.* a soldering iron with a copper point. **copper-bottomed** *a.* **1** (*Naut.*) sheathed with copper. **2** (financially) reliable. **copper butterfly** *n.* a copper (the butterfly). **copper-fastened** *a.* **1** (*Naut.*) fastened with copper bolts. **2** (of an agreement) binding. **copperhead** *n.* **1** a highly venomous N American snake, *Agkistrodon contortrix*, allied to the rattlesnake. **2** a reddish-brown venomous snake, *Denisonia superba*, found in southern Australia and Tasmania. **3** an Indian rodent-eating snake, *Elaphe radiata*. **4** (*Hist.*) a Northern sympathizer with the Confederates during the American Civil War. **copperplate** *n.* **1** neat and elegant handwriting. **2** a polished plate of copper on which something is engraved for printing. **3** an impression from such a plate. *~a.* **1** (of handwriting) neat and elegant. **2** of or relating to the art of engraving on copper. **copper pyrites** *n.* (*Mineral.*) CHALCOPYRITE. **coppersmith** *n.* a worker in copper. **copper sulphate** *n.* a copper salt, $CuSO_4$, usu. found as blue crystals, used as a fungicide, in dyeing etc. **copper vitriol** *n.* blue vitriol, hydrous copper sulphate. **coppery** *a.* made of, containing or resembling copper. [OE *copor*, L *cuprum Cyprium*, Gr. *Kuprios*, Cyprian]

copperas (kop´ərəs) *n.* a green sulphate of iron, green vitriol. [ME and OF *coperose*, L *cuprōsa*, from *cuprum*, copper]

coppice (kop´is) *n.* a small wood of small trees and undergrowth, cut periodically for firewood. *~v.t.* to cut (trees and bushes) to make a coppice. *~v.i.* **1** to form a coppice. **2** to grow new shoots from a cut stump. **coppiced** *a.* **coppicewood** *n.* COPSEWOOD (under COPSE). [OF *copeiz*, cut wood, from a late L *colpātīcium* (*colpāre*, to strike, to cut)]

copra (kop´rə) *n.* the dried kernel of the coconut, yielding coconut oil. [Port. and Sp., prob. from Malay *koppara*, coconut]

co-precipitation (kōprisipitā´shən) *n.* (*Chem.*) precipitation of more than one compound from a solution at the same time.

copresent (kōprez´ənt) *a.* present at the same time. **copresence** *n.*

copro- (kop´rō) *comb. form* of or relating to or living on or among dung. [Gr. *kopros*, dung]

coprocessor (kō´prōsesə) *n.* (*Comput.*) a microprocessor which operates in conjunction with another processor in a computer by providing supplementary functions or performing specialized operations.

co-produce (kōprədūs´) *v.t.* to produce (a film, play etc.) jointly with one or more other people. **co-producer** *n.* **co-production** *n.*

coprolalia (koprōlā´liə) *n.* (*Psych.*) the obsessive repeated use of obscene language.

coprolite (kop´rəlīt) *n.* the fossil dung of various extinct animals, chiefly saurians, largely used as fertilizer. **coprolitic** (-lit´-) *a.*

coprology (kəprol´əji) *n.* **1** lewdness. **2** filth in literature or art.

coprophagan (kəprof´əgən) *n.* any insect belonging to the Coprophagi, lamellicorn beetles feeding on or living in dung. **coprophagous** *a.* dung-eating. **coprophagy** (-ji) *n.* [Gr. *koprophagos* (*phagein*, to eat)]

coprophilia (koprəfil´iə) *n.* morbid, esp. sexual, interest in excrement. **coprophiliac** (-ak) *n.* **coprophilous** (-prof´iləs) *a.* growing in dung.

coprosma (kəproz´mə) *n.* (*pl.* **coprosmas**) any of various evergreen Australasian shrubs or small trees of the genus *Coprosma*, which bear colourful berries. [Gr. *osmē*, smell]

copse (kops) *n.* a coppice. *~v.t.* **1** to plant or preserve for copsewood. **2** to cover with copses. **copsewood** *n.* undergrowth, brushwood. **copsy** *a.* (*comp.* **copsier**, *superl.* **copsiest**). [COPPICE]

Copt (kopt) *n.* **1** an Egyptian at the time of the ancient Greek and Roman empires. **2** a Coptic Christian. **Coptic** *a.* of or relating to the Copts, or to the monophysite Egyptian Church established in the 5th cent. *~n.* the language of the Copts, now extinct except in Coptic Church liturgy. [F *Copt*, Arab. *qubt*, Copt. *gyptios*, *kyptaios*, Gr. *Aiguptios*, Egyptian]

Copt. *abbr.* Coptic.

copula (kop´ūlə) *n.* (*pl.* **copulas**) **1** (*Logic, Gram.*) the word in a sentence or proposition which links the subject and predicate together. **2** that which links or connects. **3** (*Mus.*) a brief connecting passage. **copular** *a.* [L *cōpula* (CO-, *apere*, to fasten, with dim. suf.)]

copulate[1] (kop´ūlāt) *v.i.* to have sexual intercourse. *~v.t.* to couple together. **copulation** (-lā´shən) *n.* **1** sexual intercourse. **2** the act of coupling. **3** (*Logic, Gram.*) connection. **copulative** *a.* **1** serving to unite. **2** (*Gram.*) acting as a copula. **3** (*Gram.*) having two or more words, phrases or predicates connected by a copulative conjunction. **4** of or relating to sexual union. *~n.* a copulative conjunction. **copulative conjunction** *n.* (*Gram.*) a conjunction which links words, phrases etc. that are connected in sense, e.g. *and*, as opposed to a disjunctive conjunction. **copulatively** *adv.* **copulatory** *a.* [L *cōpulātus*, p.p. of *cōpulāre*, as COPULA]

copulate[2] (kop´ūlət) *a.* joined, connected. [as COPULATE[1]]

copy (kop´i) *n.* (*pl.* **copies**) **1** a transcript or imitation of an original. **2** a thing made in imitation of or exactly like another. **3** an example of a particular work or book. **4** in journalism, material for reporting, writing articles etc. **5** something that will make a good (newspaper) story. **6** the words, as opposed to the pictures or graphic material, in an advertisement etc. **7** manuscript ready for setting. **8** an original, a model, a pattern. **9** a writing exercise. *~v.t.* **1** to make a copy of. **2** (*often with out*) to make a written copy of, to transcribe. **3** to follow as pattern or model. **4** (*with to*) to send or give a copy of (a letter etc.) to someone. *~v.i.* to make a copy, esp. illicitly. **copiable** *a.* **copier** *n.* **1** a person who copies. **2** a photocopier. **3** an imitator, a plagiarist. **4** a transcriber. **copybook** *n.* a book in which specimens of good handwriting, formerly usu. proverbs, maxims etc., are written clearly to be copied esp. by children learning to write. *~a.* **1** conventional. **2** perfect. **copycat** *n.* (*coll.*) a person who imitates someone else. *~a.* done in imitation. **copydesk** *n.* a desk in a newspaper office where copy is edited before being passed for printing. **copy editor** *n.* a person who prepares written material for printing by correcting its style, punctuation etc. **copy-edit** *v.t., v.i.* **copy-editing** *n.* **copyhold** *n.* (*Law, Hist.*) **1** a tenure for which the tenant has nothing to show but the copy of the rolls made by the steward of the lord's court. **2** property held by such tenure. *~a.* held by such tenure. **copyholder** *n.* **copyist** *n.* **copyreader** *n.* (*N Am.*) a copy editor or newspaper subeditor. **copyread** *v.t.* (*past, p.p.* **copyread** (-red)). **copyright** *n.* the exclusive right for the author of a literary or artistic production, or the author's heirs, to publish or sell copies of their work. *~a.* protected by copyright. *~v.t.* to secure copyright for (a book, music, picture etc.). **copyright library** *n.* any one of six libraries (three in England, one each in Scotland, Wales and the Republic of Ireland) entitled to receive a free copy of every book published in the United Kingdom. **copy-typist** *n.* a person who types from written copy, rather than from shorthand or tape. **copywriter** *n.* a person who writes advertisements. **copywriting** *n.* [F *copie*, L *cōpia*, abundance, med. L, a transcript]

coq au vin (kok ō vī´) *n.* a stew of chicken in red wine. [F, cock with wine]

coquelicot (kok´likō) *n.* **1** a name for any of the species of red-flowered field poppies. **2** a reddish-orange colour, the colour of the poppy flowers. [F, the poppy, orig. the cock's comb (*coq*, cock; termination onomat. from the cock's crowing)]

coquet (kəket´) *v.i.* (*pres.p.* **coquetting,** *past, p.p.* **coquetted**) **1** to flirt (with). **2** to make love. **3** to trifle. **4** to take up a task or a subject without serious intentions of carrying it on. **coquetry** (kō´-, kok´-) *n.* (*pl.* **coquetries**) **1** the practices of a coquette; affectation of encouragement to an admirer; flirtation. **2** treating serious matters lightly or frivolously. **coquette** *n.* **1** a female flirt; a jilt. **2** a hummingbird of the genus *Lophornis*. ~*v.i.* to coquet. **coquettish** *a.* **coquettishly** *adv.* **coquettishness** *n.* [F, dim. of *coq*, cock]

coquilla (kəkil´yə), **coquilla nut** *n.* the nut of *Attalea funifera*, a Brazilian palm, used in carving. [Sp., dim. of *coca*, a shell]

coquina (kōkē´nə) *n.* a type of soft, whitish limestone formed from broken shells and coral. [Sp., shellfish]

coquito (kəkē´tō) *n.* (*pl.* **coquitos**) a Chilean nut-bearing palm tree, *Jubaea chilensis*. [Sp., dim of *coco*, COCONUT (under COCO)]

Cor. *abbr.* **1** (*Bible*) Corinthians. **2** coroner.

cor[1] (kaw) *int.* (*sl.*) expressing surprise, amazement etc. **cor blimey** (blī´mi) *int.* used to express surprise, irritation etc. [corr. of *God* (*blind me*)]

cor[2] (kaw) *n.* (*Mus.*) a horn. **cor anglais** (kawr ong´glā) *n.* (*pl.* **cors anglais** (kawz ong´glā, kawr)) **1** the English horn, a woodwind instrument of the oboe family, slightly lower in pitch than the oboe. **2** a person who plays the cor anglais in an orchestra. **3** an organ stop producing the sound of a cor anglais. [F, from L *cornū*]

cor[3] (kaw) *n.* a Hebrew measure, a homer. [Heb. *kor*]

cor. *abbr.* **1** (*Mus.*) cornet. **2** coroner. **3** correction. **4** corrective. **5** correlative.

cor- (kaw) *pref.* the form of COM- used before *r*.

coracle (kor´əkəl) *n.* a light boat used in Wales and Ireland, made of wickerwork covered with leather or oiled cloth. [Welsh *corwgl* (cp. OIr. *curach*, boat)]

coracoid (kor´əkoid) *n.* **1** (*also* **coracoid process**) a hooklike process of the scapula in mammals. **2** a separate bone in the pectoral arch in birds, reptiles and monotremes. ~*a.* **1** hook-shaped. **2** resembling a crow's beak. [mod. L *coracoīdes*, Gr. *korakoeidēs* (*korax -akos*, a raven)]

coradicate (kōrad´ikət) *a.* derived from the same root. [L *rādīcātus*, from *radix*, root]

coral (kor´əl) *n.* **1** the calcareous skeletal structure secreted by certain marine polyps or zoophytes of the class Anthozoa, deposited in masses on the bottom of the sea. **2** the animal or colony of animals forming these structures. **3** a deep orange-pink colour. **4** the unfertilized eggs of a lobster or scallop (from their colour). **5** an infant's toy made of coral. ~*a.* made of or resembling coral. **coral island** *n.* an island formed by the growth and accumulation of coral. **coralliferous** (-lif´-) *a.* **coralliform** (koral´ifawm) *a.* (*Bot.*) branching like coral. **coralligenous** (-lij´in-) *a.* producing coral. **coralline** (-līn) *a.* **1** of the nature of coral. **2** containing or resembling coral. ~*n.* **1** a seaweed of the genus *Corallina* with calcareous fronds. **2** any of various coral-like aquatic animals. **corallite** (-līt) *n.* **1** a coral-shaped petrifaction. **2** the skeleton or case of a polyp. **3** coralline marble. **corallitic** (-lit´-) *a.* **coralloid** *a.* **1** resembling coral. **2** coralliform. ~*n.* an organism akin to or resembling coral. **coral rag** *n.* a coralliferous limestone of the Middle Oolite. **coral reef** *n.* a ridge or series of ridges of coral, tending to form a coral island. **coralroot** *n.* **1** a purple-flowered cruciferous woodland plant, *Cardamine bulbifera*. **2** (*also* **coralroot orchid**) any of a number of almost leafless orchids of the genus *Corallorhiza*, living mostly on dead organic matter. **coral snake** *n.* any of a large number of snakes belonging to the cobra family Elapidae, most patterned with bright bands of red, yellow, black or white. **coral tree** *n.* a tropical tree of the genus *Erythrina*, bearing blood-red flowers. [OF, from L *corallum*, Gr. *korallion*]

coram populo (kawram pop´ūlō) *adv.* in public. [L]

cor anglais COR[2].

coranto (kəran´tō) *n.* (*pl.* **corantos**) a rapid kind of dance. [from F *courante* or It. *coranta*]

corban (kaw´bən) *n.* among the ancient Jews, a thing consecrated to God. [Heb. *qorbān*, an offering]

corbeil (kaw´bəl, -bā´) *n.* **1** a sculptured basket, esp. such as forms the ornamental summit of a pillar etc. **2** in fortifications, a small basket filled with earth, and set upon parapets as a protection from the besiegers' fire. [F *corbeille*, from L *corbicula*, dim. of *corbis*, a basket]

corbel (kaw´bəl) *n.* **1** a bracket or projection of stone, wood or iron projecting from a wall to support some superincumbent weight. **2** a corbel block. ~*v.t.* (*pres.p.* **corbelling,** (*N Am.*) **corbeling,** *past, p.p.* **corbelled,** (*N Am.*) **corbeled**) **1** (*with off, out*) to support by means of corbels. **2** to lay (a stone etc.) to form a corbel. **3** (*with off, out*) to (cause to) project by constructing on corbels. **corbel block** *n.* a short timber helping to support a beam at either end. **corbel table** *n.* a projecting course, parapet etc. supported by corbels. [OF, from low L *corbellum*, from *corvellus*, dim. of *corvus*, a raven]

corbie (kaw´bi) *n.* (*Sc.*) a raven, a crow or a rook. **corbie-steps** *n.pl.* the stepped slopes of gables (common in Scottish and Flemish architecture). [OF *corbin*, dim. of *corb*, a raven]

cord (kawd) *n.* **1** thick string or thin rope composed of several strands, or a piece of this. **2** an electric flex. **3** (*Anat.*) a cordlike structure. **4** (*pl.*) corduroy trousers. **5** ribbed cloth, esp. corduroy. **6** a raised rib in woven cloth. **7** anything which binds or draws together emotionally etc. **8** a measure for cut wood, 128 cu. ft. (approx. 3.6 m^3). ~*v.t.* **1** to bind with a cord. **2** to fit a cord to. **cordage** *n.* **1** a quantity or store of ropes. **2** the ropes or rigging of a ship collectively. **3** a quantity of wood measured in cords. **corded** *a.* **1** bound or fastened with cords. **2** made with cords. **3** ribbed or twilled (like corduroy). **4** (of muscles) standing out like cords. **cordless** *a.* (of an electrical appliance) operated by stored electricity, e.g. batteries, as in *cordless telephone*. **cordwood** *n.* wood piled up to be sold by the cord. [F *corde*, L *chorda*, Gr. *chordē*]

cordate (kaw´dāt) *a.* heart-shaped. [L *cor cordis*, heart]

Cordelier (kawdəliə´) *n.* **1** a Franciscan friar of the strictest rule (from the knotted rope worn round the waist). **2** a member of a revolutionary club founded in Paris in 1790, which met in an old convent of the Cordeliers. [F, from *cordelle*, dim. of *corde*, CORD]

cordial (kaw´diəl) *a.* **1** sincere, hearty, warm-hearted. **2** cheering or comforting the heart. **3** proceeding from the heart. ~*n.* **1** a sweetened drink made with fruit juice, usu. diluted before drinking. **2** a medicine used to increase the circulation or to raise the spirits. **3** anything which cheers or comforts. **4** a liqueur. **cordiality** (-al´-) *n.* (*pl.* **cordialities**). **cordially** *adv.* [F, from med. L *cordiālis* (*cor cordis*, the heart)]

cordiform (kaw´difawm) *a.* heart-shaped. [L *cor cordis*, the heart, FORM]

cordillera (kawdilyeə´rə) *n.* a ridge or chain of mountains, esp. used (*in pl.*) of the Andes, and the continuation of these in Central America and Mexico. [Sp., from *cordilla*, a string or rope, dim. of *cuerda*, L *chorda*, cord]

cordite (kaw´dīt) *n.* a smokeless explosive, prepared in stringlike grains. [CORD]

cordoba (kaw´dəbə) *n.* **1** the basic monetary unit of Nicaragua, equal to 100 centavos. **2** a coin of this value. [Sp. *córdoba*]

cordon (kaw´dən) *n.* **1** a line or series of persons, posts or ships placed so as to guard or blockade a place. **2** a ribbon or cord worn as an ornament, a mark of rank or the badge of an order. **3** a fruit-tree trained and closely pruned to grow as a single stem. **4** a projecting band of stones in a wall, a string-course. [F, dim. of *corde*, cord]

cordon bleu (kawdõ blœ´) *a.* (of food or cookery) of the highest standard. ~*n.* (*pl.* **cordons bleus** (kawdõ blœz´)) a cook or chef of the highest calibre. [F, blue ribbon]

cordon sanitaire (kawdõ saniteə´) *n.* (*pl.* **cordons sanitaires** (kawdõ sanēteə´)) **1** a line of guards surrounding a disease-infected area, to cut off communication and so prevent the spread of the disease. **2** any similar preventative measure or set-up designed to isolate or protect. [F, sanitary cordon]

cordovan (kaw´dəvən) *n.* **1** fine leather, esp. horsehide, orig. made at Cordova (now Córdoba) in Spain. **2** cordwain.

corduroy (kaw´dəroi, -roi´) *n.* **1** a stout-ribbed cotton cloth made with a pile. **2** (*pl.*) corduroy trousers. ~*a.* made of this material. **corduroy road** *n.* a causeway of logs laid over a swamp. [prob. from F *corde du roi*, king's cord]

cordwain (kawd´wān) *n.* a kind of leather, finished as a black morocco, orig. from Córdoba in Spain. **cordwainer** *n.* **1** a worker in cordwain. **2** a shoemaker. [OF *cordoan*, late L *cordoānum*, from *Cordoa*, Córdoba)]

CORE (kaw) *abbr.* Congress of Racial Equality (in the US).

core (kaw) *n.* **1** the heart or inner part of anything. **2** the hard middle of an apple, pear or similar fruit, containing the seeds. **3** the pith, the gist, the essence. **4** the insulated conducting wires of a cable. **5** the central strand of a rope. **6** (*also* **core curriculum**) the essential part of a school curriculum, studied by all pupils. **7** the central part of the earth. **8** the round mass of rock brought up by an annular drill. **9** a piece of magnetic material, such as soft iron, inside an induction coil. **10** the part of a nuclear reactor containing the fissile material. **11** a small ring of magnetic material formerly used in a computer memory to store one bit. **12** (*also* **core memory, core store**) a computer memory which uses cores. **13** a mass of sand or something similar put into a mould in order to create a space or hollow in a casting. **14** a layer of wood supporting veneer. **15** the central portion of a flint left after flakes have been struck off. ~*v.t.* to remove the core from. **coreless** *a.* **corer** *n.* **core subjects** *n.pl.* the subjects, such as maths or science, studied as part of a core curriculum. **core time** *n.* in a flexitime system, the central part of the day when everyone is at work. [etym. uncertain (L *cor*, the heart, and OF *cor*, horn, have been suggested)]

coregent (kōrē´jənt) *n.* a joint ruler or governor.

corelation CORRELATION (under CORRELATE).

coreligionist (kōrilij´ənist) *n.* a person of the same religion.

corella (kərel´ə) *n.* any of various small Australian cockatoos of the genus *Kakatoe*. [Austral. Abor.]

coreopsis (koriop´sis) *n.* (*pl.* **coreopsises**) any of the many annual or perennial garden plants of the genus *Coreopsis*, with bright, mostly yellow flowers. [Gr. *koris*, a bug; *opsis*, appearance (from the shape of the seed)]

☒ **corespond** common misspelling of CORRESPOND.

co-respondent (kōrispon´dənt) *n.* a joint respondent in a lawsuit, esp. a divorce suit.

corf (kawf) *n.* (*pl.* **corves** (-vz)) **1** formerly a basket, now usu. a wagon, for carrying ore or coal in mines. **2** a large basket or perforated box for keeping lobsters or fish alive in the water. [prob. from LG (cp. Dut. *korf*, G *Korb*)]

CORGI (kaw´gi) *abbr.* Confederation for Registration of Gas Installers.

corgi (kaw´gi) *n.* (*pl.* **corgis**) a small, smooth-haired, short-legged dog, orig. from Wales. [Welsh, dwarf dog]

coriaceous (koriā´shəs) *a.* **1** made of or resembling leather. **2** (*Bot.*) stiff like leather. [L *coriāceus*, from *corium*, skin, leather]

coriander (korian´də) *n.* **1** an umbellifer, *Coriandrum sativum*, with aromatic and carminative seeds used as a spice in cooking. **2** the seeds of this plant. [F *coriandre*, L *coriandrum*, Gr. *koriannon*]

Corinthian (kərin´thiən) *a.* **1** of or relating to Corinth, a city of Greece. **2** licentious, dissipated. **3** (of sport, players etc.) amateur. **4** (of literary style) over-ornate. ~*n.* **1** a native or inhabitant of Corinth. **2** a debauchee. **3** a dandy. **4** an amateur in sport, esp. if wealthy. **Corinthianesque** (-esk´) *a.* **Corinthian order** *n.* (*Archit.*) the most elaborate and ornate of the three Grecian orders, the capital being enriched with graceful foliated forms added to the volutes of the Ionic capital.

Coriolis effect (koriō´lis) *n.* (*Physics*) the apparent deflection, caused by the rotation of the earth, of a body moving relative to the earth, the deflection being to the right in the northern hemisphere and to the left in the southern hemisphere. **Coriolis force** *n.* the force causing the Coriolis effect. [Gustave-Gaspard *Coriolis*, French mathematician and engineer, 1792–1843]

corium (kaw´riəm) *n.* (*pl.* **coria** (-riə)) **1** the innermost layer of the skin in mammals. **2** a kind of body-armour, composed of scales or small plates of leather, worn by Roman soldiers. [L, skin, leather]

cork (kawk) *n.* **1** a stopper for a bottle or cask. **2** the very light outer layer of bark of the cork oak, from which stoppers for bottles, floats for fishing etc. are made. **3** a float for fishing. **4** (*Bot.*) a layer of close-fitting, dead, impermeable cells protecting the living internal tissues of plants against injury and loss of water. ~*a.* made of cork. ~*v.t.* **1** to close with a cork. **2** (*often with up*) to stifle or restrain (feelings etc.). **3** to blacken with burnt cork. **corkage** *n.* **1** a charge levied at hotels and restaurants on wines consumed by guests but not supplied by the hotel. **2** the corking or uncorking of bottles. **cork cambium** *n.* PHELLOGEN. **corked** *a.* **1** stopped with a cork. **2** (of wine) supposedly tasting of the cork (but in fact tainted by a fungus growing on the cork). **3** blackened with burnt cork. **corker** *n.* (*coll.*) **1** something or somebody astounding. **2** a statement that puts an end to a discussion. **corking** *a.* (*coll.*) excellent, superb, magnificent. **cork jacket** *n.* a jacket lined with cork, to support the wearer in water. **corklike** *a.* **cork oak** *n.* an oak, *Quercus suber*, much cultivated in Spain, Portugal and France for the sake of its bark. **corkscrew** *n.* a spirally twisted, screwlike device for drawing corks. ~*v.i.* to move in a spiral or zigzag fashion. ~*v.t.* to cause to move in a spiral or zigzag fashion. ~*a.* twisted to resemble a corkscrew, spiral. **cork-tipped** *a.* (of a cigarette) having a filter of cork or a corklike material. **corkwood** *n.* **1** light, porous wood. **2** a name given to various trees with light, porous wood. **corky** *a.* (*comp.* **corkier**, *superl.* **corkiest**) **1** resembling cork in nature or appearance. **2** (*coll.*) sprightly, lively. **3** (of wine) corked. [etym. uncertain (cp. OSp. *alcorque*, a cork shoe, and Sp. *corcho*)]

corm (kawm) *n.* a bulblike, fleshy underground stem, sometimes called a solid bulb. **cormophyte** (kaw´məfīt) *n.* (*Bot.*) a plant of the division Cormophyta, comprising those with roots, stems and leaves. [Gr. *kormos*, the trimmed trunk of a tree]

cormorant (kaw´mərənt) *n.* any of the somewhat ducklike waterbirds of the genus *Phalacrocorax*, in Britain esp. *P. carbo*, a voracious seabird. [OF *cormerant*, L *corvus marīnus*, sea-crow]

Corn. *abbr.* **1** Cornish. **2** Cornwall.

corn[1] (kawn) *n.* **1** grain. **2** the seed of cereals. **3** wheat. **4** (*Sc., Ir.*) oats. **5** (*N Am., Austral., New Zeal.*) maize, sweetcorn. **6** something corny, such as a song, joke etc. **7** a single seed or grain of certain plants. ~*v.t.* **1** to preserve and season with salt. **2** †to feed with corn. **cornball** *n.* (*N Am.*) (*coll.*) a rustic person. ~*a.* unsophisticated, rustic. **cornbrash** *n.* a calcareous sandstone belonging to the Inferior Oolite. **cornbread** *n.* (*N Am.*) bread made from maize meal. **corn chandler** *n.* a retail dealer in corn etc. **corn circle** *n.* CROP CIRCLE (under CROP). **corn cob** *n.* a spike of maize. **corn-cob pipe** *n.* a tobacco-pipe with a bowl made from a corn cob. **corncockle** *n.* a plant, *Agrostemma githago*, with reddish-purple flowers, related to the campions and once common in cornfields. **corncrake** *n.* a bird, *Crex crex*, of the rail family, with brown barred plumage and a harsh grating call, inhabiting hayfields, grassland etc. **corn dolly** *n.* a decorative figure made of plaited straw. **corned beef** *n.* tinned seasoned and cooked beef. **corn exchange** *n.* a market where corn is sold from samples. **corn-factor** *n.* a dealer in corn. **cornfield** *n.* a field in which corn is growing. **cornflakes** *n.pl.* a breakfast cereal made from toasted flakes of maize. **cornflour** *n.* finely ground meal of maize or rice, used in cooking to sweeten sauces etc. **cornflower** *n.* any of several plants that grow amongst corn, esp. the blue-flowered, *Centaurea cyanus*. **Corn Laws** *n.pl.* laws designed to regulate the price of corn (abolished in England, 1846). **corn marigold** *n.* a yellow-flowered composite plant, *Chrysanthemum segetum*. **corn meal** *n.* (*N Am.*) meal of maize. **corn on the cob** *n.* maize boiled or grilled and eaten direct from the cob. **corn pone** *n.* (*N Am.*) cornbread baked or fried, esp. in small oval loaves. **cornrows** *n.pl.* a style of braiding the hair into tight plaits, adopted by some blacks. **corn salad** *n.* LAMB'S LETTUCE (under LAMB). **corn spurrey** *n.* a white-flowered plant, *Spergula arvensis*, of the pink family, found in cornfields. **cornstarch** *n.* (*N Am.*) cornflour. **cornstone** *n.* an earthy concretionary limestone forming a lower series in the Old Red Sandstone. **corn whiskey** *n.* American whiskey distilled from a mash containing at least 80% maize. **corny**[1] *a.* (*comp.* **cornier**, *superl.* **corniest**) **1** trite. **2** old-fashioned and sentimental. **3** unsophisticated. **cornily** *adv.* [OE from Gmc. *korno-* (cp. Dut. *koren*, Dan. and Swed. *korn*, Goth. *kaurn*, G *Korn*), Indo-Eur. *grnəm* (L *grānum*, GRAIN)]

corn[2] (kawn) *n.* a horny excrescence on the foot or hand, produced by pressure over a bone. **to tread on someone's corns** to upset or offend a person's feelings. **corny**[2] *a.* (*comp.* **cornier**, *superl.* **corniest**). **corniness** *n.* [OF *corn*, L *cornū*, horn]

cornea (kaw´niə) *n.* (*pl.* **corneas, corneae** (-niē)) the transparent forepart of the external coat of the eye, through which the rays of light pass. **corneal** *a.* [L, fem. of *corneus*, horny (*cornū*, horn)]

cornel (kaw´nəl) *n.* a tree or shrub of the genus *Cornus*, which includes the cornelian cherry, *C. mas*, and the dogwood, *C. sanguinea*. [ult. from L *cornus*; derivation obscure]

cornelian (kawnēl´yən), **carnelian** (kah´-) *n.* **1** a variety of semi-transparent chalcedony. **2** the reddish colour of this stone. [F *cornaline*; etym. uncertain]

corneous (kaw´niəs) *a.* **1** horny. **2** hard, like horn. [L *corneus* (*cornū*, horn)]

corner (kaw´nə) *n.* **1** the place where two converging lines or surfaces meet. **2** the space included between such lines or surfaces. **3** an angle. **4** a place enclosed by converging walls or other boundaries. **5** a place where two streets meet. **6 a** either of two opposite angles of a boxing or wrestling ring where contestants go between rounds. **b** the contestant's coach etc. who give support between rounds at the contestant's corner. **7** a region, a quarter, esp. a remote place. **8** a nook. **9** a position of difficulty or embarrassment. **10** in football and hockey, a free kick or hit from a corner. **11** a combination to buy up the available supply of any commodity, in order to raise the price, a ring. **12** a triangular cut of ham etc. ~*v.t.* **1** to drive into a corner, or into a position of difficulty. **2** to buy up (a commodity) in order to control (the market). **3** to furnish with corners. ~*v.i.* **1** (esp. of vehicles) to turn a corner. **2** to form a corner (in a commodity). **just around/ round the corner 1** (*coll.*) very close. **2** (*coll.*) imminent. **to cut corners** CUT[1]. **to turn the corner 1** to go round it into the next street. **2** to pass the crisis of an illness. **3** to get past a difficulty. **cornerback** *n.* **1** in American football, a defensive back. **2** the role or position of such a player. **cornered** *a.* **1** (*usu. in comb.*) having corners or angles. **2** (*fig.*) placed in a difficult position. **corner shop** *n.* a small neighbourhood shop, often on a street corner, selling a variety of goods. **cornerstone** *n.* **1** the stone which unites two walls of a building. **2** the principal stone. **3** the foundation. **4** something of the first importance. **cornerwise** *adv.* diagonally, with the corner in front. [OF *cornier*, late L *cornēria*, from L *cornū*, horn]

cornet[1] (kaw´nit) *n.* **1** a three-valved brass musical instrument shaped like a small trumpet. **2** a cornetist. **3** an ice-cream cone. **4** a conical paper bag; a piece of paper twisted into a conical receptacle for small wares. **5** an organ stop producing a cornet-like sound. **6** a cornetto. **7** the lower part of a horse's pastern. **cornet-à-piston** (kawnitapis´tən, kawnāapēstõ´) *n.* (*pl.* **cornets-à-piston** (kawnits-, kawnāz-), **cornets-à-pistons** (-pis´tənz)) a cornet (the musical instrument). **cornetist** (-net´-), **cornettist** *n.* a cornet-player. [OF from late L *cornetum*, L *cornū*]

cornet[2] (kaw´nit) *n.* (*Hist.*) the lowest commissioned officer in a cavalry regiment. **cornetcy** *n.* (*pl.* **cornetcies**). [F *cornette*, dim. of *corne*, from L *cornū*, horn]

cornetto (kawnet´ō), **cornett** (kaw´nit) *n.* (*pl.* **cornetti** (-tē), **cornetts**) an old woodwind instrument with finger holes and a cup-shaped mouthpiece. [It., dim. of *corno*, horn, from L *cornū*, horn]

corni CORNO.

cornice (kaw´nis) *n.* **1** a moulded horizontal projection crowning a wall, entablature, pillar or other part of a building. **2** an ornamental band of plaster between a wall and ceiling. **3** a projecting mass of snow along the top of a precipice. **corniced** *a.* **cornicing** *n.* [F *cornice* (now *corniche*), It. *cornice* (etym. uncertain)]

corniche (kawnēsh´), **corniche road** *n.* a coast road, esp. one along the face of a cliff. [F, the same as *cornice*]

cornicing CORNICE.

cornily, corniness CORNY.

Cornish (kaw´nish) *a.* of or relating to Cornwall. ~*n.* the ancient Celtic language of Cornwall. **Cornish cream** *n.* CLOTTED CREAM (under CLOT). **Cornishman** *n.* (*pl.* **Cornishmen**). **Cornish pasty** *n.* a half-moon-shaped pasty filled with seasoned meat and vegetables.

corno (kaw´nō) *n.* (*pl.* **corni** (-nē)) (*Mus.*) a horn. **corno inglese** (ing·glā´sā) *n.* (*pl.* **corni inglesi** (-sē)) COR ANGLAIS (under COR[2]). [It., from L *cornū*]

cornu (kaw´nū) *n.* (*pl.* **cornua** (-ə)) (*Anat.*) a hornlike process. **cornual** *a.* **cornuate** (-ət) *a.* [L]

cornucopia (kawnūkō´piə) *n.* (*pl.* **cornucopias**) **1** an abundant stock. **2** the horn of plenty, a goat's horn wreathed and filled to overflowing with flowers, fruit, corn etc., the symbol of plenty and peace. **3** a representation of a cornucopia. **cornucopian** *a.* [L *cornū copiae*]

cornuted (kawnū´tid) *a.* **1** horned or having hornlike projections. **2** horn-shaped.

corny[1] CORN[1].
corny[2] CORN[2].
corolla (kərol´ə) *n.* (*pl.* **corollas**) the inner whorl of two series of floral envelopes occurring in the more highly developed plants, the petals. **corollaceous** (korəlā´-) *a.* **corollate** (kor´ələt), **corollated** (-lātid) *a.* **1** like a corolla. **2** having a corolla. [L, dim. of *corōna*, a crown]
corollary (kərol´əri) *n.* (*pl.* **corollaries**) **1** (*Logic*) an additional inference from a proposition. **2** something that follows as a deduction from something else, a natural consequence. **3** something appended. ~*a.* additional, supplementary, being or following as a corollary. [L *corollārium*, the price of a garland, a gratuity, a corollary, from *corollārius*, pertaining to a garland, from *corolla*, dim. of *corōna*, a crown]
corollate COROLLA.
corona[1] (kərō´nə) *n.* (*pl.* **coronas, coronae** (-nē)) **1** a disc or halo round the sun or the moon. **2** an anthelion or disc of light opposite the sun. **3** the zone of radiance round the moon in a total eclipse of the sun. **4** a broad projecting face forming the principal member of a cornice. **5** a circular chandelier hanging from the roof, esp. in churches. **6** the circumference or margin of a compound radiated flower. **7** (*Anat.*) any structure like a crown in shape. **8** a glowing electrical discharge round a charged conductor. **coronal**[1] *a.* [L, a crown]
corona[2] (kərō´nə) *n.* (*pl.* **coronas**) a kind of long cigar with straight sides. [Sp., from L *corōna*, a crown; originally a proprietary name]
coronach (kor´ənəkh) *n.* in the Scottish Highlands and in Ireland, a dirge, a funeral lamentation. [Ir. *coránach* (cp. Gael. *corranach*), from *comh-*, together, *rànach*, an outcry, from *ràn*, to howl]
coronae CORONA[1].
coronagraph (kərō´nəgrahf), **coronograph** *n.* an optical instrument used to observe the sun's corona.
coronal[1] CORONA[1].
coronal[2] (kərō´nəl) *a.* **1** of or relating to a crown or the crown of the head. **2** (*Bot.*) of or relating to a corona. **coronal bone** *n.* the bone forming the forehead and front part of the skull. **coronally** *adv.* **coronal plane** *n.* an imaginary plane dividing the body vertically into front (ventral) and rear (dorsal) sections. **coronal suture** *n.* the suture extending over the crown of the skull and separating the frontal and parietal bones. [F, from L *corōna*]
coronal[3] (kor´ənəl) *n.* **1** a circlet or coronet. **2** a wreath or garland. [F, from L *corōna*]
coronary (kor´ənəri) *n.* (*pl.* **coronaries**) a coronary thrombosis. ~*a.* **1** (*Anat.*) denoting or involving blood vessels, nerves etc. which lie round a part of the body. **2** resembling a crown. **3** placed as a crown. **coronary artery** *n.* either of two arteries springing from the aorta before it leaves the pericardium. **coronary bypass** *n.* the bypassing of a blocked or narrowed part of a coronary artery by means of a piece of healthy blood vessel taken from elsewhere in the body and grafted round the malfunctioning section. **coronary thrombosis** *n.* (*pl.* **coronary thromboses**) the formation of a clot in one of the arteries of the heart. **coronary vessels** *n.pl.* certain vessels which furnish the substance of the heart with blood. [L *corōnārius*, from *corōna*, a crown]
coronation (korənā´shən) *n.* the act or ceremony of solemnly crowning a sovereign. **coronation oath** *n.* the oath taken by a sovereign at the coronation. [med. L *coronātio*, from L *coronāre*, to crown, from *corōna*, a crown]
coroner (kor´ənə) *n.* **1** an officer of the Crown whose duty it is to inquire into cases of sudden or suspicious death, and to determine the ownership of treasure-trove. **2** (*Hist.*) an officer in charge of the private property of the Crown. **coronership** *n.* **coroner's inquest** *n.* **1** a judicial inquiry before a coroner and a jury into death occurring suddenly, from violence, an unknown cause or in a prison. **2** a judicial inquiry before a coroner and a jury into cases of treasure trove. [A-F *coruner*, from *coruna*, L *corōna*, a crown]
coronet (kor´ənit) *n.* **1** a little crown. **2** any of various types of small crown worn by princes, princesses and the nobility, varying in style according to the rank of the wearer. **3** an ornamental fillet worn as part of a woman's headdress. **4** nobility. **5** the part of a horse's pastern where the skin turns to horn. **6** a bony ring round the base of the antler of a deer. **coroneted** *a.* **1** wearing a coronet. **2** entitled to wear a coronet, of noble birth. [OF, dim. of *corone*, from L *corōna*, a crown]
coronograph CORONAGRAPH.
co-routine (kō´rootēn) *n.* (*Comput.*) part of a computer program functioning like a subroutine but which can be left and entered at any point.
corozo (kərō´zō) *n.* (*pl.* **corozos**) **1** a S American ivory-nut tree, *Phytelephas macrocarpa*, the source of vegetable ivory. **2** any of various other palm trees. **corozo-nut** *n.* the fruit of the ivory-nut tree, used by turners for making ornaments etc. [Sp.]
corp., Corp. *abbr.* **1** corporal. **2** corporation.
corpora CORPUS.
corporal[1] (kaw´pərəl, -prəl) *n.* **1** an army non-commissioned officer of the lowest grade. **2** a sailor who attends to police matters under the master-at-arms. **3** (*N Am.*) FALLFISH (under FALL). **corporalship** *n.* [F (var. *caporal*, It. *caporale*, perh. from confusion with *capo*, head), OF *corporel*, L *corporālis* (*corpus -oris*, the body)]
corporal[2] (kaw´pərəl) *a.* **1** relating to the body. **2** material, corporeal. ~*n.* the fine linen cloth on which the elements are consecrated in the Eucharist. **corporality** (-ral´-) *n.* (*pl.* **corporalities**) **1** materiality. **2** (*pl.*) material things. **3** a body. **corporally** *adv.* **corporal punishment** *n.* punishment inflicted on the body. [OF *corporel*, L *corporālis* (*corpus -oris*, the body)]
corporate (kaw´pərət) *a.* **1** united in a body and acting as an individual. **2** collectively one. **3** of or relating to a corporation or group. **4** corporative. **5** united. ~*n.* a big industrial corporation. **corporate advertising** *n.* the advertising of the name and policies of a company or group of companies, as opposed to the promotion of a particular product. **corporate body** *n.* a group of people legally empowered to act as an individual. **corporate hospitality** *n.* (lavish) entertainment by a company of (potential) clients or customers. **corporately** *adv.* **corporate raider** *n.* a person who clandestinely builds up a shareholding in a company in order to gain some control over it. **corporate state** *n.* a system of government based on trade and professional corporations. **corporatism** (kaw´pərə-) *n.* the corporate state. **corporatist** *a.*, *n.* **corporative** (kaw´pərə-) *a.* **1** of or relating to a corporation. **2** involving, run by etc. trade and professional corporations. **corporativism** *n.* [L *corporātus*, p.p. of *corporāre* (*corpus -oris*, body)]
corporation (kawpərā´shən) *n.* **1** a united body. **2** (*Law*) CORPORATE BODY (under CORPORATE). **3** (*loosely*) a company or association for commercial or other purposes. **4** an elected body charged with the conduct of civic business. **5** (*coll.*) a prominent abdomen. **corporation tax** *n.* a tax levied on the profits of companies. **corporator** (kaw´-) *n.* a member of a corporation. [L *corporātio* (*corpus -oris*, body)]
corporatism, corporative etc. CORPORATE.
corporeal (kawpaw´riəl) *a.* **1** having a body. **2** of or relating to the body. **3** material, physical, as opposed to *mental*. **4** (*Law*) tangible, visible. **corporeality** (-al´-) *n.* **corporeally** *adv.* [L *corporeus* (*corpus -oris*, body)]
corporeity (kawpərē´əti) *n.* **1** material existence. **2**

corporeality. [med. L *corporeitās*, from *corporeus* (*corpus -oris*, body)]
corposant (kaw´pəzənt) *n.* (*Naut.*) a luminous electric body often seen on the masts and rigging on dark stormy nights; St Elmo's fire. [Port. *corpo santo*, L *corpus sanctum*, sacred body]
corps (kaw) *n.* (*pl.* **corps** (kawz)) **1** a body of troops having a specific function. **2** a grouping of two or more divisions of an army, forming a tactical unit in the field. **3** a group of people employed in the same job, working together or in the same place. **corps de ballet** (də bal´ā) *n.* a body of dancers in a ballet. **corps d'élite** (dālēt´) *n.* an elite body selected from a larger group. **corps diplomatique** (diplōmatēk´) *n.* DIPLOMATIC CORPS (under DIPLOMACY). [F]
corpse (kawps) *n.* **1** a dead body, esp. of a human being. **2** the body. **corpse-candle, corpse-light** *n.* an ignis fatuus seen in churchyards and regarded as an omen of death. [OF *cors* (F *corps*), L *corpus*, the body]
corpulent (kaw´pūlənt) *a.* excessively fat or fleshy. **corpulence, corpulency** *n.* **corpulently** *adv.* [F, from L *corpulentus* (*corpus*, body)]
corpus (kaw´pəs) *n.* (*pl.* **corpora** (-pərə), **corpuses**) **1** a body. **2** the mass of anything. **3** a collection of writings or of literature. **4** the main part of an organ or any part of an organism. **corpus callosum** (kəlō´səm) *n.* (*pl.* **corpora callosa** (-sə)) the broad band of white nerve fibres connecting the cerebral hemispheres in humans and other higher mammals. **Corpus Christi** (kris´ti) *n.* the festival of the body of Christ, held in honour of the real presence in the Eucharist on the Thursday after Trinity Sunday. **corpus delicti** (dilik´tī) *n.* (*Law*) the aggregation of facts which constitute a breach of the law. **corpus luteum** (loo´tiəm) *n.* (*pl.* **corpora lutea** (-iə)) a mass of tissue which develops in the ovary after the discharge of an ovum. [L]
corpuscle (kaw´pəsəl), **corpuscule** (-pŭs´kūl) *n.* **1** a cell, esp. a *white* or *red corpuscle*, suspended in the blood. **2** a minute body or cell forming part of an organism. **3** a minute particle of matter. **corpuscular** (-pŭs´-) *a.* **1** of or relating to corpuscles. **2** atomic. **corpuscular forces** *n.pl.* forces acting on corpuscles, and determining the forms and relations of matter. **corpuscular theory** *n.* the theory that light consists of a stream of particles. [L *corpusculum*, dim. of *corpus*, body]
corr. *abbr.* **1** correspond(ing). **2** correspondence. **3** corrupted. **4** corruption.
corrade (kərād´) *v.t.* to wear down (rocks etc.), e.g. as a river does by mechanical force and solution. **corrasion** (-zhən) *n.* **corrasive** *a.* [L *corrādere* (COR-, *rādere*, to scrape)]
corral (kərahl´) *n.* **1** an enclosure (orig. of emigrants' wagons in American Indian territory) for cattle, horses etc. or for defence. **2** an enclosure for capturing elephants and other animals. *~v.t.* (*pres.p.* **corralling,** *past, p.p.* **corralled**) **1** to pen up. **2** to form into a corral. **3** (*NAm., sl.*) to get, to acquire, to lay hold of. [Sp., from *corro*, a ring of people (*correr*(*toros*), to hold a bullfight, L *currere*, to run)]
corrasion, corrasive CORRADE.
correct (kərekt´) *v.t.* **1** to set right. **2** to remove faults or errors from. **3** to mark errors in for rectification. **4** to admonish, to punish, to chastise. **5** to obviate, to counteract. **6** to eliminate an aberration. **7** to replace (something wrong) with the right thing. **8** to adjust or reset (a measuring instrument etc.) to register accurately. *~a.* **1** true, exact, accurate. **2** right, proper, decorous. **3** conforming to a fixed standard or rule. **4** free from fault or imperfection. **to stand corrected** to acknowledge a mistake. **correctable, correctible** *a.* **correction** *n.* **1** the act of correcting. **2** that which is substituted for what is wrong. **3** amendment, improvement. **4** a quantity added or taken away to make a reading, calculation etc. more accurate. **5** punishment, chastisement. **6** criticism. **under correction** as liable to correction; perhaps in error. **correctional** *a.* **correction fluid** *n.* a liquid, usu. white, which can be painted over errors in writing etc., drying to form a hard surface which can be written etc. on again. **correctitude** *n.* correctness of behaviour. **corrective** *a.* **1** having power to correct. **2** tending to correct. *~n.* **1** that which tends to correct or counteract. **2** an antidote. **correctively** *adv.* **correctly** *adv.* **correctness** *n.* **corrector** *n.* **1** a person who or something which corrects. **2** a censor. **3** a critic. [L *correctus*, p.p. of *corrigere* (*regere*, to rule, to order)]
corregidor (kəreg´idaw) *n.* the chief magistrate of a Spanish town. [Sp. (*corregir*, L *corrigere*, to correct)]
correlate (kor´əlāt) *v.i.* (*usu. with with, to*) to be reciprocally related. *~v.t.* (*usu. with with*) to bring into mutual relation. *~a.* mutually related. *~n.* a correlative. **correlation** (-ā´shən), **corelation** *n.* **1** reciprocal relation. **2** the act of bringing into correspondence or interaction. **3** the state or degree of reciprocal dependence of usu. two variables, or a quantity indicating this. **4** (*Physics*) interdependence of forces and phenomena. **5** the mutual relation of structure, functions etc. in an organism. **correlational** *a.* **correlationist** *n.* a believer in the doctrine of universal correlation of powers and forces as the outcome of one primary force. **correlative** (-rel´ə-) *a.* **1** reciprocally connected or related to, or reciprocally implied. **2** (*Gram.*) corresponding to each other, as *either* and *or*, *neither* and *nor*. *~n.* a person who or something which is correlated with another. **correlatively** *adv.* **correlativity** (-relətiv´-) *n.*
correspond (korəspond´) *v.i.* **1** to be similar, comparable or equivalent (to). **2** to be congruous. **3** to fit (with), to suit, to agree (with) etc. **4** to communicate by letters sent and received. **correspondence** *n.* **1** mutual adaptation. **2** congruity. **3** communication by means of letters. **4** the letters which pass between correspondents. **correspondence college, correspondence school** *n.* a college or school whose students do not attend directly, but whose courses are conducted by post. **correspondence column** *n.* the part of a newspaper or magazine in which readers' letters are printed. **correspondence course** *n.* any of the courses of study conducted by post by a correspondence college. **correspondent** *a.* **1** agreeing or congruous with. **2** answering. *~n.* **1** a person with whom communication is kept up by letters. **2** a person who sends news from a particular place or on a particular subject, to a newspaper, radio or TV station etc. **3** a person or firm having business relations with another. **correspondently** *adv.* **corresponding** *a.* **1** suiting. **2** communicating by correspondence. **correspondingly** *adv.* **corresponding member** *n.* a member of a learned society who lives at a distance, generally corresponding with the society but taking no part in its affairs. [F *correspondre*, med. L *correspondēre* (COR-, *respondēre*, to RESPOND)]
corrida (kərē´də) *n.* **1** a bullfight. **2** bullfighting. [Sp.; cp. CORRAL]
corridor (kor´idaw) *n.* **1** a gallery or passage communicating with the apartments of a building. **2** a passageway along the side of a railway carriage with openings into the different compartments. **3** a narrow strip of territory belonging to one state, which passes through the territory of another state (e.g. to reach the sea). **4** a narrow strip of airspace within which aircraft must fly, e.g. over a foreign country. **5** a main traffic route. **6** a particular flight path along which a spacecraft can safely re-enter the earth's atmosphere. **7** (*N Am.*) an aisle. **8** a covered way encircling a place. **corridor carriage** *n.* a railway carriage with a corridor. **corridors of power** *n.pl.* the higher ranks in any organization, seen as the seat of power and influence. **corridor**

train *n.* a train with corridors, allowing passage between carriages. [F, from It. *corridore* (*correre*, to run, L *currere*)]

corrie (kor´i) *n.* a semicircular hollow or cirque in a mountainside, usu. surrounded in part by crags. [Gael. *coire*, cauldron]

corrigendum (korijen´dəm) *n.* (*pl.* **corrigenda** (-ə)) an error needing correction, esp. in a book. [L, ger. of *corrigere*, to correct]

corrigible (kor´ijibəl) *a.* **1** capable of being corrected. **2** punishable. **3** submissive, docile. **corrigibly** *adv.* [F, from L *corrigere*, to correct]

corroborate (kərob´ərāt) *v.t.* **1** to strengthen, to confirm, to establish. **2** to bear additional witness to. **corroborant** *a.* **1** strengthening. **2** confirming. ~*n.* a tonic. **corroboration** (-ā´shən) *n.* **1** the act of strengthening or confirming. **2** confirmation by additional evidence. **corroborative** *a.* corroborating. ~*n.* a corroborant. **corroborator** *n.* **corroboratory** (-ətəri) *a.* [L *corrōborātus*, p.p. of *corrōborāre* (COR-, *rōborāre*, to strengthen, from *rōbur -boris*, strength)]

corroboree (kərob´ərē) *n.* **1** a festive or warlike dance of the Australian Aborigines. **2** any noisy party. [Austral. Abor.]

corrode (kərōd´) *v.t.* **1** to consume gradually, esp. chemically. **2** to wear away by degrees. **3** to prey upon. ~*v.i.* to be eaten away gradually. **corrodible** *a.* **corrosion** (-zhən) *n.* **1** the act or process of corroding. **2** a corroded state or area. **corrosive** (-siv) *a.* **1** tending to corrode. **2** fretting, biting, vexing, virulent. ~*n.* anything which corrodes. **corrosively** *adv.* **corrosiveness** *n.* **corrosive sublimate** *n.* mercuric chloride, a powerful irritant poison used as a fungicide etc. [L *corrōdere* (COR-, *rōdere*, to gnaw)]

corrugate[1] (kor´əgāt) *v.t.* to contract or bend into wrinkles or folds. ~*v.i.* to become wrinkled. **corrugated** *a.* bent or shaped into folds, esp. in order to be made stronger. **corrugated iron** *n.* sheet iron pressed into folds and galvanized. **corrugation** (-a´shən) *n.* **1** the act of corrugating. **2** a wrinkle, a fold. **corrugator** *n.* a muscle which contracts the brow. [L *corrūgātus*, p.p. of *corrūgāre* (COR-, *rūgāre*, to wrinkle, from *rūga*, a wrinkle)]

corrugate[2] (kor´əgət) *a.* **1** wrinkled. **2** (*Biol.*) marked with more or less acute parallel angles. [as CORRUGATE[1]]

corrupt (kərŭpt´) *a.* **1** perverted by bribery or willing to be. **2** involving bribery or unethical practices. **3** depraved. **4** (of a computer program, or data held in a computer) containing errors caused by the hardware or software. **5** (of a text etc.) vitiated by additions or alterations. **6** not genuine. **7** unsound. **8** spoiled, tainted. **9** putrid, decomposed. ~*v.t.* **1** to change from a sound to an unsound state. **2** to infect, to make impure or unwholesome. **3** (*Comput.*) to introduce errors into (data, a program etc.). **4** to bribe. **5** to falsify. **6** to vitiate or defile. **7** to debauch, to seduce. ~*v.i.* to become corrupt. **corrupter** *n.* **corruptible** *a.* able to be corrupted, liable to corruption. **corruptibility** (-bil´-) *n.* **corruptibly** *adv.* **corruption** *n.* **1** the act of corrupting. **2** the state of being corrupt. **3** bribery or fraud. **4** moral deterioration. **5** a corrupt reading or version. **6** decomposition, putrefaction. **7** putrid matter. **8** misrepresentation. **corruptive** *a.* **corruptly** *adv.* **corruptness** *n.* **corrupt practices** *n.pl.* (*Law*) direct or indirect bribery in connection with an election. [L *corruptus*, p.p. of *corrumpere* (COR-, *rumpere*, to break)]

corsac (kaw´sak), **corsak** *n.* a small yellowish Asian fox, *Vulpes corsac*. [Turk.]

corsage (kawsahzh´) *n.* **1** a flower or small bouquet or spray of flowers, usu. worn by a woman on the bodice or lapel of her dress. **2** the bodice of a woman's dress. [OF]

corsair (kaw´seə) *n.* **1** a pirate or a privateer, esp. formerly on the Barbary coast. **2** a pirate authorized by the government of his country. **3** a pirate ship. [F *corsaire*, MIt. *corsaro*, late L *cursārius* (*cursus*, a course, from *currere*, to run)]

corsak CORSAC.

corse (kaws) *n.* (*poet.*) a corpse. [OF *cors*, CORPSE]

corselet[1] CORSLET.

corselet[2] CORSELETTE.

corselette (kawsəlet´), **corselet** (kaws´lit) *n.* a woman's one-piece supporting undergarment.

corset (kaw´sit) *n.* **1** a close-fitting stiffened or elasticated undergarment worn by women to give a desired shape to the body. **2** a similar undergarment worn by either sex to support a weakened or injured part of the body. **3** (*coll.*) a restriction on bank lending capacity imposed by the Bank of England. ~*v.t.* (*pres.p.* **corseting**, *past*, *p.p.* **corseted**) to restrain or support with a corset. **corseted** *a.* **corsetier** (kawsitie´, -tyā´) *n.* a man who makes or sells corsets. **corsetière** (kawsityeə´) *n.* a woman who makes or sells corsets. **corsetry** *n.* [F, dim. of OF *cors*, body]

Corsican (kaw´sikən) *a.* of or relating to the Mediterranean island of Corsica. ~*n.* **1** a native or inhabitant of Corsica. **2** the Italian dialect spoken in Corsica.

corslet (kaws´lit), **corselet** *n.* **1** body armour. **2** a light cuirass. **3** the thorax of insects. [F *corselet*]

cortege (kawtezh´), **cortège** *n.* **1** a procession, esp. at a funeral. **2** a train of attendants. [F, from It. *corteggio* (*corte*, a court)]

Cortes (kaw´tes) *n.* the legislative assemblies of Spain and (formerly) Portugal. [Sp. and Port., pl. of *corte*, court]

cortex (kaw´teks) *n.* (*pl.* **cortices** (-tisēz)) **1** the layer of plant tissue between the vascular bundles and the epidermis. **2** bark. **3** the outer layer of an organ, such as the kidney or brain. **cortical** (-tik-) *a.* **1** belonging to the outer part of a plant or animal. **2** of or relating to the bark or rind. **corticate** (-kət), **corticated** (-kātid) *a.* **1** coated with bark. **2** resembling bark. [L *cortex -icis*, bark]

corticin (kaw´tisin) *n.* (*Chem.*) an alkaloid obtained from the bark of the aspen.

cortico- (kaw´tikō) *comb. form* of or relating to the cortex.

corticosteroid (kawtikōstiə´roid), **corticoid** (kaw´tikoid) *n.* a steroid (e.g. cortisone) produced by the adrenal cortex, or a synthetic drug with the same actions.

corticotrophic hormone (kawtikōtrō´fik, -trof´ik), **corticotropic hormone** (-trō´pik, -trop´ik) *n.* ADRENOCORTICOTROPHIC HORMONE (under ADRENOCORTICOTROPHIC). **corticotrophin, corticotropin** *n.* ADRENOCORTICOTROPHIN (under ADRENOCORTICOTROPHIC).

cortisol (kaw´tisol) *n.* HYDROCORTISONE.

cortisone (kaw´tizōn, -sōn) *n.* a corticosteroid, natural or synthetic, used to treat rheumatoid arthritis, allergies and skin diseases. [abbr. of *corticosterone* (hormone)]

corundum (kərŭn´dəm) *n.* **1** a rhombohedral mineral of great hardness, allied to the ruby and sapphire. **2** a class of minerals including these, consisting of crystallized alumina. [Tamil *kurundam*]

coruscate (kor´əskāt) *v.i.* **1** to sparkle, to glitter in flashes. **2** to be bright, flashy or brilliant. **coruscant** (-rŭs´-) *a.* **coruscating** *a.* (esp. of writ) sparkling, brilliant. **coruscation** (-kā´shən) *n.* [L *coruscātus*, p.p. of *coruscāre*, to glitter]

corvee (kawvā´, kaw´-) *n.* **1** (*Hist.*) an obligation to perform a day's unpaid labour for a feudal lord, as the repair of roads etc. **2** work done in lieu of paying taxes. **3** forced labour. **4** any burdensome task imposed on one. [F, from late L *corrogāta* (*opera*), requisitioned work (COR-, *rogāre*, to ask)]

corves CORF.

corvette (kawvet´) *n.* **1** a small, fast escort vessel armed with anti-submarine devices. **2** (*Hist.*) a flush-decked, full-rigged ship of war, with one tier of guns. [F, from Port. *corveta*, Sp. *corbeta*, prob. from L *corbīta* (*navis*), a ship of burden (*corbis*, basket)]

corvid (kaw´vid) *a.* corvine. ~*n.* any bird belonging to the Corvidae, the crow family. [L *corvus*, a raven]

corvine (kaw´vīn) *a.* of or relating to the crows. [L *corvīnus*, from *corvus*, a raven]

corybant (kor´ibant) *n.* (*pl.* **corybants, corybantes** (-ban´tēz)) a priest of Cybele, whose rites were accompanied with wild music and dancing. **corybantian** (-ban´shən) *a.* **corybantic** (-ban´-) *a.* wild, frenzied. **corybantine** (-ban´tīn) *a.* **corybantism** *n.* [F *Corybante*, L *Corybās -ntem*, Gr. *Korubas -anta*]

corylus (kor´iləs) *n.* (*pl.* **coryluses**) any shrub of the genus *Corylus*, including the hazel. [L]

corymb (kor´imb) *n.* (*Bot.*) a raceme or panicle in which the stalks of the lower flowers are longer than those of the upper, so creating a flat-topped cluster. **corymbiate** (-rim´biət) *a.* with clusters of berries or blossoms in the form of corymbs. **corymbiferous** (-bif´-) *a.* **corymbiform** (-rim´bifawm) *a.* **corymbose** (-rim´bōs) *a.* [F *corymbe*, L *corymbus*, Gr. *korumbos*, a cluster]

coryphaeus (korifē´əs) *n.* (*pl.* **coryphaei** (-fē´ī)) **1** the leader of a chorus in a classical play. **2** a chief, a leader. [L, from Gr. *koruphaios* (*koruphē*, the head)]

coryphée (korifā´) *n.* a chief dancer in a corps de ballet. [F, from Gr. *koruphaios*, a leader]

coryza (kərī´zə) *n.* **1** nasal catarrh. **2** a cold. [L, from Gr. *koruza*, running at the nose]

COS, CoS *abbr.* Chief of Staff.

cos[1] (kos), **cos lettuce** *n.* a curly variety of lettuce introduced from the island of Cos in the Aegean. [Gr. *Kōs*]

cos[2] (koz) *abbr.* cosine.

cos[3] 'COS.

'cos (koz), **cos** *conj.* (*coll.*) short for BECAUSE.

Cosa Nostra (kōzə nos´trə) *n.* the branch of the Mafia operating in the US. [It., our thing]

cosec (kō´sek) *abbr.* cosecant.

cosecant (kōsē´kənt) *n.* (*Math.*) the secant of the complement of an arc or angle.

cosech (kō´sech, -shek´) *abbr.* hyperbolic cosecant.

coseismal (kōsīz´məl) *a.* relating to the points simultaneously affected by an earthquake. ~*n.* a coseismal line or curve. **coseismal curve** *n.* a line drawn on a map through all the points simultaneously affected by an earthquake. **coseismic** *a.*

coset (kō´set) *n.* (*Math.*) a set which forms a given larger set when added to another one.

cosh[1] (kosh) *n.* a heavy blunt weapon for hitting people with, e.g. a length of metal or hard rubber. ~*v.t.* to hit with a cosh. [perh. from Romany *kosh*, stick]

cosh[2] (kosh, kozāch´) *abbr.* hyperbolic cosine.

coshering (kosh´əring) *n.* **1** (*Hist.*) an Irish custom whereby the lord was entitled to exact from his tenant food and lodging for himself and his followers. **2** rack-rent. **cosherer** *n.* a person who practises coshering. [Ir. *coisir*, a feast, feasting]

co-signatory (kōsig´nətəri) *n.* (*pl.* **co-signatories**) a person who signs jointly with others.

cosily COSY.

cosine (kō´sīn) *n.* (*Math.*) the sine of the complement of an arc or angle.

cosiness COSY.

COSLA (koz´lə) *abbr.* Convention of Scottish Local Authorities.

cosmetic (kəzmet´ik) *a.* **1** beautifying. **2** used for dressing the hair or skin. **3** intended or used to make only superficial improvements. ~*n.* an external application for improving the complexion, beautifying esp. the face, etc. **cosmetical** *a.* **cosmetically** *adv.* **cosmetician** (kozmetish´ən) *n.* a person who makes, sells or is professionally skilled in the use of cosmetics. **cosmetic surgery** *n.* surgery to improve the appearance rather than to treat illness or injury. [F *cosmetique*, Gr. *kosmētikos* (*kosmein*, to adorn, from *kosmos*, order)]

cosmic (koz´mik) *a.* **1** of or relating to the universe, esp. as distinguished from the earth. **2** derived from some part of the solar system other than the earth. **3** of or used in space travel. **4** of worldwide importance. **5** of inconceivably long duration. **cosmical** *a.* **cosmically** *adv.* in a cosmic way. **cosmic dust** *n.* minute particles of matter distributed throughout space. **cosmic radiation** *n.* very energetic radiation falling on the earth from outer space, consisting chiefly of charged particles. **cosmic rays** *n.pl.* cosmic radiation. [Gr. *kosmikos*, from *kosmos*, order, the world]

cosmo- (koz´mō) *comb. form* of or relating to the universe. [Gr. *kosmos*, the universe]

cosmogony (kozmog´əni) *n.* (*pl.* **cosmogonies**) a theory, investigation or dissertation respecting the origin of the world. **cosmogonic** (-gon´-), **cosmogonical** *a.* **cosmogonist** *n.* [Gr. *kosmogonia*]

cosmography (kozmog´rəfi) *n.* (*pl.* **cosmographies**) a description or delineation of the features of the universe, or of the earth as part of the universe. **cosmographer** *n.* **cosmographic** (-graf´-), **cosmographical** *a.* [Gr. *kosmographia*]

cosmology (kozmol´əji) *n.* (*pl.* **cosmologies**) **1** the science which investigates the evolution and structure of the universe as an ordered whole. **2** the branch of metaphysics dealing with the origin and nature of the universe and its relation to the mind. **3** an account of the origin, evolution and structure of the universe. **cosmological** (-loj´-) *a.* **cosmologist** *n.*

cosmonaut (koz´mənawt) *n.* an astronaut, esp. in the former Soviet Union. [Gr. *nautēs*, sailor]

cosmopolis (kozmop´əlis) *n.* (*pl.* **cosmopolises**) a city inhabited by people from many different countries. [Gr. *polis*, a city]

cosmopolitan (kozməpol´itən) *a.* **1** at home in any part of the world. **2** free from national prejudices and limitations. **3** sophisticated. **4** (of plants and animals) widely distributed throughout the world. ~*n.* a cosmopolitan person. **cosmopolitanism** *n.* **cosmopolitanize, cosmopolitanise** *v.t., v.i.* **cosmopolite** (-mop´əlīt) *n.* a cosmopolitan person. ~*a.* **1** worldwide in sympathy or experience. **2** devoid of national prejudice. **cosmopolitical** (-lit´-) *a.* relating to worldwide polity. [Gr. *kosmopolitēs* (*kosmos*, the world, *politēs*, a citizen)]

cosmos[1] (koz´mos), **kosmos** *n.* **1** the universe regarded as an ordered system. **2** an ordered system of knowledge. **3** any ordered system. **4** order, as opposed to chaos. **5** totality of experience. [Gr., order, ornament]

cosmos[2] (koz´mos) *n.* (*pl.* **cosmos, cosmoses**) any plant of the tropical American genus *Cosmos*, grown in gardens for their showy flowers. [Gr., ornament]

cosmotron (kos´mətron) *n.* an electrical apparatus for accelerating protons to high energies.

COSPAR *abbr.* Committee on Space Research.

co-sponsor (kōspon´sə) *n.* a joint sponsor. ~*v.t.* to sponsor jointly.

Cossack (kos´ak) *n.* a member of a people, probably of mixed Turkish origin, living on the southern steppes of Russia, and formerly furnishing light cavalry to the Russian army. **Cossack hat** *n.* a brimless hat made of fur, sheepskin, etc. [Rus. *Kazak*, Turk. *quzzaq*, a vagabond, an adventurer]

cosset (kos´ət) *v.t.* to pet, to pamper. ~*n.* **1** a pet lamb. **2** a pet. [etym. uncertain (perh. from OE *cot-sæta*, cot-sitter, brought up within doors)]

cossie (koz´i) *n.* (*esp. Austral., coll.*) SWIMMING COSTUME (under SWIM).

cost (kost) *v.t.* (*past, p.p.* **cost**) **1** to require as the price of possession or enjoyment. **2** to cause the expenditure of.

3 to result in the loss of or the infliction of. 4 to be costly to. 5 (*past, p.p.* **costed**) to calculate or set the price of (a job etc.). ~*v.i.* to be costly. ~*n.* 1 the price charged or paid for a thing. 2 expense, charge. 3 (*pl.*) expenses of a lawsuit, esp. those awarded to the successful against the losing party. 4 expenditure of any kind. 5 penalty, loss, detriment. 6 pain, trouble. **at all costs** regardless of the cost. **at any cost** regardless of the cost. **at cost** at cost price. **at the cost of** involving or resulting in the loss or sacrifice of. **to cost someone dear/ dearly** to cause someone great expenditure, severe loss etc. **to one's cost** with consequent loss, expense, disadvantage etc. **cost accountant** *n.* an accountant who analyses and records all the expected and actual costs (labour, materials, overheads etc.) of a business enterprise etc. **cost accounting** *n.* **cost-benefit analysis** *n.* a process by which the costs of some enterprise or process are gauged against the expected resulting benefits. **cost clerk, costing clerk** *n.* a clerk who records the costs in a business enterprise. **cost-conscious** *a.* very aware of costs and expenditure, and generally trying to minimize them. **cost-consciousness** *n.* **cost-cutting** *n.* the cutting of costs. ~*a.* cutting costs, or intended to do so. **cost-effective** *a.* giving a satisfactory return on the initial outlay. **cost-effectively** *adv.* **cost-effectiveness** *n.* **cost-efficiency** *n.* **cost-efficient** *a.* cost-effective. **cost-efficiently** *adv.* **costing** *n.* 1 the system of calculating the exact cost of production, so as to ascertain the profit or loss entailed. 2 (*usu.pl.*) the results of such calculations. **costless** *a.* costing nothing. **costly** *a.* (*comp.* **costlier,** *superl.* **costliest**) 1 of high price. 2 valuable. 3 involving great loss or sacrifice. **costliness** *n.* **cost of living** *n.* the cost of those goods and services considered necessary to a reasonable standard of living. **cost-plus** *a.* used of a contract where work is paid for at actual cost, with an agreed percentage addition as profit. **cost price** *n.* the price paid by the dealer. **cost-push inflation** *n.* inflation caused by rising costs. [OF *coster* (F *coûter*), L *constāre* (CON-, *stāre,* to stand)]

costa (kos´tə) *n.* (*pl.* **costae** (-tē)) 1 a rib. 2 any process resembling a rib in appearance or function. 3 the midrib of a leaf. **costal** *a.* **costate** (-tāt) *a.* [L]

co-star (kō´stah) *n.* a star appearing (in a film) with another star. ~*v.i.* (*pres.p.* **co-starring,** *past, p.p.* **co-starred**) to be a co-star. ~*v.t.* (of a film etc.) to have as co-star(s).

costard (kos´təd) *n.* 1 a large, round apple. 2 (*sl.*) †the head. [perh. from OF *coste,* a rib (L *costa*), referring to apples with prominent ribs]

Costa Rican (kostə rē´kən) *n.* a native or inhabitant of Costa Rica in Central America. ~*a.* of or relating to Costa Rica.

costate COSTA.

coster (kos´tə), **costermonger** (kos´təmŭng·gə) *n.* a seller of fruit, vegetables etc., esp. from a street barrow. **costering, costermongering** *n.* **costermongerdom** *n.* **costermongery** *n.* [COSTARD, MONGER]

costive (kos´tiv) *a.* 1 having the motion of the bowels too slow, constipated. 2 reserved, reticent. 3 niggardly. **costively** *adv.* **costiveness** *n.* [OF *costivé, costevé,* L *constīpātus,* CONSTIPATED (under CONSTIPATE)]

costmary (kost´meəri) *n.* (*pl.* **costmaries**) an aromatic plant of the aster family, *Chrysanthemum balsamita,* cultivated for use in flavouring. [OE *cost,* L *costum,* Gr. *kostos,* Arab. *qust; Mary* (St Mary)]

costume (kos´tūm, -chəm) *n.* 1 dress. 2 the customary mode of dressing. 3 the dress of a particular time or country. 4 fancy dress. 5 the attire of an actor or actress. 6 SWIMMING COSTUME (under SWIM). 7 clothing for some purpose or activity. 8 (*dated*) a woman's, usu. tailor-made, suit consisting of jacket and skirt. 9 a set of outer garments. ~*v.t.* to provide or dress with costume. **costume drama** *n.* 1 a drama in which the actors wear historical or foreign costume. 2 such dramas as a genre. **costume jewellery** *n.* cheap and showy jewellery worn to set off one's clothes. **costume piece, costume play** *n.* a costume drama. **costumer** (-tū´mə), **costumier** (-tu´miā) *n.* a maker of or dealer in costumes. [F, from It. *costume,* late L *costūma,* L *consuētūdinem,* acc. of *consuētūdo,* CUSTOM]

cosy (kō´zi), (*N Am.*) **cozy** *a.* (*comp.* **cosier,** (*N Am.*) **cozier,** *superl.* **cosiest,** (*N Am.*) **coziest**) 1 comfortable, snug. 2 complacent. 3 warm and friendly. 4 having, showing or resulting from friendship or collaboration, usu. to the detriment of others. ~*n.* (*pl.* **cosies**) 1 a fabric covering for keeping something warm, esp. a tea cosy or egg cosy. 2 a canopied seat or corner for two people. ~*v.t.* (*3rd pers. sing. pres.* **cosies,** *pres.p.* **cosying,** *past, p.p.* **cosied**) (*usu. with along, coll.*) to reassure, often with lies and deception. **to cosy up** 1 (*coll., esp. N Am.*) to try to ingratiate oneself (with). 2 (*coll., esp. N Am.*) to snuggle up (to). **cosily** *adv.* **cosiness** *n.* [etym. uncertain]

cot[1] (kot) *n.* 1 a small bed with high barred sides for a young child. 2 a hospital bed. 3 (*N Am.*) a small folding bed, a camp bed. 4 a light or portable bedstead. 5 (*Naut.*) a swinging bed like a hammock. **cot-case** *n.* 1 a person who is too ill to get out of bed. 2 (*Austral.*) a person who is too drunk to move. **cot death** *n.* the sudden and inexplicable death of a baby while sleeping. [from Hind. *khāt*]

cot[2] (kot) *n.* 1 (*poet.*) a cottage or hut. 2 a shelter for birds or animals. ~*v.t.* (*pres.p.* **cotting,** *past, p.p.* **cotted**) to put (sheep) in a cot or fold. [OE *cot, cote* (cp. Dut. and Icel. *kot,* G *Koth*)]

cot[3] (kot) *abbr.* cotangent.

cotangent (kōtan´jənt, kō´-) *n.* (*Math.*) the tangent of the complement of an arc or angle.

cote (kōt) *n.* a sheepfold, or any small house or shelter for birds or animals. [COT[2]]

cotemporary (kōtem´pərəri) *a., n.* CONTEMPORARY.

cotenant (kōten´ənt) *n.* a joint tenant. **cotenancy** *n.* (*pl.* **cotenancies**).

coterie (kō´təri) *n.* 1 a set of people associated together for friendly conversation. 2 an exclusive circle of people in society; a clique. [F, from low L *coteria,* an association of cottars for holding land, from *cota,* a COT[2] (of Gmc. orig.)]

coterminous CONTERMINOUS.

coth (koth, kotăch´) *abbr.* hyperbolic cotangent.

cothurnus (kəthœ´nəs) *n.* (*pl.* **cothurni** (-nī)) 1 the buskin worn by actors in ancient Greek and Roman tragedy. 2 tragedy. 3 the tragic style. [L, from Gr. *kothornos*]

co-tidal (kōtī´dəl) *a.* having the tides at the same time. **co-tidal line** *n.* a line on a map joining places where high or low tides occur at the same time.

cotillion (kətil´yən), **cotillon** (kotēyō´) *n.* 1 an 18th-cent. French ballroom dance for four or eight people. 2 the music for this. 3 (*N Am.*) a ball (for dancing). 4 (*N Am.*) a dance somewhat like a quadrille. [F *cotillon,* lit. a petticoat, dim. of *cotte,* coat]

cotinga (kəting´gə) *n.* any bird of the tropical Central and South American family Cotingidae, the males of many species of which have bright plumage, naked patches of bright skin, peculiar wattles etc. [F, from Tupi *cutinga*]

cotoneaster (kətōnias´tə) *n.* an ornamental shrub of the genus *Cotoneaster,* belonging to the order Rosaceae. [L *cotonea,* quince, -ASTER]

Cotswold (kots´wəld) *n.* a breed of sheep, formerly peculiar to the counties of Gloucester, Worcester and Hereford. [Cotswolds, a range of hills in the west of England]

cotta (kot´ə) *n.* a short surplice. [med. L (see COAT)]

cottage (kot´ij) *n.* **1** a small country or suburban residence. **2** a small house, esp. for labourers on a farm. **3** (*sl.*) a public toilet. ~*v.i.* (*sl.*) to engage in homosexual acts with a partner anonymously in a public toilet. **cottage cheese** *n.* a soft white cheese made from skimmed milk curds. **cottage garden** *n.* a garden informally laid out and planted with traditional British flowers and plants rather than modern or imported varieties. **cottage hospital** *n.* a small hospital without a resident medical staff. **cottage industry** *n.* a small-scale industry in which the workers, usu. self-employed, work at home. **cottage loaf** *n.* a loaf of bread made with two rounded masses of dough stuck one above the other. **cottage piano** *n.* a small upright piano. **cottage pie** *n.* shepherd's pie made with beef. **cottager** *n.* **1** a person who lives in a cottage. **2** (*N Am.*) a person living in a country or seaside residence. **3** (*Hist.*) a cottar. **cottagey, cottagy** *a.* **cottaging** *n.* (*sl.*) the performance of homosexual acts anonymously in a public toilet. [COTE, -AGE]

cottar (kot´ə), **cotter** *n.* **1** a Scottish farm labourer living in a cottage belonging to a farm and paying rent in the form of labour. **2** a person holding a cottage and a plot of land on similar terms to Irish cottier-tenure. [COT[2] or COTE, perh. through med. L *cotārius* (*cota*, COTE)]

☒ **cotten** common misspelling of COTTON.

cotter[1] (kot´ə) *n.* **1** a key, wedge or bolt for holding part of a machine in place. **2** a cotter pin. **cotter pin** *n.* **1** a split pin that opens after being passed through a hole. **2** a tapered pin with a thread at the narrower end which allows it to be fastened in place with a nut. [etym. uncertain]

cotter[2] COTTAR.

cottier (kot´iə) *n.* **1** a peasant living in a cottage. **2** (*Hist., Ir.*) a peasant holding a piece of ground under cottier tenure (cp. COTTAR). **cottier tenure** *n.* (*Hist., Ir.*) the system, now illegal, of letting portions of land at a rent fixed yearly by public competition. [OF *cotier*, med. L *cotārius* (*cota*, COTE)]

cotton (kot´ən) *n.* **1** a downy substance resembling wool, growing in the fruit of the cotton plant, used for making thread, cloth etc. **2** thread made from this. **3** cloth made of cotton. **4** cotton plants collectively, as a crop. ~*a.* made of cotton. ~*v.i.* to get on, to agree well (with). **to cotton on 1** to be attracted (to). **2** to begin to understand. **3** to make use of. **to cotton to** (*N Am., coll.*) to take a liking to. **Cotton Belt** *n.* a region of the southern United States stretching from N and S Carolina to Texas, where cotton is a major crop. **cotton cake** *n.* cottonseed pressed into cakes as food for cattle. **cotton candy** *n.* (*N Am.*) candyfloss. **cotton gin** *n.* a device for separating the seeds from cotton. **cotton grass** *n.* any plant of the genus *Eriophorum*, growing in marshy ground and having a white downy head. **cotton mouth** *n.* WATER MOCCASIN (under WATER) (from the whitish interior of its mouth). **cotton-picking** *a.* (*esp. N Am., sl.*) despicable. **cotton plant** *n.* any of various species of plant of the genus *Gossypium*, whose seed pods yield cotton. **cottonseed** *n.* the seed of the cotton plant, yielding oil, and when crushed made into cotton cake. **cottontail** *n.* any of several common American rabbits of the genus *Sylvilagus*. **cotton waste** *n.* refuse cotton used for cleaning machinery. **cottonweed** *n.* cudweed. **cottonwood** *n.* **1** any of several kinds of N American poplar, esp. *Populus deltoides* and *P. angulata* (from the white cottony hairs on the seeds). **2** any of a number of Australian trees, esp. *Bedfordia salicina*, which has leaves covered with down. **cotton wool** *n.* **1** bleached and sterilized cotton formed into pads, balls etc. and used as dressings, for cleansing etc. **2** (*N Am.*) raw cotton. **in cotton wool** pampered, protected from hard reality. **cottony** *a.* **cotton yarn** *n.* spun cotton ready for weaving. [F *coton*, from Arab. *qutun*]

cotyledon (kotilē´dən) *n.* **1** the rudimentary leaf of an embryo in the higher plants, the seed-leaf. **2** a section of the placenta in mammals. **3** any succulent plant of the southern African genus *Cotyledon*, or of the related European genus *Umbilicus*. **cotyledonal** *a.* resembling a cotyledon. **cotyledonary** *a.* **cotyledonous** *a.* possessing cotyledons. [Gr. *kotulēdōn*, a cup-shaped hollow, from *kotulē*, cup]

couch[1] (kowch) *n.* **1** a long upholstered seat with a back, for more than one person. **2** a similar piece of furniture with a headrest but no back for a doctor's or psychiatrist's patient to lie on. **3** a bed, or any place of rest. **4** a preliminary coat of paint, size etc. **5** a layer of steeped barley germinating for malting. **6** the frame or floor for this. ~*v.t.* **1** to express in words. **2** (*in p.p.*) to cause to lie. **3** to lay (oneself) down. **4** to deposit in a layer or bed. **5** to operate on for a cataract. **6** to treat (a cataract) by displacement of the lens of the eye. **7** in brewing, to spread out (barley) on the floor for germination. **8** to imply, to veil or conceal. **9** to lower (a spear) to a horizontal position for attack. **10** to embroider by couching. ~*v.i.* **1** to lie down, to rest. **2** to lie in concealment. **3** to stoop, to bend. **4** to crouch. **5** to be laid or spread out. **couching** *n.* a form of embroidery in which some threads lie on the material and are held in place by other threads passed through the material. **couch potato** *n.* (*pl.* **couch potatoes**) (*sl.*) an inactive person who watches an excessive amount of television instead of taking part in other forms of entertainment or exercise. [F *coucher*, L *collocāre* (COL-[1], *locāre*, to place, from *locus*, place)]

couch[2] (kowch, kooch) *n.* couch grass. ~*v.t.* to clear of couch grass. **couch grass** *n.* any of various grasses of the genus *Agropyron*, esp. *A. repens*, whose long, creeping roots make them difficult to get rid of. [QUITCH]

couchant (kow´chənt) *a.* (*Her.*) (of an animal) lying down with the head raised. [F, pres.p. of *coucher*, to lie (see COUCH[1])]

couchette (kooshet´) *n.* **1** a seat in a continental train which converts into a sleeping berth. **2** a carriage with such seats. **3** a similar seat on a cross-channel ferry. [F, dim. of *couche*, couch]

coudé (koodā´) *a.* (*Astron.*) (of a reflecting telescope) in which light rays are bent by mirrors to a point of focus, e.g. on a photographic plate, off the axis of the telescope. ~*n.* such a telescope. [F, bent like an elbow (*coude*, elbow)]

Couéism (koo´āizm) *n.* a therapeutic system based on auto-suggestion. [Emil *Coué*, 1857–1926, French psychologist]

cougar (koo´gə) *n.* the puma. [F *couguar*, adapted from the Guarani name]

cough (kof) *n.* **1** a convulsive effort, accompanied by noise, to expel foreign or irritating matter from the lungs. **2** an irritated condition of the organs of breathing that causes coughing. **3** a tendency to cough or habit of coughing. ~*v.t.* to drive from the lungs by a cough. ~*v.i.* **1** to expel air from the lungs in a convulsive and noisy manner, with a cough. **2** (of an engine) to make a similar noise when malfunctioning. **3** (of a gun etc.) to make a similar noise. **to cough up 1** to eject by coughing. **2** (*sl.*) to produce (money or information), esp. under duress. **cough drop** *n.* (*also* **cough lozenge, cough sweet**) a medicinal lozenge taken to cure or relieve a cough. **cough mixture** *n.* a liquid medicine taken to cure or relieve a cough. [OE *cohhetan*, prob. representing an unrecorded *cohhian* (cp. Dut. *kuchen*, to cough, G *keuchen*, to pant); imit. in orig.]

could CAN[1].

couldn't (kud´ənt) *contr.* could not.

coulee (koo´li, -lā), **coulée** (koolā´) *n.* **1** a molten or solidified lava flow. **2** (*N Am.*) a ravine or gully. [F, fem. p.p. of *couler*, to flow]

coulis (koo´lē) *n.* (*pl.* **coulis** (koo´lēz)) a thin purée. [F, from *couler*, to flow]
coulisse (koolēs´) *n.* **1** a grooved timber in which a sluice-gate or a partition slides. **2** a side-scene in a theatre. **3** (*pl.*) the space between the side-scenes. **4** a place for informal or unofficial discussion or dealing. [F, from *couler*, to flow]
couloir (kool´wah) *n.* a steep gully or long, narrow gorge on a precipitous mountainside. [F, from *couler*, to flow]
coulomb (koo´lom) *n.* a unit of electrical charge, equal to the quantity of electricity transferred by one ampere in one second. [Charles-Augustin de *Coulomb*, 1736–1806, French physicist]
coulometry (koolom´itri) *n.* a method of quantitative chemical analysis involving the measurement of the number of coulombs used in electrolysis. **coulometric** (-met´-) *a.*
coulter (kōl´tə), (*N Am.*) **colter** *n.* the iron blade fixed in front of the share in a plough. [OE *culter*, L *culter*]
coumarin (koo´mərin) *n.* an aromatic crystalline substance extracted from the tonka bean and other plants, used in flavourings and as an anticoagulant. [F *coumarine*; Tupi *cumarú*, the tonka bean]
coumarone (koo´mərōn) *n.* (*Chem.*) a colourless aromatic liquid obtained from coal tar, used in the production of synthetic resins for use in paints and varnishes, adhesives etc. **coumarone resin** *n.* a polymer of coumarone, a thermoplastic resin. [COUMARIN]
council (kown´səl) *n.* **1** a number of people met together for deliberation, advice or some administrative purpose. **2** people acting as advisers to a sovereign, governor or chief magistrate. **3** an elected body in charge of local government in a county, parish, borough etc. **4** (*loosely*) a local bureaucracy. **5** the higher branch of the legislature in some of the states of America and formerly also in some British colonies. **6** an ecclesiastical assembly attended by the representatives of various churches. **7** the governing body of a university. **8** (*Bible*) the Jewish Sanhedrin. *~a.* **1** used by a council. **2** provided or maintained by a council. **council-chamber** *n.* the room where a council meets. **council-fire** *n.* the sacred fire kept burning by the N American Indians during their councils. **council house** *n.* **1** a house owned by a local council and rented out to tenants. **2** a building in which a council meets. **councillor,** (*N Am.*) **councilor** *n.* a member of a council. **councillorship** *n.* **councilman, councilwoman** *n.* (*pl.* **councilmen, councilwomen**) (*N Am.*) a councillor. **Council of Europe** *n.* a council set up in 1949 by W European countries to discuss matters of common concern, excluding defence. **Council of Ministers** *n.* an EU decision-making body consisting of ministers from member states. **council of war** *n.* **1** a council of officers called together in time of difficulty or danger. **2** a meeting to decide on future action. **council tax** *n.* a tax for the financing of local government, introduced in 1993 as a replacement for the community charge, calculated on the capital value of the property. [F *concile*, L *concilium* (CON-, *calāre*, to summon)]

Usage note The spellings of the nouns *council, councillor* and *counsel, counsellor* should not be confused: the first refer to an elected body or assembly, and the second to a barrister or other legal representative or professional adviser.

counsel (kown´səl) *n.* **1** advice. **2** opinion given after deliberation. **3** a consultation. **4** (*Law*) a barrister. **5** (*as pl.*) the advocates engaged on either side in a law-suit. **6** a plan of action. *~v.t.* (*pres.p.* **counselling,** (*N Am.*) **counseling,** *past, p.p.* **counselled,** (*N Am.*) **counseled**) **1** to give advice or counsel to. **2** to advise. **to keep one's own counsel** to keep a matter secret. **to take counsel (with)** to seek advice (from). **counselling,** (*N Am.*) **counseling** *n.* the giving of advice, esp. the giving of advice and information in (difficult) personal situations by a qualified adviser; the advice and information given. **counsellor,** (*N Am.*) **counselor** *n.* **1** a person who gives counsel or advice. **2** an adviser. **3** (*N Am.*) (*also* **counselor-at-law**) a lawyer, esp. one who conducts a case in court. **4** a counsellor-at-law. **5** a senior member of the diplomatic service. **counsellor-at-law** *n.* in Ireland, an advocate, a counsel, a barrister. **counsellorship** *n.* [OF *conseil*, L *consilium*, from *consulere*, to consult (see CONSUL)]

Usage note See note under COUNCIL.

count[1] (kownt) *v.t.* **1** to reckon up in numbers, to calculate or total. **2** to include. **3** to consider. **4** to esteem. *~v.i.* **1** to possess a certain value. **2** to say the numerals in order. **3** in music and dancing, to keep to the correct rhythm by counting the beats. *~n.* **1** a reckoning or numbering. **2** the sum (of). **3** (*Law*) a statement of the plaintiff's case. **4** one of several charges in an indictment. **5** any of the points in an argument or discussion. **6** in boxing and wrestling, a count of up to ten seconds by the referee, during which a boxer who has been knocked down must get up or a wrestler who has been pinned down raise part of their body or else lose the match. **7** the counting of votes after an election. **8** a measure of fineness of yarn. **9** (*Physics*) the total number of ionized particles registered by a counter. **not counting** excluding. **out for the count 1** unconscious. **2** fast asleep. **3** thoroughly dispirited or dejected. **4** in boxing, having been counted out. **to count against** to be a factor against. **to count down** to count in reverse order, towards zero, in preparing for a particular event. **to count for** to be a factor in favour of. **to count in** to include. **to count noses** NOSE. **to count one's blessings** to be thankful for the good things one has. **to count one's chickens (before they are hatched)** CHICKEN. **to count on/ upon 1** to rely on. **2** to consider as certain. **to count out 1** to reckon one by one from a number of units by counting aloud. **2** to count aloud (the number one is taking from a larger amount). **3** (*coll.*) to exclude, to not count in. **4** in children's games, to select or reject by means of a counting rhyme etc. **5** to declare (a boxer) defeated upon their failure to stand up within 10 seconds of the referee beginning to count. **6** to adjourn a meeting, esp. of Parliament, after counting those present and finding they are not sufficient to form a quorum. **to count the cost 1** to calculate the damage or loss that has resulted or would result from some action. **2** to consider the risks entailed in some action. **to count the days/ hours etc.** to wait impatiently for something. **to count up** to calculate the sum of. **to keep count** to keep an accurate record of a numerical series. **to lose count** to be unable to keep count. **to take the count** in boxing, to be counted out. **countable** *a.* **countable noun, count noun** *n.* (*Gram.*) a noun which can be used in both the singular and the plural. **countback** *n.* a way of scoring in sporting competitions by which, in the event of a tie, a winner is declared on the basis of previous scores. **countdown** *n.* **1** the counting backwards of the time left before some event, esp. the launching of a spacecraft. **2** the period of such counting. **3** the checks and other procedures carried out during this period. **4** the period of time preceding any significant event. **counting** *n.* **counting house** *n.* the house, room or office appropriated to the business of keeping accounts etc. **counting rhyme** *n.* a jingle by means of which players are selected, e.g. for teams, in children's games. **countless** *a.* **1** innumerable. **2** beyond calculation. **count noun** COUNTABLE NOUN (under COUNT[1]). [OF *conter*, L *computāre*, to COMPUTE]

count² (kownt) *n.* a foreign title of rank corresponding to a British earl. **countess** *n.* **1** the wife of an earl or count. **2** a woman holding this rank in her own right. **Count Palatine** *n.* (*pl.* **Counts Palatine**) (*Hist.*) **1** a high judicial officer under the Merovingian kings. **2** the ruler of either of the Rhenish Palatinates. **3** the lord of a County Palatine. **countship** *n.* [OF *conte*, L *comes -item*, companion]

countable COUNT¹.

countenance (kown´tənəns) *n.* **1** the face. **2** the features. **3** air, look or expression. **4** composure of look. **5** favour, support, corroboration. ~*v.t.* **1** to sanction, to approve, to permit. **2** to abet, to encourage. **in countenance 1** in favour. **2** confident, assured. **out of countenance 1** out of favour. **2** abashed, dismayed. **to change countenance** to change the expression on one's face because of emotion. **to keep in countenance** to support. **to keep one's countenance** to continue composed in look, to refrain from laughter. **to lose countenance** to become embarrassed. **to put out of countenance** to abash, to cause to feel ashamed. **countenancer** *n.* [OF *contenance*, aspect, demeanour, L *continentia* (*continēre*, to contain)]

counter¹ (kown´tə) *n.* **1** a table or desk over which business is conducted (in a shop, bank, library, cafe etc.). **2** a piece of metal, plastic etc., used for reckoning, e.g. in games. **3** an imitation coin or token. **4** a person who or something which counts. **5** a calculator. **6** (*N Am.*) a kitchen worktop. **7** a pawn in someone's plans. **over the counter 1** (of medicines) sold without prescription. **2** (of the buying and selling of shares) through a broker, because the shares are not on the official list of a stock exchange. **under the counter 1** referring to trade in black market goods. **2** secret(ly). **3** surreptitious(ly). **counter-jumper** *n.* (*dated, coll.*) a shop assistant. **countertop** *n.* (*N Am.*) a worktop. [A-F *counteour*, OF *countour*, L *computātōrium*, from *computāre*, to COMPUTE]

counter² (kown´tə) *n.* **1** the opposite, the contrary. **2** a countermove. **3** in fencing, a circular parry. **4** in boxing, a blow dealt just as the opponent is striking. **5** a horse's breast. **6** the part of a boot or shoe enclosing the wearer's heel. **7** the curved part of a ship's stern. ~*a.* **1** contrary, adverse, opposed. **2** opposing. **3** duplicate. ~*adv.* **1** in the opposite direction. **2** wrongly. **3** contrarily. ~*v.t.* **1** to oppose, to contradict. **2** to make a countermove against. **3** to return (a blow) by dealing another one. ~*v.i.* **1** to make a countermove. **2** to say something in opposition or retaliation. **3** in boxing, to give a return blow. **to act counter to** to disobey (orders etc.). **to go counter** in hunting, to go in the opposite direction to that of the quarry. **to go counter to** to disobey (orders etc.). **to hunt counter** to go counter. **to run counter** to go counter. **to run counter to 1** to disobey (orders etc.). **2** to happen, behave etc. in a way other than what is expected. [F *contre*, L *contra*, against]

counter- (kowntə) *comb. form* **1** in return, duplicating. **2** in answer, corresponding. **3** in opposition. **4** in an opposite direction. [COUNTER²]

counteract (kowntərakt´) *v.t.* **1** to act in opposition to, so as to hinder or defeat. **2** to neutralize. **counteraction** *n.* **counteractive** *a.*

counter-attack (kown´tərətak) *v.t.*, *v.i.* to make an attack after an attack by an enemy or opponent. ~*n.* such an attack.

counter-attraction (kowntərətrak´shən) *n.* **1** attraction in an opposite direction. **2** a rival attraction. **counter-attractive** *a.*

counterbalance¹ (kowntəbal´əns) *v.t.* **1** to weigh against or oppose with an equal weight or effect. **2** to countervail.

counterbalance² (kown´təbaləns) *n.* an equal weight or force acting in opposition.

counterblast (kown´təblahst) *n.* an argument or statement in opposition.

counterchange (kown´təchānj) *n.* exchange, reciprocation. ~*v.t.* **1** to exchange, to alternate. **2** to interchange, to chequer. ~*v.i.* to change places or parts.

countercharge (kown´təchahj) *n.* **1** a charge in opposition to another. **2** a counterclaim. ~*v.t.* **1** to make a charge against in return. **2** to charge in opposition to (a charge of troops).

countercheck (kown´təchek) *n.* **1** a check brought against another. **2** an opposing check. **3** a second check to check the accuracy or efficiency of a first check. **4** †a retort. ~*v.t.* to make a countercheck of, on or against.

counter-claim (kown´təklām) *n.* a claim made against another claim, esp. a claim brought forward by a defendant against a plaintiff. ~*v.t.*, *v.i.* to make a counterclaim (for).

counter-clockwise (kowntəklok´wīz) *adv.* (*N Am.*) anticlockwise.

counter-culture (kown´təkŭlchə) *n.* a way of life deliberately contrary to accepted social usages.

counter-espionage (kowntəres´piənahzh) *n.* work of an intelligence service directed against the agents of another country.

counterexample (kown´tərigzahmpəl) *n.* an example or fact that does not fit a proposed theory, and which is used as an argument against it.

counterfeit (kown´təfit, -fēt) *a.* **1** made in imitation with intent to be passed off as genuine. **2** forged. **3** pretend; false. ~*n.* **1** a counterfeit thing. **2** a person who pretends to be what they are not, an impostor. ~*v.t.* **1** (*Law*) to make a counterfeit copy of, to forge. **2** to imitate or copy without right and pass off as genuine. **3** to imitate, to mimic. **4** to pretend, to simulate. **5** to resemble. ~*v.i.* to make counterfeits. **counterfeiter** *n.* [OF *contrefait*, p.p. of *contrefaire* (L *contra*, against, *facere*, to make)]

counterfoil (kown´təfoil) *n.* the counterpart of a cheque, receipt or other document, retained by the giver.

counterfort (kown´təfawt) *n.* (*Archit.*) a buttress, arch or oblique wall built against a wall or terrace to retain, support or strengthen it. [F *contrefort*]

counter-glow (kown´təglō) *n.* GEGENSCHEIN.

counter-insurgency (kowntərinsœ´jənsi) *n.* actions taken by a government, police force, army etc. to counter rebellion etc.

counterintelligence (kowntərintel´ijəns) *n.* work of an intelligence service designed to prevent or damage intelligence gathering by an enemy intelligence service.

counter-intuitive (kowntərintū´itiv) *a.* going against what one intuitively feels to be right.

counterirritant (kowntərir´itənt) *n.* **1** an irritant applied to the body to remove or lessen some other irritation. **2** anything with a similar purpose or effect. ~*a.* acting as a counterirritant. **counterirritate** *v.t.* **counter-irritation** (-ā´shən) *n.*

countermand (kowntəmahnd´) *v.t.* **1** to revoke, to annul. **2** to recall. **3** to cancel. ~*n.* an order contrary to or revoking a previous order. [OF *contremander* (L *contra*, against, *mandāre*, to command)]

countermarch (kown´təmahch) *v.i.* **1** to march in an opposite direction. **2** to perform a countermarch. ~*v.t.* to cause to countermarch. ~*n.* **1** the action of countermarching. **2** a change in the position of the wings or front and rear of a battalion. **3** a change of measures or conduct.

countermeasure (kown´təmezhə) *n.* an action taken to counter a danger, thwart an enemy etc.

countermine (kown´təmīn) *n.* **1** a gallery or mine to intercept or frustrate a mine made by the enemy. **2** a submarine mine employed to explode the mines sunk by the enemy. **3** a stratagem to frustrate any project.

~*v.t.* to oppose by a countermine. ~*v.i.* to make or place countermines.

countermove (kown´təmoov) *n.* a movement in an opposite or contrary direction, or in opposition or retaliation. ~*v.i.* to make a countermove. **countermovement** *n.*

counter-offensive (kowntərəfen´siv) *n.* 1 a counter-attack. 2 any attack made by defenders.

counteroffer (kown´tərofə) *n.* a second, usu. lower, offer by a seller attempting to close a deal.

counterpane (kown´təpān) *n.* 1 a bedcover. 2 a quilt. [earlier *counterpoint*, OF *contrepointe*, corr. of *coultepointe*, L *culcita puncta*, stitched QUILT (*puncta*, p.p. of *pungere*, to prick)]

counterpart (kown´təpaht) *n.* 1 a person who is exactly like another in character, role etc. 2 a corresponding part. 3 a duplicate or copy. 4 anything which exactly fits another, such as a seal and the impression it makes. 5 (*Law*) one of two corresponding copies of an instrument. 6 (*Mus.*) a part written to accompany another. **counterpart fund** *n.* a fund, account etc. established for amounts in the local currency equivalent to goods and services received from abroad. [OF *contrepartie* (COUNTER-, *partie*, part)]

counterplot (kown´təplot) *n.* a plot to defeat another plot. ~*v.t.* (*pres.p.* **counterplotting,** *past, p.p.* **counterplotted**) to oppose or frustrate by another plot. ~*v.i.* to make a counterplot.

counterpoint (kown´təpoint) *n.* 1 a melodious part or combination of parts written to accompany a melody. 2 the art of constructing harmonious parts. 3 the art of harmonious composition. 4 a contrasting idea, theme, argument etc. ~*v.t.* 1 (*Mus.*) to add counterpoint to (a melody etc.). 2 to set (an idea, theme etc.) in contrast to another for effect. [F *contrepoint*, med. L *contrapunctum*, point against point (*contra*, against, *punctum*, p.p. of *pungere*, to prick)]

counterpoise (kown´təpoiz) *n.* 1 a weight in opposition and equal to another. 2 a counterbalancing force, power or influence. 3 equilibrium. ~*v.t.* 1 to oppose with an equal weight so as to balance. 2 to oppose, check or correct with an equal force, power or influence. 3 to bring into or maintain in equilibrium. [F *contrepois* (now *poids*)]

counter-productive (kowntəprədŭk´tiv) *a.* producing an opposite, or undesired, result.

counterproof (kown´təproof) *n.* in printing, a reversed impression taken from another just printed.

counterproposal (kownt´əprəpōzəl) *n.* a proposal made as an alternative to a previous proposal.

counterpunch (kown´təpŭnch) *n.* a punch given in return. ~*v.i.* to make a counterpunch or counterpunches.

counter-reformation (kowntərefəmā´shən) *n.* 1 a reformation of an opposite nature to or as a reaction to another. 2 (*Hist.*) (**Counter-Reformation**) the attempt of the Roman Church to counteract the results of the Protestant Reformation.

counter-revolution (kowntərevəloo´shən) *n.* a revolution opposed to a former one, and designed to restore a former state of things. **counter-revolutionary** *n.* (*pl.* **counter-revolutionaries**) an instigator or supporter of such a revolution. ~*a.* of or relating to such a revolution.

counterscarp (kown´təskahp) *n.* 1 the exterior wall or slope of the ditch in a fortification, opposite the *scarp*. 2 the whole covered way with the parapet and glacis. [F *contrescarpe*, It. *contrascarpa* (*contra*, against, *scarpa*, SCARP[1])]

countershaft (kown´təshahft) *n.* an intermediate shaft driven by the main shaft and transmitting motion.

countersign (kown´təsīn) *v.t.* 1 to attest the correctness of by an additional signature. 2 to ratify. ~*n.* 1 a password, a secret word or sign by which one may pass a sentry, or by which the members of a secret association may recognize each other. 2 any identifying mark. **counter-signature** (-sig´nəchə) *n.* the signature on a document certifying that of another person. [F *contresigner*]

countersink (kown´təsingk) *v.t.* (*past, p.p.* **countersunk** (-sŭngk)) 1 to chamfer (a hole) for a screw or bolt head. 2 to sink (the head of a screw etc.) into such a hole. ~*n.* 1 a chamfered hole. 2 a tool for making such a hole.

counterstroke (kown´təstrōk) *n.* a stroke made in return.

countersunk COUNTERSINK.

countertenor (kown´tətenə) *n.* 1 (a singer with) a voice higher than tenor, a male alto voice. 2 a part written for such a voice.

counterterrorism (kowntəter´ərizm) *n.* terrorism carried out to prevent or in retaliation for acts of terrorism by others.

countervail (kowntəvāl´) *v.t.* 1 to act against with equal effect or power. 2 to counterbalance. ~*v.i.* to be of equal weight, power or influence on the opposite side. **countervailing duty** *n.* an import duty imposed on goods to compensate for a subsidy in the exporting country or a tax on similar goods in the importing country. [OF *contrevail*, stem of *contrevaloir* (*contre*, against, *valoir*, L *valēre*, to avail)]

countervalue (kown´təvalū) *n.* an equivalent value.

counterweigh (kowntəwā´) *v.t.* to counterbalance. **counterweight** *n.*

counterwork (kown´təwœk) *v.t.* 1 to work against. 2 to counteract. ~*n.* 1 an opposing work or effort. 2 (*Mil.*) a work constructed to oppose those of the enemy.

countess COUNT[2].

countrified COUNTRY.

country (kŭn´tri) *n.* (*pl.* **countries**) 1 a territory or state. 2 the inhabitants of any territory or state. 3 one's native land. 4 the rural part as distinct from cities and towns. 5 the rest of a land as distinguished from the capital. 6 a region or area. 7 country music. **across country** not using roads etc. **in the country** in cricket, far from the wickets, in the outfield. **to appeal to the country** to go to the country. **to go to the country** to hold a general election, to appeal to the electors. **up country** away from the coast or from the capital city. **countrified, countryfied** *a.* rustic in manners or appearance. **country and western** *n.* country music. **country-and-western** *a.* **country club** *n.* a sporting or social club in country surroundings. **country code** *n.* a recommended code of good behaviour for those using the countryside, e.g. for recreation. **country cousin** *n.* a relation of countrified ways or appearance. **country dance** *n.* 1 a dance in which the partners are ranged in lines opposite to each other. 2 any rural English dance. 3 a gathering at which such dances are performed. **country dancing** *n.* **countryfied** COUNTRIFIED (under COUNTRY). **country gentleman** *n.* (*pl.* **country gentlemen**) a man who owns and lives on an estate in the country. **country house** *n.* a mansion in the country, esp. one belonging or having belonged for generations to a landowning family. **countryman, countrywoman** *n.* (*pl.* **countrymen, countrywomen**) 1 a person who lives in a rural district. 2 an inhabitant of any particular region. 3 a fellow countryman or countrywoman. **country music** *n.* a style of popular music based on the folk music of rural areas of the US. **country park** *n.* an area of land set aside for recreational use by the general public, e.g. for hillwalking. **country party** *n.* (*pl.* **country parties**) a political party that professes to maintain the interests of the nation as a whole, or the agricultural interests as against the industrial. **country rock** *n.* 1 (*Geol.*) the rock surrounding a mineral deposit or an igneous intrusion. **2** a blend of country music and rock music. **country seat** *n.* a country house, or the house plus the estate surrounding it. **countryside** *n.* **1** a rural district, or rural districts in general. **2** the inhabitants of this. **countrywide** *a.* extending right across a country. **countrywoman** COUNTRYMAN (under COUNTRY). [OF *cuntrée, contrée,* late L *contrāta,* a region over against, from *contrā,* against]

county (kown´ti) *n.* (*pl.* **counties**) **1** a division of land for administrative, judicial and political purposes. **2** in England, Wales and Ireland, and formerly in Scotland, the chief civil unit and chief administrative division outside the seven largest conurbations. **3** in the US, the civil division next below a state. **4** county families collectively. ~*a.* **1** of or relating to a county. **2** characteristic of county families. **county borough** *n.* (before 1974) a large borough ranking administratively as a county. **county corporate** *n.* (*Hist.*) a city or town having sheriffs and other magistrates of its own, and ranking as a county. **county council** *n.* the elected council administering the civil affairs of a county. **county councillor** *n.* **county court** *n.* a local court dealing with civil cases. **county cricket** *n.* cricket played between sides representing counties. **county family** *n.* a family belonging to the nobility or gentry with an ancestral seat in the county. **County Palatine** *n.* (*pl.* **Counties Palatine**) a county of which the Count or Earl Palatine was formerly invested with royal privileges, such as Cheshire and Lancashire. **county school** *n.* a school established and maintained by a local education authority. **county town,** (*N Am.*) **county seat** *n.* the chief town of any county. [OF *cunté, conté,* L *comitātus* (see COUNT²)]

coup¹ (koo) *n.* **1** a stroke, a telling or decisive blow. **2** a victory. **3** a successful move, piece of strategy or revolution. **4** a coup d'état. **5** in billiards, a stroke putting a ball into a pocket without its touching another. [F, from OF *colp* (It. *colpo*), late L *colpus, colapus,* L *colaphus,* Gr. *kolaphos,* a blow]

coup² (kowp) *v.t.* (*Sc.*) to upset, to overturn. ~*v.i.* to be overturned. [Sc. for COPE¹]

coup de foudre (koo də food´rə) *n.* (*pl.* **coups de foudre** (koo də food´rə)) **1** a sudden and overwhelming event. **2** love at first sight. [F, flash of lightning]

coup de grâce (koo də grahs´) *n.* (*pl.* **coups de grâce** (koo də grahs´)) **1** a finishing stroke; an action that puts an end to something. **2** a death blow administered to put an end to suffering. [F, stroke of mercy]

coup de main (koo də mā´) *n.* (*pl.* **coups de main** (koo də mī´)) a sudden and energetic attack. [F, blow with the hand]

coup de soleil (koo də solāy´) *n.* (*pl.* **coups de soleil** (koo də solāy´)) sunburn. [F, stroke of sun]

coup d'état (koo dātah´) *n.* (*pl.* **coups d'état** (koo dātah´)) a sudden and violent change of government, esp. of an illegal and revolutionary nature. [F, stroke of state]

coup de théâtre (koo də tāaht´rə) *n.* (*pl.* **coups de théâtre** (koo də tāaht´rə)) **1** a dramatic turn of events in a play. **2** a sensational dramatic effect or device. **3** a notable theatrical success. [F, stroke of theatre]

coup d'oeil (koo dœy´) *n.* (*pl.* **coups d'oeil** (koo dœy´)) **1** a quick comprehensive glance. **2** a general view. [F, blow with the eye]

coupe¹ (koop) *n.* **1** a dessert made of fruit or ice cream. **2** the shallow glass dish in which such desserts are served. [F, cup]

coupe² COUPÉ.

coupé (koo´pā), (*N Am.*) **coupe** (koop) *n.* **1** (*usu., N Am.* **coupe**) a two-doored car with an enclosed body. **2** (*Hist.*) (**coupé**) a four-wheeled closed carriage. **3** (*Hist.*) (**coupé**) a half compartment with glazed front at the end of a railway carriage. [F, p.p. of *couper,* to cut (as COUP¹)]

couple (kŭp´əl) *n.* **1** two. **2** more or less two, a few. **3** two people who are engaged, married or in a steady relationship. **4** two people who are partners in a dance, sports match etc. **5** two of anything of the same kind considered together. **6** (*pl.* **couple**) a pair or brace, esp. in hunting or coursing, a pair of dogs. **7** (*pl.*) two dog collars joined by a leash. **8** in carpentry, a pair of rafters connected by a tie. **9** a pair of equal forces acting in parallel and opposite directions so as to impart a circular movement. **10** (*Physics*) two metals etc. in electrical contact with each other. **11** that which joins two things together. ~*v.t.* **1** to connect or fasten together. **2** to unite persons together, esp. in marriage. **3** to associate. **4** (*Physics*) to connect with a coupling. ~*v.i.* to copulate. **coupler** *n.* **1** a person who or something which couples. **2** (*Mus.*) a connection between two or more organ manuals or keys, or manuals and pedals. **3** (*Mus.*) OCTAVE COUPLER (under OCTAVE). **4** (*Physics*) a transformer that connects electrical circuits. **couplet** (-lit) *n.* two, usu. rhyming, lines of running verse. **coupling** *n.* **1** a device for connecting railway carriages etc. together. **2** a device for connecting parts of machinery and transmitting motion. **3** the arrangement of songs, pieces of music etc. on a gramophone record, or any one of these songs etc. [OF *cople,* L COPULA]

coupon (koo´pon) *n.* **1** a form that may be detached or cut out e.g. from an advertisement, and used as an order form, entry form for a competition etc. **2** a football pools entry form. **3** a piece of paper which can be exchanged for goods in a shop. **4** a voucher. **5** a detachable ticket or certificate entitling to food ration etc. **6** a detachable certificate for the payment of interest on bonds. [F, a piece cut off, from *couper,* to cut]

coupure (koopūə´) *n.* in fortifications, a passage, esp. one cut through the glacis to facilitate sallies by the besieged. [F *couper,* to cut]

courage (kŭr´ij) *n.* bravery, boldness, intrepidity. **courage of one's convictions** the courage to act in accordance with one's beliefs. **to lose courage** to be overcome by fear. **to pluck up courage** to summon up boldness or bravery. **to take courage 1** to pluck up courage. **2** to derive courage (from a thought, piece of news etc.). **to take one's courage in both hands** to summon up the courage necessary to do something. **courageous** (-rā´-) *a.* **courageously** *adv.* **courageousness** *n.* [OF *corage, courage,* from L *cor,* the heart, -AGE]

courant (kurant´) *a.* (*Her.*) in a running attitude. ~*n.* (*also* **courante**) **1** an old dance with a running or gliding step. **2** the music for this. [F, pres.p. of *courir,* L *currere,* to run]

courbette (kuəbet´) *n.* CURVET.

courgette (kuəzhet´) *n.* a small kind of vegetable marrow. [F, dim. of *courge,* gourd]

courier (kur´iə) *n.* **1** an employee of a private postal company offering a fast collection and delivery service usu. within a city or internationally. **2** a person employed by a travel agency to accompany a party of tourists or to assist them at a resort. **3** a person who conveys secret information for purposes of espionage, or contraband for e.g. a drug-smuggling ring. **4** a messenger sent in great haste, an express. [ME *corour,* OF *coreor* (F *coureur*), late L *curritor -ōrem,* from L *currere,* to run (coalescing later with F *courier,* It. *corriere,* med. L *currerius,* from It. *correre,* L *currere,* to run)]

course (kaws) *n.* **1** continued progress, continued movement along a path. **2** the act of passing from one place to another. **3** the direction in which something moves. **4** the path passed along, the route. **5** the correct or intended route. **6** a period of time passed. **7** the ground on which a race is run or on which a game (such as golf) is played. **8** the act of running, a race. **9** a series (of lectures, lessons, medical treatments etc.). **10** a planned programme of study. **11** any one of a series of dishes served at one meal. **12** mode of procedure. **13** method of life or conduct. **14** a career. **15** a row or tier of bricks or stones in a building. **16** the bed, or the direction of flow, of a stream. **17** in coursing, a chase after a hare by one or more dogs. **18** in bell-ringing, the series of positions which a given bell occupies in the changing order in which a set of bells is rung. **19** (*Naut.*) any of the sails set on a ship's lower yards. **20** (*Hist.*) the charge of two mounted knights in the lists. **21** (*pl.*) the menses. *~v.t.* **1** to run after, to pursue. **2** to use in coursing. **3** to traverse. *~v.i.* **1** to chase hares with greyhounds. **2** to run or move quickly. **3** (of blood etc.) to flow or circulate. **in due course** DUE. **in (the) course of 1** in the process of. **2** during. **in the course of time 1** as time passes. **2** eventually. **of course 1** naturally. **2** admittedly. **off course** not on course. **on course** following the correct course, on target, on schedule. **to run its course** RUN. **to stay the course** to last out to the end of some difficult or demanding activity. **to take its course** to run its course. **coursebook** *n.* a book for use by a student on a particular course of academic study. **course of nature** *n.* the way in which things usually happen. **courser** *n.* **1** a swift horse, a warhorse. **2** a person who practises coursing. **3** a dog used in coursing. **4** a desert bird of the genus *Cursorius*, related to the pratincole, noted for swiftness in running. **coursework** *n.* work done, or to be done, by a student as part of an academic course, often used in assessment or grading. **coursing** *a.* that courses. *~n.* the sport of hunting hares with greyhounds or lurchers. [OF *cours*, L *cursum*, acc. of *cursus*, a running, from *currere*, to run]

court (kawt) *n.* **1** an enclosed piece of ground used for games. **2** a subdivision of a piece so enclosed or merely marked out. **3** the chamber in which justice is administered. **4** the judges or persons assembled to hear any cause. **5** any meeting or body having jurisdiction. **6** a place enclosed by buildings, or enclosing a house. **7** a narrow street. **8** a quadrangle or courtyard. **9** a subdivision of a large building. **10** a word used in the names of large houses, blocks of flats etc. **11** the sovereign and advisers regarded as the ruling power. **12** the residence of a sovereign. **13** the retinue of a sovereign. **14** the body of courtiers. **15** a State reception by a sovereign. **16** deferential attention paid in order to secure favour or regard. **17** the council of certain organizations. **18** a local branch of a friendly society. **19** a meeting of a court. **20** a court shoe. *~v.t.* **1** to seek the affections of, to woo. **2** to seek the favour of, to pay court to. **3** to look for, to try to gain. **4** to act in such a way as to bring (disaster etc.). *~v.i.* to try to gain the affections of a woman. **in court** attending legal proceedings as one of the parties to a case or as counsel. **out of court 1** without the case being heard in a civil court. **2** not entitled to be heard in court. **3** not worth considering. **to go to court** to begin legal proceedings. **to laugh out of court** LAUGH. **to pay court to** to behave flatteringly or amorously (towards someone). **court card** *n.* any king, queen or knave in a pack of cards. **court circular** *n.* an official daily report in a newspaper, of the activities and engagements of the royal family. **court cupboard** *n.* a kind of sideboard on which silver etc. could be displayed. **court dress** *n.* the formal costume proper for a royal or state occasion. **court hand** *n.* (*Hist.*) the style of handwriting (based on Norman handwriting) used in records and judicial proceedings. **courthouse** *n.* **1** a house or building containing rooms used by any court. **2** (*N Am.*) the building in which the offices of a county government are found. **Court leet** *n.* (*Hist.*) a court of record held once a year by the steward of a hundred, lordship or manor. **courtlike** *a.* elegant, polished. **court martial** *n.* (*pl.* **courts martial,** (*coll.*) **court martials**) a court for the trial of members of the armed forces, composed of officers, none of whom must be of inferior rank to the prisoner. **court-martial** *v.t.* (*pres.p.* **court-martialling,** (*N Am.*) **court-martialing,** *past, p.p.* **court-martialled,** (*N Am.*) **court-martialed**) to try by court martial. **Court of Appeal,** (*N Am.*) **Court of Appeals** *n.* a law court in which appeals against the judgements of other courts are heard. **court of cassation** *n.* the highest court of appeal in France and Belgium. **Court of Exchequer** *n.* (*Hist.*) a court for the recovery of debts due to the king and to vindicate his proprietary rights etc., but afterwards developed into an ordinary law court and in 1881 merged into the Queen's (King's) Bench Division. **court of first instance** *n.* the law court in which legal proceedings are first heard. **court of law** *n.* **1** the judges and persons assembled to hear any cause. **2** a courthouse, a courtroom. **Court of Protection** *n.* the department of the Supreme Court which looks after the affairs of those not mentally capable of doing so themselves. **court of record** *n.* a court whose proceedings are officially recorded and preserved as evidence. **court of review** *n.* a court to which sentences and decisions are submitted for judicial revision. **Court of Session** *n.* the supreme civil court of justice in Scotland. **Court of St James's** *n.* the court of the British monarch. **court of summary jurisdiction** *n.* a court which has the authority to try cases, reach judgements and make convictions in summary proceedings. **court order** *n.* a directive or order given by a judge to do or refrain from doing something. **court plaster** *n.* silk surfaced with a solution of balsam of benzoin (used in the 18th cent. by fashionable ladies for patches, and since then for cuts or slight wounds). **court roll** *n.* (*Hist.*) the record of a manorial court. **courtroom** *n.* the chamber in which justice is administered. **courtship** *n.* **1** the act or process of wooing. **2** the behaviour of male birds and animals by which they try to attract a mate. **3** a period of courting. **4** the act of seeking after anything, esp. by flattery. **5** courteous attention. **6** courtly state. **court shoe** *n.* a woman's low-cut shoe without straps etc. **court tennis** *n.* real tennis. **courtyard** *n.* an open area round or within a large building. [OF *cort*, L *cōrtem*, *cohortem*, acc. of *cohors*, an enclosure, a cohort (cp. Gr. *chortos*, a courtyard, L *hortus*, a garden)]

court bouillon (kawt boo´yon, kuə booyõ´) *n.* a stock made with vegetables, water and wine or vinegar, used especially for cooking fish in. [F, short bouillon]

Courtelle® (kawtel´) *n.* a synthetic acrylic fibre.

courteous (kœ´tiəs) *a.* polite, affable, considerate. **courteously** *adv.* **courteousness** *n.* [OF *cortois*, *curteis*]

courtesan (kaw´tizan), **courtezan** *n.* **1** a prostitute or mistress. **2** a promiscuous woman. [F *courtisane*, It. *cortigiana*]

courtesy (kœ´təsi) *n.* (*pl.* **courtesies**) **1** courteousness, politeness, graciousness. **2** an act of civility. **3** gracious disposition. **4** favour, as opposed to right. **by courtesy** as a matter of courtesy, not of right. **by courtesy of** with the permission or agreement of. **courtesy light** *n.* a small light in a motor vehicle which is switched on when a door is opened. **courtesy title** *n.* a title to which a person has no legal right (used esp. of the hereditary titles assumed by the children of peers). [OF *cortesie*, from *corteis*, COURTEOUS]

courtier (kaw´tiə) *n.* **1** a person who is in attendance or a frequenter at a royal etc. court. **2** a person of polished or distinguished manners. **3** a person who courts or flatters. **courtierism** *n.* [from OF *cortoier*, to live at court (*cort*, COURT)]

courtly (kawt´li) *a.* (*comp.* **courtlier**, *superl.* **courtliest**)

1 polished, elegant, polite. 2 flattering, obsequious. 3 of or relating to a court. **courtliness** *n.*

couscous (koos´koos) *n.* 1 a N African dish of pounded wheat steamed over meat or broth. 2 the wheat used in this dish. [F, from Arab. *kuskus*, from *kaskasa*, to pound]

cousin (kŭz´ən) *n.* 1 the son or daughter of an uncle or aunt. 2 (*usu. pl.*) a person of a related people, nation or group. 3 (*Hist.*) a title used by a sovereign in addressing another sovereign or a noble. 4 used as a familiar form of address. **first cousin** FIRST. **second cousin** SECOND[1]. **third cousin** THIRD. **to call cousins** to profess kinship with. **cousin german** *n.* (*pl.* **cousins german**) a first cousin. **cousinhood** *n.* **cousinly** *a.* **cousinry** *n.* kindred, relatives. **cousinship** *n.* [F, from late L *cosīnus*, L *consobrīnus*, a cousin german on the mother's side, from *soror*, a sister]

couth (kooth) *a.* (*facet.*) well-mannered, sophisticated. [formed from UNCOUTH]

couthie (koo´thi), **couthy** *a.* (*Sc.*) 1 friendly, kindly, genial. 2 homely. ~*adv.* in a friendly or genial way. [prob. from OE *cūth*, known]

couture (kətūə´, -tuə´) *n.* 1 dressmaking. 2 dress-designing. **couturier** (-riā) *n.* a dress-designer or dressmaker. **couturière** (-rieə) *n.* a female couturier. [F]

couvade (koovahd´) *n.* a custom among certain peoples, by which a father during the birth of his child performs certain acts and abstains from certain foods etc. [F, from *couver*, to hatch, L *cubāre*, to lie]

couvert (kooveə´) *n.* a place setting in a restaurant. [F, p.p. of *couvrir*, to cover]

couverture (koo´vətjuə) *n.* chocolate for coating cakes, sweets etc. [F, covering (*couvrir*, to cover)]

COV *abbr.* 1 in genetics, crossover value. 2 (*Math.*) covariance.

covalent (kōvā´lənt) *a.* having atoms linked by a shared pair of electrons. **covalence, covalency** *n.* **covalently** *adv.*

covariant (kōveə´riənt) *n.* (*Math.*) a function standing in the same relation to another from which it is derived as any of its linear transforms do to a transform similarly derived from the latter function. **covariance** *n.*

cove[1] (kōv) *n.* 1 a small creek, inlet or bay. 2 a nook or sheltered recess. 3 (*also* **coving**) a hollow in a cornice moulding. 4 the cavity of an arch or ceiling. ~*v.t.* 1 to arch over. 2 to cause to slope inwards. 3 to make a cove in. **coved ceiling** *n.* a ceiling with a hollow curve at the junction with the wall. [OE *cofa*, a chamber (cp. Icel. *kofi*, G *Koben*, a hut or cabin)]

cove[2] (kōv) *n.* (*esp. Austral., coll.*) a man, a fellow, a chap. [prob. from Romany *kova*, thing, person]

coven (kŭv´ən) *n.* an assembly of witches. [CONVENT]

covenant (kŭv´ənənt) *n.* 1 an agreement on certain terms, a compact. 2 a document containing the terms of agreement. 3 (*Law*) a formal agreement to pay a stated sum of money to a charity for a certain period of time. 4 (*Law*) any formal agreement under seal. 5 a clause in an agreement. 6 (*Hist.*) any of certain formal agreements in favour of the Reformation, and later (esp. in 1638 and 1643) in favour of Presbyterianism. 7 (*Bible*) an agreement between God and a people or group. ~*v.t.* to grant or promise by covenant. ~*v.i.* to enter into a covenant. **Ark of the Covenant** ARK. **covenantal** (-nan´-), **covenanted** *a.* 1 secured by or held under a covenant. 2 bound by a covenant. **Covenanter** (kŭv´ənəntə, kŭvənan´tə) *n.* (*Hist.*) an adherent of the Scottish covenants in favour of Presbyterianism. **covenanter, covenantor** *n.* a person who enters into a covenant. [OF, pres.p. of *convenir* (see CONVENE)]

Coventry (kŭv´əntri, kov´-) *n.* used only as below. **to send to Coventry** to refuse to have communication or dealings with. [town in West Midlands]

cover (kŭv´ə) *v.t.* 1 to overlay. 2 to overspread with something. 3 to overspread with something so as to protect or conceal. 4 to clothe. 5 to hide, cloak or screen. 6 to lie over so as to shelter or conceal. 7 to include or deal with. 8 to be enough to defray. 9 to travel across. 10 to protect by insurance. 11 to take precautions to protect (oneself) from a possible future problem etc. 12 to report on for a newspaper, broadcasting station etc. 13 (of a sales representative) to have as a sales territory. 14 to extend over. 15 to have range or command over. 16 to hold under aim with a firearm. 17 (*Mil.*) to protect with troops. 18 to be able to reach or protect with gunfire. 19 to protect with gunfire. 20 (of a soldier) to stand behind (someone in the front rank). 21 in cricket, to stand behind so as to stop balls that are missed. 22 in football etc., to mark (an opponent). 23 to make a cover version of. 24 to play a higher card than (one already played). 25 (of an animal such as a stallion or bull) to copulate with (a female). 26 to incubate. ~*v.i.* 1 to be spread over so as to conceal. 2 to put one's hat on. 3 to play a higher card than one already played. ~*n.* 1 anything which covers or hides. 2 a lid. 3 (*often pl.*) the outside covering of a book. 4 one side or board of this. 5 anything which serves to conceal, screen or disguise. 6 pretence, pretext. 7 shelter, protection. 8 a shelter. 9 a thicket, woods which conceal game. 10 in commerce, sufficient funds to meet a liability or ensure against loss. 11 the coverage of an insurance policy. 12 (*usu. pl.*) a bed-covering, blanket. 13 an envelope or other wrapping for a packet in the post. 14 a place setting in a restaurant. 15 protective gunfire. 16 a supporting military force. 17 COVER VERSION (under COVER). 18 a (*often pl.*) in cricket, the position of cover point. b a fielder in this position. 19 in sport, the guarding of a fellow player or part of the pitch or the marking of an opponent. 20 the outer casing of a tyre. **from cover to cover** from beginning to end (of a book). **to break cover** BREAK[1]. **to cover for** to substitute for or replace (an absent fellow worker). **to cover in** 1 to fill in. 2 to finish covering, e.g. with a roof. **to cover one's tracks** 1 to remove all signs of one's passing. 2 to remove all evidence of what one has done. **to cover up** 1 to cover completely. 2 to conceal (esp. something illegal). **to take cover** to go into shelter in a place of protection. **under cover** 1 concealed; acting under an assumed identity. 2 protected; sheltered by a roof etc. 3 enclosed in an envelope addressed to another person. **under separate cover** in another envelope or parcel. **coverable** *a.* **coverage** *n.* 1 the act of covering. 2 the extent to which anything is covered. 3 the area or the people reached by a broadcasting or advertising medium. 4 the amount of protection provided by an insurance policy. 5 the amount of publicity received by a story etc. **coverall** *a.* covering everything. ~*n.* 1 (*usu. pl.*) a one-piece garment covering limbs and body, e.g. a boiler-suit. 2 anything that covers completely. **cover charge** *n.* the amount added to a restaurant bill to cover service. **cover crop** *n.* a crop grown between main crops to provide protective cover for the soil. **cover drive** *n.* in cricket, a drive past cover point. **covered** *a.* 1 sheltered, protected. 2 concealed. 3 roofed. 4 wearing a hat. **covered wagon** *n.* a type of large wagon with a canvas roof used by American settlers to transport their families and belongings. **covered way** *n.* in fortifications, a sunken area between the counterscarp and glacis. **cover girl** *n.* a female model whose photograph is used to illustrate a magazine cover. **covering** *n.* 1 that which covers. 2 a cover. **covering letter, covering note,** (*N Am.*) **cover letter** *n.* a letter explaining an enclosure. **cover note** *n.* a note given to an insured person to certify that they have cover. **cover point** *n.* 1 in cricket, a fielder or the position behind point. 2 in lacrosse, a defending player, or the position occupied by such a player. **cover slip** *n.* a thin piece of glass placed over a specimen that is to be examined under a microscope. **cover story** *n.* the main news item or story in a magazine, which has a picture or photograph relating to it on the front cover. **cover-up** *n.* **cover version** *n.* a version of a song etc., similar to the original, recorded by a different artist. [OF *cuvrir, covrir,* L *coöperīre* (CO-, *operīre,* to shut)]

coverlet (kŭv´əlit), **coverlid** (-lid) *n.* an outer covering for a bed, a counterpane or bedspread. [A-F *coverlit* (COVER, *lit,* bed)]

covert[1] (kŭv´ət, kō´vœt) *a.* **1** disguised, secret, private. **2** covered. **3** (*Law*) under protection, as in *feme covert.* **covertly** *adv.* **covertness** *n.* **coverture** *n.* **1** covering, shelter, a hiding place. **2** secrecy. **3** (*Law, Hist.*) the state of a married woman, as being under the authority of her husband. [OF, p.p. of *covrir,* to COVER]

covert[2] (kŭv´ət, kŭv´ə) *n.* **1** a place which covers and shelters. **2** a cover for game. **3** WING COVERT (under WING). **covert coat** *n.* a short overcoat. [as COVERT[1]]

covertical (kōvœ´tikəl) *a.* (*Geom.*) having common vertices.

coverture COVERT[1].

covet (kŭv´it) *v.t.* **1** to desire (something unlawful) inordinately. **2** to long for. **covetable** *a.* **covetous** *a.* **1** eagerly desirous (of). **2** eager to obtain and possess. **3** avaricious. **covetously** *adv.* **covetousness** *n.* [A-F and OF *coveiter* (L *cupere,* to desire)]

covey (kŭv´i) *n.* (*pl.* **coveys**) **1** a brood or small flock of birds (prop. of partridges). **2** a small company, a party. [OF *covée* (F *couvée*), fem. p.p. of *couver,* to hatch, L *cubāre,* to lie down]

covin (kŭv´in) *n.* **1** (*Law*) an agreement between two or more persons to injure or defraud another. **2** †fraud, deception. [OF, from late L *covenium,* a convention (*convenīre,* to CONVENE)]

coving COVE[1].

cow[1] (kow) *n.* (*pl.* **cows,** †**kine** (kīn)) **1** the female of any bovine species, esp. of the domesticated species *Bos taurus.* **2** a female domesticated cow that has calved, as opposed to *heifer.* **3** any member of any variety of domesticated cattle. **4** a female elephant, whale or seal. **5** (*sl., derog.*) a woman. **6** (*Austral., New Zeal., sl.*) a difficult or unpleasant situation, thing etc. **till the cows come home** (*coll.*) forever. **cowbane** *n.* water hemlock. **cowbell** *n.* **1** a bell hung round a cow's neck, which rings as the cow moves and so indicates its whereabouts. **2** a similar but clapperless bell used as a percussion instrument. **cowberry** *n.* (*pl.* **cowberries**) **1** the red whortleberry, *Vaccinium vitisdaea.* **2** the bilberry or whortleberry, *V. myrtillus.* **3** the berry of either of these. **cowbird** *n.* (*N Am.*) a bird belonging to any of several species of the genus *Molothrus* (from their accompanying cattle). **cowboy** *n.* **1** a man in charge of cattle on a ranch. **2** a conventional character in stories of the Wild West, often fighting Indians and not necessarily looking after cattle. **3** (*sl.*) an unqualified or unscrupulous businessman or workman. **4** a boy who tends cattle. **cowcatcher** *n.* (*N Am.*) an inclined frame attached to the front of a locomotive etc., to throw obstructions from the track. **cowfish** *n.* **1** a sea cow or small cetacean. **2** a fish, *Lactophrys quadricornis,* with hornlike protuberances over the eyes. **cowgirl** *n.* a female equivalent of a cowboy, either as one who looks after cattle or as a conventionalized character. **cowgrass** *n.* a wild trefoil, *Trifolium medium.* **cowhand** *n.* (*N Am.*) a cowboy on a ranch. **cow-heel** *n.* the foot of a cow or ox used to make jelly. **cowherd** *n.* a person who tends cattle. **cowhide** *n.* **1** the hide of a cow. **2** leather made from this. **3** a whip made of cowhide. ~*v.t.* to thrash with a cowhide. **cowhouse** *n.* a house or shed in which cows are kept. **cowish** *a.* **cow-lick** *n.* a tuft of hair that grows up over the forehead. **cowman** *n.* (*pl.* **cowmen**) **1** a man who looks after cows on a farm. **2** (*N Am.*) the owner of a cattle ranch. **cow-parsley** *n.* a hedgerow umbelliferous plant, *Anthriscus sylvestris.* **cow-parsnip** *n.* any of various umbelliferous plants of the genus *Heracleum,* esp. *H. sphondylium.* **cow-pat** *n.* a small pile of cow dung. **cow-pock** *n.* a pustule or pock of cowpox. **cowpoke** *n.* (*N Am., sl.*) a cowboy. **cow pony** *n.* (*N Am.*) the mustang of a cowboy. **cowpox** *n.* a disease affecting the udders of cows, capable of being transferred to human beings, and conferring immunity from smallpox. **cowpuncher** *n.* (*N Am.*) a cowboy. **cow's arse** *n.* (*sl.*) a mess, muddle. **cowshed** *n.* **1** a shed providing shelter for cattle. **2** a shed where cows are milked. **cow-tree** *n.* any of various trees with milky sap, esp. the S American *Brosimum utile.* **cow-weed** *n.* cow-parsley. **cow-wheat** *n.* melampyre, *Melampyrum pratense,* or any other plant of the genus. [OE *cū,* from Gmc. *kō-* (cp. Dut. *koe,* G *Kuh,* Gael. *bo,* L *bos,* Gr. *bous*)]

cow[2] (kow) *v.t.* to intimidate, to deprive of spirit or courage, to terrify, to daunt. **cowed** *a.* [prob. from Icel. *kūga*]

cowabunga (kowəbŭng´gə) *int.* (*sl.*) **1** used to express pleasure or satisfaction. **2** a cry for or accompanying determined action. [etym. uncertain]

cowage (kow´ij), **cowhage** *n.* **1** a tropical climbing plant, *Macuna pruriens.* **2** the sharp, stinging hairs of the plant, used as an anthelmintic. [Hind. *kawānch*]

coward (kow´əd) *n.* **1** a person without courage. **2** a contemptible bully. ~*a.* **1** timid, pusillanimous. **2** (*Her.*) (of an animal) represented with the tail between the legs. **cowardice** (-dis) *n.* extreme timidity, lack of courage. **cowardlike** *a.* **cowardly** *a.* craven, faint-hearted, spiritless. ~*adv.* in the manner of a coward. **cowardliness** *n.* the quality of being cowardly. **cowardy** *a.* (*coll.*) cowardly. ~*n.* (*pl.* **cowardies**) (*also* **cowardy custard**) a coward. [OF *coart* (It. *codardo*), from *coe* (It. *coda*), a tail, L *cauda;* see -ARD]

cower (kow´ə) *v.i.* **1** to stoop, to bend, to crouch. **2** to shrink or quail through fear. [etym. uncertain (cp. Icel. *kūra,* to doze, to be quiet, Dan. *kure,* G *kauern*)]

cowhage COWAGE.

cowl (kowl) *n.* **1** a hooded garment, esp. one worn by a monk. **2** a loose hood, esp. on such a garment. **3** a large pleated robe worn by English Benedictines. **4** a hood-like chimney-top, usu. movable by the wind, to facilitate the exit of smoke. **5** COWLING (under COWL). **6** the part of the body of a motor vehicle to which the windscreen, bonnet and dashboard are attached. ~*v.t.* to cover with a cowl. **cowled** *a.* **cowling** *n.* a removable metal casing for an aircraft engine. **cowl neck** *n.* a style of neck on a woman's dress, sweater etc. consisting of a collar that hangs in folds like a monk's cowl. **cowl-neck, cowl-necked** *a.* [ME *cowle, cule,* OE *cugele,* late L *cucullа,* a frock, L *cucullus,* a hood (blended with ME *covel, cuuel,* OE *cufle,* cp. Dut. *keuvel*)]

co-worker (kōwœ´kə) *n.* a fellow worker.

cowrie (kow´ri), **cowry** *n.* (*pl.* **cowries**) a gastropod of the family Cypraeidae, esp. *Cypraea moneta,* with a small shell formerly used as money in many parts of southern Asia and Africa. [Hind. *kaurī,* Sansk. *kaparda*]

co-write (kōrīt´) *v.t.* (*past* **co-wrote** (-rōt´), *p.p.* **co-written** (-rit´ən)) to write something together with one or more other people. **co-writer** *n.*

cowry COWRIE.

cowslip (kow´slip) *n.* **1** a wild plant with fragrant flowers, *Primula veris,* growing in pastures. **2** (*N Am.*) a marsh marigold. [OE *cū-slyppe,* cow dung]

Cox (koks) *n.* COX'S ORANGE PIPPIN.

cox (koks) *n.* in rowing, the person who steers for a crew in a race. ~*v.t.* to be the cox of. ~*v.i.* to act as cox. **coxed** *a.* **coxless** *a.* [COXSWAIN]

coxa (kok´sə) *n.* (*pl.* **coxae** (-ē)) **1** (*Anat.*) the hip. **2**

(*Zool.*) the articulation of the leg to the body in arthropoda. **coxal** *a.* **coxalgia** (-al´jə) *n.* **1** pain in the hip. **2** hip disease. **coxitis** (-ī´tis) *n.* inflammation of the hip joint. [L]

coxcomb (koks´kōm) *n.* **1** a conceited person, a fop, a dandy. **2** (*Hist.*) the cap resembling a cock's comb formerly worn by jesters. **coxcombical** (-kō´mi-, -kom´i-) *a.* **coxcombically** *adv.* **coxcombly** *adv.* **coxcombry** *n.* (*pl.* **coxcombries**).

coxitis COXA.

Cox's orange pippin (koksiz orənj pip´in) *n.* a sweet-tasting variety of eating apple with a green skin tinged with reddish orange. [R. *Cox*, d. 1845, English apple-grower]

coxswain (kok´sən, kok´swān), **cockswain** *n.* **1** a person who steers a boat, esp. in a race, a cox. **2** the petty officer on board ship in charge of a boat and its crew. ~*v.t.* to be the coxswain of. ~*v.i.* to act as coxswain. **coxswainship** *n.* [COCK[2], SWAIN]

coy (koi) *a.* **1** coquettish. **2** modest, shy, shrinking from familiarity. **3** annoyingly unforthcoming. **coyly** *adv.* **coyness** *n.* [F *coi* (fem. *coite*), L *quiētus*, QUIET]

coy., Coy. *abbr.* company.

coyote (koiō´ti, kīō´-) *n.* (*pl.* **coyotes, coyote**) the N American prairie wolf. [Sp., from Nahuatl *coyotl*]

coypu (koi´poo) *n.* (*pl.* **coypus, coypu**) **1** a S American aquatic rodent, *Myocastor coypus*, naturalized in Europe. **2** its fur. [N Am. Ind. name]

coz (kŭz) *n.* (*esp. N Am.*) short for COUSIN.

cozen (kŭz´ən) *v.t.* **1** to deceive, to cheat. **2** to persuade by deception or charm. ~*v.i.* to be deceitful. **cozenage** *n.* **cozener** *n.* [perh. from COUSIN (cp. F *cousiner*, to claim kindred)]

cozy COSY.

CP *abbr.* **1** (*Mil.*) command post. **2** Common Prayer. **3** Communist Party. **4** (*S Afr.*) Conservative Party. **5** (*Austral.*) Country Party.

cp *abbr.* candlepower.

cp. *abbr.* compare.

CPA *abbr.* (*N Am.*) certified public accountant.

CPAG *abbr.* Child Poverty Action Group.

cpd *abbr.* compound.

CPI *abbr.* consumer price index.

cpi *abbr.* characters per inch.

cpl, Cpl *abbr.* corporal.

CP/M® *abbr.* Control Program Monitor (a computer operating system).

CPO *abbr.* **1** chief petty officer. **2** crime prevention officer.

CPR *abbr.* **1** Canadian Pacific Railway. **2** cardiopulmonary resuscitation.

CPRE *abbr.* Council for the Preservation of Rural England.

CPS *abbr.* Crown Prosecution Service.

cps *abbr.* **1** characters per second. **2** cycles per second.

CPSA *abbr.* Civil and Public Services Association.

CPU *abbr.* central processing unit.

CQSW *abbr.* Certificate of Qualification in Social Work.

CR *abbr.* **1** Costa Rica (IVR). **2** Community of the Resurrection.

Cr[1] *chem. symbol* chromium.

Cr[2] *abbr.* Councillor.

cr *abbr.* **1** created. **2** credit, creditor. **3** crown.

crab[1] (krab) *n.* **1** a decapod crustacean of the group Brachyura, esp. the common crab, *Cancer pagurus*, and other edible species. **2** crabmeat. **3** (**Crab**) the zodiacal sign or the constellation Cancer. **4** a kind of crane. **5** a kind of windlass for hauling ships into dock. **6** a portable capstan. **7** (*pl.*) deuce ace or two aces, the lowest throw at dice. **8** (*often pl.*) a crab louse. **to catch a crab** in rowing, to sink an oar too deep and be pushed backwards by the resistance of the water, or to miss a stroke and fall backwards. **crabgrass** *n.* any of various species of creeping grasses of the genus *Digitaria*. **crab-like** *a.* **crab louse** *n.* an insect, *Phthirus pubis*, found on the human body. **crabmeat** *n.* the flesh of crabs as meat. **crab pot** *n.* a basket or wicker trap for catching crabs and lobsters. **crabwise** *adv.* sideways. [OE *crabba* (cp. Icel. *krabbi*, Dut. *kreeft*, G *Krebs*; also Dut. and LG *krabben*, to scratch)]

crab[2] (krab) *v.t.* (*pres.p.* **crabbing,** *past, p.p.* **crabbed**) **1** (*coll.*) to criticize savagely, to pull to pieces. **2** to hinder. [cogn. with CRAB[1] (cp. Dut. and LG *krabben*)]

crab[3] (krab) *n.* **1** a crab apple. **2** a crab tree. **3** a peevish, morose person. ~*a.* sour, rough, austere. ~*v.i.* (*pres.p.* **crabbing,** *past, p.p.* **crabbed**) (*coll.*) to complain, grumble. **crab apple** *n.* a wild apple, the sour-tasting fruit of any of various trees of the genus *Malus*, esp. *M. silvestris.* **crab tree, crab-apple tree** *n.* [etym. uncertain]

crabbed (krab´id, krabd) *a.* **1** peevish, morose, sour-tempered. **2** perverse. **3** (of handwriting) cramped, indecipherable. **4** intricate, perplexing, abstruse. **5** harsh, sour. **crabbedly** (-id-) *adv.* **crabbedness** (-id-) *n.* **crabby** *a.* (*comp.* **crabbier,** *superl.* **crabbiest**) **1** (*coll.*) bad-tempered. **2** perverse. **crabbily** *adv.* **crabbiness** *n.* [CRAB[1] (influenced later in sense by CRAB[3])]

CRAC *abbr.* Careers Research and Advisory Centre.

crack (krak) *v.t.* **1** to break without entire separation of the parts. **2** to cause to give a sharp, sudden noise. **3** to cause to break with a sharp noise. **4** to cause to break down by stress, torture etc. **5** to solve (a problem, code etc.). **6** to say (a joke etc.). **7** to hit sharply and with force. **8** to open and drink (e.g. a bottle of wine). **9** to break (molecules of a compound) down into simpler molecules by the application of heat, pressure or a catalyst. **10** to say smartly or sententiously. ~*v.i.* **1** to partly break apart. **2** to make a loud, sharp sound. **3** to break with a sharp noise. **4** to break down under pressure, e.g. of stress or torture; to fail. **5** (of the voice) to change in tone because of emotion. **6** (of the voice) to change at puberty. **7** (*coll.*) to chat. **8** to be ruined. ~*n.* **1** a partial separation of parts. **2** the chink, fissure or opening so made. **3** any chink or fissure. **4** a sharp sudden sound or report. **5** a sharp blow. **6** a defect or flaw, e.g. in personality. **7** a change in the tone of voice, e.g. because of emotion. **8** the change of voice at puberty. **9** (*coll.*) a sarcastic joke. **10** (*sl.*) a highly addictive form of cocaine. **11** something or someone first-rate. **12** (*dial.*) chat. **13** (*dial.*) gossip, news. **14** (*dial.*) fun, amusement. ~*a.* **1** having qualities to be boasted of. **2** excellent, superior, brilliant. **to crack a crib** (*sl.*) to break into a house. **to crack down (on)** (*coll.*) to take very strict measures (against). **to crack it** (*coll.*) to succeed. **to crack on** (*coll.*) to boast or brag. **to crack up** **1** to extol highly, to puff. **2** to suffer a mental or physical breakdown. **3** to begin laughing uncontrollably. **to get cracking** to make a prompt and active start to something. **to have a crack at** (*coll.*) to have a try, to attempt. **crackable** *a.* **crack-brained** *a.* (*coll.*) crazy, cracked. **crackdown** *n.* **cracked** *a.* **1** having a crack or cracks. **2** (*coll.*) insane, crazy. **cracked wheat** *n.* wheat that has been coarsely ground into small grains. **cracker** *n.* **1** a paper tube containing a toy etc., that gives a sharp report in being torn open. **2** a form of explosive firework. **3** a thin, brittle, hard-baked (savoury) biscuit. **4** (*sl.*) a person who or thing which is exceptional or excellent. **5** (*often pl.*) an implement for cracking. **6** (*N Am.*) a thin, crisp biscuit. **7** a crisp biscuit made with rice flour or tapioca. **8** a person who or thing which cracks. **9** (*coll.*) a speedy pace. **10** (*N Am., derog.*) a poor white. **11** (*coll.*) a lie. **cracker-barrel** *a.* (*N Am.*) (of a person, opinions, philosophy etc.) expressing or exemplifying a simple, unsophisticated view of life (supposedly typical of opinions expressed in discussions carried on beside the barrels of crackers in N American small-town stores). **cracker-jack** *n.* (*sl.*) an excellent person or thing. **crackers** *a.* (*sl.*) crazy. **crackhead** *n.* (*sl.*) a person addicted to crack (the drug). **cracking** *a.* (*coll.*) **1** vigorous. **2** very good. *~adv.* exceptionally. **crack-jaw** *a.* applied to long or unpronounceable words. *~n.* any such word. **crack of dawn** *n.* the first light of dawn. **crack of doom** *n.* the end of the world at Judgement Day, or the noise of thunder supposed to accompany this. **crack of the whip** *n.* an opportunity or chance. **fair crack of the whip** FAIR[1]. **crackpot** *n.* (*coll.*) a crazy person. *~a.* (of persons ideas etc.) crazy, eccentric. **cracksman** *n.* (*pl.* **cracksmen**) (*sl.*) a burglar or safe-breaker. **crack-up** *n.* **crack willow** *n.* a species of willow, *Salix fragilis*, which has branches that break easily, or any of a number of similar species of *Salix*. **cracky** *a.* (*comp.* **crackier,** *superl.* **crackiest**) having many cracks. [OE *cracian* (cp. Dut. *kraken* and *krakken*, G *krachen*, imit. in orig.)]

crackle (krak´əl) *v.i.* **1** to make short, sharp crackling noises. **2** to be energetic. *~v.t.* **1** to cause to make a cracking noise. **2** to produce decorative cracks in (porcelain etc.). *~n.* **1** a rapid succession of slight, sharp noises like cracks. **2** a small crack. **3** a series of such cracks. **4** porcelain, glass or paintwork with a decoration of tiny cracks. **5** the decorative cracked surface of such porcelain, glass or paintwork. **crackle-china, crackle-ware** *n.* porcelain or glass with a crackled surface. **cracklin** (-lin) *n.* crackle-china. **crackling** *a.* making short, sharp, frequent cracking noises. *~n.* **1** the browned scored skin of roast pork. **2** (*sl., offensive*) women regarded as sexual objects. **bit of crackling** BIT[1]. **crackly** *a.* (*comp.* **cracklier,** *superl.* **crackliest**) **1** (of a sound) crackling. **2** producing or making a crackly sound. **3** crisp. [from CRACK]

cracknel (krak´nəl) *n.* a hard, brittle biscuit. [corr. of F *craquelin* (cp. dial. *crackling*)]

-cracy (krəsi) *comb. form* government or rule of, or influence of or dominance by, as in *aristocracy, democracy, plutocracy, theocracy.* [F *-cratie*, Gr. *-kratia*, from *kratos*, power]

cradle (krā´dəl) *n.* **1** a baby's bed or cot, usu. rocking or swinging. **2** place of birth or early nurture. **3** infancy. **4** a frame to protect a broken or wounded limb in bed. **5** a bed or framework of timbers to support a vessel out of water. **6** the apparatus in which sailors, etc. are brought to land along a line fastened to a ship in distress. **7** a platform or trolley in which workers are suspended to work on a ceiling, the side of a building or boat, etc. **8** the part of a telephone on which the receiver rests when not in use. **9** a tool resembling a chisel, used for scraping and preparing the plate for mezzotints. **10 a** a set of fingers in a light frame mortised into a scythe to lay the corn more evenly. **b** CRADLE-SCYTHE (under CRADLE). **11** (*Mining*) a gold-washing machine. **12** the centring for an arch, culvert etc. *~v.t.* **1** to lay or place in a cradle. **2** to rock to sleep. **3** to nurture or rear from infancy. **4** to receive or hold in or as if in a cradle. **5** to cut and lay (corn) with a cradle. **6** (*Mining*) to wash in a cradle. **7** in lacrosse, to hold (the ball) in the net of the stick. **from the cradle** from infancy. **from the cradle to the grave** throughout one's life. **cradle cap** *n.* a form of dermatitis common in young babies, causing scaly patches on the scalp. **cradle-clothes** *n.pl.* swaddling-clothes. **cradle-scythe** *n.* a broad scythe fitted with a cradle. **cradle-snatcher** *n.* BABY-SNATCHER (under BABY). **cradle song** *n.* a lullaby. **cradling** *n.* **1** the act of laying or rocking in a cradle. **2** in building, a framework of wood or iron. **3** in building, the framework in arched or coved ceilings to which the laths are nailed. [OE *cradol* (etym. uncertain)]

craft (krahft) *n.* **1** dexterity, skill. **2** cunning, deceit. **3** an art, esp. one applied to useful purposes, a handicraft, occupation or trade. **4** the members of a particular trade. **5** (*pl.* **craft**) a boat. **6** (*pl.* **craft**) an aircraft or space vehicle. **7** (**Craft**) Freemasonry, or the brotherhood of Freemasons. *~v.t.* to make with skill or by hand. **-craft** *comb. form* a profession, skill or art, as in *woodcraft, handicraft, priestcraft.* **craft-brother** *n.* a person in the same craft or guild. **craft guild** *n.* an association of workers in the same occupation or trade. **craftsman, craftswoman** *n.* (*pl.* **craftsmen, craftswomen**) **1** (*also* **craftsperson,** *pl.* **craftspeople**) a person skilled in some art or handicraft. **2** a time-served experienced worker in a skilled trade. **3** a qualified private in the REME. **craftsmanship** *n.* **craft union** *n.* a labour union for all workers in a particular craft or trade. **craftwork** *n.* the work of or produced by a craftsperson. **craftworker** *n.* [OE *cræft* (cp. Dut. *kracht*, Swed., Dan. and Norw. *kraft*, G *Kraft*, power)]

crafty (krahf´ti) *a.* (*comp.* **craftier,** *superl.* **craftiest**) artful, sly, cunning, wily. **craftily** *adv.* **craftiness** *n.* [see CRAFT]

crag[1] (krag) *n.* a rugged or precipitous rock. **crag and tail** *n.* a rock or hill with a precipitous face on one side and a gradually sloping descent on the other. **cragged** *a.* **craggedness** (-gid-) *n.* **craggy** *a.* (*comp.* **craggier,** *superl.* **craggiest**) **1** full of crags, rough. **2** (of a face) attractively rugged. **craggily** *adv.* **cragginess** *n.* **cragsman** *n.* (*pl.* **cragsmen**) a skilful rock-climber. [cp. Welsh *craig*, Gael. and Ir. *creag*]

crag[2] (krag) *n.* shelly deposits, esp. in Norfolk, Suffolk and Essex, of the Pliocene age. [perh. from CRAG[1]]

cragged, craggy etc. CRAG[1].

crake (krāk) *n.* **1** the corncrake. **2** any of various other birds of the same family, belonging to the genus *Porzana.* **3** the cry of any of these birds. *~v.i.* to cry like a crake. [imit.; cp. CROAK, CROW[1]]

cram (kram) *v.t.* (*pres.p.* **cramming,** *past, p.p.* **crammed**) **1** to stuff, push or press in so as to fill to overflowing. **2** to thrust in or into by force. **3** to eat greedily. **4** to overfeed (with). **5** to coach for examination by storing the pupil's mind with formulas and answers to probable questions. *~v.i.* **1** to eat greedily. **2** to stuff oneself. **3** to learn a subject hastily and superficially, esp. to undergo cramming for examination. *~n.* **1** the system of cramming for an examination. **2** information acquired by cramming. **3** a crush, a crowd. **cram-full** *a.* absolutely full. **crammer** *n.* **1** a person who crams. **2** a coach who crams. **3** a school which specializes in cramming. [OE *crammian*, from *crimman*, to insert (cp. OHG *chrimman*, G *krimmen*)]

crambo (kram´bō) *n.* a game in which one person says a word or line of verse to which the other person must find a rhyme. **dumb crambo** DUMB. [L *crambē*, in ref. to Juvenal's *crambē repetīta*, cabbage served up again, Sat. vii.154]

crammer CRAM.

cramp[1] (kramp) *n.* **1** a spasmodic contraction of some limb or muscle, accompanied by pain and numbness. **2** (*often pl.*) acute pain in the abdomen. *~v.t.* to affect with cramp. **cramped** *a.* **1** uncomfortably or inconveniently small. **2** (of handwriting) difficult to read. **3** contracted. **4** knotty. **crampedness** *n.* [OF *crampe* (cp. Dut. *kramp*; also OHG *krimphan*, G *krampfen*, to cramp)]

cramp[2] (kramp) *n.* **1** a cramp-iron. **2** a clamp. **3** a restraint, a hindrance. *~v.t.* **1** (*often with up*) to confine closely. **2** to hinder, to restrain. **3** to fasten with a cramp-iron. **to cramp someone's style 1** to spoil the effect a person is trying to make. **2** to impede a person's actions or self-expression. **cramp-iron** *n.* an iron with bent ends binding two stones together in a masonry course. [Dut. *kramp*, see CRAMP[1]]

crampon (kram´pon) *n.* **1** (*usu. pl.*) a plate with iron spikes worn on climbing boots to assist in climbing ice-slopes etc. **2** (*usu. pl.*) a grappling iron. **3** a hooked bar of iron. [F, from late L *crampo -ōnem*, from LG (cp. CRAMP[1] and CRAMP[2])]

cran (kran) *n.* (*Sc.*) a measure of 37½ gallons (170 l) by which herrings are sold. [Gael. *crann*]

cranage CRANE[1].

cranberry (kran´bəri) *n.* (*pl.* **cranberries**) **1** any shrub of the genus *Vaccinium*, esp. the American *V. macrocarpon* and the British *V. oxycoccos*, both with a small, red, acid fruit used in sauces etc. **2** the fruit of these shrubs. [LG *kraanbere* (G *Kranbeere*), introd. by N Am. colonists]

crane[1] (krān) *n.* a long-necked bird of the family Gruidae, esp. the common crane of Europe, *Grus grus*, a migratory wading bird. ~*v.t.* to stretch out (the neck) like a crane, esp. to see over or round an object. ~*v.i.* to stretch out the neck in this way. **crane-fly** *n.* (*pl.* **crane-flies**) any fly of the family Tipulidae, with long legs, a long body and long wings, a daddy-long-legs. **craner** *n.* a person who cranes. **cranesbill** *n.* any of various species of wild geranium. [OE *cran* (cp. Dut. *kraan*, G *Kranich*, Gr. *geranos*, L *grus*)]

crane[2] (krān) *n.* **1** a machine for hoisting and lowering heavy weights. **2** anything similar, such as an iron arm turning on a vertical axis, fixed to the back of the fireplace, on which to support a kettle etc. **3** a siphon used for drawing liquors from a cask. **4** a moving platform for a film camera. ~*v.t.* to raise or move by means of a crane. **cranage** *n.* **1** the use of, or the right to use, a crane on a wharf. **2** money paid for the use of the crane. [as CRANE[1]]

crania, cranial etc. CRANIUM.

cranio- (krā´niō) *comb. form* of or relating to the skull. **craniology** (-ol´-) *n.* the scientific study of crania. **craniological** (-loj´-) *a.* **craniologist** (-ol´-) *n.* **craniometer** (-om´itə) *n.* an instrument for measuring the cubic capacity of skulls. **craniometric** (-met´-), **craniometrical** *a.* **craniometry** (-om´-) *n.* **craniotomy** (-ot´əmi) *n.* (*pl.* **craniotomies**) **1** surgical incision into the skull or removal of a part of the skull. **2** crushing of the skull of a dead foetus to make delivery easier. [L *crānium*, Gr. *kranion*, the skull]

cranium (krā´niəm) *n.* (*pl.* **craniums, crania** (-niə)) the skull, esp. the part enclosing the brain. **cranial** *a.* **cranial index** *n.* the ratio of width to length of the skull, expressed as a percentage. **cranial nerve** *n.* any of the twelve (in mammals, birds and reptiles) or ten (in fish and amphibians) paired nerves that connect directly to the brain rather than the spinal cord. **craniate** *a.* having a cranium. [L, from Gr. *kranion*]

crank[1] (krangk) *n.* **1** an arm at right angles to an axis for converting rotary into reciprocating motion, or the converse. **2** an iron elbow-shaped brace for various purposes. **3** a handle which turns the shaft of a motor until the pistons reach the maximum of compression. ~*v.t.* **1** to move or start by means of a crank. **2** to fit or provide with a crank. **3** to fasten with a crank. **4** to shape like a crank. **to crank up 1** to start an engine with a crank handle. **2** (*coll.*) to increase (speed, power etc.). **crankcase** *n.* a metal casing for the crankshaft, connecting-rods etc. in an engine. **crank handle** *n.* a crank (for starting a motor). **crankpin** *n.* a cylindrical pin parallel to a shaft and fixed at the outer end of a crank. **crankshaft** *n.* a shaft that bears one or more cranks. [OE *cranc*, orig. past of *crincan*, a form of *cringan*, to be bent up]

crank[2] (krangk) *n.* **1** an eccentric, esp. someone who is obsessed with a theory or fad. **2** (*N Am.*) a crotchety person. **3** a whimsical turn of speech. **4** a caprice, a whim, a crotchet. [etym. uncertain; perh. conn. with CRANK[1]]

crank[3] (krangk) *a.* (*Naut.*) liable to capsize. [conn. with CRANK[1] and CRANKY]

cranky (krang´ki) *a.* (*comp.* **crankier**, *superl.* **crankiest**) **1** eccentric, esp. obsessed with a theory or fad. **2** whimsical. **3** (*esp. N Am.*) irritable, fidgety. **4** full of twists. **5** (of a machine) liable to break down. **6** (*Naut.*) liable to capsize. **7** (*dial.*) shaky, sickly. **crankily** *adv.* **crankiness** *n.*

crannied CRANNY.

crannog (kran´əg) *n.* an ancient lake-dwelling, common in Scotland and Ireland, built up from the lake bottom on brushwood and piles, and often surrounded by palisades. [Ir., from *crann*, a tree, a beam]

cranny (kran´i) *n.* (*pl.* **crannies**) **1** a crevice, a chink. **2** a corner, a hole. **crannied** *a.* [prob. from F *cran*, a notch, a chink]

crap[1] (krap) *n.* **1** (*sl.*) rubbish. **2** (*sl.*) nonsense. **3** (*taboo*) excrement. **4** (*taboo*) an act of defecating. ~*v.i.* (*pres.p.* **crapping**, *past, p.p.* **crapped**) (*taboo*) to defecate. ~*a.* (*sl.*) worthless, of poor quality. **to crap out** (*sl.*) to opt out through fear, exhaustion etc. **crappy** *a.* (*comp.* **crappier**, *superl.* **crappiest**) (*sl.*) **1** rubbishy, worthless. **2** disgusting. [ME *crappe*, chaff, from MDut., from *krappen*, to break off]

crap[2] (krap) *n.* a losing throw in the game of craps. **to crap out 1** to make a losing throw in craps. **2** to be unsuccessful. **crap game** *n.* a game of craps. **crap-shooter** *n.* **crap-shooting** *n.* CRAPS. [see CRAPS]

crape (krāp) *n.* **1** a gauzy fabric of silk or other material, with a crisped, frizzly surface, formerly usu. dyed black, used for mourning. **2** a band of this material worn round the hat as mourning. ~*v.t.* to cover, dress or drape with crape. ~*a.* made of crape. **crape fern** *n.* a handsome, large-fronded fern, *Leptopteris superba*, found in New Zealand. **crape hair** *n.* artificial hair for use in theatrical costume. **crapy** *a.* (*comp.* **crapier**, *superl.* **crapiest**). [F, CRÊPE]

craps (kraps) *n.* a gambling game played with two dice, with fixed winning and losing numbers. **to shoot craps** to play craps. [poss. from *crabs*, lowest throw at dice; see CRAB[1]]

crapulent (krap´ūlənt) *a.* (*formal*) **1** given to intemperance. **2** resulting from intemperance. **3** surfeited, drunken. **crapulence** *n.* **crapulous** *a.* [L *crāpulentus*, from *crāpula*, drunkenness, Gr. *kraipalē*, nausea, the effect of a debauch]

crash[1] (krash) *v.t.* **1** to cause (a vehicle etc.) to hit something with great force and loud noise. **2** to cause (an aircraft) to fall with great force to the ground or into the sea. **3** to hit, throw, drop etc. (something) so that it makes a loud smashing noise, and often so that it breaks. **4** to cause (a computer or computer program) to cease operating suddenly. **5** (*coll.*) to go to (a party etc.) uninvited. **6** (*coll.*) to go through (a red traffic light). ~*v.i.* **1** (of a vehicle etc.) to hit something with great force and loud noise. **2** (of an aircraft) to fall with great force to the ground or into the sea. **3** (of a person) to be in a vehicle, aircraft etc. which crashes. **4** to hit (into) or collide with great force. **5** to move (through etc.) with great force and violence. **6** to move, fall, come together etc. with a loud noise, and often also breaking. **7** (of a computer or computer program) to cease operating suddenly. **8** to fail, be ruined financially. **9** to be defeated. **10** (*sl.*) to sleep, esp. in an improvised bed in someone's house. ~*n.* **1** an act or instance of crashing. **2** a loud sudden noise, as of many things broken at once. **3** a violent smash. **4** a sudden failure, collapse, bankruptcy. **5** the sudden failure of a computer or program. ~*a.* done rapidly, with urgency, or with great intensity over a short time. ~*adv.* with a crash. **to crash out 1** (*sl.*) to fall asleep. **2** (*sl.*) to become unconsciousness. **3** (*sl.*) to sleep in improvised accommodation. **crash barrier** *n.* a metal barrier along the edge or centre of a motorway etc. to prevent crashes. **crash course** *n.* a very rapid and intensive course of study. **crash-dive** *n.* **1** (*Naut.*) a submarine's sudden and rapid dive, usu. to avoid an enemy. **2** (of an aircraft) a rapid, steep descent, ending in a crash. ~*v.i.* to perform such a dive. ~*v.t.* to cause (a submarine or an aircraft) to make such a dive. **crash-halt, crash-stop** *n.* an abrupt stop made by a vehicle. **crash helmet** *n.* a padded helmet to protect the head in the event of an accident. **crashing** *a.* (*coll.*) extreme. **crash landing** *n.* an emergency landing of an aircraft, resulting in damage. **crash-land** *v.i.* to make a crash landing. ~*v.t.* to cause (an aircraft) to make a crash landing. **crash-mat** *n.* a thick mat used to cushion the impact of a fall or jump in gymnastics etc. **crash pad** *n.* (*sl.*) a place to sleep in an emergency. **crash-stop** CRASH-HALT (under CRASH[1]). **crash-tackle** *n.* in football, a very strong tackle. **crash-test** *v.t.* to test (a new product) to its breaking point in order to ascertain its reliability or safety. [imit. (cp. CRACK, CRAZE)]

crash[2] (krash) *n.* a coarse linen cloth, sometimes with cotton or jute in it, used for towelling. [Rus. *krashenina*, coloured linen]

crasis (krā´sis), **krasis** *n.* (*pl.* **crases** (-sēz), **krases**) the contracting of the vowels of two syllables into one long vowel or diphthong. **crasial** *a.* [Gr., a mixture, a blending, from *kerannunai*, to mix]

crass (kras) *a.* **1** loutish, boorish, vulgar. **2** very great, disgraceful. **3** extremely stupid, obtuse. **4** extremely tactless or insensitive. **5** (*poet.*) thick, coarse. **crassitude** (-itūd) *n.* crassness. **crassly** *adv.* **crassness** *n.* [L *crassus*]

-crat (krat) *comb. form* **1** a partisan or supporter of something denoted by a word ending in *-cracy*, as in *democrat*. **2** a member of or participant in something denoted by a word ending in *-cracy*, as in *aristocrat*, *autocrat*. **-cratic, -cratical** *comb. form* forming adjectives. **-cratically** *comb. form* forming adverbs.

cratch (krach) *n.* (*dial.*) a manger, a hay-rack, esp. for feeding animals out of doors. [OF *creche* (F *crèche*), OHG *krippa*, rel. to CRIB]

crate (krāt) *n.* **1** a large wicker case for packing crockery. **2** an open framework of wood for packing. **3** (*dated, sl.*) an old and unreliable car, aircraft etc. ~*v.t.* to pack in a crate. **crateful** *n.* (*pl.* **cratefuls**). [L *crātes*, or Dut. *krat*]

crater (krā´tə) *n.* **1** the mouth of a volcano. **2** a bowl-shaped cavity. **3** a large cavity formed in the ground by the explosion of a shell or bomb or the impact of a meteorite. **4** (*Hist.*) in ancient Greece and modern antiquities, a large bowl for mixing wine in. ~*v.t.* to make a crater or craters in. **crateriform** (-ifawm) *a.* **craterous** *a.* [L, from Gr. *kratēr*, a bowl for mixing wine (*kerannunai*, to mix)]

craton (krat´on, krā´tən) *n.* (*Geol.*) any of the large, relatively stable and immobile parts of the earth's crust, forming the main part of a continent and continental shelf. **cratonic** (-ton´ik) *a.* [Gr. *kratos*, strength]

cravat (krəvat´) *n.* **1** a tie-like scarf worn in an open-necked shirt, esp. by men. **2** (*Hist.*) a tie. **cravatted** *a.* [F *cravate*, orig. a Croat, G *Krabat(e)*, Croatian (the cravat having been introduced into France by Croats)]

crave (krāv) *v.t.* **1** to long for. **2** to ask for earnestly and submissively; to beg, to beseech, to entreat. **3** to require. ~*v.i.* **1** to long (for). **2** to beg (for). **craver** *n.* **craving** *n.* an intense desire or longing. **cravingly** *adv.* [OE *crafian*]

craven (krā´vən) *a.* cowardly, faint-hearted. ~*n.* a coward, a recreant, a dastard. **cravenly** *adv.* **cravenness** *n.* [ME *crauant*, prob. from OF *cravant*, pres.p. of *craver* (*crever*), to burst, break, overcome]

craving CRAVE.

craw (kraw) *n.* the crop or first stomach of birds or insects. **to stick in one's craw** to be hard to accept. [cogn. with Dut. *kraag*, the neck]

crawfish CRAYFISH.

crawl[1] (krawl) *v.i.* **1** to move slowly on one's hands and knees or with one's body close to the ground. **2** (of an insect, snake etc.) to move slowly with the body on or close to the ground. **3** to move slowly. **4** to assume an abject posture or manner. **5** to get on, e.g. in a career, by obsequious servility. **6** to have a sensation as though insects were creeping over one's skin. **7** to be covered with crawling things. **8** to do the crawl in swimming. ~*n.* **1** the act of crawling. **2** a slow rate of movement. **3** a swimming stroke consisting of alternate overarm movements of the arms and kicking movements of the legs. **4** (*coll.*) a trip round a number of places of the same type, esp. one to a series of pubs. **to crawl out of the woodwork** WOODWORK (under WOOD). **crawler** *n.* **1** (*coll.*) an obsequious person. **2** a creeping or crawling insect or animal. **3** a slow-moving vehicle, esp. one that moves on caterpillar tracks. **4** (*pl., esp. NAm.*) a romper suit. **crawler lane** *n.* a lane on an uphill stretch of motorway specially reserved for slow-moving vehicles. **crawlingly** *adv.* **crawl space** *n.* space under a floor or roof that is large enough to crawl through, e.g. for maintenance purposes. **crawly** *a.* (*comp.* **crawlier,** *superl.* **crawliest**). [prob. from Scand. (cp. Icel. and Swed. *krafla*, to grope, Dan. *kravle*, to crawl)]

crawl[2] (krawl) *n.* an enclosure in shallow water for keeping fish, turtles etc. alive. [Dut. *kraal*]

cray (krā) *n.* (*Austral., New Zeal.*) CRAYFISH.

crayfish (krā´fish), **crawfish** (kraw´-) *n.* (*pl. in general* **crayfish, crawfish,** *in particular* **crayfishes, crawfishes**) **1** any of the many, mostly freshwater, species of lobster-like crustaceans of the families Astacidae and Parastacidae. **2** the spiny lobster. **3** any kind of crab. [ME *crevice*, OF *crevisse*, *crevice* (F *écrevisse*), OHG *crebiz* (cp. CRAB[1])]

crayon (krā´ən, -on) *n.* **1** a stick or pencil of coloured chalk or similar material. **2** a drawing made with crayons. **3** the carbon pencil of an electric arc lamp. ~*v.t.* **1** to draw with crayons. **2** to sketch. **crayon-drawing** *n.* the act, art or result of drawing in crayons. [F, from *craie*, L *crēta*, chalk]

craze (krāz) *v.t.* **1** to make insane. **2** to make cracks or flaws in (china etc.). ~*v.i.* **1** to go mad. **2** (of the glaze on pottery etc.) to become cracked. **3** †to become weakened or impaired. ~*n.* **1** a mania, an extravagant idea or enthusiasm, a rage. **2** madness. **3** a flaw, impaired condition. **crazed** *a.* made insane. **crazy** *a.* (*comp.* **crazier,** *superl.* **craziest**) **1** mad, deranged. **2** ridiculous. **3** (*coll.*) very enthusiastic (about). **4** (*sl.*) wild, exciting. ~*n.* (*pl.* **crazies**) (*coll.*) a crazy person or thing. **like crazy** (*sl.*) extremely. **crazily** *adv.* **craziness** *n.* **crazy bone** *n.* (*NAm.*) the funny bone. **crazy paving** *n.* paving of irregularly-shaped flat stones, e.g. on a path. [perh. from Swed. *krasa* (cp. F *écraser*)]

CRC *abbr.* camera-ready copy.

CRE *abbr.* Commission for Racial Equality.

creak (krēk) *v.t.* **1** to make a continued sharp grating or squeaking noise. **2** to move with a creaking sound. **3** to move slowly and stiffly. **4** to show signs of weakness, inadequacy or wear and tear. ~*v.i.* to cause to make a creaking noise. ~*n.* a creaking sound. **creakingly** *adv.* **creaky** *a.* (*comp.* **creakier,** *superl.* **creakiest**) **1** which creaks or is liable to creak. **2** stiff, arthritic. **3** showing signs of weakness, inadequacy or wear and tear. **4** badly made, botched. **5** poorly performed. **creakily** *adv.* **creakiness** *n.* [imit. (cp. CRAKE, CRACK)]

cream (krēm) *n.* **1 a** the fatty part of milk which rises and collects on the surface, often separated off and used in cakes, desserts etc. **b** an artificial substitute for this. **2** a dish prepared with or having the texture of cream. **3** a cosmetic, antiseptic etc. preparation with a thick consistency like cream. **4** any part of a liquid that rises to the top like the cream of milk. **5** a pale yellowish-white colour. 6 a group of the best things or people. 7 the best part of anything. 8 essence or quintessence. 9 the main point of a story. 10 a soup or sauce made with cream or milk. 11 a usu. chocolate-covered sweet with a creamy peppermint- or fruit-flavoured centre. 12 a biscuit with a creamy filling. 13 a rich, sweet sherry. 14 a cream-coloured horse. *~v.t.* 1 to skim cream from. 2 to add cream to. 3 (*often with off*) to remove (the best part) from something. 4 to make creamy, e.g. by beating. 5 to treat with a cream, put cream on. 6 (*N Am., coll.*) to beat. *~v.i.* 1 to gather cream. 2 to form a scum or froth. *~a.* 1 cream-coloured. 2 of sherry, rich and sweet. **cream bun, cream-cake** *n.* a bun or cake with a filling of real or artificial cream. **cream cheese** *n.* a soft cheese made from unskimmed milk and cream. **cream-coloured** *a.* **cream cracker** *n.* an unsweetened crisp biscuit. **creamer** *n.* 1 a flat dish used for skimming the cream off milk. 2 a cream separator. 3 (*N Am.*) a small jug for cream. 4 a substitute for milk or cream for adding to coffee or tea. **creamery** *n.* (*pl.* **creameries**) 1 a shop for the sale of dairy produce. 2 an establishment where milk and cream are made into butter and cheese. **cream-laid** *a.* applied to laid paper of a creamy colour. **cream of lime** *n.* a creamy mixture of slaked lime and water. **cream of tartar** *n.* purified potassium hydrogen tartrate, used in baking etc. **cream puff** *n.* 1 a cake of puff pastry filled with cream. 2 (*coll.*) an ineffectual person. 3 (*coll.*) an effeminate man. **cream separator** *n.* a machine for separating cream from milk. **cream soda** *n.* a soft drink flavoured with vanilla. **cream tea** *n.* an afternoon meal at which scones with cream and jam are eaten. **creamware** *n.* earthenware with a cream-coloured glaze. **cream-wove** *a.* applied to woven paper of a cream colour. **creamy** *a.* (*comp.* **creamier,** *superl.* **creamiest**). **creamily** *adv.* **creaminess** *n.* [F *crème*, OF *cresme* (see CHRISM)]

crease[1] (krēs) *n.* 1 a line or mark made by folding or doubling. 2 a wrinkle. 3 in cricket, a line on the ground marking the position of bowler and batsman at each wicket. 4 in ice hockey and lacrosse, an area marked out around the goal. *~v.t.* 1 to make a crease or creases in. 2 to graze the skin of with a bullet. 3 (*sl.*) to exhaust. 4 (*coll.*) to crease up. *~v.i.* 1 to become creased or wrinkled. 2 (*coll.*) to crease up. **to crease up** (*coll.*) to double up with laughter. **creaser** *n.* **crease-resistant** *a.* (of a fabric) not creasing when in use. **creasy** *a.* (*comp.* **creasier,** *superl.* **creasiest**). [etym. uncertain]

crease[2] KRIS.

create (kriāt´) *v.t.* 1 to cause to exist. 2 to produce, to bring into existence. 3 to be the occasion of. 4 to be the first person to act (a character in a play etc.). 5 to invest with a new character, office or dignity. 6 to cause (a disturbance). *~v.i.* (*coll.*) to make a fuss. **creatable** *a.* **creative** *a.* 1 having the ability to create. 2 imaginative. 3 original. **creative accountancy, creative accounting** *n.* (*coll.*) a liberal and usu. questionable use or interpretation of accounting procedures, usu. for financial gain, e.g. through tax evasion, or to give an unduly favourable impression of one's financial position. **creatively** *adv.* **creativeness** *n.* **creativity** (krēətiv´-) *n.* [L *creātus*, p.p. of *creāre*]

creatine (krē´ətin, -tēn) *n.* an organic compound found in muscular fibre. [Gr. *kreas -atos*, meat]

creation (kriā´shən) *n.* 1 the act of creating. 2 that which is created or produced. 3 (**Creation**) God's act of creating the world or the universe. 4 (**Creation**) the universe, the world, all created things. 5 the act of appointing, constituting or investing with a new character or position. 6 a production of art, craft, or intellect. **creational** *a.* **creationism** *n.* 1 the theory that the universe was brought into existence out of nothing by God, and that new forms and species are the results of special creations. 2 the doctrine that a human soul is created for each human being at birth. **creationist** *n.* **creation science** *n.* the belief in God's special creation of the universe etc. treated as a scientific theory or position. **creator** *n.* 1 a person who or something which creates. 2 a maker. 3 (**Creator**) God, as the maker of the universe. [F, from L *creātio -ōnem* (*creāre*, to CREATE)]

creature (krē´chə) *n.* 1 a living being. 2 an animal, esp. as distinct from a human being. 3 a person (as an epithet of pity or endearment). 4 a person who owes their rise or fortune to another. 5 that which is created. 6 an instrument. *~a.* of or relating to the body. **the creature** (*esp. Ir., coll.*) drink, liquor, esp. whiskey. **creature comforts** *n.pl.* those of or relating to the body, esp. food and drink. **creaturely** *a.* 1 of or relating to a creature. 2 having the nature or qualities of a creature. **creature of habit** *n.* a person etc. who follows the same routine every day. [F *créature*, L *creatūra* (*creāre*, to create)]

crèche (kresh) *n.* 1 a day nursery in which young children are taken care of. 2 a model of the scene of the birth of Jesus. [F, see CRATCH]

cred (kred) *n.* (*coll.*) credibility, as in *street cred.*

credal CREED.

credence (krē´dəns) *n.* 1 belief, credit. 2 reliance, confidence. 3 that which gives a claim to credit or confidence. 4 a credence table. **to give credence to** to believe, accept. **credence table** *n.* 1 a small table, shelf or niche near the (south) side of the altar (or communion table) to receive the eucharistic elements before consecration. 2 a small sideboard. **credent** *a.* 1 giving credence. 2 bearing credit. **credently** *adv.* **credential** (kriden´-) *a.* 1 giving an entitlement to confidence, trust etc. 2 accredited. *~n.* 1 anything which gives an entitlement to confidence, trust etc. 2 (*pl.*) certificates or letters introducing or accrediting any person or persons. [F, from med. L *crēdentia* (*crēdere*, to believe)]

credenza (kriden´zə) *n.* (*pl.* **credenzas**) 1 a credence table. 2 a sideboard or cupboard. [It., from med. L *crēdentia* (*crēdere*, to believe)]

credible (kred´ibəl) *a.* 1 deserving of or entitled to belief. 2 convincing; seemingly effective. **credibility** (-bil´-) *n.* **credibility gap** *n.* the discrepancy between the facts and a version of them presented as true. **credibly** *adv.*

Usage note The adjectives *credible* and *credulous* should not be confused: *credible* means believable, and *credulous* too ready to believe.

credit (kred´it) *n.* 1 belief, trust, faith. 2 credibility, trustworthiness. 3 a reputation inspiring trust or confidence, esp. a reputation for solvency or honesty. 4 an acknowledgement of merit or value, or something awarded for this. 5 anything due to any person. 6 trust with regard to goods handed over on the promise of payment at a future time. 7 the time given for payment of goods sold on trust. 8 a person's financial position, esp. with regard to money in a bank etc. account. 9 a source or cause of honour, esteem or reputation. 10 the side of an account in which payment is entered, opposed to debit. 11 an entry on this side of a payment received. 12 the sum or total entered on this side. 13 (*pl.*) CREDIT TITLES (under CREDIT). 14 an acknowledgement that a student has completed a course of study. 15 a unit of study in a degree etc. course, or a point awarded for completing the unit. 16 the passing of an examination at a mark well above the minimum required. *~v.t.* (*pres.p.* **crediting,** *past, p.p.* **credited**) 1 to believe. 2 to set to the credit of (*to* the person). 3 to give credit for (*with* the amount). 4 to believe (a person) to possess, be etc. something. 5 to ascribe to. **on credit** with an agreement to pay at some later time. **to do someone credit** to be a source or cause of honour, esteem or heightened reputation for. **to get (the) credit for** to receive credit for something done. **to give credit**

to to believe. **to give someone credit for 1** to give praise or honour for something done. **2** to ascribe (a good quality or ability) to someone. **3** to enter (an amount) in a person's account. **to one's credit** as something which can be considered praiseworthy, honourable etc. **creditable** *a.* bringing credit or honour. **creditability** (-bil´-) *n.* **creditableness** *n.* **creditably** *adv.* **credit account** *n.* a type of account in which goods and services are charged to be paid for later. **credit card** *n.* a card issued by a bank or credit company which allows the holder to buy goods and services on credit. **credit line** *n.* **1** the statement of the writer's name, source etc. in a newspaper article or film credits. **2** a line of credit. **credit note** *n.* a note of an amount owed to a customer for goods returned, which can be exchanged for other goods. **creditor** *n.* **1** a person to whom a debt is due, as distinct from *debtor.* **2** the side of an account on which receipts are entered. **credit rating** *n.* a level or assessment of creditworthiness. **credit sale** *n.* the selling of something on credit. **credit scoring** *n.* the calculation of a person's credit rating by awarding and adding up points for their age, address, occupation etc. **credit squeeze** *n.* government restrictions imposed on banks to limit their loans to clients. **credit titles** *n.pl.* a list of acknowledgements of actors, participants, contributors etc. at the beginning or end of a film etc. **credit transfer** *n.* the transferring of money directly from one bank account to another. **credit union** *n.* a cooperative non-profit-making savings association that makes loans to its members at low interest. **creditworthy** *a.* deserving credit because of income level, past record of debt repayment etc. **creditworthiness** *n.* [F *crédit*, It. *credito*, L *crēditus*, p.p. of *crēdere*, to believe]

credo (krā´dō, krē´-) *n.* (*pl.* **credos**) **1** (**Credo**) the Apostles' Creed or the Nicene Creed. **2** (**Credo**) a musical setting of either of the creeds, esp. of the Nicene Creed. **3** the statement of a belief. [L, I believe, the first word of the Latin versions of the creeds]

credulous (kred´ūləs) *a.* **1** disposed to believe, esp. without sufficient evidence. **2** characterized by or due to such disposition. **credulity** (-dū´-) *n.* **credulously** *adv.* **credulousness** *n.* [L *crēdulus* (*crēdere*, to believe)]

Usage note See note under CREDIBLE.

Cree (krē) *n.* (*pl.* **Cree, Crees**) **1** a member of a N American Indian people living in central Canada. **2** the Algonquian language of this people. ~*a.* of or relating to the Cree or their language. [F *Cri*, from earlier *Cristinaux*, from Algonquian]

creed (krēd) *n.* **1** a brief summary of the articles of religious belief. **2** (**Creed**) the Apostles' Creed or the Nicene Creed. **3** any system or solemn profession of religious or other belief or opinions. **credal, creedal** *a.* [OE *crēda*, L *crēdo*]

Creek (krēk) *n.* (*pl.* **Creek, Creeks**) **1** a member of a N American people now living mostly in Oklahoma, or of a confederacy of which the Creeks were the dominant members. **2** the language spoken by this people. ~*a.* of or relating to the Creeks or their language. [CREEK]

creek (krēk) *n.* **1** a small inlet, bay or harbour, on the coast. **2** a backwater or arm of a river or an inlet on a river bank. **3** (*N Am., Austral., New Zeal.*) a small river, esp. a tributary. **4** a narrow strip of land between mountains. **5** a narrow winding passage. **up the creek 1** (*sl.*) in trouble or difficulty. **2** (*sl.*) mad. **creeky** *a.* (*comp.* **creekier**, *superl.* **creekiest**). [ME *crīke*, cp. OF *crique*, Dut. *krēke*, *kreek*, Swed. *krik*, Icel. *kriki*]

creel (krēl) *n.* **1** an osier basket. **2** a fisherman's basket. [etym. uncertain; orig. Sc.]

creep (krēp) *v.i.* (*past, p.p.* **crept** (krept)) **1** to crawl along the ground. **2** (of a plant) to grow along the ground or up a wall. **3** to move slowly and imperceptibly, stealthily, or with timidity. **4** to gain admission unobserved. **5** to behave with servility; to fawn. **6** (of a feeling etc.) to begin or develop slowly. **7** to have a sensation of shivering or shrinking, e.g. from fear or repugnance. **8** (*Naut.*) to drag with a creeper at the bottom of the water. **9** (of a metal) to become gradually deformed under stress. ~*n.* **1** creeping. **2** a slow, almost imperceptible movement. **3** (*pl.*) a feeling of shrinking horror or disgust. **4** (*sl.*) an unpleasant or servile person. **5** a place for creeping through. **6** a low arch or passage for animals. **7** gradual deforming of a metal due to stress. **to creep up on 1** to approach slowly, stealthily and without being noticed. **2** to develop slowly and imperceptibly. **to make someone's flesh creep** FLESH. **creeper** *n.* **1** a person who or something which creeps or crawls. **2** a plant with a creeping stem. **3** the name, or an element of the name, of various birds that run up trees etc., esp., in N America, the treecreeper. **4** any animal that creeps, esp. a reptile or insect. **5** (*sl.*) a soft-soled shoe. **6** a kind of patten worn by women. **7** a small spike attached to a boot to prevent slipping on ice. **8** a four-clawed grapnel used in dragging a harbour, pond or well. **9** a board on wheels or castors on which one can lie while working under a vehicle. **10** in cricket, a ball which is bowled in such a way that it stays low. **creep-hole** *n.* **1** a hole into which an animal may creep to escape danger. **2** a subterfuge, an excuse. **creeping** *a., n.* **creeping barrage** *n.* (*Mil.*) a barrage that moves forward or backward at prearranged intervals. **creeping Jenny** *n.* any of various creeping plants, esp. the moneywort. **creeping Jesus** *n.* (*sl.*) a sly or sanctimonious person. **creepingly** *adv.* **creepy** *a.* (*comp.* **creepier**, *superl.* **creepiest**) **1** having the sensation of creeping of the flesh. **2** causing this sensation. **3** characterized by or prone to creeping. **creepily** *adv.* **creepiness** *n.* **creepy-crawly** *a.* creepy. ~*n.* (*pl.* **creepy-crawlies**) a creeping insect or small animal. [OE *crēopan*, from Gmc. *creup-* (cp. Dut. *kruipen*, Swed. *krypa*)]

creese KRIS.

†**creesh** (krēsh) *n.* (*Sc.*) **1** grease, fat. **2** a stroke, a smack. ~*v.t.* to grease. **creeshy** *a.* (*comp.* **creeshier**, *superl.* **creeshiest**). [OF *craisse*, grease]

cremate (krimāt´) *v.t.* **1** to dispose of a corpse by burning. **2** to burn. **cremation** *n.* **cremationist** *n.* **cremator** *n.* **1** a person who cremates a dead body. **2** a furnace for consuming corpses or rubbish. **crematorium** (kremətaw´riəm) *n.* (*pl.* **crematoriums, crematoria** (-iə)) a place where bodies are cremated. **crematory** (krem´-) *a.* employed in or connected with cremation. ~*n.* (*pl.* **crematories**) (*esp. N Am.*) a crematorium. [L *cremātus*, p.p. of *cremāre*, to burn]

crème (krem) *n.* cream. [F]

crème brûlée (krem broolā´) *n.* (*pl.* **crèmes brûlées** (krem broolā´), **crème brûlées** (broolāz´)) **1** a dessert consisting of cream or custard covered with caramelized sugar. **2** a portion of this dessert. [F, burnt cream]

crème caramel (krem karəmel´, kar´-) *n.* (*pl.* **crèmes caramel** (krem), **crème caramels** (-melz)) **1** a dessert consisting of a set custard coated with liquid caramel. **2** a portion of this dessert. [F, caramel cream]

crème de cacao (krem də kəkah´ō, kəkā´ō) *n.* (*pl.* **crèmes de cacao** (krem), **crème de cacaos** (kəkah´ōz, kəkā´ōz)) **1** a chocolate-flavoured liqueur. **2** a glass of this liqueur. [F, cream of cocoa]

crème de cassis (krem də kasēs´) *n.* (*pl.* **crèmes de cassis** (krem)) **1** a blackcurrant-flavoured liqueur. **2** a glass of this liqueur. [F, cream of blackcurrant]

crème de la crème (krem də la krem´) *n.* the pick, best, most select, elite. [F, cream of the cream]

crème de menthe (krem də month´, menth´) *n.* (*pl.* **crèmes de menthe** (krem), **crème de menthes** (months´, menths´)) **1** a peppermint-flavoured liqueur. **2** a glass of this liqueur. [F, cream of peppermint]

crème fraîche (krem fresh´) *n.* a type of thick, slightly soured cream. [F, fresh cream]

crenate (krē´nāt), **crenated** (krinā´tid) *a.* 1 notched. 2 (*Bot.*) (of a leaf) having the edge notched. **crenation** (krinā´shən) *n.* **crenature** (krē´nəchə, kren´-) *n.* 1 a scallop. 2 a crenel. 3 (*Bot.*) a small rounded tooth on the edge of a leaf. [late L *crēna*, a notch]

crenel (kren´əl), **crenelle** (-nel´) *n.* 1 a loophole through which to discharge musketry. 2 a battlement. 3 (*Bot.*) a crenature. **crenellate** (kren´-), **crenelate** *v.t.* to furnish with battlements or loopholes. **crenellation** (-ā´shən) *n.* [OF *crenel* (F *créneau*), dim. of *cren*, *crena* (late L *crēna*, a notch)]

crenulate (kren´ūlət) *a.* (*Biol.*) (of the edges of leaves, shells etc.) finely notched or scalloped. **crenulated** (-lātid) *a.* **crenulation** (-lā´shən) *n.* [late L *crēnula*, dim. of *crēna*, notch, -ATE[1]]

Creole (krē´ōl) *n.* 1 a person of European parentage in the W Indies or Spanish America. 2 in Louisiana, a person descended from French or Spanish ancestors. 3 a person of mixed European and black parentage. 4 (**creole**) the native language of a region, formed from prolonged contact between the original native language(s) and that of European settlers. ~*a.* relating to the Creoles or a creole language. **creolize, creolise** *v.t.* **creolization** (-zā´shən) *n.* [F *créole*, Sp. *criollo*, prob. from Port. *crioulo*, a nursling, from *criar*, from L *creāre*, to CREATE]

creophagous (kriof´əgəs) *a.* carnivorous, flesh-eating. **creophagist** (-jist) *n.* **creophagy** *n.* [Gr. *kreas -atos*, -PHAGOUS]

creosote (krē´əsōt) *n.* 1 (*also* **creosote oil**) a liquid distilled from coal tar, used for preserving wood etc. 2 an antiseptic liquid distilled from wood. ~*v.t.* to treat (woodwork, etc.) with creosote. **creosote bush, creosote plant** *n.* a Mexican shrub, *Larrea tridentata*, smelling of creosote. [Gr. *kreas -atos*, flesh, *sōtēr*, saviour, from *sōzein*, to save, preserve]

crêpe (krāp, krep), **crepe** *n.* 1 crape. 2 a crapy fabric other than mourning crape. 3 a thin pancake. 4 crêpe paper. 5 crêpe rubber. **crêpé** (krāpā´) *a.* frizzled. **crêpe de Chine** (də shēn´) *n.* crape manufactured from raw silk. **crêpe paper** *n.* thin crinkly paper, used in making decorations. **crêperie** (-əri) *n.* a restaurant or café specializing in crêpes. **crêpe rubber** *n.* rubber with a rough surface used for shoe soles etc. **crêpe Suzette** (krep soozet´), **crêpe suzette** *n.* (*pl.* **crêpes Suzette** (krep), **crêpes suzettes** (krep soozets´)) a thin pancake in a hot orange or lemon sauce, served flambéed as a dessert. **crêpey, crêpy** *a.* (of dry skin etc.) like crêpe, crinkled. [F, from L *crispa*, curled]

crepitate (krep´itāt) *v.i.* 1 to crackle. 2 to burst with a series of short, sharp reports, as salt does in fire. 3 to rattle. 4 (*Biol.*) (of a beetle) to eject an acrid fluid as a form of self-defence. **crepitant** *a.* crackling. **crepitation** (-ā´shən) *n.* **crepitus** (krep´itəs) *n.* 1 crepitation. 2 (*Med.*) a rattling sound heard in the lungs during pneumonia etc. 3 (*Med.*) the sound of the ends of a broken bone scraping against each other. [L *crepitātus*, p.p. of *crepitāre*, freq. of *crepāre*, to creak]

crept CREEP.

crepuscle (krep´əsəl), **crepuscule** (-əskūl) *n.* morning or evening twilight. **crepuscular** (-pŭs´kū-) *a.* 1 of or relating to or connected with twilight. 2 glimmering, indistinct, obscure. 3 (*Biol.*) appearing or flying about at twilight. [F *crépuscule*, L *crepusculum*]

crêpy CRÊPE.

Cres. *abbr.* (in street names) Crescent.

cres., cresc. *abbr.* (*Mus.*) crescendo.

crescendo (krishen´dō) *n.* (*pl.* **crescendos, crescendi** (-di)) 1 (a musical passage performed with) a gradual increase in the force of sound. 2 a gradual increase in force or effect. 3 a climax, high point. ~*adv.*, *a.* with an increasing volume of sound. ~*v.i.* (*3rd pers. sing. pres.* **crescendoes**, *pres.p.* **crescendoing**, *past, p.p.* **crescendoed**) to increase in loudness or intensity. [It., ger. of *crescere*, to grow (see CRESCENT)]

Usage note The use of *crescendo* to mean climax is best avoided: a crescendo is a gradual increase towards a climax, not the climax itself.

crescent (kres´ənt) *a.* 1 shaped like a new moon. 2 (*poet.*) increasing, growing. ~*n.* 1 a shape like the new moon. 2 a street or row of buildings in crescent form. 3 the increasing moon in its first quarter. 4 (*Her.*) a bearing in the form of a half-moon. 5 (**Crescent**) Islam, or Islamic power. 6 (*dated*) (**Crescent**) Turkey, or Turkish power. 7 a military order with a half-moon for a symbol. **crescentic** (-sen´tik) *a.* crescent-shaped. [L *crēscens -ntem*, pres.p. of *crēscere*, to grow (incept. of *creāre*, to CREATE)]

cresol (krē´sol) *n.* a compound, occurring in three isomers, which is found in coal tar and creosote and is used in antiseptics and as a raw material for plastics. [*creos*ote, alcoh*ol*]

cress (kres) *n.* any of various cruciferous plants with a pungent taste, e.g. watercress, garden cress. [OE *cærse*, from Gmc. *kras-* (cp. Dut. *kers*, G *Kresse*, OHG *chreson*, to creep)]

cresset (kres´it) *n.* 1 (*Hist.*) a metal cup or vessel, usu. on a pole, for holding oil for a light. 2 (*Hist.*) a frame of open ironwork to contain a fire for a beacon. 3 (*Hist.*) a torch. 4 (*poet.*) a brilliant light. [OF *cresset*, *craisset*, from *craisse*, CREESH]

crest (krest) *n.* 1 a plume or comb on the head of a bird. 2 any tuft on the head of an animal. 3 a plume or tuft of feathers, esp. affixed to the top of a helmet. 4 the apex of a helmet. 5 (*Her.*) any figure placed above the shield in a coat-of-arms. 6 the same printed on paper or painted on a building etc. 7 the summit of a mountain or hill. 8 the top of a ridge. 9 the line of the top of the neck in animals. 10 an animal's mane. 11 the ridge of a wave. 12 a ridge on a bone. ~*v.t.* 1 to ornament or furnish with a crest. 2 to serve as a crest to. 3 to attain the crest of (a hill). ~*v.i.* to rise into a crest or ridge. **on the crest of a wave** at the peak of one's success; enjoying prolonged success. **riding the crest of a wave** at the peak of one's success; enjoying prolonged success. **crested** *a.* 1 adorned with, wearing or having a crest. 2 (*Bot.*) with a crestlike part. **crestfallen** *a.* 1 dispirited, abashed. 2 with a drooping crest. **crestfallenly** *adv.* **crestfallenness** *n.* **crestless** *a.* 1 not entitled to a crest. 2 not of noble family. 3 without a crest. **crestlet** *n.* a little crest. [OF *criste*, L *crista*]

cresyl (kres´il) *n.* (*Chem.*) each of three isomeric radicals derived from a cresol. **cresylic** (krisil´ik) *a.* of or relating to cresol or creosote. **cresylic acid** *n.* cresol. [CRESOL, -YL]

cretaceous (kritā´shəs) *a.* of the nature of or abounding in chalk. **Cretaceous** *a.*, *n.* (of or formed in) the last period of the Mesozoic era. **cretaceous formation** *n.* (*Geol.*) the uppermost member of the Mesozoic rocks. [L *crētāceus*, from *crēta*, chalk]

Cretan (krē´tən) *n.* a native or inhabitant of the Greek island of Crete. ~*a.* of or relating to Crete or the Cretans. [L *Crētanus*, from *Crēta*, Crete]

cretic (krē´tik) *n.* a metrical foot consisting of a short syllable preceded and followed by a long syllable. [L *crēticus*, from *Crēta*, Crete]

cretin (kret´in) *n.* 1 a person mentally and physically disabled because of a (congenital) thyroid malfunction. 2 (*coll.*) a very stupid person. **cretinism** *n.* **cretinize, cretinise** *v.t.* **cretinous** *a.* [F *crétin*, Swiss F *crestin*, *creitin*, L *Christiānus*, Christian]

cretonne (kreton´, kret´on) *n.* a cotton fabric with

pictorial patterns, used for upholstering, frocks etc. [F, from *Creton*, a village in Normandy]

Creutzfeldt–Jakob disease (kroitsfeltyak´ob) *n.* (*Med.*) a disease of human beings, related to BSE and scrapie, which causes brain degeneration, leading to death. [Hans *Creutzfeldt*, 1885–1964, and Alfons *Jakob*, 1884–1931, German physicians]

crevasse (krəvas´) *n.* **1** a deep fissure in a glacier. **2** (*N Am.*) a break in an embankment or levee of a river. [F, see CREVICE]

Usage note The meanings of *crevasse* and *crevice* overlap, but in general a *crevasse* is a large crack, and a *crevice* a narrow one.

crevice (krev´is) *n.* a crack, a cleft, a fissure. **creviced** *a.* [ME and OF *crevace* (F *crevasse*), late L *crepātia*, from *crepāre*, to crackle, to burst]

Usage note See note under CREVASSE.

crew[1] (kroo) *n.* **1** the sailors on a ship or boat, esp. as distinct from the officers or the captain. **2** the personnel on board an aircraft, train or bus. **3** a number of persons associated for any purpose. **4** a gang, a mob. ~*v.t., v.i.* to act as, or serve in, a crew (of). **crew-cut** *n.* a very short style of haircut. **crewman** *n.* (*pl.* **crewmen**). **crew neck** *n.* a close-fitting round neckline on a jersey. **crew-necked, crew-neck** *a.* [from OF *creue*, p.p. of *croistre* (F *croître*), to grow; or from OF *acreue*, ACCRUE (*acrewe*, eventually becoming *a crew*)]

crew[2] CROW[2].

crewel (kroo´əl) *n.* **1** fine two-threaded worsted. **2** embroidery or tapestry worked with such thread. **crewel work** *n.* [etym. unknown]

crib (krib) *n.* **1** a child's cot. **2** a model of the Nativity scene (placed in churches at Christmas). **3** a plagiarism. **4** a translation of or key to an author, used by students. **5** something (such as a hidden list of dates, formulae etc.) used to cheat in an examination. **6** (*coll.*) anything stolen. **7** a rack or manger. **8** a stall for cattle. **9** (*N Am.*) a bin for grain. **10** a salt-box. **11** a timber etc. framework lining a mine shaft, forming foundations etc. **12** a small cottage, a hut, a hovel. **13** (*sl.*) a brothel. **14** a situation, place, berth. **15** a wicker salmon-trap. **16** cribbage. **17** a hand at cribbage made up of two cards thrown out by each player and given to the dealer. **18** (*Austral., New Zeal.*) food, esp. a light meal. ~*v.t.* (*pres.p.* **cribbing,** *past, p.p.* **cribbed**) **1** to plagiarize. **2** to copy from a translation. **3** (*coll.*) to steal, to appropriate. **4** to shut up in a crib. **5** to confine. ~*v.i.* **1** to cheat using a crib. **2** (of horses) to bite the crib. **3** (*coll.*) to grumble. **cribber** *n.* **cribbing** *n.* **1** stealing, plagiarizing. **2** cheating. **3** internal lining of a mine shaft to prevent caving in. **4** the act of enclosing in a crib or narrow place. **crib-biting** *n.* a bad habit in some horses of biting the crib. **crib death** *n.* (*N Am.*) cot death. [OE (cp. Dut. *krib*, OHG *krippa*, G *Krippe*, Icel. and Swed. *krubba*)]

cribbage (krib´ij) *n.* a card game for two, three or four players. **cribbage board** *n.* a board with holes and pegs on which the progress of the game is marked. [CRIB]

cribbing CRIB.

cribriform (krib´rifawm) *a.* (*Anat., Bot.*) resembling a sieve; perforated like a sieve. **cribrate** (-rāt), **cribrose** (-rōs) *a.* [L *cribrum*, a sieve]

crick (krik) *n.* a spasmodic painful stiffness, esp. of the neck or back. ~*v.t.* to cause a crick in. [prob. onomat.]

cricket[1] (krik´it) *n.* an open-air game played by two sides of 11 players, consisting of an attempt to strike, with a ball, wickets defended by the opponents with bats. ~*v.i.* (*pres.p.* **cricketing,** *past, p.p.* **cricketed**) to play cricket. **not cricket** unfair, not honest. **cricket bag** *n.* a long bag for carrying a cricket bat etc. **cricketer** *n.* [etym. uncertain (perh. from OF *criquet*, a stick serving as a mark in some game with a ball)]

cricket[2] (krik´it) *n.* **1** any grasshopper-like insect of the family Gryllidae, the males being noted for their chirping. **2** any of various similar insects not belonging to the Gryllidae, such as the mole cricket. [OF *criquet*, from *criquer*, to creak (imit.)]

cricket[3] (krik´it) *n.* (*dial.*) a low, wooden stool. [etym. unknown]

cricoid (krī´koid) *a.* (*Anat.*) ringlike. **cricoid cartilage** *n.* the cartilage at the top of the trachea. [Gr. *krikoeidēs* (*krikos, kirkos*, a ring, -OID)]

cri de coeur (krē də kœ´) *n.* (*pl.* **cris de coeur** (krē)) a heartfelt appeal or protest. [F]

crier (krī´ə), **cryer** *n.* a person who cries or proclaims. [OF *criere, crieur*, from *crier*, to CRY]

crikey (krī´ki) *int.* (*coll.*) used to express astonishment. [perh. euphem. for Christ]

crim (krim) *n., a.* (*esp. Austral., New Zeal.*) (a) criminal.

†**crim. con.** (krim kon´) *n.* short for CRIMINAL CONVERSATION (under CRIMINAL).

crime (krīm) *n.* **1** an act contrary to human or divine law. **2** a charge, the grounds for accusation. **3** (*Mil.*) any offence or breach of regulations. **4** any act of wickedness or sin. **5** wrong-doing, sin. **6** (*coll.*) something to be deplored, deprecated, regretted or ashamed of. ~*v.t.* (*Mil.*) to charge with or convict of a crime. **crime fighter** *n.* a person who fights crime. **crime-fighting** *n.* **crimeful** *a.* criminal, wicked. **crimeless** *a.* **crime of passion** *n.* CRIME PASSIONEL. **crime prevention** *n.* anything done to prevent crimes being committed, esp. actions taken to safeguard buildings, cars etc. against burglary, theft etc. **crime prevention officer** *n.* a police officer who advises the public on matters of crime prevention. **crime sheet** *n.* a record of offences. **crime wave** *n.* a sudden sharp increase in crimes committed. **crime writer** *n.* a person who writes fiction about crime and detection. [F, from L *crīmen* (*cernere*, to decide, cp. Gr. *krinein*, to separate, *krîma*, a decision)]

crime passionel (krēm pasyonel´) *n.* (*pl.* **crimes passionels** (krēm pasyonel´)) a crime, esp. murder, committed because of, usu. sexual, passion and jealousy. [F, crime of passion]

criminal (krim´inəl) *a.* **1** of the nature of a crime, relating to (a) crime. **2** contrary to duty, law or right. **3** guilty of a crime. **4** tainted with crime. **5** (*Law*) involved with or relating to criminal law as distinct from civil law etc. **6** (*coll.*) regrettable, deplorable, shameful. ~*n.* **1** a person guilty of a crime. **2** a convict. †**criminal conversation** *n.* (*Law*) adultery. **criminalistic** (-lis´-) *a.* relating to criminals. **criminalistics** *n.* (*esp. N Am.*) forensic science. **criminality** (-nal´-) *n.* **criminalize, criminalise** *v.t.* **1** to make (an activity etc.) illegal. **2** to make (a person) a criminal, e.g. by criminalizing their activities. **criminalization** (-zā´shən) *n.* **criminal law** *n.* the body of laws or practice of law dealing with criminal offences and punishment of offenders, as distinct from *civil law*. **criminal libel** *n.* (*Law*) (a) libel likely to provoke a breach of the peace. **criminally** *adv.* **criminal record** *n.* a record of crimes a person has committed. [late L *criminālis*, from L *crīmen*; see CRIME]

criminate (krim´ināt) *v.t.* **1** to accuse of a crime. **2** to prove guilty of a crime. **3** to blame, to condemn. **crimination** (-ā´shən) *n.* **criminative** (-ətiv) *a.* **criminatory** (-ətəri) *a.* [L *crimināri -ātus*; see CRIME]

criminology (kriminol´əji) *n.* the scientific study of crime and criminals. **criminological** (-loj´ikəl) *a.* **criminologically** *adv.* **criminologist** (-ol´-) *n.* [L *crīmen -inem*, crime, -LOGY]

criminous (krim´inəs) *a.* guilty of a crime, criminal. **criminousness** *n.* [OF *crimineux*, from L *criminōsus*; see CRIME]

crimp[1] (krimp) *v.t.* **1** to curl or put waves into (hair). **2** to compress into ridges or folds, to frill. **3** to corrugate, to flute, to crease. **4** to cause (the flesh of live fish) to contract and become crisp and firm, by gashing it with a knife. **5** to compress so as to shape or mould. *~n.* something crimped or crimpy. **to put a crimp in** (*N Am., coll.*) to obstruct, hinder or thwart. **crimper** *n.* a person who or something which crimps. **crimping-iron, crimping-machine** *n.* an instrument or machine for fluting cap fronts, frills etc. **crimpy** *a.* (*comp.* **crimpier**, *superl.* **crimpiest**). **crimpily** *adv.* **crimpiness** *n.* [cp. CRAMP[1]]

crimp[2] (krimp) *n.* **1** (*Hist.*) a person who decoyed men for military or naval service. **2** a decoy, a disreputable agent. *~v.t.* (*Hist.*) to decoy into the military or naval service. [etym. uncertain]

Crimplene® (krim´plēn), **crimplene** *n.* a kind of crease-resistant synthetic fibre, or a fabric made from it.

crimson (krim´zən) *n.* a deep red colour. *~a.* of this colour. *~v.t.* to dye with this colour. *~v.i.* **1** to turn crimson. **2** to blush. [Sp. *cremesin, carmesi,* Arab. *qirmazī*]

cringe (krinj) *v.i.* (*pres.p.* **cringing**) **1** to shrink back in fear. **2** to crouch, to bend humbly. **3** to fawn, behave obsequiously to. **4** (*coll.*) to wince in embarrassment. **5** (*coll.*) to feel embarrassment or distaste. *~n.* **1** an act of cringing. **2** (*coll.*) something that causes embarrassment. **3** an obsequious action, flattery, obsequiousness. **cringe-making** *a.* (*coll.*) acutely embarrassing or distasteful. **cringing** *a., n.* **cringingly** *adv.* [ME *crengen,* causal from *cringan,* to sink, to fall]

cringle (kring´gəl) *n.* an iron ring on the bolt-rope of a sail for a rope to pass through. [cp. LG *kringel,* dim. of *kring,* a circle, a ring; cogn. with CRANK[1], CRINKLE]

crinite (krī´nīt) *a.* **1** hairy. **2** (*esp. Bot.*) resembling a tuft of hair. **3** (*Zool., Bot.*) covered with hair in small tufts. **crinitory** (-ni-) *a.* relating to or consisting of hair. [L *crīnītus,* from *crīnis,* hair]

crinkle (kring´kəl) *n.* **1** a wrinkle, a crease. **2** a short bend or turn. *~v.i.* **1** to form wrinkles or creases. **2** to wind in and out. **3** to make short frequent bends and turns. *~v.t.* **1** to wrinkle or crease. **2** to form with frequent bends or turns. **3** to mould into inequalities. **crinkle-crankle** (-krangkəl) *n.* (*dial.*) a twisting, a wavy line, a zigzag. *~a., adv.* **1** zigzag. **2** (twisting) in and out. **crinkle-cut** *a.* (of vegetables) cut with wavy or scalloped edges or sides. **crinkly** *a.* (*comp.* **crinklier**, *superl.* **crinkliest**). *~n.* (*pl.* **crinklies**) (*coll.*) an old person. **crinkum-crankum** (kringkəmkrang´kəm) *n.* **1** a crooked, twisted figure. **2** a zigzag. *~a.* full of twists and turns. [OE *crinkan,* cp. CRANK[1], CRINGE]

crinoid (krin´oid, krī´-) *a.* (*Zool.*) lily-shaped. *~n.* any animal belonging to the class Crinoidea of echinoderms. **crinoidal** (-noi´-) *a.* of or relating to or containing crinoids. [Gr. *krinoeidēs* (*krinon,* a lily, -OID)]

crinoline (krin´əlin, -lēn) *n.* **1** a stiff fabric of horsehair formerly used for petticoats, etc. **2** a petticoat of this material. **3** any stiff petticoat used to expand the skirts of a dress. **4** a large hooped skirt, orig. worn in the mid-19th cent. **5** the whalebone hoops for such a skirt. **6** a series of nets extended round a warship to keep off torpedoes. [F (*crin,* L *crīnis,* hair; *lin,* L *līnum,* flax)]

criosphinx (krī´ōsfingks) *n.* (*pl.* **criosphinxes**) a sphinx with a ram's head. [Gr. *krios,* ram, SPHINX]

cripes (krīps) *int.* (*coll.*) used to express surprise. [euphem. for CHRIST]

cripple (krip´əl) *n.* **1** a lame or disabled person. **2** (*coll.*) a person who is disabled or defective in some respect (*emotional cripple*). **3** a rough staging such as is used for window-cleaning. **4** in carpentry, a makeshift contrivance. *~v.t.* **1** to make lame. **2** to deprive of the use of the limbs. **3** to deprive of or lessen the power of action. **crippled** *a.* **crippledom** *n.* **cripplehood** *n.* **crippler** *n.* **crippleware** *n.* (*Comput.*) demonstration software which has been deliberately disabled in such a way that it can be evaluated by a prospective purchaser but not used to its full capacity. **crippling** *a.* **cripplingly** *adv.* [OE *crypel,* conn. with *crēopan,* to creep, from Gmc. *kruipan*]

Usage note Using *cripple* to refer to a permanently lame or disabled person can give offence, and is best avoided.

cris KRIS.

crisis (krī´sis) *n.* (*pl.* **crises** (-sēz)) **1** a momentous juncture in war, politics, commerce, domestic affairs etc. **2** a time of great danger or difficulty. **3** something causing such danger or difficulty. **4** a turning point, esp. that of a disease indicating recovery or death. **crisis management** *n.* the policy or style of management which involves taking action only when a crisis develops. [L, from Gr. *krisis,* a separating, a decision, from *krinein,* to decide]

crisp (krisp) *a.* **1** hard, dry and brittle. **2** (of vegetables etc.) firm, crunchy. **3** (of weather etc.) cold and invigorating. **4** (of a person's manner) brisk and decisive. **5** (of wording) concise and to the point. **6** (of a person's features) neat, clean-cut. **7** (of hair) closely curled. **8** (of paper) stiff and crackly. *~v.t.* **1** to make something crisp. **2** to curl, to wrinkle, to ripple. **3** to interlace. *~v.i.* **1** to become crisp. **2** to become curly. *~n.* POTATO CRISP (under POTATO). **to burn to a crisp** to overcook something to the point where it is burnt and uneatable. **crispbread** *n.* thin, dry, unsweetened biscuits of rye or wheat flour, or one of such biscuits. **crisped** *a.* **crisper** *n.* **1** a person who or something which curls or crisps. **2** a compartment in a refrigerator for vegetables to keep them crisp. **3** an instrument for crisping the nap of cloth. **crisply** *adv.* **crispness** *n.* **crispy** *a.* (*comp.* **crispier**, *superl.* **crispiest**) **1** crisp. **2** wavy. **3** curled, curling. **4** brisk. **crispily** *adv.* **crispiness** *n.* [OE, from L *crispus,* curled]

crispate (kris´pāt) *a.* (*Biol.*) having curled, wrinkled or wavy edges. **crispation** (-pā´shən) *n.* [L *crispātus,* p.p. of *crispāre,* (*crispus,* curled)]

criss-cross (kris´kros) *a., n.* **1** (a network of lines) crossing one another. **2** repeated(ly) crossing to and fro. *~v.t., v.i.* to move in, lie in, or mark with, a criss-cross pattern. *~adv.* **1** in a criss-cross pattern. **2** at cross purposes.

crista (kris´tə) *n.* (*pl.* **cristae** (-tē)) **1** (*Anat., Zool.*) a ridge or crest. **2** (*Biol.*) a ridgelike part of a mitochondrion. **cristate** (kris´tāt) *a.* **1** having a crest. **2** tufted with hairs. [L *crista,* a crest]

☒ **cristal** common misspelling of CRYSTAL.

cristobalite (kristō´bəlīt) *n.* one of the main forms of silica, occurring e.g. as opal. [Cerro San *Cristóbal* in Mexico, where it was discovered]

crit (krit) *n.* (*coll.*) **1** a critical study or examination. **2** a formal criticism. **3** (*Physics*) critical mass.

crit. *abbr.* critical.

criterion (krītiə´riən) *n.* (*pl.* **criteria** (-ə)) a principle or standard by which anything is or can be judged. [Gr. *kritērion,* means of judging (*kritēs,* judge, from *krinein,* to judge)]

Usage note *Criteria* is commonly used as a singular noun (a *criteria*) but it should always be a plural, with *criterion* as the singular.

critic (krit´ik) *n.* **1** a judge, an examiner. **2** a censurer, a caviller. **3** a person skilled in judging of literary or artistic merit. **4** a reviewer. **5** an expert in textual criticism. **critical** *a.* **1** of or relating to criticism. **2** expressing criticism; frequently making criticisms. **3** competent to criticize. **4** fastidious, exacting, captious. **5** indicating or involving a crisis. **6** decisive, vital. **7** attended with danger or risk. **8** in literature, involving textual criticism of a text. **9** (*Physics*) of or designating a point at which a chain reaction becomes self-sustaining. **10** (*Physics*) (of a nuclear reactor) able to sustain such a chain reaction. **11** (*Math.*) relating to points of coincidence or transition. **critical apparatus** *n.* APPARATUS CRITICUS (under APPARATUS). **critical constants** *n.pl.* (*Physics*) particular values relating to the critical point or state of a substance, i.e. the critical density, pressure, temperature and volume. **critical density** *n.* (*Physics*) the density of a substance at its critical temperature and pressure. **criticality** (-kal´-) *n.* (*esp. Math., Physics*). **critically** *adv.* **critical mass** *n.* the smallest amount of fissile material that can sustain a chain reaction. †**criticalness** *n.* **critical path** *n.* the series of steps and procedures by which a complex operation can be carried out in the shortest time. **critical path analysis** *n.* the establishing of a critical path, often with the aid of a computer. **critical point** CRITICAL STATE (under CRITIC). **critical pressure** *n.* (*Physics*) the minimum pressure needed to liquefy a gas at its critical temperature. **critical state, critical point** *n.* (*Physics*) the state or condition under which a substance at its critical temperature can exist as either a liquid or a gas. **critical temperature** *n.* the temperature below which a gas cannot be liquefied. **critical volume** *n.* (*Physics*) the volume of a unit of a substance at its critical temperature and pressure. **criticaster** (-kahstə) *n.* a petty or contemptible critic. **criticism** (-sizm) *n.* **1** the act of judging, esp. literary or artistic works. **2** a critical essay or opinion. **3** the work of criticizing. **4** an unfavourable judgement. **textual criticism** TEXT. **criticize, criticise** *v.t.* **1** to examine critically and deliver an opinion on. **2** to censure. *~v.i.* to make criticisms. **criticizable** *a.* **criticizer** *n.* [L *criticus*, Gr. *kritikos* (*kritēs*, a judge, from *krinein*, to judge)]

critique (kritēk´) *n.* **1** a critical essay or judgement. **2** the art of criticism. **3** the analysis of the basis of knowledge. *~v.t.* to make a critique of. [F, from Gr. *kritikē*, of criticism (*kritēs*, a judge, see CRITIC)]

critter (krit´ə) *n.* (*esp. N Am., coll.*) a creature (an animal or, as a term of pity, a person).

CRO *abbr.* **1** cathode ray oscilloscope. **2** Community Relations Officer. **3** Criminal Records Office.

croak (krōk) *v.i.* **1** (of e.g. a frog or a raven) to make a hoarse low sound in the throat. **2** (*sl.*) to die. **3** to grumble. **4** to prophesy evil. *~v.t.* **1** to utter in a low hoarse voice. **2** (*sl.*) to kill. **3** to utter dismally. *~n.* **1** the low harsh sound made by a frog or a raven. **2** any hoarse sound similar to this. **croaker** *n.* **1** a person, animal or bird that croaks. **2** a querulous person. **3** (*sl.*) a dying person. **4** a person who prophesies evil. **croaky** *a.* (*comp.* **croakier**, *superl.* **croakiest**) croaking, hoarse. **croakily** *adv.* **croakiness** *n.* [prob. imit.]

Croat (krō´at) *n.* **1** a native or inhabitant of Croatia in SE Europe. **2** a person of Croatian descent; a person belonging to a Slav ethnic group of Croatia. **3** the language of Croatia, one of the two main dialects of Serbo-Croat. **4** (*Hist.*) a soldier in the irregular cavalry in the service of Austria (largely recruited from Croats). *~a.* of or relating to the Croats or their language, Croatian. **Croatian** (krōā´shən) *a.* of or relating to Croatia, its people or their language. *~n.* **1** a native or inhabitant of Croatia. **2** a Croat. [Serbo-Croat *Hrvat*, from OSlav. *Khruvat*]

croc (krok) *n.* (*coll.*) short for CROCODILE.

croceate (krō´siāt), **croceous** (krō´shəs) *a.* **1** of or like saffron. **2** (*Bot.*) saffron-coloured. [L *croceus*, saffron]

crochet (krō´shā, -shi) *n.* a kind of knitting done with a hooked needle. *~v.t.* to knit or make in crochet. *~v.i.* to knit in this manner. [F, dim. of *croche*, a hook]

croci CROCUS.

crocidolite (krəsid´əlīt) *n.* **1** a silky fibrous silicate of iron and sodium, also called blue asbestos. **2** a yellow form of this used as a gem or ornament. [Gr. *krokis -idos*, the nap of cloth, -LITE]

crock[1] (krok) *n.* **1** an earthenware vessel; a pot, a pitcher, a jar. **2** a potsherd. **3** soot etc. collected from combustion on pots or kettles etc. *~v.t.* to blacken with soot from a pot. **crockery** *n.* **1** earthenware. **2** earthenware or china dishes, cups, plates etc. [OE *crocca* (cp. OIr. *crocan*, Gael. *crog*, Icel. *krukka*, Dut. *kruik*, G *Krug*)]

crock[2] (krok) *n.* **1** (*coll.*) a sick, decrepit or old person. **2** (*coll.*) a fool, a worthless person. **3** (*coll.*) a broken-down machine or implement. **4** a broken-down horse. **5** an old ewe. *~v.i.* to break down, collapse, become disabled etc. *~v.t.* (*often with up*) to cause to break down, become disabled etc. [etym. uncertain; prob. cogn. with CRACK (cp. Norw. *krake*, a weak or sickly animal; MDut. *kraecke*, EFris. *krakke*, a broken-down horse, house or man)]

crockery CROCK[1].

crocket (krok´it) *n.* (*Archit.*) a carved foliated ornament on a pinnacle, the side of a canopy etc. [A-F *crocket*, var. of F CROCHET]

crocodile (krok´ədīl) *n.* **1** a large amphibian reptile of the family Crocodylidae, with the back and tail covered with large, square scales. **2** (leather made from) the skin of the crocodile. **3** a string of schoolchildren walking two by two. **4** in rhetoric, a captious sophism to ensnare an opponent. **crocodile bird** *n.* an African plover-like bird, *Pluvianus Aegyptius*, which feeds on the insect parasites of the crocodile. **crocodile clip** *n.* a clip with interlocking serrated edges, used for making connections in electrical apparatus. **crocodile tears** *n.pl.* hypocritical tears like those with which the crocodile, according to fable, attracts its victims. **crocodilian** (-dil´-) *n.* any of the large amphibian reptiles of the order Crocodilia, including crocodiles, alligators, caymans and gharials. *~a.* of or relating to the crocodilians. [F, from L *crocodīlus*, Gr. *krokodeilos*]

crocus (krō´kəs) *n.* (*pl.* **crocuses, croci** (-kī, -kē)) **1** a small bulbous plant of the genus *Crocus*, belonging to the Iridaceae, with yellow, white or purple flowers, extensively cultivated in gardens. **2** metal calcined to a deep red or yellow powder and used for polishing. [L, from Gr. *krokos*]

Croesus (krē´səs) *n.* a very wealthy man. [king of Lydia, 6th cent. BC]

croft (kroft) *n.* **1** a piece of enclosed ground, esp. adjoining a house. **2** a small farm in the Highlands and islands of Scotland or northern England. *~v.i.* to live and work on a croft. **crofter** *n.* a person who farms a croft, esp. one of the joint tenants of a farm in Scotland. **crofting** *n.* [OE]

Crohn's disease (krōnz) *n.* (*Med.*) chronic inflammation of the intestines, esp. of the small intestine, usually causing pain and diarrhoea. [Burrill B. *Crohn* 1884–1983, US physician]

croissant (krwas´õ) *n.* a crescent-shaped roll of rich flaky pastry. [F; see CRESCENT]

Cro-Magnon (krōmag´non, -man´yõ) *a.* denoting an early type of modern man, living in late Palaeolithic times, whose remains were found at Cro-Magnon, in SW France.

crombie (krom´bi) *n.* an overcoat made from a type of woollen cloth. [J. & J. *Crombie*, Sc. cloth manufacturer]

cromlech (krom´lekh) *n.* **1** a circle of standing stones. **2** a prehistoric structure in which a large flat stone rests horizontally on upright ones, a dolmen. [Welsh, from *crom*, bent, *llech*, stone, slab]

crone (krōn) *n.* **1** (*derog.*) an old woman. **2** an old ewe. [ONF *carogne*, an old woman (L *caro carnis*, see CARRION)]

cronk (krongk) *a.* (*Austral., coll.*) **1** unwell. **2** unsound. **3** fraudulent. **to cronk up** to go sick, to be ill. [CRANK[3]]

crony (krō´ni) *n.* (*pl.* **cronies**) (*sometimes derog.*) an intimate friend. [Gr. *chronios*, long-continued, from *chronos*, time]

crook (kruk) *n.* **1** a shepherd's or bishop's hooked staff. **2** a bent or curved instrument. **3** a curve, a bend, a meander. **4** (*coll.*) a thief, a swindler. **5** a short tube for altering the key on a brass wind instrument. *~a.* **1** crooked. **2** (*Austral., New Zeal., coll.*) **a** sick, unwell, injured. **b** unpleasant. **c** dishonest. **d** irritable, angry. *~v.t.* **1** to make crooked or curved. **2** to pervert, to misapply. *~v.i.* to be bent or crooked. **by hook or by crook** HOOK. **to go crook (at/ on)** (*Austral., New Zeal., coll.*) to become angry (with), to reprimand. **crookback** *n.* a person who has a deformed back. **crookbacked** *a.* **crooked** (-kid) *a.* (*comp.* **crookeder**, *superl.* **crookedest**) **1** bent, curved. **2** turning, twisting, winding. **3** deformed. **4** not straightforward. **5** perverse. **6** (*Austral., New Zeal., coll.*) crook. **7** (*with* on, *Austral., coll.*) hostile (to). **crookedly** *adv.* **crookedness** *n.* **crookery** *n.* **crookneck** *n.* (*N Am.*) a curved species of squash. [prob. from Icel. *krōkr* (cp. Swed. *krok*, Dan. *krog*, OHG *kracho*)]

Usage note In Austral. coll. senses, *crooked* is usually pronounced (krukt).

---

croon (kroon) *v.i.* to sing in a low voice. *~v.t.* **1** to sing in a low voice. **2** to mutter. *~n.* **1** singing in a low voice. **2** a hollow, continued moan. **3** a low hum. **crooner** *n.* a person who sings sentimental songs in low tones. [imit. (cp. Dut. *kreunen*, to groan)]

crop (krop) *n.* **1** (*pl.*) plants grown for food. **2** the produce of such plants. **3** the amount cut or gathered from such plants, harvest. **4** an amount produced. **5** a group of anything produced, appearing etc. at one time. **6** the craw of a fowl, constituting a kind of first stomach. **7** an analogous receptacle in masticating insects. **8** the upper part of a whip, a fishing rod etc. **9** a short whipstock with a loop instead of a lash. **10** an entire tanned hide. **11** a short haircut. **12** a piece chopped off. **13** any of various cuts of meat. **14** the outcrop of a lode, a seam or a stratum of rock. **15** the top or highest part. *~v.t.* (*pres.p.* **cropping**, *past, p.p.* **cropped**) **1** to cut off the ends of. **2** to mow, to reap, to pluck, to gather. **3** (of an animal) to bite off and eat. **4** to cut off, to cut short. **5** to sow. **6** to plant and raise crops on. **7** to reduce the margin of (a book) unduly, in binding. *~v.i.* to yield a harvest, to bear fruit. **neck and crop** NECK. **to crop out 1** to come to light. **2** (*Geol.*) (of an underlying stratum) to come out at the surface by the edges. **to crop up 1** to come up unexpectedly. **2** (*Geol.*) to crop out. **crop circle** *n.* a circle, or a pattern based on circles, appearing as flattened stalks in the middle of a field of standing corn. **crop dusting** *n.* the spreading of powdered insecticide etc. on crops, from an aeroplane. **crop-ear** *n.* a horse with cropped ears. **crop-eared** *a.* having the hair or ears cut short. **crop-full** *a.* **1** having a full crop. **2** satiated. **crop-over** *n.* in the W Indies, a harvest celebration at the end of the sugar cane harvest. **cropper** *n.* **1** a person who or something which crops. **2** a grain or plant which yields a good crop. **3** a pigeon with a long crop, a pouter. **4** (*coll.*) a heavy fall. **5** (*coll.*) a collapse or failure. **to come a cropper 1** (*coll.*) to fall. **2** (*coll.*) to fail. **croppy** *n.* (*pl.* **croppies**) **1** a person with hair cropped short. **2** (*Hist.*) a Roundhead. **3** (*Hist.*) an Irish rebel of 1798. **crop rotation** *n.* the practice of growing different crops successively in a field or piece of ground, in order to vary the nutrients taken from the earth by the crops and so preserve its fertility. [OE, a bird's crop, a swelling, a head or bunch sticking out (cp. LG and Dut. *krop*, G *Kropf*, Welsh *cropa*)]

croquet (krō´kā) *n.* **1** an open-air game played on a lawn with balls and mallets. **2** the act of croqueting an opponent's ball. *~v.t.* to drive (an opponent's ball) away in this game by placing one's own ball against it and striking. *~v.i.* to play croquet. [ONF *croket*, var. of F CROCHET, dim. of *croche*, a hook]

croquette (krəket´) *n.* a savoury ball made with meat, potato etc. fried in breadcrumbs. [F, from *croquer*, to crunch]

crore (kraw) *n.* in the Indian subcontinent, ten millions, a hundred lakhs (of rupees, people etc.). [Hind. *kror*]

crosier (krō´zhə, -ziə), **crozier** *n.* **1** the hooked pastoral staff of a bishop or abbot. **2** an archbishop's staff, which bears a cross rather than a crook. **3** a shepherd's crook. [OF *crossier*, *crocier*, from *croce*, a bishop's staff, late L *crocia* (cp. OF *croc*, a crook, a hook); confused with F *crosier*, from *crois*, L *crux crucis*, CROSS]

croslet CROSSLET (under CROSS).

cross (kros) *n.* **1** an ancient instrument of execution made of two pieces of timber set transversely at various angles. **2** (**Cross**) the cross on which Jesus Christ was executed. **3** a representation of this, generally in the shape of a Latin cross, as an emblem of Christianity. **4** (**Cross**) the Christian religion. **5** a staff with a cross at the top. **6** the sign of the cross. **7** a monument usu. but not always in the shape of a Latin cross, set up in the centre of a town etc. **8** the place in a town or village where such a monument stands or has once stood, often a market place. **9** a sign or mark formed by two short lines crossing, a + or ×. **10** an emblem, ornament etc. in the shape of a Latin cross, Greek cross or any other cross. **11** the mixture of two distinct stocks in breeding animals or plants. **12** the animal or plant resulting from such a mixture. **13** a mixture. **14** a compromise. **15** anything that thwarts or obstructs. **16** trouble, affliction. **17** (*sl.*) a swindle, a preconcerted fraud. **18** in football, a pass across the field, esp. towards the opposing goal. **19** in boxing, a punch made with the fist coming from the side. **20** a movement across a stage. **21** (*Her.*) any of various changes in which one line meets or crosses another at right angles. *~a.* **1** peevish, angry. **2** transverse, oblique, lateral. **3** intersecting. **4** adverse, contrary, perverse. **5** (*sl.*) dishonest. **6** ill-gotten. *~v.t.* **1** to draw a line or lines across. **2** to erase by cross lines, to cancel. **3** to mark parallel lines on the face of (a cheque) in order to make it payable only through a bank. **4** to pass across, to traverse. **5** to place one across another. **6** to cause to intersect. **7** to pass over or in front of. **8** to meet and pass. **9** to cause to interbreed. **10** to cross-fertilize. **11** in football etc., to pass (the ball) etc. across the pitch. **12** to thwart, to counteract. **13** to be inconsistent with. **14** (*sl.*) to cheat. **15** to make the sign of the cross on or over. **16** to bestride. *~v.i.* **1** to lie or be across or over something. **2** to pass across something, to intersect. **3** (of letters between two correspondents) to be in the process of being delivered at the same time. **4** (of a telephone line) to be connected in error to more than one telephone. **5** to move in a zigzag. **6** to be inconsistent. **7** to interbreed. **8** in football etc., to pass the ball etc. across the pitch. **cross as two sticks** very peevish; in very bad humour. **on the cross 1** diagonally. **2** (*sl.*) unfairly, fraudulently. **to cross a bridge when one comes to it** BRIDGE[1]. **to cross one's fingers 1** to put one finger across an adjacent one as a sign of wishing for good luck. **2** to wish for or hope for good luck. **to cross one's heart** HEART. **to cross one's mind** to occur to one's memory or attention. **to cross someone's palm (with silver)** to give money to (e.g. a fortune-teller) as payment. **to cross swords** to have a fight or argument (with). **to cross the floor** FLOOR. **to cross the path of 1** to meet with. **2** to thwart. **to cross wires** to get one's wires crossed. **to get one's lines crossed** to get one's wires crossed. **to get one's wires crossed 1** to have a crossed line on a telephone. **2** to have a misunderstanding, to be at cross purposes. **to keep one's fingers crossed** to hope for good luck. **to take up the cross** to sacrifice self for some pious object. **cross-** *comb. form* 1 across. 2 having a part that lies across or transverse to another. 3 cross-shaped. 4 denoting two-way action or influence. **cross-action** *n.* (*Law*) a case in which the defendant in an action brings another action against the plaintiff on points arising out of the same transaction. **cross-banded** *a.* (of veneer) with its grain contrary to the general surface. **crossbar** *n.* 1 the horizontal bar of a football etc. goal. 2 the bar between the handlebar support and saddle support on a bicycle. 3 any transverse bar. **cross battery** *n.* either of two batteries commanding the same point from different directions. **crossbeam** *n.* a large beam running from wall to wall. **cross-bearer** *n.* a person who bears a processional cross, esp. before an archbishop. **cross-bedding** *n.* (*Geol.*) false bedding. **cross-bench** *n.* in parliament, one of the benches for those independent of the recognized parties. ~*a.* impartial. **cross-bencher** *n.* **crossbill** *n.* a bird of the genus *Loxia*, the mandibles of the bill of which cross each other when closed; esp. *L. curvirostra*, an irregular British visitor. **cross-bond** *n.* bricklaying in which points of one course fall in the middle of those above and below. **crossbones** *n.pl.* the representation of two thigh bones crossed as an emblem of mortality. **cross-border** *a.* occurring etc. across the border between two states. **crossbow** *n.* a weapon for shooting, formed by placing a bow across a stock. **crossbowman** *n.* (*pl.* **crossbowmen**). **cross-bred** *a.* of a cross-breed, hybrid. **cross-breed** *n.* 1 a breed produced from a male and female of different strains or varieties. 2 a hybrid. ~*v.t.* (*past, p.p.* **cross-bred**) 1 to produce a cross-breed. 2 to cross-fertilize. **cross bun** *n.* a hot cross bun. **cross-buttock** *n.* a wrestling throw over the hip. **cross-channel** *a.* travelling etc. across a channel, esp. the English Channel. **cross-check** *v.t.* to check (a fact etc.) by referring to other sources of information. ~*n.* such a check. **cross-country** *a., adv.* 1 across fields etc. instead of along the roads. 2 on minor rather than direct main roads. ~*n.* (*pl.* **cross-countries**) a cross-country race. **cross-cultural** *a.* concerning two or more different cultures, or the differences between them. **cross-current** *n.* 1 a sea etc. current flowing across another current. 2 a trend or tendency running counter to another. **cross-cut** *n.* 1 a shortcut, a path diagonally across something. 2 a cut across. 3 a step in dancing. 4 a figure in skating. 5 in mining, a drift from a shaft. ~*v.t.* to cut across. ~*a.* cut across the grain or main axis. **cross-cut saw** *n.* a large saw for cutting timber across the grain. **cross-dating** *n.* in archaeology, a method of dating one site, level etc., or objects found there, by comparison with other sites, levels etc. **cross-dresser** *n.* a transvestite. **cross-dress** *v.i.* **cross-dressing** *n.* **cross-entry** *n.* (*pl.* **cross-entries**) 1 in bookkeeping, an entry to another account. 2 a cancelling of a former entry. **cross-examine** *v.t.* to examine systematically for the purpose of eliciting facts not brought out in direct examination, or for confirming or contradicting the direct evidence. **cross-examination** *n.* **cross-examiner** *n.* **cross-eye** *n.* a squinting eye. **cross-eyed** *a.* with both eyes squinting inwards. **cross-fade** *v.t.* in TV or radio, to fade out (one signal) while introducing another. ~*n.* the act of doing this. **cross-fertilize, cross-fertilise** *v.t.* 1 (*Bot.*) to apply the pollen of one flower to the pistil of (a flower of the same species). 2 to fertilize (an animal) with genes usu. from an individual of another species. 3 to cause an interchange of ideas from different sources in. ~*v.i.* to undergo cross-fertilization. **cross-fertilization** *n.* **cross-fire** *n.* 1 firing in directions which cross each other. 2 a rapid or lively argument. 3 criticism coming from several sources at one time. **cross-grain** *n.* the grain or fibres of wood running across the regular grain. **cross-grained** *a.* 1 having the grain or fibres running across or irregularly. 2 perverse, peevish. 3 intractable. **cross-hairs** *n.pl.* two fine wires or lines that cross each other at right angles in an optical instrument, used for focusing etc. **cross-hatch** *v.t.* to shade with parallel lines crossing regularly in drawing or engraving. **cross-head** *n.* 1 the block at the head of a piston rod communicating motion to the connecting rod. 2 (*also* **cross-heading**) a heading printed across the page or a column. **cross-infection** *n.* infection of a hospital patient with an unrelated illness from another patient. **cross-infect** *v.t.* **cross-jack** (kroj´ək, kros´jak), **cross-jack yard** *n.* (*Naut.*) 1 the yard of a square-sail occasionally carried by a cutter in running before the wind. 2 the lower yard on the mizzen-mast. **cross-legged** (-legd, -leg´id) *a.* having one leg over the other. **cross-let, croslet** *n.* a small cross. **crossleted** *a.* **cross-light** *n.* 1 a light falling at an angle or crossing another. 2 a view of a subject under a different aspect. **cross-link, cross-linkage** *n.* (*Chem.*) a bond between adjacent chains of atoms in a large molecule (such as a polymer), or the atom or atoms forming the bond. **crossmatch** *v.t.* to test (e.g. blood samples from two people) for compatibility. **crossmatching** *n.* **crossness** *n.* **crossover** *n.* 1 the act of crossing over. 2 a place of crossing over. 3 a road which crosses over another. 4 a connecting point on two main railway lines. 5 (*Biol.*) crossing over. 6 a changing over from one style of music, genre of literature etc. to another. 7 (*N Am.*) the act of voting for a candidate in a political election who belongs to a party one does not usually support. ~*a.* 1 combining two distinct styles of music, genres of literature etc. 2 (of a musician etc.) having become successful in a style of music etc. other than the one they were first successful in. 3 involving or allowing a crossing over. 4 having parts that cross over each other. **crosspatch** *n.* (*coll.*) a cross, ill-tempered person. **crosspiece** *n.* 1 a transverse piece. 2 in shipbuilding, the flooring-piece resting on the keel. 3 a bar connecting the bitt heads on a ship. **cross-ply** *a.* (of motor-vehicle tyres) having the cords crossing each other diagonally to strengthen the tread. **cross-pollination** *n.* the transfer of pollen from one flower to the stigma of another. **cross-pollinate** *v.t.* **cross purpose** *n.* 1 a contrary purpose. 2 contradiction, inconsistency, misunderstanding. 3 (*pl.*) a game carried on by question and answer. **to be at cross purposes** to misunderstand or unintentionally act counter to each other. **cross-question** *v.t.* to cross-examine. ~*n.* a question put in cross-examination. **cross-refer** *v.t., v.i.* (*pres.p.* **cross-referring,** *past, p.p.* **cross-referred**) to refer from one place in a book etc. to another. **cross-reference** *n.* a reference from one place in a book etc. to another. ~*v.t.* to provide cross-references for. **cross-rhythm** *n.* (*Mus.*) 1 the use of two or more rhythms together. 2 a rhythm used along with another. **cross-road** *n.* 1 a road that crosses another or connects two others. 2 a by-way. **crossroads** *n.* a place where two roads cross. **at a/ the crossroads** at a point at which an important decision must be made or a new direction taken. **cross-ruff** *n.* in card-playing, the play in which partners trump different suits and lead accordingly. ~*v.i.* to play in this way. **cross-sea** *n.* waves setting in contrary directions. **cross-section** *n.* 1 a cutting across the grain or at right angles to the length. 2 the surface produced in this way, or a representation of it. 3 a representative sample. 4 (*Geol.*) a cutting which shows all the strata. 5 (*Physics*) a measure of the probability that a nuclear reaction will take place between subatomic particles, usu. expressed as the size of the target area one particle presents for the other. **cross-sectional** *a.* **cross-springer** *n.* (*Archit.*) a rib which extends from one pier to another in groined vaulting.

cross-staff *n.* **1** an archbishop's staff. **2** an instrument for taking altitudes and offsets in surveying. **cross stitch** *n.* **1** a kind of stitch crossing others in series. **2** needlework done in this way. **cross-stitch** *v.t.* to sew or embroider with cross stitches. **cross-stone** *n.* HARMOTOME. **cross-subsidize, cross-subsidise** *v.t.* to subsidize out of profits made elsewhere. **cross-subsidy** *n.* (*pl.* **cross-subsidies**). **crosstalk** *n.* **1** unwanted signals in a telephone, radio etc. channel, coming in from another channel. **2** repartee. **cross-tie** *n.* (*Archit.*) a transverse supporting or connecting tie. **crosstrees** *n.pl.* (*Naut.*) timbers on the tops of masts to support the rigging of the mast above. **cross-trump** *n.* CROSS-RUFF (under CROSS). **cross-vaulting** *n.* the intersecting of two or more simple vaults of arch-work. **cross-voting** *n.* (*N Am.*) voting for a party other than the one usually supported, or voting for more than one party. **cross-walk** *n.* (*N Am., Austral.*) a pedestrian crossing. **cross-way** *n.* a road that crosses another or connects two others. **crossways, crosswise** *adv.* **1** across. **2** in the form of a cross. **crosswind** *n.* **1** an unfavourable wind. **2** a sidewind. **crossword, crossword puzzle** *n.* a puzzle in which blank squares are filled with the letters of intersecting words corresponding to clues provided. **crossed** *a.* **crossed cheque** *n.* a cheque marked as negotiable only through a bank account. **crossed line** *n.* **1** a wrongly connected telephone line. **2** a misunderstanding. **crossing** *n.* **1** a place of crossing. **2** the intersection of two roads, railways etc. **3** a place where a road etc. may be crossed. **4** the place where the nave and transepts of a church intersect. **crossing over** *n.* (*Biol.*) the interchange of segments of homologous chromosomes during meiotic cell division. **crossing-sweeper** *n.* (*Hist.*) a person who swept a street crossing. **crossly** *adv.* in an ill-humoured manner. [OE *cros*, L *crux crucis*]

crosse (kros) *n.* the long, hooked, racket-like stick used in the game of lacrosse. [F, from OF *croce*, a crook or hook]

crostini (krostē´nē) *n.pl.* small pieces of toasted or fried bread covered with a topping. [It., pl. of *crostino*, a little crust]

crotch (kroch) *n.* **1** a forking. **2** the parting of two branches. **3** the angle between the thighs where the legs meet the body, or the corresponding part of e.g. a pair of trousers. **4** a hook or crook. **5** a small space in the corner of a billiard-table. **6** (*Naut.*) any of various appliances for spars, timbers etc. **crotched** *a.* **1** having a crotch. **2** forked. [etym. uncertain (cp. CRUTCH)]

crotchet (kroch´it) *n.* **1** (*Mus.*) a note, equal in length to one beat of a bar of 4/4 time. **2** a peculiar turn of mind. **3** a whimsical fancy, a conceit. **4** (*Print.*) a square bracket. **5** a hook. **crotcheteer** (-tiə´), **crotchet-monger** *n.* a person with peculiar fads and whimsies. **crotchety** *a.* **1** irritable. **2** having crotchets. **3** whimsical. **crotchetiness** *n.* [F *crochet*, dim. of *croc*, a hook]

croton (krō´tən) *n.* **1** a plant of the genus *Croton*, euphorbiaceous medicinal trees and shrubs from the warmer parts of both hemispheres. **2** any tree or shrub of the genus *Codiaeum*, of the same family as the genus *Croton*, esp. *C. variegatum*, a plant with brightly coloured leaves. **croton oil** *n.* a strong purgative oil expressed from *Croton tiglium*. [Gr. *krotōn*, a tick (from the shape of the seeds)]

crottle (krot´əl) *n.* any of several species of lichens used for dyeing. [Gael. *crotal*, a lichen]

crouch (krowch) *v.i.* **1** to stoop, to bend low. **2** to lie close to the ground. **3** to cringe, to fawn. ~*n.* the action of crouching. [etym. uncertain]

croup[1] (kroop) *n.* **1** the rump, the buttocks (esp. of a horse). **2** the part behind the saddle. [F *croupe* (cp. CROP)]

croup[2] (kroop) *n.* inflammation of the larynx and trachea, characterized by hoarse coughing and difficulty in breathing. **croupy** *a.* (*comp.* **croupier**, *superl.* **croupiest**). **croupiness** *n.* [imit.]

croupier (kroo´piā) *n.* **1** a person who superintends a gaming table and collects the money won by the bank. **2** a vice-chairman or -chairwoman at a public dinner. [F, orig. someone who rides on the CROUP[1]]

crouton (kroo´ton) *n.* a small cube of fried or toasted bread, served with soup or salads. [F, dim. of *croûte*, CRUST]

Crow (krō) *n.* (*pl.* **Crow, Crows**) **1** a member of an American Indian people living mostly in Montana. **2** the Siouan language of this people. [from their own name for themselves *apsáaloke*, crow people]

crow[1] (krō) *n.* **1** a large black bird of the genus *Corvus*, esp. the hooded crow, and the carrion crow *C. corione*. **2** any bird of the family Corvidae, including jays, magpies, jackdaws etc. **3** (*sl., derog.*) an objectionable, old or ugly woman. **4** a crowbar. **5** (*sl.*) a confederate who keeps watch while another steals. **as the crow flies** in a direct line. **stone the crows!** (*sl.*) used to express amazement. **to eat crow** (*coll.*) to (be made to) humiliate or abase oneself. **to have a crow to pluck with someone** to have some fault to find with or an explanation to demand from someone. **to pluck a crow** to contend for trifles. **to pull a crow** to pluck a crow. **crowbar** *n.* a bar of iron bent at one end (like a crow's beak) and used as a lever. **crowberry** *n.* (*pl.* **crowberries**) **1** a heathlike plant, *Empetrum nigrum*, with black berries. **2** (*N Am.*) the cranberry. **3** the berry of either of these plants. **crow-bill** *n.* a forceps for extracting bullets etc. from wounds. **croweater** *n.* (*Austral., coll.*) a person from or living in S Australia. **crow-flower** *n.* a crowfoot (buttercup). **crowfoot** *n.* **1** (*pl.* **crowfoots**) each of several species of buttercup, *Ranunculus bulbosus*, *R. acris* and *R. repens*. **2** (*Mil.*) (*pl.* **crowfeet**) a caltrop. **3** (*Naut.*) (*also* **crowfeet**) a contrivance for suspending the ridge of an awning. **crow's-foot** *n.* (*pl.* **crow's feet**) **1** a wrinkle at the corner of the eye. **2** (*Mil.*) a caltrop. **crow's-nest** *n.* a tub or box for the lookout on a ship's mast. **crow steps** *n.pl.* CORBIE-STEPS (under CORBIE). **crow-stepped** *a.* [OE *crāwe*, from *crawan* (see CROW[2])]

crow[2] (krō) *v.i.* (*past* **crew** (kroo), **crowed**) **1** to make a loud cry like a cock. **2** to make a cry of delight like an infant. **3** to exult. **4** to brag, to boast. ~*v.t.* to proclaim by crowing. ~*n.* **1** the cry of a cock. **2** the cry of delight of an infant. **crowingly** *adv.* [OE *crāwan* (cp. Dut. *kraaijen*, G *krähen*), imit.]

crowd[1] (krowd) *n.* **1** a number of persons or things collected closely and confusedly together. **2** the mass, the mob, the populace. **3** (*coll.*) a set, a party, a lot. **4** an audience. **5** a large number (of things). **6** any group of persons photographed in a film but not playing definite parts. ~*v.t.* **1** to cause to collect in crowds. **2** to press or squeeze closely together. **3** to fill by pressing. **4** to throng or press upon. **5** to press (into or through). **6** to come close to in an aggressive or threatening way. **7** (*coll.*) to pressurize (someone). ~*v.i.* **1** to press, to throng, to swarm. **2** to collect in crowds. **to crowd out 1** to force (a person or thing) out by leaving no room. **2** to fill to absolute capacity. **to crowd sail** (*Naut.*) to carry an extraordinary force or press of sail. **crowded** *a.* **crowdedness** *n.* **crowd of sail** *n.* (*Naut.*) a press of sail. **crowd-puller** *n.* an event that attracts a large audience. [OE *crūdan*]

crowd[2] (krowd) *n.* an old instrument somewhat like a violin, but with six strings (in early times three), four played with a bow and two with the thumb. ~*v.i.* to play a crowd or fiddle. **crowder** *n.* a person who plays a crowd, a fiddler. [Welsh *crwth*]

crowdy (krow´di), **crowdie** *n.* (*Sc.*) **1** meal and water (or milk) stirred together cold to form a thick gruel. **2** a kind of soft unripened cheese made from soured milk. [etym. unknown]

crown (krown) *n.* **1** the ornamental headdress or hat worn on the head by emperors, kings or princes as a badge of sovereignty. **2** an ornament of this shape. **3** (**Crown**) royal power. **4** (**Crown**) the sovereign. **5** a garland of honour worn on the head. **6** the culmination, glory. **7** a reward, distinction. **8** the top of anything, such as a hat, a mountain or a tree. **9** the head. **10** the top of the head. **11** the vertex of an arch. **12** the upper member of a cornice. **13** the highest part of a road, bridge or causeway. **14** the portion of a tooth above the gum. **15** an artificial crown for a broken or discoloured tooth. **16** the part of a plant just above and below the ground, where root and stem meet. **17** the upper part of a cut gemstone. **18** (*Naut.*) the part of an anchor where the arms join the shank. **19** (*Hist.*) a five-shilling piece. **20** a foreign coin of certain values. **21** a size of paper, 15 in. × 20 in. (381 × 508 mm) (formerly with a crown for a watermark). *~a.* (*usu.* **Crown**) belonging to the Crown or the sovereign. *~v.t.* **1** to invest with a crown, or regal or imperial dignity. **2** (*fig.*) to surround, or top, as if with a crown. **3** to form a crown, ornament or top to. **4** to dignify, to adorn. **5** to consummate. **6** to put a crown or cap on (a tooth). **7** (*coll.*) to hit on the head. **8** in draughts, to make (a piece) into a king. **9** to fill so as to brim over. **crown agent** *n.* **1** (*Sc. Law*) the solicitor who under the Lord Advocate takes charge of criminal prosecutions. **2** (**Crown Agent**) a member of a body appointed by the Overseas Development Administration to assist foreign governments and other organizations. **crown antler** *n.* the topmost antler of a stag's horn. **crown cap, crown cork** *n.* an airtight lined metal cap used to seal beer bottles etc. **Crown Colony** *n.* a colony administered by the British Government. **crown cork** CROWN CAP (under CROWN). **Crown Court** *n.* in England and Wales, a local criminal court. **Crown Derby** *n.* a type of porcelain made at Derby in the 18th cent., often marked with a crown. **crowned** *a.* **1** having a crown. **2** invested with a crown. **3** (of hats) having a crown of a given type, as in *high-crowned*, *low-crowned*. **crown glass** *n.* **1** the finest kind of window glass, made in circular sheets without lead or iron. **2** glass used in optical instruments, containing potassium and barium in place of sodium. **crown green** *n.* a type of bowling green which slopes slightly from the sides up to the centre. **crown imperial** *n.* a tall garden flower, *Fritillaria imperialis*, with a whorl of florets round the head. **crowning** *n.* in obstetrics, the stage of labour when the baby's head is passing through the vaginal opening. **crowning glory** *n.* something that is esp. distinctive or worthy of praise. **crown jewels** *n.pl.* the regalia and other jewels belonging to the sovereign. **Crown lands** *n.pl.* lands belonging to the Crown as the head of the government. **crownless** *a.* destitute or deprived of a crown. **Crown Office** *n.* **1** a section of the Court of King's (or Queen's) Bench which takes cognizance of criminal cases. **2** the office which now transacts the common law business of the Chancery. **crown of thorns** *n.* a starfish of the genus *Acanthaster*, which feeds on coral. **crown-post** *n.* a king post. **Crown prince** *n.* in some countries, the heir apparent to the Crown. **Crown princess** *n.* **1** the wife of a Crown prince. **2** in some countries, the female heir apparent to the Crown. **crown roast** *n.* roast ribs of lamb or pork formed into a circular crownlike arrangement. **crown saw** *n.* a type of cylindrical saw for cutting a circular hole. **crown-side** *n.* the Crown Office. **crown solicitor** *n.* the solicitor who prepares the cases when the Crown prosecutes. **crown wheel** *n.* in watch- and clock-making, a contrate wheel. **crown witness** *n.* a witness for the Crown in a criminal prosecution. **crownwork** *n.* in fortifications, an extension of the main work, consisting of a bastion between two curtains. [A-F *coroune*, OF *corone*, L *corōna*, a garland, a crown (cogn. with Gr. *korōnē*, the curved end of a bow)]

croze (krōz) *n.* **1** the groove in barrel staves near the end to receive the head. **2** a cooper's tool for making this. *~v.t.* to make this groove in. [perh. from F *creux*, OF *croz*, a hollow]

crozier CROSIER.

CRT *abbr.* **1** cathode ray tube. **2** composite rate tax.

cru (kroo, krü) *n.* **1** a French vineyard or group of vineyards producing wine of a particular quality. **2** a quality of wine. [F, from *crû*, grown (*croître*, to grow, from L *crescere*, to grow, increase)]

cruces CRUX.

crucial (kroo´shəl) *a.* **1** decisive. **2** searching. **3** (*Anat.*) in the form of a cross. **4** intersecting. **5** (*loosely*) very important. **6** (*sl.*) excellent. **cruciality** (-al´iti) *n.* (*pl.* **crucialities**). **crucially** *adv.* [F, from L *crux crucis*, a cross]

crucian (kroo´shən), **crucian carp** *n.* a small colourful fish, *Carassius carassius*, without barbels. [LG *karusse*, perh. from L *coracīnus*, Gr. *korakînos*, a type of fish]

cruciate (kroo´shiāt) *a.* (*Biol.*) cruciform. **cruciate ligament** *n.* either of a pair of ligaments in the knee which connect the femur and the tibia, and which cross each other. [med. L *cruciātus* (L *crux crucis*, a cross)]

crucible (kroo´sibəl) *n.* **1** a melting pot of earthenware, porcelain or refractory metal, adapted to withstand high temperatures without softening, and sudden and great alterations of temperature without cracking. **2** a basin at the bottom of a furnace to collect the molten metal. **3** a searching test or trial. [late L *crucibulum*, perh. from *crux crucis*, a cross]

crucifer (kroo´sifə) *n.* **1** a cross-bearer. **2** a plant belonging to the Cruciferae, a natural order of plants, the flowers of which have four petals disposed crosswise. **cruciferous** (-sif´-) *a.* **1** bearing a cross. **2** belonging to the Cruciferae. [L *crucifer* (*crux crucis*, a cross, *-fer*, a bearer)]

crucifier CRUCIFY.

crucifix (kroo´sifiks) *n.* (*pl.* **crucifixes**) a cross bearing a figure of Christ. **crucifixion** (-fik´shən) *n.* **1** the act of crucifying. **2** punishment by crucifying. **3** (**Crucifixion**) the death of Christ on the cross. **4** (**Crucifixion**) a picture of this. **5** torture. **6** mortification. [OF *crucefix*, L *cruci fixus*, fixed to a cross]

cruciform (kroo´sifawm) *a.* **1** cross-shaped. **2** arranged in the form of a cross. [L *crux crucis*, a cross, and -FORM]

crucify (kroo´sifī) *v.t.* (*3rd pers. sing. pres.* **crucifies,** *pres.p.* **crucifying,** *past, p.p.* **crucified**) **1** to inflict capital punishment on by affixing to a cross. **2** to torture. **3** to mortify, to destroy the influence of. **4** to subject to scathing criticism, obloquy or ridicule. **5** to defeat utterly. **crucifier** *n.* [OF *crucifier*, late L *crucifigere* (L *cruci figere*, to fix to a cross)]

cruck (krŭk) *n.* in old buildings, either of a pair of curved timbers which support the roof and extend to the ground. [CROOK]

crud (krŭd) *n.* (*sl.*) **1** any dirty, sticky or slimy substance. **2** a contemptible person. **3** rubbish, nonsense. **cruddy** *a.* (*comp.* **cruddier,** *superl.* **cruddiest**). [var. of CURD]

crude (krood) *a.* **1** raw, in a natural state, not cooked, not refined, not polished etc. **2** rude, vulgar. **3** offensively blunt. **4** coarse, rough, unfinished, hasty, approximate. **5** imperfectly developed, immature, inexperienced. **6** (of statistics) not classified or analysed. **7** not digested. *~n.* crude oil. **crudely** *adv.* **crudeness** *n.* **crude oil** *n.* unrefined petroleum. **crude turpentine** *n.* an oleoresin exuding naturally or from incisions in several coniferous trees, esp. the terebinth. **crudity** *n.* (*pl.* **crudities**). [L *crūdus*, raw]

crudités (kroodētā´) *n.pl.* raw vegetables served as an hors d'oeuvre, often with a dip or sauce. [F, raw things (L *crūdus*, raw)]

crudity CRUDE.

cruel (kroo´əl) *a.* (*comp.* **crueller,** (*N Am.*) **crueler,** *superl.* **cruellest,** (*N Am.*) **cruelest**) **1** disposed to give pain to others. **2** inhuman, unfeeling, hard-hearted. **3** causing pain, painful. ~*v.t.* (*Austral., sl.*) to thwart, spoil, frustrate. **cruel-hearted** *a.* delighting in cruelty. **cruelly** *adv.* **cruelness** *n.* **cruelty** *n.* (*pl.* **cruelties**) **1** cruel disposition or temper. **2** a barbarous or inhuman act. **3** repeated cruel acts or behaviour. **4** (*Law*) mental or physical hurt, whether caused intentionally or unintentionally, esp. as grounds for divorce. **cruelty-free** *a.* (of household, pharmaceutical, cosmetic etc. products) produced without cruelty to animals; not tested on animals. [F, from L *crūdēlis* (cogn. with *crūdus*, CRUDE)]

cruet (kroo´it) *n.* **1** a small container for pepper, salt etc. at table. **2** a cruet-stand. **3** a small bottle for holding the wine or water in the Eucharist. **cruet-stand** *n.* a frame or stand for holding cruets. [A-F, dim. of OF *crue, cruie*, prob. from OLG *crûca* (cp. OHG *kruog*), a pot]

cruise (krooz) *v.i.* **1** to sail to and fro, for pleasure or in search of plunder or an enemy. **2** (of a motor vehicle or aircraft) to travel at a moderate but sustained speed. **3** to travel (about) at a moderate speed with no fixed purpose. **4** (*sl.*) to search the streets or other public places for a sexual partner. **5** to win or succeed without difficulty. ~*v.t.* **1** to sail about or over, visiting various places. **2** (*sl.*) to search (the streets etc.) for a sexual partner. ~*n.* the act or an instance of cruising, esp. a pleasure trip on a boat. **cruise control** *n.* an electronic device which keeps a motor vehicle travelling at a predetermined speed without the use of the accelerator. **cruise missile** *n.* a low-flying subsonic guided missile. **cruiser** *n.* **1** a person or ship that cruises. **2** a warship designed primarily for speed, faster and lighter than a battleship. **3** (*N Am.*) a police patrol car. **cruiserweight** *n.* in boxing, (a) light heavyweight. **cruising speed** *n.* a comfortable and economical speed for a motor vehicle to travel at. [Dut. *kruisen*, to cross, from *kruis*, L *crux crucis*, a cross]

cruller (krŭl´ə) *n.* (*N Am.*) a light, sweet, often ring-shaped cake, deep-fried in fat. [Dut. *cruller*, from *crullen*, to curl]

crumb (krŭm) *n.* **1** a small piece, esp. of bread. **2** the soft inner part of bread. **3** a tiny portion, a particle. **4** (*sl.*) an unpleasant or contemptible person. ~*v.t.* **1** to break into crumbs. **2** to cover with crumbs (for cooking). ~*v.i.* to crumble. **crumb-brush** *n.* a curved brush for sweeping crumbs from the table. **crumb-cloth** *n.* a cloth laid over a carpet to catch the crumbs that fall from the table. **crumby** *a.* (*comp.* **crumbier,** *superl.* **crumbiest**) **1** covered with crumbs. **2** (*sl.*) crummy. [OE *crūma* (cp. Dut. *kruim*, G *Krume*)]

crumble (krŭm´bəl) *v.t.* to break into small particles. ~*v.i.* **1** to fall into small pieces. **2** to fall into ruin. ~*n.* **1** a pudding or other dish topped with a crumbly mixture of flour, sugar and butter, e.g. *apple crumble*. **2** the crumbly topping itself. **3** anything crumbly or crumbled. **crumbly** *a.* (*comp.* **crumblier,** *superl.* **crumbliest**) apt to crumble. ~*n.* (*pl.* **crumblies**) (*coll.*) a very old person. **crumbliness** *n.* [see CRUMB]

crumbs (krŭmz) *int.* (*coll.*) used to express surprise or dismay. [euphem. for CHRIST]

crumhorn KRUMMHORN.

crummy (krŭm´i) *a.* (*comp.* **crummier,** *superl.* **crummiest**) (*sl.*) **1** unpleasant, worthless. **2** unwell. **crummily** *adv.* **crumminess** *n.*

crump (krŭmp) *n.* the sound of the explosion of a heavy shell or bomb. ~*v.i.* to make such a sound. [onomat.]

crumpet (krŭm´pit) *n.* **1** a thin, light, spongy teacake, often eaten toasted. **2** in Scotland, a type of large thin pancake. **3** (*sl., offensive*) women as objects of sexual desire. **4** (*sl., offensive*) an attractive woman, as an object of sexual desire. **5** (*sl., dated*) the head. **bit of crumpet** BIT[1]. [etym. uncertain]

crumple (krŭm´pəl) *v.t.* **1** to crush. **2** to draw or press into wrinkles. ~*v.i.* **1** (of cloth, paper etc.) to become wrinkled, to shrink. **2** to collapse, give way. ~*n.* a wrinkle or crease. **crumpled** *a.* **crumple zone** *n.* a part of a motor vehicle, generally at the front or back, that is designed to crumple easily and thereby absorb the shock of impact in the event of a crash. **crumpling** *n.* **crumply** *a.* (*comp.* **crumplier,** *superl.* **crumpliest**). [from obs. *crump*, to bend or curl up]

crunch (krŭnch) *v.t.* **1** to crush noisily with the teeth. **2** to grind with the foot. ~*v.i.* **1** to make a noise like crunching. **2** to advance with crunching. ~*n.* **1** a noise of or like crunching. **2** (*coll.*) the decisive or testing moment, crisis, difficulty etc. **when it comes to the crunch** (*coll.*) at the decisive or critical moment. **crunchy** *a.* (*comp.* **crunchier,** *superl.* **crunchiest**). **crunchiness** *n.* [imit.]

cruor (kroo´aw) *n.* (*Med.*) coagulated blood. [L, blood, gore]

crupper (krŭp´ə) *n.* **1** a strap with a loop which passes under a horse's tail to keep the saddle from slipping forward. **2** the croup or hindquarters of a horse. ~*v.t.* to put a crupper on. [OF *cropiere* (see CROUP[1])]

crural (kroo´rəl) *a.* **1** belonging to the leg. **2** shaped like a human leg. [L *crūrālis* (*crūs crūris*, the leg)]

crusade (kroosād´) *n.* **1** any of several expeditions undertaken by Christians in the Middle Ages to recover possession of the Holy Land, then in Muslim hands, or any similar expedition or war undertaken at the instigation of the Church, e.g. against heretics. **2** any campaign conducted in an enthusiastic or fanatical spirit. ~*v.i.* to engage in a crusade. **crusader** *n.* [F *croisade* (OF *croisée* and Sp. *cruzada*, med. L *cruciāta*, p.p. of *cruciāre*, to mark with a CROSS)]

†**cruse** (krooz) *n.* a small pot, cup or bottle. [cp. Icel. *krūs*, Dut. *kroes*, G *Krause*]

crush (krŭsh) *v.t.* **1** to press or squeeze together between two harder bodies so as to break, bruise or reduce to powder. **2** to crumple. **3** to overwhelm by superior power. **4** to oppress, to ruin. **5** to dismay or subdue. ~*v.i.* **1** to be pressed into a smaller compass by external force or weight. **2** to make one's way by crushing. ~*n.* **1** the act of crushing. **2** a crowd. **3** (*coll.*) a crowded meeting or social gathering. **4** (*Austral.*) the funnel of a stockyard where the cattle are got in hand. **5** (*coll.*) an infatuation or the object of this. **6** a drink made by or as if by crushing fruit. **to crush out** to extinguish. **crushable** *a.* **crush bar** *n.* a bar in a theatre which patrons may use in the intervals of a play. **crush barrier** *n.* a temporary barrier to keep back, or to separate, a crowd. **crusher** *n.* a person who or something which crushes. **crush hat** *n.* a soft hat collapsing with a spring, so that it can be carried under the arm without damage, an opera hat. **crushing** *a., n.* **crushingly** *adv.* [OF *cruisir, croissir*, from Gmc. (cp. Dan. *kryste*, Swed. *krossa*)]

crust (krŭst) *n.* **1** the hard outer part of bread. **2** a piece of crust with some bread attached. **3** the crusty end of a loaf. **4** a hard piece of bread. **5** any hard rind, coating, layer, deposit or surface covering. **6** the pastry covering a pie. **7** a scab or hard patch on the skin. **8** (*Geol.*) the solid outer portion of the earth. **9** a film deposited on the inside of a bottle of wine. **10** a (meagre) living. **11** (*sl.*) impertinence. **12** hardness of manner. ~*v.t.* **1** to cover with a crust. **2** to make into crust. ~*v.i.* to become encrusted. **crustal** *a.* of or relating to the earth's crust. **crustation** (-tā´shən) *n.* an incrustation. **crusted** *a.* **1** having a crust. **2** antiquated, hoary, venerable. **3**

denoting port or other wine that has deposited a crust in the bottle. **crustose** *a.* (*Bot.*) forming or like a crust. **crusty** *a.* (*comp.* **crustier**, *superl.* **crustiest**) **1** resembling or of the nature of crust. **2** having a crust. **3** harsh, peevish, morose. **crustily** *adv.* **crustiness** *n.* [OF *crouste*, L *crusta*]

crustacean (krŭstā´shən) *n.* any animal of the class or subphylum Crustacea, including lobsters, crabs, shrimps, woodlice etc., named from their hard shells. *~a.* of or relating to crustaceans. **crustaceology** (-shiol´-) *n.* the branch of science dealing with crustaceans. **crustaceologist** *n.* **crustaceous** *a.* **1** of the nature of shell. **2** crustacean. [mod. L, neut. pl. of *crustāceus*, a. (L *crusta*, crust, shell)]

crutch (krŭch) *n.* **1** a staff, with a crosspiece to fit under the armpit, to support a lame or injured person. **2** a support. **3** (*Naut.*) any of various appliances for spars, timbers etc. **4** the crotch of a person. **5** the corresponding part of a garment. *~v.t.* to support on or as if on crutches. *~v.i.* to go on crutches. [OE *cryce*, from Gmc. *kruk-* (cp. Dut. *kruk*, Dan. *krukke*, G *Krücke*)]

crutched (krŭcht) *a.* wearing a cross as a badge. **Crutched Friars** (krŭch´id) *n.pl.* a minor order of friars who wore a cross as their badge. [ME *crouch*, to CROSS]

crux (krŭks) *n.* (*pl.* **cruxes, cruces** (kroo´sēz)) **1** the real essential. **2** anything exceedingly puzzling. [L, CROSS]

cruzado (kroozah´dō) *n.* (*pl.* **cruzados**) a former coin and monetary unit of Brazil, replaced by the cruzeiro. [Port., from *cruz*, cross]

cruzeiro (kroozeə´rō) *n.* (*pl.* **cruzeiros**) a coin and monetary unit of Brazil, equal to 100 centavos. [Port., from *cruz*, CROSS]

crwth (krooth) *n.* CROWD[2]. [Welsh]

cry (krī) *v.i.* (*3rd pers. sing. pres.* **cries**, *pres.p.* **crying**, *past, p.p.* **cried**) **1** to weep. **2** to lament loudly. **3** to utter inarticulate sounds when weeping. **4** to make a loud exclamation, esp. because of pain or grief. **5** to call loudly, vehemently or importunately, e.g. for help. **6** to exclaim. **7** (of animals and birds) to call, to make their natural sound. **8** to make a proclamation. *~v.t.* **1** to utter loudly. **2** to proclaim, to declare publicly. **3** to announce for sale. **4** to shed (tears). **5** †to demand. *~n.* (*pl.* **cries**) **1** a loud utterance, usu. inarticulate, expressive of intense joy, pain, suffering, astonishment or other emotion. **2** an importunate call or prayer. **3** proclamation, public notification. **4** a catchword or phrase. **5** a bitter complaint of injustice or oppression. **6** weeping. **7** lamentation. **8** inarticulate noise. **9** (of hounds) yelping. **10** in hunting, a pack of hounds. **11** a pack of people, a company. **a far cry 1** a long way off (from). **2** something very different (from). **for crying out loud** (*coll.*) used to express impatience or annoyance. **in full cry** in hot pursuit. **to cry against** to exclaim loudly by way of threatening or censure. **to cry down 1** to decry, to depreciate. **2** to shout down. **to cry for the moon** to ask for something one cannot have. **to cry halves** to demand a share of something. **†to cry havoc** HAVOC. **to cry in church** to publish the banns of marriage. **†to cry mercy** to beg pardon. **to cry off** to withdraw from something promised or agreed on. **to cry one's eyes out** to weep abundantly and bitterly. **to cry one's heart out** to cry one's eyes out. **to cry out** to shout, to clamour. **to cry out against** to exclaim loudly by way of censure or reproach. **to cry out for** to require or demand. **to cry over spilt milk** to waste time regretting something that cannot be undone. **to cry quits** QUIT. **to cry shame on** to protest against. **to cry stinking fish** to decry or condemn, esp. one's own wares. **to cry up** to extol, to praise highly. **to cry wolf** WOLF. **cry-baby** *n.* (*pl.* **cry-babies**) (*coll.*) a child or person easily provoked to tears. **cryer** CRIER. **cry from the heart** *n.* an ardent and impassioned appeal. **crying** *a.* **1** that cries. **2** calling for notice or vengeance, flagrant. [F *crier*, L *quīrītāre*, lit. to cry for the help of the *Quīrītes*, or Roman citizens]

cryo- (krī´ō) *comb. form* very cold. [Gr. *kruos*, frost]

cryobiology (krīobīol´əji) *n.* the study of the effects of cold on organisms. **cryobiological** (-loj´-) *a.* **cryobiologist** *n.*

cryogen (krī´əjen) *n.* (*Physics*) a freezing-mixture, a mixture of substances used to freeze liquids. **cryogenics** (-jen´-) *n.* the branch of physics which studies very low temperatures and the phenomena associated with them. **cryogenic** *a.*

cryolite (krī´əlīt) *n.* a brittle fluoride of sodium and aluminium from Greenland.

cryometer (krīom´itə) *n.* a thermometer for measuring low temperatures.

cryonics (krīon´iks) *n.* the practice of preserving a dead body by deep-freezing it, in order to keep it until the discovery of a cure for the condition which caused the death. **cryonic** *a.* **cryonic suspension** *n.* cryonics.

cryophilic (krīəfil´ik) *a.* (*Biol.*) able to live or grow at low temperatures.

cryophysics (krīōfiz´iks) *n.* low-temperature physics.

cryoprecipitate (krīōprisip´itāt) *n.* a precipitate obtained from a substance which has been frozen and then thawed under controlled conditions.

cryopreservation (krīōprezəvā´shən) *n.* **1** preservation of human sperm etc. by freezing. **2** cryonics.

cryoprotectant (krīōprətek´tənt) *n.* (*Biol.*) a substance that stops tissues freezing or prevents damage by freezing.

cryopump (krī´əpŭmp) *n.* a vacuum pump which uses liquefied gases.

cryostat (krī´əstat) *n.* an apparatus for maintaining, or for keeping something at, a low temperature.

cryosurgery (krīōsœ´jəri) *n.* surgery involving the application of very low temperatures to specific tissues in order to cut or remove them. **cryosurgeon** *n.* a surgeon specializing in cryosurgery.

cryotherapy (krīōther´əpi) *n.* medical treatment involving the use of extreme cold.

crypt (kript) *n.* **1** a vault, esp. one beneath a church, used for religious services or for burial. **2** (*Anat.*) a small pit, cavity or depression, or a pitlike gland. [L *crypta*, Gr. *kruptē*, fem. of *kruptos*, CRYPTO-]

crypt- CRYPTO-.

cryptanalysis (kriptənal´əsis) *n.* the art of deciphering codes and coded texts. **cryptanalyst** (-an´-) *n.* **cryptoanalytic** (-lit´-), **cryptoanalytical** *a.* **cryptanalytic** (-lit´-), **cryptanalytical** *a.*

cryptic (krip´tik) *a.* **1** hidden, secret, occult. **2** hard to understand. **3** (of a crossword clue) so written that the solution is far from obvious. **4** (of a crossword) having cryptic clues. **5** (of animal coloration) serving as camouflage. **cryptically** *adv.* [late L *crypticus*, from Gr. *kruptikos*, from *kruptos*, CRYPTO-]

crypto (krip´tō) *n.* (*pl.* **cryptos**) a secret member or supporter of some organization etc. [CRYPTO-]

crypto- (krip´tō), **crypt-** *comb. form* **1** secret. **2** inconspicuous. **3** not apparent or prominent. [Gr. *kruptos*, hidden (*kruptein*, to hide)]

cryptocrystalline (kriptōkris´təlīn) *a.* (*Mineral.*) having a crystalline structure which is visible only under the microscope.

cryptogam (krip´tōgam) *n.* (*Bot.*) a plant without pistils and stamens; any seedless plant such as a fern, lichen, moss, seaweed or fungus. **cryptogamic** (-gam´-), **cryptogamous** (-tog´ə-) *a.* **cryptogamist** (-tog´ə-) *n.* **cryptogamy** *n.* concealed or obscure fructification. [F *cryptogame* (Gr. *kruptos*, hidden, *gamos*, marriage)]

cryptogram (krip´təgram) *n.* **1** a text in code. **2** cipher-writing. **cryptograph** (-grahf) *n.* **1** a system of writing in cipher. **2** secret writing. **cryptographer** (-tog´-),

cryptographist *n.* **cryptographic** (-graf´-) *a.* **cryptographically** *adv.* **cryptography** (-tog´-) *n.*

cryptology (kriptol´əji) *n.* **1** the study of codes. **2** the making and breaking of codes, cryptography and cryptanalysis together. **cryptological** (-loj´-) *a.* **cryptologically** *adv.* **cryptologist** (-tol´-) *n.*

cryptomeria (kriptəmiə´riə) *n.* a coniferous evergreen tree, *Cryptomeria japonica*, from the Far East, with many cultivated varieties. [Gr. *meros*, part (because the seeds are hidden by scales)]

cryptonym (krip´tənim) *n.* **1** a secret name. **2** the name a person bears in a secret society or brotherhood. [Gr. *onuma*, a name]

crystal (kris´təl) *n.* **1** a clear transparent mineral, transparent quartz, also called *rock crystal*. **2** a piece of this. **3** an aggregation of atoms or molecules arranged in a definite pattern which often assumes the form of a regular solid terminated by a certain number of smooth plane surfaces. **4** any solid with symmetrically-organized constituent particles. **5** a very clear kind of glass. **6** articles made of crystal. **7** anything clear as crystal. **8** the clear covering over the face of a watch. **9** a crystalline component in various electronic devices, used as an oscillator etc. *~a.* **1** clear, transparent, as bright as crystal. **2** made of crystal. **crystal ball** *n.* a ball made of glass, used in crystal-gazing. **crystal class** *n.* in crystallography, any of the 32 different forms of crystal, classified according to their rotational symmetry about axes passing through a point. **crystal clear** *a.* absolutely clear. **crystal detector** *n.* a crystal arranged in a circuit so that the modulation on a radio carrier wave becomes audible in earphones etc. **crystal-gazing** *n.* looking into a crystal ball in order to foresee the future. **crystal glass** *n.* a very clear kind of glass. **crystal healing** *n.* the use of pieces of certain crystalline minerals which are supposed to promote healing and increase well-being. **crystal lattice** *n.* in crystallography, the network of points, forming a regular repeating pattern, on which the atoms, ions or molecules of a crystal are centred. **crystalline** (-līn) *a.* **1** consisting of crystal. **2** resembling crystal. **3** clear, pellucid. **4** having the form and structure of a crystal. **crystalline lens** *n.* a lenticular, white, transparent solid body enclosed in a capsule behind the iris of the eye, the lens of the eye. **crystallinity** (-lin´-) *n.* **crystallite** (-līt) *n.* **1** any one of the particles of definite form observed in thin sections of igneous rock cooled slowly after fusion. **2** a rock consisting of such particles. **3** any small developing crystal. **4** a small crystal or particle in a metal etc. **5** (*Bot.*) a crystal-like section of cellulose etc. **crystallize, crystallise** *v.t.* **1** to cause to form crystals. **2** to coat (fruit) with sugar crystals. **3** to cause (thoughts, plans etc.) to assume a definite form. *~v.i.* **1** to assume a crystalline form. **2** to form crystals. **3** to become coated with sugar. **4** (of thoughts, plans etc.) to assume a definite form. **to crystallize out** (to cause) to assume a definite form. **crystallizable** *a.* **crystallization** (-zā´shən) *n.* **crystal set** *n.* an early form of radio receiver using a crystal detector. **crystal system** *n.* in crystallography, any of the seven different categories crystals can be grouped into on the basis of how they rotate on axes. [OF *cristal*, L *crystallum*, Gr. *krustallos*, ice, rock-crystal, from *krustainein*, to freeze (*kruos*, frost)]

crystallo- (kris´təlō) *comb. form* forming, formed of, of or relating to crystal, crystalline structure or the science of crystals. [Gr. *krustallos*, CRYSTAL]

crystallogeny (kristəloj´əni) *n.* the branch of science which studies the formation of crystals. **crystallogenic** (-jen´-) *a.*

crystallographer (kristəlog´rəfə) *n.* a person who describes or investigates crystals and their formation. **crystallographic** (-graf´-) *a.* **crystallographically** *adv.*

crystallography *n.* the science which deals with the forms of crystals.

crystalloid (kris´təloid) *a.* like a crystal in appearance or structure. *~n.* **1** a body with a crystalline structure. **2** a substance that can be crystallized. **3** a substance that in solution can pass through a semi-permeable membrane. **4** (*Bot.*) a minute crystal-like particle of protein.

crystallomancy (kris´tələmansi) *n.* divination by means of a crystal or other transparent body.

crystallometry (kristəlom´ətri) *n.* the art or process of measuring the forms of crystals.

CS *abbr.* **1** chartered surveyor. **2** Christian Science. **3** civil service. **4** Court of Session. **5** Czech Republic or (formerly) Czechoslovakia (IVR).

Cs *chem. symbol* caesium.

c/s *abbr.* cycles per second.

csardas (chah´dash), **czardas** *n.* (*pl.* **csardas, czardas**) a Hungarian national dance, moving from a slow to a quick tempo. [Hung.]

CSC *abbr.* **1** Civil Service Commission. **2** Conspicuous Service Cross.

CSCE *abbr.* Conference for Security and Cooperation in Europe.

CSE *abbr.* Certificate of Secondary Education.

CSEU *abbr.* Confederation of Shipbuilding and Engineering Unions.

CSF *abbr.* cerebrospinal fluid.

CS gas (sēes´) *n.* an irritant gas, causing tears, painful breathing etc., used in riot control. [from the initials of its US inventors Ben *C*orson and Roger *S*taughton]

CSI *abbr.* Companion of (the Order of) the Star of India.

CSIRO *abbr.* Commonwealth Scientific and Industrial Research Organization.

CSM *abbr.* **1** Company Sergeant-Major. **2** Committee on Safety of Medicines.

CSO *abbr.* **1** Central Statistical Office. **2** community service order.

CST *abbr.* Central Standard Time.

CSV *abbr.* community service volunteer.

CSYS *abbr.* Certificate of Sixth Year Studies.

CT *abbr.* **1** Central Time. **2** Connecticut.

Ct *abbr.* **1** Connecticut. **2** Court.

ct *abbr.* **1** carat. **2** cent. **3** court.

ct. *abbr.* certificate.

CTC *abbr.* **1** city technology college. **2** Cyclists' Touring Club.

ctenoid (tē´noid, ten´-) *a.* **1** comb-shaped. **2** having projections like the teeth of a comb. **3** having ctenoid scales. *~n.* a ctenoid fish. **ctenoid scales** *n.pl.* (*Zool.*) scales with projections like the teeth of a comb on the lower edge. [Gr. *ktenoeides* (*kteis ktenos*, a comb)]

ctenophore (ten´əfaw, tē-) *n.* (*Zool.*) a member of the Ctenophora, coelenterates with fringed or comblike locomotive organs. **ctenophoral** (-nof´-) *a.* **ctenophoran** (-nof´-) *n.* a ctenophore. *~a.* of or relating to the Ctenophora. [Gr. *kteis ktenos*, a comb, *-phoros*, bearing, a bearer]

CTO *abbr.* in philately, cancelled to order.

CTOL *abbr.* conventional take-off and landing.

CTR *abbr.* control traffic zone.

CT scanner (sētē´) *n.* a machine which produces X-ray photographs of sections of the body with the assistance of a computer. **CT scan** *n.* [computerized axial tomography]

CTT *abbr.* capital transfer tax.

CTV *abbr.* continuous variable transmission.

CU *abbr.* **1** Cambridge University. **2** control unit.

Cu *chem. symbol* copper. [L *cuprum*]

cu. *abbr.* cubic.

cub (kŭb) *n.* **1** the young of certain animals, e.g. the lion, bear or fox. **2** an uncouth, mannerless youth. **3** (*also* **Cub Scout**) a member of the junior section of the Scout Association. **4** a cub reporter. **5** (*N Am.*) an apprentice.

6 a novice. ~*v.i.* (*pres.p.* **cubbing,** *past, p.p.* **cubbed**) 1 to give birth to cubs. 2 to hunt young foxes. ~*v.t.* to give birth to (cubs). **cubbing** *n.* **cubbish** *a.* **cubhood** *n.* **cub-hunting** *n.* **cub reporter** *n.* an inexperienced newspaper reporter. [etym. uncertain]

cub. *abbr.* cubic.

cubage (kū´bij), **cubature** (-bəchə) *n.* the process of finding the solid contents of any body. [CUBE]

Cuban (kū´bən) *a.* of or relating to Cuba, an island and republic in the Caribbean Sea, or its people. ~*n.* a native or inhabitant of Cuba. **Cuban heel** *n.* a straight-fronted moderately high heel on a boot or shoe.

cubby (kŭb´i) *n.* (*pl.* **cubbies**) a cubby hole. **cubby hole** *n.* 1 a narrow or confined space. 2 a cosy place. [cp. obs. *cub,* a stall or pen, LG *kübbung, kübje,* a shed]

cube (kūb) *n.* 1 a solid figure contained by six equal squares, a regular hexahedron. 2 a cube-shaped block or piece. 3 (*Math.*) the third power of a number (as 8 is the cube of 2). ~*v.t.* 1 to raise to the third power, to find the cube of (a number). 2 to find the cubic content of (a solid figure). 3 to cut into cubes. **cube estimate** *n.* a builder's or architect's estimate based on the cubic dimensions of a building. **cube root** *n.* 1 the number which, multiplied by itself, and then by the product, produces the cube; thus 3 is the cube root of 27, which is the cube of 3 (3 × 3 × 3 = 27). 2 the rule for the extraction of the cube root. **cube sugar** *n.* lump sugar. **cubic** *a.* 1 (*also* **cubical**) having the properties or form of a cube. 2 being or equalling a cube, the edge of which is a given unit. 3 (*also* **cubical**) three-dimensional. 4 (*Math.*) involving the cube of one or more numbers, but no higher power. 5 (*also* **cubical**) in crystallography, having three equal axes at right angles to each other. **cubical** *a.* **cubically** *adv.* **cubic content** *n.* volume in cubic metres. **cubiform** (-ifawm) *a.* cube-shaped. **cubism** *n.* an early 20th-cent. school of painting which depicted surfaces, figures, tints, light and shade etc. by a multiplicity of representations of cubes. **cubist** *n., a.* **cuboid** *a.* resembling a cube. ~*n.* 1 (*Geom.*) a solid like a cube but with the sides not all equal, a rectangular parallelepiped. 2 (*Anat.*) the cuboid bone. **cuboidal** *a.* **cuboid bone** *n.* a bone on the outer side of the foot. [F, from late L *cubum,* acc. of *cubus,* Gr. *kubos*]

cubeb (kū´beb) *n.* the small spicy berry of *Piper cubeba,* a Javanese shrub used in medicine, cookery and medicated cigarettes. [F *cubèbe* (Sp. and It. *cubeba*), Arab. *kabābah*]

cubic, cubical etc. CUBE.

cubicle (kū´bikəl) *n.* 1 a portion of a bedroom partitioned off as a separate sleeping apartment. 2 a compartment. [L *cubiculum* (*cubāre,* to lie)]

cubiform, cubism etc. CUBE.

cubit (kū´bit) *n.* an old measure of length, from the elbow to the tip of the middle finger, but varying in practice at different times from 18 to 22 in. (0.46 to 0.5 m). **cubital** *a.* (*Anat., Zool.*) of or relating to the forearm or corresponding part of the leg in animals. [L *cubitus,* a hand, an elbow]

cuboid CUBE.

cucking-stool (kŭk´ingstool) *n.* (*Hist.*) a kind of chair, formerly used for ducking disorderly women, dishonest tradesmen etc. [prob. from obs. *cuck,* to void excrement (cp. Icel. *kúka*)]

cuckold (kŭk´əld) *n.* a man whose wife is sexually unfaithful. ~*v.t.* to make (a man) a cuckold by having a sexual relationship with his wife. **cuckoldry** *n.* [OF *cucualt,* from *cucu,* CUCKOO (cp. F. *coucou,* cuckoo, *cocu,* cuckold)]

cuckoo (kuk´oo) *n.* (*pl.* **cuckoos**) 1 a migratory bird of the family Cuculidae, esp. *Cuculus canorus,* which visits Britain in the spring and summer and lays its eggs in the nests of other birds. 2 (*coll.*) a foolish person. ~*a.* (*sl.*) crazy. **cuckoo bee, cuckoo wasp** *n.* a bee or wasp, the queen of which lays its eggs in the nests of other species. **cuckoo clock** *n.* a clock which announces the hours by emitting a sound like the note of the cuckoo. **cuckoo flower** *n.* any of various plants, esp. lady's smock, *Cardamine pratensis,* or ragged robin, *Lychnis floscuculi.* **cuckoo in the nest** *n.* an unwanted and alien person, an intruder. **cuckoo pint** *n.* the wild arum, *Arum maculatum,* lords and ladies. **cuckoo spit** *n.* an exudation on plants from the larvae of the froghopper. [F *coucou,* imit. (cp. L *cuculus,* Gr. *kokkuks*)]

cucullate (kū´kəlāt) *a.* (*Zool., Bot.*) hooded, resembling a hood. [late L *cucullātus,* p.p. of *cucullāre* (L *cucullus,* a hood)]

cucumber (kū´kŭmbə) *n.* 1 the elongated fruit *Cucumis sativus,* extensively used as a salad and pickle. 2 the plant itself. **cool as a cucumber** very unemotional, imperturbable. **cucumber tree** *n.* any of several American magnolias with fruit like small cucumbers. [orig. *cucumer,* L *cucumis -merem* (later influenced by F *cocombre,* now *concombre*)]

cucurbit (kūkœ´bit) *n.* 1 a gourd. 2 a gourd-shaped vessel used in distillation. **cucurbitaceous** (-ā´shəs) *a.* [F *cucurbite,* L *cucurbita*]

cud (kŭd) *n.* food deposited by ruminating animals in the first stomach, from which it is drawn and chewed over again. **to chew the cud** 1 to ruminate. 2 to reflect. [OE *cudu, cwidu* (cp. Icel. *kwatha,* resin, OHG *chuti, quiti,* glue)]

cudbear (kŭd´beə) *n.* a crimson dye obtained from *Roccella tinctoria* and other lichens. [named by the inventor, Dr *Cuthbert* Gordon, 18th-cent. British chemist]

cuddle (kŭd´əl) *v.i.* 1 to lie close or snug together. 2 to join in an embrace. ~*v.t.* to embrace, to hug, to fondle. ~*n.* a hug, an embrace. **cuddlesome** *a.* **cuddly** *a.* (*comp.* **cuddlier,** *superl.* **cuddliest**) 1 attractive to cuddle. 2 given to cuddling. [etym. uncertain]

cuddy[1] (kŭd´i) *n.* (*pl.* **cuddies**) 1 (*chiefly Sc.*) a donkey, an ass. 2 a fool, a lout. 3 a young coalfish. [etym. uncertain (perh. an abbreviation of *Cuthbert*)]

cuddy[2] (kŭd´i) *n.* (*pl.* **cuddies**) 1 a cabin in a ship where officers and passengers take their meals. 2 a small cabin in a boat. 3 a closet or cupboard. [etym. uncertain]

cudgel (kŭj´əl) *n.* a short club or thick stick, a bludgeon. ~*v.t.* (*pres.p.* **cudgelling,** (*N Am.*) **cudgeling,** *past, p.p.* **cudgelled,** (*N Am.*) **cudgeled**) to beat with a cudgel. **to cudgel one's brains** to try hard to recollect or find out something. **to take up (the) cudgels (for)** 1 to fight (for). 2 to defend vigorously. **cudgel-play** *n.* fighting with cudgels. **cudgel-proof** *a.* able to resist a blow with a cudgel. [OE *cycgel;* etym. uncertain]

cudweed (kŭd´wēd) *n.* 1 any plant of the genus *Gnaphalium,* esp. *G. sylvaticum,* a plant formerly administered to cattle that had lost their cud. 2 any plant of the genus *Filago,* esp. *F. germanica.*

cue[1] (kū) *n.* 1 the last words of a speech, a signal to another actor that they should begin. 2 any similar signal, e.g. in a piece of music. 3 a hint, reminder. 4 a facility for cueing audio equipment. ~*v.t.* (*3rd pers. sing. pres.* **cues,** *pres.p.* **cueing, cuing,** *past, p.p.* **cued**) 1 to give a cue to. 2 to make (audio equipment) precisely ready to play something. **on cue** at the right time. **to cue in** 1 to give a cue to. 2 to inform. **to take one's cue from** to follow the example of or take advice from. **cue-bid** *n.* in bridge, a bid designed to reveal the presence of a particular card in the bidder's hand. [etym. uncertain]

cue[2] (kū) *n.* a long straight rod used by players of snooker, pool etc. ~*v.t., v.i.* (*3rd pers. sing. pres.* **cues,** *pres.p.* **cuing, cueing,** *past, p.p.* **cued**) to strike (a ball) with a cue. **cue ball** *n.* the ball which is struck with a cue. **cueist** *n.* [OF *cue* (F *queue*), L *cauda*, a tail]

cuesta (kwes´tə) *n.* a hill ridge with a gentle slope ending in a steep scarp slope. [Sp., slope]

cuff[1] (kŭf) *n.* **1** the fold or band at the end of a sleeve. **2** a linen band worn round the wrist. **3** (*pl., coll.*) handcuffs. **4** (*N Am.*) a trouser turn-up. **off the cuff** extempore, without preparation. **cuffed** *a.* **cuff link** *n.* a usu. ornamental device consisting of a button-like disc attached to a short bar with a pivoting endpiece or a pair of buttons linked by a short chain, used to fasten a shirt cuff. [etym. uncertain]

cuff[2] (kŭf) *v.t.* to strike with the open hand. ~*n.* a blow of this kind. [cp. Swed. *kuffa*, to thrust, to push]

Cufic KUFIC.

cui bono? (kwē bō´nō, bon´ō) *adv., int.* for whose benefit?, who stands to gain? [L]

cuirass (kwiras´, kū-) *n.* **1** (*Hist.*) armour for the body, consisting of a breastplate and a backplate strapped or buckled together. **2** (*Zool.*) any analogous protective covering. **3** (*Hist.*) a sheathing of iron plates on a warship. **4** an apparatus for artificial respiration. **cuirassier** (-siə´) *n.* a soldier wearing a cuirass. [F *cuirasse*, It. *corazza*, late L *corācium*, L *coriācea*, fem. of *coriāceus*, leathern (*corium*, leather)]

cuisine (kwizēn´) *n.* **1** a style of cooking. **2** cookery. [F]

cuisse (kwis), **cuish** (kwish) *n.* (*Hist.*) a piece of thigh armour.

culchie (kŭl´shi), **culshie** (-shi) *n.* (*Ir., sl., derog.*) a country labourer, a yokel. ~*a.* rustic, provincial.

cul-de-sac (kŭl´disak) *n.* (*pl.* **culs-de-sac** (kŭl-), **cul-de-sacs**) **1** a street or lane open only at one end. **2** a route or course of activity that leads nowhere. **3** (*Anat.*) a vessel, tube or gut open only at one end. [F, bottom of a bag]

-cule (kūl) *comb. form* used to form nouns, esp. indicating smallness, as in *molecule*.

culex (kū´leks) *n.* (*pl.* **culices** (-lisēz)) (*Zool.*) a dipterous insect of the genus *Culex*, containing the gnat and the mosquito. [L, a gnat]

culinary (kŭl´inəri) *a.* relating to the kitchen or cooking. **culinarily** *adv.* [L *culīnārius* (*culīna*, a kitchen)]

cull (kŭl) *v.t.* **1** to select, to choose as the best. **2** to pick, gather (flowers, fruit etc.). **3** to select (an animal) from a group, esp. as weak or superfluous, for killing. **4** to reduce the size of (a group) in this way. ~*n.* an act of culling. **culler** *n.* **culling** *n.* [OF *cuillir*, L *colligere*, to COLLECT[1]]

cullender COLANDER.

cullet (kŭl´it) *n.* broken glass for recycling. [COLLET]

cullis (kŭl´is) *n.* **1** a roof gutter. **2** a groove or channel. [F COULISSE]

cully (kŭl´i) *n.* (*pl.* **cullies**) (*sl.*) **1** a pal, a mate. **2** a dupe. [etym. uncertain]

culm[1] (kŭlm) *n.* (*Bot.*) a stem, esp. of grass or sedge. **culmiferous**[1] (-mif´-) *a.* having a hollow jointed stem. [L *culmus*]

culm[2] (kŭlm) *n.* **1** anthracite coal, esp. if in small pieces. **2** coaldust. **3** (*Geol.*) shales, sandstones, grit etc. of the Carboniferous period. **culmiferous**[2] (-mif´-) *a.* abounding in anthracite. [prob. cogn. with COAL]

culmen (kŭl´mən) *n.* (*Zool.*) the ridge on the top of a bird's bill. [L, the top]

culmiferous[1] CULM[1].

culmiferous[2] CULM[2].

culminate (kŭl´mināt) *v.i.* **1** to reach the highest point. **2** (*Astron.*) to come to the meridian. **culminant** *a.* **1** at the highest point. **2** (*Astron.*) on the meridian. **3** supreme, predominant. **culmination** (-ā´shən) *n.* **1** the end of a series of events etc. **2** the highest point. [late L *culminātus*, p.p. of *culmināre* (see CULMEN)]

culottes (kūlots´) *n.pl.* women's flared trousers cut to resemble a skirt. [F]

culpable (kŭl´pəbəl) *a.* **1** blamable, blameworthy. **2** guilty. **culpa** *n.* (*pl.* **culpae** (-pē)) (*Law*) **1** negligence, an act of neglect. **2** fault, guilt. **culpability** (-bil´-) *n.* **culpableness** *n.* **culpably** *adv.* **culpatory** (-təri) *a.* involving or expressing blame. [OF *culpable* (F *coupable*), L *culpābilis* (*culpa*, a fault)]

culprit (kŭl´prit) *n.* **1** a person who is at fault. **2** a person who is arraigned before a judge on a charge. [from the A-F legal abbr. *cul. prit* or *prist* (prob. in full *culpable: prist* or *prest d'averrer*, guilty: I am ready to confess)]

culshie CULCHIE.

cult (kŭlt) *n.* **1** a system of religious belief. **2** the rites and ceremonies of any system of belief. **3** a sect regarded as unorthodox or harmful to its adherents. **4** an intense devotion to a person, idea etc., usu. by a specific section of society. **5** the object of such devotion. **6** an intense fad or fashion. ~*a.* **1** very fashionable (*a cult film*). **2** of or relating to a pagan cult. **cultic, cultish** *a.* **cultism** *n.* adherence to a cult. **cultist** *n.* **cultus** (-təs) *n.* a cult. [L *cultus*, from *colere*, to till, to worship]

cultivar (kŭl´tivah) *n.* (*Bot.*) a variety of a naturally-occurring species, produced and maintained by cultivation. [*culti*vated *var*iety]

cultivate (kŭl´tivāt) *v.t.* **1** to till, to prepare for crops. **2** to raise or develop by tilling. **3** to cherish, to foster, to seek the friendship of. **4** to improve by labour or study, to civilize. **cultivable** *a.* **cultivatable** *a.* **cultivated** *a.* cultured, educated. **cultivation** (-ā´shən) *n.* **1** the art or practice of cultivating. **2** the state of being cultivated. **3** a state of refinement or culture. **cultivator** *n.* **1** an implement to break up the soil and remove weeds. **2** a person who cultivates. [late L *cultīvātus*, p.p. of *cultivāre* (cp. *cultus*, CULT)]

cultrate (kŭl´trāt), **cultriform** (-trifawm) *a.* (*Bot., Biol.*) **1** shaped like a knife. **2** having a sharp edge. [L *cultrātus* (*culter*, knife)]

culture (kŭl´chə) *n.* **1** a state of intellectual and artistic development. **2** an ethos reflecting this (*enterprise culture*). **3** the experimental growing of bacteria or other micro-organisms in a laboratory. **4** the group of micro-organisms so grown. **5** intellectual or moral discipline and training. **6** the act of tilling. **7** husbandry, farming. **8** breeding and rearing. ~*v.t.* **1** to grow (micro-organisms) in a laboratory. **2** to cultivate. **cultural** *a.* **cultural desert** *n.* a place lacking in cultural activities. **culture-bound** *a.* limited in outlook by virtue of belonging to a particular culture. **cultured** *a.* **1** having good education, style, manners, refinement etc. **2** in a state of intellectual development. **3** grown artificially, as pearls or micro-organisms. **cultured pearl** *n.* a pearl formed by an oyster after it has been artificially stimulated. †**cultureless** *a.* **culture shock** *n.* feelings of disorientation caused by the transition from one culture or environment to another. **culture vulture** *n.* (*often derog.*) a person eager to acquire culture and be involved with cultural activities. **culturist** *n.* [F, from L *cultūra* (cp. *cultus*, CULT)]

cultus CULT.

†**culver** (kŭl´və) *n.* **1** a wood pigeon. **2** a pigeon, a dove. [OE *culfre*]

culverin (kŭl´vərin) *n.* (*Hist.*) a long cannon or handgun. [OF *coulevrine*, fem. of *coulevrin*, adder-like (*couleuvre*, L *colubra*, snake)]

culvert (kŭl´vət) *n.* **1** a drain or covered channel for water beneath a road, railway etc. **2** an underground channel for electric wires or cables. [etym. unknown]

cum[1] (kŭm) *prep.* combined with, together with (*bathroom cum cloakroom*). [L]

cum[2] (kŭm) *n.* (*sl.*) ejaculated semen. [COME]

Cumb. *abbr.* **1** (*Hist.*) Cumberland. **2** Cumbria.

cumber (kŭm´bə) *v.t.* **1** (*poet.*) to hamper, to clog, to hinder, to impede. **2** to perplex. **3** to embarrass. ~*n.* a hindrance, an impediment. **cumbersome** *a.* **1**

unwieldy, unmanageable. **2** burdensome, troublesome. **cumbersomely** *adv.* **cumbersomeness** *n.* **cumbrance** *n.* an encumbrance. **cumbrous** *a.* **cumbrously** *adv.* **cumbrousness** *n.* [OF *combrer*, to hinder, late L *cumbrus*, a heap (cp. G *Kummer*, trouble, dial. rubbish)]

Cumberland sausage (kŭm´bələnd) *n.* a coarse-grained savoury sausage, of a type orig. made in Cumberland.

cumbia (kŭm´biə) *n.* **1** a type of dance music similar to salsa, orig. from Colombia. **2** a dance using this music.

Cumbrian (kŭm´briən) *a.* belonging to the county of Cumbria in NW England, to the former county Cumberland, or the ancient British kingdom of Cumbria. ~*n.* a native or inhabitant of (either) Cumbria or Cumberland. [L *Cumbria*, Celt. *Cymry*, Welsh, or *Cymru*, Wales]

cumbrous CUMBER.

cum grano salis (kŭm grahnō sah´lis) *adv.* with a pinch of salt, not too seriously. [L, with a grain of salt]

cumin (kŭm´in), **cummin** *n.* **1** an umbelliferous plant of the parsley family, *Cuminum cyminum*, with aromatic and carminative seeds. **2** these seeds used as flavouring for curries etc. [OE *cymen*, L *cuminum*, Gr. *kuminon*]

cummerbund (kŭm´əbŭnd), **kummerbund** *n.* a waistband or sash, worn esp. by men with evening dress. [Hind. *kamarband* (Pers. *kamar*, the waist, *band*, a band)]

cummin CUMIN.

cumquat KUMQUAT.

cumshaw (kŭm´shaw) *n.* in China etc., a present, a tip. ~*v.t.* to give a present to, to tip. [Chin. pidgin English]

cumulate[1] (kū´mūlāt) *v.t.*, *v.i.* to accumulate. **cumulation** (-lā´shən) *n.* [L *cumulātus*, p.p. of *cumulāre*, to heap up (*cumulus*, a heap)]

cumulate[2] (kū´mūlət) *a.* heaped up, accumulated. **cumulative** *a.* **1** increasing by additions. **2** tending to accumulate. **3** (*Law*) enforcing a point by accumulated proof. **4** used of drugs which, after remaining quiescent, exert their influence suddenly. **cumulative error** *n.* in statistics, an error which increases in magnitude with the size of the sample in which it is revealed. **cumulatively** *adv.* **cumulativeness** *n.* **cumulative preference shares** *n.pl.* shares on which arrears of interest are paid before ordinary shareholders are paid any on the current year. **cumulative voting** *n.* a method of voting by which the votes of the elector can be all given to a single candidate instead of being given singly to several candidates. [as CUMULATE[1]]

cumulation CUMULATE[1].

cumulative CUMULATE[2].

cumuli CUMULUS.

cumulo- (kū´mūlō) *comb. form* (of cloud) cumulus.

cumulonimbus (kūmūlōnim´bəs) *n.* (*pl.* **cumulonimbuses, cumulonimbi** (-bī)) a very thick, dark cumulus cloud, usu. a sign of thunder or hail.

cumulostratus (kūmūlōstrah´təs) *n.* (*pl.* **cumulostrati** (-tī)) a mass of cumulus cloud with a horizontal base.

cumulus (kū´mūləs) *n.* (*pl.* **cumuli** (-lī)) **1** a round billowing mass of cloud, with a flattish base. **2** (*Anat.*) the thickened portion of a cellular layer containing the ovum. **cumulous** *a.* [L, see CUMULATE[1]]

cunctation (kŭnktā´shən) *n.* **1** cautious delaying. **2** delay, dilatoriness. **cunctative** (kŭnk´-) *a.* **cunctator** *n.* [L *cunctātio* (*cunctārī*, to delay)]

cuneate (kū´niət) *a.* wedge-shaped. **cuneal** *a.* **cuneiform** (-nifawm) *a.* **1** wedge-shaped. **2** of or relating to cuneiform writing. ~*n.* cuneiform writing. **cuneiform writing** *n.* writing in characters resembling wedges or arrowheads, used in Babylonian, Hittite, Ninevite and Persian inscriptions. [L *cuneus*, a wedge, -ATE[1]]

cunjevoi (kŭn´jəvoi) *n.* **1** an Australian plant of the arum family, *Alocasia macrorrhiza*, grown for its edible rhizome. **2** (*Austral.*) a sea squirt. [Austral. Abor.]

cunnilingus (kŭniling´gəs), **cunnilinctus** (-lingk´təs) *n.* stimulation of the female genitals by the lips and tongue. [L *cunnus*, vulva, *lingere*, *linctum*, to lick]

cunning (kŭn´ing) *a.* (*comp.* **cunninger**, *superl.* **cunningest**) **1** knowing, skilful, ingenious, artful, crafty. **2** (*N Am.*) amusingly interesting, quaint. ~*n.* **1** skill, knowledge acquired by experience. **2** artfulness, subtlety. **cunningly** *adv.* **cunningness** *n.* [pres.p. of ME *cunnen*, OE *cunnan*, to know]

cunt (kŭnt) *n.* (*taboo, sl.*) **1** the female genitalia. **2** an unpleasant or disliked person. **3** a woman regarded as a sexual object. [ME *cunte*]

CUP *abbr.* Cambridge University Press.

cup (kŭp) *n.* **1** a vessel to drink from, usu. small and with one handle. **2** the liquor contained in it. **3** an ornamental drinking vessel, usu. of gold or silver, awarded as a prize or trophy. **4** anything shaped like a cup, such as an acorn, the socket for a bone. **5** either one of two cup-shaped supports for the breasts in a brassière. **6** in golf, the hole or its metal lining. **7** one's lot in life (*my cup overflows*). **8** (*Hist.*) a cupping glass. **9** the chalice used in the Holy Communion. **10** an alcoholic mixed drink, usu. with wine or cider as a base. **11** in cooking, a measure of capacity equal to 8 fl. oz. (0·23 l). ~*v.t.* (*pres.p.* **cupping,** *past, p.p.* **cupped**) **1** (of hands) to make into a cup shape. **2** to hold as if in a cup. **3** (*Hist.*) to bleed by means of a cupping-glass. ~*v.i.* (*Bot.*) to form a cup or cups. **in one's cups** intoxicated. **one's cup of tea** one's preferred occupation, company etc. **cup-and-ball** *n.* a child's game consisting in throwing up a ball and catching it in a socket. **cup-and-ball joint** *n.* a ball-and-socket joint. **cupbearer** *n.* a person who serves wine, esp. in royal or noble households. **cupcake** *n.* a small sponge cake baked in a paper or foil case. **cup final, Cup Final** *n.* the final match of a competition to decide who wins a cup. **cupful** *n.* (*pl.* **cupfuls**). **cupgall** *n.* a cuplike gall on oak leaves. **cup lichen, cup moss** *n.* a lichen, *Cladonia pyxidata*, with cup-shaped processes rising from the thallus. **cupper**[1] *n.* a person who uses a cupping glass. **cupping** *n.* (*Hist.*) the act of bleeding with a cupping glass. **cupping glass** *n.* a partially evacuated glass vessel placed over a (usu.) scarified place to induce the flow of blood. **cup-tie** *n.* a match in a knockout competition for a cup. [OE *cuppe*, late L *cuppa*, a cup, L *cūpa*, a vat, a cask]

cupboard (kŭb´əd) *n.* **1** an enclosed case or recess with shelves to receive plates, dishes, food etc. **2** a wardrobe. **cupboard love** *n.* greedy or self-interested love.

cupel (kū´pəl) *n.* a small shallow vessel used in assaying precious metals. ~*v.t.* (*pres.p.* **cupelling,** (*N Am.*) **cupeling,** *past, p.p.* **cupelled,** (*N Am.*) **cupeled**) to assay in a cupel. **cupellation** (-ā´shən) *n.* [late L *cūpella*, dim. of *cūpa*, a cask]

Cupid (kū´pid) *n.* **1** the Roman god of love. **2** a picture or statue of Cupid, usu. as a naked boy with wings, carrying a bow and arrows. **Cupid's bow** *n.* a shape of the upper lip thought to resemble the bow carried by Cupid. **Cupid's dart** *n.* the pangs of love. [L *Cupīdo* (*cupere*, to desire)]

cupidity (kūpid´iti) *n.* an inordinate desire to possess, covetousness, avarice. [F *cupidité*, L *cupiditās -tātem*, from *cupidus*, desirous, as CUPID]

cupola (kū´pələ) *n.* **1** a little dome. **2** a lantern etc. on the summit of a dome. **3** a spherical covering to a building, or any part of it. **4** a cupola furnace. **5** a revolving dome or turret on a warship. **6** (*Biol.*) a domelike organ or part, esp. the extremity of the canal of the cochlea. **cupolaed** (-ləd) *a.* **cupola furnace** *n.* a furnace for melting metals. [It., from L *cūpula*, CUPEL]

cuppa (kŭp´ə), **cupper** *n.* (*coll.*) a cup of tea.

cupper[1] CUP.

cupper[2] CUPPA.

cupping CUP.

cupreous (kū´priəs) *a.* of, like or composed of copper. **cuprammonium** (kūprəmō´niəm) *n.* (*Chem.*) a solution of copper oxide and ammonia, able to dissolve cellulose. **cupric** *a.* (*Chem.*) having divalent copper in its composition. **cupriferous** (-prif´-) *a.* copper-bearing. **cuprite** (-prīt) *n.* red copper oxide, a mineral with cubic crystal structure. **cupro-nickel** (-prō-) *n.* an alloy of copper and nickel. **cuprous** *a.* (*Chem.*) having monovalent copper in its composition. [L *cupreus*, copper]

cupressus (kūpres´əs) *n.* any conifer of the genus *Cupressus*, which includes the cypress. [L]

cupric, cupriferous etc. CUPREOUS.

cupule (kū´pūl) *n.* **1** (*Bot.*) an inflorescence consisting of a cup, as in the oak or hazel. **2** (*Zool.*) a cuplike organ. **cupular, cupulate** *a.* **cupuliferous** (-lif´-) *a.* bearing cupules. [L, *cūpula*, CUPEL]

cur (kœ) *n.* **1** a mongrel, an aggressive dog. **2** (*coll.*) a surly or despicable man. **currish** *a.* **currishly** *adv.* **currishness** *n.* [imit. (cp. Icel. *kurra*, to murmur, grumble, LG *kurren*, to snarl)]

curable CURE.

curaçao (kūrəsah´ō, koo-), **curaçoa** (-sō´ə) *n.* (*pl.* **curaçaos, curaçoas**) a liqueur flavoured with bitter orange peel, sugar and cinnamon, orig. from Curaçao. [*Curaçao* island, north of Venezuela]

curacy CURATE[1].

curare (kūrah´ri) *n.* the dried extract of plants from the genera *Strychnos* and *Chondodendron*, used by the Indians of S America for poisoning arrows, and formerly employed in physiological investigations as a muscle relaxant. **curarine** (-rīn) *n.* an alkaloid from curare. **curarize** (kū´-), **curarise** *v.t.* [Sp. and Port., from Carib *kurari*]

curassow (kū´rəsō) *n.* any turkey-like game bird of the family Cracidae, found in S and Central America. [CURAÇAO]

curate[1] (kū´rət) *n.* **1** a member of the Church of England clergy who assists the incumbent of a parish. **2** †a clergyman with an active benefice. **curacy** *n.* (*pl.* **curacies**) the office of curate. **curate-in-charge** *n.* a priest-in-charge. **curate's egg** *n.* something of which some parts are good and some parts bad. [med. L *cūrātus* (L *cūra*, a care, charge, cure)]

curate[2] CURATOR.

curative (kū´rətiv) *a.* tending to cure. ~*n.* any medicine etc. that tends to cure. [F *curatif*; see CURE]

curator (kūrā´tə) *n.* **1** a person who has charge of a library, museum or similar establishment. **2** (*Sc. Law*) a trustee for the carrying out of any purpose, a guardian. **curate**[2] (kūrāt´) *v.t.* to act as a curator of (a museum exhibit etc.). ~*v.i.* to hold the office of curator. **curation** *n.* **curatorial** (-taw´ri-) *a.* **curatorship** *n.* **curatrix** (-triks) *n.* a female curator. [L, from *cūrāre*, to CURE]

curb (kœb) *n.* **1** a check, a restraint. **2** a chain or strap passing behind the jaw of a horse in a curb bit. **3** (*N Am.*) a kerb. **4** a kerbstone. **5** an injury to the hock-joint of a horse. ~*v.t.* **1** to put a curb on. **2** to restrain, to keep in check. **curbless** *a.* without any curb or restraint. **curb roof** *n.* a mansard roof. **curbstone** *n.* (*N Am.*) a kerbstone. [F *courbe*, from L *curvus*, bent, curved]

curch (kœch) *n.* (*Sc.*) a piece of linen formerly worn by women, a kerchief. [cp. KERCHIEF]

curculio (kœkū´liō) *n.* (*pl.* **curculios**) a weevil of the family Curculionidae, esp. *Conotrachelus nenuphar*, which attacks fruit trees. [L]

curcuma (kœ´kūmə) *n.* **1** any plant of the genus *Curcuma*, tuberous plants of the ginger family. **2** turmeric, obtained from its root. [Arab. *kurkum*, saffron (cp. CROCUS)]

curd (kœd) *n.* **1** the coagulated part of milk, used to make cheese. **2** the coagulated part of any liquid. **3** the fatty matter found in the flesh of boiled salmon. **4** a cauliflower head. ~*v.t.* to curdle. ~*v.i.* to congeal. **curd cheese** *n.* a soft mild white cheese made from skimmed milk curds, smoother in consistency than cottage cheese. **curd soap** *n.* a white soap made from tallow and soda. **curdy** *a.* **1** full of curds. **2** curdled, congealed. [perh. from OE stem *crud-*, *crūdan*, to CROWD[1]]

curdle (kœ´dəl) *v.t.* **1** to break into curds. **2** to coagulate, to congeal. ~*v.i.* to become curdled. **to make someone's blood curdle** to terrify, as with a ghost story or the like. **curdler** *n.*

cure (kūə) *n.* **1** the act of healing or curing disease. **2** a remedy, a restorative. **3** a course of remedial treatment. **4** the state of being cured or healed. **5** the care or spiritual charge of souls. **6** a parish or other sphere in which to pursue this. **7** the process of vulcanizing rubber or hardening plastic etc. ~*v.t.* **1** to heal, to restore to health, to make sound or whole. **2** to preserve or pickle. **3** to eliminate or correct (a habit or practice). **4** to vulcanize (rubber), to harden (plastic etc.). ~*v.i.* **1** to effect a cure. **2** to be cured or healed. **curable** *a.* **curability** (-bil´-) *n.* **cure-all** *n.* a panacea, a universal remedy. **cureless** *a.* without cure or remedy. **cure of souls** *n.* a benefice to which parochial duties are annexed. **curer** *n.* **1** a person who cures or heals. **2** a person who prepares preserved food (*often in comb.*, as *fish-curer*). **curing** *n.* **1** the act of curing or healing. **2** the act or process of preparing articles of food for preservation. [OF, from L *cūra*, care, whence *cūrāre*, to take care of]

curé (kū´rā) *n.* a parish priest in France etc., a French rector or vicar. [F]

curette (kūret´) *n.* (*Med.*) a surgeon's instrument used for scraping a body cavity. ~*v.t.*, *v.i.* to scrape or clean with a curette. **curettage** (-ret´ij, -ritahzh´) *n.* [F]

curfew (kœ´fū) *n.* **1** a military or civil regulation to be off the streets or indoors between stated hours. **2** the time at which this comes into force. **3** a signal announcing this. **4** (*Hist.*) **a** a regulation in the Middle Ages to extinguish fires at a stated hour. **b** the bell announcing, or the time for this. [A-F *coeverfu*, OF *couvrefeu* (*couvrir*, to COVER, *feu*, L *focus*, fire)]

Curia (kū´riə), **curia** *n.* (*pl.* **Curiae** (-ē), **curiae**) **1** the papal court. **2** the temporal administration of the Vatican. **3** (*Hist.*) **a** any of the ten subdivisions of the three Roman tribes, as instituted by Romulus. **b** the building in which they met, the Roman senate house. **Curial** *a.* of or relating to a Curia, esp. the papal Curia. **Curialism** *n.* [L]

curie (kū´ri) *n.* **1** the standard unit of radioactivity, 3.7×10^{10} disintegrations per second. **2** a quantity of radioactive material representing this. [Pierre *Curie*, 1859–1906, and Marie *Curie*, 1867–1934, French scientists]

curing CURE.

curio (kū´riō) *n.* (*pl.* **curios**) a curiosity, esp. a curious piece of art; a bit of bric-a-brac. [short for CURIOSITY (under CURIOUS)]

curiosa (kūriō´sə) *n.pl.* **1** unusual (collectable) objects. **2** erotic or pornographic books. [L, neut. pl. of *cūriōsus* (see CURIOUS)]

curious (kū´riəs) *a.* **1** inquisitive, desirous to know. **2** extraordinary, surprising, odd. **3** (of books etc.) erotic, pornographic. **4** †careful, meticulous. **5** †anxious, solicitous. **6** †fastidious. **curiosity** (-os´-) *n.* (*pl.* **curiosities**) **1** a desire to know, inquisitiveness. **2** a rarity, an object of curiosity. **3** strangeness, the quality of being curious. **curiously** *adv.* **curiousness** *n.* [OF *curios*, L *cūriōsus* (*cūra*, care)]

curium (kū´riəm) *n.* an artificially-produced transuranic metallic element, at. no. 96, chem. symbol Cm. [see CURIE]

curl (kœl) *n.* **1** a ringlet or twisted lock of hair. **2** anything coiled, twisted or spiral. **3** the state of being curled. **4** a contemptuous curving of the lip. **5** a disease in potatoes and other plants, of which curled shoots and leaves are a symptom. ~*v.t.* 1 to twine. 2 to twist into curls. 3 to dress with ringlets. 4 to curve up (the lip) in contempt. ~*v.i.* 1 to twist, to curve up. 2 to rise in curves or undulations. 3 to play at the game of curling. **to curl up** 1 to go into a curled position. 2 (*coll.*) to be embarrassed or disgusted. **curler** *n.* 1 a person who or thing which curls. 2 a device for curling the hair. 3 a person who plays at curling. **curling** (kœ'ling) *n.* 1 the act of twining, twisting etc. 2 a game played on ice in which participants slide smooth stones towards a mark. **curling stone** *n.* the stone used in the game of curling. **curling tongs, curling irons, curling pins** *n.pl.* a heated device for curling the hair. **curlpaper** *n.* paper round which hair is wound to form a curl. **curly** *a.* (*comp.* **curlier,** *superl.* **curliest**) 1 having curls. 2 wavy, undulated. 3 (*Bot.*) having curled or wavy margins. **curliness** *n.* **curly kale** *n.* a variety of kale with curly leaves. [earlier *crul, crulle* (cp. Dut. *krul,* G *Krolle*)]

curlew (kœ'lū) *n.* (*pl. in general* **curlew,** *in particular* **curlews**) a migratory wading bird of the genus *Numenius,* esp. the European *N. arquatus.* [OF *courlieus* (imit. of the cry)]

curlicue (kœ'likū) *n.* a decorative curl or twist, esp. in handwriting. [CURLY (under CURL), CUE[1] (from either F *queue,* a tail, or the letter Q)]

curmudgeon (kəmŭj'ən) *n.* a miserly or churlish person. **curmudgeonly** *adv.* [etym. unknown]

currach (kŭr'ə, -əkh), **curragh** *n.* a skiff made of wickerwork and hides, a coracle. [Ir. *curach*]

currajong KURRAJONG.

currant (kŭr'ənt) *n.* 1 the dried fruit of a dwarf seedless grape orig. from the E Mediterranean. 2 the fruit of shrubs of the genus *Ribes,* bearing black, red or white berries. 3 such a shrub. [formerly *raisins of corauns,* F *raisins de Corinthe* (L *Corinthus,* Gr. *Korinthos,* Corinth)]

currawong (kŭr'əwong) *n.* an Australian crowlike songbird of the genus *Strepera.* [Austral. Abor.]

currency (kŭr'ənsi) *n.* (*pl.* **currencies**) 1 the circulating monetary medium of a country, whether in coin or paper. 2 the state of being current. 3 the period during which anything is current. 4 prevalence, general acceptance, e.g. of an idea or theory. 5 a continual passing from hand to hand, as of money. 6 †running, rapid motion. **currency note** *n.* 1 a treasury note. 2 (*Hist.*) paper money of the value of 10 shillings or £1 (issued from 1914–1928). [L *currere,* to run]

current (kŭr'ənt) *a.* 1 belonging to the present week, month, year. 2 passing at the present time. 3 in general circulation among the public, generally received or acknowledged. 4 †running, flowing, fluent. ~*n.* 1 a flowing stream, a body of water, air etc., moving in a certain direction. 2 a general drift or tendency. 3 electrical activity regarded as the rate of flow of electrical charge along a conductor. **to pass current** to be generally accepted as true, genuine etc. **current account** *n.* a bank account which usu. does not pay interest and on which one may draw cheques. **currently** *adv.* 1 at present. 2 generally. [OF *curant,* pres.p. of *courre,* from L *currere,* to run (as CURRENCY)]

curricle (kŭr'ikəl) *n.* (*Hist.*) a two-wheeled chaise for a pair of horses. ~*v.i.* to drive in a curricle. [from CURRICULUM]

curriculum (kərik'ūləm) *n.* (*pl.* **curricula** (-lə)) 1 a fixed course of study at a school etc. 2 a programme of activities. **curricular** *a.* **curriculum vitae** (vē'tī) *n.* (*pl.* **curricula vitae, curricula vitarum** (-tah'rəm)) a brief outline of one's education, previous employment, and other achievements. [L, a racecourse, dim. from *currere,* to run]

currier (kŭr'iə) *n.* a person who curries, dresses and colours leather after it has been tanned. [OF *corier,* L *coriārius* (*corium,* hide, leather)]

currish CUR.

curry[1] (kŭr'i) *n.* (*pl.* **curries**) a highly-spiced orig. Indian dish of stewed meat, fish etc. in a sauce, usu. served with rice. ~*v.t.* (*3rd pers. sing. pres.* **curries,** *pres.p.* **currying,** *past, p.p.* **curried**) to flavour with curry. **curry paste, curry powder** *n.* a mixture of ginger, turmeric and other strong spices used in curries etc. [Tamil *kari*]

curry[2] (kŭr'i) *v.t.* (*3rd pers. sing. pres.* **curries,** *pres.p.* **currying,** *past, p.p.* **curried**) 1 to groom (a horse) with a curry-comb. 2 to dress (leather). 3 to thrash. **to curry favour** to ingratiate oneself with superiors by officiousness or flattery. **curry-comb** *n.* a comb used for grooming horses. [OF *correier, conreder* (CON-, *reder,* cp. ARRAY)]

curse (kœs) *v.t.* 1 to invoke harm or evil upon. 2 to blast, to injure, vex or torment (with). 3 to excommunicate. ~*v.i.* to swear, to utter imprecations. ~*n.* 1 a solemn invocation of divine vengeance (upon). 2 a profane oath. 3 an invocation of evil (upon). 4 the evil imprecated. 5 anything which causes evil, trouble or great vexation. 6 a sentence of excommunication. **the curse** (*coll.*) menstruation. **cursed** (-sid), **†curst** *a.* 1 troubled, burdened (with or by). 2 execrable, accursed, deserving of a curse. 3 blasted by a curse, execrated. 4 vexatious, troublesome. 5 †shrewish. **cursedly** *adv.* **cursedness** *n.* 1 the state of being under a curse. 2 †shrewishness. **curser** *n.* 1 a person who curses. 2 a blasphemer. [OE *cursian;* etym. unknown]

cursillo (kœsil'ō) *n.* (*pl.* **cursillos**) an informal spiritual retreat of members of the Roman Catholic Church, esp. in Latin America. [Sp., little course]

cursive (kœ'siv) *a.* handwritten with joined characters, esp. with looped characters. ~*n.* 1 cursive writing. 2 manuscript written in a running hand, as opposed to *uncial.* **cursively** *adv.* [late L *cursīvus* (from *cursus,* p.p. of *currere,* to run)]

cursor (kœ'sə) *n.* 1 on a VDU screen, a movable point of light or other indicator showing the position of the next action, e.g. the beginning of an addition or correction. 2 the moving part of a measuring instrument, e.g. the slide with the reference line in a slide rule. [L, a runner; see CURSIVE]

cursorial (kœsaw'riəl) *a.* (*Zool.*) adapted for running. [L, *cursor,* -IAL]

cursory (kœ'səri) *a.* hasty, superficial, careless. **cursorily** *adv.* **cursoriness** *n.* [L *cursōrius,* as CURSOR]

†curst CURSE.

curt (kœt) *a.* short, concise, abrupt, esp. rudely terse. **curtly** *adv.* **curtness** *n.* [L *curtus,* docked]

curtail (kœtāl') *v.t.* 1 to shorten, lessen or reduce. 2 to cut off the end or tail of. **curtailer** *n.* **curtailment** *n.* [CURTAL]

curtail step (kœ'tāl) *n.* the bottom step of a flight of stairs, finished at its outer extremity in a scroll. [connection with CURTAIL doubtful]

curtain (kœ'tən) *n.* 1 a length of material hanging beside a window or door, or round a bed, which can be drawn across. 2 a partition, screen, cover or protection. 3 the cloth partition in a theatre, cinema etc. separating the stage or screen from the audience. 4 the end of a scene or play, marked by the closing of the curtains. 5 a curtain wall. 6 (*pl., sl.*) death, the end. ~*v.t.* 1 to enclose with or as with curtains. 2 to furnish or decorate with curtains. **curtain call** *n.* a round of applause for an actor which calls for a reappearance before the curtain falls. **curtain fire** *n.* a concentrated sustained artillery barrage. **curtain lecture** *n.* a reproof or lecture from a wife to a husband after they have retired to bed. **curtainless** *a.* **curtainraiser** *n.* 1 in a theatre, a short piece given before the main play. 2 any short preliminary event. **curtain wall** *n.* 1 a wall that is not load-bearing. **2** in a castle, a wall between two bastions. [OF *cortine*, L *cortīna* (etym. uncertain)]

†**curtal** (kœ´təl) *n.* **1** a horse with a cropped tail. **2** anything docked or cut short. ~*a.* **1** having a cropped tail. **2** concise. **curtal friar** *n.* a friar with a short frock. [OF *cortald, courtault* (*court*, short, L *curtus*, CURT; with suf. *-ald, -ault*, from Gmc.)]

†**curtal axe** (kœ´təl), (*N Am.*) **curtal ax** *n.* a heavy sort of cutting sword, a cutlass. [corr. of CUTLASS]

curtana (kœtah´nə, -tā´-) *n.* the unpointed sword carried in front of the English sovereigns at their coronation as a symbol of mercy. [Ang.-Lat. *curtana* (prob. *curtana spada*, curtailed sword), cp. CURTAL]

☒ **curtesy** common misspelling of COURTESY.

curtilage (kœ´təlij) *n.* a piece of ground lying near and belonging to a dwelling and included within the same fence. [OF *courtillage*, dim. of *courtil*, a little court (*cort*, a COURT)]

curtsy (kœt´si), **curtsey** *n.* (*pl.* **curtsies, curtseys**) an act of respect or salutation, performed by women by slightly bending the body and knees at the same time. ~*v.i.* (*3rd pers. sing. pres.* **curtsies, curtseys,** *pres.p.* **curtsying, curtseying,** *past, p.p.* **curtsied, curtseyed**) to make a curtsy. [COURTESY]

curule (kū´rool) *a.* (*Hist.*) **1** of high civic dignity. **2** having the right to use the curule chair. **curule chair** *n.* in ancient Rome, the chair of honour of the emperor and of the higher magistrates of senatorial rank under the republic, originally ornamented with ivory, and in shape like a folding stool with crossed, curved legs. [L *curūlis* (perh. from *currus*, a chariot)]

curvaceous (kœvā´shəs) *a.* (*coll.*) (of a woman's body) generously curved. [CURVE, -ACEOUS]

curvature (kœ´vəchə) *n.* **1** deflection from a straight line. **2** a curved form. **3** (*Geom.*) the continual bending of a line from a rectilinear direction. **curvate** (-vāt) *a.* curved, bent. **curvative** *a.* (*Bot.*) having the margins slightly curved. [L *curvātūra*, from *curvātus*, p.p. of *curvāre* (from CURVE)]

curve (kœv) *n.* **1** a line of which no three consecutive points are in a straight line. **2** a continuously bending course. **3** something bent, a curved form. **4** in baseball, a ball pitched so as to deviate from a straight course. ~*v.t.* to cause to bend without angles. ~*v.i.* to form or be formed into a curve. **curved** *a.* **curvy** *a.* (*comp.* **curvier,** *superl.* **curviest**) (of a woman) having a shapely figure. **curviness** *n.* [L *curvus*, bent]

curvet (kœvet´) *n.* a particular leap of a horse raising the forelegs at once, and, as the forelegs are falling, raising the hindlegs, so that all four are off the ground at once. ~*v.i.* (*pres.p.* **curvetting, curveting,** *past, p.p.* **curvetted, curveted**) **1** to make a curvet. **2** to frolic, to frisk. [It. *corvetta*, dim. of *corvo*, a curve, as CURVE]

curvi- (kœ´vi) *comb. form* curved. [L *curvus*, bent]

curvifoliate (kœvifō´liət) *a.* (*Bot.*) having revolute leaves.

curvilinear (kœvilin´iə) *a.* **1** bounded by curved lines. **2** consisting of curved lines. **curvilinearity** (-ar´-) *n.* **curvilinearly** *adv.*

cuscus[1] (kŭs´kŭs) *n.* any of several nocturnal tree-dwelling marsupials of the genus *Phalanger* of N Australia, New Guinea etc. [name in New Guinea]

cuscus[2] KHUS-KHUS.

cusec (kū´sek) *n.* a unit of rate of flow of water, 1 cu. ft. (0.0283 m^3) per second. [abbr. of *cu*bic feet per *sec*ond]

cush (kush) *n.* (*coll.*) in snooker, pool etc., the cushion.

cushat (kŭsh´ət) *n.* (*Sc., North.*) the wood pigeon or ring-dove. [OE *cūsceote*]

cush-cush (kush´kush) *n.* a variety of yam, *Diascorea trifida* of S America.

Cushing's syndrome (kush´ingz) *n.* (*Med.*) a metabolic disorder in which the adrenal cortex produces excessive corticosteroid hormones, usu. resulting in obesity, hypertension and fatigue. **Cushing's disease** *n.* (*Med.*) Cushing's syndrome as caused by a benign tumour of the pituitary gland. [H. W. *Cushing*, 1869–1939, US neurosurgeon]

cushion (kush´ən) *n.* **1** a kind of pillow or pad for sitting, kneeling or leaning on, stuffed with feathers, wool, hair or other soft material. **2** anything padded to protect against shock etc. **3** the lining at the side of a snooker or pool table which causes the balls to rebound. **4** a flat leather bag filled with sand, used by engravers to support the plate or block. **5** a pad on which gilders and binders spread gold leaf. **6** (*Zool.*) a cushion-like organ, part or growth. **7** the body of air which supports a hovercraft etc. in motion. ~*v.t.* **1** to seat, support or protect with cushions. **2** to protect against shock. **3** to furnish with cushions. **4** to place or leave (a snooker ball) close up to the cushion. **5** to suppress or quietly ignore. **cushiony** *a.* [F *coussin*, prob. OF *coissin* (prob. from L *coxa*, hip)]

Cushitic (kushit´ik) *n.* a group of Hamitic languages of E Africa. ~*a.* belonging to this group. [*Cush*, an ancient kingdom in the Nile valley, -ITE[1], -IC]

cushy (kush´i) *a.* (*comp.* **cushier,** *superl.* **cushiest**) (*coll.*) **1** (of a job etc.) well paid and with little to do. **2** soft, easy, comfortable. **cushily** *adv.* **cushiness** *n.* [Hind. *khushi*, pleasant; also CUSHIONY (under CUSHION)]

cusp (kŭsp) *n.* **1** a point, an apex, a summit. **2** (*Astrol.*) a division between signs of the zodiac. **3** (*Archit.*) a Gothic ornament consisting of a projecting point formed by the meeting of curves. **4** (*Geom.*) the point in a curve at which its two branches have a common tangent. **5** (*Bot.*) the pointed end of a leaf or other part. **6** (*Med.*) a projection on a molar tooth. **7** (*Astron.*) either of the two points of a crescent moon. **8** (*Med.*) a flap or fold in a heart valve. **cuspate** *a.* **1** having a cusp or cusps. **2** shaped like a cusp. **cusped** *a.* **cuspid** (-pid) *a.* **cuspidal** *a.* (*Geom.*) ending in a point. **cuspidate** (-dāt), **cuspidated** (-dātid) *a.* **1** having a cusp or cusps. **2** (*Bot.*) tapering to a rigid point. [L *cuspis, -idem*]

cuspidor (kŭs´pidaw) *n.* a spittoon. [Port., a spitter, from *cuspir*, to spit, L *conspuere*]

cuss (kŭs) *n.* (*coll.*) **1** a curse. **2** (*derog.*) a person, a creature (*an awkward cuss*). ~*v.t.* to curse. **cussed** (-sid) *a.* stubborn, obstinate, perverse, resolute. **cussedly** *adv.* **cussedness** *n.* **cuss word** *n.* a swear word. [CURSE]

custard (kŭs´təd) *n.* **1** a composition of milk and eggs, sweetened and flavoured. **2** a sweet sauce made of milk, sugar and custard powder. **3** (*Hist.*) an open pie filled with egg custard. **custard apple** *n.* a W Indian fruit, *Annona reticulata*, with a soft pulp. **custard pie** *n.* **1** an open pie filled with egg custard. **2** an open pie filled with foam etc., thrown in slapstick comedy. **custard powder** *n.* a composition of cornflour, colouring and flavouring, used in the making of custard. [prob. from ME *crustade*, a pie with crust, OF *croustade*, L *crustāta*, fem. p.p. of *crustāre* (see CRUST)]

custody (kŭs´tədi) *n.* (*pl.* **custodies**) **1** guardianship, security. **2** imprisonment, confinement. **custodial** (-ō´-) *a.* of or relating to custody or guardianship. **custodian** (-ō´-) *n.* a person who has the custody or guardianship of anything. **custodianship** *n.* [L *custōdia* (*custos -todem*, a guardian)]

custom (kŭs´təm) *n.* **1** a habitual use or practice, established usage, familiarity. **2** buying of goods, business, frequenting a shop to purchase. **3** (*Law*) long established practice constituting common law. ~*a.* (*esp. N Am.*) made to a customer's specifications. †**customable** *a.* **1** customary. **2** liable to duty. **custom duties, customs duties** *n.pl.* duties imposed on certain goods imported or exported. **customed** *a.* usual, accustomed. **custom house, customs house** *n.* the office where vessels enter and clear, and where custom duties are paid. **customize, customise** *v.t.* to make to a customer's specifications. **custom-made, custom-built** *a.* made to measure, custom. **customs** *n.* 1 (*as pl.*) custom duties. 2 (*as sing. or pl.*) the department of government administering these. 3 (*as sing. or pl.*) the place at a border, port, airport etc. dealing with dutiable or illegal imports or exports. **customs union** *n.* a group of states with free trade between themselves and common tariffs towards non-member states. [OF *costume*, L *consuētūdo -dinem*, custom, from *consuētus*, p.p. of *consuescere* (CON-, *suescere*, inceptive of *suēre*, to be accustomed)]

customary (kŭs´təməri) *a.* 1 habitual, usual. 2 (*Law*) holding or held by custom, liable under custom. ~*n.* (*pl.* **customaries**) a written or printed record of customs. **customarily** *adv.* **customariness** *n.*

customer (kŭs´təmə) *n.* 1 a purchaser. 2 a person who purchases regularly from a particular shop or business. 3 (*coll.*) a person one has to do with, a fellow (*He's a strange customer*).

custos (kŭs´təs) *n.* (*pl.* **custodes** (-tō´dēz)) a keeper, a custodian. **custos rotulorum** (rotūlaw´rəm) *n.* the chief civil officer or Lord Lieutenant of a county and keeper of its records. [L]

cut[1] (kŭt) *v.t.* (*pres.p.* **cutting**, *past, p.p.* **cut**) 1 to penetrate or wound with a sharp instrument. 2 to divide or separate with a sharp-edged instrument. 3 to sever, to detach, to hew, to fell, to mow or reap. 4 to carve, to trim or clip. 5 to form by cutting. 6 to reduce by cutting. 7 to mutilate or shorten (a play, article or book). 8 to edit (a film). 9 to intersect, to cross. 10 to divide into two (as a pack of cards). 11 to hit (a cricket ball) with a downward stroke and make it glance to one side. 12 to wound deeply. 13 a to leave, to give up. b (*esp. N Am.*) not to attend, to play truant from. 14 a to ignore deliberately a person that one might be expected to greet. b to renounce the acquaintance of. 15 to reduce as low as possible. 16 (*sl.*) to dilute (a drink or drug). 17 to record a song etc. on (a master tape, disc etc.). ~*v.i.* 1 to make a wound or incision with or as with a sharp-edged instrument. 2 to have a good edge. 3 (of teeth) to come through the gums. 4 to divide a pack of cards into two, esp. to establish the dealer. 5 to intersect. 6 to be able to be cut or divided (*It will cut into three*). 7 to change abruptly from one scene to another in a film. 8 (*sl.*) to move away quickly, to run (*Cut away, Flashman!*). 9 (*Med.*) to perform an operation by cutting, esp. in lithotomy. ~*int.* ordering film or television cameras to stop. **the cut of one's jib** JIB[1]. **to be (not) cut out** to be (not) naturally fitted (for). **to cut a caper** CAPER[1]. **to cut across** 1 to pass by a shorter course so as to cut off an angle. 2 to go contrary to (usual procedure etc.). **to cut a dash** DASH. **to cut a feather** FEATHER. **to cut a figure** (usu. qualified by an adjective) to look, appear or perform in a certain style (*He cuts a bold figure*). **to cut a loss** LOSS. **to cut and come again** to help oneself and take more if one will. **to cut and run** to depart rapidly. **to cut away** 1 to detach by cutting. 2 to reduce by cutting. **to cut back** 1 to prune. 2 to reduce. **to cut both ways** to have both good and bad consequences. **to cut capers** CAPER[1]. **to cut corners** 1 to take short cuts. 2 to sacrifice quality in favour of speed. **to cut dead** to refuse to acknowledge the presence of. **to cut down** 1 to fell. 2 to compress, to reduce. **to cut in** 1 to interrupt, to intrude. 2 (*coll.*) to allow to have a share in. 3 to drive in front of another person's car so as to affect their driving. 4 (of an electrical device) to start working. 5 to insert something within something else. 6 to take a lady away from her dancing partner. **to cut into** 1 to make a cut in (something). 2 to reduce or interfere with (*It cuts into her schedule*). **to cut it fine** FINE[1]. **to cut it out** to desist from doing something annoying. **to cut loose** LOOSE. **to cut no ice** ICE. **to cut off** 1 to remove by cutting, to eradicate. 2 to intercept. 3 to prevent from access. 4 to sever. 5 to discontinue. 6 to bring to an untimely end, to kill. 7 to disinherit. **to cut off one's nose to spite one's face** NOSE. **to cut one's coat according to one's cloth** to adapt to one's personal (esp. financial) circumstances. **to cut one's eye-teeth** to become worldly-wise. **to cut one's losses** LOSS. **to cut one's stick** 1 (*coll.*) to go away. 2 (*coll.*) to run, to escape. **to cut one's teeth** to have the teeth come through the gums. **to cut one's teeth on** to gain experience through, to learn one's trade or profession through. **to cut out** 1 to shape by cutting. 2 to remove or separate by cutting. 3 to excel, to outdo. 4 to supplant. 5 to cease doing, taking or indulging in something unpleasant or harmful. 6 to cease operating suddenly and unexpectedly or by the automatic intervention of a cut-out device. 7 (*Hist., Naut.*) to enter a harbour and seize and carry off (e.g. a ship) by sudden attack. 8 to relinquish a game as the result of cutting the cards. **to cut short** 1 to hinder by interruption. 2 to abridge. **to cut someone down to size** to cause someone to feel less important or be less conceited by exposing their limitations. **to cut the ground from under someone/ someone's feet** GROUND[1]. **to cut the knot** KNOT[1]. **to cut the mustard** MUSTARD. **to cut to pieces** to exterminate, to massacre. **to cut up** 1 to cut in pieces. 2 to criticize severely. 3 to distress deeply. 4 in a vehicle, to drive across the line of travel of (another driver) unexpectedly and dangerously. **to cut up rough** (*sl.*) to become quarrelsome or savage. **to cut up well** (*coll.*) to leave plenty of money. **to have one's work cut out** WORK. **cut-and-come-again** *n.* 1 an abundant supply. 2 an opportunity to help oneself (to food etc.) and return again at will. **cut-and-cover** *n.* a tunnel made by excavating an open cutting and covering it in. **cut and dried** *a.* 1 pre-arranged, already decided, inflexible. 2 (of opinions) unoriginal, trite. **cut-and-paste** *n.* 1 a technique of assembling a page layout, montage etc. by cutting material out and pasting it in place. 2 in word processing or desk-top publishing, a technique that mimics this by which text and graphics can be moved around in a document or between windows. **cutaway** *a.* 1 denoting a drawing of an engine etc. in which part of the casing is omitted to show the workings. 2 (of a coat) having the front cut away in a diagonal direction from waist to knee. ~*n.* a coat with the skirts rounded off. **cutback** *n.* 1 a reduction esp. in expenditure. 2 an instance of cutting back. **cut-down** *a.* reduced, shortened. **cut glass** *n.* glass in which a pattern is formed by cutting or grinding. **cut-in** *n.* something that is inserted within another thing, esp. a film or video sequence. **cut-line** *n.* 1 a caption. 2 the line on the wall of a squash court above which a serve must strike. **cut-off** *n.* 1 the point at which something ceases to apply, operate etc. 2 a device for cutting off a supply of electricity, water, steam etc. 3 a passage cut by a river, affording a new channel. 4 (*N Am.*) a short cut. 5 (*pl.*) shorts with unsewn or unbound leg bottoms. ~*a.* isolated, remote. **cut-off road** *n.* (*N Am.*) a bypass. **cut-out** *n.* 1 a shape etc. cut from cardboard, fabric, paper etc. 2 a device for automatic disconnection of power, release of exhaust gases etc. 3 a switch for shutting off a light or a group of lights from an electric circuit. 4 a device in a vehicle which automatically disconnects the battery from the dynamo. **cut-out box** *n.* (*N Am.*) a fuse box. **cut-price** *a.* 1 at a reduced price. 2 at the lowest price possible. **cutpurse** *n.* 1 (*Hist.*) a person who stole purses by cutting them from the girdle to which they were fastened. 2 a highwayman, a thief. **cut-rate** *a.* CUT-PRICE (under CUT[1]). **cutter** *n.* 1 a person who or something that cuts. 2 a person who cuts out men's clothes to measure. 3 a cutting tool. 4 a film or video editor. 5 (*N Am.*) a light sledge. 6 a soft brick adapted to be rubbed down for ornamental work or arching. 7 (*Naut.*) **a** a small boat for official duties. **b** (*Hist.*) a man-of-war's boat smaller than a barge, with from four to eight oars. **c** a one-masted vessel with fore-and-aft sails. **8** in cricket, a ball delivered with a sharp turn. **cut-throat** *n.* **1** a murderer, an assassin. **2** a cut-throat razor. *~a.* **1** (of competition etc.) fierce, merciless. **2** murderous, barbarous. **cut-throat razor** *n.* a folding razor with a long single-edged blade. **cutting** *a.* **1** dividing by a sharp-edged instrument. **2** sharp-edged. **3** wounding the feelings deeply. **4** sarcastic, biting. *~n.* **1** a piece cut off or out (of a newspaper etc.). **2** an excavation for a road, railway or canal. **3** in horticulture, a piece cut from a plant for propagation, a slip. **cutting-bench** *n.* (*Hist.*) the table on which a cutter assembles and edits a film. **cutting edge** *n.* **1** the edge of a blade etc. **2** the forefront of a movement, technological development etc. **cutting-edge** *a.* leading, pioneering, innovative. **cuttingly** *adv.* in a cutting manner. **cutwater** *n.* (*Naut.*) the fore part of a ship's prow which cuts the water. **cutworm** *n.* a caterpillar which cuts off plants near the roots, esp. (*N Am.*) the larva of the genus of moths *Agrotis.* [etym. uncertain]

cut[2] (kŭt) *n.* **1** the action of cutting. **2** a stroke or blow with a sharp-edged instrument. **3** an opening, gash or wound made by cutting. **4** anything done or said that hurts the feelings. **5** the omission of a part of a play. **6** a slit, a channel, a groove, a trench. **7** a part cut off. **8 a** the place where one strip of film ends in a picture and another begins. **b** the finished version of a film, edited in a particular way. **9** a stroke with a whip. **10** a particular stroke in various ball games. **11** the act of dividing a pack of cards. **12** the shape in which a thing is cut, style. **13** the act of ignoring a former acquaintance. **14** a degree (from count being formerly kept by notches). **15 a** an engraved wood block. **b** an impression from such a block. **16** a gelding. *~a.* **1** subjected to the act or process of cutting. **2** severed. **3** shaped by cutting. **4** castrated. **a cut above** (*fig.*) superior to. **cut and thrust** *n.* **1** in a debate etc., a lively exchange of opinions. **2** in a sword fight, cutting and thrusting. **3** a hand-to-hand struggle.

cutaneous (kūtā´niəs) *a.* belonging to or affecting the skin. [L *cutāneus*, from *cutis*, skin]

cutch (kŭch) *n.* catechu. [Malay *cachu*]

cute (kūt) *a.* **1** delightful, attractive, amusing, pretty. **2** cunning, sharp, clever. **cutely** *adv.* **cuteness** *n.* **cutesy** *a.* (*comp.* **cutesier**, *superl.* **cutesiest**) (*coll.*) affectedly or excessively dainty, quaint etc. **cutie** (-ti) *n.* (*sl.*) a bright, attractive person, esp. a girl or woman. [ACUTE]

cuticle (kū´tikəl) *n.* **1** the dead skin at the edge of fingernails and toenails. **2** the epidermis. **3** (*Zool.*) the outer layer of the protective covering of many invertebrates. **4** (*Bot.*) the thin external covering of the bark of a plant. **cuticular** (-tik´ū-) *a.* [L *cutīcula*, dim. of *cutis*, skin]

cutie CUTE.

cutis (kū´tis) *n.* **1** (*Anat., Zool.*) the true skin beneath the epidermis. **2** (*Bot.*) the peridium of certain fungi. [CUTICLE]

cutlass (kŭt´ləs) *n.* (*Hist.*) a broad curved sword, esp. that formerly used by sailors. [F *coutelas*, augm. of OF *coutel* (F *couteau*), a knife, L *cultellum*, acc. of *cultellus*, COULTER]

cutler (kŭt´lə) *n.* a person who makes or deals in cutting instruments. **cutlery** *n.* **1** knives, spoons and forks used for eating. **2** the business of a cutler. **3** knives and other edged instruments or tools. [OF *coutelier*, *cotelier*, from *coutel* (see CUTLASS)]

cutlet (kŭt´lit) *n.* **1** a small slice of meat, usu. from the loin or neck, for cooking. **2** minced meat or meat-substitute shaped to look like a cutlet. [F *côtelette*, dim. of *côte*, OF *coste*, L *costa*, rib]

cutter, cutting CUT[1].

cuttle (kŭt´əl) *n.* a cuttlefish. **cuttle-bone** *n.* the internal skeleton of the cuttlefish, used as a polishing agent and as a dietary supplement for cage birds. **cuttlefish** *n.* **1** a 10-armed cephalopod, *Sepia officinalis.* **2** any of various other members of the genera *Sepia* and *Sepiola.* [OE *cudele*; etym. uncertain]

cutty (kŭt´i) *a.* (*Sc., North.*) **1** short, cut short. **2** hasty, quick. *~n.* (*pl.* **cutties**) **1** a cutty pipe. **2** a short girl. **cutty pipe** *n.* (*Hist.*) a short clay tobacco pipe. **cutty-stool** *n.* (*Hist.*) a bench in old Scottish churches on which offenders were compelled to sit and undergo public rebuke. [CUT[1]]

cuvée (koovā´) *n.* a batch or blend of wine. [F, p.p. of *cuver*, to ferment (wine) in a vat]

cuvette (kūvet´) *n.* a shallow dish for holding liquids in a laboratory. [F, dim. of *cuve*, L *cūpa*, a cask, a vat]

CV *abbr.* curriculum vitae.

CVO *abbr.* Commander of the Royal Victorian Order.

CVS *abbr.* (*Med.*) chorionic villus sampling, a test to detect chromosome abnormalities in unborn babies.

Cwlth. *abbr.* Commonwealth.

cwm (kum) *n.* **1** a valley in Wales. **2** (*Geol.*) a cirque, a corrie. [Welsh]

c.w.o. *abbr.* cash with order.

CWS *abbr.* Cooperative Wholesale Society.

cwt. *abbr.* hundredweight.

CY *abbr.* Cyprus (IVR).

-cy (si) *suf.* forming nouns of quality from adjectives, and nouns of office (cp. -SHIP) from nouns, as in *idiocy, lunacy, tenancy, residency.* [L *-cia, -tia*; Gr. *-keia, -kia, -teia, -tia* (cp. -ACY)]

cyan (sī´an) *n.* a bluish-green colour. *~a.* of this colour. [Gr. *kuanos*, dark blue]

cyan- CYANO-.

cyanamide (sīan´əmīd) *n.* **1** (*Chem.*) a colourless crystalline weak acid, an amide of cyanogen. **2** any salt of this.

cyanate (sī´ənāt) *n.* (*Chem.*) a salt of cyanic acid.

cyanic (sīan´ik) *a.* **1** derived from cyanogen. **2** blue. **cyanic acid** *n.* (*Chem.*) an unstable acidic compound of cyanogen and hydrogen.

cyanide (sī´ənīd) *n.* (*Chem.*) any (very poisonous) compound of cyanogen with a metallic element. [CYANOGEN]

cyanine (sī´ənēn) *n.* a blue dye used in photographic emulsions.

cyanite KYANITE.

cyano- (sī´ənō), **cyan-** *comb. form* **1** of a blue colour. **2** of, relating to or containing cyanogen. [Gr. *kuanos*, a dark-blue mineral]

cyanobacterium (sīənōbaktiə´riəm) *n.* (*pl.* **cyanobacteria** (-riə)) (*Biol.*) any prokaryotic organism of the division *Cyanobacteria*, containing a blue photosynthetic pigment, blue-green alga. [CYANOGEN, BACTERIUM]

cyanocobalamin (sīənōkəbal´əmin) *n.* a vitamin of the B complex occurring in the liver, the lack of which can lead to pernicious anaemia, Vitamin B_{12}. [*cyano-*, *cobal*t, vi*tamin*]

cyanogen (sīan´əjən) *n.* (*Chem.*) a colourless, poisonous gas composed of carbon and nitrogen, burning with a peach-blossom flame, and smelling like almond. **cyanogenic** (-jen´-) *a.* capable of producing cyanide.

cyanosis (sīənō´sis) *n.* (*pl.* **cyanoses** (-sēz)) (*Med.*) a condition in which the skin becomes blue or leaden-coloured owing to the circulation of oxygen-deficient blood. **cyanotic** (-not´-) *a.*

cyanotype (sīan´ətīp) *n.* **1** a photographic process in which a cyanide is employed, producing a blueprint. **2** a blueprint.

cyber- (sī´bə) *comb. form* denoting computer control systems, electronic communication networks and virtual reality. [from *cybernetics*]

cybernetics (sībənet´iks) *n.* the comparative study of control and communication mechanisms in machines and living creatures. **cybernate** (sī´-) *v.t.* to control automatically, e.g. by means of a computer. **cybernation** (-ā´shən) *n.* **cybernetic** *a.* **cybernetician** (-tish´-) *n.* **cyberneticist** *n.* [Gr. *kubernetes*, a steersman]

cyberpunk (sī´bəpŭngk) *n.* **1** a style of science fiction writing that features rebellious computer hackers in a bleak future world controlled by computer networks. **2** a writer or devotee of this.

cyberspace (sī´bəspās) *n.* virtual reality, the notional environment created by computer in which people can physically interact.

cyborg (sī´bawg) *n.* a form of robot of superhuman capabilities made from biological and mechanical parts. [*cyb*ernetics, *org*anism]

cycad (sī´kad) *n.* a tropical or subtropical palmlike plant of the order Cycadeles, an order of gymnosperms, allied to the conifers. **cycadaceous** (sīkədā´shəs) *a.* [mod. L *cycas -adem* (from a supposed Gr. *kukas*, now recognized as an error for *koïkas*, acc. pl. of *koïx*, the Egyptian doum-palm)]

Cycladic (sīklad´ik) *a.* of or relating to the Cyclades, a group of islands in the S Aegean Sea, esp. to the Bronze Age civilization that existed there. [L *Cyclades*, from Gr. *Kuklades*, from *Kuklos*, circle (of islands)]

cyclamate (sik´ləmāt, sī´-) *n.* any of several compounds derived from petrochemicals, formerly used as sweetening agents. [*cyclo*hexylsulph*amate*]

cyclamen (sik´ləmən) *n.* (*pl.* **cyclamen, cyclamens**) **1** any S European tuberous plant of the genus *Cyclamen*, having red, pink or white flowers. **2** the strong pink colour associated with these. [late L, from Gr. *kuklamīnos* (perh. from *kuklos*, a circle, with reference to the bulbous root)]

cycle (sī´kəl) *n.* **1** a series of years, events or phenomena recurring in the same order. **2** a series that repeats itself. **3** a complete series or succession. **4** the period in which a series of events is completed. **5** a bicycle. **6** a long period, an age. **7** a body of legend connected with some myth. **8** (*Physics*) each complete series of changes in a periodically varying quantity, e.g. an electric current. **9** (*Astron.*) †an imaginary circle in the heavens. ~*v.i.* **1** to ride a bicycle. **2** to revolve in a circle. **cycle of the moon** *n.* a Metonic cycle. **cycle of the sun** *n.* a Metonic cycle. **cycle track, cycleway** *n.* a path, often beside a road, reserved for cyclists. **cyclic, cyclical** *a.* **1** moving or recurring in a cycle. **2** (*Bot.*) arranged in whorls. **3** (*Chem.*) (of an organic chemical compound) containing a ring of atoms. **4** (*Math.*) of a circle or cycle. **cyclically** *adv.* **cyclist** *n.* a person who rides a bicycle. [L *cyclus*, Gr. *kuklos*, a circle]

cyclo- (sī´klō) *comb. form* **1** circular. **2** of or relating to a circle, circles or cycles. [Gr. *kuklos*, a circle]

cycloalkane (sīklōal´kān) *n.* (*Chem.*) a saturated hydrocarbon having a cyclic molecular structure, cycloparaffin.

cyclo-cross (sī´klōkros) *n.* the sport of cross-country racing on a bicycle. [CYCLE, CROSS]

cyclograph (sī´klōgrahf) *n.* an instrument for describing the arcs of large circles.

cyclohexane (sīklōhek´sān) *n.* (*Chem.*) a colourless liquid cycloalkane used as a paint remover and solvent.

cycloid (sī´kloid) *n.* the figure described by a point in the plane of a circle as it rolls along a straight line till it has completed a revolution. **cycloidal** (-kloi´-) *a.* **1** resembling a circle. **2** (*Zool.*) having concentric striations. [Gr. *kukloeides*, circular, from *kuklos*, circle]

cyclometer (sīklom´itə) *n.* an instrument for recording the revolutions of a wheel, esp. that of a bicycle, and hence the distance travelled. **cyclometry** *n.* the art or process of measuring circles.

cyclone (sī´klōn) *n.* **1** a tropical cyclone. **2** a disturbance in the atmosphere caused by a system of winds blowing spirally towards a central region of low barometric pressure. **cyclonic** (-klon´-) *a.* **cyclonically** *adv.* [Gr. *kuklos*, a circle]

cycloparaffin (sīklōpar´əfin) *n.* (*Chem.*) a cycloalkane.

Cyclopean CYCLOPS.

cyclopedia (sīkləpē´diə), **cyclopaedia** *n.* an encyclopedia. **cyclopedic** *a.*

cyclopropane (sīklōprō´pān) *n.* a colourless hydrocarbon gas used as an anaesthetic.

Cyclops (sī´klops) *n.* (*pl.* **Cyclops, Cyclopses, Cyclopes** (-ōpēz)) a member of a race of mythical one-eyed giants supposed to have lived in Sicily. **Cyclopean** (sīkləpē´ən, -klō´-), **Cyclopian** *a.* **1** of or relating to the Cyclops. **2** immense, gigantic. **Cyclopean masonry** *n.* (*Archit.*) a style of architecture of great antiquity, in which massive blocks are accurately fitted together, or rough blocks laid one on another, and the interstices filled up with small stones, no mortar being used in either form. **cyclops** *n.* (*pl.* **cyclopes** (-ōpēz), **cyclops**) **1** any crustacean of the genus *Cyclops*, having a single eye. **2** (*coll.*) a one-eyed person. [L, from Gr. *Kuklōps* (*kuklos*, a circle, *ōps*, an eye)]

cyclorama (sīklərah´mə) *n.* **1** a curved wall or cloth at the rear of a stage, film set etc. **2** (*Hist.*) a panorama painted on the inside of a large cylinder and viewed by the spectator from the middle. [Gr. *horama*, a view]

cyclosis (sīklō´sis) *n.* (*pl.* **cycloses** (-sēz)) **1** (*Biol.*) circulation, as of blood, the latex in plants, or protoplasm in certain cells. **2** (*Math.*) the occurrence of cycles. [Gr. *kuklōsis*, an encircling (*kukloein*, to move in a circle)]

cyclosporin (sīklōspaw´rin) *n.* (*Med.*) an immunosuppressant drug used after transplant surgery to prevent rejection of grafts and transplants. [CYCLO-, *-sporum*, -IN[1], part of the name of the fungus from which it is derived]

cyclostome (sī´kləstōm) *n.* any fish of the subclass Cyclostomata, with a circular sucking mouth, e.g. the lamprey and hag. **cyclostomate** (-stom´-), **cyclostomous** (-klos´-) *a.* [Gr. *stomata*, pl. of *stoma*, mouth]

cyclostyle (sī´kləstīl) *n.* (*Hist.*) a machine for printing copies of handwriting or typewriting by means of a sheet perforated like a stencil. ~*v.t.* **1** to print using this machine. **2** (*coll.*) to copy (a document) by means of a copier etc.

cyclothymia (sīklōthī´miə) *n.* (*Psych.*) a psychological condition characterized by swings between elation and depression. **cyclothymic** *a.* [Gr. *thumos*, spirit]

cyclotron (sī´klətron) *n.* (*Physics*) a particle accelerator designed to accelerate protons to high energies.

cyder CIDER.

cygnet (sig´nət) *n.* a young swan. [dim. of OF *cygne* or L *cygnus*, a swan]

cylinder (sil´ində) *n.* **1** a straight roller-shaped body, solid or hollow, and of uniform circumference. **2** (*Geom.*) a solid figure described by the revolution of a right-angled parallelogram about one of its sides which remains fixed. **3** a cylindrical member of various machines, esp. the chamber in an engine in which the piston is acted upon by internal combustion, steam etc. **4** the roller used in machine-printing. **cylinder block** *n.* the fixed casing containing the cylinders of an internal-combustion engine. **cylinder head** *n.* the detachable casing fitted on the top of a cylinder block. **cylinder press** *n.* a printing press in which the type is secured on a cylinder, or in which the impression is given by a cylinder. **cylinder saw** *n.* a crown saw. **cylinder seal** *n.* (*Hist.*) a small cylindrical seal of stone or clay bearing a cuneiform inscription. **cylindrical** (-lin´dri-) *a.* having the form of a cylinder. **cylindrically** *adv.* **cylindriform** (-lin´drifawm) *a.* **cylindroid** (-droid) *n.* (*Geom.*) a solid body differing from a cylinder in having the bases elliptical instead of circular. [L *cylindrus*, Gr. *kulindros* (*kulindein*, to roll)]

cyma (sī´mə) *n.* (*pl.* **cymas, cymae** (-mē)) **1** (*Archit.*) a convex and a concave curve forming the topmost member of a cornice. **2** (*Bot.*) a cyme. **cyma recta** (rek´tə) *n.* a curve convex above and concave below. **cyma reversa** (rəvœ´sə) *n.* a curve concave above and convex below, ogee. **cymograph** (-grahf) *n.* an apparatus for tracing the outline of mouldings. [Gr. *kuma*, anything swollen, a wave, an ogee moulding, a sprout]

cymar (simah´), **simar** *n.* (*Hist.*) a woman's light loose robe or undergarment of the 17th and 18th cents. [F *simarre*, OF *chamarre* (see CHIMER (under CHIME[1]))]

cymatium (sīmā´tiəm, -shəm) *n.* (*pl.* **cymatia** (-tiə, -shə)) a cyma. [L, from Gr. *kumation*, dim. of *kuma*]

cymbal (sim´bəl) *n.* (*Mus.*) a disc of brass or bronze more or less basin-shaped, clashed together in pairs or hit with a stick etc. to produce a sharp, clashing sound. **cymbalist** *n.* [L *cymbalum*, Gr. *kumbalon* (*kumbē*, hollow)]

cymbalo (sim´bəlō) *n.* (*pl.* **cymbalos**) (*Mus.*) the dulcimer, a stringed instrument played by means of small hammers held in the hands. [It. *cembalo*, from L *cymbalum*, as CYMBAL]

cymbidium (simbid´iəm) *n.* (*pl.* **cymbidiums, cymbidia** (-iə)) any orchid of the genus *Cymbidium* having colourful, long-lasting flowers and a recess in the flower-lip. [L, from Gr. *kumbē*, cup]

cymbiform (sim´bifawm) *a.* (*Anat.*, *Bot.*) (of certain bones and grasses) boat-shaped. [L *cymba*, a boat, -FORM]

cyme (sīm) *n.* (*Bot.*) an inflorescence in which the central terminal flower comes to perfection first, as in the guelder rose. **cymoid** *a.* resembling a cyme. **cymose** (-mōs) *a.* [F, from L *cyma*, Gr. *kuma*, see CYMA]

cymograph CYMA.

cymophane (sī´məfān) *n.* (*Mineral.*) a variety of opalescent chrysoberyl. [Gr. *kuma*, a wave, *-phanēs*, appearing (*phainein*, to appear)]

cymose CYME.

Cymric (kim´rik) *a.* of or relating to the Welsh. ~*n.* the Welsh language. [Welsh *Cymru*, Wales]

cynic (sin´ik) *n.* **1** a person who is pessimistic about human nature. **2** a person who is habitually morose and sarcastic. **3** (*Hist.*) (**Cynic**) a member of a rigid sect of Greek philosophers (of which Diogenes was the most distinguished member) founded at Athens by Antisthenes, a pupil of Socrates, who insisted on the complete renunciation of all luxury and the subjugation of sensual desires. ~*a.* (**Cynic**) of or belonging to the Cynics. **cynical** *a.* **1** bitter, sarcastic, misanthropic. **2** acting in disregard of accepted standards of conduct. **cynically** *adv.* **cynicism** (-sizm) *n.* [L *cynicus*, Gr. *kunikos* (*kun-*, stem of *kuōn*, a dog)]

cynocephalus (sīnōsef´ələs) *n.* **1** a dog-headed man in ancient mythology. **2** a flying lemur. [L, from Gr. *kunokephalos* (Gr. *kuōn kunos*, dog, *kephalē*, head)]

cynophobia (sīnəfō´biə) *n.* **1** a morbid fear of dogs. **2** a neurosis manifesting itself in symptoms resembling rabies. [Gr. *kuōn kunos*, dog]

cynosure (sin´əzūə, -shuə) *n.* **1** a centre of interest or attraction. **2** the constellation of the Lesser Bear (Ursa Minor), containing the north star. [F, from L *cynosūra*, Gr. *kunosoura*, the dog's tail, the Lesser Bear (*kuōn kunos*, dog, *oura*, tail)]

cypher CIPHER.

cy près (sē prā´) *a.*, *adv.* (*Law*) as near as practicable (referring to the principle of applying a bequest as nearly as possible to the testator's aim when that aim is impracticable). ~*n.* an approximation. [A-F (F *si près*, so near)]

cypress[1] (sī´prəs) *n.* **1** (*also* **cypress tree**) a tree of the coniferous genera *Cupressus* or *Chamaecyparis*, esp. *Cupressus sempervirens*, valued for the durability of its wood. **2** a branch of this as emblem of mourning. [OF *cyprès*, late L *cypressus*, Gr. *kupressos*]

†**cypress**[2] (sī´prəs) *n.* **1** (*Hist.*) a kind of satin that was highly valued. **2** a piece of this worn as a token of mourning. [prob. from OF *Ciprè*, *Cypre*, Cyprus]

Cyprian CYPRIOT.

cyprine (sip´rīn) *n.* of or belonging to the fish suborder Cyprinoidea, containing the carp. **cyprinoid** *a.* of or like a carp. ~*n.* a carp or related fish. [L *cyprīnus*, Gr. *kuprînos*, carp]

Cypriot (sip´riət), **Cypriote** (-ōt) *n.* a native or inhabitant of Cyprus. ~*a.* of, relating or belonging to Cyprus. **Cyprian** (sip´riən) *a.* of or belonging to Cyprus, esp. as a place where the worship of Venus especially flourished. ~*n.* **1** a Cypriot. **2** †a prostitute. [Gr. *Kupriōtēs* from *Kupros*, Cyprus]

cypripedium (sipripē´diəm) *n.* any orchid of the genus *Cypripedium*, esp. the lady's slipper, possessing two fertile stamens, the central stamen (fertile in other orchids) being represented by a shieldlike plate. [Gr. *Kupris*, Venus, *podion*, a slipper]

cypsela (sip´silə) *n.* (*pl.* **cypselae** (-lē)) (*Bot.*) the dry single-seeded fruit of the daisy and related plants. [L, from Gr. *kupselē*, hollow vessel]

Cyrenaic (sīrənā´ik, sir´-) *a.* of or relating to Cyrene, an ancient Greek colony in the north of Africa, or to the hedonistic philosophy founded at that place by Aristippus. ~*n.* a philosopher of the Cyrenaic school.

Cyrillic (siril´ik) *a.* denoting the alphabet of the Slavonic nations who belong to the Orthodox Church, now esp. Russia and Bulgaria (from the fact that it was introduced by Clement, a disciple of St Cyril). ~*n.* the Cyrillic alphabet. [St *Cyril*, d. 869]

cyst (sist) *n.* **1** (*Biol.*) a bladder, vesicle or hollow organ. **2** (*Med.*) a sac or cavity of abnormal character containing fluid or semi-solid matter. **3** (*Biol.*) a thick protective membrane enclosing an organism. **cystic** *a.* **1** of, relating to or enclosed in a cyst, esp. the gall or urinary bladder. **2** having cysts, or of the nature of a cyst. **cystic fibrosis** *n.* a hereditary disease appearing in early childhood, marked by overproduction of mucus and fibrous tissue, with consequent breathing and digestive difficulties. **cystiform** (sis´tifawm) *a.* [L *cystis*, from Gr. *kustis*, a bladder]

cysteine (sis´tēn, -tiēn, -tān, -tiin) *n.* a sulphur-containing amino acid, present in proteins and essential in the human diet. **cystine** (sis´tīn) *n.* a sulphur-containing amino acid discovered in a rare kind of urinary calculus, formed by the oxidization of cysteine.

cysti- (sis´ti), **cysto-** (-ō), **cyst-** *comb. form* **1** of or relating to the bladder. **2** bladder-shaped. [Gr. *kustē*, *kustis*, a bladder]

cystic CYST.

cystitis (sistī´tis) *n.* (*Med.*) inflammation of the urinary bladder.

cysto- CYSTI-.

cystocele (sis´təsēl) *n.* (*Med.*) hernia caused by protrusion of the bladder.

cystoscope (sis´təskōp) *n.* an instrument or apparatus for the exploration of the bladder. **cystoscopic** (-skop´-) *a.* **cystoscopy** (-tos´-) *n.*

cystotomy (sistot´əmi) *n.* (*pl.* **cystotomies**) the surgical operation of cutting into the urinary bladder.

-cyte (sīt) *comb. form* (*Biol.*) a mature cell, as in *leucocyte*. [Gr. *kutos*, a hollow, a receptacle]

Cytherean (sithərē´ən) *a.* of or relating to Venus, the goddess of love, who was connected with Cythera (the modern Kithira, an island off the Peloponnese).

cytidine (sī´tidēn) *n.* a nucleoside obtained from RNA by the condensation of ribose and cytosine. [G *Cytidin*, as -CYTE]

cyto- (sī´tō) *comb. form* (*Biol.*) **1** cellular. **2** of or relating to or composed of cells. [Gr. *kutos*, a hollow]

cytoblast (sī´təblahst) *n.* a cell nucleus.

cytochrome (sī´təkrōm) *n.* any of a group of naturally-occurring compounds consisting of a protein linked to a haem, of great importance in cell oxidization.

cytogenetics (sītōjənet´iks) *n.* the branch of genetics concerned with inheritance where related to the structure and function of cells. **cytogenetic, cytogenetical** *a.* **cytogenetically** *adv.* **cytogeneticist** *n.*

cytology (sītol´əji) *n.* the study of cells. **cytological** (-loj´-) *a.* **cytologically** *adv.* **cytologist** *n.* **cytolysis** *n.* the dissolution of cells.

cytomegalovirus (sītōmeg´əlōvīrəs) *n.* (*Med.*) a variety of herpes virus that may cause serious nerve damage in those whose immune systems are weakened, esp. babies.

cytoplasm (sī´tōplazm) *n.* the protoplasm of a cell apart from the nucleus. **cytoplasmic** (-plaz´-) *a.*

cytosine (sī´təsēn) *n.* a pyrimidine occurring in all living tissues, being a component base of RNA and DNA.

cytoskeleton (sī´tōskelitən) *n.* (*Biol.*) a network of fibrous proteins that govern the shape and movement of a living cell.

cytotoxin (sītōtok´sin) *n.* a substance which is poisonous to cells. **cytotoxic** *a.*

czar, czaritza TSAR.

czardas CSARDAS.

Czech (chek) *n.* **1** a native or inhabitant of the Czech Republic. **2** the Slavonic language of the Czechs. **3** (*Hist.*) a native or inhabitant of Czechoslovakia. ~*a.* of or relating to the Czechs, their language or the Czech Republic. **Czechoslovak** (chekōslō´vak), **Czechoslovakian** (-vak´iən) *n.* (*Hist.*) a native or inhabitant of Czechoslovakia (a former state in Central Europe). ~*a.* of or relating to Czechoslovakia. [Pol. spelling of Czech *Cech*]

D[1] (dē), **d** (*pl.* **Ds, D's**) the fourth letter of the English and other versions of the Roman alphabet, corresponding to the Greek delta (Δ, δ). It is pronounced as a voiced dental plosive, though after a voiceless consonant its reflex approaches or becomes the sound of *t*, especially in the past tenses and past participles of verbs in *-ed.* ~*symbol* **1** the fourth of a series, the fourth highest in a range, e.g. of marks, etc. **2** the fourth known quantity in an algebraic expression. **3** (*Mus.*) **a** the second note of the diatonic scale of C major. **b** the scale of a composition in which the key-note is D. **4** 500 in Roman numerals. **D-day** *n.* **1** the code name for the date of the invasion of France, 6 June 1944. **2** the date planned for the beginning of an important venture. **D-layer** *n.* the lowest layer of the ionosphere which can reflect low-frequency radio waves. **D region, D layer** *n.* the lowest part of the ionosphere, between 25 and 40 miles (40 and 65 km) above the earth's surface.

D[2] *abbr.* **1** defence (in *D-notice*). **2** Democrat. **3** density (of electric flux density). **4** department. **5** deuterium. **6** dextrorotatory. **7** dimension. **8** God (L *deus*). **9** Lord (L *dominus*). **D-notice** *n.* an official notice prohibiting publication of sensitive information.

d. *abbr.* **1** date. **2** daughter. **3** day. **4** deci-. **5** delete. **6** depart(s). **7** depth. **8** died. **9** diameter. **10** penny (before decimalization, L *denarius*).

'd (d) *contr.* (*coll.*) **1** had. **2** would.

-d (d) *suf.* forming the past tense and p.p. of some regular verbs, as in *died, heard, loved, proved.* [OE *-de* (see -ED)]

DA *abbr.* **1** Diploma of Art. **2** (*N Am.*) District Attorney. **3** (*sl.*) duck's arse.

D/A *abbr.* digital to analogue.

da *abbr.* deca-.

dab[1] (dab) *v.t.* (*pres.p.* **dabbing,** *past, p.p.* **dabbed**) **1** to strike gently with some moist or soft substance. **2** to pat. **3** to rub with a dabber. **4** to press with a soft substance. ~*n.* **1** a gentle blow. **2** a light stroke or wipe with a soft substance. **3** a small amount of a soft substance dabbed. **4** (*often pl., sl.*) fingerprints. **dabber** *n.* **dab hand** *n.* (*coll.*) an expert (at). [etym. uncertain; prob. imit. (cp. TAP[1])]

dab[2] (dab) *n.* a small flatfish, *Limanda limanda.* [perh. from DAB[1]]

dabble (dab´əl) *v.t.* **1** to keep on dabbing. **2** to wet by little dips. **3** to besprinkle, to moisten, to splash. ~*v.i.* **1** to play or splash about in water. **2** to do or practise anything in a superficial manner. **3** to dip into a subject. **dabbler** *n.* a person who dabbles with or in any subject. **dabblingly** *adv.* superficially, shallowly. [freq. of DAB[1] (cp. Norw. *dabla,* Dut. *dabbelen*)]

dabchick (dab´chik), **dobchick** (dob´-) *n.* the little grebe, *Tachybaptus ruficollis.* [earlier *dap-chick, dop-chick* (*dap,* cogn. with DIP)]

dabster (dab´stə) *n.* (*coll.*) a person who is expert at anything. [DAB[1]]

da capo (da kah´pō) *adv.* (*Mus.*) (repeat) from the beginning. [It., from the head]

dace (dās) *n.* a small river fish, *Leuciscus leuciscus.* [ME *darse,* OF *darz,* DART]

dacha (dach´ə), **datcha** *n.* (*pl.* **dachas, datchas**) a country house or cottage in Russia. [Rus., gift]

dachshund (daks´hund, dak´sənd) *n.* a short-legged long-bodied breed of dog. [G, badgerhound]

dacite (dā´sīt) *n.* a type of volcanic rock. [*Dacia,* in central Europe]

dacoit (dəkoit´), **dakoit** *n.* in the Indian subcontinent or Burma (Myanmar), a member of a band of armed robbers. **dacoity** *n.* robbery by armed gang. [Hind. *dakait* (*dākā,* robbery by a gang)]

dactyl (dak´til) *n.* a metrical foot consisting of one long followed by two short syllables, or of one stressed followed by two unstressed syllables. **dactylic** (-til´-) *a.* of or relating to dactyls. ~*n.* (*usu. pl.*) verse in dactyls. **dactylic hexameter** *n.* a hexameter having as its basic structure five dactyls and a spondee or trochee. [L *dactylus,* DACTYLO-]

dactyl-, dactylio- DACTYLO-.

dactylo- (dak´tilō), **dactyl-, dactylio-** (-iō) *comb. form* **1** having fingers or digits. **2** of or relating to fingers or digits. [Gr. *daktulos,* a finger]

dactylogram (daktil´əgram) *n.* a fingerprint. **dactylography** (-og´rəfi) *n.* the study of fingerprints.

dactylology (daktilol´əji) *n.* the art of conversing with the deaf by means of the fingers.

dad (dad) *n.* (*coll.*) father. **dada** (dad´ə, -ah) *n.* (used by or to children). **daddy** *n.* (*pl.* **daddies**). **the daddy of them all** (*coll.*) the supreme example of something. **daddy-long-legs** *n.* (*pl.* **daddy-long-legs**) **1** any of various species of crane-fly. **2** (*US*) a harvestman. [cp. Welsh *tad,* Gr. *tata,* Sansk. *tata-*]

Dada (dah´dah), **Dadaism** (-izm) *n.* an early 20th-cent. school of art and literature that aimed at suppressing any correlation between thought and expression. **Dadaist** *n., a.* **Dadaistic** (-is´tik) *a.* [F, hobby horse]

dada DAD.

daddy DAD.

dado (dā´dō) *n.* (*pl.* **dados, dadoes**) **1** an arrangement of wainscoting or decoration round the lower part of the walls of a room. **2** the cube of a pedestal between the base and the cornice. [It., a die, a cube]

daedal (dē´dəl), **dedal** *a.* **1** Daedalian. **2** skilful. **3** deceitful. **4** complicated. **Daedalian** (-dā´liən), **Daedalean, Dedalian** *a.* **1** curiously formed. **2** mazelike. [L *Daedaleus,* pertaining to *Daedalus,* the Greek artificer (cp. Gr. *daidaleos,* cunningly wrought)]

daemon DEMON.

daff[1] (daf) *n.* (*coll.*) short for DAFFODIL.

daff[2] (daf) *v.i.* (*Sc.*) to play the fool. [cp. DAFT]

daffily, daffiness DAFFY.

daffodil (daf´ədil) *n.* **1** the yellow narcissus, *Narcissus pseudonarcissus.* **2** any of various other species and garden varieties of the genus *Narcissus.* **daffodil yellow** *n., a.* (of) a pale yellow colour. [ME *affodill,* OF *asphodile,* L *asphodelus,* Gr. *asphodelos*]

daffy (daf´i) *a.* (*comp.* **daffier,** *superl.* **daffiest**) (*coll.*) crazy, daft. **daffily** *adv.* **daffiness** *n.* [DAFF[2]]

daft (dahft) *a.* **1** weak-minded, imbecile. **2** foolish, silly, thoughtless. **3** frolicsome. **daft about** (*coll.*) very fond of. **daftly** *adv.* **daftness** *n.* [OE *gedæfte,* mild, gentle]

dag (dag) *n.* (*Austral., New Zeal.*) **1** a daglock. **2** (*coll.*) an old-fashioned, unattractive person; a character. ~*v.t.* (*pres.p.* **dagging,** *past, p.p.* **dagged**) to remove daglock from (a sheep). **to rattle one's dags** (*coll.*) to hurry up.

dagger[1] *n.* **daggy** *a.* (*comp.* **daggier**, *superl.* **daggiest**) (*coll.*) old-fashioned and unattractive.

dagga (dag´ə, dakh´ə) *n.* (*S Afr.*) **1** a type of hemp used as a narcotic. **2** any plant of the genus *Leonotis* also so used. [Nama *dachab*]

dagger[1] DAG.

dagger[2] (dag´ə) *n.* **1** a short two-edged weapon adapted for stabbing. **2** (*Print.*) a reference mark (†). **at daggers drawn 1** on hostile terms. **2** ready to fight. **to look daggers** to look with fierceness or animosity. **dagger-board** *n.* a sliding centreboard on a boat. [F *dague*, infl. by ME *daggen*, to pierce]

daggy DAG.

daglock (dag´lok) *n.* the dirt-covered clumps of wool around the hindquarters of a sheep. [etym. uncertain]

dago (dā´gō) *n.* (*pl.* **dagos, dagoes**) (*offensive*) a Spaniard, Italian or Portuguese. [Sp. *Diego*, James]

dagoba (dah´gəbə) *n.* (*pl.* **dagobas**) a dome-shaped Buddhist shrine containing relics. [Sinhalese *dāgaba*]

daguerreotype (dəger´ətīp) *n.* **1** the process of photographing on copper plates coated with silver iodide, developed by exposure to mercury vapour. **2** a photograph by this process. *~v.t.* **1** to photograph by this process. **2** (*fig.*) to picture exactly. **daguerreotyper, daguerreotypist** *n.* a person who produced daguerreotypes. **daguerreotypic** (-tip´-), **daguerreotypical** *a.* of or relating to daguerreotype. [Louis Jacques Mandé *Daguerre*, 1789–1851, French inventor]

dahabeeyah (dah·həbē´yə) *n.* a type of sailing-boat on the Nile. [Arab. *dhahabīyah*, the golden one (*dhahab*, gold)]

dahl DHAL.

dahlia (dā´lyə) *n.* (*pl.* **dahlias**) a composite plant of the genus *Dahlia* from Mexico, cultivated for their flowers. [Anders *Dahl*, a Swedish pupil of Linnaeus]

daily (dā´li) *a.* **1** happening, done or recurring every day. **2** published every weekday. **3** necessary for every day. **4** ordinary, usual. *~adv.* **1** day by day. **2** often. **3** continually, always. *~n.* (*pl.* **dailies**) **1** a newspaper published every weekday. **2** a woman employed daily for housework. **daily bread** *n.* necessary food and sustenance, means of living. **daily dozen** *n.* (*coll.*) daily physical exercises. [OE *dæglic* (found only in comb.)]

daimio (dī´myō) *n.* (*pl.* **daimio, damios**) the official title of a former class of feudal lords in Japan. [Jap. (Chin. *dai*, great, *myo*, name)]

daimon (dī´mōn) *n.* a genius or attendant spirit. **daimonic** (-mon´-) *a.* [Gr., DEMON]

dainty (dān´ti) *a.* (*comp.* **daintier**, *superl.* **daintiest**) **1** pretty, delicate, elegant. **2** pleasing to the taste, choice. **3** fastidious, delicate. *~n.* (*pl.* **dainties**) a delicacy; a choice morsel. **daintily** *adv.* **daintiness** *n.* [OF *dainté*, L *dignitās -tātem* (*dignus*, worthy)]

daiquiri (dak´əri, dī´-) *n.* (*pl.* **daiquiris**) a cocktail made of rum and lime-juice. [town in Cuba]

dairy (deə´ri) *n.* (*pl.* **dairies**) **1** the place or building or department of a farm where milk is kept and converted into butter or cheese. **2** a place where milk, cream and butter are sold. *~a.* of or relating to the production of milk and its products. **dairy-farm** *n.* **dairy-farming** *n.* **dairying** *n.* dairy-farming. †**dairymaid** *n.* a woman employed in a dairy. **dairyman** *n.* (*pl.* **dairymen**) a man employed in a dairy or dealing with dairy products. **dairy products** *n.pl.* [OE *dǣge*, a maidservant -ERY]

dais (dā´is) *n.* (*pl.* **daises**) **1** a platform. **2** the raised floor at the upper end of a medieval dining-hall. [A-F *deis*, OF *dois*, L *discus -um*, a quoit, late L, a table]

daisy (dā´zi) *n.* (*pl.* **daisies**) **1** a small composite flower, *Bellis perennis*, with white petals and a yellow centre. **2** any of various other flowers resembling this. **3** (*sl.*) a first-rate person or thing. **pushing up (the) daisies** dead (and buried). **daisy-chain** *n.* a string of daisies joined together. **daisy-cutter** *n.* in cricket, a ball bowled so low that it rolls along the ground. **daisy-wheel** *n.* (*Comput.*) a wheel-shaped printer with characters on spikes round the circumference. [OE *dæges ēage*, day's eye]

Dak. *abbr.* Dakota.

dak (dahk), **dawk** (dawk) *n.* (*Hist.*) the Indian post or transport by relays of runners, horses etc. **dak-bungalow** *n.* an inn or house for travellers at a dawk station. [Hind. *dāk* (prob. conn. with Sansk. *drāk*, quickly, from *drā*, to run)]

dakoit DACOIT.

dal DHAL.

Dalai Lama *n.* the spiritual leader of Tibetan Buddhism, previously also the temporal ruler of Tibet. [Mongolian *dalai*, ocean, Tibetan *blama*, high priest]

dalasi (dəlah´si) *n.* (*pl.* **dalasi, dalasis**) the standard monetary unit of the Gambia. [Gambian word]

dale (dāl) *n.* a valley, esp. from the English midlands to the Scottish lowlands. **dalesman** *n.* (*pl.* **dalesmen**) a (male) native or inhabitant of a dale, esp. in the northern counties of England. **daleswoman** *n.* (*pl.* **daleswomen**) a female native or inhabitant of a dale. [OE *dæl*, a valley (cp. Icel. *dalr*, Dan. *dal*, Goth. *dal*, G *Thal*)]

dally (dal´i) *v.i.* (*3rd pers. sing. pres.* **dallies**, *pres.p.* **dallying**, *past, p.p.* **dallied**) **1** to trifle (with), to flirt (with), to treat frivolously. **2** to idle, to delay, to waste time. *~v.t.* to fritter or waste (away). **dalliance** *n.* [OF *dalier*, to chat]

Dalmatian (dalmā´shən) *n.* **1** a variety of hound, white with numerous black or brown spots, formerly kept chiefly as a carriage dog. **2** a native or inhabitant of Dalmatia, in Croatia. *~a.* of or relating to Dalmatia.

dalmatic (dalmat´ik) *n.* **1** an ecclesiastical vestment worn by bishops and deacons in the Roman and Greek Churches at High Mass. **2** a similar robe worn by monarchs at coronation and other ceremonies. [F *dalmatique*, L *dalmatica*, orig. a., of Dalmatia]

dal segno (dal sen´yō) *adv.* (*Mus.*) (repeat) from point indicated. [It., from the sign]

dalton (dawl´tən) *n.* an atomic mass unit. [John *Dalton*, 1766–1844, British chemist]

daltonism (dawl´tənizm) *n.* colour-blindness, esp. inability to distinguish between red and green. [John *Dalton*, 1766–1844, British chemist, who suffered from this]

dam[1] (dam) *n.* **1** a bank or mound raised to keep back water (by humans to form a reservoir etc. or by a beaver). **2** any barrier acting like a dam. **3** the water kept back by a dam. **4** a causeway. *~v.t.* (*pres.p.* **damming**, *past, p.p.* **dammed**) **1** to keep back or confine by a dam. **2** to obstruct, to hinder. [cp. OFris. *dam*, *dom*, Dut. *dam*, MHG *dam*, G *Damm*, Swed. and Dan. *dam*; also OE *fordemman*, to stop up]

dam[2] (dam) *n.* a female parent (chiefly of quadrupeds); used of a human mother in contempt. [DAME]

damage (dam´ij) *n.* **1** hurt, injury, mischief or detriment to any person or thing. **2** loss or harm incurred. **3** (*pl.*) value of injury done. **4** (*pl.*, *Law*) reparation in money for injury sustained. **5** (*sl.*) cost. *~v.t.* **1** to cause damage to. **2** to injure the reputation of. *~v.i.* to receive damage. **damageable** *a.* **1** susceptible to damage. **2** causing damage. **damaging** *a.* **damagingly** *adv.* [F, from *dam*, L *damnum*, cost, loss]

Damascene (dam´əsēn, -sēn´) *a.* of or relating to Damascus. *~n.* a native or inhabitant of Damascus.

damascene (dam´əsēn, -sēn´) *v.t.* to ornament by inlaying or incrustation, or (as a steel blade) with a wavy pattern in welding. *~a.* of or relating to this form of ornamentation. *~n.* **1** a damascened article or design. **2** a damson. [F *damasquiner* (from L *Damascēnus*, Gr. *Damaskēnos*, of Damascus)]

damask (dam´əsk) *n.* 1 a rich silk stuff with raised figures woven in the pattern, orig. made at Damascus. 2 a linen fabric, with similar figures in the pattern, used for tablecloths, dinner-napkins etc. 3 a tablecloth made of this. 4 steel made with a wavy pattern by forging iron and steel together. 5 the colour of the damask rose. ~*a.* 1 made of damask. 2 pink or red, like the damask rose. 3 of or resembling damask steel. ~*v.t.* 1 to work with figured designs, to work flowers on. 2 to damascene, to give a wavy appearance to (steel work etc.). **damask rose** *n.* an old-fashioned rose, *Rosa gallica*, var. *damascena*, used to make attar of roses. **damask steel** *n.* a laminated metal of pure iron and steel, used for Damascus blades. [It. *damasco*, DAMASCENE]

dame (dām) *n.* 1 a lady; a title of honour (now applied to the wives of knights and baronets). 2 (a title of honour given to) a female equivalent of the Knight Commander or holder of the Grand Cross. 3 †the mistress of a house. 4 †a woman advanced in years. 5 a comic old woman in pantomime, usu. played by a man. 6 (*sl.*, *esp. N Am.*) a woman. **dame-school** *n.* (*Hist.*) an elementary school kept by a woman. [OF, from L *domina*, fem. of *dominus*, lord]

damfool DAMN.

dammar (dam´ə) *n.* 1 any of various Asian and Australasian trees yielding resin. 2 a resin of this kind. [Malay *damar*]

damn (dam) *int.* (*sl.*) used to express annoyance. ~*v.t.* 1 to condemn, to criticize harshly. 2 to call down curses on. 3 to condemn to eternal punishment. 4 to reveal the guilt of; to cause the ruin of. ~*v.i.* to swear profanely. ~*n.* 1 a profane oath. 2 a negligible amount. ~*a.*, *adv.* damned. **not to give a damn** to be totally unconcerned. **to damn with faint praise** to praise with so little enthusiasm that it suggests dislike or disapproval. **damfool** *a.* (*coll.*) extremely foolish. **dammit** *int.* damn it! **damnable** (dam´nəbəl) *a.* 1 deserving damnation or condemnation. 2 atrocious, despicable. **damnably** (-nə-) *adv.* **damn all** *n.* absolutely nothing. **damnation** (-nā´shən) *n.* 1 condemnation to eternal punishment. 2 eternal punishment. 3 condemnation. ~*int.* used to express anger. **damnatory** (-nə-) *a.* causing or implying condemnation. **damned** (damd) *a.* 1 condemned. 2 condemned to everlasting punishment. ~*adv.* (*coll.*) very. **a damned good try** an exceedingly good try. **to be damned if** certainly will not. **damnedest** (dam´dist), **damndest** *n.* (*coll.*) the best. **to do one's damnedest** to do one's very best. **damnify** (-ni-) *v.t.* (*3rd pers. sing. pres.* **damnifies**, *pres.p.* **damnifying**, *past*, *p.p.* **damnified**) (*Law*) to cause damage to. **damnification** (-fikā´shən) *n.* **damning** (dam´ing) *a.* suggesting guilt. **damningly** *adv.* **damn well** *adv.* definitely; whether you like it or not. [OF *damner*, L *damnāre*, from *damnum*, loss, a fine]

Damoclean (daməklē´ən) *a.* of or resembling Damocles, who having grossly flattered Dionysius of Syracuse was placed by that tyrant at a magnificent banquet with a sword suspended over his head by a single hair, to show the dangerous nature of such exalted positions; perilous, anxious. **sword of Damocles** SWORD.

†damosel DAMSEL.

damp (damp) *a.* 1 slightly wet; clammy. 2 †dejected, depressed. ~*n.* 1 humidity, moisture in a building or article of use or in the air. 2 †discouragement. 3 dejection, depression. 4 subterranean gases met with in mines, firedamp. ~*v.t.* 1 to stifle, to restrain. 2 to moisten. 3 to check, to depress. 4 to discourage, to deaden. 5 to make burn less strongly. 6 to make vibrate less. **to damp down** 1 to stifle (an emotion etc.). 2 to fill (a furnace) with coke to prevent the fire going out. **to damp off** (of the stems of plants) to rot off from damp. **damp course** *n.* a layer of impervious material put between the courses of a wall to keep moisture from rising. **dampen** *v.t.* 1 to make damp. 2 to dull, to deaden. ~*v.i.* to become damp. **dampener** *n.* **damper** *n.* 1 a person or something which damps. 2 a valve or sliding plate in a flue for regulating a fire. 3 (*Austral.*, *New Zeal.*) bread or cake baked in hot ashes. 4 (*Mus.*) a pad in a piano for deadening the sound. 5 (*Mus.*) a mute in brass wind instruments. **to put a damper on** 1 to discourage, to stifle. 2 to reduce the chances of success of. **damping** *n.* 1 the deadening of the shock of sudden movement. 2 the rate at which an electrical oscillation dies away. **damping-off** *n.* the killing of plants from excess of moisture. **dampish** *a.* **damply** *adv.* **dampness** *n.* **damp-proof** *a.* impenetrable to moisture. ~*v.t.* to render impervious to moisture. **damp-proof course** *n.* a damp course. **damp squib** *n.* a failed attempt, a disappointing event. [cp. Dut. and Dan. *damp*, G *Dampf*]

damsel (dam´zəl), **†damosel** (dam´əzel) *n.* (*poet.*) a young unmarried woman. **damselfish** *n.* a small fish of the family Pomacentidae, found around coral reefs. **damselfly** *n.* (*pl.* **damselflies**) an insect somewhat resembling a dragonfly, of the order Odonata. [OF *damoisele*, late L *dominicella*, double dim. of L *domina*, lady, mistress]

damson (dam´zən) *n.* 1 a small dark purple plum. 2 the tree, *Prunus institia*, that bears this. 3 a dark purple colour. ~*a.* damson-coloured. **damson cheese** *n.* a conserve of damsons, pressed to the consistency of cheese. [ME or A-F *damascene*, L *Damascēnum*, of Damascus]

Dan. *abbr.* Daniel.

dan[1] (dan) *n.* 1 in martial arts, any of the black-belt grades of proficiency. 2 a person who has reached such a level. [Jap.]

dan[2] (dan), **dan buoy** *n.* a type of small deep-sea buoy. [etym. unknown]

†dan[3] (dan) *n.* a title of respect placed before personal names (and before mythological names in the archaic poets). [OF *dans*, nom. *dan*, acc., from L *dominus -um*, lord]

dance (dahns) *v.i.* 1 to move, usu. to music, with rhythmical steps, figures and gestures. 2 to skip, to frolic, to move in a lively or excited way. 3 to bob up and down. ~*v.t.* 1 to express or accomplish by dancing. 2 to perform (a particular kind of dance). 3 to toss up and down, to dandle. 4 to cause to dance. ~*n.* 1 a rhythmical stepping with motions of the body, usu. adjusted to the measure of a tune. 2 a figure or set of figures in dancing. 3 a dancing-party, a ball. 4 the tune by which dance movements are regulated. 5 a dancing motion. **to dance attendance on** to pay assiduous court to; to be kept waiting by. **to dance to a person's tune** TUNE. **to lead someone a (merry) dance** to cause someone trouble or delay. **danceable** *a.* **dance band** *n.* a band that plays dance music. **dance floor** *n.* a floor or area of floor for dancing, usu. with a polished surface. **dance hall** *n.* a public hall for dancing. **dance music** *n.* music intended for dancing to. **dance of death, danse macabre** (dās məkah´brə) *n.* in medieval art, literature and music, a representation of a dance in which Death leads people to their graves. **dancer** *n.* a person who dances, esp. one who earns money by dancing in public. **dancesport** *n.* ballroom dancing as a competitive sport. **dancing** *n.*, *a.* **dancing dervish** *n.* a whirling dervish. **dancing girl** *n.* a professional female dancer. **dancing master** *n.* a man who teaches dancing. **dancing school** *n.* a place where dancing is taught. [OF *danser*, OHG *dansōn*, to draw as in a dance]

dancette (dahnset´) *n.* 1 (*Archit.*) the chevron or zigzag moulding in Norman work. 2 (*Her.*) a fesse with three indentations. **dancetté** (-set´i) *a.* having deep indentations. [prob. corr. from OF *dant*, L *dens dentem*, a tooth]

D and C (dē ənd sē´) *n.* (*Med.*) dilatation of the cervix and curettage of the womb, performed for diagnostic or therapeutic purposes.

dandelion (dan´dilīən) *n.* a plant, *Taraxacum officinale*, with a yellow rayed flower and toothed leaves. **dandelion clock** *n.* the globular seed-head of a dandelion, with downy tufts. **dandelion coffee** *n.* (a drink made from) dandelion roots, powdered. [F *dent de lion*, lion's tooth]

dander[1] (dan´də) *n.* (*coll.*) temper, anger. **to get one's dander up** to become angry. [etym. uncertain]

dander[2] (dan´də) *v.i.* (*Sc., dial.*) **1** to wander about idly. **2** to maunder. [perh. conn. with DANDLE]

Dandie Dinmont (dandi din´mənt) *n.* a breed of short-legged, rough-coated terrier. [a character in Sir Walter Scott's *Guy Mannering*]

dandify (dan´difī) *v.t.* (*3rd pers. sing. pres.* **dandifies,** *pres.p.* **dandifying,** *past, p.p.* **dandified**) to make smart, or like a dandy. **dandification** (-fikā´shən) *n.* [DANDY[1]]

dandle (dan´dəl) *v.t.* **1** to bounce (a child) up and down on one's knees or toss (it) in one's arms. **2** to pet. **dandler** *n.* [cp. LG *dand-* (WFlem. *danderen*, to bounce up and down) and It. *dandolare*, from *dandola, dondola*, a doll or puppet]

dandruff (dan´drŭf) *n.* scaly scurf on the head. [prob. a comb. of Yorks. *dander*, scurf on the skin, and *hurf* (cp. Icel. *hrufa*, scab)]

dandy[1] (dan´di) *n.* (*pl.* **dandies**) **1** a man extravagantly concerned with his appearance; a fop, a coxcomb. **2** a sloop or cutter with a jigger-mast aft, on which a lugsail is set. ~*a.* (*comp.* **dandier,** *superl.* **dandiest**) (*esp. N Am.*) very good, superior. **dandy brush** *n.* a hard whalebone brush for cleaning horses. **dandyish** *a.* **dandyism** *n.* **dandy roll, dandy roller** *n.* a roller used to produce water marks on paper. [Sc. var. of *Andrew*]

dandy[2] (dan´di), **dandy-fever** *n.* DENGUE. [corr. of DENGUE]

Dane (dān) *n.* **1** a native or inhabitant of Denmark. **2** (*Hist.*) any of the Northmen who invaded Britain in the Middle Ages. **Great Dane** GREAT. [Dan. *Daner*, Gmc. *Daniz*, pl.]

danegeld (dān´geld) *n.* **1** an annual tax formerly levied on every hide of land in England to maintain forces against or furnish tribute to the Danes (finally abolished by Stephen). **2** money given to appease. [ODan. *Danegjeld* (*gjeld*, payment, tribute, cogn. with OE *gield*)]

dane-hole DENE-HOLE.

Danelaw (dān´law), **Danelagh** *n.* **1** the portion of England allotted to the Danes by the treaty of Wedmore (AD 878), extending north-east from Watling Street. **2** †the Danish law which held over this. [OE *Denalagu*, Danish law]

danewort (dān´wœt) *n.* the dwarf elder, *Sambucus ebulus*, the flowers, bark and berries of which are used medicinally.

danger (dān´jə) *n.* **1** risk, peril, hazard; exposure to injury or loss. **2** anything that causes peril. **3** on a railway, risk in going on owing to obstruction; the signal indicating this. **4** †servitude, power, jurisdiction. **in danger of** liable to. **danger list** *n.* a list of those dangerously ill (in hospital). **danger man** *n.* a man to beware of, esp. as a rival in a sporting event. **danger money** *n.* money paid in compensation for the risks involved in any unusually dangerous job. **dangerous** *a.* **dangerously** *adv.* [OF *dangier, dongier*, ult. from L *dominium*, from *dominus*, lord]

dangle (dang´gəl) *v.i.* **1** to hang loosely. **2** to swing or wave about. **3** to hang about, esp. to obtain some favour. **4** to hover. ~*v.t.* **1** to cause to dangle. **2** to hold out (a temptation, bait etc.). **dangler** *n.* **1** something which dangles. **2** †a person who hangs about, esp. in pursuit of women. **dangling** *a.* that dangles. **dangling participle** *n.* (*Gram.*) a participle without a subject or antecedent. **dangly** *a.* (*comp.* **danglier,** *superl.* **dangliest**). [etym. uncertain; cp. DING[1], also Dan. *dangle*]

Daniel (dan´yəl) *n.* **1** an upright judge. **2** an infallible judge. [from Daniel i.-vi. and *Merchant of Venice*, IV. SC. I]

Daniell cell (dan´yəl) *n.* a type of primary voltaic cell having a copper anode and zinc cathode. [John *Daniell*, 1790–1845, English chemist]

Danish (dā´nish) *a.* of or relating to Denmark. ~*n.* **1** the language of Denmark. **2** (*as pl.*) the Danes. **3** (*coll.*) a Danish pastry (*coffee and a Danish*). **Danish blue** *n.* a strong-tasting, blue-veined cheese. **Danish pastry** *n.* a flaky pastry, usu. filled with jam, almonds or apples, and often iced. [OE *Denisc*]

dank (dangk) *a.* **1** damp, moist. **2** chilly with moisture. **dankly** *adv.* **dankness** *n.* [cp. Swed. dial. *dank*, a marshy place, Dan. dial. *dunkel*, moist]

danse macabre DANCE OF DEATH (under DANCE).

danseur (dāsœ´) *n.* a male ballet dancer. **danseuse** (dāsœz´) *n.* a female professional dancer, a ballerina. [F]

Dantean (dan´tiən) *a.* **1** of or relating to Dante Alighieri (1265–1321), Italian poet. **2** in the style of Dante, esp. of his *Inferno*; sombre, sublime. ~*n.* **1** a student of Dante. **2** a writer in the Dantean style. **Dantesque** (-tesk´) *a.* Dantean.

danthonia (danthō´niə) *n.* (*Austral., New Zeal.*) a pasture grass of the genus *Danthonia*. [E. *Danthoine*, French botanist]

dap (dap) *v.i.* (*pres.p.* **dapping,** *past, p.p.* **dapped**) to fish by letting the bait fall gently into the water. ~*v.t.* **1** to let fall lightly. **2** to cause to bounce on the ground. ~*n.* a bounce (of a ball etc.). [cp. DIP, DAB[1]]

daphne (daf´ni) *n.* any shrub of the genus *Daphne*. [Gr. *Daphne*, one of Diana's nymphs fabled to have been changed into a laurel]

dapper (dap´ə) *a.* **1** spruce, smart. **2** brisk, active. †**dapperling** *n.* a dapper person. **dapperly** *adv.* **dapperness** *n.* [cp. Dut. *dapper*, G *tapfer*, brave]

dapple (dap´əl) *n.* **1** a spot on an animal's coat. **2** a mottled marking. **3** a horse or other animal with a mottled coat. ~*a.* spotted; variegated with streaks or spots. ~*v.t.* to spot, to streak, to variegate. ~*v.i.* to become dappled. **dapple-grey** *a., n.* (a horse etc.) with a mottled grey coat. [cp. Icel. *depill*, a spot, dim. of *dapi*, pool]

darbies (dah´biz) *n.pl.* (*sl.*) handcuffs. [from *Father Darby's bands*, an old debtors' agreement]

Darby and Joan (dahbi ənd jōn´) *n.* an elderly married couple living in domestic bliss. **Darby and Joan club** *n.* a club for elderly people. [from an 18th-cent. English song]

dare (deə), (*Sc.*) **daur** (daw) *v.i.* (*past* **dared,** †**durst** (dœst)) to venture (to); to have the courage or impudence (to) (*I wouldn't dare contradict her*). ~*v.t.* **1** to attempt, to venture on. **2** to challenge, to defy. ~*n.* **1** a challenge to do something dangerous. **2** an act of boldness. **I dare say** I suppose. **daredevil** *n.* a fearless, reckless person. ~*a.* fearless, reckless. **daredevilry** *n.* **darer** *n.* **daring** *a.* courageous, bold; fearless, reckless. ~*n.* boldness, bravery. **daringly** *adv.* [OE *durran*, to dare, pres. *dearr, durron*, past *dorste* (cp. Gr. *tharsein*, to be bold); the present is an old past tense, and consequently *dare* survives as 3rd sing. along with *dares*]

Usage note It is still conventional to write *dare say* (as in *I dare say*) as two separate words, not one (*daresay*).

daren't (deənt) *contr.* dare not.

darg (dahg) *n.* (*Sc., North. or Austral.*) **1** the quantity of work done in a day. **2** a task. [corr. of *day work*]

daric (dar´ik) *n.* a gold coin of Darius I of Persia. [Gr. *Dareikos*, a.]

daring DARE.

dariole (dar´iōl) *n.* a dish cooked in a usu. flowerpot-shaped mould. **dariole mould** *n.* a usu. flowerpot-shaped mould used in cookery. [OF]

Darjeeling (dahjē´ling) *n.* tea from Darjeeling in NE India.

dark (dahk) *a.* **1** without light. **2** almost black. **3** shaded. **4** dark-haired or dark-skinned. **5** opaque. **6** gloomy, sombre. **7** blind, ignorant. **8** obscure, ambiguous. **9** hidden, concealed. **10** without spiritual or intellectual enlightenment. **11** wicked, evil. **12** cheerless. **13** sad, sullen, frowning. **14** unknown, untried (esp. used of a horse that has never run in public). *~n.* **1** darkness. **2** absence of light. **3** night, nightfall. **4** shadow, shade. **5** dark tint, the dark part of a picture. **6** lack of knowledge. **7** doubt, uncertainty. *~†v.i.* to become dark, to be eclipsed. *~†v.t.* **1** to make dark. **2** to obscure. **in the dark 1** without light. **2** in ignorance (about). **to keep something dark** to keep silent about something. **Dark Ages, Dark Age** *n.* **1** the Middle Ages, esp. the period from the 5th to the 10th cent. (from an incorrect view of the ignorance then prevailing). **2** any period of supposed ignorance. **Dark Blues** *n.pl.* the representatives of Oxford University in sporting events. **Dark Continent** *n.* Africa, esp. in the period before it was explored by Europeans. **darken** *v.i.* **1** to become dark or darker. **2** to become obscure. *~v.t.* **1** to make dark or darker. **2** to render gloomy, ignorant or stupid. **not to darken someone's door** not to appear as a visitor. **dark-eyed** *a.* **dark glasses** *n.pl.* sunglasses. **dark horse** *n.* (*fig.*) **1** a person who keeps their opinions and thoughts secret. **2** a person of unknown capabilities. **darkish** *a.* **dark lantern** *n.* a lantern which can be covered. **darkly** *adv.* **dark matter** *n.* (*Astron.*) hypothetical non-luminous matter constituting a large part of the universe's mass but unable to be detected. **darkness** *n.* **1** the state or quality of being dark. **2** blindness. **3** obscurity. **4** ignorance. **5** wickedness. **6** the powers of hell. **darkroom** *n.* a room from which actinic light is shut out for developing photographs. **darksome** (-səm) *a.* (*poet.*) dark, gloomy. **dark star** *n.* a star emitting no light, whose existence is known only from its radio waves, infrared spectrum or gravitational effect. [OE *deorc*]

darkie (dah´ki), **darky** *n.* (*pl.* **darkies**) **1** (*offensive*) a dark-skinned person, esp. of African origin. **2** (*coll.*) a dark lantern.

†darkle (dah´kəl) *v.i.* to grow dark. **darkling** (dahk´ling) *adv.* in the dark. *~a.* **1** gloomy, dark. **2** in the dark.

darling (dah´ling) *n.* **1** a person who is dearly loved. **2** a favourite. **3** (*coll.*) a lovable, charming or pretty person or thing. *~a.* **1** dearly loved. **2** (*coll.*) charming, delightful. [OE *dēorling* (*dēor*, DEAR, -LING[1])]

darn[1] (dahn) *v.t.* **1** to mend with stitches that cross or interweave. **2** to embroider with a type of running stitch. *~n.* a place mended by darning. **darner** *n.* **1** a person who darns. **2** a needle used in darning. **darning** *n.* **1** the action of a darner. **2** garments etc. to be darned. **darning needle** *n.* a needle used in darning. [cp. OE *gedyrnan*, to hide, to stop up a hole]

darn[2] (dahn), (*N Am.*) **durn** (dœn) *int.*, *v.t.* (*coll.*, *euphem.*) damn. **darned** *a.* damned.

darnel (dah´nəl) *n.* **1** a kind of grass, *Lolium temulentum*, formerly believed to be poisonous, which grows among corn. **2** any plant of the genus *Lolium*. [etym. uncertain (cp. Walloon *darnelle*)]

dart (daht) *n.* **1** a small pointed missile used in the game of darts. **2** a short-pointed missile weapon thrown by the hand. **3** (*pl.*) an indoor game of throwing darts at a dartboard. **4** a sudden leap or rapid movement. **5** an insect's sting. **6** a needle-like structure on a snail, used during copulation. **7** in dressmaking, a V-shaped tuck. *~v.t.* **1** to throw. **2** to shoot or send forth suddenly. *~v.i.* to run or move swiftly. **dartboard** *n.* a circular marked target used in the game of darts. **darter** *n.* **1** a person who throws or hurls. **2** a person who moves with great rapidity. **3** any long-necked swimming bird of the genus *Anhinga*. **4** any bird of the order Jaculatores, comprising the kingfishers and bee-eaters. **5** any small N American freshwater fish of the family Percidae. [OF *dart* (F *dard*), prob. from LG (cp. OE *daroth*, a javelin, OHG *tart*, a dart)]

Dartmoor pony (dah´tmaw, -muə) *n.* (*pl.* **Dartmoor ponies**) a breed of small hardy English pony. [*Dartmoor*, where the breed originated]

Darwinian (dahwin´iən) *a.* of or relating to Charles Darwin (1809–82), English naturalist, or Darwinism. *~n.* a believer in Darwinism. **Darwinianism** *n.* the teaching of Charles Darwin, esp. the doctrine of the origin of species by natural selection. **Darwinism** *n.* Darwinianism. **Darwinist** *n.*, *a.* **Darwinistic** (-is´-) *a.* **Darwinite** *n.*

dash (dash) *v.i.* **1** to rush, fall or throw oneself violently. **2** to strike against something and break. **3** (usu. with *up*, *off* or *away*) to run, ride or drive quickly. *~v.t.* **1** (usu. with *to pieces*) to break by collision. **2** (usu. with *out*, *down*, *away* etc.) to smite, to strike, to knock. **3** to throw violently or suddenly. **4** to bespatter, to besprinkle. **5** to dilute or adulterate by adding some other substance. **6** (with *off*) to compose or sketch hastily. **7** to destroy; to frustrate; to confound, to abash, to discourage, to daunt. *~int.* (*dated*, *coll.*, *euphem.*) damn. *~n.* **1** a sharp collision of two bodies. **2** the sound of this, the sound of water in commotion. **3** a rapid movement. **4** a rush, a hurry. **5** a small amount. **6** a sudden stroke; a blow. **7** activity, daring; brilliancy, display, ostentation (*He performed with great dash*). **8** a mark (–) denoting a break in a sentence, a parenthesis or omission. **9** (*Mus.*) a short stroke placed above notes or chords, indicating that they are to be played staccato. **10** the long element in Morse code. **11** (*N Am.*) in athletics, a sprint. **12** (*coll.*) the dashboard of a car. **dash it (all)!** (*coll.*) used to express annoyance. **to cut a dash** to make a bold impression. **to dash down** to dash off. **to dash off** to write down or complete in a hurry. **dashboard** *n.* **1** a fascia with instruments in front of the driver of a car or the pilot of an aircraft. **2** †a splashboard. **dasher** *n.* **1** a person who or something which dashes. **2** a contrivance for agitating the contents of a churn. **3** (*fig.*) a dashing person. **dashing** *a.* **1** daring, spirited. **2** showy, smart. **dashingly** *adv.* **dashingness** *n.* **dashpot** *n.* a damping device. [cp. Dan. *daske*, to slap, Swed. *daska*, to beat, LG *daschen*, to thrash]

dashiki (dah´shiki) *n.* (*pl.* **dashikis**) a type of loose shirt worn esp. by blacks in America. [from a W Afr. language]

dassie (das´i) *n.* (*S Afr.*) **1** a hyrax, *Procavia capensis*. **2** a small fish, *Diplodus sargus*. [Dut. *dasje*, dim. of *das*, badger]

dastardly (das´tədli) *a.* cowardly and nasty. **†dastard** *n.* a coward, a cowardly villain. **dastardliness** *n.* [prob. from DAZE, -ARD]

dasypod (das´ipod) *n.* any South American armadillo of the genus *Dasypodidae*. [Gr. *dasypous*, hairy-footed]

dasyure (das´iūə) *n.* any member of the genus *Dasyurus* of small marsupials, found in Australia, Tasmania and New Guinea. [Gr. *dasus*, hairy, rough; *oura*, a tail]

DAT *abbr.* digital audio tape.

dat. *abbr.* dative.

data (dā´tə) *n.pl.* (*often sing. in constr.*, *pl. of datum*) **1** facts or information from which other things may be deduced. **2** the information operated on by a computer program. **data-bank, database** *n.* a large amount of information, usu. stored in a computer for easy access. **data capture** *n.* the conversion of information into a form which can be processed by a computer. **data processing** *n.* the handling and processing of data in computer files. **data processor** *n.* **data protection** *n.* the protection of the privacy of personal data stored in computer files. [L *data*, things given, from *dare*, to give]

Usage note (1) The use of *data* as a singular noun is sometimes disapproved of, though in computing etc. it is standard. (2) Pronunciation as (dah´tə) is best avoided.

datable DATE[1].

dataria (dəteə´riə) *n.* the papal chancery at Rome from which all bulls are issued. **datary** (dā´-) *n.* (*pl.* **dataries**) an officer of the papal chancery who affixes *datum Romae* (given at Rome) to the papal bulls. [L *datārius*, that can be given]

datcha DACHA.

date[1] (dāt) *n.* **1** a fixed point of time. **2** the time at which anything happened or is appointed to take place. **3** the specification of this in a book, inscription, document or letter. **4** (*coll.*) a social or other engagement (usu. with a romantic partner). **5** (*esp. N Am.*) a person with whom one has a date. ~*v.t.* **1** to affix the date to. **2** to note or fix the date of. **3** to reveal the age of. **4** (*esp. N Am.*) to have a romantic relationship with. ~*v.i.* **1** to begin (from). **2** to become dated. **out of date** OUT. **to date** up till now. **to make/ have a date** (*coll.*) to make or have an appointment. **up to date** UP. **datable** *a.* **datebook** *n.* (*N Am.*) an appointments diary. **dated** *a.* old-fashioned. **dateless** *a.* **1** without a date. **2** very old. **3** timeless, unlikely to grow out of date. **date-line** *n.* **1** the line on either side of which the date differs, running meridionally across the western hemisphere from the poles and theoretically 180° from Greenwich. **2** the line with date and place of sending printed above a newspaper dispatch. **date-mark** *n.* a date-stamp on goods etc. **date rape** *n.* the rape of a woman by a man during or after a date. **date-stamp** *n.* **1** an adjustable rubber stamp for imprinting a date. **2** a stamp on perishable goods showing the date before which they are best used or consumed. ~*v.t.* to mark (goods) with a date-stamp. [F, from late L *data*, given, fem. p.p. of *dare*, to give (referring to the time and place at which a letter was given)]

date[2] (dāt) *n.* **1** the fruit of the date palm, an oblong fruit with a hard seed or stone. **2** the date palm. **date palm, date tree** *n.* a tall tree, *Phoenix dactylifera*, common in N Africa and Asia Minor. [OF, from L *dactylus*, Gr. *daktulos*, a finger, a date]

dative (dā´tiv) *a.* **1** denoting the grammatical case used to represent the indirect object, or the person or thing interested in the action of the verb. **2** (*Law*) that may be parted with at pleasure. **3** (*Law*) removable (from an office). **4** (*Law*) appointed by a court. ~*n.* the dative case. **datival** (-tī´-) *a.* **datively** *adv.* [L *datīvus*, pertaining to giving (*dare*, to give)]

datum (dā´təm) *n.* (*pl.* **data**) a quantity, condition, fact or other premise, given or admitted, from which other things or results may be found. **datum-line, datum-level, datum-plane** *n.* the horizontal line, such as sea level, from which calculations are made in surveying etc. [L, neut. p.p. of *dare*, to give]

datura (dətūə´rə) *n.* any solanaceous plant of the genus *Datura*, as the thorn apple, *D. stramonium*, which yields a powerful narcotic. **daturine** (-rīn, -rin) *n.* an alkaloid obtained from the thorn apple. [Hind. *dhatūra*]

daub (dawb) *v.t.* **1** to smear or coat with a soft adhesive substance. **2** to paint coarsely. **3** to apply (colour) in a crude or inartistic style. **4** to stain, to soil. ~*v.i.* to paint in a crude or inartistic style. ~*n.* **1** a smear. **2** a crude or inartistic painting. **3** a plaster or mud wall-covering. **dauber** *n.* †**daubery** *n.* **1** daubing. **2** (*fig.*) false pretence. **daubing** *n.* [OF *dauber*, to plaster, L *dealbāre*, to whitewash (DE-, *albāre*, from *albus*, white)]

daube (dawb) *n.* a stew of meat braised with wine etc. [F]

daughter (daw´tə) *n.* **1** a female child in relation to a parent or parents. **2** a female descendant. **3** a form of address used by a confessor to a female penitent etc. **4** a female member of a family, people, city etc. **5** a female spiritual descendant (of). **6** (*Biol.*) a cell formed from another of the same type. **7** (*Physics*) a nuclide formed from another by radioactive decay. **daughterhood** *n.* **daughter-in-law** *n.* (*pl.* **daughters-in-law**) a son's wife. **daughterly** *a.* **daughterliness** *n.* **daughter of the manse** *n.* the daughter of a minister. [OE *dohtor* (cp. Dut. *dochter*, G *Tochter*, Gr. *thugatēr*, Sansk. *duhitā*)]

daunt (dawnt) *v.t.* to intimidate, to dishearten (*Nothing daunted, she continued on her journey*). **daunting** *a.* **dauntingly** *adv.* **dauntless** *a.* fearless, intrepid. **dauntlessly** *adv.* **dauntlessness** *n.* [OF *danter* (F *dompter*), L *domitāre* (freq. of *domāre*, to tame)]

dauphin (dō´fã, daw´fin) *n.* (*Hist.*) the heir apparent to the French throne (from the fact that the principality of Dauphiné was an apanage of his). **dauphine** (-fēn), **dauphiness** *n.* the wife of a dauphin. [OF *daulphin*, L *delphīnus*, DOLPHIN]

daur DARE.

davenport (dav´ənpawt), **devonport** (dev´ənpawt) *n.* **1** a small writing desk with drawers on both sides. **2** (*esp. N Am.*) a large sofa, a couch. [prob. from the first maker]

davit (dav´it) *n.* **1** a spar used as a crane for hoisting an anchor. **2** either of a pair of beams projecting over a ship's side, with tackles to hoist or lower a boat. [formerly *david*, prob. from the personal name]

Davy (dā´vi), **Davy lamp** *n.* (*pl.* **Davies, Davy lamps**) a miner's wire-gauze safety lamp. [Sir Humphry *Davy*, 1778–1829, English inventor]

Davy Jones (dāvi jōnz´) *n.* (*sl.*) **1** an imaginary malign spirit with power over the sea. **2** (*also* **Davy Jones's locker**) the sea as the tomb of the drowned. [etym. unknown]

daw (daw) *n.* **1** a jackdaw. **2** an empty-headed person. [cp. OLG *dāha*, OHG *tāha*, G *Dohle* (imit. in orig.)]

dawdle (daw´dəl) *v.i.* **1** to be slow, to linger. **2** to trifle; to idle about; to waste time. ~*n.* the act of dawdling. **dawdler** *n.* [prob. a recent var. of *daddle*]

dawk DAK.

dawn (dawn) *n.* **1** the break of day. **2** the first rise or appearance. ~*v.i.* **1** to grow light, to break (as day). **2** to begin to open, expand or appear. **to dawn upon** to be realized gradually by. **dawn chorus** *n.* the singing of birds at dawn. **dawning** *n.* **1** dawn. **2** the first beginning or unfolding. **dawn redwood** *n.* a Chinese conifer, *Metasequoia glyptostroboides*. [ME *dawnen*, earlier *dawen*, daw]

day (dā) *n.* **1** the time the sun is above the horizon. **2** a space of twenty-four hours, esp. that commencing at midnight, a practice borrowed from the ancient Romans. **3** the average time interval between two successive returns of the sun to the meridian. **4** daylight; daytime. **5** the part of a day during which work is usually done. **6** any specified point in time; a date agreed on. **7** the day in the week or month for receiving visitors. **8** an age. **9** (*often pl.*) life, lifetime, period of vigour, activity or prosperity. **10** a day appointed to commemorate any event. **11** a contest, a battle, a victory. **12** today. **13** a period on another planet corresponding to a day on earth. **all in a/ the day's work** something one has to do regularly. **all (the) day** throughout the day. **at the end of the day** eventually and inevitably, when all is said and done. **day after day** with monotonous regularity, every day continuously. **day and night** **1** throughout both day and night. **2** always. **3** by or in both day and night. **day by**

day gradually, every day. **day in, day out** every day, constantly. **from day one** from the very start. **not one's day** a day on which things go wrong for one. **one day** 1 shortly; in the near future. 2 at some unspecified time in the future. **one of these days** 1 shortly; in the near future. 2 at some unspecified time in the future. **one of those days** a day on which things go wrong for one. **one's days are numbered** NUMBER. **some day** one day. **that will be the day** (*coll.*) that day will never come. **this day and age** the present historical period. **this day week** a week forward from today. **to call it a day** to stop what one is doing, esp. work. **to have seen better days** SEE[1]. **to make a day of it** MAKE[1]. **to name the day** to fix the date for one's wedding. **to save the day** SAVE. **to win/ gain/ carry the day** to come off victor. **daybed** *n.* a couch or sofa for lying on during the day. **day-blindness** *n.* indistinct vision by day. **day-boarder** *n.* a pupil who has meals, but does not sleep, at a school. **daybook** *n.* a book in which the business transactions of the day are recorded. **day-boy** *n.* a boy attending a day-school, but differing from a day-boarder in not taking dinner there. **daybreak** *n.* the first appearance of daylight. **day-care** *n.* the daytime supervision by trained staff of pre-school children or elderly or handicapped people. **day-care centre,** (*N Am.*) **day-care center** *a.* a day centre. **day centre,** (*N Am.*) **day center** *n.* a place providing social amenities for the elderly, handicapped etc. **daydream** *n.* a romantic scheme or vain fancy voluntarily indulged in. ~*v.i.* to have daydreams. **daydreamer** *n.* a person who indulges in daydreams. **dayfly** *n.* (*pl.* **dayflies**) an insect of the genus *Ephemera*. **day-girl** *n.* a girl attending a day-school, but differing from a day-boarder in not taking dinner there. **day labour,** (*N Am.*) **day labor** *n.* work paid for by the day. **day labourer,** (*N Am.*) **day laborer** *n.* a labourer who is paid by the day. **day lily** *n.* (*pl.* **day lilies**) a liliaceous plant of the genus *Hemerocallis*, the flowers of which last one day. **daylong** *a.* lasting all day. ~*adv.* the whole day. **day nursery** *n.* a children's playroom in the daytime; a crèche. **Day of Atonement** *n.* a Jewish day of fasting, ten days after the Jewish New Year; Yom Kippur. **day off** *n.* a day's holiday from work, school etc. **Day of Judgement** *n.* JUDGEMENT DAY (under JUDGE). **day of obligation** *n.* a day on which the Church prescribes Mass or Communion for all. **day of reckoning** *n.* 1 the day of settling accounts. 2 (*fig.*) the Day of Judgement. **day of rest** *n.* the sabbath. **day out** *n.* a day-trip, a day away from home. **day-owl** *n.* an owl which hunts by day, esp. the short-eared owl. **daypack** *n.* (*N Am.*) a daysack. **day release** *n.* a system which frees people from work for some hours each week to follow part-time education relevant to their employment. **day return** *n.* a special cheap ticket for travel to a place, returning the same day. **day room** *n.* a communal living-room in a school, hospital etc. **daysack** *n.* a small rucksack suitable for a single day out. **day-school** *n.* 1 a school for pupils living at home, as distinct from *boarding school*. 2 a school held in the daytime on a weekday, as distinct from *night-school, Sunday school* etc. **day shift** *n.* 1 work during the day as distinct from *night shift* etc. 2 the group of workers undertaking such work. **dayside** *n.* 1 the side of a planet facing the sun. 2 (*N Am.*) those in an organization who work during the day, esp. on a newspaper. **day-sight** *n.* vision clear by day, but indistinct at night. **days of grace** *n.pl.* 1 (*Law*) days granted by a court for delay at the prayer of a plaintiff or defendant. 2 a customary number of days (in England three) allowed for the payment of a note, or bill of exchange, after it becomes due. **dayspring** *n.* (*poet.*) the dawn; daybreak. **daystar** *n.* 1 the morning star. 2 †the sun. **daytime** *n.* day, as opposed to night. **day trip** *n.* an excursion made to and from a place in a single day. **day tripper** *n.* **daywork** *n.* work paid for by the day. [OE *dæg* (cp. Dut., Dan. and Swed. *dag*, G *Tag*)]

Day-glo® (dā´glō) *n.* a type of fluorescent paint. ~*a.* 1 being or resembling this type of paint. 2 (*loosely*) of a glowingly bright colour (usu. pink, orange or green).

daylight (dā´līt) *n.* 1 the light of day, as opposed to that of the moon or artificial light. 2 dawn. 3 light visible through an opening; an interval, a gap, a visible space. 4 openness, publicity. **to beat/ knock the living daylights out of** to beat severely. **to scare the living daylights out of** to frighten greatly. **to see daylight** 1 to begin to understand. 2 to draw near to the end of a task. **daylight robbery** *n.* flagrant extortion or overpricing. **daylight saving** *n.* a system of advancing the clock by one hour in spring and setting back the time by one hour in autumn (introduced into Great Britain in 1919). **daylight time** *n.* (*esp. N Am.*) time adjusted for daylight saving.

daze (dāz) *v.t.* 1 to stupefy, to confuse. 2 to dazzle, to overpower with light. ~*n.* the state of being dazed. **dazed** *a.* **dazedly** (dā´zidli) *adv.* [ME *dasen*, v.t., v.i. (cp. Icel. *dasask*, to become weary, refl. of *dasa*)]

dazzle (daz´əl) *v.t.* 1 to overpower with a glare of light. 2 to daze or bewilder with rapidity of motion, brilliant display, stupendous number etc. ~*v.i.* 1 to be excessively bright. 2 †(of eyes) to be dazzled. ~*n.* something which dazzles. **dazzlement** *n.* **dazzler** *n.* **dazzling** *a.* **dazzlingly** *adv.* [freq. of DAZE]

dB *abbr.* decibel(s).

DBE *abbr.* Dame Commander of the (Order of the) British Empire.

DBS *abbr.* direct broadcasting by satellite.

DC *abbr.* 1 (*Mus.*) da capo. 2 direct current. 3 District of Columbia. 4 District Commissioner.

dc *abbr.* direct current.

DCB *abbr.* Dame Commander of the Order of the Bath.

DCL *abbr.* Doctor of Civil Law.

DCM *abbr.* Distinguished Conduct Medal.

DCMG *abbr.* Dame Commander of the Order of St Michael and St George.

DCVO *abbr.* Dame Commander of the Royal Victorian Order.

DD *abbr.* 1 direct debit. 2 Doctor of Divinity.

ddC *abbr.* dideoxycytidine, a drug.

ddI *abbr.* dideoxyinosine, a drug.

DDR *abbr.* (*Hist.*) German Democratic Republic (East Germany). [G *Deutsche Demokratische Republik*]

DDS *abbr.* Doctor of Dental Surgery.

DDT *abbr.* dichlorodiphenyltrichloroethane, an insecticide.

DE *abbr.* Delaware.

de- (dē) *pref.* 1 from. 2 down. 3 away. 4 out. 5 completely, thoroughly. 6 expressing undoing, deprivation, reversal or separation. [L *de*, prep., and *de-*, pref.; or from F *dé-* (L *dis-*, *de-*)]

deaccession (dēaksesh´ən) *v.t.* (of a library, museum etc.) to dispose of and remove from the catalogue of holdings.

deacon (dē´kən) *n.* 1 a cleric in orders next below a priest. 2 a lay officer who superintends the secular affairs of a Presbyterian church. 3 a lay officer who admits persons to membership, and assists at communion in the Congregational Church. 4 a member of a class entrusted with the care of the sick and the distribution of alms to the poor in the early Church. 5 (*Sc.*) the master of an incorporated guild of craftsmen. ~*v.t.* to appoint as a deacon. **deaconess** *n.* 1 a female deacon. 2 a member of a Lutheran sisterhood. **deaconship, deaconry** *n.* [OE, from L *diāconus*, Gr. *diakonos*, a servant]

deactivate (dēak´tivāt) *v.t.* to render harmless or less radioactive. **deactivation** (-ā´shən) *n.* **deactivator** *n.*

dead (ded) *a.* 1 having ceased to live. 2 having no life, lifeless. **3** benumbed, insensible, temporarily deprived of the power of action. **4** resembling death. **5** unconscious or unappreciative. **6** without spiritual feeling. **7** obsolete, effete, useless. **8** inanimate or inorganic, as distinct from organic. **9** extinct. **10** lustreless, motionless, soundless; not resonant. **11** flat, vapid, dull, opaque. **12** certain, unerring; complete, sudden. **13** faulty or used up and no longer transmitting sound, electric current etc. **14** no longer burning. **15** no longer effervescent. **16** (of a ball) out of play in a game. *~adv.* **1** absolutely, quite, completely. **2** (*coll.*) very. *~n.* **1** (*as pl.*) dead people. **2** the time when things are still, stillness. **dead against** absolutely opposed to. **dead as a dodo** DODO. **dead as a doornail** DOOR. **dead from the neck up** (*coll.*) completely stupid. **dead on the mark** MARK[1]. **dead set against** SET[1]. **dead set on** SET[1]. **dead to the world** WORLD. **wouldn't be seen dead in/ with** would never wear, would never be seen in the company of. **dead-and-alive** *a.* spiritless, dull. **dead-ball line** *n.* in rugby, a line behind the goal line beyond which the ball is out of play. **dead bat** *n.* a cricket bat held so that it gives no momentum to the ball. **dead beat** *a.* **1** quite exhausted. **2** without recoil. **deadbeat** *n.* **1** (*coll.*) a worthless lazy person; a person who is always in debt. **2** (*Austral.*) a ruined man, one down on his luck. **dead-beat escapement** *n.* an escapement of a clock etc. which gives no recoil to the escape wheel. **deadbolt** *n.* a bolt turned by a knob or key. **dead-born** *a.* stillborn. **dead centre,** (*N Am.*) **dead center** *n.* **1** the exact centre. **2** either of the two points at which a crank assumes a position in line with the rod which impels it. **dead certainty,** (*coll.*) **dead cert** *n.* something sure to occur. **dead colouring,** (*N Am.*) **dead coloring** *n.* the first layer of colour in a picture, usually of some shade of grey. **dead-drunk** *a.* extremely intoxicated. **dead duck** *n.* (*coll.*) a person or idea doomed to failure. **dead-end** *n.* **1** a cul-de-sac. **2** a position from which no progress can be made. *~a.* (of a job etc.) having no prospects. **deadeye** *n.* **1** (*Naut.*) any one of the flat, round blocks having eyes for the lanyards, by which the rigging is set up. **2** (*N Am., coll.*) a crack shot. **deadfall** *n.* a trap with a heavy weight which falls to crush the prey. **dead-freight** *n.* a sum paid for space reserved in a ship but not made use of for cargo. **dead gold** *n.* unburnished gold. **dead hand** *n.* a stifling or restricting influence. **deadhead** *n.* **1** a withered bloom on a plant. **2** (*coll.*) a person who has a free pass. **3** a stupid, unimaginative person. *~v.t.* to remove withered blooms from (flowers) to encourage future growth. *~v.i.* (*N Am., coll.*) to finish a journey without any passengers. **Dead Heart** *n.* (*Austral.*) the land of the Central Australian Desert. **dead heat** *n.* **1** a race resulting in a draw. **2** such a result. **dead-heat** *v.i.* to draw in a race. **dead language** *n.* a language no longer spoken, such as classical Latin. **dead letter** *n.* **1** a letter which cannot be delivered by the post office, and is opened and returned to the sender. **2** a law or anything that has become inoperative. **dead level** *n.* **1** a perfect level. **2** flat country that offers no difficulty to making a railway or road. **dead lift, dead pull** *n.* **1** a lift or pull at a dead weight. **2** a thankless effort. **deadlight** *n.* **1** a shutter placed over portholes or cabin windows in rough weather. **2** (*N Am.*) a skylight that does not open. **deadline** *n.* **1** the time of newspapers, books etc. going to press. **2** a fixed time or date terminating something. **3** a line, formerly esp. in a prison, beyond which it is not permitted to go. **deadlock** *n.* **1** a complete standstill, a position in which no progress can be made. **2** a lock worked on one side by a handle, and on the other by a key. *~v.t., v.i.* to bring or come into a deadlock. **dead loss** *n.* **1** (*coll.*) a useless person, thing or situation. **2** a loss with no compensation whatever. **dead man** *n.* (*pl.* **dead men**) (*sl.*) an empty wine or beer bottle. **dead man's fingers, dead men's fingers** *n.* a variety of orchis, *Orchis mascula*. **dead man's hand, dead man's toes** *n.* the zoophyte *Alyconium digitatum*. **dead man's handle** *n.* a device for automatically cutting off the current of an electrically-driven vehicle if the driver releases his pressure on the handle. **dead march** *n.* a piece of solemn music played at funerals, esp. of soldiers. **dead men's shoes** *n.pl.* inheritances, legacies. **deadness** *n.* **dead nettle** *n.* a non-stinging labiate plant, like a nettle, of several species belonging to the genus *Lamium*. **dead of night** *n.* the middle of the night. **dead on** *a., adv.* completely accurate. **deadpan** *a., adv.* with an expressionless face or manner. *~v.i.* (*pres.p* **deadpanning,** *past, p.p.* **deadpanned**) to look or speak deadpan. *~v.t.* to address in a deadpan manner. †**dead pay** *n.* pay drawn and appropriated by officials for subordinates who are dead or discharged. **dead point** *n.* either of the dead centres of a crank. **dead reckoning** *n.* the calculation of a ship's position from the log and compass, when observations cannot be taken. **dead ringer** *n.* (*coll.*) a person or thing exactly resembling someone or something else. **dead-ropes** *n.pl.* (*Naut.*) ropes which do not run in any blocks. **dead set** *n.* a determined attack or try. **dead shot** *n.* a marksman who never misses. **dead stock** *n.* farm equipment. **dead time** *n.* a period after taking one recording or measurement during which an instrument cannot take another. **dead wall** *n.* a wall with no windows or doors. **deadwater** *n.* **1** water that is absolutely still. **2** the eddy under the stern of a ship or boat. **dead weight** *n.* **1** a mass of inert matter, a burden that exerts no relieving force. **2** any very heavy weight or load. **3** the total weight carried on a ship. **4** an unrecoverable debt. **dead wood** *n.* **1** useless people or things. **2** (*Naut.*) the built-up timbers fore and aft above the keel. [OE *dēad,* from Gmc. stem *dau-*, to die (cp. Dut. *dood,* G *tot*)]

deaden (ded´ən) *v.t.* **1** to diminish the vitality, brightness, force or power of. **2** to make insensible, to dull; to blunt. *~v.i.* to lose vitality, strength, feeling, spirit etc. **deadener** *n.* [from DEAD]

deadly (ded´li) *a.* (*comp.* **deadlier,** *superl.* **deadliest**) **1** causing or procuring death; fatal. **2** like death. **3** very boring. **4** implacable, irreconcilable. **5** intense. *~adv.* **1** as if dead. **2** extremely, excessively, intensively. **deadliness** *n.* **deadly nightshade** *n.* a poisonous shrub with dark purple berries, *Atropa belladonna*. **deadly sin** *n.* (*Theol.*) any one of the seven mortal sins, leading to damnation. [OE *dēadlic*]

deaf (def) *a.* **1** incapable or dull of hearing. **2** unwilling to hear, disregarding, refusing to listen, refusing to comply (*They were deaf to my requests*). **3** insensible (to) (*tone-deaf*). *~n.* (*as pl.*) deaf people. **to fall on deaf ears** EAR[1]. **to turn a deaf ear to** TURN. **deaf-aid** *n.* a hearing-aid. **deaf-and-dumb alphabet, deaf-and-dumb language** *n.* a system of signs for holding communication between or with deaf people. **deaf-blind** *a.* both deaf and blind. **deafen** *v.t.* **1** to make wholly or partially deaf. **2** to stun with noise. **3** to render impervious to sound by pugging (as a floor, partition etc.). **deafening** *a.* **deafly** *adv.* **deaf mute** *n.* a person who is deaf and also unable to speak. **deaf-mutism** *n.* **deafness** *n.* [OE *dēaf* (cp. Dut. *doof,* Dan. *döv,* G *taub*; also Gr. *tuphlos,* blind)]

Usage note Organizations connected with the deaf prefer *sign language* to *deaf-and-dumb alphabet* or *language*.

---

deal[1] (dēl) *n.* **1** a bargain, a piece of business; a business transaction. **2** an indefinite quantity. **3** the distribution of cards to the players. **4** a player's turn to distribute the cards. **5** a round of play at cards. **6** the hands dealt to a card-player. **7** a share, a part, a portion. **8** a particular form of treatment at a person's hands. *~v.t.* (*past, p.p.*

dealt (delt)) 1 to distribute; to award to someone as their proper share. 2 to distribute or give in succession (as cards). ~*v.i.* to distribute cards to the players. **a deal** (*coll.*) a large amount. **a good deal** 1 a large quantity. 2 to a large extent; by much, considerably. **a great deal** 1 a large quantity. 2 to a large extent; by much, considerably. **to deal by** to act towards. **to deal in** to be engaged in; to trade in. **to deal with** 1 to take action in respect of, to handle. 2 to have to do with. 3 to behave towards. 4 to consider judicially. **dealer** *n.* 1 a trader, a merchant. 2 (*sl.*) a drug-pusher. 3 in a card game, the person who deals. 4 †a jobber on the Stock Exchange. **dealership** *n.* 1 a right or agreement to deal in something. 2 a dealer's premises. **dealings** *n.pl.* 1 conduct towards others. 2 intercourse in matters of business, trade. **to have dealings with** to deal or associate with. [OE *dǣl*, a share, a portion (cp. Dut. and Dan. *deel*, OHG *teil*, G *Teil*), whence *dǣlan*, to divide]

deal[2] (dēl) *n.* 1 a plank of fir or pine of a standard size, not more than 3 in. (7.6 cm) thick, 7 in. (17.8 cm) wide, and 6 ft. (1.8 m) long. 2 fir or pine wood, esp. when sawn into such planks. [cp. OE *thille*, THILL (prob. through LG *dele* or Dut. *deel*)]

dealt DEAL[1].

deambulatory (dēamˈbūlətəri) *n.* (*pl.* **deambulatories**) 1 a place for walking about in. 2 a cloister. 3 the passage round the screen enclosing the choir in a cathedral or other large church. [L *deambulātio*, from *deambulāre* (DE-, *ambulāre*, to walk)]

dean[1] (dēn) *n.* 1 an ecclesiastical dignitary presiding over the chapter of a cathedral or collegiate church. 2 a rural dean, a member of the clergy charged with jurisdiction over a part of an archdeaconry. 3 a title applied to the head of the establishment of a chapel royal, and to the Bishop of London (as Dean of the Province of Canterbury). 4 a resident fellow in a college with disciplinary and other functions; a university official with such functions. 5 the head of a university faculty or department; the head of a medical school. 6 a doyen. **deanery** *n.* (*pl.* **deaneries**) the office, district or official residence of a dean. **Dean of Faculty** *n.* (*Sc.*) the president of the Faculty of Advocates. **Dean of Guild** *n.* (*Sc.*) a magistrate with jurisdiction over buildings, weights and measures etc. **deanship** *n.* [OF *deien*, L *decānus -um*, one set over ten (*decem*, ten)]

dean[2] DENE[1].

dear (diə) *a.* 1 beloved, cherished; greatly esteemed; (a conventional form of address used in letter-writing). 2 precious, valuable. 3 costly, of a high price; available only at a high rate of interest. 4 characterized by high prices. 5 strongly felt (*dashed my dearest hopes*). 6 †characterized by scarcity. ~*n.* 1 a darling, a loved one. 2 a cherished person, a favourite. 3 a term of endearment. ~*adv.* dearly, at a high price (*This will cost you dear*). ~*int.* expressing distress, sympathy or mild astonishment and protest. **for dear life** LIFE. **dear heart** *n.* used as a term of endearment. **dearie me** *int.* used to express sympathy, surprise etc. **Dear John (letter)** *n.* (*esp. N Am., coll.*) a letter, esp. from a woman to a man, ending a relationship. **dearly** *adv.* 1 very much (*I would dearly love to have a holiday*). 2 with affection, sincerely. 3 at a high price. **dearness** *n.* **deary, dearie** *n.* (*dial., coll.*) dear one (a term of endearment). [OE *dēore* (cp. Dut. *dier*, OHG *tiuri*, G *teuer*)]

dearth (dœth) *n.* a scarcity; lack; want, privation. [ME *derthe*, from OE *dēore*, DEAR]

deasil (dēˈzəl), **deiseal** (dēˈshəl) *n.* (*Sc.*) motion towards the right, in the direction of the hands of a clock or of the apparent motion of the sun. [Gael. *deiseil*, right-handwise, cogn. with L *dexter*, Gr. *dexios*]

deaspirate (dēasˈpirāt) *v.t.* to remove the aspirate from.

death (deth) *n.* 1 extinction of life; the act of dying. 2 the state of being dead. 3 decay, destruction. 4 a cause or instrument of death. 5 a skull or skeleton as the emblem of mortality. 6 spiritual destruction, annihilation. **at death's door** close to death. **dance of death** DANCE. **death on** 1 deadly or ruinous to. 2 skilful at. **in at the death** present at the finish. **like death warmed up/over** (*coll.*) very ill or tired. **to be the death of** 1 to cause the death of. 2 (*coll.*) to make (someone) 'die of laughing'. 3 to be a source of great worry to. **to catch one's death of cold** to catch a very bad cold. **to death** to the greatest degree, as much as possible. **to dice with death** to take great risks. **to do to death** 1 to overuse. 2 to kill. **to put to death** to execute. **death adder** *n.* any venomous snake of the genus *Acanthophis*. **death-angel** *n.* a death-cap. **deathbed** *n.* 1 the bed on which a person dies. 2 a last illness. ~*a.* of or relating to a deathbed. **death-bell** *n.* a death-knell. **death blow** *n.* 1 a mortal blow. 2 an event that brings utter ruin or destruction. **death camp** *n.* a prison or detention centre where many people die or are killed. **death-cap** *n.* a poisonous fungus, *Amanita phalloides*. **death cell** *n.* a condemned cell. **death certificate** *n.* a document issued by a doctor certifying death and giving the cause, if known. **death duties** *n.pl.* (*Hist.*) a tax levied on property when it passed to the next heir. **deathful** *a.* 1 fraught with death. 2 mortal. **death grant** *n.* a grant of money towards funeral costs. **death-knell** *n.* 1 a passing-bell. 2 a ringing in the ears supposed to forebode death. **deathless** *a.* immortal, imperishable. **deathlessly** *adv.* **deathlessness** *n.* **deathlike** *a.* **deathly** *a.* (*comp.* **deathlier**, *superl.* **deathliest**) 1 like death. 2 deadly. ~*adv.* so as to resemble death. **death mask** *n.* a plaster cast of the face after death. **death penalty** *n.* the punishment of being executed for committing a very serious crime. **death rate** *n.* the proportion of deaths in a given period in a given district. **death-rattle** *n.* a gurgling sound in the throat of a person just before death. **death roll** *n.* (a list of) the people killed in battle, a natural disaster etc. **death row** *n.* a section of condemned cells, esp. in a US prison. **death's head** *n.* a human skull, or a representation of one, as an emblem of mortality. **death's-head moth** *n.* a large European moth, *Acherontia atropos*, with markings on the back of the thorax faintly resembling a human skull. **death squad** *n.* an organized armed group engaged in systematic killings. **death tax** *n.* (*US*) a tax levied on a property on the owner's death. **death-throe** *n.* the agony of death. **death toll** *n.* the number of people killed in battle, a natural disaster etc. **death-trap** *n.* 1 a place unsuspectedly dangerous to life through insanitary or other conditions. 2 a vehicle etc. in dangerous condition. **deathwards** *adv.* **death warrant** *n.* 1 an order for the execution of a criminal. 2 an act or measure putting an end to something. **death-watch (beetle)** *n.* a wood-boring beetle, *Xestobium rufovillosum*, which makes a clicking sound formerly thought to presage death. **death wish** *n.* a desire for one's own death. [OE *dēath*, from Gmc. stem *dau-*, to die (cp. Dut. *dood*, G *Tod*)]

deattribute (dēətribˈūt) *v.t.* to end the attribution of (a work) to a particular artist etc. **deattribution** (dēatribūˈshən) *n.*

deave (dēv), **deeve** *v.t.* (*Sc., North*) 1 to deafen. 2 to stun with noise. [OE *-dēafian* (in *ādēafian*), from *dēaf*, DEAF]

deb[1] (deb) *n.* a debutante. [abbr.]

deb[2] (deb) *n.* a debenture. [abbr.]

debacle (dābahˈkəl, di-), **débâcle** (dā-) *n.* 1 a complete failure; a rout. 2 a stampede. 3 a breaking up of ice in a river. 4 breaking up and transport of rocks and gravel by a sudden outburst of water. [F *débâcle*, n., from *débâcler*, to unbar (DE-, *bâcler*, to bar)]

debag (dēbagˈ) *v.t.* (*pres.p.* **debagging**, *past*, *p.p.* **debagged**) (*coll.*) to remove the trousers of (someone) by force.

debar (dibah´) *v.i.* (*pres.p.* **debarring,** *past, p.p.* **debarred**) **1** to hinder or exclude from approach, enjoyment or action. **2** to prohibit, to forbid.

debark[1] (dibahk´) *v.t., v.i.* to disembark. **debarkation** (dēbahkā´shən) *n.* [F *débarquer*]

debark[2] (dēbahk´) *v.t.* to remove the bark from.

debarrass (dibar´əs) *v.t.* to disembarrass. [F *débarrasser* (DE-, *barrasser*, from *barrer*, to BAR[1])]

debase (dibās´) *v.t.* **1** to lower in condition, quality or value. **2** to adulterate. **3** to degrade. **debasement** *n.* **debaser** *n.* **debasingly** *adv.*

debate (dibāt´) *v.t.* **1** to contend about by words or arguments, esp. formally or publicly; to discuss. **2** to contend for. **3** to consider. ~*v.i.* **1** to discuss or argue a point, esp. formally or publicly; to engage in argument. **2** to consider. ~*n.* a (formal or public) discussion of a question; an argumentative contest. **debatable** *a.* **1** open to discussion or argument. **2** contentious. **debatably** *adv.* **debater** *n.* a person who takes part in a debate. **debating** *n., a.* **debating point** *n.* a point made to score a point in a debate rather than further the argument. **debating society** *n.* a society established for holding debates, and to improve the extempore speaking of the members. [OF *debatre* (DE-, low L *battere*, from L *battuere*, to beat)]

debauch (dibawch´) *v.t.* **1** to corrupt in morals, to pervert. **2** to lead into sensuality or intemperance. **3** to debase. **4** †to seduce from chastity or virtue. ~*n.* an act or bout of debauchery; a carouse. **debauched** *a.* having loose morals. **debauchee** (-chē´) *n.* a person who indulges their sensual appetites. **debaucher** *n.* **debauchery** *n.* indulgence of the sensual appetites. [F *débaucher*, OF *desbaucher* (DE-, perh. *bauche*, a workshop)]

debenture (diben´chə) *n.* **1** a written acknowledgement of a debt. **2** a deed or instrument issued by a company or a public body as a security for a loan of money on which interest is payable till it is redeemed. **3** (*US*) a debenture bond. **4** a certificate issued by a customhouse to an importer entitling them to a drawback or bounty. **debenture bond** *n.* (*US*) a fixed-interest bond issued by a company or corporation and backed by general credit. **debentured** *a.* secured by debenture, entitled to drawback. **debenture stock** *n.* debentures consolidated or created in the form of stock, the interest on which constitutes the first charge on the dividend. [L *dēbentur*, they are due (*dēbēre*, to be due)]

debilitate (dibil´itāt) *v.t.* to weaken, to enfeeble; to enervate, to impair. **debilitating, debilitative** *a.* **debilitation** (-ā´shən) *n.* **debility** *n.* (*pl.* **debilities**) (a) weakness, feebleness. [L *dēbilitātus*, p.p. of *dēbilitāre*, to weaken, from *dēbilis*, weak]

debit (deb´it) *n.* **1** an amount set down as a debt. **2** in book-keeping, the left-hand side of an account, in which debits are entered. ~*v.t.* (*pres.p.* **debiting,** *past, p.p.* **debited**) **1** to charge to as a debt. **2** in book-keeping, to enter (an amount, a person owing) on the debit side. **debit card** *n.* a card issued by a bank which enables the holder to debit a purchase to their account at the point of purchase. [L *dēbitum*, DEBT]

debonair (debənea´), **debonnaire** *a.* **1** having self-assurance, carefree. **2** courteous, genial, pleasing in manner and bearing. **debonairly** *adv.* **debonairness** *n.* [OF *debonaire* (*de bon aire*, of good disposition)]

debouch (dibowch´, -boosh´) *v.i.* **1** to march out from a confined place into open ground. **2** to flow out from a narrow ravine. **debouchment** *n.* **debouchure** (dābooshuə´) *n.* the mouth of a river or channel. [F *déboucher*, lit. to unstop (DE-, *bouche*, the mouth)]

debrief (dēbrēf´) *v.t.* to gather information from (someone, such as a soldier, diplomat or spy) after a mission. **debriefing** *n.*

debris (deb´rē, dā´brē) *n.* **1** broken rubbish, fragments. **2** (*Geol.*) fragmentary matter detached by a rush of water. [F *débris*, fragments, from *débriser* (DE-, *briser*, to break)]

debruised (dibroozd´) *a.* (*Her.*) crossed or folded so as to be partly covered. [ONF *debruisier*, OF *debrisier* (DE-, *brisier*, to break)]

debt (det) *n.* **1** something which is owing from one person to another, esp. a sum of money. **2** obligation, liability. **in a person's debt** under an obligation to a person. **in debt** under obligation to pay something due. **debt collector** *n.* a person whose job is collecting debts for creditors. **debtless** *a.* **debt of honour** *n.* a debt which is morally but not legally binding, such as a gambling debt. **debt of nature** *n.* death. **debtor** *n.* a person who is indebted to another, as distinct from *creditor*. [ME and OF *dette*, L *dēbitum*, neut. p.p. of *dēbēre*, to owe (*b* the result of acquaintance with the L word)]

debug (dēbŭg´) *v.t.* (*pres.p.* **debugging,** *past, p.p.* **debugged**) **1** to find and remove hidden microphones from. **2** to find and remove the faults in (a computer program, a system etc.). **3** to remove insects from. **debugger** *n.* a computer program which debugs other programs.

debunk (dēbŭngk´) *v.t.* to dispel false sentiment about, to destroy pleasing legends or illusions about. **debunker** *n.*

debus (dēbŭs´) *v.t., v.i.* (*3rd pers. sing. pres.* **debusses,** (*N Am.*) **debuses,** *pres.p.* **debussing,** (*N Am.*) **debusing,** *past, p.p.* **debussed,** (*N Am.*) **debused**) (*Mil.*) to (cause to) alight from a motor vehicle.

debut (dā´bū, deb´ū) *n.* **1** a first appearance before the public, esp. of a performer. **2** the presentation of a debutante at court. ~*v.i.* (*pres.p.* **debuting,** *past, p.p.* **debuted**) to make a debut. **debutant** (deb´ūtant), **débutant** *n.* a male performer making his debut. **debutante** (deb´ūtahnt), **débutante** *n.* **1** a young woman who makes a debut at court. **2** a female performer making her debut. [F, from *débuter*, to make a first stroke (DE-, *buter*, to throw at, from *but*, BUTT[1])]

Dec. *abbr.* December.

dec. *abbr.* **1** declaration, declared. **2** declension. **3** declination. **4** deceased. **5** (*Mus.*) decrescendo.

deca- (dek´ə), **dec-** *comb. form* ten. [Gr. *deka*, ten]

decade (dek´ād) *n.* **1** a period of ten years. **2** a group of ten. **decadal** (dikā´dəl) *a.* [F, from L *decas -adem*, Gr. *dekasa dos*, from *deka*, ten]

decadence (dek´ədəns) *n.* moral or cultural decay, deterioration; a falling-off from a high standard of excellence. **decadent** *a.* **1** having low moral or cultural standards. **2** self-indulgent, affected. ~*n.* a decadent writer or artist, esp. one having weaknesses and affectations indicating lack of strength and originality. [F *décadence*, late L *dēcadentia* (DE-, *cadere*, to fall)]

decaf (dē´kaf), **decaff** *n.* decaffeinated coffee. ~*a.* decaffeinated.

decaffeinate (dikaf´ināt) *v.t.* **1** to remove the caffeine from (coffee, tea etc.). **2** to reduce the caffeine in. **decaffeinated** *a.*

decagon (dek´əg ən) *n.* a plane figure with ten sides and ten angles. **decagonal** (dikag´-) *a.* [Gr. *gōnos*, angled]

decagram (dek´əgram), **decagramme** *n.* a weight of 10 grams (0.353 oz).

decagynous (dikaj´inəs) *a.* (*Bot.*) having ten pistils. [Gr. *gunē*, a female]

decahedron (dekəhē´drən) *n.* (*pl.* **decahedra** (-drə), **decahedrons**) a solid figure with ten sides. **decahedral** *a.*

decal (dē´kəl) *n.* a transfer, a decalcomania.

decalcify (dēkal´sifī) *v.t.* (*3rd pers. sing. pres.* **decalcifies,** *pres.p.* **decalcifying,** *past, p.p.* **decalcified**) to clear (bone etc.) of calcareous matter. **decalcification** (-fikā´shən) *n.*

decalcomania (dikalkəmā´niə) *n.* (*pl.* **decalcomanias**)

1 the process of transferring a design. 2 a design so transferred. [F *décalcomanie*, from *décalquer*, to copy, to trace]

decalitre (dek´əlētə), (*N Am.*) **decaliter** *n.* a liquid measure of capacity containing 10 litres (nearly 2½ gallons).

Decalogue (dek´əlog) *n.* the Ten Commandments. **decalogist** (-kal´əjist) *n.* a person who studies or writes about the Decalogue. [F *décalogue*, L *decalogus*, Gr. *dekalogos* (DECA-, -LOGUE)]

decametre (dek´əmētə), (*N Am.*) **decameter** *n.* a measure of length, containing 10 metres (393.7 in).

decamp (dikamp´) *v.i.* 1 to break camp. 2 to depart quickly; to take oneself off. **decampment** *n.* [F *décamper* (DE-, CAMP[1])]

decanal (dikā´nəl, dek´ənəl) *a.* 1 of or relating to a dean or a deanery. 2 of or relating to the south side of the choir, where the dean has his seat, as distinct from *cantorial*. **decani** (-nī) *a.* (sung) by the decanal side of the choir, as distinct from *cantoris*. [L *decānus*, DEAN[1]]

decani DECANAL.

decant (dikant´) *v.t.* 1 to pour off by gently inclining, so as not to disturb the sediment. 2 to pour (wine etc.) from one container into another. 3 to move (people) from one area to another to provide better housing etc. **decantation** (dēkantā´shən) *n.* **decanter** *n.* a glass container with a stopper, for holding wine or spirits. [F *décanter*, med. L *décanthāre* (DE-, *canthus*, Gr. *kanthos*, corner of the eye, lip of a cup, CANT[2])]

decapitate (dikap´itāt) *v.t.* 1 to behead. 2 to cut the top or end from. **decapitation** (-ā´shən) *n.* **decapitator** *n.* [late L *dēcapitātus*, p.p. of *dēcapitāre* (DE-, *caput*, head)]

decapod (dek´əpod) *n.* 1 any cephalopod of the order Decapoda, having two tentacles and four pairs of arms. 2 any crustacean of the order Decapoda, having five pairs of ambulatory limbs, the first pair chelate. ~*a.* 1 of or relating to the Decapoda. 2 having ten limbs. **decapodal, decapodan, decapodous** *a.* [F *décapode*, Gr. *dekapous* (DECA-, *pous podos*, a foot)]

decarbonate (dēkah´bənāt), **decarbonize** (-īz), **decarbonise** *v.t.* to remove carbon from. **decarbonization** (-zā´shən) *n.*

decastyle (dek´əstīl) *a.* (*Archit.*) having ten columns. ~*n.* a portico with ten columns in front. [med. L *decastylus*, Gr. *dekastulos* (DECA-, *stulos*, column)]

decasyllable (dek´əsiləbəl) *n.* a word or line of ten syllables. **decasyllabic** (-lab´ik) *a.*

decathlon (dikath´lon) *n.* (*pl.* **decathlons**) an athletic contest consisting of ten events. **decathlete** *n.* [Gr. *athlon*, contest]

decay (dikā´) *v.i.* 1 to rot. 2 to decline in excellence. 3 to fall away, to deteriorate. 4 (of radioactive matter) to disintegrate. ~*v.t.* 1 to cause to rot. 2 to impair, to cause to fall away. ~*n.* 1 gradual failure or decline; deterioration. 2 a state of ruin. 3 wasting away, consumption, gradual dissolution. 4 decomposition of dead tissue, rot. 5 decayed matter. 6 disintegration of radioactive matter. [OF *decair*, folk L *decadēre* (DE-, *cadēre*, L *cadere*, to fall)]

decease (disēs´) *n.* (*formal*) death, departure from this life. ~*v.i.* to die. **deceased** *a.* dead. ~*n.* a person who has recently died. **decedent** *n.* (*N Am.*) a person who has recently died. [OF *deces*, L *dēcessus*, p.p. of *dēcēdere* (DE-, *cēdere*, to go)]

deceit (disēt´) *n.* 1 the act of deceiving. 2 a tendency to deceive. 3 trickery, deception, duplicity. 4 a stratagem, a dishonest act. **deceitful** *a.* 1 given to deceit. 2 intended to deceive. **deceitfully** *adv.* **deceitfulness** *n.* [OF *deceite*, orig. fem. p.p. of *deceveir*, to deceive, L *dēcipere* (DE-, *capere*, to take)]

deceive (disēv´) *v.t.* 1 to mislead deliberately or knowingly. 2 to cheat, to delude. 3 to be unfaithful to. 4 †to disappoint. ~*v.i.* to act deceitfully. **to be deceived** to be mistaken. **to deceive oneself** to ignore the truth. **deceivable** *a.* **deceiver** *n.* [OF *deceveir*, see DECEIT]

decelerate (dēsel´ərāt) *v.i.* to reduce speed, to slow down. ~*v.t.* to cause to decelerate. **deceleration** (-rā´shən) *n.* 1 the act of decelerating. 2 the rate of diminution of speed. [L *celer*, swift]

December (disem´bə) *n.* the twelfth and last month of the year (orig. the tenth and afterwards the twelfth month of the Roman year). **Decembrist** *n.* (*Hist.*) any one of the conspirators against Tsar Nicholas of Russia at his accession in Dec. 1825. [L *decem*, ten]

decemvir (disem´və) *n.* (*pl.* **decemviri** (-rī)) 1 any one of the various bodies of ten magistrates appointed by the Romans to legislate or rule, esp. the body appointed in 451 BC to codify the laws. 2 a member of any governing council of ten. **decemviral** *a.* **decemvirate** (-rət) *n.* 1 the (term of) office of the decemviri. 2 a governing body of ten persons. [L *decem viri*, ten men]

decency DECENT.

decennary (disen´əri) *n.* (*pl.* **decennaries**) a period of ten years. ~*a.* of or relating to a period of ten years. **decennial** *a.* 1 lasting ten years. 2 occurring every ten years. **decennially** *adv.* **decennium** (-əm) *n.* (*pl.* **decennia**) a period of ten years. [L *decennis* (*decem*, ten, *annus*, year)]

decent (dē´sənt) *a.* 1 becoming, seemly. 2 modest; decorous. 3 respectable. 4 passable, tolerable. 5 (*coll.*) kind and honest. **to be decent** (*coll.*) to be sufficiently clothed to be seen in public. **decency** (dē´sənsi) *n.* (*pl.* **decencies**) 1 propriety. 2 respectable speech or behaviour. 3 freedom from immodesty or obscenity; decorum. 4 (*pl.*) accepted standards of good behaviour. **decently** *adv.* [L *decens -entem*, pres.p. of *decēre*, to be becoming]

decentralize (dēsen´trəlīz), **decentralise** *v.t.* 1 to break up (a centralized administration etc.), transfer from central control. 2 to organize on the principle of local management rather than central government. **decentralist** *n., a.* **decentralization** (-zā´shən) *n.* **decentre,** (*N Am.*) **decenter** *v.t.* to remove the centre of.

deception (disep´shən) *n.* 1 the act of deceiving. 2 the state of being deceived. 3 something which deceives; a deceit, a fraud. **deceptive** *a.* tending or apt to deceive, easy to mistake. **deceptively** *adv.* **deceptiveness** *n.* [F *déception*, L *dēceptio -ōnem* (*dēcipere*, to DECEIVE)]

decerebrate (dēser´əbrət) *a.* having undergone the removal of the cerebrum.

decern (disœn´) *v.t.* 1 (*Sc. Law*) to decree. 2 †to discern. [F *décerner*, L *dēcernere* (DE-, *cernere*, to separate, to distinguish)]

dechristianize (dēkris´chənīz), **dechristianise** *v.t.* to pervert from Christianity; to divest of Christian sentiments and principles.

deci- (des´i) *pref.* a tenth part of. [L *decimus*, tenth]

decibel (des´ibel) *n.* a unit to compare levels of intensity, esp. of sound, $\frac{1}{10}$ of a bel.

decide (disīd´) *v.t.* 1 to come to a decision about, to determine; to adjudge. 2 to settle by adjudging (victory or superiority). 3 to bring to a decision. ~*v.i.* 1 to come to a decision. 2 to give a judgement. **decidable** *a.* **decided** *a.* 1 settled; clear, evident, unmistakable. 2 determined, resolute, unwavering, firm. **decidedly** *adv.* distinctly, downright. **decidedness** *n.* **decider** *n.* 1 a deciding heat or game. 2 a person who or something which decides. [F *décider*, L *dēcīdere* (DE-, *caedere*, to cut)]

deciduous (disid´ūəs) *a.* 1 (of leaves etc. which fall in autumn and trees which lose their leaves annually) falling, not perennial. 2 (of wings etc.) shed during the lifetime of an animal. 3 falling off, not permanent; having only a temporary existence. **decidua** (-ūə) *n.* (*pl.* **deciduas, deciduae** (-ē)) the membrane lining the internal surface of the uterus, coming away after parturition. **deciduate** (-ət) *a.* having a decidua, thrown off after birth. **deciduousness** *n.* **deciduous teeth** *n.pl.* milk teeth. [L *dēciduus*, from *dēcidere* (DE-, *cadere*, to fall)]

☒ **decieve** common misspelling of DECEIVE.

decigram (des´igram), **decigramme** *n.* a weight equal to one-tenth of a gram (1.54 grain).

decile (des´īl) *n.* in statistics, any one of nine values of a random variable dividing a frequency distribution into ten equal groups.

decilitre (des´ilētə), (*NAm.*) **deciliter** *n.* a fluid measure of capacity of one-tenth of a litre (0.176 pint).

decillion (disil´yən) *n.* a million raised to the tenth power, represented by 1 followed by 60 ciphers. **decillionth** *a.* [F, from L *decem*, ten, comb. with million, cp. BILLION]

decimal (des´iməl) *a.* **1** of or relating to ten or tenths. **2** counting by tens. ~*n.* a decimal fraction. **decimal coinage** *n.* the coinage of a decimal currency. **decimal currency** *n.* a monetary system in which the coins represent the value of a given unit in multiples of ten. **decimal fraction** *n.* a fraction having some power of 10 for its denominator, esp. when it is expressed by figures representing the numerator of tenths, hundredths etc. following a point. **decimalize, decimalise** *v.t.* to reduce or adapt to the decimal system. **decimalization** (-zā´shən) *n.* **decimally** *adv.* **decimal notation** *n.* the Arabic system of numerals. **decimal place** *n.* a position of a figure in a decimal fraction to the right of the decimal point. **decimal point** *n.* the dot to the right of the unit figure in a decimal fraction. **decimal scale** *n.* a scale progressing in multiples of ten (units, tens, hundreds, thousands etc.). **decimal system** *n.* a system of weights and measures in which the values increase by multiples of ten. [late L *decimālis*, from L *decima*, tithe, fem. of *decimus*, tenth (*decem*, ten)]

decimate (des´imāt) *v.t.* **1** to destroy a tenth or a large proportion of. **2** (*Mil.*) to punish every tenth man with death. **decimation** (-ā´shən) *n.* **decimator** *n.* [L *decimātus*, p.p. of *decimāre* (*decimus*, tenth)]

decimetre (des´imētə), (*NAm.*) **decimeter** *n.* the tenth part of a metre (3.937 in).

decipher (disī´fə) *v.t.* **1** to turn from cipher into ordinary language. **2** to discover the meaning of (something written in cipher). **3** to read or explain (bad or indistinct writing). **decipherable** *a.* **decipherment** *n.*

decision (disizh´ən) *n.* **1** the act or result of deciding. **2** the determination of a trial, contest or question. **3** resolution, firmness of character. **decision support system** *n.* a system in which computers or programs provide data to assist in decision-making. **decisive** (-sī´-) *a.* **1** determining the outcome of something. **2** able to make decisions quickly. **decisively** *adv.* **decisiveness** *n.* [F *décision*, L *dēcisio -ōnem* (*dēcīdere*, DECIDE)]

decivilize (dēsiv´ilīz), **decivilise** *v.t.* **1** to render less civilized. **2** to divest of civilization.

deck (dek) *n.* **1** the plank or iron flooring of a ship, a platform forming a floor in a ship. **2** accommodation on a deck at a particular level. **3** the floor of a bus or tramcar. **4** (*sl.*) the ground. **5** a floor or platform for sunbathing etc. **6** the floor of a pier. **7** a piece of sound-recording equipment in or on which the disc, tape etc. to be played is placed. **8** (*esp. NAm.*) a pack (of cards). **9** (*US, sl.*) a packet of narcotic drugs. ~*v.t.* **1** to adorn, to beautify. **2** to cover, to put a deck to. **3** (*sl.*) to knock to the ground. **below deck** in or to the area below the main deck of a ship. **below decks** below deck. **on deck** **1** on an uncovered deck on a ship. **2** (*esp. US*) ready for action etc. **to clear the decks** to prepare for action. **to deck out** to adorn, to beautify. **to hit the deck** (*coll.*) to fall down quickly or suddenly. **deckchair** *n.* a collapsible chair, camp-stool or long chair for reclining in. **decked** *a.* **-decker** (dek´ə) *comb. form* having a specified number of decks, as *double-decker*. **deckhand** *n.* a sailor who works primarily on deck. **deckhouse** *n.* a room erected on the deck of a ship. **deck-passenger** *n.* a steerage passenger, a passenger who has no right in the cabins. **deck quoits** *n.* a game played with rope quoits and a peg. **deck tennis** *n.* a game played with quoits and a net. [cp. Dut. *decken*, to cover, Gmc. *thakjan* (cp. OE *theccan*, to THATCH)]

deckle (dek´əl) *n.* a frame used in paper-making to keep the pulp within the desired limits. **deckle edge** *n.* the rough, untrimmed edge of paper. **deckle-edged** *a.* [G *Deckel*, dim. of *Decke*, a cover]

declaim (diklām´) *v.t.* to utter rhetorically or passionately. ~*v.i.* **1** to speak a set oration in public. **2** to protest forcefully (against). **3** to speak rhetorically or passionately. **declaimer** *n.* **declamation** (dekləmā´shən) *n.* **1** the act or art of declaiming according to rhetorical rules. **2** practice in declaiming. **3** a formal oration. **4** impassioned oratory. **5** an impassioned speech. **declamatory** (-klam´-) *a.* [L *dēclāmāre* (DE- *clāmāre*, to cry out)]

declarable, declarant DECLARE.

declaration (deklərā´shən) *n.* **1** the act of declaring or proclaiming. **2** something which is declared or proclaimed. **3** the document in which anything is declared or proclaimed. **4** a manifesto, an official announcement, esp. of constitutional or diplomatic principles, laws or intentions. **5** (*Law*) **a** a statement reduced to writing. **b** an affirmation in lieu of oath. **6** in card games, the act of naming the trump suit; an announcement of a combination in one's hand. **7** in cricket, a voluntary close of innings before all the wickets have fallen. **Declaration of Independence** *n.* (*Hist.*) the document declaring the independence of the US (1776). **Declaration of Indulgence** *n.* (*Hist.*) a proclamation granting religious liberty, esp. that of Charles II in 1672 suspending the penal laws against Nonconformists and recusants, and that of James II in 1687 in favour of Roman Catholics. **declaration of the poll** *n.* an official announcement of the number of votes cast for each candidate in an election. [as DECLARE]

declare (dikleə´) *v.t.* **1** to pronounce, to assert or affirm positively. **2** to announce publicly, to proclaim formally. **3** to state the possession of (dutiable articles). **4** in card games, to name the (trump suit). **5** in cricket, to close (an innings) voluntarily. ~*v.i.* **1** to make a declaration, to avow. **2** in card games, to name the trump suit. **3** in cricket, to announce an innings as closed before all the wickets have fallen. **I (do) declare!** used to express surprise, disbelief etc. **to declare against** to side against. **to declare an interest** INTEREST[1]. **to declare for** to side with. **to declare off** to refuse to proceed with any engagement or contract. **to declare oneself** **1** to avow one's intentions. **2** to disclose one's character or attitude. **declarable** *a.* **declarant** *n.* (*Law*) a person who makes a declaration. **declarative** (-klar´-) *a.* **1** explanatory, declaratory. **2** (*Comput.*) (of a programming language) for use in problem-solving without specification of exact procedures. ~*n.* **1** a declaratory statement. **2** a declarative sentence. **declaratively** *adv.* **declarative sentence** *n.* (*Gram.*) a sentence taking the form of a simple statement. **declaratory** (-klar´-) *a.* **1** making a declaration. **2** expressive, affirmatory. **declared** *a.* self-confessed. **declaredly** (-kleə´rid-) *adv.* by one's own admission. **declarer** *n.* [F *déclarer*, L *dēclārāre* (DE-, *clārus*, clear)]

declass (dēklas´) *v.t.* to remove from a social class.

déclassé (dāklasā´) *a.* (*fem.* **déclassée**) having lost social position or estimation. [F, p.p. of *déclasser* (DE-, *classe*, L *classis*, CLASS)]

declassify (dēklas´ifī) *v.t.* (*3rd pers. sing. pres.* **declassifies**, *pres.p.* **declassifying**, *past, p.p.* **declassified**) to remove (information) from the security list. **declassification** (-fikā´shən) *n.*

declension (diklen´shən) *n.* **1** (*Gram.*) **a** the variation of inflection of nouns, adjectives and pronouns. **b** a number of nouns declined in the same way. **c** the act of declining a noun etc. **2** declining, descent, deterioration, falling off. **declensional** *a.* [OF *declinaison*, DECLINATION]

declinable DECLINE.

declinate (dek´linät, -nət) *a.* (*esp. Bot.*) bending or bent downwards in a curve. [L *dēclīnātus*, p.p. of *dēclīnāre*, to DECLINE]

declination (deklinā´shən) *n.* **1** the act of bending or moving downwards. **2** the angular distance of a heavenly body north or south of the celestial equator. **magnetic declination** MAGNETIC (under MAGNET). **declinational** *a.* **declination of the compass** *n.* the angle between the geographic and the magnetic meridians. **declinator** (dek´-) *n.* an instrument for measuring the declination and inclination of a plane. [OF, from L *dēclīnātio -ōnem*, from *dēclīnāre*, to DECLINE]

decline (diklīn´) *v.i.* **1** to sink, to fall off, to deteriorate, to decay. **2** to refuse something politely. **3** to slope downwards. **4** to droop, to stoop. **5** (of a noun) to inflect. **6** to approach the end. ~*v.t.* **1** to refuse politely, to turn away from; to reject. **2** to recite the inflections of (a noun etc.) in order. **3** to depress, to lower. ~*n.* **1** a falling-off. **2** deterioration, decay, diminution. **3** gradual failure of strength or health, formerly esp. due to tuberculosis. **4** a fall in prices. **5** setting of the sun. **6** gradual approach to extinction or death. **to go into a decline** to deteriorate gradually in health. **declinable** *a.* **declining years** *n.* old age. [F *décliner*, L *dēclīnāre* (DE-, *clīnāre*, to lean, cp. Gr. *klīnein*, to bend)]

declinometer (deklinom´itə) *n.* **1** an apparatus for measuring the declination of the needle of the compass. **2** (*Astron.*) an instrument for registering declinations. [L *dēclīno*, I decline]

declivity (dikliv´iti) *n.* (*pl.* **declivities**) **1** an inclination, a slope or gradual descent of the surface of the ground, as distinct from *acclivity*. **2** an inclination downward. **declivitous** *a.* [L *dēclīvitās*, from *dēclīvis* (DE-, *clīvus*, a slope)]

declutch (dēklŭch´) *v.i.* to release the clutch of a vehicle.

deco (dek´ō), **Deco** *n.* art deco.

decoct (dikokt´) *v.t.* **1** to boil down in hot water. **2** to extract the essence of by boiling. **decoction** *n.* **1** the act of boiling a substance to extract its essence. **2** the liquor or substance obtained by boiling. [L *dēcoctus*, p.p. of *dēcoquere* (DE-, *coquere*, to COOK)]

decode (dēkōd´) *v.t.* to translate from code symbols into ordinary language. **decodable** *a.* **decoder** *n.* a person or thing that decodes symbols.

decoke (dēkōk´) *v.t.* to remove carbon from, to decarbonize. ~*n.* an act of decoking an engine.

†**decollate** (dēkəlāt´) *v.t.* **1** to behead. **2** to cut the top or end off. **decollated** *a.* **1** beheaded. **2** (of a spiral shell) having lost the apex. **decollation** (-ā´shən) *n.* the act of beheading, esp. the beheading of St John the Baptist. [L *dēcollātus*, p.p. of *dēcollāre* (DE-, *collum*, the neck)]

décolleté (dākol´tā) *a.* (*fem.* **décolletée**) **1** (of a dress) low-necked. **2** wearing a low-necked dress. ~*n.* a low-cut neckline. **décolletage** (-tahzh´) *n.* the low-cut neckline of a dress. [F, p.p. of *décolleter* (DE-, *collet*, a collar)]

decolonize (dēkol´ənīz), **decolonise** *v.t.* to grant independence to (a colonial state). **decolonization** (-zā´shən) *n.*

decolour (dēkŭl´ə), (*N Am.*) **decolor** *v.t.* to deprive of colour, bleach. **decolorant** *a.* bleaching, blanching. ~*n.* a bleaching substance. **decolorize** (-ərīz), **decolorise** *v.t.* to deprive of colour, to bleach. ~*v.i.* to lose colour. **decolorization** (-zā´shən) *n.*

decommission (dēkəmish´ən) *v.t.* **1** to close or dismantle (a nuclear reactor etc.) which is no longer to be used. **2** to take (a ship) out of service.

decompose (dēkəmpōz´) *v.t.* **1** to resolve into constituent elements. **2** to separate the elementary parts of, to analyse. **3** to cause to rot. ~*v.i.* to become decomposed; to putrefy. **decomposable** *a.* **decomposer** *n.* an organism which causes decomposition. **decomposition** (-kompəzish´ən) *n.* [F *décomposer* (DE-, COMPOSE)]

decompound (dēkəmpownd´) *a.* compounded of compounds. **decompound leaf** *n.* a leaf composed of compound leaves.

decompress (dēkəmpres´) *v.t.* **1** gradually to relieve pressure on. **2** to return to normal atmospheric pressure conditions. **decompression** (-presh´ən) *n.* **decompression chamber** *n.* a chamber in which a person (e.g. a diver) is gradually returned to normal pressure conditions. **decompression sickness** *n.* severe pain and breathing problems caused by sudden change in atmospheric pressure. **decompressor** *n.* a device for relieving pressure on an engine.

decongestant (dēkənjes´tənt) *a.* relieving congestion. ~*n.* a drug or medicine relieving nasal or chest congestion.

deconsecrate (dēkon´sikrāt) *v.t.* to withdraw consecrated status from; to secularize. **deconsecration** (-rā´shən) *n.*

deconstruction (dēkənstrŭk´shən) *n.* a method of literary and philosophical analysis by breaking down the structure of the language on the assumption that words have no fixed meaning outside of their relation to other words. **deconstruct** (-strŭkt´) *v.t.* **deconstructionism** *n.* **deconstructionist** *n., a.*

decontaminate (dēkəntam´ināt) *v.t.* to clear of a poisonous substance or radioactivity. **decontamination** (-ā´shən) *n.*

decontrol (dēkəntrōl´) *v.t.* (*pres.p.* **decontrolling,** *past, p.p.* **decontrolled**) to terminate government control of (a trade etc.). ~*n.* the act of decontrolling something.

decor (dā´kaw), **décor** *n.* the setting, arrangement and decoration of a room or of a scene on the stage. [F]

decorate (dek´ərāt) *v.t.* **1** to make more attractive by ornamentation. **2** to be an embellishment to. **3** to confer a medal or other badge of honour on. **4** to paint, paper etc. (a room or house). **decorated** *a.* **1** adorned, ornamented, embellished. **2** possessing a medal or other badge of honour. **3** denoting the middle pointed architecture in England (*c.* 1300–1400). **decoration** (-ā´shən) *n.* **1** the act of decorating. **2** ornamentation, ornament. **3** a medal or other badge of honour. **4** (*pl.*) flags, flowers and other adornments put up on an occasion of public rejoicing etc. **Decoration Day** *n.* (*US*) Memorial Day. **decorative** (dek´ərətiv) *a.* **decoratively** *adv.* **decorativeness** *n.* **decorator** *n.* **1** a person who adorns or embellishes. **2** a person whose business it is to paint and paper rooms or houses. [L *decorātus*, p.p. of *decorāre* (*decor-*, stem of *decus*, an ornament)]

decorous (dek´ərəs) *a.* **1** behaving in a polite and decent manner. **2** in good taste. **decorously** *adv.* **decorousness** *n.* **decorum** (dikaw´rəm) *n.* (*pl.* **decorums**) **1** decency and propriety of words and conduct. **2** etiquette, polite usage. **3** a requirement of decency or etiquette. [L *decōrus* (*decor*, seemliness, from *decēre*, to befit)]

decorticate (dēkaw´tikāt) *v.t.* to strip the bark, skin, husk or outside layer from. **decortication** (-ā´shən) *n.* **1** the removal of the outside layer. **2** the surgical removal of clotted blood and scar tissue from the chest cavity. **decorticator** *n.* [L *dēcorticātus*, p.p. of *dēcorticāre* (DE-, *cortex -icem*, bark)]

decorum DECOROUS.

découpage (dākoopahzh´) *n.* the art of decorating furniture etc. with cut-out patterns. [F *découper*, to cut out]
decouple (dēkŭp´əl) *v.t.* **1** to separate, to end the connection between. **2** in electronics, to reduce unwanted distortion on (a circuit). **decoupling** *n.*
decoy (dē´koi, dikoi´) *n.* **1** a bait, an attraction. **2** a person employed to lure or entrap; a tempter. **3** a decoy-duck. **4** a pond or enclosed water into which wildfowl are lured by means of a decoy. **5** a place for entrapping wildfowl. ~*v.t.* **1** to lure into a trap or snare. **2** to allure, to entice. **decoy-duck** *n.* a tame or imitation duck, used to lure wildfowl into a trap. [formerly *coy*, Dut. *kooi*, MDut. *koye*, *kouwe*, late L *cavea*, CAGE]
decrease[1] (dikrēs´) *v.i.* to become less, to wane, to fail. ~*v.t.* to make less, to reduce in size gradually. **decreasingly** *adv.* [A-F *decreiss-*, stem of *decreistre* (OF *descreiss-*, *descreistre*), L *dēcrēscere* (DE-, *crēscere*, to grow)]
decrease[2] (dē´krīs) *n.* **1** lessening, a diminution. **2** the amount of diminution.
decree (dikrē´) *n.* **1** an edict, law or ordinance made by superior authority. **2** (*Law*) the decision in some courts, esp. in matrimonial and Admiralty cases. **3** (*Theol.*) the predetermined purpose of God. ~*v.t.* (*3rd pers. sing. pres.* **decrees**, *pres.p.* **decreeing**, *past*, *p.p.* **decreed**) **1** to command by a decree. **2** to ordain or determine. **3** to decide by law or authoritatively. ~*v.i.* to make an edict. **decree absolute** *n.* (*pl.* **decrees absolute**) the final decree in divorce proceedings. **decree nisi** *n.* (*pl.* **decrees nisi**) a provisional decree in divorce proceedings. [OF *decret*, L *dēcrētum*, neut. of *dēcrētus*, p.p. of *dēcernere* (DE-, *cernere*, to sift, to decide)]
decrement (dek´rimənt) *n.* **1** decrease, diminution. **2** the quantity lost by diminution. **3** (*Physics*) a measure of the speed of damping-out of damped waves. [L *dēcrēmentum* (*dēcrē-*, stem of *dēcrēscere*)]
decrepit (dikrep´it) *a.* **1** broken down by age and infirmities; feeble. **2** dilapidated, decayed. **decrepitude** (-tūd) *n.* [L *dēcrepitus* (DE-, *crepitus*, p.p. of *crepāre*, to crackle)]
decrepitate (dikrep´itāt) *v.t.* to calcine in a strong heat, so as to cause a continual crackling of the substance. ~*v.i.* (of a salt) to crackle in a strong heat. **decrepitation** (-ā´shən) *n.*
decrescendo (dēkrishen´dō) *adv.*, *a.* (*Mus.*) diminuendo. ~*n.* (*pl.* **decrescendos**) a diminuendo. [It., decreasing]
decrescent (dikres´ənt) *a.* (of the moon) waning. [L *decrēscens -entem*, pres.p. of *dēcrēscere* (see DECREASE[1])]
decretal (dikrē´təl) *a.* of or relating to a decree. ~*n.* **1** a decree, esp. of the Pope. **2** (*pl.*) a collection or body of papal decrees on points of ecclesiastical law or discipline. **decretalist**, **decretist** *n.* **decretive** *a.* having the force of a decree. **decretory** *a.* **1** judicial. **2** deciding, determining. [F *décrétal*, late L *dēcrētāle*, neut. of *dēcrētālis* (L *dēcrētum*, DECREE)]
decrial, **decrier** DECRY.
decriminalize (dēkrim´inəlīz), **decriminalise** *v.t.* to make (an action) no longer illegal. **decriminalization** (-zā´shən) *n.*
decry (dikrī´) *v.t.* (*3rd pers. sing. pres.* **decries**, *pres.p.* **decrying**, *past*, *p.p.* **decried**) **1** to cry down; to clamour against. **2** to depreciate. **decrial** *n.* **decrier** *n.* [F *décrier*, OF *descrier*]
decrypt (dēkript´) *v.t.* to decipher. **decryption** *n.*
decumbent (dikŭm´bənt) *a.* **1** lying down, reclining; prostrate. **2** (*Bot.*) lying flat by its own weight. **decumbence**, **decumbency** *n.* [L *decumbens -entem*, pres.p. of *dēcumbere* (DE-, *cumbere*, to lie)]
decuple (dek´ūpəl) *a.* tenfold. ~*n.* a tenfold number. ~*v.t.*, *v.i.* to increase tenfold. [F *décuple*, L *decuplus* (*decem*, ten, *-plus*, as in *duplus*, double)]
decurion (dikū´riən) *n.* (*pl.* **decurions**) (*Hist.*) **1** a Roman officer commanding ten men. **2** a member of the council of a town in Fascist Italy. [L *decurio*, from *decem*, ten (cp. *centurio*)]
decurrent (dikŭr´ənt) *a.* (*Bot.*) attached along the side of a stem below the point of insertion (as the leaves of the thistle). **decurrently** *adv.* **decursive** (-kœ´-) *a.* **1** running down. **2** decurrent. **decursively** *adv.* [L *dēcurrens -entem*, pres.p. of *dēcurrere* (DE-, *currere*, to run)]
decurve (dēkœv´) *v.t.*, *v.i.* (*Bot.*, *Zool.*) to curve downward. **decurvature** *n.* **decurved** *a.*
decussate[1] (dikŭs´āt) *v.t.*, *v.i.* to intersect at acute angles, i.e. in the form of an X. **decussated** *a.* **decussation** (dēkŭsā´shən) *n.* [L *decussātus*, p.p. of *decussāre*, (*decussis*, figure 10, X)]
decussate[2] (dikŭs´ət) *a.* intersecting at acute angles, in the form of an X. **decussately** *adv.*
dedal DAEDAL.
dedans (dədā´) *n.* **1** an open gallery at the end of a real-tennis court. **2** the spectators in this gallery. [F, inside]
dedicate (ded´ikāt) *v.t.* **1** to apply or give up wholly to some purpose, person or thing. **2** to inscribe or address (a work of art) to a friend or patron. **3** to set apart and consecrate solemnly to God or to some sacred purpose. **dedicated** *a.* **1** devoting one's time to one pursuit or cause. **2** (of computers etc.) designed to perform a specific function. **dedicatedly** *adv.* **dedicatee** (-kətē´) *n.* the person to whom something is dedicated. **dedication** (-ā´shən) *n.* **1** the act of dedicating. **2** devotion to a pursuit or cause. **3** the words in which a book, building etc. is dedicated. **4** a dedicatory inscription. **dedicative** *a.* **dedicator** *n.* **dedicatory** *a.* [L *dēdicātus*, p.p. of *dēdicāre* (DE-, *dicāre*, to proclaim, to devote)]
deduce (didūs´) *v.t.* **1** to draw as a conclusion by reasoning, to infer. **2** †to trace down step by step; to trace the descent (from). **deducement** *n.* **deducible** *a.* **deductive** (-dŭk´tiv) *a.* deduced, or capable of being deduced, from premises. **deductively** *adv.* [L *dēdūcere* (DE-, *dūcere*, to lead)]
deduct (didŭkt´) *v.t.* **1** to take away, to subtract. **2** †to reduce. **deductible** *a.* that may be deducted. ~*n.* (*US*) the excess payment in an insurance claim. **deductibility** (-bil´-) *n.* [L *dēductus*, p.p. of *dēdūcere*, see DEDUCE]
deduction (didŭk´shən) *n.* **1** the act of deducting. **2** that which is deducted. **3** the act of deducing. **4** an inference, a consequence.
deductive DEDUCE.
dee (dē) *n.* (*pl.* **dees**) **1** the fourth letter of the alphabet, D, d. **2** anything shaped like the capital form of this letter, as a D-shaped loop or link in harness. **3** either of a pair of semicircular electrodes in a cyclotron.
deed (dēd) *n.* **1** an action, a thing done with intention. **2** an illustrious exploit, an achievement. **3** fact, reality (*in deed*). **4** (*Law*) a document containing the terms of a contract and the evidence of its due execution. ~*v.t.* (*N Am.*) to transfer or convey by deed. **deed-box** *n.* a secure box for deeds etc. **deed of association** *n.* a legal instrument in which the particulars of a limited liability company must be recorded on its formation. **deed of covenant** *n.* an undertaking to pay a regular specified sum to a charity etc. which can then also recover the tax paid on income which would provide that sum. **deed poll** *n.* (*Law*) a deed made by one person only, esp. to change their name (so called because the paper is cut or polled evenly, and not indented). [OE *dǣd* (cp. Dut. *daad*, Icel. *dāth*, OHG *tat*, G *Tat*)]
deejay (dē´jā) *n.* (*coll.*) a disc jockey. [a written form of the abbreviation *DJ*]
deem (dēm) *v.t.* (*formal*) **1** to judge, to consider. **2** to suppose, to think. **deemster** (dem´stə), **dempster** (demp´stə) *n.* either of two officers who officiate as judges, one in the north and the other in the south part

of the Isle of Man. [OE *dēman*, from Gmc. *dōm-*, DOOM (cp. Dut. *doemen*, OHG *tuomian*)]

de-emphasize (dēem´fəsīz), **de-emphasise** *v.t.* **1** to remove the emphasis from. **2** to reduce the emphasis on.

deep (dēp) *a.* **1** extending far down. **2** extending far in from the surface or away from the outside. **3** having a thickness or measurement back or down (*two feet deep*). **4** dark-coloured, intensely dark. **5** profound, penetrating, abstruse. **6** heartfelt, grave, earnest. **7** intense, extreme, heinous. **8** from far down, sonorous, low in pitch, full in tone. **9** well-versed, sagacious. **10** (*coll.*) artful, scheming, secretive. **11** distant from the batsman on a cricket pitch. **12** distant from the attacking line of a football team. ~*adv.* **1** deeply, far down. **2** far on. **3** profoundly, intensely. **4** distant from the batsman or the attacking line etc. in a game. ~*n.* **1** anything deep. **2** (*poet.*) the sea (*the deep*). **3** the deep parts of the sea. **4** a deep place, an abyss, a gulf, a cavity. **5** the abyss of space. **6** (*poet.*) the bottom of the heart, the mysterious region of personality. **7** (*pl.*, *Naut.*) the estimated fathoms between the marks on the hand lead-line. **in deep water** in trouble. **deep breathing** *n.* taking long breaths, esp. for relaxation. **deep-drawn** *a.* **1** drawn from the depths. **2** (of metal) drawn through a die when cold. **deepen** *v.t.* to make deeper. ~*v.i.* to become deeper. **deep end** *n.* the end of a swimming pool where the water is deepest. **to be thrown in at the deep end** to be given the most difficult part to do first, to be required to start without much experience. **to go (in) off the deep end** to give way to one's anger. **to jump in at the deep end** to start with the most difficult part, to start without much experience. **deep-freeze** *n.* **1** a type of refrigerator for the storage of foods and perishable goods at a very low temperature. **2** a temporary cessation. ~*v.t.* (*pres.p.* **deep-freezing,** *past* **deep-froze,** *p.p.* **deep-frozen**) to freeze in a deep-freeze. **deep-fry** *v.t.* (*3rd pers. sing. pres.* **deep-fries,** *pres.p.* **deep-frying,** *past, p.p.* **deep-fried**) to fry (food) submerged in fat or oil. **deep kiss** *n.* a kiss with contact between the kissers' tongues. **deep-laid** *a.* (of a plan) profoundly, secretly or elaborately schemed. **deep-litter eggs** *n.pl.* eggs produced by hens living in sheds whose floors are thickly covered in straw or peat. **deeply** *adv.* **deepmost** *a.* **deep mourning** *n.* mourning during which only black is worn. **deepness** *n.* **deep-read** *a.* deeply versed. **deep-rooted** *a.* firmly established. **deep sea** *n.* the deeper parts of the sea. **deep-sea** *a.* of or relating to the deep sea. **deep-seated** *a.* profound; firmly seated. **deep-set** *a.* (of eyes) deeply set in the face. **Deep South** *n.* the most traditional regions of the southern US, in the south-east. **deep space** *n.* that area of space beyond the earth and the moon or the solar system. **deep therapy** *n.* the method of treating disease by gamma rays. **deep-toned** *a.* emitting a low, full sound. [OE *dēop*, from Gmc. *deup-*, cogn. with DIP (cp. Dut. *diep*, OHG *tiuf*, G *tief*)]

deer (diə) *n.* (*pl.* **deer**) any ruminant quadruped of the family Cervidae, the males having antlers, except in the one domesticated species, the reindeer. **deer fly** *n.* any bloodsucking fly of the genus *Chrysops.* **deer forest** *n.* a tract of wild land on which red deer are bred or allowed to breed for stalking. **deerhound** *n.* a large greyhound with a rough coat, formerly used for hunting deer. **deer-lick** *n.* a wet or marshy spot impregnated with salt, where deer come to lick. **deer mouse** *n.* (*pl.* **deer mice**) any American mouse of the genus *Peromyscus.* **deer-neck** *n.* a thin, ill-formed neck in a horse. **deerskin** *n.* **1** the skin of a deer. **2** leather made from the skin of a deer. ~*a.* of this material. **deerstalker** *n.* **1** a person who hunts deer by stalking. **2** a cap with peaks in front and behind and earflaps. [OE *dēor* (cp. Dut. *dier*, Icel. *dȳr*, OHG *tior*, G *Tier*)]

de-escalate (dēes´kəlāt) *v.t.* to reduce the intensity of. **de-escalation** (-ā´shən) *n.*

deeve DEAVE.

def (def) *a.* (*comp.* **deffer,** *superl.* **deffest**) (*sl.*) very good; brilliant. [DEFINITIVE (under DEFINITE)]

def. *abbr.* **1** defendant. **2** definite. **3** definition.

deface (difās´) *v.t.* **1** to disfigure; to spoil the appearance or beauty of. **2** to erase, to obliterate. **defaceable** *a.* **defacement** *n.* **defacer** *n.*

de facto (dā fak´tō) *adv.* (*formal*) in fact. ~*a.* existing in fact. [L]

defaecate DEFECATE.

defalcate (dē´falkāt) *v.i.* to commit embezzlement. **defalcation** (-kā´shən) *n.* **1** misappropriation of money, embezzlement. **2** a sum misappropriated. **3** a defect. **4** defection. **defalcator** *n.* [late L *dēfalcātus*, p.p. of *dēfalcāre* (DE-, *falcāre*, to cut with a sickle, from *falx falcis*, sickle)]

defame (difām´) *v.t.* **1** to speak maliciously about; to slander, to libel. **2** †to accuse. **defamation** (defəmā´shən) *n.* **defamatory** (-fam´-) *a.* [OF *defamer*, *diffamer*, L *diffāmāre* (*dif-*, DIS-, *fāma*, report)]

defat (dēfat´) *v.t.* (*pres.p.* **defatting,** *past, p.p.* **defatted**) to remove fat(s) from.

default (difawlt´) *n.* **1** failure to do something, esp. to appear in court on the day assigned or to meet financial liabilities. **2** want, lack, absence. **3** an option adopted by a computer if no alternative instructions are given. **4** a fault, a defect. ~*v.i.* to fail to do something, esp. to appear in court or to meet financial liabilities. ~*v.t.* (*Law*) to enter as a defaulter and give judgement against, in case of non-appearance. **by default** (happening) only because something else has not happened (*Since no one else applied, he got the job by default*). **in default of** instead of (something wanting). **judgement by default** JUDGEMENT (under JUDGE). **to go by default** to fail by default. **defaulter** *n.* **1** a person who defaults. **2** (*Mil.*) a soldier guilty of a military offence. [OF *defaute* (DE-, late L *fallita*, fem. p.p. of L *fallere*, to fail)]

defeasance (difē´zəns) *n.* **1** the act of annulling a contract. **2** (*Law*) a condition relating to a deed which being performed renders the deed void. **defeasible** *a.* that may be annulled or forfeited. **defeasibility** (-bil´-) *n.* **defeasibly** *adv.* [OF *defesance*, from *defaire*, *desfaire* (*des-*, DE-, L *facere*, to do)]

defeat (difēt´) *v.t.* **1** to overthrow, to discomfit. **2** to resist successfully, to frustrate. **3** to baffle. **4** to reject in a ballot. **5** (*Law*) to render null. ~*n.* **1** overthrow, discomfiture, esp. of an army. **2** (*Law*) annulment. **defeatism** *n.* **1** persistent expectation of defeat. **2** behaviour reflecting this. **defeatist** *n.*, *a.* [OF *defait*, p.p. of *defaire*, *desfaire* (see defeasance)]

defecate (def´əkāt), **defaecate** *v.i.* to eject faeces from the body. ~*v.t.* to purify from lees, dregs or other impurities. **defecation** (-ā´shən) *n.* the ejection of faeces from the body. **defecator** *n.* [L *dēfaecātus*, p.p. of *dēfaecāre* (DE-, *faex faecis*, dregs)]

defect[1] (dē´fekt) *n.* **1** absence of something essential to perfection or completeness. **2** moral imperfection, failing. **3** blemish. **4** the degree to which something falls short. **defective** (difek´-) *a.* **1** imperfect, incomplete, faulty. **2** intellectually, physically or morally lacking. ~*n.* (*offensive*) a person with a mental handicap. **defectively** *adv.* **defectiveness** *n.* **defects of one's qualities** *n.pl.* (*coll.*) shortcomings that usually correspond to the particular abilities or good points one possesses. [L *dēfectus*, a want, p.p. of *dēficere*, to fail (DE-, *facere*, to do)]

Usage note The meanings of the adjectives *defective* and *deficient* overlap, but in general *defective* implies some specific fault or damage, and *deficient* a shortage of something possessed.

defect[2] (difekt´) *v.i.* to desert one's country or cause for the other side. **defection** *n.* **defector** *n.* [L *dēfectus*, a want, p.p. of *dēficere*, to fail (DE-, *facere*, to do)]

defection, defector DEFECT[2].

defective DEFECT[1].

defence (difens´), (*esp. N Am.*) **defense** *n.* **1** the state or act of defending. **2** something which defends. **3** the military resources of a country. **4** (*pl.*) fortifications, fortified posts. **5** justification, vindication. **6** excuse, apology. **7** (*Law*) **a** the defendant's reply to the plaintiff's declaration, demands or charges. **b** the defendant's lawyers. **8** in team sports, the players who defend their team's goal. **defenceless** *a.* **defencelessly** *adv.* **defencelessness** *n.* the state of being undefended. **defenceman** *n.* (*pl.* **defencemen**) a defender in ice hockey or lacrosse. **defence mechanism** *n.* (*Psych.*) a usually unconscious mental adjustment for excluding from the consciousness matters the subject does not wish to receive. [ME and OF *defens*, L *defensum*, forbidden, neut. p.p. of *dēfendere*, to defend; ME and OF *defense*, defence, L *dēfensa*, fem. p.p. of *dēfendere*]

defend (difend´) *v.t.* **1** to protect, to guard; to shield from harm. **2** to keep safe against attack. **3** to support, to maintain by argument, to vindicate. **4** (*Law*) to plead in justification of. **5** in team sports, to try to stop the opposing team scoring in (a goal etc.). **6** (of the current holder) to defend (a sports title or championship) against a challenge. *~v.i.* **1** (*Law*) **a** to plead on behalf of the defendant. **b** to contest a suit. **2** in team sports, to play in defence. **defendable** *a.* **defendant** *n.* (*Law*) **1** a person summoned into court to answer some charge. **2** a person sued in a lawsuit. *~a.* of or relating to a defendant. **defender** *n.* **1** a person who defends. **2** a member of a society formed in Ireland late in the 18th century to defend Roman Catholic interests against the Orangemen. **3** in team sports, a defence player. **Defender of the Faith** *n.* a title bestowed by Pope Leo X on King Henry VIII, in 1521, for his defence of the Roman Church against Luther, and since borne by English and British sovereigns. **defensible** *a.* **defensibility** (-bil´-) *n.* **defensibly** *adv.* **defensive** *a.* **1** serving to defend. **2** overanxious to defend oneself against (expected) criticism. **3** protective, not aggressive. *~n.* an attitude or condition of defence. **on the defensive 1** ready to defend oneself. **2** overanxious to defend oneself against (expected) criticism. **defensive end** *n.* either of two particular defensive players in American football. **defensively** *adv.* **defensive medicine** *n.* diagnostic procedures carried out by doctors whether absolutely necessary or not in order to avoid any future legal indictment. **defensiveness** *n.* [OF *defender*, L *dēfendere* (DE-, *fendere*, to strike)]

defenestration (dēfenistrā´shən) *n.* (Hist. *or facet.*) the action of throwing someone (or occasionally something) out of a window. **defenestrate** (-fen´-) *v.t.*

defense DEFENCE.

defensible, defensive etc. DEFEND.

defer[1] (difœ´) *v.t.* (*pres.p.* **deferring,** *past, p.p.* **deferred**) **1** to put off; to postpone. **2** (*US*) to postpone the conscription of. *~v.i.* to delay; to procrastinate. **deferment** *n.* **deferrable** *a.* **deferral** *n.* **deferred** *a.* **deferred pay** *n.* wages or salary, esp. of a soldier, held over to be paid at his discharge or death. **deferred payment** *n.* payment by installments. **deferred sentence** *n.* (*Law*) a sentence which is postponed for a period while the court examines the offender's behaviour. **deferred shares** *n.pl.* shares on which a reduced or no dividend is paid until a fixed date or contingent event. [OF *differer*, L *differre* (*dif-*, DIS-, *ferre*, to bear)]

defer[2] (difœ´) *v.i.* (*pres.p.* **deferring,** *past, p.p.* **deferred**) to yield to the opinion of another. **deference** (def´ər-) *n.* **1** submission to the views or opinions of another; compliance. **2** respect, regard. **deferent**[1] *a.* deferential. **deferential** (defəren´-) *a.* **deferentially** *adv.* **deferrer** *n.* [F *déférer*, L *dēferre* (DE-, *ferre*, to bring)]

deferent[1] DEFER[2].

deferent[2] (def´ərənt) *n.* **1** something which carries or conveys. **2** (*Anat.*) a vessel or duct conveying fluids. *~a.* (*Anat.*) conveying fluids. [F *déférent*, or directly from L *dēferens -entem*, pres.p. of *dēferre*, DEFER[2]]

deferrable, deferral etc. DEFER[1].

deferrer DEFER[2].

defervescence (defəves´əns) *n.* (*Med.*) a cooling down; an abatement of symptoms of fever. [L *dēfervēscens -entem*, pres.p. of *dēfervēscere* (DE-, *fervēscere*, incept. of *fervēre*, to be hot)]

defeudalize (dēfū´dəlīz), **defeudalise** *v.t.* to deprive of feudal character or form.

defiance, defiant DEFY.

defibrillator (dēfib´rilātə) *n.* a machine used to apply an electric current to the chest and heart area to stop fibrillation of the heart. **defibrillation** (-ā´shən) *n.*

deficient (difish´ənt) *a.* **1** wanting, defective; falling short. **2** not fully supplied. **3** †mentally handicapped. **deficiency** (difish´ənsi) *n.* (*pl.* **deficiencies**) **1** a falling short; deficit, lack, want, insufficiency. **2** a thing lacking. **3** the amount lacking to make complete or sufficient. **deficiency disease** *n.* a disease caused by lack or insufficiency of one or more of the essential food constituents. **deficiently** adv. [late L *dēficientia*, from L *dēficiens -entem*, pres.p. of *dēficere* (see DEFECT[1])]

Usage note See note under DEFECT[1].

deficit (def´isit) *n.* **1** a falling short of revenue as compared with expenditure. **2** the amount of this deficiency. **3** the amount required to make assets balance liabilities. **deficit spending** *n.* a remedy for economic depression whereby the government's expenditure exceeds its revenue, the resulting budget deficit being financed by loans. [F *déficit*, from L *deficit*, 3rd pers. sing. pres. of *dēficere* (see DEFECT[1])]

defier DEFY.

defilade (defilād´) *v.t.* (*Mil.*) to arrange the defences so as to shelter the interior works from an enfilade. *~n.* the act of defilading. **defilement**[1] (-fī´-) *n.*

defile[1] (difīl´) *v.t.* **1** to make foul or dirty; to soil, to stain. **2** to deprive of virginity, to violate. **3** to pollute, to desecrate, to make ceremonially unclean. **defilement**[2] *n.* **defiler** *n.* [ME *defoulen*, OF *defouler*, to trample on (DE-, late L *fullāre*, to full cloth), afterwards assimilated to BEFOUL and the obs. *befile*, OE *fȳlan*, from *fūl*, FOUL]

defile[2] (dē´fīl, difīl´) *n.* **1** a long, narrow pass or passage, as between hills, along which people can march only in file. **2** a gorge. *~v.i.* to march in a file or by files. [F *défiler* (DE-, *filer*, to FILE[1])]

defilement[1] DEFILADE.

defilement[2] DEFILE[1].

☒ **definately** common misspelling of DEFINITELY (under DEFINITE).

define (difīn´) *v.t.* **1** to give a definition of, to state the meaning of (a word etc.), to describe (a thing) by its qualities and circumstances. **2** to mark out, to fix with precision (as duties etc.). **3** to determine the limits of. **definable** *a.* **definably** *adv.* [OF *definer* (superseded by F *définir*) for *definir*, L *dēfīnīre* (DE-, *fīnīre*, to set a bound, from *fīnis*, bound)]

definite (def´init) *a.* **1** limited, determinate, fixed precisely. **2** exact, distinct, clear. **3** positive, sure. **4** (*Gram.*) indicating exactly, limiting, defining. *~n.* a definite thing; a noun with a definite referent. **definite article** *n.* the word *the* or its equivalent in other languages. **definite integral** *n.* an integral expressed as the difference between its value at upper and lower limits of a variable. **definitely** *adv.* **1** in a definite manner. **2** certainly. **definiteness** *n.* **definition** (-nish´ən) *n.* **1** the act of defining. 2 a statement of the meaning of a word etc.; an exact description of a thing by its qualities and circumstances. 3 distinctness, clearness of form, esp. of an image transmitted by a lens or a television image. **definitive** (-fin´-) *a.* 1 decisive; conclusive; positive. 2 being the best or most authoritative of its kind. 3 (of a postage stamp) of a design etc. always in use, standard. ~*n.* 1 a definitive postage stamp. 2 a word used to limit the application of a common noun, such as an adjective or pronoun. **definitively** *adv.* [L *definitus*, past part. of *definere* (see DEFINE)]

Usage note The meanings of the adjectives *definite* and *definitive* overlap, but in general something *definitive* is regarded as final and authoritative, and something *definite* is exact but may be changed, and may even be misleading or untrue.

deflagrate (def´ləgrāt) *v.t.* to consume by means of rapid combustion. ~*v.i.* to be consumed by means of rapid combustion. **deflagration** (-rā´shən) *n.* **deflagrator** *n.* an instrument for producing rapid combustion, usu. a form of the voltaic battery. [L *dēflāgrātus*, p.p. of *dēflāgrāre* (DE-, *flāgrāre*, to burn)]

deflate (diflāt´) *v.t.* 1 to let down (a pneumatic tyre, balloon etc.) by allowing the air or gas to escape. 2 to reduce the inflation of (currency). 3 to humiliate, to take away the confidence of. 4 to reduce the importance of. ~*v.i.* 1 to be emptied of air or gas. 2 to bring about economic deflation. 3 to lose confidence. **deflation** *n.* 1 reduction of size by allowing air or gas to escape. 2 the reduction and control of the issue of paper money to increase its value. 3 erosion of rock by the wind. **deflationary** *a.* **deflationist** *n., a.* **deflator, deflater** *n.* [L *dēflātus*, p.p. of *dēflāre* (DE-, *flāre*, to blow)]

deflect (diflekt´) *v.i.* 1 to turn or move to one side. 2 to deviate. ~*v.t.* 1 to cause to turn, bend, or deviate. 2 to ward off, to avoid (criticism etc.). **deflection** (diflek´shən), **deflexion** *n.* 1 the act of deflecting. 2 the fact of being deflected. 3 a turn or move to one side, a deviation. 4 displacement from a neutral or zero position. **deflective** *a.* **deflector** *n.* **deflexed** *a.* (*Zool., Bot.*) deflected, bent downward. [L *dēflectere* (DE-, *flectere*, to bend), p.p. *dēflexus*]

deflorate (dēflaw´rāt) *a.* (*Bot.*) 1 having shed its pollen. 2 having the flowers fallen. ~*v.t.* to deflower. **defloration** (-flərā´shən) *n.* deflowering. [L *dēflōrātus*, p.p. of *dēflōrāre*, see DEFLOWER]

deflower (diflow´ə) *v.t.* 1 to deprive of virginity, to ravish. 2 to ravage, to despoil. 3 to strip of flowers. **deflowerer** *n.* [OF *desfleurer* (F *défleurer*), L *dēflōrāre* (DE-, *flōs flōris*, flower)]

defocus (dēfō´kəs) *v.t.* (*pres.p.* **defocusing, defocussing,** *past, p.p.* **defocused, defocussed**) to put out of focus. ~*v.i.* to go out of focus.

defoliate (dēfō´liāt) *v.t.* to deprive of leaves, esp. in warfare. **defoliant** *n.* a chemical used to remove leaves. **defoliation** (-ā´shən) *n.* 1 the act of defoliating trees. 2 the fall or shedding of leaves. [L *folium*, a leaf]

deforce (difaws´) *v.t.* 1 to withhold with violence. 2 (*Law*) to withhold the possession of (an estate etc.) from its rightful owner. 3 (*Sc. Law*) to oppose (an officer of the law) in the execution of their duty. **deforcement** *n.* [OF *deforcier*, late L *difforciāre* (*dif-*, DIS-, *fortia*, power, L *fortis*, strong)]

deforest (dēfor´ist) *v.t.* to clear of trees. **deforestation** (-tā´shən) *n.* [OF *desforester*, DISFOREST]

deform (difawm´) *v.t.* 1 to render ugly or unshapely. 2 to disfigure, to distort. 3 to mar, to spoil. ~*v.i.* to experience deformation. **deformable** *a.* **deformation** (dēfawmā´shən) *n.* 1 the act or process of deforming. 2 a disfigurement, perversion or distortion. 3 a change in shape; a quantification of this. 4 a change for the worse, as distinct from *reformation*. 5 an altered form of a word. 6 alteration in the structure and external configuration of the earth's crust through the action of internal forces. **deformational** *a.* **deformed** *a.* 1 misshapen. 2 disfigured, ugly. **deformer** *n.* **deformity** *n.* (*pl.* **deformities**) 1 the state of being deformed. 2 a disfigurement, a malformation. 3 something which mars or spoils the beauty of a thing. [OF *deformer*, L *dēformāre* (DE-, *forma*, beauty, form)]

defraud (difrawd´) *v.t.* to deprive of what is right by deception; to cheat. **defrauder** *n.* [OF *defrauder*]

defray (difrā´) *v.t.* to pay; to bear the charge of; to settle. **defrayable** *a.* **defrayal** *n.* **defrayment** *n.* [OF *défrayer* (DE-, *frai*, sing. of *frais*, cost, expense, prob. from low L *fredum*, a fine, OHG *fridu*, peace)]

defrock (dēfrok´) *v.t.* to deprive (a priest etc.) of ecclesiastical status.

defrost (dēfrost´) *v.t.* 1 to remove frost or ice from. 2 to thaw. ~*v.i.* to become defrosted. **defroster** *n.* a device for defrosting a windscreen or a refrigerator.

deft (deft) *a.* neat in handling; dextrous, clever. **deftly** *adv.* **deftness** *n.* [OE *gedæfte*, see DAFT]

defunct (difŭngkt´) *a.* 1 dead, deceased, extinct. 2 no longer in operation or use. ~*n.* a dead person. [L *dēfunctus*, p.p. of *dēfungī* (DE-, *fungī*, to perform)]

defuse (dēfūz´), (*NAm.*) **defuze** *v.t.* 1 to render (a bomb) harmless by removing the fuse. 2 to dispel the tension of (a situation).

Usage note The verbs *defuse* and *diffuse* should not be confused: *defuse* means to remove a fuse from, and *diffuse* to disperse.

defy (difī´) *v.t.* (*3rd pers. sing. pres.* **defies,** *pres.p.* **defying,** *past, p.p.* **defied**) 1 to disregard openly. 2 to baffle (*that defies description*). 3 to challenge to do or substantiate. **defiance** *n.* 1 open disobedience; opposition; contemptuous disregard. 2 challenge to battle, single combat or any contest. **in defiance of** in disobedience or disregard of, in opposition to. **defiant** *a.* 1 openly disobedient. 2 challenging; hostile in attitude. **defiantly** *adv.* **defier** *n.* [OF *defier*, late L *diffidāre* (*dif-*, DIS-, *fīdus*, faithful)]

deg. *abbr.* degree(s) (of temperature).

dégagé (dāgah´zhā), (*fem.*) **dégagée** *a.* relaxed, casual, detached. [F, p.p. of *dégager*, to set free]

degas (dēgas´) *v.t.* (*3rd pers. sing. pres.* **degases, degasses,** *pres.p.* **degassing,** *past, p.p.* **degassed**) to remove gas from.

degauss (dēgows´) *v.t.* to neutralize the magnetization of (a ship etc.), by the installation of a current-carrying conductor.

degenerate[1] (dijen´ərət) *a.* 1 having fallen from a better to worse state. 2 having low moral standards. 3 having declined in natural or moral growth. 4 (*Biol.*) having reverted to a lower type. ~*n.* a degenerate person or animal. **degeneracy** *n.* **degenerately** *adv.* [L *dēgenerātus*, p.p. of *dēgenerāre*, from *dēgener*, base (DE- *genus -neris*, race)]

degenerate[2] (dijen´ərāt) *v.i.* 1 to fall off in quality from a better to a worse physical or moral state; to deteriorate. 2 (*Biol.*) to revert to a lower type. 3 (*Bot.*) to become wild. **degeneration** (-ā´shən) *n.* 1 the act or process of degenerating. 2 the state of being degenerated. 3 (*Bot.*) the return of a cultivated plant to the wild state. 4 (*Biol.*) gradual deterioration of any organ or class of organisms.

deglutition (dēglootish´ən) *n.* (*formal*) the act or power of swallowing. [F *déglutition* (DE-, down, L *glūtītus*, p.p. of *glūtīre*, to swallow)]

degradation (degrədā´shən) *n.* 1 the act of degrading. 2 the state of being degraded; debasement, degeneracy. 3 the wearing away of higher lands, rocks etc.

degrade (digrād´) *v.t.* 1 to reduce in rank. 2 to remove from any rank, office or dignity. 3 to debase, to lower.

4 to bring into contempt. **5** to wear away; to disintegrate. **6** (*Biol.*) to reduce from a higher to a lower type. **7** (*Chem.*) to reduce to a simpler structure. **8** (*Physics*) to reduce to a less convertible form. ~*v.i.* **1** to degenerate. **2** (*Chem.*) to disintegrate. **degradable** *a.* capable of decomposing biologically or chemically. **degradability** (-bil´-) *n.* **degradative** *a.* **degraded** *a.* **1** reduced in rank, position, value or estimation. **2** low, mean, base. **3** (*Her.*) furnished with steps. **degrader** *n.* **degrading** *a.* humiliating, debasing. **degradingly** *adv.* [OF *degrader*, late L *dēgradāre* (DE-, *gradus*, a step)]

degrease (dēgrīs´) *v.t.* to remove grease from. **degreaser** *n.*

degree (digrē´) *n.* **1** a step or stage in progression, elevation, quality, dignity or rank. **2** relative position or rank. **3** relative condition, relative quantity, quality or intensity. **4** the 90th part of a right angle; the 360th part of the circumference of the earth or of a circle. **5** the unit of measurement of temperature or hardness. **6** a rank or grade of academic proficiency conferred by universities after examination, or as a compliment to distinguished persons. **7** a certain distance or remove in the line of descent determining proximity of blood. **8** social, official or Masonic rank. **9** any one of the three grades of comparison of adjectives and adverbs (POSITIVE, COMPARATIVE, SUPERLATIVE). **10** any one of the (usu. three) grades of severity of burns. **11** a grade of severity of a crime. **12** (*Mus.*) a note's position in a scale. **13** (*Math.*) the highest power of unknowns or variables in an equation. **by degrees** gradually, step by step. **to a degree** (*coll.*) to a certain extent, somewhat. **degree day** *n.* the day on which degrees are conferred at a university etc. **degreeless** *a.* **degree of comparison** *n.* (*Gram.*) the positive, comparative or superlative form of an adjective or adverb. **degree of freedom** *n.* **1** (*Physics*) an independent component of motion of a molecule or atom. **2** (*Chem.*) any of the independent variables which define the state of a system. **3** in statistics, the number of values that can be assigned to a statistical distribution. **degrees of frost** *n.pl.* (*with number*) degrees below freezing-point. [OF *degre* (DE-, L *gradus*, a step)]

degressive (digres´iv) *a.* **1** reducing in quantity. **2** (of tax) decreasing by stages below a certain sum.

degust (digŭst´) *v.t.* (*formal*) to taste so as to relish. **degustate** *v.t.* to degust. **degustation** (dēgŭstā´shən) *n.* [L *dēgustāre* (DE-, *gustāre*, to taste)]

de haut en bas (də ōt ã bah´) *adv.* condescendingly, in a manner assuming superiority. [F, from above to below]

dehisce (dihis´) *v.i.* (of the capsules or anthers of plants) to gape, to burst open. **dehiscence** *n.* **dehiscent** *a.* [L *dēhiscere* (DE-, *hiscere*, to yawn)]

dehorn (dēhawn´) *v.t.* to remove the horns from.

dehumanize (dēhū´mənīz), **dehumanise** *v.t.* **1** to divest of human character, esp. of feeling or tenderness; to brutalize. **2** to make like an automaton. **dehumanization** (-īzā´shən) *n.*

dehumidify (dēhūmid´ifī) *v.t.* (*3rd pers. sing. pres.* **dehumidifies,** *pres.p.* **dehumdifying,** *past, p.p.* **dehumidified**) to remove humidity from. **dehumidification** (-fikā´shən) *n.* **dehumidifier** *n.*

dehydrate (dēhīdrāt´) *v.t.* to release or remove water or its elements from (the body, tissues etc.). **dehydration** *n.* **dehydrator** *n.*

dehydrogenate (dēhī droj´ənāt) *v.t.* to remove hydrogen from. **dehydrogenation** (-ā´shən) *n.*

dehypnotize (dēhip´nətīz), **dehypnotise** *v.t.* to awaken from a hypnotic condition. **dehypnotization** (-zā´shən) *n.*

de-ice (dēīs´) *v.t.* **1** to disperse or remove ice (from the wings and control surfaces of an aircraft, the windows of a car). **2** to prevent the formation of ice on. **de-icer** *n.* an apparatus or substance used for this purpose.

deicide (dē´isīd, dā´-) *n.* **1** the killing of a god. **2** a person who does this. **deicidal** (-sī´dəl) *a.* [L *deus*, god, -CIDE]

deictic (dīk´tik) *a.* (*Gram.*, *Logic*) proving or pointing directly; demonstrative as distinct from *indirect* or *refutative*. ~*n.* a deictic word. **deictically** *adv.* [Gr. *deiktikos*, from *deiktos* (*deiknunai*, to show)]

deid (dēd) *a.* (*Sc.*) dead.

deify (dē´ifī, dā´-) *v.t.* (*3rd pers. sing. pres.* **deifies,** *pres.p.* **deifying,** *past, p.p.* **deified**) **1** to make a god of. **2** to adore as a god; to idolize. **deific** (-if´-) *a.* making divine. **deification** (-fikā´shən) *n.* **deifier** *n.* **deiform** *a.* **1** of godlike form. **2** conformable to the will of God. [OF *deifier*, late L *deificāre* (*deus*, god, *facere*, to make)]

deign (dān) *v.i.* to condescend (*He wouldn't deign to join us*). ~†*v.t.* to condescend to allow or grant. [OF *degnier*, L *dignārī*, to deem worthy]

Dei gratia (dāē grah´shiə) *adv.* (*formal*) by the grace of God. [L]

deil (dēl) *n.* (*Sc.*) **1** the Devil. **2** a devil or evil sprite. [DEVIL]

deindustrialize (dēindŭs´triəlīz), **deindustrialise** *v.t.* to make (a country etc.) less industrial. **deindustrialization** (-zā´shən) *n.*

deinothere (dī´nōthiə), **dinothere** *n.* an extinct mammal resembling an elephant, with tusks that curve downwards. [Gr., *deinos*, terrible, *thērion*, wild beast]

deinstitutionalize (dēinstitū´shənəlīz), **deinstitutionalise** *v.t.* **1** to remove from an institution, esp. from a mental hospital. **2** to make less institutional in organization etc. **deinstitutionalization** (-zā´shən) *n.* **deinstitutionalized** *a.*

deionize (dēī´ənīz), **deionise** *v.t.* to remove ions from (water or air). **deionization** (-zā´shən) *n.* **deionizer** *n.*

deipnosophist (dīpnos´əfist) *n.* a person who discourses learnedly at meals, an excellent dinner table conversationalist (after the title of a work by Athenaeus). [Gr. *deipnosophistēs* (*deipnon*, dinner, SOPHIST (under SOPHISM))]

deiseal DEASIL.

deism (dē´izm, dā´-) *n.* the belief in the being of a god as the governor of the universe, on purely rational grounds, without accepting divine revelation. **deist** *n.* **deistic** (-is´-), **deistical** *a.* **deistically** *adv.* [F *déisme* (L *deus*, god, -ISM)]

deity (dē´əti, dā´-) *n.* (*pl.* **deities**) **1** divine nature, character or attributes. **2** the Supreme Being. **3** a god or goddess. [F *déité*, L *deitās -tātem*, from *deus*, god]

déjà vu (dāzhah vü´), **deja vu** *n.* **1** an illusion of already having experienced something one is experiencing for the first time. **2** lack of originality, familiarity through repetition. [F, already seen]

deject (dijekt´) *v.t.* to depress in spirit; to dishearten. **dejecta** *n.pl.* (*Med.*) human or animal excrement. **dejected** *a.* **dejectedly** *adv.* **dejection** *n.* **1** the state of being dejected; lowness of spirits. **2** (*Med.*) evacuation of the bowels, excrement. [L *dejectus*, p.p. of *dējicere* (DE-, *jacere*, to throw)]

déjeuner (dā´zhənā) *n.* breakfast, luncheon. [F *jeune*, L *jejūnus*, fasting]

de jure (dē joo´ri, dā joo´ri) *adv.* (*formal*) by right, legally. ~*a.* rightful. [L]

dekko (dek´ō) *n.* (*pl.* **dekkos**) (*coll.*) a quick look (*Have a dekko at this*). ~*v.i.* (*3rd pers. sing. pres.* **dekkos,** *pres.p.* **dekkoing,** *past, p.p.* **dekkoed**) to look. [Hind. *dekho*, imper. of *dekhna*, a look]

Del. *abbr.* Delaware.

del. *abbr.* delegate.

delaine (dilān´) *n.* **1** a kind of untwilled wool muslin. **2** a fabric of wool and cotton. [F *mousseline de laine*, woollen muslin]

†**delate** (dilāt´) *v.t.* **1** to accuse, to inform against. **2** to

cite before an ecclesiastical court. **delation** *n.* **delator** *n.* [late L *dēlātāre*, to accuse (DE-, *lātus*, p.p. of *ferre*, to bring)]

delay (dilā´) *v.t.* **1** to postpone, to put off. **2** to hinder, to make (someone) late. ~*v.i.* **1** to put off action. **2** to linger. ~*n.* **1** the act of delaying. **2** postponement, retardation. **3** time lost before action; hindrance. **delayed-action** *a.* timed to activate or operate some time after initiation (*a delayed-action bomb*). **delayer** *n.* **delaying action** *n.* **1** a military engagement to delay an enemy's advance. **2** any action intended to delay something. **delayingly** *adv.* **delay line** *n.* a device for delaying the transmission of a signal. [OF *delaier*, prob. from L *dīlātāre*, freq. of *differre* (*dif-*, DIS -, *ferre*, cp. DELATE)]

delayering (dēlā´əring) *n.* the restructuring of a company or other organization by reducing the number of hierarchical layers.

dele (dē´li) *v.t.* (*pres.p.* **deleing,** *past, p.p.* **deled**) (*Print.*) to take out, omit, expunge; to mark for deletion. ~*n.* a mark indicating deletion; a deletion. **deleble** (del´əbəl), **delible** *a.* that can be deleted. [L, 2nd pers. sing. imper. of *dēlēre*, to DELETE]

delectable (dilek´təbəl) *a.* **1** delightful, highly pleasing. **2** delicious to the taste. **delectability** (-bil´-), **delectableness** *n.* **delectably** *adv.* **delectation** (dēlektā´shən) *n.* delight, pleasure, enjoyment. [OF, from L *dēlectābilis* (*dēlectāre*, to DELIGHT)]

delegable DELEGATE².

delegate¹ (del´igət) *n.* **1** a person authorized to transact business as a representative. **2** a deputy, an agent. **3** (*US*) a deputy from a territory in Congress. **4** a member of a deputation or committee. **delegacy** *n.* (*pl.* **delegacies**) **1** a delegation. **2** an appointment as a delegate. **3** the process of delegating. [OF *delegat*, L *dēlēgātus*, p.p. of *dēlēgāre* (DE-, *lēgāre*, to send, to depute)]

delegate² (del´igāt) *v.t.* **1** to depute as a delegate, agent or representative, with authority to transact business. **2** to commit (authority to transact business) to a delegate. **3** to entrust the performance of or responsibility for (a task etc.) to another. **delegable** *a.* **delegation** (-ā´shən) *n.* **1** a body of delegates. **2** the act of delegating, a deputation. **delegator** *n.*

delete (dilēt´) *v.t.* to score out, to erase. **deletion** *n.* **deletory** *n.* (*pl.* **deletories**) something which deletes. [L *dēlētus*, p.p. of *dēlēre* (DE-, *lēre*, conn. with *linere*, to smear)]

deleterious (delitiə´riəs) *a.* harmful; injurious to health or mind. **deleteriously** *adv.* [late L *dēlētērius*, Gr. *dēlētērios*, from *dēlētēr*, a destroyer (*dēleesthai*, to destroy)]

delft (delft), **delf** (delf), **delph** *n.* glazed earthenware of a type orig. made at Delft, the Netherlands. **delftware** *n.*

deli (del´i) *n.* (*pl.* **delis**) short for DELICATESSEN.

Delian (dē´liən) *a.* of or relating to Delos, in Greece. [L *Dēlius*, Gr. *Dēlios*, from *Dēlos*]

deliberate¹ (dilib´ərət) *a.* **1** done or carried out intentionally. **2** weighing matters or reasons carefully. **3** circumspect, cool, cautious. **4** leisurely, not hasty. **deliberately** *adv.* **deliberateness** *n.* [L *dēlīberātus*, p.p. of *dēlīberāre* (DE-, *lībrāre*, to weigh, from *lībra*, a balance)]

deliberate² (dilib´ərāt) *v.i.* **1** to weigh matters in the mind, to ponder. **2** to consider, to discuss, to take counsel. ~*v.t.* to weigh in the mind. **deliberation** (-ā´shən) *n.* **1** calm and careful consideration. **2** discussion of reasons for and against; a debate. **3** freedom from haste or rashness. **4** leisurely, not hasty, movement. **deliberative** (-lib´ərətiv) *a.* of, relating to, proceeding from, or acting with, deliberation. **deliberatively** *adv.* **deliberativeness** *n.* **deliberator** *n.*

delible DELE.

delicacy (del´ikəsi) *n.* (*pl.* **delicacies**) **1** the quality of being delicate. **2** anything that is subtly pleasing to the senses, the taste or the feelings. **3** a luxury, a choice morsel. **4** fineness of texture, design, tint or workmanship. **5** subtlety and sensitiveness of construction and action. **6** weakness, fragility, susceptibility to injury. **7** accuracy of perception. **8** fineness, sensitiveness, shrinking from coarseness and immodesty. **9** gentleness, consideration for others; perceptiveness.

delicate (del´ikət) *a.* **1** exquisite in form or texture. **2** fine, smooth, not coarse. **3** subtle in colour, form or style. **4** easily injured, fragile, constitutionally weak or feeble. **5** requiring careful treatment; critical, ticklish. **6** sensitive, subtly perceptive or appreciative. **7** fastidious, tender, soft, effeminate. **8** refined, chaste, pure. **9** gentle, considerate. **10** skilful, ingenious, dexterous. **11** requiring acuteness of sense to distinguish. **12** highly pleasing to the taste. **13** dainty, palatable. **†in a delicate condition** pregnant. **delicately** *adv.* **delicateness** *n.* [L *dēlicātus* (cp. *deliciae*, delight)]

delicatessen (delikətes´ən) *n.* **1** a shop or part of a shop selling cold meats and cheeses and specialist prepared foods. **2** (*pl.*) such products. [G]

delicious (dilish´əs) *a.* giving great pleasure to the taste or senses. **deliciously** *adv.* **deliciousness** *n.* [OF, from late L *dēliciōsus*, from L *dēliciae*, delight]

delight (dilīt´) *v.t.* to please greatly, to charm. ~*v.i.* to be highly pleased; to take great pleasure (in). ~*n.* **1** a state of great pleasure and satisfaction. **2** a source of great pleasure or satisfaction (*Your daughter is a delight to look after*). **delighted** *a.* **delightedly** *adv.* **delightful** *a.* **delightfully** *adv.* **delightfulness** *n.* [OF *deliter*, L *dēlectāre*, freq. of *dēlicere*]

Delilah (dilī´lə) *n.* **1** a temptress. **2** a loose woman. [the Philistine woman who betrayed Samson (Judges xvi)]

delimit (dilim´it) *v.t.* (*pres.p.* **delimiting,** *past, p.p.* **delimited**) to fix the boundaries or limits of. **delimitate** (-mitā´-) *v.t.* to delimit. **delimitation** (-ā´shən) *n.* [F *délimiter*, L *dēlīmitāre* (DE-, *līmitāre*, to bound, from *līmes līmitem*, a boundary)]

delineate (dilin´iāt) *v.t.* **1** to draw in outline; to sketch out. **2** to describe, to depict, to portray. **delineation** (-ā´shən) *n.* **delineative** (-lin´iə-) *a.* **delineator** *n.* [L *dēlīneātus*, p.p. of *dēlīneāre* (DE-, *līneāre*, to mark out, from *līnea*, a LINE¹)]

delinquent (diling´kwənt) *n.* an offender, a culprit. ~*a.* offending, failing, neglecting. **delinquency** *n.* (*pl.* **delinquencies**) **1** a fault, an offence. **2** guilt. **3** a failure or omission of duty. **delinquently** *adv.* [L *dēlinquens -entem*, pres.p. of *dēlinquere* (DE-, *linquere*, to omit)]

deliquesce (delikwes´) *v.i.* to liquefy, to melt away gradually by absorbing moisture from the atmosphere. **deliquescence** *n.* **deliquescent** *a.* [L *dēliquēscere* (DE-, *liquēscere*, incept. of *liquēre*, to be liquid)]

delirious (dilir´iəs) *a.* **1** suffering from delirium, wandering in the mind, as a result of fever etc. **2** raving, madly excited. **3** frantic with delight or other excitement. **deliriously** *adv.*

delirium (dilir´iəm) *n.* **1** a wandering of the mind, perversion of the mental processes, the results of cerebral activity bearing no true relation to reality, characterized by delusions, illusions or hallucinations, caused by fever etc. **2** frantic excitement or enthusiasm, rapture, ecstasy. **delirium tremens** (trem´enz) *n.* an acute phase in chronic alcoholism, in which hallucinations and trembling are experienced. [L, from *dēlīrāre* (DE-, *līra*, a furrow)]

delitescent (delites´ənt) *a.* (*Med.*) **1** concealed, latent. **2** in surgery, disappearing, subsiding. **delitescence** *n.* [L *dēlitēscens -entem*, pres.p. of *dēlitēscere* (DE-, *litēscere*, incept. of *latēre*, to lie hidden)]

deliver (diliv´ə) *v.t.* **1** to distribute, to present. **2** to give over, to hand over or on. **3** to free from danger or restraint; to save, to rescue. **4** to assist at the birth of (a child); to give birth to; to assist in giving birth. **5** to discharge, to send out. **6** to utter, or pronounce formally or officially. **7** to surrender, to give up. **8** (*Law*) to hand over to the grantee. **9** to aim successfully (a blow to an opponent, a ball to a team-mate etc.). **10** (*US*) to secure the support of (voters) for a candidate. *~v.i.* (*coll.*) to fulfil a promise, to carry out an undertaking, to live up to expectations. **to be delivered of** to give birth to. **to deliver oneself of** to communicate in a speech or recitation. **to deliver over** to put into someone's hands. **to deliver the goods** (*coll.*) to fulfil a promise, to carry out an undertaking, to live up to expectations. **to deliver up** to surrender possession of. **deliverable** *a.* **deliverance** *n.* **1** the state of being saved or rescued; a rescue. **2** the act of delivering an opinion. **deliverer** *n.* **1** a person who delivers. **2** a person who releases or rescues. **3** a saviour, a preserver. **delivery** (-əri) *n.* (*pl.* **deliveries**) **1** the act of delivering. **2** setting free, rescue. **3** transfer, surrender etc. **4** a distribution of letters from the Post Office. **5** a batch of letters etc. delivered. **6** the utterance of a speech. **7** style or manner of speaking. **8** childbirth. **9** discharge of a blow or missile. **10** in cricket, the act or style of delivering a ball, style of bowling. **11** (*Law*) **a** the act of putting someone in formal possession of property. **b** the handing over of a deed to the grantee. **delivery room** *n.* a room in a hospital, where babies are delivered. [F *délivrer*, late L *dēlīberāre* (DE-, L *līberāre*, to set free)]

dell (del) *n.* a hollow or small valley, usually wooded. [OE, cp. DALE]

Della Cruscan (delə krŭs´kən) *a.* **1** of or relating to the Accademia della Crusca, at Florence, which was established to purify the Italian language and published an authoritative dictionary. **2** of or relating to the Della Cruscan school; artificial, affected in style. *~n.* **1** a member of the Accademia della Crusca. **2** a member of the Della Cruscan school. **Della Cruscan school** *n.* a group of English writers residing at Florence about 1785 and considered to have an artificial style.

delocalize (dēlō´kəlīz), **delocalise** *v.t.* **1** to remove from its proper or usual place. **2** to remove a limitation on location from. **delocalization** (-zā´shən) *n.* **delocalized** *a.* (*Chem.*) (of an electron) shared among three or more atoms.

delouse (dēlows´) *v.t.* to rid (a person or place) of vermin, esp. lice.

delph DELFT.

Delphic (del´fik), **Delphian** (-fiən) *a.* **1** of or belonging to Delphi, a town of Greece, where there was a celebrated oracle of Apollo. **2** susceptible of two interpretations, ambiguous.

delphinium (delfin´iəm) *n.* (*pl.* **delphiniums**) any plant of the genus *Delphinium*, having tall blue flowers. [L *Delphīnium*, Gr. *delphīnion*, the larkspur, dim. of *delphis*, DOLPHIN]

delphinoid (del´finoid) *a.* **1** of or relating to the division Delphinoidea, including dolphins, porpoises etc. **2** resembling a dolphin. *~n.* **1** a member of the division Delphinoidea. **2** an animal resembling a dolphin. [Gr. *delphinoeidēs*, from *delphis*, DOLPHIN]

delta (del´tə) *n.* (*pl.* **deltas**) **1** the fourth letter of the Greek alphabet (δ, Δ). **2** a delta-shaped alluvial deposit at the mouth of a river. **3** a fourth-class mark given to a student's work. **4** (**Delta**) the fourth star (in brightness or position etc.) in a constellation (*Delta Cephei*). **5** an increment in a variable. **deltaic** (-tā´-) *a.* **delta-leaved** *a.* having leaves resembling a delta. **delta rays** *n.pl.* electrons moving at relatively low speeds. **delta rhythm, delta wave** *n.* the normal activity of the brain during deep sleep. **delta wing** *n.* a triangular-shaped wing on an aeroplane. **deltoid** *a.* shaped like a delta; triangular. *~n.* a triangular muscle of the shoulder, which moves the arm. [Gr.]

deltiology (deltiol´əji) *n.* the study and collecting of postcards. **deltiologist** *n.* [Gr. *deltion*, dim. of *deltos*, a writing-tablet]

deltoid DELTA.

delude (dilood´) *v.t.* to deceive, to convince (someone) that something untrue is true. **deluded** *a.* under a false impression. **deluder** *n.* [L *dēlūdere* (DE-, *lūdere*, to play)]

deluge (del´ūj) *n.* **1** a general flood or inundation, esp. the biblical flood in the days of Noah. **2** a heavy downpour of rain. **3** a torrent of words etc. **4** a torrent or flood of anything liquid, such as lava. *~v.t.* **1** to flood, to inundate with a large number of things (*deluged with phone calls*). **2** to overflow with water. [F *déluge*, L *dīluvium*, from *dīluere*, DILUTE]

delusion (diloo´zhən) *n.* **1** the act of deluding. **2** the state of being deluded. **3** an error, a fallacy. **4** (*Psych.*) an erroneous idea in which the subject's belief is unshaken by facts. **delusional** *a.* **delusions of grandeur** *n.pl.* a false belief that one is very grand or important. **delusive** (-siv) *a.* deceptive, misleading, unreal. **delusively** *adv.* **delusiveness** *n.* **delusory** *a.* [L *dēlūsio*, from *dēlūdere*, to DELUDE]

Usage note The meanings of the nouns *delusion* and *illusion* overlap, but in general a *delusion* is generated within the mind, and an *illusion* comes through the senses.

delustre (dīlŭs´tə), (*N Am.*) **deluster** *v.t.* to remove the lustre from.

de luxe (di lŭks´) *a.* luxurious, of superior quality. [F, of luxury]

delve (delv) *v.i.* **1** to dip, to descend suddenly (into). **2** to carry on laborious research (into). *~v.t.* (*poet.*) to dig, to open up with a spade. **delver** *n.* [OE *delfan*]

Dem. *abbr.* Democrat.

demagnetize (dēmag´nitīz), **demagnetise** *v.t.* to remove magnetism from. **demagnetization** (-zā´shən) *n.* **demagnetizer** *n.*

demagogue (dem´əgog), (*N Am.*) **demagog** *n.* **1** an agitator who appeals to the passions and prejudices of the people. **2** a leader of the people. **demagogic** (-gog´-) *a.* **demagogism** *n.* **demagoguery** (-gog´-) *n.* **demagogy** *n.* [Gr. *dēmagōgos* (DEMOS, *agōgos*, leading, from *agein*, to lead)]

demand (dimahnd´) *n.* **1** an authoritative claim or request. **2** the thing demanded, esp. price. **3** a claim. **4** a peremptory question. **5** desire to purchase or possess. **6** a legal claim. *~v.t.* **1** to ask for or claim with authority or as a right. **2** to ask for in a peremptory or insistent manner. **3** to seek to ascertain by questioning. **4** to need, to require. *~v.i.* to ask something as a right. **in demand** much sought after. **on demand** whenever requested. **supply and demand** SUPPLY[2]. **demandable** *a.* †**demandant** *n.* **1** (*Law*) a plaintiff in a real-property action. **2** a person who demands. **demander** *n.* **demand feeding** *n.* the feeding of a baby whenever it wants to be fed, not at fixed times. **demanding** *a.* **demand-led** *a.* brought about by consumer demand. **demand note** *n.* **1** a final notice served for payment of a bill, taxes etc. **2** (*N Am.*) a bill to be paid immediately. **demand pull** *n.* money in circulation as a contributory factor in inflation. [F *demande*, from *demander*, L *dēmandāre* (DE- *mandāre*, to entrust, to order)]

demantoid (diman´toid) *n.* a type of green garnet. [G, †*Demant*, diamond]

demarcation (dēmahkā´shən) *n.* **1** the fixing of a boundary or dividing line. **2** the division between different types of work done by members of trade unions on a single job. **demarcate** (dē´-) *v.t.* to fix the limits of. **demarcator** *n.* **demarcation dispute** *n.* a dispute over which union's members do a particular job. [Sp. *demarcacion*, from *demarcar*, to demarcate]

démarche (dā´mahsh) *n.* 1 a diplomatic approach. 2 a method of procedure. 3 an announcement of policy. [F]

dematerialize (dēmətiə´riəlīz), **dematerialise** *v.t.* to deprive of material qualities or characteristics; to spiritualize. ~*v.i.* 1 to lose material form. 2 to vanish. **dematerialization** (-zā´shən) *n.*

deme (dēm) *n.* 1 a subdivision or township in Greece (ancient and modern). 2 (*Biol.*) a closely-related group of individual plants or animals. [Gr. *dēmos*]

demean[1] (dimēn´) *v.t.* to debase (oneself), to lower (oneself). [DE-, MEAN[3]]

demean[2] (dimēn´) *v.t.* to conduct (oneself), to behave. **demeanour** (-nə), (*N Am.*) **demeanor** *n.* conduct, carriage, behaviour, deportment. [OF *demener*(DE-, *mener*, to lead, late L *minãre*, to drive cattle, L, to threaten)]

dement (diment´) *v.t.* to madden; to deprive of reason. ~†*n.* a demented person. **demented** *a.* insane, mad. **dementedly** *adv.* **dementedness** *n.* [L *dēmentāre* (DE-, *mens mentis*, mind)]

démenti (dāmā´tē) *n.* (*pl.* **démentis**) an official contradiction of a rumour etc. [F]

dementia (dimen´shə) *n.* serious deterioration of the mental faculties, with memory loss, mood swings etc. **dementia praecox** (prē´koks) *n.* a mental disorder resulting from a turning inwards into oneself away from reality, schizophrenia.

demerara (demərah´rə, -eə´-), **demarara sugar** *n.* a type of brown sugar. [river in Guyana]

demerge (dēmœj´) *v.t.*, *v.i.* to split into separate companies again. **demerger** *n.* the separation of companies formerly acting as one.

demerit (dēmer´it) *n.* (*formal*) something which merits punishment. **demeritorious** (-taw´riəs) *a.* [L *dēmeritum*, neut. p.p. of *dēmerēre*, to deserve (DE-, *merēre*, to deserve)]

demersal (dimœ´səl) *a.* (*Zool.*) found in deep water or on the ocean bed. [L *dēmersus*, submerged, plunged into]

demesne (dimēn´, -mān´), †**demain** (-mān´) *n.* 1 an estate in land. 2 a manor-house and the lands near it, which the owner keeps in his own hands. 3 the territory of the Crown or state. 4 a region, a territory, a sphere. 5 (*Law, Hist.*) possession as one's own. **held in demesne** occupied by the owner, not tenants. [OF *demeine*, as DOMAIN]

demi- (dem´i) *pref.* half, semi-, partial, partially. [F, from L *dimidius*, half]

demi-bastion (demibas´tiən) *n.* in fortification, a single face and flank, resembling half of a bastion.

demies DEMY.

demigod (dem´igod) *n.* 1 a being who is half a god. 2 the offspring of a god and a human being. **demi-goddess** *n.* a female demi-god.

demijohn (dem´ijon) *n.* a glass bottle with a large body and small neck, enclosed in wickerwork. [corr. of F *damejeanne*, Dame Jane]

demilitarize (dēmil´itərīz), **demilitarise** *v.t.* to end military involvement in and control of. **demilitarization** (-zā´shən) *n.*

demi-mondaine (dem´imondān) *n.* a prostitute. **demimonde** (-mond´) *n.* 1 persons not recognized in society, women of dubious character. 2 the section of a profession etc. which is not wholly legal or above board.

demineralize (dēmin´ərəlīz), **demineralise** *v.t.* to remove salts or other minerals from. **demineralization** (-zā´shən) *n.*

demi-pension (demipõs´yõn) *n.* (French) hotel accommodation with half board. [F]

†**demi-rep** (dem´irep) *n.* a woman of doubtful chastity.

demise (dimīz´) *n.* 1 (*formal*) death. 2 the end of something. 3 (*Law*) a transfer or conveyance by lease or will for a term of years or in fee simple. ~*v.t.* 1 (*Law*) **a** to bequeath. **b** to transfer or convey by lease or will. **demisable** *a.* **demise of the Crown** *n.* transference of sovereignty on the death or abdication of the monarch. [OF, p.p. of *desmettre*, to DISMISS]

demisemiquaver (dem´isemikwāvə) *n.* (*Mus.*) a note with the value of half a semiquaver or one-fourth of a quaver.

demission DEMIT.

demist (dēmist´) *v.t.* to make clear of condensation. **demister** *n.*

demit (dimit´) *v.t.*, *v.i.* (*pres.p.* **demitting**, *past*, *p.p.* **demitted**) to resign, abdicate. **demission** (-mish´ən) *n.* the act of resigning or abdicating. [F *démettre* (DIS, *mettre*, L *mittere*, to send)]

demitasse (dem´itas) *n.* 1 a small coffee cup. 2 a small cup of coffee. [F, half-cup]

demiurge (dem´iœj) *n.* 1 in Platonic philosophy, the creator of the universe. 2 the Logos of the Platonizing Christians. 3 in ancient Greece, a magistrate in some of the Peloponnesian states. **demiurgic** (-œ´-) *a.* [L *dēmiūrgus*, Gr. *dēmiourgos* (*dēmios*, public, from DEMOS, *ergos*, worker)]

demi-veg (dem´ivej) *a.* not completely vegetarian, but including white meat and fish in the diet. ~*n.* a person who follows such a diet.

demivolte (dem´ivolt) *n.* an artificial motion of a horse in which it raises its legs in a particular manner.

demo (dem´ō) *n.* (*pl.* **demos**) (*coll.*) a demonstration. ~*a.* (*attrib.*) serving to demonstrate something.

demob (dēmob´) *v.t.* (*pres.p.* **demobbing**, *past*, *p.p.* **demobbed**) (*coll.*) to demobilize. ~*n.* demobilization.

demobilize (dēmō´bilīz), **demobilise** *v.t.* to disband, to dismiss (troops) from a war footing. **demobilization** (-zā´shən) *n.*

democracy (dimok´rəsi) *n.* (*pl.* **democracies**) 1 the form of government in which the sovereign power is in the hands of the people, and exercised by them directly or indirectly. 2 a democratic state. 3 any more or less democratic organization or society. 4 the people, esp. the unprivileged classes. **democrat** (dem´əkrat) *n.* a person who is in favour of democracy. **Democrat** *n.* (*US*) a member of the Democratic Party. **democratic** (deməkrat´-) *a.* 1 of or relating to a democracy. 2 governed by or maintaining the principles of democracy; favouring equality. **democratically** *adv.* **democratic centralism** *n.* central determination and control of policy by officials appointed as representatives of the people. **Democratic Party** *n.* the more liberal of the two political parties in the US, the other being the *Republican Party*. **democratize, democratise** *v.t.*, *v.i.* **democratization** (-zā´shən), **democratisation** *n.* the inculcation of democratic views and principles. [F *démocratie*, L *dēmocratia*, Gr. *dēmokratia*]

démodé (dāmōdā´) *a.* out of fashion. [F]

demodulate (dēmod´ūlāt) *v.t.* (*Phys.*) 1 to extract the original audio signal from (the modulated carrier wave by which it is transmitted). 2 to separate a modulating signal from. **demodulation** (-lā´shən) *n.* **demodulator** *n.*

Demogorgon (dēmōgaw´gən) *n.* a mysterious divinity, first mentioned by a scholiast on the *Thebaid* of Statius as one of the infernal gods. [late L, from Gr. (DEMOS, GORGON)]

demography (dimog´rəfi) *n.* the study of population statistics dealing with size, density and distribution. **demographer** *n.* **demographic** (deməgraf´-) *a.* **demographical** *a.* **demographically** *adv.* **demographics** *n.pl.* demographical data. **demographic time-bomb** *n.* a fall in the size of the national workforce, caused by an earlier decline in the birthrate.

demoiselle (demwahzel´) *n.* 1 a demoiselle crane. 2 a damselfly. 3 a damselfish. 4 †an unmarried woman. **demoiselle crane** *n.* a small N African and Asian

crane, *Anthropoides virgo*, having a graceful form and bearing. [F]
demolish (dimol´ish) *v.t.* **1** to pull down; to raze. **2** to ruin, to destroy. **3** to refute. **4** (*coll.*) to eat up. **demolisher** *n.* **demolition** (deməlish´ən) *n.* **1** the act of demolishing. **2** (*Mil.*) destruction using explosives. **demolitionist** *n.* **demolitions expert** *n.* a person who is skilled in demolition using explosives. [F *démoliss-*, stem of *démolir*, L *dēmōlīrī* (DE-, *mōlīrī*, to construct, from *mōlēs*, mass)]
demon (dē´mən), **daemon** *n.* **1** an evil spirit supposed to have the power of taking possession of human beings. **2** a malignant supernatural being, a fallen angel, a devil. **3** a very cruel or evil person. **4** (*usu. in comb., sl.*) an extremely clever or skilful person (*a demon bowler*). **5** in Greek mythology, a supernatural being, lesser divinity, genius or attendant spirit supposed to exercise guardianship over a particular individual, in many respects corresponding to the later idea of a guardian angel. **demon for work** *n.* (*coll.*) a very hard worker. **demoniac** (dimō´niak) *a.* **1** of, relating to or produced by demons. **2** possessed by a demon. **3** frantic, frenzied. ~*n.* a person possessed by a demon. **demoniacal** (dēmənī´əkəl) *a.* of or relating to possession by a devil. **demoniacally** *adv.* **demonic** (dimon´-) *a.* **1** like that of a person possessed by a demon, frenzied. **2** of or relating to a demon. **3** possessed by a demon. **4** devilish. **demonism** *n.* belief in demons. **demonist** *n.* **demonize, demonise** *v.t.* **1** to make into a demon. **2** to make devilish. **3** to bring under demonic influence. **4** to regard as evil. **demonization** (-zā´shən) *n.* [L *daemōn*, Gr. *daimōn*, a deity, a genius]
demonetize (dēmŭn´ətīz), **demonetise** *v.t.* **1** to deprive of its character as money. **2** to withdraw (a metal) from currency. **demonetization** (-zā´shən) *n.*
demono- (dē´mənō) *comb. form* demon(s).
demonolatry (dēmənol´ətri) *n.* the worship of demons or evil spirits.
demonology (dēmənol´əji) *n.* the study of demons or of evil spirits. **demonologist** *n.*
demonopolize (dēmənop´əlīz), **demonopolise** *v.t.* to end the monopoly of.
demonstrate (dem´ənstrāt) *v.t.* **1** to show by logical reasoning. **2** to prove beyond the possibility of doubt. **3** to exhibit, describe and prove by means of specimens and experiments. **4** to display, to indicate. ~*v.i.* **1** to organize or take part in a public or military demonstration. **2** to act as a demonstrator. **demonstrable** (dimon´strəbəl, dem´ən-) *a.* that may be shown or proved beyond doubt. **demonstrability** (-bil´-) *n.* **demonstrably** *adv.* **demonstration** (-strā´shən) *n.* **1** the act of demonstrating. **2** clear, indubitable proof. **3** an outward manifestation of feeling etc. **4** a public exhibition or declaration of principles, feelings etc. by any party. **5** an exhibition and description of objects for the purpose of teaching or showing how something works. **6** (*Mil.*) a movement of troops as if to attack. **demonstrative** (-mon´-) *a.* **1** manifesting one's feelings strongly and openly. **2** having the power of exhibiting and proving. **3** being proof (of). **4** conclusive. **5** serving to show and make clear. **6** (of an adjective or pronoun) used to highlight the referent(s), e.g. *this* or *that.* ~*n.* a demonstrative adjective or pronoun. **demonstratively** *adv.* **demonstrativeness** *n.* **demonstrator** *n.* **1** a person who takes part in a public demonstration of political, religious or other opinions. **2** a person who demonstrates how a piece of equipment works. **3** a person who teaches by means of exhibition and experiment. **4** a car used for test drives; a piece of equipment used in demonstrations. **demonstratorship** *n.* [L *dēmonstrātus*, p.p. of *dēmonstrāre* (DE-, *monstrāre*, to show)]
demoralize (dimor´əlīz), **demoralise** *v.t.* **1** to lower the morale of, to discourage. **2** †to subvert and corrupt the morals and principles of. **demoralization** (-zā´shən) *n.* **demoralizing** *a.* **demoralizingly** *adv.* [F *démoraliser* (DE-, MORAL, -IZE)]
demos (dē´mos) *n.* the people, as distinguished from the upper classes; the mob. [Gr., the people]
demote (dimōt´) *v.t.* to reduce in status or rank. **demotion** *n.* [L *movēre*, to move]
demotic (dimot´ik) *a.* **1** of or relating to the people. **2** popular, common, vulgar. **3** of or relating to demotic. ~*n.* **1** the spoken form of modern Greek. **2** a simplified form of ancient Egyptian writing. **demotic alphabet** *n.* the alphabet used by the laity and people of ancient Egypt as distinct from the *hieratic*, on which it was based. [Gr. *dēmotikos*, from *dēmotēs*, one of the people (see DEMOS)]
demotivate (dēmō´tivāt) *v.t.* to cause to feel lack of motivation, to discourage. **demotivation** (-ā´shən) *n.*
demount (dēmownt´) *v.t.* **1** to remove from a mounting. **2** to disassemble. **demountable** *a.*
dempster DEEMSTER (under DEEM).
demulcent (dimŭl´sənt) *a.* softening, mollifying, soothing. ~*n.* a medicine which soothes irritation. [L *dēmulcēre* (DE-, *mulcēre*, to stroke)]
demur (dimœ´) *v.i.* (*pres.p.* **demurring,** *past, p.p.* **demurred**) **1** to have or express scruples, objections or reluctance. **2** (*Law*) to take exception to any point in the pleading as insufficient. **3** †to delay, to loiter, to hesitate. ~*n.* **1** scruple, objection (*without demur*). **2** the act of demurring. **demurrable** *a.* liable to exception, esp. legal objection. **demurral** *n.* (a) demur. **demurrer** *n.* **1** (*Law*) an objection made to a point submitted by the opposing party on the grounds of irrelevance or legal insufficiency. **2** an objection. [OF *demeurer*, L *dēmorārī* (DE-, *morārī*, to delay, from *mora*, delay)]
demure (dimūə´) *a.* (*comp.* **demurer,** *superl.* **demurest**) **1** reserved and modest. **2** affectedly modest, coy. **demurely** *adv.* **demureness** *n.* [OF *de* (*bons*) *murs*, of (good) manners]
demurrable DEMUR.
demurrage (dimŭr´ij) *n.* **1** an allowance by the freighter of a vessel to the owners for delay in loading or unloading beyond the time named in the charter-party. **2** the period of such delay. **3** a charge for the detention by one company of trucks etc. belonging to another. **4** a fee charged by the Bank of England for exchanging notes or coin for bullion. [OF *demo(u)rage*, from *demorer*, see DEMUR]
demurral, demurrer DEMUR.
demutualize (dēmū´tūəlīz), **demutualise** *v.t.* to end the mutual status of (a building society etc.). **demutualization** (-zā´shən) *n.*
demy (dimī´) *n.* (*pl.* **demies**) a particular size of paper, 22½ × 17½ in. (444.5 × 571.5 mm) for printing, 20 × 15½ in. (508 × 393.7 mm) for drawing or writing (*NAm.* 21 × 16 in.).
demystify (dēmis´tifī) *v.t.* (*3rd pers. sing. pres.* **demystifies,** *pres.p.* **demystifying,** *past, p.p.* **demystified**) **1** to remove the mystery from, to clarify. **2** to make less irrational. **demystification** (-fikā´shən) *n.*
demythologize (dēmithol´əjīz), **demythologise** *v.t.* to remove the mythological elements from (something, e.g. the Bible) to highlight the basic meaning. **demythologization** (-zā´shən) *n.*
den (den) *n.* **1** the lair of a wild beast. **2** a retreat, a lurking-place; a hideout created by children. **3** a place where vice or crime is indulged in (*a den of iniquity*). **4** a hovel; a miserable room. **5** (*coll.*) a study, a sanctum, a snuggery. ~†*v.i.* (*pres.p.* **denning,** *past, p.p.* **denned**) **1** to live in a den. **2** to retreat to a den. [OE *denn*, cp. *denu*, a valley, DENE[2] (Dut. *denne*, G *Tenne*)]
denarius (dinah´riəs) *n.* (*pl.* **denarii** (-riī)) a Roman silver coin, worth 10 asses; a penny. [L *dēnārius*, containing ten (*dēnī*, pl., ten by ten, from *decem*, ten)]

denary (dē´nəri) *a.* **1** containing ten. **2** based on the number ten, decimal. **denary scale** *n.* the decimal scale. [see DENARIUS]

denationalize (dēnash´ənəlīz), **denationalise** *v.t.* **1** to transfer from public to private ownership. **2** to deprive of the rights, rank or characteristics of a nation. **3** to deprive of nationality. **denationalization** (-zā´shən) *n.*

denaturalize (dēnach´ərəlīz), **denaturalise** *v.t.* **1** to render unnatural; to alter the nature of. **2** to deprive of naturalization or citizenship. **denaturalization** (-zā´shən) *n.*

denature (dēnā´chə), **denaturize** (-rīz-), **denaturise** *v.t.* **1** to change the essential nature or character of (something) by adulteration etc. **2** to modify (a protein) by heat or acid. **3** to render (alcohol) unfit for human consumption. **4** to add non-radioactive material to (radioactive material), to prevent it being used in nuclear weapons. **denaturant** *n.* **denaturation** (dēnachərā´shən) *n.* **denatured alcohol** *n.* alcohol which has been rendered unfit according to law for human consumption. [F *dénaturer*, OF *desnaturer*]

denazify (dēnah´tsifī) *v.t.* (*3rd pers. sing. pres.* **denazifies,** *pres.p.* **denazifying,** *past, p.p.* **denazified**) to purge of Nazism and its evil influence on the mind. **denazification** (-fikā´shən) *n.*

dendriform (den´drifawm) *a.* DENDROID.

dendrite (den´drīt) *n.* **1** a stone or mineral with treelike markings. **2** any one of the branched extensions of a nerve cell which conduct impulses to the body of the cell. **3** a crystal with branched treelike growth. **4** branching or treelike markings (on a stone or mineral). **dendritic** (-drit´-), **dendritical** *a.* **1** like a tree; arborescent. **2** with treelike markings. **dendritically** *adv.*

dendro- (den´dro), **dendri-, dendr-** *comb. form* resembling a tree. [Gr. *dendron*, a tree]

dendrochronology (dendrōkrənol´əji) *n.* **1** the study of the annual growth rings in trees. **2** a system of dating timber and historical events for which timber is evidence, based on such rings. **dendrochronological** (-loj´-) *a.* **dendrochronologist** *n.*

dendrogram (den´drəgram) *n.* (*Biol.*) a type of tree diagram showing relationships between kinds of organism.

dendroid (den´droid) *a.* treelike, branching, treeshaped.

dendrology (dendrol´əji) *n.* the natural history of trees. **dendrological** (-loj´-) *a.* **dendrologist** *n.*

dendrometer (dendrom´itə) *n.* an instrument for measuring the height and diameter of trees.

dene[1] (dēn), **dean** *n.* **1** a valley. **2** a deep and narrow valley (chiefly in place names). [OE *denu*]

dene[2] (dēn) *n.* a sandy down or low hill, a tract of sand by the sea. [etym. uncertain; cp. LG and G *Düne*, Dut. *duin*, F *dune*]

denegation (dēnigā´shən) *n.* contradiction, denial. [F *dénégation*, L *dēnegātio -ōnem*, from *dēnegāre*, to DENY]

dene-hole (dēn´hōl), **dane-hole** (dān´hōl) *n.* an excavation consisting of a shaft, from 2 ft. 6 in. to 3 ft. (about 75 cm to 1 m) in diameter and 20 ft. to 90 ft. (about 6 to 27 m) in depth, ending below in a cavern in the chalk, made originally to obtain chalk. [etym. uncertain; perh. OE *denu*, DENE[1]]

de-net (dēnet´) *v.t.* (*pres.p.* **de-netting,** *past, p.p.* **de-netted**) (*Hist.*) to reduce the price of (a book) below that specified by the publisher (and protected by the Net Book Agreement).

dengue (deng´gi) *n.* an acute fever common in the tropics, characterized by severe pains, a rash and swellings. [W Indian Sp., prob. from Swahili]

deniable, denial DENY.

denier[1] (dən´iə) *n.* **1** a unit for weighing and grading silk, nylon and rayon yarn, used for women's tights and stockings. **2** a small French coin, the 12th part of a sou. **3** a coin of insignificant value. [OF, from DENARIUS]

denier[2] DENY.

denigrate (den´igrāt) *v.t.* **1** to defame. **2** to blacken. ~*n.* **denigration** (-rā´shən) *n.* **denigrator** *n.* **denigratory** *a.* [L *dēnigrātus*, p.p. of *dēnigrāre* (DE-, *niger*, black)]

denim (den´im) *n.* **1** a coarse, twilled cotton fabric used for jeans, overalls etc. **2** (*pl.*) jeans made of denim. [short for F *serge de Nîmes*, serge of Nîmes]

denitrate (dēnī´trāt) *v.t.* to remove nitric or nitrous acid or nitrate from. **denitrification** (-fikā´shən) *n.* the removal of nitrogen from the soil by the agency of bacteria. **denitrify** *v.t.* (*3rd. pers. sing. pres.* **denitrifies,** *pres.p.* **denitrifying,** *past, p.p.* **denitrified**).

denizen (den´izən) *n.* **1** a citizen, an inhabitant, a dweller, a resident. **2** (*Law*) a foreigner who has obtained letters patent to give them some of the rights of a British subject. **3** a foreign word, plant or animal, that has become naturalized. ~*v.t.* to make a denizen. **denizenship** *n.* [A-F *deinzein*, from *deinz* (F *dans*), within (L DE-, *intus*, within), -AN]

denominate (dinom´ināt) *v.t.* **1** to call, to designate. **2** to give a name, epithet or title to. **denominated in** expressed as a value in (a particular monetary unit). **denomination** (-ā´shən) *n.* **1** a religious group or sect. **2** a class, a kind, esp. of particular units (such as coins or weights). **3** a designation, title or appellation. **4** the act of naming. **5** a playing card's rank in a suit, or a suit's in a pack. **denominational** *a.* of or relating to a particular religious denomination, sectarian. **denominational education** *n.* a system of education following the principles of a religious denomination. **denominationalism** *n.* **denominationalist** *n., a.* **denominationally** *adv.* **denominative** (-nətiv) *a.* giving or constituting a distinctive name. **denominator** *n.* **1** (*Math.*) the number below the line in a fraction, which shows into how many parts the integer is divided, while the numerator, above the line, shows how many of these parts are taken. **2** †a person who or something which denominates. [L *dēnōminātus*, p.p. of *dēnōmināre*]

de nos jours (də nō juə´) *a.* (*postpositive*) of this period, of our time. [F]

denote (dinōt´) *v.t.* **1** to mark, to indicate, to signify. **2** to mark out, to distinguish. **3** (*Logic*) to be a name of, to be predicable of, as distinct from *connote*. **denotable** *a.* **denotation** (dēnōtā´shən) *n.* **1** the act of denoting. **2** meaning, signification. ~*a.* signifying, pointing out. **denotation of a term** *n.* (*Logic*) the extent of a term's application. **denotative** *a.* **denotatively** *adv.* †**denotement** *n.* a sign, an indication. [F *dénoter*, L *dēnotāre* (DE-, *notāre*, to mark, from *nota*, a mark)]

denouement (dānoo´mā), **dénouement** *n.* **1** the unravelling of a plot or story. **2** the catastrophe or final solution of a plot. **3** an outcome. [F, from *dénouer* (DIS-, L *nodāre*, to knot, from *nodus*, knot)]

denounce (dinowns´) *v.t.* **1** to accuse or condemn publicly. **2** to inform against. **3** to give formal notice of the termination of (a treaty or convention). **denouncement** *n.* denunciation. **denouncer** *n.* [OF *denoncer*, L *dēnuntiāre* (DE-, *nuntiāre*, to announce, from *nuntius*, a messenger)]

de novo (dā nō´vō) *adv.* anew. [L]

dense (dens) *a.* **1** thick, compact; having its particles closely united. **2** crowded close together. **3** (*coll.*) stupid, obtuse. **4** in photography, opaque, strong in contrast. **densely** *adv.* **denseness** *n.* **densimeter** (-sim´itə) *n.* an apparatus for measuring density or specific gravity. **densimetry** *n.* **densitometer** (-om´itə) *n.* an instrument for measuring density in photography. **density** *n.* (*pl.* **densities**) **1** denseness. **2** (*Physics*) the mass per unit volume of a substance measured, for example, in grams per cubic centimetre. **3** a crowded condition. **4** a measure of the reflection or absorption of light by a surface. **5** (*coll.*) stupidity. [L *densus*]

dent[1] (dent) *n.* **1** a depression such as is caused by a blow with a blunt instrument; an indentation. **2** a lessening or diminution (*The holiday made a dent in my savings*). ~*v.t.* **1** to make a dent in; to indent. **2** to have a diminishing or harmful effect on (*The rejection dented her self-confidence*). [DINT]

dent[2] (dent) *n.* **1** a tooth of a wheel, a cog. **2** the wire staple that forms the tooth of a card. **3** a wire of the reed-frame of a loom. [F, tooth, from L *dens dentis*]

dent- DENTI-.

dental (den´təl) *a.* **1** of or relating to or formed by the teeth. **2** of or relating to dentistry. **3** (of a consonant) formed by placing the end of the tongue against the upper teeth or the ridge of the upper teeth. ~*n.* a dental consonant. **dental floss** *n.* thread used to clean between the teeth. **dental formula** *n.* a formula used to describe the dentition of a mammal. **dentalize, dentalise** *v.t.* to pronounce as a dental; to alter to a dental sound. **dental mechanic** *n.* a maker and repairer of false teeth. **dental plaque** *n.* a deposit of bacteria and food on the teeth. **dental surgeon** *n.* DENTIST. **dentary** *a.* or for relating to the teeth. ~*n.* (*pl.* **dentaries**) the bone in the lower jaw of fishes and reptiles carrying the teeth. [L *dens dentis*, as DENT[2]]

dentalium (dentā´liəm) *n.* (*pl.* **dentalia** (-liə)) a tusk shell (the mollusc or its shell).

dentate (den´tāt), **dentated** (-tātid) *a.* (*Zool.*, *Bot.*) **1** toothed. **2** indented. **dentately** *adv.* **dentation** (-tā´shən) *n.*

denti- (den´ti), **dent-** *comb. form* of or relating to the teeth. [L *dens dentis*, a tooth]

denticle (den´tikəl) *n.* **1** a small tooth. **2** a projecting point, a dentil. **denticulate** (-tik´ūlət), **denticulated** (-lātid) *a.* **1** finely toothed. **2** formed into dentils. **denticulately** *adv.* **denticulation** (-kulā´shən) *n.* [L *denticulus*, dim. of *dens dentis*, tooth]

dentiform (den´tifawm) *a.* shaped like a tooth or teeth.

dentifrice (den´tifris) *n.* powder, paste or other material for cleansing the teeth. [F, from L *dentifricium* (DENTI-, *fricāre*, to rub)]

dentil (den´til) *n.* any one of the small square blocks or projections under the moulding of a cornice. [obs. F *dentille*, from *dent*, a tooth]

dentilingual (dentiling´gwəl) *a.* formed by the teeth and the tongue. ~*n.* a consonant so formed.

dentine (den´tēn), **dentin** (den´tin) *n.* the ivory tissue forming the body of a tooth. **dentinal** (den´tinəl) *a.*

dentist (den´tist) *n.* a person skilled in and qualified in treating and preventing disorders of the teeth and jaws. **dentistry** *n.* **dentition** (-tish´-) *n.* **1** teething. **2** the time of teething. **3** the arrangement of the teeth in any species of animal. **denture** (-chə) *n.* (*often pl.*) a plate or frame with an artificial tooth or teeth, a set of false teeth. **denturist** *n.* a maker of dentures. [F *dentiste*, from *dent*, tooth]

denuclearize (dēnū´kliərīz), **denuclearise** *v.t.* to deprive of nuclear arms. **denuclearization** (-zā´shən) *n.*

denude (dinūd´) *v.t.* **1** to make bare or naked. **2** to strip of clothing, attributes, possessions, rank or any covering. **3** (*Geol.*) to lay bare by removing whatever lies above. **denudate**[1] (dē´nūdāt) *v.t.* to denude. **denudate**[2] (-dət) *a.* made naked, stripped. **denudation** (-nūdā´shən) *n.* **denudative** *a.* [L *dēnūdāre* (DE-, *nūdāre*, to strip, from *nūdus*, bare)]

denumerable (dēnū´mərəbəl) *a.* (*Math.*) able to be put into a one-to-one correspondence with the positive integers; countable. **denumerability** (-bil´-) *n.* **denumerably** *adv.*

denunciate (dinŭn´siāt) *v.t.* to denounce. **denunciation** (-ā´shən) *n.* **denunciative** (-siətiv) *a.* **denunciator** *n.* **denunciatory** *a.* [L *dēnuntiātus*, p.p. of *dēnuntiāre*, to DENOUNCE]

deny (dinī´) *v.t.* (*3rd pers. sing. pres.* **denies,** *pres.p.* **denying,** *past, p.p.* **denied**) **1** to assert to be untrue or non-existent. **2** to disown, to reject, to repudiate. **3** to refuse to grant, to withhold from. **4** to refuse admittance to. **5** to refuse access to. **6** to say 'no' to. **to deny oneself** to refrain or abstain from pleasures, to practise self-denial. **deniable** *a.* **deniability** (-bil´-) *n.* **denial** *n.* **1** the act of denying, contradicting or refusing. **2** a refusal, a negative reply. **3** abjuration, disavowal. **4** self-denial. **5** (subconscious) suppression of unacceptable knowledge or feelings. **denier**[2] *n.* a person who denies. [F *dénier*, L *dēnegāre* (DE-, *negāre*, to deny)]

deoch an doris (dokh an dor´is), **doch an dorris** *n.* (*Sc.*, *Ir.*) a drink taken just before leaving. [Gaelic *deoch an doruis*, drink at the door]

deodand (dē´ōdand) *n.* (*Hist.*) a personal chattel which had been the immediate cause of the death of any person, and on that account was forfeited to be sold for some pious use. [A-F *deodande*, L *Deo dandum*, to be given to God (*dandum*, from *dare*, to give)]

deodar (dē´ōdah) *n.* a large Himalayan cedar, *Cedrus deodara*. [Hind. *dē'odar*, *dēwdār*, Sansk. *deva-dāru*, timber of the gods (*deva-*, a deity, *dāru*, a kind of pine)]

deodorize (diō´dərīz), **deoderise** *v.t.* to deprive of odour. **deodorant** *n.* **1** a substance used to mask the odour of perspiration. **2** a substance which counteracts any unpleasant smells. **deodorization** (-zā´shən) *n.* the act of deodorizing. **deodorizer** *n.*

Deo gratias (dāō grah´shiəs) *int.* thanks be to God. [L]

deontic (dēon´tik) *a.* (*Philos.*) of or relating to duty. **deontological** (-ontəloj´-) *a.* **deontologist** *n.* **deontology** (-tol´əji) *n.* the study of duty (the Benthamite doctrine of ethics). [Gr. *deon deontos*, duty, neut. pres.p. of *dei*, it is binding]

Deo volente (dāō volen´tā) *int.* God willing; all being well. [L]

deoxidize (dēok´sidīz), **deoxidise** *v.t.* to deprive of oxygen; to extract oxygen from. **deoxidization** (-zā´shən) *n.* **deoxidizer** *n.* a substance which deoxidizes.

deoxycorticosterone (dēoksikawtikōstiə´rōn), **deoxycortone** (-kaw´tōn) *n.* a hormone which maintains the sodium and water balance in the body.

deoxygenate (dēok´sijənāt) *v.t.* to deoxidize. **deoxygenation** (-ā´shən) *n.* **deoxygenize** *v.t.* to deoxidize.

deoxyribonucleic acid (dēoksirībōnūklē´ik), **desoxyribonucleic acid** (des-) *n.* the full name for DNA. **deoxyribose** (-rī´bōz) *n.* a sugar found in DNA nucleosides.

dep. *abbr.* **1** depart(s). **2** department. **3** departure. **4** deposed. **5** deputy.

depart (dipaht´) *v.i.* **1** to go away, to leave. **2** to diverge, to deviate (from). **3** to pass away, to die. ~*v.t.* to go away from, to quit (*to depart this life*). **departed** *a.* **1** past, bygone. **2** (*formal*) dead. **the departed** a dead person or dead people. [OF *departir* (DE-, L *partīre*, to PART, to divide)]

department (dipaht´mənt) *n.* **1** a separate part or branch of business, administration or duty. **2** a branch of study or science. **3** (*coll.*) a matter one takes an interest in, an area of knowledge. **4** any one of the administrative divisions of a country, such as France. **departmental** (dēpahtmen´-) *a.* **departmentalism** *n.* a too-rigid adherence to regulations, red tape. **departmentalize, departmentalise** *v.t.* **departmentalization** (-zā´shən) *n.* **departmentally** *adv.* **departmental store** *n.* a department store. **department store** *n.* a large shop selling a great variety of goods. [F *département* (as DEPART, -MENT)]

departure (dipah´chə) *n.* **1** the act of departing; leaving. **2** the starting of a journey. **3** death. **4** divergence, deviation. **5** (*Naut.*) **a** the distance of a ship east or west of the meridian she sailed from. **b** the position of an object from which a ship commences her dead reckoning. [OF *departeure*]

depasture (dēpahs´chə) *v.t.* 1 to graze upon. 2 to put to graze. 3 to provide pasturage for. ~*v.i.* to graze. **depasturage** *n.*

dépaysé (dāpā´sā), (*fem.*) **dépaysée** *a.* that is away from home or familiar surroundings. [F]

dépêche (dāpesh´) *n.* a message; a dispatch. [F]

depend (dipend´) *v.i.* 1 to be contingent, as to the issue or result, on something else. 2 to rely for support or maintenance. 3 to rely, to trust, to reckon (on). 4 to be grammatically dependent on. 5 to be pending. 6 †to hang down. **depending on** according to. **depend upon it!** you may rely upon it, you may be certain! **it all depends** 1 it is conditional. 2 perhaps. **that depends** 1 that is conditional. 2 perhaps. **dependable** *a.* able to be depended upon. **dependableness** *n.* **dependably** *adv.* **dependant,** (*N Am.*) **dependent** *n.* 1 a person depending upon another for support or favour. 2 a retainer, a servant. **dependence** *n.* 1 the state of being dependent. 2 something on which one depends. 3 reliance, trust, confidence. 4 addiction to alcohol or drugs. **dependency** *n.* (*pl.* **dependencies**) 1 something dependent, esp. a country or state subject to another. 2 addiction to alcohol or drugs. **dependency culture** *n.* habituation to reliance on state benefits. **dependent** *a.* 1 depending on another. 2 subject to, contingent (on), relying (on) for support, benefit or favour. 3 addicted. 4 (*Gram.*) connected in a subordinate relationship. 5 †hanging down. **dependently** *adv.* **dependent variable** *n.* a variable in a mathematical equation whose value depends on that of the independent variable. [OF *dépendre*, L *dēpendēre* (DE-, *pendēre*, to hang)]

depersonalize (dēpœ´sənəlīz), **depersonalise** *v.t.* 1 to divest of personality. 2 to regard as without individuality. **depersonalization** (-zā´shən) *n.* 1 the divesting of personality. 2 (*Psych.*) the experience of unreality feelings in relation to oneself.

depict (dipikt´) *v.t.* 1 to paint, to portray. 2 to describe or represent in words. **depicter** *n.* **depiction** *n.* **depictive** *a.* **depictor** *n.* **depicture** (-pik´chə) *v.t.* to depict, to represent, to paint. [L *dēpictus*, p.p. of *dēpingere* (DE-, *pingere*, to paint)]

depilate (dep´ilāt) *v.t.* to remove hair from. **depilation** (-ā´shən) *n.* **depilator** *n.* **depilatory** (dipil´-) *a.* having the power to remove hair. ~*n.* (*pl.* **depilatories**) an application for removing superfluous hair. [L *dēpilātus*, p.p. of *dēpilāre* (DE-, *pilāre*, to pluck away, from *pilus*, a hair)]

deplane (dēplān´) *v.i.* (*N Am.*) to disembark from an aeroplane. ~*v.t.* to remove from an aeroplane.

deplete (diplēt´) *v.t.* 1 to reduce. 2 to empty, to exhaust. 3 (*Med.*) to empty or relieve, as in blood-letting. **depletion** *n.* **depletive** *a.* causing depletion. **depletory** *a.* [L *dēplētus*, p.p. of *dēplēre* (DE-, *plēre*, to fill)]

deplore (diplaw´) *v.t.* 1 to express disapproval of, to censure. 2 to lament over; to grieve. **deplorable** *a.* **deplorability** (-bil´-) *n.* **deplorableness** *n.* **deplorably** *adv.* **deploration** (dēplawrā´shən) *n.* [L *dēplōrāre* (DE-, *plōrāre*, to wail)]

deploy (diploi´) *v.t.* 1 (*Mil.*) a to open out. b to extend from column into line. 2 to bring into action. ~*v.i.* to form a more extended front. **deployment** *n.* use, esp. of troops or weapons. [F *déployer*, OF *desployer*, L *displicāre*, to unfold (DIS-, *plicāre*, to fold)]

deplume (diploom´) *v.t.* 1 to strip of feathers. 2 to strip of honour, money, ornaments etc. **deplumation** (dēploomā´shən) *n.* [F *déplumer* (DE-, L *plūma*, feather)]

depolarize (dēpō´lərīz), **depolarise** *v.t.* 1 to free (the gas-filmed plates of a voltaic battery etc.) from polarization. 2 to deprive of polarity. 3 to remove the polarization of (a ray of light). **depolarization** (-zā´shən) *n.* **depolarizer** *n.*

depoliticize (dēpəlit´isīz), **depoliticise** *v.t.* to make non-political. **depoliticization** (-zā´shən) *n.*

depolymerize (dēpol´imərīz), **depolymerise** *v.t.* (*Chem.*) to break a polymer down into monomers. ~*v.i.* (of a polymer) to break down into monomers. **depolymerization** (-zā´shən) *n.*

depone (dipōn´) *v.t.* to declare under oath; to testify. ~*v.i.* to testify, esp. under oath. **deponent** *a.* (of a Latin or Greek verb) passive or middle in form but active in meaning. ~*n.* 1 a deponent verb. 2 (*Law*) a a witness. b a person who makes an affidavit to any statement of fact. [L *dēpōnere* (DE-, *pōnere*, to put)]

depopulate (dēpop´ūlāt) *v.t.* 1 to clear of inhabitants. 2 to reduce the population of. ~*v.i.* to become less populous. **depopulation** (-lā´shən) *n.* [L *dēpopulātus*, p.p. of *dēpopulāre*, to lay waste, late L, to divest of inhabitants (DE-, *populus*, people)]

deport (dipawt´) *v.t.* 1 to expel from one country to another. 2 to carry away, esp. to a foreign country. 3 to conduct or to behave (oneself etc.). **deportable** *a.* **deportation** (dēpawtā´shən) *n.* 1 the state of being banished. 2 the act of transporting to a foreign land. **deportee** *n.* a person who is deported. **deportment** *n.* conduct, demeanour, manners. [OF *deporter*, L *dēportāre* (DE-, *portāre*, to carry)]

depose (dipōz´) *v.t.* 1 to remove from a throne or other high office. 2 (*Law*) to bear witness (that), to testify on oath to. ~*v.i.* (*Law*) to bear witness. **deposable** *a.* **deposal** *n.* [F *déposer* (DE-, *poser*, L *pausāre*, to PAUSE, late L, to place, by confusion with *pōnere*, to DEPONE)]

deposit (dipoz´it) *v.t.* (*pres.p.* **depositing,** *past, p.p.* **deposited**) 1 to lay down, to place. 2 to entrust. 3 to lodge for safety or as a pledge. 4 to lodge in a bank account. 5 to leave behind as precipitation or accumulation. 6 to lay (eggs etc.). ~*n.* 1 anything deposited or laid down. 2 something which is entrusted to another. 3 a pledge, an earnest or first instalment, a trust, a security. 4 a sum of money lodged in a bank. 5 a sum of money paid by an election candidate and returned only if they receive a certain proportion of the vote. 6 matter accumulated or precipitated and left behind. **on deposit** 1 when buying on hire purchase, payable as a first instalment. 2 in a deposit account. **deposit account** *n.* a bank account earning interest, usu. requiring notice for withdrawals. **depositary** *n.* (*pl.* **depositaries**) a person with whom anything is deposited for safety; a trustee. **deposition** (depəzi´shən, dē-) *n.* 1 the act of depositing. 2 the act of deposing, esp. from a throne. 3 (*Law*) a a voluntary affirmation sworn before a person qualified to administer an oath. b the act of bearing witness on oath. c the evidence of a witness reduced to writing. **the Deposition** 1 the taking down of Christ from the Cross. 2 a picture of this. **depositor** *n.* a person who makes a deposit, esp. of money. **depository** *n.* (*pl.* **depositories**) 1 a place where anything, esp. furniture, is placed for safety. 2 a place where some quality is to be found. 3 a depositary. [MF *depositer*, L *dēpositum*, neut. p.p. of *dēpōnere*, to DEPONE]

Usage note The spellings of the nouns *depositary* and *depository* should not be confused: a *depositAry* is a person and a *depositOry* a place.

---

depot (dep´ō) *n.* 1 a place of deposit, a storehouse. 2 a building for the storage and servicing of buses, trains or goods vehicles. 3 (*N Am.*) a railway or bus station. 4 (*Mil.*) a a storehouse for equipment. b a station for recruits. c the headquarters of a regiment. d that portion of the battalion at headquarters while the rest are abroad. [F *dépôt*, L *dēpositum*, DEPOSIT]

deprave (diprāv´) *v.t.* 1 to make bad or corrupt. 2 to vitiate. **depravation** (deprəvā´shən) *n.* 1 the act of depraving. 2 the state of being depraved. **depraved** *a.* corrupt. **depravity** (-prav´-) *n.* (*pl.* **depravities**) 1 viciousness, profligacy; perversion, degeneracy. 2 a vicious or degenerate act. **3** a state of corruption. [OF *depraver*, L *dēprāvāre* (DE-, *prāvus*, crooked, depraved)]

deprecate (dep´rikāt) *v.t.* **1** to express disapproval of or regret for. **2** to express regret or reluctance about. **3** to argue or plead earnestly against. **4** †to try to avert by prayer. **5** to depreciate. **deprecating** *a.* **deprecatingly** *adv.* **deprecation** (-ā´shən) *n.* **deprecative** (-prikətiv) *a.* **deprecator** *n.* **deprecatory** *a.* [L *dēprecātus*, p.p. of *dēprecārī* (DE-, *precārī*, to pray)]

Usage note The meanings of *deprecate, deprecation* and *deprecatory* and *depreciate, depreciation* and *depreciatory* overlap (especially in compounds in *self-*). The basic sense of *deprecate*, however, is to express reluctance about or disapproval of, and that of *depreciate* to lower in value.

depreciate (diprē´shiāt) *v.t.* **1** to lower the value of. **2** to disparage, to undervalue, to decry. **3** to reduce the price of. **4** to lower the exchange value of (money etc.). *~v.i.* to fall in value. **depreciatingly** *adv.* **depreciation** (-a´shən) *n.* **1** the act of depreciating. **2** the state of becoming depreciated. **3** a fall in value. **4** allowance for wear and tear. **depreciatory** (-shiətəri) *a.* [L *dēpretiātus*, p.p. of *dēpretiāre* (DE-, *pretium*, price, value)]

Usage note See note under DEPRECATE.

depredation (deprədā´shən) *n.* **1** plundering, spoliation. **2** an act of plundering. **depredator** (dep´-) *n.* a pillager, a plunderer. **depredatory** (dep´-, -pred´-) *a.* [F *déprédation*, L *dēpraedātio -ōnem*, from *dēpraedārī* (DE-, *praedārī*, to rob, from *praeda*, booty)]

depress (dipres´) *v.t.* **1** to press down. **2** to lower. **3** to dispirit, to make dejected. **4** to reduce or keep down the energy or activity of. **5** to bring down; to humble, to abase. **6** to cast down. **depressant** *a.* **1** lowering the spirits. **2** sedative. *~n.* **1** a sedative. **2** a depressing event or influence. **depressed** *a.* suffering from depression, low in spirits. **depressed area** *n.* an area of very serious unemployment. **depressed classes** *n.pl.* the untouchables. **depressible** *a.* **depressing** *a.* **depressingly** *adv.* **depression** (-shən) *n.* **1** the act of depressing; the state of being depressed. **2** a mental disorder characterized by low spirits, reduction of self-esteem and lowering of energy. **3** lowering of the spirits, dejection; lowering of energy or activity. **4** slackness of business; a long economic crisis. **5** a hollow place on a surface. **6** the angular distance of a heavenly body below the horizon. **7 a** a low state of the barometer indicative of bad weather. **b** the centre of low pressure in a cyclone. **depressive** *a.* **1** causing depression. **2** characterized by depression. *~n.* a person who is subject to periods of depression. **depressor** *n.* **1** a person who or something which depresses. **2** a muscle which depresses the part to which it is attached. **3** a surgical instrument for reducing or pushing back an obtruding part. **4** a nerve that lowers blood pressure. **depressor muscle** *n.* [L *dēpressus*, p.p. of *dēprimere* (DE-, *premere*, to PRESS¹)]

depressurize (dēpresh´ərīz), **depressurise** *v.t.* to reduce the atmospheric pressure in (a pressure-controlled area, such as an aircraft cabin). **depressurization** (-zā´shən) *n.*

deprive (diprīv´) *v.t.* **1** to take from, to dispossess (of). **2** to debar. **3** to bereave. **4** †to divest of an ecclesiastical dignity or preferment. **deprivable** *a.* **deprival** *n.* **deprivation** (deprivā´shən) *n.* **1** the act of depriving. **2** the state of being deprived. **3** loss, dispossession, bereavement. **4** †the act of divesting a clergyman of his spiritual promotion or dignity. **deprived** *a.* lacking adequate social, educational and medical facilities. [OF *depriver*, late L *dēprīvāre* (DE-, *prīvāre*, to deprive, from *prīvus*, single, peculiar)]

de profundis (dā prəfun´dis) *adv.* from the depths of penitence or affliction. *~n.* a cry from the depths of penitence or affliction. [L, 'out of the depths']

deprogram (dēprō´gram) *v.t.* (*pres.p.* **deprogramming,** *past, p.p.* **deprogrammed**) **1** to remove a program from (a computer). **2** (*N Am.*) to deprogramme.

deprogramme (dēprō´gram) *v.t.* to persuade (someone) to reject obsessive beliefs, ideas and fears.

Dept. *abbr.* Department.

depth (depth) *n.* **1** deepness. **2** measurement from the top or surface downwards or from the front backwards. **3** a deep place, an abyss. **4** (*pl.*) the deepest, innermost part. **5** the middle or height of a season. **6** (*pl.*) the sea, the deep part of the ocean, deep water. **7** abstruseness, profundity, mental penetration. **8** intensity of colour, shade, darkness or obscurity. **9** profundity of thought or feeling. **10** (*pl.*) the extremity, the extreme or innermost part of a region. **11** (*pl.*) a state of depression. **in depth** thoroughly, in detail. **out of one's depth 1** in water deeper than one's height. **2** puzzled beyond one's knowledge or ability. **depth-charge, depth-bomb** *n.* a mine or bomb exploded under water, used for attacking submarines. **depthless** *a.* **1** without depth. **2** unfathomable. **depth of field** *n.* the distance in front of and behind an object focused on by a lens (such as a camera or microscope) which will be acceptably sharp. **depth psychology** *n.* the study of the unconscious.

depurate (dep´ūrāt) *v.t.* to purify. *~v.i.* to become pure. **depuration** (-rā´shən) *n.* **depurative** (dipū´-) *a.* **depurator** *n.* a person who or something which purifies. [med. L *dēpūrātus*, p.p. of *dēpūrāre* (DE-, L *pūrus*, PURE)]

depute¹ (dipūt´) *v.t.* **1** to appoint or send as a substitute or agent. **2** to give as a task. **deputation** (depūtā´shən) *n.* **1** a person or persons deputed to act as representatives for others, a delegation. **2** the act of deputing. **3** an authority or commission to do something. **deputize** (dep´-), **deputise** *v.t.* to appoint or send as a deputy. *~v.i.* to act as a deputy. [F *députer*, L *dēputāre* (DE-, *putāre*, to think, to consider, to allot)]

depute² (dep´ūt) *n.* (*Sc.*) a deputy.

deputy (dep´ūti) *n.* (*pl.* **deputies**) **1** a person who is appointed or sent to act for another or others. **2** a delegate, a member of a deputation. **3** a member of the French and other legislative chambers. **4** (*Law*) a person who exercises an office in another's right. **5** a safety officer in a coalmine. **6** (*in comb.*) acting for, vice- (*deputy speaker*). **7** acting. **by deputy** by proxy. **deputy lieutenant** *n.* the deputy of a Lord Lieutenant. **deputyship** *n.*

der., deriv. *abbr.* **1** derivation. **2** derivative. **3** derived.

deracinate (diras´ināt) *v.t.* **1** to tear up by the roots. **2** to destroy. **deracination** (-ā´shən) *n.* [F *déraciner* (DE-, *racine*, ult. from L *rādix -īcem*, root)]

derail (dirāl´) *v.t.* to cause to leave the rails. *~v.i.* to run off the rails. **derailer** *n.* **derailment** *n.* [F *dérailler*]

derailleur (dirā´lə) *n.* a bicycle gear in which the chain is moved between different sprockets. [F *dérailleur*, DERAIL]

derange (dirānj´) *v.t.* **1** to put out of line or order. **2** to disorganize. **3** to disturb, to unsettle, to disorder (esp. the intellect). **deranged** *a.* **1** insane. **2** mentally disturbed. **derangement** *n.* [F *déranger*]

derate (dērāt´) *v.t.* remove the liability for rates from. *~v.i.* remove or reduce rates.

deration (dērash´ən) *v.t.* to remove from the rationed category.

Derby (dah´bi) *n.* (*pl.* **Derbies**) **1** a race for three-year-old horses, held at Epsom in May or June, founded by the 12th Earl of Derby in 1780. **2** any similar race. **donkey derby** DONKEY. **Derby Day** *n.* the day on which the Derby is run.

derby (dah´bi) *n.* (*pl.* **derbies**) **1** any important sporting event. 2 a match between two teams from the same area. 3 a stout kind of boot. 4 (*N Am.*) a bowler hat. **local derby** LOCAL.

derecognize (dērek´əgnīz), **derecognise** *v.t.* to cease to recognize the rights of (a trade union). **derecognition** (-nish´-) *n.*

de règle (də reg´lə) *a.* (*pred.*) customary, correct. [F, of rule]

deregulate (dēreg´ūlāt) *v.t.* to remove legal or other regulations from (transport services etc.), often so as to open up to general competition. **deregulation** (-lā´shən) *n.*

derelict (der´əlikt) *a.* 1 left, forsaken, abandoned. 2 dilapidated, showing neglect. 3 (*N Am.*) negligent. ~*n.* 1 a down-and-out. 2 anything abandoned (esp. a ship at sea), relinquished or thrown away. **dereliction** (derəlik´-) *n.* 1 the act of abandoning. 2 the state of being abandoned. 3 omission or neglect (as of a duty). 4 the exposure of land by the retreat of sea. 5 land left dry by the sea. **dereliction of duty** *n.* reprehensible neglect or shortcoming. [L *dērelictus*, p.p. of *dērelinquere* (DE-, *relinquere*, to RELINQUISH)]

derequisition (dērekwizish´ən) *v.t.* to free (requisitioned property).

derestrict (dēristrikt´) *v.t.* to free from restriction, e.g. to free a road from speed limits. **derestriction** *n.*

deride (dirīd´) *v.t.* to laugh at, to mock. **derider** *n.* **deridingly** *adv.* **derisible** (diriz´əbəl) *a.* **derision** (-rizh´ən) *n.* 1 the act of deriding. 2 ridicule, mockery, contempt. **to hold in derision** to hold in contempt, to make a laughing-stock. **derisive** (-siv), **derisory** *a.* 1 scoffing, deriding, ridiculing. 2 ridiculous. **derisively** *adv.* **derisiveness** *n.* [L *dērīdēre* (DE-, *rīdēre*, to laugh)]

Usage note The uses of the adjectives *derisive* and *derisory* overlap, but in general *derisive* means scoffing, and *derisory* ridiculous.

de-rig (dērig´) *v.t.* (*pres.p.* **de-rigging,** *past, p.p.* **de-rigged**) to dismantle the rigging of. ~*v.i.* to dismantle a ship's rigging.

de rigeur (də rigœ´) *a.* required by fashion. [F]

derisible, derision etc. DERIDE.

deriv. DER..

derive (dirīv´) *v.t.* 1 to obtain, to get. 2 to deduce. 3 to draw, as from a source, root or principle. 4 to trace the origin of. 5 to deduce or determine from data. ~*v.i.* 1 to come, to proceed, to be descended. 2 to originate. **derivable** *a.* **derivation** (derivā´shən) *n.* 1 the act of deriving. 2 origin, extraction. 3 the etymology of a word, the process of tracing a word to its root. 4 (*Math.*) the process of deducing a function from another. 5 drawing off. **derivational** *a.* **derivative** (diriv´-) *a.* 1 derived. 2 copied from something else, unoriginal. 3 secondary, not original. ~*n.* 1 anything derived from a source. 2 a word derived from or taking its origin in another. 3 (*Math.*) a differential coefficient. **derivatively** *adv.* [F *dériver*, L *dērīvāre*, to draw off water (DE-, *rīvus*, a stream)]

derm (dœm), **derma** (dœ´mə), **dermis** (-mis) *n.* 1 skin. 2 (*Anat.*) true skin or corium lying beneath the epidermis. **dermal** *a.* **dermic** *a.* [Gr. *derma*, from *derein*, to flay]

derm- DERMATO-.

-derm (dœm) *comb. form* skin, as in *pachyderm*.

dermatic (dœmat´ik) *a.* of or relating to the skin.

dermatitis (dœmətī´tis) *n.* inflammation of the skin.

dermato- (dœ´mətō), **derm-** *comb. form* of or relating to the skin. [Gr. *derma dermatos*, the skin]

dermatoglyphics (dœmətōglif´iks) *n.* the science of skin markings of the hands and feet. **dermatoglyphic** *a.* **dermatoglyphically** *adv.*

dermatoid (dœ´mətoid) *a.* skinlike.

dermatology (dœmətol´əji) *n.* the science of the skin and its diseases. **dermatological** (-loj´-) *a.* **dermatologist** *n.*

dermatosis (dœmətō´sis) *n.* (*pl.* **dermatoses** (-sēz)) any disease of the skin.

dermic, dermis DERM.

dernier (dœ´niā) *a.* last. **dernier cri** (krē) *n.* the last word, the latest fashion. [F]

derogate[1] (der´əgāt) *v.i.* (*formal*) 1 to detract, to withdraw a part (from). 2 to become inferior, to lower oneself, to degenerate. ~*v.t.* 1 to lessen the effect of. 2 to detract from, to disparage. **derogation** (-ā´shən) *n.* 1 the act of derogating. 2 the act of detracting from worth, name or character; disparagement. 3 deterioration. **derogative** (dirog´-) *a.* **derogatively** *adv.* **derogatory** *a.* tending to detract from honour, worth or character; disparaging, depreciatory. **derogatorily** *adv.* [L *dērogātus*, p.p. of *dērogāre* (DE-, *rogāre*, to ask, to propose a law)]

derogate[2] (der´əgət) *a.* debased, degenerated.

derrick (der´ik) *n.* 1 a hoisting machine with a boom stayed from a central post, wall, floor, deck etc., for raising heavy weights. 2 the framework over an oil-well. [the name of a Tyburn hangman in the 17th cent.]

derrière (deriœ´) *n.* (*coll.*) the buttocks, the behind. [F]

derring-do (deringdoo´) *n.* (*poet. or facet.*) 1 courageous deeds. 2 bravery. [Chaucer, *dorring don*, daring to do, mistaken by Spenser]

derringer (der´injə) *n.* a short-barrelled large-bore pistol. [Henry *Derringer*, d. 1868, US inventor]

derris (der´is) *n.* an extract of the root of tropical trees of the genus *Derris*, which forms an effective insecticide. [mod. L from Gr., leather covering]

derry (der´i) *n.* (*Austral.*) dislike, antipathy. **to have a derry on** to be biased against. [perh. from the refrain *derry-down*]

derv (dœv) *n.* diesel engine fuel oil. [acronym for *d*iesel *e*ngine *r*oad *v*ehicle]

dervish (dœ´vish) *n.* a member of one of the various Muslim ascetic orders, whose devotional exercises include meditation and often frenzied physical exercises. [Pers. *darvish*, poor]

DES *abbr.* (*Hist.*) Department of Education and Science.

desalinate (dēsal´ināt) *v.t.* to remove salt from (sea water). **desalination** (-ā´shən) *n.* **desalinator** *n.* **desalinize** (dēsal´inīz), **desalinise** *v.t.* (*N Am.*) to desalinate. **desalinization** (-zā´shən) *n.*

desalt (desawlt´) *v.t.* DESALINATE.

descale (dēskāl´) *v.t.* to remove scale or scales from.

descant[1] (des´kant), **discant** (dis´-) *n.* 1 (*poet.*) a song, a melody. 2 a counterpoint above the plainsong, an accompaniment. 3 the upper part, esp. the soprano, in part music. 4 †a discourse branching into parts. 5 a comment. **descant recorder** *n.* (*Mus.*) a recorder with a high pitch. [ONF *descant*, OF *deschant*, med. L *discantus* (DIS-, L *cantus*, singing, song)]

descant[2] (deskant´), **diskant** (dis-) *v.i.* 1 to comment or discourse at length (on). 2 to sing in parts. 3 to compose music in parts. [ONF *descant*, OF *deschant*, med. L *discantus* (DIS-, L *cantus*, singing, song)]

descend (disend´) *v.i.* 1 to come or go down. 2 to sink, to fall. 3 to slope downwards. 4 to make an attack. 5 to originate, to descend (from); to be derived. 6 to be transmitted from one generation to the next. 7 to pass on, as from more to less important matters, from general to particular, or from more remote to nearer times. 8 to stoop; to condescend; to lower or abase. 9 (*Mus.*) to become lower. 10 (of a letter such as j, p or y) to have a part below the level of the line of type. ~*v.t.* to walk, move or pass along downwards. **to descend on** to visit unexpectedly. **descendant** *n.* a person who descends from an ancestor; offspring, issue. **descended** *a.* derived, sprung (from a race or ancestor). **to be descended from** to be a descendant of. **descendent** *a.*

descender *n.* the part of a letter (such as j, p or y) which is below the level of the line of type. **descendible, descendable** *a.* 1 able to be descended. 2 (*Law*) able to be transmitted from ancestor to heir. **descending axis** *n.* the root of a plant. [F *descendre*, L *dēscendere* (DE-, *scandere*, to climb)]

descent (disent´) *n.* 1 the act of descending. 2 a slope downwards. 3 a way of descending, a path leading down. 4 downward motion. 5 decline in rank or prosperity. 6 a sudden attack, esp. from the sea. 7 a fall. 8 pedigree, lineage, origin. 9 issue of one generation. 10 transmission by succession or inheritance. 11 (*Mus.*) a passing to a lower pitch. [F *descente*, as DESCEND]

descramble (deskram´bəl) *v.t.* to convert (a scrambled signal) to intelligible form. **descrambler** *n.*

describe (diskrīb´) *v.t.* 1 to set forth the qualities, features or properties of in words. 2 to call (*He was described as a family friend*). 3 to draw, to trace out. 4 to form or trace out by motion. **describable** *a.* **describer** *n.* **description** (-skrip´shən) *n.* 1 the act of describing. 2 an account of anything in words. 3 a kind, a sort, a species (*There was no food of any description*). **to answer/ fit the description** to have the qualities or features described. **descriptive** (-skrip´-) *a.* 1 containing description. 2 capable of describing. 3 given to description. 4 (*Gram.*) of or relating to a modifier which describes the noun modified, but is not limiting or demonstrative, e.g. 'red'. **descriptively** *adv.* **descriptiveness** *n.* [OF *descrire*, L *dēscrībere* (DE-, *scrībere*, to write)]

descry (diskrī´) *v.t.* (*3rd pers. sing. pres.* **descries,** *pres.p.* **descrying,** *past, p.p.* **descried**) to make out, to espy. [OF *descrire*, see DESCRIBE]

desecrate (des´ikrāt) *v.t.* 1 to divert from any sacred purpose; to profane. 2 to divert from a sacred to a profane purpose. **desecration** (-rā´shən) *n.* **desecrator** *n.* [L *dēsecrātus*, p.p. of *dēsecrāre* (DE-, *sacrāre*, to make sacred, *sacer*, SACRED)]

deseed (dēsēd´) *v.t.* to remove the seeds from. **deseeder** *n.* a machine used for deseeding.

desegregate (dēseg´rigāt) *v.t.* to end racial segregation in (an institution, e.g. a school). **desegregation** (-ā´shən) *n.*

deselect (dēsilekt´) *v.t.* 1 to refuse to readopt as a candidate, esp. as a prospective parliamentary candidate. 2 to drop from a group or team. **deselection** *n.*

desensitize (dēsen´sitīz), **desensitise** *v.t.* to make insensitive to (a chemical agent etc.). **desensitization** (-zā´shən) *n.* **desensitizer** *n.*

desert[1] (dez´ət) *n.* 1 a waste, uninhabited, uncultivated place, esp. a waterless and treeless region. 2 an uninteresting or dreary place. ~*a.* 1 uninhabited, waste. 2 untilled, barren. **desert boots** *n.pl.* suede ankle-boots with laces. **desertification** (dizœtifikā´shən) *n.* the process of turning from desert into fertile land. **desert island** *n.* a small, uninhabited, tropical island. **desert oak** *n.* a variety of casuarina, *Casuarina decaisneana*, of Australia. **Desert Rat** *n.* (*coll.*) a soldier of the seventh Armoured Division in N Africa (1941–42). [OF, from L *dēsertus*, p.p. of *dēserere* (DE-, *serere*, to bind, to join)]

desert[2] (dizœt´) *v.t.* 1 to forsake, to abandon. 2 to quit, to leave. 3 to fail (*His sense of humour deserted him*). ~*v.i.* (*Mil.*) to abandon the service without permission. **deserted** *a.* **deserter** *n.* **desertion** *n.* [F *déserter*, late L *dēsertāre*, as DESERT[1]]

desert[3] (dizœt´) *n.* 1 what one deserves, either as reward or punishment. 2 merit or demerit. 3 state of deserving, meritoriousness. 4 (*pl.*) deserved reward or punishment. **to get one's just deserts** to receive what one's behaviour merits. **desertless** *a.* without merit. [OF *deserte*, p.p. of *deservir*, see DESERT[1]]

deserve (dizœv´) *v.t.* to be worthy of, to merit by conduct or qualities, good or bad, esp. to merit by excellence, good conduct or useful deeds. ~†*v.i.* to be worthy or deserving (of). **deservedly** (-vid-) *adv.* **deservedness** *n.* **deserver** *n.* **deserving** *a.* merited, worthy. **deserving of** having deserved (*deserving of praise*). **deservingly** *adv.* **deservingness** *n.* [OF *deservir*, L *dēservīre* (DE-, *servīre*, to serve)]

desexualize (dēseks´ūəlīz), **desexualise, desex** *v.t.* 1 to castrate or spay. 2 to deprive of sexuality.

deshabille (dāzabē´), **déshabillé** (dezab´ēā), **dishabille** (disabē´) *n.* state of undress, state of being partly or carelessly attired. [F *déshabillé*, p.p. of *déshabiller*(DIS-, *habiller*, to dress)]

desiccate (des´ikāt) *v.t.* to dry, to remove moisture from. **desiccant** *a.* drying up. ~*n.* a drying agent. **desiccated** *a.* **desiccation** (-ā´shən) *n.* **desiccative** (-kətiv) *a.* **desiccator** *n.* 1 (*Chem.*) an apparatus for drying substances liable to be decomposed by moisture. 2 an apparatus for drying food and other commercial substances. [L *dēsiccātus*, p.p. of *dēsiccāre* (DE-, *siccāre*, to dry, from *siccus*, dry)]

†**desiderate** (dizid´ərāt) *v.t.* 1 to feel the loss of. 2 to want, to miss. **desideration** (-ā´shən) *n.* **desiderative** (-dərətiv) *a.* 1 expressing desire. 2 desiring. ~*n.* (*Gram.*) a verb formed from another, and expressive of a desire to do the action implied in that verb. [L *dēsiderātus*, p.p. of *dēsiderāre*, to DESIRE]

desideratum (dizidərah´təm) *n.* (*pl.* **desiderata** (-tə)) anything desired, esp. anything to fill a gap.

design (dizīn´) *v.t.* 1 to contrive, to formulate, to project. 2 to draw, to plan, to sketch out. 3 to purpose, to intend. 4 to appropriate, to devote or apply to a particular purpose. ~*v.i.* to work as a designer. ~*n.* 1 a plan, a scheme. 2 a purpose, an intention. 3 thought and intention as revealed in the correlation of parts or adaptation of means to an end. 4 an arrangement of forms and colours forming a pattern. 5 a preliminary sketch, a study. 6 the art of designing. 7 plot, construction, general idea. 8 an artistic creation. **by design** intentionally, deliberately. **to have designs on** to scheme to take possession of. **designer** *n.* 1 a person who designs. 2 a person who produces detailed plans for a manufacturer. 3 a person who makes designs for clothing, stage or film sets etc. ~*a.* 1 (of clothes) produced by a famous designer. 2 of or relating to anything considered extremely fashionable, unusual or expensive (*designer chairs*). **designer drug** *n.* an illegal drug made up from a mixture of legal narcotics. **designer stubble** *n.* (*coll.*) two or three days' growth of beard, considered fashionable among young men. **designing** *a.* crafty, scheming. **designingly** *adv.* [F *désigner*, to denote, to signify, L *dēsignāre* (DE-, *signāre*, to mark, from *signum*, a sign)]

designate[1] (dez´ignāt) *v.t.* 1 to indicate, to mark. 2 to describe (as). 3 to select, to nominate, to appoint. **designated driver** *n.* a member of a group of friends who is appointed to drink no alcohol at a social occasion and to drive the others home afterwards. **designation** (-nā´shən) *n.* 1 the act of designating. 2 appointment, nomination. 3 name, title, description. **designative** (-nətiv), **designatory** *a.* **designator** *n.* [L *dēsignātus*, p.p. of *dēsignāre*, as DESIGN]

designate[2] (dez´ignət) *a.* (*often placed after the noun*) nominated to but not yet holding an office (*president designate*).

desire (dizīə´) *v.t.* 1 to wish (to do). 2 to wish for the attainment or possession of. 3 to express a wish to have, to request, to beseech, to command. 4 †to invite. ~*v.i.* to have desire. ~*n.* 1 an eagerness of the mind to obtain or enjoy some object. 2 a request, an entreaty. 3 the object of desire. 4 sensual appetite, lust. **desirable** *a.* 1 worthy of being desired. 2 attractive. 3 agreeable. **desirability** (-bil´-) *n.* **desirableness** *n.* **desirably** *adv.* **desireless** *a.* **desirous** *a.* desiring, wishful (*She is desirous of meeting* *with you*). **desirously** *adv.* [OF *desirer*, L *dēsiderāre*, to long for]

desist (dizist´) *v.i.* to cease, to forbear; to leave off. **desistance** *n.* [OF *desister*, L *dēsistere* (DE-, *sistere*, to put, to stop)]

desk (desk) *n.* **1** a table for a writer or reader, often with a sloping top. **2** the place from which prayers are read; a pulpit. **3** a counter for information or registration in a public place, such as a hotel. **4** a newspaper or broadcasting department *(the news desk)*. **5** (*Mus.*) a stand for two players in an orchestra. **desk-bound** *a.* engaged in deskwork. **desktop computer** *n.* a computer small enough to use on a desk. **desktop publishing** *n.* the production of text at a desk equipped with a computer and printer capable of producing high-quality printed copy. **deskwork** *n.* [med. L *desca*, L *discus*, a DISC]

deskill (dēskil´) *v.t.* **1** to reduce the level of skill required for (a job), esp. by automation. **2** to cause (workers) to do work which does not use their skills.

desman (des´mən) *n.* (*pl.* **desmans**) either of two mole-like aquatic mammals, *Desmana moschata* of Russia and *Galemys pyrenaicus* of the Pyrenees. [short for Swed. *desmansråtta*, from *desman*, musk, *råtta*, rat]

desmid (des´mid) *n.* a member of a group of microscopic freshwater algae, differing from the diatoms in their green colour, and in having no siliceous covering. [mod. L *desmidium*, Gr. *desmos*, a bond, a chain, *eidos*, a form]

desolate[1] (des´ələt) *a.* **1** forsaken, solitary, lonely. **2** uninhabited, deserted, barren, neglected, ruined. **3** forlorn, comfortless; upset. **desolately** *adv.* **desolateness** *n.* [L *dēsōlātus*, p.p. of *dēsōlāre* (DE-, *sōlāre*, to make lonely, from *sōlus*, alone)]

desolate[2] (des´əlāt) *v.t.* **1** to deprive of inhabitants. **2** to lay waste. **3** to make very unhappy. **desolated** *a.* **desolation** (-ā´shən) *n.* **1** the act of desolating. **2** the state of being desolated. **3** neglect, ruin. **4** loneliness; bitter grief, affliction. **desolator** *n.*

desorb (dēsawb´) *v.t.* to release (an absorbed substance) from a surface. ~*v.i.* (of an absorbed substance) to become released from a surface. **desorbent** *a.*, *n.* **desorption** *n.*

desoxyribonucleic acid DEOXYRIBONUCLEIC ACID.

despair (dispeə´) *v.i.* **1** to be without hope. **2** to give up all hope. ~†*v.t.* to lose all hope of. ~*n.* **1** hopelessness. **2** a person who or something which causes hopelessness. **despairing** *a.* hopeless, desperate. **despairingly** *adv.* [OF *despeir-*, stem of *desperer*, L *dēspērāre* (DE-, *spērāre*, to hope)]

despatch DISPATCH.

desperado (despərah´dō) *n.* (*pl.* **desperadoes, desperados**) a desperate or reckless ruffian. [OSp., desperate, L *dēspērātus*, as desperate]

desperate (des´pərət) *a.* **1** hopeless, reckless, lawless, regardless of danger or consequences, fearless. **2** affording little hope of success, recovery or escape; tried as a last resource. **3** extremely dangerous. **4** very bad, awful. **5** wanting very badly to do or have to do something (*desperate for a drink*). **desperately** *adv.* **1** in a desperate manner. **2** very, extremely. **desperateness** *n.* **desperation** (-ā´shən) *n.* [L *dēspērātus*, p.p. of *dēspērāre*, to DESPAIR]

despicable (dispik´əbəl, des´-) *a.* meriting contempt; vile, nasty. **despicably** *adv.* [L *dēspicābilis*, from *dēspicārī* (DE-, *specārī*, cogn. with *specere*, see DESPISE)]

despise (dispīz´) *v.t.* to look down on; to regard with contempt; to scorn. **despiser** *n.* [OF *despis-*, stem of *despire*, L *dēspicere* (DE-, *specere*, to look at)]

despite (dispīt´) *prep.* notwithstanding; in spite of. ~†*n.* **1** spite, malice. **2** aversion, vexation. **3** contemptuous treatment, outrage. †**despite of** in spite of. †**despiteful** *a.* spiteful, malicious, malignant. †**despitefully** *adv.* †**despiteous** (-spit´iəs) *a.* spiteful. [OF *despit*, L *dēspectus*, contempt, p.p. of *dēspicere*, to DESPISE]

despoil (dispoil´) *v.t.* **1** to strip or take away from by force; to plunder. **2** to spoil or destroy (a place). **despoiler** *n.* †**despoilment, despoliation** (-spoliā´shən) *n.* **1** the act of plundering. **2** the state of being despoiled. [OF *despoiller* (F *dépouiller*), L *dēspoliāre* (DE-, *spoliāre*, to SPOIL)]

despond (dispond´) *v.i.* to be low in spirits, to lose hope. ~†*n.* unhappiness, despair. **despondency, despondence** *n.* **despondent** *a.* very unhappy, disheartened. **despondently** *adv.* **despondingly** *adv.* [L *dēspondēre* (DE-, *spondēre*, to promise)]

despot (des´pot) *n.* **1** an absolute ruler or sovereign. **2** a tyrant, an oppressor. **despotic** (dispot´-) *a.* tyrannical, unfair, cruel. **despotically** *adv.* **despotism** *n.* **1** absolute authority, tyranny. **2** arbitrary government, autocracy. **3** a country ruled by a despot. [OF, from late L *despotus*, Gr. *despotēs*]

desquamate (des´kwəmāt) *v.i.* (*Med.*) to scale or peel off, to exfoliate. **desquamation** (-ā´shən) *n.* **desquamative** (diskwam´-), **desquamatory** *a.* [L *dēsquāmātus*, p.p. of *dēsquāmāre* (DE-, *squāma*, a scale)]

des res (dez rez´) *n.* (*coll.*) a desirable residence (used by estate agents). [*des*irable *res*idence]

dessert (dizœt´) *n.* the last course of a meal, consisting of fruit or sweetmeats; the sweet course. **dessertspoon** *n.* **1** a medium-sized spoon holding half as much as a tablespoon and twice as much as a teaspoon. **2** the amount that a dessertspoon will hold. **dessertspoonful** *n.* (*pl.* **dessertspoonfuls**). **dessert wine** *n.* a sweet wine served with dessert. [F from *desservir*, to clear the table (*des-*, L DIS-, *servir*, to SERVE)]

☒ **dessicate** common misspelling of DESICCATE.

destabilize (dēstā´bilīz), **destabilise** *v.t.* **1** to make unstable. **2** to undermine the power of (a government). **destabilization** (-zā´shən) *n.*

destination (destinā´shən) *n.* **1** the place to which a person is going or to which a thing is sent. **2** the purpose for which a thing is appointed or intended. **3** the act of destining.

destine (des´tin) *v.t.* to appoint, fix or determine to a use, purpose, duty or position. **destined** *a.* foreordained. [F *destiner*, L *dēstināre*, (root of *stāre*, to stand)]

destiny (des´tini) *n.* (*pl.* **destinies**) **1** the purpose or end to which any person or thing is appointed. **2** fate, fortune, lot, events as the fulfilment of fate. **3** the power which presides over the fortunes of men. **4** invincible necessity. **the Destinies** the Fates.

destitute (des´titūt) *a.* **1** in want, deprived of the necessities of life. **2** lacking, bereft (of). **3** †forsaken, forlorn. **destitution** (-titū´-) *n.* [L *dēstitūtus*, p.p. of *dēstituere* (DE-, *statuere*, to place, from *status*, p.p. of *stāre*, to stand)]

destock (dēstok´) *v.i.* to reduce one's stock.

†**destrier** (des´triə) *n.* a warhorse, a charger. [ME and A-F *destrer* (OF *destrier*), late L *dextrārius*, from *dextra*, right hand]

destroy (distroi´) *v.t.* **1** to pull down or demolish; to pull to pieces. **2** to undo, to nullify. **3** to annihilate; to lay waste. **4** to ruin the life or situation of. **5** to kill (a sick animal) humanely. **6** to overthrow. **7** to put an end to. **destroyable** *a.* **destroyer** *n.* **1** a person who destroys. **2** a fast warship armed with torpedoes. **destroying angel** *n.* a white, poisonous toadstool, *Amanita virosa*. [OF *destruire* (F *détruire*), late L *dēstruere* (DE-, *struere*, to build)]

destruction (distrŭk´shən) *n.* **1** the act of destroying. **2** the state of being destroyed. **3** demolition, ruin. **4** something which destroys. **5** death, slaughter. **destruct** *v.t.* to destroy (a rocket or missile in flight) deliberately. ~*v.i.* to be destructed. ~*n.* the act of destructing.

destructible *a.* **destructibility** (-bil´-) *n.* **destructionist** *n.* a believer in the annihilation of the wicked. **destructive** *a.* 1 causing or tending to destruction; ruinous, mischievous, wasteful. 2 serving or tending to subvert or confute (arguments or opinions); negative, as distinct from *constructive*. ~*n.* a destroyer, esp. of existing institutions. **destructive distillation** *n.* distillation at a temperature sufficiently high to decompose the substance, and evolve new products possessing different qualities. **destructively** *adv.* **destructive metabolism** *n.* the process by which protoplasm is broken down into simpler and more stable substances. **destructiveness** *n.* **destructor** *n.* a furnace for burning up refuse. [L *dēstructus*, p.p. of *dēstruere*, to DESTROY]

desuetude (disū´itūd, des´wi-) *n.* disuse; cessation of practice or habit (*to fall into desuetude*). [F *désuétude*, L *dēsuētūdo*, from *dēsuētus*, p.p. of *dēsuēscere* (DE-, *suēscere*, incept. of *suēre*, to be used)]

desulphurize (dēsŭl´fərīz), **desulphurise**, (*esp. N Am.*) **desulfurize** *v.t.* to free (an ore) from sulphur. **desulphurization** (-zā´shən) *n.*

desultory (des´əltəri) *a.* 1 passing quickly from one subject to another. 2 loose, disjointed, discursive. **desultorily** *adv.* **desultoriness** *n.* [L *dēsultōrius*, from *dēsultor*, a circus horse-leaper, from *dēsilīre* (DE-, *salīre*, to jump)]

detach (ditach´) *v.t.* 1 to disconnect, to separate; to disengage. 2 (*Mil.*) to separate from the main body for a special service. 3 (*usu. pass.*) to free from prejudice, personal considerations etc. **detachable** *a.* **detached** *a.* 1 not personally involved, impartial. 2 (of a house) not joined to the house next door. **detachedly** (-tach´id-) *adv.* **detachedness** *n.* **detached retina** *n.* a retina which is separated from the tissue underneath, causing loss of sight. **detachment** *n.* 1 freedom from prejudice, self-interest or worldly influence; independence, isolation. 2 the act of detaching. 3 the state of being detached. 4 (*Mil.*) a body of troops or a number of ships detached from the main body and sent on a special service or expedition. [F *détacher*]

detail (dē´tāl) *n.* 1 an item. 2 a minute and particular account. 3 (*pl.*) a number of particulars. 4 small features of a work of art etc., or the treatment of these (*attention to detail*). 5 (*pl.*) minute parts of a picture, statue etc., as distinct from the work as a whole. 6 a minor matter. 7 (*Mil.*) **a** a list of names detailed for particular duties. **b** a body of men selected for a special duty. ~*v.t.* 1 to list the particular items of. 2 to relate minutely. 3 (*Mil.*) to appoint for a particular service. **in detail** minutely; item by item. **to go into detail** to mention all the particulars about something. **detailed** *a.* 1 related in detail. 2 minute, complete. [F *détailler*]

detain (ditān´) *v.t.* 1 to restrain; to keep in custody. 2 to delay, to hinder. 3 †to keep back or from; to withhold. **detainee** (-ē´) *n.* a person held in custody. **detainer** *n.* 1 a person who detains. 2 the holding possession of what belongs to another. 3 the holding of a person in custody. 4 a writ of detainer. **detainment** *n.* [OF *detenir*, L *dētinēre* (DE-, *tenēre*, to hold)]

detect (ditekt´) *v.t.* 1 to discover or find out. 2 to bring to light. 3 to observe (radiation or a signal) with a detector. **detectable** *a.* **detectably** *adv.* **detection** *n.* 1 the act of detecting. 2 the discovery of crime, guilt etc., or of minute particles. **detective** *n.* a police officer employed to investigate special cases of crime. ~*a.* employed in or suitable for detecting. **amateur detective** AMATEUR. **detector** *n.* 1 a person who detects. 2 the part of a radio receiver which demodulates the radio waves. [L *dētectus*, p.p. of *dētegere* (DE-, *tegere*, to cover)]

detent (ditent´) *n.* a pin, catch or lever forming a check to the mechanism in a watch, clock, lock etc. [F *détente*, from *détendre*, L *dētinēre* (DE-, *tenēre*, to hold)]

détente (dātāt´) *n.* relaxation of tension between nations or other warring forces. [F, as DETENT]

detention (diten´shən) *n.* 1 the act of detaining. 2 the state of being detained. 3 arrest; confinement, compulsory restraint. 4 keeping in school after hours as a punishment. **detention camp** *n.* an internment camp. **detention centre** *n.* a place where young offenders are detained. [DETAIN]

détenu (dātənü´) *n.* a person kept in custody, a prisoner. **détenue** *n.* a female détenu. [F, p.p. of *détenir*, to DETAIN]

deter (ditœ´) *v.t.* (*pres.p.* **deterring**, *past, p.p.* **deterred**) 1 to discourage or frighten (from). 2 to hinder or prevent. **deterrence** (-ter´-), **determent** *n.* the act of deterring. **deterrent** (-ter´-) *a.* tending to deter. ~*n.* 1 something which deters. 2 (*coll.*) a nuclear weapon the possession of which is supposed to deter the use of a similar weapon by another power. [L *dēterrēre* (DE-, *terrēre*, to frighten)]

detergent (ditœ´jənt) *n.* 1 a chemical cleansing agent for washing clothes etc. 2 a medicine or application which has the property of cleansing. ~*a.* cleansing, purging. [L *dētergens -entem*, pres.p. of *dētergere* (DE-, *tergere*, to wipe)]

deteriorate (ditiə´riərāt) *v.t.* 1 to make inferior. 2 to reduce in value. ~*v.i.* 1 to become worse. 2 to degenerate. **deterioration** (-rā´shən) *n.* **deteriorative** (-rət-) *a.* [L *dēteriorātus*, p.p. of *dēteriorāre* (*dēterior*, worse, from *dē*, away, down)]

Usage note Pronunciation as (ditē´riāt), as though the word were *deteriate*, is best avoided.

---

determent DETER.

determinable DETERMINE.

determinant (ditœ´minənt) *a.* determinative, decisive. ~*n.* 1 a person who or something which determines or causes to fix or decide. 2 (*Math.*) the sum of a series of products of several numbers, the products being formed according to certain laws, used in the solution of equations and other processes. **determinancy** *n.*

determinate (ditœ´minət) *a.* 1 limited, definite. 2 positive, determined, resolute. **determinate inflorescence** *n.* centrifugal flowering beginning with the terminal bud. **determinately** *adv.* **determinateness** *n.* **determinative** *a.* 1 that limits or defines. 2 directive, decisive. ~*n.* 1 that which decides, defines or specifies. 2 (*Gram.*) a determiner. 3 in hieroglyphics, a sign indicating the exact signification. **determinatively** *adv.* [DETERMINE]

determination (ditœminā´shən) *n.* 1 fixed intention, resolution, strength of mind. 2 the act of determining or settling. 3 something which is determined on. 4 (*Law*) **a** settlement by a judicial decision. **b** final conclusion. 5 (*Law*) the termination of an estate or interest. 6 †direction to a certain end, a fixed tendency.

determine (ditœ´min) *v.t.* 1 to ascertain exactly. 2 to fix, to settle finally, to decide. 3 to fix the limits of, to define. 4 to cause to decide. 5 to direct, to condition, to shape. 6 (*Law*) to bring to an end. 7 to terminate, to conclude. 8 (*Geom.*) to specify the position of. ~*v.i.* 1 to decide, to resolve. 2 to end, to reach a termination. **determinable** *a.* **determinability** (-bil´-) *n.* **determined** *a.* 1 resolute. 2 having a fixed purpose. **determinedly** *adv.* **determiner** *n.* 1 a person who or thing which determines. 2 (*Gram.*) a word that limits or modifies a noun, such as *that, my, every*. **determinism** (-minizm) *n.* the doctrine that the will is not free, but is determined by antecedent causes, whether in the form of internal motives or external necessity, the latter being the postulate of fatalism. **determinist** *a., n.* **deterministic** (-nis´tik) *a.* **deterministically** *adv.* [OF *determiner*, L *dēterminâre* (DE-, *termināre*, to bound, from *terminus*, a boundary)]

deterrence, deterrent DETER.
detest (ditest´) *v.t.* to hate exceedingly, to abhor. **detestable** *a.* **detestability** (-bil´-) *n.* **detestableness** *n.* **detestably** *adv.* **detestation** (dētestā´shən) *n.* **1** extreme hatred; abhorrence, loathing. **2** a person or thing detested. **detester** *n.* [F *détester*, L *dētestārī* (DE-, *testārī*, to testify, from *testis*, a witness)]
dethrone (dithrōn´) *v.t.* **1** to remove or depose from a throne. **2** to drive from power or pre-eminence. **dethronement** *n.* **dethroner** *n.*
detinue (det´inū) *n.* (*Law*) unlawful detention. [OF *detenue*, p.p. of *detenir*, to DETAIN]
detonate (det´ənāt) *v.t.* to cause to explode with a loud bang. *~v.i.* to explode with a loud bang. **detonation** (-ā´shən) *n.* **1** the act or process of detonating. **2** an explosion with a loud bang. **3** the spontaneous combustion in a petrol engine of part of the compressed charge after sparking. **detonative** *a.* **detonator** *n.* **1** a person who or something which detonates. **2** a fog signal on a railway line. **3** a device for causing detonation. [L *dētonātus*, p.p. of *dētonāre* (*tonāre*, to thunder)]
detour (dē´tuə) *n.* **1** a roundabout way. **2** a deviation, a digression. **3** (*N Am.*) a road diversion. *~v.t.* to send by an indirect route. *~v.i.* to make a deviation from a direct route. [F *détour*, from *détourner*, to turn aside]
detox[1] (dē´toks) *n.* (*coll., esp. N Am.*) detoxification.
detox[2] (dētoks´) *v.t.* (*coll., esp. N Am.*) to detoxify. *~v.i.* to undergo detoxification.
detoxicate (dētok´sikāt) *v.t.* to detoxify. **detoxicant** *n.* a detoxifying substance. **detoxication** (-ā´shən) *n.*
detoxify (dētok´sifī) *v.t.* (*3rd pers. sing. pres.* **detoxifies,** *pres.p.* **detoxifying,** *past, p.p.* **detoxified**) to remove poison or toxin from, esp. as a treatment for drug or alcohol addiction. **detoxification** (-fikā´shən) *n.* **detoxification centre** *n.* a place where people are treated for drug or alcohol addiction.
detract (ditrakt´) *v.i.* **1** to diminish, to reduce (*The bad publicity will detract from his wholesome image*). **2** to speak disparagingly. *~v.t.* **1** to take (a part) away from something. **2** †to take away from the reputation or credit of. **detractingly** *adv.* **detraction** *n.* **1** the act of detracting. **2** depreciation, slander. **detractive** *a.* **detractor** *n.* **1** a person who detracts. **2** a defamer, a slanderer. [L *dētractus*, p.p. of *dētrahere* (DE-, *trahere*, to draw)]
detrain (dētrān´) *v.t.* to cause to alight from a train. *~v.i.* to alight from a train. **detrainment** *n.*
detribalize (detrī´bəlīz), **detribalise** *v.t.* **1** to make (a person) no longer a tribe member. **2** to take away the tribal characteristics and customs of (a tribe). **detribalization** (-zā´shən) *n.*
detriment (det´rimənt) *n.* **1** harm, injury, damage; loss. **2** a cause of detriment. **detrimental** (-men´-) *a.* causing detriment. **detrimentally** *adv.* [F *détriment*, L *dētrīmentum*, from *dētrī-* (*dētritus*, p.p.), from *dēterere* (DE-, *terere*, to rub)]
detritus (ditrī´təs) *n.* **1** (*Geol.*) accumulated matter produced by the disintegration of rock. **2** debris, rubbish. **detrital** *a.* **detrition** (-trish´-) *n.* a wearing down or away by rubbing. [L *dētrītus*, p.p. of *dēterere*, as DETRIMENT]
de trop (də trō´) *a.* superfluous, in the way. [F, excessive]
detrude (ditrood´) *v.t.* **1** to thrust or force down. **2** to expel from. [L *dētrūdere* (DE-, *trūdere*, to thrust)]
detruncate (dētrŭng´kāt) *v.t.* **1** to lop or cut off. **2** to shorten by cutting. †**detruncation** (-kā´shən) *n.* [L *dētruncātus*, p.p. of *dētruncāre* (*truncāre*, to cut off)]
Dettol® (det´ol) *n.* a type of disinfectant.
detumescence (dētūmes´əns) *n.* the diminution of swelling. [L *tumēscere*, to swell up]
detune (dētūn´) *v.t.* to adjust (a musical instrument, car engine etc.) so that it is not tuned.
deuce[1] (dūs) *n.* **1** a card or die with two spots. **2** in tennis, a score of 40 all, requiring two successive points to be scored by either party to win. **deuce-ace** *n.* the one and two thrown at dice. [F *deux*, L *duos*, acc. of *duo*]
deuce[2] (dūs) *n.* **1** (*coll.*) the Devil, invoked as a mild oath. **2** an extreme instance of (*a/ the deuce of an argument*). **the deuce to pay** serious consequences. †**deuced** (dū´sid) *a.* (*coll., euphem.*) damned. **deucedly** *adv.* [prob. from DEUCE[1] (G *Daus*, LG *duus* is used similarly)]
deus (dā´us) *n.* god. **deus ex machina** (eks mak´inə) *n.* **1** in Greek and Roman drama, a god brought on to resolve a seemingly irresolvable plot. **2** a contrived denouement. **Deus vobiscum** (vəbis´kəm) God be with you. **Deus vult** (vŭlt) God wills it. [L]
Deut. *abbr.* Deuteronomy.
deuteragonist (dūtərag´ənist) *n.* the second actor in a classical Greek play; the next actor in importance to the protagonist. [Gr. *deuteragōnistēs* (*deuteros*, second, *agōnistēs*, actor)]
deuterate (dū´tərāt) *v.t.* to replace hydrogen in (a substance) by deuterium. **deuteration** (-ā´shən) *n.*
deuterium (dūtiə´riəm) *n.* heavy hydrogen, an isotope of hydrogen with double mass. [Gr. *deuteros*, second]
deutero- (dū´tərō), **deuto-** (-tō) *comb. form* second, secondary. [Gr. *deuteros*]
Deutero-Isaiah (dūtərōī´zīə) *n.* the supposed writer of Isaiah XL–L.
deuteron (dū´təron) *n.* a heavy hydrogen nucleus.
Deuteronomy (dūtəron´əmi) *n.* the fifth book of the Pentateuch, containing a recapitulation of the Mosaic law. **Deuteronomic** (-rənom´-) *a.* **Deuteronomist** *n.* the supposed writer or one of the supposed writers of Deuteronomy. [L *Deuteronomium*, Gr. *Deuteronomion* (DEUTERO-, *nomos*, law)]
deuteroscopy (dūtəros´kəpi) *n.* second sight.
deuto- DEUTERO-.
deutoplasm (dū´tōplazm) *n.* the portion of the yolk that nourishes the embryo, the food yolk of an ovum or egg-cell.
Deutschmark (doich´mahk), **Deutsche Mark** (doich´ə) *n.* the standard unit of currency of Germany. [G]
deutzia (dū´tsiə, doit´siə) *n.* a Chinese or Japanese shrub of the genus *Deutzia*, with clusters of pink or white flowers. [J. *Deutz*, 18th-cent. Dutch botanist]
devalue (dēval´ū), **devaluate** (-āt) *v.t.* **1** to reduce the value of. **2** to stabilize (currency) at a lower level. **devaluation** (-ā´shən) *n.*
Devanagari (dāvənah´gəri) *n.* the formal alphabet in which Sanskrit and certain vernaculars are usually written. [Sansk., Hind., Marathi (Sansk. *deva*, god, *nāgarī*, alphabet, script)]
devastate (dev´əstāt) *v.t.* **1** to lay waste, to ravage. **2** to overwhelm, to upset greatly. **devastated** *a.* **devastating** *a.* (*coll.*) overwhelming, very upsetting. **devastatingly** *adv.* **devastation** (-vəstā´shən) *n.* **devastator** *n.* [L *dēvastātus*, p.p. of *dēvastāre* (DE-, *vastāre*, to waste)]
devein (dēvān´) *v.t.* to remove the main vein from.
develop (divel´əp) *v.t.* (*pres.p.* **developing,** *past, p.p.* **developed**) **1** to unfold or uncover, to bring to light gradually. **2** to work out. **3** to bring from a simple to a complex state. **4** to evolve. **5** to bring to completion or maturity by natural growth. **6** to begin to have (*He developed a bad cough*). **7** to render visible (as the picture latent in sensitized film). **8** to build on or change the use of (land). **9** in chess, to bring (a piece) into play. **10** to elaborate on (a musical theme). *~v.i.* **1** to expand. **2** to progress. **3** to be evolved. **4** to come to light gradually. **5** to come to maturity. **developable** *a.* **developable surface** *n.* a surface which can be converted into a plane with no overlap. **developer** *n.* **1** a person who or something which develops, esp. a

person who develops land. 2 a chemical agent used to expose the latent image on film or light-sensitive paper. **developing country** *n.* a poor country which is just beginning to become industrialized. **development** *n.* 1 the act of developing. 2 the state of being developed. 3 gradual growth and advancement. 4 an event which is likely to affect a situation. 5 evolution. 6 maturity, completion. 7 the process of bringing into distinctness the picture latent in sensitized film. 8 an area of land which has been developed. 9 (*Mus.*) the section of a sonata in which the themes are developed. 10 in chess, the act of bringing a piece into play. **developmental** (-men´-) *a.* 1 of or relating to development or growth. 2 evolutionary. **developmentally** *adv.* **development area** *n.* a region where new industries are being encouraged by Government to combat unemployment. [F *développer*, etym. uncertain (cp. It. *viluppare*, to enwrap, *viluppo*, a wrapping, a bundle)]

devest (divest´) *v.t.* 1 to undress. 2 to strip. 3 to denude, to deprive. 4 (*Law*) to alienate (a right or title). [DIVEST]

deviate[1] (dē´viāt) *v.i.* 1 to turn aside. 2 to stray or swerve from the path of duty. 3 to err. ~*v.t.* to cause to stray or err. **deviance, deviancy** *n.* **deviant** *a.* deviating from what is socially acceptable. ~*n.* a person whose behaviour deviates from what is socially acceptable. **deviation** (-ā´shən) *n.* 1 the act of deviating. 2 departure from orthodox Communist doctrine. 3 in statistics, the difference between one number in a series and the mean of that series. 4 the deflection of a compass from the true magnetic meridian. **deviationist** *n.* a person who departs from orthodox Communist doctrine. **deviator** *n.* **deviatory** (-viətəri) *a.* [L *dēviātus*, p.p. of *deviāre*, from *dēvius*, out of the way (DE-, *via*, way)]

deviate[2] (dē´viət) *n.* (*Psych.*) a person who deviates from the norm. ~*a.* deviant.

device (divīs´) *n.* 1 a contrivance, an invention. 2 an explosive, a bomb. 3 a plan, a scheme; a stratagem, a trick. 4 a design, a figure, a pattern. 5 a piece of computer hardware designed for a specific purpose (*a storage device*). 6 (*Her.*) an emblem or fanciful design, a motto. 7 †make, look. **to leave someone to their own devices** to leave someone to do as they please. [OF *devis*, fem. *devise*, late L *dīvīsa*, a division, mark, device, fem. of L *dīvīsum*, neut. p.p. of *dīvīdere*, to DIVIDE (cp. DEVISE)]

devil (dev´əl) *n.* 1 (*usu.* **Devil**) Satan, the chief spirit of evil. 2 any evil spirit. 3 a wicked, malignant or cruel person. 4 a person (*You lucky devil!*). 5 something troublesome. 6 a person of extraordinary energy, ingenuity and self-will devoted to selfish or mischievous ends. 7 an unfortunate person, a wretch. 8 a personification of evil. 9 energy, dash, unconquerable spirit (*It's the devil in him that makes him irresistible*). 10 a printer's errand boy. 11 a hot grilled dish, highly seasoned. 12 a kind of firework. 13 a device for tearing fishing nets. 14 a person who does literary work for which someone else takes the credit. 15 a barrister who prepares a case for another, or who takes the case of another without fee in order to gain reputation. 16 a spiked mill for tearing rags. 17 the Tasmanian devil. 18 (*S Afr.*) a dust devil. ~*v.t.* (*pres.p.* **devilling,** (*esp. N Am.*) **deviling,** *past, p.p.* **devilled,** (*esp. N Am.*) **deviled**) 1 to prepare (food) with highly-spiced condiments. 2 (*N Am.*) to harass, to torment. 3 to tear up rags with a devil. ~*v.i.* to act as a literary or legal devil. **a devil of a** (*coll.*) difficult or trying (*a devil of a problem*). **between the devil and the deep blue sea** torn between two equally undesirable alternatives. **devil a bit** not at all. **devil a one** not a single one. **like the devil** energetically or fast. **speak/ talk of the devil** said when the person who is the subject of conversation arrives. **the devil** 1 a nuisance. 2 a dilemma, an awkward fix. 3 (*as an interjection*) an expression of surprise or annoyance (*What the devil was that?*). **the devil's own job** (*coll.*) a very difficult task. **the devil take the hindmost** one must look after one's own interests. **the devil to pay** serious consequences. **the very devil** (*coll.*) something very difficult. **to give the devil his due** to give a person one dislikes credit for their good qualities. **to go to the devil** 1 to be damned. 2 (*imper.*) go away! **to play the devil with** to worry, to ruin. **devilfish** *n.* (*pl.* **devilfish**) 1 a devil ray. 2 any of various other fish, such as the stonefish. 3 (*Hist.*) an octopus. **deviling** *n.* (*dial.*) a swift. **devilish** *a.* 1 befitting a devil; diabolical; damnable. 2 mischievous. ~*adv.* (*coll.*) extraordinarily, very. **devilishly** *adv.* **devilishness** *n.* **devil-may-care** *a.* carefree and reckless. **devilment** *n.* mischief, roguery. **devil ray** *n.* any fish of the family Mobulidae. **devilry** *n.* (*pl.* **devilries**) 1 diabolical wickedness, esp. cruelty. 2 wild and reckless mischief, revelry or high spirits. 3 an act of devilry. 4 diabolism, black magic. 5 dealings with the Devil. **devil's advocate** *n.* 1 a person who puts the opposing view in a discussion without necessarily holding that view. 2 (*Hist.*) an official of the Roman Catholic Church appointed to oppose a proposed canonization or beatification. **devil's bit** *n.* a small dark blue scabious, *Succisa pratensis*. **devil's coach-horse** *n.* a large beetle, *Staphylinus olens*. **devil's darning-needle** *n.* a dragonfly. **devil's dozen** *n.* thirteen. **devil's dust** *n.* flock torn out of wool and made into cheap cloth. **devil's food cake** *n.* (*N Am.*) rich chocolate cake. **devils-on-horseback** *n.pl.* prunes wrapped in bacon. **devil's own** *n.* 1 the 88th Regiment of the line. 2 the Inns of Court Officers' Training Corps. **devil's tattoo** *n.* a drumming with the fingers upon a table etc. by persons when unthinking or impatient. **deviltry** *n.* (*pl.* **deviltries**) DEVILRY (under DEVIL). **devil-worship** *n.* worship of the Devil or devils; Satanism.[OE *dēoful*, L *diabolus*, Gr. *diabolos*, from *diaballein*, to slander (*dia*, through, *ballein*, to throw)]

devious (dē´viəs) *a.* 1 insincere and deceitful. 2 circuitous, rambling. 3 erring. 4 †out of the way, sequestered. **deviously** *adv.* **deviousness** *n.* [L *dēvius*; see DEVIATE[1]]

devise (divīz´) *v.t.* 1 to invent, to contrive; to form in the mind, to scheme, to plot. 2 (*Law*) to give or assign (property) by will. ~*n.* 1 the act of devising. 2 a will or clause of a will bequeathing real estate. **devisable** *a.* **devisee** (-zē´) *n.* (*Law*) a person to whom anything is devised by will. **deviser** *n.* a person who devises. **devisor** *n.* (*Law*) a person who bequeaths by will. [OF *deviser*, late L *dīvīsāre*, to divide, to devise, to think, freq. of L *dīvīdere* (p.p. *dīvīsus*), to DIVIDE]

devitalize (dēvī´təlīz), **devitalise** *v.t.* to deprive of vitality or of vital power. **devitalization** (-zā´shən) *n.*

devitrify (dēvit´rifī) *v.t.* (*3rd pers. sing. pres.* **devitrifies,** *pres.p.* **devitrifying,** *past, p.p.* **devitrified**) 1 to deprive of vitreous qualities. 2 to deprive (glass or vitreous rock) of transparency by making it crystalline. **devitrification** (-fikā´shən) *n.*

devocalize (dēvō´kəlīz), **devocalise** *v.t.* to make (a sound) voiceless or nonsonant.

devoice (dēvois´) *v.t.* to pronounce without vibrating the vocal cords.

devoid (divoid´) *a.* empty (of), lacking. [short for *devoided*, p.p. of obs. *devoid*, to empty, OF *devuidier*, from *vuide*, empty, VOID]

†**devoir** (dəvwah´) *n.* 1 a duty. 2 (*usu. pl.*) politeness, courtesy. [ME *dever*, OF *deveir*, L *debēre*, to owe]

devolution (dēvəloo´shən) *n.* 1 transference or delegation of authority, esp. from central to regional government. 2 passage from one person to another. 3 descent by inheritance. 4 descent in natural succession. 5 degeneration of species. 6 lapse of a right, privilege, or authority through desuetude. **devolute** (dē´-) *v.t.* to transfer (power or authority). **devolutionary** *a.*

devolutionist *n.* [L *dēvolūtus*, p.p. of *dēvolvere* (DE-, *volvere*, to roll)]
devolve (divolv´) *v.t.* to pass, transfer (duties or power) to another. ~*v.i.* **1** to be transferred, delegated or deputed. **2** to fall by succession, to descend. **devolvement** *n.* [L *dēvolvere*, as DEVOLUTION]
Devonian (divō´niən) *a.* **1** of or relating to Devon. **2** of or relating to the fourth period of the Palaeozoic era, between the Silurian and Carboniferous periods. ~*n.* **1** a native or inhabitant of Devon. **2** (*Geol.*) the Old Red Sandstone formation, well displayed in Devon. **Devonshire cream** (dev´ənshə) *n.* clotted cream. **Devonshire split** *n.* a yeast bun with jam and cream.
devonport DAVENPORT.
devore (dəvaw´rā), **dévoré** *a.* (of a fabric, esp. velvet) having a design etched with acid. [F, eaten]
dévot (dāvō´) *n.* a devotee. **dévote** (-vot´) *n.* a female devotee. [F, OF (DEVOUT)]
devote (divōt´) *v.t.* **1** to consecrate, to dedicate; to apply; to give wholly up (to). **2** †to doom, to consign (to ruin etc.); to curse. **devoted** *a.* **1** dedicated, ardently attached. **2** dedicated, consecrated (to). **devotedly** *adv.* **devotedness** *n.* **devotee** (devətē´) *n.* **1** an enthusiast of. **2** a religious zealot. **devotion** *n.* **1** deep, self-sacrificing attachment, intense loyalty. **2** (*pl.*) prayers, religious worship. **3** religious zeal. **4** the act of devoting. **5** the state of being devoted. **devotional** *a.* of or relating to religious devotion. **devotionality** (-nal´-) *n.* **devotionally** *adv.* [L *dēvōtus*, p.p. of *dēvovēre* (DE-, *vovēre*, to vow)]
devour (divowə´) *v.t.* **1** to eat up quickly and greedily. **2** (of fire) to destroy wantonly, to waste; to swallow up, to engulf. **3** to read eagerly. **4** to absorb, to overwhelm (*devoured by jealousy*). **devourer** *n.* **devouring** *a.* **devouringly** *adv.* [OF *devorer*, L *dēvorāre* (DE-, *vorāre*, to swallow)]
devout (divowt´) *a.* **1** deeply religious. **2** pious, filled with devotion. **3** sincere, genuine. **devoutly** *adv.* **devoutness** *n.* [ME, OF *devot*, L *devotus*, p.p. of *devovēre* to DEVOTE]
dew (dū) *n.* **1** moisture condensed from the atmosphere upon surface at evening and during the night. **2** freshness (*the dew of youth*). **3** dewy moisture, such as tears. ~*v.t.* to wet with dew. **dewberry** *n.* (*pl.* **dewberries**) **1** a shrub, *Rubus caesius*, which yields berries resembling blackberries. **2** its fruit. **dewclaw** *n.* **1** one of the bones behind a deer's foot. **2** the rudimentary upper toe often found in a dog's foot. **dewdrop** *n.* **1** a drop of dew. **2** a drop of mucus at the end of one's nose. **dewfall** *n.* **1** the falling of dew. **2** the time when dew falls. **dew point** *n.* the temperature at which dew begins to form. **dew-pond** *n.* a shallow, artificial pond formed on high land where water collects at night through condensation. **dew-worm** *n.* a large earthworm. **dewy** *a.* (*comp.* **dewier**, *superl.* **dewiest**) **1** wet with or as if with dew. **2** like dew. **dewily** *adv.* **dewiness** *n.* **dewy-eyed** *a.* naive, innocent. [OE *dēaw* (cp. Dut. *daauw*, Icel. *dögg*, Dan. *dug*, G *Tau*)]
dewan (diwahn´) *n.* **1** chief financial minister of an Indian state. **2** prime minister of an Indian state. **dewani** (-wah´ni) *n.* (*pl.* **dewanis**) the office of a dewan. [Arab., Pers. *dīwān* (cp. DIVAN)]
dewar (dū´ə) *n.* a type of vacuum flask, used to keep liquids or gases warm in scientific experiments. [Sir James *Dewar*, 1842–1923, British physicist]
dewater (dēwaw´tə) *v.t.* to remove water from.
Dewey Decimal System (dū´i) *n.* a system of library classification using ten main subject classes. [Melvil *Dewey*, 1851–1931, US inventor]
dewlap (dū´lap) *n.* **1** the flesh that hangs loosely from the throat of cattle and some dogs. **2** the flesh of a person's throat become flaccid through age. **3** the wattle of a turkey. **dewlapped** *a.* [etym. of *dew* uncertain; *lap* from OE *læppa*, a skirt, a LAP[1] (cp. Dan. *doglæb*, Norw. *doglæp*)]
DEW line (dū) *n.* the radar network in the Arctic regions of N America. [*d*istant *e*arly *w*arning]
deworm (dēwœm´) *v.t.* to rid (an animal) of worms.
Dexedrine® (dek´sədrēn) *n.* a dextrorotary isomer of amphetamine. [DEXTRO-, BENZEDRINE]
dexter[1] (deks´tə) *a.* **1** (*Her.*) situated on the right of a shield (to the spectator's left) etc. **2** †of, relating to or situated on the right-hand side. [L, a comparative from the root *dex-* (cp. Gr. *dexios*, *dexiteros*, Goth. *taihswa*, Sansk. *daksha*)]
dexter[2] (deks´tə) *n.* **1** a breed of small cattle originally from Ireland. **2** a member of this breed. [perh. from name of breeder]
dexterity (dekster´iti) *n.* **1** manual skill. **2** mental skill, cleverness. **3** right-handedness. **dexterous** (deks´-), **dextrous** *a.* having dexterity. **dexterously** *adv.* **dexterousness** *n.*
dextral (deks´trəl) *a.* **1** right-handed. **2** of or relating to the right. **3** (of a spiral shell) having the whorls turning towards the right. **4** (of a flatfish) having the right side uppermost. ~*n.* a right-handed person. **dextrality** (-tral´-) *n.* **dextrally** *adv.*
dextran (deks´tran) *n.* a carbohydrate produced by the action of bacteria in sugar solutions, used as a substitute for blood plasma in transfusions.
dextrin (deks´trin) *n.* a gummy substance obtained from starch, so called from its dextrorotatory action on polarized light. [F *dextrine*, from L *dextra*, fem. of DEXTER[1]]
dextro- (deks´trō) *comb. form* (*Chem.*) turning the plane of a ray of polarized light to the right, or in a clockwise direction (as seen looking against the oncoming light). [L *dexter*, the right hand]
dextrocardia (dekstrōkah´diə) *n.* a condition in which the heart lies on the right side of the chest instead of the left. **dextrocardiac** (-ak) *n.*
dextroglucose (dekstrōgloo´kōs) *n.* dextrose.
dextrogyrate (dekstrōjī´rət) *a.* causing to turn towards the right hand.
dextrorotatary (dekstrōrōtā´təri), **dextrorotary** (dekstrōrō´təri) *a.* causing to rotate clockwise. **dextrorotation** (-tā´shən) *n.*
dextrorse (deks´traws) *a.* rising from left to right in a spiral line. **dextrorsely** *adv.* [L *dextrorsum*, *-sus* (DEXTRO-, *-vorsum*, *-versum*, turned)]
dextrose (deks´trōs) *n.* a form of glucose which rotates polarized light clockwise; grape sugar.
dextrous DEXTEROUS (under DEXTERITY).
dey (dā) *n.* the title of the old sovereigns of Algiers, Tripoli and Tunis. [F, from Turk. *dāī*, lit. a maternal uncle, a title in the janizaries]
DF *abbr.* **1** Defender of the Faith. **2** direction-finder.
DFC *abbr.* Distinguished Flying Cross.
DFE *abbr.* Department for Education.
Dfl *abbr.* Dutch florin(s).
DFM *abbr.* Distinguished Flying Medal.
DG *abbr.* **1** by the grace of God (L *Dei gratia*). **2** thanks be to God (L *Deo gratias*). **3** Director General.
dg *abbr.* decigram(me).
dhal (dahl), **dal, dahl** *n.* **1** a split grain, pulse. **2** an Asian soup of or purée made from this. [Hind. *dal*, to split, from Sansk.]
dharma (dah´mə) *n.* in Hinduism and Buddhism, the fundamental concept of both natural and moral law, by which everything in the universe acts according to its essential nature or proper station. [Sansk., habit, law]
Dharuk (dŭr´uk) *n.* an extinct Australian Aboriginal language.
dhobi (dō´bi) *n.* (*pl.* **dhobis**) in the Indian subcontinent, a washerman. **dhobi itch** *n.* a fungal skin disease.

[Hind. *dhōbī*, from *dhōb*, washing, Sansk. *dhāv-*, to wash]

dhole (dōl) *n.* an Asian wild dog, *Cuon alpinus*. [etym. unknown]

dhoti (dō´ti) *n.* (*pl.* **dhotis**) a loincloth worn by male Hindus. [Hind.]

dhow (dow) *n.* a ship with one mast, a very long yard, and a lateen sail, used on the Arabian Sea. [etym. unknown]

DHSS *abbr.* (*Hist.*) Department of Health and Social Security.

dhurra DURRA.

dhurrie DURRIE.

DI *abbr.* 1 Defence Intelligence. 2 Detective Inspector. 3 Donor Insemination.

di-[1] (dī) *pref.* form of DIS- used before *b, d, g, l, m, n, r, s, v* and sometimes *j*.

di-[2] (dī) *pref.* 1 twice, two, dis-, double. 2 (*Chem.*) containing two atoms or groups of atoms of a specified kind. [Gr. *di-*, double, two]

di-[3] (dī) *pref.* form of DIA- used before a vowel.

dia. *abbr.* diameter.

dia- (dī´ə) *pref.* 1 through. 2 apart, across. [Gr. *dia*, through]

diabase (dī´əbās) *n.* an igneous rock which is an altered form of basalt; it includes most greenstone and trap. **diabasic** (-bā´sik) *a.*

diabetes (dīəbē´tēz) *n.* a disease characterized by excessive discharge of urine containing glucose, insatiable thirst and emaciation. **diabetes insipidus** (insip´idəs) *n.* diabetes caused by a disorder of the pituitary gland. **diabetes mellitus** (milī´təs) *n.* diabetes characterized by a disorder of carbohydrate metabolism, caused by insulin deficiency. **diabetic** (-bet´-) *a.* 1 of or relating to diabetes. 2 (of food) suitable for diabetics. ~*n.* a person suffering from diabetes. [L, from Gr., from *diabainein* (DIA-, *bainein*, to go)]

diablerie (diah´bləri) *n.* 1 dealings with the devil. 2 diabolism, magic or sorcery. 3 rascality, devilry. [F, from *diable*, L *diabolus*, DEVIL]

diabolic (dīəbol´ik) *a.* 1 of, relating to, proceeding from or like the devil. 2 outrageously wicked or cruel; fiendish, devilish, satanic, infernal. **diabolical** *a.* 1 diabolic. 2 (*coll.*) very bad, unpleasant. **diabolically** *adv.* **diabolism** (-ab´əl-) *n.* 1 devil-worship. 2 belief in the devil or in devils. 3 black magic. 4 devilish conduct or character, devilry. **diabolist** *n.* **diabolize, diabolise** *v.t.* 1 to make diabolical. 2 to represent as a devil. [F *diabolique*, L *diabolicus*, Gr. *diabolikos*, from *diabolos*, DEVIL]

diabolo (diab´əlō) *n.* (*pl.* **diabolos**) a game with a double cone spun in the air by a cord on two sticks, an adaptation of the old game of the devil on two sticks. [a recent formation from L *diabolus*, devil]

diacaustic (dīəkaw´stik) *a.* formed by refracted rays. [Gr. *kaustikos*, burning, from *kaiein*, to burn]

diachronic (dīəkron´ik) *a.* of or relating to the study of the historical development of a subject, e.g. a language. **diachronically** *adv.* **diachronism** (-ak´-) *n.* **diachronistic** (-akrənis´-) *a.* **diachronous** *a.* **diachrony** (-ak´-) *n.* [Gr. *chronos*, time]

diacid (dīas´id), **diacidic** (dīəsid´ik) *a.* 1 having two replaceable hydrogen atoms. 2 capable of neutralizing two protons with one molecule.

diaconal (dīak´ənəl) *a.* of or relating to a deacon. **diaconate** (-nāt) *n.* 1 the office, dignity or tenure of the office of a deacon. 2 deacons collectively. [F, from late L]

diacoustic (dīəkoos´tik) *a.* of or relating to diacoustics. **diacoustics** *n.* the science of refracted sounds.

diacritic (dīəkrit´ik), **diacritical** (-əl) *a.* 1 distinguishing, distinctive. 2 discerning, able to perceive distinctions. ~*n.* a diacritical mark. **diacritical mark** *n.* a mark (e.g. accent, cedilla, umlaut) attached to letters to show modified phonetic value or stress. [Gr. *diakritikos*]

diactinic (dīaktin´ik) *a.* transparent to or capable of transmitting actinic rays.

diadem (diə´dem) *n.* 1 a fillet or band for the head, worn as an emblem of sovereignty. 2 a crown, a wreath, a reward. 3 a crown of glory or victory. 4 supreme power, sovereignty. ~*v.t.* to adorn with a diadem. **diadem spider** *n.* the garden spider, *Epeira diadema*, so called from its markings. [OF *dyademe*, L, Gr. *diadēma* (DIA-, Gr. *deein*, to bind)]

diaeresis (dīer´əsis), (*N Am.*) **dieresis** *n.* (*pl.* **diaereses** (-sēz), (*N Am.*) **diereses**) 1 a mark placed over the second of two vowels to show that it must be pronounced separately, as *naïve*. 2 in prosody, a pause where the end of a foot coincides with the end of the word. **diaeretic** (-ret´-) *a.* [L, from Gr. *diairesis*, from *diaireein*, to divide (DI-[2], *haireein*, to take)]

diagenesis (dīəjen´isis) *n.* (*Geol.*) the changes which occur in sediments before they consolidate into rock.

diagnosis (dīəgnō´sis) *n.* (*pl.* **diagnoses** (-nō´sēz)) 1 determination of diseases by their symptoms. 2 a summary of these. 3 a summary of the characteristics by which one species is distinguished from another. 4 differentiation of character, style etc. by means of distinctive marks. 5 an analysis of phenomena or problems in order to gain an understanding. **diagnose** (-nōz) *v.t.* 1 to distinguish, to determine. 2 to ascertain the nature and cause of (a disease) from symptoms. ~*v.i.* to make a diagnosis of a disease. **diagnosable** *a.* **diagnostic** (-nos´-) *a.* of or relating to diagnosis. ~*n.* 1 a sign or symptom by which anything is distinguished from anything else. 2 a characteristic. **diagnostically** *adv.* **diagnostician** (-tish´ən) *n.* a person who diagnoses, esp. a doctor. **diagnostics** *n.* 1 (*as pl.*) computer programs used to identify faults in a system. 2 the science of diagnosing a disease. [L, from Gr. *diagnōsis* (DIA-, *gnōsis*, inquiry, knowledge, from *gignōskein*, to learn, to recognize)]

diagometer (dīəgom´itə) *n.* an instrument for measuring the relative conductivity of substances, orig. used to detect adulteration in olive oil. [F *diagomètre* (Gr. *diagein*, to carry across)]

diagonal (dīag´ənəl) *a.* 1 extending from one angle of a quadrilateral or multilateral figure to a nonadjacent angle, or from one edge of a solid to a nonadjacent edge. 2 oblique, crossing obliquely. 3 marked by oblique lines, ridges etc. ~*n.* 1 a straight line or plane extending from one angle or edge to a nonadjacent one. 2 a diagonal row, line, beam, tie etc. 3 a fabric with diagonal twills or ridges. **diagonally** *adv.* **diagonal scale** *n.* (*Math.*) a scale in which small divisions are marked by oblique lines, so as to make minute measurements. [L *diagōnālis*, Gr. *diagōnios* (DIA-, *gōnia*, an angle)]

diagram (dī´əgram) *n.* 1 (*Geom.*) a drawing made to demonstrate or illustrate some proposition, statement or definition. 2 an illustrative figure drawn roughly or in outline. 3 a series of marks or lines representing graphically the results of meteorological, statistical or other observations, or symbolizing abstract statements. ~*v.t.* (*pres.p.* **diagramming,** (*N Am.*) **diagraming,** *past, p.p.* **diagrammed,** (*N Am.*) **diagramed**) to represent in a diagram. **diagrammatic** (-grəmat´-) *a.* **diagrammatically** *adv.* [F *diagramme*, L and Gr. *diagramma*, from Gr. *diagraphein* (DIA-, *graphein*, to write)]

diagraph (dī´əgrahf) *n.* an instrument used for mechanically drawing outline sketches, enlargements of maps etc. [F *diagraphe*]

diagrid (dī´əgrid) *n.* (*Archit.*) a structure of diagonally intercepting beams or ribs.

diaheliotropic (dīəhēliətrop´ik) *a.* (*Bot.*) growing or turning transversely to the light. **diaheliotropism** (-ot´rəp-) *n.* a tendency to grow transversely to the light.

diakinesis (dīəkinē´sis) *n.* (*pl.* **diakineses** (-sēz)) the last stage of the prophase of meiosis, when homologous chromosomes cross over and separate.

dial (dī´əl) *n.* **1** the graduated and numbered face of a timepiece. **2** a similar plate on which an index finger marks revolutions, indicates steam-pressure etc. **3** an instrument for showing the time of day by the sun's shadow. **4** the control on a radio or television set for selecting wavelength or channel. **5** a control on a washing machine, cooker etc. **6** the rotating, numbered disc on a telephone. **7** (*sl.*) the human face. **8** †a timepiece, a watch. ~*v.t.* (*pres.p.* **dialling,** (*N Am.*) **dialing,** *past, p.p.* **dialled,** (*N Am.*) **dialed**) **1** to indicate (the telephone number) one wishes to call. **2** to measure or indicate with or as with a dial. ~*v.i.* to dial a telephone number. **dialler,** (*N Am.*) **dialer** *n.* **dialling** *n.* **dialling code** *n.* a group of numbers dialled to obtain an exchange in an automatic telephone dialling system. **dialling tone,** (*N Am.*) **dial tone** *n.* the sound given by a telephone to show that the line is clear. **dial-plate** *n.* the face of a timepiece or other instrument with a dial. [med. L *diālis*, daily, from *diēs*, day]

dial. *abbr.* dialect.

dialect (dī´əlekt) *n.* a form of speech or language peculiar to a particular district or people. **dialectal** (-lek´-) *a.* **dialectally** *adv.* **dialectology** (-tol´-) *n.* the study of dialects. **dialectologist** *n.* [L *dialectus*, Gr. *dialektos*, from *dialegesthai*, to discourse (DIA-, *legein*, to speak)]

Usage note The adjectives *dialectal* and *dialectical* or *dialectic* should not be confused: *dialectal* refers to speech, and *dialectic(al)* to reasoning.

dialectic (dīəlek´tik) *n.* dialectics. ~*a.* **1** dialectal. **2** of or relating to logic. **3** logical, argumentative. **dialectical** *a.* dialectic. **dialectically** *adv.* **dialectical materialism** *n.* the economic, political and philosophical system developed by Marx and Engels, based on the idea of constant change through a dialectical process of thesis, antithesis and synthesis. **dialectician** (-tish´ən) *n.* **1** a person skilled in dialectics. **2** a logician; a reasoner. **dialectics** *n.pl.* **1** the rules and methods of reasoning. **2** discussion by dialogue. **3** the investigation of truth by analysis. **4** in Kantian philosophy, critical analysis of knowledge based on science. **5** in Hegelian philosophy, the philosophical process of reconciling the contradictions of experience in a higher synthesis, the world process which is the objective realization of this synthesis. [OF *dialectique*, L *dialectica*, Gr. *dialektikē* (*technē*), the dialectic (art), as DIALECT]

Usage note See note under DIALECT.

dialectology DIALECT.

diallage (dī´əlij) *n.* a dark-to-bright-green nonaluminous variety of pyroxene, common in serpentine rock. **diallagic** (-laj´-) *a.* [Gr. *diallagē*, from *diallassein* (DIA-, *allassein*, to change)]

dialogue (dī´əlog), (*N Am.*) **dialog** *n.* **1** a conversation or discourse between two or more persons. **2** a literary composition in conversational form. **3** the conversational part of a novel etc. **4** a political discussion between two groups or nations. ~*v.i.* to hold a dialogue. ~*v.t.* to put into the form of dialogue. **dialogic** (-loj´-) *a.* of the nature of a dialogue. **dialogically** *adv.* **dialogist** (-al´əjist) *n.* **1** a person who takes part in a dialogue. **2** a writer of dialogues. **dialogue box** *n.* a small area on a computer screen prompting the user to enter data or make selections.

dialysis (dīal´isis) *n.* (*pl.* **dialyses** (-sēz)) **1** the process of separating crystalloid from colloid ingredients in soluble substances by passing through moist membranes. **2** the filtering of blood to remove waste products, either by semi-permeable membranes in the body, or by a kidney machine in the case of kidney failure. **3** a diaeresis. **dialyse** (dī´əlīz), (*esp. N Am.*) **dialyze** *v.t.* **dialyser** *n.* the apparatus in which the process of dialysis is performed. **dialytic** (-lit´-) *a.* [Gr. *dialusis* (DIA-, *luein*, to loose)]

diam. *abbr.* diameter.

diamagnetic (dīəmagnet´ik) *a.* of, relating to or exhibiting diamagnetism. ~*n.* a diamagnetic body or substance. **diamagnetically** *adv.* **diamagnetism** (-mag´nit-) *n.* **1** the force which causes certain bodies, when suspended freely and magnetized, to assume a position at right angles to the magnetic meridian, and point due east and west. **2** the branch of magnetism treating of diamagnetic substances and phenomena.

diamanté (dēəmon´tā) *n.* material covered with glittering particles, such as sequins. ~*a.* decorated with glittering particles. **diamantiferous** (dīəməntif´ərəs) *a.* yielding diamonds. **diamantine** (-man´tīn) *a.* diamond-like. [F *diamanter*, to adorn with diamonds, from *diamant*, DIAMOND]

diameter (dīam´itə) *n.* **1** a straight line passing through the centre of any object from one side to the other. **2** a straight line passing through the centre of a circle or other curvilinear figure, and terminating each way in the circumference. **3** the length of such a line. **4** transverse measurement, width, thickness. **5** in optics, the unit of measurement of magnifying power. **diametral** *a.* **diametrally** *adv.* **diametrical** (dīəmet´-), **diametric** *a.* **1** of or relating to a diameter, diametral. **2** along a diameter, direct. **3** directly opposed. **4** as far removed as possible. **diametrically** *adv.* [OF *diametre*, L and Gr. *diametros* (DIA-, *metrein*, to measure, cp. METER[1])]

diamond (dī´əmənd) *n.* **1** the hardest, most brilliant and most valuable of the precious stones, a transparent crystal of pure carbon, colourless or tinted. **2** a facet of this when cut. **3** a figure resembling this, a rhomb. **4 a** a playing card with red figures of this shape. **b** (*pl.*) a suit of such cards. **5** a baseball field or the square formed by the four bases. **6** a glazier's cutting tool with a diamond at the point. **7** a very small type for printing. **8** a glittering point or particle. ~*a.* **1** made of or set with diamonds. **2** resembling a diamond or lozenge. ~*v.t.* to adorn with or as if with diamonds. **diamond cut diamond** a meeting of two equally clever people. **rough diamond** ROUGH. **diamondback** *n.* **1** a N American terrapin, *Malaclemys terrapin*, with a diamond-patterned shell. **2** a deadly N American rattlesnake of the genus *Crotalus*, with diamond-shaped markings. **diamond-bird** *n.* PARDALOTE. **diamond-drill** *n.* an annular drill the cutting edge of which is set with diamonds for boring very hard substances. **diamond-field** *n.* a region yielding diamonds. **diamond in the rough** *n.* (*N Am.*) a rough diamond. **diamond jubilee** *n.* the 60th anniversary of a sovereign's accession. **diamond point** *n.* **1** a stylus or cutting tool with a point tipped with a diamond, used by etchers, engravers etc. **2** (*pl.*) an oblique crossing of railway lines. **diamond snake** *n.* a diamond-marked snake, *Morelia argus*, of southern Australia and Tasmania. **diamond wedding** *n.* the 60th anniversary of a marriage. [OF *diamant*, late L *diamas -antem*, L *adamas -antem*, Gr. *adamas*, ADAMANT]

Diana (dīan´ə) *n.* a woman who hunts. **Diana monkey** *n.* a large African monkey, *Cercopithecus diana*, with a white crescent-shaped band on its forehead. [Latin name of the Greek Artemis, the goddess of hunting]

diandrous (dīan´drəs) *a.* (*Bot.*) having only two stamens. [mod. L (DI-[2], Gr. *andr-*, stem of *anēr*, man, male)]

dianoetic (dīənōet´ik) *a.* of or relating to the rational or discursive faculty. [Gr. *dianoētikos*, from *dianoētos*, conceived in the mind, from *dianoeesthai* (DIA-, *noeein*, to think)]

dianthus (dīan´thəs) *n.* (*pl.* **dianthuses**) any plant of the genus *Dianthus* including the pinks and carnations. [Gr. *Dios*, of Zeus, *anthos*, flower]

diapason (dīəpā´zən) *n.* **1** a harmonious combination of notes. **2** a melodious succession of notes. **3** either of the two foundation stops of an organ. **4** a harmonious burst of music. **5** a recognized standard of pitch among musicians. **6** range, pitch. [L *diapāsōn*, Gr. *diapasōn* (short for *dia pasōn chordōn*, through all the chords)]

diapause (dī´əpawz) *n.* a period of suspended growth in insects. [Gr. *diapausis*, pause]

diaper (dī´əpə) *n.* **1** (*N Am.*) a baby's nappy. **2** a silk or linen cloth woven with geometric patterns. **3** a towel or napkin made of this. **4** a surface decoration consisting of square or diamond reticulations. ~*v.t.* **1** to decorate or embroider with this. **2** (*N Am.*) to change the nappy of. [OF *diapre*, *diasper*, Byz. Gr. *diaspros* (DIA-, *aspros*, white)]

diaphanometer (dīəfənom´itə) *n.* an instrument for measuring the transparency of the atmosphere. [see DIAPHANOUS]

diaphanous (dīaf´ənəs) *a.* (of a fabric) fine and almost transparent. **diaphanously** *adv.* [med. L *diaphanus*, Gr. *diaphanēs* (DIA-, *phan-*, stem of *phainein*, to show)]

diaphoresis (dīəfərē´sis) *n.* (*Med.*) sweating. **diaphoretic** (-ret´ik) *a.* having the power of promoting perspiration. ~*n.* a medicine having this property. [L, from Gr. from *diaphoreō*, to 'carry through']

diaphragm (dī´əfram) *n.* **1** the large muscular partition separating the thorax from the abdomen. **2** the vibrating disc in the mouthpiece or earpiece of a telephone, or in the loudspeaker of a radio receiver. **3** a dividing membrane or partition. **4** an annular disc excluding marginal rays of light. **5** a thin rubber or plastic cap placed over the mouth of the cervix as a contraceptive. **diaphragmatic** (-fragmat´-) *a.* **diaphragmatitis** (-fragmətī´tis) *n.* inflammation of the diaphragm. **diaphragm pump** *n.* a pump with a flexible diaphragm instead of a piston. [L, from Gr. *diaphragma*, from *diaphrēgnunai* (DIA-, *phrassein*, to fence)]

diaphysis (dīaf´isis) *n.* (*pl.* **diaphyses** (-sēz)) the shaft of a bone as distinct from the ends. [Gr. *diaphusis* (DIA-, *phuein*, to bring forth, to pierce)]

diapir (dī´əpiə) *n.* (*Geol.*) an anticline in which the overlying rock has been pierced by material from below. [Gr. *diapeirainein*, to pierce through]

diapositive (dīəpoz´itiv) *n.* a positive photographic transparency; a slide.

diarchy (dī´ahki), **dyarchy, dinarchy** (-nah´-) *n.* (*pl.* **diarchies, dyarchies, dinarchies**) **1** government by two rulers. **2** an instance of diarchy. **diarchal** (-ah´kəl), **diarchic** *a.* [Gr. *archia*, rule]

diarial, diarian etc. DIARY.

diarrhoea (dīərē´ə), (*N Am.*) **diarrhea** *n.* the excessive discharge of faecal matter from the intestines. **diarrhoeal, diarrhoeic** *a.* [L, from Gr. *diarrhoia* (DIA-, *rheein*, to flow)]

diarthrosis (dīahthrō´sis) *n.* (*pl.* **diarthroses** (-sēz)) an articulation of the bones permitting them to act upon each other; free arthrosis.

diary (dī´əri) *n.* (*pl.* **diaries**) **1** an account of the occurrences of each day. **2** the book in which these are registered. **3** a daily calendar with blank spaces for notes. **diarial** (dīeə´riəl) *a.* **diarian** (-eə´-) *n.* **diarist** *n.* a person who keeps a diary. **diaristic** (-ris´-) *a.* **diarize, diarise** *v.t.*, *v.i.* [L *diārium*, from *diēs*, a day]

diascope (dī´əskōp) *n.* an optical projector for showing transparencies.

Diaspora (dīas´porə) *n.* **1** (*Hist.*) the dispersion of the Jews after the Babylonian captivity. **2** Jews living outside Palestine, or now, outside Israel. **3** a dispersion or migration of any people. [Gr. *spora*, scatter]

diastaltic (dīəstal´tik) *a.* of or relating to reflex action and the nerves governing this. [Gr. *diastaltikos*, from *diastellein*, to separate (DIA-, *stellein*, to set, to send)]

diastase (dī´əstāz) *n.* a nitrogenous substance produced during the germination of all seeds, and having the power of converting starch into dextrine, and then into sugar. **diastasic** (-stā´-), **diastatic** (-stat´ik) *a.* [F, from Gr. *diastasis*, separation (DIA-, *stasis*, a placing, from the root *sta-*, to stand)]

diastasis (dīas´təsis) *n.* (*pl.* **diastases** (-sēz)) separation of bones without fracture, or of the pieces of a fractured bone. [as DIASTASE]

diastema (dīəstē´mə) *n.* (*pl.* **diastemata** (-tə)) a space between two adjacent teeth, as in most mammals. [L, from Gr. *diastēma* (as DIASTASE)]

diastole (dīas´təli) *n.* dilatation of the heart and arteries alternating with systole. **diastolic** (dīəstol´-) *a.* [med. L, from Gr. *diastolē*, from *diastellein* (DIA-, *stellein*, to send)]

diastrophism (dīas´trəfizm) *n.* deformation of the earth's crust, giving rise to mountains etc. [Gr. *diastrophē*, a twisting]

diastyle (dī´əstīl) *n.* (*Archit.*) an arrangement of columns in which the space between them is equal to three or four diameters of the shaft. ~*a.* arranged on this plan. [L *diastylos*, Gr. *diastulus* (DIA-, *stulos*, a pillar)]

diatessaron (dītes´əron) *n.* (*pl.* **diatessarons**) **1** a harmony of the four Gospels. **2** (*Mus.*) †the interval of a fourth, composed of a greater and lesser tone and a greater semitone. [OF, from L *diatessarōn*, Gr. *dia tessarōn*, by four]

diathermancy (dīəthœ´mənsi) *n.* (*pl.* **diathermancies**) the property of being freely pervious to heat. **diathermal** *a.* **diathermaneity** (-mənē´əti) *n.* **diathermic** *a.* **diathermous** *a.* [F *diathermansie* (DIA-, Gr. *thermansis*, heating, from *thermainein*, to heat)]

diathermy (dī´əthœmi) *n.* (*Med.*) the employment of high-frequency currents for the production of localized heat in the tissues.

diathesis (dīath´əsis) *n.* (*pl.* **diatheses** (-sēz)) a constitution of body predisposing to certain diseases. **diathetic** (dīəthet´-) *a.* [Gr., from *diatithenai* (DIA-, *tithenai*, to put)]

diatom (dī´ətəm) *n.* a member of the class of algae *Bacillariophyceae*, which have siliceous coverings and which exist in immense numbers at the bottom of the sea, multiplying by division or conjugation, and occurring as fossils in such abundance as to form strata of vast area and considerable thickness. **diatomaceous** (-mā´shəs) *a.* **diatomaceous earth** *n.* KIESELGUHR. **diatomic** (-tom´-) *a.* **1** (*Chem.*) containing only two atoms. **2** containing two replaceable univalent atoms. **diatomite** (-at´əmīt) *n.* KIESELGUHR. [Gr. *diatomos*, cut through, from *diatemnein* (DIA-, *temnein*, to cut)]

diatonic (dīəton´ik) *a.* (*Mus.*) **1** of the regular scale without chromatic alteration. **2** applied to the major and minor scales, or to chords, intervals and melodic progressions. **diatonically** *adv.* [F *diatonique*, L *diatonicus*, Gr. *diatonikos*, from *diatonos* (DIA-, *tonos*, TONE)]

diatribe (dī´ətrīb) *n.* an angry speech; a piece of harsh criticism or denunciation. [F, from L *diatriba*, Gr. *diatribē*, a wearing away, a discussion, a discourse, from *diatribein* (DIA-, *tribein*, to rub)]

diazepam (dīaz´ipam) *n.* a type of tranquillizer and muscle relaxant.

diazo (dīaz´ō) *a.* **1** (of a compound) having two nitrogen atoms and a hydrocarbon radical. **2** of a photocopying technique using a diazo compound exposed to light. ~*n.* (*pl.* **diazos, diazoes**) a copy made in this way. **diazotype** *n.* a diazo.

dib[1] (dib) *v.i.* (*pres.p.* **dibbing**, *past*, *p.p.* **dibbed**) to dap. **dibber** *n.* a dibble. [var. of DAB[1]]

dib[2] (dib) *n.* **1** a sheep's knuckle-bone. **2** (*pl.*) a children's game in which these are thrown into the air and caught on the back of the hand. **3** (*pl., sl.*) money. [prob. from DIB[1]]

dibasic (dībā´sik) *a.* containing two bases or two replaceable atoms.

dibber DIB[1].

dibble (dib´əl) *n.* a pointed instrument used to make a hole in the ground for seed. ~*v.t.* **1** to make holes in (soil) with a dibble. **2** to plant with a dibble. ~*v.i.* **1** to use a dibble. **2** to dap. **dibbler** *n.* a person who or something which dibbles. [perh. from DIB[1]]

dibranchiate (dībrang´kiət) *a.* of or relating to an order of cephalopods, *Dibranchiata*, having only two gills, the shell rarely external and never chambered. [Gr. *branchia*, gills]

dicast (dik´ast), **dikast** *n.* in Greek history, one of 6000 Athenians chosen each year to act as judges. **dicastic** (-kas´-) *a.* [Gr. *dikastēs*, from *dikē*, justice]

dice (dīs) *n.* (*pl.* **dice**) **1** a small cube marked with figures on the sides, used in gambling, being thrown from a box or cup. **2** (*as pl.*) more than one such cube. **3** a game played with these. **4** small cubes of food. ~*v.i.* to play at dice. ~*v.t.* **1** to chop (food) into small cubes. **2** to gamble (away) at dice. **3** to weave into a pattern with squares. **4** to trim or ornament with such a pattern. **5** (*Austral., sl.*) to leave, to reject. **no dice** an expression of refusal or lack of success. **to dice with death** DEATH. **dicer** *n.* [pl. of DIE[2]]

dicephalous (dīsef´ələs, -kef´-) *a.* having two heads on one body. [Gr. *dikephalos* (DI-[2], *kephalē*, head)]

dicey (dī´si) *a.* (*comp.* **dicier**, *superl.* **diciest**) (*coll.*) risky, difficult. [DICE]

dichlamydeous (dīkləmid´iəs) *a.* having both corolla and calyx. [Gr. *chlamus -udos*, a cloak]

dichloride (dīklaw´rīd) *n.* a compound having two atoms of chlorine with another atom.

dichlorodiphenyltrichloroethane (dīklawrōdīfenil-trīklawroē´thān, -fēnīl-) *n.* the full name for DDT.

dichogamous (dīkog´əməs) *a.* (*Bot.*) having stamens and pistils maturing at different times, so that self-fertilization is prevented. **dichogamy** *n.* [Gr. *dicho-*, asunder, *gamos*, wedded]

dichotomy (dīkot´əmi) *n.* (*pl.* **dichotomies**) **1** a separation into two. **2** a marked contrast. **3** (*Logic*) distribution of ideas into two mutually exclusive classes. **4** (*Astron.*) the moon's phase when half the disc is illuminated. **5** (*Zool., Bot.*) a continued bifurcation or division into two parts. **dichotomic** (-kətom´-) *a.* **dichotomist** *n.* **dichotomize, dichotomise** *v.t., v.i.* **dichotomous** *a.* [Gr. *dicho-*, as DICHOGAMOUS]

Usage note *Dichotomy* is sometimes used as though it meant dilemma or ambivalence, but both are best avoided.

dichroic (dīkrō´ik) *a.* assuming two or more colours, according to the direction in which light is transmitted. **dichroism** (dī´-) *n.* **dichroitic** (-it´-) *a.* **dichroscope** (dī´-) *n.* [Gr. *dichroos* (DI-[2], *chrōs*, colour, complexion)]

dichromate (dīkrō´māt) *n.* a double chromate.

dichromatic (dīkrəmat´ik) *a.* **1** characterized by or producing two colours, esp. of animals. **2** able to distinguish only two of the three primary colours. **dichromatism** (-krō´-) *n.*

dichromic (dīkrō´mik) *a.* having or perceiving only two colours. **dichromism** *n.* a form of colour-blindness in which only two of the three primary colours are distinguished. [Gr. *dichrōmos*, two-coloured, *chrōma*, colour]

dick[1] (dik) *n.* **1** a fellow or person. **2** (*sl.*) a detective. **3** (*sl., taboo*) the penis. **clever Dick** CLEVER. **dickhead** *n.* (*sl.*) a stupid or contemptible person. [*Dick*, short for Richard]

dick[2] (dik) *n.* a declaration. **to take one's dick** to make a solemn declaration; to swear. [prob. short for DECLARATION]

dicken (dik´ən) *int.* (*Austral., sl.*) used to express disbelief or disgust. [perh. from DICKENS or see DICKENSIAN]

dickens (dik´ənz) *n.* (*coll.*) the devil, the deuce (*How the dickens did she do that?*). [perh. from *Dickon*, Richard]

Dickensian (diken´ziən) *a.* **1** of, relating to or in the style of Charles Dickens 1812–70, British novelist. **2** applied to squalid conditions as described in Dickens's novels. ~*n.* an admirer of Dickens.

dicker (dik´ə) *v.i.* **1** to barter, to haggle; to carry on a petty trade. **2** to hesitate. ~*v.t.* to barter, to exchange. ~*n.* a deal or bargain. **dickerer** *n.* [ME *dyker*, late L *dicora*, L *decŭria*, a set of ten, from *decem*, ten]

dicky[1] (dik´i), **dickey** *n.* (*pl.* **dickies, dickeys**) (*coll.*) **1** a false shirt front. **2** a bird (used by or to children). **3** a driver's seat. **4** a seat behind the body of a carriage or a motor-car. **5** a pinafore or bib. **6** an ass, a donkey. **dicky bird** *n.* (*coll.*) a little bird (used by or to children). **dicky bow** *n.* a bow tie. [etym. uncertain]

dicky[2] (dik´i) *a.* (*comp.* **dickier**, *superl.* **dickiest**) (*sl.*) unsound, weak (*a dicky heart*). [etym. unknown]

diclinous (dī´klinəs) *a.* (*Bot.*) having the stamens and the pistils on separate flowers, on the same or different plants, as distinct from *monoclinous*. **diclinism** *n.* [Gr. *klinē*, a bed]

dicotyledon (dīkotilē´dən) *n.* (*pl.* **dicotyledons**) any plant of the class *Dicotyledones* of flowering plants including all of those with two cotyledons. **dicotyledonous** *a.*

dicrotic (dīkrot´ik) *a.* (of a pulse in an abnormal state) double-beating. [Gr. *dikrotos* (DI-[2], *krotos*, a beat)]

dict. *abbr.* dictionary.

dicta DICTUM.

Dictaphone® (dik´təfōn) *n.* an apparatus for recording sounds, used for taking down correspondence etc., to be transcribed afterwards.

dictate[1] (diktāt´) *v.t.* **1** to read or recite to another (words to be written or repeated). **2** to prescribe, to lay down with authority, to impose (terms etc.). ~*v.i.* **1** to give orders. **2** to utter words to be written or repeated by another. **dictation** *n.* **1** the dictating of material to be written down or recorded. **2** an instance of this, as a school exercise. **3** the material dictated. **4** the act or an instance of giving orders. **5** a command. **dictation speed** *n.* a rate of speaking which is slow enough for dictation. **dictator** *n.* **1** a person who dictates. **2** a person invested with supreme and often tyrannical authority. **3** a Roman magistrate created in time of emergency, and invested with absolute power. **4** a ruler with similar authority appointed in a time of civil disorder or securing the supremacy after a revolution. **dictatorial** (-tətaw´ri-) *a.* **1** of or relating to a dictator. **2** imperious, overbearing. **dictatorially** *adv.* **dictatorship** *n.* **dictatress** (-tris) *n.* a female dictator. [L *dictātus*, p.p. of *dictāre*, freq. of *dīcere*, to say]

dictate[2] (dik´tāt) *n.* an order, an injunction; a direction; a precept.

dictator, dictatorial etc. DICTATE[1].

diction (dik´shən) *n.* **1** the use of words. **2** manner of expression; style. [L *dictio*]

dictionary (dik´shənəri) *n.* (*pl.* **dictionaries**) **1** a book containing the words of any language in alphabetical order, with their definitions, pronunciations, parts of speech, etymologies and uses, or with their equivalents in another language. **2** a book containing information on any subject under words arranged alphabetically. [med. L *dictiōnārium*, from DICTION]

dictum (dik´təm) *n.* (*pl.* **dicta** (-tə), **dictums**) **1** a positive or dogmatic assertion. **2** OBITER DICTUM (under OBITER). **3** a maxim, a saying. [L, neut. p.p. of *dīcere*, to say]

dicynodont (dīsin´ədont) *n.* a large fossil reptile of a lizard-like form with turtle jaws. [Gr. *kun-* (stem of *kuōn*), dog, *odont-*, tooth]

did DO[1].

didactic (didak´tik, dī-) *a.* 1 adapted or tending to teach, esp. morally. 2 containing rules or precepts intended to instruct. 3 in the manner of a teacher. **didactically** *adv.* **didacticism** (-sizm) *n.* **didactics** *n.* the science or art of teaching. [Gr. *didaktikos*, from *didaskein*, to teach]

didakai DIDICOI.

diddicoy DIDICOI.

diddle (did´əl) *v.t.* 1 to cheat; to swindle. 2 (*dial.*) to jog, to jerk to and fro. ~*v.i.* (*N Am.*) to fritter away or waste time. **diddler** *n.* [etym. unknown]

diddly-squat (did´liskwot), **doodly-squat** (doo´dli-) *n.* (*N Am., sl.*) 1 anything at all (*He doesn't know diddly-squat*). 2 nothing. [var. of doodly-squat, perh. from, sl. *doodle*, excrement, *squat*, to defecate]

diddums (did´əmz) *int.* used to express commiseration to a baby. [baby-talk, did you/he/she]

didelphian (dīdel´fiən) *a.* of or relating to the Didelphidae, a family of marsupials, including the opossums. **didelphic** *a.* [Gr. *delphus*, a womb]

didgeridoo (dijəridoo´), **didjeridoo** *n.* (*pl.* **didgeridoos, didjeridoos**) an Australian musical instrument, a long, hollow wooden tube that gives a deep booming sound when blown. [Abor.]

didicoi (did´ikoi), **didakai** (-də-), **diddicoy** *n.* (*sl.*) an itinerant traveller or tinker, who is not a true Romany. [Romany]

didjeridoo DIDGERIDOO.

didn't (did´ənt) *contr.* did not.

dido (dī´dō) *n.* (*pl.* **didoes, didos**) (*N Am., coll.*) an antic, a caper. **to cut (up) didoes** to behave extravagantly or rowdily. [sl., etym. uncertain]

didst DO[1].

†**didymium** (didim´iəm) *n.* a mixture of the two elements neodymium and praseodymium, orig. thought to be a single element. [Gr. *didumos*, twin]

didymous (did´iməs) *a.* (*Bot.*) twin, growing in pairs. [Gr. *didymos*, twin]

didynamous (dīdin´əməs), **didynamian** (didinā´miən) *a..* (*Bot.*) having four stamens. [Gr. *dunamis*, power]

die[1] (dī) *v.i.* (*3rd pers. sing. pres.* **dies**, *pres.p.* **dying**, *past, p.p.* **died**) 1 to lose life, to expire; to depart this life. 2 to come to an end; to cease to exist. 3 to wither, to lose vitality, to decay. 4 to fail, to become useless, to cease to function. 5 to go out. 6 to cease or pass away gradually. 7 to faint, to fade away, to languish with affection. 8 (*Theol.*) to suffer spiritual death, to perish everlastingly. ~*v.t.* to undergo (a specified kind of death). **never say die** never give up. **to be dying** (*fig.*) to be eager (*I'm dying for a drink*). **to die away** to become gradually less distinct. **to die back** (of a plant) to die from the tip to the root. **to die down** 1 (of plants) to die off above ground, with only the roots staying alive in winter. 2 to become less loud, intense etc., to subside. **to die for** extremely attractive (*a figure to die for*). **to die hard** to be difficult to eradicate or suppress (*old habits die hard*). **to die in harness** HARNESS. **to die in one's shoes** SHOE. **to die like a dog** DOG. **to die off** to die in large numbers. **to die out** to become extinct. **to die with one's boots on** BOOT[1]. **die-away** *a.* fainting or languishing. **die-back** *n.* a disease which causes trees or shrubs to die back. **diehard** *n.* a person who is resistant to change, or who holds an untenable position, esp. in politics. [ME *degen*, *deghen*, Icel. *deyja* (cp. OS *dōian*, OHG *touwan*, from Gmc. *tāu-*)]

die[2] (dī) *n.* (*pl.* **dice, dies**) 1 (*pl.* **dice**) a dice. 2 hazard, chance, lot. 3 (*Archit.*) (*pl.* **dies**) the cube or plinth of a pedestal. 4 (*pl.* **dies**) a machine for cutting out, shaping or stamping. 5 (*pl.* **dies**) a stamp for coining money, or for impressing a device upon metal, paper etc. **straight as a die** 1 very straight. 2 completely honest. **the die is cast** an irrevocable decision has been taken. **die-cast** *v.t.* to shape (an object) by forcing molten lead or plastic into a reusable mould. **die-casting** *n.* **die-sinker** *n.* a person who cuts or engraves dies for coins, medals etc. **die-stamping** *n.* the act of embossing with a die. **diestock** *n.* a handle or stock to hold the dies in screw-cutting. [OF *de*, *det*, late L *dătum*, neut. of *dătus*, p.p. of *dăre*, to give]

dieffenbachia (dēfənbak´iə) *n.* any plant of the tropical American evergreen genus *Dieffenbachia.* [Ernst *Dieffenbach*, d. 1855, German horticulturalist]

dieldrin (dēl´drin) *n.* an insecticide containing chlorine. [Otto *Diels*, 1876–1954, and Kurt *Alder*, 1902–58, G chemists]

dielectric (dīilek´trik) *a.* nonconductive, insulating. ~*n.* any medium, such as glass, through or across which electric force is transmitted by induction; a non-conductor; an insulator. **dielectrically** *adv.* **dielectric constant** *n.* permittivity.

diene (dī´ēn) *n.* (*Chem.*) an organic compound which has two double bonds between carbon atoms.

dieresis DIAERESIS.

dies (dē´āz) *n.* (*pl.* **dies**) a day. **dies faustus** (fows´təs) *n.* an auspicious day. **Dies irae** (ē´rī) *n.* 1 a day of wrath, the Day of Judgement. 2 a 13th-cent. Latin hymn describing the Last Judgement, used in the mass for the dead. **dies non** (non) *n.* 1 a day on which business cannot be transacted. 2 a day that does not count. [L]

diesel (dē´zəl) *n.* 1 any vehicle driven by a diesel engine. 2 diesel oil. **diesel-electric** *a.* using power from a diesel-operated electric generator. ~*n.* a locomotive so powered. **diesel engine** *n.* a type of reciprocating internal-combustion engine which burns heavy oil. **dieselize, dieselise** *v.t.* to adapt or convert (an engine) to diesel fuel. ~*v.i.* to be equipped with a diesel engine. **dieselization** (-zā´shən) *n.* **diesel oil, diesel fuel** *n.* a heavy fuel oil used in diesel engines. [Rudolf *Diesel*, 1858–1913, German engineer]

diesis (dī´əsis) *n.* (*pl.* **dieses** (-sēz)) 1 the double dagger (‡); a reference mark. 2 (*Mus.*) the difference between three true major thirds and one octave. [L, from Gr., from *diienai* (DIA-, *hienai*, to send)]

diet[1] (dī´ət) *n.* 1 a prescribed course of food followed for health reasons, or to reduce or control weight. 2 the food and drink a person usually takes. 3 regular activities (*a diet of soaps and videos*). ~*a.* with a low fat or sugar content (*diet cola*). ~*v.i.* (*pres.p.* **dieting**, *past, p.p.* **dieted**) to take food, esp. according to a prescribed regimen or to reduce or control weight. ~*v.t.* 1 to feed according to the rules of medicine. 2 to feed in a restricted way as a punishment. **to go on a diet** to begin to follow a strict plan of eating so as to lose weight. **dietary** *a.* of or relating to a rule of diet. ~*n.* (*pl.* **dietaries**) 1 a regimen; a prescribed course of diet. 2 a fixed daily allowance of food, esp. in prisons, workhouses etc. **dietary fibre** *n.* foodstuffs with a high fibre content; roughage. **dieter** *n.* **dietetic** (-tet´-), **dietitical** *a.* 1 of or relating to diet. 2 prepared according to special dietary needs. **dietetically** *adv.* **dietetics** *n.* 1 the science of diet. 2 rules of diet. **dietitian** (-tish´ən), **dietician** *n.* a professional adviser on dietetics. [OF *diete*, late L *diēta*, Gr. *diaita*, mode of life (prob. conn. with *zaein*, to live)]

diet[2] (dī´ət) *n.* 1 a legislative assembly or federal parliament holding its meetings from day to day (esp. as an English name for Continental parliaments). 2 (*Hist.*) a conference or congress, esp. on international affairs. 3 (*Sc.*) a session of a court or any assembly. **dietine** (-tin) *n.* a subordinate or local diet. [L *diēta* (as DIET[1]), confused with *diēs*, a day]

dieter, dietetic etc. DIET[1].

diethyl ether (dīē´thīl) *n.* (*Chem.*) ether.

dietine DIET[2].

dif- DIS-.

differ (dif´ə) *v.i.* **1** to be dissimilar. **2** to disagree in opinion; to dissent; to be at variance; to quarrel. **to agree to differ** to give up trying to convince each other. **to differ in kind** KIND. [F *différer*, L *differre* (DIF-, *ferre*, to bear)]

difference (dif´rəns) *n.* **1** the state of being unlike or distinct. **2** the quality by which one thing differs from another. **3** disproportion between two things. **4** the remainder of a quantity after another quantity has been subtracted from it. **5** a distinction, a differential mark, the specific characteristic or differentia. **6** a point or question in dispute, a disagreement in opinion, a quarrel, a controversy. **7** (*Her.*) a figure on a coat-of-arms which distinguishes one family from another, or shows how distant a younger branch is from the elder. ~*v.t.* **1** to distinguish; to make different. **2** (*Her.*) to mark with a difference. **to make a difference 1** to have an effect. **2** to behave differently. **to make no difference** to have no effect. **to split the difference** SPLIT. **with a difference** with something distinctive added. [as DIFFER]

different (dif´rənt) *a.* **1** unlike, dissimilar. **2** distinct, not the same. **3** (*coll.*) unusual. **a different kettle of fish** KETTLE. **differently** *adv.* **differently abled** *a.* disabled. **differentness** *n.*

Usage note *From* is the safest preposition to use after *different*: though well established, *different to* is still sometimes disapproved of, and *different than* is more usual in American than British English.

differentia (difəren´shiə) *n.* (*pl.* **differentiae** (shiē)) something which distinguishes one species from another of the same genus. [L, difference, diversity; see DIFFER]

differential (difəren´shəl) *a.* **1** differing; consisting of a difference. **2** making or depending on a difference or distinction. **3** (*Math.*) of or relating to infinitesimal difference. **4** relating to specific differences. **5** of or relating to differentials. **6** relating to the difference between sets of motions acting in the same direction, or between pressures etc. ~*n.* **1** something distinguishing between two examples of the same kind. **2** (*Math.*) an infinitesimal difference between two consecutive states of a variable quantity. **3** a differential gear. **4** the amount of difference within a wages structure between rates of pay for different classes of work. **differential coefficient** *n.* (*Math.*) the measure of the rate of change of a function relative to its variable. **differential equation** *n.* an equation containing differentials. **differential gear** *n.* a device of bevelled planetary and other wheels which permits of the relative rotation of two shafts driven by a third; applied to a car, it enables the rear (driving) wheels to rotate at different speeds when rounding a corner. **differentially** *adv.* **differential motion** *n.* a mechanical movement in which a part moves with a velocity equal to the difference between the velocities of two other parts. [as DIFFER]

Usage note The noun *differential* should not be used as though it simply meant difference (without comparison of levels of the same thing).

differentiate (difəren´shiāt) *v.t.* **1** to make different. **2** to constitute a difference between, of or in. **3** to discriminate by the differentia, to mark off as different. **4** (*Math.*) to obtain the differential coefficient of. **5** (*Biol.*) to develop variation in. **6** to specialize. ~*v.i.* to develop so as to become different, to acquire a distinct character. **differentiation** (-ā´shən) *n.* **differentiator** *n.* [mod. L *differentiātus*, p.p. of *differentiāre*; see DIFFER]

difficult (dif´ikəlt) *a.* **1** hard to do or carry out. **2** troublesome. **3** hard to please. **4** not easily managed. **5** hard to understand. **6** bad-tempered. **7** full of difficulties or problems (*a difficult time*). **difficultly** *adv.* **difficultness** *n.* **difficulty** *n.* (*pl.* **difficulties**) **1** the quality of being difficult. **2** anything difficult. **3** an obstacle; objection. **4** reluctance, scruple. **5** (*pl.*) financial problems. **with difficulty** awkwardly, not easily. [OF *difficulté*, L *difficultās -tātem*, from *difficilis*, (DIF-, *facilis*, easy)]

diffident (dif´idənt) *a.* **1** lacking confidence in oneself or one's powers. **2** bashful, modest, shy. **diffidence** *n.* **1** lack of self-confidence. **2** bashfulness, shyness. **diffidently** *adv.* [L *diffidens -entem*, pres.p. of *diffidere* (DIF-, *fidere*, to trust, from *fidēs*, faith)]

diffract (difrakt´) *v.t.* **1** to break into parts. **2** to bend or deflect (a ray of light) by passing it close to an opaque object. **diffraction** *n.* **diffraction grating** *n.* an array of fine, closely-spaced opaque lines on glass which disperses light into its component colours since the amount of diffraction differs for different-coloured rays of light. **diffractive** *a.* **diffractively** *adv.* **diffractometer** (-frak´tom-) *n.* an instrument used in measuring diffraction. [L *diffractus*, p.p. of *diffringere* (DIF-, *frangere*, to break)]

☒ **diffrent** common misspelling of DIFFERENT.

diffuse[1] (difūz´) *v.t.* **1** to pour forth. **2** to spread abroad by pouring out. **3** to circulate. **4** to cause to intermingle by diffusion. **5** to dissipate. ~*v.i.* **1** to be diffused. **2** to intermingle by diffusion. **diffused** *a.* **diffused lighting** *n.* a form of illumination in which the light is softened and spread over an area instead of being concentrated in one spot. **diffusedly** (-zid-) *adv.* **diffuser** *n.* a person who or something which diffuses or circulates. **diffusible** *a.* **diffusibility** (-bil´-) *n.* [L *diffūsus*, p.p. of *diffundere* (DIF-, *fundere*, to pour)]

Usage note See note under DEFUSE.

diffuse[2] (difūs´) *a.* **1** diffused, scattered, spread out. **2** copious, verbose, not concise. **3** (*Bot.*) diverging or spreading widely. **diffusely** *adv.* **diffuseness** *n.* **diffusion** (-zhən) *n.* **1** the act of diffusing a liquid, fluid etc. **2** the spreading abroad of news etc. **3** the state of being widely dispersed. **4** the mingling of liquids, gases or solids through contact. **5** spread of cultural elements from one community to another. **diffusionist** *n.* **diffusion-tube** *n.* an instrument for determining the rate of diffusion of different gases. **diffusive** *a.* spreading, circulating, widely distributed. **diffusively** *adv.* **diffusiveness** *n.* [as DIFFUSE[1]]

dig (dig) *v.t.* (*pres.p.* **digging,** *past, p.p.* **dug** (dŭg)) **1** to excavate or turn up with a spade or similar instrument, or with hands, claws etc. **2** to thrust or push into something. **3** to obtain by digging. **4** to make by digging. **5** to poke. **6** (*dated sl.*) to approve of or like. ~*v.i.* **1** to work with a spade. **2** to excavate or turn up ground with a spade or other implement. **3** to search, make one's way, thrust, pierce or make a hole by digging. ~*n.* **1** a piece of digging (esp. archaeological). **2** a thrust, a poke. **3** a cutting remark. **4** (*N Am., coll.*) a hard-working student. **to dig a pit for** PIT[1]. **to dig in** (*coll.*) to begin eating. **to dig oneself in 1** to take up permanent quarters; to refuse to budge. **2** to make oneself indispensable. **to dig one's heels in** HEEL[1]. **to dig out 1** to obtain by digging. **2** to obtain by research. **to dig up 1** to excavate. **2** to extract or raise by digging. **3** to break up (ground) by digging. **4** to obtain by research. **digger** *n.* **1** a person who digs, esp. a gold-miner. **2** an implement, machine or part of a machine that digs. **3** (*coll.*) an Australian or New Zealander, esp. a soldier. **4** (*Austral., coll.*) a fellow, a mate. **digger wasp** *n.* any of several wasps that dig a hole in the ground for a nest. **digging** *n.* **1** the act of excavating with a spade, etc. **2** (*pl.*) a goldmine or goldfield. **3** (*pl., coll.*) lodgings. **digs** *n.pl.* (*coll.*) lodgings. [prob. from F *diguer*, to make a dike (*digue*)]

digamist DIGAMY.

digamma (dīgam´ə) *n.* (*pl.* **digammas**) (*F*) a letter in the oldest Greek alphabet, which had the sound of *w*, named after its resemblance to two gammas placed one above the other. [L, from Gr. (DI-[2], *gamma*, the letter *g*)]

digamy (dig´əmi) *n.* (*pl.* **digamies**) marrying a second time. **digamist** *n.* **digamous** *a.* [L, Gr. *digamia*, from Gr. *digamos* (DI-[2], *gamos*, marriage)]

digastric (dīgas´trik) *a.* having a double belly or protuberance. ~*n.* the digastric muscle. **digastric muscle** *n.* a double muscle which depresses the lower jaw. [Gr. *gastēr*, belly]

digest[1] (dījest´, dij-) *v.t.* **1** to break (food) down in the stomach into forms which can be easily assimilated by the body; to promote the digestion of. **2** to assimilate, to understand. **3** to arrange under proper heads or titles, to classify; to reduce to system or order. **4** to arrange methodically in the mind; to think over. **5** to soften and prepare by heat. ~*v.i.* **1** to be digested. **2** to be prepared by heat. **digester** *n.* **1** a person who digests. **2** anything which helps to promote digestion. **3** an apparatus for cooking food by exposure to heat above boiling point. **digestible** *a.* **digestibility** (-bil´-) *n.* **digestibly** *adv.* **digestion** (-jes´chən) *n.* **1** the act or process of assimilating food in the stomach; the conversion of food into chyme. **2** the power of digesting. **3** the act of extracting the essence from a substance, stewing. **4** mental reduction to order and method. **digestive** *a.* of, relating to or promoting digestion. ~*n.* **1** any substance which aids or promotes digestion. **2** a digestive biscuit. **digestive biscuit** *n.* a semi-sweet biscuit made of wholemeal flour. **digestively** *adv.* [L *dīgestus*, p.p. of *dīgerere* (DI-[1], *gerere*, to carry)]

digest[2] (dī´jest) *n.* **1** a compendium or summary arranged under proper heads or titles. **2** a magazine containing summaries of articles etc. in current literature. **3** (*Law*) a collection of Roman laws arranged under proper heads, such as the pandects of Justinian.

digger, digging DIG.

†dight (dīt) *a.* dressed, adorned, embellished. [OE *dihtan*, L *dictāre* (cp. G *dichten*, to make poetry)]

digit (dij´it) *n.* **1** a finger or toe. **2** the measure of a finger's breadth, or three-quarters of an inch. **3** any numeral under ten (so called from the primitive habit of counting on the fingers). **4** the 12th part of the diameter of the sun or moon *(used to express the quantity or magnitude of an eclipse)*. **digital** *a.* **1** representing data in the form of a series of tiny signals. **2** showing information by displaying digits, rather than by pointers and a dial. ~*n.* (*Mus.*) a key on a keyboard instrument. **digital audio tape** *n.* a tape which is recorded using a digital sound signal. **digital clock** *n.* a clock without a traditional face, the time being indicated by a display of digits. **digital computer** *n.* a computer which uses binary or decimal notation. **digitalize, digitalise** *v.t.* to digitize. **digitally** *adv.* **digital to analog converter** *n.* a device for the conversion of digital values into analog form. **digital watch** *n.* a watch without a traditional face, the time being indicated by a display of digits. **digitize, digitise** *v.t.* to put into digital form for use in a computer. **digitization** (-zā´shən) *n.* [L *digitus*]

digitalin (dijitā´lin), **digitalia** (-liə) *n.* an alkaloid obtained from the foxglove.

digitalis (dijitā´lis) *n.* **1** the dried leaves of the foxglove, which act as a cardiac sedative. **2** any member of a genus of scrophulariaceous plants, *Digitalis*, containing the foxglove. [mod. L, pertaining to the fingers, alluding to G *Fingerhut*, thimble]

digitate (dij´itāt), **digitated** (-ātid) *a.* **1** (*Zool.*) having finger-like processes. **2** (*Bot.*) branching into distinct leaves or lobes like fingers. **digitately** *adv.* **digitation** (-ā´shən) *n.* [L *digitātus*, from *digitus*, DIGIT]

digitiform (dij´itifawm) *a.* finger-shaped.

digitigrade (dij´itigrād) *a.* (of an animal, as a cat, dog, hyena and weasel) having the heel raised above the ground and walking on their toes. ~*n.* a digitigrade animal. [F, from L *digitus*, DIGIT, *-gradus*, walking]

diglot (dī´glot) *a.* bilingual. ~*n.* a bilingual book or person.

diglyph (dī´glif) *n.* (*Archit.*) a projection like a triglyph, but with two channels instead of three. [Gr. *digluphos* (DI-[2], *gluphein*, to carve)]

dignify (dig´nifī) *v.t.* (*3rd pers. sing. pres.* **dignifies,** *pres.p.* **dignifying,** *past, p.p.* **dignified**) **1** to invest with dignity. **2** to make worthy or illustrious. **3** to give the appearance of dignity to. **dignified** *a.* invested with dignity; stately; gravely courteous. **dignifiedly** *adv.* [OF *dignifier*, late L *dignificāre* (*dignus*, worthy)]

dignity (dig´niti) *n.* (*pl.* **dignities**) **1** a calm, serious and respectable manner, stateliness. **2** worth, nobility. **3** estimation, rank. **4** the importance due to rank or position. **5** a high office, a position of importance or honour. **beneath someone's dignity** degrading, in someone's own opinion. **to stand on one's dignity** to assume a manner showing one's sense of self-importance. **dignitary** *n.* (*pl.* **dignitaries**) a person who holds a position of dignity, esp. in the Church. [OF *dignité*, L *dignitās -tātem* (*dignus*, worthy)]

digraph (dī´grahf) *n.* a combination of two letters to represent one simple sound, such as *ea* in *mead* or *th* in *thin*. **digraphic** (-graf´-) *a.* [Gr. *graphē*, a mark]

digress (dīgres´) *v.i.* **1** to deviate, to wander from the main topic. **2** to stray from the direct path. **digresser** *n.* **digression** (-gresh´ən) *n.* **digressive** *a.* **digressively** *adv.* **digressiveness** *n.* [L *dīgressus*, p.p. of *dīgredī* (DI-[1], *gradī*, to step, from *gradus*, a step)]

digs DIG.

dihedral (dīhē´drəl) *a.* (*Math.*) of the nature of a dihedron. ~*n.* a dihedral angle. **dihedral angle** *n.* an angle made by the wing of an aeroplane in relation to the horizontal axis. **dihedron** (-drən) *n.* (*pl.* **dihedra, dihedrons**) (*Geom.*) a figure with two sides or surfaces. [Gr. *hedra*, seat]

dihybrid (dīhī´brid) *n.* the offspring of parents that differ in two pairs of genes.

dihydric (dīhī´drik) *a.* (*Chem.*) containing two hydroxil groups.

dikast DICAST.

dik-dik (dik´dik) *n.* any of several small E African antelopes of the genus *Madoqua*. [from an E Afr. language]

dike DYKE.

diktat (dik´tat) *n.* **1** a settlement imposed, after a war, on the defeated. **2** an order or statement allowing no opposition. [G, dictation, from L *dictāre*, to dictate]

dilacerate (dilas´ərāt) *v.t.* to tear into pieces. **dilaceration** (-ā´shən) *n.* [L *dīlacerātus*, p.p. of *dīlacerāre*]

dilapidate (dilap´idāt) *v.t.* to damage, to bring into decay or ruin. ~*v.i.* to fall into decay or ruin. **dilapidated** *a.* ruined; shabby. **dilapidation** (-ā´shən) *n.* **1** the process of decaying owing to lack of repair. **2** a state of partial ruin, decay. **3** the action of an incumbent in suffering ecclesiastical buildings etc. to fall into disrepair. **4** charge for making this good. **dilapidator** *n.* [L *dīlapidātus*, p.p. of *dīlapidāre* (DI-[1], *lapid-*, stem of *lapis*, stone)]

dilate (dīlāt´) *v.t.* to expand, to widen, to enlarge in all directions. ~*v.i.* **1** to be extended or enlarged; to expand, to swell. **2** to speak at length on a subject. **dilatable** *a.* **dilatability** (-bil´-) *n.* **dilatancy** *n.* **dilatant** *a.*, *n.* **dilatation** (-lətā´shən) *n.* **1** expansion. **2** the act of dilating. **dilation** *n.* dilatation. **dilation and curettage** *n.* D AND C. **dilatometer** (dilətom´itə) *n.* an instrument used to measure changes in dimension. **dilator** *n.* **1** a muscle that dilates the parts on which it acts. **2** a surgical instrument for dilating the walls of a cavity. [F *dilater*, L *dīlātāre* (*lātus*, broad)]

dilatory (dil´ətəri) *a.* 1 causing or tending to cause delay. 2 addicted to or marked by procrastination. 3 slow, tardy. **dilatorily** *adv.* **dilatoriness** *n.* [L *dīlātōrius*, from *dīlātōr -tōrem*, a delayer (from *dīlāt-*, p.p. stem of *differre*, to DEFER[1])]

dildo (dil´dō) *n.* (*pl.* **dildos, dildoes**) an object serving as an erect penis, used as a sex aid. [etym. uncertain]

dilemma (dilem´ə, dī-) *n.* 1 an argument in which a choice of alternatives is presented, each of which is unfavourable; a position in which a person is forced to choose between equally unfavourable alternatives. 2 inability to decide between two alternatives. 3 a difficult situation. **the horns of a dilemma** HORN. **dilemmatic** (-limat´-) *a.* [L, from Gr. *dilēmma* (DI-[2], *lēmma*, an assumption, from *lambanein*, to take)]

Usage note *Dilemma* should not simply be used to mean a problem.

dilettante (dilətan´ti) *n.* (*pl.* **dilettanti** (-ti), **diletantes**) 1 a lover or admirer of the fine arts. 2 a superficial amateur, a would-be connoisseur, a dabbler. ~*a.* 1 amateurish, superficial. 2 art-loving. **dilettantish** *a.* **dilettantism** *n.* [It., from *dilettare*, L *dēlectāre*, to DELIGHT]

diligence[1] (dil´ijəns) *n.* 1 steady application or assiduity in business of any kind. 2 care, heedfulness. [see DILIGENCE[2]]

diligence[2] (dil´ijəns) *n.* a public stagecoach, formerly used in France and adjoining countries. [F]

diligent (dil´ijənt) *a.* 1 assiduous in any business or task. 2 persevering, industrious, painstaking. **diligently** *adv.* [F, from L *dīligens -entem*, pres.p. of *dīligere* (*legere*, to choose)]

dill (dil) *n.* 1 an annual umbellifer, *Anethum graveolens*, cultivated for its aromatic seeds, and for its flavour. 2 the leaves or seeds, used as a herb in cooking. 3 (*Austral., New Zeal., sl.*) a a fool. b a dupe. **dill pickle** *n.* a pickled cucumber flavoured with dill. **dill-water** *n.* a remedy for flatulence in children, prepared from the seeds of dill. [OE *dile* (cp. Dut. *dille*, G *Dill*)]

dilly (dil´i) *n.* (*pl.* **dillies**) (*N Am., coll.*) a remarkable person or thing. ~*a.* (*comp.* **dillier**, *superl.* **dilliest**) (*Austral., coll.*) silly.

dillybag (dil´ibag) *n.* an Australian Aboriginal basket or bag made of rushes or bark. [Austral. Abor. *dilli*]

dilly-dally (dil´i dal´i) *v.i.* (*3rd pers. sing. pres.* **dilly-dallies,** *pres.p.* **dilly-dallying,** *past, p.p.* **dilly-dallied**) (*coll.*) 1 to loiter about; to waste time. 2 to hesitate. [redupl. of DALLY]

dilute (dīloot´, dil-) *v.t.* 1 to make (a liquid) thin or weaken by adding water. 2 to reduce the strength or power of; to water down. ~*a.* 1 diluted, weakened. 2 washed out, faded, colourless. **diluent** (dil´ūənt) *a.* making thin or liquid; diluting. ~*n.* something which dilutes. **dilution** *n.* [L *dīlūtus*, p.p. of *dīluere* (DI-[1], *luere*, to wash)]

diluvial (diloo´viəl), **diluvian** (-iən) *a.* 1 of or relating to Noah's flood. 2 (*Geol.*) a produced by or resulting from a flood. b of or relating to the diluvium or glacial drift. **diluvialist** *n.* one who regards certain physical phenomena as the result of Noah's flood or a series of catastrophic floods. **diluvium** (-iəm) *n.* (*pl.* **diluvia**) an accumulation of deposits apparently the result of water action on a vast scale, formerly attributed to Noah's flood, now referred to the drift or boulder formation. [L *dīluviālis*, from *dīluvium*, a deluge, from *dīluere*, as DILUTE]

dim (dim) *a.* (*comp.* **dimmer**, *superl.* **dimmest**) 1 lacking in light or brightness; somewhat dark. 2 obscure; not clear, not bright. 3 faint, indistinct, misty. 4 without lustre, tarnished, dull. 5 not clearly seen. 6 (of eyes) unable to see clearly. 7 imperfectly heard. 8 not clearly understanding or understood. 9 (*coll.*) stupid, unintelligent. ~*v.t.* (*pres.p.* **dimming**, *past, p.p.* **dimmed**) 1 to make dim. 2 (*N Am.*) to dip (headlights). ~*v.i.* to become dim. **to take a dim view of** (*coll.*) to regard pessimistically, to view with suspicion or disfavour. **dimly** *adv.* **dimmer** *n.* 1 a device whereby an electric lamp can be switched on and off gradually. 2 (*N Am.*) a a small parking light on a vehicle. b a dipped headlight. **dimmish** *a.* **dimness** *n.* [OE (cp. Icel. *dimmr*, MHG *timmer, timbar*)]

dim. *abbr.* 1 dimension. 2 diminuendo. 3 diminutive.

dime (dīm) *n.* a silver coin of the US, worth 10 cents, or one-tenth of a dollar. **a dime a dozen** cheap, ordinary. **on a dime** 1 (*N Am., coll.*) a within a very short distance. b very quickly. **dime novel** *n.* (*N Am.*) a sensational story. [OF *dime, disme*, L *decima*, fem. of *decimus* (*decem*, ten)]

dimension (dimen´shən, dī-) *n.* 1 measurable extent or magnitude, length, breadth, height, thickness, depth, area, volume etc. 2 (*pl.*) size. 3 one of a number of unknown or variable quantities contained as factors in a given product (thus ab^2c^3 is a term of six dimensions). 4 an aspect. **dimensional** *a.* **dimensioned** *a.* 1 having dimensions. 2 (*usu. in comb.*) proportional. **dimensionless** *a.* [F, from L *dīmensio -ōnem*, from *dīmensus*, p.p. of *dīmetīrī* (DI-[1], *metīrī*, to measure)]

dimer (dī´mə) *n.* (*Chem.*) a chemical composed of two identical molecules. **dimeric**[1] (-mer´ik) *a.* **dimerize, dimerise** *v.t.* to cause to form a dimer. ~*v.i.* to form a dimer. **dimerization** (-ā´shən) *n.* [*-mer*, formed on anal. of POLYMER]

dimeric[1] DIMER.

dimeric[2] DIMEROUS.

dimerous (dim´ərəs) *a.* having two parts, joints, divisions etc., arranged in pairs. **dimeric**[2] (dīmer´-) *a.* bilaterally symmetrical.

dimeter (dim´ətə) *n.* a verse of two metrical feet. [L *dimetrus*, Gr. *dimetros* (DI-[2], *metron*, measure)]

dimethyl (dīmē´thīl) *n.* (*Chem.*) ethane, an organic compound in which two equivalents of methyl take the place of two of hydrogen. **dimethylsulphoxide** (-sŭlfok´sīd), (*N Am.*) **dimethylsulfoxide** *n.* (*Chem.*) a colourless odourless liquid, used as a solvent and in skin treatment.

dimetrodon (dī´mētrədon) *n.* a large carnivorous reptile of the genus *Dimetrodon*, of the Permian period. [Gr. *metron*, measure, *odous odent-*, tooth]

dimidiate (dimid´iət) *a.* 1 divided into two halves. 2 (*Bot.*) divided or split into parts. **dimidiation** (-ā´shən) *n.* [L *dīmidiātus*, p.p. of *dīmidiāre*, from *dīmidium*, half (*medius*, middle)]

diminish (dimin´ish) *v.t.* 1 to make smaller or less. 2 to reduce in quantity, power, rank etc. 3 to taper. 4 to disparage, to degrade. 5 to take away or subtract from. 6 (*Mus.*) to lessen by a semitone. ~*v.i.* to become less, to decrease. **diminishable** *a.* **diminished** *a.* 1 made less or smaller, reduced in size or quality. 2 (*Mus.*) lessened by a semitone. **diminished responsibility** *n.* a plea in law in which criminal responsibility is denied on the grounds of mental derangement. **diminishingly** *adv.* **diminishing returns** *n.pl.* progressively smaller increases in output in spite of increased work or expenditure. **diminution** (-nū´-) *n.* 1 the act of diminishing. 2 the amount subtracted. 3 the state of becoming less or smaller. 4 (*Mus.*) lessening by a semitone. [formed on anal. of obs. *diminue*, F *diminuer*, L *dīminuere*, to break into small pieces + e.g. minish]

diminuendo (diminūen´dō) *a., adv.* (*Mus.*) gradually decreasing in loudness. ~*n.* (*pl.* **diminuendos, diminuendi** (-di)) 1 a gradual decrease in loudness. 2 a passage characterized by this. ~*v.i.* (*3rd pers. sing. pres.* **diminuendoes**, *pres.p.* **diminuendoing**, *past, p.p.*

diminuendoed) to decrease gradually in loudness. [It., pres.p. of *diminuire*, L *dīminuere*; see DIMINISH]
diminution DIMINISH.
diminutive (dimin´ūtiv) *a.* **1** small, tiny. **2** (of a word or suffix) expressing diminution. ~*n.* **1** a word formed from another to express diminution in size or importance, or affection. **2** anything of a small size. **diminutival** (-tī´-) *a.* **diminutively** *adv.* **diminutiveness** *n.*
dimissory (dim´isəri) *a.* dismissing, discharging; giving permission to depart. **dimissory letter** *n.* a letter addressed by one bishop to another, giving permission for the bearer to be ordained by the latter. [L *dīmissōrius*, from *dīmittere* (DI-[1], *mittere*, to send)]
dimity (dim´iti) *n.* (*pl.* **dimities**) a strong cotton fabric with stripes or patterns, chiefly used for bed-hangings. [It., pl. of *dimito*, late L *dimitum*, Gr. *dimitos* (DI-[2], *mitos*, a thread)]
dimmer, dimmish DIM.
dimorphic (dīmaw´fik) *a.* having or occurring in two distinct forms. **dimorphism** *n.* **1** the power of assuming or crystallizing into two distinct forms. **2** a difference of form between members of the same species. **3** a state in which two forms of flower are produced by the same species. **dimorphous** *a.* [Gr. *dimorphos* (DI-[2], *morphē*, form)]
dimple (dim´pəl) *n.* **1** a small natural depression on the cheek or chin. **2** a little depression or hollow. **3** a shallow dell or hollow in the ground. ~*v.t.* to mark with dimples. ~*v.i.* to form dimples. **dimply** *a.* (*comp.* **dimplier**, *superl.* **dimpliest**). [ME *dympull*; etym. uncertain (cp. G *Tümpel*, a pool, OHG *dumphilo*)]
dim sum (dim sŭm´), **dim sim** (sim´) *n.* a Chinese dish of small steamed dumplings with various fillings. [Cantonese *tím sam*, from *tím*, dot, *sam* heart]
dimwit (dim´wit) *n.* (*coll.*) a stupid person. **dimwitted** (-wit´-) *a.*
DIN (din) *n.* a method of classifying the speed of photographic film by sensitivity to light (the greater the light sensitivity the higher the speed). [acronym for *D*eutsche *I*ndustrie *N*orm (G, German industry standard)]
din (din) *n.* a loud and continued noise. ~*v.t.* (*pres.p.* **dinning,** *past, p.p.* **dinned**) **1** to harass with clamour. **2** to stun with a loud continued noise. ~*v.i.* to make a din. **to din into** to teach by constant repetition. [OE *dyn, dyne* (whence *dynnan*, to make a loud noise) (cp. Icel. *dynr*, Sansk. *dhūni*)]
dinar (dē´nah) *n.* **1** the standard unit of currency in the countries which formerly made up Yugoslavia. **2** the standard unit of currency of various N African and Middle Eastern countries. [Arab., Pers. *dīnār*, late Gr. *dēnarion*, L *dēnārius*, DENARIUS]
dinarchy DIARCHY.
din-din (din´din), **din-dins** *n.* (*coll.*) dinner (used by or to children).
dine (dīn) *v.i.* to take dinner. ~*v.t.* to give or provide a dinner for. **to dine on** to eat (something) for dinner. **to dine out** to be invited out to dinner. **to dine out on** to be popular socially, because of (something interesting to recount). **diner** *n.* **1** a person who dines. **2** a railway dining car. **3** (*N Am.*) a small, inexpensive restaurant. **4** a small dining room. **diner-out** *n.* a person who is frequently invited out to dinner. **dinette** (-net´) *n.* **1** an alcove or a small part of a room set aside for eating. **2** (*N Am.*) a dining table and chairs for a dinette. **dining** *n.* **dining car** *n.* a railway coach in which meals are cooked and served. **dining hall, dining room** *n.* a room for eating dinner in. **dining table** *n.* a table for eating dinner at. [F *dîner*, prob. from a late L *disjūnāre* or *disjējūnāre* (DIS-, L *jējūnus*, fasting)]
dinero (dineə´rō) *n.* (*N Am., sl.*) money.
ding[1] (ding) *v.t.* †to strike; to beat violently. ~*v.i.* **1** to ring, keep sounding. **2** (*Sc.*) to knock or thump. ~*n.* a ringing sound. **ding-a-ling** (ding´əling) *n.* **1** the sound made by a bell. **2** (*N Am.*) a mad or silly person. [ME *dingen* (cp. Icel. *dengja*, Swed. *dänga*)]
ding[2] (ding) *n.* (*Austral., sl.*) a lively party. [perh. from DING-DONG]
Ding an sich (ding an zikh´) *n.* (*Philos.*) a thing in itself. [G]
dingbat (ding´bat) *n.* (*sl.*) **1** (*N Am., Austral.*) a stupid person. **2** (*pl., Austral., New Zeal.*) **a** madness. **b** an attack of nerves.
ding-dong (ding´dong) *n.* **1** the sound of a bell. **2** (*coll.*) a violent argument. **3** a wild party. **4** a jingle, a jingling rhyme or tune. ~*a.* **1** (of a fight or contest) intense. **2** sounding like a bell; jingling. ~*adv.* **1** vigorously, intensely. **2** like the sound of a bell. ~*v.i.* to ring; to jingle. [onomat.]
dinge (dinj) *n.* a dent. ~*v.t.* to make a dent in. [etym. unknown]
dinges (ding´əs) *n.* (*S Afr., coll.*) a name for any person or thing whose name is forgotten or unknown; a thingummy. [Afrikaans, thing]
dinghy (ding´gi) *n.* (*pl.* **dinghies**) **1** a small ship's boat. **2** any small boat. **3** a small inflatable rubber boat. **4** a rowing-boat on the Ganges. [Hind. *dēngī* or *dīngī*]
dingle (ding´gəl) *n.* a dell, a wooded valley between hills. [etym. uncertain]
dingo (ding´go) *n.* (*pl.* **dingoes, dingos**) **1** the Australian wild dog, *Canis dingo.* **2** (*Austral., sl.*) a cowardly or despicable person.
dingy (din´ji) *a.* (*comp.* **dingier,** *superl.* **dingiest**) **1** soiled, grimy. **2** of a dusky, soiled or dun colour. **dingily** *adv.* **dinginess** *n.* [perh. from DUNG]
dink (dingk) *n.* (*coll.*) DINKY[2].
dinkum (ding´kəm) *a.* (*Austral., New Zeal., coll.*) good, genuine, satisfactory. **fair dinkum** FAIR[1]. **dinkum oil** *n.* the truth.
dinky[1] (ding´ki) *a.* (*comp.* **dinkier,** *superl.* **dinkiest**) (*coll.*) **1** charming, dainty, pleasing. **2** (*N Am.*) insignificant. [etym. unknown]
dinky[2] (ding´ki) *n.* (*pl.* **dinkies**) (*coll.*) either partner of a socially upwardly mobile couple with two incomes and no children. [acronym for *d*ual *i*ncome *n*o *k*ids]
dinner (din´ə) *n.* **1** the main meal of the day. **2** a feast, a banquet. **dinner dance** *n.* a dinner followed by dancing. **dinner hour** *n.* the time set apart for dinner. **dinner jacket** *n.* a man's formal jacket, usu. black, less formal than a dress coat, without tails and worn with black tie. **dinner lady** *n.* a woman who cooks or serves school lunches. **dinnerless** *a.* **dinner party** *n.* a social gathering where guests are invited to someone's house for dinner. **dinner service, dinner set** *n.* the set of dishes, used for serving dinner. **dinner table** *n.* a dining table. **dinner time** *n.* the time when dinner is eaten. **dinner-wagon** *n.* a tray or set of trays or shelves on castors. [F *dîner*, to DINE]
dinoceras (dīnos´ərəs) *n.* (*pl.* **dinocerases**) any member of an extinct genus of gigantic mammals of N America, apparently with three pairs of horns. [Gr. *deinos*, terrible, *keras*, horn]
dinoflagellate (dīnōflaj´əlāt) *n.* any of a group of unicellular aquatic organisms with two flagella. [mod. L *Dinoflagellata*, from Gr. *dinos* whirling, L *flagellum*]
dinosaur (dī´nəsaw) *n.* **1** a gigantic Mesozoic reptile. **2** an outdated person, thing or organization. **dinosaurian** (-saw´riən) *a., n.* [Gr. *deinos*, terrible, *sauros*, lizard]
dinothere DEINOTHERE.
dint (dint) *n.* **1** the mark or dent caused by a blow. **2** †a blow, a stroke. ~*v.t.* to mark with a dint. **by dint of** by force of; by means of. [OE *dynt* (cp. Icel. *dyntr*)]
dioc. *abbr.* **1** diocesan. **2** diocese.
diocese (dī´əsis) *n.* the district under the jurisdiction of a bishop. **diocesan** (-os´-) *a.* of or relating to a diocese. ~*n.* **1** a person who has ecclesiastical jurisdiction over

a diocese; a bishop or archbishop. **2** a member of the clergy of a diocese. [OF, from L *dioecēsis*, Gr. *dioikēsis* (DI-[3], *oikeein*, to keep house, to inhabit)]

diode (dī´ōd) *n.* **1** a simple electron tube in which the current flows in one direction only between two electrodes. **2** a semiconductor with two terminals. [Gr. *hodos*, way]

dioecious (dīē´shəs) *a.* **1** (*Bot.*) having the stamens on one individual and the pistils on another. **2** (*Zool.*) having the sexes in separate individuals, as distinct from *monoecious*. [mod. L (DI-[2], Gr. *oikos*, house]

dioestrus (dīēs´trəs), **diestrus** *n.* a period between periods of oestrus.

diol (dī´ol) *n.* (*Chem.*) any alcohol with two hydroxyl groups in each molecule.

Dionysiac (dīəniz´iak), **Dionysian** (-iən) *a.* **1** of or relating to Dionysus (the Greek god of wine). **2** wild, unrestrained.

Diophantine equation (dīəfan´tin) *n.* (*Math.*) an indeterminate equation which needs an integral or rational solution. [*Diophantos*, *c.* AD 275, Alexandrian mathematician]

diopside (dīop´sīd) *n.* pyroxene, esp. the transparent variety. [F (DI-[2], Gr. *opsis*, appearance)]

dioptase (dīop´tās) *n.* an emerald-green ore of copper. [F (DI-[3], Gr. *optos*, visible)]

dioptre (dīop´tə), (*N Am.*) **diopter** *n.* a unit of refractive power, being the power of a lens with a focal distance of one metre. **dioptric** *a.* **1** affording a medium for assisting the sight in the view of distant objects. **2** refractive. **3** of or relating to dioptrics. **dioptrically** *adv.* **dioptrics** *n.* the part of optics which treats of the refraction of light in passing through different mediums, esp. through lenses. [Gr. *dioptrikos*, from *dioptra*, an optical instrument (DI-[3], *op-*, stem of verb, to see, *-tra*, instr. suf.)]

diorama (dīərah´mə) *n.* **1** a painting in which natural phenomena are depicted by means of change of colour and light. **2** a scenic representation viewed through an aperture by means of reflected and transmitted light, various alterations of colour and lighting imitating natural effects. **3** a miniature set for a film or television programme. **dioramic** (-ram´-) *a.* [Gr. *horama* (*horaein*, to see)]

diorite (dī´ərīt) *n.* a granite-like rock, consisting principally of hornblende and feldspar. **dioritic** (-rit´-) *a.* [F, from Gr. *diorizein*, to distinguish (DI-[3], *horos*, a boundary)]

Dioscuri (dīoskū´rē) *n.pl.* the twins Castor and Pollux. [Gr. *Dioskouroi* (*Dios*, gen. of *Zeus*, *kouroi koroi*, pl. of *koros*, a lad)]

dioxan (dīok´san), **dioxane** (-ān) *n.* (*Chem.*) a colourless, insoluble, toxic liquid.

dioxide (dīok´sīd) *n.* (*Chem.*) one atom of a metal combined with two of oxygen.

dioxin (dīok´sin) *n.* (*Chem.*) a highly toxic substance found in some weedkillers which causes birth defects, cancers and various other diseases.

DIP (dip) *n.* (*Comput.*) a kind of integrated circuit consisting of two rows of pins in a small piece of plastic or ceramic. **DIP switch** *n.* an electronic device with switches used to select an operating mode. [*d*ual *in*-line *p*ackage]

Dip. *abbr.* Diploma.

dip (dip) *v.t.* (*pres.p.* **dipping,** *past p.p.* **dipped**) **1** to plunge into a liquid for a short time, to immerse. **2** to baptize by immersion. **3** to wash, to dye, to coat by plunging into a liquid. **4** to lower for an instant. **5** to put (the hand or a ladle) into liquid and scoop out. **6** to lower (the headlights). **7** (*Naut.*) to salute by lowering (the flag) and hoisting it again. **8** to make (a candle) by dipping the wick in tallow. **9** to scoop up. *~v.i.* **1** to plunge into liquid for a short time. **2** to sink, e.g. below the horizon. **3** to become lower or smaller, esp. briefly. **4** to bend downwards, to bow. **5** to slope or extend downwards. **6** to dip a hand or a ladle into a liquid and scoop something out. **7** to choose a leader in a children's game by means of a rhyme. *~n.* **1** the act of dipping in a liquid. **2** a short swim. **3** a candle made by dipping a wick in melted tallow. **4** the quantity taken up at one dip or scoop. **5** a preparation for washing sheep. **6** sauce, gravy etc. into which something is to be dipped. **7** a savoury mixture into which biscuits or raw vegetables are dipped before being eaten. **8** depth or degree of submergence. **9** the angle at which strata slope downwards into the earth. **10** (*sl.*) a pickpocket. **11** (*N Am., sl.*) a foolish person. **to dip into 1** to draw upon (e.g. resources). **2** to read from cursorily. **3** to take a brief interest in. **to dip out** (*Austral., sl.*) to miss out (on). **to dip the flag** FLAG[1]. **dipchick** *n.* the dabchick. **dip-net** *n.* a small fishing net with a long handle. **dip of the horizon** *n.* the apparent angular depression of the visible horizon below the horizontal plane through the observer's eye, due to his elevation. **dip of the needle** *n.* the angle which a magnetic needle makes with the horizontal. **dipper** *n.* **1** a person who dips. **2** (*coll.*) a Baptist or Anabaptist. **3** (*Astron.*) the Great Bear. **4** popular name for several birds, esp. the water ouzel. **5** a ladle. **dipping** *n.* **dipping-needle, dipping compass** *n.* a magnetized needle which, when mounted on an axis passing at right angles through its centre of gravity, will point downwards indicating the inclination of the lines of magnetic force. **dip-pipe** *n.* a pipe bent down from a gas main with its end plunged into liquid to form a seal. **dipshit** *n.* (*N Am., sl.*) a despicable person. **dipstick** *n.* **1** a rod for measuring the level of liquid in a container, esp. oil in a vehicles engine. **2** (*sl.*) a foolish or despicable person. **dip switch** *n.* a device in a car for dipping headlights. **dip-trap** *n.* a dip-pipe. [OE *dyppan*, cogn. with *dēop*, DEEP (cp. Dut. *doopen*, G *taufen*)]

Dip. A.D. *abbr.* Diploma in Art and Design.

Dip. Ed. *abbr.* Diploma in Education.

dipeptide (dīpep´tīd) *n.* a peptide with two amino acid molecules in its structure.

dipetalous (dīpet´ələs) *a.* bipetalous.

diphase (dī´fāz), **diphasic** (-fā´zik) *a.* (*Physics*) having two phases.

Dip. H.E. *abbr.* Diploma of Higher Education.

diphosphate (dīfos´fāt) *n.* (*Chem.*) a compound containing two phosphate groups in the molecule.

diphtheria (difthiə´riə) *n.* an infectious disease characterized by acute inflammation and the formation of a false membrane, chiefly on the pharynx, nostrils, tonsils and palate, causing breathing difficulties. **diphtherial** (-ther´-), **diphtheric** *a.* **diphtheritic** (-thərit´-) *a.* **diphtheritis** (-thərīt´is) *n.* **diphtheroid** (dif´thər-) *a.* [F *diphthérie*, Gr. *diphthera*, leather, skin]

Usage note Pronunciation as (dip-) is best avoided.

diphthong (dif´thong) *n.* **1** the union of two vowels in one syllable. **2** a digraph or combination of two vowel characters to represent a vowel sound. **3** either of the vowel ligatures æ or œ. **diphthongal** (-thong´gəl), **dipthongic** (-gik) *a.* **diphthongically** *adv.* **diphthongize, dipthongise** *v.t.* **diphthongization** (-zā´shən) *n.* [F *diphthongue*, L *diphthongus*, Gr. *diphthongos* (DI-[2], *phthongos*, voice)]

diphyllous (dīfil´əs) *a.* (*Bot.*) having two leaves or sepals. [Gr. *phullon*, a leaf]

diphyodont (dif´iōdont) *a.* of or relating to mammals which have two sets of teeth, one deciduous, the other permanent. [Gr. *diphuēs*, of double nature, *odous odontos*, tooth]

dipl. *abbr.* **1** diploma. **2** diplomat. **3** diplomatic.

diplo- (dip´lō) *comb. form* double. [Gr. *diploos*]

diploblastic (diplōblas´tik) *a.* (*Bot.*) having two germ layers. [Gr. *blastos*, a sprout]
diplocardiac (diplōkah´diak) *a.* having the heart double or the two sides separated.
diplococcus (diplōkok´əs) *n.* (*pl.* **diplococci** (-kok´sī)) (*Biol.*) any coccus occurring usually in pairs.
diplodocus (diplod´əkəs) *n.* a very large dinosaur of the genus *Diplodocus*, characterized by a large tail and a small head.
diploë (dip´lōē) *n.* the spongy tissue between the plates of the skull. [Gr., double]
diploid (dip´loid) *a.* **1** having the full number of paired homologous chromosomes. **2** double, twofold. *~n.* a diploid cell or organism. **diploidic** *a.* **diploidy** *n.* the state of being diploid.
diploma (diplō´mə) *n.* (*pl.* **diplomas**) **1** a certificate of a degree, licence etc. **2** a document conveying some authority, privilege or honour. **3** a charter, a state paper. **diplomaed** (-məd), **diploma´d** *a.* **diplomaless** *a.* **diplomate** (dip´ləmāt) *n.* a person who has a diploma. [L, from Gr. *diplōma* (*diploos*, double, folded)]
diplomacy (diplō´məsi) *n.* **1** the art of conducting negotiations between nations. **2** the act of negotiating with foreign nations. **3** skill in conducting negotiations of any kind. **4** adroitness, tact. **diplomat** (dip´ləmat) *n.* **1** a professional diplomatist. **2** a person who is skilled or trained in diplomacy. **diplomatic** (-mat´-) *a.* **1** of or relating to diplomacy or ambassadors. **2** adroit, tactful. **3** (of an edition) being a faithful reproduction of the original. **diplomatically** *adv.* **diplomatic bag** *n.* a bag used for sending official mail, free of customs control, to and from embassies and consulates. **diplomatic corps** *n.* the body of diplomatic representatives accredited to any government. **diplomatic immunity** *n.* the immunity from taxation and local laws given to diplomats resident in a foreign country. **diplomatic pouch** *n.* (*NAm.*) a diplomatic bag. **diplomatic relations** *n.pl.* official relations between countries marked by the presence of diplomats in each other's country. **diplomatics** *n.* **1** the art or science of ascertaining the authenticity, date, genuineness etc. of ancient literary documents. **2** †diplomacy. **diplomatic service** *n.* that part of the Civil Service which provides diplomats to represent Britain abroad. **diplomatist** *n.* a person skilled or engaged in diplomacy. **diplomatize, diplomatise** *v.i.* **1** to act as a diplomatist. **2** to practise the arts of a diplomatist. [F *diplomatie*, from *diplomate*, from *diplomatique*, mod. L *diplōmaticus*, from DIPLOMA]
diplomate DIPLOMA.
diplont (dip´lont) *n.* (*Biol.*) an animal or plant with a diploid number of chromosomes in its cells. [Gk. *ont-*, stem of *ōn*, a being]
diplopia (diplō´piə) *n.* a disorder of the eyes in which the patient sees objects double. [Gr. *ōps*, an eye]
diplotene (dip´lōtēn) *n.* (*Biol.*) a stage of the prophase of the meiosis during which paired chromosomes separate. [Gk. *tainia*, a band]
dipnoous (dip´nōəs) *a.* of or relating to an order of fishes, the Dipnoi, breathing both by gills and true lungs. [mod. L, from Gr. *dipnoos* (DI-[2], *pnoē*, breathing)]
dipody (dip´ədi) *n.* (*pl.* **dipodies**) in prosody, a double foot. [L, Gr. *dipodia* (DI-[2], Gr. *pous podos*, foot)]
dipole (dī´pōl) *n.* **1** (*Physics*) two equal and opposite electric charges or magnetic poles a small distance apart. **2** (*Chem.*) a molecule in which the centres of positive and negative charge do not coincide. **3** an aerial made of a single metal rod with the connecting wire attached half-way down. **dipolar** (-pō´-) *a.* having two poles. **dipolarize, dipolarise** *v.t.* **dipole moment** *n.* (*Physics*) the product of the separation of the charges of a dipole and their magnitude.
dipper DIP.
dippy (dip´i) *a.* (*comp.* **dippier**, *superl.* **dippiest**) (*sl.*) slightly mad.
dipsas (dip´səs) *n.* (*pl.* **dipsades** (-sədēz)) a snake whose bite was said to produce unquenchable thirst. [L, from Gr. *dipsas* (*dipsa*, thirst)]
dipso (dip´so) *n.* (*pl.* **dipsos**) (*coll.*) a dipsomaniac, an alcoholic.
dipsomania (dipsəmā´niə) *n.* alcoholism; an irresistible craving for stimulants. **dipsomaniac** (-ak) *n.* **dipsomaniacal** (-mənī´əkəl) *a.* [as DIPSO]
dipteral (dip´tərəl) *a.* (of a temple) having a double row of columns all round. [mod. L, from Gr. *diptera* (DI-[2], *pteron*, wing)]
dipterous (dip´tərəs) *a.* **1** of or relating to the Diptera, an order of insects which have two wings and two small knobbed organs called poisers. **2** (*Bot.*) having two winglike appendages. **dipteran** *a.* of or related to the Diptera. *~n.* a dipterous insect. [mod. L, from Gr. *diptera* (DI-[2], *pteron*, wing)]
diptych (dip´tik) *n.* **1** an altarpiece or other painting with hinged sides closing like a book. **2** an ancient writing-tablet of two hinged leaves, made of carved ivory waxed on the inner side. [late L *diptycha*, Gr. *diptucha*, neut. pl. of *diptuchos*, folding (DI-[2], *ptuchē*, a fold)]
dire (dīə) *a.* (*comp.* **direr**, *superl.* **direst**) **1** dreadful, fearful. **2** dismal, lamentable, sad. **3** (*coll.*) of poor quality; terrible. **direful** *a.* **direfully** *adv.* **direfulness** *n.* **direly** *adv.* **direness** *n.* [L *dīrus*]
direct (direkt´, dī-) *a.* **1** straight. **2** in a straight line from one body or place to another; not curved or crooked. **3** not reflected or refracted. **4** nearest, shortest. **5** tending immediately to an end or result. **6** not circuitous. **7** not collateral in the line of descent. **8** exact, diametrical. **9** not contrary or retrograde. **10** immediate; personal, not by proxy. **11** honest, to the point. **12** (*Mus.*) not inverted. **13** plain, to the point, straightforward, upright. **14** from east to west (applied to the motion of a planet when in the same direction as the movement of the sun amidst the fixed stars). **15** (*Gram.*) as spoken, not in reported form. *~adv.* **1** (*coll.*) directly. **2** immediately. *~v.t.* **1** to point or turn in a direct line towards any place or object. **2** to show the right road to. **3** to inscribe with an address or direction. **4** to address, to speak or write to. **5** to aim, to point. **6** to guide, to prescribe a course to, to advise. **7** to order, to command. **8** to manage, to control, to act as leader or head of (a group of musicians, a play, film etc.). *~v.i.* to give orders or instructions. **direct access** *n.* a way of reading data in a computer file without having to read through the whole file. **direct address** *n.* (*Comput.*) an address specifying the location of data. **direct broadcasting by satellite** *n.* a system of broadcasting television programmes direct to the consumer using satellites in orbit round the earth. **direct chord** *n.* (*Mus.*) a chord in which the fundamental note is the lowest. **direct current** *n.* an electric current which flows in one direction only. **direct debit** *n.* a method by which a creditor is paid directly from the payer's bank account. **direct dialling,** (*NAm.*) **direct dialing** *n.* dialling a telephone number without going through the operator. **direct dial** *a.* **direct-grant school** *n.* (before 1979) a school funded by fees and a state grant on condition that it accepted a specified number of non-fee-paying pupils. **directive** *n.* an authoritative instruction or direction. *~a.* having the power of directing. **directly** *adv.* **1** exactly. **2** immediately. **3** at once. **4** in a direct manner. *~conj.* (*coll.*) as soon as. **direct mail** *n.* advertising leaflets and promotional material sent, unsolicited, by a company to potential customers. **direct mailing** *n.* **direct method** *n.* a system of teaching a foreign language with only minimal use of translation and formal grammar. **directness** *n.* **direct object** *n.* (*Gram.*) the word or

group of words which is acted upon by a transitive verb. **direct primary** *n.* in the US, a primary election in which voters select the candidates who are to stand for office. **direct proportion** *n.* a relation between quantities with a constant ratio. **direct question** *n.* **1** an unambiguous question going straight to the point. **2** (*Gram.*) a question that is reported in the exact words, as in *She asked me, 'Where do you live?'*. **direct speech** *n.* (*Gram.*) the reporting of spoken or written discourse by repeating the exact words, as in *He said, 'I will be late'*. **direct tax** *n.* a tax levied on the person who ultimately bears the burden of it. [L *dīrectus*, p.p. of *dīrigere* (DI-[1], *regere*, to rule)]

direction (direk´shən, dī-) *n.* **1** the act of directing. **2** the end or object aimed at. **3** the course taken. **4** the point towards which one looks. **5** (*often pl.*) **a** the name or address on a letter or parcel. **b** an order or instruction. **c** an instruction how to find a destination. **6** a directorate. **7** sphere, subject. **directional** *a.* **directional aerial** *n.* an aerial that transmits or receives radio waves from one direction. **directional drilling** *n.* nonvertical drilling of oil wells, esp. when several are drilled from the same platform. **directionality** (-nal´-) *n.* **directionally** *adv.* **direction-finder** *n.* an apparatus for finding the bearings of a transmitting station. **directionless** *a.*

Directoire (direk´twah) *a.* of or relating to the costume and furniture of the Directory period in France, 1795–99. **Directoire drawers, Directoire knickers** *n.pl.* women's kneelength knickers. [F]

director (direk´tə, dī-) *n.* **1** a person who directs or manages. **2** an instructor, a counsellor. **3** anything which controls or regulates. **4** a person appointed to direct the affairs of a company. **5** a spiritual adviser, a confessor. **6** a device for controlling the application of a knife, an electric current etc. **7** the person responsible for directing the actors etc. in a film or play. **directorate** (-rət) *n.* **1** the position of a director. **2** a body or board of directors. **director-general** *n.* (*pl.* **director-generals**) the head of a large, often noncommercial organization, such as the BBC. **directorial** (-taw´ri-) *a.* **director of public prosecutions** *n.* PUBLIC PROSECUTOR (under PUBLIC). **directorship** *n.* **directress** (-tris), **directrice** (-trēs), **directrix** (-triks) *n.* a female director. [F *directeur*]

directory (direk´təri, dī-) *n.* (*pl.* **directories**) **1** a book containing the names, addresses and telephone numbers of the inhabitants etc. of a district. **2** a list of all the files on a computer disc. **3** a book of direction for public worship. **4** a board of directors. ~*a.* directing, commanding, advising. **directory enquiries,** (*N Am.*) **directory assistance** *n.* a telephone service which provides particular telephone numbers at the request of callers.

directress, directrice DIRECTOR.

directrix[1] (direk´triks) *n.* (*pl.* **directrices**) (*Geom.*) a line determining the motion of a point or another line so that the latter describes a certain curve or surface.

directrix[2] DIRECTOR.

dirge (dœj) *n.* **1** a funeral song or hymn. **2** a mournful tune or song; a lament. **dirgeful** *a.* [L *dīrige*, direct thou, imper. of *dīrigere*, to DIRECT (first word of antiphon in the office for the dead)]

dirham (diə´həm), **dirhem** *n.* **1** the standard unit of currency of several N African and Middle Eastern countries. **2** an eastern measure of weight. [Arab. *dirham, dirhim*, L *drachma*, Gr. *drachmē*, DRACHM]

dirigible (dir´ijibəl) *a.* able to be directed or steered. ~*n.* a balloon or airship which can be steered. **dirigibility** (-bil´-) *n.* [L *dīrigere*, to DIRECT]

dirigisme (dir´izhizm) *n.* state control of economic and social affairs. **dirigiste** *a.* [F, from *diriger*, to DIRECT]

diriment (dir´imənt) *a.* (*Law*) nullifying, rendering a marriage null and void. **diriment impediment** *n.* a factor which renders a marriage null and void. [L *dirimens -entem*, pres.p. of *dirimere* (*dir-* (for DIS-), *emere*, to take)]

dirk (dœk) *n.* a dagger, esp. one worn by a Highlander. ~*v.t.* to stab with a dirk. [earlier *dork* (cp. Dut. *dolk*, G *Dolch*)]

dirndl (dœn´dəl) *n.* **1** an Alpine peasant woman's dress with tight-fitting bodice and full gathered skirt. **2** any full skirt like this. [G dial. *Dirndl*, little girl, dim. of *Dirne*]

dirt (dœt) *n.* **1** foul or unclean matter, matter that soils. **2** mud, mire, dust. **3** faeces. **4** a worthless thing, trash, refuse. **5** dirtiness. **6** earth, soil. **7** obscene or malicious talk. **8** (*Mining*) the material put into the cradle to be washed. ~*v.t.* to make dirty or filthy. **to dish the dirt** to spread gossip (about). **to do someone dirt** (*sl.*) to behave maliciously towards someone. **to eat dirt 1** to put up with insult and abuse without retaliation. **2** (*N Am.*) to make an embarrassing confession. **to throw dirt at** (*coll.*) to speak maliciously about. **to treat like dirt** to behave disrespectfully towards. **dirt bike** *n.* a motorcycle for use on unsurfaced roads or dirt tracks. **dirt cheap** *a.* (*coll.*) very cheap. **dirt-eating** *n.* a disease of the nutritive functions causing an irresistible craving to eat dirt. **dirt road** *n.* (*N Am.*) an unsurfaced road. **dirt track** *n.* a racing-track with a soft, loose surface, for motorcycle racing. **dirt-tracker** *n.* **dirty** *a.* (*comp.* **dirtier,** *superl.* **dirtiest**) **1** full of, mixed, or soiled with dirt. **2** foul, nasty, unclean. **3** offensive, obscene, sordid. **4** mean; contemptible, unfair. **5** (of weather) rough, wet and gusty. **6** (of a colour) dull, not bright or clear. **7** (of nuclear weapons) producing much radioactive fallout. ~*v.t.* (*3rd pers. sing. pres.* **dirties,** *pres.p.* **dirtying,** *past, p.p.* **dirtied**) to make dirty, to soil. ~*adv.* (*sl.*) **1** extremely (*a dirty great bill*). **2** dishonestly, unfairly. ~*v.i.* to become dirty. **to do the dirty on** (*coll.*) to play an underhand trick on. **to wash one's dirty linen in public** LINEN. **dirtily** *adv.* **dirtiness** *n.* **dirty dog** *n.* (*coll.*) a dishonest or untrustworthy person. **dirty end of the stick** *n.* (*coll.*) the most unpleasant part of a task or deal. **dirty look** *n.* (*coll.*) a glance of disapproval or dislike. **dirty money** *n.* **1** money obtained by dishonest or immoral means. **2** extra pay for unpleasant or dirty work. **dirty old man** *n.* a lewd old man. **dirty trick** *n.* **1** a contemptible or unfair act. **2** (*pl.*) underhand politics or business methods, used to discredit rivals. **dirty weekend** *n.* a weekend holiday with a sexual partner. **dirty word** *n.* **1** (*coll.*) a swear word or taboo word. **2** something currently out of favour or very much disliked (*'Smoking' is a dirty word these days*). **dirty work** *n.* **1** (*coll.*) dishonesty, trickery, foul play (*I won't do your dirty work for you*). **2** work that involves dirtying one's hands and clothes. [ME *drit*, prob. from Icel. *drit*, dirt, excrement (cp. OE *drītan*, to defecate]

dis (dis), **diss** *v.t.* (*pres.p.* **dissing,** *past, p.p.* **dissed**) (*N Am., sl.*) to treat disrespectfully, to put down. [DIS-]

dis- (dis), **dif-** (dif) *pref.* **1** asunder, apart, away. **2** between, separating, distinguishing. **3** separately. **4** utterly, exceedingly. **5** (forming negative compounds) not, the reverse of. **6** undoing, depriving or expelling from. [direct from L *dis-* (conn. with *bis*, twice, orig. *duis*, Gr. *dis*, and *duo*, two; or F *dés-*, *dé-*, OF *des-*, L *dis-*, *di-*; or late L *dis-*, L *dé-*)]

disability (disəbil´iti) *n.* (*pl.* **disabilities**) **1** weakness, incapacity, inability; handicap. **2** lack of physical or intellectual power, or pecuniary means. **3** legal disqualification. [from obs. *disable*, unable]

disable (disā´bəl) *v.t.* **1** to render unable. **2** to deprive of adequate physical or intellectual power, to incapacitate. **3** to injure so as to incapacitate, to cripple. **4** to disqualify legally. **disabled** *a.* **disablement** *n.* **disablist** *a.* discriminating against disabled people.

disabuse (disəbūz´) *v.t.* to free from error or misapprehension, to undeceive.

disaccharide (dīsak´ərīd) *n.* (*Chem.*) a sugar with two linked monosaccharides per molecule.

disaccord (disəkawd´) *n.* disagreement; lack of harmony, incongruity. ~*v.i.* to disagree; to refuse assent.

disaccustom (disəkŭs´təm) *v.t.* to do away with (a habit); to free from the force of custom.

disacknowledge (disəknol´ij) *v.t.* to disown, to deny acquaintance with.

disadvantage (disədvahn´tij) *n.* **1** an unfavourable position or condition. **2** injury, detriment, hurt. ~*v.t.* to cause disadvantage to. **at a disadvantage** in an unfavourable situation or position. **disadvantaged** *a.* **1** deprived of social or economic resources. **2** discriminated against. **disadvantageous** (-advəntā´jəs) *a.* **1** prejudicial, detrimental; unfavourable to one's interest. **2** disparaging, depreciative. **disadvantageously** *adv.* **disadvantageousness** *n.*

disaffect (disəfekt´) *v.t.* (*chiefly pass.*) to estrange, alienate the affection or loyalty of. **disaffected** *a.* **1** alienated in affection, estranged. **2** discontented, disloyal. **disaffectedly** *adv.* **disaffection** *n.* **1** alienation of feeling or affection, estrangement. **2** discontent, esp. with those in authority; disloyalty.

disaffiliate (disəfil´iāt) *v.t.* **1** to end an affiliation to. **2** to detach. ~*v.i.* to separate oneself (from). **disaffiliation** (-ā´shən) *n.*

disaffirm (disəfœm´) *v.t.* **1** to deny what has been affirmed. **2** to reverse, to repudiate. **disaffirmance** *n.* **disaffirmation** (-afəmā´shən) *n.*

disafforest (disəfor´ist) *v.t.* **1** to strip of forest. **2** to reduce from the legal status of forest to that of ordinary land. **disafforestation** (-tā´shən) *n.* [med. L *afforestāre*, to AFFOREST]

disaggregate (disag´rigāt) *v.t.* to separate into components, parts or particles. **disaggregation** (-ā´shən) *n.*

disagree (disəgrē´) *v.i.* **1** to differ in opinion. **2** to quarrel, to fall out. **3** to differ; to be different or unlike. **4** to be unsuitable or injurious to the health or digestion of (*Pickled onions disagree with me*). **disagreeable** *a.* **1** offensive, unpleasant, repugnant. **2** ill-tempered. **disagreeableness** *n.* **disagreeably** *adv.* **disagreement** *n.* **1** difference of opinion. **2** a quarrel, a falling out, dissension. **3** lack of agreement. **4** unsuitableness. [F *désagréer*]

disallow (disəlow´) *v.t.* to refuse to sanction or permit; to refuse assent to; to disavow, to reject; to prohibit. **disallowance** *n.* [OF *desalouer*]

disambiguate (disambig´ūāt) *v.t.* to make unambiguous. **disambiguation** (-ā´shən) *n.*

disamenity (disəmē´niti) *n.* (*pl.* **disamenities**) a disadvantage, a drawback.

disanchor (disang´kə) *v.t.* to weigh the anchor of. ~*v.i.* to weigh anchor, to depart.

disannul (disənŭl´) *v.t.* (*pres.p.* **disannulling**, *past, p.p.* **disannulled**) to annul, to abrogate. **disannulment** *n.*

disanoint (disənoint´) *v.t.* to annul the consecration of.

disappear (disəpiə´) *v.i.* **1** to go out of sight; to become invisible. **2** to be lost. **3** to cease to exist. **to do a disappearing act** to leave suddenly, esp. in order to avoid something unpleasant. **disappearance** *n.*

disappoint (disəpoint´) *v.t.* **1** to defeat the expectations, wishes, hopes or desires of. **2** to frustrate, hinder (a plan). **disappointed** *a.* frustrated, thwarted, deceived or defeated in one's desires or expectations. **disappointedly** *adv.* **disappointing** *a.* **disappointingly** *adv.* **disappointment** *n.* **1** the failure of one's hopes. **2** something which or a person who disappoints. [F *désappointer*]

disapprobation (disaprəbā´shən) *n.* disapproval, condemnation. **disapprobative** (-ap´-) *a.* **disapprobatory** (-ap´-) *a.*

disappropriate (disəprō´priāt) *v.t.* to remove from individual possession.

disapprove (disəproov´) *v.t.* to condemn or to reject, as not approved of (*Her father disapproved of her boyfriend*). ~*v.i.* to feel or express disapproval. **disapproval** *n.* **disapprover** *n.* **disapproving** *a.* **disapprovingly** *adv.*

disarm (disahm´) *v.t.* **1** to take the weapons away from. **2** to deprive of weapons. **3** to remove the means of defence from (a ship). **4** to defuse (a bomb). **5** to reduce to a peace footing. **6** to render harmless. **7** to subdue, to tame. ~*v.i.* **1** to reduce or abandon military and naval establishments. **2** to lay aside arms. **disarmament** *n.* reduction of armaments by mutual agreement between nations. **disarmer** *n.* **disarming** *a.* tending to allay hostility or criticism; charming. **disarmingly** *adv.* [F *désarmer*]

disarrange (disərānj´) *v.t.* **1** to put out of order. **2** to derange. **disarrangement** *n.*

disarray (disərā´) *n.* **1** disorder, confusion. **2** disorderliness of dress. ~*v.t.* **1** to throw into confusion, to rout. **2** †to undress, disrobe.

disarticulate (disahtik´ūlāt) *v.t.* to separate the joints of, to disjoint. ~*v.i.* to become disjointed or separated at the joints. **disarticulation** (-lā´shən) *n.*

disassemble (disəsem´bəl) *v.t.* to take apart. **disassembler** *n.* (*Comput.*) a program which translates machine code into assembly language. **disassembly** *n.*

disassimilation (disəsimilā´shən) *n.* the conversion of assimilated substances into such as are less complex or waste substances; catabolism.

disassociate (disəsō´shiāt, -si-) *v.t., v.i.* DISSOCIATE. **disassociation** (-ā´shən) *n.* [F *désassocier* (DIS-, *associer*, ASSOCIATE[1])]

disaster (dizah´stə) *n.* **1** a sudden misfortune, a calamity. **2** misfortune, ill luck. **3** (*coll.*) fiasco, flop. **disaster area** *n.* **1** an area which has suffered a disaster and needs emergency aid. **2** (*coll.*) a person who or a place or thing which is in disarray or is a failure. **disastrous** (-trəs) *a.* **1** causing or threatening disaster. **2** very unsuccessful. **disastrously** *adv.* [F *désastre* (DIS-, *astre*, L *astrum*, Gr. *astron*, a star)]

Usage note Pronunciation of *disastrous* as (dizas´tərəs), with an extra syllable, is best avoided.

☒ **disatisfy** common misspelling of DISSATISFY.

disavow (disəvow´) *v.t.* to deny the truth of, to disown; to disapprove; to disclaim. **disavowal** *n.* [F *désavouer* (DIS-, *avouer*, to AVOW)]

disband (disband´) *v.i.* to be disbanded; to separate, to disperse. ~*v.t.* to break up the association of a group of people who have worked together. **disbandment** *n.* [F *desbander* (DIS-, OF, BAND[3])]

disbar (disbah´) *v.t.* (*pres.p.* **disbarring**, *past, p.p.* **disbarred**) to deprive of status as a barrister; to expel from membership of the bar. **disbarment** *n.*

disbelief DISBELIEVE.

disbelieve (disbilēv´) *v.t.* to refuse credit to, to refuse to believe in. ~*v.i.* to be a sceptic. **disbelief** *n.* **disbeliever** *n.* **disbelievingly** *adv.*

disbench (disbench´) *v.t.* to deprive of status as a bencher, to dismiss from senior membership of the Inns of Court.

disbenefit (disben´ifit) *n.* a disadvantage, a drawback.

disbound (disbownd´) *a.* separated from a bound volume.

disbowel (disbow´əl) *v.t.* (*pres.p.* **disbowelling**, (*N Am.*) **disboweling**, *past, p.p.* **disbowelled**, (*N Am.*) **disboweled**) to disembowel.

disbranch (disbrahnch´) *v.t.* **1** to strip of branches. **2** to sever (a branch).

disbud (disbŭd´) *v.t.* (*pres.p.* **disbudding**, *past, p.p.* **disbudded**) to cut away (esp. superfluous) buds from.

disburden (disbœ´dən) *v.t.* **1** to remove a burden or encumbrance from. **2** to relieve, to get rid of. ~*v.i.* to unload.

disburse (disbœs´) *v.t.* **1** to pay out, to expend. **2** to defray. ~*v.i.* to pay money. **disbursal** *n.* **disbursement** *n.* **disburser** *n.* [OF *desbourser* (DIS-, BURSE (under BURSA))]

disc (disk), (*N Am. and Comput.*) **disk** *n.* **1** a flat circular plate or surface. **2** a gramophone record. **3** a compact disc. **4** any round, luminous and apparently flat object. **5** (*Astron.*) the face of a celestial body. **6** the central part of a radiate compound flower. **7** a layer of fibrocartilage between vertebrae. **8** (*Comput.* **disk**) **a** MAGNETIC DISK (under MAGNET). **b** OPTICAL DISK (under OPTIC). **disc brake** *n.* a brake consisting of a metal disc attached to the axle, on the opposite surfaces of which the pads press. **disc flower, disc floret** *n.* any one of the tubular inner flowers in a composite flower. **disc harrow** *n.* a harrow consisting of sharpened saucer-shaped discs for cutting clods of soil. **disc jockey** *n.* the presenter of a programme of popular recorded music. **disk drive** *n.* the electromechanical device in a computer which reads information from, and writes it on to, the disk. **diskette** *n.* a floppy disk. **disk file** *n.* a random-access device in which information is stored, in tracks, on magnetic disks. **diskless** *a.* **disk store** *n.* a disk file. [L *discus*, Gr. *diskos*]

Usage note In general the spelling *disc* is preferred in Britain and *disk* in the United States, but in computing *disk* is standard everywhere, complicating the British spelling of cases such as *compact disc*.

disc. *abbr.* discovered.

discalced (diskalst´) *a.* (of a friar or a nun etc.) unshod, barefoot, wearing sandals. ~*n.* a barefoot or sandalled friar or nun. [L *discalceātus*, p.p. of *discalceāre* (DIS-, *calceāre*, to shoe, from *calceus*, a shoe)]

discant[1] DESCANT[1].

discant[2] DESCANT[2].

discard[1] (diskahd´) *v.t.* **1** to throw aside or away as useless. **2** to get rid of, to reject; to cast aside; to dismiss. **3** in cards, to play (a particular card) that does not follow suit. ~*v.i.* to play a non-trump card that does not follow suit. **discardable** *a.*

discard[2] (dis´kahd) *n.* **1** the playing of useless cards. **2** a card so played. **3** rejection as useless. **4** anything so rejected.

discarnate (diskah´nāt) *a.* having no flesh, disembodied. [DIS-, L *caro carnis*, flesh]

discern (disœn´) *v.t.* **1** to perceive distinctly with the senses, to make out. **2** to recognize clearly or perceive mentally. **3** †to perceive (differences). **4** †to judge or decide between. ~*v.i.* to discriminate. **discerner** *n.* **discernible** *a.* **discernibly** *adv.* **discerning** *a.* having the power to discern; discriminating, acute, penetrating. **discerningly** *adv.* **discernment** *n.* **1** the act, power or faculty of discerning. **2** clear discrimination, accurate judgement. [F *discerner*, L *discernere* (DIS-, *cernere*, to separate)]

†**discerptible** (disœp´tibəl) *a.* separable, capable of being torn apart. **discerptibility** (-bil´-) *n.* **discerption** *n.* **1** severance, division into parts or pieces. **2** a severed portion. [L *discerptus*, p.p. of *discerpere* (DIS-, *carpere*, to pick, to pluck)]

discharge[1] (dischahj´) *v.t.* **1** to unload from a ship, vehicle etc.; to take (a load etc.) out or away. **2** to emit, to let fly. **3** to dismiss. **4** to release from confinement. **5** to relieve of a load. **6** to set free from something binding. **7** to fire (a gun). **8** to empty, to pour out. **9** to pay off; to settle. **10** to perform (a duty). **11** to remove colour from (a fabric) by process of bleaching. **12** (*Law*) †to cancel, to annul. **13** (*Physics*) to remove an electrical charge from. ~*v.i.* **1** (of a river) to unload or empty itself. **2** (of a gun) to be discharged. **3** to pour out. **dischargeable** *a.* **discharger** *n.* **1** a person who or something which discharges. **2** (*Physics*) a discharging rod. [OF *descharger*]

discharge[2] (dis´chahj) *n.* **1** the act of discharging. **2** unloading. **3** firing (of a gun). **4** payment. **5** dismissal. **6** release, acquittal, liberation. **7** (of a duty) performance. **8** a paper certifying discharge. **9** emission (of a fluid). **10** a fluid discharged. **11** (*Physics*) neutralization or loss of electric charge.

disciple (disī´pəl) *n.* **1** a pupil or adherent of a philosopher, leader etc. **2** a follower of a particular cult, area of interest etc. **3** one of the early followers, esp. one of the twelve personal followers of Christ. **discipleship** *n.* **discipular** (-sip´ū-) *a.* [OE *discipul* and OF *deciple* (L *discipulus*, from *discere*, to learn), both assim. to L spelling]

discipline (dis´iplin) *n.* **1** instruction, training, exercise, or practice of the mental, moral and physical powers to promote order, regularity and efficient obedience. **2** punishment, chastisement. **3** training supplied by adversity. **4** military training. **5** order, systematic obedience, methodical action, the state of being under control. **6** a branch of instruction. **7** in the Roman Catholic Church, penitential chastisement or the instrument by which this is applied physically. **8** control over the members of a church, the rules binding on the members of a church. ~*v.t.* **1** to bring into a state of discipline. **2** to teach, to train, to drill, esp. in obedience, orderly habits and methodical action. **3** to punish, to chastise, to bring into a state of order and obedience. **disciplinable** *a.* **disciplinal** (dis´-, -plī´nəl) *a.* †**disciplinant** *n.* a member of a Spanish religious body of the Middle Ages who used to take discipline in public. **disciplinarian** (-neə´ri-) *n.* a person who rigidly enforces discipline. ~*a.* of or relating to discipline. **disciplinary** (dis´iplinəri) *a.* of or relating to or promoting discipline. **discipliner** *n.* [F, from L *dīsciplīna*, as DISCIPLE]

discipular DISCIPLE.

disclaim (disklām´) *v.t.* **1** to deny, to repudiate. **2** to refuse to acknowledge, to disown, to disavow. **3** to reject. **4** (*Law*) to renounce, to relinquish or to disavow. ~†*v.i.* to deny all claim or participation. **disclaimer** *n.* **1** the act of disclaiming. **2** renunciation, disavowal, repudiation. [A-F *desclamer*]

disclose (disklōz´) *v.t.* **1** to make known, to reveal, to divulge. **2** to uncover; to lay bare or open. **discloser** *n.* **disclosure** (-zhə) *n.* **1** the act of disclosing. **2** something which is disclosed, a revelation. [OF *desclore* (DIS-, L *claudere*, to shut, p.p. *clausus*)]

disco (dis´kō) *n.* (*pl.* **discos**) (*coll.*) **1** a discotheque. **2** disco music. ~*a.* of or relating to discotheques, as *disco dancing*. **disco music** *n.* a type of dance music with a strong bass rhythm, suitable for disco dancing.

discobolus (diskob´ələs) *n.* (*pl.* **discobuli** (-lī)) in ancient Greece, a discus-thrower. [L, from Gr. *diskobolos* (*diskos*, quoit, *-bolos*, from *ballein*, to throw)]

discography (diskog´rəfi) *n.* (*pl.* **discographies**) **1** a catalogue or list of gramophone records or compact discs, esp. by a particular artist or band. **2** the literature and study of gramophone records or compact discs. **discographer** *n.*

discoid (dis´koid), **discoidal** (-koi´-) *a.* having the shape of a disc. **discoid flower** *n.* a composite flower not radiated by having the corollas tubular, as in the tansy. [L *discoīdēs*, Gr. *diskoeidēs* (*diskos*; -OID)]

discolour (diskŭl´ə), (*N Am.*) **discolor** *v.t.* **1** to alter the colour of. **2** to give an unnatural colour to. **3** to stain; to tarnish. ~*v.i.* **1** to become stained or tarnished in colour. **2** to fade. **discoloration, discolouration** *n.* **1** the act of discolouring. **2** the state of being discoloured. **3** a discoloured appearance, a spot, a stain. **discolourment**

n. [OF *descolorer*, med. L *discolōrāre* (DIS-, L *colōrāre*, in place of L *dēcolōrāre*)]

discombobulate (diskəmbob´ūlāt) *v.t.* (*N Am., coll.*) to confuse, to disconcert. [etym. uncertain]

discomfit (diskŭm´fit) *v.t.* (*pres.p.* **discomfiting**, *past, p.p.* **discomfited**) **1** to embarrass and confuse. **2** to thwart, to frustrate. **3** †to defeat, to rout; to scatter in fight. **discomfiture** (-fichə) *n.* **1** embarrassment and confusion. **2** defeat, overthrow. [OF *desconfit*, p.p. of *desconfire*, late L *disconficere* (DIS-, *conficere*, to finish, to preserve)]

discomfort (diskŭm´fət) *n.* **1** lack of ease or comfort. **2** uneasiness, disquietude, distress. ~*v.t.* **1** to cause pain or uneasiness to. **2** to deprive of comfort. †**discomfortable** *a.* **1** causing discomfort. **2** causing disquiet or discouragement. [OF *desconforter*]

discommend (diskəmend´) *v.t.* to blame, to censure; to disapprove of; to disparage. **discommendable** *a.*

discommode (diskəmōd´) *v.t.* to cause inconvenience to. **discommodious** *a.* [obs. v. *commode*, L *commodāre*, to suit, from *commodus*, suitable]

discommon (diskom´ən) *v.t.* **1** to prevent from being common land. **2** to deprive of the use of a common. **3** to deprive of a privilege (esp. tradesmen in an English university town who may be debarred from serving undergraduates).

discompose (diskəmpōz´) *v.t.* **1** to disturb, to destroy the composure of. **2** to agitate, to vex, to disquiet. **3** †to disarrange, to disorder. **discomposedly** (-zid-) *adv.* **discomposingly** *adv.* **discomposure** (-zhə) *n.*

disconcert (diskənsœt´) *v.t.* **1** to discompose, to disquiet. **2** to throw (plans) into confusion. **disconcertedly** *adv.* **disconcerting** *a.* **disconcertingly** *a.* **disconcertion** *n.* **disconcertment** *n.* [MF *disconcerter*]

disconfirm (diskənfœm´) *v.t.* (*formal*) to show or suggest the falseness of. **disconfirmation** (-fəmā´shən) *n.*

disconformity (diskənfaw´miti) *n.* **1** a lack of conformity or agreement; inconsistency. **2** (*Geol.*) the junction between two parallel sets of strata, where there has been a long gap before the deposit of the more recent strata.

disconnect (diskənekt´) *v.t.* **1** to remove (an electrical device) from its source of power, esp. by unplugging it. **2** to separate; to disunite, to sever. **disconnected** *a.* **1** incoherent, ill-connected. **2** separated. **disconnectedly** *adv.* **disconnectedness** *n.* **disconnection, disconnexion** *n.* **1** the act of disconnecting. **2** the state of being separated, ill-connected or incoherent.

disconsolate (diskon´sələt) *a.* inconsolable, dejected, forlorn; unable to be consoled or comforted. **disconsolately** *adv.* **disconsolateness** *n.* **disconsolation** (-səlā´shən) *n.* [late L *disconsōlātus*, p.p. of *disconsōlārī* (DIS-, *consōlārī*, to CONSOLE[1])]

discontent (diskəntent´) *n.* **1** lack of content; dissatisfaction. **2** cause of dissatisfaction, a grievance. **3** †a discontented person. ~*a.* not content, dissatisfied. ~*v.t.* to make discontented, dissatisfied or uneasy. **discontented** *a.* dissatisfied, uneasy, disquieted. **discontentedly** *adv.* **discontentedness** *n.* **discontentment** *n.*

discontiguous (diskəntig´ūəs) *a.* not contiguous; having the parts not in contact.

discontinuance, discontinuation DISCONTINUE.

discontinue (diskəntin´ū) *v.t.* **1** to stop producing (*a discontinued line*). **2** to break off, to interrupt. **3** to leave off, to cease to use. **4** to give up. ~*v.i.* to cease. **discontinuance** *n.* †**discontinuation** (-ā´shən) *n.* **discontinuity** (-kontinū´-) *n.* **discontinuous** *a.* **1** not continuous, disconnected. **2** intermittent, gaping. **discontinuously** *adv.* [F *discontinuer*, late L *discontinuāre* (DIS-, L *continuāre*)]

discophile (dis´kōfīl) *n.* a person who collects gramophone records or compact discs. [Gr. *philos*, loving]

discord[1] (dis´kawd) *n.* **1** lack of concord or agreement; disagreement, contention, strife. **2** disagreement or opposition in quality, esp. in sounds. **3** (*Mus.*) **a** a lack of harmony in a combination of notes sounded together. **b** the sounding together of two or more inharmonious or inconclusive notes. **c** the interval or the chord so sounded. **d** a note that is out of harmony with another. [OF *descord*, from *descorder*, L *discordāre* (DIS-, *cor cordis*, heart)]

discord[2] (diskawd´) *v.i.* **1** to be out of harmony (with). **2** to disagree (with). **3** to be inconsistent, to clash (with). **discordant** *a.* **1** disagreeing, not in accord, unpleasing, esp. to the ear. **2** opposite, contradictory. **3** inconsistent. **discordance, discordancy** *n.* **discordantly** *adv.*

discotheque (dis´kətek) *n.* **1** a club or public place where people dance to recorded pop music. **2** mobile apparatus for playing records at a discotheque. **3** a party. [F, a record library, from Gr. *diskos*, quoit, *thēkē*, case]

discount[1] (dis´kownt) *n.* **1** a deduction from the amount of a price or an account for early or immediate payment. **2** a deduction at a certain rate from money advanced on a bill of exchange which is not yet due. **3** the deduction of a sum for payment in advance. **4** the act of discounting. **5** the rate of discount. **at a discount** **1** depreciated. **2** below par. **3** not held in much esteem. **discount house** *n.* **1** a company engaged in discounting bills of exchange on a large scale. **2** (*N Am.*) a discount store. **discount rate** *n.* (*N Am.*) the minimum lending rate. **discount store** *n.* a shop which sells most of its merchandise at below the recommended retail price. [OF *desconter*, late L *discomputāre* (DIS-, L *computāre*, to COMPUTE)]

discount[2] (diskownt´) *v.t.* **1** to deduct a certain sum or rate per cent from (an account or price). **2** to lend or advance (an amount), deducting interest at a certain rate per cent from the principle. **3** to leave out of account. **4** to anticipate, to enjoy beforehand. **5** to make allowance for, to make little account of, to disregard. ~*v.i.* to advance money on bills and other documents due at some future date, deducting the interest at the time of the loan. **discountable** *a.* **discounter** *n.*

discountenance (diskown´tənəns) *v.t.* **1** to disconcert, to abash. **2** to discourage; to express disapprobation of. ~*n.* discouragement, disfavour. [MF *descontenancer*]

discourage (diskŭr´ij) *v.t.* **1** to deprive of courage; to dishearten, to dispirit. **2** to dissuade; to deter. **discouragement** *n.* **discourager** *n.* **discouraging** *a.* **discouragingly** *adv.* [OF *descoragier*]

discourse[1] (dis´kaws) *n.* **1** talk, conversation, exchange of ideas. **2** a dissertation, a formal treatise. **3** a lecture or sermon. **4** a text consisting of more than one sentence, used for linguistic analysis. [F *discours*, L *discursus*, p.p. of *discurrere* (DIS-, *currere*, to run)]

discourse[2] (diskaws´) *v.i.* **1** to talk, to speak, to converse. **2** to talk formally, to hold forth (on). ~†*v.t.* to utter, to give forth.

discourteous (diskœ´tiəs) *a.* impolite, uncivil, rude. **discourteously** *adv.* **discourteousness** *n.* **discourtesy** *n.* (*pl.* **discourtesies**) **1** discourteous behaviour. **2** a discourteous act.

discover (diskŭv´ə) *v.t.* **1** to gain the first sight of. **2** to find out by exploration. **3** to ascertain, to realize suddenly. **4** to detect. **5** †to disclose, to reveal, to make known, to betray. **6** in chess, to remove an obstructing piece (to give check). **7** to discover (an unknown entertainer) and help them to become successful. **discoverable** *a.* **discoverer** *n.* [OF *descovrir*, med. L *discooperīre* (DIS-, L *cooperīre*, to COVER)]

discovert (diskŭv´ət) *a.* (*Law*) not having a husband, unmarried, widowed or divorced. **discoverture** (-əchə) *n.* [OF *descovert*, p.p. of DISCOVER]

discovery (diskŭv´əri) *n.* (*pl.* **discoveries**) **1** the act of discovering. **2** something which is made known for the first time. **3** something which is found out. **4** revelation; disclosure; manifestation. **5** the unravelling of the plot of a play. **6** (*Law*) compulsory disclosure of facts and documents essential to the proper consideration of a case.

discredit (diskred´it) *n.* **1** lack or loss of credit. **2** disrepute, disgrace. **3** the cause of disrepute or disgrace. **4** disbelief; lack of credibility. **5** loss of commercial credit. *~v.t.* (*pres.p.* **discrediting,** *past, p.p.* **discredited**) **1** to disbelieve. **2** to bring into disrepute. **3** to deprive of credibility. **discreditable** *a.* tending to discredit; disreputable, disgraceful. **discreditably** *adv.*

discreet (diskrēt´) *a.* **1** prudent, wary, circumspect. **2** judicious, careful in choosing the best means of action. **3** subtle, unobtrusive (*discreet aftershave*). **4** †discrete. **discreetly** *adv.* **discreetness** *n.* [F *discret*, L *discrētus*, p.p. of *discernere*, to DISCERN (differentiated from DISCRETE by late L sense, discerning, distinguishing, judicious)]

Usage note The spellings of the adjectives *discreet* (circumspect) and *discrete* (distinct) should not be confused.

discrepancy (diskrep´ənsi) *n.* (*pl.* **discrepancies**) a difference; an inconsistency, esp. between two figures or claims. **discrepant** *a.* [*discrepāre*, to be discordant (DIS-, *crepāre*, to sound)]

discrete (diskrēt´) *a.* **1** distinct, discontinuous, detached, separate. **2** (*Philos.*) not concrete, abstract. **discretely** *adv.* **discreteness** *n.* **discretive** *a.* disjunctive, separating. **discretively** *adv.* [L *discrētus*, see DISCREET]

Usage note See note under DISCREET.

discretion (diskresh´ən) *n.* **1** the power or faculty of distinguishing things that differ, or discriminating correctly between what is right and wrong, useful and injurious. **2** discernment, judgement, circumspection. **3** freedom of judgement and action. **4** (*Law*) the authority of a court to decide sentences etc. **at discretion** according to one's own judgement. **at the discretion of** according to the judgement of. **to surrender at discretion** to surrender unconditionally. **to use one's discretion** to make decisions based on one's own judgement. **discretional** *a.* **discretionally** *adv.* **discretionary** *a.*

discretive DISCRETE.

☒ **discribe** common misspelling of DESCRIBE.

discriminate[1] (diskrim´ināt) *v.i.* **1** to make a distinction or difference. **2** to treat (unfairly) a group of people either worse or better than other groups. **3** to mark the difference between things. *~v.t.* **1** to distinguish. **2** to mark or observe the difference or distinction between. **3** to distinguish by marks of difference, to differentiate. **to discriminate against** to distinguish or deal with unfairly or unfavourably. **discriminating** *a.* **1** exercising discrimination, discerning. **2** distinguishing clearly, distinctive. **3** distinguishing unfairly or unfavourably. **discriminating duties, discriminating rates** *n.pl.* duties or rates which fall unequally on different parties according to their country, position etc.; differential duties or rates. **discriminatingly** *adv.* **discrimination** (-ā´shən) *n.* **1** power or faculty of discriminating. **2** discernment, penetration, judgement. **3** the act of discriminating. **4** unfair treatment of an individual or group of people on the grounds of race, religion, sex, age etc. **discriminative**(-nət-) *a.* **discriminatively** *adv.* **discriminator** *n.* **discriminatory**(-nət-) *a.* **1** discriminating against or in favour of certain groups of people. **2** observing fine distinctions. [L *discrīminātus*, p.p. of *discrīmināre* (*discrīmen*, separation, distinction, from *discernere*, to DISCERN)]

discriminate[2] (diskrim´inət) *a.* distinctive; having the difference clearly marked. **discriminately** *adv.*

discrimination, discriminative etc. DISCRIMINATE[1].

discrown (diskrown´) *v.t.* to divest or deprive of a crown; to depose.

disculpate (diskŭl´pāt) *v.t.* to free from blame. [L *disculpātus*, p.p. of *disculpāre* (DIS-, *culpāre*, to blame)]

discursive (diskœ´siv) *a.* **1** passing from one subject to another; rambling, desultory. **2** (*Philos.*) rational, argumentative, as distinct from *intuitive*. **discursively** *adv.* **discursiveness** *n.* **discursory** *a.* [L *discurs-*, p.p. stem of *discurrere*, see DISCOURSE[1]]

discus (dis´kəs) *n.* (*pl.* **discuses**) **1** in ancient Greece, a metal disc thrown in athletic sports, a quoit. **2** a similar disc, with a thick, heavy middle, thrown in modern field events. [L, from Gr. *diskos*]

discuss (diskŭs´) *v.t.* **1** to debate. **2** to consider or examine by argument. **3** (*facet.*) to try the flavour of (a dish, wine etc.). **discussant** *n.* **discusser** *n.* **discussible, discussable** *a.* **discussion** (-shən) *n.* **1** consideration or investigation by argument for and against. **2** (*Med.*) the scattering or dispersion of a tumour etc. [L *discussus*, p.p. of *discutere*, to shake asunder, late L, to discuss (DIS-, *quatere*, to shake)]

discutient (diskū´shənt) *a.* (*Med.*) having power to disperse tumours etc. *~n.* a discutient preparation.

disdain (disdān´) *n.* scorn, a feeling of contempt combined with haughtiness and indignation. *~v.t.* **1** to regard as unworthy of notice. **2** to despise or repulse as unworthy of oneself. **disdainful** *a.* **disdainfully** *adv.* **disdainfulness** *n.* [OF *desdein*, from *desdaigner* (F *dédaigner*), to scorn, from L *dēdignārī* (DE- *dignārī*, to deem worthy, from *dignus*, worthy)]

disease (dizēz´) *n.* **1** any alteration of the normal vital processes of humans, the lower animals or plants, under the influence of some unnatural or hurtful condition. **2** any disorder or morbid condition, habit or function, mental, moral, social etc. **diseased** *a.* **1** affected with disease. **2** morbid, unhealthy, deranged. [OF *desaise*]

diseconomy (disikon´əmi) *n.* the state of being uneconomic or unprofitable.

disembark (disimbahk´) *v.i.* to leave a ship, aircraft, train etc. at the end of a journey. *~v.t.* to remove from a ship, aircraft, train etc. at the end of a journey. **disembarkation** (-embahkā´shən) *n.* [F *désembarquer*]

disembarrass (disimbar´əs) *v.t.* **1** to free from embarrassment or perplexity. **2** to disencumber (of); to liberate (from). **disembarrassment** *n.*

disembellish (disimbel´ish) *v.t.* to divest of ornament.

disembody (disimbod´i) *v.t.* (*3rd pers. sing. pres.* **disembodies,** *pres.p.* **disembodying,** *past, p.p.* **disembodied**) **1** to divest of body or the flesh; to free from a concrete form. **2** †to disband. **disembodiment** *n.*

disembogue (disimbōg´) *v.t.* (of a stream) to pour out or discharge (water) at the mouth; to pour forth or empty itself. *~v.i.* **1** to flow out. **2** †to flow into the mouth of a river, bay, gulf etc. **disemboguement** *n.* [Sp. *desembocar* (*des-*, DIS -, *em-*, IN-[1], *boca*, the mouth, L *bucca*, cheek, mouth)]

disembowel (disimbow´əl) *v.t.* (*pres.p.* **disembowelling,** (*N Am.*) **disemboweling,** *past, p.p.* **disembowelled,** (*N Am.*) **disemboweled**) **1** to lacerate so as to let the bowels protrude. **2** to take out the bowels of, to eviscerate. **disembowelment** *n.*

disembroil (disimbroil´) *v.t.* to free from confusion or perplexity.

☒ **disemminate** common misspelling of DISSEMINATE.

disemploy (disimploi´) *v.t.* to cease to employ, to remove from employment. **disemployed** *a.* **disemployment** *n.*

disempower (disimpow´ə) *v.t.* to deprive of the power to act. **disempowerment** *n.*

disenable (disinābʹəl) *v.t.* to disable, to incapacitate.
disenchant (disinchahntʹ) *v.t.* **1** to free from enchantment or glamour, to free from a spell. **2** to disillusion. **disenchanter** *n.* **disenchantingly** *adv.* **disenchantment** *n.* [F *désenchanter*]
disencumber (disinkŭmʹbə) *v.t.* to free from encumbrance. **disencumberment** *n.* **disencumbrance** *n.* [F *désencombrer*]
disendow (disindowʹ) *v.t.* to strip of endowments. **disendowment** *n.*
disenfranchise (disinfranʹchīz) *v.t.* **1** to deprive of electoral privilege. **2** to withdraw the rights of citizenship from. **disenfranchisement** (-chiz-) *n.*
disengage (disingājʹ) *v.t.* **1** to separate; to loosen, to detach. **2** (*Mil.*) to withdraw from a battle. **3** in fencing, to pass the point of one's foil to the other side of one's adversary's. **4** to release. **5** to set free from any engagement. ~*n.* in fencing, the act of disengaging. **disengaged** *a.* **1** at leisure, having the attention unoccupied. **2** free from any engagement. **3** detached, uncommitted. †**disengagedness** (-jid-) *n.* **disengagement** *n.* **1** the act of disengaging. **2** extrication. **3** the state of being disengaged. **4** detachment. **5** ease, freedom of manner. **6** dissolution of an engagement to be married. **7** in fencing, a disengage.
disentail (disintālʹ) *v.t.* (*Law*) to free from or break the entail of.
disentangle (disintangʹgəl) *v.t.* **1** to unravel, to free from entanglement. **2** to disengage, to disembarrass. ~*v.i.* to be disentangled. **disentanglement** *n.*
†**disenthral** (disinthrawlʹ), (*N Am.*) **disenthrall** *v.t.* (*pres.p.* **disenthralling,** *past, p.p.* **disenthralled**) to set free from thraldom, to emancipate. **disenthralment,** (*N Am.*) **disenthrallment** *n.*
disentitle (disintīʹtəl) *v.t.* to deprive of a right. **disentitlement** *n.*
†**disentomb** (disintoomʹ) *v.t.* **1** to remove from a tomb. **2** to discover, to bring to light. **disentombment** *n.*
disequilibrium (disēkwilibʹriəm, -ek-) *n.* a lack of balance or equilibrium, esp. in economic affairs.
disestablish (disistabʹlish) *v.t.* **1** to annul the establishment of, esp. to deprive (a Church) of its connection with the state. **2** to depose from established use or position. **disestablishment** *n.*
disesteem (disistēmʹ) *n.* a lack of esteem or regard. ~*v.t.* to look upon without esteem; to despise.
diseur (dēzœʹ) *n.* a reciter. **diseuse** (-zœzʹ) *n.* a female reciter. [F]
disfame (disfāmʹ) *n.* disrepute, dishonour.
disfavour (disfāʹvə), (*N Am.*) **disfavor** *n.* **1** a feeling of dislike or disapprobation. **2** disesteem; displeasure. ~*v.t.* to treat or regard with disfavour, to discountenance.
disfeature (disfēʹchə) *v.t.* **1** to deface, disfigure. **2** to deprive of a feature.
disfellowship (disfelʹōship) *n.* lack of fellowship. ~*v.t.* to exclude from fellowship, esp. of a church.
disfigure (disfigʹə) *v.t.* to spoil the beauty or appearance of; to deform, to mar. **disfiguration** (-gūrāʹshən) *n.* **disfigurement** *n.* **disfigurer** *n.* [OF *desfigurer* (*des-*, DIS, *figurer*, L *figūrāre*, to fashion; from *figūra*, FIGURE]
disforest (disforʹist) *v.t.* to disafforest, to clear of forest. **disforestation** (-ristāʹshən) *n.* [OF *desforester*]
disform (disfawmʹ) *v.i.* to alter in form.
disfranchise (disfranʹchīz) *v.t.* to disenfranchise. **disfranchisement** (-chiz-) *n.*
disfrock (disfrokʹ) *v.t.* **1** to strip of clerical attire. **2** to depose from the clerical office.
disgarnish (disgahʹnish) *v.t.* to disfurnish, to despoil. [OF *desgarniss-*, *desgarnir* (DIS-, *garnir*, to GARNISH)]
disgorge (disgawjʹ) *v.t.* **1** to eject from the mouth or stomach; to vomit. **2** to pour forth, empty out. ~*v.i.* to yield, give up, surrender. **disgorgement** *n.* [OF *desgorger* (DIS-, GORGE)]
disgrace (disgrāsʹ) *n.* **1** the state of being out of favour; disesteem, discredit, ignominy, shame; infamy. **2** the cause or occasion of discredit or shame. ~*v.t.* **1** to dishonour; to bring disgrace on. **2** to dismiss from favour; to degrade. **in disgrace** having lost respect, out of favour. **disgraceful** *a.* shameful, dishonourable. **disgracefully** *adv.* **disgracefulness** *n.* [F *disgrâce*, It. *disgrazia*, med. L *disgrātia* (DIS-, L *grātia*, GRACE)]
disgruntle (disgrŭnʹtəl) *v.t.* to annoy, to disappoint. **disgruntled** *a.* (*coll.*) annoyed, disappointed, discontented. **disgruntlement** *n.* [DIS-, *gruntle*, obs. freq. of GRUNT]
disguise (disgīzʹ) *v.t.* **1** to conceal or alter the appearance of, with a mask or unusual dress. **2** (*fig.*) to hide by a counterfeit appearance; to alter, to misrepresent. ~*n.* **1** a dress, mask or manner put on to disguise or conceal. **2** a pretence or show. **in disguise** wearing a disguise. **disguisedly** (-zid-) *adv.* **disguisement** *n.* **disguiser** *n.* **disguising** *n.* [OF *deguisier*]
disgust (disgŭstʹ) *v.t.* **1** to cause loathing or aversion in. **2** to offend the taste of. ~*n.* **1** aversion, loathing, repulsion. **2** a strong feeling of distaste or nausea. **in disgust** with a felling of disgust. **disgustedly** *adv.* **disgustful** *a.* **1** causing disgust, disgusting. **2** full of or inspired by disgust. **disgusting** *a.* **disgustingly** *adv.* **disgustingness** *n.* [MF *desgouster* (DIS-, L *gustāre*, to taste)]
dish (dish) *n.* **1** a broad, shallow, open vessel for serving up food at table. **2** the food so served. **3** any particular kind of food. **4** (*pl.*) the dirty dishes, cutlery and pots and pans which have been used for a meal. **5** any dishlike utensil, receptacle or concavity. **6** a dish-shaped concave reflector used as a directional aerial for radio or TV transmissions. **7** (*sl.*) an attractive person. ~*v.t.* **1** to put into or serve in a dish. **2** to make concave. **3** (*coll.*) to foil, to disappoint, to frustrate. **to dish the dirt** DIRT. **to dish up 1** to serve up. **2** (*coll.*) to present in an attractive or new way. **dishcloth,** (*dial.*) **dishclout** *n.* a cloth used for washing up dishes etc. **dishcloth gourd** *n.* a loofah. **dish-cover** *n.* a metal or earthenware cover for keeping food warm in a dish. **dished** *a.* concave. **dished wheel** *n.* a wheel that has been made concave, the spokes slanting outwards from the nave. **dishful** *n.* (*pl.* **dishfuls**) the amount in a dish. **dishpan** *n.* (*N Am.*) a washing-up bowl. **dishrag** *n.* a dishcloth. **dishtowel** *n.* a towel for drying dishes, cutlery etc. which have been washed. **dishwasher** *n.* **1** a machine for washing dishes and cutlery. **2** a person employed to wash dishes etc. **dishwater** *n.* water in which dishes, cutlery etc. have been washed. **dishy** *a.* (*comp.* **dishier,** *superl.* **dishiest**) (*sl.*) good-looking. [OE *disc*, L *discus*, DISC]
dishabille DESHABILLE.
dishallow (dis·halʹō) *v.t.* to make unholy; to profane.
disharmony (dis·hahʹməni) *n.* lack of harmony; discord, incongruity. **disharmonious** (-mōʹniəs) *a.* **disharmoniously** *adv.* **disharmonize, disharmonise** *v.t., v.i.*
dishearten (dis·hahʹtən) *v.t.* to discourage, to disappoint. **disheartening** *a.* **dishearteningly** *adv.* **disheartenment** *n.*
†**disherit** (dis·herʹit) *v.t.* (*pres.p.* **disheriting,** *past, p.p.* **disherited**) to disinherit; to dispossess. [OF *desheriter* (*des-*, DIS-, *heriter*, L *hērēditāre*, to inherit, from *hērēditās*, heirship)]
dishevel (dishevʹəl) *v.t.* (*pres.p.* **dishevelling,** (*N Am.*) **disheveling,** *past, p.p.* **dishevelled,** (*N Am.*) **disheveled**) **1** to disorder (the hair). **2** to let (the hair) down. ~*v.i.* to be spread in disorder. **dishevelled** *a.* **1** (of hair) flowing in disorder; hanging loosely and negligently. **2** (of a person) with disordered hair. **3** (of

a person) untidy, unkempt. **dishevelment** *n.* [OF *descheveler* (*des-*, DIS-, *chevel*, L *capillus*, hair)]
dishonest (dison´ist) *a.* 1 destitute of honesty, probity or good faith. 2 fraudulent, deceitful, insincere, untrustworthy. 3 †unchaste, lewd. **dishonestly** *adv.* **dishonesty** *n.* (*pl.* **dishonesties**) 1 lack of honesty or uprightness. 2 fraud, cheating, violation of duty or trust. 3 a dishonest act. [OF *deshoneste*, L *dehonestus* (DE-, *honestus*, HONEST)]
dishonour (dison´ə), (*N Am.*) **dishonor** *n.* 1 lack of honour. 2 disgrace, discredit, ignominy. 3 reproach, disparagement. 4 the cause of this. 5 refusal to honour a cheque etc. ~*v.t.* 1 to bring disgrace or shame on; to damage the reputation of. 2 to treat with indignity. 3 to refuse to accept or pay (a cheque or bill). 4 †to violate the chastity of. **dishonourable** *a.* 1 causing dishonour; disgraceful, ignominious. 2 unprincipled, mean, base; without honour. **dishonourableness** *n.* **dishonourably** *adv.* **dishonourer** *n.* [OF *deshonneur* (DIS-, L *honor -ōrem*, HONOUR)]
dishorn (dis·hawn´) *v.t.* to deprive of horns.
dishorse (dis·haws´) *v.t.* to unhorse.
disillusion (disiloo´zhən) *v.t.* to free or deliver from an illusion; to undeceive. ~*n.* disenchantment; release from illusion. **disillusioned** *a.* freed from deception or illusion. **disillusionize, disillusionise** *v.t.* **disillusionment** *n.*
☒ **disimilar** common misspelling of DISSIMILAR.
disimpassioned (disimpash´ənd) *a.* dispassionate; tranquillized.
disimprison (disimpriz´ən) *v.t.* to release from captivity; to liberate.
disimprove (disimproov´) *v.t.* to make worse. ~*v.i.* to become worse.
disincentive (disinsen´tiv) *n.* 1 something which discourages. 2 in economics, something which discourages productivity. ~*a.* discouraging.
disincline (disinklīn´) *v.t.* to make averse or indisposed (to). **disinclination** (-klinā´shən) *n.* a lack of inclination, desire or propensity; unwillingness.
disincorporate (disinkaw´pərāt) *v.t.* 1 to deprive of the rights, powers or privileges of a corporate body. 2 to dissolve (such a body). **disincorporation** (-ā´shən) *n.*
disindividualize (disindivid´ūəlīz), **disindividualise** *v.t.* to take away the individuality of.
disinfect (disinfekt´) *v.t.* to free or cleanse from infection, often by chemical means. **disinfectant** *n.* a substance which removes infection by destroying its causes. **disinfection** *n.* **disinfector** *n.*
disinfest (disinfest´) *v.t.* to rid of vermin, e.g. rats or lice. **disinfestation** (-festā´shən) *n.*
disinflation (disinflā´shən) *n.* a return to normal economic conditions after inflation, without a reduction in production. **disinflationary** *a.*
disinformation (disinfəmā´shən) *n.* the deliberate propagation or leaking of misleading information.
disingenuous (disinjen´ūəs) *a.* 1 not ingenuous. 2 lacking in frankness, openness or candour. 3 underhand, insincere. **disingenuously** *adv.* **disingenuousness** *n.*
disinherit (disinher´it) *v.i.* (*pres.p.* **disinheriting,** *past, p.p.* **disinherited**) 1 to cut off from a hereditary right. 2 to deprive of an inheritance. **disinheritance** *n.*
disintegrate (disin´tigrāt) *v.t.* 1 to separate into component parts; to reduce to fragments or powder. 2 to cause to lose cohesion. ~*v.i.* 1 to fall to pieces, to crumble. 2 to lose cohesion. 3 to deteriorate mentally or emotionally. **disintegrable** (-grəbəl) *a.* **disintegration** (-rā´shən) *n.* 1 the separation of a solid body into its component parts. 2 the wearing down of rocks by the action of the weather. **disintegrative** (-rətiv) *a.* **disintegrator** *n.* a machine for grinding bones etc.
disinter (disintœ´) *v.t.* (*pres.p.* **disinterring,** *past, p.p.* **disinterred**) 1 to dig up, esp. from a grave. 2 to discover, bring to light. **disinterment** *n.* [F *désenterrer*]
disinterest (disin´trist) *n.* 1 impartiality, disinterestedness. 2 (*loosely*) lack of interest. ~*v.t.* to divest of personal interest, to make disinterested. **disinterested** *a.* 1 without personal interest or prejudice; unbiased, impartial, unselfish. 2 (*loosely*) uninterested. **disinterestedly** *adv.* **disinterestedness** *n.*

Usage note *Disinterested* is often thought to mean the same as *uninterested*, but the commonly accepted distinction is that *disinterested* means impartial, while *uninterested* means not interested.

disinvest (disinvest´) *v.i.* to reduce or withdraw one's investment (in). **disinvestment** *n.*
disinvolve (disinvolv´) *v.t.* 1 to disentangle. 2 to remove from involvement.
disjecta membra (disjektə mem´brə) *n.pl.* scattered fragments of a written work. [L, corr. of *disjecti membra poetae*, limbs of a dismembered poet]
disjoin (disjoin´) *v.t., v.i.* to separate, to part. **disjoinable** *a.* [OF *desjoign-*, *desjoindre*, L *disjungere* (DIS-, *jungere*, to JOIN)]
disjoint (disjoint´) *v.t.* 1 to put out of joint, to dislocate. 2 to separate at the joints. 3 to put out of working order. 4 to break the connection of. ~*a.* disjointed, disconnected, out of order. **disjointed** *a.* 1 broken up, incoherent. 2 out of joint. **disjointedly** *adv.* **disjointedness** *n.* [OF *desjoint*, p.p. of *desjoindre*, as DISJOIN]
disjunction (disjŭngk´shən) *n.* 1 the act of disjoining; separation. 2 (*Logic*) a disjunctive proposition. **disjunct** *a.* disjoined (in various technical applications). **disjunctive** *a.* 1 separating, disjoining. 2 marking separation. ~*n.* 1 (*Gram.*) a disjunctive conjunction. 2 (*Logic*) a disjunctive proposition. **disjunctive conjunction** *n.* (*Gram.*) a conjunction (e.g. *or, but, though*) which unites sentences or clauses in composition, but divides them in sense, as opposed to a copulative conjunction. **disjunctively** *adv.* **disjunctive proposition** *n.* (*Logic*) a proposition with alternative predicates united by *or*. **disjuncture** *n.* the state of being disjointed; a separation. [L *disjunctio*, from *disjungere*, as DISJOIN]
disk DISC.
dislike (dislīk´) *v.t.* to regard with repugnance or aversion. ~*n.* 1 a feeling of repugnance; aversion. 2 a person or thing disliked. **dislikable, dislikeable** *a.* **dislikeful** *a.* disagreeable, unpleasant.
disload (dislōd´) *v.t.* to unload.
dislocate (dis´ləkāt) *v.t.* 1 to put out of joint. 2 to disturb, derange. 3 to break the continuity of (strata), to displace. **dislocation** (-ā´shən) *n.* [late L *dislocātus*, p.p. of *dislocāre* (*locāre*, to place, from *locus*, place)]
dislodge (disloj´) *v.t.* 1 to eject from a place of rest, retirement or defence. 2 to drive out, to expel. ~*v.i.* to quit a place. **dislodgement, dislodgment** *n.* [OF *desloger*]
disloyal (disloi´əl) *a.* 1 not true to allegiance. 2 unfaithful to the sovereign, disaffected towards the government. **disloyalist** *n.* **disloyally** *adv.* **disloyalty** *n.* [OF *desloial*]
dismal (diz´məl) *a.* 1 dark, cheerless, depressing, doleful, dreary. 2 depressingly poor (*a dismal record*). ~*n.pl.* low spirits, the blues. **dismally** *adv.* **dismalness** *n.* **dismal science** *n.* (*facet.*) political economy of the old-fashioned deductive kind. [OF *dis mal*, L *diēs mali*, evil days, unlucky days]
disman (disman´) *v.t.* (*pres.p.* **dismanning,** *past, p.p.* **dismanned**) to unman; to divest of men.
dismantle (disman´təl) *v.t.* 1 to strip of covering, equipment or means of defence. 2 to take to pieces. 3 to remove the defences (of a fortress). 4 to unrig (a ship etc.). **dismantlement** *n.* **dismantler** *n.* [MF *desmanteller*]

dismask (dismahsk´) *v.t.* to unmask. [OF *desmasquer*]

dismast (dismahst´) *v.t.* to deprive (a ship) of a mast or masts.

dismay (dismā´) *v.t.* 1 to deprive of courage; to dispirit. 2 to terrify, to daunt. ~*n.* 1 utter loss of courage or resolution. 2 a state of terror or fear. [prob. OF *des-*, DIS-, *mayer*, OHG *magan*, to be able, to have power, cogn. with OE *magan*, MAY[1] (cp. *esmayer*, to lose power, to faint, also Sp. *desmayer*, to DISMAY)]

dismember (dismem´bə) *v.t.* 1 to separate limb from limb. 2 to divide, to distribute, to partition. **dismemberment** *n.* [OF *desmembrer*]

dismiss (dismis´) *v.t.* 1 to send away; to dissolve; to disband; to allow to depart. 2 to discharge from office or employment. 3 to put aside, reject. 4 to cast off, discard. 5 (*Law*) to discharge from further consideration. 6 in cricket, to bowl out. ~*v.i.* (*imper.*, *Mil.*) break ranks! disperse! **dismissal** *n.* **dismissible** *a.* **dismissive** *a.* **dismissively** *adv.* **dismissiveness** *n.* [L *dīmittere* (DI-[1], *mittere*, to send), *dis-*, due to influence of OF *desmettre* (p.p. *dismit*)]

dismount (dismownt´) *v.i.* 1 to alight from a horse or bicycle. 2 to descend. ~*v.t.* 1 to throw down or remove (a cannon etc.) from a carriage or support. 2 to unhorse. 3 to take down or to pieces. 4 to bring down, to lower. ~*n.* the act of dismounting. [prob. from OF *desmonter*]

disnature (disnā´chə) *v.t.* to render unnatural. **disnaturalize** (-nach´ərəlīz), **disnaturalise** *v.t.* to denaturalize. [OF *desnaturer*]

Disneyesque (dizniesk´) *a.* 1 of or relating to the type of cartoon film or character created by US film producer Walt Disney, 1901–66. 2 of or relating to fantasy, whimsical.

disobedient (disəbē´diənt) *a.* refusing or neglecting to obey; refractory. **disobedience** *n.* **disobediently** *adv.* [OF *desobedient*]

disobey (disəbā´) *v.t.* 1 to neglect or refuse to obey. 2 to violate, to transgress. ~*v.i.* to be disobedient. **disobeyer** *n.* [F *désobéir*]

disoblige (disəblīj´) *v.t.* 1 to act in a way contrary to the wishes or convenience of. 2 to inconvenience. †**disobligation** (-obligā´shən) *n.* 1 a disobliging act. 2 freedom from obligation. **disobligement** *n.* **disobliging** *a.* 1 not obliging, not disposed to gratify the wishes of another. 2 churlish, ungracious. **disobligingly** *adv.* **disobligingness** *n.* [F *désobliger*]

☒ **disolve** common misspelling of DISSOLVE.

disorder (disaw´də) *n.* 1 lack of order; confusion, irregularity. 2 tumult, commotion. 3 disease, illness. 4 neglect or infraction of laws or discipline. ~*v.t.* 1 to throw into confusion. 2 to derange the natural functions of. **disordered** *a.* **disorderly** *a.* 1 confused, disarranged. 2 unlawful, irregular. 3 turbulent, causing disturbance, unruly. **disorderliness** *n.* **disorderly conduct** *n.* (*Law*) public misconduct leading to distress or harassment. **disorderly house** *n.* (*Law*) a term including brothels, gaming-houses, betting-houses and certain unlicensed places of entertainment. [F *désordre*]

disorganize (disaw´gənīz), **disorganise** *v.t.* to throw into confusion; to destroy the systematic arrangement of. **disorganization** (-zā´shən) *n.* **disorganized, disorganised** *a.* lacking order, confused. [F *désorganiser*]

disorientate (disaw´riəntāt), **disorient** (disaw´riənt) *v.t.* 1 to cause to lose one's sense of direction. 2 to confuse. 3 to turn from the east. **disorientation** (-tā´shən) *n.* [F *désorienter* (DIS-, *orienter*, to ORIENT)]

disown (disōn´) *v.t.* 1 to disclaim, to renounce, to repudiate. 2 to refuse to own. **disowner** *n.* **disownment** *n.*

☒ **dispair** common misspelling of DESPAIR.

disparage (dispar´ij) *v.t.* 1 to treat or speak of slightingly; to depreciate. 2 to discredit, to disgrace. 3 to think lightly of, to undervalue. **disparagement** *n.* **disparagingly** *adv.* [OF *desparagier* (*parage*, lineage, rank, late L *parāgium*, from *par*, equal)]

disparate (dis´pərət) *a.* 1 dissimilar, discordant. 2 having nothing in common, not coordinate. ~*n.* (*usu. pl.*) things so unlike that they admit of no comparison with each other. **disparately** *adv.* **disparateness** *n.* [L *disparātus*, p.p. of *disparāre* (DIS-, *parāre*, to make ready), assimilated in sense to *dispar*, unequal]

disparity (dispar´iti) *n.* (*pl.* **disparities**) 1 (an) inequality. 2 (a) difference in degree. 3 unlikeness. [F *disparité*]

dispart (dispaht´) *n.* the difference between the external semidiameter of a gun at the muzzle and at the breech. [etym. uncertain]

dispassionate (dispash´ənət) *a.* free from passion; calm, temperate; impartial. **dispassion** *n.* **dispassionately** *adv.* **dispassionateness** *n.*

dispatch (dispach´), **despatch** *v.t.* 1 to send off to some destination, esp. to send with celerity and haste. 2 to transact quickly; to settle, to finish. 3 to put to death. 4 to eat quickly. 5 †to deliver (from), to relieve (of). 6 †to deprive. 7 †to get rid of. ~*n.* 1 the act of dispatching or being dispatched. 2 prompt action. 3 promptitude, quickness, speed. 4 a message or letter dispatched, esp. an official communication on state affairs. 5 the act or an instance of killing someone. **hatches, matches and dispatches** HATCH[2]. **mentioned in dispatches** cited for bravery or valuable services. **dispatch case** *n.* (*Mil.*) a leather case for carrying papers. **dispatcher** *n.* **dispatch rider** *n.* a motorcyclist who carries dispatches. [Sp. *despachar* (DIS-, late L *pactāre*, to make an agreement, from L *pactum*, an agreement, neut. p.p. of *pangere*, to fasten)]

dispel (dispel´) *v.t.* (*pres.p.* **dispelling,** *past, p.p.* **dispelled**) to dissipate, to disperse; to drive away, to banish. **dispeller** *n.* [L *dispellere* (DIS-, *pellere*, to drive)]

dispensable (dispen´səbəl) *a.* 1 able to be dispensed with, inessential. 2 (of a law etc.) able to be relaxed. 3 †for which a dispensation may be granted, pardonable. **dispensability** (-bil´-) *n.*

dispensary (dispen´səri) *n.* (*pl.* **dispensaries**) 1 a place where medicines are dispensed. 2 an establishment where medicines and medical advice are given free to the poor. [see DISPENSE]

dispensation (dispensā´shən) *n.* 1 the act of dispensing; distribution. 2 something distributed. 3 scheme, plan, economy. 4 the government of the universe. 5 the management of the world by Providence. 6 (*Theol.*) God's dealings with humans, esp. the divine relation at a particular period (as the Mosaic dispensation). 7 a system of principles, rights and privileges enjoined. 8 in the Roman Catholic Church, a licence to omit or commit something enjoined or forbidden by canon law. 9 the act of dispensing with or doing without something. 10 management, administration. **dispensational** *a.* **dispensatory** *a.* granting dispensation. ~*n.* (*pl.* **dispensatories**) a book listing medical prescriptions, their composition and use. [L *dispensātio*, as DISPENSE]

dispense (dispens´) *v.t.* 1 to deal out, to distribute. 2 to administer. 3 to prepare and give out (medicine). 4 to grant a dispensation to. **to dispense with** 1 to do without. 2 to grant exemption from. **dispenser** *n.* 1 a person who or something which dispenses. 2 a machine which dispenses money, soap etc. 3 (*Med.*) a person who dispenses medicines. 4 †a steward. **dispensing** *n.*, *a.* **dispensing chemist** *n.* a chemist who is qualified to prepare and dispense medicines. **dispensing optician** *n.* an optician who is qualified to supply and fit spectacles and contact lenses. [OF *dispenser*, L *dispensāre*, freq. of *dispendere* (DIS- *pendere*, to weigh)]

disperse (dispœs´) *v.t.* 1 to scatter; to send, drive or throw in different directions. 2 to dissipate, to cause to vanish. 3 to distribute, to diffuse. 4 to disseminate. 5

(*Physics*) to divide (white light) into its component colours. **6** (*Chem.*) to put (particles) into a colloidal state, to distribute evenly in a fluid. ~*v.i.* **1** to be scattered in different directions. **2** to break up, to vanish. **3** to become spread over a wide area. **dispersable** *a.* **dispersal** *n.* **dispersant** *n.* (*Chem.*) a liquid or gas used to disperse particles in a medium. **dispersedly** (-sid-) *adv.* **disperser** *n.* **dispersible** *a.* **dispersive** *a.* **dispersively** *adv.* **dispersiveness** *n.* [F *disperser*, from L *dispersus*, p.p. of *dispergere* (DIS-, *spargere*, to scatter)]

dispersion (dispœ´shən) *n.* **1** the act of dispersing. **2** the state of being dispersed. **3** (*Chem.*) a mixture containing one substance dispersed in another. **4** (*Med.*) the removal of inflammation. **5** (*Math.*) in statistics, the scattering of variables around the arithmetic mean or median. **6** in ecology, the pattern of distribution of an animal or plant population. **the Dispersion** (*Hist.*) the scattering of the tribes of Israel, esp. the Babylonian captivity. **dispersion of heat, dispersion of light** *n.* (*Physics*) the separation produced by the refraction at different angles of rays of different wavelengths. [L *dispersio*, as DISPERSE]

dispirit (dispir´it) *v.t.* **1** to deprive of spirit or courage. **2** to discourage, to dishearten, to deject. **dispirited** *a.* **dispiritedly** *adv.* **dispiritedness** *n.* **dispiriting** *a.* **dispiritingly** *adv.*

displace (displās´) *v.t.* **1** to remove from the usual or proper place. **2** to remove from a position of dignity; to dismiss. **3** to take the place of, to put something in the place of, to supersede. **4** to banish. **displaced persons** *n.pl.* refugees who for any reason cannot be repatriated. **displacement** *n.* **1** the act of displacing. **2** the state of being displaced. **3** removal by superseding. **4** change of position. **5** the water displaced by a floating body, such as a ship, the weight of which equals that of the floating body at rest. **6** (*Physics*) the amount by which anything is displaced. **7** (*Geol.*) a fault. **8** (*Psych.*) the unconscious transferring of strong emotions from the original object to another. **9** the state of being superseded by something else. **displacement activity** *n.* (*Psych.*) a kind of behaviour which seems to have no relevance to the situation, such as scratching one's head when confused. **displacement ton** a unit used to measure the amount of water displaced by a vessel, equivalent to 2240 lbs or 35 cu. ft. (0.99 m^3) of sea water.

display (displā´) *v.t.* **1** to exhibit, to expose, to show. **2** to exhibit ostentatiously, to parade. **3** to make known, to unfold, to reveal. **4** to make prominent. ~*n.* **1** displaying. **2** show, exhibition. **3** the kind of behaviour displayed by some birds and fish, esp. to attract a mate. **4** (*Comput.*) **a** the information displayed on a screen. **b** the screen itself. **5** ostentatious behaviour. **6** setting in prominent type. **displayer** *n.* [OF *despleier* (DIS-, *pleier*, L *plicāre*, to fold)]

displease (displēz´) *v.t.* to dissatisfy, to offend; to vex, to annoy; to be disagreeable to. ~*v.i.* to cause displeasure or offence. **to be displeased at/ with** to be annoyed or vexed at or with; to disapprove. **displeasing** *a.* **displeasingly** *adv.* [OF *desplaisir*]

displeasure (displezh´ə) *n.* **1** a feeling of annoyance, vexation, irritation or anger. **2** †injury, offence. ~†*v.t.* to displease, to annoy. [OF *desplaisir*, as DISPLEASE (assim. to PLEASURE)]

displume (disploom´) *v.t.* to strip of plumes, feathers or decorations.

dispone (dispōn´) *v.t.* **1** to dispose, dispose of. **2** (*Sc. Law*) to make over or convey (property). **disponee** (-nē´) *n.* (*Sc. Law*) a person to whom property is disponed. **disponer** *n.* (*Sc. Law*) a person who dispones property. [L *dispōnere* (DIS-, *pōnere*, to place)]

disport (dispawt´) *v.t.* to amuse (oneself), to divert (oneself); to enjoy (oneself). ~*v.i.* to play, to amuse or divert oneself; to gambol. ~†*n.* **1** sport, play, diversion, relaxation. **2** a hobby, a pastime. [OF *desporter* (*des-*, DIS-, *porter*, L *portāre*, to carry)]

disposal (dispō´zəl) *n.* **1** the act of disposing. **2** distributing, bestowing, giving away or dealing with things in some particular way. **3** disposition. **4** control, management, command. **5** order or arrangement in which things are disposed. **6** the act of getting rid of rubbish. **7** (*N Am.*) a waste disposal unit. **at the disposal of 1** available for the use of. **2** in the power of, at the command of. [as DISPOSE]

dispose (dispōz´) *v.t.* **1** to arrange, to set in order; to place. **2** to settle. **3** to adjust, to direct, to incline. **4** to hand over, to bestow. ~*v.i.* to determine or arrange affairs. **to dispose of 1** to put into the hands of someone else. **2** to get rid of. **3** to sell. **4** to finish, to settle. **5** to kill. **6** to prove wrong. **7** to use up. **disposable** *a.* **1** capable of being disposed of. **2** designed for disposal after use, as *disposable razors*. ~*n.* any item intended for disposal after use. **disposability** (-bil´-) *n.* **disposable income** *n.* net income after payment of tax, available for use. **disposed** *a.* inclined (*I didn't feel disposed to help her*). **disposer** *n.* **disposure** *n.* **1** disposal. **2** disposition. [OF *disposer* (DIS-, *poser*, L *pausāre*, to cease, to POSE[1], substituted for *pōnere*, to place)]

disposition (dispəzish´ən) *n.* **1** the act of disposing, ordering, arranging or bestowing. **2** disposal. **3** †the state or manner of disposal. **4** arrangement in general. **5** aptitude; inclination, temperament, natural tendency. **6** a humour, caprice, fancy. **7** (*Sc. Law*) the disposal of property. **8** (*Law*) any unilateral writing by which a person makes over to another a piece of heritable or movable property. **9** (*usu. pl.*) arrangement, plan, preparation. **10** (*usu. pl.*) the posting of troops in the most advantageous position. **dispositional** *a.* **dispositioned** *a.* [F, from L *dispositio -ōnem*, from *dispositus*, p.p. of *dispōnere* (DIS-, *pōnere*, to place)]

dispossess (dispəzes´) *v.t.* **1** to oust from possession, esp. of real estate. **2** to eject, to dislodge. **3** to deprive (of). **dispossession** (-zesh´ən) *n.* **dispossessor** *n.* [OF *despossesser*]

disposure DISPOSE.

dispraise (disprāz´) *v.t.* to censure, to express disapprobation of. ~*n.* blame, disapprobation, disparagement. **dispraiser** *n.* **dispraisingly** *adv.* [OF *despreisier*, L *dēpretiāre*, to DEPRECIATE]

†**dispread** (dispred´) *v.t.* to spread in different directions. ~*v.i.* to be spread out. [DIS-, SPREAD]

disproof (disproof´) *n.* **1** refutation. **2** something which proves error or falsehood.

disproportion (disprəpaw´shən) *n.* **1** lack of proportion between things or parts. **2** an inadequacy, a disparity. **3** lack of symmetry. ~*v.t.* **1** to make out of proportion. **2** †to make inconsistent. **disproportionably** *adv.* **disproportional** *a.* **disproportionally** *adv.* **disproportionate** *a.* **1** not duly proportioned. **2** too large or too small in relation to something. **disproportionately** *adv.* **disproportionateness** *n.*

disprove (disproov´) *v.t.* to prove to be erroneous or unfounded; to refute. **disprovable** *a.* **disproval** *n.* [OF *desprover*]

dispute (dispūt´) *v.i.* **1** to contend in argument; to quarrel in opposition to another. **2** to quarrel, to wrangle. **3** to debate, to discuss. ~*v.t.* **1** to contend about in argument; to oppose, to question, to challenge or deny the truth of. **2** to reason upon, to discuss, to argue. **3** to contend or strive for, to contest. **4** to strive against, to resist. ~*n.* **1** contention or strife in argument; debate, controversy. **2** a difference of opinion; a falling out, a quarrel. **3** a dispute between management and trade union. **4** contest, strife, struggle. **beyond/ past/ without dispute** without the possibility of being disputed. **disputable** *a.* open to dispute; questionable, uncertain. **disputability** (-bil´-) *n.* **disputableness** *n.*

disputably *adv.* **disputant** *n.* a person who disputes; a person who engages in controversy. ~*a.* engaged in disputation or controversy. **disputation** (-tā´shən) *n.* **1** the act of disputing. **2** controversy, discussion. **3** an exercise in arguing both sides of a question for the sake of practice. **disputatious** *a.* given to dispute or controversy; cavilling, contentious. **disputatiously** *adv.* **disputatiousness** *n.* †**disputative** *a.* inclined to argument. **disputer** *n.* [OF *desputer*, L *disputāre* (DIS-, *putāre*, to think)]

disqualify (diskwol´ifī) *v.t.* (*3rd pers. sing. pres.* **disqualifies,** *pres.p.* **disqualifying,** *past, p.p.* **disqualified**) **1** to render unfit, to disable, to debar. **2** to render or declare legally incompetent for any act or post. **3** to disbar from a competition on account of an irregularity. **disqualification** (-fikā´shən) *n.* **1** the act of disqualifying. **2** something which disqualifies.

disquiet (diskwī´ət) *v.t.* to disturb, to make uneasy, to harass, to vex. ~*n.* lack of quiet or peace; uneasiness, restlessness, anxiety. **disquieting** *a.* **disquietingly** *adv.* **disquietness** *n.* **disquietous** *a.* **disquietude** (-tūd) *n.* the state of being disquieted; anxiety, uneasiness.

disquisition (diskwizish´ən) *n.* **1** a formal discourse or treatise. **2** a formal and systematic inquiry, an investigation. **disquisitional** *a.* **disquisitive** (-kwiz´-) *a.* [L *disquīsītio*, from *disquīsitus*, p.p. of *disquīrere* (DIS-, *quaerere*, to seek)]

disrate (disrāt´) *v.t.* (*Naut.*) to degrade or reduce in rating or rank.

disregard (disrigahd´) *v.t.* **1** to take no notice of; to neglect. **2** to ignore as unworthy of regard. ~*n.* lack or omission of attention or regard; slight, neglect. **disregarder** *n.* **disregardful** *a.* **disregardfully** *adv.*

disrelish (disrel´ish) *n.* a distaste or dislike; aversion, antipathy. ~*v.t.* **1** to feel dislike for or aversion to. **2** to dislike the taste of.

disremember (disrimem´bə) *v.t.* (*coll.*) to be unable to remember; to forget.

disrepair (disripeə´) *n.* a state of being out of repair; dilapidation.

disreputable (disrep´ūtəbəl) *a.* **1** not reputable; of bad repute, not respectable; discreditable, mean. **2** dirty or shabby in appearance. **disreputableness** *n.* **disreputably** *adv.* **disrepute** (-ripūt´) *n.* a loss or lack of reputation; discredit.

disrespect (disrispekt´) *n.* lack of respect or reverence; rudeness, incivility. **disrespectable** *a.* **disrespectful** *a.* lacking in respect; uncivil, rude. **disrespectfully** *adv.* **disrespectfulness** *n.*

disrobe (disrōb´) *v.t.* **1** to strip of a robe or dress; to undress (oneself). **2** to divest of authority. ~*v.i.* to undress. **disrober** *n.*

disrupt (disrŭpt´) *v.t.* **1** to interrupt, to prevent from continuing. **2** to tear apart, to break in pieces. **disrupter** *n.* **disruption** (-shən) *n.* **disruptive** *a.* tending to cause disruption. **disruptively** *adv.* **disruptiveness** *n.* **disruptor** *n.* [L *disruptio*, from *disruptus*, p.p. of *disrumpere* (DIS-, *rumpere*, to break)]

diss DIS.

☒ **dissapear** common misspelling of DISAPPEAR.

☒ **dissapoint** common misspelling of DISAPPOINT.

dissatisfy (disat´isfī) *v.t.* (*3rd pers. sing. pres.* **dissatisfies,** *pres.p.* **dissatisfying,** *past, p.p.* **dissatisfied**) **1** to make discontented, to displease. **2** to fall short of the expectations of. **dissatisfaction** (-fak´shən) *n.* **dissatisfactory** (-fak´-) *a.* **dissatisfiedly** *adv.*

dissect (disekt´, dī-) *v.t.* **1** to cut in pieces. **2** to anatomize; to cut up (an organism) so as to examine the parts and structure. **3** to analyse, to criticize in detail. **dissected** *a.* **1** (*Bot.*) cut into narrow segments. **2** (*Geol.*) of or relating to hills and valleys cut by erosion. **dissectible** *a.* **dissecting** *n.* **dissecting microscope** *n.* a microscope allowing dissection of the object being examined. **dissecting room, dissecting table** *n.* a room or table where dissection is carried out. **dissection** (-sek´shən) *n.* **dissector** *n.* [L *dissectus*, p.p. of *dissecāre* (DIS-, *secāre*, to cut)]

Usage note The pronunciation (dī-) is sometimes disapproved of.

disseise (dis·sēz´), **disseize** *v.t.* to deprive of possession of estates etc.; to dispossess wrongfully. **disseisin** (-zin) *n.* unlawful dispossession. **disseisor** *n.* [A-F *disseiser*, OF *dessaisir*]

dissemble (disem´bəl) *v.i.* to hide one's feelings, opinions or intentions; to play the hypocrite. ~*v.t.* **1** to pretend, to feign, to simulate. **2** to hide under a false appearance. **dissemblance** *n.* **1** the act of dissembling. **2** unlikeness, dissimilarity. **dissembler** *n.* **dissemblingly** *adv.* [OF *dissimuler*, L *dissimulāre* (DIS-, *simulāre*, to simulate), assim. to RESEMBLE]

disseminate (disem´ināt) *v.t.* **1** to spread (information) about. **2** to scatter (seed) about with a view to growth or propagation. **disseminated** *a.* **disseminated sclerosis** *n.* multiple sclerosis. **dissemination** (-ā´shən) *n.* **disseminator** *n.* [L *dissēminātus*, p.p. of *dissēmināre* (DIS-, *sēmināre*, to sow, from *sēmen*, seed)]

dissension (disen´shən) *n.* disagreement of opinion; discord, contention, strife. [F, from L *dissentio -ōnem*, as DISSENT]

dissent (disent´) *v.i.* **1** to differ or disagree in opinion; to hold opposite views. **2** to withhold assent or approval. **3** to differ from an established Church, esp. from the Church of England. ~*n.* **1** difference or disagreement of opinion. **2** a declaration of disagreement or nonconformity. **3** a protest by a minority. **dissenter** *n.* **1** a person who dissents or disagrees, esp. one who dissents from an established Church. **2** (**Dissenter**) a member of a sect that has separated from the Church of England. †**dissentious,** †**dissensious** *a.* [L *dissentīre* (DIS-, *sentīre*, to feel)]

dissentient (disen´shənt) *a.* disagreeing or differing in opinion; holding or expressing contrary views. ~*n.* **1** a person who holds or expresses contrary views. **2** a dissenter from the views of a political or other party. **dissentience, dissentiency** *n.* [L *dissentiens -entem*, pres.p. of *dissentīre*, as DISSENT]

dissepiment (disep´imənt) *n.* (*Zool., Bot.*) a division or partition in an organ or part. [L *dissaepīmentum*, *dissaepīre* (DIS-, *saepīre*, to hedge off, from *saepēs*, a hedge)]

dissertation (disətā´shən) *n.* a formal discourse on any subject; a disquisition, treaty or exile. †**dissert** (disœt´), †**dissertate** *v.i.* **1** to discourse in a formal manner. **2** to write a dissertation. †**dissertational** *a.* [L *dissertus*, p.p. and *dissertāre*, freq. of *disserere* (DIS-, *serere*, to join)]

disservice (disœ´vis) *n.* a harmful act, a bad turn. †**disserve** *v.t.* to do a disservice to; to injure.

dissever (disev´ə) *v.t.* to sever, to separate. **disseverance, disseveration** (-vərā´shən) *n.* **disseverment** *n.*

dissident (dis´idənt) *a.* not in agreement; disagreeing, dissenting. ~*n.* **1** a person who dissents from or votes against any motion. **2** a person who disagrees with the government; a dissenter. **dissidence** *n.* [L *dissidens -entem*, pres.p. of *dissidēre* (DIS-, *sedēre*, to sit)]

dissimilar (disim´ilə) *a.* not similar; unlike in nature, properties or appearances; discordant. **dissimilarity** (-lar´-) *n.* (*pl.* **dissimilarities**). **dissimilarly** *adv.*

dissimilate (disim´ilāt) *v.t.* to make (sounds) unlike. ~*v.i.* (of sounds) to become unlike. **dissimilation** (-ā´shən) *n.* the rendering of two similar sounds unlike, or two dissimilar sounds identical, when such sounds come together. **dissimilatory** (-lətəri) *a.* [L *similus*, after ASSIMILATE]

dissimilitude (disimil´itūd) *n.* unlikeness, dissimilarity.

dissimulate (disim´ūlāt) *v.t., v.i.* to dissemble, to

conceal, to disguise. **dissimulation** (-lā´shən) *n.* **dissimulator** *n.* [L *dissimulātus*, p.p. of *dissimulāre* (DIS-, *simulāre*, to SIMULATE)]

dissipate (dis´ipāt) *v.t.* **1** to scatter; to drive in different directions. **2** to disperse, to dispel. **3** to squander, to waste, to fritter away. *~v.i.* **1** to be dispersed, to vanish. **2** to indulge in dissolute or frivolous enjoyment. **dissipated** *a.* **1** given to dissipation, dissolute. **2** wasted in dissipation. **3** scattered, dispersed. **dissipater** *n.* **dissipation** (-pā´shən) *n.* **1** the act of dissipating or scattering. **2** the state of being dispersed or scattered. **3** excessive indulgence in luxury, frivolity or vice; dissoluteness. **4** wasteful expenditure, extravagance. **5** disintegration, dispersion, diffusion. **dissipative** *a.* **dissipator** *n.* [L *dissipātus*, p.p. of *dissipāre* (DIS-, obs. *sipāre*, to throw)]

dissociate (disō´shiāt, -si-) *v.t.* **1** to separate, to disconnect. **2** (*Chem.*) to decompose, esp. by the action of heat. **3** (*Psych.*) to cause to undergo dissociation. *~v.i.* to become separated or disconnected. **to dissociate oneself from** to deny any connection or association with. **dissociated personality** *n.* (*Psych.*) a personality which is temporarily taken control of by unconscious complexes, causing a loosening of control over consciousness. **dissociation** (-shiā´shən, -siā´-) *n.* **1** separation, disconnection. **2** (*Psych.*) a loosening of control over consciousness in which the personality is temporarily taken control of by unconscious complexes. **dissociative** (-shiətiv, -siətiv) *a.* [L *dissociātus*, p.p. of *dissociāre* (DIS-, *sociāre*, to associate, from *socius*, a comrade)]

dissoluble (disol´ūbəl) *a.* able to be dissolved, decomposed or disconnected. **dissolubility** (-bil´-) *n.* **dissolubly** *adv.* [L *dissolūbilis*, from *dissolvere*, to DISSOLVE]

dissolute (dis´əloot) *a.* given to dissipation, loose in morals; licentious, debauched. *~n.* a dissolute person. **dissolutely** *adv.* **dissoluteness** *n.* [L *dissolūtus*, p.p. of *dissolvere*, to DISSOLVE]

dissolution (disəloo´shən) *n.* **1** the act or process of dissolving, separating, disintegrating, decomposing; liquefaction. **2** the destruction of any body by the separation of its parts. **3** death, the separation of soul and body. **4** separation of a meeting, assembly or body. **5** the official ending of a marriage, partnership or other relationship. **6** gradual disappearance. **7** dissoluteness, corruption, depravity. **dissolution of parliament** *n.* the end of a parliament, to be followed by a general election. [L *dissolūtio*, as DISSOLUTE]

dissolve (dizolv´) *v.t.* **1** to diffuse the particles of (a substance) in a liquid. **2** to convert from a solid to a liquid state by heat or moisture. **3** to cause to disappear gradually. **4** to separate; to break up. **5** to put an end to (as a meeting etc.); to dismiss, to disperse. *~v.i.* **1** to become liquefied. **2** to decompose, to disintegrate. **3** to break up, to separate. **4** to fade away, to melt away. **5** to melt by the action of heat. **6** to vanish. **7** (*coll.*) to be emotionally overcome (*She dissolved into tears*). **8** in films and TV, to fade out one scene and merge in the next. *~n.* a scene in a film or TV programme which is dissolved. **dissolvable** *a.* **dissolvent** *a.* having the power to melt or dissolve. *~n.* anything which has the power of dissolving or melting, a solvent. **dissolver** *n.* [L *dissolvere* (DIS-, *solvere*, to loosen)]

dissonant (dis´ənənt) *a.* **1** (*Mus.*) discordant, inharmonious. **2** harsh, incongruous. **dissonance, dissonancy** *n.* **dissonantly** *adv.* [L *dissonans -antem*, pres.p. of *dissonāre*, to be unlike in sound, from *dissonus*, discordant]

dissuade (diswād´) *v.t.* **1** to try to persuade not to do some act. **2** to advise against. **3** to divert from a purpose by argument. **dissuader** *n.* **dissuasion** (-zhən) *n.* **dissuasive** (-siv) *a.* **1** tending to dissuade. **2** dehortatory. *~n.* a dissuasive argument or reason. **dissuasively** *adv.* [L *dissuādēre* (DIS-, *suādēre*, to persuade)]

dissyllable DISYLLABLE.

dissymmetry (disim´itri) *n.* (*pl.* **dissymmetries**) **1** lack of symmetry between objects or parts. **2** an instance of dissymmetry. **3** the fact of two objects or parts of being mirror images of each other. **dissymmetrical** (-met´-) *a.* **dissymmetrically** *adv.*

dist. *abbr.* **1** distant. **2** distinguish(ed). **3** district.

distaff (dis´tahf) *n.* **1** a cleft stick about 3 ft. (0.91 m) long, on which wool or carded cotton is wound for spinning. **2** women's work. **distaff side** *n.* the female side of a family or descent. [OE *distæf* (cp. LG *diesse*, a bunch of flax)]

distal (dis´təl) *a.* **1** applied to the extremity of a bone or organ farthest from the point of attachment or insertion. **2** situated at the farthest point from the centre. **distally** *adv.* [formed from DISTANCE]

distance (dis´təns) *n.* **1** the space between two objects measured along the shortest line. **2** extent of separation however measured. **3** the quality of being distant, remoteness. **4** a distance point (*from a distance*). **5** a set interval. **6** the length of a course run in a competition. **7** reserve, coolness; avoidance of familiarity; unfriendliness. **8** remoteness in time (past or future). **9** the remoter parts of a view or the background of a picture. **10** a point on a racecourse 204 yd. (219.5 m) from the winning post. *~v.t.* **1** to place far off. **2** to leave behind in a race; to outstrip, to outdo. **3** to cause to seem remote. **at a distance** from a long way off. **to go the distance 1** to complete something one has started. **2** to endure to the end of a game or bout in sport. **to keep at a distance** not to become too friendly with. **to keep one's distance 1** to behave respectfully. **2** to behave with reserve or coldness. **distance learning** *n.* an educational system by which students study at home, by means of a correspondence course, videos, etc. **distance post** *n.* in athletics, a post at the end of a race, used for the disqualification of runners who do not pass it. **distance runner** *n.* in athletics, a runner who competes in long-distance or middle-distance races. [OF, from L *distantia* (see DISTANT)]

distant (dis´tənt) *a.* **1** separated by intervening space. **2** remote in space, time (past or future), succession, relationship, resemblance, kind or nature. **3** at a certain distance (*four miles distant*). **4** not plain or obvious; faint, slight. **5** reserved, cool. **6** distracted, absent (*a distant look*). **distant early warning** *n.* (*N Am.*) a radar system for detecting a missile attack. **distantly** *adv.* **distantness** *n.* **distant signal** *n.* a railway signal reached before the home signal and indicating whether that is at danger or not. [F, from L *distans -ntem*, pres.p. of *distāre* (DIS-, *stāre*, to stand)]

distaste (distāst´) *n.* **1** disrelish, aversion of the taste. **2** dislike, disinclination. **distasteful** *a.* **1** offensive, displeasing; repulsive. **2** unpleasant to the taste. **distastefully** *adv.* **distastefulness** *n.*

distemper[1] (distem´pə), **destemper** *n.* **1** a method of painting with colours soluble in water, mixed with chalk or clay, and diluted with size instead of oil. **2** the coloured preparation used in this style of painting. *~v.t.* to paint or colour with distemper. [L *temperāre*, to TEMPER, to mix in due proportions (cp. OF *destempré*, immoderate)]

distemper[2] (distem´pə) *n.* a catarrhal disorder affecting dogs, foxes etc. *~†v.t.* **1** to disturb, to vex. **2** to derange (the mental or bodily functions of). **distempered** *a.* **1** disordered in mind or body. **2** intemperate, immoderate. [OF *destemprer*, as DISTEMPER[1]]

distend (distend´) *v.t.* to spread or swell out; to inflate. *~v.i.* to swell out. **distensible** *a.* **distensibility** *n.* **distension** (-shən) *n.* **1** the act of distending. **2** the state of being distended. 3 breadth, expansion. [L *distendere* (DIS-, *tendere*, *tentum* or *tēnsum*, to stretch)]

disthrone (disthrōn´) *v.t.* to dethrone.

distich (dis´tik) *n.* a couplet; two lines of poetry making complete sense. [L *distichus*, *distichon*, Gr. *distichon* (DI-[2], *stichos*, a row)]

distichous (dis´tikəs) *a.* (*Bot.*) 1 having two rows (of leaves etc.). 2 arranged in two rows. [as DISTICH]

distil (distil´), (*NAm.*) **distill** *v.t.* (*pres.p.* **distilling**, *past, p.p.* **distilled**) 1 to extract by means of vaporization and condensation. 2 to extract the essence of. 3 to make or obtain by this process. 4 to purify by this process. 5 to let fall in drops, to shed. ~*v.i.* 1 to fall in drops; to trickle. 2 to flow forth gently, to exude. 3 to undergo the process of distillation. **distillable** *a.* **distillate** (dis´tilāt) *n.* the product of distillation. **distillation** (-ā´shən) *n.* 1 the act of distilling. 2 the act or process of heating a solid or liquid in a vessel so constructed that the vapours thrown off from the heated substance are collected and condensed. 3 the product of this process, a distillate. **destructive distillation** DESTRUCTIVE (under DESTRUCTION). **fractional distillation** FRACTIONAL (under FRACTION). **vacuum distillation** VACUUM. **distillatory** *a.* **distiller** *n.* a person who distils, esp. a manufacturer of whisky or another spirit by distillation. **distillery** *n.* (*pl.* **distilleries**) a building where whisky or another spirit is produced by distillation. [L *distillāre* (DI-[1], *stillāre*, to trickle, from *stilla*, a drop)]

distinct (distingkt´) *a.* 1 clearly distinguished or distinguishable, different, separate. 2 standing clearly apart, not identical. 3 unmistakable, clear, plain, evident, definite. 4 (*coll.*) decided, positive. **distinction** (-tingk´shən) *n.* 1 a mark or note of difference. 2 a distinguishing quality, a characteristic difference. 3 the act of distinguishing, discrimination. 4 something which differentiates. 5 honour, title, rank. 6 eminence, superiority. 7 an examination grade signifying excellence (*a pass with distinction*). 8 in literary criticism, individuality. **distinction without a difference** *n.* a superficial distinction. **distinctive** *a.* 1 serving to mark distinction or difference, characteristic. 2 separate, distinct. **distinctively** *adv.* **distinctiveness** *n.* **distinctly** *adv.* **distinctness** *n.* [L *distinctus*, p.p. of *distinguere*, to DISTINGUISH]

Usage note The meanings of the adjectives *distinct* and *distinctive* overlap, but in general *distinct* means clearly distinguished or separate, and *distinctive* serving to distinguish or characteristic.

distingué (dēstãgā´), (*fem.*) **distinguée** *a.* having an air of nobility or dignity. [F, p.p. of *distinguer*, to DISTINGUISH]

distinguish (disting´gwish) *v.t.* 1 to discriminate, to differentiate. 2 to indicate the difference of from others by some external mark. 3 to classify. 4 to tell apart, to discriminate between. 5 to perceive the existence of by means of the senses; to recognize. 6 to be a mark of distinction or characteristic property of. 7 to separate from others by some token of honour or preference. 8 to make eminent, prominent, or well known. ~*v.i.* to differentiate; to draw distinctions. **distinguishable** *a.* **distinguishably** *adv.* **distinguished** *a.* 1 having an air of nobility or dignity. 2 eminent, celebrated, remarkable. **Distinguished Conduct Medal** *n.* a medal awarded to warrant officers and other ranks for gallantry in the field. **Distinguished Flying Cross** *n.* a medal for gallantry awarded to officers and warrant officers of the RAF. **Distinguished Service Medal, Distinguished Service Cross** *n.* a medal awarded for gallantry to RN officers and warrant officers, and CPOs and other ratings. **Distinguished Service Order** *n.* a medal for meritorious service awarded to officers in the three services. **distinguisher** *n.* **distinguishing** *a.* **distinguishingly** *adv.* [L *distinguere* (DI-[1], *stinguere*, prob. cogn. with Gr. *stizein*, to prick)]

distort (distawt´) *v.t.* 1 to twist or alter the natural shape or direction of. 2 to pervert from the true meaning. 3 to distort (an electrical sign) during transmission or application. **distortedly** *adv.* **distortedness** *n.* **distortion** (-taw´shən) *n.* 1 the act of distorting. 2 the state of being distorted. 3 a writhing, a contortion. 4 a perversion of meaning, a misrepresentation. 5 deviation from strict reproduction in a radio receiver or loudspeaker. **distortional** *a.* **distortionless** *a.* **distortive** *a.* [L *distortus*, p.p. of *distorquēre* (DIS-, *torquēre*, to twist)]

distract (distrakt´) *v.t.* 1 to draw or turn aside, to divert the mind or attention of. 2 to draw in different directions, to confuse, to bewilder, to perplex. 3 (*usu. p.p.*) to drive mad, to trouble. 4 to amuse. **distracted** *a.* 1 disturbed mentally, crazed, maddened. 2 worried, harassed, perplexed. **distractedly** *adv.* **distracting** *a.* **distractingly** *adv.* **distraction** (-trak´shən) *n.* 1 diversion of the mind or attention. 2 the thing that diverts; an interruption, a diversion. 3 relaxation, relief, amusement. 4 a lack of concentration. 5 confusion, perplexity, agitation, violent mental excitement arising from pain, worry etc. 6 mental aberration, madness, frenzy. **to drive to distraction** to cause intense irritation to. **distractive** *a.* **distractively** *adv.* **distractor** *n.* [L *distractus*, p.p. of *distrahere* (DIS-, *trahere*, to draw)]

distrain (distrān´) *v.t.* (*Law*) to seize for debt; to take the personal property of, in order to satisfy a demand or enforce the performance of an act. ~*v.i.* to levy a distress. **distrainable** *a.* **distrainee** (-nē´) *n.* a person whose property is distrained. ~*n.* **distrainer** *n.* **distrainment** *n.* **distrainor** *n.* **distraint** *n.* the act of seizing goods for debt. [OF *destreign-*, stem of *destreindre*, L *distringere* (DI-[1], *stringere*, to STRAIN[1], compress)]

distrait (distrā´), (*fem.*) **distraite** (-trāt´) *a.* absent-minded, abstracted, inattentive. [F, p.p. of *distraire*, to DISTRACT]

distraught (distrawt´) *a.* bewildered, agitated, distracted. [DISTRACT, *a.*, distracted, assim. to CAUGHT, TAUGHT etc.]

distress (distres´) *n.* 1 extreme anguish or pain of mind or body. 2 misery, poverty, destitution. 3 exhaustion, fatigue. 4 calamity, misfortune. 5 a state of danger. 6 (*Law*) **a** the act of distraining. **b** goods taken in distraint. ~*v.t.* 1 to afflict with anxiety, unhappiness or anguish, to vex. 2 to exhaust, to tire out. 3 (*Law*) to distrain. **in distress** 1 in a state of anguish or danger. 2 (of a ship) in a disabled or perilous condition. **distressed** *a.* 1 afflicted with pain or anxiety. 2 destitute, poor. 3 (of furniture, fabric etc.) having been artificially made to look old or worn. **distressed area** *n.* an industrial area where there is high unemployment and poverty. **distressful** *a.* **distressfully** *adv.* **distressing** *a.* **distressingly** *adv.* **distress rocket** *n.* a signal for help from a ship in imminent danger. **distress signal** *n.* a radio or light signal, e.g. from a ship in need of prompt assistance. **distress warrant** *n.* a writ authorizing the seizure and compulsory sale of household effects etc. in settlement of a debt. [OF *destrece*, from *destrecier*, late L *districtiāre*, from *districtus*, p.p. of *distringere*, to DISTRAIN]

distribute (distrib´ūt) *v.t.* 1 to divide or deal out amongst a number. 2 to spread about, to disperse. 3 in hot-metal printing, to separate and return (type) to the cases. 4 to arrange, to allocate, to classify. 5 (*Logic*) to use (a term) in its fullest extent, so as to include every individual of the class. **distributable** *a.* **distributary** *a.* distributive. **distributed system** *n.* two or more computers which are linked by a network. **distribution**

(-bū´shən) *n.* **1** the act of distributing. **2** apportionment, division. **3** the apportionment of wealth among the various classes of the community. **4** the dispersal of commodities among the consumers. **5** dispersal, arrangement of a number of scattered units. **6** an assigning to different positions, the act of dividing or arranging into classes etc. **7** (*Logic*) the application of a term to all the members of a class individually, as distinct from collective application. **distributional** *a.* **distributive** (-trib´ūtiv) *a.* **1** distributing or allotting the proper share to each. **2** of or relating to distribution. **3** (*Gram.*) expressing distribution, separation or division. **4** (*Logic*) indicating distribution, as distinguished from collective terms. ~*n.* a distributive word such as *each, every, either* or *neither.* **distributively** *adv.* **distributiveness** *n.* **distributor** *n.* **1** a person who or something which distributes. **2** a wholesaler or agent who distributes goods to retailers. **3** the device in a petrol engine which distributes current to the sparking plugs. [L *distribūtus*, p.p. of *distribuere* (DIS-, *tribuere*, to divide, allot)]

Usage note Pronunciation as (dis´-), with stress on the first syllable, is best avoided.

district (dis´trikt) *n.* **1** a portion of territory specially defined for judicial, administrative, fiscal or other purposes. **2** a division having its own representative in a legislature, its own district council, a church or chapel of its own or a separate magistrate. **3** a region, tract of country. ~*v.t.* (*N Am.*) to divide into districts. **District Attorney** *n.* (*N Am.*) the prosecuting officer of a district. **district court** *n.* (*N Am.*) a court having cognizance of cases arising within a defined district. **district heating** *n.* a supply of heating from a central source to a district. **district nurse** *n.* a nurse employed by a local authority to visit and look after patients in their own homes. **district visitor** *n.* a church worker who visits the sick etc. in a section of a parish. [F, from late L *districtus*, p.p. of *distringere*, to DISTRAIN]

distrust (distrŭst´) *v.t.* **1** to have no confidence in. **2** to doubt, to suspect. **3** to question the reality, truth or sincerity of. **4** †to be anxious about. ~*n.* **1** lack of confidence, reliance or faith (in). **2** suspicion, discredit. **distruster** *n.* **distrustful** *a.* **distrustfully** *adv.* **distrustfulness** *n.*

disturb (distœb´) *v.t.* **1** to agitate, to disquiet. **2** to change the position of. **3** to worry, unsettle, to make uneasy. **4** to hinder, to interrupt, to inconvenience. **disturbance** *n.* **1** interruption of a settled state of things. **2** agitation, public agitation or excitement, tumult, disorder, uproar, an outbreak. **3** (*Law*) the interruption of a right; the hindering and disquieting of a person in the lawful and peaceable enjoyment of their right. **4** a minor earthquake. **5** a small atmospheric depression. **6** a mental or emotional disorder. **7** any interruption from unwanted stations, atmospherics etc. in the reception of a radio signal. **disturbed** *a.* emotionally or mentally unstable. **disturber** *n.* **disturbing** *a.* **disturbingly** *adv.* [OF *destourber*, L *disturbāre* (DIS-, *turbāre*, to trouble, from *turba*, a crowd, a tumult)]

distyle (dī´stīl) *n.* (*Archit.*) a portico having two columns. [DI-², Gr. *stulos*, a pillar]

disulphide (dīsul´fīd), (*esp. N Am.*) **disulfide** *n.* a compound in which two atoms of sulphur are united to another element or radical. **disulphate** (-fāt) *n.* a salt of sulphuric acid, containing two equivalents of the acid to one of the base.

disunion (disūn´yən) *n.* the state of being disunited; disagreement, discord.

disunite (disūnīt´) *v.t.* **1** to disjoin, to divide. **2** to put at variance. ~*v.i.* to become divided. **disunity** (-ū´ni-) *n.* **1** disunion. **2** a state of variance.

disuse¹ (disūs´) *n.* a cessation of use, practice or exercise; the state of being disused; desuetude. **to fall into disuse** to stop being used.

disuse² (disūz´) *v.t.* to cease to use. **disused** *a.* no longer in use.

disutility (disūtil´iti) *n.* (*pl.* **disutilities**) **1** harmfulness. **2** a disadvantage, a drawback.

disyllable (dīsil´əbəl), **dissyllable** (dis-) *n.* a word or metrical foot of two syllables. **disyllabic** (-lab´-) *a.* **disyllabism** *n.* [F *dissyllabe* (DI-², SYLLABLE)]

dit¹ (dit) *n.* a word representing the dot in Morse code when this is spoken.

dit² (dē) *a.* **1** named. **2** reputed. [F]

dital (dī´təl) *n.* (*Mus.*) a thumb stop on a guitar or lute for raising the pitch of a string by a semitone. [It. *dito*, finger]

ditch (dich) *n.* **1** a trench made by digging to form a boundary or for drainage. **2** a stream. **3** a trench or fosse on the outside of a fortress, serving as an obstacle to assailants. ~*v.t.* **1** to make a ditch, trench or drain in. **2** to surround with a ditch. **3** (*coll.*) to abandon, to get rid of. **4** (*coll.*) to make an emergency landing in (an aircraft). **5** (*coll.*) to crash (a vehicle) intentionally in order to avoid a more serious collision. **6** (*N Am., coll.*) to derail (a train). ~*v.i.* **1** to dig or repair ditches. **2** (of an aircraft) to be brought down by an emergency landing. **ditcher** *n.* **ditchwater** *n.* stagnant water in a ditch. **dull as ditchwater** very uninteresting or unentertaining. [OE *dīc*, cp. DYKE]

ditheism (dī´thiizm) *n.* the theory of two co-equal gods or opposing powers of good and evil, the basic principle of Zoroastrianism and Manichaeism. **ditheist** *n.* **ditheistic** (-is´-) *a.*

dither (didh´ə) *v.i.* **1** to be distracted or uncertain; to hesitate, to be indecisive. **2** to quiver, thrill. ~*n.* (*coll.*) **1** agitation. **2** indecisiveness. **all of a dither** (*coll.*) very agitated or indecisive. **ditherer** *n.* **dithery** *a.* [rel. to DODDER¹]

dithyramb (dith´iram, -ramb) *n.* **1** in ancient Greece, a choric hymn in honour of Bacchus, full of frantic enthusiasm. **2** any wild, impetuous poem or song. **dithyrambic** (-ram´bik) *a.* [L *dīthyrambus*, Gr *dīthurambos* (etym. unknown)]

ditriglyph (dītrī´glif) *n.* (*Archit.*) the interval between two triglyphs. [F *ditriglyphe*]

ditrochee (dītrō´kē) *n.* a metrical foot of two trochees. [L *ditrochaeus*, Gr. *ditrochaios*]

ditsy DITZY.

dittany (dit´əni) *n.* (*pl.* **dittanies**) **1** a herb, *Origanum dictamnus*, which was prized by the ancients for its medicinal properties. **2** (*N Am.*) a small herb, *Cunila origanoides*, growing in the Eastern US. **3** the bastard dittany, *Dictamnus fraxinella.* [OF *ditain*, L *dictamnum*, Gr. *diktamnon*, from *Diktē*, in Crete]

ditto (dit´ō) *n.* (*pl.* **dittos**) **1** what has been said before. **2** the same thing. **3** a similar thing. ~*a.* similar. ~*v.t.* (*3rd pers. sing. pres.* **dittoes**, *pres.p.* **dittoing**, *past, p.p.* **dittoed**) to repeat (what someone else has said or done). **suit of dittos** SUIT. **to say ditto** to repeat, endorse. **dittography** (-tog´rəfi) *n.* (*pl.* **dittographies**) **1** repetition of words or letters in copying. **2** an example of dittography. **dittographic** (-graf´-) *a.* **dittology** (-tol´-) *n.* a double reading of a text. **ditto marks** *n.pl.* a mark consisting of two dots, placed under a word to show that it is to be repeated on the next line. [It., from L *dictus*, p.p. of *dīcere*, to say]

ditty (dit´i) *n.* (*pl.* **ditties**) a little poem, a song. ~*v.t.* (*3rd pers. sing. pres.* **ditties**, *pres.p.* **dittying**, *past, p.p.* **dittied**) to fit to music. [OF *dité*, L *dictātum*, a thing dictated, neut. p.p. of *dictāre*, to DICTATE¹]

ditty bag (dit´i) *n.* (*Naut.*) a sailor's bag for needles, thread and odds and ends. **ditty box** *n.* a box similarly used by fishermen. [etym. uncertain]

ditzy (dit´si), **ditsy** *a.* (*comp.* **ditzier, ditsier,** *superl.*

ditziest, ditsiest) (*NAm., sl.*) 1 scatterbrained. 2 overelaborate.

diuresis (dīūrē´sis) *n.* (*Med.*) an excess of urine secretion. **diuretic** (-ret´ik) *a.* (*Med.*) causing the secretion of urine. ~*n.* a diuretic medicine. [mod. L, from Gr. (*ourēsis*, urination)]

diurnal (dīœ´nəl) *a.* 1 of or relating to a day or the day-time. 2 performed in a day. 3 daily, of each day. 4 of common occurrence. 5 (*Zool.*) of the day, as distinct from *nocturnal*. ~*n.* 1 †a journal, a day-book. 2 in the Roman Catholic Church, a book containing the little hours of the divine office. **diurnally** *adv.* [L *diurnālis*, from *diurnus*, daily (*diēs*, day)]

Div. *abbr.* Division.

div. *abbr.* 1 divide(d). 2 dividend. 3 divine. 4 division. 5 divorce(d).

diva (dē´və) *n.* (*pl.* **divas**) a famous female singer, a prima donna. [It., from L *dīva*, a goddess, fem. of *dīvus*, divine, a deity]

divagate (dī´vəgāt) *v.t.* to ramble, to diverge, to digress. **divagation** (-ā´shən) *n.* [L *dīvagātus*, p.p. of *dīvagārī* (DI-[1], *vagārī*, to wander)]

divalent (dīvā´lənt) *a.* (*Chem.*) with a valency of two. [DI-[2], L *valens -entem*, pres.p. of *valēre*, to be worth]

divan (divan´) *n.* 1 in oriental countries, a court of justice, the highest council of state. 2 (*poet.*) a council, a council chamber. 3 a cigar shop. 4 a smoking saloon. 5 a thickly-cushioned backless seat or sofa against the wall of a room. 6 †a collection of poems by one author. 7 a restaurant. **divan-bed** *n.* a mattress bed that can be converted into a sofa by day. [Turk. *divān*, Pers. *dīvān*, a brochure, a collection of poems, a tribunal, a custom house (cp. DOUANE)]

divaricate[1] (dīvar´ikāt) *v.i.* 1 to diverge into branches or forks. 2 (*Bot.*) to branch off from the stem at a right or obtuse angle. **divarication** (-ā´shən) *n.* [L *dīvāricātus*, p.p. of *dīvāricāre* (DI-[1], *vāricāre*, to spread apart, to straddle, from *vāricus*, straddling)]

divaricate[2] (dīvar´ikət) *a.* 1 spreading irregularly and wide apart. 2 branching off at a right or obtuse angle.

dive (dīv) *v.i.* (*pres.p.* **diving**, *past, p.p.* **dived**, (*NAm.*) **dove** (dōv)) 1 to plunge, esp. head first, under water. 2 to descend quickly. 3 to descend quickly and disappear. 4 to thrust one's hand rapidly (into something). 5 (*fig.*) to enter deeply (into any question, science or pursuit). ~*v.t.* to thrust (one's hand) rapidly into something. ~*n.* 1 a sudden plunge head first into water. 2 a sudden plunge or dart. 3 (*coll.*) a disreputable bar or pub. 4 an underground room in a restaurant or bar. 5 the submerging of a submarine. 6 (of an aircraft) a steep descent with the nose down. 7 (*sl.*) in boxing, a faked knockout. **dive-bomber** *n.* a military aeroplane which releases its bombs while in a steep dive. **dive-bombing** *n.* diving suddenly on a target to release bombs. **diver** *n.* 1 a person who dives, esp. someone who dives for pearls, or to work on sunken vessels etc. 2 any waterbird of the family Gaviidae, remarkable for their habit of diving. **diving** *n., a.* **diving beetle** *n.* a water beetle of the family Dytiscidae, which has flattened hind legs, used for diving and swimming. **diving bell** *n.* a hollow vessel, orig. bell-shaped, in which one may remain for a time under water, air being supplied through a flexible tube. **diving board** *n.* a platform from which one may dive into a swimming pool. **diving dress** *n.* a diving suit. **diving duck** *n.* a duck which can dive and swim under water, esp. a member of the tribe Aythini. **diving suit** *n.* waterproof clothing and breathing-helmet for divers working at the bottom of the sea. [OE *dūfan*, to dive, to sink, and *dyfan*, to dip (eventually combined)]

diverge (dīvœj´, div-) *v.i.* 1 to go in different directions from a common point or from each other; to branch off. 2 to vary from a normal form. 3 to deviate, to differ. ~*v.t.* to cause to diverge. **divergement** *n.* **divergence, divergency** *n.* **divergent** *a.* **divergently** *adv.* **divergent series** *n.* an infinite series the sum of which becomes indefinitely greater as more terms are added. **divergent thinking** *n.* thinking in which several different ideas emanate from a single idea or problem. **divergingly** *adv.* [L *vergere*, to VERGE[1]]

†divers (dī´vəz) *a.* several, sundry. [OF, from L *dīversus*, various, p.p. of *dīvertere*, to DIVERT]

diverse (dīvœs´) *a.* 1 different, unlike, distinct. 2 varying, made up of a variety of things. **diversely** *adv.* **diverseness** *n.* **diversiform** *a.* of divers or varied forms. **diversify** *v.t.* (*3rd pers. sing. pres.* **diversifies**, *pres.p.* **diversifying**, *past, p.p.* **diversified**) 1 to make different from others; to give variety to; to variegate. 2 to invest in securities of different types of (enterprise). ~*v.i.* to be engaged in the manufacture of several types of manufactured goods etc. **diversification** (-fikā´shən) *n.* **diversity** *n.* (*pl.* **diversities**) 1 difference, unlikeness; variance. 2 variety, distinctness. [as DIVERS]

diversion (dīvœ´shən, div-) *n.* 1 the act of diverting or turning aside. 2 something which tends or serves to divert the mind or attention from care, business or study. 3 a relaxation, distraction, amusement. 4 a redirection of traffic owing to the temporary closing of a road. 5 (*Mil.*) the act of diverting the attention of the enemy from any design by demonstration or feigned attack. **diversional** *a.* **diversionary** *a.* **diversionist** *n.* a subversive person, a dissident. [med. L *dīversio*, from *dīvertere*, to DIVERT]

diversity DIVERSE.

divert (dīvœt´, div-) *v.t.* 1 to turn from any course or direction, to turn aside, to deflect. 2 to draw off, to distract. 3 to entertain, to amuse. **diverter** *n.* **divertible** *a.* **divertimento** (divœtimen´tō) *n.* (*pl.* **divertimenti** (-tē), **divertimentos**) a piece of entertaining music. **diverting** *a.* entertaining, amusing. **divertingly** *adv.* **divertissement** (dēvœtēs´mā) *n.* an interlude, ballet, light entertainment. [MF *divertir*, L *dīvertere* (DI-[1], *vertere*, to turn), to turn aside, *dēvertere* (DE-, *vertere*), to turn away]

diverticulum (dīvətik´ūləm) *n.* (*pl.* **diverticula** (-lə)) an abnormal sac or pouch on the wall of a tubular organ, esp. the intestine. **diverticular** *a.* **diverticular disease** *n.* a condition characterized by abdominal pain caused by muscular spasms in diverticula. **diverticulitis** (-lī´tis) *n.* inflammation of the diverticula. **diverticulosis** (-lō´sis) *n.* the condition of having several diverticula. [L, bypath]

divertimento, divertissement etc. DIVERT.

Dives (dī´vēz) *n.* a wealthy man (after the parable of Lazarus and the rich man in Luke xvi.19–31). [L, rich]

divest (dīvest´, div-) *v.t.* 1 to strip of clothing. 2 to deprive, rid (of). **divestiture** (-chə) *n.* **divestment** *n.* [formerly *devest*, OF *devestir*, *desvestir*, late L *disvestīre*, *dīvestīre* (DI-[1], *vestīre*, from *vestis*, a garment)]

divi DIVVY[1].

divide (divīd´) *v.t.* 1 to cut or part in two; to sever, to partition. 2 to cause to separate, to break into parts. 3 to distribute, to deal out. 4 to form the boundary between. 5 to part or mark divisions on (mathematical instruments etc.). 6 to distinguish the different kinds of, to classify. 7 to share, to take a portion of with others. 8 to separate (Parliament or a meeting) by taking opinions on, for and against. 9 to destroy unity amongst, to disunite feelings. 10 (*Math*) **a** to separate into factors. **b** to perform the operation of division. ~*v.i.* 1 to be parted or separated. 2 to share. 3 to diverge. 4 (of a legislative house) to express decision by separating into two parts. 5 (*Math.*) to be an exact division of a number. ~*n.* **1** a marked distinction between two groups of people (*the North–South divide*). **2** (*Geog.*) a watershed. **to divide against itself** to split into opposing groups. **dividable** *a.* **divide and rule** *n.* a policy of causing divisions between people or groups who otherwise might unite in opposition to those in power. **divided** *a.* **divided highway** *n.* (*NAm.*) a dual carriageway. **dividedly** *adv.* **divided skirt** *n.* culottes. **divider** *n.* **1** a person who or something which divides. **2** a screen, a partition. **3** (*pl.*) compasses used to divide lines into a given number of equal parts. [L *dīvidere* (DI-[1], *-videre*, cp. *vidua*, WIDOW)]

dividend (div´idend) *n.* **1** the share of the interest or profit which belongs to each shareholder in a company, bearing the same proportion to the whole profit that the shareholder's capital bears to the whole capital. **2** a sum of money paid to football-pools winners. **3** (*Law*) the fractional part of the assets of a bankrupt paid to a creditor, in proportion to the amount of the debt. **4** (*Math.*) a number to be divided by a divisor. **5** an advantage, a bonus. **dividend-stripping** *n.* a method of evading tax on dividends arranged between a company liable to pay tax and one which is able to claim repayment of tax. **dividend warrant** *n.* the authority on which shareholders receive the amount of a dividend from the bankers of a company. **dividend yield** *n.* a dividend in terms or percentage of a share price. [F *dividende*, L *dīvidendum*, gerund of *dīvidere*, as DIVIDE]

divider DIVIDE.

divi-divi (div´idivi) *n.* (*pl.* **divi-divis**) **1** a tropical American tree, *Caesalpinia coriaria*. **2** the seed pods of the divi-divi, used for tanning and dyeing. [Carib]

divination, divinatory DIVINE[2].

divine[1] (divīn´) *a.* **1** of, relating to, proceeding from or of the nature of God, a god, or gods. **2** appropriated to the service of the Deity, religious, sacred. **3** above the nature of man, superhuman, godlike, celestial. **4** (*coll.*) wonderful. ~*n.* **1** a clergyman, an ecclesiastic. **2** a theologian. **the Divine** God. **divinely** *adv.* **divineness** *n.* **divine office** *n.* the office of the Roman breviary, consisting of matins with lauds, prime, tierce, sext, none, vespers and compline, the recitation of which is obligatory on all clerics holding a benefice, on all persons in Holy Orders and on all monastics of both sexes professed for the service of the choir. **divine right** *n.* the claim of kings to hold their office by divine appointment, and hence to govern absolutely without any interference on the part of their subjects. **divine service** *n.* the worship of God according to established forms. **divinize** (divin-), **divinise** *v.t.* to treat as divine; to deify. **divinization** (-zā´shən) *n.* [OF *devin*, L *dīvīnus*, cogn. with *dīvus*, *deus*, god]

divine[2] (divīn´) *v.t.* **1** to find out by inspiration, intuition or magic. **2** to foresee, to presage. **3** to conjecture, to guess. ~*v.i.* **1** to practise divination. **2** to have a presentiment. **3** to guess. **divination** (-vinā´shən) *n.* **1** the art of predicting or foretelling events, or of discovering hidden or secret things by real or by alleged supernatural means. **2** an omen, an augury. **3** a prediction or conjecture as to the future. **divinatory** (-vin´-) *a.* **diviner** *n.* **divining rod** *n.* a dowsing rod. [F *deviner*, L *dīvīnāre*, from *dīvīnus*, as DIVINE[1]]

diving DIVE.

divinity (divin´iti) *n.* (*pl.* **divinities**) **1** the quality of being divine. **2** the Divine Being; God. **3** a deity, a god. **4** the science of divine things. **5** theology.

divinize DIVINE[1].

☒ **divise** common misspelling of DEVISE.

divisible (diviz´ibəl) *a.* **1** capable of division. **2** (*Math.*) able to be divided into equal parts by a divisor without a remainder. **divisibility** (-bil´-) *n.* **divisibly** *adv.* [L *dīvīsibilis*, from *dīvīsus*, p.p. of *dīvidere*, to DIVIDE]

division (divizh´ən) *n.* **1** the act of dividing. **2** the state of being divided; separation. **3** distribution. **4** something which divides or separates. **5** a boundary, a partition. **6** a separate or distinct part. **7** a district, an administrative unit. **8** a separate group of people. **9** a distinct sect or body. **10** disunion, disagreement, variance. **11** each of the groups of teams of a similar standard which make up a football league. **12** (*Biol.*) a separate class, kind, species or variety; a distinction. **13** the part of a county or borough returning a Member of Parliament. **14** the separation of Members of Parliament for the purpose of voting. **15** a formal vote in Parliament. **16** (*Math.*) the process of dividing one number by another. **17** (*Logic*) the separation of a genus into its constituent species; classification; analysis of meaning. **18** (*Mil.*) a body of soldiers, usu. three brigades, under the command of a general officer, applied loosely to smaller bodies. **19** in the navy, a number of ships under one command. **20** (*Mus.*) variation. **long division** LONG[1]. **short division** SHORT. **divisional, divisionary** *a.* **divisionally** *adv.* **division lobby** *n.* either of the two corridors in Parliament in which the members vote. **division of labour** *n.* distribution of parts of industrial and other work among different people in order to secure specialization on particular processes and to save time. **division sign** *n.* (*Math.*) the sign ÷, indicating division. **divisor** (-vī´zə) *n.* **1** (*Math.*) a number by which a dividend is divided. **2** a number that divides another without a remainder. [DIVIDE]

divisive (divī´siv) *a.* **1** forming or noting separation or division, analytical. **2** tending to division or dissension. **divisively** *adv.* **divisiveness** *n.*

divorce (divaws´) *n.* **1** the dissolution of the marriage tie by competent authority. **2** the separation of husband and wife by judicial sentence of a secular or ecclesiastical court. **3** a separation of things closely connected. ~*v.t.* **1** to dissolve by legal process the bonds of marriage between. **2** to separate (a married pair) by divorce. **3** to obtain a divorce from. **4** to remove, to separate. **5** †to dissolve (a union). ~*v.i.* to become divorced. **divorcé** (-sā´) *n.* a man who has been divorced. **divorcée** (-sā´) *n.* a woman who has been divorced. **divorceable** *a.* **divorcee** (-sē´) *n.* a person who has been divorced. **divorcement** *n.* a divorce; a dissolution of the marriage contract. **divorcer** *n.* [F, from L *dīvortium*, from *dīvortere*, old form of *dīvertere*, to DIVERT]

divot (div´ət) *n.* **1** (*Sc.*, *North.*) a turf, a sod used for roofing or capping dry walls. **2** a piece of turf torn up by the head of a golf club when driving. [etym. unknown]

divulge (dīvŭlj´, div-) *v.t.* **1** to make known; to reveal, disclose. **2** to publish. **divulgement** *n.* **divulgence** *n.* **divulger** *n.* [prob. from F *divulguer* or directly from L *dīvulgāre* (DI-[1], *vulgāre*, to publish, from *vulgus*, the people)]

divvy[1] (div´i), **divi** *n.* (*pl.* **divvies, divis**) (*coll.*) **1** a dividend; a share. **2** a distribution. ~*v.t.* (*3rd pers. sing. pres.* **divvies**, *pres.p.* **divvying**, *past, p.p.* **divvied**) to divide (up).

divvy[2] *n.* (*pl.* **divvies**) (*sl.*) a stupid person; an idiot. ~*a.* (*sl.*) stupid, foolish. [etym. uncertain]

Diwali (diwah´li) *n.* a Hindu festival honouring Lakshmi, the goddess of wealth, celebrated from October to November and marked by the lighting of lamps. [Hind. *dīwalī*, from Sansk. *dīpāvalī*, a row of lights, from *dipa*, a lamp]

Dixie (dik´si) *n.* the US southern states. **Dixieland** (dik´siland) *n.* **1** Dixie. **2** an early type of jazz music played by small combinations of instruments. [etym. uncertain]

dixie (dik´si) *n.* a pot for cooking over an outdoor fire. [Hind. *degshi*, a pot]

DIY *abbr.* do-it-yourself.

dizzy (diz´i) *a.* (*comp.* **dizzier**, *superl.* **dizziest**) **1** giddy, dazed, vertiginous. **2** causing dizziness, confusing. **3** whirling; reeling. **4** (*coll.*) foolish, scatterbrained. ~*v.t.* (*3rd pers. sing. pres.* **dizzies**, *pres.p.* **dizzying**, *past, p.p.* **dizzied**) **1** to make dizzy. **2** to confuse, to confound. **dizzily** *adv.* **dizziness** *n.* [OE *dysig*, foolish, stupid, *dysigian*, to be foolish]

DJ *abbr.* **1** dinner jacket. **2** disc jockey.

djellaba (jəl´əbə), **djellabah, jellaba** *n.* a cloak with wide sleeves and a hood, worn by men in N Africa and the Middle East. [Arab. *jallabah*]

djibba, djibbah JIBBA.

Djiboutian (jiboo´tiən) *a.* of or relating to Djibouti, in E Africa. ~*n.* a native or inhabitant of Djibouti.

djinn JINNEE.

DK *abbr.* Denmark (IVR).

DL *abbr.* Deputy Lieutenant.

dl *abbr.* decilitre(s).

D.Litt. *abbr.* Doctor of Literature, Doctor of Letters. [L *Doctor Litterarum*]

DM *abbr.* Deutschmark.

dm *abbr.* decimetre(s).

DMA *abbr.* (*Comput.*) direct memory access.

D-mark (dē´mahk) *n.* short for DEUTSCHMARK.

DMs (dēemz´) *n.pl.* Dr Martens (boots).

DMSO *abbr.* dimethylsulphoxide.

D. Mus. *abbr.* Doctor of Music.

DMZ *abbr.* (*N Am.*) demilitarized zone.

DNA *abbr.* deoxyribonucleic acid, the main constituent of chromosomes, in the form of a double helix, which is self-replicating and transmits hereditary characteristics. **DNA fingerprinting** *n.* GENETIC FINGERPRINTING (under GENETIC).

DNase (dēenāz´) *n.* an enzyme which hydrolyses DNA.

DNB *abbr.* Dictionary of National Biography.

do[1] (doo) *v.t.* (*2nd pers. sing. pres.* †**doest** (doo´ist), *aux.* †**dost** (dŭst), *3rd pers. sing. pres.* **does** (dŭz), †**doeth** (doo´ith), †**doth** (dŭth), *pres.p.* **doing,** *past* **did** (did), *2nd pers. sing. past* †**didst** (didst), *p.p.* **done** (dŭn)) **1** to execute, perform, effect, transact, carry out (a work, thing, service, benefit, injury etc., or the action of any verb understood. **2** to produce, to make. **3** to bring to an end, to complete, to finish, to accomplish. **4** to produce, to cause, to render (good, evil, honour, justice, injury etc.). **5** to work. **6** to deal with. **7** to translate. **8** to prepare, to cook. **9** to play the part of. **10** to satisfy, to be adequate for. **11** to travel at a speed of. **12** to put on (a play). **13** (*coll.*) to rob, to burgle. **14** (*coll.*) to cheat, to swindle, to humbug. **15** (*coll.*) to convict. **16** (*coll.*) to injure, to kill. **17** (*coll.*) to spoil. **18** (*sl.*) to entertain, to feed. **19** (*coll.*) to serve (a period of time) in prison. **20** (*coll.*) to tire out, to fatigue, to exhaust. **21** (*coll.*) to visit and see the sights of. **22** (*taboo, sl.*) to have sexual intercourse with. **23** (*sl.*) to take (a drug). ~*v.i.* **1** to act, to behave, to conduct oneself. **2** to perform deeds. **3** to finish, to make an end, to cease. **4** to fare, to get on (in an undertaking or in health etc.). **5** to serve, to suffice, to be enough, to answer the purpose. ~*v.aux.* **1** in neg. and interrog. sentences, as *I do not play, Do you play?*. **2** with inf. for special emphasis, as *I do believe, They do love him.* **3** in the imper., as *Do give him my regards, Do not disturb.* **4** in inverted sentences, as *Seldom do I get so angry.* **5** poetically, as *It did appear.* **6** as a substitute for a verb expressing any action, usu. to avoid repetition, as *I walked there in the same time as he did; You play whist as well as he does; Did he catch the train? I did; He often comes here, I seldom do.* ~*n.* (*pl.* **dos, do's**) **1** (*coll.*) a party, a celebration. **2** (*sl.*) a swindle, a fraud. **anything doing** anything going on. **no can do** NO[2]. **nothing doing** NOTHING. **to be done with** DONE. **to be nothing to do with 1** to be no concern or business of. **2** not to be connected with. **to be to do with** to be connected with, to be about. **to do about** to do (something) to deal with. **to do away with** (*coll.*) to remove, to abolish. **to do by** to treat, to deal with (*hard done by*). **to do down 1** (*coll.*) to get the better of, to cheat. **2** (*coll.*) to humiliate. **to do for 1** to suit (*That dress does nothing for her*). **2** to put an end to; to ruin, to kill. **3** (*coll.*) to do domestic work for. **to do in 1** (*sl.*) to kill. **2** (*coll.*) to exhaust. **to do one's best** to exert one's best efforts. **to do one's diligence** to do one's best. **to do or die** to make a last, desperate attempt. **to do out** (*coll.*) to decorate (a room). **to do out of** (*coll.*) to deprive unfairly of (*I was done out of my chance to speak*). **to do over 1** (*sl.*) to attack, to beat. **2** (*sl.*) to decorate a room. **3** (*N Am.*) to perform a second time. **to do someone proud** PROUD. **to do time** TIME. **to do to** to do by. **to do to death** DEATH. †**to do unto** to do by. **to do up 1** to renovate, to decorate. **2** to dress up or make oneself up. **3** to fasten. **4** to pack in a parcel. **5** to cause the downfall. **6** to attack, to beat. **7** to tire out. **to do well** to prosper, to profit. **to do with 1** to need, to want (*I could do with a drink*). **2** to have business or connection with. **3** to dispose of. **4** to handle, to treat. **to do without** to dispense with. **to have done** DONE. **to have done with** DONE. **to have (something) to do with** to have business or connection with. **to make do** MAKE[1]. **doable** *a.* †**do-all** *n.* a factotum. **doer** *n.* **do-good** *a., n.* **do-gooder** *n.* a person who tries to help others, often in a meddlesome or ineffectual way. **do-goodery** *n.* **do-goodism** *n.* **do-it-yourself** *n.* decorating, household repairs and building as a hobby. **do-nothing** *n.* an idler. **do-or-die** *a.* denoting a reckless determination to succeed. **dos and don'ts** *n.pl.* rules. [OE *dōn*, past *dyde*, p.p. *gedōn*, from Gmc. *dō-* (Dut. *doen, deed, gedaan*, G *tun, tat, taten, getan*)]

do[2] DOH.

do. *abbr.* ditto.

DOA *abbr.* dead on arrival.

dob (dob) *v.t.* (*pres.p.* **dobbing,** *past, p.p.* **dobbed**) (*Austral., sl.*) to betray. [var. of DAB[1]]

dobbin (dob´in) *n.* a draught horse. [familiar form of *Robert*, cp. ROBIN]

dobby (dob´i) *n.* (*pl.* **dobbies**) **1** a brownie. **2** an attachment to a loom for weaving small figures. [cp. DOBBIN]

dobchick DABCHICK.

dobe (dō´bi) *n.* (*N Am., coll.*) an adobe.

Dobermann (dō´bəmən), **Dobermann pinscher** (pin´shə) *n.* a large breed of dog with a smooth black and tan coat, used as a guard dog. [L. *Dobermann*, 19th-cent. German dog breeder, G *Pinscher*, terrier]

dobra (dō´brə) *n.* (*pl.* **dobras**) the standard monetary unit of Sao Tomé e Principe.

dobsonfly (dob´sənflī) *n.* (*pl.* **dobsonflies**) a large N Am. neuropterous insect of the family Corydalidae, esp. *Corydalis cornutus*, whose larvae are used as fishing bait. [etym. unknown]

doc (dok) *n.* (*coll.*) a doctor.

Docetae (dōsē´tē) *n.pl.* a sect in the early Church who maintained that Christ had not a natural but only a phantasmal or celestial body. **Docetic** (-sē´-, -set´-) *a.* **Docetism** (dō´sitizm) *n.* **Docetist** *n.* [Gr. *Dokētai*, from *dokeein*, to seem]

doch-an-dorris DEOCH AN DORIS.

docile (dō´sīl) *a.* **1** tractable; easily managed. **2** †teachable; willing or ready to learn. **docilely** *adv.* **docility** (-sil´-) *n.* [F, from L *docilis*, from *docēre*, to teach]

dock[1] (dok) *n.* **1** an artificial basin in which ships are built or repaired. **2** (*often pl.*) an artificial basin for the reception of ships to load and unload; a dockyard.

3 (*N Am.*) a wharf. 4 a dry dock. 5 a scene dock. 6 in a railway station, an enclosure between platforms where lines terminate. ~*v.t.* 1 to bring into dock. 2 to place in a dry dock. 3 to equip with docks. 4 to join (a spacecraft) with another. ~*v.i.* 1 to come into a dock. 2 (of a spacecraft) to join with another spacecraft. **to be in dock** to be away for repairs. **to put into dock** to send away for repairs. **dockage** *n.* 1 accommodation in docks. 2 dock-dues. 3 the practice of berthing ships. **dock-dues** *n.pl.* dues payable by ships using docks. **docker** *n.* a labourer at docks. **dock-glass** *n.* a large glass, orig. used for sampling wine at the docks. **dockize, dockise** *v.t.* to convert (a river) into a floating harbour or range of docks. **dockization** (-zā´shən) *n.* **dockland** *n.* the land around docks. **dock-master** *n.* the officer in charge of docks or of a dockyard. **dock-side** *n.* the area beside a dock. **dockyard** *n.* a large enclosed area with wharves, docks etc. where vessels are built or repaired, usually in connection with the Navy. [cp. MDut. *docke, dokke* (mod. Dut. *dok*), also E dial. *doke*, a hollow]

dock[2] (dok) *n.* the enclosure for prisoners in a criminal court. **in the dock** charged with an offence. **dock brief** *n.* (*Law*) a brief undertaken without a fee for a prisoner who would not otherwise be defended. [perh. through thieves' cant from *dok*, a hutch, a pen]

dock[3] (dok) *n.* a common name for various species of the genus *Rumex*, perennial herbs, most of them troublesome weeds, esp. the common dock, *R. obtusifolius.* [OE *docce*]

dock[4] (dok) *v.t.* 1 to cut the tail off. 2 to cut short (an animal's tail). 3 to abridge, to curtail. 4 to deduct a part from; to deprive a part of. ~*n.* 1 the solid bony part of an animal's tail. 2 the tail after being cut short. 3 the divided part of a crupper through which a horse's tail is put. **dock-tailed** *a.* [cp. Icel. *dockr*, a short, stumpy tail, LG *dokke*, a bunch, a stump, G *Docke*, a plug, a peg]

docket (dok´it) *n.* 1 a summary or digest. 2 (*Law*) a register of judgements. 3 (*N Am.*) an alphabetical list of cases for trial. 4 (*N Am.*) a similar summary of business to be dealt with by a committee or assembly. 5 an endorsement of a letter or document summarizing the contents. 6 a warrant certifying payment of duty, issued by a custom house. 7 a certificate from the clearing house entitling to delivery of cotton goods. 8 a ticket or label showing the address of a package etc. ~*v.t.* (*pres.p.* **docketing,** *past, p.p.* **docketed**) 1 to make an abstract or note of the contents of (a document) on the back. 2 (*Law*) to make an abstract, digest or summary of judgements and enter in a docket. [etym. uncertain]

Doc Martens® (dok mah´tinz) *n.pl.* DR MARTENS.

doctor (dok´tə) *n.* 1 a qualified practitioner of medicine or surgery. 2 (*N Am.*) a qualified dentist or veterinary surgeon. 3 †a teacher, a learned man. 4 a person who has been awarded the highest degree in a faculty at a university etc. either for proficiency or as a compliment. 5 a person who repairs things. 6 a name for various mechanical devices. 7 an artificial fly for salmon fishing. 8 (*dated, sl.*) a loaded die. 9 (*dated, sl.*) brown sherry, from its being doctored. 10 a ship's cook. 11 a camp cook. ~*v.t.* 1 to treat medically. 2 to confer the degree of doctor on. 3 to patch up, to mend. 4 to adulterate. 5 to falsify. 6 to castrate or spay (a dog or cat). ~*v.i.* to practise as a physician. **just what the doctor ordered** exactly what was needed. **to go for the doctor** 1 (*Austral., sl.*) to make a supreme effort. 2 to bet all one's money. **doctoral** *a.* **doctorate** (-rət) *n.* the degree, rank or title of a doctor; doctorship. **doctorial** (-taw´ri-) *a.* **doctoring** *n.* 1 practising as a physician. 2 adulteration, falsification. **doctorly** *a.* **Doctor Martens** *n.pl.* Dr Martens boots. **Doctor of Philosophy** *n.* 1 a person who holds the highest university degree in any faculty except medicine, law or theology. 2 the degree held by a Doctor of Philosophy. **Doctor of the Church** *n.* any of certain early Fathers, esp. Ambrose, Augustine, Jerome and Gregory in the Western Church, and Athanasius, Basil, Gregory of Nazianzus and Chrysostom in the Eastern. **doctorship** *n.* **doctor's stuff** *n.* medicine. [OF *doctour*, L *doctor -ōrem*, from *docēre*, to teach]

doctrinaire (doktrineə´) *a.* visionary, theoretical, impractical. ~*n.* a person who theorizes in politics without regard to practical considerations; a theorizer, an ideologist. **doctrinairism** *n.* **doctrinarian** *n.* **doctrinarianism** *n.* [F, from L *doctrīna*, DOCTRINE]

doctrine (dok´trin) *n.* 1 what is taught. 2 the principles, tenets or dogmas of any church, sect, literary or scientific school, or party. **doctrinal** (-trī´-) *a.* 1 of or relating to doctrine. 2 of the nature of or containing a doctrine. **doctrinally** *adv.* **doctrinism** *n.* **doctrinist** *n.* [F, from L *doctrīna*, from DOCTOR]

docudrama (dok´ūdrahmə) *n.* a television film of a dramatized version of a true story.

document[1] (dok´ūmənt) *n.* 1 a written or printed paper containing information for the establishment of facts. 2 †any mark, fact, deed or incident furnishing evidence or illustration of a statement or view. 3 †an example, a warning. **documental** (-men´-) *a.* **documentalist** (-men´-) *n.* a person whose work is documentation. **documentary** (-men´-) *n.* (*pl.* **documentaries**) a film which represents real events or phases of life. ~*a.* 1 relating to documents. 2 presenting facts or reality. **documentarian** (-teə´riən) *n.* 1 a documentary photographer or film-maker. 2 an analyst of historical documents. **documentarily** (-men´-) *adv.* **documentarist** (-men´-) *n.* a documentary film-maker. [F, from L *documentum*, from *docēre*, to teach]

document[2] (dok´ūment) *v.t.* 1 to furnish with the documents necessary to establish any fact. 2 to prove by means of documents. 3 to record in a document. **documentation** (-mentā´-) *n.* 1 the preparation or use of documents. 2 the documents or references given. 3 (*Comput.*) the written instructions etc. which are supplied with a program or a software system.

DOD *abbr.* (*N Am.*) Department of Defence.

dodder[1] (dod´ə) *v.i.* 1 to shake, to tremble, to totter. 2 to be feeble and worn out. **dodderer** *n.* **dodder-grass** *n.* quaking-grass. **doddery** *a.* **dodderiness** *n.* [etym. uncertain; cp. TOTTER[2]]

dodder[2] (dod´ə) *n.* a plant of the genus *Cuscuta*, which consists of slender, twining, leafless parasites, enveloping and destroying the plants on which they grow. [ME *doder*, cp. Dan. *dodder*, G *Dotter*]

doddered (dod´əd) *a.* (of an aged oak etc.) having lost its top or its branches. [prob. from obs. *dod*, to poll, to top]

doddle (dod´əl) *n.* (*coll.*) something very easily accomplished.

dodeca- (dōdek´ə) *pref.* twelve. [Gr. *dōdeka*]

dodecagon (dōdek´əgon) *n.* (*pl.* **dodecagons**) (*Geom.*) a plane figure of 12 equal angles and sides. [Gr. *dōdekagōnon*]

dodecagynian (dōdekəjin´iən), **dodecaginous** (-kaj´in-) *a.* of or relating to the Dodecagynia, a Linnaean order of plants containing those having from 12–19 free styles. [Gr. *gunē*, a woman, a female]

dodecahedron (dōdekəhē´drən) *n.* (*pl.* **dodecahedra, dodecahedrons**) (*Geom.*) a solid figure of 12 equal sides, each of which is a regular pentagon. **dodecahedral** *a.* [Gr. *dōdekaedron* (*hedra*, a seat)]

dodecandrous (dōdikan´drəs) *a.* of or relating to the Dodecandria, a Linnaean class of plants, comprising those having 12–19 free stamens. [Gr. *anēr andros*, a male]

dodecaphonic (dōdekəfon´ik) *a.* twelve-note. **dodecaphonist** (-kaf´ən-) *n.* a composer of twelve-note music.

dodecasyllable (dōdekəsil´əbəl) *n.* a metrical line of 12 syllables.

dodge (doj) *v.i.* **1** to move aside suddenly. **2** to change place by a sudden movement. **3** to move rapidly from place to place so as to elude pursuit etc. **4** in change-ringing, to change the order of the ringing of two bells. *~v.t.* **1** to escape from by quickly moving aside. **2** to evade by cunning or deceit. **3** (*Austral., sl.*) to obtain dishonestly. *~n.* **1** a sudden movement to one side. **2** a trick, an artifice. **3** an evasion. **4** a skilful contrivance or expedient. **5** in change-ringing, a particular change or order. **to dodge the column** COLUMN. **dodger** *n.* **1** a person who dodges or evades. **2** a trickster, a cheat. **3** a screen on the bridge of a ship to protect against rough weather. **4** (*N Am.*) an advertising leaflet. **5** (*sl.*) food, esp. bread. **dodgery** *n.* **dodging** *n.* **1** the act of dodging. **2** the process of lightening or darkening a particular part of a photograph using an enlarger. **dodgy** *a.* (*comp.* **dodgier,** *superl.* **dodgiest**) (*coll.*) **1** full of dodges; crafty, artful, tricky. **2** uncertain, risky. [etym. uncertain]

Dodgem® (doj´əm) *n.* a bumper car in an amusement ground.

dodo (dō´dō) *n.* (*pl.* **dodos, dodoes**) **1** a large extinct bird, *Raphus cucullatus*, formerly found in Mauritius. **2** a stupid person. **dead as a dodo** completely obsolete or defunct. [Port. *doudo*, silly, foolish]

Dodonaean (dōdōnē´ən) *a.* of or relating to Jupiter, worshipped in the temple of Dodona, in Epirus, where there was a famous oracle. [L *Dōdōnaeus*, Gr. *Dōdōnaios*]

DoE *abbr.* Department of the Environment.

doe (dō) *n.* **1** the female of the fallow deer. **2** the female of the rabbit, hare etc. **doe-eyed** *a.* having large, dark eyes, like a doe's. **doeskin** *n.* **1** the skin of a doe. **2** leather made from doeskin. **3** an untwilled fine woollen cloth resembling this. [OE *dā*, cp. L *dāma*]

doek (duk) *n.* (*S Afr.*) a head-cloth, worn by married women.

doer, does DO[1].

doesn't (dŭz´ənt) *contr.* does not.

doest, doeth DO[1].

doff (dof) *v.t.* to take off (clothing, esp. one's hat). **doffer** *n.* **1** a part of a carding machine for stripping the cotton or wool from the cylinder. **2** a person who removes the full bobbins or spindles. [contr. of *do off*]

dog (dog) *n.* **1** a domesticated mammal of numerous breeds classed together as *Canis familiaris*. **2** any wild animal of the genus *Canis*, which includes wolves, jackals and coyotes, or of the family Canidae, which includes foxes. **3** the male of the dog, wolf or fox. **4** a surly fellow; a contemptible person. **5** (*N Am., Austral., sl.*) an informer. **6** either of two southern constellations. **7** a name given to various mechanical contrivances acting as holdfasts. **8** a device with a tooth which penetrates or grips an object and detains it. **9** (*N Am., sl.*) something of poor quality. **10** an andiron or firedog. **11** (*sl.*) a horse which is difficult to control. *~v.t.* (*pres.p.* **dogging,** *past, p.p.* **dogged**) **1** to follow like a dog; to track the footsteps of. **2** to fasten or secure with a dog. **hot dog** HOT. **not a dog's chance** not the slightest chance. **the dogs** (*coll.*) greyhound races. **the tail wags the dog** WAG[1]. **to die like a dog** to die miserably or shamefully. **to dog it** (*N Am., coll.*) to be lazy, to slack. **to give to the dogs** to throw away. **to go to the dogs** (*sl.*) to go to ruin. **to lead a dog's life** **1** to lead a life of continual wretchedness. **2** to be continually bickering. **to let sleeping dogs lie** to leave well alone. **to put on the dog** (*N Am., coll.*) to behave in a pretentious manner. **to throw to the dogs** to throw away. **dogbane** *n.* a plant with a bitter root, belonging to the genus *Apocynum*, supposed to be poisonous to dogs. **dog-belt** *n.* a belt with a chain attached, worn by people who draw sledges in mines. **dogbiscuit** *n.* a coarse biscuit for dogs. **dog box** *n.* (*Austral., sl.*) a compartment in a railway carriage which has no corridor. **dog cart** *n.* a light, two-wheeled, double-seated, one-horse cart. **dog-cheap** *a.* extremely cheap. **dog-clutch** *n.* a clutch in which teeth in one part fit into slots in another part. **dog collar** *n.* **1** a leather or metal collar worn by dogs. **2** a clerical collar. **3** a high, straight shirt collar. **dog days** *n.pl.* the period in July and August during which the dog-star rises and sets with the sun, a conjunction formerly supposed to account for the high temperatures common at that season. **dog-eared** *a.* (of a book) having the corners turned down or torn. **dog-eat-dog** *a.* involving ruthless pursuit of one's own interests. **dog-end** *n.* (*sl.*) a cigarette end. **dogface** *n.* (*N Am., sl.*) a US soldier. **dog-fall** *n.* a fall in which both wrestlers touch the ground together. **dog-fancier** *n.* a person who keeps and breeds dogs for sale. **dog fennel** *n.* MAYWEED. **dogfight** *n.* **1** a fight between dogs. **2** a wrangle, a struggle. **3** a duel in the air between two aircraft. **dogfighter** *n.* **dogfighting** *n.* **dogfish** *n.* (*pl.* **dogfish, dogfishes**) any small shark of the families Scylorhinidae and Squalidae, which follow their prey in packs. **dogfox** *n.* a male fox. **doggie** *n.* a dog (used by or to children). **doggish** *a.* **doggishly** *adv.* **doggishness** *n.* **doggo** *a.* hidden. **to lie doggo** (*coll.*) to wait silently and motionlessly. **dog-grass** *n.* couch grass. **doggy** *n.* (*pl.* **doggies**) a dog (used by or to children). *~a.* (*comp.* **doggier,** *superl.* **doggiest**) **1** of or relating to a dog. **2** fond of dogs. **3** flashy, raffish. **dogginess** *n.* **doggy bag** *n.* (*coll.*) a bag for taking home uneaten food after a restaurant meal. **doggy-paddle** *n.* the dog-paddle. **dog-handler** *n.* a person, such as a police officer, who works with a trained dog. **dog-handling** *n.* **dog-head** *n.* the hammer of a gunlock. **doghole** *n.* a place fit only for dogs. **doghouse,** (*N Am.*) **doghutch** *n.* a dog-kennel. **in the doghouse** (*sl.*) in disfavour. **dog in the manger** *n.* a person who prevents other people from enjoying what they cannot enjoy themselves; a churlish person. **dog-kennel** *n.* a house or hut for a dog. **dog Latin** *n.* spurious, ungrammatical Latin. **dog-leg** *n.* a sharp bend, like a dog's hind leg. *~a.* bent like a dog's hind leg. *~v.i.* (*pres.p.* **dog-legging,** *past, p.p.* **dog-legged**) to bend sharply. **dog-leg fence** (*Austral.*) a fence made of logs laid horizontally on X-shaped supports. **dog-legged** *a.* (of a staircase) constructed in zigzags without a well-hole. **dog-leg hole** *n.* in golf, a hole where players cannot take direct aim at the hole from the tee. **doglike** *a.* like a dog. **dogman** (-mən) *n.* (*pl.* **dogmen**) (*Austral.*) a person directing the operator of a crane while sitting on the load being lifted by the crane. **dog-paddle** *n.* a simple swimming stroke in which the arms imitate the front legs of a swimming dog. **dog rose** *n.* the wild brier, *Rosa canina*. **dogsbody** *n.* (*pl.* **dogsbodies**) **1** (*coll.*) someone made use of by others; a useful person treated as a drudge. **2** (*Naut., sl.*) a junior officer. **dog's breakfast** *n.* (*coll.*) a mess. **dog's dinner** *n.* (*sl.*) a mess. **dressed up like a dog's dinner** dressed too flamboyantly. **dog's disease** *n.* (*Austral., sl.*) influenza. **dog's-ear** *n.* a corner of a page of a book turned down. *~v.t.* to turn the corners of (a book) by careless handling. **dogshore** *n.* either of two struts that hold the cradle of a ship from sliding on the slipways when the keel-blocks are taken out. **dog-sick** *a.* exceedingly sick; vomiting. **dogskin** *n.* **1** the skin of a dog tanned for gloves. **2** an imitation of this. *~a.* made of dogskin. **dog sled** *n.* a sled pulled by a team of dogs. **dogsleep** *n.* a light, fitful sleep. **dog's meat** *n.* coarse meat, given as food to dogs. **dog's mercury** *n.* a common poisonous plant, *Mercurialis perennis*. **dog's-nose** *n.* a mixture of gin and beer. **dogs of war** *n.pl.* (*poet.*) the chaos or disorder which results from war. **dog's-tail** *n.* a pasture-grass, *Cynosurus cristatus.* **dog-star** *n.* Sirius, the principal star in the constellation Canis major. **dog's-tongue** *n.* hound's tongue. **dog's tooth** *n.* **1** any plant of the genus *Erythronium*, esp. *E. dens-canis*, which has purple flowers. **2** a broken-check pattern used in tweed. **dog's tooth violet** *n.* any plant of the genus *Erythronium*, esp. *E. dens-canis*, which has purple flowers. **dog-tag** *n.* a metal disc attached to a dog's collar, showing the owner's address. **dog-tail** *n.* dog's-tail. **dog-tired** *a.* worn out. **dog-tooth** *n.* **1** (*Archit.*) a kind of ornament used in Early English mouldings. **2** a broken-check pattern used in tweed. **dogtooth-spar** *n.* a kind of calcareous spar crystallizing in pointed rhombohedral forms. **dog trials** *n.pl.* (*Austral., New Zeal.*) a competition to test the skills of sheepdogs. **dogtrot** *n.* a gentle, easy trot; a jog-trot. **dogvane** *n.* (*Naut.*) a small vane of cork and feathers, placed on the weather-rail as a guide to the man at the wheel. **dog-violet** *n.* the scentless wild violet, *Viola riviniana.* **dogwatch** *n.* (*Naut.*) either one of two watches of two hours each between 4 and 8 p.m. [OE *docga*]

dogate DOGE.

Dogberry (dog´bəri) *n.* (*pl.* **Dogberries**) **1** an officious constable or policeman. **2** an incapable and overbearing magistrate. [an ignorant but good-natured constable in Shakespeare's *Much Ado About Nothing*]

dogberry (dog´bəri) *n.* (*pl.* **dogberries**) the fruit of the dogwood.

doge (dōj) *n.* (*Hist.*) the title of the chief magistrate of the republics of Venice and Genoa. **dogate** (dō´gāt) *n.* the position, office or rank of a doge. [It. *doge*, L *ducem*, acc. of *dux*, leader (cp. DUKE)]

dogged (dog´id) *a.* stubborn, obstinate, persistent, tenacious. **it's dogged as does it** (*coll.*) it pays to be persistent. **doggedly** *adv.* **doggedness** *n.*

dogger[1] (dog´ə) *n.* a Dutch fishing boat with bluff bows like a ketch, employed in the North Sea in the cod and herring fishery. [A-F *doggere*; etym. unknown]

dogger[2] (dog´ə) *n.* (*Geol.*) a large concretion occurring in some sedimentary rocks. [dial., a kind of ironstone, perh. from DOG]

doggerel (dog´ərəl) *n.* verses written with little regard to rhythm or rhyme. *~a.* of or relating to doggerel. [etym. unknown]

doggish, doggo etc. DOG.

doggone (dog´on) *a., adv.* (*N Am., sl.*) damned. *~int.* used to express annoyance. **doggoned** *a.* goddamned. [GOD, DAMN]

dogie (dō´gi) *n.* (*N Am.*) a motherless calf. [etym. unknown]

dogma (dog´mə) *n.* (*pl.* **dogmas**) **1** an established principle, tenet or system of doctrines put forward to be received on authority, esp. that of a Church, as opposed to one deduced from experience or reasoning. **2** a positive, magisterial or arrogant expression of opinion. **dogmatic** (-mat´-), **dogmatical** *a.* **1** of or relating to dogma, doctrinal. **2** based on theory not induction. **3** asserted with authority, positive, authoritative. **4** magisterial, arrogant, dictatorial. **dogmatically** *adv.* **dogmatics** *n.* **1** doctrinal theology, the science which deals with the statement and definition of Christian doctrine. **2** a system of dogma. **dogmatism** *n.* dogmaticalness; arrogance or undue positiveness in assertion. **dogmatist** *n.* **dogmatize, dogmatise** *v.i.* to make dogmatic assertions; to lay down principles with undue positiveness and confidence. *~v.t.* to lay down as a dogma. [L, from Gr. *dogma -matos*, from *dokeein*, to seem, to think, cogn. with L *docēre*, to teach]

dogwood (dog´wud) *n.* **1** any shrub of the genus *Cornus*, esp. *C. sanguinea*, the wild cornel, with white flowers and purple berries. **2** any of various similar shrubs, esp. *Euonymus europaeus* or *Rhamnus frangula.* **3** the wood of the dogwood.

DoH *abbr.* Department of Health.

doh (dō), **do** *n.* (*pl.* **dohs, dos**) (*Mus.*) **1** the first note of a major scale in the tonic sol-fa system of notation. **2** the note C in the fixed-doh system. [arbitrary]

doily (doi´li), **doyley** *n.* (*pl.* **doilies, doyleys**) a small ornamental mat or napkin on which to place cakes, sandwiches, bottles, glasses etc. [*Doily*, an 18th-cent. London haberdasher]

doing (doo´ing) *n.* **1** something done or performed; an event, transaction, proceeding, affair. **2** effort. **3** (*coll.*) a beating. **4** (*pl.*) objects whose name one has forgotten or does not want to say. **5** (*pl.*) behaviour, conduct.

†**doit** (doit) *n.* **1** a small Dutch copper coin worth about half a farthing. **2** any small piece of money, a trifle. [Dut. *duit*; perh. conn. with OE *thwitan*, to cut]

doited (doi´tid) *a.* crazed; mentally affected, esp. by old age. [perh. a var. of doted, see DOTE]

dojo (dō´jō) *n.* (*pl.* **dojos**) **1** a room where martial arts are practised. **2** a mat on which martial arts are practised. [Jap., from *dō*, a way, *jō*, a place]

dol. *abbr.* dollar(s).

dolabriform (dōlab´rifawm) *a.* (*Bot.*) having the form of an axe; hatchet-shaped. [L]

Dolby® (dol´bi) *n.* a system used to cut down interference on broadcast or recorded sound. [R. *Dolby*, b.1933, US engineer]

dolce (dol´chā) *adv.* sweetly, softly. *~a.* (of music) sweet, soft. **dolce far niente** (fah nien´ti) *n.* sweet idleness. **dolce vita** (vē´tə) *n.* a life of luxury and self-indulgence. [It.]

Dolcelatte (dolchālat´i) *n.* a kind of soft, blue-veined, Italian cheese. [It., sweet milk]

doldrums (dol´drəmz) *n.pl.* **1** low spirits, the dumps. **2** a state of inactivity. **3** that part of the ocean near the equator between the regions of the trade winds where calms and variable winds prevail. [prob. a slang deriv. of DULL]

dole[1] (dōl) *n.* **1** (*coll.*) unemployment benefit. **2** distribution, esp. in charity. **3** alms, money or food distributed in charity. **4** †fortune, lot. **5** †a share, a lot, a portion. *~v.t.* to distribute. **on the dole** (*coll.*) receiving unemployment benefit. **to dole out** to distribute in small quantities. **dole-bludger** *n.* (*Austral., sl.*) a person on unemployment benefit who makes no attempt to find work. [OE *dāl*, var. of *dæl*, DEAL[1]]

dole[2] (dōl) *n.* (*poet.*) sorrow, lamentation. **doleful** *a.* **1** sorrowful, sad. **2** dismal, gloomy. **dolefully** *adv.* **dolefulness** *n.* [OF *doel* (F *deuil*), late L *dolium*, L *dolor*]

dolerite (dol´ərīt) *n.* a variety of trap-rock consisting of feldspar and pyroxene. [F *dolérite*, Gr. *doleros*, deceptive, from the difficulty of discriminating the compounds]

dolichocephalic (dolikōsifal´ik, -kef-), **dolicephalous** (-sef´ələs, -kef´-) *a.* long-headed (applied to skulls in which the width from side to side bears a less proportion to the width from front to back than 80%). **dolichocephalism** (-sef´-) *n.* [Gr. *dolichos*, long]

dolichos (dol´ikos) *n.* any plant of the genus *Dolichos*, having long pods allied to the kidney bean. [Gr., long]

dolichosaurus (dolikōsaw´rəs) *n.* (*pl.* **dolichosauruses**) a small snakelike reptile from the Cretaceous era. [Gr. *dolichos*, as DOLICHOS, *sauros*, a lizard]

dolina (dolē´nə), **doline** (dolēn´) *n.* (*Geol.*) a funnel-shaped depression in the earth. [Rus., a valley]

doll (dol) *n.* **1** a child's toy representing a human figure. **2** (*coll.*) a pretty but silly young woman. **3** (*esp. N Am., coll.*) a term of endearment to a woman. **to doll up** (*coll.*) to dress up, to make oneself look smart. **doll-house** *n.* (*N Am.*) a doll's house. **dollish** *a.* **dollishly** *adv.* **dollishness** *n.* **doll's house** *n.* **1** a small toy house for dolls. **2** a very small house. [pet name for *Dorothy*]

dollar (dol´ə) *n.* 1 the chief unit of currency of the US, Canada, Australia, New Zealand etc. 2 any of various coins of different values. 3 (*Hist., sl.*) five shillings (25p); a crown piece. **dollar area** *n.* the area in which currency is linked to the US dollar. **dollar diplomacy** *n.* 1 diplomacy dictated by financial interests abroad. 2 diplomacy which uses financial power as a weapon. **dollar gap** *n.* the excess of imports over exports in trade with a dollar-area country. **dollarization** (-īzā´-), **dollarisation** *n.* the domination of the US dollar over another country's economy. **dollar mark, dollar sign** *n.* the sign $, used to represent a dollar. **dollar spot** *n.* 1 a fungal disease of lawns. 2 a discoloured patch caused by dollar spots. [LG *daler*, G *Thaler*, abbr. of *Joachimsthaler*, coins of silver from a mine in the *Joachimsthal*]

dollop (dol´əp) *n.* (*coll.*) 1 a shapeless lump. 2 a heap, quantity. ~*v.t.* (*pres.p.* **dolloping,** *past, p.p.* **dolloped**) to serve in dollops. [etym. uncertain]

dolly (dol´i) *n.* (*pl.* **dollies**) 1 a doll (used by or to children). 2 (*coll.*) a simple catch in cricket. 3 a stick with which dirty clothes are agitated in a washtub. 4 a corn dolly. 5 (*coll.*) a dolly-bird. 6 an appliance used in pile-driving. 7 a perforated board placed over a tub to wash ore in. 8 a hoisting platform; a trolley. ~*v.t.* to dress up, to make (oneself) look smart. ~*v.i.* to move a dolly camera closer to or away from a subject. ~*a.* (*comp.* **dollier,** *superl.* **dolliest**) attractive, glamorous. **dolly-bird** *n.* (*coll.*) an attractive, glamorous young woman. **dolly camera** *n.* a cine-camera moving on a type of trolley. **dolly mixture** *n.* a mixture of tiny coloured sweets. **dolly-shop** *n.* (*Hist.*) an unlicensed pawnshop, a marine-store (from a black doll being used as a sign). **dolly shot** *n.* a shot taken with a dolly camera. **dolly switch** *n.* a switch for an electric light etc., consisting of a lever to be pushed up and down. **dolly tub** *n.* a washing tub.

Dolly Varden (doli vah´dən) *n.* 1 a large-patterned print dress. 2 a wide-brimmed woman's hat with one side bent down. 3 a N American char, *Salvelinus malma*. [a character in Dickens's *Barnaby Rudge*]

dolma (dol´mə) *n.* (*pl.* **dolmas, dolmades** (-mah´dhez)) a vine leaf stuffed with rice and meat. [Turk., from *dolmak*, to fill, to be filled]

dolman (dol´mən) *n.* (*pl.* **dolmans**) 1 a long Turkish robe, open in front, and with narrow sleeves. 2 a woman's loose mantle with dolman sleeves. 3 a hussar's jacket or cape with the sleeves hanging loose. **dolman sleeve** *n.* a sleeve which tapers from a wide armhole to a tightly-fitting wrist. [F, from G, from Hung. *dolmany*, Turk. *dōlān*]

dolmen (dol´mən) *n.* a cromlech; the megalithic framework of a chambered cairn, consisting usually of three or more upright stones supporting a roof-stone. [F, prob. from Corn. *dolmēn, tolmēn* (*doll, toll*, hole, *mēn*, stone)]

dolomite (dol´əmīt) *n.* a brittle, subtransparent or translucent mineral consisting of the carbonates of lime and magnesia. **dolomitic** (-mit´-) *a.* **dolomitize, dolomitise** *v.t.* to change into dolomite. **dolomitization** (-zā´shən) *n.* [Déodat de *Dolomieu*, 1750–1801, French geologist. Nothing to do with the Dolomite Mts in Tyrol]

dolor DOLOUR.

doloroso (dolərō´sō) *a., adv.* (*Mus.*) (to be performed) in a soft, dolorous manner.

dolorous (dol´ərəs) *a.* 1 full of pain or grief. 2 causing or expressing pain or grief, doleful. **dolorously** *adv.* **dolorousness** *n.* [OF *dolerus*, from DOLOUR]

dolour (dol´ə), (*N Am.*) **dolor** *n.* pain, suffering, distress; grief, sorrow, lamentation. [OF, from L *dolor dolōrem*, from *dolēre*, to grieve]

dolphin (dol´fin) *n.* 1 any sea mammal of the family Delphinidae, having a beaklike snout. 2 the dorado, *Coryphaena hippuris*. 3 (*N Am.*) **a** a mooring-post. **b** an anchored spar with rings, serving as a mooring-buoy. 4 a protective structure on a bridge. 5 (*Her. etc.*) a conventional representation of a curved fish. **dolphinarium** (-eə´riəm) *n.* (*pl.* **dolphinariums**) an aquarium for dolphins, often one for public displays. **dolphin-fly** *n.* (*pl.* **dolphin-flies**) an insect, *Aphis fabae*, which infests bean plants. [ME *delfyn*, L *delphīnus*, see DAUPHIN, OF *daulphin*, which affected the later spelling]

dolt (dōlt) *n.* a stupid person; a numskull. **doltish** *a.* **doltishly** *adv.* **doltishness** *n.* [prob. *dult*, dulled, see DULL]

DOM[1] *abbr.* to God the best and greatest. [L *Deo optimo maximo*]

DOM[2] *abbr.* Dominican Republic (IVR).

Dom (dom) *n.* 1 in the Roman Catholic Church, a title given to members of the Benedictine and Carthusian orders. 2 the Portuguese equivalent of the Spanish *Don*. [abbr. of L *dominus*, lord]

dom. *abbr.* 1 domain. 2 domestic.

-dom (dəm) *suf.* denoting power, jurisdiction, office or condition, a group of people, as in *earldom, kingdom, officialdom, freedom*. [OE *dōm*, judgement, cogn. with G *-tum*]

domain (dəmān´) *n.* 1 territory, district or space over which authority, jurisdiction or control is or may be exercised. 2 one's landed property, estate. 3 (*fig.*) sphere, province, field of influence, thought or action. 4 (*Physics*) the part of a ferromagnetic solid where all the atoms are magnetically aligned. 5 (*Math.*) the aggregate to which a variable belongs. **domainal, domanial** (-mā´niəl) *a.* [F *domaine*, late L *dominicum*, L *dominium*, from *dominus*, lord]

domaine (dəmān´) *n.* a vineyard. [F, see DOMAIN]

domanial DOMAIN.

dome[1] (dōm) *n.* 1 a roof, usually central, the base of which is a circle, an ellipse or a polygon, and its vertical section a curved line, concave towards the interior; a cupola. 2 the revolving dome-shaped roof of an observatory, which can be opened up. 3 a natural vault, arching canopy or lofty covering. 4 a rounded hilltop. 5 (*poet.*) a mansion, temple or other building of a stately kind. 6 (*Geol.*) any dome-shaped object or structure. 7 a termination of a prism by two planes meeting above in a horizontal edge. 8 (*sl.*) the head. ~*v.t.* to cover with or shape into a dome. ~*v.i.* to swell into a domelike shape. **domed** *a.* 1 furnished with a dome. 2 dome-shaped. **domelike** *a.* [MF *dome*, It. *duomo*, L *domus*, a house]

†**dome**[2] (doom) *n.* doom.

Domesday (doomz´dā), **Domesday Book, Doomsday Book** *n.* a register of the lands of England compiled (1084–86) by order of William the Conqueror. [ME DOOMSDAY (under DOOM)]

domestic (dəmes´tik) *a.* 1 employed or kept at home. 2 fond of home. 3 tame, not wild. 4 relating to the internal affairs of a nation; not foreign. 5 made in one's own country. 6 of or relating to the home or household. ~*n.* 1 a household servant. 2 (*pl.*) articles of home (as opposed to foreign) manufacture, esp. (*N Am.*) cotton cloth. **domesticable** *a.* **domestically** *adv.* **domestic architecture** *n.* the architecture of dwelling houses. **domesticate** *v.t.* 1 to naturalize (foreigners etc.). 2 to accustom to domestic life and the management of household affairs. 3 to tame. 4 to bring (a plant) into cultivation from a wild state. **domesticated** *a.* 1 tamed. 2 content with home life. 3 used to household chores. **domestication** (-ā´shən) *n.* **domestic economy** *n.* the economical management of household affairs. **domestic science** *n.* the study of household skills, including cookery, needlework etc. **domestic trade** *n.* the trade carried on within a country. [F *domestique*, L *domesticus*, from *domus*, home]

domesticity (domestis´iti, dō-) *n.* (*pl.* **domesticities**) 1 the state of being domestic. 2 domestic character, homeliness. 3 home life. 4 (*pl.*) domestic affairs, family matters.

domical DOME[1].

domicile (dom´isīl), **domicil** (-sil) *n.* 1 a house, a home. 2 (*Law*) a a place of permanent residence. b length of residence (differing in various countries) necessary to establish jurisdiction in civil actions. 3 the place at which a bill of exchange is made payable. ~*v.t.* 1 to establish in a place of residence. 2 to make payable at a certain place. ~*v.i.* to be established in a place of residence. **domiciled** *a.* **domiciliary** (-sil´-) *a.* of or relating to a domicile or residence. **domiciliary visit** *n.* a visit under legal authority to a private house to search for suspected persons or things. **domiciliate** (-sil´-) *v.t.* to establish in a residence. **domiciliation** (-siliā´shən) *n.* [F, from L *domicilium*, from *domus*, home]

dominant (dom´inənt) *a.* 1 predominant, ruling, governing. 2 overshadowing, prominent. 3 (of a gene) producing a particular feature even if inherited from only one parent, as distinct from *recessive*. 4 (*Mus.*) of or relating to the fifth note of a scale. ~*n.* 1 (*Mus.*) the fifth note of the scale of any key, counting upwards. 2 a prevalent species in a plant community. **dominance** *n.* **dominancy** *n.* **dominantly** *adv.* [F, from L *dominans -antem*, pres.p. of *dominārī*, from *dominus*, lord]

dominate (dom´ināt) *v.t.* 1 to predominate over. 2 to overlook (as a hill). 3 to influence controllingly, to rule, govern. ~*v.i.* 1 to predominate, to prevail. 2 to be the most influential or the chief or most conspicuous. **domination** (-ā´shən) *n.* 1 the exercise of power or authority. 2 rule, sway, control, dominion. 3 (*pl.*) the fourth order of angels. **dominative** *a.* **dominator** *n.* **dominatrix** (dominā´triks) *n.* (*pl.* **dominatrices** (-trisēz)) a dominant woman, esp. in a sadomasochistic relationship. [L *dominātus*, p.p. of *dominārī*, from *dominus*, lord]

dominee (doo´mini) *n.* a minister in any of the Afrikaner Churches in South Africa. [from Dut.]

domineer (dominiə´) *v.i.* to exercise authority arrogantly and tyrannically; to assume superiority over others. **domineering** *a.* **domineeringly** *adv.* [MDut. *domineren*, OF *dominer*, L *dominārī*, see DOMINANT]

dominical (dəmin´ikəl) *a.* among Christians, of or relating to the Lord or the Lord's Day. **dominical letter** *n.* one of the seven letters A–G which denotes Sunday in any particular year. [med. L *dominicālis*, L *dominicus*, from *dominus*, lord]

Dominican (dəmin´ikən) *n.* 1 a member of an order of preaching friars, founded in 1216 by Domingo de Guzman (canonized as St Dominic); a Black Friar. 2 a nun in one of the orders founded by St Dominic. 3 a native or inhabitant of the Dominican Republic. 4 a native or inhabitant of Dominica. ~*a.* 1 of or relating to the Dominicans. 2 of or relating to the Dominican Republic. 3 of or relating to Dominica. [med. L *Dominicānus*, from *Dominicus*, Domingo]

dominie (dom´ini) *n.* (*Sc.*) 1 a teacher, a schoolmaster. 2 a minister, a clergyman. [L *domine*, sir, voc. of *dominus*, lord]

dominion (dəmin´yən) *n.* 1 sovereign authority, lordship; control, rule, government. 2 (*Law*) uncontrolled right of possession or use. 3 a district, region or country under one government. 4 (*Hist.*) a self-governing country of the British Commonwealth, esp. Canada. **Dominion Day** *n.* (*Hist.*) CANADA DAY (under CANADIAN). [OF, from late L *dominio -ōnem*, L *dominium*, from *dominus*, lord]

domino (dom´inō) *n.* (*pl.* **dominoes**) 1 any of 28 oblong dotted pieces, orig. of bone or ivory, used in playing dominoes. 2 a masquerade dress worn for disguise by both sexes, consisting of a loose black cloak or mantle with a small mask. 3 a kind of half mask. **domino effect** *n.* the theory that a single event leads to many similar events elsewhere as a chain reaction, like the fall of a long row of dominoes, all standing on end, caused by pushing the first domino in the row. **dominoes** *n.* any of various games played with dominoes, often involving pairing up matching values. **domino theory** *n.* the domino effect. [Sp. or F, from L *dominus*, lord (orig. perh. the hood worn by a master)]

Don (don) *n.* 1 a title formerly restricted to Spanish noblemen and gentlemen, now common to all men in Spain, Sir, Mr. 2 a Spanish gentleman. 3 a Spaniard. 4 (*N Am., sl.*) an important member of the Mafia. **Don Juan** (ju´ən, wahn) *n.* a male flirt; a would-be rake (from the hero of Byron's poem). **Don Quixote** (kihō´ti, kwik´sōt) *n.* a man who is excessively idealistic or chivalrous, esp. one who goes to foolish extremes (from the hero of Cervantes' *Don Quixote de la Mancha*, 1605).

don[1] (don) *n.* 1 a fellow or tutor of a college, esp. at Oxford or Cambridge. 2 (*Austral., New Zeal., sl.*) an adept, an expert. 3 †a person of distinction. **donnish** *a.* **donnishly** *adv.* **donnishness** *n.* [Sp., from L *dominus*, lord]

don[2] (don) *v.t.* (*pres.p.* **donning,** *past, p.p.* **donned**) to put on (clothing). [contr. of *do on*]

dona (dō´nə) *n.* (*sl.*) 1 a woman. 2 a sweetheart. [Sp. *doña* or Port. *dona*, from L *domina*, lady]

donate (dōnāt´) *v.t.* to bestow as a gift, esp. on a considerable scale for public or religious purposes. **donator** *n.* a donor. **donatory** *n.* (*pl.* **donatories**) the recipient of a donation. [L *dōnāre*, to give]

donation (dōnā´shən) *n.* 1 the act of giving. 2 something which is given, a gift, a presentation, a contribution, esp. to a public institution. 3 (*Law*) an act or contract by which any thing, or the use of and the right to it, is transferred as a free gift to any person or corporation. [F, from L *dōnātio -ōnem*, from *dōnāre*, to give, from *dōnum*, a gift]

Donatism (dō´nətizm) *n.* the doctrine of an Arian sect, founded in AD 311 by *Donatus*, a Numidian bishop who denied the infallibility of the Church and insisted on individual holiness as a condition of membership. **Donatist** *n.* **Donatistic** (-tis´-), **Donatistical** *a.* [med. L *Donatismus*]

donative (dō´nətiv) *n.* 1 a gift, a present, a gratuity, esp. an official donation. 2 (*Hist.*) a benefice directly given by a patron without presentation to or institution by the ordinary. ~*a.* vested or vesting by this form of presentation. [L *dōnātivus*, from *dōnāre*, to give]

donator, donatory DONATE.

done (dŭn) *a.* 1 performed, executed. 2 socially acceptable (*not the done thing*). ~*int.* accepted (used to express agreement to a proposal, as a wager, or a bargain). **done brown** (*sl.*) cheated completely. **to be done with** to have finished with. **to have done** to have finished. **to have done with** to have no further concern with. **done for** *a.* (*coll.*) ruined, killed, exhausted. **done in, done up** *a.* (*coll.*) worn out, exhausted. [DO[1]]

donee (dōnē´) *n.* 1 the person to whom anything is given. 2 (*Law*) the person to whom lands or tenements are given gratuitously or conveyed in fee tail. [L *dōnum*, a gift, -EE]

doner kebab (don´ə) *n.* spit-roasted lamb served in pitta bread, usually with salad. [Turk. *döner*, rotating]

dong[1] (dong) *v.i.* to make the sound of a large bell. ~*v.t.* (*Austral., New Zeal., coll.*) to punch hard. ~*n.* 1 the sound of a large bell. 2 (*Austral., New Zeal., coll.*) a hard punch. 3 (*taboo, sl.*) a penis. [imit.]

dong[2] (dong) *n.* the standard unit of currency of Vietnam. [Vietnamese]

donga (dong´gə) *n.* (*S Afr., Austral.*) a gully, a watercourse with steep sides. [Nguni]

dongle (dong´gəl) *n.* (*Comput.*) an electronic device used to protect software from unauthorized use.

donjon (dŭn´jən) *n.* the grand central tower or keep of a castle, esp. a medieval Norman one, the lower storey generally used as a prison. [DUNGEON]

donkey (dong´ki) *n.* **1** a long-eared member of the horse family, an ass. **2** (*coll.*) a stupid person. **to talk the hind legs off a donkey** to talk a lot. **donkey derby** *n.* a race in which the competitors ride donkeys. **donkey engine** *n.* an auxiliary engine for light work on board steamships. **donkey jacket** *n.* a short, thick jacket worn by workmen. **donkey-pump** *n.* a steam-pump, worked independently of the main engine, for supplying boilers with water and for other purposes. **donkey's years** *n.pl.* (*coll.*) a long time. **donkey vote** *n.* (*Austral.*) one where the voter's preference follows the order in which the candidates are listed. **donkey work** *n.* drudgery, routine work. [perh. a double dim. of DUN[1], from the colour]

donna (don´ə) *n.* **1** an Italian lady. **2** (**Donna**) an Italian title for, or form of address to, a lady, Madame, madam. [It., from L *domina*, lady]

donnée (don´ā), **donné** *n.* **1** a subject, a theme. **2** an assumption, a fact. [F, p.p. of *donner*, to give]

donnish DON[1].

donnybrook (don´ibruk) *n.* a rowdy brawl. [*Donnybrook* Fair, held annually near Dublin until 1855]

donor (dō´nə) *n.* **1** a giver. **2** a person who gives blood, semen or an organ for the medical treatment of another person. **3** (*Chem.*) an atom which supplies the electrons in a coordinate bond. **4** (*Physics*) an impurity in semiconductor material which contributes free electrons to increase its conductivity. **5** (*Law*) a person who grants an estate. **donor card** *n.* a card carried by a person willing to have parts of their body used for transplant after their death. [OE *donour*, OF *doneur*, L *dōnātōr -ōrem*, from *dōnāre*, to give]

don't (dōnt) *contr.* do not. ~*n.* a prohibition (*dos and don'ts*). **don't know** *n.* **1** a person without a firm opinion on any matter. **2** an answer given by a person with such a lack of opinion.

donut DOUGHNUT (under DOUGH).

doodah (doo´dah), (*N Am.*) **doodad** (-dad) *n.* (*coll.*) any small decorative article or gadget. **all of a doodah** flustered, in a state of confusion.

doodle (doo´dəl) *v.i.* to draw pictures or designs absent-mindedly while thinking or listening. ~*n.* a picture drawn in this way. **doodler** *n.* [imit.]

doodlebug (doo´dəlbŭg) *n.* **1** (*coll.*) the earliest type of flying bomb used by the Germans in the war of 1939–45, the V-1. **2** (*N Am.*) the larva of the ant-lion. **3** (*N Am.*) a diviner's rod. **4** (*N Am.*) any scientific or unscientific instrument for locating minerals.

doodly-squat DIDDLY-SQUAT.

doohickey (doo´hiki), **doojigger** (doo´jigə) *n.* (*N Am., coll.*) any small mechanical device.

doolally (doolal´i) *a.* (*sl.*) insane, eccentric. [*Deolali*, a town near Bombay, India]

doolie (doo´li) *n.* a covered litter of bamboo. [Hind. *dōlī*]

doom (doom) *n.* **1** fate or destiny (usu. in an evil sense). **2** ruin, destruction, perdition. **3** judgement; judicial decision or sentence. **4** condemnation, penalty. **5** the Day of Judgement. **6** †an enactment, statute or law. ~*v.t.* **1** to condemn (to do something). **2** to predestine. **3** to consign to ruin or calamity. **4** to pass sentence upon. **crack of doom** CRACK. **doom-laden** *a.* suggesting disaster or tragedy. **doomsayer** *n.* a person who predicts disaster. **doomsaying** *n.* **doomsday** *n.* **1** the Day of Judgement; the end of the world. **2** a day of judgement or reckoning. **till doomsday** for ever. **Doomsday Book** DOMESDAY. **doomster** *n.* a doomsayer. **doomwatch** *n.* **1** pessimism, esp. about the future of the environment. **2** observation of the environment to prevent its destruction by pollution etc. **doomwatcher** *n.* [OE *dōm*, from Gmc. *dōmo* (Dan., Swed. *dom*, OHG *tuom*, cp. Gr. *themis*, law)]

Doona® (doo´nə) *n.* (*Austral.*) a duvet. [etym. unknown]

door (daw) *n.* **1** a frame of wood or metal, usually on hinges, closing the entrance to a building, room, safe etc. **2** an opening for entrance and exit. **3** entrance, exit, access, means of approach. **4** a house, a room (*She lives two doors down from us*). **5** (*fig.*) the entrance or beginning; means of access (to). **out of doors** outside the house; in or into the open. **to close the door to** to exclude the possibility of. **to lay at the door** to blame. **to leave the door open** to ensure that an opportunity remains available to one. **to lie at the door of** to be the fault or responsibility of. **to open the door to** to allow the possibility of. **to show the door** to turn out; to send away unceremoniously. **within doors** inside the house. **doorbell** *n.* a bell inside a building actuated by a button outside a door. **doorcase** *n.* the structure in which a door swings. **doored** *a.* **door frame** *n.* a doorcase. **door head** *n.* the top of a doorcase. **doorkeeper** *n.* a doorman. **doorknob** *n.* a handle on a door. **doorknock** *n.* (*Austral.*) a door-to-door collection for charity. **doorknocker** *n.* **1** a hinged device attached to a door, for knocking. **2** a person who sells, collects or canvasses from door to door. **doorman** *n.* (*pl.* **doormen**) a porter, a person employed to open doors. **doormat** *n.* **1** a mat for removing dirt from the shoes, placed inside or outside a door. **2** (*coll.*) a submissive person, often imposed on by others. **doornail** *n.* a large nail formerly used for studding doors. **dead as a doornail** DEAD. **doorplate** *n.* a metal plate on a door bearing the name of the occupant. **doorpost** *n.* side-piece or jamb of a doorway. **doorsill** *n.* the wooden plank or flat stone forming the bottom of a doorcase. **doorstep** *n.* **1** a step leading up to an outer door. **2** (*sl.*) a thick slice of bread. ~*v.i.* (*pres.p.* **doorstepping,** *past, p.p.* **doorstepped**) to go from door to door to canvass during a political campaign, or to try to sell goods, often intrusively. ~*v.t.* **1** (of a journalist) to wait outside the house of (a person) to try to obtain a photograph or interview. **2** to leave in someone's care. **on one's doorstep** very close to one's home. **doorstepping** *n.* **doorstone** *n.* a slab in front of a door; the threshold. **doorstop** *n.* a device which stops a door from moving. **door-to-door** *a.* **1** from one house to the next. **2** (of a journey) direct. **doorway** *n.* **1** an opening in a wall fitted with a door. **2** (*fig.*) a means of access (to). **dooryard** *n.* (*N Am.*) a garden immediately outside the door of a house. [OE *dor*, fem. *duru* (cp. Dan. *dor*, Icel. *dyrr*, G *Tür*, Gr. *thura*, L *fores*)]

☒ **doormouse** common misspelling of DORMOUSE.

doozy (doo´zi) *n.* (*pl.* **doozies**) (*N Am., sl.*) something wonderful or excellent. [etym. uncertain]

dop (dop) *n.* (*S Afr.*) **1** a kind of cheap brandy. **2** a measure of any spirit. [Afrikaans]

dopa (dō´pə) *n.* an amino acid, a precursor of dopamine. [G, from *D*i*o*xy*p*henyl*a*lanine, its former name]

dopamine (dō´pəmēn) *n.* a chemical found in the brain, acting as a neurotransmitter, a precursor of adrenalin.

dopant (dō´pənt) *n.* a substance used to dope a semiconductor.

dope (dōp) *n.* **1** a varnish used for waterproofing, protecting and strengthening the fabric parts of an aircraft. **2** any thick liquid or semi-fluid used for food or as a lubricant. **3** an antiknock compound added to petrol. **4** an absorbent material used for holding liquid. **5** the material used to hold nitroglycerine and other explosives. **6** a drug given to a horse or greyhound, or taken by an athlete, to affect the outcome of a race; any illegal drug, esp. cannabis. **7** (*sl.*) a stupefying drug. **8** (*sl.*) a stupid person. **9** (*sl.*) **a** inside information, particulars. b misleading information. ~*v.t.* **1** to drug, to stupefy with drugs. **2** to add impurities to. **3** to apply dope to, to smear. ~*v.i.* to take illegal drugs. ~*a.* (*sl.*) excellent. **to dope out** (*sl.*) to devise, to discover. **doper** *n.* **dopey** *a.* (*comp.* **dopier,** *superl.* **dopiest**) (*coll.*) **1** stupid. **2** drugged. **3** sleepy, sluggish. **doping** *n.* the adding of impurities to a semiconductor to produce a modification of its properties. **dopy** *a.* dopey. **dopily** *a.* **dopiness** *n.* [Dut. *doop*, dipping, sauce, from *doopen*, to dip]

doppelgänger (dop´əlgengə, -gangə) *n.* the apparition of a living person; a wraith. [G *Doppelgänger*, double-goer]

Dopper (dop´ə) *n.* a member of the Reformed Church of South Africa, characterized by extreme simplicity of manners and dress. [Afrikaans, etym. unknown]

dopplerite (dop´lərīt) *n.* a black substance found in peat beds.

Doppler's principle (dop´ləz) *n.* (*Physics*) the principle that when the source of any wave motion is approached, the frequency appears greater than it would to an observer moving away. **Doppler effect, Doppler shift** *n.* an observed shift in the frequency of light according to Doppler's principle. [C. J. *Doppler*, 1803–53, Austrian physicist]

dopy DOPE.

dor (daw), **dor-beetle** *n.* any of several insects that make a loud humming noise in flying, esp. the black dung-beetle, *Geotrupes stercorarius.* [OE *dora*, bumble-bee, prob. onomat.]

dorado (dərah´dō) *n.* (*pl.* **dorados**) **1** a fish, *Coryphaena hippurus*, of brilliant colouring. **2** a gold-coloured S American river fish. **3** (*Astron.*) a southern constellation, the Swordfish. [Sp., gilded, from L *deaurātus*, p.p. of *deaurāre* (DE-, *aurum*, gold)]

Dorcas Society (daw´kəs) *n.* a charitable association for providing clothes for the poor. [Gr., gazelle, transl. of Aram. *Tabitha* (Acts ix.36)]

doree DORY[1].

Dorian (daw´riən) *n.* **1** an inhabitant of Doris, in ancient Greece. **2** a member of one of the four great ethnic divisions of the ancient Greeks. ~*a.* of or relating to Doris or its inhabitants. **Dorian mode** *n.* (*Mus.*) a simple, solemn form of music, the first of the authentic Church modes. **Doric** (dor´-) *n.* **1** (*Archit.*) the Doric order. **2** a broad, rustic dialect, esp. Scots. **Doric dialect** *n.* **1** the broad, rustic dialect of the natives of Doris. **2** any broad, rustic dialect, esp. Scots. **Doric order** *n.* the earliest, strongest and most simple of the three Grecian orders of architecture.

dork (dawk) *n.* (*sl.*) **1** a stupid or socially awkward person. **2** a penis. **dorkish** *a.* **dorky** *a.* (*comp.* **dorkier,** *superl.* **dorkiest**).

Dorking (daw´king) *n.* a breed of domestic fowl, orig. from Dorking. [town in Surrey]

dorm (dawm) *n.* short for DORMITORY.

dormant (daw´mənt) *a.* **1** in a state resembling sleep, torpid, inactive. **2** undeveloped, inoperative. **3** not asserted or claimed. **4** in abeyance. **5** (of a plant) alive but not currently growing. **6** (*Her.*) lying with the head on the paws. **dormancy** *n.* [F, pres.p. of *dormir*, L *dormīre*, to sleep]

dormer (daw´mə) *n.* a dormer window. **dormer bungalow** *n.* a two-storeyed bungalow with dormer windows upstairs. **dormer window** *n.* a window piercing a sloping roof and having a vertical frame and a gable (orig. used in sleeping chambers). [OF *dormeor*, L *dormītōrium*, as DORMANT]

dormie DORMY.

dormitive (daw´mitiv) *a.* promoting sleep; narcotic, soporific. [L *dormit*, p.p. stem of *dormīre*, to sleep]

dormitory (daw´mitri) *n.* (*pl.* **dormitories**) **1** a sleeping room, esp. in a school or public institution, containing a number of beds. **2** (*N Am.*) a students' hall of residence. **3** a resting place. **dormitory town, dormitory suburb** *n.* a town or suburb whose inhabitants work elsewhere, often in a nearby city. [L *dormītōrium*, DORMER]

Dormobile® (daw´məbēl) *n.* a van equipped for living in while travelling.

dormouse (daw´mows) *n.* (*pl.* **dormice** (-mīs)) **1** a small British hibernating rodent, *Myoxus avellanarius.* **2** any of various other members of the family Gliridae, resembling both a mouse and a squirrel. [dial. Eng. *dorm*, to sleep, F *dormir* (see DORMANT)]

dormy (daw´mi), **dormie** *a.* in golf, of or relating to a player who is as many holes ahead of their opponent as there remain holes to play. [etym. uncertain, perh. F *dormi*, p.p. of *dormir*, to sleep]

dornick (daw´nik) *n.* a stout damask linen cloth, orig. made at Tournai. [Flem. *Doornik*, Tournai, in Flanders]

doronicum (dəron´ikəm) *n.* leopard's bane. [mod. L, ult. from Arab. *darānaj*]

dorp (dawp) *n.* (*S Afr.*) a small town. [Dut.]

dors- DORSO-.

dorsa DORSUM.

dorsal (daw´səl) *a.* **1** of or relating to the back. **2** situated on the back. **3** shaped like a ridge. **dorsal fin** *n.* the fin on the back of a fish which aids balance. **dorsally** *adv.* [F, from late L *dorsālis*, from *dorsum*, the back]

dorsiferous (dawsif´ərəs), **dorsiparous** (-sip´-) *a.* (*Bot.*) (of ferns) having seeds at the back of the frond. [-FEROUS; L *-parus*, bringing forth]

dorsiflexion (dawsiflek´shən) *n.* (*Med.*) a bending backwards.

dorsigrade (daw´sigrād) *a.* walking on the back of the toes.

dorsiparous DORSIFEROUS.

dorso- (daw´sō), **dors-, dorsi-** (-si) *comb. form* of, relating to or situated on the back. [L *dorsum*, back]

dorsum (daw´səm) *n.* (*pl.* **dorsa**) (*Zool., Anat.*) the back. [L, the back]

dory[1] (daw´ri), **doree** *n.* (*pl.* **dories, dorees**) a golden-yellow sea fish of the family Zeidae, esp. the John Dory. [F *dorée*, fem. p.p. of *dorer*, to gild (cp. DORADO)]

dory[2] (daw´ri) *n.* (*pl.* **dories**) (*N Am.*) a small, flat-bottomed boat. [etym. unknown]

doryphore (dor´ifaw) *n.* a self-righteous critic. [F, a Colorado beetle, from Gr. *doruphoros*, a spear-carrier]

DOS® (dos) *n.* (*Comput.*) a particular computer operating system. [*d*isk *o*perating *s*ystem]

dos-à-dos (dōzədō´) *a.* (of two books) bound together but facing in opposite directions. ~*n.* (*pl.* **dos-à-dos**) a seat designed for sitting back-to-back. [F, back to back]

dose (dōs) *n.* **1** the amount of any medicine which is taken or prescribed to be taken at one time. **2** (*fig.*) a quantity or amount of anything offered or given. **3** anything unpleasant which one has to take. **4** the amount of ionizing radiation absorbed by a person or thing. **5** (*sl.*) a venereal infection, esp. gonorrhoea. ~*v.t.* **1** to administer doses to. **2** to adulterate, to mix (spirits with wine). **a dose of one's own medicine** MEDICINE. **like a dose of salts** very quickly and thoroughly. **dosage** *n.* the process or method of dosing; the application of doses, for example of spirits to wine. **dosimeter** (-sim´itə), **dosemeter** (dōs´mētə) *n.* an instrument which measures radiation. **dosimetric** (-met´-) *a.* **dosimetry** (-sim´-) *n.* [F, from med. L and Gr. *dosis*, a giving, from *didonai*, to give]

do-se-do (dōsidō´, -zi-), **do-si-do** *n.* (*pl.* **do-se-dos, do-si-dos**) a square dance in which dancers pass each other back to back. [corr. of DOS-À-DOS]

dosh (dosh) *n.* (*sl.*) money. [etym. uncertain]

do-si-do DO-SE-DO.

dosimeter DOSE.

doss (dos) *v.i.* (*sl.*) **1** to sleep. **2** to sleep in a cheap lodging house. **3** to go to bed. **4** to spend time aimlessly. *~n.* a bed or a sleeping place in a cheap lodging house. **dosser** *n.* **1** a person who sleeps in cheap lodging houses or hostels. **2** a doss-house. **3** (*Ir. dial.*) a lazy, idle person. **to doss down** to go to sleep in a makeshift bed. **doss-house** *n.* a cheap lodging house. [prob. from F *dos*, back, L *dorsum*]

dossal (dos´əl) *n.* an ornamental hanging at the back of an altar or a stall, or round the sides of a chancel. [med. L *dossāle*, L *dorsum*]

dossier (dos´iā, -iə) *n.* a collection of papers and other documents relating to a person, a thing or an event. [F, from *dos*, L *dorsum*, back (from its bulging shape)]

dost DO[1].

DoT *abbr.* Department of Transport.

dot[1] (dot) *n.* **1** a little mark, spot or speck made with a pen or pointed instrument. **2** a period mark, a full point, a point over *i* or *j*, or used as a diacritic. **3** (*Mus.*) a point used as a direction, in various senses. **4** the short element in Morse code. **5** a tiny thing. *~v.t.* (*pres.p.* **dotting,** *past, p.p.* **dotted**) **1** to mark with a dot or dots. **2** to mark or scatter with small detached objects like dots. **3** (*sl.*) to hit. *~v.i.* to make dots or spots. **on the dot (of)** (*coll.*) precisely (at). **the year dot** YEAR. **to dot and carry one** to put down the units and transfer the tens to the next column in a sum (used by or to schoolchildren). **to dot the i's and cross the t's 1** (*coll.*) to be precisely exact. **2** (*coll.*) to put the finishing touches to an undertaking. **dot matrix** *n.* (*Comput.*) a matrix consisting of lines of pins which are used selectively to create the characters. **dot matrix printer** *n.* (*Comput.*) a printer which operates by means of a dot matrix. **dotted line** *n.* a row of dots, esp. to indicate the place on a form where one should sign one's name. **dotter** *n.* [OE *dott*, the head of a boil (cp. Dut. *dot*, a little bundle, LG *dutte*, a plug)]

dot[2] (dot) *n.* a dowry. [F, from L *dōtem*, acc. of *dōs*]

dotage (dō´tij) *n.* **1** impairment of the intellect by age. **2** silliness, infatuation. **dotard** (-təd) *n.* **1** a person whose intellect is impaired by age. **2** a person who is foolishly and excessively fond of someone or something. [F *radoter*, to talk nonsense]

dote (dōt) *v.i.* to be silly or deranged, infatuated or feeble-minded. **to dote on** to be foolishly fond of. **doter** *n.* **dotingly** *adv.*

doth DO[1].

dotterel (dot´ərəl) *n.* **1** a small migratory plover, *Endromias morinellus* (said to be so foolishly fond of imitation that it mimics the actions of the fowler, and so suffers itself to be taken). **2** (*dial.*) a dupe, a gull, a dotard. [from DOTE]

dottily, dottiness DOTTY.

dottle (dot´əl) *n.* a plug of tobacco left unsmoked in a pipe. [prob. from DOT[1]]

dotty (dot´i) *a.* (*comp.* **dottier,** *superl.* **dottiest**) **1** marked with dots, dotlike. **2** (*coll.*) **a** unsteady of gait, shaky. **b** imbecile. **c** eccentric. **d** ridiculous. **dotty about/ on** (*coll.*) excessively or foolishly fond of. **dottily** *adv.* **dottiness** *n.* [DOT[1]]

douane (dooahn´) *n.* a Continental custom house. **douanier** (dwahnyā´) *n.* a custom-house officer. [F, from Arab. *dīwān*, DIVAN]

Douay Bible (doo´ā), **Douay version** *n.* an English version of the Vulgate, made by the students of the Roman Catholic college at Douai, in N France, and published 1582–1609. [old form of *Douai*, town in N France]

double[1] (dŭb´əl) *a.* **1** composed of two, in a pair or in pairs. **2** forming a pair, twofold. **3** folded, bent back or forward. **4** twice as much, as great or as many. **5** of twice the strength or value. **6** designed for two people (*a double bed*). **7** (of a domino) having an equal number of spots on each half. **8** of two kinds, aspects or relations; ambiguous. **9** (*fig.*) hypocritical, treacherous, deceitful. **10** (*Mus.*) an octave lower in pitch. **11** (of a flower) having the stamens more or less petaloid. *~adv.* **1** twice. **2** in two ways. **3** in twice the number, quantity, amount, strength etc. **4** two together. **bent double** stooping. **double acrostic** *n.* an acrostic in which the first and last letters of each line are used. **double act** *n.* two comedians or other entertainers who have a joint act. **double-acting** *a.* exerting power in two directions. **double agent** *n.* a spy working for two opposing sides at the same time. **double axe** *n.* a double-headed axe, a religious symbol in Minoan Crete. **double-banked** *a.* (of a boat or galley) having two men to work the same oar, or two tiers of oars. **double-banking** *n.* **1** double parking. **2** (*Austral., New Zeal.*) the act of riding two on a horse or cycle. **double bar** *n.* (*Mus.*) two single bars together, to denote the end of a part. **double-barrelled** *a.* **1** (of a gun) having two barrels. **2** (of a surname) having two parts. **double bass** *n.* the largest and lowest-toned of the stringed instruments, played with a bow. **double bassoon** *n.* the largest instrument in the oboe class, with the lowest pitch. **double bill** *n.* a theatre or cinema programme featuring two main items. **double bind** *n.* a dilemma. **double-blind** *a.* (of an experiment) having neither the tester nor the subject knowing details which could prejudice the results. *~n.* a double-blind experiment. **double bluff** *n.* an attempt to deceive by making a true statement appear false. **double boiler** *n.* two saucepans, one fitting into the other, food being cooked gently in the inner pan by the heat of boiling water in the outer one. **double bond** *n.* a pair of bonds linking two atoms in a molecule. **double-book** *v.t.* to make two reservations for (a room etc.) for the same time. **double-breasted** *a.* (of a jacket etc.) lapping over and buttoning on either side. **double-charge** *v.t.* **1** to entrust with a double share. **2** to charge (a gun) with a double quantity. **double-check** *v.t.* to check a second time. **double chin** *n.* a fold of fat below the chin. **double-chinned** *a.* **double coconut** *n.* the nut of the coco-de-mer. **double concerto** *n.* a concerto for two solo instruments. **double cream** *n.* thick cream, with a higher fat content than single cream. **double-cross** *v.t.* (*coll.*) to betray, to cheat. *~n.* the act of double-crossing. **double-crosser** *n.* **double dagger** *n.* (*Print.*) a double obelus. **double-dealer** *n.* **double-dealing** *n.* deceitful behaviour, esp. in business. *~a.* deceitful, tricky. **double-decker** *n.* **1** a bus with two decks. **2** anything with two layers. **double-declutch** *v.i.* to change to a different gear by moving into neutral and then into the desired gear. **double decomposition** *n.* a reaction in which two chemical compounds exchange some of their constituents. **double density** *a.* (*Comput.*) denoting a disk which has twice the basic storage capacity. **double-dotted** *a.* **double-dotted note** *n.* (*Mus.*) a note increased in length by three-quarters, as shown by two dots placed after it. **double-dotted rhythm** *n.* (*Mus.*) a rhythm characterized by double-dotted notes. **double drummer** *n.* (*Austral.*) a large cicada. **double dummy** *n.* in bridge, play in which two hands are revealed. **double Dutch** *n.* **1** gibberish, jargon; a language not understood by the hearer. **2** (*N Am.*) a skipping game in which one rope is turned clockwise and the other anticlockwise, the skipper jumping over each rope in turn. **double-dye** *v.t.* to dye with double intensity. **double-dyed** *a.* stained or tainted with infamy; doubly infamous. **double-eagle** *n.* **1** a representation, as in the imperial arms of Russia and Austria, of an eagle with two heads. **2** (*N Am.*) in golf, an albatross. **3** (*Hist.*) an American gold coin worth 20 dollars. **double-edged** *a.* **1** having two cutting edges. **2** having two meanings or effects, one positive and one negative. **double entry** *n.* a method of bookkeeping in which every transaction is entered twice, once on the credit side of the account, and once on the debit side. **double exposure** *n.* **1** the recording of two superimposed images on a single piece of film. **2** the picture resulting from this. **double fault** *n.* in tennis, two faults in succession, resulting in the loss of a point. **double-fault** *v.i.* in tennis, to serve a double fault. **double feature** *n.* two full-length feature films shown in a single programme. **double figures** *n.pl.* a number greater than 9 but less than 100. **double first** *n.* **1** first-class honours in two subjects or examinations for a degree. **2** a person who achieves a double first. **double flat** *n.* (*Mus.*) a sign indicating a drop of two semitones. **double-fronted** *a.* (of a house) having main windows on each side of the front door. **double-gild** *v.t.* **1** to gild with a double coating. **2** to excuse. **double glazing** *n.* **1** the fitting of a double layer of glass in a window to act as a form of insulation. **2** the double layer of glass itself. **double-glaze** *v.t.* **double Gloucester** *n.* a rich hard cheese orig. made in Gloucestershire. **double-headed** *a.* **1** having two heads. **2** (of a train) drawn by two locomotives. **3** (*Bot.*) having flowers growing close to one another. **double header** *n.* **1** a train drawn by two locomotives. **2** (*N Am.*) two games played consecutively. **3** (*Austral.*) a coin with a head on each side. **double-hearted** *a.* deceitful, treacherous. **double helix** *n.* two helices coiled round the same axis, the molecular structure of DNA. **double-hung** *a.* a term applied to the sashes of a window when both are movable and fitted with lines and weights. **double jeopardy** *n.* (*N Am.*) a second trial for the same offence. **double-jointedness** *n.* abnormal mobility of joints not associated with injury or disease, nor causing symptoms. **double knit** *n.* a fabric knitted on a double set of needles to give a double thickness. **double knitting** *n.* a knitting yarn of medium thickness. **double-lock** *v.t.* to fasten by turning the lock twice. **double-manned** *a.* furnished or equipped with twice the usual number of men. **double-minded** *a.* unsettled, wavering; fickle, undetermined. **double napoleon** *n.* (*Hist.*) a coin worth 40 francs. **double-natured** *a.* having a double or twofold nature. **double negative** *n.* an ungrammatical sentence construction with two negatives where only one is needed, such as *I don't need nothing.* **doubleness** *n.* **double obelus, double obelisk** *n.* (*Print.*) a reference mark (‡). **double-park** *v.t.* to park (a vehicle) parallel with one already parked at the kerb. **double play** *n.* in baseball, a play in which two runners are put out. **double pneumonia** *n.* pneumonia affecting both lungs. **double quick** *adv.* very quickly. ~*n.* (*Mil.*) the quickest pace next to a run. ~*a.* very quick. **double-reed** *a.* denoting a wind instrument with a set of two reeds in the mouthpiece which vibrate against each other. **double refraction** *n.* the formation of two unequally refracted rays of light from a single unpolarized ray. **double rhyme** *n.* a two-syllable rhyme. **double salt** *n.* a salt which, when dissolved, gives two different salts in solution. **double saucepan** *n.* a double boiler. **double sharp** *n.* (*Mus.*) a sign indicating a rise of two semitones. **double shuffle** *n.* a scraping dance step made twice with each foot in turn. **double-sided** *a.* able to be used on both sides. **double-space** *v.t.* to type with a line space between the lines. **doublespeak** *n.* talk that sounds sensible though it is actually a compound of sense and gibberish. **double standard** *n.* **1** a single moral principle applied in different ways to different groups of people and unfairly allowing different behaviour to the different groups. **2** bimetallism. **doublestar** *n.* two stars so near each other that they appear to be one when seen with the naked eye. **double-stop** *v.i.* (*pres.p.* **double-stopping,** *past, p.p.* **double-stopped**) (*Mus.*) to play chords on a violin on two stopped strings. **double stop** *n.* **double take** *n.* a delayed reaction. **double-talk** *n.* doublespeak. **doublethink** *n.* the holding of two contradictory beliefs at the same time. **double time** *n.* **1** pay at twice the usual rate, esp. for overtime. **2** a marching step at the rate of 165 steps to the minute, or (*US*) of 180 steps to the minute. **double-tongue** *v.i.* (*Mus.*) to apply the tongue rapidly to the teeth and the palate alternately, as in staccato passages played on the flute or cornet. ~*v.t.* to play with double-tonguing. **double-tongued** *a.* **1** giving contrary accounts of the same thing at different times. **2** deceitful, double-dealing. **double top** *n.* a score of double twenty in darts. **double vision** *n.* a disorder of the eyes in which the patient sees objects double. **double whammy** *n.* (*coll.*) a twofold blow or misfortune. **doubly** *adv.* [OF from L *duplus* (*duo*, two, *-plus*, cogn. with Gr. *-plos*, -fold)]

double[2] (dŭb´əl) *n.* **1** twice as much or as many, a double quantity. **2** a drink of spirits which is twice the usual measure. **3** a bend or twist (in a road or river). **4** a wraith, a doppelgänger. **5** a person who almost exactly resembles someone else. **6** an understudy in a dramatic production. **7** (*Mil.*) running, the pace for charging. **8** a turn in running to escape pursuit. **9** (*fig.*) a trick, an artifice. **10** (*pl.*) in tennis etc., a game between two pairs. **11** in sport, two successive wins against the same team. **12** in bridge, the act of doubling an opponent's bid. **13** a bet on two races, the stake and winnings on the first being applied to the second race. **14** in darts, a throw between the two outer circles. ~*v.t.* **1** to increase by an equal quantity, amount, number, value etc., to multiply by two. **2** to fold down or over, to bend, to turn upon itself. **3** to be twice as much as. **4** (*Mus.*) to add the upper or lower octave to. **5** to act two (parts) in the same play. **6** (*Naut.*) to sail round or by. **7** in bridge, to raise the scores at stake in. **8** to clench (one's fist). **9** in billiards, to cause to rebound. ~*v.i.* **1** to become twice as much or as great. **2** to be folded over. **3** to be an understudy. **4** to play a dual role. **5** to play more than one musical instrument. **6** in bridge, on the strength of one's own hand, to double the number of points an opponent may gain or lose. **7** to turn or wind to escape pursuit. **8** to run. **9** in billiards, to rebound. **at the double 1** very fast. **2** at twice the normal speed. **on the double** (*N Am.*) at the double. **to double back** to go back in the direction one has come from. **to double up 1** to bend one's body into a stooping or folded posture. **2** to collapse with pain or laughter. **3** to make (another person) double up. **4** to share a room or bed with someone. **5** to use the winnings from a bet to make another bet. **6** to clench. **7** to fold or become folded. **double or quits** *n.* a game such as pitch and toss to decide whether the person owing shall pay twice their debt or nothing. **doubler** *n.* [as DOUBLE[1]]

double-entendre (dooblãtã´drə) *n.* **1** a word or phrase with two interpretations, one of which is usually indelicate. **2** a humour which relies on double entendres. [obs. F, double understanding]

doublet (dŭb´lit) *n.* **1** either of a pair. **2** either of two words from the same root, but differing in meaning. **3** a word or passage printed twice by mistake. **4** (*Physics*) a combination of two lenses. **5** (*pl.*) a pair of thrown dice showing the same number. **6** (*Physics*) a closely spaced pair of spectral lines. **7** (*Hist.*) a close-fitting garment covering the body from the neck to a little below the waist. **8** a historical account which occurs twice in different contexts, usually originating from different sources. **9** a counterfeit gem made of two pieces of crystal with a coloured substance between them. **doublet and hose** *n.* regular masculine attire in the Tudor period; an undress attire suitable for active exertion (implying the absence of a cloak). [F, dim. of DOUBLE[1]]

doubletree (dŭb´əltrē) *n.* the horizontal bar on a vehicle to which the swingletree for harnessing horses is attached.

doubloon (dəbloon´) *n.* **1** (*Hist.*) a Spanish and S American gold coin (orig. the double of a pistole). **2** (*pl.*, *sl.*) money. [F *doublon*, or Sp. *doblon* (*doble*, DOUBLE[1])]

doublure (dooblua´) *n.* an ornamental lining for a book cover. [F, lining, from *doubler*, to DOUBLE[2], to line]

doubt (dowt) *v.t.* **1** to hold or think questionable. **2** to hesitate to believe or assent to. **3** †to distrust, suspect or fear. *~v.i.* to be in uncertainty about the truth, probability or propriety of anything. *~n.* **1** uncertainty of mind upon any point, action or statement. **2** an unsettled state of opinion. **3** indecision, hesitation, suspense. **4** distrust, inclination to disbelieve. **5** a question, a problem, an objection. **beyond doubt** definitely true. **in doubt** uncertain. **no doubt** certainly, very unlikely, admittedly. **without (a) doubt** definitely. **doubtable** *a.* **doubter** *n.* **doubtful** *a.* **1** liable to doubt. **2** uncertain, admitting of doubt. **3** ambiguous, not clear in meaning. **4** uncertain, undecided, hesitating. **5** suspicious. **doubtfully** *adv.* **doubtfulness** *n.* **doubting** *n.*, *a.* **doubtingly** *adv.* assuredly, certainly, admittedly. **Doubting Thomas** *n.* a person who persists in doubt until they have tangible evidence (from Thomas the apostle who would not believe in the Resurrection until he had seen Jesus (John, xx.24–25)). **doubtless** *a.* **1** sure, confident, certain. **2** †free from fear. **doubtlessly** *adv.* **doubtlessness** *n.* [OF *douter*, L *dubitāre*, from *dubius*, doubtful]

douce (doos) *a.* (*Sc.*) sober, sedate, peaceable, sweet, pleasant. **doucely** *adv.* **douceness** *n.* [OF *doux*, fem. *douce*, *dolz*, L *dulcis*, sweet]

douceur (doosœ´) *n.* a small present; a gift, a bribe. [F, as DOUCE]

douche (doosh) *n.* **1** a jet of water or vapour directed upon some part of the body. **2** an instrument for applying this. *~v.t.* to apply a douche to, esp. to flush out (the vagina or other cavity). *~v.i.* to take a douche. [F, from It. *doccia*, a conduit, from L *ductus*, p.p. of *ducere*, to lead]

dough (dō) *n.* **1** the paste of bread etc. before baking; a mass of flour or meal moistened and kneaded. **2** anything resembling this in appearance or consistency. **3** (*sl.*) money. **dough-baked** *a.* deficient in intellect. **doughboy** *n.* **1** a flour dumpling boiled in salt water. **2** (*N Am.*) a private soldier in the US Army. **doughfaced** *a.* (*N Am.*) cowardly, weak, pliable. †**dough-kneaded** *a.* soft like dough. **doughnut,** (*N Am.*) **donut** *n.* **1** a cake, often ring-shaped, made of sweetened dough and fried in fat. **2** any ring-shaped object. **doughnutting** *n.* (*coll.*) the practice of MPs sitting in the seats around a speaker during a televised debate to give the impression of a crowded house. **doughy** *a.* (*comp.* **doughier,** *superl.* **doughiest**) **1** like dough; soft. **2** pale, pasty. **doughiness** *n.* [OE *dāh* (cp. Dut. *deeg*, Dan. *deig*, G *Teig*, also Sansk. *dih-*, to smear, L *fingere*, to shape, Gr. *teichos*, an earth wall]

†**doughty** (dow´ti) *a.* (*comp.* **doughtier,** *superl.* **doughtiest**) brave, valiant. **doughtily** *adv.* **doughtiness** *n.* [OE *dohtig* (cp. *dugan*, to be strong, G *taugen*, to be worth, whence *tüchtig*, able)]

Douglas fir (dŭg´ləs), **Douglas pine, Douglas spruce** *n.* any tall American conifer of the genus *Pseudotsuga*, grown for ornament and timber. [David *Douglas*, 1798–1834, British botanist]

Doukhobor DUKHOBOR.

douleia DULIA.

doum (doom), **doum-palm** *n.* an Egyptian palm, *Hyphaene thebaica*, remarkable for the dichotomous division of the trunk and branches. [Arab. *daum*, *dūm*]

dour (duə) *a.* (*Sc.*, *North.*) hard, bold, sullen; stern, severe, obstinate. **dourly** *adv.* **dourness** *n.* [L *dūrus*]

doura DURRA.

douroucouli (doorəkoo´li) *n.* (*pl.* **dourocoulis**) a nocturnal ape of the genus *Aotus*, of Central America.

douse[1] (dows), **dowse** *v.t.* **1** to plunge into water, to dip. **2** to throw water over, to drench. **3** (*Naut.*) **a** to strike or slacken (a sail) suddenly. **b** to close (a porthole). **4** to extinguish. *~v.i.* to be plunged into water. **to douse the glim** (*sl.*, *dated*) to put out the light. [etym. uncertain]

douse[2] DOWSE[1].

dove[1] (dŭv) *n.* **1** any bird of the family Columbidae, resembling a pigeon, but smaller and paler. **2** an emblem of gentleness and innocence. **3** the symbol of the Holy Ghost. **4** in politics, an advocate of peaceable and conciliatory policies towards opponents, as distinct from *hawk*. **5** a gentle person (a term of endearment). **dove-coloured** *a.* grey with a tinge of pink. **dovecote, dovecot** (-kot) *n.* a small house or box for domestic pigeons. **to flutter the dovecots** to throw peaceful people into alarm; to scandalize conventional circles. **dove-eyed** *a.* having eyes like a dove; meek, gentle-looking. **dove grey** *n.* **dove-grey** *a.* **dovekie** (-ki) *n.* the little auk. **dovelet** (-lit) *n.* a young dove. **dovelike** *a.* **dove's-foot** *n.* one of the cranesbills, *Geranium molle*. **dove tree** *n.* a tree native to China, *Davidia involucrata*, which has white flowers resembling doves' wings. [OE *dūfe* (only in *dūfe-doppa*), from *dūfan*, to dive (cp. G *Taube*, and for sense L *columba*, dove, Gr. *kolumbos*, diver)]

dove[2] DIVE.

Dover's powder (dō´vəz) *n.* a sweat-inducing compound, with opium, potassium sulphate and ipecacuanha. [Thomas *Dover*, 1660–1742, British physician]

dovetail (dŭv´tāl) *n.* **1** a mode of fastening boards together by fitting tenons, shaped like a dove's tail spread out, into corresponding cavities. **2** a tenon or a joint of this kind. *~v.t.* **1** to fit together by means of dovetails. **2** to fit exactly. *~v.i.* to fit exactly. **dovetail joint** *n.* a joint fastened by such tenons.

dowager (dow´əjə) *n.* **1** a widow in possession of a dower or jointure. **2** a title given to a widow to distinguish her from the wife of her husband's heir. **3** (*sl.*) a dignified old lady. [OF *douagere*, from *douage*, dowry, *douer*, to DOWER]

dowdy (dow´di) *a.* (*comp.* **dowdier,** *superl.* **dowdiest**) dull, unfashionable. *~n.* (*pl.* **dowdies**) a dull, unfashionably dressed woman. **dowdily** *adv.* **dowdiness** *n.* **dowdyish** *a.* **dowdyism** *n.* [ME *dowd*, a shabby or untidily dressed person, etym. uncertain]

dowel (dow´əl) *n.* a pin or peg for connecting two stones or pieces of wood, being sunk into the side of each. *~v.t.* (*pres.p.* **dowelling,** (*N Am.*) **doweling,** *past*, *p.p.* **dowelled,** (*N Am.*) **doweled**) to fasten by dowels. **dowel-joint** *n.* a junction by means of a dowel. **dowelling,** (*N Am.*) **doweling** *n.* a long, thin rod of wood etc., for cutting into dowels. **dowel-pin** *n.* a dowel. [perh. from F *douille*, a socket (but cp. LG *dovel*, G *Döbel*, plug or tap, OF *douelle*, a barrel-stave)]

dower (dow´ə) *n.* **1** the part of a husband's property which his widow enjoys during her life. **2** †dowry. **3** an endowment, a natural gift, a talent. *~v.t.* **1** to endow (with). **2** †to give a dowry to. **dower house** *n.* a house on an estate reserved for the widow of the late owner. **dowerless** *a.* [OF *doaire*, late L *dōtārium*, from *dōtāre*, to endow (*dōs dōtis*, cp. Gr. *dōs*, a gift)]

dowie (dow´i) *a.* (*Sc.*) dull, low-spirited, dreary. [prob. from OE *dol*, DULL]

dowitcher (dow´ichə) *n.* a wading bird of the genus *Limnodromus*, found on the shores of arctic and subarctic N America. [Iroquoian]

Dow–Jones index (dow jōnz´), **Dow–Jones average** *n.* an index of the prices of stocks and shares on the New

York Stock Exchange. [Charles *Dow*, 1851–1902, and Edward *Jones*, 1856–1920, US economists]

down[1] (down) *adv.* (*superl.* **downmost**) **1** towards the ground. **2** from a higher to a lower position. **3** on the ground. **4** below the horizon. **5** from former to later times. **6** from north to south. **7** away from the capital or a university. **8** (*Naut.*) **a** with a stream or current. **b** to leeward. **9** (of a crossword clue) to fit a word leading downwards in the grid. **10** into less bulk. **11** to finer consistency. **12** into quiescence (*Settle down!*). **13** in writing. **14** paid as a deposit. **15** to or in a state of subjection, disgrace or depression. **16** at a low level. **17** prostrate, in a fallen position or condition. **18** losing or beaten (*two goals down*). **19** temporarily out of action. **20** over one's throat. **21** downstairs, out of bed. **22** reduced in price. **23** in American football, out of play. ~*prep.* **1** along, through, or into, in a descending direction. **2** from the top or the upper part to the bottom or a lower part of. **3** at a lower part of. **4** along. ~*a.* (*superl.* **downmost**) **1** moving, sloping or directed towards a lower part or position. **2** of or relating to rail travel out of a city. **3** depressed, downcast. ~*v.t.* (*coll.*) **1** to put, strike or throw down, to overcome. **2** to eat or drink. ~*v.i.* to descend. ~*n.* **1** the act of putting down. **2** in American football, one of up to four chances to advance the ball for a score. **3** (*coll.*) a state of depression. **4** the act of playing the first piece in a game of dominoes. **5** (*esp. pl.*) a reverse. **6** (*coll.*) a grudge, dislike. **down on one's luck** LUCK. **down the hatch!** HATCH[1]. **down to earth** EARTH. **down to the ground** GROUND[1]. **down with** abolish (*Down with the terrorists!*). **to be down on** to disapprove of, to be severe towards. **to down tools** **1** to stop work. **2** to strike. **to down with** to put down. **to have a down on** (*coll.*) to have a grudge against. **down!** *int.* (*ellipt.*) get, lie, put or throw down! **down and out** *a.* **1** utterly destitute and without resources. **2** in boxing, unable to continue the fight. **down-and-out** *n.* an utterly destitute person. **down at heel** *a.* **1** having worn heels. **2** shabby, disreputably dressed. **downbeat** *n.* **1** a downward movement of a conductor's baton. **2** an accented beat marked in this way. ~*a.* **1** depressed, pessimistic. **2** casual, relaxed. **downcast** *a.* **1** looking downward. **2** dejected, sad. ~*n.* **1** a ventilating shaft. **2** (*Geol.*) a downthrow. **down draught** *n.* a downward current of air. **downer** *n.* (*sl.*) **1** a tranquillizing drug, esp. a barbiturate. **2** a depressing experience. **3** a downturn. **on a downer** depressed, pessimistic. **downfall** *n.* **1** a sudden loss of prosperity, rank, reputation; ruin, overthrow. **2** a fall of rain, snow etc. **3** a cause of someone's downfall. **downfield** *adv.* UPFIELD (under UP- (+ C–H WORDS)). **downfold** *n.* (*Geol.*) a syncline. **downgrade**[1] (-grād´) *v.t.* **1** to lower in status. **2** to disparage. **downgrade**[2] (down´-) *n.* **1** a downward gradient on a railway. **2** decadence. **3** an instance of lowering in rank. **on the downgrade** (*N Am.*) in decline. **downhaul** *n.* (*Naut.*) a rope for hauling down a sail. **downhearted** *a.* dispirited, dejected. **downheartedly** *adv.* **downheartedness** *n.* **downhill** (downhil´) *adv.* **1** on a descending slope. **2** towards ruin or disgrace. *a.* descending, sloping downwards, declining. ~*n.* **1** a declivity, a downward slope. **2** a decline. **3** a downhill race in skiing. **to go downhill** to deteriorate physically or morally. **downhole** *a.* of or relating to any equipment in the oil industry which is used in the well itself. **down-home** *a.* (*N Am.*) homely, rustic, unsophisticated. **down in the mouth** *a.* (*coll.*) unhappy, fed up. **downlighter** *n.* a lamp or spotlight whose light is directed downwards. **down-line** *n.* a railway line for trains going away from a main terminus. **download** *v.t.* to transfer (data) directly from one computer to another. ~*n.* an instance of downloading. **down-lying** *n.* (*dial.*) **1** lying down or going to bed. **2** childbed, confinement. **downmarket** *a.* of or relating to cheaply produced goods of poor quality. **down payment** *n.* a deposit paid on an article bought on hire purchase. **downpipe** *n.* a drainpipe which carries water from a roof to the ground. **down platform** *n.* the platform adjoining a down-line. **downplay** *v.t.* to play down the importance of. **downpour** *n.* a heavy, persistent fall of rain. **downrange** *a., adv.* in the flight path of a rocket or missile. **downrate** *v.t.* to lower in value or importance. **downright** *a.* **1** directly to the point; plain, unequivocal; outspoken, artless, blunt. **2** complete, utter (*downright rudeness*). ~*adv.* thoroughly, absolutely. **downrightness** *n.* **downriver**[1] (downriv´ə) *adv.* towards or near the mouth of a river. **downriver**[2] (down´rivə) *a.* located or taking place downriver. **downscale** *v.t.* (*N Am.*) to reduce in scale or size. ~*a.* inferior, esp. socially. **downshift** *n.* the act of changing to a lower gear when driving. ~*v.i.* to make a downshift. **downside** *n.* **1** a negative aspect of any situation; the negative side, adverse aspect; disadvantage. **2** a downward swing of share prices. **down-sitting** *n.* the act of sitting down, repose, rest. **downsize** *v.t., v.i.* to reduce in size (esp. the workforce of a company). **downspout** *n.* (*N Am.*) a downpipe. **downstage** *a., adv.* at or to the front of the stage in a theatre. **downstair** *a.* downstairs. **downstairs** *adv.* **1** down the stairs. **2** on or to a lower floor. ~*a.* relating to a lower floor. ~*n.* **1** the lower part of a building. **2** the servant's quarters. **downstate** *a.* (*N Am.*) of or in a part of a state which is far from the large cities, esp. in the south of the state. ~*n.* a downstate part of a state. ~*adv.* in or to the downstate part of a state. **downstream** *a., adv.* in the direction of the current of a river. **downstroke** *n.* a downward stroke in handwriting. **downswing** *n.* **1** a downward trend in trade statistics etc. **2** the part of a swing in golf when the club is moving downwards towards the ground. **downthrow** *n.* (*Geol.*) the casting down, by earthquake or other action, of the strata on one side of a fault to a lower level. **down time** *n.* the time during a normal working day when a computer, or other machinery, is inoperative. **down-to-earth** *a.* realistic, practical, sensible. **downtown** *n.* the business and commercial centre of a city. ~*a.* situated in (belonging to) this area. ~*adv.* in or towards this area. **down-train** *n.* a train travelling away from a main terminus. **downtrodden** *a.* **1** oppressed; tyrannized over. **2** trodden under foot. **downturn** *n.* a downward trend, esp. in business. **down under** *n., adv.* (*coll.*) (in or to) Australia or New Zealand. **downward** *a.* moving, directed or tending from higher, superior or earlier to lower, inferior or later. ~*adv.* downwards. **downwardly** *adv.* **downwards** *adv.* **1** from a higher to a lower position, level, condition or character. **2** from earlier to later. **3** from superior to inferior. **downwarp** *n.* (*Geol.*) a wide depression, a syncline. **downwind** *a., adv.* in the direction in which the wind is blowing. [ME *adown*, OE *of- dūne*, off the down or hill]

down[2] (down) *n.* **1** the fine soft plumage of young birds or the plumage found under the feathers. **2** fine soft hair, esp. on the human face or on leaves, fruits etc. **3** any soft, fluffy substance. **Downie**® *n.* a duvet. **downy** *a.* (*comp.* **downier**, *superl.* **downiest**) **1** covered with down. **2** made of down. **3** resembling down. **4** soft, placid, soothing. **5** (*sl.*) cunning, knowing, artful. **downily** *adv.* **downiness** *n.* [Icel. *dūnn* (cp. LG *dûne*, G *Daune*)]

down[3] (down) *n.* **1** a tract of upland, esp. the chalk uplands of southern England, used for pasturing sheep. **2** a bank of sand etc. cast up by the sea. **downland** (-lənd) *n.* [OE *dūn* (cp. ODut. *dúna*, whence Dut. *duin*, LG *düne*, F *dune*)]

downer DOWN[1].

Downie® DOWN[2].

downmost DOWN[1].

Down's syndrome (downz) *n.* a genetic disorder characterized by lower than average intelligence, short stature, sloping eyes and flattened facial features. [John Langdon-*Down*, 1828–96, British physician]

downy DOWN[2].

dowry (dow´ri) *n.* (*pl.* **dowries**) **1** the property which a wife brings to her husband. **2** an endowment, gift or talent. [A-F *dowarie*, as DOWER]

dowse[1] (dows), **douse** *v.i.* to use a dowsing rod for the discovery of subterranean waters or minerals. **dowser** *n.* **dowsing-rod** *n.* a forked twig or other stick used by dowsers to discover subterranean waters or minerals. [etym. unknown]

dowse[2] DOUSE[1].

doxology (doksol´əji) *n.* (*pl.* **doxologies**) a brief formula or hymn of praise to God. **doxological** (-səloj´-) *a.* [late L, Gr. *doxologia* (*doxa*, glory, -LOGY)]

†**doxy**[1] (dok´si) *n.* (*pl.* **doxies**) **1** a female lover. **2** a prostitute. [etym. uncertain]

doxy[2] (dok´si) *n.* (*pl.* **doxies**) (*facet.*) opinion, esp. in religious matters. [from ORTHODOXY (under ORTHODOX) etc.]

doyen (doi´en) *n.* the senior member of a body of people. **doyenne** (doi´en, -en´) *n.* a female doyen. [F, from L *decānus*, DEAN[1]]

doyley DOILY.

doz. *abbr.* dozen.

doze (dōz) *v.i.* **1** to sleep lightly. **2** to be drowsy. ~*v.t.* to spend in drowsy inaction. ~*n.* a light sleep; a nap. **to doze off** to fall into a light sleep. **dozer** *n.* **dozy** *a.* (*comp.* **dozier**, *superl.* **doziest**). **dozily** *adv.* **doziness** *n.* [cp. Dan. *döse*, Icel. *dūsa*, LG *dussen*]

dozen (dŭz´ən) *n.* (*pl.* **dozen, dozens**) **1** an aggregate of twelve things or people. **2** about twelve, an indefinite number. **3** (*pl.*) a large number (of). ~*a.* twelve. **by the dozen** in large numbers. **the dozens** a game of exchanged verbal insults, indulged in by some African Americans. **to talk nineteen to the dozen** to talk incessantly. **dozenth** *a.* [OF *dozaine* (*doze*, L *duodecim*, twelve, -*aine*, L -*ēna*, as in *centēna*)]

dozer, dozy DOZE.

DP *abbr.* **1** data processing. **2** displaced person.

D.Phil. *abbr.* Doctor of Philosophy.

DPP *abbr.* Director of Public Prosecutions.

dpt *abbr.* department.

Dr *abbr.* **1** debit. **2** debtor. **3** Doctor. **4** Drive.

dr. *abbr.* **1** drachm(s). **2** drachma(s). **3** drain. **4** dram(s).

drab[1] (drab) *a.* (*comp.* **drabber**, *superl.* **drabbest**) **1** of a dull brown or dun colour. **2** dull, commonplace, monotonous. ~*n.* **1** drab colour. **2** monotony. **drabbet** (-it) *n.* a coarse drab linen. **drably** *adv.* **drabness** *n.* [F *drap*, cloth]

drab[2] (drab) *n.* a prostitute, a slut. ~*v.i.* to associate with drabs. **drabber** *n.* a person who associates with drabs. **drabbish** *a.* [cp. Irish *drabog*, Gael. *drabach*]

drab[3] DRIBS AND DRABS (under DRIB).

drabber DRAB[2].

drabbet DRAB[1].

drabbish DRAB[2].

drabble (drab´əl) *v.t.* to draggle; to make wet and dirty, as by dragging through filth. ~*v.i.* to become wet and dirty. [ME *drabelen*, cp. LG *drabeln*]

dracaena (drəsē´nə) *n.* (*pl.* **dracaenas**) any shrub or tree of the genera *Dracaena* or *Cordyline*. [mod. L, from Gr. *drakaina*, fem. of *drakōn*, dragon]

drachm (dram) *n.* **1** an apothecaries' weight of 60 grains (⅛ oz, 3.542 g). **2** an avoirdupois 27 ⅓ grains (1/16 oz, 1.771g). **drachma** (drak´mə) *n.* (*pl.* **drachmas, drachmae** (-mē)) **1** the chief unit of currency of modern Greece. **2** the principal silver coin of the ancient Greeks, worth six obols. **3** an Attic weight, about 60 gr. avoirdupois (3.542 g). [F *drachme*, L *drachma*, Gr. *drachmē* (*drassesthai*, to grasp), cp. *dragma*, a grasp, handful]

drack (drak) *a.* (*Austral.*, *sl.*) unattractive. [etym. uncertain]

dracone (drak´ōn) *n.* a large, flexible container for liquids, towed by a ship.

draconian (drəkō´niən), **draconic** (-kon´ik) *a.* inflexible, severe, cruel. [*Dracōn*, an Athenian legislator (about 621 BC), whose laws were extremely severe]

draff (draf) *n.* refuse, lees, esp. of malt after brewing or distilling. [ME *draf* (cp. Dut., Icel., Swed. *draf*)]

draft (drahft) *n.* **1** the first outline of any writing or document. **2** a rough copy. **3** a rough sketch of work to be executed. **4** a written order for the payment of money. **5** a cheque or bill drawn, esp. by a department or a branch of a bank upon another. **6** a demand (on). **7** a number of people selected for some special purpose, a detachment, a contingent. **8** the selection of people for some special purpose. **9** (*N Am.*) conscription for the army etc. **10** a reinforcement. **11** (*N Am.*) a draught. ~*v.t.* **1** to draw up an outline of, to compose the first form of, make a rough copy of. **2** to select (some of a larger number of people) for some special purpose. **3** (*N Am.*) to conscript for the army etc. **4** (*Austral.*) to separate and sort out (cattle). **draft dodger** *n.* (*N Am.*) a person who tries to avoid doing compulsory military service. **draft dodging** *n.* **draftee** (drahftē´) *n.* (*N Am.*) a conscript. **drafter** *n.* **drafting** *n.* **draftsman** *n.* (*pl.* **draftsmen**) **1** a person who draws up documents. **2** a draughtsman. **drafty** *a.* (*comp.* **draftier**, *superl.* **draftiest**). [DRAUGHT]

drag (drag) *v.t.* (*pres.p.* **dragging**, *past*, *p.p.* **dragged**) **1** to pull along the ground by main force. **2** to draw by force; to haul. **3** to draw along with difficulty. **4** to force (someone) to go somewhere. **5** to break (a soil) surface with a harrow. **6** to search (a river etc.) with a grapnel. **7** to put a drag on (a wheel). **8** to perform too slowly. ~*v.i.* **1** (of a dress etc.) to trail along the ground. **2** to search a river etc. with a grapnel, nets etc. **3** to move slowly or heavily. **4** (*coll.*) to draw on a cigarette. **5** to go on at great length. ~*n.* **1** anything which retards movement. **2** an iron shoe or skid fastened on a wheel of a vehicle to check the speed. **3** (*Hist.*) a kind of open four-horse coach. **4** a dredge. **5** a four-clawed grapnel for dragging or dredging under water. **6** a dragnet. **7** a draw on a cigarette. **8** a heavy kind of harrow; an implement to spread manure. **9** the total resistance of an aeroplane along its line of flight. **10 a** in hunting, an artificial scent. **b** the trail of a fox. **c** a hunt in which a drag is used. **d** the action of using a drag. **11** laborious movement, slow process. **12** (*coll.*) something or someone boring or irritating. **13** (*sl.*) **a** clothes appropriate to the opposite sex, esp. women's clothes worn by men. **b** a party where the people wear drag. **c** clothes generally. **14** the act of dragging. **15** (*sl.*) a motor car. **16** (*N Am.*, *sl.*) influence. **17** (*sl.*) a road, a street (*the main drag*). **18** an impediment. **to drag anchor** (of a ship) to trail the anchor along the bottom when it will not take firm hold. **to drag in** to introduce (a subject) gratuitously or irrelevantly. **to drag one's feet/ heels** (*coll.*) to go slowly deliberately. **to drag out** to make (something) last longer than necessary. **to drag something out of someone** to get information from someone with difficulty. **to drag up** (*coll.*) **1** to mention (an unpleasant event or story). **2** to bring up or rear in a careless fashion. **drag-anchor** *n.* a sea anchor. **draggy** *a.* (*comp.* **draggier**, *superl.* **draggiest**) (*coll.*) boring or unpleasant. **drag-hound** *n.* a hound used in a drag hunt. **drag hunt** *n.* **1** a hunt in which a drag is used. **2** a club devoted to this kind of hunting. **dragline** *n.* an excavator which is dragged by cables at the end of an arm. **dragman** *n.* (*pl.* **dragmen**) a fisherman who uses a dragnet. **dragnet** *n.* **1** a net dragged along the bottom of a river etc. for catching fish. 2 a net drawn over a field to enclose game. 3 a systematic police search of an area for criminals. **drag queen** *n.* a man who wears women's clothing, esp. as a theatrical act. **drag race** *n.* a race in which specially modified cars race over a timed course. **drag racing** *n.* **dragsman** *n.* (*pl.* **dragsmen**) the driver of a drag or coach. **dragster** *n.* a car modified for drag racing. [prob. a var. of DRAW]

dragée (drazh´ā) *n.* 1 a sweetmeat consisting of a nut, fruit etc. with a hard sugar coating. 2 a small silver-coloured sugar ball for decorating cakes. 3 a chocolate-covered sweet. 4 a pill with a hard sugar coating. [F]

dragger DRAG.

draggle (drag´əl) *v.t.* to make wet and dirty by dragging on the ground. ~*v.i.* 1 to become dirty by being trailed along the ground. 2 to trail along the ground. 3 (*fig.*) to lag, to straggle. **draggletail** *n.* a slut. **draggle-tailed** *a.* sluttish; draggling. **draggling** *a.*

draggy DRAG.

dragoman (drag´əmən), **drogman** (drog´mən), **drogoman** (-əmən) *n.* (*pl.* **dragomans, dragomen, drogmans, drogmen, drogomans, drogomen**) a person who acts as guide, interpreter and agent for travellers in the Middle East. [F, from It. *dragomanno*, med. Gr. *dragoumanos*, OArab. *targumān*, interpreter]

dragon (drag´ən) *n.* 1 a fabulous monster found in the mythology of nearly all nations, generally as an enormous winged lizard with formidable claws etc. 2 (*Astron.*) a constellation in the northern hemisphere. 3 a flying lizard. 4 a violent, spiteful person, esp. a woman. **to chase the dragon** (*sl.*) to smoke heroin. **dragonet** (-nit) *n.* 1 any sea fish of the family Callionymidae. 2 a little dragon. **dragonfish** *n.* (*pl.* **dragonfish**) any sea fish of the order Stomiiformes, having a barbel on the chin. **dragonfly** *n.* any insect of the order Odonata, having a long brilliant body and two pairs of large wings. **dragonish** *a.* shaped, or otherwise like, a dragon. **dragon's blood** *n.* a red resin exuding from various trees, much used for staining and colouring. **dragon's teeth** *n.pl.* 1 (*coll.*) concrete antitank obstacles which point upwards from the ground. 2 seeds or causes from which wars and disputes spring. **dragon tree** *n.* a palmlike tree, *Dracaena draco*, of W Africa and the adjacent islands. [F, from L *draco -ōnem*, Gr. *drakōn*, serpent (*drak-*, stem of *derkesthai*, to see)]

dragonnade (dragənād´) *n.* 1 (*usu. pl.*) the persecutions of Protestants in France during the reign of Louis XIV by means of dragoons who were quartered upon them. 2 a persecution by means of troops. ~*v.t.* to persecute by this means. [F, from *dragon*, DRAGOON]

dragoon (drəgoon´) *n.* 1 a cavalry soldier, orig. a mounted infantryman armed with a short musket or carbine called a dragon. 2 in the British army, a soldier in any of certain regiments that were formerly mounted infantry. 3 a tough, belligerent man. 4 a kind of pigeon. ~*v.t.* 1 to subdue by military force. 2 to compel by violent measures. [F *dragon*, orig. a kind of musket, DRAGON]

dragsman, dragster DRAG.

drail (drāl) *n.* a piece of lead on the shank of the hook of a fishing rod. ~*v.i.* to draggle. [perh. *draggle, tail*]

drain (drān) *v.t.* 1 to draw off gradually. 2 to cause to run off by tapping etc. 3 to empty by drawing away moisture from. 4 to drink up. 5 to exhaust or to deprive (of vitality, resources etc.). ~*v.i.* 1 to flow off gradually. 2 to be emptied of moisture. ~*n.* 1 a strain, heavy demand. 2 a channel for conveying water, sewage etc. 3 (*Med.*) a tube for drawing off pus etc. 4 (*sl.*) a drink. **down the drain** (*coll.*) wasted. **to drain to the dregs** DREG. **to laugh like a drain** LAUGH. **drainable** *a.* **drainage** *n.* 1 the act, practice or science of draining. 2 the natural or artificial system by which land or a town is drained. 3 sewage etc. which is carried away through drains. **drainage basin, drainage area** *n.* the region drained by a river and its tributaries. **drainage-tube** *n.* a tube introduced into a suppurating wound or chronic abscess to allow free discharge of putrid accumulations. **drainboard** *n.* (*N Am.*) a draining board. **draincock** *n.* a tap for emptying a tank or other vessel. **drainer** *n.* 1 a person who or something which drains. 2 a person who constructs drains. 3 a device on which wet things are put to drain. **draining board** *n.* a board beside a sink on which washed-up crockery is put to dry. **drainpipe** *n.* 1 a pipe for draining superfluous or waste water, particularly from a roof or gutter. 2 (*pl.*, *coll.*) trousers with very narrow legs. ~*a.* (of trousers) having very narrow legs. [OE *dreahnian*, cogn. with *drȳge*, DRY]

drake[1] (drāk) *n.* the male of the duck. **drakestone** *n.* a flat stone thrown so as to skim over water in the game of ducks and drakes. [etym. uncertain (cp. G dial. *draak*, OHG *antrahho*, G *Enterich*, dial. *endedrach*, from *Ente, Ende*, duck)]

drake[2] (drāk) *n.* 1 the mayfly. 2 †a dragon. [OE *drāca*, L *draco*, DRAGON]

Dralon® (drā´lon) *n.* an acrylic fibre, or a fabric made from it, usu. used in upholstery.

dram (dram) *n.* 1 a drachm in apothecaries' weight. 2 (*fig.*) a small quantity of spirits, as much as is drunk at once. 3 the chief unit of currency in Armenia. ~*v.i.* (*pres.p.* **dramming**, *past*, *p.p.* **drammed**) to drink drams. ~*v.t.* to ply with stimulants. [DRACHM]

drama (drah´mə) *n.* 1 a play, usually intended for performance by living actors on the stage. 2 an exciting or distressing event. 3 dramatic art, the composition and presentation of plays. 4 dramatic aspect. 5 the dramatic literature or theatrical art of a particular country or period. **drama-doc** *n.* (*sl.*) a drama-documentary. **drama-documentary** *n.* a film, play etc. composed of a mixture of fact and fiction. **dramatic** (drəmat´-), †**dramatical** *a.* 1 of, relating to or of the nature of drama. 2 of or relating to the stage, theatrical. 3 intended or suitable for representation on the stage. 4 striking, catastrophic, impressive. 5 over-emotional, flamboyant, meant for effect. **dramatically** *adv.* **dramatic irony** *n.* tragic irony. **dramatics** *n.pl.* 1 a display of exaggerated behaviour. 2 (*as sing.*) the producing or study of plays. [late L *drāma*, Gr. *drāma -atos* (*draein* to do, to act)]

dramatis personae (dramətis pəsō´nī) *n.pl.* 1 the set of characters in a play. 2 a list of these. [L, characters of the play]

dramatist (dram´ətist) *n.* a writer of plays.

dramatize (dram´ətīz), **dramatise** *v.t.* 1 to set forth in the form of a drama. 2 to describe dramatically. 3 to exaggerate. 4 to convert (a story, novel etc.) into a play. ~*v.i.* (of a novel, story etc.) to be dramatized. **dramatizable** *a.* **dramatization** (-zā´shən) *n.*

dramaturge (dram´ətœj) *n.* a dramatist, a playwright. **dramaturgic** (-tœ´jik), **dramaturgical** *a.* **dramaturgist** *n.* **dramaturgy** *n.* the technique of writing or producing plays. [F, from Gr. *dramatourgos* (*drāma -atos*, DRAMA, *ergein*, to work)]

Drambuie® (dramboo´i, -bū´-) *n.* a liqueur with a Scotch whisky base. [Gael. *dram buidheach*, a satisfying drink]

drank DRINK.

drape (drāp) *v.t.* 1 to cover, clothe or decorate with cloth etc. 2 to adjust or arrange the folds of (a dress, curtains etc.). ~*n.* 1 a hanging which drapes a curtain. 2 the way that a garment hangs. **draper** *n.* a person who sells cloth and other fabrics. **drapery** *n.* (*pl.* **draperies**) 1 the trade of a draper. 2 cloth and other fabrics. 3 something with which an object is draped, hangings, tapestry etc. 4 a curtain. 5 the arrangement of dress in sculpture, painting etc. **draperied** *a.* draped. [F *draper*, from *drap*, cloth]

drastic (dras´tik, drah´-) *a.* acting vigorously; effective, efficacious. **drastically** *adv.* [Gr. *drastikos*, from *drasteos*, to be done (*draein*, to do)]

drat (drat) *int.* (*euphem.*) damn. **dratted** *a.* [said to be a corr. of *god rot*]

draught (drahft), (*N Am.*) **draft** *n.* **1** a current of air. **2** the act of pulling. **3** the load being pulled. **4** the act of dragging with a net. **5** the quantity of fish taken in one sweep of a net. **6** the act of drinking. **7** the quantity of liquor drunk at once. **8** a dose of medicine. **9** the depth to which a ship sinks in water. **10** a draft, a preliminary drawing, design or plan for a work to be executed. **11** the drawing of beer from a cask. **12** (*pl.*) a game played by two persons on a draughtboard with twelve round pieces of different colours on each side. *~v.t.* to draft. **on draught** (of beer) able to be obtained by drawing off from a cask. **to feel the draught** (*coll.*) to be aware of, or affected by, adverse (economic) conditions. **draught beer** *n.* beer drawn from the cask, as distinguished from bottled or canned beer. **draughtboard** *n.* a chequered board on which draughts is played. **draught-engine** *n.* an engine for raising ore, water etc. **draught-hook** *n.* an iron hook on a gun carriage to manoeuvre it. **draught horse** *n.* a horse used for pulling heavy loads. **draught-proof** *a.* proof against draughts. *~v.t.* to make proof against draughts. [ME *drahte*, as if from OE *dragan*, to DRAW (cp. Dut. *dragt*, G *Tracht*)]

draughtsman (drahfts´mən), (*N Am.*) **draftsman** *n.* (*pl.* **draughtsmen,** (*N Am.*) **draftsmen**) **1** a person who draws, designs or plans. **2** a person skilled in drawing. **3** a piece used in the game of draughts. **4** a person who draws up documents. **draughtsmanship** *n.* **draughtswoman** *n.* (*pl.* **draughtswomen**) a woman skilled in drawing.

draughty (drahf´ti), (*N Am.*) **drafty** *a.* (*comp.* **draughtier,** (*N Am.*) **draftier,** *superl.* **draughtiest,** (*N Am.*) **draftiest**) full of draughts or currents of air. **draughtily** *adv.* **draughtiness** *n.*

Dravidian (drəvid´iən) *n.* **1** a member of the people of S India and Sri Lanka speaking Tamil, Telugu, Canarese and Malayalam. **2** any of these languages. *~a.* of or relating to the Dravidians or any of their languages.

draw (draw) *v.t.* (*past* **drew** (droo), *p.p.* **drawn** (drawn)) **1** to draft, to picture, to portray. **2** to drag or pull. **3** to pull after one; to haul. **4** to pull out or up. **5** to extract or remove by pulling. **6** to cause to flow or come forth. **7** to elicit. **8** to induce to do something, esp. to reveal information. **9** in cards, to cause to be played. **10** to take, to receive, to derive. **11** to infer, to deduce. **12** to take in, to inhale. **13** to lengthen, to pull out, to stretch, to protract. **14** to extract. **15** to disembowel. **16** to take (tickets) out of a box or wheel. **17** to unsheathe (a sword). **18** to allure, attract, to cause to follow one. **19** to cause to come out. **20** in hunting, to search for game. **21** to write (a cheque etc.) for payment by (a bank). **22** to drag (an animal such as a badger) from a hole. **23** to compose (a document). **24** to note (a comparison). **25** to make (wire) by pulling a piece of metal through a series of small holes. **26** in golf, to drive to the left (or right if left handed). **27** in bowls, to bowl in a curve. **28** (*Naut.*) to need (a specified depth of water) to float. **29** to pull (curtains) open or shut. **30** to finish (a game) with equal scores. *~v.i.* **1** to practise the art of delineation. **2** to breathe in the smoke from a cigarette. **3** to pull, to haul. **4** (of a chimney, pipe etc.) to allow a free motion, current etc. **5** (of tea) to infuse. **6** to unsheathe a sword or take a pistol from its holster. **7** to draw lots. **8** to make demands (on). **9** to move, to approach. **10** to finish a game with equal scores. **11** to write out a draft for payment. **12** (of a sail) to swell tightly. **13** (*Naut.*) to require a certain depth of water. *~n.* **1** the act or power of drawing. **2** a pull, a strain. **3** an attraction, a lure. **4** the act of drawing lots. **5** a lot or chance drawn. **6** a drawn game or contest. **7** a puff on a cigarette. **8** the act of pulling a gun quickly out of its holster to shoot. **9** (*N Am.*) the part of a drawbridge that can be moved. **quick on the draw** QUICK. **to draw a bead on** BEAD. **to draw a blank** not to succeed in finding what one is looking for. **to draw and quarter** (*Hist.*) to disembowel and dismember after hanging, as a penalty. **to draw back** **1** to move back. **2** to withdraw; to be unwilling to fulfil a promise. **to draw bit** BIT². **to draw breath** **1** to pause, to have a break. **2** to breathe, to live. **to draw bridle** to draw rein. **to draw fire** to attract criticism to oneself, away from someone else. **to draw in** **1** to contract. **2** to entice, to inveigle. **3** (of days) to close in, to shorten. **4** (of a train) to arrive at a station. **to draw in one's horns** HORN. **to draw it mild** (*coll.*) to state, describe or ask moderately, not to exaggerate or be exorbitant. **to draw lots** LOT. **to draw near** to approach. **to draw off** **1** to withdraw, to retire, to retreat. **2** to rack (wine etc.). **to draw on** **1** to lead to as a consequence. **2** to allure, attract, entice. **3** to approach. **4** to put on (clothes or shoes). **to draw one's sword against** to attack. **to draw out** **1** to lengthen; to protract. **2** to set in order for battle. **3** to induce to talk, to elicit. **4** to write out. **5** (of days) to become longer. **6** (of a train) to leave the station. **to draw rein** REIN. **to draw stumps** to stop playing cricket for the day. **to draw the line at** to refuse to go as far as. **to draw the long bow** to tell incredible stories. **to draw the short straw** STRAW. **to draw the shot** in bowls, to bowl closest to the jack. **to draw the teeth of** to render harmless. **to draw up** **1** to compose. **2** to put into proper form. **3** to put (oneself) into a stiff erect attitude. **4** to come to a stop. **to draw up with** to overtake. **drawback** *n.* **1** money paid back, esp. excise or import duty remitted or refunded on goods exported. **2** a deduction, a rebate. **3** a disadvantage; an inconvenience; an obstacle. **drawback lock** *n.* a lock having a spring-bolt that can be drawn back by a knob inside the door. **drawbar** *n.* a bar to connect a locomotive with a tender. **drawbridge** *n.* **1** a bridge that may be raised on hinges at one or both ends to allow ships to pass or to prevent passage across. **2** a game of bridge for two. **drawcord** *n.* a drawstring. **drawdown** *n.* the act of borrowing money. **draw-gate** *n.* the valve or door of a sluice or lock. **draw gear** *n.* a railway-carriage coupling. **drawknife** *n.* (*pl.* **drawknives**) a cutting blade with a handle at each end, for shaving wood. **draw-net** *n.* a net with wide meshes for catching large birds; a seine. **drawplate** *n.* a drilled steel plate through which wire is drawn to reduce and equalize its thickness. **drawshave** *n.* a drawknife. **draw-sheet** *n.* (*Med.*) an extra sheet doubled lengthwise and placed across the bed so that it may be pulled beneath the patient as required. **drawstring** *n.* a cord or thread, threaded through or otherwise attached to fabric, which can be pulled together in the fabric. **draw-well** *n.* a deep well from which water is drawn by means of a rope and bucket. [OE *dragan*, cp. Dut. *dragen*, G *tragen*]

drawee (drawē´) *n.* the person on whom a bill of exchange or order for payment in money is drawn.

drawer¹ (draw) *n.* a sliding boxlike receptacle in a table etc. **top drawer** TOP¹. **drawerful** *n.* (*pl.* **drawerfuls**). **drawers** (drawz) *n.pl.* (*facet.*) an undergarment covering the lower body with holes for the legs.

drawer² (draw´ə) *n.* **1** a person who draws. **2** a person who draws a bill or order for the payment of money. **3** a person who or something which has the quality of attracting. **4** †a barman.

drawing (draw´ing) *n.* **1** the act of drawing. **2** the art of representing objects on a flat surface by means of lines drawn with a pencil, crayon etc. **3** a delineation of this kind. **4** a sketch in black and white, or monochrome. **5** the distribution of prizes in a lottery. **out of drawing** incorrectly drawn. **drawing board** *n.* a large rectangular frame for holding a sheet of paper while drawing. **back to the drawing board** back to start again after an unsuccessful attempt. **drawing-knife** *n.* a blade having a handle at each end, used by coopers etc. **drawing paper** *n.* thick paper for drawing on. **drawing pin** *n.* a flat-headed tack for securing drawing paper to a board etc. **drawing room** *n.* **1** a room for the reception of company. **2** a formal reception by a sovereign or person of high official rank. **3** (*N Am.*) a private compartment in a railway coach. **drawing-room** *a.* suitable for a drawing room.

drawl (drawl) *v.t.* to utter in a slow, lengthened tone. ~*v.i.* to speak with a slow, prolonged utterance. ~*n.* a slow, lengthened manner of speaking. **drawler** *n.* **drawling** *a.* **drawlingly** *adv.* [prob. from DRAW (cp. Dut. *dralen*)]

drawn (drawn) *a.* **1** haggard. **2** (of butter) melted. **3** (of a position in chess) likely to result in a draw. **4** (of a sword) pulled out. **5** (of a fowl) eviscerated. **at daggers drawn** DAGGER[2]. **drawn game** *n.* a game in which neither side can claim any decided advantage. **drawn out** *a.* long-drawn. **drawn work, drawn-thread work** *n.* fancy work in which some of the threads of a fabric are pulled out and some fastened, so as to form a pattern. [p.p. of DRAW]

dray[1] (drā) *n.* **1** a low cart, generally of strong and heavy construction, used by brewers etc. **2** (*Austral.*, *New Zeal.*) a cart with two wheels. **dray horse** *n.* a strong, heavy horse used for pulling a dray. **drayman** *n.* (*pl.* **draymen**) a driver in charge of a dray. [from OE *dragan*, to DRAW (cp. *dræge*, a draw-net)]

dray[2] DREY.

dread (dred) *v.t.* **1** to fear greatly. **2** to anticipate with terror and shrinking. **3** to be apprehensive or anxious about, to doubt. ~*n.* **1** great fear or terror. **2** apprehension of evil. **3** awe, reverence. **4** the person or thing dreaded. ~*a.* **1** exciting great fear or terror, frightful. **2** †awe-inspiring, to be reverenced. **dreaded** *a.* **1** greatly to be feared. **2** (*coll.*) annoying, inconvenient, unwelcome (*the dreaded hiccups*). **dreadful** *a.* **1** inspiring dread; terrible; awe-inspiring. **2** (*coll.*) annoying, disagreeable, troublesome, frightful, horrid. **3** (*coll.*) bad, extreme (*a dreadful mistake*). **penny dreadful** PENNY. **dreadfully** *adv.* **dreadfulness** *n.* **dreadlocks** (dred´loks) *n.pl.* long hair worn in many tight plaits by Rastafarians. **dreadlocked** *a.* **dreadnought** *n.* **1** †a person totally devoid of fear. **2** †a heavy, woollen, felted cloth. **3** †a heavy overcoat made of this material. **4** (*Hist.*) a type of battleship, first built 1905–06, with its main armament composed of big guns. [OE *drǣdan* (in *on-drǣdan*, *of-drǣdan* etc.)]

dream (drēm) *n.* **1** a vision. **2** thoughts and images that pass through the mind of a sleeping person. **3** the state of mind in which these occur. **4** a visionary idea, a fancy, reverie. **5** someone or something beautiful or enticing. **6** the condition of being divorced from reality. ~*v.i.* (*past*, *p.p.* **dreamed, dreamt** (dremt)) **1** to have visions. **2** to think, to imagine as in a dream. **3** to conceive as possible. **4** to waste time in idle thoughts. **5** to indulge in a daydream. ~*v.t.* **1** to see, hear, feel etc. in a dream. **2** to imagine or conceive in a visionary fashion, to picture in hope or imagination. **like a dream** very smoothly; very successfully. **to dream away** to spend (time) idly. **to dream up** (*coll.*) to invent (an idea or excuse). **waking dream** WAKING (under WAKE[1]). **dreamboat** *n.* (*coll.*) **1** a very desirable person, esp. of the opposite sex. **2** a very desirable thing. **dreamer** *n.* **1** a person who dreams. **2** an impractical, unrealistic person. **dreamful** *a.* **dreamingly** *adv.* **dreamland** *n.* the region of fancy or imagination. **dreamless** *a.* **dreamlessly** *adv.* **dreamlike** *a.* **dreamscape** *n.* a dreamlike scene. **dream ticket** *n.* two electoral candidates regarded as the ideal combination. **dreamtime** *n.* the alcheringa. **dream-world** *n.* a world of illusions. **dreamy** *a.* (*comp.* **dreamier**, *superl.* **dreamiest**) **1** habitually daydreaming. **2** visionary. **3** (*poet.*) full of or causing dreams. **4** dreamlike, soft and gentle. **5** (*coll.*) extremely attractive. **dreamily** *adv.* **dreaminess** *n.* [ME *dream*, OE *drēam*, music, joy, mirth, appear to be distinct and to have caused a non-extant *drēam*, vision, to be avoided in favour of *swefn*, to sleep (cp. OS *drōm*, a dream, G *Traum*)]

dreary (driə´ri) *a.* (*comp.* **drearier**, *superl.* **dreariest**) dismal, gloomy; cheerless, tiresome, dull. ~†*n.* dreariness. **drear** (driə) *a.* (*poet.*) dreary. **drearly** *adv.* **drearily** *adv.* **dreariness** *n.* **drearisome** (-səm) *a.* [OE *drēorig*, from *drēor*, gore]

dredge[1] (drej) *n.* **1** an apparatus for dragging under water to bring up objects from the bottom for scientific purposes. **2** a bucket or scoop for scraping mud etc. from the bed of a pond etc. **3** a dragnet for catching oysters. ~*v.t.* **1** to gather or bring up with a dredge. **2** to remove or clear away by means of a dredge. **3** to clean or deepen (a river or harbour) with a dredging-machine. ~*v.i.* to use a dredge. **to dredge up 1** to lift with a dredge. **2** to find (something) previously obscure or well hidden. **dredger**[1], **drudger** *n.* **1** a ship for dredging. **2** a dredging-machine. **3** a person who fishes with a dredge. [Sc. *dreg*, ME *drege*, prob. from OE *dragan*, to DRAW, DRAG]

dredge[2] (drej) *v.t.* **1** to sprinkle (flour etc.). **2** to sprinkle with flour etc. **dredger**[2] *n.* a box with a perforated lid for sprinkling. **dredging-box** *n.* [ME *dragie*, later *dredge*, a comfit, from OF *dragee*, late L and Gr. *tragēmata*, spices, condiments]

dredger[1] DREDGE[1].

dredger[2] DREDGE[2].

dree (drē) *v.t.* (*3rd pers. sing. pres.* **drees**, *pres.p.* **dreeing**, *past, p.p.* **dreed**) (*Sc.*) to suffer, to endure. **to dree one's weird** to abide by one's lot. [A-S *drēogan*, to perform, to endure]

dreg (dreg) *n.* (*usu. pl.*) **1** the sediment or lees of liquor. **2** worthless refuse. **3** the lowest class. **4** the most undesirable part. **not a dreg** not a drop, not the least part (left). **to drain/ drink to the dregs** to enjoy to the full. **dreggy** *a.* (*comp.* **dreggier**, *superl.* **dreggiest**). [cp. Icel. *dregg*, pl. *dreggjar*, Swed. *dragg*]

dreich (drēkh) *a.* (*Sc.*) **1** tedious, wearisome, long. **2** bleak. [DREE]

drench (drench) *v.t.* **1** to wet thoroughly. **2** to soak, to saturate. **3** to cause to swallow (esp. a medicinal draught). ~*n.* **1** a liquid medicine for horses or cattle. **2** a soaking, a flood. **3** †a large draught, a potion. **4** in tanning, a solution for bating etc. **drencher** *n.* [OE *drencan*, causal of *drincan*, to drink]

Dresden china (drez´dən), **Dresden porcelain, Dresden ware** *n.* fine, delicately decorated china made at Meissen, near Dresden, Germany. ~*a.* delicate and pretty.

dress (dres) *v.t.* **1** to clothe, to attire. **2** to adorn, to decorate. **3** (*Naut.*) to decorate with flags etc. **4** to cleanse, trim, brush, comb etc. **5** to curry or rub down. **6** to cleanse and treat (a wound). **7** to prepare for use, to cook. **8** to cover (a salad etc.) with dressing. **9** to make straight. **10** (*Mil.*) to form (ranks) into a straight line. **11** to order, arrange, array. **12** to prune, to cut. **13** to manure. **14** to square and give a smooth surface to (stone etc.). **15** to arrange goods attractively in (a shop window). **16** to smooth and give a nap to (cloth). ~*v.i.* **1** to clothe oneself. **2** to put on evening clothes. **3** to attire oneself elaborately. **4** (*Mil.*) to arrange oneself in proper position in a line. ~*n.* **1** that which is worn as clothes, esp. outer garments. **2** garments, apparel. **3** a lady's gown, a frock. **4** the art of adjusting dress. **5** an external covering, as plumage. **6** external appearance, outward form. **dressed to kill** KILL. **dressed up like a**

dog's dinner DOG. **to dress down 1** (*coll.*) to chastise, to reprimand severely. **2** (*coll.*) to dress casually or informally. **to dress up 1** to clothe elaborately. **2** to invest with a fictitious appearance. **3** to wear fancy dress. **dress circle** *n.* the first tier of seats above the pit in a theatre. **dress coat** *n.* a man's coat with narrow pointed tails, worn as evening dress. **dress-goods** *n.pl.* fabrics for women's and children's outer garments. **dress length** *n.* enough fabric to make a dress. **dressmaker** *n.* a person who makes women's dresses. **dressmaking** *n.* **dress parade** *n.* **1** a formal military parade in full uniform. **2** a fashion show. **dress preserver** *n.* a protector, usu. of waterproof materials, fitted under the armpits of a woman's dress to prevent staining by perspiration. **dress rehearsal** *n.* the final rehearsal of a play etc., with costumes and effects. **dress sense** *n.* a knowledge of style in dress and the ability to pick clothes which suit one. **dress shield** *n.* a dress preserver. **dress shirt** *n.* **1** a man's shirt worn with formal evening dress. **2** (*N Am.*) any long-sleeved shirt. **dress-tie** *n.* a tie for wearing with formal evening dress. **dress uniform** *n.* a full ceremonial military uniform. **dressy** *a.* (*comp.* **dressier**, *superl.* **dressiest**) **1** fond of showy dress. **2** wearing rich or showy dress. **3** showy. **4** stylish, smart. **dressiness** *n.* [OF *dresser*, ult. from L *dīrectus*, DIRECT]

dressage (dres´ahzh) *n.* the training of a horse in deportment, obedience and response to signals given by the rider's body. [F]

dresser[1] (dres´ə) *n.* **1** a kitchen sideboard with a set of shelves for displaying plates etc. **2** (*N Am.*) a chest of drawers. **3** †a bench or table on which meat was prepared or dressed for use. [OF *dresseur*, from *dresser*, as DRESSAGE]

dresser[2] (dres´ə) *n.* **1** a person who dresses another, esp. an actor for the stage. **2** a surgeon's assistant in operations etc. who dresses wounds etc. **3** a person who dresses in a specified manner (*a smart dresser*).

dressing (dres´ing) *n.* **1** the act of dressing. **2** gum, starch etc. used in sizing or stiffening fabrics. **3** sauce, salad dressing. **4** (*N Am.*) stuffing. **5** manure applied to soil. **6** ointment, liniment, a bandage etc. applied to a wound or sore. **7** a thrashing, a scolding. **8** (*pl.*) the mouldings and sculptured decorations on a wall or ceiling. **dressing case** *n.* a small case for toilet requisites. **dressing down** *n.* (*coll.*) a severe telling-off. **dressing gown** *n.* a loose robe worn over nightclothes. **dressing room** *n.* **1** a room next to a bedroom, for dressing in. **2** the room where actors put on costumes and stage make-up. **dressing station** *n.* a military, naval, or air-force first-aid post. **dressing table** *n.* a table fitted with drawers and a mirror, used while dressing, making up etc.

dressy DRESS.

drew DRAW.

drey (drā), **dray** *n.* a squirrel's nest. [etym. unknown]

drib (drib) *n.* a driblet, a petty amount or quantity. **driblet** (-lit) *n.* a small or petty portion or sum. **dribs and drabs** (drabz) *n.pl.* (*coll.*) small numbers at a time (*They arrived in dribs and drabs*). [prob. onomat., or from OE *drepan*, to hit]

dribble (drib´əl) *v.i.* **1** to fall in a quick succession of small drops. **2** to drip, to trickle. **3** to slaver, to drivel. **4** to manoeuvre a football in a forward direction by slight kicks from alternate sides. ~*v.t.* **1** to allow to drip. **2** to give out slowly by drops. **3** to dribble (a football). ~*n.* **1** a trickling stream. **2** saliva dribbling from the mouth. **3** in football, a piece of dribbling. **dribbler** *n.* **dribbly** *a.* (*comp.* **dribblier**, *superl.* **dribbliest**). [freq. of DRIB]

drice (drīs) *n.* frozen carbon dioxide in granular form. [*dry ice*]

drier, dried DRY.

drift (drift) *n.* **1** something which is driven along by a wind or current. **2** a driving. **3** a current, a driving or compelling force. **4** the course of drifting or movement. **5** meaning, aim, tenor (*Do you catch my drift?*). **6** a mass (of snow, leaves, sand etc.) driven together. **7** a loose accumulation of sand and debris deposited over the surface by the action of water or ice. **8** deviation of a ship, aircraft or projectile from a direct course caused by a current or wind. **9** a mass of flowering plants. **10** (*Mining*) a horizontal passage following a lode or vein. **11** a drive of cattle, esp. to a particular place on a given day for determination of ownership etc. **12** a drift-net. **13** (*S Afr.*) a ford. **14** a tool for enlarging or aligning holes. **15** a controlled skid for taking bends at high speed. **16** a gradual change in a supposedly constant piece of equipment. ~*v.i.* **1** to be driven into heaps. **2** to float or be carried along by or as if by a current. **3** to be carried along by circumstances. **4** (*Mining*) to make a drift. ~*v.t.* **1** to drive along or into heaps. **2** (of a current) to carry along. **3** to cover with drifts or driftage. **4** to shape or enlarge (a hole). **driftage** *n.* **1** drifting or drifted substances. **2** the distance to which a ship drifts in bearing up against wind and currents. **drift anchor** *n.* a drag-anchor. **drift-bolt** *n.* a steel rod used to drive out a bolt. **drifter** *n.* **1** a trawler or fishing boat using a drift-net to fish, esp. for enemy mines. **2** a person who wanders aimlessly from place to place. **drift-ice** *n.* floating masses of ice drifting on the sea. **driftless** *a.* without clear meaning or aim. **drift-net** *n.* a large fishing net. **drift-netter** *n.* **drift-netting** *n.* **drift-way** *n.* **1** (*Mining*) a drift. **2** (*dial.*) a common way for driving cattle. **driftwood** *n.* wood carried by water onto the shore. **drifty** *a.* (*comp.* **driftier**, *superl.* **driftier**) forming snowdrifts. [from OE *drīfan*, to DRIVE (cp. Dut., Icel., Swed. *drift*, G *Trift*)]

drill[1] (dril) *n.* **1** a metal tool for boring holes in hard material. **2** constant practice or exercise in any art or business. **3** the act of drilling soldiers or sailors, the series of exercises by which they are rendered efficient. **4** rigorous training or discipline. **5** (*coll.*) correct procedure, the right way to do something. **6** any mollusc, esp. *Urosalpinx cinerea*, which bores into oyster shells. ~*v.t.* **1** to bore or pierce with a pointed tool, to perforate. **2** to make holes in, by this means. **3** to train by repeated exercise. **4** to train to the use of arms, to exercise in military exercises. **5** to shoot (someone). ~*v.i.* **1** to bore holes with a drill. **2** to go through a course of military exercise. **driller**[1] *n.* **drilling-machine** *n.* a machine for drilling holes in metal. **drilling platform** *n.* a platform which is either mobile or attached to the seabed, used as a base for equipment during the drilling of an oil well. **drilling rig** *n.* **1** the machinery needed to drill an oil well. **2** an offshore mobile drilling platform. **drillmaster** *n.* **1** a military drill instructor. **2** a person who instructs in a strict, militaristic manner. **drill press** *n.* an upright drilling-machine. **drill-sergeant** *n.* **1** a non-commissioned officer who drills soldiers or school pupils. **2** a martinet, a narrow-minded devotee of routine. **drill stem** *n.* a rotating rod used in drilling. **drillstock** *n.* a handle or holder for a metal drill. [cp. MDut. *drillen*, to bore, to turn round, to form to arms, to exercise]

drill[2] (dril) *n.* **1** a small trench or furrow, or a ridge with a trench along the top, for seeds or small plants. **2** a row of plants in such a furrow. **3** a machine for sowing grain in rows. ~*v.t.* to sow (seed) or plant in rows. ~*v.i.* to sow or plant in this manner. **drill-barrow** *n.* a manual machine for drilling and sowing. **driller**[2] *n.* **drill-harrow** *n.* a harrow for crushing the earth and removing weeds between the rows of plants. **drill-plough** *n.* a plough for sowing grain in drills. [etym. uncertain; perh. from DRILL[1]]

drill[3] (dril) *n.* a baboon from W Africa, *Mandrillus leucophaeus.* [perh. from local name]

drill[4] (dril) *n.* a heavy cotton twilled cloth used for trousers etc. [earlier *drilling*, corr. of G *Drillich*, corr. of L *trilix trilīcem* (*tri-*, three, *līcium*, a thread)]

driller[1] DRILL[1].

driller[2] DRILL[2].

drily (drī´li), **dryly** *adv.* **1** amusingly and cleverly. **2** in a dry manner.

drink (dringk) *v.t.* (*past* **drank** (drangk), *p.p.* **drunk** (drŭngk)) **1** to swallow (a liquid). **2** to imbibe, absorb, suck in. **3** to swallow up, to empty. **4** to take in by the senses. **5** to pledge, to toast. **6** to cause (oneself) to be in a particular condition by drinking too much alcohol (*He drank himself into oblivion*). **7** to waste (money, wages or property) on indulgence in alcohol. *~v.i.* **1** to swallow a liquid. **2** to drink alcohol habitually, esp. to excess. *~n.* **1** something to be drunk. **2** a draught, a potion. **3** intoxicating liquor. **4** an alcoholic drink. **5** excessive indulgence in intoxicating liquors, intemperance. **in drink** intoxicated. **the drink** (*coll.*) the sea. **to drink deep** to take a long draught. **to drink in** to absorb readily; to receive greedily, as with the senses; to gaze upon, listen to etc. with delight. **to drink like a fish** FISH[1]. **to drink off** to swallow at a single draught. **to drink someone under the table** to drink and remain comparatively sober while one's drinking companion gets completely drunk. **to drink the health of** to wish health to in drinking; to toast. **to drink to** to salute in drinking; to drink the health of. **to drink to the dregs** DREG. **to drink up** to swallow completely. **drinkable** *a.* **1** able to be drunk. **2** fit for drinking. **drinkableness** *n.* **drink-driving** *n.* the act of driving after drinking alcohol. **drink-driver** *n.* **drinker** *n.* **1** a person who drinks. **2** a person who habitually drinks alcohol, esp. to excess. **3** a large, brownish moth, *Euthrix potatoria*, whose caterpillar drinks dew. **drinking** *n.* **drinking-bout** *n.* a session of drinking alcohol; a revel. **drinking fountain** *n.* a device erected in a public place which supplies a jet of drinking water. **drinking-horn** *n.* a drinking vessel made of horn. **drinking song** *n.* a song in praise of drinking parties. **drinking-up time** *n.* the time between the call for last orders and closing time, in which to finish drinks. **drinking water** *n.* water suitable for drinking. **drink-money** *n.* money given to buy liquor; a tip. **drink-offering** *n.* a Jewish offering of wine; a libation. [OE *drincan*, from Gmc. *drenk-* (cp. Dut. *drinken*, G *trinken*)]

Usage note In standard English, the past tense of the verb *drink* is *drank*, not *drunk*.

drip (drip) *v.i.* (*pres.p.* **dripping,** *past, p.p.* **dripped**) **1** to fall in drops. **2** to throw off moisture in drops. *~v.t.* to let fall in drops. *~n.* **1** the act of dripping, a falling in drops. **2** a drop of liquid. **3** a dripping sound. **4** (*coll.*) a stupid or insipid person. **5** drip-feed. **6** (*Archit.*) the projecting edge of a moulding or corona over a door or window. **drip-dry** *a.* (of clothing) made of such a material that, when hung up to drip, it dries quickly without wringing and needs no ironing. *~v.i., v.t.* (*3rd pers. sing. pres.* **drip-dries,** *pres.p.* **drip-drying,** *past, p.p.* **drip-dried**) to dry in this way. **drip-feed** *v.t.* (*past, p.p.* **drip-fed**) to feed nutrients to (a patient) in liquid form, using a drip-feed. *~n.* **1** the apparatus for the intravenous administration of some liquid, drop by drop. **2** the feeding of nutrients to a patient in this way. **3** the nutrients administered in this way. **dripless** *a.* **drip-mat** *n.* a small mat put under a glass to soak up drips. **drip-moulding** *n.* **1** a corona or projecting tablet or moulding over the heads of doorways, windows etc. to throw off rain. **2** a filtering-stone. **dripping** *n.* **1** the fat which falls from roasting meat. **2** (*pl.*) water, grease etc. falling or trickling from anything. **to be dripping with** to have a large number or amount of. **dripping pan** *n.* a pan for catching the fat which drips from roasting meat. **dripping wet** *a.* extremely wet. **drippy** *a.* (*comp.* **drippier,** *superl.* **drippiest**) **1** inclined to drip. **2** insipid, inane. **drippily** *adv.* **drippiness** *n.* **drip stone** *n.* a drip-moulding. [OE *dryppan* (cp. OS *driopan*, G *triefen*)]

drive (drīv) *v.t.* (*pres.p.* **driving,** *past* **drove** (drōv), †**drave** (drāv), *p.p.* **driven** (driv´ən)) **1** to push or urge by force. **2** to guide or direct (a vehicle or horse). **3** to convey in a vehicle. **4** to be licensed to drive. **5** to constrain, to compel. **6** to force into a particular state (*She drives me mad*). **7** to operate (a computer). **8** to prosecute, to carry on. **9** to chase, hunt, esp. to frighten (game) into an enclosure or towards guns. **10** to overwork. **11** to throw, to propel. **12** in golf, to propel (the ball) with the driver. **13** in cricket, to hit (the ball) to or past the bowler with a swift free stroke. **14** to force (a nail etc.) with blows. **15** to propel (machinery etc.). **16** to bore (a tunnel etc.). **17** to press (an argument). **18** †to hold a drift in. *~v.i.* **1** to be urged forward by violence. **2** to dash, to rush violently, to hasten. **3** to drift, to be carried. **4** to travel in a vehicle, esp. under one's own direction or control. **5** to control or direct a vehicle, engine etc. **6** to hold a driving licence. **7** to aim a blow, to strike furiously. **8** to tend, to aim, to intend. **9** in golf, to hit the ball with the driver. *~n.* **1** a ride in a vehicle. **2** a road for driving on, esp. a private carriageway to a house. **3** a forward stroke at cricket etc. **4** a concerted effort made for charity etc. **5** transmission of power to the wheels of a vehicle etc. **6** the position of the steering wheel in a vehicle (*left-hand drive*). **7** a driving of game, cattle, or of an enemy. **8** push, energy. **9** energy, motivation. **10** a disk drive. **11** a series of competitive games of whist, bridge etc. **12** (*Austral., New Zeal.*) a line of trees on a hillside, cut down when one falls on another. **to drive a coach and horses through** (*coll.*) to demolish (an argument or idea) by pointing out the obvious faults. **to drive a hard bargain** to be hard in making a bargain. **to drive at** (*fig.*) to hint at. **to drive home 1** to force (something) completely in. **2** to explain (something) emphatically and make sure it is understood. **to drive out 1** to expel; to oust. **2** to take the place of. **to drive up the wall** (*coll.*) to madden, to annoy greatly. **to let drive** to strike furiously, to aim a blow. **what are you driving at?** what exactly do you mean? **drivable, driveable** *a.* **drive-by** *a.* (of a crime, esp. a shooting) committed from a moving vehicle. **drive-in** *n.* a café, cinema etc. where customers are served or can watch a film without leaving their cars. *~a.* denoting a drive-in café, cinema etc. **drive-on, drive-on/drive-off** *a.* (of a ship) able to be driven onto and off by motor vehicles. **driver** *n.* **1** a person who or something which drives. **2** a person who drives a vehicle or an engine. **3** an electronic device which provides power for output. **4** something which communicates motion to something else, as a wheel. **5** (*Comput.*) a program which controls a device. **6** a wooden-headed golf club used to propel the ball from the tee. **in the driver's seat** in control. **driver ant** *n.* a W African ant of the family Dorylinae. **driverless** *a.* **driver's license** *n.* (*N Am.*) a driving licence. **driver's test** *n.* (*N Am.*) a driving test. **drive-shaft** *n.* a shaft which transmits torque. **drive-through** *a.* **1** (*esp. N Am.*) denoting a restaurant etc. where customers are served at a window without leaving their cars. **2** (*esp. N Am.*) able to be driven through. **drive-time** *a.* of or relating to the times of day when people are driving to or from work. **driveway** *n.* a path large enough for a car, from a road to a house. **driving** *a.* having great force (*driving rain*). **driving-band** *n.* **1** the strap or belt for connecting and communicating motion to parts of machinery. **2** a soft metal band at the end of a projectile which engages with the rifling of the gun and causes the fired shell to rotate. **driving licence** *n.* a permit to drive, granted to a person who has passed a driving test. **driving mirror** *n.* the small mirror inside a car which enables a driver to see what is behind. **driving range** *n.* a place for practising driving golf balls. **driving seat** *n.* **1** the seat for the driver in a vehicle. **2** a position of authority or control. **driving-shaft** *n.* a shaft transmitting motion from the driving wheel. **driving test** *n.* an examination in the driving and handling of a motor vehicle. **driving wheel** *n.* **1** the wheel which communicates motion to other parts of the machinery. **2** a large wheel of a locomotive, a cycle-wheel or motor-wheel to which motive force is applied directly. [OE *drīfan* (cp. Dut. *drijven*, Goth. *dreiban*, G *treiben*)]

drivel (driv´əl) *n.* **1** slaver; spittle flowing from the mouth. **2** silly, nonsensical talk; twaddle. ~*v.i.* (*pres.p.* **drivelling,** (*N Am.*) **driveling,** *past* **drivelled,** (*N Am.*) **driveled**) **1** to slaver, to allow spittle to flow from the mouth, as a child, idiot or dotard. **2** to talk nonsense. **3** to be weak or silly. ~*v.t.* to fritter (away). **driveller,** (*N Am.*) **driveler** *n.* [OE *dreflian*, from same stem as DRAFF]

driven, driver etc. DRIVE.

drizzle (driz´əl) *n.* **1** fine, small rain. **2** in cookery, small, fine drops of a liquid sprinkled over something. ~*v.i.* to rain slightly. ~*v.t.* **1** to shed in small, fine drops. **2** to sprinkle. **drizzly** *a.* (*comp.* **drizzlier,** *superl.* **drizzliest**). [freq. of ME *dresen*, OE *drēosan*, to fall in drops]

Dr Martens® (doktə mah´tinz) *n.pl.* heavy lace-up boots with thick, cushioned soles.

drogue (drōg) *n.* **1** a bag drawn behind a boat to prevent her broaching to. **2** a drag attached to a harpoon line to check the progress of a whale when struck. **3** a windsock. **4** a parachute which reduces the speed of a falling object or landing aircraft. **5** a target for firing practice, pulled along by an aircraft. **6** a cone-shaped device on the end of the refuelling hose of a tanker aircraft into which the probe of the receiving aircraft fits. [prob. var. of DRAG]

droguet (drōgā´) *n.* a ribbed woollen fabric, a kind of rep. [F, DRUGGET]

droit (droit) *n.* **1** a right, a due. **2** a legal right. **droit de seigneur** (drwah də senyœ´) *n.* (*Hist.*) the supposed right of a lord to have sexual intercourse with a vassal's bride on their wedding night. [F, from late L *drictum*, L *dīrēctum*, DIRECT, late L, a right, a law]

droll (drōl) *a.* odd, facetious, ludicrous, comical, laughable. ~†*n.* a facetious person, a jester, a buffoon. **drollery** *n.* (*pl.* **drolleries**) idle sportive jocularity, buffoonery. **drollness** *n.* **drolly** (drōl´li) *adv.* [F *drôle*, etym. uncertain]

drome (drōm) *n.* (*coll.*) an aerodrome.

-drome (drōm) *comb. form* a large area specially prepared for some specific purpose, as *aerodrome*, *hippodrome*.

dromedary (drom´idəri) *n.* (*pl.* **dromedaries**) **1** an Arabian camel. **2** a swift variety of the species, used for riding on. [OF *dromedaire*, late L *dromedārius*, L *dromas -adem*, Gr. *dromas -ada*, running, runner, from *dramein*, to run]

dromond (drom´ənd) *n.* a large medieval ship. [A-F *dromund*, OF *dromon*, late L *dromō -ōnem*, Gr. *dromōn*, from *dromos*, racing, a course]

-dromous (drəməs) *comb.form* running, as *anadromous*. [Gr. *dromos*, race, racecourse]

drone (drōn) *n.* **1** the male of the bee, larger than the worker, which makes the honey. **2** an idler, a lazy person who lives on the industry of others. **3** a deep, humming sound. **4** the unchanging bass produced from the three lower pipes of a set of bagpipes. **5** any of these lower pipes. **6** a string which produces a droning sound on a stringed instrument. **7** a person with a low, monotonous speaking voice. **8** a monotonous speech. **9** a radio-controlled aircraft. ~*v.i.* **1** to make a monotonous, humming noise. **2** to talk in a monotonous tone. **3** to live in idleness. ~*v.t.* **1** to read or say in a monotonous tone. **2** to spend (time) idly. **drone-pipe** *n.* the drone of a set of bagpipes. **droning** *a.* **droningly** *adv.* [OE *drān*, *dræn*, a bee, cogn. with ME *drounen*, Sansk. *dhran*, to sound]

drongo (drong´gō) *n.* (*pl.* **drongos**) **1** any glossy, black, insect-eating bird of the family Dicruridae. **2** (*Austral.*, *New Zeal.*, *sl.*) a slow-witted person. [Malagasy]

droob (droob) *n.* (*Austral.*, *sl.*) an ineffectual person. [perh. from DROOP]

drool (drool) *v.i.* **1** to drivel, to slaver. **2** to show excessive or lascivious pleasure in something. ~*n.* saliva trickling from the mouth. [contr. of DRIVEL]

droop (droop) *v.i.* **1** to hang, lean or bend down. **2** (of the eyes) to look downwards. **3** to sink. **4** to fail, to flag, to languish, to decline; to be dejected, to despond, to lose heart. ~*v.t.* to let fall or hang down. ~*n.* **1** the act of drooping. **2** a drooping attitude. **3** loss of heart. **droopingly** *adv.* **droop snoot** *n.* (*coll.*) an adjustable nose (of an aircraft). **droopy** *a.* (*comp.* **droopier,** *superl.* **droopiest**). **droopily** *adv.* **droopiness** *n.* [cp. Icel. *drūpa*, see DROP]

drop (drop) *n.* **1** a globule or small portion of liquid in a spherical form, which is falling, hanging or adhering to a surface. **2** a very small quantity of a fluid. **3** (*Med.*) the smallest separable quantity of a liquid. **4** (*pl.*) liquid medicine applied in such units with a dropper. **5** a minute quantity, an infinitesimal particle. **6** (*coll.*) a delivery. **7** (*sl.*) a cache, a hiding place. **8** (*sl.*) a bribe. **9** (*coll.*) a glass or drink of alcohol. **10** anything resembling a drop, or hanging as a drop, such as an earring, or other pendent ornament. **11** any of various sweetmeats (*chocolate drops*). **12** the act of dropping, a fall, a descent, a collapse. **13** a reduction, a lowering. **14** a thing that drops or is dropped. **15** the unloading of troops from an aircraft by parachute. **16** a painted curtain suspended on pulleys which is let down to conceal the stage in a theatre. **17** a falling trapdoor. **18** the part of a gallows contrived so as to fall from under the feet of persons to be hanged. **19** an abrupt fall in a surface. **20** the amount of this. **21** (*N Am.*) a slot in a receptacle through which things can be dropped. ~*a.* lowered (*a drop waist*). ~*v.t.* (*pres.p.* **dropping,** *past*, *p.p.* **dropped**) **1** to allow or cause to fall in drops, as a liquid. **2** to cause to fall, to fell. **3** to take off (one's trousers or underpants). **4** to lower, to let down. **5** to dismiss, to give up. **6** to set down (a passenger) from a vehicle. **7** to let fall, to utter casually, to mention casually. **8** to write to in an informal manner. **9** to bear (a foal, calf etc.). **10** to omit. **11** to stop (doing something), to have done with. **12** to let go. **13** to sprinkle with drops. **14** (*coll.*) to bring down, to kill. **15** (*coll.*) to lose. **16** to unload from an aircraft by parachute. **17 a** in rugby, to hit (a ball) by a drop kick. **b** to score (a goal) with a drop kick. **18** to stop seeing or associating with (someone). ~*v.i.* **1** to fall in drops; to drip, to discharge itself in drops. **2** to fall. **3** to collapse suddenly, to sink as if exhausted, to faint. **4** to die. **5** to be uttered. **6** to cease, to lapse, to come to an end. **7** to fall (behind). **8** to jump down. **9** (of a card) to be played along with a card of a higher value. **at the drop of a hat** immediately. **drop dead!** (*sl.*) used to express contempt or dismissal. **drop it!** (*sl.*) stop doing, or talking about, that! **fit to drop** completely exhausted. **ready to drop** completely exhausted. **to drop a brick** BRICK. **to drop a curtsy** to curtsy. **to drop anchor** to let down the anchor. **to drop asleep** to fall asleep. **to drop astern 1** to move or pass towards the stern. **2** to reduce speed so as to allow another to pass ahead. **to drop a stitch** in knitting, to let a stitch fall off the end of the needle. **to drop away** to depart. **to drop back** to fall behind, to be overtaken. **to drop back into** to revert to (a former habit). **to drop behind** to drop back. **to drop by** to drop in. **to drop down 1** to descend a hill. **2** to sail down a river towards the sea. **to drop in 1** to make an informal visit. **2** to call unexpectedly. **to drop into 1** (*coll.*) to make an informal visit to (a place). **2** (*coll.*) to develop (a habit). **to drop off 1** to decrease, to become less. **2** (*coll.*) to fall gently asleep. **3** to set down (a passenger) from a vehicle. **to drop on** to scold, to punish. **to drop one's aitches/ hs** not to pronounce the *h*'s at the beginnings of words. **to drop out** (*coll.*) to refuse to follow a conventional lifestyle, esp. to leave school or college early. **to drop to** (*sl.*) to become aware of. **to drop to the rear** to drop back. **to have had a drop too much** (*coll.*) to have had slightly too much to drink. **to have the drop on** (*coll.*) to have an advantage over. **to let drop** to disclose, seemingly without any intention of so doing. **drop curtain** *n.* a drop scene. **drop-dead gorgeous** *a.* (*sl.*) stunningly attractive. **drop-drill** *n.* a contrivance for simultaneously manuring and sowing in drills. **drop forge** *n.* a forge for metal with two dies, one of them fixed, the other acting by force or gravity. **drop-forge** *v.t.* **drop-forging** *n.* **drop goal** *n.* a goal scored in rugby with a dropkick. **drop hammer** *n.* a drop forge. **drop-handlebars** *n.pl.* curving, lowered handlebars on a bicycle. **drophead** *n.* the folding roof of a convertible car. **drop-in centre** *n.* a day centre, usu. run by the social services, where clients may call informally for advice etc. **drop in the ocean, drop in a bucket** *n.* a proportionately tiny amount. **drop kick** *n.* in rugby, a kick made by letting the ball drop and kicking it on the rise. **drop-leaf** *a.* (of a table) having a hinged flap which can be lowered or raised. **droplet** (-lit) *n.* a tiny drop. **drop-off** *n.* **1** the act of dropping someone or something off. **2** a decrease. **3** (*N Am.*) a sheer cliff or slope. **drop-out** *n.* (*coll.*) a person who rejects conventional society. **dropper** *n.* **1** a person who or something which drops. **2** a small glass tube with a rubber bulb at one end, for administering medicinal drops. **3** in angling, an artificial fly set at some distance from the end of a cast. **4** (*Austral., New Zeal., S Afr.*) a vertical stave in a fence. **dropping** *n.* **droppings** *n.pl.* **1** something which falls or has fallen in drops. **2** the dung of animals or birds. **drop scene** *n.* a painted curtain suspended on pulleys which is let down to conceal the stage in a theatre. **drop scone** *n.* a small, thick pancake cooked on a hot griddle. **drop shot** *n.* a shot in tennis, squash or badminton which falls to the ground immediately after crossing the net or hitting the wall. **drop test** *n.* in engineering, a test carried out by dropping under typical conditions. **drop-test** *v.t.* to carry out a drop test on. **dropwort** *n.* **1** a plant with tuberous root fibres, *Spiraea filipendula*. **2** any of various other species of spiraea. **3** any of various species of *Oenanthe*, esp. *O. fistulosa*. **drop zone** *n.* an area set aside for parachutists to land in. [OE *dropa*, whence *dropian*, to drop (cogn. with DRIP, DROOP)]

dropsy (drop´si) *n.* (*pl.* **dropsies**) **1** oedema. **2** (*sl.*) a tip, a bribe. **dropsical** *a.* **dropsically** *adv.* **dropsied** *a.* suffering from dropsy. [ME *dropesie, ydropesie*, MF *hydropisie*, L *hydrōpisis*, Gr. *hudrōps -ōpos* (*hudōr*, water)]

droshky (drosh´ki), **drosky** (dros´-) *n.* (*pl.* **droshkies, droskies**) **1** a Russian open four-wheeled vehicle in which the passengers ride astride a bench, their feet resting on bars near the ground. **2** a public cab in Germany. [Rus. *drozhki*, dim. of *drozi*, a wagon]

drosometer (drosom´itə) *n.* an instrument for measuring the quantity of dew collected on a surface during the night. [Gr. *drosos*, dew]

drosophila (drosof´ilə) *n.* (*pl.* **drosophilas**) any of the small fruit flies of the genus *Drosophilia*, used in laboratory genetic experiments. [Gr. *drosos*, dew, *-phila*, -PHILE]

dross (dros) *n.* **1** the scum or useless matter left from the melting of metals. **2** anything utterly useless, refuse, rubbish. **3** anything impure. **drossy** *a.* (*comp.* **drossier,** *superl.* **drossiest**). **drossiness** *n.* [OE *drōs* (cp. MDut. *droes*, G *Drusen*, lees, dregs)]

drought (drowt), (*Sc., Ir., N Am., poet.*) †**drouth** (drooth, drowth) *n.* **1** dryness, dry weather; long-continued rainless weather. **2** an absence of rain or moisture. **3** a protracted lack of something. **4** thirst. **droughty** *a.* (*comp.* **droughtier,** *superl.* **droughtiest**). †**drouthy** *a.* (*comp.* **drouthier,** *superl.* **drouthiest**).

drouk (drook) *v.t.* (*Sc., North.*) to drench; to duck. **droukit** (-it) *a.* [etym. uncertain (cp. Icel. *drukna*, to be drowned, DRUNK)]

drouth DROUGHT.

drove[1] DRIVE.

drove[2] (drōv) *n.* **1** a collection of animals driven in a body. **2** a road for driving cattle on. **3** a shoal, a crowd, a mass of people, esp. when moving together. **4** a narrow channel for draining or irrigation. **5** a stonemason's broad chisel. ~*v.t.* to dress (stone) with a drove. ~*v.i.* to drive cattle in droves. **drover** *n.* a person who drives cattle or sheep to market; a cattle-dealer. **drove road** *n.* (*esp. Sc.*) an old grassy track used by droves of cattle. **droving** *n.* [OE *drāf*, from *drīfan*, to DRIVE]

drown (drown) *v.i.* **1** to be suffocated in water or other liquid. **2** to perish in this manner. ~*v.t.* **1** to suffocate by submersion in water or other liquid. **2** to submerge, to drench, to overwhelm with water, to overflow, to deluge. **3** to overpower (by a volume of sound). **4** to overwhelm, to quench, to put an end to. **like a drowned rat** soaked to the skin. **to drown one's sorrows** to drink alcohol in order to forget one's problems and sorrows. **to drown out** to drive out by a flood. **drowned valley** *n.* a valley which has been submerged by a rise of sea level or a depression of the land. **drowner** *n.* a person who is drowning. [OE *druncnian*, to become intoxicated, to drown, from *druncen*, p.p. of *drincan*, to DRINK]

drowse (drowz) *v.i.* **1** to be sleepy or half asleep. **2** to doze. **3** to be heavy and dull. ~*v.t.* **1** to make drowsy. **2** to spend (time) in an idle or sluggish way. ~*n.* **1** the state of being half asleep. **2** drowsiness, heaviness. **drowsy** *a.* (*comp.* **drowsier,** *superl.* **drowsiest**) **1** inclined to sleep, sleepy. **2** disposing to sleep. **3** sluggish, stupid. **drowsiness** *n.* [OE *drūsian*, to become languid]

drub (drŭb) *v.t.* (*pres.p.* **drubbing,** *past, p.p.* **drubbed**) **1** to beat with a stick; to cudgel. **2** to beat thoroughly in a fight or contest. **to drub into** to instil into. **drubber** *n.* **drubbing** *n.* [prob. from Arab. *darb*, a beating]

drudge (drŭj) *n.* **1** a person employed in menial work. **2** a person who toils at uncongenial work and is ill-paid; a slave; a hack. ~*v.i.* to perform menial work; to work hard with little reward; to slave. **drudger** *n.* a drudge. **drudgery** *n.* hard, menial or tedious work. **drudgingly** *adv.* [prob. cogn. with OE *drēogan*, to DREE]

drudger DREDGER.

drug (drŭg) *n.* **1** any substance, mineral, vegetable or animal, used as the basis or as an ingredient in medical preparations. **2** a narcotic causing addiction. ~*v.t.* (*pres.p.* **drugging,** *past, p.p.* **drugged**) **1** to mix drugs with, esp. to make narcotic. **2** to administer drugs, esp. narcotics, to. **3** to render insensible with drugs. **4** (*fig.*) to deaden. ~*v.i.* to take drugs, esp. narcotics. **drug addict, drug fiend** *n.* a person who is addicted to the use of narcotics. **druggist** *n.* **1** (*N Am.*) a pharmaceutical chemist. **2** a person who deals in drugs. **druggy, druggie** *n.* (*pl.* **druggies**) (*coll.*) a drug addict. ~*a.* of or relating to drugs, esp. narcotics. **drug on the market** *n.*

a commodity which is so common as to be unsaleable. **drug pusher** *n.* a person who sells narcotic drugs illegally. **drug squad** *n.* a division of a police force which investigates drug-related crime. **drugstore** *n.* (*N Am.*) a chemist's shop where pharmaceuticals and other small articles are sold, often including refreshments. [F *drogue*, etym. uncertain]

drugget (drŭg´it) *n.* **1** a coarse woollen fabric, felted or woven, used as a covering or as a substitute for carpet. **2** a covering or carpet made of drugget. [F *droguet*, etym. uncertain]

druggist, druggy DRUG.

Druid (droo´id) *n.* **1** one of the priests or teachers of the early Gauls and Britons or perh. of pre-Celtic peoples, who taught the transmigrating of souls, frequently celebrated their rites in oak groves, and are alleged to have offered human sacrifices. **2** a member of the Ancient Order of Druids, a benefit society, established in 1781. **3** an officer of the Welsh Gorsedd. **4** a member of any of several movements trying to revive Druidic practices. **Druidess** (-dis) *n.* a female Druid. **Druidic** (-id´-), **Druidical** *a.* **Druidism** *n.* [F *druide*, L *druidae*, *-des*, pl., from OCelt. (cp. OIr. *druid-*, Gael *draoi*, *draoidh*, *druidh*, a magician, a sorcerer)]

drum[1] (drŭm) *n.* **1** a musical instrument made by stretching parchment over the head of a hollow cylinder or hemisphere. **2** (*often pl.*) a drummer or the percussion section of an orchestra. **3** the sound of a drum beating, or a sound resembling this. **4** the tympanum or hollow part of the middle ear. **5** the membrane across this. **6** anything drum-shaped, esp. a small cylindrical box for holding fruit, fish etc. **7** the quantity contained in such a box. **8** (*Austral.*, *New Zeal.*, *coll.*) a swag, a bundle, a tramp's roll, a bluey. **9** (*Archit.*) **a** the solid part of the Corinthian and the composite capitals. **b** the upright part of a cupola, either above or below the dome. **c** the cylindrical block forming part of a column. **10** in machinery, a revolving cylinder over which a belt or band passes. **11** any sea fish of the family Sciaenidae, which emits a drumming or grunting noise. **12** (*Hist.*) †an evening or afternoon party at which card-playing was carried on. **13** a cylindrical instrument on which computer data can be stored. **14** (*Austral.*, *sl.*) sound information. **15** (*sl.*) **a** a house. **b** a night club. **c** a brothel. ~*v.i.* (*pres.p.* **drumming,** *past, p.p.* **drummed**) **1** to beat or play a tune on a drum. **2** to beat rapidly or thump, on a table, the floor, a piano etc. **3** (of certain insects, birds etc.) to make a sound like the beating of a drum. **4** (*N Am.*) to tout for customers. ~*v.t.* **1** to perform on a drum. **2** to beat rapidly or thump one's fingers etc. on a table, the floor, a piano etc. **3** (*Austral.*, *sl.*) to give sound information. **4** to summon. **to beat the drum for** (*coll.*) to try to raise interest in. **to drum into** to instil into. **to drum out** to expel from a regiment with disgrace; to cashier. **to drum up** to canvass (aid or support). **drumbeat** *n.* the sound made by a beating drum. **drum brake** *n.* a type of brake with shoes which rub against a brake drum. **drumfire** *n.* **1** (*Mil.*) rapid, continuous gunfire. **2** a hail of criticism or complaints. **drumfish** *n.* any sea fish of the family Sciaenidae, which emits a drumming or grunting noise. **drumhead** *n.* **1** the membrane stretched at the top of a drum. **2** the membrane across the drum of the ear. **3** the top of the capstan. **drumhead court martial** *n.* a court martial held in the field (orig. round the drumhead in wartime). **drum kit** *n.* a set of drums and cymbals. **drum machine** *n.* an electronic device programmed to reproduce the sound of drums and other percussion instruments. **drum major** *n.* a non-commissioned officer in charge of the drums of a regiment, or who leads the band on the march. **drum majorette** *n.* (*esp. N Am.*) a girl or young woman who marches in a procession dressed in a uniform and twirling a baton. **drummer** *n.* **1** a person who performs on a drum or a drum kit. **2** (*esp. N Am.*, *coll.*) a commercial traveller. **3** (*sl.*) a thief. **4** the member of an orchestra in charge of the percussion instruments. **drumstick** *n.* **1** the stick with which a drum is beaten. **2** anything resembling such a stick, esp. the leg of a cooked fowl. [cp. MDut. *tromme* and Dut. *trom*, MHG *trumme*, orig. a trumpet]

drum[2] (drŭm), **drumlin** (-lin) *n.* (*Geol.*) a long, narrow ridge of drift or alluvial formation. **drumlinoid** *n.* [Gael. and Ir. *druim*]

drummer DRUM[1].

Drummond light (drŭm´ənd) *n.* limelight or oxy-hydrogen light. [Capt. T. *Drummond*, 1797–1840, inventor]

drunk (drŭngk) *a.* **1** intoxicated, stupefied or overcome with alcoholic liquors. **2** inebriated, highly excited (with joy etc.). ~*n.* (*sl.*) **1** a habitually drunken person. **2** a period of drunkenness. **drunk as a lord** very drunk. **drunkard** (-kəd) *n.* a person who is habitually or frequently drunk. **drunken** *a.* **1** habitually intoxicated; given to drunkenness. **2** caused by drunkenness. **3** characterized by intoxication. **drunken driving** *n.* drink-driving. **drunkenly** *adv.* **drunkenness** *n.* [p.p. of DRINK]

drupe (droop) *n.* a fleshy fruit containing a stone with a kernel, such as the peach or plum. **drupaceous** (droopā´shəs) *a.* **1** bearing drupes. **2** of or related to drupes. **3** resembling a drupe. **drupel** (droo´pəl), **drupelet** (droop´lit) *n.* a succulent fruit formed by an aggregation of small drupes, for example the raspberry. [L *drūpa*, Gr. *druppa*, an overripe olive]

Druse (drooz), **Druze, Druz** *n.* a member of a politico-religious sect of Islamic origin, inhabiting the region of Mt Lebanon in Syria. [Arab. *Durūz*, said to be from Ismail al-*Darazi*, or the Tailor, founder of the sect in 1040]

druse (drooz) *n.* **1** a cavity in a rock lined or studded with crystals. **2** the crystalline lining of this. **drusy** *a.* (*comp.* **drusier,** *superl.* **drusiest**). [G, from Czech *druza*]

Druz, Druze DRUSE.

dry (drī) *a.* (*comp.* **drier,** *superl.* **driest**) **1** devoid of moisture. **2** arid. **3** without sap or juice, not succulent. **4** lacking rain, having an insufficient rainfall. **5** thirsty. **6** dried up, removed by evaporation, draining or wiping. **7** not giving milk. **8** not yielding juice. **9** (of land, a shore etc.) not under water. **10** (of wine etc.) not sweet. **11** (of bread) without butter. **12** (of groceries etc.) not liquid. **13** prohibiting by law the sale of alcoholic liquors. **14** (esp. of an addict) not drinking alcohol or taking drugs. **15** (*fig.*) lifeless, insipid, lacking interest, dull. **16** meagre, bare, plain. **17** sarcastic, cynical, ironical, sly. **18** without sympathy or cordiality, cold, discouraging, harsh. **19** holding dry political views. **20** exhibiting a sharp, frigid preciseness in execution or the want of a delicate contour in form. ~*n.* (*pl.* **dries**) **1** the act of drying. **2** a dry place (*the dry*). **3** (*coll.*) a Conservative politician who holds very strong right-wing views. **4** a dry ginger ale, wine, sherry etc. ~*v.t.* (*3rd pers. sing. pres.* **dries,** *pres.p.* **drying,** *past, p.p.* **dried**) **1** to free from or deprive of water or moisture. **2** to deprive of juice, sap or succulence. **3** to drain, to wipe. **4** to cause to cease yielding milk. ~*v.i.* **1** to lose or be deprived of moisture. **2** to grow dry. **3** to cease yielding milk. **4** (of an actor) to forget one's lines. **the Dry 1** (*Austral.*) the dry season. **2** (*Austral.*) the inland desert. **to dry out 1** to become dry. **2** to undergo treatment for alcohol or drug abuse. **to dry up 1** to deprive totally of moisture. **2** to dry dishes after they have been washed. **3** (of moisture) to disappear. **4** to cease to flow, to cease to yield water. **5** (of an actor) to forget one's lines. **6** (*sl.*) to stop talking or doing something. **to go**

dry to prohibit the sale of alcoholic liquors. **to run dry** RUN. **dry battery** *n.* a battery made up of dry cells. **dry-bulb thermometer** *n.* one of a pair of thermometers the other of which is always kept moist, the two together indicating the degree of humidity of the air. **dry cell** *n.* a battery cell in which the electrolyte is a paste and not a fluid. **dry-clean** *v.t.* to clean with a petrol-based solvent or other detergent. *~v.i.* to be suitable for cleaning with a petrol-based solvent or other detergent. **dry-cleaner** *n.* **dry cough** *n.* a cough which does not produce phlegm. **dry cure** *v.t.* to cure by drying and salting, as distinguished from pickling. **dry dock** *n.* a dock which can be emptied of water for ship repairs. **dry-dock** *v.t.* to put in dry dock. **dryer, drier** *n.* **1** an apparatus for drying the hair, hands, clothes etc. after washing. **2** a clothes horse. **3** a material added to oil paints and printers' ink to make them dry. **dry-eyed** *a.* not shedding tears. **dry farming** *n.* a method of growing crops in semi-arid regions by reducing the moisture lost through evaporation. **dry fly** *n.* an angler's fly which floats on the surface, as distinguished from one that is allowed to sink. **dry-fly** *a.* of or relating to fishing with a dry fly. *~v.i.* (*3rd pers. sing. pres.* **dry-flies,** *pres.p.* **dry-flying,** *past, p.p.* **dry-flied**) to fish with a dry fly. **dry-goods** *n.pl.* **1** any non-liquid goods. **2** (*N Am.*) cloths, silks, drapery, haberdashery etc., as distinguished from groceries. **dry hole** *n.* an oil well which does not produce a viable amount of oil. **dry ice** *n.* solid carbon dioxide used in refrigeration. **dryish** *a.* **dry land** *n.* land, as distinguished from the sea. **dryland** *n.* (*usu. pl., esp. N Am.*) an area with low rainfall. *~a.* of or relating to drylands. **dryly** DRILY. **dry measure** *n.* a measure for dry goods, for example a bushel. **dry milk** *n.* (*N Am.*) dried milk. **dry monsoon** *n.* the monsoon that blows from the north-east in winter. **dryness** *n.* **dry-nurse** *n.* a nurse who rears a child without breastfeeding. *~v.t.* to rear without breastfeeding. **dry plate** *n.* a photographic plate with a hard, dry, sensitized film, adapted for storing and carrying about. **dry-point** *n.* **1** a needle for engraving on a copper plate without acid. **2** an engraving so produced. **dry riser** *n.* a vertical, empty pipe with connections on every floor of a building, to which a fireman's hose can be attached. **dry rot** *n.* **1** decay in timber caused by fungi which reduce it to a dry brittle mass. **2** the fungi which cause dry rot. **dry run** *n.* **1** shooting practice without live ammunition. **2** (*coll.*) a practice run, a rehearsal. **dry-salt** *v.t.* to dry cure. **dry-salter** *n.* (*Hist.*) **1** a dealer in dried and salted meat, pickles etc. **2** a dealer in dyestuffs, chemical products etc. **dry-saltery** *n.* **dry-shod** *a., adv.* without wetting the feet. **dry ski** *n.* a specially adapted ski for use on a dry surface. **dry skiing** *n.* **dry slope** *n.* an artificial ski slope used for practising. **drystone** *a.* (of a wall) built without mortar. **drywall** *n.* (*esp. N Am.*) a plasterboard. [OE *drȳge* (cp. Dut. *droog*, G *trocken*)]

dryad (drīʹəd) *n.* (*pl.* **dryads**) in mythology, a nymph of the woods. [L *dryas*, pl. *-ades*, Gr. *druas -ades* (*drūs*, a tree)]

dryer, dryish etc. DRY.

dryopithecine (drīōpithʹəsēn) *n.* any member of the genus *Dryopithecus* of extinct apes, thought to be the ancestors of modern apes. [Gr. *drūs*, tree, *pithēkos*, ape]

DS *abbr.* **1** dal segno. **2** disseminated sclerosis.

DSC *abbr.* Distinguished Service Cross.

D.Sc. *abbr.* Doctor of Science.

DSM *abbr.* Distinguished Service Medal.

DSO *abbr.* Distinguished Service Order.

DSS *abbr.* Department of Social Security.

DST *abbr.* **1** daylight saving time. **2** double summer time.

DT *abbr.* delirium tremens.

D.T. *abbr.* Department of Transport.

DTI *abbr.* Department of Trade and Industry.

DTP *abbr.* desktop publishing.

DT's, DTs *abbr.* delirium tremens.

duad DYAD.

dual (dūʹəl) *a.* **1** consisting of two. **2** twofold, binary, double. **3** (*Gram.*) expressing two (applied to an inflection of a verb, adjective, pronoun or noun, which, in certain languages, expresses two persons or things, as distinct from the plural which expresses more than two). *~n.* (*Gram.*) a dual form. *~v.t.* (*pres.p.* **dualling,** *past, p.p.* **dualled**) to convert into a dual carriageway. **dual carriageway** *n.* a road which has at least two lanes in each direction, with traffic travelling in opposite directions separated by a central reservation. **dual control** *a.* able to be operated by either of two people. **dual in-line package** *n.* DIP. **dualism** *n.* **1** duality, the state of being twofold. **2** a system or theory based on a radical duality of nature or animating principle, for example mind and matter, good and evil in the universe, divine and human personalities in Christ, independence of the cerebral hemispheres. **dualist** *n.* **dualistic** (-lisʹ-) *a.* **dualistically** *adv.* **duality** (-alʹ-) *n.* (*pl.* **dualities**). **dualize, dualise** *v.t.* **dually** *adv.* **Dual Monarchy** *n.* the former union of Austria-Hungary. **dual number** *n.* (*Gram.*) a dual form. **dual personality** *n.* a psychological condition in which a single person has two distinct characters. **dual-purpose** *a.* having, or intended for, two separate purposes. [L *duālis*, from *duo*, two]

duan (dooʹahn) *n.* a canto. [Gael.]

dub[1] (dŭb) *v.t.* (*pres.p.* **dubbing,** *past, p.p.* **dubbed**) **1** to confer knighthood upon by a tap with a sword on the shoulder. **2** to confer any dignity, rank, character or nickname upon. **3** to dress or trim. **4** to smear (leather) with grease so as to soften. **to dub a cock** to trim the hackles and cut off the comb and gills of a cock for cockfighting. **to dub a fly** to dress an artificial fly for fishing. [late OE *dubbian*, perh. from OF (cp. *adober, adouber*, It. *addobare*), etym. unknown]

dub[2] (dŭb) *v.t.* (*pres.p.* **dubbing,** *past, p.p.* **dubbed**) **1** to give a new soundtrack, esp. in a different language, to (a film). **2** to add (music etc.) to a film. **3** to combine (soundtracks). **4** to make a copy of (a recording). **dubbing**[1] *n.* [abbr. of DOUBLE[1]]

dub[3] (dŭb) *n.* (*N Am., sl.*) a clumsy or unskilful person. *~v.t.* (*pres.p.* **dubbing,** *past, p.p.* **dubbed**) in golf, to bungle (a shot). [perh. from DUB[1]]

dub[4] (dŭb) *v.i.* (*pres.p.* **dubbing,** *past, p.p.* **dubbed**) (*sl.*) to pay (up). [etym. uncertain]

dub[5] (dŭb) *n.* (*Sc., North.*) a deep pool in a stream; a puddle. [etym. uncertain]

dubbin (dŭbʹin) *n.* a preparation of grease for preserving and softening leather. *~v.t.* to put dubbin on (boots and shoes). **dubbing**[2] *n.* dubbin.

dubbing[1] DUB[2].

dubbing[2] DUBBIN.

dubious (dūʹbiəs) *a.* **1** undetermined; doubtful; wavering in mind. **2** of uncertain result or issue. **3** questionable. **4** open to suspicion. **dubiety** (-bīʹə-) *n.* (*pl.* **dubieties**). **dubiously** *adv.* **dubiousness** *n.* [L *dubiōsus*, from *dubius*, doubtful (*duo*, two)]

dubitation (dūbitāʹshən) *n.* doubt, hesitation, uncertainty. **dubitative** (duʹbitətiv) *a.* **1** tending to doubt. **2** expressing doubt. **dubitatively** *adv.* [F, from L *dubitātio -ōnem*, from *dubitāre*, to DOUBT]

Dublin Bay prawn (dŭbʹlin) *n.* **1** a Norway lobster. **2** a large prawn, usu. cooked as scampi.

Dubonnet® (doobonʹā) *n.* **1** a sweet, red, French aperitif. **2** a glass of Dubonnet.

ducal (dūʹkəl) *a.* of or relating to a duke or duchy. **ducally** *adv.* [F, from late L *ducalis*, from *dux ducis*, DUKE]

ducat (dŭkʹət) *n.* **1** (*Hist.*) a coin, of gold or silver, formerly current in several European countries. **2** any coin. **3** (*pl., sl.*) money, cash. **ducatoon** (-toon´) *n.* an old silver coin, originally Venetian, formerly circulating in the Netherlands. [F, from It. *ducato*, late L *ducātus*, a DUCHY (under DUCHESS)]

Duce (doo´chi) *n.* the official title of Benito Mussolini, 1883–1945 when head of the Fascist state in Italy. [It., leader]

Duchenne muscular dystrophy (dooshen´) *n.* a severe form of muscular dystrophy, which affects mainly boys. [Guillaume *Duchenne*, 1806–75, French neurologist]

duchess (dŭch´is) *n.* **1** the wife or widow of a duke. **2** a woman who holds a duchy in her own right. **3** (*coll.*) a woman of imposing appearance. **4** a size of roofing slate. **duchesse** (dooshes´, dŭch´is) *n.* **1** a heavy satin. **2** a dressing table with a tilting mirror. **3** a table cover or centrepiece. **duchesse lace** *n.* Flemish lace with designs in cord outline. **duchesse potatoes** *n.pl.* mashed potatoes mixed with butter, milk and egg yolk, piped onto a dish and baked. **duchesse set** *n.* a set of covers for a dressing table. **duchy** *n.* (*pl.* **duchies**) **1** the territory, jurisdiction or dominions of a duke. **2** the royal dukedom of Cornwall or Lancaster. **duchy court** *n.* the court of a duchy, esp. the duchy of Lancaster in England. [F *duchesse*]

duck[1] (dŭk) *n.* (*pl.* **duck, ducks**) **1** a web-footed waterbird of the family Anatidae, esp. the domestic duck. **2** the female of this species, as distinct from a *drake*. **3** duck flesh, eaten as food. **4** (*coll.*) darling. **5** in cricket, a score of nothing. **6** (*Mil.*) popular name for an amphibious motor vehicle. **lame duck** LAME[1]. **like water off a duck's back** (*coll.*) completely without effect. **to break one's duck** to score one's first run in a game of cricket. **to make ducks and drakes of** to squander. **to play ducks and drakes with** to squander. **to take to (something) like a duck to water** to discover a natural aptitude for (something). **duckbill** *n.* a duck-billed platypus. **duck-billed** *a.* having a bill like a duck. **duck-billed platypus** *n.* PLATYPUS. **duck board** *n.* (*usu. pl.*) planking used to cover muddy roads or paths. **duck-hawk** *n.* **1** (*dial.*) a marsh harrier, *Circus aeruginosus*. **2** (*N Am.*) a peregrine. **duckling** *n.* a young duck. **duck-pond** *n.* **ducks** *n.* (*coll.*) a term of familiarity or endearment. **ducks and drakes** *n.* a game of making a flat stone skip along the surface of water. **duck's arse,** (*N Am.*) **duck's ass** *n.* (*sl.*) a hairstyle in which the hair at the back of the neck is cut to look like a duck's tail. **duck's-egg** *n.* in cricket, a score of no runs. **duck-shot** *n.* small shot for shooting wild duck. **duck soup** *n.* (*N Am.*) anything easy to do. **duckweed** *n.* any of several floating waterweeds of the genus *Lemna*, which are eaten by duck and geese. **ducky** *n.* (*pl.* **duckies**) (*coll.*) a term of familiarity or endearment. ~*a.* sweet, delightful. [OE *dūce*, cogn. with DUCK[2]]

duck[2] (dŭk) *v.i.* **1** to dive, dip or plunge under water. **2** to bob the head. **3** to bow. **4** (*coll.*) to avoid (a responsibility etc.). **5** in bridge, to lose a trick by deliberately playing a low card when holding a higher one. ~*v.t.* **1** to dip under water and suddenly withdraw. **2** to bob (the head). ~*n.* **1** a quick plunge or dip under water. **2** a bob or sudden lowering of the head. **to duck out of** to dodge (a responsibility etc.). **ducker** *n.* a diving bird, esp. the dabchick or little grebe, or the water ouzel. **ducking** *n.* **ducking-stool** *n.* (*Hist.*) a kind of stool or chair on which scolds were tied and ducked. [ME *duken*, *douken*, as from an OE *dūcan* (cp. Dut. *duiken*, Dan. *dukke*, G *tauchen*)]

duck[3] (dŭk) *n.* **1** a kind of untwilled linen or cotton fabric, lighter and finer than canvas, used for jackets, aprons etc. **2** (*pl.*) trousers or a suit made of this. [prob. from Dut. *dock* (cp. Dan. *dug*, Swed. *duk*, G *Tuch*)]

duct (dŭkt) *n.* **1** a tube, canal or passage by which a fluid is conveyed. **2** (*Anat.*) a tubular passage for conveying chyle, lymph and other fluids. **3** (*Bot.*) a canal or elongated cell holding water, air etc. ~*v.t.* to convey by means of a duct. **ducting** *n.* **1** a system of ducts. **2** material in the form of ducts. **ductless** *a.* **ductless gland** *n.* an endocrine gland. [L *ductus*, p.p. of *ducere*, to lead]

ductile (dŭk´tīl) *a.* **1** able to be drawn out into threads or wire; malleable, not brittle. **2** capable of being moulded, plastic. **3** (*fig.*) pliant, tractable, yielding to persuasion or advice. **ductility** (-til´-), **ductileness** *n.* [F, from L *ductilis*, as DUCT]

ducting, ductless DUCT.

dud (dŭd) *n.* **1** (*sl.*) a useless person or thing. **2** a counterfeit coin or cheque; a forgery. **3** a shell that has failed to explode. ~*a.* **1** useless, worthless. **2** counterfeit. **duds** *n.pl.* clothes. [etym. uncertain]

dude (dūd) *n.* **1** a fop, an affected person; an aesthete. **2** (*N Am.*) a city-bred person, esp. one having a holiday on a dude ranch. **3** a man, a guy (*a cool dude*). **dude ranch** *n.* (*N Am.*) a ranch run as a pleasure resort by city people. **dudish** *a.* **dudishly** *adv.* **dudism** *n.* [LG *duden-dop*, *dudenkop*, a lazy fellow]

dudeen (doodēn´) *n.* (*Ir.*) a short clay tobacco pipe. [etym. unknown]

dudgeon[1] (dŭj´ən) *n.* anger, sullen resentment, indignation. **in high dudgeon** angry or resentful. [etym. uncertain]

†dudgeon[2] (dŭj´ən) *n.* **1** the root of the box tree. **2** the handle of a dagger formerly made of this wood. **3** a small dagger. [etym. unknown]

dudish, dudism etc. DUDE.

due (dū) *a.* **1** owed, owing, that ought to be paid, rendered or done to someone. **2** claimable, proper, suitable, appropriate. **3** expected, appointed to arrive, calculated to happen. **4** ascribable, that may be attributed (to). **5** planned or arranged. ~*adv.* exactly, directly. ~*n.* **1** what is owed or owing to one. **2** what one owes. **3** a debt, an obligation, tribute, toll, fee or other legal exaction. **due to** because of. **in due course** when the right time comes. **to become due** to fall due. **to fall due** to become payable; to mature as a bill. **to give someone their due** to be fair to someone. **to give the devil his due** DEVIL. **to pay one's dues** PAY[1]. **due date** *n.* the date by which a payment must be made. **†dueful** *a.* due, suitable. [OF *deū*, p.p. of *devoir*, to owe, L *debēre*]

Usage note It is best to avoid the use of *due to* for 'because of' (as a compound preposition): *The delay was due to the weather* is generally acceptable, but *They were delayed due to the weather* is not.

duel (dū´əl) *n.* **1** (*Hist.*) a combat between two persons with deadly weapons to decide a private quarrel, usu. an affair of honour. **2** any contest or struggle between two persons, parties, causes, animals etc. ~*v.i.* (*pres.p.* **duelling,** (*N Am.*) **dueling,** *past, p.p.* **duelled,** (*N Am.*) **dueled**) to fight in a duel; to contest. **dueller,** (*N Am.*) **dueler** *n.* **duellist,** (*N Am.*) **duelist** *n.* [F, from It. *duello*, L *duellum*, archaic form of *bellum*, war (cp. *duo*, two)]

duello (dūel´ō) *n.* (*pl.* **duellos**) **1** a duel. **2** the rules of duelling. [It., see DUEL]

☒ **duely** common misspelling of DULY.

duende (dooen´dā) *n.* **1** a demon, an evil spirit. **2** inspiration, magnetism. [Sp.]

duenna (dūen´ə) *n.* (*pl.* **duennas**) an elderly woman employed as companion and governess to young women, a chaperone. [Sp. *dueña*, L *domina*, a lady]

duet (dūet´), **duetto** (dooet´to) *n.* **1** a composition for two performers, vocal or instrumental. **2** any performance by two people. **3** a dialogue. ~*v.i.* (*pres.p.* **duetting,** *past, p.p.* **duetted**) to perform a duet. **duettist** *n.* **duetto** (dooet´ō) *n.* (*pl.* **duettos, duetti** (-tē)) a duet. [It. *duetto*, dim. of *duo* (L *duo*, two)]

duff[1] (dŭf) *n.* (*dial., coll.*) a stiff, flour pudding boiled in a bag. **up the duff** (*Austral., sl.*) pregnant. [DOUGH]

duff[2] (dŭf) *v.t.* (*sl.*) 1 in golf, to bungle (a shot). 2 to fake up (rubbishy articles) for sale. 3 (*Austral.*) to steal (cattle) by altering the brands. ~*a.* useless, not working. **to duff up** to beat up. [perh. from DUFFER]

duffel (duf´əl), **duffle** *n.* 1 a thick, coarse kind of woollen cloth, with a thick nap. 2 (*N Am.*) a camper's change of clothes, outfit, kit. **duffel bag** *n.* a cylindrical, canvas bag with a drawstring used to close it and carry it. **duffel coat** *n.* a three-quarter-length coat usu. made from duffel, hooded and fastened with toggles. [*Duffel*, town in Belgium]

duffer (dŭf´ə) *n.* 1 (*sl.*) a stupid, awkward or useless person. 2 (*Austral., sl.*) a person who steals cattle. 3 (*Austral., sl.*) an unproductive mine. 4 (*dial.*) a pedlar, a hawker of women's dress, or of cheap and flash jewellery, sham smuggled goods etc. [etym. uncertain (cp. DUFF[2])]

dug[1] (dŭg) *a.* that has been dug. **dugout** *n.* 1 a canoe made of a single log hollowed out, or of parts of two logs thus hollowed out and afterwards joined together. 2 a rough cabin cut in the side of a bank or hill. 3 a cellar, cave or shelter used as a protection against enemy shelling. 4 (*sl.*) a retired army officer recalled for service. 5 the enclosure at a sports ground occupied by the manager, trainer and reserve players. [p.p. of DIG]

dug[2] (dŭg) *n.* 1 a teat, a nipple of an animal. 2 (*derog.*) a woman's breast. [etym. obscure (cp. Sansk. *duh*, to milk)]

dugong (doo´gong) *n.* (*pl.* **dugong, dugongs**) a large herbivorous aquatic mammal, *Dugong dugon*, with two forelimbs only, belonging to the Sirenia, and inhabiting the Indian seas. [Malay *dūyōng*]

duiker (dī´kə), **duyker** *n.* 1 any of several small African antelopes of the genus *Cephalophus*. 2 a southern African cormorant, *Phalacrocorax africanus*. [Dut. *duiker*, diver]

duke (dūk) *n.* 1 a noble holding the highest hereditary rank outside the royal family. 2 the sovereign prince of a duchy. 3 (*pl., sl.*) fists; hands. 4 a cross between the sweet cherry and the sour cherry. **dukedom** *n.* the territory, title or rank of a duke. **dukeship** *n.* [F *duc*, L *dux ducis*, a leader]

Dukhobor (doo´kəbaw), **Doukhobar** *n.* a member of a Russian mystical sect who were oppressed for their passive resistance to militarism, and migrated in large numbers from their homes in the Caucasus to Canada. [Rus. *dukhoborets*, spirit-wrestler, *dukh*, spirit, soul, *borets*, fighter]

dulcet (dŭl´sit) *a.* sweet to the ear. **dulcetly** *adv.* [OF *doucet*, dim. of *doux*, L *dulcis*, sweet; assim. to L]

†**dulcify** (dŭl´sifī) *v.t.* (*3rd pers. sing. pres.* **dulcifies,** *pres.p.* **dulcifying,** *past, p.p.* **dulcified**) 1 to make sweet or gentle. 2 to sweeten; to free from acidity, acrimony or saltness. **dulcification** (-fikā´shən) *n.* [L *dulcificāre*, as DULCET]

dulcimer (dŭl´simə) *n.* a musical instrument with strings of wire, which are struck with rods. [OF *doulcemer*, Sp. *dulcemele*, perh. from L *dulce melos*, a sweet song]

dulcitone (dŭl´sitōn) *n.* a keyboard instrument with graduated tuning forks which are struck with hammers.

dulia (dū´liə), **douleia** (doolī´ə) *n.* the lowest of the three degrees of adoration recognized in the Roman Catholic Church, the reverence paid to angels, saints etc. [med. L, from Gr. *douleia*, slavery, servitude, from *doulos*, slave]

dull (dŭl) *a.* 1 slow of understanding; stupid, not quick in perception. 2 without sensibility. 3 blunt, obtuse. 4 not sharp or acute. 5 lacking keenness in any of the senses. 6 sluggish, inert, slow of movement. 7 stagnant. 8 (of trade) not brisk or active. 9 not bright, dim, tarnished. 10 cloudy, overcast, gloomy, depressing. 11 uninteresting, tedious, wearisome. 12 hard of hearing, deaf. 13 not loud or clear. ~*v.t.* 1 to make dull or stupid. 2 to stupefy. 3 to make blunt. 4 to render less acute, sensitive, interesting or effective. 5 to make heavy or sluggish, to deaden. 6 to tarnish, to dim. ~*v.i.* to become dull, blunt, stupid or inert. **to dull the edge of** to make less intense. **dullard** (-ləd) *n.* a blockhead; a dunce. **dullish** *a.* **dullness, dulness** *n.* **dull-witted** *a.* stupid. **dully** *adv.* [ME *dul* (cp. OE *dol*, stupid, Dut. *dol*, G *toll*, mad)]

dulse (dŭls) *n.* an edible kind of seaweed, *Rhodymenia palmata*. [Ir., Gael. *duileasg*]

duly (dū´li) *adv.* 1 in a suitable manner; properly; becomingly; regularly. 2 punctually. [DUE]

Duma (doo´mə) *n.* 1 a legislative body in Russia and some other republics formerly in the USSR. 2 (*Hist.*) the old Russian parliament or chamber of representatives, a legislative and revising body whose authority was limited by the veto of the Tsar, first summoned in 1906. [Rus., thought, a council]

dumb (dŭm) *a.* 1 unable to utter articulate sounds. 2 unable to speak, esp. through deafness or some other physical cause. 3 silent, (temporarily) speechless. 4 refraining from speaking, reticent, taciturn. 5 soundless. 6 (*coll.*) stupid, unintelligent. 7 having no say. 8 (*Comput.*) able only to transmit or receive data, not able to be programmed, as distinct from *intelligent*. ~*v.t.* to make dumb; to silence. **to dumb down** (*N Am., sl.*) to bring or come down to a lower level of understanding. **to strike dumb** to confound; to astonish; to render speechless by astonishment. **dumb animal** *n.* an animal, esp. seen as defenceless. **dumb-bell** *n.* 1 one of a pair of weights connected by a short bar or handle, swung in the hand for exercise. 2 (*sl.*) a stupid person. **dumb blonde** *n.* an attractive but stupid woman with fair hair. **dumb cluck** *n.* (*coll.*) a fool. **dumb crambo** *n.* a game similar to crambo in which the rhymes are expressed in dumbshow. **dumbhead** *n.* (*N Am., sl.*) a stupid person. **dumb-iron** *n.* in a motor vehicle, the curved forward end of the frame to which a front spring is made fast. **dumbly** *adv.* **dumbness** *n.* **dumbo** *n.* (*pl.* **dumbos**) (*sl.*) a stupid person. **dumb piano** *n.* a silent keyboard for exercising the fingers. **dumbshow** *n.* 1 gestures without speech. 2 part of a play acted in pantomime. **dumbstruck** *a.* temporarily shocked into silence. **dumb terminal** *n.* a computer terminal which can only receive data and has no processing power. **dumb waiter** *n.* 1 a movable framework for conveying food etc. from one room to another, a service lift. 2 a dining-room apparatus with revolving shelves for holding dishes etc. [OE; cp. Dut. *dom*, Swed. *dumb*, Dan. *dum*, OHG *tump*, G *dumm*, mute, stupid]

Usage note Using *dumb* to refer to a person unable to speak through deafness etc. can give offence, and is best avoided.

dumbfound (dŭm´fownd), **dumfound** *v.t.* to strike dumb; to confound, to confuse, to perplex, to astound.

dumdum (dŭm´dŭm), **dumdum bullet** *n.* a soft-nosed expanding bullet that lacerates the flesh. [*Dum-Dum*, town and military station near Calcutta]

dumfound DUMBFOUND.

dummy (dŭm´i) *n.* (*pl.* **dummies**) 1 a ventriloquist's doll. 2 a figure for showing off clothes in a shop window. 3 a figure used as a target in shooting practice. 4 any sham article. 5 a sham package displayed in a shop. 6 a prototype of a book. 7 the design layout of a page. 8 a feigned pass in rugby or football. 9 (*coll.*) a stupid person. 10 (*derog., sl.*) a person who cannot speak. 11 a person who is a mere tool of another person. 12 a rubber teat for a baby to suck. 13 the fourth exposed hand when three persons are playing at whist etc. **14** in bridge, the hand of the declarer's partner, exposed after the first lead, or the declarer's partner. **15** (*Mil.*) a blank round of ammunition, used for training. ~*a.* counterfeit, feigned. ~*v.t.* (*3rd pers. sing. pres.* **dummies,** *pres.p.* **dummying,** *past, p.p.* **dummied**) to pretend to pass (the ball) in rugby or football. ~*v.i.* to feign a pass in rugby or football. **double dummy** DOUBLE[1]. **to dummy up** (*N Am., sl.*) to say nothing. **to sell a dummy** to feign a pass or move in rugby or football. **dummy run** *n.* a trial run, a rehearsal.

dump[1] (dŭmp) *n.* **1** a pile of refuse. **2** a place for depositing rubbish. **3** (*coll.*) an unpleasant place, esp. a house. **4** an army storage depot. **5** a pile of earth or ore. **6** the act of dumping computer data. ~*v.t.* **1** to put down carelessly. **2** to unload. **3** to dispose of. **4** (*coll.*) to end a relationship with. **5** (*Mil.*) to leave (ammunition) in a dump. **6** to send (surplus produce, esp. manufactured goods that are unsaleable at home) to a foreign market for sale at a low price. **7** to get rid of (unwanted) things or people. **8** to record (the data on an internal computer memory) on an external storage device during a computer run. **to dump on** (*esp. N Am.*) to treat badly. **dumpbin** *n.* a container in a shop for e.g. sale and bargain items. **dumper** *n.* **1** a person who or something which dumps. **2** a vehicle which tips up at the back to dump its load. **3** (*Austral., New Zeal.*) a heavy wave dangerous to swimmers. **dumper truck, dump truck, dump wagon** *n.* a vehicle which tips up at the back to dump its load. [ME *dumpen*, to fall flat, prob. from Scand. (cp. Norw. *dumpa*, to thump, Swed. dial. *dompa*, Dan. *dumpe*, to fall plump)]

dump[2] (dŭmp) *n.* **1** a leaden counter used in playing chuck-farthing. **2** a small coin. **3** a short, thick and heavy object. **4** a stocky person. [etym. uncertain; perh. from DUMPY]

dumpling (dŭmp´ling) *n.* **1** a mass of dough or pudding, boiled or baked, often enclosing fruit etc. **2** a short, fat person. [prob. dim. of DUMP[2]]

dumps (dŭmps) *n.pl.* sadness, depression, melancholy. **in the dumps** low-spirited, depressed. **dumpish** *a.* sad, gloomy, melancholy; depressed in spirits. [etym. uncertain; cp. DAMP]

dumpy (dŭm´pi) *a.* (*comp.* **dumpier,** *superl.* **dumpiest**) **1** short and thick; plump. **2** depressed. ~*n.* a short-legged Scottish breed of domestic fowl. **dumpily** *adv.* **dumpiness** *n.* **dumpy level** *n.* a spirit level with a short telescope and a compass attached, used in surveying. [etym. uncertain; cp. DUMP[2]]

dun[1] (dŭn) *a.* (*comp.* **dunner,** *superl.* **dunnest**) **1** of a dull brown or brownish-grey colour. **2** (*poet.*) dark, gloomy. ~*n.* **1** a dun colour. **2** a dun-fly. **3** a dun horse. ~*v.t.* (*pres.p.* **dunning,** *past, p.p.* **dunned**) (*N Am.*) to preserve or cure (cod etc.), so as to give it a dark colour. **dun-bird** *n.* the pochard. **dun-diver** *n.* the female or young male of the goosander. **dunning** *n.* [OE *dunn*, cp. Ir., Gael. *donn*, Welsh *dwn*]

dun[2] (dŭn) *v.t.* (*pres.p.* **dunning,** *past, p.p.* **dunned**) **1** to demand payment from with persistence. **2** to press, to plague, to pester. ~*n.* **1** a creditor who presses persistently for payment. **2** a debt-collector. **3** an importunate demand for the payment of a debt. [perh. a var. of DIN]

dun[3] (dŭn) *n.* a hill, a mound, an earthwork (largely used in place-names). [Ir. Gael.]

dunce (dŭns) *n.* a stupid person, a person who is slow in learning. **duncehood** *n.* **dunce's cap** *n.* a conical paper cap formerly worn by a school pupil to indicate slowness of learning. [a word introduced by the Thomists or disciples of Thomas Aquinas, in ridicule of the followers of John *Duns* Scotus, d. 1308]

dunch (dŭnsh) *v.t.* (*Sc., North.*) to push with the elbow. ~*n.* a jog, a smart push or blow. [etym. unknown]

Dundee cake (dŭndē´) *n.* a fruit cake decorated with almonds. [*Dundee*, city in Scotland]

dunderhead (dŭn´dəhed) *n.* a stupid person. **dunderheaded** *a.* **dunderpate** *n.* a dunderhead. [etym. uncertain]

dune (dūn) *n.* a hill, mound or ridge of sand on the seashore. **dune buggy** *n.* a beach buggy. [F, from MDut. *dūne*, cogn. with OE *dūn*]

dung (dŭng) *n.* **1** the excrement of animals; manure. **2** anything filthy. ~*v.t.* to manure or dress with dung. ~*v.i.* to void excrement. **dung-beetle** *n.* a beetle of the family Scarabaeidae, the larvae of which develop in dung. **dung-fly** *n.* a two-winged fly of the family Scatophagidae, which feeds upon dung. **dung-fork** *n.* a fork for spreading manure. **dunghill, dungheap** *n.* **1** a heap of dung. **2** an accumulation of dung and refuse in a farmyard. **3** (*fig.*) a filthy place. **4** any vile or contemptible situation, position or condition. **dung-worm** *n.* a worm or larva found in dung and used as bait for fish. **dungy** *a.* (*comp.* **dungier,** *superl.* **dungiest**). [OE (cp. G *Dung*, Swed. *dynga*, Dan. *dynge*)]

dungaree (dŭng·gərē´) *n.* **1** a coarse kind of calico used for overalls. **2** (*pl.*) trousers with a bib. [Hind. *dungrī*]

dungeon (dŭn´jən) *n.* **1** a prison or place of confinement, esp. one that is dark and underground. **2** †a donjon or keep of a medieval castle. ~†*v.t.* to confine in a dungeon. [F *donjon*, late L *domnio*, *-ōnem*, L *dominio*, from *dominus*, lord (cp. DOMINION)]

dunite (dŭn´īt) *n.* a rock consisting essentially of olivine, frequently accompanied by chromite. [Mt *Dun*, New Zealand]

duniwassal (doo´niwahsəl) *n.* a Highland gentleman of inferior rank, a yeoman. [Gael. *duine vasal* (*duine*, a man, *vasal*, noble, cp. Welsh *uchel*)]

dunk (dŭngk) *v.t.* **1** to dip (a cake or biscuit) in what one is drinking, e.g. tea or coffee. **2** to dip, to immerse. [G *tunken*, to dip]

Dunker (dŭng´kə) *n.* a member of a sect of German-American Baptists. [G *Tunker*, from *tunken*, to dip]

dunlin (dŭn´lin) *n.* a small sandpiper, *Calidira alpina*, a common shorebird. [DUN[1], -LING[1]]

dunnage (dŭn´ij) *n.* **1** (*Naut.*) loose wood, faggots, boughs etc., laid in the hold to raise the cargo above the bilge-water, or wedged between the cargo to keep it from rolling when stowed. **2** (*coll.*) assorted luggage. [formerly *dinnage*; etym. uncertain]

dunning DUN[1].

dunno (dənō´) *contr.* (*coll.*) (I) don't know.

dunnock (dŭn´ək) *n.* the hedge sparrow, *Prunella modularis* (from its colour).

dunny[1] (dŭn´i) *n.* (*pl.* **dunnies**) **1** (*Sc., Austral.*) an outside lavatory. **2** (*Sc.*) a basement.

dunny[2] (dŭn´i) *a.* (*comp.* **dunnier,** *superl.* **dunniest**) (*coll.*) hard of hearing. [etym. uncertain (perh. conn. with DIN)]

dunt (dŭnt) *n.* (*Sc.*) **1** a blow or stroke. **2** a dint or wound. **3** a bump, a jolt. ~*v.t.* to thump, push or prod. [perh. a var. of DINT]

duny DUNE.

duo (dū´ō) *n.* (*pl.* **duos**) **1** a pair of performers who work together. **2** (*Mus.*) a duet. [It., DUET]

duodecennial (dūōdisen´iəl) *a.* occurring once every 12 years. [L *duodecim*, twelve, *annus*, year]

duodecimal (dūōdes´iməl) *a.* proceeding in computation by twelves (applied to a scale of notation in which the local value of the digits increases twelvefold as they proceed from right to left). ~*n.* **1** the duodecimal system. **2** duodecimal notation. **duodecimally** *adv.* **duodecimo** *n.* (*pl.* **duodecimos**) **1** a book consisting of sheets of 12 leaves or 24 pages. **2** the size of such a book (written 12mo and called 'twelvemo'). ~*a.* consisting of 12 leaves to the sheet. [L *duodecimus*, twelfth, *duodecim*, twelve (DUO-, *decem*, ten)]

duodenal DUODENUM.

duodenary (dūədē´nəri) *a.* **1** of or relating to the number 12. **2** proceeding by twelves. [L *duodenarius*, from *duodēnī*, 12 apiece, as DUODECIMAL]

duodenum (dūodē´nəm) *n.* (*pl.* **duodenums**) the first portion of the small intestine (so called from being about the length of 12 fingers' breadths). **duodenal** *a.* **duodenectomy** (-ek´təmi) *n.* (*pl.* **duodenectomies**) excision of the duodenum. **duodenitis** (-ī´tis) *n.* inflammation of the duodenum. [med. L, as DUODENARY]

duologue (dū´əlog) *n.* **1** a dialogue for two persons. **2** a dramatic composition for two actors.

duomo (dwō´mō) *n.* (*pl.* **duomos**) an Italian cathedral. [It. (see DOME[1])]

duopoly (dūop´əli) *n.* (*pl.* **duopolies**) an exclusive trading right enjoyed by two companies. [L *duo*, two, Gr. *pōleein*, to sell]

duotone (dū´ətōn) *n.* **1** an illustration in two tones or colours. **2** the process of producing a duotone. *~a.* in two tones or colours. [L *duo*, two]

dupe (dūp) *n.* a person who is easily deceived; a credulous person. *~v.t.* to trick, to cheat, to make a dupe of. **dupable** *a.* **dupability** (-bil´-) *n.* **duper** *n.* **dupery** (-əri) *n.* [F, etym. unknown]

dupion (dū´piən) *n.* **1** a double cocoon formed by two or more silkworms. **2** silk made from such cocoons. **3** an imitation of this silk. [F *doupion*, from It. *doppione*, from *doppio*, L *duplus*, DOUBLE[1]]

duple (dū´pəl) *a.* **1** double, twofold. **2** (*Mus.*) having two beats to the bar. **duple ratio** *n.* the ratio of two to one, six to three etc. **duplet** *n.* (*Mus.*) two equal notes played in the time of three. **duple time** *n.* musical time with two beats to the bar. [L *duplus*, double (*duo*, two, *-plus*, -fold)]

duplex (dū´pleks) *n.* (*N Am.*) a duplex apartment or house. *~a.* double, twofold. **duplex apartment** *n.* (*N Am.*) a two-storey apartment. **duplex gas burner** *n.* a gas burner with two jets that coalesce into a single flame. **duplex house** *n.* (*N Am.*) a house split into two dwellings. [L (*duo*, two, *plic-*, see DUPLICATE[1])]

duplicable DUPLICATE[2].

duplicate[1] (dū´plikət) *a.* **1** double, twofold, existing in two parts exactly corresponding. **2** corresponding exactly with another. *~n.* **1** one of two things exactly similar in material and form. **2** a reproduction, a replica, a copy. **3** a copy of an original legal document having equal binding force. **4** a form of bridge or whist in which the players keep the hands that they are dealt and the same hands are played by different players in turn. **5** †a pawn ticket. **in duplicate** in the original plus a copy. **duplicate bridge** *n.* a form of bridge in which the players keep the hands they are dealt and the same hands are played by different players in turn. **duplicate ratio** *n.* the ratio of the squares of two numbers. **duplicate whist** *n.* a form of whist in which the players keep the hands they are dealt and the same hands are played by different players in turn. [L *duplicātus*, p.p. of *duplicāre* (*duo*, two, *plicāre*, to fold)]

duplicate[2] (dū´plikāt) *v.t.* **1** to make or be a reproduction of. **2** to double. **3** to make in duplicate. **4** to make copies of on a machine. **5** to do twice, esp. unnecessarily. **6** (*Biol.*) to divide and form into two parts or organisms. **duplicable** (-plikəbəl) *a.* **duplication** (-ā´shən) *n.* **duplicative** (-ətiv) *a.* **duplicator** *n.* a machine for duplicating typescript.

duplicity (dūplis´iti) *n.* **1** double-dealing, dissimulation. **2** †doubleness of speech or action. **duplicitous** *a.* [F *duplicité*, L *duplicitās -tātem*, from DUPLEX]

dupondius (dūpon´diəs) *n.* (*pl.* **dupondii** (-diī)) a coin in ancient Rome, worth two asses. [L]

duppy (dŭp´i) *n.* (*pl.* **duppies**) a malevolent ghost in W Indian folklore. [prob. from an Afr. language]

dura DURRA.

durable (dūə´rəbəl) *a.* **1** having the quality of endurance or continuance. **2** lasting, permanent, firm, stable. **durability** (-bil´-) *n.* **durableness** *n.* **durably** *adv.* [F, from L *dūrābilis*, from *dūrāre*, to last, from *dūrus*, hard]

Duralumin® (dūral´ūmin) *n.* an alloy of aluminium, copper and other metals, having great strength and lightness. [L *dūrus*, hard]

dura mater (dūərə mā´tə) *n.* the first of three lining membranes of the brain and spinal cord. [med. L, the hard mother, a trans. of an Arabic phrase]

duramen (dūrā´men) *n.* the heartwood or central wood in the trunk of exogenous trees. [L, hardness, from *dūrāre*, to harden]

†durance (dūə´rəns) *n.* **1** imprisonment. **2** endurance, durability. [F, from *durer*, to last, as DURAMEN]

duration (dūrā´shən) *n.* **1** continuance. **2** length of time of continuance. **3** power of continuance. **4** a specific length of time. **for the duration** (*sl.*) so long as a situation or war lasts. **durative** (dūə´rətiv) *a.* denoting the aspect of a verb which implies continuance of action in time, as in the imperfect and progressive tenses. *~n.* a verb in this aspect. [OF, from late L *dūrātio -ōnem*, from L *dūrāre*, to last]

durbar (dœ´bah) *n.* (*Hist.*) **1** an Indian ruler's court. **2** a state reception by an Indian ruler or by a British governor. **3** a hall of audience. [Pers., Hind. *darbār*, a court]

durchkomponiert (duəkh´komponiət) *a.* (*Mus.*) having different music for each stanza. [G, *durch*, through, *komponiert*, composed]

duress (dūres´) *n.* **1** constraint, compulsion, restraint of liberty, imprisonment. **2** (*Law*) restraint of liberty or threat of violence to compel a person to do some act of exculpation by one who has been so restrained or threatened. [OF *duresce*, L *dūritia*, from *dūrus*, hard]

Durex® (dūə´reks) *n.* a condom.

durian (dūə´riən) *n.* **1** a large tree, *Durio zibethinus*, grown in the Malay archipelago. **2** the globular pulpy fruit of this. [Malay *durian*, from *durī*, prickle]

duricrust (dūə´rikrŭst) *n.* (*Geol.*) a hard, mineral crust found near the surface of soil in semi-arid regions.

during (dūə´ring) *prep.* **1** in or within the time of. **2** throughout the course or existence of. [orig. pres.p. of dure]

durmast (dœ´mahst) *n.* a Eurasian oak, *Quercus petraea*. [etym. uncertain]

durn DARN[2].

durned DARNED (under DARN[2]).

durra (dur´ə), **dari** (dah´ri), **dura, dhurra, doura** *n.* a kind of sorghum, *Sorghum bicolor*, cultivated for grain and fodder. [Arab. *durah, durrah*]

durrie (dŭr´i), **dhurrie** *n.* a coarse cotton fabric, made in squares, and used in the Indian subcontinent for carpets, curtains, coverings for furniture etc. [Hind. *darī*]

†durst DARE.

durum (dūə´rəm) *n.* a variety of spring wheat, *Triticum durum*, with a high gluten content, used mainly for the manufacture of pasta. [L *dūrum*, neut. of *dūrus*, hard]

durzi (dœ´zi) *n.* (*pl.* **durzis**) an Indian tailor. [Urdu, from Pers. *dārzi*, from *darz*, sewing]

dusk (dŭsk) *n.* **1** shade, gloom. **2** partial darkness, twilight. *~a.* (*poet.*) **1** shadowy, dim, obscure. **2** dark. *~v.t.* (*poet.*) to make somewhat dark; to obscure. *~v.i.* (*poet.*) to grow or to appear dark. **duskish** *a.* **dusky** *a.* (*comp.* **duskier**, *superl.* **duskiest**) **1** dark. **2** shadowy. **duskily** *adv.* **duskiness** *n.* [ME *dose*, dark, dim, OE *dox* (cp. Swed. *dusk*, a shower, Norw. *dusk*, mist)]

dust (dŭst) *n.* **1** earth or other matter reduced to such small particles as to be easily raised and carried about by the air. **2** a stirring of such fine particles. **3** household refuse. **4** pollen. **5** the decomposed bodies of the dead. **6** †the human body. **7** the grave. **8** the ground. **9** a low or despised condition. **10** turmoil, excitement, confusion, commotion, a row. **11** (*sl.*) money. *~v.t.* **1** to brush or sweep away the dust from. **2** to sprinkle or cover with powdered chocolate, icing sugar etc. **3** to make dusty. **4** to clean by brushing or beating. *~v.i.* **1** to dust furniture or a room. **2** to have a dust-bath. **in the dust 1** humiliated. **2** dead. **not to see (someone) for dust** to be suddenly left abandoned by (someone). **to bite the dust 1** to fail. **2** to die. **to dust down 1** to remove dust from. **2** (*coll.*) to scold, to reprimand. **3** to dust off. **to dust off 1** to remove dust from. **2** to reuse (an old idea or plan). **to dust someone's jacket** to give someone a beating. **to kick up/ raise a dust** to make a disturbance. **to shake the dust off one's feet** to leave angrily. **to throw dust in the eyes of** to mislead, to deceive, to delude. **when the dust settles** when a situation calms down. **dust and ashes** *n.pl.* something disappointing. **dust-bath** *n.* the rubbing of dust into their feathers by birds, prob. to get rid of parasites. **dustbin** *n.* a receptacle for household refuse. **dust bowl** *n.* an area reduced to aridity by drought and over-cropping. **dustcart** *n.* a vehicle for removing refuse from houses, streets etc. **dust-coat** *n.* a light overcoat. **dust cover** *n.* **1** a dust sheet. **2** a dust jacket. **dust devil** *n.* (*S Afr.*) a small whirlwind which whips up dust, leaves and litter. **duster** *n.* **1** a cloth used to remove dust. **2** a person who dusts. **3** (*N Am.*) a dust-coat. **dusting** *n.*, *a.* **dusting powder** *n.* very fine powder, esp. talcum powder. **dust jacket** *n.* a protective printed paper cover for a book. **dustless** *a.* **dustman** *n.* (*pl.* **dustmen**) **1** a person whose occupation is to remove refuse from dustbins. **2** a sandman. **dustpan** *n.* a small container into which dust is swept. **dust sheet** *n.* a sheet thrown over furniture while a room is being dusted or while it is unused. **dust-shot** *n.* shot of the smallest size. **dust storm** *n.* a windstorm which whips up clouds of dust as it travels through arid areas. **dust-trap** *n.* an object on which dust gathers. **dust-up** *n.* (*coll.*) a row, a heated quarrel, a fight. **dust-wrapper** *n.* a dust jacket. **dusty** *a.* (*comp.* **dustier,** *superl.* **dustiest**) **1** covered with or full of dust. **2** like dust. **3** dull, uninteresting. **4** (of a colour) dull. **not so dusty** (*sl.*) pretty good. **dustily** *adv.* **dustiness** *n.* **dusty answer** *n.* an unsatisfactory or bad-tempered response. **dusty miller** *n.* **1** any of various plants, esp. *Artemisia stelleriana*, whose leaves and flowers have a dusty appearance. **2** an artificial fly for fishing. [OE *dūst* (cp. Dut. *duist*, G *Dunst*)]

Dutch (dŭch) *a.* **1** of or relating to the Netherlands. **2** †of or relating to the Low Germans, or to the German peoples. **3** (*S Afr.*) of Dutch origin. **4** (*N Am., sl.*) of German extraction. *~n.* **1** the language of the Netherlands. **2** (*S Afr., derog.*) Afrikaans. **3** †the German language, esp. Low German. **4** (*as pl.*) **a** the people of the Netherlands. **b** (*S Afr.*) Afrikaans-speaking people. **double Dutch** DOUBLE[1]. **to go Dutch** to share the cost of an outing. **Dutch auction** *n.* an auction sale in which the auctioneer keeps reducing prices until a buyer is found. **Dutch bargain** *n.* a bargain concluded over a glass of liquor. **Dutch barn** *n.* a barn for storage, with open sides and a steel frame supporting a curved roof. **Dutch cap** *n.* **1** a moulded rubber cap fitting over the cervix to act as a contraceptive barrier. **2** a woman's white lace cap, part of the Dutch national dress. **Dutch cheese** *n.* a small round cheese manufactured in Holland from skim milk. **Dutch courage** *n.* false courage, inspired by stimulants. **Dutch doll** *n.* a wooden doll. **Dutch door** *n.* (*N Am.*) a stable door. **Dutch elm disease** *n.* a disease of elms caused by the fungus *Ceratocytis ulmi* and carried by beetles, causing withering and defoliation, and often fatal. **Dutch gold, Dutch foil** *n.* Dutch metal. **Dutch hoe** *n.* a garden hoe with a blade. **Dutch interior** *n.* a painting of a domestic scene by a Dutch artist, esp. Pieter de Hooch. **Dutchman** *n.* (*pl.* **Dutchmen**) **1** a male native inhabitant of the Netherlands, or a male descendant of one. **2** a Dutch ship. **3** (*N Am., sl.*) a German. **if so, I'm a Dutchman** used to express denial or disbelief. **Dutchman's breeches** *n.* a N American plant, *Dicentra cucullaria*, with finely divided leaves and white or pink flowers. **Dutchman's pipe** *n.* a N American climbing plant, *Aristolochia durior*, with flowers shaped like a curved pipe. **Dutch medicine** *n.* (*S Afr.*) patent medicine, esp. made from herbs. **Dutch metal** *n.* a highly malleable copper alloy with zinc, used instead of gold leaf. **Dutch oven** *n.* **1** a cooking chamber suspended in front of a fire so as to cook by radiation. **2** a heavy container with a lid, used for stewing, braising etc. **Dutch pink** *n.* a yellow pigment obtained from quercitron bark. **Dutch Reformed Church** *n.* the Afrikaans-speaking branch of the Calvinist church in South Africa. **Dutch rush** *n.* the scouring rush, *Equisetum hyemale*, used for cleaning and polishing wood. **Dutch tile** *n.* a variegated or painted glazed tile made in the Netherlands, formerly used for lining large fireplaces. **Dutch treat** *n.* (*coll.*) an outing with each person paying their own share. **Dutch uncle** *n.* a person who criticizes in a stern, blunt manner. **Dutchwoman** *n.* (*pl.* **Dutchwomen**) a female native or inhabitant of the Netherlands, or a female descendant of one. [MDut. *Dutsch*, Hollandish, or G *Deutsch*, German]

dutch (dŭch) *n.* (*Cockney sl.*) a wife. [perh. short for DUCHESS]

duty (dū´ti) *n.* (*pl.* **duties**) **1** something which is bound or ought to be paid, done or performed. **2** something which a particular person is bound morally or legally to do. **3** moral or legal obligation. **4** the course of conduct prescribed by ethics or religion, the binding force of the obligation to follow this course. **5** obedience or submission due to parents or superiors. **6** any service, business or office. **7** a toll, tax, impost or custom charged by a government on the importation, exportation, manufacture or sale of goods or on transfer of property etc. **8** office, function, occupation, work. **9** any of the various acts entailed in this. **10** the useful work done by an engine or motor, measured in units against units of fuel. **11** the performance of church services. **off duty** not engaged in one's appointed duties. **on duty** engaged in performing one's appointed duties. **to do duty for 1** to serve in lieu of someone or something else. **2** to serve as a makeshift for. **†duteous** (-tiəs) *a.* obedient, dutiful. **†duteously** *adv.* **†duteousness** *n.* **dutiable** *a.* liable to the imposition of a duty or custom. **dutied** *a.* charged with duty. **dutiful** *a.* careful in performing the duties required by law, justice or propriety; reverential, deferential. **dutifully** *adv.* **dutifulness** *n.* **duty-bound** *a.* obliged by one's sense of duty (to do something). **duty-free** *a.* not liable to duty, tax or custom. **duty-free shop** *n.* a shop, usu. on a ship or at an airport, where duty-free goods are for sale. **duty officer** *n.* the officer on duty at any particular time. **duty-paid** *a.* on which duty has been paid. **duty visit** *n.* a visit paid out of a sense of duty rather than for pleasure. [A-F *dueté*]

duumvir (dūŭm´və) *n.* (*pl.* **duumvirs**) either of two officers or magistrates in ancient Rome appointed to carry out jointly the duties of any public office. **duumviral** (-virəl) *a.* **duumvirate** (-virət) *n.* [L (*duo*, two, *viri*, men)]

duvet (doo´vā) *n.* a quilt stuffed with down or man-made fibres, used as a bed covering instead of blankets and a sheet. [F, down, earlier *dumet*, dim. of OF *dum* (cp. Icel. *dūnn*)]

dux (dŭks) *n.* (*Sc., Austral., New Zeal.*) the top pupil of a school. [L, leader]

duyker DUIKER.

DV *abbr.* God willing (L *Deo volente*).

Dvr. *abbr.* Driver.
dwale (dwāl) *n.* the deadly nightshade, *Atropa belladonna.* [ME *dwale* (cp. Dan. *dvale*, Swed. *dwala*, a trance, OE *dwala*, an error, stupefaction)]
dwam (dwahm), **dwalm** *n.* (*Sc., North.*) a daydream, absent-mindedness. *~v.i.* to become ill. [cp. OE *dwolma*, confusion]
dwarf (dwawf) *n.* (*pl.* **dwarfs, dwarves** (-vz)) **1** a human being, animal or plant much below the natural or ordinary size. **2** a supernatural being of small stature. **3** any relatively small star with high density and ordinary luminosity, e.g. the sun. *~a.* **1** below the ordinary or natural size. **2** stunted, puny, tiny. *~v.t.* **1** to stunt the growth of. **2** to cause to look small or insignificant by comparison. *~v.i.* to become stunted in growth. **dwarfed** *a.* **dwarfed tree** *n.* a bonsai tree. **dwarfish** *a.* **dwarfishly** *adv.* **dwarfishness** *n.* **dwarfism** *n.* the condition of being a dwarf. **dwarf star** *n.* any relatively small star with high density and ordinary luminosity, e.g. the sun. [OE *dweorg, dweorh*, from Gmc. *dwerg-* (Dut. *dwerg*, Swed., Dan. *dverg*, G *Zwerg*)]
dweeb (dwēb) *n.* (*N Am., sl.*) a stupid or contemptibly weak man or boy. [etym. unknown]
dwell (dwel) *v.i.* (*past, p.p.* **dwelt** (-t), **dwelled**) **1** (*formal*) to reside, to abide (in a place); to live, to spend one's time. **2** to linger, pause, tarry. *~n.* a pause; a slight regular stoppage of the movement of a machine while a certain operation is effected. **to dwell on/ upon 1** to think for a long time or continually about (something unpleasant). **2** to speak or write at length about. **3** to prolong (a sound). **dweller** *n.* (*formal*) a resident, an inhabitant. **dwelling** *n.* (*formal*) a residence, an abode, a habitation. **dwelling house** *n.* a house for residence, as distinguished from a place of business, an office, a warehouse etc. **dwelling-place** *n.* (*formal*) a place of residence. [OE *dwellan*, to lead astray (later, *dwelian*, to lead astray, to err, to be delayed)]
DWEM (dwem) *n.* a dead White European male, esp. one who has been regarded as being of undue historical or literary importance because of belonging to a dominant section of society.
dwindle (dwin´dəl) *v.i.* **1** to shrink, to diminish, to become smaller; to waste away. **2** to degenerate, to decline. [OE *dwinan*]
d.w.t. *abbr.* dead-weight tonnage.
dwt. *abbr.* (*Hist.*) pennyweight.
DX (dēeks´) *n.* long-range radio transmissions.
Dy *chem. symbol* dysprosium.
dyad (dī´ad), **duad** (dū´ad) *n.* **1** (*Math.*) an operator which is two vectors combined. **2** two units treated as one; a group of two, a pair, a couple. **3** (*Chem.*) a diatomic element, atom or radical. **dyadic** (-ad´-) *a.* [L *dyas dyadis*, Gr *duas duados* (*duo*, two)]
Dyak (dī´ak), **Dayak** *n.* a person belonging to the aboriginal race inhabiting Borneo, probably related to the Malays. [Malay *dayak*, up country]
dyarchy DIARCHY.
dybbuk (dib´uk) *n.* (*pl.* **dybukkim** (-kim), **dybbuks**) in Jewish folklore, the soul of a dead sinner which enters the body of a living person and takes control of their actions. [Heb. *dibbūk*, devil]
dye (dī) *v.t.* (*pres.p.* **dyeing,** *past, p.p.* **dyed**) **1** to stain, to colour. **2** to impregnate with colouring matter. **3** to cause (a material) to take a certain colour. *~v.i.* (of a material that is being dyed) to take a colour. *~n.* **1** a substance used for dyeing, colouring-matter. **2** a colour, tinge or hue, produced by or as if by dyeing. **3** a substance which yields a dye. **to dye in grain** GRAIN. **to dye in the wool** to dye (the wool) before spinning, to give a more permanent result. **dyeable** *a.* **dyed** *a.* **dyed in the wool** *a.* fixed in one's opinions, uncompromising. **dye-house** *n.* a building where dyeing is carried on. **dyeing** *n.* **dye-line** *n.* a diazo print. **dyer** *n.* a person whose business is dyeing. **dyer's greenweed, dyer's broom** *n.* a small Eurasian shrub, *Genista tinctoria*, with yellow flowers formerly used to make a green dye. **dyer's oak** *n.* a Mediterranean oak, *Quercus infectoria*, with galls formerly used to make a yellow dye. **dyer's-weed** *n.* any of various plants yielding dyestuff, such as dyer's greenweed or dyer's broom, dyer's rocket, which yields a yellow dye, and dyer's woad. **dyestuff** *n.* a substance which yields a dye. **dyewood** *n.* any wood from which a dye is extracted. **dye-works** *n.* a dye-house. [OE *dēagian*, from *dēag*, a dye]
dying (dī´ing) *a.* **1** about to die. **2** mortal, perishable. **3** done, given or uttered just before death. **4** associated with death. **5** drawing to an end, fading away. *~n.* the act of dying, death. **to one's dying day** for the rest of one's life. **dying declaration** *n.* a legal declaration made by a person on the point of death. **dyingly** *adv.* **dying oath** *n.* an oath made on the point of death, or as seriously as if on the point of death. [DIE[1]]
dyke (dīk), **dike** *n.* **1** a wall built to protect low-lying lands from being flooded. **2** a ditch, a moat, a watercourse or channel, either natural or artificial. **3** a wall or fence of turf or stone without cement. **4** a causeway. **5** (*fig.*) a barrier, a defence. **6** a wall-like mass of cooled and hardened volcanic or igneous rock, occupying rents and fissures in sedimentary strata. **7** (*Austral., sl.*) a lavatory. **8** (*sl.*) a lesbian. *~v.t.* to defend with dykes or embankments. [OE *dīc* (cp. Dut. *dijk*, G *Teich*)]
dyn *abbr.* dyne.
dynameter (dīnam´itə) *n.* an instrument for measuring the magnifying powers of a telescope.
dynamic (dīnam´ik) *a.* **1** of or relating to forces not in equilibrium, as distinct from *static.* **2** motive, active, energetic. **3** of or relating to dynamics. **4** (*Mus.*) of or relating to levels of loudness. **5** involving or dependent upon mechanical activity, like the dynamic theory of Kant. *~n.* **1** the motive force of any action. **2** (*Mus.*) dynamics. **dynamical** *a.* **1** dynamic. **2** (*Theol.*) inspiring or animating, not impelling mechanically. **dynamical geology** *n.* dynamic geology. **dynamically** *adv.* **dynamic equilibrium** *n.* a balance between continuing processes. **dynamic geology** *n.* the study of the forces that have brought about geological changes. **dynamicist** (-nam´isist) *n.* **dynamics** *n.pl.* **1** (*as sing.*) **a** the branch of mechanics which deals with the behaviour of bodies under the action of forces which produce changes of motion in them. **b** the branch of any science which deals with forces or changes. **2** the opposing forces in any situation which cause it to change. **3** (*Mus.*) degrees of levels of loudness. **dynamic viscosity** *n.* a measurement of the force required to overcome internal friction. [F *dynamique*, Gr. *dunamikos*, from *dunamis*, power, *dunamai*, I am strong]
dynamism (dī´nəmizm) *n.* **1** the restless energy of a forceful personality. **2** a system or theory explaining phenomena as the ultimate result of some immanent force, such as the doctrine of Leibnitz that all substance involves force. **dynamist** *n.* **dynamistic** (-mis´-) *a.*
dynamite (dī´nəmīt) *n.* **1** a powerful explosive compound, extremely local in its action, consisting of nitroglycerine mixed with an absorbent material. **2** an exciting or impressive person or thing. **3** (*sl.*) a narcotic, esp. heroin. *~v.t.* to blow up with dynamite. **dynamiter** *n.* [Gr. *dunamis*, see DYNAMIC]
dynamo (dī´nəmō) *n.* (*pl.* **dynamos**) **1** a machine for converting mechanical energy into electricity by means of electromagnetic induction. **2** (*coll.*) a very energetic person.
dynamo- (dī´nəmō) *comb. form* of or relating to force or power. [Gr. *dunamis*, power]
dynamoelectric (dīnəmōilek´trik) *a.* of or relating to the conversion of mechanical into electric energy or the reverse. **dynamoelectrical** *a.*

dynamograph (dīnam´əgrahf) *n.* a dynamometer used for recording speed, power, adhesion etc. on electric railways.

dynamometer (dīnəmom´itə) *n.* an instrument for the measurement of power, force or electricity.

dynamotor (dī´nəmōtə) *n.* an electrical machine capable of acting as a motor and a generator which converts direct current into alternating current.

dynast (din´əst, dī´nəst) *n.* **1** a ruler, a monarch. **2** a member or founder of a dynasty. **dynastic** (-nas´-) *a.* **dynastically** *adv.* **dynasty** (din´-) *n.* (*pl.* **dynasties**) **1** a line, race or succession of sovereigns of the same family. **2** a family with several generations dominant in any field of activity. [late L *dynastēs*, Gr. *dunastēs*, a lord, from *dunatos*, able (*dunamai*, I am strong)]

dynatron (dī´nətron) *n.* (*pl.* **dynatrons**) a four-electrode thermionic valve which generates continuous oscillation.

dyne (dīn) *n.* (*Physics*) a unit for measuring force, the amount that, acting upon a gram for a second, generates a velocity of one centimetre per second. [F, from stem of Gr. *dunamai*, see DYNAST]

dys- (dis) *comb. form* (*esp. Med.*) diseased, difficult or bad. [Gr. *dus-*, bad]

dysaesthesia (disəsthē´ziə), (*N Am.*) **dysesthesia** *n.* (*Med.*) insensibility.

dysentery (dis´əntri) *n.* an infectious tropical febrile disease, causing inflammation in the large intestines, and accompanied by mucous and bloody evacuations. **dysenteric** (-ter´-) *a.* [OF *dissenterie*, L *dysenteria*, Gr. *dusenteria* (*entera*, bowels)]

dysesthesia DYSAESTHESIA.

dysfunction (disfŭngk´shən) *n.* impaired or abnormal functioning, esp. of any organ or part of the body. **dysfunctional** *a.*

dysgenic (disjen´ik) *a.* unfavourable to the hereditary qualities of any stock or people. **dysgenics** *n.* the study of hereditary factors contributing to the degeneration of any stock or people.

dysgraphia (disgraf´iə) *n.* inability to write. **dysgraphic** *a.* [Gr. *graphein*, to write]

dyslexia (dislek´siə) *n.* an impaired ability in reading and spelling caused by a neurological disorder. **dyslexic** *a., n.* [Gr. *lexis*, word]

dyslogistic (disləjis´tik) *a.* disparaging, disapproving, censuring. **dyslogistically** *adv.*

dysmenorrhoea (dismenərē´ə), (*N Am.*) **dysmenorrhea** *n.* difficult or painful menstruation. **dysmenorrhoeal, dysmenorrhoeic** *a.*

dyspepsia (dispep´siə), **dyspepsy** (-si) *n.* indigestion.

dyspeptic (-tik) *a.* of, relating to, of the nature of, or suffering from dyspepsia. ~*n.* a person who is subject to dyspepsia. [L, from Gr. *duspepsia*, from *duspeptos*, hard to digest (*peptein*, to cook)]

dysphagia (disfā´jiə) *n.* (*Med.*) difficulty of swallowing. **dysphagic** (-faj´ik) *a.* [Gr. *phagein*, to eat]

dysphasia (disfā´ziə) *n.* (*Med.*) difficulty in speaking or understanding speech, caused by injury to or disease of the brain. **dysphasic** *a.* [Gr. *phasis*, speech]

dysphemism (dis´fəmizm) *n.* **1** the use of an offensive word or phrase in place of an inoffensive or mild one. **2** the offensive word or phrase used. **dysphemistic** (-mis´-) *a.* [after eu*phemism*]

dysphonia (disfō´niə) *n.* a difficulty in speaking arising from disease or malformation of the organs. [Gr. *dusphōnia*, harshness of sound (*phōnē*, sound)]

dysphoria (disfaw´riə) *n.* a morbid uneasiness; feeling unwell. **dysphoric** (-for´ik) *a.* [Gr. *pherein*, to bear]

dysplasia (displā´ziə) *n.* (*Med.*) abnormal growth of tissues. **dysplastic** (-plas´tik) *a.* [Gr. *plasis*, formation]

dyspnoea (dispnē´ə), (*N Am.*) **dyspnea** *n.* difficulty of breathing. **dyspnoeal** *a.* **dyspnoeic** *a.* [L, from Gr. *duspnoia* (*pnoē*, breathing)]

dysprosium (disprō´ziəm) *n.* a rare silvery-white metallic element, at. no. 66, chem. symbol Dy, of the rare earth group, used in laser materials etc. [Gr. *dysprositos*, difficult of access]

dysthymia (disthī´miə) *n.* (*Med.*) anxiety and depression. **dysthymiac** (-ak) *n.* a person who suffers from dysthymia. **dysthymic** *a.* [Gr. *dusthumos*, desponding (*thumos*, spirit)]

dystocia (distō´shə) *n.* (*Med.*) difficult childbirth. [Gr. *tokos*, childbirth]

dystopia (distō´piə) *n.* an imaginary wretched place, the opposite of a utopia. **dystopian** *a., n.*

dystrophy (dis´trəfi) *n.* **1** any of various disorders characterized by the wasting away of muscle tissue. **2** the condition of lake water when it is too acidic to support life. **dystrophic** (-trof´-) *a.* [Gr. *trophē*, nourishment]

dysuria (disū´riə), **dysury** (dis´-) *n.* difficulty and pain in passing urine. **dysuric** *a.* [OF *dissurie*, L *dysūria*, Gr. *dusouria* (*ouron*, urine)]

DZ *abbr.* Algeria (IVR).

dziggetai (dzig´itī) *n.* (*pl.* **dziggetais**) a variety of wild ass, *Equus hemionus*, somewhat resembling the mule, native to Central Asia. [Mongolian]

dzo (zhō, zō), **dzho, zho** *n.* (*pl.* **dzo, dzos, dzho, dzhos, zho, zhos**) a hybrid breed of Himalayan cattle developed from crossing the yak with common horned cattle. [Tibetan *mdso*]

E

E[1] (ē), **e** (*pl.* **Es, E's**) the fifth letter of the English and other versions of the Roman alphabet, corresponding to the Greek epsilon (Ε, ε). It has four principal sounds in stressed syllables: (1) high and long as in *me*, marked in this dictionary ē; (2) mid and short as in *men, set*, left unmarked, e; (3) central and long where historically an *r* followed as in *her*, marked œ; (4) front and diphthongized or long as in *there*, marked eə. In unstressed syllables it has two principal sounds: (1) reduced or indeterminate as in *camel, garment*, marked ə; (2) high and short as in *begin*, marked i. At the end of words it is usu. silent as in *mane, cave*, serving to indicate that the preceding syllable is long. After *c* and *g* it denotes that those letters are to be pronounced as soft, as *s* and *j* respectively. In conjunction with other vowels *e* also represents a variety of sounds, as in *death, ear, eerie, foetus, glue, health, pear, seize* etc. *~symbol* **1** the fifth of a series, the fifth highest in range, e.g. of marks, etc. **2** the fifth known quantity in an algebraic expression. **3** (*Mus.*) **a** the third note of the diatonic scale in C major. **b** the scale of composition in which the keynote is E. **4** (*Math.*) the basis of Naperian logarithms, approximately equalling 2.718.

E[2], **e** *abbr.* **1** East, Eastern. **2** Ecstasy (the drug). **3** Egyptian. **4** electron. **5** electronic. **6** (*Physics*) energy ($E = mc^2$). **7** English. **8** Europe, European. **E-free** *a.* (of a foodstuff) containing no food additives (with E numbers). **E-layer, E-region** *n.* a region of the ionosphere which is able to reflect medium-frequency radio waves. **e-mail, email** *n.* electronic mail. *~v.t.* **1** to send electronic mail to. **2** to send by electronic mail. **E number** *n.* a number preceded by the letter E denoting a certain food additive in accordance with EU regulations.

e- (i, e) *pref.* EX-, as in *elocution, emend, evade, evolve.*

ea. *abbr.* each.

each (ēch) *a., pron.* every one (of a limited number) considered separately. **each and every** *a.* all, every single. **each other** *pron.* one another, reciprocally (*They hate each other*). **each way** *adv.* in betting, for either a win or a place in the first three (*bet £5 each way*). **each-way** *a.* [OE *ǣlc*, from Gmc., ever alike]

eager (ē´gə) *a.* **1** excited by an ardent desire to attain, obtain or succeed (*eager to learn; eager for news*). **2** keen, enthusiastic. **3** ardent, vehement, impatient (*an eager wish*). **4** †sharp, acrid. **eager beaver** *n.* (*coll.*) a person who is always active or eager for work. **eagerly** *adv.* **eagerness** *n.* [A-F *egre*, OF *aigre*, L *ācer ācrem*, keen]

eagle (ē´gəl) *n.* **1** any of various large birds of prey of the family Accipitridae, esp. of the genus *Aquila*, such as the golden eagle. **2** a figure or symbol representing an eagle. **3** (*Her.*) a noble armorial bearing, emblematic of power and fortitude, and adopted as a national emblem by the USA, Prussia, Austria, Russia and France. **4** a military standard carrying a figure of an eagle. **5** a US colonel's shoulder insignia. **6** (*Hist.*) the emblem of a Roman or French ensign. **7** a golf score of two strokes under par for a particular hole. **8** a former US gold coin worth ten dollars. **9** a lectern in the form of an eagle with spread wings. *~v.t.* to achieve a golf score of two strokes under par for (a particular hole). **eagle eye** *n.* sharp sight, watchfulness. **eagle-eyed** *a.* **1** sharp-sighted as an eagle. **2** quick in understanding. **eagle owl** *n.* any of various large European or Asian owls with large ear tufts, esp. the European *Bubo bubo*. **eagle ray** *n.* a large ray of the family Myliobatidae with long, narrow pectoral fins. **eaglestone** *n.* a hollow oval nodule of clay ironstone (from the ancient belief that the eagle carried such a nodule to her nest to facilitate the laying of her eggs). **eaglet** (-lit) *n.* a young eagle. **eaglewood** *n.* **1** an Asian tree, *Aquilaria agallocha*, whose wood yields a fragrant resin used in perfumes. **2** the wood of this tree. [A-F *egle*, OF *aigle*, L *aquila*]

eagre (ē´gə) *n.* a tidal wave or bore in an estuary. [etym. unknown]

ealdorman (awl´dəmən) *n.* (*pl.* **ealdormen** (-mən)) the highest royal official of a shire in Anglo-Saxon times, responsible for law and order and for levying and leading the local fyrd.

-ean (ēən, iən), **-aean, -eian** *suf.* **1** belonging to, as in *European*. **2** like, as in *plebeian*. [-AN, embodying the end of the stem in L words in *-aeus, -eius*; Gr. words in *-aios, -eios*; and Eng. words in *-ey* and *-y*]

E. & O. E. *abbr.* errors and omissions excepted.

ear[1] (iə) *n.* **1** the organ of hearing and balance, consisting of the external ear, middle ear and internal ear. **2** the external part of the ear; the pinna. **3** the sense of hearing. **4** a delicate perception of the differences of sounds and judgement of harmony (*He has an ear for languages*). **5** notice or attention (esp. favourable consideration). **6** a small earlike projection from a larger body, usu. for support or attachment, such as the handle of a jug. **all ears** (*coll.*) listening carefully and with great interest. **inner ear** INNER. **in one ear and out the other** heard but making no lasting impression. **middle ear** MIDDLE. **out on one's ear** (*coll.*) sent away ignominiously. **to believe one's ears** BELIEVE. **to bring (down) about one's ears** to be responsible for causing oneself (trouble etc.). **to fall on deaf ears** (of a request etc.) to be ignored. **to give (an) ear** to listen (to). **to have/ keep one's ear to the ground** to be well informed about trends, rumours, opinions etc. **to have someone's ear** to be able to speak to and influence somebody. **to lend an ear** to listen (to). **to make a pig's ear of** PIG. **to play by ear** PLAY. **to play it by ear** PLAY. **to prick up one's ears 1** to begin to listen attentively. **2** (of dogs etc.) to raise the ears as if listening. **to set by the ears** to incite or cause strife between. **to turn a deaf ear to** TURN. **up to one's ears** (*coll.*) completely, so as to be overwhelmed (*up to her ears in debt*). **wet behind the ears** WET. **with a flea in one's ear** (*coll.*) with a sharp or contemptuous rebuke (*She sent me away with a flea in my ear*). **earache** *n.* pain in the middle or internal ear. **earbash** *v.t.* (*Austral., New Zeal., sl.*) to talk excessively to; to harangue. *~v.i.* to earbash someone. **earbasher** *n.* **earbashing** *n.* †**eardrop** *n.* **1** a jewel for hanging from the ear. **2** (*usu. in pl.*) a medicinal drop for inserting into the ear. **eardrum** *n.* the tympanum or tympanic membrane. **eared** *a.* having ears (*a long-eared owl*). **eared seal** *n.* any seal of the family Otariidae, with visible earflaps and hind limbs developed for locomotion on land. **earflap** *n.* **1** either of two flaps of cloth or fur attached to the sides of a hat, that can be let down to keep the ears warm. **2** (*Zool.*) a small flap of skin forming the external ear of some seals and similar animals. **earful** *n.* (*coll.*) **1** a severe and lengthy rebuke or reprimand (*to give somebody an earful*). **2** an excessively long conversation or talk. **earhole** *n.* the aperture of an ear. **earless** *a.* **earless seal** *n.* any seal of the family Phocidae, with no external earflaps and only rudimentary hind limbs. **earlike** *a.* **ear lobe** *n.* the soft lower part of the external ear. **earmark** *n.* **1** a mark on the ear by which a sheep or other animal can be identified. **2** any distinctive mark or feature. ~*v.t.* **1** to mark (a sheep etc.) by cutting or slitting the ear. **2** to set a distinctive mark upon. **3** to set aside (funds etc.) for a particular purpose. **earmuffs** *n.pl.* a pair of pads worn over the ears to protect them from cold, noise etc. **earphone** *n.* a part of a radio, telephone etc. which converts electrical signals into audible speech, worn or held close to the ear. **earpiece** *n.* the part of a telephone etc. that is held to the ear. **ear-piercing** *a.* painfully loud and shrill. ~*n.* the making of a small hole in the ear lobe from which an earring can be hung. **earplug** *n.* a piece of soft material placed in the ear to keep out sound, water etc. **earring** *n.* an ornament for the ear, usu. clipped onto or attached through the ear lobe. **ear shell** *n.* ABALONE. **earshot** *n.* hearing distance (*within earshot*; *out of earshot*). **ear-splitting** *a.* painfully loud. **earstopple** *n.* (*N Am.*) an earplug. **ear-trumpet** *n.* a trumpet-shaped tube to be held to the ear, formerly used as a hearing aid. **earwax** *n.* a waxlike substance secreted by the ear, cerumen. [OE *ēare* (cp. Dut. *oor*, Icel. *eyra*, G *Ohr*, L *auris*, Gr. *ous*)]

ear[2] (iə) *n.* a seed-bearing head of corn (*an ear of wheat*). ~*v.i.* to form ears (of corn). [OE *ēar*, pl. (cp. Dut. *aar*, Icel., Dan. and Swed. *ax*, G *Ähre*; cogn. with L *acus*, *aceris*, husk of corn)]

earing (iə´ring) *n.* (*Naut.*) a small line for fastening the corner of a sail to a yard in reefing. [see also EARRING (under EAR[1])]

earl (œl) *n.* a British nobleman ranking next below a marquess and next above a viscount, equivalent to a COUNT[2]. **belted earl** BELT. **earldom** *n.* the rank, title or position of an earl. **Earl Grey** *n.* a type of black tea flavoured with bergamot. **Earl Marshal** *n.* an English officer of state, head of the College of Heralds, with ceremonial duties on various royal occasions and jurisdiction in questions relating to arms and grants of arms. **Earl Palatine** *n.* (*Hist.*) an earl exercising royal authority within his domain. [OE *eorl*, a warrior (cp. Icel. *jarl*, *earl*, OS *erl*, a man)]

early (œ´li) *adv.* (*comp.* **earlier**, *superl.* **earliest**) **1** before the proper, expected or usual time (*The train arrived early*). **2** in good time (*Shop early for Christmas*). **3** soon after the beginning of a period (*Come early next week*). **4** quickly, promptly (*Reply early*). ~*a.* **1** before the proper, expected or usual time (*I was early for work*). **2** in good time (*We were early for the bus*). **3** soon after the beginning of a day, month etc. (*early evening*; *an early riser*). **4** happening or situated near the beginning of a period of development, existence etc. (*early settlers*; *at the earliest opportunity*). **5** primitive, in the distant past (*early man*). **6** quick, prompt (*early payment*). **7** occurring or relating to young childhood (*early learning*; *her early years*). **8** immature, of a person's younger years (*his early novels*). **9** ripening, flowering etc. before other similar plants (*early potatoes*). ~*n.* (*pl.* **earlies**) an early fruit or vegetable. **at the earliest** not before (*next week at the earliest*). **earliness** *n.* **early bird** *n.* (*coll.*) a person who gets up or arrives very early. **early closing** *n.* the British custom of shutting shops etc. on one afternoon of each week. **early-closing day** *n.* the day of early closing at a particular shop, town etc. **early day motion** *n.* a motion laid before the British House of Commons for discussion at an early date, usu. merely to draw attention to a matter without a full debate. **early days** *n.pl.* **1** early in the course of something, before it is clear how it will progress. **2** (*Austral.*, *New Zeal.*) during the settlement period in the 19th cent. **early door** *n.* admission to a theatre before the official time for opening on payment of an extra charge. **Early English** *n.*, *a.* **1** (*Archit.*) (of) the first of the pointed or Gothic styles of English architecture (12th–13th cent.), characterized by lancet windows, clustered pillars and vaulted roofs with moulded groins on the ribs only (*an Early-English church*). **2** (of) Old and Middle English. **early grave** *n.* a premature or untimely death (*He went to an early grave*). **early hours** *n.pl.* the very early morning. **early music** *n.* music from before the classical period, i.e. up to *c.* 1750. **early musician** *n.* **early night** *n.* an occasion when a person goes to bed early. **early on** *adv.* at an early stage (*early on in history*). **earlier on** *adv.* before. **early retirement** *n.* retirement from work by choice before the statutory retirement age. **early warning** *n.* advance notice of a problem or military attack. **early warning system** *n.* a system of advance notice, esp. of danger such as a nuclear attack. [OE *ǣrlīce* (*ǣr*, sooner, *līc*, like, *līce*, -LY[1])]

earn (œn) *v.t.* **1** to gain (money etc.) as the reward of labour. **2** (of an investment) to bring in (income) as interest or profit. **3** to merit, deserve or become entitled to as the result of any action or course of conduct (*You have earned a rest*; *He earned himself a name for duplicity*). **to earn an honest penny** HONEST. **earned income** *n.* income from paid employment. **earner** *n.* **1** a person who earns (*a wage earner*). **2** (*coll.*) a profitable job or business (*a nice little earner*). **earnings** *n.pl.* **1** money earned, wages. **2** profits from an investment. **earnings-related** *a.* (of a pension, benefit etc.) whose amount is based on present or past earnings. [OE *earnian* (cp. OHG *arnōn*, also G *ernten*, to reap, from *Ernte*, harvest)]

Usage note In standard English, the past tense and participle of *earn* is *earned*, not *earnt*.

---

earnest[1] (œ´nist) *a.* **1** serious, grave (*an earnest expression*). **2** serious, not trifling or joking (*an earnest plea*). **3** ardent, eager or zealous in the performance of any act or the pursuit of any object (*an earnest student*; *earnest endeavour*). **4** heartfelt, sincere (*my earnest desire*). ~*n.* seriousness, reality, not a pretence. **in earnest 1** seriously, sincerely, not jokingly (*I say this in earnest*). **2** with determination (*get down to work in earnest*). **earnestly** *adv.* **earnestness** *n.* [OE *eornost*, whence *eorneste*, a., adv. (cp. Dut. and G *ernst*)]

earnest[2] (œ´nist) *n.* **1** earnest-money. **2** a pledge, an assurance or token of something to come (*in earnest of my intentions*). **earnest-money** *n.* an instalment paid to seal a contract or agreement. [ME *ernes*, prob. a corr. of *erles*, *arles*, prob. from L *arr(h)a*, pledge]

EAROM (iə´rom) *abbr.* (*Comput.*) electronically alterable read-only memory.

earth (œth) *n.* **1** (*often* **(the) Earth**) the globe, the planet on which we live. **2** the ground, the visible surface of the globe (*to fall to earth*). **3** dry land, as opposed to the sea. **4** this world, as opposed to other possible worlds such as heaven or hell. **5** the people of the world (*The whole earth rejoiced*). **6** soil; the soft material in which plants grow, composed of clay, mould etc. **7** dead, inert matter. **8** the human body, as opposed to the soul or spirit. **9** the hole of a fox, badger etc. **10 a** plates or wires of an electric circuit, aerial etc. connected to the ground, providing a point of zero voltage or an escape for electrical surges. **b** the part of the ground where such an electrical connection is made. **11** an earthlike metallic oxide, such as alumina (*rare earth*; *alkaline earth*). ~*v.t.* **1** to complete a circuit by connecting (an electrical device) to the earth. **2** (*usu. with up*) to cover (plants, roots etc.) with earth as protection against cold, light etc. **3** to drive (a fox etc.) to its earth. **4** †to hide or place under the earth. ~*v.i.* (of a fox) to go to its earth, to go to ground. **down to earth** realistic, practical, sensible. **gone to earth** in hiding. **on earth 1** (*coll.*) **a** used as an intensifier after question words (*what on earth?*; *who on earth?*). **b** (*after superlatives*) in the world, of all (*the greatest show on earth*). **the earth** (*coll.*) an excessive amount, everything (*to want/cost the earth*). **to come back/ down to earth** to come back to reality from daydreams or fantasy. **to run to earth** RUN. **earthborn** *a.* **1** (*chiefly poet.*) born from or on the earth. **2** human, mortal. **earthbound** *a.* **1** moving towards the earth. **2** restricted to the earth. **3** fixed or fastened in or to the earth. **4** (*fig.*) fixed on earthly objects; dull, lacking in imagination or refinement. **earthcloset** *n.* a lavatory in which earth is used to cover the excreta. **earthen** *a.* made of earth, baked clay or similar substance. **earthenware** *n.* **1** coarse pottery made of baked clay (*an earthenware jug*). **2** vessels made of earthenware. **earth-friendly** *a.* environment-friendly, nonpolluting. **earthlight** *n.* earthshine. **earthlike** *a.* **earthling** (-ling) *n.* **1** (esp. in science fiction) an inhabitant of the earth, a human being. **2** †an earthly-minded person. **earthly** *a.* (*comp.* **earthlier,** *superl.* **earthliest**) **1** of or relating to this world, terrestrial. **2** of or relating to this life, as opposed to heaven or a future life. **3** mortal, human (*earthly remains*). **4** carnal, material or materialistic, as opposed to spiritual. **5** (*coll.*) possible, conceivable (*What earthly use is it?*). **not an earthly** (*coll.*) not a chance. **earthliness** *n.* **earthly paradise** *n.* in the Bible, the Garden of Eden, the abode of Adam and Eve before the Fall. **earthman** *n.* (*pl.* **earthmen**) (esp. in science fiction) an inhabitant of the earth, a human being. **earth mother** *n.* **1** in mythology, a female deity personifying the earth and viewed as the source of fertility. **2** a sensual and fertile woman. **earth mover** *n.* a large vehicle for digging and moving earth. **earth-moving** *n.* removal of earth in road-building etc. **earthnut** *n.* **1 a** a perennial umbelliferous plant of Europe and Asia, *Canopodium majus*, with edible dark-brown tubers, also called pignut. **b** the tuber of this plant. **2** any of various plants with roundish edible roots or tubers, such as the truffle. **3** a peanut. **earthpig** *n.* AARDVARK. **earth pillar** *n.* a column of soft rock or clay protected from erosion by a stone cap. **earthquake** *n.* **1** a movement of a portion of the earth's crust produced by volcanic forces. **2** (*fig.*) a major social, political or other disturbance. **earth science** *n.* any science dealing with the earth or its atmosphere, e.g. geography, geology, meteorology. **earth-shaking** *a.* (*coll.*) momentous, of profound or devastating effect. **earth-shakingly** *adv.* **earth-shattering** *a.* (*coll.*) earthshaking. **earth-shatteringly** *adv.* **earth shifter** *n.* an earth mover. **earth-shifting** *n.* **earthshine** *n.* (*Astron.*) earthlight, faint light visible upon the dark part of the moon, caused by light reflected from the earth. **earthstar** *n.* any of various woodland fungi of the genus *Geastrum*, esp. *G. triplex*, with a brown, onion-shaped body which splits to form a star shape when releasing spores. **earth tremor** *n.* a slight earthquake. **earthward** *a., adv.* moving towards the earth. **earthwards** *adv.* **earth wax** *n.* OZOCERITE. **earthwork** *n.* **1** mounds, ramparts etc. made of earth used for defensive purposes. **2** embankments, cuttings etc. in civil engineering. **earthworm** *n.* **1** a burrowing annelid worm, esp. of the genus *Lumbricus* or *Allolobophora*. **2** a grovelling or sordid person. **earthy** *a.* (*comp.* **earthier,** *superl.* **earthiest**) **1** consisting of, composed of or resembling earth or soil. **2** coarse, crude, unrefined (*earthy humour*). **3** robust, lusty. **earthily** *adv.* **earthiness** *n.* [OE *eorthe* (cp. Dut. *aarde*, Icel. *jörth*, Goth. *airtha*, G *Erde*)]

earwig (iə´wig) *n.* **1** any of various insects of the order Dermaptera, esp. *Forficula auricularia*, with curved forceps at its tail. **2** (*N Am.*) a small centipede. ~*v.i.* (*pres.p.* **earwigging,** *past, p.p.* **earwigged**) (*coll.*) to eavesdrop. ~†*v.t.* to attempt to influence by private importuning. **earwigging** *n.* (*coll.*) a serious scolding or reprimand. [OE *ēar-wicga*, ear-beetle, insect (*wicga*, from *wegan*, to move, allied to L *vehere, vec-*, to carry), from the erroneous belief that it crept into the ear]

ease (ēz) *n.* **1** a state of freedom from labour, trouble or pain. **2** freedom from constraint or formality. **3** facility, readiness. **4** absence of effort. ~*v.t.* **1** to free from pain, anxiety, labour or trouble. **2** to relieve or free from a burden. **3** to make easier or lighter. **4** to assuage, to mitigate. **5** to render less difficult. **6** to make looser, to relax, to adjust. **7** (*Naut.*) to slacken (a rope, sail, speed etc.). ~*v.i.* to relax one's efforts or exertions. **at (one's) ease** in a state free from anything likely to disturb, annoy or cause anxiety. **ease her** (*Naut.*) the command to reduce the engine speed of a steamer. **ill at ease** ILL. **to ease away 1** (*Naut.*) to slacken (a rope etc.) gradually. **2** to become less oppressive. **to ease down** to ease away. **to ease off** to ease away. **to ease oneself 1** to empty the bowels. **2** to urinate. **to stand at ease** (*Mil.*) to stand with the legs apart and hands behind the back. **easeful** *a.* promoting ease, quiet or repose; comfortable. **easement** *n.* **1** the act of easing; alleviation, mitigation. **2** a convenience. **3** (*Law*) a liberty, right or privilege, without profit, which one proprietor has in or through the estate of another, as a right of way, light, air etc. **easer** *n.* [OF *aise*, etym. uncertain (cp. It. *agio*)]

easel (ē´zəl) *n.* a wooden frame used to support a picture, blackboard, open book etc. [Dut. *ezel*, a little ass (cp. G *Esel*)]

easily, easiness EASY.

east (ēst) *a.* **1** situated towards the point where the sun rises when in the equinoctial. **2** coming from this direction. ~*n.* **1** the point of the compass where the sun rises at the equinox; 90° to the right of north. **2** the eastern part of a country. **3** the countries to the east of Europe. **4** the east wind. **5** (**East**) in bridge, a player in a position to the left of 'North'. ~*adv.* towards, at or near the quarter of the rising sun. ~*v.i.* **1** to move towards the east. **2** to veer from the north or south towards the east. **3** (*reflex.*) to find one's east, to orientate oneself. **eastbound** *a.* travelling eastwards. **East End** *n.* the east (and unfashionable) end of London or of other cities. **East-Ender** *n.* **easterly** *a.* **1** situated or in the direction of the east. **2** looking towards the east. **3** coming from the east, or parts lying towards the east; blowing from the east. ~*adv.* **1** towards the direction of the east. **2** in or from the east. ~*n.* (*pl.* **easterlies**) a wind from the east. **East Germanic** *n., a.* (of) the group of Germanic languages represented by Gothic, and some like Burgundian and Vandal of which mere vestiges survive. **East Indies** *n.pl.* (*Hist.*) the countries of SE Asia; the islands of the Malay archipelago. **East Indiaman** *n.* (*pl.* **East Indiamen**) (*Hist.*) a ship sailing to and from SE Asia. **East Indian** *a.* **easting** *n.* **1** (*Naut.*) distance traversed on an easterly course. **2** distance east of a given meridian. **3** movement to the east. **east-north-east** *n.* the point of the compass halfway between east and north-east. **east-south-east** *n.* the point of the compass halfway between east and south-east. **eastward** *a., adv.* towards the east. ~*n.* an eastward direction; the parts lying towards the east. **eastward ho!** HO. **eastwardly** *a., adv.* **eastwards** *adv.* **East–West** *a.* of or relating to relations, talks etc. between eastern and western countries. **east wind** *n.* a wind coming from an easterly direction. [OE *ēast*, adv., in the east, eastwards, *ēastan*, from the east (cp. Dut. *oost*, Icel. *austr*, G *osten*)]

Easter (ēs´tə) *n.* **1** the festival in commemoration of the resurrection of Christ, taking place on the Sunday after the full moon that falls on or next after 21 Mar. **2** the period around Easter. **Easter Day** *n.* Easter Sunday. **Easter dues, Easter offerings** *n.pl.* payments or offerings to the parson of a parish at Easter. **Easter egg** *n.* **1** an egg-shaped present, often made of chocolate, given at Easter. **2** an egg boiled hard and stained or gilded, to symbolize the resurrection. **Easter eve** *n.* the day before Easter Day. **Easter Sunday** *n.* the Sunday of the festival of Easter. **Eastertide** *n.* **1** the time round about Easter. **2** the time between Easter and Whitsun. **Easter week** *n.* the week beginning with Easter Sunday. [*OE ēastre* (*Eastre, Eostre*, Gmc. dawn-goddess)]

eastern (ēs´tən) *a.* **1** situated in the east. **2** of or relating to the east. **3** blowing from the east. **4** (**Eastern**) of or relating to the Far East, Middle East, or Near East. **Eastern Church** *n.* **1** the Christian Church in eastern Europe or the Middle East. **2** the Orthodox Church. **Eastern Empire** *n.* the eastern division of the Roman Empire having Constantinople as capital, after the division into an Eastern and Western Empire by Theodosius in 395. **easterner** *n.* **1** an inhabitant of the eastern part of any country or region. **2** in the US, a native or inhabitant of the eastern or New England States. **eastern hemisphere** *n.* the hemisphere of the earth containing Europe, Africa and Asia. **easternmost** *a.* **Eastern Orthodox Church** *n.* the Orthodox Church. **Eastern question** *n.* the political question in the late 19th and early 20th cents. as to the distribution of political power in Eastern Europe, esp. those parts under the actual or nominal rule of Turkey. **Eastern (Standard) Time** *n.* **1** the standard time established for the eastern US and parts of Canada. **2** the standard time established for eastern Australia. [OE *ēasterne*]

easy (ē´zi) *a.* (*comp.* **easier,** *superl.* **easiest**) **1** not difficult, not requiring great labour, exertion or effort. **2** free from pain, trouble, care or discomfort. **3** in comfortable circumstances, well-to-do. **4** at ease. **5** not strict. **6** free from embarrassment, constraint or affectation. **7** smooth, flowing, fluent. **8** easily persuaded, compliant. **9** indulgent, not exacting. **10** (of money) not hard to get (as distinct from *tight*). **11** fitting loosely. **12** slight, trivial. *~adv.* in an easy manner. *~n.* a relaxation of effort or a pause in rowing. **easy!** move or go gently. **easy ahead!** move or steam at a moderate speed. **easy all!** stop rowing. **easy as pie** (*coll.*) very easy. **easy as winking** (*coll.*) very easy. **easy come easy go** what is obtained easily is just as easily spent or lost. **easy does it!** move or go gently. **easy of access** easy to get to or into. **easy on the ear** agreeable to listen to. **easy on the eye** agreeable to look at. **honours easy** HONOUR. **I'm easy** I have no particular preference or strong opinion. **of easy virtue** (of a woman) promiscuous. **stand easy!** (an order to) stand at ease. **to go easy** to be careful, to slow down. **to go easy on/ with** to use only a little of. **to take it easy** to take one's time, to relax. **easily** *adv.* **easiness** *n.* **easy care** *a.* (of fabrics) not needing any special treatment during washing etc. **easy chair** *n.* an armchair stuffed and padded for resting or reclining in. **easy circumstances** *n.pl.* prosperity. **easygoing** *a.* **1** taking things in an easy manner. **2** indolent. **3** moving easily. **easy listening** *a.* (of music) popular, requiring no effort of the listener. *~n.* this category of music. **easy mark, easy meat, easy touch** *n.* (*coll.*) a gullible person. **easy money** *n.* (*coll.*) money acquired without much effort. **easy-osy** (-ōzi) *a.* indolent, easy-going. **easy over** *a.* (*N Am.*) (of a fried egg) done on both sides. **easy-peasy** *a.* (*coll.*) childishly easy or uncomplicated. **Easy Street** *n.* (*coll.*) a position of financial good fortune or security. **easy terms** *n.pl.* a hire purchase arrangement in which the payments are not too onerous. [OF *aisié* (F *aisé*), p.p. of *aiser*, to EASE]

EAT *abbr.* (East Africa) Tanzania (IVR).

eat (ēt) *v.t.* (*past* **ate** (āt, et), *p.p.* **eaten** (ē´tən)) **1** to chew and swallow as food. **2** to devour. **3** to destroy by eating. **4** (*fig.*) to corrode. **5** to consume. **6** to wear away, to waste. **7** (*coll.*) to vex. *~v.i.* **1** to take food. **2** to be eaten. **3** to taste, to relish. **to eat away** to destroy, to rust, to corrode. **to eat crow** CROW[1]. **to eat dirt** DIRT. **to eat humble pie** HUMBLE[1]. **to eat in** to eat at home or where one is staying. **to eat into** to corrode. **to eat like a horse** HORSE. **to eat one's hat** (*coll.*) to admit that one's prediction has been mistaken. **to eat one's heart out 1** to pine away. **2** to be extremely envious. **to eat one's words** to retract what one has said. **to eat out** to eat in a restaurant, café or hotel. **to eat out of house and home** to ruin (someone) by consuming all they have. **to eat out of someone's hand** to be totally compliant or willing to obey a person. **to eat someone's salt** SALT. **to eat up 1** to eat completely, to finish. **2** to consume in (unnecessarily) large quantities. **3** to absorb. **eatable** *a.* fit to be eaten. *~n.* **1** anything fit or proper for food. **2** (*pl.*) the solid materials of a meal. **eater** *n.* **1** a person who eats. **2** a fruit suitable for eating uncooked. **eatery** *n.* (*pl.* **eateries**) (*coll.*) a restaurant, café etc. **eating** *a.* **1** (esp. of apples) suitable for eating without being previously cooked. **2** of or relating to food or eating. **eating house** *n.* **1** a restaurant. **2** a shop where provisions are sold ready for eating. **eats** *n.pl.* (*coll.*) food. [OE *etan* (cp. Dut. *eten*, G *essen*; also L *edere*, Gr. *edein*)]

EAU *abbr.* (East Africa) Uganda (IVR).

eau (ō) *n.* water (used in compounds to designate various spirituous waters and perfumes). **eau-de-Cologne** (dəkəlōn´) *n.* a scent consisting of a solution of volatile oils in alcohol, orig. made in Cologne. **eau-de-Nil** (dənēl´) *n., a.* (of) a pale greenish colour, said to be like Nile water. **eau de vie** (dəvē´) *n.* brandy. [F]

eaves (ēvz) *n.pl.* the lower edge of the roof which projects beyond the wall, and serves to throw off the water which falls on the roof. **eavesdrop** *n.* an act of eavesdropping. *~v.i.* (*pres.p.* **eavesdropping,** *past, p.p.* **eavesdropped**) to listen secretly so as to overhear confidences. **eavesdropper** *n.* [OE *efes*, sing., prob. cogn. with OVER (now taken as pl. and *eave* sometimes used as sing.)]

EAZ *abbr.* East Africa Zanzibar, i.e. Tanzania (IVR).

ebb (eb) *n.* **1** the flowing back or going out of the tide. **2** the draining away of flood water. **3** decline, failure, decay. *~v.i.* **1** to flow back. **2** to recede, to decline, to decay. **at a low ebb** weak, in a state of decline. **ebb and flow** the continual improvement and deterioration of circumstances etc. **on the ebb 1** receding. **2** declining. **to ebb and flow 1** to rise and fall. **2** to increase and decrease, to improve and deteriorate. **ebb tide** *n.* the retiring tide. [OE *ebba*, the ebb, whence *ebbian*, to ebb (cp. Dut. *ebbe, eb*)]

EBCDIC (eb´sidik) *n.* (*Comput.*) a code for alphanumeric characters. [acronym for *e*xtended *b*inary-*c*oded *d*ecimal *i*nterchange *c*ode]

Ebola (ebō´lə) *n.* a virus occurring in parts of Africa, infection with which causes a serious illness.

ebonics (ibon´iks) *n.* American black street slang. [blend of EBONY, PHONICS (under PHONIC)]

ebony (eb´əni) *n.* (*pl.* **ebonies**) **1** the wood of various species of *Diospyros*, noted for its solidity and black colour, capable of a high polish, and largely used for mosaic work and inlaying. **2** a tree of the genus *Diospyros*. *~a.* **1** made of ebony. **2** intensely black. **ebon** *a.* (*formal*) **1** consisting of or like ebony. **2** black. *~n.* ebony. **ebonist** *n.* a worker in ebony. **ebonite** (-nīt) *n.* vulcanite. **ebonize, ebonise** *v.t.* to make the colour of ebony. [OF and L *ebenus*, Gr. *ebenos* (prob. of eastern origin)]

ebracteate (ibrak´tiāt) *a.* (*Bot.*) without bracts. [E-, BRACT, -ATE[2]]

EBRD *abbr.* European Bank for Reconstruction and Development.

ebriety (ibrī´əti) *n.* drunkenness, intoxication. **ebriose** (-ōs), **ebrious** (-əs) *a.* **1** drunk. **2** addicted to drink. **3** characteristic of drunkenness. **ebriosity** (ēbrios´-) *n.* **1** habitual drunkenness. **2** (*fig.*) exhilaration. [L *ēbriātus*, p.p. of *ēbriāre*, to intoxicate, from *ēbrius*, drunk]

EBU *abbr.* European Broadcasting Union.

ebullient (ibŭl´yənt) *a.* **1** overflowing with high spirits or enthusiasm, exuberant. **2** boiling (over). **ebullience, ebulliency** *n.* **ebulliently** *adv.* **ebullition** (ebəlish´ən) *n.* **1** the boiling or bubbling of a liquid. **2** effervescence. **3** a sudden outburst (of feeling). [L *ēbulliens -ntem*, pres.p. of *ēbullīre* (*bullīre*, to boil)]

eburnation (ebənā´shən), *n.* an excessive deposition of bony matter, sometimes found in a diseased state of the joints. [L *eburnus*, ivory]

EC *abbr.* **1** East Central. **2** Ecuador (IVR). **3** European Commission. **4** European Community. **5** executive committee.

ecad (ē´kad) *n.* in ecology, an organism which has been modified by the environment. [ECO-, -AD[2]]

écarté (ākah´tā) *n.* **1** a game of cards played by two people with 32 cards. **2** a ballet position in which one arm and leg are extended. [F, from *écarter*, to discard]

ecbolic (ekbol´ik) *n.* an ecbolic drug. ~*a.* stimulating uterine contractions and promoting the expulsion of the foetus. [Gr. *ekbolē*, a throwing out]

Ecce Homo (eki hō´mō) *n.* a painting or sculpture representing Christ crowned with thorns, as before Pilate (John xix.5). [L, behold the man]

eccentric (iksen´trik) *a.* **1** peculiar or odd in manner or character. **2** erratic, irregular, anomalous. **3** departing from the usual practice or established forms or laws. **4** not placed centrally. **5** (*Geom.*) (of circles and spheres) not having the same centre, not concentric. ~*n.* **1** a person of odd or peculiar habits. **2** an oddity. **3** a mechanical contrivance for converting circular into reciprocating rectilinear motion, such as that operating the slide-valve of a steam engine or the cam in an internal-combustion engine. **eccentrically** *adv.* **eccentricity** (eksəntris´iti) *n.* (*pl.* **eccentricities**) **1** whimsical conduct or character. **2** departure from what is usual, regular or established. **3** an oddity, a peculiarity. **4** the state of not being concentric. **5** deviation from a central position. **6** (*Astron.*) a measure of the departure from circularity of the orbit of a planet. [late L *eccentricus*, Gr. *ekkentros* (*ek*, out, *kentron*, CENTRE)]

ecchymosis (ekimō´sis) *n.* (*pl.* **ecchymoses** (-sēz)) a bruise, a discoloration of the skin due to the effusion of blood from blood vessels ruptured by a blow. [Gr. *ek*, out, *chumos*, CHYME]

Eccles. *abbr.* Ecclesiastes.

Eccles cake (ek´əlz kāk) *n.* a small cake made of pastry and filled with dried fruit. [*Eccles*, a town in Lancashire]

ecclesiastic (iklēzias´tik) *n.* a person in holy orders, a member of the clergy. ~*a.* ecclesiastical. **ecclesia** (iklē´ziə) *n.* **1** an assembly of free citizens, esp. the legislative assembly of ancient Athens. **2** a church; a religious assembly, a congregation. **ecclesial** *a.* **ecclesiastical** *a.* of or relating to the Church or the clergy. **ecclesiastically** *adv.* **ecclesiasticism** (-sizm) *n.* [med. L, from Gr. *ekklēsia*, from *ekkalein* (*ek*, out, *kalein*, to call)]

ecclesiolatry (iklēziol´ətri) *n.* excessive reverence for ecclesiastical forms and traditions. **ecclesiolater** *n.*

ecclesiology (iklēziol´əji) *n.* **1** the study of all matters connected with churches, esp. church architecture, decoration and antiquities. **2** theology in relation to the Church. **ecclesiological** (-loj´-) *a.* **ecclesiologist** *n.*

Ecclus. *abbr.* Ecclesiasticus.

eccrine (ek´rin, -rīn) *a.* denoting a gland that secretes externally, esp. the sweat glands. **eccrinology** (-nol´-) *n.* the branch of physiology relating to secretions. [Gr. *ek*, out of, *krīnein*, to separate, secrete]

ecdysis (ek´disis, ekdī´sis) *n.* the casting of the skin, as by snakes, insects and crustaceans. [Gr. *ekdusis*, from *ekduein* (*ek*, off, *duein*, to put)]

ECG *abbr.* **1** electrocardiogram. **2** electrocardiograph.

echelon (esh´əlon) *n.* **1** (a group of persons in) a level, stage or grade of an organization etc. **2** the arrangement of troops, ships, aircraft etc. as in the form of steps, with parallel divisions one in advance of another. ~*v.t.* to form in echelon. [F, from *échelle*, L *scāla*, a ladder]

echeveria (echiviə´riə) *n.* a succulent plant of the genus *Echeveria*, found in Central and S America. [M. *Echeveri*, 19th-cent. Mexican botanical artist]

echidna (ikid´nə) *n.* a mammal of the genus *Tachyglossus* or *Zaglossus*, popularly known as the spiny anteater, which lays eggs instead of giving birth to live young like other mammals. [Gr., viper]

echinoderm (ikī´nədœm) *n.* any individual of the Echinodermata, a phylum of animals containing the sea urchins, starfish and sea cucumbers. **echinodermal** (-dœ´məl), **echinodermatous** *a.* [Gr. *echīnos*, sea urchin, hedgehog, *derma*, skin, pl. *dermata*]

echinus (ikī´nəs) *n.* (*pl.* **echini** (-nī), **echinuses**) **1** a sea urchin of the genus *Echinus*. **2** the convex projecting moulding below the abacus of an Ionic column and in the cornices of Roman architecture. **echinate** (-nāt), **echinated** *a.* having numerous rigid hairs or straight prickles; bristly or spiny like a hedgehog or sea urchin. **echinite** (-nīt) *n.* (*Geol.*) a fossil echinoderm or sea urchin. **echinoid** (-noid) *n.* a sea urchin. ~*a.* like a sea urchin. [L, *echīnus*, a hedgehog; see ECHINODERM]

echo (ek´ō) *n.* (*pl.* **echoes**) **1** the repetition of a sound caused by its being reflected from some obstacle. **2** a sound reflected from some obstacle; a reflected radio or radar beam. **3** a close imitation in words or sentiment; a hearty response. **4** a slavish imitator. **5** a reminder of something else. **6** (*Mus.*) a repetition of a phrase in a softer tone. **7** repetition of the last syllables of a verse in the next line, so as to give a continuous sense. **8** in whist etc., a response to a partner's call for trumps. ~*v.i.* (*3rd pers. sing. pres.* **echoes**, *pres.p.* **echoing**, *past*, *p.p.* **echoed**) **1** to give an echo; to resound. **2** to be sounded back. ~*v.t.* **1** to return or send back (as a sound). **2** to repeat with approval. **3** to imitate closely. **echocardiogram** *n.* the record produced by an echocardiograph. **echocardiograph** *n.* (*Med.*) a machine using ultrasound to investigate the heart for disease. **echocardiographer** *n.* **echocardiography** *n.* **echo chamber** *n.* a room whose walls echo sound for recording or radio effects or for measuring acoustics. **echoencephalogram** *n.* (*Med.*) the record produced by encephalography. **echoencephalography** *n.* the use of ultrasound to investigate brain tissues. **echoer** *n.* **echoey** (ek´ōi) *a.* **1** like an echo. **2** full of echoes. **echogram** *n.* a recording made by an echo sounder. **echograph** *n.* a machine which records echograms. **echoic** *a.* **1** of, relating to or like an echo. **2** imitative, onomatopoeic. **echoically** *adv.* **echoism** *n.* onomatopoeia. **echolalia** (-lā´liə) *n.* (*Psych.*) the automatic repetition of another person's utterances, a symptom of some forms of mental illness. **echoless** *a.* **echolocation** *n.* finding the position of objects by means of reflected sound waves. **echometer** (ikom´itə) *n.* an instrument for measuring the duration of sounds. **echo sounder** *n.* (*Naut.*) an apparatus for sounding the depth of water beneath the keel of a ship. **echo-sounding** *n.* **echo verse** *n.* verse in which the last syllable of each line is repeated in the next. [L, from Gr. *ēchō* (cp. *ēchos*, *ēchē*, sound)]

echovirus (ek´ōvīrəs), **ECHO virus** *n.* (*pl.* **echoviruses,**

ECHO viruses) (*Med.*) any of a group of viruses which can cause meningitis or intestinal or respiratory illnesses. [acronym for *e*nteric *c*ytopathogenic *h*uman *o*rphan; see VIRUS]

echt (ekht) *a.* genuine, authentic. [G]

eclair (ikleə´) *n.* an iced, finger-shaped cream-filled pastry. [F, lightning]

†**éclaircissement** (ikleəsēs´mā) *n.* an explanation or clearing up of a subject of dispute or misunderstanding. [F, from *éclaircir*, to clear up]

eclampsia (iklamp´siə) *n.* (*Med.*) convulsions or fits, particularly of the type that occur with acute toxaemia in pregnancy. **eclamptic** (-tik) *a.* [Gr. *ek*, out, *lampein*, to shine]

éclat (āklah´) *n.* 1 brilliant success. 2 acclamation, applause. 3 splendour, striking effect. [F, from *éclater*, OHG *skleizan*, to burst into fragments]

eclectic (iklek´tik) *a.* 1 broad, not exclusive. 2 selecting, choosing, picking out at will from the (best of) doctrines, teachings etc. of others. 3 containing or consisting of selections from the works of others. ~*n.* 1 a person who derives opinions, tastes or practical methods from various sources. 2 a philosopher who borrows doctrines from various schools. **eclectically** *adv.* **eclecticism** (-tisizm) *n.* [Gr. *eklektikos* (*eklegein*, see ECLOGUE)]

eclipse (iklips´) *n.* 1 the total or partial obscuration of the light from a heavenly body by the passage of another body between it and the eye or between it and the source of its light. 2 a temporary failure or obscuration. 3 a loss of brightness, glory, honour or reputation. 4 a moulting phase during which a bird's distinctive markings are obscured. ~*v.t.* 1 to cause an eclipse of (a heavenly body) by passing between it and the spectator or between it and its source of light. 2 to intercept the light of, to obscure. 3 to outshine, surpass, excel. ~*v.i.* 1 to suffer an eclipse. 2 to be eclipsed. **in eclipse** 1 having been outshone, in decline. 2 (of a bird) having lost its distinctive plumage. **eclipsing binary** *n.* (*Astron.*) a binary star whose components eclipse each other as they pass in front of one another. **ecliptic** (-tik) *a.* 1 of, constituting or relating to the sun's apparent path in the sky. 2 of or relating to an eclipse. ~*n.* 1 the apparent path of the sun round the earth. 2 the plane passing through the sun's centre which contains the orbit of the earth. 3 a great circle on the terrestrial globe answering to, and falling within, the plane of the celestial ecliptic. [OF, from L *eclipsis*, Gr. *ekleipsis*, from *ekleipein* (*ek*, out of, *leipein*, to leave)]

eclogue (ek´log) *n.* an idyll or pastoral poem, esp. one containing dialogue. [L *ecloga*, Gr. *eklogē*, from *eklegein* (*ek*, out of, *legein*, to pick)]

eclosion (iklō´zhən) *n.* emergence, esp. of a larva from an egg or of an insect from a pupa-case. [F *éclosion*, from *éclore*, to hatch]

eco- (ē´kō, ek´ō) *comb. form* concerned with ecology, habitat or the environment. [Gr. *oikos*, a house]

ecocide (ē´kōsīd, ek´-) *n.* the destruction of an environment, or of aspects of an environment. **ecocidal** (-sī´dəl) *a.*

ecoclimate (ē´kōklīmət, ek´-) *n.* the climate of an area, perceived as of ecological importance.

ecofreak (ē´kōfrēk, ek´-) *n.* (*coll.*) a person who attaches (too much) importance to the well-being of the environment.

eco-friendly (ē´kōfrendli, ek´-) *a.* not damaging to the environment.

ecolabel (ē´kōlābəl, ek´-) *n.* a label on a food or household product asserting that the product contains nothing damaging to the environment. **ecolabelling**, (*N Am.*) **ecolabeling** *n.*

E. coli (ē kō´lī) *abbr.* Escherichia coli, a bacterium causing food poisoning.

ecology (ikol´əji), **oecology** *n.* 1 the branch of biology dealing with the relations between organisms and their environment. 2 the study of the relations between people and their environment, human ecology. **ecological** (ēkəloj´-, ek-) *a.* **ecologically** *adv.* **ecologist** *n.*

Econ. *abbr.* Economics.

econometrics (ikonəmet´riks) *n.* statistical and mathematical analysis of economic theories. **econometric** *a.* **econometrical** *a.* **econometrician** (-mətrish´ən) *n.* **econometrist** (-met´rist) *n.* [see METRE[1]]

economic (ēkənom´ik, ek-) *a.* 1 relating to the science of economics. 2 of or relating to industrial concerns or commerce. 3 maintained for the sake of profit or for the production of wealth. 4 capable of yielding a profit, financially viable. 5 frugal, thrifty, economical. 6 practical in application. **economical** *a.* 1 characterized by economic management; careful, frugal, thrifty. 2 economic. **economically** *adv.* **economic geography** *n.* the branch of geography concerned with the geographical distribution of resources and their use. **economic geology** *n.* the study of the rocks and minerals that are of use to mankind, and their geological relations. **economic refugee** *n.* a person who seeks refuge in another country because of poverty rather than persecution. **economics** *n.* 1 the science of the production and distribution of wealth, political economy. 2 the financial aspects of an activity, business etc. 3 (*as pl.*) the condition of a country, community or individual, with regard to material prosperity. **economic zone** *n.* a coastal area which a country claims as its own territory for purposes of fishing etc. [L *oeconomicus*, Gr. *oikonomikos*, see ECONOMY]

Usage note The meanings of the adjectives *economic* and *economical* overlap, but in general *economic* refers to economics, and *economical* refers to thrift or frugality. The corresponding negatives in *un-* are similarly distinguished.

economy (ikon´əmi) *n.* (*pl.* **economies**) 1 the totality of goods and services produced and consumed by a community or state; the wealth or financial resources of a community etc. 2 an organized or formalized system for the production and consumption of wealth. 3 the management, regulation and government of an economy. 4 a frugal and judicious use or expenditure of money or resources; carefulness, frugality. 5 (*usu. pl.*) a saving or reduction of expense. 6 careful and judicious use of anything, as of time. 7 the disposition, arrangement or plan of any work. 8 †the management of the affairs of a household. **economies of scale** *n.pl.* the savings that are possible when operating on a large scale. **economist** *n.* 1 a person skilled in the science of economics. 2 a person who manages with economy. **economize**, **economise** *v.i.* to manage domestic or financial affairs with economy. ~*v.t.* 1 to use, administer or expend with economy. 2 to use sparingly, to turn to the best account. **economization** (-zā´shən) *n.* **economizer** *n.* **economy class** *n.* the cheapest class of travel, with no luxuries. **economy-size** *a.* of a large size offering a proportionately lower cost. [L *oeconomia*, Gr. *oikonomia*, from *oikonomein*, to manage a household (*oikos*, a house, *nemein*, to deal out)]

écorché (ākawshā´) *n.* an anatomical figure with the muscular system exposed for the purpose of study. [F, p.p. of *écorcher*, to flay]

ECOSOC *abbr.* United Nations Economic and Social Council.

ecospecies (ē´kōspēshiz, ek´-) *n.* (*pl.* **ecospecies**) a taxonomic species regarded as an ecological unit.

ecosphere (ē´kōsfiə, ek´-) *n.* 1 the parts of the universe, esp. the earth, where life can exist. 2 the biosphere.

écossaise (ākosez´) *n.* **1** a Scottish dance in duple time. **2** the music to it. [F, fem. of *écossais*, Scottish]
ecosystem (ē´kōsistəm, ek´-) *n.* a system consisting of a community of organisms and its environment.
ecoterrorism (ēkōter´ərizm, ek-) *n.* terrorist acts threatened or carried out in order to help environmentalist causes. **ecoterrorist** *n.*
ecotourism (ēkōtuə´rizm, ek-) *n.* tourism managed on a small scale and in environmentally friendly ways. **ecotourist** *n.*
ecotype (ē´kotīp, ek´-) *n.* (*Biol.*) a distinctive group within a species which has adapted to its particular environment.
écraseur (ākrazœ´) *n.* an instrument for removing tumours etc. without effusion of blood. [F, a crusher, from *écraser*, to crush]
ecru (ek´roo, ākrü´) *a.* of the colour of unbleached linen. ~*n.* this colour. [F, raw, unbleached]
ECS *abbr.* European Communications Satellite.
ECSC *abbr.* European Coal and Steel Community.
ecstasy (ek´stəsi) *n.* (*pl.* **ecstasies**) **1** a state of mental exaltation. **2** excessive emotion, rapture, excessive delight, or excessive grief, distress or pain. **3** prophetic or poetic frenzy. **4** a trance. **5** (**Ecstasy**) methylenedioxymethamphetamine (MDMA), a synthetic stimulant and hallucinogenic drug based on amphetamine. **6** a morbid state of the nervous system in which the mind is completely absorbed by one idea. **7** †madness, distraction. **ecstasize, ecstasise** *v.t.* to fill with ecstasy, to enrapture. ~*v.i.* to go into ecstasies. **ecstatic** (-stat´-) *a.* **1** of, relating to or producing ecstasy; ravishing, entrancing, rapturous. **2** subject to ecstasy. **3** ravished, entranced. **ecstatically** *adv.* [OF *extasie*, med. L *ecstasis*, Gr. *ekstasis* (*ek*, out, *stasis*, a standing, from *histanai*, to place)]
ECT *abbr.* electroconvulsive therapy.
ecthyma (ekthī´mə) *n.* a skin disease characterized by an eruption of pimples. [Gr. *ekthuma*, from *ekthuein* (*ek*, out, *thuein*, to boil)]
ecto- (ek´tō) *comb. form* (*Biol.*) of or relating to the outside of something. [Gr. *ektos*, outside]
ectoblast (ek´təblahst) *n.* the membrane composing the walls of a cell. **ectoblastic** (-blahs´tik) *a.* [Gr. *blastos*, a sprout]
ectoderm (ek´tədœm) *n.* **1** the outer layer of the ectoblast. **2** the external integument of the Coelenterata. **ectodermal** (-dœ´məl) *a.*
ectogenesis (ektōjen´əsis) *n.* the growth of an organism or part outside the body instead of inside. **ectogenetic** (-jənet´ik) *a.* **ectogenic** (-jen´ik) *a.* **ectogenous** (-toj´ənəs) *a.*
ectomorph (ek´təmawf) *n.* a person of slight or thin build. **ectomorphic** *a.* **ectomorphy** *n.* [Gr. *morphē*, form]
-ectomy (ek´təmi) *suf.* denoting the surgical removal of a part of the body, as *tonsillectomy*. [Gr. *ektomē* (*ek*, out, *temnein*, to cut)]
ectoparasite (ektōpar´əsīt) *n.* an organism parasitic on the outside of the host.
ectopia (ektō´piə) *n.* congenital displacement of an organ or part. **ectopic** (-top´-) *a.* out of place. **ectopic pregnancy** *n.* the abnormal development of a foetus outside the womb, usu. in a Fallopian tube. [Gr. *ek*, out of, *topos*, place]
ectoplasm (ek´təplazm) *n.* **1** the outer layer of protoplasm or sarcode of a cell. **2** a substance supposed to emanate from the body of a spiritualist medium during a trance. **ectoplasmic** *a.* **ectoplasmically** *adv.*
ectosarc (ek´təsahk) *n.* the outer transparent sarcode-layer of certain protozoa, as the amoeba.
ectozoon (ektəzō´on) *n.* (*pl.* **ectozoa** (-zōə)) an animal parasitic on the outside of other animals.
ectype (ek´tīp) *n.* a copy, as distinguished from an original. **ectypal** (-ti-) *a.* **ectypography** (-tipog´rəfi) *n.* a mode of etching which leaves the design in relief. [Gr. *ektupon* (*ek*, out, *tupos*, a figure)]
ecu (ek´ū, ā´kū), **ECU** *n.* (*pl.* **ecu, ecus, ECU, ECUs**) a currency unit used as a unit of account in the European Union, its value based on the value of several different European currencies. [acronym for *E*uropean *C*urrency *U*nit]
écu (ākū´, akü´) *n.* (*Hist.*) **1** a French silver coin of varying value, usu. considered as equivalent to the English crown. **2** a French 5-franc piece. [F, from L *scutum*, a shield]
ecumenical (ēkūmen´ikəl, ek-), **oecumenical** *a.* **1** belonging to the Christian Church or Christian world as a whole. **2** of or relating to the ecumenical movement. **3** general, universal, worldwide. **ecumenically** *adv.* **ecumenical movement** *n.* a movement in the Christian Church encouraging and promoting unity on issues of belief, worship etc. **ecumenicism** (-sizm), **ecumenism** (ekū´-) *n.* the principles of the ecumenical movement. **ecumenics** *n.* the study of the ecumenical movement. [L *oecumenicus*, from Gr. *oikoumenikos* (*oikoumenē* (*gē*), the inhabited (world))]
eczema (ek´simə) *n.* an inflammatory disease of the skin, characterized by blisters and itching. **eczematous** (-sem´-) *a.* [Gr., a pustule, from *ekzeein* (*ek*, out, *zeein*, to boil)]
ed. *abbr.* **1** edited. **2** edition. **3** editor. **4** educated. **5** education.
-ed (id, d) *suf.* **1** forming the past tense and participle of regular verbs (used also as participial adjectives). **2** forming adjectives from nouns or noun phrases, as in *cultured, good-natured, moneyed, talented*. [OE *-ed, -ad, -od*; in sense 2 representing OE *-ede*]
edacious (idā´shəs) *a.* greedy, voracious, ravenous. **edaciously** *adv.* **edaciousness, edacity** (-das´i-) *n.* [L *edax edācis*, from *edere*, to eat]
Edam (ē´dam) *n.* a kind of pressed, yellow cheese with a red outer skin of wax. [*Edam*, a town in the Netherlands]
edaphic (idaf´ik) *a.* of or relating to the soil. **edaphically** *adv.* [Gr. *edaphos*, the ground]
EDC *abbr.* **1** ethylene dichloride. **2** European Defence Community.
Edda (ed´ə) *n.* the title of either of two Icelandic books, the Elder or Poetic Edda and the Younger or Prose Edda (see ELDER[1], YOUNG). **Eddaic** (-dā´ik) *a.* **Eddic** *a.* [Icel.]
eddo (ed´ō) *n.* (*pl.* **eddoes**) taro. [W Afr.]
eddy (ed´i) *n.* (*pl.* **eddies**) **1** a small whirlpool. **2** a current of air, fog, smoke etc. moving in a circle, whirling. ~*v.i., v.t.* (*3rd pers. sing. pres.* **eddies,** *pres.p.* **eddying,** *past, p.p.* **eddied**) to whirl in an eddy. **eddy current** *n.* electrical current circulating in the mass of a conductor caused by a change in the magnetic field. [etym. uncertain]
edelweiss (ā´dəlvīs) *n.* a small white composite plant, *Gnaphalium alpinum*, growing in rocky places in the Alps. [G *edel*, noble, *weiss*, white]
edema OEDEMA.
Eden (ē´dən) *n.* **1** the region in which Adam and Eve were placed at their creation, according to the Bible. **2** a region or abode of perfect bliss. **3** a state of complete happiness. **the Garden of Eden** Eden. **Edenic** (ēden´-) *a.* [Heb. *'ēden*, pleasure, delight]
edentate (ēden´tāt) *a.* **1** having no incisor teeth. **2** belonging to the Edentata, an order of mammals with no front teeth or no teeth whatsoever, containing the armadillos, sloths and anteaters. ~*n.* an edentate animal. **edental** *a.* edentate. ~*n.* an edentate animal. **edentulous** (-tū´ləs) *a.* edentate. [L *ēdentātus*, p.p. of *ēdentāre*, to render toothless (E-, *dens dentem*, a tooth)]
EDF *abbr.* European Development Fund.
edge (ej) *n.* **1 a** the sharp or cutting part of an instrument,

such as a sword. **b** the sharpness of this. **2** anything edge-shaped, the crest of a ridge, the line where two surfaces of a solid meet. **3** a boundary-line. **4** the brink, border, margin or extremity of anything. **5** sharpness, keenness, of mind or appetite. **6** acrimony, bitterness. *~v.t.* **1** to sharpen, to put an edge on. **2** to make an edge or border to. **3** to be a border to. **4** to incite, to egg on, to instigate. **5** to move or put forward little by little. *~v.i.* **1** to move forward or away little by little. **2** to move sideways, to sidle (up). **on edge** irritable. **on the edge of** very nearly (doing or being involved in). **to edge out** to get rid of gradually. **to have the edge on/ over** to have an advantage over. **to set one's teeth on edge 1** to cause a tingling or grating sensation in the teeth. **2** to cause a feeling of irritation or revulsion. **to take the edge off** to weaken, to lessen the force of. **edge-bone** *n.* AITCHBONE. **edgeless** *a.* **edger** *n.* **edge-rail** *n.* **1** a form of rail which bears the rolling stock on its edge. **2** a rail placed by the side of the main rail at a switch. **edge tool, edged tool** *n.* **1** any of the heavier varieties of cutting tool. **2** anything dangerous to deal or play with. **edgeways, edgewise** *adv.* **1** with the edge turned up, or forward in the direction of the edge. **2** sideways. **to get a word in edgeways** to say something with difficulty because of someone else talking. **edging** *n.* **1** that which forms the border or edge of anything, such as lace, trimming etc. on a dress. **2** a border or row of small plants set along the edge of a bed. **edging shears** *n.pl.* long-handled shears used to neaten the edge of a lawn. **edgy** *a.* (*comp.* **edgier**, *superl.* **edgiest**) **1** having or showing an edge. **2** irritable, nervy. **3** sharp in temper. **4** in art, too sharply defined. **edgily** *adv.* **edginess** *n.* [OE *ecg*, cp. Dut. *egge*, G *Ecke*; also L *aciēs*, Gr. *akis*, a point]

edh ETH.

edible (ed´ibəl) *a.* fit for food, eatable. *~n.* anything fit for food; an eatable. **edibility** (-bil´-) *n.* **edibleness** *n.* [late L *edibilis*, from *edere*, to eat]

edict (ē´dikt) *n.* a proclamation or decree issued by authority. **edictal** (idik´-) *a.* [L *ēdictum*, neut. p.p. of *ēdīcere* (E-, *dīcere*, to speak)]

edifice (ed´ifis) *n.* **1** a building, esp. one of some size and pretension. **2** a complicated organization or structure. [F *édifice*, L *aedificium* (*aedes*, a building, *-ficium*, from *facere*, to make)]

edify (ed´ifī) *v.t.* (*3rd pers. sing. pres.* **edifies**, *pres.p.* **edifying**, *past, p.p.* **edified**) **1** to build up spiritually; to improve, to instruct. **2** to enlighten. **3** †to build, to construct. **4** †to organize, to establish. **edification** (-fikā´shən) *n.* **edificatory** (-fikā´-) *a.* **edifying** *a.* morally improving. **edifyingly** *adv.* [F *édifier*, L *aedificāre* (as EDIFICE)]

edit (ed´it) *v.t.* (*pres.p.* **editing**, *past, p.p.* **edited**) **1** to prepare for publication or processing by compiling, selecting, revising etc. **2** to censor, to alter; to reword, to improve or correct. **3** to conduct or manage (a periodical etc.) by selecting and revising the literary matter. *~n.* **1** an act or instance of editing. **2** something edited. **3** an editing facility. **to edit out** to remove during editing. **edition** (idish´ən) *n.* **1** the form in which a literary work is published. **2** the whole number of copies published at one time. **3** one particular broadcast forming part of a regular series. **4** a person or thing that closely resembles another except in one specified aspect (*a smaller edition of his brother*). **édition de luxe** (ādēsyō də lüks´) *n.* (*pl.* **éditions de luxe** (ādēsyō)) a handsomely printed and bound edition of a book. **editio princeps** (idish´iō prin´seps) *n.* (*pl.* **editiones principes** (-ō´nēz, -sipēz)) the first printed edition of a book. **editor** *n.* **1** a person who prepares the work of others for publication or broadcasting. **2** a person who conducts or manages a newspaper or periodical or a section of one. **3** a person who cuts and makes up the shots for the final sequence of a film. **4** (*Comput.*) a program that facilitates the alteration of text already stored in a computer. **editorial** (-taw´-) *a.* **1** of or relating to an editor or editing. **2** written by or proceeding from an editor. *~n.* an article written by or proceeding from an editor, a leading article. **editorialist** *n.* **editorialize, editorialise** *v.i.* to introduce personal opinions into reporting. **editorially** *adv.* **editorship** *n.* **editress** (-tris) *n.* a woman editor. [L *ēditus*, p.p. of *ēdere* (E-, *dare*, to give)]

-edly (idli) *suf.* forming adverbs from the p.p. of verbs, as *markedly*, *guardedly*.

EDP *abbr.* electronic data processing.

EDT *abbr.* Eastern Daylight Time.

EDTA *abbr.* ethylenediamine tetra-acetic acid, a chelating agent.

educate (ed´ūkāt) *v.t.* **1** to train and develop the intellectual and moral powers of. **2** to provide with schooling. **3** to train or develop (an organ or a faculty). **4** to train (an animal). **5** to bring up (a child or children). **educable** (-kəbəl) *a.* **educability** (-bil´-) *n.* **educatable** *a.* **educated** *a.* **1** having been educated to a high standard. **2** cultured. **3** informed (*an educated guess*). **education** (-kā´shən) *n.* **1** the process of educating, systematic training and development of the intellectual and moral faculties. **2** a type of educating or instruction. **3** a stage in the process of educating. **4** a course of instruction. **5** the result of a systematic course of training and instruction. **educational** *a.* **educationalist, educationist** *n.* **1** a person who is versed in educational methods. **2** an advocate of education. **educationally** *adv.* **educative** (ed´ūkətiv) *a.* **educator** *n.* [L *ēducātus*, p.p. of *ēducāre*, rel. to *ēdūcere*, to EDUCE]

educe (idūs´) *v.t.* **1** to bring out, evolve, develop. **2** to deduce, infer. **3** (*Chem.*) to extract. **educible** *a.* **educt** (ē´dŭkt) *n.* **1** that which is educed. **2** an inference, a deduction. **3** (*Chem.*) a substance separated by the decomposition of another substance in which it had previously existed. **eduction** (idŭk´-) *n.* the act of educing. **eduction pipe** *n.* the pipe which carries off the exhaust steam from the cylinder of an engine. **eductive** *a.* [L *ēdūcere* (E-, *dūcere*, to lead)]

edulcorate (idŭl´kərāt) *v.t.* **1** to sweeten. **2** to remove acidity from. **3** to free from acids, salts or impurities by washing. **edulcoration** (-ā´shən) *n.* **edulcorator** *n.* **1** a person who or thing which sweetens or removes acidity. **2** a dropping-tube for applying small quantities of water to test tubes, watch-glasses etc. [L *ēdulcorātus*, p.p. of *ēdulcorāre* (E-, *dulcor*, sweetness)]

edutainment (edūtān´mənt) *n.* infotainment.

Edw. *abbr.* Edward.

Edwardian (edwawd´iən) *a.* **1** of or relating to the periods of any of the kings of England named Edward, esp. that of Edward VII (1901–10). **2** characteristic of the manners, architecture etc. of the period of Edward VII. *~n.* a person belonging to, or affecting the style of, this period. **Edwardian prayer book** *n.* the prayer book authorized by Edward VI in 1549.

ee (ē) *n.* (*pl.* **een** (ēn)) (*Sc.*) EYE[1].

-ee (ē) *suf.* **1** denoting the recipient, as in *grantee*, *legatee*, *payee*, *vendee*. **2** denoting the direct or indirect object, as in *addressee*, *employee*. **3** denoting something small in its class, as in *bootee*. **4** used arbitrarily, as in *bargee*, *devotee*. [A-F *-é*, p.p. used as noun (e.g. *apelé*, summoned, corr. to *apelour*, summoner)]

EEC *abbr.* European Economic Community.

EEG *abbr.* **1** electroencephalogram. **2** electroencephalograph.

eejit (ē´jit) *n.* (*Ir., Sc.*) IDIOT.

eel (ēl) *n.* **1** a snakelike fish of the genus *Anguilla*, esp. the common European species, *A. anguilla*. **2** an eel-like fish. **3** a slippery or evasive person. **4** an eelworm. **eel-buck, eel-pot** *n.* a basket trap for catching eels. **eel-fare** *n.* **1** the passage of young eels up streams. **2** a brood of young eels. **eel-fork, eel-spear** *n.* a pronged instrument or fork for spearing eels. **eelgrass** *n.* 1 GRASS-WRACK (under GRASS). 2 any plant of the genus *Vallisneria*, living submerged in fresh water. **eel-like** *a.* **eelpout** *n.* 1 any fish of the family Zoarcidae. 2 the burbot, *Lota lota.* 3 a blenny. **eelworm** *n.* a minute eel-like worm esp. of a kind found in vinegar or in plant roots. **eely** *a.* [OE *ael* (cp. Dut. *aal*, G *Aal*, Icel. *āll*)]

een EE.

†**e'en**[1] (ēn) *n.* EVEN[1]. [contr.]

e'en[2] (ēn) *a.* (*Sc.*) EVEN[2]. ~*adv.* EVEN[4]. [contr.]

-een (ēn) *suf.* forming feminine diminutive nouns, as in *colleen.* [Ir. dim. suf. *-ín*]

†**e'er** (eə) *adv.* EVER. [contr.]

-eer (iə) *suf.* 1 denoting an agent or a person concerned with or dealing in, as in *charioteer, musketeer, pamphleteer, sonneteer.* 2 forming verbs with the meaning 'to perform activities associated with', as in *electioneer, profiteer.* [F *-ier*, L *-iārius*, or F *-air*, L *-ārius*]

eerie (iə'ri) *a.* (*comp.* **eerier**, *superl.* **eeriest**) 1 strange, weird. 2 causing fear. **eerily** *adv.* **eeriness** *n.* [ME *eri*, prob. from OE *earg, earh*, timid, cowardly]

EETPU *abbr.* Electrical, Electronic, Telecommunications and Plumbing Union.

EETS *abbr.* Early English Text Society.

ef- (ef, if) *pref.* EX- used before *f*, as in *efface, effigy.*

eff (ef) *v.i.*, *v.t.* (*sl.*) a euphemism for FUCK. **effing and blinding** swearing copiously. **effing** *a.* **eff off!** *int.* [pronunc. of the letter *f*]

efface (ifās') *v.t.* 1 to rub out, to wipe out, obliterate. 2 to cast into the shade. 3 to make not noticeable. 4 to render negligible. **effaceable** *a.* **effacement** *n.* [F *effacer* (EF-, L *facies*, face)]

effect (ifekt') *n.* 1 the result or product of a cause or operation, the consequence. 2 efficacy, power of producing a required result. 3 accomplishment, fulfilment. 4 purport, aim, purpose. 5 the impression created by a work of art. 6 a combination of colours, forms, sounds, rhythm etc., calculated to produce a definite impression. 7 (*pl.*) goods, movables, personal estate. 8 a physical phenomenon. ~*v.t.* 1 to produce as a consequence or result. 2 to bring about, to accomplish. 3 †to give effect to. **for effect** in order to produce a striking impression. **in effect** 1 in reality, substantially. 2 practically. **of no effect** 1 without validity or force. 2 without result. **to bring/ carry into effect** to accomplish. **to give effect to** 1 to carry out. 2 to make operative. **to no effect** in vain, uselessly. **to take effect** to operate, to produce its effect. **to that effect** having that result. **to the effect that** such that. **with effect from** taking effect from (a specified date). **without effect** invalid, without result. **effective** *a.* 1 producing its proper effect. 2 producing a striking impression. 3 fit for duty or service. 4 real, actual. ~*n.* a person who is fit for duty. **effectively** *adv.* **effectiveness** *n.* **effectivity** (-tiv'iti) *n.* **effectless** *a.* **effector** *n.* an organ that effects response to stimulus, e.g. a muscle, gland. ~*a.* of or relating to such an organ. **effectual** (-chuəl) *a.* 1 productive of an intended effect. 2 adequate, efficacious. 3 valid. **effectuality** (-chual'-) *n.* **effectually** *adv.* **effectualness** *n.* **effectuate** *v.t.* to effect, to bring to pass, to accomplish. **effectuation** (-ā'shən) *n.* [OF *effect*, L *effectus*, p.p. of *efficere* (EF-, *facere*, to make)]

Usage note The adjectives *effective* and *effectual* should not be confused: *effective* involves actual performance or achievement, and *effectual* only potential; unlike *effective, effectual* is not used of people (though *ineffectual* is). The meaning of *effectual* also overlaps with that of *efficacious*, but *efficacious* implies an established purpose and reliable performance. See also notes under AFFECT[1], EFFICIENT.

effeminate (ifem'inət) *a.* (of a man) womanish; unmanly, weak. **effeminacy** *n.* **effeminately** *adv.* [L *effēminātus*, p.p. of *effēmināre* (EF-, *fēmina*, woman)]

effendi (ifen'di) *n.* (*pl.* **effendis**) 1 a learned man or a man of social standing in the eastern Mediterranean. 2 (*Hist.*) master, as a title of respect in Turkey. [Turk. *efendī*, sir, lord (corr. of Gr. *authentēs*)]

efferent (ef'ərənt) *a.* 1 (*Med.*) conveying outwards. 2 discharging. ~*n.* 1 an efferent vessel or nerve. 2 a stream carrying off water from a lake etc. [L *efferens -ntem*, pres.p. of *efferre* (EF-, *ferre*, to carry)]

effervesce (efəves') *v.i.* 1 to bubble up, from the escape of gas, as fermenting liquors. 2 to escape in bubbles. 3 to boil over with excitement. **effervescence, effervescency** *n.* **effervescent** *a.* [L *effervescere* (EF-, *fervescere*, incept. of *fervēre*, to boil)]

effete (ifēt') *a.* 1 decadent. 2 having lost all vigour and efficiency. 3 worn out or exhausted. 4 sterile, barren. **effeteness** *n.* [L *effētus*, weakened by bringing forth young (EF-, *fētus*, FOETUS)]

efficacious (efikā'shəs) *a.* producing or having power to produce the effect intended. **efficaciously** *adv.* **efficaciousness** *n.* **efficacy** (ef'ikəsi) *n.* [L *efficax -ācis*, from *efficere*, to EFFECT]

efficient (ifish'ənt) *a.* 1 causing or producing effects or results. 2 competent, capable. **efficiency** *n.* (*pl.* **efficiencies**) 1 the quality or state of being efficient. 2 power to produce a desired result. 3 the ratio of the output of energy to the input of energy. **efficient cause** *n.* (*Philos.*) something which initiates an action or process of change. **efficiently** *adv.* [F, from L *efficiens -ntem*, pres.p. of *efficere*, to EFFECT]

Usage note The meanings of *efficient* overlap with those of *effective* and *efficacious*, but *efficient* implies skill or economy of effort.

effigy (ef'iji) *n.* (*pl.* **effigies**) a representation or likeness of a person, as on coins, medals etc. **to burn/ hang in effigy** to burn or hang an image of, to show hatred, dislike or contempt of. [L *effigiēs* (EF-, *fingere*, to fashion)]

effleurage (eflərahzh') *n.* in massage, a stroking movement of the hand. ~*v.i.* to use such a movement. ~*v.t.* to massage (a person) using such a movement. [F, from *effleurer*, to touch lightly]

effloresce (efləres') *v.i.* 1 to burst into flower, to blossom. 2 (*Chem.*) to crumble to powder through loss of water or crystallization on exposure to the air. 3 (of salts) to form crystals on the surface. 4 (of a surface), to become covered with saline particles. 5 to fulfil promise, to mature. **efflorescence** *n.* **efflorescent** *a.* [L *efflōrescere*, incept. of *efflōrēre*, to blossom (EF-, *flōrēre*, to blossom, from *flōs flōris*, a flower)]

effluent (ef'luənt) *a.* flowing or issuing out; emanating. ~*n.* 1 the liquid that is discharged from a sewage tank. 2 a river or stream which flows out of another or out of a lake. **effluence** *n.* 1 the act or state of flowing out. 2 that which flows out, an emanation. [L *effluens -ntem*, pres.p. of *effluere* (EF-, *fluere*, to FLOW)]

effluvium (ifloo'viəm) *n.* (*pl.* **effluvia** (-viə)) an emanation affecting the sense of smell, esp. a disagreeable smell and vapour as from putrefying substances etc. [late L, as EFFLUENT]

efflux (ef'lŭks) *n.* 1 the act of flowing out or issuing. 2 outflow, effusion. 3 an emanation, that which flows out. **effluxion** (iflŭk'shən) *n.* [L *effluxus*, p.p. of *effluere*; see EFFLUENT]

effort (ef'ət) *n.* 1 an exertion of physical or mental power, a strenuous attempt, an endeavour. 2 a display of power, an achievement. 3 (*coll.*) the result of an effort, something achieved. **effortful** *a.* **effortfully** *adv.* **effortless** *a.* **effortlessly** *adv.* **effortlessness** *n.* [F, from OF *esforcier*, to force, from L *ex*, out, *fortis*, strong]

effrontery (ifrŭn'təri) *n.* (*pl.* **effronteries**) 1 impudence, shamelessness, insolence. 2 an impudent speech or act. [F *effronterie*, from *effronté*, shameless (EF-, *frons*, *-ntis*, forehead)]

effulgent (ifŭl´jənt) *a.* 1 shining brightly. 2 diffusing radiance. **effulge** (ifŭlj´) *v.i.* (*formal*) 1 to shine out. 2 to become famous or illustrious. **effulgence** *n.* **effulgently** *adv.* [L *effulgēre* (EF-, *fulgēre*, to shine)]

effuse[1] (ifūz´) *v.t.* 1 to pour out, to emit. 2 to diffuse. **effusion** (-zhən) *n.* 1 the act of pouring out. 2 that which is poured out. 3 a shedding, as of blood. 4 (*facet.*) an outpouring of genius or emotion. 5 frank expression of feeling, effusiveness. 6 the escape of any fluid out of the proper part of the body into another. **effusive** (-siv) *a.* 1 gushing, exuberant, demonstrative. 2 (of rock) volcanic, poured out when molten and then solidifying. **effusively** *adv.* **effusiveness** *n.* [L *effūsus*, p.p. of *effundere* (EF-, *fundere*, to pour)]

effuse[2] (ifūs´) *a.* 1 (*Bot.*) (of an inflorescence) spreading loosely. 2 (of a shell) having the lips separated by a groove. ~†*n.* effusion, outpouring. [see EFFUSE[1]]

E-fit (ē´fit) *n.* a computerized form of photofit with a wide range of possible facial features, usu. used in helping police and witnesses build up a picture of suspects. [acronym for *e*lectronic *f*acial *i*dentification *t*echnique]

EFL *abbr.* English as a foreign language.

eft (eft) *n.* the common newt. [OE *efete* (etym. uncertain)]

EFTA (ef´tə), **Efta** *abbr.* European Free Trade Association.

EFTPOS (eft´pos), **Eftpos** *abbr.* electronic funds transfer at point of sale (a method of payment in which funds are transferred directly at the shop till through a computer network, using a debit or credit card).

EFTS *abbr.* electronic funds transfer system.

†**eftsoon** (eftsoon´), **eftsoons** (-z) *adv.* 1 soon after, speedily, forthwith. 2 presently, by and by. [OE *eftsōna*, again (AFT, SOON)]

e.g. *abbr.* for example. [L *exempli gratia*]

Usage note The abbreviations *e.g.* and *i.e.* should not be confused: *e.g.* introduces an example, and *i.e.* an identification or paraphrase.

---

egad (igad´) *int.* (*Hist.*, *facet.*) by God (a minced oath). [prob. *a*, AH, GOD]

egalitarian (igaliteə´riən) *a.* believing in the principle of human equality. ~*n.* a person who advocates equality for all humankind. **egalitarianism** *n.* **egality** (-gal´-) *n.* [F *égalitaire*, from *égal*, EQUAL]

egence (ē´jəns) *n.* (*formal*) the state of being needy. [L *egens -ntem*, pres.p. of *egēre*, to be in need]

egest (ijest´) *v.t.* 1 to eject. 2 to void as excrement. **egesta** (-tə) *n.pl.* 1 waste matter thrown out. 2 excreta. **egestion** (-chən) *n.* [L *ēgestus*, p.p. of *ēgerere* (E-, *gerere*, to carry)]

egg[1] (eg) *n.* 1 the ovum of birds, reptiles, fishes and many of the invertebrates, usu. enclosed in a spheroidal shell, and containing the embryo of a new individual. 2 the egg of a bird, esp. of domestic poultry, largely used as food. 3 an ovum or germ-cell. 4 the early stage of anything; the germ, the origin. 5 something spheroidal. 6 (*coll.*) a person or thing (to be) dealt with. ~*v.t.* (*N Am.*) to pelt with rotten eggs. ~*v.i.* to collect eggs. **as sure as eggs is eggs** (*coll.*) quite certainly. **bad egg** BAD. **egg and spoon race** a race in which the runners carry eggs in spoons. **good egg!** GOOD. **to have egg on one's face** to be mistaken, to look foolish. **egg and anchor**, **egg and dart**, **egg and tongue** *n.* (*Archit.*) various kinds of moulding carved alternately with egg-shapes and anchors etc. **egg-beater** *n.* 1 a device for whisking eggs. 2 (*N Am.*, *coll.*) a helicopter. **egg-bird** *n.* a sea bird, the eggs of which are collected for food etc., esp. a W Indian tern, *Hydrochelidon fuliginosum*. **egg-bound** *a.* (of the oviduct of a bird) obstructed by an egg. **egg-cleavage** *n.* the first process of germination, in which the fertilized cell of the ovum becomes divided. **egg cosy** *n.* (*pl.* **egg cosies**) a fabric covering for keeping a boiled egg warm. **eggcup** *n.* a cup-shaped vessel used to hold a boiled egg at table. **egg custard** *n.* a flavoured custard made with eggs. **egg-dance** *n.* 1 a dance by a blindfold person among eggs. 2 (*fig.*) a task of extreme intricacy. **egger**, **eggar** *n.* a person who gathers eggs. **egger-moth**, **eggar-moth** *n.* any of various British moths of the family Lasiocampidae. **egg-flip**, **egg-nog** *n.* a drink compounded of eggs beaten up, sugar, and beer, cider, wine or spirits. **egghead** *n.* (*coll.*) an intellectual. **eggless** *a.* **eggplant** *n.* (*N Am.*) the *Solanum esculentum*, or aubergine. **eggs-and-bacon** *n.* any of several plants with yellowish flowers. **eggshell** *n.* the calcareous envelope in which an egg is enclosed. **eggshell china** *n.* very thin porcelain. **eggshell paint** *n.* paint with a slightly glossy finish. **egg-slice** *n.* a kitchen utensil for removing eggs, omelettes etc. from the pan. **egg-spoon** *n.* a small spoon used for eating eggs. **egg-timer** *n.* a device for timing the boiling of an egg. **egg-tooth** *n.* a hard point or knob on the bill-sheath or snout of an embryo bird or reptile, for cracking the containing shell. **egg-whisk** *n.* a kind of wire utensil used for beating up eggs. **egg white** *n.* the albuminous part of an egg surrounding the yolk. **eggy** *a.* (*comp.* **eggier**, *superl.* **eggiest**). [ON *egg* (cp. OE *æg*, Dan. *æg*, Dut. *ei*, G *Ei*)]

egg[2] (eg) *v.t.* to incite, to urge (on). [Icel. *eggja*, to EDGE]

eggar, **egger** EGG[1].

eglandulose (iglan´dūlōs), **eglandular** (-dūlə) *a.* (*Bot.*) without glands.

eglantine (eg´ləntīn, -tin) *n.* the sweet-brier. [F *églantine*, from OF *aiglant*, prob. from L *acus*, needle, *-lentus*, -LENT]

ego (ē´gō, eg´ō) *n.* (*pl.* **egos**) 1 individuality, personality. 2 the self-conscious subject, as contrasted with the non-ego, or object. 3 (*Psych.*) the conscious self, which resists on the one hand the threats of the super-ego, and on the other the impulses of the id. 4 (*coll.*) self-confidence or self-conceit. **egocentric** (-sen´trik) *a.* self-centred. **egocentrically** *adv.* **egocentricity** (-tris´-) *n.* **egocentrism** *n.* **ego-ideal** *n.* (*Psych.*) one's own picture of what one would like to be, developed as one learns social standards. **egoism** *n.* 1 egotism. 2 pure self-interest, systematic selfishness. 3 the theory that a person's chief good is the complete development and happiness of self, and that this is the proper basis of morality. 4 the doctrine that human beings can be absolutely certain of nothing but their own existence and the operations of their own mind. **egoist** *n.* **egoistic** (-is´-), **egoistical** *a.* **egoistically** *adv.* **egomania** (-mā´niə) *n.* excessive or pathological egotism. **egomaniac** *n.* **egomaniacal** (-mənī´əkəl) *a.* **egotism** (-tizm) *n.* 1 the habit of too frequently using the word I in writing or speaking. 2 a too frequent mention of oneself in writing or conversation. 3 self-glorification, self-conceit, self-absorption. **egotist** *n.* **egotistic** (-tis´-), **egotistical** *a.* **egotistically** *adv.* **egotize** (-tīz), **egotise** *v.i.* **ego trip** *n.* (*coll.*) an action or experience which adds to a person's self-important feelings. **ego tripper** *n.* [L, I]

egregious (igrē´jəs) *a.* 1 conspicuously bad, flagrant. 2 notable, notorious. 3 extraordinary, out of the common, remarkable, exceptional. **egregiously** *adv.* **egregiousness** *n.* [L *ēgregius* (E-, *grex gregis*, flock)]

egress (ē´gres) *n.* 1 departure. 2 a means or place of exit. 3 the act or power of going out. 4 (*Astron.*) the end of a transit or eclipse. **egression** (igresh´ən) *n.* [L *ēgressus*, p.p. of *ēgredī* (E-, *gradī*, to go)]

egret (ē´gret) *n.* 1 a heron of those species that have long and loose plumage over the back, of the genus *Egretta* or *Bulbulcus*. 2 the feathery or hairy down of seeds. 3 an aigrette. [OF *egrette*, *aigrette*, AIGRETTE]

Egyptian (ijip´shən) *a.* of or relating to Egypt or the Egyptians. *~n.* **1** a native or inhabitant of Egypt. **2** the language of ancient Egypt. **3** †a gypsy. **4** (*Print.*) type with thick stems. **Egyptianize, Egyptianise** *v.t.* **Egyptianization** (-zā´shən) *n.* **Egyptian pebble, Egyptian jasper** *n.* a variety of jasper with zones of brown and yellow, found between Cairo and Suez, in Egypt. **Egyptian thorn** *n.* the tree *Acacia vera*, which yields gum arabic. **Egyptology** (-tol´əji) *n.* the study of the antiquities, language etc. of ancient Egypt. **Egyptological** (-loj´-) *a.* **Egyptologist** (-tol´-) *n.*

eh (ā) *int.* used to express doubt, inquiry, surprise etc. [ME *ey*, OE *ēa*]

EHF *abbr.* extremely high frequency.

EHO *abbr.* environmental health officer.

EI *abbr.* **1** East Indies. **2** East Indian.

-eian (ēən) *suf.* forming adjectives and nouns from nouns ending in *-ey*, as *Harleian, Bodleian.*

EIB *abbr.* European Investment Bank.

Eid (ēd), **Id** *n.* a Muslim festival. **Eid ul-Adha** (ŭlah´də) *n.* the festival marking the culmination of the haj. **Eid ul-Fitr** (ŭlfit´rə) *n.* the festival marking the end of Ramadan. [Arab.]

eider (ī´də) *n.* **1** a large Arctic duck, *Somateria mollissima.* **2** eiderdown. **eiderdown** *n.* **1** the soft and elastic down from the breast of this bird. **2** a quilt filled with eiderdown or similar material. **eider duck** *n.* [Icel. *æthar*, gen. of *æthr*, an eider duck (as in *æthar-dūn*, eiderdown)]

eidetic (īdet´ik) *a.* able to reproduce a vivid image of something previously seen or imagined. *~n.* a person who can reproduce eidetic images. **eidetically** *adv.* [Gr. *eidētikos*, belonging to an image, from *eidos*, form]

eidograph (ī´dəgrahf) *n.* an instrument for copying plans or drawings on an enlarged or reduced scale. [Gr. *eidos*, form]

eidolon (īdō´lon) *n.* (*pl.* **eidolons, eidola** (-lə)) **1** an image, likeness or representation. **2** an apparition, a spectre. [Gr., see IDOL]

eigen- (īgən) *comb. form* characteristic, own. [G]

eigenfrequency (ī´gənfrēkwənsi) *n.* (*pl.* **eigenfrequencies**) any of the natural frequencies of vibration of a system.

eigenfunction (ī´gənfŭngkshən) *n.* (*Physics*) the function that satisfies a particular differential equation, esp. in wave mechanics.

eigenvalue (ī´gənvalū) *n.* (*Physics*) a value for which a particular differential equation has an eigenfunction, esp. in wave mechanics.

eight (āt) *n.* **1** the number or figure 8 or VIII. **2** the age of eight. **3** a set of eight things or people. **4** in rowing, a crew of eight in a boat. **5** in skating, a curved outline resembling the figure 8. **6** an article of attire such as a shoe etc. denoted by the number 8. **7** a card with eight pips. **8** a score of eight points. **9** the eighth hour after midday or midnight. *~a.* consisting of one more than seven. **figure (of) eight** FIGURE. **one over the eight** (*coll.*) slightly drunk. **eight-day** *a.* (of clocks) going for eight days. **eightfold** *a.* **eighth** (ātth) *n.* **1** any one of eight equal parts. **2** (*Mus.*) the interval of an octave. *~n., a.* **1** (the) last of eight (people, things etc.). **2** the next after the seventh. **eighthly** *adv.* **eighth note** *n.* (*Mus., N Am.*) a quaver. **eightsome, eightsome reel** *n.* a form of Scottish reel for eight dancers. [OE *eahta* (cp. Dut. and G *acht*, L *octo*, Gr. *oktō*, Gael. *ochd*, Sansk. *ashtau*)]

eighteen (ātēn´) *n.* **1** the number or figure 18 or XVIII. **2** the age of 18. *~a.* **1** 18 in number. **2** aged 18. **eighteenmo** (-mō) *n.* (*pl.* **eighteenmos**) (*coll.*) an octodecimo, a book whose sheets are folded to form 18 leaves, written 18mo. **eighteenth** *n.* any one of 18 equal parts. *~n., a.* **1** (the) last of 18 (people, things etc.). **2** (the) next after the 17th. [OE *eahtatȳne*]

eighty (ā´ti) *n.* (*pl.* **eighties**) **1** the number or figure 80 or LXXX. **2** the age of 80. *~a.* **1** 80 in number. **2** aged 80. **eighties** *n.pl.* **1** the period of time between a person's 80th and 90th birthdays. **2** the range of temperature between 80 and 90 degrees. **3** the period of time between the 80th and 90th years of a century. **eightieth** *n.* any one of 80 equal parts. *~n., a.* **1** (the) last of 80 equal parts. **2** the next after the 79th. **eightyfold** *a., adv.* [OE *eahtatig*]

☒ **eigth** common misspelling of EIGHTH (under EIGHT).

einkorn (īn´kawn) *n.* a variety of wheat, *Triticum monococcum*, used for feeding animals. [G, *ein*, one, *Korn*, seed]

einsteinium (īnstī´niəm) *n.* a radioactive element, at. no. 99, chem. symbol Es, artificially produced from plutonium. [Albert *Einstein*, 1879–1955, German-American physicist]

eirenic IRENIC.

eirenicon (īrē´nikon), **irenicon** *n.* a measure or proposal intended to make or restore peace. [Gr. *eirēnikon*, neut. of *eirēnikos*, from *eirēnē*, peace]

eisteddfod (īstedh´vod, -ted´fod) *n.* (*pl.* **eisteddfods, eisteddfodau** (-vodī)) a competitive congress of Welsh bards and musicians held annually to encourage native poetry and music. **eisteddfodic** *a.* [Welsh, a sitting, from *eistedd*, to sit]

either (ī´dhə, ē´-) *a., pron.* **1** one or the other of two. **2** each of two. *~adv., conj.* **1** in one or the other case (as a disjunctive correlative). **2** any more than the other (with neg. or interrog., as *If you don't I don't either*). **either-or** *a.* of or relating to a situation in which a choice must be made between two alternatives. [OE *ægther*, contr. of *æghwæther* (*ā*, aye, *ge-*, pref., *hwæther*, WHETHER)]

eiusdem generis (āūsdem jen´əris) *a.* (*Law*) of the same kind. [L]

ejaculate[1] (ijak´ūlāt) *v.t.* **1** to utter suddenly and briefly; to exclaim. **2** to eject. *~v.i.* **1** to utter ejaculations. **2** to emit semen. **ejaculation** (-lā´shən) *n.* **1** an abrupt exclamation. **2** the emission of seminal fluid. **ejaculative** *a.* **ejaculatory** *a.* [L *ējaculātus*, p.p. of *ējaculārī* (E-, *jaculārī*, to cast, from *jaculum*, a dart, see EJECT[1])]

ejaculate[2] (ijak´ūlət) *n.* semen which has been ejaculated. [see EJACULATE[1]]

eject[1] (ijekt´) *v.t.* **1** to discharge, to emit. **2** to drive away, to expel. **3** (*Law*) to oust or dispossess. **ejecta** (-ə) *n.pl.* matter thrown out, esp. from a volcano. **ejection** (-shən) *n.* **ejective**[1] *a.* tending to eject. **ejectment** *n.* **1** the act of casting out or expelling. **2** ejection, expulsion. **3** dispossession. **4** (*Law*) an action to recover possession. **ejector** *n.* **1** a person who ejects, drives out, or dispossesses. **2** an appliance by which a jet of elastic fluid, such as steam or air, is made to exhaust a fluid of the same or a different kind. **3** a contrivance for removing a spent cartridge from a breech-loading gun. **ejector seat** *n.* a seat that can be shot clear of the vehicle in an emergency. [L *ējectus*, p.p. of *ējicere* (E-, *jacere*, to throw)]

eject[2] (ē´jekt) *n.* (*Psych.*) something that is not an object of our own consciousness but inferred to have actual existence. **ejective**[2] (-jek´-) *a.* [see EJECT[1]]

ejective[1] EJECT[1].

ejective[2] EJECT[2].

eke (ēk) *v.t.* **1** (*coll.*) to produce, support or maintain with difficulty. **2** to make up for or supply deficiencies in (with *out*). [OE *īecan* (cp. Goth. *aukan*, L *augēre*)]

ekka (ek´ə) *n.* (*Ang.-Ind.*) a small one-horse carriage. [Hind.]

el[1] (el) *n.* **1** the 12th letter of the alphabet, L, l. **2** anything shaped like the capital form of this letter.

el[2] (el) *n.* (*US*) an elevated railway.

-el -LE[2].

elaborate[1] (ilab´ərət) *a.* **1** carefully or highly wrought. **2** highly finished. **elaborately** *adv.* **elaborateness** *n.* [L *ēlabōrātus*, p.p. of *ēlabōrāre* (E-, *labōrāre*, to work (*labor*, LABOUR))]

elaborate[2] (ilab´ərāt) *v.t.* 1 to develop in detail. 2 to work up and produce from its original material (as the food of animals or plants, so to adapt it for nutrition). 3 to produce by labour. ~*v.i.* to go into more detail (on). **elaboration** (-ā´shən) *n.* **elaborative** *a.* **elaborator** *n.*

élan (ilan´, ālā´), **elan** *n.* dash, vigour and style. [F, prob. from ELAND]

eland (ē´lənd) *n.* a large oxlike antelope, *Tragelaphus derbianus*, from S Africa. [Dut., an elk (cp. G *Elen*, also Welsh *elain*, a hind)]

elapse (ilaps´) *v.i.* (esp. of time) to glide or pass away. [L *ēlapsus*, p.p. of *ēlābī* (E-, *lābī*, to glide)]

elasmobranch (ilaz´məbrangk) *n.* a fish of the subclass Elasmobranchii, having platelike gills, containing the sharks, rays and chimeras. **elasmobranchiate** (-brang´kiət) *a.* [Gr. *elasmos*, a metal plate, *branchia*, gills]

elasmosaurus (ilazməsaw´rəs) *n.* (*pl.* **elasmosauruses**, **elasmosauri** (-rī)) an extinct marine reptile with platelike gills and a tough skin. [Gr. *sauros*, a lizard]

elastane (ilas´tān) *n.* a polyurethane with elastic properties, used in the manufacture of close-fitting clothing.

elastic (ilas´tik) *a.* 1 having the quality of returning to that form or volume from which it has been compressed, expanded or distorted; springy, rebounding. 2 flexible, adaptable. 3 admitting of extension. 4 readily recovering from depression or exhaustion, buoyant. 5 (*Physics*) (of a collision) involving no reduction in kinetic energy. ~*n.* a strip of elastic substance, a string or cord woven with India rubber threads. **elastically** *adv.* **elasticate** *v.t.* to render elastic. **elasticated** *a.* **elastic band** *n.* a rubber band for holding things together. **elastic bitumen**, **elastic pitch** *n.* elaterite. **elasticin** (-las´tisin), **elastin** *n.* (*Chem.*) the substance forming the fibres of elastic tissue. **elasticity** (ēlastis´iti) *n.* **elasticize** (-īz), **elasticise** *v.t.* to make elastic. **elastic tissue** *n.* yellow fibrous tissue occurring in the ligaments of the vertebrae, the jaw etc. [Gr. *elastikos*, propulsive, from *ela-*, stem of *elaunein*, to drive]

elastomer (ilas´tōmə) *n.* a synthetic rubberlike substance. **elastomeric** (-mer´ik) *a.*

Elastoplast® (ilas´təplahst) *n.* 1 a gauze surgical dressing on a backing of adhesive tape, suitable for small wounds, cuts and abrasions. 2 (**elastoplast**) a temporary measure used in an emergency etc.

elate (ilāt´) *v.t.* 1 to raise the spirits of, to stimulate. 2 to make exultant. 3 †to raise, to elevate. ~*a.* lifted up, in high spirits, exultant. **elatedly** *adv.* **elatedness** *n.* **elation** (ilā´shən) *n.* [L *ēlātus* (E-, *lātus*, p.p. of *ferre*, to bear, to raise)]

elater (el´ətə) *n.* 1 a coleopterous insect of the genus *Elater*, called click beetles or skipjacks, from their ability to spring up and alight on their feet. 2 (*Bot.*) an elastic spiral filament attached to spores. [ELASTIC]

elaterin ELATERIUM.

elaterite (ilat´ərīt) *n.* a soft elastic mineral, elastic bitumen.

elaterium (elətiə´riəm) *n.* a powerful purgative obtained from the fruit of the squirting cucumber. **elaterin** (ilat´ərin) *n.* the active principle of elaterium. [L, from Gr. *elatērios*, driving away; see ELASTIC]

elbow (el´bō) *n.* 1 the joint uniting the forearm with the upper arm. 2 the part of a sleeve covering the elbow. 3 an elbow-shaped (usu. obtuse) angle, bend or corner. 4 an elbow-shaped piece of piping etc. ~*v.t.* 1 to push or thrust with the elbows, to jostle. 2 to force (a way or oneself into, out of etc.) by pushing with the elbows. ~*v.i.* 1 to make one's way by pushing with the elbows. 2 to jostle. 3 to go out of one's way. 4 to zig-zag. **at one's elbow** near at hand. **more power to your elbow** POWER. **out at (the) elbows** 1 shabby in dress; in needy circumstances. 2 (of a coat etc.) worn through at the elbows, shabby. **to give someone the elbow** to dismiss or reject someone. **to jog someone's elbow** to give a reminder. **to rub elbows with** RUB[1]. **up to the elbows** deeply engaged in business. **elbow-chair** *n.* an armchair. **elbow grease** *n.* hard and continued manual exercise. **elbow-pipe** *n.* a pipe with an end resembling an elbow. **elbow room** *n.* ample room for action. [OE *elboga*, *elnboga* (*eln*, ELL, *boga*, BOW[1])]

†**eld** (eld) *n.* 1 old age. 2 former ages; antiquity. [OE *ield*, *ieldo*, from *eald*, OLD]

elder[1] (el´də) *a.* 1 older. 2 senior in position. 3 of or relating to former times. 4 in card-playing, having the right to play first. ~*n.* 1 a senior in years. 2 a person whose age entitles them to respect. 3 (*pl.*) persons of greater age. 4 a member of a senate, a counsellor. 5 an officer in the Jewish synagogue, in the early Christian, and in the Presbyterian and other churches. **elder brethren** *n.pl.* the masters of Trinity House, London, an organization that supplies lighthouses, buoys etc. **Elder Edda** *n.* a collection of ancient Icelandic poems (*c.* 1200), ascribed to Saemund, dealing with Norse mythology and heroic traditions. **elder hand** *n.* in cards, the person on the dealer's left, who has the right to play first. **elderly** *a.* bordering on old age. **elderliness** *n.* **eldership** *n.* **elder statesman** *n.* 1 a retired or experienced and respected politician or administrator. 2 any one of the confidential advisers of the Emperor of Japan. **eldest** *a.* 1 oldest. 2 first born of those surviving. 3 †of earliest date, of longest standing. **the eldest** the oldest person of the three or more in question. **eldest hand** *n.* ELDER HAND (under ELDER[1]). [OE *ieldra*, comp. of *eald*, OLD]

elder[2] (el´də) *n.* a tree of the genus *Sambucus*, esp. *S. nigra*, a small tree bearing white flowers and dark purple berries. **elderberry** *n.* (*pl.* **elderberries**) 1 the elder tree. 2 the fruit of the elder tree. **elderflower** *n.* the flower of the elder tree. **elder gun** *n.* a popgun made of the hollow stem of the elder. **elder wine**, **elderberry wine** *n.* a wine made from elderberries and elderflowers. [OE *ellen*, *ellern*]

El Dorado (el dərah´dō), **eldorado**, **Eldorado** *n.* 1 any place where money or profit is easily obtained. 2 an inexhaustible mine. 3 an imaginary land of gold in South America, between the Orinoco and Amazon. [Sp., the gilded]

eldritch (el´drich) *a.* (*Sc.*, *N Am.*) strange, weird, ghastly, frightful. [etym. uncertain]

Eleatic (eliat´ik) *a.* 1 of or relating to Elea, a town of Magna Graecia (in S Italy). 2 relating to the school of philosophy founded by Xenophanes at Elea. ~*n.* a follower of the philosophy of Xenophanes, Parmenides and Zeno. **Eleaticism** (-sizm) *n.* [L *Eleāticus*]

elecampane (elikampān´) *n.* 1 a composite plant, *Inula helenium*, used in cooking and medicinally. 2 the candied root-sticks of this used as a sweetmeat. [F *enule-campane*, L *inula campāna* (*enule*, assim. to OE *eolone*, *elene*, a perversion of L *inula*, *elecampane*; *campāna*, either growing in the fields or Campanian)]

elect (ilekt´) *v.t.* 1 to choose for any office or employment. 2 to choose by vote. 3 to determine on any particular course of action. 4 (*Theol.*) to choose for everlasting life. 5 †to pick out. ~*a.* 1 chosen, picked out. 2 (*placed after the noun*) designated to an office, but not yet in possession of it, as *president elect*. 3 (*Theol.*) chosen by God for everlasting life. **the elect** 1 the people chosen by God etc. 2 highly select or self-satisfied people. **electable** *a.* **election** (ilek´shən) *n.* 1 the act of choosing out of a number, esp. by vote. 2 the ceremony or process of electing. 3 power of choosing or selection. 4 (*Theol.*) the selection of certain individuals from humankind to be eternally saved (the characteristic doctrine of Calvinism). **by-election** BY. **general**

election GENERAL. **electioneer** (-niə´) *v.i.* **1** to work at an election in the interests of some particular candidate. **2** (*derog.*) to say what one thinks voters want to hear to get elected. **electioneering** *n.* **elective** *a.* **1** appointed, filled up or bestowed by election. **2** of or relating to election or choice. **3** having or exercising the power of choice. **4** optional. **5** involving some not all, selective. ~*n.* (*N Am.*) an optional course of study. **electively** *adv.* **elector** *n.* **1** a person who has the right, power or privilege of electing. **2** (*Hist.*) (**Elector**) any one of the princes of Germany who were entitled to vote in the election of the Emperor. **electoral** *a.* **electoral college** *n.* **1** in the US, the body of people who elect the president and the vice-president, having been themselves elected by vote. **2** a body of electors. **electorally** *adv.* **electoral register**, **electoral roll** *n.* an official list of the people entitled to vote in a borough, district etc. **electorate** (-rət) *n.* **1** the whole body of electors. **2** (*Austral.*, *New Zeal.*) the area represented by a Member of Parliament. **3** (*Hist.*) the dignity or territory of an elector of the German Empire. **electorship** *n.* **Electress** *n.* **1** (*Hist.*) the wife of a German Elector. **2** (**electress**) a female elector. [L *ēlectus*, p.p. of *ēligere* (E-, *legere*, to choose)]

Electra complex (ilek´trə kompleks) *n.* (*Psych.*) attraction of a daughter to her father accompanied by hostility to her mother. [in Gr. tragedy *Electra* incited her brother Orestes to murder their mother who had already murdered their father, Agamemnon]

electret (ilek´trit) *n.* (*Physics*) a permanently polarized piece of dielectric material. [*elec*tric, magn*et*]

electric (ilek´trik) *a.* **1** containing, generating or operated by electricity. **2** resembling electricity, magnetic. **3** dramatic, highly charged with emotion etc. ~*n.* **1** a non-conductor, in which electricity can be excited by means of friction. **2** (*pl.*) electric circuits or equipment. **electrical** *a.* of or relating to electricity; electric. **electrical engineer** *n.* an engineer dealing with the design and construction of electrical engines and equipment. **electrical engineering** *n.* **electrically** *adv.* **electricals** *n.pl.* **1** shares in electricity companies. **2** electric circuits or equipment. **electric bell** *n.* a bell in which the hammer is operated electrically by means of a solenoid. **electric blanket** *n.* a blanket containing an electrically-heated element. **electric blue** *n.* a steely blue. ~*a.* of this colour. **electric cable** *n.* an insulated wire or flexible conductor for conveying a current. **electric chair** *n.* a chair in which persons condemned to death are electrocuted. **electric charge** *n.* the accumulation of electrical energy in an electric battery. **electric circuit** *n.* **1** the passage of electricity from a body in one electric state to a body in another by means of a conductor. **2** a conductor passing electricity in this way. **electric clock** *n.* a clock worked by electricity, esp. one operated by a synchronous motor working off AC mains. **electric cooker** *n.* an assembly of electrically-heated boiling-plates, grill and oven for commercial or domestic cooking. **electric current** *n.* the continuous transition of electricity from one place to another. **electric eel** *n.* a large S American eel, *Electrophorus electricus*, able to give an electric shock. **electric eye** *n.* **1** a photocell. **2** a miniature cathode ray tube. **electric fence** *n.* a wire fence charged with electricity, used for purposes of security. **electric field** *n.* a region in which forces are exerted on any electric charge present there. **electric fire**, **electric heater**, **electric radiator** *n.* an apparatus which uses electricity to heat a room. **electric furnace** *n.* a furnace used for industrial purposes heated by electricity. **electric guitar** *n.* an electrically amplified guitar. **electric hare** *n.* an artificial hare made to run by electricity, used in greyhound racing. **electrician** (eliktrish´ən) *n.* **1** a person who installs or maintains electrical equipment. **2** a person skilled in the science and application of electricity. **electricity** (eliktris´iti) *n.* **1** a form of energy which makes its existence manifest by attractions and repulsions, by producing light and heat, chemical decomposition and other phenomena. **2** the branch of physics dealing with the laws and phenomena of electricity. **3 a** an electric charge. **b** an electric current. **4** strong excitement or emotional tension. **electric jar** *n.* a Leyden jar. **electric light** *n.* a light produced by the passage of an electric current. **electric locomotive** *n.* a locomotive in which the power is derived from a battery, a generator or a contact wire or rail. **electric organ** *n.* **1** (*Mus.*) an organ operated electrically. **2** (*Biol.*) in some fishes, an organ which can produce and discharge electricity. **electric railway** *n.* a system employing electricity to drive trains. **electric ray** *n.* a flatfish of the genus *Torpedo* which can give an electric shock. **electric razor**, **electric shaver** *n.* an appliance for removing bristles, hair etc. by the rapid movement of a protected blade actuated by electricity. **electric shock** *n.* the sudden pain felt from the passing of an electric current through the body. **electric storm** *n.* a violent disturbance of electric conditions of the atmosphere. **electric strength** *n.* the maximum electric field strength that can be applied to an insulator without causing breakdown. **electric torch** *n.* a small lamp carried in the hand, containing an electric battery and bulb. **electrify** (ilek´trifī) *v.t.* (*3rd pers. sing. pres.* **electrifies**, *pres.p.* **electrifying**, *past*, *p.p.* **electrified**) **1** to charge with electricity. **2** to thrill with joy, surprise or other exciting emotion. **3** to give an electric shock to. **electrification** (-fikā´shən) *n.* **1** the act or process of electrifying. **2** the state of being electrified. **3** conversion of a steam or other mechanical system into one worked by electricity. **electrifier** *n.* **electrize** (ilek´trīz), **electrise** *v.t.* to electrify. **electrization** (-zā´shən) *n.* [L *ēlectrum*, Gr. *ēlektron*, amber, conn. with *ēlektōr*, shining]

electro (ilek´trō) *n.* (*pl.* **electros**) **1** an electrotype. **2** electroplate. ~*v.t.* (*3rd pers. sing. pres.* **electroes**, *pres.p.* **electroing**, *past*, *p.p.* **electroed**) **1** to electrotype. **2** to electroplate.

electro- (ilektrō) *comb. form* **1** having electricity for its motive power. **2** of, relating to or resulting from electricity. [Gr. *ēlektron*, amber]

electrobath (ilek´trōbahth) *n.* a solution of a metallic salt used in electrotyping and electroplating.

electrobiology (ilektrōbīol´əji) *n.* electrophysiology, the science of the electric phenomena of living organisms. **electrobiologist** *n.*

electrocardiograph (ilektrōkah´diəgrahf) *n.* an instrument which indicates and records the manner in which the heart muscle is contracting. **electrocardiogram** *n.* a record so produced.

electrochemistry (ilektrōkem´istri) *n.* the science of the chemical effects produced by electricity. **electrochemical** *a.* **electrochemically** *adv.* **electrochemist** *n.*

electroconvulsive (ilektrōkənvŭl´siv) *a.* (of a therapy for mental or nervous disorders) using electric shocks to the brain.

electrocopper (ilektrōkop´ə) *v.t.* to give a copper coating to by electrolysis.

electroculture (ilek´trokŭlchə) *n.* the application of electricity to horticulture.

electrocute (ilek´trəkūt) *v.t.* **1** to kill by an electric shock. **2** to carry out a judicial sentence of death by administering a powerful electric shock. **electrocution** (-kū´shən) *n.* [EXECUTE]

electrode (ilek´trōd) *n.* **1** any one of the poles of a galvanic battery, or of an electrical device. **2** an anode, cathode, grid, collector, base etc.

electrodialysis (ilektrōdīal´isis) *n.* dialysis in which an electric field is applied across a semi-permeable membrane.

electrodynamics (ilektrōdīnam´iks) *n.* the branch of mechanics concerned with electricity in motion. **electrodynamic** *a.* **electrodynamometer** (-nəmom´itə) *n.* an instrument for measuring the strength of an electric current.

electroencephalograph (ilektrōensef´ələgrahf, -kef´-) *n.* an instrument recording small electrical impulses produced by the brain. **electroencephalogram** *n.* the record produced by an electroencephalograph. **electroencephalography** *n.*

electroengraving (ilektrōengrā´ving) *n.* engraving by means of electricity.

electrograph (ilek´trəgrahf) *n.* a recording electrometer.

electrokinetics (ilektrōkinet´iks) *n.* ELECTRODYNAMICS.

electroluminescence (ilektrōloomines´əns) *n.* luminescence produced by the application of an electric current. **electroluminescent** *a.*

electrolyse (ilek´trəlīz), (*N Am.*) **electrolyze** *v.t.* **1** to decompose by direct action of electricity. **2** to subject to electrolysis. **3** to remove (hair) by electrolysis. **electrolyser** *n.* **electrolysis** (-ol´isis) *n.* **1** the decomposition of chemical compounds by the passage of an electric current through them. **2** the science dealing with this process and its phenomena. **3** the removal of unwanted body hair by applying an electrically charged needle to the hair follicles. **electrolyte** (ilek´trəlīt) *n.* a compound which may be decomposed by an electric current. **electrolytic** (-lit´ik) *a.* **electrolytical** *a.* **electrolytically** *adv.*

electromagnet (ilektrōmag´nit) *n.* a bar of soft iron rendered magnetic by the passage of a current of electricity through a coil of wire surrounding it. **electromagnetic** (-net´ik) *a.* **electromagnetically** *adv.* **electromagnetic radiation** *n.* radiation with electric and magnetic fields at right angles to each other, visible light, radio waves, X-rays etc. **electromagnetic spectrum** *n.* the whole range of wavelengths, from long radio waves to short gamma rays, over which electromagnetic radiation occurs. **electromagnetism** (-mag´-) *n.* **1** magnetism produced by an electric current. **2** the science which treats of the production of magnetism by electricity, and the relations between magnetism and electricity.

electromechanical (ilektrōmikan´ikəl) *a.* of or relating to the use of electricity in mechanical processes etc. **electromechanically** *adv.*

electrometallurgy (ilektrōmet´alœji) *n.* the separation of metals from their alloys by means of electrolysis.

electrometer (eliktrom´itə) *n.* an instrument for measuring the amount of electrical force, or for indicating the presence of electricity. **electrometric** (ilektrōmet´-) *a.* **electrometrical** *a.* **electrometry** (-trom´itri) *n.*

electromotion (ilektrōmō´shən) *n.* **1** the passage of an electric current in a circuit. **2** mechanical motion produced by means of electricity. **electromotive** *a.* **electromotive force** *n.* difference in potential giving rise to an electric current. **electromotor** *n.* a machine for converting electric into mechanical energy.

electromuscular (ilektrōmŭs´kūlə) *a.* of or relating to the action of the muscles under electric influence.

electron (ilek´tron) *n.* (*Physics*) a particle bearing a negative electric charge, the most numerous constituent of matter and probably the cause of all electrical phenomena. **electron beam** *n.* a stream of electrons in a gas etc. **electron camera** *n.* a device which converts an optical image into an electric current by electronic means. **electron diffraction** *n.* the study of crystal structures by the diffraction of an electron beam by the atoms or molecules of the crystal. **electron gun** *n.* a device for producing an electron beam from a cathode. **electron lens** *n.* a device for focusing an electron beam by means of electrodes etc. **electron microscope** *n.* a thermionic tube in which a stream of electrons is focused on to a cathode and thence casts a magnified image of the cathode on to a screen, capable of very high magnification. **electron pair** *n.* **1** two electrons sharing the same orbit. **2** an electron and a positron. **electron spin resonance** *n.* a technique for finding electrons in a paramagnetic substance by the use of high-frequency radiation in a magnetic field. **electron-volt** *n.* a unit of energy in atomic physics, the increase in energy of an electron when its potential is raised by 1 volt.

electronegative (ilektrōneg´ətiv) *a.* **1** passing to the positive pole in electrolysis. **2** of or relating to, or producing, negative electricity. ~*n.* an electronegative element.

electronic (ilektron´ik) *a.* **1** of or relating to electronics. **2** operated or produced by means of electronics. **electronically** *adv.* **electronic brain** *n.* an electronic computer. **electronic data interchange** *n.* a process whereby information is transferred by linked computer terminals, telephones, fax machines etc. **electronic engineer** *n.* an engineer dealing with the design and construction of electronic equipment. **electronic engineering** *n.* **electronic flash** *n.* a flash for high-speed photography produced from a gas-discharge tube. **electronic mail** *n.* messages sent from one computer or fax machine to another by means of linked terminals. **electronic publishing** *n.* publishing of books etc. by electronic means, i.e. on disk etc. rather than on paper. **electronics** (eliktron´iks) *n.* the science of applied physics that deals with the conduction of electricity in a vacuum, or a semiconductor, and with other devices in which the movement of electrons is controlled. **electronic tagging** *n.* the tracking of people, goods etc. by attaching a tag with a transmitter.

electropathy (ilek´trōpathi) *n.* ELECTROTHERAPEUTICS.

electrophilic (ilektrōfil´ik) *a.* having an affinity for electrons. **electrophile** (ilek´trəfīl) *n.*

electrophorus (ilektrof´ərəs) *n.* an instrument for generating static electricity by induction. **electrophoresis** (-fərē´sis) *n.* the movement of charged particles under the influence of an electric field.

electrophysiology (ilektrōfiziol´əji) *n.* the study of electric phenomena in living organisms. **electrophysiological** (-loj´ikəl) *a.*

electroplate (ilek´trōplāt) *v.t.* to cover with a coating of silver or other metal by exposure in a solution of a metallic salt, which is decomposed by electrolysis. ~*n.* articles so produced. **electroplater** *n.*

electroplexy (ilek´trəpleksi) *n.* electroconvulsive therapy.

electropolar (ilektrōpō´lə) *a.* denoting a conductor positively electrified at one end and negatively at the other.

electroporation (ilektrōpərā´shən) *n.* (*Biol.*) the introduction of DNA etc. into bacteria by opening the pores of the cell membranes with an electric pulse. [PORE[1]]

electropositive (ilektrōpoz´itiv) *a.* **1** having a tendency to pass to the negative pole in electricity. **2** of or relating to, or producing, positive electricity. ~*n.* an electropositive element.

electroscope (ilek´trəskōp) *n.* an instrument for detecting the presence and the quality of electricity. **electroscopic** (-skop´ik) *a.*

electroshock (ilektrōshok´) *a.* (of medical treatment) using electric shocks.

electrostatic (ilektrōstat´ik) *a.* **1** of or relating to electrostatics. **2** produced by electricity at rest. **electrostatics** *n.* the science of static electricity. **electrostatic units** *n.pl.* a system of units based on the forces between static electric charges.

electrotechnology (ilektrōteknol´əji) *n.* the use of electricity in technology. **electrotechnic** *a.* **electrotechnical** *a.* **electrotechnics** *n.*

electrotherapeutics (ilektrōtherəpū´tiks), **electrotherapy** (-ther´əpi) *n.* (*Med.*) the use of electricity to treat paralysis etc. **electrotherapeutic** *a.* **electrotherapeutical** *a.* **electrotherapist** (-ther´əpist) *n.*
electrothermancy (ilektrōthœ´mənsi) *n.* the science of the relations of electric currents and the temperature of bodies. **electrothermal** *a.* **electrothermic** *a.*
electrotonus (ilektrot´ənəs) *n.* the alteration in the activity of a nerve or muscle under the action of a galvanic current. **electrotonic** (-ton´ik) *a.* [L *tonus*, tone]
electrotype (ilek´trətīp) *n.* **1** the process of producing copies of medals, woodcuts, type etc., by the electric deposition of copper upon a mould. **2** the facsimile so produced. *~v.t.* to copy by this process. **electrotyper** *n.* **electrotypist** *n.*
electrovalent (ilektrōvā´lənt) *a.* (*Chem.*) of or relating to bonding caused by electrostatic attraction between ions. **electrovalence** *n.* **electrovalency** *n.*
electroweak (ilektrōwēk´) *a.* (*Physics*) of or relating to a combination of electromagnetic and weak interactions.
electrum (ilek´trəm) *n.* **1** an alloy of gold and silver in use among the ancients. **2** native gold containing silver. **3** an alloy of copper, zinc and nickel, also called *German silver.* [L *ēlectrum*, Gr. *ēlektron*, amber, conn. with *ēlektōr*, shining]
electuary (ilek´tūəri) *n.* (*pl.* **electuaries**) a purgative medicine mixed with some sweet confection. [late L *ēlectuārium*, prob. from Gr. *ekleikton* (*ekleichein*, to lick away, cp. LICK)]
eleemosynary (eliəmos´inəri) *a.* (*formal*) **1** given or done by way of alms. **2** devoted to charitable purposes. **3** supported by or dependent on charity. [med. L *eleēmosynārius*, Gr. *eleēmosunē*, ALMS]
elegant (el´igənt) *a.* **1** pleasing to good taste. **2** graceful, well-proportioned, delicately finished, refined. **3** excellent, first-rate. **4** (of an apparatus, experiment etc.) simple and ingenious. **elegance** *n.* **elegantly** *adv.* [F *élégant*, L *ēlegans, -ntem*, conn. with *ēligere*, to choose, see ELECT]
elegy (el´əji) *n.* (*pl.* **elegies**) **1** a lyrical poem or a song of lamentation. **2** a poem written in elegiac couplets. **3** a poem of a plaintive, meditative kind. **elegiac** (-jī´-) *a.* **1** mournful. **2** of or relating to, or of the nature of elegies. **3** suited to elegy; used for elegies. **elegiacally** *adv.* **elegiac couplet** *n.* a couplet consisting of a hexameter and a pentameter. **elegiacs** *n.pl.* verse written in elegiac couplets, as were many of the elegies of the Greeks and Romans. **elegist** *n.* a composer of an elegy or elegies. **elegize** (el´əjīz), **elegise** *v.t.* to compose an elegy upon. *~v.i.* **1** to compose an elegy. **2** to write in a plaintive strain. [F *élégie*, L *elegīa*, Gr. *elegeia* (*elegos*, a lament)]
element (el´əmənt) *n.* **1** any one of the fundamental parts of which anything is composed. **2** a substance which cannot be resolved by chemical analysis into simpler substances. **3** a contributory factor; an aspect of a whole. **4** (*pl.*) earth, air, fire and water, formerly considered as fundamental substances. **5** the natural habitat of any creature, as water of fish. **6** the proper or natural sphere of any person or thing. **7** (*pl.*) violent atmospheric agencies. **8** (*pl.*) the rudiments of any science or art. **9** the resistance wire of an electric heater. **10** any one of the electrodes of a primary or secondary cell. **11** (*pl.*) the bread and wine used in the Eucharist. **12** a sole member constituting a set. **elemental** (-men´-) *a.* **1** of or relating to the four elements of which the world was supposed to be formed. **2** of or relating to the primitive forces of nature; like the primitive forces of nature. **3** ultimate, simple, uncompounded. **4** of, relating to or arising from first principles. *~n.* an elemental spirit. **elementalism** *n.* the theory which resolves the gods of antiquity into the forces and aspects of nature. **elementally** *adv.* in an elemental manner. **elemental spirit** *n.* any of those spirits identified with natural forces, such as salamanders, sylphs, gnomes and undines, said to inhabit respectively fire, air, earth and water. **elementary** (-men´-) *a.* **1** rudimentary, treating of first principles, introductory. **2** easy, simple. **3** consisting of one element; primary, uncompounded. **elementarily** *adv.* **elementariness** *n.* **elementary particle** *n.* any of several particles, such as electrons, protons or neutrons, which are less complex than atoms, so called because believed to be incapable of subdivision. **elementary school** *n.* **1** (*esp. Hist.*) a primary school. **2** (*N Am.*) a school attended by children for the first six to eight years of education. [OF, from L *elementum* (etym. uncertain)]
elemi (el´əmi) *n.* a gum resin obtained from the Philippine tree, *Canarium luzanicum*, used in pharmacy. [Arab. *al-lāmī*]
elenchus (ileng´kəs) *n.* (*pl.* **elenchi** (-kī)) (*Logic*) a refutation. **elenctic** (ilengk´tik) *a.* [L, from Gr. *elenchos*]
elephant (el´ifənt) *n.* (*pl. in general* **elephant**, *in particular* **elephants**) **1** a large pachydermatous animal, four-footed, with flexible proboscis and long curved tusks, of which two species now exist, *Elephas maximus* and *Loxodonta africana*, the former partially domesticated and used as a beast of draught and burden. **2** a size of paper (28 × 23 in.; double, 40 × 26¾ in.) (71.1 × 58.4 cm; 101.6 × 67.9 cm). **African elephant** AFRICAN. **Indian elephant** INDIAN. **white elephant** WHITE. **elephant beetle** *n.* a large W African beetle, *Goliathus giganteus* or *G. cacicus.* **elephant-bird** *n.* an aepyornis. **elephant fish** *n.* the southern chimera, *Callorhyncus antarcticus*, found off New Zealand, S Australia and Tasmania, so called from its prehensile snout. **elephant grass** *n.* any of several very tall tropical grasses, esp. *Pennisetum purpureum.* **elephantiasis** (eləfəntī´əsis) *n.* a cutaneous disease occurring in tropical countries, in which the skin of the patient becomes hardened and the part affected greatly enlarged. **elephantine** (-fan´tīn) *a.* **1** of or relating to elephants. **2** resembling an elephant. **3** huge, immense. **4** unwieldy, clumsy. **elephantoid** (-fan´toid) *a.* **elephant seal** *n.* the sea elephant. **elephant shrew** *n.* a small African insectivorous mammal with a long snout, of the family Macroscelididae. [ME *olifaunt*, OF *olifant*, L *elephas, -ntem* Gr. *elephas* (etym. uncertain)]
Eleusinian (elūsin´iən) *a.* **1** relating to Eleusis, in ancient Attica, or to the mysteries in honour of Demeter celebrated there annually. **2** darkly mysterious. [L *Eleusīnius*, Gr. *Eleusinios*]
elevate (el´əvāt) *v.t.* **1** to lift up; to raise aloft. **2** to raise from a lower to a higher place. **3** to exalt in position or dignity. **4** to make louder or higher. **5** to raise in character or intellectual capacity. **6** to refine, to improve. **7** to elate, to animate, to exhilarate. **elevated** *a.* **1** raised. **2** at or on a higher level. **3** (*coll.*) slightly intoxicated. **elevated railway** *n.* a city railway raised on pillars above the street-level. **elevation** (elivā´shən) *n.* **1** the act of elevating. **2** the state of being elevated. **3** an elevated position or ground. **4** height above sea level, or any other given level. **5** the height of a building. **6** a side or end view of an object or building drawn with or without reference to perspective. **7** (*Astron.*) the angular altitude of a heavenly body above the horizon. **8** in gunnery, the angle of the line of fire with the plane of the horizon. **9** (*fig.*) exaltation, grandeur, dignity. **10** in ballet, the ability to leap and seem to remain suspended in the air. **11** the tightening of elevators to raise the body. **elevator** *n.* **1** a person who or something which elevates. **2** a hinged flap on the tailplane to provide vertical control of an aircraft. **3** a muscle whose function it is to raise any part of the body. **4** a machine for hoisting, as to raise grain from a

car or ship to a high level, whence it can be discharged into any other receptacle. **5** (*N Am.*) a lift for moving between floors or levels. **6** (*N Am.*) a place to which grain is lifted for storage. **elevatory** *a.* [L *ēlevātus*, p.p. of *ēlevāre* (E-, *levāre*, to lift, from *levis*, light)]

eleven (ilev´ən) *n.* **1** the number or figure 11 or XI. **2** the age of 11. **3** a set of eleven things or people. **4** an article of attire, such as a shoe etc., denoted by the number 11. **5** a score of 11 points. **6** the 11th hour after midday or midnight. **7** in cricket or association football, the eleven people selected to play for a particular side. ~*a.* **1** 11 in number. **2** aged 11. **the eleven** the disciples of Christ without Judas. **elevenfold** *a., adv.* **eleven plus (examination)** *n.* (*Hist.*) a school examination taken by children of about 11 to determine the particular type of secondary education they were to be given by the state. **elevenses** (-ziz) *n.pl.* (*coll.*) a snack taken in the middle of the morning. **eleventh** *n.* **1** any one of 11 equal parts. **2** (*Mus.*) the interval of an octave and a fourth. ~*n., a.* **1** (the) last of 11 (people, things etc.). **2** (the) next after the 10th. **at the eleventh hour** at the last moment (in allusion to the parable of the labourers, Matthew xx). **eleven year period** *n.* (*Astron.*) the cycle of periodic changes in the occurrence of sunspots. [OE *endlufon*, *endleofan*, from Gmc. *ainlif-* (cp. Dut. and G *elf*, Goth. *ainlif*, Icel. *ellifu*)]

elevon (el´ivon) *n.* a wing-flap on a delta wing aircraft. [*elev*ator, ailer*on*]

ELF *abbr.* extremely (or extra) low frequency.

elf (elf) *n.* (*pl.* **elves** (elvz)) **1** a tiny supernatural being supposed to inhabit groves and wild and desolate places and to exercise a mysterious power over humans. **2** a fairy. **3** a mischievous person. **4** an imp. **5** a tiny creature, a dwarf. **6** (a pet name for) a child. **elf-arrow**, **elf-bolt**, **elf-dart** *n.* a flint arrowhead used in the Stone Age, popularly thought to be shot by fairies. **elf-child** *n.* (*pl. elf-children*) a child supposed to be left by fairies in exchange for one taken away by them. **elfin** *a.* elfish. ~*n.* **1** a little elf. **2** a sprite, an urchin. **elfish**, **elvish** *a.* **1** like an elf. **2** of the nature of an elf. **3** proceeding from or caused by elves. **4** mischievous. **elvishly** *adv.* **elvish-marked** *a.* marked by the fairies. **elf-lock** *n.* hair tangled in a knot, as if done by elves. **elf-struck** *a.* bewitched by elves. [OE *ælf* (cp. Icel. *ālfr*, G *Elf*, also *Alp*, a nightmare)]

elicit (ilis´it) *v.t.* (*pres.p.* **eliciting**, *past, p.p.* **elicited**) **1** to draw out, evoke. **2** to educe, extract. **elicitation** (-ā´shən) *n.* **elicitor** *n.* [L *ēlicitus*, p.p. of *ēlicere* (E-, *lacere*, to entice)]

Usage note The spellings of the verb *elicit* and the adjective *illicit* (pronounced the same) should not be confused.

elide (ilīd´) *v.t.* **1** to strike out, omit, delete. **2** esp. in grammar, to cut off (as the last syllable). **3** to annul. **elision** (ilizh´ən) *n.* **1** the suppression of a letter or syllable for the sake of euphony, metre etc. **2** the suppression of a passage in a book or a discourse. [L *ēlīdere* (E-, *laedere*, to dash)]

eligible (el´ijibəl) *a.* **1** fit or deserving to be chosen. **2** desirable, suitable. **3** fit or qualified to be chosen to any office or position. **4** desirable for marriage. **eligibility** (-bil´-) *n.* **eligibly** *adv.* [F *éligible*, L *ēligibilis*, from *ēligere*, see ELECT]

eliminate (ilim´ināt) *v.t.* **1** to cast out, expel. **2** to cast aside, remove, get rid of. **3** to exclude, to ignore (certain considerations). **4** to expel (waste matter) from the body. **5** (*sl.*) to murder. **6** (*Math.*) to cause to disappear from an equation. **7** to disengage, to isolate. **eliminable** *a.* **elimination** (-ā´shən) *n.* **1** the act of eliminating. **2** expulsion, ejection. **3** leaving out or passing over. **4** (*Math.*) removal of a quantity from an equation. **eliminator** *n.* a device for supplying a battery radio receiving-set with electricity from the mains. **eliminatory** *a.* [L *ēliminātus*, p.p. of *ēlimināre* (E-, *līmin-*, stem of *līmen*, threshold)]

ELINT (elint´), **Elint** *n.* gathering intelligence by electronic means. [*el*ectronic *int*elligence]

eliquation (elikwā´shən) *n.* **1** liquefaction. **2** in metallurgy, the separation of a fusible substance from another less fusible by heating to a degree sufficient to melt the former but not the latter. [L *ēliquatio -ōnem*]

elision ELIDE.

elite (ālēt´), **élite** *n.* **1** the pick, the flower, the best part. **2** a type size for typewriters of 12 characters per in. (2.54 cm). **elitism** *n.* (*often derog.*) **1** the favouring of the creation of an elite. **2** a sense of pride or conceit at belonging to an elite. **elitist** *n., a.* [F, from L *ēlecta*, fem. of *ēlectus*, ELECT]

elixir (ilik´sə) *n.* **1** the alchemists' liquor for transmuting metal into gold. **2** a potion for prolonging life. **3** a cordial, a sovereign remedy. **4** †the essential principle or quintessence. **5** †a distillation or concentrated tincture. **elixir vitae** (vī´tē), **elixir of life** *n.* a potion which was supposed to prolong life. [med. L, from Arab. *al-iksīr* (*al*, the, Gr. *xērion*, dry powder for wounds)]

Elizabethan (ilizəbē´thən) *a.* **1** of or relating to Queen Elizabeth I or Queen Elizabeth II or the time of either of these. **2** in the style characterizing the literature, architecture, dress etc. of the time of Elizabeth I. ~*n.* a personage or writer of the time of Elizabeth I or II.

elk (elk) *n.* (*pl. in general* **elk**, *in particular* **elks**) **1** the largest animal of the deer family, *Alces alces*, a native of northern Europe and of N America, where it is called the moose. **2** the wapiti. **3** the eland. **Irish elk** IRISH. **elk-hound** *n.* **1** a large breed of hunting dog of the spitz type, orig. used for hunting elk. **2** a dog of this breed. **Elks** *n.pl.* a US fraternal society. [OE *elh*, *elch* (cp. Icel. *elgr*, OHG *elaho*, L *alces*, Gr. *alkē*)]

ell (el) *n.* (*Hist.*) a measure of length, varying in different countries, for measuring cloth: the English ell is 45 in. (114.3 cm). **ell-wand** *n.* a measuring rod an ell long. [OE *eln* (cp. Dut. *el*, G *Elle*, Goth. *aleina*, Swed. *aln*, Gr. *ōlenē*, L *ulna*, whence F *aune*)]

ellagic (ilaj´ik) *a.* of or relating to gall-nuts or to gallic acid. **ellagic acid** *n.* an acid obtained from gallic acid, bezoars, certain barks etc. [F *ellagique*, from *ellag*, anagram of *galle*, gall-nut]

ellipse (ilips´) *n.* **1** a regular oval; a plane curve of such a form that the sum of two straight lines, drawn from any point in it to two given fixed points called the foci, will always be the same. **2** a conic section formed by a plane intersecting a cone obliquely. **3** ellipsis. **ellipsis** (-sis) *n.* (*pl.* **ellipses** (-sēz)) **1** omission of one or more words necessary to the complete construction of a sentence. **2** (*Print.*) a set of three dots indicating omitted matter. **3** †a mark denoting the omission of one or more words or letters, as in *d——d* for 'damned'. **ellipsograph** *n.* an instrument for describing ellipses. **ellipsoid** (-soid) *n.* **1** a solid figure of which every plane section through one axis is an ellipse and every other section an ellipse or a circle. **2** †a solid figure produced by the revolution of an ellipse about its axis. ~*a.* ellipsoidal. **ellipsoidal** (elipsoi´-) *a.* of or relating to an ellipsoid. **elliptic** (-tik), **elliptical** (-kəl) *a.* **1** of or relating to an ellipse. **2** of or relating to ellipsis. **elliptically** *adv.* **ellipticity** (eliptis´-) *n.* **1** the quality of being elliptic. **2** the extent to which any ellipse differs from a circle, or any ellipsoid from a sphere. [L *ellipsis*, Gr. *elleipsis*, from *elleipein* (*el-*,*en*, in, *leipein*, to leave)]

elm (elm) *n.* **1** any tree of the genus *Ulmus*. **2** ENGLISH ELM (under ENGLISH). **3** the wood of the elm. **elmen** *a.* of or relating to the elm. **elm tree** *n.* **elmwood** *n.* **elmy** *a.* [OE (cp. Icel. *ālmr*, Swed. and Dan. *alm*, G *Ulm*, L *ulmus*)]

El Niño (el nē´nyō) *n.* a warm ocean current in the

southern Pacific, arising every few years, which affects the S American coast directly and climatic disturbance over a much larger area. [Sp., the (Christ) child, because often arising around Christmas]

elocution (eləkū´shən) *n.* **1** the art, style or manner of speaking or reading. **2** effective oral delivery. **3** appropriate language in speaking or writing. **4** a particular style of speaking. **elocutionary** *a.* **elocutionist** *n.* [L *ēlocūtio -ōnem*, from *ēloquī* (E-, *loquī*, to speak)]

eloge (ālōzh´) *n.* an encomium, a panegyric, esp. a discourse in honour of a deceased person. **elogist** (el´əjist) *n.* [F *éloge*, L *ēlogium*, a short saying (Gr. *logos*, a saying, a word), confused with *eulogium*, EULOGY]

Elohim (ilō´him) *n.* the ordinary name of God in the Hebrew Scriptures. **Elohist** *n.* a Biblical writer or one of the writers of parts of the Hexateuch, where the word *Elohim* is habitually used for *Yahveh*, Jehovah. **Elohistic** (eləhis´-) *a.* [Heb. *elōhim*, pl. used in sing. sense, God]

†**eloin** (iloin´), **eloign** *v.t.* **1** to remove. **2** to remove or seclude (oneself). **3** to carry off. **4** (*Law*) to remove beyond the jurisdiction of a court or sheriff. [OF *esloignier* (F *éloigner*), late L *exlongāre*, *ēlongāre*, as ELONGATE]

elongate (ē´lɒnggāt) *v.t.* **1** to extend. **2** to make longer. ~*v.i.* **1** to grow longer. **2** (*Bot.*) to increase in length, to taper. **3** to recede. ~*a.* **1** lengthened, extended. **2** (*Zool.*, *Bot.*) very slender in proportion to length. **elongated** *a.* slender in proportion to length. **elongation** (-gā´shən) *n.* **1** the act of lengthening or extending. **2** the state of being elongated. **3** a prolongation, an extension. **4** (*Astron.*) the angular distance of a planet from the sun or of a satellite from its primary. [late L *ēlongātus*, p.p. of *ēlongāre*, to remove (E-, *longus*, long)]

elope (ilōp´) *v.i.* **1** to run away with a lover, with a view to clandestine marriage, in defiance of social or moral restraint. **2** to run away in a clandestine manner, to abscond. **elopement** *n.* **eloper** *n.* [*aloper*, perh. from a ME *alope* or *ilope*, p.p. of *aleapen* or *leapen*, to LEAP (cp. the later MDut. *ontlōpen* and G *entlaufen*)]

eloquence (el´əkwəns) *n.* **1** fluent, powerful and appropriate verbal expression, esp. of emotional ideas. **2** eloquent language. **3** rhetoric. **eloquent** *a.* **1** having the power of expression in fluent, vivid and appropriate language. **2** full of expression, feeling or interest. **eloquently** *adv.* [F *éloquence*, L *ēloquentia*, *ēloquens -ntem*, pres.p. of *ēloquī* (E-, *loquī*, to speak)]

Elsan® (el´san) *n.* a type of chemical lavatory.

else (els) *adv.* **1** besides, in addition, other. **2** instead. **3** otherwise, in the other case, if not. **elsewhere** *adv.* in or to some other place. [OE *elles*, gen. sing. used as adv. (cp. OHG *elles*, *alles*, also L *alius*, other)]

ELT *abbr.* English language teaching.

eluant, eluate ELUTE.

elucidate (iloo´sidāt) *v.t.* **1** to make lucid, throw light on. **2** to render intelligible; to explain. **elucidation** (-ā´shən) *n.* **elucidative** (-loo´-) *a.* **elucidator** *n.* **elucidatory** *a.* [late L *ēlūcidātus*, p.p. of *ēlūcidāre* (E-, *lūcidus*, bright)]

elude (ilood´) *v.t.* **1** to escape from by artifice or dexterity. **2** to evade, to dodge, to shirk. **3** to remain undiscovered or unexplained by. **4** to baffle (search or inquiry). **5** †to delude. **eluder** *n.* **eludible** *a.* **elusion** (-zhən) *n.* **elusive** (-siv) *a.* **1** difficult to catch or locate. **2** difficult to remember. **elusively** *adv.* **elusiveness** *n.* **elusory** *a.* [L *ēlūdere* (E-, *lūdere*, to play, p.p. *lūsus*)]

Usage note The spellings of adjectives *elusive*, *elusory* (from *elude*) and *illusive* and *illusory* (deceptive, pronounced the same) should not be confused.

eluent ELUTE.

Elul (ē´lul) *n.* the sixth month of the Jewish ecclesiastical, and the 12th of the civil year, beginning with the new moon of September. [Heb. *ălal*, to reap]

elusion, elusive ELUDE.

elute (iloot´) *v.t.* to wash out by the action of a solvent. **eluate** *n.* a liquid obtained by elution. **eluent** (el´ū-), **eluant** *n.* a liquid used for elution. **elution** (iloo´shən) *n.* purification or separation by washing. [L *ēlūtio -ōnis*, washing]

elutriate (iloo´triāt) *v.t.* (*Chem.*) to purify by straining or washing so as to separate the lighter and the heavier particles. **elutriation** (-ā´shən) *n.* **elutriator** *n.* [L *ēlutriātus*, p.p. of *ēlutriāre*, to wash out]

ELV *abbr.* expendable launch vehicle.

elvan (el´vən) *n.* **1** intrusive igneous rock penetrating sedimentary strata in Cornwall, Devon and Ireland. **2** a vein or dike of this. **elvanite** (-nīt) *n.* **elvanitic** (-nit´-) *a.* [etym. uncertain (perh. Corn. *elven*)]

elver (el´və) *n.* a young eel, esp. a young conger. [EELFARE (under EEL)]

elvish, elves ELF.

Elysium (iliz´iəm) *n.* **1** in Greek mythology, the abode of the souls of heroes after death. **2** a place or state of perfect happiness. **Elysian** *a.* **Elysian Fields** *n.* the paradise of Greek mythology. [L, from Gr. *Elusion* (*pedion*), (the plain) of the blessed]

elytron (el´itron) *n.* (*pl.* **elytra** (-trə)) each of the horny sheaths which constitute the anterior wings of beetles. **elytriform** (ilit´rifawm) *a.* [Gr. *elutron*, a sheath, from *eluein*, to roll round]

Elzevir (el´zəviə, -və) *a.* of or relating to, or resembling the type used by the Elzevirs in their editions of Latin classics. [*Elzevir*, a celebrated family of printers, of Amsterdam, 1595–1680]

em (em) *n.* **1** the 13th letter of the alphabet, M, m. **2** (*Print.*) the square of the body of any size of type, used as the unit of measurement for printed matter. **3** a printers' general measure of 12 points or ⅙ in. (0.42 cm). **em dash, em rule** *n.* a dash one em long (—), used in punctuation.

em- (em, im) *pref.* EN- used before *b*, *p* and sometimes *m*, as in *embank*, *empanoply*, *emmarble*.

'em (əm) *pron.* (*coll.*) THEM. [ME *hem*]

EMA *abbr.* European Monetary Agreement.

emaciate (imā´siāt) *v.t.* **1** to cause to lose flesh or become lean. **2** to reduce to leanness, to impoverish (soil etc.). **emaciated** *a.* abnormally and unhealthily thin. **emaciation** (-ā´shən) *n.* [L *ēmaciātus*, p.p. of *ēmaciāre* (E-, *maciēs*, leanness, from *macer*, lean)]

email E-MAIL (under E[2]).

emanate (em´ənāt) *v.i.* **1** to issue or flow as from a source, to originate. **2** to proceed (from). ~*v.t.* to emit, send out. **emanation** (-ā´shən) *n.* **1** the act of emanating from something, as from a source. **2** that which emanates, an efflux, an effluence. **3** the theory that all things are outflowings from the essence of God. **4** any product of a process of emanating. **emanative** *a.* **emanator** *n.* **emanatory** *a.* [L *ēmānātus*, p.p. of *ēmānāre*, to flow out]

emancipate (iman´sipāt) *v.t.* **1** to release from bondage, slavery, oppression, or legal, social or moral restraint. **2** to set free, to liberate. **3** in Roman law, to liberate from parental authority. **emancipation** (-ā´shən) *n.* **1** the releasing from slavery, oppression, restraint or legal disabilities. **2** the state of being freed from any bond or restraint. **emancipationist** *n.* an advocate of emancipation of slaves. **emancipator** (-man´-) *n.* **emancipatory** *a.* **emancipist** *n.* (*Hist.*) in Australia, a convict who had served their term. [L *ēmancipātus*, p.p. of *ēmancipāre* (E-, *mancipāre*, to transfer property, from *manceps*, from *manus*, hand, *capere*, to take)]

emarginate[1] (imah´jināt) *v.t.* **1** to take away the edge or margin of. **2** to emphasize the contour lines of (a microscopic object embedded in jelly) through unequal refraction. **emarginated** *a.* EMARGINATE[2]. **emargination** (-ā´shən) *n.* [L *ēmargінātus*, p.p. of *ēmargināre* (E-, *margināre*, to furnish with a border, from *margo -ginis*, MARGIN]

emarginate[2] (imah´jinət) *a.* **1** with the margin notched. **2** (*Bot.*) notched at the apex. [see EMARGINATE[1]]

emasculate[1] (imas´kūlāt) *v.t.* **1** to castrate. **2** to deprive of masculine strength or vigour; to make effeminate, to weaken. **3** to deprive (as language) of force or energy. **4** to enfeeble (a literary work) by undue expurgation or excision. **5** to remove coarse expressions from (a literary production). **emasculation** (-ā´shən) *n.* **emasculative** (-mas´-) *a.* **emasculator** *n.* **emasculatory** *a.* [L *ēmasculātus*, p.p. of *ēmasculāre* (E-, *masculus*, male)]

emasculate[2] (imas´kūlət) *a.* **1** castrated. **2** enfeebled, effeminate, weak. [see EMASCULATE[1]]

embalm (imbahm´) *v.t.* **1** to preserve (e.g. a body) from putrefaction by means of spices and aromatic drugs. **2** (*poet.*) to imbue with sweet scents. **3** (*fig.*) to preserve from oblivion. **embalmer** *n.* **embalmment** *n.* [F *embaumer*]

embank (imbangk´) *v.t.* to confine or defend with a bank or banks, dikes, masonry etc. **embankment** *n.* **1** a bank or stone structure for confining a river etc. **2** a raised mound or bank for carrying a road etc. **3** the act or process of embanking.

☒ **embarass** common misspelling of EMBARRASS.

embarcation EMBARKATION (under EMBARK).

embargo (imbah´gō) *n.* (*pl.* **embargoes**) **1** a prohibition by authority upon the departure of vessels from ports under its jurisdiction. **2** a complete suspension of foreign commerce or of a particular branch of foreign trade. **3** a hindrance, check, impediment. **4** a prohibition or restraint, as on publication. ~*v.t.* (*3rd pers. sing. pres.* **embargoes**, *pres.p.* **embargoing**, *past, p.p.* **embargoed**) **1** to lay an embargo upon. **2** to seize for purposes of state. **3** to requisition, seize, confiscate. **4** to prohibit, to forbid. [Sp., from *embargar*, to arrest, hinder, prob. from late L *imbarricāre* (*im-*, IN-[1], *barra*, BAR[1])]

embark (imbahk´) *v.t.* **1** to put on board ship. **2** to invest (e.g. money) in any business. ~*v.i.* **1** to go on board ship. **2** (*fig.*) to engage or enter (upon any undertaking). **embarkation** (embahkā´shən), **embarcation** *n.* **1** the act of putting or going on board a ship or vessel. **2** a cargo, anything that is embarked. [F *embarquer*, late L *imbarcāre*]

embarras de choix (ãbara də shwa´) *n.* a perplexing number of things to choose from. **embarras de richesse** (rēshes´), **embarras de richesses** *n.* a perplexing abundance of wealth, more than one needs or can manage. [F]

embarrass (imbar´əs) *v.t.* **1** to confuse, perplex, disconcert. **2** to encumber, hamper, entangle, impede, hinder. **3** to involve in pecuniary difficulties. **4** to complicate, render difficult. ~*n.* (*N Am.*) a place where navigation is rendered difficult by accumulations of driftwood etc. **embarrassed** *a.* **1** feeling self-conscious, awkward, disconcerted. **2** in financial difficulties. **embarrassedly** *adv.* **embarrassing** *a.* causing embarrassment. **embarrassingly** *adv.* **embarrassment** *n.* **1** perplexity of mind, discomposure, uneasiness, perturbation arising from bashfulness. **2** confusion or intricacy of affairs. **3** pecuniary difficulties. **4** an impediment, a hindrance. [F *embarrasser*, to hamper, from *embarras*, conn. with *embarrer*, to bar in]

embassy (em´bəsi) *n.* (*pl.* **embassies**) **1** the official residence or offices of an ambassador. **2** the body of persons sent as ambassadors; an ambassador and their suite. **3** the function, office or mission of an ambassador. **4** an official deputation or mission. †**embassade** (-sād) *n.* an embassy. [OF *ambassée*, late L *ambactiāta*, *ambasciāta*, orig. fem. p.p. of *ambactiāre*, to go on a mission (see AMBASSADOR)]

embattle[1] (imbat´əl) *v.t.* **1** to array in order of battle. **2** to prepare for battle. **3** to fortify. ~*v.i.* to be drawn up in battle array. **embattled**[1] *a.* **1** prepared for battle. **2** involved in a battle or in conflict of another kind. [OF *embataillier*]

embattle[2] (imbat´əl) *v.t.* to furnish with battlements. **embattled**[2] *a.* (*Her.*) shaped like battlements. [BATTLEMENT]

embattled[1] EMBATTLE[1].

embattled[2] EMBATTLE[2].

embay (imbā´) *v.t.* **1** to enclose (a vessel) in a bay, to landlock. **2** to force (a vessel) into a bay. **3** to shut in, confine, enclose, surround. **embayment** *n.*

embed (imbed´), **imbed** *v.t.* (*pres.p.* **embedding**, **imbedding**, *past, p.p.* **embedded**, **imbedded**) **1** to lay as in a bed. **2** to set firmly in surrounding matter. **3** to enclose firmly (said of the surrounding matter). **embedment** *n.*

embellish (imbel´ish) *v.t.* **1** to beautify, to adorn. **2** to add incidents or imaginary accompaniments so as to heighten (a narrative). **embellisher** *n.* **embellishment** *n.* [OF *embellir* (EM-, *bel*, L *bellus*, handsome)]

ember[1] (em´bə) *n.* **1** a smouldering piece of coal or wood. **2** (*often pl.*) smouldering remnants of a fire or of passion, love etc. [OE *ǣmerge* (cp. Dan. *emmer*, OHG *eimurja*)]

ember[2] (em´bə) *n.* an anniversary, a recurring time or season. **Ember days** *n.pl.* in the Christian Church, certain days set apart for fasting and prayer, the Wednesday, Friday and Saturday next following the first Sunday in Lent, Whit-Sunday, Holy Cross Day (14 Sept.), and St Lucy's Day (13 Dec.). **Ember-tide** *n.* the season at which Ember days occur. **Ember weeks** *n.pl.* the weeks in which the Ember days fall. [OE *ymbren*, prob. corr. of *ymbryne*, a period, revolution (*ymb*, about, *ryne*, running)]

ember-goose (em´bəgoos), **ember-diver** *n.* (*pl.* **ember-geese**, **ember-divers**) the northern diver or loon, *Gavia immer.* [Norw. *emmer-gaas*]

embezzle (imbez´əl) *v.t.* to appropriate fraudulently (what is committed to one's care). ~*v.i.* to commit embezzlement. **embezzlement** *n.* **embezzler** *n.* [A-F *enbeseler*, OF *besillier*, to maltreat, to ravage, prob. from *bes-*, late L *bis-*, a pejorative pref. (cp. OF *besil*, ill-treatment, torture), influenced by L *imbecillāre*, to weaken]

embitter (imbit´ə) *v.t.* **1** to cause (a person) to be bitterly resentful or hostile. **2** to make bitter, or more bitter. **3** to render harder or more distressing, to aggravate. **4** to add poignancy or sharpness to. **embitterment** *n.*

†**emblaze** (imblāz´) *v.t.* **1** to set in a blaze, to kindle. **2** (*fig.*) to light up, to cause to glitter. **3** to emblazon, to set forth by heraldic devices. **4** to glorify.

emblazon (imblā´zən) *v.t.* **1** to blazon; to adorn with heraldic figures or armorial designs. **2** to decorate; to make brilliant. **3** to celebrate, to make illustrious. **emblazoner** *n.* **emblazoning** *n.* emblazonment. **emblazonment** *n.* **1** the act or art of blazoning. **2** blazonry. **emblazonry** *n.* blazonry.

emblem (em´bləm) *n.* **1** a symbolic figure; a picture, object or representation of an object symbolizing some other thing, class, action or quality, as a crown for royalty or a balance for justice. **2** a symbol, a type, a personification. **3** a heraldic device. ~†*v.t.* to symbolize, to represent or show forth by an emblem. **emblema** (-blē´mə) *n.* (*pl.* **emblemata** (-mətə)) (*usu. in pl.*) a figure with which the ancients decorated gold, silver and copper vessels, and which could be fixed on or taken off at pleasure. **emblematic** (-mat´-), **emblematical** (-kəl) *a.* **emblematically** *adv.* **emblematist** (-blem´-) *n.* a writer of allegories or inventor of emblems. **emblematize**, **emblematise** *v.t.* **1** to represent by or as an emblem. **2** to symbolize. **emblematology**

(-tol´-) *n.* [L and Gr. *emblēma*, from *emballein* (EM-, *ballein*, to throw)]

emblements (em´bləmənts) *n.pl.* **1** (*Law*) growing crops annually produced by the cultivator's labour, which belong to the tenant, though the lease may terminate before harvest. **2** the natural products of the soil. [OF *emblaement*, from *emblaer* (F *emblaver*), to sow with corn, med. L *imbladāre* (IN-[1], *bladum*, L *ablatum*, the gathered-in harvest, hence corn)]

embody (imbod´i) *v.t.* (*3rd pers. sing. pres.* **embodies**, *pres.p.* **embodying**, *past, p.p.* **embodied**) **1** to incarnate or invest with a material body. **2** to express in a concrete form. **3** to be a concrete expression of, to form into a united whole. **4** to incorporate, include. **embodier** *n.* **embodiment** *n.*

embog (imbog´) *v.t.* (*pres.p.* **embogging**, *past, p.p.* **embogged**) **1** to plunge into a bog. **2** to encumber in or as in a bog.

embogue (imbōg´) *v.i.* (*3rd pers. sing. pres.* **embogues**, *pres.p.* **emboguing**, *past, p.p.* **embogued**) to disembogue, to discharge (as a river into the sea). [Sp. *embocar* (EM-, *boca*, mouth)]

embolden (imbōl´dən) *v.t.* **1** to give boldness to. **2** to encourage.

embolism (em´bəlizm) *n.* **1** partial or total blocking-up of a blood vessel by a clot of blood, bubble of air etc. **2** an intercalation; the insertion of days, months or years in the calendar in order to produce regularity. **3** anything intercalated, such as a period of time, a prayer in the order of public worship etc. **embolectomy** (-ek´təmi) *n.* (*pl.* **embolectomies**) the surgical removal of an embolus. **embolic** (-bol´ik) *a.* **embolismic** (-liz´-) *a.* **embolus** (-ləs) *n.* (*pl.* **emboli** (-lī)) a clot which causes embolism. [L *embolismus*, late Gr. *embolismos*, from *embolē*, a throwing in (EM-, *ballein*, to throw)]

embonpoint (ãbõpwã´) *n.* plumpness of person or figure. *~a.* **1** plump, well-nourished. **2** stout. **3** (*euphem.*) fat. [F, orig. *en bon point*, in good condition]

embosom (imbuz´m) *v.t.* (*formal*) **1** to place or hold in or as in the bosom of anything. **2** to enclose, surround. **3** to embrace, to cherish.

emboss (imbos´) *v.t.* **1** to engrave or mould in relief. **2** to decorate with bosses or raised figures. **3** to cause to stand out in relief. **embossed** *a.* **embosser** *n.* **embossment** *n.* [OF *embosser* (EM-, *bosse*, BOSS[1])]

embouchure (ãbooshuə´) *n.* **1** the shaping of the lips to the mouthpiece of a brass or wind instrument. **2** the mouthpiece of such an instrument. **3** the mouth of a river etc. [F, from *emboucher*, to put in the mouth, to discharge by a mouth (EM-, *bouche*, mouth)]

embow (imbō´) *v.t.* **1** to arch, to vault. **2** to bend, to curve like a bow. **embowed** *a.* **embowment** *n.*

embowel (imbow´əl) *v.t.* (*pres.p.* **embowelling**, (*N Am.*) **emboweling**, *past, p.p.* **embowelled**, (*N Am.*) **emboweled**) to disembowel. **embowelment** *n.* **1** the act of disembowelling. **2** the inward parts of anything. [OF *enboweler* (EM-, *bouel*, BOWEL)]

embower (imbow´ə) *v.t.* (*formal*) **1** to enclose in or as in a bower. **2** to shelter, to surround (as with trees or shrubs).

embox (imboks´) *v.t.* to set or shut in or as in a box.

embrace[1] (imbrās´) *v.t.* **1** to enfold in the arms. **2** to clasp and hold fondly. **3** (of, e.g., a creeping plant) to clasp or twine round. **4** to enclose, encircle, surround. **5** to include, contain, comprise. **6** to receive, adopt, accept eagerly. **7** to take in with the eye, to comprehend. **8** †to have sexual intercourse with. *~v.i.* **1** to join in an embrace. **2** †to join in sexual intercourse. *~n.* **1** a clasping in the arms. **2** (*pl., dated*) sexual intercourse. **embraceable** *a.* **embracement** *n.* **embracer**[1] *n.* **embracing** *a., n.* **embracingly** *adv.* **embracingness** *n.* **embracive** *a.* [OF *embracer* (EM-, *brace*, L *bracchia*, pl., the arms)]

†**embrace**[2] (imbrās´) *v.t.* to fasten or fix with a brace.

embracer[1] EMBRACE[1].

embracer[2] (imbrā´sə) *n.* (*Law*) a person who endeavours to corrupt a jury by embracery. **embracery** *n.* (*Law*) the offence of attempting to influence a jury by threats, bribery etc. [OF *embraceor*, from *embraser*, to set on fire (EM -, *braise*, hot charcoal)]

embranchment (imbrahnch´mənt) *n.* **1** a branching out, as of the arm of a river. **2** that part of a tree where the branches diverge. **3** a ramification.

embrangle (imbrang´gəl) *v.t.* **1** to entangle, to complicate. **2** to confuse, perplex. **embranglement** *n.*

embrasure (imbrā´zhə) *n.* **1** the inward enlargement, bevelling or splaying of the sides of a window or door. **2** an opening in a parapet or wall to fire guns through. **embrasured** *a.* [MF, from *embraser* (F *ébraser*), to splay or chamfer (EM-, *braser*, to splay or chamfer)]

embrave (imbrāv´) *v.t.* **1** to inspire with courage, to embolden. **2** to adorn, beautify, embellish.

embreathe (imbrēdh´) *v.t.* **1** to breathe into, inspire. **2** to breathe in, inhale.

embrittle (imbrit´əl) *v.t.* to make brittle. **embrittlement** *n.*

embrocate (em´brəkāt) *v.t.* to moisten, bathe or foment (as a diseased part of the body). **embrocation** (-ā´shən) *n.* **1** a preparation for application by rubbing or fomenting. **2** the act of bathing or fomenting. [med. L *embrocātus*, p.p. of *embrocāre*, from *embrocha*, Gr. *embrochē*, from *embrechein* (EM-, *brechein*, to wet)]

embroglio IMBROGLIO.

embroider (imbroi´də) *v.t.* **1** to ornament with figures or designs in needlework. **2** to variegate, to diversify. **3** to embellish with additions, esp. a narrative with exaggerations or fiction. *~v.i.* to do embroidery. **embroiderer** *n.* **embroidery** *n.* (*pl.* **embroideries**) **1** the act, process or art of embroidering. **2** ornamentation done with the needle. **3** the fabric ornamented. **4** additional embellishment. **5** exaggeration or fiction added to a narrative. [A-F *enbroyder* (OF EM-, *broder*, prob. rel. to *bord*, edge, border)]

embroil (imbroil´) *v.t.* **1** to throw into confusion. **2** to entangle, to confuse. **3** to involve (someone) in a quarrel or contention (with another). **embroiler** *n.* **embroilment** *n.* [F *embrouiller* (EM-, *brouiller*, see BROIL[1])]

embrue IMBRUE.

embry- EMBRYO-.

embryectomy (embriek´təmi) *n.* (*pl.* **embryectomies**) the surgical operation of removing the foetus through an incision in the abdomen.

embryo (em´briō) *n.* (*pl.* **embryos**) **1** an unborn offspring. **2** the human offspring up to the end of the second month of development. **3** the rudimentary plant in the seed after fertilization. **4** the beginning or first stage of anything. *~a.* undeveloped, rudimentary. **in embryo** **1** in the first or earliest stage. **2** in a rudimentary or undeveloped state. **embryoid** *a.* **embryonal** *a.* **embryonic** (-on´ik) *a.* **embryonically** *adv.* [med. L *embryo -ōnis*, Gr. *embruon* (EM-, *bruon*, neut. of *bruōn*, pres.p. of *bruein*, to be full of a thing, to swell with it)]

embryo- (embriō), **embry-** *comb. form* of or relating to the embryo or embryos. [see EMBRYO]

embryoctony (embriok´təni) *n.* the destruction of the foetus in the womb. [Gr. *embruoktonos* (*ktenein*, to kill)]

embryogenesis (embriəjen´isis, embriōjənē´sis), **embryogeny** (-oj´əni) *n.* the formation of an embryo.

embryogony (embriog´əni) *n.* the formation of an embryo. [Gr. *-gonia*, production]

embryology (embriol´əji) *n.* the science of the embryo and the formation and development of organisms. **embryological** (-loj´-) *a.* **embryologically** *adv.* **embryologist** *n.*

embryotomy (embriot´əmi) *n.* (*pl.* **embryotomies**) the cutting up of an embryo or foetus in the uterus to aid removal.

embus (imbŭs´) *v.t.* (*pres.p.* **embussing**, (*N Am.*) **embusing**, *past, p.p.* **embussed**, (*N Am.*) **embused**) (*Mil.*) to put troops into buses or lorries for transport. ~*v.i.* (of troops) to mount a bus or lorry.

emcee (emsē´) *n.* (*coll.*) a master of ceremonies. ~*v.t., v.i.* (*3rd pers. sing. pres.* **emcees**, *pres.p.* **emceeing**, *past, p.p.* **emceed**) to act as emcee (for an occasion). [pron. of the initials MC]

-eme (ēm) *suf.* in linguistics, forming nouns, meaning a smallest possible, indivisible unit, as *morpheme, phoneme.* [F *-ème*, from Gr. *-ēma*]

emend (imend´) *v.t.* **1** to correct, remove faults from. **2** to improve (as the result of criticism). **emendable** *a.* **emendals** *n.pl.* (*Hist.*) the sum total in the bank or in stock (orig. prob. set aside for making up losses), still used in the books of the Society of the Inner Temple. **emendation** (ēmendā´shən) *n.* **emendator** (ē´men-) *n.* **emendatory** (imen´də-) *a.* [L *ēmendāre* (E-, *menda*, a fault)]

Usage note The meanings of the verbs *emend* and *amend* overlap, but *emend* is used mainly of corrections in texts being edited, and *amend* of correction and improvement more generally.

emerald (em´ərəld) *n.* **1** a variety of beryl, distinguished by its beautiful green colour. **2** the colour of this. **3** (*Her.*) the green colour in coat armour, vert. **4** †a small type, between nonpareil and minion. ~*a.* of a bright green colour. **emerald-copper** *n.* dioptase, an emerald green crystallized mineral. **emerald green** *n.* **1** a bright green colour. **2** a bright green pigment, produced from arsenate of copper. **emeraldine** (-dīn, -din) *a.* **Emerald Isle** *n.* (*formal*) the island of Ireland. **emerald moth** *n.* any of several green-coloured geometrid moths. [OF *emeraude, esmeralde*, L *smaragdum -dus*, Gr. *smaragdos* (Sansk. *asmā*, a stone, *marakata*, emerald)]

emerge (imœj´) *v.i.* **1** to rise up out of anything in which a thing has been immersed or sunk. **2** to appear in sight (from below the horizon or from a place of concealment). **3** to appear, to come out (such as facts on an inquiry). **4** to crop up, become apparent. **5** to issue from a state of depression, suffering or obscurity. **emergence** *n.* **emergent** *a.* **1** coming into being, evolving. **2** arising or appearing unexpectedly. **3** (of a country etc.) having recently acquired independence. **emergent year** *n.* the epoch or date from which any people begin to compute their time. [L *ēmergere* (E-, *mergere*, to dip)]

emergency (imœ´jənsi) *n.* (*pl.* **emergencies**) **1** a sudden occurrence or situation demanding immediate action, a crisis. **2** a person requiring immediate medical attention. **3** (*Austral., New Zeal.*) a reserve player to substitute for an injured player in a team. **emergency exit** *n.* in a theatre or other public building, a door specially provided for exit in case of fire or other contingency. **emergency landing** *n.* a forced descent by a plane due to engine trouble etc. [late L *ēmergentia*, as EMERGE]

emeritus (imer´itəs) *a.* **1** (*placed after the noun*) having served one's term of office and retired with an honorary title (*professor emeritus*). **2** in ancient Rome, retired from public service. ~*n.* (*pl.* **emeriti** (-tī)) a person who has served their term and retired from an office. [L, p.p. of *ēmerērī* (E-, *merērī*, to earn)]

emerods (em´ərods) *n.pl.* (*Bible*) haemorrhoids. [HAEMORRHOIDS]

emersion (imœ´shən) *n.* **1** the action of emerging, esp. from water. **2** the reappearance of a heavenly body from behind another at the end of an eclipse or occultation. **emerse** (imœs´) *a.* (*Bot.*) (of the leaves of an aquatic plant) reaching above the water surface. **emersed** *a.*

emery (em´əri) *n.* a coarse variety of corundum, of extreme hardness, and black or greyish-black colour, used for polishing hard substances. **emery board** *n.* a strip of card or wood, coated with crushed emery and used to file fingernails. **emery cloth, emery paper** *n.* cloth or paper brushed with liquid glue and dusted with powdered emery. **emery wheel** *n.* a wheel faced with emery, used for grinding and polishing metal articles. [F *émeri*, MF *emeril, esmeril*, It. *smeriglio* (or late L *smericulum*), Gr. *smēris*]

emetic (imet´ik) *a.* inducing vomiting. ~*n.* a preparation for causing vomiting. **emesis** (em´əsis) *n.* the action of vomiting. **emetically** *adv.* **emetine** (em´ətīn, -tin) *n.* an alkaloid obtained from ipecacuanha, of which it forms the chief active principle. **emetocathartic** (emitōkəthah´tik) *a.* producing vomiting and purging. **emetology** (emitol´-) *n.* [L *emeticus*, Gr. *emetikos*, from *emeein*, to vomit]

émeute (imūt´) *n.* **1** a seditious or revolutionary outbreak. **2** a riot or popular disturbance. [F, from *émouvoir*, L *ēmovēre* (E-, *movēre*, to move)]

EMF *abbr.* **1** electromagnetic field. **2** (*often* **emf**) electromotive force. **3** European Monetary Fund.

EMI *abbr.* electromagnetic interference.

-emia -AEMIA.

emiction (imik´shən) *n.* **1** the discharge of urine. **2** urine. **emictory** *n., a.* [L *ēmictio*, from *ēmict-*, p.p. stem of *ēmingere* (E-, *mingere*, to make water)]

emigrate (em´igrāt) *v.i.* **1** to leave one's country in order to settle in another. **2** (*coll.*) to leave one's place of abode for another. ~*v.t.* to send (emigrants) out of the country. **emigrant** *a.* **1** emigrating. **2** of or relating to emigration. ~*n.* a person who emigrates. **emigration** (-rā´shən) *n.* **emigrationist** *n.* an advocate for or promoter of emigration. **emigratory** *a.* [L *ēmigrātus*, p.p. of *ēmigrāre* (E-, *migrāre*, to MIGRATE)]

émigré (em´igrā), **emigre** *n.* an emigrant, esp. one of the royalists who left France at the time of the French Revolution. [F]

éminence grise (eminãs grēz´) *n.* (*pl.* **éminences grises** (eminãs grēz´)) a man in the background exercising power unofficially. [F, grey eminence, name applied to Cardinal Richelieu's private secretary, Père Joseph, d.1638]

eminent (em´inənt) *a.* **1** distinguished. **2** (of services, qualities etc.) remarkable. **3** rising above others; high, lofty, prominent. **eminence, eminency** *n.* **1** loftiness, height. **2** a part rising above the rest, or projecting above the surface. **3** high rank, superiority. **4** distinction, celebrity. **5** †supreme degree. **6** (**Eminence**) a title of honour applied to cardinals. **†to have the eminence of** to be better than. **eminent domain** *n.* the right of the state to confiscate private property for public use, payment usu. being made in compensation. **eminently** *adv.* [L *ēminens -ntem*, pres.p. of *ēminēre*, to stand out, project (E-, *minae*, threats, projections)]

emir (imiə´) *n.* **1** in the Middle East and N Africa, a prince, chieftain, governor or commander. **2** a title given to the descendants of Muhammad through Fatima, his daughter. **emirate** (em´ərət) *n.* the jurisdiction, office or territory of an emir. [Arab. *amīr*, AMIR (*amara*, he commanded)]

emissary (em´isəri) *n.* (*pl.* **emissaries**) a messenger or agent, esp. one sent on a secret, dangerous or unpleasant mission. ~*a.* **1** of or relating to a messenger or agent. **2** serving as an outlet, esp. of or relating to a vein which draws blood from sinuses. [L *ēmissārius*, from *ēmiss-*, p.p. stem of *ēmittere*, to EMIT]

emission (imish´ən) *n.* **1** the act or process of emitting or being emitted. **2** the thing given off or out. **3** (*Physics*) energy emitted from any source. **4** electrons emitted from atoms in a cathode or electron gun. **5** a discharge of fluid (esp. semen) from the body. **6 a** the act of issuing banknotes etc. **b** the number and value of the notes etc. sent out. **emission spectrum** *n.* ELECTROMAGNETIC SPECTRUM (under ELECTROMAGNET). **emission theory** *n.* Isaac Newton's theory that light consists of particles emitted by luminous bodies. **emissive** *a.* **emissivity** (emisiv´-) *n.* **emissory** *a.* [L *ēmissio*, see EMISSARY]

emit (imit´) *v.t.* (*pres.p.* **emitting**, *past, p.p.* **emitted**) **1** to give out, to give vent to, to issue, to discharge, to utter. **2** to print and send into circulation (as banknotes). **emitter** *n.* **1** somebody or something that emits. **2** an electrode of a transistor. [L *ēmittere* (E-, *mittere*, to send)]

emmenagogue (imen´əgog) *n.* (*Med.*) a medicine that induces or restores the menses. **emmenology** (emənol´-) *n.* the study of menstruation. [Gr. *emmēna*, menses, *agōgos*, drawing forth]

Emmental (em´əntahl), **Emmenthal** *n.* a type of Swiss cheese with holes in it. [*Emmenthal*, a valley in Switzerland]

emmer (em´ə) *n.* a variety of wheat, *Triticum dicoccum*, grown in Europe largely as livestock fodder. [G]

emmet (em´it) *n.* **1** †an ant. **2** (*coll.*) a tourist in Cornwall. [OE *ǣmete*, see ANT]

Emmy (em´i) *n.* (*pl.* **Emmys, Emmies**) the television equivalent of an Oscar, awarded by the American Academy of Television Arts and Sciences. [etym. uncertain]

emollient (imol´iənt) *a.* **1** softening, relaxing. **2** making soft or supple. ~*n.* **1** a substance which softens the part to which it is applied, and soothes and diminishes irritation. **2** anything intended to soothe or comfort. **emollience** *n.* [L *ēmolliens -ntem*, pres.p. of *ēmollīre*, to soften (E-, *mollis*, soft)]

emolument (imol´ūmənt) *n.* **1** the profit arising from any office or employment. **2** remuneration. **emolumentary** (-men´-) *a.* [OF, from L *ēmolumentum*, profit, from *ēmolere* (E-, *molere*, to grind) or *ēmōlīrī* (E-, *mōlīrī*, to work)]

emotion (imō´shən) *n.* **1** agitation of the mind. **2** a state of excited feeling of any kind, whether of pain or pleasure. **3** excitement. **emote** *v.i.* (*coll.*) to show or express exaggerated emotion as in acting. **emoter** *n.* **emotional** *a.* **1** of or relating to emotion. **2** easily affected with emotion. **3** arousing emotion. **4** based on emotion, using emotion rather than reason. **emotionalism** *n.* **emotionalist** *n.* **emotionality** (-nal´-) *n.* **emotionalize, emotionalise** *v.t.* **emotionally** (-mō´-) *adv.* **emotionless** *a.* **emotive** *a.* **1** of or relating to emotion. **2** tending to produce emotion. **emotively** *adv.* **emotiveness** *n.* [L *ēmōtio -ōnem*, from *ēmovēre* (E-, *movēre*, to move)]

Usage note The uses of *emotional* and *emotive* overlap, but only *emotional* means easily affected with emotion; *emotive* is more usual of arousing emotion.

Emp. *abbr.* **1** Emperor. **2** Empire. **3** Empress.

empanel (impan´əl), **impanel** *v.t.* (*pres.p.* **empanelling, impanelling**, (*N Am.*) **empaneling, impaneling**, *past, p.p.* **empanelled, impanelled**, (*N Am.*) **empaneled, impaneled**) **1** to enter on the list of jurors. **2** to enrol as a jury. **empanelment** *n.*

empathy (em´pəthi) *n.* **1** the capacity for identifying with the experience of others, or appreciating things or emotions outside ourselves. **2** the losing of one's identity in, e.g. a work of art. **empathetic** (-thet´-) *a.* **empathetically** *adv.* **empathic** (-path´-) *a.* **empathically** *adv.* **empathist** *n.* **empathize, empathise** *v.t.* [Gr. *empathēs*, in a state of emotion]

empennage (impen´ij) *n.* the stabilizing parts at the rear of an aeroplane, including the rudder, the fin and the elevator. [F, the feathering of an arrow (L *penna*, a feather)]

emperor (em´pərə) *n.* **1** the sovereign of an empire. **2** the highest dignity (superior to king). **3** the sovereign of the Holy Roman Empire. **emperor moth** *n.* a large British moth, *Saturnia pavonia*. **emperor penguin** *n.* the largest type of penguin, *Aptenodytes forsteri*. **emperorship** *n.* †**empery** *n.* (*pl.* **emperies**) **1** sovereignty, empire. **2** the territory of an emperor. [OF *empereor*, nom. *emperere*, L *imperātor -ōrem*, from *imperāre*, to command (IM-[1], *parāre*, to prepare, order)]

emphasis (em´fəsis) *n.* (*pl.* **emphases** (-sēz)) **1** a special prominence or significance put on an idea, policy etc. **2** a particular stress laid upon a word or words, to indicate special significance. **3** accent, stress on a word or syllable in speaking. **4** force or intensity of expression, language, feeling, gesture etc. **emphasize, emphasise** *v.t.* **1** to give special prominence to, to distinguish. **2** to pronounce (a word or syllable) with particular stress. **emphatic** (-fat´ik) *a.* **1** speaking or behaving forcibly, with emphasis. **2** (of words or syllables) carrying the accent. **3** (of words or phrases) spoken with emphasis, significant. **emphatical** *a.* **emphatically** *adv.* [L, from Gr. (EM-, *phasis*, from *phainein*, to show)]

emphractic (imfrak´tik) *a.* having the quality of closing the pores of the skin. ~*n.* an emphractic medicine. [Gr. *emphraktikos*, from *emphrattein* (EM-, *phrattein*, to block)]

emphysema (emfisē´mə) *n.* **1** distension in the tissue of the lung, causing breathing difficulties. **2** the pressure of air causing distension in the cellular tissue. **emphysematous** *a.* [Gr. *emphusēma*, from *emphusaein* (EM-, *phusaein*, to blow, puff)]

empire (em´pīə) *n.* **1 a** the group of states or nations over which an emperor rules. **b** a state in which the sovereign is an emperor. **2 a** supreme and extensive dominion. **b** absolute power. **3** a large business conglomerate controlled by one person or company. **4** the period or duration of an empire. ~*a.* indicating the style of costume and furniture of the First or Second French Empire. **the Empire 1** (*Hist.*) the British Empire. **2** (*Hist.*) the first Napoleonic empire (1804–15). **3** (*Hist.*) the Holy Roman Empire. **empire builder** *n.* a person who seeks added power and authority, esp. by increasing the number of their staff. **empire building** *n.* **Empire Day** *n.* the former name of Commonwealth Day. **empire gown** *n.* a high-waisted gown after the style of those worn during the First Empire. **Empire State** *n.* (a nickname for) the state of New York. [OF, from L *imperium*, conn. with *imperāre* (see EMPEROR)]

empirical (impir´ikəl) *a.* **1** founded on experience or observation, not theory. **2** acting on this. **3 a** of the nature of a quack, charlatanic. **b** of or relating to quackery. ~*n.* **1** a person who relies solely on experience or observation. **2** a medical practitioner without scientific training, a quack, a charlatan. **empiric** *a.* empirical. **empirical formula** *n.* (*Chem.*) a formula which gives the proportions of the atoms in a molecule, but not the exact numbers. **empirically** *adv.* **empiricism** (-sizm) *n.* **1** (*Philos.*) the theory that knowledge can only be derived from experience or observation. **2** the use of empirical methods. **empiricist** (-sist) *n., a.* **empirism** (em´-) *n.* **1** a conclusion attained on empirical grounds. **2** empiricism. **empiristic** (empiris´-) *a.* [F *empirique*, L *empīricus*, Gr. *empeirikos*, from *empeiros*, experienced (EM-, *peira*, trial)]

emplacement (implās´mənt) *n.* **1** a setting in position. **2** a fortified platform for guns. **3** location, situation, position.

emplane (implān´), **enplane** (in-) *v.i.* to go on board an aeroplane. ~*v.t.* to place in an aeroplane.

employ (imploi´) *v.t.* **1** to use, to exercise. **2** to set at work. **3** to keep in one's service, esp. for pay. **4** to spend or pass (time, oneself etc.) in any occupation.

~*n.* **1** the state of being employed. **2** occupation, business, profession. **in the employ of** employed by. **employable** *a.* **employability** (-bil´-) *n.* **employee** (imploi´ē, emploiē´), (*N Am.*) **employe** *n.* a person who is employed regularly in some task or occupation for salary or wages. **employer** *n.* a person who employs people for salary or wages. **employment** *n.* **1** the act of employing. **2** the state of being employed. **3** regular occupation, trade or profession. **employment agency** *n.* (*pl.* **employment agencies**) a private agency used by people looking for work and by employers seeking employees. **employment exchange** *n.* (*Hist.*) an employment office. **employment office** *n.* a government office which advises the unemployed about job vacancies. [OF *employer,* L *implicāre* (IM-[1], *plicāre,* to fold)]

emplume (imploom´) *v.t.* to adorn with or as with plumes. [F *emplumer* (EM-, PLUME)]

empoison (impoi´zən) *v.t.* **1** to mix poison with. **2** to taint, vitiate, corrupt. **3** to make hostile, embitter. **4** †to administer poison to; to kill with or as with poison. **empoisonment** *n.* [F *empoisonner* (EM-, POISON)]

empolder IMPOLDER.

emporium (impaw´riəm) *n.* (*pl.* **emporiums, emporia** (-riə)) **1** a large shop where many kinds of goods are sold. **2** a commercial centre, a market. [L, from Gr. *emporion,* neut. of *emporios,* commercial, from *emporos,* a passenger, a merchant (EM-, *poros,* a way)]

empoverish IMPOVERISH.

empower (impow´ə) *v.t.* **1** to authorize. **2** to enable. **3** to give power or self-determination to. **empowerment** *n.*

empress (em´pris) *n.* **1** the wife or widow of an emperor. **2** a female ruler of an empire. [OF *emperesse,* fem. of *empereor,* EMPEROR]

empressement (āpres´mā) *n.* cordiality, goodwill, eagerness. [F, from *empresser,* to urge, *s'empresser,* to be eager]

†**emprise** (imprīz´) *n.* an adventurous or chivalrous undertaking. [OF, orig. fem. of *empris,* p.p. of *emprendre* (EM-, *prendre,* L *prehendere,* to take)]

empty (emp´ti) *a.* (*comp.* **emptier,** *superl.* **emptiest**) **1** void, containing nothing. **2** devoid (of). **3** vacant, unoccupied. **4** unloaded. **5** destitute, desolate. **6** meaningless, unsubstantial, shadowy. **7** senseless, inane. **8** without intelligence, ignorant. **9** hungry, unsatisfied. ~*n.* (*pl.* **empties**) an empty packing-case, trunk, barrel, crate, bottle etc. ~*v.t.* (*3rd pers. sing. pres.* **empties,** *pres.p.* **emptying,** *past, p.p.* **emptied**) **1** to remove the contents from, to make vacant. **2** to deprive (of). **3** to remove from a receptacle (into another). **4** to pour out, discharge. ~*v.i.* **1** to become empty. **2** to discharge (as a river). **on an empty stomach** STOMACH. **emptier** *n.* **emptily** *adv.* **emptiness** *n.* **empty-handed** *a.* **1** bringing nothing. **2** carrying away nothing. **empty-headed** *a.* silly, witless. **empty-hearted** *a.* heartless. **emptyings** *n.pl.* (*N Am.*) the lees of beer, cider etc., used as yeast. **empty-nester** *n.* a parent whose children have grown up and left home. **empty purse** *n.* a state of poverty, lack of resources. [OE *æmtig,* from *æmetta,* leisure]

empurple (impœ´pəl) *v.t.* **1** to tinge or colour with purple. **2** to make angry.

empyema (empīē´mə) *n.* a collection of pus in a body cavity, esp. in the pleura. [Gr. *empuēma,* from *empueein* (EM-, *pueein,* to suppurate)]

empyrean (empirē´ən) *n.* **1** the highest and purest region of heaven, where the element of fire was supposed by the ancients to exist without any admixture of grosser matter. **2** the upper sky. ~*a.* of or relating to the highest heaven or the upper sky. **empyreal** (-pir´i-) *a.* [med. L *empyraeus,* Gr. *empuros,* fiery (EM-, *pur,* fire)]

empyreuma (empiroo´mə) *n.* (*pl.* **empyreumata** (-mətə)) the disagreeable smell and taste produced when animal and vegetable substances are burned. **empyreumatic** (-mat´-), **empyreumatical** (-kəl) *a.* **empyreumatize** (-roo´-), **empyreumatise** *v.t.* [Gr. *empureuma,* from *empureuein,* to set on fire]

EMS *abbr.* European Monetary System.

EMU *abbr.* **1** economic and monetary union. **2** electromagnetic unit.

emu[1] (ē´mū) *n.* (*pl.* **emus**) a large Australian cursorial bird of the genus *Dromaius,* esp. *D. Novaehollandiae,* resembling the cassowary but different in having no casque. **emu-wren** *n.* a small Australian bird, *Stipiturus malachurus,* having the tail feathers loose-webbed, and somewhat resembling those of the emu. [Port. *ema,* ostrich]

emu[2] *abbr.* electromagnetic unit.

emulate (em´ūlāt) *v.t.* **1** to try to equal or excel. **2** to imitate with intent to equal or excel. **3** to rival. **4** (*Comput.*) to imitate the functions of (another computer) so as to be able to use the same software etc. **emulation** (-lā´shən) *n.* **1** the act of emulating. **2** ambition to equal or excel the action of others. **3** rivalry, envy, jealousy. **emulative** (-lətiv) *a.* **emulatively** *adv.* **emulator** *n.* **1** a person who emulates. **2** a rival. **3** †a disparager. †**emulatress** (-tris) *n.* a woman who emulates. [L *aemulātus,* p.p. of *aemulārī,* from *aemulus,* EMULOUS]

emulgent (imŭl´jənt) *a.* **1** milking or draining out. **2** (*Med.*) denoting the renal arteries and veins (the ancients assuming that they milked out the serum by means of the kidneys). [L *ēmulgens -ntem,* pres.p. of *ēmulgēre* (E-, *mulgēre,* to milk)]

emulous (em´ūləs) *a.* **1** desirous of equalling or excelling others. **2** engaged in rivalry or competition. **3** desirous of fame or honour. **4** envious, factious, contentious. **emulously** *adv.* **emulousness** *n.* [L *aemulus*]

emulsion (imŭl´shən) *n.* **1** a colloidal suspension of one liquid in another. **2** a light-sensitive substance held in suspension in collodion or gelatine, used for coating plates or films. **3** emulsion paint. ~*v.t.* to apply emulsion paint to. **emulsify** (-mul´sifī) *v.t.* (*3rd pers. sing. pres.* **emulsifies,** *pres.p.* **emulsifying,** *past, p.p.* **emulsified**) to convert into an emulsion. **emulsification** (-fikā´shən) *n.* **emulsifier** *n.* something which emulsifies, esp. a food additive which prevents the ingredients of processed food from separating. **emulsin** *n.* a neutral fermenting substance found in almonds. **emulsionize, emulsionise** *v.t.* **emulsion paint** *n.* a water-thinnable paint made from an emulsion of a resin in water. **emulsive** *a.* [L *ēmūls-,* p.p. stem of *ēmulgēre,* to drain out (see EMULGENT)]

emunctory (imŭngk´təri) *a.* **1** serving to wipe the nose. **2** serving to carry noxious or useless particles out of the body. ~*n.* (*pl.* **emunctories**) an excretory duct. [L *ēmunct-,* p.p. stem of *ēmungere,* to wipe the nose]

emys (em´is) *n.* (*pl.* **emydes** (-idēz)) (*Zool.*) the freshwater tortoise. [Gr. *emus*]

en (en) *n.* **1** the 14th letter of the alphabet, N, n. **2** (*Print.*) the unit of measurement for casting-off copy, an en being the average width of a letter. **en dash, en rule** *n.* a dash one en long (–), used in punctuation.

en- (in, en, ən) *pref.* forming verbs with the meanings in, on, into, upon, as *enambush, encamp, encourage, engulf, enjewel, enslave, enlighten, encomium, energy, enthusiasm.* [F *en-, em-,* L *in-, im-,* in; also Gr. *en-, em-*]

-en[1] (ən) *suf.* forming diminutives of nouns, as *chicken, maiden.* [OE, from Gmc. *-înom*]

-en[2] (ən) *suf.* forming feminine nouns, as *vixen.* [OE, from Gmc. *-inî* (G *-in*)]

-en[3] (ən) *suf.* forming adjectives from nouns, meaning pertaining to, made of, of the nature of, as *earthen, flaxen, golden, woollen.* [OE, from Gmc. *-īno* (cp. G and L *-ino-*)]

-en[4] (ən) *suf.* forming the pl. of nouns, as *oxen.* [OE *-an,* pl. of weak decl.]

-en[5] (ən) *suf.* forming verbs from adjectives or nouns, meaning to become or cause to become, as *deepen, fatten, heighten.* [OE *-nan, -nian*]
-en[6] (ən) *suf.* forming the p.p. of strong verbs, as *broken, fallen, spoken.* [OE *-en*]
enable (inā´bəl) *v.t.* 1 to make able. 2 to authorize, empower (to). 3 to supply with means (to do any act). 4 (*Comput.*) to render (a device) operational. **enablement** *n.* **enabler** *n.* **enabling act** *n.* legislation conferring specified powers on a person or organization.
enact (inakt´) *v.t.* 1 to decree. 2 to pass, as a bill into a law. 3 to represent, act, play. ~†*n.* 1 that which is enacted. 2 (*fig.*) a purpose, a resolution. **enactable** *a.* **enacting clause** *n.* (*usu. in pl.*) a clause in a bill which contains new enactments. **enaction** *n.* **enactive** *a.* **enactment** *n.* 1 the act or fact of enacting. 2 something enacted, as a law. **enactory** *a.*
enallage (inal´əjē) *n.* a change of words, or a substitution of one mood, tense, number, case or gender of the same word for another. [L, from Gr., conn. with *enallassein* (EN-, *allassein*, to change)]
enamel (inam´əl) *n.* 1 a vitreous, opaque or semi-transparent material with which metal, porcelain and other vessels, ornaments etc. are coated by fusion, for decorative or preservative purposes. 2 any smooth, hard, glossy coating. 3 a lacquer, a varnish, a paint, a cosmetic. 4 the ivory-like substance which covers the surface of the teeth. 5 a work of art made with enamel. 6 a bright smooth surface. ~*v.t.* (*pres.p.* **enamelling**, (*N Am.*) **enameling**, *past, p.p.* **enamelled**, (*N Am.*) **enameled**) 1 to coat with enamel. 2 to paint, encrust or inlay with enamel. 3 to portray in enamel. 4 to form a smooth glossy surface upon. 5 to decorate with various colours. ~*v.i.* to practise the art of enamelling. **enameller**, (*N Am.*) **enameler** *n.* **enamellist**, (*N Am.*) **enamelist** *n.* **enamel paint** *n.* **enamelware** *n.* kitchen utensils coated with enamel. **enamelwork** *n.* [ME *enamayl*, OF *esmail*, med. L *smaltum*, from Gmc. (cp. OHG *smalzjan*, Dut. *smelten*, to SMELT[1])]
enamour (inam´ə), (*N Am.*) **enamor** *v.t.* 1 to captivate, to charm. 2 to inflame with love. **to be enamoured** 1 to be in love. 2 to be fond (of). [OF *enamorer*]
enanthema (enənthē´mə) *n.* (*Med.*) an ulcer or other eruption on a mucus-secreting surface. [mod. L (EN-, EXANTHEMA)]
enanthic OENANTHIC.
enantio- (inantiō) *comb. form* opposite, mirror image. [Gr. *enantios*]
enantiomer (inan´tiōmə) *n.* (*Chem.*) a molecule which is the mirror image of another. **enantiomeric** (-mer´ik) *a.*
enantiomorph (inan´tiōmawf) *n.* a crystal structure which is the mirror image of another. **enantiomorphic** *a.* **enantiomorphism** *n.* **enantiomorphous** *a.*
enantiosis (inantiō´sis) *n.* a figure of speech by which one says (usually ironically) the reverse of what one means. [Gr., from *enantioesthai*, from *enantios*, contrary]
enarch (inahch´) *v.t.* 1 to arch over. 2 (*Her.*) to arch with a chevron. 3 in horticulture, to inarch.
†**enarration** (ēnərā´shən) *n.* a narration or description. [L *ēnārrātio -ōnem*, *īnārrāre* (E-, *nārrāre*, to NARRATE)]
enarthrosis (enahthrō´sis) *n.* (*pl.* **enarthroses** (-sēz)) a ball-and-socket joint. **enarthrodial** (-diəl) *a.* [Gr., from *enarthros*, jointed (EN-, *arthron*, a joint)]
enation (inā´shən) *n.* (*Bot.*) the production of outgrowths upon the surface of an organ. **enate** (ē´nate) *a.* growing out. [L *ēnātus*, born]
en avant (ān avā´) *int.* forward! [F]
en barbette (ān bahbet´) *a.* (of guns) so mounted as to allow of their being fired over a parapet without embrasures or port-holes. [F, *en*, in, BARBETTE]
en bloc (ā blok´) *adv.* as one unit, all together. [F]
en brosse (ā bros´) *a.* (of hair) cut very short so that it stands on end. [F *brosse*, a brush]
enc. *abbr.* 1 enclosed. 2 enclosure.
en cabochon (ān kab´əshon) *a.* (of a precious stone) polished, but without facets. [F, *en*, in, CABOCHON]
encaenia (insē´niə) *n.pl.* 1 a festival to commemorate the dedication of a church, the founding of a city etc. 2 the annual commemoration of founders and benefactors of Oxford University. [L, from Gr. *enkainia* (EN-, *kainos*, new)]
encage (inkāj´) *v.t.* to shut in or as in a cage.
encamp (inkamp´) *v.i.* 1 to form an encampment. 2 to settle down temporarily in tents. ~*v.t.* 1 to settle (troops) in an encampment. 2 to lodge (troops) in tents. **encampment** *n.* 1 a camp. 2 the place where troops are encamped. 3 the act of encamping.
encapsulate (inkap´sūlāt) *v.t.* 1 to enclose in a capsule. 2 to capture the essence of. 3 to put in a shortened form. 4 to isolate. **encapsulation** (-ā´shən) *n.*
encarnalize (inkah´nəlīz), **encarnalise** *v.t.* 1 to make carnal. 2 to make fleshly. 3 to embody in the flesh.
encase (inkās´), **incase** *v.t.* 1 to put into a case. 2 to enclose in a case. 3 to protect with a case. **encasement** *n.* [F *encaisser* (EN-, *caisse*, CASE[2])]
encash (inkash´) *v.t.* 1 to cash, to convert (bills etc.) into cash. 2 to realize, to obtain in the form of cash. **encashable** *a.* **encashment** *n.*
encaustic (inkaw´stik) *n.* 1 a mode of painting in which the colours are fixed by heat (now chiefly of painting on vitreous or ceramic ware in which the colours are burnt in). 2 a painting done by this method. ~*a.* of or relating to or executed by this method. **encaustically** *adv.* **encaustic brick**, **encaustic tile** *n.* a brick or tile which is inlaid with clay patterns burnt in. [F *encaustique*, L *encausticus*, Gr. *enkaustikos*, from *enkaiein* (EN-, *kaiein*, to burn)]
encave (inkāv´) *v.t.* to hide in a cellar. [OF *encaver*, to put in a cellar]
-ence (əns) *suf.* 1 forming abstract nouns meaning a state or quality, as *existence, corpulence.* 2 forming abstract nouns meaning an action, as *appearance, emergence.* [F *-ence*, or directly from L *-entia*, from pres.p. in *-ens -entis* (rarely from neut. pl. of adjectives)]
enceinte (āsīnt´) *a.* pregnant. ~*n.* the space within the ramparts of a fortification. [F, fem. of *enceint*, L *incinctus*, p.p. of *incingere* (IN-[1], *cingere*, to girdle)]
encephal- ENCEPHALO-.
encephala, **encephalic** ENCEPHALON.
encephalin ENKEPHALIN.
encephalitis (insefəlī´tis, -kef-) *n.* inflammation of the brain. **encephalitic** (-lit´ik) *a.* **encephalitis lethargica** (lithah´jikə) *n.* acute inflammation of the brain, commonly called sleepy sickness.
encephalo- (insef´əlō, -kef´-), **encephal-** *comb. form* brain. [Gr. *enkephalos* (EN-, *kephalē*, a head)]
encephalocele (insef´əlōsēl, -kef´-) *n.* hernia of the brain.
encephalography (insefəlog´rəfi, -kef-) *n.* radiography of the brain. **encephalogram** (-sef´əlōgram, -kef-) *n.* an X-ray photograph of the brain. **encephalograph** (-grahf) *n.* an apparatus for making an X-ray photograph of the brain.
encephalomyelitis (insefəlōmīəlī´tis, -kef-) *n.* (*Med.*) acute inflammation of the brain and spinal cord.
encephalon (insef´əlon, -kef´-) *n.* (*pl.* **encephala** (-lə)) 1 the brain. 2 the contents of the skull. **encephalic** (ensifal´ik, -kef-) *a.* **encephaloid** *a.* of or relating to or resembling brain matter. **encephalous** *a.* having a distinct brain or head, used of certain molluscs. [Gr. *enkephalon* (EN-, *kephalē*, the head)]
encephalopathy (insefəlop´əthi, -kef-) *n.* (*pl.* **encephalopathies**) any degenerative disease referable to a disorder of the brain. **encephalopathic** (-path´-) *a.*

encephalotomy (insefəlot´əmi, -kef-) *n.* (*pl.* **encephalotomies**) **1** the operation of cutting into the brain. **2** dissection of the brain.

encephalous ENCEPHALON.

enchain (inchān´) *v.t.* **1** to bind with chains. **2** to chain up. **3** to hold fast, to rivet (attention etc.). **enchainment** *n.* [OF *enchainer*]

enchant (inchahnt´) *v.t.* **1** to influence by magic, to bewitch. **2** to fascinate, to charm. **3** to delight in the highest degree. **enchanted** *a.* **1** greatly delighted. **2** fascinated, captivated. **3** under the influence of magic or a magician. **enchantedly** *adv.* **enchanter** *n.* **1** a person who practises enchantment; a magician. **2** a person who delights or fascinates. **enchanter's nightshade** *n.* a woodland plant of the genus *Circaea*, esp. *C. lutetiana*. **enchanting** *a.* delightful, charming. **enchantingly** *adv.* **enchantment** *n.* **enchantress** *n.* a female enchanter. [F *enchanter*, L *incantāre* (IN-[1], *cantāre*, to sing)]

enchase (inchās´) *v.t.* **1** to set or encase within any other material, such as a gem in precious metal. **2** to serve as a setting for, to encircle. **3** to adorn with embossed work. **4** to decorate with figures. **5** to enshrine, to enclose. [F *enchâsser* (EN-, *châsse*, shrine, L *capsa*, CASE[2])]

enchilada (enchilah´də) *n.* a Mexican dish of a meat-filled tortilla served with chilli sauce. [Sp., fem. p.p. of *enchilar*, to season with chilli]

enchiridion (enkīrid´iən) *n.* (*pl.* **enchiridions, enchiridia** (-diə)) (*formal*) a handbook or manual, a small guide or book of reference. [Gr. *encheiridion* (EN-, *cheir*, hand, *-idion*, dim. suf.)]

enchorial (inkaw´riəl) *a.* **1** belonging to or used in a country. **2** popular, common; applied to the demotic characters formed from Egyptian hieroglyphics. **enchoric** (-kor´-) *a.* [Gr. *enchorios* (EN-, *chora*, country)]

encipher (insī´fə) *v.t.* to put (a message etc.) into cipher, to encode. **encipherer** *n.* **encipherment** *n.*

encircle (insœ´kəl) *v.t.* **1** to enclose or surround (with). **2** to take up a position round. **3** to embrace, to encompass. **encircling** *n.*, *a.*

encl. *abbr.* **1** enclosed. **2** enclosure.

en clair (ã kleə´) *a.*, *adv.* (of telegrams etc.) not in code or cipher. [F]

enclasp (inklahsp´) *v.t.* to enfold in a clasp, to embrace.

enclave (en´klāv) *n.* **1** a territory completely surrounded by that of another state; an enclosure, as viewed from outside it. **2** a group of people whose behaviour and opinions differ from those of the people they live among. **enclavement** (-klāv´-) *n.* [F, from *enclaver*, late L *inclāvāre* (IN-[1], *clāvus*, nail, or *clāvis*, key)]

enclitic (inklit´ik) *a.* (*Gram.*) of or relating to a word which cannot, as it were, stand by itself, but is pronounced as part of the preceding word, on which it throws its accent, e.g. *thee* in *prithee*. *~n.* an enclitic word or particle. **enclitically** *adv.* [L *encliticus*, Gr. *enklitikos* (EN-, *klīnein*, to lean)]

enclose (inklōz´), **inclose** *v.t.* **1 a** to shut in. **b** to surround or hem in on all sides. **2** to surround by a fence. **3** to put one thing inside another for transmission or carriage, esp. an extra sheet in a letter. **4** to contain. **5** (*Math.*) to surround on all sides. **enclosable** *a.* **enclosed order** *n.* a Christian contemplative order which does not allow its members to go into the outside world. **encloser** *n.* **enclosure** (-zhə) *n.* **1** the act of enclosing, esp. the act of enclosing common land so as to make it private property. **2** that which is enclosed. **3** a space of ground enclosed or fenced in. **4** that which encloses, as a fence. **5** anything enclosed in an envelope, wrapper etc.

encode (inkōd´) *v.t.* to translate a message into code. **encoder** *n.*

encomiast (inkō´miast) *n.* **1** a person who composes an encomium, a panegyrist. **2** a flatterer. **encomiastic** (-as´-) *a.* bestowing praise; laudatory, panegyrical. **encomiastical** *a.* **encomiastically** *adv.* [Gr. *enkōmiastēs*, from *enkōmiazein*, to praise, as ENCOMIUM]

encomium (inkō´miəm) *n.* (*pl.* **encomiums, encomia** (-miə)) **1** a formal eulogy or panegyric. **2** high commendation. **3** high-flown praise. [L, from Gr. *enkōmion*, neut. of *enkōmios*, laudatory (EN-, *kōmos*, revelry)]

encompass (inkŭm´pəs) *v.t.* **1** to surround, to invest. **2** to go round, to encircle. **3** to include, contain. **4** to make happen, to bring about. **encompassment** *n.*

encore (ong´kaw) *int.* used as a call for a repetition at a concert, theatre etc. *~n.* **1** a demand for a repetition of a song etc. **2** the repetition itself. *~v.t.* **1** to call for a repetition of. **2** to call back (a performer). *~v.i.* to call for an encore. [F, again, L (*in*) *hanc horam*, to this hour]

encounter (inkown´tə) *v.t.* **1** to meet face to face. **2** to meet with, come across, esp. unexpectedly. **3** to meet in a hostile manner. **4** to confront resolutely, to oppose. *~n.* **1** a meeting face to face. **2** a hostile meeting, a skirmish, a battle. **3** an unplanned or unexpected meeting. **4** a meeting of an encounter group. **encounterer** *n.* **1** a person who encounters another. **2** an adversary, an opponent. **encounter group** *n.* a group of people who meet to develop self-awareness and understanding of others by frank exchange of feelings, opinions and contact. [OF *encontrer*, late L *incontrāre* (IN-[1], *contra*, against)]

encourage (inkŭr´ij) *v.t.* **1** to give courage or confidence to. **2** to animate, embolden. **3** to urge, to incite (to do). **4** to stimulate, to promote, to foster (trade, opinion etc.). **encouragement** *n.* **encourager** *n.* **encouraging** *a.* **encouragingly** *adv.* [OF *encoragier* (EN-, COURAGE)]

encrinite (en´krinīt) *n.* a fossil crinoid. **encrinal** (-krin´-), **encrinic, encrinital** (-nī´-) *a.* of or relating to or containing encrinites. [Gr. EN-, *krinon*, lily; -ITE[1]]

encroach (inkrōch´) *v.i.* **1** to intrude (upon) what belongs to another. **2** to infringe (upon). **3** to get possession of anything gradually or by stealth. **encroacher** *n.* **encroaching** *a.* **encroachingly** *adv.* **encroachment** *n.* **1** the act of encroaching. **2** that which is taken by encroaching. **3** (*Law*) the act of unlawfully trespassing upon or interfering with the rights, property or privileges of another. [OF *encrochier* (EN-, *croc*, hook, cp. MDut. *kroke*, Icel. *krōkr*, crook)]

encrust (inkrŭst´), **incrust** *v.t.* **1** to cover with a crust or hard coating. **2** to form a crust upon the surface of. **3** to apply a decorated layer or lining to the surface of. *~v.i.* to form a crust. **encrustation** (enkrəstā´shən) *n.* **encrustment** *n.* [prob. through F *incruster*, from L *incrustāre* (IN-[1], *crusta*, CRUST)]

encrypt (inkript´) *v.t.* **1** to put (information or a message) into code. **2** to conceal (information or a message) thus. **encryption** (-krip´shən) *n.*

encumber (inkŭm´bə) *v.t.* **1** to hamper, impede or embarrass by a weight, burden or difficulty; to burden. **2** to weigh down with debt. **3** to load or fill with rubbish or superfluous things. **encumberment** *n.* **encumbrance** *n.* **1** a hindrance to freedom of action or motion. **2** a burden, a hindrance, a clog. **3** (*Law*) a liability upon an estate, such as a mortgage, a claim etc. **4** a dependent person, esp. a child. **encumbrancer** *n.* (*Law*) a person who holds an encumbrance upon another person's estate. [OF *encombrer*, late L *incumbrāre* (IN-[1], *cumbrus*, an obstacle, see CUMBER)]

-ency (ənsi) *suf.* forming abstract nouns meaning state or quality, as *efficiency*, *emergency*, *presidency*. [-ENCE]

encyclical (insik´likəl, -sī´-), **encyclic** *n.* a circular letter, esp. a letter from the Pope to the bishops or to the Church at large. *~a.* (of a letter) sent about to many persons or places. [late L *encyclicus*, Gr. *enkuklios* (EN-, *kuklos*, a ring, a circle)]

encyclopedia (insīklōpē´diə), **encyclopaedia** *n.* a book containing information on all branches of knowledge, or on a particular branch, usu. arranged alphabetically. **encyclopedian** *a.* **encyclopedic** *a.* **1** of or relating to an encyclopedia. **2** (of knowledge) comprehensive; wide ranging. **encyclopedical** *a.* **encyclopedically** *adv.* **encyclopedism** *n.* **1** the compilation of an encyclopedia. **2** the possession of a large range of knowledge and information. **encyclopedist** *n.* [late L, from pseudo-Gr. *enkuklopaideia*, a false reading for *enkuklios paideia*, general instruction (see ENCYCLICAL, and *paideia*, from *paideuein*, to educate, from *pais, paidos*, a child)]

encyst (insist´) *v.t.* to enclose in a cyst, bladder or vesicle. ~*v.i.* to become thus enclosed. **encystation** (ensistā´shən) *n.* **encystis** (-is) *n.* (*Med.*) an encysted tumour. **encystment** *n.*

end (end) *n.* **1** the extreme point or boundary of a line or of anything that has length. **2** the termination, limit or last portion. **3** the last part of a period. **4** the conclusion of a state or action. **5** a ceasing to exist. **6** the final lot or doom. **7** abolition. **8** death. **9** the cause of death. **10** a result, a natural consequence, a necessary outcome. **11** a purpose, an object, a designed result. **12** a reason for (a thing's) existence, a final cause. **13** the half of a sports court or pitch occupied by one player or team. **14** in bowls, the part of a game played from one of the ends of the green to the other. **15** in American football, a player on the wing. **16** (*usu. pl.*) a remnant. ~*a.* **1** final. **2** farthest. **3** last. ~*v.i.* **1** to come to an end, to cease. **2** to result (in). ~*v.t.* **1** to bring to an end. **2** to put to an end, to destroy. **3** (*fig.*) †to harvest, to get in (corn). **all ends up** completely. **at a loose end** (*coll.*) with nothing in particular to do. **at an end 1** finished, completed. **2** exhausted, used up. **at loose ends** (*N Am.*) at a loose end. **at one's wits' end** WIT[1]. **at the end of one's tether** at the limit of one's strength, endurance or patience. **at the end of the day** DAY. **be-all and end-all** BE. **end of story** (*coll.*) that is all, there is no more. **end on** with the end pointing towards one. **end to end** with the ends touching, lengthwise. **in the end 1** finally. **2** after all. **no end** (*coll.*) plenty, much, many. **odds and ends** ODD. **on end 1** upright, erect. **2** continuously. **the end** (*coll.*) something unendurably bad, the last straw. **to come to a bad end** to have an unpleasant or disgraceful future. **to come to an end** to end, to be finished, to be exhausted. **to end it all** to commit suicide. **to end up** to arrive at or become at last. **to keep one's end up** (*coll.*) to stand one's ground. **to make an end of** to bring to a close, to finish. **to make (both) ends meet** to keep expenditure within income. **to put an end to 1** to terminate, to stop. **2** to abolish. **to that end** for that purpose. **without end 1** everlasting. **2** very long. **3** inexhaustible. **end-around** *n.* in American football, a play in which an end carries the ball around the opposite end. **endgame** *n.* the last part of a game of chess etc., when only a few pieces remain in play. **ending** *n.* **1** a conclusion, a termination. **2** the latter part of a story, an occurrence etc. **3** (*Gram.*) the terminating syllable of a word. **end-iron** *n.* a movable plate in a kitchen range for enlarging or contracting the fire space. **endless** *a.* **1** having no end. **2** infinite, unlimited, perpetual. **3** incessant. **4** innumerable. **endless band, endless cable, endless chain** *n.* a band with ends fastened together for conveying mechanical motion. **endlessly** *adv.* **endlessness** *n.* **endless screw** *n.* a screw conveying motion to a wheel in the teeth of which the threads engage. **endlong** *adv.* **1** lengthwise as distinguished from crosswise. **2** straight along. **3** †continuously. ~†*a.* standing on end, vertical. **end matter** *n.* (in a book) the parts after the end of the main text, e.g. appendices, bibliography, index. **endmost** *a.* the nearest to the end, the furthest. **endnote** *n.* a note at the end of a book or a section of a book. **end of the line** *n.* the point at which something stops or beyond which it cannot continue. **end of the road** *n.* the point beyond which a person or thing can no longer go on or survive. **endpaper** *n.* any one of the blank pages placed between the cover and the body of a book. **end-play** *n.* (in bridge) a way of playing the last tricks of a hand so as to force one's opponents to make a bad lead. **end point** *n.* the point at which any process is seen as completed, esp. that where titration etc. shows an effect. **end product** *n.* the final product obtained after a series of processes. **end result** *n.* the final outcome. **end run** *n.* **1** (*N Am.*) an evasive tactic. **2** (in American football) a play in which the ball carrier runs round their own end. **ends of the earth** *n.pl.* the remotest parts of the earth. **end standard** *n.* a metal bar acting as a standard of length, of which the ends are the specified distance apart. **end-stopped** *a.* (of poetry) having a pause in sense at the end of a line. **end-user** *n.* the person, firm etc. in receipt of a manufactured product being sold. **endways** *adv.* **1** on end. **2** with the end foremost or uppermost. **3** end to end. **4** lengthwise. **endwise** *adv.* **end zone** *n.* the rectangular area at the end of an American football pitch. [OE *ende* (cp. Dut. *einde*, Icel. *endi*, Dan. *ende*, G *Ende*)]

-end (ənd) *suf.* forming nouns with the meaning somebody or something to be perceived or treated in a particular way, as *reverend*. [L gerundive ending *-endus*]

endamage (indam´ij) *v.t.* **1** to damage. **2** to prejudice.

endanger (indān´jə) *v.t.* to expose to danger, to put in hazard. **endangered species** *n.* a species whose numbers are declining and which is at risk of extinction. **endangerment** *n.*

endear (indiə´) *v.t.* **1** to make dear (to). **2** to cause to be loved. **endearing** *a.* **endearingly** *adv.* **endearment** *n.* **1** the act of endearing. **2** the state of being endeared. **3** words or a gesture expressing affection.

endeavour (indev´ə), (*N Am.*) **endeavor** *v.i.* **1** to strive (after) a certain end. **2** to try, to make an effort (to). ~*n.* **1** an effort, an attempt. **2** exertion for the attainment of some object. **endeavourer** *n.* [ME *endeveren* (EN-, *dever* (F *devoir*), duty)]

endeictic (indīk´tik) *a.* showing, exhibiting. **endeixis** (-dīk´sis) *n.* a symptom. [Gr. *endeiktikos*, from *endeiknunai* (EN-, *deiknunai*, to show)]

endemic (indem´ik) *a.* peculiar to a particular locality or people. ~*n.* **1** an endemic disease. **2** an endemic plant. **endemically** *adv.* **endemic disease** *n.* a disease common from local causes in a particular district or among a particular people or class, beyond which it shows no tendency to spread. **endemicity** (endəmis´-) *n.* **endemiology** (indēmiol´əji) *n.* the scientific study of endemic diseases. **endemism** *n.* [EN-, Gr. *dēmos*, people (cp. *endēmios*)]

Usage note The adjectives *endemic* and *epidemic* should not be confused: an endemic disease is one common in a particular place or among a particular people, and an epidemic disease is one common at a particular time.

endermic (indœ´mik) *a.* acting upon or through the skin, as an unguent applied after blistering. **endermically** *adv.*

enderon (en´dəron) *n.* (*Med.*) the inner derm or true skin. [EN-, Gr. *deros*, *derma*, skin]

☒ **endevour** common misspelling of ENDEAVOUR.

ending END.

endive (en´div, -dīv) *n.* **1** a kind of chicory, *Cichorium endivia*, much cultivated for use in salads, or *C. intybus*, the wild endive. **2** (*N Am.*) chicory in general. [F, from L *intibus*]

endo- (en´dō) *comb. form* of or relating to the inside of anything. [Gr. *endon*, within]
endocardium (endōkah´diəm, endə-) *n.* (*pl.* **endocardia** (-diə)) a membrane lining the interior of the human heart. **endocardiac** (-ak) *a.* **endocarditis** (-dī´tis) *n.* inflammation of the endocardium. **endocarditic** (-dit´ik) *a.* [Gr. *kardia*, heart]
endocarp (en´dōkahp) *n.* (*Bot.*) the inner layer of a pericarp. **endocarpic** (-kah´pik) *a.*
endocranium (endōkrā´niəm) *n.* (*pl.* **endocrania** (-iə)) the thick membrane lining the cranial cavity.
endocrine (en´dōkrīn, -krin) *a.* (of a gland) having no duct and secreting directly into the bloodstream. ~*n.* the internal secretion of a gland. **endocrine gland** *n.* **endocrinology** (-krinol´əji) *n.* the scientific study of the endocrine glands. **endocrinological** (-log´-) *a.* **endocrinologist** (-nol´-) *n.*
endoderm (en´dōdœm) *n.* **1** the inner layer of the blastoderm. **2** the membrane lining the internal cavity of certain organisms, esp. the Coelenterata. **endodermal** *a.* **endodermic** *a.*
endogamous (endog´əməs) *a.* necessarily marrying within the tribe. **endogamy** *n.* **1** the custom of taking a wife only within the tribe. **2** pollination between two flowers on the same plant. [Gr. *gamos*, marriage]
endogen (en´dōjən) *n.* an endogenous plant. **endogenesis** (-jen´-) *n.* **endogenous** (-doj´-) *a.* growing from within. **endogeny** *n.*
endolymph (en´dōlimf) *n.* the serous fluid in the membranous labyrinth of the ear.
endometrium (endōmē´triəm) *n.* (*pl.* **endometria** (-triə)) the membrane lining the cavity of the womb. **endometrial** *a.* **endometriosis** (-ō´sis) *n.* the presence of endometrial tissue outside the womb. **endometritis** (-mitrī´tis) *n.* inflammation of the endometrium. [Gr. *metra*, womb]
endomorph (en´dōmawf) *n.* **1** a person of plump, thickset build. **2** a mineral enclosed inside another. **endomorphic** *a.* **endomorphy** *n.*
endoparasite (endōpar´əsīt), **entoparasite** *n.* (*Zool.*) a parasite living in the interior of its host. **endoparasitic** (-sit´-) *a.*
endophyllous (indof´iləs) *a.* denoting leaves evolved from a sheath.
endoplasm (en´dōplazm) *n.* the partially fluid inner layer of protoplasm. **endoplasmic** (-plaz´mik) *a.* **endoplasmic reticulum** *n.* (*pl.* **endoplasmic reticula** (-lə)) a membranous network within the cytoplasm of a cell, in which proteins are synthesized.
endorphin (endaw´fin) *n.* any of a group of chemicals occurring naturally in the brain which have a similar effect to morphine.
endorse (indaws´), **indorse** *v.t.* **1** to write (one's name) on the back of (a cheque) to specify oneself as the payee. **2** to assign by writing on the back of (a negotiable document). **3 a** to ratify, confirm, approve. **b** to declare one's approval of (a product), by way of advertising. **4** to record a conviction on (an offender's driving licence). **to endorse over** to transfer one's rights in (a bill etc.) to another person. **endorsable** *a.* **endorsee** (-sē´) *n.* the person to whom a negotiable document is assigned by endorsing. **endorsement** *n.* **endorser** *n.* [ME *endosse*, OF *endosser*, med. L *indorsāre* (IN-[1], L *dorsum*, the back)]
endoscope (en´dōskōp) *n.* an instrument for inspecting internal parts of the body. **endoscopic** (-skop´ik) *a.* **endoscopically** *adv.* **endoscopy** (endos´kəpi) *n.*
endoskeleton (endōskel´itən) *n.* the internal bony and cartilaginous framework of the vertebrates.
endosmosis (endozmō´sis), **endosmose** (en´dozmōs) *n.* the passage of a fluid from outside inwards through a porous diaphragm. **endosmotic** (-mot´-), **endosmic** (-doz´-), **endosmosmic** (-moz´-) *a.* **endosmically** *adv.* **endosmotically** *adv.*
endosperm (en´dōspœm) *n.* the albumen of a seed. **endospermic** (-spœ´-) *a.*
endospore (en´dōspaw) *n.* **1** the inner layer of the wall of a spore. **2** a small spore produced by some algae and bacteria.
endothelium (endōthē´liəm) *n.* (*pl.* **endothelia** (-liə)) a membrane lining blood vessels, tubes, cavities etc. **endothelial** *a.*
endothermic (endōthœ´mik) *a.* **1** (*Chem.*) occurring, or formed, with the absorption of heat. **2** (*Zool.*) characterized by the generation of heat internally. **endothermal** *a.* **endothermically** *adv.* **endothermism** *n.* **endothermy** *n.*
endotoxin (endōtok´sin) *n.* a toxin present within a bacterium and only released at death. **endotoxic** *a.*
endow (indow´) *v.t.* **1** to bestow a permanent income upon. **2** to invest (with talents, qualities etc.). **3** to invest with goods, estate, privileges etc. **endower** *n.* **endowment** *n.* **1 a** the act of making permanent provision for the support of any person, institution etc. **b** the fund or property so appropriated. **2** (*pl.*) natural gifts, qualities or ability. **endowment assurance**, **endowment insurance** *n.* an assurance to provide a fixed sum at a specified age or on death before that age. **endowment mortgage** *n.* a form of mortgage in which the capital repayments go into a life assurance policy. [EN-, F *douer*, L *dōtāre*, to DOWER]
endozoic (endōzō´ik) *a.* **1** living inside an animal. **2** (*Bot.*) of or relating to a method of seed-dispersal in which the seed is swallowed by an animal and then passed out in its excreta.
endue (indū´), **indue** *v.t.* (*formal*) **1** (*usu. p.p.*) to endow, to furnish. **2** to put on (as clothes). **3** to clothe, to invest (with). [OF *enduire*, L *indūcere* (IN-[1], *dūcere*, to lead, draw), in certain senses confused with ENDOW and also with L *induere*, to put on]
endure (induə´) *v.t.* **1** to undergo, to suffer. **2** to tolerate (a person). **3** to bear, to stand (a test or strain). **4** to submit to. ~*v.i.* **1** to last, to continue to exist. **2** to stay in the same state. **3** to bear sufferings with patience and fortitude. **endurable** *a.* **endurability** (-bil´-) *n.* **endurableness** *n.* **endurance** *n.* **1** the act or state of enduring or suffering. **2** the capacity of bearing or suffering with patience. **3** continuance, duration. **endurer** *n.* **enduring** *a.* **1** durable, permanent. **2** long-suffering. **enduringly** *adv.* **enduringness** *n.* [OF *endurer*, L *indūrāre* (IN-[1], *dūrus*, hard)]
ENE *abbr.* east-north-east.
-ene (ēn) *suf.* **1** (*Chem.*) denoting a hydrocarbon, such as *benzene*, *naphthalene*. **2** denoting an inhabitant of a place, as *Cairene*. [L *-ēnus*, adj. suf.]
en effet (ãn efe´) *adv.* in effect. [F]
enema (en´əmə) *n.* (*pl.* **enemas, enemata** (-mətə)) **1** a fluid injected into the rectum. **2** an injection. **3** the apparatus with which an injection is made. [Gr. *enēma*, from *enienai* (EN-, *hienai*, to send)]
enemy (en´əmi) *n.* (*pl.* **enemies**) **1** someone hostile to another person, or to a cause etc. **2** an adversary, one opposed to any person, subject or cause. **3** a hostile army, military force or ship. **4** (a member of) a hostile force or nation. **how goes the enemy?** (*coll.*) what is the time? **the Enemy** the Devil. [OF *enemi*, L *inimīcus* (*in*, UN-[1], *amīcus*, friend)]
energetic, **energize** ENERGY.
energumen (enəgū´mən) *n.* **1** an enthusiast, a fanatic. **2** a person possessed by a spirit, esp. an evil spirit, a demoniac. [late L *energūmenus*, Gr. *energoumenos*, p.p. of *energeein*, to work in or upon, see ENERGY]
energy (en´əji) *n.* (*pl.* **energies**) **1** internal or inherent power. **2** force, vigour. **3** capability of action or performing work by the use of physical or other

resources, as *nuclear energy*. 4 active operation. 5 emphasis. 6 (*Physics*) a body's power of performing mechanical work. **kinetic energy** KINETIC. **latent energy** LATENT. **potential energy** POTENTIAL (under POTENT[2]). **energetic** (enəjet´ik) *a*. 1 active, vigorously operative. 2 forcible, powerful. **energetically** *adv*. **energetics** *n*. physical, as distinct from vital, dynamics. **energize** (en´-), **energise** *v.t.* to give energy to. ~*v.i.* to act energetically and vigorously. **energizer** *n*. **energy tax** *n*. a range of possible taxes on the use of non-renewable energy sources, to reduce their use and so protect the environment. [late L *energīa*, Gr. *energeia* (EN-, *ergon*, work)]

enervate (en´əvāt) *v.t.* 1 to deprive of force or strength; to weaken. 2 to render effeminate. ~*a*. weakened; wanting in spirit, strength or vigour. **enervating** *a*. **enervation** (enəvā´shən) *n*. **enervative** *a*. **enervator** *n*. [L *ēnervātus*, p.p. of *ēnervāre* (E-, *nervus*, sinew)]

enface (infās´) *v.t.* to write, print or stamp the face of (a document). **enfacement** *n*.

en face (ã fas´) *adv*. 1 opposite, facing. 2 facing forwards. [F]

en famille (ã famēy´) *adv*. 1 at home with one's family. 2 informally. [F]

enfant gâté (ãfã gatā´) *n*. (*pl*. **enfants gâtés** (ãfã gatā´)) someone whose character has been spoiled by over-indulgence. [F, spoilt child]

enfant terrible (ãfã terēb´lə) *n*. (*pl*. **enfants terribles** (ãfã terēb´lə)) 1 a person who embarrasses people by behaving indiscreetly, unconventionally etc. 2 a child who makes embarrassing remarks. [F, terrible child]

enfeeble (infē´bəl) *v.t.* to make feeble or weak. **enfeeblement** *n*.

enfeoff (infēf´, -fef´) *v.t.* 1 (*Law*) to invest with a fief. 2 to bestow or convey an estate in fee simple or fee tail. 3 to grant (someone) possession. **enfeoffment** *n*. 1 (*Law*) the act of enfeoffing. 2 the deed by which the fee simple is conveyed. [A-F *enfeoffer*, OF *enfeffer* (EN-, FIEF)]

en fête (ã fet´) *adv*. dressed for a holiday, celebrating a holiday. [F]

enfetter (infet´ə) *v.t.* (*formal*) 1 to fetter. 2 to enslave (to).

enfilade (enfilād´) *n*. 1 a fire that may rake a position, line of works or body of troops, from end to end. 2 a position liable to a raking fire. ~*v.t.* to pierce or rake with shot from end to end. **enfilading battery** *n*. a battery that rakes a whole line with its fire. [F, from *enfiler*, to thread (EN-, *fil*, L *fīlum*, a thread)]

enfold (infōld´), **infold** *v.t.* 1 to wrap up, to enwrap, to enclose. 2 to clasp, to embrace. 3 to arrange or shape in folds. **enfoldment** *n*.

enforce (infaws´) *v.t.* 1 to compel obedience to (a law etc.). 2 to force or impose (loyalty, obedience, some form of activity etc.). 3 to press or urge forcibly (an argument etc.). **enforceable** *a*. **enforceability** (-bil´-) *n*. **enforced** *a*. forced, not voluntary. **enforcedly** (-sid-) *adv*. **enforcement** *n*. **enforcement notice** *n*. an official notice served on someone who has breached planning regulations. **enforcement officer** *n*. a government official employed to report on infringements of regulations. **enforcer** *n*. [OF *enforcer*, late L *infortiāre* (IN-[1], L *fortis*, strong)]

enfranchise (infran´chīz) *v.t.* 1 to give (someone) the right to vote. 2 to give (a town, constituency etc.) full municipal or parliamentary rights and privileges. 3 to set free. **enfranchisement** (-chiz-) *n*. 1 the act of enfranchising. 2 the state of being enfranchised. 3 admission to the municipal or the parliamentary franchise. **enfranchisement of copyhold lands** *n*. (*Law*) the conversion of such lands into freeholds. **enfranchiser** *n*. [OF *enfranchiss-*, stem of *enfranchir* (EN-, *franc*, FRANK)]

ENG *abbr*. electronic news gathering.

Eng. *abbr*. 1 England. 2 English.

eng. *abbr*. 1 engineer. 2 engineering. 3 engraver. 4 engraving.

engage (ingāj´) *v.t.* 1 to bind by a promise or contract, esp. by promise of marriage. 2 to hire, order, bespeak. 3 to employ, to occupy the time or attention of. 4 to attack, to come into conflict with. 5 to cause to interlock (parts of a gear etc.). ~*v.i.* 1 to promise (to do something). 2 to take part (in). 3 to enter into, embark (on). 4 to begin to fight, to enter into conflict (with). 5 to interlock (with). **engaged** *a*. 1 pledged to marry. 2 booked or occupied. 3 busy, employed. 4 (of a telephone line) already being used. **engaged column** *n*. (*Archit.*) a column fastened into a wall so that it is partly concealed. **engaged couple** *n*. two persons who have exchanged promises of marriage. **engaged signal**, **engaged tone** *n*. a tone heard on a telephone line to indicate that it is already being used. **engaged wheels** *n.pl.* wheels interlocking with each other by means of cogs etc. **engagement** *n*. 1 the act of engaging. 2 an obligation, a contract. 3 a mutual promise of marriage. 4 employment or occupation of time or attention. 5 an appointment. 6 a hiring, a contract to employ. 7 the state of being hired. 8 an enterprise embarked on. 9 an action or battle between armies or fleets. 10 (*pl.*) the contracts entered into by a trader. **engagement ring** *n*. a ring worn on the third finger of the left hand by a woman engaged to be married. **engaging** *a*. winning, pleasing, attractive (used of manners or address). **engagingly** *adv*. **engagingness** *n*. [F *engager* (EN-, *gage*, a pledge)]

engagé (ãgazhā´, ong·gazh´ā) *a*. (of a writer, artist etc.) committed to a moral or political cause. [F, ENGAGED (under ENGAGE)]

en garde (ã gahd´) *int*. (in fencing) used as a warning to be ready to receive attack. ~*a*. ready for attack. [F, on guard]

engender (injen´də) *v.t.* 1 to be the cause of, to bring about. 2 (*formal*) to beget. ~†*v.i.* to come into existence. **engenderer** *n*. **engenderment** *n*. [F *engendrer*, L *ingenerāre* (IN-[1], *genus*, a race, a brood)]

engine (en´jin) *n*. 1 an apparatus consisting of a number of parts for applying mechanical power, esp. one that converts energy into motion. 2 a machine or instrument used in war. 3 an instrument, a tool. 4 means to effect a purpose. 5 †native wit. 6 understanding. ~*v.t.* 1 †to torture by means of an engine. 2 to furnish (a ship) with engines. **engine driver** *n*. a person who drives a locomotive. **engine house** *n*. a building containing an engine. **engine lathe** *n*. a lathe driven by machinery. **engine man** *n*. (*pl*. **engine men**) a person who drives or manages a locomotive. **engine plane** *n*. (*Mining*) an underground passage along which an endless chain or rope worked by an engine hauls tubs and trucks. **engine room** *n*. a room, esp. in a ship, where the engines are housed. **enginery** (-jin´ri) *n*. (*pl*. **engineries**) 1 engines. 2 apparatus, mechanism, machinery. **engine-sized** *a*. (of paper) sized by machinery. **engine-turning** *n*. complex ornamental turning, as on the outside of watch-cases, done by machinery. **engine-turned** *a*. [OF *engin*, L *ingenium*, genius (see INGENIOUS)]

engineer (enjiniə´) *n*. 1 a person who is trained or qualified in a branch of engineering. 2 a person who designs or carries out construction work of mechanical, electrical or civic nature. 3 a person who maintains and repairs machinery, a mechanic. 4 (*N Am.*) someone who manages or attends to a locomotive, an engine driver. 5 a member of that part of an army which attends to engineering work. 6 (*fig.*) someone who carries through any undertaking skilfully or ingeniously. ~*v.t.* 1 to direct or carry out, as an engineer, the formation or execution of (as railways, canals etc.). 2 to contrive, to manage by tact or ingenuity. ~*v.i.* to act as an engineer. **engineering** *n.* **1** the skill or profession of an engineer. **2** the application of scientific principles to the design and construction of machinery, public works etc. **engineering science** *n.* [OF *engigneor*, late L *ingeniātor -ōrem*, from *ingeniāre*, as ENGINE]

enginery ENGINE.

engird (ingœd´) *v.t.* (*past*, *p.p.* **engirt** (-gœt´)) to encircle, to encompass with or as if with a girdle.

engirdle (ingœ´dəl) *v.t.* to surround with or as with a girdle.

engirt ENGIRD.

English (ing´glish) *a.* **1** of or relating to England or its inhabitants. **2** spoken or written in the English language. **3** characteristic of or becoming an English person. ~*n.* (*pl.* **English**) **1** the language of the British Isles, N America, Australasia, parts of Southern Africa, and other parts of the British Commonwealth. **2** (*Print.*) a size of type between great primer and pica. **3** (*pl.*) the people of England (sometimes of Britain). **4** (*pl.*) the soldiers fighting on the English side. **5** (*N Am.*) side on a billiard ball. ~*v.t.* **1** to translate into the English language. **2** to express in plain English. **English bond** *n.* bonding brickwork by means of alternate courses of headers and stretchers. **English elm** *n.* the elm *Ulmus procera*. **English galingale** *n.* a rare English sedge, *Cyperus longus*. **English horn** *n.* COR ANGLAIS (under COR[2]). **Englishism** *n.* **Englishman** *n.* (*pl.* **Englishmen**) a man who is a native or a naturalized inhabitant of England. **Englishness** *n.* **English Pale** *n.* (*Hist.*) the part of Ireland in which English authority was recognized. †**Englishry** *n.* **1** the quality or state of being an English person. **2** the part of the population of a country that is of English ancestry, esp. the English settlers in Ireland and their descendants. **3** the English population, the English quarter. **Englishwoman** *n.* (*pl.* **Englishwomen**) a woman who is a native or naturalized inhabitant of England. [OE *Englisc*, *Ǣnglisc*, from *Engle*, the Angles]

englut (inglŭt´) *v.t.* (*pres.p.* **englutting**, *past*, *p.p.* **englutted**) **1** to swallow. **2** to gulp down, to glut, to satiate. [OF *englotir*, L *ingluttīre* (IN-[1], *gluttīre*, to swallow); and in later senses formed from EN-, GLUT]

engorge (ingawj´) *v.t.* **1** (*Med.*) to congest (with blood). **2** (*in p.p.*) to fill to excess. **3** to swallow up, to devour (food). **engorged** *a.* **1** (*Med.*) congested with blood. **2** filled to excess, crammed. **engorgement** *n.* [F *engorger* (EN-, *gorge*, GORGE)]

engraft (ingrahft´), **ingraft** *v.t.* **1** to graft upon, to insert (a scion of one tree) upon or into another. **2** to incorporate. **3** to implant, instil. **engraftment** *n.*

engrail (ingrāl´) *v.t.* (*chiefly Her.*) to indent in curved lines, to make ragged at the edges as if broken with hail. **engrailment** *n.* [OF *engresler*, perh. from *gresle* (F *grêle*), hail]

engrain INGRAIN[1].

engram (en´gram) *n.* (*Psych.*) the physical trace of a memory in the brain. **engrammatic** (-mat´ik) *a.* [G *Engramm* (Gr. EN-, *gramma*, a letter, *graphein*, to write)]

en grande tenue (ã grãd tənü´) *adv.* in full evening dress. [F]

en grand seigneur (ã grã senyœ´) *adv.* like a lord, using or having a grand or arrogant manner. [F]

engrave (ingrāv´) *v.t.* **1** to cut figures, letters etc. (on), with a chisel or graver. **2** to represent on wood, metal etc., by carving with a graver. **3** to inscribe or decorate (a surface) with figures etc. **4** to imprint on the mind, to impress deeply. ~*v.i.* to practise the art of engraving. **engraver** *n.* **engraving** *n.* **1** the act, process or art of cutting figures, letters etc. on wood, stone or metal. **2** that which is engraved. **3** an impression from an engraved plate, a print.

engross (ingrōs´) *v.t.* **1** to monopolize, to occupy the attention entirely, to absorb. **2** to write or type out formally, e.g. a legal document. **3** to write out in large, bold letters. **engrossed** *a.* absorbed (in, as in reading a book). **engrosser** *n.* **engrossing** *a.* absorbing, occupying the attention completely. **engrossment** *n.* **1** a document which has been engrossed. **2** the act of engrossing documents. **3** the state of having one's attention wholly taken up. **4** exorbitant appropriation or acquisition. [A-F *engrosser* (EN-, *grosse*, late L *grossa*, large writing)]

engulf (ingŭlf´), **ingulf**, †**engulph** *v.t.* **1** to cast, as into a gulf. **2** to swallow up, as in a gulf or whirlpool. **engulfment** *n.*

enhance (inhahns´) *v.t.* **1** to raise in importance, degree etc. **2** to improve. **3** to augment, to intensify. **4** to raise in price. **5** to exaggerate. **enhanced radiation weapon** *n.* a neutron bomb. **enhancement** *n.* **enhancer** *n.* **enhancive** *a.* [A-F *enhauncer*, OF *enhaucer* (IN-[1], late L *altiāre*, to heighten, from *altus*, high)]

enharmonic (enhahmon´ik) *a.* (*Mus.*) having intervals less than a semitone, as between G sharp and A flat. ~*n.* enharmonic music. **enharmonical** *a.* **enharmonically** *adv.* **enharmonic modulation** *n.* change as to notation, but not as to sound. [L *enharmonicus*, Gr. *enarmonikos* (EN-, *harmonia*, HARMONY)]

enhearten (inhah´tən) *v.t.* to encourage, cheer, strengthen.

enigma (inig´mə) *n.* **1** an inexplicable or mysterious proceeding, person or thing. **2** a saying in which the meaning is concealed under obscure language, a riddle. **enigmatic** (enigmat´-), **enigmatical** (-əl) *a.* **enigmatically** *adv.* **enigmatist** (inig´-) *n.* a maker of or dealer in enigmas or riddles. **enigmatize**, **enigmatise** *v.i.* **1** to speak or write enigmatically. **2** to deal in enigmas. [L *aenigma*, Gr. *ainigma -atos*, from *ainissesthai*, to speak obscurely or allusively, from *ainos*, fable]

enjambment (injamb´mənt), **enjambement** *n.* the continuation of a sentence or clause, without a pause in sense, from one line of verse or couplet into the next. [F *enjambement*, from *enjamber* (EN-, *jambe*, leg)]

enjoin (injoin´) *v.t.* **1** to direct, prescribe, impose (an act or conduct). **2** to direct or command (a person to do something). **3** to instruct (that). **4** (*Law*) to prohibit or restrain (a person) from doing something. **enjoinment** *n.* [OF *enjoindre*, L *injungere* (IN-[1], *jungere*, to join)]

enjoy (injoi´) *v.t.* **1** to take pleasure or delight in. **2** to have the use or benefit of. **3** to experience or have. **4** †to have sexual intercourse with. **to enjoy oneself** (*coll.*) to experience pleasure or happiness. **enjoyable** *a.* **enjoyability** (-bil´-) *n.* **enjoyableness** *n.* **enjoyably** *adv.* **enjoyment** *n.* [OF *enjoier*]

enkephalin (enkef´əlin), **encephalin** (-sef´-, -kef´-) *n.* a chemical found in the brain, having a pain-killing effect similar to that of morphine. [Gr. *en*, in, *kephalē*, head]

enkindle (inkin´dəl) *v.t.* (*formal*) **1** to kindle, to set on fire. **2** to inflame, to rouse into passion, action etc.

enlace (inlās´) *v.t.* **1** to encircle tightly, to surround. **2** to embrace, enfold, entwine. **3** to entangle. **enlacement** *n.* [F *enlacer* (EN-, *lacer*, ult. from L *laqueāre*, to ensnare, from *laqueus*, a noose)]

enlarge (inlahj´) *v.t.* **1** to make greater; to extend in dimensions, quantity or number. **2** to expand, to widen. **3** to make more comprehensive. **4** to reproduce (a photographic negative) on a larger scale. ~*v.i.* **1** to become bigger. **2** to expatiate (upon). **enlargeable** *a.* **enlargement** *n.* **1** the act or process of extending or increasing. **2** an increase in size or bulk. **3** something added on, an addition. **4** release from confinement. **5** diffuseness of speech or writing. **6** a photographic print or negative of a larger size taken from another. **enlarger** *n.* an apparatus for making enlargements of photographs. [OF *enlarger*]

enlighten (inlī´tən) *v.t.* **1** to give mental or spiritual light to, to instruct. **2** to release from ignorance, prejudice or superstition. **3** to give (someone) information (on). **4** to supply with light. **5** (*poet.*) to shed light upon. **enlightener** *n.* **enlightenment** *n.* **1** the act of enlightening. **2** the state of being enlightened. **3** (**Enlightenment**) an 18th-cent. philosophical movement which stressed the importance of rationality and questioned tradition.

enlist (inlist´) *v.t.* **1** to enrol, esp. to engage for military service. **2** to gain the interest, assistance, participation or support of. *~v.i.* to engage oneself for military service. **enlisted man** *n.* (*pl.* **enlisted men**) (*US*) a soldier or sailor who is not an officer. **enlister** *n.* **enlistment** *n.*

enliven (inlī´vən) *v.t.* **1** to give spirit or animation to. **2** to impart life to, to stimulate. **3** to brighten, render cheerful in appearance. **enlivener** *n.* **enlivenment** *n.*

en masse (ã mas´) *adv.* in a group, all together. [F]

enmesh (inmesh´) *v.t.* **1** to entangle or catch in or as if in a net. **2** to entrap. **enmeshment** *n.*

enmity (en´miti) *n.* (*pl.* **enmities**) **1** the state or quality of being an enemy. **2** hatred, hostility. **3** an instance of this. [A-F *enemité*, OF *enemistié*, late L *inimīcitas -tātem*, from L *inimīcus*, enemy]

ennea- (en´ia) *comb. form* nine. [Gr. *enneas -ados*]

ennead (en´iad) *n.* a set of nine things, esp. of nine books or discourses. [Gr.]

enneagynous (eniaj´inəs) *a.* (*Bot.*) having nine pistils. [Gr. *gunē*, woman]

enneahedron (eniəhē´drən) *n.* (*pl.* **enneahedrons, enneahedra** (-drə)) (*Geom.*) a solid figure with nine sides. **enneahedral** (-drəl) *a.* having nine sides.

enneandrian (enian´driən), **enneandrous** (-drəs) *a.* (*Bot.*) having nine stamens. [Gr. *anēr andros*, man]

enneapetalous (eniəpet´ələs) *a.* (*Bot.*) having nine petals.

enneaphyllous (eniəfil´əs) *a.* (*Bot.*) having nine leaflets composing a compound leaf.

ennoble (inō´bəl) *v.t.* **1** to make a noble of. **2** to make noble; to elevate in character or dignity. **ennoblement** *n.* **ennobling** *a.* [OF *ennoblir* (EN-, NOBLE)]

ennui (onwē´) *n.* **1 a** listlessness. **b** lack of interest in things. **2** boredom. **ennuyé** (-yā´) *a.* (*fem.* **ennuyée**) affected with ennui. [F, from OF *enui*, L *in odio* (cp. ANNOY)]

ENO *abbr.* English National Opera.

eno-, en- OENO-.

enormous (inaw´məs) *a.* **1** huge, immense. **2** exceedingly great in size, number or quantity. **3** †extremely wicked. **enormity** *n.* (*pl.* **enormities**) **1** a monstrous crime, an outrage, an atrocity. **2** the state or quality of being excessively wicked. **3** enormousness. **enormously** *adv.* **enormousness** *n.* [earlier *enorm*, MF *enorme*, L *enormis* (E-, *norma*, pattern, NORM)]

Usage note The use of *enormity* of size (rather than *enormousness*) is sometimes disapproved of, though it is quite common.

enosis (en´ōsis, enō´-) *n.* the proposal for the political union of Cyprus with Greece. [Gr.]

enough (inŭf´), †**enow** (inow´) *a.* (*usu. placed after the noun*) sufficient for or adequate to need or demand. *~pron.* **1** a sufficiency; a quantity or amount which satisfies requirement or desire. **2** that which is equal to the powers or abilities. *~int.* used to denote sufficiency or satisfaction. *~adv.* sufficiently, tolerably, passably. **to have had enough of 1** to have had sufficient of. **2** to have had too much of, to be tired of. **well enough** tolerably well. [OE *genōh*, *genōg*, allied to impers. *geneah*, it suffices (cp. Goth. *ganohs*, enough, *ganah*, it suffices, also Icel. *gnogr*, Dan. *nok*, G *genug*, enough, Sansk. *naç*, to attain, L *nancisci*, to obtain, p.p. *nactus*)]

enounce (inowns´) *v.t.* **1** (*formal*) **a** to enunciate, state definitely. **b** to pronounce. **enouncement** *n.* [F *énoncer*, L *ēnuntiāre*, to ENUNCIATE]

†**enow** ENOUGH.

en papillote (ã papēyot´) *adv.* baked in an envelope of foil or greased paper. [F]

en passant (ã pas´ã) *adv.* **1** by the way. **2** in chess, applied to the taking of a pawn that has moved two squares as if it had moved only one. [F, in passing]

en pension (ã pāsyō´) *adv.* as a lodger, with meals provided. [F, see PENSION[2]]

enplane EMPLANE.

enprint (en´print) *n.* an enlarged photographic print.

en prise (ã prēz´) *a.* in chess, of or relating to a piece which is exposed to capture.

enquire INQUIRE.

enrage (inrāj´) *v.t.* **1** to put in a rage. **2** to exasperate. **3** to provoke to fury. **enragement** *n.* [OF *enrager*]

en rapport (ã rapaw´) *adv.* in sympathy (with). [F]

enrapture (inrap´chə) *v.t.* to fill with rapture, to delight.

enrich (inrich´) *v.t.* **1** to make rich or richer. **2** to add to the quality or value of. **3** to fertilize. **4** to add to the contents of. **5** (*Physics*) to increase the proportion of a particular isotope in (an element, esp. uranium). **enriched** *a.* **enricher** *n.* **enrichment** *n.* [F *enrichir*]

enrobe (inrōb´) *v.t.* **1** to put a robe upon, to attire. **2** to put a coating on. **enrober** *n.*

enrol (inrōl´), (*N Am.*) **enroll** *v.t.* (*pres.p.* **enrolling**, *past, p.p.* **enrolled**) **1** to write down on or enter in a roll. **2** to record, to register, to celebrate. **3** to include as a member, to record the admission of. *~v.i.* to enrol oneself (as a member, student etc.). **enrollee** (-ē´) *n.* **enroller** *n.* a person who enrols or registers. **enrolment**, (*N Am.*) **enrollment** *n.* **1** the act of enrolling. **2** the state of being enrolled. **3** the total number of people enrolled. [OF *enroller*]

enroot (inroot´) *v.t.* **1** to fix by the root. **2** to implant deeply. **3** to entangle by or as by the roots.

en route (ã root´) *adv.* on the way; on the road. [F]

Ens. *abbr.* Ensign.

ens (enz) *n.* (*pl.* **entia** (en´shiə)) (*Philos.*) **1** entity, being, existence. **2** any existing being or thing. [late L *ēns*, pres.p. of *esse*, to be]

Ensa (en´sə) *n.* an official organization for entertaining men and women in the armed services during World War II. [acronym for *e*ntertainments *n*ational *s*ervices *a*ssociation]

†**ensample** (insahm´pəl) *n.* an example, a pattern, a model. *~v.t.* **1** to exemplify. **2** to show by example. [A-F, corr. of OF *essample*, EXAMPLE]

ensanguine (insang´gwin) *v.t.* (*formal*) **1** (*now only in p.p.*) to smear or cover with blood. **2** to make crimson. [EN-, L *sanguis -inis*, blood]

ensate (en´sāt) *a.* (*Bot.*) shaped like a sword with a straight blade. [L *ensis*, a sword]

ensconce (inskons´) *v.t.* **1** to settle (oneself) comfortably or securely. **2** to hide. [SCONCE[2]]

ensemble (āsā´blə, onsom´bəl) *n.* **1** all the parts of anything taken together. **2** the general effect of things taken together. **3** an outfit consisting of several (matching) garments. **4** (*Mus.*) the joint effort of all the performers. **5** (*Mus.*) a combination of two or more performers or players. **6** a group of supporting players or performers. **7** (*Physics*) a set of systems having the same constitution but behaving in different ways. *~adv.* **1** all together. **2** all at once. [F, from late L *insimul* (*in simul*, at the same time)]

enshrine (inshrīn´) *v.t.* **1** to place in or as if in a shrine. **2** to enclose and cherish (something) as if it is sacred. **3** to act as a shrine for. **enshrinement** *n.*

enshroud (inshrowd´) *v.t.* (*formal*) **1** to cover with or as if with a shroud. **2** to conceal.

ensiform (en´sifawm) *a.* sword-shaped, as the leaf of an iris. **ensiform cartilage, ensiform process** *n.* the cartilaginous part at the end of the sternum or breastbone. [L *ensis*, a sword]

ensign (en´sīn, -sin) *n.* **1** a national banner, a standard, a regimental flag, the flag with distinguishing colours carried by ships. **2** a badge of rank or office. **3** (*Hist.*) the lowest rank of commissioned officers in an infantry regiment, by the senior of whom the colours were carried. **4** the lowest ranking commissioned officer in the US navy. **5** a sign or symbol. ~*v.t.* **1** to distinguish by a badge. **2** to be the distinguishing mark of. **3** (*Her.*) to distinguish by any mark or ornament, borne on or over a charge. **ensign-bearer** *n.* the soldier who carries the colours; an ensign. **ensigncy, ensignship** *n.* [OF *enseigne*, late L *insignia*, orig. neut. pl. of *insignis*, remarkable, from *signum*, a SIGN]

ensilage (en´silij, insī´lij) *n.* **1** a method of preserving forage crops whilst moist and succulent, without previously drying, by storing them en masse in pits or trenches. **2** fodder so preserved, silage. ~*v.t.* to preserve by the process of ensilage. **ensile** (insīl´) *v.t.* **1** to put into a silo for this purpose. **2** to ensilage. **ensilability** (-əbil´iti) *n.* [F, from *ensiler*, Sp. *ensilar*, to preserve grain in a pit, see SILO]

enslave (inslāv´) *v.t.* **1** to make a slave of, to reduce to bondage. **2** to bring under the domination of some influence, habit, vice etc. **enslavement** *n.* servitude. **enslaver** *n.* a person who or thing which enslaves.

ensnare (insneə´) *v.t.* **1** to entrap. **2** to overcome by treachery. **ensnarement** *n.*

ensphere (insfiə´) *v.t.* **1** to place in or as if in a sphere. **2** to form into a round body.

enstatite (en´stətīt) *n.* a rock-forming mineral, magnesium silicate. [Gr. *enstatēs*, adversary]

ensue (insū´) *v.i.* (*3rd pers. sing. pres.* **ensues**, *pres.p.* **ensuing**, *past, p.p.* **ensued**) **1** to follow in course of time, to succeed. **2** to result (from). **ensuing** *a.* coming next after. [OF *ensu-*, stem of *ensuivre*, late L *insequere*, L *insequī* (IN-[1], *sequī*, to follow)]

en suite (ã swēt´) *adv.* in succession, as part of a set. ~*a.* forming a unit, as *en suite bathroom.* [F]

ensure (inshooə´) *v.t.* **1** to make certain (that). **2** to make safe (against or from any risk). **3** to assure or guarantee (something to or for). **4** †to insure. **ensurer** *n.* [A-F *enseurer*, from OF *seur*, SURE]

enswathe (inswādh´) *v.t.* to enwrap, to bandage. **enswathement** *n.*

ENT *abbr.* ear, nose and throat.

ent- ENTO-.

-ent (ənt) *suf.* **1** forming adjectives meaning causing or performing some action, or being in a condition, as *astringent, inherent.* **2** forming nouns denoting an agent, as *recipient, student.* [L *-entem*, acc. of *-ens*, pres.p. ending]

entablature (intab´ləchə) *n.* (*Archit.*) the upper part of a classical building supported upon the columns, consisting in upward succession of the architrave, frieze and cornice. [ult. from late L *intabulāre*, to form an *intabulātum* or flooring (cp. It. *intavolatura*)]

entablement (intā´bəlmənt) *n.* **1** the platform or series of platforms supporting a statue, above the dado and base. **2** an entablature. [F, from *entabler*]

entail (intāl´) *v.t.* **1** to involve, to necessitate. **2** to bestow or settle (a possession) inalienably on a certain person and their heirs. **3** to restrict (an inheritance) to a particular class of heirs. **4** to impose (certain duties, expenses etc. upon someone). ~*n.* **1** an estate in fee limited in descent to a particular heir or heirs. **2** the limitation of inheritance in this way. **3** (*fig.*) anything that is inherited as an inalienable possession. **entailer** *n.* **entailment** *n.* [EN-, F *taille*, TAIL[2]]

entamoeba (entəmē´bə), (*esp. N Am.*) **entameba** *n.* (*pl.* **entamoebas, entamoebae** (-bē), (*esp. N Am.*) **entamebas, entamebae**) any amoeba of the *Entamoeba* genus, which causes amoebic dysentery in humans.

entangle (intang´gəl) *v.t.* **1** to ensnare, as in a net. **2** to involve in difficulties, obstacles, contradictions etc. **3** to twist together so that unravelling is difficult. **entanglement** *n.* **1** the act of entangling. **2** the state of being entangled. **3** a thing or set of circumstances that entangles. **4** an embarrassing or compromising relationship, esp. sexual. **5** (*Mil.*) an obstruction made using barbed wire etc. **entangler** *n.*

entasis (en´təsis) *n.* (*pl.* **entases** (-sēz)) (*Archit.*) the almost imperceptible convex curvature given to a shaft or a column. [Gr., from *enteinein* (EN-, *teinein*, to strain)]

entelechy (intel´əki) *n.* (*pl.* **entelechies**) (*Philos.*) **1** (in Aristotle's philosophy) the complete realization or full expression of a function or potentiality. **2** (in Leibnitz's philosophy) a monad. [Gr. *entelecheia* (EN-, *telei*, dat. of *telos*, the end, perfection, *echein*, to have)]

entellus (intel´əs) *n.* (*pl.* **entelluses**) (*Zool.*) an Indian monkey, the hanuman. [*Entellus*, a person in Virgil's *Aeneid* v.437–72]

entente (ãtãnt´, ontont´) *n.* **1** a friendly understanding. **2** a group of states having such an understanding. **Entente Cordiale** (kawdiahl´) *n.* **1** the understanding between France and Britain reached in 1904. **2** (*also* **entente cordiale**) any such understanding between states or other powers. [F, understanding]

enter (en´tə) *v.t.* **1** to go or come into. **2** to pierce, to penetrate. **3** to associate oneself with, become a member of. **4** to insert, to set down in writing, a list, book etc. **5 a** to put down the name of as a competitor for a race etc. **b** to become a competitor in (a race etc.). **6** to initiate into a business etc. **7** to present or submit (a proposal, a protest etc.). **8** to join in, participate in. **9** to cause to be inscribed upon the records of a court or legislative body. **10** to admit into the regular pack (said of a young dog). **11** to admit as a pupil or member, to procure admission as such. **12** (*Law*) to take possession of. **13** to report a vessel's arrival at the custom house. **14** †to initiate, to introduce. ~*v.i.* **1** to go or come in. **2** to become a competitor. **3** (of an actor) to appear on stage. **to enter an appearance** to show oneself. **to enter into 1** to form a part of. **2** to join. **3** to engage or take an interest in, to sympathize with. **4** to become a party to (an agreement, treaty, recognizances etc.). **to enter on** to begin, to set out upon. **to enter one's head** HEAD[1]. **to enter up 1** to set down in a regular series. **2** to complete a series of entries. **to enter upon 1** to begin, set out upon. **2** to begin to treat of (a subject etc.). **3** to take legal possession of. **enterable** *a.* **enterer** *n.* [F *entrer*, L *intrāre*, from *intrā*, within]

enter- ENTERO-.

enteral (en´tərəl) *a.* of or relating to the intestines.

enterectomy (entərek´təmi) *n.* (*pl.* **enterectomies**) surgical removal of part of the small intestine.

enteric (inter´ik) *a.* of or relating to the intestines. ~*n.* enteric fever. **enteric fever** *n.* typhoid fever. [Gr. *enterikos*, from *enteron*, intestine]

enteritis (entərī´tis) *n.* inflammation of the small intestine, usu. causing diarrhoea.

entero- (en´tərō), **enter-** *comb. form* of or relating to the intestines. [Gr. *enteron*, from *entos*, within]

enterocele (en´tərōsēl) *n.* a hernia containing part of the intestines.

enterolite (en´tərōlīt) *n.* a stony calculus.

enterology (entərol´əji) *n.* (*pl.* **enterologies**) a treatise or discourse on the intestines, often extended to all the internal parts of the human body.

enteropathy (entərop´əthi) *n.* disease of the small intestine.

enterostomy (entəros´təmi) *n.* (*pl.* **enterostomies**) the surgical formation of an opening to the small intestine through the abdominal wall.

enterotomy (entərot´əmi) *n.* (*pl.* **enterotomies**) the surgical opening up of the intestines.

enterovirus (entərōvī´rəs) *n.* (*pl.* **enteroviruses**) a virus which enters the body through the intestinal tract.

enterprise (en´təprīz) *n.* **1** an undertaking, esp. a bold or difficult one. **2** spirit of adventure, boldness, readiness to attempt. **3** a business concern. **enterprise culture** *n.* a commercial mindset which is encouraging to business initiative and adventurousness. **enterpriser** *n.* **enterprise scheme** *n.* a government scheme to encourage the setting up of small firms with state financial support. **enterprise zone** *n.* a depressed area given special government financial etc. backing to encourage commercial etc. improvement. **enterprising** *a.* **1** ready to undertake schemes involving difficulty or hazard. **2** energetic, adventurous. **3** full of enterprise. **enterprisingly** *adv.* [OF *entreprise*, from *entrepris*, p.p. of *entreprendre*, late L *interprendere*, to undertake (L *inter*, among, *prendere*, *prehendere*, to take in hand)]

entertain (entətān´) *v.t.* **1** to receive and treat as a guest. **2** to occupy agreeably; to divert, to amuse. **3** to hold in mind, cherish. **4** to consider favourably. ~*v.i.* to exercise hospitality, to receive company. **entertainer** *n.* a person who entertains, esp. a person who performs amusingly at an entertainment. **entertaining** *a.* amusing. **entertainingly** *adv.* **entertainment** *n.* **1** the act of entertaining. **2** receiving guests with hospitality. **3** a public performance intended to amuse. **4** accommodation for a traveller or guest. **5** a banquet. **6** the art of entertaining, amusing or diverting. **7** the pleasure afforded to the mind by anything interesting, amusement. **8** hospitality. [F *entretenir*, late L *intertenēre* (*inter*, among, *tenēre*, to hold)]

enthalpy (en´thəlpi, -thalpi) *n.* (*Physics*) the heat content of a substance per unit mass. [Gr. *thalpos*, heat]

enthral (inthrawl´), (*N Am.*) **enthrall, inthrall** *v.t.* (*3rd pers. sing. pres.* **enthrals**, (*N Am.*) **enthralls, inthralls**, *pres.p.* **enthralling**, (*N Am. also*) **inthralling**, *past, p.p.* **enthralled**, (*N Am. also*) **inthralled**) **1** to enslave, to captivate. **2** to reduce to the condition of a thrall. **enthraller** *n.* **enthralling** *a.* **enthralment**, (*N Am.*) **enthrallment, inthrallment** *n.*

enthrone (inthrōn´) *v.t.* **1** to place on a throne or place of dignity. **2** to invest with sovereign power. **3** to induct or install (as an archbishop or bishop) into the powers or privileges of a see. **enthronement** *n.*

enthronize (inthrō´nīz), **enthronise** *v.t.* to enthrone, to induct. **enthronization** (-zā´shən) *n.* [OF *intronizer*, late L *inthronīzāre*, Gr. *enthronizein* (EN-, *thronos*, THRONE)]

enthusiasm (enthū´ziazm, -thoo´-) *n.* **1** intense and passionate zeal. **2** ardent admiration. **3** fervour. **4** †an ecstatic feeling arising from supposed inspiration or possession by a divinity. **enthuse** *v.i.* **1** (*coll.*) to manifest enthusiasm. **2** to speak gushingly. **enthusiast** *n.* **1** a person filled with or prone to enthusiasm. **2** a person whose mind is completely possessed by any subject. **3** a visionary. **4** †a person who believes themselves possessed or inspired. **enthusiastic** (-as´-) *a., n.* **enthusiastically** *adv.* [late L *enthūsiasmus*, Gr. *enthousiasmos*, from *enthousiazein*, to be inspired, from *enthousia*, from *entheos*, possessed by a god (EN-, *theos*, god)]

enthymeme (en´thimēm) *n.* (*Logic*) a syllogism of which one premise is suppressed, and only an antecedent and a consequent expressed in words. **enthymematic** (-mat´-), **enthymematical** (-kəl) *a.* [L *enthȳmēma*, Gr. *enthumēma -atos*, from *enthumeesthai*, to think (EN-, *thumos*, mind)]

entia ENS.

entice (intīs´) *v.t.* **1** to attract, esp. by offering a reward or other inducement. **2** to tempt, seduce (from). **enticeable** *a.* **enticement** *n.* **enticer** *n.* **enticing** *a.* alluring, seductive. **enticingly** *adv.* [OF *enticier*, prob. from late L *intitiāre*, to kindle, set on fire (EN-, L *titio*, a firebrand)]

entire (intīə´) *a.* **1** whole, complete, perfect. **2** unbroken, undivided. **3** unmixed, pure. **4** unqualified, unreserved. **5** (of a horse) not castrated. **6** (*Bot.*) having the edges (as of a leaf) unbroken or unserrated. **7** unfeigned, earnest. **8** †honest, sincere. **9** †unimpaired, fresh. ~*n.* **1** an uncastrated horse. **2** a kind of porter or stout. **entirely** *adv.* **1** wholly, in every part; fully, completely. **2** exclusively. **entireness** *n.* **entirety** (-rəti) *n.* (*pl.* **entireties**) **1** entireness, completeness. **2** the entire amount, quantity or extent. **in its entirety** completely, as a whole. [OF *entier*, L *integrum*, acc. of *integer* (*in-*, not, *tāg-*, root of *tangere*, to touch)]

entitative ENTITY.

entitle (intī´təl) *v.t.* **1** to give a right, title or claim to anything. **2** to give a certain name or title to, to designate. **3** to dignify (someone) by a title. **entitlement** *n.* **1** the state of being entitled (to). **2** something to which one is entitled. [OF *entiteler*, L *intitulāre* (IN-[1], *titulus*, TITLE)]

entity (en´titi) *n.* (*pl.* **entities**) **1** anything that has real existence, a being. **2** essence, existence, as distinguished from qualities or relations. **3** the essential nature of a thing, that which constitutes its being. **entitative** *a.* [late L *entitās -tātem*, from ENS]

ento- (en´tō), **ent-** *comb. form* of or relating to the inside of anything. [Gr. *entos*, within]

entoblast (en´tōblahst) *n.* (*Biol.*) the nucleus of a cell. **entoblastic** *a.* [Gr. *blastos*, a sprout]

entom- ENTOMO-.

entomb (intoom´) *v.t.* **1** to place in a tomb, to bury. **2** to be a grave or tomb for. **entombment** *n.* [F *entomber* (EN-, *tombe*, TOMB)]

entomic (intom´ik) *a.* relating to insects.

entomo- (en´təmō), **entom-** *comb. form* of or relating to insects. [Gr. *entomon*, an insect, neut. of *entomos*, cut into, from *entemnein* (EN-, *temnein*, to cut)]

entomoid (en´təmoid) *a.* resembling an insect. ~*n.* anything resembling an insect.

entomology (entəmol´əji) *n.* the scientific study of insects. **entomologic** (-loj´-), **entomological** *a.* **entomologically** *adv.* **entomologist** (-mol´-) *n.*

Usage note See note under ETYMOLOGY.

entomophagous (entəmof´əgəs) *a.* (*Zool.*) feeding on insects. **entomophagy** (-fəji) *n.*

entomophilous (entəmof´iləs) *a.* (*Bot.*) **1** attractive to insects. **2** (of a flower) in which the pollen is carried by insects from the male to the female flowers.

entomostracous (entəmos´trəkəs) *a.* belonging to the Entomostraca, a division of crustaceans, small in size, with the body segments usu. distinct, and gills attached to the feet or organs of the mouth. **entomostracan** *a., n.* [Gr. *ostrakon*, shell]

entoparasite (entōpar´əsīt) *n.* ENDOPARASITE.

entophyte (en´təfīt) *n.* any parasitic plant growing in the interior of animal or vegetable structures. **entophytal** (-fī´-) *a.* **entophytic** (-fit´ik) *a.*

entourage (ãtoorahzh´, on-) *n.* **1** retinue, people following or attending on an important person. **2** surroundings, environment. [F, from *entourer*, to surround, from *entour* (EN-, *tour*, circuit)]

entozoon (entəzō´on) *n.* (*pl.* **entozoa** (-zō´ə)) (*Zool.*) an animal living within the body of another animal. **entozoal, entozoic** *a.* **entozoology** (-ol´əji) *n.* the study of the entozoa. **entozoologist** *n.* [Gr. *zōon*, animal]

entr'acte (ãtrakt´) *n.* **1** the interval between the acts of a play. **2** music, dancing or other performance between the acts of a play. [F *entre*, between, *acte*, act]

entrails (en´trālz) *n.pl.* **1** the internal parts of animals; the intestines. **2** the internal parts (as of the earth). [OF *entraile*, late L *intrālia*, from *inter*, among]

entrain[1] (intrān´) *v.t.* to draw after, to bring as a consequence. **entrainment**[1] *n.* [F *entraîner* (*en-*, L *inde*, away, *traîner*, to drag, see TRAIN)]

entrain[2] (intrān´) *v.t.* to put into a railway train. *~v.i.* to get into a train. **entrainment**[2] *n.*

entrain[3] (ãtrī´) *n.* enthusiasm, high spirits. [F]

en train (ã trī´) *adv.* in progress, under way. [F]

entrainment[1] ENTRAIN[1].

entrainment[2] ENTRAIN[2].

entrammel (intram´əl) *v.t.* (*pres.p.* **entrammelling**, (*N Am.*) **entrammeling**, *past, p.p.* **entrammelled**, (*N Am.*) **entrammeled**) to entangle, hamper, fetter.

entrance[1] (en´trəns) *n.* **1** the act of entering, or an instance of entering. **2** the power, right or liberty of entering. **3** the passage or doorway by which a place is entered. **4** the means of entering into. **5** the act of coming on to the stage. **6** entering into or upon. **7** the right of admission. **8** entrance fee, or fee paid for admission, as to an entertainment, club, race etc. **9** (*Mus.*) an entry. **10** the entering of a ship or goods at the custom house. **11** (*Naut.*) the bow of a vessel. **entrance fee**, **entrance money** *n.* money paid for entrance or admission. **entrant** *n.* **1** a person who enters. **2** a person entering upon or into a new profession, sphere, competition etc. [ENTER]

entrance[2] (intrahns´) *v.t.* **1** to throw into a state of ecstasy. **2** to carry away, transport, enrapture. **3** to overwhelm (with some strong emotion). **entrancement** *n.* **entrancing** *a.* [EN-, TRANCE]

entrant ENTRANCE[1].

entrap (intrap´) *v.t.* (*pres.p.* **entrapping**, *past, p.p.* **entrapped**) **1** to catch in or as in a trap. **2** to lure into making a compromising statement or into committing a (criminal) offence. **3** to entangle in contradictions, difficulties etc. **entrapment** *n.* **entrapper** *n.* [OF *entraper* (EN-, *trape*, a trap)]

entreat (intrēt´) *v.t.* **1** to beseech, to ask earnestly. **2** to ask for (something) earnestly. **3** †to treat, to act towards. **4** †to treat of, to discuss. *~v.i.* to make entreaties. **entreatingly** *adv.* **entreatment** *n.* **1** entreaty. **2** †conversation, interview. **3** †treatment. **entreaty** *n.* (*pl.* **entreaties**) **1** an urgent request. **2** importunity. [OF *entraiter* (EN-, *traiter*, to TREAT)]

entrechat (ã´trəsha) *n.* a leap in dancing, esp. one including a striking of the heels together several times. [F]

entrecôte (on´trəkōt, -kot) *n.* a beefsteak cut from between two ribs. [F, *entre*, between, *côte*, rib (L *costa*)]

entrée (ã´trā, on´-) *n.* **1** freedom or right of entrance. **2** (*orig. N Am.*) the main course of a meal. **3** a dish served between the fish and the meat courses. [F, entry]

entremets (ã´trəmā) *n.* (*pl.* **entremets**) **1** a light dish served between courses. **2** a sweet dish. [F, from OF *entremès* (*entre*, between, *mès*, viands)]

entrench (intrench´), **intrench** *v.t.* **1** to put (oneself) in a defensible position, as if with trenches. **2** (*Mil.*) to surround with trenches. **3** to make furrows in. *~v.i.* **1** to entrench oneself. **2** to trespass or encroach (upon). **entrenched** *a.* (of a person's attitude etc.) fixed, difficult to change by argument etc. **entrenchment** *n.* **1** the act of entrenching. **2** an instance of being entrenched. **3** (*Mil.*) a position fortified with trenches.

entre nous (ãtrə noo´) *adv.* between ourselves, in private. [F]

entrepôt (ã´trəpō) *n.* **1** a warehouse for the temporary deposit of goods. **2** a free port where foreign merchandise is kept in bond till re-exported. **3** a commercial centre to which goods are sent for distribution. [F, from L *interpositum*, neut. p.p. of *interpōnere* (*inter*, between, *pōnere*, to put)]

entrepreneur (ãtrəprənœ´, on-) *n.* **1** a person who undertakes a (financial) enterprise, esp. one with an element of risk. **2** a contractor, or commercial intermediary. **3** an organizer of entertainments for the public. **entrepreneurial** (-nœ´riəl) *a.* **entrepreneurialism** *n.* **entrepreneurially** *adv.* **entrepreneurism** *n.* **entrepreneurship** *n.* [F, from *entreprendre*, to undertake (see ENTERPRISE)]

entresol (ãtrəsol´) *n.* a low storey between two higher ones, usu. between the first and the ground floor, a mezzanine. [F (*entre*, between, *sol*, the ground)]

entrism ENTRYISM (under ENTRY).

entropion (intrō´piən) *n.* introversion of the eyelids. [Gr. *entropē*, rel. to *entrepein* (EN-, *trepein*, to turn)]

entropy (en´trəpi) *n.* (*pl.* **entropies**) (*Physics*) the property of a substance, expressed quantitatively, which remains constant when the substance changes its volume or does work with no heat passing into or from it, thus forming an index of the availability of the thermal energy of a system for mechanical work. **entropic** (-trop´ik) *a.* **entropically** *adv.* [Gr. *tropē*, a transformation or turning, from *trepein*, to turn]

entrust (intrŭst´), **intrust** *v.t.* **1** to commit or confide (something or someone) to a person's care. **2** to charge with (a duty, care etc.). **entrustment** *n.*

entry (en´tri) *n.* (*pl.* **entries**) **1** the act of entering. **2** the passage, gate, opening or other way by which anything is entered. **3** the act of entering or inscribing in a book etc. **4** an item so entered. **5** a ceremonial entrance into a place. **6** (*Mus.*) **a** the coming in of an instrument or voice in ensemble music. **b** the point in a piece of ensemble music where this happens. **7 a** a person, animal or thing competing in a race or competition. **b** a list of competitors etc. **8** the exhibiting of a ship's papers at the custom house to procure leave to land goods. **9** (*Law*) the act of taking possession by setting foot upon land or tenements. **10** the depositing of a document in the proper office. **11** unauthorized entrance into premises, thus one of the acts necessary to constitute burglary or trespass. **12** the mouth of a river. **13** in bridge, (a card which provides) a chance to transfer the lead from oneself to one's partner or the dummy. **entry form** *n.* an application form for a competition, a club etc. **entryism**, **entrism** *n.* the policy of joining a political party etc., in order to influence policy from within. **entryist** *n., a.* **entry permit** *n.* a document authorizing a person to enter a building etc. [F *entrée*, late L *intrāta*, from *intrāre*, to ENTER]

Entryphone® (en´trifōn) *n.* a telephonic device at the entrance to a block of flats etc., which allows visitors to communicate with the flat occupier.

entwine (intwīn´), **intwine** *v.t.* **1** to twine or twist together. **2** (*fig.*) to interlace, to mingle together. **3** to embrace, clasp, enfold. *~v.i.* to become twined or twisted together. **entwinement** *n.*

enucleate (inū´kliāt) *v.t.* **1** to bring to light, elucidate, solve. **2** to extract (a tumour) surgically from its covering. **enucleation** (-ā´shən) *n.* [L *ēnucleātus*, p.p. of *ēnucleāre*]

enumerate (inū´mərāt) *v.t.* **1** to reckon up one by one, to count. **2** to specify the items of. **enumerable** *a.* **enumeration** (-ā´shən) *n.* **enumerative** (-ətiv) *a.* **enumerator** *n.* **1** a person who enumerates. **2** a person who deals with population census forms. [L *ēnumerātus*, p.p. of *ēnumerāre*]

enunciate (inŭn´siāt) *v.t.* **1** to pronounce distinctly, articulate clearly. **2** to express definitely, state or announce with formal precision. *~v.i.* **1** to pronounce words or syllables. **2** to speak. **enunciable** *a.* **enunciation** (-ā´shən) *n.* **1** a declaring or announcing. **2** the manner of pronunciation or utterance. **3** a statement, formal expression. **4** the statement of a proposition. **5** a proposition, esp. one that has not been proved or disproved. **enunciative** *a.* **enunciatively** *adv.* **enunciator** *n.* **enunciatory** *a.* [L *ēnuntiātus*, p.p. of *ēnuntiāre* (E-, *nuntius*, a messenger)]

enure INURE.

enuresis (enūrē´sis) *n.* involuntary urinating, incontinence of urine. **enuretic** (-ret´ik) *a.* [Gr. *en*, in, *ouron*, urine]

enveigle INVEIGLE.

envelop (invel´əp) *v.t.* (*pres.p.* **enveloping**, *past, p.p.* **enveloped**) **1** to enwrap, to enclose, to surround so as to hide, to enshroud. **2** to wrap in or as in an envelope or covering. **3** to surround (an enemy) with troops or offensive works. **envelopment** *n.* [OF *enveloper* (etym. uncertain; cp. DEVELOP)]

envelope (en´vəlōp, on´-) *n.* **1** a folded paper wrapper to contain a letter. **2** anything which wraps or envelops. **3** (*Astron.*) the nebulous covering of the head of a comet. **4** (*Bot.*) a whorl of altered leaves surrounding the organs of fructification. **5** the gas-bag of a balloon. **6** the outer glass covering of a light bulb, or the metal covering of a valve etc. **7** (*Math.*) a surface or curve which is tangential to each of a group of surfaces or curves. [F *enveloppe*, as ENVELOP]

envenom (inven´əm) *v.t.* **1** to make poisonous, to impregnate with poison. **2** (*fig.*) to make bitter or spiteful. [OF *envenimer*]

enviable, **envious** ENVY.

environ (invīə´rən) *v.t.* **1** to surround, to be or extend round, to encircle. **2** to surround so as to attend or protect, to beset. **3** to surround (with persons or things). **environage** *n.* environment. **environs** *n.pl.* the parts or districts round any place. [F *environner*, from *environ*, round about (EN-, *virer*, to veer, to turn)]

environment (invīə´rənmənt) *n.* **1** the act of surrounding. **2** that which encompasses, surrounding objects, scenery, circumstances etc. **3** the sum of external influences affecting an organism. **4** living conditions. **5** (*usu.* **the environment**) the whole of the natural world inhabited by living organisms, esp. considered as vulnerable to pollution etc. **6** (*Comput.*) the whole operating system used by a computer for a particular application. **environmental** (-men´-) *a.* of or relating to the environment. **environmental health officer** *n.* an official employed to investigate and prevent potential public health hazards, such as lack of hygiene. **environmentalism** *n.* **1** the belief that the environment is the main influence on people's behaviour and development. **2** concern for the environment and its preservation from pollution etc. **environmentalist** *n.* **1** a person who believes in environmentalism. **2** a person who is concerned with or involved in the protection and preservation of the environment. **environmentally** *adv.* **environmental terrorism** *n.* eco-terrorism. **environment-friendly** *a.* not damaging to the environment.

envisage (inviz´ij) *v.t.* **1** to conceive of as a possibility. **2** to contemplate, esp. a particular aspect of. **3** (*Philos.*) to perceive by intuition. **4** †to look into the face of, to look directly at. **5** †to face, confront. **envisagement** *n.* [F *envisager*]

envision (invizh´ən) *v.t.* to visualize, to envisage.

envoi (en´voi), **envoy** *n.* a postscript to a collection of poems, or a concluding stanza to a poem. [OF *envoié*, properly, a message, p.p. of *envoyer*, to send (*en voie*, L *in via*, on the way)]

envoy[1] (en´voi) *n.* **1** a diplomatic agent, next in rank below an ambassador, sent by one government to another on some special occasion. **2** a messenger, a representative. **envoyship** *n.* [as ENVOI]

envoy[2] ENVOI.

envy (en´vi) *n.* (*pl.* **envies**) **1** ill-will at the superiority, success or good fortune of others, a grudging sense of another's superiority to oneself. **2** the object of this feeling. ~*v.t.* (*3rd pers. sing. pres.* **envies**, *pres.p.* **envying**, *past, p.p.* **envied**) **1** to regard with envy. **2** to covet. ~*v.i.* to have envious feelings. **enviable** *a.* **1** capable of exciting envy. **2** of a nature to be envied. **3** greatly to be desired. **enviably** *adv.* **envier** *n.* **envious** *a.* **1** feeling envy. **2** instigated by envy. **enviously** *adv.* **enviousness** *n.* [OF *envie*, L *invidia*, from *invidus*, rel. to *invidēre*, to envy (IN-[1], *vidēre*, to see)]

enweave INWEAVE.

enwind (inwīnd´) *v.t.* (*past, p.p.* **enwound** (-wownd´)) (*formal*) to wind or coil around.

enwrap (inrap´), **inwrap** *v.t.* (*pres.p.* **enwrapping**, **inwrapping**, *past, p.p.* **enwrapped**, **inwrapped**) (*formal*) **1** to wrap or enfold. **2** to envelop. **3** to engross, to absorb. **4** to involve, implicate.

enwreathe (inrēth´), **inwreathe** *v.t.* (*formal*) to encircle with or as with a wreath.

Enzed (enzed´) *n.* (*coll.*) **1** New Zealand. **2** a New Zealander. **Enzedder** *n.* [pron. of the letters *n, z*]

enzootic (enzōot´ik) *a.* of or relating to a disease which affects animals in a certain district either constantly or periodically; endemic among animals. ~*n.* an enzootic disease. [EN-, Gr. *zōon*, animal]

enzyme (en´zīm) *n.* a protein produced by living cells which acts as a catalyst, esp. in the digestive system. **enzymic** (-zī´-, -zim´-), **enzymatic** (-mat´-) *a.* **enzymology** (-mol´-) *n.* the scientific study of enzymes. **enzymological** (-loj´-) *a.* **enzymologist** (-mol´-) *n.* [Gr. *enzumos*, unfermented]

e.o. *abbr.* ex officio.

EOC *abbr.* Equal Opportunities Commission.

Eocene (ē´əsēn) *a.* of or relating to the lowest division of the Tertiary strata. ~*n.* **1** the Eocene period. **2** the Eocene strata. [Gr. *ēōs*, dawn, *kainos*, new]

eod *abbr.* every other day.

eohippus (ēəhip´əs) *n.* (*pl.* **eohippuses**) an extinct forerunner of the horse, the earliest known form of horse-like mammal. [Gr. *ēōs*, dawn, *hippos*, horse]

Eolian AEOLIAN.

eolipile, **eolipyle** AEOLIPILE.

eolith (ē´əlith) *n.* a roughly-chipped flint dating from the very early palaeolithic age, found abundantly in parts of the North Downs, but not accepted as artificial by many archaeologists. **Eolithic** (-lith´-) *a.* of or relating to the early palaeolithic age. [Gr. *ēōs*, dawn]

eon AEON.

eosin (ē´əsin) *n.* a red fluorescent dye, sometimes used in biology. **eosinic** (-sin´ik) *a.* **eosinophil** (-sin´-) *a.* readily staining with eosin. ~*n.* a white blood cell which does this. [Gr. *ēōs*, dawn]

-eous (iəs) *suf.* forming adjectives meaning of the nature of, as *arboreous*, *ligneous*, *righteous*. [L *-eus*, pertaining to, of the nature of]

eozoon (ēəzō´on) *n.* a member of a hypothetical genus of Protozoa found in the Laurentian strata in Canada, the supposed remains of which are now believed to be inorganic. **eozoic** *a.* [Gr. *ēōs*, dawn, *zōon*, animal]

EP *abbr.* **1** electroplated. **2** extended play (record). **3** extreme pressure.

Ep. *abbr.* epistle.

e.p. *abbr.* en passant (in chess).

ep- (ep) *pref.* EPI- used before a vowel, as in *epact*, *epoch*.

EPA *abbr.* (*US*) Environmental Protection Agency.

epact (ē´pakt) *n.* **1** the moon's age at the beginning of the year. **2** the excess (in days) of the solar year above the lunar year. [MF *epacte*, late L *epacta*, Gr. *epaktē*, from *epagein*, to intercalate (EP-, *agein*, to bring)]

epagoge (epəgō´gi) *n.* (*Logic*) **1** the bringing forward of particular examples to prove a universal conclusion. **2** argument by induction. **epagogic** (-goj´-) *a.* [Gr. *epagōgē*, from *epagein* (EP-, *agein*, to bring)]

epana- (ep´ənə, ip´anə), **epan-** *comb. form* denoting repetition, doubling. [Gr. EP-, *ana*, up, again]

epanadiplosis (ipanədiplō´sis) *n.* (*pl.* **epanadiploses** (-sēz)) a rhetorical figure by which a sentence ends with the same word with which it begins. [Gr. *diplōsis*, a doubling]
epanalepsis (ipanəlep´sis) *n.* a figure of speech by which the same word or clause is repeated after other words intervening. **epanaleptic** *a.* [Gr. *lēpsis*, from *lambanein*, to take]
epanodos (ipan´ədos) *n.* **1** a rhetorical figure in which the second member of a sentence is an inversion of the first. **2** resumption after a digression. [Gr. *hodos*, way]
epanorthosis (ipanawthō´sis) *n.* (*pl.* **epanorthoses** (-sēz)) a rhetorical figure by which a person retracts what they have said for the purpose of putting it more forcibly. **epanorthotic** (-ot´ik) *a.* [Gr. *orthōsis*, a setting straight, from *orthos*, straight]
eparch (ep´ahk) *n.* **1** a governor or prefect of an eparchy. **2** in the Russian Church, the bishop of an eparchy. **3** a governor of a province in modern Greece. **eparchy** *n.* (*pl.* **eparchies**) **1** (*Hist.*) a prefecture. **2** a diocese in the Russian Church. **3** a province of modern Greece. [Gr. *eparchos* (EP-, *archos*, a ruler)]
epaulette (ep´əlet), (*N Am.*) **epaulet** *n.* **1** an ornamental badge worn on the shoulder in military, naval and certain civil full dress uniforms. **2** (*pl.*, *fig.*) the rank of officer. **epauletted** (-let´-) *a.* [F *épaulette*, from *épaule*, shoulder]
épée (ep´ā) *n.* **1** a duelling sword. **2** a fencing foil. **épéeist** *n.* [F, a sword]
epeirogenesis (ipīrōjen´əsis), **epeirogeny** (-oj´əni) *n.* (*Geol.*) the making of a continent by the pushing up of parts of the earth's crust. **epeirogenetic** (-gənet´ik), **epeirogenic** (-jen´ik) *a.* [Gr. *epeiros*, mainland, GENESIS]
epencephalon (epənsef´əlon, -kef´-) *n.* (*pl.* **epencephala** (-lə)) the hindmost division of the brain. **epencephalic** (-fal´ik) *a.*
epenthesis (ipen´thəsis) *n.* (*pl.* **epentheses** (-sēz)) **1** (*Gram.*) the addition of a letter or letters in the middle of a word, as in *alitium* for *alitum*. **2** the phonetic change resulting from the transference of a semivowel to the preceding syllable. **epenthetic** (epənthet´-) *a.* [late L, from Gr. (EP-, *en-*, in, *thesis*, a placing, from *tithenai*, to place)]
epergne (ipœn´) *n.* an ornamental stand, usu. branched, for the centre of a table etc. [poss. F *épargne*, a saving]
epexegesis (ipeksəjē´sis) *n.* (*pl.* **epexegeses** (-sēz)) **1** words added to elucidate something which has gone before. **2** the act of adding such words. **epexegetic** (-jet´-), **epexegetical** *a.* [Gr. *epexēgēsis* (EP-, EXEGESIS)]
Eph. *abbr.* Ephesians.
eph- (ef) *pref.* EPI- used before *h*, as in *ephemera*, *ephor*.
ephebe (ifēb´, ef´ēb) *n.* in ancient Greece, a freeborn youth between the ages of 18 and 20, qualified for citizenship. **ephebic** *a.* **1** (*Zool.*) adult, mature, at the maximum of development. **2** of or relating to an ephebe. [L *ephēbus*, Gr. *ephēbos* (EPI-, *hēbē*, early manhood)]
ephedra (ef´ədrə, efed´rə) *n.* any evergreen shrub of the genus *Ephedra*, growing in America and Eurasia. **ephedrine** *n.* an alkaloid drug obtained from some plants of the genus, used to treat asthma, hay fever etc. [L, from Gr. (EPH-, *hedra*, a seat)]
ephemera (ifem´ərə) *n.* (*pl.* **ephemeras**, **ephemerae** (-rē)) **1** a member of a genus of ephemeropterous insects, the *Ephemera*, containing the mayfly. **2** the mayfly. **3** (*pl. of* **ephemeron**) items, such as newspapers, packaging etc., of transient usefulness or interest. **4** a fever of only one day's continuance. **ephemeral** *a.* **1** beginning and ending in a day. **2** short-lived, transient. **ephemerality** (-ral´-) *n.* **ephemerally** *adv.* **ephemeralness** *n.* **ephemeris** (-ris) *n.* (*pl.* **ephemerides** (efəmer´idēz)) **1** (*Astron.*) a table or data showing the daily position of the planets. **2** a collection of such tables, an astronomical almanac. **3** †a journal, an account of daily transactions. **4** ephemera. **ephemeris time** *n.* (*Astron.*) time as measured by the orbit of the earth round the sun, rather than by the rotation of the earth on its axis. **ephemerist** *n.* a collector of ephemera. **ephemeron** (-rən) *n.* **1** (*pl.* **ephemerons**) an insect of the *Ephemera*. **2** (*usu. in pl.* **ephemera**) anything short-lived. [Gr. *ephēmeros* (EPI-, *hēmera*, day)]
Ephes. *abbr.* Ephesians.
Ephesian (ifē´zhən) *a.* of or relating to Ephesus. ~*n.* **1** an inhabitant of Ephesus. **2** †a jolly companion. [L *Ephesius*, Gr. *Ephesios*]
ephod (ef´od, ē´-) *n.* **1** an emblematic short coat covering the shoulders and breast of the Jewish High Priest. **2** a similar but less splendid garment worn by the ordinary priests. [Heb. *āphad*, to put on]
ephor (ef´aw) *n.* (*pl.* **ephors**, **ephori** (-ərī)) any one of the five magistrates chosen at Sparta and invested with the highest power, controlling even the kings. **ephoralty** *n.* **ephorate** *n.* [Gr. *ephoros* (EPI-, *horaein*, to see)]
epi (ā´pē) *n.* (*pl.* **epis**) **1** a tuft of hair, esp. on a horse's forehead. **2** a cowlick. [F]
epi- (ep´i) *pref.* upon, at, to, besides, in addition, as *epigram*, *episode*. [Gr.]
epiblast (ep´iblahst) *n.* (*Biol.*) the outermost of the layers in the blastoderm. **epiblastic** (-las´-) *a.* [Gr. *blastos*, sprout]
epic (ep´ik) *a.* **1** narrating some heroic event in a lofty style. **2** large-scale. **3** impressive. **4** (*coll.*) very good. ~*n.* **1** a long poem narrating the history, real or fictitious, of some notable action or series of actions, accomplished by a hero or heroes. **2** a work of art associated with some aspect of the epic poem, such as a long adventure novel, a long historical film. **epical** *a.* **epically** *adv.* **epic dialect** *n.* the ancient Greek dialect in which the *Iliad* and the *Odyssey* were composed. [L *epicus*, Gr. *epikos*, from *epos*, a word]
epicalyx (epikā´liks) *n.* (*pl.* **epicalyxes**, **epicalyces** (-lisēz)) a whorl of leaves forming an additional calyx outside the true calyx.
epicanthus (epikan´thəs) *n.* (*pl.* **epicanthi** (-thī)) a fold of skin over the inner angle of the eye, characteristic of Chinese and other eastern Asian peoples. **epicanthic** *a.* **epicanthic fold** *n.* [Gr. *kanthos*]
epicarp (ep´ikahp) *n.* **1** (*Bot.*) the outermost layer of fruits. **2** peel, rind, skin. [Gr. *karpos*, fruit]
epicedium (episē´diəm), **epicede** (ep´isēd) *n.* (*pl.* **epicediums**, **epicedia** (-iə), **epicedes**) **1** a dirge. **2** a funeral ode. **epicedial** (-sē´-), **epicedian** *a.* [L *epicēdīum*, Gr. *epikēdeion* (EPI-, *kēdos*, care)]
epicene (ep´isēn) *a.* **1** (*Gram.*) of common gender, having only one form for both sexes. **2** of or relating to both sexes. **3** hermaphrodite. **4** sexless. **5** effeminate. ~*n.* **1** (*Gram.*) a noun common to both genders, as *sheep*. **2** a person having the characteristics of both sexes. [L *epicoenus*, Gr. *epikoinos* (EPI-, *koinos*, common)]
epicentre (ep´isentə), (*N Am.*) **epicenter**, **epicentrum** (-sen´trəm) *n.* **1** the point on the earth's surface over the focus of an earthquake. **2** (*fig.*) the focus of a quarrel, a difficulty etc. **epicentral** *a.* [Gr. *epikentron* (EPI-, *kentron*, centre)]
epicontinental (epikontinen´təl) *a.* (esp. of a sea) situated over a continental shelf.
epicotyl (epikot´il) *n.* (*Bot.*) the part of the stem of an embryonic plant above the cotyledons.
epicure (ep´ikūə) *n.* **1** a person devoted to sensual pleasures, esp. those of the table. **2** †an Epicurean. **Epicurean** (-rē´ən) *a.* **1** of or relating to Epicurus or his system of philosophy, which taught that pleasure is the supreme good and the basis of morality. **2** (**epicurean**) devoted to pleasure, esp. the more refined varieties of

sensuous enjoyment. ~*n.* **1** a follower of Epicurus. **2** (**epicurean**) a person devoted to pleasure. **3** a sensualist, a gourmet. **epicureanism** *n.* **epicurism** *n.* [*Epicūrus*, Gr. *Epikouros* d. 270 BC, Greek philosopher]

epicycle (ep´isīkəl) *n.* a small circle the centre of which is carried round upon another circle. **epicyclic** (-sī´-, -sik´-) *a.* **epicycloid** (-sī´kloid) *n.* a curve generated by the revolution of a point in the circumference of a circle rolling along the exterior of another circle. **epicycloidal** (-sīkloi´-) *a.* [L *epicyclus*, Gr. *epikuklos* (EPI-, *kuklos*, circle)]

epideictic (epidīk´tik) *a.* **1** showing off. **2** done for effect, in order to display one's skill (applied to set orations). [Gr. *epideiktikos*, from *epideiknunai* (EPI-, *deiknunai*, to show)]

epidemic (epidem´ik) *a.* affecting at once a large number in a community. ~*n.* **1** a disease attacking many persons at the same time, and spreading with great rapidity. **2** an outbreak of such a disease. **3** a widespread and rapid outbreak of an activity, type of behaviour etc. **epidemical** *a.* **epidemically** *adv.* **epidemiology** (-dēmiol´-) *n.* the study and treatment of epidemic diseases. **epidemiological** (-loj´-) *a.* **epidemiologist** *n.* [F *épidémique*, from *épidémie*, late L and Gr. *epidēmia*, from *epidēmios* (EPI-, *dēmos*, people)]

Usage note See note under ENDEMIC.

epidermis (epidœ´mis) *n.* **1** (*Zool.*) the cuticle or skin constituting the external layer in animals. **2** (*Bot.*) the exterior cellular coating of the leaf or stem of a plant. **epidermal**, **epidermic** *a.* of or relating to the epidermis. **epidermoid** (-moid), **epidermoidal** *a.*

epidiascope (epidī´əskōp) *n.* an optical projector which may be used for opaque objects or transparencies. [Gr. *epi*, upon, *dia*, through, *skopeein*, to view]

epididymis (epidid´imis) *n.* (*pl.* **epididymides** (-didim´idēz)) a mass of sperm-carrying tubes at the back of the testes.

epidote (ep´idōt) *n.* a brittle mineral, a silicate of alumina and lime, of vitreous lustre and of various colours, mostly found in crystalline rocks. **epidotic** (-dot´-) *a.* [F *épidote*, formed from Gr. *epididonai* (EPI-, *didonai*, to give)]

epidural (epidū´rəl) *a.* situated on, or administered outside, the lower portion of the spinal canal. ~*n.* the epidural injection of an anaesthetic, e.g. in childbirth. **epidural anaesthetic**, (*N Am.*) **epidural anesthetic** *n.* an epidural. **epidurally** *adv.* [DURA MATER]

epifauna (epifaw´nə) *n.* the animals which live on the surface of submerged ground, or attached to underwater objects etc. **epifaunal** *a.*

epifocal (epifō´kəl) *a.* epicentral.

epigastrium (epigas´triəm) *n.* (*pl.* **epigastria** (-triə)) the upper part of the abdomen, esp. that part above the stomach. **epigastric** *a.* [Gr. *epigastrion* (EPI-, *gastēr*, stomach)]

epigeal (epijē´əl) *a.* **1** (*Bot.*) **a** growing close to the ground. **b** having the cotyledons above ground. **epigean** *a.* **epigeous** *a.*

epigene (ep´ijēn) *a.* (*Geol.*) originating on the surface of the earth. [F *épigène*, Gr. *epigenēs* (EPI-, *genēs*, born)]

epigenesis (epijen´əsis) *n.* (*Biol.*) the theory that in reproduction the organism is brought into being by the union of the male and female elements. **epigenesist** *n.* **epigenetic** (-net´-) *a.* **1** of or relating to epigenesis. **2** (of minerals) formed later than the surrounding rocks. **3** produced by external influences, not genetic. **epigenous** (ipij´-) *a.* (*Bot.*) growing upon the surface of a part, as do many fungi.

epigeous EPIGEAL.

epiglottis (epiglot´is) *n.* (*pl.* **epiglottises**, **epiglottides** (-dēz)) (*Anat.*) a leaflike cartilage at the base of the tongue which covers the glottis during the act of swallowing. **epiglottal** *a.* **epiglottic** *a.* [Gr. *epiglōttis* (EPI-, *glōssa*, tongue)]

epigone (ep´igōn) *n.* (*pl.* **epigones**, **epigoni** (ipig´ənī)) a person belonging to a later and less noteworthy generation. [Gr.]

epigram (ep´igram) *n.* **1** a short poem or composition of a witty or pointed character. **2** a pithy or witty saying or phrase. **3** the use of such phrases. **epigrammatic** (-mat´-), **epigrammatical** *a.* **epigrammatically** *adv.* **epigrammatist** (-gram´-) *n.* **epigrammatize** (-gram´-), **epigrammatise** *v.t.* to write or express by way of epigrams. [F *épigramme*, L and Gr. *epigramma* (EPI-, -GRAM)]

epigraph (ep´igrahf) *n.* **1** a quotation, in verse or prose, placed at the beginning of a work, or of divisions in a work, as a motto. **2** an inscription placed on buildings, statues, tombs, coins and the like, denoting their use and appropriation. **epigraphic** (-graf´-), **epigraphical** *a.* **epigraphically** *adv.* **epigraphy** (ipig´-) *n.* **1** the deciphering and explanation of inscriptions. **2** inscriptions taken collectively. **epigraphist** *n.* [Gr. *epigraphē* (EPI-, *graphein*, to write)]

epigynous (ipij´inəs) *a.* (*Bot.*) (of the stamens or corolla) growing on the top of the ovary, with only the upper portions free. **epigyny** *n.* [EPI-, Gr. *gunē*, woman]

epilate (ep´ilāt) *v.t.* to remove hair by the roots (from), by any method. **epilation** (-ā´shən) *n.* **epilator** *n.* [F *épiler*, from L *ex*, from, out, *pilus*, hair]

epilepsy (ep´ilepsi) *n.* a functional disorder of the brain which involves convulsions of varying intensity, with or without loss of consciousness. **epileptic** (-lep´-) *a.* **1** suffering from epilepsy. **2** of or relating to or indicating the presence of epilepsy. ~*n.* a person who has epilepsy. **epileptical** *a.* [MF *epilepsie*, L and Gr. *epilēpsia*, from *epilambanein* (EPI-, *lambanein*, to take)]

epilimnion (epilim´niən) *n.* (*pl.* **epilimnia** (-iə)) the upper, warmer layer of water in a lake. [Gr. *limnion*, dim. of *limnē*, lake]

epilogue (ep´ilog), (*N Am.*) **epilog** *n.* **1** the concluding part of a book, essay or speech, a peroration. **2 a** a short speech or poem addressed to the spectators at the end of a play. **b** the actor who delivers this. **3** (*with* **the**) a short programme of a usu. religious nature, at the end of the day's broadcasting. **epilogist** (ipil´əjist) *n.* **epilogize** (ipil´əjīz), **epilogise**, **epiloguize** (-gīz), **epiloguise** *v.i.* to pronounce or deliver an epilogue. ~*v.t.* to put an epilogue to. [F, from L *epilogus*, Gr. *epilogos* (EPI-, *logos*, speech)]

epimer (ep´imə) *n.* (*Chem.*) either one of the two differing isomers which can form around asymmetric carbon atoms. **epimeric** (-mer´-) *a.* **epimerism** (epim´-) *n.* **epimerize** (epim´-), **epimerise** *v.t.* to convert from one epimer to the other.

epinasty (ep´inasti) *n.* (*pl.* **epinasties**) (*Bot.*) curving of an organ through more rapid growth of the upper surface. **epinastic** (-nas´-) *a.* **epinastically** *adv.* [Gr. *nastos*, from *nassein*, to squeeze close]

epinephrine (epinef´rin, -rēn) *n.* (*N Am.*) adrenalin. [Gr. *nephros*, kidney]

epipetalous (epipet´ələs) *a.* (*Bot.*) (of stamens) growing separately on the corolla.

Epiph. *abbr.* Epiphany.

epiphany (ipif´əni) *n.* (*pl.* **epiphanies**) **1** (**Epiphany**) the manifestation of Christ to the Magi at Bethlehem. **2** (**Epiphany**) the annual festival, held on 6 January, the 12th day after Christmas, to commemorate this. **3** the appearance or manifestation of a divinity. **epiphanic** (epifan´ik) *a.* [F *épiphanie*, from late L, from Gr. *epiphania*, neut. pl., from *epiphainein* (EPI-, *phainein*, to show), used as equivalent to *epiphaneia*, appearance, manifestation, from *epiphanēs*, manifest]

epiphenomenon (epifinom´inən) *n.* (*pl.* **epiphenomena** (-nə)) a phenomenon that is secondary and incidental, a mere concomitant of some effect, esp. a secondary symptom of a disease. **epiphenomenal** *a.*

epiphragm (ep´ifram) *n.* (*Zool.*) the disclike secretion with which snails and other molluscs close their shells during hibernation. [Gr. *epiphragma*, a lid, from *epiphrassein* (EPI-, *phrassein*, to fence)]

epiphyllous (epifil´əs) *a.* (*Bot.*) growing on a leaf.

epiphysis (ipif´əsis) *n.* (*pl.* **epiphyses** (-sēz)) (*Anat.*) **1** a process formed by a separate centre of ossification. **2** the pineal body. [Gr. *phusis*, growth]

epiphyte (ep´ifit) *n.* **1** a plant growing upon another, usu. not deriving its nourishment from this. **2** a fungus parasitic on an animal body. **epiphytal** (-fī´-), **epiphytic** (-fit´-) *a.*

episcopacy (ipis´kəpəsi) *n.* (*pl.* **episcopacies**) **1** government of a Church by bishops, the accepted form in the Latin and Greek communions and the Church of England; prelacy. **2** (**the episcopacy**) the bishops taken collectively. **episcopal** *a.* **1** of or relating to a bishop or bishops. **2** (of a Church) constituted on the episcopal form of government. **Episcopal Church** *n.* the Anglican Church in Scotland or the United States. **episcopalian** (-pā´-) *n.* **1** (**Episcopalian**) a member of an Episcopal Church. **2** a supporter of episcopal Church government and discipline. ~*a.* **1** episcopal. **2** (**Episcopalian**) belonging to one of the Episcopal Churches. **episcopalianism** *n.* **episcopalism** *n.* **episcopally** *adv.* **episcopate** (-pət) *n.* **1** the office or see of a bishop. **2** the term during which any bishop holds office. **3** (**the episcopate**) bishops collectively. [late L *episcopātus*, *episcopus*, bishop]

episcope (ep´iskōp) *n.* an optical projector used for projecting on a screen an enlarged image of an opaque object. [Gr. *skopeein*, to look]

episematic (episimat´ik) *a.* (*Zool.*) (of coloration) serving to facilitate recognition by animals of the same species. [Gr. *sēma*, *-atos*, a sign, token]

episiotomy (epēziot´əmi) *n.* (*pl.* **episiotomies**) the cutting of the perineum during childbirth in order to prevent its tearing. [Gr. *epision*, pubic region]

episode (ep´isōd) *n.* **1** an incident or series of events in a story, separable though arising out of it. **2** an incident or closely connected series of events in real life. **3** one part of a series on radio or television. **4** (*Mus.*) a portion of a fugue deviating from the main theme. **5** the parts in dialogue between the choric parts in Greek tragedy, which were primarily interpolations. **episodic** (-sod´-), **episodical** *a.* **1** occurring as separate incidents. **2** irregular, sporadic. **episodically** *adv.* [Gr. *epeisodion*, addition, episode (EPI-, *eisodos*, entering)]

epispastic (epispas´tik) *a.* drawing, exciting action in the skin; blistering. ~*n.* a preparation for producing counterirritation, a blister. [Gr. *epispastikos* (EPI-, *spaein*, to draw)]

epistaxis (epistak´sis) *n.* bleeding from the nose. [Gr. *epistazein*, to shed in drops]

epistemology (ipistəmol´əji) *n.* (*Philos.*) the science which deals with the origin and method of knowledge. **epistemic** (-stē´-, -stem´-) *a.* of or relating to knowledge or epistemology. **epistemically** *adv.* **epistemics** *n.* the study of knowledge, and how it is acquired and processed. **epistemological** (-loj´-) *a.* **epistemologically** *adv.* **epistemologist** (-mol´-) *n.* [Gr. *epistēmē*, knowledge]

episternum (epistœ´nəm) *n.* (*pl.* **episterna** (-nə)) the upper part of the sternum or breast-bone in mammals, or that portion of an articulate animal immediately adjoining the sternum. **episternal** *a.*

epistle (ipis´əl) *n.* **1** a written communication, a letter (now only in a formal or facetious sense). **2** a literary work (usu. in verse) in the form of a letter. **3** (**Epistles**) letters written by Apostles to the Churches, now forming part of the New Testament. **4** a lesson in the Church service, so called as being taken from the apostolic epistles. ~†*v.t.* **1** to write or communicate by a letter. **2** to write an introduction or preface. **epistler** (ipis´-, ipist´-), **epistoler** (-tələ) *n.* **1** a writer of letters. **2** the person who reads the epistle in a church service. **epistle side** *n.* the south side of the altar at which the epistle is read, as distinct from the *gospel side*. **epistolary** (-tə-) *a.* **1** in the form or style of a letter or letters. **2** of or relating to or suitable for letters. **3** contained in or carried on by means of letters. ~*n.* a book containing the epistles. [OF, from L *epistola*, Gr. *epistolē*, from *epistellein* (EPI-, *stellein*, to send)]

epistrophe (ipis´trəfi) *n.* a rhetorical figure in which several sentences or clauses end with the same word.

epistyle (ep´istīl) *n.* (*Archit.*) the architrave. [L *epistylium* (Gr. *stulos*, pillar)]

epitaph (ep´itahf) *n.* **1** a commemorative inscription in prose or verse, as for a tomb or monument. **2** an inscription on a tomb. **epitaphian** (-taf´-) *a.* **epitaphic** (-taf´-) *a.* **epitaphist** *n.* [L *epitaphium* (directly or through F *épitaphe*), Gr. *epitaphion*, neut. of *epitaphios*, a., over a tomb (EPI-, *taphos*, tomb)]

epitasis (ipit´əsis) *n.* (*pl.* **epitases** (-sēz)) the portion of a classical drama in which the plot is developed, between the protasis or introduction and the catastrophe. [Gr., from *epiteinein* (EPI-, *teinein*, to stretch)]

epitaxy (ep´itaksi) *n.* the growth of one layer of crystals on another so that they have the same structure. **epitaxial** (-tak´-) *a.* [Gr. *taxis*, arrangement]

epithalamium (epithəlā´miəm) *n.* (*pl.* **epithalamiums**, **epithalamia** (-miə)) a song or poem celebrating a marriage. **epithalamial** *a.* **epithalamic** (-lam´-) *a.* [L, from Gr. *epithalamion*, neut. of *epithalamios*, a. (EPI-, *thalamos*, bridal chamber)]

epithelium (epithē´liəm) *n.* (*pl.* **epitheliums**, **epithelia** (-liə)) the cell tissues lining the alimentary canal and forming the outer layer of the mucous membranes. **epithelial** *a.* **epithelioma** (-liō´mə) *n.* (*pl.* **epitheliomas**, **epitheliomata** (-mətə)) (*Med.*) a tumour affecting epithelial tissue. **epitheliomatous** *a.* [mod. L (EPI-, Gr. *thēlē*, teat)]

epithem (ep´ithem) *n.* (*pl.* **epithems**, **epithemata** (-ətə)) (*Med.*) any external application, except ointment or plasters. [Gr. *epithema*, from *epitithenai* (EPI-, *tithenai*, to place)]

epithet (ep´ithet) *n.* **1** an adjective or phrase denoting any quality or attribute. **2** a descriptive term. **3** (*coll.*) an abusive expression. **4** a nickname. **epithetic** (-thet´-), **epithetical** *a.* **epithetically** *adv.* [L and Gr. *epitheton*, from *epitithenai* (as EPITHEM)]

epitome (ipit´əmi) *n.* **1** a brief summary of a book, document etc. **2** a perfect example, a person or thing that embodies the characteristics of a group, class etc. **3** (*fig.*) a representation in miniature of something else. **epitomic** (-tom´ik), **epitomical** *a.* **epitomist** *n.* **epitomize**, **epitomise** *v.t.* **1** to make an abstract, summary or abridgement of. **2** to represent in miniature. **3** †to cut down, curtail. **epitomization** (-zā´shən) *n.* **epitomizer** *n.* [L, from Gr. *epitomē* (EPI-, *temnein*, to cut)]

epizoon (epizō´on) *n.* (*pl.* **epizoa** (-zō´ə)) an animal parasitic upon the exterior surface of another. **epizoan** *a.* **epizootic** (-ot´-) *a.* of or relating to diseases epidemic among animals. ~*n.* **1** an epizootic disease. **2** an epidemic among cattle. [Gr. *zōon*, animal]

e pluribus unum (ā pluəribəs oo´nəm) *n.* one out of many (the motto of the USA). [L]

EPNS *abbr.* **1** electroplated nickel silver. **2** English Place Name Society.

epoch (ē´pok) *n.* **1** a fixed point from which succeeding years are numbered, a memorable date. **2** a period in history or of a person's life characterized by momentous events, an era. **3** a subdivision of geological time, the period during which a set of strata is formed. **4**

(*Astron.*) the moment when a certain event takes place or a certain position is reached. **5** (*Astron.*) the longitude of a planet at any given time. **epochal** (ep´-, ē´-) *a.* **epochally** *adv.* **epoch-making** *a.* of such importance as to mark an epoch. [late L *epocha*, Gr. *epochē*, a stop, check, pause, from *epechein* (EP-, *echein*, to have, to hold)]

epode (ep´ōd) *n.* **1** (in Greek lyric poetry) the part after the strophe and antistrophe. **2** lyric poetry in which a shorter line follows a longer one. **epodic** (ipod´-) *a.* [OF, from L *epōdos*, Gr. *epōdos*, from *epadein* (EP-, *adein*, *aeidein*, to sing)]

eponym (ep´ənim) *n.* **1 a** a name given to a people, place or institution, after some person. **b** the person (real or imaginary) whose name is used. **2** the name of a mythical person made to account for the name of a country or people. **3** a character whose name is the title of a play or book. **eponymic** (-nim´-), **eponymous** (ipon´-) *a.* **eponymously** *adv.* [Gr. *epōnumos* (EP-, *onoma*, Aeolic *onuma*, name)]

epopee (ep´əpē), **epopoeia** (-pē´ə) *n.* **1** an epic or heroic poem. **2** epic poetry, the series of events forming the material for an epic. [F *épopée*, Gr. *epopoiia*, from *epopoios* (*epos*, word, song, *poios*, maker, from *poieein*, to make)]

EPOS *abbr.* electronic point-of-sale (a sales-recording system in which bar codes are read by a laser scanner).

epos (ep´os) *n.* (*pl.* **eposes**) **1** an epopee. **2** unwritten narrative poetry embodying heroic traditions.

epoxy (ipok´si) *a.* containing oxygen plus two other atoms, frequently carbon, themselves already attached. ~*n.* (*pl.* **epoxies**) any of a group of synthetic resins containing epoxy groups and used for coatings and adhesives. **epoxide** *n.* an epoxy compound. **epoxide resin** *n.* **epoxy resin** *n.*

EPROM (ē´prom) *n.* (*Comput.*) a kind of read-only memory which can be erased and reprogrammed. [acronym for *e*rasable *p*rogrammable *r*ead-*o*nly *m*emory]

eps *abbr.* earnings per share.

epsilon (ep´silon) *n.* the fifth letter of the Greek alphabet (Ε, ε). [Gr. *e psilon*, bare or mere e]

Epsom salts (ep´səm) *n.pl.* sulphate of magnesia, a saline purgative. **epsomite** (-īt) *n.* native sulphate of magnesia. [*Epsom*, town in Surrey where the salts were formerly prepared from a mineral spring]

EPSRC *abbr.* Engineering and Physical Sciences Research Council.

Epstein–Barr virus (epstīnbah´) *n.* (*Med.*) a virus which causes glandular fever, and is associated with several human cancers. [M. A. *Epstein*, b. 1921, and Y. M. *Barr*, b. 1932, British virologists]

epyllion (ipil´iən) *n.* (*pl.* **epyllia** (-iə)) a poem like an epic but shorter. [Gr., dim. of *epos*, a word, song]

equable (ek´wəbəl) *a.* **1** characterized by evenness or uniformity. **2** smooth, level, even. **3** not varying, not irregular. **4** not subject to irregularities or disturbance. **5** even-tempered. **equability** (-bil´-) *n.* **equableness** *n.* **equably** *adv.* [L *aequābilis*, from *aequāre*, to make level, from *aequus*, equal]

Usage note The adjectives *equable* and *equitable* should not be confused: *equable* means even or unvarying, and *equitable* fair or just.

equal (ē´kwəl) *a.* **1** the same in size, number, quality, degree etc. **2** even, uniform, not variable. **3** evenly balanced. **4** having the same status or rights. **5** impartial, unbiased, fair, just. **6** having adequate power, ability or means (to). ~*n.* **1** a person or thing not inferior or superior to another. **2** a person of the same or similar age, rank, office, talents or the like. **3** a match. ~*v.t.* (*pres.p.* **equalling**, (*N Am.*) **equaling**, *past*, *p.p.* **equalled**, (*N Am.*) **equaled**) **1** to be equal to. **2** to become equal to, to match. **3** to return a full equivalent for. **to be equal to** to have the courage, intelligence etc. for. **to equal out** to become equal or balanced. **equalitarian** (-teə´riən) *a.*, *n.* (an) egalitarian. **equalitarianism** *n.* **equality** (ikwol´-) *n.* (*pl.* **equalities**) **1** the state of being equal. **2** †evenness. **3** †equability. **on an equality with** on equal terms with. **equalize**, **equalise** *v.t.* to make equal (to, with). **equalization** (-zā´shən) *n.* **equalizer** *n.* **1** something that equalizes, esp. a score in a game. **2** (*sl.*) a gun. **3** a connection in an electric system which compensates for undesirable frequencies. **equally** *adv.* **equalness** *n.* **equal opportunity** *n.* (*pl.* **equal opportunities**) the right to equality (with those of different sex, race etc.) in obtaining employment and in treatment as an employee. ~*a.* (of an employer) not discriminating on grounds of sex, race etc. **equal-opportunities** *a.* **equal sign**, **equals sign** *n.* (*Math.*) the sign =, used to show that two quantities etc. are of equal value. **equal temperament** *n.* (*Mus.*) a system of tuning an instrument so that the octave is divided into twelve equal intervals or semitones. [L *aequālis*, see EQUABLE]

Usage note It is best not to use *equally as*: preferred alternatives are *equally with* (a noun) and *just as* (an adjective).

equanimity (ekwənim´iti, ē-) *n.* **1** evenness or composure of mind. **2** a temper not easily disturbed. **3** resignation. **equanimous** (ikwan´-) *a.* **1** of an even frame of mind. **2** not easily elated or depressed. **equanimously** *adv.* **equanimousness** *n.* [F *équanimité*, L *aequanimitās -tātem*, from *aequanimis* (*aequus*, equal, *animus*, mind)]

equate (ikwāt´) *v.t.* **1** to regard as equal (to). **2** to equalize. ~*v.i.* to be equal. **equatable** *a.* **equatability** (-bil´-) *n.* [L *aequatus*, p.p. of *aequāre*, from *aequus*, equal]

equation (ikwā´shən) *n.* **1** the act of making equal. **2** equality. **3** (*Math.*) a statement consisting of two algebraic expressions equal to one another, and connected by the sign =. **4** (*Astron.*) a sum added or subtracted to allow for any special circumstance affecting the exactness of a calculation. **5** (*Chem.*) a formula which expresses a chemical reaction and notes the proportions of the chemicals involved. **equational** *a.* **equationally** *adv.* **equation of light** *n.* (*Astron.*) the allowance made in determining the position of a heavenly body for the time occupied in the transmission of its light to the eye of the observer. **equation of payments** *n.* a rule for ascertaining at what time a person should pay the whole of a debt contracted in different portions to be repaid at different times. **equation of the first order** *n.* an equation which involves the first derivative only. **equation of the second order** *n.* an equation which involves the second derivative only. **equation of time** *n.* the difference between mean and apparent time. [L *aequātio -ōnem*, from *aequāre*, as EQUATE]

equator (ikwā´tə) *n.* **1** a great circle on the earth's surface, equidistant from its poles, and dividing it into the northern and southern hemispheres. **2** (*Astron.*) CELESTIAL EQUATOR (under CELESTIAL). **equatorial** (ekwətaw´-) *a.* **1** of or relating to the equator. **2** situated on or near the equator. **equatorially** *adv.* **equatorial mount**, **equatorial mounting** *n.* (*Astron.*) a mounting for an equatorial telescope. **equatorial telescope** *n.* a telescope mounted on an axis parallel to that of the earth, used for noting the course of the stars as they move through the sky. [late L, as EQUATION]

equerry (ek´wəri, ikwer´i) *n.* (*pl.* **equerries**) **1** an officer of a royal household. **2** an officer having the care of the horses of nobles or princes. [F *écurie*, med. L *scūria*, a stable, OHG *scûr*, *sciura*, a shed (G *Scheuer*, barn), confused with L *equus*, horse]

equestrian (ikwes´triən) *a.* **1** of or relating to horses or horsemanship. **2** mounted on horseback. **3** †given to or skilled in horsemanship. ~*n.* **1** a rider on horseback. **2** a person who performs feats of horsemanship. **3** a circus-rider. **equestrianism** *n.* **equestrienne** (-en´) *n.* a female rider or performer on horseback. [L *equestris*, from *eques*, horseman, from *equus*, horse]

equi- (ēk´wi, ek´wi) *comb. form* equal. [L *aequus*, equal]

equiangular (ēkwiang´gūlə, ek-) *a.* (*Math.*) having or consisting of equal angles.

equidistant (ēkwidis´tənt, ek-) *a.* **1** equally distant from some point or place. **2** separated from each other by equal distances. **equidistance** *n.* **equidistantly** *adv.*

equilateral (ēkwilat´ərəl, ek-) *a.* having all the sides equal. ~*n.* a figure having all its sides equal. **equilaterally** *adv.*

equilibrate (ēkwilī´brāt, ek-, ikwil´i-) *v.t.* **1** to balance (two things) exactly. **2** to counterpoise. ~*v.i.* **1** to balance (each other) exactly. **2** to be a counterpoise (to). **equilibration** (-rā´shən) *n.* **equilibrator** *n.*

equilibrium (ēkwilib´riəm, ek-) *n.* (*pl.* **equilibriums, equilibria** (-riə)) **1** a state of equal balance, equipoise. **2** equality of weight or force. **3** mental or emotional balance or stability. **4** due proportion between parts. **5** (*Physics*) a state of rest or balance due to the action of forces which counteract each other. **equilibrist** (ikwil´-) *n.* a person who balances in unnatural positions, esp. a tight-rope walker, an acrobat. [L *aequilībrium* (EQUI-, *lībrāre*, to balance, from *lībra*, a balance)]

equine (ek´wīn) *a.* **1** of or relating to a horse or horses. **2** resembling a horse. **equinely** *adv.* **equinia** (ikwin´iə) *n.* a contagious disease to which equine animals are subject, glanders. [L *equīnus*, from *equus*, a horse (cp. Gr. *hippos*, *hikkos*, OE *eoh*)]

equinox (ek´winoks, ē´-) *n.* **1** the moment at which the sun crosses the equator and renders day and night equal throughout the world, now occurring (vernal equinox) on 21 March and (autumnal equinox) on 23 September. **2** (*Astron.*) one of two points at which the sun in its annual course crosses the celestial equator. **3** †an equinoctial gale. **equinoctial** (-nok´shəl) *a.* **1** of or relating to the equinoxes, or the regions or climates near the terrestrial equator. **2** designating an equal length of day and night. **3** happening at or about the time of the equinoxes. ~*n.* **1** the equinoctial line. **2** (*pl.*) equinoctial gales. **equinoctial gale** *n.* a gale happening at or near either equinox. **equinoctial line** *n.* (*Astron.*) the celestial equator. **equinoctially** *adv.* in the direction of the equinoctial line. **equinoctial point** *n.* either of the two points wherein the equator and ecliptic intersect each other. **equinoctial time** *n.* time reckoned from the moment when the sun passes the vernal equinox. **equinoctial year** *n.* an astronomical year. [F *équinoxe*, L *aequinoctium* (EQUI-, *nox noctis*, night)]

equip (ikwip´) *v.t.* (*pres.p.* **equipping**, *past*, *p.p.* **equipped**) **1** to furnish, accoutre, esp. to supply with everything needed for some profession or activity. **2** to fit out (as a ship), to prepare for any particular duty. **3** to qualify. **equipage** (ek´wipij) *n.* **1** that with which a person is equipped. **2** a carriage with horses and attendants. **3** the outfit of a ship for a voyage. **4** (*Hist.*) the arms and general outfit of a body of troops, including baggage, provisions etc. **5** †a retinue, attendance, train of followers. **equipaged** *a.* **equipment** *n.* **1** the act of equipping. **2** the state of being equipped. **3** that which is used in equipping or fitting out. **4** outfit, furniture, apparatus required for work, intellectual and other qualifications. **equipper** *n.* [F *équiper*, *esquiper* (A-F *eskiper*), prob. from Icel. *skipa*, to arrange, to man (a ship), from *skip*, ship]

équipe (ākēp´) *n.* (esp. in motor racing) a team. [F]

equipment EQUIP.

equipoise (ek´wipoiz) *n.* **1** a state of equality of weight or force, equilibrium. **2** that which counterbalances. ~*v.t.* **1** to counterbalance. **2** to hold in equilibrium.

equipollent (ēkwipol´ənt, ek-) *a.* **1** having equal force, power, significance etc. **2** equivalent. ~*n.* something that is equipollent. **equipollence, equipollency** *n.* **1** equality of force etc. **2** (*Logic*) equivalence between two or more propositions. **equipollently** *adv.* [OF *equipolent*, L *aequipollens -ntem* (EQUI-, *pollens*, pres.p. of *pollēre*, to be strong)]

equiponderate (ēkwipon´dərāt, ek-) *v.t.* **1** to counterpoise. **2** to put into equipoise. **equiponderance, equiponderancy** *n.* **equiponderant** *a.* [med. L *aequiponderātus*, p.p. of *aequiponderāre* (EQUI-, *ponderāre*, to weigh, from *pondus*, weight)]

equipotential (ēkwipəten´shəl, ek-) *a.* (*Physics*) having the same, or being at the same, potential at all points (of a line, surface or region). ~*n.* an equipotential line, surface or region.

equiprobable (ēkwiprob´əbəl, ek-) *a.* equally probable. **equiprobability** (-bil´-) *n.*

equisetum (ekwisē´təm) *n.* (*pl.* **equiseta** (-tə), **equisetums**) (*Bot.*) a plant of the genus of cryptogams *Equisetum*, containing the horsetails and constituting the order Equisetaceae. **equisetaceous** (-sitā´shəs) *a.* **equisetic** (-set´-) *a.* of or relating to, or derived from any species of *Equisetum*. [L (*equus*, horse, *saeta*, bristle)]

equitable (ek´witəbəl) *a.* **1** acting or done with equity; fair, just. **2** (*Law*) of or relating to a court or the rules of equity. **equitableness** *n.* **equitably** *adv.* [F *équitable*]

Usage note See note under EQUABLE.

equitant (ek´witənt) *a.* overlapping, astride or overriding (of leaves etc.). [L *equitans -ntem*, pres.p. of *equitāre*, see EQUITATION]

equitation (ekwitā´shən) *n.* **1** the act or art of riding on horseback. **2** horsemanship. **equitative** (ek´witətiv) *a.* [L *equitātio -ōnem*, from *equitāre*, from *eques -itis*, horseman, from *equus*, horse]

equity (ek´witi) *n.* (*pl.* **equities**) **1** justice, fairness. **2** the application of principles of justice to correct the deficiencies of law. **3** (*Law*) the system of law, collateral and supplemental to statute law, administered by courts of equity. **4** the net value of mortgaged property. **5 a** (*pl.*) stocks and shares not bearing a fixed rate of interest. **b** the value of all the shares in a company. **6** (**Equity**) the actors' trade union. **equity capital** *n.* the share capital of a company which is owned by ordinary shareholders. **equity-linked** *a.* (of an insurance policy) of which part or all of the premiums are invested in shares. **equity of redemption** *n.* (*Law*) the right allowed to a mortgagor to a reasonable time within which to redeem his estate when mortgaged for a sum less than it is worth. [OF *equité*, L *aequitās -tātem*, from *aequus*, fair]

equivalent (ikwiv´ələnt) *a.* **1** of equal value, force or weight (to). **2** alike in meaning, significance or effect. **3** interchangeable, corresponding. **4** having the same result. **5** (*Geom.*) having equal areas or dimensions. **6** (*Chem.*) having the same combining power. **7** (*Geol.*) corresponding in position, and, within certain limits, in age. ~*n.* **1** anything which is equal to something else in amount, weight, value, force etc. **2** (*Chem.*) (*also* **equivalent weight**) the weight of an element or compound which will combine with or displace one gram of hydrogen or eight grams of oxygen. **equivalence, equivalency** *n.* **equivalently** *adv.* [MF, from late L *aequivalens -ntem* (EQUI-, *valēre*, to be worth)]

equivocal (ikwiv´əkəl) *a.* **1** doubtful of meaning, ambiguous, capable of a twofold interpretation. **2** of uncertain origin, character etc. **3** (of a person) open to doubt or suspicion. **4** †equivocating. **equivocality** (-kal´-) *n.*

equivocally *adv.* **equivocalness** *n.* [late L *aequivocus* (EQUI-, *voc-*, root of *vocāre*, to call)]

equivocate (ikwiv´əkāt) *v.i.* **1** to use words in an ambiguous manner. **2** to speak ambiguously so as to deceive. **3** to prevaricate. **equivocation** (-ā´shən) *n.* **equivocator** *n.* **equivocatory** *a.* [late L *aequivocātus*, p.p. of *aequivocāre*, see EQUIVOCAL]

equivoque (ek´wivōk), **equivoke** *n.* **1** an ambiguous term or phrase, an equivocation. **2** a pun or other play upon words. [ME, from late L *aequivocus*, EQUIVOCAL]

ER *abbr.* **1** Queen Elizabeth. **2** King Edward. [L]

Er *chem. symbol* erbium.

er (œ) *int.* used to express a hesitation in speech. [imit.]

-er[1] (ə) *suf.* **1 a** forming nouns, denoting an agent or doer, as *hatter, player, singer.* **b** sometimes doubled, as *caterer, poulterer.* **2** forming nouns, denoting a resident or native of, as *Londoner, Lowlander.* [OE *-ere*, from Gmc. *-ârjoz* (cp. L *-arius*)]

-er[2] (ə) *suf.* forming nouns, denoting a person or thing connected with, as *butler, officer, teenager.* [OF *-er*, L *-ar -ārem*; or A-F *-er*, OF *-ier*, L *-arius*; or OF *-eüre*, L *-ātūram*]

-er[3] (ə) *suf.* forming adjectives, denoting the comparative, as *richer, taller.* [ME *-er, -ere, -re*, OE *-ra*]

-er[4] (ə) *suf.* forming nouns, denoting an action, as *disclaimer, user.* [F *-er, -re*, the infinitive ending]

-er[5] (ə) *suf.* forming verbs, with a frequentative meaning, as *chatter, slumber, twitter.* [OE *-rian*, Gmc. *-rûjan*]

-er[6] (ə) *suf.* forming nouns, with diminutive and colloquial meanings, as *soccer.* [poss. -ER[1]]

ERA *abbr.* (*US*) Equal Rights Amendment.

era (iə´rə) *n.* **1** a historical period or system of chronology running from a fixed point of time marked by an important event such as the birth of Christ, the Hegira etc. **2** the date from which this is reckoned. **3** a long period of time having a unifying characteristic, as *Christian era.* **4** (*Geol.*) any one of the main divisions of geological time. [late L *aera*, a number, orig. pl. of *aes*, money]

eradiate (irā´diāt) *v.i.* (*formal*) to shoot out, as rays of light. ~*v.t.* to emit (as rays). **eradiation** (-ā´shən) *n.*

eradicate (irad´ikāt) *v.t.* **1** to root up. **2** to destroy or get rid of completely. **eradicable** *a.* **eradication** (-ā´shən) *n.* **eradicator** *n.* [L *ērādīcātus*, p.p. of *ērādīcāre* (E-, *rādix*, root)]

erase (irāz´, irās´) *v.t.* **1** to rub out. **2** to obliterate, to expunge. **3** (*fig.*) to raze. **erasable** *a.* **erasement** *n.* **eraser** *n.* **1** something that erases. **2** a piece of rubber etc. used to erase pencil or ink marks from paper. **erasion** (-zhən) *n.* **erasure** (-zhə) *n.* [L *ērāsus*, p.p. of *ērādere* (E-, *rādere*, to scrape)]

ERASMUS (iraz´məs) *abbr.* European Community Action Scheme for the Mobility of University Students.

Erastian (iras´tiən) *n.* a person holding the opinions on ecclesiastical matters attributed to Erastus, that the State has supreme authority over the Church. ~*a.* of or relating to Erastus or holding his doctrines. **Erastianism** *n.* **Erastianize, Erastianise** *v.t.* **1** to imbue with Erastian doctrines. **2** to organize (a Church system) on these principles. ~*v.i.* to hold Erastian views. [Thomas *Erastus*, 1524–83, Swiss physician and theologian]

erbium (œ´biəm) *n.* (*Chem.*) a rare metallic element, at. no. 68, chem. symbol Er, forming a rose-coloured oxide. [*Ytterby*, in Sweden]

ere (eə) *prep.* (*formal or poet.*) before, sooner than. ~*conj.* before that, sooner than. **ere long** before long, soon. **erewhile** *adv.* some time ago, formerly. [OE *aer* (cp. Dut. *eer*, OHG *ēr*, G *eher*, sooner) from Gmc. *airiz*, orig. comp. of *air*, early]

erect (irekt´) *a.* **1** upright, vertical. **2** standing up straight. **3** not bending or stooping. **4** (of the penis, clitoris etc.) distended and stiff, as a result of sexual excitement. **5** (*Bot.*) pointing straight up (as leaves). **6** (of hair) standing up from the skin, bristling. **7** attentive, alert. ~*v.t.* **1** to set upright; to raise. **2** to construct, to build. **3** (*fig.*) to elevate, to exalt. **4** to set up, to establish. **erectable** *a.* **erectile** (-tīl) *a.* susceptible of erection. **erectile tissue** *n.* tissue formed of blood vessels intermixed with nervous filaments, and capable of dilatation under excitement. **erectility** (-til´-) *n.* **erection** *n.* **1** the act of setting upright, building, constructing, establishing etc. **2** the state of being erected. **3** a building, a structure. **4** the distension of a part consisting of erectile tissue, esp. the penis. **5** an instance of such distension. **erectly** *adv.* **erectness** *n.* **erector** *n.* [L *ērectus*, p.p. of *ērigere* (E-, *regere*, to rule, to set)]

eremite (er´əmīt) *n.* a hermit or recluse. **eremitic** (-mit´-), **eremitical** *a.* [late L *erēmīta*, HERMIT]

erethism (er´əthizm) *n.* **1** undue excitation of an organ or tissue. **2** a state of abnormal mental excitement or irritability. [F *éréthisme*, Gr. *erethismos*, from *erethizein*, to irritate]

erewhile ERE.

erg[1] (œg), **ergon** (-gon) *n.* the unit of work done in moving a body through 1 cm of space against the resistance of 1 dyne. **ergograph** (-gəgrahf) *n.* an instrument which measures the work done by a contracting muscle. **ergometer** (-gom´itə) *n.* a dynamometer. [Gr. *ergon*, work]

erg[2] (œg) *n.* (*pl.* **ergs, areg** (ah´reg)) an area of shifting sand dunes, esp. in the Sahara. [Arab *'irj*]

ergative (œ´gətiv) *a.* (*Gram.*) **1** of or relating to a case in some languages used to denote the doer of an action as the object of the verb. **2** of or relating to a language which uses the ergative case. ~*n.* **1** the ergative case. **2** a noun in this case. [Gr. *ergatēs*, a workman, from *ergon*, work]

ergo (œ´gō) *adv.* (*formal*) **1** therefore. **2** consequently. [L]

ergocalciferol (œgōkalsif´ərol) *n.* vitamin D_2, calciferol. [ERGOT]

ergonomics (œgənom´iks) *n.* the scientific study of the relationship between workers, their environment and machinery. **ergonomic** *a.* **ergonomically** *adv.* **ergonomist** (-gon´əmist) *n.* [Gr. *ergon*, work, and (ec)*onomics*]

ergosterol (œgos´tərol) *n.* a plant sterol which is converted to vitamin D_2 by ultraviolet radiation. [ERGOT]

ergot (œ´gət) *n.* **1** a disease in various grains and grasses, esp. in rye, caused by a fungus, *Claviceps purpurea*, whose presence can cause food poisoning. **2** this dried fungus, used medicinally. **3** a preparation of ergot of rye used in midwifery to produce contraction of the uterus. **4** a small horny bump on the back of a horse's fetlock. **ergotine** (-tin) *n.* a slightly bitter substance, forming the active principle of ergot of rye. **ergotism**[1] *n.* **1** the disease of ergot in grasses. **2** food poisoning produced by eating grain affected with ergot. [F, from OF *argot*, a cock's spur, hence spurred rye; etym. uncertain]

ergotism[1] ERGOT.

ergotism[2] (œ´gətizm) *n.* arguing, wrangling. [ERGO]

erica (er´ikə) *n.* a member of the genus *Erica* of shrubby plants forming the heath family. **ericaceous** (-kā´shəs) *a.* **1** of or relating to the family of plants Ericaceae, including heathers, azaleas etc. **2** (of compost) acidic, suitable for growing ericaceous plants. [L, from Gr. *ereikē*]

erigeron (irij´ərən) *n.* a member of the genus *Erigeron* of plants resembling the aster. [Gr. *ērigerōn* (*ēri*, early, *gerōn*, old man)]

eringo ERYNGO.

Erinys (erin´is) *n.* (*pl.* **Erinyes** (erin´iēz)) in Greek mythology, a Fury. [Gr.]

eristic (iris´tik) *a.* **1** of or relating to controversy or disputation. **2** (of an argument) designed to win rather than to reach the truth. ~*n.* **1** a controversialist. **2** the art of disputation. **eristically** *adv.* [Gr. *eristikos*, from *erizein*, to contend, from *eris*, strife]

Eritrean (eritrā´ən) *a.* of or relating to Eritrea, a country in north-east Africa. ~*n.* a native or inhabitant of Eritrea. [It. *Eritrea*, from L *Mare Erythraeum*, Red Sea, from Gr. *eruthros*, red]

erk (œk) *n.* (*sl.*) **1** a naval rating. **2** (*dated*) an aircraftman. **3** a despicable or disliked person. [*aircraftman*]

erl-king (oel´king) *n.* in German and Scandinavian folklore, a bearded goblin harmful to children. [G *Erl-könig*, alder-king, after Dan. *ellerkonge*, king of the elves]

ERM *abbr.* exchange rate mechanism.

ermine (œ´min) *n.* (*pl. in general* **ermine**, *in particular* **ermines**) **1** the stoat, *Mustela erminea*, hunted in winter for its fur, which then becomes snowy white, with the exception of the tip of the tail which is always black. **2** the fur of this used for the robes of judges, peers etc. **3** (*Her.*) a fur represented by triangular black spots on white. **4** (*fig.*) the office of judge. **ermined** *a.* clothed with or wearing ermine. [OF (F *hermine*, cp. Prov. *ermini*), prob. from L (*mūs*) *armenius*, lit. (mouse) of Armenia]

ern ERNE.

-ern (ən) *suf.* forming adjectives, as in *northern*, *southern*. [OE, from Gmc. *-rônjo-* (*-ro-*, *-ônjo-*, cp. L *-āneus*)]

erne (œn), (*N Am.*) **ern** *n.* an eagle, esp. the sea eagle. [OE *earn* (cp. Dut. *arend*, Icel. *orn*; also Gr. *ornis*, bird)]

Ernie (œ´ni) *n.* the device employed for drawing the prize-winning numbers of Premium Bonds. [acronym for electronic *r*andom *n*umber *i*ndicator *e*quipment]

erode (irōd´) *v.t.* **1** to eat into or away. **2** to corrode. **3** (*Geol.*) to wear away; to eat out (a channel etc.). **4** (*Med.*) (of an ulcer etc.) to destroy (tissue) gradually. ~*v.i.* to be worn away or gradually eaten away. **erodible** *a.* **erose** (irōs´) *a.* **1** gnawed. **2** (*Bot.*) irregularly indented, as if bitten away. **erosely** *adv.* **erosion** (-zhən) *n.* **1** the act of eroding, or process of being eroded. **2** (*Geol.*) the wearing away of rock by water, wind or ice. **erosional** *a.* **erosive** (-siv) *a.* [F *éroder*, L *ērōdere* (E-, *rōdere*, to gnaw, p.p. *rōsus*)]

erogenous (iroj´inəs) *a.* **1** sensitive to sexual stimulation. **2** producing sexual desire. [Gr. *erōs*, love]

☒ **eroneous** common misspelling of ERRONEOUS.

erose, **erosion** etc. ERODE.

erotic (irot´ik) *a.* of or relating to, caused by or causing sexual desire; amatory. ~*n.* **1** a person with strong sexual desires. **2** an amatory poem. **erotica** *n.pl.* erotic art or literature. **erotically** *adv.* **eroticism** (-sizm) *n.* **1** erotic nature or quality. **2** the use, in art or literature, of erotic language or imagery. **3** sexual excitement. **4** (*Psych.*) an exaggerated display of sexual feelings. **eroticize**, **eroticise** *v.t.* **erotism** (er´ə-) *n.*

eroto- (irot´ō) *comb. form* erotic, eroticism. [Gr. *erōs erōtos*, love]

erotogenic (irotōjen´ik), **erotogenous** (erətoj´ənəs) *a.* erogenous.

erotology (erətol´əji) *n.* the study of eroticism or of sexual behaviour. **erotological** (-loj´-) *a.* **erotologically** *adv.* **erotologist** (-tol´-) *n.*

erotomania (irotōmā´niə) *n.* **1** abnormal or excessive sexual desire. **2** a preoccupation with sexual desire. **erotomaniac** *n., a.*

err (œ) *v.i.* **1** to blunder, to miss the truth, right or accuracy; to be incorrect. **2** to deviate from duty. **3** to sin. **to err on the right side** to deviate from strict accuracy or the prescribed course of action so as to ensure a better outcome. **to err on the side of** to favour (a specified side, aspect etc.) in one's actions. [OF *errer*, L *errāre* (cogn. with Goth. *airzjan*, whence G *irren*)]

errancy ERRANT.

errand (e´rənd) *n.* **1** a short journey to carry a message or perform some other commission, esp. on another's behalf. **2** the object or purpose of such a journey. **errand boy**, **errand girl** *n.* a boy or girl employed to run on errands. **errand of mercy** *n.* a charitable mission. [OE *ærende* (cp. OS *ārundi*, Icel. *eyrindi*, *ōrindi*, *erindi*, OHG *ārunti*); etym. uncertain]

errant (er´ənt) *a.* **1** erring. **2** wandering, roving, rambling, esp. roaming in quest of adventure as a knight errant. **knight errant** KNIGHT. **errancy**, **errantry** *n.* (*pl.* **errancies**, **errantries**). [OF, wandering, pres.p. of *errer*, low L *iterāre*, L *iter*, a journey; or L *errans -ntem*, pres.p. of *errāre*, see ERR]

errata ERRATUM.

erratic (irat´ik) *a.* **1** irregular in movement, eccentric, unpredictable. **2** wandering, straying (formerly applied to the planets in contradistinction to the fixed stars). **3** (*Med.*) shifting from one place to another. **4** (*Geol.*) (of boulders) transported by ice from their original situation. ~*n.* **1** †a rogue, a vagabond. **2** (*Geol.*) an erratic block, a boulder transported by ice. **erratically** *adv.* **erraticism** *n.* [L *errāticus*, from *errāre*, see ERR]

erratum (irah´təm) *n.* (*pl.* **errata** (-tə)) **1** an error or mistake in printing or writing. **2** (*pl.*) a list of corrections appended to a book. [L, neut. p.p. of *errāre*, see ERR]

erroneous (irō´niəs) *a.* mistaken, incorrect. **erroneously** *adv.* **erroneousness** *n.* [L *errōneus*, from *erro -ōnis*, a vagabond (see ERR)]

error (er´ə) *n.* **1** a mistake in writing, printing etc. **2** deviation from truth or accuracy. **3** a wrong opinion. **4** a false doctrine or teaching. **5** a transgression, a sin of a venial kind. **6** (*Astron.*) the difference between the positions of the heavenly bodies as determined by calculation and by observation. **7** in statistics, a measure of the difference between some quantity and an approximation of it, usu. expressed as a percentage. **error-free** *a.* **errorless** *a.* [OF *errour*, L *errōrem*, acc. of *error*, a wandering, from *errāre* (see ERR)]

ersatz (œ´zats, eə´-) *a.* **1** imitation. **2** artificial. ~*n.* a substitute (in a pejorative sense). [G]

Erse (œs) *n.* the Gaelic dialect of Ireland or the Scottish Highlands. ~*a.* Irish or Scottish Gaelic. [early Sc. var. of *Irish*]

erst (oest) *adv.* once, formerly, of yore. **erstwhile** *adv.* some while ago. ~*a.* previous, former. [OE *ærest*, superl. of *ær*, soon]

erubescent (erəbes´ənt) *a.* **1** reddening, blushing. **2** reddish. **erubescence** *n.* [L *ērubescens -ntem*, pres.p. of *ērubescere* (E-, *rubescere*, incept. of *rubēre*, to be red)]

eruca (iroo´kə) *n.* a member of the genus *Eruca*, herbs of the family Cruciferae. **erucic acid** (-sik) *n.* a crystalline fatty acid found in rape seed, wallflower seed and mustard seed. [L *ērūca*, ROCKET[2]]

eructation (ērŭktā´shən) *n.* **1** the act or an instance of belching. **2** that which is ejected by belching. **3** any sudden ejection of gases or solid matter from a volcano. **eructate** (irŭk´tāt) *v.t.* **eructative** (-tətiv) *a.* [L *ēructātio -ōnem*, from *ēructāre* (E-, *ructāre*, to belch)]

erudite (er´ədīt) *a.* **1** learned, well-read, well-informed. **2** (of a book etc.) displaying great scholarship. **eruditely** *adv.* **eruditeness** *n.* **erudition** (-dish´-) *n.* **1** learning, extensive knowledge gained by study. **2** scholarship. [L *ērudītus*, p.p. of *ērudīre* (E-, *rudis*, rude)]

erupt (irŭpt´) *v.t.* **1** to emit violently, as a volcano, geyser etc. **2** to force through (as teeth through the gums). ~*v.i.* **1** to burst out. **2** to break through (of teeth etc.). **3 a** (of pimples etc.) to appear (on the skin). **b** (of the skin) to produce pimples etc. **4** (of a volcano) to emit lava, gases etc. **eruption** *n.* **1** the act of bursting forth. **2** a sudden emission. **3** that which breaks out. **4** (*Med.*) the breaking out of vesicles, pimples, rash etc. upon the skin. **5** the breaking through of teeth. 6 an outburst of lava etc. from a volcano or other vent. **eruptive** *a.* **eruptively** *adv.* **eruptiveness** *n.* **eruptivity** (erŭptiv´iti) *n.* [L *ēruptus*, p.p. of *ērumpere* (E-, *rumpere*, to break)]

-ery (əri) *suf.* used with nouns and adjectives, and sometimes with verbs, to form nouns, generally abstract or collective, meaning a business, place of business, cultivation etc., conduct, things connected with or of the nature of etc.; orig. confined to Romance words, but now used with those of Gmc. origin, e.g., *foolery, grocery, pinery, rockery, tannery, witchery.* [F *-erie* (L *-ārio-*, *-ia*; or L *-ātor -ōrem*)]

eryngo (iring´gō), **eringo** *n.* (*pl.* **eryngoes, eryngos, eringoes, eringos**) (*Bot.*) any plant of the genus *Eryngium*, umbelliferous plants, including the sea holly. [L *ēryngion*, Gr. *ērungion*, dim. of *ērungos*, goat's beard]

erysipelas (erisip´iləs) *n.* a streptococcal infection of the skin in which the affected parts are of a deep red colour, with a diffused inflammation of the underlying cutaneous tissue and cellular membrane. **erysipelatous** (-pel´ətəs) *a.* [L, from Gr. *erusipelas* (*erusi-*, rel. to *eruthros*, red, *pella*, skin)]

erythema (erithē´mə) *n.* a superficial redness of the skin, occurring in patches. **erythemal, erythematic** (-mat´-), **erythematous** *a.* [Gr. *eruthēma*, from *eruthainein*, to be red, from *eruthros*, red]

erythr- ERYTHRO-.

erythrism (irith´rizm) *n.* an abnormal red coloration, esp. of fur or plumage.

erythrite (irith´rīt) *n.* a red or greenish-grey variety of feldspar. [Gr. *eruthros*, red]

erythro- (irith´rō), **erythr-** *comb. form* red. [Gr. *eruthros*, red]

erythroblast (irith´rōblahst) *n.* a cell in the bone marrow that will develop into an erythrocyte.

erythrocyte (irith´rəsīt) *n.* a red blood cell in vertebrates. **erythrocytic** (-sit´ik) *a.*

erythroid (irith´roid) *a.* of or relating to erythrocytes.

erythromycin (irithrōmī´sin) *n.* an antibiotic used to treat bacterial infections. [Gr. *mukēs*, fungus]

erythropoiesis (irithrōpoiē´sis) *n.* the formation of red blood cells. [Gr. *poiēsis*, a making, production, from *poieein*, to make]

ES *abbr.* El Salvador (IVR).

Es *chem. symbol* einsteinium.

-es[1] (iz) *suf.* forming the pl. of nouns that end in a sibilant sound, as *kisses, witches, axes*; also of some nouns that end in *-o*, as *tomatoes.*

-es[2] (iz) *suf.* forming the 3rd pers. sing. pres. of verbs that end in a sibilant sound, as *kisses, watches*; also of some verbs that end in *-o*, as *goes.*

ESA *abbr.* European Space Agency.

ESB *abbr.* electrical stimulation of the brain.

escadrille (eskədril´) *n.* **1** a French squadron of aircraft. **2** a flotilla. [F, a flotilla]

escalade (eskəlād´) *n.* an attack on a fortified place in which ladders are used to mount the ramparts etc. *~v.t.* to storm by means of ladders. **escalader** *n.* [F, from Sp. *escalada*, fem. p.p. of *escalar*, med. L *scalāre*, to scale, from *scāla*, ladder]

escalate (es´kəlāt) *v.i.* to increase (rapidly) in scale, intensity or magnitude. *~v.t.* to cause to escalate. **escalation** (-ā´shən) *n.* [see ESCALATOR]

escalator (es´kəlātə) *n.* a conveyor for passengers consisting of a continuous series of steps on an endless chain, ascending or descending and arranged to give facilities for mounting or leaving at either end; a moving staircase. [F *escalader*, to scale, to climb]

escallonia (eskəlō´niə) *n.* an evergreen shrub of the S American flowering genus *Escallonia*, of the saxifrage family. [*Escallon*, an 18th-cent. Spanish traveller]

escallop (iskal´əp) *n.* **1** an escalope. **2** a scallop. **3** (*Her.*) a scallop shell.

escalope (es´kəlop, iskal´əp) *n.* a thin boneless slice of meat, esp. veal or pork. [F]

escapade (eskəpād´, es´-) *n.* an exciting or daring prank or adventure. [F, from Sp. or Prov. *escapada*, from *escapar*, to ESCAPE]

escape (iskāp´) *v.t.* **1** to get safely away from. **2** to flee so as to be free from. **3** to evade, to avoid (a thing or act). **4** to slip away from, elude attention or recollection of. **5** to find an issue from. **6** to slip from unawares or unintentionally. *~v.i.* **1** to get free. **2** to get safely away. **3** to find an issue, to leak. **4** to evade punishment, capture, danger, annoyance etc. *~n.* **1** the act or an instance of escaping. **2** the state of having escaped, a means of escaping. **3** evasion, flight, deliverance. **4** a means of escaping. **5** a leakage (from a gas or water pipe, electric main etc.). **6** a plant from a garden apparently growing wild. **7** (*Law*) violent or privy evasion out of lawful restraint. **8** (*Comput.*) a function key which can cancel a command, end the current operation etc. **escapable** *a.* **escape clause** *n.* a clause in a contract which specifies the circumstances which free one of the parties from any or all obligations. **escapee** (eskəpē´) *n.* a person who has escaped, esp. an escaped prisoner. **escape hatch** *n.* a means of exit from a submarine in an emergency. **escapement** *n.* **1** a device in a clock or watch for checking and regulating the movement of the wheels. **2** (in a piano) the mechanism which removes the hammer from the string immediately after striking. **3** (in a typewriter) the mechanism which regulates the movement of the carriage. **4** a means of escaping. **escape pipe, escape valve** *n.* an outlet for steam, water etc. in case of necessity. **escaper** *n.* **escape road** *n.* a short piece of roadway leading off a steep downward slope or a sharp bend to enable out-of-control vehicles to stop safely. **escape shaft** *n.* a shaft provided in case of emergency for the escape of miners. **escape velocity** *n.* the minimum velocity needed to escape from a gravitational field. **escape warrant** *n.* (*Law*) a warrant addressed to sheriffs etc. to retake an escaped prisoner. **escape wheel** *n.* a toothed wheel in the escapement of a watch or clock. **escapism** *n.* the shirking of unpleasant facts and realities by filling the mind with pleasing irrelevancies. **escapist** *a.*, *n.* **escapologist** (eskəpol´əjist) *n.* a performer whose act is escaping from locked handcuffs, chains, boxes etc. **escapology** *n.* [A-F *escaper*, OF *eschaper* (F *échapper*), prob. from a late L *excappāre* (EX-, *cappa*, cloak)]

escargot (iskah´gō) *n.* an edible snail. [F]

escarp (iskahp´) *n.* **1** a steep slope below a plateau. **2** the slope on the inner side of a ditch, below a rampart, opposite the counterscarp. *~v.t.* **1** to scarp. **2** in fortification, to cut or form into a slope. **escarpment** *n.* **1** the precipitous face of a hill or ridge. **2** an escarp in a fortification. [F *escarpe*, SCARP[1]]

-esce (es) *suf.* forming inceptive verbs, as *acquiesce, coalesce, effervesce.* [L *-escere*, infin. ending of inceptive verbs]

-escence (es´əns) *suf.* forming abstract nouns from inceptive verbs, as *acquiescence, coalescence, opalescence.* **-escent** (es´ənt) *suf.* forming adjectives from inceptive verbs, as *acquiescent, coalescent, iridescent, opalescent.* [L *-escens -entem*, pres.p. ending of inceptive verbs]

eschalot (esh´əlot, -lot´) *n.* a shallot.

eschatology (eskətol´əji) *n.* the doctrine of the final issue of things, death, the last judgement, the future state etc. **eschatological** (-loj´-) *a.* **eschatologist** (-tol´-) *n.* [Gr. *eschatos*, last]

escheat (ischēt´) *n.* (*Hist.*) **1** the reverting of property to the Crown or the state, on the death of the owner intestate without heirs. 2 the property so reverting. ~*v.t.* 1 to confiscate. 2 to forfeit (to). ~*v.i.* to revert by escheat. **escheatable** *a.* **escheatage** *n.* **escheator** *n.* an officer formerly appointed in every county to register the escheats of the Crown. [OF *eschete*, fem. p.p. of *escheoir* (F *échoir*), late L *excadere* (EX-, L *cadere*, to fall)]

eschew (ischoo´) *v.t.* (*formal*) 1 to avoid; to shun. 2 to abstain from. 3 to flee from. **eschewal** *n.* **eschewer** *n.* [OF *eschiver*, OHG *sciuhan* (G *scheuen*), cogn. with OE *sceoh*, SHY[1]]

eschscholtzia (esholt´siə) *n.* a member of the genus of flowering herbs, *Eschscholtzia*, comprising the California poppy. [J. F. von *Eschscholtz*, 1793–1831, German naturalist]

escort[1] (es´kawt) *n.* 1 an armed guard attending a person or persons, baggage etc. which are being conveyed from one place to another, as a protection against attack or for compulsion or surveillance. 2 a guard of honour. 3 a person or persons accompanying another for protection or guidance. 4 a person of the opposite sex who accompanies one on a social occasion. **escort agency** *n.* (*pl.* **escort agencies**) a company which provides people, usu. of the opposite sex, to act as hired escorts on social occasions. [F *escorte*, It. *scorta*, fem. p.p. of *scorgere*, to guide, conduct (EX-, L *corrigere*, to CORRECT)]

escort[2] (iskawt´) *v.t.* 1 to act as escort to. 2 to attend upon. [see ESCORT[1]]

escribe (iskrīb´) *v.t.* to draw (a circle) so as to touch one side of a triangle exteriorly and the other two produced. [L *scrībere*, to write]

escritoire (eskritwah´) *n.* a writing desk with drawers etc. for papers and stationery, a bureau. [F, now *écritoire*, L *scriptōrium*, from *scriptus*, p.p. of *scrībere*, to write]

escrow (eskrō´) *n.* (*Law*) a fully-executed deed or engagement to do or pay something, put into the custody of a third party until some condition is fulfilled. ~*v.t.* to place (a document) in escrow. **in escrow** (of a document) executed and placed in the custody of a third party. [OF *escroue*, a scroll]

escudo (eskū´dō) *n.* (*pl.* **escudos**) 1 the standard unit of currency in Portugal. 2 a coin representing an escudo. [Port., from L *scutum*, a shield]

esculent (es´kūlənt) *a.* (*formal*) 1 fit or good for food. 2 edible. ~*n.* a thing suitable for food. [L *esculentus*, from *esca*, food]

escutcheon (iskŭch´ən) *n.* 1 a shield or shield-shaped surface charged with armorial bearings. 2 any similar surface or device. 3 a perforated plate to finish an opening, as a keyhole etc. 4 part of a ship's stern bearing her name. **blot on the escutcheon** BLOT[1]. **escutcheoned** *a.* [A-F and ONF *escuchon*, OF *escusson*, prob. from a late L *scūtiō -ōnem*, from L *scūtum*, a shield]

Esd. *abbr.* Esdras (Aprocrypha).

ESE *abbr.* east-south-east.

-ese (ēz) *suf.* 1 forming adjectives and nouns, meaning belonging to a country etc. as inhabitant(s) or language, as *Maltese*, *Chinese*. 2 forming nouns, meaning the style, language, theme etc. of a particular writer, writing etc. as *Johnsonese*, *journalese*. [OF *-eis*, L *-ensis*, pl. *-enses*]

esemplastic (esəmplas´tik) *a.* moulding, shaping or fashioning into one, unifying. [Gr. *es*, into, *hen*, neut. of *heis*, one, *plastikos*, from *plassein*, to mould]

☒ **esential** common misspelling of ESSENTIAL.

esker (es´kə), **eskar** *n.* a bank or long mound of glacial drift such as are found abundantly in Irish river valleys. [Ir. *eiscir*]

Eskimo (es´kimō), **Esquimau** *n.* (*pl.* **Eskimo, Eskimos, Esquimaux** (-mōz)) 1 a member of a group of peoples inhabiting Greenland and the adjacent parts of N America, the Aleutian Islands and Siberia. 2 any of the languages spoken by this group. ~*a.* of or relating to these peoples or their language or culture. **Eskimo dog** *n.* a breed of dog with a thick coat and curled tail, used to draw sledges. **Eskimo roll** *n.* (in canoeing) a full-circle roll under water. [N Am. Indian, eaters of raw flesh]

Usage note The word *Eskimo* can give offence, especially in Canada. *Inuit* is the preferred name for the Canadian group, and can also be used to refer to the people as a whole.

Esky® (es´ki) *n.* (*pl.* **Eskies**) in Australia, a portable container or chest for cooled drinks or food.

ESL *abbr.* English as a second language.

ESN *abbr.* (*Hist.*) educationally subnormal.

esophag-, esophago- OESOPHAG-.

esoteric (esəter´ik, ē-) *a.* 1 of philosophical doctrines, religious rites etc., meant for or intelligible only to the initiated. 2 recondite, secret, confidential. **esoterical** *a.* **esoterically** *adv.* **esotericism** (-sizm) *n.* **esotericist** *n.* [Gr. *esōterikos*, from *esōteros*, inner, compar. of *esō*, within, from *eis*, into]

ESP *abbr.* extrasensory perception.

esp. *abbr.* especially.

espadrille (espədril´) *n.* a rope-soled shoe with a cloth upper. [F, from Prov. *espardilho*, from *espart*, esparto]

espagnolette (ispanyəlet´) *n.* a bolt used for fastening a french window, one turn of the knob securing the sash both at top and bottom. [F, from *espagnol*, Spanish]

espalier (ispal´iə) *n.* 1 a lattice-work on which shrubs or fruit trees are trained flat against a wall. 2 a tree so trained. ~*v.t.* to train (a tree or shrub) in this way. [F, from It. *spalliera*, from *spalla*, a shoulder, L *spatula*, a blade]

esparto (ispah´tō) *n.* (*pl.* **espartos**) a kind of coarse grass or rush, *Stipa tenacissima*, growing in the sandy regions of northern Africa and Spain, largely used for making paper, mats etc. **esparto grass** *n.* [Sp., from L *spartum*, Gr. *sparton*, a rope made of a plant called *spartos*]

especial (ispesh´əl) *a.* 1 distinguished in a certain class or kind. 2 pre-eminent, exceptional, particular. 3 of or relating to a particular case, not general or indefinite. **especially** *adv.* [OF, from L *speciālis*, SPECIAL]

†**esperance** (es´pərəns) *n.* hope. [F, ult. from L *sperans -ntis*, pres.p. of *sperāre*, to hope]

Esperanto (espəran´tō) *n.* an international artificial language invented in 1887, based on the chief European languages. **Esperantist** *n.* [*Esperanto*, hopeful, pseudonym of the inventor, L. L. Zamenhof, 1859–1917, Polish linguist]

espial ESPY.

espiègle (espieg´lə) *a.* roguish, frolicsome. **espièglerie** (-glərē´) *n.* [F, corr. of G Till *Eulenspiegel*, a legendary German peasant with a reputation for impish practices]

espionage (es´piənahzh) *n.* 1 the act or practice of spying. 2 the employment of spies. [F, from *espionner*, from *espion*, a spy]

esplanade (esplənād´, -nahd´) *n.* 1 a level space, esp. a level walk or drive by the seaside etc. 2 a clear space between the citadel and the houses of a fortified town. [MF, from *esplaner*, to level (as Sp. *esplanada* and It. *spianata*), L *explānāre* (EX-, *plānus*, level)]

espouse (ispowz´) *v.t.* 1 to adopt, to support, defend (a cause etc.). 2 (of a man) to marry. 3 to give in marriage (to). **espousal** *n.* 1 the adoption (of a cause etc.). 2 (*usu. in pl.*) the act or ceremony of contracting a man and woman to each other; betrothal, marriage. **espouser** *n.* [OF *espouser*, from *espouse*, SPOUSE, wife, L *sponsa*, fem. p.p. of *spondēre*, to promise]

espressivo (espresē´vō) *a.* (*Mus.*) with expression. [It.]

espresso (ispres´ō), **expresso** (iks-) *n.* (*pl.* **espressos, expressos**) 1 very strong black coffee made by a machine which uses steam pressure. 2 a coffee-making machine using steam pressure for high extraction. 3 an espresso bar. **espresso bar** *n.* a coffee bar where espresso is served. [It.]

esprit (isprē´, es-) *n.* 1 wit. 2 sprightliness. **esprit de corps** (də kaw´) *n.* the spirit of comradeship, loyalty and devotion to the body or association to which one belongs. **esprit de l'escalier** (də leskal´yā) *n.* 1 the thinking of an apt or witty answer after the moment for it has passed. 2 such an answer. **esprit fort** (faw) *n.* (*pl.* **esprits forts** (isprē faws, es-)) a strong-minded person, esp. a determined freethinker in religious matters. [F, from L *spīritus*, SPIRIT]

espy (ispī´) *v.t.* (*3rd pers. sing. pres.* **espies**, *pres.p.* **espying**, *past, p.p.* **espied**) (*formal*) 1 to catch sight of. 2 to detect, to discern. **espial** (ispī´əl) *n.* 1 the act or an instance of espying. 2 spying, observation. **espier** *n.* [OF *espier*, OHG *spehōn* (G *spähen*), to SPY]

Esq. *abbr.* Esquire.

-esque (esk) *suf.* forming adjectives, meaning like, in the manner or style of, as *arabesque, burlesque, Dantesque, picturesque.* [F, from It. *-esco*, med. L *-iscus* (cp. OHG *-isc*, G *-isch*, -ISH[1])]

Esquimau, **Esquimaux** ESKIMO.

esquire (iskwīə´) *n.* 1 a title of respect, placed after a man's surname in the addresses of letters. 2 the armour-bearer or attendant on a knight, a squire. 3 a title of dignity next in degree below a knight. 4 (*US*) a title used after a lawyer's surname. ~*v.t.* to attend upon as an escort. [OF *escuyer*, L *scūtārius*, from *scūtum*, shield]

ESR *abbr.* electron spin resonance.

ESRC *abbr.* Economic and Social Research Council.

ESRO *abbr.* European Space Research Organization.

ess (es) *n.* 1 the 19th letter of the alphabet, S, s. 2 anything shaped like this. **collar of esses** COLLAR. [OE]

-ess[1] (is) *suf.* forming nouns, denoting the feminine, as *empress, murderess, seamstress, songstress* (the last two are double feminines formed on the OE fem. *-ster*, as in *spinster*). [F *-esse*, L *-issa*]

-ess[2] (es) *suf.* forming abstract nouns from adjectives, as *largess, duress.* [ME, from F *-esse*, from L *-itia*]

essay[1] (es´ā) *n.* 1 a short informal literary composition or disquisition, usu. in prose. 2 (*formal*) an attempt. **essayist** *n.* a writer of essays. [OF *essai*, ASSAY]

essay[2] (esā´) *v.t.* (*formal*) 1 to try, to attempt. 2 to test. 3 to test the quality or nature of. ~*v.i.* to make an endeavour. [see ESSAY[1]]

essence (es´əns) *n.* 1 the distinctive quality of a thing. 2 that which makes a thing what it is. 3 that which differentiates a thing from all other things, or one thing of a kind from others of the same kind. 4 an ethereal or immaterial being. 5 a solution or extract obtained by distillation. 6 the essential oil or characteristic constituent of a volatile substance. 7 perfume, scent. ~*v.t.* to perfume, to scent. **in essence** fundamentally. **of the essence** of the greatest importance. [F, from L *essentia*, from *essens -ntis*, pres.p. of *esse*, to be]

Essene (esēn´, es´-) *n.* a member of an ancient Jewish sect of religious mystics who cultivated poverty, community of goods and asceticism of life. **Essenism** (es´ə-) *n.* [L *Esseni*, pl., Gr. *Essēnoi* (etym. uncertain)]

essential (isen´shəl) *a.* 1 important in the highest degree. 2 necessary to the existence of a thing, indispensable (to). 3 real, actual, distinguished from accidental. 4 of or relating to the essence of a thing. 5 containing the essence or principle of a plant etc. 6 (*Med.*) idiopathic, not connected with another disease. 7 (of an amino or fatty acid) necessary for the normal growth of the body, but not synthesized by the body. ~*n.* 1 that which is fundamental or characteristic. 2 an indispensable element. 3 a point of the highest importance. **essential character** *n.* the quality which serves to distinguish one genus, species etc. from another. **essential element** *n.* any chemical element which is necessary for the normal growth of an organism. **essential harmony** *n.* (*Mus.*) a harmony belonging to one particular key. **essentialism** *n.* (*Philos.*) the doctrine that things have essential characteristics which define their nature. **essentialist** *n., a.* **essentiality** (-shial´-) *n.* **essentially** *adv.* **essentialness** *n.* **essential oil** *n.* a volatile oil containing the characteristic constituent or principle of a plant, usu. obtained by distillation with water. **essential proposition** *n.* a proposition that predicates of a subject something entailed in its definition. [late L *essentiālis*, see ESSENCE]

Essex man (esiks man´) *n.* the stereotypical southern English working class man, lacking in style but with a large disposable income. **Essex girl** *n.* Essex man's female equivalent.

EST *abbr.* 1 Eastern Standard Time. 2 electro-shock treatment.

est. *abbr.* 1 established. 2 estimated.

-est[1] (ist) *suf.* forming the superlative degree of adjectives and adverbs, as *richest, tallest, liveliest.* [OE *-est, -ast, -ost, -st*, Gmc. *-isto-* (cp. Gr. *-isto-*)]

†-est[2] (ist), **-st** (st) *suf.* forming the 2nd pers. sing. of verbs, as *givest, gavest, canst, didst.* [OE *-est, -ast, -st*]

establish (istab´lish) *v.t.* 1 to set upon a firm foundation, to found, institute. 2 to settle or secure firmly (in office, opinion etc.). 3 to make firm or lasting (as a belief, custom, one's health etc.). 4 **a** to ascertain. **b** to substantiate, verify, put beyond dispute. 5 to ordain officially and settle on a permanent basis (as a Church). **to establish a suit** (in cards) to exhaust all higher cards of a particular suit that are in the hands of opponents. **established Church** *n.* the Church established by law, the State Church. **establisher** *n.* **establishment** (-mənt) *n.* 1 the act of establishing. 2 the state of being established. 3 a permanent organization such as the army, navy or civil service, a staff of servants etc. 4 a public institution, business organization or private household. 5 (*often* **Establishment**) the group of people who are in positions of power and influence in society and the State, usu. perceived as being middle-aged and conservative. **establishmentarian** (-teə´ri-) *n.* an advocate or supporter of an established Church. ~*a.* advocating or supporting an established Church. **establishmentarianism** *n.* [OF *establiss-*, stem of *establir*, L *stabilīre* (*stabilis*, firm)]

estaminet (estam´inā) *n.* a small cafe in which wine etc. is sold. [F, etym. uncertain]

estancia (istan´siə, -thiə) *n.* 1 in Spanish America, a cattle-farm, ranch or country estate. 2 the residence on this. **estanciero** (estansieə´rō, -thyeə´rō) *n.* (*pl.* **estancieros**) a Spanish-American cattle-farmer. [Sp., from med. L *stantia*, from *stare*, to stand]

estate (istāt´) *n.* 1 property, esp. a landed property. 2 (*Law*) a person's interest in lands and tenements (*real estate*) or movable property (*personal estate*). 3 a person's assets and liabilities taken collectively. 4 land built on either privately or by a local authority for housing (*a housing estate*) or for factories and businesses (*an industrial estate*). 5 a property given over to the growing of a particular crop, as *rubber estate.* 6 (*formal*) state, condition, circumstances, standing, rank. 7 a class or order invested with political rights (in the United Kingdom the three estates are the Lords spiritual, the Lords temporal and the Commons). 8 (*coll.*) an estate car. **estate agent** *n.* 1 an agent concerned with the renting or sale of real estate. 2 the manager of a landed property. **estate car** *n.* a car with a large open space behind the passenger seats, and a rear door. **estate duty** *n.* death duty on property (until 1976). **estate of the realm** *n.* any of the social or political estates in a monarchy, esp. in the United Kingdom. [OF *estat*, L *statum*, acc. of *status*, STATE]

esteem (istēm´) *v.t.* 1 to hold in high estimation, to regard with respect; to prize. 2 (*formal*) to consider, to reckon. ~*n.* opinion or judgement as to merit or demerit, esp. a favourable opinion; respect, regard. [OF *estimer*, L *aestimāre*, to ESTIMATE[1]]

ester (es´tə) *n.* (*Chem.*) an organic compound derived by the replacement of hydrogen in an acid by an organic radical. **esterify** (-ter´ifī) *v.t.* (*3rd pers. sing. pres.* **esterifies**, *pres.p.* **esterifying**, *past*, *p.p.* **esterified**) to change into an ester. **esterification** (-fikā´shən) *n.* [coined word]

Esth. *abbr.* Esther (Old Testament and Apocrypha).

esthesia, esthesis AESTHESIA.

esthete, esthetic AESTHETE.

estimable (es´timəbəl) *a.* worthy of esteem or regard. **estimably** *adv.*

estimate[1] (es´timāt) *v.t.* 1 to compute the value of, to appraise. 2 to form an opinion about. 3 †to esteem. **estimation** (-ā´shən) *n.* 1 the act of estimating. 2 opinion or judgement. 3 esteem. **estimative** *a.* **estimator** *n.* [L *aestimātus*, p.p. of *aestimāre*, to value]

estimate[2] (es´timət) *n.* 1 an approximate calculation of the value, number, extent etc. of anything. 2 the result of this. 3 a contractor's statement of the sum for which he would undertake a piece of work. 4 (*pl.*) a statement of probable expenditure submitted to Parliament or other authoritative body. 5 a judgement respecting character, circumstances etc.

estival, estivate AESTIVAL.

Estonian (estō´niən, is-) *a.* of or relating to Estonia, one of the Baltic republics, its language or its people. ~*n.* 1 a native or inhabitant of Estonia. 2 the language of Estonia, related to Finnish and Hungarian.

estop (istop´) *v.t.* (*pres.p.* **estopping**, *past*, *p.p.* **estopped**) (*Law*) to bar, preclude, prevent (from). **estoppage** (-ij) *n.* **estoppel** (-əl) *n.* 1 (*Law*) **a** an act or statement that cannot legally be denied. **b** a plea alleging such an act or statement. [A-F *estopper*, OF *estouper* (late L *stuppāre*, to stuff with tow, from L *stuppa*, tow)]

estovers (istō´vəz) *n.pl.* (*Hist.*) 1 necessaries or supplies allowed by law, esp. wood which a tenant could take from a landlord's estate for repairs etc. 2 an allowance to a person out of an estate for support. [OF *estover*, *estovoir*, to be necessary]

estrade (istrahd´) *n.* a slightly raised platform, a dais. [F, from Sp. *estrado*, L *strātum*, neut. p.p. of *sternere*, to spread]

estrange (istrānj´) *v.t.* 1 to alienate, to make indifferent or distant in feeling. 2 to cut off from friendship. 3 to make (oneself) a stranger to. **estranged** *a.* 1 having been estranged. 2 (of a husband or wife) no longer living with their spouse. **estrangement** *n.* **estranger** *n.* [OF *estranger*, L *extrāneāre*, from *extrāneus*, STRANGE]

estray (istrā´) *n.* a domestic animal, as a horse, ox etc. found straying or without an owner. [A-F, from *estraier*, to stray, see ASTRAY]

estreat (istrēt´) *n.* 1 (*Law*) a true copy of an original writing, esp. of penalties set down in a court record. 2 to enforce (a fine or a recognizance). ~*v.t.* 1 to extract or copy from the records of a court. 2 to levy a fine under estreat. [A-F *estrete*, OF *estraite*, fem. p.p. of *estraire*, L *extrahere*, to EXTRACT[1]]

estrogen OESTROGEN.

estrus, estrum OESTRUS.

estuary (es´chuəri) *n.* (*pl.* **estuaries**) the mouth of a river etc. in which the tide meets the current; a firth. **estuarial** (-eə´riəl), **estuarian** *a.* **estuarine** (-rīn) *a.* **Estuary English** *n.* an informal form of English spoken esp. by young people in London, Kent, Essex and other parts of the Home Counties. [L *aestuārium*, from *aestuāre*, to surge, from *aestus*, heat, surge, tide]

e.s.u. *abbr.* electrostatic unit.

esurient (isū´riənt) *a.* (*formal or facet.*) 1 hungry. 2 needy. **esurience** *n.* **esuriently** *adv.* [L *ēsuriens -ntem*, pres.p. of *ēsurīre*, desiderative from *ēsus*, p.p. of *edere*, to eat]

-et[1] (it) *suf.* forming diminutive nouns, as *chaplet*, *circlet*, *coronet*, *dulcet*, *russet*, *violet*. [OF *-et*, *-ette*, etym. uncertain (cp. It. *-etto*, *-etta*)]

-et[2] (it), **-ete** (ēt) *suf.* forming nouns denoting a person involved in some activity as *poet*, *athlete*. [Gr. *-ētēs*]

ETA[1] *abbr.* estimated time of arrival.

ETA[2] (et´ə) *n.* a Basque separatist terrorist organization. [initials of the Basque name *Euzkadi ta Azkatasuna*]

eta (ē´tə, ā´-) *n.* the seventh letter of the Greek alphabet (Η, η). [Gr. *ēta*]

étagère (ātazheə´) *n.* a stand with open shelves for ornaments etc. [F, from *étage*, shelf]

et al. (et al´) *abbr.* and others. [L *et alii*, *aliae* or *alia*]

etalon (et´əlon) *n.* (*Physics*) a device which measures wavelengths by means of reflections from silvered glass or quartz plates. [F, a standard]

etc. *abbr.* etcetera.

etcetera (itset´ərə), **et cetera** *adv.* and the rest, and so on. **etceteras** *n.pl.* 1 sundries, extras. 2 things unspecified. [L *et cetera*, and (the) rest]

Usage note Pronunciation as (ek-) is best avoided.

etch (ech) *v.t.* 1 to produce or reproduce (a picture) on a metal plate, for printing copies, by engraving with an acid through the lines previously drawn with a needle on a coated surface. 2 to engrave (a metal plate) in this way. 3 to corrode or eat away. 4 to impress on the mind. ~*v.i.* to practise this art. **etchant** *n.* an acid or other corrosive used in etching. **etcher** *n.* **etching** *n.* 1 the act of etching. 2 an impression taken from an etched plate. **etching ground** *n.* the coating (of wax etc.) of the plate for etching. **etching needle** *n.* a sharp-pointed instrument for making lines in the etching ground. [Dut. *etsen*, G *ätzen*, OHG *ezjan*, Gmc. *atjan* (causal), to make eat]

ETD *abbr.* estimated time of departure.

-ete -ET[2].

eternal (itœ´nəl) *a.* 1 without beginning or end. 2 everlasting, perpetual. 3 unchanging. 4 (*coll.*) incessant, constant. **the Eternal** the everlasting God, the Deity. **Eternal City** *n.* the city of Rome. **eternality** (-nal´iti) *n.* †**eternalize, eternalise, eternize, eternise** *v.t.* 1 to make eternal. 2 to prolong indefinitely. 3 to immortalize. **eternally** *adv.* **eternalness** *n.* **eternal triangle** *n.* a sexual or emotional relationship involving three people, usu. two of one sex and one of the other, often resulting in tension or conflict. [OF *eternel*, late L *aeternālis*, from *aeternus* (*aeviternus*, from *aevum*, age)]

eternity (itœ´niti) *n.* (*pl.* **eternities**) 1 eternal duration. 2 endless past or future time. 3 unchangeableness of being. 4 future life after death. 5 immortality of fame. 6 (*coll.*) a very long time. 7 (*pl.*) the eternal realities. **eternity ring** *n.* a ring set all round with stones, signifying continuity. [OF *eternité*, L *aeternitas -tātem*, from *aeternus* (see ETERNAL)]

etesian (itē´zhiən) *a.* 1 annual. 2 blowing periodically. **Etesian winds** *n.pl.* periodical winds, esp. northwesterly winds blowing for about six weeks in summer in the eastern Mediterranean. [L *etēsius*, Gr. *etēsios*, from *etos*, year]

ETH *abbr.* Ethiopia (IVR).

eth (edh), **edh** *n.* a letter (Ð, ð) used in Icelandic and in Old English (= th).

-eth[1] -TH[1].

†**-eth**[2] (ith), **-th** *suf.* forming the 3rd pers. sing. pres. of verbs, as *goeth*, *saith*. [OE *-eth*, *-ath*, *-th*]

ethanal (eth´ənal) *n.* (*Chem.*) acetaldehyde.

ethane (ē´thān, eth´-) *n.* (*Chem.*) a colourless and odourless gaseous compound of the paraffin series. **ethanediol** (-dīol) *n.* ethylene glycol. [*ether*]

ethanoate (ēthan´ōāt) *n.* (*Chem.*) a salt or ester of acetic acid, acetate. **ethanoic acid** (ethənō´ik) *n.* acetic acid.
ethanol (eth´ənol) *n.* (*Chem.*) a colourless liquid produced by fermenting sugars and constituting the intoxicating agent in various drinks, alcohol.
ethene (eth´ēn) *n.* (*Chem.*) ethylene.
ether (ē´thə) *n.* **1** (*Chem.*) a light, volatile and inflammable fluid, produced by the distillation of alcohol with an acid, esp. sulphuric acid, and used as an anaesthetic or a solvent. **2** any of a class of similar compounds, with an oxygen atom joined to two alkyl groups. **3** (*also* **aether**) a fluid of extreme subtlety and elasticity (formerly) assumed to exist throughout space and between the particles of all substances, forming the medium of transmission of light and heat. **4** (*also* **aether**) the upper air, the higher regions of the sky, the clear sky. **ethereal** (ithiə´riəl), **etherial** *a.* **1** of the nature of ether. **2** resembling celestial ether, light, airy, tenuous, subtle, exquisite, impalpable, spiritual. **3** (*Chem.*) of or relating to ether. **ethereality** (-al´-) *n.* **etherealize**, **etherealise** *v.t.* **1** to convert into ether. **2** to render spiritual. **etherealization** (-zā´shən) *n.* **ethereally** *adv.* **ethereal oil** *n.* (*Chem.*) an essential oil produced by distillation. †**ethereous** (ithiə´riəs) *a.* ethereal. **etheric** (ither´ik) *a.* **etherify** (ē´thərifī) *v.t.* (*3rd pers. sing. pres.* **etherifies**, *pres.p.* **etherifying**, *past, p.p.* **etherified**) (*Chem.*) to make or convert into an ether. **etherification** (-fikā´shən) *n.* **etherism** *n.* (*Med.*) the effects produced by the administration of ether as an anaesthetic. **etherize**, **etherise** *v.t.* **1** (*Chem.*) to convert into ether. **2** (*Med.*) to anaesthetize with ether. **etherization** (-zā´shən) *n.* [L *aether*, Gr. *aithēr*, from root of *aithein*, to burn]
Ethernet® (ē´thənet) *n.* (*Comput.*) a type of local area network.
ethic (eth´ik) *n.* a moral principle or a set of principles. ~*a.* ethical. **ethical** *a.* **1** treating of or relating to morals. **2** dealing with moral questions or theory. **3** conforming to a recognized standard. **4** (*Med.*) (of a drug) not advertised to the public and available only on prescription. **ethical dative** *n.* ETHIC DATIVE (under ETHIC). **ethical investment** *n.* the practice of investing money only in those companies which are not involved in racial discrimination or in products causing potential harm to health, life or the environment, as cigarettes, nuclear weapons. **ethicality** (-kal´-) *n.* **ethically** *adv.* **ethic dative** *n.* (*Gram.*) the dative of a personal pronoun indicating indirect interest in the fact stated, e.g. 'I will buy *me* a hat'. **ethicism** (-sizm) *n.* **ethicist** *n.* **ethicize** (-sīz), **ethicise** *v.t.* **1** to make ethical. **2** to treat ethically. **ethics** *n.pl.* **1** the science of morals. **2** a system of principles and rules of conduct. **3** the whole field of moral science, including political and social science, law, jurisprudence etc. [L *ēthicus*, Gr. *ēthikos*, from ETHOS]
Ethiopian (ēthiō´piən) *a.* **1** of or relating to Ethiopia, a country in north-eastern Africa, or its inhabitants. **2** of or relating to a biogeographical region consisting of Africa south of the Sahara. ~*n.* **1** a native or inhabitant of Ethiopia. **2** †a person of African descent. †**Ethiop** (ē´thiop) *n.* **Ethiopic** (-op´-) *a.* of or relating to modern Ethiopia. ~*n.* **1** the liturgical language of the Church in Ethiopia. **2** the group of modern Semitic languages spoken in the region of Ethiopia, incl. Amharic. [L *Aethiops -pis*, Gr. *Aithiops -pos* (etym. uncertain)]
ethmoid (eth´moid), **ethmoidal** (-moi´-) *a.* resembling a sieve. ~*n.* the ethmoid bone. **ethmoid bone** *n.* a cellular bone situated between the orbital processes at the root of the nose, through which the olfactory nerves pass. [Gr. *ēthmoeidēs* (*ēthmos*, sieve)]
ethn- ETHNO-.
ethnarch (eth´nahk) *n.* (*Hist.*) the governor of a people or district in the Roman and Byzantine empires. **ethnarchy** *n.* [Gr. *ethnos*, nation, *archos*, ruler]
ethnic (eth´nik) *a.* **1** of or relating to or characteristic of a race, people or culture. **2** of or relating to the culture or traditions of a particular people. **3** of or relating to a group within a community which has a racial or cultural identity different from that of the majority group. **4** of or relating to the food, clothing etc. used by such a group. **5** belonging to a nation by birth or origin rather than by acquired nationality. **6** †not Jewish nor Christian. ~*n.* **1** a member of an ethnic minority. **2** a heathen or pagan. **ethnical** *a.* of or relating to ethnology. **ethnically** *adv.* **ethnic cleansing** *n.* the systematic persecution of a distinct ethnic group within a community, members of which are killed, imprisoned, forced to move to another area etc. †**ethnicism** (-sizm) *n.* **1** heathenism, paganism. **2** a non-Jewish and non-Christian religion. **ethnicity** *n.* **ethnic minority** *n.* (*pl.* **ethnic minorities**) a (relatively) small group within a community of different racial or cultural origin, and remaining unassimilated. **ethnics** *n.* ethnology. [L *ethnicus*, Gr. *ethnikos*, from *ethnos*, nation]
ethno- (eth´nō), **ethn-** *comb. form* ethnic, ethnological. [Gr. *ethnos*, nation]
ethnoarchaeology (ethnōahkiol´əji), (*N Am.*) **ethnoarcheology** *n.* the scientific study of the cultural institutions of a society, through the examination of its buildings, artefacts etc. **ethnoarchaeological** (-loj´-) *a.* **ethnoarchaeologically** *adv.* **ethnoarchaeologist** (-ol´-) *n.*
ethnobotany (ethnōbot´əni) *n.* (the study of) the knowledge and use of plants by traditional societies. **ethnobotanical** (-botan´ikəl) *a.* **ethnobotanically** *adv.* **ethnobotanist** (-bot´-) *n.*
ethnocentrism (ethnōsen´trizm) *n.* the mental habit of viewing the world solely from the perspective of one's own culture. **ethnocentric** *a.* **ethnocentrically** *adv.* **ethnocentricity** (-tris´iti) *n.*
ethnography (ethnog´rəfi) *n.* the scientific study and description of different human societies. **ethnographer** *n.* **ethnographic** (-graf´-), **ethnographical** *a.* **ethnographically** *adv.*
ethnology (ethnol´əji) *n.* the science which treats of the varieties of the human race. **ethnologic** (-loj´-), **ethnological** *a.* **ethnologically** *adv.* **ethnologist** (-nol´-) *n.* a student of ethnology.
ethnomethodology (ethnōmethədol´əji) *n.* the study of everyday human communication by speech. **ethnomethodological** (-loj´-) *a.* **ethnomethodologist** (-dol´-) *n.*
ethnomusicology (ethnōmūzikol´əji) *n.* the study of the music of different societies. **ethnomusicological** (-loj´-) *a.* **ethnomusicologically** *adv.* **ethnomusicologist** (-kol´-) *n.*
ethogram (ē´thəgram) *n.* (*Zool.*) the typical behaviour and activities of an animal, noted in a list. [Gr. *ethos*, ETHOS]
ethology (ēthol´əji) *n.* **1** the science of animal behaviour. **2** the scientific study of the formation of patterns of human behaviour. **ethologic** (-loj´-), **ethological** *a.* **ethologist** *n.* [L and Gr. *ēthologia*]
ethos (ē´thos) *n.* the characteristic spirit, character, disposition or genius of a people, community, institution, system etc. [Gr., character, disposition]
ethoxyethane (ēthoksiē´thān) *n.* (*Chem.*) ether, as used as an anaesthetic.
ethyl (eth´il, ē´thīl) *n.* (*Chem.*) a monovalent fatty hydrocarbon radical of the paraffin series, forming the base of common alcohol and ether, acetic acid etc. **ethyl alcohol** *n.* the ordinary alcohol of commerce. **ethylate** *v.t.* to introduce an ethyl group into (a molecule). **ethylene** (eth´ilēn) *n.* a hydrocarbon gas found in petroleum and natural gas, used in the manufacture of polythene etc. **ethylene glycol** *n.* a colourless soluble liquid used as an antifreeze and in

the manufacture of polyesters. **ethylenic** (-lē´nik) *a.* [ether]

ethyne (ē´thīn, eth´-) *n.* (*Chem.*) acetylene.

-etic (et´ik) *suf.* forming nouns and adjectives, meaning (a person or thing) of the nature of or serving as, as *athletic, ascetic, prosthetic.* [Gr. *-ētikos, -etikos*]

etiolate (ē´tiəlāt) *v.t.* **1** to blanch (a plant) by keeping in the dark. **2** to make (a person) pale and unhealthy. *~v.i.* to become blanched by deprivation of light. **etiolation** (-ā´shən) *n.* [F *étioler*, Norm. F *s'étieuler*, to grow into haulm, from *éteule*, OF *esteule*, L *stipula*, straw]

etiology AETIOLOGY.

etiquette (et´iket) *n.* **1** the conventional rules of behaviour in polite society. **2** the established rules of precedence and ceremonial in a court. **3** the codes of formal behaviour between members of a profession etc. [F *étiquette*, a TICKET]

Etonian (itō´niən) *n.* a person educated or being educated at Eton College. *~a.* of or relating to Eton College. **Eton collar** *n.* a wide, starched collar worn outside the jacket. **Eton crop** *n.* a woman's haircut, very short and flat. **Eton fives** *n.* a form of the game of fives in which the court has three walls. **Eton jacket** *n.* a boy's untailed dress coat.

étrier (ā´triā) *n.* a small rope ladder used in mountaineering. [F, a stirrup]

Etrurian (itroo´riən) *a.* of or relating to Etruria, an ancient country in central Italy. *~n.* a native or inhabitant of Etruria. [L *Etrūria*]

Etruscan (itrŭs´kən) *a.* Etrurian. *~n.* **1** an Etrurian. **2** the language of Etruria. **Etruscan vases** *n.pl.* vases found in Etruscan tombs, but which are of Grecian design. [L *Etruscus*, from as ETRURIAN]

et seq., et seqq. *abbr.* and the following (passage(s), page(s) etc.). [L *et sequentes, et sequentia*]

-ette (et) *suf.* **1** forming nouns meaning diminutive, as *cigarette, kitchenette.* **2** forming female nouns, as *brunette*, often offensive, as *jockette.* **3** forming nouns meaning imitation, as *flannelette, leatherette.* [OF *-ette*, fem. of *-et* (dim. suf.)]

étude (ātūd´, -tūd´) *n.* (*Mus.*) a short composition written mainly to test or develop a player's technical skill. [Fr, a study]

etui (ātwē´, et-) *n.* a small case for pins, needles etc. [F, a case, sheath]

-etum (ē´təm) *suf.* forming nouns meaning (a place or garden containing) a collection of plants, as *arboretum, pinetum.* [L]

etyma ETYMON.

etymology (etimol´əji) *n.* (*pl.* **etymologies**) **1** the branch of linguistics that treats of the origin and history of words. **2** the history of the origin and modification of a particular word; derivation. **3** an account of the derivation of a word or words. **etymologic** (-loj´-), **etymological** *a.* **etymologically** *adv.* **etymologist** *n.* **etymologize, etymologise** *v.t.* to give or trace the etymology of. *~v.i.* **1** to study etymology. **2** to search into the source of words. **3** to propose etymologies for words. [OF *ethimologie*, L *etymologia*, Gr. *etumologia* (*etumos*, real, rel. to *eteos*, true)]

Usage note The subjects *etymology* and *entomology* should not be confused: *etymology* is concerned with words, and *entomology* with insects.

etymon (et´imon) *n.* (*pl.* **etymons, etyma** (-mə)) the primitive or root form of a word. [L from Gr., neut. of *etumos*, see ETYMOLOGY]

EU *abbr.* European Union.

Eu *chem. symbol* europium.

eu- (ū) *comb. form* good, well, pleasant, as in *eulogy, euphony.* [Gr., well]

eucaine (ūkān´) *n.* a form of local anaesthetic. [*co*caine]

eucalyptus (ūkəlip´təs) *n.* (*pl.* **eucalyptuses, eucalypti** (-tī)) **1** (*also* **eucalypt**) any evergreen myrtaceous tree belonging to the Australasian genus *Eucalyptus*, comprising the gum-trees. **2** eucalyptus oil. **eucalyptus oil** *n.* an aromatic oil obtained from eucalyptus leaves, used medicinally. [Gr. *kaluptos*, covered, from *kaluptein*, to cover (the flower being protected by a cap)]

eucaryon, eucaryote EUKARYON.

eucharis (ū´kəris) *n.* a bulbous plant from S America of the genus *Eucharis*, cultivated in hothouses for its pure white bell-shaped flowers. [Gr. *eucharis* (*charis*, grace)]

Eucharist (ū´kərist) *n.* **1** the sacrament of the Lord's Supper. **2** the elements, bread and wine, given in this sacrament. **Eucharistic** (-ris´-), **Eucharistical** *a.* [OF *eucariste*, late L and Gr. *eucharistia*, from *eucharistos*, grateful (EU-, *charizesthai*, to show favour to, from *charis*, grace)]

euchlorine (ūklaw´rēn), **euchlorin** (-rin) *n.* a yellow explosive gas with bleaching properties, obtained from a mixture of chlorate of potash and dilute hydrochloric acid. [Gr. *chlōros*, green, -INE (on analogy of CHLORINE)]

euchre (ū´kə) *n.* an orig. American card game for several persons, usu. four, with a pack from which the cards from the twos to the nines have been excluded. *~v.t.* **1** to beat by taking three of the five tricks at euchre. **2** (*Austral., coll.*) to beat thoroughly, to ruin. **3** to outwit. [etym. uncertain]

Euclidean (ūklid´iən) *a.* of or relating to Euclid or to the axioms and postulates of his geometry. [*Euclid* (L *Euclideus*, Gr. *Eukleideios*, fl. 300 BC Alexandrian mathematician)]

eudemonism (ūdē´mənizm), **eudaemonism** *n.* the system of ethics which makes the pursuit of happiness the basis and criterion of moral conduct. **eudemonic** (-mon´-) *a.* **eudemonics** *n.pl.* eudemonism. **eudemonist** *n.* **eudemonistic** (-nis´-) *a.* [Gr. *eudaimōn*, happy]

eudiometer (ūdiom´itə) *n.* an instrument, consisting of a graduated glass jar with wires for electric sparking, used to measure changes in volume of gases during chemical reactions. **eudiometric** (-met´-), **eudiometrical** *a.* **eudiometrically** *adv.* **eudiometry** (-diom´-) *n.* the measurement of the composition of a gaseous mixture by means of the eudiometer. [Gr. *eudios* (EU-, *Di-*, stem of *Zeus*, gen. *Dios*, the God of the sky)]

eugenic (ūjen´ik) *a.* of or relating to the development and improvement of offspring, esp. human offspring, through selective breeding. **eugenically** *adv.* **eugenics** *n.* the science or political beliefs relating to this. **eugenicist** *n.* **eugenism** (ū´-) *n.* **eugenist** *n.*

euglena (ūglē´nə) *n.* a single-celled aquatic animal of the genus *Euglena*, with a single flagellum. [Gr. *glēnē*, eyeball]

euhemerism (ūhē´mərizm) *n.* the theory formulated by Euhemerus of Messenia in Sicily (about 300 BC), that the classic gods are merely deified national kings and heroes, and their miraculous feats exaggerated traditions of actual events. **euhemerist** *n.* **euhemeristic** (-ris´-) *a.* **euhemerize, euhemerise** *v.i.* to follow euhemerism. *~v.t.* to treat or explain (myths) rationalistically.

eukaryon (ūkar´iən), **eucaryon** *n.* a highly organized cell nucleus, with DNA in the form of chromosomes, characteristic of higher organisms. **eukaryote** (-riōt) *n.* an organism which has such cell nuclei. **eukaryotic** (-iot´ik) *a.* [Gr. *karuon*, kernel]

eulachon (ū´ləkən) *n.* the candlefish of the N Pacific. [Chinook *ulâkân*]

eulogy (ū´ləji) *n.* (*pl.* **eulogies**) **1** praise, encomium, panegyric. **2** a writing or speech in praise of a person. **3** (*N Am.*) a funeral oration. **eulogist** *n.* **eulogistic** (-jis´-), **eulogistical** *a.* **eulogistically** *adv.* **eulogium** (ūlō´jiəm) *n.* (*pl.* **eulogiums, eulogia** (-iə)) eulogy.

eulogize, eulogise *v.t.* **1** to speak or write of in praise. **2** to commend, to extol. [late L *eulogium*, Gr. *eulogia*]

eunuch (ū´nək) *n.* **1** a castrated man, esp. an attendant in a harem, or a state functionary in Oriental palaces and under the Roman emperors. **2** an ineffectual or powerless person. ~*a.* **1** castrated; emasculate. **2** unproductive. ~†*v.t.* to make into a eunuch. **eunuchize, eunuchise** *v.t.* [L *eunūchus*, Gr. *eunouchos*, one in charge of a bedchamber (*eunē*, bed, *och-*, stem of *echein*, to hold)]

euonymus (ūon´iməs) *n.* any tree or shrub of the genus *Euonymus*, containing the spindle tree. [L, from Gr. *euonumos*, of good name, luck (*onoma*, Aeolic *onuma*, name)]

eupatrid (ūpat´rid) *n.* (*pl.* **eupatrids, eupatridae** (-dē)) a member of the hereditary aristocracy of Attica, a patrician. [Gr. *eupatridēs* (*patēr*, father)]

eupeptic (ūpep´tik) *a.* **1** having a good digestion. **2** of or relating to or characteristic of good digestion. **eupepsia** (-siə), **eupepsy** *n.* **eupepticity** (-tis´-) *n.* [Gr. *eupeptos* (*peptein*, to digest)]

euphemism (ū´fəmizm) *n.* **1** the use of a soft or pleasing term or phrase for one that is harsh or offensive. **2** such a term or phrase. **euphemist** *n.* **euphemistic** (-mis´-) *a.* **euphemistically** *adv.* **euphemize, euphemise** *v.t.* **1** to speak of euphemistically. **2** to express in euphemism. ~*v.i.* to speak in euphemism. [Gr. *euphēmismos*, from *euphēmos* (*phēmē*, speaking, fame)]

Usage note The linguistic practices of *euphemism* and *euphuism* should not be confused: *euphemism* is expressing something in alternative, more acceptable, terms, and *euphuism* using high-flown language.

euphonium (ūfō´niəm) *n.* (*pl.* **euphoniums**) (*Mus.*) a brass instrument related to the tuba. [see EUPHONY]

euphony (ū´fəni) *n.* (*pl.* **euphonies**) **1** an agreeable sound. **2** smoothness or agreeableness of sound in words and phrases. **3** a pleasing pronunciation. **4** the tendency towards greater ease of pronunciation in phonetic change. **euphonic** (ūfon´-), **euphonical** *a.* **euphonically** *adv.* **euphonious** (ūfō´-) *a.* **euphoniously** *adv.* **euphoniousness** *n.* **euphonize, euphonise** *v.t.* [F *euphonie*, Gr. *euphōnia* (*phōnē*, voice)]

euphorbia (ūfaw´biə) *n.* any plant of the genus *Euphorbia*, including the spurges, comprising about 700 species, many of which are poisonous while others have medicinal qualities. **euphorbiaceous** (-ā´shəs) *a.* [L *euphorbea*, from *Euphorbus*, Greek physician]

euphoria (ūfaw´riə) *n.* a feeling of well-being, supreme content, esp. exaggerated or baseless. **euphoriant** *a.* inducing euphoria. ~*n.* a euphoriant drug. **euphoric** (-for´ik) *a.* **euphorically** *adv.* [Gr.]

euphrasy (ū´frəsi) *n.* (*pl.* **euphrasies**) the eyebright. [med. L and Gr. *euphrasia*, cheerfulness]

euphuism (ū´fūizm) *n.* a pedantic affectation of elegant and high-flown language. **euphuist** *n.* **euphuistic** (-is´-) *a.* **euphuistically** *adv.* †**euphuize, euphuise** *v.i.* [from *Euphues* (1578–80), a work by John Lyly, which brought the style into vogue (Gr. *euphuēs*, well-grown or well-endowed (*phuein*, to produce))]

Usage note See note under EUPHEMISM.

Eur. *abbr.* European.

Eur- EURO-.

Eurasian (ūrā´zhən) *a.* **1** of mixed European and Asian descent; esp. formerly in British India etc., born of a European father and an Asian mother. **2** of or relating to both Europe and Asia. ~*n.* a person of European and Asian descent.

Euratom (ūrat´əm) *n.* the European Atomic Energy Community of 1958 in which France, Belgium, West Germany, Italy, the Netherlands and Luxembourg united for the peaceful development of nuclear energy.

eureka (ūrē´kə) *int.* used to express exultation over a discovery. ~*n.* **1** an exclamation of 'eureka'. **2** a discovery, an invention. [Gr. *heurēka*, I have found (Archimedes' exclamation on discovering a test for the purity of the gold in Hiero's crown, involving the displacement of water)]

eurhythmics (ūridh´miks), (*N Am.*) **eurythmics** *n.* the scientific use or art of rhythmical movement, esp. as applied to dancing and gymnastic exercises. **eurhythmic, eurhythmical** *a.* **1** of or relating to eurhythmics. **2** having a pleasing harmony or rhythm. **eurhythmy** (-mi) *n.*

Euro (ū´rō) *n.* (*pl.* **Euros**) **1** a European. **2** a Eurodollar. ~*a.* European.

Euro- (ū´rō), **Eur-** *comb. form* of or relating to Europe or Europeans, or the European Union.

euro[1] (ū´rō) *n.* (*pl.* **euros**) (*Austral.*) a wallaby of S and Central Australia, *Macropus robustus*. [Austral. Abor.]

euro[2] (ū´rō) *n.* (*pl.* **euros**) the proposed European Union unit of currency. [*Europe*]

Eurobond (ū´rōbond) *n.* a bond issued in a European country, but in one of the other European currencies.

Eurocentric (ūrōsen´trik) *a.* perceiving European culture, history etc. as of central importance in the world. **Eurocentrism** *n.*

Eurocheque (ū´rōchek) *n.* **1** a type of cheque able to draw on certain banks in other European countries on receipt of the appropriate card. **2** the banking system enabling the use of these cheques.

Eurocommunism (ūrōkom´ūnizm) *n.* the form of Communism followed by western European Communist parties, more pragmatic than, and independent of, the Soviet version. **Eurocommunist** *n., a.*

Eurocrat (ū´rəkrat) *n.* an official involved in the administration of any part of the European Union.

Euro-currency (ū´rōkŭrənsi) *n.* (*pl.* **Euro-currencies**) currency of a country outside Europe held on deposit in a European bank.

Eurodollar (ū´rōdolə) *n.* a US dollar held in European banks to ease the financing of trade.

Euro-election (ū´rōilekshən) *n.* an election for the European Parliament.

Euromarket (ū´rōmahkit) *n.* **1** the money markets of the European Union collectively. **2** the market of any one of the Euro-currencies. **3** the European Union considered as a unified market for goods and services.

European (ūrəpē´ən) *a.* **1** of or relating to, happening in, or extending over, Europe. **2** native to Europe. **3** of or relating to, or concerning, Europe as a whole, rather than an individual country. **4** of or relating to the European Union. **5** in favour of, or supporting the European Union, Europhile. ~*n.* **1** a native or inhabitant of Europe. **2** a person of European descent. **3** a person who is interested in or supports the European Union. **European Community** *n.* the official name of the European Union before November 1993. **European Economic Community** *n.* the orig. free trade association of 6 countries, founded in 1957, which expanded and became the European Community in 1967. **Europeanism** *n.* **Europeanize, Europeanise** *v.t.* **Europeanization** (-zā´shən) *n.* **European plan** *n.* (*N Am.*) the system of charging for a hotel room without including meals. **European Union** *n.* an economic and political association of 15 W European countries, based on free trade among all the members, which developed out of the European Economic Community and the European Community.

Europhile (ū´rōfīl) *n.* (*coll.*) a person who is in favour of the European Union and its institutions. ~*a.* of or relating to the opinions and attitudes of a Europhile.

Europhobe (ū´rōfōb) *n.* (*coll.*) a person who dislikes the European Union and its institutions and who is against further links with Europe. ~*a.* of or relating to the opinions and attitudes of a Europhobe. **Europhobia** *n.* **Europhobic** *a.*

europium (ūrō´piəm) *n.* (*Chem.*) an extremely rare metallic element, soft and silvery white, at. no. 63, chem. symbol Eu.

Euro-rebel (ū´rōrebəl) *n.* a politician who disagrees with their party's official line on the European Union.

Eurosceptic (ū´rōskeptik) *n.* a person who is sceptical about the benefits to the UK of membership of the European Union, and who is opposed to further integration into the Union. **Euroscepticism** (-tisizm) *n.*

Eurotunnel (ū´rōtŭnəl) *n.* the Channel tunnel.

Eurovision (ū´rəvizhən) *n.* the network of European television production and relay run by the European Broadcasting Union.

eurythmics EURHYTHMICS.

Euskarian (ūskeə´riən) *a.* Basque. ~*n.* **1** the Basque language. **2** a Basque. [*Euskara*, the name applied by the Basques to their own language]

Eustachian (ūstā´shən, -kiən) *a.* of or relating to Eustachius, an Italian physician of the 16th cent. **Eustachian tube** *n.* a duct leading to the cavity of the tympanum of the ear from the upper part of the pharynx.

eustasy (ūs´təsi) *n.* changes in the world shoreline level or sea level caused by melting ice, tectonic movements etc. **eustatic** (ūstat´-) *a.* [Gr. *stasis*, a standing]

eutectic (ūtek´tik) *a.* (*Chem.*) of or relating to the mixture of two or more substances with a minimum melting point. ~*n.* a eutectic mixture. **eutectic point, eutectic temperature** *n.* the minimum melting point of a eutectic mixture. [Gr. *eu*, well, *tektos*, molten]

euterpe (ūtœ´pi) *n.* **1** (*Bot.*) a palm of the S American genus *Euterpe*. **2** (*Astron.*) (**Euterpe**) the 27th asteroid. **Euterpean** *a.* of or relating to music. [Gr., the muse of music (*terpein*, to please)]

euthanasia (ūthənā´ziə) *n.* **1** easy, painless death. **2** a method of producing this. **3** putting to death in this manner, esp. in cases of extreme or terminal human suffering. [Gr., from *euthanatos* (*thanatos*, death)]

euthenics (ūthen´iks) *n.* the study of the improvement of human living standards by control of the environment. **euthenist** *n.* [Gr. *euthēneein*, to flourish]

eutherian (ūthiə´riən) *n.* a member of the subclass of mammals, Eutheria, which nourish their unborn young through a placenta. ~*a.* of or relating to this subclass, which includes most mammals. [Gr. *thēr*, a beast]

eutrophic (ūtrof´ik, -trō´-) *a.* (of a body of water) rich in dissolved nutrients and supporting an abundance of plant life whose decomposition deoxygenates the water, harming the animal populations. **eutrophicate** *v.t.* **eutrophication** (-ā´shən) *n.* **eutrophy** (ū´trəfi) *n.* [Gr. *eutrophos*, well-fed]

eV *abbr.* electronvolt.

EVA *abbr.* extravehicular activity.

evacuate (ivak´ūāt) *v.t.* **1 a** to remove inhabitants from (a danger zone). **b** to remove (people) temporarily from a danger zone. **2** to withdraw from (esp. of troops). **3** to form a vacuum. **4** to make empty, esp. to eject from or to empty the excretory passages. **5** (*fig.*) to divest of its meaning. **evacuant** *a.* **1** producing evacuation. **2** purgative. ~*n.* a medicine producing this effect. **evacuation** (-ā´shən) *n.* **1** the act of evacuating. **2** the transfer of people from a danger zone. **evacuative** *a.* **evacuator** *n.* **evacuee** (-ē´) *n.* a person, esp. a child, evacuated from a danger zone. [L *ēvacuātus*, p.p. of *ēvacuāre* (*vacuus*, empty)]

evade (ivād´) *v.t.* **1** to avoid or elude by artifice, stratagem or sophistry. **2** to avoid (doing something), to shirk. **3** to avoid answering (a question). **4** to avoid paying (taxes), e.g. by concealing income or falsifying accounts. **5** to defeat, baffle, foil. ~*v.i.* **1** to escape. **2** to practise sophistry. **3** to act evasively. **evadable** *a.* **evader** *n.* [F *évader*, L *ēvādere* (*vādere*, to go)]

evaginate (ivaj´ināt) *v.t.* (*Med.*) to turn inside out, to unsheathe (as a tubular organ). **evagination** (-ā´shən) *n.* [L *ēvaginātus*, p.p. of *ēvagināre* (*vagina*, sheath)]

evaluate (ival´ūāt) *v.t.* **1** to determine the value or worth of, to appraise. **2** (*Math.*) to find a numerical expression for. **evaluation** (-ā´shən) *n.* **evaluative** (-val´-) *a.* **evaluator** *n.* [F *évaluer*]

evanesce (evənes´) *v.i.* **1** to disappear, to vanish. **2** to fade away, as if in vapour. **evanescence** *n.* **evanescent** *a.* **1** disappearing gradually. **2** fading, fleeting. **evanescently** *adv.* [L *ēvānescere* (*vānescere*, from *vānus*, vain)]

evangel (ivan´jəl) *n.* **1** †the Gospel. **2** †any one of the four Gospels. **3** †a gospel, a doctrine of political or social reform. **4** (*N Am.*) an evangelist.

evangelical (ēvənjel´ikəl) *a.* **1** of or relating to the Gospel. **2** according to the doctrine of the Gospel. **3** proclaiming or maintaining the truth taught in the Gospel. **4** of or relating to a tradition in the Protestant churches which emphasizes the importance of the fundamental teaching of Scripture, the doctrines of the Fall, Christ's atonement, and salvation by faith not works. **5** belonging to an evangelical church or party. **6** firmly believing in and actively promoting a cause. ~*n.* a member of the evangelical branch of Protestantism. **evangelic** *a.*, *n.* evangelical. **evangelicalism** *n.* **evangelically** *adv.*

evangelism (ivan´jəlizm) *n.* **1** the preaching of the Gospel. **2** evangelicalism. **3** enthusiastic promotion of any cause. **evangelist** *n.* **1** (*also* **Evangelist**) any one of the four writers of the Gospels (Matthew, Mark, Luke and John). **2** a preacher of the Gospel. **3** a lay preacher. **4** a person who evangelizes or believes in evangelism. **5** an enthusiastic and active supporter of a cause. **evangelistic** (-lis´-) *a.* **1** of or relating to the four Evangelists. **2** of or relating to preaching of the Gospel. **3** evangelical. **evangelize, evangelise** *v.t.* **1** to preach the Gospel to. **2** to convert to Christianity. **3** to try to persuade (people) to join or support a cause. ~*v.i.* **1** to preach the Gospel. **2** to campaign energetically for a cause. **evangelization** (-zā´shən) *n.* **evangelizer** *n.* [Of *evangile*, eccles. L *ēvangelium*, Gr. *euangelion* (*angellein*, to announce)]

evanish (ivan´ish) *v.i.* (*formal*) to vanish, to disappear. **evanishment** *n.* **evanition** (evənish´ən) *n.* [OF *evaniss-*, stem of *evanir*, L *ēvānescere*, to EVANESCE]

evaporate (ivap´ərāt) *v.t.* **1** to convert into vapour, to vaporize. **2** to drive off the moisture from by heating or drying. **3** to cause to vanish. ~*v.i.* **1** to become vapour. **2** to pass away in vapour. **3** to exhale moisture. **4** (*coll.*) to disappear, to vanish. **evaporable** *a.* **evaporated milk** *n.* unsweetened milk from which some of the water has been evaporated. **evaporation** (-ā´shən) *n.* **evaporative** (-ətiv) *a.* **evaporator** *n.* **evaporimeter** (-rim´itə) *n.* an instrument which measures the rate of evaporation of water. **evaporite** *n.* (*Geol.*) a rock, a salt etc. formed by the evaporation of water. [L *ēvaporātus*, p.p. of *ēvaporāre*]

evasion (ivā´zhən) *n.* **1** the act of evading or escaping (as from a question, argument or charge). **2** a subterfuge, an equivocation. **3** an evasive answer. **evasive** (-siv) *a.* **1** seeking to evade. **2** facilitating evasion or escape. **3** (of a person) not straightforward, devious. **4** elusive. **evasively** *adv.* **evasiveness** *n.* [F *évasion*, late L *ēvāsio -ōnem*, from *ēvādere*, to EVADE]

eve (ēv) *n.* **1** the evening before a holiday or other event or date. **2** the period immediately preceding some important event. **3** †evening. [OE *æfen*, *ēfen* (cp. OHG *ābant*, G *Abend*)]

evection (ivek´shən) *n.* (*Astron.*) an inequality in the longitude of the moon, due to the action of the sun. [L *ēvectio*, from *ēvehere* (*vehere*, to carry, p.p. *vectus*)]

even[1] (ē´vən), (*poet.*) **e'en** (ēn) *n.* evening. **evenfall** *n.* (*poet.*) early evening. **evensong** *n.* **1** a form of worship for the evening, esp. in Anglican churches. **2** the time for evening prayer. **eventide** *n.* (*poet.*) evening. **eventide home** *n.* a home for elderly people. [as EVE]

even[2] (ē´vən) *a.* **1** level, smooth, uniform. **2** on the same level, in the same plane (with). **3** parallel. **4** capable of being divided by the number 2 without any remainder, as opposed to *odd.* **5** (of numbers) round, not including fractions or remainders. **6** equal. **7** equally balanced, fair, impartial. **8** uniform or unvarying in quality. **9** unvarying, equable, unruffled. **on an even keel 1** (*Naut.*) (of a ship) drawing the same water fore and aft. **2** (of a person) well-balanced, emotionally, mentally or financially. **to be/ get even with 1** to revenge oneself on. **2** to be quits with. **to even out** to become even or equal. **to even up** to balance, to make equal. **to make even 1** †to square accounts with. **2** (*Print.*) to space out the lines, so that a given passage may end with a full line. **even break** *n.* an even chance. **even chance** *n.* an equal likelihood of success or failure. **even date** *n.* **1** in commercial use, today. **2** the same date. **even-handed** *a.* impartial, equitable, fair. **even-handedly** *adv.* **even-handedness** *n.* **evenly** *adv.* **even-minded** *a.* even-tempered. **even-mindedly** *adv.* **even money** *n.* evens. ~*a.* just as likely to be or happen as not. **evenness** *n.* †**even-pleached** *a.* smoothly or evenly intertwined. **evens** *n.pl.* odds quoted on a racehorse etc. such that if it wins the person betting gains an amount equal to the stake. **even-tempered** *a.* not easily upset or angered, placid. [OE *efen, efn* (cp. Dut. *even,* OHG *eban,* G *eben*)]

even[3] (ē´vən) *v.t.* **1** to make smooth or level. **2** to place on a level. **3** †to treat as equal, to compare. ~*v.i.* to be or become equal. **to even out** to make or become even or level. **to even up** to bring or come up to the same level. **evener** *n.* [OE *efnan,* as EVEN[2]]

even[4] (ē´vən) *adv.* **1** to a like degree, equally. **2** as much as, so much as (expressing unexpectedness, surprise, concession or emphasis, a comparison being implied). **3** evenly. **4** exactly, just, simply, neither more nor less than. **5** unexpectedly; in an extreme case. **even as** at the very same time that. **even now 1** at this very moment. **2** now and before. **even so 1** exactly; yes. **2** nevertheless. **3** in that case also. **even though** in spite of the fact that. [OE *efne,* as EVEN[2]]

evening (ēv´ning) *n.* **1** the close or latter part of the day. **2** the period from sunset to dark, or from sunset to bed-time. **3** (*fig.*) the close or decline, as of life. **4** the latter part. ~*a.* of or relating to, or happening in the evening. ~*int.* (*coll.*) GOOD EVENING (under GOOD). **evening class** *n.* a class held in the evenings, usu. for adults. **evening dress** *n.* the dress prescribed by convention for wearing for a formal occasion in the evening. **evening primrose** *n.* any plant belonging to the genus *Oenothera,* the yellow flowers of which usu. open in the evening. **evening primrose oil** *n.* an oil obtained from the seeds of the evening primrose, used as a food supplement. **evenings** *adv.* (*coll.*) during most evenings. **evening star** *n.* Jupiter, Mercury or esp. Venus when visible in the west in the evening. [OE *æfnung,* from *æfnian,* to grow towards evening, from *æfen,* EVEN[1]]

evens EVEN[2].

event (ivent´) *n.* **1** anything that happens, as distinguished from a thing that exists. **2** an occurrence, esp. one of great importance. **3 a** the fact of an occurrence. **b** the contingency or possibility of an occurrence. **4** the consequence of any action. **5** the issue or conclusion. **6** any of several possible occurrences regarded as having a probability of its own. **7** any item in a programme of games, contests etc., esp. one on which money is wagered. **8** (*Physics*) a single occurrence of a particular process. ~*v.i.* to take part in one-day or three-day events. **at all events** in any case, whatever happens. **in any event** at all events. **in the event 1** as it turns out, or turned out. **2** if it should so turn out. **in the event of** if so, if it so happens. **in the event that** if it turns out that. **one-day event** ONE. **three-day event** THREE. **eventer** *n.* **1** a horse that takes part in one- or three-day events. **2** a person who takes part in such events. **eventful** *a.* **1** full of events. **2** attended by important changes. **eventfully** *adv.* **eventfulness** *n.* **event horizon** *n.* (*Astron.*) the boundary of the gravitational field of a black hole, from which no electromagnetic radiation can escape. **eventing** *n.* taking part in one- or three-day events. **eventless** *a.* lacking (important) events. [OF, from L *ēventus,* p.p. of *ēvenīre,* to happen (*venīre,* to come)]

eventide EVEN[1].

eventual (iven´chuəl) *a.* finally resulting, ultimate, final. **eventuality** (-al´-) *n.* (*pl.* **eventualities**) a possible event or result. **eventually** *adv.* **eventuate** *v.i.* (*formal*) **1** to happen, to come to pass, to result. **2** to turn out (well or ill). **eventuation** (-ā´shən) *n.* [EVENT]

ever (ev´ə), (*poet.*) **e'er** (eə) *adv.* **1** at all times; always. **2** continually. **3** at any time. **4** in any degree. **did you ever?** (*coll.*) did you ever see or hear anything like this? **ever after** continually after a certain time. **ever and anon** now and then; at one time and another. **ever since** continually after a certain time. **ever so** to any degree or extent conceivable. **ever such a** (*coll. or dial.*) a very. **everglade** *n.* **1** (*US*) a low, marshy tract of country, interspersed with patches covered with high grass. **2** (*pl.* **Everglades**) the region of this character in Florida. **evergreen** *a.* **1** always green. **2** retaining its verdure throughout the year. **3** always young or fresh. ~*n.* **1** a plant which retains its verdure through the year. **2** a person, book, song etc. which stays fresh or popular for many years. **everlasting** *a.* **1** lasting for ever, eternal, perpetual. **2** continual, unintermittent. **3** interminable, tiresome. **4** of flowers, not changing colour when dried. ~*n.* **1** eternity. **2** IMMORTELLE. **the Everlasting** God. **everlastingly** *adv.* **everlastingness** *n.* **evermore** *adv.* always, eternally, continually. [OE *æfre* (etym. uncertain, perh. rel. to OE *ā, āwa,* AYE[2], cp. Gr. *aiōn,* L *aevum*)]

evert (ivœt´) *v.i.* **1** to turn outwards, to turn inside out. **2** †to overthrow. **eversible** *a.* **eversion** (-shən) *n.* [L *ēvertere* (*vertere,* to turn)]

every (ev´ri) *a.* **1** each of a group or collection, all separately. **2** each one at a specified interval from the one before, as *every fourth person.* **3** the greatest possible, as *every hope of succeeding.* **every bit 1** quite (as). **2** the whole. **every last** the total number of. **every now and again** from time to time. **every now and then** from time to time. **every one** each one. **every other** OTHER. **every so often** intermittently. **every time 1** on each occasion, with no exception. **2** (*coll.*) yes, certainly. **every which way 1** (*N Am., coll.*) in all directions or ways. **2** (*N Am., coll.*) in a disorderly fashion. **on every hand** HAND. **everybody** *pron.* every person. **everybody else** (*collectively*) all other persons. **every day** *adv.* **1** on each or every day. **2** continually. **everyday** *a.* **1** met with or happening daily. **2** worn or used on ordinary occasions. **3** common, usual. **4** commonplace. **Everyman** *n.* **1** a figure in a medieval morality play who represents everyone or mankind. **2** (**everyman**) the person in the street, everyone. **everyone** *pron.* everybody. **every one** *n.* each person or thing, without exception. **everyplace** *adv.* (*N Am.*) everywhere. **everything** *pron.* **1** all things collectively. **2** all of the things making up a whole. **3** (*coll.*) a great deal. **4** (*fig.*) something of the highest importance. **to have everything** (*coll.*) to have every advantage, wealth, attractiveness etc. **everyway** *adv.* in every way, in every respect. **everywhere** *adv.* **1** in every place. **2**

(*coll.*) in many places. [ME *everi, everich* (OE *æfre*, ever, *ælc*, each)]

evict (ivikt´) *v.t.* **1** to eject from lands, tenements or property by law. **2** to dispossess by legal process. **eviction** *n.* **evictor** *n.* [L *ēvictus*, p.p. of *ēvincere* (*vincere*, to conquer)]

evidence (ev´idəns) *n.* **1** anything that makes clear or obvious; ground for knowledge, indication, testimony. **2** that which makes truth evident, or renders evident to the mind that it is truth. **3** (*Law*) information by which a fact is proved or sought to be proved, or an allegation proved or disproved. **4** such statements, proofs etc. as are legally admissible as testimony in a court of law. **5** obviousness. ~*v.t.* to make evident; to be evidence of, to attest. **in evidence 1** received or offered as tending to establish a fact or allegation in a court of law. **2** (*coll.*) plainly visible, conspicuous. **evident** *a.* open or plain to the sight; manifest, obvious. **evidential** (-den´-) *a.* **1** of or relating to evidence. **2** affording evidence. **3** proving conclusively. **evidentially** *adv.* **evidentiary** (-den´shəri) *a.* of or relating to, or of the nature of evidence. **evidently** *adv.* **1** obviously. **2** apparently. **3** it is obvious that. **4** yes, it would appear so. [F *évidence*, L *ēvidentia*, from *ēvidens -ntem*, pres.p. of *ēvidēre* (*vidēre*, to see)]

evil (ē´vəl) *a.* **1** bad, injurious, mischievous, worthless, morally bad, wicked. **2** calamitous, agitated, sorrowful. **3** unlucky, producing disastrous results. **4** malicious, slanderous. ~*adv.* in an evil manner; badly, foully, as *evil-smelling*. ~*n.* **1** an evil thing. **2** that which injures or displeases, calamity, harm. **3** sin, depravity, malignity. **4** †a malady, a disease. **to speak evil of** to slander, defame. **evil days** *n.pl.* a period of misfortune. **evil-disposed**, **evil-affected** *a.* unkindly and injuriously disposed. **evildoer** *n.* a person who does evil, a wrong-doer, a malefactor. **evildoing** *n.* **evil eye** *n.* a supposed power of fascinating, bewitching or materially injuring by staring at. **evil-eyed** *a.* **1** malicious. **2** looking malicious. **3** having the power of the evil eye. **evilly** *adv.* **evil-minded** *a.* having evil thoughts, spiteful, malicious. **evil-mindedly** *adv.* **evil-mindedness** *n.* **evilness** *n.* **Evil One** *n.* the Devil. **evil-speaking** *n.* slander, calumny, defamation. **evil-tempered** *a.* having a bad temper, unpleasant. [OE *yfel* (cp. Dut. *euvel*, OHG *upil*, G *Übel*)]

evince (ivins´) *v.t.* **1** to show clearly. **2** to indicate, to make evident. **3** to demonstrate, to show possession of. **evincible** *a.* **evincive** *a.* [L *ēvincere* (*vincere*, to conquer)]

Usage note The verb *evince* is occasionally used as though it meant to attest (confused with the verb *evidence*) or to call up (*evoke*), but both are best avoided.

---

eviscerate (ivis´ərāt) *v.t.* (*formal*) **1** to disembowel. **2** to empty of all that is vital. **3** to empty, to gut. **evisceration** (-ā´shən) *n.* [L *ēviscerātus*, p.p. of *ēviscerāre* (*viscera*, bowels)]

evitable (ev´itəbəl) *a.* (*formal*) that can be avoided. [F *éviter*, L *ēvītāre* (*vītāre*, to shun)]

evoke (ivōk´) *v.t.* **1** to call up, to summon forth (a memory etc.) esp. from the past. **2** to elicit or provoke. **3** to cause (spirits) to appear. **†evocate** (ev´əkāt) *v.t.* **evocation** (evəkā´shən) *n.* **evocative** (ivok´ətiv) *a.* tending to evoke, esp. feelings or memories. **evocatively** *adv.* **evocativeness** *n.* **evocator** (ev´əkātə) *n.* **evoker** *n.* [F *évoquer*, L *ēvocāre* (*vocāre*, to call)]

evolute (ev´əloot) *n.* (*Geom.*) a curve from which another is described by the end of a thread gradually wound upon or unwound from the former, thus forming the locus of the centres of curvature of the other (the *involute*). [L *ēvolūtus*, p.p. of *ēvolvere*, to EVOLVE]

evolution (ēvəloo´shən, ev-) *n.* **1** the gradual cumulative change in the characteristics of organisms over many generations, which results in new species. **2** this process of gradual change, which accounts for the development from simpler to more complex forms. **3** any development from a simpler to a more complex or advanced form. **4** the act of unrolling, unfolding, opening or growing. **5** a series of things unrolled or unfolded. **6** development, as of an argument, plot, design, organism or political, social or planetary system etc. **7** (*Math.*) the opening or unfolding of a curve. **8** (*Math.*) the extraction of roots from any given power, the reverse of *involution*. **9** the evolving or giving off of gas, heat etc. **10** doubling of ranks or files, countermarching or other changes of position, by which the disposition of troops or ships is changed. **11** (*pl., fig.*) movements, changes of position etc. in dancing etc. **evolutional, evolutionary** *a.* of or relating to or produced by evolution. **evolutionally, evolutionarily** *adv.* **evolutionism** *n.* the theory or doctrine of evolution as the origin of species. **evolutionist** *n.* **1** a person who believes in or advocates evolutionism. **2** a person skilled in evolutions. **evolutionistic** (-nis´-) *a.* **evolutive** *a.* **1** tending to or promoting evolution. **2** evolutionary. [L *ēvolūtio -ōnem*, see EVOLUTE]

evolve (ivolv´) *v.t.* **1** to unfold, to expand. **2** to develop, to bring to maturity. **3** to give off (gas, heat etc.). **4** to bring forth, work out, set forth (an argument etc.) in an orderly manner. ~*v.i.* **1** to open. **2** to develop. **evolvable** *a.* **evolvement** *n.* **evolver** *n.* [L *ēvolvere* (*volvere*, to roll)]

evulsion (ivŭl´shən) *n.* (*formal*) the act of forcibly plucking or extracting. [L *ēvulsio -ōnem*, from *ēvulsus*, p.p. of *ēvellere* (*vellere*, to pluck)]

evzone (ev´zōn) *n.* a member of an elite Greek infantry regiment. [mod. Gr. *euzōnos*, Gr., dressed for action (*zōnē*, a girdle)]

ewe (ū) *n.* a female sheep. **ewe lamb** *n.* (*fig.*) a dearest possession. **ewe-neck** *n.* **1** a condition in horses in which the neck is thin and concave. **2** a horse having this condition. **ewe-necked** *a.* [OE *eowu* (cp. Dut. *ooi*, OIr. *oi*, Gr. *ois*, L *ovis*, Sansk. *avi*)]

ewer (ū´ə) *n.* a kind of pitcher or large jug for water with a wide mouth. [A-F, from OF *aiguier*, L *aquārium*, from *aqua*, water]

Ex. *abbr.* Exodus (Old Testament).

ex[1] (eks) *n.* **1** the 24th letter of the alphabet, X, x. **2** anything shaped like this.

ex[2] (eks) *prep.* **1** from, out of, sold from. **2** without. [L, out of]

ex[3] (eks) *n.* (*pl.* **exes, ex's**) (*coll.*) a former spouse, boyfriend or girlfriend.

ex. *abbr.* **1** examination, examined. **2** example. **3** except, exception. **4** exchange. **5** excursion. **6** executed, executive. **7** export. **8** express. **9** extra.

ex- (eks) *pref.* **1** out, forth, out of, as *exceed, exclude, exit, extend, extol.* **2** thoroughly, as *exacerbate, excruciate.* **3** without, -less, as *exonerate, expatriate, exalbuminous, exstipulate.* **4** formerly, previously occupying the position of, as *ex-chancellor, ex-president.* [L *ex-, ex*, out of, from, or Gr. *ex, ek*]

exa- (ek´sə) *pref.* (*Math.*) a factor of 10^{18}. [perh. Gr. *hex*, six]

exacerbate (igzas´əbāt, eksas´-) *v.t.* **1** to irritate, to exasperate, to embitter. **2** to aggravate, to increase the violence of (as a disease). **exacerbation** (-ā´shən) *n.* [L *exacerbātus*, p.p. of *exacerbāre* (*acerbus*, bitter)]

exact[1] (igzakt´) *a.* **1** precisely agreeing in amount, number or degree. **2** accurate, strictly correct. **3** precise, strict, punctilious. **4** consummate, perfect. **exactitude** (-titūd) *n.* exactness, precision. **exactly** *adv.* **1** in an exact manner. **2** quite so, precisely, just so (in answer to a question or affirmation). **3** in express terms. **not**

exactly 1 (*iron.*) not at all. 2 not precisely. **exactness** *n.* the quality of being exact. **exact sciences** *n.pl.* those in which mathematical accuracy is attainable. [L *exactus*, p.p. of *exigere* (*agere*, to drive)]

exact[2] (igzakt´) *v.t.* 1 to compel (money etc.) to be paid or surrendered. 2 to demand as of right, to insist on, to require authoritatively. **exactable** *a.* **exacting** *a.* 1 severe or excessive in demanding. 2 urgently requiring. 3 requiring much effort or skill. **exactingly** *adv.* **exactingness** *n.* **exaction** *n.* 1 the act of exacting, or an instance of exacting. 2 a forcible, illegal or exorbitant demand, extortion. 3 that which is exacted. 4 a compulsory or oppressive impost or service. **exactor**, **exacter** *n.* [see EXACT[1]]

exaggerate (igzaj´ərāt) *v.t.* 1 to heighten, to overstate, to represent as greater than is in fact the case. 2 to increase, intensify, aggravate. 3 to represent (features, colours etc.) in a heightened manner. ~*v.i.* to use or be given to exaggeration. **exaggeratedly** *adv.* **exaggeratingly** *adv.* **exaggeration** (-ā´shən) *n.* **exaggerative** (-aj´-) *a.* **exaggeratively** *adv.* **exaggerator** *n.* **exaggeratory** *a.* [L *exaggerātus*, p.p. of *exaggerāre* (*agger*, a heap)]

exalbuminous (eksalbū´minəs) *a.* (*Bot.*) (of seeds) without albumen.

exalt (igzawlt´) *v.t.* 1 to raise in dignity, rank, power or position. 2 to elevate in character, spirits, diction or sentiment, to ennoble, to dignify. 3 to elate. 4 to praise, extol, glorify. 5 to increase in force, to intensify. **exaltation** (egzawltā´shən) *n.* 1 the act of exalting, or an instance of exalting. 2 elevation in power, rank, dignity or position. 3 elation, rapture, ecstasy. 4 intensification, augmentation. 5 (*Astrol.*) the position of a planet in the zodiac where it exerts the maximum of influence. 6 a flock of larks. **exalted** *a.* lofty, noble. **exaltedly** *a.* **exaltedness** *n.* †**exalter** *n.* [L *exaltāre* (*altus*, high)]

exam (igzam´) *n.* (*coll.*) an examination.

examine (igzam´in) *v.t.* 1 to inquire into, to investigate, scrutinize. 2 to consider critically, to weigh and sift (as arguments for and against). 3 to inspect, to explore. 4 (*Law*) to question (e.g. the accused or a witness). 5 to test the capabilities, qualifications, knowledge of etc., by questions and problems. 6 to inspect ((a part of) a patient's body) with a view to diagnosing possible illness. ~*v.i.* to make inquiry or research. **examen** (-zā´mən) *n.* (in the Roman Catholic Church) an examination of one's conscience. **examinable** *a.* that may be examined. **examination** (-ā´shən) *n.* 1 **a** the act of examining, or an instance of examining. **b** the state of being examined. 2 careful inspection, scrutiny or inquiry. 3 **a** the process of testing the capabilities or qualifications of a candidate for any post, or the progress, attainments or knowledge of a student. **b** a test of this kind. 4 the act or an instance of inspecting a patient's body to diagnose possible illness. 5 (*Law*) a careful inquiry into facts by taking evidence. **examinational** *a.* **examination-in-chief** *n.* (*Law*) questioning in court of one's own witness, as distinct from *cross-examination*. **examine-in-chief** *v.t.* **examination paper** *n.* 1 a paper containing questions for candidates, pupils etc. 2 a series of answers to such questions by an examinee. **examinee** (-nē´) *n.* **examiner** *n.* [F *examiner*, L *exāmināre*, from *exāmen* (*exagmen*, the tongue of a balance, conn. with *exigere*, to weigh out (*agere*, to drive))]

example (igzahm´pəl) *n.* 1 a sample, a specimen. 2 a copy, model or pattern. 3 any person, fact or thing illustrating a general rule. 4 a person, course of conduct etc. seen as worthy of imitation. 5 a person, a punishment, or the person punished serving as a warning. 6 a problem or exercise (in mathematics etc.) for the instruction of students. ~*v.t.* 1 (*usu. passive*) **a** to exemplify. **b** to serve as an example to. **c** to give a precedent for. **for example** as an illustration. **to make an example of** to punish as a deterrent to others. [OF, from L *exemplum* (*emere*, to take, to buy, see EXEMPT)]

exanimate (igzan´imət) *a.* 1 lifeless, dead. 2 without animation, depressed, spiritless. **exanimation** (-ā´shən) *n.* [L *exanimātus*, p.p. of *exanimāre* (*anima*, life)]

ex ante (eks an´ti) *a.* based on the prediction of results. [L]

exanthema (iksan´thimə, eksanthē´mə) *n.* (*pl.* **exanthemas**) 1 a skin rash accompanying a disease. 2 any disease which is accompanied by a skin rash, e.g. measles. **exanthematic** (-mat´ik) *a.* **exanthematous** (-thē´mətəs) *a.* [Gr. *antheein*, to blossom]

exarch (ek´sahk) *n.* 1 in the Greek Church, a grade in the ecclesiastical hierarchy instituted by Constantine the Great, formerly equivalent to patriarch or metropolitan, later a bishop in charge of a province, and also a legate of a patriarch. 2 a governor of a province under the Byzantine Empire. **exarchate** (ek´sahkāt, -sah´-) *n.* **exarchy** *n.* (*pl.* **exarchies**). [L *exarchus*, Gr. *exarchos* (*archein*, to rule)]

exasperate (igzas´pərāt) *v.t.* 1 to irritate to a high degree; to provoke. 2 to aggravate, to embitter. 3 †to incite. **exasperated** *a.* irritated. **exasperatedly** *adv.* **exasperating** *a.* **exasperatingly** *adv.* **exasperation** (-ā´shən) *n.* [L *exasperātus*, p.p. of *exasperāre* (*asper*, rough)]

☒ **exaust** common misspelling of EXHAUST.

Exc. *abbr.* Excellency.

exc. *abbr.* 1 excellent. 2 except, exception. 3 excursion.

ex cathedra (eks kəthē´drə) *a.* authoritative, to be obeyed. ~*adv.* authoritatively. [L, from the (bishop's) chair]

excaudate (ekskaw´dāt) *a.* (*Zool.*) having no tail. [L *cauda*, a tail]

excavate (eks´kəvāt) *v.t.* 1 to hollow out. 2 to form by digging or hollowing out. 3 to remove (from the ground) by digging. 4 to uncover by digging, to dig out, esp. for archaeological research. 5 to investigate (an archaeological site) by digging. ~*v.i.* to conduct archaeological research by digging. **excavation** (-ā´shən) *n.* **excavator** *n.* [L *excavātus*, p.p. of *excavāre* (*cavus*, hollow)]

exceed (iksēd´) *v.t.* 1 to go or pass beyond. 2 to be more or greater than. 3 to do more than is warranted by. 4 to surpass, to outdo, to excel. **exceedable** *a.* **exceeding** *a.* 1 very great in amount, duration, extent or degree. 2 pre-eminent. ~†*adv.* exceedingly. **exceedingly** *adv.* 1 very much. 2 pre-eminently. [F *excéder*, L *excēdere* (*cēdere*, to go)]

excel (iksel´) *v.t.* (*pres.p.* **excelling**, *past, p.p.* **excelled**) 1 to surpass in qualities. 2 to exceed, to outdo. ~*v.i.* to be superior, distinguished or pre-eminent (in or at). **to excel oneself** to do better than one (or others) had thought possible. **excellence** (ek´-) *n.* 1 the state of excelling. 2 superiority, pre-eminence. 3 surpassing virtue, goodness or merit. 4 that in which any person or thing excels. 5 an excellent quality, feature or trait. **excellency** *n.* (*pl.* **excellencies**) 1 excellence. 2 (**Excellency**) a title of honour given to a governor, an ambassador, a commander-in-chief and certain other officers. **excellent** *a.* 1 surpassing others in some good quality. 2 of great virtue, worth etc. 3 †exceeding, remarkable. 4 superior or pre-eminent in bad or neutral qualities. **excellently** *adv.* [F, from L *excellere* (*cellere*, in *antecellere*, rel. to *celsus*, high)]

excelsior (iksel´siaw) *int.* used to express an intention of climbing higher. **Excelsior®** *n.* (*N Am.*) packing material composed of thin wood-shavings. [L, comp. of *excelsus*, lofty (*celsus*, high)]

excentric (eksen´trik) *a.*, *n.* ECCENTRIC (in technical uses).

except (iksept´) *v.t.* to leave out, to omit, to exclude. ~*v.i.* to make objection (to or against). ~*prep.* not including, exclusive of, omitting, but. ~*conj.* unless. **X excepted** not including X. **excepting** *prep.* (*usu. after not*) omitting, with the exception of. ~*conj.* unless. **exception** *n.* **1 a** the act, or an instance, of excepting. **b** the state of being an exception. **2** that which is excepted. **3** an instance of that which is excluded from or is at variance with a rule, class or other generalization. **4** an objection, disapproval. **to take exception 1** to object, to find fault. **2** to express disapproval. **with the exception of** omitting; not including. **exceptionable** *a.* **1** liable to objection. **2** objectionable. **3** unusual. **exceptionableness** *n.* **exceptionably** *adv.* **exceptional** *a.* **1** forming an exception. **2** unusual, extraordinarily good, unprecedented. **exceptionality** (-nal´-) *n.* **exceptionally** *adv.* **exceptionary** *a.* indicating an exception. **exceptive** *a.* **1** forming an exception. **2** tending to make objections. [OF *excepter*, L *exceptāre*, freq. of *excipere* (*capere*, to take)]

Usage note The adjectives *exceptionable* and *exceptional* should not be confused: *exceptionable* means objectionable, and *exceptional* outstanding. The corresponding negatives in *un-* are similarly distinguished.

excerpt[1] (iksœpt´) *v.t.* **1** to make an extract of or from. **2** to cite, to quote. **excerptible** *a.* **excerption** *n.* [L *excerptus*, p.p. of *excerpere*, to select (*carpere*, to pluck)]

excerpt[2] (ek´sœpt) *n.* (*pl.* **excerpts, excerpta** (-tə)) an extract or selection from a book, play, film etc., esp. an article printed off separately from the proceedings of a learned society. [see EXCERPT[1]]

excess (ikses´, ek´-) *n.* **1** that which exceeds what is usual or necessary. **2** an instance of exceeding. **3** the quality, state or fact of exceeding the ordinary measure, proportion or limit. **4** the amount by which one number or quantity exceeds another. **5** (*usu. pl.*) transgression of due limits. **6** intemperance, over-indulgence, extravagance. **7** (*pl.*) outrageous behaviour. **8** a specified amount which must be paid by the policy-holder towards the amount of a claim. ~*a.* more than is usual or permitted. **in excess** to excess. **in excess of** more than. **to excess** more than is normal or proper. **excess baggage, excess luggage** *n.* a quantity above the weight allowed free carriage. **excess fare** *n.* the amount paid for travelling beyond the point for which a ticket has been taken or in a higher class. **excessive** (-ses´-) *a.* **1** more than normal or proper. **2** too much. **excessively** *adv.* **excessiveness** *n.* **excess postage** *n.* payment due when not enough stamps have been put on a letter or package. [OF *exces*, L *excessus -cessum*, a going out, from *excēdere*, to EXCEED]

exch. *abbr.* **1** exchange. **2** exchequer.

exchange (ikschānj´) *v.t.* **1** to give or receive in return for something else. **2** to hand over for an equivalent in kind. **3** to give and receive in turn, to interchange. **4** to give, resign or abandon (as one state or condition for another). ~*v.i.* **1** to be given or received in exchange. **2** to be received as of equal value. **3** to pass from one office or institution to another by taking the place of another person. ~*n.* **1** the act, or an instance, of exchanging; a parting with one article or commodity for an equivalent in kind. **2** the act of giving and receiving reciprocally, interchange. **3** the act of resigning one state for another. **4** something given or received in exchange. **5** a short argument or quarrel. **6** a short correspondence by letter. **7 a** exchanging money for its value in money of the same or another country. **b** the commission charged for such a transaction. **8** the system by which goods or property are exchanged and debts settled, esp. in different countries, without the transfer of money. **9** the place where merchants, brokers etc. meet to transact business. **10** a place where people are introduced to each other to exchange services or information, e.g. an employment exchange. **11** an apparatus or an office in which telephone lines are connected. **12** (*coll.*) an exchange student or teacher. **13** (in chess) the capture of a piece by each player in consecutive moves. **in exchange (for)** as something exchanged (for), in return (for). **to exchange blows** to quarrel physically, to have a fight. **to exchange words** to quarrel verbally, to have an argument. **exchangeable** *a.* **1** that may be exchanged (for). **2** rateable by what can be procured in exchange. **exchangeability** (-bil´-) *n.* **exchangeably** *adv.* **exchanger** *n.* **exchange rate** *n.* the ratio at which the currency of one country can be exchanged for that of another. **exchange rate mechanism** *n.* an arrangement for regulating the fluctuation of exchange rates of the European Union currencies against each other or against the euro. **exchange student, exchange teacher** *n.* a student or teacher who exchanges posts with a corresponding person from another country. [OF *eschangier*, late L *excambiāre* (*cambiāre*, L *cambīre*, to CHANGE)]

exchequer (ikschek´ə) *n.* **1** a State treasury. **2** (*Hist.*) the Government department dealing with the public revenue. **3** finances or pecuniary resources. **4** the Court of Exchequer. **exchequer bill** *n.* a bill for money, or a promissory bill, issued from the Exchequer by authority of Parliament. [ME *eschekere*, OF *eschequier*, med. L *scaccārium*, a chessboard]

excide (iksīd´) *v.t.* **1** to cut out. **2** to extirpate. [L *excīdere* (*caedere*, to cut)]

excimer (ek´simə) *n.* (*Chem.*) a dimer in an excited state, consisting of an excited and an unexcited molecule. [*exci*ted di*mer*]

excise[1] (ek´siz, iksīz´) *n.* **1** a tax or duty on certain articles produced and consumed in a country (in the United Kingdom on e.g. alcoholic drinks and tobacco). **2** a tax on licences to carry out certain activities. **3** the branch of the Civil Service which collects and manages the excise duties, called the Board of Customs and Excise. **4** †a tax of any kind. **excise laws** *n.pl.* (*N Am.*) licensing laws. **excise officer, exciseman** *n.* (*pl.* **excise officers, excisemen**) (*Hist.*) an officer who collected the excise duties, and tried to prevent any evasion of the excise laws. [prob. from MDut. *excijs*, OF *acceis*, late L *accēnsum*, from *accensāre*, to tax (*ac-*, AD-, *census*, tax)]

excise[2] (iksīz´) *v.t.* **1** to impose an excise duty on (goods). **2** to compel (a person) to pay excise duty. **excisable** *a.* subject or liable to excise duty. [see EXCISE[1]]

excise[3] (iksīz´) *v.t.* to cut out (part of a book or of the body). **excision** (-sizh´ən) *n.* [L *excīsus*, p.p. of *excīdere*, to EXCIDE]

excite (iksīt´) *v.t.* **1** to rouse, to stir into action, energy or agitation. **2** to stimulate, to bring into activity. **3** to stir up the feelings or emotions of (a person). **4** to arouse sexually. **5** to provoke, to bring about by stimulating. **6** to produce electrical activity in. **7** to supply electric current to the coils of (an electromagnet). **8** to supply a signal to (a transistor etc.). **9** (*Physics*) to raise (an atom) from its normal to a higher energy level. **10** to cause the emission of radiation from (a substance). **11** to cause a substance to emit (radiation). **excitable** *a.* **1** susceptible to stimulation. **2** characterized by excitability. **excitability** (-bil´-) *n.* **excitably** *adv.* **excitant** (ek´si-) *a.* **1** stimulating. **2** tending to excite. ~*n.* **1** that which excites increased action in an organism. **2** a stimulant. **excitation** (eksitā´shən) *n.* **1** the act, or an instance, of being excited. **2** the state of being excited. **excitative** *a.* **excitatory** *a.* **excitedly** *adv.* **excitedness** *n.* **excitement** *n.* **exciter** *n.* **1** a person who or thing which excites. **2** a stimulant. **3** any agent which produces electrical activity. **4** any agent which excites an atom etc. **exciting** *a.* **1** stimulating. **2** producing excitement or enthusiasm. **excitingly** *adv.* **excitingness** *n.* **excitive** *a.*

excitor *n.* an afferent nerve belonging to the spinal group. [OF *exciter*, L *excitāre*, freq. of *exciēre* (*ciēre*, to summon)]

exciton (ek´siton, iksī´ton, ek-) *n.* (*Physics*) a mobile entity in a crystal, formed by an excited electron bound to its associated hole.

excl. *abbr.* **1** exclamation. **2** excluding. **3** exclusive.

exclaim (iksklām´) *v.i.* to cry out abruptly or passionately. ~*v.t.* to utter in an abrupt or passionate manner. **exclaimer** *n.* [F *exclamer*, L *exclāmāre* (*clāmāre*, to cry aloud)]

exclamation (eksklәmā´shәn) *n.* **1** the act of exclaiming. **2** an expression of surprise, pain etc. **exclamation mark,** (*N Am.*) **exclamation point** *n.* a sign (!) indicating emotion etc. **exclamatory** (-klam´ә-) *a.* **1** containing or expressing exclamation. **2** using exclamation. [L *exclāmātio -ōnem*; see EXCLAIM]

exclave (eks´klāv) *n.* part of a country disjoined from the main part and surrounded by foreign territory, where it is considered an enclave. [L *ex*, out, *clavis*, a key]

exclosure (iksklō´zhә) *n.* an area shut off from entry or intrusion, esp. a forested area fenced to keep out animals.

exclude (ikslood´) *v.t.* **1** to shut out, to prevent from coming in. **2** to prevent from participating. **3** to debar; to expel and keep out. **4** to reject, to except, to leave out. **5** to prevent the possibility of. **excludable** *a.* **excluded middle** *n.* (*Logic*) the principle that a proposition must be either true or false, with no third truth value. **exclusion** (-zhәn) *n.* **1** the act, or an instance, of excluding. **2** the state of being excluded. **to the exclusion of** so as to exclude. **exclusionary** *a.* tending to exclude. **exclusion clause** *n.* a clause in a contract which excludes one of the parties from liability in specified circumstances. **exclusionist** *n.* **1** a person who would exclude another from any privilege, position etc. **2** a person who supported the Bill, introduced in the reign of Charles II, to exclude the Duke of York (afterwards James II) from the throne. **3** one of the free settlers of Australia who opposed the granting of the franchise to ex-convicts. ~*a.* favouring exclusion. **exclusionism** *n.* **exclusion order** *n.* an order preventing the entry into the United Kingdom of anyone known to be involved in terrorism. **exclusion principle** *n.* PAULI EXCLUSION PRINCIPLE. **exclusive** (-siv) *a.* **1** shutting out or tending to shut out. **2** desiring to shut out. **3** fastidious in the choice of associates, snobbish. **4** available only from a specified source, a shop etc. **5** serving, allowing entry to a few selected people. **6** not inclusive (of). **7** excluding all else. **8** excluding all that is not specified. ~*adv.* not taking into account or not inclusively (of). ~*n.* **1** a story published only by one newspaper, radio station etc. **2** a person who is exclusive in their manners or tastes. **3** a person who excludes all but a very few from their society, a snob. **Exclusive Brethren** *n.pl.* the stricter section of the Plymouth Brethren, having very restricted contact with non-members. **exclusively** *adv.* **exclusiveness** *n.* **exclusive zone** *n.* an area of a country's territorial waters in which exploitation by other countries is officially banned. **exclusivism** *n.* **1** the act or practice of excluding. **2** systematic exclusiveness. **exclusivist** *n.* **exclusivity** (-siv´-) *n.* [L *exclūdere*, p.p. *exclūsus* (*claudere*, to shut)]

excogitate (ekskoj´itāt) *v.t.* **1** to think out. **2** to devise by thinking. **excogitation** (-ā´shәn) *n.* [L *excōgitātus*, p.p. of *excōgitāre* (*cōgitāre*, to COGITATE)]

excommunicate[1] (ekskәmū´nikāt) *v.t.* **1** to exclude from the communion and privileges of the Church. **2** to expel. **excommunication** (-ā´shәn) *n.* **excommunicative** *a.* **excommunicator** *n.* **excommunicatory** *a.* [late L *excommūnicātus*, p.p. of *excommūnicāre* (*commūnis*, COMMON)]

excommunicate[2] (ekskәmū´nikәt) *a.* excommunicated. ~*n.* a person who has been excommunicated. [as EXCOMMUNICATE[1]]

ex-con (ekskon´) *n.* (*coll.*) an ex-convict, a person who has served their sentence and been released from prison.

excoriate (ekskaw´riāt) *v.t.* **1** to strip the skin from. **2** to gall or tear off the skin by abrasion. **3** to criticize severely. **excoriation** (-ā´shәn) *n.* **1** the act of excoriating. **2** an abrasion. [L *excoriātus*, p.p. of *excoriāre* (*corium*, skin, hide)]

excrement (eks´krәmәnt) *n.* **1** refuse matter discharged from the body after digestion, faeces. **2** excretion. **excremental** (-men´-) *a.* **excrementitious** (-tish´әs) *a.* [F *excrément*, L *excrēmentum*, from *excernere*, as EXCRETE]

excrescence (ikskres´әns) *n.* **1** an abnormal, useless or disfiguring outgrowth. **2** an ugly and superfluous addition. **excrescent** *a.* growing abnormally or redundantly, superfluous, redundant. **excrescential** (-en´shәl) *a.* [L *excrescentia*, from *excrescere* (*crescere*, to grow)]

excrete (ikskrēt´) *v.t.*, *v.i.* to separate and discharge (superfluous matter) from the organism. **excreta** (-tә) *n.pl.* matter discharged from the body, esp. faeces and urine. **excreter** *n.* **excretion** *n.* **1** the ejection of waste matter from the body. **2** that which is excreted. **excretive** *a.* having the quality or power of excretion. **excretory** *a.* of or relating to excretion, conveying excreted matter. [L *excrētus*, p.p. of *excernere* (*cernere*, to sift)]

excruciate (ikskroo´shiāt) *v.t.* **1** to inflict severe pain or mental agony upon. **2** to torture. **excruciating** *a.* **excruciatingly** *adv.* **excruciation** (-ā´shәn) *n.* [L *excruciātus*, p.p. of *excruciāre* (*crux*, *crucis*, cross)]

exculpate (eks´kәlpāt, iks´kŭl-) *v.t.* (*formal*) **1** to clear from a charge. **2** to free from blame, exonerate. **3** to vindicate. **exculpation** (ekskŭlpā´shәn) *n.* **exculpatory** (ikskŭl´pә-) *a.* [L *exculpātus*, p.p. of *exculpāre* (*culpa*, fault)]

excurrent (ekskŭr´әnt) *a.* **1** running or passing out. **2** flowing out (as blood from the heart). **3** forming a passage outward. **4** (*Bot.*) projecting beyond the edge or point. [L *excurrens -ntem*, pres.p. of *excurrere* (see EXCURSIVE)]

excursion (ikskœ´shәn) *n.* **1 a** a journey or ramble for health or pleasure. **b** a short tour, a trip by an individual or a body of persons. **2** a wandering from the subject, a digression. **3** (*Astron.*) a deviation from the fixed course. **4** †a sally, a sortie, an expedition. **excursional, excursionary** *a.* of or relating to an excursion. **excursion fare** *n.* a special cheap fare allowed on some journeys on public transport. **excursionist** *n.* **1** a person who goes on an excursion. **2** a person who organizes excursions. **excursion train** *n.* a train carrying excursionists at a reduced fare. [as EXCURSIVE]

excursive (ikskœ´siv) *a.* rambling, deviating, exploring. **excursively** *adv.* **excursiveness** *n.* [L *excurs-*, p.p. stem of *excurrere* (*currere*, to run)]

excursus (ikskœ´sәs) *n.* (*pl.* **excursuses, excursus**) **1** a dissertation appended to a work, containing an exposition of some point raised or referred to in the text. **2** a digression during a narrative. [L, verbal n. of *excurrere*, as EXCURSIVE]

excuse[1] (ikskūz´) *v.t.* **1** to free from blame or guilt, to lessen the blame or guilt attaching to. **2** to pardon, to acquit (a person). **3** to ask pardon or indulgence for. **4** to serve as a vindication or apology for, to justify. **5** to relieve of or exempt from an obligation or duty. **6** to remit, not to exact (e.g. a debt). **7** to dispense with. **to be excused** (*euphem.*) to go to the lavatory. **to excuse oneself** **1** to (try to) justify one's actions. **2** to ask permission to leave. **excusable** *a.* **excusableness** *n.* **excusably** *adv.* †**excusator** *n.* **excusatory** *a.* **excuse me** *int.* used to express apology or disagreement. **excuse-me** *n.*

a dance during which partners may be changed on request. **excuser** *n.* [OF *excuser*, L *excūsāre* (*causa*, CAUSE)]

excuse[2] (ikskūs´) *n.* **1** a plea offered in extenuation of a fault or for release from an obligation, duty etc. **2** an apology, a justification. **3** the ground or reason for excusing. **4** a pretended reason. **5** the act of excusing, an exculpation. **excuse for** (*coll.*) a bad example of, a botched attempt at. [as EXCUSE[1]]

ex-directory (eksdirek´təri) *a.* **1** (of a telephone number) not listed in a telephone directory and not revealed to inquirers. **2** (of a person) having such a telephone number.

ex div. *abbr.* ex dividend.

ex dividend (eks div´idend) *a.*, *adv.* not including the next dividend.

exeat (ek´siat) *n.* **1** leave of absence, as to a student at school or university. **2** permission granted by a bishop to a priest to go out of his diocese. **exeant** (-ant) *n.* leave of absence to several persons. [L *exeat*, let him go out, *exeant*, let them go out, 3rd pers. subj. of *exīre*, to go out]

exec (egzek´) *n.* **1** an executive. **2** an executor.

execrate (ek´sikrāt) *v.t.* **1** to curse, to imprecate evil upon. **2** to detest. **3** to denounce as accursed. ~*v.i.* to utter curses. **execrable** *a.* **1** detestable, accursed. **2** abominable. **3** very bad, of very poor quality. **execrableness** *n.* **execrably** *adv.* **execration** (-ā´shən) *n.* **execrative** *a.* **execratively** *adv.* **execratory** *a.* [L *execrātus*, p.p. of *execrārī*, *exsecrārī* (*sacrāre*, to consecrate, from *sacer*, sacred, accursed)]

execute (ek´sikūt) *v.t.* **1** to carry into effect, to put in force. **2** to perform, to accomplish, complete. **3** to perform what is required to give validity to any legal instrument, as by signing and sealing. **4** to discharge (a duty, function, office etc.). **5** to play or perform (a piece of music, a part in a play). **6** to make or produce (a movement, drawing etc.). **7** to carry out a sentence of death on. **executable** *a.* **executant** (igzek´ū-) *n.* **1** a person who performs or carries into effect. **2** (*Mus.*) a performer on any instrument. **execution** (-kū´shən) *n.* **1** the act, or an instance, of executing. **2** performance, accomplishment. **3** the act of carrying into effect. **4** the carrying out of a death sentence. **5** the mode of performing a work of art, skill, dexterity. **6** the act of giving validity to a legal instrument, as by signing. **7** the carrying into effect of the judgement of a court. **8** a warrant empowering an officer to carry a judgement into effect, esp. one authorizing the seizure of a debtor's goods in default of payment. **executionary** *a.* **executioner** *n.* **1** a person who carries out a death sentence. **2** a person who kills, esp. a contract killer. **executive** (igzek´ūtiv) *a.* **1** having the function or power of executing. **2** of or relating to performance or carrying into effect. **3** carrying laws, decrees etc. into effect. **4** of or relating to, or suitable for the use of, a business executive. **5** (*coll.*) large, expensive or sophisticated. ~*n.* **1** the person or body of persons carrying laws, ordinances, sentences etc. into effect. **2** the administrative branch of a government or of a business. **3** (in business) a senior manager or administrator. **executively** *adv.* **executive order** *n.* (*US*) the equivalent to an Order in Council. **executive session** *n.* **1** (*US*) a meeting of the Senate to discuss executive business, formerly held in private. **2** any meeting held in private. [OF *executer*, med. L *execūtāre*, L *execūtus*, *exsecūtus*, p.p. of *exsequī* (*sequī*, to follow)]

executor (igzek´ūtə) *n.* a person who executes, esp. one appointed by a testator to carry out the provisions of their will. **executorial** (-taw´ri-) *a.* **executorship** *n.* **executory** *a.* **executrix** (-triks) *n.* (*pl.* **executrixes**, **executrices** (-trī´sēz)) a woman executor. [A-F *executour*, L *exsecūtor -ōrem*, as EXECUTE]

exedra (ek´sidrə, -sē´-) *n.* (*pl.* **exedrae** (-drē)) **1** the portico of the Grecian palaestra in which discussions were held. **2** a hall for conversation. **3** an elevated seat, a bishop's throne, a porch, a projecting chapel. **4** a recess. [L, from Gr. (*hedra*, a seat)]

exegesis (eksijē´sis) *n.* (*pl.* **exegeses** (-sēz)) exposition, interpretation, esp. of the Scriptures. **exegete** (ek´sijēt) *n.* a person skilled in the exegesis of the Scriptures. **exegetic** (-jet´-) *a.* of or relating to exegesis, expository. **exegetical** *a.* **exegetically** *adv.* **exegetics** *n.pl.* **1** scientific interpretation, esp. of Scripture. **2** hermeneutics. **exegetist** *n.* [Gr. *exēgēsis*, from *exēgeisthai* (*hēgeisthai*, to lead)]

exempla EXEMPLUM.

exemplar (igzem´plə) *n.* **1** a pattern or model to be copied. **2** a noted example. **3** a typical example. **4** a parallel instance. **5** a copy, as of a book. **exemplary** *a.* **1** serving as a pattern or model. **2** worthy of imitation. **3** typical, serving to exemplify, illustrative. **4** serving as a warning. **exemplarily** *adv.* **exemplariness** *n.* **exemplary damages** *n.pl.* damages given in excess of the loss suffered by the plaintiff, in order to act also as punishment to the defendant. [OF *exemplaire*, L *exemplārium*, from *exemplāris*, from *exemplum*, an EXAMPLE]

exemplify (igzem´plifī) *v.t.* (*3rd pers. sing. pres.* **exemplifies**, *pres.p.* **exemplifying**, *past*, *p.p.* **exemplified**) **1** to illustrate by example. **2** to be an example of, to prove by an attested copy. **3** (*Law*) to make an authenticated copy of (a document). **exemplifiable** *a.* **exemplification** (-fikā´shən) *n.* **exemplifier** *n.* [med. L *exemplificāre*]

exemplum (igzem´pləm) *n.* (*pl.* **exempla** (-plə)) **1** an example. **2** a short story or anecdote which illustrates a moral. [L, example]

exempt (igzempt´) *a.* **1** free (from). **2** not liable or subject to (a tax, obligation etc.). ~*n.* **1** a person who is exempted or freed (from). **2** an exon. ~*v.t.* **1** to free or allow to be free. **2** to grant immunity (from). **exemption** *n.* **1** the state or an instance of being exempt. **2** immunity. **3** freedom from the obligation of doing compulsory military service. [OF, from L *exemptus*, p.p. of *eximere* (*emere*, to take)]

exenterate (iksen´tərāt) *v.t.* to disembowel, eviscerate. **exenteration** (-ā´shən) *n.* [L *exenterātus*, p.p. of *exenterāre* (Gr. *enteron*, intestine)]

exequatur (eksikwā´tə) *n.* **1** a written recognition of a consul or commercial agent, given by the government to which he is accredited. **2** official authority or permission to execute some act. **3** an authorization by a sovereign or government for the exercise of episcopal functions under papal authority or the promulgation of a papal bull. [L, he may perform, 3rd sing. subj. of *exequī*, see EXECUTE]

exequies (ek´sikwiz) *n.pl.* (*formal*) funeral rites; the ceremony of burial. **exequial** (-sē´-) *a.* [OF *exeques*, L *exequias*, acc. of *exequiae* (*sequī*, to follow)]

exercise (ek´səsīz) *n.* **1** systematic exertion of the body for the sake of health. **2** physical exertion for the training of the body. **3** (*often pl.*) drill, athletics. **4** mental practice designed to develop a faculty or skill. **5** a composition designed to improve the technique of a player or singer. **6** the act of using, employing or exerting (a skill, a right etc.). **7** practice (of a function, virtue, occupation, art etc.). **8** (*pl.*) military manoeuvres, simulated battles, for training purposes. **9** a course of action designed to demonstrate a specified fact or quality (*an exercise in diplomacy*). **10** (*pl,, N Am.*) a ceremony to mark a stage in an academic year. **11** a devotional observance, an act of public or private worship. ~*v.t.* **1** to employ, to exert, to put in practice or operation. **2** to perform the duties of, to fulfil. **3** to train (a person). **4** to keep employed or busy. **5** to make anxious or solicitous, to perplex, worry. **6** to exert (muscles, brain, memory etc.) so as to develop their power. **7** to give (an animal) physical exercise. ~*v.i.* **1** †to use action or exertion (upon). **2** to take (regular) physical exercise; to do exercises. **greatly exercised about** deeply anxious regarding. **exercisable** *a.* **exercise bicycle**, **exercise bike** *n.* an exercising machine, at a gymnasium etc., like a bicycle without wheels. **exercise book** *n.* **1** a book for writing notes etc. in. **2** a printed book containing exercises. **exerciser** *n.* [OF *exercice*, L *exercitium*, from *exercitus*, p.p. of *exercēre*, to keep at work (*arcēre*, to shut up)]

exercitation (igzœsitā´shən) *n.* **1** exercise, practice. **2** a dissertation, a literary or rhetorical display of skill. [L *exercitātio -ōnem*, from *exercitāre*, freq. of *exercēre* (as EXERCISE)]

exergonic (eksœgon´ik) *a.* (of a biochemical reaction) accompanied by the release of energy, and therefore able to occur spontaneously. [as EXERGUE]

exergue (ek´sœg) *n.* **1** the small space beneath the base line of a subject engraved on a coin or medal. **2** the name, date or inscription placed there. **exergual** (-œ´gəl) *a.* [F, prob. from Gr. EX-, *ergon*, work]

☒ **exerpt** common misspelling of EXCERPT.

exert (igzœt´) *v.t.* to apply or use (strength, power, ability etc.) with effort, to put in action or operation. **to exert oneself** to strive, to use effort. **exertion** (-shən) *n.* [L *exsertus*, p.p. of *exserere*, to put forth (*serere*, to bind, to put)]

exes[1] EX[3].

exes[2] (ek´siz) *n.pl.* (*coll.*) (reimbursable) expenses.

exeunt (ek´siunt) *v.i.* they go off the stage, they retire (stage direction). **exeunt omnes** (omnāz´) they all go off the stage. [L, they go out]

exfiltrate (eks´filtrāt) *v.t.* to withdraw (spies etc.) secretly, as distinct from *infiltrate*. ~*v.i.* to move out of a place secretly. **exfiltration** (-trā´shən) *n.*

exfoliate (eksfō´liāt) *v.i.* **1** (of skin, rocks etc.) to shed or come off in flakes or scales. **2** to separate into flakes. **3** (of a tree) to shed its bark in layers. ~*v.t.* **1** to remove in flakes. **2** to cause to come off in flakes. **exfoliation** (-ā´shən) *n.* **exfoliative** *a.* [L *exfoliātus*, p.p. of *exfoliāre* (*folium*, a leaf)]

ex gratia (eks grā´sha) *a.*, *adv.* as an act of favour, and with no acceptance of liability. [L]

exhalation (eksəlā´shən) *n.* **1** the act or process of exhaling. **2** evaporation. **3 a** that which is exhaled. **b** a puff of breath. **4** a breathing out. **5** vapour, mist. **6** effluvium, an emanation. [L *exhalātio -ōnem*, see EXHALE]

exhale (iks·hāl´, igzāl´) *v.t.* **1** to breathe out. **2** to emit, or cause to be emitted, in vapour. **3** to draw up in vapour. ~*v.i.* **1** to be given off as vapour. **2** to pass off as an emanation. **3** to make an expiration, as distinct from *inhale*. **exhalable** *a.* **exhalant** *a.* having the quality of exhaling or evaporating. ~*n.* an organ or a vessel that exhales or emits vapour. [F *exhaler*, L *exhālāre* (EX-, *hālāre*, to breathe)]

exhaust (igzawst´) *v.t.* **1** to use up the whole of, to consume. **2** to wear out by exertion. **3** to draw off. **4** to empty by drawing out the contents. **5** to drain of resources, strength or essential properties. **6** to study, discuss, treat the whole of a subject. ~*n.* **1** the discharge of steam, gas, vapour etc. from an engine after it has performed its work. **2** the gases etc. so discharged. **3** the pipe or system which removes these gases. **4** an apparatus for withdrawing air by means of a partial vacuum. **5** the outward current of air so produced. **exhausted receiver** *n.* the receiver of an air pump after the air has been pumped out. **exhauster** *n.* **exhaustible** *a.* **exhaustibility** (-bil´-) *n.* **exhausting** *a.* tending to exhaust or tire out completely. **exhaustion** (-chən) *n.* **1** the act, or an instance, of exhausting. **2** the state of being exhausted. **3** a complete loss of strength. **4** a method of proving a point by showing that all alternatives are absurd or impossible. **exhaustive** *a.* tending to exhaust (esp. a subject), comprehensive. **exhaustively** *adv.* **1** so as to exhaust. **2** by the process of exhaustion. **exhaustiveness** *n.* [L *exhaustus*, p.p. of *exhaurīre* (*haurīre*, to draw)]

exhibit (igzib´it) *v.t.* **1** to offer to public view. **2** to present for inspection. **3** to show, to display, to manifest. **4** to furnish an instance of. **5** to bring forward officially. ~*n.* **1** anything exhibited. **2** an article or collection of articles sent to an exhibition. **3** a document or other item produced in court and used as evidence. **exhibiter** *n.* **exhibition** (eksibish´ən) *n.* **1** the act, or an instance, of exhibiting. **2** a display. **3** a public display of works of art or manufacture, natural products etc. **4** the act of allowing to be seen, as temper. **5** the production of documents etc. before any tribunal in proof of facts. **6** an allowance to a student in college, school etc., orig. maintenance, support, pecuniary assistance. **7** (*Sc. Law*) an action for compelling delivery of documents. **to make an exhibition of oneself** to behave so as to appear foolish or contemptible. **exhibitioner** *n.* a student who has obtained an exhibition at a college or school. **exhibitionism** *n.* **1** a tendency to show off, to attract attention to oneself. **2** (*Psych.*) a compulsive desire to exhibit one's genitals in public. **exhibitionist** *n.* **exhibitionistic** (-ist´ik) *a.* **exhibitionistically** *adv.* **exhibitor** (eksib´-) *n.* **exhibitory** *a.* [L *exhibitus*, p.p. of *exhibēre* (*habēre*, to have)]

exhilarate (igzil´ərāt) *v.t.* to gladden, to enliven, to animate. **exhilarant** *a.*, *n.* **exhilarating** *a.* **exhilaratingly** *adv.* **exhilaration** (-ā´shən) *n.* **exhilarative** (-ətiv) *a.* [L *exhilarātus*, p.p. of *exhilarāre* (*hilaris*, glad, cheerful)]

exhort (igzawt´) *v.t.* **1** to incite by words (to good deeds). **2** to admonish. **3** to urge, to advise or encourage by argument. ~*v.i.* to deliver an exhortation. ~†*n.* an exhortation. **exhortation** (egzawtā´shən) *n.* **1** the act or practice of exhorting. **2** an admonition, earnest advice. **3** a formal address, esp. in church. **exhortative** (-awt´-) *a.* **exhortatory** *a.* **exhorter** *n.* [OF *exhorter*, L *exhortārī* (*hortārī*, to urge)]

exhume (igzūm´, eks·hūm´) *v.t.* **1** to dig out, esp. a corpse from its grave. **2** (*fig.*) to unearth, to discover. **exhumation** (eks·hūmā´shən, egzū-) *n.* **exhumer** *n.* [F *exhumer*, late L *exhumāre* (*humus*, the ground)]

ex hypothesi (eks hīpoth´əsī) *adv.* according to the hypothesis stated; following the hypothesis. [L]

exigeant (egzēzhã´) *a.* (*fem.* **exigeante** (-ãt)) exacting. [F, p.p. of *exiger*, L *exigere*, as EXIGENCE]

exigence (ek´sijəns, -sij´-), **exigency** (iksij´-, igzij´-) *n.* (*pl.* **exigences**, **exigencies**) **1** urgent need, demand, necessity. **2** a state of affairs demanding immediate action or remedy, an emergency. [F *exigence*, L *exigentia*, from *exigere* (*agere*, to drive)]

exigent (ek´sijənt) *a.* **1** urgent, pressing. **2** demanding more than is reasonable, exacting. **exigently** *adv.* **exigible** *a.* that may be exacted (from or against). [L *exigens -ntem*, pres.p. of *exigere* (see EXIGENCE)]

exiguous (igzig´ūəs, iksig´-) *a.* small, slender, scanty. **exiguity** (eksigū´iti) *n.* **exiguously** *adv.* **exiguousness** *n.* [L *exiguus*, small, as EXIGENCE]

exile (eg´zīl, ek´sīl) *n.* **1** banishment, expatriation. **2** long absence from one's native country, whether voluntary or enforced. **3** a person who is banished, or has been long absent from their native country. **4** (**Exile**) the captivity of the Jews in Babylon. ~*v.t.* to banish from one's native country, town etc. **exilement** *n.* **exilian** (-il´-), **exilic** (-il´-) *a.* of or relating to exile or banishment, esp. to that of the Jews in Babylon. [OF *exil*, L *exilium*, *exsilium* (*salīre*, to leap)]

eximious (egzim´iəs) *a.* excellent, illustrious. **eximiously** *adv.* [L *eximius*, select, from *eximere*, to EXEMPT]
ex int. *abbr.* ex interest.
ex interest (eks in´trəst) *a.*, *adv.* not including interest. [L]
exist (igzist´) *v.i.* **1** to be, to have actual being. **2** to live. **3** to continue to be. **4** to live or have being under specified conditions. **5** (of inanimate objects or circumstances) to be found, to occur. **6** to carry on living, after a fashion, in unfavourable circumstances. **existence** *n.* **1** the state of being or existing. **2** continuance of being. **3** life. **4** mode of existing. **5** a thing that exists; a being, an entity. **6** all that exists. **existent** *a.* having being or existence, existing, actual. **existential** (egzisten´shəl, eksi-) *a.* **1** of or relating to or consisting in existence. **2** (*Logic*) (of a proposition etc.) asserting the existence of something. **3** (*Philos.*) of or relating to human existence or to existentialism. **existentialism** *n.* a philosophical theory which considers human beings as morally free, and responsible for making their own system of values in an otherwise meaningless universe. **existentialist** *n.*, *a.* **existentially** *adv.* **existible** (-ist´-) *a.* **existibility** (-bĭl´) *n.* [F *exister*, L *existere*, *esistere* (*sistere*, causal of *stare*, to stand)]
exit[1] (ek´sit, eg´zit) *n.* **1** a passage or door, a way out. **2** a going out. **3** freedom to go out. **4** a place where vehicles can enter or leave a motorway. **5** the departure of an actor from the stage. **6** departure, esp. from this life; death, decease. **exit permit** *n.* a written authorization to leave a country. **exit poll** *n.* an unofficial poll taken by asking people leaving a polling station how they have voted. **exit visa** *n.* an exit permit. [L *exitus*, a going out, from *exīre* (*īre*, to go)]
exit[2] (ek´sit) *v.i.* **1** to depart, to leave a place. **2** goes off the stage (stage direction). **3** (*formal*) to die. **4** (in bridge, whist etc.) to lose the lead deliberately. **5** (*Comput.*) to leave a subroutine, a program etc., to go out or away from. *~v.t.* (*N Am.*) to leave. [L, he goes out, 3rd pers. sing. pres. of *exīre*]
☒ **exite** common misspelling of EXCITE.
ex-lib. *abbr.* ex-libris.
ex-libris (ekslib´ris) *n.* (*pl.* **ex-libris**) a bookplate, a label bearing an owner's name, crest, device etc. [L *ex librīs*, out of the books, from the library (of)]
☒ **exma** common misspelling of ECZEMA.
ex nihilo (eks nī´hilō) *adv.* out of nothing (*creation ex nihilo*). [L]
exo- (ek´sō) *comb. form* of or relating to the outside of anything, external. [Gr. *exō*, outside]
exobiology (eksōbīol´əji) *n.* the branch of biology which studies the possibility of extraterrestrial life, and what forms this might take. **exobiologist** *n.*
exocarp (ek´sōkahp) *n.* (*Bot.*) the outer layer of a pericarp. **exocarpic** (-kah´pik) *a.*
Exocet® (ek´səset) *n.* **1** a French-built surface-skimming missile that can be launched from surface or air. **2** (**exocet**) an exceptionally effective weapon.
exocrine (ek´səkrīn, -krin) *a.* (of a gland) producing secretions that are released through a duct. *~n.* an exocrine gland. [Gr. *krīnein*, to separate]
Exod. *abbr.* Exodus.
exoderm (eks´ədœm) *n.* (*Anat.*) the epidermis, the outer layer of the blastoderm. **exodermal** (-dœ´-) *a.*
exodus (eks´ədəs) *n.* **1** a departure, esp. of a large body of persons. **2** (**Exodus**) the departure of the Israelites from Egypt under Moses. **3** (**Exodus**) the second book of the Old Testament, narrating this event. [Gr. *exodos*]
ex off. *abbr.* ex officio.
ex officio (eks əfish´iō) *adv.* by virtue of one's office. *~a.* official. [L *ex*, out of, *officiō*, abl. of *officium*, duty, OFFICE]
exogamy (eksog´əmi) *n.* **1** the custom of marrying outside one's own tribe. **2** (*Biol.*) the union of reproductive cells not related or only distantly related to each other. **exogamic** (-gam´-), **exogamous** (-og´-) *a.* [Gr. *gamos*, marriage]
exogenous (eksoj´inəs) *a.* **1** of or relating to an exogen. **2** developing externally. **3** having external origins (*exogenous depression*). **exogen** (ek´səjən) *n.* **1** a plant whose stem increases by an annual layer growing on the outside of the wood, as distinct from *endogen*. **2** a dicotyledon. **exogenously** *adv.* [Gr. *gen-*, root of *gignesthai*, to be born or produced]
exon[1] (ek´son) *n.* any one of the four officers of the Yeomen of the Guard ranking as corporals. [prob. representing F pron. of EXEMPT]
exon[2] (ek´son) *n.* (*Biol.*) any segment of a gene which consists of codons. [L *ex*, out of, Gr. neut. suf. *-on*]
exonerate (igzon´ərāt) *v.t.* **1** to free from a charge or blame, to exculpate. **2** to relieve from a duty, obligation or liability. **3** †to relieve of a weight or burden. **exoneration** (-ā´shən) *n.* **exonerative** (-ətiv) *a.* [L *exonerātus*, p.p. of *exonerāre* (*onus oneris*, a burden)]
exoparasite (eksōpar´əsīt) *n.* an ectoparasite. **exoparasitic** (-sit´ik) *a.*
exophagy (eksof´əji) *n.* cannibalism in which only persons of a different tribe are eaten. **exophagous** (-gəs) *a.*
exophthalmia (eksofthal´miə), **exophthalmos** (-məs), **exophthalmus** *n.* (*Med.*) abnormal protrusion of the eyeball. **exophthalmic** *a.* **exophthalmic goitre** *n.* Graves' disease.
exoplasm (ek´səplazm) *n.* (*Biol.*) the denser outer layer of the cuticular protoplasm of certain protozoans, ectoplasm.
exor. *abbr.* executor.
exorable (ek´sərəbəl) *a.* that can be persuaded by pleading. **exorability** (-bil´-) *n.* **exorably** *adv.*
exorbitant (igzaw´bitənt) *a.* out of all bounds, grossly excessive, inordinate, extravagant. **exorbitance** *n.* **exorbitantly** *adv.* [L *exorbitans -ntem*, pres.p. of *exorbitāre*, to fly out of the track (*orbita*, a track)]
exorcize (ek´sawsīz), **exorcise** *v.t.* **1** to expel (as an evil spirit) by prayers and ceremonies. **2** to free or purify from unclean spirits. **exorcist** *n.* **1** a person who exorcizes. **2** a member of one of the minor orders in the Roman Catholic Church, to whom the function of exorcism (now restricted to priests) was formerly committed. **exorcism** *n.* **exorcization** (-zā´shən) *n.* **exorcizer** *n.* [late L *exorcizāre*, Gr. *exorkizein* (*horkos*, oath)]
exordium (igzaw´diəm) *n.* (*pl.* **exordiums**, **exordia** (-diə)) the beginning of anything, esp. the introductory part of a literary work or discourse. **exordial** *a.* [L, from *exordīrī* (*ordīrī*, to begin)]
exoskeleton (eksōskel´itən) *n.* an external skeleton, e.g. in arthropods, formed by a hardening of the integument. **exoskeletal** *a.*
exosmosis (eksozmō´sis), **exosmose** (ek´sozmōs) *n.* (*Biol.*) passage of a liquid through a porous membrane from within outwards to mix with an external fluid. **exosmotic** (-mot´-) *a.* [Gr. *ōsmos*, a pushing]
exosphere (ek´sōsfiə) *n.* the outermost layer of the earth's atmosphere. [Gr. *sphaira*, sphere]
exospore (ek´sōspaw) *n.* (*Biol.*) **1** the outer layer of the wall of a spore. **2** a spore released by the formation of a septum.
exostosis (eksōstō´sis) *n.* (*pl.* **exostoses** (-sēz)) **1** a tumour of a bony nature growing upon and arising from a bone or cartilage. **2** a morbid growth of hard wood projecting like warts or tumours from the stem or roots of a plant.
exoteric (eksəter´ik), **exoterical** *a.* **1** external, public, fit to be imparted to outsiders. **2** comprehensible to the general public, as distinct from *esoteric*. **3** (of disciples) not admitted to esoteric doctrines. **4** ordinary, popular.

~*n.* 1 an uninitiated person. 2 (*pl.*) truths or doctrines suitable for popular instruction. **exoterically** *adv.* **exotericism** (-sizm) *n.* [Gr. *exōterikos*, from *exōterō*, comp. of *exō*, outward, from ex, out]

exothermic (eksōthœ´mik), **exothermal** (-məl) *a.* (*Chem.*) involving the evolution of heat. **exothermically, exothermally** *a.* [Gr. *thermē*, heat]

exotic (igzot´ik) *a.* 1 introduced from a foreign country. 2 romantically strange, glamorous. 3 (*coll.*) rare, unusual. 4 (of a fuel etc.) new and high-energy. ~*n.* 1 anything foreign. 2 anything introduced from a foreign country, as a plant. **exotica** (-kə) *n.pl.* rare or unusual objects, esp. when forming a collection. **exotically** *adv.* **exotic dancer** *n.* a striptease or belly dancer. **exoticism** (-sizm) *n.* [L *exōticus*, Gr. *exōtikos*, from *exō*, as EXOTERIC]

exotoxin (eksōtok´sin) *n.* a toxin released from within a living bacterium into the surrounding medium. **exotoxic** *a.*

exp. *abbr.* 1 expenses. 2 experiment(al). 3 expired. 4 exponential. 5 export(er). 6 express.

expand (ikspand´) *v.t.* 1 to open or spread out. 2 to distend, to cause to increase in bulk. 3 to widen, to extend, to enlarge. 4 to write out in full (what is condensed or abbreviated). 5 (*Math.*) to develop into a series, to state in a fuller form. ~*v.i.* 1 to become opened or spread out, distended, or enlarged in bulk, not mass. 2 to become more relaxed, to talk more openly. **expandable** *a.* **expanded** *a.* **expanded metal** *n.* sheet metal cut and formed into a lattice, used for reinforcing concrete etc. **expanded plastic** *n.* foam plastic or polystyrene. **expander** *n.* **expanding universe** *n.* the universe regarded as ever expanding, according to a theory based on the Doppler effect in the light from stars and galaxies. **expansible** (-sibəl) *a.* **expansibility** (-bil´-) *n.* **expansile** (-sīl) *a.* 1 of or relating to expansion. 2 capable of expanding, expansible. [L *expandere* (*pandere*, to spread (p.p. *pansus*), rel. to *patēre*, see PATENT]

expanse (ikspans´) *n.* 1 a wide, open extent or area. 2 expansion or extension. 3 amount of expansion. [L *pans-*, p.p. stem of *pandere*, see EXPAND]

expansion (ikspan´shən) *n.* 1 the act, or an instance, of expanding. 2 the state of being expanded. 3 enlargement, extension, distension. 4 extension of business, increase of liabilities, extension of the currency or of territory. 5 increase of volume, as of fuel in a cylinder. **expansionary** *a.* **expansion bolt** *n.* a bolt that expands when it is tightened, so that it can be fixed firmly in a crack etc. **expansion card, expansion board** *n.* (*Comput.*) a printed circuit board that can be inserted in a computer to give extra facilities. **expansionism** *n.* **expansionist** *n.* a person who advocates territorial or economic expansion. **expansionistic** *a.* **expansion joint** *n.* a joint between metal rails, concrete pieces etc., which allows for expansion when heated. **expansion slot** *n.* (*Comput.*) a connector in a computer into which an expansion card can be fitted. [late L *expansio -ōnem*, as EXPANSE]

expansive (ikspan´siv) *a.* 1 having the power of expanding. 2 able or tending to expand. 3 extending widely, comprehensive. 4 frank, effusive. **expansively** *adv.* **expansiveness** *n.* **expansivity** (-iv´iti) *n.* [as EXPANSE]

ex parte (eks pah´ti) *adv.* (*Law*) 1 proceeding from one side only. 2 in the interests of one side. **ex-parte** *a.* one-sided. [L, from one side]

expat EXPATRIATE².

expatiate (ikspā´shiāt) *v.i.* 1 to dilate. 2 to speak or write copiously (on a subject). 3 to wander at large. **expatiation** (-ā´shən) *n.* **expatiatory** *a.* [L *expatiātus*, p.p. of *expatiārī* (*spatiārī*, to roam, from *spatium*, space)]

expatriate¹ (ekspā´triāt) *v.t.* 1 to exile. 2 to drive into banishment. 3 to exile (oneself), or withdraw (oneself) from citizenship. ~*v.i.* 1 to emigrate. 2 to renounce one's citizenship in one's country. **expatriation** (-ā´shən) *n.* [L *expatriātus*, p.p. of *expatriāre* (*patria*, one's native land)]

expatriate² (ekspā´triət), (*coll.*) **expat** (ekspat´) *n.* a person living away from their own country. ~*a.* 1 living abroad. 2 exiled.

expect (ikspekt´) *v.t.* 1 to look forward to. 2 to regard as certain or likely to happen, to anticipate. 3 to require as due. 4 (*coll.*) to think, to suppose (that). **expectable** *a.* **expectably** *adv.* **expectancy, expectance** *n.* (*pl.* **expectancies, expectances**) 1 the act or state of expecting, expectation. 2 the state of being expected. 3 prospect of possessing, enjoying etc. 4 a thing which is expected. **expectant** *a.* 1 expecting, waiting in expectation (of). 2 anticipating, presumptive. 3 pregnant. ~*n.* a person who waits in expectation of something, as a candidate for an office etc. **expectantly** *adv.* **expectation** (ekspiktā´shən) *n.* 1 the act or state of expecting, anticipation, a confident awaiting (of). 2 (*pl.*) prospects (of inheriting). 3 the ground for confident anticipation (of). 4 the probability of a future event. 5 something expected. **expectation of life** *n.* LIFE EXPECTANCY (under LIFE). **expectative** *a.* of or relating to, or giving rise to expectation. ~*n.* the object of expectation. **expecter** *n.* a person who expects. **expecting** *a.* (*coll.*) pregnant. **expectingly** *adv.* [L *expectāre* (*spectāre*, freq. of *specere*, to see)]

expectorate (ikspek´tərāt) *v.t.* to discharge from the lungs or throat by coughing, hawking or spitting. ~*v.i.* 1 to discharge matter from the lungs or throat by coughing etc. 2 to spit. **expectorant** *a.* having the quality of promoting expectoration. ~*n.* a medicine promoting expectoration. **expectoration** (-ā´shən) *n.* **expectorative** (-spek´-) *a.* **expectorator** *n.* [L *expectorātus*, p.p. of *expectorāre* (*pectus -oris*, the breast)]

expedient (ikspē´diənt) *a.* 1 promoting the object in view. 2 advantageous, convenient. 3 conducive to personal advantage. 4 appropriate, suitable. 5 politic as opposed to just. ~*n.* 1 that which promotes an object. 2 an advantageous way or means. 3 a shift, a contrivance. **expedience, expediency** *n.* **expediential** (-en´-) *a.* **expediently** *adv.* [F *expédient*, L *expediens -ntem* (pres.p. of *expedīre*, as EXPEDITE)]

Usage note The adjectives *expedient* and *expeditious* should not be confused: *expedient* means advantageous or convenient, and *expeditious* speedy.

expedite (ek´spədīt) *v.t.* 1 to facilitate, to assist or accelerate the progress of. 2 to dispatch, accomplish quickly. ~†*a.* 1 easy, disencumbered. 2 speedy, ready, expeditious, active, light-armed. **expediter** *n.* **expeditious** (-dish´əs) *a.* 1 speedy, ready, active. 2 done with efficiency and rapidity. **expeditiously** *adv.* **expeditiousness** *n.* [L *expedītus*, p.p. of *expedīre* (*pēs pedis*, the foot)]

expedition (ekspədish´ən) *n.* 1 any journey or voyage by an organized body for some definite object. 2 the persons with their equipment engaged in this. 3 a march or voyage of an army or fleet to a distance with hostile intentions. 4 speed, promptness, dispatch. **expeditionary** *a.* relating to, constituting or used in an expedition. **expeditionist** *n.* [as EXPEDITE]

expeditious EXPEDITE.

expel (ikspel´) *v.t.* (*pres.p.* **expelling,** *past, p.p.* **expelled**) 1 to drive or force out. 2 to eject, to banish. 3 to turn out formally (as from a school, college, or society). **expellable** *a.* **expellant, expellent** *a.* **expellee** (-ē´) *n.* **expeller** *n.* [L *expellere* (*pellere*, to drive, p.p. *pulsus*)]

expend (ikspend´) *v.t.* 1 to spend, to lay out. 2 to consume, to use up. **expendable** *a.* 1 likely to be or intended to be wasted. 2 that can be sacrificed in order to attain some purpose. **3** unimportant, not worth saving. **4** that need not be reused. ~*n.* something that is expendable. **expendability** (-bil´-) *n.* **expendably** *adv.* **expenditure** (-dichə) *n.* **1** the act of expending; disbursement, consumption. **2** the amount expended. [L *expendere* (*pendere*, to weigh, p.p. *pensus*)]

expense (ikspens´) *n.* **1** a laying out or expending. **2** cost, charge, outlay, price paid. **3** (*pl.*) outlay in performance of a duty or commission. **4** (*pl., coll.*) money reimbursed for this. **5** something on which money has to be spent. **at the expense of 1** at the cost of. **2** to the discredit or detriment of. **expense account** *n.* an account of expenses refunded to an employee by an employer. **expensive** *a.* **1** costly, causing or requiring a large expenditure. **2** extravagant, lavish. **expensively** *adv.* **expensiveness** *n.* [A-F, from late L *expensa*, fem. of *expensus*, p.p. of *expendere*, see EXPEND]

experience (ikspiə´riəns) *n.* **1** practical acquaintance with any matter. **2** knowledge gained by observation or trial. **3** a particular instance of such knowledge. **4** something undergone of an affecting or impressive nature. **5** the fact of being so affected or impressed. ~*v.t.* **1** to gain a practical knowledge of by trial or observation. **2** to undergo, to feel, to meet with. **3** to make trial or proof of. **4** to train. **to experience religion** (*N Am.*) to be converted. **experienceable** *a.* **experienced** *a.* **1** taught by experience. **2** practised, skilled. **experience table** *n.* an actuarial table, based on past statistics. [OF, from L *experientia*, from *experīrī*, to go through, to try, *perītus*, skilled)]

experiential (ikspiərien´shəl) *a.* of or relating to, or derived from experience. **experientialism** *n.* (*Philos.*) experiential philosophy. **experientialist** *a.* **experientially** *adv.* **experiential philosophy** *n.* a philosophy which states that all knowledge and ideas are derived from experience. [L *experientia*]

experiment (iksper´imənt) *n.* **1** a trial, proof or test of anything. **2** an act, operation or process designed to discover some unknown truth, principle or effect, to test a hypothesis or to test a fact. **3** †experience. ~*v.i.* **1** to make an experiment or trial (on or with). **2** to investigate by this means. **3** to search by trial. **experimental** (-men´-) *a.* **1** pertaining to, derived from, or founded upon experiment. **2** practising experiments. **3** empirical. **4** based on an (unfinished) experiment; provisional. **experimentalism** *n.* **experimentalist** *n.* **experimentalize, experimentalise** *v.i.* **experimentally** *adv.* **experimental philosophy** *n.* philosophy based on induction and insisting on experiment and observation as indispensable to reasoned knowledge. **experimentation** (-tā´shən) *n.* the act or practice of making experiments. **experimentative** (-men´-) *a.* **experimenter** *n.* **experimenter effect** *n.* the effect that an experimenter's assumptions and expectations have on the results of the experiment. [OF, from L *experīmentum*, from *experīrī*, to EXPERIENCE]

expert (ek´spœt) *a.* **1** experienced, dexterous from use and experience. **2** practised, skilful (at or in). **3** based on, or resulting from, special skill or knowledge. ~*n.* **1** a person who has special skill or knowledge. **2** a scientific or professional witness. ~†*v.t.* **1** to make trial of. **2** to experience. **expertise**[1] (-tēz´) *n.* expert skill, opinion or knowledge. **expertise**[2] EXPERTIZE (under EXPERT). **expertize** (eks´pœtīz), **expertise** *v.t., v.i.* to give an expert opinion (on). **expertly** *adv.* **expertness** *n.* **expert system** *n.* a computer system designed using expert knowledge and artificial intelligence techniques, so that it can solve problems and make intelligent decisions. [OF, from L *expertus*, p.p. of *experīrī*, as EXPERIMENT]

expiate (ek´spiāt) *v.t.* **1** to atone for. **2** to make reparation or amends for. **3** to pay the penalty of. **expiable** *a.* **expiation** (-ā´shən) *n.* **expiator** *n.* **expiatory** *a.* [L *expiātus*, p.p. of *expiāre* (*piāre*, to propitiate, from *pius*, devout)]

expire (ikspīə´) *v.t.* **1** to breathe out from the lungs. **2** to send forth, to emit, to exhale. **3** †to bring to an end. ~*v.i.* **1** to come to an end. **2** (of a guarantee, authorization etc.) to come to an end through passage of time, to lose validity. **3** to emit the last breath; to die. **4** to breathe out. **expiration** (ekspirā´shən) *n.* **1** the act of breathing out. **2** cessation, termination. **expiratory** (-spī´-) *a.* of or relating to the emission of breath from the lungs. **expirer** *n.* **expiry** *n.* **1** expiration, termination. **2** death. [F *expirer*, L *expīrāre* (*spīrāre*, to breathe)]

explain (iksplān´) *v.t.* **1** to make clear, plain or intelligible. **2** to expound and illustrate the meaning of. **3** to account for. **4** to state, as an explanation. ~*v.i.* to give explanations. **to explain away 1** to get rid of (difficulties) by explanation. **2** to modify or do away with (a charge etc.) by explanation. **to explain oneself 1** to make one's meaning clear. **2** to give an account of one's motives, intentions, conduct etc. **explainable** *a.* **explainer** *n.* [MF *explaner*, L *explānāre* (*plānāre*, to flatten, from *plānus*, flat)]

explanation (eksplənā´shən) *n.* **1** the act, or an instance, of explaining. **2** the sense or definition given by an interpreter or expounder. **3** the process of arriving at a mutual understanding or reconciliation. **4** that which accounts for anything. **explanatory** (-plan´-) *a.* **1** containing an explanation. **2** serving to explain. **explanatorily** *adv.*

explant[1] (eksplahnt´) *v.t.* to remove (living tissue) to a medium for tissue culture. **explantation** (-ā´shən) *n.* [L *explantāre*, to plant out]

explant[2] (eks´plahnt) *n.* a piece of living tissue removed for culture. [as EXPLANT[1]]

expletive (iksplē´tiv) *a.* **1** serving to fill out or complete. **2** introduced merely to fill a gap or vacancy. ~*n.* **1** a word, not necessary to the sense, introduced to fill up a line or a sentence. **2** an interjection or word added for emphasis, esp. a swear word. **expletory** *a.* [L *explētīvus*, from *explētus*, p.p. of *explēre* (*plēre*, to fill)]

explicate (eks´plikāt) *v.t.* **1** to unfold the meaning of. **2** to make clear, explain the difficulties of (a text etc.). **3** to develop (the contents of an idea, proposition etc.). **explicable** *a.* capable of being explained. **explication** (-ā´shən) *n.* **explicative, explicatory** *a.* serving to explain or interpret. **explicator** *n.* [L *explicātus*, p.p. of *explicāre* (*plica*, a fold)]

explicit[1] (iksplis´it) *a.* **1** plainly expressed, distinctly stated, as distinct from *implicit*. **2** definite. **3** (of a person) unreserved, outspoken. **4** showing or describing nudity or sexual activity quite plainly. **explicitly** *adv.* **explicitness** *n.* [F *explicite*, L *explicitus*, old form of *explicātus*, as EXPLICATE]

explicit[2] (iksplis´it) *n.* (*Hist.*) a word formerly written at the end of manuscript books, and equivalent to 'finis', 'the end'. [med. L, here ends, orig. abbr. of *explicitus*, see EXPLICIT[1]]

explode (iksplōd´) *v.t.* **1** to cause to burst with a loud noise. **2** to refute, expose, discredit (a theory, fallacy etc.). **3** †to cry down, to hoot or hiss away. ~*v.i.* **1** to burst with a loud noise. **2** to give vent suddenly to strong feelings, esp. anger. **3** (*fig.*) to come to an end as if by bursting, to collapse. **4** (of population) to increase suddenly and dramatically. **exploded** *a.* (of a drawing) depicting all the outer parts (of a machine, organism etc.) as lifted off the inner parts, so that all may be shown, with their relationships. **exploder** *n.* a person who explodes or rejects. **exploding** *n., a.* **exploding star** *n.* (*Astron.*) a nova or supernova. [MF *exploder*, L *explōdere*, p.p. *explōsus* (*plaudere*, to clap)]

exploit[1] (ek´sploit) *n.* **1** a feat, a great or noble achievement. **2** an adventure. [OF *esploit*, profit, achievement, L *explicitum*, neut. p.p. of *explicere*, see EXPLICATE]

exploit[2] (eksploit´) *v.t.* 1 to make use of, derive benefit from. 2 to utilize, esp. to make use of or take advantage of for one's own profit. **exploitable** *a.* **exploitation** (-ā´shən) *n.* **exploitative** *a.* **exploiter** *n.* **exploitive** *a.* [as EXPLOIT[1]]

explore (iksplaw´) *v.t.* 1 to search or inquire into. 2 to investigate, to examine. 3 to travel over (a country etc.) in order to examine or discover. 4 (*Med.*) to investigate (an organ etc.) in detail. **exploration** (eksplərā´shən) *n.* **explorational** *a.* **explorative** (-plor´-) *a.* **exploratory** *a.* **exploratory operation** *n.* a surgical operation carried out for purposes of diagnosis. **explorer** *n.* 1 a person who explores. 2 a traveller into unknown or little-known parts. [F *explorer*, L *explōrāre*, to search out (prob. *plōrāre*, to make to flow, from *pluere*, to flow)]

explosion (iksplō´zhən) *n.* 1 a bursting or exploding with a loud noise. 2 a sudden and violent noise. 3 a sudden and violent outbreak, as of physical forces, anger etc. 4 a sudden and very rapid increase or expansion. **explosion welding** *n.* the welding of metals with different melting points using the pressure created by an explosion. **explosive** (-siv) *a.* 1 bursting or driving out with great force and noise. 2 liable to explode or cause explosion. 3 (of a situation) tense, potentially violent. 4 (of consonants) plosive. ~*n.* 1 an explosive agent or substance, as gunpowder, dynamite etc. 2 a plosive consonant. **explosively** *adv.* **explosiveness** *n.* [L *explōsio -ōnem*, from *explōdere*, EXPLODE]

Expo (eks´pō), **expo** *n.* (*pl.* **Expos, expos**) a large public exhibition. [*expo*sition]

exponent (ikspō´nənt) *a.* 1 setting forth or explaining. 2 exemplifying. ~*n.* 1 a person who sets forth or explains. 2 a person who or thing which advocates or promotes a party, principle or cause. 3 a type, a representative. 4 a number or quantity written to the right of and above another number or quantity, to show how many times the latter is to be taken as a factor (thus, in the expression a^3, ^{3} is an exponent, and shows that *a* is to be taken three times as a factor thus, $a \times a \times a$). **exponential** (ekspənen´-) *a.* 1 (*Math.*) of or relating to an exponent or exponents. 2 involving variable exponents. 3 (*coll.*) very rapid. **exponential curve** *n.* a relationship between two quantities such that as one quantity increases by equal steps the other increases by equal percentages of its previous value. **exponential equation** *n.* an equation into which the unknown quantity enters as an exponent. **exponential function** *n.* a function containing a quantity raised to an exponent. **exponential growth** *n.* growth at an ever-increasing rate as the total size or number increases. **exponential horn** *n.* a horn-shaped loudspeaker in which the sides of the horn follow an exponential curve. **exponentially** *adv.* **exponential quantity** *n.* a quantity with a variable exponent. [L *expōnens -ntem*, pres.p. of *expōnere* (*pōnere*, to put, p.p. *positus*)]

export[1] (ikspawt´) *v.t.* to carry or send (goods) to foreign countries. **invisible exports** INVISIBLE. **visible exports** VISIBLE. **exportable** (-spaw´-) *a.* **exportability** (-bil´-) *n.* **exportation** (ekspawtā´shən) *n.* the act or practice of exporting goods. **exporter** *n.* [L *exportāre* (*portāre*, to carry)]

export[2] (eks´pawt) *n.* 1 the act or process of exporting, exportation. 2 a commodity sent to a foreign country. 3 (*pl.*) the quantity or value of goods exported. ~*a.* suitable for export, of good quality. **export duty** *n.* a duty paid on goods exported. **export reject** *n.* an item sold in its country of origin because it is not of high enough quality to export. [as EXPORT[1]]

expose (ikspōz´) *v.t.* 1 to lay bare or open. 2 to leave unprotected or vulnerable. 3 to subject (to any influence or action). 4 to turn out and abandon (as a child). 5 to exhibit, to display, esp. for sale. 6 to disclose, lay bare, reveal. 7 to unmask, reveal the identity of. 8 to subject (a photographic film in a camera) to light. ~*n.* (*N Am.*) an exposé. **to expose oneself** 1 to display one's genitals in public so as to shock or embarrass others. 2 to reveal one's faults, weaknesses etc. **exposable** *a.* **exposal** *n.* **exposé** (-zā) *n.* 1 a formal declaration or recital of facts. 2 a disclosure, an exposure (of damning or sensational information). **exposer** *n.* **exposition** (ekspəzi´shən) *n.* 1 the act of exposing. 2 an explanation, an account (of). 3 an explanation or interpretation of the meaning of an author or a work, a commentary. 4 †exposure. 5 a public exhibition. 6 (*Mus.*) the first statement of the themes in a sonata movement etc. **expositional** *a.* **expositive** (-spoz´-) *a.* **expositor** (-spoz´-) *n.* 1 a person who expounds or explains. 2 a commentator. **expository** (-spoz´-) *a.* **exposure** (ikspō´zhə) *n.* 1 the act of exposing. 2 the state of being exposed to view, inconvenience, danger etc. 3 the state of being unsheltered from cold, heat, sun etc. 4 physical illness resulting from prolonged coldness. 5 abandonment (of a child, aged person etc.). 6 display, esp. of goods for sale. 7 a disclosure, revelation, unmasking. 8 situation (of a property) with respect to the points of the compass, or free access of light and air; outlook, aspect. 9 **a** the act of allowing light from an object to fall upon a sensitized photographic plate. **b** the duration of this exposure. **c** the piece of film thus exposed. 10 appearance in public, esp. on stage or television or in the press. **exposure meter** *n.* a device attached to a camera which measures the strength of the light so that the length of exposure etc. can be adjusted. [F *exposer* (*poser*, L *pausāre*, to rest, to lay down), confused with L *expōnere*, to put out (cp. COMPOSE)]

ex post (eks pōst´) *a.* (*Econ.*) based on actual results. [L]

ex post facto (eks pōst fak´tō) *a.*, *adv.* having retrospective force. [L, from (what is) done after]

expostulate (ikspos´tūlāt) *v.i.* to reason earnestly (with a person), to remonstrate. **expostulation** (-ā´shən) *n.* **expostulative** *a.* **expostulator** *n.* **expostulatory** *a.* [L *expostulātus*, p.p. of *expostulāre* (*postulāre*, to demand)]

exposure EXPOSE.

expound (ikspownd´) *v.t.* 1 to set out the meaning of in detail. 2 to explain, to interpret. **expounder** *n.* [ME *expounen*, OF *espondre*, L *expōnere* (see EXPONENT)]

express[1] (ikspres´) *a.* 1 set forth or expressed distinctly. 2 direct, explicit, definitely shown or stated, not merely implied. 3 intended, prepared, done, made, sent for a special purpose. 4 (of a likeness) exact. 5 (of goods etc.) delivered by express messenger or post. ~*adv.* 1 at high speed. 2 by express messenger, train or post. 3 †specially, on purpose. ~*n.* 1 an express train. 2 an express messenger. 3 an express rifle. 4 (*N Am.*) a company which organizes express deliveries. ~*v.t.* to send by express messenger or post. **expressage** *n.* 1 the sending or carrying of goods by express messenger or post. 2 a charge for this. **express bullet** *n.* a bullet with a hollow point causing it to spread on striking. **express delivery** *n.* delivery by special messenger. **expressly** *adv.* **express rifle** *n.* a sporting rifle with a high muzzle-velocity and low trajectory. **express train** *n.* a fast train with few intermediate stops. **expressway** *n.* (*Austral.*, *N Am.*) a motorway. [OF *expres*, L *expressus*, p.p. of *exprimere* (*primere*, to press)]

express[2] (ikspres´) *v.t.* 1 to set out, to represent, to put into words or symbolize by gestures etc. 2 to reveal, to exhibit. 3 (*Math.*) to represent (by symbols, in terms etc.). 4 to squeeze or press out; to emit, to exude. **to express oneself** to declare one's opinions or feelings in words (well, strongly etc.). **expresser** *n.* **expressible** *a.* **expression** (-shən) *n.* 1 the act, or an instance, of expressing. **2** that which is expressed, an utterance, saying, statement of a thought. **3** a word, a phrase. **4** (*Math.*) a combination of symbols representing a quantity or meaning. **5** mode of expression. **6** the aspect of the face as indicative of feeling and character, purpose etc. **7** intonation of voice. **8** the exhibition of character and feeling (in a picture, statue etc.). **9** (*Mus.*) the mode of execution that expresses the spirit and feeling of a passage. **10** expressiveness. **expressional** *a.* **1** of or relating to expression. **2** having the power of expression, esp. in language, painting etc. **expressionism** *n.* a movement in literature and the visual arts in which artists express emotional experiences and reactions rather than representing external reality. **expressionist** *a.* of or relating to expressionism. ~*n.* an artist who devotes himself to the expression of feeling, character etc. **expressionistic** *a.* **expressionistically** *adv.* **expressionless** *a.* **expressionlessly** *adv.* **expressionlessness** *n.* **expression mark** *n.* (*Mus.*) a word or sign indicating the way in which a passage is to be expressed. **expression stop** *n.* a harmonium stop regulating the wind pressure and force of the notes. **expressive** *a.* **1** serving to express. **2** significant. **3** vividly indicating any expression or emotion. **expressively** *adv.* **expressiveness** *n.* **expressivity** (-siv´iti) *n.* **expressure** (-shə) *n.* **1** the act of expressing. **2** expression. **3** a mark, impression. **4** an image, a picture. [OF *expresser* (as EXPRESS[1])]

expresso ESPRESSO.

expropriate (iksprō´priāt) *v.t.* **1** (of the state) to take from an owner, esp. for public use. **2** to dispossess. **expropriation** (-ā´shən) *n.* **expropriator** (-prō´-) *n.* [late L *expropriātus*, p.p. of *expropriāre* (*proprium*, property, neut. of *proprius*, own)]

expulsion (ikspŭl´shən) *n.* **1** the act, or an instance, of expelling. **2** the state of being expelled. **3** ejection. **expulsive** *a.* serving or tending to expel. [L *expulsio -ōnem*, from *expellere*, to EXPEL]

expunge (ikspŭnj´) *v.t.* **1** to blot or rub out. **2** to efface, to erase. **expunction** (-pŭngk´-) *n.* **expunger** *n.* [L *expungere* (*pungere*, to prick, p.p. *punctus*)]

expurgate (ek´spœgāt) *v.t.* **1** to free from anything offensive, obscene or noxious (used esp. of books). **2** to remove (such parts). **expurgation** (-ā´shən) *n.* **expurgator** *n.* **expurgatorial** (-pœgətaw´-) *a.* **expurgatory** (-pœ´-) *a.* serving to expurgate. **expurgatory index** *n.* INDEX EXPURGATORIUS (under INDEX). [L *expurgātus*, p.p. of *expurgāre* (*purgāre*, to cleanse)]

exquisite (ek´skwizit, ikskwiz´it) *a.* **1** fine, delicate, dainty; delicately beautiful; very beautiful. **2** delicate or refined in perception, keenly sensitive, nice, fastidious. **3** acute; poignant. **4** intensely pleasurable or painful. ~*n.* a fop; a person who dresses or behaves finically. **exquisitely** *adv.* **exquisiteness** *n.* [L *exquīsītus*, choice, p.p. of *exquīrere* (*quaerere*, to seek)]

exr *abbr.* executor.

exsanguinate (eksang´gwināt) *v.t.* (*formal*) to drain of blood. **exsanguination** (-ā´shən) *n.* **exsanguine** *a.* **1** bloodless. **2** suffering from poorness of blood. **exsanguinity** (-gwin´-) *n.* lack or deficiency of blood. **exsanguinous** *a.* [L *exsanguinātus*, p.p. of *exsanguināre* (*sanguis -inis*, blood)]

exscind (iksind´) *v.t.* to cut off or out, to sever, to excise. [L *exscindere* (*scindere*, to cut)]

exsect (iksekt´) *v.t.* (*formal*) to cut out. **exsection** (-shən) *n.* [L *exsectus*, p.p. of *exsecāre* (*secāre*, to cut)]

exsert (iksœt´) *v.t.* to thrust out, protrude. **exserted** *a.* **1** (*Biol.*) protruding, thrust out, unsheathed. **2** (*Bot.*) (of stamens) longer than the corolla. [L *exsertus*, p.p. of *exserere*, to put forth]

ex-service (eks·sœ´vis) *a.* **1** having formerly been a member of one of the armed forces. **2** of or relating to, or serving, ex-servicemen or -women. **ex-serviceman** *n.* (*pl.* **ex-servicemen**). **ex-servicewoman** *n.* (*pl.* **ex-servicewomen**).

exsiccate (ek´sikāt) *v.t.* **1** to dry up. **2** to evaporate. **3** to drain dry. **exsiccation** (-ā´shən) *n.* **exsiccative** (-sik´ətiv) *a.* **exsiccator** (ek´-) *n.* an apparatus for drying moist substances. [L *exsiccātus*, p.p. of *exsiccāre* (*siccus*, dry)]

ex silentio (eks silen´shiō) *a.*, *adv.* based on a lack of contrary evidence. [L, from silence]

exstipulate (ikstip´ūlət) *a.* (*Bot.*) without stipules. [L *stipula*, a stalk]

ext. *abbr.* **1** extension. **2** exterior(ly). **3** external(ly). **4** extra. **5** extract.

extant (ikstant´) *a.* **1** (of a species, document etc.) still existing. **2** surviving. **3** †standing out, protruding. [L *extans -ntem*, pres.p. of *exstāre* (*stāre*, to stand)]

☒ **extasy** common misspelling of ECSTASY.

extemporaneous (ikstempərā´niəs) *a.* uttered, made, composed or done without preparation. **extemporaneously** *adv.* **extemporaneousness** *n.* **extemporary** (-tem´-) *a.* extemporaneous. **extemporarily** *adv.* **extemporariness** *n.*

extempore (ikstem´pəri) *adv.* without premeditation or preparation. ~*a.* unstudied, delivered without preparation. **extemporize**, **extemporise** *v.t.* to compose or produce without preparation. ~*v.i.* to speak without notes or previous study. **extemporization** (-zā´shən) *n.* [L *ex tempore*, from the time]

extend (ikstend´) *v.t.* **1** to stretch out; to make larger in space, time or scope. **2** to prolong (as a line, a period etc.). **3** to amplify, to expand, to write out in full. **4** to cause to reach (to, over or across). **5** to enlarge. **6** to hold out, offer, grant. **7** to value, to assess, to seize under a writ of extent. **8** to stretch out, to unbend (of muscles). **9** to exert, to strain to the utmost. ~*v.i.* to stretch, to reach (in space, time or scope). **to extend a welcome (to)** to welcome cordially. **extendable** *a.* **extendability** (-bil´-) *n.* **extended** *a.* **1** spread out. **2** (of type) having a broad face. **extended credit** *n.* a form of buying on credit in which the item becomes the property of the buyer immediately, as distinct from *hire purchase*. **extended family** *n.* (*pl.* **extended families**) a social unit comprising more than a couple and their children, including e.g. grandparents, aunts, uncles etc. **extendedly** *adv.* **extended-play** *a.* (of a gramophone record) of the same size as a single, but playing for longer, typically two tracks per side instead of one. **extender** *n.* **1** a person or thing that extends. **2** a substance added to paint, ink etc. to give it extra bulk. **extendible**, **extensible** *a.* **extendibility** (-bil´-), **extensibility** *n.* **extensile** (-sīl) *a.* capable of being stretched out or protruded. [L *extendere*, p.p. *extensus* (*tendere*, to stretch)]

extensimeter EXTENSOMETER.

extension (əksten´shən) *n.* **1** the act or process of extending. **2** the state of being extended; prolongation, enlargement. **3** extent, range, space. **4** an increase of dimension, an addition, an additional part. **5** an additional wing or annexe of a house. **6 a** an additional telephone using the same line as the main one. **b** the number of this telephone. **7** an extra period of time allowed to complete some activity. **8** a variation to a licence allowing the sale of alcoholic drinks later than usual. **9** words amplifying the subject or predicate of a sentence. **10** the property by virtue of which every body occupies a limited portion of space in three dimensions. **11** (*Med.*) the pulling of the broken part of a limb in a direction away from the trunk, to bring the ends of the bone into their proper position. **12** (*Logic*) the extent of the application of a general term, as distinct from *intension*. **extensional** *a.* **extensionist** *n.* **1** a promoter of university extension. **2** a student connected with this. [L *extentio -ōnem*, *extensio -ōnem*, as EXTEND]

extensive (iksten´siv) *a.* **1** widely spread or extended, large. **2** comprehensive. **3** depending on cultivation of a large area, as opposed to *intensive.* **extensively** *adv.* **extensiveness** *n.* [late L *extensīvus,* see EXTEND]

extensometer (ekstensom´itə), **extensimeter** (-im´-) *n.* **1** an instrument which measures small changes in length etc. of metal under stress. **2** an instrument which measures stresses and deformation in other materials. [L *extensus,* p.p. of *extendere,* to EXTEND]

extensor (iksten´sə) *n.* a muscle which serves to extend or straighten any part of the body. **extensor muscle** *n.* [late L, see EXTEND]

extent (ikstent´) *n.* **1** the space, dimension or degree to which anything is extended. **2** size, width, compass, scope, comprehension, distribution, degree. **3** a large space. **4** a writ of execution against the body, lands and goods of a debtor. **5** seizure of lands etc., execution. **6** (*Logic*) extension. [A-F *extente, estente,* p.p. of *estendre,* L *extendere*]

extenuate (iksten´ūāt) *v.t.* **1** to lessen, to diminish the seriousness of, by showing mitigating circumstances. **2** to offer excuses for. **extenuating** *a.* **extenuating circumstances** *n.pl.* those which make an act seem less wrong or less criminal. **extenuatingly** *adv.* **extenuation** (-ā´shən) *n.* **extenuator** (-ten´-) *n.* **extenuatory** *a.* extenuating, palliating. [L *extenuātus,* p.p. of *extenuāre* (*tenuis,* thin)]

exterior (ikstiə´riə) *a.* **1** external, outer. **2** situated on the outside. **3** coming from without, extrinsic. **4** outward, visible. **5** (of a scene in a film or TV programme) filmed in the open air. ~*n.* **1** the outer surface. **2** the external features. **3** the outward or visible aspect, dress, conduct, deportment etc. **exterior angle** *n.* an angle between any side of a rectilinear figure and the adjacent side produced. **exteriority** (-rior´iti) *n.* **exteriorize, exteriorise** *v.t.* **1** to realize in outward form. **2** to externalize. **exteriorization** (-ā´shən) *n.* **exteriorly** *adv.* [L, comp. of *exter* or *exterus,* outer]

exterminate (ikstœ´mināt) *v.t.* **1** to eradicate, to destroy utterly, esp. living creatures. **2** to get rid of, eliminate. **extermination** (-ā´shən) *n.* **exterminator** *n.* **exterminatory** *a.* [L *exterminātus,* p.p. of *extermināre* (*terminus,* a boundary)]

extern (ek´stœn) *n.* **1** (*N Am.*) a student or pupil who does not reside in a college or seminary. **2** †the outward appearance. ~†*a.* external.

external (ikstœ´nəl) *a.* **1** situated on the outside. **2** of or relating to the outside, superficial. **3** derived from outside. **4** belonging to the world of phenomena as distinguished from the conscious mind, objective. **5** (*Theol.*) consisting in outward acts. **6** (*Med.*) applied to the outside of the body. **7** of or relating to relations with foreign countries. **8** extraneous, extrinsic. ~*n.* **1** an exterior or outer part. **2** (*pl.*) outward features, symbols, rites, circumstances. **3** (*pl.*) non-essentials. **external degree** *n.* a degree taken without actually attending the university that awards it, studying being done elsewhere. **external ear** *n.* the outer part of the ear, consisting of the pinna and the canal leading to the eardrum. **external evidence** *n.* evidence which is independent of the matter under discussion. **external examiner** *n.* an examiner from another educational institution brought in to ensure that examinations are fairly marked etc. **externalism** *n.* **externality** (ekstœnal´-) *n.* (*pl.* **externalities**). **externalize, externalise** *v.t.* **1** to give external shape or objective existence to. **2** to treat as consisting of externals. **externalization** (-ā´shən) *n.* **externally** *adv.* **external student** *n.* a student studying for an external degree. [L *externus,* from *exter,* see EXTERIOR]

exteroceptor (ek´stərōseptə) *n.* a sensory organ which receives impressions from outside the body, e.g. the eye. **exteroceptive** *a.*

exterrestrial (ekstəres´triəl) *a., n.* EXTRATERRESTRIAL.

exterritorial (eksteritaw´riəl) *a.* EXTRATERRITORIAL. **exterritoriality** (-al´-) *n.*

extinct (ikstingkt´) *a.* **1** extinguished, put out. **2** (of a volcano) that has permanently ceased eruption. **3** worn out, ended, finished. **4** come to an end, that has died out (as a family, species etc.). **5** (of an office, title etc.) obsolete. ~†*v.t.* to extinguish. [L *extinctus,* p.p. of *extinguere* (*stinguere,* to quench)]

extinction (ikstingk´shən) *n.* **1** the act of extinguishing or of making extinct. **2** the state of being extinguished or extinct. **3** extermination, destruction, annihilation. **4** the paying off of a debt, a mortgage etc. **5** (*Physics*) the absorption of light or other radiation by the earth's atmosphere. **extinctive** *a.* [L *extinctio -ōnem,* see EXTINCT]

extine (ek´stin, -stēn, -stīn) *n.* (*Bot.*) the outer coat of a grain of pollen. [L *exterus,* outer]

extinguish (iksting´gwish) *v.t.* **1** to put out, to quench (as a light, hope, passion, life etc.). **2** to eclipse, to cloud, to obscure, to throw into the shade. **3** to destroy, to annihilate. **4** to suppress. **5** to pay off (a debt, mortgage etc.). **6** (*Law*) to render void. **extinguishable** *a.* **extinguisher** *n.* **1** a person or thing that extinguishes. **2** a conical cap for extinguishing a candle (or, formerly, a link). **3** a device for putting out a fire. **extinguishment** *n.* [L *extinguere* (*stinguere,* to quench)]

extirpate (ek´stəpāt) *v.t.* **1** to root out, to destroy utterly, to exterminate. **2** to cut out or off. **extirpation** (-ā´shən) *n.* **extirpator** *n.* [L *extirpātus,* p.p. of *extirpāre, exstirpāre* (*stirps, -pis,* a stem)]

extol (ikstōl´, -tol´), (*N Am.*) **extoll** *v.t.* (*3rd pers. sing. pres.* **extols,** (*N Am.*) **extolls,** *pres.p.* **extolling,** *past, p.p.* **extolled**) to praise in the highest terms, to glorify. **extoller** *n.* **extollingly** *adv.* **extolment** *n.* [L *extollere* (*tollere,* to raise)]

extort (ikstawt´) *v.t.* **1** to wrest or wring (from) by force, threats, importunity etc. **2** (*Law*) to exact illegally under colour of a public office. **3** (*fig.*) to extract arbitrarily or subjectively (a meaning from a passage, data etc.). **extorter** *n.* **extortion** *n.* **1** the act of extorting. **2** oppressive or illegal exaction. **3** something extorted. **4** a gross overcharge. †**extortionary** *a.* **extortionate** (-ət) *a.* **1** (of prices) exorbitant. **2** characterized by extortion; oppressive. **extortionately** *adv.* **extortioner** *n.* **extortionist** *n.* **extortive** *a.* [L *extortus,* p.p. of *extorquēre,* to twist]

extra (ek´strə) *a.* **1** beyond what is absolutely necessary. **2** larger or better than is usual; of superior quality. **3** supplementary, additional. ~*adv.* **1** over and above what is usual. **2** more than usually. **3** additionally. ~*n.* **1** something beyond what is absolutely necessary or usual, esp. something not covered by the ordinary fee. **2** an addition. **3** in cricket, a run scored otherwise than off the bat. **4** an actor temporarily engaged as one of a crowd etc. **5** a special edition of a newspaper containing late news. **extra cover** *n.* (in cricket) a fielding position, or a fielder, between cover point and mid-off. **extra-special** *a.* latest (edition of an evening paper). **extra time** *n.* additional time allowed at the end of a sports match to compensate for time lost through injury etc. **extra-virgin** *a.* of or relating to olive oil of the highest quality, extracted by pressing and not by chemical extraction. [L *extrā,* beyond, from outside, or short for EXTRAORDINARY]

extra- (ekstrə) *comb. form* **1** on the outside, without. **2** outside the bounds of. **3** beyond the scope of. [L]

extracanonical (ekstrəkənon´ikəl) *a.* not part of the canon of the Bible.

extracellular (ekstrəsel´ūlə) *a.* (*Biol.*) situated or occurring outside a cell or cells. **extracellularly** *adv.*

extracorporeal (ekstrəkawpaw´riəl) *a.* outside the body.

extract[1] (ikstrakt´) *v.t.* **1 a** to draw or pull out. **b** to draw out by mechanical or chemical means. **2** to select a part from, to copy out or quote (as a passage from a book etc.). **3 a** to obtain with difficulty. **b** (*coll.*) to extort. **4** to derive (from). **5** †to deduce (from). **to extract the root of** to find the root of (a number or quantity). **extractable** *a.* **extractability** (-bil´-) *n.* **extraction** *n.* **1** the act, or an instance, of extracting. **2** the process of being extracted. **3** descent, family, lineage, derivation. **4** the act of drawing anything from a substance by chemical or mechanical process. **5** the removal of a tooth. **extractive** *a.* **1** tending or serving to extract. **2** capable of extraction. ~*n.* **1** an extract. **2** (*Chem.*) the principle forming the basis in extracts. **extractive industries** *n.pl.* those (e.g. mining, agriculture, fishing) concerned with obtaining natural resources. **extractor** *n.* **1** a person or thing that extracts. **2** an extractor fan. **extractor fan** *n.* an electric fan which extracts air, gas etc. from a room. [L *extractus*, p.p. of *extrahere* (*trahere*, to draw)]

extract[2] (eks´trakt) *n.* **1** that which is extracted by distillation, solution etc. **2** a passage quoted from a book or writing. **3** an essential obtained from a substance. **4** a preparation containing the essence of a substance. [as EXTRACT[1]]

extra-curricular (ekstrəkərik´ūlə) *a.* (of an activity) outside or in addition to the normal course of study.

extradition (ekstrədish´ən) *n.* **1** the surrender of fugitives from justice by a government to the authorities of the country where the crime was committed. **2** (*Psych.*) in perception, the localizing of sensations at a distance from the centre of sensation. **extradite** (ek´-) *v.t.* **1** to surrender under a treaty of extradition. **2** to secure the extradition of. **extraditable** (-dī´-) *a.* subject to extradition, rendering one liable to extradition. [F (L *traditio -ōnem*, TRADITION)]

extrados (ikstrā´dos) *n.* (*pl.* **extrados** (-dōz), **extradoses**) the exterior curve of an arch, esp. measured on the top of the voussoirs (cp. INTRADOS). [F (*dos*, L *dorsum*, the back)]

extragalactic (ekstrəgəlak´tik) *a.* being or occurring outside the Milky Way.

extrajudicial (ekstrəjoodish´əl) *a.* **1** taking place outside the court, not legally authorized. **2** outside the ordinary course of law or justice. **extrajudicially** *adv.*

extralinguistic (ekstrəling·gwis´ tik) *a.* outside the area of language or of linguistics.

extramarital (ekstrəmar´itəl) *a.* (esp. of sexual relations) outside marriage. **extramaritally** *adv.*

extramundane (ekstrəmŭn´dān) *a.* of or relating to, or existing in a region outside our world or outside the material universe.

extramural (ekstrəmū´rəl) *a.* **1** situated beyond or outside the walls or boundaries of a place. **2** (of a course or department) connected with a university or college, but additional to the usual courses. **3** taking place, or taught, off the premises of a college etc.

extraneous (ikstrā´niəs) *a.* **1** foreign, not belonging to a class, subject etc. **2** not intrinsic, external. **3** not essential. **extraneity** (-nē´iti) *n.* **extraneously** *adv.* **extraneousness** *n.* [L *extrāneus*, from *extrā*, outside]

extranuclear (ekstrənū´kliə) *a.* (*Biol.*) situated or occurring outside the nucleus of a cell.

extraordinary (ikstraw´dinəri, ekstrəaw´-) *a.* **1** beyond or out of the ordinary course, unusual. **2** of an uncommon degree or kind, remarkable, rare, exceptional, surprising. **3** additional, extra. **4** sent, appointed, or convened for a special purpose or occasion. ~*n.* **1** an extraordinary thing. **2** (*pl.*) †extra allowances or receipts, esp. to troops. **extraordinarily** *adv.* **extraordinariness** *n.* [L *extraordinārius* (*extrā ordinem*, outside the usual order)]

extraparochial (ekstrəpərō´kiəl) *a.* beyond, outside of, or not reckoned within the limits of, any parish.

extra-physical (ekstrəfiz´ikəl) *a.* not subject to or bound by physical laws or processes.

extrapolate (ikstrap´əlāt) *v.t.* **1** (*Math.*) to estimate (the value of a function etc.) beyond the known values by the extension of a curve. **2** to infer, conjecture from what is known. **extrapolation** (-ā´shən) *n.* **extrapolative** (-trap´-) *a.* **extrapolator** *n.* **extrapolatory** *a.* [L *extrā*, and inter*polate*]

extra-professional (ekstrəprəfesh´ənəl) *a.* not coming within the ordinary duties of a profession.

extrasensory (ekstrəsen´səri) *a.* beyond the ordinary senses. **extrasensory perception** *n.* the supposed ability of some people to know things by means other than normal sense data.

extra-spectral (ekstrəspek´trəl) *a.* lying outside the visible spectrum.

extraterrestrial (ekstrətəres´triəl) *a.* **1** situated or occurring outside the earth or its atmosphere. **2** originating outside the earth, alien. ~*n.* (in science fiction) a being from outer space.

extraterritorial (ekstrəteritaw´riəl) *a.* **1** beyond the jurisdiction of the laws of the country in which one is living. **2** situated, or valid, outside a country's territory. **extraterritoriality** (-al´-) *n.* **extraterritorially** *adv.*

extra-tropical (ekstrətrop´ikəl) *a.* beyond or outside of the tropics, north or south.

extra-uterine (ekstrə·ū´tərīn) *a.* (*Med.*) outside the uterus.

extravagant (ikstrav´əgənt) *a.* **1** exceeding due bounds, unrestrained by reason, immoderate. **2** visionary, fantastic, showy. **3** spending money immoderately or unrestrainedly, wasteful. **4** (of prices etc.) exorbitant. **extravagance** *n.* **1** the state or quality of being extravagant. **2** an extravagant act, statement or conduct. **3** excessive expenditure, prodigality. **extravagancy** *n.* (*pl.* **extravagancies**). **extravagantly** *adv.* **extravagate** *v.i.* **1** to wander or roam at will. **2** to go beyond reasonable bounds. **3** to go to extremes. [L *extrāvagans -ntem*, pres.p. of *extrāvagārī* (*vagārī*, to wander)]

extravaganza (ekstravəgan´zə) *n.* **1** a fantastic composition in drama, fiction, poetry, music or other literary form. **2** an expensive and spectacular light entertainment production. **3** a fantastic piece of conduct, sentiment or imagination. [It. *estravaganza*]

extravasate (ikstrav´əsāt) *v.t.* to force or let out of the proper vessels (as blood). ~*v.i.* to flow out of the proper vessels. **extravasation** (-ā´shən) *n.* [L *vās*, a vessel]

extravascular (ekstrəvas´kūlə) *a.* outside the vascular system.

extravehicular (ekstrəvēhik´ūlə) *a.* taking place outside a vehicle, esp. a spacecraft.

extravert EXTROVERT.

extrema, extremal EXTREMUM.

extreme (ikstrēm´) *a.* **1** of the highest degree, most intense. **2** beyond what is reasonable, immoderate. **3** outermost, farthest. **4** at the utmost limit, at either end. **5** last, final. **6** very strict or rigorous. **7** at the furthest right or left politically. **8** (*Mus.*) the highest and lowest (of parts), augmented (of intervals). ~*n.* **1** the utmost or farthest point or limit, the extremity. **2** the utmost or highest degree. **3** (*Math.*) the first or the last term of a ratio or series. **4** the subject or the predicate of a proposition as distinguished from the copula, the major or the minor term in a syllogism as distinguished from the middle. **5** either one of two things or qualities as different or as far removed from each other as possible. **6** (*Mus.*) the highest and lowest parts. **in the extreme 1** in the highest degree. **2** extremely. **to extremes** (resorting) to the most severe or drastic measures. **to the other extreme** to the opposite opinion, course of action etc. **extremely** *adv.* very, greatly, to a great degree. **extremeness** *n.* **extreme unction** *n.* in the Roman Catholic Church, the former name for the sacrament of Annointing the Sick. **extremist** *n.* **1** a person ready to go to extremes. **2** a person holding extreme opinions and ready to undertake extreme actions. ~*a.* of or relating to an extremist. **extremism** *n.* **extremity** (-strem´-) *n.* (*pl.* **extremities**) **1** the utmost point, side or limit. **2** the greatest degree. **3** the remotest part, the end. **4** a condition of the greatest difficulty, danger or distress. **5** (*pl.*) the hands and feet. **6** (*pl.*) extreme measures. [OF, from L *extrēmus*, superl. of *exterus*, outward]

extremum (ikstrē´məm) *n.* (*pl.* **extremums, extrema** (-mə)) (*Math.*) the maximum or the minimum value of a function. **extremal** *a.* [L, neut. of *extrēmus*, see EXTREME]

extricate (ek´strikāt) *v.t.* **1** to disentangle, to set free from any perplexity, difficulty or embarrassment. **2** to cause to be given off (as a gas from a state of combination). **extricable** *a.* **extrication** (-ā´shən) *n.* [L *extrīcātus*, p.p. of *extrīcāre* (*tricae*, impediments)]

extrinsic (ikstrin´sik) *a.* **1** being outside or external. **2** proceeding or operating from without. **3** not inherent or contained in a body. **4** not essential. **extrinsicality** (-kal´-) *n.* **extrinsically** *adv.* [F *extrinsèque*, L *extrinsecus*, adv., from without (*extrin*, from *exter*, outward, *secus*, beside)]

☒ **extrordinary** common misspelling of EXTRAORDINARY.

extrorse (ikstraws´) *a.* (*Bot.*) (of anthers) turned outwards from the axis of growth. **extrorsal** *a.* [F, from L *extrorsus* (*versus*, towards)]

extrovert (ek´strəvœt), **extravert** *n.* **1** a person having a type of temperament which is predominantly engaged with the external world. **2** (*coll.*) a lively, sociable person. ~*a.* of or relating to (the personality of) such a person. **extroversion** *n.* **extroversive** *a.* **extroversively** *adv.* **extroverted** *a.* [L *extrā*, outside; *vertere*, to turn]

extrude (ikstrood´) *v.t.* **1** to thrust or push out or away. **2** to expel. **3** to shape (metal or plastic) by melting and forcing through a die. **4** to make (tubes etc.) by this method. **extrusion** (-zhən) *n.* **extrusive** (-siv) *a.* **1** thrusting out or tending to thrust out. **2** poured out on the surface (as volcanic rocks). [L *extrūdere*, p.p. *extrūsus* (*trūdere*, to thrust)]

exuberant (igzū´bərənt) *a.* **1** effusive, overflowing with vitality, spirits or imagination. **2** exceedingly fruitful; luxuriant in growth. **3** characterized by abundance or richness. **4** overflowing, copious, superabundant. **exuberance** *n.* **exuberantly** *adv.* **exuberate** *v.i.* **1** to abound, to overflow. **2** to indulge freely (in). [L *exūberans -ntem*, pres.p. of *exūberāre* (*ūber*, fertile, cp. *ūber*, an udder)]

exude (igzūd´) *v.t.* **1** to emit or discharge through pores, as sweat, moisture, or other liquid matter. **2** to give out slowly. **3** to show freely (a feeling, mood etc.). ~*v.i.* to ooze or flow out slowly through pores etc. **exudate** (eg´zūdāt) *n.* something exuded. **exudation** (eksūdā´shən) *n.* **exudative** *a.* [L *exūdāre* (*sūdāre* to sweat)]

exult (igzŭlt´) *v.i.* **1** to rejoice exceedingly. **2** to triumph (over). **exultant** *a.* **1** rejoicing, triumphing. **2** feeling or displaying exultation. **exultancy** *n.* **exultantly** *adv.* **exultation** (egzŭltā´shən) *n.* **exultingly** *adv.* [F *exulter*, L *exultāre*, *exsultāre*, freq. of *exsilere* (*salīre*, to leap)]

exurbia (eksœ´biə) *n.* residential areas outside the suburbs of a town or city. **exurb** (eks´-) *n.* such an area. **exurban** *a.* **exurbanite** *n.*, *a.*

exuviae (igzū´viē) *n.pl.* (*also constr. as sing.*) **1** the cast or shed skin, shells, teeth etc. of animals. **2** fossil remains of animals in a fragmentary state. **3** things cast off or relinquished. **exuvial** *a.* **exuviate** *v.t.* to cast off, to shed. ~*v.i.* to cast the old shell, skin etc. **exuviation** (-ā´shən) *n.* [L, cast skins of animals, spoils of an enemy, from *exuere*, to put off]

ex-voto (eksvō´tō) *adv.* in pursuance of a vow. ~*n.* (*pl.* **ex-votos**) anything offered to a divinity in gratitude for an exemplary favour. **ex-votive** *a.* [L *ex vōtō*, out of a vow]

EXW *abbr.* ex works.

ex works (eks wœks´) *a.*, *adv.* **1** direct from the factory. **2** (of a price) not including a delivery charge.

-ey -Y[3].

eyas (ī´əs) *n.* **1** an unfledged hawk. **2** in falconry, a hawk taken from the nest for training or whose training is not complete. [earlier *nyas*, F, *niais*, a nestling, ult. from L *nīdus*, nest]

eye[1] (ī) *n.* **1** the organ of vision. **2** the eyeball, iris or pupil. **3** the socket or part of the face containing this organ. **4 a** sight, ocular perception, view, public observation. **b** the power of seeing, discernment, acuteness of vision. **5** careful observation, oversight, care, attention. **6** look, mien, expression. **7** mental perception, way of regarding. **8** (*pl.*) estimation, judgement (of conduct etc.). **9** consciousness, awareness. **10** (*coll.*) a private eye. **11** anything more or less eye-shaped. **12** the bud of a plant. **13** a spot on some feathers, as those of the peacock and argus pheasant. **14** the centre of a target, a bull's-eye. **15** the centre of some flowers. **16** a small opening or perforation. **17** the thread-hole of a needle. **18** the loop or catch in which the hook of a dress is fastened. **19** the hole in the head of an eye bolt. **20** a circular or oval window. **21** the circular aperture at the summit of a dome, the central point or circle in an Ionic volute. **22** the calm place at the very centre of a storm or hurricane. **23** †a slight tinge, a shade. **all my eye (and Betty Martin)** all humbug, rubbish. **an eye for an eye** strict retaliation. **before one's (very) eyes** right in front of one, in plain view. **eyes front** turn your head and eyes in front. **eyes left** turn your head and eyes to the left. **eyes right** turn your head and eyes to the right. **in one's mind's eye** in one's imagination. **in the eye/ eyes of 1** in the regard, estimation or judgement of. **2** from the point of view of. **in the twinkling of an eye** TWINKLE. **in the wind's eye** WIND[1]. **mind your eye** take care, look out. **more than meets the eye** MEET[1]. **my eye!** (*sl.*) used to express astonishment. **one in the eye** ONE. **to be all eyes** to watch intently. **to believe one's eyes** BELIEVE. **to catch one's eye** to attract one's attention. **to close/ shut one's eyes to** to refuse to or pretend not to see. **to cry one's eyes out** CRY. **to do someone in the eye** to defraud someone. **to get one's eye in** to gain skill or proficiency. **to have an eye for 1** to pay due regard to. **2** to appreciate. **3** to be on the lookout for. **to have an eye to** to regard, to have designs on. **to have eyes for** to be interested in. **to hit one between the eyes** to astonish or shock one. **to hit one in the eye** to astonish or shock one. **to keep an eye on** to watch carefully or narrowly. **to keep an eye open/ out** to keep a lookout (for). **to keep one's eye in** to retain skill or proficiency. **to keep one's eyes open/ peeled/ skinned** to watch carefully, to be careful. **to look someone in the eye/ eyes** LOOK. **to lower one's eyes** to look down towards the ground. **to make eyes at** to regard amorously. **to meet someone's eye** MEET[1]. **to open someone's eyes** OPEN. **to pipe one's eye** PIPE. **to put someone's eye out** to make someone jealous. **to raise one's eyes 1** to look up from the ground. **2** to look upwards (to). **to remove the scales from someone's eyes** SCALE[1]. **to see eye to eye** to be in complete agreement (with). **to set/ lay/ clap eyes on** to have sight of, to see. **to take one's eyes off** to look away from, to take one's attention off. **to turn a blind eye to** TURN. **to view with a friendly/ jealous eye** to regard with these feelings. **to wipe one's eyes** to stop weeping. **to wipe the eye of 1** to show up the foolishness of. **2** to shoot what someone has missed. **under the eye of** watched or supervised by. **up to the eyes** deeply (immersed, engaged, in debt etc.). **with one eye on** directing part of one's mind to. **with one eye shut** without needing to pay much attention. **with one's eyes open** aware of all the facts. **with one's eyes shut 1** not aware of all the facts. **2** very easily, without having to pay much attention. **eyeball** *n.* the globe of the eye. *~v.t.* (*esp. N Am., sl.*) to stare at. *~v.i.* to stare. **eyeball to eyeball** (of discussions etc.) at close quarters, face to face. **(up) to the eyeballs** (*coll.*) completely immersed (in work etc.). **eye bank** *n.* (*Med.*) a place where corneas are stored for use in grafts. **eyebath** *n.* a small vessel for bathing the eyes. **eyeblack** *n.* mascara. **eye bolt** *n.* a bolt having an eye or loop at one end for the reception of a ring, hook etc. **eyebright** *n.* any plant of the genus *Euphrasia*, formerly much used as a remedy for diseases of the eye. **eyebrow** *n.* the fringe of hair above the orbit of the eyes. **to raise an eyebrow** to raise one's eyebrows to show surprise or disapproval. **eyebrow pencil** *n.* a pencil applied to the eyebrows to alter their shape or colour. **eye-catching** *a.* striking. **eye contact** *n.* a direct look between people. **eyecup** *n.* (*N Am.*) an eyebath. **eyed** *a.* having eyes (*esp. in comb.* as *blue-eyed*). **eye-drop** *n.* **1** a tear. **2** (**eye drop**) a medication for the eye, administered as drops. **eyeful** *n.* (*pl.* **eyefuls**) **1** as much as the eye can take in at a look, long look. **2** (*sl.*) an attractive woman. **3** a foreign body in the eye. **eyeglass** *n.* **1** a lens to aid the sight. **2** (*pl.*) a pair of these fastened over the nose or held in the hand. **3** (*pl., N Am.*) spectacles. **4** the lens nearest the eye in an optical instrument. **5** a glass for applying lotion to the eyes. **eyehole** *n.* **1** a hole to look through. **2** the cavity containing the eye. **eye language** *n.* communication by means of looks. **eyelash** *n.* **1** the row of hairs edging the eyelids. **2** a single hair from the edge of the eyelid. **by an eyelash** by a small margin. **eyeless** *a.* **1** destitute of eyes. **2** blind, sightless. **eye level** *n.* the same height above the ground as a person's eyes. **eye-level** *a.* at the same height above the ground as a person's eyes. **eyelid** *n.* a fold of skin above or below the eye that can be moved to open or close the eye. **eyeliner** *n.* a cosmetic used to draw a line along the edge of the eyelid. **eye mask** *n.* a covering for the eyes, esp. one soaked with a soothing lotion. **eye of a needle** *n.* a needle's eye. **eye of day** *n.* the sun. **eye-opener** *n.* **1** something that furnishes enlightenment or astonishment. **2** (*N Am., coll.*) an alcoholic drink taken in the early morning. **eye-opening** *a.* **eyepatch** *n.* a covering to protect an injured eye. **eyepiece** *n.* the lens or combination of lenses at the end nearest the eye in an optical instrument. **eye rhyme** *n.* similarity of words in spelling but not in sound. **eye-salve** *n.* salve or ointment for the eyes. **eye-shade** *n.* a shade worn above the eyes to protect them from glare. **eyeshadow** *n.* a coloured cosmetic for the eyelids. **eyeshot** *n.* sight, range of vision, view. **eyesight** *n.* **1** vision, the ability to see. **2** view, observation. **eyesore** *n.* anything offensive to the sight. **eye-splice** *n.* (*Naut.*) a splice made by turning the end of a rope back on itself, and interlacing the strands of this with those of the standing part, leaving a loop. **eye-spot** *n.* **1** a light-sensitive spot on the body of some simple organisms. **2** a fungal disease of plants marked by eye-shaped spots. **eye-stalk** *n.* a movable stalk in crustaceans etc., bearing an eye. **eye strain** *n.* fatigue or irritation of the eyes. **eye-tooth** *n.* (*pl.* **eye-teeth**) either one of the upper canine teeth of humans. **to cut one's eye-teeth** CUT[1]. **eyewash** *n.* **1** a lotion for the eyes. **2** (*coll.*) deception, humbug, a fraudulent pretence, a covering up of unpleasant facts. **eye-water** *n.* **1** a medicated bath or water for the eyes. **2** tears. **eyewitness** *n.* a person who sees an event with their own eyes and is able to give evidence. **eye-worm** *n.* an African nematode worm, *Loa loa*, that infects the eye. [OE *ēage* (cp. Dut. *oog*, Icel. *auga*, Goth. *augō*, G *Auge*, also L *oculus*)]

eye[2] (ī) *v.t.* (*pres.p.* **eyeing**, **eying**, *past, p.p.* **eyed**) to watch, to observe (fixedly, suspiciously, jealously etc.). **to eye askance** to look at with suspicion or distrust. **to eye up** (*coll.*) to assess visually, esp. admiringly. [from EYE[1]]

eyelet (ī´lit) *n.* **1 a** a small hole or opening, an aperture like an eye, for a cord etc. to pass through. **b** a reinforcement for such a hole. **2** a loophole. **3** a small hole with stitched edges, in embroidery. **4** a small eye. *~v.t.* (*pres.p.* **eyeleting**, *past, p.p.* **eyeleted**) to provide with eyelets. **eyelet-hole** *n.* a hole made as an eyelet for looking or shooting through or for fastening a hook etc. [ME *oilet*, OF *oeillte*, dim. of *oeil*, L *oculus*, eye]

Eyetie (ī´tī) *n., a.* (*sl., offensive*) (an) Italian. [mispronunciation of *Ita*lian]

eyot AIT.

eyra (eə´rə) *n.* a reddish-coloured variety of jaguarundi. [Tupi *eirara*]

eyre (eə) *n.* **1** a journey or circuit. **2** a court of itinerant justices. **justices in eyre** JUSTICE. [OF *eire*, *erre*, from *errer*, late L *iterāre*, to journey, from L *iter*, a journey]

eyrie (īə´ri, iə´-, eə´-), **aery** (eə´ri, iə´-), **aerie** (eə´ri) *n.* **1** the nest of any bird of prey, esp. of an eagle. **2** the young of a bird of prey. **3** a human dwelling or retreat perched on a high and inaccessible place. [med. L *aeria*, F *aire* (from L *ārea*, a spot of level ground, or *ātrium*, an open hall)]

Ez. *abbr.* Ezra.

Ezek. *abbr.* Ezekiel.

F

F[1] (ef), **f** (*pl.* **Fs, F's**) the sixth letter of the English and other versions of the Roman alphabet. It is pronounced as a voiceless labiodental fricative. *~symbol* **1** the sixth of a series, the sixth highest in a range, e.g. of marks etc. **2** the sixth known quantity in an algebraic expression. **3** (*Mus.*) **a** the fourth note of the diatonic scale of C major. **b** the key of a composition in which the keynote is F. **F clef** *n.* the bass clef. **F-layer** *n.* the highest layer of the ionosphere, having the greatest concentration of free electrons. **f-number** *n.* **1** the ratio of the focal length to the true diameter of a lens. **2** a number expressing the size of the aperture of a camera lens. **f-stop** *n.* in photography, a setting on a camera corresponding to a certain f-number. **F-word** *n.* a taboo word beginning with the letter *f*, usu. *fuck*.

F[2] *abbr.* **1** Fahrenheit. **2** fail, failure(s). **3** farad. **4** faraday. **5** filial generation. **6** force. **7** France. **F_1, F_2** *abbr.* first and second filial generations.

F[3] *chem. symbol* fluorine.

f *abbr.* **1** fathom(s). **2** female. **3** feminine. **4** femto. **5** filly. **6** (of pencil lead) fine. **7** folio. **8** following. **9** forte. **10** franc(s). **11** frequency. **12** (in the Netherlands) guilder.

FA *abbr.* **1** Fanny Adams (*euphem.* for *fuck all*). **2** Football Association. **FA Cup** *n.* in England, an annual knockout competition, open to all members of the Football Association.

fa FAH.

FAA *abbr.* **1** Federal Aviation Administration. **2** Fleet Air Arm.

fab (fab) *a.* (*coll.*) wonderful, very good. [short for *fabulous*]

fabaceous (fəbā´shəs) *a.* leguminous, beanlike. [late L *fabāceus*, from L *faba*, a bean]

Fabian (fā´biən) *a.* **1** cautious, avoiding open conflict (from the behaviour of Fabius Maximus Cunctator, who harassed Hannibal in the second Punic war by his cautious and dilatory strategy). **2** of or relating to the Fabians. *~n.* a member of the Fabian Society, an organization of Socialists relying on moral force rather than revolution. **Fabianism** *n.* **Fabianist** *n.* [L *Fabiānus*, from Q. *Fabius* Maximus, d. 203 BC, Roman general]

fable (fā´bəl) *n.* **1** a story, esp. one in which animals are represented as endowed with speech in order to convey a moral lesson. **2** a legend, a myth. **3** a fabrication, a falsehood. **4** the plot of a drama or epic poem. **5** gossip. *~v.i.* **1** to write fables or fictitious tales. **2** to tell falsehoods. **3** to romance. *~v.t.* **1** to feign, to invent. **2** to describe or narrate fictitiously or falsely. **fabled** *a.* **1** celebrated in fable, mythical, fictitious. **2** legendary, famous. **fabler** *n.* a person who composes fables. [F, from L *fābula*, from *fārī*, to speak]

fabliau (fab´liō) *n.* (*pl.* **fabliaux** (-ōz)) a metrical tale, dealing usually with ordinary life, composed by the trouvères in the 12th and 13th cents., and intended for recitation. [F, from OF *fablel*, through the pl. *fabliaux* (dim. of FABLE)]

Fablon® (fab´lon) *n.* an adhesive-backed plastic sheeting used for covering shelves, table mats etc.

fabric (fab´rik) *n.* **1** woven, felted or knitted material. **2** the basic structure of a building, its stonework, timbers etc. **3** mode of construction or manufacture, workmanship, texture. **4** a building, an edifice. **5** the basic structure, a system of correlated parts (*the fabric of society*). **fabric conditioner** *n.* a liquid added when washing clothes to make them feel softer. [F *fabrique*, L *fabrica*, rel. to *faber*, artificer]

fabricate (fab´rikāt) *v.t.* **1** to build, to construct. **2** to form by art or manufacture. **3** to forge, to invent, to trump up. **fabrication** (-ā´shən) *n.* **1** forgery, a forgery, a falsehood. **2** manufacture, construction. **fabricator** *n.* [see FABRIC]

fabulist (fab´ūlist) *n.* **1** a writer or inventor of fables. **2** a liar. **fabulize, fabulise** *v.i.* to write or speak in fables. [F *fabuliste* (see FABLE, -IST)]

fabulous (fab´ūləs) *a.* **1** (*coll.*) wonderful, very good, very enjoyable. **2** beyond belief, incredible. **3** exaggerated, absurd. **4** feigned, fictitious, invented. **5** given to fabling. **6** related or described in fables; mythical, legendary, unhistorical. **fabulosity** (-los´-), **fabulousness** *n.* **fabulously** *adv.* [F *fabuleux* (see FABLE, -OUS)]

facade (fəsahd´), **façade** *n.* **1** the front of a building, the principal face. **2** an outward appearance, esp. one put on for show or to deceive, a front. [F, from *face*, after It. *facciata*, from *faccia*, FACE]

face (fās) *n.* **1** the front part of the head, from the chin to the top of the forehead. **2** a facial expression, a look (*have a sad face*). **3** a grimace (*pull a face*). **4** a person, esp. one communicating a quality (*nice to see some fresh faces*). **5** that part of anything which presents itself to the view, the front, the upper or main surface. **6** the plane surface of a solid. **7** an exposed surface of rock on a cliff or mountain, or in a mine or quarry. **8** the dial of a watch, clock etc. **9** the working side of a tool or instrument. **10** the printed surface of a playing card. **11** the printing surface of type. **12** a design or style of type. **13** the striking surface of a bat, racket or golf club. **14** the outward visible state of things, the appearance, aspect (*the unacceptable face of capitalism*). **15** dignity, reputation (*lose face*). **16** the obverse of a coin. **17** composure, coolness. **18** (*coll.*) impudence, effrontery, cheek. **19** (*coll.*) make-up. *~v.t.* **1** to turn the face towards. **2** to meet in front. **3** to confront boldly, to stand up to. **4** to acknowledge without evasion (*to face facts*). **5** to bring face to face with. **6** to stand opposite to. **7** to put a coating or covering on; to put facings on (a garment). **8** to cause to turn in any direction. **9** (*Golf*) to strike (the ball) with the face of the club full in the middle, in driving from the tee. *~v.i.* **1** to look in a certain direction. **2** to be situated with a certain aspect. **3** to turn the face in a certain direction. **about face** ABOUT. **black in the face** livid with annoyance, exertion etc. **face as long as a fiddle** a sad, dismal face. **face down** with the face or front pointing downwards. **face downwards** face down. **face to face (with)** **1** in someone's or each other's actual presence. **2** opposite; in confrontation. **3** clearly, without anything interposed. **face up** with the face or front pointing upwards. **face upwards** face up. **in (the) face of** **1** in spite of. **2** when encountering. **in your face** IN-YOUR-FACE (under IN). **left face** (*Mil.*) turn left without moving from the same position. **let's face it** (*coll.*) let us look at the matter honestly and realistically. **on the face of it** to judge by appearances. **right face** (*Mil.*) turn right without moving from the same position. **to face down** **1** to confront sternly or defiantly. **2** to force to give way. **to face off** **1** to drop the puck or ball to start or restart a game of ice hockey or lacrosse. **2** to have a confrontation. **to face out** to carry off by boldness or effrontery. **to face the enemy** to meet the enemy with determination. **to face the music** to suffer unpleasant consequences of something, esp. punishment or criticism. **to face up to** to meet courageously. **to fly in the face of** **1** to defy openly. **2** to act in direct opposition to. **to have the face** to be impudent, cool or composed enough (to). **to lose face** **1** to be humiliated. **2** to suffer loss of personal prestige. **to make/ pull a face** **1** to distort the features. **2** to grimace. **to put a bold/ brave/ good face on** **1** to make the best of, to pretend that one is not unduly upset by. **2** to adopt a confident air. **to put a new face on** to alter the appearance of. **to put one's face on** (*coll.*) to put on make-up. **to save (one's) face** to save oneself from disgrace or humiliation. **to set one's face against** to oppose, to withstand firmly. **to show one's face** to appear. **to shut one's face** (*esp. imper., sl.*) to be quiet. **to someone's face** **1** openly. **2** in plain words. **until one is blue in the face** for ever without success. **face-ache** *n.* neuralgia. **face card** *n.* a court card. **face cloth, face flannel** *n.* a cloth used to wash the face. **face cream** *n.* a cosmetic cream that is rubbed into the face to moisturize the skin. **faced** *a.* smoothed on the surface, as stone. **-faced** *comb. form* **1** having a face of a certain kind. **2** having a certain number of faces. **faceguard** *n.* a guard to protect the face in fencing, welding etc. **faceless** *a.* **1** (of bureaucrats etc.) remote from and unmoved by the concerns of ordinary citizens. **2** anonymous. **3** without a face. **facelessness** *n.* **facelift** *n.* **1** an operation to remove wrinkles and make the face look younger and smoother. **2** renovations, repairs carried out to improve or modernize the appearance of something. **face mask** *n.* **1** a mask covering part of the face. **2** a face pack. **face-off** *n.* **1** the dropping of the puck or ball between two opposing players to start or restart a game of ice hockey or lacrosse. **2** a confrontation. **face pack** *n.* a creamy cosmetic mixture applied to the face. **face paint** *n.* paint that is applied to the face. **face-painting** *n.* **face-plate** *n.* **1** a disc on or attachment to a lathe, on which work can be mounted. **2** a protective guard for the face, esp. the glass panel of a diver's helmet. **face powder** *n.* cosmetic powder for the face. **facer** *n.* **1** a blow in the face. **2** a sudden difficulty, a dilemma. **face-saving** *a.* intended to prevent humiliation or loss of one's prestige. **face-saver** *n.* **face-to-face** *a.* having the people concerned talking to or looking at one another. **face value** *n.* **1** the nominal value shown on coins, banknotes etc. **2** the apparent value of anything. **faceworker** *n.* a miner who works at the coal face. [F, from pop. L *facia*, L *faciēs*]

facet (fas´it) *n.* **1** an aspect or part of something. **2** a small face or surface. **3** any one of the small planes which form the sides of a crystal, a cut diamond or other gem. **4** a flat surface with a definite boundary as a segment of a compound eye. **5** (*Archit.*) a flat projection between the flutings of a column. ~*v.t.* (*pres.p.* **faceting,** (*N Am.*) **facetting,** *past, p.p.* **faceted,** (*N Am.*) **facetted**) to cut a facet or facets on. **faceted,** (*N Am.*) **facetted** *a.* [F *facette*, dim. of *face*, FACE]

facetiae (fəsē´shiē) *n.pl.* **1** humorous or witty sayings. **2** curious, comic, or esp. indecent books. [L, pl. of *facētia*, wit, from *facētus*, elegant, urbane]

facetious (fəsē´shəs) *a.* **1** given to or characterized by levity; flippant, waggish, jocular. **2** intended to be amusing. **facetiously** *adv.* **facetiousness** *n.* [F *facétieux*, from *facétie*, L *facētia*, see FACETIAE]

facia (fā´shə), **fascia** *n.* **1** the instrument board of a car. **2** the nameboard above a shop.

facial (fā´shəl) *a.* of or relating to the face. ~*n.* a beauty treatment for the face. **facial angle** *n.* the angle formed by lines drawn from the nostrils to the ear and to the forehead. **facially** *adv.* [F, from med. L *faciālis*]

-facient *comb. form* added to the stems of Latin and English verbs to give the sense of producing the action expressed in the verb, as *calefacient, liquefacient.* [L *faciens entem*, pres.p. of *facere*, to make]

facies (fā´shiēz) *n.* (*pl.* **facies**) **1** the general aspect of an assembly of organisms characteristic of a particular locality. **2** the characteristics of a rock or a geological formation. [L, face]

facile (fas´īl) *a.* **1** easily done; easily surmountable. **2** ready, fluent. **3** glib, superficial, shallow. **4** †easy-tempered, gentle. **facilely** *adv.* **facileness** *n.* [F, from L *facilis*, from *facere*, to do]

facilitate (fəsil´itāt) *v.t.* **1** to make easy or less difficult. **2** to further, to help forward. **facilitation** (-ā´shən) *n.* **facilitative** (-tətiv) *a.* **facilitator** *n.* [as FACILE]

Usage note *Facilitate* should not be used of helping a person (with a person as its direct object).

facility (fəsil´iti) *n.* (*pl.* **facilities**) **1** easiness in performing or in being performed; freedom from difficulty. **2** ease, readiness, fluency (of speech etc.). **3** quickness, dexterity, aptitude. **4** (*usu. pl.*) means or equipment provided to facilitate any activity (*recreational facilities*). **5** a service. **6** (*chiefly N Am.*) a building or plant serving a particular purpose. **7** a sum made available for borrowing. **8** (*often pl., coll.*) a lavatory. **9** †readiness to be persuaded or led, pliability. [F, from L *facilis*, from *facere*, to do]

facing (fā´sing) *n.* **1** a covering in front for ornament, strength or other purposes. **2** a coating of a different material, on a wall etc. **3** (*pl.*) the trimmings on the collar, cuffs etc. of a uniform, serving to distinguish one regiment from another.

façon de parler (fas´õ də pah´lā) *n.* manner of speaking; phrase, phrasing. [F]

facsimile (faksim´ili) *n.* **1** an exact copy of handwriting, printing, a picture etc. **2** the transmission by electronic scanning and reproduction of written or pictorial material. ~*v.t.* (*pres.p.* **facsimileing,** *past, p.p.* **facsimiled**) to make a facsimile of. **in facsimile** exactly like. **facsimilist** *n.* [L (*fac*, imper. of *facere*, to make, *simile*, neut. of *similis*, like)]

fact (fakt) *n.* **1** something that has really occurred or been done; something known to be true or existing, as distinct from an inference or conjecture. **2** (*usu. pl.*) a piece of information that can be discovered. **3** reality, actuality, the concrete basis of experience. **4** (*Law*) an act or deed. **after the fact** after the actual committing of a crime. **as a matter of fact** actually, in fact. **before the fact** before the actual committing of a crime. **in (point of) fact** in reality, actually, independently of theory or argument. **fact-finding** *a.* investigative, appointed to establish the facts of a situation. **fact sheet** *n.* a printed document containing information. **facts of life** *n.pl.* **1** the details of esp. human reproduction. **2** the (often unpleasant) realities of a situation. [L *factum*, a thing done, orig. neut. p.p. of *facere*, to do]

facta FACTUM.

factice (fak´tis) *n.* (*Chem.*) a rubber-like material made by treating vegetable oils with sulphur. [L *facticius*, factitious]

faction[1] (fak´shən) *n.* **1** a body of persons combined or acting in union, esp. a party within a party combined to promote their own views or purposes at the expense of order and the public good. **2** partisanship, discord, dissension. **factional** *a.* **factionalism** *n.* **factionalize, factionalise** *v.t., v.i.* **factionally** *adv.* **factious** *a.* **1** given to faction or party; seditious, turbulent. **2** opposed to the established government. **factiously** *adv.* **factiousness** *n.* [F, from L *factio -ōnem*, a doing, a way of making (cp. FASHION), a class, a party, from *facere*, to do, p.p. *factus*]

Usage note The adjectives *factious* and *fractious* should not be confused: *factious* means given to dissent, and *fractious* peevish.

faction² (fak´shən) *n.* literary etc. work which blends factual events and characters with fiction. [from *fact* and fict*ion*]

-faction (fak´shən) *comb.form* denoting making, turning or converting, as in *rarefaction, satisfaction, tumefaction.* [L *-factio -ōnem*, n. of action of verbs in *-facere*; or, occasionally, from verbs in *-ficāre*, as in *petrifaction*]

factitious (faktish´əs) *a.* 1 artificial, not natural. 2 affected; unreal, bogus. **factitiously** *adv.* **factitiousness** *n.* [L *facticius*, from *factus*, p.p. of *facere*, to make]

Usage note The adjectives *factitious* and *fictitious* should not be confused: *factitious* means artificial, and *fictitious* imaginary.

factitive (fak´titiv) *a.* 1 causing, effecting. 2 (*Gram.*) applied to that relation existing between two words, as between an active verb and its object, when the action expressed by the verb causes a new state or condition in the object, as in *The people made him king.* [L *factus*, as FACTITIOUS]

factoid (fak´toid) *n.* 1 an item of information that is considered to be true because it is repeated frequently. 2 (*N Am.*) a piece of trivial information. *~a.* relating to or of the nature of a factoid. [from FACT and -OID]

factor (fak´tə) *n.* 1 any circumstance, fact or influence which contributes to a result. 2 each of the quantities that multiplied together make up a given number or expression. 3 an agent, a deputy. 4 (*Sc.*) a steward or agent of an estate. 5 a business that buys a manufacturer's invoices and collects payment from customers. 6 an agent employed to sell goods on commission. *~v.t.* 1 to act as factor for or to look after (property). 2 to manage. 3 to factorize. *~v.i.* to work as a factor. **factorable** *a.* **factorage** *n.* the commission given to a factor by their employer. **factor analysis** *n.* a statistical method of identifying a fewer number of underlying variables from a larger number of variables. **factorial** (-taw´-) *a.* 1 of or relating to a series of mathematical factors. 2 of or relating to a factor or land agent. *~n.* 1 the product of a series of factors in arithmetical progression, as $(x+2)(x+4)(x+6)$. 2 the product of an integer multiplied into all its lower integers, e.g. the factorial of $4 = 4 \times 3 \times 2 = 24$. **factorially** *adv.* **factoring** *n.* 1 the work of a factor. 2 the buying up of trade debts or lending money on the security of them. **factorize** (-taw´-), **factorise** *v.t.* to express (a number) in terms of its factors. *~v.i.* to be expressible in terms of its factors. **factorization** (-zā´shən) *n.* **factor of safety** *n.* the ratio of the breaking stress to the greatest stress likely to be applied. **factor VIII, factor eight** *n.* a blood-clotting agent used in the treatment of haemophiliacs. [F *facteur*, L *factōr-em*, as FACT]

factory (fak´təri, -tri) *n.* (*pl.* **factories**) 1 a building in which any manufacture is carried out, a works, a workshop, a mill. 2 a trading station established in a foreign place by a company of merchants. **Factory Acts** *n.pl.* acts to provide for the health and safety of those employed in factories. **factory farm** *n.* a farm practising factory farming. **factory farming** *n.* the intensive rearing of animals for milk, egg or meat production in a largely artificial environment. **factory floor** *n.* workers in a factory in contrast to the management. **factory ship** *n.* a vessel in a fishing fleet which processes the catches. **factory shop** *n.* an outlet in which manufactured goods that are surplus, slightly damaged etc. are sold to the public. [med. L *factōria*, as FACTOR]

factotum (faktō´təm) *n.* (*pl.* **factotums**) 1 a person employed to do all sorts of work, a handyman. 2 a servant who manages all their employer's concerns. [med. L (L *fac*, imper. of *facere*, to do, *totum*, neut. a., all)]

factual (fak´chuəl) *a.* concerned with or containing facts; actual or real. **factuality** (-al´iti) *n.* **factually** *adv.* **factualness** *n.*

factum (fak´təm) *n.* (*pl.* **factums, facta** (-tə)) 1 a thing done; an act or deed. 2 (*Law*) a deed, a sealed instrument. 3 a report of facts or points in a controversy. [L, FACT]

facula (fak´ūlə) *n.* (*pl.* **faculae** (-lē)) (*Astron.*) a luminous spot or streak on the sun's disc. **facular, faculous** *a.* [L, dim. of *fax, facis*, a torch]

faculty (fak´əlti) *n.* (*pl.* **faculties**) 1 a natural power of the mind, such as the will, reason, sense etc.; capacity for any natural action, such as seeing, feeling, speaking. 2 power or ability of any special kind. 3 (*N Am.*) the ability to do or manage. 4 the members collectively of any of the learned professions. 5 any one of the departments of instruction in a university. 6 the professors and lecturers in such a department. 7 an authorization or licence to perform certain functions, esp. ecclesiastical. **facultative** (-əltətiv) *a.* 1 imparting a faculty or power; empowering, permissive, as opposed to compulsory. 2 optional; that may or may not occur. 3 of or relating to a faculty. 4 able to live under more than one set of environmental conditions. **facultatively** *adv.* **facultize, facultise** *v.t.* **Faculty of Advocates** *n.* the college or incorporated body of barristers in Scotland. [F *faculté*, L *facultās -tātem*, contr. from *facilitās*, see FACILE]

FAD *abbr.* flavin adenine dinucleotide.

fad (fad) *n.* 1 a whim, a passing fancy, taste or fashion, a craze. 2 an idiosyncratic taste or distaste for something. 3 a hobby; a favourite theory or idea. **faddish** *a.* **faddishly** *adv.* **faddishness** *n.* **faddism** *n.* **faddist** *n.* **faddy** *a.* (*comp.* **faddier,** *superl.* **faddiest**) fussy as regards likes and dislikes, esp. in food. **faddily** *adv.* **faddiness** *n.* [etym. uncertain]

fade (fād) *v.i.* 1 to grow lighter in colour, pale, dim or indistinct. 2 to wither, as a plant; to lose freshness, brightness, vigour or beauty; to languish. 3 to disappear gradually. 4 (of a person) to grow weaker, to decline. 5 (of electronic signals) to decrease in strength or volume. 6 (of brakes) to lose their effectiveness gradually. 7 (of an athlete, team etc.) to perform less well, to cease to mount a serious challenge. 8 to perform a fade-in or fade-out. 9 (of a golf ball) to deviate from a straight flight. *~v.t.* 1 to cause to grow lighter in colour. 2 to cause to wither or decay. 3 to cause to decrease in strength or volume. 4 in golf, to slice (a shot) slightly. *~n.* 1 an instance of fading in or out or both simultaneously. 2 a dimming of stage lighting. 3 in golf, a slight (often deliberate) slice. **to do a fade** (*sl.*) to go away, to leave. **to fade away** 1 to fade. 2 (*coll.*) to grow very thin. **to fade in** to cause (sound or a picture) to appear gradually. **to fade out** to cause (sound or a picture) to disappear gradually. **fade-in, fade-up** *n.* an act of fading sound or a picture in. **fadeless** *a.* unfading. **fadelessly** *adv.* **fade-out, fade-down** *n.* an act of fading sound or a picture out. **fadingly** *adv.* [OF *fader*, from *fade*, dull, tasteless, L *vapidum*, acc. of *vapidus*]

fadge (faj) †*v.i.* 1 to suit, to fit. 2 to agree. 3 to get on, to prosper. *~n.* (*Austral., New Zeal.*) a package of wool in a bale. [etym. uncertain]

fado (fah´dō) *n.* (*pl.* **fados**) a type of esp. melancholy Portuguese folk song. [Port. fate]

faeces (fē´sēz), (*esp. N Am.*) **feces** *n.pl.* excrement from the bowels. **faecal** (fē´kəl) *a.* [L, pl. of *faex*, dregs]

†**faerie** (feə´ri), †**faery** *n.* fairyland, esp. the imaginary realm depicted in Spenser's *Faerie Queene.* *~a.* visionary, beautiful but unsubstantial. [var. of FAIRY]

Faeroese (feərōēz´) *a.* of or relating to the Faeroes, a group of islands in the N Atlantic between Iceland and the Shetland Islands. ~*n.* (*pl.* **Faeroese**) **1** a native or inhabitant of the Faeroes. **2** (*as pl.*) the people of the Faeroes. **3** the language of the Faeroes.

faff (faf) *v.i.* (*coll.*) to dither, to fuss (often with *about*). ~*n.* a fuss. [imit.]

fag[1] (fag) *n.* **1** (*coll.*) a cigarette. **2** (*coll.*) a boring, tiresome or unwelcome task. **3** fatigue, exhaustion. **4** laborious drudgery, toil. **5** a junior at a public school who has to perform certain duties for a senior boy. ~*v.i.* (*pres.p.* **fagging,** *past, p.p.* **fagged**) **1** to toil wearily; to work till one is weary. **2** to act as a fag in a public school. ~*v.t.* **1** to tire, to exhaust, to weary (often with *out*). **2** to use as a fag or drudge in a public school. **fag end** *n.* **1** (*coll.*) a cigarette butt. **2** the unimportant or worthless remaining part of anything. **3** the fringed or untwisted end of a rope. **4** the loose end of a web of cloth, generally of coarser texture. [etym. uncertain (perh. corr. of FLAG[1])]

fag[2] (fag) *n.* (*chiefly N Am., offensive*) a male homosexual. [abbr. of *faggot*]

faggot (fag´ət) *n.* **1** a cake or ball of chopped liver, herbs etc. **2** (*N Am.* **fagot**) **a** a bundle of sticks or small branches of trees, used for fuel, filling ditches, road-making etc. **b** a bundle of steel or wrought-iron rods. **c** a bundle of any material. **3** (*chiefly N Am., offensive*) a male homosexual. ~*v.t.* (*pres.p.* **faggoting,** (*N Am.*) **fagoting,** *past, p.p.* **faggoted,** (*N Am.*) **fagoted**) **1** to bind or tie up in a faggot or bundle. **2** to join as in faggoting. **3** †to collect together. **faggoting,** (*N Am.*) **fagoting** *n.* **1** a type of embroidery in which some horizontal threads are tied together in hourglass shapes. **2** the joining together of materials like this. **faggoty** *a.* [F *fagot*, etym. uncertain (perh. from Norw. *fagg*, a bundle)]

fagotto (fəgot´ō) *n.* (*pl.* **fagotti** (-ē)) a bassoon. [It.]

fah (fah), **fa** *n.* **1** the fourth note of a major scale in the tonic sol-fa system of notation. **2** the note F in the fixed-doh system. [It.]

Fahr. *abbr.* Fahrenheit.

Fahrenheit (far´ənhīt) *a.* of or relating to the temperature scale on which the freezing point of water is marked at 32° and the boiling point at 212°. [Gabriel Daniel *Fahrenheit*, 1686–1736, who devised it]

faience (fayãs´) *n.* **1** tin-glazed earthenware of a particular kind. **2** glazed blocks of terracotta used as facings. [F *faïence*; It. *Faenza*, city in Italy famous in the 15th and 16th cent. for pottery made there]

fail[1] (fāl) *v.i.* **1** not to succeed (in). **2** not to succeed in the attainment (of). **3** not to pass an examination. **4** to be or become deficient or wanting; to run short; to come short of the due amount or measure. **5** to lose strength or spirit, to sink, to decline. **6** to die away. **7** to be or become ineffective or inoperative. **8** to become bankrupt or insolvent. ~*v.t.* **1** not to pass (an examination). **2** to cause not to pass. **3** to be insufficient for; to come short of. **4** to deceive, to disappoint, to desert. **5** to neglect or omit (to do something). ~*n.* **1** failure, default. **2** a failure grade in an examination. **3** a person who fails an examination. **without fail** certainly, assuredly, in spite of all hindrances. **failed** *a.* **1** unsuccessful. **2** deficient, worn-out. **failing** *n.* **1** a deficiency, shortcoming. **2** the act of becoming insolvent or bankrupt. **3** an imperfection, a weakness, a foible. ~*prep.* if not; in default of. **fail-safe** *a.* (of a mechanism) incorporated in a system to render it safe in the event of failure or malfunction. **failure** (-yə) *n.* **1** lack of success. **2** an unsuccessful person or thing. **3** an omission, non-performance, non-occurrence. **4** a failing or coming short. **5** decay, breaking down. **6** insolvency, bankruptcy. [OF *faillir*, to miss, pop. L *fallīre*, to be wanting, to disappoint, L *fallere*, to deceive]

fail[2] (fāl) *n.* (*Sc.*) a turf, sod. [prob. from Gael. *fàl*, a sod]

†**fain** (fān) *a.* **1** glad, well-pleased; desirous. **2** content or compelled (to) for lack of a better alternative. ~*adv.* gladly, readily. [OE *fægen*, rel. to *gefēan*, to rejoice]

fainéant (fā´niənt, -ã) *a.* do-nothing; idle, sluggish. ~*n.* a do-nothing, an idler. [F, as if formed of *fait-néant*, do nothing; actually from OF *faignant*, sluggard, pres.p. of *faindre*, to skulk, see FAINT]

faint (fānt) *a.* **1** (of sound or brightness) dim, indistinct, slight, feeble. **2** weak, feeble. **3** giddy, inclined to faint. **4** slight, remote (*a faint chance*). **5** timid, fearful. **6** (of smells) sickly, oppressive. **7** with light lines to guide writing. ~*v.i.* to lose consciousness because of hunger, shock etc. ~*n.* **1** a fainting fit. **2** (*pl.*) crude spirit produced at the beginning and end of distillation in the manufacture of whisky, sold as spirit of an inferior grade. **not to have the faintest (idea)** (*coll.*) not to know at all. **to damn with faint praise** DAMN. **faint heart** *n.* a cowardly or timid nature. **faint-hearted** *a.* cowardly, timid, spiritless. **faint-heartedly** *adv.* **faint-heartedness** *n.* **faintish** *a.* **faintly** *adv.* **faintness** *n.* [OF *feint*, p.p. of *feindre, faindre*, to FEIGN]

fair[1] (feə) *a.* **1** just, reasonable, legitimate. **2** light in colour or complexion; blond. **3** passably good, not bad, of moderate quality; satisfactory. **4** beautiful, attractive, pleasing to the eye. **5** clear, pure, clean. **6** not effected by unlawful or underhand means, above board. **7** free from spot, blemish or cloud, serene. **8** (of the weather) fine and sunny, not raining. **9** favourable, auspicious, promising. **10** open, unobstructed. **11** civil, obliging, polite. **12** legible, plain. **13** specious. **14** †orderly, neat. **15** †liberal, kind, mild. ~*adv.* **1** according to the rules, straight, clean. **2** completely, absolutely. **3** courteously, civilly, plausibly. **4** openly, honestly, justly. **5** on equal terms. ~*n.* †a beautiful woman. ~†*v.t.* to make fair or beautiful. ~*v.i.* (of the weather) to become fair. **by fair means or foul** MEANS. **fair enough** (*coll.*) (indicating at least partial assent to a proposition, terms etc.) all right, OK. **fair's fair** (*coll.*) used as a protest or reminder that everyone is entitled to fair or equal treatment. **fair to middling** (*coll.*) not bad, about average. **for fair** (*US, sl.*) absolutely. **to be in a fair way** to stand a good chance. **to bid fair** BID. **fair and square** *a.* honourable, straightforward, above board. ~*adv.* **1** fairly, honestly, without trickery or deceit. **2** exactly on target. **fair cop** *n.* a justified arrest. **fair copy** *n.* a copy (of a document etc.) not defaced by corrections. **fair crack of the whip** *n.* a fair opportunity or chance. **fair dinkum** *a.* (*Austral., New Zeal., coll.*) fair, genuine. ~*n.* fair play. **fair dos** (dooz) *n.pl.* (*coll.*) fair play, equal shares etc., fair treatment. **fair game** *n.* a legitimate target for attack, criticism or ridicule. **fair-haired** *a.* having hair of a light colour, blond. **fairing** *n.* **1** a structure to provide streamlining of an aircraft, car etc. **2** the process of streamlining. **fairish** *a.* **1** pretty fair. **2** tolerably large. **fairlead** *n.* (*Naut.*) a device for guiding a rope etc., to keep it clear of obstructions, reduce chafing etc. **fair leather** *n.* leather with its natural colour. **fairly** *adv.* **1** in a fair manner. **2** moderately, passably. **3** completely, absolutely, utterly. **4** †softly, gently. **fairly and squarely** *adv.* fair and square. **fair-minded** *a.* honest, impartial, just. **fair-mindedly** *adv.* **fair-mindedness** *n.* **fair name** *n.* a good reputation. **fairness** *n.* **in all fairness** it is only right or just that, being strictly honest. **fair play** *n.* reasonable behaviour; just or equal conditions for all. **fair rent** *n.* a rent set in accordance with official guidelines. **fair-seeming** *a.* **1** superficially favourable or equitable. **2** plausible, specious. **fair sex** *n.* women. **fair-spoken** *a.* **1** using courteous language. **2** bland, polite, plausible. **fair trade** *n.* reciprocity, the granting of free trade only to nations that allow it in return. **fair treat** *n.* (*coll.*)

something or someone very pleasing. **fairwater** *n.* a structure to assist a ship's smooth passage through water. **fairway** *n.* **1** the navigable part of a river, channel or harbour. **2** the smooth passage of turf between holes on a golf course. **fair-weather** *a.* appearing only in times of prosperity; not good in times of need (*a fair-weather friend*). [OE *fæger* (cp. Icel. *fagr*, OHG *fagar*)]

fair[2] (feə) *n.* **1** a funfair. **2** a market or gathering for trade in a particular town or place. **3** a trade show. **fairground** *n.* an open space where fairs, exhibitions etc. are held. [OF *feire* (F *foire*), L *fēria* or pl. *fēriae*, a holiday]

Usage note The pseudo-archaic spelling *fayre* is used especially of bazaars and trade shows.

---

fairing FAIR[1].

Fair Isle (feə) *a.* applied to woollen articles knitted in coloured patterns typical of Fair Isle (one of the Shetland Islands).

fairy (feə´ri) *n.* (*pl.* **fairies**) **1** an imagined small supernatural being having magical powers, supposed to assume human form and to meddle for good or for evil in human affairs. **2** (*sl., offensive*) an effeminate man or homosexual. ~*a.* **1** of, relating to or connected with fairies; fairy-like; fanciful, imaginary. **2** small, delicate or dainty. **fairily** *adv.* **fairy armadillo** *n.* (*pl.* **fairy armadillos**) a very small burrowing armadillo, *Chlamyphorus truncatus.* **fairy cake** *n.* a small individual soft cake, esp. with icing. **fairy cycle** *n.* a child's small bicycle. **fairydom** *n.* **fairy godmother** *n.* a (usu. unexpected) benefactress. **fairyhood** *n.* **fairyism** *n.* **fairyland** *n.* **1** the imaginary home of the fairies. **2** a region of enchantment. **fairy lights** *n.pl.* small lights of many colours used for decoration. **fairy-like** *a.* **fairy ring** *n.* a circular band of turf greener than the rest caused by the growth of fungi (formerly supposed to be caused by the dancing of fairies). **fairy-stones** *n.pl.* **1** the fossil remains of sea urchins. **2** recent concretions of hardened clay occurring near the source of some chalybeate springs. **fairy story, fairy tale** *n.* **1** a tale about fairies. **2** a fanciful or highly improbable story. ~*a.* **1** as in a fairy tale. **2** extremely beautiful or wonderful. [OF *faerie*, enchantment (F *féerie*), from *fée*, a fairy]

fait accompli (fāt, fet əkom´plē) *n.* (*pl.* **faits accomplis** (fāt, fet əkom´plē)) an accomplished fact. [F]

faith (fāth) *n.* **1** firm and earnest belief, conviction, complete confidence, reliance, trust. **2** the assent of the mind to what is stated or put forward by another. **3** a system of religious belief. **4** spiritual apprehension or voluntary acceptance of divine revelation apart from absolute proof. **5** active belief in the doctrines and moral principles forming a system of religion. **6** commitment to keep a promise etc., fidelity, constancy, loyalty. **7** a promise, pledge or engagement. **8** credibility, reliability, trustworthiness. **9** a philosophical, scientific or political creed or system of doctrines. ~†*int.* in faith, indeed. **in faith** in truth. **in good faith** with honest intentions. **on the faith of 1** in reliance on. **2** on the warrant of. **the faith** the true religion. **to keep faith with** to be loyal to. **faithful** *a.* **1** loyal to one's promises, duty or engagements; conscientious, trustworthy. **2** upright, honest. **3** truthful, worthy of belief. **4** exact, accurate. **the faithful** true believers in a particular creed or religious system. **faithfully** *adv.* in a faithful manner. **yours faithfully** a conventional way of ending a formal or business letter. **faithfulness** *n.* **faith healing** *n.* curing of disease by means of prayer and faith, without the use of drugs etc. **faith-healer** *n.* **faithless** *a.* **1** lacking faith, unbelieving. **2** disloyal, unfaithful, not true to promises or duty, unreliable. **3** treacherous. **faithlessly** *adv.* **faithlessness** *n.* [OF *fei*, *feid*, L *fides*, *fidem* (cp. Gr. *pistis*, faith, *peithein*, to persuade)]

Usage note In closing letters, *Yours faithfully* is a formal style, and goes with an opening in which an unknown or unfamiliar person is addressed as 'Sir' or 'Madam' (*Dear Sirs, Dear Madam* etc.).

---

faits accomplis FAIT ACCOMPLI.

fajita (fəhē´tə) *n.* a kind of tortilla wrapped around meat, chillies, onions etc.

fake[1] (fāk) *v.t.* **1** to pretend, to simulate. **2** to do up, to cover up defects and faults so as to give a more valuable appearance to, to doctor; to contrive, to fabricate, to make up from defective material. **3** to cheat, to defraud, to deceive. ~*n.* **1** a thing, e.g. a manufactured antique made to deceive, a sham. **2** a swindle, a dodge. ~*a.* bogus, sham, counterfeit. **faker** *n.* **fakery** *n.* [etym. uncertain]

fake[2] (fāk) *n.* (*Naut.*) one of the coils in a rope or cable when laid up. ~*v.t.* to coil (a rope). [etym. uncertain]

fakir (fā´kiə, fəkiə´), **faquir** *n.* **1** a Muslim religious mendicant. **2** a Hindu mendicant, ascetic or wonder-worker. **3** a very holy man. [Arab. *faqīr*, orig. poor, indigent]

falafel FELAFEL.

Falange (fəlanj´) *n.* the Fascist movement in Spain, founded in 1933. **Falangism** *n.* **Falangist** *n.* [Sp., from Gr. *phalanx*]

Falasha (fəlah´shə) *n.* (*pl.* **Falasha, Falashas**) a member of an Ethiopian people who practise a form of Judaism. [Amharic, immigrant]

falbala (fal´bələ) *n.* **1** a trimming, a flounce. **2** a furbelow. [etym. unknown, cp. FURBELOW]

falcate (fal´kāt) *a.* (*Anat.*) hooked; bent or curved like a sickle or scythe. **falcated** *a.* (*Astron.*) sickle-shaped, applied to the moon in the first and fourth quarters. [L *falcātus*, from *falx falcis*, sickle]

falchion (fawl´chən, -shən) *n.* a short, broad sword with a slightly curved blade. [OF *fauchon*, late L *falcio -ōnem*, L *falx falcis*, a sickle]

falciform (fal´sifawm) *a.* having the form of a sickle. [L *falx falcis*, sickle]

falcon (fawl´kən, fal´-) *n.* **1** any diurnal bird of prey of the family *Falconidae* having pointed wings, esp. the peregrine falcon and others trained to hawk game. **2** a female falcon, esp. the peregrine (cp. TIERCEL). **falconer** *n.* **1** a person who keeps and trains hawks for hawking. **2** a person who hunts with hawks. **falconet** (-nit) *n.* **1** a small falcon. **2** †a small cannon. **falconry** *n.* **1** the art of training falcons to pursue and attack game. **2** the sport of hawking. [OF *faucon*, late L *falco -ōnem*, perh. as FALCIFORM]

falderal (fal´dəral), **folderol** (fol´dərol) *n.* **1** a trifle, a gewgaw. **2** a nonsensical refrain in a song. **3** foolish nonsense. [refrain to a song]

faldstool (fawld´stool) *n.* **1** a portable folding seat, stool or chair, used by a bishop. **2** a desk at which the Litany is said. **3** a desk or stool to kneel at during prayer. [OE *fældestōl*, med. L *faldistolium*, OHG *faldstuol* (*faldan*, to fold, *stuol*, cp. G *Stuhl*, a chair)]

fall (fawl) *v.i.* (*past* **fell** (fel), *p.p.* **fallen** (faw´lən)) **1** to descend from a higher to a lower place or position by the force of gravity. **2** to descend suddenly, to drop. **3** to sink, to flow down, to be poured down, to become lower in level of surface. **4** to hang down, to droop. **5** to come down, to become prostrate. **6** to be hit or wounded. **7** to be killed (esp. in battle). **8** to be overthrown, to lose power. **9** to be taken by the enemy. **10** in cricket, to be taken by the bowling side. **11** to decrease in number, amount, value, weight, loudness etc. **12** to become lower in pitch. **13** to subside, to abate, to ebb, to languish, to die away. **14** to fail, to be degraded or disgraced. **15** to sink into sin, vice, error, to give away to temptation. **16** to lose one's virginity. **17** (of the face) to assume a despondent expression. **18** to become, to pass into a specified state, as in *fall asleep, fall ill.* **19** to be transferred by chance, lot, inheritance, or otherwise. **20** to turn out, to result, to happen. **21** to be uttered or dropped, as a chance remark. **22** to be born (said of certain animals). ~*v.t.* to cut down, to fell; to let fall, to drop. ~*n.* **1** the act of falling. **2** a bout at wrestling or a throw in this. **3** a decrease in number, amount etc. **4** the degree of inclination, the gradient or slope. **5** a downward slope. **6** the amount of descent, the distance through which anything falls. **7** the discharging of a river. **8** (*chiefly N Am.*) autumn. **9** (*usu. pl.*) a cataract, a cascade, a waterfall. **10** the amount of rain, snow etc. in a district. **11** downfall, degradation, declension from greatness or prosperity, ruin, disgrace. **12** death, destruction, overthrow. **13** the surrender or capture of a town. **14** the act of felling or cutting down. **15** the amount of timber cut down. **16** the number of certain animals, such as lambs, born. **17** a lapse from virtue; a yielding to temptation. **18** a long false hair-piece. **19** a veil. **20** that part of the rope in hoisting-tackle to which the power is applied. **21** (*Mus.*) a cadence. **the Fall** the sin of disobedience of Adam, and through him, of all the human race. **to fall about** (*coll.*) to laugh hysterically. **to fall afoul of** AFOUL. **to fall among** to come among accidentally. **to fall apart** to collapse, to become unstitched, unstuck etc., to go to pieces. **to fall astern** (*Naut.*) to drop behind. **to fall away 1** to desert; to revolt; to apostatize; to fall into wickedness. **2** to extend or slope downwards, esp. suddenly. **3** to pine, to become thin. **4** to decay, to languish. **to fall back** to recede, to give way, to retreat. **to fall back on/ upon** to have recourse to. **to fall behind 1** to be passed by, to lag behind. **2** to become in arrears with. **to fall between two stools 1** to fail through being unable to choose between two alternatives. **2** to be neither one thing or the other. **to fall by the ears** EAR[1]. **to fall down 1** to be thrown down, to drop. **2** to prostrate oneself. **3** to fail, to be inadequate. **to fall down on** to fail to carry out. **to fall flat** FLAT[1]. **to fall for 1** (*coll.*) to be impressed by, to fall in love with. **2** to be fooled by. **to fall foul of** FOUL. **to fall from** to drop away from, to desert, to forsake. **to fall from grace** GRACE. **to fall home** (*Naut.*) to curve inwards, as the timbers or sides of a ship. **to fall in 1** (*Mil.*) to take one's place in line. **2** to give way inwards. **to fall in love** LOVE. **to fall into** to come into the range of; to be classed with. **to fall into line** LINE[1]. **to fall into place** PLACE. **to fall in with 1** to meet with accidentally. **2** to agree to, to concur in. **3** to coincide with. **to fall off 1** to decrease in quality, quantity or amount, to become depreciated. **2** to withdraw, to recede. **3** to prove faithless; to revolt. **4** (of a ship) to fail to keep its head to the wind. **to fall on deaf ears** EAR[1]. **to fall on one's feet** FOOT. **to fall on/ upon 1** (of the eyes, glance etc.) to alight on, to be directed towards. **2** to attack. **3** to meet or discover by chance, to come across. **to fall out 1** to happen, to come to pass, to turn out, to result. **2** to quarrel. **3** (of the hair etc.) to become separate from the body. **4** (*Mil.*) to leave the ranks. **to fall over 1** to tumble or be knocked down. **2** to trip or stumble over. **to fall over backwards** BACKWARDS. **to fall over oneself 1** (*coll.*) to be eager, or overeager (to do something). **2** (*coll.*) to stumble clumsily. **to fall short 1** to be deficient. **2** to drop before reaching the mark or target. **to fall short of** to fail to attain. **to fall through** to fail, to miscarry, to come to nothing. **to fall to** to begin hastily or eagerly, to set to, e.g. to begin eating. **to fall to pieces** to fall apart, to go to pieces. **to fall to the ground** GROUND[1]. **to fall under 1** to be subject to. **2** to come within the range of; to be classed with or reckoned with or under. **to fall within** to be included in. **fall-back** *a.* **1** used as an alternative if plans fail or something unexpected happens. **2** (of a wage) being a minimum amount that is paid when no work is available. ~*n.* a reserve; a fall-back wage. **fallen** *a.* **1** killed, esp. in battle. **2** seduced; morally degraded. **3** overthrown. **fallenness** *n.* **faller** *n.* **1** a racehorse which falls during a race. **2** a share or stock which falls in value. **fallfish** (fawl´fish) *n.* (*pl. in general* **fallfish,** *in particular* **fallfishes**) a N American freshwater fish, *Semotilus corporalis*, similar to the chub. **fall guy** *n.* **1** a person who is easily duped. **2** a scapegoat, a cat's paw. **falling-away** *n.* apostasy. **falling-off** *n.* a decrease. **falling-out** *n.* a quarrel or disagreement. **falling star** *n.* a meteor appearing to fall rapidly to the earth. **fall-off** *n.* a decrease. **fallout** *n.* **1** the deposit of radioactive dust after a nuclear explosion. **2** secondary consequences, by-products. **fall-pipe** *n.* a downpipe. **fall-trap** *n.* a trap with a door which falls and imprisons. [OE *feallan*, cp. Dut. *vallen*, Icel. *falla*, G *fallen*, also L *fallere*, to deceive]

fallacy (fal´əsi) *n.* (*pl.* **fallacies**) **1** a prevalent but mistaken belief, based on unsound reasoning or incorrect information. **2** (*Logic*) a delusive mode of reasoning, an example of such. **3** an error, a sophism; sophistry, delusiveness. **fallacious** (fəlā´shəs) *a.* **fallaciously** *adv.* **fallaciousness** *n.* [L *fallăcia*, from *fallax*, deceptive, from *fallere*, to deceive]

fallal (fal·lal´) *n.* a gaudy ornament or trinket, a gewgaw. [cp. KNICK-KNACK; perh. conn. with FALBALA]

fallen FALL.

fallible (fal´ibəl) *a.* likely to make mistakes; liable to err. **fallibility** (-bil´-) *n.* **fallibly** *adv.* [late L *fallibilis*, from *fallere*, to deceive]

Fallopian tube (fəlō´piən) *n.* either of two ducts or canals in female mammals by which ova are conveyed to the uterus. [Gabriel *Fallopius*, 1523–62, Italian anatomist, who first described them]

fallow[1] (fal´ō) *a.* **1** (of land) ploughed and tilled but not sown; uncultivated. **2** unused, neglected. **3** (of a sow) not pregnant. ~*n.* land ploughed and harrowed but left unsown; land left uncultivated for a period. ~*v.t.* to plough and harrow and leave unsown. **fallowness** *n.* [ME *falwe*, ploughed land, OE *fælging*; *fealga*, harrows for breaking crops]

fallow[2] (fal´ō) *a.* of a pale brownish or reddish-yellow colour. **fallow deer** *n.* a small species of deer, *Dama dama*, having a white-spotted fawn coat in summer. [OE *fealu* (cp. Dut. *vaal*, G *fahl*, also L *pallidus*, pale, Gr. *polios*, grey)]

false (fawls) *a.* **1** not true, contrary to truth, not conformable to fact; deceptive, misleading; erroneous, wrong, incorrect. **2** uttering untruth, lying, deceiving; deceitful, treacherous, faithless (to). **3** feigned, sham, spurious, counterfeit, not genuine. **4** forced, unconvincing. **5** artificial, man-made. **6** fitting over or replacing a main part. **7** (esp. of plants) resembling a different species. **8** (*Mus.*) out of tune. ~*adv.* **1** falsely; wrongly. **2** (*Mus.*) out of tune. **under false colours** COLOUR. **false alarm** *n.* a needless warning, a cause of unnecessary anxiety or excitement. **false bedding** *n.* (*Geol.*) strata in which the layers are not parallel through disturbance by currents whilst they were being laid down. **false bottom** *n.* a partition inserted above the true bottom, often concealing a secret compartment. **false colour** *n.* a colour used in the production of an image to help the interpretation of that image. **false colours** *n.pl.* **1** flags to which a ship has no right, raised to deceive an enemy. **2** misleading pretence or deceit. **to sail under false colours** to assume a false character. **false concord** *n.* (*Gram.*) a breaking of the rules of agreement in number, gender, tense etc. **false dawn** *n.* **1** light appearing just before sunrise. **2** a promising sign of change, progress etc. that in the end fails. **false gharial**

n. an Indonesian and Malaysian crocodile, *Tomistoma schlegelii.* †**false-hearted** *a.* treacherous, betraying. †**false-heartedness** *n.* **falsehood** (-hud) *n.* **1** untruthfulness, falseness, lying, lies. **2** a lie, an untruth. **3** deceitfulness, unfaithfulness. **false imprisonment** *n.* illegal imprisonment. **false keel** *n.* a supplementary keel fastened below the true keel of a ship for protection and to promote stability. **falsely** *adv.* **false move** *n.* an unwise or thoughtless action. **falseness** *n.* **false position** *n.* an awkward position that may lead to misrepresentation or misunderstanding. **false pregnancy** *n.* a psychosomatic condition producing symptoms of pregnancy. **false pretences** *n.pl.* (*Law*) misrepresentations made with intent to deceive or defraud. **false rib** *n.* FLOATING RIB (under FLOAT). **false roof** *n.* a roof-shaped ceiling below the actual roof. **false scent** *n.* **1** a series of scents left in order to mislead. **2** misleading clues etc. aimed at deceiving followers. **false scorpion** *n.* an arachnid of the order Pseudoscorpiones. **false start** *n.* **1** a disallowed start to a race, usu. caused by a competitor moving away too early. **2** an unsuccessful beginning to any activity. **false step** *n.* **1** a stumble or slip. **2** an imprudent action. **false teeth** *n.pl.* artificial teeth, dentures. **false topaz** *n.* CITRINE. **falsework** *n.* a temporary structure supporting actual construction work. **falsies** (-siz) *n.pl.* (*coll.*) pads used to improve the shape of the breasts. **falsity** *n.* (*pl.* **falsities**). [OE and OF *fals*, L *falsus*, p.p. of *fallere*, to deceive]

falsetto (fawlset´ō) *n.* (*pl.* **falsettos**) **1** a pitch or range of (usu. the male) voice higher than the natural register. **2** a singer using this range. ~*a.* **1** of, relating to or produced by such a voice. **2** artificial, affected. [It., dim. of *falso*, FALSE]

falsies FALSE.

falsify (fawl´sifī) *v.t.* (*3rd pers. sing. pres.* **falsifies,** *pres.p.* **falsifying,** *past. p.p.* **falsified**) **1** to make false. **2** to give a false or spurious appearance to (a document, statement etc.). **3** to misrepresent. **4** to counterfeit, to forge. **5** to disappoint (expectations), to confute, to disprove. **falsifiable** *a.* **falsifiability** (-fīəbil´iti) *n.* **falsification** (-fikā´shən) *n.* [F *falsifier*, late L *falsificāre*, from *falsificus* (*falsus*, FALSE, *ficus*, rel. to *facere*, to make)]

falsity FALSE.

Falstaffian (fawlstahf´iən) *a.* fat, coarsely humorous, convivial, dissolute. [*Falstaff*, a character in Shakespeare's *Henry IV* and *V* and *Merry Wives of Windsor*]

falter (fawl´tə) *v.i.* **1** to stumble, to totter, to waver, to be unsteady. **2** to stammer, to stutter. **3** to hesitate in action; to act with irresolution. **4** to tremble, to flinch. ~*v.t.* to utter with hesitation or stammering. **falterer** *n.* **falteringly** *adv.* [etym. uncertain]

fam. *abbr.* **1** familiar, familiarly. **2** family.

fame (fām) *n.* **1** the state of being well-known, renown, celebrity. **2** †reputation, esp. good reputation. **3** †public report or rumour. ~*v.t.* **1** to make famous or renowned. **2** to celebrate. **famed** *a.* **1** much talked of; renowned, celebrated. **2** †circulating as a report. [F, from L *fāma* (*fārī*, to speak), cp. Gr. *phēmē*]

familial FAMILY.

familiar (fəmil´yə) *a.* **1** of one's own acquaintance, well-known, intimate. **2** knowing or understanding a thing well; intimate (with). **3** easily understood, not obscure. **4** usual, common, ordinary, not novel. **5** sexually intimate. **6** too informal; presumptuous. **7** unconstrained, free, unceremonious. **8** †of or relating to one's family. ~*n.* **1** an intimate or close friend or companion. **2** a familiar spirit. **3** a confidential servant in the household of the Pope or a bishop. **4** †the assistant of a magician or witch. **familiarity** (-lia´r-) *n.* (*pl.* **familiarities**) **1** the state of being familiar. **2** close friendship, intimacy. **3** (*sometimes pl.*) (an act of) sexual intimacy. **4** presumptuous behaviour. **familiarize** (fəmil´yərīz), **familiarise** *v.t.* **1** to make well acquainted (with), to accustom. **2** to make well-known. **familiarization** (-zā´shən) *n.* **familiarly** *adv.* **familiar spirit** *n.* a demon or spirit supposed to attend at call. [OF *familier*, L *familiāris* from *familia*, FAMILY]

famille (famē´, famēy´) *n.* a Chinese enamelled porcelain. **famille jaune** (zhōn) *n.* a Chinese enamelled porcelain in which the background of the design is yellow. **famille noire** (nwah) *n.* a Chinese enamelled porcelain in which the background of the design is black. **famille rose** (rōz) *n.* a Chinese enamelled porcelain in which the background of the design is pink. **famille verte** (veət) *n.* a Chinese enamelled porcelain in which the background of the design is green. [F]

family (fam´ili) *n.* (*pl.* **families**) **1** a group of people related to one another, esp. parents and their children. **2** children, as distinguished from their parents. **3** those people who can trace their descent from a common ancestor; a house, kindred, lineage. **4** a race, a group of peoples from a common stock. **5** a group of persons or peoples united by bonds of civilization, religion etc. **6** a group of related things or beings having common characteristics. **7** a group of related languages. **8** honourable descent, noble lineage. **9** (*Math.*) a group of curves or surfaces that differ only by one quality. **10** a group of genera. **11** (*Zool.*) a subdivision of an order. **12** (*Bot.*) an order. **13** (*Chem.*) a group of compounds having a common basic radical. ~*a.* **1** of, relating to or belonging to the family (*the family home*). **2** designed to be enjoyed or used by parents and (esp. young) children (*family viewing*). **3** providing for the needs of families (*a family butcher*). **in the family way** pregnant. **to keep something in the family** to ensure that something, e.g. a possession or piece of information, does not pass outside the family or a select group. **to run in the family** RUN. **familial** (fəmil´iəl) *a.* characteristic of or relating to a family. **family allowance** *n.* the former name for CHILD BENEFIT (under CHILD). **family Bible** *n.* a large Bible in which the names and dates of birth, marriage and death of members of a family are entered. **family credit** *n.* in Britain, a social security benefit paid to people in low-income work who have at least one child. **Family Division** *n.* a division of the High Court dealing with divorce, the custody of children etc. **family doctor** *n.* a general practitioner who treats a family. **family income supplement** *n.* in Britain, a social security benefit formerly paid to families with earnings below a set level. **family likeness** *n.* physical or other resemblance between near relations. **family man** *n.* a man who has a wife and children, esp. a man who is fond of home life. **family name** *n.* a surname. **family planning** *n.* regulating the number of, and intervals between, children, usu. by means of contraceptives. **family therapy** *n.* a form of psychotherapy in which the members of a family meet together to try to improve the ways in which they communicate to and relate with one another. **family tree** *n.* a genealogical chart. [L *familia*, from *famulus*, a servant]

famine (fam´in) *n.* **1** extreme shortage of food. **2** a period of this. **3** an extreme scarcity of anything. **4** †hunger, starvation. [F, from late L *famīna*, L *famēs*, hunger, whence F *faim*]

famish (fam´ish) *v.i.* **1** to suffer extreme hunger; to die of hunger. **2** †to faint. ~*v.t.* to starve; to reduce to extreme hunger. **famished, famishing** *a.* (*coll.*) feeling extremely hungry. [obs. v. *fame*, L *famēs*, as FAMINE, -ISH[1]]

famous (fā´məs) *a.* **1** very well-known; renowned, celebrated; illustrious; noted. **2** (*coll.*) first-rate, very good, excellent. **famously** *adv.* **1** (*coll.*) in a very friendly way (*get on famously*). **2** in a famous way. **famousness** *n.* [A-F, from OF *fameus*, L *fāmōsus*, from *fāma*, FAME]

famulus (fam´ūləs) *n.* (*pl.* **famuli** (-lī)) an assistant or servant of a magician or scholar. [L, a servant]

fan[1] (fan) *n.* **1** an apparatus with revolving blades to give a current of air for ventilation. **2** an instrument, usu. flat, with radiating sections opening out in a wedge-shape for agitating the air and cooling the face. **3** an implement, object or structure shaped like an open fan. **4** a bird's tail, a wing, a leaf shaped like a fan. **5** (*Geol.*) a fan-shaped deposit of alluvium. **6** a winnowing implement or machine. **7** a small sail or vane for keeping the sails of a windmill to the wind. **8** (*Naut.*) the blade of a screw propeller. ~*v.t.* (*pres.p.* **fanning,** *past, p.p.* **fanned**) **1** to cool with a fan. **2** to move or stimulate with or as with a fan. **3** to agitate (the air) with a fan. **4** to stir up. **5** to spread like a fan. **6** to winnow; to winnow or sweep away (chaff). ~*v.i.* **1** to move or blow gently. **2** to spread out like a fan. **to fan out** to radiate outwards in a fan-shape, to move off in divergent directions. **fan belt** *n.* a belt which drives the radiator cooling fan and generator in a car engine. **fan dance** *n.* a dance by an (apparently) nude solo performer in which large fans are manipulated in front of the body. **fan heater** *n.* an electric heater in which the heat from an element is dispersed by a fan. **fan-jet** TURBOFAN (under TURBO-). **fanlight** *n.* a small (originally semicircular) window above a door or another window. **fanlike** *a.* **fanner** *n.* **fanning-machine, fanning-mill** *n.* a winnowing-machine. **fan palm** *n.* any of various palm trees having fan-shaped leaves, such as *Chamaerops humilis*, esp. the genus *Corypha*, typified by the talipot, *C. umbraculifera*, from Sri Lanka and Malabar. **fantail** *n.* **1** a variety of the domestic pigeon with a large tail. **2** a flycatcher of the genus *Rhipidura*. **3** a fan-shaped tail. **4** a form of gas-burner giving a broad, flat flame. **5** a fan on a windmill. **6** the overhanging stern of a ship. **fantailed** *a.* **fan vaulting** *n.* (*Archit.*) vaulting in which the tracery spreads out like a fan. [OE *fann*, L *vannus*, a winnowing-fan]

fan[2] (fan) *n.* an enthusiastic admirer; a devotee. **fan club** *n.* an organized group of devotees. **fandom** *n.* the world of enthusiastic devotees of a particular person or interest. **fan mail** *n.* letters to a famous person from admirers. **fanzine** (-zēn) *n.* a magazine for fans of a particular interest, activity or person, written by amateurs. [abbr. of FANATIC]

fanatic (fənat´ik) *a.* **1** enthusiastic in the extreme. **2** holding extravagant or extremely dogmatic or bigoted views. ~*n.* a person who has an extreme enthusiasm for something. **fanatical** *a.* **fanatically** *adv.* **fanaticism** (-sizm) *n.* **fanaticize** (-sīz), **fanaticise** *v.t.* to make fanatical. ~*v.i.* to become a fanatic. [F *fanatique*, L *fānāticus*, from *fānum*, a temple]

fancy (fan´si) *v.t.* (*3rd pers. sing. pres.* **fancies,** *pres.p.* **fancying,** *past, p.p.* **fancied**) **1** (*coll.*) to want to have or do. **2** (*coll.*) to be attracted, esp. sexually, to. **3** (*coll.*) to have an excessively high opinion of (oneself etc.). **4** to like the idea of being or doing (*fancy yourself as the boss*). **5** to choose (a person, team etc.) as the probable winner. **6** to breed as a hobby or sport. ~*int.* used to express surprise or amazement. ~*n.* (*pl.* **fancies**) **1** a personal inclination, liking or attachment. **2** a liking that does not last long, a caprice, a whim. **3** an imaginary, unreal or improbable idea, a delusion. **4** something favoured. **5** the faculty or the act of forming images, esp. those of a playful, frivolous or capricious kind. **6** the power to conceive imagery. **7** a mental image. **8** a fad, a hobby. ~*a.* (*comp.* **fancier,** *superl.* **fanciest**) **1** elaborate, not plain; ornamental, decorative. **2** (*sometimes iron.*) extravagant or fine; expensive or impressive (*a fancy price*). **3** arising in or based on the imagination. **4** needing skill to be performed; complex. **5** (of flowers) particoloured. **6** (of animals) bred for particular qualities. **(just) fancy!** used to express surprise or disbelief. **the fancy** those who follow a certain sport, esp. boxing or dog fanciers etc. **to take a fancy to** to develop a liking or an affection for, to desire. **to take someone's fancy** to attract someone. **to tickle someone's fancy** to attract someone. **fanciable** *a.* (*coll.*) (of a person) sexually attractive. **fancier** *n.* **1** a person who breeds or sells birds, dogs, rabbits etc. for their special qualities. **2** a connoisseur or follower of an activity (*usu. in comb.*, as *pigeon fancier*). **fanciful** *a.* **1** arising from the imagination; baseless, unreal, imaginary. **2** indulging in fancies; whimsical. **3** unusually elaborate and ornamented. **fancifully** *adv.* **fancifulness** *n.* **fancily** *adv.* **fanciness** *n.* **fancy dress** *n.* fanciful clothes worn at a party, representing a famous person from history, a story etc. **fancy-dress party, fancy-dress ball** *n.* **fancy fair** *n.* a sale of fancy goods, a bazaar. **fancy-free** *a.* not in love, not involved in a relationship, and without responsibilities or commitments (*footloose and fancy-free*). **fancy goods** *n.pl.* articles of a showy rather than a useful kind; ornamental fabrics such as ribbons and coloured silks. **fancy man** *n.* (*sl., derog.*) **1** a woman's lover. **2** a prostitute's pimp, a ponce. **fancy woman** *n.* (*sl., derog.*) a mistress. **fancy-work** *n.* ornamental knitting, embroidery, crocheting etc. [corr. of FANTASY]

fandangle (fandang´gəl) *n.* **1** a gaudy trinket, a gewgaw. **2** a nonsensical idea or nonsensical behaviour. [prob. coined from FANDANGO]

fandango (fandang´gō) *n.* (*pl.* **fandangoes, fandangos**) **1** a lively Spanish dance in triple time, for two people who beat time with castanets. **2** the musical accompaniment of such a dance. [Sp., from an Afr. language]

fane (fān) *n.* (*poet.*) a temple, a place of worship, a sanctuary. [L *fānum*]

fanfare (fan´feə) *n.* **1** a short, loud sounding of trumpets, bugles etc. **2** fuss or publicity to accompany something such as an announcement or welcome. [F, prob. onomat.]

fanfaronade (fanfərənād´, -nahd´) *n.* **1** arrogant boasting, swaggering or blustering. **2** a fanfare. ~*v.i.* to make a flourish or noisy display. [F *fanfaronnade*, from *fanfaron*, a braggart, as FANFARE]

fang (fang) *n.* **1** a large pointed tooth, esp. the canine tooth of a dog or wolf. **2** the long, hollow or grooved tooth of a poisonous snake through which it injects its venom. **3** the biting part of a spider. **4** the part of a tooth embedded in the gum. **5** (*coll.*) a person's tooth. **fanged** *a.* furnished with fangs. **fangless** *a.* [OE, a taking or seizing (cp. Dut. *vangen*, G *fangen*, to catch)]

fanner FAN[1].

fanny (fan´i) *n.* (*pl.* **fannies**) **1** (*taboo*) the female genitals. **2** (*N Am., sl.*) the buttocks. **fanny pack** *n.* (*N Am.*) BUMBAG (under BUM[1]). [*Fanny*, nickname for *Frances*]

Fanny Adams (ad´əmz), (*usu.*) **sweet Fanny Adams** *n.* **1** (*sl.*) nothing at all (euphem. for *fuck all*). **2** (*Naut., sl.*) tinned mutton; stew. [from the name of a young murder victim *c.* 1870, whose body was cut up into small pieces]

fanon (fan´ən) *n.* in the Roman Catholic Church, a maniple or napkin used by the officiating priest at Mass; an embroidered band attached to the wrist of the celebrant. [F, from med. L *fanō fanōnem*, a napkin, OHG *fano*]

fan-tan (fan´tan) *n.* **1** a Chinese gambling game involving guessing a number of objects. **2** a card game in which the cards are played in a sequence. [Chin.]

fantasia (fantā´ziə, -təzē´ə) *n.* a musical or other composition that is not governed by traditional fixed form; a composition based on several popular tunes. [It., FANTASY]

fantasist, fantasize FANTASY.

†**fantasm** PHANTASM.

fantast (fan´tast), **phantast** *n.* a dreamer or visionary. [L, from Gr. *phantasia*, see FANTASY]

fantastic (fantas´tik) *a.* **1** (*coll.*) wonderful, very good, very enjoyable. **2** (*coll.*) very great; extravagant. **3** fanciful, strange or whimsical, capricious. **4** odd, grotesque. **to trip the light fantastic** TRIP. **fantastical** *a.* **fantasticality** (-kal´-) *n.* **fantastically** *adv.* **fantasticalness** *n.* **fantasticate** *v.t.* **fantastication** (-ā´shən) *n.* **fantasticism** (-sizm) *n.* [as FANTASY]

fantasy (fan´təsi), **phantasy** *n.* (*pl.* **fantasies, phantasies**) **1** a fanciful mental image or daydream. **2** an extravagant, whimsical or bizarre fancy, image or idea. **3** the faculty of inventing or forming fanciful images. **4** a fanciful or whimsical invention or design. **5** a novel, drama, film etc. characterized by strange, unrealistic, alien or grotesque characters and settings; such works collectively. **6** (*Mus.*) a fantasia. **7** a synthetic hallucinogenic drug, a mixture of ecstasy and LSD or mescalin. **8** †a hallucination, a delusive vision. ~*v.t.* (*3rd pers. sing. pres.* **fantasies,** *pres.p.* **fantasying,** *past, p.p.* **fantasied**) to fantasize. **fantasist** *n.* **fantasize, fantasise** *v.i.* **1** to conjure up and indulge in gratifying mental images. **2** to dream up fantastic (and usu. impracticable) schemes, ideas etc. ~*v.t.* to dream up fantastic ideas about. **fantasy football** *n.* a competition in which players make up their own teams from different players and score points according to how well their players perform in reality. [OF *fantasie*, L, from Gr. *phantasia*, from *phantazein*, to make visible, from *phainein*, to show]

Fanti (fan´ti), **Fante** *n.* (*pl.* **Fanti, Fantis, Fante, Fantes**) **1** a member of a Ghanaian people. **2** the language of this people.

fantom PHANTOM.

fanzine *n.* FAN².

FAO *abbr.* Food and Agriculture Organization (of the United Nations).

faquir FAKIR.

far (fah) *a.* (*comp.* **farther, further,** *superl.* **farthest, furthest**) **1** distant, a long way off; separated by a wide space. **2** extending or reaching a long way. **3** more distant of two, other, opposite. **4** remote from or contrary to one's purpose, intention or wishes. ~*adv.* **1** at or to a great distance in space, time or proportion. **2** to a great degree or extent, very greatly, by a great deal. **3** by a great interval, widely. **a far cry** CRY. **as far as 1** to the distance of (a certain point). **2** to the extent that. **by far** in a very great measure; very greatly; exceedingly. **far and away** AWAY. **far and near** everywhere. **far and wide** over a large number of places; everywhere. **far be it from me** I would not even consider; I am very reluctant (to do something). **far from 1** anything but, not at all. **2** (*followed by pres.p.*) used to indicate that the speaker's actions or intentions are the opposite of those stated. **far from it** on the contrary. **far to seek** SEEK. **how far** to what extent, distance etc. **so far 1** up to a specified point. **2** up to now. **so far as** as far as. **so far so good** used to express satisfaction with how something has progressed or developed up to now. **to go far 1** to be successful (esp. in one's career). **2** (*esp. in neg.*) to be sufficient for. **to go too far** to exceed reasonable limits. **faraway** *a.* **1** remote in time, place or relationship, distant. **2** dreamy, absent-minded. **far between** *a.* at long intervals, infrequent. **Far East** *n.* the region including China, Japan, North and South Korea and other countries in E Asia. **far-fetched** *a.* (of a story or explanation) improbable, unrealistic, unconvincing. **far-flung** *a.* extending to far-off places. **far gone** *a.* **1** in an advanced state (of exhaustion, illness, wear etc.). **2** (*coll.*) very drunk. **far left** *n.* the extreme left wing of a political party etc. ~*a.* holding very left-wing views. **farness** *n.* **Far North** *n.* the Arctic regions. **far-off** *a.* distant, remote. ~*adv.* at or to a great distance. **far out** *a.* (*sl.*) **1** unconventional, eccentric, weird. **2** (*also int.*) wonderful, great. **far-reaching** *a.* having broad influence, effects or implications, extensive, thoroughgoing. **far right** *n.* the extreme right wing of a political party etc. ~*a.* holding very right-wing views. **far-seeing** *a.* considering what will happen in the future and so making wise judgements. **far-sighted** *a.* **1** considering what will happen in the future and so making wise judgements. **2** (*N Am.*) LONG-SIGHTED (under LONG¹). **far-sightedly** *adv.* **far-sightedness** *n.* **Far South** *n.* the Antarctic regions. **Far West** *n.* the part of the United States lying west of the Great Plains. **Far Western** *a.* [OE *feor* (cp. Dut. *ver*, Icel. *fjarri*, G *fern*, also Gr. *peran*, beyond)]

Usage note See note under FURTHER¹

---

farad (fa´rəd) *n.* the derived SI unit of capacitance, the capacity of a capacitor in which the electrical potential is raised 1 volt by the presence of 1 coulomb of charge on each plate. **faradaic** (farədā´ik), **faradic** (farad´-) *a.* (of an electric current) inductive. **faradize, faradise** *v.t.* to stimulate (the muscles) with faradic currents. **faradization** (-zā´shən) *n.* [Michael *Faraday*, 1791–1867, British chemist and physicist]

faraday (far´ədā) *n.* a quantity of electric charge numerically equal to Faraday's constant. **Faraday cage** *n.* a container used to shield electrical equipment against electrostatic fields. **Faraday effect** *n.* the phenomenon in a magnetic field in which the plane of polarization of electromagnetic waves rotates. **Faraday's constant** *n.* the quantity of an electric charge equivalent to 1 mole of electrons, 96.49 coulombs per mole.

farandine FERRANDINE.

farandole (farəndōl´) *n.* **1** a lively Provençal dance. **2** a piece of music for this dance. [Prov. *farandoulo*]

farce (fahs) *n.* **1** a humorous play in which the actors are involved in ridiculously complex and improbable situations. **2** drama of this kind. **3** a ridiculously futile or disorganized situation or action; a pretence, mockery, hollow formality. **farcical** (-ikəl) *a.* **1** of or relating to farce; ludicrous, droll, comical. **2** ridiculous, absurd, contemptible. **farcicality** (-kal´-) *n.* **farcically** *adv.* [F, orig. stuffing, hence an interlude or an inserted jest, from *farcer*, L *farcīre*, to stuff]

farceur (fahsœ´) *n.* **1** a joker, a jester, a wag. **2** a performer in or writer of farces. **farceuse** (-sœz´) *n.* a female farceur. [F, as FARCE]

farcical FARCE.

farcy (fah´si) *n.* a disease in horses, closely allied to glanders, in which the lymph vessels become inflamed. **farcy bud, farcy button** *n.* a little tumour on the face, neck or inside of the thigh in horses, generally the first indication of farcy. [F *farcin*, L *farcīminum*, from *farcīre*, to stuff]

†**farded** (fah´did) *a.* rouged, painted with cosmetics. [obs. v. *fard*, from F, prob. from or rel. to OHG *gifarwit*, p.p. of *farwjan*, to paint]

fare (feə) *n.* **1** the sum of money to be paid by a passenger for a journey by bus, train etc. **2** a passenger who pays to travel in a taxi etc. **3** food provided in a restaurant or café. ~*v.i.* (*formal*) **1** to get on, progress. **2** to be in any state, to happen, to turn out (well or badly). **3** to go, to travel. **fare stage** *n.* **1** a section of a bus route for which a certain charge is made. **2** a bus stop marking this. [OE *faran* (cp. Dut. *varen*, OHG *faran*, G *fahren*, also Gr. *poros*, a way, L *portāre*, to carry)]

farewell (feəwel´) *int.* goodbye, adieu. ~*n.* **1** words said at another person's leave-taking. **2** departure; leave-taking. ~*a.* expressing leave-taking (*a farewell speech*). [as FARE]

farina (fərē´nə) *n.* **1** flour or meal of cereal; the powder obtained by grinding nuts, roots etc. 2 any powdery substance. 3 starch. **farinaceous** (farinā´-) *a.* **farinose** (far´i-) *a.* 1 producing farina. 2 (*Bot.*) covered with a meal-like dust, floury, mealy. [L, from *far*, corn, spelt]

farl (fahl) *n.* a thin cake of oatmeal or flour, orig. a quarter of such a cake. [corr. of obs. *fardel*, OE *fēortha*, FOURTH]

farm (fahm) *n.* 1 an area of land together with its buildings, used for growing crops or rearing animals. 2 a farmhouse. 3 an area of land or water where a particular kind of animal or fish is bred. 4 a place for storage. ~*v.t.* 1 to use (land) for growing crops or rearing animals. 2 to breed (animals or fish) on a farm. 3 to let out (labourers) on hire. 4 to contract for the feeding, lodging etc. of (children) at so much per head. 5 to lease or let out (taxes, offices etc.) at a fixed sum or rate per cent; to take the proceeds of (taxes, offices etc.) for such a fixed sum or rate. ~*v.i.* to be a farmer. **to farm out** 1 to delegate, to contract out. 2 to put (esp. a child) into someone's care. **farmable** *a.* **farmer** *n.* a person who runs or owns a farm. **farmer-general** *n.* (*pl.* **farmers-general**) in France before 1789, a person who contracted for the right of levying certain taxes in a particular district. **farmhand** *n.* an agricultural labourer employed on a farm. **farmhouse** *n.* a dwelling house attached to a farm. **farmhouse loaf** *n.* a large rectangular white loaf with a slightly curved top. **farming** *n.* the business of growing crops or rearing animals. **farmstead** (-sted) *n.* a farm with the dwelling and other buildings on it. **farmyard** *n.* a yard or open area surrounded by or adjacent to farm buildings. ~*a.* crude or vulgar. [A-F and OF *ferme* (*à ferme*, on lease), med. L *firma*, orig. a fixed payment (cp. FIRM[1]), L *firmus*, firm, durable]

faro (feə´rō) *n.* a game of cards in which players bet against the dealer. [PHARAOH]

Faroese FAEROESE.

farouche (fəroosh´) *a.* 1 unsociable, shy, sullen. 2 wild, untamed. [F, from L *foras*, out of doors]

farrago (fərah´gō) *n.* (*pl.* **farragos**, (*N Am.*) **farragoes**) a confused mixture, a medley. **farraginous** (-raj´i-) *a.* [L, mixed fodder, a medley, from *far*, spelt]

farrier (far´iə) *n.* 1 a person who shoes horses. 2 a person who treats diseases and injuries in horses. 3 a non-commissioned officer in charge of the horses in a cavalry regiment. **farriery** *n.* (*pl.* **farrieries**) 1 the occupation of a farrier. 2 a farrier's shop, a smithy. [OF *ferrier*, L *ferrārius*, from *ferrum*, iron]

farrow (far´ō) *n.* 1 a litter of pigs. 2 the act of giving birth to a litter of pigs. ~*v.t.* to give birth to (pigs). ~*v.i.* to farrow pigs. [OE *fearh*, a pig (cp. Dut. *varken*, OHG *farah*, also L *porcus*)]

farruca (fəroo´kə) *n.* a type of flamenco dance. [Sp.]

Farsi (fah´sē) *n.* modern Persian, the Indo-European language of Iran. [Pers., cp. *Parsee*]

fart (faht) *v.i.* (*sl.*, *taboo*) to break wind through the anus. ~*n.* 1 (*sl.*, *taboo*) a discharge of wind from the anus. 2 (*sl.*) an unpleasant, stupid or boring person. **to fart about** (*sl.*) to behave foolishly, to waste time. [OE *feortan*, cp. OHG *verzen*, G *farzen*, also Gr. *perdein*]

farther FURTHER[1].

farthest FURTHEST (under FURTHER[1]).

farthing (fah´dhing) *n.* 1 a quarter part of an old penny, the smallest British copper coin (withdrawn in 1961). 2 the smallest possible amount. [OE *fēorthing*, *fēortha*, FOURTH]

farthingale (fah´dhing·gāl) *n.* (esp. in the 16th cent.) a woman's hooped skirt used to extend the wide gown and petticoat. [OF *verdugale*, corr. of Sp. *verdugado*, from *verdugo*, a rod]

fartlek (faht´lek) *n.* a method of athletic training, mixing fast and slow running. [Swed. *fart*, speed and *lek*, play]

fasces (fas´ēz) *n.pl.* 1 the ancient insignia of the Roman lictors, consisting of a bundle of elm or birch rods, in the middle of which was an axe. 2 in Fascist Italy, an emblem of authority. [L, pl. of *fascis*, a bundle (see FASCIA)]

fascia (fā´shə, fash´iə) *n.* (*pl.* **fasciae** (-shiē), **fascias**) 1 (*Archit.*) a flat surface in an entablature or elsewhere. 2 a band, stripe belt, sash, fillet. 3 a thin, tendon-like sheath surrounding the muscles and binding them in their places. 4 FACIA. **fascial** *a.* **fasciate** (fa´shiāt), **fasciated** (-ātid) *a.* 1 (*Bot.*) flattened by the growing together of several parts. 2 striped. **fasciation** (-ā´shən) *n.* an abnormal growing together of parts into a ribbon-like structure. [L, a band, conn. with *fas*, that which is binding]

fascicle (fas´ikəl) *n.* 1 any one of the parts of a book that is published in instalments. 2 a small bundle, cluster or group; a cluster of leaves, flowers etc., a tuft. 3 (*Anat.*) a bundle of fibres. **fascicled** *a.* clustered together in a fascicle. **fascicular** (-sik´ū-) *a.* **fasciculate** (-sik´ūlət), **fasciculated** (-lātid) *a.* collected in clusters, small bundles or bunches. **fasciculation** (-lā´shən) *n.* **fascicule** (-kūl) *n.* a fascicle, esp. of a book. **fasciculus** (fəsik´ūləs) *n.* (*pl.* **fasciculi** (-lī)) (*Anat.*) a bundle of fibres, a fascicle. [L, dim. of *fascis*, see FASCES]

fasciitis (fashiī´tis) *n.* inflammation of the fascia of a muscle.

fascinate (fas´ināt) *v.t.* 1 to exercise an irresistible influence over; to captivate, to attract irresistibly, to enchant, to charm. 2 (of snakes) to make (prey) motionless by means of a look or presence. **fascinating** *a.* irresistibly attractive, charming, bewitching. **fascinatingly** *adv.* **fascination** (-ā´shən) *n.* **fascinator** *n.* a person or thing that fascinates. [L *fascinātus*, p.p. of *fascināre*, from *fascinum*, a spell]

fascine (fasēn´) *n.* a cylindrical faggot of brushwood used in building earthworks, for filling trenches, protecting riverbanks etc. [F, from L *fascīna*, a bundle of sticks, from *fascis*]

Fascism (fash´izm) *n.* 1 the extreme right-wing theory of government introduced into Italy by Benito Mussolini in 1922, the object of which was to oppose socialism and communism by controlling every form of national activity. 2 (*usu.* **fascism**) any ideology or system regarded as brutal, repressive, excessively nationalistic or militaristic. **Fascist, fascist** *a.*, *n.* **fascistic** (-shis´tik), **Fascistic** *a.* [It. *Fascismo*, from *fascio*, L *fascis*, a bundle]

fashion (fash´ən) *n.* 1 the activity or business concerned with the style of clothes. 2 the current popular style of clothes or way of behaving. 3 a way or style of doing something; manner, way, pattern. 4 the form, make, style or external appearance of any thing. 5 fashionable or genteel society. ~*v.t.* 1 to give shape and form to; to frame, to mould. 2 to fit, to adapt. **after a fashion** satisfactorily, but not very well. **after the fashion of** in the same way as; like. **in a fashion** after a fashion. **in fashion** popular and favoured at a particular time. **out of fashion** unpopular and disapproved of at a particular time. **to set the fashion** to set the example in a new style of clothes or behaviour. **-fashion** *comb. form* forming adverbs in the sense 'in the manner of, like'. **fashionable** *a.* 1 popular and favoured at a particular time. 2 characteristic of, approved by, or patronized by people of fashion. **fashionability** (-bil´-), **fashionableness** *n.* **fashionably** *adv.* **-fashioned** *comb. form* forming adjectives in the sense 'made or shaped (in a certain way)'. **fashioner** *n.* a person who fashions or gives shape to anything. **fashion victim** *n.* a person who slavishly follows trends in fashion. [OF *faceon*, L *factiōnem*, nom. *-tio*, a making, from *facere*, to make (cp. FACTION[1])]

☒ **fasinate** common misspelling of FASCINATE.

fast[1] (fahst) *a.* 1 swift, rapid, moving quickly. 2 taking a short time. **3** intended for high speed (*a fast road*). **4** imparting quick motion, as a bowler, pitcher etc. **5** promoting quick motion, as a billiard table, cricket pitch etc. **6** (of a clock etc.) showing a time ahead of the correct time. **7** (of photographic film) needing only a short exposure time. **8** (of a camera shutter) permitting short exposure times. **9** firmly fixed, firm, tight. **10** firmly adhering, faithful, steady, close. **11** (of a colour) lasting, durable, permanent, unfading, not washing out. **12** (of a person) immoral, dissipated, pleasure-seeking, promiscuous. **13** acquired with little effort or by shady means. *~adv.* **1** quickly, swiftly, in rapid succession; without delay. **2** firmly, tightly, securely. **3** soundly, completely, thoroughly (*fast asleep*). **fast and furious** quickly, energetically; vigorous and eventful, noisy or heated. **to make fast** to fasten securely, to tie. **to play fast and loose** PLAY. **to pull a fast one** (*coll.*) to trick, to deceive, to use underhand methods. **fastback** *n.* (a car with) a back which forms a continuous slope from roof to bumper. **fast breeder, fast breeder reactor** *n.* a nuclear reactor which produces at least as much fissionable material as it consumes. **fast buck** *n.* a lot of money easily earned. **fast food** *n.* food, e.g. burgers and chicken pieces, which can be prepared and served very quickly, esp. in certain types of restaurant. **fast-food** *a.* serving fast food. **fast forward** *n.* a control that enables video or recording tape to be wound on very rapidly. *~v.t.* to wind on by means of a fast-forward control. **fast-forward** *a.* relating to such a control. **fastish** *a.* rather fast. **fast lane** *n.* a part of the carriageway used by fast-moving traffic, esp. the outer lane of a motorway. **in the fast lane** (*coll.*) where the pace of life is particularly fast, exciting or risky. **fastness** *n.* **1** the quality or state of being fast or secure. **2** a fortress, a stronghold, esp. in a remote and inaccessible place. **fast neutron** *n.* a neutron with high kinetic energy. **fast reactor** *n.* a nuclear reactor using mostly fast neutrons. **fast-talk** *v.t.* (*chiefly N Am., coll.*) to persuade by fast, clever, deceptive talk. **fast track** *n.* the quickest route to achieve a particular goal or position. **fast-track** *a.* being or related to the fast track. *~v.t.* to promote (an employee) by this route. **fast-tracker** *n.* **fast train** *n.* an express train. **fast-wind** *v.t.* (*past, p.p.* **fast-wound**) to wind (video or recording tape) very rapidly. **fast worker** *n.* (*coll.*) a person who makes rapid progress in relations with the opposite sex. [OE *fæst* (cp. Dut. *vast*, Icel. *fastr*, G *fest*, and FAST[2])]

fast[2] (fahst) *v.i.* to abstain from food, esp. as a religious observance for the mortification of the body or as a sign of grief, affliction or penitence. *~n.* **1** a (period of) total or partial abstinence from or deprivation of food, esp. from religious motives. **2** a time set apart for fasting. **3** any holy time or season. **fast day** *n.* **1** a day appointed as a fast. **2** (*Sc.*) a day of humiliation and prayer in preparation for Holy Communion. **fasting** *n.* [OE *fæstan* (cp. Dut. *vasten*, Icel. *fasta*, G *fasten*, from Goth. *fastan*, in the sense of to be firm, strict)]

fasten (fah´sən) *v.t.* **1** to fix firmly, to make secure, to attach. **2** to secure, as by a bolt, a lock, a tie, knot etc. **3** to fix or set firmly or earnestly. *~v.i.* **1** to become fast. **2** to seize, to lay hold (upon). **to fasten on 1** to lay hold on. **2** to become aware of and concentrate (one's attention) on (something). **3** to attach (blame, responsibility, a nickname etc.) to. **fastener** *n.* a device that fastens, makes fast or secures. **fastening** *n.* **1** the act of making fast or secure. **2** anything which makes fast or secure, such as a bolt, bar, strap or catch. [OE *fæstnian* (as FAST[1], -EN[1])]

fastidious (fastid´iəs) *a.* **1** extremely careful, delicate, refined, esp. in matters of taste; fussy. **2** difficult to please. **3** squeamish, easily disgusted. **fastidiously** *adv.* **fastidiousness** *n.* [L *fastīdiōsus*, from *fastīdium*, loathing, from *fastus*, arrogance]

fastigiate (fəstij´iət) *a.* (*Bot.*) tapering to a point like a pyramid. [L *fastīgium*, the apex of a gable]

fat (fat) *a.* (*comp.* **fatter**, *superl.* **fattest**) **1** having a lot of flesh and overweight; plump, fleshy, corpulent, full-fed. **2** (of animals) fed up for killing. **3** oily, greasy, unctuous; resinous. **4** prosperous, thriving, rich, affluent. **5** fertile, fruitful, rich. **6** (of a book) thick, substantial. **7** substantial, rewarding (*fat profits*). **8** (of coal) bituminous. **9** (of clay etc.) sticky, plastic. **10** (*coll., iron.*) very little (*a fat chance*). **11** (of printing type) thick, broad-faced. *~n.* **1** a natural substance of a more or less oily character that occurs esp. in animals. **2** the fat part of anything. **3** the best or choicest part of anything. **4** that part of anything which is considered redundant or excessive. **5** a part that gives an actor opportunity to display their powers. **6** an organic compound of glycerol with one of a group of acids. *~v.t.* (*pres.p.* **fatting**, *past, p.p.* **fatted**) **1** to make fat or plump. **2** to fatten. *~v.i.* to become fat, to gain flesh. **the fat is in the fire** (*coll.*) there's going to be trouble. **to kill the fatted calf** CALF[1]. **to live off/ on the fat of the land** to have the best of everything. **fat cat** *n.* (*chiefly N Am., coll.*) a very wealthy or influential person. **fat-faced** *a.* having a plump round face. **fat farm** *n.* (*N Am., sl.*) a health farm where people go to slim. **fat-head** *n.* (*coll.*) a stupid person. **fat-headed** *a.* **fat-headedness** *n.* **fat hen** *n.* the white goosefoot, *Chenopodium album*. **fatless** *a.* **fatling** (-ling) *n.* a young animal fattened for slaughter; a fattened animal. **fatly** *adv.* **fatness** *n.* **fatso** (-sō) *n.* (*pl.* **fatsoes**) (*sl., offensive*) a fat person. **fatstock** *n.* livestock fattened for slaughter. **fatten** *v.t.* **1** to make (esp. animals) fat, to feed for the table. **2** to make (ground) fruitful, to fertilize. *~v.i.* to grow or become fat, to gain flesh. **fattening** *a.* (of food) easily making people fat. **fattish** *a.* somewhat fat. **fattism, fatism** *n.* discrimination against fat people. **fattist, fatist** *n., a.* **fatty** *a.* (*comp.* **fattier**, *superl.* **fattiest**) **1** consisting of or having the qualities of fat. **2** oily; greasy, unctuous. **3** of or relating to fat; adipose. *~n.* (*pl.* **fatties**) (*coll.*) a fat person. **fattiness** *n.* **fatty acid** *n.* any of a class of aliphatic, carboxylic acids, e.g. palmitic acid, acetic acid. **fatty degeneration** *n.* the abnormal conversion of the protein elements into a granular fatty matter. **fatty oil** *n.* FIXED OIL (under FIX). [OE *fæt, fætt*, OFris. *fat*, Dut. *vet*, G *fett* (orig. p.p. of a v. to fatten)]

fatal (fā´təl) *a.* **1** causing death, destruction or ruin. **2** having very undesirable consequences. **3** fateful, decisive. **4** decreed by fate, inevitable. **fatalism** *n.* **1** the belief that all events are predetermined and beyond human control. **2** submission to fate. **fatalist** *n.* **fatalistic** (-lis´-) *a.* **fatalistically** *adv.* **fatality** (fətal´-) *n.* (*pl.* **fatalities**) **1** a (person who suffers) death by accident or violence. **2** a fixed and unalterable course of things. **3** predetermination by fate esp. to death or disaster. **4** a fatal influence; deadliness. **fatally** *adv.* [see FATE]

fata Morgana (fah´tə mawgah´nə) *n.* **1** a mirage observed from the harbour of Messina and adjacent places, and supposed by Sicilians to be the work of the fairy Morgana. **2** a mirage; a figment of the imagination. [It. *fata*, a fairy, *Morgana*, the legendary half-sister of King Arthur, famed for her magical powers]

fate (fāt) *n.* **1** a power considered to control and decide events unalterably. **2** destiny, lot, fortune; one's ultimate condition as brought about by circumstances and events; what is destined to happen. **3** death, destruction. **4** (*pl.*) **(the Fates)** three Greek goddesses supposed to preside over human birth, life and fortunes. *~v.t.* (*usu. pass.*) **1** to decree by fate or destiny. **2** to destine to destruction. **fated** *a.* **1** doomed to destruction. **2** decreed by fate, predetermined. **3** fatal, fateful. **fateful** *a.* **1** having momentous, often catastrophic, consequences. **2** bringing death or destruction. **fatefully** *adv.* **fatefulness** *n.* **fate worse than death** *n.* a calamitous experience. [L *fātum*, orig. neut. p.p. of *fārī*, to speak]

father (fah´dhə) *n.* **1** a male parent. **2** a man who begets a child. **3** a man who exercises paternal care. **4** a stepfather. **5** a father-in-law. **6** any male animal considered as regards its offspring. **7** a male ancestor, a patriarch. **8** the first to practise any art; an originator, author, contriver, an early leader. **9** a respectful mode of address to an old man or any man deserving great reverence. **10** a priest, a confessor, the superior of a convent, a religious teacher etc. **11** (*Theol.*) the first person of the Trinity. **12** the senior member of any profession or body. **13** (*pl.*) elders, senators, the leading men (of a city etc.). *~v.t.* **1** to beget. **2** to be or act as father of. **3** to adopt as a child. **4** to originate. **5** to adopt or assume as one's own child, work etc. **6** to accept responsibility for. **adoptive father** ADOPTIVE (under ADOPT). **to father on/ upon** to suggest that (someone) is responsible for. **Father Christmas** *n.* SANTA CLAUS. **father confessor** *n.* **1** a priest who hears confessions. **2** a person to whom one confides intimate matters. **father figure** *n.* an older man whom one looks to for advice and support. **fatherhood** *n.* **1** the condition of being a father. **2** the character or authority of a father. **father-in-law** *n.* (*pl.* **fathers-in-law**) the father of a person's husband or wife. **fatherland** *n.* a person's native country. **fatherless** *a.* **fatherlessness** *n.* **fatherlike** *a.* **fatherly** *a.* **1** like a father; kind, caring, loving. **2** proper to or becoming a father. *~adv.* in the manner of a father. **fatherliness** *n.* **father of lies** *n.* Satan. **father of (the) chapel** *n.* the president of a branch of a printers' or journalists' trade union. **Father's Day** *n.* a day (in Britain the third Sunday in June) observed as a day to honour fathers. **fathership** *n.* **Fathers of the Church** *n.* the ecclesiastical writers of the early church. **Father Superior** *n.* the head of a religious house. **Father Time** *n.* time personified, esp. as a bearded old man with a scythe and an hourglass. [OE *fæder* (cp. Dut. *vader*, G *Vater*, L *pater*, Gr. *patēr*)]

fathom (fadh´əm) *n.* (*pl.* **fathoms,** (*esp. after a number*) **fathom**) **1** a measure of length, six ft. (1.8 m) used principally in nautical and mining measurements. **2** six ft. (1.8 m) square, as a measure of wood in cross-section independently of length. *~v.t.* **1** (often with *out*) to penetrate, to comprehend, to get to the bottom of. **2** to measure the depth of. **fathomable** *a.* **fathometer** (-om´itə) *n.* an instrument for measuring the depth of the sea by sound waves. **fathomless** *a.* not to be fathomed. **fathomlessly** *adv.* **fathom line** *n.* (*Naut.*) a sounding line. **fathom wood** *n.* waste timber sold by fathom lots. [OE *fæthm*, the space enclosed by the arms outstretched (cp. Dut. *vadem*, G *Faden*, also L *patēre*, to extend, Gr. *petannunai*)]

fatigue (fətēg´) *n.* **1** weariness, exhaustion from bodily or mental exertion. **2** METAL FATIGUE (under METAL). **3** the reduction in response of a muscle, organ etc. as a result of overactivity. **4** exertion or an activity causing weariness or exhaustion. **5** labour not of a military nature performed by soldiers. **6** (*pl.*) military overalls. *~v.t.* (*3rd pers. sing. pres.* **fatigues,** *pres.p.* **fatiguing,** *past, p.p.* **fatigued**) to tire, to weary; to exhaust the strength of by bodily or mental exertion. **fatiguable, fatigable** *a.* **fatiguability** (-gəbil´iti), **fatigability** *n.* **fatigued** *a.* **fatigue-dress** *n.* the dress worn by soldiers on fatigue duty. **fatigueless** *a.* **fatiguing** *a.* [OF *fatiguer*, L *fatīgāre*, to tire]

Fatiha (fah´tiə, fat´-), **Fatihah** *n.* the short first sura of the Koran, used by Muslims as a prayer.

Fatimid (fat´imid), **Fatimite** (-mīt) *n.* **1** a descendant of Fatima, daughter of Muhammad. **2** a member of the Muslim dynasty that ruled over N Africa 909–1171. *~a.* **1** of or relating to a descendant of Fatima. **2** of or relating to this dynasty and its members.

fatness FAT.

fatuous (fat´ūəs) *a.* **1** idiotic, inane, silly. **2** stupid, imbecile, foolish. **fatuity** (fətū´iti) *n.* (*pl.* **fatuities**). **fatuitous** *a.* **fatuously** *adv.* **fatuousness** *n.* [L *fatuus*]

fatwa (fat´wah) *n.* a religious edict issued by a Muslim leader. [Arab.]

faubourg (fō´buəg) *n.* a suburb of a city or town. [F]

fauces (faw´sēz) *n.pl.* the area from the cavity at the back of the mouth to the pharynx. **faucial** (-shəl), **faucal** (-kəl) *a.* **1** of or relating to the fauces or gullet. **2** deeply guttural. [L]

faucet (faw´sit) *n.* **1** (*chiefly N Am.*) a tap. **2** the tap on a barrel. [F *fausset*, Prov. *falset*, from *falsar*, to bore]

faucial FAUCES.

fault (fawlt) *n.* **1** a defect, blemish, imperfection. **2** an error, failing, mistake or blunder. **3** a slight offence or deviation from right or propriety. **4** responsibility for a mistake or wrongdoing, blame. **5** an improper service at tennis. **6** a penalty point in showjumping. **7** a defect in an electric circuit. **8** (*Geol.*) a fracture in the earth's surface, together with a break in the continuity of the strata. **9** loss of the scent in hunting. *~v.t.* **1** to find a fault in, to criticize. **2** (*Geol.*) to cause to undergo a fault. *~v.i.* **1** to commit a fault, to blunder. **2** (*Geol.*) to undergo a fault. **at fault** to blame, in error. **to a fault** excessively. **to find fault with** to complain of, to blame, to censure, esp. in a carping manner. **fault-finding** *a.* constantly criticizing; censorious. *~n.* constant criticism; censoriousness. **fault-finder** *n.* a person given to fault-finding. **faultless** *a.* without fault; perfect, flawless. **faultlessly** *adv.* **faultlessness** *n.* **faulty** *a.* (*comp.* **faultier,** *superl.* **faultiest**) having faults; imperfect, defective, flawed. **faultily** *adv.* **faultiness** *n.* [ME and OF *faute*, pop. L *fallita*, a defect, fem. p.p. of *fallere*, to FAIL[1]]

faun (fawn) *n.* one of a kind of rural deities, with a human body and the horns and legs of a goat, bearing a strong resemblance to the satyrs, with whom they are generally identified. [L *Faunus*, a Latin rural deity whose attributes bear a strong analogy to those of Pan, with whom he is identified]

fauna (faw´nə) *n.* (*pl.* **faunae** (-nē), **faunas**) **1** the animals found in or belonging to a certain region or time. **2** a treatise upon or list of these. **faunal** *a.* **faunist** *n.* **faunistic** (-nis´tik) *a.* [L, a Roman goddess, sister of Faunus]

faute de mieux (fōt də mjœ´) *adv.* for lack of anything better. [F]

fauteuil (fōtœy´) *n.* an easy, upholstered armchair. [F, from MF *fauldeteuil*, low L *faldistolium*, see FALDSTOOL]

fauvism (fō´vizm) *n.* a 20th-cent. art movement, characterized by vivid use of colour and a free treatment of form. **fauve** (fōv) *n.* a person who practises or advocates fauvism. **fauvist** *n.* [F *fauvisme*, from *fauve*, a wild beast]

faux (fō) *a.* imitation, false. [F, 'false']

faux pas (fō pah´) *n.* (*pl.* **faux pas** (pahz´)) **1** a blunder, a slip. **2** a social indiscretion. [F]

fave (fāv) *n., a.* (*sl.*) favourite. [abbr.]

favela (fav´elə) *n.* in Brazil, a shack or shanty town. [Port.]

favour (fā´və), (*N Am.*) **favor** *n.* **1** a kind or indulgent act. **2** friendly regard, kindness, goodwill; approval. **3** partiality, preference, excessive kindness or indulgence. **4** aid, support, furtherance, facility, convenience for doing something; behalf, advantage (of). **5** (*dated*) leave, consent. **6** (*dated*) a letter, a communication. **7** (*pl., formal*) a woman's consent to sexual activity. *~v.t.* **1** to regard or behave towards with kindness. **2** to approve, to prefer, to show partiality to. **3** to befriend, to support. 4 to facilitate. 5 to promote. 6 to oblige (with). 7 to be propitious or fortunate for. 8 to resemble in features. 9 to avoid using, to treat with special care (as an injured limb). **in favour** 1 approved. 2 approving. **in favour of** 1 approving, on the side of. 2 to the advantage of. 3 to the account of. 4 in preference to. **out of favour** disapproved. **to curry favour** CURRY[2]. **favourable** *a.* 1 approving, commending, consenting. 2 friendly, well-disposed, encouraging; propitious. 3 tending to promote or to encourage. 4 convenient, advantageous. **in a favourable light** LIGHT[1]. **favourableness** *n.* **favourably** *adv.* **favoured** *a.* **-favoured** *comb. form* having a certain look or appearance, as in *ill-favoured, well-favoured.* **favouredly** *adv.* **favouredness** *n.* [OF, from L *favor, -ōrem,* from *favēre,* to show goodwill to]

favourite (fā´vərit), (*N Am.*) **favorite** *a.* 1 preferred before all others. 2 regarded with special favour. 3 beloved. ~*n.* 1 a person or thing regarded with special affection, preference or partiality. 2 a person chosen as a companion and intimate by a superior and unduly favoured. 3 in sport, the competitor considered to have the best chance of winning. **favourite son** *n.* (*N Am.*) a person chosen as a candidate for presidency by the delegates from their home state. **favouritism** *n.* showing an unfair special preference for a person or group, partiality. [OF *favorite,* fem. p.p. of *favorir,* to FAVOUR]

favus (fā´vəs) *n.* (*Med.*) a disease of the scalp, characterized by pustules succeeded by cellular crusts bearing some resemblance to a honeycomb. [L, honeycomb]

fawn[1] (fawn) *n.* 1 a young deer; a buck or doe in its first year. 2 the colour of a young deer, light yellowish brown. ~*a.* like a fawn in colour, light yellowish brown. ~*v.t.* (of deer) to bring forth. ~*v.i.* to bring forth a fawn. **in fawn** (of deer) pregnant. [OF *fan, faon,* through low L from L *foetus,* FOETUS]

fawn[2] (fawn) *v.i.* 1 (*usu. with on or upon*) to court in a servile manner, to grovel, to cringe. 2 (of animals, esp. dogs) to show affection by cringing, licking the hand etc. **fawner** *n.* **fawning** *a.* 1 courting servilely. 2 flattering by cringing or meanness. ~*n.* servile flattery. **fawningly** *adv.* [OE *fahnian,* from *fægen,* see FAIN]

fax (faks) *n.* 1 a system for electronically scanning, transmitting and reproducing documents etc. via a telephone line. 2 a document etc. sent in this way. 3 (*also* **fax machine**) a machine for sending or receiving documents in this way. ~*v.t.* to send (a document) in this way. [abbr. of *facsimile*]

fay (fā) *n.* a fairy. [OF *fae* (F *fée*), L *fata,* the Fates]

fayre FAIR[2].

faze (fāz) *v.t.* (*coll.*) to disconcert, to put off one's stroke. **fazed** *a.* [var. of *feeze,* to drive off, OE *fēsian*]

FBA *abbr.* Fellow of the British Academy.

FBI *abbr.* (in the US) Federal Bureau of Investigation.

FC *abbr.* 1 Football Club. 2 Forestry Commission.

FCA *abbr.* Fellow of the Institute of Chartered Accountants.

FCC *abbr.* (in the US) Federal Communications Commission.

FCO *abbr.* Foreign and Commonwealth Office.

fcp *abbr.* foolscap.

FD *abbr.* Defender of the Faith. [L *Fidei Defensor*]

FDA *abbr.* 1 First Division (Civil Servants) Association. 2 (in the US) Food and Drug Administration.

FDR *abbr.* (*Hist.*) Free Democratic Republic (the former West Germany).

FE *abbr.* further education.

Fe *chem. symbol* iron. [L *ferrum*]

fealty (fē´əlti) *n.* (*pl.* **fealties**) 1 fidelity of a vassal or feudal tenant to a lord. 2 fidelity, loyalty, allegiance. [OF *fealte,* L *fidēlitās -tātem,* FIDELITY]

fear (fiə) *n.* 1 an unpleasant feeling caused by impending danger, pain etc. 2 dread, a state of alarm. 3 a cause of fear. 4 anxiety, worry. 5 awe, reverence. 6 risk, possibility (of something unpleasant happening) (*no fear of being misunderstood*). ~*v.t.* 1 to be afraid of, to dread. 2 to suspect, to doubt. 3 to shrink from, to hesitate (to do). 4 to show reverence towards, to venerate. ~*v.i.* 1 to be afraid. 2 to feel anxiety or worry. 3 to doubt, to mistrust. **for fear** 1 in order that not; lest. 2 in dread (that or lest). **never fear** there is no need to worry or be afraid. **no fear** (*coll.*) not likely; certainly not. **without fear or favour** showing no partiality. **feared** *a.* 1 regarded with fear. 2 †afraid. **fearful** *a.* 1 apprehensive, afraid (lest). 2 timid, timorous. 3 terrible, awful, frightful. 4 (*coll.*) extraordinary, unusual, annoying. **fearfully** *adv.* **fearfulness** *n.* **fearless** *a.* not afraid; courageous, intrepid. **fearlessly** *adv.* **fearlessness** *n.* **fearnought, fearnaught** *n.* a heavy, shaggy, woollen fabric, used for seamen's coats, for lining portholes, doors of powder magazines etc. **fearsome** (-səm) *a.* fearful, terrible, alarming, formidable. **fearsomely** *adv.* **fearsomeness** *n.* [OE *fær,* danger, calamity (cp. G *Gefahr,* also L *perīculum*)]

feasible (fē´zibəl) *a.* 1 that may or can be done, practicable, probable. 2 (*coll.*) manageable. 3 likely, plausible. **feasibility** (-bil´-) *n.* **feasibility study** *n.* a study of the practicability of a suggested scheme. †**feasibleness** *n.* **feasibly** *adv.* [OF *faisable,* from *fais,* stem of *faire,* L *facere,* to do]

Usage note The uses of *feasible* to mean likely, plausible or probable are sometimes disapproved of.

feast (fēst) *n.* 1 a large and sumptuous meal enjoyed by a great number of people; a banquet. 2 an anniversary or periodical celebration of some great event or person, esp. a religious anniversary. 3 anything giving great enjoyment to body or mind. ~*v.t.* 1 to entertain sumptuously. 2 to gratify or please greatly, as with something delicious or luscious. ~*v.i.* 1 to eat and drink sumptuously. 2 to be highly gratified or pleased. **to feast one's eyes on** to look at with great delight. **feast day** *n.* a day on which a feast, esp. a religious feast, is held; a festival. **feaster** *n.* a person who eats sumptuously; a guest, a partaker of a feast. **Feast of Tabernacles** *n.* SUCCOTH. [OF *feste* (F *fête*), late L *festa,* orig. neut. pl. of L *festus,* joyful]

feat[1] (fēt) *n.* 1 a notable act or performance, esp. one displaying great strength, skill or daring. 2 an exploit, an accomplishment. [OF *fait,* L *factum,* FACT]

†**feat**[2] (fēt) *a.* 1 dexterous, skilful. 2 nimble. 3 smart, neat, trim. **featly** *adv.* [OF *fait,* made, L *factus,* p.p. of *facere,* to make]

feather (fedh´ə) *n.* 1 a plume or quill, one of the appendages growing from a bird's skin, forming collectively the soft covering of a bird. 2 such a plume worn as an ornament, esp. in the hat. 3 a strip of a feather attached to an arrowshaft. 4 (*usu. pl.*) a hairy fringe on a dog's tail or legs, a tuft of long hair on a horse's leg. 5 a tongue on the edge of a board fitting into a groove on the edge of another board. 6 in rowing, the act of feathering. 7 something extremely light. 8 (*pl.*) plumage. 9 (*pl.*) game birds considered collectively. ~*v.t.* 1 to dress, cover or provide with feathers. 2 to decorate with or as with feathers. 3 to turn (an oar) so that the blade passes horizontally through the air. 4 to change the angle or allow free rotation of (a propeller blade) to minimize wind resistance. ~*v.i.* 1 to move as feathers. 2 to have a feathery appearance. 3 in rowing, to turn the oar and carry through the air edgeways. 4 to change the angle of a propeller blade. 5 in hunting, to set hounds directly on the trail. 6 (of hounds) to make a quivering movement with the tail when searching for traces of deer etc. **birds of a feather** BIRD. **in fine/ high feather** in high spirits, elated. **to feather one's nest** 1 to accumulate wealth for oneself. **2** to make provision for oneself. **to show the white feather** to show signs of cowardice or timidity (said to be derived from the belief that a white feather in the tail of a gamecock was a sign of cowardice). **feather bed** *n.* a mattress stuffed with feathers. **feather-bed** *v.t.* (*pres.p.* **feather-bedding,** *past, p.p.* **feather-bedded**) **1** to pamper, to spoil. **2** to give financial assistance to (an industry). **feather-bedding** *n.* the practice of protecting jobs by allowing overmanning or inefficient or slow working. **feather-boarding** *n.* a roof or other covering of boards that thin off at the top and overlap like a bird's feathers. **feather-brain, feather-head, feather-pate** *n.* a silly, frivolous person. **feather-brained, feather-headed, feather-pated** *a.* **feather duster** *n.* a long-handled brush of feathers. **feathered** *a.* **1** covered with feathers (*also in comb.*, as *well-feathered*). **2** winged. **3** fitted, fringed or adorned with a feather or feathers. **4** having feather appendages. **5** feathery, featherlike. **6** swift, rapid. **feathered game** *n.* game birds. **feather edge** *n.* **1** an edge like a feather. **2** the thinner edge of a wedge-shaped board or plank. **feather-edged** *a.* (of boards) having one edge thinner than the other. **feather grass** *n.* a perennial grass, *Stipa pennata*, with graceful, feathered awns. **feathering** *n.* **1** plumage. **2** the feathers on an arrow. **3** a feathery fringe or coat (of setters etc.). **4** (*Archit.*) an arrangement of small arcs or foils separated by projecting points or cusps. **feather in one's cap** *n.* an honour, a distinction that one can be proud of. **featherless** *a.* without feathers; deprived of feathers; unfledged. **featherlet** (-lit) *n.* **feather-light** *a.* extremely light. **feather stitch** *n.* an embroidery stitch producing a zigzag line somewhat like feathers. **feather-stitch** *v.t.* to embroider with a feather stitch. **featherweight** *n.* **1** an extremely light person or thing. **2** a boxer, weightlifter etc. in the weight category intermediate between bantamweight and lightweight. **3** this weight category. **4** a jockey of the lightest weight allowed to be carried by a horse in a handicap, 4 st. 7 lb. (28 kg). **feathery** *a.* **1** covered, fringed or adorned with or as with feathers. **2** featherlike, resembling feathers. **3** (*Bot.*) plumose. **4** (*fig.*) light, flimsy, fickle. **featheriness** *n.* [OE *fether* (cp. Dut. *veder*, G *Feder*, L *penna*, Gr. *pteron*, wing, *petesthai*, to fly)]

feature (fē´chə) *n.* **1** a distinctive, characteristic or prominent part of anything. **2** (*usu. pl.*) a part of the face, such as the eyes, nose or mouth. **3** a special article in a newspaper or magazine on a particular topic. **4** (*also* **feature film**) a full-length film, esp. the main film in a programme. **5** (*also* **feature programme**) a radio or television documentary. *~v.t.* **1** to give prominence to, to make a feature of. **2** to have as a characteristic. **3** to present in an important role or as an important subject. *~v.i.* to be a characteristic, to figure prominently. **featured** *a.* **-featured** *comb. form* having a certain kind of features or form of face. **featureless** *a.* **1** without any distinct or distinctive features. **2** shapeless. [OF *faiture*, L *factūra*, from *facere*, to make]

Feb. *abbr.* February.

febrifacient (febrifā´shənt) *a.* causing fever. *~n.* anything which causes fever. **febriferous** (-brif´-) *a.* inducing fever. **febrific** (-brif´-) *a.* **1** productive of fever. **2** feverish. [L *febris*, FEVER, -FACIENT]

febrifuge (feb´rifūj) *n.* a medicine which has the property of dispelling or mitigating fever. **febrifugal** (-brif´ūgəl, -fūg´əl) *a.* [F *fébrifuge* (L *febris*, FEVER, *fugāre*, to drive away)]

febrile (fē´brīl) *a.* of, relating to, proceeding from or indicating fever. **febrility** (fibril´iti) *n.* [F, from L *febrīlis*, see FEBRIFUGE]

February (feb´ruəri, feb´ūəri) *n.* (*pl.* **Februaries**) the second month of the year, containing in ordinary years 28 days, and in leap years 29. [L *Februārius*, from *februa*, pl., a festival of purification, sing. *februum*, purification]

Usage note The pronunciation with (ū) and only one (r) is sometimes disapproved of.

fec. *abbr.* he/she made it. [L *fecit*]

fecal FAECAL (under FAECES).

feces FAECES.

fecial FETIAL.

feck (fek) *n.* (*Sc.*) **1** efficacy, strength, vigour. **2** space, value, quantity, number. **3** the bulk, the greatest part. [etym. uncertain; perh. corr. of EFFECT]

feckless (fek´lis) *a.* **1** weak, feeble, ineffective. **2** incompetent, irresponsible. **fecklessly** *adv.* **fecklessness** *n.* [as FECK]

fecula (fek´ūlə) *n.* (*pl.* **feculae** (-lē)) lees, sediment, from vegetable infusions, esp. starch. [as FECULENT]

feculent (fek´ūlənt) *a.* **1** filthy, foul. **2** full of dregs, lees or sediment. **3** muddy, turbid. **feculence, feculency** *n.* [F *féculent*, L *faeculentus*, from *faex, faeces*, FAECES]

fecund (fē´kənd, fek´-) *a.* (*formal*) fruitful, prolific, fertile, productive. **fecundability** (fikŭndəbil´iti) *n.* **fecundate** *v.t.* (*formal*) to make fruitful or prolific. **fecundation** (-dā´shən) *n.* **fecundity** (-kŭn´-) *n.* (*formal*) **1** the quality of being fruitful or prolific. **2** the power or property of producing young or germinating. **3** power of production or creation. **4** richness of invention. **fecundize, fecundise** *v.t.* [F *fécond*, L *fēcundus*]

Fed (fed) *n.* The Federal Reserve.

Fed., fed. *abbr.* **1** Federal. **2** Federation.

fed[1] (fed) *a.* that has been fed. **fed up** *a.* (*coll.*) unhappy or bored (with). **to be fed up (to the back teeth) with** to have had more than enough of, to be sick of. [p.p. of FEED[1]]

fed[2] (fed) *n.* (*coll.*) (in the US) a federal agent or official, esp. a member of the FBI.

fed[3] FEED[1].

fedayee (fedah´yē) *n.* (*pl.* **fedayeen** (-yēn)) a member of an Arab commando group, esp. fighting against Israel. [Arab. *fidāī*, one who sacrifices himself]

federal (fed´ərəl) *a.* **1** (*also* **Federal**) relating to, arising from or supporting a system of government formed by the union of several states. **2** relating to such a central government as distinguished from the government of the separate states. **3** (**Federal**) supporting the cause of the Union in the American Civil War. **4** of, relating to or based upon a treaty, league or contract. *~n.* **1** a supporter of the principle of federation. **2** (**Federal**) a supporter of the American Union in the Civil War. **federacy** *n.* (*pl.* **federacies**) a federation of states. **Federal Bureau of Investigation** *n.* a branch of the US Department of Justice concerned with internal security, espionage and sabotage. **federalism** *n.* **federalist** *n.* **federalize, federalise** *v.t.* to bring together in a political confederacy. *~v.i.* to combine into a political confederacy. **federalization** (-zā´shən) *n.* **federally** *adv.* **Federal Party** *n.* (*Hist.*) a US party existing from 1787 to *c.* 1830, orig. under the leadership of Alexander Hamilton, supporting the Federal constitution and centralization of government. **Federal Reserve Bank** *n.* any one of 12 US banks holding reserves and performing functions similar to those of the Bank of England. **federate**[1] (-ərāt) *v.t.* **1** to organize as a federal group of states. **2** to federalize. **3** to bring together for a common object. *~v.i.* **1** to combine and form a federal group. **2** to come together for a common object. **federate**[2] (-ərət) *a.* **1** united under a federal government or organization. **2** leagued together. **federation** (-ā´shən) *n.* **1** a federal government or group of states. **2** a confederated body. **3** the act of uniting in a confederacy. **federationist** *n.* **federative** *a.* **federatively** *adv.* [F *fédéral*, from L *faedus -eris*, a treaty, covenant, cogn. with *fidēs*, FAITH]

fedora (fidaw´rə) *n.* (*N Am., coll.*) a soft felt hat with a curled brim. [*Fédora*, title of a play (1882) by V. Sardou]

fee (fē) *n.* **1** payment or remuneration to a public officer, a professional person or an organization for the execution of official functions or for the performance of a professional service. **2** a charge paid for a privilege, such as admission to a society, public building etc. **3** (*often pl.*) charge, payment (*school fees*). **4** †a gratuity. **5** (*Law*) inherited ownership of land. **6** †ownership, property. **7** (*Hist.*) land and estate held of a feudal superior. ~*v.t.* (*past, p.p.* **fee'd, feed**) **1** to pay a fee or reward to. **2** to engage for a fee, to hire. **to hold in fee** (*Law*) to own absolutely. **feeless** *a.* **fee simple** *n.* (*Law*) ownership of land that is without limitation to any particular class of heirs. **fee tail** *n.* (*Law*) ownership of land that is limited to a particular class of heirs. [A-F *fee*, OF *fé*, *fieu*, *fief*, prob. through med. L *feodum*, *feudum* or *fevum*, from OHG *fehu*, payment, wages, money, property, cattle (cp. OE *feoh*, Dut. *vee*, L *pecus*, cattle, *pecunia*, money)]

feeble (fē´bəl) *a.* (*comp.* **feebler**, *superl.* **feeblest**) **1** weak, destitute of physical strength; infirm, debilitated. **2** lacking in force, vigour or energy. **3** lacking in moral or intellectual power. **4** dim, faint. **5** ineffective, pointless, insipid. **6** unconvincing, lame. **feeble-minded** *a.* **1** stupid, unintelligent. **2** mentally deficient, imbecile. **feeble-mindedly** *adv.* **feeble-mindedness** *n.* **feebleness** *n.* **feeblish** *a.* **feebly** *adv.* [A-F *feble*, OF *foible* (F *faible*), L *flēbilis*, mournful, from *flēre*, to weep]

feed[1] *v.t.* (*past, p.p.* **fed** (fed)) **1** to give food to. **2** to put food into the mouth of. **3** to supply with that which is necessary to existence, continuance or development. **4** to cause (cattle) to graze. **5** to serve as food or nourishment for. **6** to nourish, to cause to grow or develop. **7** to cause (land) to be grazed. **8** to cause to pass (e.g. a rope or tape) through or into something. **9** to supply (a machine etc.) with material. **10** to supply (a machine etc.) with (the necessary material) for its operation. **11** to supply (a signal, power) to an electric circuit. **12** to cue in a response from (another performer). **13** to pass the ball or puck to (another player). **14** to provide (information) to. **15** to gratify. **16** †to entertain, to edify. ~*v.i.* **1** to take food; to eat. **2** to subsist (on or upon). **3** to grow fat. **4** to support oneself. **5** to indulge or gratify oneself mentally. **6** (of a river etc.) to flow into a larger river etc. ~*n.* **1** food, fodder, pasturage. **2** the act of feeding or giving food. **3** an amount of food given to babies or provender given to horses, cattle etc. at a time. **4** (*coll.*) a meal, a feast. **5** the operation of supplying a machine with material, or of bringing a tool into operation. **6** the machinery for this. **7** the amount supplied. **8** the charge of a gun. **9** a performer who supplies cues, esp. a straight man. **to feed back** to produce or provide feedback. **to feed the fishes** FISH[1]. **to feed up 1** to give plenty to eat, to fatten. **2** to satiate. **feedback** *n.* **1** the return of part of the output of a system, circuit or mechanical process to the input. **2** the return of part of the sound output of a loudspeaker to the microphone, producing a high-pitched whistle. **3** the modification produced by the effects of a biological etc. process on another stage of the same pattern. **4** reactions and comments from customers, consumers, audience etc. **feeder** *n.* **1** a person who supplies food or nourishment. **2** a person who fattens cattle. **3** a person who eats, esp. one who eats in a certain manner, as a *quick feeder*. **4** a feeding bottle. **5** a child's bib. **6** a tributary stream. **7** an artificial channel supplying a canal etc. **8** a railway, bus service etc. that links outlying areas to the main system. **9** a wire, usu. in pairs, carrying electricity to various points in a system. **10** the apparatus feeding a machine; a hopper. **11** a theatrical feed. **12** a person who nourishes, encourages or supports. **feeding** *n.* **1** eating. **2** that which is eaten; food. **feeding bottle** *n.* a bottle with a rubber teat for supplying liquid food to infants. **feeding-ground** *n.* a place where animals or fish resort for food. **feedstock** *n.* raw material used in a manufacturing or industrial process. **feedstuff** *n.* fodder. [OE *fēdan* (cp. Dut. *voeden*, Goth. *fōdjan*, OHG *fuotan*, see also FOOD]

feed[2] FEE.

feel (fēl) *v.t.* (*past, p.p.* **felt** (felt)) **1** to perceive by touch. **2** to examine or explore by touch. **3** to touch, to handle, to try or find out by handling or groping. **4** to have a sensation of, otherwise than by the senses of sight, hearing, taste or smell. **5** to be conscious of. **6** to have the emotions stirred by. **7** to experience, to undergo. **8** to be affected by. **9** to know in one's inner consciousness, to be convinced (that); think, consider. ~*v.i.* **1** to have perception by the sense or act of touching. **2** to be conscious of a certain sensation (as cold, wet, hungry or tired). **3** (*reflex.*) to be conscious of (oneself) as in a certain state (as afraid, anxious, busy etc.). **4** to be stirred in one's emotions. **5** to seem to the sense of touch, to produce a certain sensation (*the air feels cold*). ~*n.* **1** the sense of touch. **2** the characteristic sensation of something, esp. one related to that of touch; general impression. **3** perception, esp. of an emotional kind. **to feel after** to try to find out by the sense of touch, to search for as by groping. **to feel for 1** to feel after. **2** to have sympathy or compassion for. **to feel free** not to hesitate (to do something). **to feel like** to wish to, to be in the mood for. **to feel one's oats** OAT. **to feel one's way** to move ahead cautiously. **to feel out** to try to discover the opinions of, esp. indirectly; sound out. **to feel strange** to feel unwell. **to feel the draught** DRAUGHT. **to feel up** (*sl.*) to touch (someone) in such a way as to arouse oneself or the other person sexually. **to feel up to** (*coll.*) to feel able or strong enough to. **to feel with** to have sympathy for. **to get the feel of** to become familiar with. **to make one's presence/influence felt** to do something that causes people to become aware of one's presence etc. **feel-bad** *a.* of or relating to a set of circumstances that together contribute to a feeling of dissatisfaction and pessimism (*the feel-bad factor*). **feeler** *n.* **1** an organ of touch in invertebrate animals. **2** a tentative enquiry (*to put out feelers*). **3** a person who or thing that feels. **feeler gauge** *n.* a thin metal strip of a known thickness used to measure a gap. **feel-good** *a.* of or relating to a set of circumstances that together contribute to a feeling of satisfaction and optimism (*the feel-good factor*). **feeling** *n.* **1** the sense of touch; the sensation produced when a material body is touched. **2** a physical sensation of any kind. **3** an emotional state or reaction; emotion such as anger or joy. **4** (*pl.*) susceptibilities, sympathies. **5** sympathy or love. **6** an impression, a sense, an intuition. **7** a sentiment, belief or conviction (usu. nonrational). **8** the emotional content or mood of a work of art; the emotional response produced by such a work; emotional sensibilities shown in such a work. ~*a.* **1** perceiving by the touch. **2** easily affected or moved, sensitive, of great sensibility. **3** expressive of or manifesting great sensibility. **4** affecting. **feelingless** *a.* **feelingly** *adv.* [OE *fēlan* (cp. Dut. *voelen*, OHG *fuolan*, G *fühlen*, also OE *folm*, L *palma*, Gr. *palamē*, palm of the hand)]

feet FOOT.

feign (fān) *v.t.* **1** to invent, to pretend, to simulate, to counterfeit. **2** †to imagine, to represent in fiction. ~*v.i.* to make pretences; to dissimulate. [OF *feindre*, L *fingere*]

feijoa (fā´jōə) *n.* **1** any evergreen shrub or tree of the genus *Feijoa*. **2** the aromatic edible fruit of this shrub or tree. [J. de Silva *Feijo*, d. 1824, Brazilian naturalist]

feint[1] (fānt) *n.* **1** a pretence of aiming at one point while another is the real object. **2** a feigned or sham attack. **3** a pretence. *~v.i.* to make a feint or pretended attack (upon, against or at). [F *feinte*, from *feindre*, see FEIGN]

feint[2] (fānt) *a.* (of ruled lines on paper) light, faint. [alt. of FAINT]

☒ **feirce** common misspelling of FIERCE.

feisty (fīs´ti) *a.* (*comp.* **feistier**, *superl.* **feistiest**) (*chiefly N Am., coll.*) **1** spirited, tough. **2** irritable, touchy. **feistily** *adv.* **feistiness** *n.* [from N Am. dial. *feist*, a small dog]

felafel (felah´fəl), **falafel** *n.* a spicy ball or cake of mashed chickpeas or beans. [Arab. *falāfil*]

feldspar (feld´spah), **felspar** (fel´spah) *n.* (*Mineral.*) any of a group of silicates of aluminium combined with a mineral, e.g. potassium, sodium or calcium, that are the most important group of rock-forming minerals and the major constituent of igneous rocks. **feldsparization, feldsparisation** *n.* (*Geol.*) alteration of other material into feldspar. **feldspathic** (-spath´-), **feldspathoid** (feld´spəthoid), **feldspathose** (feld´spəthōs) *a.* **1** of or relating to feldspar. **2** having feldspar in the composition. [G *Feldspath* (*Feld*, field, *Spath*, spar)]

felicity (fəlis´iti) *n.* (*pl.* **felicities**) **1** happiness, blissfulness. **2** a source of happiness, a blessing. **3** appropriateness, neatness. **4** a happy turn or expression. **5** a happy way or faculty of expressing, behaving etc. **felicific** (fēlisif´-) *a.* producing happiness. **felicitate**[1] (filis´itāt) *v.t.* **1** to congratulate. **2** †to confer happiness upon. †**felicitate**[2] (fəlis´itət) *a.* **felicitation** (-ā´shən) *n.* (*usu. pl.*) congratulation. **felicitous** *a.* **1** well-suited, apt, well-expressed. **2** charming in manner, operation etc. **3** happy, delightful, prosperous. **felicitously** *adv.* **felicitousness** *n.* [L *fēlīcitās -tātem*, good fortune, *fēlīcitātus*, p.p. of *fēlīcitāre*, from *fēlix -līcis*, happy]

felid (fē´lid) *n.* a member of the Felidae, the cat family, containing lions, tigers, leopards, pumas and cats. [L *fēlis*, a cat]

feline (fē´līn) *a.* **1** of or relating to cats, catlike; belonging to the Felidae, the cat family. **2** sly, stealthy. **3** graceful, sinuous. *~n.* an animal of the cat family, the Felidae. **felinity** (-lin´-) *n.* [L *felinus* from *feles*, cat]

fell[1] FALL.

fell[2] (fel) *v.t.* **1** to hew or cut down. **2** to knock down; to bring to the ground. **3** to finish with a fell in sewing. *~n.* **1** a quantity of timber felled. **2** a seam or hem in which one edge is folded over another and sewed down. **feller**[1] *n.* a person who fells or cuts down trees. [OE *fiellan*, causal, from *feallan*, to FALL (cp. Dut. *vellen*, Icel. *fella*, G *fällen*, all causatives)]

fell[3] (fel) *n.* **1** the hide or skin of an animal, esp. if covered with hair; a fleece. **2** a thick woolly or hairy covering. **3** a dense, matted growth (of hair etc.). **fellmonger** *n.* a dealer in hides and skins. [OE *fel*, skin (cp. Dut. *vel*, G *Fell*, also L *pellis*, Gr. *pella*)]

fell[4] (fel) *n.* (*North.*) **1** a rocky hill. **2** a high stretch of barren moorland. **fell walking** *n.* the activity or recreation of walking on the fells. **fell walker** *n.* [Icel. *fjall*, prob. conn. with G *Fels*, a rock]

fell[5] (fel) *a.* **1** (*poet.*) cruel, savage, fierce. **2** (*poet.*) destructive, terrible, deadly, dire. **3** (*Sc.*) huge. **at one fell swoop** in a single action, on a single occasion. **felly** *adv.* [OF *fel*, late L *fello*, *felo*, FELON[1]]

fella (fel´ə) *n.* **1** (*coll.*) fellow, man. **2** (*dial.*) a male sweetheart. [alteration of FELLOW]

fellah (fel´ə) *n.* (*pl.* **fellahin** (-əhēn´)) an Egyptian agricultural labourer or peasant. [Arab. *fellāh*]

fellatio (fəlā´shiō, -lah´t-) *n.* oral stimulation of the penis. **fellate** (filāt´) *v.t.* **fellator** *n.* [L *fellātus*, p.p. of *fellāre*, to suck]

feller[1] FELL[2].

feller[2] (fel´ə) *n.* **1** (*coll.*) fellow, man. **2** (*dial.*) a male sweetheart. [alteration of FELLOW]

felloe (fel´ō), **felly** (fel´i) *n.* (*pl.* **felloes, fellies**) **1** any one of the curved segments of a wheel, to which the spokes are attached. **2** the whole rim of a wheel. [OE *felg* (cp. Dut. *velg*, G *Felge*)]

fellow (fel´ō) *n.* **1** a man, a boy. **2** (*derog.*) a person considered as unimportant. **3** (*usu. pl.*) an associate, a comrade; a partner; a companion. **4** a contemporary. **5** one of the same kind or species. **6** an equal in rank, a peer, a compeer. **7** one of a pair. **8** a person or thing like or equal to another, a counterpart, a match. **9** a member of a learned or an incorporated society. **10** an incorporated member of a college. **11** the holder of a fellowship or stipendiary position endowed for purposes of research. **12** a member of a university governing body; one of the trustees of a college. *~a.* (*attrib.*) associated with oneself or of the same class or relationship (*one's fellow workers*). *~v.t.* to match, to pair with, to suit. **fellow commoner** *n.* a person who has the right to dine with the fellows at certain universities. **fellow countryman, fellow countrywoman** *n.* a native of the same country as another. **fellow-craft** *n.* a Freemason of the second degree. **fellow-creature** *n.* a creature like oneself, the work of the same Creator. **fellow feeling** *n.* sympathy esp. from sharing similar experiences; joint interest. **fellowship** *n.* **1** companionship, association, close friendship, friendliness, warmth of feeling, community of interest, participation. **2** a body of associates. **3** a brotherhood, a fraternity. **4** a company, a corporation, a guild. **5** the condition or state of being a fellow. **6** the position of fellow in a college or learned society. **7** an endowment for maintaining a graduate engaged in research; the status of such a graduate. **8** sharing in membership of a community partaking of Holy Communion together. **9** the rule by which profit or loss is divided among partners in proportion to the capital invested. *~v.t.* (*pres.p.* **fellowshipping,** (*N Am.*) **fellowshiping,** *past, p.p.* **fellowshipped,** (*N Am.*) **fellowshiped**) to admit to religious fellowship. *~v.i.* (*chiefly N Am.*) to religiously associate (with), to unite with. **fellow-traveller** *n.* **1** a person who travels with another person on a journey. **2** (*usu. derog.*) a person who, without declaring themselves to be a member, sympathizes with the aims of the Communist Party or other similar organization. [Icel. *fēlagi*, a partner, one who lays down fee or goods in partnership, from *fē*, property, cogn. with OE *feoh*, cattle, see FEE]

felly FELLOE.

felo de se (fē´lō di sē, fel´ō) *n.* (*pl.* **felones de se** (filō´nēz di sē´), **felos de se** (fē´lōz, fel´ōz)) **1** a person who commits felony by suicide. **2** self-murder, suicide. [A-L, felon upon himself (see FELON[1])]

felon[1] (fel´ən) *n.* a person who has committed a felony. *~a.* cruel, malignant, malicious; wicked, murderous. **felonious** (filō´-) *a.* **1** of the nature of a felony. **2** (*Law*) done with deliberate purpose to commit a crime. **3** (*Law*) that has committed felony. **feloniously** *adv.* **feloniousness** *n.* **felonry** *n.* (*pl.* **felonries**) **1** a body of felons. **2** (*Hist.*) convicts in a penal colony in Australia. **felony** *n.* (*pl.* **felonies**) **1** in US law and in Engish law until 1967, an offence of graver character than a misdemeanour. **2** an offence of a very serious character, conviction for which formerly involved loss of lands and goods. [OF from late L *fellōnem*, nom. *fello*, *felo* (perh. from L *fel*, gall)]

felon[2] (fel´ən) *n.* a whitlow or abscess close to the nail. [med. L *fello*, a score]

felones de se, felos de se FELO DE SE.

felsite (fel´sīt) *n.* (*Mineral.*) felstone. **felsitic** (-sit´-) *a.* [from *fels-*, corr. form, see FELDSPAR]

felspar FELDSPAR.

felstone (fel´stōn) *n.* (*Mineral.*) feldspar occurring in compact masses. [G *Felsstein* (*Fels*, rock, *Stein*, stone)]

felt[1] FEEL.

felt[2] (felt) *n.* **1** a kind of cloth made of wool or wool and cotton compacted together by rolling, beating and pressing; similar cloth or material made from other fibres. 2 a piece of this material. ~*a.* made of this material (*a felt hat*). ~*v.t.* 1 to make into felt. 2 to cover with felt. 3 to press into a compact mass. ~*v.i.* to become matted together. **felter** *n.* 1 a maker of or worker in felt. 2 a bird that makes its nest with or as with felt. ~*v.t.*, *v.i.* to mat or clot together like felt. **felt hat** *n.* a hat made of felt. **felting** *n.* the act or process of making felt. **felt-maker** *n.* **felt tip pen, felt-tipped pen, felt tip** *n.* a pen with a writing point made of pressed felt or similar fibres. **felty** *a.* [OE, cp. Dut. *vilt*, G *Filz*]

felucca (felŭk´ə) *n.* a small vessel used in the Mediterranean, propelled by oars or lateen sails or both. [It., prob. from Arab.]

felwort (fel´wœt) *n.* a gentian with purple flowers, *Gentianella amarella*. [OE *feldwyrt*, see FIELD, WORT]

fem. *abbr.* feminine.

female (fē´māl) *a.* 1 denoting the sex which gives birth to young or lays eggs from which new individuals are developed. 2 (*Bot.*) having a pistil, but no stamens, capable of being fertilized and producing fruit; bearing fruit. 3 of, relating to or characteristic of woman or womanhood or female animals and plants; womanly, feminine. 4 designed for receiving a correlative mechanical part designated male (*a female screw*). ~*n.* 1 (*sometimes derog.*) a woman or girl. 2 (*Zool.*) an individual of the female sex. **female condom** *n.* a contraceptive device worn in the vagina. **female die** *n.* the concave die, into which the male or convex die is struck. **female impersonator** *n.* a male performer who dresses as and imitates a woman. **femaleness** *n.* [OF *femelle*, L *fēmella*, dim. of *fēmina*, a woman]

feme (fēm, fem) *n.* (*Law*) a woman or wife. **feme covert** (kŭv´ət), **feme couvert** (fam kooveə´) *n.* (*Law*) a married woman. **feme sole** (sōl) *n.* (*Law*) 1 an unmarried woman, spinster or widow. 2 a married woman having rights of property or trade independent of her husband. [A-F and OF]

feminine (fem´inin) *a.* 1 of, relating to or characteristic of women or the female sex. 2 womanly; effeminate. 3 having qualities associated with women; gentle, tender, pretty. 4 (*Gram.*) belonging to the gender denoting or classified as females. 5 (of rhymes) having two syllables, the first accented. †**feminal** *a.* womanly. **feminality** (-nal´-) *n.* 1 the quality of being female. 2 the characteristic nature of woman or the female sex. 3 something characteristic of female nature. †**femineity** (-nē´i-) *n.* 1 womanliness. 2 womanishness. **feminine caesura** *n.* a caesura following an unstressed syllable, as in '*And eat our pot of honey on the grave*'. **femininely** *adv.* **feminineness, feminity** (-min´-) *n.* the qualities or manners becoming a woman. **feminine rhyme** *n.* a rhyme on a word ending with an unstressed syllable, e.g. *fable, table*; *notion, motion*. **femininity** (-nin´-) *n.* **feminism** *n.* 1 the advocacy of the rights of women to political, economic and social equality with men. 2 the development of female characteristics in a male person. **feminist** *n.*, *a.* **feministic** (-nis´-) *a.* **feminize, feminise** *v.t.* to make feminine. ~*v.i.* to become feminine. [OF *feminin*, L *fēminīnus*, from *fēmina*, a woman]

femme (fem) *n.* (*sl.*) 1 a particularly feminine or effeminate person. 2 the less dominant or more feminine partner in a lesbian or male homosexual relationship. [F, woman]

femme de chambre (fam də shā̃´brə) *n.* (*pl.* **femmes de chambre** (fam də shā̃´brə)) 1 a chambermaid. 2 a lady's maid. [F, bedroom woman]

femme fatale (fam fatahl´) *n.* (*pl.* **femmes fatales** (fam fatahl´)) a seductive woman, esp. one who lures men to their downfall. [F, fatal woman]

femmes de chambre FEMME DE CHAMBRE.

femmes fatales FEMME FATALE.

femto- (fem´tō) *pref.* a thousand million millionth (10^{-15}). [Dan. or Norw. *femten*, fifteen]

femur (fē´mə) *n.* (*pl.* **femurs, femora** (fem´ərə)) 1 the thigh bone. 2 the third joint of the leg in insects. **femoral** (fem´ərəl) *a.* of or belonging to the thigh. ~*n.* the femoral artery. [L *femur -oris*, the thigh]

fen[1] (fen) *n.* low, flat and marshy land; a marsh, a bog. **the Fens** the low-lying districts in the east of England, partially drained and abounding in broads or lakes. **fen-berry** *n.* (*pl.* **fen-berries**) the cranberry, *Vaccinium oxycoccos*. **fen-duck** *n.* the shoveller. **fen-fire** *n.* the will-o'-the-wisp. **fenland** *n.* a fen; fen country. **fenlander** *n.* an inhabitant of the fens. **fenman** *n.* (*pl.* **fenmen**) an inhabitant of fen country. **fenny** *a.* [OE *fenn* (cp. Dut. *ven, veen*, G *Fenne*)]

fen[2] (fŭn, fen) *n.* (*pl.* **fen**) a Chinese monetary unit worth one-hundredth of a yuan; a coin of this value. [Chin. *fēn*, a hundredth part]

fence (fens) *n.* 1 a structure serving to enclose and protect a piece of ground, or to keep cattle from straying, e.g. a wall, a hedge or a line of rails or posts etc. 2 an obstacle in steeplechasing or showjumping. 3 a guardplate, guide or gauge of various kinds in machinery etc. 4 (*sl.*) a purchaser or receiver of stolen goods, or a place where such goods are purchased or deposited. 5 the art of fencing or swordplay. ~*v.t.* 1 to enclose, encircle or protect with or as with a fence. 2 to separate (off) with a fence. 3 to defend, shield or protect. 4 to parry, to ward off. 5 (*sl.*) to deal in (stolen goods). ~*v.i.* 1 to practise the art of swordplay. 2 to use a sword skilfully. 3 to defend oneself or repel attack skilfully. 4 (of a horse) to jump over fences. 5 to parry enquiries adroitly, to equivocate. 6 (*sl.*) to deal in stolen goods. **over the fence** (*Austral.*, *coll.*) unreasonable, utterly indecent. **to mend fences** to restore good relations (with someone), to make up differences. **to sit on the fence** to remain neutral in respect to opposing policies. **fenced** *a.* 1 enclosed with a fence. 2 fortified. **fenceless** *a.* 1 unenclosed. 2 undefended, defenceless. **fence post** *n.* a post that supports a fence. **fencer** *n.* 1 a person skilled in fencing. 2 a builder of fences. 3 a horse good at jumping over fences. **fencing** *n.* 1 the act of making fences. 2 a fence or fences, a railing or railings. 3 material for making fences. 4 the act or art of using a sword or foil in attack or defence. 5 a protection or guard round any dangerous piece of machinery. [short for DEFENCE]

fencible (fen´sibəl) *n.* (*Hist.*) a soldier enlisted for home defence. ~*a.* 1 (*chiefly Sc.*) capable of defence or of being defended. 2 belonging to the fencibles. [short for DEFENSIBLE (under DEFEND)]

fend (fend) *v.t.* (*Sc.*) to provide for, to support. ~*v.i.* (*Sc.*) to strive, to resist, to offer opposition. **to fend for** to provide or to get a living for. **to fend off** to keep off, ward off. [short for DEFEND]

fender (fen´də) *n.* 1 a piece of furniture, usu. of iron or brass, placed on the hearth to keep in falling coals, ashes etc. 2 a piece of timber or plastic or mass of rope to protect the side of a vessel from injury by collision. 3 a person or thing that serves to defend, protect or ward off anything hurtful or dangerous. 4 (*N Am.*) the wing or mudguard of a motor vehicle. 5 (*N Am.*) the bumper of a motor vehicle. **fender bender** *n.* (*N Am.*, *sl.*) a collision between motor vehicles, esp. one involving only minor damage. **fenderless** *a.* **fender pile** *n.* a piece of timber placed in front of dock walls and similar structures to protect against blows from vessels. [from FEND]

fenestella (fenistel´ə) *n.* (*Archit.*) a niche on the south side of the altar containing the piscina, and often the credence. [L, dim. of *fenestra*, a window]

fenestra (fines´trə) *n.* (*pl.* **fenestrae** (-trē)) 1 a window-like aperture in a bone. 2 a transparent spot or aperture in a wing, leaf etc. 3 a tiny hole in a surgical instrument. 4 a hole made by fenestration. **fenestral** *a.* 1 †of or relating to a window. 2 (*Biol.*) having small transparent spots or fenestrae. **fenestra ovalis** (ōvah´lis) *n.* the oval opening between the middle ear and the cavity of the inner ear. **fenestra rotunda** (rōtŭn´də) *n.* the round opening between the middle ear and the cochlea of the inner ear. **fenestrate** (-trət, fen´əs-) *a.* 1 (of leaves) having only a network of filamentous cells formed. 2 relating to the naked hyaline transparent spots on the wings of butterflies. **fenestrated** (-trātid, fen´is-) *a.* 1 furnished with windows. 2 (*Anat.*) having fenestrae. 3 perforated. 4 fenestrate. **fenestration** (-trā´shən) *n.* 1 (*Archit.*) the construction, arrangement or method of design of windows. 2 the formation of fenestrae. 3 a surgical operation in which an artificial opening is made in the bony labyrinth of the inner ear, esp. to improve hearing. 4 the condition of having fenestrae. [L, a window]

feng shui (feng´ shooi, fŭng´) *n.* in Chinese philosophy, a system of good and bad influences in the environment, used when deciding where to locate buildings etc.

Fenian (fē´niən) *n.* 1 a member of an Irish secret society which was formed in America in about 1858, having as its object the overthrow of the British government in Ireland, and the establishment of an independent republic. 2 (*offensive*) an (esp. Irish) Roman Catholic. ~*a.* 1 of or relating to this society or to Fenianism. 2 (*offensive*) (Irish) Roman Catholic. **Fenianism** *n.* [OIr. *Fēne*, a name of the ancient Irish, confused with *Fīann*, the warriors who defended Ireland in the time of Finn]

fennec (fen´ek) *n.* a small fox, *Vulpes zerda*, common in Africa. [Arab. *fenek*]

fennel (fen´əl) *n.* 1 a fragrant umbelliferous plant with yellow flowers, *Feniculum vulgare*, whose seeds and leaves are used as flavourings. 2 the seeds of this. 3 (*also* **Florence fennel, sweet fennel**) a variety of this with thickened stalks that are eaten as a vegetable. **fennel flower** *n.* a herb of the genus *Nigella*, such as ragged lady, *N. damascena*, or the nutmeg flower, *N. sativa.* [OE *finol, finugl*, L *faeniculum*, dim. of *faenum*, hay]

fent (fent) *n.* 1 the opening left in a garment (as in a shirtsleeve) for convenience of putting it on. 2 a crack, a rift. 3 a remnant. [F *fente*, from *fendre*, L *findere*, to cleave]

fenugreek (fen´ūgrēk) *n.* a leguminous plant, *Trigonella foenum-graecum*, the seeds of which are used as a flavouring or in animal fodder. [F *fenugrec*, L *faenugræcum* (*faenum*, hay, *Graecum*, neut. a., Greek)]

feoff (fēf, fef) *v.t.* (*Law, Hist.*) to grant possession to, to enfeoff. ~*n.* a fief. **feoffee** (-ē´) *n.* a person who is invested with an estate by feoffment. **feoffment** *n.* 1 the conveyance of a fief to another, accompanied by actual delivery of possession. 2 the mode of such conveyance. **feoffor** *n.* a person who grants a fief. [OF *feoffer, fieffer*, from *fief*, FEE]

ferae naturae (fiə´rē nətū´rē, fer´ē) *a.* (of deer, hares, pheasants etc.) wild, as distinguished from domesticated. [L, of a wild nature]

feral (fiə´rəl, fer´) *a.* 1 wild, savage, brutal. 2 changed from a domesticated into a wild state. 3 uncultivated. [L *fera*, a wild beast]

fer de lance (feə də lãs´) *n.* (*pl.* **fers de lance** (feə də lãs´), **fer de lances** (feə də lãs´)) the yellow viper of Central and S America, *Bothrops atrox.* [F, lancehead (*fer*, iron)]

feretory (fer´ətəri) *n.* (*pl.* **feretories**) 1 the bier or shrine in which relics of saints were carried in procession. 2 a reliquary, a chapel or place in a church in which shrines were kept. [OF *fiertre*, L *feretrum*, Gr. *pheretron*, from *pherein*, to bear]

ferial (fiə´riəl, fe´-) *a.* 1 in the Church calendar, of or relating to ordinary weekdays as opposed to festival or fast days. 2 of or relating to holidays. [F *férial*, L *fēriālis*, from *fēria*, a holiday, see FAIR[2]]

ferine (fiə´rīn) *a.* feral. [L *ferīnus*, from *fera*, wild animal]

fermata (fœmah´tə) *n.* (*pl.* **fermatas**) (*Mus.*) 1 a continuation of a note or rest beyond its usual length; pause. 2 a sign indicating this. [It. *fermare*, to stop]

ferment[1] (fœ´ment) *n.* 1 commotion, tumult, agitation, excitement, uproar. 2 any substance, organic or inorganic, which causes fermentation. 3 leaven. 4 fermentation; internal motion of the constituent parts of a fluid. [as FERMENT[2]]

ferment[2] (fəment´) *v.t.* 1 to excite fermentation in, to subject to fermentation. 2 to rouse, to agitate, to excite. ~*v.i.* 1 to be in a state of fermentation, to effervesce. 2 to be agitated, as by violent emotions. **fermentable** (-men´-) *a.* **fermentability** (-bil´-) *n.* **fermentation** (fœmentā´shən) *n.* 1 a process that takes place in certain substances or liquids by living organisms or chemical agents, with the production of heat, effervescence and chemical decomposition, esp. the change of sugar to ethyl alcohol. 2 commotion, agitation, excitement. **fermentative** (-tativ) *a.* causing, produced by or of the nature of fermentation. **fermenter** (-men´-) *n.* **fermentescible** (fœmentes´ibəl) *a.* 1 able to cause fermentation. 2 capable of fermentation. [F, from L *fermentum*, from root of *fervēre*, to boil]

fermeture (fœ´məchə) *n.* the mechanism for closing the breech of a gun or other firearm. [F, from *fermer*, to shut]

fermi (fœ´mi) *n.* (*pl.* **fermis**) a unit of length equal to 10^{-15} metre. **fermion** (-ən) *n.* any of a group of subatomic particles, e.g. a nucleon, that has half-integral spin and obeys the exclusion principle. **fermium** (-əm) *n.* an element, at. no. 100, chem. symbol Fm, artificially produced from plutonium. [Enrico *Fermi*, 1901–54, Italian physicist]

fern (fœn) *n.* (*pl.* **fern, ferns**) a non-flowering plant springing from a rhizome, and having the reproductive organs on the lower surface of fronds or leaves, which are often divided in a graceful, feathery form. **fern bird** *n.* the grass bird or New Zealand pipit. **fernery** *n.* (*pl.* **ferneries**) a place where ferns are grown. **fernless** *a.* **fern seed** *n.* the seeds or spores of ferns, formerly supposed to render a person invisible. **ferny** *a.* [OE *fearn* (cp. Dut. *varen*, G *Farn*, also Sansk. *parna* and Gr. *pteron*, wing, feather)]

ferocious (fərō´shəs) *a.* 1 fierce, savage, cruel, barbarous. 2 (*esp. N Am., coll.*) intense, extreme. **ferociously** *adv.* **ferociousness** *n.* **ferocity** (-ros´-) *n.* (*pl.* **ferocities**) 1 the state or quality of being ferocious; savageness, fierceness, wildness, fury. 2 a ferocious act. [L *ferōci-*, stem of *ferox*, cogn. with *ferus*, wild]

-ferous (fərəs), **-iferous** (if´ərəs) *suf.* bearing, producing, having, as in *auriferous, fossiliferous.* **-ferously** *suf.* **-ferousness** *suf.* [L *fer-*, stem of *ferre*, to bear, -OUS]

†**ferrandine** (fer´əndēn), †**farandine** (far´-) *n.* a mixed cloth of silk and other materials. [prob. from F. *Ferrand*, name of inventor, *c.* 1630]

ferrara (fərah´rə) *n.* a broadsword of special excellence. [perh. from native of It. town *Ferrara*, or from It. *ferrajo*, cutter, L *ferrārius*, from *ferrum*, iron]

ferrate (fer´āt) *n.* (*Chem.*) a salt of the hypothetical ferric acid. **ferreous** (-iəs) *a.* of or relating to iron; of the nature of iron; made of iron. [L *ferrum*, iron]

ferrel FERRULE.

ferret[1] (fer´it) *n.* 1 a partially tamed variety of polecat, *Mustela putorius furo*, used for killing rats and driving rabbits out of their holes. 2 a sharp-eyed searcher or investigator. ~*v.t.* (*pres.p.* **ferreting,** *past, p.p.* **ferreted**) 1 to drive out of a hole or clear (ground) with ferrets. 2 to hunt or take with ferrets. 3 to search (out) by persevering investigation. ~*v.i.* 1 to hunt rabbits etc. with a ferret. 2 to search or rummage about (for). **ferreter** *n.* a person who ferrets. **ferrety** *a.* [OF *furet*, late L *fūrētus*, identified with *fūrō -ōnem*, L *fūr*, robber]

ferret[2] (fer´it) *n.* a tape made of silk or cotton. **ferret silk** *n.* floss silk. [prob. from It. *fioretti*, a kind of silk, pl. of *fioretto*, dim of *fiore*, flower, L *flōrem*, nom. *flōs*]

ferri- (fer´i) *comb. form* (*Chem.*) denoting a compound of iron in the ferric state. [L *ferrum*, iron]

ferriage (fer´iij) *n.* 1 conveyance by a ferry. 2 the fare paid for this.

ferric (fer´ik) *a.* 1 of, relating to or extracted from iron. 2 containing trivalent iron. [L *ferrum*, iron]

ferricyanic (ferisīan´ik) *a.* of or relating to a compound of iron in its ferric state with cyanogen.

ferriferous (ferif´ərəs) *a.* yielding iron.

ferrimagnetism (ferimag´nitizm) *n.* the spontaneous magnetization of a substance in which one group of magnetic atoms is arranged in an opposite direction to the other. **ferrimagnetic** (-magnet´ik) *a.*

Ferris wheel (fer´is) *n.* a big, upright revolving fairground wheel with seats suspended from its rim. [G.W.G. *Ferris*, 1859–96, US engineer]

ferrite (fer´īt) *n.* a sintered ceramic consisting of a mixture of ferric oxide and other metallic oxides, which possesses magnetic properties.

ferro- (fer´ō) *comb. form* 1 (*Mineral.*) denoting a substance containing iron. 2 (*Chem.*) denoting a compound of iron in the ferrous state. [L *ferrum*, iron]

ferrocalcite (ferōkal´sīt) *n.* calcite containing carbonate of iron and turning brown on exposure.

ferroconcrete (ferōkong´krēt) *n.* concrete strengthened by incorporation of iron bars, strips etc.; reinforced concrete. ~*a.* made of reinforced concrete.

ferrocyanic (ferōsīan´ik) *a.* (*Chem.*) of or relating to iron in the ferrous state and cyanogen. **ferrocyanic acid, ferrocyanhydric acid** (-hī´-) *n.* a white crystalline powder derived from iron and cyanogen. **ferrocyanide** (-sī´ənīd) *n.* a salt of ferrocyanic acid.

ferroelectric (ferōilek´trik) *a.* (of materials) showing spontaneous electric polarization, but not conducting electric current. ~*n.* a ferroelectric material. **ferroelectricity** (-tris´iti) *n.*

ferromagnetism (ferōmag´nitizm) *n.* the magnetic properties of certain materials, e.g. iron and cobalt, that are easily magnetized, vary in their degree of magnetization depending on the strength of the applied magnetizing field, and in some cases retain their magnetization when that field is withdrawn. **ferromagnetic** (-magnet´ik) *a.*

ferrosilicon (ferōsil´ikən) *n.* (*Chem.*) a compound of silicon and iron added to molten iron to give it a larger proportion of silicon.

ferrotype (fer´ōtīp) *n.* 1 a positive photograph on a sensitized film laid on a thin iron plate. 2 the iron plate used in this process.

ferrous (fer´əs) *a.* 1 containing iron. 2 (*Chem.*) of, relating to or containing divalent iron. [L *ferrum*, iron]

ferruginous (fəroo´jinəs) *a.* 1 containing iron or iron rust. 2 of the colour of iron rust. **ferruginate** *v.t.* **ferruginous deposits** *n.pl.* rocks containing sufficient iron ore to make mining worthwhile. **ferruginous duck** *n.* a European duck, *Aythya nyroca*, with a reddish brown plumage. [L *ferrūginus*, from *ferrūgo -inis*, from *ferrum*, iron]

ferrule (fer´ool, -əl), **ferrel** *n.* 1 a metallic ring or cap on the handle of a tool, the end of a stick, the joint of a fishing rod, a post etc. to strengthen it. 2 a short piece of pipe screwed into a main to form a connection with a service-pipe. **ferruled** *a.* [formerly *verrel* (OF *virelle* F *virole*), late L *virola*, L *viriola*, dim. of *viriae*, bracelets]

ferry (fer´i) *v.t.* (*3rd pers. sing. pres.* **ferries,** *pres.p.* **ferrying,** *past, p.p.* **ferried**) to transport over a river, strait or other narrow expanse of water, in a boat, barge etc. ~*v.i.* to go or pass across narrow water in a boat etc. ~*n.* (*pl.* **ferries**) 1 a boat, or occasionally an aeroplane etc., used for carrying passengers across a river, strait or other narrow expanse of water. 2 the provision of such a method of transport. 3 the right of ferrying and charging a toll for so doing. 4 the passage where a ferryboat plies. **ferryboat** *n.* a boat used as a ferry. **ferrybridge** *n.* 1 a large vessel used for carrying trains across a river etc. where a ferry operates. 2 (*N Am.*) the landing stage at a river etc. where a ferry operates, esp. on a tidal river where it rises and falls with the tide. **ferryman** *n.* (*pl.* **ferrymen**). [OE *ferian*, from *faran*, to FARE]

fers de lance FER DE LANCE.

fertile (fœ´tīl) *a.* 1 able to support abundant growth. 2 able to bear offspring, fruitful. 3 capable of growing or developing. 4 productive, fruitful. 5 (of the mind) inventive, resourceful. 6 able to be transformed into fissionable material. **Fertile Crescent** *n.* the area of fertile land in the E Mediterranean, from Israel to the Persian Gulf. **fertility** (-til´-) *n.* **fertility drug** *n.* a drug given to apparently infertile women to stimulate ovulation. **fertility rite** *n.* a pagan religious ceremony intended to ensure the fertility of the soil, animals or human population. **fertility symbol** *n.* **fertilize** (-ti-), **fertilise** *v.t.* 1 to make fertile or productive. 2 to provide (an egg, a female animal or plant) with male reproductive material to form a new individual. 3 to make (esp. soil) rich. **fertilizable** *a.* **fertilization** (-zā´shən) *n.* **fertilizer** *n.* 1 a fertilizing agent. 2 a chemical applied to the soil to make it more fertile and modify its acidity or alkalinity. [OF *fertil*, L *fertilis*, from *ferre*, to bear]

ferula (fer´ūlə) *n.* (*pl.* **ferulas, ferulae** (-lē)) 1 any umbelliferous plant of the Mediterranean genus *Ferula*, esp. the giant fennel *F. communis* with a thick stem. 2 a ferule. **ferulaceous** (-lā´-) *a.* 1 of or relating to canes or reeds. 2 having a reedlike stem. [L, a rod, orig. giant fennel]

ferule (fer´ool, -əl) *n.* a rod or cane formerly used to punish children in school. ~*v.t.* to punish with a ferule. [see FERULA]

fervent (fœ´vənt) *a.* 1 ardent, earnest, zealous, vehement. 2 hot, boiling, glowing. **fervency** *n.* **fervently** *adv.* **fervid** (-vid) *a.* 1 ardent, impassioned. 2 burning, very hot. **fervidly** *adv.* **fervidness** *n.* **fervour** (-və), (*N Am.*) **fervor** *n.* 1 ardour, intensity of feeling, vehemence; zeal. 2 heat, warmth. [OF, from L *fervens -ntem*, pres.p. of *fervēre*, to boil]

fescennine (fes´ənīn) *a.* scurrilous, licentious. **fescennine verses** *n.pl.* extempore dialogues in verses, characterized by broad and licentious satire. [L *Fescennīnus*, relating to the ancient festivals of *Fescennia*, a town of Etruria]

fescue (fes´kū) *n.* a grass of the genus *Festuca*, important for pasture. **fescue-grass** *n.* *Festuca ovina*, an important pasture grass. [ME, OF *festu*, L *festūca*, a stalk, a stem]

fess[1] (fes), **fesse** *n.* (*Her.*) 1 a broad band of metal or colour crossing the shield horizontally, and occupying one-third of it. 2 any of the nine honourable ordinaries, representing a knight's girdle. **in fess** arranged horizontally. **fess point** *n.* the midpoint of a shield. [OF, from L *fascia*, see FASCIA]

fess[2] (fes) *v.i.* (*coll.*) to confess. [CONFESS]

-fest (fest) *comb. form* an event or gathering for a particular activity, as *songfest*. [G *Fest*, a celebration]

festal (fes´təl) *a.* 1 festive, joyous, gay, merry. 2 actively involved in holiday pursuits. 3 of or relating to a feast or holiday. **festally** *adv.* [OF, from L *festum*, FEAST]

fester (fes´tə) *v.i.* **1** to become septic or infected. **2** to cause persistent annoyance or resentment; to rankle. **3** to become rotten; to decay. **4** to form pus. *~v.t.* to make septic or infected. *~n.* **1** a tumour or sore containing pus. **2** the act or state of festering or rankling. [OF *festre* (whence *festrir*, to fester), L *fistula*, see FISTULA]

festina lente (fes´tinə len´ti) *v.i.* (*imper.*) make haste slowly, do not be impetuous. [L]

†**festinate**[1] (fes´tinət) *a.* hasty, hurried. **festinately** *adv.* [as FESTINATE[2]]

†**festinate**[2] (fes´tināt) *v.i.* to hasten. *~v.t.* to hurry, accelerate. **festination** (-ā´shən) *n.* an involuntary speeding-up of the gait, experienced by some sufferers from Parkinson's disease. [L *festīnātus*, p.p. of *festīnāre*, to hasten]

festival (fes´tivəl) *n.* **1** a day or period of celebration or holiday, often with religious significance. **2** a series of concerts, plays etc., in a town. **3** a merrymaking. *~a.* of, relating to or characterizing a festival or feast; festal. **festival of lights** *n.* **1** Hanukkah. **2** Diwali. **festive** *a.* **1** of, relating to or used for a feast or festival. **2** joyous, gay, celebratory. **3** (of a person) enjoying feasting. **festively** *adv.* **festiveness** *n.* **festivity** (-tiv´-) *n.* (*pl.* **festivities**) **1** gaiety, mirth, joyfulness. **2** a feast, a festival, a joyous celebration or entertainment. **3** (*pl.*) celebrations; merrymaking. [OF, from late L *festīvālis*, L *festīvus*, from *festum*, FEAST]

festoon (festoon´) *n.* **1** a decorative chain or garland of flowers, foliage, drapery etc. suspended by the ends to hang as a curve. **2** a carved ornament in the form of a garland or wreath. *~v.t.* to form into or adorn with or as with festoons; to decorate in a showy manner. **festoonery** *n.* [F *feston*, It. *festone*, prob. from *festum*, see FESTIVAL]

Festschrift (fest´shrift), **festschrift** *n.* (*pl.* **Festschriften** (-tən), **Festschrifts, festschriften, festschrifts**) a collection of learned writings by various authors, published in honour of a scholar. [G *Fest*, a celebration and *Schrift*, writing]

feta (fet´ə), **fetta** *n.* a firm white Greek cheese made from sheep's or goat's milk. [mod. Gr. (*tyri*) *pheta*, from *tyri*, cheese, *pheta*, It. *fetta*, slice]

fetal FOETUS.

fetch[1] (fech) *v.t.* **1** to go for and bring back. **2** to cause to come. **3** to draw forth (breath), to heave (a sigh). **4** (*coll.*) to strike. **5** (*coll.*) to delight, to charm. **6** to bring in, to sell for (a price). **7** to derive, to elicit. **8** to bring to any state, condition or position. **9** (*Naut.*) to reach, to arrive at. *~v.i.* (*Naut.*) to reach a place, to bring up. *~n.* **1** an act of fetching. **2** a stratagem, a trick, a dodge. **3** striving after, a powerful effort. **4** a deep breath, a sigh. **5** (*Naut.*) the distance travelled, esp. by wind or waves, across open water without obstruction. **to fetch and carry** to go to and fro with things; to perform menial tasks. **to fetch out** to bring out, to cause to appear. **to fetch up** **1** (*coll.*) to end up. **2** to vomit. **3** to recall, to bring to mind. **4** (*Naut.*) to stop suddenly, to come to a stand. **5** (*coll.*) to bring up, raise, rear (children). **to fetch up all standing** to stop suddenly with sails set. **fetcher** *n.* **fetching** *a.* (*coll.*) attractive, charming, taking. **fetchingly** *adv.* [OE *feccan*, *fetian*, prob. rel. to *fæt*, step, journey]

fetch[2] (fech) *n.* a wraith or double. **fetch-candle,** †**fetch-light** *n.* a light appearing at night, believed by the superstitious to portend the death of some person. [etym. unknown]

fête (fāt, fet), **fete** *n.* **1** an outdoor event with stalls and entertainments, usu. locally organized to raise money for charity. **2** a festival, an entertainment. **3** the festival of the saint after whom a person is named. *~v.t.* to entertain, to feast; to honour lavishly. **fête champêtre** (shāpet´rə) *n.* (*pl.* **fêtes champêtres** (fāt shāpet´rə)) an open-air festival. **fête galante** (gal´ãt) *n.* (*pl.* **fêtes galantes** (fāt galã´t)) **1** an early 18th-cent. genre of French painting showing figures in a pastoral setting. **2** a painting in this genre. [F *fête*, OF *feste*, L *festum*, FEAST]

fetial (fē´shəl), **fecial** *a.* **1** of or relating to the fetiales. **2** ambassadorial, heraldic. *~n.* (*pl.* **fetiales** (fēshiā´lēz)) any of a college of priests in ancient Rome, who presided over the ceremonies connected with the ratification of peace or the formal declaration of war. [L *fetiālis* (etym. unknown)]

feticide FOETUS.

fetid (fet´id, fē´-), **foetid** *a.* having an offensive smell; stinking. **fetidly** *adv.* **fetidness** *n.* **fetor** (fē´tə) *n.* a strong or offensive smell; a stench. [L *fētidus*, from *fētēre*, to stink]

fetish (fet´ish) *n.* **1** (*Psych.*) an object providing sexual gratification. **2** any material object supposed to be the vessel, vehicle or instrument of a supernatural being, the possession of which gives supposed special powers. **3** an object of devotion, an idol, a fixation. **fetishism** *n.* **1** (*Psych.*) a condition in which sexual gratification is obtained from parts of the body other than the genital parts. **2** belief in fetishes; worship of them. **fetishist** *n.* **fetishistic** (-shis´-) *a.* **fetishize, fetishise** *v.t.* **fetishization** (-zā´shən) *n.* [F *fétiche*, Port. *feitiço*, sorcery, L *factītius*, artificial]

fetlock (fet´lok) *n.* **1** the back projecting part of a horse's leg, between the pastern and the cannon-bone. **2** the joint at this part of the leg. **3** the tuft of hair growing at this projection. [etym. obscure (cp. LG *fitlock*, G *Fissloch*)]

fetor FETID.

fetta FETA.

fetter (fet´ə) *n.* **1** a chain for the feet. **2** (*usu. pl.*) a shackle, a bond. **3** (*pl.*) captivity. **4** anything which restrains or confines. *~v.t.* **1** to put fetters upon, to bind with fetters. **2** to confine, restrain; to hamper, impede. **fettered** *a.* **1** chained, bound. **2** hampered, impeded. **3** of or relating to the feet of animals, e.g. seals, when the feet stretch backwards so as to be unfit for walking. **fetterless** *a.* **fetterlock** *n.* **1** a shackle for a horse when turned out to grass. **2** (*Her.*) a figure of a shackle and padlock. **3** a fetlock. [OE *fetor* (cp. Dut. *veter*, race, G *Fesser*, from Gmc. *fet-*, rel. to *fōt-*, foot, also L *pedica*, Gr. *pedē*, fetter)]

fettle (fet´əl) *v.t.* **1** to clean, trim or put right. **2** to remove (the rough edge of a metal casting etc.). **3** to line (a furnace). *~v.i.* to fuss about, to be busy. *~n.* condition, order, trim. **in fine fettle** in good condition or health. **in good fettle** in fine fettle. **fettler** *n.* **1** (*Austral.*) a person whose job is to maintain railway tracks. **2** a person who fettles. [perh. from OE *fetel*, a girdle, belt]

fettuccine (fetuchē´ni), **fettucini** *n.* tagliatelle. [It., pl. of *fettuccina*, dim. of *fettuccia*, a small slice]

fetus FOETUS.

feu (fū) *n.* **1** (*Sc. Law*) a perpetual lease at a fixed rent. **2** (*Hist.*) tenure on condition of the performance of certain services or certain returns in money or kind. **3** the land, houses or other real estate so held. *~v.t.* (*3rd pers. sing. pres.* **feus,** *pres.p.* **feuing,** *past, p.p.* **feued**) (*Sc. Law*) to give or take in feu. **feuar** (-ə) *n.* a person who holds real estate on feu. **feu duty** *n.* the annual rent for such a holding. [var. of FEE]

feud[1] (fūd) *n.* **1** hostility between two tribes or families in revenge for an injury, often carried on for several generations. **2** a long and bitter dispute or quarrel. **3** enmity, quarrel, contention, animosity. *~v.i.* to carry on a feud. **feudist** *n.* (*N Am.*) a person who is carrying on a feud. [ME *fede*, OF *faide*, OHG *fēhida*, cogn. with OE *fæhth*, enmity]

feud[2] (fūd) *n.* **1** land held on condition of performing certain services; a fief. **2** the right to such land. **feudal** *a.* **1** according to or resembling the feudal system. **2** of, relating to, consisting of or founded upon a feud or fief. 3 old-fashioned. **feudality** (-dal´-) *n.* (*pl.* **feudalities**) 1 feudal principles; the feudal system. 2 the quality or state of being feudal. 3 a fief, a feudal holding. **feudalize, feudalise** *v.t.* to reduce to feudal tenure. **feudalization** (-zā´shən) *n.* **feudally** *adv.* **feudal system** *n.* the social system in Europe during the Middle Ages, by which the ownership of land was vested in the lord, with possession or tenancy being granted to the vassal in return for military service. **feudalism** *n.* the feudal system. **feudalist** *n.* 1 a supporter of feudalism. 2 a person familiar with feudal law. **feudalistic** (-lis´-) *a.* **feudary** *a.* of, relating to or held by feudal tenure. ~*n.* (*pl.* **feudaries**) a feudatory. **feudatory** *a.* 1 holding or held by feudal tenure. 2 subject to overlordship. ~*n.* (*pl.* **feudatories**) 1 a person who holds lands of another by feudal tenure; a vassal. 2 a fief, a dependent lordship. [med. L *feudum*, see FEE]

feu de joie (fœ də zhwah´) *n.* (*pl.* **feux de joie** (fœ də zhwah´)) the firing of guns in token of public rejoicing. [F, fire of joy]

feuilleton (fœy´tõ) *n.* 1 that part of a newspaper which is devoted to light literature, criticism or fiction. 2 an article or a serial story in this part of a newspaper. [F, from *feuillet*, dim. of *feuille*, L *folia*, pl. of *folium*, leaf]

feuter FEWTER.

feux de joie FEU DE JOIE.

fever (fē´və) *n.* 1 an abnormally high body temperature and quickened pulse, often accompanied by delirium. 2 any one of a group of diseases, e.g. scarlet fever or yellow fever, characterized by this. 3 a state of nervous excitement; agitation. ~*v.t.* to affect with or put into a fever. ~*v.i.* to become feverish. **fevered** *a.* **fever heat** *n.* the abnormally high temperature of the body characteristic of fever. **feverish** *a.* 1 suffering from or affected with fever. 2 indicating fever; resembling a fever. 3 infested with fever. 4 excited, restless, hectic. **feverishly** *adv.* **feverishness** *n.* **feverous** *a.* 1 infested with fever. 2 causing a fever. 3 †feverish. **fever pitch** *n.* a state of extreme excitement or activity. **fever tree** *n.* 1 a tree that produces a febrifuge, esp. *Pickneya pubens* of the south-east USA. 2 a tall flowered swamp tree of southern Africa, *Acacia xanthophloea*. [OE *fēfor*, L *febris*]

feverfew (fē´vəfū) *n.* a bushy strong-scented plant, *Tanacetum parthenium*. [corr. of OE *fēferfuge*, L *febrifuga* (*febris*, *fugāre*, to put to flight)]

few (fū) *a.* 1 not many. 2 small, limited or restricted in number. ~*pron.* a small number (of). **a few** a small number (of). **a good few** (*coll.*) a considerable number (of). **every few** once in every series of a few (days, hours etc.). **few and far between** rare, occurring very infrequently. **no fewer than** as many as (a surprisingly large number). **not a few** a considerable number. **of few words** reserved, habitually saying little (*a woman of few words*). **some few** not a great number. **the Few** the fighter pilots of the Royal Air Force who flew in the Battle of Britain in 1940. **the few** 1 the minority. 2 the elect. **to have a few** to consume several alcoholic drinks. **fewness** *n.* [OE *fēa*, *fēawe* (cp. OHG *fao*, L *paucus*, Gr. *pauros*)]

Usage note See note on *fewer* under LESS.

fewter (fū´tə), **feuter** *n.* a rest for the lance attached to the saddle (orig. lined with felt). [OF *feutre*, med. L *filtrum*, cogn. with FELT[2], see FILTER]

fey (fā) *a.* 1 eccentric, odd in a whimsical, other-worldly way. 2 (*chiefly Sc.*) in unnaturally high spirits. 3 (*chiefly Sc.*) fated, doomed, on the verge of death (implying both the nearness of this event and the impossibility of avoiding it). 4 (*chiefly Sc.*) clairvoyant, psychic. **feyly** *adv.* **feyness** *n.* [OE *fǣge* (cp. Icel. *feigr*, Dut. *veeg*, about to die, G *feige*, cowardly)]

Feynman diagram (fīn´mən) *n.* a graphical representation of the interactions between subatomic particles. [Richard *Feynman*, 1918–88, US physicist]

fez (fez) *n.* (*pl.* **fezzes**) a flat-topped conical usu. red cap without a brim, fitting close to the head, with a tassel of silk, wool etc., worn by men in the Middle East. [F, prob. from *Fez*, a city in Morocco, where they were orig. manufactured]

ff *abbr.* 1 folios. 2 (and those e.g. pages) following. 3 fortissimo.

Fg. Off. *abbr.* Flying Officer.

fiacre (fiah´krə) *n.* a small four-wheeled horse-drawn carriage. [F, named after the Hôtel de St *Fiacre*, Paris, where such vehicles were first hired out]

fiancé (fiā´sā, -on´-) *n.* the man to whom a woman is engaged to be married. **fiancée** *n.* the woman to whom a man is engaged to be married. [F, p.p. of *fiancer*, to betroth]

fianchetto (fiənchet´ō, -ket´-) *n.* (*pl.* **fianchettoes**) in chess, the development of a bishop to a long diagonal of the board. ~*v.t.* (*3rd pers. sing. pres.* **fianchettoes**, *pres.p.* **fianchettoing**, *past*, *p.p.* **fianchettoed**) to develop (a bishop) in this way. [It., dim. of *fianco*, flank]

Fianna Fáil (fiana foil´) *n.* one of the major political parties in the Republic of Ireland. [Ir. *fianna*, a band of warriors, and *Fáil*, gen. of *Fál*, ancient poetic name for Ireland]

fiar (fē´ə) *n.* (*Sc. Law*) a person who has the fee simple or reversion of property. [perh. from FEE, -ER[1]]

fiasco (fias´kō) *n.* (*pl.* **fiascos**) a complete and humiliating failure; a ridiculous breakdown; an ignominious result; a debacle. [It., a flask, a bottle (sense obscure)]

fiat (fī´ət, -at) *n.* 1 an order, command, decree, esp. an arbitrary one. 2 (*Law*) the order or warrant of a judge or other constituted authority sanctioning or allowing certain processes; an authorization. **fiat money** *n.* (*N Am.*) paper currency made legal tender by a Government order, but not convertible into coins. [L, let it be done]

fib (fib) *n.* a harmless or venial lie; a white lie. ~*v.i.* (*pres.p.* **fibbing**, *past*, *p.p.* **fibbed**) to tell a fib. **fibber, fibster** *n.* a person who tells fibs. [perh. from FABLE or obs. redupl. *fible-fable*, nonsense]

fiber FIBRE.

Fibonacci series (fēbanah´chi), **Fibonacci sequence** *n.* a series of numbers, e.g. 1, 1, 2, 3, 5, in which each number is the sum of the preceding two numbers. **Fibonacci number** *n.* a number in the Fibonacci series. [Leonardo *Fibonacci*, *c.* 1170–*c.* 1250, Italian mathematician]

fibr- FIBRO-.

fibre (fī´bə), (*N Am.*) **fiber** *n.* 1 a slender filament; a thread, string or filament, of which the tissues of animals and plants are made. 2 the substances composed of animal or vegetable tissue forming the raw material in textile manufacture. 3 a structure composed of filaments. 4 a piece of glass in the form of a filament. 5 DIETARY FIBRE (under DIET[1]). 6 essence, nature, material, character, nerve, strength (*moral fibre*). **fibreboard** *n.* a building material made of compressed wood or plant fibres. **fibred,** (*N Am.*) **fibered** *a.* composed of or having fibres (*esp. in comb.*, as *finely-fibred*). **fibrefill** *n.* a synthetic material used as a filling for pillows, cushions etc. **fibreglass** *n.* 1 very fine filaments of molten glass worked into a synthetic fibre. 2 a plastic reinforced by glass fibres. **fibreless** *a.* **fibre optics** *n.* 1 (*as sing.*) a technology based on the transmission of light along bundles of very thin glass or plastic fibres, used esp. in telecommunications and exploratory medicine. 2 (*as pl.*) the fibres used in this technology. **fibrescope** *n.* a flexible instrument using fibre optics which enables the operator to see into otherwise inaccessible areas. **fibriform** (-brifawm) *a.* **fibrous** *a.* consisting of, containing or resembling fibres. **fibrously** *adv.* **fibrousness** *n.* [F, from L *fibra*]

fibril (fīˊbril), **fibrilla** (-brilˊə) *n.* (*pl.* **fibrils, fibrillae** (-lē)) **1** a little fibre. **2** (*Bot.*) any one of the minute subdivisions in which a branching root terminates. **3** a minute subdivision of a fibre in a nerve, muscle etc. **fibrillar** *a.* **fibrillary** *a.* **fibrilliform** (-brilˊifawm) *a.* **fibrillose** *a.* [dim. of L *fibra*, as FIBRE]

fibrillate[1] (fīˊbrilāt, fibˊ-) *v.i.* **1** (of a fibre) to split into fibrils. **2** (of the muscle fibres in the heart) to undergo irregular contractions. ~*v.t.* to split (a fibre) into fibrils. **fibrillation** (-āˊshən) *n.*

fibrillate[2] (fīˊbrilət) *a.* of or relating to fibrils or a fibrous structure.

fibrin (fīˊbrin, fibˊ-) *n.* a protein contained in the blood, causing it to clot. **fibrino-** *comb. form* **fibrinogen** (-brinˊəjən) *n.* a protein entering into the formation of fibrin and into coagulation. **fibrinolysin** (-olˊisin) *n.* an enzyme that promotes the breakdown of blood clots. **fibrinous** *a.* composed of or of the nature of fibrin. [as FIBRE, -IN[1]]

fibro (fīˊbrō) *n.* (*pl.* **fibros**) (*Austral.*) **1** a cement mixed with asbestos fibre, used in sheets for building. **2** a house built mainly of this. [use of FIBRO-]

fibro- (fīˊbrō), **fibr-** *comb. form* denoting a substance consisting of or characterized by fibres. [FIBRE]

fibroblast (fīˊbrōblahst) *n.* a cell that contributes to the formation of connective tissue fibres.

fibroid (fīˊbroid) *a.* of the nature or form of fibre or fibrous tissue. ~*n.* a benign tumour.

fibroin (fīˊbrōin) *n.* the protein that is the chief constituent of silk, cobwebs, the horny skeleton of sponges etc.

fibroline (fīˊbrəlēn) *n.* a yarn spun from waste in hemp, flax and jute, used for backing carpets, rugs etc.

fibroma (fībrōˊmə) *n.* (*pl.* **fibromas, fibromata** (-mətə)) a benign fibrous tumour.

fibrosis (fībrōˊsis), **fibrositis** (-sīˊtis) *n.* muscular rheumatism. **fibrositic** (-sitˊik) *a.* **fibrotic** (-brotˊik) *a.* [mod. L, as FIBRE]

fibrous FIBRE.

fibula (fibˊūlə) *n.* (*pl.* **fibulae** (-lē), **fibulas**) **1** the outer and smaller bone of the leg. **2** a clasp, buckle or brooch. **fibular** *a.* [L, a brooch, from *fivere*, var. of *figere*, to fix]

-fic (fik) *suf.* forming adjectives from nouns, verbs etc., as *honorific, horrific, malefic*. **-fically** *suf.* [L *-ficus*, from weakened root of *facere*, to make]

-fication (fikāˊshən) *suf.* forming nouns from verbs in -FY, as *purification*. [L *-ficātio -ōnem*, from *-ficāre*, see -FY]

fiche (fēsh) *n.* (*pl.* **fiche, fiches**) a microfiche. [F *fiche*, a sheet of paper]

fichu (fēˊshoo) *n.* a light shawl or scarf worn by women over the neck and shoulders. [F, from *ficher*, to fix, to put on]

fickle (fikˊəl) *a.* changeable, inconstant. **fickleness** *n.* **fickly** *adv.* [OE *ficol*, rel. to *befician*, to deceive]

†**fico** (fēˊkō), **figo** (fēˊgō) *n.* (*pl.* **ficoes, figoes**) **1** a fig; a worthless thing. **2** a gesture of contempt shown by putting the thumb between the second and third fingers. [It., from L *ficus*, FIG[1]]

fictile (fikˊtīl) *a.* **1** capable of being moulded; moulded by art. **2** made of earth or clay. **3** manufactured by or suitable for the potter; of or relating to pottery. [L *fictilis*, from *fingere*, to fashion]

fiction (fikˊshən) *n.* **1** an invented statement or narrative; a story, a romance. **2** literature, esp. in prose, describing imaginary people and events. **3** a falsehood. **4** the act or art of feigning or inventing. **5** that which is feigned, imagined or invented. **6** any point or thing assumed for the purposes of justice or convenience (*legal fiction*). **fictional** *a.* **fictionality** (-nalˊ-) *n.* **fictionalize, fictionalise** *v.t.* to introduce fictional elements into (a narrative of real events). **fictionalization** (-zāˊshən) *n.* **fictionally** *adv.* **fictionist** *n.* a writer of fiction; a novelist. **fictitious** (-tishˊəs) *a.* **1** feigned, imaginary, counterfeit, false, assumed. **2** of or relating to novels. **3** having no real existence. **4** accepted by a conventional or legal fiction. **fictitiously** *adv.* **fictitiousness** *n.* **fictive** *a.* **1** imaginative, creative. **2** imaginary, fictitious, feigned, counterfeit. [F, from L *fictio -ōnem*, from *fingere*, to fashion]

Usage note See note on *fictitious* under FACTITIOUS.

ficus (fēˊkəs, fīˊ-) *n.* any plant of the genus *Ficus*, including the fig tree and the rubber plant. [L, fig]

fid (fid) *n.* **1** (*Naut.*) a bar of wood or iron to support a topmast. **2** (*Naut.*) a pointed wooden pin used to open the strands of a rope in splicing. **3** a small piece or wedge of an object. [etym. uncertain]

-fid (fid) *comb. form* divided into parts. [L *-fidus*, from *findere*, to split]

Fid. Def. *abbr.* Defender of the Faith. [L *Fidei defensor*]

fiddle (fidˊəl) *n.* **1** (*coll.*) a violin or stringed instrument with a bow. **2** (*coll.*) a swindle, a dishonest practice. **3** (*coll.*) an awkward or tricky operation. **4** (*Naut.*) a frame of bars and strings, to keep things from rolling off the cabin table in bad weather. ~*v.i.* **1** to make restless movements with the hands or fingers. **2** to move aimlessly; to waste time in aimless activity. **3** to play on a fiddle. **4** to tinker (with), to fuss (with), to tamper (with). ~*v.t.* **1** (*coll.*) to falsify (accounts etc.). **2** (*coll.*) to contrive to do or obtain (something) by underhand means. **3** to play (e.g. a tune) on a fiddle. **fit as a fiddle** in good condition, ready for anything. **on the fiddle** (*coll.*) cheating, being dishonest, falsifying accounts etc. for one's own advantage. **to fiddle about 1** to tinker, to fuss (with). **2** to interfere or tamper (with). **to fiddle around** to fiddle about (with). **to play first fiddle** to take a leading part. **to play second fiddle** to take a subordinate part. **fiddle-back** *n.* **1** a fiddle-shaped back of a chair. **2** a chasuble with a fiddle-shaped front. **fiddle block** *n.* (*Naut.*) a block with two sheaves. **fiddle-de-dee** (-didēˊ) *n., int.* nonsense. **fiddle-faddle** (-fadəl) *n.* trifling talk; nonsense. ~*int.* nonsense. ~*a.* **1** trifling. **2** making a fuss about trifles. ~*v.i.* **1** to trifle. **2** to make a fuss about trifles. **fiddle-faddler** *n.* **fiddle-head** *n.* an ornamental scroll-like carving at the bows of a ship. **fiddle pattern** *n.* a fiddle-shaped pattern for the heads of spoons and forks. **fiddler** *n.* **1** a person who plays the fiddle. **2** (*coll.*) a cheat or swindler. **3** a person who makes a fuss about trifles. **4** a small crab of the genus *Uca* having one large claw and one very small one. **fiddlestick** *n.* **1** a violin bow. **2** (*pl.*) rubbish, something absurd. ~*int.* (*pl.*) nonsense; rubbish. **fiddlewood** *n.* any one of several tropical American trees of the genus *Citharexylum* yielding hard wood. **fiddling** *a.* **1** trifling, fussy. **2** petty, contemptible. **3** fiddly. **fiddly** *a.* (*comp.* **fiddlier**, *superl.* **fiddliest**) **1** tricky, awkward. **2** small, difficult to manipulate. **3** fiddling. [OE *fithele*, etym. uncertain (cp. Dut. *vedel*, G *Fiedel*)]

fiddley (fidˊli) *n.* (*Naut.*) **1** the iron framework enclosing the deckhatch leading to the stokehole of a steamer. **2** the space below this. [etym. unknown]

fideicommissum (fidiīkəmisˊəm) *n.* (*pl.* **fideicommissa**) **1** a testator's bequest to trustees. **2** a trust or trust estate. **fideicommissary** (-komˊisəri) *n.* (*pl.* **fideicommissaries**) a beneficiary by such a bequest or trust. **fideicommissor** *n.* a person who creates a fideicommissum. [L, neut. p.p. of *fideicommittere* (*fidei*, dat. of *fidēs*, faith, *committere*, to entrust, COMMIT)]

Fidei Defensor (fidiī difenˊsaw) *n.* Defender of the Faith. [L]

fideism (fī´diizm) *n.* the religious doctrine that knowledge can be attained only by faith not by reason. **fideist** *n.* **fideistic** (fidiis´tik) *a.* [L *fides*, faith, and -ISM]

fidelity (fidel´iti) *n.* **1** careful and loyal observance of duty; faithful adherence to an agreement, a set of beliefs etc. **2** loyalty, faithfulness, esp. to one's husband or wife. **3** honesty, veracity, reliability. **4** accurate correspondence (of a copy, description, picture etc.) to the original. **5** exactness in sound reproduction (*high fidelity*). **fidelity insurance** *n.* insurance taken out by an employer to cover losses arising from an employee's dishonesty etc. [F *fidélité*, L *fidēlitās -tātem*, from *fidēlis*, from *fidēs*, faith]

fidget (fij´it) *v.i.* (*pres.p.* **fidgeting,** *past, p.p.* **fidgeted**) **1** to move about restlessly. **2** to worry, to be uneasy. ~*v.t.* to worry or make (others) uncomfortable. ~*n.* **1** a state of nervous restlessness. **2** a person who fidgets. **3** a person who worries or makes others uncomfortable. **4** (*pl.*) restless movements. **fidgety** *a.* **fidgetiness** *n.* [from dial. *fidge*, to twitch]

Fido (fī´dō) *n.* an apparatus that allows aircraft to land by dispersing fog, using petrol burners positioned on the ground. [acronym for *F*og *I*ntensive *D*ispersal *O*peration]

fiducial (fidū´shəl) *a.* **1** denoting a fixed point or line used as a basis for measurement or comparison. **2** confident, sure, firm. **3** of the nature of a trust. **fiducially** *adv.* **fiduciary** *a.* **1** of or relating to a trust, trustee or trusteeship. **2** held or given in trust. **3** depending on public confidence for its value. ~*n.* (*pl.* **fiduciaries**) a trustee. [L *fidūciālis*, from *fidūcia*, trust, from *fidēre*, to trust, *fidēs*, faith]

fidus Achates (fīdəs əkā´tēz) *n.* a trusty friend, a faithful companion. [L, the faithful Achates, the devoted follower of Aeneas in Virgil's *Aeneid*]

fie (fī) *int.* used to express contempt, irony, disgust, shame or impatience. [ME and OF *fi*, L *fī*]

fief (fēf) *n.* **1** an estate held under the feudal system or in fee. **2** feudal tenure. **3** a person's realm of operations. **fiefdom** *n.* a fief. [OF, from L *fevum*, see FEE]

field (fēld) *n.* **1** a piece of land, esp. one enclosed for crops or pasture. **2** a region that is rich in some natural product (such as an *oilfield* or *coalfield*). **3** the area of grass on which cricket, football or other games are played. **4** in cricket, the fielders collectively, especially with respect to their positions. **5** all the competitors in a race, or all except the favourite. **6** all the entrants, candidates etc. in a contest. **7** the open country. **8** a wide expanse, e.g. of sea or sky. **9** the place where a battle is fought. **10** the battle itself. **11** the scene of military operations. **12** the participants in a hunt. **13** a sphere of activity or knowledge; an interest or speciality. **14** the sphere of practical operations away from the office, laboratory etc. (*a field naturalist*). **15** the surface on which the figures in a picture are drawn. **16** a field of force; the force exerted in such an area. **17** the range of view or perception. **18** (*Comput.*) a set of characters comprising a unit of information as part of a record. **19** (*Her.*) the surface of a shield or one of its divisions. **20** (*Math.*) a set of mathematical elements subject to two binary operations, addition and multiplication, such that the set is a commutative group under addition and also under multiplication if zero is excluded. **21** each of two or more sets of scanning lines forming a television picture. ~*v.t.* **1** in cricket etc., to catch or stop (the ball) and return it. **2** to assemble (a team, an army) ready for action. **3** to deal with (questions etc.), esp. off the cuff. **4** to retrieve (something or someone liable to go astray). ~*v.i.* **1** to act as a fielder in cricket and other games. **2** to back the field against the favourite in a race etc. **in the field 1** working away from the office, laboratory etc. **2** campaigning. **to hold the field 1** to maintain one's ground against all comers. **2** to surpass all competitors. **to keep the field** to continue a campaign. **to play the field** to diversify one's interests or activities, esp. not to commit oneself to a steady boyfriend or girlfriend. **to take the field 1** to commence active military operations. **2** to begin a campaign. **3** to go on to the field of play. **field allowance** *n.* an extra payment to officers on a campaign to meet the increased cost of living etc. **field artillery** *n.* light ordnance suitable for use in the field. **field bed** *n.* **1** a folding bed; a camp bed. **2** †a bed in the open air. **field-book** *n.* a book used by surveyors, engineers etc., in which the memoranda of surveys taken in the field are set down. **field-cornet** *n.* (*Hist.*) a minor S African magistrate. **field day** *n.* **1** a day of unusual importance, excitement or display. **2** a day on which troops are exercised in manoeuvres, esp. in front of an audience. **3** a day spent working in the natural environment, away from the laboratory, office etc. **to have a field day** to take gleeful advantage of. **field dressing** *n.* medical appliances for use on the battlefield. **field-effect transistor** *n.* a semiconductor unipolar device in which the electric current flows through a narrow channel between two electrodes from one region to another. **fielder** *n.* a player who fields at cricket etc. **field events** *n.pl.* athletic events other than racing, e.g. discus-throwing and jumping etc. **field glasses** *n.pl.* binoculars. **field goal** *n.* **1** in American football, a score made by kicking the ball over the crossbar from ordinary play. **2** in basketball, a score made while the ball is in play. **field gun** *n.* a light artillery piece for service in the field. **field hockey** *n.* (*N Am.*) hockey played on grass. **field hospital** *n.* an ambulance or temporary hospital near a battlefield. **field ice** *n.* ice formed in the polar regions in fields or floes, as distinct from icebergs. **field marshal** *n.* an officer of the highest rank in the British army. **field meeting** *n.* a secret open-air meeting for worship or preaching, a conventicle. **field mouse** *n.* any of several species of mice of the genus *Apodemus* living in fields etc. **field mushroom** *n.* the common edible mushroom, *Agaricus campestrus.* **field mustard** *n.* charlock. **field notes** *n.pl.* notes made on the spot during fieldwork. **field officer** *n.* (*Mil.*) an officer above the rank of captain, but below that of general (such as a major, a colonel etc.). **field of force** *n.* (*Physics*) the space within which a certain force is present, e.g. a magnetic field. **field of honour** *n.* the scene of a battle or duel. **field of view** *n.* **1** the space visible in an optical instrument at one view. **2** the area in front of the eyes that can be seen without moving the eyes. **field of vision** *n.* field of view. **field-piece** *n.* a light artillery piece for use in a battle. **field preacher** *n.* a person who preaches at religious meetings in the open air. **field rank** *n.* any army rank above that of captain but below that of general. **fieldsman** *n.* (*pl.* **fieldsmen**) a fielder. **field sport** *n.* an outdoor sport, such as hunting, shooting or coursing. **fieldstone** *n.* natural stone used in building. **field strength** *n.* the power of an electric (magnetic) field at some precise point. **field telegraph** *n.* a movable telegraph system for use on campaign, manoeuvres etc. **field train** *n.* a department of the Royal Artillery for the supply of ammunition to the army at the front. **field trial** *n.* (*often pl.*) a test on a new invention, design etc. carried out under actual operating conditions. **field trip** *n.* a visit undertaken by schoolchildren or students to study phenomena or collect information in situ. **fieldwards** *adv.* **field winding** *n.* a coil of wire wound on iron in order to make a strong electromagnetic field when the current is passing. **fieldwork** *n.* **1** observations or operations carried out in situ by students, researchers, anthropologists, surveyors etc. **2** (*pl.*) temporary fortifications thrown up by besiegers or besieged. **fieldworker** *n.* [OE *feld* (cp. Dut. *veld*, G *Feld*)]

fieldfare (fēld´feə) *n.* a species of thrush, *Turdus pilaris*, a winter visitant in England. [OE *feldefare*; prob. field-goer]

fiend (fēnd) *n.* **1** a demon, a devil, an evil spirit. **2** a person of extreme wickedness or cruelty. **3** (*coll.*) an addict (*a fresh-air fiend*). **4** something disagreeable. **the fiend** Satan. **fiendish** *a.* **1** wicked, cruel or unpleasant. **2** very difficult; challenging. **fiendishly** *adv.* **fiendishness** *n.* **fiendlike** *a.* [OE *fēond*, from *fēogan*, to hate (cp. G *Feind*)]

fierce (fiəs) *a.* (*comp.* **fiercer,** *superl.* **fiercest**) **1** savage, furiously hostile or aggressive; raging, violent. **2** vehement, ardent, eager, impetuous. **3** intense or strong in an unpleasant way. **4** (of a machine) not operating smoothly. **fiercely** *adv.* **fierceness** *n.* [OF *fers, fiers*, nom. of *fer, fier*, L *ferus*, wild]

fieri facias (fī´ərī fā´shias) *n.* (*Law*) a writ to the sheriff to order a levy on the goods and chattels of the defendant in order to pay a sum or debt. [L, cause it to be done]

fiery (fī´ri) *a.* (*comp.* **fierier,** *superl.* **fieriest**) **1** consisting of fire, on fire, flaming with fire. **2** hot, like fire; producing a burning sensation. **3** glowing or red, like fire. **4** (of skin or a sore) inflamed. **5** (of a mine etc.) highly inflammable, liable to explosions. **6** (of curry etc.) hot-tasting. **7** vehement, ardent, eager; passionate, hot-tempered, irascible. **8** pugnacious, mettlesome, untamed. **9** (of a cricket pitch) making the ball rise dangerously high. **fierily** *adv.* **fieriness** *n.* **fiery cross** *n.* **1** a wooden cross, the ends of which had been set on fire, formerly sent round the Scottish Highlands to summon a clan to war. **2** a flaming cross used as a symbol by the Ku Klux Klan. **fiery-red** *a.* red as fire.

fiesta (fies´tə) *n.* **1** a holiday or festivity. **2** (esp. in Spain and Latin America) a religious holiday or festival esp. on a saint's day. [Sp.]

FIFA (fē´fə) *abbr.* International Football Federation. [F, *F*édération *I*nternationale de *F*ootball *A*ssociation]

fi. fa. *abbr.* fieri facias.

fife (fīf) *n.* **1** a small flutelike pipe, chiefly used in military music. **2** a player of this instrument. *~v.i.* to play upon a fife. *~v.t.* to play (tunes) on the fife. **fife-major** *n.* a non-commissioned officer who formerly superintended the fifers of a regiment. **fifer** *n.* **fife-rail** *n.* (*Naut.*) a rail on the quarter-deck and poop or around the mast of a vessel (perhaps so called because a fifer sat on this whilst the anchor was being weighed). [either from F *fifre* or through G *Pfeife*, pipe, from OHG *pfīfa*, a PIPE, from *pfīfan*, to PIPE]

fifish (fī´fish) *a.* disturbed in one's mind, cranky. [*Fife*, Scotland]

fifteen (fif´tēn, -tēn´) *n.* **1** the number or figure 15 or XV. **2** the age of 15. **3** a team of 15 players, esp. in rugby football. **4** a set of 15 things. **5** a size measuring 15. **6** (of films) classified as suitable to be watched by people of 15 years and over. *~a.* **1** 15 in number. **2** aged 15. **the Fifteen** the Jacobite rising of 1715. **fifteenth** *n.* **1** any one of 15 equal parts. **2** (*Mus.*) the interval of a double octave. **3** an organ stop sounding two octaves above the open diapason. *~a., n.* **1** (the) last of 15 (people, things etc.). **2** (the) next after the 14th. [OE *fīftȳne*]

fifth (fifth) *n.* **1** any one of five equal parts. **2** (*Mus.*) **a** a diatonic interval of five notes, equal to three tones and a semitone. **b** the resulting concord. **c** two notes separated by this interval sounded together. **3** (*N Am., coll.*) **a** a fifth part of a US gallon of liquor or spirits (about 750 ml). **b** a bottle containing this. *~a., n.* **1** (the) last of five (people, things etc.). **2** (the) next after the fourth. **to take the fifth 1** to exercise the right guaranteed under the Fifth Amendment. **2** (*N Am., coll.*) to avoid answering a question so as not to get oneself into trouble. **Fifth Amendment** *n.* the amendment to the US Constitution allowing defendants the right to refuse to testify against themselves and prohibiting a second trial for an offence of which a person has been acquitted. **fifth column** *n.* a group of people in a country who, whether as individuals or as members of an organization, are ready to give help to an enemy (from the reference of General Mola who, in the Spanish Civil War in 1936 said that he had four columns encircling Madrid and a fifth column in the city, being sympathizers ready to assist the attacking party). **fifth columnist** *n.* **fifth-generation** *a.* of or relating to a type of computer that uses artificial intelligence. **fifthly** *adv.* in the fifth place. **Fifth Monarchy** *n.* the last of the five great empires referred to in Daniel ii.44, identified with the millennial reign of Christ prophesied in the Apocalypse. **Fifth-monarchy man** *n.* (*Hist.*) a member of a sect of enthusiasts in the time of Cromwell, who declared themselves 'subjects only of King Jesus', and believed that a fifth universal monarchy (after those of Assyria, Persia, Greece and Rome) would be established shortly on earth under the personal reign of Christ, and that no other government ought to rule until Christ's second coming. **fifth wheel** *n.* **1** (*chiefly N Am.*) a spare wheel. **2** a superfluous person or thing. **3** a horizontal steering bearing placed above the front axle of a carriage enabling it to turn freely. [OE *fīfta* (cp. G *fünfte*, Gr. *pemptos*, L *quinctus*)]

fifty (fif´ti) *n.* (*pl.* **fifties**) **1** the number or figure 50 or L. **2** the age of 50. *~a.* **1** 50 in number. **2** aged 50. **fifties** *n.pl.* **1** the period of time between one's 50th and 60th birthdays. **2** the range of temperatures between 50 and 60 degrees. **3** the period of time between the 50th and 60th years of a century. **fiftieth** (-tiəth) *n.* any one of 50 equal parts. *~n., a.* **1** (the) last of 50 (people, things etc.). **2** (the) next after the 49th. **fifty-fifty** *adv.* in equal shares, half each. *~a.* **1** with equal shares, equal. **2** equally likely to happen or not to happen. **fifty-first, fifty-second etc.** *n., a.* the ordinal numbers corresponding to fifty-one etc. **fiftyfold** (-fōld) *a., adv.* **fifty-one, fifty-two etc.** *n., a.* the cardinal numbers between 50 and 60. [OE *fīftig* (cp. G *fünfzig*)]

fig[1] (fig) *n.* **1** the pear-shaped fleshy fruit of the genus *Ficus*, esp. *F. carica*. **2** the tree bearing this, noted for its broad leaves. **3** other trees bearing similar fruit; the fruit of these. **4** anything valueless, a trifle. **5** a spongy excrescence on a horse's frog, consequent on a bruise. **6** †a gesture of contempt shown by putting the thumb between the second and third fingers. *~†v.t.* (*pres.p.* **figging,** *past, p.p.* **figged**) to insult with ficoes or contemptuous snapping motions of the fingers. **not to care a fig** not to care at all. **fig leaf** *n.* **1** the leaf of a fig tree. **2** a flimsy covering to hide something (from Gen. iii.7 and the use made of the fig leaf in statues to cover genitals). **fig tree** *n.* **1** *Ficus carica*, a tropical tree or shrub which produces the edible fig. **2** any other tree bearing similar fruit. **figwort** *n.* **1** any plant of the genus *Scrophularia*, esp. *S. aquatica* and *S. nodosa* (from their being popular remedies for piles). **2** the pilewort, *Ranunculus ficaria*. [F *figue*, L *ficus*]

fig[2] (fig) *v.t.* (*pres.p.* **figging,** *past, p.p.* **figged**) to dress, deck, rig (up or out). *~n.* dress, array, outfit, equipment. **in full fig** in full dress. **in good fig** in good form or condition. **to fig out** to make (a horse) lively. **to fig up** to fig out. **figgery** *n.* elaborate ornament. [var. of FEAGUE]

fig. *abbr.* **1** figure. **2** figurative(ly).

fight (fīt) *v.i.* (*past, p.p.* **fought** (fawt)) **1** to contend in arms or in battle, or in single combat (with, against). **2** to strive for victory or superiority, to war. **3** to strive in a determined way to achieve something. **4** to oppose, to offer resistance. **5** (*chiefly N Am.*) to quarrel, to disagree. *~v.t.* **1** to contend with, to struggle against (*to fight* poverty). 2 to engage in, to carry on or wage (a contest, battle, lawsuit, campaign etc.). 3 to maintain by conflict. 4 to contend over. 5 to gain or win by conflict. 6 to manage, lead or manoeuvre in battle. 7 to take part in (a boxing match). 8 to set on or cause (dogs or cocks) to fight. ~*n.* 1 a struggle between individuals, armies or animals, to injure each other or obtain the mastery. 2 a battle, a combat. 3 a contest of any kind, contention. 4 a boxing match. 5 a determined effort to achieve something. 6 a quarrel, a row. 7 power of or inclination for fighting. **to fight back** 1 to resist. 2 to counter-attack. 3 to hold back (tears, an emotion) with an effort. **to fight down** to hold back or suppress. **to fight for** 1 to campaign or strive on behalf of. 2 to try with determination to gain or achieve. **to fight (it) out** to decide (a contest or wager) by fighting. **to fight off** to repel. **to fight shy of** to avoid from a feeling of mistrust, dislike or fear. **to fight to the finish** FINISH. **to fight with the gloves off** GLOVE. **to make a fight of it** to offer resistance. **to put up a fight** to offer resistance. **fightback** *n.* a counterattack; retaliation; recovery. **fighter** *n.* 1 a person or animal that fights. 2 a boxer. 3 a combative person, one who does not give in easily. 4 a fast military aircraft equipped to attack other aircraft. **fighter-bomber** *n.* a military aircraft designed to be both a fighter and a bomber. **fighting** *n.* **fighting chair** *n.* (*N Am.*) a chair mounted in a fixed position on a boat, used when catching a large fish. **fighting chance** *n.* a chance of success if every effort is made. **fighting-cock** *n.* a game cock. **to live like fighting-cocks** to get the best of food and drink. **fighting-fish** *n.* SIAMESE FIGHTING FISH (under SIAMESE). **fighting fit** *a.* in peak condition. **fighting fund** *n.* money raised to support a campaign by, e.g. workers on strike. **fighting-man** *n.* (*pl.* **fighting-men**). **fighting-top** *n.* one of the gun platforms on the mast of a sailing warship. **fighting words** *n.pl.* (*coll.*) words that show a readiness to engage in a fight. [OE *feohtan* (cp. Dut. *vechten*, OHG *fehtan*, G *fechten*)]

figment (fig´mənt) *n.* a fiction, an invented statement, something that exists only in the imagination, a fabrication, a fable. [L *figmentum* (*fig-*, base of *fingere*, to feign, -MENT)]

figuline (fig´ūlīn) *a.* 1 made of clay; earthenware. 2 fictile. ~*n.* an object made from clay; pottery. [L *figulīnus*, from *figulus*, a potter]

figura (figūə´rə) *n.* a person or thing that is representative or symbolic. [as FIGURE]

figure (fig´ə) *n.* 1 the external form or shape of a person or thing. 2 bodily shape, esp. from the point of view of its attractiveness. 3 an unidentified person seen in outline. 4 a personage, a character. 5 the mental impression that a person makes, appearance, distinction. 6 the representation of any form, as by carving, modelling, painting, drawing, embroidery, weaving or any other process. 7 a statue, an image, a likeness. 8 a combination of lines or surfaces enclosing a space, such as a triangle, sphere etc. 9 a diagram, an illustrative drawing, a pattern. 10 an emblem, a type, a simile. 11 a fancy, a creation of the imagination, an idea. 12 a symbol representing a number, esp. any one of the 10 Arabic numerals; a number expressed in this way. 13 a sum, an amount. 14 a value, a price (*a high figure*). 15 (*pl.*) arithmetical calculations. 16 the several steps or movements which a dancer makes in accord with the music. 17 a certain movement or division in a set dance. 18 in skating, a movement or combination of movements beginning and ending at a fixed point. 19 any way of speaking or writing in which words are deflected from their literal or ordinary sense, such as metaphor, ellipsis, hyperbole. 20 (*Gram.*) a recognized deviation from the ordinary form or construction. 21 (*Mus.*) a phrase, a short series of notes producing a single impression. 22 (*Logic*) the form of a syllogism with respect to the position of the middle term. 23 (*Astrol.*) a horoscope. ~*v.t.* 1 to form an image, likeness or representation of. 2 to represent, to picture, to imagine. 3 to symbolize, to typify. 4 to cover, adorn or ornament a pattern with figures. 5 to work out in figures, to calculate, to reckon. 6 to mark with numbers or prices. 7 to express by a metaphor or image. 8 (*Mus.*) to mark with figures indicating the harmony. 9 (*chiefly N Am.*) to believe, to consider, to conclude. ~*v.i.* 1 to appear, to be conspicuous. 2 to do arithmetical calculations. 3 (*coll.*) to seem rational, to accord with expectation; to be likely. 4 to make or cut a figure. **to cut a figure** CUT[1]. **to figure on** (*coll.*) to plan to; to base one's plans or calculations on; to bargain on. **to figure out** 1 to ascertain by computation, to work out; to estimate. 2 to understand, to fathom out. **to figure up** to add up, to reckon. **to keep one's figure** to remain slim and attractive. **to lose one's figure** to become rather fat. **to put a figure on** (*coll.*) to state the exact number or amount of. **figural** *a.* 1 represented by a figure or delineation. 2 relating to figures and shapes. 3 (*Mus.*) figurate. **figurant** (fig´ūərənt) *n.* a ballet dancer who merely appears as one of a group. **figurante** (fig´ūərənt) *n.* a female figurant. †**figurate** (-rət) *a.* 1 of a fixed and determinate form. 2 (*Mus.*) florid or decorative. **figuration** *n.* 1 the act of giving a certain determinate form to. 2 form, shape, conformation, outline. 3 a figurative representation. 4 ornamentation. 5 (*Mus.*) florid or figured counterpoint. **figurative** (fig´ərətiv, -ūə-) *a.* 1 representing something by a figure or type, typical. 2 emblematic, symbolic, metaphorical, not literal. 3 full of figures of speech. 4 flowery, ornate. 5 pictorial in representation. **figuratively** *adv.* **figurativeness** *n.* **-figure** *comb. form* (of a number) made up of a specified number of figures. **figured** *a.* 1 adorned with figures or devices; decorative or ornamental. 2 represented by figures, pictured. 3 (of wood) with variegated or ornamental grain. 4 shaped in a (certain) fashion. **-figured** *comb. form* having a certain or specified kind of figure. **figured bass** *n.* (*Mus.*) a bass having the accompanying chords indicated by numbers above or below the notes; continuo. **figure-dance** *n.* a dance or dancing with elaborate figures. **figure-dancer** *n.* **figure eight**, *n.* a shape or movement resembling the Arabic numeral eight (8). **figurehead** *n.* 1 a nominal leader or head without real authority. 2 the ornamental bust or full-length carving on the prow of a ship. **figureless** *a.* shapeless. **figure of eight** *n.* a shape or movement resembling the Arabic numeral eight (8). **figure of fun** *n.* a person considered as being ridiculous. **figure of speech** *n.* a figurative use of language. **figure skating** *n.* skating in prescribed patterns. **figure skater** *n.* **figure-weaving** *n.* the process of weaving figured fabrics. **figurine** (fig´ərēn, -ūə-) *n.* a statuette in clay or metal. †**figurist** *n.* a person who makes use of or interprets figures. [F, from L *figūra*, from *fig-*, stem of *fingere*, see FEIGN]

figwort FIG[1].

Fijian (fējē´ən) *n.* 1 a native or inhabitant of the Fiji islands. 2 the language of the Fijians. ~*a.* of or relating to Fiji, the Fijians or their language.

†**filaceous** (filā´shəs) *a.* consisting of threads. [L *filum*, a thread, -ACEOUS]

filagree FILIGREE.

filament (fil´əmənt) *n.* 1 a slender, threadlike process, a fibre or fibril, such as those of which animal and vegetable tissues are composed. 2 the thread of carbon or metal in an incandescent electric lamp. 3 the heater wire of a thermionic valve. 4 that part of the stamen which supports the anther. 5 †a hypothetical chain of air, light etc. particles. **filamentary** (-men´-) *a.* of the nature of or formed by a filament or filaments. **filamented** *a.* furnished with filaments. **filamentose**

(-men´-), **filamentous** (-men´-) *a.* **1** like a filament. **2** composed of filaments. **3** bearing filaments. [F, from late L *filāmentum*, from *filāre*, to spin, L *filum*, a thread]

filar (fī´lə) *a.* **1** of or relating to a thread. **2** furnished with threads. [L *filum*, a thread]

filaria (fileə´riə) *n.* (*pl.* **filariae** (-riē)) any of the genus of threadlike parasitic nematode worms producing live embryos which find their way into the bloodstream of the human host. **filarial** *a.* **filariasis** (fileəriā´sis, filərī´əsis) *n.* (*pl.* **filariases** (-riā´sez, -rī´əsēz)) a tropical disease caused by filarial infection, esp. in the lymph vessels. [L *filum*, a thread]

filature (fil´əchə) *n.* **1** the reeling of silk from cocoons. **2** the apparatus used for this. **3** an establishment for reeling silk. **4** floss silk. [F, from L *filāre*, to spin]

filbert (fil´bət) *n.* **1** the nut of the cultivated hazel, *Corylus maxima*. **2** the shrub bearing these nuts. **3** (*also* **filbert brush**) an oval brush used in oil painting. [F *noix de filbert*, from St *Philibert*, whose feast day is on 22 Aug. when they are ripe]

filch (filch) *v.t.* to steal, to pilfer. *~n.* **1** that which is filched. **2** a filcher. **3** the act of filching. **filcher** *n.* a petty thief, a pilferer. [etym. uncertain]

file[1] (fīl) *n.* **1** a box or folder, a string or wire, or similar devices in or on which documents are kept in order, for preservation and convenience of reference. **2** the set of papers kept in this way. **3** (*Comput.*) an organized collection of data with a unique name by means of which it can be accessed. **4** a set of periodicals arranged in order of publication. **5** a row of people or things arranged one behind the other from front to back. **6** a row of soldiers ranged in this way. **7** a collection of papers arranged in order of date or subject for ready reference, esp. in a court of law in connection with a case. **8** in chess, a line of squares extending from player to player. **9** †a roll, list or catalogue. **10** †a rank, series or class. *~v.t.* **1** to place in or on a file. **2** to arrange in order and endorse. **3** (*Law*) to place on the records of a court, to initiate (charges, a lawsuit) (*to file a petition for divorce*). **4** to send in (a story) to a newspaper. *~v.i.* **1** to walk in file or line. **2** to place in file. **3** to initiate a lawsuit. **in file** drawn up or marching in a line or lines of people one behind another. **on file** preserved and catalogued for reference. **rank and file** RANK[1]. **to file away 1** to preserve or catalogue in a file. **2** to make a mental note of. **3** to go off in a military file. **to file off** to go off in a military file. **file-leader** *n.* the soldier placed in front of a file. **filer**[1] *n.* **file server** *n.* (*Comput.*) a device that manages and controls access to stored files. **filing cabinet** *n.* a cabinet with drawers for storing files. [F *fil*, L *filum*, a thread]

file[2] (fīl) *n.* **1** a steel instrument with a ridged surface, used for cutting and smoothing metals, ivory, wood, fingernails etc. **2** anything used to polish or refine. *~v.t.* **1** to smooth or polish with a file. **2** to cut (the surface) away with a file. **3** to polish, to elaborate. **to file away** to remove (roughness etc.) from a surface by means of a file. **file-cutter** *n.* a maker of files. **filefish** *n.* (*pl. in general* **filefish,** *in particular* **filefishes**) **1** any fish of the family Balistidae with a toothed dorsal spine. **2** (*New Zeal.*) an edible, thick-skinned fish. **filer**[2] *n.* [OE *fēol* (cp. Dut. *vijl*, G *Feile*)]

filer[1] FILE[1].

filer[2] FILE[2].

filet (fī´lā, fil´it) *n.* **1** a kind of net or lace having a square mesh. **2** a fillet of meat. **filet mignon** (fē´lā mē´nyō) *n.* a small, very tender steak cut from the tail end of a fillet of beef. [F, thread]

filial (fil´iəl) *a.* **1** of or relating to a son or daughter. **2** befitting a child in relation to parents. **3** (*Biol.*) bearing the relation of a son or daughter. **filial generation** *n.* a generation following a parental generation. **filiality** (-al´-) *n.* **filially** *adv.* †**filiate** *v.t.* to affiliate. **filiation** (filiā´shən) *n.* **1** the relation of a child to its parents. **2** descent, transmission (from). **3** genealogical relation. **4** (*Law*) affiliation. **5** the development of offshoots. **6** a branch of something, e.g. a society. [late L *filiālis*, from *filius*, son, *filia*, daughter]

filibeg (fil´ibeg), **fillibeg, philabeg** (-əbeg) *n.* a kilt. [Sc., from Gael. *feileadh-beag* (*feileadh*, fold, *beag*, little)]

filibuster (fil´ibŭstə) *n.* **1** (*esp. N Am.*) a parliamentary obstructionist, a person who seeks to hinder legislation by prolonged speeches. **2** an instance of obstructing a political process in this way. **3** a lawless military adventurer, esp. one in quest of plunder, a freebooter, a buccaneer. **4** a person who takes part in an unauthorized military expedition into a foreign state. *~v.i.* to act as a filibuster. *~v.t.* to obstruct legislation in this way. **filibusterism** *n.* **filibusterous** *a.* [Sp., corr. from Dut. *vrijbuiter*, a freebooter (*vrij*, free, *buit*, booty)]

filiform (fil´ifawm, fī´-) *a.* **1** having the form of a thread. **2** long, slender, round and equally thick throughout. [L *filum*, a thread]

filigree (fil´igrē), **filagree** (-əgrē), †**filigrane** (-grān) *n.* **1** ornamental work, executed in fine gold or silver wire, plaited, and formed into delicate openwork or tracery. **2** any ornamental tracery or openwork. **3** anything delicate and fancy, showy and fragile. *~a.* **1** of or relating to filigree. **2** composed of or resembling filigree. **filigreed** *a.* ornamented with filigree. [F *filigrane*, It. *filigrana* (*filo*, L *filum*, a thread, *grano*, L *grānum*, GRAIN)]

filings (fī´lingz) *n.pl.* the fine particles cut or rubbed off with a file.

Filipino (filipē´nō) *n.* (*pl.* **Filipinos**) a native or inhabitant of the Philippine Islands. *~a.* of or relating to the Philippines or the Filipinos. [Sp., from *Felipe*, Philip II, of Spain]

fill (fil) *v.t.* **1** to put or pour into until all the space is occupied, to make full (with). **2** to occupy the whole capacity or space of, to pervade, to spread over or throughout. **3** to block up (a crack with putty, a hollow tooth with stopping etc.). **4** to appoint a person to discharge the duties of. **5** to hold. **6** to discharge the duties of. **7** to occupy (time). **8** to satisfy, to glut. **9** to fulfil, to meet. **10** to stock or store abundantly. **11** to cause to be filled or crowded. **12** in poker, to complete (a full house) by drawing the cards needed. **13** (*N Am.*) to make up (a prescription). **14** to distend (as sails). **15** to trim (a sail) to catch the wind. *~v.i.* **1** to become or grow full. **2** to be satisfied. **3** to pour out liquor, to give to drink. **4** (of a sail) to be distended. *~n.* **1** as much as will satisfy (*eat one's fill*). **2** a full supply. **3** as much as will fill. **4** material used for filling. **to fill a gap** GAP. **to fill in 1** to insert, so as to fill a vacancy. **2** to complete (anything that is unfinished, such as an outline or a form). **3** (*coll.*) to provide with necessary or up-to-date information. **4** to occupy (time). **5** to act as a temporary substitute (for). **6** to fill (a hole) completely. **7** (*sl.*) to beat up. **to fill out 1** to become bigger or fatter, to become distended. **2** to enlarge. **3** (*chiefly N Am.*) to complete (a form etc.). **to fill the bill** BILL[1]. **to fill up 1** to fill or occupy completely. **2** to complete (a form etc.). **3** to fill the petrol tank of (a car etc.). **4** to become full. **5** to make up the deficiencies in, to supply what is wanting in. **6** to supply, to discharge; to fulfil, to satisfy. **7** to stop up by filling. **to have one's fill of** to have rather too much of. **filler** *n.* **1** material used to fill cracks and holes in plaster, woodwork etc. **2** an item used to fill a space between more important items (as in a newspaper, a TV programme, a schedule etc.). **3** the filling opening of a petrol tank, gearbox, crankcase etc. **4** a funnel used in filling casks, bottles etc. **5** a person or thing that fills. **filler cap** *n.* a cap closing the opening of a petrol tank on a car etc. **filling** *a.* **1**

occupying the whole space or capacity. 2 (esp. of food) satisfying. ~*n.* 1 anything serving to fill up. 2 gold or other material used to fill up a cavity in a tooth. 3 a substance used to fill up holes, cavities or defects. 4 a food mixture filling sandwiches, cakes etc. 5 inferior material used to fill up space in goods of better quality. 6 rubble and other rough material filling up the interior of a stone- or brick-faced wall. 7 (*chiefly N Am.*) the weft of a woven fabric. **filling station** *n.* a roadside establishment supplying petrol, oil etc. to motorists. **fill-up** *n.* 1 a thing that fills up something. 2 an act of filling up the petrol tank of a car etc. [OE *fyllan*, OS *fullian*, cogn. with FULL[1]]

fille de joie (fē də zhwah´) *n.* (*pl.* **filles de joie** (fē də zhwah´)) a prostitute. [F, daughter of joy]

fillet (fil´it) *n.* 1 a fleshy portion or slice of meat. 2 the fleshy part of an animal from near its loin used for meat (*fillet steak*). 3 portions of meat or fish removed from the bone and served either flat or rolled together and tied round. 4 a band of metal, a string or ribbon for binding the hair or worn round the head. 5 a ribbon, a narrow band or strip. 6 a bandage. 7 a raised rim or moulding. 8 **a** a plain liner band on the back of a book. **b** a tool used to impress this. 9 (*pl.*) the loins of a horse. 10 a narrow, flat band between mouldings. 11 the projection between the flutes of a column. 12 any small scantling less than a batten. 13 a small horizontal division of a shield. ~*v.t.* (*pres.p.* **filleting,** *past, p.p.* **filleted**) 1 to remove bones from (fish or meat); to make into fillets. 2 to bind with a fillet or bandage. 3 to adorn with a fillet or fillets. **filleter** *n.* [ME and OF *filet*, dim. of *fil*, L *fīlum*, a thread]

fillibeg FILIBEG.

fillip (fil´ip) *n.* 1 a stimulus, an incentive, a boost. 2 a sharp, sudden blow with the finger jerked from under the thumb. 3 anything of small moment, a trifle. ~*v.t.* (*pres.p.* **filliping,** *past, p.p.* **filliped**) 1 to stimulate, incite, encourage. 2 to strike with the nail of the finger by a sudden jerk from under the thumb. 3 to propel with such a blow. ~*v.i.* to make a fillip. [prob. var. of FLIP]

fillis (fil´is) *n.* a kind of loosely-twisted string used to tie up plants etc. [F *filasse*]

fillister (fil´istə) *n.* 1 the rabbet on the outer edge of a sash bar. 2 a plane for making a rabbet. [etym. unknown]

filly (fil´i) *n.* (*pl.* **fillies**) 1 a female foal. 2 (*dated*) a lively girl or young woman. **filly-foal** *n.* [cogn. with FOAL]

film (film) *n.* 1 a series of connected moving images projected on a screen; a story represented in this way. 2 in photography, a thin coating of sensitized material spread over a plate for receiving a negative or positive image. 3 a thin plate or strip of celluloid or other material supporting such a coating. 4 (*pl.*) the cinema industry generally. 5 a thin skin, coating or layer. 6 a fine thread or filament. 7 a thin, slight covering or veil. 8 a dimness or opaqueness affecting the eyes. 9 a thin sheet of plastic or similar material used for packaging. ~*v.t.* 1 to record on a photographic film. 2 to make a film of (a book etc.). 3 to cover with a film. ~*v.i.* 1 to match a photographic film of a book etc. 2 to be reproduced as a film in a certain way (*The story films well*). 3 to become covered with or as with a film. **film clip** *n.* a short extract from a film. **filmgoer** *n.* a person who often goes to the cinema. **film-going** *n.* **filmic** *a.* of or relating to films or the cinema. **film-maker** *n.* a person who makes films, esp. a director or producer. **film-making** *n.* **filmography** (-mog´-) *n.* (*pl.* **filmographies**) a list of films by a particular artist or director or on a particular subject. **film recorder** *n.* the apparatus which records sound on film. **film recording** *n.* the process by which sound is recorded on the edge of a film for synchronous reproduction. **filmset** *v.t.* (*pres.p.* **filmsetting,** *past, p.p.* **filmset**) to expose (type characters) on to photographic film from which printing plates are made. **filmsetter** *n.* **filmsetting** *n.* **film star** *n.* a leading cinema actor or actress. **filmstrip** *n.* a sequence of images on a strip of photographic film, projected as stills. **filmy** *a.* (*comp.* **filmier,** *superl.* **filmiest**) 1 thin and gauzy, transparent. 2 covered with or as if with film; misted, blurred. **filmily** *adv.* **filminess** *n.* [OE *filmen*, membrane, prepuce, cogn. with *fel*, FELL[3]]

filo (fē´lō), **phyllo** *n.* a kind of flaky pastry, usually layered in thin leaves. [mod. Gr. *phullo*, a leaf]

Filofax® (fī´lōfaks) *n.* a small ring-binder with a leather or similar cover into which the owner can insert sheets at will to make up e.g. a diary, an address list etc., intended as a personal, portable compendium of information.

filoplume (fil´əploom, fī´-) *n.* a thread feather, one having an almost invisible stem. **filoplumaceous** (-mā´-) *a.* [mod. L *filoplūma* (L *fīlum*, a thread, *plūma*, a feather)]

filose (fī´lōs) *a.* (*Biol.*) having or ending in a threadlike process. [L *fīlum*, a thread]

filoselle (filəsel´, fil´əsel) *n.* floss silk. [F, from It. *filosello* (L *follis*, a bag, or *fīlum*, a thread)]

fils[1] (fils) *n.* (*pl.* **fils**) a monetary unit of Bahrain, Iraq, Jordan, Kuwait and Yemen. [Arab.]

fils[2] (fēs) *n.* the son; junior; added to a French surname to distinguish a son from a father with the same name. [F, son]

filter (fil´tə) *n.* 1 an apparatus for straining liquids and freeing them from impurities, usu. by means of layers of sand, charcoal or other material through which they are passed. 2 the layer of porous material through which the liquids are passed. 3 the material so used. 4 an apparatus for purifying air or another gas by a similar process. 5 a filter tip. 6 a device for altering the relative intensity of the wavelengths in a beam of light, X-rays etc. 7 a circuit for altering the relative intensity of different frequencies of an alternating current. 8 **a** an auxiliary traffic light at a road junction in the form of a green arrow, which permits a stream of traffic to turn left or right while the main stream is held up. **b** an arrangement or lane that has such a traffic light. ~*v.t.* 1 to pass (liquid etc.) through a filter. 2 to strain, to purify by passing through a filter. ~*v.i.* 1 to pass through a filter. 2 to pass gradually. 3 to percolate. **to filter out** to remove by filtering. **to filter through** 1 to pass through in diffused or diluted form. 2 to become known by degrees. **filterable, filtrable** (fi´ltrəbəl) *a.* 1 that can be filtered. 2 (*Med.*) (of a virus) capable of passing through the pores of a fine filter. **filter-bed** *n.* a reservoir with a layer of sand or other filtering material at the bottom through which water is allowed to flow. **filter-feeding** *n.* (*Zool.*) a method of feeding used by many aquatic invertebrates in which minute particles of food are filtered from the surrounding water. **filter-feeder** *n.* **filter-paper** *n.* a porous paper used for filtering liquids. **filter tip** *n.* (a cigarette with) an attached tip made of a porous substance to trap impurities. **filter-tipped** *a.* [OF *filtre*, med. L *filtrum*, OLG *filt*, FELT[2]]

filth (filth) *n.* 1 anything dirty or foul; foulness, corruption, pollution. 2 anything that defiles morally. 3 foul language, obscenity. **the filth** (*sl.*, *offensive*) the police. **filthy** *a.* (*comp.* **filthier,** *superl.* **filthiest**) 1 dirty, foul, unclean. 2 morally impure; obscene. 3 (of weather) cold, wet and windy. 4 disgraceful, unpleasant. **filthily** *adv.* **filthiness** *n.* **filthy lucre** *n.* 1 gain obtained by dishonest methods. 2 (*facet.*) money. [OE *fȳlth*, from *fūl*, FOUL]

filtrable FILTER.

filtrate (fil´trāt) *n.* any liquid that has passed through a filter. ~*v.t., v.i.* to filter. **filtration** (-trā´shən) *n.* 1 the act or result of filtering. 2 the absorption of traffic from a secondary road into the traffic of a main road; the holding-up of main-road traffic while this is done.

fimbria (fim´briə) *n.* (*pl.* **fimbriae** (-briē)) the radiated fringe of the Fallopian tube. **fimbriate** (-ət) *a.* fringed. **fimbriated** (-ātid) *a.* 1 fringed. 2 (*Biol.*) having fimbriae or fringes. [L, a thread, fibre or fringe]

Fin. *abbr.* 1 Finland. 2 Finnish.

fin (fin) *n.* 1 the organ by which fish propel, balance and steer themselves, consisting of a membrane supported by rays (*the anal fin*). 2 a part or appendage resembling a fin, such as the flipper of a seal. 3 a flat part that projects from an aircraft, rocket or motor vehicle to give stability. 4 a paddle-shaped device worn for underwater swimming. 5 a projecting rib that dissipates heat on a radiator, engine cylinder etc. 6 a sharp projection on a ploughshare. 7 (*sl.*) the hand. ~*v.t.* (*pres.p.* **finning,** *past, p.p.* **finned**) 1 to provide with fins. 2 to carve or cut up (a chub). ~*v.i.* 1 to swim under water. 2 (of a whale) to beat the water with fins. **fin-back** FIN WHALE (under FIN). **fin-footed** *a.* web-footed. **fin-keel** *n.* 1 a fin-shaped keel. 2 a vessel with such a keel. **finless** *a.* **finlike** *a.* **finned** *a.* 1 having fins. 2 having broad edges on either side. **-finned** *comb. form* having a certain kind of fins, as *prickly-finned, red-finned.* **finny** *a.* (*comp.* **finnier,** *superl.* **finniest**) 1 having fins. 2 like a fin. 3 (*poet.*) abounding in fish. **fin-ray, fin-spine** *n.* a spinous ray in the fin of a fish. **fin-toed** *a.* web-footed. **fin whale, fin-back, finner, finner-whale** *n.* a rorqual, *Balaenoptera physalus,* with a dorsal fin. [OE *finn* (cp. Dut. *vin,* also L *pinna*)]

fin. *abbr.* 1 finance. 2 financial.

finable FINE[2].

finagle (finā´gəl) *v.i.* (*coll.*) to behave dishonestly. ~*v.t.* (*coll.*) to get or obtain dishonestly. **finagler** *n.* [dial. *fainaigue*]

final (fī´nəl) *a.* 1 of, occurring at or relating to the end or conclusion; ultimate, last. 2 that cannot be changed or questioned; conclusive, decisive. 3 concerned with the end or purpose. ~*n.* 1 the last game or contest in a series that decides the overall winner of a sports or other competition. 2 the edition of a newspaper that is published at the very latest time in a day. 3 (*usu. pl.*) the last series of examinations in a degree course. 4 (*N Am.*) an examination at the end of each university class. 5 (*Mus.*) the tonic note of a mode. **in the final analysis** ANALYSIS. **final cause** *n.* (*Philos.*) the end or aim, esp. the ultimate object of the creation of the universe. **final clause** *n.* (*Gram.*) a clause expressing the object or purpose. **final drive** *n.* the last section of the transmission section in a motor vehicle. **finalism** *n.* (*Philos.*) the doctrine that everything exists or was created by a determinate cause. **finalistic** (-lis´tik) *a.* **finalist** *n.* a competitor in the finals of examinations, sports etc. **finality** (-nal´-) *n.* (*pl.* **finalities**) 1 the state or quality of being final. 2 the belief that something is final. 3 the state of being finally and completely settled. 4 the end of everything, completeness. 5 a final and decisive act, event, statement etc. **finalize, finalise** *v.t.* 1 to put in final form. 2 to complete; to settle. 3 to give approval to the final arrangements for or details of. **finalization** (-zā´shən) *n.* **finally** *adv.* **final solution** *n.* the Nazi policy of the extermination of all the Jews in Europe. [OF, from L *fīnālis,* from *finis,* the end]

finale (finah´li) *n.* 1 the last section or movement of a musical composition. 2 the last part, piece, scene or action in any performance or exhibition. 3 the last piece in a programme. 4 the close, end, conclusion. [It., as FINAL]

finality, finalism etc. FINAL.

finance (finans´, fī´-) *n.* 1 the science or system of management of revenue and expenditure, esp. public revenue and expenditure. 2 (*pl.*) monetary affairs, the income of a state, sovereign, firm or individual. 3 obtaining money, esp. to fund purchases etc. 4 money. ~*v.t.* 1 to provide with capital. 2 to manage the financial arrangements of. ~*v.i.* 1 to manage financial operations. 2 to obtain capital by borrowing. **finance company, finance house** *n.* a company that specializes in making loans, esp. for hire purchase. **financial** (-nan´shəl) *a.* 1 of or relating to finance or revenue. 2 monetary, fiscal. 3 (*Austral., New Zeal., sl.*) having money. **financialist** (-nan´-) *n.* a financier. **financially** *adv.* **Financial Times Index** *n.* an indicator of prices on the London Stock Exchange based on the average daily prices of a selected list of ordinary shares. **financial year** *n.* the period for which public or official accounts are made up, e.g. 6 April to 5 April for income-tax purposes in Britain; the tax year. **financier** (-nan´siə) *n.* 1 a person who is skilled in finance, esp. the management of public revenues. 2 a person engaged in large-scale monetary dealings. 3 a capitalist. ~*v.i.* 1 to manage financial affairs. 2 to raise money by negotiation. ~*v.t.* 1 to manage the financial affairs of. 2 to finance. [OF, from late L *financia,* from *fīnāre,* to pay a fine or tax, from *finis,* a final payment, L, the end]

finch (finch) *n.* any songbird of the family Fringillidae, including the bullfinch, chaffinch and canary, with a short conical beak that is used to crack seeds. **finch-backed, finched** *a.* (of cattle) striped or spotted on the back. [OE *finc* (cp. Dut. *vink,* G *Fink*)]

find (fīnd) *v.t.* (*past, p.p.* **found** (fownd)) 1 to chance on, to meet with, to come across. 2 to discover, learn or acquire by search, study or other effort. 3 to rediscover (something lost). 4 to ascertain by experience or experiment. 5 to perceive, to recognize. 6 to consider, to be of the opinion that. 7 to reach, to arrive at. 8 to succeed in obtaining. 9 to reach the feelings of, to come home to. 10 to gain or regain the use of. 11 to summon up. 12 to supply, to furnish, to provide. 13 to discover to be present. 14 to maintain, to support. 15 (*Law*) to decide, to determine; to declare by verdict. 16 to invent. 17 (*sl.*) to steal. ~*v.i.* 1 to discover anything by searching or seeking. 2 to arrive at a decision in a cause. 3 to discover a fox or other game. ~*n.* 1 the discovery of anything valuable. 2 the thing so found. 3 the finding of a fox. **all found** (of a worker's wages) with food and lodging included free. **to find against** (*Law*) to reach a verdict on (a person), judging them to be guilty or to have lost the case. **to find a ship's trim** (*Naut.*) to ascertain how the ship will sail best. **to find a (true) bill** BILL[1]. **to find a way** WAY. **to find fault with** FAULT. **to find favour (in the eyes of)** 1 to be considered acceptable (by). 2 to be graciously received and treated (by). **to find for** (*Law*) to reach a verdict on (a person), judging them to be innocent or to have won the case. **to find it in one's heart** to be willing out of kindness (to do something). **to find one's bearings** BEAR[2]. **to find oneself** 1 to be or perceive oneself to be (in a certain situation). 2 to be or feel as regards health. 3 to provide oneself with the necessaries of life. 4 to realize one's own capabilities or vocation. **to find one's feet** FOOT. **to find one's way** 1 to succeed in reaching a place. 2 to come, esp. by chance. **to find out** 1 to discover. 2 to get information. 3 to unravel, to solve. 4 to invent, to devise. 5 to detect, to discover the dishonesty of. **findable** *a.* **finder** *n.* 1 a person who finds. 2 a discoverer, an inventor. 3 a small telescope fixed to the tube and parallel to the axis of a larger one, for finding objects to be examined by the larger telescope. 4 the viewfinder of a camera. **finders keepers** (*coll.*) whoever finds something has the right to keep it. **finding** *n.* 1 a discovery. 2 the act of returning a verdict; a verdict. 3 (*usu. pl.*) the result of an investigation. 4 (*pl.*) tools and materials which some workers have to furnish at their own expense. 5 (*pl., N Am.*) shoemaker's tools and other requisites. **6** (*pl., coll.*) things found. **find-spot** *n.* the place where an archaeological object is found. **find the lady** *n.* THREE-CARD TRICK (under THREE). [OE *findan* (cp. Dut. *vinden*, Swed. and Icel. *finna*, G *finden*)]

fin de siècle (fĩ də syek´lə) *a.* **1** of, relating to or characteristic of the close of the nineteenth century. **2** decadent. ~*n.* the end of the century, esp. the nineteenth. [F, end of the age]

fine[1] (fīn) *a.* **1** excellent in quality, form or appearance. **2** good, satisfactory, enjoyable, pleasant. **3** well, in good health. **4** free from clouds or rain; bright, clear and sunny. **5** refined, pure, free from dross or extraneous matter. **6** (of silver or gold) containing a certain proportion of pure metal. **7** (of feelings, taste, differences, distinctions etc.) delicate, subtle, nice, fastidious, dainty. **8** in small grains or particles. **9** thin, small, slender, tenuous. **10** (of print) small. **11** keen, sharp. **12** of delicate texture or material. **13** finished, consummate, accomplished, brilliant. **14** handsome, beautiful. **15** showy, smart, decorative, pretentious. **16** well expressed. **17** dignified, impressive. **18** complimentary; euphemistic. **19** (*iron.*) unpleasant or unsatisfactory (*We're in a fine mess*). **20** in cricket, at or through a position close to the line of the stumps. ~*adv.* **1** finely. **2** (*coll.*) very well. ~*v.t.* **1** to refine, purify, clear from impurities. **2** to make finer, to sharpen, to taper. **3** to make less coarse. ~*v.i.* **1** to become finer, purer, clarified. **2** to taper, to dwindle (away). ~*n.* **1** fine weather (*in rain or fine*). **2** very fine or powdery particles in mining etc. ~*int.* good! all right! well done! **a fine kettle of fish** KETTLE. **in fine feather** FEATHER. **in fine fettle** FETTLE. **not to put too fine a point on it** speaking frankly. **one of these fine days** at some unspecified date in the future. **to cut/ run it fine** to reduce to the minimum; to take a risk by allowing little margin. **to fine down 1** to clear or to become clear of grossness, opacity or impurities. **2** to reduce and improve by the removal of superfluous matter. **to fine up** (*Austral., coll.*) (of the weather) to become fine. **to get something down to a fine art** to learn to do something in a skilful way. **fine arts** *n.pl.* the arts, such as poetry, music, painting, sculpture and architecture, that appeal to the mind or sense of beauty. **fine chemicals** *n.pl.* chemicals that have a high purity and are produced in small quantities. **fine-draw** *v.t.* (*past* **fine-drew,** *p.p.* **fine-drawn**) to draw together the edges of and mend (a tear) so that no trace remains visible. **fine-drawn** *a.* **1** drawn out finely or thinly. **2** excessively subtle. **3** (of features) slim, delicate. **fine-grained** *a.* having a fine grain; made up of small particles. **finely** *adv.* **fineness** *n.* **1** the quality or state of being fine. **2** the quantity of pure metal in an alloy expressed in fractions or in carats. **fine print** *n.* text typeset in small print, esp. the details of a contract. †**finer** *n.* a refiner of metals. **fine-spoken** *a.* using fine phrases. **fine-spun** *a.* **1** delicate, flimsy. **2** drawn or spun out to minuteness. **3** over-refined or elaborate. **4** unpractical. **fine-tooth comb, fine-toothed comb** *n.* a comb with thin teeth set very close together. **to go over with a fine-tooth comb** to examine minutely, to investigate very thoroughly. **fine-tune** *v.t.* to make delicate adjustments to. **fine-tuning** *n.* **fining** *n.* **1** the process of refining metals, esp. of making cast iron malleable. **2** the clarifying of wines, malt liquors etc. **3** (*pl.*) the preparation, generally a solution of gelatin or isinglass, used to fine or clarify liquors. **fining-pot** *n.* a crucible in which metals are refined. [OF *fin*, late L *fīnus*, prob. from L *fīnītus*, well-rounded, finished, from *fīnīre*, to end, *fīnis*, as FINE[2]]

fine[2] (fīn) *n.* **1** a sum of money imposed as a penalty for an offence. **2** a fee paid by an incoming tenant to the landlord. **3** (*Hist., Law*) a fee paid by a tenant or vassal on the transfer or alienation of the tenant right. ~*v.t.* **1** to impose a financial penalty upon. **2** to punish by fine. ~*v.i.* **1** to pay a fine or monetary consideration. **2** †to pay a penalty or ransom. **in fine 1** in conclusion, in short, finally. **2** to sum up. **finable** *a.* deserving or liable to a fine. [OF *fin*, L *fīnis*, end]

fine[3] (fēn), **fine champagne** (fēn shāpahn´yə) *n.* old liqueur brandy. [F, fine (brandy from) Champagne (vineyards in Charente, France)]

Fine Gael (fēnə gāl´) *n.* one of the major political parties in the Republic of Ireland. [Ir., tribe of Gaels]

finery[1] (fī´nəri) *n.* **1** fine clothes, showy decorations. **2** †the quality of being fine or showy.

finery[2] (fī´nəri) *n.* (*pl.* **fineries**) a hearth for converting cast iron into wrought iron. [F *finerie*, from *finer*, to refine]

fines herbes (fēnz eəb´) *n.pl.* a mixture of finely chopped herbs used as flavouring. [F, fine herbs]

finesse (fines´) *n.* **1** elegance, refinement. **2** artifice, stratagem or artful manipulation; a subtle contrivance to gain an end. **3** skill, dexterity, adroitness, esp. in handling difficult situations. **4** in whist etc., an attempt to take a trick with a lower card, so as to retain a higher one for later tricks. ~*v.i.* **1** to use artifice to gain an end. **2** to try to win a trick with a lower card than a card possibly in one's opponent's hand, while one has a higher card in one's own. ~*v.t.* **1** to play (a card) in this manner. **2** to manipulate, to manage by means of trickery or stratagem. [F, rel. to FINE[1]]

finger (fing´gə) *n.* **1** any of the five digits or parts at the end of the hand; any of the four longer digits as distinguished from the thumb. **2** the part of a glove that covers a finger. **3** anything resembling or serving the purpose of a finger, an index, a gripper, a catch, a guide shaped like a finger. **4** the width of a finger, a measure of length or of the quantity of liquid in a glass. **5** (*sl.*) **a** an informer. **b** a pickpocket. **c** a police officer. **6** (*pl.*) the hand, the instrument of work or art. **7** (*pl.*) skill in using the fingers, as in playing on a keyed instrument. ~*v.t.* **1** to touch with or turn about in the fingers. **2** to meddle or interfere with. **3** to pilfer. **4** to perform with the fingers. **5** to play (a musical instrument) with the fingers. **6** to mark (a piece of music) so as to indicate which fingers should be used. **7** (*sl.*) to identify (to the police). ~*v.i.* to use the fingers esp. skilfully in playing an instrument. **all fingers and thumbs** clumsy or awkward. **not to lift a finger** to do nothing, to stand idly by. **one's fingers all thumbs** THUMB. **one's fingers itch** ITCH. **to burn one's fingers** to hurt or bring trouble on oneself by meddling. **to get/ pull one's finger out** (*sl.*) to start making an effort, to get cracking. **to give someone the finger** to make an obscene gesture to someone, as a sign of contempt, by raising the middle finger. **to have a finger in** to be concerned in or mixed up with. **to have a finger in every pie** to be involved in everything. **to lay/ put a finger (up)on** to touch, to interfere with in the slightest. **to let slip through one's fingers** SLIP[1]. **to point the finger (at) 1** to accuse, to blame. **2** to censure. **to put one's finger (up)on** to detect or point out precisely (the cause, meaning etc.). **to put the finger on** (*sl.*) to identify or inform against. **to twist/ wind/ wrap around one's little finger** to have someone in one's power, to be able to do as one likes with someone. **to work one's fingers to the bone** WORK. **finger alphabet** *n.* a form of sign language using signs made on the fingers for talking to the deaf. **finger-board** *n.* the board at the neck of a stringed instrument, against which the fingers are pressed on the strings. **finger bowl, finger glass** *n.* a bowl or glass in which to rinse the fingers during a meal. **finger-dry** *v.t.* (*3rd pers. sing. pres.* **finger-dries,** *pres.p.* **finger-drying,** *past, p.p.* **finger-dried**) to dry and shape (the hair) by moving one's fingers through it. **fingered** *a.* **1** having fingers. **2** (*Bot.*) digitate. **-fingered** *comb. form* having a certain kind of fingers. **fingerer** *n.* **1** a person who fingers. **2** a pilferer. **fingering**[1] *n.* **1** the act of touching with the fingers. **2** (*Mus.*) a method of using the fingers in playing upon a keyed, stringed or holed instrument. **3** marks upon a piece of music to guide the fingers in playing. **4** delicate work done with the fingers. **finger language** *n.* a language that uses the finger alphabet. **fingerless** *a.* **fingerling** (-ling) *n.* the young of the salmon or trout, a parr. **fingermark** *n.* a dirty mark left by fingers. **fingernail** *n.* the nail at the end of each finger. **finger-paint** *n.* thickish paint for applying with the fingers, hand etc., used esp. by children. ~*v.i.* to apply finger-paint. **finger-painting** *n.* **fingerpick** *n.* a plectrum that is worn on a finger. ~*v.i., v.t.* to play with a fingerpick. **finger-plate** *n.* a plate on the side of a door, near the handle, to preserve the paint from finger-marks. **finger-post** *n.* a signpost where roads cross or divide, pointing out directions. **fingerprint** *n.* **1** an impression of the whorls of lines on fingers, used for purposes of identification. **2** an identifying characteristic. ~*v.t.* to take the fingerprints of. **finger ring** *n.* a ring worn on the finger. **finger-stall** *n.* a cover for protecting a finger during dissections, or when injured or diseased. **fingertip** *n.* the end or tip of a finger. **to have at one's fingertips** to know thoroughly, to be well versed in. **to the fingertips** completely. [OE (cp. Dut. *vinger*, Icel. *fingr*, Dan., Swed. *finger*, G *Finger*)]

fingering[1] FINGER.

fingering[2] (fing´gəring) *n.* a thick, loose, woollen yarn used for knitting. [earlier *fingram*, perh. from F *fin grain*, fine grain]

finial (fin´iəl, fī´-) *n.* **1** a terminal ornament on top of the apex of a gable, pediment, roof, canopy etc. **2** the highest part of a pinnacle. [var. of FINAL]

finical (fin´ikəl) *a.* finicky. **finicality** (-kal´-) *n.* **finically** *adv.* **finicalness** *n.* **finicky** *a.* **1** affecting great nicety, precision or delicacy. **2** overnice, fussy, fastidious. **3** particular about details or trifles. **4** crotchety. **finickiness** *n.* **finicking** *a.* [prob. from FINE[1]]

fining FINE[1].

finis (fin´is, fē´-) *n.* **1** the end, finish, conclusion (printed at the end of a book). **2** the end of all things, death. [L]

finish (fin´ish) *v.t.* **1** to bring to an end. **2** to complete. **3** to arrive at the end of. **4** to perfect. **5** to give the final touches to, to treat the surface of, to trim, to polish. **6** to consume, to get through. **7** to kill, to defeat, to render powerless. **8** to complete the social education of (a girl). ~*v.i.* **1** to come to the end, to reach the end, to cease, to expire. **2** to end up. **3** to leave off. ~*n.* **1** the act of finishing. **2** the termination, the final stage; the end of a race when the competitors reach the winning post; the killing of the fox at the end of a hunt. **3** the last touches, what gives the effect of perfect completeness; the final stage of any work. **4** the appearance, texture etc. of the surface of wood, cloth etc. **5** grace, elegance, polish, refinement. **to fight to the finish** to continue fighting until one of the parties is killed or completely defeated. **to finish off 1** to complete. **2** to consume or use up the remainder of. **3** to kill or destroy (someone or something already wounded or facing defeat or ruin). **to finish up 1** to consume or use up entirely. **2** to arrive, come to rest or end up. **to finish with** to stop one's association with. **finisher** *n.* **1** a person or thing that finishes. **2** a worker or a machine that performs the final operation in a process of manufacture. **3** a crushing blow that settles a contest. **finishing** *n., a.* **finishing coat** *n.* the last coat in painting or plastering. **finishing school** *n.* a private school where girls are taught social graces in preparation for entry into fashionable society. **finishing stroke** *n.* a final, destructive action or event. **finishing touch** *n.* (*usu. pl.*) the last detail that is necessary to complete something perfect. [OF *finiss-*, base of *finir*, L *finīre*, to end, see FINIS]

finite (fī´nīt) *a.* **1** having limits or bounds, not infinite. **2** (*Gram.*) applied to those parts of a verb which are limited by number and person, such as the indicative, subjunctive, imperative. **finitely** *adv.* in a finite manner. **finiteness, finitude** (fin´itūd) *n.* **finitism** (fī´nītizm) *n.* the belief in the finiteness of the world, God etc. **finitist** *n.* [L *finītus*, p.p. of *finīre*, to finish]

fink (fingk) *n.* (*chiefly N Am., sl.*) **1** an informer. **2** a strike-breaker. **3** a contemptible person. ~*v.t.* (*chiefly N Am., sl.*) to inform on (someone) to the police. **to fink out** (*chiefly N Am., sl.*) to go back on (something); let (someone) down. [etym. unknown]

Finn (fin) *n.* a native inhabitant of Finland. **Finlandization** (finləndizā´shən), **Finlandisation** *n.* the pursuit by a non-communist country, e.g. Finland, of an economic policy of accommodation with the former Soviet Union. **Finlandize** *v.t.* **Finnic** *a.* **1** belonging to the Finnish group of peoples. **2** the group of languages including Finnish and Estonian. **Finnish** *a.* of or relating to Finland, the Finns or their language. ~*n.* the language of the Finns. **Finno-Ugric** (finōoo´grik, -ū´grik), **Finno-Ugrian** (-oo´griən, -ū´griən) *n.* the family of languages including Magyar, Lapp, Finnish and Estonian. ~*a.* of or relating to these languages. [OE *Finnas*, pl. (Icel. *Finnr*, Swed., Dan. and G *Finne*)]

finnan haddock (fin´ən), **finnan** *n.* a kind of smoke-dried haddock. [etym. uncertain; perh. corr. of *Findhorn*, a fishing village in Scotland]

finned FIN.

finnesko (fin´əskō) *n.* (*pl.* **finnesko**) a boot made of the tanned skin of reindeer, having the hair on the outside. [Norw. *Finn* and *sko*, a shoe]

☒ **finnish** common misspelling of FINISH.

fino (fē´nō) *n.* (*pl.* **finos**) a light-coloured very dry sherry. [Sp., fine]

fiord FJORD.

fiorin (fī´ərin) *n.* white bent grass, *Agrostis stolonifera*. [Ir. *fiorthan*]

fioritura (fyawrituə´rə) *n.* (*pl.* **fioriture** (-rə)) (*Mus.*) a decorative phrase or turn, a flourish added by the performer. [It., FLOURISH]

fipple (fip´əl) *n.* an arrangement of a block and a sharp edge, the sound-producing mechanism in e.g. a recorder. **fipple flute** *n.* an end-blown flute with a fipple. [etym. unknown]

fir (fœ) *n.* **1** any coniferous tree of the genus *Abies* with single needlelike leaves. **2** the wood of these. **fir cone** *n.* the cone-shaped fruit of the fir. **fir-needle** *n.* the spinelike leaf of the fir. **firry** *a.* consisting of or containing firs. [ME *firre*, prob. from Scand. (cp. Icel. *fyri-*, Dan. *fyr*), perh. cogn. with OE *furh*, OHG *forha*, G *Föhre*, and also L *quercus*, oak]

fire (fīə) *n.* **1** the production of heat and light by combustion. **2** combustion, flame, incandescence. **3** fuel in a state of combustion, as in a furnace or grate. **4** a radiant gas or electric heater. **5** anything burning. **6** a conflagration. **7** a light, glow or luminosity resembling fire. **8** a spark or sparks emitted when certain substances are struck violently. **9** intense heat, fever. **10** the discharge of firearms. **11** ardent emotion, fervour. **12** liveliness of imagination, vigour of fancy, poetic inspiration. **13** a severe affliction, torture, persecution. ~*v.t.* **1** to discharge, to cause to explode; to propel from a gun. **2** to set on fire, to kindle, to ignite. **3** (*coll.*) to dismiss, to discharge from employment. **4** to deliver in rapid succession. **5** to supply (e.g. a furnace) with fuel. **6** to inflame, to irritate. **7** to stimulate, to enthuse, to excite, to animate, to inspire. **8** to bake (pottery etc.). **9** to cure (tea or tobacco). **10** in veterinary medicine, to cauterize. ~*v.i.* **1** to catch fire, to be kindled. **2** (of an internal-combustion engine) to be in operation. **3** to discharge firearms. **4** to shoot (at) with firearms. **5** to ring (e.g. a peal of bells) simultaneously. *~int.* a word of command for soldiers to discharge their firearms. **fire away!** begin! **Greek fire** GREEK. **on fire 1** burning, in flames. **2** excited, ardent, eager. **to catch fire 1** to ignite. **2** to become excited. **to fire away** to begin, to proceed. **to fire off 1** to discharge (a firearm). **2** to shoot (a round, a shell). **3** to utter in rapid succession. **to fire out** to expel forcibly, to chuck out. **to fire up 1** to start up (an engine etc.). **2** to fill with enthusiasm. **3** to kindle a fire. **4** to be inflamed with passion, to be irritated. **to go through fire and water** to expose oneself to all dangers. **to play with fire** to expose oneself to risk. **to set fire to** to set on fire. **to set on fire 1** to kindle. **2** to excite, to inflame. **to set the world/ Thames on fire** to do something remarkable or striking. **to take fire** to catch fire. **under fire 1** exposed to the enemy's fire-arms. **2** exposed to one's opponent's questions or criticism. **fire alarm** *n.* an automatic apparatus for communicating warning of a fire. **fire and brimstone** *n.* the torments of hell. **firearm** *n.* (*usu. pl.*) a weapon that projects a missile by the explosive force of gun-powder etc., esp. a rifle or pistol. **fireback** *n.* **1** the rear wall of a furnace or fireplace. **2** an iron slab for this. **3** any pheasant of the genus *Lophura* of SE Asia. **fireball** *n.* **1** a large meteor or shooting star. **2** the luminous cloud of hot gases at the centre of a nuclear explosion. **3** an enthusiastic or energetic person. **4** globular lightning. **5** †a ball or sack filled with combustible materials, a grenade. **fire-balloon** *n.* a balloon that rises because of the heat of a fire that burns at its mouth. **fire-bar** *n.* any of the bars in a furnace on which the fuel rests. **firebasket** *n.* a small portable grate. **firebird** *n.* any of various songbirds with a bright red plumage, esp. the Baltimore oriole. **fire blight, fire blast** *n.* a disease of plants, esp. hops and fruit trees, giving leaves and blossoms a scorched appearance. **firebomb** *n.* an incendiary bomb. *~v.t.* to attack with a firebomb. **firebox** *n.* the chamber in which the fuel is burned in a locomotive etc. **firebrand** *n.* **1** a piece of wood kindled or on fire. **2** a person who causes trouble or inflames passions. **3** an arsonist. **firebreak** *n.* a strip of land in a forest etc. kept clear of trees or vegetation to stop the spread of fire. **firebrick** *n.* a brick capable of withstanding fire, used for fireplaces, furnaces and all kinds of work exposed to intense heat. **fire brigade** *n.* a body of people organized by a public authority etc. for the extinguishing of fires. **fire-bucket** *n.* a bucket (filled with water or sand) kept in readiness in case of fire. **firebug** *n.* (*coll.*) an arsonist. **fireclay** *n.* a kind of clay consisting of nearly pure silicate of alumina, capable of standing intense heat, used in the manu-facture of firebricks. **fire company** *n.* **1** a fire brigade. **2** a fire-insurance company. **fire-control** *n.* the system of controlling gunfire from one spot. **firecracker** *n.* (*chiefly N Am.*) an explosive firework. **firecrest** *n.* a European warbler, *Regulus ignicapillus*, with a red and orange crest. **fire-cross** *n.* FIERY CROSS (under FIERY). **firedamp** *n.* the explosive mixture of hydrocarbons, esp. methanes, that accumulates in coal mines. **fire department** *n.* (*N Am.*) a fire brigade. **firedog** *n.* an andiron. **fire door** *n.* **1** a fire-resistant door that has the aim of preventing a fire from spreading through a building. **2** an emergency exit. **fire-drake** *n.* **1** a fiery dragon or serpent. **2** an ignis fatuus. **3** a firework. **fire drill** *n.* **1** a practice of the routine to be observed in case of fire. **2** an instrument used by the Australians and Tasmanians for producing fire, consisting of two pieces of soft dry wood, one of which is made to revolve quickly upon the other till they ignite. **fire-eater** *n.* **1** a juggler who pretends to swallow fire. **2** a belligerent person, a person who is fond of fighting. **fire engine** *n.* a vehicle equipped with fire-fighting equipment. **fire escape** *n.* an emergency staircase or apparatus for enabling people to escape from the upper parts of buildings that are on fire. **fire extinguisher** *n.* a port-able apparatus for extinguishing fires by spraying them with water or chemicals. **firefight** *n.* an exchange of fire between military units. **firefighter** *n.* a person who is employed to extinguish fires. **fire-fighting** *n.* **1** the extinguishing of fires. **2** (*fig.*) dealing with emergencies or unplanned critical situations. *~a.* of or relating to fire-fighting. **firefly** *n.* (*pl.* **fireflies**) any small luminous winged insect of the family Lampyridae. **fireguard** *n.* **1** a wire frame placed before an open fire as a safeguard against accidental fire or injury to children etc. **2** (*N Am.*) **a** a fire-watcher. **b** a firebreak. **fire hose** *n.* a hosepipe used for extinguishing fires. **firehouse** *n.* (*N Am.*) a fire station. **fire insurance** *n.* insurance against loss by fire. **fire-irons** *n.pl.* the implements for tending a domestic fire, poker, tongs and shovel. **fireless** *a.* destitute of or without fire. **firelight** *n.* the light from a fire in a fireplace. **firelighter** *n.* a flammable substance used to help start a fire in a grate, barbecue etc. **fire-lock** *n.* an old-fashioned musket or other gun having a lock with a flint and steel, by means of which the priming was ignited. **fireman** *n.* (*pl.* **firemen**) **1** a person who is employed to extinguish fires. **2** a stoker. **3** a person employed in a coal mine to see that no firedamp is present. **fire marshal** *n.* (*N Am.*) an official responsible for investigating the causes of fires and for fire-prevention measures. **fire-office** *n.* a fire-insurance office. **fire-opal** *n.* GIRASOL. **fire-pan** *n.* **1** a pan for holding fire, a brazier. **2** †the receptacle for the priming in a firelock. **fireplace** *n.* **1** a place for a fire in a room, esp. the grate and the hearth. **2** the structure surround-ing this. **3** the space around this. **fireplug** *n.* a hydrant for connecting a fire hose with a water main. **fire policy** *n.* (*pl.* **fire policies**) a policy or certificate guaranteeing compensation up to a stated limit in case of damage by fire. **firepower** *n.* **1** the effective capabi-lity of weaponry, missiles etc. **2** influence or strength from the point of view of something, e.g. finances or intelligence. **fire practice** *n.* a fire drill. **fireproof** *a.* capable of resisting fire; incombustible. *~v.t.* to make fireproof. **fireproof curtain** *n.* SAFETY CURTAIN (under SAFETY). **fireproofing** *n.* **1** the process of making some-thing fireproof. **2** material used for this purpose. **firer** *n.* **1** a person or thing that fires. **2** (*in comb.*) a gun with one or more barrels, as a *single-firer*. **fire-raising** *n.* **1** the act of setting on fire. **2** incendiarism, arson. **fire-raiser** *n.* **fire-resistant** *a.* tending not to catch fire and resistant to the effects of fire to a required degree. **fire risk** *n.* risk of accidental damage by fire. **fire screen** *n.* **1** a fireguard. **2** a screen placed between a person and the fire to keep off the direct rays. **3** a decorative screen placed in front of a fireplace. **fireship** *n.* a vessel loaded with combustibles and explosives, and sent among an enemy's ships in order to set them on fire. **fireside** *n.* **1** the space around a fireplace, the hearth. **2** a person's home or home life. *~a.* home, domestic. **fireside chat** *n.* an informal talk. **fire station** *n.* a build-ing from which fire engines and firefighters operate. **fire-step** FIRING-STEP (under FIRE). **fire-stone** *n.* **1** a stone capable of bearing a high degree of heat, used in furnaces etc. **2** a stone used for striking fire, such as a flint or iron pyrites. **firestorm** *n.* a huge fire, esp. one started by bombing, which causes and is kept ablaze by violent inrushing winds. **firethorn** *n.* pyracantha. **firetrap** *n.* a building without adequate means of exit in case of fire. **fire-walking** *n.* the ritual of walking barefoot over white-hot ashes, stones etc. **fire-walker** *n.* **fire warden** *n.* (*N Am.*) a person employed to prevent or control fires. **fire-watcher** *n.* a person who watches for the outbreak of fires, esp. during an air raid. **fire-watching** *n.* **firewater** *n.* (*coll.*) strong alcohol.

fireweed *n.* any of several plants that spring up on burnt-over areas of land, esp. the rosebay willowherb. **firewood** *n.* wood for burning used as fuel. **firework** *n.* 1 a preparation of various kinds of combustible chemicals and explosives for producing a brilliant display for public entertainment, at times of public rejoicing etc. 2 similar preparations used for illumination, signalling, incendiary purposes or in war. 3 (*pl.*) a display of bad temper. 4 (*pl.*) a spectacular display of wit or virtuosity. **fire-worship** *n.* worship of fire as a living being or deity. **fire-worshipper** *n.* a person who worships fire, e.g. a Parsee. **firing** *n.* 1 the act of discharging firearms. 2 material for a fire; fuel. 3 the baking of ceramic products in a kiln. 4 the ignition of an explosive mixture in an internal-combustion cylinder. 5 the adding of fuel to a boiler furnace. **firing charge** *n.* the explosive used for detonating the charge in a torpedo, mine etc. **firing line** *n.* a line of troops engaging the enemy with firearms. **to be in the firing line** to be at the forefront of any activity and exposed to greatest risk. **firing party** *n.* a detachment detailed to fire over a grave at a military funeral, or to shoot a condemned man. **firing pin** *n.* a sliding pin in firearms that strikes the detonator and explodes the charge. **firing-point** *n.* FLASHPOINT (under FLASH). **firing squad** *n.* 1 a detachment which carries out executions by shooting. 2 a firing party. **firing-step, fire-step** *n.* a raised ledge inside a trench on which soldiers stand to fire. [OE *fȳr* (cp. Dut. *vuur*, Dan. and Swed. *fyr*, G *Feuer*, also Gr. *pūr*)]

firkin (fœ´kin) *n.* 1 a measure of capacity; one quarter of a barrel or nine gallons (about 41 l). 2 a small wooden cask used for butter, tallow etc., of no fixed capacity. [formerly *ferdekyn*, prob. from MDut. (*vierde*, fourth, *ken*, -KIN)]

†**firlot** (fœ´lət) *n.* (*Sc.*) a dry measure, one quarter part of a boll. [perh. corr. of FOUR or FOURTH and LOT]

firm[1] (fœm) *a.* 1 fixed, stable, steady. 2 difficult to move or disturb; not shaking. 3 solid, compact, unyielding. 4 securely established, unchanging, definite, immutable. 5 steadfast, determined, constant. 6 staunch, enduring, resolute. 7 (of prices etc.) constant, unwavering, not changing in level. ~*adv.* firmly. ~*v.t.* 1 to fix firmly. 2 to make firm, to consolidate. 3 to fix firmly in the soil. 4 †to confirm. ~*v.i.* 1 to become firm. 2 to solidify. **firmly** *adv.* **firmness** *n.* **firm offer** *n.* a definite offer. **firmware** *n.* a computer program or data stored in a read-only memory. [OF *ferme*, L *firmus*]

firm[2] (fœm) *n.* 1 a business partnership. 2 the partners in such a business. 3 a group of doctors and assistants. [late L *firma*, a signature, L *firmāre*, to confirm, as FIRM[1] (cp. FARM)]

firmament (fœ´məmənt) *n.* (*poet.*) the sky regarded as an arch or vault. **firmamental** (-men´-) *a.* of or relating to the firmament; celestial; of the upper regions. [OF, from L *firmāmentum*]

firman (fœ´mən, -mahn) *n.* a decree, mandate or order of an Eastern monarch, issued for any purpose, such as a passport, grant, licence etc. [Pers. *fermān*]

firn (fœn) *n.* névé, snow on the higher slopes of lofty mountains, not yet consolidated into ice. [G, last year's snow (*firne*, of last year)]

firry FIR.

first (fœst) *a.* 1 foremost in order, time, place, rank, importance or excellence. 2 earliest in occurrence. 3 nearest, coming next (to something specified or implied). 4 chief, highest, noblest. 5 basic, fundamental. 6 most willing (*be the first to admit the mistake*). 7 (*Mus.*) of the highest vocal part or principal player of a specified instrument. ~*adv.* 1 before all others in order, time, place, rank, importance or excellence. 2 before some time, act or event (specified or implied). 3 sooner, rather, in preference. 4 for the first time. 5 first-class (when travelling). ~*n.* 1 the person or thing that comes first. 2 the first mentioned. 3 the beginning; the first day of a month. 4 an important event that has not happened before. 5 a place in the first class of an examination list; a candidate winning this. 6 the first place in a race; the winner of this. 7 (*pl.*) the best quality of a commodity such as flour. 8 the upper part in a duet, trio etc. 9 first gear. **at first** 1 at the beginning. 2 originally. **at first sight** SIGHT. **at (the) first blush** BLUSH. **first and last** essentially; generally. **first off** (*coll.*) firstly, first of all. **first or last** sooner or later. **first things first** things must be done in order with the most important things first. **first up** (*esp. Austral.*) first of all. **from first to last** 1 throughout. 2 altogether. **from the first** from the outset. **in the first flight** FLIGHT[1]. **in the first place** as the first reason or point. **not to know the first thing about** to be entirely ignorant of. **of the first magnitude** among the best, worst, most important etc. of its kind. **to get to first base** BASE[1]. **to make first base** BASE[1]. **to play first fiddle** FIDDLE. **first aid** *n.* assistance rendered to an injured person before a doctor comes. **first aider** *n.* **first-begot, first-begotten** *a.* first-born among offspring (applied esp. to Jesus Christ as the offspring of God the Father). ~*n.* the eldest child. **first blood** *n.* 1 in boxing etc., the initial issue of blood. 2 the first point, goal etc. scored in a competition. **first-born** *a.* born first, eldest. ~*n.* the first in order of birth. **First Cause** *n.* the Creator of all things. **first-class** *a.* 1 first-rate, of the highest quality or degree. 2 of, belonging to or travelling by first class. 3 (of postage) charged at a higher rate for quicker delivery. ~*adv.* by first class. **first class** *n.* 1 the group of the best people or things. 2 first-class post. 3 the first or best class of railway carriage or other accommodation. 4 a the highest division in an examination list. b a place in this. **first comer** *n.* the person who arrives first. **first costs** *n.pl.* the original costs, as distinguished from the price which includes profit. **first cousin** *n.* the child of an uncle or aunt. **first day** *n.* Sunday, as being the first day of the week. **first-day cover** *n.* an envelope postmarked on the first day of issue of new stamps. **first-degree** *a.* (*Med.*) of burns that affect only the surface of the skin, making it painful and red. **First Empire** *n.* the empire of Napoleon I (1804–15). **first finger** *n.* the finger next to the thumb. **First Fleet** *n.* (*Hist.*) the ships that brought the original convicts to Australia in 1788. **First Fleeter** *n.* one of these convicts. **first floor** *n.* 1 the floor or storey of a building next above the ground floor. 2 (*N Am.*) the ground floor. **first-foot** *n.* 1 (*Sc.*) the first caller at a house on New Year's Day. 2 the first person met in setting out on some important business. ~*v.t.* to enter as first-foot. ~*v.i.* to be a first-foot. **first form** *n.* the lowest class in schools. **first-fruits** *n.pl.* 1 the fruit or produce first gathered in any season, esp. as offered to God. 2 the first effects or results. 3 the first profits of any office, paid to a superior. **first gear** *n.* the lowest forward gear on a motor vehicle. **first-hand** *a.* 1 obtained directly from the first or original source. 2 direct. ~*adv.* directly. **at first hand** as the original purchaser, owner, hearer etc. **first intention** *n.* 1 (*Med.*) the natural healing of a wound. 2 (*pl., Logic*) a person's basic conception of material things. **First Lady** *n.* (*pl.* **First Ladies**) 1 the wife of or official hostess for the US president or a state governor. 2 any woman pre-eminent in her field. **first lieutenant** *n.* (*N Am.*) an officer in the army or air force that is next below a captain. **first light** *n.* the time when light first appears in the morning. **firstling** (-ling) *n.* 1 the first-born, the first-born in a season. 2 (*pl.*) the first-fruits. **firstly** *adv.* in the first place, to begin with. **first mate** *n.* the chief officer of a merchant vessel, next in rank to the captain. **first meridian** *n.* a prime meridian. **first name** *n.* a Christian name or first forename. **first night** *n.* the first public performance of a play etc. **first-nighter** *n.* a person who makes a point of attending first performances of plays etc. **first offender** *n.* a person not previously convicted. **first officer** *n.* the chief officer of a merchant vessel, next in rank to the captain. **first past the post** *a.* **1** of an electoral system in which each voter casts a single vote and only the candidate who polls the highest number of votes is returned. **2** winning a race by being the first to reach the post. **first person** *n.* (*Gram.*) the form of a pronoun, verb etc. indicating or including the speaker. **first post** *n.* (*Mil.*) the first of two bugle calls announcing the time of retiring for the night. **first-rate** *a.* of the first or highest class or quality; of the highest excellence. *~adv.* excellently, very well. **first reading** *n.* the introduction and presentation of a Bill in a legislative assembly. **first refusal** *n.* the choice or option of accepting or refusing something before it is offered to others. **First Reich** *n.* the Holy Roman Empire, AD 962–1806. **first school** *n.* a primary school for children aged 5 to 8 or 9. **first sergeant** *n.* (*N Am.*) the highest-ranking non-commissioned officer in a military subdivision. **first strike** *n.* an initial, unprovoked or pre-emptive attack with nuclear missiles. **first-strike** *a.* **first-string** *a.* of regular team members as opposed to substitutes. **first thing** *adv.* early, as the first action of the day; before doing other things. **first time** *adv.* immediately. **first-time** *a.* doing something for the first time. **first water** *n.* **1** the purest quality (of diamonds etc.). **2** the finest quality. [OE *fyrst* (cp. Icel. *fyrstr*, Dan. *förste*, also G *Fürst*, prince), superl. from stem *fur-*, *for-*, see FORE, FORMER[1]]

firth (fœth), **frith** (frith) *n.* (*Sc.*) an estuary, a narrow inlet of the sea. [prob. from Icel. (cp. Norw. FJORD)]

fisc (fisk) *n.* **1** the treasury of the State, the public purse or exchequer. **2** (*facet.*) one's purse. [L *fiscus*, a basket, a purse, the treasury]

fiscal (fis´kəl) *a.* of or relating to the public revenue or exchequer or to taxes, financial. *~n.* **1** a public functionary with legal or financial duties in various foreign countries. **2** a procurator fiscal. **3** †a treasurer. **fiscality** (fiskal´iti) *n.* (*pl.* **fiscalities**) **1** (*pl.*) fiscal matters or arrangements. **2** undue concern for these. **fiscally** *adv.* **fiscal year** *n.* the financial year.

fish[1] (fish) *n.* (*pl. in general* **fish,** *in particular* **fishes**) **1** a cold-blooded vertebrate animal with gills and fins, living wholly in water. **2** an invertebrate creature, e.g. a jellyfish, living wholly in water. **3** the flesh of fish used as food. **4** (*coll.*) a certain kind of person, e.g. an *odd fish.* **5** a person who is being angled for. **6** (*Naut., sl.*) a torpedo or submarine. *~v.i.* **1** to try to catch fish, esp. with a line or net. **2** to search for something under water. **3** to grope or feel around for. **4** to seek to learn or obtain anything by indirect means or finesse. *~v.t.* **1** to attempt to catch (fish) in. **2** to lay hold of and retrieve or drag up from under water or from inside something. **3** to search (water etc.) by sweeping, dragging etc. **neither fish, flesh nor good red herring** nondescript; neither fish, flesh nor fowl. **neither fish, flesh nor fowl** nondescript; of a vague indefinite character. **other fish to fry** OTHER. **the Fish** the zodiacal sign or constellation Pisces. **the Fishes** the Fish, Pisces. **to drink like a fish** to drink to excess. **to feed the fishes** to be drowned. **to fish for compliments** to lead people to pay compliments. **to fish out 1** to find and draw out. **2** to ascertain by cunning enquiry. **to fish the anchor** to draw up the flukes to the bulwarks after the anchor has been catted. **fish and chips** *n.* fried fish and fried potato chips. **fish ball, fish cake** *n.* a fried cake of chopped fish and mashed potatoes. **fish-basket** *n.* a basket for serving fish. **fishbowl** *n.* a usu. spherical glass bowl in which fish are kept as pets. **fish eagle** *n.* any eagle, esp. of the genus *Haliaetus*, that catches and feeds on fish. **fisher** *n.* **1** †a person who is employed in fishing; a fisherman. **2** an animal that catches fish, esp. the pekan, a N American marten, *Martes pennanti*, having valuable fur. **fisherfolk** *n.pl.* people whose livelihood is fishing. **fisherman** *n.* (*pl.* **fishermen**) **1** a person whose job is to catch fish. **2** an angler. **3** a boat or vessel used in catching fish. **fisherman's bend** *n.* a kind of knot. **fishery** *n.* (*pl.* **fisheries**) **1** the business of catching or rearing fish. **2** any place where fishing is carried on. **3** (*Law*) permission to fish in reserved water. **fish-eye** *a.* of a wide-angle photographic lens with a convex front which covers up to 180°. **fish farm** *n.* an installation for the rearing of fish, usu. in ponds or tanks. **fish farmer** *n.* **fish farming** *n.* **fish finger** *n.* a small bar-shaped portion of fish coated in breadcrumbs or batter. **fish-garth** *n.* a staked or dammed enclosure on a river for taking or preserving fish. **fish-gig** (-gig) *n.* a spear with several barbed prongs used in taking fish. **fishglobe** *n.* a small globular aquarium for goldfish etc. **fish-glue** *n.* **1** a glue made of the entrails and skin of fish. **2** isinglass. **fish-hawk** *n.* the osprey. **fish-hook** *n.* **1** a barbed hook for catching fish. **2** (*Naut.*) the hook in tackle for raising an anchor. **fishing** *n.* **1** the business of catching fish. **2** the sport or hobby of angling. **3** a place where angling is carried on. **4** a fishery. **fishing boat** *n.* a boat used in catching fish. **fishing-fly** *n.* (*pl.* **fishing-flies**) a fly, either natural or synthetic, used as a bait in fishing. **fishing frog** *n.* the angler fish. **fishing line** *n.* a line with a baited hook attached for catching fish. **fishing net** *n.* a net for catching fish. **fishing rod** *n.* a long, slender, tapering rod, usu. in sections jointed together, for angling. **fishing tackle** *n.* all the apparatus required by an angler. **fish kettle** *n.* a long oval pan for boiling fish. **fish-knife** *n.* (*pl.* **fish-knives**) a broad-bladed knife for eating or serving fish with. **fish ladder** *n.* a series of pools arranged in steps to enable fish swimming upstream to bypass dams etc. **fishlike** *a.* **fish louse** *n.* (*pl.* **fish lice**) a small crustacean parasitic upon fishes and other aquatic animals. **fishmeal** *n.* ground dried fish that is used as animal feed or as a fertilizer. **fishmonger** *n.* a retail dealer in fish. **fishnet** *n.* open mesh fabric resembling netting. **fish-oil** *n.* oil obtained from fish and other marine animals such as whales. **fish out of water** *n.* anyone out of their element, in a strange or bewildering situation. **fish pond** *n.* **1** a pond in which fish are kept. **2** (*facet.*) the sea. **fishpot** *n.* a trap made of wicker that is used to catch eels, lobsters etc. **fish slice** *n.* **1** a broad-bladed utensil used by cooks for turning fish or other fried foods or taking them out of the pan etc. **2** a broad-bladed knife, usually of silver, for serving fish at table. **fish-sound** *n.* the swim-bladder of a fish. **fish-spear** *n.* a spear or dart, usu. with barbs, for striking fish. **fish stick** *n.* (*N Am.*) a fish finger. **fish-strainer** *n.* **1** a metal colander with handles, used for taking fish out of a fish kettle. **2** a perforated slab at the bottom of a dish to drain cooked fish. **fishtail** *n.* anything that is like a fish's tail in shape or movement. *~v.i.* to move the rear part of a motor vehicle from side to side. *~a.* shaped like the tail of a fish. **fishtail burner** *n.* a gas burner producing a jet of flame that broadens. **fish-torpedo** *n.* (*pl.* **fish-torpedoes**) a fish-shaped, self-propelled torpedo. **fishway** *n.* FISH LADDER (under FISH[1]). **fishwife** *n.* (*pl.* **fishwives**) **1** a coarse, foul-mouthed woman. **2** a woman that sells fish. **fishy** *a.* (*comp.* **fishier,** *superl.* **fishiest**) **1** like, consisting of, relating to or suggestive of fish. **2** inhabited by or abounding in fish. **3** (*coll.*) of a doubtful character, questionable, dubious. **fishily** *adv.* **fishiness** *n.* [OE *fisc* (cp. Dut. *visch*, Icel. *fiskr*, G *Fisch*, also L *piscis*)]

fish[2] (fish) *n.* **1** a flat piece of wood or iron etc. used to strengthen a beam etc. **2** (*Naut.*) a strip of wood for mending or strengthening a spar. **3** a counter used in various games. *~v.t.* **1** (*Naut.*) to mend or strengthen a spar with a fish. **2** to join with a fish-plate. **fish-bolt** *n.*

a bolt that is used for fastening fish-plates to rails. **fish-joint** *n.* a joint made with fish-plates on a railway line. **fish-plate** *n.* 1 a plate of iron etc. used to fasten rails end to end. 2 a flat piece of metal having ends that resemble a fish's tail, used in positioning masonry. [F *fiche*, a peg, from *ficher*, prob. L *figere*, to fix]

fisk[1] (fisk) *n.* the Crown Treasury of Scotland. [var. of *fisc*]

†**fisk**[2] (fisk) *v.i.* 1 to bustle. 2 to frisk (about). [perh. from OE *fȳsan*, to hurry]

†**fisnomy** (fiz´nəmi) *n.* PHYSIOGNOMY. [corr.]

fissi- (fis´i) *comb. form* divided; dividing; by division. [L *fissus*, p.p. of *findere*, to split, cleave]

fissidactyl (fisidak´til) *a.* having the digits divided. [Gr. *daktulos*, finger]

fissile (fis´ īl) *a.* 1 capable of undergoing nuclear fission. 2 that may be cleft or split, esp. in the direction of the grain, as wood, or along natural planes of cleavage, as rock. **fissility** (-sil´-) *n.* [L *fissilis*, from *findere*, to cleave]

fission (fish´ən) *n.* 1 the act or process of cleaving, splitting or breaking up into parts. 2 nuclear fission. 3 a form of asexual reproduction in certain simple organisms, the individual cell dividing into new cells. **fissionable** *a.* **fission bomb** *n.* atom bomb.

fissiparous (fisip´ərəs) *a.* 1 reproducing by fission. 2 tending to split or cleave. **fissiparity** (-par´-) *n.* **fissiparously** *adv.* **fissiparousness** *n.*

fissiped (fis´iped) *a.* having the toes separate. ~*n.* a fissiped animal.

fissirostral (fisiros´trəl) *a.* having a deeply cleft beak; belonging to the group of birds, Fissirostres.

fissure (fish´ə) *n.* 1 a cleft or opening made by the splitting or parting of any substance. 2 a slit or narrow opening, such as the deep narrow depression between the anterior and middle lobes of the brain on each side. ~*v.t.* to cleave, to split. ~*v.i.* to become split or cleft. [F, from L *fissūra*, as FISSILE]

fist (fist) *n.* 1 the clenched hand, esp. in readiness to strike a blow. 2 handwriting. 3 (*coll.*) the hand. 4 a typographical hand pointing. ~*v.t.* 1 to strike or grip with the fist. 2 (*Naut.*) to handle (ropes, sails etc.). **to make a good fist** (*coll.*) to make a good attempt (at). **to make a poor fist** (*coll.*) to make a poor attempt (at). **fisted** *a.* **-fisted** *comb. form* having a certain kind of fist. **fist fight** *n.* a fight using one's bare fists. **fistful** *n.* (*pl.* **fistfuls**). **fistic, fistical** *a.* (*facet.*) of or relating to pugilism. **fisticuffs** (-tikŭfs) *n.pl.* 1 a fight in which the fists are used. 2 a boxing match. [OE *fyst* (cp. Dut. *vuist*, G *Faust*)]

fistula (fis´tūlə) *n.* (*pl.* **fistulas, fistulae** (-lē)) 1 an abnormal or surgically made opening between a hollow organ and the skin surface or between two hollow organs. 2 a narrow pipelike passage, duct or spout, in insects, whales etc. 3 a kind of ancient Roman flute made of reeds. **fistular, fistulate** (-lət) *a.* 1 hollow like a reed. 2 of or relating to a fistula. **fistulose, fistulous** *a.* 1 hollow like a pipe or reed. 2 of the form or nature of a fistula. [L, a pipe, a flute]

fit[1] (fit) *a.* (*comp.* **fitter**, *superl.* **fittest**) 1 adapted, suitable, appropriate. 2 qualified, competent. 3 ready, prepared, in a suitable condition (to do or for). 4 in good physical condition. 5 (*coll.*) as if, in such an extreme mood or condition as (*fit to drop*). 6 becoming, proper, right. ~*v.t.* 1 to be of the right size, measure and shape for. 2 to adapt to any shape, size or measure. 3 to make suitable, to accommodate, to find room for. 4 to insert or fix. 5 to qualify, to prepare. 6 to be adapted, suitable or proper for. 7 to supply, to furnish, to equip. 8 to try on (a garment). 9 to be in harmony with. 10 to correspond to exactly. ~*v.i.* 1 to be adjusted or adapted to the right shape, measure, form etc. 2 to be proper, suitable, convenient or becoming. ~*n.* 1 exact adjustment, as of a dress to the body. 2 the manner in which anything fits, the style in which a garment fits. ~*adv.* as if in such an extreme condition, appropriately. **fit to be tied** TIE. **fit to drop** DROP. **to fit in** 1 to find room or time for. 2 to be esp. socially accommodating or suitable. **to fit like a glove** GLOVE. **to fit on** to try on (a garment). **to fit out** to equip, to furnish with things that are necessary or suitable. **to fit the bill** BILL[1]. **to fit the description** DESCRIPTION (under DESCRIBE). **to fit up** 1 to furnish with the things suitable or necessary. 2 (*sl.*) to frame. **to see fit to** SEE[1]. **to think fit to** to decide to (do something). **fitly** *adv.* **fitment** *n.* 1 a piece of furniture. 2 (*usu. pl.*) fittings. 3 an accessory part of a machine. **fitness** *n.* 1 suitability. 2 good physical condition or health. **fitness walker** *n.* a person who walks regularly not only for pleasure but also as a form of keep-fit exercise. **fitted** *a.* 1 adapted, suitable (for). 2 shaped or built to fit exactly into or over a certain space, and usu. permanently attached. 3 furnished with fitted, matching cupboards etc., built-in. **fitter** *n.* 1 a person who or thing that fits. 2 a person who supervises the cutting, fitting etc. of garments. 3 a person who puts together the several parts of machinery. 4 a person who fits or repairs certain kinds of apparatus (*a gas-fitter*). **fitting** *a.* suitable, appropriate, right, proper. ~*n.* 1 preliminary trying on of a garment. 2 the act of making fit. 3 a small, removable part or attachment (*electric light fitting*). 4 (*pl.*) apparatus, furniture used in equipping a house, shop etc. **fittingly** *adv.* **fittingness** *n.* **fitting shop** *n.* a workshop in which machinery is fitted up. **fitting-up** *n.* the act or process of furnishing with the necessary fittings or fixtures. **fit-up** *n.* (*sl.*) 1 a temporary stage. 2 a travelling theatre company. [ME *fyt*, etym. uncertain]

fit[2] (fit) *n.* 1 a sudden attack of epilepsy or other disease characterized by unconsciousness or convulsions. 2 a violent seizure or paroxysm. 3 a sudden transitory attack of illness. 4 a spasm, a seizure, a short burst. 5 a transient state of impulsive action, a mood, a caprice. **by/ in fits and starts** intermittently. **in fits** laughing uncontrollably. **to give someone a fit** (*coll.*) to surprise or shock a person. **to have a fit** (*coll.*) to be very angry or shocked. **fitful** *a.* 1 spasmodic, capricious, wavering. 2 acting by fits and starts. **fitfully** *adv.* **fitfulness** *n.* [OE *fitt*, etym. and sense doubtful (perh. as FIT[3])]

†**fit**[3] (fit), †**fytte** *n.* a short canto or division of a poem. [OE *fitt*, a song, part of a poem]

fitch (fich) *n.* 1 a polecat. 2 **a** the fur of the polecat. **b** a brush made of this. **fitch-brush** *n.* [cp. MDut. *fisse*, a polecat]

fitchew (fich´oo) *n.* a polecat. [as FITCH]

fitter, fitting etc. FIT[1].

FitzGerald contraction (fitsjer´əld), **FitzGerald–Lorentz contraction** *n.* the contraction that a moving body shows when its speed comes close to that of light. [G. F. *Fitzgerald*, 1851–1901, Irish physicist and H. A. *Lorentz*, 1853–1928, Dutch physicist]

five (fīv) *n.* 1 the number or figure 5 or V. 2 the age of five. 3 a set of five things; a team of five players. 4 the fifth hour after midnight or midday. 5 a card, counter etc. with five pips. 6 (in cricket etc.) a hit scoring five runs. 7 a size measuring five. ~*a.* 1 five in number. 2 aged five. **bunch of fives** BUNCH. **to take five** (*coll.*) to take a few minutes' break. **five-a-side** *a.* of a football game with five players in each team. ~*n.* a five-a-side football game. **five-corner, five-corners** *n.* (*Austral.*) a shrub of the genus *Styphelia* that produces a five-sided fruit; this fruit. **five-eighth** *n.* (*Austral.*) a player in rugby football posted between the half-backs and three-quarter backs. **five-figure tables** *n.pl.* tables of five-figure logarithms. **five-finger** *n.* 1 any of various plants, esp. *Potentilla reptans* and *Lotus corniculatus*. 2 a species of starfish, *Uraster rubens* or *Solaster papposus*. **five-finger exercise** *n.* 1 an exercise to improve the touch in playing the piano. **2** a simple task. **fivefold** *a., adv.* **1** five times as much or as many. **2** consisting of five parts. **five hundred** *n.* a form of euchre in which the aim is to reach 500 points. **five o'clock shadow** *n.* beard growth which becomes visible on a man's shaven face late in the day. **fivepence, fivepence piece, fivepenny piece** *n.* a coin worth five pence. **five-penny** (fiv´pəni, fip´ni) *a.* priced at five pence. **five-per-cents** *n.pl.* stocks or shares paying 5%. **fiver** *n.* (*coll.*) **1** a five-pound note. **2** (*N Am.*) a five-dollar bill. **3** anything that counts as five, such as a stroke for five at cricket etc. **fives** *n.* a game in which a ball is struck against a wall by the open hand or a small wooden bat. **Eton fives** ETON. **Rugby fives** RUGBY. **fives court** *n.* a court with two, three or four walls where the game of fives is played. **five senses** *n.pl.* the senses of sight, hearing, taste, smell and touch. **five-star** *a.* of the highest class, e.g. of hotels. **fivestones** *n.* the game of jacks played with five metal pieces, usu. without a ball. **five wits** *n.pl.* the five senses, the mental faculties. **five-year plan** *n.* **1** a government plan in socialist countries for economic development over a five year period. **2** a business plan covering five years' projected development. [OE *fīf* (cp. Dut. *vijf*, G *fünf*, Gr. *pente*, L *quinque*)]

fix (fiks) *v.t.* **1** to make firm or stable; to fasten, attach, secure firmly. **2** to settle, to determine, to decide (on). **3** to establish, to implant. **4** to attract and hold (a person's eyes, attention etc.). **5** to direct steadily. **6** to mend or repair. **7** to adjust, to identify a definite position for. **8** (*coll.*) to adjust, to arrange properly, to set to rights. **9** (*chiefly N Am.*) to prepare (food or drink). **10** (*coll., usu. pass.*) to provide with (*How are you fixed for money?*). **11** to make rigid. **12** to absorb (e.g. nitrogen) by forming a non-gaseous mixture. **13** to stop a change in. **14** to calculate the rate of occurrence in. **15** to deprive of volatility, to make permanent or stable (e.g. colours, a photographic image etc.). **16** to solidify. **17** (*sl.*) to punish, to get even with. **18** (*sl.*) to influence illicitly. **19** (*sl.*) to inject (esp. oneself) with a drug. **20** (*euphem.*) to spay or castrate (an animal). *~v.i.* **1** to become fixed or rigid. **2** to lose volatility. **3** to become congealed. **4** (*chiefly N Am., coll.*) to be about to, to be set to. **5** to settle down permanently. **6** †to take up one's position. **7** (*sl.*) to receive an injection of a drug. *~n.* **1** an awkward predicament, a dilemma. **2** the position of a ship, aircraft etc. as determined by radar etc. **3** the determination of such a position. **4** (*sl.*) an injection of heroin or a similar drug. **5** (*sl.*) an act or instance of bribery. **to fix on/ upon** to determine on; to choose, to select. **to fix up 1** (*coll.*) to arrange, to organize; to settle. **2** to accommodate. **3** to assemble or construct. **4** to provide. **fixable** *a.* **fixed** *a.* **1** fast, firm. **2** established, settled, unalterable. **of no fixed abode** (*formal*) having no regular home or address, vagrant. **fixed assets, fixed capital** *n.* business assets of a relatively permanent nature, such as buildings or plant etc. **fixed-doh** *a.* (*Mus.*) of a notation used in sight-singing in which C is called 'doh', regardless of the key, as distinct from *movable-doh*. **fixed focus** *n.* a camera focus that cannot be altered. **fixed idea** *n.* a rooted idea, one tending to become a monomania, an idée fixe. **fixed income** *n.* income gained from a pension or investments yielding unchanging interest. **fixed link** *n.* a permanent means of crossing a stretch of water, e.g. a bridge or tunnel, as opposed to e.g. a ferry. **fixedly** (fik´sid-) *adv.* **1** steadfastly, firmly. **2** intently. **fixedness** (fik´sid-) *n.* **1** the quality or state of being fixed. **2** immobility, steadfastness. **3** absence of volatility. **fixed odds** *n.pl.* odds at the start of a race that are already determined. **fixed oil, fixed alkali** *n.* any oil or alkali that is not easily volatilized. **fixed-penalty** *a.* involving the payment of a predetermined and invariable fine. **fixed point** *n.* (*Physics*) a reproducible unchanging temperature. **fixed property** *n.* landed estate, houses etc. **fixed star** *n.* a star which apparently maintains the same relative position to other stars in the sky, as distinct from planets. **fixed-wing** *a.* having permanently attached wings, in contrast to e.g. a helicopter. **fixer** *n.* **1** a person or thing that fixes. **2** a substance used to make a photographic image permanent. **3** (*coll.*) a person adept at finding esp. crafty or illicit solutions to problems. **fixing** *n.* a way or means of fixing. **fixings** *n.pl.* (*N Am.*) **1** equipment. **2** trimmings. [orig. an a., from OF *fixe*, L *fixus*, p.p. of *figere*, to fix]

fixate (fik´sāt) *v.t.* **1** to render fixed. **2** to fix the gaze upon. **3** (*Psych.*) to arrest the psychological development of at an immature stage. **4** (*usu. pass.*) to cause to be obsessed. **fixation** (fiksā´shən) *n.* **1** the act of fixing. **2** the act of fixating. **3** an obsession. **4** the process of making non-volatile, as causing a gas to combine with a solid. **5** the process of ceasing to be fluid and becoming firm. **6** (*Psych.*) an emotional arrest of development of the personality. **fixative** *a.* serving or tending to fix. *~n.* **1** a substance used to make colours permanent or prevent crayon or pastel drawings from becoming blurred. **2** a substance used for holding e.g. hair or false teeth in place.

fixity (fiks´iti) *n.* **1** coherence of parts. **2** fixedness, stability, permanence. **3** the quality of being able to resist the tendency to lose weight or become volatilized through heat.

fixture (fiks´chə) *n.* **1** anything fixed in a permanent position. **2** (*coll.*) a person or thing regarded as permanently established and immovable. **3** a sporting event arranged for a particular date; the date arranged for this. **4** (*Law*) articles attached to a house or land and regarded as part of it.

fizgig (fiz´gig) *n.* **1** †a gadding, flirting girl. **2** †a firework of damp powder that fizzes. **3** (*Austral., sl.*) a police informer. *~*†*a.* flighty. [etym. obscure (perh. from FIZZ and GIG[1])]

fizz (fiz) *v.i.* **1** to make a hissing or spluttering sound. **2** (of a drink) to effervesce. *~n.* **1** a hissing, spluttering sound. **2** effervescence. **3** (*coll.*) champagne. **4** (*coll.*) gingerbeer, lemonade etc. **fizzy** *a.* (*comp.* **fizzier**, *superl.* **fizziest**) effervescent. **fizzily** *adv.* **fizziness** *n.* [imit.]

fizzle (fiz´əl) *v.i.* to fizz. *~n.* **1** the sound or action of fizzing or fizzling. **2** (*sl.*) a feeble ending. **to fizzle out** to end in a feeble or disappointing way. [freq. of FIZZ]

FJI *abbr.* Fellow of the Institute of Journalists.

fjord (fyawd), **fiord** *n.* a long, narrow inlet of the sea, bounded by high cliffs, as in Norway. [Norw.]

FL *abbr.* Florida.

fl. *abbr.* **1** floor. **2** florin. **3** floruit. **4** flourished. **5** fluid.

Fla. *abbr.* Florida.

flab FLABBY.

flabbergast (flab´əgahst) *v.t.* to overwhelm with wonder and amazement; to astound, to stagger with surprise. **flabbergasted** *a.* [etym. uncertain]

flabby (flab´i) *a.* (*comp.* **flabbier**, *superl.* **flabbiest**) **1** hanging loosely; limp, flaccid. **2** lacking in fibre or nerve; languid, feeble, wasteful. **flab** *n.* (*coll.*) loose, hanging, fat body tissue, a sign of being overweight or out of condition. **flabbily** *adv.* **flabbiness** *n.* [var. of obs. *flappy*, a., see FLAP]

flabellate (fləbel´ət) *a.* fan-shaped. **flabellation** (flabəlā´shən) *n.* (*Med.*) cooling with a fan or similar contrivance. **flabelliform** (-fawm) *a.*

flabellum (fləbel´əm) *n.* (*pl.* **flabella** (-ə)) **1** a fan, esp. one used in the Greek Church to drive away flies from the chalice or in the Roman Catholic Church to carry in religious processions. **2** (*Biol.*) a fan-shaped part or organ. [L, a fan]

flaccid (flak´sid, flas´id) *a.* 1 lacking firmness or vigour. 2 limp, flabby, drooping. 3 relaxed, feeble. **flaccidity** (-sid´-) *n.* **flaccidly** *adv.* **flaccidness** *n.* [F *flaccide*, L *flaccidus*, from *flaccus*, flabby]

flack[1] (flak) *n.* (*N Am., sl.*) a publicity agent. [etym. unknown]

flack[2] FLAK.

flacon (flakõ´) *n.* a small bottle, esp. a scent-bottle. [F, see FLAGON]

flag[1] (flag) *n.* 1 a piece of cloth, usu. square or oblong, and plain or bearing a design, attached by one edge to a staff or rope by which it can be hoisted on a pole or mast, and displayed as a banner, ensign or signal. 2 a child's toy or device similar to a flag. 3 an indicator that may be raised to show that a taxi is for hire. 4 (*Naut.*) a flag carried by a flagship to show that the admiral is in command. 5 the flagship itself. 6 the bushy part of a dog's tail, as of a setter. ~*v.t.* (*pres.p.* **flagging,** *past, p.p.* **flagged**) 1 to put a flag over. 2 to decorate with flags. 3 to mark out with or as if with flags. 4 to signal or communicate by means of a flag or flags. 5 to mark (a passage in a book or document etc.) for someone's attention. 6 to code (computer data) so as to make it easily retrievable. **to dip the flag** (*Naut.*) to lower and then raise a flag as a salute. **to flag down** to signal to (a vehicle) to stop. **to keep the flag flying** to continue to represent or stand up for e.g. a country or principles. **to lower the flag** to strike the flag. **to put the flag out** to celebrate a triumph, success etc. **to show the flag** 1 to send an official representative or military unit to a place as a courtesy or a means of asserting a claim etc. 2 (*coll.*) to put in an appearance. **to strike the flag** 1 to pull the flag down in token of surrender or submission. 2 (of an admiral) to relinquish the command. **flag-boat** *n.* a boat serving as a mark in sailing matches. **flag-captain** *n.* the commanding officer of a flagship. **Flag Day** *n.* in the US, 15 June, the annual holiday to celebrate the adoption in 1777 of the Stars and Stripes. **flag day** *n.* a day on which street collections are made for a specific charity, a small flag being worn as a token of having given money. **flagger** *n.* **flag-lieutenant** *n.* an admiral's aide-de-camp. **flag-list** *n.* the roll or register of flag-officers. **flagman** *n.* (*pl.* **flagmen**) a person who makes signals with or as if with flags. **flag of convenience** *n.* a foreign flag under which a vessel is registered to escape taxation etc. in its real country of origin. **flag-officer** *n.* 1 a commander of a squadron. 2 a commodore, admiral, vice admiral or rear admiral. **flag of truce** *n.* 1 a white flag indicating that the enemy has some peaceful communication to make. 2 an offer of peace. **flagpole** *n.* FLAGSTAFF (under FLAG[1]). **to run (something) up the flagpole** to sound out (an idea etc.); to test reactions to (something). **flagship** *n.* 1 the ship which carries the admiral, and on which his flag is displayed. 2 the most important of a group, esp. something regarded as embodying e.g. a company's prestige. **flagstaff** *n.* (*pl.* **flagstaffs**) the pole or staff on which a flag is displayed. **flag-station** *n.* a railway station at which trains stop only when signalled. **flag-wagging** *n.* 1 (*Mil., sl.*) signalling or signalling-drill with hand-held flags. 2 flag-waving. **flag-waving** *n.* showy expression of patriotic feeling. **flag-waver** *n.* [perh. imit. (cp. FLAG[2], also Dut. *vlag*, Dan. *flag*, Norw. and Swed. *flagg*, G *Flagge*)]

flag[2] (flag) *v.i.* (*pres.p.* **flagging,** *past, p.p.* **flagged**) 1 to lose strength or vigour. 2 to become spiritless or dejected; to lose interest. 3 to hang loosely, to droop. 4 to become limp. [prob. imit. in origin (cp. ME *flakken*, to waver, flutter, OF *flaquir*, to hang down, become flaccid, L *flaccus*, limp; also FLABBY, FLICKER[1])]

flag[3] (flag) *n.* 1 a broad flat stone used for paving. 2 (*pl.*) a pavement made of such stones. 3 a fine-grained rock which can be split into slabs for paving. ~*v.t.* (*pres.p.* **flagging,** *past, p.p.* **flagged**) to pave with flags. **flagging** *n.* 1 the act of paving with flagstones. 2 flagstones. 3 a pavement of flagstones. **flagstone** *n.* a flag. **flagstoned** *a.* [prob. a form of FLAKE[1]]

flag[4] (flag) *n.* 1 any of various herbaceous plants with long bladelike leaves growing in moist places, chiefly belonging to the genus *Iris*. 2 the long bladelike leaf of such a plant. 3 (*pl. or coll.*) a coarse, reedy kind of grass. **flaggy** *a.* **flag-worm** *n.* a worm or grub found in the roots of flags and used as bait by anglers. [prob. rel. to FLAG[1], from its waving or fluttering (cp. Dut. *flag*, mod. Dan. *flaeg*)]

flag[5] (flag), **flag-feather** (flag´fedhə) *n.* a quill-feather of a bird's wing. [perh. *fag*, a loose flap, cp. FLAG[1]]

flagellate[1] (flaj´əlāt) *v.t.* to whip, to beat, to scourge. **flagellant** *n.* 1 a person who scourges themselves or others as part of a religious discipline. 2 a person who thrashes themselves or others for sexual gratification. ~*a.* of or relating to flagellation; given to scourging. **flagellation** (-ā´shən) *n.* a scourging or flogging; thrashing of oneself or others, esp. as part of a religious discipline or for sexual gratification. **flagellator** *n.* **flagellatory** *a.* [L *flagellātus*, p.p. of *flagellāre*, to scourge, from *flagellum*, dim. of *flagrum*, a scourge]

flagellate[2] (flaj´ələt, -lāt) *a.* having whiplike outgrowths or flagella. ~*n.* a flagellate protozoan. **flagellar** *a.* **flagelliform** (-jel´ifawm) *a.* whiplike in shape or form. **flagellum** (-jel´əm) *n.* (*pl.* **flagella** (-ə)) 1 a minute whiplike appendage. 2 a trailing shoot; a runner.

flageolet[1] (flajəlet´, flaj´-) *n.* 1 a small wind instrument blown from a mouthpiece at the end, with two thumb holes and producing a shrill sound similar to but softer than that of the piccolo. 2 an organ stop producing a similar sound. 3 a tin whistle. [F, dim. of OF *flageol*, etym. uncertain]

flageolet[2] (flajəlet´, -lā´) *n.* a kind of French bean. [F, corr. of *fageolet*, dim. of *fageol*, L *faseolus*, bean]

flagitate (flaj´itāt) *v.t.* to demand with importunity. **flagitation** (-ā´shən) *n.* [L *flāgitātus*, p.p. of *flāgitāre*]

flagitious (fləjish´əs) *a.* 1 heinous, flagrant, villainous. 2 deeply criminal. **flagitiously** *adv.* **flagitiousness** *n.* [L *flāgitiōsus*, from *flāgitium*, a disgraceful act (rel. to FLAGON)]

flagon (flag´ən) *n.* 1 a large squat bottle usually holding about 2 pints (1.13 litres), in which wine is sold. 2 a large vessel with a handle, narrow mouth or spout and a lid, used for liquors. 3 a similar vessel used to hold the wine in the Eucharist. [OF *flacon*, late L *flasco -ōnem*, *flasca*, FLASK]

flagrant (flā´grənt) *a.* glaring, notorious, outrageous, scandalous. **flagrancy** *n.* **flagrantly** *adv.* [L *flagrans -ntem*, pres.p. of *flagrāre*, to blaze]

flail (flāl) *n.* a wooden instrument consisting of a short heavy bar hinged to a longer staff or handle, used for threshing grain by hand. ~*v.t.* 1 to swing or beat wildly. 2 to strike with or as if with a flail. ~*v.i.* to thresh around. [OE *fligel*, prob. from L FLAGELLUM (under FLAGELLATE[2]) (form influ. by the cognate OF *flael*, whence F *fléau*)]

flair (fleə) *n.* 1 a natural aptitude or gift; talent. 2 stylishness; panache. 3 keen perception, discernment. 4 a keen sense of smell. [F, from *flairer*, to smell, pop. L *flāgrāre*, L *frāgrāre*]

flak (flak), **flack** *n.* 1 fire from anti-aircraft guns. 2 adverse criticism, dissent. **flak jacket** *n.* a reinforced jacket worn by soldiers, police etc. as protection against gunshot etc. [initials of G *Flug(zeug)abwehrkanone*, anti-aircraft gun]

flake[1] (flāk) *n.* 1 a loosely cohering mass, a fleecy particle (as of snow). 2 a thin piece peeled off. 3 a thin scalelike fragment. 4 in archaeology, a fragment of hard stone chipped off and used as a tool or weapon. 5 a natural part of the edible tissue of some fish. 6 dogfish etc. considered as food. 7 (*N Am., sl.*) an eccentric person. ~*v.t.* 1 to form into flakes or loose particles. 2 to chip flakes off, to chip off in flakes. 3 to sprinkle with flakes, to fleck. ~*v.i.* to peel or scale off in flakes. **to flake out** (*coll.*) to collapse or fall asleep from exhaustion. **flake white** *n.* English white lead in the form of scales, used as a pigment. **flaky** *a.* (*comp.* **flakier,** *superl.* **flakiest**) 1 consisting of flakes. 2 liable to flake. 3 (*N Am., sl.*) unstable, unreliable. 4 (*N Am., sl.*) eccentric; crazy. 5 not with it. **flakily** *adv.* **flakiness** *n.* **flaky pastry** *n.* pastry in the form of very thin light layers. [etym. obscure]

flake[2] (flāk) *n.* 1 a rack for drying fish. 2 a frame for storing provisions, esp. oatcake. 3 a light platform or rack. 4 a stage hung over a ship's side, for the use of painters etc. 5 (*dial.*) a hurdle, esp. one used for a fence. [perh. from Icel. *flake, fleke*, a hurdle, rel. to L *plectere*, and Gr. *plekein*, to plait]

flam (flam) *n.* a false pretext, a sham, a deception, a lie. ~*v.t.* (*pres.p.* **flamming,** *past, p.p.* **flammed**) to deceive, to impose upon. [etym. uncertain]

flambé (flā´bā, flom´-) *v.t.* (*3rd pers. sing. pres.* **flambés,** *pres.p.* **flambéing,** *past, p.p.* **flambéed**) to sprinkle with brandy etc. and ignite. ~*a.* served in ignited brandy. [from F *flamber*, to flame]

flambeau (flom´bō) *n.* (*pl.* **flambeaus, flambeaux**) 1 a torch, esp. one made of thick wicks covered with wax or pitch. 2 a large ornamental candlestick. [F, dim. of OF *flambe*]

flamboyant (flamboi´ənt) *a.* 1 exuberant, extravagant, showy. 2 florid, highly decorated. 3 gorgeously coloured. 4 (of hair etc.) wavy or flamelike. 5 (*Archit.*) of or relating to the decorated French Gothic style, having flamelike tracery. **flamboyance** *n.* **flamboyancy** *n.* **flamboyantly** *adv.* [F, pres.p. of *flamboier*, as FLAMBEAU]

flame (flām) *n.* 1 a mass or stream of vapour or gas in a state of combustion. 2 a blaze; fire. 3 a glow, a bright light. 4 a blaze of colour. 5 a strong reddish-orange colour. 6 ardour, excitement, passion. 7 (*coll.*) a boyfriend or girlfriend, a sweetheart. ~*v.t.* 1 to apply a flame to. 2 †to inflame, to excite. 3 to send (a signal) with or as if with flame. ~*v.i.* 1 to burn with a flame. 2 to send out flame, to blaze, to burst into flames. 3 (*fig.*) to break (out) or blaze (up) in violent passion. 4 to shine, to glow, to flash. 5 (*poet.*) to move like flame. **to flame out** 1 (of a jet engine) to lose power because of the extinction of the flame. 2 (*esp. N Am.*) to fail, esp. in an obvious way. **to go up in flames** to be destroyed by a fierce fire. **flame-colour** *n.* a strong reddish-orange colour. **flame-coloured** *a.* **flame gun** *n.* a device that projects a stream of burning liquid to destroy garden weeds. **flameless** *a.* **flamelet** (-lit) *n.* **flamelike** *a.* **flameout** *n.* 1 the extinction of the flame in a jet engine, causing loss of power. 2 (*esp. N Am.*) an utter or obvious failure. **flameproof** *a.* treated so as to withstand heat or fire without being damaged. ~*v.t.* to make flameproof. **flame-thrower, flame-projector** *n.* a weapon that projects a stream of burning liquid. **flaming** *a.* 1 burning, blazing. 2 intensely hot. 3 intensely bright. 4 inflaming, exciting, passionate. 5 vehement, violent. 6 exaggerated, florid, extravagant. 7 (*sl.*) used to express annoyance; bloody. **flamingly** *adv.* **flamy** *a.* [OF *flambe*, L *flamma*, prob. from the base *flag-*, to burn (*flagrāre*, to blaze) or *flāre*, to blow]

flamen (flā´men) *n.* (*pl.* **flamens, flamines** (flam´inēz)) an ancient Roman priest devoted to some special deity. **flaminical** (fləmin´-) *a.* [L, prob. as FLAME]

flamenco (fləmeng´kō) *n.* (*pl.* **flamencos**) 1 a kind of music played on the guitar or sung by gypsies. 2 a dance performed to such music. [Sp., Flemish]

flamines, flaminical FLAMEN.

flamingo (fləming´gō) *n.* (*pl.* **flamingos, flamingoes**) a long-necked web-footed wading bird, with a small body and very long legs, its feathers rose or scarlet in colour, belonging to the family Phoenicopteridae. [Port. *flamengo*, Sp. *flamenco*]

flammable (flam´əbəl) *a.* that can catch fire and burn easily. **flammability** (-bil´iti) *n.* [L *flammare*, from *flamma*, a flame]

Usage note See note under INFLAMMABLE.

flan (flan) *n.* 1 an open pastry or sponge base with fruit or savoury filling. 2 a plain metal disc from which a coin is made. **flan-case** *n.* [F]

flanch[1] (flahnch) *n.* 1 a flange. 2 (*Her.*) a subordinary or part of a shield enclosed by an arc from the upper corners to the base, and always borne in pairs. [perh. a var. of FLANGE OR FLANK]

flanch[2] (flahnch), **flaunch** (flawnch) *v.i.* to slope inwards towards the top of a chimney. ~*v.t.* to cause to flanch. **flanching** *n.* [prob. from OF *flanche*]

flaneur (flanœ´) *n.* a lounger, an idler. **flanerie** (-nərē´) *n.* the practice or habit of sauntering or idling. [F, from *flâner*, to saunter]

flange (flanj) *n.* a projecting rib or rim affixed to a wheel, tool, pipe etc., for strength, as a guide, or for attachment to something else. ~*v.t.* to supply with a flange. **flanged** *a.* **flangeless** *a.* **flange rail** *n.* a rail having a bent-up flange to keep the wheel on the metals. [prob. from OF *flanche*]

flank (flangk) *n.* 1 the fleshy or muscular part of the side between the hips and the ribs. 2 the cut of meat from the flank of an animal. 3 either side of a building, mountain etc. 4 the side of an army or body of troops. ~*v.t.* 1 to stand or be at the flank or side of, to border. 2 to attack, turn or threaten the flank of. 3 to direct sweeping gunfire at. 4 to secure or guard the flank of. ~*v.i.* 1 to border, to touch. 2 to be posted on the flank or side. **in flank** at the side. **flanker** *n.* 1 a person or thing that flanks, or is posted, stationed or placed on the flanks. 2 a fortification projecting so as to command the flank of an assailing body. 3 (*also* **flank forward**) in rugby, a wing forward. 4 in American football, an offensive back who lines up outside an end. 5 (*pl.*) skirmishers thrown out on the flanks of an army when marching. 6 (*sl.*) a swindle or trick. **flank-movement** *n.* a manoeuvre directed at turning the enemy's flank. [F *flanc*; perh. from Gmc. (cp. OHG *hlanca*, the loin, the side, also OE *hlanc*, slender)]

flannel (flan´əl) *n.* 1 a soft woollen fabric, with a light nap. 2 (*pl.*) garments made of this material, esp. trousers. 3 a piece of flannel used for washing the face etc. 4 (*coll.*) flattery, soft soap. 5 (*coll.*) evasive waffling, nonsense. ~*v.t.* (*pres.p.* **flannelling,** (*N Am.*) **flanneling,** *past, p.p.* **flannelled,** (*N Am.*) **flanneled**) 1 to wrap in or rub with flannel or a flannel. 2 (*coll.*) to flatter. ~*v.i.* 1 to speak in a flattering way. 2 (*coll.*) to waffle on evasively. **flannelboard, flannelgraph** *n.* a piece of flannel attached to a piece of paper or board, on which pictures etc. can be stuck when pressed on, used as a toy or in teaching as a visual aid. **flannelette** (flanəlet´) *n.* a cotton fabric made to imitate flannel. **flannel flower** *n.* an Australian plant of the genus *Actinotus*, with white flannel-like bracts below the flowers. **flannelled,** (*N Am.*) **flaneled** *a.* 1 covered with or wrapped up in flannel. 2 wearing flannel trousers. **flannelly** *a.* **flannel-mouth** *n.* (*N Am., sl.*) a braggart. [from Welsh *gwlanen*, from *gwlan*, wool, or from OF *flaine*, blanket, coverlet]

flap (flap) *v.t.* (*pres.p.* **flapping,** *past, p.p.* **flapped**) 1 to move (wings, one's arms etc.) rapidly up and down or to and fro. 2 to beat, strike or drive away with anything broad and flexible. 3 to let fall (as the brim of a hat). ~*v.i.* 1 to be moved loosely to and fro, to flutter, swing about or oscillate. 2 to move the wings rapidly up and down or to and fro. 3 (*coll.*) to be in a state of anxiety or confusion. 4 (*coll.*) (of the ears) to listen eagerly. 5 to hang down, as the brim of a hat. 6 to strike a loose blow or blows. ~*n.* 1 anything broad and flexible, hanging loosely, or attached by one side only, usu. used to cover an opening. 2 the hinged leaf of a table or shutter. 3 the motion or act of flapping. 4 a light stroke or blow with something broad and loose. 5 a slap. 6 an implement for driving flies away. 7 a movable control surface on the wing of an aircraft to increase lift on take-off and drag on landing. 8 (*coll.*) a state of anxiety or confusion. 9 an open mushroom-top. 10 (*pl.*) a disease in the lips of horses. **flapdoodle** *n.* rubbish, nonsense. **flapjack** *n.* 1 a biscuit made of oat flakes and syrup. 2 (*esp. N Am.*) a kind of pancake. **flapper** *n.* 1 a person or thing that flaps. 2 a partridge or wild duck not yet able to fly. 3 a flap, a part or organ loosely attached or hanging. 4 a device that is flapped, e.g. to kill flies. 5 (*sl.*) in the 1920s, a flighty young woman. **flappy** *a.* [prob. imit.]

flare (fleə) *v.i.* 1 to open or spread outwards at one end. 2 to blaze, to flame up or to glow, esp. with an unsteady light. 3 to burst into anger. 4 to be gaudy, glaring or too showy in dress. 5 (*sl.*) to bounce, to swagger. ~*v.t.* 1 to provide with a flare or flares (as a skirt or trousers). 2 to cause to flare up. 3 to burn off (excess gas or oil). ~*n.* 1 a large unsteady light, a glare. 2 a sudden outburst. 3 (a device producing) a blaze of light used for illumination, signalling or to attract attention. 4 in dressmaking, material cut on the cross to give additional fullness. 5 a widening or spreading out. 6 (a thing with) a flared shape. 7 (*pl.*) wide-bottomed trousers. 8 (*Astron.*) a powerful eruption of radiation from a star. 9 the curving motion of a ship's bows, pushing water outwards. 10 unwanted light on a film as a result of reflections within the optical instrument. **to flare up** 1 to blaze out. 2 to become angry suddenly. **flared** *a.* having a flare or flares, flare-shaped. **flare-path** *n.* an area that is illuminated so that aircraft can land and take off. **flare-up** *n.* 1 a sudden outbreak into flame. 2 an outburst of anger, violence, hostilities etc. 3 a showy but transient display. **flaring** *a.* 1 flaming, dazzling. 2 gaudy, too showy or ostentatious. **flaringly** *adv.* **flary** *a.* gaudy, showy. [cp. Norw. *flara*; also G *flattern*, to flicker]

flash (flash) *v.i.* 1 to send out a quick, sudden or regular gleam. 2 to appear with a sudden and transient gleam. 3 to reflect light, to glitter, to burst forth, appear or occur suddenly. 4 to burst suddenly into flame, light or perception. 5 to rush swiftly, to dash, break or splash, as water or waves. 6 to signal using e.g. a torch or the headlights of a car. 7 (*sl.*) to expose oneself indecently. ~*v.t.* 1 to emit or send forth in flashes or like flashes. 2 to cause to gleam. 3 to signal (a message) to (someone) using light. 4 (*often with out or up, coll.*) to display or expose suddenly and briefly. 5 to display ostentatiously. 6 to convey or transmit instantaneously (as news by radio). 7 to send swiftly along. 8 to send a rush of water down (a river, weir etc.). 9 in glass-making, to expand into a dish or sheet, to cover (plain glass) with a thin coating of coloured glass. ~*n.* 1 a sudden and transitory blaze or gleam of bright light. 2 the space of time taken by this, an instant. 3 a sudden occurrence or display of feeling or understanding. 4 a sudden outburst, as of anger, wit, merriment etc. 5 in photography, flashlight, an apparatus for producing flashlight. 6 a newsflash. 7 an area of bright colour. 8 the momentary photographic exposure of a view. 9 vulgar show, ostentation. 10 a body of water driven along with violence. 11 a device such as a sluice for producing this. 12 a label with regimental name etc. sewn on the uniform shoulder. 13 a sticker on goods etc. advertising e.g. a reduction in price. 14 thieves' jargon; cant, slang. 15 a ridge of excess thin plastic or metal formed during moulding. 16 a preparation of capsicum, burnt sugar etc., used for colouring and giving a fictitious strength to rum and brandy. 17 †a showy person, a fop. ~*a.* 1 gaudy, vulgarly showy. 2 counterfeit, forged. 3 occurring or carried out very quickly. 4 slang, cant. 5 of or relating to thieves or vagabonds. **to flash over** to make an electric circuit by discharging over or across an insulator. **flashback** *n.* an interruption in the narrative of e.g. a film or novel to show past events. **flash-board** *n.* a hatch for releasing water from a mill-dam. **flash-bulb** *n.* a (usu. disposable) bulb used to produce flashlight. **flash burn** *n.* a burn suffered as the result of momentary exposure to intense heat. **flashcard** *n.* a card with e.g. words or numbers printed on it for children to look at briefly as an aid to learning. **flash-cube** *n.* a plastic cube containing four flash-bulbs. **flasher** *n.* 1 (*sl.*) a man who exposes himself indecently. 2 a person or thing that flashes. 3 a device that causes a light to flash. 4 a vehicle indicator light. **flash flood** *n.* a sudden flood, caused by heavy local rainfall. **flashgun** *n.* a device which holds and fires a flashbulb. **flashing** *n.* a watertight joint used in roofing with sheet metal, a strip of lead carrying water into a gutter. **flashing point** *n.* FLASHPOINT (under FLASH). **flash in the pan** *n.* an abortive attempt (from a flash produced by the hammer of a gun on a flint which then fails to explode the powder). **flash lamp** *n.* a portable flashing electric torch. **flashlight** *n.* 1 a brilliant light for taking (usu. indoor) photographs. 2 an electric battery torch. 3 a flashing light. **flash memory** *n.* (*Comput.*) a kind of device in which data is kept even when the power supply fails. **flash-over** *n.* an instance of electricity flashing over. **flashpoint** *n.* 1 the degree of temperature at which the vapour from oil or spirit ignites. 2 the point at which tension erupts into violence. 3 a place or region where such eruptions are likely to occur. **flash unit** *n.* a flashgun. **flashy** *a.* (*comp.* **flashier**, *superl.* **flashiest**) 1 gaudy, tawdry, cheap and showy. 2 showy but empty, brilliant but shallow. **flashily** *adv.* **flashiness** *n.* [prob. onomat. in sense of dashing or flapping like water]

flask (flahsk) *n.* 1 a small bottle or similar vessel. 2 a flat bottle, usu. mounted in metal, for carrying spirits in the pocket. 3 a vacuum flask. 4 a thin, long-necked bottle, encased in wicker, for wine or oil. 5 a large reinforced metal container for transporting nuclear waste. 6 POWDER FLASK (under POWDER). [F *flasque* or It. *flasco* (cp. G *Flasche*, OHG *flasca*, OE *flasce*, *flaxe*), ult. perh. from L *vasculum*, dim. of *vas*, a vessel]

flasket (flahs´kit) *n.* 1 a long shallow basket with two handles. 2 a small flask. [OF *flasquet*, dim. of *flasque*, as FLASK]

flat[1] (flat) *a.* (*comp.* **flatter**, *superl.* **flattest**) 1 having a level and even surface. 2 horizontal, level. 3 even, smooth, having few or no elevations or depressions. 4 having little depth or thickness. 5 level with the ground, lying prone, prostrate. 6 having a surface or side in continuous contact with another surface. 7 plain, positive, absolute, downright. 8 monotonous, dull, uninteresting, insipid, pointless, spiritless. 9 having lost sparkle or freshness. 10 depressed, dejected. 11 (of a tyre) deflated. 12 (of a battery) having little or no charge. 13 (of shoes) not having a raised heel. 14 (of feet) having little or no arch. 15 uniform, without variety of contrast, tint or shading. 16 (*Mus.*) a below the true pitch. b (of a key) containing a flat or flats. c being a semitone lower than the specified note. d minor (applied to intervals). 17 having only a small rise, as some arches. 18 a (of prices) low. b (of a market) inactive. 19 (of a rate or price) fixed or standard. 20 in painting, wanting relief or prominence of the figures. 21 (of paint) not glossy; matt. 22 of or relating to flat racing. ~*adv.* 1 flatly, positively. 2 prostrate, level with the ground. 3 (*Mus.*) below the true pitch. 4 exactly, completely (*in ten seconds flat*). ~*n.* 1 a flat, plain surface. 2 a level plain or low tract of land. 3 a plot of ground laid down level. 4 a shallow, a low tract flooded at high tide. 5 a flat part of anything; anything that is flat. 6 a broad, flat-bottomed boat. 7 the palm of the hand. 8 in a theatre, scenery on a wooden frame pushed on to the stage from the sides. 9 (*N Am.*) a broad-brimmed straw hat. 10 **a** a note that is a semitone lower than the one from which it is named. **b** the sign indicating this lowering of pitch. 11 a punctured tyre. 12 (*sl.*) a foolish person. ~*v.i.* (*pres.p.* **flatting,** *past, p.p.* **flatted**) 1 to flatten, to make flat and smooth. 2 (*Mus., N Am.*) to lower in pitch. **flat as a pancake** very flat. **flat broke** (*coll.*) having no money, skint. **flat out** at full speed, with maximum effort; using all one's resources. **in a flat spin** SPIN. **that's flat!** (*coll.*) that is final, irrevocable. **the flat** 1 the flat-racing season. 2 flat racing. **to fall flat** to be unsuccessful. **flat boat, flat-bottomed boat** *n.* a large boat with a flat bottom, used for transport on rivers in the US. **flat cap** *n.* a cap with a low, flat crown. **flatcar** *n.* a railway wagon that does not have raised sides. **flat-chested** *a.* (of a woman) with small breasts. **flatfish** *n.* (*pl. in general* **flatfish,** *in particular* **flatfishes**) any fish (such as the sole, plaice, turbot etc.) of the Pleuronectidae, distinguished by their laterally highly compressed body, absence of coloration on the under side, and the position of both eyes on the upper side. **flat foot** *n.* a foot that has an arch which is lower than normal. **flatfoot** *n.* (*pl.* **flatfoots, flatfeet**) (*derog.*) a police officer. **flat-footed** *a.* 1 with the feet not arched. 2 awkward. 3 ponderous, unimaginative. 4 (*coll.*) off guard. 5 (*coll.*) downright, resolute, determined. **flat-footedly** *adv.* **flat-footedness** *n.* **flat-four** *a.* (of an engine) with four cylinders mounted horizontally. ~*n.* a flat-four engine. **flat-head** *n.* 1 a food fish of the family Platycephalidae, with a flattened body and both eyes on the upper side. 2 (*sl.*) a silly person. **flat iron** *n.* an instrument for smoothing clothes etc. **flatly** *adv.* **flatness** *n.* **flat-pack** *n.* an item of furniture designed for self-assembly at home, packed in a flat box to be transported relatively easily. ~*v.t.* to pack flat in a box. **flat-packed** *a.* **flat race** *n.* a horse race on level ground without obstacles. **flat racing** *n.* **flat rate** *n.* an invariable rate. **flat-screen** *a.* of or relating to a television system that uses a flat rather than a curved screen, avoiding distortion of picture. **flat spin** *n.* 1 a spin in which the aircraft is almost horizontal. 2 (*coll.*) a confused and frantic state. **flatsquare** *a.* (of a television screen) flat, not convex, with reduced distortion. **flatten** *v.t.* 1 to make flat, to level. 2 to lay flat. 3 to knock down or out. 4 to defeat resoundingly. 5 (*Mus.*) to depress or lower in pitch. 6 to make vapid, dull or insipid. 7 to deject, to dispirit. ~*v.i.* 1 to become flat or level. 2 to lose force or interest, to pall. 3 to depress the voice, to fall in pitch. **to flatten out** (of an aircraft) to change from the gliding approach to the position to alight, when approaching to land. **flattener** *n.* **flattie** *n.* (*pl.* **flatties**) (*coll.*) 1 a shoe with a flat heel. 2 a flat boat. 3 a police officer. **flatting** *n.* 1 the act or process of flattening. 2 a covering of size over gilding. 3 the process of rolling out metal into sheets. 4 a style of inside house-painting in which the colours are not glossy. **flatting-mill** *n.* a mill for rolling out metal by cylindrical pressure. **flattish** *a.* **flat-top** *n.* 1 (*N Am., sl.*) an aircraft carrier. 2 (*sl.*) a man's short flat style of haircut. **flatworm** *n.* any worm of the phylum Platyhelminthes, including tapeworms and planarians, with a flattened body. [Icel. *flatr*, etym. uncertain]

flat[2] (flat) *n.* 1 a set of rooms on one floor forming a separate residence. 2 a floor or storey of a house. ~*v.i.* (*pres.p.* **flatting,** *past, p.p.* **flatted**) (*Austral.*) to share a house (with). **flatlet** (-lit) *n.* a small flat. **flatmate** *n.* a person with whom one shares a flat. [OE *flet*, a floor, cogn. with FLAT[1]]

flatten FLAT[1].

flatter[1] (flat´ə) *v.t.* 1 to praise falsely or unduly. 2 to persuade (oneself concerning one's achievement or ability). 3 to display to advantage. 4 to represent too favourably. 5 to court, cajole or gratify by compliment, adulation or acclaim. 6 to raise false hopes in. ~*v.i.* to use flattery. **flatterer** *n.* **flattering** *a.* **flattering unction** *n.* consolation that one gives one's own conscience or self-respect. **flatteringly** *adv.* **flattery** *n.* (*pl.* **flatteries**) 1 the act or practice of flattering. 2 false or uncritical praise; adulation, cajolery. [etym. obscure; prob. from OF *flater*, to flatten, smooth, caress, cogn. with FLAT[1] (*-er* not from OF infin., but from the derivative *flaterie*, or from assim. to or substitution for the obs. v. *flatter*, to flutter or float)]

flatter[2], **flattish** FLAT[1].

flatulent (flach´ələnt) *a.* 1 affected with or troubled by wind or gases generated in the alimentary canal. 2 generating or likely to generate wind in the stomach. 3 pretentious, turgid. 4 inflated, empty, vain. **flatulence, flatulency** *n.* **flatulently** *adv.* **flatus** (flā´təs) *n.* wind in the stomach or bowels; flatulence. [F, from late L *flātulens -ntem*, from *flātus*, a blowing, from *flāre*, to blow]

flaught (flawht) *n.* (*Sc.*) 1 a flapping, a commotion. 2 a flight (as of birds). 3 a flash (as of lightning). [var. of FLIGHT[1]]

flaunch FLANCH[1].

flaunt (flawnt) *v.i.* 1 to make an ostentatious or gaudy show. 2 to behave cheekily or saucily. 3 to wave or flutter in the wind. ~*v.t.* 1 to display ostentatiously or impudently; to parade, to show off. 2 to wave or flutter in the wind. ~*n.* 1 the act of flaunting; impudent parade. 2 a boasting or vaunting. 3 finery. **flauntingly** *adv.* **flaunty** *a.* flaunting, ostentatious. [etym. uncertain]

Usage note The meanings of the verbs *flaunt* and *flout* should not be confused: *flaunt* means to display ostentatiously, and *flout* to disregard or defy. Rules are flouted, not flaunted.

flautist (flaw´tist) *n.* a player of the flute. [It. *flautista*, from *flauto*, a flute]

flavescent (fləves´ənt) *a.* 1 yellowish. 2 turning yellow. [L *flāvescens -ntem*, pres.p. of *flāvescere*, to become yellow, from *flāvus*, yellow]

flavin (flā´vin), **flavine** (-vēn) *n.* 1 any of various chemical compounds containing nitrogen that form the nucleus of certain natural yellow pigments. 2 a yellow pigment, obtained formerly from dyer's oak. **flavin adenine dinucleotide** *n.* a chemical compound containing riboflavin in its molecular structure, with important functions in biochemical reactions. **flavine** (flā´vēn, -vin) *n.* 1 an antiseptic derived from acridine. 2 FLAVIN. **flavone** *n.* any of a class of yellow pigments derived from a crystalline compound occurring in plants. **flavoprotein** (flāvōprō´tēn) *n.* any of a group of enzymes containing derivatives of riboflavin that are important in oxidation reactions in cells. [L *flāvus*, yellow]

flavour (flā´və), (*N Am.*) **flavor** *n.* 1 that quality in any substance which affects the taste, or the taste and smell. 2 a characteristic or distinctive quality. 3 a faint mixture of a usu. unpleasant quality. 4 (*esp. N Am.*) flavouring. ~*v.t.* 1 to impart a flavour to, to season. 2 to render pleasing to the palate. **flavorous, flavoursome** (-səm) *a.* pleasing to taste or smell. **flavoured** *a.* 1 having a distinct flavour. 2 (*in comb.*) having a particular flavour, as *full-flavoured*. **flavour enhancer** *n.* a salt, e.g. monosodium glutamate, that enhances the flavour of food. **flavourful** *a.* **flavouring** *n.* an (artificial) substance that gives flavour to food and drink. **flavourless** *a.* **flavour of the month, flavour of the week** *n.* (*often facet.*) a person or thing much in favour at a particular time. [ME *flauor, flavoure*, prob. from OF *flaur, fraar*, smell (L *frāgrāre*, to smell sweet, or *flāre*, to blow)]

flaw[1] (flaw) *n.* **1** a defect, an imperfection. **2** a crack, a slight fissure. **3** (*Law*) a defect in a document, evidence etc., rendering it invalid. ~*v.t.* **1** to break, to crack. **2** to mar, to spoil. **3** to render invalid. ~*v.i.* to crack. **flawless** *a.* **flawlessly** *adv.* **flawlessness** *n.* **flawy**[1] *a.* full of flaws; defective. [perh. from Icel. *flaga*, a slab (cp. Swed. *flaga*, flake, flaw)]

flaw[2] (flaw) *n.* **1** a sudden puff or gust. **2** a squall, a violent but brief storm. **3** †a tumult. **4** †a mental commotion. **flawy**[2] *a.* gusty. [perh. cogn. with FLAW[1] or with FLAY (cp. Dut. *vlaag*)]

flawy[1] FLAW[1].

flawy[2] FLAW[2].

flax (flaks) *n.* **1** a plant of the genus *Linum*, esp. *L. usitatissimum*, the common flax, the fibre of which is made into yarn, and woven into linen cloth. **2** the fibrous part of the plant prepared for manufacture. **3** any of various kinds of similar plants. **4** †cloth or fabric of flax. **flax-comb** *n.* a comb or hackle for dressing flax. **flax-dresser** *n.* a person who prepares flax for the spinner. **flaxen** *a.* **1** made of flax. **2** like flax in softness, silkiness or colour. **3** light yellow or straw-coloured. **flaxen-haired, flaxen-headed** *a.* **flax-lily** *n.* (*pl.* **flax-lilies**) a New Zealand flax bush, *Phormium tenax*, that yields valuable fibre. **flax-mill** *n.* a mill or place where flax is spun. **flaxseed** *n.* linseed. **flaxy** *a.* [OE *fleax* (cp. Dut. *vlas*, G *Flachs*; perh. cogn. with Gr. *plekein*, and L *plectere*, to weave)]

flay (flā) *v.t.* **1** to strip the skin from. **2** to peel, to pare. **3** to strip, to plunder. **4** to criticize severely. [OE *flēan* (cp. Icel. *flā*, MDut. *vlaen*; cogn. with Gr. *plēssein*, to strike)]

flea (flē) *n.* **1** a small wingless blood-sucking insect belonging to the order Siphonaptera, parasitic on mammals and birds and noted for its leaping powers. **2** flea beetle. **3** WATER FLEA (under WATER). **with a flea in one's ear** EAR[1]. **fleabag** *n.* (*sl.*) **1** a dirty or neglected person. **2** a shabby or dirty thing. **3** a sleeping bag. **4** (*chiefly N Am.*) an inferior lodging house. **fleabane** *n.* any of various plants of the genus *Pulicaria* or *Inula*, supposed to drive away fleas. **flea beetle,** (*N Am.*) **flea-bug** *n.* a small leaping beetle of the family Halticidae, very destructive to hops and other plants. **flea bite** *n.* **1** the bite of a flea. **2** the red spot caused by the bite. **3** the smallest trifle, a trifling inconvenience. **4** a tiny amount. **flea-bitten** *a.* **1** bitten by a flea. **2** full of fleas. **3** coloured, as some horses, with small red spots on a lighter ground. **4** dirty, shabby. **flea circus** *n.* a show of performing fleas. **flea collar** *n.* a collar for pets with a substance used for killing insects. **flea market** *n.* an open-air market selling usu. second-hand goods. **fleapit** *n.* (*coll., facet.*) a shabby cinema or theatre. **fleawort** (-wœt) *n.* a plant of the genus *Tephroseris*, supposed to drive away fleas. [OE *flēah* (cp. Dut. *vloo*, G *Floh*; prob. cogn. with FLEE)]

fleam (flēm) *n.* a lancet for bleeding horses and cattle. [OF *flieme*, med. L *flētoma*, abbr. of L *phlebotomum*, Gr. *phlebotomon*, see PHLEBOTOMY]

flèche (flāsh, flesh) *n.* **1** a spire, esp. a slender one, usu. of wood covered with lead, over the intersection of the nave and transepts of a church. **2** a simple kind of redan, usu. constructed at the foot of the glacis, consisting of a parapet with faces. [F, orig. an arrow]

fleck (flek) *n.* **1** a dot, stain or patch of colour or light. **2** a spot, a freckle, a stain, a speck. ~*v.t.* to spot, to streak, to dapple, to variegate with spots or flecks. **flecker** *v.t.* **1** to fleck, to spot, to dapple. **2** to scatter (light) in flakes or patches. **fleckless** *a.* spotless, stainless, blameless. [cp. Icel. *flekkr*, Dut. *vlek*, G *Fleck*]

flection FLEXION (under FLEXIBLE).

fled FLEE.

fledge (flej) *v.t.* **1** to provide with feathers or plumage. **2** to rear (a young bird) until it can fly. **3** to feather (an arrow). **4** to deck or cover with anything resembling feathers. ~*v.i.* to acquire feathers or plumage for flight. **fledged** *a.* **1** feathered. **2** able to fly. **3** mature, developed. **fledgeless** *a.* **fledgling** (-ling), **fledgeling** *n.* **1** a young bird just fledged. **2** a raw and inexperienced person. ~*a.* newly fledged. [OE *flycge* (found in *unflycge*, unfledged), cp. Dut. *vlug*, G *Flügge* (cogn. with FLY[2])]

flee (flē) *v.i.* (*past, p.p.* **fled** (fled)) **1** to run away, as from danger to a place of safety. **2** to vanish, to disappear. **3** to pass away. ~*v.t.* **1** to run away from. **2** to shun. [OE *flēon*, cp. G *fliehen*, Goth. *thliuhan*]

fleece (flēs) *n.* **1** the woolly covering of a sheep or similar animal. **2** the quantity of wool shorn from a sheep at one time. **3** anything resembling a fleece, such as a woolly head of hair, a fleecy cloud or fall of snow. **4** soft warm material with a pile, used as a hanging. **5** (*Her.*) a representation of a fleece hanging from a ring. ~*v.t.* **1** to rob, to plunder, to swindle, to overcharge. **2** to shear the wool from. **3** to furnish with a fleece. **4** to cover with anything fleecy. **fleeceable** *a.* **fleeced** *a.* **fleeceless** *a.* **fleece-picker** *n.* (*Austral., New Zeal.*) FLEECY[2]. **fleecer** *n.* a person who fleeces or plunders. [OE *flēos* (cp. Dut. *vlies*, G *Fliess*)]

fleech (flēch) *v.t.* (*Sc.*) **1** to flatter. **2** to beg, to entreat. [etym. uncertain]

fleecie FLEECY[2].

fleecy[1] (flēˊsi) *a.* (*comp.* **fleecier**, *superl.* **fleeciest**) **1** woolly, wool-bearing. **2** resembling a fleece in appearance or qualities. **3** covered with fleece. **fleecily** *adv.* **fleeciness** *n.*

fleecy[2] (flēˊsi), **fleecie** *n.* (*pl.* **fleecies**) (*Austral., New Zeal.*) a person whose job is to pick up fleeces after shearing.

fleer (fliə) *v.i.* **1** to grin or laugh in contempt or scorn. **2** to gibe, to sneer. ~*v.t.* to laugh or sneer at. ~*n.* mockery or scorn expressed by words or looks. **fleeringly** *adv.* [cp. Norw. *flira*, Swed. *flissa*, to titter]

fleet[1] (flēt) *n.* **1** a number of ships or smaller vessels with a common object, esp. a body of warships under one command. **2** the entire body of warships belonging to one government, a navy. **3** a collection of aircraft or road vehicles used for a common purpose and usu. under one ownership. **Fleet Admiral** *n.* (*N Am.*) Admiral of the Fleet. **Fleet Air Arm** *n.* the aviation branch of the Royal Navy. [OE *flēot*, a ship, from *flēotan*, to float]

fleet[2] (flēt) *a.* (*poet.*) swift of pace, nimble, rapid, speedy. ~*v.i.* **1** to move swiftly. **2** to pass swiftly. **3** (*fig.*) to glide away, to vanish. ~*v.t.* **1** (*Naut.*) to change the position of, to shift. **2** †to pass (the time) quickly or pleasantly. **fleet-footed** *a.* able to run with great speed. **fleeting** *a.* passing quickly, transient. **fleetingly** *adv.* **fleetly**[1] *adv.* **fleetness** *n.* [OE *flēotan* (cp. Dut. *vlieten*, G *fliessen*, Icel. *fljōta*, also Gr. *pleein*, to sail)]

fleet[3] (flēt) *a.* (*dial.*) shallow. ~*adv.* at or to no great depth. **fleetly**[2] *adv.* [prob. cogn. with FLEET[2] (cp. Dut. *vloot*)]

fleet[4] (flēt) *n.* a creek, an inlet. **the Fleet** **1** a stream or ditch, now a sewer, emptying into the Thames east of Fleet St. **2** (*Hist.*) the prison that stood near this. **Fleet Street** *n.* **1** the former centre of newspaper offices in London. **2** British journalism or journalists. **Fleet-Streeter** *n.* a journalist. [OE *flēot* (cp. Dut. *vliet*, G *Fliess*, Icel. *fljōt*; cogn. with FLEET[3])]

fleetly[1] FLEET[2].

fleetly[2] FLEET[3].

Fleming (flem´ing) *n.* **1** a native of Flanders. **2** a member of a Flemish-speaking people of N and W Belgium. **3** a person of Belgian or Dutch descent. **Flemish** *a.* of or relating to Flanders. ~*n.* **1** the Flemish language. **2** (*as pl.*) Flemings. **Flemish bond** *n.* in brickwork, a bond that has alternating stretchers and headers in each course. **Flemish brick** *n.* a kind of brick used for paving, of a yellowish colour, and harder than ordinary bricks. [MDut. *Vlâming*, whence *Vlaemisch*, from *Flân-*, whence Flanders]

flench FLENSE.

flense (flens), **flench** (flench), **flinch** (flinch) *v.t.* **1** to strip the blubber or the skin from (a whale or seal). **2** to cut up (a whale or seal). [Dan. *flense*]

flesh (flesh) *n.* **1** the soft part of an animal body, esp. the muscular tissue, between the bones and the skin. **2** excess weight; fat. **3** †animal tissue used as food, as distinct from vegetable, fish, and sometimes from poultry. **4** the soft pulpy part of a fruit or plant. **5** the body, as distinguished from the soul, esp. when considered to be sinful. **6** carnal appetites; that which is carnal; a carnal, unrenewed state. **7** the present state of existence. **8** the human race. **9** flesh colour. **10** kindred. ~*v.t.* **1** to embody in flesh. **2** to encourage by giving flesh to (hawks, dogs etc.). **3** to initiate. **4** to exercise or use for the first time. **5** to harden, to inure or accustom to any practice or habit. **arm of flesh** ARM[1]. **in the flesh** in person; in bodily form. **the way of all flesh** WAY. **to be made flesh** to become incarnate. **to flesh out** to elaborate, to give more substance or detail to. **to lose flesh** to lose plumpness, to become thin. **to make someone's flesh creep** to arouse (a physical sense of) horror in someone. **to put on flesh** to grow fatter. **flesh and blood** *n.* **1** the body. **2** human nature, esp. as alive, not imaginary, or as liable to infirmities. **3** one's children or near relatives. **flesh-brush** *n.* a brush or glove for stimulating the action of the skin by friction. **flesh colour** *n.* the colour of flesh; yellowish pink. **flesh-coloured** *a.* **flesher** *n.* (*Sc.*) a butcher. **flesh-fly** *n.* (*pl.* **flesh-flies**) a carnivorous insect of the genus *Sarcophaga*, esp. *S. carnaria*, the larvae of which feed on decaying flesh. **flesh-hook** *n.* a hook to take meat out of a pot. **fleshings** *n.pl.* light flesh-coloured tights to represent the skin, worn by actors, dancers etc. **fleshless** *a.* without flesh, lean, scraggy. **fleshling** *n.* a person devoted to carnal pleasures. **fleshly** *a.* (*comp.* **fleshlier**, *superl.* **fleshliest**) **1** of or relating to the flesh, corporeal, sensual, lascivious. **2** human, as distinct from spiritual. **3** mortal, material; not divine or supernatural. **4** worldly. **fleshliness** *n.* **fleshpots** *n.pl.* **1** sumptuous living (Exod. xvi.3). **2** nightclubs etc. offering lavish or sexually titillating entertainment. **flesh pottery** *n.* **flesh side** *n.* the side of the hide next to the flesh. **flesh tints** *n.pl.* the colours which best represent the human skin. **flesh wound** *n.* a wound not reaching the bone or any vital organ. **fleshy** *a.* (*comp.* **fleshier**, *superl.* **fleshiest**) **1** like flesh. **2** fat, plump, corpulent. **3** (of flesh) without bone. **4** (of fruit etc.) pulpy. **fleshiness** *n.* [OE *flǣsc* (cp. Dut. *vleesch*, G *Fleisch*; also Icel. and Dan. *flesk*, pork, bacon)]

†**fletch** (flech) *v.t.* to feather (as an arrow). †**fletcher** *n.* a person who feathered arrows, a maker of bows and arrows. [corr. of FLEDGE]

fleur-de-lis (flœdəlē´), **fleur-de-lys** *n.* (*pl.* **fleurs-de-lis** (flœdəlē´), **fleurs-de-lys**) **1** the iris flower. **2** (*Her.*) **a** a lily with three petals. **b** (*Hist.*) the royal arms of France. **fleury** (fluə´ri), **flory** (flaw´-) *a.* (*Her.*) adorned with fleurs-de-lis. [F, lily flower]

fleuret (fluə´rət, flœ´-) *n.* an ornament like a small flower. [F *fleurette*, dim. of *fleur*]

fleuron (fluə´ron, flœ´-) *n.* a flower-shaped ornament, used for a tailpiece, in architecture, on coins etc. [F, from *fleur*]

fleurs-de-lis, fleurs-de-lys FLEUR-DE-LIS.

fleury FLEUR-DE-LIS.

flew FLY[2].

flews (flooz) *n.pl.* the large lips of a deep-mouthed hound. [etym. uncertain]

flex[1] (fleks) *v.t.* **1** to bend or cause to bend. **2** (*Geol.*) to subject (strata) to fracture or distortion. **3** in archaeology, to position (a dead body) with legs raised under chin. ~*v.i.* **1** to be bent. **2** (of a muscle) to contract. **to flex one's muscles 1** to contract the muscles, esp. of the arm, in order to display them or as a preliminary to a trial of strength. **2** (*fig.*) to put on a show of power or strength. [L *flexus*, p.p. of *flectere*]

flex[2] (fleks) *n.* **1** flexible insulated wire. **2** a piece of this, used to connect an electrical appliance to the mains. [short for FLEXIBLE]

flexible (flek´sibəl) *a.* **1** pliant, easily bent. **2** tractable, easily persuaded, manageable. **3** variable, adaptable, versatile. **flexibility** (-bil´iti) *n.* **flexibly** *adv.* in a flexible manner. †**flexile** (-īl) *a.* **1** easily bent, supple. **2** pliant, tractable. **3** versatile. **flexility** (-sil´iti) *n.* **flexion** (-shən), **flection** *n.* **1** the act or process of bending. **2** a condition of being bent. **3** a bending movement of a joint or limb. **4** a bend, a curve. **5** (*Gram.*) inflection. **6** (*Math.*) flexure of a line. **flexional** *a.* **flexionless** *a.* **flexor, flexor muscle** *n.* a muscle that causes a limb or part to bend. **flexuose** (-ūōs) *a.* **1** winding, serpentine. **2** crooked, zigzag. **flexuosity** (-os´-) *n.* **flexuoso-** (fleksūō´sō), **flexuos-** *comb. form* **flexuous** *a.* **1** full of bends or turns, winding. **2** wavering, unsteady. **3** (*Zool., Bot. etc.*) presenting alternating curvatures in opposite directions. **flexuously** *adv.* **flexure** (-shə) *n.* **1** the act, process or manner of bending. **2** the state of being bent. **3** a bend, a curve, a turn, curvature. **4** (*Math.*) curving of a line, surface or solid. **5** (*Geol.*) the bending or folding of strata under pressure. **flexure of a curve** *n.* the bending of a curve towards or from a straight line. **flexural** *a.* [L *flexus* p.p. of *flectere*]

flexitime (flek´sitīm), (*N Am.*) **flex time** (fleks´tīm) *n.* **1** a system of working which allows workers some freedom to choose the times when they arrive for and leave work, usu. so long as they are present during a stipulated period (core time). **2** the hours worked in this way. [*flexi*ble *time*]

flexography (fleksog´rəfi) *n.* a form of letterpress printing that uses flexible rubber or plastic plates and synthetic inks, used for printing on paper, packaging, plastics etc. **flexographic** (-səgraf´ik) *a.*

flexuose, flexure etc. FLEXIBLE.

fley (flā) *v.t.* (*Sc., North.*) to frighten. [OE *flȳgan* (found in *a-flȳgan*), causative of *flēogan*, to FLY[2]]

flibbertigibbet (flib´ətijibit) *n.* **1** a chatterer. **2** a flighty, thoughtless person. **3** a fiend. [onomat., or meaningless jargon]

flick (flik) *n.* **1** a smart, light blow or flip, as with a whip. **2** the short sudden release of a bent finger or the wrist. **3** a short sudden movement. **4** a light sharp sound. **5** (*coll.*) a film, a movie. ~*v.t.* **1** to strike or move with a flick. **2** to jerk or flip (dust etc.) away. **3** to give a flick with. ~*v.i.* to make a flicking movement. **the flicks** (*coll.*) the cinema. **to flick through** to read through quickly or inattentively, to turn over (pages etc.) quickly. **flick knife** *n.* a knife with a blade that springs out when a button in the handle is pressed. [onomat.]

flicker[1] (flik´ə) *v.i.* **1** to shine unsteadily, to burn unsteadily, to waver. **2** to move quickly to and fro, to quiver, to flutter. **3** (of hope etc.) to appear faintly and briefly. ~*n.* **1** the act of flickering. **2** an unsteady or dying light. **3** a brief and faint feeling etc. **4** discontinuity of cinema projection caused by too few flashes of the pictures per second. **to flicker out** to die away after an unsteady brightness. **flickeringly** *adv.* [OE *flicerian*, imit.]

flicker[2] (flik´ə) *n.* any N American woodpecker of the genus *Colaptes*. [onomat.]

flicker-mouse (flik´əmows) *n.* (*pl.* **flicker-mice** (-mīs)) a bat; cp. FLITTER-MOUSE (under FLITTER).

flier FLYER[1].

flight[1] (flīt) *n.* **1** the act, manner or power of flying through the air. **2** an air or space journey, esp. a scheduled trip made by a commercial airline. **3** the basic tactical unit of an airforce. **4** swift movement or passage, such as the motion of a projectile or the passing of time. **5** a trajectory. **6** a soaring, a sally, an excursion, a sustained effort (*a flight of fancy*). **7** the distance to which anything can fly. **8** a number of birds or insects moving together. **9** a migration. **10** a volley (of arrows, spears etc.). **11** a series of steps mounting in one direction. **12** a line of hurdles on a course. **13** in angling, a device for causing the bait to spin rapidly. **14** the pursuit of game by a hawk. **15** a feather or vane attached to the tail of an arrow or dart. *~v.t.* **1** to shoot at wildfowl flying overhead. **2** to give a high, slow trajectory to (a ball etc.). **3** to put a feather or vane on (an arrow or dart). **in the first/ top flight** taking a leading position; outstanding. **to take/ wing one's flight** to fly. **flight arrow** *n.* a light, blunt, well-feathered arrow for long-distance shooting. **flight attendant** *n.* a steward or stewardess who looks after passengers on an aircraft. **flight bag** *n.* a small zipped shoulder bag carried by travellers in an aeroplane. **flight control** *n.* a system that controls the movement of an aeroplane. **flight deck** *n.* **1** an aircraft carrier's deck on which aircraft take off and land. **2** the compartment at the front of a large aircraft housing the controls, navigation equipment etc. **flight engineer** *n.* a member of the crew of an aeroplane in charge of the engines. **flight feather** *n.* any of the large feathers that cover the wings of a bird and provide lift and control in flying. **flightless** *a.* unable to fly. **flight lieutenant** *n.* a commissioned rank in the RAF next below squadron leader. **flight officer** *n.* (*Hist.*) a rank in the WRAF, equivalent to flight lieutenant. **flight of stairs** *n.* a set of stairs, as from one landing to another. **flight path** *n.* the planned course of an aircraft or spacecraft. **flight plan** *n.* the proposed route and schedule of an aircraft flight. **flight recorder** *n.* an instrument which records details of an aircraft's performance in flight, used to provide evidence in the event of an accident. **flight sergeant** *n.* a non-commissioned rank in the RAF, ranking above chief technician. **flight shooting** *n.* **1** shooting with flight arrows. **2** shooting at flocks of wild fowl on the wing. **flight-test** *v.t.* to test (an aircraft, spacecraft etc.) during a flight. **flighty** *a.* (*comp.* **flightier,** *superl.* **flightiest**) **1** capricious, volatile; frivolous, fickle. **2** mentally unstable; crazy. **flightily** *adv.* **flightiness** *n.* [OE *flyht*, from Gmc. *fleugan*, to FLY[2]]

flight[2] (flīt) *n.* **1** the act of fleeing or running away. **2** a hasty departure, retreat or evasion. **to put to flight** to cause to run away or disappear. **to take (to) flight** to run away, to flee. [ME *fliht*, *fluhte*, OHG *flucht*, from Gmc. *thliuhan*, to FLEE]

flighty FLIGHT[1].

flimflam (flim´flam) *n.* **1** nonsense, rubbish. **2** humbug, deception. **3** a piece of deception. *~v.t.* (*pres.p.* **flimflamming,** *past, p.p.* **flimflammed**) to deceive, to swindle. **flimflammer** *n.* **flimflammery** *n.* (*pl.* **flimflammeries**). [prob. onomat.]

flimsy (flim´zi) *a.* (*comp.* **flimsier,** *superl.* **flimsiest**) **1** without strength or solidity; insubstantial. **2** easily torn or damaged. **3** (of an excuse etc.) weak, ineffective, unconvincing. **4** thin, slight, frail. **5** frivolous, trivial, superficial, paltry. *~n.* (*pl.* **flimsies**) **1** very thin paper. **2** a copy made on this. **3** (*sl.*) an old-style £5 banknote. **flimsily** *adv.* **flimsiness** *n.* [etym. uncertain, prob. onomat.]

flinch[1] (flinch) *v.i.* **1** to shrink from (an undertaking, suffering etc.). **2** to wince, to give way, to fail. *~n.* an act or instance of flinching. **flincher** *n.* **flinchingly** *adv.* [OF *flenchir*, etym. uncertain]

flinch[2] FLENSE.

flinder (flin´də) *n.* (*usu. pl.*) a fragment, a piece, a splinter. [Norw. *flindra*, a chip, a splinter, Dut. *flenter*]

fling (fling) *v.t.* (*past, p.p.* **flung** (flŭng)) **1** to cast or throw with sudden force; to hurl. **2** to move (part of one's body) forcefully. **3** to send or put suddenly and unceremoniously. **4** to utter hastily or violently. **5** to send forth, to emit. **6** to throw to the ground, to defeat. *~v.i.* **1** to rush violently, to flounce. **2** (of horses) to kick, struggle, plunge (out). **3** to flout, sneer, to throw invective or aspersions (at). *~n.* **1** a cast or throw from the hand. **2** a gibe, a sneer. **3** a period of unrestrained behaviour or enjoyment. **4** a lively Scottish, esp. Highland dance. **5** a kick, plunge or jump. **to fling away** to discard, to reject. **to fling down** to cast or throw to the ground, to demolish, to ruin. **to fling off** to abandon, discard, disown. **to fling oneself into** **1** to rush into. **2** to undertake (an activity) enthusiastically. **to fling oneself on** to throw oneself on the mercy of. **to fling open** to throw open suddenly or violently. **to fling out** **1** to be violent or unruly. **2** to make violent or insulting remarks. **3** to utter hastily or violently. **to have a fling at** **1** to make a passing attempt at. **2** to gibe or scoff at. **to have one's fling** **1** to give oneself up to unrestrained behaviour or enjoyment. **2** to have one's own way. **flinger** *n.* [cp. Icel. *flengja*, Swed. *flänga*]

flint (flint) *n.* **1** a variety of quartz, usu. grey, smoke-brown or brownish-black and encrusted with white, easily chipped into a sharp cutting edge. **2** a nodule of flint, a flint pebble. **3** a piece of flint shaped for use in a gun, a tinderbox, lighter or a primitive tool or weapon. **4** a piece of iron alloy used to make a spark in a cigarette lighter. **5** anything extremely hard. **6** extreme hardness. **flint corn** *n.* a kind of maize with hard translucent grains. **flint glass** *n.* a very pure and lustrous kind of glass, orig. made with calcined flints. **flint implements** *n.pl.* a generic name for flint tools or weapons etc. made by prehistoric humans. **flint-knapper** *n.* a person who flakes flints or makes flints for guns. **flintlock** *n.* **1** a lock for an obsolete kind of gun in which the cock holds a piece of flint, and comes down upon the steel cap of the pan containing the priming, which is ignited by the spark so caused. **2** a gun having such a lock. **flintwood** *n.* (*Austral.*) the blackbutt tree. **flinty** *a.* (*comp.* **flintier,** *superl.* **flintiest**) **1** composed of flint. **2** of the nature of or resembling flint. **3** cruel, pitiless, hard-hearted. **flintiness** *n.* [OE (cp. Dan. *flint*, Swed. *flinta*); perh. Gr. *plinthos*, brick]

flip (flip) *v.t.* (*pres.p.* **flipping,** *past, p.p.* **flipped**) **1** to flick, jerk or toss (e.g. a coin) quickly to make it spin in the air. **2** to strike lightly. **3** to move (about or away) with a light blow. **4** to turn over. *~v.i.* **1** to strike lightly, to flap or flick (at). **2** to make a flicking noise. **3** to move with a sudden jerky motion. **4** (*sl.*) to lose control of oneself, to become very angry. **5** (*sl.*) to become wildly enthusiastic. *~n.* **1** a quick, light blow. **2** an act of flipping, a somersault. **3** a short trip in an aeroplane. **4** a short quick tour. **5** a mixed alcoholic drink containing beaten egg. **6** a drink of heated beer and spirit. *~a.* **1** (*coll.*) flippant. **2** (*coll.*) impertinent. **to flip one's lid** (*coll.*) to lose self-control. **to flip over** to (cause to) turn over. **to flip through** to read through quickly or carelessly. **flip chart** *n.* a large blank pad placed on a stand and bound at the top so that one page can be turned over to show the next page in the sequence of information. **flip-flap, flip-flop** *adv.* with (a noise as of) repeated flapping. **flip-flop** *n.* 1 a kind of sandal consisting simply of a sole and a strap held between the toes. 2 (*N Am.*) a backward handspring. 3 (*esp. N Am.*) a complete reversal (of opinion etc.). 4 an electronic device or circuit capable of assuming either of two stable states. ~*v.i.* (*pres.p.* **flip-flopping,** *past, p.p.* **flip-flopped**) to move about with a flapping noise. **flipper** *n.* 1 the broad fin of a fish. 2 the flat broad limb or paddle of a turtle, penguin etc. 3 a paddle-shaped shoe worn for esp. underwater swimming. 4 (*dated, sl.*) the hand. **flipping** *a., adv.* (*sl., euphem.*) used to express annoyance; bloody. **flipside** *n.* 1 the less important side of a popular single record on which material additional to the title number is recorded. 2 the opposite or less familiar side of a person or thing. [prob. onomat.]

flippant (flip´ənt) *a.* 1 trifling, lacking in seriousness. 2 impertinent, disrespectful. **flippancy** *n.* **flippantly** *adv.* [perh. from FLIP]

flipper, flipping FLIP.

flirt (flœt) *v.i.* 1 to make sexual advances for amusement or self-gratification. 2 to play at lovemaking. 3 to move with jerks, short flights or springs. 4 †to flit about. ~*v.t.* 1 to jerk (away). 2 to wave or jerk to (a fan etc.) and fro rapidly. ~*n.* 1 a person who flirts a lot. 2 a flirting motion, a jerk, a fling. **to flirt with** 1 to treat lightly, to risk carelessly. 2 to entertain thoughts of superficially, to toy with. **flirtation** (-tā´shən) *n.* 1 a playing at courtship; coquetry. 2 a casual involvement or interest. **flirtatious** (-tā´-) *a.* **flirtatiously** *adv.* **flirtatiousness** *n.* **flirtingly** *adv.* **flirtish** *a.* **flirty** *a.* (*comp.* **flirtier,** *superl.* **flirtiest**). [prob. imit.]

flisk (flisk) *v.i.* (*Sc.*) 1 to frisk. 2 to be restive. ~*n.* a whim, a freak. [onomat., cp. WHISK]

flit (flit) *v.i.* (*pres.p.* **flitting,** *past, p.p.* **flitted**) 1 to move, to pass from place to place. 2 to fly about lightly and rapidly. 3 to depart. 4 to leave one's house, usu. secretly to escape one's creditors or responsibilities. 5 (*Sc., North.*) to move from one place of abode to another. 6 †to flutter. ~*n.* 1 the act of flitting. 2 a stealthy departure. **flitter** *n.* [cogn. with FLEET[2], cp. Icel. *flytja*, Swed. *flitta*]

flitch (flich) *n.* 1 a side of pork salted and cured. 2 a steak from a fish, esp. halibut. 3 a board or plank from a tree trunk, usu. from the outside. 4 (*also* **fitch-plate**) a strengthening plate in a beam. ~*v.t.* to cut into flitches. **flitch beam** *n.* a beam made up of an iron plate between two pieces of wood. [OE *flicce* (cp. Icel. *flikki*, Dan. *flik*)]

flite (flīt) *v.i.* 1 †to contend. 2 (*Sc., North.*) to brawl, to scold, to wrangle. ~*n.* (*Sc.*) a scolding, a heated dispute. [OE *flītan*]

flitter (flit´ə) *v.i.* 1 to flit about. 2 to flutter. **flitter-mouse** *n.* (*pl.* **flitter-mice**) a bat; cp. FLICKER-MOUSE.

flivver (fliv´ə) *n.* (*N Am., dated, sl.*) 1 a cheap small motor car or aircraft. 2 a failure. [etym. uncertain]

flix (fliks) *n.* fur, esp. the down of the beaver. [etym. unknown]

flixweed (fliks´wēd) *n.* a plant *Descurainia sophia*, formerly supposed to cure dysentery. [earlier *fluxweed*]

float (flōt) *v.i.* 1 to be supported on the surface of or in a fluid. 2 to swim or get afloat on water. 3 to hover in the air. 4 to move or glide without effort. 5 to move in a fluid or gas, to drift. 6 to move aimlessly, e.g. in the mind. 7 (of a currency) to be free to find its own level on foreign exchange markets. 8 to circulate. ~*v.t.* 1 to support on the surface of or in a fluid. 2 (of water) to bear up or bear along. 3 to convey, to carry on or as if on water. 4 to set afloat, to launch. 5 to flood with a liquid. 6 to waft through the air. 7 to put into circulation. 8 to be or become financially current. 9 to form a limited company with a view to making a public issue of shares. 10 to offer for sale on the Stock Exchange. 11 to cause (a currency) to float. 12 to suggest (an idea etc.) for consideration. ~*n.* 1 anything buoyed up on the surface of a liquid. 2 a buoyant device designed to keep a person afloat. 3 the cork or quill on a fishing line. 4 a cork on a fishing net. 5 the bladder supporting fish, animals etc. in the water. 6 a floating mechanism in a ballcock etc. regulating a supply-tap. 7 a timber raft, a floating wharf. 8 the gear of an aircraft for alighting on water. 9 a small delivery vehicle with a flat platform for goods. 10 (a vehicle carrying) a tableau or exhibit in a parade. 11 (*usu. pl.*) the footlights of a theatre. 12 a kind of trowel for smoothing the plastering on walls. 13 a float-board. 14 a drink with a lump of ice cream floating in it. 15 a small sum of money used to provide change at the start of business. 16 a small sum of money for expenditure on minor items. 17 an act of floating. **floatable** *a.* 1 able to float. 2 navigable. **floatability** *n.* **floatage, flotage** *n.* 1 anything found floating, flotsam. 2 the right to appropriate flotsam. 3 floating power, buoyancy. 4 ships and other vessels on a river. 5 the part of a ship above the waterline. **floatation** FLOTATION. **float-board** *n.* one of the boards of an undershot waterwheel or a paddle wheel. **float-bridge** *n.* a bridge of boats or rafts. **float-carburettor** *n.* a carburettor in which the feed is controlled by a float. **floater** *n.* 1 a person or thing that floats. 2 a person who frequently changes jobs. 3 (*sl.*) a mistake. **float-feed** *n.* a feed in a control system regulated by a float. **float glass** *n.* a type of glass hardened while floating on the surface of a liquid. **floating** *a.* 1 resting on the surface of a fluid. 2 at sea. 3 unattached, free, disconnected. 4 circulating, not fixed or invested. 5 fluctuating, variable, of uncertain amount. **floating anchor** *n.* a sea anchor. **floating assets** *n.pl.* assets held for the purpose of being subsequently converted into money. **floating axle** *n.* a live axle in which the revolving part turns the wheels, while the weight of the vehicle is supported on the ends of a fixed axle housing. **floating battery** *n.* an armoured vessel, heavily armed, for bombarding fortresses, defending harbours etc. **floating bridge** *n.* 1 a bridge of rafts and timber floating on the surface of the water. 2 a ferry that uses chains. **floating capital** *n.* CIRCULATING CAPITAL (under CIRCULATE). **floating debt** *n.* the portion of the national debt repayable at a stated time or on demand. **floating dock** *n.* a large iron or wooden structure into which a vessel can be floated, the internal water then being pumped out to result in a floating dry dock. **floating kidney** *n.* 1 a condition in which the kidney is unusually mobile. 2 such a kidney. **floating light** *n.* 1 a lightship. 2 a lifebuoy to which a light is attached, to attract attention to a person in the water, and to direct the boat's crew coming to the rescue. **floatingly** *adv.* **floating pier** *n.* a landing stage which rises and falls with the tide. **floating point** *n.* a decimal point that does not hold a fixed position in a mathematical rotation. **floating-point** *a.* **floating rib** *n.* either of the lowest two pairs of ribs, which are not attached to the breastbone. **floating voter** *n.* a person of no fixed party-political allegiance. **float process** *n.* the process used in making float glass. **float roll calender** *n.* an ironing machine in which articles with buttons can be ironed and pressed without damage. **float-stone** *n.* a spongy variety of opal light enough to float on the surface of water. **floaty** *a.* (*comp.* **floatier,** *superl.* **floatiest**) (of material or clothes) light and airy. [OE *flotian*, cogn. with FLEET[2]; influ. by OF *floter* (F *flotter*)]

floatel (flōtel´), **flotel** *n.* a boat or platform providing accommodation for offshore oil-rig workers. [*float*ing *hotel*]

floc (flok) *n.* (*Chem.*) matter in woolly or loose floating masses precipitated in a solution.

floccus (flok´əs) *n.* (*pl.* **flocci** (flok´si)) 1 a tuft of woolly hair. **2** the down of unfledged birds. **floccillation** (-silā´shən) *n.* a picking of the bedclothes by a delirious patient. **floccose** (-ōs) *a.* covered with little woolly tufts. **floccosely** *adv.* **flocculate** (-ūlāt) *v.t.*, *v.i.* to form into a flocculent mass. **flocculation** (-lā´shən) *n.* **floccule** (-ūl) *n.* **1** a loose tuft. **2** a small woolly or tuftlike portion. **flocculence** *n.* **flocculent** *a.* **1** in small flakes, woolly, tufted. **2** (*Chem.*) (of precipitates) loosely aggregated in cloudlike masses. **flocculose, flocculous** *a.* **flocculus** (-ləs) *n.* (*pl.* **flocculi** (-lī)) **1** a floccule. **2** a lobe on the undersurface of the human cerebellum. **3** a cloudy marking on the surface of the sun. [L *floccus*, a lock of wool, dim. *flocculus*]

flock[1] (flok) *n.* **1** a company or collection of animals, esp. sheep, goats or birds. **2** a crowd, a large body. **3** a congregation, considered in relation to their minister. **4** a group of children or pupils. ~*v.i.* **1** to come together in a flock, to congregate, to assemble. **2** to move or go in crowds. ~*v.t.* **1** to crowd. **2** to press by crowding. [OE *flocc* (cp. Icel. *flokkr*)]

flock[2] (flok) *n.* **1** a lock or tuft of wool, cotton, hair etc. **2** (*usu. pl.*) wool-dust used in coating certain portions of the patterns in some wallpapers. **3** fibrous material, made by tearing up woollen rags by machinery, used to stuff upholstery, mattresses etc. **flock-bed** *n.* a bed stuffed with flocks of wool, hair or torn-up rags. **flock paper, flock wallpaper** *n.* wallpaper, to which flock is attached with size. **flocky** *a.* [prob. from OF *floc*, L *floccus*]

floe (flō) *n.* a large sheet of floating ice. [prob. from Norse *flo*, a layer]

flog (flog) *v.t.* (*pres.p.* **flogging,** *past, p.p.* **flogged**) **1** to beat with a whip or stick as punishment. **2** to whip, to lash (e.g. the water in fly-fishing). **3** to urge or drive by beating. **4** to repeat or labour to the point of tedium. **5** (*sl.*) to sell. ~*v.i.* to make progress by forceful or painful means. **to flog a dead horse 1** to try to revive interest in something stale. **2** to pursue a hopeless task. **to flog to death** (*coll.*) to talk about to the point of tedium. **flogger, flogster** *n.* **flogging** *n.* punishment by whipping. [perh. corr. of L *flagellāre*, see FLAGELLATE[1]]

flong (flong) *n.* (*Print.*) prepared paper used for the matrices in stereotyping. [F *flan*, flawn]

flood (flŭd) *n.* **1** an abundant flow of water. **2** a body of water rising and overflowing land not usually covered with water, an inundation. **3** the inflow of the tide. **4** a downpour, a torrent. **5** (*poet.*) a river, the sea. **6** an overflowing abundance. **7** (*coll.*) a floodlight. ~*v.t.* **1** to overflow, to inundate, to deluge. **2** to supply copiously (with). **3** to irrigate. **4** to supply too much petrol to (the carburettor). ~*v.i.* **1** (of the sea) to be at its highest. **2** to rise and overflow. **3** to arrive in large numbers (*enquiries flooded in*). **4** to have uterine haemorrhage. **5** to have excessive menstrual discharge. **the Flood** the flood recorded in Genesis. **to flood out** to drive from one's home etc. because of a flood. **flood and field** *n.* (*poet.*) sea and land. **floodgate** *n.* **1** a gate in a waterway arranged to open when the water attains a certain height, and so allow it to escape freely to prevent floods, a sluice. **2** the lower gate of a lock. **3** a restraint against an esp. emotional outburst. **flooding** *n.* **1** the act of inundating. **2** the state of being flooded, an inundation. **3** an abnormal discharge of blood from the uterus. **floodlight** *n.* **1** a powerful beam of artificial light used esp. in the theatre, in sports stadiums or to illuminate buildings. **2** a lamp producing such light. ~*v.t.* (*pres.p.* **floodlighting,** *past, p.p.* **floodlit**) to illuminate with floodlight. **floodlighting** *n.* **floodmark** *n.* high water mark. **flood plain** *n.* an area of flat land near a river, formed by sediment deposited during floods. **flood tide** *n.* the rising tide. **flood water** *n.* water left by flooding. [OE *flōd* (cp. Icel. *flōd*, Dut. *vloed*, G *Flut*), cogn. with FLOW]

floor (flaw) *n.* **1** the bottom surface of a room, on which people walk and which supports the furniture. **2** the boards or other material of which this is made. **3** the bottom of the sea, a cave etc. **4** a storey in a building. **5** a suite of rooms on the same level. **6** the part of the house assigned to members of a legislative assembly. **7** the trading hall of a stock exchange. **8** the (area occupied by) people attending a meeting or debate as the audience. **9** the right to address a meeting, assembly etc. **10** any level area corresponding to the floor of a room. **11** the flat portion of a vessel's hold. **12** the bottom of a coal seam. **13** the lowest limit of prices, wages etc. ~*v.t.* **1** to furnish with a floor. **2** to be or serve as a floor (to). **3** to knock down. **4** (*coll.*) to baffle or confound, to put to silence (as in argument). **5** (*coll.*) to get the better of, to defeat. **to cross the floor** (of an MP etc.) to change party-political allegiance. **to have the floor** to be given the right to address a meeting, assembly etc. **to mop the floor with someone** to defeat someone completely. **to take the floor 1** to rise to speak, to take part in a debate. **2** (*Ir.*) to get up to dance. **to wipe the floor with someone** (*coll.*) to defeat someone completely. **floorboard** *n.* any of the planks making up a floor. **floorcloth** *n.* **1** a piece of soft fabric used for washing floors. **2** a substitute for a carpet. **floorer** *n.* **1** (*coll.*) something which floors or defeats. **2** a knock-down blow. **3** a poser, a baffling question. **4** a decisive retort. **floor exercises** *n.pl.* gymnastic exercises that do not require equipment. **flooring** *n.* **1** material for floors. **2** a floor, a platform. **floor lamp** *n.* (*N Am.*) a lamp, usu. portable, that stands on the floor. **floor leader** *n.* (*N Am.*) the leader of a party in a legislative assembly. **floor-length** *a.* (of garments) that reach to the floor. **floorless** *a.* **floor manager** *n.* **1** the stage manager of a television programme. **2** the manager of a floor in a large store. **floor plan** *n.* a diagram showing the arrangement of rooms on one storey of a building. **floor polish** *n.* a manufactured substance used for polishing floors. **floor show** *n.* a performance on the floor of a restaurant, nightclub etc. **floor timbers** *n.pl.* the main timbers on which a floor is laid. **floorwalker** *n.* (*N Am.*) a shopwalker. [OE *flōr* (cp. Dut. *vloer*, G *Flur*)]

floozie (floo´zi), **floozy** *n.* (*pl.* **floozies**) (*derog.*) a woman who is attractive in a common sort of way and thought to be free with her company and favours. [etym. uncertain]

flop (flop) *v.i.* (*pres.p.* **flopping,** *past, p.p.* **flopped**) **1** to tumble about or fall loosely and heavily. **2** to sway about heavily, to flap. **3** to make a dull sound as of a soft body flapping. **4** to move or walk about (in an ungainly manner). **5** to move or sit suddenly. **6** (*coll.*) to fail dismally. **7** (*sl.*) to go to bed. ~*v.t.* **1** to let fall negligently or noisily. **2** to cause to strike with a heavy dull sound. ~*n.* **1** the act or motion of flopping. **2** the noise of a soft outspread body falling suddenly to the ground. **3** (*coll.*) a complete failure. **4** (*esp. N Am., sl.*) a place to sleep. ~*adv.* **1** with a flop. **2** suddenly. **flophouse** *n.* (*esp. N Am., sl.*) a doss-house, a cheap lodging house. **floppy** *a.* (*comp.* **floppier,** *superl.* **floppiest**) soft and flexible, limp. ~*n.* (*pl.* **floppies**) a floppy disk. **floppily** *adv.* **floppiness** *n.* **floppy disk** *n.* (*Comput.*) a flexible magnetic disk for data storage. [var. of FLAP]

-flop (flop) *comb. form* floating-point operations per second, as in *megaflop*. [acronym]

floptical (flop´tikəl) *a.* of, relating to or designed for a kind of floppy disk drive that uses a laser to set the read-write head. [*floppy*, *optical*]

flor. *abbr.* floruit.

flora (flaw´rə) *n.* (*pl.* **floras, florae** (-rē)) **1** the whole vegetation of a country, district or geological period. **2** a book dealing with the vegetation of a country or district. **floral** *a.* **1** of or relating to flowers. **2** of or relating to floras. **3** consisting of, or decorated with, flowers. **floral envelope** *n.* the perianth or parts surrounding the stamens and pistils, generally consisting of calyx and corolla. **florally** *adv.* [L, Flora, the Roman goddess of flowers and gardens, from *flōs flōris*, FLOWER]

Floréal (flor´āal) *n.* the eighth month of the French revolutionary calendar, from 21 April to 20 May. [F from L *floreus*, of flowers]

floreat (flo´riat) *v.i.* may (a person, situation etc.) flourish. [L]

Florence (flo´rəns) *n.* a kind of red wine from Florence, the chief city of Tuscany, in northern Italy. **Florence fennel** FENNEL. **Florence flask** *n.* a thin glass flask, with large globular body and long narrow neck. [F, from L *Flōrentia* (It. *Firenze*)]

Florentine (flo´rəntīn) *a.* **1** of or relating to Florence. **2** (**florentine** (-tēn)) served or prepared with spinach. *~n.* **1** a native or inhabitant of Florence. **2** a biscuit containing nuts and dried fruit, coated on one side with chocolate. **3** a kind of durable silk fabric. **4** a kind of pie or tart, esp. a meat pie without under-crust. **Florentine iris, Florentine flower-de-luce** *n.* a white or pale-blue iris, *Iris florentina.* [L *Flōrentīnus*, from *Flōrentia*, see FLORENCE]

florescence (flawres´əns) *n.* **1** the flowering of a plant. **2** the season when a plant flowers. **florescent** *a.* [L *flōrescens -ntem*, pres.p. of *flōrescere*, incept. of *flōrēre*, see FLOURISH, -ENCE]

floret (flor´it, flaw-) *n.* **1** a small flower. **2** a small flower forming part of a composite one. **3** any one of the flowering stems on the head of a cauliflower etc. [OF *florete*, dim. of *fleur*]

floriate (flaw´riāt) *v.t.* to adorn with floral ornaments or designs. **floriated** *a.* **floriation** (-iā´shən) *n.* [L *flōs flōris*]

floribunda (floribŭn´də, flaw-) *n.* a plant, esp. a rose, whose flowers grow in dense clusters. [mod. L *floribundus*, flowering freely]

floriculture (flo´rikŭlchə, flaw´-) *n.* the cultivation of flowers or flowering plants. **floricultural** (-kŭl´-) *a.* **floriculturist** (-kŭl´-) *n.*

florid (flo´rid) *a.* **1** flushed with red, ruddy. **2** bright in colour. **3** flowery, highly embellished, elaborately ornate. **4** covered with or abounding in flowers; showy. **floridity** (-rid´iti) *n.* **floridly** *adv.* **floridness** *n.* [L *flōridus*]

floriferous (florif´ərəs, flaw-) *a.* bearing many flowers. [L *flōrifer*]

floriform (flo´rifawm) *a.* having the shape of a flower.

florilegium (florilē´jiəm, flaw-) *n.* (*pl.* **florilegia** (-jiə), **florilegiums**) an anthology. [L *flōs flōris*, FLOWER, *legere*, to cull]

florin (flo´rin) *n.* **1** a former British coin, orig. silver, worth the equivalent of 10p, a two-shilling piece. **2** a foreign gold or silver coin, of various values according to country and period. **3** an English gold coin of Edward III, worth 6s. 8d. (33p). **4** orig. a Florentine coin, stamped with the lily flower, the national badge of Florence. [OF, from It. *fiorino*, dim. of *fiore*, L *flōrem*]

florist (flo´rist) *n.* **1** a person who sells flowers. **2** a person skilled in growing flowers; a cultivator of flowers. **floristic** (-ris´-) *a.* of or relating to flowers or their distribution. **floristically** *adv.* **floristics** *n.* **floristry** *n.*

floruit (flor´uit, flaw´-) *v.i.* (he or she) was alive and actively working; flourished, used to express the period during which a person, e.g. a painter or writer, was most active (in the absence of exact dates of birth and death). *~n.* the period during which a person was alive and actively working. [L, he or she flourished, 3rd sing. perf. of *flōrēre*, see FLOURISH]

flory FLEURY (under FLEUR-DE-LIS).

floscular (flos´kūlə), **flosculous** *a.* **1** having little flowers. **2** bearing many florets or composite flowers. **floscule** *n.* a floret. [L *flōsculus*, dim. of *flōs*, FLOWER]

flos ferri (flos fe´ri) *n.* (*Mineral.*) a spicular variety of aragonite. [L, flower of iron]

floss (flos) *n.* **1** the exterior rough silk envelope of a silkworm's cocoon. **2** the downy substance on the husks of certain plants, such as the bean. **3** dental floss. **4** untwisted silk thread used in embroidery. *~v.t., v.i.* to use dental floss. **floss silk** *n.* untwisted filaments of the finest silk, used in embroidery etc. **flossy** *a.* (*comp.* **flossier**, *superl.* **flossiest**) **1** of, resembling or relating to floss. **2** (*coll.*) showily stylish; fancy. [perh. from OF *flosche*, down, cp. FLOCK²]

flotage FLOATAGE (under FLOAT).

flotant (flō´tənt) *a.* (*Her.*) floating, as a flag, bird, or anything swimming. [F *flottant*, pres.p. of *flotter*, see FLOTATION]

flotation (flōtā´shən), **floatation** *n.* **1** the floating of a company on the Stock Exchange. **2** the act or state of floating. **3** the science of floating bodies. **4** the separation of the particulars of a material, e.g. powdered ore, by their relative capacities to float. **flotative** (flō´-) *a.* **1** capable of floating. **2** tending to float.

flotel FLOATEL.

flotilla (flətil´ə) *n.* **1** a small fleet. **2** a fleet of small vessels. [Sp., dim. of *flota*, a fleet]

flotsam (flot´səm) *n.* goods lost in shipwreck and found floating. **flotsam and jetsam** *n.* **1** wreckage or any property found floating or washed ashore. **2** odds and ends. **3** vagrants etc. [A-F *floteson*, OF *flotaison*, from *floter*, to FLOAT]

flounce¹ (flowns) *v.i.* **1** to move abruptly or violently. **2** to exaggerate one's movements as a means of calling attention to oneself or one's impatience etc. *~n.* a flouncing movement. [prob. cogn. with Norw. *flunsa*, to hurry, Swed. dial. *flunsa*, to plunge]

flounce² (flowns) *n.* a gathered or pleated strip of cloth sewed to a petticoat, dress etc., with the lower border hanging loose. *~v.t.* **1** to attach flounces to. **2** to deck or trim with flounces. [ME *frounce*, OF *fronce*, from *froncer*, to wrinkle, L *frons*, the forehead]

flounder¹ (flown´də) *n.* **1** a flatfish, *Pleuronectes flesus*, resembling the plaice, but with paler spots. **2** any small flatfish of the family Pleuronectidae or Bothidae. [OF *flondre* (cp. Norw. *flundra*, Dan. *flynder*)]

flounder² (flown´də) *v.i.* **1** to struggle or stumble about violently, as when stuck in mud. **2** to struggle along with difficulty. **3** to blunder along, to do things badly. *~n.* **1** a stumbling or blundering effort. **2** the motion or act of floundering. **flounderer** *n.* [prob. cogn. with Norw. *flundra*, Dut. *flodderen*]

flour (flow´ə) *n.* **1** the finer part of meal, esp. of wheatmeal. **2** fine soft powder of any substance. *~v.t.* **1** to sprinkle flour upon. **2** (*N Am.*) to grind into flour. **flour bolt, flour dresser** *n.* a machine for bolting or bolting and dressing flour. **flour mill** *n.* a mill for grinding and sifting flour. **floury** *a.* (*comp.* **flourier**, *superl.* **flouriest**) **1** covered with flour. **2** like flour. **flouriness** *n.* [var. of FLOWER (ME *flour of whete*, the finest meal)]

flourish (flŭr´ish) *v.i.* **1** to grow in a strong and healthy way. **2** to thrive, to prosper, to increase in wealth, honour or happiness. **3** to be in good health. **4** to be in a state of complete development. **5** to be alive or at work (at or about a certain date). **6** to use florid language. **7** to make bold and fanciful strokes in writing. **8** to move about fantastically. **9** (*Mus.*) to play in a bold, dashing style, with ornamental notes. **10** to sound a fanfare. **11** †to brag. **12** †to blossom. *~v.t.* **1** to brandish, fling or wave about. **2** to flaunt, to show ostentatiously. **3** to embellish with ornamental or fantastic figures. *~n.* **1** a brandishing or waving of a weapon or other thing. **2** a figure formed by strokes or lines fancifully drawn. **3** rhetorical display, a florid expression. **4** (*Mus.*) **a** a passage played for display. **b** a fanfare of trumpets etc. **c** an improvised prelude or other addition. **5** †a flourishing condition, prosperity. **flourished** *a.* **1** adorned with flourishes. **2** (*Her.*) fleury. **flourisher** *n.* **flourishing** *a.* **1** thriving, prosperous. **2** making a show. **flourishingly** *adv.* **flourish of trumpets** *n.* **1** the sounding of trumpets when receiving any person of distinction. **2** an ostentatious announcement. **flourishy** *a.* [OF *floriss-*, stem of *florir*, L *flōrēre*, from *flōs flōris*, FLOWER]

flout (flowt) *v.t.* **1** to mock, to insult. **2** to treat with contempt, to disregard, to defy. *~v.i.* **1** to sneer. **2** to behave with contempt or mockery. *~n.* **1** a word or act of contempt. **2** a sneer, an insult. **flouter** *n.* **floutingly** *adv.* [prob. var. of FLUTE (cp. MDut. *fluyten*, to play the flute, to jeer)]

Usage note See note under FLAUNT.

---

flow (flō) *v.i.* **1** (of a fluid) to move, run or spread. **2** (of blood etc.) to circulate. **3** (of the tide) to rise. **4** to issue, to spring, to gush out. **5** to sway, glide, hang or float, to move easily or freely, to undulate. **6** to be poured out abundantly, to abound, to come or go in abundance or great numbers. **7** to result, to issue, to be descended (from). **8** (of talk etc.) to proceed smoothly without hesitation. **9** (of a rock) to yield to pressure without breaking so that the shape is changed. **10** to discharge blood in excess from the uterus. **11** †to melt, to become liquid. **12** to overflow. *~†v.t.* to overflow, to flood. *~n.* **1** the act, state, manner or motion of flowing. **2** the quantity that flows. **3** a flowing liquid, a stream. **4** a copious stream, abundance, a plentiful supply. **5** the rise of the tide. **6** an overflowing. **7** menstruation. **8** the change in shape of a rock under pressure. **9** (*Sc.*) a wet or marshy tract. **10** undulation (of drapery etc.). **11** a quicksand. **to go with the flow** to do the same as others, not trying to do something different. **†flowage** *n.* the act or state of flowing. **flow chart, flow diagram, flowsheet** *n.* a diagram showing the sequence of operations in a complex process or computer program. **flowing** *a.* **1** moving as a stream. **2** copious, fluent, easy. **3** smooth, unbroken, not abrupt or stiff. **4** hanging loose and waving. **5** (of a fore-and-aft sail) slackened, with the wind across the vessel's course. **flowingly** *adv.* **flowingness** *n.* **flowing sheet** *n.* (*Naut.*) a sheet that is slackened to allow it greater movement in the wind. **flow lines** *n.pl.* lines in igneous rocks resulting from the flow of the material before consolidation. **flowmeter** *n.* a device that measures the rate of flow of a liquid or gas in a pipe. **flow-on** *n.* (*Austral.*) an adjustment to wages or salary, given as a result of one already made to another group of workers undertaking similar work. **flowstone** *n.* rock that has been deposited in a thin sheet by flowing water. [OE *flōwan* (cp. Dut. *vloeijen*, Icel. *flōa*), cogn. with Gr. *pleein*, to sail, L *pluere*, to rain (not *fluere*, to flow)]

flower (flow´ə) *n.* **1** the organ or growth comprising the organs of reproduction in a plant. **2** a flowering plant. **3** the blossom, the bloom. **4** the finest, choicest or best individual, part, period etc. **5** the prime; the period of youthful vigour. **6** (*pl.*) decorative phrases; figures of speech. **7** (*pl., Chem.*) substances of a powdery consistency or form, esp. if produced by sublimation. **8** (*pl.*) †the menstrual discharge. *~v.i.* **1** to produce flowers, to bloom, to blossom. **2** to be in the prime. *~v.t.* **1** to embellish with flowers. **2** to cause to blossom. **in flower** with the flowers appeared and opened. **flowerage** *n.* **1** the state of being in flower. **2** flowers in general. **flower-bearing** *a.* producing flowers. **flower bed** *n.* a plot of ground in a garden or park in which flowers are grown. **flower-bud** *n.* a bud which develops into a flower. **flower-de-luce** (-dəloos´) *n.* (*pl.* **flowers-de-luce** (-dəloos´)) FLEUR-DE-LIS. **flowered** *a.* **1** having or embellished with flowers or figures of flowers. **2** (*in comb.*) bearing flowers, as *blue-flowered, six-flowered.* **flowerer** *n.* a plant that flowers at a particular time or in a particular way (*spring flowerer*). **floweret** (-rit) *n.* a little flower. **flower garden** *n.* a garden devoted to the cultivation of flowers. **flower girl** *n.* a girl or woman selling flowers, esp. in the street. **flower-head** *n.* CAPITULUM. **flowering** *a.* **1** that flowers. **2** flowery, in bloom. **flowering plant** *n.* an angiosperm. **flowering rush** *n.* a water plant, *Butomus umbellatus*, with an umbel of pink flowers. **flowerless** *a.* **flowerlessness** *n.* **flower-like** *a.* **flower people** *n.pl.* colourfully dressed hippies of the late 1960s who wore or carried flowers as symbols of peace and love. **flowerpot** *n.* an earthenware pot to hold plants. **flower power** *n.* a youth culture of the late 1960s which rejected materialism and advocated peace and love. **flower show** *n.* a horticultural exhibition, usu. competitive. **flowers of sulphur** *n.pl.* a form of sulphur obtained by distillation from other forms. **flowers of zinc** *n.pl.* zinc oxide. **flower-stalk** *n.* the peduncle supporting the flowers of a plant. **flowery** *a.* **1** abounding in or full of flowers or blossoms. **2** highly figurative or decorative, florid. [OF *flour*, L *flōrem*, nom. *flōs*, cogn. with BLOW[3]]

flown FLY[2].

fl. oz. *abbr.* fluid ounce.

FLQ *abbr.* (in Canada) Front de Libération du Quebec.

Flt. Lt. *abbr.* Flight Lieutenant.

Flt. Off. *abbr.* (*Hist.*) Flight Officer.

flu (floo) *n.* (*coll.*) a highly contagious viral disease marked by fever aches and catarrhal inflammation of the respiratory passages. [short for *influenza*]

flub (flŭb) *v.t., v.i.* (*pres.p.* **flubbing**, *past, p.p.* **flubbed**) (*N Am., coll.*) to botch or bungle. *~n.* a bungle; blunder. [etym. unknown]

fluctuate (flŭk´chūāt) *v.i.* **1** to vary, to change irregularly in degree, to be unsettled. **2** to rise and fall like waves. **3** to hesitate, to waver. *~†v.t.* to cause to move or roll about like waves. **fluctuant** *a.* **1** unsteady, wavering. **2** †undulating, moving like a wave. **fluctuating** *a.* unsteady, wavering. **fluctuation** (-ā´shən) *n.* [L *fluctuātus, p.p.* of *fluctuāre*, from *fluctus*, a wave]

flue[1] (floo) *n.* **1** a passage or tube by which smoke can escape or hot air be conveyed. **2** †a chimney. **flue-cure** *v.t.* to cure (tobacco) by means of heat from artificial flues. **flue pipe** *n.* an organ pipe in which the sound is produced by air passing through a fissure and striking an edge above. **flue stop** *n.* an organ stop controlling a rank of flue pipes. **flue work** *n.* the flue stops of an organ as distinct from the reed-stops. [etym. doubtful, perh. from obs. *flue*, shallow, or from FLUE[4]]

flue[2] (floo) *n.* **1** light down or fur. **2** fluff. **fluey** *a.* [etym. unknown, perh. cogn. with FLY[2] (cp. Norw. *flu*, G *flug*, flight)]

flue[3] (floo) *n.* a kind of fishing net. [etym. uncertain, cp. Dut. *flouw*]

flue[4] (floo) *v.i.* (*3rd pers. sing. pres.* **flues**, *pres.p.* **flueing,** *past, p.p.* **flued**) **1** to widen or spread out. **2** to splay. *~v.t.* to cause (a window, jambs etc.) to splay. [prob. from obs. a. *flue*, see FLUE[1]]

fluence (floo´əns) *n.* (*coll.*) influence. **to put the fluence on** to hypnotize. [short for *influence*]

fluent (floo´ənt) *a.* **1** able to speak a foreign language easily, accurately and without hesitation (*fluent in Spanish*). **2** ready and natural in the use of words. **3** eloquent, copious, voluble. **4** moving or curving smoothly, graceful. **5** fluid, mobile, changeable. **6** †flowing, liquid. *~n.* (*Math.*) the variable quantity in fluxions. **fluency** *n.* **1** fluent command of a foreign language. **2** readiness and easy flow (of words or ideas).

3 the quality of being fluent. **fluently** *adv.* [L *fluens -entem*, pres.p. of *fluere*, to flow]

fluff (flŭf) *n.* 1 light down or fur. 2 flocculent matter. 3 the nap of anything. 4 (*sl.*) a mistake made esp. in delivering lines, reading a text or playing a game or a piece of music. 5 something insubstantial. ~*v.t.* 1 to cover with fluff or give a fluffy surface to. 2 to shake or spread (feathers out, as a bird). 3 (*coll.*) to bungle. ~*v.i.* 1 to become a soft mass. 2 (*coll.*) to make a mistake in performing. **bit of fluff** BIT[1]. **fluffy** *a.* (*comp.* **fluffier,** *superl.* **fluffiest**) 1 of, like or relating to fluff. 2 covered with fluff. **fluffily** *adv.* **fluffiness** *n.* [prob. from FLUE[2]]

flugelhorn (floo´gəlhawn) *n.* a valved brass instrument resembling, but slightly larger than, a cornet. [G *Flügel*, wing, *Horn*, horn]

fluid (floo´id) *n.* 1 a liquid or gas, not a solid. 2 a substance whose particles readily move and change their relative positions. ~*a.* 1 capable of flowing, as water. 2 composed of particles that move freely in relation to each other. 3 liquid, gaseous. 4 not rigid or stable. 5 smooth and graceful. 6 using liquid for the transmission of power. **fluid drive** *n.* a system of transmitting power through a change in the momentum of oil. **fluidics** *n.* the study and use of fluids flowing in channels simulating the flow of electricity in conductors, used in applications usu. performed by electronic devices. **fluidic** *a.* **fluidify** (-id´-) *v.t.* (*3rd pers. sing. pres.* **fluidifies,** *pres.p.* **fluidifying,** *past, p.p.* **fluidified**). **fluidity** (-id´-) *n.* **fluidize, fluidise** *v.t.* to make (a solid) a fluid by pulverizing it and moving it in a rapidly flowing upward stream of gas. **fluidization** (-zā´shən) *n.* **fluidized bed** *n.* a layer of fluidized solids, used as a medium in a heat exchanger. **fluidly** *adv.* **fluid measure** *n.* apothecaries' measure of capacity of the British pharmacopoeia. **fluid mechanics** *n.* the study of the forces and flow within liquids. **fluidness** *n.* **fluid ounce** *n.* 1 a British unit of liquid capacity equal to 1/20 of an imperial pint (28.4 ml). 2 (*also* **fluidounce**) a unit equal to 1/16 of a US pint (29.5 ml). **fluidram** *n.* (*N Am.*) a fluid drachm. [OF *fluide*, L *fluidus*, from *fluere*, to flow]

fluke[1] (flook) *n.* 1 an accidentally successful stroke; any lucky chance. 2 a chance breeze. ~*v.i.* to score by luck. ~*v.t.* to hit or obtain in this way. **fluky**[1] *a.* (*comp.* **flukier,** *superl.* **flukiest**) 1 obtained by chance, not skill. 2 unsteady, variable. **flukily** *adv.* **flukiness** *n.* [etym. uncertain]

fluke[2] (flook) *n.* 1 a parasitic worm belonging to the Trematoda, found chiefly in the livers of sheep. 2 a flounder or other flatfish. 3 a kind of potato. **fluky**[2] *a.* (of sheep) infested with flukes. [OE *flōc*; cogn. with G *flach*, flat]

fluke[3] (flook) *n.* 1 the broad holding portion of an anchor. 2 either of the flat lobes of a whale's tail. 3 a barb of a lance, harpoon etc. 4 a tool for cleansing a hole previous to blasting. [prob. from FLUKE[2]]

fluky[1] FLUKE[1].

fluky[2] FLUKE[2].

flume (floom) *n.* 1 an artificial channel for conveying water to a mill or for some other industrial use. 2 a deep ravine traversed by a torrent. 3 a water chute or water slide at a swimming pool or amusement park. ~*v.t.* 1 to carry down a flume. 2 to drain by means of a flume. ~*v.i.* to make flumes. **to be up the flume** (*N Am., sl.*) to be done for. **to go up the flume** (*N Am., sl.*) to come to grief. [OF *flum*, L *flumen*, a river, from *fluere*, to flow]

flummery (flŭm´əri) *n.* (*pl.* **flummeries**) 1 nonsense, humbug. 2 empty compliments. 3 anything insipid or out of place. 4 a food made of oatmeal or bran boiled to a jelly. 5 a kind of blancmange. [Welsh *llymru*]

flummox (flŭm´əks) *v.t.* (*coll.*) to perplex, confound. [prob. onomat.]

flump (flŭmp) *v.i.* 1 to fall down heavily. 2 to flop. 3 to sit down with a flop. ~*v.t.* to throw down with a dull, heavy noise. ~*n.* 1 a dull, heavy noise, as of something let fall. 2 the action of flumping. [imit.]

flung FLING.

flunk (flŭngk) *v.t.* (*chiefly N Am., coll.*) to (cause to) fail a subject, course etc. ~*v.i.* to fail, esp. in an examination or course. ~*n.* an instance of flunking. **to flunk out** (*chiefly N Am., coll.*) to be expelled for failure. [cp. FLINCH[1] and FUNK[1]]

flunkey (flŭng´ki), **flunky** *n.* (*pl.* **flunkeys, flunkies**) 1 a servant in livery, a footman. 2 a lackey. 3 a toady; a snob. 4 (*N Am.*) a person who does menial work. **flunkeydom** *n.* **flunkeyish** *a.* **flunkeyism** *n.* [Sc., prob. from FLANKER (under FLANK) (cp. F *flanquer*, to run at the side of)]

fluor (floo´aw), **fluorspar** (fluə´spah, flaw´-), **fluorite** (fluə´rīt) *n.* an isometric, transparent or subtranslucent brittle mineral, having many shades of colour, composed of calcium fluoride. [L, flow, from *fluere*, to flow]

fluor- FLUORO-.

fluorate FLUORINE.

fluorescence (fluəres´əns, flaw-) *n.* 1 a quality existing in certain substances of giving out light of a different colour from their own or that of the light falling upon them. 2 the coloured luminosity thus produced, esp. the visible light produced by the action of ultraviolet rays. **fluoresce** *v.i.* 1 to be or become fluorescent. 2 to exhibit fluorescence. **fluorescein** (-sēn, -sin) *n.* an orange dye with a greenish-yellow fluorescence in alkaline. **fluorescent** *a.* having the quality of fluorescence. **fluorescent lamp, fluorescent bulb** *n.* a lamp consisting of a glass tube with a fluorescent coating of phosphor inside, which emits light on the passage through the tube of an electric current. **fluorescent screen** *n.* a screen coated on one side with a phosphor that fluoresces when exposed to X-rays etc.

fluorhydric (fluəhī´drik, flaw´-) *a.* HYDROFLUORIC ACID.

fluorine (fluə´rēn, flaw´-) *n.* a non-metallic gaseous element, at. no. 9, chem. symbol F, forming with chlorine, bromine and iodine the halogen group. **fluorate** (-rāt) *n.* a salt of fluoric acid. **fluoric** (-o´-) *a.* containing fluorine. **fluoric acid** *n.* **fluoridate** *v.t.* to add traces of fluoride to (water) to prevent or reduce tooth decay. **fluoridation** (-dā´shən), **fluoridization** (-zā´shən), **fluoridisation** *n.* **fluoride** (-rīd) *n.* a compound of fluorine with an element or radical.

fluorite FLUOR.

fluoro- (fluə´rō, flaw´ə), **fluor-** *comb. form* 1 fluorine. 2 fluorescence. [FLUOR]

fluorocarbon (fluərōkah´bən, flaw-) *n.* any of a series of compounds of fluorine and carbon, which are chemically inert and highly resistant to heat.

fluoroscope (fluə´rəskōp, flaw-) *n.* an apparatus consisting of a lightproof box with a fluorescent screen, for observing the effects of X-rays. **fluoroscopy** (-ros´kəpi) *n.*

fluorosis (fluərō´sis, flaw-) *n.* poisoning by fluorine or its compounds.

fluorspar FLUOR.

flurry (flŭ´ri) *n.* (*pl.* **flurries**) 1 a squall. 2 a sudden and violent shower of rain, snow etc. 3 a short and intense period of activity. 4 commotion, agitation, bustle, confusion. 5 nervous excitement. ~*v.t.* (*3rd pers. sing. pres.* **flurries,** *pres.p.* **flurrying,** *past, p.p.* **flurried**) to agitate, to fluster, to upset, to bewilder with noise or excitement. [onomat.; cp. HURRY]

flush[1] (flŭsh) *v.i.* to colour as if with a rush of blood, to redden up, to blush, to glow. ~*v.t.* 1 to cause to colour or become red. 2 to redden. 3 to inflame. 4 to encourage, to excite, as with passion. ~*n.* 1 a sudden flow or rush of blood to the face causing a redness. 2 any warm colouring or glow. 3 a sudden rush of emotion, elation, excitement. **4 a** (*also* **hot flush**) a sudden feeling of heat during the menopause. **b** a hot fit in fever. **5** vigour. **6** bloom, blossoming. **flushed** *a.* [perh. the same as FLUSH², influ. by BLUSH (but cp. Swed. dial. *flossa*, to blaze, to flare)]

flush² (flŭsh) *v.i.* **1** to flow swiftly. **2** to rush. **3** to become filled (as pipes) with a sudden rush of water. **4** to become suffused. **5** (of a plant) to grow fresh shoots. ~*v.t.* **1** to cleanse by a rush of water. **2** to remove an object. **3** to flood. ~*n.* **1** a sudden flow of water. **2** the run or race from a mill-wheel. **3** the cleansing of a drain, lavatory etc. with a rush of water. **4** a morass, a bog. **flusher** *n.* a person or thing that flushes drains etc. **flushing-box, flushing-cistern, flushing-tank** *n.* a cistern for supplying lavatories or urinals with a rush of water. [perh. from FLUSH⁵, or a form of FLASH]

flush³ (flŭsh) *a.* **1** level, even, on the same plane (with). **2** plentifully supplied, esp. with money. **3** abundant; filled up. **4** full to overflowing. **5** copious, abounding. **6** filled up. ~*v.t.* **1** to make even. **2** to level (up). **3** to fill in (a joint) so as to make even with the surface. **flush deck** *n.* a deck with a level floor from stem to stern. **flushness** *n.* **1** fullness. **2** abundance. [prob. from FLUSH²]

flush⁴ (flŭsh) *n.* a hand of cards all of one suit. [perh. from F *flux*, L *fluxus*, from *fluere*, to flow]

flush⁵ (flŭsh) *v.i.* **1** to take wing. **2** (of game birds) to start up suddenly. ~*v.t.* to cause to take wing; to put up. **to flush out** to find and force to come out. [prob. imit.; cp. *flisk*, var. of FRISK, RUSH¹]

fluster (flŭs´tə) *v.t.* **1** to flurry or confuse. **2** to agitate, to make nervous. **3** to befuddle, to make tipsy, to intoxicate. ~*v.i.* to be in an agitated or confused state. ~*n.* confusion of mind, agitation. [conn. with Icel. *flaustra*, to be flustered (cp. EFris. *flostern*, *flustern*, to rustle)]

flustra (flŭs´trə) *n.* (*pl.* **flustrae** (-trē)) (*Zool.*) a sea-mat, an individual of the genus of Polyzoa called *Flustridae*. [mod. L, substituted by Linnaeus for *eschara*]

flute (floot) *n.* **1** a tubular wind instrument with a blowhole near the end and holes stopped by the fingers or with keys for producing variations of tone, esp. a transverse flute. **2** an organ stop with a similar tone. **3** a flute-player. **4** a long vertical groove, semicircular in section, esp. in the shaft of a column. **5** a similar groove or corrugation in a dress etc. **6** a long thin French roll of bread. **7** a tall, narrow wine glass. ~*v.i.* **1** to play a flute. **2** to whistle or sing with a flutelike sound. ~*v.t.* **1** to play, sing or utter with flutelike tones. **2** to play (a tune etc.) on a flute. **3** to form flutes or grooves in. **fluted** *a.* **1** (*Archit.*) channelled, furrowed. **2** (of the upper notes, of a soprano) clear and mellow. **flutelike** *a.* **fluting** *n.* **1** a groove, a channel. **2** fluted work in pillars etc. **flutist** *n.* a person who plays the flute, a flautist. **fluty** *a.* resembling a flute in tone. [OF *fleute*, *flaute*, *flahute* (prob. imit.; perh. conn. with L *flāre*, to blow)]

flutter (flŭt´ə) *v.i.* **1** to flap the wings rapidly. **2** to hover, flit or move about in a fitful, restless way. **3** to move with quick, irregular motions. **4** to quiver, to vibrate. **5** to fall in a quivering manner. **6** (of the pulse etc.) to beat spasmodically. **7** to be agitated or uncertain. **8** to wander. **9** to act frivolously. ~*v.t.* **1** to cause to move about with quick vibrations. **2** to vibrate, to cause to quiver or flap about rapidly. **3** to agitate or alarm. ~*n.* **1** the act of fluttering. **2** quick, short and irregular vibration. **3** a state of excitement, anxiety, or agitation. **4** disorder, stir. **5** (*coll.*) a gamble, a bet. **6** a toss or spin (as of a coin). **7** a venture or speculation. **8** a spasmodic beating of the heart etc. **9** a quick movement of the tongue when playing the flute or other wind instrument. **10** a variation or distortion in pitch occurring at higher frequencies in sound reproduction. **11** potentially dangerous oscillation set up in something, e.g. part of an aircraft, by natural forces. **to flutter the dovecotes** DOVE¹. **flutterer** *n.* **flutteringly** *adv.* **fluttery** *a.* [OE *flotorian*, from *flēotan*, to FLEET²]

fluvial (floo´viəl), **fluviatic** (-at´-), **fluviatile** (-tīl, -til) *a.* **1** of or belonging to a river. **2** (*Geol.*) caused by a river. **3** living in rivers. [F *fluvial*, L *fluvialis*, F *fluviatile*, L *fluviātilis*; from *fluvium*, river]

fluvio- (floo´viō) *comb. form* relating to a river or rivers.

fluvioglacial (flooviō´glāshəl, -siəl) *a.* of, relating to or caused by rivers from glacial ice or rivers and glaciers.

fluviomarine (flooviōmərēn´) *a.* of, relating to or produced by the joint action of a river and the sea (as deposits at a river mouth).

fluviometer (flooviom´itə) *n.* an apparatus for measuring the rise and fall in a river.

flux (flŭks) *n.* **1** the act or state of flowing. **2** the motion of a fluid. **3** a state of movement or continual change. **4** an issue or flowing out, a discharge. **5** (*Physics*) **a** the rate of flow of a fluid etc. across a given surface. **b** the amount of fluid crossing a surface at a given time. **6** the flow of the tide, as opposed to the ebb. **7** an abnormal discharge of fluid matter from the body. **8** any substance which assists the fusion of minerals or metals. **9** fusion. **10** the amount of radiation or particles falling on an area. **11** the strength of a magnetic field. **12** (*Math.*) continuous motion (as a line considered as the flux of a point). ~*v.t.* **1** to melt, to fuse. **2** to facilitate fusion with a flux. **3** (*Med.*) †to purge. ~*v.i.* **1** to flow. **2** (of the tide etc.) to rise. **3** to issue in a flux. **4** to melt. **fluxion** (-shən) *n.* **1** (*Math.*) the rate of variation of a variable quantity. **2** the act or state of flowing. **3** something which flows. **4** continuous variation. **5** fusion of metals. **6** an unnatural flow of blood or humour towards any organ. **fluxional, fluxionary** *a.* of or relating to fluxions. [OF, from L *fluxus*, from *fluere*, to flow]

fly¹ (flī) *n.* (*pl.* **flies**) **1** a two-winged insect of the order Diptera, esp. the housefly *Musca domestica*. **2** any other winged insect. **3** a disease in turnips, hops etc. caused by various flies. **4** an artificial fly used as bait in fishing. **like flies** in vast numbers and offering no resistance. **there are no flies on (a person)** the specified person is no fool. **fly agaric** *n.* a poisonous scarlet mushroom, *Amanita muscaria*, growing in woods. **flyblow** *v.t.* (*past* **flyblew**, *p.p.* **flyblown**) **1** to deposit eggs in, as the blowfly in meat. **2** to corrupt, to taint. ~*n.* the egg of a blow-fly. **flyblown** *a.* **1** tainted by flies or maggots. **2** impure, corrupt, tainted. **flybook** *n.* a book or case for anglers' flies. **flycatcher** *n.* **1** a flytrap. **2** any of various passerine birds that catch flying insects, esp. of the family Muscicapidae or Tyrannidae. **fly-fish** *v.i.* to angle with natural or artificial flies for bait. **fly-fisher** *n.* **fly-flap** *n.* an instrument to drive away flies. **fly in the ointment** *n.* a slight flaw, or minor disadvantage, that spoils the quality of something. **fly on the wall** *n.* an intimate, but unnoticed, observer of events. **fly-paper** *n.* paper prepared to catch or poison flies. **fly powder** *n.* a powder usu. consisting of arsenic mixed with sugar, used to kill flies. **fly-rod** *n.* a flexible resilient rod used in fly-fishing. **fly speck** *n.* **1** the small speck of a fly's excrement. **2** any small speck. **flyspecked** *a.* **flyspray** *n.* (an aerosol containing) insecticide. **flytrap** *n.* **1** a trap for catching flies. **2** any of various plants that catch flies, esp. the Venus flytrap. **fly-tying** *n.* preparing angler's flies. **flyweight** *n.* **1** a boxer, wrestler, weightlifter etc. in the weight category below bantam weight. **2** this weight category. **fly-whisk** *n.* a whisk for driving away flies. [OE *flēoge*, from FLY²]

fly² (flī) *v.i.* (*3rd pers. sing. pres.* **flies**, *pres.p.* **flying**, *past* **flew** (floo), *p.p.* **flown** (flōn)) **1** to move through the air with wings. **2** to pilot or ride in an aircraft. **3** to flutter or wave in the air. **4** to pass or be driven through the air with great speed or violence. **5** (of time) to pass very swiftly. **6** to depart in haste. **7** to flee, to run away, to try to escape. **8** to burst or break violently (in pieces). **9** to start, to pass suddenly or violently, to spring, to hasten, to burst (as to arms or into a rage) (*to fly into a temper*). ~*v.t.* **1** to cause to fly or float in the air. **2** to pilot (an aircraft). **3** to travel over by air. **4** to transport by air. **5** to use (e.g. an airline) for air travel. **6** to flee from, to avoid, to quit by flight. **7** to hunt with a hawk. **8** to make (a hawk, pigeon etc.) fly. **9** to set or keep (a flag) flying. ~*n.* (*pl.* **flies**) **1** the act or state of flying. **2** the distance that something flies. **3** (*usu. pl.*) **a** a flap covering buttonholes. **b** the fastening in a such a flap. **4** a loose flap for covering the entrance to a tent. **5** (*pl.*) a gallery over the proscenium in a theatre where the curtains or scenes are controlled. **6** (*pl. usu.* **flys**) a one-horse carriage, a hackney coach. **7** a flywheel or a regulating device acting on the same principle. **8** the portion of a vane that shows the direction of the wind. **9** the length of a flag from the staff to the outer edge. **10** the part of a flag furthest from the staff. **on the fly** in baseball, in the air, without bouncing. **to fly a kite** KITE. **to fly at 1** to attack suddenly, to rush at with violence or fierceness. **2** to criticize severely. **3** (of a hawk) to soar at and attack. **to fly blind** BLIND. **to fly high 1** to be ambitious. **2** to succeed, to excel. **to fly in the face of** FACE. **to fly off 1** to become suddenly detached. **2** †to revolt, to desert. **to fly off the handle** HANDLE. **to fly open** to open suddenly and violently. **to let fly 1** to shoot or throw out. **2** to direct a violent blow (at). **3** to use violent language. **4** (*Naut.*) to let go suddenly and entirely. **flyable** *a.* **fly-away** *a.* **1** streaming, loose. **2** (of hair) tending not to stay in place. **3** flighty, volatile. ~*n.* a runaway. **flyball** *n.* a baseball hit high into the air. **fly boy** *n.* (*N Am., sl.*) a member of the US Air Force, esp. a pilot. **fly-by** (-bī) *n.* (*pl.* **fly-bys**) an observation flight, esp. by a spacecraft, past a target at close range. **fly-by-night** *a.* unreliable, untrustworthy. ~*n.* **1** an unreliable or untrustworthy person. **2** a runaway debtor. **3** a person who goes out at night to a place of entertainment. **fly-by-wire** *n.* a system of aircraft control that uses electronic rather than mechanical connections between the controls and the aircraft parts. ~*a.* of or relating to such a system. **fly-drive** *a.* of or relating to a holiday that includes the cost of the flight and also car rental. ~*v.i.* (*past* **fly-drove,** *p.p.* **fly-driven**) to go on such a holiday. **flyer**[1], **flier** *n.* **1** a pilot or aviator. **2** (*in comb.*) a person or thing that flies in a particular way, as a *high-flyer.* **3** an animal, vehicle, train etc. that goes with exceptional speed. **4** a small handbill. **5** a flying jump. **6** (*coll.*) a flying start. **7** a flywheel. **8** (*Austral.*) the kangaroo. **9** a speculative attempt or venture. **10** (*pl.*) a straight flight of stairs. **11** (*Print.*) a vibratory rod with fingers to carry the sheet from the tapes to the delivery table. **fly-front** *n.* a concealed closing on the front of a garment. **fly-half** *n.* (*pl.* **fly-halves**) in rugby, a stand-off half. **fly-kick** *n.* a kick made while running. **flyleaf** *n.* (*pl.* **flyleaves**) a blank leaf at the beginning or end of a book. **flyman** *n.* (*pl.* **flymen**) **1** the driver of a fly. **2** the person who works the ropes of scenes etc. in a theatre. **flyover** *n.* **1** an intersection, esp. of two roads or railways at which one is carried over the other on a bridge. **2** (*N Am.*) a fly-past. **fly-past** *n.* a ceremonial flight by aircraft over a certain point. **fly-pitcher** *n.* (*sl.*) a street trader. **fly-pitching** *n.* **fly-posting** *n.* unauthorized affixing of posters. **flysheet** *n.* **1** a two- or four-page tract. **2** a handbill; a prospectus. **3** an extra sheet of canvas that can be fitted over the roof of a tent. **flywheel** *n.* a heavy-rimmed wheel attached to a machine for regulating the speed by its inertia. [OE *flēogan* (cp. Dut. *vliegen*, Icel. *fljūga*, G *fliegen*), not conn. with FLEE]

fly[3] (flī) *a.* (*comp.* **flyer,** *superl.* **flyest**) **1** (*sl.*) clever, sharp, wide-awake. **2** (*N Am., sl.*) stylish, fine. **flyness** *n.* [etym. doubtful]

flyer[1] FLY[2].

flyer[2] FLY[3].

flying (flī´ing) *a.* **1** fluttering in the air, streaming, loose. **2** brief, hurried. **3** moving with or as if with wings. **4** moving or adapted to move swiftly. **with flying colours** COLOUR. **flying bedstead** *n.* a framework resembling a bedstead raised vertically from the ground by jet propulsion. **flying boat** *n.* a large seaplane with a buoyant fuselage. **flying bomb** *n.* a jet-propelled, pilotless aeroplane with a charge of explosive in the head which is detonated when the plane falls. **flying bridge** *n.* a temporary bridge for military purposes. **flying buttress** *n.* an arched or slanting structure springing from solid masonry and serving to support another part of a structure. **flying doctor** *n.* a doctor in remote areas who uses an aircraft to answer calls. **flying dragon** *n.* a flying lizard. **Flying Dutchman** *n.* **1** a legendary mariner condemned to sail against the wind till the Day of Judgement. **2** his spectral ship. **flying fish** *n.* a marine fish esp. of the family Exocoetidae with enlarged winglike pectoral fins used for gliding through the air. **flying fox** *n.* **1** a large fruit bat, esp. belonging to the genus *Pteropus*, having a fox-like head. **2** (*Austral.*) a conveyor on a suspended wire. **flying gurnard** *n.* a fish with large pectoral fins, *Dactylopterus volitans.* **flying jib** *n.* a sail extending beyond the standing jib. **flying jib-boom** *n.* an extension of the jib-boom. **flying jump** *n.* a jump taken with a running start. **flying lemur** *n.* either of two mammals of the genus *Cynocephalus* of SE Asia, whose fore and hind limbs are connected by a fold of skin enabling the animal to take flying leaps from tree to tree. **flying lizard** *n.* any lizard of the SE Asian genus *Draco*, which can make gliding leaps. **flying machine** *n.* a machine for flying through the air. **flying officer** *n.* a junior commissioned rank in the RAF next below flight lieutenant. **flying party** *n.* a detachment of soldiers employed in skirmishing round an enemy. **flying phalanger** *n.* any of various Australian marsupials of the genus *Petaurus* or *Petauroides* whose fore and hind limbs are connected by a fold of skin enabling the animal to move with gliding leaps. **flying picket** *n.* (a member of) a mobile band of pickets who reinforce local pickets during a strike. **flying saucer** *n.* an unidentified flying object, esp. in the shape of a large disc. **flying squad** *n.* a mobile detachment of police. **flying squirrel** *n.* a squirrel of the subfamily Pteromyinae with a patagium or fold of skin like that of the flying lemurs, by which it makes flying leaps. **flying start** *n.* **1** the start of a race etc. in which the competitors are already travelling at speed as they pass the starting point. **2** a promising strong start giving initial advantage. **flying suit** *n.* a one-piece garment worn by aircrew. **flying wing** *n.* an aircraft that consists mainly of one large wing and little or no fuselage or tailplane.

FM *abbr.* **1** Field Marshal. **2** frequency modulation.

Fm *chem. symbol* fermium.

fm., fm *abbr.* fathom(s).

FO *abbr.* **1** Field Officer. **2** Flying Officer. **3** Foreign Office.

fo. *abbr.* folio.

foal (fōl) *n.* the young of a horse or related animal; a colt, a filly. ~*v.i.* (of a mare) to give birth to young. ~*v.t.* to give birth to (a foal). **with foal** (of a mare etc.) pregnant. **foalfoot** *n.* the coltsfoot, *Tussilago farfara.* [OE *fola* (cp. Dut. *veulen*, G *Fohlen*), cogn. with L *pullus*, Gr. *pōlos*]

foam (fōm) *n.* **1** a mass of bubbles produced in liquids by violent agitation or fermentation. **2** the similar formation produced by saliva in an animal's mouth. **3** froth, spume. **4** chemical froth used in fire-fighting. **5** a light, cellular solid, produced by aerating and then solidifying a liquid. 6 (*poet.*) the sea. ~*v.i.* 1 to gather, produce or emit foam. 2 to be covered or filled with foam. 3 to move (along, against etc.) with production of foam. 4 to pass (away) in foam. ~†*v.t.* 1 to cause to foam. 2 to throw out or express with violence. **to foam at the mouth** to be very angry. **foamingly** *adv.* **foamless** *a.* **foam plastic** *n.* plastic of foamlike consistency. **foam rubber** *n.* rubber of foamlike consistency largely used in upholstery etc. **foamy** *a.* (*comp.* **foamier,** *superl.* **foamiest**). [OE *fām* (cp. G *Feim*); prob. cogn. with L *spūma*]

fob[1] (fob) *n.* 1 (*also* **fob chain**) a chain by which a pocket watch is carried in a waistband pocket. 2 a small pocket for carrying a watch. 3 a tab on a keyring. ~*v.t.* (*pres.p.* **fobbing,** *past, p.p.* **fobbed**) to put into one's pocket. [etym. uncertain (cp. G dial. *Fuppe*)]

fob[2] (fob) *v.t.* (*pres.p.* **fobbing,** *past, p.p.* **fobbed**) to cheat, to impose upon. **to fob off** to put off with lies or excuses. **to fob off with** to delude into accepting by a trick. [prob. from LG *foppen* (cp. G *foppen*, to befool)]

f.o.b. *abbr.* free on board.

focaccia (fəkach´ə) *n.* (*pl.* **focaccias**) 1 a kind of Italian bread sprinkled before baking with olive oil, salt and often herbs. 2 a loaf of this. [It.]

focal, foci FOCUS.

fo'c'sle FORECASTLE.

focus (fō´kəs) *n.* (*pl.* **focuses, foci** (fō´sī)) 1 a point at which rays of light, heat, electrons etc. meet after reflection, deflection or refraction, or from which they appear to diverge. 2 the relation between the eye or lens and the object necessary to produce a clear image. 3 a state of clear definition. 4 the point from which any activity (such as a disease or an earthquake wave) originates. 5 the point on which attention or activity is concentrated. 6 (*Geom.*) one of two points having a definite relation to an ellipse or other curve. ~*v.t.* (*pres.p.* **focusing, focussing,** *past, p.p.* **focused, focussed**) 1 to bring (rays) to a focus or point. 2 to adjust (eye or instrument) so as to be at the right focus. 3 to bring into focus. 4 to concentrate. 5 to cause to converge to a focus. ~*v.i.* 1 to concentrate. 2 to converge to a focus. **in focus** 1 adjusted so as to obtain a clear image. 2 clearly perceived or defined. **focal** *a.* of, relating to or situated at a focus. **focalize, focalise** *v.t.* to focus. **focalization** (-zā´shən) *n.* **focal length, focal distance** *n.* the distance between the centre of a lens and the point where initially parallel rays converge. **focal plane** *n.* the plane that is perpendicular to the axis of a lens and passes through the focus. **focal point** *n.* 1 the focus of reflected rays of lights etc. 2 the focus of attention or activity. [L, hearth]

fodder (fod´ə) *n.* 1 food such as straw or hay fed to cattle. 2 (*facet.*) food. ~*v.t.* 1 to feed or supply with fodder. 2 †to feed. **fodderer** *n.* a person who fodders cattle. **fodderless** *a.* [OE *fōdor*, from *fōda*, FOOD (cp. Dut. *voeder*, G *Futter*)]

FOE *abbr.* Friends of the Earth.

foe (fō) *n.* (*esp. formal or poet.*) 1 a personal enemy; an opponent, an adversary. 2 an enemy in war. 3 an ill-wisher. **foelike** *a.* like a foe. **foeman** *n.* (*pl.* **foemen**) an enemy in war. [OE *fāh*, *fāg*, hostile (*gefā*, an enemy, *fēon*, *fēogan*, to hate)]

foehn FÖHN.

foetid FETID.

foetus (fē´təs), (*esp. N Am.*) **fetus** *n.* (*pl.* **foetuses,** (*esp. N Am.*) **fetuses**) the young of animals in the womb, and of vertebrates in the egg, after the parts are distinctly formed, esp. an unborn human more than eight weeks after conception. **foetal** *a.* of or relating to a foetus. **foetation** (-tā´shən) *n.* the formation of a foetus. **foeticide** (-tisīd) *n.* 1 the destruction of a foetus. 2 abortion. [L *fētus*, offspring, rel. to *fu-*, *fuī*, I was, *futurus*, to be, Gr. *phuein*, to beget]

fog[1] (fog) *n.* 1 a dense watery vapour rising from land or water and suspended near the surface of land or sea, reducing or obscuring visibility. 2 a dense cloud of smoke with similar effect. 3 a cloudiness on a photographic negative. 4 a state of confusion, uncertainty or perplexity. ~*v.t.* (*pres.p.* **fogging,** *past, p.p.* **fogged**) 1 to surround or cover with or as if with a fog. 2 to perplex, to bewilder. 3 to make (a photographic negative) cloudy. ~*v.i.* 1 to become foggy. 2 in photography, to become cloudy. **in a fog** confused, in a state of uncertainty. **fog bank** *n.* a dense mass of fog at sea. **fogbound** *a.* 1 immobilized by fog. 2 covered in fog. **fog-bow** *n.* a faint bow, resembling a rainbow, produced by light on a fog. **foggy**[1] *a.* 1 thick, murky. 2 full of or subject to fog. 3 of, relating to or resembling fog. 4 confused, vague, obscure, perplexed, indistinct. **not to have the foggiest** (*coll.*) not to have the slightest notion. **foggily** *adv.* **fogginess** *n.* **foghorn** *n.* 1 an instrument to give warning to ships in a fog. 2 (*coll.*) a loud deep resounding voice. **fog lamp, foglight** *n.* a strong light fitted to a vehicle to facilitate driving in fog. **fog signal** *n.* a detonator placed on a railway for the guidance of engine drivers. [etym. doubtful]

fog[2] (fog) *n.* 1 a second growth of grass after first cutting, aftermath. 2 coarse grass remaining through the winter. 3 (*Sc.*) moss. ~*v.t.* (*pres.p.* **fogging,** *past, p.p.* **fogged**) 1 to leave (land) as a fog. 2 to feed (cattle) with fog. ~†*v.i.* to grow mossy. **foggy**[2] *a.* (*comp.* **foggier,** *superl.* **foggiest**) 1 full of coarse, rank grass. 2 consisting of or resembling rank grass. 3 (*Sc.*) covered with moss, mossy. [etym. uncertain]

fogey (fō´gi), **fogy** *n.* (*pl.* **fogeys, fogies**) an old-fashioned eccentric person. **fogeydom** (-dəm) *n.* **fogeyish** *a.* **fogeyism** *n.*

foggy[1] FOG[1].

foggy[2] FOG[2].

fogy FOGEY.

föhn (fœn), **foehn** *n.* 1 the warm south wind in the Alps. 2 a warm dry wind on the lee side of mountains. [G, perh. ult. from L *Favōnius*]

foible (foi´bəl) *n.* 1 a weak point in a person's character. 2 the part of a sword blade between the middle and point. [F, now *faible*, FEEBLE]

foie gras (fwah grah´) *n.* PÂTÉ DE FOIE GRAS (under PÂTÉ).

foil[1] (foil) *n.* 1 very thin sheet metal. 2 an amalgam of quicksilver and tin at the back of a mirror. 3 a thin leaf of metal put under gems to increase their lustre or brighten or alter their colour. 4 something that serves to set off something else to advantage. 5 a rounded leaflike space or arc in window tracery. ~*v.t.* 1 to back (glass, crystal etc.) with foil. 2 to set off by contrast. 3 (*Archit.*) to decorate or design with foils. [OF *foil* (F *feuille*), L *folium*, a leaf (cp. Gr. *phullion*)]

foil[2] (foil) *v.t.* 1 to baffle, to frustrate. 2 to throw off the scent, to spoil or obliterate (the scent of a hunted animal) by crossing. 3 to defeat, to repulse, to parry. ~*v.i.* (of an animal) to spoil the scent of a hunted animal. ~*n.* 1 the trail of hunted game. 2 †a defeat, a frustration, a failure when success seems certain. [OF *fouler*, to tread, to stamp or full (cloth), late L *fullāre*, from L *fullo*, a fuller (perh. influ. by ME *fylen*, to make foul)]

foil[3] (foil) *n.* a straight thin sword, blunted by means of a button on the point, used in fencing. **foilist** *n.* [etym. unknown]

foil[4] (foil) *n.* HYDROFOIL.

†**foin** (foin) *v.t.* to thrust at. ~*v.i.* to lunge or thrust. ~*n.* 1 a thrust or lunge. 2 a stroke, as in fencing. **foiningly** *adv.* [OF *foine*, *foisne*, L *fusana*, a fish-spear]

†**foison** (foi´zən) *n.* 1 plenty, abundance. 2 power, strength. 3 (*pl.*) resources. [OF, from L *fūsio -ōnem*, from *fundere*, to pour]

foist (foist) *v.t.* 1 to impose (an unwelcome thing or

person) (on). **2** to palm off (on or upon) as genuine. **3** to introduce surreptitiously or wrongfully. **foister** *n.* [orig. to palm or conceal in the hand, prob. from Dut. prov. *vuisten*, from *vuist*, fist]

fol. *abbr.* **1** folio. **2** following.

folacin FOLIC ACID.

fold[1] (fōld) *n.* **1** a pen or enclosure for sheep. **2** a flock of sheep. **3** a group of believers or members of a church. **4** the Church, the flock of Christ. *~v.t.* to put or enclose in or as if in a fold. **foldless**[1] *a.* [OE *fald* (cp. Dut. *vaalt*, Dan. *fold*)]

fold[2] (fōld) *v.t.* **1** to double or lay one part of (a flexible thing) over another. **2** to bring together and entwine (e.g. arms, legs). **3** to clasp (arms etc.) round. **4** to embrace. **5** to enfold, to envelop. **6** to make compact by folding. **7** to close (e.g. wings, petals). **8** †to enswathe, to conceal. *~v.i.* **1** to become folded or doubled. **2** to shut in folds. **3** (*Geol.*) to be doubled up. **4** to fail, to cease operations, to go bankrupt. *~n.* **1** the act or an instance of folding. **2** a part doubled or laid on another. **3** a line made by folding. **4** a bend or doubling, a pleat. **5** a hollow between two parts (as of a fabric). **6** a coil, a folding, an embrace. **7** (*Geol.*) a flexure in strata. **to fold in** in cookery, to mix in gradually and carefully. **foldable** *a.* **foldaway** *a.* designed to be folded away when not in use. **folding** *n.*, *a.* **folding chair** *n.* a collapsible chair. **folding door** *n.* a door with vertical jointed sections that can be folded against one another. **folding machine** *n.* **1** a machine for folding printed sheets for newspapers or books. **2** a machine which shapes pans and tinware by pressure. **folding money** *n.* (*esp. N Am., coll.*) banknotes. **folding stool** *n.* a portable collapsible stool. **foldless**[2] *a.* **fold-out** *n.* an oversize page in a book or magazine that is folded out by the reader. [OE *fealdan* (cp. Icel. *falda*, G *falten*, also Gr. *plassein*, *plekein*, L *plicāre*)]

-fold (fōld) *suf.* forming adjectives and adverbs denoting multiplication, as *fourfold*, *manifold*, or composition of a number of parts, as *sixfold*. [OE *feald*, cogn. with FOLD[2] (cp. Gr. *-plasios*, L *-plex*)]

folder (fōl´də) *n.* **1** a person who or thing that folds. **2** a holder for loose papers. **3** a folded leaflet. **4** a bone or ivory blade used in folding papers.

folderol FALDERAL.

foldless[1] FOLD[1].

foldless[2] FOLD[2].

foliaceous (fōliā´shəs) *a.* **1** having the texture, structure or organs of or as of leaves. **2** leaf-shaped. **3** furnished with leaves. **4** consisting of thin laminae; laminated. **5** splitting into thin laminae. [L *foliāceus*, from *folium*, a leaf]

foliage (fō´liij) *n.* **1** leaves in the aggregate. **2** in art, architecture etc. the representation of leaves or clusters of leaves, as ornament. **foliage leaf** *n.* (*pl.* **foliage leaves**) a leaf excluding petals, modified leaves etc. **foliar** *a.* of, consisting of or relating to leaves. **foliar feed** *n.* feed provided for plant leaves. **foliose** (-ōs), **folious** *a.* **1** leafy, abounding in or of the nature of leaves. **2** having a leaflike shape. [MF *fueillage*, *foillage* (F *feuillage*), from *fueille*, L *folia*, leaves]

foliate[1] (fō´liāt) *v.i.* to split or disintegrate into thin laminae. *~v.t.* **1** to decorate with leaf-patterns, foils, leaflike tracery etc. **2** to number the leaves of (a manuscript, book etc.). **3** †to beat into a leaf or thin plate. **4** †to cover over (e.g. a mirror) with a thin coat or sheet of tin, quicksilver etc. **foliation** (-ā´shən) *n.* **1** foliating. **2** (*Archit.*) ornamentation by trefoil, quatrefoil, cinquefoil, and similar tracery based on the form of a leaf.

foliate[2] (fō´liət, -iāt) *a.* **1** leaflike, leaf-shaped. **2** furnished with leaves. **3** having a particular number of leaves.

folic acid (fō´lik, fo´-), **folacin** (fō´ləsin) *n.* a vitamin of the vitamin B complex found esp. in green vegetables and liver and used in the treatment of anaemia.

folie (folē´) *n.* madness, folly. **folie à deux** (a dœ´) *n.* the presence of similar delusions in the minds of two closely associated people. **folie de grandeur** (də grādœ) *n.* delusions of grandeur. [F]

folio (fō´liō) *n.* (*pl.* **folios**) **1** a leaf of paper or other material for writing etc., numbered on the front. **2** a page of manuscript. **3** a sheet of paper folded once. **4 a** a book of the largest size, whose sheets are folded once. **b** any large volume or work. **5** a page in an account book, or two opposite pages numbered as one. **6** the number of a page. **7** 72 words of manuscript in legal documents, 90 words in Parliamentary proceedings. *~a.* (of a book) of, relating to or having the format of a folio. **in folio** made or composed of folios. [abbr. of L *in foliō*, in the form of a sheet folded once]

foliole (fō´liōl) *n.* a leaflet, one of the separate parts of a compound leaf. **foliolate** (-lāt) *a.* [F, from L *foliolum*, dim. of *folium*, a leaf]

foliose, folious FOLIAGE.

folk (fōk) *n.* (*pl.* **folk, folks**) **1** (*pl. in constr.*) people, people collectively. **2** (*pl. in constr.*) a particular class of people, as *old folk*. **3** (*usu.* **folks**) members of one's own family; also used as a familiar form of address to a group of assembled people. **4** a people, nation or ethnic group. **5** folk music. **6** (*in comb.*) people of a specified kind, as *menfolk*, *kinsfolk*. *~a.* **1** originating among the common people. **2** based on or employing traditional or popular motifs. **folk custom** *n.* a custom of the people. **folk dance** *n.* **1** a traditional dance of countryfolk. **2** the music for such a dance. **folk etymology** *n.* (*pl.* **folk etymologies**) a popular but often erroneous derivation of a word. **folkie** (fōk´i) *n.* (*coll.*) a devotee of folk music. *~a.* (*coll.*) of or relating to folk music. **folkish** *a.* traditional, popular. †**folkland** *n.* in feudal law, the land of the people as distinguished from land held by deed. **folklore** *n.* **1** popular beliefs, tales, traditions or legends. **2** the systematic study of such beliefs etc. **folkloric** *a.* **folklorism** *n.* **folklorist** *n.* a student of folklore. **folkloristic** (-ris´tic) *a.* **folk memory** *n.* (*pl.* **folk memories**) a memory of a distant event passed down through several generations of a community. †**folkmoot** *n.* **1** an assembly of the people of a shire, city or town. **2** a Court leet or local court. **folk music** *n.* **1** the traditional popular music of the common people. **2** modern popular music in the style of this. **folk singer** *n.* a person who sings folk songs. **folk song** *n.* **1** a song or ballad, supposed to have originated among the people and to have been handed down by tradition. **2** a modern song in this style. **folksy** *a.* (*comp.* **folksier**, *superl.* **folksiest**) **1** (*chiefly N Am., coll.*) informal, casual, sociable, friendly. **2** (affectedly) traditional in style. **folksiness** *a.* **folk tale** *n.* a traditional or popular legend or story. **folkways** *n.pl.* traditional social customs. **folkweave** *n.* a loosely woven fabric. **folky** *a.* (*comp.* **folkier**, *superl.* **folkiest**) traditional or popular in style. **folkiness** *n.* [OE *folc* (cp. Icel. *fōlk*, Dan. and Swed. *folk*, Dut. *volk*, G *Volk*)]

foll. *abbr.* following.

follicle (fol´ikəl) *n.* **1** a small cavity, sac or gland. **2** HAIR FOLLICLE (under HAIR). **3** GRAAFIAN FOLLICLE. **4** a dry fruit that consists of one compartment containing many seeds which opens on one side only. **follicular** (-lik´ū-), **folliculate** (-lik´ū-), **folliculated** (-lik´ū-) *a.* [F, from L *folliculus*, a little bag, dim. of *follis*, bellows]

follow (fol´ō) *v.t.* **1** to go or come after. **2** to move behind. **3** to pursue (e.g. an enemy). **4** to go along (a path, road etc.). **5** to come or happen after in point of time, order, rank or importance. **6** to imitate, to pattern oneself upon. **7** to go after as an admirer or disciple. **8** to engage in, to practise (as a profession). **9** to conform to, act upon (a rule, policy etc.). **10** to watch the course of. **11**

to keep the mind or attention fixed on. **12** to understand, to grasp the meaning of. **13** to result, to be the consequence of. **14** to seek after, to try to attain. **15** to provide (with a successor). **16** to accompany, to attend upon, to serve. **17** to adhere to, to side with, to support the cause of. **18** †to follow up, to prosecute (an affair). ~*v.i.* **1** to come or go after another person or thing. **2** to pursue. **3** to be the next thing to be done or said. **4** to be a natural consequence, to ensue. **5** to be the logical consequence, to be deducible. **as follows** used as an introductory formula to a statement, list etc. **to follow on 1** to continue without a break. **2** to continue from where somebody else left off. **3** in cricket, to bat again immediately after completing one's first innings because one is more than a certain number of runs behind. **to follow one's nose** NOSE. **to follow out** to implement (an idea, instructions etc.). **to follow suit** SUIT. **to follow through 1** in golf, cricket etc., to continue the swing after hitting the ball. **2** to take further action consequent upon an initial act. **3** to follow to a conclusion. **to follow up 1** to pursue closely and steadily. **2** to pursue an advantage. **3** to make further efforts to the same end. **4** to take appropriate action about. **5** (*Med.*) to re-examine a patient, or check progress, at intervals after treatment. **follower** *n.* **1** a person who follows. **2** a devotee, a disciple, an imitator or adherent. **3** a companion. **4** a subordinate, a servant, an attendant. **5** one of the same party. **6** a machine part that is driven by another part. **following** *a.* **1** coming next after, succeeding, now to be mentioned. **2** (of wind) blowing in the direction one is travelling. ~*prep.* after. ~*n.* a body of followers or adherents. **the following** the person(s) or thing(s) now to be mentioned. **follow-on** *n.* an act of following on. **follow-the-leader, follow-my-leader** *n.* a game in which those behind must follow the steps and imitate the actions of the leader. **follow-through** *n.* the act of following through. **follow-up** *n.* **1** a reminding circular sent by an advertiser. **2** (*Med.*) a check or checks on a patient's progress. **3** a further or consequent action. [ME *folwan*, OE *folgian* (cp. Dut. *volgen*, G *folgen*)]

folly (fol´i) *n.* (*pl.* **follies**) **1** foolishness, lack of understanding or judgement, senselessness. **2** a foolish act, idea or conduct. **3** an object of foolish attention or imitation. **4 a** a structure built for picturesque effect or to gratify the builder's whim. **b** (*derog.*) any building which seems more grand, elaborate or expensive than its purpose warrants. **5 a** a revue in which the performers wear elaborate costumes. **b** the performers in such a revue. **6** †wantonness, immorality, depravity. [OF *folie*, from *fol*, FOOL[1]]

foment (fəment´) *v.t.* **1** to cause (trouble or a riot) to develop. **2** to nourish, to foster, to encourage, to promote. **3** to apply warm or medicated lotions to. **4** to warm. **5** to poultice. **fomentation** (fōmentā´shən) *n.* **1** the act of fomenting. **2** the lotion, poultice, warm cloths etc. applied. **fomenter** *n.* [F *fomenter*, L *fōmentāre*, from *fōmentum* (for *fovimentum*), from *fovēre*, to warm, cherish]

fomes (fō´mēz) *n.* (*pl.* **fomites** (-mitēz)) a substance of a porous kind liable to absorb and retain contagious substances and so spread disease. [L, touchwood]

fond (fond) *a.* **1** doting on, delighting in (*fond of children*). **2** tender or loving, affectionate. **3** foolishly naive. **to be fond of** to like very much, to love. **fondly** *adv.* affectionately. **fondness** *n.* [ME *fonned*, p.p. of obs. v. *fon*, to be foolish]

fondant (fon´dənt) *n.* a sweet paste made of sugar and water. **fondant icing** *n.* icing made of this paste. [F, from *fondre*, to melt, L *fundere*, to pour]

fondle (fon´dəl) *v.t.* **1** to caress. **2** †to treat with great kindness or indulgence. ~*v.i.* to indulge in caresses (with). **fondler** *n.* [freq. of FOND]

fondue (fon´doo, -dū) *n.* a dish consisting of a hot sauce (usu. of cheese and white wine) into which pieces of bread etc. are dipped, or of cubes of meat which are cooked by dipping into hot oil at table and eaten with a variety of spicy sauces. [F fem. of *fondu*, p.p. of *fondre*, to melt]

font[1] (font) *n.* **1** the vessel or basin to contain water for baptism. **2** the oil reservoir for a lamp. **fontal** *a.* of or relating to a fount or source, to a baptismal font, or to baptism. **font-stone** *n.* a baptismal font. [OE *fant*, *font*, L *fontem*, nom. *fons*, a FOUNT[1]]

font[2] (font), **fount** (fownt) *n.* a set of type of one face and size. [F *fonte*, from *fondre*, to found]

fontanelle (fontənel´), (*N Am.*) **fontanel** *n.* an interval between the bones of the infant cranium. [F *fontanelle*, dim. of *fontaine*, FOUNTAIN]

food (food) *n.* **1** any substance, esp. solid in form, which, taken into the body, assists in sustaining or nourishing the living being. **2** victuals, provisions; aliment, nutriment. **3** nutriment for plants. **4** that which nourishes, sustains or is material for. **5** anything that provides stimulus for thinking (*food for thought*). **food additive** *n.* a substance used to preserve food or to enhance its colour, flavour etc. **food chain** *n.* a community of organisms thought of as a hierarchy in which each eats the one below and is eaten by the one above. **food court** *n.* an area in a shopping mall containing several fast-food outlets with seating accommodation. **food for worms** *n.* a dead person, esp. after burial. **foodie, foody** *n.* (*pl.* **foodies**) (*coll.*) a person with an intense interest in (esp. more exotic kinds of) food. **foodism** *n.* **foodless** *a.* **food poisoning** *n.* a severe gastrointestinal condition caused by eating food which is naturally poisonous or has been contaminated. **food processor** *n.* an electrical appliance which chops, shreds or blends etc. food. **foodster** *n.* a foodie. **foodstuff** *n.* any thing or material used for food. **food value** *n.* a measure of the nourishment of a food, measured in calories, vitamins or minerals. [OE *foda*, from root *fōd-*, *fad*, cp. Gr. *pateesthai*, L *pāscere*, to feed, *pānis*, bread]

fool[1] (fool) *n.* **1** a person without common sense or judgement; a silly person. **2** a dupe. **3** (*Hist.*) a jester, a buffoon. **4** †an idiot, an imbecile. ~*a.* (*esp. N Am., coll.*) foolish, silly. ~*v.t.* **1** to make a fool of. **2** to dupe, to cheat, to impose upon, to play tricks upon, to trick. **3** to waste (time away). ~*v.i.* **1** to play the fool. **2** to trifle, to idle. **to act the fool** to behave in a foolish, playful way. **to fool around/ about 1** to behave foolishly or irresponsibly. **2** to waste time. **3** to trifle (with). **to fool with** to meddle with in a careless and risky manner. **to make a fool of 1** to cause to appear ridiculous. **2** to deceive, to disappoint. **to play the fool** to act the fool. **foolery** *n.* (*pl.* **fooleries**) **1** habitual folly. **2** the act of playing the fool. **3** folly, absurdity. **fooling** *n.* buffoonery. **foolish** *a.* **1** silly, not sensible, not wise. **2** absurd or ridiculous. **foolishly** *adv.* **foolishness** *n.* **foolproof** *a., adv.* secure against any ignorant mishandling. **fool's errand** *n.* an absurd or fruitless errand or quest; the pursuit of what cannot be found. **fool's gold** *n.* iron pyrites. **fool's mate** *n.* the simplest mate in chess. **fool's paradise** *n.* a state of unreal or deceptive joy or good fortune. **fool's parsley** *n.* a poisonous umbelliferous herb, *Aethusa cynapium*. [OF *fol* (F *fou*), L *follem*, acc. of *follis*, bellows, windbag, late L fool]

fool[2] (fool) *n.* a dish made of fruit, esp. gooseberries, stewed and crushed with cream etc. [prob. from FOOL[1]]

foolhardy (fool´hahdi) *a.* (*comp.* **foolhardier**, *superl.* **foolhardiest**) daring without sense or judgement, foolishly bold; rash, reckless. **foolhardihood, foolhardiness** *n.* **foolhardily** *adv.* [OF *folhardi* (*fol*, fool, *hardi*, bold)]

foolscap (foolz´kap) *n.* **1** a size of writing paper 17 × 13½ in. (43.2 × 34.3 cm) or of printing paper, folio, 13½

× 8½ in. (34.3 × 21.6 cm), quarto, 8½ × 6¾ in. (21.6 × 17.1 cm), octavo, 6¾ × 4¼ in. (17.1 × 10.8 cm). 2 a pointed cap with bells, formerly worn by professional jesters. [named from the paper's original watermark of a fool's cap and bells]

foot (fut) *n.* (*pl.* **feet** (fēt)) 1 the part of the leg which treads on the ground in standing or walking, and on which the body is supported; the part below the ankle. 2 that which serves to support a body. 3 that part of an article of dress which receives the foot. 4 a pace or step. 5 (*pl.* **feet, foot**) a measure of 12 in. (30.5 cm), named as being roughly the length of a man's foot. 6 the lowest part, the base, the lower end of e.g. a table, chair or bed; the bottom. 7 foot soldiers, infantry. 8 in prosody, a set of syllables forming the rhythmical unit in verse, speech etc. 9 an attachment on a sewing machine that holds the material in position. 10 (*Zool.*) the locomotive organ of invertebrate animals, the tube-foot of an echinoderm. 11 (*Bot.*) the part by which a petal is attached. 12 †basis, footing, status. ~*v.i.* 1 to walk, to dance. 2 to pace. 3 to go or travel on foot. ~*v.t.* to travel over by walking. **at the feet of** 1 humbly adoring or supplicating. 2 submissive to. 3 as a disciple or student of. **my foot!** used to express disbelief, contradiction etc. **not to put a foot wrong** to not make a mistake. **off one's feet** in such a state that one can hardly stand (*be rushed off one's feet*). **on foot** 1 walking. 2 in motion, action or process of execution. **on one's feet** 1 standing up. 2 in good health. 3 thriving, getting on well. **to catch on the wrong foot** to take unprepared or at a disadvantage. **to drag one's feet** DRAG. **to fall on one's feet** to emerge safely or successfully. **to find one's feet** to become accustomed to, and able to function effectively in, new circumstances. **to foot a bill** (*coll.*) to pay a bill. **to foot it** 1 to go on foot. 2 to dance. **to foot up to** (of items in an account) to mount or total up to. **to get off on the wrong foot** to make a bad start, esp. in personal relations with someone. **to get one's feet wet** to begin to join in an activity. **to have one foot in the grave** to be near death, very old or moribund. **to have one's/ both feet on the ground** to be realistic, sensible or practical. **to keep one's feet** not to fall. **to keep on foot** to maintain in a state of readiness (as a standing army). **to put one's best foot forward** 1 to step out briskly. 2 to try to show oneself at one's best. **to put one's feet up** (*coll.*) to rest. **to put one's foot down** 1 to be firm, determined. 2 to go faster in a car etc. **to put one's foot in it** to blunder, to get into a scrape. **to run off one's feet** RUN. **to set foot** to tread (on), to enter (in). **to set foot on/ in** to go into, to enter. **to set on foot** 1 to put in motion. 2 to originate. **to sweep off one's feet** to enrapture, to make a complete and sudden conquest of. **to think on one's feet** to react to situations as they arise. **under foot** on the ground. **under one's feet** in the way. **feet of clay** *n.pl.* serious weakness in a person who is admired. **footage** *n.* 1 length or distance measured in feet. 2 the length of a film (in feet). **foot-and-mouth disease** *n.* a contagious eczematous viral disease chiefly affecting cattle. **footbath** *n.* 1 a vessel in which to wash the feet. 2 the act of washing the feet. **footbed** *n.* an insole in a shoe, used to make the shoe fit more comfortably. **footboard** *n.* 1 a board to support the feet. 2 a board at the foot of a bed. 3 a step for getting into or out of a vehicle. 4 a footplate. 5 a treadle. 6 a platform for a footman behind a carriage. **footboy** *n.* a page, a boy in livery. **footbrake** *n.* a brake operated by the foot in a motor vehicle. **footbridge** *n.* a narrow bridge for foot passengers. †**footcloth** *n.* the housings of a horse, reaching down to the ground. **footed** *a.* 1 having feet. 2 (*usu. in comb.*) having a particular kind of feet, as *swift-footed*. **footer** (fut´ə) *n.* 1 (*in comb.*) **a** a person or thing of a particular number of feet in length or height (*a six-footer*). **b** a particular kind of kick of a football (*a right-footer*). 2 a line of text printed at the foot of a page. 3 (*coll.*) the game of football. **footfall** *n.* the sound of a footstep. **foot-fault** *n.* in tennis etc. the act of overstepping the baseline when serving. ~*v.i.* to make a foot-fault. ~*v.t.* to award a foot-fault against. **footguards** *n.pl.* regiments of infantry. **foothill** *n.* a hill lying at the base of a range of mountains. **foothold** *n.* 1 something which sustains the foot. 2 support at the foot. 3 a position of stability or security. 4 a basis of operations; a secure position from which further progress can be made. **footie** FOOTY. **foot in both camps** *n.* a connection with both of two mutually antagonistic groups. **foot in the door** *n.* 1 a first step towards a desired end. 2 a favourable position from which to advance. **footless** *a.* **footlights** *n.pl.* a row of lights, screened from the audience, in front of the stage of a theatre. **footloose** *a.* free, unbound by ties (*footloose and fancy free*). **footman** *n.* (*pl.* **footmen**) 1 a male domestic servant in livery. 2 (*Hist.*) a foot soldier. 3 a stand for holding a kettle before the fire. **footmark** *n.* a footprint. **foot muff** *n.* a covering lined with fur, to keep the feet warm. **footnote** *n.* a note at the bottom of the page of a book. ~*v.t.* to provide with footnotes. **footpad** *n.* (*Hist.*) a highwayman who robs on foot. **footpage** *n.* a footboy. **foot passenger** *n.* a person who travels on e.g. a ferry on foot, a pedestrian. **footpath, footway** *n.* a narrow path or way for pedestrians only. **footplate** *n.* a platform for the driver and fireman on a locomotive. **foot-pound** *n.* (*pl.* **foot-pounds**) a unit of energy, the amount that will raise one pound avoirdupois one foot. **foot-pound-second system** *n.* a system of measurements that has the foot, pound and second as its basic units. **footprint** *n.* 1 the mark or print of a foot or shoe. 2 any sign of the presence of a person. 3 the area of the earth's surface within which the signal of a geostationary communications satellite can be received. 4 the area within which a spacecraft is to land. 5 the space on a desktop occupied by a computer. **foot-race** *n.* a running match on foot. **foot-rest** *n.* a support for a foot or the feet. **foot-rope** *n.* (*Naut.*) 1 a rope to which the lower edge of a sail is sewn. 2 a rope for sailors to stand on, below a yard. **foot-rot** *n.* a disease in the feet of sheep and cattle, characterized by an abnormal growth. **foot-rule** *n.* a ruler 12 in. (30.5 cm) long. **foots** *n.pl.* 1 sediment, dregs, oil refuse etc. 2 coarse sugar. **footsie** (-si) *n.* (*coll.*) amorous or flirtatious touching with the feet. **footslog** *v.i.* (*pres.p.* **footslogging,** *past, p.p.* **footslogged**) to march or tramp, esp. laboriously. ~*n.* a laborious march or walk. **footslogger** *n.* **foot soldier** *n.* an infantry soldier. **footsore** *a.* having the feet sore or tender. **footstalk** *n.* 1 (*Bot.*) **a** the petiole of a leaf. **b** the peduncle of a flower. 2 (*Zool.*) the attachment of a crinoid etc. **footstall** *n.* a stirrup on a side-saddle. **footstep** *n.* 1 the act of stepping or treading with the feet; tread. 2 a footprint. 3 the sound of the step of a foot. 4 (*pl.*) traces of a course pursued or actions done (*She followed in her father's footsteps and became a butcher*). **footstone** *n.* a stone placed at the foot of a grave, distinguished from the headstone. **footstool** *n.* a stool for resting the feet. **foot-warmer** *n.* 1 a metal vessel containing hot water for warming the feet. 2 a hot-water bottle. **footwear** *n.* shoes, boots, socks etc. **footwell** *n.* a space for the feet in front of the front seats of a car. **footwork** *n.* 1 skilful use of the feet in boxing, dancing etc. 2 clever manoeuvring, esp. of an evasive kind. **footworn** *a.* footsore. **footy**[1] *n.* (*coll.*) the game of football. [OE *fōt* (cp. Dut. *voet*, Icel. *fōtr*, G *Fuss*, also Gr. *pous podos*, L *pes pedis*)]

football (fut´bawl) *n.* 1 any of several games played between two teams with a ball that is kicked, or handled and kicked, to score goals or points. 2 a large ball used in the game of football. 3 a contentious issue, esp. one which is bandied about between opposing groups. **Football Association** *n.* the body founded in 1863 to make rules, supervise and preside over Association Football in Britain. **footballer** *n.* **football hooligan** *n.* a hooligan at a football match or one travelling to or from a football match. **Football League** *n.* an organized collection of Association Football clubs founded in 1888 to arrange matches and supervise the business arrangements of its constituents. **football pools** *n.pl.* a form of gambling based on forecasting the results of football matches.

footing (fut´ing) *n.* **1** a place for standing or putting the feet on. **2** foothold. **3** a firm or secure position. **4** relative position, status or condition; relationship. **5** entrance into a new sphere, society, profession, trade etc. **6** the adding up of a column of figures and putting the total at the foot. **7** (*Archit.*) a course at the base or foundation of a wall. **8** (*pl.*) foundations, bases. **9** †a footprint, a track. **to keep one's footing** not to fall. **to pay one's footing** to pay a sum of money on doing anything for the first time, as on being admitted to a trade etc.

footle (foo´təl) *v.i.* (*coll.*) to trifle; to potter about aimlessly. *~n.* rubbish, twaddle; nonsense, foolery. **footling** *a.* trivial; silly. [etym. uncertain]

Footsie (fut´si) *n.* (*coll.*) the Financial Times–Stock Exchange 100 Index. [the initial letters *FTSE*]

footy[1] FOOT.

†**footy**[2] (fu´ti) *a.* **1** musty. **2** paltry, contemptible, worthless. [earlier *foughty*, prob. from OE *fūht*, damp]

foo yong (foo yong´) *n.* a Chinese dish made with egg mixed with chicken, meat and other ingredients, cooked like an omelette. [Cantonese]

foozle (foo´zəl) *v.i.* to waste time, to fool about. *~v.t.* **1** to make a mess of. **2** in golf, to bungle. *~n.* **1** a fogey. **2** in golf, a bungled stroke. **foozler** *n.* **foozling** *a.* [cp. G prov. *fuseln*, to work slowly]

fop (fop) *n.* a man overfond of dress; a dandy, a coxcomb. †**fopling** (-ling) *n.* a petty fop. **foppery** *n.* (*pl.* **fopperies**). **foppish** *a.* **foppishly** *adv.* **foppishness** *n.* [ME *foppe* (cp. Dut. and G *foppen*, to cheat, to hoax)]

for (faw, fə) *prep.* **1** in the place of, instead of. **2** in exchange against, as the equivalent of. **3** as the price or requital or payment of. **4** in consideration of, by reason of. **5** because of, on account of, in favour of, on the side of. **6** in order to, with a view to. **7** appropriate or suitable to. **8** toward, tending toward, conducive to. **9** to fetch, to get, to save. **10** to attain, to reach, to arrive at. **11** (*sl.*) against. **12** on behalf of, for the sake of. **13** with regard to, in relation to. **14** as regards. **15** so far as. **16** as, as being, in the character of. **17** to the amount or extent of. **18** at the cost of. **19** in spite of, notwithstanding. **20** in comparison of, contrast with. **21** during. **22** to prevent. **23** because of. **24** so as to start promptly at. *~conj.* **1** since, because. **2** seeing that. **3** in view of the reason that. **4** †on this account that. **5** †in order that. **as for** AS[1]. **for all that** **1** nevertheless. **2** in spite of all that. **for all the world** WORLD. **for as much as** FORASMUCH. **for ever** FOREVER. **for evermore** FOREVERMORE (under FOREVER). **for good** GOOD. **for short** SHORT. **o/ oh for** used to express a desire for something. **to be for it** (*coll.*) to be marked for reprimand or punishment. [OE, prob. abbr. from *fore* (cp. Dut. *voor*, G *vor*, also L *prō*, Gr. *pro*)]

f.o.r. *abbr.* free on rail.

for- (faw) *pref.* **1** away, off, as *forget, forgive.* **2** negative, prohibitive or privative, as *forbear, forbid, forsake.* **3** amiss, badly, as *fordo.* **4** intensive, as *forlorn.* [OE *for-* (cp. Icel. and Dan. *for-*, Dut. and G *ver-*), cogn. with Gr. *peri-*, *pro-*, *para-*, L *per-*, *pro-*]

forage (for´ij) *n.* **1** food for horses and cattle. **2** the act of foraging. *~v.i.* **1** to seek for or to collect forage. **2** to hunt for supplies. **3** to rummage (about). **4** to carry out a raid. *~v.t.* **1** to overrun in order to collect forage. **2** to ravage, to plunder. **3** to obtain for forage. **4** to supply with forage or food. **forage cap** *n.* a military undress cap. **forager** *n.* [OF *fourrage*, from *forre* (F *feurre*), low L *fōdrum*, from Gmc., cogn. with FODDER]

foramen (fərā´men) *n.* (*pl.* **foramina** (-ram´inə)) a small natural opening, passage or perforation in parts of plants and animals. **foramen magnum** (mag´nŭm) *n.* the opening at the base of the skull through which the spinal cord passes. **foraminate** (-ram´inət), **foraminated** (-nātid) *a.* **foraminifer** (forəmin´ifə), **foraminiferan** (-nif´ərən) *n.* any protozoan of the order Foraminifera with a shell perforated by pores, through which slender pseudopodia protrude. **foraminiferous** (-nif´-) *a.* **foraminous** (-ram´i-) *a.* [L, from *forāre*, to bore]

forasmuch (forəzmŭch´), †**forasmuch as** *conj.* seeing that; since; in consideration that.

foray (for´ā) *n.* a sudden attacking expedition, a raid. *~v.t.* **1** to pillage, to ravage. **2** to make a raid on. *~v.i.* **1** to make a raid. **2** to go foraging or pillaging. [Sc., prob. from ME *forreyer*, a forager, OF *forrier*, from *forre*, FORAGE]

forbade, forbad FORBID.

forbear[1] (fawbeə´) *v.t.* (*past* **forbore** (-baw´), *p.p.* **forborne** (-bawn´)) **1** to refrain or abstain from. **2** to bear with, to treat with patience. *~v.i.* **1** to refrain or abstain (from). **2** to be patient, to refrain from feelings of resentment. **forbearance** *n.* patience, self-control. **forbearingly** *adv.* [OE *forberan*]

Usage note The spellings of the verb *forbear* (to refrain) and the noun *forebear* (an ancestor) should not be confused.

forbear[2] FOREBEAR.

forbid (fəbid´) *v.t.* (*pres.p.* **forbidding,** *past* **forbade** (-bad´, -bād´), **forbad** (-bad), *p.p.* **forbidden** (-bid´ən)) **1** to order not to do. **2** to interdict, to prohibit. **3** to exclude, to oppose. **forbiddance** *n.* the act of forbidding. **forbidden** *a.* prohibited. **forbidden degrees** *n.pl.* the number of degrees of descent from the same ancestor within which marriage between two related people is prohibited. **forbidden fruit** *n.* anything desired but pronounced unlawful (from the fruit of the tree of the knowledge of good and evil, which Adam was commanded not to eat (Gen. ii.17)). **forbidden ground** *n.* an area or subject that must be avoided. †**forbiddenly** *adv.* **forbidder** *n.* **forbidding** *a.* **1** repulsive, disagreeable. **2** giving rise to aversion or dislike. **3** threatening, formidable. **forbiddingly** *adv.* **forbiddingness** *n.* [OE *forbēodan*]

forbore, forborne FORBEAR[1].

forbye (fəbī´, faw-), **forby** *prep.* (*Sc., dial.*) **1** besides, in addition to. **2** †near, past. *~adv.* besides, moreover.

force[1] (faws) *n.* **1** strength, energy, active power. **2** military or naval strength. **3** violence, coercion, compulsion. **4** unlawful violence. **5** an organized body of e.g. soldiers, police officers or workers; an army or part of an army. **6** (*pl.*) troops. **7** efficacy, validity. **8** significance, weight, import, full meaning. **9** persuasive or convincing power; a person or thing considered as having this. **10** energy, vigour, animation, vividness. **11** power exerted on a person or object. **12** (*Physics*) **a** that which produces or tends to produce a change of velocity in a body at rest or in motion. **b** a measure of the intensity of this. *~v.t.* **1** to constrain (a person) by force or against their will; to compel. **2** to use violence to. **3** to strain, to distort. **4** to impose or impress (upon) with force. **5** to bring about, to accomplish, or to make a way by force. **6** to drive or push violently or against resistance. **7** to stimulate artificially. **8** to cause to grow or ripen by artificial heat. **9** to cause to ripen prematurely. **10** in card playing, to compel (a player) to play in a certain way, to compel (a certain card) to be played. **by force** by compulsion. **by force of** by means of. **in force** 1 in operation, valid, enforced. 2 in large numbers, in great strength. **the Force** the police. **to come into force** 1 to become valid. 2 to be enforced or carried out. **to force from** 1 to elicit by force. 2 to wrest from. **to force one's way** to push through obstacles by force. **to force out** to drive out. **to force someone's hand** HAND. **to force the bidding** to make bids at an auction in order to increase the price quickly. **to force the issue** to cause a decision to have to be taken immediately. **to force the pace** PACE[1]. **to join forces** to work together in a combined manner. **forceable** *a.* **forced** *a.* 1 constrained, affected. 2 brought about by force. 3 unnatural. **forced labour,** (*N Am.*) **forced labor** *n.* involuntary labour. **forced landing** *n.* an unavoidable landing of an aircraft in an emergency, e.g. because of mechanical failure. **forcedly** (-sid-) *adv.* **forced march** *n.* a march in which the physical capacity of troops is exerted to the utmost. **force-feed** *v.t.* (*past, p.p.* **force-fed**) to feed forcibly. **force field** *n.* an invisible barrier created by a force. **forceful** *a.* 1 full of or possessing force, forcible, strong, powerful. 2 impelled with force. 3 violent, impetuous. **forcefully** *adv.* **forcefulness** *n.* **force-land** *v.t., v.i.* to make a forced landing. **forceless** *a.* **force-pump, forcing-pump** *n.* a pump which delivers water under pressure, so as to raise it to an elevation above that attainable by atmospheric pressure. **forcer** *n.* **forcible** *a.* 1 done or brought about by force. 2 having force, powerful, efficacious, impressive. **forcible detainer** *n.* (*Law*) the keeping of houses, land etc., from the owner by force. **forcible entry** *n.* (*Law*) a violent taking possession of or entering into or upon houses or lands. **forcibleness** *n.* **forcibly** *adv.* **forcing** *n., a.* **forcing-house** *n.* a hothouse. **forcing-pit** *n.* a sunk hotbed containing fermenting materials to produce bottom heat for forcing plants. [OF, from late L *fortia*, from L *fortis*, strong]

force[2] (faws) *n.* (*North.*) a waterfall. [Icel. and Norw. *foss*]

force majeure (faws mazhœ´) *n.* 1 superior power. 2 circumstances not under a person's control, so excusing them from fulfilling a contract. [F]

forceps (faw´səps, -sips) *n.* (*pl.* **forceps**) 1 a surgical instrument in the form of a pair of tongs, pincers or pliers for holding or extracting anything. 2 (*Anat., Zool.*) an organ shaped like a pair of forceps. **forcipate** (-pāt), **forcipated** *a.* formed like a forceps, to open and enclose something such as the chelae of a lobster. [L *forceps -cipis*]

forcible FORCE[1].

forclose FORECLOSE.

ford (fawd) *n.* a shallow part of a river where it may be crossed by wading or in a vehicle. ~*v.t.* to cross (water) at a ford. ~*v.i.* to cross water by wading at a ford. **fordable** *a.* **fordless** *a.* [OE, cogn. with FARE (cp. G *Furt*, also L *portus*, a harbour)]

fordo (fawdoo´) *v.t.* (*3rd pers. sing. pres.* **fordoes** (-dŭz), *pres.p.* **fordoing** (-doo´ing), *past* **fordid** (-did), *p.p.* **fordone** (-dŭn)) 1 to destroy, to ruin, to kill, to put an end to. 2 (*usu. p.p.*) to wear out, to exhaust. [OE *fordōn*]

fore (faw) *a.* 1 being in front. 2 being in front of some other thing. 3 being the front part. 4 front. 5 anterior, prior, former, first. ~*n.* 1 the front part. 2 (*Naut.*) the bow. 3 the foremast. ~*int.* in golf, before, beware in front (warning to persons standing in the direction of a drive). ~†*prep.* 1 before. 2 (chiefly now in oaths) for, in the presence of, as *fore God.* 3 in preference to. ~*adv.* 1 †previously. 2 in the front part. 3 (*Naut.*) in or towards the bows. **at the fore** (*Naut.*) displayed on the foremast. **to come to the fore** to become important or popular. **to the fore** 1 to the front, prominent, conspicuous. 2 ready, available, forthcoming. 3 (*Sc.*) still surviving. **fore and aft** *adv.* at, along or over the whole length of a ship. **fore-and-aft** *a.* at, along or over the whole length of a ship from stem to stern. **fore-and-aft rigged** *a.* having sails set lengthwise to the ship, as opposed to square sails set on yards. [OE, for, before, prep., beforehand, adv. (see FOR, with which it is radically identical)]

fore- (faw) *pref.* 1 before, in front, beforehand, chiefly with verbs, as in *foreordain.* 2 in front, the front or front part, as in *forecourt, forerunner.* 3 (*Naut.*) of, near or at the bow or the foremast.

forearm[1] (fawrahm´) *v.t.* to prepare beforehand for attack or defence.

forearm[2] (faw´rahm) *n.* 1 the anterior part of the arm, between the wrist and elbow. 2 the equivalent part in a foreleg or a wing.

forebear (faw´beə), **forbear** *n.* an ancestor.

Usage note See note under FORBEAR[1].

forebode (fawbōd´) *v.t.* 1 to foretell, predict. 2 to be an advance warning of, to foreshadow. 3 to feel a presentiment of something, esp. evil. ~*v.i.* to prognosticate, esp. evil. **forebodement** *n.* **foreboder** *n.* **foreboding** *n.* prophecy, presage or anticipation, esp. of evil. **forebodingly** *adv.*

fore-body (faw´bodi) *n.* (*pl.* **fore-bodies**) that part of a vessel's hull forward of midship.

forebrace (faw´brās) *n.* a rope on the fore yardarm for shifting the sail.

forebrain (faw´brān) *n.* the front part of the brain, including the cerebrum, thalamus and hypothalamus.

forecabin (faw´kabin) *n.* a forward cabin, usu. for second-class passengers.

forecast (faw´kahst) *v.t.* (*past, p.p.* **forecast, forecasted**) 1 to foresee, to predict. 2 to be an early sign of. 3 to calculate beforehand. ~*n.* 1 a statement or calculation of probable events, esp. regarding future weather. 2 foresight, prevision. **forecaster** *n.*

forecastle (fōk´səl, faw´kahsəl), **fo'c'sle** *n.* 1 in merchant ships, a forward space below deck where the crew live. 2 (*also* **forecastle deck**) a short upper deck forward, formerly raised to command the enemy's decks. **forecastle deck** *n.* a short deck at the end of a vessel.

foreclose (fawklōz´), **forclose** *v.t.* 1 to shut out, exclude or bar. 2 to preclude. 3 to put an end to or settle beforehand (e.g. an arguable matter). ~*v.i.* to foreclose a mortgage. **to foreclose a mortgage** to deprive the mortgager of equity of redemption on failure to pay money due on a mortgage. **foreclosure** (-zhə) *n.* the act of foreclosing. [OF *forclos*, p.p. of *forclore* (*for-*, L *foris*, outside, *clore*, to CLOSE[2])]

forecourt (faw´kawt) *n.* 1 an open or paved area in front of a building, esp. a filling station. 2 the first or outer court, that immediately inside the entrance to the precincts of a building. 3 (in tennis etc.) the part of the court between the service line and the net.

foredeck (faw´dek) *n.* 1 the forepart of a deck. 2 the deck in the forepart of a ship.

foredge FORE-EDGE.

foredoom (fawdoom´) *v.t.* 1 to doom beforehand. 2 to predestinate.

fore-edge (faw´rej), **foredge** *n.* the front or outer edge of a book or of a leaf in a book.

forefather (faw´fahdhə) *n.* 1 an ancestor. 2 a member of a previous generation of a people or family.

forefend FORFEND.

forefinger (faw´fing·gə) *n.* the finger next to the thumb.

forefoot (faw´fut) *n.* (*pl.* **forefeet**) 1 either of the front feet of a four-footed animal. 2 the forward end of a vessel's keel.

forefront (faw´frŭnt) *n.* 1 the extreme front. 2 a leading or influential part or position.

foregather (fawgaʹdhə), **forgather** *v.i.* **1** to meet together, to assemble. **2** to meet or associate (with).
forego[1] (fawgōʹ) *v.t., v.i.* (*3rd pers. sing. pres.* **foregoes** (-gōzʹ), *pres.p.* **foregoing** (-gōʹing), *past* **forewent** (-went), *p.p.* **foregone** (-gonʹ)) to go before, to precede in time, order or place. **foregoer** *n.* **1** a person who goes before another, a predecessor. **2** †an ancestor. **foregoing** *a.* preceding, previously mentioned. **foregone** (fawʹgon) *a.* **1** past, preceding. **2** determined before. **foregone conclusion** *n.* **1** a conclusion determined beforehand or arrived at in advance of evidence or reasoning. **2** a result that might be foreseen.

Usage note The spellings of the verbs *forego* (to precede) and *forgo* (to go without) should not be confused.

forego[2] FORGO.
foreground (fawʹgrownd) *n.* **1** the nearest part of a view. **2** the part of a picture which seems to lie nearest the spectator. **3** the most prominent position. *~v.t.* **1** to put in the foreground. **2** to make prominent.
forehand (fawʹhand) *n.* **1** a forehand stroke. **2** the side on which such strokes are made. **3** that part of a horse in front of the rider. *~a.* **1** (in tennis etc.) of, relating to or being a stroke made with the palm of the hand facing in the direction of the stroke. **2** foremost, leading. **3** †anticipative, in advance. **forehanded** *a.* **1** in tennis etc., forehand. **2** (*N Am.*) thrifty, well-off. **3** (*N Am.*) done in good time; timely.
forehead (forʹid, fawʹhed) *n.* **1** the part of the face which reaches from the eyebrows upwards to the hair. **2** the front part, the brow. [OE *forhēafod* (FORE-, HEAD[1])]
forehock (fawʹhok) *n.* a foreleg cut of pork or bacon.
forehold (fawʹhōld) *n.* the forepart of a ship's hold.
forehorse (fawʹhaws) *n.* the foremost horse in a team.
foreign (forʹən) *a.* **1** belonging to, connected with or derived from a country or nation other than one's own. **2** dealing with other countries. **3** introduced from outside. **4** unfamiliar, strange, extraneous, dissimilar, not belonging (to). **5** having no connection with, irrelevant, impertinent, inappropriate. **foreign aid** *n.* economic assistance, food etc. given by one country to another. **Foreign and Commonwealth Office** *n.* the British government department that is concerned with foreign affairs. **foreign body** *n.* (*pl.* **foreign bodies**) a substance occurring in an organism or tissue where it is not normally found. **foreign-built** *a.* built in a foreign country. **foreign correspondent** *n.* a representative of a newspaper sent to a foreign country to report on its politics etc. **foreigner** *n.* **1** a person born or belonging to a foreign country or speaking a foreign language. **2** a foreign ship, an import or product from a foreign country. **3** a stranger, an outsider. **foreign exchange** *n.* (trading in) foreign currencies. **foreignism** *n.* **foreignize, foreignise** *v.t., v.i.* **foreign legion** *n.* a unit of foreign volunteers serving within a national regular army, esp. the French. **foreign minister** *n.* a foreign secretary. **foreignness** *n.* **Foreign Office** *n.* **1** the government department for foreign affairs. **2** the building occupied by this. **foreign secretary** *n.* (*pl.* **foreign secretaries**) a cabinet minister in charge of relations with foreign countries. **foreign service** *n.* (*esp. N Am.*) DIPLOMATIC SERVICE (under DIPLOMACY). **foreign trade** *n.* interchange of commodities by importation or exportation with other countries. [OF *forain*, late L *forāneus*, from L *forās*, out of doors, conn. with *foris*, a door]
forejudge (fawjŭjʹ) *v.t.* to judge before trial or decide before hearing the evidence. **forejudgement, forejudgment** *n.*
foreknow (fawnōʹ) *v.t.* (*pres.p.* **foreknowing**, *past* **foreknew** (-nū), *p.p.* **foreknown** (-nōnʹ)) to know beforehand. **foreknowable** *a.* **foreknower** *n.* †**foreknowingly** *adv.* **foreknowledge** (-nolʹij) *n.* knowledge of a thing before it happens, prescience.
†**forel** (foʹrəl), **forrel** *n.* a kind of parchment used for book covers. [OF *forrel* (F *fourreau*), dim. of *forre*, a sheath]
forelady (fawʹlādi) *n.* (*pl.* **foreladies**) (*N Am.*) a forewoman.
foreland (fawʹlənd) *n.* **1** a point of land extending into the sea, a promontory. **2** a strip of land outside of or in front of an embankment etc.
foreleg (fawʹleg) *n.* a front leg of an animal, chair etc.
forelock[1] (fawʹlok) *n.* a lock of hair growing over the forehead. **to take time by the forelock** to grasp an opportunity. **to touch/ tug one's forelock** to raise one's hand to one's forehead as a sign of deference to a person of a higher social class.
forelock[2] (fawʹlok) *n.* a pin or wedge passing through the end of a bolt to prevent this from being withdrawn. *~v.t.* to secure by a forelock.
foreman (fawʹmən) *n.* (*pl.* **foremen**) **1** a worker supervising others. **2** the person who acts as chairperson and spokesperson for a jury.
foremast (fawʹmahst) *n.* the mast nearest the bow of a vessel. **foremastman** *n.* a common sailor.
forementioned (fawmenʹshənd) *a.* already mentioned.
foremost (fawʹmōst) *a.* **1** first in time, place, order, rank or importance. **2** chief, most notable. *~adv.* **1** in the first place. **2** first, before anything else. [OE *foremost*, *fyrmest*, double superl. from *forma*, first, old superl. of *fore*, before, above; assim. to MOST[1]]
foremother (fawʹmŭdhə) *n.* a female ancestor or predecessor.
forename (fawʹnām) *n.* a name preceding the surname, a Christian name.
forenamed (fawnāmdʹ) *a.* named or mentioned before.
forenight (fawʹnīt) *n.* (*Sc.*) the evening.
forenoon (fawnoonʹ) *n.* (*esp. Sc.*) the early part of the day, from morning to noon.
forensic (fərenʹsik) *a.* **1** of or relating to courts of law, crime detection or to public debate. **2** of, used in or relating to forensic science. **3** used in debates or legal proceedings. *~n.* **1** (*usu. pl., coll.*) forensic science. **2** (*N Am.*) an argumentative thesis at a college. **forensically** *adv.* **forensic medicine** *n.* the science of medicine in its relation to law, medical jurisprudence. **forensic science** *n.* the application of scientific techniques to the investigation and detection of crimes. [L *forensis*, of or relating to the forum, see FORUM]
foreordain (fawrawdānʹ) *v.t.* to ordain beforehand, to predestinate. **foreordination** (-dināʹshən) *n.*
forepart (fawʹpaht) *n.* **1** the first or most advanced part. **2** the earlier part.
forepaw (fawʹpaw) *n.* either of the front paws of a four-footed animal.
forepeak (fawʹpēk) *n.* the part of a vessel's hold in the angle of the bow.
foreplay (fawʹplā) *n.* sexual stimulation preceding intercourse.
forequarter (fawʹkwawtə) *n.* **1** the front half of the side of a carcass, as of beef. **2** (*pl.*) the forelegs, shoulders and chest of a horse or similar quadruped.
foreran FORERUN.
forerank (fawʹrangk) *n.* **1** the foremost rank. **2** the front.
forereach (fawrēchʹ) *v.t.* (*Naut.*) to gain upon, to get ahead of. *~v.i.* to shoot ahead (on), esp. on a ship going in stays.
foreread (fawrēdʹ) *v.t.* (*past, p.p.* **foreread** (-redʹ)) **1** to tell beforehand. **2** to signify by tokens. **forereading** *n.* a previous perusal.
forerun (fawrŭnʹ) *v.t.* (*pres.p.* **forerunning**, *past* **foreran** (-ranʹ), *p.p.* **forerun**) **1** to precede, to go before. **2** to betoken, to usher in. **forerunner** (fawʹ-) *n.* **1** a

predecessor, an ancestor. **2** a precursor, herald. **3** a messenger sent before. **4** †an omen, a prognostic.

foresail (faw´sāl, -səl) *n.* the principal sail on the foremast.

foresaw FORESEE.

foresee (fawsē´) *v.t.* (*pres.p.* **foreseeing,** *past* **foresaw** (-saw´), *p.p.* **foreseen** (-sēn´)) **1** to see beforehand. **2** to know beforehand, to have prescience of. **foreseeable** *a.* **foreseeability** (-bil´iti) *n.* **foreseeably** *adv.* **foreseeing** *a.* exercising foresight. **foreseeingly** *adv.* **foreseer** *n.*

foreshadow (fawshad´ō) *v.t.* **1** to show or be a sign or warning of beforehand. **2** to typify beforehand, to prefigure. *~n.* a foreshadowing or prefiguration of something.

foresheet (faw´shēt) *n.* **1** the rope holding the lee corner of a foresail. **2** (*pl.*) the space in a boat forward of the foremost thwart, usu. covered with a grating.

foreship (faw´ship) *n.* the forepart of a ship, the prow. [OE *forscip* (as FORE-, SHIP)]

foreshock (faw´shok) *n.* a comparatively small earthquake that precedes a much larger earthquake.

foreshore (faw´shaw) *n.* **1** the part of the shore lying between high- and low-water marks. **2** the ground between the sea and land that is cultivated or built upon.

foreshorten (fawshaw´tən) *v.t.* in drawing or painting, to represent (figures or parts of figures that project towards the spectator) so as to give a correct impression of form and proportions. **foreshortened** *a.*

foreshow (fawshō´) *v.t.* (*past* **foreshowed,** *p.p.* **foreshown** (-shōn´)) **1** to predict, to represent beforehand. **2** to foreshadow. [OE *fore-scēawian*]

foresight (faw´sīt) *n.* **1** consideration beforehand, forethought. **2** provident care for the future, prudence, precaution. **3** the front sight of a gun. **foresighted** (fawsītid) *a.* **foresightedly** *adv.* **foresightedness** *n.* †**foresightful** *a.*

foreskin (faw´skin) *n.* the prepuce, the loose skin covering the end of the penis.

†**forespeak** (fawspēk´) *v.t.* (*pres.p.* **forespeaking,** *past* **forespoke** (-spōk), *p.p.* **forespoken** (-spō´kən)) **1** to predict, to foretell. **2** (*Sc.*) to bespeak.

forest (for´ist) *n.* **1** an extensive wood or area of wooded country. **2** the trees growing in such an area. **3** a wild uncultivated tract of ground partly covered with trees and underwood. **4** (*Hist.*) a large tract of country set apart for game and hunting, in many cases orig. a royal hunting ground. **5** something resembling a forest, because having a dense mass of tall vertical objects. *~v.t.* **1** to plant with trees. **2** to convert into a forest. †**forestage** *n.* **1** a tribute payable to the sovereign's foresters. **2** an ancient service paid by foresters to the sovereign. **3** the right to take estovers from a forest. †**forestal** *a.* **forestation** (foristā´shən) *n.* the planting of a forest. **forester** *n.* **1** a person who is in charge of a forest. **2** an inhabitant of a forest. **3** a bird, beast or tree of a forest. **4** a person who looks after the trees on an estate. **5** (*usu.* **Forester**) a member of the Ancient Order of Foresters, a friendly society. **6** (*Austral.*) the largest variety of kangaroo. **forest-fly** *n.* (*pl.* **forest-flies**) a fly frequenting woodlands, *Hippobosca equina*, troublesome to horses. **forest-oak** *n.* an Australian genus of timber trees, the *Casuarina.* **forestry** *n.* **1** the science of cultivating trees and managing forests. **2** the management of growing timber. **3** (*poet.*) woodland, a multitude of trees. **4** (*Sc. Law*) the privileges of a royal forest. **forest tree** *n.* a large tree that is suitable to be grown in a forest. [OF (F *forêt*), from late L *foresta*, a wood, *forestis* (*silva*), the outside or open (wood), from L *foris*, outside]

forestall (fawstawl´) *v.t.* **1** to hinder by anticipation; to act beforehand in order to prevent. **2** to anticipate. **3** to deal beforehand with. **4** to buy up (commodities) beforehand so as to control the sale. **to forestall the market** to engross or buy up commodities, so as to obtain control of the market. **forestaller** *n.* [OE *forsteall*, interference, interception]

forestay (faw´stā) *n.* (*Naut.*) a strong rope, reaching from the foremast head to the bowsprit end, to support the mast.

forester, forestry FOREST.

foretaste[1] (faw´tāst) *n.* **1** experience or enjoyment (of) beforehand. **2** anticipation.

foretaste[2] (fawtāst´) *v.t.* **1** to taste beforehand. **2** to anticipate enjoyment (of).

foreteeth FORETOOTH.

foretell (fawtel´) *v.t.* (*past, p.p.* **foretold** (-tōld)) **1** to predict, to prophesy. **2** to foreshadow. **foreteller** *n.*

forethought (faw´thawt) *n.* **1** consideration beforehand. **2** deliberate intention beforehand. **3** foresight, provident care. **forethoughtful** *a.*

foretime (faw´tīm) *n.* **1** time past. **2** early times.

foretoken[1] (fawtō´kən) *v.t.* to foreshadow, to prognosticate.

foretoken[2] (faw´tōkən) *n.* a token beforehand, an omen.

foretold FORETELL.

foretooth (faw´tooth) *n.* (*pl.* **foreteeth**) a front tooth.

foretop (faw´top, -təp) *n.* **1** (*Naut.*) the top or platform at the head of the foremast. **2** the fore-topgallant-masthead. **fore-topgallant-mast** *n.* the mast above the fore-topmast. **fore-topgallant-sail** *n.* the sail above the fore-topsail. **foretopman** *n.* (*pl.* **foretopmen**) a man stationed in the foretop. **fore-topmast** *n.* the mast at the head of the foremast. **fore-topsail** *n.* the sail above the foresail.

forever (fəre´və) *adv.* **1** (**for ever**) for all future time, eternally. **2** continually, persistently. *~n.* (*poet.*) eternity. **forevermore** *adv.* (*N Am.*) used to add more emphasis than *forever* or *for ever.*

forewarn (faw·wawn´) *v.t.* **1** to warn or caution beforehand. **2** to give notice to beforehand. **forewarner** *n.*

forewent FOREGO[1].

forewind (faw´wind) *n.* a favourable wind.

forewoman (faw´wumən) *n.* (*pl.* **forewomen** (-wimin)) **1** a woman who supervises other workers. **2** the woman who acts as a chairperson and spokesperson for a jury.

foreword (faw´wœd) *n.* a short introduction at the beginning of a book, often written by someone other than the author.

foreyard (faw´yahd) *n.* (*Naut.*) the lowest yard on a foremast.

forfeit (faw´fit) *n.* **1** a penalty, a fine, esp. a stipulated sum to be paid in case of breach of contract. **2** something which is lost through fault, crime, omission or neglect. **3** (*pl.*) a game in which for every breach of the rules the players have to give up some article or perform a playful task or ceremony. **4** the article given up or task etc. performed in this way. **5** the process of forfeiting. **6** †a misdeed, a crime. *~a.* **1** lost or surrendered through fault or crime. **2** †subject, liable. *~v.t.* (*pres.p.* **forfeiting,** *past, p.p.* **forfeited**) **1** to lose the right to or possession of by fault, crime, omission or neglect. **2** to lose. **to forfeit bail** BAIL[1]. **forfeitable** *a.* **1** that may be forfeited. **2** subject to forfeiture. **forfeiter** *n.* a person who incurs a penalty. **forfeiture** (-chə) *n.* **1** the act of forfeiting. **2** something which is forfeited. **3** a penalty or amercement. [OF *forfait*, orig. p.p. of *forfaire*, late L *foris facere*, to transgress, lit. to act beyond or outside]

forfend (fawfend´), **forefend** *v.t.* **1** †to avert, to ward off. **2** (*N Am.*) to secure or protect.

forfex (faw´feks) *n.* a pair of scissorlike anal appendages in earwigs. **forficate** (-fikət), **forficated** *a.* [L, scissors]

☒ **forfit** common misspelling of FORFEIT.

forgather FOREGATHER.

forgave FORGIVE.

forge[1] (fawj) *v.t.* **1** to make, invent, or imitate fraudulently, to counterfeit (*to forge money*). **2** to fabricate, esp. to counterfeit or alter a signature or document with intent to defraud. **3** to make or construct. **4** to form or fabricate by heating and hammering. *~v.i.* to commit forgery. *~n.* **1** the workshop of a smith. **2** a blacksmith's open fireplace or hearth where iron is heated by forced draught. **3** a furnace or hearth for making wrought iron. **4** a place where anything is made. **5** a workshop. **forgeable** *a.* **forger** *n.* **1** a person who commits forgery. **2** a smith, a person who forges metal. **forgery** (-jə-) *n.* (*pl.* **forgeries**) **1** the act of forging, counterfeiting or falsifying. **2** a fraudulent imitation. **3** a deception. **forging** *n.* **1** something which is forged. **2** a piece of forged metal work. [OF, ult. from L *fabrica*, FABRIC]

forge[2] (fawj) *v.i.* **1** to move steadily (forward or ahead). **2** to move at an increased speed (forward or ahead). [etym. uncertain]

forget (fəget´) *v.t.*, *v.i.* (*pres.p.* **forgetting**, *past* **forgot** (-got´), *p.p.* **forgotten** (-got´ən), (*NAm.*) **forgot**) **1** to lose remembrance of. **2** to fail to remember or bring through inadvertence. **3** to neglect (to do something). **4** to put out of mind purposely. **to forget oneself 1** to lose one's self-control, to behave unbecomingly. **2** to act unselfishly. **forgetful** *a.* **1** tending to be absent-minded. **2** neglectful, forgetting. **forgetfully** *adv.* **forgetfulness** *n.* **forget-me-not** (fəget´minot) *n.* a small plant of the genus *Myosotis*, esp. *M. scorpoides*, with small bright blue flowers. **forgettable** *a.* **forgetter** *n.* **forgettery** *n.* (*pl.* **forgetteries**) (*coll.*) a bad memory. **†forgettingly** *adv.* [OE *forgitan* (FOR-, GET[1])]

forgive (fəgiv´) *v.t.* (*pres.p.* **forgiving**, *past* **forgave** (-gāv´), *p.p.* **forgiven** (-giv´ən)) **1** to cease to feel anger or resentment towards. **2** to pardon, not to punish (a person or offence). **3** not to exact the penalty for. **4** to pardon or remit (an offence or debt). *~v.i.* to show forgiveness. **forgivable** *a.* **forgivably** *adv.* **forgiveness** *n.* **1** the act of forgiving. **2** the tendency to forgive. **3** the state of being forgiven. **4** remission, pardon. **forgiver** *n.* **forgiving** *a.* inclined to forgive; merciful, gracious. **forgivingly** *adv.* **forgivingness** *n.* [OE *forgifan* (FOR-, GIVE)]

forgo (fawgō´, fə-), **forego** *v.t.* (*3rd pers. sing. pres.* **forgoes, foregoes,** *pres.p.* **forgoing, foregoing,** *past* **forwent** (-went´), **forewent,** *p.p.* **forgone** (-gon´), **foregone**) **1** to go without, to refrain from. **2** to give up, deny oneself, renounce, relinquish, decline; to quit. [OE *forgān*]

Usage note See note under FOREGO[1].

forgone FORGO.

forgot, forgotten FORGET.

☒ **foriegn** common misspelling of FOREIGN.

forint (for´int) *n.* the monetary unit of Hungary since 1946, equivalent to 100 fillér. [Hung.]

forjudge (fawjŭj´) *v.t.* (*Law*) to deprive, dispossess or exclude by a judgement. **forjudgement, forjudgment** *n.* **forjudger** *n.* [OF *forjuger*]

fork (fawk) *n.* **1** an instrument with two or more prongs, used in eating or cooking. **2** an agricultural implement terminating in two or more prongs, used for digging, impaling, lifting, carrying or throwing. **3** anything of a similar form (*a tuning fork*). **4** a forking or bifurcation. **5** a diverging branch. **6** a confluent, a tributary. **7** a point where a road divides into two. **8** a forked support into which a bicycle wheel fits. **9** the crutch, the bifurcation of the human body. **10** in chess or draughts, a simultaneous attack on two pieces. **11** a flash of forked lightning. **12** †a barbed point, e.g. of an arrow. *~v.t.* **1** to raise or pitch with a fork. **2** to dig or break up (ground) with a fork. **3** to make sharp or pointed. **4** in chess or draughts, to attack two pieces so that only one can escape. *~v.i.* **1** to divide into two. **2** to send out branches. **3** to take one or other branch at a fork in the road etc. **to fork out/ up** (*coll.*) to hand over or pay (money), esp. unwillingly. **to fork over 1** to turn over (soil) using a fork. **2** (*coll.*) to hand over (money), esp. unwillingly. **forked** *a.* **1** dividing into branches, branching, cleft, bifurcated. **2** terminating in points or prongs. **3** having a certain number of prongs (*two-forked*). **forked lightning** *a.* lightning in the form of a jagged or branching line. **†forkedly** (-kid-) *adv.* **†forkedness** (-kid-) *n.* **fork-lift truck** *n.* a vehicle which raises and transports by means of two power-driven horizontal steel prongs. **forklike** *a.* **fork lunch, fork supper** *n.* a buffet at which food is eaten using a fork. **forktail** *a.* having a forked tail. **forky** *n.* forked, forklike. [OE *forc*, L *furca*]

forlorn (fəlawn´) *a.* **1** lonely and sad. **2** deserted, abandoned, uncared-for. **3** helpless, wretched, hopeless. **4** deprived, bereft (of). **forlornly** *adv.* **forlornness** *n.* [OE *forloren*, p.p. of *forlēosan* (FOR-, LOSE)]

forlorn hope (fəlawn´ hōp) *n.* **1** a bold, desperate enterprise. **2** a faint hope. [after Dut. *verloren hoop*, lit. lost troop (from *hoop*, heap, see HEAP), cp. F *enfans perdus*]

form (fawm) *n.* **1** the shape or external appearance of anything apart from its colour. **2** configuration, figure, outline, esp. of the human body. **3** particular arrangement, disposition, organization or constitution. **4** a document with blanks to be filled in. **5** a document that is regularly drawn. **6** established practice or method. **7** a rule of procedure, ceremony or ritual. **8** the mode in which anything is perceptible to the senses or intellect. **9** kind, specific state, species, variety, variation. **10** a specific shape of a word as regards inflection, spelling or pronunciation. **11** the outward aspects of words, in contrast to their meaning. **12** a shape, mould or model upon which a thing is fashioned. **13** a customary method or formula. **14** a fixed order of words. **15** literary nature of a book etc., as distinct from the subject. **16** artistic style or mode of expression, as opposed to content or subject matter. **17** orderly arrangement of parts, order, symmetry. **18** behaviour according to accepted rules or conventions. **19** good physical condition or fitness, a good state of health or training; general state or inclination. **20** in sport, the performance of a person or animal over a period of time. **21** (*sl.*) a criminal record. **22** a long seat without a back. **23** a class in a school considered as an administrative unit, all the pupils in a particular year or a subdivision of a year group. **24** the seat or bed of a hare. **25** the structure of a mathematical expression. **26** (*esp. NAm.*) FORME. **27** (*also* **formwork**) a temporary mould that is used to hold concrete while setting. **28** that which differentiates matter and generates species. **29** (*Philos.*) **a** the essential nature of something. **b** that which the mind contributes, the mode of knowing, the subjective element in perception. **30** in Kantian philosophy, the categories or subjective elements by which the mind apprehends objects. *~v.t.* **1** to give form or shape to. **2** to arrange in any particular manner. **3** to make, construct or create. **4** to model or mould to a pattern. **5** to train, to instruct, to mould or shape by discipline. **6** to develop, conceive, devise, construct (ideas etc.). **7** to be the material for. **8** to be or constitute (a part or one of). **9** to organize or embody. **10** to articulate. **11** to become. **12** (*Mil.*) to combine into (a certain order). **13** (*Gram.*) to make by derivation or by affixes or prefixes. *~v.i.* **1** to assume a form. **2** (*Mil.*) to combine (into a certain order). **in/ on form** showing one's talent to advantage, playing, running or performing well. **off form** playing or performing below one's usual standard. **out of form** not playing, running or performing well. **form class** *n.* a group of words that share the same grammatical or syntactic features. **form criticism** *n.* literary criticism of the Bible in which the structural forms of the text are analysed into proverbs, stories etc. and related to their historical background. **formless** *a.* **1** without form, shapeless. **2** having no regular form. **formlessly** *adv.* **formlessness** *n.* **form letter** *n.* (a copy of) a standard letter sent to many different people, often with relevant individual details added. **form master** *n.* a male form teacher. **form mistress** *n.* a female form teacher. **form teacher** *n.* the teacher with general administrative and tutelary responsibility for a form. [OF *forme*, L *forma*]

form- (fawm) *comb. form* (*Chem.*) containing formyl as a radical. [FORMYL (under FORMIC)]

-form (fawm), **-iform** (ifawm) *suf.* **1** like, having the shape of, as *cruciform, dendriform.* **2** having a certain number of forms, as *multiform, uniform.* [F *-forme*, L *-formis*, from *forma*, FORM]

formal (faw´məl) *a.* **1** made, performed, held or done according to established forms. **2** observant of established form, ceremonious, serious, punctilious, precise. **3** conventional, perfunctory. **4** explicit, definite. **5** orderly, regular. **6** in a set form. **7** of or relating to the outward form as opposed to reality, content or subject matter, outward. **8** (*Logic*) of or relating to form as opposed to matter. **9** (*Philos.*) of or relating to the formative essence that makes a thing what it is, essential, not material. ~*n.* (*N Am.*) **1** a social occasion at which formal dress is worn. **2** an evening gown. **formalism** *n.* **1** the quality of being formal, esp. without consideration of the inner reality or content. **2** formality, esp. in religion. **3** (*Math.*) **a** the notation or structure in which information is expressed. **b** a mathematical description of a physical situation. **4** a stylistic method of theatrical production. **formalist** *n.* **formalistic** (-lis´-) *a.* **formality** (-mal´-) *n.* (*pl.* **formalities**) **1** conventionality, mere form. **2** an established order or method, an observance required by custom or etiquette, esp. without having any real effect. **3** conformity to custom, rule or established method. **4** the condition or quality of being formal. **5** artistic precision, observance of rule as opposed to originality. **formalize, formalise** *v.t.* **1** to make or render formal. **2** to give legal formality to, to formulate. **formalization** (-zā´shən) *n.* **formally** *adv.* [L *formālis*, from *forma*, FORM]

formaldehyde (fawmal´dihīd) *n.* formic aldehyde, a colourless gas generated by the partial oxidation of methyl alcohol, and used as an antiseptic and disinfectant.

formalin (fawm´əlin) *n.* a solution of formaldehyde used as an antiseptic, for the destruction of disease germs, and as a food preservative.

formant (faw´mənt) *n.* **1** a component of a sound, esp. which gives it its particular tone, colour or quality. **2** in linguistics, a morpheme that occurs only in combination in a word or stem. [G, from L *formans*, pres.p. of *formare*, to shape, fashion]

format (faw´mat) *n.* **1** the external form and size of a book, magazine etc. **2** the general plan, arrangement and style of e.g. a television programme. **3** (*Comput.*) the arrangement of data on a disk etc. ~*v.t.* (*pres.p.* **formatting,** *past, p.p.* **formatted**) **1** to arrange in a specific format. **2** (*Comput.*) to prepare a disk etc. for the reception of data. [F, from L *formātus*, from *forma*, FORM]

formate FORMIC.

formation (fawmā´shən) *n.* **1** the act or process of forming or creating. **2** the state of being formed or created. **3** the manner in which anything is formed. **4** conformation, arrangement, disposition of parts, structure. **5** a thing formed, regarded in relation to form or structure. **6** a group of rocks or strata of common origin, structure or physical character. **7** an arrangement of troops, aircraft, ships etc. (*formation flying*). **formational** *a.* **formative** (faw´mə-) *a.* **1** having the power of giving form, shaping. **2** plastic. **3** of or relating to formation, growth or development. **4** (of combining forms, prefixes etc.) serving to form words. ~*n.* **1** a formative combining form, prefix etc. **2** a word formed in accordance with some rule or usage. **formatively** *adv.* [L *formātio -ōnem*, from *forma*, FORM]

forme (fawm) *n.* **1** a body of type composed and locked in a chase for printing. **2** (*Print.*) a quantity of film arranged for making a plate. [FORM]

former[1] (faw´mə) *a.* **1** preceding in time. **2** mentioned before something else, the first-mentioned (of two). **3** past, earlier, ancient, bygone. **one's former self** SELF. **formerly** *adv.* **1** in former times. **2** of the past or earlier times. [formed from ME *formest*, FOREMOST, double superl. from OE *forma*, first]

Usage note The *former* should not be used to mean the first-mentioned of more than two (*the first*).

former[2] (faw´mə) *n.* **1** a person or thing that forms. **2** in electrical engineering, a frame or core on which a coil can be wound. **3** a structural part of an aircraft that helps to maintain the shape of the fuselage, a wing etc. **4** (*in comb.*) a member of a certain school form (*a sixth-former*).

formic (faw´mik) *a.* (*Chem.*) of, relating to or produced by ants. **formate** (-māt) *n.* a salt or ester of formic acid. **formic acid** *n.* an acid found in the fluid emitted by ants, in stinging nettles etc., and now obtained from oxalic acid distilled with glycerine. **formicant** *a.* (of the pulse) weak, almost imperceptible, creeping like an ant. **formicary** *n.* (*pl.* **formicaries**) an anthill. **formicate** (-kət) *a.* resembling an ant. **formication** (-ā´shən) *n.* irritation of the skin that feels like the crawling of ants. **formyl** (-mīl) *n.* (*Chem.*) the radical theoretically constituting the base of formic acid. [short for *formicic*, from L *formīca*, an ant]

Formica® (fawmī´kə) *n.* a hard, long-lasting laminated plastic used for surfacing materials and other purposes.

formidable (faw´midəbəl, -mid´-) *a.* **1** tending to excite fear or respect. **2** to be feared. **3** dangerous to encounter. **4** difficult to resist, overcome or accomplish. **formidability** (-bil´-) *n.* **formidableness** *n.* **formidably** *adv.* [F, from L *formīdābilis*, from *formīdāre*, to dread]

Usage note The pronunciation (-mid´-), with stress on the second syllable, is sometimes disapproved of.

formula (faw´mūlə) *n.* (*pl.* **formulas, formulae** (-lē)) **1** (*Chem.*) (*pl.* **formulae**) an expression by means of symbols of the elements of a compound. **2** (*pl.* **formulae**) the expression of a rule or principle in algebraic symbols. **3** a prescribed form of words. **4** a fixed rule, a set form, a conventional usage. **5** a formal enunciation of faith, doctrine, principle etc. **6** a compromise solution to a dispute, an agreed form of words. **7** a prescription, a recipe. **8** a milk mixture or substitute used as baby food. **9** a technical specification which determines the class in which a racing car competes. **formulaic** (-lā´ik) *a.* **formularize, formularise** *v.t.* to formulate. **formularization** (-zā´shən) *n.* **formulary** *a.* **1** stated, prescribed. **2** of the nature of a formula; using formulae. **3** formal, ritual. ~*n.* (*pl.* **formularies**) **1** a book containing stated and prescribed forms, esp. relating to religious belief or ritual. **2** a collection of formulae used in preparation of medicinal drugs. **3** a formula. **formulate** *v.t.* **1** to express in a formula. **2** to set forth in a precise and systematic form. **formulation** (-lā´shən) *n.* **formulator** *n.* **formulism** *n.* strict observance of or dependence upon formulas. **formulist** *n.* **formulistic** (-lis´-) *a.* **formulize, formulise** *v.t.* to formulate. **formulization** (-zā´shən) *n.* [L, dim. of *forma*, FORM]

formyl FORMIC.

fornent (fənent´), **fornenst** (-nenst´) *prep.* (*Sc.*) right opposite to. ~*adv.* opposite. [FORE, ANENT]

fornicate (faw´nikāt) *v.i.* (*formal or facet.*) to commit fornication. **fornication** (-kā´shən) *n.* **1** voluntary sexual intercourse between two unmarried people or between people not married to each other. **2** (*Bible*) sexual immorality, esp. adultery. **fornicator** *n.* †**fornicatress** *n.* a female fornicator. [L *fornicātus*, p.p. of *fornicārī*, from *fornix -icis*, an arch, a brothel]

fornix (faw´niks) *n.* (*pl.* **fornices** (-nisēz)) **1** (*Anat.*) **a** the arch of the vagina. **b** the roof of the pharynx. **c** an arch-shaped formation in the brain. **2** a similar part or organ in a plant or shell. [L, an arch]

forrader (for´ədə) *a., adv.* (*coll.*) more or further forward. [comp. of FORWARD]

forrel FOREL.

forsake (fəsāk´) *v.t.* (*pres.p.* **forsaking,** *past* **forsook** (-suk), *p.p.* **forsaken** (-sāk´ən)) **1** to leave, to abandon, to withdraw from. **2** to renounce, to cast off, to reject, to give up. **forsaker** *n.* [OE *forsacan* (FOR-, *sacan*, to quarrel, see SAKE[1])]

forsook FORSAKE.

forsooth (fəsooth´) *adv.* (*chiefly iron.*) in truth, certainly, doubtless.

†**forspeak** (fawspēk´) *v.t.* (*past* **forspoke** (-spōk´), *p.p.* **forspoken** (-spōk´ən)) **1** to forbid, to speak against. **2** to bewitch, to charm.

†**forspend** (fəspend´) *v.t.* (*past, p.p.* **forspent** (-spent´)) (*usu. p.p.*) to wear out, to exhaust with toil.

†**forspoke,** †**forspoken** FORSPEAK.

forswear (fəsweə´) *v.t.* (*past* **foreswore** (-swaw´), *p.p.* **foresworn** (-swawn´)) **1** to abjure, to renounce upon oath or with protestations. **2** to swear falsely. **3** †to break (an oath, allegiance, etc.). *~v.i.* to swear falsely. **to forswear oneself** to perjure oneself. **forswearer** *n.* a perjurer. **forswornness** *n.* **1** the state of being forsworn. **2** perjury. [OE *forswerian*]

forsythia (fawsī´thiə) *n.* any oleaceous shrub of the genus *Forsythia* bearing numerous yellow flowers in early spring before the leaves. [William *Forsyth*, 1737–1804, English botanist]

fort (fawt) *n.* **1** a fortified place, esp. a detached outwork or an independent fortified work of moderate extent. **2** (*Hist.*) a trading station in N America. **forted** *a.* guarded by forts, fortified. **fortlet** (fawt´lit) *n.* a small fort. [OF, from L *fortis* (*domus*, strong (house)]

fortalice (faw´təlis) *n.* **1** an outwork of a fortification. **2** a small fort. [med. L *fortalitia*, from *fortis*, strong]

forte[1] (faw´tā, faw´ti, fawt) *n.* **1** a person's strong point. **2** that in which a person excels. **3** the strong part of a sword blade, i.e. from the hilt to the middle. [F fem. a., strong, as FORT (fem. unmeaningly adopted instead of masc.)]

forte[2] (faw´ti) *adv.* (*Mus.*) with loudness or force. *~a.* performed with loudness or force. *~n.* a passage to be performed with loudness or force. **forte forte** *adv.* very loud. **fortepiano** *n.* (*pl.* **fortepianos**) an early form of piano. **forte piano** *adv.* loudly, then softly. *~a.* loud, then soft. [It., strong, from L *fortis*]

forth (fawth) *adv.* **1** forward. **2** out. **3** out into view. **4** out from home or another starting point. **5** out of doors. **6** forwards in place, time or order. **7** indefinitely forward in time. *~*†*prep.* out of, away from. **and so forth** SO[1]. **back and forth** to and fro. **forthcoming** *a.* **1** coming forth, ready to appear or to be produced, published etc. **2** approaching, soon to take place. **3** available. **4** (of a person) communicative, responsive. *~*†*n.* **1** coming forth. **2** (*Sc. Law*) an action by which an assessment is made effectual. **forthcomingness** *n.* **forthright** *a.* **1** outspoken, direct, to the point. **2** going straight forward. *~adv.* **1** in a direct or outspoken manner. **2** straight forward. **3** at once, straightaway. **forthrightly** *adv.* **forthrightness** *n.* **forthwith** (-with´, -widh´) *adv.* immediately, without delay. [OE, from *fore*, see FORE (cp. Dut. *voort*, G *fort*)]

forties, fortieth FORTY.

fortify (faw´tifī) *v.t.* (*3rd pers. sing. pres.* **fortifies,** *pres.p.* **fortifying,** *past, p.p.* **fortified**) **1** to strengthen or secure by forts, ramparts etc. **2** to make defensible against the attack of an enemy. **3** to make strong, to give power or strength to, to invigorate, to encourage. **4** to strengthen the structure of. **5** to add alcoholic strength to. **6** to enrich (a food) by adding vitamins etc. **7** to confirm, to corroborate. *~v.i.* to raise fortifications. **fortifiable** *a.* **fortification** (-fikā´shən) *n.* **1** the act, process, art or science of fortifying a place or position against the attacks of an enemy. **2** a defensive work, a fort. **3** (*pl.*) works erected to defend a place against attack. **4** increasing the strength of wine with alcohol. **5** †an accession of strength, a strengthening. **fortifier** *n.* [OF *fortifier*, L *fortificāre* (*fortis*, strong, *-ficāre*, from *facere*, to make)]

fortissimo (fawtis´imō) *adv.* (*Mus.*) very loudly. *~a.* performed very loudly. *~n.* (*pl.* **fortissimos, fortissimi** (-mē)) a passage that is to be performed very loudly. [It., superl. of *forte*, see FORTE[2]]

fortitude (faw´titūd) *n.* strength, esp. that strength of mind which enables one to meet danger or endure pain with calmness. **fortitudinous** (-tū´din-) *a.* [F, from L *fortitūdo*, from *fortis*, strong]

fortnight (fawt´nīt) *n.* **1** a period of two weeks or 14 days. **2** two weeks from a certain day (*on Thursday fortnight*). **fortnightly** *a.* happening or produced once a fortnight. *~adv.* **1** once a fortnight. **2** every fortnight. *~n.* (*pl.* **fortnightlies**) a fortnightly publication. [ME *fourtenight*, OE *fēowertȳne niht*, 14 nights]

Fortran (faw´tran), **FORTRAN** *n.* a high-level computer language used esp. for mathematical and scientific purposes. [*for*mula *tran*slation]

fortress (faw´tris) *n.* a fortified place, esp. a strongly fortified town accommodating a large garrison and forming a permanent stronghold. *~v.t.* (*poet.*) to furnish with or serve as a fortress, to defend. [OF *forteresse*, var. of *fortalesce*, *fortalice*]

fortuitous (fawtū´itəs) *a.* happening by chance; casual, accidental. **fortuitism** *n.* (*Philos.*) the doctrine that mere chance, not design, is the principle governing the operation of natural causes. **fortuitist** *n.* **fortuitously** *adv.* **fortuitousness** *n.* **fortuity** *n.* (*pl.* **fortuities**) **1** a chance occurrence; an accident. **2** fortuitousness. [L *fortuitus*, from *fors fortis*, chance]

Usage note *Fortuitous* is sometimes used as though it meant fortunate or opportune, but this is best avoided.

fortunate (faw´chənət) *a.* **1** lucky, prosperous. **2** happening by good luck. **3** bringing or indicating good fortune, auspicious. **fortunately** *adv.* **1** luckily. **2** it is fortunate that. **fortunateness** *n.* [L *fortūnātus*, p.p. of *fortūnāre*, from *fortūna*, see FORTUNE]

fortune (faw´choon, -chən) *n.* **1** wealth. **2** a large property or sum of money. **3** chance, luck, that which happens as if by chance. **4** that which brings good or ill, a personification of this, a supernatural power supposed to control one's lot and to bestow good or evil (*Fortune smiled on them*). **5** good luck, prosperity. **6** a person's future destiny. **7** (*pl.*) the progress or history of a person or thing. *~*†*v.t.* **1** to control the fortunes of. **2** to provide with a fortune. *~*†*v.i.* to happen, to chance. **to make a/ one's fortune** to gain great wealth. **to tell a person's fortune** to make predictions about a person's future, by looking e.g. at the lines on their hand. **Fortune 500** *a.* of or relating to the 500 most profitable US industrial corporations. **fortune cookie** *n.* (*N Am.*) a biscuit with a slip of paper inside it, which has a prediction, proverb, joke etc. written on it. **fortune hunter** *n.* (*coll.*) a person who seeks to gain wealth, esp. through marriage. **fortune-hunting** *n., a.* **fortuneless** *a.* **1** luckless. **2** without a dowry. **fortune-teller** *n.* a person who makes predictions about a person's future. **fortune-telling** *n.* [F, from L *fortūna*, cogn. with *fors fortis*, chance, and *ferre*, to bring]

forty (faw'ti) *n.* (*pl.* **forties**) **1** the number or figure 40 or XL. **2** the age of 40. **3** a set of 40 people or things. ~*a.* **1** 40 in number. **2** aged 40. **forties** (faw'tiz) *n.pl.* **1** the period of time between one's 40th and 50th birthdays. **2** the range of temperature between 40 and 50 degrees. **3** the period of time between the 40th and 50th years of a century. **roaring forties** ROARING (under ROAR). **the Forties** the area of sea between the NE coast of Scotland and the SW coast of Norway. **fortieth** (faw'tiəth) *n.* any one of 40 equal parts. ~*n.*, *a.* **1** (the) last of 40 (people, things etc.). **2** the next after the 39th. **forty-first, forty-second etc.** *n.*, *a.* the ordinal numbers corresponding to forty-one etc. **forty-five** *n.* a record played at 45 r.p.m. **the Forty-five** the Jacobite rebellion of 1745–46. **fortyfold** *a.*, *adv.* **forty-niner** *n.* any of the adventurers who went to California at the time of the gold rush in 1849. **forty-one, forty-two etc.** *n.* the cardinal numbers between forty and fifty. **forty winks** *n.pl.* a nap. [OE *fēowertig* (FOUR, -TY[1]), cp. Dut. *veertig*, G *vierzig*]

forum (faw'rəm) *n.* (*pl.* **forums, fora** (-rə)) **1** a place of assembly for public discussion or judicial purposes. **2** a meeting to discuss matters of public interest. **3** a medium, e.g. a magazine, for open discussion. **4** a tribunal, a court of law. **5** a market place. **6** (*Hist.*) the public place in Rome in which were the courts of law, public offices etc. and where orations were delivered. **7** in the Roman Catholic Church, the sphere in which the Church exercises jurisdiction. [L]

forward (faw'wəd) *a.* **1** at or near the forepart of anything. **2** in front. **3** towards the front. **4** onward. **5** in advance, advancing or advanced. **6** well advanced, progressing, early, premature, precocious. **7** eager, prompt. **8** pert, presumptuous. **9** of or relating to future commercial dealings, products etc. ~*n.* a mainly attacking player at football etc. stationed at the front of a formation. ~*v.t.* **1** to help onward, to promote. **2** to hasten the growth of. **3** to send on or ahead, to send to a further destination. **4** to send. ~*adv.* **1** (*also* **forwards**) **a** towards the front. **b** onward in place or time. **c** onward so as to make progress. **d** towards the future. **e** to an earlier time. **f** ahead, in advance. **g** to the front, to a prominent position. **2** towards, at or in the forepart of a vessel or aircraft. **forwarder** *n.* **1** a person who helps forward. **2** a promoter. **3** a person who transmits goods. **4** a person or firm whose business is to facilitate the onward shipment of goods to their destination. **5** a person who prepares a sewed book for the finisher by plain covering. **forward-looking** *a.* **1** progressive. **2** looking to, or planning for, the future. **forwardly** *adv.* **forwardness** *n.* **1** the quality or state of being forward. **2** assurance. **3** pertness, presumption. [OE *foreweard* (FORE, -WARD)]

forwent FORGO.

fossa (fos'ə) *n.* (*pl.* **fossae** (fos'ē)) (*Anat.*) a shallow depression, pit or cavity. **fossiform** (-fawm) *a.* [L, a ditch, orig. fem. p.p. of *fodere*, to dig]

fosse (fos) *n.* **1** a ditch, a trench, esp. around a fortification, commonly filled with water. **2** a canal. **3** a fossa. **fossette** (-et') *n.* a dimple, a small fossa. [F, from L FOSSA]

fossick (fos'ik) *v.i.* **1** (*Austral.*, *New Zeal.*, *coll.*) to search for gold or precious stones, esp. in abandoned workings. **2** to rummage about. **fossicker** *n.* [cp. dial. *fussock*, to bustle about]

fossiform FOSSA.

fossil (fos'əl) *n.* **1** the hardened remains of a prehistoric animal or plant found inside a rock etc. **2** (*coll.*) an antiquated, out-of-date or inflexible person or thing. **3** a word or phrase once current but now found only in a few special contexts. ~*a.* **1** preserved in the strata of the earth's crust, esp. if mineralized. **2** of, like or relating to fossils. **3** antiquated. **4** found underground. **5** dug up. **fossilate** *v.t.*, *v.i.* to fossilize. **fossilation** (-ā'shən) *n.* **fossil fuel** *n.* a naturally-occurring fuel formed by the decomposition of prehistoric organisms. **fossiliferous** (-lif'-) *a.* **fossilify** (-sil'-) *v.t.* (*3rd pers. sing. pres.* **fossilifies,** *pres.p.* **fossilifying,** *past, p.p.* **fossilified**) to fossilize. **fossil ivory** *n.* ivory from the tusks of a mammoth. **fossilize, fossilise** *v.t.* **1** to convert into a fossil. **2** to render antiquated or inflexible. ~*v.i.* **1** to be converted into a fossil. **2** to become antiquated or inflexible. **fossilization** (-zā'shən) *n.* [OF, from L *fossilis*, from *fossus*, p.p. of *fodere*, to dig]

fossor (fos'aw) *n.* (*Hist.*) a member of an order of inferior clergy charged with the burial of the dead. **fossorial** (-saw'riəl) *a.* **1** adapted for digging. **2** (*Zool.*) being or relating to a burrowing animal. [late L, grave-digger, from *fossus*, see FOSSIL]

foster (fos'tə) *v.t.* **1** to nourish, to support, to encourage, to promote the growth of. **2** to bring up or nurse (esp. a child not one's own). **3** to place in the charge of foster parents. **4** (of circumstances) to be favourable to. **5** to harbour (an ill feeling). ~*a.* of or relating to fostering (*a foster home*). **fosterage** *n.* **1** the act or custom of fostering. **2** the state of being a foster child. **3** the care of a foster child. **4** fostering or encouraging. **foster brother** *n.* a brother by fostering, not by birth. **foster child** *n.* a child brought up or nursed by someone other than their natural parent(s). **foster daughter** *n.* a female foster child. **fosterer** *n.* **foster father** *n.* a male foster parent. **fosterling** (-ling) *n.* a foster child. **foster mother** *n.* a female foster parent. †**foster-nurse** *n.* a wet-nurse. **foster parent** *n.* a person who takes the place of a parent in rearing a child. **foster sister** *n.* a sister by fostering, not by birth. **foster son** *n.* a male foster child. [OE *fōstrian*, from *fōstor*, nourishment, cogn. with *fōda*, FOOD]

fou (foo) *a.* (*Sc.*) drunk. [FULL[1]]

foudroyant (foodroi'ənt) *a.* **1** (of a disease) beginning in a sudden and intense form. **2** †overwhelming, thundering or flashing, like lightning. [F, pres.p. of *foudroyer*, to strike with lightning, from *foudre*, ult. from L *fulgur*, lightning]

fouetté (fwet'ā) *n.* a step in ballet in which the dancer stands on one foot and makes a whiplike movement with the other. [F p.p. of *fouetter*, to whip]

fought, †foughten FIGHT.

foul (fowl) *a.* **1** dirty, filthy, unclean. **2** loathsome, offensive to the senses. **3 a** covered or filled with noxious matter. **b** overgrown with weeds, clogged, choked. **4** (*coll.*) disgusting, revolting. **5** morally offensive, obscene, disgusting. **6** polluted. **7** unfair, unlawful, dishonest, against the rules. **8** stormy, cloudy, rainy. **9** (of a rope) entangled. **10** (of the bottom of a vessel) covered with barnacles, weeds etc. **11** (of a proof) full of printer's errors, dirty, inaccurate. ~*adv.* irregularly, against the rules. ~*n.* **1** in sport, a foul stroke, any breach of the rules of a game or contest. **2** an entanglement, blockage or collision, e.g. in sailing, riding or fishing. **3** foul weather or fortune. **4** a foul thing. ~*v.t.* **1** to make foul or dirty. **2** to defile, to soil, to pollute. **3** in sport, to commit a foul against. **4** to come into collision with, to impede, block or entangle. **5** to dishonour. ~*v.i.* **1** to become foul or dirty. **2** to come into collision. **3** to become clogged or entangled. **4** in sport, to commit a foul. **to fall foul of 1** to come or run against with force. **2** to come into collision, entanglement or conflict with. **3** to quarrel with. **4** to be contrary to, to go against. **to foul up 1** to make dirty, to pollute. **2** to block, to entangle. **3** to become blocked or entangled. **4** (*coll.*) to blunder. **5** (*coll.*) to spoil or cause to break down by making mistakes etc. **to play foul** to hit or deal with an opponent or competitor in a manner forbidden by the rules. **to run foul of** to fall foul of. **foul brood** *n.* a bacterial disease of bee larvae. **foul fish** *n.* a fish in or just after the spawning season. **foully** *adv.* 1 in a foul manner. 2 abominably, treacherously, wickedly. **foul mouth** *n.* a person who uses offensive language. **foul-mouthed, foul-spoken, foul-tongued** *a.* (of a person) often using offensive language. **foulness** *n.* **foul play** *n.* 1 unfair behaviour in a game or contest, a breach of the rules. 2 dishonest or treacherous conduct. 3 violence, murder. **foul-up** *n.* a bungled or blundered situation. [OE *fūl* (cp. Dut. *vuil*, Icel. *fūll*, G *faul*, also Gr. *puon*, stinking, L *pus*, see PUS) whence *fūlian*, to decay]

foulard (foolah´, -lahd´) *n.* 1 a soft, thin material of silk or silk mixed with cotton. 2 something made of this, e.g. a silk handkerchief. [F, etym. unknown]

foumart (foo´mət, -maht) *n.* the polecat. [ME *fulmart*, *folmard*, OE *fūl*, FOUL, *mearth*, a marten]

found[1] FIND.

found[2] (fownd) *v.t.* 1 to set up or establish (an institution, organization etc.) by providing the necessary money, to endow. 2 to lay the foundation or basis of. 3 to begin to erect or build. 4 to originate, to give origin to. 5 to construct or base (upon). 6 to fix firmly. ~*v.i.* to rest (upon) as a foundation or basis. **founder**[1] *n.* a person who founds or originates anything, esp. one who endows a permanent fund for the support of an institution. **founder member** *n.* any of the original members who combined to establish a society etc. **foundership** *n.* **founder's share** *n.* a share of stock allotted to a promoter of a corporation as part payment for goodwill, plant etc. **founding** *n., a.* **founding father** *n.* 1 a member of the American Constitutional Convention of 1787. 2 a person who establishes or institutes something. **foundress** *n.* a female founder. [F *fonder*, L *fundāre*, from *fundus*, bottom, base]

found[3] (fownd) *v.t.* 1 to cast by melting (metal) or fusing (material for glass) and pouring it into a mould. 2 to make of molten metal or glass. **founder**[2] *n.* a person who casts metal. **foundry** *n.* (*pl.* **foundries**) 1 a building where metals are cast. 2 the act or art of casting metals. [F *fondre*, L *fundere*, to pour]

foundation (fowndā´shən) *n.* 1 the natural or artificial base of a structure. 2 (*pl.*) the part of a structure below the surface of the ground. 3 the grounds, principles or basis on which anything stands. 4 the reasons on which an opinion etc. is founded. 5 the act of founding or establishing. 6 that on which anything is established or by which it is sustained. 7 permanent basis. 8 the fund or endowment which supports an institution. 9 that which is founded or endowed. 10 an endowed institution. 11 (*also* **foundation garment**) a woman's undergarment that supports the figure, e.g. a corset. 12 a cosmetic used as a base for other facial make-up. 13 the stiff fabric forming the basis of various articles of clothing. **foundational** *a.* **foundation course** *n.* a basic, general course, taught e.g. in the first year at some universities and colleges. **foundation cream** *n.* a cream over which cosmetics are applied. **foundationless** *a.* without foundation. **foundation-muslin, foundation-net** *n.* openwork, gummed fabrics for stiffening dresses and bonnets. **foundation school** *n.* an endowed school. **foundation stone** *n.* 1 a stone laid with ceremony to commemorate the founding of a building. 2 the basis of something on which future success depends. [L *fundātio* (FOUND[2])]

founder[1] FOUND[2].

founder[2] FOUND[3].

founder[3] (fown´də) *v.i.* 1 (of a ship) to fill with water and sink. 2 to fail, to break down. 3 to be ruined. 4 to fall in, to give way. 5 (of a horse) to fall lame. ~*v.t.* 1 to sink (a ship) by making it fill with water. 2 to lame by causing soreness or inflammation in the feet of (a horse). ~*n.* 1 inflammation of the sensitive parts of a horse's foot from overwork. 2 rheumatism of horses' chest muscles. [OF *fondrer*, to sink in, from *fond*, L *fundus*, the bottom]

foundling (fownd´ling) *n.* a deserted child of unknown parents. **foundling hospital** *n.* a charitable institution where deserted children are brought up. [FOUND[1], -LING[1]]

foundry FOUND[3].

fount[1] (fownt) *n.* 1 a spring, a fountain, a well. 2 a source. **fountful** *a.* [F *font*, L *fons fontis*]

fount[2] FONT[2].

fountain (fown´tin) *n.* 1 an ornamental jet of water driven high into the air by pressure. 2 the structure for producing such a jet. 3 a public structure with a drinking supply. 4 a spring of water, natural or artificial. 5 the source of a river or stream. 6 a source, a first principle. 7 a reservoir to contain a liquid, as in a lamp, printing press, fountain pen etc. 8 (*Her.*) a roundel divided into six spaces by waved lines across the shield. 9 a soda fountain. **fountained** *a.* (*esp. in comb.*) having fountains, as *many-fountained*. **fountainhead** *n.* an original source or spring. **fountainless** *a.* **fountain pen** *n.* a pen with a reservoir or cartridge containing ink. [OF *fontaine*, late L *fontāna*, L *fons fontis*]

four (faw) *n.* 1 the number or figure 4 or IV. 2 the age of four. 3 the fourth hour after midnight or midday. 4 a set of four persons or things, a team of four horses, a four-oared boat or its crew. 5 a card or domino with four spots. 6 in cricket, (a score of four runs from) a shot which crosses the boundary after hitting the ground. 7 a size measuring four. 8 (*Mil.*) a marching column four men wide. ~*a.* four in number, aged four. **on all fours** 1 crawling on the hands and feet or knees. 2 agreeing precisely (with). **the four freedoms** freedom of speech and religion and freedom from fear or want. **the four seas** the seas surrounding Great Britain on N, S, E and W. **the four winds** the four cardinal points. **four-ball** *n.* a game of golf between two pairs, in which the better individual score at each hole is counted. **four-centred** *a.* (of an arch) having the curve described from four centres. **four-dimensional** *a.* **four-eyes** *n.* (*sl.*) a person wearing glasses. **four-flush** *n.* a worthless poker hand in which only four of the five cards are of the same suit. **four-flusher** *n.* (*N Am., sl.*) a bluffer. **fourfold** *a.* 1 four times as many or as much, quadruple. 2 consisting of four parts. ~*adv.* in fourfold measure. **four-footed** *a.* having four feet, quadruped. **four-foot way** *n.* the space between the metals (actually 4ft 8½in., 1.435 m) on a railway. **four-handed** *a.* 1 having four hands, quadrumanous. 2 (of games) for four players. 3 (of music) for two performers. **four-horse** *a.* drawn by four horses. **four hundred** *n.* (*N Am.*) the most exclusive social group of people in a particular area. **four-in-hand** *a.* drawn by four horses. ~*adv.* with four horses driven by one driver. ~*n.* 1 a vehicle so drawn and driven. 2 (*N Am.*) a long necktie tied in a skip-knot with the ends left dangling. **four-leaf, four-leaved** *a.* (of a clover leaf) with four leaflets instead of three, supposed to bring good luck. **four-letter word** *n.* any of a number of short English words referring to the body, sex or excrement and considered vulgar or obscene. **four-oar** *a.* propelled by four oars. **four o'clock** *n.* the marvel of Peru, *Mirabilis jalapa*, so named from its flowers opening at four o'clock in the afternoon. **fourpence** (faw´pəns) *n.* the sum of four pence. **fourpenny** *a.* worth fourpence, costing fourpence. ~*n.* (*pl.* **fourpennies**) a old silver coin worth 4d. **fourpenny one** *n.* (*dated sl.*) a blow, a cuff. **four-ply** *a.* having four strands, thicknesses etc. ~*n.* plywood of four layers. **four-post** *a.* (of a bed etc.) having four high posts at the corners to support a canopy and curtains. **four-poster** *n.* a (usu. large) bedstead with a canopy and curtains. †**fourscore** *a.* 1

4 times 20, 80. 2 80 years old. ~*n.* the number of 4 times 20. **foursome** (-səm) *a.* done by four persons. ~*n.* **1** a group of four people. **2** a game of golf between two pairs, the partners playing their ball alternately. **four-square** *a.* **1** having four sides and angles equal. **2** square-shaped. **3** firmly established. **4** immovable, resolute, forthright. ~*adv.* resolutely. **four-stroke** *a.* **1** (of an internal-combustion engine) firing once every four strokes of movement of the piston. **2** (of a vehicle) having a four-stroke engine. ~*n.* a four-stroke engine or vehicle. **four-way** *a.* allowing passage in any one of four directions. **four-wheel, four-wheeled** *a.* having four wheels. **four-wheel drive** *n.* a system whereby power is transmitted to all four wheels of a motor vehicle. **four-wheeler** *n.* a vehicle having four wheels, esp. a horse-drawn cab. [OE *fēower* (cp. Dan. *fire*, Dut. and G *vier*, Welsh *pedwar*, L *quatuor*, Gr. *tessares*)]

fourchette (fuəshet´) *n.* **1** (*Anat.*) a thin fold of skin at the back of the vulva. **2** a fork-shaped piece between the fingers of gloves. **3** a forked surgical instrument formerly used for cutting the fraenum in tongue-tied infants. [F, dim. of *fourche*, L *furca*, FORK]

fourgon (fuə´gõ) *n.* a French baggage-wagon. [F, etym. unknown]

Fourier analysis (foo´riə, -riā) *n.* (*Math.*) the analysis of periodic function into its harmonic components, using a Fourier series. **Fourier series** *n.* (*Math.*) an infinite trigonometric series used to represent a periodic function. [Baron Jean Baptiste Joseph *Fourier*, 1768–1830, French mathematician]

Fourierism (furi´ərizm) *n.* a system of social reorganization advocated by Fourier, based on the principle of natural affinities. **Fourierist, Fourierite** *n.* [F. M. Charles *Fourier*, 1772–1837, French socialist]

fourteen (faw´tēn, -tēn´) *n.* **1** the number or figure 14 or XIV. **2** the age of 14. **3** a size measuring 14. ~*a.* **1** 14 in number. **2** aged 14. **fourteenth** *n.* **1** any one of 14 equal parts. **2** an interval of an octave and a seventh. **3** a note separated from another by this interval, two such notes sounded together. ~*n., a.* **1** (the) last of 14 (people, things etc.). **2** (the) next after the 13th. [OE *fēowertȳne*]

fourth (fawth) *n.* **1** any one of four equal parts, a quarter. **2** the person or thing in fourth position. **3** the fourth forward gear of a motor vehicle. **4** (*Mus.*) **a** an interval of four diatonic notes, comprising two whole tones and a semitone. **b** two notes separated by this interval sounded together. ~*n., a.* **1** (the) last of four (people, things etc.). **2** (the) next after the third. **fourth dimension** *n.* the extra coordinate (time) needed to locate a point in space. **fourth-dimensional** *a.* **fourth estate** *n.* the newspaper press; journalism or journalists collectively. **fourthly** *adv.* in the fourth place. **fourth-rate** *n.* (*Hist.*) **1** a 50- to 70-gun vessel. **2** a gunboat carrying from one to four guns. ~*a.* **1** fourth best, as a grade of quality in various commodities. **2** (*coll.*) mediocre, poor, inferior.

☒ **fourty** common misspelling of FORTY.

fovea (fō´viə) *n.* (*pl.* **foveae** (-viē)) **1** (*Anat.*) a small pit or depression. **2** a small depression in the back of the retina of the eye, for sharpest vision. **foveal** *a.* **foveate** (-āt) *a.* [L]

foveola (fōvē´ələ) *n.* (*pl.* **foveolae** (-lē)) (*Anat.*) a small depression. **foveolate** (-əlāt), **foveolated** (-lā´tid) *a.* [L, dim. of FOVEA]

fowl (fowl) *n.* (*pl. in general* **fowl**, *in particular* **fowls**) **1** (*also* **domestic fowl**) a cock or hen of the domestic or poultry kind, kept mainly for its eggs and flesh. **2** any other domesticated bird e.g. the turkey or duck, kept for its eggs and flesh. **3** their flesh used as food. **4** a bird. **5** birds collectively. ~*v.i.* to hunt, catch or kill wild birds for sport. **fowl cholera** *n.* CHICKEN CHOLERA (under CHICKEN). **fowler** *n.* a person who pursues wildfowl for sport. **fowling** *n.* **fowling-piece** *n.* a light smooth-bore gun adapted for shooting wildfowl. **fowl pest** *n.* a contagious virus disease of fowls. **fowl run** *n.* **1** an enclosure in which domestic fowls can run about. **2** a breeding establishment for fowls. [OE *fugol* (cp. Dut. *vogel*, G *Vogel*, Icel. and Dan. *fugl*), from Gmc. *flug-*, to FLY[1]]

fox (foks) *n.* **1** any of various doglike mammals of the genus *Vulpes* or a related genus with a pointed snout, erect ears and a straight bushy tail, esp. the reddish brown *V. vulpes*. **2** the fur of a fox. **3** a sly, cunning person. **4** (*chiefly N Am., sl.*) a physically attractive woman. ~*v.t.* **1** to baffle, to perplex. **2** to trick, to outwit. **3** (*chiefly p.p.*) to discolour (pages of a book etc.). **4** (*N Am.*) to repair (boots) by adding an outer covering over the upper. **5** †to intoxicate. ~*v.i.* **1** to be crafty. **2** (of paper etc.) to become discoloured, esp. to turn reddish. **foxed** *a.* **1** stained with spots, as a book or print. **2** (*sl.*) drunk. **foxglove** *n.* any tall plant of the genus *Digitalis*, esp. *D. purpurea*, with purple flowers resembling the fingers of a glove, the leaves of which are used as a sedative. **foxhole** *n.* **1** (*Mil.*) a small trench. **2** a place of refuge or hiding. **foxhound** *n.* a hound bred and trained to hunt foxes. **fox-hunt** *n.* **1** the hunting of a fox with hounds. **2** a group of people involved with this. ~*v.i.* to hunt foxes with hounds. **fox-hunter** *n.* a person who hunts foxes. **fox-hunting** *a.* of, relating to, or fond of hunting foxes. ~*n.* the act or practice of hunting foxes with a pack of hounds. **foxing** *n.* **foxlike** *a.* **foxshark** *n.* the thresher, *Alopias vulpinus*, a shark about 15 ft. (4.5 m) long, with a long rough tail. **foxtail** *n.* **1** the tail of a fox. **2** any of several grasses of the genus *Alopecurus*, with soft cylindrical spikes of flowers, esp. *Alopecurus pratensis*. **fox terrier** *n.* a short-haired breed of dog, orig. employed to unearth foxes, now chiefly as a pet. **fox-trap** *n.* a snare to catch foxes. **foxtrot** *n.* **1** a ballroom dance with a combination of slow and quick steps. **2** the music for this dance. **3** short steps taken by a horse when changing its pace. ~*v.i.* (*pres.p.* **foxtrotting**, *past, p.p.* **foxtrotted**) to perform this dance. **foxy** *a.* (*comp.* **foxier**, *superl.* **foxiest**) **1** foxlike, tricky, crafty. **2** foxed. **3** (*chiefly N Am.*) physically attractive. **4** reddish-brown in colour. **5** (of a painting) having too much of this colour. **foxily** *adv.* **foxiness** *n.* [OE (cp. Dut. *vos*, G *Fuchs*)]

foyer (fo´yā, -yə) *n.* the entrance hall or other large public area where people meet or wait in a hotel, theatre etc. [F, from low L *focārum*, from *focus*, see FOCUS]

fp *abbr.* **1** fortepiano. **2** (*also* **FP**) freezing point.

FPA *abbr.* Family Planning Association.

FPS *abbr.* Fellow of the Pharmaceutical Society.

fps, f.p.s. *abbr.* **1** feet per second. **2** foot-pound-second. **3** frames per second.

Fr *chem. symbol* francium.

Fr. *abbr.* **1** Father. **2** France. **3** French. **4** Friar.

fr. *abbr.* **1** franc(s). **2** from.

Fra (frah) *n.* brother, a title given to an Italian monk or friar. [It., short for *frate*, from L *frater*, brother]

frabjous (frab´jəs) *a.* joyous. **frabjously** *adv.* [devised by Lewis Carroll, supposedly *fair* and *joyous*]

fracas (frak´ah) *n.* (*pl.* **fracas** (-ahz)) a disturbance, a row, an uproar, a noisy quarrel. [F, from *fracasser*, It. *fracassare*, to break in pieces]

fractal (frak´təl) *n.* a computer-generated figure produced from a simpler figure by applying a fixed set of rules, and itself giving rise to more complex figures by repeated application of the same rules and so on. ~*a.* of or relating to a fractal. **fractality** (-tal´-) *n.* **fracted** *a.* broken. **fractile** (-tīl) *a.* **1** liable to break. **2** (*Geol.*) indicating breakage or cleavage. [L *fractus*, see FRACTION]

fraction (frak´shən) *n.* **1** a number that is not a whole number, e.g. ¼, 0.7. **2** a very small amount or portion.

3 a component of a mixture separated by a fractional process such as fractional distillation. 4 an organized dissenting political group. 5 †dissension, a rupture. 6 the rite of breaking the bread in the Eucharist. **fractional, fractionary** *a.* 1 of or relating to fractions. 2 constituting a fraction. 3 forming but a small part, insignificant. **fractional distillation** *n.* the separation of liquids having different boiling points. **fractionalize, fractionalise** *v.t.* **fractionally** *adv.* **fractionate** (-nāt) *v.t.* to separate (a mixture) into portions having different properties, by distillation or analogous process. **fractionation** (-ā´shən) *n.* **fractionize, fractionise** *v.t.* to break up into fractions or divisions. [OF *fraccion*, from eccles. L *fractio -ōnem*, from *fractus*, p.p. of *frangere*, to break]

fractious (frak´shəs) *a.* 1 apt to quarrel. 2 snappish, cross, fretful, peevish. 3 unruly. **fractiously** *adv.* **fractiousness** *n.* [from FRACTION, in the sense of dissension]

Usage note See note under FACTION[1].

fracture (frak´chə) *n.* 1 the act of breaking by violence. 2 a break, a breakage. 3 the result of breaking. 4 the breakage of a bone or cartilage. 5 (*Mineral.*) the irregularity of surface produced by breaking a mineral across, as distinguished from splitting it along the planes of cleavage. 6 in linguistics, the substitution of a diphthong for an originally simple vowel, esp. under the influence of a following consonant. 7 a diphthong substituted in this way. ~*v.t.* 1 to break across. 2 to separate the continuity of the parts of. ~*v.i.* to break or crack. [OF, from L *fractūra*, as FRACTION]

fraenum (frē´nəm), **frenum** *n.* (*pl.* **fraena** (-nə), **frena**) a band or ligament restraining the action of an organ, as that of the tongue. **fraenulum** (-nūləm), **frenulum** *n.* (*pl.* **fraenula, frenula** (-lə)) a small fraenum. [L, a bridle]

fragile (fraj´īl) *a.* 1 brittle, easily broken. 2 weak, frail, delicate. **fragilely** *adv.* **fragility** (-jil´-) *n.* [F, from L *fragilis*, from *frag-*, root of *frangere*, to break]

fragment[1] (frag´mənt) *n.* 1 a piece broken off. 2 a small detached portion. 3 an incomplete or unfinished portion. 4 the surviving portion of a whole work of art etc. that has been destroyed. **fragmental** (-men´-) *a.* 1 of, relating to or consisting of fragments, fragmentary. 2 disconnected. **fragmentally, fragmentarily** *adv.* **fragmentary** *a.* fragmental. **fragmentariness** *n.* **fragmentary rocks** *n.pl.* (*Geol.*) rocks made up of fragments, as breccias, conglomerates etc. **fragmentize, fragmentise** *v.t.* [F, or directly from L *fragmentum*, as FRAGILE]

fragment[2] (fragment´) *v.t.*, *v.i.* (to cause) to break into fragments. **fragmentation** (-tā´shən) *n.* 1 the breaking into fragments. 2 (*Biol.*) the breaking-up of a chromosome. **fragmentation bomb** *n.* a bomb whose casing is designed to shatter in small, deadly fragments on explosion. **fragmented** (-men´-) *a.*

fragrant (frā´grənt) *a.* emitting a pleasant perfume, sweet-smelling, odorous. **fragrance** *n.* 1 a sweet smell. 2 the particular scent of a perfume, toilet water etc. **fragranced** *a.* **fragrancy** *n.* (*pl.* **fragrancies**) a fragrance. **fragrantly** *adv.* [F, from L *frāgrans -ntem*, pres.p. of *frāgrāre*, to emit a perfume]

frail[1] (frāl) *a.* 1 fragile, delicate. 2 infirm, in weak health. 3 weak in character or resolution, liable to be led astray. 4 perishable, insubstantial. 5 (*euphem.*) unchaste. ~*n.* (*N Am., sl.*) a woman. **frailish** *a.* **frailly** *adv.* **frailness** *n.* **frailty** *n.* (*pl.* **frailties**) 1 the condition of being frail. 2 the weakness of fault. 3 a liability to be led astray. [OF *fraile*, L *fragilis*, FRAGILE]

frail[2] (frāl) *n.* 1 a rush basket used for packing figs etc. 2 a certain quantity of figs or raisins, about 75 lb. (34 kg), contained in a frail. [OF *frayel*, *freël*, perh. from earlier *fleël*, L *flagellum*, a whip, a vine-shoot]

fraise (frāz) *n.* 1 a ruff. 2 a horizontal or sloping palisade round a rampart. 3 a tool for enlarging a drill hole etc. [F, a ruff]

Fraktur (frak´tuə) *n.* a style of typeface formerly used for typesetting German. [G]

framboesia (frambē´ziə), (*N Am.*) **frambesia** *n.* (*Med.*) the yaws, a contagious eruption characterized by swellings like raspberries. [F *framboise*, a raspberry]

frame (frām) *n.* 1 a case or border to enclose or surround a picture, a pane of glass etc. 2 a structure that gives strength and shape to something. 3 a fabric or structure composed of parts fitted together. 4 the structure of a human body. 5 the rigid part of a bicycle. 6 the construction, constitution or build of anything. 7 (*pl.*) the structure of a pair of glasses, holding the lenses. 8 the established order or system (of society or the body politic). 9 disposition of mind (*a frame of mind*). 10 any of various machines in the form of framework used in manufacturing, mining, building, printing etc. 11 a structure on which embroidery is worked. 12 a single exposure on a film. 13 a single, complete television picture. 14 a a triangular structure used to set up the balls for a break in snooker etc. b the balls so arranged. c a single round of a game of snooker etc. 15 a glazed portable structure for protecting plants from frost. 16 one of the sections of which a beehive is composed, esp. one for a honeycomb. 17 (*N Am., sl.*) a frame-up. ~*v.t.* 1 to surround with a frame; to serve as a frame to. 2 to form or construct by fitting parts together. 3 to fit, adapt or adjust. 4 to contrive. 5 to devise, to invent. 6 to compose, to express. 7 to plan, to arrange. 8 to form in the mind, to conceive, imagine. 9 to articulate, to form with the lips. 10 (*coll.*) to (conspire to) incriminate. **framable** *a.* **frame aerial** *n.* a radio aerial consisting of wire wound on a frame. **frame house** *n.* a house with a wooden framework covered with boards. **frameless** *a.* **frame of reference** *n.* 1 a set or system of standards, derived from an individual's experience, to which they refer when making judgements etc. 2 a set of axes used to describe the location of a point. **framer** *n.* 1 a person who frames. 2 a maker, a contriver. **frame-saw** *n.* a flexible saw blade stretched in a frame to stiffen it. **frame-up** *n.* (*coll.*) an attempt to incriminate, a false criminal charge. **framework** *n.* 1 the frame of a structure. 2 the fabric for enclosing or supporting anything, or forming the substructure to a more complete fabric. 3 (*fig.*) structure, arrangement (of society etc.). **framing** *n.* 1 a frame, framework. 2 a setting. [OE *framian*, to avail, to further, from *fram*, adv., forward]

franc (frangk) *n.* the standard unit of currency in France, Belgium, Switzerland and various other countries. [F, said to be from *Francorum Rex*, King of the Franks, the inscription on the earliest coins]

franchise (fran´chīz) *n.* 1 the right to vote. 2 the qualification for this. 3 citizenship. 4 a licence to market a company's goods or services in a specified area. 5 a right, privilege, immunity or exemption granted to an individual or to a body. 6 the district or territory to which a certain privilege or licence extends. ~*v.t.* to grant a franchise to. **franchisee** (-zē´) *n.* the holder of a franchise. **franchisement** (-chiz-) *n.* **franchizer, franchiser** *n.* 1 a person having the elective franchise. 2 a person who grants a franchise. [OF, from *franchiss-*, stem of *franchir*, to free oneself, from *franc*, FRANK]

Franciscan (fransis´kən) *a.* of or relating to St Francis of Assisi, or the order of mendicant friars founded by him in 1209. ~*n.* a member of the Franciscan order, a grey friar. [med. L *Franciscus*, Francis, St *Francis* of Assisi, 1182–1226]

francium (fran´siəm) *n.* a radioactive chemical element of the alkali metal group, at. no. 87, chem. symbol Fr. [mod. L, from *France*]

Franco- (frang´kō), **franco-** *comb. form* of or relating to

France or the French, as in *Franco-German, Franco-Russian.* [med. L *Francus,* FRANK]

francolin (frang´kəlin) *n.* a partridge of the genus *Francolinus.* [F, from It. *francolino*]

Francophile (frang´kōfīl) *n.* an admirer of France or the French.

Francophobe (frang´kōfōb) *n.* a disliker or fearer of France or the French.

Francophone (frang´kōfōn) *a.* French-speaking, having French as the native or an official language. ~*n.* a Francophone person.

franc-tireur (frãtērœ´) *n.* (*pl.* **francs-tireurs** (frãteroe´)) a French light-infantry soldier belonging to an irregular corps. [F, free-shooter (*franc,* FRANK, *tirer,* to shoot)]

frangible (fran´jibəl) *a.* that may be easily broken. **frangibility** (-bil´-) *n.* **frangibleness** *n.* [late L *frangibilis,* from *frangere,* to break]

frangipane (fran´jipān) *n.* **1** a kind of pastry made with cream, almonds and sugar; a flan filled with this. **2** frangipani. [as FRANGIPANI]

frangipani (franjipah´ni) *n.* (*pl.* **frangipanis**) **1** a shrub or tree of the tropical American genus *Plumeria* with clusters of fragrant white or pink flowers. **2** the perfume prepared from this plant. [prob. from the inventor of the perfume, the Marquis *Frangipani,* 16th-cent. Italian nobleman]

franglais (frã´glā) *n.* an informal version of French which contains a high proportion of English words. [F *français,* French and *anglais,* English]

Frank (frangk) *n.* **1** a member of the ancient Germanic peoples or tribes who conquered France in the 6th cent. **2** a name given by inhabitants of the eastern Mediterranean region to a W European. **Frankish** *a., n.* [L *Francus,* OHG *Franko,* prob. from the name of a weapon (cp. OE *franca,* a javelin)]

frank (frangk) *a.* **1** open, ingenuous, sincere, candid. **2** generous, liberal, profuse, free, unrestrained. **3** (*Med.*) unmistakable. ~*v.t.* **1** to mark (a letter etc.) in such a way as to indicate that postage has been paid. **2** (*Hist.*) to send or cause to be sent under an official privilege, such as, formerly, the signature of a member of Parliament, so as to pass free. **3** †to secure the free passage of (a person or thing). ~*n.* **1** a signature authorizing a letter to go through the post free of charge. **2** the right to send letters etc. in this manner. **3** the letter or package sent in this way. **frankable** *a.* **franker** *n.* **franking machine** *n.* a machine that franks letters etc. **frankly** *adv.* **1** in a frank manner. **2** to be frank. **frankness** *n.* [OF *franc,* low L *francus,* free, from FRANK]

frankalmoign (frang´kəlmoin) *n.* (*Law*) a tenure by which a religious body holds lands with no obligations except such as prayers, almsgiving etc. [OF *franc,* FRANK, A-F *almoine,* OF *almosne* (F *aumône*), alms]

Frankenstein (frang´kənstīn), **Frankenstein's monster** *n.* **1** a work that brings disaster to its creator. **2** a destructive monster in human form. [character in the novel *Frankenstein* by Mary Shelley]

frankfurter (frangk´fœtə) *n.* a small, smoked sausage of beef and pork. [short for G *Frankfurter Wurst,* a sausage made in Frankfurt am Main]

frankincense (frang´kinsens) *n.* a gum or resin burning with a fragrant smell, used as incense, obtained from trees of the genus *Boswellia.* [OF *franc encens*]

franklin (frang´klin) *n.* in the 14th and 15th cents., an English freeholder, not liable to feudal service. [A-F *fraunclein,* low L *francus,* free, -LING[1]]

frantic (fran´tik) *a.* **1** mad, distracted; wildly excited or desperately worried. **2** marked by extreme haste, agitation or desperation. **3** (*coll.*) intense, very great. **frantically, franticly** *adv.* **franticness** *n.* [OF *frenetique,* late L *phrenēticus,* Gr. *phrenitikos,* from *phrenitis,* inflammation of the brain, from *phrēn,* brain]

frap (frap) *v.t.* (*pres.p.* **frapping,** *past, p.p.* **frapped**) (*Naut.*) to draw together by ropes crossing each other, to secure and strengthen, to bind the end of a rope with string. [OF *fraper,* to strike]

frappé (frap´ā) *a.* iced. ~*n.* **1** an iced drink. **2** a soft water ice. [F, p.p. of *frapper,* to strike, to ice]

frascati (fraskah´ti) *n.* (*pl.* **frascatis**) an esp. white wine from the Frascati region of Italy.

frass (fras) *n.* **1** excrement of larvae. **2** refuse left by a wood-boring insect. [G *Frasz,* cogn. with *fressen,* to devour]

fratch (frach) *v.i.* (*chiefly North.*) **1** to quarrel. **2** to worry. ~*n.* a quarrel. **fratchety, fratching** *a.* fratchy. **fratchy** *a.* (*comp.* **fratchier,** *superl.* **fratchiest**) **1** quarrelsome. **2** irritable. [prob. onomat.]

†**frater** (frā´tə) *n.* a refectory in a monastery. [OF *fraitur,* short for *refreitor,* from low L *refectorium*]

fraternal (frətœ´nəl) *a.* **1** brotherly. **2** of, relating to or suitable for brothers. **3** existing between brothers. **4** (of twins) from two separate ova. **5** (*N Am.*) of or relating to a fraternity. **fraternally** *adv.* **fraternity** *n.* (*pl.* **fraternities**) **1** a brotherhood, a group of men associated for a common interest or for religious purposes. **2** a group of men associated or linked together by similarity of rank, profession, interests etc. **3** (*N Am.*) a college association of male students. **4** the state of being a brother; brotherliness. **fraternize** (frat´-), **fraternise** *v.i.* **1** to associate or hold fellowship with others of like occupation or tastes. **2** to associate (with members of a hostile group) on friendly terms. **fraternization** (-zā´shən) *n.* **fraternizer** *n.* [OF *fraternel,* late L *frāternālis,* L *frāternus,* from *frāter,* brother]

fratricide (frat´risīd) *n.* **1** the murder of a brother or sister. **2** a person who murders their brother or sister. **fratricidal** (-sīd´-) *a.* [OF, from L *frātricīda* (*frāter,* brother, -CIDE)]

Frau (frow) *n.* (*pl.* **Frauen** (frow´ən)) a German woman, wife or widow; Mrs. **Fräulein** (froi´līn, fraw´-, frow´-) *n.* (*pl.* **Fräulein**) a young lady, a German spinster; Miss. [G]

fraud (frawd) *n.* **1** an act or course of deception deliberately practised to gain unlawful or unfair advantage. **2** (*Law*) such deception directed to the detriment of another. **3** a deception, a trick, trickery. **4** (*coll.*) a deceitful person or thing. **fraudful** *a.* **fraudster** *n.* a person who commits fraud. **fraudulence** *n.* **fraudulent** (-ūlənt) *a.* **1** practising fraud. **2** characterized by or containing fraud. **3** intended to defraud, deceitful. **fraudulently** *adv.* [OF *fraude,* L *fraudem,* nom. *fraus*]

fraught (frawt) *a.* **1** involving, entailing, attended by, filled (with). **2** tense, characterized by or inducing anxiety or stress. **3** freighted, laden, stored (with). ~†*n.* **1** a cargo, a burden. **2** (*Sc.*) a load, two pails (of water). [p.p. of obs. v. *fraught,* to load, from obs. n. *fraught,* cargo, from LG (see EFris. *fracht,* G *Fracht,* MDut. and MLG *vracht*), cp. FREIGHT]

Fraülein FRAU.

Fraunhofer lines (frown´hōfə) *n.pl.* the dark lines in spectra of the sun or stars. [Joseph von *Fraunhofer,* 1787–1826, German physicist]

fraxinella (fraksinel´ə) *n.* a kind of rue or dittany, esp. *Dictamnus albus,* cultivated for its leaves and flowers which give off an inflammable vapour. [dim. of L *fraxinus,* ash]

fray[1] (frā) *v.t.* **1** to wear away by rubbing. **2** to fret, to chafe. **3** to make strained or irritated. **4** †to rub. ~*v.i.* (of a garment, cloth etc.) to become rubbed or worn, esp. so as to become unravelled or ragged at the edges. [OF *freier,* L *fricāre,* to rub]

fray[2] (frā) *n.* **1** an affray; fighting. **2** a noisy quarrel, a brawl, a riot. **3** a combat, a contest. **4** †anxiety, fear. ~†*v.t.* to frighten. ~†*v.i.* to fight. [from AFFRAY]

frazil (frā´zil, frəzil´) *n.* (*N Am.*) ice crystals formed in turbulent water. [Can. F, perh. from F *fraisil,* cinders]

frazzle (fraz´əl) *v.t.* 1 to reduce to a state of physical or nervous exhaustion. 2 to burn thoroughly, to char. 3 to fray at the edge, to unravel. ~*v.i.* to be worn out, nervous. ~*n.* an exhausted or charred state (*worn/burnt to a frazzle*). [from E dial. *fazle*, to fray]

freak (frēk) *n.* 1 an abnormal or deformed person or thing (*a freak of nature*). 2 (*coll.*) an unconventional or eccentric person. 3 (*coll.*) an unrestrained enthusiast for a certain thing (*a computer freak*). 4 a highly unusual or abnormal occurrence. 5 (*coll.*) a person who has hallucinations from the use of or addiction to drugs. 6 a sudden wanton whim or caprice; a humour, a vagary. ~*a.* highly unusual, abnormal, esp. in magnitude or intensity. ~*v.t.* 1 (*coll.*) to freak out. 2 (*usu. p.p.*) to variegate, to streak. ~*v.i.* (*coll.*) to freak out. **to freak out** 1 (*coll.*) (to cause) to hallucinate. 2 (*coll.*) (to cause) to be in a highly emotional, excited or angry state. 3 to assume a strikingly unconventional lifestyle. **freakful** *a.* **freakish** *a.* 1 eccentric, unconventional. 2 abnormal. 3 whimsical. **freakishly** *adv.* **freakishness** *n.* **freak-out** *n.* (*coll.*) 1 an act or instance of freaking out. 2 a highly emotional or hallucinatory experience. **freak show** *n.* a sideshow at a fair where people with physical abnormalities can be seen. **freaky** *a.* (*comp.* **freakier,** *superl.* **freakiest**) (*coll.*) freakish. **freakily** *adv.* **freakiness** *n.* [etym. uncertain (perh. conn. with OE *frec*, bold, rash, or *frīcian*, to dance)]

freckle (frek´əl) *n.* 1 (*usu. pl.*) a yellowish or light-brown spot on the skin, caused by sunburn or other causes. 2 any small spot or discoloration. ~*v.t.* (*usu. p.p.*) to mark with freckles. ~*v.i.* to become marked with freckles. **freckle-faced** *a.* with a freckled face. **freckling** *n.* 1 marking with freckles. 2 a mark like a freckle. **freckly** *a.* [earlier *frecken*, cp. Icel. *freknur*, pl.]

free[1] (frē) *a.* (*comp.* **freer** (frēə), *superl.* **freest** (frē´ist)) 1 at liberty; not in bondage or under restraint. 2 living under a government based on the consent of the citizens. 3 (of a government) not arbitrary or despotic. 4 (of a state) not under foreign domination. 5 released from authority or control. 6 not confined, restricted, checked or impeded. 7 at liberty to choose or act, permitted (to do). 8 independent, unattached, unconnected with the State. 9 available without payment or charge, costing nothing. 10 not subject to (charges, duties, fees etc.). 11 without restriction, open, gratuitous. 12 liberal, generous. 13 released, clear, exempt (from). 14 unconstrained, not bound or limited (by rules, conventions etc.). 15 not containing a certain thing. 16 spontaneous, unforced. 17 unoccupied, vacant. 18 clear, unobstructed. 19 not busy, having no obligations or commitments. 20 not fixed or joined. 21 (of a translation) not literal. 22 unconventional, unceremonious, careless, reckless. 23 forward, impudent. 24 indelicate, broad. 25 unreserved, frank, ingenuous. 26 admitted to or invested with certain privileges (of). 27 (*Physics*) **a** not charged by an external force. **b** not bound in an atom or molecule. 28 (of energy) available. 29 (*Zool.*) unattached. 30 (*Chem.*) not combined with another body. 31 (*Bot.*) not adhering, not adnate. ~*adv.* 1 freely. 2 without cost or charge. 3 (*Naut.*) not close-hauled. **for free** (*coll.*) gratis, for nothing. **free alongside ship** delivered free on the dock or wharf. **free of charge** CHARGE. **free on board** (of goods) delivered on board or into conveyance free of charge. **free on rail** (of goods) delivered free to a railway wagon. **to make free** MAKE[1]. **-free** *comb. form* free from, not containing. **free agency** *n.* the state of acting freely or without constraint upon the will. **free agent** *n.* a person who is free to act according to their own opinions and wishes. **free alms** *n.pl.* FRANKALMOIGN. **free and easy** *a.* 1 unconstrained, unceremonious, informal. 2 careless. ~*n.* (*pl.* **free and easies**) an unceremonious kind of social gathering or other entertainment. **free arts** LIBERAL ARTS (under LIBERAL). **free association** *n.* (*Psych.*) the bringing to consciousness of unconscious processes through words and ideas which the subject spontaneously associates with keywords provided by a psychoanalyst. **freebase** *v.t.*, *v.i.* (*sl.*) 1 to purify (cocaine). 2 to smoke (cocaine) so purified. ~*n.* purified cocaine produced by freebasing. **freeboard** *n.* the space between the water-line on a vessel and the upper side of the deck, or the uppermost full deck. **free-born** *a.* 1 born free. 2 inheriting the right and liberty of a citizen. **Free Church** *n.* a Protestant Church dissenting or seceding from an established Church, a Nonconformist Church. **Free Churchism** *n.* **free city, free town** *n.* a city or town independent in its government and franchise, and virtually forming an independent state. **free collective bargaining** *n.* negotiations between trade unions and employers unhampered by government guidelines or legal restraints. **free enterprise** *n.* an economic system in which commercial companies compete for profit, largely without state interference or control. **free fall** *n.* 1 the motion of an unrestrained or unpropelled body in a gravitational field. 2 the part of a parachute jump before the parachute opens. 3 the movement of a spacecraft in space, without power from the engines. 4 a state of fast, esp. uncontrollable, falling (*prices going into free fall*). **free-fall** *v.i.* (*past* **free-fell,** *p.p.* **free-fallen**) to move into a free fall. **free fight** *n.* a fight in which anyone can join. **free flight** *n.* the flight of a rocket etc. when its motor has ceased to produce thrust. **free-floating** *a.* unattached, having no specific object, uncommitted. **Freefone, Freephone, freefone, freephone** *n.* a telephone service in which callers can telephone a company free of charge, with the company paying the cost of the calls. **free-for-all** *n.* a free fight, a disorganized brawl or argument. **free-form** *a.* having an irregular shape or structure. **free hand** *n.* complete freedom to act as one wishes. **free-hand** *a.* (of a drawing etc.) executed by the hand without the aid of instruments. ~*adv.* in a freehand manner. **free-handed** *a.* generous, liberal. **free-handedly** *adv.* **free-handedness** *n.* **free-hearted** *a.* 1 frank, open, unreserved. 2 liberal. **free-heartedly** *adv.* **free-heartedness** *n.* **free house** *n.* a public house that is free to buy beer or liquor from any supplier. **free kick** *n.* in football, a kick with which an opponent may not interfere, awarded for a foul or infringement by the other side. **free labour,** (*N Am.*) **free labor** *n.* workers not belonging to trade unions. **free-labourer** *n.* **freelance** *n.* 1 (*also* **freelancer**) a self-employed person hired by others for specific (usu. short-term) assignments. 2 (*Hist.*) (*usu.* **free lance**) a member of one of the free companies of mercenaries in the Middle Ages. ~*a.*, *adv.* not bound to a particular employer. ~*v.i.* to work freelance. **free library** *n.* a public library. **free-liver** *n.* 1 a person who indulges their appetites, esp. at table. 2 (*Biol.*) an organism which is neither parasitic nor symbiotic. **free-living** *n.*, *a.* **freeload** *v.i.* (*coll.*) to sponge, to live at another's expense. **freeloader** *n.* **free love** *n.* sexual intercourse without marriage or without formal or legal commitments. **free lover** *n.* a person who advocates or practises free love. **freely** *adv.* **free market** *n.* an economic market in which prices are regulated by supply and demand. **free-minded** *a.* having the mind free from care, trouble or perplexity. **freeness** *n.* **free pardon** *n.* a complete or partial remission of the legal consequences of crime. **free pass** *n.* an official authorization, entitling the holder to travel or to enter an exhibition, theatre etc. without having to pay. **free port** *n.* 1 a port or section of a port where goods are received and shipped free of duty. 2 a port where ships of all nations may load or unload free of duty. **Freepost** *n.* a postal service in which letters etc. can be sent to a company free of charge, with the company paying the postage. **free radical** *n.* an atom, or group of atoms, containing at least one unpaired electron. **free-range** *a.* kept or produced in natural conditions. **free school** *n.* **1** (*Hist.*) a school where no fees are charged. **2** a school that does not impose restrictions on the pupils. **free selection** *n.* (*Hist.*) in Australia, the legal right to select Crown lands. **free sheet** *n.* a newspaper distributed free. **free skating** *n.* that part of a figure-skating competition in which the competitors have partial or complete freedom to organize their programmes. **free speech** *n.* the right to express one's opinions publicly. **free spirit** *n.* an independent or unconventional person. **free-spoken** *a.* **1** speaking without reserve. **2** blunt, candid, frank. **free-spokenness** *n.* **free-standing** *a.* not attached to, supported by or integrated with other objects. **Free States** *n.pl.* those States of the American Union in which slavery never existed, or was abolished before the Civil War. **freestone** *n.* **1** a stone which can be cut freely in any direction. **2** a kind of peach or other fruit easily freed from its stone when ripe. **freestyle** *n.* **1** a race, in swimming, skiing etc. in which each competitor can choose which style to use. **2** all-in wrestling. *~a.* of or relating to such a race or style of wrestling. **freestyler** *n.* **free-thinker** *n.* **1** a rationalist, sceptic or agnostic. **2** a person who rejects authority in religious belief. **free-thinking** *a., n.* **free-thought** *n.* **free throw** *n.* **1** an unimpeded throw awarded because of a foul by an opponent. **2** in basketball, an unimpeded shot at the basket from a marked line. **free-tongued** *a.* free-spoken. **free town** FREE CITY (under FREE[1]). **free trade** *n.* international trade, free interchange of commodities without protection by customs duties. **free-trader** *n.* **1** a person who advocates free trade. **2** †a smuggler. **free verse** *n.* unrhymed verse with no set metrical pattern. **free vote** *n.* a parliamentary vote left to the individual's choice, free from party discipline. **freeway** *n.* (*N Am.*) **1** a motorway. **2** a toll-free highway. **free wheel** *n.* **1** a driving wheel on a bicycle that can be disconnected from the driving gear and allowed to revolve while the pedals are at rest. **2** a bicycle with such a wheel. **freewheel** *v.i.* **1** to run down a hill (on a bicycle or in a motor car) without using engine power or brakes. **2** to move or live in an unconstrained or irresponsible fashion. **freewheeling** *n., a.* **free will** *n.* **1** the power of directing one's own actions without constraint by any external influence. **2** voluntariness, spontaneity. **free-will** *a.* given freely, voluntary. **Free World** *n.* (*esp. Hist.*) the non-Communist countries collectively. [OE *frēo* (cp. Dut. *vrij*, G *frei*, cogn. with Sansk. *priya*, beloved)]

free[2] (frē) *v.t.* (*3rd pers. sing. pres.* **frees,** *pres.p.* **freeing,** *past, p.p.* **freed**) **1** to set at liberty, to emancipate. **2** to rid or relieve (of or from). **3** to extricate, to clear, to disentangle. **to free up 1** (*coll.*) to make available. **2** (*coll.*) to cause to operate with fewer restrictions. **freedman** *n.* (*pl.* **freedmen**) an emancipated slave. [from FREE[1]]

freebie (frē´bi) *n.* (*coll.*) something given for which a person does not have to pay. [from *freeby*, obs. sl., gratis]

freebooter (frē´bootə) *n.* a pirate or buccaneer, an adventurer who makes a business of plundering. **freeboot** *v.i.* **freebootery** *n.* **freebooting** *a.* [Dut. *vrijbuiter*, from *vrijbuit* (FREE[1], BOOTY)]

freedom (frē´dəm) *n.* **1** the state of being free, liberty, independence. **2** personal liberty, non-slavery, civil liberty. **3** liberty of action, free will. **4** exemption, immunity (from). **5** lack of conventionality, frankness, excessive familiarity. **6** violation of the rules of good breeding, a liberty. **7** ease or facility in doing anything. **8** participation in certain privileges, exemptions, and immunities of or relating to citizenship of a city or membership of a company. **9** free use (of). **10** boldness in form. **freedom fighter** *n.* a person who fights (esp. as an irregular soldier) for the liberation of a nation etc. from foreign rule or a tyrannical regime. †**freedomless** *a.* **freedom of conscience** *n.* the right of individuals to decide on moral, religious etc. matters for themselves. **freedom of religion** *n.* the right of individuals to choose to follow whichever religion they want. **freedom of the press** *n.* the right to print and publish statements, opinions etc., without censorship. [OE *frēodōm* (as FREE[1], -DOM)]

freehold (frē´hōld) *n.* **1** an estate held in fee simple, fee tail or for life. **2** the tenure by which such an estate is held. **3** an office held for life. *~a.* of, being or related to the nature of a freehold. **freeholder** *n.* the possessor of a freehold.

freeman (frē´mən) *n.* (*pl.* **freemen**) **1** a person who is not a slave or serf. **2** a person who holds the franchise of a citizen or a particular privilege, esp. the freedom of a city, company etc. **freewoman** *n.* (*pl.* **freewomen**) a female freeman.

freemartin (frē´mahtin) *n.* a sexually imperfect cow, usu. born as twin with a bull calf. [etym. unknown]

Freemason (frē´māsən) *n.* a member of an association of 'Free and Accepted Masons', a secret order or fraternity (probably originating as a fraternity of skilled masons, with right of free movement, about the 14th cent.). **Freemasonry** *n.* **1** the system, rites and principles of Freemasons. **2** (*usu.* **freemasonry**) a secret understanding, community of interests, or instinctive sympathy among a number of people.

freesia (frē´ziə, -zhə) *n.* any of a S African genus of bulbous flowering plants allied to the iris. [mod. L, from Freidrich Heinrich Theodor *Freese*, d. 1876, German physician]

freeze (frēz) *v.i.* (*pres.p.* **freezing,** *past* **froze** (frōz), *p.p.* **frozen** (frō´zən)) **1** to be turned from a fluid to a solid state by cold. **2** (*impers.*) to be at that degree of cold at which water turns to ice or becomes covered with ice. **3** to become covered or clogged by ice. **4** to become attached (to) or fastened (together) by frost. **5** to feel very cold. **6** to die of cold. **7** to be chilled (by fear). **8** to become motionless or paralysed. **9** to respond with sudden detachment. *~v.t.* **1** to congeal by cold. **2** to form ice upon or convert into ice. **3** to injure, overpower or kill with cold. **4** to preserve (food) by freezing and storing at a temperature below freezing point. **5** to chill with fear. **6** to anaesthetize (as if) by cold. **7** to render motionless or paralysed. **8** to cause to respond with sudden detachment. **9** to stop at a particular stage or state. **10** to stop (a moving film) at a particular frame. **11** in finance, to prohibit the use of or dealings in. **12** to fix or stabilize (prices etc.). *~n.* **1** the act or state of freezing. **2** a frost. **to freeze on to** (*sl.*) to seize or hold tightly. **to freeze out** (*coll.*) to compel the retirement of from business, competition, society etc., by boycotting, contemptuous treatment or similar methods. **to freeze up** to (cause to) be obstructed by the formation of ice. **freezable** *a.* **freeze-dry** *v.t.* (*3rd pers. sing. pres.* **freeze-dries,** *pres.p.* **freeze-drying,** *past, p.p.* **freeze-dried**) to dehydrate while in a frozen state in a vacuum, esp. for preservation. **freeze-frame** *n.* **1** a single frame of a film repeated to give the effect of a still photograph. **2** a single frame of a video recording viewed as a still. **3** the facility to produce a freeze-frame. *~v.t.* to use freeze-frame on. **freezer** *n.* an apparatus for freezing food etc., a room or cabinet, or a compartment in a refrigerator for the long-term storage of perishable foodstuffs. **freezing** *a.* **1** (*also* **freezing cold**) very cold. **2** distant, chilling. **freezingly** *adv.* **freezing-mixture** *n.* a mixture of salt and snow, or pounded ice, or a combination of chemicals with or without ice, for producing intense cold. **freezing point** *n.* **1** the point at which water freezes, marked 32° on the Fahrenheit scale, and 0° on the Celsius and Réaumur scales. **2** the temperature at which a substance freezes. **freezing works** *n.pl.* (*Austral., New Zeal.*) a slaughterhouse at which animal carcasses are frozen for export. [OE *frēosan* (cp. Dut. *vriezen*, G *frieren*, also L *pruīna*, hoar frost)]

freight (frāt) *n.* **1** the transportation of goods by road, railway, sea or air. **2** goods transported, a cargo. **3** the money due or paid for the transportation of goods, esp. for water. **4** ordinary transportation, as distinct from express. **5** the hire of a ship, aircraft etc. for transporting goods. **6** a burden or load. *~v.t.* **1** to transport (goods) as freight. **2** to load with goods for transportation. **3** to hire or charter for this purpose. **4** to load, to fill. **freightage** *n.* **1** the transporting of goods. **2** money paid for the hire of a ship or the transportation of goods. **3** freight. **freight car** *n.* (*N Am.*) a railway wagon for goods. **freighter** *n.* **1** a ship or aircraft designed for transporting goods. **2** a person who hires or loads a ship. **3** a person who contracts to receive and forward goods. **4** (*Hist.*) in the US, a person who transported goods in a wagon across the plains. **freightless** *a.* **Freightliner®** *n.* a train designed for the rapid transportation of containerized cargo. **freight note** *n.* a statement supplied to ship owners by dock authorities giving weights, measurements etc. of cargo. **freight ton** *n.* a unit of weight or volume of cargo equivalent to a metric ton (2, 205 lb., 1000 kg) or 40 cu. ft. **freight train** *n.* (*N Am.*) a goods train. [cp. MDut. *vrecht*, *vracht*, OF *fret*, OHG *frēht*, see also FRAUGHT]

☒ **freind** common misspelling of FRIEND.

fremitus (frem´itəs) *n.* (*Med.*) a movement or vibration perceptible externally, as on the walls of the chest when a patient speaks. [L, a roaring, from *fremere*, to roar]

frena FRAENUM.

French (french) *a.* **1** of or relating to France, its inhabitants or language. **2** belonging to or native to France. *~n.* **1** the language spoken by the people of France, also an official language in Belgium, Switzerland, Canada and other countries. **2** (*as pl.*) the people of France. **3** (*coll.*) dry vermouth. **excuse/ pardon my French** excuse my bad language. **French bean** *n.* **1** the kidney or haricot bean, *Phaseolus vulgaris.* **2** the pod or seed of this used as food. **French bread** *n.* crusty white bread in a thin, long loaf. **French Canadian** *n.* a Canadian whose main language is French. **French-Canadian** *a.* of or relating to the French-speaking part of Canada or its people. **French chalk** *n.* a variety of talc, steatite or soapstone used for marking cloth, and in powder as a dry lubricant for tight boots etc. **French cricket** *n.* a children's version of cricket in which the legs of the person who is batting serve as the wicket. **French cuff** *n.* a wide band of material turned back to make a cuff of double thickness. **French curve** *n.* an instrument designed to assist in drawing curved lines. **French door** *n.* FRENCH WINDOW (under FRENCH). **French dressing** *n.* **1** a salad dressing made of oil and vinegar or lemon juice with seasoning. **2** a creamy, often sweet, salad dressing. **French fries, French fried potatoes** *n.pl.* (potato) chips. **French horn** *n.* a metal wind instrument of circular shape with a gradual taper from the mouthpiece to a large flaring bell. **Frenchify** *v.t.* (*3rd pers. sing. pres.* **Frenchifies,** *pres.p.* **Frenchifying,** *past, p.p.* **Frenchified**) **1** to make French. **2** to influence with French tastes or manners. **Frenchification** (-fikā´shən) *n.* **French kiss** *n.* a kiss in which one partner's tongue is inserted into the other partner's mouth. **French knickers** *n.pl.* wide-legged knickers. **French leave** *n.* absence without permission. **French letter** *n.* (*coll.*) a contraceptive sheath, a condom. **Frenchlike** *a.* **French loaf** *n.* (*pl.* **French loaves**) a loaf of French bread. **Frenchman** *n.* (*pl.* **Frenchmen**) a male native or inhabitant of France. **French mustard** *n.* a type of mustard mixed with vinegar etc. **Frenchness** *n.* **French pink** *n.* a yellow pigment. **French polish** *n.* **1** a solution of resin or gum resin in alcohol or wood naphtha, for polishing wood. **2** the polish produced. *~v.t.* to polish with this. **French polisher** *n.* **French roll** *n.* a light kind of fancy bread. **French roof** *n.* (*pl.* **French roofs**) a mansard roof or one having portions of two different pitches. **French seam** *n.* a double seam, stitched first on the wrong, then on the right side, so that the edges are invisible. **French toast** *n.* **1** bread toasted one side only. **2** bread dipped in beaten egg and lightly fried. **French vermouth** *n.* dry vermouth. **French window** *n.* (*usu. pl.*) a pair of doors with full-length glazing, opening onto a garden, balcony etc. **Frenchwoman** *n.* (*pl.* **Frenchwomen**) a female native or inhabitant of France. [OE *Frencisc* (FRANK, -ISH[1])]

frenetic (frənet´ik), †**phrenetic** *a.* **1** frantic, frenzied. **2** fanatic. **frenetically** *adv.* [ME and OF *frenetike*, L *freneticus*, Gr. *phrenitikos*, see FRANTIC]

frenulum, frenula FRAENULUM (under FRAENUM).

frenum FRAENUM.

frenzy (fren´zi) *n.* (*pl.* **frenzies**) **1** a violent bout of wild or unnatural excitement, agitation or fury. **2** delirium, madness. **3** temporary mental derangement. **4** extravagant folly. *~v.t.* (*3rd pers. sing. pres.* **frenzies,** *pres.p.* **frenzying,** *past, p.p.* **frenzied**) **1** (*usu. p.p.*) to drive to madness. **2** to infuriate. **frenzical** *a.* **frenzied** *a.* **frenziedly** *adv.* [OF *frenesie*, late L and late Gr. *phrenēsis*, Gr. *phrenitis*, inflammation of the brain (cp. FRANTIC)]

Freon® (frē´on) *n.* any of various gaseous and liquid fluorine-containing chemicals used in aerosols, refrigerants etc.

freq. *abbr.* **1** frequent. **2** frequently. **3** frequentative.

frequency (frē´kwənsi), **frequence** (-ns) *n.* (*pl.* **frequencies, frequences**) **1** the quality of occurring frequently. **2** common occurrence. **3** repetition at short intervals. **4** rate of occurrence. **5** the comparative number of occurrences in a given time. **6** in statistics, the number or proportion of individuals or things in a single class. **7** in electricity, a term referring to the speed of variations of alternating currents, alternating electromotive forces, and electromagnetic waves. **8** (*Physics*) rate of repetition or recurrence. **frequency band** *n.* a range of frequencies or wavelengths in the radio spectrum. **frequency distribution** *n.* in statistics, an arrangement of data which shows the frequency of occurrence of the different values of a variable. **frequency modulation** *n.* **1** in electronics, the varying of the frequency of the carrier wave in accordance with the frequency of speech or music, for example. **2** the broadcasting system using this. **frequency response** *n.* the ability of an audio amplifier or other device to deal with the different frequencies applied to it. [as FREQUENT[1]]

frequent[1] (frē´kwənt) *a.* **1** occurring often, common. **2** repeated at short intervals. **3** occurring near together, abundant. **4** constant, habitual. **frequentative** (-kwen´-) *n., a.* (*Gram.*) (a verb or verbal form) expressing frequent repetition or intensity of an action. **frequently** *adv.* often, commonly, at frequent intervals. **frequentness** *n.* [L *frequens*, *-ntem*, pres.p. of lost v. *frequēre*, allied to *farcīre*, to cram, see FARCE]

frequent[2] (frikwent´) *v.t.* to visit or resort to often or habitually. **frequentage** *n.* **frequentation** (-tā´shən) *n.* **frequenter** *n.*

fresco (fres´kō) *n.* (*pl.* **frescos, frescoes**) a kind of watercolour painting on fresh plaster or on a wall covered with mortar not quite dry. *~v.t.* (*3rd pers. sing. pres.* **frescoes,** *pres.p.* **frescoing,** *past, p.p.* **frescoed**) to paint (a picture) or decorate (a wall etc.) in fresco. **frescoed** *a.* **fresco secco** *n.* SECCO. [It., orig. a. FRESH]

fresh (fresh) *a.* **1** new. **2** not known, met with or used previously, recent. 3 other, different, additional. 4 newly produced, not withered or faded, not stale, decayed or tainted. 5 pure, not salt, drinkable. 6 not preserved with salt, or by pickling, tinning, freezing etc. 7 raw, inexperienced. 8 just arrived (from). 9 looking young or healthy. 10 bright and clean in appearance. 11 vividly and distinctly retained in the mind. 12 refreshed, reinvigorated. 13 (of a horse) frisky. 14 brisk, active, vigorous, fit. 15 (of air, a breeze etc.) refreshing, reviving, cool. 16 (*coll.*) cheeky, impertinent, amorously impudent. 17 quarrelsome. ~*adv.* 1 (*esp. in comb.*) freshly, as *fresh-cut*. 2 recently. 3 coolly, refreshingly. 4 with fresh vigour. ~*n.* 1 (*ellipt.*) the fresh part (of the day, season etc.). 2 a freshet. 3 a day of open weather. 4 a freshwater river or spring. 5 (*Sc.*) a thaw, open weather. **fresh out of** (*coll.*) having recently (completely) run out of. **to get fresh** (*coll.*) to take undesired liberties with someone of the opposite sex. **to have/ gather fresh way** (*Naut.*) to go at increased speed. **freshen** *v.t.* 1 to make fresh. 2 to enliven, to revive. 3 to make less salty. 4 (*Naut.*) to relieve (something such as a rope) by altering the position of a part subject to friction. ~*v.i.* 1 to become fresh. 2 to lose saltiness. 3 to become brisk, to gain strength. 4 (of cattle) to come into milk. **to freshen up** 1 to refresh oneself, to have a wash or shower, change one's clothes etc. 2 to revive, to give a fresher, more attractive appearance to. 3 to replenish (a drink). **fresher** *n.* (*coll.*) a freshman. **freshet** (-it) *n.* 1 a sudden flood caused by heavy rains or melted snow. 2 a freshwater stream. **fresh-faced** *a.* having a clean, young-looking complexion. †**freshish** *a.* **fresh-looking** *a.* appearing fresh. **freshly** *adv.* **freshman** *n.* (*pl.* **freshmen**) 1 a novice, a beginner, esp. a student in the first year at a university or college. 2 (*N Am.*) a student in the first year at high school. **freshmanship** *n.* **freshness** *n.* **fresh-run** *a.* (of salmon, sea trout etc.) newly come up from the sea. **freshwater** *a.* 1 of or relating to, found in or produced by fresh water. 2 (of a sailor) used to river or coasting trade. 3 (*N Am.*) (esp. of a college) small or little known. 4 †raw, unskilled. **freshwater flea** *n.* any of several waterfleas of the genus *Daphnia*, having a transparent shell and prominent eyes. **fresh-watered** *a.* 1 supplied with fresh water. 2 newly watered. **freshwoman** *n.* (*pl.* **freshwomen**) a female freshman. [OE *fersc* (cp. Dut. *versch*, G *frisch*, OHG *frisc*, assim. to the cognate OF *fresche*, fem. of *freis*)]

fresnel (frā´nel), **Fresnel** *n.* a photographic lens that has a surface of stepped concentric circles which are thinner and flatter than an ordinary lens of equivalent focal length. [Augustin Jean *Fresnel*, 1788–1827, French physicist]

fret[1] (fret) *v.i.* (*pres.p.* **fretting**, *past, p.p.* **fretted**) 1 to be worried, irritated, vexed or troubled. 2 to be in a state of agitation or commotion. 3 to grieve, to be discontented. 4 to be worn or eaten away. 5 to flow in little waves or ripples. 6 to make way by attrition or corrosion. ~*v.t.* 1 to irritate, vex, annoy. 2 to make uneasy or distressed. 3 to eat away, to corrode. 4 to wear away, to rub or chafe. 5 to make (a way or passage) by rubbing. 6 to make rough or disturb (as water). 7 †to devour. ~*n.* 1 a state of irritation or vexation. 2 the act or process of fretting or rubbing away. 3 a spot abraded or corroded. 4 an agitation of the surface of a fluid. 5 a chafing of the skin. **fretful** *a.* 1 worried, distressed; angry, irritable. 2 captious. **fretfully** *adv.* **fretfulness** *n.* [OE *fretan* (cp. Dut. *vreten*, G *fressen*), from *ētan*, to EAT, with pref. *fra-*, FOR-]

fret[2] (fret) *v.t.* (*pres.p.* **fretting**, *past, p.p.* **fretted**) 1 to ornament, to decorate. 2 to ornament (esp. a ceiling) with carved work. 3 to variegate. ~*n.* 1 an ornament formed by small bands or fillets intersecting each other at right angles, used in classical architecture. 2 (*Her.*) a figure composed of bars crossed and interlaced. 3 fretwork. 4 ornamental work. **fretsaw** *n.* a small saw with a long thin narrow blade on a frame, used in cutting fretwork. **fretted**[1] *a.* 1 ornamented with fretwork. 2 having raised or sunken ornamentation in rectangular forms. 3 (*Her.*) (of charges or ordinaries) interlaced with each other. **fretwork** *n.* 1 carved or open woodwork in ornamental patterns and devices. 2 a variegated pattern composed of interlacing lines of various patterns. [prob. from OF *freter*, found in p.p. *frete*, adorned with interlaced work]

fret[3] (fret) *n.* any of several small pieces of metal, wood, or ivory placed upon the fingerboard of certain stringed instruments to regulate the pitch of the notes. ~†*v.t.* (*pres.p.* **fretting**, *past, p.p.* **fretted**) to put such a fret on (a musical instrument). **fretboard** *n.* a fingerboard with frets. **fretless** *a.* **fretted**[2] *a.* [etym. uncertain; perh. from OF *frete*, a ferrule]

fretted[1] FRET[2].

fretted[2] FRET[3].

Freudian (froi´diən) *a.* of or relating to the psychological theories of Freud. ~*n.* a follower of Freud or his methods. **Freudianism** *n.* **Freudian slip** *n.* an unintentional action, such as a slip of the tongue, held to betray an unconscious thought. [Sigmund *Freud*, 1856–1939, Austrian psychologist]

FRG *abbr.* (*Hist.*) Federal Republic of Germany.

Fri. *abbr.* Friday.

friable (frī´əbəl) *a.* 1 capable of being easily reduced to powder. 2 readily crumbled. **friability** (-bil´-), **friableness** *n.* [F, from L *friābilis*, from *friāre*, to rub, to crumble]

friar (frī´ə) *n.* 1 a member of a monastic order, esp. one of the four mendicant orders, Augustinians or Austin Friars, Franciscans or Grey Friars, Dominicans or Black Friars, and Carmelites or White Friars. 2 a patch in a printed sheet that has not received the ink. **friarbird** *n.* (*Austral.*) a honeyeater with a bald head and neck. **friarlike, friarly** *a.* **friar's balsam, friars' balsam** *n.* a tincture of benzoin used esp. as an inhalant. **friar's cowl** *n.* the wake-robin, *Arum arisarum* or *A. maculatum*. **friar's lantern** *n.* the ignis fatuus. **friary** *n.* (*pl.* **friaries**) a monastery of a mendicant order. [ME and OF *frere*, L *frātrem*, nom. *frāter*, brother]

fribble (frib´əl) *v.i.* to act frivolously. ~*v.t.* to waste or trifle (away). ~*a.* frivolous, silly. ~*n.* 1 a trifler. 2 a frivolous, contemptible person. **fribbledom** *n.* **fribbler** *n.* **fribblish** *a.* [prob. onomat.]

fricandeau (frik´andō) *n.* (*pl.* **fricandeaux** (-dōz)) 1 a larded veal cutlet, braised or roasted and glazed. 2 a dish made with this, served with a sauce. ~*v.t.* (*3rd pers. sing. pres.* **fricandeaus**, *pres.p.* **fricandeauing**, *past, p.p.* **fricandeaued**) to make into a fricandeau. [F, etym. unknown]

fricassee (frik´əsē, -sē´) *n.* small pieces of meat, esp. chicken or veal, fried, stewed and served in a usu. white sauce. ~*v.t.* (*3rd pers. sing. pres.* **fricassees**, *pres.p.* **fricasseeing**, *past, p.p.* **fricasseed**) to cook as a fricassee. [F *fricassée*, orig. fem. p.p. of *fricasser*, etym. unknown]

fricative (frik´ətiv) *n.* a consonant, such as *f*, *sh*, *th*, produced by the friction of the breath issuing through a narrow opening. ~*a.* produced by such friction. [L *fricāre*, to rub, -ATIVE]

friction (frik´shən) *n.* 1 the act of two bodies rubbing together. 2 (*Physics*) resistance which any body meets with in moving over another body. 3 conflict, disagreement, lack of harmony. 4 (*in comb.*) of devices that transmit motion by friction between surfaces (*friction clutch*; *friction gear*). 5 chafing or rubbing a part of the body to promote circulation. **frictional** *a.* **frictionally** *adv.* **frictionless** *a.* [F, from L *frictiōnem*, nom. *frictio*, from *fricāre*, to rub]

Friday (frī´di) *n.* the sixth day of the week, following Thursday. ~*adv.* (*coll.*) on Friday. **Fridays** *adv.* (*coll.*) on Fridays, each Friday. [OE *frīgedæg* (cp. OHG *Frīatag*, G *Freitag*) dedicated by Germanic peoples to Frig, the wife of Odin, as a translation of the late L *dies Veneris*, day of the planet Venus]

fridge (frij), **frig** *n.* short for REFRIGERATOR (under REFRIGERATE). **fridge-freezer** *n.* an upright kitchen unit consisting of a refrigerator and a freezer.

friend (frend) *n.* **1** a person known well to another and regarded with affection, usually excluding sexual or familial relationships. **2** an acquaintance. **3** a person of the same nation or party, one who is not an enemy. **4** a person on the same side, an adherent, a sympathizer, a patron or promoter (of a cause, institution etc.). **5** (**Friend**) a member of the Society of Friends. **6** anything that helps one, esp. in an emergency. **7** a term of salutation. **8** (*pl.*) †one's near relations. **9** (*euphem.*) a lover. ~†*v.t.* to befriend. **my honourable friend** used in the House of Commons to refer to another member of one's own party. **my learned friend** used in a court of law by one lawyer to refer to another lawyer. **my noble friend** used in the House of Lords to refer to another member of one's own party. **Society of Friends** SOCIETY. **to be/ keep friends with** to be friendly with. **to make friends** to become intimate or reconciled (with). **friend at court** *n.* a person who has influence to help another. **friended** *a.* (*esp. in comb.*) having friends, as *well-friended.* **friendless** *a.* **friendlessness** *n.* †**friendlike** *a.* **friendly** *a.* (*comp.* **friendlier,** *superl.* **friendliest**) **1** having the disposition of a friend, good-natured. **2** acting as a friend. **3** characteristic of friends or of kindly feeling. **4** amicable, not hostile. **5** favourable, propitious. **6** played for amusement or entertainment, not as part of a competition. **7** useful, convenient, opportune. **8** user-friendly. ~*adv.* in the manner of a friend. ~*n.* (*pl.* **friendlies**) a game played for entertainment or practice, not a league or competition fixture. **friendlily** *adv.* **friendliness** *n.* **-friendly** *comb. form* **1** helpful to (*reader-friendly*). **2** favouring, protecting. **friendly action, friendly suit** *n.* a legal action instituted between two parties not at variance to obtain a judicial decision upon a certain point. **friendly fire** *n.* (*Mil.*) gunfire from one's own side that accidentally causes casualties or damage to one's own forces. **friendly match** *n.* a match played for entertainment or practice, a friendly. **Friendly Society** *n.* (*pl.* **Friendly Societies**) a society for the purpose of mutual assurance against sickness, old age etc. **friendship** *n.* **1** a relationship between friends. **2** the state of being friends. **3** an act of personal kindness or goodwill. **4** †aptness to unite or combine. [OE *frēond*, cp. Dut. *vriend*, G *Freund*, Goth. *frijōnds*, pres.p. of *frijōn*, to love (cp. OE *frēon, frēogan*, see FREE[1])]

frier FRYER (under FRY[1]).

Friesian (frē´zhən) *n.* **1** any of a breed of large black and white dairy cattle originally from Friesland. **2** this breed of cattle. **3** Frisian. **4** a Frisian. ~*a.* of or relating to Friesians. [var. of FRISIAN]

frieze[1] (frēz) *n.* **1** the middle division of an entablature, between the architrave and the cornice, usu. enriched by sculpture. **2** the band of sculpture occupying this. **3** a horizontal band or strip, either plain or decorated, elsewhere in a wall. [F *frise* (cp. Sp. *friso*), perh. from It. *fregio*, a fringe, L *Phrygium* (*opus*), Phrygian (work)]

frieze[2] (frēz) *n.* a coarse woollen cloth, with a rough nap on one side. **friezed** *a.* made rough like the nap of frieze. [F *frise* (in *drap de frise*, cloth of Friesland, from Dut. *Vries*, a Frieslander)]

frig[1] (frig) *v.t., v.i.* (*pres.p.* **frigging,** *past, p.p.* **frigged**) (*taboo, sl.*) **1** to masturbate. **2** to have sexual intercourse (with). ~*n.* **1** an act of sexual intercourse. **2** (*sl.*) a least amount. **to frig about** to potter or mess about. **frigging** *a.* used as an intensive to express one's annoyance with something. ~*adv.* very, extremely. [dial. *frig*, to rub]

frig[2] FRIDGE.

frigate (frig´ət) *n.* **1** a naval escort vessel between a corvette and a destroyer in size. **2** (*N Am.*) a similar vessel between a destroyer and cruiser in size. **3** (*Hist.*) a warship next in size below a ship of the line. **frigate bird** *n.* a large tropical bird of the family Fregitidae with a long bill, a wide wingspan and a forked tail. [MF *fregate*, It. *fregata*, etym. uncertain]

frigatoon (frigətoon´) *n.* a Venetian vessel with a square stern, and only a mainmast and mizzen-mast. [It. *fregatone*, as FRIGATE]

fright (frīt) *n.* **1** sudden and violent fear or alarm; an instance of this. **2** a state of terror. **3** a person who or thing that presents a ridiculous or grotesque appearance in person or dress. ~*v.t.* (*poet.*) to frighten. **to take fright** to become frightened. **frighten** *v.t.* **1** to alarm, terrify, scare; to throw into a state of fright. **2** to drive (away, out of, or into) by fright. ~*v.i.* to become frightened. **frightener** *n.* (*sl.*) someone or something intended to frighten a person, esp. for criminal purposes. **to put the frighteners on** to (attempt to) coerce or deter someone with threats (of violence). **frightful** *a.* **1** dreadful, fearful, shocking. **2** horrible, hideous, very disagreeable. **3** causing fright. **4** (*coll.*) awful, extreme, extraordinary. **frightfully** *adv.* **frightfulness** *n.* **1** being frightful. **2** the terrorizing of civilians, as a military tactic. [OE *fyrhto*, cogn. with *forht*, afraid, cp. OS *foroht, forht*, G *Furcht*]

frigid (frij´id) *a.* **1** lacking warmth or feeling or ardour. **2** stiff, formal, forbidding. **3** without animation or spirit, dull, flat. **4** (esp. of a woman) sexually unresponsive. **5** cold, lacking heat or warmth. **frigidity** (-jid´-) *n.* **1** the state of being frigid. **2** (*Psych.*) the decrease or absence of sexual response esp. in a woman. **frigidly** *adv.* **frigidness** *n.* **frigid zone** *n.* either of the two parts of the earth between the Arctic Circle and the North Pole or between the Antarctic Circle and the South Pole. [L *frīgidus*, from *frīgēre*, to be cold, from *frīgus*, cold]

frigorific (frigərif´ik) *a.* (*Physics*) producing cold (from an old theory that cold is due to an imponderable substance called *frigoric* (cp. CALORIC)). [F *frigorifique*, L *frīgorificus*, from L *frīgus -oris*, cold]

frijol (frihōl´) *n.* (*pl.* **frijoles** (-hō´les)) a bean resembling the kidney bean, used in Mexican cookery. [Mex. Sp.]

frill (fril) *n.* **1** a pleated or fluted strip of cloth sewn upon one edge only. **2** a ruffle, a flounce. **3** a ruff or frill-like fringe of hair, feather etc. on an animal, bird or plant. **4** a similar paper decoration on a chop or other cut of meat. **5** (*pl., coll.*) finery, frippery, decorative non-essentials. **6** (*pl., coll.*) airs, affectations. **7** the puckering of a film at the edge of a negative. ~*v.t.* **1** to furnish with a frill, to form into a frill. **2** to serve as a frill to. ~*v.i.* in photography, to pucker at the edge of a plate. **with no frills** plain, unornamented, no-nonsense. **without frills** plain, ornamented, no-nonsense. **frilled** *a.* furnished with a frill or frills. **frillies** *n.pl.* (*coll.*) women's underwear. **frilling** *n.* **1** material for frills. **2** a group or set of frills. **frill lizard, frilled lizard, frill-necked lizard** *n.* a large Australian lizard, *Chlamydosaurus kingli*, with an erectile fold of skin around its neck. **frilly** *a.* (*comp.* **frillier,** *superl.* **frilliest**) **1** having many frills. **2** resembling a frill. **frilliness** *n.* [etym. uncertain; prob. from LG (cp. WFlem. *frul, frulle*)]

Frimaire (frimeə´) *n.* the third month of the French revolutionary calendar, from 22 November to 21 December. [F from *frimas*, hoarfrost]

fringe (frinj) *n.* **1** an ornamental border to dress or furniture, consisting of loose threads or tassels. **2** a border, an edging, a margin. **3** the front hair cut short with a straight edge along the forehead. **4** (*Bot.*) a row of long filiform processes. 5 (*Zool.*) a border of hairs or other processes. 6 (*Physics*) **a** any of the alternating light or dark bands produced by the interference or diffraction of light. **b** a strip of false colour in an image. 7 something marginal or additional. 8 a group with marginal or extreme views. 9 (*N Am.*) a fringe benefit. *~v.t.* 1 to border with or as if with a fringe. 2 to serve as a fringe to. *~a.* 1 existing alongside mainstream or conventional forms, institutions etc. 2 marginal, secondary, peripheral. **the Fringe** that part of an arts festival, the London theatre etc. which presents new, experimental or avant-garde works away from the main venues. **fringe benefit** *n.* something additional to wages or salary regularly received as part of an employee's remuneration from an employer. **fringeless** *a.* **fringelike** *a.* **fringe medicine** *n.* the treatment of illnesses by methods that are considered to be unconventional by the medical profession. **fringing** *n.* material for a fringe. **fringing reef** *n.* a coral reef fringing the shore. **fringy** *a.* [OF *frenge* (F *frange*), L *fimbria*]

fringilline (frin´jilīn) *a.* finchlike, belonging to the genus *Fringilla* or family Fringillidae of small singing birds containing the finches. [L]

frippery (frip´əri) *n.* (*pl.* **fripperies**) 1 worthless, needless or showy adornments. 2 tawdry finery. 3 mere display. 4 **a** knick-knacks, gewgaws. **b** a knick-knack. *~a.* 1 tawdry, trifling. 2 contemptible. [OF *freperie*, from *frepe*, a rag, prob. from L *fibra*, FIBRE]

Frisbee® (friz´bi) *n.* a plastic disc, used in throwing and catching games.

frisée (frē´zā) *n.* ENDIVE. [F, from *chocorée frisée*, curly endive]

frisette (frizet´) *n.* a front or band of artificial curls worn on the forehead. [F, from *friser*, to FRIZZ]

friseur (frēzœ´) *n.* a hairdresser. [F, as FRISETTE]

Frisian (friz´iən) *a.* 1 of or relating to Friesland. 2 a native or inhabitant of Friesland. *~n.* 1 the language of Friesland. 2 a native or inhabitant of Friesland. [L *Frisii*, pl., OFris. *Frise*]

frisk (frisk) *v.i.* to leap, skip or gambol about, to frolic. *~v.t.* (*coll.*) to search (a person) for firearms etc. *~n.* a gambol, a frolic. **frisker** *n.* a person who frisks. **friskful** *a.* **frisky** *a.* (*comp.* **friskier**, *superl.* **friskiest**) playful, lively. **friskily** *adv.* **friskiness** *n.* [from obs. a. *frisk*, OF *frisque*, lively, OHG *frisc*, FRESH]

frisket (fris´kit) *n.* a light frame by which a sheet of paper to be printed is held in place. [F *frisquette*]

frisson (frē´sõ) *n.* a shudder, a thrill. [F]

frit[1] (frit) *n.* 1 a calcined mixture of sand and fluxes ready to be melted in a crucible to form glass. 2 a vitreous composition used in the manufacture of porcelain, enamel etc. *~v.t.* (*pres.p.* **fritting**, *past, p.p.* **fritted**) to expose to dull red heat so as to decompose and fuse. [F *fritte*, It. *fritta*, fem. p.p. of *friggere*, to FRY[1]]

frit[2] (frit) *a.* (*dial.*, *coll.*) frightened.

frit-fly (frit´flī) *n.* (*pl.* **frit-flies**) a small fly, *Oscinella frit*, that arrests the growth of wheat and other cereals by boring into the bud. [etym. unknown]

frith FIRTH.

fritillary (fritil´əri) *n.* (*pl.* **fritillaries**) 1 any plant of the liliaceous genus *Fritillaria*, esp. snake's head (*F. meleagris*), with drooping bell-like flowers speckled with dull purple. 2 any of various butterflies of the genus *Argynnis*, with brownish wings chequered with black and silver. [late L *fritillāria*, from L *fritillus*, a dice-box]

frittata (fritah´tə) *n.* an Italian dish made with fried beaten eggs. [It.]

fritter[1] (frit´ə) *n.* a piece of fruit, meat etc. dipped in a light batter and fried. [OF *friture*, L *frictus*, p.p. of *frīgere*, to FRY[1]]

fritter[2] (frit´ə) *n.* (*pl.*) fragments, bits, shreds. *~†v.t.* to break into small pieces. **to fritter away** to waste (esp. time or money). [etym. uncertain; perh. from obs. *fitters*, n.pl., cogn. with G *Fetzen*, a rag, a scrap; or from OF *fretura*, L *fractūra*, FRACTURE; or from FRITTER[1]]

fritto misto (fritō mis´tō) *n.* a dish of fried food, esp. seafood. [It., mixed fry]

fritz (frits) *n.* the process of failing (only as below). **on the fritz** (*N Am.*, *sl.*) not in working order. [etym. unknown]

frivolous (friv´ələs) *a.* 1 trifling, trumpery, of little or no importance or significance. 2 lacking seriousness, inclined to trifling or silly behaviour. **frivol** *v.i.* (*pres.p.* **frivolling**, (*N Am.*) **frivoling**, *past, p.p.* **frivolled**, (*N Am.*) **frivoled**) to trifle. *~v.t.* to trifle (away); to spend foolishly. **frivolity** (-vol´-) *n.* (*pl.* **frivolities**). **frivolously** *adv.* **frivolousness** *n.* [L *frīvolus*, prob. cogn. with *friāre*, *fricāre*, to rub]

frizz (friz) *v.t.* 1 to curl, to crisp. 2 to form (the hair) into a mass of small tight curls. 3 to raise a nap on (cloth). 4 to treat (chamois leathers) with pumice etc. *~v.i.* (of hair) to form into small tight curls. *~n.* 1 frizzed hair, a mass or row of curls. 2 a frizzed state. **frizzy** *a.* (*comp.* **frizzier**, *superl.* **frizziest**) in a mass of small tight curls. **frizziness** *n.* [F *friser*, from *frise*, FRIEZE[2]]

frizzle[1] (friz´əl) *v.t.*, *v.i.* to form (into) crisp, tight curls. *~n.* 1 a curled or crisped lock of hair. 2 frizzed hair. **frizzly** *a.* [etym. uncertain, older than but prob. conn. with FRIZZ]

frizzle[2] (friz´əl) *v.t.* to fry (bacon etc.) with a hissing noise. *~v.i.* to make a hissing noise while being fried. **to frizzle up** to burn or shrivel. [prob. from earlier *frizz*, imit. adaptation of FRY[1]]

Frl. *abbr.* Fräulein.

fro (frō) *adv.* away, backwards (only as below). **to and fro** 1 forwards and backwards. 2 repeatedly from one place to another and back again. [Icel. *frā*, FROM; cp. OE *fram*]

frock (frok) *n.* 1 a woman's or girl's dress. 2 the long upper garment with loose sleeves worn by monks. 3 the office of a priest. 4 a frock coat. 5 a military coat of similar shape. 6 a smock. 7 a woven woollen tunic worn by sailors. *~v.t.* to invest with priestly status or office. **frock coat** *n.* a close-fitting coat, with long broad skirts of the same length in front and behind. **frocked** *a.* **frocking** *n.* material for smocks. **†frockless** *a.* [F *froc*, prob. from late L *frocus*, *floccus*, FLOCK[2]]

froe (frō), **frow** *n.* (*N Am.*) a cleaving tool, with a handle set at right angles to the wedge-shaped blade. [from *forward*, turned away]

Froebel system (frœ´bəl, frō´-) *a.* a form of kindergarten in which the child's senses are developed by handwork etc. **Froebelian** (-bē´liən), **Froebelism** *n.* [Friedrich Willhelm August *Froebel*, 1782–1852, German educator]

frog[1] (frog) *n.* 1 a squat, smooth-skinned, tailless amphibian of the order Anura with the back legs developed for jumping. 2 (*derog.*) (*often* **Frog**) a French person. 3 a grooved piece of iron or steel to guide train wheels over an intersection in the track. 4 the hollow in one or both faces of a brick. 5 the block by which the hair is attached to the heel of a violin etc. bow. **frog in one's/the throat** (*coll.*) phlegm on the vocal chords impeding speech. **frogbit** *n.* a small aquatic plant, *Hydrocharis morsusranae*. **frogfish** *n.* (*pl. in general* **frogfish**, *in particular* **frogfishes**) an angler fish, esp. of the family Antennariidae. **froggery** *n.* (*pl.* **froggeries**) a place where frogs are kept or are numerous. **froggy** *a.* 1 abounding with frogs. 2 of, like or relating to frogs. 3 (*derog.*) French. **Froggy** *n.* (*pl.* **Froggies**) (*derog.*) a French person. **froghopper** *n.* a genus of small insects of the family Cercopidae remarkable for their leaping powers, and whose larvae secrete a protective spittle-like substance. **frogman** *n.* (*pl.* **frogmen**) an underwater swimmer equipped with rubber suit, flippers, face mask etc. and an oxygen supply. **frogmarch** *v.t.* 1 to carry face downwards between four people each holding a limb. 2 to move (a person) by force, usu. by seizing from behind and propelling forwards while the arms are pinioned, or by dragging backwards between two people each grasping an arm. ~*n.* the act of frogmarching a person. **frogmouth** *n.* any of various Australian and SE Asian birds of the family Podargidae with large broad mouths. **frogspawn** *n.* 1 a gelatinous mass of frogs' eggs. 2 certain freshwater algae. [OE *frogga, frox* (cp. Icel. *froskr,* G *Frosch*)]

frog[2] (frog) *n.* 1 a spindle-shaped button or toggle used for fastening military cloaks and coats. 2 the loop of a scabbard. **frogged** *a.* **frogging** *n.* [Port. *froco,* L *floccus,* FLOCK[2]]

frog[3] (frog) *n.* a tender horny substance in the middle of the sole of a horse's foot. [etym. unknown; perh. corr. of FORK]

froideur (frwodœ´) *n.* coolness in a relationship between people. [F]

frolic (frol´ik) *v.i.* (*pres.p.* **frolicking,** *past, p.p.* **frolicked**) 1 to play pranks. 2 to frisk. 3 to indulge in merrymaking. ~†*a.* 1 gay, merry, sportive. 2 full of pranks. ~*n.* 1 a wild prank. 2 an outburst of gaiety and mirth. 3 a merrymaking. 4 a light-hearted entertainment. **frolicful** *a.* **frolicker** *n.* †**frolicky** *a.* **frolicsome** *a.* **frolicsomely** *adv.* **frolicsomeness** *n.* [prob. from MDut. *vrolick* (Dut. *vrolijk*), cp. G *fröhlich* (*vrō-* or *froh-,* merry, joyous, -LIKE)]

from (from) *prep.* 1 away, out of (expressing separation, departure, point of view, distinction or variation). 2 beginning with, after (expressing the starting point or lower limit in time or space). 3 arriving, coming, deriving (indicating the original location, source or model). 4 by means of, because of, by reason of (expressing instrumentality, cause, reason or motive). **from a child** from childhood. **from day to day** as the days pass; daily. **from hour to hour** as the hours pass; hourly. **from now on** from this time onwards. **from out** out from, forth from. **from time to time** at intervals, now and then. **from year to year** as the years pass; yearly. [OE *from, fram* (cp. Icel. *frā,* FRO, OS and OHG *fram,* Goth. *framis*), orig. forward]

fromage blanc (fromahzh blã´) *n.* a kind of soft French cheese made from cow's milk, with a creamy sour taste. [F, white cheese]

fromage frais (fromahzh frā´) *n.* a kind of smooth low-fat soft cheese with a light texture. [F, fresh cheese]

frond (frond) *n.* 1 (*Bot.*) a leaflike expansion in which the functions of stem and foliage are not entirely differentiated, often bearing the organs of fructification, as in many cryptogams, esp. the ferns. 2 the leaflike thallus of some algae. 3 (*Zool.*) a leaflike expansion, as in many zoophytes. **frondage** *n.* **frondescence** (-des´-) *n.* coming into leaf. **frondescent** *a.* **frondiferous** (-dif´-) *a.* **frondlet** *n.* **frondose** *a.* **frondous** *a.* [L *frons -ndis,* a leaf]

Fronde (frond) *n.* 1 (*Hist.*) the French party, 1648–57, who attacked Mazarin and the Court during the minority of Louis XIV. 2 any party of malcontents. **Frondeur** (-dœ´) *n.* 1 a member of the Fronde. 2 (**frondeur**) an opponent of the government, an irreconcilable. [F, a sling]

front (frŭnt) *n.* 1 the forward part or side of anything. 2 the most conspicuous part. 3 the beginning, the first part. 4 the part of a garment covering the chest. 5 a face of a building, esp. the principal face. 6 a frontage. 7 a seaside promenade. 8 a position directly ahead, or in the foremost part of something. 9 the position of leadership. 10 the vanguard. 11 the main forward positions of an army etc. 12 the lateral space occupied by a military unit. 13 the direction in which a line of troops faces. 14 a line of battle. 15 the place where a battle is fought. 16 a particular sphere of activity. 17 a group of people or organizations who make common cause together. 18 the line of separation between air masses of different density and temperature. 19 the auditorium in a theatre. 20 outward appearance or bearing. 21 impudence, boldness. 22 something which serves as a cover or disguise for secret or illegal activities. 23 a frontman. 24 a set of false hair or curls worn over the forehead. 25 a dicky. 26 (*poet.*) the forehead. 27 the face. ~*a.* 1 relating to or situated in or at the front. 2 articulated at or towards the front of the mouth. ~*v.t.* 1 to stand or be situated opposite to. 2 to face, to look (to or towards). 3 †to confront, to meet face to face, to oppose. 4 to furnish with a front. 5 to be the leader or head of. 6 to be the presenter of (a TV programme etc.). ~*v.i.* 1 to face, to look, to be situated with the front (towards). 2 (*coll.*) to act as a front or cover (for). 3 †to be foremost. 4 †to be opposed. **in front** 1 in an advanced or the leading position. 2 facing or ahead of one. **in front of** 1 before. 2 in advance of; ahead of. 3 in the presence of. **on the front burner** BURNER (under BURN[1]). **out front** in a theatre, in the audience or auditorium. **to come to the front** to take a prominent position. **to front up** (*Austral.*) to turn up. **frontage** *n.* 1 a the front part of a building. b the extent of this. c land between this and a road. 2 land facing a road or water. 3 the direction in which anything faces, an outlook. **frontager** *n.* 1 the owner of a frontage. 2 a person who lives on the frontier. **frontage road** *n.* (*N Am.*) a service road. **frontal** *a.* 1 situated on, of or relating to the front. 2 belonging to the forehead. ~*n.* 1 a small pediment over a door or window. 2 an ornamental hanging or panel in front of an altar. 3 the façade of a building. 4 a bandage or application for the forehead. **frontal attack** *n.* an attack on the front of an army, in contrast to an attack on the flank. **frontal lobe** *n.* the front lobe of either side of the brain. **frontally** *adv.* **frontate** (-tāt), **frontated** *a.* (*Bot.*) increasing in breadth. **front bench** *n.* the foremost bench in the House of Commons, assigned to leaders of the government or opposition. **frontbencher** *n.* **front door** *n.* 1 the principal entrance to a building. 2 the main means of access to a situation etc. **fronted** *a.* 1 formed with a front, as troops. 2 changed into or towards a front sound. **-fronted** *comb. form* having a front of a specified type. **frontless** *a.* 1 without a front. 2 †full of effrontery, shameless. **front line** *n.* 1 the positions closest to the enemy in a battle. 2 the most advanced and active, or most exposed and dangerous positions in any field of activity. **front-line** *a.* 1 of, relating to or suitable for the front line in battle. 2 neighbouring a hostile state or a scene of (armed) conflict. **front-line states** *n.pl.* (*Hist.*) the countries bordering on South Africa and opposed to its policy of apartheid. **frontman** *n.* (*pl.* **frontmen**) 1 a nominal leader or figurehead. 2 the leader of a group of musicians etc. 3 the presenter of a TV programme. 4 a person with the role of covering for illegal activities. **front matter** *n.* the preliminary pages of a book, consisting of the title-page, table of contents etc. before the main part of the book. **front office** *n.* a main office, e.g. a headquarters of the police. **front of house** *n.* in a theatre, those activities which involve direct contact with the public, e.g. box office, selling programmes. **front-of-house** *a.* **front page** *n.* the first page of a newspaper, containing important or noteworthy news. **front-page** *a.* (worthy of) figuring on the front page of a newspaper. **front passage** *n.* (*coll.*) the vagina. **front piece** *n.* in a theatre, a small play acted in front of the curtain. **front room** *n.* a room in the front of a house, esp. a living room. **front runner** *n.* 1 the leader or most favoured contestant in a race, election etc. 2 a person or horse that runs or performs best when in the lead. **frontward** *a., adv.* **frontwards**

adv. **front-wheel drive** *n.* transmission of power to the front wheels of a motor vehicle. [OF, from L *frontem*, nom. *frons*, the forehead]

frontier (frŭn´tiə, -tiə´) *n.* **1 a** that part of a country which fronts or borders upon another. **b** the line marking a boundary between states or areas. **2** (*chiefly N Am.*) the margins of settled and unsettled territory. **3** (*often pl.*) the current limit of knowledge or attainment in a particular sphere. ~*a.* of, relating to or situated on the frontier. **frontierless** *a.* **frontiersman** *n.* (*pl.* **frontiersmen**) a person living in the margins of settled and unsettled territory. **frontierswoman** *n.* (*pl.* **frontierswomen**) a female frontiersman. [OF, late L *frontēria*, *-tāria*, as FRONT]

frontispiece (frŭn´tispēs) *n.* **1** a picture facing the title-page of a book. **2** a façade, a decorated front or chief entrance. **3** a pediment above a door, window etc. ~*v.t.* to furnish with, to serve or put as, or to supply a frontispiece (to a book). [F *frontispice*, late L *frontispicium* (*frons -ntis*, the forehead, *specere*, to look), assim. to PIECE]

frontlet (frŭnt´lit) *n.* **1** a small band or fillet worn on the forehead. **2** a phylactery. **3** the decorated border of an altar frontal. **4** the forehead in birds. [OF *frontlet*]

fronto- (frun´tō) *comb. form* of or relating to the forehead, the frontal bone of the forehead, or the frontal region. [L *frons -ntis*, the forehead]

fronton (frŭn´tən) *n.* (*Archit.*) a pediment, frontal. [F, from It. *frontone*, as FRONTO-]

†**frore** (fraw) *a.* (*poet.*) frozen, frosty. [OE *froren*, p.p. of *frēosan*, to FREEZE]

frost (frost) *n.* **1** (*also* **white frost**) minute crystals of frozen dew or vapour, rime or hoar frost, esp. covering the ground at night. **2** the act or state of freezing, the congelation of fluids by the abstraction of heat. **3** temperature below freezing point. **4** the state of the atmosphere that produces freezing. **5** frosty weather. **6** coldness of manner or attitude. **7** (*sl.*) a disappointment, a fiasco, a failure. ~*v.i.* to become covered with frost. ~*v.t.* **1** to cover with or as if with frost. **2** to injure by frost. **3** to give a fine-grained, slightly roughened appearance to (glass, metal etc.). **4** (*chiefly N Am.*) to ice (a cake). **5** to whiten (as the hair). **6** to dredge with fine sugar. **7** to sharpen (the nails of a horse's shoes) in frosty weather. **degrees of frost** DEGREE. **Jack Frost** JACK[1]. **frostbite** *n.* inflammation often resulting in gangrene, usu. of the fingers or toes, caused by exposure to extreme cold. **frostbitten** *a.* **frost-bound** *a.* confined by frost. **frosted** *a.* **1** covered with frost or any substance resembling frost. **2** damaged by frost. **3** having a rough, granulated surface. **4** (*chiefly N Am.*) covered with icing. **frosting** *n.* **1** (*chiefly N Am.*) icing. **2** a rough, granulated surface produced on glass, metal etc. in imitation of frost. **frostless** *a.* **frost-nail** *n.* a projecting nail driven into a horse's shoe to prevent slipping in frosty weather. **frost-work** *n.* the figures formed by frost on glass etc. **frosty** *a.* (*comp.* **frostier**, *superl.* **frostiest**) **1** producing frost. **2** excessively cold. **3** attended with frost. **4** affected or injured by frost. **5** covered with or as if with frost. **6** cool, unfriendly, unenthusiastic. **frostily** *adv.* **frostiness** *n.* [OE *forst* (cp. Dut. *vorst*, Dan., Swed. *fros*, G *Frost*); cogn. with FREEZE]

froth (froth) *n.* **1** foam, spume, the mass of small bubbles caused in liquors by shaking or fermentation. **2** foamy excretion, scum. **3** empty display of ideas or talk. **4** light, insubstantial matter. ~*v.t.* **1** to cause to foam. **2** to cover with froth. ~*v.i.* to form or emit froth. **froth-blower** *n.* (*coll.*) a beer drinker. **frothless** *a.* **frothsome** (-səm) *a.* **frothy** *a.* (*comp.* **frothier**, *superl.* **frothiest**). **frothily** *adv.* **frothiness** *n.* [cogn. with Icel. *frotha* (cp. OE *āfrēothan*, to froth)]

frottage (frotahzh´) *n.* **1** the technique of producing images or textures by rubbing with e.g. a pencil on a sheet of paper placed on top of an object. **2** sexual gratification obtained by rubbing against another person's clothed body. [F, from *frotter*, to rub]

frou-frou (froo´froo) *n.* **1** a rustling, as of a silk dress. **2** elaborate dress, frills. [F, imit.]

frow[1] (frow) *n.* **1** a Dutchwoman. **2** a housewife. [Dut. *vrouw*, cp. FRAU]

frow[2] FROE.

†**froward** (frō´əd) *a.* not willing to comply, refractory, perverse, mutinous. †**frowardly** *adv.* †**frowardness** *n.* [ME *fraward*]

frown (frown) *v.i.* **1** to express displeasure, worry or seriousness by contracting the brows. **2** to look gloomy, threatening or with disfavour. **3** to scowl, to lour. **4** to express displeasure (at or upon). ~*v.t.* **1** to repress, repel or rebuke with a frown. **2** to express with a frown. ~*n.* **1** a knitting of the brows in displeasure, worry or mental absorption. **2** any sign of displeasure. **frowner** *n.* **frowningly** *adv.* [OF *frongnier* (cp. F *renfrogner*, *refrogner*), from Gmc. (cp. Swed. dial. *fryna*, to make a wry face)]

frowst (frowst) *n.* (*coll.*) **1** stuffiness. **2** an unwholesome smell (in a room). ~*v.i.* to remain indoors or to enjoy frowst. **frowster** *n.* **frowsty** *a.* (*comp.* **frowstier**, *superl.* **frowstiest**). **frowstiness** *n.* [etym. unknown]

frowzy (frow´zi), **frowsy** *a.* (*comp.* **frowzier, frowsier**, *superl.* **frowziest, frowsiest**) **1** musty, fusty, close. **2** slovenly, unkempt, dirty. **frowziness** *n.* [etym. uncertain]

froze FREEZE.

frozen (frō´zən) *a.* **1** preserved by freezing. **2** very cold. **3** fixed, immobilized. **4** (of prices etc.) pegged at a certain level. **5** (of assets etc.) not convertible. **6** frigid, aloof, disdainful. **frozenly** *adv.* **frozen mitt** *n.* (*coll.*) hostility, rejection. **frozenness** *n.* **frozen shoulder** *n.* painful stiffness in the shoulder joint. [p.p. of FREEZE]

FRS *abbr.* Fellow of the Royal Society.

FRSE *abbr.* Fellow of the Royal Society of Edinburgh.

Fructidor (frŭk´tidaw) *n.* **1** in the French Revolutionary calendar, the 12th month of the republican year (18 Aug. to 16 Sept.). **2** the coup d'état that occurred in Fructidor in 1797. [F, from L *frūctus*, fruit, Gr. *dōron*, gift]

fructify (frŭk´tifī) *v.t.* (*3rd pers. sing. pres.* **fructifies**, *pres.p.* **fructifying**, *past, p.p.* **fructified**) **1** to make fruitful or productive. **2** to fertilize. ~*v.i.* to bear fruit. **fructiferous** (-tif´-) *a.* bearing fruit. **fructification** (-fikā´shən) *n.* **1** the act or process of fructifying. **2** any spore-bearing structure in ferns, mosses, fungi etc. **3** the fruit of a seed-bearing plant. **fructiform** (-tifawm) *a.* **fructose** (-tōz, tōs) *n.* the very sweet soluble form of sugar that occurs esp. in fruit juices and honey. **fructuate** *v.i.* to bear fruit, to come to fruit. **fructuation** (-chooā´shən) *n.* coming to fruit; fruition. **fructuous** (-chu-) *a.* **1** fruitful, fertile. **2** full of fruit. [F *fructifier*, L *frūctificāre* (*frūctus*, FRUIT, *-ficāre*, *facere*, to make)]

frugal (froo´gəl) *a.* **1** thrifty, sparing. **2** not profuse or lavish. **3** economical in the use or expenditure of food, money etc. **frugality** (-gal´-) *n.* **1** economy, thrift. **2** a sparing use of anything. **frugally** *adv.* **frugalness** *n.* [L *frūgālis*, from *frūgi*, dat. of *frūx*, fruit, profit]

†**frugiferous** (froojif´ərəs) *a.* bearing fruit, fruitful. **frugivorous** (-jiv´-) *a.* feeding on fruit. [L *frūgifer*]

fruit (froot) *n.* **1 a** the edible succulent product of a plant or tree in which the seeds are enclosed. **b** (*collect. sing.*) these in quantity. **2** (*Bot.*) the matured ovary or seed vessel with other parts adhering thereto. **3** the spores of cryptogams. **4** (*pl.*) the vegetable products yielded by the earth, serving for food to humans and animals. **5** (*Bible*) offspring. **6** product, result or consequence. **7** (*usu pl.*) benefit, profit. **8** (*chiefly N Am.*, *sl.*, *offensive*) a male homosexual. ~*v.i.* to bear fruit. ~*v.t.* to cause to produce fruit. **fruitage** *n.* **fruitarian** (-teə´ri-) *n.* a person who eats only fruit. **fruit bar** *n.* a piece of dried pressed fruit. **fruitbat** *n.* any large Old World fruit-eating bat of the suborder Megachiroptera found in tropical and subtropical regions. **fruit-body** *n.* (*pl.* **fruit-bodies**) FRUITING BODY (under FRUIT). **fruit bud** *n.* a bud which produces fruit. **fruitcake** *n.* (*sl.*) an eccentric or insane person. **fruit cake** *n.* a cake containing currants and other dried fruit. **fruit cocktail** *n.* a fruit salad, esp. one of small finely chopped fruit. **fruited** *a.* **fruiter** *n.* **1** a tree that bears fruit, esp. considered with reference to its quality. **2** a ship that carries fruit. **3** a fruit-grower. **fruiterer** *n.* a person who deals in fruits. **fruit fly** *n.* (*pl.* **fruit flies**) any of various flies, esp. of the genus *Drosophila*, with larvae which feed on fruit. **fruitful** *a.* **1** producing fruit in abundance. **2** successful, productive, fertile. **3** bearing children, prolific. **fruitfully** *adv.* **fruitfulness** *n.* **fruiting** *a.* bearing fruit. **fruiting body** *n.* (*pl.* **fruiting bodies**) the part of a fungus that bears spores. **fruit knife** *n.* (*pl.* **fruit knives**) a knife with a silver blade for paring and cutting fruit. **fruitless** *a.* **1** not bearing fruit, unproductive. **2** unsuccessful, unprofitable, useless, vain, idle. **fruitlessly** *adv.* **fruitlessness** *n.* **fruitlet** (-lit) *n.* a drupel. **fruit machine** *n.* a coin-in-the-slot gambling machine which spins symbols (as of fruit) and pays out if certain combinations are visible when it stops. **fruit salad** *n.* **1** a mixture of fruits cut up and sweetened. **2** (*sl.*) a displayed arrangement of medals etc. **fruit-spur** *n.* a small branch of which the growth is arrested for the development of fruit-buds. **fruit sugar** *n.* fructose. **fruit tree** *n.* a tree cultivated for its fruit. **fruitwood** *n.* the wood of a fruit tree, esp. when used in making furniture. **fruity** *a.* (*comp.* **fruitier,** *superl.* **fruitiest**) **1** of or like fruit, in taste, smell etc. **2** (of wine) tasting of the grape. **3** rich, full-flavoured. **4** (of a voice) round, mellow and rich. **5** salacious, risqué. **6** (*N Am., sl.*) crazy. **7** (*chiefly N Am., sl., offensive*) homosexual. **fruitily** *adv.* **fruitiness** *n.* [OF, from L *frūctum*, nom. *-us*, from *fruī*, to enjoy]

fruition (frooish´ən) *n.* **1** the bearing of fruit. **2** attainment, fulfilment. **3** pleasure or satisfaction derived from attainment of a desire. [OF, from *fruitiōnem*, nom. *-tio*, from *fruī*, to enjoy (cp. FRUIT)]

frumentaceous (froomәntā´shəs) *a.* of the nature of, resembling or composed of wheat or other cereal. [L *frūmentāceus*, from *frūmentum*, corn]

frumenty (froo´mənti), **furmenty** (fœ´mənti), **furmety** (-məti) *n.* a dish made of wheat boiled in milk and flavoured with spices. [OF *frumentée*, from *frument*, L *frūmentum*, as FRUMENTACEOUS]

frump (frŭmp) *n.* an old-fashioned, unattractive or dowdy-looking woman. **frumpish** *a.* **frumpishly** *adv.* **frumpy** *a.* (*comp.* **frumpier,** *superl.* **frumpiest**) old-fashioned, unattractive or dowdy. **frumpily** *adv.* **frumpiness** *n.* [etym. uncertain]

frusta FRUSTUM.

frustrate[1] (frustrāt´) *v.t.* **1** to make ineffective. **2** to prevent from succeeding, to defeat, to thwart, to baulk. **3** to nullify, to disappoint. **4** to cause feelings of dissatisfaction or discouragement. **frustrated** *a.* **1** thwarted. **2** dissatisfied, discouraged. **3** sexually unfulfilled. **frustratedly** *adv.* **frustrater** *n.* **frustrating** *a.* **frustratingly** *adv.* **frustration** (-strā´shən) *n.* [L *frustrātus*, p.p. of *frustrārī*, from *frustrā*, in vain]

frustrate[2] (frŭs´trāt) *a.* vain, of no effect.

frustule (frŭs´tūl) *n.* the covering or shell, usu. in two valves, of a diatom. [F, from late L *frustulum*, dim. of FRUSTUM]

frustum (frŭs´təm) *n.* (*pl.* **frusta** (-tə), **frustums**) **1** the part of a regular solid next to the base, formed by cutting off the top. **2** the part of a solid between two planes. [L, a fragment]

frutex (froo´teks) *n.* (*pl.* **frutices** (-tisēz)) a woody plant smaller than a tree, a shrub. **frutescent** (-tes´-) *a.* shrubby. **frutescence** *n.* **fruticetum** (-sē´təm) *n.* (*pl.* **fruticetums, fruticeta**) an arboretum for fruit trees and shrubs. **fruticose** *a.* **1** of the nature of a shrub, shrubby. **2** (*Zool.*) shrublike in appearance (as certain zoophytes). [L]

fry[1] (frī) *v.t.* (*3rd pers. sing. pres.* **fries,** *pres.p.* **frying,** *past, p.p.* **fried**) **1** to cook with hot fat or oil in a pan. **2** to burn or overheat. **3** (*sl.*) to electrocute. ~*v.i.* **1** to be cooked with hot fat or oil in a pan. **2** to be burnt or overheated. **3** (*sl.*) to be electrocuted. ~*n.* (*pl.* **fries**) **1** a dish of anything fried. **2** the liver, lights, heart etc. of pigs, sheep, calves or oxen. **3** (*pl.*) potato chips. **4** (*N Am.*) a social gathering at which the main food is fried. **5** a state of worry, agitation or excitement. **to fry up** to heat or reheat in a frying pan. **fried** *a.* (*sl.*) drunk. **fryer, frier** *n.* **1** a vessel or pan for frying. **2** a person who fries. **3** (*N Am.*) a young chicken suitable for frying. **frying pan,** (*N Am.*) **frypan** *n.* a shallow metal pan with a long handle, in which food is fried. **out of the frying pan into the fire** out of one trouble into another that is worse. **fry-up** *n.* (*coll.*) a dish of various fried food. [OF *frire*, L *frīgere*, cp. Gr. *phrugein*, to parch]

fry[2] (frī) *n.pl.* **1** young fish, esp. those fresh from the spawn, also yearling salmon. **2** the young of certain other creatures, e.g. frogs. **3** a swarm of children. **4** †a quantity of trifling objects. [cp. Icel. *friō*, Dan. and Swed. *frō*]

FS *abbr.* Flight Sergeant.

FSA *abbr.* Fellow of the Society of Antiquaries.

FSH *abbr.* follicle-stimulating hormone.

FT *abbr.* Financial Times. **FT Index** *n.* any of a number of indicators of the general trend in share prices, based on the movements of selected shares and published daily in the Financial Times.

ft. *abbr.* **1** foot, feet. **2** fort.

FTC *abbr.* (*N Am.*) Federal Trade Commission.

fth, fthm *abbr.* fathom.

ft lb *abbr.* foot-pound.

FTP *abbr.* (*Comput.*) file-transfer protocol.

FT–SE *abbr.* Financial Times–Stock Exchange.

fubsy (fŭb´zi), **fubby** (-i) *a.* (*comp.* **fubsier, fubbier,** *superl.* **fubsiest, fubbiest**) fat, squat. [from obs. *fub*, chubby, onomat.]

fuchsia (fū´shə) *n.* any garden plant of the genus *Fuchsia*, with hanging purple, red or white funnel-shaped flowers. [L *Fuchs*, German botanist, 1501–66]

fuchsine (fook´sēn) *n.* a magenta dye of the rosaniline series. [from FUCHSIA, owing to resemblance to flower]

fuci FUCUS.

fuck (fŭk) *v.i., v.t.* (*taboo., sl.*) to have sexual intercourse (with). ~*n.* (*taboo., sl.*) **1** an act of sexual intercourse. **2** a partner in sexual intercourse. ~*int.* (*taboo., sl.*) used to express violent displeasure or one's disregard or defiance of someone. **fuck all** nothing at all. **not to give a fuck** not to care in the least. **to fuck about/around** **1** to waste time, to mess around. **2** to treat inconsiderately. **to fuck off** to go away. **to fuck up** **1** to botch, to damage. **2** to make a mess of. **3** to disturb emotionally. **fucked** *a.* **1** broken, damaged, kaput. **2** exhausted. **fucker** *n.* a (stupid) person, fellow. **fucking** *n.* sexual intercourse. ~*a.* used as an expletive to express one's annoyance with something. ~*adv.* very, extremely. **fuck-up** *n.* a muddle or mess. [etym. uncertain; perh. G *ficken*, to strike, to fuck]

fucus (fū´kəs) *n.* (*pl.* **fuci** (fū´sī)) **1** a genus of algae, containing some of the commonest seaweeds. **2** any species of this genus. **fucivorous** (-siv´-) *a.* feeding on seaweed, as the sirenians. **fucoid** *a.* resembling a fucus. ~*n.* a fossil plant, like a fucus. **fucoidal** (-koi´-) *a.* [L, rock-lichen, red dye, rouge]

fuddle (fŭd´əl) *v.t.* **1** to make stupid with drink, to intoxicate. **2** to confuse. ~†*v.i.* to tipple, to get drunk.

~*n.* **1** a drinking bout. **2** intoxication. **3** the state of being muddled. **fuddler** *n.* a drunkard, a sot. [cp. LG *fuddeln*, to work lazily]

fuddy-duddy (fŭd´idŭdi) *a.* (*coll.*) **1** old-fogeyish, old-fashioned. **2** stuffy, pompous. **3** fussy, prim, censorious. ~*n.* (*pl.* **fuddy-duddies**) a fuddy-duddy person.

fudge[1] (fŭj) *n.* **1** a soft sweet of chocolate, candy etc. **2** a made-up or nonsensical story. **3** nonsense. ~*int.* used to express mild annoyance. [onomat., or same as FUDGE[2]]

fudge[2] (fŭj) *v.t.* **1** to deal with in a makeshift, careless way. **2** to falsify, to fake, to make imprecise, esp. as a means of covering up unpalatable facts. **3** to dodge, to evade. **4** to patch or make up, to fake. ~*v.i.* **1** to do things in a makeshift way. **2** to be evasive and imprecise. **3** to cheat. ~*n.* **1** a makeshift compromise. **2** an evasion. **3** an item of late news inserted into a newspaper. **4** an attachment on a printing machine for the insertion of this. **fudgy** *a.* [etym. uncertain; perh. var. of FADGE]

fuehrer FÜHRER.

fuel (fū´əl) *n.* (*pres.p.* **fuelling,** (*N Am.*) **fueling,** *past, p.p.* **fuelled,** (*N Am.*) **fueled**) **1** combustible matter, such as wood, coal or peat burnt to provide heat or power. **2** fissile material for use in a nuclear reactor. **3** food considered as a source of energy. **4** anything which serves to feed or increase passion or excitement. ~*v.t.* **1** to supply or store with fuel. **2** to feed, increase or sustain. ~*v.i.* to get or receive fuel. **fuel cell** *n.* a cell in which chemical energy is continuously converted into electrical energy. **fuel element** *n.* a can containing nuclear fuel for use in a reactor. **fuel injection** *n.* a system whereby fuel is introduced directly into the combustion chamber of an internal-combustion engine, without the need for a carburettor. **fuel-injected** *a.* **fuelless** *a.* **fuelling,** (*N Am.*) **fueling** *n.* fuel, firing. **fuel oil** *n.* an oil that is used for fuel, esp. in engines and furnaces. **fuel rod** *n.* a rod-shaped fuel element in a nuclear reactor. [A-F *fewaile*, OF *fouaille*, low L *focālia*, neut. pl. of *focālis*, from *focus*, a hearth]

fuero (fweə´rō) *n.* (*pl.* **fueros**) (*Hist.*) **1** in Spain, a code, charter, grant of privileges or custom having the force of law. **2** a tribunal or a place where justice is administered. [Sp., L *forum*, see FORUM]

fug (fŭg) *n.* (*coll.*) the close atmosphere of an unventilated room. ~*v.i.* (*pres.p.* **fugging,** *past, p.p.* **fugged**) to remain in or enjoy a fug. **fuggy** *a.* [etym. unknown]

fugacious (fūgā´shəs) *a.* **1** fleeting, lasting only a short time, transitory, ephemeral. **2** (*Bot.*) falling off early. **fugaciously** *adv.* **fugaciousness** *n.* **fugacity** (-gas´-) *n.* **1** fleetingness, transience. **2** (*Chem.*) the tendency to expand or escape. [L *fugax -ācis*, from *fugere*, to flee]

fugal, fugato FUGUE.

-fuge (fūj) *comb. form* expelling, driving out, as in *febrifuge*. [L *-fugus*, from *fugere*, to flee, but altered in meaning to *fugāre*, to put to flight]

fugitive (fū´jitiv) *a.* **1** fleeing, running away, having taken flight, runaway. **2** transient, not stable or durable, volatile, easily wafted or carried away. **3** fleeting, evanescent, ephemeral, of only passing interest. ~*n.* **1** a person who flees from danger, pursuit, justice, bondage or duty. **2** a runaway, a deserter, a refugee. **3** a person or thing hard to be caught or detained. **fugitively** *adv.* **fugitiveness** *n.* [F *fugitif -tive*, L *fugitīvus*, from *fugere*, to flee]

fugleman (fū´gəlmən) *n.* (*pl.* **fuglemen**) **1** a soldier who takes up a position in front of a company as a guide to the others in their drill. **2** a person who sets an example for others to follow, a leader, a ringleader. **3** a spokesman. **fugle** *v.i.* to out as a fugleman. [G *Flügelmann* (*Flügel*, wing, *Mann*, man)]

fugue (fūg) *n.* **1** a musical composition on one or more short subjects, which are repeated by successively entering voices and developed contrapuntally. **2** (*Psych.*) an attempt to escape from reality. **3** (*Psych.*) loss of memory coupled with disappearance from one's usual environments. ~*v.i.* (*3rd pers. sing. pres.* **fugues,** *pres.p.* **fuguing,** *past, p.p.* **fugued**) to compose or play a fugue. **fugal** *a.* in the style or nature of a fugue. **fugally** *adv.* **fugato** (foogah´tō, fū-) *adv., a.* in the fugue style but not in strict fugal form. **fugued** *a.* in the style of a fugue. **fuguist** *n.* a writer or performer of fugues. [F, from It. *fuga*, L *fuga*, flight, cogn. with *fugere*, to flee]

führer (fū´rə, fü´-), **fuehrer** *n.* **1** a leader, esp. one who exerts tyrannical authority. **2** (**Führer, Fuehrer**) the head of the National–Socialist German government, the title assumed by Adolf Hitler from 1934. [G, leader]

-ful (ful, fəl) *suf.* **1** full of, abounding in, having, able to, as in *artful, beautiful, sinful, mournful, wilful.* **2** (*pl.* **-fuls**) the quantity or number required to fill, as in *cupful, handful, houseful.* [OE *full*, see FULL[1]]

Fulah (foo´lah), **Fula** (foo´lə) *n.* (*pl.* **Fulah, Fula, Fulahs, Fulas**) **1** a member of one of the peoples of W and central Africa. **2** the language of this people. [Afr. name]

fulcrum (ful´krəm, fŭl´-) *n.* (*pl.* **fulcra** (-krə), **fulcrums**) **1** the fixed point on which the bar of a lever rests or about which it turns. **2** a means of making any kind of force or influence effective. **3** (*Zool., Bot.*) an additional organ, such as a stipule, scale, spine etc. **fulcraceous** (-krā´-), **fulcral, fulcrant** *a.* **fulcrate** (-krət) *a.* (*Bot.*) furnished with or supported by fulcra. [L, a support, from *fulcīre*, to prop]

fulfil (fulfil´), (*N Am.*) **fulfill** *v.t.* (*pres.p.* **fulfilling,** *past, p.p.* **fulfilled**) **1** to accomplish, to carry out, to execute, to perform. **2** to satisfy, to correspond to, to comply with. **3** to fill out. **4** to finish, to complete (a term of office etc.). **5** (*also reflex.*) to realize the potential of. **fulfillable** *a.* **fulfilled** *a.* happy and satisfied. **fulfiller** *n.* **fulfilment, fulfilling** *n.* [OE *fullfyllan* (as FULL[1], FILL)]

fulgent (fŭl´jənt) *a.* (*poet.*) shining, dazzling, exceedingly bright. **fulgently** *adv.* **fulgid** (-jid) *a.* **fulguration** (-gūrā´shən) *n.* **1** in surgery, the destruction of tissue by means of high-frequency electric sparks. **2** (*usu. pl.*) flashing of lightning. **3** †in assaying, the sudden brightening of gold or silver in the crucible as the last traces of dross leave the surface. **fulgurite** (-gūrīt) *n.* (*Geol.*) a vitrified tube in sand, supposed to be produced by the action of lightning. [L *fulgens -ntem*, pres.p. of *fulgēre*, to shine]

fuliginous (fūlij´inəs) *a.* **1** sooty, smoky, soot-coloured. **2** dusky, gloomy. **fuliginosity** (-nos´-) *n.* **fuliginously** *adv.* [L *fūlīginōsus*, from *fūlīgo -inis*, soot]

full[1] (ful) *a.* (*comp.* **fuller,** *superl.* **fullest**) **1** filled up, replete. **2** having no space empty, containing as much as the limits will allow. **3** well supplied, having abundance (of). **4** filled to repletion, satisfied with. **5** charged or overflowing (with feeling etc.). **6** preoccupied or engrossed with. **7** plentiful, copious, ample. **8** complete, perfect, at the height of development. **9** ample or intense in volume or extent, swelling, plump. **10** strong, sonorous. **11** (of clothes etc.) made of a large amount of material. **12** visible in its entire dimensions. **13** (of the moon) having the whole disc illuminated. **14** (of the tide) high. **15** pregnant. **16** (*sl.*) drunk. ~*adv.* **1** quite, equally. **2** completely, exactly, directly. **3** very. **4** more than adequately. ~*n.* **1** complete measure or degree. **2** the utmost or fullest extent. **3** the highest state or point. **4** a state of satiety. **5** the state or time of a full moon. ~*v.t.* to fill (out), to give fullness to, to make full. ~*v.i.* to become full. **at full blast** BLAST. **at full length** LENGTH. **at full pelt** PELT[1]. **at full stretch** STRETCH. **at**

full tilt TILT. **at the full 1** at the height or the highest condition. **2** (of the moon) with the whole disc illuminated. **full and by** (*Naut.*) close-hauled but with the sails filling. **full as a goog** very drunk. **full of beans** BEAN. **full of oneself** having an exaggerated view of one's own importance. **full speed/ steam ahead** used as an order to go or work as fast as possible. **in full** completely, without abridgement, abatement or deduction. **in full cry** CRY. **in full face** with all the face visible towards the spectator. **in full fig** FIG[2]. **in full rig** RIG[1]. **in full swing** SWING. **in full view** completely visible. **not the full quid** QUID[1]. **on a full stomach** STOMACH. **(the) full whack** WHACK. **to come full circle** CIRCLE. **to the full** to the utmost extent. **full age** *n.* the status of being an adult, with responsibilities and rights. **full-back** *n.* in football, hockey etc., a defensive player, usu. the rearmost in any on-field formation. **full beam** *n.* the brightest setting of the headlights of a car or other motor vehicle. **full blast** *adv.* at full blast. **full-blooded** *a.* **1** vigorous. **2** sensual. **3** of pure blood, not hybrid. **full-bloodedly** *adv.* **full-bloodedness** *n.* **full-blown** *a.* **1** fully expanded, as a flower. **2** mature, perfect, fully developed. **3** fully qualified. **full board** *n.* the provision by a hotel etc. of accommodation and all meals. **full-bodied** *a.* having a full, rich flavour or quality. **full-bottomed** *a.* (of a wig) long at the back. **full-bound** *a.* (of books) bound entirely in leather. **full brother** *n.* a brother having both parents in common. **full colour,** (*N Am.*) **full color** *n.* the complete range of colours. **full-colour, full-coloured** *a.* **full-cream** *a.* (of milk) not skimmed. **full dress** *n.* **1** formal dress worn on ceremonial occasions. **2** evening dress. **full-dress** *a.* at which full dress is to be worn. **full-dress debate** *n.* a debate previously arranged on some important question, in contrast to one arising casually. **full employment** *n.* the condition in which the labour force and other resources in a community are used to their greatest extent. **full face** *adv.* with all the face visible towards the spectator. **full-faced** *a.* **1** having a broad chubby face. **2** with all the face visible towards the spectator. **3** (of type) having the heavy lines very thick. **full-fashioned** *a.* FULLY-FASHIONED (under FULL[1]). **fullflavoured,** (*N Am.*) **full-flavored** *a.* **1** strongly flavoured, highly spiced. **2** (*sl.*) (of a story) indecent. **full-fledged** FULLY-FLEDGED (under FULL[1]). **full flood** *n.* **1** the tide at its highest level. **2** speaking with great speed and fluency (*in full flood*). **full-frontal** *a.* **1** (of a nude) with the genitals fully revealed. **2** unrestrained, omitting no detail. **full-grown** *a.* mature, fully developed. **full growth** *n.* the most mature, fully developed stage. **full hand** FULL HOUSE (under FULL[1]). **full-hearted** *a.* **1** brave, confident, courageous. **2** full of feeling, deeply stirred. **full-heartedly** *adv.* **full-heartedness** *n.* **full house** *n.* **1** (*also* **full hand**) (in poker) three of a kind and a pair. **2** in bingo etc., the set of numbers needed to win. **3** an auditorium filled to capacity. **fullish** *a.* **full-length** *a.* **1** of or showing the entire figure. **2** of the standard or greatest length. ~*n.* a full-length portrait. ~*adv.* stretched to the full extent. **full lock** *n.* **1** maximum turn imparted to the front wheels of a vehicle. **2** the full extent to which the front wheels will turn. **full marks** *n.pl.* the highest score in a test, examination or other assessment. **full moon** *n.* **1** the moon with its whole disc illuminated. **2** the time at which this occurs. **full-mouthed** *a.* **1** (of livestock) having a full set of teeth. **2** (of a dog) baying loudly. **3** spoken loudly. **full nelson** *n.* in wrestling, a form of nelson in which both arms are passed under the opponent's arms. **fullness, fulness** *n.* **1** the state or quality of being full. **2** completeness, satiety. **3** largeness, richness, volume, force. **4** everything contained in (the earth etc.). **in the fullness of time** at the eventual time. **the fullness of the heart** full, true feelings. **full out** *adv.* **1** at full power. **2** fully, completely. **3** (*Print.*) adjoining the margin, not indented. **full-page** *a.* taking up a whole page. **full pelt** *adv.* at full pelt. **full pitch** *n., adv.* FULL TOSS (under FULL[1]). **full point** FULL STOP (under FULL[1]). **full professor** *n.* a professor of the highest academic grade at a university etc. **full sail** *adv.* with all sails set and a fair wind. **full-scale** *a.* **1** of the same size as the original. **2** using all available resources. **3** all-out. **full score** *n.* the complete score of a musical composition, showing the part for each performer separately. **full sister** *n.* a sister having both parents in common. **full stop** *n.* **1** (*also* **full point**) a punctuation mark (.), used at the end of a sentence or an abbreviation. **2** an abrupt finish. **full term** *n.* the normal or expected end date for a pregnancy. **full-term** *a.* **full-throated** *a.* with the full power of the voice. **full tilt** *adv.* at full tilt. **full time** *n.* **1** the end of play in a sports match. **2** the total usual duration of work. **full-time** *adv.* for the whole of the (standard) working week. ~*a.* working or using the whole of the (standard) working week. **full-timer** *n.* **full toss** *n.* in cricket, a delivery which reaches the batsman without touching the ground. ~*adv.* without the delivery touching the ground. **full up** *adv.* completely full, with no room for more. **fully** *adv.* **1** completely, entirely, quite. **2** not less than. **-fully** (fuli, fəli) *suf.* forming adverbs, as in *dreadfully.* **fully-fashioned, full-fashioned** *a.* shaped to the lines of the body. **fully-fledged, full-fledged** *a.* **1** (of a bird) having all its feathers. **2** fully qualified, having full status as. **3** fully developed, mature. [OE *full* (cp. Dut. *vol*, Icel. *fullr*, Goth. *fullo*, G *voll*, Sansk. *pūrna*, L *plēnus*, Gr. *plērēs*)]

full[2] (ful) *v.t.* to cleanse and thicken (cloth). **fuller**[2] *n.* a person whose occupation is to full cloth. **fuller's earth** *n.* a kind of clay that absorbs grease, esp. used in fulling cloth. **fullery** *n.* (*pl.* **fulleries**) a place where cloth is fulled. **fulling-mill** *n.* [OF *fouler*, late L *fullāre*, from L *fullo*, a fuller]

fuller[1] FULL[1].

fuller[2] FULL[2].

fuller[3] (ful´ə) *n.* **1** a blacksmith's tool for making grooves. **2** a groove made by this. ~*v.t.* to form a groove or channel in with this. [etym. unknown]

fullerene (ful´ərēn) *n.* (*Chem.*) a molecule consisting of 60 carbon atoms arranged in spherical shape, with possible uses as a lubricant, superconductor etc., also called a *Buckyball.* [Buckminster *Fuller*, 1895–1963, US inventor of the geodesic dome]

☒ **fullfil** common misspelling of FULFIL.

fulmar (ful´mə) *n.* a seabird of the genus *Fulmaris glacialis*, allied to the petrels, abundant in the Arctic seas. [prob. Scand. (cp. Icel. *fūll*, FOUL, *mar*, a MEW[2])]

fulminate[1] (fŭl´mināt, ful´-) *v.i.* **1** to lighten or thunder. **2** to explode with a loud noise or report, to detonate. **3** to express denunciations very loudly. **4** (of a disease) to develop suddenly. ~*v.t.* **1** to cause to explode. **2** to utter (threats, denunciations or censures). **fulminant** *a.* **1** fulminating. **2** (of diseases) developing suddenly. **fulminating** *a.* thundering, explosive. **fulminating powder** *n.* an explosive compound. **fulmination** (-ā´shən) *n.* **fulminatory** *a.* **fulminous** *a.* **1** severely critical. **2** relating to thunder and lightning. [L *fulminātus*, p.p. of *fulmināre*, from *fulmen*, lightning]

fulminate[2] (fŭl´minət) *n.* **1** a salt of fulminic acid. **2** an explosive containing this. **fulminic** (-min´-) *a.* of, relating to or capable of detonation. **fulminic acid** *n.* an unisolated acid that unites with certain metals to form explosive fulminates.

fulness FULLNESS (under FULL[1]).

fulsome (ful´səm) *a.* **1** (esp. of compliments, flattery etc.) disgusting by excess or grossness, coarse, excessive, satiating. **2** abundant, copious. **fulsomely** *adv.* **fulsomeness** *n.*

Usage note The use of *fulsome* in a favourable sense is now widely disapproved of, though in fact it is the oldest use of the word.

fulvous (fŭl´vəs) *a.* tawny, reddish yellow. **fulvescent** (-ves´-) *a.* [L *fulvus*]

fumarole (fū´mərōl) *n.* **1** a hole in the ground in a volcanic region forming an exit for subterranean vapours. **2** a smoke vent. **fumarolic** (-rol´-) *a.* [It. *fumaruolo*, L *fūmāriolum*, dim. of *fūmārium*, from *fūmāre*, to smoke]

fumatorium (fūmətaw´riəm) *n.* (*pl.* **fumatoriums, fumatoria** (-riə)) **1** a room or apparatus for fumigating. **2** a chamber in a conservatory etc. for destroying insects by chemical fumes. [L *fūmāre*, to smoke]

fumatory (fū´mətəri) *n.* (*pl.* **fumatories**) a place for smoking or fumigation.

fumble (fŭm´bəl) *v.i.* **1** to grope about. **2** to act, esp. to use one's hands, in an uncertain, aimless or awkward manner. **3** to bungle in any business. **4** †to stammer, to be confused. ~*v.t.* **1** to handle or manage awkwardly. **2** to fail to catch or hold. **3** to deal with in an uncertain or hesitating manner. ~*n.* an act or instance of fumbling. **fumbler** *n.* **1** a person who acts awkwardly. **2** a fumbling attempt. **fumblingly** *adv.* [perh. from Dut. *fommelen* (cogn. with OE *folm*, L *palma*, the palm of the hand)]

fume (fūm) *n.* **1** (*usu. pl.*) a smoke, vapour or gas, esp. an unpleasant or toxic one. **2** mental agitation, esp. an angry mood. **3** anything empty, fleeting or unsubstantial. **4** †incense. **5** †smoke. ~*v.i.* **1** to emit smoke or vapour. **2** to pass off in smoke or vapour. **3** to show irritation, to fret, to chafe. ~*v.t.* **1** to dry, perfume, stain or cure with smoke, esp. to darken (oak, photographic plates etc.) with chemical fumes, as of ammonia. **2** to dissipate in vapour. **3** to flatter. **4** to perfume. **5** to fumigate. **fume cupboard, fume chamber, fume hood** *n.* a ventilated enclosure for experimenting with or storing chemicals with harmful vapours. **fumeless** *a.* **fumingly** *adv.* **1** angrily. **2** with passion. **fumy** *a.* **1** full or composed of fumes. **2** causing fumes. **3** smoky, vaporous. [OF *fum*, L *fūmus*, smoke]

fumet (fūmet´), **fumette** *n.* **1** the smell of game or meat when high. **2** a concentrated, esp. game, stock. [F, from *fumer*, L *fūmāre*, to smoke, as FUME]

fumigate (fū´migāt) *v.t.* **1** to subject to the action of smoke or vapour, esp. for the purpose of disinfection. **2** †to perfume. **fumigant** *n.* **fumigation** (-gā´shən) *n.* **fumigator** *n.* a person or thing that fumigates, esp. an apparatus for applying smoke, gas etc. for the purpose of cleansing, disinfecting, or perfuming. [L *fūmigātus*, p.p. of *fūmigāre* (*fūmus*, smoke, *-ig-*, *ag-*, base of *agere*, to drive)]

fumingly FUME.

fumitory (fū´mitəri) *n.* (*pl.* **fumitories**) a herb belonging to the genus *Fumaria*, esp. *F. officinalis*, formerly used for skin diseases. [ME and OF *fumeterre* (*fume de terre*), late L *fūmus terræ*, smoke of the earth]

fumy FUME.

fun (fŭn) *n.* **1** (a source of) amusement, enjoyment, pleasure. **2** hectic activity or argument. ~*a.* (*coll.*) **1** enjoyable. **2** amusing, entertaining. **for fun** for pleasure simply. **for the fun of it** for fun. **in fun** as a joke. **like fun 1** (*coll.*) energetically. **2** (*coll.*) thoroughly. **3** (*coll., iron.*) not at all. **to be great/ good fun** to be very enjoyable or amusing. **to have fun** to enjoy oneself. **to make fun of 1** to hold up to or turn into ridicule, to mock. **2** to banter. **to poke fun at** to make fun of. **what fun!** how enjoyable. **fun and games** *n.* (*iron.*) frivolous activity, trouble. **funboard** *n.* in windsurfing, a kind of board that is less steady but faster than a normal board. **funfair** *n.* a usu. outdoor show with rides, sideshows, games of skill and other amusements. **fun fur** *n.* inexpensive, artificial fur (often dyed) for clothes, seat covers etc. **fun run** *n.* (*coll.*) a long-distance run organized not as a competition but for enjoyment, to raise money for charity etc. **funster** (fŭn´stə) *n.* a person who makes fun; a teaser or joker. [prob. corr. of *fon*, to make a fool of]

funambulist (fūnam´būlist) *n.* a rope-walker or rope-dancer; a performer on the tight or slack rope. **funambulate** *v.i.* to walk or dance on a rope. **funambulation** (-lā´shən) *n.* **funambulatory** *a.* performing like a rope-dancer. [earlier *funambule*, L *fūnambulus* (*fūnis*, rope, *ambūlare*, to walk)]

function (fŭngk´shən) *n.* **1** the specific activity, operation or power belonging to an agent. **2** duty, occupation, office. **3** a public or official ceremony. **4** a social entertainment of some importance. **5** the specific purpose of any animal or plant organ. **6** (*Comput.*) a part of a program corresponding to a single value. **7** (*Math.*) a quantity dependent for its value on another or other quantities so that a change in the second correspondingly affects the first. ~*v.i.* **1** to perform a function or duty. **2** to operate. **functional** *a.* **1** of or relating to some office or function; official. **2** formal. **3** practical, utilitarian, avoiding ornament. **4** able to perform (its function), working. **5** of, relating to or affecting the action or functions of an organ, not its substance or structure. **6** (of a mental disorder) not having a direct organic cause. **7** (*Math.*) relating to or depending on a function. **functional disease** *n.* derangement of some function of the body, as distinguished from organic or structural disease. **functional food** *n.* a food that contains additives which contribute to good health. **functional group** *n.* (*Chem.*) the group of atoms in a compound that determines the chemical behaviour of the compound. **functionalism** *n.* emphasis on the practical usefulness of a thing. **functionalist** *n.* **functionality** (-al´-) *n.* **functionally** *adv.* **functionary** *n.* (*pl.* **functionaries**) a person who holds any office or trust; an official. ~*a.* **1** of or relating to a function or functions. **2** official. **function key** *n.* (*Comput.*) a key that generates special instructions. **functionless** *a.* **function word** *n.* (*Gram.*) a word whose purpose is to connect or modify the meaning of other words rather than express meaning itself. [OF (F *fonction*), L *functiōnem*, nom. *functio*, from *fungī*, to perform]

fund (fŭnd) *n.* **1** a sum of money or stock of anything available for use or enjoyment. **2** (*pl.*) assets, capital. **3** a sum of money set apart for a specific purpose, permanent or temporary. **4** (*pl.*) **a** money lent to a government and constituting a national debt. **b** the stock of a national debt regarded as an investment. **c** (*coll.*) money, finances, financial resources. **5** †the bottom. ~*v.t.* **1** to provide money for. **2** to amass, collect, store. **3** to place in a fund. **4** to convert into a single fund or debt, esp. to consolidate into stock or securities bearing interest at a fixed rate. **in funds** (*coll.*) provided with cash, flush with money. **fundable** *a.* **funded** *a.* **1** invested in public funds. **2** forming part of the national debt of a country, existing in the form of bonds bearing regular interest. **funded debt** *n.* the portion of the national debt converted into bonds and annuities. **fundholder** *n.* **1** a person who has property invested in the public funds. **2** a general practitioner who is provided with and controls their own budget. **fundholding** *n., a.* **funding** *n.* financial provision, support. **fundless** *a.* **fund-raiser** *n.* a person who raises money for an (often charitable) organization, project etc. **fund-raising** *n., a.* [F *fond*, L *fundus*, the bottom; later assim. to L]

fundament (fŭn´dəmənt) *n.* **1** (*facet.*) the lower part of the body, the buttocks. **2** (*facet.*) the anus. **3** a foundation. [ME and OF *fondement*, L *fundāmentum*, from *fundāre*, to found (later form directly from L)]

fundamental (fŭndəmen´təl) *a.* **1** of, relating to or serving as a foundation or base. **2** basic, essential, primary, original, indispensable. *~n.* **1** (*usu. pl.*) a principle, rule or article forming the basis or groundwork. **2** (*Mus.*) the lowest note of a chord. **fundamental bass** *n.* (*Mus.*) a bass consisting of a succession of fundamental notes. **fundamentalism** *n.* **1** in Christianity, strict belief in the literal truth of the Bible. **2** in Islam, strict observance of the teachings of the Koran and of Islamic law. **3** strict adherence to the fundamental principles of any religion. **fundamentalist** *n., a.* **fundamentality** (-tal´-) *n.* **fundamentally** *adv.* **fundamental note** *n.* (*Mus.*) the lowest note of a chord. **fundamental particle** *n.* a subatomic particle. **fundamental tone** *n.* (*Mus.*) the tone produced by the vibration of the whole of a string etc. [as FUNDAMENT]

fundi FUNDUS.

fundus (fŭndəs) *n.* (*pl.* **fundi** (-dī)) (*Anat.*) the base of an organ or the part furthest away from its opening. [L, bottom]

funeral (fū´nərəl) *n.* **1** the ceremony held at the burial or cremation of a dead person. **2** a procession of people at a funeral. **3** (*coll.*) someone's concern or affair in which they alone will be (adversely) affected (*that's your funeral!*). *~a.* of, relating to or connected with the committal of the dead. **funebrial** (-nē´bri-) *a.* funerary. **funeral director** *n.* an undertaker. **funeral home** *n.* (*N Am.*) funeral parlour. **funeral honours,** (*N Am.*) **funeral honors** *n.pl.* marks of respect paid to the deceased at a funeral. **funeral parlour,** (*N Am.*) **funeral parlor** *n.* a place where the dead are prepared for burial or cremation and funerals may be held. **funeral pile, funeral pyre** *n.* a pile of wood etc. on which a dead body is burnt. **funeral urn** *n.* an urn that holds the ashes of a cremated corpse. **funerary** *a.* of, used at or relating to funerals. **funereal** (-niə´ri-) *a.* **1** of, relating to or suitable for a funeral. **2** dismal, sad, mournful. **3** gloomy, dark. **funereally** *adv.* [OF, from late L *fūnerālis*, from *fūnus fūneris*, a funeral procession]

fungi FUNGUS.

fungible (fŭn´jibəl) *a.* (*Law*) of such a nature that it may be replaced by another thing of the same class. *~n.pl.* movable goods which may be valued by weight or measure. **fungibility** (-bil´-) *n.* [med. L *fungibilis*, from *fungī*, to perform, operate, see FUNCTION]

fungus (fŭng´gəs) *n.* (*pl.* **fungi** (-gī, -jī), **funguses**) **1** a mushroom, toadstool, mould, mildew, or other cryptogamous plant, without chlorophyll and feeding on organic matter. **2** a morbid growth or excrescence of a spongy nature. **3** something of rapid or parasitic growth. **4** (*sl.*) a beard. **fungaceous** (-gā´-) *a.* **fungal** *a.* of, relating to or of the nature of a fungus. *~n.* a fungus. **fungic** (-jik) *a.* obtained from fungi. **fungicide** (-jisīd) *n.* anything that destroys fungi or their spores. **fungicidal** *a.* **fungiform** (-jifawm), **fungiliform** (-jil´-) *a.* having a termination like the head of a fungus. **fungistatic** (-jistat´ik) *a.* slowing down the growth of fungi. **fungistatically** *adv.* **fungivorous** (-jiv´-) *a.* feeding on fungi. **fungoid** (-goid) *a.* of the nature of or like a fungus. *~n.* a fungoid plant. **fungology** (-gol´-) *n.* the science of fungi. **fungological** (-loj´-) *a.* **fungologist** (-gol´-) *n.* **fungosity** (-gos´-) *n.* **fungous** *a.* **1** like or of the nature of a fungus. **2** excrescent, springing up suddenly, ephemeral. **3** spongy, unsubstantial. **fungusy** *a.* [L, prob. cogn. with Gr. *sphongos*, a SPONGE]

funicular (fūnik´ūlə, fən-) *a.* **1** of, relating to, consisting of, or depending on a rope or cable. **2** (of a mountain railway) operated by means of a cable. *~n.* a railway worked by means of a cable, usu. a mountain railway. **funicle** (fū´nikəl) *n.* (*Bot.*) a funiculus. **funiculus** (-ləs) *n.* (*pl.* **funiculi** (-lī)) **1** the umbilical cord. **2** a number of nerve fibres enclosed in a tubular sheath. **3** (*Bot.*) a cord connecting the seed with the placenta. [L *fūniculus*, dim. of *fūnis*, a rope, -AR[1]]

funk[1] (fŭngk) *n.* (*sl.*) **1** a state of fear or panic. **2** a coward. *~v.i.* **1** to be in a state of terror. **2** to flinch, to shrink in fear or cowardice. *~v.t.* **1** to be afraid of. **2** to shirk, to try to evade through fear or cowardice. **3** (*usu. p.p.*) to frighten, to scare. **in a funk** (*N Am.*) in a state of despondency or depression. **funker** *n.* **funkhole** *n.* **1** a dugout. **2** any refuge someone can retreat to. **funky**[1] *a.* (*comp.* **funkier,** *superl.* **funkiest**) **1** very fearful, terrified. **2** cowardly. [etym. uncertain]

funk[2] (fŭngk) *n.* **1** (*N Am., sl.*) a stink. **2** funky music. *~†v.t.* to blow smoke upon so as to stifle or annoy. *~v.i.* †to smoke. **funky**[2] *a.* (*comp.* **funkier,** *superl.* **funkiest**) **1** (of jazz, pop etc.) having a strong rhythmical beat, earthy, unsophisticated, soulful, like early blues. **2** fashionable. **3** unconventional, odd, quaint. **4** smelly, stinking. **funkily** *adv.* **funkiness** *n.* [etym. uncertain (perh. from OF *funkier*, ult. from L *fūmigāre*, see FUMIGATE)]

funkia (fŭng´kiə) *n.* HOSTA. [former genus name, from H. C. *Funck*, 1771–1839, German botanist]

funky[1] FUNK[1].

funky[2] FUNK[2].

funnel (fŭn´əl) *n.* **1** a conical vessel usu. terminating below in a tube, for pouring liquids etc. into vessels with a small opening. **2** a tube or shaft for ventilation, lighting etc. **3** something resembling a funnel in shape or function. **4** the chimney of a steamship or steam-engine. **5** the inside of a chimney, a flue. *~v.t.* (*pres.p.* **funnelling,** (*N Am.*) **funneling,** *past, p.p.* **funnelled,** (*N Am.*) **funneled**) to pour or pass (as if) through a funnel. *~v.i.* to move (as if) through a funnel. **funnel-form, funnel-shaped** *a.* (*Bot.*) (of a calyx, corolla etc.) having the tube gradually enlarging upwards so as to constitute a funnel. **funnelled,** (*N Am.*) **funneled** *a.* **1** having a funnel or funnels. **2** funnel-shaped. **funnel-like** *a.* **funnel-net** *n.* a tapering, funnel-shaped net. **funnel-web spider** *n.* (*Austral.*) a large venomous spider, *Atrax robustus*, found in New South Wales. [ME *fonel*, prob. through OF (cp. Prov. *founil*, Sp. *fonil*, Port. *funil*), from late L *fundibulum* (L *infundibulum*), from *fundere*, to pour]

funny[1] (fŭn´i) *a.* (*comp.* **funnier,** *superl.* **funniest**) **1** amusing, causing mirth or laughter. **2** droll, comical, laughable. **3** strange, curious, odd, puzzling. **4** suspicious; underhand, involving trickery. **5** (*coll.*) slightly unwell. *~n.* (*pl.* **funnies**) (*coll.*) **1** a joke. **2** (*pl.*) comic strips or the comics section of a newspaper. **funnily** *adv.* **funniness** *n.* **funniosity** (-os´-) *n.* (*pl.* **funniosities**) **1** a comical thing. **2** comicality. **funny bone** *n.* the lower part of the elbow over which the ulnar nerve passes, a blow on which causes a curious tingling sensation. **funny business** *n.* **1** (*coll.*) dubious or suspicious goings-on; trickery. **2** jokes, drollery. **funny-face** *n.* (*coll.*) used as an affectionate form of address. **funny farm** *n.* (*sl.*) a mental hospital. **funny-ha-ha** *a.* (*coll.*) funny in its amusing or comical sense. **funnyism** *n.* **funny man** *n.* (*pl.* **funny men**) **1** a clown. **2** a buffoon or wag. **funny money** *n.* (*coll.*) counterfeit or inflated money. **funny paper** *n.* a newspaper or magazine that contains comical matter. **funny-peculiar** *a.* (*coll.*) funny in its strange or odd sense. [see FUN]

funny[2] (fŭn´i) *n.* (*pl.* **funnies**) a narrow, clinker-built pleasure boat, for a pair of sculls. [etym. uncertain, perh. from FUNNY[1]]

funster FUN.

fur (fœ) *n.* **1** the soft fine hair growing thickly upon certain animals, distinct from ordinarily longer hair. **2** (*pl.*) the skins, esp. dressed skins, of such animals. **3** the skin of such animals used for lining or trimming garments. **4** a lining, trimming or garment made of fur.

5 (*as pl.*) fur-bearing animals. 6 the downy covering on the skin of a peach. 7 a coat or crust deposited by a liquid. 8 a deposit from wine. 9 a coat of morbid matter collected on the tongue. 10 a crust deposited on the interior of kettles etc. by hard water. 11 (*Her.*) a patched or tufted tincture. ~*v.t.* (*pres.p.* **furring,** *past, p.p.* **furred**) 1 to cover, provide, line or trim with fur. 2 to cover or coat with morbid matter. 3 to nail pieces of timber to (as joists or rafters) in order to bring them into a level. ~*v.i.* to become encrusted with fur or scale, as the inside of a boiler. **the fur will fly** there will be an argument. **to make the fur fly** to create a scene, to start a row. **fur and feather** *n.pl.* fur-bearing animals and game birds. **furless** *a.* **furred** *a.* 1 lined or ornamented with fur. 2 coated with fur or scale. **furrier** (fŭr´iə) *n.* 1 a dealer in furs. 2 a person who prepares and sells furs. **furriery** *n.* the work of a furrier. **furring** *n.* 1 trimming or lining with furs. 2 a deposit of scale on the inside of boilers etc. 3 thin pieces fixed on the edge of timber to make the surface even. 4 a lining on a brick wall to prevent dampness. 5 double planking on the sides of a ship. **furry** *a.* (*comp.* **furrier,** *superl.* **furriest**) 1 covered in fur, wearing fur. 2 made of fur. 3 of or resembling fur. 4 coated with a scale or deposit. **furriness** *n.* **fur seal** *n.* a seal yielding a fur valuable commercially. [OF *forrer*, to line, to sheathe (F *fourrer*), from Gmc. (cp. OE *fōdor*, G *Futter*, Icel. *fōthr*)]

fur. *abbr.* furlong(s).

furbelow (fœ´bilō) *n.* 1 a piece of material, plaited and puckered, used as trimming on skirts and petticoats, a flounce. 2 (*pl.*) finery (*frills and furbelows*). ~*v.t.* to furnish or trim with furbelows. [var. of FALBALA]

furbish (fœ´bish) *v.t.* 1 to rub so as to brighten, to polish up. 2 to renovate, to restore the newness or brightness of. 3 to clean or brighten (up). **furbisher** *n.* [OF *forbiss-*, stem of *forbir*, OHG *furban*]

furcate[1] (fœ´kāt, -kət) *a.* forked, dividing into branches like the prongs of a fork. [L *furcātus*, from *furca*, a FORK]

furcate[2] (fœ´kāt, fœkāt´) *v.i.* to fork, to divide into branches. **furcation** (-kā´shən) *n.*

furcula (fœ´kūlə) *n.* (*pl.* **furculae** (-lē)) the two clavicles of birds joined together so as to form one V-shaped bone, the wishbone. **furcular** *a.*

furfur (fœ´fə) *n.* (*pl.* **furfures** (fœ´fūrēz, -fərēz)) 1 scurf or dandruff. 2 (*pl.*) particles of scurf, branlike scales of skin. **furfuraceous** (-rā´-) *a.* **furfuration** (-rā´shən) *n.* **furfurous** *a.* [L]

furfurol (fœ´fərol, -fū-) *n.* (*Chem.*) an oil formed in the dry distillation of sugar, or by distilling bran with dilute sulphuric acid. [as FURFUR, -OL]

furioso (fūriō´sō) *adv.* (*Mus.*) with fury or vehemence. ~†*n.* (*pl.* **furiosos**) a furious or impetuous person. [It., as FURIOUS]

furious (fū´riəs) *a.* 1 extremely angry; full of fury, raging, violent, frantic. 2 rushing with vehemence or impetuosity, tempestuous. 3 vehement, eager. **furiosity** (-os´-) *n.* **furiously** *adv.* **furiousness** *n.* [OF *furieus* (F *furieux*), L *furiōsus*, from *furia*, FURY]

furl (fœl) *v.t.* 1 to roll up (a sail) and wrap about a yard, mast or stay. 2 to roll, wrap, fold or close (up). 3 to give up (hopes). ~*v.i.* to become rolled or folded up. **furlable** *a.* [OF *ferler, ferlier*]

furlong (fœ´long) *n.* 1 a measure of length, the eighth part of a mile, 220 yd. (201 m). 2 a group of strips of land in the open-field system of agriculture. [OE *furlang* (*furh*, FURROW, *lang*, LONG[1])]

furlough (fœ´lō) *n.* leave of absence, esp. from military duty or from missionary service. ~*v.t.* (*N Am.*) to grant leave of absence to. ~*v.i.* (*N Am.*) to spend furlough. [Dut. *verlof* (cp. Dan. *forlov*, G *Verlaub*), as FOR-, LEAVE[2]]

furmenty, furmety FRUMENTY.

furnace (fœ´nis) *n.* 1 a chamber or structure containing a chamber in which fuel is burned for the production of intense heat, esp. for melting ores, metals etc. 2 a closed fireplace for heating a boiler, hot water or hot-air pipes etc. 3 a very hot place. 4 a time, place or occasion of severe trial or torture. ~*v.t.* 1 to cast into or heat in a furnace. 2 †to exhale like a furnace. [OF *fornais* (F *fournaise*) L *fornācem*, nom. *-nax*, *for-*, *furnus*, oven]

furnish (fœ´nish) *v.t.* 1 to equip, to fit up, esp. (a house or room) with movable furniture. 2 to provide or supply (with). 3 to supply, to afford, to yield. 4 †to provide with what is necessary. 5 †to decorate. ~*v.i.* (*sl.*) (of a horse) to fill out, to improve in strength and appearance. **furnished** *a.* (of a house, flat etc.) rented or let with furniture. **furnisher** *n.* 1 a dealer in furniture. 2 a person who furnishes. **furnishings** *n.pl.* furniture, carpets, curtains etc. [OF *fourniss-*, stem of *fournir*, ult. from OHG *frumjan*, to perform, provide (cogn. with *fruma*, profit, advantage, G *fromm*, good, Eng. FORMER[1])]

furniture (fœ´nichə) *n.* 1 movable articles, e.g. beds, chairs, tables etc. with which a house or room is furnished. 2 equipment, equipage, outfit. 3 the masts and rigging of a ship. 4 an ornamental addition. 5 (*Print.*) the material, of wood, metal or plastic, which keeps the pages firmly fixed in the chase, and separates them so as to allow a uniform margin when printed. 6 locks, door and window trimmings etc. 7 the mountings of a gun. 8 the trappings of a horse. **furniture beetle** *n.* a beetle, *Anobium puncatatum*, the larvae of which bore into wood. **furniture van** *n.* a large high-sided van for transporting furniture, esp. when moving house. [F *fourniture*, as FURNISH]

furor (fū´raw) *n.* 1 (*N Am.*) FURORE. 2 †rage, fury, madness. [L, from *furere*, to rage]

furore (fūraw´ri, fū´raw) *n.* 1 an uproar, an outburst of public indignation. 2 great excitement or enthusiasm. 3 a craze, a rage. [It., as FUROR]

furphy (fœ´fi) *n.* (*Austral., sl.*) a groundless rumour, a false report (orig. circulated by the drivers of Furphy's military water and sanitary carts). **furphy merchant** *n.* a person who circulates groundless rumours. [J. *Furphy*, maker of the cart in the First World War]

furrier, furring FUR.

furrow (fŭr´ō) *n.* 1 a trench in the earth made by a plough. 2 a narrow trench, groove or hollow. 3 a rut. 4 the track of a ship. 5 a wrinkle on the face. ~*v.t.* 1 to plough. 2 to make grooves, furrows or wrinkles in. 3 to mark (the face) with deep wrinkles. ~*v.i.* to become furrowed. **furrowless** *a.* **furrow-slice** *n.* the strip of earth thrown up from a furrow by the plough. **furrowy** *a.* [OE *furh* (cp. Dut. *voor*, Icel. *for*, G *Furche*)]

furry FUR.

further[1] (fœ´dhə), **farther** (fah´-) *a.* 1 more remote. 2 more advanced. 3 going or extended beyond that already existing or stated, additional. ~*adv.* 1 at or to a greater distance, degree or extent. 2 at or to a more advanced point. 3 moreover, in addition, also. **further to** (*formal*) with reference to (an earlier letter etc.). **till further notice** to continue until clearly changed. **till further orders** till further notice. **to see no further than one's nose** NOSE. **further education** *n.* formal, post-school education usu. below degree level. **furthermore** *adv.* moreover, besides. **furthermost** *a.* furthest, most remote. **furthest** *a.* most remote in time or place. ~*adv.* at or to the greatest distance or extent. **at (the) furthest** at the greatest distance; at most. [OE *furthra*, adv. *furthor* (cogn. with FORE, *-ther* is the comp. suf.), cp. Dut. *vorders*, G *vorder*, Gr. *proteros*, comp. of *pro*]

Usage note The forms *farther* and *farthest*, rather than *further* and *furthest*, are now used only occasionally and restricted to physical distance.

further[2] (fœ´dhə) *v.t.* to help forward, to advance, to promote. **furtherance** *n.* promotion, help, assistance, advancement. **furtherer** *n.*

furtive (fœ´tiv) *a.* **1** stealthy, sly. **2** secret, surreptitious, designed to escape attention. **3** obtained by or as if by theft. **furtively** *adv.* **furtiveness** *n.* [F *furtif*, fem. *furtive*, L *furtīvus*, from *furtum*, theft (*fūr*, a thief, cp. Gr. *phōr*)]

furuncle (fū´rŭngkəl) *n.* a superficial inflammatory tumour, with a central core, a boil. **furuncular** (-rŭng´-), **furunculoid, furunculous** *a.* **furunculosis** (-kyəlōsis) *n.* **1** a skin condition characterized by the presence of many boils. **2** a bacterial disease of salmon and trout. [L *fūrunculus*, orig. dim. of *fūr*, thief]

fury (fū´ri) *n.* (*pl.* **furies**) **1** vehement, uncontrollable anger, rage. **2** a fit of rage. **3** impetuosity, uncontrolled violence. **4** intense, ecstatic passion, inspiration, enthusiasm. **5** (**Fury**) each of the three avenging goddesses of classical mythology. **6** an avenging spirit. **7** a furious woman, a virago. **like fury** (*coll.*) with furious energy. **furylike** *a.* raging, frenzied. [OF *furie*, L *furia*, from *furere*, to rage]

furze (fœz) *n.* gorse. **furzy** *a.* [OE *fyrs*]

fusarole (fū´zərōl) *n.* a moulding placed immediately under the echinus in Doric, Ionic or composite capitals. [F *fusarolle*, It. *fusaruola*, L *fūsus*, a spindle]

fuscous (fŭs´kəs) *a.* brown tinged with grey or black; dingy. [L *fuscus*]

fuse[1] (fūz) *v.t.* **1** to melt. **2** to reduce to a liquid or fluid state by heat. **3** to unite by or as if by melting together. **4** to provide with a fuse. **5** to cause to fail by blowing a fuse. ~*v.i.* **1** to melt. **2** to become fluid. **3** to become united by or as if by melting together. **4** to fail because of a blown fuse. ~*n.* **1** (a device containing) a strip of fusible wire or metal which melts if the current in an electric circuit exceeds a certain value. **2** the melting of wire etc. caused by a short circuit. **to blow a fuse** to lose one's temper. **fuse box** *n.* a box containing one or more fuses. **fuse wire** *n.* the wire used in a fuse. **fusible** *a.* capable of being easily fused or melted. **fusibility** (-bil´-) *n.* **fusible alloy, fusible metal** *n.* an alloy, usually of lead, tin and bismuth, compounded in definite proportions to melt at a given temperature. **fusible plug** *n.* a plug of fusible metal used in a steam boiler or an electric circuit to prevent an excessive increase of temperature. **fusile** (-īl) *a.* **1** fusible. **2** fluid through heat. **3** produced by melting or casting. **fusing point** *n.* the temperature at which a given substance melts. **fusion** (-zhən) *n.* **1** the act of melting or rendering liquid by heat. **2** the state of being so melted or liquefied. **3** union by or as if by melting together, blending. **4** a product of such melting or blending; a fused mass. **5** the combination at very high temperature of atomic nuclei of hydrogen or deuterium to form helium nuclei and liberate nuclear energy (*nuclear fusion*). **6** coalescence or coalition (as of political parties). **fusional** *a.* **fusion bomb** *n.* a bomb, e.g. the hydrogen bomb, whose energy results from nuclear fusion. **fusionism** *n.* **fusionist** *n.* a person who advocates political fusion. **fusion reactor** *n.* a nuclear reactor operating on the fusion principle. [L *fūsus*, p.p. of *fundere*, to pour]

fuse[2] (fūz), **fuze** *n.* **1** a tube, cord or casing filled or saturated with combustible material, and used for igniting a charge in a mine or projectile. **2** a detonating device in a bomb or shell. ~*v.t.* to provide with a fuse or fuses. **fuseless** *a.* [It. *fuso*, L *fūsus*, a spindle]

fusee[1] (fūzē´), (*N Am.*) **fuzee** *n.* **1** the cone round which the chain is wound in a clock or watch. **2** a fuse. **3** a match with a mass of inflammable material at its head, used for lighting pipes etc. in a wind. **4** (*N Am.*) a railway red flare light, used as a warning signal. [F *fusée*, L *fūsāta*, spindleful, orig. fem. p.p. of *fūsāre*, from *fūsus*, a spindle]

†**fusee**[2] FUSIL[1].

fuselage (fū´zəlahzh) *n.* the main body of an aeroplane. [F *fuselé*, spindle-shaped, -AGE]

fusel oil (fū´zəl) *n.* a poisonous oily product, composed chiefly of amyl alcohol, formed during the manufacture of corn, potato or grape spirits. [G *Fusel*, spirits of inferior quality]

fusible FUSE[1].

fusiform (fū´zifawm) *a.* shaped like a spindle, tapering at both ends.

fusil[1] (fū´zil), †**fusee** (-zē´) *n.* an obsolete firelock, lighter than a musket. **fusilier** (-liə´), (*also, N Am.*) **fusileer** *n.* **1** (*Hist.*) a soldier armed with a fusil. **2** a soldier in any of several regiments formerly armed with fusils. **fusillade** (-lād´) *n.* **1** a continuous, rapid discharge of firearms. **2** a rapid succession of blows, critical comments etc. ~*v.t.* to shoot down or storm by fusillade. [F *fusil*, It. *focile*, a fire-steel, ult. from L *focus*, a hearth]

fusil[2] (fū´zil) *n.* (*Her.*) a bearing resembling a lozenge, longer in proportion to breadth. [OF *fusel* (F *fuseau*), from L *fūsus*, a spindle]

fusile FUSE[1].

fusilier FUSIL[1].

fusilli (fuzil´i) *n.pl.* pasta in the form of short, thick spirals. [It.]

fusion FUSE[1].

fuss (fŭs) *n.* **1** excessive activity, labour or trouble, taken or exhibited. **2** unnecessary bustle or commotion, too much ado. **3** undue importance given to trifles or petty details. **4** a quarrel, dispute or protest. **5** a person who fusses. ~*v.i.* **1** to make a fuss. **2** to be very busy with trifles or petty details. **3** to move fussily. **4** to worry, to be nervous or restless. ~*v.t.* to worry, to agitate. **to kick up a fuss** to make a fuss. **to make a fuss** to cause a commotion, esp. by complaining. **to make a fuss of** to lavish attention on as a sign of affection. **fusser** *n.* **fusspot, fussbudget** *n.* (*coll.*) a person who fusses. **fussy** *a.* (*comp.* **fussier**, *superl.* **fussiest**) **1** nervous, excitable, esp. over small details. **2** finicky, fastidious. **3** over-elaborate, over-ornate. **fussily** *adv.* **fussiness** *n.* [prob. onomat.]

fustanella (fŭstənel´ə) *n.* a type of short white kilt worn by men in Greece and Albania. [It., dim. of mod. Gr. *phoustani*, It. *fustagno*, FUSTIAN]

fustian (fŭs´chən) *n.* **1** a coarse twilled cotton or cotton and linen cloth, with short velvety pile. **2** inflated or pompous writing or speaking; bombast; claptrap, mere verbiage. **3** †a kind of egg flip. ~*a.* **1** made of fustian. **2** bombastic, pompous, pretentious, inflated. **3** using bombastic language. **4** worthless. **fustianed** *a.* **fustianist** *n.* a person who uses bombastic language in writing or speaking. **fustianize, fustianise** *v.i.* [ME *fustane*, OF *fustaigne*, It. *fustagno*, low L *fustāneum*, neut. a. masc. *fustāneus*, prob. from Arab. *Fustāt*, a suburb of Cairo]

fustic (fŭs´tik) *n.* a yellow wood used in dyeing, from either of two kinds of tree, esp. *old fustic*. [F and Sp. *fustoc*, Arab. *fustuq*, Gr. *pistakē*, PISTACHIO]

†**fustigate** (fŭs´tigāt) *v.t.* **1** to beat with a cudgel. **2** to cane. †**fustigation** (-gā´shən) *n.* [late L *fūstīgātus*, p.p. of *fūstīgāre*, from *fūstis*, a cudgel]

fusty (fŭs´ti) *a.* (*comp.* **fustier**, *superl.* **fustiest**) **1** mouldy, musty. **2** rank, smelling unpleasant. **3** close, stuffy. **4** old-fashioned. **fustily** *adv.* **fustiness** *n.* [OF (F *fût*), L *fūstem*, nom. *fūstis*, a stick, a log]

fut. *abbr.* future.

futchel (fŭch´əl) *n.* any of the timbers set lengthwise in the framework of a carriage, to support the splinter-bar and the shafts or pole. [etym. unknown]

futhorc (foo´thawk), **futhark** (foo´thahk), **futhork** (-thawk) *n.* the runic alphabet. [from the first six letters *f u þ o r k*]

futile (fū´tīl) *a.* **1** useless, of no effect. **2** trifling, worthless, frivolous. **futilely** *adv.* **futility** (-til´-) *n.* [L *fūtilis*, *futtilis*, leaky, easily poured out, prob. from root of *fundere*, to pour]

futon (foo´ton) *n.* **1** a Japanese floor-mattress used as a bed. **2** a kind of low wooden sofa bed with such a mattress. [Jap.]

futtock (fŭt´ək) *n.* (*Naut.*) any of the timbers in the compound rib of a vessel. **futtock-plate** *n.* an iron plate at the head of a lower mast, to which the futtock-shrouds and the deadeyes of the topmast shrouds are secured. **futtock-shrouds** *n.pl.* the short shrouds from this to a band on the mast below. [prob. corr. of *foot hook*]

future (fū´chə) *a.* **1** that will be. **2** that is to come or happen after the present. **3** that is to come or happen after death. **4** (*Gram.*) expressing action yet to happen. **5** that will be something specified (*our future king*). ~*n.* **1** time to come. **2** what will be or will happen in the future. **3** prospective condition, state, career, etc. **4** likelihood of success. **5** (*Gram.*) the future tense. **6** (*pl.*) **a** goods, stocks etc., bought or sold for future delivery. **b** contracts for these. **for the future** from now onwards. **in the future** from now onwards. **to deal in futures** to speculate for a rise or fall. **futureless** *a.* **futureness** *n.* **future perfect** *n., a.* (the tense) expressing an action as completed in the future, as *it will have been.* **future shock** *n.* a state of stress, disorientation and inability to cope caused by an excess of significant and rapid change in society. **futurism** *n.* an early 20th-cent. movement in painting, poetry, sculpture, music and literature, aiming at expressing the movement and development of objects, instead of the picture they present at a given moment. **futurist** *n.* **1** a follower of futurism. **2** a student of the future. **3** a believer in human progress. **4** a person who holds that a great part of Scripture prophecy (esp. of the book of Revelation) is still to be fulfilled. **futuristic** (-ris´-) *a.* **1** of the future or futurism. **2** (of design, architecture etc.) ultra-modern, apparently anticipating styles of the future. **futuristically** *adv.* **futurity** (-tūə´-) *n.* (*pl.* **futurities**) **1** the state of being future. **2** future time, esp. eternity. **3** (*often pl.*) future events, things to come. **futurity stakes** *n.pl.* (*N Am.*) stakes at which the entrants have been selected long before the race is run. **futurology** (-rol´-) *n.* the prediction of future developments from current, esp. sociological and technological, trends. **futurological** (-loj´-) *a.* **futurologist** (-rol´-) *n.* [OF *futur*, fem. *future*, L *futurus*, fut.p. of *esse*, to be]

fuze FUSE[2].

fuzee FUSEE[1].

fuzz (fŭz) *v.i.* **1** to fly off in minute particles. **2** to become fluffy. ~*v.t.* to make fluffy. ~*n.* **1** minute light fibres or particles of down or similar matter, fluff. **2** fluffy or frizzled hair. **3** fuzziness. **the fuzz 1** (*sl.*) the police. **2** (*sl.*) a police officer. **fuzz-ball** *n.* a puffball. **fuzzbox** *n.* an electronic device that breaks up the sound, esp. of guitars, that passes through it, esp. by adding a buzzing. **fuzz-wig** *n.* a wig of frizzed curls. **fuzzy** *a.* (*comp.* **fuzzier**, *superl.* **fuzziest**) **1** covered with fuzz, fluffy. **2** having many small, tight curls. **3** blurred, indistinct. **4** (*Math.*) of or relating to a form of set theory in which membership of the set depends on probability functions (*fuzzy logic*). **fuzzily** *adv.* **fuzziness** *n.* **fuzzy-wuzzy** (-wŭzi) *n.* (*pl.* **fuzzy-wuzzies**) (*sl., offensive*) **1** a black person, esp. one with tightly curled hair. **2** (*Hist.*) a Sudanese, a Sudanese fighter. **3** (*Austral.*) a native of New Guinea. [prob. echoic of blowing]

fwd *abbr.* **1** front-wheel drive. **2** four-wheel drive.

fwd. *abbr.* forward.

FX *abbr.* (*coll.*) (visual) effects.

FY *abbr.* (*N Am.*) fiscal year.

-fy (fī) *suf.* forming verbs, meaning to bring into a certain state, to make, to produce, as in *beautify, deify, horrify, petrify, sanctify, terrify, speechify.* [F *-fier*, L *-ficāre*, *facere*, to make]

fyke (fīk) *n.* (*N Am.*) a fish trap consisting of a net that is open at one end so as to allow fish to enter but opposing their exit. [Dut. *fuik*]

fylfot (fil´fot) *n.* a swastika. [borrowed by mod. antiquaries from a MS. (*c.* 1500) where it prob. means *fill-foot*]

fyrd (fœd, fiəd) *n.* **1** a militia at the command of the king in Anglo-Saxon times, able to bear arms. **2** the duty to serve in this. [OE, cogn. with FARE]

fytte FIT[3].

fz *abbr.* sforzando.

G

G[1] (jē), **g** (*pl.* **Gs, G's**) the seventh letter of the English and other versions of the Roman alphabet, corresponding to the Greek gamma (Γ, γ). It has two sounds: (1) hard, a voiced velar plosive, before *a, o, u*, as in *gate, god, gun* (except in *gaol*), and when initial, always before *e* and *i* in words of English origin, as in *get, give*, and when final as in *bag*; also before the consonants *l* and *r*, as in *glove, grove*; (2) soft, a voiced palatal affricate, like that of *j*, in words of Greek or Latin origin before *e* or *i*. *~symbol* **1** the seventh of a series, the seventh highest in a range, e.g. of marks, etc. **2** (*Mus.*) **a** a fifth note of the diatonic scale of C major. **b** the scale of composition in which the keynote is G. **G-clef** *n.* (*Mus.*) **1** the treble clef. **2** a sign indicating the position of G above middle C. **G-string** *n.* **1** a garment consisting of a small piece of cloth covering the pubic area and attached front and back to a waistband, worn e.g. by an entertainer when performing striptease. **2** a loincloth.

G[2] *abbr.* **1** gauss. **2** giga-. **3** Government. **4** grand, i.e. a thousand dollars or pounds. **5** gravitational constant. **6** Group. **G7** *n.* Group of Seven, the seven leading Western industrial nations (Canada, France, Italy, Japan, UK, USA and Germany), whose finance ministers hold periodic summit meetings. **G-man** *n.* (*pl.* **G-men**) (*US, sl.*) a Government man, a member of the Federal Bureau of Investigation specially selected for intrepidity as a criminal-hunter.

g *abbr.* **1** gas. **2** gelding. **3** gram(s). **4** gravity; acceleration due to this.

GA *abbr.* Georgia.

Ga *chem. symbol* gallium.

gab (gab) *n.* **1** idle talk, chatter. **2** (*Sc.*) the mouth. *~v.i.* (*pres.p.* **gabbing,** *past, p.p.* **gabbed**) to talk glibly, to chatter, to prate. **the gift of the gab** (*coll.*) a talent for speaking, fluency. **gabber** *n.* (*coll.*) a talkative person, gossip. **gabby** *a.* (*comp.* **gabbier,** *superl.* **gabbiest**) (*coll.*) talkative, loquacious. **gabfest** *n.* **1** (*chiefly N Am., coll.*) a prolonged session of speeches, discussion or gossip. **2** a gathering for this. [perh. onomat; perh. variant of GOB[1]]

gabardine (gab´ədēn, -dēn´), **gaberdine** *n.* **1** a cloth with a corded effect, used largely for raincoats. **2** a rainproof coat made of this. **3** (*usu.* **gabardine**) a long coarse gown or cloak, worn in the Middle Ages by Jews and others. [from Sp. *gabardina* or OF *gauvardine*, prob. a pilgrim's garment]

gabber GAB.

gabble (gab´əl) *v.i.* **1** to utter inarticulate sounds rapidly. **2** to talk rapidly and incoherently. *~v.t.* to utter noisily or inarticulately. *~n.* **1** rapid, incoherent or inarticulate talk. **2** cackle, chatter. **gabblement** *n.* **gabbler** *n.* [prob. imit. (cp. BABBLE)]

gabbro (gab´rō) *n.* (*pl.* **gabbros**) (a) rock composed of feldspar and diallage, sometimes with serpentine or mica. **gabbroic** (-rō´ik), **gabbroid** *a.* **gabbronite** (-nīt) *n.* a bluish-green or grey variety of scapolite somewhat resembling gabbro. [It.]

gabby GAB.

gabelle (gəbel´) *n.* a tax or duty, esp. the tax on salt in France before the Revolution, 1789. [F, from med. L *gabella, gablum*, from Gmc. (cp. GAVEL[2])]

gaberdine GABARDINE.

gabfest GAB.

gabion (gā´biən) *n.* a cylindrical basket of wickerwork or metal, filled with earth or stones, used for foundations etc. in engineering work and (esp. formerly) for shelter against an enemy's fire while trenches are being dug. **gabionade** (-nād´) *n.* a work formed of gabions. **gabionage** *n.* gabions collectively. **gabioned** *a.* furnished with, formed of or protected with gabions. [F, from It. *gabbione*, augm. form of *gabbia*, cage]

gable (gā´bəl) *n.* **1** the triangular upper portion of the end of a building, between the sloping sides of the roof. **2** a wall with the upper part shaped like this. **3** a canopy or other architectural member with this shape. **gabled** *a.* having gables. **gable end** *n.* the end wall of a building with a gabled upper part. **gable roof** *n.* a ridge roof ending in a gable. **gablet** (gā´blit) *n.* a small gable, esp. forming an ornamental canopy over a tabernacle or niche. **gable window** *n.* a window in a gable or with a gable over it. [OF, from Gmc. (cp. Icel. *gafl*, Dut. *gevel*, pinnacle, Gr. *kephalē*, head; also OHG *gabala*, G *Gabel*, fork)]

gad[1] (gad) *v.i.* (*pres.p.* **gadding,** *past, p.p.* **gadded**) **1** to rove or wander idly (about, out etc.). **2** to ramble or straggle (as a plant). *~n.* gadding or roaming about. **gadabout** *n.* a person who gads about habitually. **gadder** *n.* **gaddingly** *adv.* [etym. uncertain (perh. from gadfly, or from obs. *gadling*, OE *gædling*, a companion, from *gæd*, fellowship)]

gad[2] (gad) *int.* used to express surprise etc. **by gad** used as an oath or to express surprise etc. **gadzooks** (-zooks´) *int.* used as an oath or to express surprise etc. [minced pron. of GOD]

gad[3] (gad) *n.* **1** a miner's iron wedge sharply pointed for splitting stone etc. **2** a pointed tool of iron or steel. **3** an iron punch with a wooden handle. **4** a goad or pointed stick for driving cattle. **†gadling** (-ling) *n.* a boss or small spike of steel on the knuckles of gauntlets. **†gadman, †gadsman** *n.* (*pl.* **gadmen, gadsmen**) (*Sc.*) a person who uses a goad. [Icel. *gaddr*, cogn. with L *hasta*, a spear]

Gadarene (gad´ərēn) *a.* involving or taking part in a chaotic or suicidal rush, flight etc. [from *Gadara* in ancient Palestine, with ref. to Matthew viii.28–32]

gadder, gaddingly etc. GAD[1].

gadfly (gad´flī) *n.* (*pl.* **gadflies**) **1** a bloodsucking insect of the genus *Tobanidae* or *Oestrus*, which bites cattle and other animals, a horsefly. **2** a person, thing or impulse that irritates or torments. **3** †a mischievous or irritating gadabout. [etym. uncertain; perh. GAD[1] or OE *gād*, GOAD]

gadget (gaj´it) *n.* **1** a small tool, an appliance. **2** an ingenious device for making a job easier. **gadgeteer** (-iə´) *n.* a person interested in gadgets. **gadgetry** *n.* **gadgety** *a.* [etym. uncertain]

Gadhelic (gədel´ik) *a., n.* GOIDELIC (under GOIDEL). [Ir. *Gaedheal*, pl. *Gaedhil*, a Gael]

gadoid (gā´doid) *n.* any fish of the cod family Gadidae. *~a.* of or belonging to the cod family Gadidae. [Gr. *gados*, COD[1], -OID]

gadolinite (gad´əlinīt) *n.* a black, vitreous silicate of yttrium, beryllium and iron, formed in crystals. **gadolinium** (gadəlin´iəm) *n.* a soft metallic element, at. no. 64, chem. symbol Gd, of the rare-earth group. [J. *Gadolin*, 1760–1852, Finnish mineralogist]

gadroon (gədroon´), **godroon** *n.* (*usu. pl.*) an ornament consisting of a series of convex curves, used in architecture and metalwork for edgings, mouldings etc. **gadrooned** *a.* having a moulding in the form of a gadroon. [F *godron*]

gadwall (gad´wawl) *n.* a large freshwater duck, *Anas strepera*, of N Europe and America. [perh. corr. of *gadwell* (GAD², WELL²)]

gadzooks GAD².

Gael (gāl) *n.* 1 a Scottish Celt. 2 (*less commonly*) an Irish Celt. **Gaelic** (gā´lik, gal´ik) *a.* of or relating to the Gaels or their language. ~*n.* 1 the language spoken by the Gaels. 2 (*less commonly*) the language of the Irish and Manx Celts. **Gaelic coffee** *n.* a drink made of sweetened coffee mixed with Irish whiskey and topped with cream. **Gaelic football** *n.* a game involving two teams of 15 players, the object of which is to kick, bounce or punch a ball into a net stretched between two posts or over a crossbar above the net. **Gaelic League** *n.* an association formed to further the revival of the Irish language and ancient culture. **Gaeltacht** (gāl´təkht) *n.* any of the regions in Ireland where Irish Gaelic is the vernacular language. [Gael. *Gaidheal*]

gaff¹ (gaf) *n.* 1 a stick with a metal hook at the end, used by anglers to land heavy fish. 2 on a sailing boat, the spar which extends the upper edge of fore-and-aft sails not set on stays. ~*v.t.* to seize or land with a gaff. **gaff-topsail** *n.* a sail spread by a gaff above the mainsail of a fore-and-aft rigged vessel. [OF *gaffe* (cp. LG *gaffel*, G *Gabel*, a fork)]

gaff² (gaf) *n.* (*sl.*) foolish talk, nonsense, outcry. **to blow the gaff** to let out the secret, to give information. [etym. uncertain]

gaff³ (gaf) *n.* 1 (*sl.*) a person's home. 2 †a theatre or other place of cheap entertainment. [etym. uncertain]

gaff⁴ (gaf) *v.i.* (*sl.*) 1 to gamble. 2 †to toss, esp. for liquor. [etym. unknown]

gaffe (gaf) *n.* a social blunder, esp. a tactless comment. **to make a gaffe** to put one's foot in it. [F]

gaffer (gaf´ə) *n.* 1 (*coll.*) a foreman, an overseer. 2 the chief lighting electrician on a television or film set. 3 an old fellow, esp. an aged rustic (formerly a term of respect, now of familiarity). [corr. of GRANDFATHER (under GRAND)]

gag (gag) *v.t.* (*pres.p.* **gagging**, *past, p.p.* **gagged**) 1 to stop the mouth of (a person) by thrusting something into it or tying something round it, so as to prevent speech. 2 to silence. 3 to deprive of freedom of speech. 4 to apply the gag-bit to a horse. 5 to cause to choke or retch. 6 (*sl.*) to deceive. ~*v.i.* 1 to struggle for breath, choke, retch. 2 (*sl.*) to practise deception or fraud. 3 to crack jokes. 4 (of an actor) to introduce interpolations into a part. ~*n.* 1 something thrust into the mouth to prevent one from speaking. 2 a joke, esp. a rehearsed one. 3 an interpolation introduced by an actor into their part. 4 (*sl.*) an imposture, a lie. 5 an instrument for holding the mouth open during a surgical operation. 6 in Parliament, a closure or guillotine. **gag-bit** *n.* a very powerful bit used in horse-breaking. **gagger** *n.* 1 a person who gags. 2 a light T-shaped lifter used in iron-founding. **gagman** *n.* (*pl.* **gagmen**) 1 a person who writes jokes. 2 a comedian. **gag-rein** *n.* a rein used for pulling the bit upward or backward. **gagster** *n.* GAGMAN (under GAG). [prob. imit.]

gaga (gah´gah) *a.* (*coll., derog.*) foolish, senile, fatuous. [F]

gage¹ (gāj) *n.* 1 something laid down as security, to be forfeited in case of non-performance of some act; a pledge, a pawn. 2 (*Hist.*) a glove or other symbol thrown down as a challenge to combat. 3 †a challenge. ~*v.t.* 1 to deposit as a pledge or security for some act. 2 †to stake, to risk, to wager. 3 †to guarantee. **gagelike** *a.* [OF *gage, gauge, wage*, from Gmc. (cp. WED, also WAGE)]

gage² (gāj) *n.* a greengage. [Sir William *Gage*, *c.* 1725, the introducer]

gage³ GAUGE.

☒ **gaget** common misspelling of GADGET.

gagger GAG.

gaggle (gag´əl) *v.i.* 1 to make a noise like a goose. 2 to cackle, to chatter. ~*n.* 1 a collection of geese on land. 2 (*coll.*) a group of people, usu. disorganized or animated. [imit.; cp. CACKLE]

Gaia (gī´ə) *n.* the earth as a self-regulating organism. [Gr.]

gaiety (gā´əti) *n.* (*pl.* **gaities**) 1 mirth, merriment. 2 a state of lively happiness. 3 a gay appearance, a brave show. 4 (*pl.*) †amusements, festivities. **to add to/ increase the gaiety of nations** to cause general pleasure or amusement. [OF *gayeté*]

gaijin (gījin´) *n.* in Japan, a foreigner. ~*a.* foreign, alien. [Jap. *gaikaku*, foreign country, *jin*, person]

gaillardia (gālah´diə) *n.* any plant of the genus *Gaillardia*, the daisy family. [*Gaillard* de Marentonneau, 18th-cent. French botanist]

gaily GAY.

gain (gān) *n.* 1 anything obtained as an advantage or in return for labour. 2 profit. 3 increase, growth, accession. 4 amount of increase, growth. 5 (*pl.*) profits, emoluments (*ill-gotten gains*). 6 the acquisition of wealth. 7 the ratio of the output power of an amplifier to the input power usu. measured in decibels, volume. ~*v.t.* 1 to obtain through effort. 2 to earn, to win, to acquire. 3 to progress, to advance, to get more of. 4 to reach, to attain to. 5 to win (over). 6 to obtain as a result, to incur, e.g. a penalty. 7 (of a clock etc.) to become fast to the extent of. ~*v.i.* 1 to advance in interest, possessions or happiness. 2 to gain ground, to encroach (upon). 3 to get the advantage (on or upon). 4 (of a clock etc.) to become fast. **to gain ground** 1 to advance in any undertaking. 2 to make progress. **to gain ground upon** to get nearer (to one pursued). **to gain on/ upon** 1 to get nearer to (an object of pursuit). 2 to encroach upon. **to gain over** to win over to any side, party or view. **to gain the day** DAY. **to gain the ear of** to secure favourable consideration from. **to gain the upper hand** to be victorious. **to gain the wind** to get to the windward side (of another ship). **to gain time** to obtain delay for any purpose. **gainable** *a.* **gain-control** *n.* the volume control in an amplifier or receiving set. **gainer** *n.* a person who gains profit, return or advantage. **gainful** *a.* 1 profitable, advantageous, remunerative. 2 devoted to gain. **gainfully** *adv.* **gainfulness** *n.* **gainings** *n.pl.* profits, gains. **gainless** *a.* unprofitable. **gainlessness** *n.* [OF, from *gaigner, gaaignier* (cp. F *gagne, gagner*), OHG *weidenēn*, to pasture, to graze, from *weida*, pasturage]

gaine (gān) *n.* a metal tube containing explosive which is screwed to a fuse. [F *guine*, a sheath]

gainly (gān´li) *a.* 1 suitable, gracious. 2 comely, shapely. [Icel. *gegn*, straight, ready, serviceable, -LY¹]

gainsay (gānsā´) *v.t.* (*past, p.p.* **gainsaid** (-sed´)) 1 to contradict, to deny. 2 to controvert, to dispute, to hinder. ~†*n.* contradiction. **gainsayer** *n.* **gainsaying** *n.*

†**gainst** (gānst, genst), **'gainst** *prep.* AGAINST.

gait (gāt) *n.* manner of walking or going, carriage. **to go one's (own) gait** to go one's own way. **gaited** *a.* (*usu. in comb.*) having a particular gait (*crab-gaited*). [Icel. *gata*, GATE²]

gaiter (gā´tə) *n.* 1 a covering for the ankle or the leg below the knee, usu. fitting down upon the shoe. 2 (*N Am.*) a half-boot with a cloth top or elastic sides. ~*v.t.* to dress with gaiters. **gaitered** *a.* **gaiterless** *a.* [F *guêtre*, etym. unknown]

☒ **gaity** common misspelling of GAIETY.

Gal. *abbr.* Galatians.

gal¹ (gal) *n.* (*coll., N Am.*) a girl.

gal[2] (gal) *n.* (*Physics*) a unit of acceleration equal to 1 cm per second per second. [from *Gal*ileo; see GALILEAN[1]]
gal. *abbr.* gallons.
gala (gah´lə, gā´-) *n.* **1** a festivity, a fête. **2** a sporting occasion involving several events (*swimming gala*). **gala day** *n.* a holiday with sports or festivities. **gala dress** *n.* festive attire. [F, from It., conn. with *galante*, gay]
galact- GALACTO-.
galactagogue (gəlak´təgog) *a.* promoting the flow of milk. ~*n.* a medicine which promotes the flow of milk. [Gr. *agōgos*, leading, from *agein*, to lead]
galactic (gəlak´tik) *a.* **1** (*Astron.*) of or relating to a galaxy, esp. the Milky Way. **2** of or relating to milk or the secretion of milk, lactic. ~*n.* the great circle of the celestial sphere which contains the galactic plane. **galactic plane** *n.* the geometrical plane that passes though the spiral arms of the Galaxy. **galactic poles** *n.pl.* the two opposite points on the celestial sphere that are the furthest N and S and which can be joined by an imaginary line perpendicular to the galactic plane. **galactin** (-tin) *n.* a nitrogenous substance obtained from milk, and existing in the juices or the seeds of certain plants. **galactonic** (galəkton´-) *a.* [Gr. *galaktikos*, from *gala galaktos*, milk]
galacto- (gəlak´tō), **galact-** *comb. form* milk or milky. [Gr. *gala galaktos*, milk]
galactometer (galaktom´itə) *n.* a lactometer.
galactophorous (galaktof´ərəs) *a.* producing milk.
galactopoietic (gəlaktōpoiet´ik) *a.* increasing the flow of milk. ~*n.* a substance which increases the flow of milk. [Gr. *poētikos*, from *poiein*, to make]
galactorrhoea (gəlaktərē´ə), (*N Am.*) **galactorrhea** *n.* an excessive flow of milk. [Gr. *rhoia*, a flowing]
galactose (gəlak´tōs) *n.* a sweet crystalline glucose obtained from milk-sugar by treatment with dilute acid.
galago (gəlā´gō) *n.* (*pl.* **galagos**) the bushbaby, one of an African genus of lemurs. [from Afr. name]
galah (gəlah´) *n.* (*Austral.*) **1** the grey, rose-breasted cockatoo, *Eulophus roseicapillus*. **2** (*coll.*) a silly person, a simpleton. [Austral. Abor.]
Galahad (gal´əhad) *n.* a chivalrous person, noted for courtesy, integrity etc. [Sir *Galahad*, one of King Arthur's legendary knights]
galantine (gal´əntēn) *n.* a dish of white meat, freed from bone, tied up, sliced, boiled, covered with jelly and served cold. [F, from low L *galatina*, corr. of *gelatina*, GELATIN (n. due to conf. with *galant*, GALLANT[1])]
galatea (galətē´ə) *n.* a blue-and-white striped cotton fabric. [from *HMS Galatea*, 19th-cent. warship]
Galatian (gəlā´shən) *a.* belonging to Galatia. ~*n.* a native or inhabitant of Galatia. [*Galatia*, in Asia Minor, -AN]
galaxy (gal´əksi) *n.* (*pl.* **galaxies**) **1** a star system held together in a symmetrical or asymmetrical shape by gravitational attraction. **2** a brilliant assemblage of persons or things. **3** (**Galaxy**) the disc-shaped system of stars that contains our solar system; it is known as the Milky Way from its appearance as a luminous band consisting of innumerable stars indistinguishable to the naked eye, stretching across the sky. [OF *galaxie*, L *galaxiam*, nom. *-ias*, Gr. *galaxias*, from *gala*, milk]
galbanum (gal´bənəm) *n.* a bitter, odorous gum resin obtained from Persian species of *Ferula*, esp. *F. galbaniflua*, an ingredient in the anointing-oil used by Jewish people. [L, from Gr. *chalbanē*, prob. from an Oriental word]
gale[1] (gāl) *n.* **1** a wind stronger than a breeze but less violent than a storm. **2** a wind with a velocity of 40 m.p.h. (64 k.p.h.) or over, registering force eight on the Beaufort scale. **3** an outburst (*gales of laughter*). **4** a quarrel, a disturbance. [cp. Dan. *gal*, Norw. *galen*, mad, furious, Icel. *gola*, a breeze]
gale[2] (gāl) *n.* the bog myrtle, *Myrica gale*, a twiggy shrub growing on marshy ground, sweet-gale. [OE *gagel* (cp. Dut. and G *gagel*)]
gale[3] (gāl) *n.* (*Hist.*) a periodic payment of rent. **gale-day** *n.* rent-day. [prob. from OE *gafol*, GAVEL[1]]
galea (gā´liə) *n.* (*pl.* **galeae** (gā´liē), **galeas**) **1** (*Biol.*) a helmet-like organ or part. **2** (*Bot.*) the arched upper lip in some labiates. **3** (*Anat.*) the amnion. **4** a bandage for the head. **galeate** (-ət), **galeated** (-ātid) *a.* [L, a helmet]
Galen (gā´lən) *n.* a physician. **Galenic** (gəlen´ik), **Galenical** *a.* of or according to Galen, esp. applied to medicines prepared from vegetable substances by infusion or decoction, as opposed to chemical remedies. ~*n.* a medicine prepared in this manner. **Galenism** *n.* **Galenist** *n.* [Claudius *Galēnus*, AD 130–200, a Greek physician of Pergamos]
galena (gəlē´nə) *n.* native sulphide of lead or lead-ore. **galenic** (-len´-), **galenical** *a.* **galenite** (-nīt) *n.* galena. [L]
galeopithecus (galiōpithē´kəs, -pith´i-) *n.* a flying lemur. **galeopithecine** (-sin), **galeopithecoid** (-koid) *a.* [Gr. *galeē*, weasel, *pithēkos*, an ape]
galette (gəlet´) *n.* a flat, round cake. [F, from *galet*, a pebble, Bret. *kalet*, hard as a stone]
galia melon (gah´liə) *n.* a small round melon with orange flesh and rough skin.
Galibi (gəlē´bi) *n.* (*pl.* **Galibi, Galibis**) **1** a member of an Indian people of French Guiana. **2** the Carib language of the Galibi. ~*a.* of or relating to the Galibi or their language.
Galician (gəlish´iən) *a.* of or relating to either of the regions called Galicia, one in NW Spain, the other in central Europe. ~*n.* a native or inhabitant of Galicia.
Galilean[1] (galilē´ən) *a.* of or according to Galileo, esp. applied to the simple telescope developed and used by him. [*Galileo*, 1564–1642, the astronomer]
Galilean[2] GALILEE.
Galilee (gal´ilē) *n.* a porch or chapel at the entrance of a church (prob. so called because, like Galilee in respect to Judaea, it was less sacred than the body of the church, or in allusion to Matt. iv.15, 'Galilee of the Gentiles'). **Galilean**[2] (-lē´-) *a.* of or relating to Galilee. ~*n.* **1** a native or inhabitant of Galilee. **2** a Christian (applied contemptuously by pagans at the time of Christ). **the Galilean** (*derog.*) Jesus Christ. [a Roman province, comprising the north of Palestine west of the Jordan]
galingale (gal´ing·gāl), **galangal** (-əng·gal) *n.* **1** the aromatic rootstock of certain E Asian plants of the ginger family and of the genus *Alpinia* and *Kaempferia*, formerly used for culinary purposes. **2** ENGLISH GALINGALE (under ENGLISH). [OF *galingal*, Arab. *qalanjān*, prob. through Pers. from Chin. *Ko-liang-Kiang*, mild ginger from *Ko*, in Canton]
galiot GALLIOT.
galipot[1] (gal´ipot) *n.* a yellowish-white, sticky resin exuding from the pine tree *Pinus maritimus* and hardening into a kind of turpentine, called, after refining, white, yellow or Burgundy pitch. **galipot varnish** *n.* [F, etym. uncertain]
galipot[2] GALLIPOT.
galium (gal´iəm) *n.* bedstraw, a genus of slender herbaceous plants, containing goosegrass, lady's bedstraw etc. [Gr. *galion*]
gall[1] (gawl) *n.* **1** self-assurance, cheek, impudence. **2** bile, the bitter, yellowish fluid secreted by the liver. **3** anything exceedingly bitter. **4** rancour, malignity, bitterness of mind. **5** the gall bladder. **gall and wormwood** all that is hateful, exasperating and unwelcome. **gall bladder** *n.* a pear-shaped membraneous sac, lodged on the undersurface of the liver, which receives the bile. **gall duct, gall passage, gall pipe** *n.* a duct which conveys the bile. **gall-less** *a.* without bitterness; free from rancour. **gall stone** *n.* an abnormal calcareous concretion formed in the gall bladder. [OE *gealla* (cp.

Dut. *gal*, Icel. *gall*, G *Galle*, also L *fel*, Gr. *cholē*), cogn. with YELLOW]

gall[2] (gawl) *n.* an abnormal growth on plants, esp. the oak, caused by the action of some insect. ~*v.t.* to impregnate with a decoction of galls. **gall-fly, gall-insect, gall-louse, gall-wasp** *n.* an insect, chiefly belonging to the genus *Cynips*, that causes the production of galls. **gallnut, gall apple** *n.* a gall produced on the oak, esp. by the puncture by *C. gallae tinctoria* of the leaf-buds of the gall-oak, used (esp. formerly) in the making of ink and for other purposes. **gall-oak** *n.* the oak, *Quercus infectoria*. [OF *galle*, L *galla*]

gall[3] (gawl) *n.* **1** a sore, swelling, or blister, esp. one produced by friction or chafing on a horse. **2** soreness, irritation. **3** someone who or something that causes soreness or irritation. **4** †a bare place in a field or a crop. **5** †a blemish, a defect. **6** (*US*) a marshy lowland (in the southern states). ~*v.t.* **1** to annoy, to harass, to vex. **2** to chafe, hurt or injure by rubbing. **3** to make sore by friction. ~*v.i.* **1** to fret. **2** †to act in an irritating manner. **galling** *a.* vexing, irritating, chafing. **gallingly** *adv.* [OE *gealla*, perh. cogn. with GALL[2]]

gall. *abbr.* gallon(s).

gallant[1] (gal´ənt) *a.* **1** brave, high-spirited, courageous, chivalrous. **2** fine, stately. **3** showy, well-dressed. **gallantry**[1] *n.* courage of a bold, dashing, magnanimous kind. [OF *gallant*, *galant*, pres.p. of *galer*, to make merry, from G]

gallant[2] (gal´ənt, gəlant´) *n.* **1** a man of fashion, a beau. **2** a man who is attentive and polite to women. **3** †a bold and dashing fellow. **4** a lover, a wooer; a paramour. ~*a.* **1** specially attentive to women. **2** of or relating to love. ~*v.t.* **1** to attend as a gallant or cavalier, to escort. **2** to pay court to. **3** to flirt with. ~*v.i.* **1** to play the gallant. **2** to flirt. **gallantly** *adv.* **gallantry**[2] *n.* (*pl.* **gallantries**) **1** politeness and deference to women, with or without evil intent. **2** a polite or deferential act. **3** amorous intrigue. **4** †showy appearance, a brave show.

gallantry[1] GALLANT[1].

gallantry[2] GALLANT[2].

galleass (gal´ias) *n.* (*pl.* **galleasses**) a heavy, low-built type of galley propelled by both sails and oars, usu. with three masts and about 20 guns. [OF *galeace*, It. *galeazza*, late L *galea*, GALLEY[1]]

galleon (gal´iən) *n.* a large ship, with three or four decks, much used in 15th–17th cents., esp. by the Spaniards in trade with their American possessions. [Sp. *galeon*, late L *galeo -ōnem*, from *galea*, GALLEY[1]]

galleria (galərē´a) *n.* a number of small independent shops in one building, on one floor or arranged in galleries on several floors. [It.]

gallery (gal´əri) *n.* (*pl.* **galleries**) **1** an elevated floor or platform projecting from the wall toward the interior of a church, hall, theatre, or other large building, commonly used for musicians, singers or part of the congregation or audience. **2** a corridor, a passage, a long and narrow room. **3** a room or building used for the exhibition of pictures and other works of art; a collection of works of art. **4** a passage open at one side, usu. projecting from the wall of a building and supported on corbels or pillars. **5** the highest and cheapest tier of seats in a theatre, concert hall etc. **6** a body of spectators. **7** (*derog.*) an unrefined section of an audience. **8** a portico or colonnade, a balcony, a veranda. **9** a covered passage in a fortification, either for defence or communication. **10** an adit, drift, or heading, within a mine. **11** a room or area, often soundproof, overlooking a theatre, studio etc. used by the director, lighting or other technical personnel. ~*v.t.* (*3rd pers. sing. pres.* **galleries**, *pres.p.* **gallerying**, *past*, *p.p.* **galleried**) to furnish or pierce with a gallery or galleries. **to play to the gallery** to court popular applause. **galleried** *a.* **gallery forest** *n.* a stretch of forest, esp. beside a river, in open country. **galleryite** (-īt) *n.* a regular playgoer, a member of the audience in the gallery. [OF *galerie*, late L *galeria*, etym. uncertain]

galley[1] (gal´i) *n.* **1** the cook-house on board a ship, boat or aircraft. **2** (*Hist.*) a low, flat vessel, with one deck, navigated with sails and oars, that were usu. worked by slaves or convicts. **3** an ancient Greek or Roman war-vessel of this type with one or more tiers of oars. **4** a row-boat of large size, esp. one larger than the gig, used by the captain of a man-of-war. **5** a state barge. **galley slave** *n.* **1** in ancient times, a criminal condemned to the galleys. **2** a drudge. [OF *galie*, late L *galea*, a galley]

galley[2] (gal´i) *n.* **1** in the traditional method of printing by hot-metal composition, an oblong tray on which compositors placed type as it was set up. **2** a galley proof. **galley-press** *n.* a press at which galley proofs were pulled. **galley-proof** *n.* a proof taken from type in a galley, usu. in one column on a long strip of paper as distinct from that arranged in pages. [F *galée*]

galley-west (galiwest´) *adv.* (*esp. US, sl.*) to put (somebody or something) into a state of confusion, unconsciousness or inaction, esp. in *to knock galley-west*. [Eng. dial. *colly-west*, awry]

galliambic (galiam´bik) *n.* **1** a literary metre, technically a tetrameter catalectic composed of Ionics, a minore (˘˘) with variations and substitutions – the metre of the *Attis* of Catullus and of Tennyson's *Boadicea*. **2** (*pl.*) verses in this metre. ~*a.* in this metre. [L *galliambus*, the metre used by the Galli or priests of Cybele in their chants]

galliard (gal´yəd) *n.* **1** a lively dance, common in the 16th and 17th cents. **2** the music to this. **3** †a merry or lively person. ~†*a.* merry, jaunty. [F *gaillard* (fem. *gaillarde*, whence the n.)]

Gallic (gal´ik) *a.* **1** French; characteristic of the French. **2** of or relating to ancient Gaul. **gallice** (-isi) *adv.* in French. **Gallicism** (-sizm) *n.* a French expression or idiom. **Gallicize** (-sīz), **Gallicise** *v.t., v.i.* to make or become French in style, attitude, language etc. [L *Gallicus*, from *Gallus*, a GAUL]

gallic (gal´ik) *a.* of, relating to, or from plant galls. **gallic acid** *n.* a crystalline substance present in plant galls, also in tea and other plants, used as a tanning agent and in inks and dyes. [GALL[1]]

Gallican (gal´ikən) *a.* **1** of or relating to the ancient Church of Gaul or France. **2** ultramontane, claiming autonomy for the Church in France and repudiating papal control. ~*n.* a member of the French Church who held Gallican views. **Gallicanism** *n.* **Gallicanist** *n.* [L *Gallicānus*, as GALLIC]

galligaskins (galigas´kinz) *n.pl.* **1** loose breeches popular in the 16th and 17th cents. **2** gaiters worn by sportsmen in the 19th cent. [corr. of F *garguesques*, corr. of *greguesques*, It. *Grechesca*, orig. fem. of *Grechesco*, Greekish]

gallimaufry (galimaw´fri) *n.* (*pl.* **gallimaufries**) **1** a hash, a hotchpotch. **2** an inconsistent or ridiculous medley. [F *gallimafrée*, stew, etym. unknown]

gallinaceous (galinā´shəs) *a.* of or relating to the order Galliformes of birds, containing pheasants, partridges, grouse, turkeys, domestic fowls, and allied forms. **gallinacean** *a.* gallinaceous. ~*n.* a gallinaceous bird. [L *gallīnāceus*, from *gallīna*, a hen]

gallinule (gal´inūl) *n.* **1** any bird of the genus *Gallinula*, esp. *G. chloropus*, the moorhen. **2** any of the various similar birds of the genus *Porphyrula* or *Porphyrio*. [late L *gallīnula*, dim. of L *gallina*, hen]

galliot (gal´iət), **galiot** *n.* **1** a small, swift galley propelled by sails and oars. **2** a one- or two-masted Dutch or Flemish merchant vessel. [OF *galiote*, late L *galeota*, from *galea*, GALLEY[1]]

gallipot (gal´ipot), **galipot** *n.* a small glazed earthenware pot used to contain ointments, medicines, preserves etc. [prob. GALLEY[1], POT[1]]

gallium (gal´iəm) *n.* a soft, grey metallic element of extreme fusibility, at. no. 31, chem. symbol Ga, used in semiconductors. [from L *gallus*, a cock, alluding to the name of its discoverer, M. *Lecoq* de Boisbaudran]

gallivant (galivant´) *v.i.* **1** to gad about, to go around seeking pleasure. **2** to flirt. [prob. from GALLANT[2]]

galliwasp (gal´iwosp) *n.* a small harmless W Indian lizard, *Diploglossus monotropis*, erroneously reputed to be venomous. [etym. uncertain]

Gallo- (gal´ō) *comb. form* **1** French. **2** Gaulish. [L *Gallus*, a Gaul]

gallo- (gal´ō) *comb. form* of or relating to gallic acid, gallic.

galloglass (gal´ōglahs) *n.* an armed soldier or retainer of an ancient Irish chieftain. [Ir. *gallóglách* (*gall*, a foreigner, *óglách*, a youth, a warrior)]

Gallomania (galōmā´niə) *n.* a mania for French fashions, habits, or practices, literature etc. **Gallomaniac** *n.*

gallon (gal´ən) *n.* **1** a British liquid measure of capacity equal to eight pints (4.55 l). **2** a British dry measure equal to one-eighth of a bushel (4.55 l). **3** a US liquid measure of capacity equal to 3.79 l. **4** (*pl.*) a large quantity. **imperial gallon** IMPERIAL. **Winchester gallon** WINCHESTER. **gallonage** *n.* [OF *galon*, *jalon*, gallon, prob. cogn. with F *jale*; etym. unknown]

galloon (gəloon´) *n.* **1** a narrow braid of silk, worsted or cotton, with gold or silver thread interwoven, for binding uniforms, dresses etc. **2** any of various other materials used for binding or edging. [F *galon*, prob. from OF *gall*, see GALA]

gallop (gal´əp) *v.i.* (*pres.p.* **galloping**, *past*, *p.p.* **galloped**) **1** to run in a series of springs, as a horse at its fastest pace. **2** to ride at a gallop. **3** to go or do anything at a very rapid pace. *~v.t.* to make (a horse) gallop. *~n.* **1** the motion of a horse at its fastest speed, with all the feet off the ground at one point in the progressive movement of the four limbs. **2** the act of riding or a ride at this pace. **3** an area set aside for this. **4** a galop. **at a gallop** at the fastest speed. **the gallops** horse-racing over flat ground. **gallopade** (-pād´) *n.* **1** a sidelong or curvetting kind of gallop. **2** a brisk dance, of Hungarian origin. *~v.i.* to dance a gallopade. **galloper** *n.* **1** a horse that gallops. **2** a person who gallops on a horse, or who makes great haste. **3** an aide-de-camp. **4** a light field-gun attached to cavalry. **galloping** *a.* progressing rapidly, out of control (*galloping inflation*; *galloping consumption*). [OF *galoper*, prob. from Gmc. (cp. Flem. *walop*, gallop, OS *hlōpan*, to LEAP]

Gallophile (gal´ōfīl) *n.* a devotee of French customs etc., a Francophile.

Gallophobe (gal´ōfōb) *n.* a person who hates French ways or fears the French. **Gallophobia** (-fō´biə) *n.*

Gallovidian (galəvid´iən) *a.* of or belonging to Galloway in SW Scotland. *~n.* a native of Galloway. [med. L *Gallovidia* from Welsh *Gallwyddel*, Galloway]

galloway (gal´əwā) *n.* **1** a black breed of cattle, orig. bred in Galloway. **2** a small, hardy variety of horse. [*Galloway*, in SW Scotland]

gallows (gal´ōz) *n.sing.* **1** a framework, usu. consisting of timber uprights and a crosspiece, on which criminals are executed by hanging. **2** execution by hanging. **3** a similar framework used for gymnastics, for hanging things on, in printing, cookery etc. **gallows-bird** *n.* a person who deserves hanging. **gallows-bitts** *n.pl.* (*Naut.*) a strong frame erected amidships on the deck of a sailing ship to hold spare spars. **gallowses** GALLUSES. **†gallows-free** *a.* saved from hanging. **gallows humour** *n.* macabre, ironic humour. **†gallows-ripe** *a.* ready to be hanged. **gallows-top** *n.* (*Naut.*) a crosspiece of timber placed at the less top of the gallows-bitts. **gallows-tree** *n.* the gallows. [OE *galga* (cp. Icel. *gālgi*, Dut. *galg*, G *Galgen*)]

Gallup poll (gal´əp) *n.* **1** a method of ascertaining the trend of public opinion by questioning a representative cross-section of the population. **2** a poll according to this method. [G. H. *Gallup*, 1901–84, US statistician]

galluses (gal´əsiz), **†gallowses** *n.pl.* (*N Am., Sc., coll.*) braces for trousers. [GALLOWS]

galoot (gəloot´) *n.* (*coll.*) **1** an awkward, uncouth person. **2** a clumsy soldier. [etym. uncertain]

galop (gal´əp, gəlop´) *n.* **1** a lively dance in 2/4 time. **2** the music to the dance. *~v.i.* (*pres.p.* **galoping**, *past*, *p.p.* **galoped**) to dance this. [F, see GALLOP]

galore (gəlaw´) *adv.* in plenty, abundantly (*There was food galore at the feast*). [Ir. *go leor* (*go*, to, *leor*, sufficient)]

galoshes (gəlosh´əz) *n.pl.* a pair of waterproof overshoes, usu. of vulcanized rubber, for protecting a person's boots or shoes in wet weather. [F *galoche*, prob. through L from Gr. *kalopodion*, dim. of *kalopous*, a shoemaker's last (*kalon*, wood, *pous podos*, foot)]

galtonia (gawltō´niə) *n.* any plant of the genus *Galtonia* of the lily family, native to S Africa, esp. *G. candicans*, with lanceolate leaves, waxy white flowers and a fragrant scent. [after Sir Francis *Galton*, 1822–1911, British scientist]

galumph (gəlŭmf´) *v.i.* **1** to move noisily and clumsily. **2** to prance exultantly. **galumphing** *a.* [coined by Lewis Carroll, prob. from GALLOP and TRIUMPH]

galvan- GALVANO-.

galvanism (gal´vənizm) *n.* **1** electricity produced by chemical action, esp. that of acids on metals. **2** the branch of science dealing with the galvanic process. **galvanic** (galvan´ik) *a.* **1** of, relating to or produced by galvanism. **2** (of movements, expression etc.) forced and spasmodic, as if caused by the action of an electric current. *~n.* a number of connected galvanic cells for producing an electric current. **galvanically** *adv.* **galvanist** *n.*

galvanize (gal´vənīz), **galvanise** *v.t.* **1** to rouse into life or activity as by a galvanic shock. **2** to apply galvanism to, esp. to stimulate muscular action etc. by galvanism. **3** to plate with gold or other metal by galvanism. **galvanization** (-zā´shən) *n.* **galvanized iron** *n.* iron coated with zinc (orig. by galvanic deposition), to protect it from moisture. **galvanizer** *n.* [L. *Galvani*, 1737–98, Italian physician and its discoverer]

galvano- (gal´vənō), **galvan-** *comb. form* galvanic current.

galvanometer (galvənom´itə) *n.* a delicate apparatus for determining the existence, direction, and intensity of electric currents. **galvanometric** (-met´rik), **galvanometrical** *a.* **galvanometry** *n.*

galvanoscope (gal´vənōskōp) *n.* an instrument for detecting the presence and showing the direction of electric currents.

galvanotropism (galvənot´rəpizm) *n.* the directional movement in a growing plant induced by an electric stimulus.

Galwegian (galwē´jən) *a.* **1** of or belonging to Galloway, SW Scotland; Gallovidian. **2** of or belonging to Galway, Ireland. *~n.* a native or inhabitant of Galloway or Galway. [assim. to NORWEGIAN]

gam[1] (gam) *n.* **1** a group, or school, of whales. **2** †a keeping company or exchange of visits among whalers at sea. *~v.i.* (*pres.p.* **gamming**, *past*, *p.p.* **gammed**) **1** to congregate or form a school (as whales). **2** to exchange courtesies (as ships at sea). *~v.t.* to call on or exchange visits with (another ship and its crew at sea). [etym. uncertain]

gam[2] (gam) *n.* (*sl.*) a human leg, esp. female. [perh. F dial. *gambe*, leg]

gam- GAMO-.

gama grass (gah´mə) *n.* a fodder grass, *Tripsacum dactyloides*, with culms from 4–7 ft. (1–2 m) high, growing in the south of the US. [perh. var. of *grama grass*]

gamb (gam) *n.* (*Her.*) a figure of an animal's leg on a coat of arms. [OF *gambe* (F *jambe*)]

gamba (gam´bə) *n.* **1** a viola da gamba. **2** an organ stop with a tone like that of the violin or cello. [for VIOLA DA GAMBA (under VIOLA[1])]

gambade (gambād´), **gambado** (-dō) *n.* (*pl.* **gambades, gambados, gambadoes**) **1** a bound or spring of a horse. **2** a caper, a fantastic movement, a freak, a frolic. [F *gambade* or Sp. *gambada*, GAMBOL]

gambado[1] GAMBADE.

gambado[2] (gambā´dō) *n.* (*pl.* **gambados, gambadoes**) a leather legging or large boot for horse riders. [It. *gamba*, the leg]

Gambian (gam´biən) *a.* of or relating to The Gambia in W Africa. *~n.* a native or inhabitant of The Gambia.

gambier (gam´biə) *n.* an extract from the leaves of *Uncaria gambir*, used in medicine as an astringent, and also for dyeing and tanning. [Malay *gambir*]

gambit (gam´bit) *n.* **1** an opening in chess, in which a pawn is sacrificed in order to obtain a favourable position for attack (*King's gambit*; *Queen's gambit*; *Steinitz gambit*). **2** an opening move or manoeuvre in any strategy, campaign, battle of wits etc. **gambit-pawn** *n.* a pawn sacrificed at the opening of a chess game. [ult. from It. *gambetto*, a tripping up, from *gamba*, leg]

gamble (gam´bəl) *v.i.* **1** to play, esp. a game of chance, for money. **2** to risk large sums or other possessions on some contingency. **3** to speculate financially. **4** to knowingly take any sort of serious risk. *~v.t.* to bet (a sum etc.) in gambling. *~n.* **1** gambling. **2** a gambling venture or speculation. **to gamble away** to squander or lose in gambling. **gambler** *n.* [prob. from OE *gamenian*, to play, from *gamen*, a GAME[1], with freq. suf. -LE[1]]

gamboge (gambōj´, -boozh´) *n.* a gum resin, from E Asia, used as a yellow pigment and in medicine. [mod. L *Gambogium*, Cambodia]

gambol (gam´bəl) *v.i.* (*pres.p.* **gambolling,** (*N Am.*) **gamboling,** *past, p.p.* **gambolled,** (*N Am.*) **gamboled**) to frisk or skip about; to frolic. *~n.* a frolic; a skipping or playing about. [earlier *gambold*, *gambalde*, OF *gambade*, It. *gambata*, from *gamba*, leg]

gambrel (gam´brəl) *n.* **1** a horse's hock. **2** a bent piece of wood used for suspending carcasses. **3** a gambrel roof. **gambrel roof** *n.* **1** a curved or double-pitched roof. **2** a roof with inclined sides and gable-like ends. [etym. uncertain (cp. CAMBREL)]

game[1] (gām) *n.* **1** an exercise for diversion, usu. with other players, a pastime. **2** a contest played according to specified rules and decided by chance, strength, skill or a combination of these. **3** (*pl.*) athletic contests, esp. such as are held at periodical dates, as the Olympic Games etc. **4** (*pl.*) athletics and sports on a school curriculum. **5** (*N Am.*) a match, e.g. baseball. **6** a single round in a sporting or other contest. **7** the number of points required to win a game. **8** the score in a game. **9** a project, plan, or scheme designed to defeat others. **10** a success in a game or contest. **11** (*coll.*) **a** (*pl.*) tricks, dodges, subterfuges. **b** a lark, an amusing incident. **12** sport, merriment, diversion. **13** jest, as opposed to being serious. **14** wild animals or birds pursued or shot in field sports, as hares, grouse, partridges, pheasants. **15** the flesh of animals or birds pursued or shot in field sports. **16** an object of pursuit. **17** a flock of swans that are not wild. *~a.* **1** of or relating to game. **2** plucky, spirited. **3** ready, willing (to do etc.). *~v.i.* **1** to play at games of chance. **2** to play for a stake. **3** to gamble. *~v.t.* to gamble (away). **game, set and match** (*coll.*) a final and convincing victory. **off one's game** off form. **on one's game** on form. **the game** (*coll.*) prostitution. **the game is not worth the candle** CANDLE. **the game is up** **1** everything has failed. **2** the game (bird or animal) has started up. **to be off one's game** to be playing poorly, not giving one's best performance. **to be on the game** (*coll.*) to be earning a living as a prostitute. **to die game** to maintain a resolute attitude to the last. **to give the game away** **1** to reveal a secret or strategy. **2** (*coll.*) to reject or abandon a competition etc. **to have the game in one's hands** **1** to be sure of winning. **2** to have success in any contest, undertaking etc. at one's command. **to make (a) game of** to turn into ridicule. **to play a waiting game** WAIT. **to play the game** **1** to abide by the rules. **2** to act in an honourable way. **game bag** *n.* a bag to hold the game killed or taken by a sportsman. **game ball** *n.* GAME POINT (under GAME[1]). **game bird** *n.* **1** a bird hunted for sport or food. **2** a bird of the order of Galliformes, which includes many of those hunted for sport. **gamebook** *n.* a book for recording game killed. **Game Boy**® *n.* a hand-held computer game with a small screen. **game chips** *n.pl.* thinly-cut potato slices often fried and served with game. **gamecock** *n.* a cock bred and trained for fighting. **game-egg** *n.* an egg from which game birds are bred. **game fish** *n.* a large fish that is caught for sport. **gamefowl** *n.* GAME BIRD (under GAME[1]). **gameful** *a.* **1** full of sport or mirth. **2** sportive. **gamekeeper** *n.* a person employed to look after game, coverts etc., and to prevent poaching on a private estate or game reserve. **gamekeeping** *n.* **game laws** *n.pl.* **1** laws for the preservation of game. **2** the regulation of the seasons for killing game etc. **game licence** *n.* a licence giving the right to kill or deal in game. **gamely** *adv.* pluckily, with spirit. **gameness** *n.* spirit, pluck, courage. **game of chance** *n.* a game depending on luck rather than skill. **game plan** *n.* **1** the tactics etc. of a football team, prearranged before a match. **2** any carefully planned strategy. **game point** *n.* a situation in a game of tennis etc. when one point is enough to determine the game. **gamer** *n.* a person who plays a game, esp. a role-playing game or a computer game. **game reserve** *n.* **1** an area of land stocked with game preserved for sport. **2** an area of land set aside for the protection of wild animals. **game show** *n.* a television programme, esp. a quiz show, in which selected contestants compete for prizes. **gamesman** *n.* (*pl.* **gamesmen**) a person who practises gamesmanship. **gamesmanship** *n.* the art or practice of winning games by disconcerting the opponent (by talking etc.) but without actually cheating. **gamesome** (-səm) *a.* **1** inclined to play. **2** merry, gay. **gamesomely** *adv.* **gamesomeness** *n.* **gamester** *n.* a person who is addicted to gaming, a gambler. **game theory, games theory** *n.* the analysis of all choices and strategies available by means of a game or military, social etc. conflict in order to choose the best possible course of action. **game warden** *n.* a person employed to look after game, esp. on a game reserve. **gaming** *n.* gambling. **gaming house** *n.* **1** a house where gambling is carried on. **2** a house of ill-repute, a brothel. **gaming table** *n.* a table for gambling games. **gamy** *a.* (*comp.* **gamier,** *superl.* **gamiest**) **1** having the flavour or odour of game, high. **2** abounding in game. **3** plucky, spirited, game. **4** (*N Am.*) suggestive of scandal. **gamily** *adv.* **gaminess** *n.* [OE *gamen* (cp. Icel. and OHG *gaman*, Dut. *gammen*)]

game[2] (gām) *a.* **1** lame, crippled. **2** (of the arm or leg) crooked. **gammy** (gam´i) *a.* (*comp.* **gammier,** *superl.* **gammiest**) (*coll.*) **1** crippled, crooked (*gammy leg*). **2** wrong, spurious. *~n.* (*pl.* **gammies**) a lame person. [etym. uncertain]

gamelan (gam´əlan) *n.* **1** a SE Asian percussion instrument similar to a xylophone. **2** an orchestra made up of a number of gamelans or similar instruments. [Javanese]

gamet- GAMETO-.
gametangium (gamitan´jiəm) *n.* (*pl.* **gametangia** (-jiə)) a cell or organ in which gametes are formed.
gamete (gam´ēt, -mēt´) *n.* a sexual reproductive cell, either of the two germ cells that unite to form a new organism – in the male, a spermatozoon, in the female an ovum. **gametal** (gam´ətəl, -ē´-), **gametic** (-et´-, -ē´-) *a.* **gamete intra-fallopian transfer** *n.* a treatment for infertile women in which eggs and sperm (the gametes) are injected directly into the Fallopian tubes via a catheter. [Gr. *gametes*, husband, *gamete*, wife]
gameto- (gamē´tō), **gamet-** *comb. form* gamete.
gametocyte (gamē´tōsīt) *n.* a cell that breaks up into gametes.
gametogenesis (gamētōjen´əsis) *n.* the formation of gametes.
gametophyte (gamē´tōfīt) *n.* a plant of the generation that produces gametes in plant species which show alternation of generations. **gametophytic** (-fit´ik) *a.*
gamic (gam´ik) *a.* **1** (*Biol.*) of or relating to sex, sexual, sexually produced. **2** (of ova) capable of development after sexual fertilization. [Gr. *gamikos*, from *gamos*, marriage]
gamily GAMY (under GAME[1]).
gamin (gam´in, -mã´) *n.* **1** a homeless child, an urchin. **2** a cheeky child. [F, perh. from G *Gemein*, a common soldier]
gamine (gam´ēn, -ēn´) *n.* **1** a small boylike girl or woman. **2** a female gamin. ~*a.* (esp. of a girl or woman) having a boyish look. [F]
gaminess GAMY (under GAME[1]).
gamma (gam´ə) *n.* **1** the third letter of the Greek alphabet (Γ, γ). **2** a third-class mark given for a student's work. **3** (**Gamma**) the third star (in brightness or position etc.) in a constellation. **gamma camera** *n.* a device which detects gamma radiation, used for imaging parts of the body into which a radioactive substance has been introduced. **gamma globulin** *n.* any of a group of proteins that are carried in blood and serum and include most known antibodies. **gamma radiation, gamma rays** *n.* short-wavelength, penetrating electromagnetic rays emitted by radioactive substances, used in the treatment of cancer and in radiography of metals. **gamma securities, gamma stocks** *n.pl.* Stock Exchange stocks which are rarely traded. [Gr.]
gammadion (gəmad´iən), **gammation** (-matiən) *n.* (*pl.* **gammadia** (-iə), **gammatia**) **1** an ornament composed of the gamma singly or in combination, formerly used in sacerdotal vestments in the Greek Church. **2** a cruciform ornament composed of four gammas, placed back to back, forming a voided Greek cross. **3** a fylfot, a swastika. [late Gr., from GAMMA]
†**gammer** (gam´ə) *n.* an old woman. [prob. a corr. of GRANDMOTHER (under GRAND)]
gammon[1] (gam´ən) *n.* **1** the buttock or thigh of a hog salted and dried. **2** a cured ham. ~*v.t.* **1** to make into bacon. **2** to salt and dry in smoke. [OF *gambon* (F *jambon*), from *gambe*, a leg]
gammon[2] (gam´ən) *n.* **1** nonsense, humbug. **2** a fraud, a hoax. ~*int.* nonsense, humbug. ~*v.t.* to hoax, to impose upon. ~*v.i.* **1** to pretend. **2** to talk deceptively, to chaff. [orig. thieves' slang, prob. from ME and OE *gamen*, GAME[1]]
gammon[3] (gam´ən) *n.* **1** a defeat at backgammon in which the winner's score is equivalent to two games. **2** †backgammon. ~*v.t.* to win a gammon against (an opponent in backgammon). [prob. from OE *gamen*, GAME[1]]
gammon[4] (gam´ən) *v.t.* (*Naut.*) to make fast (the bowsprit) to the stem of a ship. ~*n.* the lashing used. **gammoning** *n.* **gammoning-hole, gammoning-plate** *n.* the hole through which or to which the gammoning is fastened. [etym. uncertain]
gammy GAME[2].
gamo- (gam´ō) *comb. form* (*Biol.*) **1** sexual. **2** having certain parts united. [Gr. *gamos*, marriage]
gamogenesis (gamōjen´əsis) *n.* (*Biol.*) sexual reproduction. **gamogenetic** (-jinet´ik) *a.* **gamogenetically** *adv.*
gamopetalous (gamōpet´ələs) *a.* (*Bot.*) having the petals united.
gamophyllous (gamōfil´əs) *a.* (*Bot.*) having the leaves united.
gamosepalous (gamōsep´ələs) *a.* (*Bot.*) having the sepals united.
gamp (gamp) *n.* (*coll.*) an umbrella, esp. a large and clumsy one. [Mrs *Gamp*, a nurse in Dickens's *Martin Chuzzlewit*]
gamut (gam´ət) *n.* **1** the whole range, compass or extent. **2** the whole series of notes recognized by musicians. **3** a major diatonic scale. **4** †the first or lowest note in Guido's scale equivalent to G on the lowest line of the modern bass stave. **to run the gamut of** to go through the complete range of. [med. L *gamma ut* (*gamma*, the third letter of the Greek alphabet, used by Guido of Arezzo to mark the first or lowest note in the medieval music scale, combined with *ut*, the first word in a mnemonic stanza from a hymn beginning *Ut queant laxis resonare fibris*, containing the six names of the hexachord *Ut re mi fa sol la*)]
gamy GAME[1].
-gamy (gəmi) *comb. form* marriage or kind of marriage, as in *bigamy*, *endogamy*, *misogamy*. [Gr. *gamos*, marriage]
gander (gan´də) *n.* **1** the male of the goose. **2** a simpleton, a noodle. **3** (*coll.*) a quick look. ~*v.i.* to look quickly. **ganderism** *n.* behaviour suited to a gander. **gander party** *n.* STAG-NIGHT (under STAG). [OE *gandra*, earlier *ganra* (*d* inserted as in Dut. *gander*), perh. cogn. with GOOSE]
G and S, G & S *abbr.* Gilbert and Sullivan.
g and t *abbr.* gin and tonic.
gang[1] (gang) *n.* **1** a number of persons associated for a particular purpose (often in a bad sense). **2** a number of workmen under a foreman, or of slaves or convicts. **3** a set of tools operating together. **4** a course or vein in a mine. ~*v.i.* to act in concert with. **to gang up** to join with others (in doing something). **to gang up on** to join with others to make an attack on (someone). **gang-bang** *n.* (*sl.*) an occasion on which a number of males have successive sexual intercourse with one female. **gang-banger** *n.* (*esp. N Am., sl.*) a member of an urban teenage gang. **ganger** *n.* the overseer or foreman of a gang of labourers. **gangland** *n.* the world of organized crime. **gang mill** *n.* a saw mill with gang saws. **gang plug** *n.* an electrical adaptor with several sockets. **gang rape** *n.* successive rapes by a number of people committed on one victim on one occasion. **gang-rape** *v.t.* to carry out a gang rape on. **gang saw** *n.* a saw with several blades fitted in a frame, producing parallel cuts. **gang show** *n.* a variety entertainment performed by members of the Scout Association and Guide Association. **gangsman** *n.* (*pl.* **gangsmen**) a ganger. **gangsta** (-stə) *n.* **1** (*sl.*) a gangster. **2** (*also* **gangsta rap**) a type of rap music with lyrics often inspired by gangsters. **gangster** (-stə) *n.* a member of a criminal gang. **gangsterland** *n.* gangland. **gang switches** *n.pl.* electrical switches connected together in order to be operated simultaneously.
gang[2] (gang) *v.i.* (*Sc.*) to go. **gangplank** *n.* a plank, usu. with cleats, used for boarding or landing from a vessel. **gangway** *n.* **1** an opening in the bulwarks affording entrance to or exit from a vessel. **2** a temporary bridge affording means of passage from a ship to the shore. **3** a passage into or out of a building or between rows of seats. **4** a passage connecting different parts of a vessel. **5** in a mine, a main level. **6** in the House of Commons,

a narrow cross passage giving access to the back benches, and dividing the more independent members from the immediate supporters of the Government and the opposition. ~*int.* clear the way! [OE *gangan* (cp. Icel. *ganga*, OHG *gangan*)]

gang[3] GANGUE.

gangling (gang´gling) *a.* loosely built, lanky, awkward.

gangle *v.i.* to move awkwardly. **gangly** *a.* (*comp.* **ganglier**, *superl.* **gangliest**). [OE *gangan*, to go]

ganglion (gang´gliən) *n.* (*pl.* **ganglia** (-ə)) **1** in pathology, a globular growth in the sheath of a tendon. **2** an enlargement in the course of a nerve forming a local centre for nervous action. **3** an aggregation of nerve cells forming a nucleus in the central nervous system. **4** a glandiform organ such as the spleen or the thyroid body. **gangliac** (-ak), **gangliar, ganglionic** (-on´-) *a.* of or relating to a ganglion or ganglia. **gangliated** (-ātid), **gangliform** (-fawm), **ganglionary** (-əri), **ganglionated** *a.* composed of ganglia. [Gr.]

gangrene (gang´grēn) *n.* **1** death or decay in a part of the body, the first stage of mortification, as a result of poor blood supply to the part. **2** moral corruption, social decay. ~*v.t.* **1** to cause gangrene in. **2** to infect with decay or vice; to corrupt. ~*v.i.* to become gangrenous. **gangrenescent** (-grənes´-) *a.* **gangrenous** (-grə-) *a.* [L *gangraena*, Gr. *gangraina*]

gangsta, gangster GANG[1].

gangue (gang), **gang** *n.* the earthy matter or matrix in which ores are embedded. [F, from G *Gang*, vein, lode, cogn. with GANG[1]]

gangway GANG[2].

ganister (gan´istə) *n.* **1** a kind of grit or hard sandstone from the lower coal-measures. **2** a mixture of ground quartz and fire-clay used for lining Bessemer converters. [etym. uncertain]

ganja (gan´jə) *n.* marijuana, a dried preparation of *Cannabis sativa* or Indian hemp, smoked as an intoxicant and narcotic. [Hind. *gānjhā*]

gannet (gan´it) *n.* **1** a seabird, *Sula bassana*, also called *solan goose*. **2** (*coll.*) a greedy person. **gannetry** *n.* (*pl.* **gannetries**) a gannet colony. [OE *ganot* (cp. Dut. *gent*, MHG *ganze*, GANDER]

ganoid (gan´oid) *a.* **1** (of fish scales) bright, smooth, like enamel. **2** (of fish) having such scales. ~*n.* any fish having ganoid scales. **ganoidal** (-oi´dəl), **ganoidean** (-oi´diən) *a.* **ganoin** (-ō´in) *n.* a calcareous substance that forms a shiny, enamel-like coating on ganoid scales. [F *ganoïde* (Gr. *ganos*, brightness, -OID)]

gansey (gan´zi) *n.* a woollen pullover or jersey. [var. of GUERNSEY]

gantlet GAUNTLET[2].

gantry (gan´tri), **gauntry** (gawn´-) *n.* (*pl.* **gantries, gauntries**) **1** (*only* **gantry**) a structure surrounding a rocket on the launch pad, for carrying railway signals, a travelling crane etc. **2** a wooden frame for standing a barrel upon. [etym. uncertain (perh. from OF *gantier*, also *chantier*, L *canterium*)]

gaol JAIL.

gap (gap) *n.* **1** an opening, a breach, as in a hedge, a fence etc. **2** a chasm, a break in a mountain ridge. **3** a breach of continuity, a blank, hiatus, interruption. **4** a deficiency. **5** a wide divergence. ~*v.t.* (*pres.p.* **gapping**, *past, p.p.* **gapped**) to make a gap in. **to stand in the gap** to expose oneself for the protection of others. **to stop/ fill/ supply a gap** to repair a defect or make up a deficiency. **gapped** *a.* **gappy** *a.* **gap-toothed** *a.* having spaces between the teeth. [Icel., from *gapa*, see GAPE]

gape (gāp) *v.i.* **1** to stare with open mouth in wonder, surprise or perplexity. **2** to open the mouth wide. **3** to yawn. **4** to open in a fissure or chasm, to split or stand open. ~*n.* **1** the act of gaping; a fit of staring open-mouthed. **2** a stare with open mouth. **3** a yawn; a fit of yawning. **4** the width of the mouth when opened, as of birds etc. **5** the part of a beak that opens. **6** the opening between the shells of a bivalve that does not shut completely. **7** (*pl.*) a disease in young poultry caused by the gapeworm and characterized by much gaping. **to gape at** to open the mouth and gaze at with astonishment. **to gape for/ after** to desire eagerly, to crave. **gaper** *n.* someone who or something which gapes, esp. various kinds of birds, fish and molluscs. **gapeworm** *n.* a nematode worm of the family Syngamidae, that causes gapes in poultry. **gapingly** *adv.* [Icel. *gapa* (cp. Dut. *gapen*, G *gaffen*)]

gapped, gappy GAP.

gar (gah), **garfish** *n.* (*pl. in general* **gar, garfish,** *in particular* **gars, garfishes**) **1** any fish of the family Belonidae with a long pointed snout, esp. *Belone belone*. **2** (*NAm.*) a garpike. **garpike** *n.* (*NAm.*) any fish of the American genus *Lepisosteus*. [OE *gār*, a spear, FISH[1]]

garage (gar´ahzh, -ij) *n.* **1** a building for housing or repairing motor vehicles. **2** an establishment where this is done as a business or where motor fuels etc. are sold. **3 a** GARAGE ROCK (under GARAGE). **b** a type of house music. ~*v.t.* to put or keep in a garage. ~*a.* (*coll.*) rough-and-ready, amateurish, improvised. **garage rock** *n.* a type of unsophisticated rock music. **garage sale** *n.* a sale of second-hand goods held on the grounds of a private home, esp. in a garage. [F, from *garer*, to put into dock, from Gmc. (cp. Goth. *warjan*, OE *werian*, to defend)]

garam masala (gŭrəm məsah´lə) *n.* a mixture of spices often used in Indian cookery. [Urdu]

☒ **garantee** common misspelling of GUARANTEE.

garb[1] (gahb) *n.* **1** dress, costume. **2** distinctive style of dress. **3** outward appearance. ~*v.t.* **1** to put garments upon. **2** to put in a distinctive dress. [through F *garbe* (now *galbe*) or directly from It. *garbo*, grace, elegance, from Gmc. (cp. OHG *garwī*, *garawī*, cogn. with GEAR)]

garb[2] (gahb) *n.* (*Her.*) a sheaf of grain. [A-F *garbe* (F *gerbe*), from Gmc. (cp. OHG *garba*, G *Garbe*)]

garbage (gah´bij) *n.* **1** kitchen waste. **2** anything worthless or offensive, sordid rubbish. **3** nonsense. **4** irrelevant or invalid data. **5** animal refuse, esp. the entrails, offal. **garbage in, garbage out** (*Comput.*) if poor-quality or irrelevant data is entered or programmed, the results are worthless. **garbage bin** *n.* (*esp. Austral.*) a dustbin. **garbage can** *n.* (*N Am.*) a dustbin. **garbage disposal unit** *n.* (*N Am.*) a waste disposal unit. [etym. uncertain]

garble (gah´bəl) *v.t.* **1** to jumble, give a confused version of (a story, quotation etc.). **2** to distort or mutilate (an account, story etc.) deliberately, in such a way as to convey a false impression. **3** to pervert, to falsify. **4** †to separate the fine or valuable parts off from the coarse and worthless. **garbler** *n.* [perh. through OF *garbeller*, from It. *garbellare*, to garble spices, from Arab. *gharbala*, to sift]

garbo (gah´bō) *n.* (*pl.* **garbos**) (*Austral.*, *coll.*) a refuse collector. [GARBAGE]

garboard (gah´bawd) *n.* (*Naut.*) the first plank fastened on either side of a ship's keel. **garboard-strake** *n.* **1** the row of planks next to the keel on a ship's bottom. **2** the row of plates corresponding to this in an iron ship. [obs. Dut. *gaarboord*]

garbologist (gahbol´əjist) *n.* (*US, coll. or facet.*) a refuse collector. [GARBAGE]

garçon (gah´son) *n.* a waiter (usu. used as a form of address: *Garçon!*). [F, dim. of *gars*, lad]

Garda (gah´də) *n.* the police force of the Irish Republic. **garda** *n.* (*pl.* **gardai** (-dē)) a member of the Irish police force.

gardant GUARDANT (under GUARD).

garden (gah´dən) *n.* **1** an enclosed piece of ground appropriated to the cultivation of fruit, flowers or vegetables, often with a lawn. **2** (*pl.*) a public pleasure-ground adorned with trees, flower-beds etc. **3** (*US*) a hall for public assemblies. ~*a.* **1** of or relating to a garden. **2** cultivated, not wild. ~*v.i.* **1** to cultivate a garden. **2** (*coll.*) in cricket, to smooth out bumps etc. in the pitch with the bat, often as a delaying tactic. **common or garden** (*coll.*) the ordinary (sort). **everything in the garden is lovely** everything appears to be well. **the Garden** the philosophical school of Epicurus or its tenets. **to lead (someone) up the garden path** LEAD[1]. **garden balsam** *n.* the plant *Impatiens balsamina*, a fast-growing annual with lance-shaped leaves and pink or white flowers. **garden centre** *n.* a place where plants, fertilizers and garden tools and equipment are sold. **garden city, garden suburb, garden village** *n.* a planned town or suburb in rural surroundings. **garden cress** *n.* a pepperwort, *Lepidium sativum*. **gardened** *a.* **1** cultivated like a garden. **2** furnished with gardens. **garden-engine** *n.* a pump and tank on wheels for watering plants. **gardener** *n.* a person who gardens, esp. one whose occupation is to attend to or to manage gardens. **gardenesque** (-esk´) *a.* **garden flat** *n.* a flat that opens onto a garden. **garden frame** *n.* a glazed frame for protecting plants during the winter or for forcing. **garden glass** *n.* a bell-glass for protecting plants. **gardening** *n.* **1** horticulture. **2** work in a garden. **garden party** *n.* a social meeting or a company entertained on a lawn or in a garden. **garden plot** *n.* a piece of ground used as a garden. **garden seat** *n.* a seat, esp. a long one for several persons, for use in a garden. **garden warbler** *n.* a European woodland bird, *Sylvia borin*. [A-F *gardin* (F *jardin*), from Gmc. (cp. OS *gardo*, OE *geard*, YARD[1], Icel. *garthr*, GARTH, G *Garten*)]

gardenia (gahdē´niə) *n.* any shrub or tree of the tropical genus *Gardenia*, usu. cultivated in greenhouses for its large fragrant flowers. [Dr Alexander *Garden*, d. 1791, US botanist]

☒ **gardian** common misspelling of GUARDIAN.

garfish GAR.

garganey (gah´gəni) *n.* (*pl.* **garganeys**) a small duck of Europe and Asia, *Anas querquedula*, the male of which has a white stripe over each eye. [It. dial. *garganello*]

gargantuan (gahgan´tūən) *a.* immense, enormous, incredibly big. **gargantuism** *n.* [*Gargantua*, the giant of Rabelais' satire *Gargantua and Pantagruel*]

garget (gah´git) *n.* **1** an inflammation of the throat in cattle. **2** an inflammation of the udder of cows or ewes. **3** (*US*) pokeweed. **gargety** *a.* [OF *gargate*, the throat (etym. uncertain; cp. GARGOYLE)]

gargle (gah´gəl) *v.t.* to rinse (the mouth or throat) with some medicated liquid, which is prevented from passing down the throat by the breath. ~*v.i.* **1** to rinse the mouth or throat in this way. **2** to make a sound like that in gargling. ~*n.* **1** a liquid used for washing the mouth or throat. **2** (*sl.*) an alcoholic drink. [F *gargouiller*]

gargoyle (gah´goil), **gurgoyle** (gœ´-) *n.* a grotesque spout, usu. carved to represent a human or animal figure, projecting from Gothic buildings, esp. churches, to throw rainwater clear of the wall. [F *gargouille*, windpipe (cp. F *gorge*, throat, Gr. *garg-*, base of *gargarizein*, GARGARIZE (under GARGARISM))]

garibaldi (garibawl´di) *n.* (*pl.* **garibaldis**) **1** a loose kind of blouse worn by women or children and popular in the 1860s, like the red shirts worn by Garibaldi and his men. **2** a garibaldi biscuit. **3** a small red fish, *Hypsypops rubicundus*, of California. **garibaldi biscuit** *n.* a sandwich-type biscuit with a layer of currants. [Giuseppe *Garibaldi*, 1807–82, liberator of Italy]

garish (geə´rish) *a.* **1** gaudy, showy, flashy. **2** excessively or extravagantly decorated. **3** dazzling, glaring. **garishly** *adv.* **garishness** *n.* [earlier *gaurish*, from obs. *gauren*, to stare, etym. uncertain]

garland (gah´lənd) *n.* **1** a wreath or festoon of flowers, leaves etc. worn round the neck or hung up. **2** a festoon of metal, stone, ribbons or other material used for decoration etc. **3** the prize, the chief honour. **4** a collection of choice pieces, esp. of poems. ~*v.t.* to deck with a garland. [OF *garlande*, etym. uncertain (F *guirlande*, from It. *ghirlanda*)]

garlic (gah´lik) *n.* any of various bulbous-rooted plants of the genus *Allium*, esp. *A. sativum*, with a strong odour and a pungent taste, used in cookery. **garlic bread** *n.* a long thin bread roll sliced, spread with garlic butter and heated. **garlic butter** *n.* butter flavoured with garlic. **garlic-eater** *n.* **garlicky** *a.* **garlic mayonnaise** *n.* mayonnaise flavoured with garlic, aioli. **garlic mustard** *n.* a plant, *Alliaria petiolata*, of the mustard family with small white flowers and a garlic smell. [OE *gārlēac* (as GAR, LEEK)]

garment (gah´mənt) *n.* **1** an article of clothing, esp. one of the larger articles, such as a coat or gown. **2** (*pl.*) clothes. **3** a visible covering. ~*v.t.* (*usu. p.p., poet.*) to attire with or as with a garment. **garmentless** *a.* [ME and OF *garnement*, from *garnir*, see GARNISH]

garner (gah´nə) *v.t.* to store in or as in a granary, to gather. ~*n.* **1** a place for storing grain, a granary. **2** a store, a repository. [OF *gernier*, *grenier*, L *grānārium*, GRANARY]

garnet (gah´nit) *n.* a vitreous mineral of varying composition, colour and quality, the deep red, transparent kinds of which are prized as gems. [OF *grenat*, *granat*, late L *grānātus*, from (*mālum*) *grānātum*, POMEGRANATE, from the resemblance to its seeds]

garni (gah´nē) *a.* in cooking, garnished, trimmed, esp. with salad. [F]

garnish (gah´nish) *v.t.* **1** to adorn; to embellish (as a dish of food) with something laid round it. **2** to supply, to furnish. **3** (*Law*) **a** to warn to appear in court. **b** to give notice to, not to pay money to a defendant. ~*n.* an ornament, a decoration, especially things put round a dish of food as embellishment. **garnishee** (-shē´) *n.* a person who has received notice not to pay any money which they owe to a third person, who is indebted to the person giving notice. ~*v.t.* (*p.p.* **garnisheed**) (*Law*) **1** to garnish. **2** to attach (money etc.) to prevent payment to a defendant. **garnisher** *n.* **garnishing** *n.* **1** the act of ornamenting. **2** things used for decoration, esp. of dishes of food. **garnishment** *n.* **1** an ornament, an embellishment. **2** (*Law*) a warning to a party to appear in court, or not to pay money etc. to a defendant. [OF *garniss-*, stem of *garnir*, *guarnir*, *warnir*, to defend, to fortify, from Gmc. (cp. OHG *warnōn*, G *warnen*, to WARN)]

garniture (gah´nichə) *n.* **1** ornamental appendages, trimmings, ornament, embellishment. **2** furniture, appurtenances. **3** costume, dress.

garotte GARROTTE.

garpike GAR.

garret (gar´it) *n.* **1** an upper room or storey immediately under the roof, an attic. **2** †a turret, a watch-tower. **3** (*sl.*) †the head. [OF *garite* (F *guérite*), from *garir*, *warir*, to defend, from Gmc. (cp. OHG *warjan*, OE *werian*)]

garrison (gar´isən) *n.* **1** a body of troops stationed in a fort or fortified place. **2** a fortified place manned with soldiers, guns, etc., a stronghold. ~*v.t.* **1** to furnish (a fortress) with soldiers. **2** to occupy as a garrison. **3** to place on duty defending a garrison. **garrison town** *n.* a town in which a garrison is regularly stationed. [F *garison*, defence, safety, from *garir*, to defend]

garron (gar´ən) *n.* a small horse bred in Galloway, the Highlands and Ireland. [Gael. *gearran*, a gelding]

garrotte (gərot´), **garotte**, (*N Am.*) **garrote** *n.* **1** (*Hist.*) a method of execution in which the victim was fastened by an iron collar to an upright post, and a knob operated by a screw or lever dislocated the spinal column, or a small blade severed the spinal cord at the base of the brain (orig. the method was strangulation by a cord twisted with a stick). **2** killing with a length of wire around the throat. **3** robbery with strangling of the victim. *~v.t.* **1** to execute or kill by this means. **2** to render helpless or insensible by strangulation in order to rob. **garrotter** *n.* [Sp. *garrote*, a stick, etym. uncertain]

garrulous (gar´ələs) *a.* **1** talkative, loquacious, chattering. **2** wordy. **garrulity** (-roo´-) *n.* **garrulously** *adv.* **garrulousness** *n.* [L *garrulus*, from *garrīre*, to chatter]

garter (gah´tə) *n.* **1** a band round the leg for holding a stocking up. **2** (*N Am.*) a suspender for a stocking or sock. *~v.t.* **1** to fasten (a stocking etc.) with a garter. **2** to put a garter upon. **3** †to invest with the Order of the Garter. **the Garter 1** the badge of the highest order of British knighthood, instituted by Edward III, about 1348. **2** the order itself. **3** membership of this. **garter belt** *n.* (*N Am.*) a suspender belt. **Garter Principal King-of-Arms** *n.* the chief herald of the Order of the Garter. **garter snake** *n.* a harmless American snake belonging to the genus *Thamnophis.* **garter stitch** *n.* plain knitting. [OF *gartier* (F *jarretiere*), from *garet* (F *jarret*), the leg, perh. from Celt. (cp. Bret. and Welsh *gar*, the shank of the leg)]

garth (gahth) *n.* **1** the grass plot surrounded by the cloisters of a cathedral, monastery etc. **2** a close, a yard. **3** a garden, croft or paddock. **4** a fish weir. [Icel. *garthr*, cogn. OE *geard*, YARD[2]]

gas (gas) *n.* (*pl.* **gases,** (*esp. N Am.*) **gasses**) **1** a substance in the form of air, possessing the condition of perfect fluid elasticity. **2** a gaseous substance used for lighting and heating, esp. that obtained from gas-bearing rock structures or from coal. **3** (*esp. N Am., coll.*) gasolene, petrol. **4** in coal-mining, an explosive mixture of firedamp and air. **5** a gas used as an anaesthetic. **6** empty talk, frothy eloquence. **7** boasting, bragging. **8** (*dated coll. or dial.*) something great or wonderful (*It's a gas!*). *~v.i.* (*pres.p.* **gassing,** *past, p.p.* **gassed**) **1** to indulge in empty talk. **2** to boast. *~v.t.* **1** to attack, to stupefy or kill by means of poison gas. **2** to supply gas to, to treat or inflate with gas. **3** to subject (a fabric, such as lace) to the action of burning gas in order to remove loose fibres. **to step on the gas 1** to accelerate a motor vehicle. **2** to hurry. **gasbag** *n.* **1** a bag for holding gas or stopping an escape from a gas main. **2** (*coll.*) a talkative person. **gas black** *n.* the fine black powder produced by burning natural gas and used as a pigment in paints. **gas bottle** *n.* a steel cylinder for holding compressed gas. **gas bracket** *n.* a pipe projecting from a wall and fitted with a burner or burners. **gas burner** *n.* the tube or jet at which the gas issues and is ignited. **gas cap** *n.* gas found above the liquid in an oil-bearing rock structure. **gas chamber, gas oven** *n.* an airtight place designed for killing animals or humans by means of a poisonous gas. **gas chromatography** *n.* a method of analysing a mixture of volatile substances which depends on the relative speeds at which the various components of the mixture pass through a long narrow tube that contains an inert gas and a solvent. **gas-coal** *n.* bituminous coal from which gas for heating and illuminating purposes can be made. **gas coke** *n.* coke left as a residuum after gas has been extracted from gas-coal. **gas cooker** *n.* a cooking stove using gas as a fuel. **gas-cooled** *a.* cooled by a flow of gas. **gas-cooled reactor** *n.* a nuclear reactor that uses a gas as the coolant. **gas engine** *n.* an engine in which the motive power is obtained from the explosion of gas. **gaseous** (gā´siəs, gas´-) *a.* **1** in the form of gas. **2** like gas. **gaseousness** *n.* **gas escape** *n.* a leakage of gas. **gas field** *n.* a region in which natural gas occurs. **gas fire** *n.* a device for heating a room etc. by burning gas. **gas-fired** *a.* fuelled by a gas or gases. **gas-fitter** *n.* a person employed to lay pipes and put up fixtures for gas. **gas-fittings** *n.pl.* brackets, stoves, fires and other apparatus for lighting and heating by gas. **gas gangrene** *n.* a gangrenous infection in deep wounds caused by bacteria which produce gases in the surrounding tissues. **gas gauge** *n.* an instrument for testing gas pressure. **gas-guzzler** *n.* (*N Am., coll.*) a (usu. large) car that uses a lot of petrol. **gasholder** *n.* a large structure for storing gas. **gasiform** *a.* of the nature or form of gas. **gasify** *v.t.* (*3rd pers. sing. pres.* **gasifies,** *pres.p.* **gasifying,** *past, p.p.* **gasified**) to convert into gas. **gasifiable** *a.* **gasification** (-fikā´shən) *n.* **gas jet** *n.* **1** a gas burner. **2** a jet of flame from it. **gas lamp** *n.* a lamp that burns gas. **gasless** *a.* **gaslight** *n.* **1** the light produced by the combustion of coal gas. **2** a gas jet. **gaslit** *a.* **gas lighter** *n.* a cigarette lighter that uses gas as a fuel. **gas main** *n.* a principal pipe leading from a gasworks and having branches and distributing pipes. **gasman** *n.* (*pl.* **gasmen**) **1** a person employed to read household gas meters. **2** a gas-fitter. **3** a person employed at a gasworks. **4** †a collector of money due for the supply of gas. **gas mantle** *n.* a chemically-prepared incombustible gauze hood for a gas lamp, that becomes incandescent when heated. **gas mask** *n.* a mask with a chemical filter to protect the wearer against poisonous gases and fumes. **gas meter** *n.* a machine for measuring and recording the quantity of gas consumed. **gasohol** *n.* a fuel made by mixing petrol and ethyl alcohol. **gas oil** *n.* an oil distilled from crude petroleum used as a fuel for heating etc. **gas-permeable** *a.* allowing gases to pass, esp. to the cornea of the eye. **gas plant** *n.* fraxinella. **gas ring** *n.* a circular hollow pipe with perforations that serve as gas jets, used for cooking. **gasser** *n.* **1** (*coll.*) a person who talks a lot, a gossip. **2** (*sl.*) an attractive or impressive person or thing. **gas shell** *n.* an artillery shell containing a chemical mixture that produces or diffuses poison gas on explosion. **gas show** *n.* an expression on the surface of natural gas escaping from underground reservoirs. **gas station** *n.* (*N Am., coll.*) a filling station, petrol station. **gassy** *a.* (*comp.* **gassier,** *superl.* **gassiest**) **1** (of carbonated drinks etc.) very effervescent. **2** like gas. **3** gaseous. **4** full of empty talk. **5** (*coll.*) quick to flare up, touchy, irascible. **gassiness** *n.* **gas tank** *n.* **1** (*N Am., coll.*) the petrol tank of a motor vehicle. **2** a gasometer. **gas tar** *n.* coal tar. **gas thermometer** *n.* a device for measuring temperature by observing the volume of gas at a constant pressure, or the pressure of gas at a constant volume. **gas-tight** *a.* (of pipes etc.) not allowing gas to escape, not leaky. **gas trap** *n.* in plumbing, a double curve or U-shaped section of a pipe in which water remains and forms a seal that blocks the escape of foul gases. **gas turbine** *n.* an internal-combustion engine in which air is heated under pressure; the hot, expanding gas drives a turbine, which in turn powers the compressor. **gas welding** *n.* the welding of metals with a hot flame produced by the burning of gases, usu. oxyacetylene. **gas well** *n.* a well that yields natural gas. **gasworks** *n.* an industrial plant where gas, esp. coal gas, is produced. [Dut., invented by the chemist J. B. van Helmont, 1577–1644, from Gr. *chaos*, see CHAOS]

Gascon (gas´kən) *n.* **1** a native of Gascony, France. **2** (**gascon**) a boaster. *~a.* of or relating to Gascony. **gasconade** (-nād´) *n.* boasting, bravado, bragging. *~v.i.* to boast, to brag. **gasconader** (-nā´də) *n.* [F]

gaselier (gasəliə´), **gasolier** *n.* an ornamental metalwork pendant with branches carrying gas burners for lighting a room etc. [*gas*, chand*elier*]

gaseous GAS.

gash[1] (gash) *n.* **1** a long, deep, open cut, esp. in flesh; a flesh wound. **2** a cleft. **3** an act of gashing someone or something. *~v.t.* to make a long, deep, gaping cut

in. [earlier *garsh*, *garse*, OF *garser*, perh. from late L *caraxāre*, Gr. *charassein*, to scratch, incise]
gash[2] (gash) *a.* (*sl.*) spare, extra, surplus to requirements. ~*n.* rubbish, surplus material. [etym. uncertain]
gash[3] (gash) *v.i.* (*Sc.*) to gossip, to tattle. [etym. uncertain]
gasiform, gasify etc. GAS.
gasket (gas´kit) *n.* **1** a strip of tough but flexible material for packing or caulking joints in pipes, engines etc. to make them airtight or watertight. **2** a plaited cord by which the sails, when furled, are bound close to the yards or gaffs. **to blow a gasket** (*coll.*) to lose one's temper. [etym. uncertain]
gaskin (gas´kin) *n.* the part of a horse's hind leg between the stifle and the hock, lower thigh.
gaso- (gas´ō) *comb. form* of, relating to or using gas.
gasohol GAS.
gasolene GASOLINE.
gasolier GASELIER.
gasoline (gas´əlēn), **gasolene** *n.* **1** a volatile inflammable product of the distillation of petroleum, used for heating and lighting. **2** (*N Am.*) petrol.
gasometer (gəsom´itə) *n.* **1** (*Chem.*) an apparatus for measuring, collecting, preserving or mixing different gases. **2** (*coll.*) a gasholder. **gasometric** (-met´-) *a.* **gasometry** *n.* the science, act or practice of measuring gases.
gasoscope (gas´əskōp) *n.* an instrument for detecting the presence of carburetted hydrogen in mines, buildings etc.
gasp (gahsp) *v.i.* to breathe in a convulsive manner, as from exhaustion or astonishment. ~*v.t.* to emit or utter with gasps. ~*n.* a short painful catching of the breath. **at the last gasp 1** at the last extremity. **2** at the point of death. **to gasp out/ away** to breathe out (one's life etc.) convulsively. **gasper** *n.* **1** a person who gasps. **2** (*dated sl.*) a cigarette. **gaspingly** *adv.* [prob. from Icel. *geispa*, to yawn (cp. Dut. *gijpen*, OE *gipian*, in *gipung*, a gaping)]
gasser, gassy etc. GAS.
Gastarbeiter (gast´ahbītə) *n.* (*pl.* **Gastarbeiters, Gastarbeiter**) a person with temporary permission to work in a foreign country. [G, from *Gast*, guest, *Arbeiter*, worker]
gasteral GASTRIC.
gasteropod GASTROPOD.
gasthaus (gast´hows) *n.* (*pl.* **gasthäuser** (-hoizə)) a German guest house or small hotel. [G, from *Gast*, guest, *Haus*, house]
gasthof (gast´hof) *n.* (*pl.* **gasthöfe** (-hœfə)) a (relatively large) German hotel. [G, *Hof*, hotel]
☒ **gastly** common misspelling of GHASTLY.
gastr- GASTRO-.
gastral GASTRIC.
gastralgia (gastral´jə) *n.* pain in the stomach. **gastralgic** *a., n.*
gastrectomy (gastrek´təmi) *n.* (*pl.* **gastrectomies**) the surgical removal of (part of) the stomach.
gastric (gas´trik) *a.* of or relating to the stomach. **gastral, gasteral** (gas´tərəl) *a.* **gastric acid** *n.* gastric juice. **gastric fever** *n.* inflammation of the stomach, enteric or typhoid fever. **gastric flu** *n.* (*coll.*) any of several types of stomach disorder, with symptoms including nausea, diarrhoea, abdominal cramps and high temperature. **gastric juice** *n.* a clear, colourless acid secreted by the stomach, one of the principal agents in digestion. **gastric ulcer** *n.* an ulcer of the inner wall of the stomach. **gastrin** (-trin) *n.* a hormone produced in the stomach that stimulates the secretion of gastric juice. **gastritis** (-trī´tis) *n.* inflammation of the stomach. [late L *gastricus*, from Gr. *gastēr -eros*, stomach]
gastro- (gas´trō), **gastr-** *comb. form* stomach. [Gr. *gastēr -eros*, stomach]
gastrocnemius (gastroknē´miəs) *n.* (*pl.* **gastrocnemii** (-iī)) the large muscle in the calf of the leg which helps to extend the foot. [Gr. *gastroknēmia* (as GASTRO-, *knēmē*, leg)]
gastroenteric (gastrōenter´ik) *a.* of or relating to the stomach and the intestines. **gastroenteritis** (-tərī´tis) *n.* inflammation of the stomach and of the intestines. **gastroenterology** (-tərol´əji) *n.* the study of diseases of the stomach and the intestines. **gastroenterological** (-loj´-) *a.* **gastroenterologist** *n.* **gastroenterostomy** (-təros´təmi) *n.* (*pl.* **gastroenterostomies**) the surgical formation of an opening between the stomach and the small intestine.
gastrointestinal (gastrōintestī´nəl) *a.* of or relating to the stomach or the intestines.
gastrolith (gas´trəlith) *n.* **1** (*Zool.*) a small stone swallowed by birds, reptiles and fish to aid digestion in the gizzard. **2** (*Med.*) a stone formed in the stomach, a calculus.
gastronomy (gastron´əmi) *n.* the art or science of good eating, epicurism. **gastronome** (gas´trənōm) *n.* **1** a lover and connoisseur of good food and drink, a gourmet. **2** an epicure. **gastronomic** (-nom´-), **gastronomical** *a.* of or relating to eating and drinking. **gastronomically** *adv.* [F *gastronomie*, Gr. *gastronomia* (from *gastēr -eros*, stomach, on anal. of *astronomia*, ASTRONOMY)]
gastrophile (gas´trəfīl) *n.* a lover of their stomach or of good eating. **gastrophilism** (-trof´i-) *n.* **gastrophilist** *n.* **gastrophilite** (-trof´ilīt) *n.*
gastropod (gas´trəpod), **gasteropod** (-tər-) *n.* an individual of the Gastropoda, a class of molluscs usu. inhabiting a univalve shell (as the snails), of which the general characteristic is a broad muscular ventral foot. ~*a.* gastropodous. **gastropodous** (-trop´-) *a.* belonging to or characteristic of the Gastropoda. [Gr. *gastēr -eros*, stomach, *pous podos*, foot]
gastroscope (gas´trəskōp) *n.* a medical instrument for examining the interior of the stomach. **gastroscopy** (gastros´kəpi) *n.* an examination of the stomach in order to discover disease.
gastrostomy (gastros´təmi) *n.* (*pl.* **gastrostomies**) a surgical operation to introduce food directly into the stomach, where it cannot be taken by mouth.
gastrotomy (gastrot´əmi) *n.* (*pl.* **gastrotomies**) the surgical operation of cutting into or opening the abdomen. **gastrotomic** (gastrətom´-) *a.*
gastrovascular (gastrōvas´kūlə) *a.* **1** of or relating to the vascular system and the stomach. **2** serving both for circulation and the digestion of food.
gastrula (gas´trələ) *n.* (*pl.* **gastrulae** (-lē)) an embryonic form or stage in the development of a metazoon, consisting of a double-walled sac enclosing a cuplike cavity. **gastrular** *a.* **gastrulation** (-lā´shən) *n.* the formation of a gastrula. [mod. L, dim. from Gr. *gastēr -eros*, stomach]
gat[1] (gat) *n.* **1** a narrow passage between sandbanks, a strait, a channel. **2** an opening in cliffs. [prob. Icel.]
gat[2] (gat) *n.* (*N Am., sl.*) a revolver. [abbr. of GATLING]
gat[3] GET[1].
gate[1] (gāt) *n.* **1** a movable barrier, consisting of a frame of wood or iron, swinging on hinges or sliding, to close a passage or opening, usu. distinguished from a door by openwork instead of solid panels. **2** an opening in a wall or fence affording entrance and exit to an enclosure, a gateway. **3** an entrance, an opening, an opportunity. **4** in an airport, any one of the designated points for boarding or disembarking from aircraft, usu. numbered. **5** a natural opening, as a strait, a mountain pass etc. **6** a sluice admitting water to or shutting it off from a lock or dock. **7** either of a pair of barriers that close a road at a level-crossing. **8** a part of a gearbox, having slots into which the gear lever is moved to engage a particular gear. **9** in a film projector, the mechanism to guide and gain access to the film as it

passes the light source. **10** in horseracing, a device to start racing usu. consisting of a set of stalls with barriers that are simultaneously removed at the moment of starting, a starting gate. **11** the number of people attending a race-meeting, football match etc. **12** the amount of money taken at the gates, gate money. **13** (*coll.*) the starting moments of a race (*to get a good gate*). **14** an electronic circuit (in a computer) that controls the passage of information signals when permitted by another independent source of similar signals. **15** (*sl.*) the mouth. ~*v.t.* **1** to furnish with a gate. **2** to confine (a student) to the grounds of a school or college. **to get/ be given the gate** (*NAm., sl.*) to be dismissed. **gateage** *n.* **1** the gates used in controlling a flow of water. **2** the area of a gate-opening, as in the case of a turbine gate. **gate-change** *n.* in motor vehicles, the mechanism on the gear lever in which the latter is held for change in an H-shaped rack. **gatecrash** *v.t., v.i.* to attend a function or entertainment without an invitation. **gate-crasher** *n.* **gatefold** *n.* a folded insert in a book or magazine that exceeds the size of the other pages; fold-out. **gatehouse** *n.* **1** a lodge, house or defensive structure at or over a gate. **2** a toll gate cottage. **gatekeeper** *n.* **1** a person in charge of a gate. **2** the lessee or collector of tolls at a toll gate. **3** a brown butterfly, *Pyronia tythonus*. **gateleg** *a., n.* (a folding table) with legs that swing in to permit the leaves to be shut down. **gate-legged** *a.* **gateman** *n.* (*pl.* **gatemen**) a person in charge of a gate. **gate money** *n.* entrance money taken at a sports ground etc. **gatepost** *n.* a post on which a gate is hung or against which it shuts. **between you and me and the gatepost** BETWEEN. **gate valve** *n.* a sliding valve which opens the full area of a pipe. **gateway** *n.* **1** an opening or passage that may be closed by a gate. **2** an entrance, a means of ingress or egress. **3** a location through which one has access to an area (*Carlisle, gateway to Scotland*). **4** a device connecting two different computer networks. [OE *geat*]

gate[2] (gāt) *n.* **1** a street (*usu. in comb.*, as *Boargate, Friargate*). **2** †a way, a road. **3** (*Sc.*) one's way or manner of doing (see GAIT). **any gate** (*dial.*) anywhere. **some gate** (*dial.*) somewhere. **that gate** (*dial.*) there. [Icel. *gata*, see GAIT]

-gate (gāt) *comb. form* added to the name of a place or person to denote a scandal connected with that place or person, as *Billygate, Irangate*. [from WATERGATE]

gateau (gat´ō) *n.* (*pl.* **gateaus** (-ōz), **gateaux** (-ō, -ōz)) a rich cake filled with cream and decorated with icing etc. [F, OF *gastel* (cp. OHG *wastel*)]

gather (gadh´ə) *v.t.* **1** to bring together, to collect, to cause to assemble. **2** to accumulate, to acquire. **3** to cull, to pluck. **4** to pick (up). **5** to get in, as harvest. **6** to deduce, to infer, to conclude. **7** to draw together, to contract, to pucker, to draw into folds or pleats. **8** to summon (up). **9** (*Print.*) to arrange (pages) in their proper sequence. ~*v.i.* **1** to come together, to assemble, to congregate, to unite. **2** to grow by addition, to increase. **3** to concentrate, to generate pus or matter. **4** to ripen. ~*n.* a pleat or fold of cloth, made by drawing together. **to gather fresh way** FRESH. **to gather head 1** to gain strength. **2** to ripen (as a boil etc.). **to gather (one's) breath** to recover one's wind, to have respite. **to gather oneself together** to concentrate all one's strength or faculties, as on an effort. **to gather speed** to increase speed. **to gather way** (of a vessel) to begin to move, to gain impetus, so as to answer to the helm. **gatherable** *a.* **gathered** *a.* (*euphem.*) dead. **gatherer** *n.* **gathering** *n.* **1** the act of collecting or assembling together. **2** an assembly, a meeting, a party. **3** an abscess, a boil. **4** a group of leaves bound together in a book. **gathering cry** *n.* a rallying cry, a summons to war. **gathering ground** *n.* **1** the region from which a river and its tributaries draw their supplies. **2** the area feeding a reservoir. **gathers** *n.pl.* small pleats. [OE *gædrian, gaderian*, from *geador*, together (cp. Dut. *gaderen*, from *gader*)]

Gatling (gat´ling), **Gatling gun** *n.* a machine-gun with a series of parallel barrels each having its own lock actuated by a crank at the breech, capable of firing more than 1000 shots a minute. [US inventor, Dr R. J. *Gatling*, 1818–1903]

gator (gā´tə) *n.* (*NAm.*) an alligator.

GATT (gat), **Gatt** *abbr.* General Agreement on Tariffs and Trade.

gauche (gōsh) *a.* **1** awkward, clumsy. **2** tactless, uncouth, boorish. **gaucherie** (-əri, -ərē´) *n.* **1** awkwardness. **2** a blunder, esp. a social mistake or awkwardness. **3** awkward manners. [F, left-handed, awkward (cp. OHG *welk*, orig. awkward, weak)]

gaucho (gow´chō) *n.* (*pl.* **gauchos**) a cowboy of the pampas of Uruguay and Argentina, noted for their horse-riding skills. [Sp., prob. from Quechuan]

gaudeamus igitur (gowdiah´mus ig´ituə) *int.* let us therefore rejoice. [L]

gaudy[1] (gaw´di) *a.* (*comp.* **gaudier**, *superl.* **gaudiest**) vulgarly and tastelessly brilliant and ornate, garish, flashy. **gaud** *n.* **1** a showy ornament or trinket, finery. **2** (*pl.*) †showy ceremonies, festivities. **3** †a trick. **gaudery** *n.* cheap finery, showy ornament, show. **gaudily** *adv.* **gaudiness** *n.*

gaudy[2] (gaw´di) *n.* (*pl.* **gaudies**) a grand festival or entertainment, esp. one held annually at an English college in commemoration of some event. **gaudy day** *n.* **1** the day on which a gaudy is held. **2** a holiday. [OF *gaudir*, L *gaudēre*, to rejoice]

gauffer GOFFER.

gauge (gāj), (*Naut., NAm.*) **gage** *v.t.* **1** to ascertain the dimensions, quantity, content, capacity or power of. **2** to test the content or capacity of (casks etc.) for excise purposes. **3** to estimate or appraise (abilities, character etc.), judge. **4** to reduce to a standard size. **5** in dress-making, to gather into a uniform series of puckers. ~*n.* **1** a standard of measurement. **2** an instrument for regulating or determining dimensions, amount, capacity etc. according to a fixed standard. **3** a graduated instrument showing the height of a stream, quantity of rainfall, force of the wind, steam-pressure in a boiler etc. **4** the distance between the two rails of a railway track. **5** the diameter of the barrel of a gun. **6** the thickness of a sheet of plastic, film, metal etc. **7** the diameter of wire, screws, needles etc. **8** the depth to which a vessel sinks in the water. **9** the position of a ship with reference to another and the wind. **10** extent, capacity, scope. **11** a criterion. **12** in the traditional method of printing, a piece of hard wood, variously notched, used to adjust the dimensions, slopes etc. of the various sorts of letters in type-founding. **13** a strip for regulating length of pages, width of margins etc. **14** in carpentry, an instrument for scoring a line parallel to the straight side of a board. **broad gauge** GAUGE. **lee gauge** LEE. **narrow gauge** NARROW. **standard gauge** STANDARD. **to take the gauge of** to estimate. **weather gauge** WEATHER. **gaugeable** *a.* **gauge glass** *n.* a tube to indicate the height of water in a boiler. **gauge pressure** *n.* the amount by which the pressure within a fluid exceeds that of the surrounding atmosphere. **gauger** *n.* a person who gauges, esp. one who gauges casks etc., a customs officer. **gauge theory** *n.* (*Physics*) a type of quantum theory of elementary particles designed to describe subatomic interactions in terms of exchange of virtual particles. **gauging rod, gauging rule, gauging ruler, gauging stick** *n.* a customs officer's measuring instrument. [OF *gauger* (F *jauger*), etym. unknown]

Gaul (gawl) *n.* **1** a native or inhabitant of the ancient Roman province of Gaul (at the centre of which was France). **2** (*loosely*) a Frenchman or Frenchwoman.

Gaulish *a.* **1** of or relating to Gaul. **2** French. *~n.* the language of ancient Gaul. [F *Gaule*, L *Gallus*, prob. conn. with OE *wealh*, a foreigner]

gauleiter (gow´lītə) *n.* **1** the chief official of a district in Germany under the Nazi regime. **2** (*coll.*) someone in a position of petty authority who behaves in an overbearing and excessively authoritarian manner.

Gaullist (gō´list) *n.* a person who adheres to the policies and principles associated with General Charles de Gaulle, president of France 1959–69. **Gaullism** *n.* [F]

gault (gawlt) *n.* **1** a series of geological beds of stiff dark-coloured clay and marl between the upper and lower greensand. **2** clay or marl from these beds. [etym. uncertain]

gaultheria (gawlthiə´riə) *n.* a plant of the genus *Gaultheria*, evergreen aromatic shrubs of the heath family, containing the wintergreen, *Gaultheria procumbens.* [Dr J. F. *Gaultier*, d. 1756, Canadian botanist]

gaumless GORMLESS.

gaunt (gawnt) *a.* thin, emaciated, haggard, pinched, attenuated. **gauntly** *adv.* **gauntness** *n.* [etym. uncertain (cp. Norw. *gaud*, a thin stick, a tall, thin man)]

gauntlet[1] (gawnt´lit) *n.* **1** a long stout glove covering the wrists. **2** a long glove covered with plate-metal, worn with armour. **3** the part of a glove covering the wrists. **to take up the gauntlet** to accept a challenge. **to throw down the gauntlet** to challenge, to defy. **gauntleted** *a.* wearing gauntlets. [OF *gantelet*, dim. of *gant*, a glove, prob. from Scand. (cp. OSwed. *wante*)]

gauntlet[2] (gawnt´lit), (*US*) **gantlet** (gant´-) *n.* a military (and sometimes a naval) punishment, in which a prisoner had to run between two files of men armed with sticks, knotted cords or the like, with which they struck him as he passed. **to run the gauntlet 1** to suffer this punishment. **2** to be exposed to an ordeal, severe criticism etc. [Swed. *gatlopp* (*gata*, GATE[2], *lopp*, a course, from *löpa*, to run, cogn. with LEAP)]

gauntry GANTRY.

gaup GAWP.

gaur (gow´ə) *n.* a large fierce Indian ox, *Bos gaurus.* [Hind.]

gauss (gows) *n.* (*pl.* **gauss, gausses**) the cgs unit of magnetic flux density. [K. F. *Gauss*, 1777–1855, German mathematician]

Gaussian distribution (gows´iən) *n.* in statistics, normal distribution.

gauze (gawz) *n.* **1** a surgical dressing of an openwork mesh such as muslin. **2** a light, transparent silk or cotton fabric. **3** a thin veil or haze. **4** in a theatre, a scenery cloth of openwork fabric, usu. painted, which becomes translucent when the stage behind is lit. **gauzy** *a.* (*comp.* **gauzier**, *superl.* **gauziest**). **gauzily** *adv.* **gauziness** *n.* [F *gaze*, perh. from *Gaza*, in the Middle East]

gavage (gav´ahzh) *n.* **1** the fattening of poultry by forced feeding. **2** the feeding of a patient unable or unwilling to eat by means of a tube through the mouth into the stomach. [pop. F, from *gaver*, from *gave*, the crop of a bird]

gave GIVE.

gavel[1] (gav´əl) *n.* **1** a small mallet, esp. one used by a chairman for demanding attention or by an auctioneer. **2** a mason's setting-maul. *~v.i.* (*pres.p.* **gavelling**, (*N Am.*) **gaveling**, *past, p.p.* **gavelled**, (*N Am.*) **gaveled**) to use a gavel. *~v.t.* to use a gavel to end or dismiss. [etym. uncertain]

gavel[2] (gav´əl) *n.* (*Hist.*) partition of land among the whole tribe or clan at the holder's death. **gavelkind** (-kīnd) *n.* (*Law, Hist.*) a system of land tenure prevalent in Kent and Wales whereby the lands of a person dying intestate descended to all the sons in equal shares, or in default of sons, to all the daughters. **gavelman** *n.* (*pl.* **gavelmen**) a tenant holding land by this tenure. [OE *gafol*, tribute, toll, cogn. with GIVE; or from the first part of *gavelkind*]

gavial GHARIAL.

gavotte (gəvot´) *n.* **1** a dance of a lively yet dignified character resembling the minuet. **2** the music for this. **3** a dance-tune in common time and in two parts, each repeated. [F, from Prov. *gavoto*, from *Gavot*, an inhabitant of *Gap*, in Dauphiné]

Gawd (gawd) *n., int.* (*sl.*) God.

gawk (gawk) *n.* a clumsy, awkward, shy person. *~v.i.* to stare (at or about) stupidly. **gawkish** *a.* [etym. uncertain]

gawky (gaw´ki) *a.* (*comp.* **gawkier**, *superl.* **gawkiest**) awkward, clownish. *~n.* (*pl.* **gawkies**) **1** an awkward or clownish person. **2** a simpleton. **gawkihood** *n.* **gawkily** *adv.* **gawkiness** *n.*

gawp (gawp), **gaup** *v.i.* to gape, esp. in astonishment. **gawpus** (-pəs) *n.* (*pl.* **gawpuses**) a simpleton. **gawpy** *a.* [dial., cogn. with YELP]

gay (gā) *a.* (*comp.* **gayer**, *superl.* **gayest**) **1** full of mirth; light-hearted, cheerful, merry. **2** given over to pleasure or cheerfulness. **3** showy, brilliant in appearance, dressed in bright colours. **4** (*coll.*) homosexual. **5** (*coll.*) of, relating to or frequented by homosexuals. **6** (*coll.*) licentious, immoral. *~n.* a homosexual, esp. a male. **gaily** *adv.* **gay bar** *n.* a bar frequented by homosexuals. **gay-bashing** *n.* (*coll.*) violent victimization of homosexuals. **Gay Gordons** *n.* a traditional Scottish dance that involves alternate walking and polka steps. **gay liberation, gay lib** *n.* **1** the securing of gay rights. **2** the movement for this. †**gayness** *n.* **gay plague** *n.* (*coll., offensive*) the illness Aids. **gay rights** *n.pl.* legal and social rights for homosexuals, esp. to achieve equal treatment with heterosexuals. [OF *gai*, prob. from OHG *wāhi*, fine]

gayal (gīyahl´, -yal´) *n.* an ox, *Bos frontalis*, with horns depressed at the base and extended outwards, widely domesticated in Asia. [Hind. *gayāl*]

gaz. *abbr.* gazette, gazetteer.

gazania (gəzā´niə) *n.* any plant of the S African genus *Gazania*, with bright yellow or orange flowers that close up in the afternoon. [Theodore of *Gaza*, 1398–1478, botanist]

gazar (gəzah´) *n.* a stiff gauzy silk fabric. [F, from *gaze*, GAUZE]

gaze (gāz) *v.i.* to fix the eye intently (at or upon). *~n.* **1** a fixed look. **2** a look of curiosity, attention, admiration or anxiety. **gazehound** *n.* a hound which hunts by sight, as a greyhound. **gazer** *n.* [etym. uncertain; cp. Swed. dial. *gasa*]

gazebo (gəzē´bō) *n.* (*pl.* **gazebos, gazeboes**) **1** an ornamental turret, lantern or summer house with a wide prospect, often erected in a garden. **2** a belvedere. **3** a balcony or projecting window. [prob. a facetious coinage from GAZE on anal. of LAVABO]

gazelle (gəzel´) *n.* a swift and very graceful antelope of Africa and Asia, esp. *Gazella dorcas*, noted for its large, soft black eyes. [F *gazelle*, earlier *gazel*, Arab. *ghazāl*]

gazette (gəzet´) *n.* **1** an official journal containing lists of appointments to any public office or commission, legal notices, lists of bankrupts etc. **2** a newspaper. *~v.t.* to publish in a gazette, esp. to announce the appointment or bankruptcy of (*usu. in p.p.*). **gazetteer** (gazətiə´) *n.* a dictionary of place names, a geographical index. *~v.t.* to include in a gazetteer. [F, from It. *gazzetta*, prob. after a Venetian coin, the price of the first newspaper or of the privilege of reading it]

gazpacho (gaspach´ō) *n.* (*pl.* **gazpachos**) a spicy Spanish soup made with tomatoes, chopped onion, cucumber, green peppers, garlic etc. and usu. served cold. [Sp.]

gazump (gəzŭmp´) *v.t., v.i.* (*coll.*) **1** to raise the price of a property etc. after accepting an offer from (a buyer) but before contracts have been signed, usu. because other parties have made a subsequent higher offer. **2** to swindle. **gazumper** *n.* [prob. Yiddish *gezumph*, to swindle]

gazunder (gəzŭn´də) *v.t., v.i.* (*coll.*) to lower the sum offered to (a seller) on a property etc. just before the contracts are signed. [GAZUMP, UNDER]

GB *abbr.* Great Britain.

GBA *abbr.* (Great Britain) Alderney, Channel Islands (IVR).

GBE *abbr.* (Knight or Dame) Grand Cross of the British Empire.

GBG *abbr.* (Great Britain) Guernsey, Channel Islands (IVR).

GBH, gbh *abbr.* grievous bodily harm.

GBJ *abbr.* (Great Britain) Jersey, Channel Islands (IVR).

GBM *abbr.* (Great Britain) Isle of Man (IVR).

GBZ *abbr.* (Great Britain) Gibraltar (IVR).

GC *abbr.* George Cross.

GCA *abbr.* ground control (or controlled) approach system, ground control apparatus.

GCB *abbr.* (Knight or Dame) Grand Cross of the Bath.

GCE *abbr.* General Certificate of Education.

GCHQ *abbr.* Government Communications Headquarters.

gcm *abbr.* greatest common measure (in mathematics).

GCMG *abbr.* (Knight or Dame) Grand Cross of the Order of St Michael and St George.

GCSE *abbr.* the General Certificate of Secondary Education in England, Wales and N Ireland, designed to suit a range of academic abilities and based on both coursework and examinations.

GCVO *abbr.* (Knight or Dame) Grand Cross of the Royal Victorian Order.

Gd *chem. symbol* gadolinium.

Gdn. *abbr.* Garden.

Gdns. *abbr.* Gardens.

GDP *abbr.* gross domestic product.

GDR *abbr.* (*Hist.*) German Democratic Republic.

gds *abbr.* goods.

Gdsm. *abbr.* Guardsman.

Ge *chem. symbol* germanium.

gean (gēn) *n.* **1** the wild cherry, *Prunus avium*. **2** the fruit of this. [F *guigne*, etym. unknown]

gear (giə) *n.* **1** apparatus, tools, mechanical appliances, harness, tackle, equipment, dress. **2** a set of cog-wheels, links, levers etc. **3** a connection by which an engine, motor etc. is brought into work. **4** the arrangement by which the driving-wheel of a cycle, motor vehicle etc. performs more or fewer revolutions relatively to the pedals, piston etc. **5** the gear ratio in use (*Engage low gear*). **6** on a vessel, the ropes, blocks etc. belonging to any particular sail or spar. **7** (*coll.*) clothes. **8** goods, movables. **9** (*coll.*) illegal drugs, esp. marijuana. **10** (*Sc.*) property, wealth. *~v.t.* **1** to harness, to put gear on. **2** to put (a machine or motor vehicle) into gear. **3** to furnish with gearing. *~v.i.* **1** to come or be in gear (with). **2** to fit (into) exactly (as a cog-wheel). **high gear** HIGH. **in gear** (of a machine or motor vehicle) connected up and ready for work. **low gear** LOW[1]. **out of gear 1** (of gearing or couplings) disconnected. **2** out of working order. **3** disturbed, upset. **to change gear 1** to engage a different gear in a motor vehicle. **2** to change pace. **to gear down** to decrease activity, facilities etc., usu. industrial, in response to a change in situation. **to gear up** to increase activity, facilities etc., usu. industrial, in response to a change in situation. **gearbox** *n.* **1** the casing in which gears are enclosed in a motor vehicle. **2** a set of gears and its casing. **gear case** *n.* the casing in which gears are enclosed on a bicycle etc. **gear change** *n.* **1** an act of changing gear, usu. in a motor vehicle. **2** (*N Am.*) a gear lever. **geared-up** *a.* fully equipped and ready. **gearing** *n.* **1** gear, working parts. **2** a series of wheels etc. for transmitting motion. **3** (*Naut.*) tackle. **4** the ratios of a particular system of gears in comparison with other systems. **5** in company finance, the ratio of the amount a company has borrowed to its share capital, usu. expressed as a percentage. **gearless** *a.* **gear lever,** (*esp. N Am.*) **gear shift, gearstick** *n.* in a motor vehicle, a device for selecting or connecting gears. **gearwheel** *n.* a wheel with cogs, esp. the wheel transmitting motion in a cycle. [ME *gere*, prob. from Icel. *gervi* (cp. OHG *garvawī*, OE *gearu*)]

GEC *abbr.* General Electric Company.

†**geck** (gek) *n.* a dupe, a fool. *~v.i.* to toss the head. [cp. LG *geck*, Dut. *gek*, G *Geck*]

gecko (gek´ō) *n.* (*pl.* **geckos, geckoes**) any of various lizards with adhesive toes, by which means they can walk on a wall or ceiling. [Malay *gēkoq*, from its cry]

geddit (ged´it) *int.* (*sl.*) (do you) get it?, do you see the joke etc.?

gee[1] (jē), **gee-up** (jēŭp´) *int.* go on, move faster (a command to a horse etc.). *~v.t.* (*past, p.p.* **geed**) **1** to command (a horse etc.) to move faster. **2** to encourage, hearten. **gee-gee** *n.* a horse (used by or to children).

gee[2] (jē) *n.* (*pl.* **gees**) **1** the letter G. **2** (*usu. pl., US, sl.*) a thousand dollars. **gee-string** *n.* a G-string.

gee[3] (jē), **gee-whizz** (jēwiz´) *int.* (*coll.*) an exclamation expressing surprise, delight etc. [euphem. var. of JESUS]

geebung (jē´bŭng) *n.* any shrub or tree of the proteaceous genus *Persoonia*, or its fruit. [Austral. Abor.]

geek (gēk) *n.* **1** (*sl.*) an odd or eccentric person, a misfit, an inept person. **2** (*Austral., sl.*) a look. **geeky** *a.* [GECK]

geep (gēp) *n.* a cross between a goat and a sheep produced artificially by combining genetic material from both.

geese GOOSE.

gee-up GEE[1].

gee-whizz GEE[3].

geezer (gē´zə) *n.* (*coll.*) **1** a man. **2** an old man or woman. [perh. from F *guiser*, masquerader]

gefilte fish (gəfil´tə), **gefüllte fish** *n.* in Jewish cookery, cooked chopped fish mixed with matzo meal, egg and seasonings and then poached, either stuffed back into the skin of the fish or as dumplings. [Yiddish, filled fish]

gegenschein (gā´gənshīn) *n.* a faint glow in the night sky at a position opposite to that of the sun, counterglow. [G *gegen*, against, counter, *Schein*, shine]

Gehenna (gəhen´ə) *n.* hell, a place of torment. [L, from Gr. *geenna*, late Heb. *gēhinnōm*, the valley of Hinnom, a valley near Jerusalem, where (Jer. xix.) men sacrificed their children to Baal or Moloch]

gehlenite (gā´lənīt) *n.* a green mineral silicate of aluminium and calcium occurring in tetragonal crystalline form. [A. A. *Gehlen*, 1775–1815, German chemist]

Geiger counter (gī´gə) *n.* a device for the detection and counting of particles from radioactive materials. [inventor H. *Geiger*, 1882–1945, German physicist]

geisha (gā´shə) *n.* (*pl.* **geisha, geishas**) **1** a Japanese girl or woman trained in the art of being a hostess for men, with skills in conversation, dancing, music. **2** a Japanese prostitute. **geisha girl** *n.* [Jap.]

Geissler tube (gīs´lə) *n.* a sealed, gas-filled glass or quartz tube with electrodes at each end, producing visible or ultraviolet light, used in spectroscopy. [Heinrich *Geissler*, 1814–79, German inventor]

Geist (gīst) *n.* the spirit, principle or tendency of an age, time-spirit. [G, spirit]

gel (jel) *n.* **1** the jelly-like material formed when a colloidal solution is left standing. **2** a transparent sheet of solid gelatin etc. placed in front of spotlights in a theatre, studio etc. to change the colour of the light. *~v.i.* (*pres.p.* **gelling,** *past, p.p.* **gelled**) **1** to become a gel. **2** (*coll.*) to form a friendship or satisfactory working relationship with someone. **3** (*coll.*) (of a situation, relationship etc.) to begin to function co-operatively and satisfactorily. ~*v.t.* to make into a gel, to cause to gel. [JELLY]

gelada (jəlahʹdə) *n.* (*pl.* **gelada, geladas**) a baboon from NE Africa, *Theropithecus gelada*, with long mane, bare red chest and ridged muzzle. [Arab. *qilādah*, mane]

gelatin (jelʹətin), **gelatine** (-tēn) *n.* a transparent substance forming a jelly in water, obtained from connective animal tissue, such as skin, tendons, bones, horns etc. **gelatinate** (-latʹ-) *v.i.*, *v.t.* GELATINIZE (under GELATIN). **gelatinize** (-latʹ-), **gelatinise** *v.i.* to be converted into jelly, or a substance like jelly. ~*v.t.* to convert into a substance like jelly. **gelatinizable** *a.* **gelatinization** (-zāʹshən) *n.* **gelatinizer** *n.* **gelatinoid** (-latʹ-) *a.*, *n.* (a substance) resembling gelatin. **gelatinous** (-latʹ-) *a.* of the nature of or consisting of gelatin, jelly-like. **gelatin paper** *n.* photographic paper coated with sensitized gelatin. [F *gélatine*, It. *gelatina*, L *gelata*, JELLY]

gelation (jəlāʹshən) *n.* solidification into a gel by cooling or freezing. [L *gelātio*, from *gelāre*, to freeze]

geld[1] (geld) *v.t.* (*past, p.p.* **gelded, gelt** (gelt)) **1** to castrate (esp. a horse), to emasculate, to spay. **2** to deprive of any essential part. **3** †to expurgate excessively. **gelder** *n.* a person who gelds animals. **gelding** *n.* **1** a castrated animal, esp. a castrated horse. **2** the act of castrating, castration. **3** †a eunuch. [Icel. *gelda*, from *geldr* (cp. G *Gelt*), barren]

geld[2] (geld) *n.* the tax paid by land holders to the Crown under the Saxon and early Norman kings. [OE *gield*, from *gieldan*, see YIELD (cp. Icel. *giald*, OHG *gelt*, G *Geld*)]

gelid (jelʹid) *a.* **1** extremely cold. **2** icy. **gelidity** (-lidʹ-) *n.* **gelidly** *adv.* [L *gelidus*, from *gelu*, frost]

gelignite (jelʹignīt) *n.* an explosive containing nitroglycerin. **gelly** *n.* (*coll.*) gelignite. [GELATIN, L *ign-is*, fire, -ITE[1]]

gell JELL.

gelsemium (jelsēʹmiəm) *n.* (*pl.* **gelsemiums**) any plant of the genus of climbing shrubs *Gelsemium*, which contains three species, of which the best known is the American yellow jasmine, *Gelsemium sempervirens*, the poisonous root of which yields a medicinal substance. [mod. L, from It. *gelsomino*, JASMINE]

gelt[1] (gelt) *n.* (*sl.*) money, cash. [G or Dut. *geld*, money, cogn. with GELD[2]]

gelt[2] GELD[1].

gem (jem) *n.* **1** a precious stone, such as the diamond, ruby, emerald etc. **2** a person or object of great rarity, beauty or value. **3** a treasure, the most prized or the choicest part. **4** (*pl.*) minute green cellular bodies in the fructification of liverworts, and in some mosses etc., gemmae. **5** a geometrid moth. ~*v.t.* (*pres.p.* **gemming,** *past, p.p.* **gemmed**) to adorn with or as with gems. ~*v.i.* to bud. **gemlike** *a.* **gemmy** *a.* **1** full of or set with gems. **2** bright, glittering. **3** (*sl.*) spruce, smart, neat. **gemstone** *n.* a precious stone cut or polished for ornamental purposes. [OF *gemme*, L *gemma*, a bud, a jewel]

Gemara (gəmahʹrə) *n.* the second portion of the Talmud, consisting of a commentary on the first part of the Mishna, or text. **Gemaric** *a.* of or relating to the Gemara. **Gemarist** *n.* [Aram.]

gemeinschaft (gəmīnʹshaft) *n.* (*pl.* **gemeinschaften** (-tən)) a social group united by kinship, common beliefs etc. [G, community]

gemel (jemʹəl) *n.* **1** (*Her.*) a pair of parallel bars. **2** a gemel-ring. **3** †either of twins. **gemel hinge** *n.* a hinge formed of a hook and loop. **gemel-ring** *n.* a kind of finger-ring formed of two (or more) rings. **gemel window** *n.* a window with two bays. [OF (F *jumeau*), L *gemellus*, dim. of *geminus*, twin]

geminal (jemʹinəl) *a.* (*Chem.*) (of molecules) having two functional groups attached to the same atom. **geminally** *adv.*

geminate[1] (jemʹinət) *a.* united or arranged in pairs. **geminative** *a.* [L *geminātus*, p.p. of *gemināre*, to double, from *geminus*, twin]

geminate[2] (jemʹināt) *v.t.* to double, to arrange in pairs. ~*v.i.* to occur in pairs.

Gemini (jemʹinī) *n.* (*pl.* **Gemini, Geminis**) **1** (*as pl.*) a constellation, the Twins, containing the two conspicuous stars, Castor and Pollux. **2 a** the third sign of the zodiac. **b** a person born under Gemini. **Geminids** (-idz) *n.pl.* meteoric bodies radiating, usu. in early December, from the constellation Gemini. **geminous** *a.* double, in pairs, twin. [L, twins, pl. of *geminus*, see GEMINATE[1]]

gemma (jemʹə) *n.* (*pl.* **gemmae** (-ē)) **1** (*Zool.*) a budlike outgrowth in polyps, ascidians etc., which separates from the parent organism and develops into an individual. **2** a leaf-bud. **3** (*pl.*) minute green cellular bodies in the fructification of liverworts, and in some mosses etc. **gemmaceous** (-āʹ-) *a.* like a bud, of, relating to or of the nature of leaf-buds. [L, see GEM]

gemmate (jemʹāt) *a.* **1** (*Zool.*) reproducing by gemmation. **2** (*Bot.*) having buds. ~*v.i.* **1** to bud. **2** to reproduce by gemmation. **gemmation** (-aʹshən) *n.* **1** (*Zool.*) reproduction by the development of gemmae from the parent body. **2** the act of budding. **3** vernation, or the arrangement of the leaf in the bud. **4** the time of budding. **5** the disposition of buds on the plant. **gemmative** *a.* [L *gemmātus*, p.p. of *gemmāre*, to bud, from *gemma*, see GEMMA]

gemmiferous (jemifʹərəs) *a.* **1** producing gems. **2** producing or propagating by buds or gemmae.

gemmiparous (jemipʹərəs) *a.* **1** (*Zool.*) propagating by gemmation. **2** (*Bot.*) producing buds. **gemmiparously** *adv.*

gemmule (jemʹūl) *n.* **1** any one of the small reproductive bodies thrown off by sponges. **2** a small gemma or reproductive bud. **3** a reproductive cell of a cryptogam. [F, from L *gemmūla*, dim. of GEMMA]

gemmy GEM.

gemote (gəmōtʹ) *n.* (*Hist.*) a public meeting or assembly, esp. the court held in Anglo-Saxon England in each shire or hundred before the Norman Conquest. [OE *gemōt* (*ge-*, together, MOOT)]

gemsbok (gemzʹbok), **gemsbuck** (-bŭk) *n.* a large antelope of W and E Africa, *Oryx gazella*, with long straight horns. [Dut., from G *Gemsbock* (*Gemse*, chamois, *Bock*, buck)]

gemütlich (gəmooʹtlikh) *a.* **1** comfortable, cosy. **2** friendly, genial. [G]

Gen. *abbr.* **1** General. **2** Genesis.

gen (jen) *n.* (*coll.*) full particulars (of), information (about). ~*v.i.* (*pres.p.* **genning,** *past, p.p.* **genned**) to read up about (*I'm genning up on the subject*). **genned-up** *a.* (*coll.*) well informed, armed with the right information. [*gen*eral information]

gen. *abbr.* **1** gender. **2** general. **3** generally. **4** generic. **5** genitive. **6** genus.

-gen (jən) *comb. form* **1** producing (*antigen*). **2** produced (*oxygen*). **3** growth (*endogen*). [F *-gène*, Gr. *genēs*, born of a certain kind, from *gen-*, root of *gignesthai*, to be born, *gennaein*, to beget etc.]

genco (jenʹkō) *n.* (*pl.* **gencos**) a company generating and selling power, esp. electricity. [*gen*erating *co*mpany]

gendarme (zhãʹdahm) *n.* **1** an armed policeman, in France and some other Continental countries. **2** a pinnacle of rock blocking a mountain ridge. **gendarmerie** (-mərēʹ), **gendarmery** (-dahʹ-) *n.* (*pl.* **gendarmeries**) **1** the armed police of France. **2** a body of gendarmes. **3** the headquarters of a body of gendarmes. [F, from pl. *gens d'armes*, men of arms]

gender (jenʹdə) *n.* **1** (*Gram.*) any one of the classes (usually *masculine*, *feminine* and *common* or *neuter*) into which words referring to people or things are divided, often coinciding with their sex or sexlessness. 2 classification of words into genders according to their forms etc. 3 (*loosely*) sex (*an issue of gender, the male gender*). **gender bender** *n.* (*coll.*) a person whose appearance and behaviour is of a kind usu. associated with members of the opposite sex. **gender-bending** *n.* sexually ambiguous appearance or behaviour, e.g. bisexuality or transvestism. **gendered** *a.* GENDER-SPECIFIC (under GENDER). **gender gap** *n.* lack of communication, understanding etc. between the sexes. **genderless** *a.* 1 not having or indicating one specific sex. 2 suitable for either sex. **gender person** *n.* (*esp. N Am.*) a deliberately non-sexist term for a human being of either sex. **gender reassignment** *n.* sex change by surgery. **gender role** *n.* the set of attitudes and behaviour that a particular culture considers appropriate for each sex. **gender-specific** *a.* belonging to or limited to either one sex or the other. [ME *gendre*, OF *genre*, L *genere*, abl. of GENUS]

gene (jēn) *n.* 1 the unit of heredity, one of the units of DNA occupying a fixed linear position on the chromosome. 2 the factor in a gamete which determines the appearance of an hereditary characteristic. **gene bank** *n.* a collection of seeds, plants, tissue cultures etc. for future use, esp. for breeding of crops. **gene flow** *n.* the movement and exchange of genes between interbreeding populations. **gene frequency** *n.* the frequency of a particular allele of a gene within a population. **gene locus** *n.* (*pl.* **gene loci**) the position of a gene on the chromosome. **gene pool** *n.* the entire stock of different genes in an interbreeding population. **gene splicing** *n.* the artificial introduction of DNA from one organism into that of another. **gene therapy** *n.* the treatment of certain diseases by the insertion of new genes into non-reproductive cells in a patient (such new genes not being inherited by the patient's offspring). **genic** (jen´-) *a.* [Gr. *genos*, born of a certain kind]

genealogy (jēnial´əji) *n.* (*pl.* **genealogies**) 1 the history or investigation of the descent of families. 2 a record or exhibition of a person's or family's descent in the natural order of succession. 3 pedigree, lineage. 4 the course of a plant's or an animal's development from earlier forms. **genealogical** (-niəloj´-) *a.* 1 of or relating to genealogy. 2 exhibiting the successive stages of family descent. **genealogically** *adv.* **genealogical tree** *n.* the genealogy of a family or species drawn out in an inverted figure resembling a tree, with a root, branches etc. **genealogist** *n.* **genealogize, genealogise** *v.i.* to investigate descent, to prepare genealogies. ~*v.t.* 1 to investigate the descent of, to trace a pedigree of. 2 to prepare a genealogy of. [OF *genealogie*, late L *geneālogia*, Gr. *genealogia* (*genea*, race)]

genera GENUS.

generable GENERATE.

general (jen´ərəl) *a.* 1 common, universal. 2 ordinary, usual, widespread, prevalent. 3 not special, particular, partial or local. 4 (*Biol.*) relating to a whole genus, kind, class or order. 5 not limited in scope or application. 6 indefinite, vague. 7 not specialized or restricted. 8 taken or viewed as a whole. 9 added to words expressive of rank or office, indicating that the office holder is chief or supreme within a certain sphere (*director-general, postmaster-general*). ~*n.* 1 an officer ranking next below a field marshal, usu. extended to lieutenant generals and major generals. 2 the commander of an army. 3 a strategist (*a midfield general*). 4 in the Roman Catholic Church, the chief of a religious order, or of all the houses or congregations having the same rule. 5 the chief part, the majority. 6 (*pl.*) general facts or principles. 7 (*coll.*) †a general servant. 8 (*Hist.*) a general drum-call beaten in the morning to give notice to the infantry to be ready to march. 9 †the whole. 10 †the public, the common people. **as a general rule** in most cases or in all ordinary cases. **in general** 1 in the main, generally. 2 in most cases or in all ordinary cases, for the most part. **General American** *n.* American English of a form that is not distinctively regional or local. **general anaesthetic,** (*N Am.*) **general anesthetic** *n.* a drug which anaesthetizes the whole body, with loss of consciousness. **General Assembly** *n.* 1 the main debating forum of the United Nations. 2 the body of representatives that directs the affairs of the Church of Scotland. **general average** *n.* in marine insurance, loss shared by the shipowner and all cargo owners. **General Certificate of Education** *n.* a certificate for secondary school pupils in England, Wales and N Ireland, based on an examination at advanced level. **general confession** *n.* in a church service, a statement of repentance in which the whole congregation joins. **general council** *n.* a council called together by the authority of the Church at large. **general dealer** *n.* a person who deals in many articles of daily use. **general delivery** *n.* (*N Am.*) the equivalent of poste restante. **general election** *n.* an election for representatives for all constituencies in a state. **general headquarters** *n.* the headquarters of a military commander. **general hospital** *n.* a hospital that takes patients whatever their disease or injury. **generalia** (jenərā´liə) *n.pl.* general principles. **generalism** *n.* a general conclusion, statement or opinion. **generalist** *n.* a person knowledgeable in many fields as distinct from a specialist. **generality** (jenəral´əti) *n.* (*pl.* **generalities**) 1 the state of being general, as opposed to specific. 2 a general statement or principle. 3 a vague statement, vagueness. 4 the main body, the majority. **generalize** (jen´ərəlīz), **generalise** *v.i.* 1 to draw general inferences. 2 to speak vaguely, to employ generalities. 3 to form general ideas. 4 to reason inductively. 5 in paintings, to represent typical not particular features. **generalizable** *a.* **generalizability** (-bil´-) *n.* **generalization** (-zā´shən) *n.* 1 a general statement or inference. 2 the act or process of generalizing. 3 the act of making general, or of bringing several objects, agreeing in some point, under one head or class. 4 an induction. **generalizer, generaliser** *n.* **generally** *adv.* 1 for the most part, in most cases. 2 ordinarily, commonly, usually. 3 without minute detail, without specifying. **general meeting** *n.* a meeting open to all members of an institution, society etc. **generalness** *n.* **general officer** *n.* an officer above the rank of colonel. **general post office** *n.* a chief or head post office. **general practice** *n.* 1 the state of being a general practitioner. 2 the surgery, patients, staff etc. of a general practitioner. **general practitioner** *n.* a physician or surgeon treating all kinds of cases, a GP. **general-purpose** *a.* useful for several different functions. **general reader** *n.* a person who reads miscellaneous books etc., as distinct from one following a course of special study. †**general servant** *n.* a female servant whose duties are not special, a maid-of-all-work. **generalship** *n.* 1 the office or rank of a general. 2 skill in the management of troops and the conduct of war, strategy. 3 skilful leadership, management or organization. 4 tactful diplomacy. **general staff** *n.* in the army, officers assigned to advise senior officers on operations and policy. **general strike** *n.* a strike by all or most workers in most parts of a city, province or country. **General Synod** *n.* the governing body of the Church of England, made up of bishops, clergy and lay representatives. **general term** *n.* (*Logic*) a term which is the sign of a general conception or notion. **General Thanksgiving** *n.* a form of thanksgiving used in the Church of England. **general theory of relativity** *n.* 1 an extension of the special theory of relativity to consider the effects of acceleration and gravitation. 2 the fact or condition of being relative. 3 (*Philos.*) the state of being dependent on or determined by something else. **general warrant** *n.* (*Law*) a warrant (now illegal) to apprehend all suspected persons, without naming any particular individual. [OF, from L *generālis*, from GENUS]

generalissimo (jenərəlis´imō) *n.* (*pl.* **generalissimos**) **1** the chief commander of a force furnished by several powers, or military and naval in combination. **2** a commander-in-chief. **3** (*coll.*) any esp. autocratic leader. [It., superl. of *generale*, GENERAL]

generate (jen´ərāt) *v.t.* **1** to produce or bring into existence; to cause to be. **2** to produce, to evolve, to originate. **3** to beget, to procreate. **4** to produce by rule from a given set. **5** (*Math.*) to trace out or form by the motion of a point or a magnitude of inferior order. **generable** *a.* **generant** *a.* generating, producing. ~*n.* **1** something which generates. **2** (*Math.*) a point, line or surface that, by its motion, traces out a line, surface or solid. **generating plant** *n.* all the equipment needed for generating electrical energy. **generation** (-ā´shən) *n.* **1** a single succession or step in natural descent or in development. **2** the people of the same period or age. **3** an age or period between one succession and another; a stage in development. **4** the average time in which the child takes the place of the parent (usu. estimated at about ⅓ of a century). **5** the act of generating. **6** production, creation, bringing into existence. **7** propagation of the species. **8** reproduction, propagation. **9** †progeny, offspring, issue. **10** †a family, a race. **11** †pedigree, lineage. **generation gap** *n.* the difference in opinions and understanding between members of different generations. **generative** (-ərətiv) *a.* **1** having the power of generating. **2** of or relating to generation or production. **3** productive, fruitful. **generative grammar** *n.* **1** a set of rules by which all the sentences of a language may be generated. **2** grammar based on such rules. **generator** *n.* **1** an apparatus for producing electrical energy from mechanical energy. **2** someone who or something which generates or produces. **3** any apparatus for the production of gas, steam, electricity etc. **4** (*Chem.*) a compound from which a more complex substance is moulded. **5** (*Mus.*) the principal sound or fundamental tone of a chord etc. **generator unit** *n.* an independent generator in an electrical plant capable of working or stopping without affecting the rest of the machinery. **generatrix** (-ā´triks) *n.* (*pl.* **generatrixes, generatrices** (-trisēz)) **1** a female parent. **2** (*Math.*) a generant. [L *generātus*, p.p. of *generāre*, from *genus generis*, kind]

generic (jəner´ik), **generical** (-əl) *a.* **1** of or relating to a class or kind, as opposed to specific. **2** of or relating to a genus. **3** comprehensive, applied to large classes of goods or drugs, identified by the product itself and not by a brand name, not having a trademark. **generically** *adv.* **generic name** *n.* **1** the name of a genus, e.g. Saxifraga in *Saxifraga longifolia*. **2** a general name for a product, not a brand name or trademark. [L *genus generis*, see GENUS, -IC]

generous (jen´ərəs) *a.* **1** open-handed, bountiful, liberal, munificent. **2** magnanimous, high-spirited. **3** overflowing, abundant, fertile. **4** strong, stimulating (as wine). **generosity** (-ros´-) *n.* **generously** *adv.* **generousness** *n.* [F *généreux*, L *generōsus*, as GENERIC]

genesis (jen´əsis) *n.* (*pl.* **geneses** (-sēz)) **1** the act of begetting, producing or giving origin to. **2** creation, beginning, origination, mode of production or formation. **Genesis** *n.* the first book of the Bible, in which the story of the Creation is told. [L, from Gr. *genesis*, from *gen-*, root of *gignesthai*, to become, to be born]

genet (jen´it), **genette** (jinet´) *n.* **1** a small mammal, *Genetta vulgaris*, related to the civet. **2** its fur, or catskin dressed in imitation of this fur. [OF *genete*, Sp. *jineta*, Arab. *jarnait*]

genetic (jənet´ik) *a.* **1** of or relating to genes or genetics. **2** of or relating to the origin, generation or creation of a thing. **genetic affinity** *n.* affinity founded on resemblances existing from a very early age, and therefore presumed to imply a common origin. **genetical** *a.* **genetically** *adv.* **genetic code** *n.* the system, based on the molecular arrangement of the chromosomes, that ensures the transmission of hereditary characteristics. **genetic counselling** *n.* advice given to prospective parents on the likelihood of inherited disorders in their children, or the course and management of these disorders. **genetic engineering** *n.* the artificial alteration of the genes of an organism in order to control the transmission of certain hereditary characteristics. **genetic fingerprint** *n.* the particular DNA pattern that is unique to an individual and can be used to identify that individual or their offspring. **genetic fingerprinting, genetic profiling** *n.* the act or process of taking a genetic fingerprint from an individual's saliva, blood or sperm, used in forensic science etc. **geneticist** (-sist) *n.* a student of genetics. **genetic map** *n.* a graphic representation of the order of genes within chromosomes. **genetic parents** *n.pl.* the parents whose genes a child carries. **genetics** *n.* **1** the study of heredity and variation in organisms. **2** the inherited characteristics of an organism, species or group. [from GENESIS (cp. ANTITHETIC (under ANTITHESIS) from ANTITHESIS)]

Usage note See note under CONGENITAL.

Geneva (jənē´və) *a.* of, originating from or relating to Geneva, Switzerland. **Geneva bands** *n.pl.* a pair of white linen strips hanging from the front of a clerical collar, such as those worn by Swiss Calvinist clergy. **Geneva Bible** *n.* a translation of the Bible into English, made and published at Geneva in 1560. **Geneva Convention** *n.* a convention made between the great powers (1864–5) to ensure the neutrality of ambulances, military hospitals and those in charge of them, in time of war. **Geneva cross** *n.* a red Greek cross on a white ground, the distinguishing mark of military ambulances etc., and symbol of the Red Cross Society. **Geneva gown** *n.* the black preaching gown worn by Presbyterian ministers and Low Church clergy in England. **Genevan** *a.* of or relating to Geneva. ~*n.* a Genevese, a Calvinist. **Genevese** (jenəvēz´) *a.* Genevan. ~*n.* (*pl.* **Genevese**) **1** a native or inhabitant of Geneva. **2** (*as pl.*) the people of Geneva. [town in Switzerland]

genever (jənē´və), **geneva** *n.* Dutch gin. [Dut. *genever*, OF *genèvre*, L *juniperus*, JUNIPER]

genial¹ (jē´niəl) *a.* **1** of a cheerful and kindly disposition, cordial, sympathetic, enlivening. **2** conducive to life and growth, soft, mild. **3** †of or relating to marriage or procreation, generative. **geniality** (-al´-) *n.* **genialize, genialise** *v.t.* to give geniality to. **genially** *adv.* **genialness** *n.* [from F or directly from L *geniālis*]

genial² (jinē´əl) *a.* of, relating to or near the chin. [Gr. *geneion*, chin, from *genus*, jaw]

genic GENE.

-genic (jen´ik) *comb. form* **1** of or relating to generation, as in *antigenic*. **2** suited for, as in *photogenic*. **-genically** *comb. form* forming adverbs.

geniculate (jənik´ūlāt), **geniculated** (-lātid) *a.* **1** having knee joints. **2** having a joint or joints capable of bending sharply. **3** (*Bot.*) bent abruptly like a knee, as the stems of many grasses. ~*v.t.* to form a knot or joint in. **geniculation** (-lā´shən) *n.* **1** the quality of having knots or joints. **2** †the act of kneeling. [L *geniculātus*, from *geniculum*, dim. of *genu*, knee]

genie (jē´ni) *n.* **1** in fairy stories etc., a magical being who appears suddenly to carry out a person's wishes. **2** JINNEE. [F *génie*, L GENIUS]

genii GENIUS.

genio- (jē´niō) *comb. form* chin. [Gr. *geneion*, chin, see GENIAL²]

genipap (jen´ipap) *n.* **1** the fruit of the W Indian tree *Genipa americana*, about the size of an orange, with a winy taste. **2** this tree. [Port. *genipapo*, from Tupi]

genista (jənis´tə) *n.* any shrub of the genus *Genista* with few, simple leaves and yellow flowers. [L]

genital (jen´itəl) *a.* **1** of or relating to the reproductive organs. **2** of or relating to generation or procreation. **genitals, genitalia** (-tā´liə) *n.pl.* the external reproductive organ(s). [OF, from L *genitālis*, from *genit-*, part. stem of *gignere*, to beget]

genitive (jen´itiv) *a.* denoting a grammatical case indicating origin, possession or the like, applied to a case in inflected languages and also to the Eng. possessive. ~*n.* **1** the genitive case. **2** a word or form in the genitive case. **genitival** (-tī´-) *a.* **genitivally** *adv.* [L *genetīvus*, of generation, as GENITAL (a mistranslation of Gr. *genikē*, generic)]

genito- (jen´itō) *comb. form* genital.

genitor (jen´itə) *n.* a biological father, sire. [F *geniteur*, L *genitōrem*, nom. *-tor*, as GENITAL]

genito-urinary (jenitōū´rinəri) *a.* of or relating to the genital and urinary organs.

genius (jē´niəs) *n.* (*pl.* **geniuses, genii** (-niī)) **1** a person of extraordinary intellectual, imaginative, expressive or inventive ability. **2** an extraordinary endowment of ability. **3** the dominant character, spirit or sentiment (of). **4** natural bent or inclination of the mind. **5** a person who exercises powerful influence over another for good or ill. **6** in mythology, a guardian deity or spirit, supposed to preside over the destinies of an individual, place, nation etc. **7** in mythology, either of two spirits attendant on a person through life, one good, the other evil. **genius loci** (lō´sī) *n.* **1** the spirit or associations predominant in a locality, community or institution. **2** the presiding deity of a place. [L, from *gen-*, root of *gignere*, to beget]

genizah (gənē´zə) *n.* a room attached to a synagogue for storing old books, documents etc. [Heb.]

genoa (jen´ōə), **genoa jib** *n.* in yachting, a large triangular jib sail. **Genoa cake** *n.* a rich fruit cake with almonds on the top. **Genoese** (-ēz´) *a.* of or relating to Genoa, a city in N Italy. ~*n.* (*pl.* **Genoese**) **1** a native or inhabitant of Genoa. **2** (*pl.*) the people of Genoa. [L *Genua*, It. *Genova*]

genocide (jen´əsīd) *n.* the (attempted) intentional and systematic destruction of a national, ethnic or religious group, e.g. the Jews by the Nazi Germans during World War II. **genocidal** (-sī´-) *a.* [Gr. *genos*, born of a certain kind, -CIDE]

Genoese GENOA.

genome (jē´nōm) *n.* the complete set of chromosomes that is contained in any single cell. **genomic** (-nom´-) *a.* [G *Genom*, from *Gen*, gene, chromo*some*]

genotype (jen´ətīp) *n.* **1** the basic genetic structure of an organism. **2** a group of organisms with the same genetic structure. **genotypic** (-tip´-), **genotypical** *a.* **genotypically** *adv.*

-genous (jinəs) *comb. form* **1** born (*indigenous*). **2** bearing, producing (*endogenous*). [L *-genus*, born, from *gen-*, root of *gignere*, to beget]

genre (zhā´rə, zhon´rə) *n.* **1** a kind, sort, class, particularly in the field of the arts. **2** a style, manner, esp. artistic. **3** a type of painting, the subject of which is some scene in everyday life. **genre painting** *n.* the painting of scenes from everyday life. **genre piece** *n.* an example of genre painting. [F, kind, see GENDER]

genro (genrō´) *n.pl.* (*Hist.*) elder statesmen in Japan who were on occasion consulted by the Emperor. [Jap.]

gens (jenz) *n.* (*pl.* **gentes** (jen´tēz)) **1** in anthropology, a tribe, clan or group of families. **2** a clan, house, or sept among the ancient Romans or ancient Greeks. [L, from *gen-*, stem of *gignere*, to beget]

gent (jent) *n.* **1** (*coll.*) a gentleman. **2** a would-be gentleman. **3** (*pl.*) men (in trade descriptions of goods). **the gents/ gents'** a public lavatory for males.

genteel (jentēl´) *a.* **1** (*now coll. or facet.*) gentlemanly or ladylike. **2** elegant in appearance, manners or dress, stylish. **3** well-bred, refined, free from vulgarity. ~†*n.* a genteel person. **genteelish** *a.* **genteelism** *n.* a word or phrase used in place of another word that is perceived to be coarse or vulgar. **genteelly** *adv.* **genteelness** *n.* [earlier *gentile*, F *gentil*, see GENTILE]

gentian (jen´shən) *n.* **1** any plant of the genus *Gentiana* or *Gentianella* of bitter herbs, usu. having blue flowers, common in mountain regions. **2** gentian bitter. **gentianaceous** (-ā´shəs) *a.* of or belonging to the family of flowering plants that includes the felwort and the gentian. **gentian bitter** *n.* a liquor made from gentian roots. **gentianella** (-nel´ə) *n.* a dwarf gentian, *Gentiana acaulis*, with flowers of intense blue. **gentianic** (-shian´-) *a.* **gentianin** (-nin), **gentianic acid** *n.* a bitter compound extracted from gentian-root. **gentian violet** *n.* a greenish crystalline substance that forms a violet solution in water and is used in the treatment of burns and boils, as an antiseptic and as a biological stain. [L *gentiāna*, from *Gentius*, king of Illyria]

gentile (jen´tīl) *a.* **1** Christian, as opposed to Jewish. **2** non-Jewish. **3** heathen, pagan. **4** not of one's religious faith, esp. not Mormon. **5** of or relating to a people or tribe. **6** (*Gram.*) denoting nationality, country, or locality. ~*n.* **1** a Christian, as opposed to a Jew. **2** a non-Jewish person. **3** a heathen, a pagan. **4** a person who is not a Mormon. **5** (*Gram.*) a word denoting nationality, country or locality. [OF *gentil*, L *gentīlis*, from *gens gentis*, see GENS]

gentility (jəntil´əti) *n.* **1** social superiority, polite good breeding. **2** respectable manners and habits associated with good society. **3** people of noble birth. **4** the state of belonging to a gens or clan. [OF *gentilité*]

gentle (jen´təl) *a.* (*comp.* **gentler**, *superl.* **gentlest**) **1** mild, tender, kindly. **2** not rough, coarse, violent or stern. **3** moderate, not severe, not energetic. **4** not steep (*a gentle slope*). **5** (*Her.*) of noble breeding, having the right to bear arms. ~*n.* the larva of the meat-fly or bluebottle, used as bait in angling. ~*v.t.* **1** to handle gently but firmly. **2** to tame (as a colt). **3** to make gentle, amiable or kind. **of gentle birth** of honourable birth, belonging to the gentry, having good breeding. **gentle craft, gentle art** *n.* **1** the practice of angling. **2** †the trade of shoemaking. **gentlefolk, gentlefolks** *n.pl.* (*poet.*) people of good position, of gentle birth. **gentleness** *n.* **gentle sex, gentler sex** *n.* the female sex, women. **gently** *adv.* [OF *gentil*, see GENTILE]

gentleman (jen´təlmən) *n.* (*pl.* **gentlemen**) **1** a man of good breeding, kindly feelings and high principles, a man of honour. **2** (*pl.*) men, esp. the male members of an audience. **3** a man who by education, occupation or income holds a good social position. **4** a man of respectable position who follows no occupation. **5** a man entitled to bear arms. **6** (*coll.*) the personal attendant of a man of rank. **7** †a man of gentle birth, a man above the rank of yeoman. **8** †a man belonging to the gentry, or following the profession of arms, the church or the law. **gentleman-at-arms** *n.* (*pl.* **gentlemen-at-arms**) a member of a company forming a bodyguard to the sovereign on state occasions. **gentleman farmer** *n.* (*pl.* **gentlemen farmers**) a man of property who occupies his own farm. **gentleman-in-waiting** *n.* (*pl.* **gentlemen-in-waiting**) a man of noble birth attached to the royal household. **gentlemanlike** *a.* **gentlemanly** *a.* **1** like a gentleman in appearance, feeling or behaviour. **2** of or relating to or becoming a gentleman. **gentlemanliness** *n.* **gentleman of fortune** *n.* (*euphem.*) an adventurer. **gentleman of the bedchamber** *n.* (*pl.* **gentlemen of the bedchamber**) an officer of the Royal

Household who waits upon a male sovereign. **gentleman's agreement, gentlemen's agreement** *n.* an agreement binding in honour but not legally. **gentleman's gentleman** *n.* a valet, a personal servant. **gentleman-usher** *n.* a gentleman who officiates as usher to a sovereign or other person of high rank.

gentlewoman (jen´təlwumən) *n.* (*pl.* **gentlewomen** (-wimən)) **1** a woman of good birth or breeding. **2** a woman who waits upon a lady of high rank. **gentlewomanly** *a.* **gentlewomanliness** *n.*

gentoo (jen´too) *n.* (*pl.* **gentoos**) a penguin, *Pygoscelis papua*, found esp. in the Falkland Islands. [Hind., from Port. *gentio*, gentile]

gentry (jen´tri) *n.* **1** people of high birth and social standing. **2** the social class immediately below the nobility in position and birth. **3** (*coll.*) people, folks. **gentrification** (-fikā´shən) *n.* the process by which the character of an esp. inner urban area formerly lived in by working-class people is changed by an influx of middle-class people, with a consequent increase in property values. **gentrify** (-fī) *v.t.* (*3rd pers. sing. pres.* **gentrifies,** *pres.p.* **gentrifying,** *past, p.p.* **gentrified**) to change by gentrification. **gentrifier** *n.* [OF *genterise*, from *gentil*, gentle]

genu (jen´ū) *n.* (*pl.* **genua** (-ūə)) (*Anat.*) **1** the technical name for the knee. **2** any kneelike part or bend in a structure. **genual** *a.* of or relating to the knee. [L *genu*, knee]

genuflect (jen´ūflekt) *v.i.* to bend the knee, esp. in worship. **genuflection** (-flek´shən), **genuflexion** *n.* **genuflector** *n.* **genuflectory** (-flek´-) *a.* [late L *genuflectere* (*genu*, the knee, *flectere*, to bend)]

genuine (jen´ūin) *a.* **1** natural, belonging to or coming from the true source. **2** real, true. **3** not counterfeit, false, spurious or adulterated. **4** (*Zool.*) true to type, not aberrant. **genuinely** *adv.* **genuineness** *n.* [L *genuīnus*, from the root *gen-*, to beget]

genus (jē´nəs) *n.* (*pl.* **genera** (jen´ərə)) **1** (*Biol.*) a class or kind of objects containing several subordinate classes or species. **2** a group or class of plants or animals differentiated from all others by certain common characteristics and comprising one or more species. **3** a kind, group, class, order, family. [L, as GENUINE; cogn. with KIN]

-geny (jəni) *comb. form* production or mode of production, as *ontogeny, philogeny.* [F *génie*, from Gr. *geneia* or L *gen-*, stem of *genesis*]

Geo. *abbr.* George.

geo (jē´ō), **gio** *n.* (*pl.* **geos, gios**) (*Sc.*) a narrow inlet, a creek, esp. in Orkney and Shetland. [Sc., from Icel. *gja*]

geo- (jē´ō) *comb. form* of or relating to the earth. [Gr. *geo-*, from *gē*, earth]

geobotany (jēōbot´əni) *n.* the study of the geographical distribution of plants. **geobotanist** *n.*

geocarpy (jē´ōkahpi) *n.* (*Biol.*) the ripening of a plant's fruit below the ground.

geocentric (jēōsen´trik), **geocentrical** (-kəl) *a.* **1** having the earth as centre. **2** viewed from the earth as centre. **3** having reference to the centre of the earth, as distinguished from any spot on its surface. **geocentrically** *adv.* **geocentricism** (-sizm) *n.* belief that the earth is the centre of the universe. **geocentric latitude** *n.* the latitude at which a planet would appear if viewed from the centre of the earth. **geocentric system** *n.* the obsolete doctrine that the earth is the centre of the planetary system.

geochemistry (jēōkem´istri) *n.* the study of the chemical composition of the crust of the earth. **geochemical** *a.* **geochemist** *n.*

geochronology (jēōkrənol´əji) *n.* the measuring of geological time. **geochronological** (-kronəloj´-) *a.* **geochronologist** *n.*

geod. *abbr.* geodesy.

geode (jē´ōd) *n.* **1** a hollow nodule of any mineral substance, often lined with crystals. **2** the cavity in such a nodule. **geodic** (-od´-) *a.* [F *géode*, from L *geōdes*, from Gr. *geōdēs*, earthy, from *gē*, earth]

geodesy (jēod´əsi), **geodetics** (-det´-) *n.* the science or art of measuring the earth's surface or large portions of it, as distinguished from surveying, which deals only with limited tracts. **geodesic** (-dē´-, -des´-), **geodetic** (-det´-) *a.* **1** of or relating to geodesy. **2** carried out or determined by means of geodesy. **geodesic dome** *n.* a light, strong dome built from a latticework of polygons so that the pressure load is evenly distributed throughout the structure. **geodesic line, geodetic line** *n.* the shortest line between two points on the earth's surface or that of a geometrical solid. **geodesist** *n.* **geodetically** *adv.* **geodetic surveying** *n.* a method of surveying large areas which takes into account the curvature of the earth. [F *géodésie*, from Gr. *geōdaisia* (as GEO-, *-daisia*, division, from *daiein*, to divide)]

geodynamic (jēōdīnam´ik), **geodynamical** *a.* relating to the latent forces of the earth. **geodynamicist** (-isist) *n.* **geodynamics** *n.* the branch of geology which deals with the forces and processes within the earth.

geog. *abbr.* **1** geographer. **2** geographical, geographic. **3** geography.

geogeny (jēoj´əni) *n.* the science or study of the formation of the crust of the earth.

geognosy (jēog´nəsi) *n.* **1** knowledge of the structure of the earth, structural geology. **2** knowledge of the mineral and structural character of rocks. **geognostic** (-nos´-), **geognostical** *a.* [F *géognosie* (GEO-, Gr. *gnōsis*, knowledge, from *gignōskein*, to know)]

geogony (jēog´əni) *n.* the science of the formation of the earth. **geogonic** (jēəgon´ik) *a.*

geography (jēog´rəfi) *n.* **1** the science of the surface of the earth, its physical features, natural productions, inhabitants, political divisions, commerce etc. **2** a book dealing with the subject of geography. **3** the layout and locations of a limited area (*the geography of a building*). **economic geography** ECONOMIC. **human geography** HUMAN. **mathematical geography** MATHEMATICAL. **physical geography** PHYSICAL. **political geography** POLITICAL. **geographer** *n.* **geographic** (-graf´-) *a.* **1** of or relating to geography. **2** relating to or containing a description of the earth. **geographical** *a.* geographic. **geographical concentration** *n.* in marketing, the degree to which the demand for a particular product or service is limited to particular geographical areas. **geographical determinism** *n.* the social theory that human activity is determined by geographical factors. **geographical latitude** *n.* the angle between the plane of the equator and a perpendicular to the surface of the earth at a given point. **geographically** *adv.* **geographical mile** *n.* one minute of longitude measured at the equator, also called a nautical mile (see MILE). **geographical variation** *n.* the alteration in form, habits etc. of a species or variety of plant or animal due to a change of habitat. [F *géographie*, L *geographia*, Gr. *geōgraphia*]

geoid (jē´oid) *n.* **1** the shape of the earth, an oblate spheroid. **2** the surface the earth would have if all parts of it were the same height as the mean sea level of the oceans. **geoidal** (-oi-) *a.* [G from Gr. *geoeidēs*, earthlike]

geol. *abbr.* **1** geological, geologic. **2** geologist. **3** geology.

geology (jēol´əji) *n.* **1** the science of the earth's crust, its composition, its structure, and the history of its development. **2** a treatise on this subject. **3** the geological structure of a particular area. **dynamic geology** DYNAMIC. **economic geology** ECONOMIC. **structural geology** STRUCTURAL (under STRUCTURE). **geologic** (jēəloj´-) *a.* forming part of the subject matter of geology. **geological** *a.* of or relating to geology. **geologically** *adv.* **geological time** *n.* the time occupied by the development of the planet earth to the present. **geologist** *n.* **geologize, geologise** *v.i.* 1 to study geology. 2 to make geological investigations, esp. in a particular district. ~*v.t.* to study the geology of. [med. L *geōlogia*]

geom. *abbr.* 1 geometer. 2 geometrical. 3 geometry.

geomagnetism (jēōmag´nətizm) *n.* 1 the magnetic field of the earth. 2 the study of the earth's magnetism. **geomagnetic** (-net´-) *a.* **geomagnetically** *adv.* **geomagnetist** *n.*

geomancy (jē´ōmansi) *n.* 1 the art of siting buildings by a form of divination. 2 divination by means of lines, figures or dots on the earth or on paper, or by the shape formed by particles of earth cast on the ground. **geomancer** *n.* **geomantic** (-man´-) *a.* [F *géomancie*, L *geōmantīa*, Gr. *geōmanteia*]

geometer (jēom´itə) *n.* 1 a geometrician. 2 a geometrid. **geometer moth** *n.* a geometrid moth. **geometrid** (-trid) *n.* a moth or its caterpillar belonging to the family called Geometridae on account of their seeming to measure the ground as they move along, a looper. ~*a.* of or relating to the Geometridae. [L and G *geōmetrēs* (GEO-, *metrēs*, measurer, from *metrein*, to measure)]

geometry (jiom´ətri) *n.* 1 the branch of mathematics concerned with the properties and relationships of points, lines, curves, surfaces and solids. 2 the relative arrangement of points, lines etc. **plane geometry** PLANE[1]. **solid geometry** SOLID. **geometric** (jēəmet´-) *a.* 1 of or relating to geometry. 2 (of architecture, design etc.) composed of or decorated by regular lines or shapes such as circles, triangles or rectangles. **geometrical** *a.* geometric. **geometrically** *adv.* **geometrical progression** *n.* a progression in which the terms increase or decrease by a common ratio, as 1, 3, 9, 27; 144, 72, 36, 18. **geometrical proportion** *n.* a proportion based on equal ratios in its two parts, as 2: 4:; 6: 12. **geometrical series** *n.* a series in geometrical progression. **geometrician** (jēəmətrish´ən), **geometrist** *n.* **geometric mean, geometrical mean** *n.* the central number of a geometrical progression, which can be calculated, where there are *n* numbers, as the *n*th root of their product. **geometric tracery, geometrical tracery** *n.* window tracery of which the openings are simple geometrical patterns. **geometrize, geometrise** *v.i.* 1 to work or construct according to the rules or methods of geometry. 2 to proceed geometrically. [OF *geometrie*, L and Gr. *geōmetria*]

geomorphic (jēōmaw´fik) *a.* of or relating to the form of the earth or the solid features of its surface.

geomorphology (jēōmawfol´əji) *n.* the study of the origin, development and characteristics of land forms. **geomorphologic** (-fəloj´-), **geomorphological** *a.* **geomorphologically** *adv.* **geomorphologist** *n.*

geophagy (jēof´əgi) *n.* the act or habit of eating earth. **geophagist** *n.* [GEO-, Gr. *phagein*, to eat]

geophones (jē´ōfōnz) *n.pl.* a device for deflecting sound waves, shock waves etc. in the ground. [GEO-, Gr. *phōnē*, voice, sound]

geophysics (jēōfiz´iks) *n.* the science that deals with the physical characteristics of the earth. **geophysical** *a.* **geophysicist** (-sist) *n.*

geophyte (jē´ōfit) *n.* a perennial plant that propagates by having buds (i.e. bulbs, corms etc.) below the surface of the soil. **geophytic** (-fit´ik) *a.* [GEO-, Gr. *phyton*, plant]

geopolitics (jēōpol´itiks) *n.* 1 the study of how the political views and aims of a nation are affected by its geographical position. 2 (*as pl.*) the combination of the geographical and political factors that affect a country or area. **geopolitical** (-lit´-) *a.* **geopolitician** (-tish´ən) *n.*

geoponics (jēōpon´iks) *n.* the art and science of agriculture. **geoponic** *a.* [Gr. *geoponikos*, from GEO-, *ponos*, labour]

Geordie (jaw´di) *n.* 1 (*coll.*) a native of Tyneside, NE England. 2 (*coll.*) the dialect spoken by the people of NE England. ~*a.* of or relating to Tyneside, its people, dialect, culture etc. [Sc. and North., dim. of GEORGE]

George (jawj) *n.* (*coll.*) an automatic aircraft pilot. **by George!** used to express surprise mixed with admiration. **George Cross, George Medal** *n.* either of two decorations instituted in 1940, primarily for civilians in recognition of acts performed with the greatest heroism or most conspicuous courage in circumstances of extreme danger. [L *Georgius*, Gr. *Geōrgios*, a saint said to have been martyred under Diocletian]

georgette (jawjet´) *n.* a plain semi-transparent dress material usually of silk or crêpe. [Mme *Georgette*, a French dressmaker]

Georgian[1] (jaw´jən) *a.* 1 relating to the period of George I–IV in Great Britain, 1714–1830. 2 relating to the reign of George V, 1910–36.

Georgian[2] (jaw´jən) *a.* 1 of or relating to Georgia, a republic of SE Europe. 2 of or relating to Georgia, one of the southern states of the US. ~*n.* a native or inhabitant of either Georgia.

georgic (jaw´jik) *n.* 1 a poem on husbandry or rural affairs. 2 any one book of Virgil's *Georgics*, a poem in four books on husbandry. ~†*a.* of or relating to agriculture or rural affairs. [L *geōrgicus*, Gr. *geōrgikos*, from *geōrgos*, a husbandman (GEO-, *ergein*, to work)]

geoscience (jēōsī´əns) *n.* 1 any of the sciences that are concerned with the earth, e.g. geology, geophysics or geodesy. 2 earth sciences collectively. **geoscientist** *n.*

geosphere (jē´əsfiə) *n.* 1 the solid part of the earth, the lithosphere. 2 any one of the concentric regions of the earth and its atmosphere.

geostatic (jēəstat´ik) *a.* 1 able to resist or support the pressure of earth from all sides. 2 denoting or relating to the pressure exerted by a mass of rock, earth etc. **geostatics** *n.* the branch of physics concerned with the statics of rigid bodies, esp. the balance of forces within the earth.

geostationary (jēōstā´shənəri) *a.* (of a satellite) orbiting the earth at the same speed as the earth rotates so remaining above the same spot on the earth's surface.

geostrophic (jēəstrof´ik) *a.* of or caused by the force produced by the rotation of the earth. **geostrophic wind** *n.* a wind the direction and force of which are influenced by the earth's rotation.

geosynchronous (jēōsing´krənəs) *a.* GEOSTATIONARY.

geosyncline (jēōsing´klīn) *n.* a part of the earth's crust that has sunk inwards, resulting in a usu. long and broad depression containing deep thicknesses of rock or sediment.

geotaxis (jēōtak´sis) *n.* the response of an organism or a plant to the stimulus of gravity.

geotectonic (jēōtekton´ik) *a.* of or relating to the structure of the earth.

geothermal (jēōthœ´məl) *a.* of or relating to the internal heat of the earth. **geothermal energy** *n.* energy from the natural heat of the earth, e.g. hot springs. **geothermic** *a.*

geothermometer (jēōthəmom´itə) *n.* an instrument for measuring the earth's heat at different depths, as in mines or wells.

geotropism (jēot´rəpizm) *n.* the tendency exhibited by the organs of a plant to turn towards the centre of the earth. **negative geotropism** NEGATIVE (under NEGATE). **positive geotropism** POSITIVE. **geotropic** (-trop´-) *a.* **geotropically** *adv.*

Ger. *abbr.* 1 German. 2 Germany.

ger. *abbr.* 1 gerund. 2 gerundive.

gerah (giə´rə) *n.* the smallest ancient Hebrew weight and coin, equivalent to 1⁄20 of a shekel. [Heb.]

geraniol (jərā´niol) *n.* an alcohol with the odour of roses, found in many essential oils and used in perfumery.

geranium (jərā´niəm) *n.* **1** any hardy herbaceous plant or shrub of the genus *Geranium*, natives of all temperate regions, such as the cranesbill. **2** a cultivated plant of the allied genus *Pelargonium*. [L, from Gr. *geranion*, from *geranos*, a crane (from the shape of the seed-pod)]

geratology (jerətol´əji) *n.* the branch of knowledge dealing with the phenomena of ageing and decay. **geratologic** (-təloj´-) *a.* [Gr. *gēras gēratos*, old age, -LOGY]

gerbe (jœb) *n.* (*Her.*) a figure resembling a wheatsheaf. [F]

gerbera (gœ´bərə, j-) *n.* any plant of the genus *Gerbera*, esp. *G. jamesonii*, the Transvaal daisy from S Africa. [Traugott *Gerber*, d.1743, naturalist]

gerbil (jœ´bil) *n.* any of numerous small, burrowing, mouselike rodents of the subfamily Gerbillinae, from desert regions of Asia and Africa, often kept as pets. [F *gerbille*, from mod. L *gerbillus*, a little JERBOA]

gerenuk (ger´ənook) *n.* an antelope, *Litocranius walleri*, of E Africa, characterized by a long neck and long legs. [Somali]

gerfalcon GYRFALCON.

geriatrics (jeriat´riks) *n.* the branch of medicine dealing with old age and its diseases. **geriatric** *a.* **1** of or relating to geriatrics or to elderly people. **2** (*coll.*, *derog.*) old, senile, worn out, useless. **geriatrician** (-riətrish´ən) *n.* a specialist in geriatrics. [Gr. *geras*, old age, *iatros*, a physician]

germ (jœm) *n.* **1** a micro-organism, esp. the type that is supposed to cause disease, a microbe. **2** (*Biol.*) **a** the portion of living matter from which an organism develops. **b** the embryo of an animal or plant. **c** a partially-developed organism. **3** the origin, source or elementary principle (*the germ of an idea*). **in germ** existing in an undeveloped state. **germ cell** *n.* the parent cell from which a new individual develops, usu. distinguished as the female element in reproduction from the sperm cell or male element. **germicide** (-misīd) *n.* a substance used for destroying germs. ~*a.* destroying germs, esp. disease-germs. **germicidal** (-si´dəl) *a.* **germ layer** *n.* (*Biol.*) any of the three layers of cells (ectoderm, mesoderm, endoderm) formed in an embryo. **germless** *a.* **germ line** *n.* (*Biol.*) a series of germ cells continuing through successive generations of an organism. **germ line therapy** *n.* (*Med.*) the treatment of certain diseases by the insertion of new genes into the reproductive cells of a patient, such genes then being passed on to all future generations. **germ plasm** *n.* the part of the protoplasm in which the power of reproduction is supposed to reside and which is transmitted from one generation to its offspring. **germ theory** *n.* the theory that certain diseases are caused by the development of micro-organisms introduced into the body through germs or spores. **germ tube** *n.* the tubelike growth issuing from a germinating spore. **germ warfare** *n.* the use of bacterial weapons to cause disease in enemy troops and populations. **germy** *a.* [F *germe*, L *germen -inis*]

German (jœ´mən) *a.* of or relating to Germany or its inhabitants. ~*n.* **1** a native or inhabitant of Germany. **2** the language of Germany, spoken also in Austria and parts of Switzerland. **German alloy** *n.* an aluminium alloy comprising aluminium, copper and zinc. **German Empire** *n.* **1** the empire established in 1871 by the union of the North German Confederation, Baden, Hesse, Bavaria and Württemberg. **2** WESTERN EMPIRE (under WESTERN). **Germanesque** (-nesk´) *a.* **Germanic** (jəman´-) *a.* **1** characteristic of Germans or Germany. **2** of or relating to the peoples originating in the area which became Germany (Anglo-Saxons, Scandinavians and Germans). **3** of or relating to the branch of Indo-European languages including German, Dutch, English and the Scandinavian languages. ~*n.* **1** the Germanic branch of Indo-European languages. **2** the unrecorded ancestor of this branch. **Germanist** *n.* an expert in the German language or other matters relating to Germany. **Germanism** *n.* **Germanity** (-man´-) *n.* **Germanize, Germanise** *v.t.* to assimilate or make to conform to German ideas, customs, idioms etc. ~*v.i.* to conform to these. **Germanization** (-zā´shən) *n.* **Germanizer** *n.* **German measles** *n.* rubella, a mild infectious disorder resembling measles which if contracted by a pregnant woman may cause birth deformities in her unborn child. †**German Ocean** *n.* the North Sea. **German sausage** *n.* a large kind of highly spiced sausage stuffed with partly-cooked meat. **German shepherd (dog)** *n.* an Alsatian dog. **German silver** *n.* a white alloy of nickel, copper and zinc, used for mathematical instruments, tableware etc. **German text** *n.* a black-letter text closely resembling old English and modern German. [L *Germānus*, perh. from Celt. (cp. OIr. *gair*, neighbour)]

german (jœ´mən) *a.* **1** having both parents the same (*brother german*). **2** having both grandparents the same on one side (*cousin german*). **3** †closely connected, relevant, pertinent (cp. GERMANE). [OF *germain*, L *germānus*, having the same parents (cogn. with GERMAN)]

germander (jœman´də) *n.* any plant of the genus *Teucrium*. **germander speedwell** *n.* an English wild plant with blue flowers, *Veronica chamaedrys*. [F *germandrée*, late L *germandra, gamandria*, late Gr. *chamandrua*, corr. of Gr. *chamaidrus* (*chamai*, on the ground, *drûs*, tree)]

germane (jœmān´) *a.* **1** relevant (to), appropriate. **2** closely related (to).

germanium (jəmā´niəm) *n.* a metallic element of a greyish-white colour, at. no. 32, chem. symbol Ge, used in the construction of transistors because of its electrical properties. **germanic** (-man´-) *a.* containing germanium, esp. in the tetravalent state. **germanous** (jœ´mənəs) *a.* containing germanium in the divalent state. [L *Germānus*, GERMAN]

Germano- (jœman´ō) *comb. form* German.

Germanomania (jœmənōmā´niə) *n.* enthusiasm for Germany or German things.

Germanophile (jœman´əfīl) *n.* an admirer of Germany and the Germans.

Germanophobe (jœman´əfōb) *n.* a hater of Germany or Germans. **Germanophobia** (-fō´biə) *n.* **Germanophobic** *a.*

germen (jœ´mən) *n.* (*pl.* **germens, germina** (jœ´minə)) (*Biol.*) the ovary or rudimentary seed-vessel of a plant. **germinal** (-mi-) *a.* **1** relating to or of the nature of a germ. **2** germinative. **3** in the earliest stage of development, embryonic. **4** productive of new ideas. **germinally** *adv.* **germinal vesicle** *n.* the large nucleus of an oocyte before it develops into an ovum. [L, see GERM]

germicide GERM.

germinal GERMEN.

germinate (jœ´mināt) *v.i.* **1** to sprout, to shoot, to bud. **2** to develop. ~*v.t.* **1** to cause to sprout or bud. **2** to put forth. **3** to cause to develop or produce. **germinable** *a.* **germinant** *a.* sprouting, growing, developing. **germination** (-ā´shən) *n.* **1** the first act of growth in an embryo plant, ovum etc. **2** the act or process of germinating. **germinative** (-nətiv) *a.* **germinator** *n.* [L *germinātus*, p.p. of *germināre*, from *germen*, see GERM]

germon (jœ´mən) *n.* ALBACORE. [F]

Geronimo (jəron´imō) *int.* used to express excitement, bravado etc. when about to leap, go into energetic action etc. [an Apache chief]

geronto- (jəron´tō), **geront-** *comb. form* of or relating to old age. **gerontic** (jəron´tik) *a.* of or relating to old people, senile. [as GERONTOCRACY]

gerontocracy (jerəntok´rəsi) *n.* (*pl.* **gerontocracies**) **1** government by old men or old people. **2** a government of old men or old people. **3** a state so governed.

gerontocrat (jəron´-) *n.* **gerontocratic** (-krat´-) *a.* [Gr. *gerōn gerontos*, an old man]

gerontology (jerəntol´əji) *n.* the science dealing with old age, the ageing process and the problems special to old people. **gerontological** (-loj´-) *a.* **gerontologist** *n.*

geropiga (jerəpē´gə), **jerupiga** *n.* a mixture sometimes added to port wine, made of unfermented grape juice with brandy, sugar and colouring matter. [Port., corr. of *hiera-picra*, a purgative]

-gerous (jərəs) *comb. form* bearing, having, as in *armigerous.* [L *-ger* from *gerere*, to bear]

gerrymander (jer´imandə) *v.t.* **1** to tamper with the boundaries of (an electoral district or constituency) so as to secure unfair advantages for a particular candidate, party or class. **2** to tamper with or manipulate to secure advantage. *~n.* an unfair rearrangement of a constituency in this manner; an act of gerrymandering. **gerrymanderer** *n.* [Elbridge *Gerry*, governor of Massachusetts, *-mander* (SALAMANDER, which the map of one district rearranged by Gerry was supposed to resemble)]

gerund (jer´ənd) *n.* a form of a verb acting as a noun: in English a form ending in *-ing*, in Latin, a part of the verb used as a noun instead of the infinitive in cases other than the nominative. **gerundial** (-rŭn´-) *a.* **gerundive** (-rŭn´div) *n.* in Latin, a form of a verb acting as an adjective, ending in *-ndus* and declinable, giving the sense of *must* and *should* (be done). *~a.* of or relating to or of the nature of a gerund or gerundive. **gerundival** (-dī´-) *a.* of or relating to a gerund or gerundive. **gerundively** *adv.* [L *gerundium*, from *gerundum*, neut. ger. of *gerere*, to do]

gesellschaft (gəzel´shahft) *n.* (*pl.* **gesellschaften** (-tən)) a social group, held together by practical concerns and not by ties of kinship, as distinct from *gemeinschaft.* [G, society]

gesso (jes´ō) *n.* (*pl.* **gessoes**) **1** plaster of Paris used for painting, sometimes for sculpture. **2** a ground made of this. [It., from L GYPSUM]

†gest (jest), **geste** *n.* **1** a deed, an exploit, an achievement. **2** a tale or history of the exploits of a hero or heroes, esp. a medieval ballad or metrical romance. *~v.i.* to compose or recite gests or legendary tales. [OF *geste*, from L *gesta*, exploits, orig. neut. pl. of *gestus*, p.p. of *gerere*, to carry on, to perform]

gestalt (gəstalt´) *n.* (*Psych.*) an organized whole in which each part affects every other part. **gestaltism** *n.* **gestaltist** *n.* **gestalt psychology** *n.* a system of thought maintaining that all perceptions, reactions etc. are gestalts or organized wholes. **gestalt therapy, gestalt psychotherapy** *n.* a therapy in which patients are led towards self-discovery by concentrating on the immediate present and expressing their true feelings. [G, form, pattern]

Gestapo (gəstah´pō) *n.* **1** the body of secret police formed to secure strict obedience to the government of Nazi Germany. **2** (*derog.*) any similar organization. [first letters of G *Geheime Staats Polizei*, secret state police]

gestation (jestā´shən) *n.* **1** the process of being carried in the uterus from the time of conception to that of birth. **2** the period between conception and birth. **3** the process of being developed or elaborated in private thought. **4** the period during which a plan, idea, etc. is conceived and developed. **gestate** *v.t.* **1** to carry (a foetus) in gestation. **2** to develop (an idea, plan etc.) usu. privately. **gestational** *a.* **gestative** *a.* **gestatorial** (jestətaw´riəl) *a.* for carrying. **gestatorial chair** *n.* the state chair in which the Pope is carried on special occasions. **gestatory** (jes´tətəri) *a.* **1** of or relating to gestation or pregnancy. **2** †that may be carried or worn. [through F, or directly from L *gestātiōnem*, nom. *gestātio*, from *gestāre*, freq. of *gerere*, to carry]

geste GEST.

gesticulate (jestik´ūlāt) *v.i.* to make expressive gestures or motions, as in speaking or instead of speaking. *~v.t.* to express or represent by gestures. **gesticulation** (-lā´shən) *n.* **1** the act or art of gesticulating to express emotion or illustrate an argument. **2** a gesture. **gesticulative** (-lətiv), **gesticulatory** *a.* of, relating to or represented by gesticulation. **gesticulator** *n.* [L *gesticulātus*, p.p. of *gesticulārī*, from *gesticulus*, dim. of *gestus*, gesture]

gesture (jes´chə) *n.* **1** a motion of the face, body or limbs, used to express emotion or to illustrate or enforce something that is said. **2** a significant move or act, usu. of a friendly nature. **3** the art of using gesture for rhetorical or dramatic purposes. **4** †bearing, deportment. **5** †posture. *~v.i.* to gesticulate. *~v.t.* to accompany or represent with gestures or action. **gestural** *a.* **gesturer** *n.* [late L *gestūra*, from *gestus*, p.p. of *gerere*, to carry, to deport (oneself)]

gesundheit (gəzunt´hīt) *int.* your health (said after someone has sneezed). [G]

get[1] (get) *v.t.* (*pres.p.* **getting,** *past* **got** (got), **†gat** (gat), *p.p.* **got,** (*esp. N Am.*) **gotten** (got´ən)) **1** to procure, to obtain, to gain possession of by any means, to acquire (*to get a new car*). **2** to earn, to win (*to get first prize*). **3** to receive, to obtain (*to get a letter*). **4** to receive as one's portion or penalty, to suffer (*to get a £20 fine*). **5** to understand, learn, commit to memory (*Do you get what I mean?*). **6** (*coll., in p.p.*) to have, to possess (*I have got a car*). **7** (*coll.*) to be obliged (to) (*You have got to do it*). **8** to beget, to procreate (*She has got three children*). **9** to succeed in obtaining, bringing, putting etc. (*to get a train*). **10** to induce, to persuade (to) (*Get him to accept*). **11** to betake (oneself) (*I got myself to the doctor's*). **12** (*coll.*) to catch, to outwit, to nonplus (*I got him with a slower ball*). *~v.i.* **1** to arrive at any place, condition or posture (*to get there*). **2** to go, to depart (*Go away! get!*). **3** (*coll.*) to succeed, to find the way or opportunity (to) (*I got to be manager*). **4** to be a gainer, to profit (*to give as good as you get*). **get along!** used to express mild disbelief. **get away!** used to express mild disbelief. **get knotted!** KNOT[1]. **get lost!** go away. **get on!** used to express mild disbelief. **get ready, get set, go!** used as a command to start a race. **to be getting on for** to approach in time or age. **to get about 1** to be able to move or walk about (after an illness). **2** to become known, to be reported abroad. **3** to travel from place to place. **to get across 1** to communicate, to make oneself understood. **2** to be communicated. **to get ahead 1** to prosper. **2** to come in advance (of). **to get along 1** to proceed, to advance. **2** to succeed, to fare, to manage (well or badly). **3** (*coll.*) to go away. **4** (*coll.*) to have a friendly relationship. **to get among 1** to become one of. **2** (*coll.*) to acquire, become involved with, esp. in a disruptive way (*to get among the wickets*). **to get around** to get about. **to get around to** to get round to. **to get at 1** to be able to reach. **2** to ascertain (*to get at the truth*). **3** (*sl.*) to banter, to tease, usu. in a spiteful way. **4** to influence, corrupt, bribe (a jockey etc.). **5** to drug or illegally tamper with (a racehorse). **6** to imply, to hint at. **to get away 1** to escape. **2** to disengage oneself (from). **3** to quit. **to get away with 1** to make off with. **2** to escape discovery in connection with (something wrong or illegal). **to get back 1** to receive back, to recover. **2** to return, to come back. **3** to contact again. **to get back at** to retaliate against. **to get behind 1** to go back into the rear. **2** to lag. **3** to fall into arrears. **4** to penetrate, to unravel. **to get by 1** (*coll.*) to just cope, despite difficult circumstances. **2** to elude. **3** to be good enough. **to get by heart** HEART. **to get clear 1** to disengage oneself. **2** to be released. **to get cracking** CRACK. **to get done with** (*coll.*) to finish with. **to get down 1** to alight, to descend. **2** to swallow. **3** (*coll.*) to make unhappy, to depress. **4** to write down. **to get**

down to 1 to concentrate upon. **2** to start work on. **to get even 1** to revenge oneself. **2** to equalize (with). **to get forward** to make progress, to advance. **to get free** to escape, to disengage oneself. **to get going 1** to begin. **2** to make haste. **to get high 1** to reach a state of pleasure or euphoria. **2** to become pleasurably affected by drugs etc. **to get his/ hers/ etc. 1** (*sl.*) to get one's deserts. **2** (*sl.*) to be killed. **to get hold of** HOLD[1]. **to get home 1** to arrive at one's home. **2** to arrive at the winning post. **to get in 1** to enter. **2** to collect and place under cover (as crops). **3** to make room for. **4** to be elected. **5** to arrive home. **to get in on the act** ACT. **to get in the road (of)** (*esp. Sc.*) to be an obstruction (to), to get in the way (of). **to get into 1** to put on (as clothes etc.). **2** (*coll.*) to become involved in. **3** to possess, dominate or take over (a person's mood, personality etc.). **to get it** (*sl.*) to be in trouble, to be punished. **to get it in the neck** NECK. **to get it into one's head** to become convinced (that). **to get it together** to become well organized, to take control. **to get laid** (*sl.*) to have sexual intercourse. **to get loose** to escape, to disengage oneself. **to get near** to approach within a small distance. **to get off 1** to dismount, to alight (from). **2** to escape, to be released (from). **3** to be acquitted, to be let off (with or for). **4** to start. **5** to go to sleep. **6** to take off, to remove. **7** to procure the acquittal of. **8** to cause to go to sleep. **to get off on 1** (*coll.*) to be impressed by. **2** (*coll.*) to enjoy. **to get off one's bike** (*esp. Austral.*) to become angry. **to get off with 1** (*coll.*) to behave flirtatiously with. **2** (*coll.*) to begin or have a sexual relationship with. **3** (*coll.*) to escape blame or punishment for. **to get on 1** to put or pull on. **2** to move on. **3** to advance. **4** to succeed or prosper. **5** to grow late. **6** to grow old. **7** to have a friendly relationship. **8** to do, fare or manage (with or without). **9** to mount. **to get one's act together** ACT. **to get one's bearings** BEARING (under BEAR[2]). **to get one's eye in** EYE[1]. **to get one's goat** GOAT. **to get one's hand in** to get into practice. **to get one's head down** HEAD[1]. **to get one's head together** HEAD[1]. **to get one's knickers in a twist** KNICKERS. **to get one's leg over** LEG. **to get one's own back** OWN[1]. **to get on one's nerves** NERVE. **to get on one's wick** WICK[1]. **to get on to 1** to make contact with. **2** to become aware of, discover. **to get out 1** to pull out, to extract. **2** to escape from any place of confinement or restraint. **3** to be divulged. **4** to publish or say finally, after difficulties. **5** to complete the solution of. **to get out of 1** to avoid (doing something). **2** to obtain (something) from, with some difficulty. **to get outside (of)** (*sl.*) to eat or drink, to ingest. **to get over 1** to surmount, overcome (a difficulty etc.). **2** to recover from (illness, surprise, disappointment etc.). **3** to make intelligible. **4** (*coll.*) to persuade. **5** to finish (a task etc.) with relief. **to get over with** to finish (a task etc.) with relief. **to get rid of** RID[1]. **to get round** ROUND. **to get round to** to deal with in due course. **to get set** (*esp. Austral. coll.*) to place a bet. **to get somewhere** SOME. **to get stuck in 1** to start doing a task vigorously. **2** (*coll.*) to eat hungrily. **to get stuck into 1** to start doing vigorously. **2** (*coll.*) to eat (something) hungrily. **3** to attack (someone) physically or verbally. **to get the best of** BEST. **to get the better of** BETTER. **to get the gate** GATE[1]. **to get the hang of** HANG. **to get the hump** HUMP. **to get there 1** (*coll.*) to succeed. **2** (*coll.*) to understand. **to get the worst of it** WORST. **to get through 1** to reach a point beyond, to reach one's destination. **2** to succeed in doing, to complete, to finish (with). **3** to pass (an examination). **4** to pass (as a bill). **5** to use up. **6** to make a telephone connection. **to get through to 1** to make a telephone connection with. **2** (*coll.*) to make understand or pay attention. **to get to 1** to reach, to arrive at. **2** to begin (a task etc.). **3** (*coll.*) to annoy or irritate. **4** (*coll.*) to affect emotionally. **to get together 1** to meet, to assemble. **2** to bring together, to amass. **to get to sleep** SLEEP. **to get under one's skin** SKIN. **to get up 1** to rise (as from a bed etc.). **2** to mount. **3** to dress up, to disguise. **4** to begin to rage or be violent (as the wind, waves etc.). **5** to prepare, to get ready. **6** to learn, to work up. **7** to invent, to devise. **to get up one's nose** NOSE. **to get up to** (*coll.*) to be doing, to be involved in, esp. wrongly. **to get wind of** WIND[1]. **to get with child** (*dated*) to make pregnant. **to have got it bad/ badly** (*sl.*) to be infatuated or obsessed. **get-at-able** *a.* accessible. **getaway** *n.* (*coll.*) an escape, esp. from the scene of a crime. ~*a.* used in a getaway. **get-out** *n.* a means of avoiding something. **get-rich-quick** *a.* with the purpose of making a lot of money in a short time (*a get-rich-quick scheme*). **gettable** *a.* obtainable. **getter** *n.* **1** a person or thing that gets. **2** a substance for removing residual gas from a vacuum tube etc. ~*v.t.* **1** to remove with a getter. **2** to remove from with a getter. **getting on** *a.* (*coll.*) growing old, advanced in years. **get-together** *n.* (*coll.*) an informal gathering. **get-up** *n.* **1** a person's dress and other accessories. **2** the manner in which anything is presented, as on the stage. **3** the style or format (of a book). **get-up-and-go** *n.* **1** energy and enthusiasm. **2** ambition. [Icel. *geta* (cp. OE *-gietan*, in *forgietan*, *engietan* etc., also Goth. *-gitan*, G *vergessen*, cogn. with L *-hendere*, in *prehendere*, to seize, Gr. *chandanein*, to seize)]

get[2] (get) *n.* **1** the act of begetting. **2** that which is begotten, offspring, progeny. **3** (*Sc.*) a brat. **4** (*sl., offensive*) a bastard. [from GET[1]]

geta (gā´tə) *n.* (*pl.* **geta, getas**) a Japanese wooden sandal. [Jap.]

gettable, getter etc. GET[1].

geum (jē´əm) *n.* any plant of the genus *Geum*, the rose family, comprising the avens or herb-bennet. [L]

GeV *abbr.* (*Physics*) giga-electron-volt.

gewgaw (gū´gaw) *n.* a showy trifle; a toy, a bauble. ~*a.* showy without value, gaudy. [perh. from ME *givegove*, a reduplication of GIVE]

gey (gī) *a.* (*Sc.*) considerable, middling (in amount). ~*adv.* considerably, very. [var. of GAY]

geyser (gē´zə) *n.* **1** a hot spring throwing up a column of water at intervals (as in SW Iceland, the Yellowstone region in N America, and New Zealand). **2** an apparatus for heating a stream of water supplying a bath etc. **geyserite** (-īt) *n.* an opal-like silica deposited from the waters of geysers and hot springs, sinter. [Icel. *geysir*, gusher, name of a hot spring in Iceland, from *geysa*, to gush]

GG *abbr.* **1** Girl Guides. **2** Governor-General. **3** Grenadier Guards.

GH *abbr.* Ghana (IVR).

Ghanaian (gahnā´ən) *n.* a native or inhabitant of Ghana in W Africa. ~*a.* of or relating to Ghana.

gharial (gar´iahl), **gavial** (gā´viəl) *n.* a large Indian crocodile, *Gavialis gangeticus*, with a long, slender muzzle. [Hind. *ghariyāl*]

gharry (ga´ri), **gharri** *n.* (*pl.* **gharries, gharris**) a variety of wheeled carriage in the Indian subcontinent. [Hind. *gārī*]

ghastly (gahst´li) *a.* (*comp.* **ghastlier**, *superl.* **ghastliest**) **1** horrible, frightful, shocking. **2** (*coll.*) awful, unpleasant (*a ghastly mistake*). **3** pale, deathlike, haggard. ~*adv.* in a ghastly manner. **ghastlily** *adv.* **ghastliness** *n.* [*gast*, to terrify, -LY[1]]

ghat (gaht, gawt), **ghaut** (gawt) *n.* (*Ind.*) **1** a flight of steps descending to a river, a landing-place. **2** a range of mountains (*Eastern and Western Ghats*). **3** a mountain pass. [Hind. *ghāt*]

ghazal (gaz´əl) *n.* an Oriental lyric poem, usu. erotic, convivial or religious in subject, having a limited number of couplets, all with the same rhyme. [Arab., an ode]

Ghazi (gah´zi) *n.* (*pl.* **Ghazis**) a person who has fought for Islam against non-Muslims. **Ghazism** *n.* [Arab. *ghāzi*, p.p. of *ghazā*, to fight]

GHB *abbr.* gamma hydroxy butyrate, a designer drug with anaesthetic properties.

ghee (gē), **ghi** *n.* butter, usu. prepared from buffalo-milk, clarified into an oil, which can be kept for a long time. [Hind. *ghī*]

gherao (gerow´) *n.* (*pl.* **gheraos**) in the Indian subcontinent, a form of industrial action in which a person, e.g. an employer, is imprisoned in a room, building etc. until certain demands are met. [from Hind. *gherna*, to surround, besiege]

gherkin (gœ´kin) *n.* a young and green small variety of cucumber, used for pickling. [Dut. *agurkken* (now *agurkje*), ult. from late Gr. *angourion*, Pers. *angārah*]

ghetto (get´ō) *n.* (*pl.* **ghettos, ghettoes**) **1** a poor, densely populated area of a city, esp. inhabited by an ethnic minority. **2** the quarter of a town formerly inhabited by Jews. **3** a segregated area, a place apart. **4** a group confined to such an area. ~*v.t.* (*3rd pers. sing. pres.* **ghettoes,** *pres.p.* **ghettoing,** *past, p.p.* **ghettoed**) to confine to a ghetto. **ghetto-blaster** *n.* a large portable stereo radio-cassette or CD player. **ghettoize, ghettoise** *v.t.* to make into a ghetto. **ghettoization** (-zā´shən) *n.* [It., perh. abbr. of *borghetto*, dim. of *borgo*, BOROUGH]

ghi GHEE.

Ghibelline (gib´əlīn, -lēn) *n.* a person who sided with the German Emperors in their contests with the Guelphs or partisans of the Popes, in Italy during the Middle Ages. [It. *ghibellino*, said to be a corr. of *Waiblingen*, an estate in Württemberg belonging to the Hohenstaufen family, from which sprang several Emperors during the 12th and 13th cents.]

ghilgai GILGAI.

ghillie GILLIE.

ghost (gōst) *n.* **1** the spirit or soul of a dead person appearing to the living, an apparition. **2** the soul of a dead person in the other world. **3** the soul or spirit, the vital principle. **4** a mere shadow or semblance. **5** the remotest likelihood (*a ghost of a chance*). **6** a person who does literary or artistic work for which another takes the credit. **7** in optics, a spot, gleam or secondary image caused by a defect in a lens. **8** in television reception, a duplicated image. ~*v.i.* **1** to be a ghost writer. **2** to appear as or like a ghost. ~*v.t.* **1** to ghost-write (a book etc.). **2** to haunt as a ghost. **to give up the ghost** to die, to expire. **ghostbuster** *n.* (*coll.*) a person supposed to banish ghosts etc. **ghost dance** *n.* a N American Indian religious dance aspiring to reunion with the dead and a return to the past. **ghost gum** *n.* a eucalyptus of inland Australia having a smooth white trunk. **ghosting** *n.* the phenomenon of duplicated images in television reception. **ghostlike** *a.* **ghostly** *a.* (*comp.* **ghostlier,** *superl.* **ghostliest**) **1** of or relating to ghosts or apparitions. **2** dismal, gloomy. **3** of or relating to the spirit or soul, spiritual. ~*adv.* spiritually. **ghostliness** *n.* **ghost moth** *n.* a nocturnal moth of the family Hepialidae, the caterpillars of which wreak havoc on the roots of hop plants. **ghost story** *n.* a tale concerned with the supernatural, esp. one of a terrifying character. **ghost town** *n.* a deserted or semi-deserted town, such as a formerly flourishing mining town. **ghost train** *n.* a fairground miniature railway in a dark space, where the rider is confronted by ghostly apparitions. **ghost word** *n.* a word perpetuated in dictionaries etc. but due to the errors of copyists, printers etc. **ghost-write** *v.t., v.i.* to write (a speech, autobiography etc.) for another person. **ghost writer** *n.* a person who writes (speeches, books etc.) for someone else who is presumed to be the author. [OE *gāst* (cp. Dut. *geest*, G *Geist*), prob. cogn. with Icel. *geisa*, to rage, Goth. *usgaisjan*, to terrify]

ghoul (gool) *n.* **1** an evil spirit supposed, in Eastern tales, to devour human corpses. **2** a person who robs graves. **3** a person interested in morbid things. **ghoulish** *a.* **1** like a ghoul. **2** excessively interested in morbid things. **ghoulishly** *adv.* **ghoulishness** *n.* [Arab. *ghūl*]

GHQ *abbr.* General Headquarters.

ghyll GILL².

GHz *abbr.* gigahertz.

GI (jēī´) *n.* (*pl.* **GIs, GI's**) (*N Am., coll.*) a soldier in the US Army, esp. a private. ~*a.* **1** of or relating to US servicemen. **2** (of equipment etc.) conforming to US Army regulations. [abbr. of *government issue*]

giant (jī´ənt) *n.* **1** a mythical being of human form but superhuman size. **2** (*pl.*) in Greek mythology, the offspring of Uranus and Ge (heaven and earth) who rebelled against the gods. **3** a man of extraordinary size. **4** any person, animal, plant etc. of abnormal size. **5** a person of extraordinary powers, ability etc. (*a literary giant*). **6** GIANT STAR (under GIANT). ~*a.* **1** gigantic. **2** very large of its class, type, species etc. **3** like a giant. **giantess** *n.* (*pl.* **giantesses**) a female giant. **giant fibres** *n.pl.* the large nerve fibres of the ventral nerve cord of many invertebrates. **giant hogweed** *n.* a tall cow parsley, *Heracleum mantegazzianum*, which can cause a severe reaction if handled. **gianthood** (-hud) *n.* †**giantish** *a.* **giantism** *n.* abnormal development in size esp. as caused by dysfunction of the pituitary gland. **giant-killer** *n.* **1** in folklore, a person who overcomes giants. **2** in sport, a lowly person or team that beats a bigger one. **giant-killing** *a., n.* **giant-like** *a.* **giant panda** *n.* a large, black-and-white, bearlike mammal, *Ailuropoda melanoleuca*, from China and Tibet. **giant powder** *n.* a form of dynamite, consisting of infusorial earth saturated with nitroglycerine. **giant sequoia** *n.* the sequoia *Sequoiadendron giganteum*. **giant slalom** *n.* a slalom of greater distance and with more widely spaced obstacles than the standard. **giant star** *n.* a star of great brightness and a very low mean density. [OF *geant*, L *gigantem*, nom. *gigas*, from Gr. *gigas -antos*, etym. uncertain]

giaour (jow´ə) *n.* (*derog.*) a non-Muslim, esp. a Christian. [Pers. *gāwr*]

giardiasis (jiahdī´əsis) *n.* (*Med.*) stomach infection with the protozoa of the genus *Giardia*, esp. *G. lamblia* causing nausea, diarrhoea etc., often caused by drinking contaminated water.

Gib (jib) *n.* (*coll.*) Gibraltar.

gib¹ (gib) *n.* a metal wedge, pin or bolt to hold a machine part etc. in place. ~*v.t.* (*pres.p.* **gibbing,** *past, p.p.* **gibbed**) to fasten with a gib. [etym. unknown]

†**gib²** (gib) *n.* **1** a cat, esp. a tom-cat. **2** a cat that has been castrated. **gib-cat** *n.* a tom-cat. [short for *Gilbert*]

gibber¹ (jib´ə), **jibber** *v.i.* to jabber, to talk rapidly and inarticulately. ~*n.* talk or noise of this kind. **gibberish** *n.* **1** inarticulate sounds. **2** unmeaning or unintelligible language, jargon. ~*a.* unmeaning. [imit.]

gibber² (jib´ə) *n.* (*Austral.*) a stone, a boulder. [Austral. Abor.]

gibberellic acid (jibərel´ik) *n.* a product extracted from the fungus *Gibberella fujikuroi*, used to stimulate plant growth. **gibberellin** *n.* any of several plant growth regulators produced by the fungus *Gibberella*.

gibbet (jib´it) *n.* **1** an upright post with a crosspiece from which the bodies of executed criminals were formerly hung on display. **2** a gallows. **3** the gallows, death by hanging. ~*v.t.* (*pres.p.* **gibbeting,** *past, p.p.* **gibbeted**) **1** to execute by hanging. **2** to hang or expose on or as on a gibbet. **3** to expose to public contempt and derision. [OF *gibet*, dim. of *gibe*, a staff or club; cp. JIB¹]

gibbon (gib´ən) *n.* any individual of the genus *Hylobates*, long-armed anthropoid apes from E Asia. [F, prob. from Eng. GIB² (conferred by Buffon)]

gibbous (gib´əs), **gibbose** (-ōs) *a.* **1** protuberant, convex, swelling into inequalities. **2** (of the illuminated portion of the moon or of a planet) exceeding a semicircle but falling short of a circle. **3** hunch-backed, humped, crook-backed. **gibbosity** (-bos´-) *n.* **gibbously** *adv.* **gibbousness** *n.* [L *gibbōsus*, from *gibbus*, a hump]

gibe (jīb), **jibe** *v.i.* **1** to use sneering or taunting expressions. **2** to jeer, to scoff (at), to rail, to flout. ~*n.* a sneer, a scoff, a taunt. **giber** *n.* **gibingly** *adv.* [etym. uncertain (cp. Icel. *geipa*, to talk nonsense, from *geip*, nonsense; also OF *giber*, to play rude pranks)]

Gibeonite (gib´iənīt) *n.* **1** any of the inhabitants of Gibeon, condemned for their duplicity to be 'hewers of wood and drawers of water' (Joshua ix.23). **2** a drudge, the lowest of servants. [*Gibeon*, a city in ancient Palestine]

giblets (jib´lits) *n.pl.* the feet, neck, and internal eatable parts of a fowl, such as the heart, liver, gizzard etc., which are removed before cooking. [OF *gibelet*, cogn. with *gibier*, game, and *gibelotte*, rabbit-stew]

Gibraltarian (jibrawlteə´riən) *n.* an inhabitant of Gibraltar. ~*a.* of or relating to Gibraltar. [*Gibraltar*, a rock, seaport and fortified town at the southern extremity of Spain, since 1704 a British possession]

†**Gibson girl** (gib´sən) *n.* a girl conforming to the tastes in fashion and beauty of around 1900. [C. D. *Gibson*, 1867–1944, US artist]

gibus (jī´bəs) *n.* (*pl.* **gibuses**) a crush-hat, an opera hat. [name of original maker]

gid (gid) *n.* a disease causing vertigo in sheep, sturdy. [short for GIDDY]

giddy (gid´i) *a.* (*comp.* **giddier**, *superl.* **giddiest**) **1** having a whirling, swimming or dizziness in the head. **2** reeling, tending to stagger or fall. **3** causing the sensation of giddiness (as a precipice, a dance, success etc.). **4** inconstant, changeable, fickle, flighty. **5** elated, excited, rash. ~*v.t.* (*3rd pers. sing. pres.* **giddies**, *pres.p.* **giddying**, *past, p.p.* **giddied**) to make giddy. ~*v.i.* to become giddy. **to play the giddy goat** to act the fool. **giddily** *adv.* **giddiness** *n.* †**giddy-go-round** *n.* a roundabout or merry-go-round. [OE *gydig*, prob. cogn. with GOD (cp. Gr. *entheos*, possessed by the god)]

giddy-up (gidiŭp´) *int.* used as a command to a horse to make it start moving or go faster. [corr. of *get up*]

gidgee (gij´ē) *n.* a small Australian tree, *Acacia cambagei.*

gie (gē) *v.t.*, *v.i.* (*Sc.*) to give.

GIFT (gift) *abbr.* (*Med.*) gamete intra-fallopian transfer (see GAMETE).

gift (gift) *n.* **1** a thing given, a present, a contribution. **2** a natural quality, talent or endowment. **3** the act, right, or power of giving. **4** (*Law*) the voluntary bestowal of property without consideration. **the gift of the gab** GAB. **to look a gift-horse in the mouth** to find fault with what cost one nothing. **gifted** *a.* **1** given, bestowed. **2** largely endowed with intellect, talented. **giftedly** *adv.* **giftedness** *n.* **gift of tongues** *n.* the power of speaking in unknown tongues, esp. as conferred on the Apostles at Pentecost. **giftshop** *n.* a shop selling gifts etc. **gift token, gift voucher** *n.* a voucher worth a specified amount, given as a gift, which can be exchanged for goods etc. by the recipient. **giftware** *n.* goods suitable as gifts. **gift-wrap** *v.t.* (*pres.p.* **gift-wrapping**, *past, p.p.* **gift-wrapped**) to wrap (a gift) in attractive paper. **giftwrap** *n.* paper for wrapping gifts. [from OE or Icel. *Gift* (cp. Dut. and G *Gift*, from the verb GIVE]

gig[1] (gig) *n.* **1** a light two-wheeled vehicle drawn by one horse. **2** a light clinker-built boat, 20–28 ft. (6–9 m) long, rowed by 4, 6 or 8 alternate oars. **3** a machine for raising a nap on cloth by passing it over rotary cylinders furnished with wire teeth. **gig-lamps** *n.pl.* (*dated sl.*) spectacles. [orig. a whipping-top (cp. Norw. *giga*, to totter)]

gig[2] (gig) *n.* (*coll.*) a job, esp. a booking for a musician to perform. ~*v.i.* (*pres.p.* **gigging**, *past, p.p.* **gigged**) to perform at a gig.

gig[3] (gig) *n.* a type of fishing spear. [from *fishgig*, earlier *fizgig*, Sp. *fisga*, harpoon]

giga- (gig´ə, gī´gə) *comb. form* denoting 10^9, as *gigawatt*, or 2^{30}, as *gigabyte.*

gigabyte (gig´əbīt) *n.* a unit of computer memory capacity equal to 1,024 megabytes.

giga-electron-volt (gigəilek´tronvōlt) *n.* a unit of energy equal to 1,000 million electron-volts.

gigaflop (gig´əflop, gī´-) *n.* a unit of computer processing speed equal to 1,000 million floating-point operations per second. [GIGA-, *flo*ating-*p*oint]

gigahertz (gig´əhœts, gī´-) *n.* (*pl.* **gigahertz**) a unit of frequency equal to 10^9 hertz.

gigametre (gig´amētə, gī´-) *n.* a unit of distance equal to 10^9 metres.

gigantic (jīgan´tik) *a.* **1** huge, enormous, giant-like; immense, extraordinary. **2** suitable for a giant. **gigantesque** (-tesk´) *a.* **gigantically** *adv.* **gigantism** (jī´-) *n.* **1** abnormal largeness. **2** GIANTISM (under GIANT). **3** abnormal largeness due to polyploidy. [L *gigas- -ntis*, GIANT]

gigawatt (gig´awot, gī´-) *n.* a unit of power equal to 10^9 watts.

giggle (gig´əl) *v.i.* **1** to laugh in a silly or affected manner, to titter. **2** to laugh in a nervous, catchy way, with attempts to restrain oneself. ~*n.* a silly or nervous laugh. **giggler** *n.* **giggly** *a.* (*comp.* **gigglier**, *superl.* **giggliest**) given to giggling, inclined to giggle. [imit., freq. in form (cp. Dut. *giggelen*)]

giglet (gig´lit), **giglot** (-lət) *n.* a flighty, giddy girl. ~*a.* fickle, inconstant, wanton. [prob. cogn. with GIG[1]]

GIGO (gī´gō) *abbr.* (*Comput.*) garbage in, garbage out.

gigolo (zhig´əlō) *n.* (*pl.* **gigolos**) **1** a young man paid by an older woman to be a sexual partner or escort. **2** a professional dance-partner or escort. [F, sl., a low fellow]

gigot (jig´ət) *n.* a leg of mutton or lamb. **gigot sleeve** *n.* a leg-of-mutton sleeve. [F, dim. of *gigue*, a leg]

gigue (zhēg) *n.* a piece of dance music, usu. in 6/8 time.

Gila monster (hē´lə) *n.* a large poisonous lizard, *Heloderma suspectum*, found in Arizona and New Mexico. [from *Gila*, on Arizona River]

gilbert (gil´bət) *n.* the cgs unit for measuring magnetomotive force. [William *Gilbert*, 1544–1603, English scientist]

Gilbertian (gilbœ´tiən) *a.* absurdly topsy-turvy. [Sir W. S. *Gilbert*, 1836–1911, writer of comic operas]

gild (gild) *v.t.* (*past, p.p.* **gilded, gilt** (gilt)) **1** to coat, overlay or wash thinly with gold. **2** to impart a golden colour or appearance to. **3** to make brilliant, to brighten. **4** to give a specious or agreeable appearance to, to gloss over. **to gild the lily** to spoil beauty by overembellishing. **to gild the pill** PILL. **gilded** *a.* **gilded cage** *n.* an environment of wealth and luxury in which a person is obliged by others or by circumstance to spend a restricted life. **Gilded Chamber** *n.* the House of Lords. **gilded youth** *n.* young people of wealth and fashion. **gilder** *n.* a person whose occupation it is to coat articles with gold. **gilding** *n.* **1** the act, process or art of overlaying with gold. **2** gilding-metal in leaf, powder, or liquid, for application to any surface. **3** outward decoration, covering, or disguise designed to give a fair appearance to anything. [OE *gyldan*, in *begyldan*, see GOLD]

Usage note The spellings of the verb *gild* (with gold) and the noun *guild* (a society) should not be confused.

gilet (jilā´) *n.* **1** a woman's light sleeveless top resembling a waistcoat. **2** a sleeveless padded jacket.

gilgai (gil´gī) *n.* (*pl.* **gilgais**) in Australia, a saucer-shaped depression containing a pool of water, a water hole. [Austral. Abor.]

gill[1] (gil) *n.* (*usu. pl.*) **1** each of the organs of respiration, or branchiae, of fishes and some amphibia. **2** in fish etc., a double row of long slender lamellae, extending, like the teeth of a comb, from the convex side of a branchial arch, and supported by a delicate membrane. **3** each of the hair or leaflike respiratory processes projecting from the body of some aquatic insects. **4** each of the vertical lamellae under the cap of mushrooms and other fungi. **5** each of the loose fleshy appendages, or wattles, at a fowl's throat. **6** (*pl., facet.*) the flesh about a person's jaws and chin. **green/ white about the gills** pale in the face because of nausea, fear, exhaustion etc. **gill cover** *n.* the external bony covering of a fish's gills. **gilled** *a.* **gill-net** *n.* a net, usu. set vertically, for entangling fish by the gills. **gill pouch** *n.* any of a series of paired linear outgrowths on the pharynx of all cyclostomes, and present at the embryonic stage of all vertebrates; in fish and some animals these are gill slits. **gill slit, gill opening** *n.* any one of the openings by which water passes into the gills. [cp. Dan. *gicælle*, Swed. *gāl*, also Gr. *cheilos*, lip]

gill[2] (gil), **ghyll** *n.* **1** a deep and narrow ravine, often wooded. **2** a gully or stream bed on a precipitous hillside. [Icel. *gil*]

gill[3] (jil) *n.* **1** a liquid measure, usu. one quarter of a pint (about 140 cl). **2** (*dial.*) half a pint (about 280 cl). [OF *gille, gelle*, low L *gillo, gella*, etym. uncertain]

gill[4] (jil), **Gill, jill, Jill** *n.* **1** †a girl, a lass; a sweetheart. **2** (*dial.*) a female ferret. **3** †ground ivy. [short for *Gillian*, F *Juliane*, L *Juliana*, from *Julius*]

gillie (gil´i), **ghillie** *n.* **1** a man or boy who attends a person fishing or hunting, esp. in the Scottish highlands. **2** (*Hist.*) an attendant on a Highland clan chief. [Gael. *gille*]

gillion (gil´yən, jil´-) *n.* (*dated*) in Britain, one thousand million, now superseded by the term *billion*. [GIGA-, MILLION]

gillyflower (jil´iflowə) *n.* **1** the clove-scented pink, *Dianthus caryophyllus*. **2** any of various flowers with a similar scent, esp. the white stock and the wallflower. [earlier *gylofre*, OF *girofle*, late L *caryophyllum*, Gr. *karuophullon* (*karuon*, nut, *phullon*, leaf), ending assim. to FLOWER]

gilt[1] (gilt) *a.* **1** gilded. **2** adorned with something resembling gold, gold-coloured. ~*n.* **1** gold laid over the surface of a thing, gilding. **2** (*pl.*) gilt-edged securities. **3** money, gold. **to take the gilt off the gingerbread** GINGERBREAD. **gilt-edged** *a.* having the edges gilded. **gilt-edged securities** *n.pl.* investments of the most reliable character. **gilthead** *n.* any of several fishes with golden spots or lines on their heads, including the dorado, the striped tuna or bonito, and the golden wrasse. [GILD]

gilt[2] (gilt) *n.* a young sow. [Icel. *gyltr*]

gimbals (jim´bəlz, gim´-) *n.pl.* forms of universal joint for securing free motion in suspension, or for suspending anything, such as a lamp, a compass, a chronometer etc., so that it retains a horizontal or other required position, or is in equilibrium. [alt. form of *gimmal*, GEMEL]

gimcrack (jim´krak), **jimcrack** *n.* **1** a pretty but useless or flimsy article, a worthless knick-knack. **2** †a showy person, a dandy, a fop. ~*a.* showy but flimsy and worthless. **gimcrackery** *n.* **gimcracky** *a.* [etym. uncertain, perh. in first sense from obs. *gim, jimp*, spruce, and *crack*, a lively boy]

gimlet (gim´lit) *n.* **1** a small boring-tool with a worm or screw for penetrating wood, and a wooden crosspiece for a handle. **2** a cocktail of gin and lime juice. ~*v.t.* **1** to bore or pierce with a gimlet. **2** to turn round (as an anchor) with a motion like the turning of a gimlet. **gimlet eye** *n.* a piercing eye. [OF *guimbelet*, dim. of *guimble*]

gimme (gim´mē) *n.* (*coll.*) in golf, a small putt that is unlikely to be missed and that an opponent would normally concede without the necessity of one playing it. **gimme cap, gimme hat** *n.* (*N Am., coll.*) a peaked baseball-style cap bearing a company name, logo etc., usu. given away free as advertising material. [*give me*]

gimmick (gim´ik) *n.* a trick, device or oddity of behaviour used to attract extra interest, attention or publicity. **gimmickry** *n.* **gimmicky** *a.* [etym. unknown]

gimp[1] (gimp), **guimp, gymp** *n.* **1** silk, wool, or cotton twist interlaced with wire or coarse cord. **2** a silk fishing line whipped with thin wire to protect it against injury from the teeth of large fish. ~*v.t.* to trim or whip with gimp or with fine wire. [etym. uncertain, cp. Dut. *gimp*, F *guimpe*]

gimp[2] (gimp) *n.* (*esp. N Am., sl.*) **1** a lame or crippled person, esp. an old one. **2** an awkward, clumsy or ineffectual person. [poss. comb. of *grandfather* and *limp*]

gin[1] (jin) *n.* an alcoholic drink, distilled usu. from grain, and flavoured with juniper berries. **gin and it** *n.* a drink consisting of gin mixed with Italian vermouth. **gin fizz** *n.* a drink composed of gin, lemon juice and soda water etc. **gin palace** *n.* (*derog.*) a gaudily-decorated public house or bar. **gin rummy** *n.* a form of the card game rummy. **gin shop** *n.* (*Hist.*) a tavern or drinking saloon where spirits were sold. **gin sling** *n.* a cold drink, composed of gin, soda water, lemon, and sugar. [short for GENEVER]

gin[2] (jin) *n.* **1** a trap, a snare for small mammals and birds. **2** a machine for separating cotton-fibre from the seeds, a cotton gin. **3** a portable hoisting-machine usu. having a tripod frame, one leg being movable. ~*v.t.* (*pres.p.* **ginning**, *past, p.p.* **ginned**) **1** to clean (as cotton) of the seeds by means of a gin. **2** to snare, to entrap. **gin house** *n.* a house where cotton is ginned. **ginner** *n.* **ginning** *n.* the operation by which cotton is cleared of its seeds. [contraction of OF *engin*, ENGINE]

gin[3] (jin) *n.* an Aboriginal woman of Australia. [Austral. Abor.]

ginger (jin´jə) *n.* **1** the hot spicy root of the ginger plant used, either whole or powdered, in cookery, as a preserved sweet, in drinks or in medicine. **2** a plant, *Zingiber officinale*, with a pungent, spicy rootstock. **3** the light reddish colour of powdered ginger. **4** (*coll.*) a red-haired person. **5** mettle, dash, go. **6** stimulation. ~*v.t.* **1** to liven (up), to stimulate, to put on one's mettle. **2** to flavour with ginger. **gingerade** (-ād) *n.* ginger beer or ginger ale. **ginger ale** *n.* a carbonated drink, prepared by dissolving sugar in water, flavouring with ginger or essence of ginger, and colouring with a solution of caramel. **ginger beer** *n.* a fermented, carbonated soft drink prepared from ginger, white sugar, water and yeast. **ginger beer plant** *n.* a system, usu. in the home, by which yeast is fermented with ginger to make ginger beer. **ginger cordial** *n.* a cordial or liqueur made with raisins, lemon rind, and ginger and water strengthened with spirits. **ginger group** *n.* a group of people within an organization such as a political party who share a specialized interest or viewpoint and who seek to influence the main body of the organization through their enthusiasm. **ginger nut** *n.* a ginger-flavoured biscuit. **ginger snap** *n.* a crisp thin ginger-flavoured biscuit; a brandy snap. **ginger wine** *n.* a wine made by the fermentation of sugar, water and ginger. **gingery** *a.* **1** spiced with ginger; suggestive of ginger. **2** (*coll.*) red-haired. **3** stimulating. [earlier *gingivere*, OE *gingifere*, late L *gingiber*, L *zingiber*, Gr. *zingiberis*, Sansk. *çrngavera* (*çrnga*, horn, *vera*, body)]

gingerbread (jin´jəbred) *n.* a dark-coloured cake or biscuit made of flour, treacle or molasses, ground ginger and other spices. ~*a.* **1** made of gingerbread. **2** showy, tawdry, flimsy and fantastic (in allusion to the fanciful shapes, often gilded, in which gingerbread used to be moulded). **to take the gilt off the gingerbread** to reveal the unattractive reality behind something which appears to be glamorous. **gingerbread man** *n.* (*pl.* **gingerbread men**) a flat cake made of gingerbread shaped, roughly, like a human being. **gingerbread tree, gingerbread palm** *n.* **1** the doum-palm. **2** a W African tree, *Parinarium macrophyllum*, with a farinaceous stone-fruit. **gingerbreadwork** *n.* work cut or carved in fanciful shapes.

gingerly (jin´jəli) *adv.* daintily, fastidiously, cautiously, so as to move without noise or risk of hurting oneself or anything trodden upon. *~a.* dainty, fastidious, cautious. **gingerliness** *n.* [perh. from OF *gensor*, compar. of *gent*]

gingham (ging´əm) *n.* a kind of linen or cotton fabric woven of dyed yarn, usu. in stripes or checks. [F *guingan*, Malay *ginggang*, orig. striped]

gingili (jin´jili) *n.* **1** sesame, *Sesamum orientale*. **2** sesame oil. [Hind. *jingalī*, ult. from Arab. *juljulān*]

gingival (jinjī´vəl) *a.* of or relating to the gums. **gingivitis** (-jivī´təs) *n.* inflammation of the gums. [L *gingīva*, the gum]

gingko GINKGO.

ginglymus (jing´gliməs, ging´-) *n.* (*pl.* **ginglymi** (-mī)) (*Anat.*) a hinge joint admitting only of flexion and extension in one plane, such as the elbow. [Gr. *ginglumos*, hinge]

gink (gingk) *n.* (*sl.*) **1** an awkward, clumsy or foolish person. **2** fellow, man, person.

ginkgo (gingk´gō), **gingko** (ging´kō), **jingko** *n.* (*pl.* **ginkgos, ginkgoes, gingkos, gingkoes**) a Japanese tree, *Ginkgo biloba*, with fan-shaped leaves, also called *maidenhair tree*. [Jap. *ginkyo*, from Chin. *yin-hing* (*yin*, silver, *hing*, apricot)]

ginnel (gin´əl) *n.* (*dial.*) a narrow passage, alley.

ginner, ginning GIN².

ginormous (jīnaw´məs) *a.* (*coll.*) huge, enormous. [*gi*ant, e*normous*]

ginseng (jin´seng) *n.* **1** any of several herbs belonging to the genus *Panax*, esp. *P. schinseng* of China and *P. quinquefolius* of N America, the root of which has a sharp, aromatic taste, and is highly esteemed as a medicine or tonic by the Chinese etc. **2** this root. [Chin. *jên shên* (*jên*, man, *shên*, meaning doubtful)]

giocoso (jokō´sō) *adv.*, *a.* (*Mus.*) (played) in a lively, joking manner. [It.]

Giottesque (jotesk´) *a.* in the style of or after Giotto. *~n.* the style established by Giotto and his school. [*Giotto* di Bondone, 1276–1337, Italian painter]

gip¹ (gip) *v.t.* (*pres.p.* **gipping**, *past, p.p.* **gipped**) to take out the entrails of (herrings etc.). [etym. unknown]

gip² GYP¹.

gip³ GYP³.

gippo (jip´ō) *n.* (*pl.* **gippos**) **1** (*sl., offensive*) a gypsy or similar person. **2** (*derog.*) an Egyptian, esp. an Egyptian soldier. [abbr. of *Egyptian*]

gippy tummy (jip´i), **gyppy tummy** *n.* (*coll.*) an upset stomach, diarrhoea etc. [as GIPPO]

gipsy GYPSY.

giraffe (jirahf´, -raf´) *n.* (*pl.* **giraffe, giraffes**) an African ruminant, *Giraffa camelopardalis*, with an extremely long neck, and two bony excrescences on the head, light fawn in colour with darker spots. [F (now *girafe*), Sp. *girafa*, Arab. *zarāfah*]

girandole (jir´əndōl) *n.* **1** a revolving firework discharging rockets. **2** a branching chandelier or candlestick. **3** a rotating jet of water. **4** a pendent jewel, usu. for the ears, with a large set encircled by smaller ones. [F, from It. *girandola*, from *girare*, L *gȳrare*, to turn in a circle, from *gȳrus*, Gr. *guros*, circle]

girasol (jir´əsol), **girasole** (-sōl) *n.* a variety of opal with reddish refractions, also called *fire-opal*. [It. *girasole*, orig. sunflower; *girare*, as GIRANDOLE, *sole*, sun]

gird¹ (gœd) *v.t.* (*past, p.p.* **girded, girt** (gœt)) **1** to bind round (usu. the waist) with some flexible band, esp. in order to secure or confine the clothes. **2** to secure (one's clothes) with a girdle, belt etc. **3** to fasten (a sword on or to) with a girdle or belt. **4** to invest or equip (with). **5** to surround or encircle with or as with a girdle, to encompass, to besiege. **6** †to dress, to clothe. **to gird (up) one's loins** **1** to get ready to do something. **2** to prepare oneself for (vigorous) action. **girding** *n.* **1** something that girds. **2** †a girdle. **3** †a covering. **4** (*Sc.*) a saddle-girth. [OE *gyrdan* (cp. Dut. *gorden*, G *gürten*), cogn. with GIRTH, GARDEN, YARD¹]

gird² (gœd) *v.i.* to sneer, to mock (at). *~n.* a sarcasm, a sneer. [etym. unknown]

girder (gœ´də) *n.* a principal beam, esp. a compound structure of iron, steel, wood or metal, spanning the distance from wall to wall, or pier to pier, used to support joints, walls, roof, roadway, or other similar load. **girder bridge** *n.* a bridge consisting of girders.

girdle¹ (gœ´dəl) *n.* **1** a lightweight elasticated undergarment worn by women about the hips and thighs. **2** a belt, zone or cord for securing a loose garment round or encircling the waist. **3** anything that encircles as a belt or zone. **4** the bones by which the limbs are united to the trunk in vertebrate animals. **5** a small circular band or fillet round the shaft of a column. **6** the line of greatest marginal circumference of a gemstone, at which it is grasped by the setting. **7** (*Bot.*) a zonelike ring on a stem etc. *~v.t.* **1** to gird or surround with or as with a girdle. **2** to make a cut round (the trunk of a tree) through the bark, in order to kill it or in some cases to make it fruit better. **girdler** *n.* **1** a person or thing that girdles. **2** a maker of girdles. [OE *gyrdel*, from *gyrdan*, to GIRD¹]

girdle² (gœ´dəl) *n.* (*Sc., North*) a round flat plate of iron for baking cakes etc. (*girdle scones*). [var. of GRIDDLE]

girl (gœl) *n.* **1** a female child, a young and unmarried woman. **2** a female waitress or servant. **3** a girlfriend. **the girls** **1** the daughters of a family. **2** girls collectively. **3** (*often offensive*) women collectively. **girl Friday** *n.* a female secretary and general assistant in an office. **girlfriend** *n.* **1** a regular female companion, esp. one with whom there is a romantic relationship. **2** a female friend. **Girl Guide** *n.* a member of the Guides Association, an international organization founded with the aim of developing health, character and practical skills. **girlhood** *n.* **girlie, girly** *n.* (*pl.* **girlies**) a girl (esp. as a term of endearment). *~a.* **1** (*derog.*) girlish. **2** denoting or relating to magazines containing pictures of women in erotic poses. **girlish** *a.* like a girl. **girlishly** *adv.* **girlishness** *n.* **girl power** *n.* power exercised by young women. **Girl Scout** *n.* a girl belonging to the Scout Association. [ME *gerle*, a young person, cp. LG *gör*, a child]

girn GURN.

giro (jī´rō) *n.* (*pl.* **giros**) **1** in the UK, a system operated by banks and post offices whereby, when the required instructions have been issued, payments can be made by transfers from one account to another. **2** a giro cheque. *~v.t.* (*3rd pers. sing. pres.* **giroes**, *pres.p.* **giroing**, *past, p.p.* **giroed**) to pay by giro. **giro cheque** *n.* in the UK, a benefit cheque for people who are ill, unemployed etc. that can be cashed at a post office or bank.

Girondist (zhērō´dist) *n.* in French history, a member of the moderate Republican party in the French Assembly (1791–3) (so named because its leaders represented the department of the Gironde). *~a.* of or relating to the Girondists. [*Gironde*, a maritime department in SW France, on the Bay of Biscay]

☒ **girrafe** common misspelling of GIRAFFE.

girt¹ (gœt) *a.* **1** girded, bound. **2** (of a vessel) moored so taut by cables fixed in opposite directions as to prevent her swinging. [p.p. of GIRD¹]

†**girt**[2] GIRTH.

girth (gœth), †**girt** (gœt) *n.* **1** the measurement round anything, the circumference e.g. of one's waist, of a tree. **2** the band by which a saddle or burden is made fast and kept secure on a horse's back by passing round its belly. **3** a circular bandage or anything that encircles or girds. *~v.t.* **1** to secure on (a horse) with a girth. **2** to fit with a girth. **3** to measure the girth of. **4** to measure (a certain amount) in girth. **5** to surround, to encompass. [Icel. *gjörth*, a girdle, cp. Goth. *gairda*]

gisarme (jēzahm´) *n.* a long-shafted battleaxe with a point on the back of the axe head, carried by foot soldiers. [OF *guisarme*, prob. from OHG *getisarn*, weeding tool]

gismo GIZMO.

gist (jist) *n.* **1** the essence or main point of a question. **2** (*Law*) the real ground of an action. [OF (F *gît*), it lies, 3rd pers. sing. pres. of *gésir*, L *jacēre*, to lie]

git (git) *n.* (*sl.*) an unpleasant or worthless person; a bastard. [alteration of GET[2]]

gitano (jitah´nō) *n.* (*pl.* **gitanos**) a male gypsy. **gitana** (-nə) *n.* a female gypsy. [Sp., ult. from L *Ægyptiānus* (cp. GYPSY)]

gîte (zhēt) *n.* in France, a privately-owned, self-contained, self-catering apartment or cottage available for holiday lets. [F *gîte*, OF *giste*, as GIST]

gittern (git´œn) *n.* a medieval instrument like a guitar, a cittern. [OF *guiterne*, as CITTERN]

giusto (joos´tō) *a., adv.* (*Mus.*) (of musical tempo) regular(ly), strict(ly), accurate(ly). [It., from L *justus*, JUST[1]]

give (giv) *v.t.* (*past* **gave** (gāv), *p.p.* **given** (giv´ən)) **1** to hand over or transfer the possession of or right to without price or compensation. **2** to bestow, to confer, to present. **3** to grant, to concede, to allow, to put in one's power. **4** to hand over, to deliver. **5** to commit, to consign, to put in someone's keeping. **6** to transfer as price or in exchange, to pay, to sell. **7** to return, to render as due. **8** to surrender, to relinquish. **9** to yield up, to devote. **10** to yield as product. **11** to communicate, to impart. **12** to be the source or author of. **13** to occasion, to cause. **14** to offer, to hold out, to show or exhibit. **15** to care to the extent of (*I don't give a damn*). **16** to assign, to suppose, to assume (as conditions or circumstances). *~v.i.* **1** to part with freely and gratuitously. **2** to yield to pressure, to collapse. **3** to move back, to recede. **4** to make way or room. **5** to lead, to open (upon). **6** (*coll.*) to be forthcoming. *~n.* **1** the state of yielding or giving away. **2** elasticity. **3** adaptability, compliance. **give me** I prefer (*Give me radio, any day!*). **give or take** (*coll.*) if you add or subtract (an amount or number) in making an estimate. **give you good day/ even/ morrow** (*dated*) a way of greeting (for *God give you good day* etc.). **to be given to** to have a habit of, to be fond of. **to give and take 1** to be fair, to act fairly. **2** to exchange. **to give as good as one gets** to be a match for an opponent throughout a contest, argument etc. **to give away 1** to make over as a gift, to transfer. **2** to hand over in marriage to a bridegroom during the wedding ceremony. **3** to let out or divulge inadvertently. **4** to give or concede to an opposing player or side by mistake. **5** (*Austral.*) to abandon, to lose interest in. **to give back** to restore, return something to someone. **to give birth (to)** to bring forth, to have a baby, young etc. **to give chase to** to pursue. **to give down** (of a cow) to give milk. **to give forth 1** to emit. **2** †to publish, to tell. **to give in 1** to yield. **2** to hand in. **to give in charge** CHARGE. **to give in marriage** to permit the marriage of (a daughter). **to give into** to afford a prospect into, to face. **to give into custody** to hand over or consign to the police etc. **to give it to** (*coll.*) to scold, punish severely, beat. **to give of** to contribute. **to give off** to emit. **to give oneself** (of a woman) to yield to sexual intercourse. **to give oneself up to** to abandon or addict oneself to. **to give on to** to afford a prospect on or into, to face. **to give out 1** to emit. **2** to publish, to proclaim. **3** to distribute. **4** (*coll.*) to show, to profess. **5** to break down. **6** to run short. **7** in cricket (of an umpire) to indicate that a batsman is out. **to give over 1** to hand over, to transfer. **2** to abandon, to despair of. **3** (*in p.p.*) to devote or addict (*given over to gambling*). **4** to cease (from), to desist (*Give over!*). **5** to yield. **to give to understand** to inform authoritatively; to lead to believe. **to give up 1** to surrender. **2** to resign. **3** to commit. **4** to despair of. **5** to stop doing. **to give way 1** to yield, to fail to resist. **2** to make concessions. **3** to make room. **4** to be superseded. **5** to break down, to collapse. **6** to abandon (oneself to). **7** to be depreciated in value. **8** to begin to row. **9** to row with increased energy. **to give wings to** WING. **what gives?** (*coll.*) what is happening? **give and take** *n.* **1** mutual concession or forbearance. **2** fair measure on either side. **give-away** *n.* **1** (*coll.*) an unintentional revelation. **2** something given free. **given** *a.* **1** that has been given. **2** assumed or specified. **3** signed and dated. *~n.* a known fact, a thing to be assumed. **given that** granted that. **given name** *n.* a forename, a baptismal name. **giver** *n.* [OE *giefan* (cp. Dut. *geven*, Icel. *gefa*, Goth. *giban*, G *geben*)]

gizmo (giz´mō), **gismo** *n.* (*pl.* **gizmos, gismos**) (*coll.*) a gadget. **gizmology** (-mol´-) *n.* (*sl.*) technological gadgetry. [etym. unknown]

gizzard (giz´əd) *n.* **1** a strong muscular division of the stomach, esp. the second stomach in birds. **2** a thickened muscular stomach in certain fish, insects and molluscs. **to stick in one's gizzard** (*coll.*) to be very disagreeable to one. [ME *giser*, OF *giser*, *gezier* (F *gésier*), L *gigeria*, pl., cooked entrails of poultry]

Gk. *abbr.* Greek.

gl. *abbr.* **1** glass. **2** gloss.

glabella (gləbel´ə) *n.* (*pl.* **glabellae** (-ē)) (*Anat.*) the smooth flat area of bone between the eyebrows. **glabellar** *a.*

glabrous (glā´brəs), **glabrate** (glā´brāt, -brət) *a.* **1** smooth. **2** devoid of hair or pubescence.

glacé (glas´ā) *a.* **1** (of fruit etc.) preserved in sugar, candied (and usu. glossy). **2** (of leather goods etc.) polished, smooth. **3** iced. **glacé icing** *n.* icing that sets with a shiny surface. [F, p.p. of *glacer*, to ice, from *glace*, ice]

glacial (glā´shəl, glā´siəl) *a.* **1** (of geological formations) due to or characterized by glaciers, ice sheets or floating ice. **2** due to or like ice, icy. **3** of or relating to ice. **4** (*Chem.*) crystallizing at ordinary temperatures. **glacialist** *n.* a glaciologist. **glacially** *adv.* **glacial period, glacial epoch, glacial era** *n.* a period during which a large part of the northern hemisphere was covered with an ice sheet, an ice age. **glaciate** (glā´siāt) *v.t.* **1** to scratch, polish or wear down by means of ice. **2** to cover with ice in the form of sheets or glaciers. *~v.i.* to be converted into ice. **glaciated** *a.* **glaciation** (-ā´shən) *n.* the subjection of an area to glacial conditions. [F, from L *glaciālis*, from *glacies*, ice]

glacier (glas´iə, glā´-) *n.* a streamlike mass of ice, formed by consolidated accumulations of snow at high altitudes, slowly descending to lower regions. **glacier table** *n.* a block of stone left standing on a pillar of ice which it has sheltered from the sun's rays while all the ice around has melted away. [F, from *glace*, L *glacies*, ice]

glacio- (glā´siō, glas´-) *comb. form* **1** glacial. **2** glacier.

glaciology (glāsiol´əji, glas-) *n.* the study of glacial action and its geological effects. **glaciologic** (-loj´-), **glaciological** *a.* **glaciologist** *n.*

glaciometer (glāsiom´itə, glas-) *n.* an apparatus or device for measuring the rate of movement of glaciers.

glacis (glas´is, -ē, glā´-) *n.* (*pl.* **glacis** (-is, -ēz)) a sloping bank in a fortification, e.g. in front of a rampart, where assailants would be exposed to fire. [F, orig. a slippery place, from OF *glacer*, from *glace*, ice]

glad[1] (glad) *a.* (*comp.* **gladder**, *superl.* **gladdest**) **1** pleased, gratified. **2** indicating pleasure or satisfaction. **3** affording pleasure, joy or satisfaction (*glad tidings*). **4** bright, cheerful (*glad expression*). ~†*v.t.* (*pres.p.* **gladding**, *past, p.p.* **gladded**) to make glad. **gladden** *v.t.* **1** to make glad or joyful. **2** to cheer up. ~*v.i.* to become glad or joyful, to rejoice. **glad eye** *n.* (*coll.*) ogling (*to give someone the glad eye*). **glad hand** *n.* (*coll.*) a welcome, esp. a fulsome one. ~*v.t.* to welcome, esp. by shaking hands. **glad-hand** *v.t.* **glad-hander** *n.* a person keen to win many people over by greeting them effusively, e.g. a vote-seeking politician. **gladhanding** *n.* **gladly** *adv.* **gladness** *n.* **glad rags** *n.* (*coll.*) **1** one's best or smartest clothes. **2** evening dress. †**gladsome** (-səm) *a.* †**gladsomely** *adv.* †**gladsomeness** *n.* [OE]

glad[2] (glad), (*Austral.*) **gladdie** (glad´i) *n.* (*coll.*) a gladiolus.

gladden GLAD[1].

gladdie GLAD[2].

gladdon (glad´ən) *n.* a purple iris, *Iris foetidissima*, also called *stinking iris* because of its unpleasant odour when bruised.

glade (glād) *n.* **1** an open space in a wood or forest. **2** (*N Am.*) an opening in the ice of rivers or a tract of smooth ice. **3** an everglade. [prob. from Scand. (cp. Icel. *glathr*)]

gladiate (glad´iət) *a.* (*Bot.*) sword-shaped. [as GLADIATOR]

gladiator (glad´iātə) *n.* **1** in Roman times, a man employed to fight in the amphitheatre. **2** a political combatant. **3** a controversialist. **gladiatorial** (-iətaw´riəl) *a.* **gladiatorism** *n.* **1** the act or practice of fighting as gladiators. **2** prize-fighting. **gladiatorship** *n.* [L, from *gladius*, a sword]

gladiolus (gladiō´ləs) *n.* (*pl.* **gladioli** (-lī), **gladioluses**) any iridaceous plant of the genus *Gladiolus*, with a fleshy bulb, sword-shaped leaves and spikes of bright-coloured flowers. [L, dim. of *gladius*, sword]

Gladstone (glad´stən), **Gladstone bag** *n.* a light leather bag with flexible sides, opening along the middle and secured with a clasp and straps. **Gladstonian** (-stō´-) *a.* of or relating to the British statesman W. E. Gladstone, 1809–98, esp. a supporter of his Home Rule policy.

Glagolitic (glagəlit´ik) *a.* of or relating to the earliest Slavonic alphabet, principally used in Istria and Dalmatia, in the offices of the Roman Catholic Church. [OSlav. *glagolŭ*, word]

glair (gleə), **glaire** *n.* **1** white of egg, or a preparation made with this, used as size or varnish. **2** any similar viscous, transparent substance. ~*v.t.* to smear or overlay with glair. **glaireous** (-riəs) *a.* **glairy** *a.* [OF *glaire*, prob. from L *clāra*, fem. of *clārus*, clear, bright]

Glam. *abbr.* Glamorgan.

glam (glam) *a.* (*coll.*) glamorous. ~*v.t.* (*pres.p.* **glamming**, *past, p.p.* **glammed**) to glamorize. **glam rock** *n.* (*coll.*) a type of pop or rock music distinguished by performers in showy, glamorous clothes, hairstyles etc. [abbr.]

glamour (glam´ə), (*esp. N Am.*) **glamor** *n.* **1** fascinating attractiveness due largely to grooming, expensive clothes, or other artifice. **2** †magic, enchantment. **3** †bewitching delusive charm or illusion. ~*v.t.* **1** (*coll.*) to make glamorous. **2** †to bewitch, enchant. **to cast a glamour over** to bewitch, enchant. **glamorize, glamorise** *v.t.* to make glamorous. **glamorization** (-zā´shən) *n.* **glamorous** *a.* **glamorously** *adv.* **glamorousness** *n.* **glamour boy, glamour girl** *n.* a young man or woman with a glamorous appearance or lifestyle. **glamourpuss** *n.* (*coll.*) a glamorous woman. [Sc.]

glance[1] (glahns) *v.i.* **1** to give a quick or cursory look (at). **2** to glide off or from (as a blow). **3** to dart or flash a gleam of light or brightness. **4** to touch, to allude, to hint (at). **5** to move about rapidly. **6** to give only cursory consideration (to). ~*v.t.* **1** to strike obliquely. **2** to direct (a look or the eye) rapidly or cursorily. **3** †to shoot or dart swiftly or suddenly. **4** †to hint at, to allude to. ~*n.* **1** a quick or transient look, a hurried glimpse (at). **2** in cricket, a hit with the bat turned obliquely to the ball. **3** an oblique impact of an object on another causing it to be deflected. **4** a flash, a gleam. **at a glance** immediately, at a first look. **glancing** *a.* **glancingly** *adv.* [prob. from OF *glacier*, to slip, to glide, from *glace*, ice (influ. by ME *glenten*, to glide, to glance, cogn. with OHG *glanz*, bright, clear)]

glance[2] (glahns) *n.* any mineral with a metallic lustre, usu. a sulphide, selenide or telluride (*copper glance*, *silver glance*). **glance-coal** *n.* anthracite. [prob. from OF *glacier*, to slip, to glide, from *glace*, ice (influ. by ME *glenten*, to glide, to glance, cogn. with OHG *glanz*, bright, clear)]

gland (gland) *n.* **1** an organ secreting certain constituents of the blood, either for extraction and specific use or for elimination as waste products. **2** a cellular organ in plants, usu. secreting oil or aroma. **3** a sleeve employed to press packing tight on or around a piston-rod etc. **glandless** *a.* **glandular** *a.* **1** characterized by the presence of a gland or glands. **2** consisting or of the nature of a gland or glands; affecting the glands. **glandular fever** *n.* an infectious disease characterized by the swelling of the lymph nodes. **glandularly** *adv.* **glandule** (glan´dūl) *n.* a small gland. †**glandulation** (-lā´shən) *n.* the arrangement and structure of the glandules in plants. **glanduliferous** (-lif´-) *a.* **glandulous** *a.* [F *glande*, OF *glandre*, L *glandula*, dim. of *glans -ndis*, acorn]

glanders (glan´dəz) *n.pl.* a very dangerous and contagious disease in horses, characterized by a running discharge from the nostrils, and enlargement and hardening of the glands of the lower jaw. **glandered** *a.* **glanderous** *a.* [from OF *glandre*, as GLAND]

glandes GLANS.

glandiferous (glandif´ərəs) *a.* bearing acorns or other nutlike fruits. **glandiform** (glan´difawm) *a.* **1** having the form of an acorn. **2** in physiology, resembling a gland. [L *glandifer* (*glans -ndis*, see GLAND)]

glandular, glandule etc. GLAND.

glans (glanz) *n.* (*pl.* **glandes** (glan´dēz)) **1** the nutlike fruit of some forest trees, an acorn, a beech-nut, a chestnut etc. **2** a structure of a similar shape to an acorn, such as the extremity of the penis. **3** a cushion-like swelling. [GLAND]

glare[1] (gleə) *v.i.* **1** to shine with a dazzling or overpowering light. **2** to look with fierce, piercing eyes, to stare. **3** to be obtrusively overdressed or gaudy. **4** to be very conspicuous. ~*v.t.* to send out or express with a glare. ~*n.* **1** an intense, fierce look or stare. **2** a fierce overpowering light, disagreeable brightness. **3** exposure to attention. **4** tawdry splendour. **glaring** *a.* **1** shining with dazzling brightness. **2** staring. **3** too conspicuous or overcoloured. **4** notorious, barefaced, infamous. **glaringly** *adv.* **glaringness** *n.* **glary** *a.* of dazzling brightness. [prob. cogn. with GLASS, cp. OE *gloer*, a transparent substance]

glare[2] (gleə) *a.* (*N Am.*) smooth and glassy (as ice). [etym. uncertain]

glasnost (glaz´nost) *n.* esp. of the USSR government of the later 1980s, a willingness to be more open and accountable. [Rus., frankness]

glass (glahs) *n.* (*pl.* **glasses**) **1** a hard, brittle, transparent substance, formed by fusing together mixtures of the silicates of potash, soda, lime, magnesia, alumina and lead in various proportions, according to the quality or kind required. **2** a substance of vitreous structure or composition. **3** a drinking vessel of glass. **4** the quantity which a drinking glass will hold. **5** an instrument for indicating atmospheric changes, a barometer. **6** a mirror, a looking-glass. **7** a lens. **8** an optical instrument composed partly of glass, an eyeglass, a telescope. **9** a sand-glass, an hourglass. **10** a thermometer. **11** a window pane. **12** (*pl.*) spectacles, also called *pair of glasses.* **13** (*collect.*) ornaments or utensils made of glass; greenhouses; windows. *~v.t.* **1** to fit or cover with or as with glass, to glaze. **2** to case in glass. **3** to mirror, to reflect (oneself or itself) in or as in a glass. **4** to make (the eye) glassy. **people who live in glass houses** critical people susceptible to criticism through their own pursuits or opinions. **glass-blowing** *n.* the art or process of shaping molten or softened glass into vessels. **glass-blower** *n.* **glass case** *n.* a case or shallow box having a glass lid or sides to show the contents. **glass ceiling** *n.* a situation in an organization where promotion appears to be possible but is prevented by discrimination etc. **glass cloth** *n.* **1** a cloth for wiping and cleaning glasses. **2** cloth covered with powdered glass, like sandpaper. **3** a fabric woven of fine-spun glass threads. **glass coach** *n.* a kind of horse-drawn carriage with glass windows instead of curtains. **glass-cutting** *n.* the art or process of cutting, grinding and polishing glassware. **glass-cutter** *n.* a worker or a tool that cuts glass. **glass eye** *n.* **1** an artificial eye of glass. **2** a type of blindness in horses. **glass fibre** *n.* FIBRE-GLASS (under FIBRE). **glassful** *n.* as much as a drinking glass will hold. **glass-gall** *n.* SANDIVER. **glass-grinding** *n.* glass-cutting. **glass harmonica** *n.* a set of musical glasses. **glasshouse** *n.* **1** a greenhouse or conservatory. **2** (*sl.*) a military prison. **3** (*esp. N Am.*) a house or building where glass is made. **glassine** (glas´ēn) *n.* a glossy transparent paper used for covering books. **glass jaw** *n.* esp. in boxing, a jaw that cannot take punches. **glassless** *a.* **glasslike** *a.* **glass-making** *n.* the manufacture of glass. **glass-maker** *n.* **glass-painting** *n.* the art of painting designs on glass with colours which are burnt in. **glasspaper** *n.* paper covered with finely-powdered glass used for rubbing down and smoothing rough surfaces of wood etc. **glass snake** *n.* an American lizard without limbs, *Ophisaurus ventralis.* **glass soap** *n.* oxide of manganese and other substances used in the manufacture of glass to remove colour due to ferrous salts etc. **glass-staining** *n.* the art or process of colouring glass during manufacture. **glass-stainer** *n.* **glassware** *n.* (*collect.*) articles made of glass. **glass wool** *n.* fine fibres of glass used for packing and insulation. **glasswork** *n.* **1** glass manufacture. **2** glassware. **glassworker** *n.* **glassworks** *n.* a place or building where glass is manufactured. **glasswort** *n.* any of various maritime herbs of the genus *Salicornia* or *Salsola*, containing alkali formerly used in glass-making, marsh samphire. **glassy** *a.* (*comp.* **glassier**, *superl.* **glassiest**) **1** hard, dull, lacking fire, fixed (of the eye). **2** like glass, vitreous. **3** lustrous, smooth, mirror-like (of water). *~n.* (*Austral.*) (*also* **glassie**) a glass marble. **(just) the glassy** just the job, the best. **glassily** *adv.* **glassiness** *n.* [OE *glæs* (cp. Dut. *glas*, Icel. *gler*, G *Glas*, perh. from Gmc. root rel. to OE *glōwan*, to GLOW)]

Glaswegian (glāzwē´jən, glas-) *n.* a native or inhabitant of Glasgow in Scotland. *~a.* of or relating to Glasgow. [mod. L *Glaswegiānus*, from *Glasgow*]

Glauber's salt (glow´bəz, glaw´-), **Glauber's salts** *n.* sodium sulphate, a strong laxative. [J. R. *Glauber*, 1604–68, German chemist]

glaucescent (glawses´ənt) *a.* tending to become or becoming glaucous. **glaucescence** *n.* [L *glaucus*]

glaucoma (glawkō´mə) *n.* a disease of the eye in which the pressure within the eyeball causes dimness and ultimately loss of vision. **glaucomatous** *a.* **glaucosis** (-sis) *n.* [Gr., from *glaukos*]

glauconite (glaw´kənīt) *n.* an amorphous green hydrous silicate of iron, potassium etc. [G *Glauconit*, from Gr. *glaukon*, neut. of *glaukos*, as GLAUCOUS]

glaucous (glaw´kəs) *a.* **1** sea-green, pale greyish-blue. **2** (*Bot.*) covered with a bloom or down of this tinge (as with grapes). **glaucous gull** *n.* a large grey and white gull, *Larus hyperboreus*, found in N and Arctic regions. [L *glaucus*, Gr. *glaukos*]

glaze (glāz) *v.t.* **1** to furnish, fit or cover with glass. **2** to fit with a sheet or panes of glass. **3** to furnish with windows. **4** to overlay (pottery) with a vitreous substance. **5** to cover (a surface) with a thin glossy coating. **6** to make smooth and glossy. **7** †to cover (the eyes) with a film. *~v.i.* to become glassy (as the eyes). *~n.* **1** a smooth, lustrous coating. **2** a coating, formed of various substances, used to glaze earthenware, pictures, paper, confectionery etc. **3** a glazed surface. **4** (*US*) a thin sheet of ice. **glazed** *a.* **1** having been glazed. **2** (esp. of a person's expression) vacant, bored. **glazed frost** *n.* a coating of ice caused by the freezing of rain or by refreezing after thawing. **glazer** *n.* **1** a person who glazes earthenware. **2** a wheel for grinding or polishing cutlery. **3** a calico-smoothing wheel. **glazier** (-ziə, -zhə) *n.* a person whose business it is to set glass in windows etc. **glaziery** *n.* **glazing** *n.* **1** the act or process of setting glass in window frames, picture frames etc. **2** covering with a glaze, or giving a glazed or glossy surface to pottery and other articles. **3** the glaze or other material used to give something a glazed finish. **4** glasswork. **5** glazed windows. **6** the process of applying semi-transparent colours thinly over other colours to tone down roughness. **glazy** *a.* [ME *glasen*, from OE *glæs*, GLASS]

GLC *abbr.* **1** gas-liquid chromatography. **2** (*Hist.*) Greater London Council.

Gld *abbr.* guilder(s).

gleam (glēm) *n.* a flash, a beam, a ray, esp. one of a faint or transient kind. *~v.i.* **1** to send out rays of a quick and transient kind. **2** to shine, to glitter. **gleamingly** *adv.* **gleamy** *a.*

glean (glēn) *v.t.* **1** to collect bit by bit, to pick up here and there (*to glean information*). **2** to gather (ears of corn which have been passed over) from a cornfield. **3** to gather ears of corn from. **4** †to strip, so as to leave nothing behind. *~v.i.* to gather the ears of corn left on the ground. **gleaner** *n.* **gleaning** *n.* **gleanings** *n.pl.* **1** snippets of information etc. collected here and there. **2** the useful remnants of a crop gathered up after harvest. [OF *glener* (F *glaner*), etym. uncertain]

glebe (glēb) *n.* **1** the land furnishing part of the revenue of an ecclesiastical benefice. **2** (*Mining*) †land containing ore. **3** †land, soil, ground. **4** †a piece of cultivated ground. **glebe-house** *n.* a vicarage, manse etc. **glebe land** *n.* land attached to a parish church etc. that brings in income. **glebeless** *a.* [OF, from L *glēba*, a clod of earth, the soil]

glede (glēd) *n.* (*Sc., North.*) the kite, *Milvus regalis.* [OE *glida*, cogn. with GLIDE]

glee (glē) *n.* **1** joy, mirth, gladness, delight. **2** a musical composition for several voices in harmony, consisting usu. of two or more contrasted movements and without instrumental accompaniment. **glee club** *n.* a club or society devoted to singing glees and other choral music. **gleeful** *a.* merry, joyous. **gleefully** *adv.* †**gleeman** *n.* (*pl.* **gleemen**) a minstrel or singer. [OE *glēo*, *glīw* (cp. Icel. *glȳ*)]

gleet (glēt) *n.* **1** (*Med.*) a viscous discharge from the urethra in gonorrhoea. **2** a similar discharge from a sore, ulcer etc. **gleety** *a.* [OF *glette*, slime, filth]

Gleichschaltung (glīkh´shaltung) *n.* the enforced standardization of political, cultural, economic institutions etc. in authoritarian states. [G]

glen (glen) *n.* a narrow valley, esp. in Scotland, a dale. [Gael. *gleann* (cp. Welsh *glyn*)]

glene (glē´nē) *n.* (*Anat.*) **1** the ball or pupil of the eye. **2** a socket or cavity. **glenoid, glenoidal** (-noi´-) *a.* socket-shaped, cupped. **glenoid cavity** *n.* a small socket or cavity in a bone receiving a projection from another bone to form a joint. [Gr.]

glengarry (glengar´i), **glengarry bonnet** *n.* (*pl.* **glengarries, glengarry bonnets**) a woollen cap, high in front with ribbons hanging down behind, worn by some Highland regiments. [*Glengarry*, valley in Scotland]

gley (glā) *n.* a sticky, waterlogged clay, bluish-grey in colour. [Rus.]

glia (glī´ə, glē´ə) *n.* NEUROGLIA. **glial** *a.* [Gr., glue]

gliadin (glī´ədin) *n.* gluten. [F *gliadine*, from Gr. *glia*, glue]

glib (glib) *a.* **1** voluble, fluent, not very weighty or sincere. **2** offhand. **3** †smooth, slippery, moving easily. ~†*adv.* glibly. **glibly** *adv.* **glibness** *n.* [prob. imit. (cp. Dut. *glibberig*, slippery)]

glide (glīd) *v.i.* **1** to move smoothly and gently. **2** to slip or slide along, as on a smooth surface. **3** to pass rapidly, smoothly and easily. **4** to pass imperceptibly (away) (*Time glided away*). **5** (*Mus.*) to pass from tone to tone without a perceptible break. **6** to fly an engineless heavier-than-air aeroplane which is catapulted or launched from a height, and makes use of rising air currents. ~*v.t.* to cause something to glide. ~*n.* **1** the act of gliding. **2** (*Mus.*) a passage from one tone to another without a break. **3** in phonetics, a continuous sound produced in passing from one position of the organs of speech to another. **4** in cricket, a hit with the bat turned obliquely to the ball, a glance. **glide path** *n.* the path followed by an aircraft as it descends to a landing. **glider** *n.* **1** a heavier-than-air flying-machine with no motive power. **2** someone or something that glides. **gliding** *n.* the sport of piloting a glider. **glidingly** *adv.* [OE *glīdan* (cp. Dut. *glijden*, G *gleiten*)]

glim (glim) *n.* **1** a faint light. **2** (*sl.*) †a lantern, candle etc. **to douse the glim** DOUSE[1]. [orig. obscure, cogn. with GLEAM and GLIMPSE]

glimmer (glim´ə) *v.i.* **1** to emit a faint or feeble light. **2** to shine faintly. ~*n.* **1** a faint, uncertain or unsteady light. **2** a faint vestige, an uncertain sign (*a glimmer of hope, intelligence, sense*). **3** a glimpse. **4** (*pl.*, *sl.*) the eyes. **glimmering** *n.* a glimmer, a twinkle. **glimmeringly** *adv.* [as GLIM]

glimpse (glimps) *n.* **1** a momentary look, a rapid and imperfect view (of). **2** a passing gleam, a faint and transient appearance. **3** †a faint resemblance, a slight tinge. ~*v.t.* **1** to catch a glimpse of. **2** to see for an instant. ~*v.i.* **1** to appear for an instant. **2** to glance (at). **3** to appear faintly, to glimmer. **glimpsing** *n.* a glimpse. [ME *glimsen*, as GLIM]

glint (glint) *v.i.* **1** to gleam, to flash. **2** to glitter, to sparkle. ~*v.t.* to reflect, to flash back. ~*n.* **1** a gleam, a flash, a sparkle. **2** †a glimpse. [prob. from the earlier *glent*, ME *glenten*, cogn. with G *glänzen*, to make bright, from *Glanz*, brightness]

glissade (glisahd´, -sād´) *n.* **1** a method of sliding down a steep snow slope, usu. with an ice axe or alpenstock held as rudder and support. **2** a gliding step in ballet. ~*v.i.* to slide down a steep snow slope using an ice axe etc. for support. [F from *glisser*, to slip or slide, OF *glier*, from Gmc. (cp. G *gleiten*, to GLIDE)]

glissando (glisan´dō) *a.*, *n.* (*pl.* **glissandos, glissandi** (-dē)) (of) a rapid sliding of the finger(s) up and down the musical scale. [F from *glisser*, slide]

glissé (glē´sā) *n.* (*pl.* **glissés** (glē´sā)) in ballet, a sliding step esp. using the flat of the foot. [F from *glisser*, slide]

glisten (glis´ən) *v.i.* to gleam, to sparkle, usu. by reflection. ~*n.* **1** a glitter or sparkle, esp. by reflection. **2** a gleam. **glistening** *a.* **glisteningly** *adv.* [ME *glistnen*, OE *glisnian*, from *glisian*, to shine]

†**glister** (glis´tə) *v.i.* to glitter, to sparkle. ~*n.* glitter, lustre, brightness. **glisteringly** *adv.* [ME *glisteren*, OE *glisian*, as GLISTEN]

glitch (glich) *n.* (*sl.*) **1** an unexpected problem, malfunction etc., technical hitch, hiccup. **2** an extraneous electric current or false signal, esp. one that disrupts the smooth operation of a system. [prob. from G *glitschen*, to slip]

glitter (glit´ə) *v.i.* **1** to gleam, to sparkle. **2** to shine with a succession of brilliant gleams or flashes. **3** to be brilliant, showy or specious. ~*n.* **1** a bright sparkling light. **2** brilliancy, splendour. **3** speciousness, attractiveness. **4** tiny glittering particles used for decoration. **glitteringly** *adv.* **glittery** *a.* [Icel. *glitra*, freq. of *glita* (cogn. with G *gleissen*, OE *glitenian*), from Gmc. *glis*, to shine]

glitterati (glitərah´ti) *n.pl.* (*sl.*) fashionable people, such as media personalities, artists, jet-setters etc., as a social group.

glitz (glits) *n.* (*coll.*) ostentation, conspicuous showiness. **glitzy** (glit´si) *a.* (*comp.* **glitzier**, *superl.* **glitziest**). **glitzily** *adv.* **glitziness** *n.* [*gl*amour and R*itz*, perh. influ. by G *Glitzern*, glitter]

gloaming (glō´ming) *n.* (*poet.*) evening twilight. [OE *glōmung*, cogn. with GLOW]

gloat (glōt) *v.i.* to look or dwell (on or over) with exultant feelings of malignity, lust, greed etc. ~*n.* **1** the act of gloating. **2** an unpleasant look of triumphant satisfaction. **gloater** *n.* **gloatingly** *adv.* [cp. Icel. *glotta*, to grin; G *glotzen*, to stare]

glob (glob) *n.* a rounded lump of something soft, a dollop. [perh. blend of BLOB and GLOBE]

globe (glōb) *n.* **1** a ball, a sphere, a round or spherical body. **2** the earth. **3** a sphere on which are represented the land and sea, and usu. the political divisions of the world. **4** anything of a globular or nearly globular shape. **5** an orb borne as emblem of sovereignty. **6** an almost spherical vessel, such as an aquarium, lampshade etc. **7** the eyeball. **8** (*Austral.*) **a** an electric light bulb. **b** a body of men etc. drawn up in a circle. ~*v.t.* to form into a globe. ~*v.i.* to become globular. **celestial globe** CELESTIAL. **terrestrial globe** TERRESTRIAL. **global** (glō´bəl) *a.* **1** worldwide. **2** relating to the globe as an entirety. **3** across the board. **4** taking in entire groups or classes (*global search-and-replace*). **globalism** *n.* **globalize, globalise** *v.t.* to make global in scope or application. **globalization** (-zā´shən) *n.* **globally** *adv.* **global positioning system** *n.* a system for locating the exact position of ships, planes etc. anywhere in the world by means of signals sent to and from orbiting satellites. **global village** *n.* the world viewed as an integrated system, esp. as linked by means of instant (mass) communication. **global warming** *n.* the potential increase in the temperature of the earth's atmosphere caused by pollution, the greenhouse effect. **globate** (glō´bāt), **globated** *a.* spherical, spheroidal. **globe artichoke** *n.* a type of artichoke, *Cynara scolymus*, cultivated for food. **globe-fish** *n.* any tropical fish of the family *Tetradontidae*, one having the power of inflating its skin till it becomes nearly globular. **globe flower** *n.* any plant of the ranunculaceous genus *Trollius*, esp. the British *T. europaeus*, with yellow, almost spherical flowers. **globe lightning** *n.* BALL LIGHTNING (under BALL[1]). **globe-like** *a.* globoid. **globe-thistle** *n.* any plant of various species of the genus *Echinops*, a thistle-like genus of composite plants belonging to the aster family. **globe-trotter** *n.* a traveller who hurries from place to place sight-seeing or who visits many foreign countries. **globe-trotting** *a.*, *n.* **globigerina** (glōbijərī´nə) *n.* (*pl.* **globigerinae** (-nē)) a minute marine invertebrate of the genus *Globigerina*, with a many-chambered spiral shell. **globigerinal** *a.* **globigerina mud, globigerina ooze** *n.* a light-coloured calcareous mud or ooze in places in the ocean 3000 fathoms (5500 m) deep, consisting of shells of globigerinae. **globoid** *a.* like a globe in shape. ~*n.* a globular granule or concretion of mineral matter found in aleuron. **globose** *a.* spherical, globular. **globosity** (-bos´-) *n.* [L *globātus*, p.p. of *globāre*, to make into a ball; *globōsus*, spherical (OF *globe*), from *globus*]

globin (glō´bin) *n.* a colourless protein of the blood. [L *globus*, a globe]

globoid, globose GLOBE.

globule (glob´ūl) *n.* **1** a particle of matter in the form of a small globe. **2** a minute drop or pill. **globular** *a.* **1** having the shape of a small globe or sphere. **2** composed of globules. **globular cluster** *n.* (*Astron.*) a spherical cluster of stars usu. in the outer regions of a galaxy. **globularity** (-lar´-) *n.* shaped like a globe or globule. **globularly** *adv.* **globularness** *n.* **globuliferous** (-lif´-) *a.* producing, containing or having globules. **globulin** (-lin) *n.* **1** any of a group of single proteins obtained from animals and plants, esp. forming a large part of blood serum protein, usu. insoluble in water but soluble in salt solution. **2** the starchy granules in the cells of plants. **globulite** (-īt) *n.* a minute globular body representing the most rudimentary stage in the formation of crystals. **globulous** *a.* [F, from L *globulus*, dim. of *globus*, GLOBE]

glochidium (glōkid´iəm) *n.* (*pl.* **glochidia** (-ə)) any of the barbed hairs among the spores of some ferns and on certain plants. **glochidiate** (-iət) *a.* (*Bot.*) barbed (of hairs etc.). [Gr. *glōchidion*, dim. of *glochis*, arrow-point]

glockenspiel (glok´ənshpēl) *n.* a musical instrument consisting of hanging metal bars or tubes, to be struck with a hammer. [G, *Glocken*, bells, *spielen*, to play]

glom (glom) *v.t.* (*pres.p.* **glomming**, *past, p.p.* **glommed**) **1** (*esp. N Am, sl.*) to snatch, seize. **2** to steal. **3** to look at, to eye. **to glom on to 1** to take possession of. **2** to grab hold of. [etym. uncertain; perh. Sc. *glaum*, to snatch]

glome GLOMERULE.

glomerate (glom´ərət) *a.* **1** (*Anat.*) compactly clustered (as glands, vessels etc.). **2** (*Bot.*) congregated into a head. **glomeration** (-ā´shən) *n.* [L *glomerātus*, p.p. of *glomerāre*, as GLOMERULE]

glomerule (glom´ərool) *n.* **1** (*Bot.*) a flower-cluster forming a compact head. **2** (*Anat.*) a convoluted mass of blood vessels, tissues etc. **glome** (glōm) *n.* a glomerule. **glomerulate** (gləmœ´rūlət) *a.* **glomerulus** (glomer´ūləs) *n.* (*pl.* **glomeruli** (-lī)) a cluster of nerve fibres, spores, small blood vessels etc., esp. those projecting into the end of a kidney tubule. [L *glomus*, a ball]

gloom (gloom) *n.* **1** obscurity, partial darkness. **2** depression, dejection, melancholy. **3** circumstances that occasion melancholy or despondency. **4** †a dark or dismal place. ~*v.i.* **1** to appear obscurely or dimly. **2** to look dismal, sullen or frowning. **3** to lour, to be or become cloudy or dark. ~*v.t.* **1** to fill or cover with darkness or obscurity. **2** to render dark, sullen or dismal. **gloomful** *a.* **gloomfully** *adv.* **gloomy** *a.* (*comp.* **gloomier**, *superl.* **gloomiest**) **1** dark, obscure. **2** sad, melancholy, dispiriting, louring. **3** sullen, morose, threatening. **gloomily** *adv.* **gloominess** *n.* [ME *gloumen*, to lour, cogn. with GLUM]

gloop (gloop) *n.* (*coll.*) a thick, sticky liquid. [imit. of GLOP]

glop (glop) *n.* (*N Am., sl.*) a soft, gooey mush, esp. unpalatable food of this consistency. [perh. comb. of GLUE and SLOP[1]]

Gloria (glaw´riə) *n.* (*pl.* **Glorias**) **1** a song or versicle of praise, forming part of the English Church service or the Mass, or the music to this, esp. *Gloria in excelsis Deo*. **2** a doxology. **Gloria in excelsis** (ekschel´sis), **Gloria Patri** (pah´tri), **Gloria Tibi** (tib´i) *int.*, *n.* [L, glory]

gloria (glaw´riə) *n.* (*pl.* **glorias**) **1** a halo. **2** a closely-woven fabric of silk, cotton etc. used for umbrellas. [L]

glorify (glaw´rifī) *v.t.* (*3rd pers. sing. pres.* **glorifies**, *pres.p.* **glorifying**, *past, p.p.* **glorified**) **1** to magnify, to make glorious, to pay honour and glory to in worship, to praise, to extol. **2** to exalt to celestial glory. **3** to make splendid, to beautify. **glorifiable** *a.* **glorification** (-fikā´shən) *n.* **1** the act of glorifying. **2** (*coll.*) an exaggerated or overembellished version of a story, account etc. **3** (*coll.*) a riotous celebration, festivity. **glorified** *a.* (*coll.*) seeming to be more splendid than it really is (*This room is just a glorified cupboard*). **glorifier** *n.* [F *glorifier*, L *glōrificāre* (*gloria*, GLORY, *-ficāre*, to make)]

gloriole (glaw´riōl) *n.* a glory, halo or nimbus. [F, from L *glōriola*, dim. of *glōria*, GLORY]

glory (glaw´ri) *n.* (*pl.* **glories**) **1** high honour, honourable distinction. **2** fame, renown. **3** an occasion of praise, a subject for pride or boasting. **4** illustriousness, splendour of estate, magnificence, grandeur. **5** brilliance, effulgence, splendour. **6** a state of exaltation. **7** adoration or praise ascribed in worship. **8** the divine presence or its manifestations. **9** the felicity of heaven. **10** a combination of the nimbus and aureola. **11** a halo. **12** †arrogance, ambition. ~*v.i.* (*3rd pers. sing. pres.* **glories**, *pres.p.* **glorying**, *past, p.p.* **gloried**) to boast, to feel pride, to exult. ~†*v.t.* to glorify. **in (all) one's glory** (*coll.*) in full enjoyment of one's doings, idiosyncrasies etc. **in glory** enjoying the felicity of heaven. **to glory in** to be proud of. **to go to glory** (*sl.*) to die, disintegrate, go wrong etc. (*That shot has gone to glory!*). **glorious** (glaw´riəs) *a.* **1** full of glory, illustrious. **2** worthy of admiration or praise. **3** entitling one to fame or honour. **4** splendid, magnificent. **5** (*coll.*) hilarious, uproarious (*the glorious expression on his face*). **6** very amusing. **7** completely satisfactory. **gloriously** *adv.* **gloriousness** *n.* **glorious twelfth** *n.* 12 Aug., when grouse-shooting begins. **glory be!** *int.* used to express surprise. **glory box** *n.* (*Austral.*) a box, chest etc. in which a young woman stores her trousseau etc., bottom drawer. **glory flower, glory pea** *n.* any evergreen New Zealand tree of the papilionaceous genus *Clianthus*. **glory hole** *n.* **1** (*coll.*) a room, cupboard etc. where rubbish and odds and ends have been stowed away anyhow. **2** an opening through which one can look into the interior of a furnace. **gloryingly** *adv.* †**gloryless** *a.* **glory-of-the-snow** *n.* the liliaceous plant *Chionodoxa luciliae*, native to W Asia and cultivated for its blue flowers. [OF *glorie* (F *glorie*), L *glōria*]

Glos. *abbr.* Gloucestershire.

gloss[1] (glos) *n.* **1** the brightness or lustre from a polished surface. **2** polish, sheen. **3** a specious or deceptive outward appearance. ~*v.t.* **1** to make glossy or lustrous. **2** to render specious or plausible. **to gloss over** to seek to avoid drawing attention to by mentioning only briefly or misleadingly. **glosser** *n.* **glossing** *n.* the steaming, drying and twisting of silk thread, so as to develop a gloss. **gloss paint** *n.* paint containing a varnish that gives it a shiny finish. **glossy** *a.* (*comp.* **glossier**, *superl.* **glossiest**) having a smooth, lustrous surface. **glossily** *adv.* **glossiness** *n.* **glossy magazine** *n.* a magazine printed on glossy paper with many colour illustrations. [prob. from Scand. (cp. Icel. *glossi*, a blaze, Norw. *glosa*, to glow)]

gloss[2] (glos) *n.* **1** an explanatory word or note in the margin or between the lines of a book, as an explanation of a foreign or strange word. **2** a comment, interpretation or explanation. **3** a superficial or misleading interpretation etc. **4** a glossary, translation, or commentary. ~*v.t.* **1** to explain by note or comment. **2** to annotate. **3** to comment upon, esp. in a censorious way. ~*v.i.* to make comments, to annotate, to write glosses. **glossator** (-sā´-), †**glossatist** *n.* a writer of glosses. [ME and OF *glose*, med. L *glosa*, L and Gr. *glōssa*, the tongue, a word requiring explanation]

glossa (glos´ə) *n.* (*pl.* **glossae** (-ē)) tongue. **glossal** *a.* of or relating to the tongue, lingual. **glossitis** (-sī´tis) *n.* an inflammation of the tongue. [Gr. *glōssa*, tongue]

glossary (glos´əri) *n.* (*pl.* **glossaries**) **1** a list, vocabulary or dictionary of explanations of technical, obsolete, rare or dialectal words or forms. **2** a collection of glosses or notes. **glossarial** (-seə´ri-) *a.* **glossarist** *n.* [L *glōssārium*, from *glōssa*, GLOSS[2]]

glosseme (glos´ēm) *n.* a unit or feature of a language which has a meaning but which cannot be analysed in terms of any smaller unit.

glosso- (glos´ō) *comb. form* **1** of or relating to the tongue. **2** linguistic. [Gr. *glōssa*, the tongue, language]

glossography (glosog´rəfi) *n.* (*pl.* **glossographies**) **1** the writing of glosses or comments. **2** a treatise on the tongue. **glossographer** *n.* **glossographical** (-səgraf´-) *a.*

glossolalia (glosəlā´liə) *n.* speech in an unknown language, occurring in religious ecstasy, trances etc.

glossology (glosol´əji) *n.* **1** the explanation of technical terms, as of a science. **2** †linguistics, the science of language. **glossological** (-səloj´-) *a.* **glossologist** *n.*

glossopharyngeal (glosōfərin´jiəl) *a.* of or relating to the tongue and the pharynx. ~*n.* either of the glossopharyngeal nerves, a pair of cranial nerves supplying the tongue and pharynx.

glottis (glot´is) *n.* (*pl.* **glottises, glottides** (-dēz)) the mouth of the windpipe forming a narrow aperture covered by the epiglottis when one holds the breath or swallows, contributing, by its dilatation and contraction, to the modulation of the voice. **glottal** *a.* **glottal stop** *n.* a speech sound produced by closing and suddenly opening the glottis. **glottic** *a.* [GLOSSO-]

glove (glŭv) *n.* **1** a covering for the hand, usu. with a separate division for each finger. **2** a boxing glove. ~*v.t.* to cover with or as with a glove. **to fight with the gloves off** to fight or contend in earnest, to show no mercy. **to fit like a glove** to fit perfectly in size and shape. **to take up the glove** to accept a challenge. **to throw down the glove** to make a challenge. **glove box** *n.* **1** a glove compartment in a car. **2** a sealed glass box for handling radioactive materials using built-in gloves. **glove compartment** *n.* a small storage compartment in a car, usu. set into the dashboard. **gloved** *a.* **gloveless** *a.* **glove puppet** *n.* a puppet that fits on to the hand. **glover** *n.* a person who makes or sells gloves. **glove-stretcher** *n.* an instrument for stretching the fingers of gloves so that they may be drawn on easily. [OE *glōf*, prob. from Gmc. *lōf-*, cogn. with *loof*, the hand]

glow (glō) *v.i.* **1** to radiate light and heat, esp. without flame. **2** to be incandescent. **3** to be bright or red with heat, to show a warm colour. **4** to feel great bodily heat. **5** to be warm or flushed with passion or fervour. **6** to be ardent. ~*n.* **1** incandescence, red or white heat. **2** brightness, redness, warmth of colour. **3** vehemence, ardour. **4** heat produced by exercise. **glow discharge** *n.* a luminous electrical discharge in gas at low pressure. **glowing** *a.* **1** radiating light, heat etc. **2** enthusiastic, ardent (*a glowing tribute*). **glowingly** *adv.* **glow plug** *n.* a plug fitted to the cylinder block of a diesel engine. **glow-worm** *n.* a beetle, *Lampyris noctiluca* or *L. splendidula*, the female of which is phosphorescent. [OE *glōwan* (cp. Icel. *glōa*, Dut. *gloeijen*, G *glüten*)]

glower (glow´ə) *v.i.* to scowl, to stare fiercely or angrily. ~*n.* a savage stare, a scowl. **gloweringly** *adv.* [etym. uncertain, cp. LG *gluren*]

gloxinia (gloksin´iə) *n.* any tropical plant of the genus *Gloxinia*, with large bell-shaped flowers, from tropical America. [B. P. *Gloxin*, 18th-cent. German botanist]

gloze (glōz) *v.t.* **1** to explain away, to palliate, to extenuate. **2** †to explain by note or comment. **3** †to flatter, to wheedle. ~*v.i.* **1** to comment. **2** †to use flattery. ~*n.* **1** flattery, wheedling. **2** specious show. **3** †a gloss, a comment. **4** (*pl.*) †specious talk. †**to gloze over** to explain away. **glozer** *n.* **1** a glosser. **2** a flatterer. [F *gloser*, from *glose*, GLOSS[2]]

glucagon (gloo´kəgon) *n.* a hormone produced in the pancreas which aids the breakdown in the liver of glycogen to glucose.

glucinum (gloosī´nəm), **glucinium** (gloosin´iəm) *n.* beryllium (from the sweet taste of the salts). †**glucina** (-nə) *n.* oxide of glucinum. [F *glucine*, Gr. *glukus*, sweet]

glucohaemia (glookōhē´miə), (*N Am.*) **glucohemia** *n.* GLUCOSURIA.

glucose (gloo´kōs) *n.* **1** a fermentable sugar, less sweet than cane sugar, obtained from dried grapes and other fruits, dextrin etc. and occurring in the urine of persons suffering from glucosuria. **2** any of the group of sweet compounds including dextrose, laevulose etc. **glucic acid** *n.* a colourless, honey-like compound obtained from glucose or cane sugar by the action of acids or alkalis. **glucosic** (-kos´ik), **glucic** (-sik) *a.* derived from, of or relating to glucose. **glucoside** (-sīd) *n.* a vegetable substance yielding glucose when decomposed. **glucosidic** (-sid´ik) *a.* [Gr. *glukus*, sweet]

glucosuria (glookəsū´riə) *n.* one form of diabetes, the principal characteristic of which is the occurrence of sugar in the urine. **glucosuric** *a.* [Gr. *ouron*, URINE]

glue (gloo) *n.* **1** an adhesive or sticky substance. **2** an impure gelatin made of the chippings of hides, horns and hoofs, boiled to a jelly, cooled in moulds, and used hot as a cement. ~*v.t.* (*3rd pers. sing. pres.* **glues**, *pres.p.* **gluing, glueing**, *past*, *p.p.* **glued**) **1** to join or fasten with glue. **2** to unite, to attach firmly. ~†*v.i.* **1** to stick together. **2** to be firmly attached. **glue ear** *n.* (*Med.*) a blocking of the Eustachian tube by mucus, caused by infection and perh. resulting in deafness. **glue-pot** *n.* a vessel for heating glue, with an outer vessel to hold water and prevent burning. **gluer** *n.* **glue-sniffing** *n.* the inhalation of the fumes of certain glues for their narcotic effects. **glue-sniffer** *n.* **gluey** *a.* (*comp.* **gluier**, *superl.* **gluiest**). **glueyness** *n.* †**gluish** *a.* [OF *glu*, late L *glūtem*, nom. *glūs*, cogn. with GLUTEN]

glug (glŭg) *n.* (*coll.*) the sound of liquid being poured, esp. out of or into a narrow opening. [imit.]

glühwein (gloo´vīn) *n.* hot, spiced sweetened red wine, mulled wine, as prepared in Germany. [G *glühen*, to glow, *Wein*, wine]

glum (glŭm) *a.* sullen, moody, dejected, dissatisfied. ~†*v.i.* (*pres.p.* **glumming**, *past*, *p.p.* **glummed**) to look sullen or gloomy. **glumly** *adv.* **glumness** *n.* [var. of GLOOM]

glume (gloom) *n.* **1** a chafflike scale or bract forming part of the inflorescence in grasses. **2** a husk. **glumaceous** (-mā´-) *a.* **glumiferous** (-mif´-) *a.* **glumose, glumous** *a.* [L *glūma*, from *glūbere*, to peel, cp. Gr. *gluphein*, to hollow out]

gluon (gloo´on) *n.* (*Physics*) a hypothetical subatomic particle, thought of as passing between quarks, binding them together to form particles.

glut (glŭt) *n.* **1** an oversupply of a market. **2** a surfeit. **3** a superabundance. ~*v.t.* (*pres.p.* **glutting**, *past*, *p.p.* **glutted**) **1** to fill to excess, to stuff, to gorge, to sate. **2** to fill with an oversupply (as a market). **3** to swallow, to swallow down. [OF *gloutir*, L *glūtīre*, to swallow, to devour]

glutamate (gloo´təmāt) *n.* a salt or ester of glutamic acid, esp. a sodium salt used as a flavour enhancer in some foods.

glutamic acid (glootam´ik) *n.* an amino acid occurring in proteins which plays an important part in the nitrogen metabolism of plants and animals.

glutamine (gloo´təmēn) *n.* an amino acid present in many proteins.

gluten (gloo´tən) *n.* **1** a yellowish-grey, elastic albuminous substance, left in wheat flour which has been washed in water. 2 a sticky substance, glue. **gluten-bread** *n.* bread containing a large quantity of gluten, largely used in the diet of those suffering from diabetes. **glutin** (-tin) *n.* vegetable gelatin, gliadin. †**glutinate** *v.t.* 1 to cement with glue. 2 to glue. †**glutination** (-ā´shən) *n.* **glutinative** (-nətiv) *a.* [L *glūten -tinis*]

gluteus (gloo´tiəs) *n.* (*pl.* **glutei** (-tiī)) each of the three large muscles forming the buttock. **gluteal** *a.* [L, from Gr. *gloutos*, rump]

glutin GLUTEN.

glutinous (gloo´tinəs) *a.* 1 viscous, gluey, sticky. 2 covered with a sticky exudation. **glutinize, glutinise** *v.t.* to render viscous or gluey. **glutinosity** (-nos´-) *n.* **glutinously** *adv.* [L *glūten -tinis*]

glutton (glŭt´ən) *n.* 1 a person who eats to excess. 2 a gormandizer, a gourmand. 3 a person who indulges in anything to excess, as a voracious reader, worker etc. 4 a carnivorous animal of the weasel tribe, the wolverine, formerly supposed to be a voracious feeder. ~†*v.i.* to gluttonize. **glutton for punishment** *n.* a person eager to take on hard or unpleasant tasks. †**gluttonish** *a.* **gluttonize, gluttonise** *v.i.* to eat to excess, to gorge. **glutton-like** *a.* **gluttonous** *a.* **gluttonously** *adv.* **gluttony** *n.* [OF *glutun, glouton*, L *glūtōnem*, nom. *glūto*, from *glūtīre*, to swallow, see GLUT]

glyc- GLYCO-.

glycerol (glis´ərol) *n.* a sticky, sweet, colourless liquid obtained from animal and vegetable fats and oils, used in the manufacture of soaps, medicines, confectionery, antifreeze etc. **glyceral** *n.* one of a series of compounds obtained by heating glycerol with aldehydes. **glycerate** (-rāt) *n.* 1 a salt of glyceric acid. 2 a solution in glycerol. **glyceric** (-ser´-) *a.* of or relating to glycerol. **glyceride** (-rīd) *n.* any fatty acid ester of glycerol. **glycerine** (-rin, -rēn), **glycerin** (-rin) *n.* glycerol. **glycerinate** *v.t.* to treat (esp. vaccine lymph) with glycerol. **glyceroid** *n.* **glyceryl** (-ril) *n.* the radical of glycerol and the glycerides. [F *glycérine*, Gr. *glukeros, glukus*, sweet]

glycine (glī´sēn), **glycin** (-sin) *n.* a crystalline, sweetish amino acid occurring in proteins, glycocoll.

glyco- (glī´kō), **glyc-** *comb. form* containing glycerol or compounds producing sugars. [Gr. *glukus*, sweet]

glycocoll (glī´kōkol) *n.* GLYCINE.

glycogen (glī´kəjən) *n.* a white insoluble, starchlike compound occurring in animal tissues such as the liver and convertible into dextrose. **glycogenesis** (-jen´-) *n.* the formation of glycogen from sugar. **glycogenic** (-jen´-) *a.*

glycol (glī´kōl) *n.* a diatomic alcohol of the fatty group typified by ethyl glycol, used as an antifreeze in car engines and for de-icing aircraft wings. **glycolic** (-kol´-), **glycollic** *a.* **glycollate** (-āt) *n.* [*glycerine* and *alcohol*]

glycolysis (glīkol´isis) *n.* the breakdown of glucose by enzymes into acids, with the release of energy.

glyconic (glīkon´ik) *a.* applied to varieties of classic verse consisting of three trochees and a dactyl. ~*n.* a glyconic verse. [*Glukōn*, a Gr. poet]

glycoprotein (glīkōprō´tēn) *n.* any of a group of complex proteins containing a carbohydrate mixed with a simple protein.

glycosuria (glīkōsū´riə) *n.* GLUCOSURIA.

glyph (glif) *n.* 1 in a computer or word processor, a character or symbol beyond the normal range of characters. 2 a hieroglyph. 3 (*Archit.*) a fluting or channel, usu. vertical. **glyphic** *a.* carved, sculptured. ~*n.* a hieroglyph. [Gr. *gluphē*, from *gluphein*, to carve]

glyphography (glifog´rəfi) *n.* the process of making engravings for printing in which an electrotype with the design in relief is obtained from an intaglio etching. **glyphograph** (glif´əgraf) *n.* 1 a plate prepared by glyphography. 2 an impression from such a plate. ~*v.t., v.i.* to engrave by glyphography. **glyphographer** *n.* **glyphographic** (-graf´-) *a.*

glyptal (glip´təl) *n.* an alkyd resin used for surface coatings, esp. one formed from glycerol and phthalic acid or anhydride. [perh. from *gly*cerol, *phthal*ic]

glyptic (glip´tik) *a.* relating to carving or engraving, esp. on gems. ~*n.* (*usu. pl.*) the art of engraving, esp. on gems. [Gr. *gluptikos*, from *gluptos*, carved, from *gluphein*, see GLYPH]

glyptodont (glip´tədont) *n.* any extinct edentate mammal of the genus *Glyptodon* from S America, similar to but larger than the armadillo. [Gr. *gluptos*, carved, as GLYPTIC, *odous, odontos*, tooth]

glyptography (gliptog´rəfi) *n.* the art of engraving on gems. **glyptograph** (glip´təgraf) *n.* an engraving on a gem. **glyptographer** *n.* **glyptographic** (-graf´-) *a.* [Gr. *gluptos*, see GLYPTIC, -GRAPHY]

glyptotheca (gliptəthē´kə) *n.* a room or building for the preservation of sculpture. [Gr. *gluptos*, see GLYPTIC, *thēkē*, a repository]

GM *abbr.* 1 George Medal. 2 general manager. 3 grant-maintained. 4 General Motors. 5 Grand Master.

GMB *abbr.* General and Municipal Boilermakers' (Union).

GMC *abbr.* General Medical Council.

Gmc. *abbr.* Germanic.

GMS *abbr.* grant-maintained status.

GMT *abbr.* Greenwich Mean Time.

GMWU *abbr.* General and Municipal Workers' Union.

gnamma (nam´ə), **namma** *n.* a waterhole in a rock. **gnamma hole** *n.* [Austral. Abor.]

gnaphalium (nəfā´liəm) *n.* any woolly plant of the genus *Gnaphalium*, typified by the cudweed, having a small sessile flower-head. [Gr. *gnaphalion*, a downy plant]

gnar KNAR.

gnarled (nahld) *a.* rugged, lined, weather-beaten, twisted. **gnarl** *v.t.* to twist or contort. ~*n.* a protuberance, a twisted growth or contorted knot, in a tree. **gnarly** *a.* 1 full of knots or gnarls. 2 peevish, perverse. [var. of KNURL]

gnash (nash) *v.t.* 1 to strike or grind (the teeth) together. 2 to grind or champ. ~*v.i.* 1 to grind the teeth together, as in rage, despair etc. 2 to rage. **gnashers** *n.pl.* (*sl.*) teeth, esp. false teeth. **gnashingly** *adv.* [ME *gnasten*, onomat. in orig. (cp. Icel. *gnastan*, a gnashing, G *knastern*, to gnash)]

gnat (nat) *n.* any small two-winged fly of the genus *Culex*, the females of which have a blood-sucking proboscis, esp. *C. pipiens*, the common gnat. **to strain at a gnat and swallow a camel** to be scrupulous about trifles and lax in matters of great moment (Matt. xxiii.24). [OE *gnæt*]

gnathic (nath´ik), **gnathal** (nā´thəl) *a.* (*Anat., Zool.*) of or relating to the jaw. **gnathion** (nā´-, nath´-) *n.* (*Anat.*) the lowest point of the midline of the lower jaw, used as a reference point in craniometry. **gnathism** *n.* classification of mankind according to measurements of the jaw. **gnathitis** (-thī´-) *n.* inflammation of the upper jaw or cheek. [Gr. *gnathos*, jaw]

gnatho- (nā´thō) *comb. form* of or relating to the jaw or cheek.

†**gnathonic** (nəthon´ik), **gnathonical** (nəthon´ikəl) *a.* flattering, sycophantic, parasitical. **gnathonism** (nā´-) *n.* [L *Gnathōnicus*, from *Gnatho*, the chief character in Terence's *Gnatho*, from Gr. *gnathos*, jaw]

gnathoplasty (nath´əplasti) *n.* the formation of a cheek by plastic surgery.

gnathopod (nath´əpod) *n.* (*pl.* **gnathopoda** (-thop´ədə)) the foot-jaw of crustaceans.

-gnathous (nəthəs) *comb. form* having a jaw of a certain kind, as in *prognathous*.

gnaw (naw) *v.t.* (*p.p.* **gnawed, gnawn** (nawn)) 1 to bite or eat away by degrees. **2** to bite repeatedly or persistently. **3** to bite in agony, rage or despair. **4** to corrode. **5** to consume or wear away by degrees (*gnawed by indecision*). ~*v.i.* **1** to use the teeth in biting repeatedly or persistently (at or into). **2** to cause corrosion or wearing away. **to gnaw a file** FILE[2]. **gnawer** *n.* **gnawing** *n.* **gnawingly** *adv.* [OE *gnagen*]

GNB *abbr.* Good News Bible.

gneiss (nīs) *n.* a laminated metamorphic rock consisting of feldspar, quartz and mica. **gneissic** *a.* **gneissoid** *a.* **gneissose** *a.* [G, from OHG *gneistan*, to sparkle]

gnocchi (nok´i, nyok´i) *n.* an Italian dish consisting of small potato or semolina dumplings, served with a sauce or used to garnish soup etc. [It., *lumps*]

gnome[1] (nōm) *n.* **1** an imaginary being, a kind of misshapen sprite, dwarf, goblin, supposed to inhabit the interior of the earth, and to be the guardian of mines, quarries etc. **2** an ornamental garden figure in the supposed shape of a gnome. **Gnomes of Zurich** *n.pl.* (*coll.*) international bankers thought to have great power and exercise a sinister and mysterious effect on world economics. **gnomish** *a.* [F, from L *gnomus* (used by Paracelsus), perh. from GNOME[2], or *gēnomos* (Gr. *gē*, earth, *-nomos*, dweller)]

gnome[2] (nōm) *n.* a pithy saying expressing a general truth, a maxim, an aphorism. **gnomic** *a.* dealing in maxims, sententious, didactic. **gnomic aorist** *n.* in Greek grammar, a use of the aorist tense to express, not the past, but a general truth, as in proverbs etc. [Gr. *gnōmē*, from *gignōskein*, to know]

gnomo- (nō´mō) *comb. form* of or relating to a maxim.

gnomology (nōmol´əji) *n.* (*pl.* **gnomologies**) **1** a collection of maxims or sententious reflections or sayings. **2** the sententious element in writing and literature. **gnomologic** (-loj´-), **gnomological** *a.* **gnomologist** (-mol´-) *n.*

gnomon (nō´mon) *n.* **1** a rod, pillar, pin or plate on a sundial, indicating the time of day by its shadow. **2** a vertical pillar used in an analogous way for determining the altitude of the sun. **3** the index of the hour-circle of a globe. **4** (*Geom.*) the figure remaining when a parallelogram has been removed from the corner of a larger one of the same form. **gnomonic** (-mon´-), **gnomonical** *a.* of or relating to the art of making and using dials. **gnomonically** *adv.* **gnomonic projection** *n.* the projection of the lines of a sphere from the centre. **gnomonics** *n.* the art or science of making and using dials. [Gr. *gnōmōn*, an inspector, gnomon of a dial, as GNOME[2]]

gnosiology (nōziol´əji) *n.* the philosophy dealing with cognition, the theory of knowledge, or the operation of the cognitive faculties. [Gr. *gnōsis*, see -GNOSIS]

gnosis (nō´sis) *n.* (*pl.* **gnoses** (-sēz)) **1** knowledge, esp. of mysteries. **2** gnostic philosophy. [Gr., GNOME[2]]

-gnosis (nō´sis) *comb. form* esp. in medicine, recognition, as in *diagnosis.* [mod. L from Gr., knowledge]

gnostic (nos´tik) *a.* **1** relating to knowledge or cognition, intellectual. **2** (*facet.*) knowing, shrewd, worldly-wise. **3** having esoteric knowledge. **4** of or belonging to the Gnostics or Gnosticism. ~*n.* an adherent of Gnosticism. **gnostically** *adv.* **Gnosticism** (-sizm) *n.* a system of religious philosophy flourishing in the first six centuries of the Church, that combined ideas from Greek and Oriental philosophy with Christianity, which it professed to expound as a mystical philosophy or gnosis. **gnosticize** (-sīz), **gnosticise** *v.t.*, *v.i.* **gnosticizer** *n.* [Gr. *gnōstikos*, from *gnōstos*, known, as GNOSIS]

GNP *abbr.* Gross National Product.

Gnr. *abbr.* Gunner.

gns *abbr.* guineas.

gnu (noo) *n.* (*pl.* **gnus, gnu**) any large-horned antelope of the genus *Connochaetes*, native to S Africa, also called *wildebeest.* [Nama]

GNVQ *abbr.* General National Vocational Qualification, a qualification designed to fit students for training or advanced study in a specific field.

go[1] (gō) *v.i.* (*2nd pers. sing. pres.* †**goest** (-ist), *3rd pers. sing. pres.* **goes** (gōz), *pres.p.* **going,** *past* **went** (went), *p.p.* **gone** (gon)) **1** to move, to move from one place, condition, or station to another. **2** to begin to move, to start to move from a place, to depart, to pass away, as opposed to come (*I am going now*). **3** to keep up a movement, to be moving, to be acting, operating, or working (*Is the clock going?*). **4** to travel (*We are going to Australia*). **5** to proceed, to advance (*to go for goal*). **6** to end, to come out, to succeed, to turn out (well or ill) (*How did it go?*). **7** to take a certain course (*The verdict went for him*). **8** to be habitually (*to go hungry*; *to go barefoot*). **9** to be used, said etc., habitually, to pass, to be circulated or current (*the going rate of exchange*). **10** to average. **11** to extend, to reach, to point in a certain direction (*The road goes west from here*). **12** to tend, to conduce (*It all goes to show...*). **13** to run, to have a certain tenor (*The song goes like this*). **14** to be applicable, to fit, to suit (with) (*The bag goes with your hat*). **15** to belong, to be harmonious (with a tune etc.). **16** to be released, to get away (*You may go*). **17** to be given up, to be abandoned, abolished, or lost (*My watch has gone*). **18** to fail, to give way, break down (*That roof is going!*). **19** (*usu. in. p.p.*) to die. **20** to pass into a certain state, to become (*to go wild*; *to go mad*). **21** to be sold (*Going at £30!*). **22** to be spent (*His wages had gone on drink*). **23** (*as aux. verb*) to be about (to do), to intend (*She is going to get up shortly*). **24** to make a certain noise (*go 'bang'*). **go ahead** start, proceed without hesitation. **go on** used to express mild disbelief, come now, come come! **go to hell/ blazes/ Jericho/ Bath/ Putney** be off! **have gone and done it** (*coll.*) have been foolish enough to do it. **to go** (*coll.*) (of food) for taking away from the restaurant. **to go about** **1** to get to work at. **2** to go from place to place. **3** to take a circuitous course. **4** (of a vessel) to tack, to change course. **5** to wear. **to go abroad** **1** to go to a foreign country. **2** to go out of doors. **3** †to be disclosed. **to go against** to be in opposition to. **to go ahead** **1** to proceed in advance. **2** to make rapid progress. **3** to start. **to go a long way (towards)** LONG[1]. **to go aside** **1** to withdraw apart from others. **2** to go wrong. **to go astray** to wander from the right path. **to go at** **1** to attack. **2** to work at vigorously. **to go away** to depart. **to go back on** to fail to keep (one's word). **to go bail** **1** to act as bail for. **2** (*coll.*) to vouch. **to go begging** BEG[1]. **to go behind** **1** to call in question. **2** to look beyond (the apparent facts etc.). **to go between** to mediate between. †**to go beyond** to cheat, to outdo. **to go bush** (*Austral.*) to take to the bush, to go to a place where one cannot be contacted. **to go by** **1** to pass by or near to. **2** to pass by. **3** to pass unnoticed or disregarded. **4** to take as a criterion. **to go by default** DEFAULT. **to go down** **1** to descend. **2** to set. **3** to founder (as a ship). **4** to fall (before a conqueror). **5** to be beaten in a sports match. **6** to be set down in writing. **7** esp. in the UK, to leave university. **8** to be swallowed, to be palatable or acceptable. **to go down (with)** to fall ill (with). **to go dry** (*coll.*) to adopt prohibition; to give up drinking or having alcoholic liquor on the premises. **to go Dutch** DUTCH. **to go far** **1** to be very successful. **2** to attain distinction. **to go for** **1** to go somewhere to obtain something. **2** to attack. **3** to be true for, include (*and that goes for her as well*). **4** to be attracted by. **5** to be sold for. **to go for nothing** to count for nothing. **to go forth** **1** to issue or depart from a place. **2** to be published or spread abroad. **to go forward** to advance. **to go great guns** GUN. **to go halves** HALF. **to go hard with** (*dated, impers.*) to cause great trouble, danger or difficulty to. **to go ill with** (*impers.*) to happen or fare badly or evil with. **to go in** **1** to enter. **2** (of the sun) to go behind clouds. **3** in cricket, to have an innings. †**to go in and out** to be perfectly at liberty. **to go in for 1** to be in favour of. **2** to follow as a pursuit or occupation. **to go into 1** to enter. **2** to frequent. **3** to take part in. **4** to investigate or discuss. **to go it 1** to carry on. **2** to keep a thing up. **3** to conduct oneself recklessly or outrageously. **to go it alone** to carry on single-handedly. **to go native** to adopt the ways and customs of a place. **to go off 1** to depart. **2** to be fired, explode (as a gun, firework etc.). **3** to rot, perish, putrefy. **4** to fall away. **5** to become unconscious. **6** to die. **7** to cease to be perceptible. **8** to fare, to succeed (well or badly). **to go off one's head** (*coll.*) to become insane. **to go on 1** to proceed, to continue, to persevere. **2** to grumble, to complain. **3** to talk at length. **4** (*coll., imper.*) rubbish, nonsense. **5** (*coll.*) to behave (badly etc.). **6** to appear on the stage. **7** at cricket, to begin a spell of bowling. **8** †to become chargeable (to the parish etc.). **to go one better** to excel, to cap. **to go out 1** to depart, to leave (a room etc.). **2** to be extinguished. **3** to vacate office. **4** to leave home and enter employment. **5** to go into society. **6** to go on strike. **7** to lose consciousness. **to go out with** to have a sexual relationship with. **to go over 1** to cross, to pass over. **2** to rat, to change one's party or opinions. **3** to read, to examine. **4** to rehearse. **5** to retouch. **to go phut** PHUT. **to go round 1** to pay a number of visits. **2** to encompass or be enough to encompass, to be enough for (the whole party etc.). **to go shares** SHARE[1]. **to go sour** SOUR. **to go steady** to go about regularly with the same boyfriend or girlfriend. **to go the whole hog** HOG. **to go through 1** to pass through. **2** to undergo. **3** to suffer. **4** to examine. **5** (*coll.*) to overhaul, to ransack, to strip. **6** to discuss thoroughly. **7** to perform (a duty, ceremony etc.). **8** to be completed. **to go through with** to perform thoroughly, perh. despite reluctance, to complete. **to go together** to harmonize, to be suitable to or match each other. **to go to one's head** HEAD[1]. **to go to prove** PROVE. **to go to show** SHOW. **to go to the country** COUNTRY. **to go under 1** to be known as (a title or a name). **2** to sink. **3** to be submerged or ruined. **4** to perish. **to go up 1** to climb, pass upwards. **2** to rise, increase. **3** to be constructed. **4** to be destroyed, as by fire or explosion. **to go upon** to act upon as a principle. **to go well with 1** to be approved (by). **2** to complement, suit, match etc. **3** to happen or fare well with. **to go west 1** (*sl.*) to be destroyed, irretrievably damaged etc. **2** (*sl.*) to die. **to go with 1** to accompany. **2** to follow the meaning of, to understand. **3** to be with (child). **4** to side or agree with. **5** to suit, to match. **to go without** to be or manage without, to put up with the want of. **to go with the flow** FLOW. **go-ahead** *a.* characterized by energy and enterprise. **go-as-you-please** *a.* unceremonious, untroubled by rules etc. **go-between** *n.* a person who acts as an intermediary between two parties. **go-by** *n.* **1** the act of passing without notice. **2** intentional failure to notice. **3** evasion, deception. **to give the go-by to 1** to evade. **2** to cut, to slight. **3** to pass or outstrip. **4** to dismiss as of no moment. **go-cart** *n.* **1** a small handcart. **2** a child's toy wagon. **3** †a small framework without a bottom, running on casters, for teaching infants to walk. **4** GO-KART (under GO[1]). **go-devil** *n.* (*N Am.*) a jointed instrument used to clean the inside of pipes, pipelines etc. **go-getter** *n.* a bustling, pushing person. **go-kart** *n.* a small light racing car with a low-powered engine. **go-off** *n.* (*coll.*) the start. **go-slow** *n.* a deliberate curtailment of the rate of production by organized labour in an industrial dispute. **go-to-meeting** *a.* (of clothes) suitable for church or chapel. [OE *gān* (cp. Dut. *gaan*, G *gehen*)]

go[2] (gō) *n.* (*pl.* **goes**) **1** a turn, a bout (of doing something). **2** one's turn in a game. **3** a try, an attempt. **4** rush, energy, enterprise. **5** spirit, life, animation. **6** the act of going. **7** (*coll.*) a fix, a scrape, an awkward turn of affairs. **8** (*coll.*) fashion, the mode. **9** a spree. **10** in cribbage, a player's turn at which they are unable to play, counting one to their opponent. **11** †a drink of liquor, esp. of gin. **all the go** entirely in the fashion. **from the word go** (*coll.*) from the very beginning. **on the go 1** vigorously in motion. **2** on the move. **quite the go** entirely in the fashion. **to go to glory** GLORY. **to have a go** (*coll.*) to make an attempt. **to have a go at someone** (*coll.*) to attack someone, physically or verbally. [from GO[1]]

go[3] (gō) *n.* a Japanese board game for two people, its aim being to capture one's opponent's counters (or stones) in order to occupy a greater amount of the board. [Jap.]

goa (gō´ə) *n.* a Tibetan gazelle, *Procapra picticaudata*, grey-brown in colour with backward-curving horns. [Tibetan *dgoba*]

goad (gōd) *n.* **1** a pointed instrument to urge oxen to move faster. **2** (*fig.*) anything that stings, spurs or incites. ~*v.t.* **1** to prick, drive or urge on with a goad. **2** to stimulate, to incite. **3** to drive (on, to, into etc.). **goadsman, goadster** (-stə) *n.* a person who drives an animal with a goad. [OE *gād* (cp. Lombardic *gaida*, arrowhead, OIr. *gai*, spear)]

goal (gōl) *n.* **1** in football, hockey etc., the posts connected by a crossbar between which the ball must be driven to win a point. **2** the act of kicking the ball between such posts or over such a bar. **3** destination, purpose, aim. **4** the ultimate aim of a person's ambition. **5** the winning post or mark indicating the end of a race. **goal area** *n.* in football, a defined rectangular area in front of each goal. **goal average** *n.* in sport, the ratio of the number of goals scored for a team to those scored against. **goalball** *n.* a ball game played between teams of visually handicapped people. **goal difference** *n.* in sport, the difference between the number of goals scored for and against a team. **goalie** *n.* (*coll.*) a goalkeeper. **goalkeeper** *n.* in sport, esp. football, a player stationed near to guard the goal. **goal kick** *n.* in football, a free kick from the goal area taken by the defence side after the ball has been put out of play over the goal line by a member of the attacking side. **goal kicker** *n.* in rugby football, a player assigned to kick for goal when penalties or conversions arise. **goal kicking** *n.* **goal line** *n.* a line drawn through the goalposts to form the boundary at each end of the field of play in football. **goalmouth** *n.* in sport, the area immediately in front of a goal. **goalpost** *n.* in football etc., either of the two upright posts marking the goal. **to move the goalposts** (*coll.*) to change the conditions, regulations, limits etc. applying to a particular matter or action. **goalscorer** *n.* in sport, a player who scores a goal. **goaltender, goalminder** *n.* (*N Am.*) in sport, esp. ice hockey, a player stationed near to guard the goal. [etym. uncertain, perh. from an OE *gāl*, conn. with *gœlan*, to impede]

goanna (gōan´ə) *n.* **1** (*Austral.*) a large monitor lizard. **2** (*New Zeal.*) the tuatara. [corr. *iguana*]

goat (gōt) *n.* **1** a hairy, horned and bearded domesticated ruminant belonging to the genus *Capra*, esp. *C. hircus*, of which there are many varieties. **2** (*pl.*) the genus *Capra*. **3** a bad or inferior person or thing. **4** a fool. **5** a lascivious person, a lecher. **the Goat** the sign of the zodiac Capricorn. **to get one's goat** to make one angry. **to play the giddy goat** GIDDY. **goat antelope** *n.* a ruminant mammal of the subfamily *Rupicaprini*, including the chamois, goral and Rocky Mountain goat. **goat-god** *n.* Pan. **goatherd** *n.* a person who tends goats. **goatish** *a.* **1** resembling a goat. **2** of a rank smell. **3** lecherous. **goatishly** *adv.* **goatishness** *n.* **goatling** (-ling) *n.* **goat moth** *n.* any large moth of the family *Cossidae*, esp. *Cossus cossus* and *C. ligniperda*. **goat's-beard** *n.* **1** a meadow plant with large yellow flowers, *Tragopogou pratensis*. **2** a white-flowered herbaceous plant of the rose family, *Aruncus dioicus*. **goatskin** *n.*

the skin of a goat. ~*a.* made of goatskin. **goat's-rue** *n.* a leguminous plant, *Galega officinalis.* **goat's-thorn** *n.* the plants *Astragalus tragacantha,* the great, and *A. poterium,* the small goat's-thorn. **goatsucker** *n.* the nightjar, any bird of the genus *Caprimulgus,* chiefly nocturnal and insectivorous, once falsely thought to milk goats, esp. *C. europaeus,* a British summer visitant. **goaty** *a.* [OE *gāt* (cp. Dut. *geit,* G *Geiss,* also L *hœdus*)]

goatee (gōtē′), **goatee beard** *n.* a small beard like a goat's on the point of the chin.

gob[1] (gob) *n.* **1** the mouth. **2** a mouthful. **3** a clot of something slimy, such as saliva. ~*v.i.* (*pres.p.* **gobbing,** *past, p.p.* **gobbed**) to spit. **gobbin** (-in), **gobbins** *n.* in coal-mining, waste material used to pack into spaces from which the coal has been removed. **gobsmacked, gobstruck** *a.* (*sl.*) amazed, dumbfounded. **gobstopper** *n.* a large boiled sweet. [from OF *gobe,* mouthful (*gober,* to swallow), or perh. directly from Celt. (cp. Gael. and Ir. *gob,* beak, mouth)]

gob[2] (gob) *n.* (*sl.*) a US sailor. [etym. uncertain]

gobang (gōbang′) *n.* a game played on a chequer-board, with 50 coloured counters, the object being to get five into a row. [Jap. *goban,* chess-board]

gobbet (gob′it) *n.* **1** a mouthful, a lump, a piece, esp. of meat. **2** an extract from a text, esp. one used for educational purposes. [OF *gobet,* dim. of *gobe,* GOB[1]]

gobbin, gobbins GOB[1].

gobble (gob′əl) *v.t.* to swallow down hastily and greedily or noisily. ~*v.i.* **1** to swallow food in this manner. **2** to make a noise in the throat as a turkeycock. ~*n.* **1** a noise made in the throat like that of a turkeycock. **2** in golf, a rapid stroke in putting which sends the ball straight into the hole. **gobbler** *n.* **1** a person who gobbles food. **2** a gormandizer. **3** a turkeycock. [perh. from GOB[1], later adapt. as imit. of turkey]

gobbledegook (gob′əldigook), **gobbledygook** *n.* (*coll.*) pretentious, esp. unintelligible, language characterized by jargon and circumlocution. [perh. from GOBBLE]

Gobelin (gō′bəlin, gob′lī) *a.* applied to a superior kind of French tapestry made at the Gobelins or imitated from this. **Gobelin blue** *n.* the shade of blue that appears a good deal in Gobelin tapestry. **Gobelin tapestry** *n.* [*Gobelins,* factory in Paris founded by the *Gobelin* family]

gobemouche (gōb′moosh) *n.* (*pl.* **gobemouches** (gōb′moosh)) a gullible, credulous person, someone who will believe anything. [F, lit. fly-catcher (*gober,* to swallow, *mouche,* fly, L *musca*)]

gobioid (gō′bioid) *a.* of or relating to the Gobiidae family of fishes that includes the goby.

goblet (gob′lit) *n.* **1** a drinking vessel, usu. of glass, with a stem, a foot and without a handle. **2** a drinking cup, usu. bowl-shaped and of glass or metal. [OF *gobelet,* dim. of *gobel,* cup, etym. uncertain, but perh. from L *cūpellum,* nom. *-us,* dim. of *cūpa,* cask]

goblin (gob′lin) *n.* a mischievous spirit of ugly or grotesque shape; an elf, a gnome. **goblinism** *n.* [F *gobeline,* low L *gobelīnus,* perh. from Gr. *kobālos,* a rogue, a goblin (but cp. KOBOLD)]

gobo (gō′bō) *n.* (*pl.* **gobos, goboes**) **1** in television, film etc., a shield placed around a camera to exclude unwanted light. **2** a device on a microphone to exclude unwanted sound. [etym. unknown]

goby (gō′bi) *n.* (*pl.* **gobies**) a small fish belonging to the genus *Gobius,* characterized by the union of the ventral fins into a disc or sucker. [L *gōbius, cōbius,* Gr. *kōbios*]

GOC *abbr.* General Officer Commanding.

god (god) *n.* **1** a superhuman or supernatural being regarded as controlling natural forces and human destinies and worshipped or propitiated by humans. **2** a deity, a divinity. **3** (**God**) in monotheistic religions, the Supreme Being, the self-existent and eternal creator and ruler of the universe. **4** a personification of any of the forces of nature. **5** a person formally recognized as divine and entitled to worship. **6** an image, animal etc., worshipped as an embodiment or symbol of supernatural power, an idol. **7** (*fig.*) a person or thing greatly idolized. **8** (*pl.*) the upper gallery in a theatre. ~*v.t.* (*pres.p.* **godding,** *past, p.p.* **godded**) to deify. **for God's sake** SAKE[1]. **God almighty!** used to express surprise or anger. **God bless me!** BLESS. **God bless you!** BLESS. **God forbid** used to express the hope that a certain event etc. will not happen. **God help you/ her/ etc. 1** used to express sympathy, concern etc. **2** (*iron.*) used to imply that a person's situation is not to be envied. **God knows 1** a mild oath expressing apathy or annoyance. **2** God is my (etc.) witness that. **God's truth** STREWTH. **God willing** if circumstances permit. **to god it** to behave as if one were godlike. **to play God** PLAY. **ye gods!** used to express frustration, annoyance etc. **ye gods and little fishes!** used to express surprise, protest etc. **god-awful** *a.* (*coll.*) terrible, dreadful. **godchild** *n.* (*pl.* **godchildren**) someone for whom a person stands sponsor at baptism. **goddam, goddamn, goddamned** *a.* **1** damned. **2** hateful. ~*int.* (*esp. N Am., coll.*) used to express annoyance. **goddaughter** *n.* a female godchild. **goddess** (-is) *n.* **1** a female deity. **2** (*fig.*) a woman of pre-eminent beauty, goodness or charm. **goddess-like** *a., adv.* **goddess-ship** *n.* **godfather** *n.* **1** a male godparent. **2** a man who gives a name to any person or thing. **3** the head of a Mafia family or other criminal organization. **God-fearing** *a.* worshipping or reverencing God, moral, upright. **God-forsaken** *a.* **1** (of a place) forlorn, deserted, unwelcoming. **2** (of a person) wretched, miserable, depraved. **3** abandoned by God. **God-given** *a.* **1** received from God. **2** possessed from birth or by divine authority. **Godhead** *n.* **1** a deity. **2** divine nature or essence. **the Godhead** God. **Godhood** *n.* **godkin** (-kin), **godlet** (-lit) *n.* a petty god. **godless** *a.* **1** acknowledging no god. **2** without God. **3** impious, irreligious. **4** wicked. **godlessly** *adv.* **godlessness** *n.* **godlike** *a.* **godly** *a.* (*comp.* **godlier,** *superl.* **godliest**) God-fearing, pious, devout. ~†*adv.* piously, religiously. **godliness** *n.* **godmother** *n.* a female godparent. **godparent** *n.* a person who is a sponsor for a child at a baptism. **God's acre** *n.* a burial ground. **godsend** *n.* an unlooked-for acquisition or gain, a piece of good fortune. **God's gift** *n.* (*iron.*) a person of utmost importance (to). **godship** *n.* **godson** *n.* a male godchild. **God's (own) country, Godzone country** *n.* (*Austral., New Zeal., coll.*) any country seen as being ideal, usu. that of the speaker. **God speed** *n.* the wish 'God speed you' to a person starting on a journey, undertaking etc. **God squad** *n.* (*sl.*) a religious group or organization, usu. evangelical in its outlook and behaviour. **godward** *adv., a.* **godwards** *adv.* [OE (cp. Dut. *god,* G *Gott*), prob. from root *ghu-,* to worship (not conn. with GOOD)]

godet (gō′dā, -det′) *n.* in dressmaking, a piece of cloth inserted in a skirt, so that it hangs in folds suggestive of a flare. [F]

godetia (gədē′shə) *n.* any plant of the genus *Godetia,* a flowering herb allied to the evening primroses. [M. *Godet,* d. 1879, Swiss botanist]

godown (gōdown′, gō′-) *n.* an E Asian or Indian warehouse. [Malay *godong*]

godroon GADROON.

godwit (god′wit) *n.* a marsh or shore bird of the genus *Limosa,* resembling the curlew but having a slightly upturned bill. [etym. unknown]

Godwottery (godwot′əri) *n.* affected, over-elaborate, archaic speech or writing. [*God wot,* in poem on gardens by T. E. Brown, 1876]

goer (gō′ə) *n.* **1** a person who attends regularly (*usu. in comb.* as in *churchgoer*). **2** (*Austral., coll.*) a person or thing that is likely to succeed, a proposal etc. that is acceptable. **3** (*coll.*) a lively dynamic person. **4** (*coll.*) a sexually promiscuous person, usu. female. **5** someone who or something which goes (*usu. in comb.* as in *fast-goer*). [GO[1], -ER[1]]

Goethian (gœ´tiən), **Goethean** *a.* of, relating to or characteristic of Goethe. ~*n.* a follower or admirer of Goethe. [J. W. von *Goethe*, 1749–1832, German poet]

gofer[1] (gō´fə), **gopher** *n.* (*coll.*) a person employed to run errands, give general assistance etc. [*go for*, influ. by GOPHER[1]]

gofer[2] (gō´fə) *n.* a waffle, a thin batter cake baked between two hinged plates that imprint a honeycomb pattern on both sides. [F *gaufre*, honeycomb, wafer, from Gmc. (cp. WAFER)]

goffer (gō´fə, gof´ə), **gauffer** (gof´ə) *v.t.* **1** to plait, to crimp (edges of lace etc.) with a heated iron. **2** to raise in relief, to emboss (edges of books). ~*n.* **1** a plaiting, fluting, or ruffle. **2** a tool for goffering. **goffering** *n.* **1** this process of plaiting, crimping etc. **2** a plait or ruffle produced by goffering. **3** an embossed design on the edge of a book. [F *gauffrer* (now *gaufrer*), to print with a pattern, as GOFER[2]]

goggle (gog´əl) *v.i.* **1** to strain or roll the eyes. **2** to stare. **3** (of the eyes) to protrude, to bulge. ~*v.t.* to roll (the eyes) about, to turn (the eyes) sideways. ~*a.* **1** prominent, staring, full (*goggle eyes*). **2** rolling from side to side. ~*n.* a strained or staring rolling of the eyes. **goggle-box** *n.* (*coll.*) a television set. **goggled** *a.* (of the eyes) staring, prominent. **goggle-dive** *n.* an underwater dive, using goggles. **goggle-eyed** *a.* **goggles** *n.pl.* **1** protective spectacles, as those worn in swimming, welding etc. **2** (*sl.*) spectacles worn to correct defective eyesight. **3** (*sl.*) the eyes. **4** blinkers for horses that are apt to take fright. **5** a disease of sheep, staggers. **goggly** *a.* [etym. uncertain, perh. imit. (cp. Gael, *gog*, a nodding of the head)]

goglet (gog´lit) *n.* an earthenware vessel, a water-cooler used esp. in the Indian subcontinent. [Port. *gorgoleta* (cp. F *gargoulette*)]

go-go (gō´gō), **gogo** *a.* (*coll.*) **1** active, lively. **2** alert to opportunities. **go-go dancer** *n.* (*dated*) a (scantily clad) dancer who performs gyrating, usu. erotic routines in nightclubs etc.

Goidel (goi´dəl) *n.* a member of the Celtic people of Ireland, Scotland and the Isle of Man. **Goidelic** (-del´-) *n.* the group of Celtic languages comprising Scottish and Irish Gaelic and Manx. ~*a.* of or relating to Goidelic or the Goidels. [OIr., a Gael]

going (gō´ing) *n.* **1** the act of moving or walking. **2** departure. **3** the condition of ground, roads, racecourse, track etc., as regards walking, riding, etc. (*also in comb.* as in *slow-going*, *rough-going*). **4** (*Bible*) †course of life. **5** †pregnancy, gestation. ~*a.* **1** working, in actual operation. **2** existing, to be had (*the best that are going*). **going on** (esp. of the time, one's age etc.) almost, nearly (*I am 16, going on 17*). **to go while the going's good** to seize the chance of getting away, to put into action. **going away** *n., a.* (for) leaving, departure, esp. on honeymoon (*going-away outfit*). **going concern** *n.* a business etc., in actual operation. **going down** *n.* setting, sunset. **going order** *n.* order or condition suitable for working. **going-over** *n.* (*pl.* **goings-over**) (*coll.*) **1** a thorough inspection, overhaul etc. **2** a beating, mugging, thrashing. **3** (*N Am.*) a scolding, telling-off. **goings-on** *n.pl.* behaviour, conduct (usu. in a bad sense). **going-train** *n.* the train of wheels turning the hands in a clock. **going-wheel** *n.* a ratchet arrangement for keeping a clock going while it is being wound up.

goitre (goi´tə), (*N Am.*) **goiter** *n.* a morbid enlargement of the thyroid gland, causing an unsightly deformity of the neck. **goitred** *a.* affected with goitre. **goitrous** *a.* **1** of or relating to, affected with, or resembling a goitre. **2** (of places) characterized by cases of goitre. [F *goître*, from *goitreux*, affected with goitre, ult. from L *guttur*, the throat]

Golconda (golkon´də) *n.* an inexhaustible mine of wealth. [a ruined city lying NW of Hyderabad, India]

gold (gōld) *n.* **1** a precious metallic element, at. no. 79, chem. symbol Au, of a bright yellow colour, the most ductile, malleable, and one of the heaviest of metals, much used for coins, jewellery etc. **2** the metal gold in the form of coin, money. **3** wealth, riches. **4** anything very precious or valuable and genuine or pure. **5** the metal gold used as a coating or wash, gilding. **6** the colour of gold. **7** a gold medal. **8** the centre of an archery target. ~*a.* **1** made of gold, consisting of gold. **2** coloured like gold. **good as gold** GOOD. **gold amalgam** *n.* gold combined with mercury in a soft plastic state. **gold-beater** *n.* a person who beats out gold for gilding. **gold-beater's skin** *n.* a prepared membrane of the caecum of the ox, used for separating the leaves of gold under the hammer, and also as an application to cuts. **gold-beating** *n.* the act or trade of beating out gold for gilding. **gold bloc** *n.* in economics, a group of countries having a gold standard. **gold brick** *n.* **1** something with a bogus display of value, a fraud. **2** a lazy person. **gold-bug** *n.* (*coll.*) a millionaire, wealthy person, plutocrat. **gold card** *n.* a credit card issued only to people with a high credit rating, offering superior benefits. **gold-cloth** *n.* cloth interwoven with gold thread, cloth of gold. **gold-digger** *n.* **1** (*sl.*) a person who forms an intimate relationship only for material gain. **2** a person who mines for gold. **gold-digging** *n.* **gold disc** *n.* an award given to a recording artist, group etc. for the high sales of a particular record, CD etc., often presented in the form of a golden replica disc. **gold dust** *n.* gold in very fine particles. **gold-fever** *n.* a mania for gold-seeking, esp. the gold rush to California in 1848–9. **goldfield** *n.* a district where gold is found. **goldfinch** *n.* any songbird of the genus *Carduelis*, esp. the European *C. carduelis* which has a yellow band across the wings. **goldfish** *n.* (*pl. in general* **goldfish,** *in particular* **goldfishes**) a golden-red carp, *Carassius auratus*, kept in ponds, aquariums etc. **goldfish-bowl** *n.* **1** a fish-bowl. **2** (*coll.*) a state or situation of exposure to public curiosity, a place lacking in privacy. **gold foil** *n.* a thicker kind of gold leaf. **gold lace** *n.* lace made of gold wire. **gold leaf** *n.* gold beaten into a very thin sheet. **gold medal** *n.* an award for first place in a race or competition, esp. in the Olympic Games (as distinct from *silver medal* or *bronze medal*). **gold mine** *n.* **1** a place where gold is mined. **2** (*coll.*) a source of wealth or profit. **gold of pleasure** *n.* a yellow-flowered plant, *Camelina sativa*. **gold plate** *n.* vessels, dishes etc. of gold. **gold record** *n.* GOLD DISC (under GOLD). **gold reserve** *n.* the total amount of gold held by a central bank to make national and international payments and to protect the value of currency. **gold rush** *n.* a rush to a place where gold has been discovered. **goldsize** *n.* an adhesive used in gilding. **goldsmith** *n.* **1** a worker in gold. **2** a dealer in gold plate. **3** †a banker. **goldsmithy, goldsmithery, goldsmithry** *n.* goldsmith's work. **gold standard** *n.* a system which defines the currency of a nation in terms of its value in gold. **Gold Stick** *n.* **1** a gilt rod carried by a court official (colonel of the Life Guards or captain of the gentlemen-at-arms) attending the sovereign on state occasions. **2** the official carrying this rod. **gold thread** *n.* **1** a flattened silver-gilt wire, laid over a thread of silk. **2** a bitter plant, *Coptis trifolia*. **gold-washer** *n.* **1** a person who washes the refuse dirt from gold ore. **2** the implement used for separating gold from dirt. **gold wire** *n.* gold drawn to the form of wire. [OE (cp. Dut. *goud*, Icel. *gull*, G *Gold*), cogn. with YELLOW]

golden (gōl´dən) *a.* **1** of the colour or lustre of gold. **2**

made or consisting of gold. **3** bright, shining, resplendent. **4** excellent, precious, most valuable (*a golden moment*). **5** most favourable (*a golden opportunity*). **6** rich in or yielding gold. **golden age** *n.* **1** a fabled primeval period of perfect human happiness and innocence, in which the earth yielded her fruits without toil, and all creatures lived in peace. **2** the most illustrious period of a nation's literature or prosperity, esp. the first part of the Classical age of Latin literature. **golden ager** *n.* (*N Am.*) an old person. **golden balls** *n.pl.* the three balls displayed as the emblem of a pawnbroker. **golden boy, golden girl** *n.* a popular or successful person in a particular field. **golden calf** *n.* (*fig.*) money as an aim in itself (Ex. xxxii.4). **golden chain** *n.* another name for the laburnum. **golden delicious** *n.* a variety of sweet, green-skinned apple. **golden eagle** *n.* a large eagle, *Aquila chrysaetos*, found in the mountainous parts of Britain, esp. Scotland. **golden-eye** *n.* any marine duck of the genus *Bucephala.* **Golden Fleece** *n.* **1** in Greek mythology, the fleece of gold taken from the ram on which Phryxus was carried through the air to Colchis, and in quest of which the Argonauts sailed under Jason. **2** an order of knighthood instituted in 1429 in Spain and Austria. **golden girl** GOLDEN BOY (under GOLDEN). **golden goal** *n.* in soccer, a goal scored in extra time which brings the match to an immediate end, giving victory to the scoring team (under the arrangements in some tournaments etc.). **golden goose** *n.* a reliable and continuing source of wealth and profit. **golden hamster** *n.* the hamster *Mesocricetus auratus*, kept as a pet. **golden handcuff** *n.* (*coll.*) a payment or benefit given to an employee as an inducement to continue working for the same company. **golden handshake** *n.* (*coll.*) a payment or benefit given to an employee when leaving a job, esp. on retirement. **golden hello** *n.* (*coll.*) a payment or benefit given to an employee on joining a company. **Golden Horde** *n.* the Tartar horde that devastated E Europe in the 13th cent. **Golden Horn** *n.* an inlet of the Bosporus forming the harbour at Istanbul. **golden jubilee** *n.* the 50th anniversary of an event of public importance. **golden mean** *n.* **1** the principle of neither too much nor too little, moderation. **2** GOLDEN SECTION (under GOLDEN). **golden number** *n.* the number denoting the year's place in a Metonic lunar cycle of 19 years, used in calculating the movable feasts, such as Easter. **golden oldie** *n.* (*coll.*) **1** an old recording or film that is still popular. **2** an old person who is still popular, successful, sprightly etc. **golden opinions** *n.pl.* high regard. **golden orfe** *n.* a yellow aquarium variety of the orfe fish. **golden oriole** *n.* a European bird, *Oriolus oriolus*, the male of which has yellow and black, the female green plumage. **golden parachute** *n.* (*coll.*) a clause in the contract of a company executive guaranteeing financial recompense in the event of redundancy following a merger, takeover etc. **golden perch** *n.* CALLOP. **golden rain** *n.* a kind of firework. **golden retriever** *n.* a retriever with a golden-coloured or dark cream coat. **golden rod** *n.* a tall yellow-flowered plant of the genus *Solidago*, esp. *S. virgaurea.* **golden rule** *n.* **1** any important rule or principle. **2** the rule that we should do as we would be done by (Matt. vii.12). **golden section** *n.* in fine arts, the division of a line, plane figure etc. into two sections where the proportion of the smaller to the larger section is the same as that of the larger section to the whole. **golden share** *n.* a controlling share (block), esp. as held by the government in a privatized company, that can be used to prevent a takeover by an unacceptable party. **Golden State** *n.* (*N Am.*) California. **golden syrup** *n.* a pale-coloured treacle. **golden wedding** *n.* the 50th anniversary of a marriage.

goldilocks (gōl´diloks) *n.* **1** a person with golden hair. **2** a buttercup, *Ranunculus auricomus.* **3** any of various other plants with bright yellow flowers, esp. *Aster linosyris*, a plant of the daisy family.

golem (gō´ləm) *n.* in Jewish legend, a figure constructed in the form of a human being and brought to life by supernatural means.

golf (golf) *n.* a game played by two persons or couples with clubs and small hard balls on commons, moorlands, fields or links with short grass, consisting of hitting the balls into a series of small holes in the ground in as few strokes as possible. ~*v.i.* to play golf. **golf bag** *n.* a tall, cylindrical bag used for carrying clubs, balls etc. **golf ball** *n.* **1** a small, hard, white ball used in playing golf. **2** (an electric typewriter that has) a small metal ball bearing the type that moves to press them on to the paper (as distinct from *daisy-wheel*). **golf cart** *n.* **1** a motorized cart for carrying golfers and equipment. **2** a hand-pulled trolley used for carrying golf equipment. **golf club** *n.* **1** any of the clubs used in playing golf. **2** a golfing establishment usu. with a golf course and a clubhouse, which golfers join as members. **golf course** *n.* the course of 9 or 18 holes on which golf is played. **golfer** *n.* a person who plays golf. **golf links** *n.pl.* **1** a golf course set in undulating rough country by the sea. **2** (*dated*) any golf course. [perh. from Dut. *kolf* (cp. LG *kulf*, G *Kulbe*, club)]

Golgi body (gol´ji, -gi), **Golgi apparatus** *n.* (*Biol.*) a structure of vesicles, vacuoles and folded membranes within the cytoplasm of most cells, involved esp. in the secretion and transport of substances.

†**Golgotha** (gol´gəthə) *n.* a burial place, a charnel house. [Gr., a place near Jerusalem, where Christ was crucified, from Aram. *gulgalta*, Heb. *gulgōleth*, skull]

†**goliard** (gō´liəd) *n.* **1** any of various authors of satirical and ribald Latin verses (12th–13th cents.), some of which were signed by a mythical *Golias.* **2** a buffoon, a jester. **goliardic** (-ah´-) *a.* **goliardy, goliardery** *n.* [OF, a glutton, from *gole* (F *gueule*), L *gula*, gluttony]

Goliath (gəlī´əth) *n.* **1** a giant. **2** a gigantic person or thing. **Goliath beetle** *n.* any large beetle of the genus *Goliathus*, esp. the huge tropical beetle, *G. giganteus.* **Goliath frog** *n.* the largest living frog, *Rana goliath*, of Africa. [the Philistine giant of Gath (I Sam.xvii)]

golliwog (gol´iwog) *n.* a black-faced doll with fuzzy hair and bright clothes. [*Golliwogg*, character in children's books first published by US writers Florence and Bertha Upton]

gollop (gol´əp) *v.t.* (*pres.p.* **golloping**, *past, p.p.* **golloped**) to swallow greedily and hurriedly. ~*n.* a hasty gulp. [perh. from GULP]

golly[1] (gol´i) *int.* used to express surprise. [euphem. for GOD]

golly[2] (gol´i) *n.* (*pl.* **gollies**) (*coll.*) a gollywog.

GOM *abbr.* Grand Old Man, orig. applied to W. E. Gladstone, 1809–98, British statesman.

gombeen (gombēn´) *n.* (*Ir.*) usury. **gombeenism** *n.* **gombeen man, gombeen woman** (*pl.* **gombeen men, gombeen women**) *n.* a moneylender. [Ir. *gaimbin*, said to be from same OCelt. root as L *cambium*, CHANGE]

gombroon (gombroon´) *n.* Persian semi-transparent white pottery imitated in Chelsea ware. [town on Persian Gulf]

gomeril (gom´əril) *n.* (*Sc., North.*) a simpleton. [etym. obscure]

Gomorrah (gəmor´ə) *n.* a dissolute town. [Gr., from Heb. *'Amōrā*, one of the cities of the plain (Gen. xvii–xix)]

gomphosis (gomfō´sis) *n.* (*Anat.*) a kind of articulation by which the teeth are firmly implanted in their sockets. [Gr., from *gomphoein*, to bolt together, from *gomphos*, bolt]

gomuti (gəmoo´ti) *n.* a black hairlike fibre, not decaying in water, obtained from the sago palm, and used for cordage, thatching etc. [Malay]

gon- GONO-.

-gon (gən) *comb. form* used to form nouns denoting a figure with a number of angles, as in *hexagon, octagon, pentagon*. [Gr. *-gōnos*, angled]

gonads (gō´nadz, gon´-) *n.pl.* undifferentiated sex glands, the embryonic sexual apparatus, with rudiments of both sexes which later develop into either ovaries or testes. **gonadal** (-nad´-), **gonadic** *a.* **gonadotrophic** (-dətrō´fik), **gonadotropic** (-pik) *a.* stimulating the gonads. **gonadotrophin, gonadotrophic hormone** *n.* the hormone that stimulates the gonads. [Gr. *gonē*, cogn. with *gignesthai*, to become, to be born, -AD[1]]

gondola (gon´dələ) *n.* **1** a long, narrow Venetian boat with peaked ends, propelled by one oar. **2** the car of an airship, balloon, ski lift etc. **3** a free-standing block of shelves used to display goods in a supermarket etc. **4** (*N Am.*) **a** a large, light, flat-bottomed freight-boat. **b** (*also* **gondola car**) a flat railway wagon. **gondolier** (-liə´) *n.* a person who rows a gondola. [It.]

gone (gon) *a.* **1** past (*It is gone eight*). **2** dead. **3** (*sl.*) enthralled, entranced, usu. on music, drugs etc. **4** (*coll.*) pregnant (*six months gone*). **5** lost, beyond hope. **6** ruined, undone. **gone on** (*sl.*) infatuated with. **gone coon** *n.* (*N Am., sl.*) a person who is hopelessly ruined. **gone goose, gone gosling** *n.* (*coll.*) someone who or something that is doomed, beyond hope etc. **goner** *n.* (*coll.*) a person who or something that is ruined or ill beyond recovery. [p.p. of GO[1]]

gonfalon (gon´fələn) *n.* an ensign or banner, usu. displayed from a crossyard on a pole, with streamers, such as the standard of certain Italian republics. **gonfalonier** (-niə´) *n.* **1** a gonfalon or standard bearer. **2** (*Hist.*) the title of the chief magistrate in certain medieval Italian republics. **gonfanon** (-nən) *n.* (*Hist.*) a gonfalon. [It. *gonfalone*, OHG *gundfano* (*gund*, Gmc. *gunthja*, war, *fano*, banner)]

gong (gong) *n.* **1** a tambourine-shaped metal instrument which when struck with a padded stick emits a loud sonorous note, used as a signal for meals etc. **2** a flattish bell struck with a hammer. **3** (*sl.*) a medal. *~v.t.* (*coll.*) to stop a person or activity by sounding a gong. **gong metal** *n.* a sonorous metal, 100 parts copper, 25 parts tin. [Malay]

gongoozler (gong·goo´zlə) *n.* a person who stares idly or curiously at something. [Eng. dial.]

Gongorism (gong´gərizm) *n.* a florid and affected style of writing somewhat analogous to euphemism, introduced by Góngora. **gongoresque** (-resk´) *a.* **Gongorist** *n.* [Lius de *Góngora* y Argote, 1561–1627, Spanish poet]

goniatite (gō´niətīt) *n.* any extinct cephalopod mollusc of the Palaeozoic genus *Goniatites*, similar to an ammonite. [mod. L *gōniatītēs*, from Gr. *gōnia*, angle]

gonidium (gənid´iəm) *n.* (*pl.* **gonidia** (-iə)) **1** a reproductive cell produced asexually in algae. **2** one of the green algal cells or buds in the thallus of lichens. **gonidial, gonidic, gonidioid, gonidiose** *a.* [from Gr. *gonē*, offspring, seed]

goniometer (gōniom´itə) *n.* an instrument for measuring angles, esp. of crystals. **goniometric** (-əmet´-), **goniometrical** *a.* **goniometry** *n.* [F *goniomètre*]

gonk (gongk) *n.* a soft round toy with arms and legs, popular in the 1960s.

gonna (gon´ə) *contr.* (*coll.*) going to (*I'm gonna be strong*).

gono- (gon´ō), **gon-** *comb. form* sexual or reproductive, as in *gonorrhoea*.

gonococcus (gonōkok´əs) *n.* (*pl.* **gonococci** (-kok´sī, -kok´ī)) the organism that causes gonorrhoea. **gonococcal** *a.*

gonocyte (gon´ōsīt) *n.* **1** a germ cell. **2** an oocyte. **3** a spermatocyte.

gonophore (gon´əfaw) *n.* **1** (*Bot.*) a stalk holding the pistil and stamens above the floral envelope in certain plants. **2** (*Zool.*) one of the zooids containing the reproductive elements in Hydrozoa. [Gr. *gonos*, offspring, generation, cogn. with GONOCYTE, -PHORE]

gonorrhoea (gonərē´ə), (*N Am.*) **gonorrhea** *n.* a venereal disease affecting the urethra and other mucous surfaces, accompanied by inflammation and purulent discharge. **gonorrhoeal** (-əl) *a.* [med. L, from Gr. *gonorrhoia* (*gonos*, seed, *rhoia*, a flowing]

gonzo (gon´zō) *a.* (*N Am., coll.*) bizarre, crazy, esp. of an exaggerated journalistic writing style. [perh. It., foolish or Sp. *ganso*, goose, fool]

goo (goo) *n.* (*coll.*) sticky matter. **gooey** *a.* (*comp.* **gooier**, *superl.* **gooiest**). **gooeyness, gooiness** *n.*

good (gud) *a.* (*comp.* **better**, *superl.* **best**) **1** having such qualities as are useful, proper, and satisfactory. **2** fit, proper, suitable, expedient (*a good match of colours*). **3** conducive to the end desired, profitable, serviceable (*The car has good brakes*). **4** adequate, satisfactory, competent (*a good worker; good at spelling*). **5** advantageous, beneficial (*good value*). **6** genuine, sound, valid, wholesome (*You need a good meal; The ticket is good for three games*). **7** perfect, complete, thorough (*a good clean*). **8** reliable, safe, sure (*a good driver*). **9** sound financially (*a good investment*). **10** ample, considerable (*a good way away*). **11** possessed of moral excellence, righteous, virtuous (*a good deed; a good person*). **12** kind, benevolent, friendly, amiable, courteous (*That was good of you*). **13** pleasant, acceptable, palatable (*good food; a good time*). **14** well-behaved (*a good child*). *~n.* **1** that which contributes to happiness, advantage etc. **2** that which is right, useful etc. **3** welfare. **4** prosperity. **5** benefit, advantage. **6** goodness, good qualities, virtuous and charitable deeds. **7** (*pl.*) movable property, chattels, effects. **8** wares, merchandise. **as good as** not less than, the same as, practically, virtually. **as good as one's word 1** fulfilling one's promises. **2** trustworthy. **3** not to be deterred. **for good (and all)** finally, definitely, completely. **for good measure** MEASURE. **good as gold** (esp. of children) very well behaved. **good for you!** used to express approval, encouragement etc. **good on you!** good for you! **in a good light** LIGHT[1]. **in good case** CASE[1]. **in good fettle** FETTLE. **in good fig** FIG[2]. **in good heart** HEART. **in good odour** ODOUR. **in good order** ORDER. **in good repair** REPAIR[1]. **†in good sooth** SOOTH. **in good time** TIME. **in good voice** VOICE. **in someone's good books** BOOK. **on a good wicket** WICKET. **on one's good behaviour** BEHAVIOUR (under BEHAVE). **to be good for** to be relied on to pay or bring in (a stated amount). **to come good 1** (*coll.*) esp. after a setback, to succeed or improve. **2** to recover one's health after illness etc. **to hold good** HOLD[1]. **to make good 1** to perform, to fulfil, to become successful. **2** to supply a deficiency. **3** to replace. **4** to compensate (for). **5** to confirm. **to see good** SEE[1]. **to stand a good chance** CHANCE. **to stand good** STAND. **to take in good part** not to take offence. **to the good** extra, over and above, as a balance or profit (*We are £5 to the good*). **good afternoon** *n., int.* a form of salutation at meeting or parting in the afternoon. **good beggar** *n.* a successful fundraiser for charity etc. **Good Book** *n.* the Bible. **good breeding** *n.* courteous manners formed by nurture and education. **good company** *n.* **1** a pleasant companion. **2** a pleasant group of friends. **†good-conditioned** *a.* being in a good state. **good day** *n., int.* a form of salutation at meeting or parting. **good egg!** *int.* (*sl.*) excellent! **good evening, good even, †good e'en** *n., int.* a form of salutation at meeting or parting in the evening. **good faith** *n.* honest intentions. **in good faith** FAITH. **good fellow** *n.* **1** a person of a good easy nature. **2** a genial, sociable person. **good-fellowship** *n.* **1** sociability. **2** pleasant company. **3** conviviality. **good folk, good people** *n.pl.* (*euphem.*) the fairies. **good form** *n.* **1** good manners. **2** breeding. **good-for-nothing, †good-for-nought** *a.* of no value, worthless. *~n.* an idle person, a vagabond. **Good Friday** *n.* the Friday of Holy Week, a solemn day commemorating the Crucifixion. **good hand** *n.* an expert (at). **good-hearted** *a.* kind, well-meaning. **good heavens!** *int.* used to express surprise, dismay, irritation etc. **good humour,** (*N Am.*) **good humor** *n.* a cheerful temper, amiability. **good-humoured** *a.* **good-humouredly** *adv.* **goodie** GOODY. **goodish** *a.* (*coll.*) moderately good. **good job** *n.* (*coll.*) a satisfactory turn of affairs. **Good King Henry** *n.* a weed of the goosefoot family, *Chenopodium bonus-henricus*, found in the northern hemisphere. **good lady** *n.* (usu. patronizing) wife. **good-looking** *a.* **1** handsome. **2** appearing to be good or virtuous. **good-looker** *n.* **good looks** *n.pl.* handsomeness. **good luck** *n.*, *int.* good fortune, prosperity. **goodly** *a.* **1** handsome, comely, graceful, kind. **2** large, considerable. **3** (*iron.*) poor, rubbishy. ~†*adv.* kindly. **goodliness** *n.* **†goodman** *n.* (*pl.* **goodmen**) **1** (a respectful mode of address to) a man below the rank of gentleman. **2** the head of a family. **3** the master of a house. **4** a husband. **good money** *n.* **1** real money, money that might have been spent elsewhere (*to throw good money after bad*). **2** (*coll.*) high earnings. **good morning, †good morrow** *n.*, *int.* a form of salutation at meeting or parting in the morning. **good nature** *n.* **1** kindness of disposition. **2** freedom from selfishness. **good-natured** *a.* **good-naturedly** *adv.* **good-neighbourliness** *n.* friendliness, kindly conduct between neighbours. **goodness** *n.* **1** the quality or state of being good. **2** that which is good. **3** moral excellence, virtue. **4** kindness, good nature, generosity. **5** the virtue or essence of anything. **6** (*euphem.*) God. **for goodness' sake** SAKE[1]. **goodness gracious!** used to express surprise etc. **goodness knows!** used to express lack of knowledge etc. **good night** *n.*, *int.* a form of salutation on parting at night or at bedtime. **goodo** (gud´ō) *a.* (*Austral.*, *New Zeal.*, *coll.*) good. **good offices** *n.pl.* mediating influence. **good-oh** (gudō´) *int.* used to express enthusiasm. **good oil** *n.* (*Austral.*, *coll.*) reliable information, true report. **good old days** *n.pl.* **1** better or happier former times. **2** the past viewed nostalgically. **good one** *n.* **1** (*coll.*) a funny joke. **2** an implausible or unbelievable statement or assertion. **good patch** *n.* (*coll.*) a sequence of good experiences or achievements. **good riddance** *n.*, *int.* a welcome relief from someone or something undesirable. **goods** *n.pl.* merchandise. **the goods 1** (*sl.*) just what is wanted. **2** (*esp. N Am.*, *coll.*) evidence (against someone). **to deliver the goods** DELIVER. **goods and chattels** *n.pl.* personal belongings of all kinds. **goods train** *n.* a train carrying merchandise only, a freight train. **goods truck** *n.* a truck for goods only. **good sailor** *n.* a person who is not liable to be seasick. **good Samaritan** *n.* a person who helps another in need or other adversity (alluding to Luke x.30–37). **good sense** *n.* sound judgement. **Good Shepherd** *n.* Jesus Christ. **good temper** *n.* freedom from irritability. **good-tempered** *a.* good-humoured. **good-temperedly** *adv.* **good thing** *n.* **1** a favourable bargain or speculation. **2** a witty remark or story. **3** (*pl.*) delicacies, good fare, creature comforts. **good-time girl** *n.* **1** a woman who recklessly pursues pleasure. **2** (*euphem.*) a prostitute. **good times** *n.pl.* a period of prosperity, happiness etc. **good turn** *n.* a kindly helpful act. **good value** *n.* something or someone worth the money, time, attention etc. expended on it. **†goodwife** *n.* (*pl.* **goodwives**) the mistress of a house. **goodwill** *n.* **1** kindly feeling or disposition. **2** benevolence, favour. **3** acquiescence, ready consent. **4** the established popularity or custom of a business sold with the business itself. **good wishes** *n.pl.* best wishes. **good word** *n.* a recommendation or endorsement (*to put in a good word for*). **good works** *n.pl.* acts of charity. **goody**[1] *int.* (*coll.*) used, esp. by children, to express delight. **goody**[2], **goodie** *n.* (*pl.* **goodies**) (*coll.*) **1** a person on the side of what is right and truthful, esp. a good character in fiction, cinema, television or radio. **2** (*usu. in pl.*) an object, gift etc. which is especially desirable. **3** a goody-goody. **4** †an elderly woman below the rank of gentlewoman. **goody-goody** *n.* (*pl.* **goody-goodies**) (*coll.*, *usu. derog.*) a priggishly good person. ~*a.* priggishly good. [OE *gōd* (cp. Dut. *goed*, Icel. *gōthr*, G *gut*), cogn. with GATHER]

goodbye (gudbī´), (*N Am.*) **goodby** *n.*, *int.* (*pl.* **goodbyes,** (*N Am.*) **goodbys**) (a) farewell. [corr. of *God be with you!*]

goof (goof) *n.* (*coll.*) **1** a foolish mistake, a blunder. **2** a stupid person. ~*v.i.*, *v.t.* to blunder. **goof ball** *n.* (*N Am.*, *sl.*) **1** a barbiturate pill. **2** a fool. **goofy** *a.* (*comp.* **goofier,** *superl.* **goofiest**) (*coll.*) **1** silly. **2** (of front teeth) protruding. **3** infatuated. **goofily** *adv.* **goofiness** *n.*

goog (gug) *n.* (*Austral.*, *sl.*) an egg. **full as a goog** FULL[1]. [etym. unknown]

googly (goo´gli) *n.* (*pl.* **googlies**) in cricket, a ball bowled in a disguised manner to break a different way from that expected, an off-break ball bowled with a leg-break action.

googol (goo´gol) *n.* (*coll.*) ten raised to the power of one hundred, 10^{100}. **googolplex** (-pleks) *n.* (*coll.*) ten raised to the power of a googol. [20th cent., coined by E. Kasner, N American mathematician]

gook (gook, guk) *n.* (*N Am.*, *sl.*, *offensive*) a foreigner, esp. a person from E Asia. [etym. unknown]

goolie (goo´li), **gooly** *n.* (*pl.* **goolies**) **1** (*sl.*, *usu. pl.*) a testicle. **2** (*Austral.*, *sl.*) a stone, pebble. [from Hind. *goli*, bullet, ball, pill]

goombah (goom´bah) *n.* (*N Am.*, *sl.*) **1** a member of a criminal gang. **2** a boss, mentor, crony etc.

goon (goon) *n.* **1** a stupid person. **2** a thug hired to terrorize others, esp. in an industrial or political context. [etym. unknown]

goonda (goon´də) *n.* a desperado, a hooligan. [Hind.]

goop[1] (goop) *n.* (*sl.*) a rude or foolish person. **goopy** *a.* (*comp.* **goopier,** *superl.* **goopiest**). **goopiness** *n.*

goop[2] (goop) *n.* a thick, sticky liquid, gloop.

goosander (goosan´də) *n.* a large diving duck, *Mergus merganser.* [etym. uncertain (perh. GOOSE, *-ander*, cp. Icel. *önd*, a duck, pl. *andir*)]

goose (goos) *n.* (*pl.* **geese** (gēs)) **1** a web-footed bird intermediate in size between the duck and the swan, belonging to the family Anatidae. **2** the female of this, as distinct from gander. **3** a silly person, a simpleton. **4** (*pl.* **gooses**) a tailor's smoothing iron. **5** (*sl.*) a prod between the buttocks. ~*v.t.* (*sl.*) to prod between the buttocks. **to cook someone's goose** COOK. **goose-fish** *n.* (*N Am.*) the angler fish or monkfish, *Lophius piscatorius.* **goose-flesh,** (*N Am.*, *Sc.*) **goose bumps, goose pimples, goose-skin** *n.* a peculiar roughness of the human skin produced by cold, fear etc. **goosefoot** *n.* (*pl.* **goosefoots**) any herb of the genus *Chenopodium* with leaves shaped like a goose's foot. **goosegrass** *n.* **1** the Eurasian plant cleavers, *Galium aparine.* **2** the plant silverweed, *Potentilla anserina.* **gooseherd** *n.* a person who tends geese. **gooseneck** *n.* **1** on a sailing boat, a bent iron fitted at the end of a yard or boom for various purposes. **2** a piece of iron shaped like the neck of a goose. **goose-quill** *n.* a quill-feather of a goose, esp. (formerly) used as a quill pen. **goose-step** *n.* **1** a marching step in which the legs are raised almost parallel with the ground without bending the knees. **2** marking time by raising the feet alternately, as a balancing drill for recruits. **goose-wing** *n.* a lower corner of a sailing boat's mainsail or foresail when the middle part is furled. **goose-winged** *a.* on a vessel with fore and aft sails, having the mainsail on one side and the foresail on the other, thus giving the appearance of outstretched 'wings'. **goosey** *n.* a goose (used by or to children). **goosy** *a.* **1** of or like a goose. **2** having goose-flesh. [OE *gōs* (cp. Dut. and G *Gans*, Icel. *gās*, L *anser*, Gr. *chēn*, perh. conn. with *chainein*, to gape)]

gooseberry (guz´bəri, goos´-) *n.* (*pl.* **gooseberries**) **1** the thorny shrub *Ribes grossularia.* **2** the fruit of this shrub. **to play gooseberry** to act as an unwanted third party to a pair of lovers. [prob. GOOSE, BERRY]

goosegog (goos´gog, guz´-) *n.* (*coll.*) a gooseberry.

GOP *abbr.* (*US*) Grand Old Party (the Republican Party).

gopak (gō´pak) *n.* a folk dance from Ukraine characterized by high leaps, performed by men. [Rus.]

gopher[1] (gō´fə) *n.* any of various American burrowing animals of the family *Geomyidae.* [etym. uncertain]

gopher[2] (gō´fə) *n.* (*Bible*) the wood of which Noah's ark was made. [Heb.]

goral (gaw´rəl) *n.* a Himalayan goatlike antelope, *Nemorhedus goral.* [Hind., prob. from Sansk.]

goramy GOURAMI.

gorblimey (gawblī´mi) *int.* (*coll.*) used to express surprise, indignation etc. ~*n.* (*pl.* **gorblimeys**) a soft cap worn by members of the armed forces.

gorcock (gaw´kok) *n.* (*Sc., North.*) the moorcock or male of the red grouse. [etym. uncertain]

Gordian (gaw´diən) *a.* intricate, complicated. **Gordian knot** *n.* **1** any apparently inextricable difficulty or deadlock. **2** a knot in the harness of Gordius, a king of Phrygia, which Alexander the Great is said to have cut with his sword upon hearing the promise of the oracle that whoever could untie it should possess the empire of Asia. **to cut the Gordian knot** to remove a difficulty by drastic measures.

Gordon setter (gaw´dən) *n.* a black and tan breed of setter, used as gun dogs. [after the 4th Duke of *Gordon*, 1743–1827]

gore[1] (gaw) *n.* blood from a wound, esp. thick, clotted blood. **gory** *a.* (*comp.* **gorier,** *superl.* **goriest**) **1** covered with gore. **2** bloody, involving bloodshed and killing. **gorily** *adv.* **goriness** *n.* **gory dew** *n.* a minute freshwater alga, *Palmella cruenta*, coating damp walls in shady places with rosy gelatinous patches. [OE *gor*, dirt, filth (cp. Icel. *gor*, Dut. *goor*)]

gore[2] (gaw) *v.t.* **1** to pierce, to stab. **2** to pierce with a horn, point etc. [OE *gār*, a spear (cp. Icel. *geirr*, and perh. OIr. *gár*)]

gore[3] (gaw) *n.* **1** a triangular piece in a dress, sail, balloon, umbrella etc. **2** a triangular piece of land. **3** (*Her.*) a curved section cut from a shield, orig. denoting cowardice. ~*v.t.* **1** to make into or shape as a gore. **2** to fit with a gore. [OE *gāra*, cogn. with GORGE]

gorge (gawj) *n.* **1** a narrow pass between cliffs or hills. **2** (*dated*) the throat, gullet. **3** the contents of the stomach. **4** a heavy meal, a surfeit. **5** in a fortification, the narrow entrance into a bastion or other outwork. **6** in angling, a bait to be swallowed by a fish. ~*v.t.* **1** to swallow, to devour greedily. **2** to glut, to satiate, to choke up. ~*v.i.* to feed greedily. **one's gorge rises at** one is nauseated or disgusted by. **gorged** *a.* (*Her.*) bearing a crown or the like round the neck. **gorger** *n.* [OF, etym. uncertain]

gorgeous (gaw´jəs) *a.* **1** splendid, richly decorated, magnificent. **2** ornate. **3** (*coll.*) very fine, beautiful etc. **gorgeously** *adv.* **gorgeousness** *n.* [OF *gorgias*, etym. uncertain]

gorget (gaw´jit) *n.* **1** a piece of armour for defending the throat or neck. **2** a metallic ornament formerly worn on the breast by officers on duty. **3** a ruff or wimple formerly worn by women. **4** a necklace. [OF *gorgete*, dim. of *gorge*, see GORGE]

Gorgio (gaw´jō) *n.* (*pl.* **Gorgios**) (among gypsies) someone who is not a gypsy. [Romany]

gorgon (gaw´gən) *n.* **1** in Greek mythology, any one of three snake-haired female monsters so terrible in appearance that the sight of them was fabled to turn beholders to stone. **2** a person of frightening appearance, esp. a repulsive-looking woman. **gorgoneion** (-nī´on) *n.* (*pl.* **gorgoneia** (-nī´ə)) a mask or other representation of a gorgon's head, often used as a keystone. **gorgonian**[1] (-gō´niən), **gorgonesque** (-nesk´) *a.* **gorgonize, gorgonise** *v.t.* to gaze at so as to paralyse or turn to stone. [L *Gorgō -ōnis*, Gr. *Gorgō*, pl. *-ones*, from *gorgos*, terrible]

gorgonian[1] GORGON.

gorgonian[2] (gawgō´niən) *n.* any brightly-coloured horny coral of the order Gorgonacea, having flexible polyps growing in the form of shrubs, feathers etc., such as the sea fan. ~*a.* of or relating to the Gorgonacea. [from GORGON, in allusion to their petrified character]

Gorgonzola (gawgənzō´lə) *n.* a soft blue-veined Italian cheese. [village near Milan]

gorilla (gəril´ə) *n.* **1** a large vegetarian African anthropoid ape, *Gorilla gorilla*, growing to about 5½ ft. (1.6 m) in height. **2** (*coll.*) a threateningly large man. [Gr. form of alleged Afr. name for a wild man in account of Hermo the Carthaginian's travels in 5th or 6th cent. BC]

gormandize (gaw´məndīz), **gormandise** *v.t.* to eat greedily, to gorge. ~*v.i.* to eat food greedily. ~*n.* **1** taste in the provision and appreciation of table delicacies. **2** †indulgence in eating, gluttony. **gormandizer** *n.* **gormandizing** *n.* [OF *gourmandise*, gluttony, from GOURMAND]

gormless (gawm´lis), **gaumless** *a.* witless, clumsy, stupid. **gormlessly** *adv.* **gormlessness** *n.* [ON *gaumr*, care, attention]

☒ **gorrila** common misspelling of GORILLA.

gorse (gaws) *n.* any yellow-flowered, prickly shrub of the genus *Ulex*, furze, whin. **gorsy** *a.* [OE *gorst* (cogn. with G *Gerst*, L *hordeum*, barley, L *horridus*, bristly)]

Gorsedd (gaw´sedh) *n.* a meeting of bards and Druids in Wales, esp. associated with the eisteddfod. [Welsh]

gory GORE[1].

gosh (gosh) *int.* used to express surprise. [GOD]

goshawk (gos´hawk) *n.* a large, short-winged hawk, *Accipiter gentilis.* [OE *gos-hafuc* (as GOOSE, HAWK[1])]

Goshen (gō´shən) *n.* a land of plenty. [the land in Egypt given by Pharaoh to the Israelites to dwell in (Gen. xlv)]

gosling (goz´ling) *n.* a young goose.

gospel (gos´pəl) *n.* **1** the teaching or revelation of Jesus Christ. **2** the doctrine preached by Christ and the Apostles. **3** (**Gospel**) **a** any one of the canonical books ascribed respectively to Matthew, Mark, Luke and John. **b** a selection from these books read in the Church service. **4** anything accepted as infallibly true. **5** the principle that one adopts as a guide to life or action. **6** the creed of a party etc. **gospeller,** (*N Am.*) **gospeler** *n.* **1** a person who claims that their religious beliefs are based exclusively on the Gospels (often applied contemptuously to Protestants, Puritans etc.). **2** a person who reads the Gospel in the Communion service. **gospel side** *n.* in a church, the north side of the chancel where the Gospel is read. **gospel truth** *n.* the absolute truth, something completely true. [OE *godspell*, good tidings]

gossamer (gos´əmə) *n.* **1** the slender cobweb-like threads floating in the air in calm weather, produced by small spiders. **2** thin, filmy gauze. **3** anything exceedingly flimsy or unsubstantial. **gossamered** *a.* **gossamery** *a.* [ME *gossomer*, lit., goose-summer, i.e. St Martin's summer (early Nov.), when geese were eaten, the time of its prevalence]

gossip (gos´ip) *n.* **1** idle talk, tittle-tattle. **2** mere rumour. **3** informal chat or writing, esp. about persons or incidents of the day. **4** a person who regularly indulges in tittle-tattle. ~*v.i.* (*pres.p.* **gossiping,** *past, p.p.* **gossiped**) **1** to tattle, to chat. **2** to talk or write in an informal easy-going way. **gossip column** *n.* a section of a newspaper devoted to information and rumour about well-known personalities. **gossip columnist** *n.* **gossiper** *n.* **gossipmonger** *n.* a spreader of gossip. **gossipy**

a. [OE *godsibb*, orig. related in God, a sponsor in baptism]

gossoon (gosoon´) *n.* (*Ang.-Ir.*) a boy, a lad. [corr. of F GARÇON]

gossypium (gəsip´iəm) *n.* a tropical genus of herbs and shrubs belonging to the *Malvaceae* or mallow family, including three species from which commercial cotton is obtained. [L *gossypion*]

got (got), **got-up** *a.* dressed up, disguised, prepared for effect or to take in. [p.p. of GET[1]]

Goth (goth) *n.* **1** a member of an ancient Germanic tribe which invaded southern Europe in the 3rd–5th cents., establishing kingdoms in Italy, southern France and Spain. **2** a rude, ignorant person. **3** (**goth**) a member of a subculture identified by black clothing, striking black and white make-up, metallic jewellery and a preference for a particular form of rock music. **Gothish** *a.* [late L *Gothī*, Gr. *Gothoi*, Goth. *Gutōs* or *Gutans*, pl.]

Goth. *abbr.* Gothic.

†**Gothamist** (gō´təmist, got´-, -th-) *n.* a foolish person, someone easily taken in. **Gothamite** (-īt) *n.* **1** a Gothamist. **2** (*US, facet.*) a New Yorker. [*Gotham*, a village in Nottinghamshire, said to be noted for its foolish inhabitants]

Gothic (goth´ik) *a.* **1** in the style of architecture characterized by pointed arches, clustered columns etc. **2** (of a novel, film etc.) in a style characterized by gloomy, menacing surroundings in which supernatural or horrifying events take place. **3** of or relating to the Goths or their language. **4** rude, barbarous. *~n.* **1** the Gothic style of architecture. **2** the language of the Goths. **3** (*Print.*) a heavy black-letter typeface, old-fashioned German or sans serif. **4** (**gothic**) a goth. **Gothically** *adv.* **Gothicism** (-sizm) *n.* **1** conformity to the Gothic style of architecture. **2** a Gothic idiom. **3** rudeness of manners. **Gothicist** (-sist) *n.* **Gothicize** (-sīz), **Gothicise** *v.t.* **1** to make Gothic. **2** to bring back to barbarism. *~v.i.* to go back to barbarism. **Gothic revival** *n.* the wave of interest in Gothic culture that occurred in the late 18th and the first half of the 19th cent. [GOTH]

gotta (got´ə) *contr.* (*coll.*) **1** have got to (*I gotta go*). **2** have got a (*I gotta horse*).

gotten GET[1].

Götterdämmerung (gœtədem´ərung) *n.* in German mythology, the final destruction of the world. [G, twilight of the gods]

gouache (gooahsh´) *n.* a method of painting with opaque colours mixed with water, honey and gum. [F, from It. *guazzo*]

Gouda (gow´də) *n.* a round mild cheese originally made at Gouda, in the Netherlands.

gouge (gowj) *n.* **1** a chisel with a concave blade, used to cut holes or grooves. **2** a groove, cut etc. made with this tool. **3** (*sl.*) a swindle, a fraud. *~v.t.* **1** to cut, force or scoop (out) with or as with a gouge. **2** (*N Am.*) to cheat. **gouger** *n.* [F, late L *guvia*, etym. uncertain]

goujon (goo´zhon) *n.* a small strip of chicken or fish, usu. deep-fried in a coating of breadcrumbs etc. [F, as GUDGEON[1]]

goulash (goo´lash) *n.* **1** a stew of meat and vegetables highly seasoned with paprika. **2** in contract bridge, a method of dealing again with unshuffled cards in threes and fours, used when no player has bid on the previous deal. [Hung. *gulyas*, herdsman]

gourami (goo´rəmi), **goramy** (gaw´-) *n.* (*pl.* **gouramis, goramies**) a nest-building Oriental fish, *Osphrenemus goramy*, much valued for food. [Javanese]

gourd (guəd) *n.* **1** a large fleshy fruit of climbing or trailing plants belonging to the Cucurbitaceae, the hard outer coat of which can serve as a container for water, wine etc. **2** a bottle, cup etc. made from a gourd. **3** a vessel of a similar shape. **4** (*pl.*) hollow dice employed for cheating. **gourdful** *n.* **gourd-worm** *n.* a fluke-worm resembling a gourd seed. [F *gourde*, ult. from L *cucurbita*]

gourmand (guə´mənd) *n.* **1** a glutton. **2** (*dated*) a person who loves delicate fare, a gourmet. *~a.* gluttonous, fond of eating. **gourmandism, gourmandise** (-ēz) *n.* gluttony, the habits of a gourmand. [F, etym. uncertain]

Usage note The nouns *gourmand* and *gourmet* should not be confused: a *gourmand* is a glutton, and a *gourmet* a connoisseur.

gourmet (guə´mā) *n.* a connoisseur of good food, an epicure. *~a.* **1** of or relating to a gourmet. **2** of a standard considered appropriate to a gourmet (*a gourmet meal*). [F, orig. a wine-taster]

Usage note See note under GOURMAND.

gout (gowt) *n.* **1** a disease affecting the joints, esp. the big toe and foot, with inflammation, pain and irritability being the leading symptoms. **2** †a drop, a clot, esp. of blood. **gouty** *a.* (*comp.* **goutier,** *superl.* **goutiest**) **1** affected with or relating to gout. **2** swollen. **goutily** *adv.* **goutiness** *n.* [OF *goute*, L *gutta*, a drop]

goût (goo) *n.* **1** taste, relish. **2** good taste, artistic discernment. [F, earlier *goust*, L *gustus*]

Gov. *abbr.* **1** Governor. **2** Government.

gov. *abbr.* governor.

govern (gŭv´ən) *v.t.* **1** to direct and control. **2** to rule with authority, esp. to administer the affairs of a state. **3** to exercise military command over. **4** to regulate, to sway, to influence, to determine. **5** to conduct (oneself) in a specific way. **6** to restrain, to curb. **7** (*Gram.*) (of a verb or preposition) to require a particular case in (a word following it), to have (a noun or case) dependent upon it. *~v.i.* **1** to exercise authority. **2** to administer the law. **3** to have the control (over). **governable** *a.* **governability** (-bil´-) *n.* **governably** *adv.* **governance** (-əns) *n.* **1** the action, manner or system of governing. **2** government, authority, control. **governing body** *n.* a board, committee etc. of people who collectively oversee an institution. [OF *governer*, L *gubernāre*, to steer, guide, from Gr. *kubernân*, to steer]

governess (gŭv´ənis) *n.* a woman employed to teach children in a private household. **governess-car, governess-cart** *n.* a light two-wheeled horse-drawn vehicle with two seats only, facing each other. **governessy** *a.* [earlier *governeress*, OF *gouverneresse*, fem. of *gouverneur*, GOVERNOR]

government (gŭv´ənmənt, gŭv´əmənt) *n.* **1** control, direction, regulation, exercise of authority, esp. authoritative administration of public affairs. **2** the form or system of such administration. **3** the body of persons in charge of the government of a state at any particular time, an administration, a ministry. **4** self-control, manageableness. **5** the power of controlling. **6** the form of policy in a state. **7** the right of governing. **8** the executive power. **9** the territory under a governor, a province. **10** (*Gram.*) the influence of a word in determining the case or mood of another. **governmental** (-men´-) *a.* **governmentalism** *n.* **governmentalist** *n.* **governmentally** *adv.* **Government House** *n.* the official residence of a governor, esp. a British one overseas. **government issue** *a.* (*esp. US*) supplied by the government. **government man** *n.* (*Austral.*) a 19th-cent. convict, an assigned servant. **government paper** *n.* bonds, securities etc. issued by a government. **government pension** *n.* (*N Am.*) a state pension. **government surplus** *n.* unused government equipment for disposal by sale. [OF *governement*]

Usage note The pronunciation with the first *n* silent is sometimes disapproved of.

governor (gŭv´ənə) *n.* **1** a person who governs, esp. someone invested with authority to execute the laws and administer the affairs of a state, province etc. **2** a ruler, a head of the executive. **3** the Crown representative in a colony or dependency. **4** (*US*) the elective chief magistrate of a state. **5** the commander in a fortress or garrison. **6** (*sl.*) a term used by a person to refer to their employer, father etc. **7** an unceremonious mode of address (*Look here, governor!*). **8** a device for limiting the speed of an engine, motor etc., or the flow or pressure of a fluid or gas. **governor-general** *n.* (*pl.* **governors-general**) a chief of the executive in a large dependency, having subordinate deputy governors. **governor-generalship** *n.* **governorship, governorate** (-rət) *n.* [OF *governeur*]

Gov.-Gen. *abbr.* Governor-General.

Govt. *abbr.* Government.

gowan (gow´ən) *n.* (*Sc., North.*) the daisy or similar white or yellow field-flower. [perh. conn. with Icel. *gulr*, YELLOW, or with OE *golde*, GOLD]

gowk (gowk) *n.* (*Sc., North.*) **1** a fool, a simple or awkward person. **2** †the cuckoo. [Icel. *gaukr* (cp. G *Gauch*, OE *gēak*)]

gown (gown) *n.* **1** a woman's loose, long, outer garment, a dress, esp. a handsome or stylish one. **2** a long, loose robe worn by members of the clergy, judges, lawyers, university graduates etc. **3** a protective garment as worn by surgeons during an operation. **4** a Roman toga. **town and gown** the townspeople and the university staff and students in a university town, as opposed to or contrasted with each other. **gownboy** *n.* a boy wearing a gown, esp. a foundation scholar in an endowed school. **gowned** *a.* wearing a gown. **gownsman** *n.* (*pl.* **gownsmen**) **1** a person whose professional dress is a gown, such as a member of a university or a lawyer. **2** a person wearing a gown as emblem of peace, a civilian. [OF *gaune, gonne*, late L *gunna*, a skin, a fur garment]

gowpen (gow´pən) *n.* **1** a handful, a double handful, as much as can be held in the hollow of the two hands. **2** †a perquisite of meal allowed to a miller's man. [Sc., from Icel. *gaupn*]

goy (goi) *n.* (*pl.* **goyim** (-im), **goys**) (*sl., offensive*) among Jews, a name for a non-Jewish person. [Heb., a nation]

GP *abbr.* **1** General Practitioner. **2** Grand Prix.

gp. *abbr.* group.

Gp. Capt. *abbr.* Group Captain (in the RAF).

GPI *abbr.* general paralysis of the insane.

GPMU *abbr.* Graphical, Paper and Media Union.

GPO *abbr.* **1** General Post Office. **2** (*US*) Government Printing Office.

GPS *abbr.* Global Positioning System.

GR *abbr.* King George. [L *Georgius Rex*]

Gr. *abbr.* **1** Grand. **2** Greece. **3** Greek.

gr. *abbr.* **1** grain(s). **2** gram(s). **3** grey. **4** gross.

Graafian follicle (grah´fiən) *n.* a small sac in which the ova are matured in the ovary of mammals. [Regnier de *Graaf*, 1641–73, Dutch anatomist]

grab (grab) *v.t.* (*pres.p.* **grabbing,** *past, p.p.* **grabbed**) **1** to seize, snatch or grasp suddenly. **2** to take possession of violently or lawlessly. **3** (*coll.*) to capture, to arrest. **4** (*coll.*) to interest (*How does that grab you?*). *~v.i.* to grasp, snatch, or clutch (at). *~n.* **1** a sudden snatch, grasping or seizing (at). **2** an implement for clutching, a grip. **3** rapacious or dishonest acquisition, esp. in commerce or the foreign policy of a government. **up for grabs 1** (*coll.*) on offer. **2** for sale. **3** ready for the taking. **grab bag** *n.* (*N Am.*) a lucky dip. **grabber** *n.* **grabby** *a.* (*coll.*) greedy, grasping, eager to grab. **grab handle, grab rail** *n.* a handle, rail etc. to steady passengers in a moving vehicle. [prob. orig. Eng., perh. from GRIP[1] (cp. Swed. *grabba*, MDut. and MLG *grabben*)]

grabble (grab´əl) *v.i.* **1** to grope, to feel about (for). **2** to sprawl on all fours (after, for etc.). [freq. of GRAB]

graben (grā´bən) *n.* (*Geol.*) an elongated depression where the earth's surface has subsided between two fault lines. [19th cent., from OHG *graban*, to dig]

grace (grās) *n.* **1** the quality which makes form, movement, expression or manner elegant, harmonious, refined and charming. **2** a natural gift or endowment. **3** an acquired accomplishment, charm or attraction. **4** a courteous or affable demeanour. **5** free, unmerited favour or goodwill. **6** clemency, mercy. **7** a boon, a benefaction. **8** (*Mus.*) an ornamental note or passage introduced as an embellishment. **9** (*Theol.*) the free, unmerited favour of God. **10** a divine, regenerating and invigorating influence. **11** the state of being forgiven by and reconciled to God, with participation in the favours granted through the merits of Christ. **12** a spiritual favour or excellence. **13** a short prayer before a meal invoking a blessing or expressing thanks. **14** a privilege or indulgence, esp. an extension of time legally allowed after a payment falls due. **15** (**Grace**) used as part of a formula for addressing or referring to a duke, duchess or archbishop (*Your Grace*). **16** at a university, a vote, decree, a licence to take a degree, a dispensation from statutes etc. **17** (*pl.*) †thanks. **airs and graces** AIR. **her grace** a courteous phrase adopted in speaking of a duchess and formerly of a female sovereign. **his grace** a courteous phrase adopted in speaking of an archbishop or duke, and formerly of a male sovereign. **the Graces** in Greek mythology, three goddesses embodying and conferring beauty and charm. **to be in the good graces of** to enjoy the favour of. **to fall from grace** FALL. **with a bad grace** reluctantly. **with a good grace** willingly. **your grace** a courteous phrase adopted in speaking to an archbishop, duke or duchess, and formerly to a sovereign. **grace-and-favour** *a.* (of a house, flat etc.) granted free of rent by the sovereign as a mark of gratitude. **grace cup** *n.* a cup, usu. of wine, passed round after a meal for drinking the concluding health or healths. **graceful** *a.* full of grace, elegance or beauty, esp. of form or movement. **gracefully** *adv.* **gracefulness** *n.* **graceless** *a.* **1** lacking in grace, elegance etc., ungraceful. **2** lacking in propriety or decency, mannerless. **3** depraved, abandoned. **4** †out of favour, unfortunate. **gracelessly** *adv.* **gracelessness** *n.* **grace note** *n.* (*Mus.*) an extra note introduced for embellishment. [OF *grace* (F *grâce*), L *grātia*, from *grātus*, pleasing]

gracile (gras´īl) *a.* slender, lean, thin, esp. in an anthropological sense. **gracility** (grəsil´-) *n.* **1** slenderness. **2** unadorned simplicity.

gracious (grā´shəs) *a.* **1** exhibiting grace, favour or kindness. **2** benevolent, kind. **3** courteous, condescending, affable. **4** graceful, pleasing, bland. **5** proceeding from divine grace. **6** benignant, merciful. **gracious living** *n.* an elegant way of life. **graciously** *adv.* **gracious me!** *int.* used to express surprise or protest. **graciousness, graciosity** (-os´-) *n.* [OF (F *gracieux*), L *gratiōsus*, as GRACE]

grackle (grak´əl), **grakle** *n.* **1** any American oriole of the genus *Quiscalus*, also called *blackbird* in N America. **2** any mynah bird of the genus *Gracula*, allied to the starlings. [L *grāculus*, a jackdaw]

grad (grad) *n.* (*coll.*) a graduate.

gradable GRADE.

gradation (grədā´shən) *n.* **1** an orderly arrangement, succession or progression step by step. **2** (*usu. in pl.*) a step, stage or degree in order, rank, quality, merit etc. **3** in art, the gradual blending of one tint, tone etc. with another. **4** (*Mus.*) an ascending or descending succession of chords. **5** in philology, ablaut. **gradate** *v.t.* to arrange or blend (colours etc.) by imperceptible gradation. *~v.i.* to pass from one tint to another by such gradations. **gradational** *a.* **gradationally** *adv.* **gradationed** *a.* formed by gradation. **gradatory** (grā´də-) *a.* proceeding by gradations. [L *gradātio -ōnem*, from *gradus*, a step]

grade (grād) *n.* **1** a degree or step in rank, quality, value, order etc. **2** a class of people of similar rank, ability, proficiency etc. **3** a mark given to a student's work as an indication of its quality. **4** class (at school). **5** an animal or class of animals (such as cattle or sheep) produced by crossing a common stock with some better breed. **6** (*Zool.*) a group supposed to have branched off from a parent stem at a certain stage of development. **7** degree of intensity (of a disease). **8** gradient, the degree of slope in a road. **9** a sloping road, track etc. **10** in philology, the position of a vowel or root in an ablaut series. *~v.t.* **1** to arrange in grades. **2** to gradate. **3** to adjust the rate of slope in, as a road. **4** (of cattle) to cross (a stock) with a better breed. **at grade** (*N Am.*) at the same level (as of a place where two roads cross each other). **to grade up** to improve (stock) by crossing with a better breed. **to make the grade** to succeed. **gradable** *a.* **grade cricket** *n.* in Australia, competitive cricket played between teams arranged in grades. **grade crossing** *n.* (*N Am.*) a level crossing. **grader** *n.* **1** a person who or thing which grades. **2** a motor-driven vehicle with a blade for pushing earth, rubble etc., used in road construction etc. **3** (*N Am.*) a pupil at a particular grade (*in comb.*, as *seventh grader*). **grade school** *n.* (*N Am.*) primary school. [F, from L *gradum*, nom. *-us*, see GRADATION]

-grade (grād) *comb. form* of a kind or manner of movement or progression, as in *retrograde.*

gradely (grād´li) *a.* (*dial.*) **1** decent, respectable, worthy. **2** well. **3** proper, suitable. **4** good-looking. *~adv.* decently, properly, well, becomingly. [ME *graythly*, Icel. *greithliga* (cp. GRAITH, OE *gerǣde*, G *gerade*, ready)]

gradient (grā´diənt) *n.* **1** the rate of ascent or descent in a railway or road, degree of slope, inclination. **2** a stretch of sloping road, railway etc. **3** in civil engineering, grade. **4** rate of variation or increase or decrease in height of thermometer or barometer over a large area or the diagrammatic line denoting such variation. [from GRADE, after L *gradiens -ntem*, p.p. of *gradi*, to walk]

gradine (grədēn´), **gradin** (grā´din) *n.* **1** each in a series of rising steps or a tier of seats. **2** a shelf or step at the back of an altar. [F *gradin*, It. *gradino*, from *grado*, GRADE]

gradual (grad´ūəl, graj´əl) *a.* **1** regular and slow, as opposed to abrupt, steep, rapid. **2** proceeding by steps or degrees. *~n.* **1** in church music, an antiphon sung between the reading of the Epistle and the Gospel. **2** a book containing such antiphons or the music for them. **gradualism** *n.* esp. regarding political policy, the principle of making change slowly and gradually rather than quickly or by violent means. **gradualist** *n.* **gradually** *adv.* **gradualness** *n.*

graduate[1] (grad´ūāt, graj´-) *v.i.* **1** to be awarded a first degree from a university. **2** to alter, change or pass by degrees. *~v.t.* **1** to mark with degrees. **2** to divide into or arrange by gradations. **3** to apportion (a tax etc.) according to a scale of grades. **4** to temper or modify by degrees. **5** (*N Am.*) to confer an academic degree upon. **6** (*Chem.*) to bring (a fluid) to a certain degree of consistency, as by evaporation. **graduand** (-and) *n.* a person who is about to graduate from a university. **graduated pension** *n.* a system of pension contributions deducted from an employee's salary in proportion to their earnings. **graduation** (-ā´shən) *n.* **1** regular progression by successive degrees. **2** a division into degrees or parts. **3** the conferring or receiving of academical degrees. **4** (*Chem.*) the reduction of a liquid to a certain consistency by evaporation. **graduator** *n.* an instrument for dividing lines into minute equal parts. [late L *graduātus*, p.p. of *graduāre*, as GRADE]

graduate[2] (grad´ūət, graj´-) *n.* **1** a person who has received a degree from a university. **2** (*Chem.*) a graduated vessel for measuring liquids. **graduate school** *n.* a university department for advanced work by graduates. **graduateship** *n.*

gradus (grā´dəs) *n.* (*pl.* **graduses**) a dictionary of Greek or Latin prosody formerly used in public schools. [short for *Gradus ad Parnassum*, steps to Parnassus]

Graecism (grē´sizm), **Grecism** *n.* **1** a Greek idiom, style or mode of expression. **2** cultivation of the Greek spirit, style or mode of expression. **Graecize, Graecise** *v.t.* to give a Greek form or character to. *~v.i.* to cultivate or follow the Greek spirit, ideas, ways of expression etc. [F *grécisme*, med. L *Graecismus*, from *Graecus*, GREEK]

graeco- (grē´ko, grī´-), **greco-** (grē´kō) *comb. form* Greek.

graffiti (grəfē´ti) *n.pl.* (*sing.* **graffito** (-tō)) **1** (*pl.*) drawings or words, sometimes obscene, sometimes political, painted or written on walls etc. in public view. **2** (*pl.*) drawings or inscriptions scratched on an ancient wall or other surface. **3** a piece of graffiti. **4** SGRAFFITO. [It., from *graffio*, a scratch]

Usage note As a mass or collective noun *graffiti* can be either singular or plural (*Graffiti cover(s) the walls*), though the singular construction is less widely acceptable. As a countable noun it should always be a plural, however, with *graffito* as the singular.

graft[1] (grahft) *n.* **1** a small shoot of a tree or plant inserted into another tree of a different stock which supplies the sap to nourish it. **2** living tissue from a person or animal transplanted to another. **3** incorporation with a foreign stock. **4** (*coll.*) hard work, unremitting labour. *~v.t.* **1** to insert (a shoot or scion) in or upon another plant or tree. **2** to insert as a graft. **3** to insert grafts upon. **4** to plant (a tree or stock) thus with another variety. **5** to transplant (as living animal tissue). **6** to incorporate with another stock. **7** to insert or implant (upon) so as to form a vital union. **8** on a vessel, to cover (a ring-bolt etc.) with spun yarn or a weaving of thin cord. *~v.i.* **1** to insert grafts or scions in or on other stocks. **2** (*coll.*) to work hard. **grafter**[1] *n.* **1** a person who carries out the process of grafting. **2** (*coll.*) a hard worker. **3** †a tree from which a graft was taken. **4** grafting clay. **grafting clay, grafting wax** *n.* a composition used for covering grafted parts of plants and trees to exclude air. [earlier *graff*, OF *grafe* (F *greffe*), low L *graphium*, Gr. *graphion*, a stylus, from *graphein*, to write]

graft[2] (grahft) *n.* **1** acquisition of money etc. by taking advantage of an official position. **2** manipulation of state or municipal business in order to secure illicit profits or influence. **3** illicit gains so obtained. **4** bribery. **5** a swindle. **grafter**[2] *n.* [etym. uncertain]

grafter[1] GRAFT[1].

grafter[2] GRAFT[2].

Grail (grāl) *n.* **1** a dish or cup said to have been used by Christ at the Last Supper, and employed by Joseph of Arimathea to collect Christ's blood while on the cross, *Saint Grail, Sangreal.* **2** the object of a quest. [OF *graal*, *greal*, late L *gradālis*, etym. uncertain]

grain (grān) *n.* **1** a single seed of a plant, particularly of food plants. **2** a collective term for corn in general or the fruit of cereal plants, such as wheat, barley, rye etc. **3** (*N Am.*) wheat. **4** (*pl.*) the husks or refuse of malt after brewing or of any grain after distillation. **5** any small, hard particle. **6** the smallest particle or amount. **7** the smallest unit of weight in the troy and avoirdupois system, approx. equivalent to 0.0648 grams. **8** a unit of weight for pearls equal to 50 mg or ¼ of a carat, also called *metric grain.* **9** in photography, any one of the particles in a photographic emulsion of a film or plate the size of which limits the extent to which the projected image can be enlarged. **10** granular texture, degree of roughness or smoothness of surface. **11** texture, arrangement of particles, esp. the arrangement of the fibres of wood or other fibrous substance. **12** the lines of fibre in wood or, in stone, of cleavage planes, forming a pattern. **13** a red dye made from cochineal or kermes insects. **14** any fast dye, esp. red, crimson or purple. **15** temper, disposition, natural tendency. ~*v.t.* **1** to form into grains, to granulate. **2** to treat so as to bring out the natural grain. **3** to paint or stain in imitation of this. **4** to give a granular surface to. **5** to scrape the hair off (hides) with a grainer. ~*v.i.* to form grains, to become granulated. **against the grain** contrary to inclination, reluctantly, with aversion. **in grain** downright, thorough, absolute, inveterate. **to dye in grain 1** to dye in a fast colour, esp. in kermes. **2** to dye deeply or into the fibre. **with a grain of salt** SALT. **grain alcohol** *n.* alcohol made by the fermentation of grain. **grained** *a.* (*esp. in comb.*, as *fine-grained*). **grain elevator** *n.* a machine that raises grain to a higher floor, esp. one having an endless belt fitted with scoops. **grainer** *n.* **1** a person who paints or stains in imitation of the grain of wood. **2** the brush that a grainer uses. **3** an infusion of pigeon's dung for giving flexibility to skins in tanning. **4** a tanner's knife. **graining** *n.* **1** the act of producing a grain. **2** milling on the edge of a coin. **3** a process in tanning. **grain leather** *n.* leather dressed with the grain side outwards. **grainless** *a.* **grain side** *n.* the side (of leather) from which the hair has been removed. **grains of Paradise** *n.pl.* the seeds of *Aframomum melegueta*, a tropical W African spice, used in stimulants, diuretics and spirituous liquors. **grain whisky** *n.* a whisky made using other cereals in addition to malted barley, as distinct from malt whisky. **grainy** *a.* (*comp.* **grainier**, *superl.* **grainiest**) **1** granular in composition or appearance, esp. in a photographic image or television picture. **2** resembling the grain of wood. **graininess** *n.* [OF, from L *grānum*, rel. to CORN[1]]

graith (grāth) *n.* (*Sc.*) **1** equipment, attire. **2** apparatus, gear. **3** armour. **4** harness. **5** goods, possessions. ~*a.* ready. ~*v.t.* **1** (*North.*) to make ready. **2** to array. [Icel. *greithe*, cogn. with OE *gerǣde*, trappings, gear]

grakle GRACKLE.

grallatorial (gralətaw´riəl) *a.* (*Zool.*) of or relating to long-legged wading birds such as storks, flamingoes etc. [L *grallātor*, one who walks on stilts, from *grallae*, stilts]

gralloch (gral´əkh) *n.* the entrails of a deer. ~*v.t.* to disembowel (a deer). [Gael. *grealach*, viscera]

gram[1] (gram), **gramme** *n.* the standard unit of mass in the metric system, defined as the mass of one cubic centimetre of distilled water at its maximum density weight equalling a thousandth of a kilogram (about 0.04 oz.). **gram-equivalent** *n.* (*Chem.*) the amount of a substance equal to its atomic or molecular weight in grams. [F *gramme*, late L and Gr. *grammā*, a small weight, see -GRAM]

gram[2] (gram) *n.* the chick-pea, *Cicer arietinum*, or other kinds of pulse, used esp. in Asia as food. [perh. from Port. *grão*, L *grānum*, GRAIN]

gram. *abbr.* grammar, grammatical.

-gram (gram) *comb. form* forming compounds with prepositional prefixes, numerals etc., to denote something written, as in *epigram*, *monogram*, *anagram*. [Gr. *gramma -atos*, a letter, something written, from *graphein*, to write]

grama (grah´mə), **grama grass** *n.* any of various species of low pasture grass in the western and south-western US. [Sp. *grama*, L *grāmen*, grass]

†**gramercy** (grəmœ´si) *int.* (*Hist.*) used to express thanks or surprise. ~*n.* an expression of thanks. [OF *grant merci*, great thanks]

graminaceous (graminā´shəs), **gramineous** (-min´-) *a.* of or relating to grass or the tribe of grasses. **gramineae** (grəmin´iē) *n.pl.* the botanical order of endogens, containing the grasses. **graminifolious** (graminifō´liəs) *a.* having leaves like grass. **graminivorous** (graminiv´ərəs) *a.* feeding on grass. [mod. L, from *grāmen -inis*, grass]

grammalogue (gram´əlog) *n.* **1** in shorthand writing, a word represented by a single sign. **2** a logogram, or letter or character standing for a word. [Gr. *gramma*, -GRAM, *logos*, word]

grammar (gram´ə) *n.* **1** a system of principles and rules for speaking and writing a language. **2** a person's manner of applying these rules, or speech or writing considered with regard to its correctness (*His grammar is awful!*). **3** the study of the way a language shows the relationship between words, including its inflectional systems, syntax and phonology. **4** a book containing the principles and rules of grammar. **5** the elements of an art or science, a treatise on these. **grammarian** (-meə´ri-) *n.* **1** an expert in grammar, esp. one who writes about or teaches grammar. **2** a philologist. **grammarless** *a.* **grammar school** *n.* **1** a selective secondary school with a mainly academic curriculum. **2** a school originally established (mostly in the 16th cent.) for teaching Latin. **grammatical** (-mat´ikəl), †**grammatic** *a.* **1** of or relating to grammar. **2** according to the rules of grammar. **grammatical gender** *n.* gender based on the forms of words, not sex. **grammatically** *adv.* **grammaticalness** *n.* **grammatical sense** *n.* the literal sense. **grammatical subject** *n.* the literal as distinct from the logical subject. **grammaticism** (-mat´isizm) *n.* a point in grammar. **grammaticize** (-mat´isīz), **grammaticise** *v.t.* to make grammatical. [OF *gramaire*, L *grammatica*, Gr. *grammatikē -kos*, pertaining to letters, from *gramma*, a letter, from *graphein*, to write]

gramme GRAM[1].

gramophone (gram´əfōn) *n.* **1** (*dated*) a record-player. **2** a device for reproducing sounds stored on disc (invented by E. Berliner, 1887). **3** (*N Am.*) a phonograph. [Gr. *gramma*, a letter, *phonē*, sound (cp. PHONOGRAM)]

grampus (gram´pəs) *n.* (*pl.* **grampuses**) **1** the dolphin *Grampus griseus*, characterized by a blunt snout and pointed black flippers. **2** the killer whale. **3** (*coll.*) a person who breathes heavily and loudly. [A-F *grampais*, OF *grapois*, L *crassum piscem*, nom. *crassus piscis*, fat fish]

Gram stain (gram), **Gram's stain** *n.* (*Biol.*) a technique used to classify bacteria, based on their ability to retain or lose a violet stain. **Gram-positive, Gram-negative** *a.* (of bacteria) retaining or not retaining the first dye of a Gram stain. [H. C. J. *Gram*, Danish physician, 1853–1938]

gran (gran) *n.* (*coll.*) grandmother.

granadilla GRENADILLA.

granary (gran´əri) *n.* (*pl.* **granaries**) **1** a storehouse for grain. **2** a country or district producing and exporting an abundance of corn. **granary bread** *n.* brown bread containing whole grains of wheat. [L *grānārium*]

grand (grand) *a.* **1** great or imposing in size, character or appearance. **2** magnificent, fine, splendid. **3** dignified, lofty, noble. **4** (*coll.*) highly satisfactory, excellent. **5** morally impressive, inspiring (*a grand gesture*). **6** (*Mus.*) great, of full compass, for full orchestra, or with all accessory parts and movements. **7** (*coll.*) distinguished, fashionable or aristocratic (society). **8** pre-eminent in rank etc., chief (*Grand Master*). **9** (*Law*) principal, as opposed to petty, common etc. (*grand larceny*). **10** main, comprehensive, complete, final (*grand total*). **11** in the second degree (of relationships) (*grandmother*, *grandchild*). ~*n.* (*sl.*) 1,000 dollars or pounds. **grandad** (gran´dad), **granddad, grandaddy** *n.* (*coll.*) grandfather. **grand air** *n.* an air of distinction. †**grandam, grandame** *n.* **1** a grandmother. **2** an animal's dam's dam. **3** an old woman. **grand assize, grand inquest** *n.* (*Law*) an assize or inquest of great or chief importance, as opposed to petty or common. **grand-aunt** *n.* GREAT-AUNT (under GREAT). **grandchild** (*pl.* **grandchildren**) (gran´chīld) *n.* the child of a son or daughter. **grand committee** *n.* any of several standing committees of the House of Commons appointed every session to consider bills relating to law or trade. **granddaughter** (gran´daw-) *n.* the daughter of a son or daughter. **grand duke, grand duchess** *n.* a sovereign of lower rank than a king, the ruler in certain European states. **grand ducal** *a.* **grand duchy** *n.* a state, province etc. ruled by a grand duke or duchess. **grandfather** *n.* the father of a parent. **grandfather clock** *n.* an old-fashioned clock worked by weights, in a tall wooden case. **grandfatherly** *a.* **Grand Fleet** *n.* (*Hist.*) the portion of the British Navy employed in British and northern seas. **Grand Inquisitor** *n.* in some countries, the director of a court of inquisition. **grand jury** *n.* a jury whose duty is to enquire if there is sufficient ground for a prisoner to be tried by a petty or ordinary jury. **grand juror** *n.* a member of a grand jury. **grand larceny** *n.* (*Hist.*) theft of anything over a value fixed by statute (in England before 1827, one shilling). **grandly** *adv.* **grandma** (gran´mah), †**grandmama** (-məmah) *n.* (*coll.*) grandmother. **grand master** *n.* **1** in chess or bridge, an outstanding player, winner of many international tournaments, competitions etc. **2** the head of a military order of knighthood, the head of the Freemasons, Good Templars etc. **grandmother** *n.* the mother of a parent. **to teach one's grandmother to suck eggs** to seek presumptuously to advise a more experienced or knowledgeable person. **grandmother clock** *n.* a clock similar to but slightly smaller than a grandfather clock. **grandmotherly** *a.* **1** like a grandmother. **2** fussy. **Grand National** *n.* an annual steeplechase run at Aintree, Liverpool. **grand-nephew** *n.* GREAT-NEPHEW (under GREAT). **grandness** *n.* **grand-niece** *n.* GREAT-NIECE (under GREAT). **grand opera** *n.* an opera with a serious plot that is sung throughout, as opposed to comic opera. **grandpa** (gram´pah, gran´-), †**grandpapa** (-pəpah), **grandpappy** (-papi) *n.* (*coll.*) grandfather. **grandparent** *n.* a grandfather or grandmother. **grand passion** *n.* an overwhelming love affair. **Grand Penitentiary** *n.* a cardinal who presides over a religious court, the penitentiary. **Grand Pensionary** *n.* (*Hist.*) the first minister of Holland and Zeeland in the 17th and 18th cents. **grand piano** *n.* a large piano with horizontal framing. **Grand Remonstrance** *n.* the statement of grievances presented by Parliament to Charles I in 1641. **grandsire** *n.* **1** a grandfather. **2** an animal's sire's sire. **3** a male ancestor. **4** in bell-ringing, a method of change-ringing. **grand slam** *n.* **1** in auction bridge, the winning of 13 tricks by a side. **2** in contract bridge, a fulfilled contract to take all 13 tricks. **3** in tennis, golf etc., the winning of all the major competitions in a season. **4** in baseball, a home run hit when all three bases are occupied by members of the batting team allowing all of them to score. **grandson** *n.* the son of a son or daughter. **grandstand** *n.* the principal stand for spectators on a racecourse etc. ~*v.i.* (*coll.*) to behave in an ostentatious way in order to impress. **grandstand finish** *n.* a close and exciting finish in a sporting contest. **grand total** *n.* the total of all subordinate sums. **grand tour** *n.* **1** a tour through the countries of continental Europe, esp. as formerly undertaken as an essential part of the education of young people of wealthy families. **2** any extended esp. educational sightseeing tour. **grand-uncle** *n.* GREAT-UNCLE (under GREAT). **grand unified theory** *n.* (*Physics*) any of several theories attempting to give a single mathematical formalism to the electromagnetic, strong and weak interactions of elementary particles. **Grand Vizier** *n.* formerly, the prime minister of the Ottoman Empire, or of any eastern monarchy. [L *grandis*, great]

grand cru (grã krü) *n.*, *a.* (a wine) from a top-ranking vineyard. [F, great growth]

grande dame (grã dam´) *n.* (*pl.* **grandes dames** (grã dam´)) **1** an aristocratic lady. **2** a dignified and socially important old lady. [F, great lady]

grandee (grandē´) *n.* **1** a Spanish or Portuguese nobleman of the highest rank. **2** a person of high rank or power. **grandeeship** *n.* [Sp. and Port. *grande*, grand]

grandeur (gran´dyə) *n.* **1** the quality of being grand. **2** greatness, nobility, impressiveness, sublimity, majesty. **3** splendour, magnificence, dignity, splendid or magnificent appearance or effect. [F, from *grand*, GRAND]

Grand Guignol (grã gēnyol´) *n.* a theatrical programme consisting of short sensational blood-curdling pieces. [F, from the name of a theatre in Paris]

grandiflora (grandiflaw´rə) *a.* (of a plant etc.) bearing large flowers. [L *grandis*, great, FLORA]

grandiloquent (grandil´əkwənt) *a.* **1** using lofty or pompous language. **2** bombastic. **grandiloquence** *n.* **grandiloquently** *adv.* [L *grandiloquus* (GRAND, L *-loquus*, speaking, from *loqui*, to speak), assim. to ELOQUENT (under ELOQUENCE)]

grandiose (gran´diōs) *a.* **1** imposing, impressive, producing the effect of grandeur. **2** intended to produce the effect of grandeur, affecting impressiveness, pompous. **3** great in style or scale. **grandiosely** *adv.* **grandioseness** *n.* **grandiosity** (-os´-) *n.* [F, from It. *grandioso*, L *grandis*, GRAND]

grand mal (grã mal´) *n.* a major epileptic attack, as opposed to *petit mal*. [F, great illness]

Grand Marnier® (grã mah´niā) *n.* a French liqueur with an orange flavour, based on brandy. [F]

Grand Prix (grã prē´) *n.* (*pl.* **Grands Prix** (grã prē´)) **1** any of several international motor or motorcycle races taking place annually in locations round the world. **2** any of various other major international competitive events, e.g. in horse racing. [F, great prize]

grand seigneur (grã senyœ´) *n.* (*pl.* **grands seigneurs** (grã senyœ´)) **1** a person of high rank. **2** a noble gentleman. [F, great lord]

grand siècle (grã siek´lə) *n.* the golden age, esp. the 17th cent. in France. [F, great century, age]

Grands Prix GRAND PRIX.

grands seigneurs GRAND SEIGNEUR.

grange (grānj) *n.* **1** a farmhouse with the outbuildings etc., esp. if occupied as a country residence. **2** †a barn. **3** (*N Am.*) a farmers' organization. [OF, from L *grānea*, *grānica*, from L *grānum*, GRAIN]

grangerize (grān´jərīz), **grangerise** *v.i.*, *v.t.* to add illustrations to (a book) that have been taken from other books. **grangerism** *n.* **grangerite** (-īt), **grangerizer** *n.* **grangerization** (-ā´shən) *n.* [James *Granger*, 1716–76, author of a *Biographical History of England* (1769), published with blank leaves for illustration]

graniferous (grənif´ərəs) *a.* bearing grain or seed of grainlike form. **graniform** (gran´ifawm) *a.* **granivorous** (-niv´-) *a.* feeding on grain. [L *grānifer* (as GRAIN)]

granite (gran´it) *n.* **1** a granular, igneous rock consisting of feldspar, quartz and mica, confusedly crystallized. **2** the personal quality of endurance, determination, toughness etc. **granite ware** *n.* an enamelled ironware or hard pottery with speckled surface resembling granite. **granitic** (-nit´-), **granitoid** *a.* resembling granite. **granitification** (-fikā´shən) *n.* formation into granite. **granitiform** (-nit´ifawm) *a.* [It. *granito*, p.p. of *granire*, to speckle, from *grano*, L *grānum*, GRAIN]

grannie GRANNY.

grannom (gran´əm) *n.* **1** a four-winged fly frequenting streams. **2** an imitation of this used in fly-fishing. [etym. uncertain]

granny (gran´i), **grannie** *n.* (*pl.* **grannies**) **1** a grandmother. **2** an old woman. **granny bond** *n.* (*coll.*) a National Savings certificate available to old-age pensioners only. **granny dumping** *n.* (*esp. N Am.*) the practice of abandoning a confused, aged relative outside a hospital etc. because care has become too burdensome or expensive. **granny flat, granny annexe** *n.* a self-contained flat added to or part of a house, designed to accommodate an elderly relative. **granny-knot, granny's bend** *n.* a badly-tied reef-knot having the tie crossed the wrong way. **Granny Smith** *n.* a green-skinned apple suitable for cooking or eating.

granodiorite (granədī´ərīt) *n.* a coarse-grained igneous rock with elements of granite and diorite in its composition.

granolith (gran´əlith) *n.* artificial stone consisting of crushed granite and cement. **granolithic** (-lith´-) *n., a.* [Gr. *lithikos*, from *lithos*, stone]

grant (grahnt) *v.t.* **1** to bestow, concede or give, esp. in answer to a request. **2** to allow as a favour or indulgence. **3** (*Law*) to transfer the title to, to confer or bestow (a privilege, charter etc.). **4** to admit as true, to concede or allow (as premises to an argument). ~†*v.i.* to agree, to consent. ~*n.* **1** a sum of money bestowed or allowed. **2** a gift, an assignment, a formal bestowal. **3** the act of granting. **4** the thing granted. **5** a concession or admission of something as true. **6** (*Law*) a conveyance in writing. **7** the thing conveyed. **to take for granted 1** to assume as admitted basis of an argument. **2** to cease to show appreciation for another's help, work etc. due to familiarity. **grantable** *a.* **grant aid, grant-in-aid** *n.* a central government grant to a local government authority or to an institution. **grant-aid** *v.t.* **grantee** (-tē´) *n.* (*Law*) the person to whom a grant or conveyance is made. **granter** *n.* a person who grants (a wish etc.). **grant-maintained** *a.* (of a school) self-governing and funded by central government as opposed to local authority. **grantor** *n.* (*Law*) a person who makes a conveyance. [OF *graunter, greanter, creanter*, late L *crēantāre* for *crēdentāre*, from *crēdent-*, part. stem. of *crēdere*, to trust, see CREED]

Granth (grŭnt), **Granth Sahib** (sah´hib) *n.* the sacred scriptures of the Sikhs. [Hind., book]

granule (gran´ūl) *n.* **1** a little grain. **2** a small particle. **granular** *a.* composed of or resembling granules. **granularity** (-lar´-) *n.* **granularly** *adv.* **granulate** (-lāt) *v.t.* **1** to form into granules or small particles. **2** to make rough on the surface. ~*v.i.* to collect or be formed into grains. **granulated sugar** *n.* coarse-grained white sugar. **granulation** (-ā´shən) *n.* **1** the act of forming into granules. **2** healing by the formation of little grainlike bodies or projections, in sores or wounds. **3** (*pl.*) the prominences thus formed. **4** a granulated surface. **5** the process of rendering a metal granular, e.g. by pouring it in a melted state on to a rapidly rotating disk. **granulative** (-lətiv) *a.* **granulator** *n.* **granuliferous** (-lif´-) *a.* bearing or full of granules. **granuliform** (-ifawm) *a.* **granulitic** (-lit´-) *a.* **granulize, granulise** *v.t.* [late L *grānulum*, dim. of *grānum*, grain]

granulo- (gran´ūlō) *comb. form* of or relating to granules.

granulocyte (gran´ūləsīt) *n.* a white blood cell that ingests bacteria etc. and that has granular cytoplasm. **granulocytic** (-sit´-) *a.*

granulometric (granūlōmet´rik) *a.* relating to the distribution of grain sizes in sand etc.

grape (grāp) *n.* **1** a berry, the fruit of the vine. **2** grapeshot. **3** (*pl.*) a tumour shaped like a bunch of grapes, on the legs of horses. **the grape** (*coll.*) wine. **grape brandy** *n.* brandy distilled from grapes or wine. **grapefruit** *n.* (*pl.* **grapefruit**) **1** a large round yellow citrus fruit, growing in bunches. **2** the tree, *Citrus paradisi*, which bears this fruit. **grape hyacinth** *n.* a bulbous plant belonging to the genus *Muscari* with usu. blue flowers. **grapery** *n.* (*pl.* **graperies**) a building or place where grapes are grown. **grape scissors** *n.pl.* scissors for thinning out bunches of grapes on the vines, or for dividing bunches at the table. **grapeseed** *n.* the seed of the vine. **grapeseed oil** *n.* the oil pressed from grapeseeds, used in cooking. **grapeshot** *n.* (*Hist.*) small balls for a cannon, loaded in tiers so as to scatter when fired. **grapestone** *n.* a pip or seed of the grape. **grape-sugar** *n.* dextrose. **grapevine** *n.* **1** any vine of the genus *Vitis*, esp. *V. vinifera*. **2** in skating, a figure in which the feet, which are both on the ice simultaneously, cut interlacing lines. **3** (*coll.*) ill-defined unofficial sources of intelligence by which news, rumour etc. is conveyed. **grapey, grapy** *a.* made of or like grapes.

graph[1] (grahf, graf) *n.* a diagram representing a mathematical or chemical relationship and based on two graduated scales. ~*v.t.* to plot on a graph. **graphical** (-ikəl) *a.* **1** in the form of a graph or graphs. **2** indicating by means of diagrams etc. instead of numbers, statistics etc. **3** graphic. **graph paper** *n.* squared paper used for drawing graphs, diagrams etc. [short for GRAPHIC]

graph[2] (grahf, graf) *n.* in linguistics, a visual symbol, usu. a letter or letters that represents a unit of spoken sound etc. [Gr. *graphe*, writing]

-graph (grahf, graf) *comb. form* written, writing, writer, as in *autograph, lithograph, seismograph, tachograph*. **-grapher** (grəfə) *comb. form* a person versed in a particular science, technique etc. [Gr. *-graphos*, from *graphein*, to write]

grapheme (graf´ēm) *n.* **1** a letter or combination of letters representing a unit of spoken sound, e.g. *sh* in *shut*. **2** a feature of a written expression that cannot be explained in terms of smaller units. **graphematic** (-mat´ik), **graphemic** (grəfē´mik) *a.* **graphemically** (-əli) *adv.* [GRAPH[2], -EME]

graphic (graf´ik) *a.* **1** of or relating to the art of writing, delineating, engraving, painting etc. **2** well delineated (*graphic art*). **3** vividly or forcibly descriptive (*graphic detail*). **4** having the faculty of vivid description. **5** (*pl.*) the art of drawing, esp. in mathematics, engineering etc. **6** (*pl.*) the production of designs and images by computer. **7** (*pl.*) designs produced in this way. **-graphic, -graphical** *comb. form* forming adjectives. **graphicacy** *n.* the ability to create, interpret or work with diagrams. **graphically** *adv.* **graphicalness, graphicness** *n.* **graphical user interface** *n.* (*Comput.*) utility software that displays icons and that the user operates with a mouse rather than by typing written words. **graphic arts** *n.pl.* the visual and technical arts, such as drawing, printing, design etc. **graphic artist** *n.* **graphic equalizer** *n.* an electronic device for adjusting the output of various sound frequencies from a tape player, CD or similar source. **graphic formula** *n.* (*Chem.*) a formula representing the relations of the atoms of a molecule to each other. **graphic granite** *n.* a compound of quartz and feldspar, in which the quartz is disposed through the matrix roughly like Hebrew characters. **graphic novel** *n.* an adult novel presented in comic strip format. **graphics pad, graphics tablet** *n.* (*Comput.*) a flat board on which one draws with a stylus, the pattern traced being transferred directly to the screen. [L *graphicus*, Gr. *graphikos*, from *graphein*, to write]

graphite (graf´īt) *n.* a form of carbon used in pencils, as a lubricant and in nuclear reactors, blacklead, plumbago. **graphitic** (-fit´-) *a.* **graphitoid** (-i-) *a.* [G *Graphit*, as GRAPHIC]

grapho- (graf´ō) *comb. form* of, relating to or for writing. [Gr., from *graphē*, writing, from *graphein*, to write]

graphology (grəfol´əji) *n.* **1** the study of handwriting. **2** the art of inferring character from handwriting. **3** graphic formulae or notation. **graphologic** (grafəloj´-), **graphological** *a.* **graphologist** *n.*

graphomania (grafōmā´niə) *n.* a psychological urge to write or scribble (sometimes senseless) words.

-graphy (grəfi) *comb. form* 1 denoting a particular style of writing, drawing etc., as in *lithography*. 2 denoting a particular area of study, writing etc., as in *geography*. [see GRAPHO-]

grapnel (grap´nəl) *n.* 1 an instrument with several flukes or claws for seizing, grasping or lifting. 2 a grappling iron. 3 an anchor with flukes for mooring boats, balloons etc. [ME *grapenel*, dim., from OF *grapin* (F *grappin*), from *grape*, a hook]

grappa (grap´ə) *n.* a coarse Italian brandy distilled from the residue of a wine press. [It., grape stalk]

grapple (grap´əl) *v.i.* 1 to contend or struggle (with or together) in close fight. 2 to get to close quarters (with a task, subject etc.) and strive to accomplish etc. ~*n.* 1 a grappling iron. 2 a grapnel or similar clutching device. 3 a close hold or grip in wrestling or other contest. 4 a close struggle. ~*v.t.* 1 to lay fast hold of, to seize, to clutch. 2 to come to close quarters with. **grappler** *n.* **grappling iron, grappling hook** *n.* an iron instrument with claws or hooks for seizing and holding fast. [MF *grappil*, a ship's grapnel, dim. of *grape*, see GRAPE]

graptolite (grap´təlīt) *n.* an extinct marine invertebrate with a solid axis somewhat resembling a pencil or quill pen, found as a fossil. **graptolitic** (-lit´-) *a.* [Gr. *graptos*, painted, marked, from *graphein*, to write, draw]

grasp (grahsp) *v.t.* 1 to seize and hold fast. 2 to lay hold of and keep possession of, esp. with eagerness or greed. 3 to comprehend with the mind. ~*v.i.* 1 to clutch (at). 2 to attempt to lay hold. ~*n.* 1 a fast grip, clutch or hold. 2 ability to seize and hold. 3 forcible possession, mastery. 4 intellectual comprehension. **to grasp at** 1 to try to seize. 2 to be eager to accept. **to grasp at straws/a straw** STRAW. **to grasp the nettle** NETTLE. **graspable** *a.* **grasper** *n.* **grasping** *a.* greedy. **graspingly** *adv.* **graspingness** *n.* **grasping reflex** *n.* the response by an infant's fingers or toes to grasp an object that touches them. [ME *grapsen*, cogn. with OE *grāphan*, to GROPE]

grass (grahs) *n.* 1 the green-bladed herbage on which cattle, sheep etc. feed. 2 any plant of the family Gramineae, distinguished by simple, sheathing leaves, a stem usu. jointed and tubular, and flowers enclosed in glumes, including the cereals, reeds and bamboos, as well as the plants pop. known as grasses. 3 pasture, grazing. 4 (*coll.*) marijuana. 5 (*sl.*) an informer. 6 (*Mining*) the surface of the ground. 7 (*pl.*) heads or spires of grass flowers gathered. ~*v.t.* 1 to cover with grass or turf. 2 to lay on the grass to bleach. 3 to bring to grass, to land (as a fish). 4 (*sl.*) to fall, to knock down. 5 to discharge. ~*v.i.* (*sl.*) to inform against. **to bring to grass** (*Mining*) to bring up to the surface. **to go out to grass** 1 to go out to pasture. 2 to go out from work, on a holiday, into retirement etc. **to go to grass** to be knocked down. **to let the grass grow under one's feet** to waste time and so lose an opportunity. **to put out to grass** to send out to grass. **to send out to grass** 1 to send out to pasture. 2 to send out from work, on a holiday, into retirement etc. **to send to grass** to knock down. **to turn out to grass** to send out to grass. **grass bird** *n.* 1 any of various Australian warblers, esp. of the genus *Megalurus*. 2 a warbler from S Africa, *Sphenoeacus afer*. **grass box** *n.* a container attached to a lawnmower to catch grass cuttings. **grasscloth** *n.* a fine soft Eastern fabric made from the fibres of the inner bark of *Boehmeria nivea*. **grass court** *n.* a tennis court with a surface of closely mown grass. **grass-cutter** *n.* a mowing machine. **grassed** *a.* (of a golf club) with the face slightly filed back. **grass-green** *a.* verdant, dark green. ~*n.* the colour of grass. †**grass hand** *n.* (*Print.*) a compositor who filled a temporary vacancy. **grassland** *n.* land kept under grass, esp. a large open area of grazing land. **grassless** *a.* destitute of grass. **grasslike** *a.* **grass of Parnassus** *n.* a white-flowered plant, *Parnassia palustris*, belonging to the saxifrage order, growing in moist places. **grass-oil** *n.* a fragrant volatile oil distilled from various Indian grasses. **grass parakeet** *n.* an Australian parakeet, esp. of the genus *Neophema*, commonly found in grassland. **grass-plot** *n.* a plot of ground covered with grass. **grass roots** *n.pl.* 1 the ordinary people. 2 the basic essentials, foundation, origin. **grass skirt** *n.* a skirt made of long grass fastened to a waistband. **grass skis** *n.pl.* short skis with wheels or rollers for skiing on grassy slopes. **grass skiing** *n.* **grass snake** *n.* a harmless Eurasian snake, *Natrix natrix*. **grass tree** *n.* an Australasian tree belonging to the *Xanthorrhaea* or other genera, having spearlike stalks etc., black boy. **grass widow, grass widower** *n.* 1 a person whose husband or wife is away for a lengthy period. 2 (*Hist.*) a divorced woman or man. **grass-widowhood** *n.* **grass-wrack** *n.* a seaweed belonging to the genus *Zostera*, also called *eelgrass*. **grassy** *a.* (*comp.* **grassier**, *superl.* **grassiest**) 1 covered with grass. 2 like grass. 3 green. **grassiness** *n.* [OE *gærs*, *græs* (cp. Dut., Icel., and G *Gras*, cogn. with GREEN, GROW and L *grāmen*, grass)]

grasshopper (grahs´hopə) *n.* a grass-eating, chirping insect of the order Orthoptera, with hind legs formed for leaping. ~*a.* (of a person's mind etc.) constantly moving from subject to subject. **knee-high to a grasshopper** (*coll.*) young, small. **grasshopper-beam** *n.* on a steam engine, a working-beam pivoted at the end instead of the centre, and acting on the principle of parallel motion. **grasshopper warbler** *n.* a small warbler, esp. *Locustella naevia*, whose song resembles the noise made by a grasshopper.

grate[1] (grāt) *n.* 1 a frame of iron bars for holding fuel for a fire. 2 the recess of a fireplace, boiler etc. 3 a grating. **grated** *a.* **grateless** *a.* [late L *grāta*, var. of *crāta*, L *crātes*, hurdle]

grate[2] (grāt) *v.t.* 1 to rub against a rough surface so as to reduce to small particles. 2 to rub, as one thing against another, so as to cause a harsh sound. 3 to grind down. 4 to produce (as a hard, discordant sound) by the collision or friction of rough bodies. 5 to irritate, to vex, to offend (one's nerves). ~*v.i.* 1 to rub (upon) so as to emit a harsh, discordant noise. 2 to have an irritating effect (upon). **grater** *n.* a kitchen utensil with a rough surface for reducing a substance to small particles. **grating**[1] *a.* harsh, discordant, irritating. **gratingly** *adv.* [OF *grater* (F *gratter*), from Gmc. (cp. Dan. *kratte*, G *kratzen*, to scratch)]

grateful (grāt´fəl) *a.* 1 thankful, marked by or indicative of gratitude. 2 pleasing, agreeable, acceptable, refreshing. **gratefully** *adv.* **gratefulness** *n.* [obs. *grate*, agreeable, L *grātus*, -FUL]

graticule (grat´ikūl) *n.* 1 a grid of intersecting lines in a telescope or other optical instrument to aid viewfinding or to measure the scale of the object viewed. 2 a grid of intersecting lines on which a map is drawn. **graticulation** (grətikūlā´shən) *n.* the division of a design or drawing into squares for the purpose of reducing or enlarging it. [F, from *graticuler*, to divide with squares, from *graticule*, L *grāticula*, var. of *crāticula*, dim. of *crātes*, see GRATE[1]]

gratify (grat´ifī) *v.t.* (*3rd pers. sing. pres.* **gratifies**, *pres.p.* **gratifying**, *past, p.p.* **gratified**) 1 to please, to delight. 2 to humour, to satisfy the desire of. 3 to indulge, to give free rein to. 4 to reward. 5 (*coll.*) to give a present, gratuity or bribe to. **gratification** (-fikā´shən) *n.* 1 the act of gratifying. 2 something which gratifies. 3 an enjoyment, a satisfaction. 4 a reward, a recompense, a gratuity. **gratifier** *n.* **gratifying** *a.* **gratifyingly** *adv.* [F *gratifier*, L *grātificārī* (as *grātus*, pleasing, -FY)]

gratin (grat´ī) *n.* 1 in cookery, a light crust on a dish, usu. made by browning breadcrumbs and cheese. 2 a dish prepared in this way with breadcrumbs and grated cheese. [F, from *gratter*, to grate, see GRATE[2]]

gratiné (grä´tēnā) *a.* AU GRATIN.

grating[1] GRATE[2].

grating[2] (grā´ting) *n.* **1** an open framework or lattice of metal bars or wooden slats, parallel or crossed. **2** a series of parallel wires or lines ruled on glass or the like for producing spectra by diffraction. [GRATE[1]]

gratis (grat´is) *adv., a.* for nothing, without charge, free. [L, for *grātiis*, abl. of *grātia*, favour]

gratitude (grat´itūd) *n.* **1** thankfulness, appreciation of kindness. **2** grateful feeling towards a benefactor. [F, from late L *grātitūdinem*, nom. *-tūdo*, from *grātus*, pleasing]

gratuitous (grətū´itəs) *a.* **1** uncalled for, unnecessary. **2** without cause, motive or warrant. **3** granted without claim or charge. **4** free, voluntary. **gratuitously** *adv.* **gratuitousness** *n.* [L *grātuītus*, freely or spontaneously given, as GRATITUDE]

gratuity (grətū´iti) *n.* (*pl.* **gratuities**) **1** a gift, a present voluntarily given in return for a service, a tip. **2** a bonus or bounty paid to service personnel on retirement, discharge etc. [OF *gratuité*, late L *grātuitātem*, nom. *-tas*, cogn. with GRATUITOUS]

gratulatory (grat´ūlātəri) *a.* congratulatory, complimentary, expressing joy. [from L *grātulārī*, to CONGRATULATE]

graunch (grawnch) *v.i.* (*coll.*) to make a crunching, grating or grinding sound. *~v.t.* to cause (something) to make this sound.

graupel (grow´pəl) *n.* soft hail, snow pellets. [G]

gravadlax GRAVLAX.

gravamen (grəvā´men) *n.* (*pl.* **gravamens, gravamina** (-minə)) **1** the most serious part of a charge. **2** (*Law*) the part of an action which weighs most heavily against the defendant. [late L, from *gravāre*, to load, from *gravis*, heavy]

grave[1] (grāv) *n.* **1** a hole in the earth for burying a dead body in. **2** a place of burial, a sepulchre. **3** a monument over this, a tomb. **4** mortality, death, destruction. **5** a place of destruction, extinction, or abandonment. *~v.t.* **1** to form or shape by cutting or carving into a surface, to engrave. **2** to produce (a figure, inscription etc.) by engraving or carving. **3** †to dig or bury. **to have one foot in the grave** FOOT. **to turn in one's grave** (of a dead person) to be (thought to be) shocked or distressed by some modern event. **grave clothes** *n.pl.* wrappings in which the dead are buried. **gravedigger** *n.* **1** a person who digs graves. **2** an insect that buries dead insects etc., to feed its larvae. **graven** *a.* carved or inscribed. **graven image** *n.* an idol. **graver** *n.* **1** an engraver. **2** an engraving tool, a burin. **gravestone** *n.* a stone, usu. inscribed, set over or at the head or foot of a grave. **graveyard** *n.* a burial ground. [OE *grafan*, whence *græf*, a grave (cp. Dut. *graven*, G *Graben*), cogn. with GROOVE]

grave[2] (grāv) *a.* **1** important, serious, momentous. **2** sedate, solemn, dignified. **3** sombre, plain, not gaudy. **4** (*Mus.*) low in pitch. **5** slow in movement. **grave accent** (grahv) *n.* a mark (`) placed over a vowel in some languages to indicate a change in pronunciation from that of the normal letter, originally to a lower pitch. **gravely** *adv.* [F, from L *gravis*, heavy]

grave[3] (grāv) *v.t.* to clean (a ship's bottom) by scraping or burning, and (formerly) by covering it with pitch and tallow. **graving dock** *n.* a dry dock into which vessels are floated for this purpose. [etym. uncertain, perh. from OF *grave* (F *grève*), a strand or shore]

gravel (grav´əl) *n.* **1** small water-worn stones or pebbles mixed with sand etc. **2** fragments of water-worn rock larger than sand, a stratum of this. **3** a bed of such material bearing gold. **4** a disease characterized by the presence of minute concretions in the urine. *~v.t.* (*pres.p.* **gravelling,** (*N Am.*) **graveling,** *past, p.p.* **gravelled,** (*N Am.*) **graveled**) **1** to cover, lay or strew with gravel. **2** to embarrass, to confound, to perplex. **gravelling** *n.* a covering of gravel. **gravelly** *a.* **1** of or like gravel. **2** (of a voice) deep and rough in sound. **gravel pit** *n.* a pit out of which gravel is dug. **gravel-walk** *n.* a path laid with gravel. [OF *gravele*, dim. of *grave*, strand, gravel, cp. GRAVE[3]]

graven GRAVE[1].

†**graveolent** (grəvē´ələnt) *a.* (of plants) smelling strongly and offensively. **graveolence** *n.* [L *graveolens -ntem* (*grave*, adv., from *gravis*, GRAVE[2], *olens -ntem*, pres.p. of *olēre*, to smell)]

Graves (grahv) *n.* a light usu. white wine, pressed in the Graves district. [F]

Graves' disease (grāvz) *n.* a disease characterized by an overactive thyroid gland, resulting in swelling of the neck and protruding eyes. [R. J. *Graves*, Irish physician]

gravid (grav´id) *a.* **1** (*Zool., formal*) pregnant. **2** (*Zool.*) containing a foetus. [L *gravidus*, from *gravis*, GRAVE[2]]

gravimeter (grəvim´itə) *n.* an instrument for determining variations in gravity at different points of the earth's surface. **gravimetric** (-met´-) *a.* **gravimetrically** *adv.* **gravimetry** *n.*

gravitate (grav´itāt) *v.i.* **1** to be powerfully drawn (towards). **2** to be attracted, to tend (towards). **3** to be acted on by gravity. **4** to tend downwards, to sink, to settle down. **gravitation** (-tā´shən) *n.* **1** the act or process of gravitating. **2** the force of gravity. **gravitational** *a.* **gravitational constant** *n.* in Newton's law of gravitation, the factor (*G*) relating force to mass and distance. **gravitational field** *n.* the region around a body in space within which it exerts a gravitational pull. **gravitationally** *adv.* **gravitative** *a.* produced by gravitation. [mod. L *gravitāre*, from *gravis*, GRAVE[2]]

gravity (grav´iti) *n.* **1** (*Physics*) the force causing bodies to tend towards the centre of the earth. **2** the degree of intensity of this force. **3** the similar tendency towards the centre of other bodies. **4** importance, seriousness, enormity. **5** solemnity, sedateness, sobriety, grave demeanour. **6** weight, heaviness. **graviton** (-on) *n.* (*Physics*) a hypothetical quantum of gravitational energy. **gravity feed** *n.* a feed or supply in which the material (oil, grain etc.) runs downhill. [from *gravité*, or directly from L *gravitātem*, nom. *-tas*, from *gravis*, GRAVE[2]]

gravlax (grav´laks), **gravadlax** (grav´ədlaks) *n.* dry-cured salmon marinated in salt, sugar, herbs and spices, originally from Scandinavia. [Swed. *grav*, trench, *lax*, salmon]

gravure (grəvūə´) *n.* **1** (short for) photogravure. **2** an engraving. [F, from *graver*, to ENGRAVE]

gravy (grā´vi) *n.* **1** the fat and juice from meat during and after cooking. **2** a sauce made with this or other ingredients. **3** (*sl.*) money acquired with little effort. **gravy boat** *n.* a boat-shaped bowl or dish for holding gravy. **gravy dish** *n.* **1** a meat-dish with a hollow for gravy. **2** a dish in which gravy is served. **gravy train** *n.* (*sl.*) a job, course of action etc. requiring little effort in return for easy money, benefits etc. [etym. uncertain, perh. OF *grané*, L *grānātus*, full of grains (*grānum*, GRAIN), misread *graué*]

gray GREY.

grayling (grā´ling) *n.* **1** any freshwater fish of the genus *Thymallus* with a large dorsal and an adipose fin. **2** any butterfly of the genus *Hipparchia*, esp. *H. semele*, which has grey or grey-brown wings. [GREY, -LING[1]]

graze[1] (grāz) *v.i.* **1** to eat growing grass. **2** (of land, fields etc.) to supply grass for grazing. **3** to feed, to browse. **4** to move along devouring. **5** (*coll.*) to eat snacks etc. standing up or moving around (as at a party, gathering etc.) rather than sitting down to a meal. *~v.t.* **1** to feed (cattle, etc.) on growing grass. **2** to supply with pasturage. **3** to tend (cattle etc.) at pasture. **4** to pasture. **5** to feed on, to eat. **grazer** *n.* an animal that grazes. **grazing** *n.* **1** the act of pasturing or feeding on grass. **2** a pasture. [OE *grasian*, from *græs*, GRASS]

graze² (grāz) *v.t.* **1** to touch, rub or brush slightly in passing. **2** to scrape or abrade in rubbing past. ~*v.i.* **1** to touch some person or thing lightly in passing. **2** to pass (along, by, past etc.) in light or momentary contact. ~*n.* **1** a slight abrasion. **2** a slight touch or rub in passing. [etym. uncertain, prob. from GRAZE¹]

grazier (grā´ziə) *n.* **1** a person who pastures cattle, and rears and fattens them for market. **2** (*Austral.*) a large-scale cattle or sheep farmer. **graziery** *n.*

grazioso (gratsiō´sō) *a.* (*Mus.*) graceful, elegant. **graziosamente** (-səmen´ti) *adv.* elegantly. [It.]

grease¹ (grēs) *n.* **1** oily or fatty matter of any kind. **2** animal fat in a melted or soft state. **3** inflammation of a horse's heels. **grease cup** *n.* a cup-shaped vessel through which grease is driven into machinery. **grease gun** *n.* a syringe for injecting grease or oil into machinery. **grease monkey** *n.* (*coll.*) a mechanic. **greasepaint** *n.* a paste used for painting the face in theatrical make-up. **greaseproof paper** *n.* paper which will not allow grease to penetrate, used for wrapping food, lining tins etc. **greaser** *n.* **1** someone who or something that greases, a mechanic. **2** (*N Am.*, *offensive*) a Mexican or Spanish-American. **grease trap** *n.* a contrivance fixed in drains for catching grease from sinks etc. [OF *graisse*, L *crassus*, a., fat]

grease² (grēs, -z) *v.t.* **1** to smear, lubricate or soil with grease. **2** to cause to go smoothly. **3** to infect (horses) with grease. **like greased lightning** (*coll.*) very quickly. **to grease someone's palm** (*coll.*) to bribe someone.

greasy (grē´zi, -si) *a.* (*comp.* **greasier**, *superl.* **greasiest**) **1** smeared, saturated or soiled with grease. **2** made of or like grease. **3** unctuous, oily, exuding grease. **4** slimy or slippery with something having the effect of grease. **5** (of horses) affected with the disease called grease. **6** corpulent, fat. **7** gross, unpleasantly unctuous. **8** †indelicate, indecent. **greasily** *adv.* **greasiness** *n.* **greasy pole** *n.* **1** a light-hearted contest between two people astride a horizontal pole smeared with grease in which the aim is to unseat an opponent by hitting them with a pillow etc. **2** (*coll.*) a difficult route to success, with many potential pitfalls. **greasy spoon** *n.* (*coll.*) a cheap restaurant, esp. one selling mainly fried foods.

great (grāt) *a.* (*comp.* **greater**, *superl.* **greatest**) **1** large in bulk, number, amount, extent or degree. **2** very large, big, vast. **3** beyond the ordinary, extreme. **4** important, weighty, momentous, critical. **5** of the highest importance, capital (of letters), pre-eminent, the chief. **6** of exceptional ability, highly gifted, possessing genius. **7** (*coll.*) very skilful, experienced or knowing (at). **8** having lofty moral qualities, magnanimous, noble. **9** grand, majestic, sublime. **10** pregnant. **11** excessive, grievous, burdensome. **12** notorious. **13** denoting a step of ascending or descending consanguinity (*great-grandfather*). ~*n.* **1** (*collect.*) great people (*the great*). **2** †the mass, the bulk, the gross. **a great deal** DEAL¹. **no great shakes** SHAKE. **the great and the good** (*often iron.*) worthy and distinguished people. **the great mass** MASS². **the great unpaid** UNPAID (under UN- (+ O–P WORDS)). **the great unwashed** UNWASHED (under UN- (+ U–W WORDS)). **to be great at** to be skilful at. **to have a great mind** MIND. **great ape** *n.* **1** any of the larger apes, such as the gorilla, chimpanzee etc. **2** (*coll.*) a clumsy or foolish person. **great auk** *n.* a flightless bird, *Alca impennis*, now extinct. **great-aunt** *n.* the sister of a grandfather or grandmother. **Great Bear** *n.* (*Astron.*) the constellation Ursa Major. **Great Charter** *n.* MAGNA CARTA. **great circle** *n.* a circle on a sphere (such as the earth) formed by a plane passing through the centre of the sphere, representing the shortest distance between two points on the sphere. **great coat** *n.* an overcoat. **Great Council** *n.* (*Hist.*) the assembly of tenants-in-chief and important churchmen which corresponded to the Saxon witenagemot, and was superseded by the House of Lords. **great crested grebe** *n.* a large Eurasian diving bird, *Podiceps cristatus*. **Great Dane** *n.* **1** a breed of large short-haired dog. **2** any dog of this breed. **Great Divide** *n.* **1** the boundary between life and death. **2** (*usu.* **great divide**) any boundary between two contrasting regions, cultures etc. **greaten** *v.t.* **1** to make greater, to enlarge. **2** to magnify. ~*v.i.* to become greater, to dilate. **Greater, greater** *a.* (of a city) used to describe the whole city including outer suburbs and adjacent urban areas. **Greater Bairam** *n.* the four-day Muslim festival which falls at the end of the Islamic year. **greater celandine** *n.* a yellow-flowered plant related to the poppy, *Chelidonium majus*. **greatest common measure** *n.* (*Math.*) the highest number that will divide into two or more numbers exactly, the highest common factor. **great go** *n.* (*Hist.*) in some UK universities, the final examinations for degrees. **great-grandchild** *n.* (*pl.* **great-grandchildren**) a grandchild's son or daughter. **great-granddaughter** *n.* a grandchild's daughter. **great-grandfather** *n.* a grandparent's father. **great-grandmother** *n.* a grandparent's mother. **great-grandparent** *n.* a grandparent's parent. **great-grandson** *n.* a grandchild's son. **great gross** *n.* 144 dozen. **great gun** *n.* **1** a cannon. **2** a distinguished person. **to blow great guns** (of wind) to blow tempestuously. **to go great guns** (*coll.*) to make vigorous and successful progress. **great-hearted** *a.* **1** high-spirited, magnanimous. **2** brave. **great house** *n.* the hall, mansion or principal residence in a country place. **great inquest** *n.* the Last Judgement. **Great Lakes** *n.pl.* five lakes on the border between the US and Canada, Lakes Superior, Huron, Michigan, Erie and Ontario. **greatly** *adv.* **1** to a great degree, much, exceedingly. **2** nobly, magnanimously. **3** †grandly, illustriously. **great majority** *n.* (*euphem.*) the dead. **Great Mogul** *n.* any of the emperors of Delhi, 1526–1857, formerly sovereigns of the greater part of Hindustan. **great-nephew** *n.* the grandson of a brother or sister. **greatness** *n.* **great-niece** *n.* the granddaughter of a brother or sister. **great northern diver** *n.* a seabird, *Gavia immer*, of the northern hemisphere. **great organ** *n.* the principal manual of a large organ with its pipes and mechanism. **Great Powers** *n.pl.* the leading states of the world collectively. **Great Russian** *n.* the Russian language. ~*a.* of or relating to the Russian people or their language. **greats** *n.pl.* the course of study in *Literae Humaniores* (Greek and Roman history, literature and philosophy) at Oxford University. **Great Scott, Great Scot** *int.* used to express surprise etc. **Great Seal** *n.* the official seal of the United Kingdom used to seal treaties, writs summoning Parliament, and other state documents of great importance. **Great Spirit** *n.* the deity of N American Indians. **great tit** *n.* a Eurasian bird, *Parus major*, with a black-and-white head and yellow underparts. **great toe** *n.* the big toe. **great-uncle** *n.* the brother of a grandfather or grandmother. **Great War** *n.* the First World War, 1914–18. **great wen** *n.* London. **great year** *n.* a supposed year, estimated by early Greek and Hindu astronomers to occur in about 26,000 years, at the end of which all the heavenly bodies were imagined to return to the same places as they occupied at the Creation. [OE *grēat* (cp. Dut. *groot*, G *gross*)]

☒ **greatful** common misspelling of GRATEFUL.

greave (grēv) *n.* (*usu. pl.*) armour for the legs. [OF *greve*, shin; etym. uncertain]

greaves (grēvz) *n.pl.* fibrous scraps or refuse of melted tallow. [cp. LG *greven*]

grebe (grēb) *n.* a diving bird of the family Podicipedidae with lobed feet and no tail. [F *grèbe*, etym. uncertain]

Grecian (grē´shən) *a.* **1** of or relating to Greece. **2** in the Greek style, esp. in being classically simple in appearance. ~*n.* **1** a Greek. **2** a Greek scholar. **Grecianize, Grecianise** *v.t.*, *v.i.* **Grecian nose** *n.* a straight nose continuing the line of the forehead. [L *Græcia*, Greece, -AN]

Grecism, Grecize GRAECISM.

greco- GRAECO-.

grecque (grek) *n.* 1 (*Archit.*) an ornamental Greek fret. 2 a coffee-strainer or a coffee-pot fitted with a strainer. [F, fem. of *grec*, GREEK]

greed (grēd) *n.* avarice, insatiable desire or covetousness. **greedy** *a.* (*comp.* **greedier,** *superl.* **greediest**) 1 having an inordinate desire for food or drink, voracious, gluttonous. 2 eager to obtain, covetous, desirous (of). **greedily** *adv.* **greediness** *n.* [OE *grædig* (cp. Dut. *gretig*, Dan. *graadig*)]

Greek (grēk) *n.* 1 a native or inhabitant of Greece. 2 a person of Greek descent. 3 the language of Greece. 4 something one does not understand (*It's all Greek to me*). ~*a.* of or relating to Greece or its people. **when Greek meets Greek** when one champion meets another, when equals encounter each other. **Greek Church** *n.* the Orthodox or Eastern Church, including most of the Christians in Greece, Russia, the Balkan States and the Turkish Empire, which separated from Rome in the 9th cent. **Greek cross** *n.* an upright beam with a transverse beam of the same length, the shape of a + sign. **Greek fire** *n.* an artificial combustible used by the Byzantines in their wars with the Saracens for setting hostile ships on fire. **Greek gift** *n.* a gift bestowed with some treacherous motive (in allusion to Virgil's *Aeneid* ii.49). **greeking** *n.* in desktop publishing, advertising etc., the representation of text by roughly drawn characters that have no meaning in themselves. [OE *Grēcas*, *Crēcas*, pl., L *Graecus*, from Gr. *Graikos*, ancient name for the Hellenes]

green (grēn) *a.* 1 having a colour like growing herbage, of the colour in the spectrum between blue and yellow. 2 unripe, immature. 3 undeveloped, inexperienced, easily imposed on. 4 fresh, not withered, not dried, seasoned, cured, dressed or tanned. 5 (of a wound) not healed. 6 pale, sickly. ~*n.* 1 the colour of growing herbage. 2 a colour composed of blue and yellow. 3 a green pigment or dye. 4 a grassy plot or piece of land (*village green*). 5 (*coll.*) a person who is concerned about environmental issues. 6 (*pl.*) fresh leaves or branches of trees. 7 (*pl.*) the young leaves and stems of plants of the cabbage kind, used for food. 8 vigour, youth, prime. ~*v.i.* to become or grow green. ~*v.t.* 1 to make green. 2 to make (urban areas) more attractive by the addition of trees, gardens and parks. 3 (*sl.*) to hoax. **green about the gills** GILL[1]. **green as grass** naive, inexperienced, immature. **green in one's eye** a sign that one is gullible. **greenback** *n.* 1 (*coll.*) a legal-tender banknote first issued by the US in 1862, the back being printed in green. 2 a note issued by any national bank in the US. **green ban** *n.* (*Austral.*) the refusal by trade unionists to work on a construction project that would necessitate the destruction of something of natural, historical or social significance. **green belt** *n.* an area around a city in which building is restricted. **Green Beret** *n.* a commando, esp. in the US. **greenbottle** *n.* any fly of the genus *Lucilia*, esp. *L. sericata* which lays eggs on the skin of sheep. **green card** *n.* 1 an international car insurance document. 2 (*US*) a permit allowing foreign nationals to live and work in the US. **green cheese** *n.* 1 unripened cheese, whey cheese. 2 cheese coloured with sage. **Green Cloth** *n.* a department in the royal household under the Lord Steward, chiefly concerned with food and provisions. **green cloth** *n.* a gaming table. **green-coloured,** (*N Am.*) **green-colored** *a.* pale, sickly. **green crop** *n.* a crop of fodder used in the green state. **green drake** *n.* the common mayfly. **green earth** *n.* a hydrous silicate of potassium, iron and other metals, glauconite. **greenery** *n.* green plants and trees, fresh green growth. **green-eyed** *a.* 1 having green eyes. 2 seeing things with jealous eyes. **the green-eyed monster** jealousy. **green eye** *n.* jealousy. **green fat** *n.* the green gelatinous part of the turtle, much esteemed by gourmets. **green fee,** (*N Am.*) **greens fee** *n.* the fee paid to play a round of golf, esp. by non-members of a golf club. **greenfeed** *n.* (*Austral., New Zeal.*) crop grown to be fed fresh to livestock, green crop. **greenfield** *a.* (of a building site, development area etc.) previously unbuilt, undeveloped. **greenfinch** *n.* a common British songbird, *Carduelis chloris*, with green and gold plumage. **green fingers** *n.pl.* skill at growing plants. **green-fingered** *a.* **greenfly** *n.* (*pl.* **greenfly, greenflies**) any of several small green insects that are destructive to plants, esp. the green aphid. **green goose** *n.* (*pl.* **green geese**) a goose killed under four months old and eaten without stuffing. **greengrocer** *n.* a retailer of vegetables, fruit etc. **greengrocery** *n.* (*pl.* **greengroceries**). **greenhead** *n.* 1 any biting fly of the genus *Chrysops*. 2 an Australian stinging ant, *Chalcoponera metallica*. **greenheart** *n.* 1 a hard-timbered W Indian tree, *Ocotea rodiaei*. 2 the wood of this, used for dock gates, shipbuilding, fishing rods etc. **greenhorn** *n.* an inexperienced or foolish person. **greenhouse** *n.* a glasshouse for cultivating and preserving tender plants. **greenhouse effect** *n.* the increased temperature of the earth caused by its atmosphere acting as the glass of a greenhouse does due to high levels of carbon dioxide, ozone etc. **greenhouse gas** *n.* any of the gases, esp. carbon dioxide, whose emission causes the greenhouse effect. **greenie** (-ni) *n.* (*coll.*) a conservationist. **greening** *n.* 1 the act of becoming green. 2 greenness. 3 the planting of greenery in urban or desert areas. 4 a kind of apple which is green when ripe. **greenish** *a.* **greenishness** *n.* **greenkeeper,** (*N Am.*) **greenskeeper** *n.* the person in charge of a golf course. **green label, green labelling** *n.* ECOLABEL. **green leek** *n.* any of several Australian parrots, green or mainly green in colour. **greenlet** *n.* the vireo, a small American songbird. **green light** *n.* a signal to proceed. **to get the green light** (*coll.*) to get permission to go ahead with a project. **green linnet** *n.* GREENFINCH (under GREEN). **greenly** *adv.* **greenmail** *n.* a business tactic whereby a company buys a large number of shares in another company with the threat of a takeover, thereby forcing the threatened company to repurchase the shares at a higher price. ~*v.i.* to practise this tactic. **greenmailer** *n.* **green man** *n.* 1 the symbol shown at pedestrian road crossings etc. to indicate that it is safe to cross. 2 the image of an old man surrounded by greenery, used at least since medieval times as a symbol of fertility, plenty etc. **green manuring** *n.* the cultivation and ploughing-in of a crop of vetch, rape etc. **green manure** *n.* **greenness** *n.* **Green Paper** *n.* a set of policy proposals issued by the government. **green pepper** *n.* the green unripe fruit of the sweet pepper, *Capsicum annuum*, eaten raw or cooked. **green plover** *n.* a lapwing. **green pound** *n.* an agreed exchange rate for certain agricultural produce within the European Union. **green revolution** *n.* 1 agricultural advances in developing countries based on fertilizers, pesticides etc. 2 the rise in concern for the environment in industrialized countries. **green room** *n.* a room in which actors or musicians wait before or during the performance. **greensand** *n.* two series of beds of sandstone (largely consisting of green earth or glauconite) called the Upper and Lower greensand, in the Cretaceous series. **greenshank** *n.* a large sandpiper, *Tringa nebularia*, breeding in northern Eurasia. **green shoots** *n.pl.* evidence of growth or renewal, used esp. in describing economic recovery. **greensickness** *n.* chlorosis, severe anaemia. **greensick** *a.* **greenskeeper** GREENKEEPER (under GREEN). **green snake** *n.* either of two harmless N American snakes. **green-stick fracture** *n.* a form of fracture to which children are very liable, in which one side of the bone is broken and the other merely bent. **greenstone** *n.* **1** a greenish igneous rock consisting of a crystalline granular mixture of feldspar and hornblende. **2** a fine-grained stone used for putting a very keen edge on surgical instruments. **3** a kind of jade. **greenstuff** *n.* green vegetables for culinary use. **greensward** *n.* (*formal*) turf covered with grass. **green tea** *n.* tea prepared by drying leaves with steam, as opposed to fermenting them. **green thumb** *n.* GREEN FINGERS (under GREEN). †**green vitriol** *n.* crystallized ferrous sulphate, copperas. **greenweed** *n.* DYER'S GREENWEED (under DYE). **greenwood** *n.* a wood in summer. ~*a.* of or relating to a greenwood. **green woodpecker** *n.* the green and yellow European woodpecker *Picus viridis*, with a red crown. **greeny** *a.* (*comp.* **greenier,** *superl.* **greeniest**). **greenyard** *n.* an enclosure, pound etc. for stray animals. [OE *grēne* (cp. Dut. *groen*, G *grün*, cogn. with *grōwan*, to GROW)]

greengage (grēn´gāj) *n.* a green, sweet variety of plum, *Prunus domestica italica.* [Sir William *Gage* who introduced it *c.* 1725]

Greenwich Mean Time (grin´ij, gren´ich) *n.* mean time for the meridian of Greenwich, adopted as the standard time in Great Britain and several other countries. [*Greenwich*, a borough in SE London, where an astronomical observatory was situated, 1646–1958]

greet[1] (grēt) *v.t.* **1** to address with a salutation at meeting. **2** to hail. **3** to receive at meeting or on arrival (with speech, gesture etc.). **4** to receive (*The news was greeted with applause*). ~*v.i.* to exchange greetings. **greeting** *n.* **1** the act of saluting or welcoming. **2** a salutation, a welcome. **greetings card, greeting card** *n.* a decorative card conveying congratulations, good wishes etc. [OE *grētan* (cp. Dut. *groeten*, G *grüssen*)]

greet[2] (grēt) *v.i.* (*chiefly Sc.*) to weep, to cry, to lament. ~*n.* weeping, lamentation. [OE *grætan* (cp. Icel. *grāta*, Goth. *grētan*, to weep) blended with *grēotan*, etym. uncertain]

gregarious (grigeə´riəs) *a.* **1** tending to associate with others, sociable. **2** living or going in flocks, herds etc. **3** growing in clusters or in association with others. **gregariously** *adv.* **gregariousness** *n.* [L *gregārius*, from *grex gregis*, flock, herd]

Gregorian (grigaw´riən) *a.* of or relating to or established or produced by Gregory. **Gregorian calendar** *n.* the reformed calendar introduced by Pope Gregory XIII in 1582. **Gregorian chant** *n.* plainsong, choral music arranged by Gregory I, Pope 590–604. **Gregorian telescope** *n.* the first form of reflecting telescope, invented by James Gregory, 1638–75. [late L *Gregōrius*, Gr. *Grēgorios*, Gregory, -AN]

Gregory powder (greg´əri) *n.* the compound powder of rhubarb, magnesium carbonate and ginger, used as a laxative. [James *Gregory*, 1758–1822, Scottish physician]

greige (grāzh) *a.* of a colour midway between grey and beige.

☒ **greivance** common misspelling of GRIEVANCE.

☒ **greive** common misspelling of GRIEVE.

gremial (grē´miəl) *n.* in the Roman Catholic Church, an episcopal vestment covering the lap, orig. to prevent drops of chrism falling on the vestments during ordination etc. ~†*a.* **1** fully resident in a university, college etc. **2** of or relating to the lap or bosom. [late L *gremiālis*, from *gremium*, the lap]

gremlin (grem´lin) *n.* **1** (*sl.*) an imaginary mischievous sprite, jokingly held to be responsible for problems in mechanical, electronic equipment, systems etc. **2** any source of mischief. [etym. unknown]

grenade (grənād´) *n.* **1** a small explosive shell thrown by hand (also known as a *hand grenade*) or fired from a rifle. **2** a glass shell containing chemicals for extinguishing fires, discovering leakages in drains etc. [F, from Sp. *granada*, orig. POMEGRANATE]

grenadier (grenədiə´) *n.* **1** (*pl.*) (**Grenadiers**) the Grenadier Guards, the first regiment of the royal household infantry. **2** any deep-sea fish of the family Macrouridae, with a large head and body and a long tapering tail. **3** †a foot soldier armed with grenades. **4** †a member of what used to be the first company of every battalion of foot, chosen for long service and approved courage.

grenadilla (grenədil´ə), **granadilla** (gran-) *n.* **1** any of various species of passion flower, *Passiflora.* **2** its edible fruit. [Sp., dim. of *granada*, a pomegranate, L *grānātus*, from *grānum*, GRAIN]

grenadine[1] (gren´ədēn) *n.* a pomegranate syrup. [F *grenadin*, etym. uncertain]

grenadine[2] (gren´ədēn) *n.* a thin, gauzy, silk or woollen fabric for women's dresses etc. [F, perh. from *Granada*, city in Spain]

Gresham's law (gresh´əmz) *n.* the tendency for currency superior in intrinsic worth to be hoarded and to circulate less than currency of lower intrinsic worth. [Sir T. *Gresham*, English financier, d. 1579]

gressorial (gresaw´riəl) *a.* (*Zool.*) adapted for walking, applied to the feet of birds having three toes in front (two of them connected) and one behind. [L *gressor*, walker, from *gradī*, to walk, -IAL]

grew GROW.

grey (grā), (*N Am.*) **gray** *a.* **1** of a colour between white and black, ash-coloured. **2** dull, clouded, dim. **3** dark, dismal, depressing. **4** having grey hair. **5** old, aged, of or relating to old age, ancient. **6** (*coll.*) nondescript, lacking in charisma. ~*n.* **1** a grey colour, grey pigment. **2** grey light, twilight, cold, sunless light. **3** grey clothes. **4** a grey or white animal, esp. a horse. ~*v.t.* to make grey. ~*v.i.* to become grey. **grey area** *n.* an issue or situation that is not clear-cut. **greybeard** *n.* **1** an old man. **2** a large earthen jar for spirit. ~*a.* having a grey beard. **grey-bearded** *a.* **grey-coated** *a.* having a grey coat. **grey eminence** *n.* ÉMINENCE GRISE. **Grey Friar** *n.* a Franciscan friar. **grey goose** *n.* (*pl.* **grey geese**) any grey-coloured goose of the genus *Anser*, esp. the greylag. **grey-haired, grey-headed** *a.* **1** having grey hair. **2** old, time-worn. **3** of long service (in). **greyhead** *n.* a person with grey hair. **greyhen** *n.* the female of the black grouse. **greyish** *a.* **greylag** *n.* the European wild goose, *Anser anser*, the original of the domestic goose. **greyly** *adv.* **grey market** *n.* the unofficial, but not necessarily illegal, selling of products, alongside selling on the official market. **grey matter** *n.* **1** (*coll.*) intellect, intelligence. **2** the greyish tissue of the brain and spinal cord containing the nerve cells. **grey meerkat** *n.* a grey-and-black meerkat, *Suricata suricatta.* **grey mullet** *n.* any food fish of the family Mugilidae, found near coasts. **greyness** *n.* **Greys** *n.pl.* a British cavalry regiment, the 2nd Dragoons (orig. Scottish), so called from all the horses being greys. **grey seal** *n.* the large N Atlantic seal, *Halichoerus grypus.* **grey squirrel** *n.* the squirrel *Sciurus carolinensis*, introduced to Europe from N America in the 19th cent. **greystone** *n.* a compact volcanic grey or greenish rock, composed of feldspar and augite. **greywether** *n.* (*usu. pl.*) detached blocks of sarsen or sandstone occurring chiefly in SW England, often in the form of circles. **grey wolf** *n.* (*pl.* **grey wolves**) the N American timber wolf. [OE *græg* (cp. Dut. *grauw*, Icel. *grār*, G *grau*)]

greyhound (grā´hownd) *n.* a variety of dog characterized by its tall slender form, keen sight, and swiftness. **greyhound racing** *n.* the sport of racing greyhounds on an oval track in pursuit of an electrically-propelled dummy hare. [OE *grīgund* cf. ON *greyhundr* (*grey*, dog, bitch, *hundr*, hound)]

greywacke (grā´wakə), (*N Am.*) **graywacke** *n.* (*Geol.*) a gritstone or conglomerate, usu. consisting of small fragments of quartz, flinty slate etc. cemented together, occurring chiefly in Silurian strata. [G *Grauwacke* (*grau*, GREY, WACKE)]

grice (grīs) *n.* **1** (*esp. Sc.*) a young or sucking pig. **2** (*Her.*) a wild boar. [Icel. *grīss*]

grid (grid) *n.* **1** a grating of parallel bars. **2** a system of intersecting horizontal and vertical lines on a map, plan etc., used to identify locations. **3** a system of principal routes for the transmission of power, supply of gas etc. **4** an electrode placed in a thermionic tube between two other electrodes for the purpose of controlling the flow of current between them. **5** a perforated or ridged plate used in a storage battery. **6** (*Mining*) a griddle. **7** a gridiron for docking ships. **8** in a theatre, a framework above the stage for supporting lights, scenery etc. **9** in motor racing, a system of markings on the track to indicate starting positions. **grid bias** *n.* voltage applied to the grid of a valve. **grid circuit** *n.* the circuit connected between grid and cathode. **grid current** *n.* the current passing between grid and cathode. **grid leak** *n.* a fixed resistance for the leakage of electrons from the grid circuit. **grid potentiometer** *n.* a mechanism to facilitate critical adjustment of grid potential or grid bias. [short for GRIDIRON]

griddle (grid´əl) *n.* **1** a heated metal plate for cooking, usu. commercially, eggs, burgers etc. **2** a circular iron plate for baking cakes. **3** (*Mining*) a wire-bottomed sieve or screen. *~v.t.* (*Mining*) to screen with a griddle. **griddle-cake** *n.* a cake baked on a griddle. [A-F *gridil*, OF *greil* (F *grille*), perh. from L *crātīcula*, dim. of *crātes*, a hurdle]

gride (grīd) *v.i.* **1** to grind, scrape or jar (along, through etc.). **2** to grate. *~*†*v.t.* **1** to pierce, to cut. **2** to cause to grate. *~n.* a grating sound. [metathesis of GIRD[2]]

gridelin (grid´əlin) *n.* a colour of mixed white and red, a grey-violet or purple. [F *gris-de-lin*, flax-grey]

gridiron (grid´ īən) *n.* **1** a grated iron utensil for broiling fish, meat etc. **2** a framework of parallel timbers or iron beams for supporting a ship in dry dock. **3** in a theatre, a framework above the stage for supporting the apparatus for drop-scenes etc. **4** a series of parallel lines for shunting goods trains. **5** wire network between cathode and anode. **6** (*N Am.*) an American football field. **gridiron manoeuvre** *n.* a naval movement in which ships in two parallel columns cross each to the opposite column. **gridiron pendulum** *n.* a compensation pendulum constructed with parallel bars of different metals. [ME *gredire*, as GRIDDLE (assim. to IRON)]

gridlock (grid´lok) *n.* a large-scale traffic jam where a whole area of intersecting roads is at a standstill. **gridlocked** *a.* [perh. from GRID, DEADLOCK (under DEAD)]

grief (grēf) *n.* **1** deep sorrow or mental distress due to loss, disaster or disappointment. **2** regret, sadness. **3** something which causes sorrow or sadness. **4** bodily pain. **to come to grief 1** to meet with disaster. **2** to fail. **3** to come to ruin. **griefless** *a.* **grieflessness** *n.* **grief-stricken** *a.* suffering great sorrow. [OF, from *grever*, to GRIEVE[1]]

grievance (grē´vəns) *n.* **1** a cause for complaint. **2** a wrong, an injustice. **3** something which causes grief. **to air a grievance** to state a cause of complaint. **grievance-monger** *n.* a confirmed grumbler. [OF *grevance*, from GRIEVE[1]]

grieve[1] (grēv) *v.t.* **1** to lament, to sorrow over. **2** to cause pain or sorrow to. **3** to annoy. *~v.i.* to feel grief, to mourn, to sorrow. **grievingly** *adv.* **grievous** *a.* **1** causing grief or pain, hurtful, injurious. **2** hard to be borne, distressing, oppressive. **3** flagrant, atrocious, heinous. **grievous bodily harm** *n.* (*Law*) a serious injury to one person caused by another. **grievously** *adv.* **grievousness** *n.* [OF *grever*, L *gravāre*, to burden, from *gravis*, GRAVE[1]]

Usage note The word *grievous* is sometimes heard pronounced (grē´viəs), as though it were *grievious*, but this is best avoided.

grieve[2] (grēv) *n.* **1** an overseer, steward or bailiff. **2** †a sheriff. [Sc., North., from ONorthum. *græfa*, OE *gerēfa*, REEVE[1]]

griffin (grif´in), **griffon** (-ən), **gryphon** *n.* **1** a fabulous creature, with the body and legs of a lion, the head and wings of an eagle and listening ears, emblematic of strength, agility and watchfulness. **2** (*sl.*) a betting tip. **3** a hint. **4** †a watchful guardian, a duenna. **griffin-like** *a.* [F *griffon*, L *grȳphus*, *gryps*, Gr. *grups*, from *grupos*, hooked, hook-beaked]

griffon[1] (grif´ən) *n.* a variety of dog like a terrier, with short, coarse hair. [F, ident. with *griffon*, GRIFFIN]

griffon[2] (grif´ən), **griffon vulture** *n.* a vulture, *Gyps fulvus*, of Eurasia and N Africa.

griffon[3] GRIFFIN.

grift (grift) *v.i.* (*esp. N Am., sl.*) to swindle. **grifter** *n.* a con-man, a swindler.

grig (grig) *n.* **1** a sand eel or a young eel. **2** a cricket or grasshopper. **3** a lively or merry person. [etym. uncertain (perh. the later senses distinct and onomat. in orig.)]

Grignard reagent (grēn´yah, -yahd) *n.* any of a class of organic magnesium compounds used in the synthesis of organic compounds. [V. *Grignard*, d. 1935, French organic chemist]

grike (grīk), **gryke** *n.* (*Geol.*) a vertical fissure in an exposed limestone surface, formed by the action of rainwater. [N dial., etym. uncertain]

grill[1] (gril) *v.t.* **1** to cook under a grill, broil on a gridiron. **2** (*coll.*) to interrogate severely. **3** to subject to extreme heat. *~n.* **1** a device on a cooker which radiates heat. **2** a gridiron. **3** meat etc. grilled. **griller** *n.* **grill room** *n.* a room in a restaurant where meat etc. is grilled and served. [F *griller*, from *gril*, OF *graïl*, prob. as GRIDDLE]

grill[2] GRILLE.

grillage (gril´ij) *n.* a structure of sleepers and cross-beams forming a foundation in marshy soil for a pier, wharf or the like. [GRILLE, -AGE]

grille (gril), **grill** *n.* **1** an open grating, railing or screen of lattice-work, to enclose or shut a sacred or private place, or to fill an opening in a door etc. **2** a metal grid etc. allowing ventilation (*radiator grille*). **3** in fish culture, a frame with glass tubes for fish eggs during incubation. [F, as GRIDDLE (cp. GRILL[1])]

grilse (grils) *n.* a young salmon when it first returns from the sea, usu. in its second year. [etym. uncertain (perh. a corr. of OF *grisle*, grey)]

grim (grim) *a.* (*comp.* **grimmer**, *superl.* **grimmest**) **1** stern, relentless, severe, unyielding. **2** of a forbidding aspect. **3** savage, cruel. **4** hideous, ghastly. **like grim death** tenaciously. **the Grim Reaper** REAPER (under REAP). **grim-looked** *a.* **grimly** *a.* grim, stern-looking. *~adv.* in a grim manner. **grimness** *n.* [OE (cp. G *grimm*), cogn. with obs. *grame*, angry]

grimace (grimās´, grim´əs) *n.* a distortion of the features, a wry face, expressing disgust, contempt, affectation etc. *~v.i.* to make grimaces. **grimaced** *a.* distorted. **grimacer** *n.* [F, etym. uncertain]

†**grimalkin** (grimal´kin) *n.* **1** an old cat, esp. a she-cat. **2** a jealous or spiteful old woman. [GREY, *Malkin*, dim. of *Maud*, *Matilda*]

grime (grīm) *n.* **1** dirt, smut. **2** dirt deeply engrained. *~v.t.* to dirty, to begrime. **grimy** *a.* (*comp.* **grimier**, *superl.* **grimiest**). **grimily** *adv.* **griminess** *n.* [cp. W Flem. *grijm*, Dan. *grim*, Swed. dial. *grima*, a spot or smut]

Grimm's law (grimz) *n.* a law formulated by Grimm

concerning the modification of consonants in the most important of the Indo-European languages. [Jakob *Grimm*, 1785–1863, German philologist]

grin (grin) *v.i.* (*pres.p.* **grinning,** *past, p.p.* **grinned)** **1** to show the teeth as in laughter, derision or pain. **2** to smile in a malicious, sickly or affected manner. *~v.t.* to express by grinning. *~n.* **1** the act of grinning. **2** a smile with the teeth showing. **to grin and bear it** to endure pain etc. with stoicism. **to grin like a Cheshire cat** CHESHIRE. **grinningly** *adv.* [OE *grennian*, cp. OHG *grînnan*, to mutter (prob. the sense was influenced by the root seen in OHG *grînan*, to distort the face)]

grind (grīnd) *v.t.* (*past, p.p.* **ground** (grownd)) **1** to reduce to powder or fine particles by crushing and friction. **2** to produce (flour etc.) by this process. **3** to wear down, sharpen, smooth or polish by friction, esp. on a grindstone. **4** to grate. **5** to oppress with laws, taxes etc. **6** to work (a mill). **7** to turn the handle of (various appliances). **8** to study laboriously. **9** to teach (a pupil in a subject) laboriously. *~v.i.* **1** to perform the act of grinding. **2** to be rubbed together. **3** to be ground. **4** to grate, to rub gratingly. **5** to toil hard and distastefully. **6** to study laboriously. *~n.* **1** the act or process of grinding. **2** hard and monotonous work (*the daily grind*). **3** hard study, esp. for an examination. **4** a turn at the handle of a machine or instrument. **to grind to a halt** to stop gradually, esp. because of a breakdown, failure etc. **grinder** *n.* **1** a person who or something that grinds. **2** a grinding machine. **3** a molar tooth, a tooth generally. **4** (*sl.*) a crammer. **5** a person who studies hard. **grindery** *n.* (*pl.* **grinderies)** **1** a place where tools etc. are ground. **2** materials and tools for leather-workers. **grindingly** *adv.* **grindstone** *n.* **1** a flat circular stone, used for grinding tools. **2** †a millstone. **to keep one's nose to the grindstone** to stick to one's work. [OE *grindan* (cp. Dut. *grendan*, and perh. L *frendere*, to gnash, grind)]

gringo (gring´gō) *n.* (*pl.* **gringos**) (*esp. N Am., derog.*) an English-speaking foreigner. [Mex. Sp.]

grip[1] (grip) *v.t.* (*pres.p.* **gripping,** *past, p.p.* **gripped)** **1** to seize hold of. **2** to grasp or hold tightly. **3** to hold the attention of. *~v.i.* to take firm hold. *~n.* **1** the act of seizing or holding firmly. **2** a firm grasp, a clutch. **3** the power of grasping. **4** a particular mode of clasping hands, holding a bat, club etc. **5** the part of a weapon, instrument etc. that is held in the hand. **6** a grasping or clutching part of a machine, a clutch. **7** a tool for gripping. **8** (*pl.*) on a film set or in the theatre, a person employed to carry equipment, shift scenery, props etc. **9** (*pl.*) close combat, hand-to-hand conflict. **10** the power of holding the attention. **11** a suitcase, a hold-all, handgrip. **in the grip of** dominated by, affected by, esp. in a negative way. **to come to grips with** to deal with, tackle (a problem etc.). **to get a grip on oneself** to bring oneself under control, to discipline oneself. **to get to grips with** to come to grips with. **gripper** *n.* **gripping** *a.* having the power of holding the attention, absorbing, compelling. **grippy** *a.* **gripsack** *n.* (*N Am.*) a travelling bag, suitcase. [OE *gripa*, a handful, and *gripe*, a clutch, both cogn. with GRIPE]

grip[2] (grip) *n.* a small ditch or furrow. *~*†*v.t.* (*pres.p.* **gripping,** *past, p.p.* **gripped)** to trench, to drain. [OE *grӯpe*, *grēpe*, a trench, a burrow]

gripe (grīp) *v.i.* **1** to complain, esp. in a persistent, peevish way. **2** (of the stomach etc.) to be painful with colic. **3** (of a vessel) to come up too close to the wind against the helm as in sailing close-hauled. **4** †to get money by extortion. *~v.t.* **1** to affect with severe spasmodic gastric or intestinal pain. **2** to seize and hold firmly. **3** to clutch, to pinch. *~n.* **1** a complaint, esp. of a minor nature. **2** the act of complaining. **3** (*pl.*) severe, sporadic pains in the abdomen. **4** a grasp, a firm hold with the hands, a pinch, a squeeze. **5** a series of ropes, dead-eyes and hooks, fastened to ring-bolts in the deck, for securing boats. **6** one of a pair of bands passing round a boat when suspended from the davits. **7** the forefoot of a ship, the forward end of the keel. **8** a clutch, a brake applied to the wheel of a cable car, crane, derrick etc. **9** a mean, niggardly person. **10** clutch, power, control, bondage. **griper** *n.* a person who persistently complains. **gripe water** *n.* a solution given to a baby to ease the pain of colic. **griping** *a.* **1** (of a pain) severe, spasmodic. **2** persistently complaining. **3** grasping, greedy. **gripingly** *adv.* [OE *grīpan* (cp. Dut. *grӯpen*, Goth. *greipan*, G *greipen*)]

gripper, gripping etc. GRIP[1].

Griqua (grē´kwə), **Grikwa** (grik´wə) *n.* (*pl.* **Griqua, Griquas, Grikwa, Grikwas**) a member of a people descended from Dutch settlers and the Nama of southern Africa.

grisaille (grizāl´, -zī´) *n.* a style of painting or staining in grey monochrome, esp. on stained glass, representing solid bodies in relief, such as ornament of cornices etc. [F, from *gris*, grey, OHG *grīs*, etym. unknown]

griseofulvin (griziōful´vin) *n.* an antibiotic used to treat fungal infections. [mod. L, from *Penicillium griseofulvin* (the fungus from which it was obtained), from ML *griseus*, grey, and L *fulvus*, reddish-yellow]

griseous (griz´iəs, gris´-) *a.* (*Zool., Bot.*) bluish-grey. [med. L *griseus*, OHG *grīs*, see GRISAILLE]

grisette (grizet´) *n.* **1** a lively and attractive girl or young woman of the French working classes. **2** †a grey woollen fabric, used for dresses by women of the working classes. [F, from *gris*, see GRISAILLE]

griskin (gris´kin) *n.* the lean part of the loin of a bacon pig. [GRICE, -KIN]

grisly (griz´li) *a.* (*comp.* **grislier,** *superl.* **grisliest)** horrible, terrible, fearful, grim. *~*†*adv.* horribly, terribly, fearfully. **grisliness** *n.* [OE *grīslīc* (*grīs-* in *ā-grīsan*, to shudder, *-līc*, -LY[1])]

grison (griz´ən, grī´zən) *n.* any carnivorous mammal of the genus *Galactis*, like a large weasel with grey fur and a white stripe across the forehead.

grist[1] (grist) *n.* **1** corn to be ground. **2** corn which has been ground. **3** malt for brewing or distilling. **gristmill** *n.* a mill for grinding corn. **grist to the mill** *n.* something advantageous or profitable. [OE *grīst*, cogn. with GRIND]

grist[2] (grist) *n.* a size of rope as denoted by the number and thickness of the strands. [etym. uncertain; perh. conn. with GIRD[1]]

gristle (gris´əl) *n.* cartilage, esp. when found in meat. **gristly** *a.* [OE, etym. uncertain (cp. OFris. and MLG *gristal*)]

grit[1] (grit) *n.* **1** coarse rough particles such as sand or gravel. **2** gritstone, a compact sandstone of sharp siliceous grain. **3** (*coll.*) firmness, determination, pluck. **4** the character of a stone as regards texture or grain. *~v.i.* (*pres.p.* **gritting,** *past, p.p.* **gritted)** **1** to be ground together. **2** to give out a grating sound. **3** to grate. *~v.t.* **1** to grind or grate (as the teeth). **2** to apply salt, grit etc. to (an icy road etc.). **gritstone** *n.* a coarse-grained sandstone. **gritter** *n.* a person who or machine which applies grit etc. to icy roads. **gritty** *a.* (*comp.* **grittier,** *superl.* **grittiest**). **grittily** *adv.* **grittiness** *n.* [OE *grēot* (cp. Icel. *grjōt*, G *Griess*), allied to GROUT[1]]

grit[2] (grit) *a.* (*comp.* **gritter,** *superl.* **grittest**) (*Sc.*) great.

grits (grits) *n.pl.* **1** (*N Am.*) coarsely-ground grain, esp. corn. **2** husked and granulated but unground meal, esp. coarse oatmeal. [OE *gryttan* (cp. MDut. *grutte*, barley, G *Grütze*, also GROATS)]

grizzle[1] (griz´əl) *v.i.* (usu. of a child) to cry, complain etc. in a fretful way. *~n.* **1** a person who grizzles. **2** the act of grizzling. [dial., etym. uncertain]

grizzle[2] (griz´əl) *n.* **1** a grey colour. **2** grey hair. **3** a kind of wig. **4** †a grey-haired man. **5** †roan-coloured.

grizzled *a.* **1** grey, grey-haired. **2** interspersed with grey. **grizzly** *a.* grey, greyish. *~n.* (*pl.* **grizzlies**) a grizzly bear. **grizzly bear** *n.* a N American bear, *Ursus horribilis*, of great size and strength. [OF *grisel*, from *gris*, grey, see GRISAILLE]

gro. *abbr.* gross (144).

groan (grōn) *v.i.* **1** to utter a deep moaning sound, as in pain or grief. **2** to be burdened. **3** to grieve. **4** to suffer hardship. *~v.t.* **1** to utter with groans. **2** to silence or express disapproval of by groans. *~n.* **1** a low moaning sound, as of someone in pain or sorrow. **2** such a sound simulated in derision or disapproval. **to groan inwardly** to feel disappointment etc. without expressing it. **groaner** *n.* **groaningly** *adv.* [OE *grānian* (cp. G *greinen*, to GRIN)]

groat (grōt) *n.* **1** (*Hist.*) a small silver coin, value 4 old pence. **2** (*dated*) any trifling sum. **not worth a groat** worthless. [ME and LG *grote* (cp. MDut. *groot*), cogn. with GREAT]

groats (grōts) *n.pl.* husked oats or wheat. [cp. OE *grūt*, coarse meal, cogn. with GRITS]

Gro-bag® GROW.

grocer (grō´sə) *n.* a dealer in food and miscellaneous household supplies. **grocery** *n.* (*pl.* **groceries**) **1** (*usu. pl.*) the food, provisions etc. sold by a grocer. **2** the grocer's trade or shop. **3** (*N Am.*) a food and liquor shop. [OF *grossier*, one who sells in the gross, med. L *grossārius*, from *grossus*, GROSS]

grockle (grok´əl) *n.* (*coll.*, *often derog.*) a tourist (as described by a resident of the host region). [invented]

grog (grog) *n.* **1** a mixture of rum and cold water, orig. issued in the Royal Navy. **2** (*Austral.*, *coll.*) any esp. cheap alcoholic drink. *~*†*v.t.* (*pres.p.* **grogging**, *past*, *p.p.* **grogged**) **1** to make grog by adding water to (spirits). **2** to extract spirits (from an emptied cask) by pouring in hot water. *~*†*v.i.* to drink grog. **to grog on** (*Austral.*, *coll.*) to take part in a session of heavy drinking. **grog-blossom** *n.* a redness or eruption on the nose or face, due to excessive drinking. †**groggery** *n.* (*pl.* **groggeries**) (*N Am.*) a grog-shop. **groggy** *a.* (*comp.* **groggier**, *superl.* **groggiest**) **1** dazed, unsteady through illness, exhaustion, drink etc. **2** (of a horse) moving uneasily, as with tender feet or forelegs. **groggily** *adv.* **grogginess** *n.* **grog on** *n.* (*Austral.*, *coll.*) a drinking party. **grog-shop** *n.* a place where alcholic liquor is sold. [said to be from a nickname 'Old Grog' of Admiral Vernon, from his wearing a GROGRAM cloak; about 1745 he ordered his sailors to dilute their rum with water]

grogram (grog´rəm) *n.* a coarse cloth of silk and mohair or silk and wool. *~a.* made of grogram. [F *gros grain*, coarse grain]

groin[1] (groin) *n.* **1** the hollow in the human body where the thigh and the trunk unite. **2** (*Archit.*) the edge formed by an intersection of vaults. **3** the fillet or moulding covering this. *~v.t.* **1** to form (a roof) into groins. **2** to furnish with groins. **groin-centring** *n.* the centring of timber during construction. **groined** *a.* **groining** *n.* [earlier *grine*, *grynae*, prob. from OE *grynde*, an abyss or depression, cogn. with G *Grund*, valley, GROUND[1]]

groin[2] GROYNE.

Grolier (grō´liə, -iā) *n.* a book or binding from Grolier's collection. **Grolier design** *n.* in bookbinding, the geometrical or arabesque ornament that characterized Grolier's bindings. **Grolieresque** (-əresk´) *a.* [Jean *Grolier*, 1479–1565, French bibliophile]

grommet (grom´it), **grummet** (grŭm´-) *n.* **1** a ring or eyelet of metal, rubber or plastic designed to strengthen or protect the opening of a hole. **2** (*Med.*) a tube inserted in the ear to allow air to enter the middle ear. **3** (*Naut.*) a ring formed of rope laid round and spliced, used as a rowlock etc. **4** †a wad made of rope, rammed between the ball and the charge in a muzzle-loading gun. [OF *gromette* (F *gourmette*), a curb, from *gourmer*, to curb, etym. unknown]

gromwell (grom´wəl) *n.* any trailing herb of the genus *Lithospermum* of the borage family, esp. *L. officinale*, the hard stony seeds of which were formerly used in medicine. [earlier *gromil*, OF (etym. uncertain)]

groom (groom) *n.* **1** a person in charge of horses or a stable. **2** a bridegroom. **3** any of several officers in the royal household (*groom-in-waiting*). *~v.t.* **1** to tend or care for, esp. in a very careful way. **2** to prepare and train (a person). **grooming** *n.* **1** a person's training, appearance etc. **2** the act of tending, caring for. **groom of the bedchamber** *n.* (*pl.* **grooms of the bedchamber**) an officer of the Royal Household who waits upon a male sovereign. **groom of the stole** *n.* (*pl.* **grooms of the stole**) the first lord of the bedchamber. **groomsman** *n.* (*pl.* **groomsmen**) an unmarried friend of the bridegroom who assists in the arrangements of a wedding. [perh. from OF *gromet*, *groumet* (F *gourmet*, see GOURMET), dim. of *groume*, a boy, a servant]

groove (groov) *n.* **1** a channel, furrow or long hollow, esp. cut with a tool for something to fit into or work in. **2** natural course or events of one's life, a rut. **3** (*dated sl.*) an exalted state (*It's a groove!*). **4** (*dial.*) a shaft or pit. *~v.t.* to cut or form a groove or grooves in. *~v.i.* (*dated sl.*) to be delighted, pleased, satisfied etc. **grooved** *a.* **groover** *n.* **groovy** *a.* (*comp.* **groovier**, *superl.* **grooviest**) **1** of a groove. **2** (*dated*, *sl.*) up to date, excellent, very good, pleasant. **grooviness** *n.* [Dut. *groeve*, cogn. with OE *grafan*, to GRAVE[1]]

grope (grōp) *v.i.* **1** to search (after) something as in the dark, by feeling about with the hands. **2** to feel about with the hands. **3** to feel one's way. **4** to seek blindly. *~v.t.* **1** (*sl.*) to fondle for sexual gratification. **2** to seek out by feeling with the hands in the dark, or as a blind person. **3** †to seek into. **4** †to inquire into. **groper**[1] *n.* **gropingly** *adv.* [OE *grāpian* (cogn. with *grīpan*, to GRIPE)]

groper[1] GROPE.

groper[2] GROUPER.

grosbeak (grōs´bēk) *n.* any of several finches and cardinals having thick bills and bright plumage. [F *grosbec* (GROSS, BEAK)]

groschen (grō´shən) *n.* **1** an Austrian coin worth one-hundredth of a schilling. **2** (*coll.*) a German 10-pfennig piece. **3** an old German silver coin. [G]

groset (grō´zit), **grossart** (-sət) *n.* (*Sc.*) a gooseberry. [earlier *groser*, F *groseille*]

grosgrain (grō´grān) *n.* a heavy ribbed silk, rayon etc. fabric or ribbon. [F, large grain]

gros point (grō pwī´) *n.* a stitch in embroidery covering two horizontal and two vertical threads, as distinct from *petit point*. [F, large point]

gross (grōs) *a.* **1** big, rank. **2** fat, bloated, overfed. **3** flagrant, glaring (*gross misconduct*). **4** total, not net (*gross income*). **5** coarse, indelicate, obscene. **6** lacking fineness, dense, thick, material. **7** dull, unrefined. **8** general, not specific. **9** †plain, palpable. *~n.* **1** 12 dozen. **2** the sum total. **3** the main body, the mass. **by the gross** in gross. **in gross 1** in bulk, wholesale. **2** in a general way, on the whole. **to gross up** to convert (a net figure) to a gross figure (as net income to its pre-tax value). **gross domestic product** *n.* the total annual value of all goods and services produced domestically in a country. **gross-headed** *a.* thick-headed, stupid. **grossly** *adv.* **gross national product** *n.* the total annual value of all goods and services produced in a country, including net investment incomes from foreign nations. **grossness** *n.* **gross ton** *n.* a unit measuring gross internal capacity, equivalent to 100 cu. ft. (2.83 m^3). **gross weight** *n.* the weight of goods with their container included. [OF *gros*, fem. *grosse*, late L *grossus*, thick, etym. uncertain]

grossular (gros´ūlə) *a.* of or belonging to a gooseberry. ~*n.* a Siberian variety of garnet, sometimes called the gooseberry garnet. [mod. L *grossulāria*, from OF *groselle*, gooseberry]

grot (grot) *n.* (*coll.*) rubbish, junk, dirt, filth. ~*a.* dirty. [back-formation from GROTTY]

grotesque (grōtesk´) *a.* **1** distorted, irregular, extravagant or fantastic in appearance. **2** ludicrous through these qualities, absurd, bizarre. ~*n.* **1** a grotesque person or thing. **2** whimsically designed ornamentation consisting of figures of plants and animals of fanciful invention. **3** (*pl.*) whimsical figures or scenery. **4** (*Print.*) a group of related sans serif typefaces. **grotesquely** *adv.* **grotesqueness** *n.* **grotesquerie** (-kəri) *n.* [OF, from It. *grottesca*, antique work (GROTTO, -ESQUE)]

grotto (grot´ō) *n.* (*pl.* **grottoes, grottos**) **1** a small cave, esp. one that is picturesque. **2** an artificial cave or cave-like room decorated with rocks, shells and the like. **grottoed** *a.* **grotto-work** *n.* ornamental rockery etc. in a garden to imitate a grotto. [It. *grotta*, late L *crupta*, L *crypta*, Gr. *kruptē*, CRYPT]

grotty (gro´ti) *a.* (*comp.* **grottier,** *superl.* **grottiest**) **1** (*coll.*) unattractive. **2** (*coll.*) dirty, filthy. **3** inferior, substandard. **grottily** *adv.* **grottiness** *n.* [by shortening and alteration from *grotesque*]

grouch (growch) *v.i.* to grumble, to grouse. ~*n.* **1** a discontented mood. **2** an irritable and complaining person, a grumbler. **grouchy** *a.* [GRUDGE]

ground[1] (grownd) *n.* **1** the surface of the earth as distinct from the air or the heavens. **2** a floor, pavement or other supporting surface. **3** a region or tract of land. **4** land, landed estates. **5** (*pl.*) private enclosed land attached to a house. **6** an area of land designated for a special purpose (*sports ground, showground*). **7** the firm, solid earth. **8** the bottom of the sea. **9** the substratum, the base or foundation. **10** the background, the surface on which a picture or design is laid, the prevailing colour or tone. **11** the reason, motive, origin, cause. **12** (*pl.*) basis, valid reason, pretext, the first or fundamental principles. **13** the extent of an inquiry or survey, area, scope. **14** (*pl.*) sediment, dregs, esp. of coffee. **15** the position occupied by an army. **16** an acid-resisting composition spread over the surface of the metal to be etched. **17** strata containing a mineral lode or coal-seam. **18** in fine art, the first layer of paint, the flat surface from which the figures rise. **19** in sport, the area allotted to a single player or to a side. ~*v.t.* **1** to set or place upon or in the ground. **2** to base or establish (on). **3** to instruct thoroughly (in) the elementary principles of. **4** to run (a ship) aground. **5** to prevent (an aeroplane) from taking to the air. **6** to withhold permission for (a person, esp. a young one) to go out socially, usu. as a punishment. ~*v.i.* (of a vessel) to strike the ground. **above ground** ABOVE. **below ground** BELOW. **down to the ground 1** (*coll.*) thoroughly. **2** (*coll.*) in every respect. **on one's own ground** in familiar and comfortable circumstances, on one's own subject or terms. **on the ground** in practical conditions, the place of operations as distinct from a place where related administrative decisions are made. **to cut the ground from under someone/ someone's feet** (*coll.*) to anticipate someone's arguments or actions etc., and thereby render them meaningless or ineffective. **to fall to the ground 1** to come to naught. **2** to fail. **to gain ground** to advance, to meet with success, to prevail. **to get off the ground** (*coll.*) to make a start, esp. one that is successful. **to give ground** to give way, to retire, to yield. **to have one's/ both feet on the ground** FOOT. **to hold one's ground** HOLD[1]. **to lose ground 1** to be driven back, to give way. **2** to lose advantage or credit. **3** to decline, to fall off. **to run into the ground** RUN. **to run to ground** RUN. **to shift one's ground 1** to change the basis or premises of one's reasoning. **2** to try a different plan. **to stand one's ground** STAND. **groundage** *n.* dues paid for space occupied by a ship on a beach or in port. **ground-angling** *n.* angling without a float, with the weight placed close to the hook. **ground ash** *n.* an ash sapling. **groundbait** *n.* bait thrown into the water to attract fish. ~*v.t.* to put groundbait into in preparation for angling. **ground bass** *n.* a bass passage of a few bars constantly repeated, with a varied melody and harmony. **ground control** *n.* control of landing an aircraft or spacecraft by information transmitted from the ground. **ground cover** *n.* **1** low-growing plants and shrubs, esp. as used to cover a whole area. **2** air support for ground troops. **ground crew** *n.* the people who supervise an aircraft's progress etc. from the ground. **grounded** *a.* **1** that has been grounded. **2** having a solid foundation to one's life, having strong roots. **groundedly** *adv.* **1** in a grounded manner. **2** on good grounds, with good reason. **grounder** *n.* (*esp. N Am.*) in sport, a ball that is hit or passed along the ground. **ground floor** *n.* the storey or rooms level with the exterior ground (in the US called the first floor). **to get in on the ground floor** to become involved with a (potentially) successful enterprise in its early stages. **ground frost** *n.* a ground temperature on grass of 0°C (32°F) or under. **ground game** *n.* running game, as hares, rabbits etc., as distinct from birds. **groundhog** *n.* the American marmot, *Marmota monax*, the woodchuck. **ground ice** *n.* ice formed at the bottom of the water before the surface freezes, also called *anchor ice*. **grounding** *n.* instruction in the elements of a subject. **ground ivy** *n.* a labiate creeping plant, *Glechoma hederacea*, with purple-blue flowers. **groundless** *a.* without foundation, reason or warrant, baseless. **groundlessly** *adv.* **groundlessness** *n.* **groundling** *n.* **1** a creeping plant. **2** a fish that keeps at the bottom, esp. the loach and the gudgeon. **3** (*Hist.*) a spectator who stood on the floor of a theatre; one of the common people. **groundnut** *n.* **1** the peanut. **2** the American wild bean, *Apios tuberosa*, having an edible tuber. **3** the edible tuber of this. **ground oak** *n.* an oak sapling. **ground pine** *n.* a herb, *Ajuga chamaepitys*, with a resinous odour. **ground plan** *n.* **1** a horizontal plan of a building at the ground level. **2** an outline or general plan of anything. **ground rent** *n.* rent paid by a leaseholder to the owner of the land built on. **ground rule** *n.* (*often pl.*) a basic rule of a game, procedure etc. **groundsheet** *n.* a waterproof sheet spread on the ground to give protection against dampness, esp. inside a tent. **groundskeeper** *n.* (*N Am.*) a groundsman. **groundsman** *n.* (*pl.* **groundsmen**) a person employed to look after a sports ground. **ground speed** *n.* the speed of an aircraft relative to the earth's surface. **ground squirrel** *n.* any burrowing rodent resembling a squirrel, esp. one of the genus *Spermophilus*. **ground staff** *n.* **1** the non-flying staff of an airport or airbase. **2** the people employed to maintain a sports ground. **ground state** *n.* (*Physics*) the lowest (or normal) energy state of an atom etc. **ground stroke** *n.* a stroke (as in tennis) made by hitting a ball that has bounced up off the ground. **groundswell** *n.* **1** a long, deep swell or rolling of the sea, caused by a past or distant storm or earthquake. **2** the increasingly apparent presence of an intangible phenomenon such as a public feeling or opinion. **ground tackle** *n.* the ropes and tackle connected with the anchors and mooring apparatus of a vessel. **groundwater** *n.* underground water consisting mainly of surface water that has seeped down. **groundwork** *n.* **1** preliminary work necessary before further work can be undertaken, a foundation or basis. **2** a fundamental principle. **groundy** *a.* full of sediment or dregs. **ground zero** *n.* the point on the ground directly below a nuclear explosion in the air. [OE *grund* (cp. Dut. *grond*, G *Grund*)]

ground[2] (grownd) *a.* having been ground. **ground glass** *n.* glass with the surface ground to make it obscure. **ground-glass** *a.* [p.p. of GRIND]

ground[3] GRIND.

groundsel (grownd´səl) *n.* any plant of the genus *Senecio* with pinnatifid leaves and small yellow flowers, esp. the common weed, *S. vulgaris*, which is used for feeding cage birds. [OE *gund-* or *grundeswylige* (perh. *gund*, pus, *swylige*, from *swelgan*, to SWALLOW[1], lit. pus-swallower, from use in poultices)]

group (groop) *n.* **1** the combination of several figures or objects to form a single mass. **2** a number of persons or things stationed near each other, a cluster, an assemblage. **3** a number of persons or things classed together on account of certain resemblances. **4** a grade in classification not corresponding precisely to any regular division or subdivision. **5** a series of minerals agreeing essentially in chemical composition. **6** a series of rocks or strata deposited about the same period. **7** in the RAF, the highest subdivision of a command. *~v.t.* **1** to form into or place in a group. **2** to put (an object) in close relation or contact (with). **3** to bring together so as to produce a harmonious whole or effect. *~v.i.* to form or fall into a group. **groupage** *n.* **group captain** *n.* a commissioned rank in the RAF equivalent to that of colonel in the army. **group dynamics** *n.* **1** (*sing.*) the field of psychology concerned with the development and interaction of human groups. **2** (*pl.*) the interaction of people in groups. **groupie** *n.* (*sl.*) **1** a (usu. female) fan who travels with and is sexually available to the members of a pop group. **2** an enthusiast, follower etc. of a particular sport or activity. **group practice** *n.* a medical practice run by a partnership of general practitioners. **group therapy** *n.* in psychiatry, the treatment of a group of patients in regular sessions where problems are shared in group discussion. **groupthink** *n.* (*esp. N Am., derog.*) decision-making by groups. **group velocity** *n.* the speed at which the energy of a wave or wave group travels. **groupware** *n.* computer software that enables collective working by several different users. **group work** *n.* work organized to be done by people working in groups (esp. pupils in a class). [F *groupe*, It. *groppo*, prob. from Gmc. (cp. CROP)]

grouper (groo´pə), (*esp. Austral., New Zeal.*) **groper** (grō´) *n.* any marine fish of the family Serranidae, characterized by a heavy body, big head and large mouth. [Port. *garupa*, perh. from S Am. word]

grouse[1] (grows) *n.* (*pl.* **grouse**) **1** any gallinaceous game bird of the family Tetraonidae with a plump body and feet more or less feathered, esp. *Lagopus scoticus*, the red grouse, moor fowl or moor game, *Lyrurus tetrix*, the black game or heath fowl, *Tetrao urogallus*, the capercaillie, wood or great grouse, and *Lagopus mutus*, the ptarmigan or rock grouse. **2** the flesh of these, esp. of the red grouse. *~v.i.* to hunt or shoot grouse. **grousy** *a.* [etym. uncertain]

grouse[2] (grows) *v.i.* to grumble. *~n.* a grievance. **grouser** *n.* [cp. GRUDGE]

grout[1] (growt) *n.* **1** a thin, coarse mortar to run into the joints of masonry and brickwork. **2** a finishing coat of fine stuff for ceilings. **3** coarse meal. **4** (*pl.*) dregs, grounds. *~v.t.* to fill up with grout. **grouting** *n.* **1** the act or process of filling in or finishing with grout. **2** the grout filled in. **3** the injection of cement grout into foundations etc. for strengthening. **grouty** *a.* muddy, dirty. [OE *grūt*, cogn. with GRIT[1]]

grout[2] (growt) *v.t.* (of a pig) to turn (up) with the snout. *~v.i.* to turn up the ground with the snout. [perh. conn. with GROUT[1], or from ROOT[1]]

grove (grōv) *n.* **1** a small wood. **2** a cluster of trees shading an avenue or walk. **3** a wood or forest sacred to a divinity. **groved** *a.* **groveless** *a.* **groves of Academe** *n.pl.* a university environment. **grovy** *a.* [OE *grāf*, etym. unknown]

grovel (grov´əl) *v.i.* (*pres.p.* **grovelling,** (*N Am.*) **groveling,** *past, p.p.* **grovelled,** (*N Am.*) **groveled**) **1** to make an abject apology. **2** to behave in an obsequious manner. **3** to lie or move with the body prostrate on the earth. **groveller** *n.* **grovellingly** *adv.* [erron. formed from obs. adv. *grovelling* (obs. *groof* in *on groof* or *grufe*, face downwards, Icel. *āgrūfu*, -LING[2]]

grow (grō) *v.i.* (*past* **grew** (groo), *p.p.* **grown** (grōn)) **1** to increase in bulk by the assimilation of new matter into the living organism. **2** to develop. **3** to increase in number, degree, power etc. **4** to exist as a living thing. **5** to spring up, to be produced, to arise. **6** to pass into a certain state. **7** to adhere. **8** to become rooted. *~v.t.* to cultivate, to raise by cultivation, to produce. **to grow downward** to diminish. **to grow on one** to increase in one's estimation, to impress one more and more. **to grow on trees** TREE. **to grow out of 1** to issue from. **2** to develop or result from. **3** to become too big or mature for, outgrow. **to grow together** to become closely united, to become incorporated in each other. **to grow up 1** to arrive at manhood or womanhood. **2** to advance to full maturity. **3** to arise, to become prevalent or common. **4** to begin to behave sensibly. **Gro-bag®, growbag, growing bag** *n.* a large plastic bag, containing a growing medium (such as compost) in which seeds can be germinated and plants grown to full size. **growable** *a.* **grower** *n.* **1** a person who or something that grows. **2** a cultivator. **growing** *n., a.* **growingly** *adv.* **growing pains** *n.pl.* **1** neuralgic pains in the limbs felt by young children (not in fact caused by growing). **2** (*coll.*) difficulties experienced in the early stages of a project, business etc. **Growmore** *n.* a standard type of vegetable fertilizer. **grown** *a.* **grown-up** *a.* adult. *~n.* an adult. **growth** (grōth) *n.* **1** the act or process of growing. **2** increase, development, in number, extent, bulk, stature etc. **3** cultivation of vegetable produce. **4** something which grows or is grown. **5** (*Med.*) an abnormal formation, such as a tumour. **6** a product, a result. **growth hormone** *n.* a substance which stimulates growth in plants, animals and human beings. **growth industry** *n.* a commercial activity that is growing rapidly. **growth ring** *n.* a concentric layer of new growth, esp. on a tree, representing a year's development. **growth stock** *n.* stock that is invested in for capital value rather than high income yield. [OE *grōwan* (cp. Dut. *groeijen*, Icel. *grōa*), cogn. with GRASS, GREEN]

growl (growl) *v.i.* **1** to make a deep guttural sound as of anger. **2** to murmur. **3** to grumble. **4** to speak angrily or gruffly. **5** to rumble. *~v.t.* to utter or express by a growl. *~n.* **1** a deep guttural sound like that made by an angry dog. **2** a grumbling. **3** a complaint. **growler** *n.* **1** a person or animal that growls. **2** a grumbler. **3** an American fish, the black bass, of the genus *Micropterus*, from the sound it emits when landed. **4** a small iceberg. **5** (*coll.*) †a four-wheeled horse-drawn cab. **growlery** *n.* (*pl.* **growleries**) a place to grumble in, a person's private room or den. **growlingly** *adv.* [prob. onomat.]

grown, growth GROW.

groyne (groin), **groin** *n.* a structure of piles, concrete etc., acting as a breakwater on a foreshore, and causing sand and shingle to be retained. *~v.t.* to furnish with groynes. [etym. uncertain, perh. from GROIN[1]; but cp. F *groin*, snout, from *grogner*, L *grunnīre*, to grunt]

grub (grŭb) *v.i.* (*pres.p.* **grubbing,** *past, p.p.* **grubbed**) **1** to dig by scratching or tearing up the ground superficially. **2** to search, to rummage. **3** to drudge, to toil, to do manual work. *~v.t.* **1** to dig (up or out). **2** to clear (ground) of roots etc. **3** to find by searching. **4** (*sl.*) to provide with food. *~n.* **1** the larva of an insect, esp. of bees and wasps, with a distinct head but no legs. **2** (*sl.*)

food. **3** a drudge, a hack. **4** in cricket, a ball bowled along the ground. **5** †a short thick-set person, a dwarf. **to grub along** (*coll.*) to plod or drudge along. **to grub up** to dig up by the roots. **grub axe, grub hoe, grub hook, grub tool, grub machine** *n.* implements for grubbing up roots, stumps etc. **grubber** *n.* **1** (*derog.*) a person who is excessively and demeaningly devoted to amassing wealth, votes etc. (*money-grubber*). **2** an instrument for stirring up the soil and clearing out weeds, a grub hoe. **3** a machine to pull up stumps and roots. **4** a grub kick. **grubbing** *a., n.* **grubbing axe, grubbing hoe, grubbing hook, grubbing machine, grubbing tool** *n.* implements for grubbing up roots, stumps etc. **grubby** *a.* (*comp.* **grubbier,** *superl.* **grubbiest**) **1** dirty, grimy. **2** full of grubs. **grubbily** *adv.* **grubbiness** *n.* **grub kick** *n.* (*Austral., coll.*) in football, a kick that sends the ball along the ground. **grub-screw** *n.* a small headless screw. **grubstake** *n.* provisions etc., given to a prospector in return for a share of the finds. ~*v.i.* (*sl.*) to supply food in return for a share of profit. [prob. cogn. with OE *grafan*, to GRAVE[1]]

Grub Street (grŭb) *n.* (*derog.*) the work and milieu of hack writers. ~*a.* of or relating to this kind of writer. [a street (now Milton Street) near Moorfields, London, once much inhabited by literary hacks]

grudge (grŭj) *v.t.* **1** to feel discontent or envy at. **2** to give or take unwillingly or reluctantly. ~*v.i.* **1** †to murmur, to complain, to grumble, to grieve. **2** to be unwilling or reluctant. **3** to be envious, to cherish ill-will. ~*n.* **1** ill-will, a feeling of malice or malevolence. **2** unwillingness, reluctance. **grudger** *n.* **grudging** *a.* **grudgingly** *adv.* [ME *grachen*, OF *groucier* (low L *groussāre*), etym. uncertain]

grue (groo) *v.i.* (*Sc., North.*) **1** to shudder. **2** to feel horror or dread. [cogn. with Dan. *grue*, Dut. *gruwen*, G *grauen*]

gruel (groo´əl) *n.* **1** semi-liquid food made by boiling oatmeal or other meal in water or milk. **2** any food of similar consistency. **to give someone their gruel** (*coll.*) to defeat, punish severely, or kill someone. **gruelling,** (*N Am.*) **grueling** *a.* arduous, demanding, requiring fortitude. ~*n.* severe or harsh treatment or experience. **gruellingly** *adv.* [OF, from late L *grūtellum*, dim. of *grūtum*, from Gmc. (cp. OLG and OE *grūt*, GROATS)]

gruesome (groo´səm) *a.* frightful, horrible, repulsive. **gruesomely** *adv.* **gruesomeness** *n.* [GRUE, -SOME[1]]

gruff (grŭf) *a.* **1** of a rough, surly or harsh aspect. **2** sour, rough, harsh, hoarse-voiced. **gruffish** *a.* **gruffly** *adv.* **gruffness** *n.* [cp. Dut. *grof*, G *grov*]

grumble (grŭm´bəl) *v.i.* **1** to murmur with discontent. **2** to complain in a surly or muttering tone. **3** to growl, to mutter, to rumble. ~*v.t.* to express or utter in a complaining manner. ~*n.* **1** the act of grumbling. **2** a complaint. **3** (*pl.*) a discontented disposition. **grumbler** *n.* **1** a person who grumbles. **2** a discontented person. **grumbling** *a.* causing intermittent discomfort or discontent (*a grumbling appendix*). **grumblingly** *adv.* [etym. uncertain (cp. F *grommeler*, Dut. *grommelen*, freq. of *grommen*, and G *grummelen*)]

grume (groom) *n.* **1** a fluid of a thick, sticky consistency. **2** a clot, as of blood. **grumous** *a.* **1** (of blood) thick, clotted, coagulated. **2** (*Bot.*) divided into little clustered grains. **grumousness** *n.* [OF, from late L *grūmus*, a small heap]

grummet GROMMET.

grumous GRUME.

grumpy (grŭm´pi) *a.* (*comp.* **grumpier,** *superl.* **grumpiest**) surly, cross, peevish, ill-tempered. **grump** *n.* **1** a bad-tempered person. **2** (*pl.*) a fit of bad temper or sulkiness. **grumpily** *adv.* **grumpiness** *n.* **grumpish** *a.* **grumpishly** *adv.* [imit., cp. GRUNT]

Grundyism (grŭn´diizm) *n.* **1** prudishness. **2** a slavish respect for conventions in matters of sex. **Grundified** *a.* **Grundy** *n.* **Grundyish** *a.* **Grundyist** *n.* [Mrs *Grundy*, a character in Morton's *Speed the Plough*, 1798, adopted as the type of conventional respectability]

grunge (grŭnj) *n.* (*orig. N Am., sl.*) a style of rock music, fashion etc. emphasizing discordant, often ugly elements, the music being characterized by raucous, distorted guitar, the fashion by loose-fitting uncoordinated outfits. **grungy** (grŭn´ji) *a.* squalid, seedy. [etym. unknown]

grunion (grŭn´yən) *n.* a small Californian sea fish, *Leuresthes tenuis*, that spawns on shore.

grunt (grŭnt) *v.i.* **1** to make a deep guttural noise like a pig. **2** to grumble, to growl, to complain. ~*v.t.* to express or utter in a grunting manner. ~*n.* a deep guttural sound, as of a hog. **grunter** *n.* **1** a person or animal that grunts. **2** a hog. **3** any of several fishes that grunt when caught. **gruntingly** *adv.* **gruntle** (-təl) *n.* (*Sc.*) **1** a snout, esp. of a pig. **2** a face or muzzle. **gruntling** (-ling) *n.* a young pig or hog. [OE *grunnettan*, freq. of *grunian* (cp. Dan. *grynte*, G *grunzen*, also L *grunnīre*)]

Gruyère (groo´yeə, grē´-) *n.* a Swiss or French cheese made from cows' milk, pale-coloured, firm and full of cavities. [town in Switzerland]

gr. wt. *abbr.* gross weight.

gryke GRIKE.

gryphon GRIFFIN.

grysbok (grīs´bok) *n.* any small, straight-horned antelope of the genus *Raphicerus*, found in Central and S Africa. [Dut. *grijsbok* (*grijs*, GREY, BUCK[1])]

GS *abbr.* **1** General Secretary. **2** General Staff.

gs *abbr.* guineas.

GT *abbr.* *gran turismo*, a touring car, usu. a fast sports car. [It.]

Gt *abbr.* Great.

GTi *abbr.* *gran turismo* injection, a GT car with fuel injection.

GU *abbr.* genitourinary.

guacamole (gwahkəmō´li) *n.* a Mexican dish of mashed avocado, citrus juice and seasonings. [Sp., from S Am. Indian *ahuaca*, avocado, *molli*, sauce]

guacharo (gwah´chərō) *n.* (*pl.* **guacharos**) OIL-BIRD (under OIL).

guaco (gwah´kō) *n.* (*pl.* **guacos**) a tropical American plant, *Mikania guaco*, and others, said to cure snakebites. [Sp., from S Am. Indian language]

☒ **guage** common misspelling of GAUGE.

guaiacum (gwī´əkəm) *n.* **1** any tree of the genus *Guaiacum*, W Indian and tropical N American trees, one of which, *G. officinale*, furnishes *lignum vitae*, while its bark, wood and resin, with those of *G. sanctum*, are used in medicine. **2** the wood of this genus. **3** a drug made from the resin used as a stimulant and nutritional alterative. **guaiac** (-ak) *n.* **1** the wood of the guaiacum. **2** the resin from this, used medicinally. **guaiacol** (-kol) *n.* a phenol obtained by distillation from guaiacum resin and found in wood tar. [Sp. *guayaco*, from Haitian]

guan (gwahn) *n.* a bird similar to a pheasant of the family Cracidae, esp. of the genus *Penelope*, found in the tropical rainforests of S America. [S Am. Indian name]

guanaco (gwənah´kō) *n.* (*pl.* **guanacos**) a wild mammal, *Lama guanicoe*, related to the llama and inhabiting the chain of the Andes to their most southerly point. [S Am. Indian *huanaco*]

guano (gwah´nō) *n.* (*pl.* **guanos**) **1** a valuable manure, composed chiefly of the excrement of seabirds found esp. on islands off S America and in the Pacific. **2** an artificial manure, esp. fish manure or fish guano. ~*v.t.* (*3rd pers. sing. pres.* **guanoes,** *pres.p.* **guanoing,** *past, p.p.* **guanoed**) to manure or fertilize with guano. **guaniferous** (-nif´-) *a.* producing guano. **guanine** (-nēn) *n.* a white amorphous substance found in guano and in the liver and pancreas of animals. [Sp., from Quechua *huanu*, dung]

guarana (gwərah´nə) *n.* the powdered seeds of *Paullinia cupana*, a Brazilian shrub. **guarana bread, guarana paste** *n.* bread or paste made from guarana by the Brazilian Indians for food and medicinal purposes. [S Am. Indian language]

Guarani (gwərah´nē) *n.* (*pl.* **Guarani, Guaranis**) **1** a member of a S American Indian people of Paraguay, S Brazil and Bolivia. **2** the language of this people. **3** (**guarani**) the chief monetary unit of Paraguay. ~*a.* of or relating to the Guarani or their language. [Sp.]

guarantee (garəntē´) *n.* **1** a formal promise to see an agreement, duty or liability fulfilled, esp. with regard to the quality etc. of a bought product. **2** any security, warranty or surety given. **3** the act of guaranteeing. **4** guaranty. **5** the person to whom the guarantee is given. **6** a person who becomes surety for the performance of certain acts by another. ~*v.t.* **1** to undertake responsibility for the fulfilment of a promise, contract etc. **2** to pledge oneself or engage (that). **3** to become guarantor or surety for. **4** to assure the continuance or permanence of. **5** to undertake to secure (to another). **6** to assure or secure against or from risk or damage. **guaranteed** *a.* warranted. **guarantee fund** *n.* a sum subscribed to provide an indemnity in case of loss. **guarantor** *n.* a person who gives a guarantee or guaranty. [GUARANTY (perh. the orig. sense, one who guarantees, from Sp. *garante*, WARRANT)]

guaranty (gar´ənti) *n.* (*pl.* **guaranties**) **1** the act of guaranteeing, esp. an undertaking to be responsible for a debt or obligation of another person. **2** that which guarantees, that on which a guarantee or security is based. [A-F *guarantie*, from OF *garantir*, to WARRANT]

guard (gahd) *v.t.* **1** to watch over, to protect, to defend (from or against). **2** to stand guard over, to prevent the escape of. **3** to secure the safety of. **4** to secure (against criticism etc.). ~*v.i.* to be cautious or take precautions (against). ~*n.* **1** defence, protection, a state of vigilance, watch against attack, surprise etc. **2** a person or body of people on guard. **3** a screen to prevent accident placed in front of a fireplace etc. **4** a contrivance to prevent injury, accident or loss. **5** a sentry, an escort. **6** a person in charge of a railway train or a coach. **7** a state, posture or act of defence, esp. in boxing, fencing, cricket etc. **8** (*N Am.*) a prison warder. **9** the part of a sword-hilt which protects the hand. **10** a watch-chain. **11** an ornamental edging or border. **off guard** off one's guard. **off one's guard** unprepared for attack, surprise etc. **on guard** on one's guard. **on one's guard** prepared for attack, surprise etc. **to guard against** to take precautionary action to try to prevent (something happening). **to mount guard** to go on guard. **to raise one's guard** to become vigilant against danger. **to stand guard** (of a sentry) to keep watch. **guardant** (-dənt) *a.* (*Her.*) (of an animal etc.) presenting the full face to the spectator. **guard cell** *n.* (*Bot.*) either of the two cells that border the pore of a stoma and cause it to open and close. **guarded** *a.* (of a comment, remark etc.) cautious, avoiding commitment. **guardedly** *adv.* **guardedness** *n.* **guarder** *n.* **guardhouse, guardroom** *n.* a house or room for those on guard or for prisoners. **guardless** *a.* **guard rail** *n.* **1** a rail to protect against falling off a deck etc. **2** a rail fixed inside the inner rail at curves, points etc., to prevent derailment. **guard ring** *n.* **1** a ring-shaped electrode used to counteract distortion of electric fields at the edges of other electrodes, esp. in a capacitor. **2** a ring that keeps another ring from slipping off the finger. **Guards** *n.pl.* household troops responsible for ceremonial duties and guarding the head of state. **Guardsman** *n.* (*pl.* **Guardsmen**) an officer or private in the Guards. **guard's van** *n.* a compartment or carriage usu. at the rear of a train for the use of the guard, caboose. [OF *garder*, from Gmc., see WARD]

guardian (gah´diən) *n.* **1** a person who has the charge, care or custody of any person or thing. **2** a protector. **3** the superior of a Franciscan convent. **4** (*Law*) a person who has the charge, custody and supervision of a person not legally capable of managing their own affairs. ~*a.* **1** guarding. **2** acting as a guardian or protector. **guardian angel** *n.* an angel or spirit supposed to be assigned to a person as guardian and protector. **guardian of the poor** *n.* (*Hist.*) any of the members of a board elected by the ratepayers to administer the Poor Laws in a particular parish or district. **guardianship** *n.* **1** the office of a guardian. **2** care, protection, esp. legal tutelage. [OF *gardien*, from *garde*, as GUARD]

guava (gwah´və) *n.* **1** the luscious fruit of various species of the tropical American myrtaceous genus *Psidium*, esp. *P. guajava*. **2** any of the trees on which they grow. [Sp. *guayaba*, from S Am. Indian]

guayule (gwīoo´li) *n.* **1** a silver-leaved Mexican shrub, *Parthenium argentatum*. **2** a rubber substitute derived from the sap of this plant. [S Am. Sp., from Nahautl]

gubbins (gŭb´inz) *n.* **1** (*coll.*) **a** a small device, gadget etc. **b** paraphernalia, odds and ends. **c** something of little value. **2** †a foolish person. [perh. rel. to GOBBET]

gubernatorial (gūbənətaw´riəl) *a.* of or relating to a governor, esp. of a US state. [L *gubernātor*, from *gubernāre*, to steer, to GOVERN]

guddle (gŭd´əl) *v.i.* (*Sc.*) to grope for fish with the hands. ~*v.t.* to catch (fish) by groping and tickling. ~*n.* (*coll.*) a muddle, confusion. [etym. uncertain]

gude (gid) *a., n.* (*Sc.*) GOOD.

gudgeon[1] (gŭj´ən) *n.* **1** a small freshwater fish, *Gobio gobio*, easily caught and largely used as bait. **2** a person who is easily taken in. [F *goujon*, L *gōbiōnem*, nom. *gōbio*, GOBY]

gudgeon[2] (gŭj´ən) *n.* **1** any of several types of pivot at the centre of a wheel, bell mechanism etc. **2** the tubular 'sleeve' part of a hinge into which a pin fits. **3** an eye or socket in which a rudder turns. **gudgeon pin** *n.* a metal pin that links the piston of an internal combustion engine to the little-end bearing of the connecting rod. [OF *gougeon*, perh. as GUDGEON[1]]

guelder rose (gel´də) *n.* a shrubby plant, *Viburnum opulus*, bearing ball-shaped bunches of white flowers, also called the *snowball tree*. [*Guelderland*, province of the Netherlands, formerly a German duchy with Guelders as its capital]

Guelph (gwelf), **Guelf** *n.* (*Hist.*) a member of the popular party in medieval Italy which aimed at national independence, and supported the Pope against the Ghibellines. **Guelphic** *a.* of or belonging to the Guelphs. **Guelphic order** *n.* an order of knighthood instituted for Hanover in 1815. [It. *Guelfo*, MHG *Welf*, name of the Dukes of Bavaria, a distinguished princely family now represented by the ducal house of Brunswick and the royal family of Great Britain, used as a war-cry in 1140 at the battle of Weinsberg against the Emperor Conrad III]

guenon (gənon´) *n.* any of various long-tailed African monkeys of the genus *Cercopithecus*. [F]

guerdon (gœ´dən) *n.* (*poet.*) a reward, a recompense. ~†*v.t.* to reward. [OF, from med. L *widerdōnum*, OHG *widarlōn* (*wider*, against, *lōn*, LOAN, assim. to L *dōnum*, gift)]

guereza (ger´izə) *n.* a black Ethiopian monkey, of the genus *Colobus*, with a fringe of white hair and a bushy tail. [Afr.]

guerilla GUERRILLA.

guerite (gārēt´) *n.* (*Mil.*) a small loopholed tower, usu. on the point of a bastion, to hold a sentinel. [F, GARRET]

Guernsey (gœn´zi) *n.* (*pl.* **Guernseys**) **1** a Guernsey cow. **2** a close-fitting knitted or woven woollen sweater, usu. blue, originally worn by seamen. 3 (*Austral.*) a similar garment, sometimes sleeveless, worn by football players. **to get a guernsey** 1 (*Austral.*) to be selected for a football team. 2 (*Austral.*, *coll.*) to win approval, succeed. **Guernsey cow** *n.* a breed of dairy cattle originating from Guernsey. **Guernsey lily** *n.* a southern African or Japanese nerine, *Nerine sarniensis*, pink in colour, cultivated in Guernsey for the market. [one of the Channel Islands]

guerrilla (gəril´ə), **guerilla** *n.* a member of a small independent fighting band carrying out irregular warfare, esp. against an army, and usu. politically motivated. **guerrilla strike** *n.* a sudden industrial strike. **guerrilla tactics** *n.* the pursuit of a campaign by using sudden unpredictable offensive actions. **guerrilla warfare** *n.* fighting with guerrillas. [Sp., dim. of *guerra*]

guess (ges) *v.t.* 1 to judge or estimate on imperfect grounds, to conjecture. 2 to imagine, to suppose on probable grounds, to divine (one to be). 3 to conjecture rightly. 4 (*N Am.*, *coll.*) to suppose. 5 to believe. *~v.i.* 1 to form a conjecture, to judge at random. 2 to hazard a supposition (that). *~n.* 1 a conjecture. 2 an opinion, estimate or supposition based on imperfect grounds. **anybody's guess** anyone's guess. **anyone's guess** something that is difficult to determine or predict. **I guess** (*N Am.*, *coll.*) I suppose so, I think it likely. **to keep someone guessing** (*coll.*) to make another person remain in a state of uncertainty by withholding information. **guessable** *a.* **guesser** *n.* **guessingly** *adv.* **guess-rope** *n.* GUEST-ROPE. **guesstimate**[1] (-timət), **guestimate** *n.* (*coll.*) an estimate made by guessing. **guesstimate**[2] (-āt), **guestimate** *v.t.* to estimate by guessing. **guesswork** *n.* 1 action or calculation based on guess. 2 procedure by guessing. [ME *gessen* (cogn. with Dut. *gissen*, Dan. *gisse*, prob. from OE *gitan*, to GET[1])]

guest (gest) *n.* 1 a person invited by another to a meal, party etc. or to stay at their house. 2 a person who stays temporarily at a hotel, guest house etc. 3 an entertainer, actor etc. invited to perform in the show, film etc. of other people. 4 a parasitic animal or vegetable. *~v.i.* 1 to appear as a guest on a television or radio show etc. 2 to be a guest. **be my guest** 1 please make use of the facilities available. 2 do whatever you wish. **paying guest** PAY[1]. **guest house** *n.* a boarding house, a small hotel. **guest night** *n.* a night when visitors are entertained by a club etc. **guest of honour** *n.* the most important guest at a function. **guest room, †guest chamber** *n.* a room for the accommodation of a guest. [OE *gœst*, *giest* (cp. Icel. *gestr*, Dut. and G *Gast*, also L *hostis*, foe, orig. stranger)]

guestimate GUESSTIMATE.

guest-rope (gest´rōp), **guess-rope** (ges´-) *n.* 1 a hawser carried by a boat to a distant object for warping a vessel towards this. 2 a rope for making fast a boat to a ship. [etym. unknown]

guff (gŭf) *n.* (*coll.*) nonsense, humbug. [prob. imit.]

guffaw (gəfaw´) *n.* a burst of loud or coarse laughter. *~v.i.* to laugh loud or coarsely. *~v.t.* to say with such a laugh. [imit.]

GUI (goo´i) *abbr.* (*Comput.*) graphical user interface.

guide (gīd) *v.t.* 1 to direct, lead or conduct. 2 to rule, to regulate, to govern. 3 to direct the course of. 4 to be the object, motive or criterion of (action, opinion etc.). *~n.* 1 a person who leads another or points the way. 2 a leader, a conductor, esp. a person employed to conduct a party of tourists etc. 3 an adviser. 4 (**Guide**) a Girl Guide. 5 anything adopted as a sign or mark of direction or criterion of accuracy. 6 a guidebook. 7 a soldier acting as a pivot to regulate an evolution or alignment in a manoeuvre. 8 a ship by which a squadron or fleet regulate their movements. 9 a bar, rod, bearing surface or other device acting as indicator or regulating motion. **guidable** *a.* **†guidage** *n.* (*Law*) pay for safe conduct through a strange country. **guidance** *n.* 1 the act of guiding. 2 direction. 3 government. **guidebook** *n.* a book for tourists, describing places of interest, means of transit etc. **guided missile** *n.* a rocket- or jet-propelled projectile with a warhead, electronically guided to its target by remote control. **guide dog** *n.* a dog trained to lead a blind person. **Guide Guider** *n.* the adult leader of a company of Guides. **guideless** *a.* **guideline** *n.* 1 a statement setting out future policy, courses of action etc. 2 a line drawn as a guide for further drawing or writing. **guide-post** *n.* a finger-post to show the way, a signpost. **guider** *n.* **guide-rope** *n.* GUY[2]. **†guideship** *n.* **guideway** *n.* on a machine, a groove, track or frame directing the motion of a part. **guiding light, guiding star** *n.* a person or thing used as a guide or model. [OF *guider*, earlier *guier*, prob. from Gmc. (cogn. with OE *wītan*, to know, whence *wīsian*, to guide)]

guidon (gī´dən) *n.* 1 the forked or pointed pennant of a troop of light cavalry. 2 the flag of a guild or fraternity. 3 a standard-bearer. [F, from It. *guidone*, prob. from *guida*, GUIDE]

guild (gild) *n.* a society or corporation belonging to the same class, trade or pursuit, combined for mutual aid and protection of interests. **guild-brother** *n.* a fellow-member of a guild. **guildhall** *n.* 1 a hall where a guild or corporation meets. 2 a town hall. 3 the hall where the corporation of a city meets. **guildsman** *n.* (*pl.* **guildsmen**). **Guild Socialism** *n.* a form of socialism under which every industry would be organized as an autonomous guild, holding the factories etc. from the central government, but managing its own affairs through representatives of the workers. **guildswoman** *n.* (*pl.* **guildswomen**). [OE *gild*, a payment from *gildan*, to YIELD (cp. Dut. and G *Geld*, money)]

Usage note See note under GILD.

guilder (gil´də) *n.* 1 the chief monetary unit of the Netherlands. 2 GULDEN. [corr. of Dut. GULDEN]

guile (gīl) *n.* deceit, craft, cunning. **guileful** *a.* **guilefully** *adv.* **guilefulness** *n.* **guileless** *a.* **guilelessly** *adv.* **guilelessness** *n.* [OF, from Gmc., cp. WILE]

guillemot (gil´imot) *n.* any swimming seabird of the genus *Uria* or *Cepphus*, with a short tail and pointed wings. [F, dim. of *Guillaume*, OHG *Wilhelm*, William]

guilloche (gilōsh´) *n.* an ornament of intertwisted or interlaced bands. [F]

guillotine (gil´ətēn) *n.* 1 an apparatus for beheading a person at a stroke, consisting of an upright frame, down which a weighted blade slides in grooves. 2 a machine for cutting thicknesses of paper etc. 3 a surgical instrument for cutting tonsils etc. 4 in Parliament, the curtailment of debate by fixing beforehand the hours when parts of a bill must be voted on. *~v.t.* 1 to execute by guillotine. 2 to cut with a guillotine. [F, after Dr J. I. *Guillotin*, 1738–1814, who introduced it (1792) during the French Revolution]

guilt (gilt) *n.* 1 the state of having committed a crime or offence. 2 criminality, culpability. 3 the feeling that one is to blame. **guilt complex** *n.* a (real or imagined) obsessive feeling of guilt or responsibility. **guiltless** *a.* 1 free from guilt. 2 innocent. 3 having no knowledge (of), inexperienced. 4 clear (of). **guiltlessly** *adv.* **guiltlessness** *n.* **guilty** *a.* (*comp.* **guiltier**, *superl.* **guiltiest**) 1 having committed a crime. 2 criminal, culpable (of). 3 characterized by guilt (*a guilty expression*). **guiltily** *adv.* **guiltiness** *n.* [OE *gylt*]

guimp GIMP[1].

guinea (gin´i) *n.* 1 (*Hist.*) a gold coin formerly current in Great Britain, coined 1663–1813, orig. of gold from Guinea, with the nominal value of 20s. (£1) until 1717, when this was fixed at 21s. 2 a sum of money equivalent to a guinea, £1.05. **Guinea corn** *n.* Indian millet *Sorghum vulgare*, also called *durra*. **guinea fowl,**

guinea hen *n.* a gallinaceous bird of the family Numididae, esp. *Numida meleagris*, something like the turkey, of a dark grey colour with white spots, orig. from Africa. **Guinea grains** *n.pl.* GRAINS OF PARADISE (under GRAIN). †**guinea pepper** *n.* a variety of the pepper plant, *Capsicum frutescens*, from which cayenne pepper is obtained. **guinea pig** *n.* **1** a small domesticated cavy, *Cavia porcellus*, native to Brazil. **2** a person or thing used as a subject for a medical or other experiment. **Guinea worm** *n.* a whitish or dark brown nematode worm, *Dracunculus medinensis*, parasitic in the skin of the human feet etc. [*Guinea*, Port. *Guiné*, country on W coast of Africa]

guipure (gipūə´) *n.* **1** a lace without a ground or mesh, the pattern being held in place by threads. **2** a kind of gimp. [F, from OF *guiper*, from Gmc. (cp. Goth. *weipan*, to crown, G *weifen*, to wind)]

guise (gīz) *n.* **1** external appearance. **2** semblance, pretence. **3** manner, way, fashion. **4** habit, dress. ~*v.t.* to dress up. ~†*v.i.* to go mumming. **guiser** *n.* (*chiefly Sc.*) **1** a person in disguise. **2** a masker, a mummer, esp. at Halloween. [OF, from Gmc. (cp. OHG *wīsa*, WISE[2])]

guitar (gitah´) *n.* a (usu. six-)stringed instrument, somewhat like the violin in shape, but larger, with frets stopped by one hand, the strings being plucked with the fingers of the other or with a plectrum. **guitarfish** *n.* a tropical sea-fish of the family Rhinobatidae, one of the rays, shaped like a guitar. **guitarist** *n.* [Sp. *guitarra*, ult. from Gr. *kithara* (cp. CITTERN, GITTERN)]

guiver (gī´və), **gyver** *n.* (*Austral.*, *New Zeal.*, *sl.*) **1** plausible talk. **2** affected speech or manner.

Gujarati (goojərah´ti), **Gujerati** *n.* **1** the language of Gujarat in W India. **2** a native or inhabitant of Gujarat. ~*a.* of or relating to Gujarat or its language.

gula (gū´lə) *n.* **1** (*Zool.*) a large plate on the underside of the head in some insects. **2** †the throat. **gular** *a.* [L]

gulag (goo´lag) *n.* the system of forced labour camps in the former USSR, esp. as used to correct dissidents. [Rus. *G*lavnoye *U*pravleniye Ispravitelno-Trudovykh *Lag*erei, Main Administration for Corrective Labour Camps, described by Russian writer A. Solzhenitsyn, b. 1918, in *The Gulag Archipelago*]

gulch (gŭlch) *n.* a deep ravine caused by the action of water. ~†*v.t.* to swallow greedily. [etym. uncertain (n. prob. from v., the latter imit.)]

gulden (gul´dən) *n.* **1** any of various gold coins of Germany or the Netherlands. **2** a silver coin, the florin of Austria and Hungary, and the guilder of Holland. [Dut. and G]

gules (gūlz) *n.* (*Her.*) a red colour, represented on an engraved escutcheon by vertical lines. ~*a.* red (*a griffin gules*). †**guly** *a.* [ME and OF *goules* (F *gueules*), med. L *gulæ* ermine, dyed red, etym. uncertain]

gulf (gŭlf) *n.* **1** an inlet of the sea, deeper and narrower proportionately than a bay. **2** a deep hollow, chasm or abyss. **3** a whirlpool, anything that swallows or engulfs. **4** a profound depth, as of the ocean. **5** an impassable difference between two opinions, negotiating positions etc. **6** (*Mining*) a large deposit of ore in a lode. ~†*v.t.* **1** to swallow up, to engulf. **2** to form gulfs in. ~*v.i.* to flow like a gulf or eddy. **the Gulf 1** the Persian Gulf. **2** the Gulf of Mexico. **Gulf Stream** *n.* an ocean current carrying warm water from the Gulf of Mexico across the Atlantic to the British Isles and Scandinavia. **gulfweed** *n.* SARGASSO. **gulfy** *a.* **1** full of whirlpools. **2** deep as a gulf. [F *golfe*, ult. from late Gr. *kolphos*, Gr. *kolpos*]

gull (gŭl) *n.* **1** any long-winged, web-footed bird of the family Laridae, mostly marine in habitat. **2** a simpleton, a dupe. ~*v.t.* **1** to fool, to trick. **2** to impose upon. **gullery** *n.* (*pl.* **gulleries**) a breeding place for gulls. **gullish** *a.* **gull-wing** *a.* **1** (of an aircraft wing) having a short inner section that slopes up from the fuselage and a long horizontal outer section. **2** (of a car door) opening upwards. [prob. Corn. *gullan*, cp. Welsh *gwylan*, Bret. *gwelan*, prob. from root, to wail]

Gullah (gŭl´ə) *n.* **1** a member of a black people living on the coast of S Carolina and neighbouring islands. **2** the Creole language spoken by them. ~*a.* of or relating to the Gullahs or their language. [perh. from *Angola*]

gullet (gŭl´it) *n.* **1** the throat. **2** the oesophagus. **3** a water-channel. [OF, dim. of *gole*, L GULA]

gullible (gŭl´ibəl) *a.* credulous, easily deceived. **gullibility** (-bil´-) *n.* **gullibly** *adv.* [GULL, -IBLE]

gully[1] (gŭl´i), **gulley** *n.* (*pl.* **gullies, gulleys**) **1** a channel or ravine worn by water. **2** a ditch, drain or gutter. **3** a gully-hole. **4** in cricket, (a fielder in) the position between slips and point. ~*v.t.* (*3rd pers. sing. pres.* **gullies**, *pres.p.* **gullying**, *past, p.p.* **gullied**) to wear a channel by water action. **gully-hole** *n.* **1** an opening into a drain at the side of a street. **2** a manhole. [F *goulet*, GULLET]

gully[2] (gŭl´i) *n.* (*pl.* **gullies**) (*Sc.*, *North.*) a large knife. [perh. orig. a knife for the GULLET]

†**gulosity** (gūlos´iti) *n.* gluttony, greediness. [late L *gūlōsitās*, from L *gūlōsus*, gluttonous, from GULA]

gulp (gŭlp) *v.t.* to swallow (down) eagerly or in large draughts. ~*v.i.* to make a noise in swallowing or trying to swallow, to gasp or choke. ~*n.* **1** the act of gulping. **2** a large mouthful. **3** an effort to swallow, a catching or choking in the throat. **to gulp back** to keep back or suppress (esp. tears). **gulper** *n.* **gulpingly** *adv.* **gulpy** *a.* [imit. (cp. Dut. *gulpen*, Norw. *glupa*)]

gum[1] (gŭm) *n.* the fleshy tissue around the roots of the teeth. **gumboil** *n.* a boil or small abscess on the gums. **gummy**[1] *a.* (*comp.* **gummier**, *superl.* **gummiest**) toothless. ~*n.* (*pl.* **gummies**) **1** (*Austral.*) a sheep that has lost its teeth. **2** a small shark, *Mustelus antarcticus*, found off coasts of Tasmania and Victoria. **gummily** *adv.* **gumshield** *n.* a pad worn by boxers etc. to protect the gum and teeth. [OE *gōma* (cp. Icel. *gomr*, G *Gaumen*, palate)]

gum[2] (gŭm) *n.* **1** a sticky substance which exudes from certain trees, and hardens, but is more or less soluble in water, used for sticking things together. **2** a gum tree or other plant or tree exuding this. **3** (*coll.*) chewing gum. ~*v.t.* (*pres.p.* **gumming**, *past, p.p.* **gummed**) **1** to cover or stiffen with gum. **2** to fasten or stick (down, in, together, up) with or as with gum. ~*v.i.* **1** to exude gum. **2** (of an axle etc.) to become sticky or clogged with disuse, dirt etc. **to gum up the works** (*coll.*) to interfere with, spoil or delay something. **gum ammoniac** *n.* an ammoniac gum resin. **gum benjamin** *n.* BENZOIN. **gumboot** *n.* a rubber boot, either of a pair of wellingtons. **gumdrop** *n.* a gelatinous sweet containing gelatine or gum arabic. **gum elastic** *n.* rubber. **gum-juniper** *n.* sandarac. **gummiferous** (-mif´-) *a.* producing gum. **gumming** *n.* a disease in trees bearing stonefruit, characterized by a morbid exudation of gum. **gummous** *a.* of the nature of gum. **gummosity** (-mos´-) *n.* **gummy**[2] *a.* (*comp.* **gummier**, *superl.* **gummiest**) **1** sticky, viscous, adhesive. **2** productive of or covered with gum. **3** (of legs, ankles etc.) puffy, swollen. **gumminess** *n.* **gum nut** *n.* (*Austral.*) the woody seed capsule of the eucalyptus. **gum resin** *n.* a vegetable secretion consisting of a gum and a resin, e.g. gamboge. **gumshoe** *n.* **1** (*esp. N Am.*) a rubber overshoe, either of a pair of galoshes. **2** (*N Am.*, *coll.*) a policeman or detective. ~*v.i.* (*N Am.*, *coll.*) to go about silently, to move or act stealthily. **gum tree** *n.* **1** (*Austral.*) any of several species of eucalyptus. **2** any of various trees. **to be up a gum tree** (*coll.*) to be cornered, in a fix, brought to bay. **gum turpentine** *n.* an oleoresin exuding naturally or from incisions in several coniferous trees, esp. the terebinth. [ME and OF *gomme*, L *gommi*, Gr. *kommi*, prob. from Egypt.]

gumbo (gŭm´bō) *n.* (*pl.* **gumbos**) **1** the okra, *Abelmoschus esculentus.* **2** a soup or a dish made of young capsules of this, seasoned, stewed and served with melted butter. **3** a patois of black and Creole people in Louisiana etc. **4** a silty soil of the W and S US prairies that becomes very sticky when wet. [Am. F, from Bantu]

gumma (gŭm´ə) *n.* (*pl.* **gummas, gummata** (-ətə)) a tumour with gummy contents, usu. due to syphilis. **gummatous** *a.* [mod. L, from GUM²]

gummiferous, gumming etc. GUM².

gummy¹ GUM¹.

gummy² GUM².

gumption (gŭmp´shən) *n.* **1** common sense, practical shrewdness, acuteness, tact, capacity for getting on. **2** †in painting, the art of preparing colours. **gumptious** *a.* [Sc., etym. uncertain]

gun (gŭn) *n.* **1** a tubular weapon from which projectiles are shot by means of gunpowder or other explosive force, a cannon, musket, rifle or carbine. **2** a person with a gun, a member of a shooting party. ~*v.t.* (*pres.p.* **gunning,** *past, p.p.* **gunned**) to accelerate a vehicle rapidly. ~†*v.i.* to use a gun, esp. to go fowling. ~*a.* (*Austral., coll.*) (of a person) skilled, expert. **to beat the gun** to jump the gun. **to give (something) the gun 1** (*coll.*) to increase the speed of (a car etc.). **2** to give (a task etc.) one's maximum effort. **to go great guns** to make vigorous and successful progress. **to gun for 1** (*coll.*) to seek to kill, harm or destroy. **2** to strive to obtain. **to jump the gun 1** to begin (a race) before the starting pistol has fired, to make a false start. **2** (*coll.*) to begin prematurely. **to spike someone's guns** SPIKE¹. **to stick to one's guns** to maintain an opinion in the face of opposition. **gun barrel** *n.* the barrel or tube of a gun. **gunboat** *n.* a warship of small size carrying heavy guns, formerly armed with a single heavy gun. **gunboat diplomacy** *n.* the use of naval or military threats as part of international negotiations. **gun carriage** *n.* the apparatus upon which a cannon is mounted for service. **gun cotton** *n.* a highly explosive substance made by soaking cotton in nitric and sulphuric acids, and then carefully drying. **gun dog** *n.* a dog which is trained to locate and retrieve game. **gunfight** *n.* a fight using firearms. **gunfighter, gunslinger** *n.* (*esp. Hist., N Am.*) a person known for their skill in fighting with firearms. **gunfire** *n.* the repeated firing of guns. **gunflint** *n.* a flint used for firing an old-fashioned flintlock gun. **gunhouse** *n.* a shelter for a gun and the gunners against the enemy's fire. **gunlayer** *n.* the gunner whose duty it is to sight and elevate a gun or howitzer. **gunless** *a.* **gunlock** *n.* the mechanism by which the charge in a gun is exploded. **gunman** *n.* (*pl.* **gunmen**) an armed gangster. **gunmetal** *n.* **1** a dull blue-grey colour. **2** an alloy of copper and tin or zinc from which cannon were formerly cast. **gunner** *n.* **1** in the army, an artillery soldier, esp. a private. **2** in the navy, a warrant officer in charge of ordnance or ordnance stores. **3** in an aircraft crew, a member who operates a gun. **4** a person shooting game. †**to kiss/marry the gunner's daughter** (*Naut., sl.*) to be lashed to a gun and flogged. **gunnery** *n.* **1** the art of managing heavy guns. **2** the science of artillery. **3** the firing of heavy guns. **gunning** *n.* shooting game with a gun. **gunplay** *n.* the use of guns. **gunpoint** *n.* the muzzle of a gun. **at gunpoint** being under the threat of being shot. **gunpowder** *n.* **1** a mixture of saltpetre, carbon and sulphur, reduced to a fine powder, then granulated and dried, used as an explosive. **2** gunpowder tea. **Gunpowder Plot** *n.* a plot to blow up the Houses of Parliament by gunpowder on 5 Nov. 1605, and at one blow destroy King James I, the Lords and the Commons. **gunpowder tea** *n.* a fine kind of green tea, each leaf of which is rolled up. **gunpower** *n.* the strength or number of available guns. **gunroom** *n.* **1** a room on one of the lower decks of a warship to accommodate junior officers. **2** a room where guns are stored. **gun-runner** *n.* a person who smuggles any kind of firearms into a country. **gun-running** *n.* **gunshot** *n.* **1** a shot fired from a gun. **2** the range of a gun (*within gunshot*). **gun-shy** *a.* (of a dog, horse etc.) frightened at the sound of firearms. **gun-site** *n.* a gun emplacement, usu. fortified. **gunslinger** GUNFIGHTER (under GUN). **gunsmith** *n.* a person who makes or repairs small firearms. **gunstock** *n.* the shaped block of wood to which the barrel of a gun is fixed. [short for Icel. *Gunnhildr* (*gunn-*, war, *hildr*, battle), a woman's name given to a war machine]

gunge (gŭnj) *n.* (*coll.*) an unpleasant sticky substance, a dirty encrustation. **gungy** *a.*

gung-ho (gŭnghō´) *a.* **1** uninhibited, over-eager. **2** enthusiastic. [Chin. *gonghe*, to work together, slogan adopted by US marines in World War II]

gunk (gŭngk) *n.* (*coll.*) an unpleasant sticky or slimy substance, gunge. [orig. trademark of a grease solvent]

gunnel¹ (gŭn´əl) *n.* any small eel-like sea fish of the family Pholidae, esp. *Pholis gunnellus*, the butterfish, common on the British coasts and on the N American shores of the Atlantic. [etym. unknown]

gunnel² GUNWALE.

gunnera (gŭn´ərə, gŭniə´rə) *n.* any plant of the genus *Gunnera*, a large-leaved ornamental herb.

gunny (gŭn´i) *n.* (*pl.* **gunnies**) **1** a heavy coarse sackcloth, usu. of jute or hemp, of which bags etc. are made. **2** a bag made of this. [Hind. *gōnī*, Sansk. *gōnī*]

Gunter (gŭn´tə) *n.* **1** a Gunter's scale. **2** on a vessel, an arrangement of topmast and rigging, in which the former slides up and down the lower mast on rings or hoops, so called from the resemblance to a sliding variety of Gunter's scale. **Gunter's chain** *n.* a surveyor's chain, 22 yd. (approx. 20 m) in length. **Gunter's scale** *n.* a flat rule having scales of chords, tangents etc. and logarithmic lines, engraved on it, by which questions in navigation and surveying were solved mechanically. [Edmund *Gunter*, 1581–1626, English mathematician and astronomer]

gunwale (gŭn´əl), **gunnel** *n.* **1** the upper edge of a ship's side next to the bulwarks. **2** a strip forming the upper edge of a boat. [GUN, WALE]

gunyah (gŭn´yah) *n.* an Aboriginal bush hut, usu. built of twigs and bark. [Austral. Abor.]

guppy (gŭp´i) *n.* (*pl.* **guppies**) a small brightly-coloured W Indian freshwater fish, now a common aquarium fish. [R. J. L. *Guppy*, 19th-cent. naturalist who first presented specimens to the British Museum]

gurdwara (guə´dwahrə, gœdwah´rə) *n.* a Sikh temple. [Punjabi, from Sansk. *guru*, teacher]

gurgitation (gœjitā´shən) *n.* the movement of a liquid in a whirlpool or in boiling. [L *gurges, -itis*, a whirlpool]

gurgle (gœ´gəl) *v.i.* **1** to make a bubbling sound, as water poured from a bottle or running over a stony stream bottom. **2** to run or flow with such a sound. ~*v.t.* to utter with such a sound. ~*n.* **1** a gurgling sound. **2** a purling noise. [prob. after It. *gorgogliare*, from L *gurgulio*, the gullet]

Gurkha (gœ´kə) *n.* **1** a member of the dominant ethnic group in Nepal, of Hindu descent, expelled from Rajputana by the Mohammedan invasion. **2** (*pl.*) Indian soldiers of this ethnic group serving in the British army. [Hind.]

gurn (gœn), **girn** *v.i.* **1** to pull a face. **2** to pull as ugly a face as possible, esp. in a competition. [var. of GRIN]

gurnard (gœ´nəd), **gurnet** (gœ´nət) *n.* the popular name of any sea fish of the family Triglidae, characterized by a large angular head, covered with bony plates, and three free pectoral rays. [prob. from F *grognard*, from *grogner*, to grunt]

guru (gur´oo) *n.* **1** a Hindu spiritual teacher or guide. **2**

a mentor with particular expertise or knowledge. [Sansk., heavy, weighty]

gush (gŭsh) *v.i.* **1** to flow or rush out copiously or with violence. **2** to be effusive or affectedly sentimental. **3** to be filled with water, tears etc. **4** to be uttered rapidly and copiously. *~v.t.* to pour (out) rapidly or copiously. *~n.* **1** a violent and copious issue of a fluid. **2** the fluid thus emitted. **3** an outburst. **4** extravagant affectation of sentiment. **gusher** *n.* **1** an oil well that discharges with great force or without requiring pumps. **2** a person who or something that gushes. **gushing** *n., a.* **gushingly** *adv.* **gushy** *a.* (*comp.* **gushier,** *superl.* **gushiest**) effusive or affectedly sentimental. **gushily** *adv.* **gushiness** *n.* [cp. EFris. *gūsen*, LG *gusen*, Icel. *gusa*, G *giessen*]

gusset (gŭs´it) *n.* **1** a small triangular piece of cloth inserted in a dress to enlarge or strengthen some part. **2** an angle-iron or bracket for stiffening an angle in construction work. **3** (*Her.*) a gore. **gusseted** *a.* [OF *gousset*, a flexible piece of armour filling up a joint, dim. of *gousse*, a nutshell]

gussy (gŭs´i) *v.t.* (*3rd pers. sing. pres.* **gussies,** *pres.p.* **gussying,** *past, p.p.* **gussied**) (*coll.*) to smarten (up), to dress (up) (*She's gussied up*). [poss. from dim. of name *Augustus*]

gust (gŭst) *n.* **1** a short but violent rush of wind, a squall. **2** an outburst of passion. **gusty** *a.* **gustily** *adv.* [Icel. *gustr*, cogn. with GUSH]

gustation (gŭstā´shən) *n.* **1** the act of tasting. **2** the sense of taste. **gustative** (gŭs´tətiv) *a.* **gustatory** *a.* of or relating to gustation. **gustatory nerve** *n.* the lingual nerve upon which taste depends. [L *gustātio*, tasting, from *gustus*, taste]

gusto (gŭs´tō) *n.* **1** zest, enjoyment, pleasure (*to eat with gusto*). **2** flavour, relish. [see GUSTATION]

gut (gŭt) *n.* **1** the intestinal canal. **2** (*pl.*) the intestines. **3** an intestine or a part of the alimentary canal. **4** the belly or the stomach as a symbol of gluttony. **5** (*pl.*) the core or essential part of something. **6** (*pl., coll.*) stamina, courage, persistence. **7** catgut, the prepared intestines of animals used for the strings of musical instruments. **8** fibre drawn from a silkworm before it spins its cocoon, used for fishing lines. **9** a narrow passage of water, esp. a sound or strait. *~v.t.* (*pres.p.* **gutting,** *past, p.p.* **gutted**) **1** to eviscerate, to draw the entrails out of. **2** (of fire etc.) to plunder, to remove or destroy the contents of. *~a.* of or relating to instinctive feelings, intuition (*a gut feeling*). **to hate someone's guts** (*coll.*) to dislike someone intensely. **to have guts** (*coll.*) to be courageous. **to work/ slog one's guts out** (*coll.*) to work extremely hard. **gutful** *n.* (*Austral., coll.*) more than enough of an unacceptable situation etc. **gutless** *a.* cowardly. **gutlessly** *adv.* **gutlessness** *n.* **gut-rot** *n.* (*sl.*) **1** a stomach upset. **2** cheap, harmful liquor, rot-gut. **guts** *n.* (*sl.*) a glutton. *~v.i.* to gormandize. **gut-scraper** *n.* (*coll.*) a fiddler. **gutser** *n.* (*sl.*) a glutton. **to come a gutser 1** (*Austral., coll.*) to fall over. **2** to fail. **gutsy** *a.* (*comp.* **gutsier,** *superl.* **gutsiest**) **1** greedy. **2** plucky. **gutsiness** *n.* **gutted** *a.* (*sl.*) fed up, disappointed. **gutty**[1] *a.* corpulent. [OE *gutt*, in pl. *guttas* (cp. G *Gosse*), prob. cogn. with *gēotan*, to pour]

gutta (gŭt´ə) *n.* (*pl.* **guttae** (-ē)) **1** (*Med.*) a drop. **2** in the Doric order of architecture, an ornament resembling a drop. **gutta rosacea** (rōzā´siə), **gutta rosea** (rō´ziə), **gutta rubea** (roo´biə) *n.* (*Med.*) inflammation of the face, with redness and pimples. **gutta serena** (sərē´nə) *n.* (*Med.*) amaurosis. **guttate** (-tāt) *a.* (*Bot.*) besprinkled or speckled. **gutté** (-ā), **guttee** (-tē´) *a.* (*Her.*) sprinkled with drops. **guttiferous** (-tif´-) *a.* (*Bot.*) yielding gum or resinous sap. **guttiform** (-fawm) *a.* drop-shaped. [L]

gutta-percha (gŭtəpœ´chə) *n.* a tough, waterproof rubber substance obtained from the latex of various Malaysian trees. **†gutty**[2] *n.* (*pl.* **gutties**) a gutta-percha golf ball. [Malay *gatah*, gum, *percha*, name of the tree]

gutté GUTTA.

gutter (gŭt´ə) *n.* **1** a channel at the side of a street or a trough below eaves for carrying away water. **2** a channel worn by water. **3** a trench, conduit etc. for the passage of water or other fluid. **4** (*Print.*) the space between the printed matter in two adjacent pages. **5** either of the two channels at the sides of a ten-pin bowling lane. **6** (*usu. pl., Sc.*) dirt, mire. *~v.t.* **1** to form channels or gutters in. **2** to provide with gutters. *~v.i.* **1** to become channelled or worn with hollows, as a burning candle. **2** to stream (down). **guttering** *n.* **1** material for gutters. **2** a gutter or arrangement of gutters. **3** the act of forming gutters. **4** the act of falling in drops. **gutter press** *n.* cheap and sensationalist newspapers. **guttersnipe** *n.* a street urchin. [OF *gutiere*, from *goute*, see GOUT]

guttiform GUTTA.

guttural (gŭt´ərəl) *a.* **1** (of a sound, voice etc.) throaty, harsh, raucous. **2** produced or formed in the throat. **3** of or relating to the throat. *~n.* a sound or combination of sounds produced in the throat or the back part of the mouth, such as *k*, *q*, hard *c* and *g*, *ng* and the German *ch*. **gutturalism** *n.* **gutturalize, gutturalise** *v.t.* **1** to form in the throat. **2** to speak in a harsh, raucous tone. **gutturally** *adv.* [F, from L *guttur*, throat]

gutturo- (gŭt´ərō) *comb. form* of the throat. **gutturo-nasal** *a.* of, relating to or produced by the throat and the nose.

gutty[1] GUT.

gutty[2] GUTTA-PERCHA.

guv (gŭv) *n.* (*coll., esp. dial.*) used as a term of address to a man (usu. in authority). [contr. of *guv*nor, var. of governor]

guy[1] (gī) *n.* **1** (*coll.*) a man, a fellow, a person. **2** an effigy of Guy Fawkes burnt on 5 Nov. in memory of the Gunpowder Plot. **3** (*coll.*) a ridiculously dressed person. *~v.t.* **1** to ridicule. **2** to display in effigy. *~v.i.* (*dated*) to carry a guy round on 5 Nov.

guy[2] (gī) *n.* a rope, chain etc., to steady a load in hoisting or to act as a stay. *~v.t.* to guide or steady by means of a guy or guys. **guy-rope** *n.* [OF *guie*, from *guier*, see GUIDE]

guzzle (gŭz´əl) *v.i.* to drink or eat greedily. *~v.t.* **1** to drink or eat (something) greedily. **2** to waste (one's income) in guzzling. *~n.* **1** a drinking bout. **2** †drink. **guzzler** *n.* [perh. from OF *gosiller*, to vomit, cogn. with *gosier*, the throat]

gwyniad (gwin´iad) *n.* a freshwater salmonoid fish, *Coregonus pennantii*, found in Lake Bala, Wales and the Lake District. [Welsh, from *gwyn*, white]

gybe (jīb), (*N Am.*) **jibe** *v.i.* (*Naut.*) **1** to take the wind on the other quarter (of a sailing boat). **2** to swing from one side of the mast to the other (of a fore-and-aft sail). *~v.t.* **1** to make (a vessel) take the wind on the opposite quarter. **2** to shift (a sail) in this way. *~n.* the act or process of gybing. [prob. from Dut *gijben* (now *gijpen*)]

gym (jim) *n.* **1** short for GYMNASIUM. **2** short for GYMNASTICS. **gym shoe** *n.* a plimsoll. **gymslip** *n.* a tunic worn by schoolgirls as part of a school uniform. *~a.* (*coll.*) of or relating to a school-age girl (*gymslip mums*).

gymkhana (jimkah´nə) *n.* a meeting for equestrian sports and games, orig. a place for athletic sports. [Hind. *gend-khāna*, ball-house, racket-court, assim. to GYMNASTICS]

gymnasium (jimnā´ziəm) *n.* (*pl.* **gymnasiums, gymnasia** (-ə)) **1** a building or room where gymnastics, indoor sports etc. are done. **2** in Germany or Scandinavia, a school of the highest grade preparatory to the universities. **gymnasial** *a.* **gymnasiarch** (-ahk) *n.* **1** in ancient Greece, a public official who superintended athletes. **2** †a leading athlete. **3** †a head instructor in an academy. **gymnasiast** (-ast) *n.* a pupil in a gymnasium. [L, from Gr. *gumnasion*, from *gumnazein*, to exercise naked, from *gumnos*, naked]

gymnastics (jimnas´tiks) *n.* **1** (*as sing. or pl.*) a course of instruction, discipline or exercise for the development of body or mind. **2** (*as pl.*) exercises for the development of bodily strength and agility. **3** (*as sing.*) the gymnastic art. **gymnast** (jim´-) *n.* a person skilled in gymnastics. **gymnastic** *a.* **1** of or relating to exercises for the development of the body. **2** involving athletic effort. **3** involving great mental effort or discipline. **gymnastically** *adv.* [Gr. *gymnastēs*, as GYMNASIUM]

gymno- (jim´nō) *comb. form* naked, destitute of protective covering. [Gr. *gumnos*, naked]

gymnosophist (jimnos´əfist) *n.* a member of an ancient Hindu sect of philosophic hermits who wore little or no clothing and lived a life of contemplation and asceticism. **gymnosophy** *n.* [*gymnosophistae*, pl., Gr. *gumnosophistai* (GYMNO-, SOPHIST (under SOPHISM))]

gymnosperm (jim´nōspœm) *n.* any one of a class of plants having naked seeds, such as the pine. **gymnospermous** (-spœ´məs) *a.*

gymp GIMP[1].

gyn- GYNO-.

gynaeceum GYNOECIUM.

gynaeco- (gī´nikō, jī´-), (*N Am.*) **gyneco-** *comb. form* of or relating to women. [Gr. *gunē gunaikos*, woman]

gynaecocracy (gīnikok´rəsi, jī-), (*N Am.*) **gynecocracy** *n.* government by women or a woman. **gynaecocrat** (-kəkrat) *n.* **gynaecocratic** (-krat´-) *a.*

gynaecology (gīnikol´əji), (*N Am.*) **gynecology** *n.* the science dealing with the functions and diseases of women and girls. **gynaecological** (-kəloj´-) *a.* **gynaecologist** *n.*

gynaecomastia (gīnikōmas´tiə), (*N Am.*) **gynecomastia** *n.* (*Med.*) the enlargement of a man's breasts usu. due to hormone imbalance or hormone therapy.

gynandrous (jinan´drəs, gin-) *a.* (of a plant) having the stamens and pistil together in a single column. **gynandromorph** (-drəmawf) *n.* (*Biol.*) an individual with both male and female characteristics, esp. of insects. **gynandromorphically** *adv.* **gynandromorphism** (-maw´-) *n.* **gynandromorphous** (-maw´-) *a.* **gynandry** *n.* a tendency in the female towards a male body. [Gr. *gunandros* (*gunē*, woman, *anēr andros*, man)]

gyneco- GYNAECO-.

gynecocracy GYNAECOCRACY.

gynecology GYNAECOLOGY.

gynecomastia GYNAECOMASTIA.

gyniolatry (jīniol´ətri) *n.* excessive devotion to women. [Gr. *gunē*, woman, -LATRY]

gyno- (jī´nō, gī´nō), **gyn-** *comb. form* **1** distinctively feminine. **2** (*Bot.*) of or relating to the female organs of plants. [Gr. *gunē*, woman]

gynoecium (jīnisē´əm, gī-), **gynaeceum** *n.* (*pl.* **gynoecia** (-siə), **gynaecea**) **1** (*Bot.*) the female organs in a plant. **2** in ancient Greece and Rome, the part of a house reserved for the women. [L, from Gr. *gunaikeion*, from *gunē gunaikos*, woman]

gynophobia (jīnōfō´biə, gī-) *n.* an abnormal fear of women.

gynophore (jī´nōfaw, gī´-) *n.* (*Bot.*) a stalk supporting an ovary above the level of other parts of the flower, as in the passion flower.

-gynous (jinəs) *comb. form* **1** of or relating to women, as in *androgynous*, *misogynous*. **2** (*Bot.*) (of a plant) having female organs or pistils. [Gr. *-gunos*, from *gunē*, woman]

gyp[1] (jip), **gip** *n.* a male servant in some colleges at Cambridge and Durham Universities. [perh. short for GYPSY (or for obs. *gippo*, scullion, orig. man's short tunic, from obs. F *jupeau*)]

gyp[2] (jip) *v.t.* (*pres.p.* **gypping**, *past, p.p.* **gypped**) (*coll.*) to cheat, swindle. ~*n.* a swindle. [perh. from *gypsy*]

gyp[3] (jip), **gip** *n.* (*coll.*) pain. **to give someone gyp** to cause someone pain.

gyppy tummy GIPPY TUMMY.

gypsophila (jipsof´ilə) *n.* any plant of the genus *Gypsophila*, a hardy perennial with small white and pink flowers, related to the pinks. [Gr. *gupsos*, chalk]

gypsum (jip´səm) *n.* a mineral consisting of hydrous sulphate of lime, used to make plaster, paint, glass, fertilizer etc. ~*v.t.* to manure with gypsum. **gypseous** *a.* **gypsiferous** (-sif´-) *a.* [L, from Gr. *gupsos*, chalk]

gypsy (jip´si), **gipsy** *n.* (*pl.* **gypsies, gipsies**) **1** a member of a nomad people (calling themselves Romany), prob. of Hindu extraction, dark in complexion and hair, and speaking a language descended from Sanskrit. **2** a person resembling a gypsy, esp. in dark complexion. **3** an itinerant traveller, wanderer. ~*v.i.* (*3rd pers. sing. pres.* **gypsies**, *pres.p.* **gypsying**, *past, p.p.* **gypsied**) to picnic or camp out in the open air. **gypsify** *v.t.* (*3rd pers. sing. pres.* **gypsifies**, *pres.p.* **gypsifying**, *past, p.p.* **gypsified**). **gypsy-bonnet, gypsy-hat** *n.* a bonnet or hat with a large brim or side flaps, often tied down to the side of the head. **gypsy cart, gypsy van, gypsy wagon** *n.* a large horse-drawn van such as Romanies live and travel in from place to place. **gypsydom, gypsyhood, gypsyism** *n.* the habits, practices or life of Romanies. **gypsy-flower, gypsy-rose** *n.* SCABIOUS. **gypsyish** *a.* **gypsy moth** *n.* a moth, *Lymatria dispar*, whose hairy caterpillar is destructive of trees. **gypsy table** *n.* a light round table on a tripod made orig. of sticks roughly tied together. [earlier *gypcian*, *Egypcien*, OF *Egyptien*, late L *Aegyptiānus*, from L *Aegyptius*, an inhabitant of Egypt]

gyrate (jīrāt´) *v.i.* to rotate, revolve, whirl, in either a circle or a spiral. ~*a.* **1** circular, convoluted. **2** (*Bot.*) arranged in rings, curved in a coil. **3** moving round in a circle. **gyration** (-ā´shən) *n.* **gyrational** *a.* **gyratory** (jī´rətəri) *a.* **gyre** *n.* a gyration, a revolution. ~*v.t.* **1** to turn round. **2** to whirl. ~*v.i.* to turn or move in a circle. **gyral** *a.* **gyrally** *adv.* **gyrose** (jī´rōz) *a.* **1** (*Bot.*) marked with wavy lines. **2** circinate. [L *gȳrātus*, p.p. of *gȳrāre*, from GYRUS]

gyrfalcon (jœ´fawlkən), **gerfalcon, jerfalcon** *n.* **1** a large and powerful falcon of northern regions, *Falco rusticolus*. **2** a large falcon used for hawking at herons etc. [OF *gerfaucon*, med. L *gēro- gīrefalco*, MHG *gīrvalke*]

gyri GYRUS.

gyro (jī´rō) *n.* (*pl.* **gyros**) (*coll.*) **1** a gyroscope. **2** a gyrocompass.

gyro- (jī´rō) *comb. form* **1** round, curved. **2** relating to revolutions. [Gr. *guros*, circle, ring]

gyrocompass (jī´rōkŭmpəs) *n.* a navigating compass consisting of an electrically driven gyroscope, the axle of which orientates the sensitive element.

gyromagnetic (jīrōmagnet´ik) *a.* **1** (*Physics*) of or caused by the magnetic and mechanical properties resulting from the spin of a rotating charged particle. **2** (of a compass) combining a gyroscope and a magnetic compass.

gyromancy (jī´rōmansi) *n.* divination performed by walking round in a circle or ring until one falls from dizziness.

gyron (jī´ron) *n.* (*Her.*) a triangular charge formed by two lines meeting at the fesse-point. **gyronny** *a.* [F]

gyropilot (jī´rōpīlət) *n.* a gyrocompass used in ships, aircraft etc. for automatic steering.

gyroplane (jī´rōplān) *n.* an aeroplane deriving its lift from the reaction of the air on freely rotating rotors in a horizontal plane, an autogiro.

gyroscope (jī´rəskōp) *n.* a heavy flywheel rotated (usu. electrically) at very high speed and supported on an axis at right angles to the plane of the wheel, used as a controlling or stabilizing device or as a compass in ships, aeroplanes etc. **gyroscopic** (-skop´-) *a.* **gyroscopically** *adv.*

gyrose GYRATE.

gyrostabilizer (jī´rōstābilīzə), **gyrostabiliser** *n.* a gyroscopic device for steadying the roll of a vessel.

gyrostat (jī´rōstat) *n.* Lord Kelvin's modification of the gyroscope, for illustrating the dynamics of rotating bodies. **gyrostatic** (-stat´-) *a.*

gyrus (jī´rəs) *n.* (*pl.* **gyri** (-rī)) (*Med.*) a fold, a ridge between two grooves, esp. of the brain. [L, from Gr. *guros*, a ring]

gyte[1] (gīt) *a.* (*Sc.*) mad, crazy. [etym. unknown]

gyte[2] (gīt) *n.* (*Sc.*) a child. [corr. of GET[1]]

gytrash (gī´trash) *n.* (*Sc.*) a ghost, spectre, apparition. [etym. uncertain]

gyttja (jich´ə) *n.* (*Geol.*) a usu. black organic sediment deposited in a lake. [Swed., mud]

gyve (jīv) *n.* (*usu. in pl.*) a fetter, shackle. ~†*v.t.* to fetter, enchain, entangle. [ME *guive*, etym. uncertain]

gyver GUIVER.

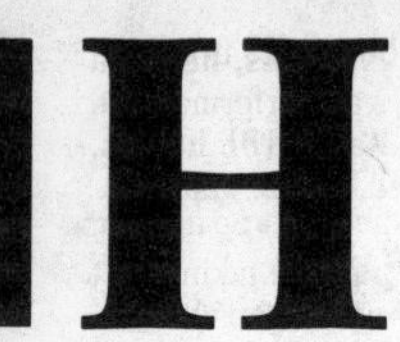

H[1] (āch), **h** (*pl.* **Hs, H's**) the eighth letter of the English and other versions of the Roman alphabet. It is pronounced mostly as a simple breathing at the beginning of a word or syllable, as in *help, hard, hope* etc., but is also commonly joined to other consonants to form digraphs, as *ch* in *child, chill, sh* in *shin, th* in *this, that, think*. Joined with *p*, and sometimes with *g*, it gives the sound of *f*, as in *philosophy, enough*; sometimes the latter digraph is silent, as in *bough, plough. Ch* is common in words derived from Greek, and in such cases is usu. pronounced as *k* in *chemistry, chyle* etc.; the Scottish and German *ch*, marked in this dictionary kh, is a velar fricative corresponding to the Greek χ, as in *clachan, Reichstag. ~symbol* **1** magnetic field strength. **2** (**h**) Planck's constant. **to drop one's hs** DROP. **H-girder** *n.* a girder having a crosspiece, in the shape of a capital letter H.

H[2] *chem. symbol* hydrogen. **H-bomb** *n.* a hydrogen bomb.

H[3] *abbr.* **1** (of a pencil lead) hard. **2** henry(s). **3** (*sl.*) heroin. **4** hospital (on signs). **5** Hungary (IVR). **6** hydrant. **H-hour** *n.* the hour at which a military operation etc. is scheduled to begin (H for *hour*).

h *abbr.* **1** hecto-. **2** height. **3** high. **4** horse. **5** hot. **6** hour(s). **7** husband.

Ha. *chem. symbol* hahnium.

ha[1] (ha, hah), **hah** *int.* **1** used to express surprise, joy, suspicion or other sudden emotion. **2** an inarticulate sound expressive of hesitation. *~v.i.* **1** to express surprise, wonder etc. **2** to hesitate. **ha ha! 1** used to express the sound of laughter. **2** used to express surprise, joy, suspicion or other sudden emotion. [onomat., common to Gmc., Gr., L etc.]

ha[2] *abbr.* hectare(s).

haaf (hahf) *n.* a deep-sea fishing ground (off Orkney and Shetland). [Icel. *haf*, the high sea]

haar (hah) *n.* (*dial., esp. Sc.*) a wet mist, esp. a sea-fog. [perh. from Icel. *hārr*]

Hab. *abbr.* Habakkuk (in the Old Testament).

habanera (habəneə´rə) *n.* **1** a Cuban dance in slow duple time. **2** the music for this dance. **3** a dance from Havana. [Sp.]

habdabs (hab´dabz) *n.pl.* (*sl.*) a feeling of anxiety, apprehension or irritation (*the screaming habdabs*). [etym. uncertain]

habeas corpus (hābiəs kaw´pəs) *n.* a writ to produce a prisoner before a court, with details of the day and cause of the arrest and detention, in order that the justice of this may be determined. [L, you may have the body]

haberdasher (hab´ədashə) *n.* **1** a seller of small articles of apparel, as ribbons, laces, silks etc. **2** (*N Am.*) a person who sells men's clothing. **3** †a pedlar. **4** †a hatter. **haberdashery** *n.* (*pl.* **haberdasheries**) **1** a haberdasher's shop or business. **2** the type of goods sold by a haberdasher. [from obs. *haberdash*, haberdashery, A-F *hapertas*, etym. unknown]

habergeon (hab´əjən) *n.* a sleeveless coat of mail or armour to protect the neck and breast. [OF *haubergeon*, dim. of *hauberc*, HAUBERK]

habiliment (həbil´imənt) *n.* (*usu. pl.*) an item of clothing. [OF *habillement*, from *habiller*, to dress]

habilitate (həbil´itāt) *v.i.* to become qualified (for). *~v.t.* to furnish with means, to finance. **habilitation** (-ā´shən) *n.* **habilitator** *n.* a person who supplies means. [L *habilitātus*, p.p. of *habilitāre*, to make fit, from *habilitās*, ABILITY]

habit (hab´it) *n.* **1** a permanent tendency to perform certain actions. **2** a settled inclination, disposition or trend of mind. **3** a manner, practice, use or custom, acquired by frequent repetition. **4** an addiction. **5** (*Zool., Bot.*) a characteristic manner of growth. **6** physical constitution. **7** garb, dress or costume, esp. one of a distinctive kind, as of a religious order. **8** RIDING HABIT (under RIDING[1]). *~v.t.* to dress, to clothe. **creature of habit** CREATURE. **to be in the habit of** to do (something) usually or regularly. **to make a habit of** to do (something) usually or regularly. **habited** *a.* clothed, dressed. **habit-forming** *a.* tending to become a habit or an addiction. [OF, from L *habitum*, nom. *-tus*, from *habēre*, to have, refl. to be constituted, to be]

habitable (hab´itəbəl) *a.* that may be lived in or inhabited. **habitability** (-bil´-), **habitableness** *n.* **habitably** *adv.* **habitant** *n.* **1** an inhabitant of Lower Canada of French origin. **2** †an inhabitant. **habitation** (-ā´shən) *n.* **1** the act of inhabiting. **2** the state of being inhabited. **3** a place of abode. **4** a natural region or locality. [F, from L *habitābilis*, from *habitāre*, to dwell, freq. of *habēre*, see HABIT]

habitat (hab´itat) *n.* **1** the natural home or locality of an animal or plant. **2** the place where a person or group is at home or usually found.

habitual (habit´ūəl) *a.* **1** formed or acquired by habit. **2** according to habit, usual. **3** customary, constant. **4** rendered permanent by use. **habitually** *adv.* **habitualness** *n.* **habituate** *v.t.* **1** to accustom (to). **2** to make familiar by frequent repetition. **habituation** (-ā´shən) *n.* **habitude** (hab´itūd) *n.* **1** a customary manner or mode, habit, aptitude, tendency, propensity. **2** customary relation, familiarity. [late L *habituālis*, from *habitus*, HABIT]

habitué (həbit´ūā) *n.* a person who habitually frequents a place, esp. a place of amusement. [F, a regular (customer or visitor)]

háček (hah´chek) *n.* a diacritical mark (ˇ) placed above a letter to modify its pronunciation, esp. in Slavonic languages. [Czech]

hachure (hashooə´) *n.* (*usu. pl.*) any one of a series of short lines employed to represent half-tints and shadows, and on maps to denote hill slopes. *~v.t.* to cover or mark with hachures. [F, from *hacher*, to HATCH[3]]

hacienda (hasien´də) *n.* **1** in Spain, Latin America etc., an estate, a farm or plantation, an establishment in the country for stock-raising etc., esp. with a residence for the proprietor. **2** a (Spanish or Latin American) factory. [Sp., from OSp. and L *facienda*, things to be done, neut. pl. gerund of *facere*, to do]

hack[1] (hak) *v.t.* **1** to cut irregularly or into small pieces. **2** to chop, to notch. **3** to cut unskilfully. **4** to kick (a player's shins) at football. **5** (*sl.*) to mangle in uttering. **6** (*sl.*) to tolerate. **7** (*sl.*) to cope with. **8** to gain access to (a computer system or data) illegally. *~v.i.* **1** to cut or chop away at anything. **2** to emit a short dry cough. **3** to use computers as a hobby, esp. in order to manipulate another computer system illegally. *~n.* **1** an irregular cut, a gash, a notch, a dent. **2** a kick (on the shins etc.).

3 the result of this. 4 a mattock or large pick. 5 a miner's pick with a chisel edge at one end. **hacker** *n.* 1 a person who writes computer programs as a hobby. 2 a person who uses a computer to gain access to another computer system, often for illegal purposes. **hacking** *a.* 1 slashing, chopping, mangling. 2 (of a cough) short, dry and intermittent. **hacksaw** *n.* a handsaw used for cutting metal. ~*v.t.* (*past, p.p.* **hacksawed, hacksawn**) to cut with a hacksaw. [ME *hakken*, OE *-haccian* (cp. Dut. *hakken*, Dan. *hakke*, G *hacken*)]

hack[2] (hak) *n.* 1 a hackney, a horse for hire. 2 a horse for general purposes, esp. as distinct from a hunter or racer. 3 (*N Am.*) a hackney carriage. 4 a person who earns money from routine literary or journalistic work. ~*v.t.* 1 to ride (a horse) for pleasure. 2 to let out for hire. 3 to make common or hackneyed. ~*v.i.* 1 to go riding for pleasure. 2 to be let out for hire. 3 to ride at the pace of an ordinary hack. **hackette** (haket´) *n.* (*derog.*) a female journalist. **hacking jacket, hacking coat** *n.* a short jacket with a vent or vents at the back, worn for riding. **hackwork** *n.* work done by a literary or journalistic hack. [abbr. of HACKNEY]

hack[3] (hak) *n.* 1 a rack or grated frame, a hatch. 2 a feeding-rack or manger. 3 a frame for drying bricks. 4 a drying-frame for fish. 5 a feeding-board for hawks. 6 the state of partial liberty in which young hawks are kept. **at hack** (of a hawk) at liberty but obedient to the falconer. [var. of HATCH[1]]

hackamore (hak´əmaw) *n.* a rope with a loop used instead of a bit on a horse unused to a bridle. [Sp. *jáquima*]

hackberry (hak´bəri) *n.* (*pl.* **hackberries**) 1 a N American tree of the genus *Celtis*, related to the elms. 2 its purple berry. [var. of HAGBERRY]

hackbut (hak´bŭt), **hagbut** (hag´bŭt) *n.* HARQUEBUS. **hackbuteer** (-tiə´), **hackbutter** *n.* [MF *haquebute*, OF *haquebusche*, see HARQUEBUS]

hackery (hak´əri) *n.* (*pl.* **hackeries**) in the Indian subcontinent, a simple two-wheeled car, drawn by bullocks. [prob. from Hind.]

hackle[1] (hak´əl) *n.* 1 a long shining feather on or from a cock's neck. 2 a fly for angling, dressed with this. 3 a feather in a Highland soldier's bonnet. 4 the hairs on a cat's or dog's neck. 5 an instrument with sharp steel spikes for dressing or combing (flax etc.). 6 fibrous substance unspun, as raw silk. ~*v.t.* 1 to tie a hackle on (an artificial fly). 2 to dress or comb (flax or hemp) with a hackle. **to make someone's hackles rise** to make someone angry. **with its hackles up** (of a dog, cock etc.) ready to fight. [ME *hachele*, cogn. with MHG *hachele* (G *Hechel*, cp. Dut. *hekel*)]

hackle[2] (hak´əl) *v.t.* to hack, to mangle. **hackler** *n.* [rel. to HACK[1]]

hackney (hak´ni) *n.* (*pl.* **hackneys**) 1 a horse kept for riding or driving. 2 a horse kept for hire. 3 a hackney carriage. **hackney carriage, hackney coach** *n.* a passenger road vehicle licensed for hire. **hackneyed** *a.* (of a phrase) used so often that it has become stale, trite and ineffective. [ME *Hakeney*, Hackney, in E London]

had HAVE.

haddock (had´ək) *n.* (*pl. in general* **haddock,** *in particular* **haddocks**) a sea fish, *Melanogrammus aeglefinus*, allied to the cod and fished for food. [ME *haddok*, etym. uncertain]

hade (hād) *n.* the inclination of a fault or vein from the vertical, complementary to the dip. ~*v.i.* to incline from the vertical. [etym. uncertain]

Hades (hā´dēz) *n.* in Greek mythology, the lower world, the abode of the spirits of the dead. [Gr. *Hadēs, Aidēs*, the god of the lower world]

Hadith (had´ith) *n.* tradition, esp. the body of tradition relating to the sayings and doings of Muhammad. [Arab.]

hadji (haj´i), **hajji, haji** *n.* (*pl.* **hadjis, hajjis, hajis**) (a title conferred on) a Muslim who has performed the pilgrimage to Mecca. **hadj, hajj, haj** *n.* (*pl.* **hadjes, hajjes, hajes**) a pilgrimage to Mecca. [Arab. *hājī*]

hadn't (had´ənt) *contr.* had not.

hadron (had´ron) *n.* an elementary particle taking part in strong nuclear interactions. **hadronic** (-ron´-) *a.* [Gr. *hadros*, heavy]

hadrosaur (had´rəsaw) *n.* a gigantic fossil saurian of the family Hadrosauridae, from the Cretaceous strata of N America. [mod. L *hadrosaurus* (Gr. *hadros*, thick, *sauros*, lizard)]

†**hadst** HAVE.

hae (hā) *v.t.* (*Sc.*) to have.

haecceity (heksē´iti) *n.* (*Philos.*) the quality of being a particular thing, individuality. [med. L *hæcceitas*, thisness (Duns Scotus), from *haec*, fem. of *hīc*, this]

haem (hēm), (*N Am.*) **heme** *n.* a red organic compound containing iron, found in haemoglobin. [as HAEMA-]

haema- (hē´mə), (*N Am.*) **hema-** *comb. form* blood. [Gr. *haima haimatos*, blood]

haemal (hē´məl), (*N Am.*) **hemal** *a.* 1 of or relating to the blood. 2 on, of or relating to the side of the body containing the heart and great blood vessels. [as HAEMA-]

haematemesis (hēmətem´isis), (*N Am.*) **hematemesis** *n.* a vomiting of blood.

haematic (hēmat´ik), (*N Am.*) **hematic** *a.* 1 of or relating to the blood. 2 containing blood. 3 acting on the blood. 4 blood-coloured. ~*n.* a medicine acting on the blood. **haematics** *n.* the branch of physiology concerned with the blood.

haematin (hē´mətin), (*N Am.*) **hematin** *n.* 1 an amorphous substance associated with haemoglobin in the blood. 2 haemotoxylin.

haematite (hē´mətīt), **hematite** *n.* a native sesquioxide of iron, occurring in two forms, red and brown, a valuable iron ore. **haematitic** (-tit´-) *a.* [from Gr. *haimatitēs*, like blood]

haemato- (hē´mətō), (*N Am.*) **hemato-** *comb. form* blood. **haematoblast** (hēmat´əblast) *n.* any one of the minute colourless disks, smaller than the ordinary corpuscles, found in the blood. **haematoblastic** (-blas´-) *a.* **haematocele** (hē´mətəsēl, hem´-) *n.* a cavity containing blood. **haematocrit** (hē´mətəkrit, hem´-) *n.* 1 an instrument for separating blood cells from plasma to measure their relative proportions. 2 the relative proportions of blood cells and plasma. **haematoid** (hē´mətoid, hem´-) *a.* having the appearance of blood. **haematology** (hēmətol´əji, hem´-) *n.* the branch of physiology dealing with blood. **haematologic** (-loj´ik), **haemotological** *a.* **haematologist** *n.* **haematoma** (hēmətō´mə, hem´-) *n.* (*pl.* **haematomas, haematomata** (-mətə)) a lump of clotted blood. **haematophagous** (hēmətof´əgəs) *a.* that feeds on blood. **haematosis** (hēmətō´sis, hem´-) *n.* 1 the formation of blood or of blood corpuscles. 2 the conversion of venous into arterial blood. **haematoxylin** (hēmətok´silin, hem´-) *n.* a red dye obtained from logwood. **haematoxylic** (-toksil´ik) *a.* **haematozoa** (hēmətəzō´ə, hem´-) *n.pl.* parasites found in the blood. [as HAEMA-]

haematuria (hēmətū´riə, hem-), (*N Am.*) **hematuria** *n.* the presence of blood in the urine.

-haemia -AEMIA.

haemo- (hē´mō, hem´ō), (*N Am.*) **hemo-** *comb. form* short form of HAEMATO-. **haemochrome** *n.* the colouring matter of the blood. **haemocoel** (-sēl) *n.* the main body cavity of many invertebrate creatures. **haemocyanin** (-sī´ənin) *n.* an oxygen-bearing substance containing copper, found in arthropods and molluscs. **haemocyte** *n.* a blood cell, esp. of an invertebrate animal. **haemodialysis** (hēmōdīal´əsis, hem´-) *n.* dialysis (of blood). **haemodynamics** (hēmōdīnam´iks) *n.* the dynamics of the circulation of the blood. **haemoglobin** (hēməglō´bin) *n.* the colouring matter of the red corpuscles of the blood. **haemoid** (hē´moid, hem´-) *a.* haematoid. **haemolymph** (hē´mōlimf, hem´-) *n.* the fluid in invertebrate creatures having a similar function to that of blood. **haemolysis** (hēmol´isis, hem-) *n.* the release of haemoglobin from red blood cells. **haemolytic** (-lit´-) *a.* **haemophilia** (hēməfil´iə, hem-) *n.* a constitutional tendency to bleed heavily because the clotting mechanism does not function normally. **haemophiliac** (-ak) *n.* a person suffering from this. *~a.* suffering from haemophilia. **haemophilic** *a.* **haemoptysis** (hēmop´tisis) *n.* a spitting or coughing up of blood from the lungs. **haemostatic** (hēməstat´ik, hem-) *a.* serving to stop bleeding. *~n.* **1** a medicine for doing this. **2** (*pl.*) the branch of physiology relating to the hydrostatics of blood. **haemostasis** (hēmōstā´sis, hem-), **haemostasia** (-stā´ziə) *n.* **1** congestion of blood. **2** stoppage of the flow of blood by means of constriction or compression of an artery.

haemorrhage (hem´ərij), (*N Am.*) **hemorrhage** *n.* **1** an abnormal discharge of blood from the heart, arteries, veins or capillaries. **2** an extensive loss of people, resources etc. *~v.i.* **1** to have a haemorrhage of blood. **2** to lose people, resources etc. extensively. **3** to be lost extensively. *~v.t.* to lose in large numbers or quantities. **haemorrhagic** (-raj´-) *a.* [MF *hemorrhagie*, late L *haemorrhagia*, Gr. *haimorrhagia* (HAEMO-, *-rhagia*, from stem of *rhēgnunai*, to break)]

haemorrhoids (hem´əroidz), (*N Am.*) **hemorrhoids** *n.pl.* (*Med.*) swollen veins around the anus. **haemorrhoidal** (-roi´-) *a.* [formerly *emorods*, *emoroydes*, OF *emoroyde*, L *haemorrhoidae*, pl. of *haemorrhoida*, Gr. *haimorrhoïdēs*, pl. of *haimorrhoïs*, a., discharging blood (HAEMO-, *-rhoos*, flowing, from *rheein*, to flow)]

haeremai (hī´rəmī), **haere mai** *int.* (*New Zeal.*) welcome! [Maori]

hafiz (hah´fiz) *n.* (a Muslim title for) a person knowing the Koran by heart. [Pers.]

hafnium (haf´niəm) *n.* a metallic element occurring in zirconium ores, symbol Hf, at. no. 72. [L *Hafniae*, Copenhagen]

haft (hahft) *n.* a handle, esp. of a dagger, knife or tool. *~v.t.* to set in or fit with a handle. [OE *hæft*, from root of *hebban*, to HEAVE]

Hag. *abbr.* Haggai (in the Old Testament).

hag[1] (hag) *n.* **1** a witch. **2** a fury. **3** an ugly old woman. **4** a hagfish. **hagfish** *n.* (*pl. in general* **hagfish**, *in particular* **hagfishes**) an eel-like fish, of the family Myxinidae, that feeds on the bodies or remains of other fish. **haggish** *a.* **haggishly** *adv.* **hag-ridden** *a.* suffering from nightmares. [perh. shortened from OE *haegtesse*]

hag[2] (hag) *n.* (*Sc., North.*) **1** a break or soft place in a bog. **2** any one of the turfy hillocks of firmer ground in a bog. [perh. from Icel. *hogg*, a cut or gap, from *hoggva*, cogn. with OE *heawan*, to HEW]

hagberry (hag´bəri) *n.* (*pl.* **hagberries**) **1** the bird cherry, *Prunus padus*. **2** (*N Am.*) the hackberry. [from Scand. (cp. Dan. *haeggebaer*)]

hagbut HACKBUT.

Haggadah (həgah´də) *n.* **1** the legendary part of the Talmud. **2** a book recited at Seder. **Haggadic** (-gad´-), **Haggadical** *a.* **Haggadist** *n.* a person who studies the Haggadah. **Haggadistic** (-dis´-) *a.* [Heb., a tale, a story]

haggard[1] (hag´əd) *a.* **1** anxious, careworn or gaunt from fatigue, trouble etc. **2** wild-looking. **3** (of a hawk) caught wild. *~n.* a wild or untrained hawk. **haggardly** *adv.* **haggardness** *n.* [F *hagard* (perh. conn. with OHG *haga*, HEDGE, whence *faucon hagard*, hedge-falcon)]

haggard[2] (hag´əd) *n.* (*Ireland, Isle of Man*) a stack-yard. [cp. Icel. *heygarthr* (*hey*, hay, *garthr*, GARTH)]

haggis (hag´is) *n.* a Scottish dish traditionally made of liver, lights, heart etc. minced with onions, suet, oatmeal etc., enclosed in a sheep's stomach. [Sc., etym. uncertain]

haggish HAG[1].

haggle (hag´əl) *v.i.* **1** to wrangle, esp. over a bargain. **2** (*Sc.*) to struggle onwards. *~v.t.* to hack, to mangle. *~n.* a wrangle about terms. **haggler** *n.* [prob. freq. of HAG[2]]

hagiarchy (hag´iahki) *n.* (*pl.* **hagiarchies**) **1** government by priests. **2** an order of priests or holy men. [as HAGIO-, + Gr. *archē*, rule, from *archein*, to reign]

hagio- (hag´iō) *comb. form* of or relating to saints or to holy things. [Gr. *hagios*, holy]

hagiocracy (hagiok´rəsi) *n.* (*pl.* **hagiocracies**) government by priests or holy persons.

hagiography (hagiog´rəfi) *n.* (*pl.* **hagiographies**) **1** the writing of the biography of saints. **2** a series of lives of saints. **3** any biography that treats its subject as excessively good, noble etc. **4** †the Hagiographa. **Hagiographa** (hagiog´rəfə) *n.pl.* the third and last of the Jewish divisions of the Bible, comprising the books not included in 'the Law' and 'the Prophets'; also called *Writings*. **hagiographer** *n.* **1** a writer of a hagiography or hagiographies. **2** any one of the writers of the Hagiographa. **hagiographic** (-graf´-), **hagiographical** *a.* **hagiographist** *n.* [Gr. (HAGIO-, *graphē*, writing)]

hagiolatry (hagiol´ətri) *n.* the worship of saints. **hagiolater** *n.*

hagiology (hagiol´əji) *n.* (*pl.* **hagiologies**) **1** literature relating to the lives and legends of saints. **2** a work on the lives of saints. **hagiologic** (-loj´-), **hagiological** *a.* **hagiologist** *n.*

hagioscope (hag´iəskōp) *n.* an oblique opening in the wall of a church to enable people in the transept or aisles to see the high altar.

hah HA[1].

ha-ha (hah´hah), **haw-haw** (haw´haw) *n.* (*pl.* **ha-has**, **haw-haws**) a hedge, fence or wall sunk between slopes. [F *haha*, a sudden obstacle that laughs at one]

hahnium (hah´niəm) *n.* a radioactive element, chem. symbol Ha, at. no. 105, produced artificially from californium. [Otto *Hahn*, 1879–1968, German chemist]

Haida (hī´də) *n.* (*pl.* **Haida, Haidas**) **1** a member of a N American Indian people of British Columbia. **2** the language of this people. *~a.* of or relating to the Haida or their language.

haiduk (hī´duk), **heyduck** *n.* a member of a class of mercenaries in Hungary who were granted lands and the rank of nobles in 1605. [Czech, Pol. *hajduk*, from Hung. *hajdú*, pl. *-duk*, orig. robber, brigand]

haik[1] (hīk, hāk), **haick** *n.* a strip of woollen or cotton cloth worn as an upper garment by Arabs over the head and body. [Arab. *hayk*, from *hak*, to weave]

haik[2] HAKE[2].

haiku (hī´koo) *n.* (*pl.* **haiku**) **1** a Japanese verse of 17 syllables, in 3 parts. **2** an imitation of this in English etc. [Jap.]

hail[1] (hāl) *n.* **1** frozen rain or particles of frozen vapour falling in showers. **2** (*fig.*) a great number of violent or abusive words etc. *~v.i.* **1** (*impers.*) to pour down hail. **2** to come down with swiftness or violence. *~v.t.* to pour down or out (abuse, blows etc.), as hail. **hailstone** *n.* a single pellet of hail. **hailstorm** *n.* **haily** *a.* [OE *hagol* (cp. Icel. *hagl*, Dut., Dan. and G *Hagel*)]

hail[2] (hāl) *v.t.* **1** to call or signal to (a person, taxi etc.) from a distance. **2** to designate or acclaim (as). **3** to welcome, to salute. *~v.i.* to come (from a particular place) originally or as one's home (*She hails from Manchester*). *~int.* used to express welcome or salutation. *~n.* **1** a salutation. **2** a shout to attract attention. **within hail** within hailing distance. **within hailing distance** close enough to be heard if one shouts. **hailer** *n.* **hail-fellow-well-met** *a.* on easy, familiar terms. **Hail Mary** *n.* (*pl.* **Hail Marys**) AVE MARIA (under AVE). [Icel. *heill*,

HALE[1], used ellipt. as a greeting (cp. OE *wes hāl*, be whole, good health)]

hair (heə) *n.* **1** a filament composed of a tube of horny, fibrous substance, with a central medulla enclosing pigment cells, growing from the skin of an animal. **2** (*collect.*) the mass of such filaments forming a covering for the head or the whole body. **3** hairlike cellular processes on the surface of plants. **4** a hairlike strand in a hairbrush etc. **5** the mass of such strands. **6** (*fig.*) something very small or fine; a very minute distance. **7** †haircloth. **against the hair** against the grain. **by a hair** by a very small margin. **keep your hair on!** (*coll.*) don't lose your temper. **not to turn a hair** not to show any sign of fatigue or alarm. **to a hair** to an extreme nicety, exactly. **to get in one's hair** to become a nuisance, to make one irritated. **to let one's hair down** **1** (*coll.*) to talk without restraint. **2** (*coll.*) to forget ceremony, to behave uninhibitedly. **to make someone's hair curl** (*coll.*) to shock or scandalize someone greatly. **to make someone's hair stand on end** to make someone very frightened or horrified. **to split hairs** to quibble about trifles, to be overnice. **hairbreadth, hair's breadth** *n.* **1** the breadth of a hair. **2** a very minute distance. **hairbrush** *n.* a brush for the hair. **hair-brush** *n.* a brush made of hair. **haircare** *n.* the process of keeping hair clean and in good condition. **haircloth** *n.* cloth made wholly or in part of hair. **haircut** *n.* **1** the act of cutting a person's hair. **2** the style in which a person's hair is cut. **hairdo** *n.* (*pl.* **hairdos**) (*coll.*) **1** a woman's hairstyle when it has been curled or put up. **2** an act or process of so styling hair. **hairdresser** *n.* **1** a person who styles and cuts hair. **2** a hairdresser's shop or business. **hairdressing** *n.* **hair-dryer, hairdrier** *n.* an electric device for drying the hair, either a hand-held one that blows warm air, or a hood that covers the head. **haired** *a.* having hair (*usu. in comb.*, as *grey-haired*). **hair follicle** *n.* the gland or cavity at the root of a hair. **hair gel** *n.* a sticky substance like clear jelly, used for styling hair. **hair-grass** *n.* any tall, tufted grass of the genera *Aira*, *Deschampsia*, *Corynephorus* etc. **hairgrip** *n.* a narrow hairpin with ends that spring tightly together. **hair lacquer** *n.* a chemical substance used to keep a hairstyle in place. **hairless** *a.* **hairlike** *n.* **hairline** *n.* **1** the edge of the hair on a person's head, esp. the forehead. **2** (*usu. attrib.*) a very thin crack or narrow line. **3** (*Print.*) a very thin stroke or line in a typeface. **4** a fishing-line of horsehair. **hairnet** *n.* a net, sometimes almost invisible, to keep the hair in place. **hair of the dog** *n.* (*coll.*) a small amount of what has proved harmful, esp. of alcohol during a hangover. **hair oil** *n.* oil for dressing the hair. **hairpiece** *n.* a piece of artificial hair worn to change the style of the natural hair. **hairpin** *n.* a pin for fastening the hair. **hairpin bend** *n.* a sharp V-shaped turn in a road. **hair-raising** *a.* very frightening. **hair-raisingly** *adv.* **hair's breadth** HAIRBREADTH (under HAIR). **hair shirt** *n.* a shirt made of horsehair, worn as a penance. **hairslide** *n.* a decorative clip for holding hair in place. **hair-space** *n.* (*Print.*) the thinnest space used. **hair-splitting** *n.* the practice of making distinctions that are too minute to be significant. ~*a.* quibbling. **hair-splitter** *n.* **hairspray** *n.* lacquer for the hair sprayed from an aerosol can. **hairspring** *n.* the fine steel spring regulating the balance wheel in a watch. **hairstreak** *n.* any butterfly marked with fine streaks, belonging to the genera *Callophrys*, *Strymonidia* etc. **hair-stroke** *n.* a hairline in penmanship or on type, a serif. **hairstyle** *n.* a particular way of arranging the hair. **hairstyling** *n.* **hairstylist** *n.* **hair-trigger** *n.* a secondary trigger for releasing a main trigger by very slight pressure. **hair-wave** *n.* a wavelike appearance given to the hair. **hair-worm** *n.* a member of a genus of simple threadlike nematoid worms found in stagnant and slow-running water. **hairy** *a.* (*comp.* **hairier**, *superl.* **hairiest**) **1** covered with hair. **2** consisting of or resembling hair. **3** (*coll.*) difficult, exciting or dangerous. **4** (*sl.*) clumsy. **hairily** *adv.* **hairiness** *n.* [OE *hǣr*, *hēr* (cp. Dut. and G *Haar*, Icel. *hār*)]

haji, hajjii HADJI.

haka (hah´kə) *n.* **1** a ceremonial Maori dance. **2** a similar display by a New Zealand rugby team before a match. [Maori]

hake[1] (hāk) *n.* (*pl. in general* **hake**, *in particular* **hakes**) a fish belonging to the genus *Merlucius*, allied to the cod. ~*v.i.* to fish for hake. [etym. uncertain (cp. obs. *haked*, OE *hacod*, the pike)]

hake[2] (hāk), **haik** *n.* **1** a wooden frame for drying. **2** a cheese-rack. **3** a manger. **4** a hatch in a weir for a mill. [HACK[3]]

hakeem HAKIM[1].

hakenkreuz (hah´kənkroits) *n.* the swastika, the Nazi symbol. [G, *Haken*, hook, *Kreuz*, cross]

hakim[1] (həkēm´), **hakeem** *n.* (in Muslim countries) a physician. [Arab. *hakīm*, wise, from *hakama*, to exercise authority]

hakim[2] (hah´kim) *n.* **1** (in Muslim countries) a governor. **2** a judge. [Arab. *hākim*, as HAKIM[1]]

hal- HALO-.

Halachah (həlah´kə, halahkhah´), **Halakah** (-k-) *n.* a body of traditional laws, supposed to be of Mosaic origin, included in the Mishna. **Halachic** *a.* **Halachist** *n.* [Heb. *halākāh*, the rule one walks by, from *hālak*, to walk]

halal (həlahl´) *n.* meat which is prepared in accordance with Muslim law. ~*v.t.* (*pres.p.* **halalling**, *past*, *p.p.* **halalled**) to prepare (meat) in this way. ~*a.* (of meat) prepared in this way. [Arab. *halāl*, lawful]

halation (həlā´shən) *n.* a blurring in a photographic negative caused by the reflection of a strong light from the back of the plate during exposure. [HALO, -ATION]

halberd (hal´bəd), **halbert** (hal´bət) *n.* a weapon consisting of a combination of spear and battleaxe, mounted on a pole 5 to 7 ft. (1.5 to 2m) in length. **halberdier** (-diə´) *n.* a person armed with a halberd. [OF *halebarde*, MHG *helmbarde* (*helm*, helmet, or perh. *helm*, handle, *barde*, a broad axe)]

halcyon (hal´siən) *n.* **1** a tropical (esp. Australasian) kingfisher of the genus *Halcyon*. **2** a bird, supposed by the ancients to make a floating nest at the winter solstice, and to have the power of calming the sea while it was breeding. **3** calm, peace. ~*a.* peaceful, happy, pleasant, prosperous. **halcyon days** *n.pl.* a time of prosperity, peace and happiness (from the period of time (about a fortnight) during which the halcyon was traditionally supposed to breed). [L, from Gr. *alkuōn*, kingfisher]

hale[1] (hāl) *a.* (esp. of an elderly man) sound and vigorous, robust (*hale and hearty*). **haleness** *n.* [North., from OE *hāl*, WHOLE]

hale[2] (hāl) *v.t.* to drag, to draw violently. [OF *haler*, from OHG *halōn* (G *holen*, cp. Dut. *halen*, OE *ge-holian*)]

haler (hah´lə) *n.* (*pl.* **haler, halers, haleru** (hah´ləroo)) a unit of currency of the Czech Republic. [Czech]

half (hahf) *n.* (*pl.* **halves** (hahvz)) **1** either of two equal parts into which a thing or quantity is or may be divided. **2** a half part or share. **3** (*coll.*) a half-pint. **4** †a half-year, a term. **5** HALF-BACK (under HALF). **6** a half-price travel ticket. **7** a score for a golfer that is the same as their opponent's. ~*a.* consisting of or forming a half. ~*adv.* **1** to the extent or degree of a half. **2** to a certain extent or degree. **3** partially, imperfectly (*often in comb.*). **4** (*coll.*) half past (*It's half three*). ~†*v.t.* to halve. **by halves** badly, imperfectly. **half a** one half of a; roughly one half of a. **half a crown** HALF-CROWN (under HALF). **half a dozen** HALF-DOZEN (under HALF). **half an hour** HALF-HOUR (under HALF). **half past** half an hour past, as in *half past three*. **half the battle** BATTLE. **half the time** (*coll.*) as often as not. **not half** 1 (*iron.*) rather. 2 (*sl.*) not at all. **not to know the half of it** to have only a vague notion of the truth. **other half** OTHER. **to cry halves** CRY. **to go halves** to share equally (with another or in). **to have half a mind** MIND. **too clever by half** far too clever. **too cocky by half** far too cocky. **half a chance** *n.* (*coll.*) even the slightest chance or opportunity. **half-and-half** *n.* 1 a mixture of equal parts of two drinks, esp. beer and stout or bitter and mild. 2 (*N Am.*) a mixture of milk and cream for tea or coffee. ~*a.* languid, spiritless. ~*adv.* using two equal parts. **half an eye** *n.* 1 some part of one's attention or perceptiveness. 2 a modicum of perceptiveness or intelligence. **half-back** *n.* 1 in football, hockey etc., a position behind the forwards. 2 a person who plays in this position. **half-baked** *a.* 1 not thorough. 2 (*sl.*) half-witted, silly. 3 inexperienced. 4 not quite baked. **half-beak** *n.* any sea or freshwater fish of the family Hemiramphidae, having a lower jaw that is longer than the upper jaw. **half-binding** *n.* a bookbinding in which the backs and corners are of leather and the sides are of paper or cloth. **half-blood** *n.* 1 the relationship between two people who have only one parent in common. 2 a person so related. 3 a person with parents of different racial origins. ~*a.* 1 born of the same father or mother. 2 half-blooded. **half-blooded** *a.* born of parents of different racial origins. **half-blue** *n.* 1 a person who has represented Oxford or Cambridge University at a minor sport or as a substitute. 2 the distinction of doing this. **half board** *n.* in hotels etc., the provision of bed, breakfast and one main meal per day. **half-boot** *n.* a boot reaching high up the ankle. **half-bottle** *n.* 1 a bottle that is half the full standard size. 2 a quantity equal to the contents of this. **half-bound** *a.* (of a book) bound in half-binding. **half-bred** *a.* 1 imperfectly bred. 2 lacking in refinement. 3 of mixed breed, mongrel. **half-breed** *n.* (*offensive*) an offspring of parents of different racial origins. ~*a.* half-blooded. **half-brother** *n.* a brother by one parent only. **half-butt** *n.* a billiard or snooker cue intermediate in length between an ordinary cue and a butt. **half-caste** *n.* (*offensive*) a person with parents of different racial origins, esp. with one parent from the Indian subcontinent and one from Europe. **half-century** *n.* (*pl.* **half-centuries**) 1 fifty years. 2 a score of fifty in cricket. **half-cock** *n.* the position of the cock of a firearm when retained by the first notch, so that it cannot be moved by the trigger. **to go off at half-cock** to fail as a result of being too impetuous. **to go off half-cocked** to fail as a result of being too impetuous. **half-crown, half a crown** *n.* a former British silver coin, value two shillings and sixpence (approx. 12p). **half-cut** *a.* (*sl.*) quite drunk. **half-dead** *a.* 1 almost dead. 2 (*coll.*) nearly exhausted. **half-deck** *n.* the part of a merchant ship where cadets and apprentices are quartered. **half-dime** *n.* (*N Am.*) five cents. **half-dozen, half a dozen** *n., a.* six or slightly more. **half-duplex** *a.* allowing a communication signal to be sent in only one direction at a time. **half-face** *n.* the face as seen in profile. **half-hardy** *a.* (of a plant) able to survive outside except in severe frosts. **half-hear** *v.t.* (*past, p.p.* **half-heard**) to hear indistinctly. **half-hearted** *a.* 1 lukewarm, indifferent. 2 poor-spirited, weak. **half-heartedly** *adv.* **half-heartedness** *n.* **half-hitch** *n.* a knot made by passing the end of a rope over a higher part of it and up through the resulting loop. **half holiday** *n.* 1 the latter half of a working day taken as a holiday. 2 a day on which this is allowed. **half-hose** *n.* socks. **half-hour, half an hour** *n.* thirty minutes. **on the half-hour** at half past each hour, at 30 minutes past the hour. **half-hourly** *adv., a.* **half-hunter** *n.* a watch that has a hinged cover with a hole allowing you to see part of the face and the approximate time. **half-inch** *n.* a unit of length equal to half an inch. ~*v.t.* (*sl.*) to steal, to purloin (rhyming slang, from *pinch*). **half-integer** *n.* the product of dividing an odd integer by two. **half-integral** *a.* **half-landing** *n.* a landing halfway up a flight of stairs. **half-lap** *n.* LAP JOINT (under LAP[2]). **half-length** *n.* a portrait showing only the upper half of the body. ~*a.* consisting of only half the full length. **half-life** *n.* the time taken for the radiation from a radioactive substance to decay to half its initial value. **half-light** *n.* a dim light as at dawn or dusk. **half-litre,** (*N Am.*) **half-liter** *n.* a quantity consisting of half a litre. **half-marathon** *n.* a running race of 13 miles 352 yards (21.243 km). **half mast** *n.* the middle of or halfway up the mast, the position of a flag denoting respect for a dead person. **at half mast** (*coll.*) (of trousers etc.) around the knees, having slipped down. **half measures** *n.pl.* methods of dealing with a problem that are not satisfactory or effective. **half-moon** *n.* 1 the moon when only half of its surface can be seen from earth. 2 the time when a half-moon is visible. 3 something in the shape of a half-moon. ~*a.* (*attrib.*) shaped like a half-moon (*half-moon spectacles*). **half-mourning** *n.* a mourning costume of black relieved by grey. **half nelson** *n.* in wrestling, a form of nelson in which one arm is passed under one of the opponent's. **half note** *n.* (*Mus.*) 1 a minim. 2 a semitone. **half pay** *n.* a reduced salary esp. because of sickness or retirement. **half-pay** *a.* entitled to half pay, on half pay. **halfpenny** (hāpˊni), **ha'penny** *n.* (*pl.* **halfpennies, halfpence, ha'pennies, ha'pence**) 1 a former British copper coin, half the value of a penny. 2 †a small fragment. ~*a.* 1 of the value or price of a halfpenny. 2 almost worthless. **halfpenny-worth, ha'p'orth** (hāˊpəth) *n.* 1 as much as can be bought for a halfpenny. 2 a very small amount. **half-pie** *a.* (*New Zeal.*) not very satisfactory or effective; half-baked. **half-plate** *n.* a photographic plate 16.5 cm by 10.8 cm in size. **half price** *n.* a reduced charge of half the normal price for admission to an entertainment or for rail travel etc. **half-price** *a., adv.* at or for half the normal price. **half-relief** *n.* 1 relief in moulding or carving etc. in which the design stands out half as much as the true proportion of the objects depicted. 2 a sculpture, carving etc. in this. **half-seas-over** *a.* (*sl.*) slightly drunk. **half-shift** *n.* (*Mus.*) a move of the hand upward on a violin to reach a high note. **half-sister** *n.* a sister by one parent only. **half-size** *n.* a size in clothing that is halfway between two normal sizes. **half-sole** *n.* a sole covering the front half of a shoe. **half-sovereign** *n.* a former British gold coin worth ten shillings (50p). **half-shaft** *n.* the cam shaft of a four-stroke cycle combustion engine, rotating at half the rate of the crank shaft. **half-starved** *a.* poorly fed, not having sufficient food. **half-step** *n.* (*Mus.*) a semitone. **half term** *n.* a short holiday halfway through a school term. **half the battle** *n.* an immense advantage. **half-tide** *n.* 1 half the time of a tide, about six hours. 2 the tide midway between flow and ebb. **half-timbered** *a.* (*Archit.*) having the foundations and principal supports of timber, and the spaces filled with plaster or brickwork to form the walls. **half-time** *n.* 1 the time at which the first half of a game is completed. 2 an interval in play at this time. 3 half the ordinary time allotted. **half-title** *n.* 1 a short title of a book, printed on the recto preceding the title page. 2 a title printed on the recto preceding a separate section of a book. **half-tone** *a.* of or relating to a process by which printing blocks are made with the shaded portions in small dots, by photographing on to a prepared plate through a finely ruled screen or grating. ~*n.* 1 a reproduction made by this process. 2 (*Mus., US*) a semitone. **half-track** *n.* 1 a vehicle running on one pair of wheels and one pair of Caterpillar tracks or similar. 2 this type of propulsion mechanism. **half-truth** *n.* a statement suppressing part of the truth. **half-volley** *n.* (*pl.* **half-volleys**) a stroke in tennis in which a ball is hit immediately after it bounces. **halfway** *adv.* 1 in the middle. 2 at half the distance. 3 more or less. ~*a.* situated in the middle or at half the distance; equidistant from two extremes. **halfway house** *n.* 1 a compromise. 2 a place providing short-term accommodation for people leaving institutions such as prisons or mental hospitals to provide rehabilitation before going back into the community. 3 the midpoint in a progression. 4 an inn halfway between two towns etc. **halfway line** *n.* a line across the middle of a football pitch etc., from which the game starts. **halfwit** *n.* 1 a silly person. 2 (*often offensive*) a mentally handicapped person. **half-witted** *a.* **half-wittedly** *adv.* **half-wittedness** *n.* **half-yearly** *a.* happening every six months. ~*adv.* once in every six months. [OE *healf, half* (cp. Dut. *half*, Icel. *hālfr*, G *halb*)]

Usage note Use of *a half a(n)*, with an extra indefinite article (as in *a half an hour*) is best avoided.

hali- HALO-.

halibut (hal´ibət) *n.* (*pl. in general* **halibut,** *in particular* **halibuts**) a large flat fish of the N Atlantic, *Hippoglossus hippoglossus*, sometimes weighing from 300 to 400 lb. (135–180 kg), used for food. **halibut oil** *n.* extract from the liver of this fish, rich in vitamins A and D. [ME *hali*, holy, and *butte*, a flounder, perh. cogn. with BUTT[1]]

halide (hā´lid, hal´-) *n.* a binary salt of halogen.

halieutic (haliū´tik) *a.* (*formal*) of or relating to fishing. [L *halieuticus*, Gr. *halieutikos*, from *halieutēs*, a fisherman, from *halieuein*, to fish, from *hals halos*, the sea]

haliotis (haliō´tis) *n.* any gastropod belonging to the genus *Haliotis*, having a shell lined with mother-of-pearl. [Gr. *hals halos*, sea, *ous otos*, ear, after the shape of the shell]

halite (hā´līt) *n.* rock salt. [L *halites*]

halitosis (halitō´sis) *n.* offensive breath. **halituous** (-lit´ū-) *a.* 1 like breath. 2 vaporous. 3 produced by breathing. **halitus** (hal´itəs) *n.* (*pl.* **halituses**) a vapour, an exhalation. [L *halitus*, breath, from *halāre*, to breathe]

hall (hawl) *n.* 1 a large room, esp. one in which public meetings or concerts are held, the large public room in a palace, castle etc. 2 a large building in which public business is transacted. 3 a room or passage forming the entry area of a house. 4 (*N Am.*) a connecting passage between rooms, a landing. 5 a residential building for undergraduates or other students. 6 **a** a large room in which members of a college etc. dine in common. **b** dinner in such a room. 7 a college or department of a university. 8 a manor house or mansion. 9 the room in a mansion in which the servants dine etc. 10 the building occupied by a guild etc. 11 (*pl.*) †music halls. **hall of Eblis** *n.* pandemonium (*Eblis* being the chief evil jinnee of Muslim mythology). **Hall of Fame** *n.* (*esp. N Am.*) 1 a building containing memorials to famous people. 2 a group of people who are famed for a particular reason. **hall of residence** *n.* a residential building for students. **hall porter** *n.* a person who carries bags for guests in a hotel. **hall stand,** (*N Am.*) **hall tree** *n.* a piece of furniture with pegs for coats and a place for umbrellas, sometimes with a mirror. **hallway** *n.* an entrance hall. [OE *heall* (cp. Dut. and Dan. *hal*, Icel. *hall*), cogn. with *helan*, to cover]

hallah CHALLAH.

hallelujah ALLELUIA.

halliard HALYARD.

hallmark (hawl´mahk) *n.* 1 an official stamp stamped by the Goldsmiths' Company and Government assay offices on gold and silver articles to guarantee the standard. 2 any mark of genuineness. ~*v.t.* 1 to stamp with a hallmark. 2 to mark or label as genuine or excellent.

hallo[1] HALLOO.

hallo[2] HELLO.

halloo (həloo´), **hallo** (həlō´), **halloa** *v.i.* (*past, p.p.* **hallooed, halloed, halloaed**) 1 to cry, to call attention. 2 to cheer dogs on with cries. ~*v.t.* 1 to shout loudly to. 2 to cheer or urge on. 3 to chase with shouts. ~*n., int.* a call to cheer on dogs. [imit., cp. OF *halloer*]

hallow (hal´ō) *v.t.* 1 to make sacred or worthy of reverence. 2 to revere. 3 to consecrate, to sanctify. ~†*n.* a saint. **Hallowe'en** (-ēn´) *n.* 31 October, the eve of All Saints' Day. †**Hallowmas** (-məs) *n.* the feast of All Saints' Day. [OE *hālgian*, from *hālig*, HOLY]

Hallstatt (hal´stat, -shtat), **Hallstattian** (-iən) *a.* denoting the first period of the Iron Age, typified by weapons found in the necropolis of Hallstatt which illustrate the transition from the use of bronze to that of iron. [*Hallstatt*, near Salzburg, Austria]

halluces HALLUX.

hallucinate (həloo´sināt) *v.i.* to have hallucinations. ~*v.t.* to affect with hallucinations. **hallucinant** *a., n.* **hallucination** (-ā´shən) *n.* an apparent sense perception or appearance of an external object that is not present in reality, an illusion. **hallucinator** *n.* **hallucinatory** *a.* **hallucinogen** (-əjən) *n.* a drug etc. that induces hallucinations. **hallucinogenic** (-jen´-) *a.* inducing hallucinations. [L *hallūcinātus*, p.p. of *hallūcinārī, alūcinārī*]

hallux (hal´əks) *n.* (*pl.* **halluces** (-ləsēz)) 1 the big toe. 2 the digit corresponding to this (as in some birds). [L *allex*]

halm HAULM.

halma (hal´mə) *n.* a game for two or four played on a board with 256 squares. [Gr., leap, from *allesthai*, to leap]

halo (hā´lō) *n.* (*pl.* **haloes, halos**) 1 a luminous circle round the sun or moon caused by the refraction of light through mist. 2 a nimbus or bright disc surrounding the heads of saints etc. 3 a concept of glory associated with an object. ~*v.t.* (*3rd pers. sing. pres.* **haloes,** *pres.p.* **haloing,** *past, p.p.* **haloed**) to surround with or as with a halo. ~*v.i.* to be formed into a halo. [F, from L *halō*, acc. of *halōs*, orig. a round threshing-floor]

halo- (hal´ō), **hali-** (-i), **hal-** *comb. form* 1 of or relating to salt or the sea. 2 of or relating to a halogen. [Gr. *hals*, salt]

halogen (hal´əjən) *n.* an element or other radical which by combination with a metal forms a salt (fluorine, chlorine, bromine, iodine and astatine). **halogenate** (həloj´-) *v.t.* to combine or treat with halogen. **halogenated** *a.* **halogenation** (-ā´shən) *n.* **halogenic** (-jen´-) *a.* **halogen lamp** *n.* a lamp with a filament surrounded by halogen. **halogenous** (-loj´-) *a.*

haloid (hal´oid) *a.* resembling common salt. ~*n.* a salt formed by the union of a halogen with a metal.

halon (hā´lon) *n.* any of various halogens, used in fire extinguishers. [from HALOGEN]

haloperidol (halōper´idol) *n.* a drug used in the treatment of mania and other psychotic disorders. [from HALOGEN and PIPERIDINE]

halophyte (hal´əfīt, hā´-) *n.* a plant suited to growing in salty conditions. [Gr. *hals, halos* salt]

halothane (hal´əthān) *n.* a volatile liquid used as a general anaesthetic. [HALO-, ETHANE]

halt[1] (hawlt) *n.* 1 a stop or interruption in activity or motion. 2 a minor stopping-place on a railway line. ~*v.i.* to come to a stop, esp. of soldiers. ~*v.t.* to cause to stop. **to call a halt (to)** to bring some activity to an end. [G *Halt*, a stoppage, cogn. with HOLD[1]]

halt[2] (hawlt) †*a.* limping, lame, crippled. ~*v.i.* 1 to limp, to be lame. **2** to doubt, to hesitate. **3** to fall or come short. **4** to be faulty in measure or rhyme. ~*n.* **1** (*collect.*) †lame persons generally. **2** †the act of limping; lameness. **3** a disease in sheep. **halting** *a.* **haltingly** *adv.* [OE *healt, halt* (cp. Icel. *haltr*, Dan. *halt*)]

halter[1] (hawl´tə) *n.* **1** a headstall and strap or rope by which an animal is fastened. **2** a rope to hang criminals. **3** death by hanging. **4** the strap of a halter-neck top. ~*v.t.* **1** to put a halter on. **2** to tie up with a halter. **3** to hang with a halter. **halter-break** *v.t.* to train (a horse) to submit to the halter. **halter-neck** *n., a.* (a style of neckline, bodice or top) with a piece of fabric around the neck, leaving the back and shoulders bare. [OE *hælfter* (cp. G *Halfter*), cogn. with HELVE]

halter[2] HALTERE.

haltere (hal´tiə), **halter** (-tə) *n.* (*pl.* **halteres** (-tiə´rēz)) either of two modified hind wings on dipterous insects, used for maintaining balance in flight. [Gr., a balancing weight held by jumpers, from *hallesthai*, to leap]

halutz CHALUTZ.

halva (hal´və, -vah), **halvah** *n.* a sweet made from sesame seeds and honey, typically from the Eastern Mediterranean. [Yiddish; Turkish *helva*]

halve (hahv) *v.t.* **1** to divide into two equal parts. **2** to share equally. **3** to lessen by half, to reduce to half. **4** to join (timbers) together by chopping away half the thickness of each. **5** in golf, to win the same number of holes, or to reach a hole in the same number of strokes, as the other side. [ME *halven*, from HALF]

halves HALF.

halyard (hal´yəd), **halliard** *n.* a rope or tackle for hoisting or lowering yards, sails or flags. [ME *halier* (HALE[1]), assim. to YARD[1]]

ham[1] (ham) *n.* **1** the hind part of the thigh. **2** (*usu. in pl.*) the thigh and buttock. **3** the thigh of an animal, esp. of a hog, salted and dried in smoke, or otherwise cured. **4** an amateur radio operator, a radio ham. **5** a ham actor. **6** the acting of a ham actor. ~*v.t., v.i.* (*pres.p.* **hamming,** *past, p.p.* **hammed**) (*sl.*) to act in a clumsy or exaggerated way. **to ham up** (*sl.*) to overact. **ham actor** *n.* **1** a bad, inexperienced actor. **2** an amateur actor. **3** a beginner, a novice. **ham-fisted** *a.* (*coll.*) **1** clumsy. **2** inept. **ham-fistedly** *adv.* **ham-fistedness** *n.* **ham-handed** *a.* HAM-FISTED (under HAM[1]). **ham-handedly** *adv.* **ham-handedness** *n.* **hammy** *a.* (*comp.* **hammier,** *superl.* **hammiest**) **1** of or relating to ham. **2** like ham. **3** (*sl.*) like a ham actor, over-theatrical. [OE *hamm* (cp. Dut. *ham*, Icel. *höm*, G *Hamme*)]

ham[2] (ham) *n.* (*Hist.*) a village, a town (now only in place names, as *Cheltenham*). [OE *hām*, HOME[1]]

hamadryad (hamədrī´əd, -ad) *n.* (*pl.* **hamadryads, hamadryades** (-ədēz)) **1** in Greek and Roman mythology, a dryad or wood nymph, who lived and died with the tree in which she lived. **2** an Indian venomous snake, *Naja bungarus*. [L *hamadryas*, pl. *-ades*, Gr. *hamadruades* (*hama*, with, *drus*, tree)]

hamadryas (hamədrī´əs, -as) *n.* (*pl.* **hamadryases**) an Arabian and NE African baboon, *Papio hamadryas*. [L *hamadryas*, cp. HAMADRYAD]

hamamelis (haməmē´lis) *n.* (*pl.* **hamamelises**) a shrub, such as the witch hazel, belonging to the genus *Hamamelis*. [L from Gr., medlar]

hamartia (həmah´tiə) *n.* the tragic flaw which destroys the principal character in a Greek tragedy. [Gr., fault, guilt]

hamartiology (həmahtiol´əji) *n.* (*pl.* **hamartiologies**) **1** (*Theol.*) the doctrine of sin. **2** a treatise on sin. [Gr. *hamartia*, sin]

hamate (hā´māt) *a.* **1** hook-shaped. **2** having a hook. [L *hāmātus*, from *hāmus*, a hook]

hamba (ham´bə) *int.* (*S Afr., offensive*) go away. [Nguni *ukuttamba* to go]

hamburger (ham´bœgə) *n.* a flat cake of minced beef, fried or grilled and often served in a bun. [G, of Hamburg]

hame[1] (hām) *n.* (*usu. in pl.*) either of the pair of curved bars of wood or metal fixed on the collar of a draught horse, to which the traces are connected. [cogn. with Dut. *haam*]

hame[2] (hām) *n.* (*Sc.*) home.

hamesucken (hām´sŭkən) *n.* (*Sc. Law*) the crime or felony of assaulting someone in their own house. [OE *hāmsōcn* (*hām*, HOME[1], *sōcn*, seeking, assault)]

Hamite (ham´īt) *n.* a member of a group of peoples in Egypt and N Africa, supposedly descended from Noah's son Ham. **Hamitic** (-mit´-) *a.* **1** of or relating to a group of N African languages including ancient Egyptian and Berber. **2** of or relating to the Hamites. ~*n.* the Hamitic group of languages. [*Ham*, second son of Noah]

hamlet (ham´lit) *n.* a small village, a little cluster of houses in the country. [OF *hamelet*, dim. of *hamel* (F *hameau*), from Gmc. (cp. OFris. and OE *hām*, HOME[1])]

hammal (həmahl´) *n.* **1** an Oriental porter. **2** a palanquin-bearer. [Arab. *hammāl*, from *hamala*, to carry]

hammam (həmahm´) *n.* **1** an Oriental bathhouse. **2** a Turkish bath. [Arab. *hāmmam*]

hammer (ham´ə) *n.* **1** a tool for driving nails, beating metals etc., consisting of a head, usu. of steel, fixed at right angles on a handle. **2** a machine, part of a machine or other appliance, performing similar functions, as a steam-hammer or the block striking the strings of a piano. **3** the part of a gunlock for exploding the charge. **4** the striker of a bell etc. **5** an auctioneer's mallet. **6** a metal ball, approx. 16 lb. (7.3 kg) in weight, attached to a handle by a long wire and thrown in an athletics contest. **7** the contest in which this is thrown. **8** MALLEUS. ~*v.t.* **1** to strike, beat or drive with or as with a hammer. **2** to forge or form with a hammer. **3** to work hard or persistently. **4** (*coll.*) to defeat easily. **5** in the Stock Exchange, to declare a defaulter. ~*v.i.* **1** to work or beat with or as with a hammer. **2** to make a noise like a hammer. **3** to work hard (at). **hammer and tongs 1** with great noise and vigour. **2** violently. **to bring to the hammer** to put up for auction. **to come under the hammer** to be sold by auction. **to hammer down** to fasten down by hammering. **to hammer home** to stress greatly. **to hammer in 1** to drive in with a hammer. **2** to stress greatly. **to hammer out 1** to flatten with a hammer. **2** to work out laboriously in the mind. **3** to play (a tune) heavy-handedly. **up to the hammer** first-rate. **hammer and sickle** *n.* the emblem symbolic of worker and peasant adopted on the flag etc. of the former USSR. **hammerbeam** *n.* (*Archit.*) a short beam projecting horizontally from a wall, in place of a tie-beam, to support the timbers of a roof. **hammer drill** *n.* an electric drill in which the bit moves backwards and forwards as well as rotating, used for drilling masonry. **hammerer** *n.* **hammer-harden** *v.t.* to harden (a metal) by hammering it in the cold state. **hammerhead** *n.* **1** the head of a hammer. **2** a S African marsh bird, *Scopus umbretta*. **3** (*also* **hammerhead shark**) a shark of the family Sphyrnidae, with a head like a hammer. **hammer-headed** *a.* **hammering** *n.* **1** the act of using a hammer. **2** the noise of a hammer being used. **3** (*coll.*) a clear defeat. **hammerless** *a.* **hammerlock** *n.* a grip in wrestling in which one person's arm is held twisted and bent behind their back by their opponent. **hammer-toe** *n.* a malformation of the foot consisting of permanent angular fixing of one or more toes. [OE *hamor* (cp. Dut. *hamer*, Icel. *hamarr*, G *Hammer*)]

hammock (ham´ək) *n.* a swinging or suspended bed made of canvas or netting, and hung by hooks from a roof, ceiling, tree etc. [Sp. *hamaca*, prob. from Carib]

hammy HAM[1].

hamper[1] (ham´pə) *n.* **1** a large wickerwork basket, with a cover. **2** this and its contents, usu. food for a picnic. **3** a package of groceries etc. put together for a special occasion. **4** (*N Am.*) a laundry basket. [formerly *hanaper, hanper*, OF *hanapier*, cp. hanap, a medieval drinking vessel]

hamper[2] (ham´pə) *v.t.* **1** to impede the movement or free action of. **2** to obstruct or impede (movement etc.). **3** to hinder, to shackle, to fetter. **4** †to put out of order. ~*n.* **1** anything which hampers or impedes free action. **2** (*Naut.*) rigging, equipment or other gear of a cumbrous kind. [etym. uncertain (cp. LG *hampern*, Dut. *haperen*, to stop, to fail)]

hamshackle (ham´shakəl) *v.t.* to fasten the head of (an ox, horse etc.) to one of its forelegs. [etym. uncertain, perh. conn. with HAMPER[2]]

hamsin KHAMSIN.

hamster (ham´stə) *n.* a ratlike rodent of the subfamily Cricetinae, with large cheek pouches in which it carries grain for food during hibernation. **common hamster** COMMON. **golden hamster** GOLDEN. [G]

hamstring (ham´string) *n.* **1** any of the tendons of the thigh muscle behind the knee. **2** (in quadrupeds) the large tendon at the back of the hock in the hind leg. ~*v.t.* (*past, p.p.* **hamstrung** (-strŭng), **hamstringed**) **1** to lame or disable by cutting or severing the hamstring. **2** to prevent (someone) from carrying out their plan. [HAM[1], STRING]

hamulus (ham´ūləs) *n.* (*pl.* **hamuli** (-lī)) (*Anat.*) a hook-like process. **hamular, hamulose** (-ōz) *a.* [L, dim. of *hāmus*, hook]

hamza (ham´zə), **hamzah** *n.* the sign used for a glottal stop in Arabic script. [Arab. *hamzah*, lit. compression]

Han (han) *n.* (*pl.* **Han**) a member of one of the peoples indigenous to China, as distinct from Manchus, Mongols etc.

hance (hans) *n.* (*Archit.*) the haunch of an arch. [perh. through an A-F *haunce*, from OF *hauce*, from *haucer* (F *hausser*), late L *altiāre*, from *altus*, high]

hand (hand) *n.* **1** the part of the body used for grasping and holding, consisting of the palm and fingers, at the extremity of the human arm. **2** a similar body part of monkeys and other primates. **3** the end of a limb, esp. a forelimb, in other animals, when serving as a prehensile organ. **4** a direction to one side (right or left). **5** the power of execution, skill, performance, handiwork. **6** a person having skill. **7** a pledge of marriage. **8** (*often in pl.*) possession, control, authority, power. **9** a source, a person giving information etc. **10** (*pl.*) operatives, labourers, the crew of a ship, players, people engaged in a game etc. **11** a part, a share, a turn, an innings. **12** an act of helping. **13** a game at cards. **14** the cards held by a player. **15** a part in a game of cards. **16** one of the players in a game of cards. **17** a player's turn to serve the ball at tennis, rackets etc. **18** a style of workmanship, handwriting etc. **19** a signature. **20** a lineal measure of 4 ins. (10 cm), a palm (for measuring horses). **21** a handful. **22** a handle. **23** the pointer or index finger of a watch, clock or counter. **24** five of any articles for sale. **25** a bunch of bananas. **26** a bundle of tobacco leaves. **27** a shoulder (of pork). **28** a round of applause. ~*v.t.* **1** to give, deliver or transmit with the hand. **2** to assist or conduct with the hand (into, out of etc.). **3** to deliver verbally. **4** (*coll.*) to deliver readily or inappropriately. **5** (*Naut.*) to furl. **6** †to seize, to lay hands on. **7** †to handle. **all hands** ALL. **at first hand** FIRST-HAND (under FIRST). **at hand 1** close by. **2** available. **3** about to happen. **at/ on all hands 1** by all parties. **2** from all quarters. **at second hand** SECOND-HAND (under SECOND[1]). **at the hands/ hand of 1** from or through (a person). **2** by the means or instrumentality of. **by hand 1** by a person, with the hands (as distinct from instruments or machines). **2** by messenger or agent. **3** by artificial rearing (of children or the young of animals). **for one's own hand** (to play or act) for one's personal advantage. **from hand to hand** from one person to another, bandied about. **from hand to mouth** without provision for the future. **hand and foot** completely, attending to every need (*She waits on him hand and foot*). **handed to one on a plate** PLATE. **hand in glove** on most intimate terms (with). **hand in hand 1** holding hands (with each other). **2** in union, unitedly. **hand over fist** (*coll.*) with rapid, unchecked progress. **hand over hand 1** by passing the hands alternately one above or before the other, as in climbing. **2** with rapid, unchecked progress. **hands off!** stand off, don't touch. **hands up! 1** raise hands, those who assent etc. **2** raise hands to assure surrender. **hand to hand 1** at close quarters. **2** in close fight. **heavy on hand** (of a horse etc.) hard to manage. **in hand 1** in a state of preparation or execution. **2** in possession. **3** under control. **light on hand** (of a horse etc.) easy to manage. **not to do a hand's turn** (*coll.*) to do no work at all. **off one's hands 1** finished with. **2** no longer one's responsibility. **on all hands** everywhere, on all sides. **on every hand** everywhere, on all sides. **on hand 1** present, nearby. **2** in stock. **on one's hands 1** (left) to one's responsibility. **2** (left) unsold. **on the one hand ...on the other** from this point of view...from that point of view. **out of hand 1** done, ended, completed. **2** without further consideration; at once, directly, extempore. **3** out of control. **to ask the hand of** to ask permission to marry (a woman). **to bear a hand** to lend assistance. **to come to hand 1** to be received. **2** to arrive. **to force someone's hand** to make someone take action against their will. **to give a (big) hand to** to clap, to applaud. **to give a hand** to help, to lend a hand. **to give one's hand** to agree to marry. **to give the hand of** to give permission to marry (a woman). **to hand 1** near. **2** available. **to hand down 1** to transmit, to give in succession. **2** to bequeath. **3** to pass on after use. **4** (*US*) to express authoritatively in court. **to hand in** to deliver to an office etc. **to hand it to** to give credit to, to acknowledge the superiority, victory etc. of. **to hand off 1** to push off with the hand. **2** in American football, to pass the ball by hand. **to hand on** to transmit, to give in succession. **to hand out 1** to distribute. **2** to allocate. **to hand over** to deliver (to a person). **to hand round/ around** to distribute. **to have a hand for** to be skilful at. **to have a hand in 1** to have a share in. **2** to be mixed up with. **to have one's hands full** to be fully occupied. **to have one's hands tied** to have no freedom of action. **to hold hands** to hold each other's hand. **to hold hands with** to hold the other person's hand. **†to hold one's hand** to refrain from action. **to hold someone's hand** to make something easier for someone by helping and supporting them, showing them how to do something etc. **to keep one's hand in** to keep oneself in practice. **to lay hands on 1** to touch. **2** to assault. **3** to seize. **4** to lay the hands on the head of (in ordination, confirmation etc.). **to lay one's hands on 1** to get, to acquire, to seize. **2** to find. **to lend a hand** to help, to give assistance. **to shake hands** to clasp each other's right hand in token of friendship etc. **to show one's hand** to disclose one's designs (orig. of cards). **†to stay one's hand** to refrain from action. **to take a hand** to take part in a game, esp. of cards. **to take a hand in 1** to take a share in. **2** to get mixed up with. **to take by the hand** to take (someone) under one's protection, care or guidance. **to take in hand 1** to undertake, attempt. **2** to deal with, to manage. **3** to discipline. **to tie someone's hands** to prevent someone from taking action. **to win hands down** to win without an effort, easily. **under one's hand** with one's proper signature. **handbag** *n.* **1** a small bag for carrying money and personal things. **2** (*also* **handbag music**) a commercialized development of house music. ~*v.t.*

(*pres.p.* **handbagging**, *past, p.p.* **handbagged**) (of a woman) to abuse or reprimand publicly, to treat insensitively. **handbagging** *n.* **handball** *n.* **1** in football, a ball illegally played with the hand. **2** a game similar to football, played by throwing the ball between the goals. **3** a game played in a walled court, hitting the ball against the wall with the hand. **handbarrow** *n.* a kind of stretcher, having a pair of handles at each end, adapted to be carried by two people. **handbasin** *n.* a basin for washing the hands in a bathroom. **handbell** *n.* a small bell rung with the hand, esp. one of a series played musically. **handbill** *n.* a small printed sheet for circulating information. **handbook** *n.* a small book or treatise on any subject, a compendium, a manual. **hand brace** *n.* a hand tool for boring. **handbrake** *n.* a brake worked by a hand lever, esp. on a motor vehicle. **handbrake turn** *n.* a sharp U-turn caused by deliberate application of the handbrake at speed. **hand-breadth** HAND'S-BREADTH (under HAND). **handcar** *n.* a small hand-propelled truck running on a railway line, used by workers on the line. **handcart** *n.* a two-wheeled vehicle for carrying parcels or goods, pushed or drawn by hand. **handclap** *n.* an act of clapping. **hand cream** *n.* cream for moisturizing the hands. **handcuff** *n.* (*usu. pl.*) a manacle for the wrists, consisting of a chain and locking-rings. ~*v.t.* to secure with handcuffs. **-handed** *comb. form* **1** having a hand of a certain kind. **2** involving the number of hands specified (*a one-handed vault*). **3** using or made for the hand specified (*left-handed scissors*). **-handedly** *adv.* **-handedness** *n.* **-hander** *n.* (*in comb.*) a blow, stroke etc. using the stated hand, part of the hand or number of hands. **handful** *n.* (*pl.* **handfuls**) **1** as much or as many as can be held in the hand. **2** a small number or quantity. **3** (*coll.*) a troublesome person or task. **handglass** *n.* **1** a small mirror with a handle. **2** a magnifying glass for holding in the hand. **3** a bell-glass or glazed frame, for the protection of plants. **4** (*Naut.*) a small sandglass, formerly used to time the running out of the log-line. **hand grenade** *n.* a grenade for throwing by hand. **handgrip** *n.* **1** a grasp or seizure with the hands. **2** a convenient handle. **3** (*esp. NAm.*) a suitcase, a large bag for holding luggage, equipment etc. **handgun** *n.* a gun that can be held and fired in one hand. **hand-held** *a.* held in the hands when in use. ~*n.* a hand-held computer. **handhold** *n.* something for the hand to hold on by (in climbing etc.). **hand-hot** *a.* (of water etc.) of a degree of heat that the hands can still be put into. **hand lead** *n.* (*Naut.*) a small lead for sounding. **handless** *a.* **hand line** *n.* a line worked by the hand, esp. a fishing line without a rod. **handlist** *n.* a brief list for reference. **hand loom** *n.* a loom worked by hand. **handmade** *a.* produced by hand, not by machinery. †**handmaid, handmaiden** *n.* a female servant or attendant. **hand-me-downs** *n.pl.* (*coll.*) second-hand clothes. **hand mill** *n.* **1** a small mill worked by hand. **2** a quern. **hand organ** *n.* a barrel organ worked by a handle. **handout** *n.* **1** a short informal document given to students, an audience etc. to help them understand a particular lesson, lecture etc. **2** a statement handed out to the press. **3** a gift of money etc. esp. to the poor. **handover** *n.* an act of handing over, a transfer. **handpick** *v.t.* to choose carefully. **hand press** *n.* a press, esp. for printing, worked by the hand, as distinct from one worked by steam, water etc. **handpump** *n.* a pump worked by the hand. **hand puppet** *n.* a glove puppet. **handrail** *n.* a rail alongside stairs, landings etc. **handsaw** *n.* a saw riveted at one end to a handle, and designed to be used by one hand. **hand's-breadth, hand-breadth** *n.* a linear measurement equal to the breadth of the hand. **hand-screw** *n.* **1** a screw-jack for raising heavy weights. **2** a screw, generally for brake adjustment, which can be turned by hand. **handset** *n.* the receiver of a telephone. **handsewing** *n.* sewing with the needle in the hand, as distinct from by machine. **handsewn** *a.* **handsfree** *a.* (of a telephone etc.) that does not need to be held during operation or use. **handshake** *n.* a shake of another's hand as a greeting. **hands-off** *a.* without interfering or controlling someone directly. **hands-on** *a.* **1** having or through practical experience. **2** requiring practical involvement. **handspike** *n.* a bar, usu. of wood shod with steel, used as a lever for lifting, heaving etc. **handspring** *n.* a somersault done by springing first onto the hands, then over on to the feet. **handstand** *n.* the act of balancing upright on one's hands. **hand-to-hand** *a.* (of fighting) at close quarters, using swords, fists etc. **hand tool** *n.* a tool worked with the hand, without electricity etc. **hand towel** *n.* a small towel for drying the hands. **handwork** *n.* work done with the hands, as distinct from that done by machinery etc. **handworked** *a.* **handwriting** *n.* **1** writing done by hand. **2** the style of writing peculiar to a person. **handwritten** *a.* written by hand, as distinct from printed etc. [OE *hand, hond* (cp. Dut. and G *Hand*, Icel. *hönd, hand*)]

h & c *abbr.* hot and cold (water).

handicap (han´dikap) *n.* **1** any physical or mental disability. **2** a disadvantage. **3** a race or contest in which an allowance of time, distance or weight is made to the inferior competitors. **4** the more difficult conditions imposed on a superior competitor. **5** a golfer's average number of strokes above par. ~*v.t.* (*pres.p.* **handicapping**, *past, p.p.* **handicapped**) **1** to impose heavier weight or other disadvantageous conditions on (a competitor). **2** to put at a disadvantage. **handicapped** *a.* having a physical or mental disability. **handicapper** *n.* [from the drawing of lots out of a hat or cap]

handicraft (han´dikrahft) *n.* **1** skill in working with the hands. **2** a manual occupation or trade requiring both skill and art. ~*a.* of or relating to manual skills or labour. **handicraftsman** *n.* (*pl.* **handicraftsmen**) a person employed in a handicraft. [OE *handcræft*]

handily, handiness HANDY.

handiwork (han´diwœk), **handywork** *n.* **1** work done by the hands. **2** the product of one's hands, labour or effort. [OE *handgeweorc* (HAND, *weorc*, collect. WORK)]

handkerchief (hang´kəchif) *n.* (*pl.* **handkerchiefs, handkerchieves** (-chēvz)) **1** a piece of cloth, silk, linen or cotton, carried for wiping the nose, face etc. **2** a neckcloth, a neckerchief. [HAND, KERCHIEF]

Usage note The plural *handkerchiefs* is preferred to *handkerchieves*.

handle (han´dəl) *v.t.* **1** to touch, to feel with, to wield or use with the hands. **2** to treat (well etc.). **3** to deal with, to manage. **4** to deal in. **5** to treat of. ~*v.i.* (of a vehicle) to respond in a specified way to control by a driver. ~*n.* **1** that part of a vessel, tool or instrument, by which it is grasped and held in the hand. **2** an instrument or means by which anything is done. **3** the quality of fabric in respect of how it feels and how easy it is to work with. **4** (*sl.*) a name, title, a call sign. **to fly off the handle** to become angry suddenly, to go into a rage. **to get a handle on** (*coll.*) to find a means of understanding etc. **to give a handle to** to furnish an occasion or advantage that may be utilized. **handleable** *a.* **handleability** (-bil´-) *n.* **handlebar** *n.* a horizontal bar with grips at each end for steering a bicycle, motorcycle etc. **handlebar moustache** *n.* a thick, wide moustache that curls upwards at each end. **handled** *a.* **handler** *n.* **1** a person who handles or deals in something. **2** a person who trains and controls an animal, as a police dog. **3** in tanning, a tan-pit containing a weak ooze. **handling** *n.* **1** the action of touching, feeling etc. with the hand. **2** in drawing, the art of managing the pencil. **3** a characteristic style of painting, composing, manipulating etc. **4** the responsiveness of a vehicle to a driver's control. [OE *handlian*, from HAND (cp. Dut. *handelen*, G *handeln*)]

†handsel (han´səl), **hansel** *n.* **1** a gift for luck, esp. on the first Monday in the New Year. **2** an instalment paid to seal a bargain. **3** the first sale, present, use etc. **4** (*fig.*) a foretaste. *~v.t.* (*pres.p.* **handselling, hanselling,** (*N Am.*) **handseling, hanseling,** *past, p.p.* **handselled, hanselled,** (*N Am.*) **handseled, hanseled**) **1** to give a handsel to. **2** to use for the first time. **3** to be the first to use. [perh. from Scand. (cp. Icel. *handsal*, Dan. *handsel*, OE *handselen*, delivery into the hand)]

handsome (han´səm) *a.* (*comp.* **handsomer,** *superl.* **handsomest**) **1** good-looking, well formed, finely featured. **2** liberal, generous. **3** ample, large. **4** (*N Am.*) showing skill and cleverness, adroit. **5** noble. **6** †handy, convenient, suitable. **handsomely** *adv.* **1** in a handsome manner. **2** (*Naut.*) carefully. **handsomeness** *n.*

handy (han´di) *a.* (*comp.* **handier,** *superl.* **handiest**) **1** useful and easy to use. **2** close at hand, near, convenient. **3** dexterous, skilful with the hands. **handily** *adv.* **handiness** *n.* **handy-dandy** *n.* a children's game in which one child has to guess in which hand of the other some small article is held. **handyman** *n.* (*pl.* **handymen**) **1** a person who does odd jobs. **2** a person who is good at DIY.

handywork HANDIWORK.

hang (hang) *v.t.* (*past, p.p.* **hung** (hŭng)) **1** to attach to a point of support higher than its own height. **2** to attach loosely to a point of support above the centre of gravity. **3** to fasten so as to leave movable (as a bell, gate, the body of a coach etc.). **4** (*past, p.p.* **hanged**) to suspend by the neck on a gallows as capital punishment. **5** to place (a painting etc.) on view on a wall. **6** to attach (wallpaper) in vertical strips to a wall. **7** to suspend (game) from a hook to mature. **8** to cover or decorate with anything suspended. **9** to attach, to fasten. **10** (*coll.*) to attach the blame for. **11** to cause to droop (*hung her head*). *~v.i.* **1** to be hung or suspended. **2** to dangle. **3** (of clothing) to drape or fall. **4** to be immobile in the air. **5** to be executed by hanging. **6** to droop, to bend forwards. **7** to be fixed or suspended with attention. **8** to depend on future events. **9** to be in suspense; to be stuck. *~n.* **1** a slope, a declivity. **2** the way that something hangs. **3** a general tendency, drift or bent. **hang (it)!** used to express annoyance or surprise. **I'll be hanged** hang it! **not to care/ give a hang** (*coll.*) to be totally unconcerned. **to get the hang of 1** to understand the drift or connection of. **2** to get the knack of. **to go hang** (*coll.*) to do one's worst without anyone caring. **to hang about/ around 1** to loiter, to loaf. **2** to stay near, to frequent. **3** to wait. **4** to associate (with). **to hang back 1** to act reluctantly, to hesitate. **2** to stay behind. **to hang by a thread** THREAD. **to hang down** to droop. **to hang fire 1** to hesitate. **2** (of a charge in a firearm) not to ignite immediately. **to hang heavy/ heavily** (of time) to go slowly. **to hang in 1** (*esp. N Am., coll.*) to persist. **2** (*esp. N Am., coll.*) to linger. **to hang in doubt** to be in suspense. **to hang in effigy** EFFIGY. **to hang in the balance** BALANCE. **to hang loose** LOOSE. **to hang on 1** to grasp or hold. **2** to persist. **3** to depend on. **4** (*coll.*) to wait. **to hang on to 1** to keep holding. **2** to retain. **to hang on/ upon 1** to be dependent on. **2** to listen closely to. **3** to adhere closely to. **4** to be a weight or drag on. **5** to rest, to dwell upon. **to hang out 1** to suspend from a window etc. **2** (of a tongue) to protrude loosely. **3** (*sl.*) to live (in a particular place); to spend a lot of time (somewhere). **to hang over 1** to be hanging or immobile above. **2** to be oppressively present to. **3** to be overhanging. **to hang together 1** to be consistent, to make sense. **2** to be closely united. **to hang up 1** to suspend. **2** to replace a telephone receiver and so end the call. **3** to put aside, to leave undecided. **4** to defer indefinitely. **5** (*sl.*) to cause neurosis or anxiety in. **to hang up one's hat** HAT. **to let it all hang out** (*sl.*) to be completely relaxed, to abandon inhibition. **hangbird** *n.* a bird that builds a hanging nest, esp. the Baltimore oriole. **hang-dog** *n.* a guilty-looking person. *~a.* sullen, guilty-looking. **hanger** *n.* **1** a person who hangs or causes to be hanged. **2** that on which a thing is hung or suspended. **3** a coat-hanger. **4** a pot-hook. **5** a short, curved sword or cutlass, orig. hung from the belt. **6** a sloping wood or grove (largely in place-names). **hanger-on** *n.* (*pl.* **hangers-on**) a person who hangs on or sticks to a person, place etc., a dependant, a parasite. **hang-glider** *n.* **1** a type of large kite controlled by a person suspended beneath it in a harness. **2** a person who flies a hang-glider. **hang-glide** *v.i.* **hang-gliding** *n.* **hanging** *n.* **1** the act of suspending etc. **2** an execution by the gallows. **3** an exhibition of paintings etc. **4** (*pl.*) fabrics hung up to cover or drape a room. *~a.* **1** suspended, dangling. **2** steep, inclined. **3** punishable by hanging. **hanging-bird** *n.* HANGBIRD (under HANG). **hanging buttress** *n.* a buttress supported on a bracket or projection. **hanging committee** *n.* a committee appointed to choose and arrange pictures in an exhibition. **hanging garden** *n.* a garden rising in terraces one above the other. **hanging valley** *n.* a valley that joins another at a higher level. **hanging valve** *n.* a hinged valve falling by the action of gravity. **hangman** *n.* (*pl.* **hangmen**) **1** a public executioner who hangs people. **2** a guessing-game in which suggestions of letters not in the word to be guessed are recorded by drawing the lines of a gallows and hanged person. **hangnail** *n.* an agnail. **hang-nest** *n.* **1** a bird constructing a pendulous nest. **2** the nest of such a bird. **3** HANGBIRD (under HANG). **hang-net** *n.* a net with a large mesh hanging vertically on stakes. **hang-out** *n.* (*coll.*) a haunt. **hangover** *n.* **1** the after-effects of drinking too much alcohol. **2** a survival from an earlier time. **hang-up** *n.* (*coll.*) **1** a neurosis or anxiety. **2** the source of this. [from two OE verbs. *hangian*, intr., and the causal *hōn*, and in North. Eng. from Icel. *hengja*, whence the p.p. *hung*]

hangar (hang´ə) *n.* a large shed, esp. for aircraft. **hangarage** *n.* [F, etym. uncertain]

Hang Seng index (hang seng´ indeks) *n.* an indicator giving relative prices of major shares on the Hong Kong Stock Exchange. [from the name of a Hong Kong bank]

hank (hangk) *n.* **1** a coil or skein. **2** a unit of measurement of two or more skeins of yarn, silk, wool or cotton, tied together (840 yd. (750 m) of cotton yarn, 560 yd. (500 m) of worsted). **3** (*Naut.*) any one of the hoops or rings to which a fore-and-aft sail is bent. *~v.t.* **1** (*Naut.*) to fasten to a hank. **2** †to form into hanks. [cp. Icel. *hōnk*, Dan. and LG *Hank*]

hanker (hang´kə) *v.i.* to have strong desire or longing (after). **hankerer** *n.* **hankering** *n.* **hankeringly** *adv.* [etym. uncertain, prob. cogn. with Dut. *hunkeren*]

☒ **hankerchief** common misspelling of HANDKERCHIEF.

hanky (hang´ki), **hankie** *n.* (*pl.* **hankies**) (*coll.*) a handkerchief. **hanky-panky** (hangkipang´ki) *n.* (*coll.*) **1** improper activity esp. of a sexual kind. **2** jugglery, trickery, fraud. [coined on anal. of HOCUS-POCUS (under HOCUS)]

Hanoverian (hanəviə´riən, -veə´-) *a.* of or relating to Hanover or the Hanoverians. *~n.* **1** a native or inhabitant of Hanover. **2** an adherent of the House of Hanover, the dynasty holding the throne of Great Britain and Ireland from 1714 to 1901. [G *Hanover*, state and capital city]

Hansa HANSE.

Hansard (han´sahd) *n.* the official report of the proceedings of the British Parliament (from the name of the compilers and printers, 1774–1889). **Hansardize,**

Hansardise *v.t.* to produce the official record of the former utterances of (an MP) in order to confute them. [Messrs. *Hansard*]

Hanse (hans), **Hansa** (han´sə) *n.* **1** a corporation or guild of merchants. **2** the entrance-fee of a medieval guild. **Hanseatic** (-siat´-) *a.* **Hanseatic League** *n.* a medieval confederacy between certain German towns for the protection of commerce. **Hanse Towns** *n.pl.* the towns which confederated to form the Hanseatic League. [OF, from OHG *hansa*, a company]

hansel HANDSEL.

Hansen's disease (han´sənz) *n.* leprosy. [G. H. A. *Hansen*, 1841–1912, Norwegian physician and bacteriologist]

hansom (han´səm), **hansom cab** *n.* a two-wheeled horse-drawn cab in which the driver's seat is behind the body, the reins passing over the hooded top. [J. A. *Hansom*, 1803–82, patentee in 1834]

Hantavirus (han´tə) *n.* an often-fatal virus whose symptoms are similar to those of flu. [the *Hantaan* river in Korea, where a number of related viruses were first isolated]

Hants (hants) *abbr.* Hampshire.

Hanukkah (han´əkə, -nukə), **Chanukah, Chanukkah** *n.* the Jewish festival of lights in commemoration of the rededication of the temple (165 BC). [Heb., consecration]

hanuman (han´uman) *n.* **1** a lemur, *Presbytis entellus*, sacred to Hindus. **2** (**Hanuman**) the Hindu monkey-god, a helper of Rama. [Hind. *hanumān*, Hindu monkey-god]

†**hap**[1] (hap) *n.* **1** chance, luck. **2** that which happens or chances. **3** a casual event. ~*v.i.* (*pres.p.* **happing,** *past, p.p.* **happed**) to befall, to happen by chance. †**haply** *adv.* **1** by chance. **2** perhaps. [prob. from Icel. *happ* (cp. OE *gehæp*, fit)]

hap[2] (hap) *v.t.* (*pres.p.* **happing,** *past, p.p.* **happed**) (*Sc.*) **1** to cover over. **2** to wrap up. ~*n.* a covering. [etym. unknown]

hapax legomenon (hapaks ligom´inon) *n.* (*pl.* **hapax legomena** (-minə)) a word or expression that has only been used once; a nonce-word. [Gr., something said only once]

ha'penny HALFPENNY (under HALF).

haphazard (haphaz´əd) *a.* **1** happening by chance. **2** random. ~†*n.* mere chance, accident. ~*adv.* at random. **haphazardly** *adv.* **haphazardness** *n.*

hapless (hap´lis) *a.* unhappy, unfortunate, luckless. **haplessly** *adv.* **haplessness** *n.* [HAP[1]]

haplo- (hap´lō) *comb. form* single, simple. [Gr.]

haplography (haplog´rəfi) *n.* inadvertent writing of a word or letter once which should be written twice, as *superogatory* for *supererogatory.*

haploid (hap´loid) *a.* **1** having half the usual number. **2** having a single set of unpaired chromosomes. **3** composed of haploid cells. ~*n.* a haploid cell or organism.

haplology (haplol´əji) *n.* the omission in speech of one or more similar sounds or syllables.

haply HAP[1].

ha'p'orth HALFPENNY (under HALF).

happen (hap´ən) *v.i.* **1** to occur. **2** to befall, to occur by chance. **3** to chance (to). **4** to light (upon). ~*adv.* (*North.*) perhaps. **as it happens** actually, in fact. **happening** *n.* **1** (*usu. in pl.*) something that happens, a chance occurrence. **2** (*coll.*) a spontaneous event, performance etc. ~*a.* (*esp. N Am., sl.*) trendy, modern. **happenstance** (-stans) *n.* (*esp. N Am.*) **1** chance, luck. **2** something that happens by chance.

happi (hap´i), **happi-coat** *n.* (*pl.* **happis, happi-coats**) a loose casual coat worn in Japan. [Jap.]

happy (hap´i) *a.* (*comp.* **happier,** *superl.* **happiest**) **1** enjoying pleasure from something good. **2** contented, satisfied. **3** lucky, fortunate. **4** prosperous, successful. **5** apt, felicitous. **6** favourable. **7** dexterous, ready, skilful. **8** (*coll.*) slightly drunk. **9** (*in comb.*) in a dazed state. ~†*v.t.* (*3rd pers. sing. pres.* **happies,** *pres.p.* **happying,** *past, p.p.* **happied**) to make happy. **happy as a sandboy** SANDBOY (under SAND). **happily** *adv.* **happiness** *n.* **happy dispatch** *n.* HARA-KIRI. **happy event** *n.* (*coll.*) the birth of a baby. **happy families** *n.* a card game with a pack having representatives of family members instead of suits. **happy-go-lucky** *a.* careless, thoughtless, improvident. **happy hour** *n.* a period when a bar etc. sells drinks at reduced prices to attract customers. **happy hunting ground** *n.* (*coll.*) an area of activity offering easy rewards. **happy medium** *n.* a compromise; a state of affairs avoiding extremes. **happy thought** *n.* an apposite or timely suggestion, idea etc. [HAP[1], -Y[1]]

haptic (hap´tik) *a.* relating to the sense of touch. [Gr. *haptein*, to touch]

hapuka (həpoo´kə) *n.* a New Zealand fish, the grouper. [Maori]

hara-kiri (harəkē´ri, -kir´-), **hari-kari** (harikar´i) *n.* a Japanese method of suicide by disembowelling. [Jap. *hara*, belly, *kiri*, cutting]

Usage note The spelling *hari-kari* and pronunciation (harikar´i) are best avoided.

---

harangue (hərang´) *n.* **1** a declamatory address to a large assembly. **2** a noisy and vehement speech, a tirade. ~*v.t.* (*pres.p.* **haranguing,** *past, p.p.* **harangued**) to address in an angry, vehement way. **haranguer** *n.* [MF, from med. L *harenga* or It. *aringa*, prob. from OHG *hring*, a ring (of people)]

harass (har´əs, həras´) *v.t.* **1** to torment. **2** to molest. **3** to tire out with care or worry. **4** (*Mil.*) to worry by repeated attacks. **harassed** *a.* **harasser** *n.* **harassingly** *adv.* **harassment** *n.* **1** the act of harassing. **2** the state of being harassed. [MF *harasser*, perh. from OF *harer*, to hound a dog on]

Usage note The pronunciation (-ras´), with the stress on the second syllable, is sometimes disapproved of.

---

harbinger (hah´binjə) *n.* **1** a person who announces the approach of another. **2** a person who or thing which foretells what is coming. **3** a precursor. **4** †a person sent ahead to find lodgings. ~*v.t.* **1** to precede as harbinger. **2** to announce the approach of. [ME *herbergeour*, OF *herbergere*, from *herberge* (F *auberge*), OHG *heriberga* (*hari*, army, *bergan*, to shelter)]

harbour (hah´bə), (*N Am.*) **harbor** *n.* **1** a refuge, esp. a refuge or shelter for ships. **2** a port or haven. **3** †an asylum, a place of shelter or security. **4** †a lodging, an inn. ~*v.t.* **1** to shelter. **2** to keep in mind, esp. secretly. **3** †to entertain, to cherish, to foster. **4** †to trace (a hart or hind) to its covert. ~*v.i.* **1** to come to anchor in a harbour. **2** †to take shelter, to lodge. **harbourage** (-rij) *n.* a shelter, harbour, refuge. **harbour dues** *n.pl.* charges for mooring or accommodating a ship in a harbour. **harbourer** *n.* **harbourless** *a.* **harbour master** *n.* an official having charge of the berthing and mooring of ships in a harbour. **harbour seal** *n.* (*N Am.*) the common greyish-black seal, *Phoca vitulina.* [ME *hereberge*, perh. from OE (*here*, army, *beorg*, shelter), cp. HARBINGER]

hard (hahd) *a.* **1** firm, solid, compact. **2** not yielding to pressure. **3** difficult to accomplish, understand or explain. **4** laborious, fatiguing, strenuous. **5** intricate, perplexing. **6** harsh, severe; galling, inflexible, cruel, unfeeling. **7** sordid, miserly, stingy. **8** ideologically rigid. **9** not open to dispute, definite. **10** difficult to bear, oppressive, unjust. **11** high in alcohol. **12** (of a drug) highly addictive and harmful. **13** coarse, unpalatable. **14** rough and harsh to the palate, the touch etc. **15** (of water) containing mineral salts making it difficult to use for washing. **16** in phonetics, sounded gutturally (as *c* and *g* when not pronounced like *s* and *j*); aspirated (as *k, t, p*, compared with *g, d, b*). **17** (of stocks and shares) stable in value. *~adv.* **1** forcibly, violently. **2** strenuously, severely. **3** with effort or difficulty. **4** close, near. **5** so as to be firm or solid. **6** as hard or as far as possible, to the utmost limit. *~n.* **1** a firm landing place, jetty or roadway. **2** (*coll.*) hard cash. **3** (*sl.*) hard labour. **4** something that is hard. **hard as nails 1** callous, unsympathetic. **2** physically tough. **hard by 1** close by. **2** close at hand. **hard of hearing** having defective hearing. **hard on 1** difficult for. **2** unkind to, unpleasant to. **3** critical of. **4** close behind. **hard put to** unlikely to find it easy to. **hard put to it** in difficulties. **hard row to hoe** ROW[1]. **hard upon** close behind. **to go hard with** to cause problems or difficulties for someone. **to play hard to get** PLAY. **to put the hard word on** (*Austral., New Zeal., sl.*) to ask or pressurize (someone) to do something. **hard and fast** *a.* strict; that must be strictly adhered to. **hardback** *n.* a book with a stiff binding. *~a.* having a stiff binding. **hardbacked** *a.* **hardbag (music)** *n.* a development of house music, less commercialized than handbag. **hardbake** *n.* a kind of toffee containing blanched almonds. **hard-baked** *a.* cooked until hard. **hardball** *n.* (*N Am.*) **1** a baseball. **2** (*sl.*) severe or uncompromising tactics. *~v.t.* (*sl.*) to put pressure on (a person). **hardbitten** *a.* tough and not easily shocked. **hardboard** *n.* thin board made of compressed woodchips bound together with resin. **hardbody** *n.* (*pl.* **hardbodies**) (*sl.*) **1** a muscular body developed through exercise. **2** a person with such a body. **hard-boiled** *a.* **1** boiled until hard. **2** (*coll.*) hard-headed, unemotional, callous, shrewd. **hard case** *n.* **1** a tough or violent person. **2** (*Austral., New Zeal.*) an amusing or eccentric person. **3** a difficult case. **4** a case of hardship. **hard cash** *n.* actual coin; ready money. **hard cheese** *n., int.* (*coll.*) hard luck. **hard coal** *n.* anthracite, non-bituminous coal. **hard copy** *n.* printout, or a paper version, of a computer document. **hardcore** *n.* **1** rubble, refuse stone etc. crushed to form the substratum of a road. **2** an experimental form of rock music with a fast, aggressive style. **hard core** *n.* **1** a group within a larger group, devoted to their beliefs and resistant to change. **2** an irreducible central core. **hard-core** *a.* **1** loyal to beliefs and resistant to change. **2** (of pornography) sexually explicit. **hard court** *n.* a tennis court with a surface of tarmac, concrete etc. **hardcover** *n., a.* (*esp. N Am.*) HARDBACK (under HARD). **hard currency** *n.* **1** coin, metallic money. **2** a currency unlikely to depreciate suddenly or fluctuate in value. **hard disk** *n.* a rigid magnetizable disk for computer storage. **hard doer** *n.* (*Austral.*) a smart Alec, a tough nut. **hard-done-by** *a.* treated unfairly or badly. **hard drinker** *n.* a person who drinks heavily, a drunkard. **hard-earned** *a.* earned or acquired with difficulty. **hard error** *n.* (*Comput.*) an irreversible error. **hard-faced** *a.* **1** having a harsh or stern face. **2** brazen, insolent. **hard-favoured, hard-featured** *a.* of harsh features; ill-looking, ugly. **hard feelings** *n.pl.* feelings of bitterness and resentment. **hard fern** *n.* a fern, *Blechnum spicant*, with dark-green erect leaves. **hard-fought** *a.* closely contested. **hard going** *n.* something or someone difficult to deal with, a laborious task. **hardhack** *n.* (*N Am.*) a New England shrub, *Spiraea tomentosa*. **hard hat** *n.* **1** a protective helmet of a type worn on construction sites. **2** a reactionary. **hardhead** *n.* **1** a hard-headed person. **2** HARDHEADS (under HARD). **hard-headed** *a.* practical, not sentimental, matter-of-fact. **hard-headedly** *adv.* **hard-headedness** *n.* **hardheads** *n.* a knapweed, *Centaurea nigra*, with purple flower heads. **hard-hearted** *a.* cruel, unfeeling, pitiless. **hard-heartedly** *adv.* **hard-heartedness** *n.* **hard hit** *a.* seriously damaged or affected, esp. by monetary losses. **hard-hitting** *a.* forceful, effective, outspoken. **hardish** *a.* **hard labour,** (*N Am.*) **hard labor** *n.* enforced labour, esp. when added to imprisonment. **hard landing** *n.* **1** an awkward, bumpy aircraft landing. **2** a spacecraft landing which destroys the vehicle. **hard line** *n.* an approach that is without compromise; an unyielding attitude. **hardline** *a.* (of a policy) uncompromising, extreme. **hardliner** *n.* a person following a hardline policy. **hard lines** *n.pl., int.* (*coll.*) hard luck. **hard luck** *n.* misfortune, undeserved lack of success. *~int.* used to express commiseration. **hard-mouthed** *a.* **1** (of a horse) insensible to the action of the bit. **2** obstinate, difficult to manage. **hardness** *n.* **hard-nosed** *a.* (*coll.*) unsentimental, tough, realistic. **hard nut** *n.* (*sl.*) an aggressive person. **hard nut to crack** *n.* **1** a problem that is difficult to solve. **2** something that is difficult to understand. **3** a person who is not easily convinced. **hard-on** *n.* (*sl.*) an erect penis, an erection. **hard pad** *n.* a form of distemper in dogs. **hard palate** *n.* the front part of the palate. **hardpan** *n.* a layer of hard clay below the soil. **hard-paste** *a.* denoting, of or relating to porcelain made from clay and stone and fired at a high temperature. **hard porn, hard pornography** *n.* sexually explicit pornography. **hard-pressed** *a.* closely pressed, in difficulties. **hard radiation** *n.* highly penetrating radiation. **hard rock** *n.* (*coll.*) rock music with an aggressive style and heavy beat. **hard roe** *n.* the roe of a female fish. **hard sauce** *n.* a firm mixture of butter and sugar, often flavoured with rum, brandy etc. **hard sell** *n.* (*coll.*) **1** aggressive selling, advertising etc. **2** an instance of this. **hard-set** *a.* **1** rigid, stony, inflexible. **2** beset by problems. **hardshell** *a.* **1** (of a crab etc.) having a hard shell. **2** rigid, unyielding, uncompromising. **hard shoulder** *n.* an extra lane beside the nearside lane of a motorway etc. used for stopping in emergencies. **hardstanding** *n.* a hard surface of tarmac etc. on which a vehicle may stand when not in use. **hard stuff** *n.* (*coll.*) the strongest alcoholic drink, spirits, esp. whisky. **hard tack** *n.* coarse ship's biscuit. **hard top** *n.* a car with a roof of metal or other rigid material, esp. when this is detachable. **hard up** *a.* in need, esp. of money, very poor. **hard up for** in need of, short of. **hardware** *n.* **1** items of metal, ironmongery etc. **2** items of machinery, heavy weaponry etc. **3** the physical apparatus of a computer system. **hard-wearing** *a.* durable. **hard wheat** *n.* a type of wheat with hard kernels that are high in gluten, used for making bread and pasta. **hard-wired** *a.* (of an electronic circuit) involving a permanent connection, and having a specific function. **hard-won** *a.* won or achieved with difficulty. **hardwood** *n.* close-grained wood from deciduous trees, as distinct from that from pines etc. **hardwooded** *a.* **hard-working** *a.* given to working hard and diligently. [OE *heard* (cp. Dut. *hard*, Icel. *harthr*, G *hart*, also Gr. *kratus*, strong)]

harden (hah´dən) *v.t.* **1** to make hard or harder. **2** to temper (tools). **3** to confirm (in effrontery, wickedness, obstinacy etc.). **4** to make insensible, unfeeling or callous. *~v.i.* **1** to become hard or harder. **2** to become unfeeling or callous. **3** to become confirmed (in vice). **4** (of prices) to become stable. **to harden off** to make (a plant) more able to withstand cold conditions by increasing periods of exposure. **hardener** *n.* **1** a person who or thing which hardens. **2** a chemical placed in photographic negatives to prevent the film melting in hot weather. **hardening** *n.* **1** an act of making hard; the process of becoming hard. **2** an instance of this. **hardening of the arteries** *n.* ARTERIOSCLEROSIS (under ARTERY).

hardihood, hardiness etc. HARDY.

hardly (hahd´li) *adv.* **1** scarcely, not quite. **2** harshly, rigorously. **3** unfavourably. **4** with difficulty. **hardly**

any very few, very little. **hardly ever** very seldom.

Usage note (1) A clause with the word *hardly* is a negative one, and so should not contain another negative word: *They couldn't hardly think* and *without hardly a thought* are not standard English. (2) When *hardly* refers to time ('only just'), a following *when* is preferable to *than* (so *She hardly got in when the phone rang*).

hards (hahdz), **hurds** (hœdz) *n.pl.* the coarse or refuse part of flax or wool. [OE *heordan* (cp. MDut. *heerde, herde*), not cogn. with HARD]

hardship (hahd´ship) *n.* **1** that which is hard to bear, as privation, suffering, toil, fatigue, oppression, injury, injustice. **2** the conditions or occasion causing this.

hardy (hah´di) *a.* (*comp.* **hardier**, *superl.* **hardiest**) **1** unaffected by fatigue; robust. **2** (of plants) capable of bearing exposure to winter weather. **3** bold, overconfident, audacious. ~*n.* an ironsmith's chisel fixed upright, usu. in a hole or socket in an anvil, for cutting metal etc. **hardihood** *n.* **1** boldness, daring. **2** audacity, effrontery. **hardily** *adv.* in a daring or audacious manner. **hardiness** *n.* **hardy annual** *n.* **1** an annual plant that may be sown in the open. **2** a question that crops up annually or periodically. [F *hardi*, orig. p.p. of *hardir*, from Gmc. (OHG *hartjan*, to make strong, cp. OE *heard*, HARD)]

hare (heə) *n.* **1** a long-eared short-tailed mammal of the genus *Lepus*, similar to but larger than the rabbit and with longer hind legs. **2** ELECTRIC HARE (under ELECTRIC). **3** the flesh of the hare as food. ~*v.i.* to run swiftly. **to run with the hare and hunt with the hounds** to keep in with both sides. **to start a hare** to raise a topic of conversation. **hare and hounds** *n.* a paper-chase. **harebell** *n.* the bluebell of Scotland, *Campanula rotundifolia*. **hare-brained** *a.* (*coll.*) rash, giddy, flighty. **harelip** *n.* (*perh. offensive*) a congenital fissure of the upper lip, a cleft lip. **hare-lipped** *a.* **hare's-foot, hare's-foot clover** *n.* a species of clover, *Trifolium arvense*. [OE *hara* (cp. Dut. *haas*, Dan. and Swed. *hare*, G *Hase*)]

Usage note Using *harelip* can give offence: the term *cleft lip* is preferred.

Hare Krishna (hari krish´nə, hahrā) *n.* **1** a sect devoted to the Hindu god Krishna. **2** a member of this sect. [Sansk., Vishnu Krishna (a chant)]

harem (heə´rəm, hah´rēm, -rēm´), **hareem** (hah´rēm, -rēm´) *n.* **1** the apartments reserved for the women in a Muslim household. **2** the occupants of these. **3** a group of female animals that share the same mate. [Arab. *haram*, from *harama*, be prohibited]

harewood (heə´wud) *n.* stained sycamore, used for furniture. [G dial. *Ehre* (from L *acer*, maple), alt. after HARE]

haricot (har´ikō), **haricot bean** *n.* the kidney or French bean, often dried. [F, etym. uncertain]

Harijan (hŭr´ijən, har´-) *n.* a member of a class of people in India, formerly considered to be inferior and untouchable. [Sansk., *Hari*, Vishnu, *jana*, person]

hari-kari HARA-KIRI.

hark (hahk) †*v.i.* to listen (*usu. in imper.*). **to hark back to** to return to some point or matter from which a temporary digression has been made (orig. to call hounds back when they have passed the scent). [ME *herkien* (cogn. with OFris. *herkia*, G *horchen*)]

harken HEARKEN.

harl[1] (hahl), **harle, herl** (hœl) *n.* **1** filaments of flax or hemp. **2** a barb of a feather, esp. one from a peacock's tail, used in making artificial fishing flies. [cp. MLG *Herle, Harl*, LG *Harl*]

harl[2] (hahl) *v.t.* (*Sc., North.*) **1** to drag along the ground. **2** to roughcast (a wall) with lime. ~*v.i.* **1** to drag oneself. **2** in angling, to troll. ~*n.* **1** the act of harling. **2** a small amount or quantity. **3** roughcast. [etym. unknown]

harlequin (hah´likwin) *n.* **1** (*also* **Harlequin**) **a** a leading character in a pantomime or harlequinade, dressed in a mask and parti-coloured and spangled clothes. **b** the character in Italian commedia dell'arte on which the pantomime character was based. **2** a buffoon. **3** the harlequin duck. ~*a.* parti-coloured, variegated. **harlequinade** (-nād´) *n.* **1** that part of a pantomime in which the harlequin and clown play the principal parts. **2** an extravaganza. **3** a piece of fantastic conduct. **harlequin duck** *n.* a sea duck with variegated plumage, *Histronicus histronicus*, of the northern hemisphere. **harlequinesque** (-nesk´) *a.* [OF *Herlequin*, leader of demon horse-riders]

†**harlot** (hah´lət) *n.* a prostitute; a promiscuous woman. **harlotry** *n.* **1** prostitution. **2** promiscuity in a woman. [OF, orig. masc., vagabond, rogue, cp. It. *arlotto* (etym. uncertain)]

harm (hahm) *n.* hurt, injury, damage, evil. ~*v.t.* to injure, hurt or damage. **out of harm's way** safe. **harmful** *a.* hurtful, injurious, detrimental. **harmfully** *adv.* **harmfulness** *n.* **harmless** *a.* **1** not hurtful or injurious. **2** inoffensive. **harmlessly** *adv.* **harmlessness** *n.* [OE *hearm* (cp. Icel. *harmr*, G *Harm*)]

harmattan (hahmat´ən) *n.* a dry hot wind blowing from the interior of Africa to the western coast in December, January and February. [Fanti *haramata*]

harmonic (hahmon´ik) *a.* **1** of or relating to harmony or music. **2** concordant, harmonious. ~*n.* (*usu. in pl.*) **1** a harmonic tone. **2** a radio frequency which is a multiple of a main frequency. **harmonica** (hahmon´ikə) *n.* **1** a mouth organ. **2** GLASS HARMONICA (under GLASS). **harmonical** *a.* **harmonically** *adv.* **harmonic motion** *n.* a type of symmetrical oscillatory motion. **harmonic progression** *n.* a series of numbers whose reciprocals are in arithmetical progression, as ⅕, ⅐, ⅑. **harmonic proportion** *n.* the relation of three consecutive terms of a harmonic progression. **harmonic quantities** *n.pl.* numbers or quantities having this relation. **harmonics** *n.* the science of musical sounds. **harmonic series** *n.* HARMONIC PROGRESSION (under HARMONIC). **harmonic tone** *n.* (*usu. in. pl.*) an overtone accompanying a fundamental note at a fixed interval. [L *harmonicus*, Gr. *harmonikos*, from *harmonia*, HARMONY]

harmonious, harmonist HARMONY.

harmonium (hahmō´niəm) *n.* a keyed musical wind instrument whose tones are produced by the forcing of air through free reeds. [F]

harmony (hah´məni) *n.* (*pl.* **harmonies**) **1** the adaptation of parts to each other, so as to form a complete, symmetrical or pleasing whole. **2** the agreeable combination of simultaneous sounds, the production of musical chords or chord progressions. **3** an arrangement of musical parts for combination with an air or melody. **4** the science dealing with the musical combination of sounds. **5** concord or agreement in views, sentiments etc. **6** a literary work showing the agreement between parallel or corresponding passages of different authors, esp. of the Gospels. **in harmony 1** producing musical chords or chord progressions. **2** in agreement. **harmonious** (-mō´-) *a.* **1** musical, tuneful. **2** concordant, having harmony. **3** having parts adapted and proportioned to each other, symmetrical. **4** without discord or dissension. **harmoniously** *adv.* **harmoniousness** *n.* **harmonist** *n.* **1** a person skilled in harmony or harmonizing. **2** a person who studies and shows the agreement between corresponding passages of different authors. **harmonistic** (-nis´-) *a.* **harmonize, harmonise** *v.t.* **1** to make harmonious. **2** to arrange in musical concord, to add the proper accompaniment to. **3** to adjust in proper proportions. **4** to cause to agree (with). ~*v.i.* **1** to agree in sound or effect. **2** to live in peace and concord. **3** to correspond, to be congruous (with). **harmonization** (-āˊshən) *n.* **harmonizer** *n.* **harmony of the spheres** *n.* in Pythagorean theory, the natural harmonies said to be produced by the movement of the celestial spheres or of the heavenly bodies set in them. [F *harmonie*, L and Gr. *harmonia* (*harmos*, a fitting or joining, from the root *ar-*, to fit)]

harmotome (hahˊmətōm) *n.* a vitreous hydrous silicate of aluminium and barium characterized by cross-shaped crystals. [F, from Gr. *harmos*, joint, *-tomos*, cutting, from *temnein*, to cut]

harness (hahˊnis) *n.* **1** the working gear of a horse or other draught animal. **2** an arrangement of straps etc. to hold a person or thing safely, e.g. in a pram, hang-glider etc. **3** the electrical wiring system of a vehicle or aircraft. **4** †the equipment of a knight or man-at-arms, arms and armour. **5** a device in a loom for raising and lowering the warp threads. *~v.t.* **1** to put a harness on (a horse etc.). **2** to utilize (natural forces, e.g. water) for motive power. **3** to attach by a harness (to). **4** †to equip with armour. **in harness** at one's work. **to die in harness** to continue to the last in one's business or profession. **harnesser** *n.* **harness racing** *n.* a type of trotting with horses harnessed to a two-wheeled trap. [MG and OF *harneis*, etym. uncertain]

harp (hahp) *n.* a musical instrument of triangular shape, with strings which are plucked by the fingers with the frame upright. *~v.i.* **1** to play on a harp. **2** to dwell incessantly (on) (*Stop harping on about it!*). **harper, harpist** *n.* a player on the harp. **harp seal** *n.* an Arctic seal, *Phoca groenlandica*, with dark bands on its back suggestive of the shape of a harp. **harp-shell** *n.* a mollusc of the tropical genus *Harpa*. [OE *hearpe* (cp. Dut. *harp*. Icel. *harpa*, G *Harfe*)]

harpings (hahˊpingz), **harpins** (-pinz) *n.pl.* the strengthening planks that encompass the bow or extensions of the rib-bands of a vessel. [prob. from HARP]

harpoon (hahpoonˊ) *n.* a barbed, spearlike missile weapon with a line attached, used for striking and killing whales etc. *~v.t.* to strike, catch or kill with a harpoon. **harpooneer** (-niəˊ), **harpooner** *n.* **harpoon gun** *n.* a gun for firing a harpoon. [F *harpon*, from *harpe*, a claw, late L and Gr. *harpē*, a sickle]

harpsichord (hahpˊsikawd) *n.* a stringed instrument with a keyboard moving quills that pluck instead of hammers that strike, similar in form to the pianoforte. [OF *harpechorde* (*harpe*, HARP, *chorde*, CHORD[2])]

harpy (hahˊpi) *n.* (*pl.* **harpies**) **1** in Greek and Roman mythology, a monster represented with the face of a woman, the body of a vulture and fingers armed with sharp claws. **2** an extortioner, a rapacious person or animal. **3** a harpy eagle. **harpy eagle** *n.* a crested eagle, *Harpia harpyja*, from S America. **harpy-footed** *a.* with claws like a harpy. [OF *harpie*, L *harpyiae*, Gr. *harpuiai* (pl.), from the root *harp-*, to seize]

harquebus (hahˊkwibəs), **arquebus** (ahˊ-) *n.* (*pl.* **harquebuses, arquebuses**) an old kind of musket fired from a forked hand rest or tripod. **harquebusier** (-siəˊ) *n.* [F *harquebuse*, It. *arcobugio* (*arco*, bow, *bugio*, a hole), a pop. corr. of MHG *haekbüsse*]

☒ **harrass** common misspelling of HARASS.

harridan (harˊidən) *n.* **1** an ill-tempered or bullying (old) woman. **2** a worn-out haggard old woman. [prob. from MF *haridelle*, a worn-out horse]

harrier[1] (harˊiə) *n.* **1** a variety of dog, smaller than the foxhound, orig. used for hare-hunting. **2** (*pl.*) a pack of such hounds with huntsmen. **3** a member of a club of cross-country or hare-and-hounds runners. [HARE, -ER[1]]

harrier[2] (harˊiə) *n.* **1** a person who harries or plunders. **2** a bird of prey of the genus *Circus*. [HARRY, -ER[1]]

Harris Tweed® (harˊis) *n.* a type of tweed woven in the Outer Hebrides.

Harrovian (hərōˊviən) *a.* of or relating to Harrow School. *~n.* a person educated or being educated at Harrow School. [*Harrow*-on-the-Hill, Middlesex]

harrow[1] (harˊō) *n.* a large rake or frame with teeth, drawn over ground to level it, stir the soil, destroy weeds or cover seed. *~v.t.* **1** to draw a harrow over. **2** to torment, to cause anguish or suffering to. **under the harrow** in distress or tribulation. **harrower** *n.* **harrowing** *a.* causing anguish or torment. **harrowingly** *adv.* [MG *harwe*, etym. uncertain]

†**harrow**[2] (harˊō) *v.t.* to plunder, to spoil, to harry, to pillage. **harrowing of hell** *n.* the descent of Christ into hell to rescue the righteous. [HARRY]

harrumph (hərŭmfˊ) *v.i.* to make a sound as if clearing one's throat, often to indicate disapproval. *~v.t.* to say in such a manner. [imit.]

harry (harˊi) *v.t.* (*3rd pers. sing. pres.* **harries,** *pres.p.* **harrying,** *past, p.p.* **harried**) **1** to plunder, to pillage, to lay waste. **2** to harass. *~v.i.* to make plundering excursions. [OE *hergian*, cogn. with *here*, army]

harsh (hahsh) *a.* **1** rough to the touch or other senses. **2** discordant, irritating. **3** austere, morose, severe. **4** rigorous, inclement. **5** unfeeling. **harshen** *v.t.* to make harsh or harsher. *~v.i.* to become harsh or harsher. **harshly** *adv.* **harshness** *n.* [ME *harsk*, from Scand. (cp. Dan. *harsk*, Swed. *härsk*, G *harsch*)]

harslet HASLET.

hart (haht) *n.* a stag, esp. a male red deer, from its fifth year onwards. **hart of ten** *n.* a hart with ten tines on its antlers. **hart's tongue** *n.* a fern, *Phyllitis scolopendrium*, with tongue-shaped leaves. [OE *heort*, *heorot*, from Gmc. *herut*, horned (cp. L *cervus*, stag, *keras -atos*, horn)]

hartal (hahˊtəl) *n.* (*Ind.*) a boycott or protest carried out by closing shops. [Hind. *hāt*, shop, *tālā*, bolt]

hartebeest (hahˊtibēst) *n.* a large African antelope of the genus *Alcephalus*, with horns that bend at the tips. [Afrikaans (*hert*, hart, *beest*, beast)]

†**hartshorn** (hahtsˊhawn) *n.* **1** a preparation from shavings or chippings of the horns of the hart. **2** spirit of hartshorn. **salt of hartshorn** SALT. **spirit of hartshorn** SPIRIT.

harum-scarum (heərəmskeəˊrəm) *a.* giddy, hare-brained, reckless. *~n.* a giddy, hare-brained or reckless person. [prob. compounded from HARE and SCARE]

haruspex (hərŭsˊpeks) *n.* (*pl.* **haruspices** (-pisēz)) an ancient Etruscan or Roman soothsayer who divined the will of the gods by inspecting the entrails of victims. **haruspicy** (-pisi) *n.* [L, lit. inspector of entrails (root from Sansk. *hird*, entrails, L *spic-*, to behold)]

Harvard classification (hahˊvəd) *n.* a system for classifying stars based on their spectral type. [*Harvard*, the observatory in Massachusetts where the system was invented]

harvest (hahˊvist) *n.* **1** the process of reaping and gathering crops, esp. of corn. **2** the season for this. **3** ripe corn or other agricultural products gathered and stored. **4** the yield of any natural product for the season. **5** the product or result of any labour or effort. *~v.t.* **1** to reap and gather in (corn, grain etc.). **2** to garner, to lay up. **3** to receive as payment, penalty etc. **harvestable** *a.* **harvest bug, harvest louse, harvest mite, harvest tick** *n.* a minute tick, mite or acaridan which burrows in or attaches itself to the skin during late summer and autumn, setting up an irritating itch. **harvester** *n.* **1** a reaper. **2** a reaping and binding machine. **3** a harvest mite. **harvest festival** *n.* a religious service of thanksgiving for the harvest. **harvest home** *n.* **1** the close of harvesting. **2** a merrymaking in celebration of this. **harvestless** *a.* **harvestman** *n.* (*pl.* **harvestmen**) **1** an arachnid with long slender legs. **2** a labourer in the harvest. **harvest moon** *n.* the moon at its full about the time of the autumnal equinox. **harvest mouse** *n.* a very small fieldmouse, *Micromys minutus*, which makes a nest usu. among wheat stalks. [OE *hærfest* (cp. Dut. *herfst*, Icel. *haust*, G *Herbst*), from Gmc. root *harb-* (cp. L *carpere*, to pluck)]

has HAVE.

has-been (haz´bēn) *n.* (*coll.*) a person or idea that is no longer important, influential or useful.

hash[1] (hash) *n.* **1** a dish of meat that has already been cooked, cut into small pieces and recooked, often mixed with vegetables etc. **2** (*N Am.*) shepherd's pie. **3** (*coll.*) a mess, a muddle. **4** a second preparation of old matter. **5** reused material. **6** (*in full* **hash sign**) the # symbol. ~*v.t.* **1** to cut or chop up in small pieces. **2** to mince. **to make a hash of** (*coll.*) to make a mess of. **to settle someone's hash** (*coll.*) to defeat a person completely. **hash browns** *n.pl.* a fried mixture of chopped potatoes and onion. [OF *hachis*]

hash[2] (hash) *n.* (*coll.*) hashish. [abbr.]

hashish (hash´ēsh), **hasheesh** *n.* the tender tops and sprouts of Indian hemp, *Cannabis indica*, used as a narcotic for smoking, chewing etc. [Arab. *hashīsh*]

Hasid (has´id) *n.* (*pl.* **Hasidim** (-im)) a member of any of several mystical Jewish sects. **Hasidic** (-sid´-) *a.* [Heb. *hāsid*, pious]

haslet (haz´lit), **harslet** (hah´-) *n.* mixed pieces of the entrails, liver, heart etc. of an animal, usu. a hog, cooked and pressed into a loaf. [ME and OF *hastelet*, from *haste*, a spit, L *hasta*, a spear]

hasn't (haz´ənt) *contr.* has not.

hasp (hahsp) *n.* **1** a fastening, esp. a clamp or bar hinged at one end, the other end passing over a staple, where it is secured by a pin, key or padlock. **2** a skein of yarn. ~*v.t.* to fasten, shut or secure with a hasp. [OE *hæpse* (cp. Dut. *haspel*, Icel. *hespa*, G *Haspe*)]

hassle (has´əl) *n.* (*coll.*) **1** something causing difficulty or problems. **2** an argument. ~*v.t.* **1** to cause difficulty or problems for. **2** to harass. ~*v.i.* **1** to argue. **2** to behave in a difficult or destructive way. [etym. uncertain]

hassock (has´ək) *n.* **1** a small stuffed footstool or cushion for kneeling on in church. **2** a matted tuft of rank grass, a tussock. [OE *hassuc*, etym. uncertain, not from Welsh *hesg*, sedges]

†hast HAVE.

hastate (has´tāt) *a.* (*Bot.*) triangular, like the head of a spear. [L *hastātus*, from *hasta*, spear]

haste (hāst) *n.* hurry, speed of movement or action; urgency, precipitance. ~†*v.i.* to make haste. **in haste** speedily, precipitately. **to make haste 1** to be quick. **2** to be in a hurry. **hasten** (hā´sən) *v.i.* to move with haste or speed. ~*v.t.* **1** to cause to hurry. **2** to expedite. **3** to urge or press on. **hastener** *n.* **hasty** *a.* (*comp.* **hastier,** *superl.* **hastiest**) **1** hurried, quick. **2** eager, precipitate. **3** rash, inconsiderate. **4** irritable. **hastily** *adv.* **hastiness** *n.* **hasty pudding** *n.* a pudding made from flour, semolina etc. stirred into boiling milk. [OF *haste* (F *hâte*), whence *haster*, from WG *Haisti-*, violence (cp. OE *hæst*)]

hat (hat) *n.* **1** a covering for the head, usu. having a crown or top and a continuous brim. **2** the dignity of a cardinal (from the broad-brimmed scarlet hat worn by cardinals). **3** a specified function or occupation (*wearing my teacher's hat, I would say yes, but as a parent, no*). ~*v.t.* (*pres.p.* **hatting,** *past, p.p.* **hatted**) to provide, fit or cover with a hat. **hats off to** used to express admiration for or approval of. **out of a hat 1** (selected) at random. **2** as if by a clever trick or magic. **to hang up one's hat** to make oneself at home (in another house). **to keep under one's hat** (*coll.*) to keep secret. **to pass (round) the hat** to ask for contributions of money, donations etc. **to send round the hat** to pass round the hat. **to take off one's hat to** (*coll.*) to express admiration for or approval of. **to talk through one's hat** to talk about something one does not understand. **to throw one's hat into the ring** to enter a contest, election etc. **hatband** *n.* a ribbon or band of fabric round a hat. **hat block** *n.* a block or mould for shaping or ironing hats. **hatbox** *n.* a box for carrying or storing a hat in. **hatful** *n.* (*pl.* **hatfuls**). **hatless** *a.* **hatpin** *n.* a long pin, often with a decorative head, used to hold a hat in place by pinning it to the hair. **hat stand** *n.* a set of hooks or a piece of furniture for hanging hats on. **hatter** *n.* **1** a person who makes or sells hats. **2** (*Austral.*) a miner who lives and works by himself. **hat-trick** *n.* **1** the feat at cricket of taking three wickets with consecutive balls (from its being held to entitle the bowler to the reward of a new hat). **2** the feat of one player scoring three goals etc. in one match. **3** three successes in any area of activity. [OE *hæt*, cogn. with HOOD[1]]

hatable HATE.

hatch[1] (hach) *n.* **1** an opening in a wall between two rooms. **2** a small door in a spacecraft, aircraft etc. **3** an opening in a roof for access to the outside. **4** (*Naut.*) a hatchway, or a trapdoor or shutter to cover this. **5** a floodgate or a grated opening in a weir used as a fish trap. **down the hatch!** (*coll.*) drink up! (as a toast). **under hatches 1** (*Naut.*) confined below; out of sight. **2** in a state of bondage or repression. **3** dead. **hatchback** *n.* a car with a door at the back that opens upwards. **hatchway** *n.* a large opening in the deck of a ship for lowering cargo etc. [OE *hæce* (cp. Dut. *hek*, Swed. *häck*), prob. conn. with OE *haca*, the bolt of a door]

hatch[2] (hach) *v.t.* **1** to produce (young) from eggs by incubation or artificial heat. **2** to produce young from (eggs). **3** to evolve, to contrive, to devise (a plan, plot etc.). ~*v.i.* **1** to come out of the egg. **2** (of eggs) to produce young. ~*n.* **1** the act of hatching. **2** a brood hatched. **to count one's chickens before they are hatched** CHICKEN. **hatchery** *n.* (*pl.* **hatcheries**) a place where eggs are hatched artificially, esp. those of fish or poultry. **hatches, matches and dispatches** *n.* (*coll.*) newspaper announcements of births, marriages and deaths. **hatchling** *n.* a young bird, fish or reptile that has just hatched. [ME *hacchen* (cp. Swed. *häcka*, Dan. *hække*)]

hatch[3] (hach) *v.t.* **1** to mark with fine lines, parallel or crossing each other. **2** to inlay with thin strips of another material. **hatched moulding** *n.* (*Archit.*) ornamentation with a series of cuts or grooves crossing each other, common in Norman work. **hatching** *n.* lines crossing each other at more or less acute angles, esp. as shading on a drawing, or as road markings. [F *hacher*, see HASH[1]]

hatchel (hach´əl) *v.t.* (*pres.p.* **hatchelling,** (*N Am.*) **hatcheling,** *past, p.p.* **hatchelled,** (*N Am.*) **hatcheled**) **1** to dress (flax). **2** to heckle, to worry. [HACKLE[1]]

hatchet (hach´it) *n.* a small axe with a short handle for use with one hand. **to bury the hatchet** to forgive and forget, to effect a reconciliation (in allusion to an American Indian custom of burying a tomahawk on the conclusion of peace). **hatchet-faced** *a.* having a narrow face with sharp, prominent features. **hatchet job** *n.* (*coll.*) a fiercely critical speech or piece of writing. **hatchet man** *n.* (*pl.* **hatchet men**) **1** a person hired to carry out violent or illegal tasks. **2** a person appointed to sack people in an organization. **hatchety** *a.* [F *hachette*, dim. of *hache*, OHG *happja*, a sickle]

hatchment (hach´mənt) *n.* a funeral escutcheon or panel bearing the coat of arms of a deceased person placed on the front of the person's house, in a church etc. [corr. of ACHIEVEMENT (under ACHIEVE)]

hate (hāt) *n.* **1** extreme dislike or aversion, hatred. **2** (*coll.*) a hated thing or person (*a pet hate*). ~*v.t.* **1** to dislike exceedingly; to abhor, to detest. **2** (*coll.*) to dislike. **3** to be unwilling or reluctant (to do something). **hatable, hateable** *a.* **hateful** *a.* **1** causing hate; odious, detestable. **2** †feeling hatred. **hatefully** *adv.*

hatefulness *n.* **hate mail** *n.* a series of unpleasant or aggressive letters, usu. from an anonymous writer. **hater** *n.* **hatred** (-rid) *n.* **1** great dislike or aversion. **2** active malevolence, animosity, enmity. [OE *hete*, from Gmc. root *hat-*, whence *hatian*, to hate]

†**hath** HAVE.

hatha yoga (hathə yō´gə) *n.* a form of yoga involving physical exercises and breathing control. [Sansk. *hatha*, force, YOGA]

hatred HATE.

hatter, hat-trick HAT.

hauberk (haw´bœk) *n.* a coat of mail, sometimes without sleeves, formed of interwoven steel rings. [OF *hauberc*, OHG *halsberg* (*hals*, neck, cp. *hals*, *bergan*, cogn. with OE *beorgan*, to protect, see BURY)]

haughty (haw´ti) *a.* (*comp.* **haughtier**, *superl.* **haughtiest**) **1** proud, arrogant, disdainful, supercilious. **2** proceeding from or expressing disdainful pride. **haughtily** *adv.* **haughtiness** *n.* [earlier *haught*, F *haut*, L *altus*, high]

haul (hawl) *v.t.* **1** to pull or drag with force. **2** to transport by dragging or in a lorry etc. **3** to bring unceremoniously or forcibly (*hauled before the judge*). ~*v.i.* **1** to alter the course of a ship. **2** to pull or drag (at or upon) with force. ~*n.* **1** a hauling, a pull. **2** the drawing of a net. **3** an amount that is taken or stolen at once. **4** a distance travelled. **to haul over the coals** COAL. **to haul up** (*coll.*) to bring for trial in a court of law. **haulage** (-ij) *n.* **1** transporting of goods. **2** the charge for this. **hauler** *n.* **1** a person who or thing which hauls. **2** HAULIER (under HAUL). **haulier** *n.* **1** a person or business that transports goods by lorry. **2** a worker who hauls trucks to the bottom of the shaft in a coal mine. [var. of HALE[2]]

haulm (hawm), **halm** *n.* **1** a stem, a stalk. **2** (*collect.*) the stems or stalks of peas, beans, potatoes etc. [OE *healm* (cp. Dut. and G *Halm*, Icel. *hālmr*, also L *culmus*, Gr. *kalamos*, reed)]

haunch (hawnch) *n.* **1** that part of the body between the ribs and the thigh; the buttock, the basal joint. **2** the leg and loin of an animal used as meat. **3** (*Archit.*) the shoulder of an arch. **4** †the rear, the hind part. **haunch bone** *n.* the hip bone. **haunched** *a.* having haunches. [OF *hanche*, from Gmc. (cp. OHG *anchā*, leg)]

haunt (hawnt) *v.t.* **1** to visit (a place or person) frequently as a ghost or spirit. **2** to frequent, to resort to often; to frequent the company of. **3** to recur to the mind of (a person) frequently in an irritating way. ~*v.i.* to stay or be frequently (about, in etc.). ~*n.* **1** a place which one often visits or frequents. **2** a den, a feeding place for animals etc. **haunted** *a.* **haunter** *n.* **haunting** *a.* having a lasting effect on the emotions; poignant. **hauntingly** *adv.* [OF *hanter*, etym. uncertain]

Hausa (how´zə) *n.* (*pl.* **Hausa, Hausas**) **1** a member of a people of W Africa and central Sudan. **2** their Hamitic language. ~*a.* of or relating to the Hausa or their language. [Afr. name]

hausfrau (hows´frow) *n.* a German housewife. [G]

haustellum (hawstel´əm) *n.* (*pl.* **haustella** (-lə)) the sucking organ of certain insects and crustaceans. **haustellate** (haw´stələt) *a.* [dim. from L *haustrum*, from *haurīre*, to draw (water)]

haustorium (hawstaw´riəm) *n.* (*pl.* **haustoria** (-riə)) a rootlet or sucker of a parasitic plant. [from L *haustor*, a drawer, as HAUSTELLUM]

hautboy (hō´boi) *n.* **1** †an oboe. **2** (*also* **hautbois strawberry, hautbois**) a tall species of strawberry, *Fragaria moschata*. [F *hautbois* (*haut*, L *altus*, high, *bois*, late L *boscus*, wood)]

haute couture (ōt kutūə´, -tuə´) *n.* **1** the designing and making of exclusive trend-setting fashions. **2** the designers and houses creating such fashions. [F *haute*, high, *couture*, sewing]

haute cuisine (ōt kwizēn´) *n.* cooking of a very high standard. [F *haute*, high, *cuisine*, cooking]

haute école (ōt ākōl´) *n.* **1** difficult feats of horsemanship. **2** a method of teaching these. [F]

hauteur (ōtœ´) *n.* haughtiness, lofty manners or demeanour. [F, from *haut*, high]

haut monde (ō mõd´) *n.* high society. [F *haut*, high, *monde*, world]

haut-relief (ōrilēf´) *n.* **1** high relief. **2** carving in high relief.

Havana (həvan´ə) *n.* a cigar made at Havana or elsewhere in Cuba.

have (hav) *v.t.* (*3rd pers. sing. pres.* **has** (haz), †**hath** (hath), *pres.p.* **having**, *past, p.p.* **had** (had), *2nd pers. sing. pres.* †**hast** (hast), *past* †**hadst** (hadst)) **1** to possess, to hold as owner. **2** to hold at one's disposal. **3** to enjoy, to suffer, to experience. **4** to engage in. **5** to give birth to; to have given birth to. **6** to receive, to get, to obtain. **7** to take for consumption; to eat or drink. **8** to require, to claim. **9** to hold mentally, to retain. **10** to feel as an emotion. **11** to show as an action. **12** (*usu. neg.*) to tolerate, to entertain. **13** to maintain. **14** to hold as part, appurtenance, quality etc., to contain, to comprise. **15** to know, to understand, to be engaged in. **16** to know as a language. **17** to vanquish, to hold at one's mercy. **18** (*coll.*) to circumvent, to cheat, to bring forth, to bear. **19** (*sl.*) to engage in sexual intercourse with. ~*v.i.* (*usu. in imper.*) to go, to get (at, after, with etc.). ~*v.aux.* **1** used with past participles to denote the completed action of verbs. **2** used with past participles in conditional clauses (*had I known*; *if I had known*). ~*n.* **1** (*usu. in pl., coll.*) a wealthy person. **2** (*sl.*) a deception, a swindle. †**have at** (*imper.*) attack, encounter. **let someone have it** **1** (*coll.*) punish, censure or abuse them. **2** give it to them. **to be had** to be taken in. **to have got to** (*coll.*) to have to. **to have had it** **1** (*coll.*) to have let one's opportunity or moment go by. **2** (*coll.*) to have done something that will have serious consequences for one. **3** (*coll.*) to have been killed or overcome. **4** (*coll.*) to be too old. **to have it** **1** to have found the solution. **2** to win a vote etc. **to have it in for** to want to harm. **to have it in one** to be capable, to have the ability. **to have it off/ away** (*sl.*) to have sexual intercourse. **to have it out** to settle a quarrel or dispute by fighting, debate etc. **to have it that** to maintain or argue that. **to have nothing on someone** **1** to have no evidence that a person has done something wrong. **2** to have no advantage over another person. **to have on** **1** to be wearing (something). **2** to have (something) planned. **3** to deceive (someone), to trick (someone). **to have one's hand in** to be in practice. **to have out** to have (a tooth etc.) removed or extracted. **to have something on someone** **1** to have evidence that a person has done something wrong. **2** to have an advantage over another person. **to have to** to be obliged to. **to have up** (*coll.*) to cause to be prosecuted in court. **have-not** *n.* (*usu. pl., coll.*) a poor person. [OE *habban* (cp. Dut. *hebban*, Icel. *hafa*, G *haben*, and perh. L *habēre*)]

Usage note It is incorrect to write *of* for *have* in *could have, should have* etc. (informal *could've, should've*).

havelock (hav´lok) *n.* a light covering for the cap hanging over the neck, worn as a protection against sunstroke. [General Sir H. *Havelock*, 1795–1857]

haven (hā´vən) *n.* **1** a port, a harbour. **2** a station or refuge for ships. **3** a refuge, an asylum. ~*v.t.* to shelter. [OE *hæfene* (cp. Dut. *haven*, Icel. *höfn*, G *Hafen*)]

have-not HAVE.

haven't (hav´ənt) *contr.* have not.

haver[1] (hā´və) *v.i.* **1** to talk nonsense. **2** to hesitate, to dither. ~*n.* (*usu. pl., Sc.*) nonsense, foolish talk. **haverel** (-rəl) *n.* (*Sc., North.*) a person who is foolish. **haverer** *n.* [etym. unknown]

haver[2] (hav´ə) *n.* (*Sc. Law*) a person who holds a deed or document.

haversack (hav´əsak) *n.* a strong bag carried over the shoulder or on the back to hold provisions etc. when walking. [F *havresac*, G *Habersack* (*Haber*, oats, *Sack*, SACK[1])]

Haversian canal (həvœ´siən, -shən) *n.* any one of the canals forming a network in bone, conveying and protecting the blood vessels. [Clopton *Havers*, d. 1702, English physician]

haversine (hav´əsīn), **haversin** *n.* (*Math.*) a value equal to half of a versed sine. [from HALF, VERSED SINE (under VERSED)]

havildar (hav´ildah) *n.* a sergeant of an Indian regiment of infantry. [Pers. *hawāl-dār*, from Arab. *hawālah*, charge, Pers. *dār*, holding]

having HAVE.

havoc (hav´ək) *n.* **1** widespread destruction; devastation, waste. **2** chaos. ~*v.t.* (*pres.p.* **havocking**, *past, p.p.* **havocked**) to lay waste; to devastate. †**to cry havoc** to give the signal for violence or devastation. **to play havoc with 1** to damage. **2** to upset. [A-F *havok*, OF *havot*, plunder, prob. from Gmc. and cogn. with HEAVE]

haw[1] (haw) *n.* **1** the berry or fruit of the hawthorn. **2** the hawthorn itself. **3** †a hedge, an enclosed field or yard. [OE *haga* (cp. Icel. *hagi*, Dut. *haag*, G *Hag*)]

haw[2] (haw) *int., n.* a sound expressive of hesitation in speaking. ~*v.i.* to utter this sound, to speak with hesitation (*hum and haw*). [imit.]

haw[3] (haw) *n.* **1** the nictitating membrane or third eyelid (of a horse etc.). **2** (*often in pl.*) a disease of this, characterized by inflammation, enlargement etc. [etym. unknown]

Hawaiian (həwī´ən) *a.* of or relating to Hawaii, its people or their language. ~*n.* **1** a native or inhabitant of Hawaii. **2** the Austronesian language of Hawaii. [*Hawaii*, island in the N Pacific]

hawfinch (haw´finch) *n.* a large European finch, *Coccothraustes coccothraustes*, with a sturdy beak.

haw-haw HA-HA.

hawk[1] (hawk) *n.* **1** a bird of prey belonging to the family Accipitridae, having a long tail, short rounded wings and a curved beak. **2** a rapacious or aggressive person. **3** an advocate of an aggressive foreign policy. ~*v.i.* **1** to hunt birds etc. by means of trained hawks or falcons. **2** to attack on the wing, to soar (at). ~*v.t.* to pursue or attack on the wing. **to know a hawk from a handsaw** to be intelligent and discriminating. **hawkbit** *n.* a plant with yellow daisy-like flowers, of the genus *Leontodon*. **hawk-eyed** *a.* having sharp sight. **hawking** *n.* falconry. **hawkish** *a.* **hawkishness** *n.* **hawklike** *a.* **hawkmoth** *n.* a moth of the family Sphingidae, the flight of which is not unlike that of a hawk in quest of prey. **hawk-nosed** *a.* having a hooked nose. **hawk's-beard** *n.* any plant of the composite genus *Crepis*, related to the hawkweeds. **hawksbill, hawksbill turtle** *n.* a small turtle, *Eretmochelys imbricata*, living in tropical climates and having curved beaklike jaws. **hawkweed** *n.* any daisy of the composite genus *Hieracium*. [OE *hafoc, heafoc* (cp. Dut. *havic*, Icel. *haukr*, G *Habicht*), prob. from Gmc. root *haf-*, to seize, cp. L *capere*]

hawk[2] (hawk) *v.i.* to clear or try to clear the throat in a noisy manner. ~*v.t.* to force (up) phlegm from the throat. ~*n.* an effort to force up phlegm from the throat. [prob. imit.]

hawk[3] (hawk) *v.t.* **1** to carry about for sale, to try to sell. **2** to carry or spread about. [HAWKER[2]]

hawk[4] (hawk) *n.* a plasterer's board with handle underneath, for carrying plaster, mortar etc. [etym. uncertain]

hawker[1] (haw´kə) *n.* **1** a person who practises the sport of hawking. **2** a falconer.

hawker[2] (haw´kə) *n.* a person who travels around selling goods in the street or from house to house. [prob. from G (cp. LG *Höker*, Dut. *heuker*, G *Höker*)]

hawk's-beard, hawksbill HAWK[1].

hawse (hawz) *n.* (*Naut.*) **1** that part of the bow in which the hawse-holes are situated. **2** the distance between a ship's head and the anchors by which she rides. **3** the situation of the cables when a ship is moored from the bows with two anchors. **hawse-hole** *n.* a hole in each bow through which a cable or hawser can be passed. **hawse-pipe** *n.* a metal lining for a hawse-hole. [prob. from Icel. *hals*, neck]

hawser (haw´zə), **halser** *n.* (*Naut.*) a cable, used in towing and mooring. [OF *haucier* (F *hausser*), late L *altiāre*, to raise, from L *altus*, high]

hawthorn (haw´thawn) *n.* a thorny, rosaceous shrub or tree belonging to the genus *Crataegus*, bearing white or pink flowers which develop into haws. [OE *hægthorn* (HAW[1], THORN)]

hay[1] (hā) *n.* grass cut and dried for fodder. ~*v.t.* **1** to make (grass etc.) into hay. **2** to sow (land) with grass to make hay. **3** to supply or feed with hay. ~*v.i.* to make hay. **to hit the hay** (*coll.*) to go to bed, to sleep. **to make hay** to turn, toss and expose mown grass to the sun for drying. **to make hay of** to throw into confusion. **to make hay while the sun shines** to take advantage of every favourable opportunity. **haybox** *n.* an airtight box, with a thick layer of hay, used for keeping food hot, and for continuing the process of slow cooking after the food has been removed from the fire. **haycock** *n.* a conical heap of hay. **hay fever** *n.* a severe catarrh with asthmatic symptoms, frequent in summer and caused by a reaction to pollen, dust etc. **hayfield** *n.* a field where hay is being made. **hayfork** *n.* a fork for turning over or pitching hay. **hayknife** *n.* a large, broad knife with a handle set crosswise, used for cutting hay out of a stack. **hayloft** *n.* a loft for storing hay. **haymaker** *n.* **1** a person employed in making hay. **2** a machine for tossing hay. **3** (*coll.*) a swinging punch. **haymaking** *n.* **haymow** *n.* **1** a hayrick. **2** a mass of hay laid up in a barn. **hayrick** *n.* HAYSTACK (under HAY[1]). **hayseed** *n.* **1** grass seed from hay. **2** (*N Am., Austral., New Zeal.*) a yokel, a rustic. **haystack** *n.* a pile of hay in the open air, built with a conical or ridged top, traditionally thatched to keep it dry. **haywire** *a.* (*coll.*) **1** crazy, mad. **2** chaotic, disordered. [ME *hey*, OE *hīeg*, cogn. with HEW]

hay[2] (hā), **hey** *n.* **1** a country dance with a winding movement. **2** a dance figure following a weaving pattern. [etym. uncertain]

haywire HAY[1].

hazard (haz´əd) *n.* **1** a danger, a risk. **2** chance. **3** a game at dice; the stake in gaming. **4** any one of the winning openings in a real-tennis court. **5** a difficulty, obstacle, bunker etc. on a golf course. **6** in billiards, a stroke putting a ball into a pocket. ~*v.t.* **1** to risk; to expose to chance or danger. **2** to run the risk of. **3** to venture (an act, statement etc.). ~*v.i.* to run a risk, to venture. **hazardable** *a.* **hazard light, hazard warning light** *n.* a flashing light on a vehicle indicating that it has stopped in an emergency or is doing something unexpected. **hazardous** *a.* **1** full of hazard, danger, or risk. **2** depending on chance. **hazardously** *adv.* **hazardousness** *n.* **hazard pay** *n.* (*N Am.*) danger money, extra money paid to compensate for risks taken. [OF *hasard*, perh. from Arab. *al zahr*, the die]

haze[1] (hāz) *n.* **1** lack of transparency in the air, a very thin mist or vapour, usu. due to heat. **2** obscurity or indistinctness of perception, understanding etc. ~*v.t.* to make hazy. **hazy** *a.* (*comp.* **hazier**, *superl.* **haziest**) **1** misty; thick with haze. **2** dim, vague, indistinct, obscure. **3** muddled. **hazily** *adv.* **haziness** *n.* [etym. unknown]

haze[2] (hāz) *v.t.* **1** (*Naut.*) to harass or punish with overwork. **2** (*N Am.*) to bully, to tease. **hazer** *n.* **hazing** *n.* [etym. uncertain, cp. OF *haser*, to irritate, to annoy]

hazel (hā´zəl) *n.* **1** a shrub or small tree of the genus *Corylus*, esp. the European *C. avellana*, bearing the hazelnut. **2** the wood of this tree. **3** a stick made from this. **4** a reddish-brown or greenish-brown colour, esp. of eyes. *~a.* (esp. of eyes) reddish-brown or greenish-brown. **hazel-grouse** *n.* a grouse, *Tetrastes bonasia*, living in woodland. **hazelnut** *n.* the fruit of the hazel, the cobnut, a round nut with a reddish-brown shell. [OE *hæsel* (cp. Icel. *hasl*, Dut. *hazel*, G *Hasel*)]

hazing HAZE[2].

hazy HAZE[1].

HB *abbr.* hard and black (of pencil lead).

Hb *abbr.* haemoglobin.

HBM *abbr.* Her (or His) Brittanic Majesty.

HC *abbr.* **1** Holy Communion. **2** House of Commons.

h.c. *abbr.* honoris causa.

HCF *abbr.* **1** highest common factor. **2** Honorary Chaplain to the Forces.

HCFC *abbr.* hydrochlorofluorocarbon.

hdqrs *abbr.* headquarters (now replaced by HQ for military uses).

HDTV *abbr.* high-definition television.

HE *abbr.* **1** Her Excellency, His Excellency. **2** His Eminence. **3** high explosive.

He *chem. symbol* helium.

he (hē) *pron.* (*obj.* **him,** *poss.* **his**) **1** the male person or animal referred to. **2** the person of unknown or unspecified sex, esp. referred to in an antecedent indefinite pronoun or noun (*If anyone insults you, punch him*). *~n.* **1** a male person. **2** a children's game of chasing to touch another player. **3** the chaser in this game. **he-cat, he-goat etc.** *n.* a male cat, goat, etc. **he-man** *n.* (*pl.* **he-men**) (*coll.*) a virile man. [OE *hē* cogn. with OFris. and OS *hi, he*]

Usage note *He* is sometimes used as an objective pronoun (after a verb or preposition), especially when joined by *and* to a personal name or pronoun, *he and X*, but this is best avoided. See also note under THEY.

---

head[1] (hed) *n.* **1** the foremost part of the body of an animal, the uppermost in a human, consisting of the skull, with the brain and the special sense organs. **2** any part, organ or thing of an analogous kind. **3** a measure of length equal to a head, esp. in a horse race. **4** the upper part of anything, the top. **5** the upper end of a valley, lake, gulf etc. **6** the front part of a ship, plough, procession, column of troops etc. **7** the first or most honourable place, the forefront, the place of command. **8** a chief, a ruler, a principal or leader. **9** a head teacher of a school. **10** the more honourable end of a table etc. **11** the part of a bed where the head rests. **12** the obverse of a coin or medal. **13** the knobbed end of a nail etc. **14** the striking part of a tool. **15** the globular cluster of flowers or leaves at the top of a stem. **16** the ripened part of an ulcer or boil. **17** froth on liquor. **18** the part of a machine tool etc. that holds a drill or cutter. **19** the device on a tape recorder that can record sound, or play back or erase recorded sound. **20** a promontory. **21** the capital of a pillar etc. **22** a person, an individual, esp. as counted. **23** a single one (as of cattle). **24** a main division, a topic, a category. **25** a culmination, a crisis, a pitch. **26** pressure of water available for driving mills; available steam-pressure. **27** liberty, licence, freedom from restraint. **28** an aptitude for something specified. **29** the mind, the understanding, the intellect, esp. as distinguished from the feelings. **30** one's life. **31** a ship's toilet. **32** a bundle of flax about 2 ft. (60 cm) long. **33** (*sl.*) an addict, a devotee, a fan. **34** (*coll.*) a headache. **35** (*sl.*) a headline. *~a.* (*attrib.*) chief, principal. **above someone's head** over someone's head. **a head for** an ability to understand or tolerate. **from head to foot/toe** over the whole person. **head and ears 1** the whole person. **2** completely. **head and shoulders 1** by the height of the head and shoulders. **2** by a great margin. **head over heels 1** turning upside down. **2** completely (in love). **heads will roll** ROLL. **in one's head 1** by thinking only, without physical aids. **2** in one's mind. **off one's head 1** out of one's mind. **2** wildly excited, demented. **off the top of one's head** TOP[1]. **on one's (own) head** being one's own responsibility; at one's own risk. **out of one's head 1** off one's head. **2** out of one's own head. **out of one's own head 1** by one's own invention. **2** of one's own accord. **over head and ears** deeply (immersed). **over someone's head 1** beyond someone's understanding. **2** appealing to a higher authority than someone. **3** without regard for one's higher status. **to be unable to make head or tail of** to be unable to understand at all. **to bite someone's head off** (*coll.*) to snap at someone; to be irritable. **to come into one's head** to enter one's head. **to come to a head 1** to reach a crisis or culminating point. **2** (of an ulcer or boil) to suppurate. **3** to ripen. **to enter one's head** to occur as a thought in one's mind. **to get it into one's head** GET[1]. **to get one's head down 1** (*sl.*) to start working seriously. **2** (*sl.*) to go to sleep. **to get one's head together** to collect one's thoughts, to achieve a more balanced state of mind. **to give someone their head 1** to give liberty or licence to. **2** to let (a horse) go as it pleases. **to go to one's head 1** (of alcoholic drink) to make one slightly drunk. **2** (of success etc.) to make one vain, arrogant etc. **to have a head like a sieve** SIEVE. **to have one's head screwed on the right way** to be sensible or well-balanced. **to hide one's head** HIDE[1]. **to keep one's head** to remain calm. **to keep one's head above water** WATER. **to keep one's head down** (*coll.*) to avoid being noticed when there are problems. **to let someone have their head** to give someone their head. **to lose one's head 1** to be carried away by excitement. **2** to lose one's presence of mind. **3** to be decapitated. **to make head 1** to push forward. **2** to struggle (against) effectually. **to make head or tail of** to have the slightest understanding of (usu. in neg. and interrog. contexts). **to put one's heads together** to consider (a problem) together. **to raise its (ugly) head** to become apparent, esp. in an ominous way. **to rear its (ugly) head** to become apparent, esp. in an ominous way. **to take it into one's head 1** to fix on the idea or belief (that), esp. with no supporting evidence. **2** to resolve (to do something). **to turn someone's head** to cause someone to be vain or infatuated. **with one's head in the clouds** being unrealistic; daydreaming. **headache** *n.* **1** a neuralgic or other persistent pain in the head. **2** (*coll.*) a source of worry. **headachy** *a.* suffering from or tending to cause headache. **headage** (-ij) *n.* **1** the number of head of cattle etc. **2** a payment per capita for animals. **headband** *n.* **1** a band for the hair. **2** a band at the top and bottom inside the back of a book. **headbanger** *n.* (*sl.*) **1** a person who makes violent head movements in time to pop music. **2** a stupid, crazy or violent person. **headbanging** *n.* (*sl.*) **1** the making of violent head movements in time to pop music. **2** forcing people to cooperate. **headboard** *n.* a panel at the head of a bed. **head boy** *n.* the (elected or appointed) senior male pupil at a school. **head-butt** *n.* a forceful attack made by thrusting the top of the head at another person. *~v.t.* to strike (a person) using a head-butt. **head case** *n.* (*coll.*) a mad or foolish person. **headcheese** *n.* (*N Am.*) portions of the head and feet of swine cut up fine, boiled and pressed into a mass; brawn. **head cold** *n.* a cold affecting the head, not the chest. **headcount** *n.* a count of all the people etc. present, employed etc. **headdress** *n.* a covering or decoration for the head. **headed** *a.* **1** having a head. **2** having intellect or mental faculties (*esp. in comb.*, as *hard-headed*). **headfast** *n.* a rope to make fast the head of a vessel to some fixed object. **head first, head foremost** *adv.* 1 with the head in front (of a plunge). 2 precipitately. **headgear** *n.* 1 what is worn on the head; covering or ornaments for the head. 2 a bridle. 3 machinery at the top of a mine shaft or boring. **head girl** *n.* the (elected or appointed) senior female pupil at a school. **headhunt** *v.t.* to seek and recruit for a vacancy as a business executive etc. ~*v.i.* to engage in headhunting. **headhunter** *n.* 1 a person or agency that specializes in seeking and recruiting business executives etc. 2 a member of a people, notably the Dyaks of Borneo and Celebes, who make or made hostile raids in order to secure human heads as trophies. **headhunting** *n.* **headlamp** *n.* HEADLIGHT (under HEAD[1]). **headland** *n.* 1 a point of land projecting into the sea, a cape, a promontory. 2 a ridge or strip of unploughed land at either end of a field, where the plough is turned. **headless** *a.* †foolish, rash, obstinate, groundless. **headlight** *n.* 1 a lamp at the front of a vehicle, locomotive etc. 2 a beam of light from this. **headlike** *a.* **headline** *n.* 1 the line at the head of a page or paragraph giving the title etc. 2 (*pl.*) news set out in large, heavy type. 3 (*pl.*) the main news summarized in a broadcast news bulletin. ~*v.t.* to give a headline to, to include among the headlines. ~*v.i.* to appear as the main act or performer, to star. **to hit/ make the headlines** to gain notoriety, to get notice in the press. **headliner** *n.* (*N Am.*) the main act or performer; a star. **headlock** *n.* a wrestling hold with an arm locked around the opponent's head. **headlong** *adv.* 1 head first. 2 violently, hastily, rashly. ~*a.* 1 steep, precipitous. 2 violent, precipitate. 3 rash, thoughtless. **head louse** *n.* (*pl.* **head lice**) a louse which infests human hair. **headman** *n.* (*pl.* **headmen**) a chief, a leader, a head worker. **headmaster** *n.* a male head teacher. **headmasterly** *a.* **headmastership** *n.* **headmistress** *n.* a female head teacher. **headmistressly** *a.* **headmistress-ship** *n.* **headmost** *a.* most forward, most advanced. **head of hair** *n.* the particular quality of hair on a person's head. **head of state** *n.* (*pl.* **heads of state**) the leader of a government, or a monarch. **head-on** *a.*, *adv.* 1 (of a collision) with the front of one vehicle hitting that of another. 2 head-to-head. **headphones** *n.pl.* a set of earphones for listening to music etc. **headpiece** *n.* 1 an ornamental engraving at the head of a chapter etc. 2 armour for the head, a helmet. 3 (*coll.*) the head, the intellect. **headrace** *n.* a race that leads water to a water wheel. **headrest** *n.* a padded support for the head, esp. at the top of a seat in a vehicle. **head restraint** *n.* an extension of or addition to the top of a seat in a vehicle, to prevent the head from jolting backwards. **headroom** *n.* room or space for the head in a low tunnel etc.; the amount of space above a vehicle passing under a bridge etc. **headsail** *n.* a sail on the foremast or forward of this. **headscarf** *n.* (*pl.* **headscarves, headscarfs**) a scarf worn over the head. **head sea** *n.* a heavy sea running directly against a ship's course. **headset** *n.* a set of earphones joined by a band over the head. **head-shake** *n.* a significant shake of the head. **headship** *n.* the office of head teacher, a post as a head teacher. **headshrinker** *n.* (*sl.*) a psychiatrist. **headsman** *n.* (*pl.* **headsmen**) a person who cuts off heads, an executioner. **headspring** *n.* 1 the source of a stream. 2 the source or origin of something. **headsquare** *n.* a headscarf. **headstall** *n.* the bridle without the bit and reins. **head start** *n.* 1 an advantage given or taken at the beginning of a race etc. 2 an advantageous beginning to any enterprise. **headstock** *n.* 1 the part supporting the end or head, esp. the end of a revolving spindle. 2 the portion of a lathe that contains the mandrel. 3 the part which supports the cutters in a planing-machine. **headstone** *n.* 1 a stone at the head of a grave. 2 the principal stone in a building. 3 a cornerstone. **headstrong** *a.* ungovernable, obstinate, intractable, self-willed. **head teacher** *n.* the principal teacher at a school. **head-to-head** *n.* a direct debate or contest between two people or teams. ~*adv.* directly confronting the opposition. ~*a.* involving direct confrontation. **head-up** *n.* (of an instrument display) visible without the driver, pilot etc. having to look down at instruments. **head voice** *n.* (in singing etc.) sounds produced above the chest register. **headward** *a.*, *adv.* **headwater** *n.* (*usu. pl.*) the upper part of a stream near its source. **headway** *n.* 1 motion ahead, rate of progress. 2 headroom. **to make headway** to advance, to make progress. **headwind** *n.* a contrary wind. **headword** *n.* a word constituting a heading, esp. in a dictionary. **headwork** *n.* 1 mental work. 2 (*Archit.*) a headlike ornament on the keystone of an arch. **heady** *a.* (*comp.* **headier,** *superl.* **headiest**) 1 headstrong, precipitate. 2 violent, impetuous, intoxicating, inflaming, exhilarating. 3 headachy. [OE *hēafod* (cp. Dut. *hoofd*, Icel. *haufoth*, G *Haupt*)]

head[2] (hed) *v.t.* 1 to lead, to be the leader to, to direct. 2 to move or travel in (a specified direction). 3 to be or form a head to. 4 to provide with a head. 5 to put or to be a heading to a chapter, etc. 6 to get ahead of. 7 to lop (as trees). 8 to oppose, to check. 9 to strike (a ball) with the head. 10 †to behead. ~*v.i.* 1 to go or tend in a direction. 2 to form a head. **to head back** 1 to intercept, to get ahead of and turn back or aside. 2 to return to one's starting point. **to head off** 1 to intercept, to get ahead of and turn back or aside. 2 to leave, to set off. 3 to forestall. **to head the bill** BILL[1]. **to head up** to be in charge of (a team of people etc.). [from HEAD[1]]

-head (hed) *suf.* denoting state or quality, as in *godhead*, *maidenhead*. [OE *-hād* (ME *-hod*), cogn. with Goth. *haidux*, manner, way]

header (hed´ə) *n.* 1 (*coll.*) an act of heading a ball. 2 a plunge or dive head first. 3 a person who puts or fixes a head on anything. 4 a machine for heading nails, rivets etc. 5 a reaper that clips off the corn heads only. 6 a brick or stone laid with its end in the face of the wall. 7 a running title or rubric. 8 a header tank. 9 a tube or water-chamber in a steam boiler into which either end of a stack of water tubes is secured in such a manner that the steam and water can go from one tube or coil to another. **header tank** *n.* a water tank that feeds or maintains pressure in a plumbing system.

heading (hed´ing) *n.* 1 an inscription at the head of an article, chapter etc. 2 a running title. 3 a division of the topics of a discourse. 4 the band of fabric at the top of a curtain onto which tape for the hooks is sewn. 5 the end or the beginning of a drift or gallery in a mine; a gallery, drift or adit. 6 a passage built along the line of a tunnel under construction. 7 the compass bearing of an aircraft etc. 8 the pieces which compose a cask head.

headquarters (hedkwaw´təz) *n.* (*in constr. sing. or pl.*) 1 the residence of the commander-in-chief of an army. 2 the main office of an organization. 3 the centre of authority.

heal (hēl) *v.t.* 1 to make sound or whole again, to restore to health; to cure of (disease etc.). 2 to cause to skin over. 3 to reconcile (differences etc.). 4 to end the suffering caused by. 5 to free from guilt, to purify. ~*v.i.* 1 to grow or become sound or whole again. 2 to skin over. **healable** *a.* **heal-all** *n.* 1 a universal remedy. 2 any of various medicinal herbs. **healer** *n.* **healing** *a.* 1 tending to heal. 2 soothing, mollifying. **healingly** *adv.* [OE *hǣlan*, cogn. with HALE[1], WHOLE]

heald (hēld) *n.* a heddle. [etym. uncertain]

health (helth) *n.* 1 a state of bodily or organic soundness, freedom from bodily or mental disease or decay. 2 physical condition (good, bad etc.). 3 the condition with respect to finances, morals etc. 4 a toast wishing that someone may be well, prosperous etc. **health centre** *n.* a building where several doctors see patients, and where other health services are available. **health certificate** *n.* a certificate confirming good health. **health farm** *n.* an establishment, often in the country, where clients can diet, exercise, relax etc. **health food** *n.* types of food, e.g. organically grown or with no synthetic ingredients, regarded as promoting health. **healthful** *a.* **1** promoting health, either physical or spiritual. **2** healthy, salubrious. **healthfully** *adv.* **healthfulness** *n.* **health physics** *n.* the branch of physics dealing with the protection of workers from the effects of radioactive materials. **health resort** *n.* a place where sick, delicate or convalescent people stay for the benefit of their health. **health service** *n.* a medical service provided by the State. **health visitor** *n.* a nurse specializing in preventive medicine, who visits people in their own homes. **healthy** *a.* (*comp.* **healthier,** *superl.* **healthiest**) **1** enjoying good health. **2** hale, sound. **3** promoting health, salubrious, salutary. **4** ample. **healthily** *adv.* **healthiness** *n.* [OE *hǣlth*, from *hāl*, WHOLE]

heap (hēp) *n.* **1** a pile or accumulation of many things placed or thrown one on another. **2** (*esp. in pl., coll.*) a large number, a lot, a crowd, a good many times, a good deal. **3** an old thing in very bad condition; a wreck. ~*v.t.* **1** to throw (together) or pile (up) in a heap. **2** to load or overload (with). **3** to pile (upon). **to heap coals of fire on someone's head** COAL. **heaped** *a.* (of a spoonful etc.) with more above the brim than in the bowl. [OE *hēap* (cp. Dut. *hoop*, Swed. *hop*, G *Haufe*)]

hear (hiə) *v.t.* (*past, p.p.* **heard** (hœd)) **1** to perceive by the ear, to perceive the sound of. **2** to listen to, to attend to. **3** to listen to as a judge etc. **4** to understand by listening. **5** to be a hearer of. **6** to pay regard to, to heed, to obey. **7** to be informed of by report. **8** to receive a communication (from). ~*v.i.* **1** to have the sense of hearing. **2** to be told, to be informed (of, about etc.). **hear! hear!** used to express agreement or approval. **to hear someone out** to listen to what a person has to say without interrupting. **to hear tell/ say** to have been told (of something). **will not hear of** will not consider allowing or agreeing. **hearable** *a.* **hearer** *n.* **1** a person who hears. **2** a member of an audience. **hearing** *n.* **1** the act of perceiving sound. **2** the sense by which sound is perceived. **3** audience, attention. **4** a judicial trial or investigation. **5** earshot (*within hearing*). **hard of hearing** HARD. **hearing aid** *n.* a device for assisting a person with a hearing problem to hear. **hearing-impaired** *a.* having defective hearing. [OE *hīeran* (cp. Dut. *hooren*, Icel. *heyra*, G *hören*)]

†**hearken** (hah´kən), **harken** *v.i.* to listen attentively (to). ~*v.t.* to hear, to regard. **hearkener** *n.* [OE *heorcnian*, as HARK]

hearsay (hiə´sā) *n.* common talk, report or gossip. ~*a.* told or given at second hand. **hearsay evidence** *n.* evidence given in a court of law based on what was reported to the witness.

hearse (hœs) *n.* a vehicle in which the dead are taken to the place of burial or cremation. ~*v.t.* to carry in or on a hearse at a funeral. [OF *herce*, It. *erpice*, L *hirpicem*, nom. *hirpex*, a harrow]

heart (haht) *n.* **1** the muscular central organ of the circulation of the blood, which keeps going by its rhythmical contraction and dilation. **2** the breast, the position of the heart. **3** capacity for feeling; the emotions or affections, esp. the passion of love. **4** sensibility, tenderness. **5** zeal, ardour, courage, spirit. **6** the central or innermost part. **7** the essential or most important part. **8** the round head of a cabbage etc. **9** strength, efficacy, fertility. **10** a conventional representation of a heart, as on a valentine. **11** anything heart-shaped. **12 a** (*pl.*) a suit of cards marked with figures like hearts. **b** a card of this suit. **c** (*pl.*) a card game involving the taking of tricks, those of hearts being disadvantageous. ~*v.i.* (of a plant etc.) to grow into a compact head or mass. ~†*v.t.* to hearten. **after one's own heart** exactly as one desires; as one feels or thinks oneself. **at heart 1** in reality, truly, at bottom. **2** in one's inmost feelings. **by heart** by rote, by or from memory. **close to one's heart 1** very dear to one. **2** that has a strong emotional effect on one. **dear heart** DEAR. **from (the bottom of) one's heart 1** with absolute sincerity. **2** fervently. **have a heart!** be more considerate; do not be so harsh. **heart and hand** with enthusiastic energy. **heart and soul** with full commitment, devotedly. **in (good) heart 1** in good spirits. **2** in good condition, fertile. **in one's heart** inwardly, secretly. **near one's heart** close to one's heart. **out of heart 1** in low spirits, depressed. **2** (of land) exhausted of fertility. **to break someone's heart** to cause someone overwhelming grief. **to cross one's heart** to promise or aver something solemnly. **to cry one's heart out** CRY. **to eat one's heart out** EAT. **to find it in one's heart to** to be able to bring oneself to (do); to be willing to. **to get by heart** to learn by heart. **to give one's heart to** to fall deeply in love with. **to have at heart** to be earnestly set upon, to cherish (a design etc.). **to have one's heart in** (*usu. neg.*) to be fully committed or devoted to. **to have one's heart in one's mouth** to be violently frightened or startled. **to have one's heart in the right place** to have a kind nature; to have good intentions. **to have the heart to** (*usu. neg.*) to be able or have the courage to (do something unkind or unpleasant). **to learn by heart** to commit to memory. **to lose heart** to become discouraged. **to lose one's heart to** to fall deeply in love with. **to make one's heart bleed** (*iron.*) to distress. **to one's heart's content** as much as one likes. **to pluck up heart** to pluck up courage. **to put one's heart into** to become fully committed or devoted to, to do whole-heartedly. **to set one's heart on** to want very much. **to set someone's heart at rest** to tranquillize, to console. **to shut one's heart to** SHUT. **to speak to someone's heart** to comfort, to encourage, to cheer. **to take heart** to pluck up courage. **to take to heart** to be greatly affected by. **to wear one's heart on one's sleeve 1** to be excessively frank and unreserved. **2** to reveal one's inmost feelings and thoughts. **with all one's heart 1** very willingly. **2** completely, utterly. **with one's whole heart 1** very willingly. **2** completely, utterly. **heartache** *n.* anguish of mind. **heart attack** *n.* an acute loss of normal function in the heart, a coronary thrombosis. **heartbeat** *n.* **1** a pulsation of the heart. **2** an emotion. **heart-block** *n.* a condition in which the atria and the ventricles of the heart do not beat in coordination. **heartbreak** *n.* overpowering sorrow. **heartbreaker** *n.* a person who or thing which breaks the heart. **heartbreaking** *a.* **heartbreakingly** *adv.* **heartbroken** *a.* **heartburn** *n.* a burning pain in the stomach arising from indigestion. **heart disease** *n.* disease of the heart, of any kind. **hearted** *a.* **-hearted** *a.* (*in comb.*) having emotions or a nature of the specified kind (*kind-hearted*). **heart failure** *n.* a condition in which the heart fails to function normally, often leading to death. **heartfelt** *a.* deeply felt, sincere. **heartland** *n.* (*often pl.*) the central or most important part of a country etc. **heartless** *a.* having or showing no feeling or affection; insensible, pitiless, cruel. **heartlessly** *adv.* **heartlessness** *n.* **heart-lung machine** *n.* a machine that adopts the function of a patient's heart and lungs during heart surgery. **heart of gold** *n.* a kind and generous nature. **heart of oak** *n.* **1** a person of courage. **2** a courageous nature. **heart of stone** *n.* an unfeeling or unyielding nature. **heart-rending** *a.* heartbreaking, intensely afflictive. **heart-rendingly** *adv.* **heart's-blood** *n.* **1** the lifeblood. **2** life. **3** †the soul, essence. **heart-searching** *n.* an anguished examination of one's feelings etc. **heartsick** *a.* 1 pained in mind. 2 deeply afflicted. **heartsickness** *n.* **heartsome** *a.* (*Sc.*) 1 encouraging, inspiring. 2 merry, cheerful. †**heart-sore** *a.* grieved at heart. **heartstrings** *n.pl.* 1 the sensibilities; pity, compassion. 2 one's deepest affections. **heart-throb** *n.* 1 the beating of the heart. 2 a person, e.g. a film star, adulated by many. **heart-to-heart** *n., a.* (a conversation) of a searching and intimate nature. **heart-warming** *a.* inspiring emotional approval. **heart-whole** *a.* 1 having the affections free, not in love. 2 undaunted. 3 sincere. **heartwood** *n.* the hardest, inner section of a tree trunk; duramen. [OE *heorte* (cp. Dut. *hart*, Icel. *hjarta*, G *Herz*; also L *cordis*, Gr. *kardia*)]

hearten (hah´tən) *v.t.* to encourage, to inspire, to stir up. ~*v.i.* to cheer (up). **heartener** *n.* **heartening** *a.* **hearteningly** *adv.* [OE *hiertan*, as HEART]

hearth (hahth) *n.* 1 the floor of a fireplace; the area around a fireplace. 2 the fireside as a symbol of the domestic circle, the home. 3 that part of a reverberatory furnace in which the ore is laid, or in a blast furnace the lowest part through which the metal flows. **hearthbrush** *n.* a small brush for sweeping up ashes. †**hearth-money, hearth-tax** *n.* a tax on domestic hearths imposed in the 16th cent. **hearthrug** *n.* a rug placed in front of a fireplace. **hearthstone** *n.* 1 a stone forming a hearth. 2 a soft kind of stone for whitening hearths etc. [OE *hearth* (cp. Dut. *haard*, Swed. *hard*, G *Herd*)]

heartsease (hahts´ēz), **heart's-ease** *n.* 1 the wild pansy, *Viola tricolor*. 2 peace of mind.

hearty (hah´ti) *a.* (*comp.* **heartier**, *superl.* **heartiest**) 1 proceeding from the heart, sincere. 2 cordial, good-natured, kindly. 3 healthy (*hale and hearty*). 4 of keen appetite. 5 full, abundant, satisfying. 6 boisterous. 7 irritatingly cheerful. ~*n.* 1 a brave, hearty person, esp. a sailor; a fellow sailor. 2 an extrovert person, esp. a sporty one. **heartily** *adv.* **heartiness** *n.*

heat (hēt) *n.* 1 a form of energy capable of melting and decomposing matter, and transmissible by means of radiation, conduction or convection. 2 hotness, the sensation produced by a hot body. 3 hot weather. 4 an inflamed condition of the skin, flesh etc. 5 redness, flush, high colour. 6 hotness or pungency of flavour. 7 violence, vehemence, fury; anger. 8 intense excitement. 9 warmth of temperament; animation, fire. 10 sexual receptiveness in animals, esp. in female mammals. 11 any one of a series of courses in a race or other contest. 12 (*sl.*) coercive pressure. 13 (*sl.*) searches etc. by police after a crime. ~*v.t.* 1 to make hot. 2 to inflame, to cause to ferment; to excite. ~*v.i.* 1 to become hot. 2 to become inflamed or excited. **in the heat of the moment** without thinking; without prior consideration (because of the pressure of events). **more heat than light** more anger or vehemence than enlightenment. **on heat** (of a female mammal) ready for mating. **to take the heat out of** to make (a situation) less emotional or tense. **to turn the heat on** (*coll.*) to put (a person) under pressure; to direct criticism at (a person). **heat barrier** *n.* the heating effect of air friction, making flight at high speeds difficult. **heat death** *n.* the state of uniform distribution of energy in a closed system. **heated** *a.* 1 passionate, angry. 2 made hot. **heatedly** *adv.* **heat engine** *n.* an engine driven by hot air, steam or other agent for converting heat into mechanical energy. **heater** *n.* 1 a device that heats. 2 (*sl.*) a pistol. **heat-exchanger** *n.* a device that transfers heat from one fluid to another. **heat exhaustion** *n.* a condition characterized by weakness, dizziness etc., caused by exposure to excessive heat. **heating** *n.* 1 the action of making hot. 2 the means of provision of heat to a building etc. **heat lamp** *n.* a lamp providing heat as well as light. **heat-proof** *a.* designed to be able to resist heat. ~*v.t.* to make heatproof. **heat pump** *n.* a machine for transferring heat from a low temperature to a higher temperature, for the purpose of space or water heating. **heat rash** *n.* prickly heat. **heat-resistant** *a.* heatproof. **heat-seeking** *a.* (of a missile) guided by an infra-red detector. **heat shield** *n.* a shield that protects from high temperatures, e.g. those produced by a spacecraft re-entering the earth's atmosphere. **heat sink** *n.* 1 a device that conducts heat away from an electrical component. 2 (in a high-speed aircraft) a layer of material that absorbs heat. **heatspot** *n.* 1 an urticarious pimple attributed to heat. 2 a freckle. **heatstroke** *n.* a condition characterized by a high temperature, faintness etc., caused by exposure to excessive heat. **heat treatment** *n.* the application of heat to change the properties of metals, to ease damaged muscles etc. **heat-treat** *v.t.* **heatwave** *n.* 1 an unbroken spell of hot weather. 2 a wave of radiant heat. [OE *hætu*, from *hāt*, HOT]

heath (hēth) *n.* 1 an open space of country, esp. one covered with shrubs and coarse herbage. 2 (*Bot.*) an area with many ericaceous shrubs. 3 any plant belonging to the genus *Erica*, or the allied genus *Calluna*, consisting of narrow-leaved evergreen shrubs with wiry stems and red or reddish flowers. **heath bell** *n.* a flower growing on a heath, esp. on heather. **heathberry** *n.* (*pl.* **heathberries**) a berry growing on low shrubs common on heaths, such as the bilberry, cranberry etc. **heath cock** *n.* the male of the black grouse. **heath fowl, heath game** *n.* the black grouse. **heath hen** *n.* the female of the black grouse. **heathland** *n.* an area of heath. **heathy** *a.* [OE *hǣth* (cp. Dut. and G *Heide*, Icel. *heithr*)]

heathen (hē´dhən) *n.* 1 a person who is not Christian, Jewish or Muslim. 2 a non-believer, a pagan, an idolater. 3 an unenlightened or barbarous person. 4 (*Bible*) a Gentile. ~*a.* 1 that is a heathen. 2 of or relating to heathens. **the heathen** (*collect.*) heathen people. **heathendom** *n.* 1 the portion of the world in which heathenism is dominant. 2 heathens collectively. 3 heathenism. **heathenish** *a.* 1 of or belonging to the heathens. 2 barbarous, rapacious, cruel. **heathenishly** *adv.* **heathenishness** *n.* **heathenism, heathenry** *n.* the moral or religious state or practices of heathens. **heathenize, heathenise** *v.t.* to make heathen. [OE *hǣthen* (cp. Dut. *heiden*, Icel. *heithimr*, G *Heide*), cogn. with HEATH]

heather (hedh´ə) *n.* 1 a low-growing ericaceous plant, *Calluna vulgaris*, with narrow leaves, wiry stems and purple, pink or white flowers. 2 any of various similar plants. **heather mixture** *n.* 1 a fabric of a speckled colour supposed to resemble heather. 2 the speckled colour of this. **heathery** *a.* 1 abounding in heather. 2 suggestive of heather. [etym. uncertain]

Heath Robinson (hēth rob´insən) *a.* (of a device) ingenious and extremely complex. [W. *Heath Robinson*, 1872–1944, English cartoonist who drew such devices]

†**heaume** (hōm) *n.* a large helmet coming down to the shoulders. [F, from OF *helme*, HELM[2]]

heave (hēv) *v.t.* (*past, p.p.* **heaved**, (*esp. Naut.*) **hove** (hōv)) 1 to lift, to raise, with effort. 2 to utter or force from the breast (*heave a sigh*). 3 (*coll.*) to throw, to cast (something heavy). 4 (*Naut.*) to hoist (as the anchor), to haul. 5 (*Geol.*) to fracture and displace (strata). ~*v.i.* 1 to rise and fall with alternate or successive motions. 2 to pant. 3 to retch, to vomit. ~*n.* 1 an upward motion or swelling. 2 the act of heaving. 3 a sigh. 4 an effort to vomit. 5 the amount of displacement of a vein or stratum, esp. measured in a horizontal direction. **to heave down** to turn (a ship) on one side in order to clean it. **to heave in/ into sight** to come into sight. **to heave out** to throw out. **to heave to** 1 (*Naut.*) to bring a ship to a standstill. 2 (*Naut.*) to bring the head (of a ship) to the wind and so stop its motion. **heave-ho** *int.* used by sailors in hauling up the anchor. ~*n.* 1 a cry of 'heave-ho'. 2 dismissal, removal. **to get the heave-ho** (*coll.*) to be dismissed from employment. **to give the heave-ho** (*coll.*) to dismiss from employment. **heaver** *n.* a person who or thing which heaves (*esp. in comb.*, as *coal-heaver*). [OE *hebban* (cp. Dut. *heffen*, Icel. *hefja*, G *heben*, also L *capere*, to take, Gr. *kōpē*, handle)]

heaven (hev´ən) *n.* 1 (*often in pl.*) the sky, the firmament; the atmosphere enveloping the earth regarded as the region in which the clouds float, the winds blow etc. 2 (*also* **Heaven**) the abode of God or the gods and the blessed. 3 (*usu.* **Heaven**) God, providence. 4 any place or state of extreme joy or pleasure. 5 (*coll.*) something extremely pleasing. 6 according to ancient cosmology, any one of several revolving spheres in which the heavenly bodies were carried round the earth. *~int.* (*sing. or pl.*) used to express surprise, irritation etc. **for heaven's sake** SAKE[1]. **heaven forbid** may it never happen (that). †**heaven forfend** may it never happen (that). **heaven knows** used to reinforce the seriousness or sincerity of a statement. **heavens above!** used to express surprise, dismay, irritation etc. **host of heaven** HOST[2]. **to move heaven and earth** MOVE. **heavenly** *a.* 1 of or relating to the heavens, celestial. 2 inhabiting heaven; divine. 3 situated in the heavens (as the planets, stars etc.). 4 supremely blessed or excellent. 5 (*coll.*) highly pleasing, delicious. **heavenliness** *n.* **heavenly body** *n.* a sun, star, planet or other mass of matter, as distinct from the earth. **heavenly host** *n.* the host of heaven. **heaven of heavens** *n.* SEVENTH HEAVEN (under SEVENTH). **heaven-sent** *a.* (of an opportunity etc.) coming at an opportune moment. **heavenward** *a.*, *adv.* **heavenwards** *adv.* [OE *heofon*, *hefon* (etym. uncertain)]

heaves (hēvz) *n.pl.* (*also sing. in constr.*) an asthmatic disease in horses, broken wind. [HEAVE]

heavily, heaviness HEAVY.

Heaviside layer (hev´isīd), **Heaviside-Kennelly layer** (-ken´əli) *n.* a layer in the upper atmosphere that reflects radio waves, thus enabling reception round the curved surface of the earth, the E-layer. [British physicist O. *Heaviside*, 1850–1925, US physicist A. E. *Kennelly*, 1861–1939]

heavy (hev´i) *a.* (*comp.* **heavier**, *superl.* **heaviest**) 1 having great weight, weighty, ponderous. 2 of great density or specific gravity, dense. 3 of a larger and weightier kind than the usual or standard (as metal, artillery etc.). 4 great, powerful, forcible, violent. 5 concerned with large amounts or dealings. 6 requiring great effort. 7 unwieldy, clumsy. 8 plentiful, abundant; large in amount. 9 hard to digest. 10 weighed down, loaded (with). 11 not easily borne. 12 oppressive, grievous, severe; burdensome, obstructive, clogging; difficult. 13 stern, strict. 14 drowsy, dull, sluggish, stupid. 15 tedious. 16 doleful, depressing, depressed. 17 excessively serious, sombre. 18 (of the ground) soft and wet. 19 (of the sky, clouds etc.) threatening, louring. 20 (of bread, cakes etc.) not properly raised. 21 (of wine etc.) of full body. 22 armed with heavy weapons. 23 †deep, loud. 24 †pregnant. *~n.* (*pl.* **heavies**) 1 (*coll.*) a thug, a villain. 2 a villainous or tragic role in a play. 3 (*usu. in pl., coll.*) a serious, broadsheet newspaper, rather than a popular tabloid. 4 anything large or weighty of its kind. 5 (*Sc.*) a type of strong beer. *~adv.* heavily, with great weight. **heavy on** 1 using a lot of. 2 unduly strict with or harsh to. 3 giving hard wear to. **heavy on hand** HAND. **to make heavy weather** WEATHER. **with a heavy hand** 1 oppressively. 2 unstintingly, without sparing. **heavily** *adv.* **heaviness** *n.* **heavy breather** *n.* 1 a person who breathes audibly. 2 a person who makes obscene telephone calls, panting audibly while doing so. **heavy breathing** *n.* audible breathing, esp. resulting from physical exertion or to suggest sexual excitement. **heavy chemicals** *n.pl.* chemicals produced in bulk for agriculture and industry. **heavy-duty** *a.* 1 designed to sustain more than usual wear. 2 (*N Am.*, *coll.*) larger than usual in size, amount etc. **heavy-footed** *a.* walking heavily or clumsily, ponderous. **heavy going** *pred. a.* difficult to get through, laborious. **heavy-handed** *a.* 1 clumsy, awkward. 2 oppressive. **heavy-handedly** *adv.* **heavy-handedness** *n.* **heavy-headed** *a.* headachy, stupid, drowsy. **heavy-hearted** *a.* dejected. **heavy hydrogen** *n.* deuterium. **heavy industry** *n.* industry involved in the manufacturing of large machinery, vehicles etc., or the extraction and processing of raw materials. **heavyish** *a.* **heavy metal** *n.* 1 a metal with a high specific gravity. 2 a type of loud rock music with a strong beat. 3 heavy artillery. **heavy mob** *n.* (*coll.*) the people with the power to frighten or coerce. **heavy petting** *n.* close sexual contact without intercourse. **heavy purse** *n.* a state of wealth, riches. **heavy sleeper** *n.* a person who sleeps very deeply and is not easy to wake. **heavy spar** *n.* barytes. **heavy water** *n.* deuterium oxide, a liquid similar to ordinary water, with density about 10% greater. **heavyweight** *n.* 1 a person or animal of more than average weight. 2 a boxer, wrestler, weightlifter etc. in the highest main weight category. 3 this weight category. 4 a jockey above the average weight. 5 (*coll.*) a person of great power, influence or intellect. [OE *hefig*, cogn. with HEAVE]

Heb. *abbr.* 1 Hebrew (the language). 2 Hebrews (in the New Testament).

hebdomad (heb´dəmad) *n.* (*formal*) 1 a week, a period of seven days (alluding to Daniel's prophecy (Dan. ix.27)). 2 a group of seven things. 3 in Gnosticism, a group of seven spirits dwelling in the seven planets. **hebdomadal** (-dom´-) *a.* 1 meeting or occurring weekly. 2 consisting of seven days. **hebdomadally** *adv.* **hebdomadary** (-dom´-) *a.* hebdomadal. [L and Gr. *hebdomasados* (*hegdomos*, seventh, from *hepta*, seven)]

hebe (hē´bi) *n.* an evergreen shrub of the genus *Hebe*, with spikes of purple or white flowers. [Gr. *Hēbē*, goddess of youth, from as HEBETIC]

hebetate (heb´ətāt) *v.t.* 1 to make blunt or dull. 2 to stupefy. *~v.i.* to become blunt or dull. **hebetation** (-ā´shən) *n.* [L *hebetātus*, p.p. of *hebetāre*, from *hebes -etis*, blunt]

hebetic (hibet´ik) *a.* of or relating to youth or pubescence. [Gr. *hēbē*, youthful prime]

Hebraic (hibrā´ik) *a.* 1 of or relating to the Hebrews. 2 of or relating to Hebrew. **Hebraically** *adv.* **Hebraism** (hē´-) *n.* 1 the thought or religion of the Hebrews. 2 a Hebrew characteristic. 3 a Hebrew idiom or expression. **Hebraist** *n.* 1 a person learned in Hebrew language and literature. 2 a person who conforms or adheres to Jewish ideas or religious observances. **Hebraistic** (-is´-), **Hebraistical** *a.* **Hebraistically** *adv.* **Hebraize, Hebraise** *v.t.* 1 to convert into a Hebrew idiom. 2 to give a Hebrew character to. *~v.i.* 1 to become Hebrew. 2 to act according to Hebrew manners or fashions. [late L *Hebraicus*, Gr. *Hebraikos*]

Hebrew (hē´broo) *n.* 1 the Semitic language of the ancient Jews and, in a modern form, of the State of Israel. 2 an Israelite. 3 (*often offensive*) a Jew. *~a.* 1 of or relating to Hebrew. 2 of or relating to the Israelites or Jews. **Hebrew Scriptures** *n.pl.* the sacred writings of Judaism, comprising the Law, the Prophets and the Hagiographa or Writings. [F *hébreu*, L *Hebraeus*, Gr. *Hebraios*, Aram. *ebrai*, Heb. *'ibrī*, prob. one from the other side, an immigrant]

Hebridean (hebridē´ən) *n.* a native or inhabitant of the Hebrides. *~a.* of or relating to the Hebrides, islands off the west coast of Scotland. [*Hebrides*, erron. for L *Hebudes* (Pliny), *Hebudae*, Gr. *Heboudai*]

hecatomb (hek´ətoom) *n.* 1 in ancient Greece or Rome,

the sacrifice of 100 oxen or other beasts. **2** any great sacrifice. [L *hecatombē*, Gr. *hekatombē* (*hekaton*, a hundred, *bous*, ox)]

heck[1] (hek) *int.* (*coll.*) used to express irritation, dismay etc. ~*n.* hell (*What the heck do you think you're up to?*). [used instead of *hell*]

heck[2] (hek) *n.* (*Sc., North.*) **1** a grated contrivance in a stream, used as a fish trap or to obstruct the passage of fish. **2** a rack for fodder. **3** a hatch. [var. of HATCH[1]]

heckelphone (hek´əlfōn) *n.* a baritone oboe. [W. *Heckel*, 1856–1909, German instrument maker]

heckle (hek´əl) *v.t.* **1** to interrupt and worry (a public speaker) by deliberately inconvenient questions, taunts etc. **2** to hackle. ~*n.* an act of heckling a speaker. **heckler** *n.* **heckling** *n.*

hectare (hek´teə, -tah) *n.* a measure of area equal to 10,000 sq. metres or 2.471 acres. **hectarage** *n.* [F]

hectic (hek´tik) *a.* **1** full of excitement, exciting, wild; very busy. †**2** (*Med.*) **a** (of fever) habitual, continual, esp. as symptomatic of tuberculosis. **b** of, relating to or suffering from such a fever. ~†*n.* (*Med.*) **1** a hectic fever or flush. **2** a patient suffering from this. **hectically** *adv.* †**hectic fever, hectic flush** *n.* (*Med.*) a fever associated with tuberculosis, dysentery etc. [F *hectique*, late L *hecticus*, Gr. *hektikos*, from *hexis*, habit of body, from *hexein*, fut. of *echein*, to have, to hold]

hecto- (hek´tō) *comb. form* a hundred. **hectogram** (hek´təgram), **hectogramme** *n.* a weight of 100 grams or 3.52 oz. **hectograph** (hek´təgrahf) *n.* a machine for multiplying copies of writings or drawings. **hectographic** (-graf´-) *a.* **hectolitre** (hek´təlētə), (*N Am.*) **hectoliter** *n.* a liquid measure 100 litres or 3.531 cu. ft. **hectometre** (hek´təmētə), (*N Am.*) **hectometer** *n.* a measure of length equal to 100 metres or 109.3633 yds. [Gr. *hekaton*, a hundred]

hector (hek´tə) *v.t.* to bully, to treat with insolence. ~*v.i.* to play the bully, to bluster. ~*n.* a bully, a blusterer. **hectorer** *n.* **hectoringly** *adv.* [Gr. *Hectōr*, the son of Priam and Hecuba, the bravest of the Trojan warriors in Homer's *Iliad*]

he'd (hēd) *contr.* **1** he had. **2** he would.

heddle (hed´əl) *n.* one of the sets of parallel cords or wires forming loops for the warp threads of a loom. [perh. from an OE *hefedl*, earlier form of *hefeld*]

hedera (hed´ərə) *n.* a climbing plant of the genus *Hedera*, an ivy. [L]

hedge (hej) *n.* **1** a fence of bushes or small trees. **2** a barrier of any kind. **3** a means of securing oneself against loss. **4** a shifty or non-committal statement. ~*v.t.* **1** to fence (in) with or separate (off) by a hedge. **2** to surround or enclose with or as with a hedge. **3** to secure oneself against loss (on a speculation etc.) by transactions that would provide some compensation. ~*v.i.* **1** to plant or repair hedges. **2** to act in a shifty way, to avoid making a decisive statement. **hedge-hop** *v.i.* (*pres.p.* **hedge-hopping**, *past, p.p.* **hedge-hopped**) to fly very low over fields etc. **hedge-hopper** *n.* **hedge hyssop** *n.* a N American scrophulareous plant, *Gratiola aurea*, believed to have medicinal properties. **hedge laying** *n.* the practice of maintaining a hedge by cutting into the stems and laying them over to encourage new growth and create a strong barrier. **hedgeless** *a.* **hedger** *n.* **hedgerow** *n.* a row of shrubs planted as a hedge. **hedge-school** *n.* (*Hist.*) a poorly staffed and equipped school such as was formerly conducted in the open air in country parts of Ireland. **hedge-schoolmaster** *n.* **hedge sparrow** *n.* a common European bird, *Prunella modularis*, one of the warblers; the dunnock. **hedge trimmer** *n.* a power tool with a cutter for trimming hedges. [OE *hecg* (cp. Dut. *hegge*, Icel. *heggr*, G *Hecke*), cogn. with *hāga*, HAW[1]]

hedgehog (hej´hog) *n.* **1** a small insectivorous mammal, *Erinaceus europaeus*, covered above with spines, and able to roll itself up into a ball. **2** any other animal covered with spines, such as the porcupine.

hedonism (hē´dənizm, hed´-) *n.* **1** the doctrine or belief that pleasure is the chief good. **2** behaviour motivated by this. **hedonic** (-don´-) *a.* **1** of or relating to pleasure. **2** (*Psych.*) of or relating to sensations in general. **hedonics** *n.pl.* (*also sing. in constr.*) **1** the scientific study of pleasure. **2** the branch of ethics dealing with the relations of duty and pleasure. **hedonist** *n.* **hedonistic** (-nis´-) *a.* **hedonistically** *adv.* [Gr. *hēdonē*, pleasure]

-hedron (hē´drən, hed´-) *comb. form* (*pl.* **-hedra** (-drə), **-hedrons**) a solid figure having the specified number of sides. **-hedral** *comb. form* having the specified number of sides.

heebie-jeebies (hēbijē´biz) *n.pl.* (*coll.*) nervous anxiety, apprehension (*suffering from the heebie-jeebies*). [coined by W. DeBeck, 1890–1942, American cartoonist]

heed (hēd) *v.t.* to pay attention to, to take notice of. ~*n.* **1** care, attention. **2** careful consideration. **to take/ give/ pay heed** to pay attention (to). **heedful** *a.* **1** attentive, regardful (of). **2** circumspect, wary. **heedfully** *adv.* **heedfulness** *n.* **heedless** *a.* **1** careless. **2** thoughtless. **3** negligent (of). **heedlessly** *adv.* **heedlessness** *n.* [OE *hēdan* (cp. Dut. *hoeden*, G *hüten*, from *Hut*, protection), prob. cogn. with HOOD[1]]

hee-haw (hē´haw) *v.i.* to bray like a donkey. ~*n.* **1** a donkey's bray. **2** a loud and foolish laugh. [imit.]

heel[1] (hēl) *n.* **1** the rounded hinder part of the human foot. **2** the corresponding part of the hind limb in quadrupeds, often above the foot. **3** the part of a shoe, stocking etc. covering the heel. **4** a block built up of pieces of leather to raise the hinder part of a boot or shoe from the ground. **5** a heel-like protuberance, knob or part, such as the lower end of a mast, the hindermost part of a ship's keel, the cusp of a molar tooth, the crook in the head of a golf club. **6** the crusty end of a loaf of bread. **7** the rind of a cheese. **8** the latter part, the tail-end of anything. **9** (*coll.*) a contemptible person. ~*v.t.* **1** to add a heel to; to repair a heel of. **2** in rugby, to pass the ball with the heels. **3** in golf, to hit the ball with the heel of a club. ~*v.i.* to dance on the heels. ~*int.* used to instruct a dog to walk close behind. **at heel** (of a dog) close behind. **at the heels of** close behind. **down at heel** DOWN[1]. **head over heels** HEAD[1]. **on the heels of** following closely after. **to come to heel** (of a dog) to walk close beside in a controlled manner. **to cool one's heels** COOL. **to dig one's heels in** to be obstinate. **to drag one's heels** DRAG. **to heel 1** (of a dog) close behind. **2** (of a person) under control. **to kick one's heels** KICK[1]. **to show a clean pair of heels (to)** to run away (from). **to take to one's heels** to run away. **to turn on one's heel** to turn round sharply. **heelball** *n.* a composition of hard wax and lampblack, used to give a smooth surface to heels, and for taking rubbings of inscriptions etc. **-heeled** *a.* (*in comb.*) having heels of the specified type, e.g. *high-heeled*; see also WELL-HEELED (under WELL[1]). **heeler** *n.* **1** a person who puts heels on boots. **2** (*N Am., sl.*) a political hanger-on. **heelless** *a.* **heelpiece** *n.* a piece of leather on the heel of a shoe. **heeltap** *n.* **1** a thickness of leather in the heel of a shoe. **2** a small quantity of liquor left in the bottom of a glass. [OE *hēla* (cp. Dut. *hiel*, Icel. *hœll*), allied to *hōh*, HOUGH]

heel[2] (hēl) *v.i.* of a ship, to incline or cant over to one side. ~*v.t.* to make (a ship) do this. ~*n.* an inclination to one side (of a ship, etc.). [ME *helden*, OE *hyldan*, cogn. with *heald*, sloping]

heel[3] (hēl) *v.t.* to plant in the ground and cover the roots. **to heel in** to plant in a temporary position and firm the soil. [OE *helian*, from Gmc.]

heft (heft) *v.t.* to try the weight of by lifting. ~*n.* **1** (*dial.*,

N Am.) weight, heaviness. **2** †the act of heaving. [from HEAVE]

hefty (hef´ti) *a.* (*comp.* **heftier**, *superl.* **heftiest**) **1** strong, muscular, powerful. **2** big. **heftily** *adv.* **heftiness** *n.* [HEFT]

Hegelian (higā´liən, hāgē´-) *a.* of or relating to Hegel or his philosophy. ~*n.* an adherent of the teaching of Hegel. **Hegelianism** *n.* the philosophical system of Hegel. [George Frederick William *Hegel*, 1770–1831, German philosopher]

hegemony (higem´əni, -jem-) *n.* leadership, predominance, esp. applied to the relation of one state to another or to a confederation. **hegemonic** (hegəmon´-, hej-) *a.* [Gr. *hēgemonia*, from *hēgemōn*, leader, from *hēg-*, stem of *agein*, to lead]

Hegira (hej´irə), **Hejira, Hijra** (hij´rə) *n.* **1** the flight of Muhammad from Mecca to Medina, in AD 622, from which the Muslim era is computed. **2** a hurried escape from a dangerous situation. [med. L, from Arab. *hijrah*, from *hajara*, to separate]

hegumen (higū´mən), **hegumenos** (-minōs) *n.* the head of a monastery in the Greek Church. [med. L *hēgūmenus*, Gr. *hēgoumenos*, orig. pres.p. of *hegeisthai*, to lead]

heifer (hef´ə) *n.* **1** a young cow that has not yet calved. **2** (*sl.*, *offensive*) a woman. [OE *hēahfore*, etym. uncertain]

heigh (hā) *int.* used to call attention or express enquiry or encouragement. **heigh-ho** (-hō´) *int.* used to express disappointment, weariness or regret. [imit.]

heighday HEYDAY.

height (hīt) *n.* **1** the distance of the top above the foot, basis or foundation. **2** altitude above the ground, sea level or other recognized level. **3** the quality or state of being high. **4** an elevated position. **5** an eminence, a summit. **6** stature. **7** elevation in rank, office, society etc. **8** the fullest extent or degree. **at its height 1** at its highest degree. **2** at the culminating point. **heighten** *v.t.* **1** to make high or higher, to raise, to elevate. **2** to increase, to enhance, to intensify, to accentuate, to emphasize. ~*v.i.* **1** to rise. **2** to increase, to augment. **3** to intensify. **height of land** *n.* (*N Am.*) a watershed. [OE *hīehtho*, from *hēah*, HIGH]

heinous (hā´nəs, hē´-) *a.* abominable, flagrant, atrocious; wicked in the highest degree. **heinously** *adv.* **heinousness** *n.* [OF *haïnos*, from *haïne*, hate, from *haïr*, to hate]

heir (eə) *n.* **1** a person who by law succeeds or is entitled to succeed another in the possession of property or rank. **2** a person who succeeds to any gift, quality etc. **3** †a child, offspring. ~*v.t.* to be heir to, to inherit. **heir apparent** *n.* (*pl.* **heirs apparent**) the heir who will succeed on the death of the present possessor and whose right to succeed cannot be challenged. **heir-at-law** *n.* (*pl.* **heirs-at-law**) a person who inherits property by right of descent. **heirdom** *n.* **heiress** *n.* a female heir. **heirless** *a.* **heirloom** *n.* **1** an item of property which descends with an estate to an heir. **2** any possession that has remained in a family for several generations. **heir presumptive** *n.* (*pl.* **heirs presumptive**) an heir whose actual succession may be prevented by the birth of someone else. **heirship** *n.* [OF, from late L *hērem*, L *hērēdem*, acc. of *hērēs*]

Heisenberg uncertainty principle (hī´zənbœg) *n.* (*Physics*) the principle that the position and velocity of a subatomic particle cannot both be ascertained at the same time. [W. K. *Heisenberg*, 1901–76, German physicist]

heist (hīst) *n.* (*N Am.*, *sl.*) a burglary, a robbery. ~*v.t.* to rob, to steal.

hei-tiki (hātik´i) *n.* (*New Zeal.*) a neck decoration made of greenstone.

Hejira HEGIRA.

HeLa cell (hē´lə) *n.* a human cultured epithelial cell used in virological research. [from *He*nrietta *La*cks, from whom the original cells came]

held HOLD[1].

Heldentenor (hel´dəntenə) *n.* (*pl.* **Heldentenors, Heldentenöre** (-nœ´rə)) (a singer with) a strong tenor voice, suitable for Wagnerian roles. [G, hero tenor]

helenium (helē´niəm) *n.* any plant belonging to the genus *Helenium*, having daisy-like flowers and often growing up to 5 ft. (1.6 m) tall. [L]

heli- (hel´i) *comb. form* helicopter.

heliacal (hilī´əkəl) *a.* **1** closely connected with the sun. **2** rising just before the sun. **heliacally** *adv.* **heliacal rising, heliacal setting** *n.* the apparent rising or setting of a star when it first becomes perceptible or invisible in the rays of the sun. [late L *hēliacus*, Gr. *hēliakos*, from *hēlios*, sun]

helianthemum (hēlianth´iməm) *n.* any low-growing evergreen plant of the genus *Helianthemum*, having yellow or orange saucer-shaped flowers. [L]

helianthus (hēlian´thəs) *n.* any plant, such as the sunflower, belonging to the genus *Helianthus*, typically having large daisy-like flowers. [Gr. *anthos*, flower]

helical (hel´ikəl) *a.* like a helix; spiral. **helical gears** *n.pl.* gearwheels in which the teeth are set at an angle to the axis. **helically** *adv.* **helicity** (hēlis´iti) *n.* **1** the quality or nature of a helix. **2** the projection of the spin of a subatomic particle on the direction of its linear momentum. **helicograph** (-kəgrahf) *n.* an instrument for describing spirals. **helicoid** (-koid) *a.* **helicoidal** *a.* [from L *helix -icis*, see HELIX]

helices HELIX.

helichrysum (helikrī´səm) *n.* any plant of the genus *Helichrysum*, having daisy-like flowers with papery petals. [L]

helicity HELICAL.

helicon (hel´ikən) *n.* a bass tuba that coils behind the player's head. [L, from Gr. *Helikōn*, see HELICONIAN]

Heliconian (helikō´niən) *a.* of or relating to Helicon or the Muses. [L *Helicōnius*, Gr. *Helikōnios*, from *Helikōni*, a mountain in Boeotia, the fabled seat of Apollo and the Muses]

helicopter (hel´ikoptə) *n.* an aircraft with one or more power-driven airscrews mounted on vertical axes by the aid of which it can take off and land vertically. ~*v.t.* to transport by helicopter. ~*v.i.* to fly in a helicopter. **helicopter gunship** *n.* a heavily armed helicopter for attacking ground forces. **helicopter pad** *n.* an area, e.g. on the roof of a building, where helicopters can take off and land. [HELIX, Gr. *pteron*, a wing]

helio- (hē´liō) *comb. form* **1** of or relating to the sun. **2** produced by the rays of the sun. [Gr. *hēlios*, the sun]

heliocentric (hēliōsen´trik) *a.* **1** having reference to the sun as centre. **2** regarded from the point of view of the sun. **heliocentrically** *adv.*

Heliochrome® (hē´liəkrōm) *n.* a photograph representing an object in the natural colours. **heliochromic** (-krō´-) *a.* of or relating to heliochromy. **heliochromotype** (-krō´mətīp) *n.* a Heliochrome. **heliochromy** *n.* a photographic process by which the natural colours of objects are reproduced. [Gr. *chrōma*, colour]

heliograph (hē´liəgrahf) *n.* **1** an apparatus for signalling by reflecting flashes of sunlight. **2** a heliogram. **3** an instrument for obtaining photographs of the sun. **4** an engraving obtained by a process in which a prepared plate is exposed to the light. ~*v.i.*, *v.t.* to signal with a heliograph; to photograph by a heliographic process. **heliogram** (-gram) *n.* a message transmitted by heliograph. **heliographic** (-graf´-), **heliographical** *a.* **heliography** (-og´rə-) *n.* (*pl.* **heliographies**) **1** the operation of signalling with the heliograph. **2** the process of engraving by exposure by light.

heliogravure (hēliōgrəvūə´) *n.* photogravure.

heliolatry (hēliol´ətri) *n.* sun-worship. **heliolater** *n.* **heliolatrous** *a.* [HELIO-, -LATRY]
heliolithic (hēliōlith´ik) *a.* of or relating to a civilization known for sun-worship and the erection of megaliths.
heliology (hēliol´əji) *n.* the science of the sun.
heliometer (hēliom´itə) *n.* an instrument for measuring small angles in the heavens, such as the angular distance between stars, the diameter of stars etc. (orig. for measuring the diameter of the sun). **heliometric** (-əmet´-), **heliometrical** *a.*
heliophilous (hēliof´iləs) *a.* attracted by or turning towards the sunlight.
heliophobic (hēliōfō´bik) *a.* disliking or turning away from the sunlight.
heliostat (hē´liəstat) *n.* an instrument, comprising a mirror turned by clockwork, by which the rays of the sun are continuously reflected in a fixed direction. **heliostatic** (-stat´ik) *a.* [Gr. *statos*, standing, from *sta-*, stem of *histanai*, to stand]
heliotherapy (hēliəther´əpi) *n.* curative treatment by exposing the body to the rays of the sun.
heliothermometer (hēliōthəmom´itə) *n.* a thermometer with a blackened bulb for registering the effect of atmospheric absorption on solar radiation.
heliotrope (hē´liətrōp) *n.* **1** any plant of the borage family belonging to the genus *Heliotropium*, having scented purple flowers. **2** any of various plants whose flowers turn with the sun. **3** a purple colour characteristic of heliotrope flowers. **4** a red-spotted variety of quartz, bloodstone. **5** a surveying apparatus for reflecting the sun's rays, a kind of heliograph. *~a.* of the purple colour of heliotrope flowers. **heliotropic** (-trop´-), **heliotropical** *a.* of, relating to or manifesting heliotropism. **heliotropism** (-ot´rə-), **heliotropy** (-ot´rəpi) *n.* movement of leaves or flowers towards the sun. [L *heliotropium*, Gr. *heliotropion* (*trop-*, stem of *trepein*, to turn)]
heliotype (hē´liətīp) *n.* **1** a picture obtained by printing from a gelatin surface in the same way as from a lithographic stone. **2** this process. **heliotypic** (-tip´-) *a.* **heliotypography** (-tīpog´-), **heliotypy** (-tīpi) *n.*
heliozoan (hēliəzō´ən) *a.* (*Zool.*) of or relating to the order Heliozoa, a group of protozoans with threadlike radiating processes. *~n.* a protozoan of this class. **heliozoic** *a.* [Gr. *zōā*, pl. of *zōon*, animal]
helipad (hel´ipad) *n.* a helicopter pad.
heliport (hel´ipawt) *n.* an airport for the landing and departure of helicopters.
heli-skiing (hel´iskēing) *n.* skiing from a starting point reached by helicopter.
helispheric (helisfer´ik), **helispherical** (-əl) *a.* winding round a globe spirally. [HELIX, SPHERICAL (under SPHERE)]
helium (hē´liəm) *n.* a gaseous inert element, chem. symbol He, at. no. 2. [Gr. *hēlios*, sun (the element being first discovered in the atmosphere of the sun)]
helix (hē´liks) *n.* (*pl.* **helices** (-lisēz)) **1** a spiral or coiled curve, as of wire or rope. **2** a curve cutting a line at a constant angle with the axis of a cylinder or solid cone. **3** the rim or fold of the external ear. **4** a small volute under the abacus of a Corinthian column, and other spiral ornaments. **5** a gastropod of the genus *Helix*, containing the common snails. [L, from Gr.]
hell (hel) *n.* **1** the place of punishment for the wicked after death in Christianity, Judaism and Islam; the place or state of the dead. **2** a place of extreme misery, pain or suffering; torment, torture. **3** †a gambling-house. *~int.* used to express anger, annoyance etc. **a hell of a/ helluva** (*coll.*) a very good, bad, remarkable etc. (thing of its kind). **as hell** (*coll.*) extremely. **come hell or high water** (*coll.*) whatever may happen. **for the hell of it** for amusement, just for fun. **hell for leather** (*coll.*) very fast. **hell to pay** very unpleasant consequences. **like hell 1** (*coll.*) very hard, much etc. **2** (*coll.*) used to deny a statement made by another. **not to have a hope in hell** not to have any chance at all. **to beat/ scare etc. the hell out of** to beat, scare etc. severely. **to catch hell** to get hell. **to get hell** to be severely scolded or punished. **to give someone hell 1** to scold someone severely. **2** to make life very difficult for someone. **to play (merry) hell with 1** (*coll.*) to harm or damage. **2** (*coll.*) to scold. **what the hell?** what does it matter? **what/ where/ why etc. the hell?** (*coll.*) used as an intensifier. **hellbender** *n.* a salamander, *Cryptobranchus alleganiensis*, of N America. **hell-bent** *a.* recklessly intent (on). **hell-cat** *n.* a witch, a hag; a vicious woman. **hellfire** *n.* the torments of hell. **hell-hole** *n.* a terrible place. **hell-hound** *n.* **1** a fiend of hell. **2** an agent of hell. **hellish** *a.* **1** of or relating to hell. **2** detestable. **3** atrociously wicked. *~adv.* (*coll.*) very; terribly (*hellish difficult*). **hellishly** *adv.* **hellishness** *n.* **hell-like** *a.* **hellraiser** *n.* a troublemaker. **hellraising** *a.*, *n.* **Hell's Angel** *n.* a member of a gang wearing leather and riding motorcycles, often with a reputation for causing trouble. **hell's bells, hell's teeth** *int.* used to express anger, annoyance etc. **hellward** *a.*, *adv.* [OE *hel* (cp. Dut. and Icel. *hel*, OHG *Hella*, G *Hölle*), from *hel-*, to hide, whence OE *hēlan*, as hele]
hellebore (hel´ibaw) *n.* **1** any plant of the ranunculaceous genus *Helleborus*, containing *H. niger*, the Christmas rose, and the hellebore of the ancients, *H. officinalis*. **2** a lily, *Veratrum alba*. **3** any of various other plants supposed by the ancients to be a cure for insanity. **helleborine** (-rēn, -rīn) *n.* any temperate orchid of the genus *Epipactis* or *Cephalanthera*. †**helleborism** *n.* [L *helleborus*, Gr. *helleboros*]
Hellene (hel´ēn) *n.* (*pl.* **Hellenes**) **1** an ancient Greek, a person of Greek descent whether inhabiting Europe or Asia Minor. **2** a citizen of modern Greece. **Hellenic** (-len´-, -lē´-), †**Hellenian** (-lē´-) *a.* **Hellenism** (hel´ə-) *n.* **1** Greek civilization or culture. **2** cultivation of Greek ideas, language, style etc. **3** Greek nationalism. **4** a Greek idiom, phrase, peculiarity or custom. **Hellenist** *n.* **1** a person who is learned in Greek language and literature. **2** a person who adopted the Greek language, dress, customs etc., esp. a Greek Jew in the early days of Christianity. **Hellenistic** (-nis´-) *a.* **Hellenistically** *adv.* **Hellenize** (hel´ə-), **Hellenise** *v.i.* **1** to adopt or follow Greek habits. **2** to use or study the Greek language. *~v.t.* **1** to permeate with Greek ideas, culture etc. **2** to make Greek. **Hellenization** (-ā´shən) *n.* [Gr. *Hellēn*]
hellgrammite (hel´grəmīt) *n.* (*N Am.*) the aquatic larva of the *Corydalus cornutus*, used as bait in fishing. [etym. unknown]
hellion (hel´yən) *n.* (*N Am.*) a naughty child; a mischievous person. [prob. from *hellion* (dial.) a rogue, a good-for-nothing]
hello (həlō´), **hallo, hullo** *int.* **1** an informal greeting. **2** a preliminary summons and answer when telephoning. **3** an exclamation of surprise. **4** a call for attention. *~n.* (*pl.* **hellos, hallos, hullos**) a cry of 'hello'. *~v.i.* (*3rd pers. sing. pres.* **helloes, halloes, hulloes**, *past, p.p.* **helloed, halloed, hulloed**) to cry 'hello'.
helm[1] (helm) *n.* **1** the instrument or apparatus by which a vessel is steered; the rudder and its operative parts, such as the tiller or wheel; the tiller. **2** turning of the helm. **3** a position of management or direction. **4** †a helmsman. *~v.t.* **1** to guide, to steer. **2** to manage. **at the helm** steering, in control, at the head. **to put down the helm** (*Naut.*) to bring the rudder to windward. **to put up the helm** (*Naut.*) to bring the rudder to leeward. **helmage** (-ij) *n.* **1** guidance; direction. **2** management. **helmless**[1] *a.* **helmsman** *n.* (*pl.* **helmsmen**) the person who steers a vessel. [OE *helma* (cp. Icel. *hjalm*)]
helm[2] (helm) *n.* **1** a helmet. **2** (*dial.*) a cloud gathering

over the northern Pennines before or during a storm. **helmed** *a.* helmeted. **helmless**[2] *a.* [OE, Dut., G, cogn. with *helan*, as hele]

helmet (hel´mit) *n.* **1** a piece of defensive armour for the head. **2** a protective covering for the head worn by police officers, cyclists etc. **3** the hooded upper lip of some flowers. **4** a helmet shell. **helmeted** *a.* wearing a helmet. **helmet shell** *n.* a tropical mollusc belonging to the genus *Cassis.* [obs. F *healmet*, dim. of *helm*, HELM[2]]

helminth (hel´minth) *n.* a worm, esp. a parasitic intestinal worm. **helminthiasis** (-thī´əsis) *n.* a condition in which the body is infested with parasitic worms. **helminthic** (-min´-) *a.* relating to intestinal worms. **helminthite** (-min´-) *n.* (*Geol.*) a sinuous mark on sandstone supposed to be a fossil worm-track. **helminthoid** (-min´-) *a.* **helminthology** (-thol´-) *n.* the study of intestinal worms. **helminthological** (-əloj´-) *a.* **helminthologist** (-thol´-) *n.* **helminthous** (-min´-) *a.* [Gr. *helmins -minthos*, worm]

helmless[1] HELM[1].

helmless[2] HELM[2].

helot (hel´ət) *n.* **1** (*also* **Helot**) a serf or bond slave in ancient Sparta. **2** a slave or serf. **helotism** *n.* the system of serfdom in Sparta or elsewhere. **helotry** *n.* **1** helots collectively; bond slaves or serfs. **2** slavery. [L *Hēlōtēs*, Gr. *Heilōtes*, pl. of *Hielōs*, prob. orig. an inhabitant of *Helos*, a Laconian town whose inhabitants were enslaved by the Spartans]

help (help) *v.t.* (*past* **helped, †holp** (holp), *p.p.* **helped, †holpen** (hol´pən)) **1** to provide with something needed or wanted to achieve an end; to assist, to aid. **2** to contribute to. **3** to improve (a situation etc.). **4** to supply succour or relief to in an emergency. **5** to remedy, to prevent. *~v.i.* **1** to lend aid or assistance. **2** to be of use. **3** to be an improvement. *~n.* **1** aid, assistance, the act of helping; the fact of being helped. **2** a person or thing that helps. **3 a** a person hired for a job, esp. a farm worker or domestic servant. **b** several employees collectively. **4** an escape, a remedy. **5** succour, relief. **6** a helping (of food etc.). **it cannot be helped 1** there is no remedy. **2** it cannot be prevented or avoided. **so help me (God)** a strong oath or asseveration. **to help along 1** to help (an infirm person etc.) to walk. **2** to advance (negotiations etc.). **to help down** to help (a person) in descending. **to help off 1** to help (a person) to remove or take off (a garment etc.). **2** to help (a person) to alight from (a step etc.). **to help on 1** to forward, to advance. **2** to help (a person) put on (a garment etc.). **to help oneself** to refrain from acting (*He tried not to laugh, but couldn't help himself*). **to help oneself to** to take for oneself without waiting for offer or permission. **to help out** to help to complete or to get out of a difficulty. **to help over** to enable to surmount. **to help to** to supply with, to furnish with. **to help up** to help (a person) in rising or getting up (a stair etc.). **helpdesk** *n.* an information point or telephone line offering technical support etc. within an organization. **helper** *n.* **helpful** *a.* **1** giving help, useful. **2** obliging. **helpfully** *adv.* **helpfulness** *n.* **helping** *a.* giving help or support. *~n.* a portion of food given at table. **helping hand** *n.* an act of assisting. **helpless** *a.* **1** lacking power to help oneself. **2** without help. **3** made powerless or weak. **helplessly** *adv.* **helplessness** *n.* **helpline** *n.* **1** a telephone line operated by a charity etc. for people in distress. **2** a telephone line operated by a commercial organization to provide assistance or information. **help screen** *n.* (*often. pl.*) instructions displayed on a visual display unit. [OE *helpan* (cp. Dut. *helpen*, Icel. *hjālpa*, G *helfen*)]

helpmate (help´māt) *n.* **1** a helper. **2** a partner or helpful companion, esp. a spouse. **helpmeet** (-mēt) *n.* a helpmate (formed by a misunderstanding of Gen. ii.18, 'help meet for him').

helter-skelter (heltəskel´tə) *adv.* in great hurry and confusion. *~a.* hurried and confused. *~n.* **1** hurry or confusion. **2** a funfair amusement consisting of a tower with a spiral slide. [imit.]

helve (helv) *n.* the handle of a weapon or tool. *~v.t.* to fit a helve to. [OE *hielfe* (cp. MDut. *helve*), cogn. with HALTER[1]]

Helvetian (helvē´shən) *a.* Swiss. *~n.* **1** a Swiss. **2** a member of the ancient Helveti, a Celtic tribe. **Helvetic** (-vet´-) *a.* Helvetian. *~n.* a Swiss Protestant, a Zwinglian. [L *Helvētia*, Switzerland]

hem[1] (hem) *n.* the edge or border of a garment or piece of cloth, esp. when doubled and sewn in to strengthen it. *~v.t.* (*pres.p.* **hemming**, *past, p.p.* **hemmed**) **1** to double over and sew in the border of. **2** to enclose or shut (in, about or round). **hemline** *n.* the hemmed bottom edge of a skirt or dress etc. **hemmer** *n.* **1** a person who or that which hems. **2** an attachment on a sewing machine for hemming. **hemstitch** *n.* an ornamental stitch made by drawing out parallel threads and fastening the cross threads. *~v.t.* to hem with this stitch. **hemstitcher** *n.* [OE *hemm*, *hem* (cp. G *hemmen*, to stop, to check)]

hem[2] (hem) *int.*, *n.* a voluntary short cough, uttered by way of warning, encouragement etc. *~v.i.* (*pres.p.* **hemming**, *past, p.p.* **hemmed**) **1** to utter this sound. **2** to hesitate in speech. **to hem and haw** to hum and haw. [imit.]

hema- HAEMA-.

hemal HAEMAL.

hematemesis HAEMATEMESIS.

hematic HAEMATIC.

hematin HAEMATIN.

hematite HAEMATITE.

hemato- HAEMATO-.

hematuria HAEMATURIA.

heme HAEM.

hemeralopia (hemərəlō´piə) *n.* a pathological condition in which the eyes see badly by daylight and better by night or artificial light. [from Gr. *hēmeralops* (*hēmera*, day, *alaos*, blind, *ōps*, eye)]

hemerocallis (hemərōkal´is) *n.* (*pl.* **hemerocallises**) the day lily. [from Gr. *hēmerokalles* (*hēmera*, day, *kallos*, beauty)]

hemi- (hem´i) *comb. form* **1** half, halved. **2** of or relating to one half. [Gr. *hēmi-*]

-hemia -AEMIA.

hemianopsia (hemiənop´siə), **hemianopia** (-ō´piə), **hemiopia** (hemiō´piə), **hemiopsia** (-op´siə) *n.* blindness over half the field of vision. **hemianoptic, hemiopic** (-op´-) *a.* [Gr. *an-*, privative, *opsis*, sight]

hemicellulose (hemisel´ūlōs) *n.* any of a group of polysaccharides occurring chiefly in the cell wall.

hemichordate (hemikaw´dāt) *n.* any small wormlike marine animal of the phylum Hemichordata, having numerous gill slits in the pharynx. *~a.* of or belonging to this phylum.

hemicycle (hem´isīkəl) *n.* **1** a semicircle. **2** a semicircular arena, room or division of a room. [F *hémicycle*, L *hēmicyclium*, Gr. *hemikuklion*]

hemidemisemiquaver (hem´idemisemikwāvə) *n.* a musical note equal in time to half a demisemiquaver.

hemihedral (hemihē´drəl) *a.* in crystallography, having only half the normal number of planes or facets. [Gr. *hedra*, seat, base]

hemiopia, hemiopsia HEMIANOPSIA.

hemiplegia (hemiplē´jə) *n.* paralysis of one side of the body. **hemiplegic** (-plej´-, -plē´-) *a.*, *n.* [Gr. *hēmiplēgia* (*plēgē*, stroke, from *plēssein*, to strike)]

hemipterous (hemip´tərəs) *a.* of or belonging to the order Hemiptera of insects with piercing or sucking mouthparts, and usu. having four wings, the upper pair partly horny and partly membranous, comprising bugs, lice etc. **hemipteral** *a.* **hemipteran** *n.*, *a.* **hemipteron**

(-ən) *n.* (*pl.* **hemiptera** (-rə)) a hemipterous insect. [HEMI-, Gr. *pteron*, wing]

hemisphere (hem´isfiə) *n.* **1** the half of a sphere or globe, divided by a plane passing through its centre. **2** half of the terrestrial or the celestial sphere. **3** a map or projection of either of these. **4** CEREBRAL HEMISPHERE (under CEREBRUM). **hemispheric** (-sfer´-), **hemispherical** *a.* **hemispheroid** (-sfiə´-) *n.* **hemispheroidal** (-roi´-) *a.* [F *hémisphère*, Gr. *hēmisphaira*]

hemistich (hem´istik) *n.* **1** half a verse, usu. as divided by the cæsura. **2** an imperfect verse. **hemistichal** *a.* [L *hēmistichium*, Gr. *hēmistichion* (*stichos*, a line)]

hemitrope (hem´itrōp) *a.* (of a crystal) looking as if one half were turned round upon the other. ~*n.* a crystal of this form. **hemitropic** (-trop´-) *a.* hemitrope. [F *hémitrope* (Gr. *-tropos*, turning, from *trepein*, to turn)]

hemlock (hem´lok) *n.* **1** any poisonous umbelliferous plant of the genus *Conium*, esp. *C. maculatum*, having finely divided leaves, spotted stems and small white flowers. **2** a poison derived from this. **3** HEMLOCK SPRUCE (under HEMLOCK). **hemlock spruce, hemlock fir** *n.* **1** any coniferous tree of the genus *Tsuga*, having short flat needles. **2** the wood of any of these trees. [OE *hymlic*, etym. uncertain]

hemmer HEM[1].

hemo- HAEMO-.

hemorrhage HAEMORRHAGE.

hemorrhoids HAEMORRHOIDS.

hemp (hemp) *n.* **1** an Asian herbaceous plant, *Cannabis sativa.* **2** the fibre of this, used for making ropes, coarse fabrics etc. **3** any of several narcotic drugs derived from the hemp plant, esp. cannabis or marijuana. **4** any of various other vegetable fibres used for cloth or cordage. **Indian hemp** INDIAN. **hemp agrimony** *n.* a composite plant, *Eupatorium cannabinum*, having small clusters of reddish flowers. **hempen** *a.* made of or resembling hemp. **hemp-nettle** *n.* a coarse plant of the labiate genus *Galeopsis.* [OE *henep* (cp. Dut. *hennep*, Icel. *hampr*, G *Hanf*, also Gr. *kannabis*)]

hen (hen) *n.* **1** the female of any bird, esp. the domestic fowl. **2** a female of certain other animals such as the lobster, crab or salmon. **3** (*Sc., dial.*) a term of address (often affectionate) to a woman. **hen and chickens** *n.* (*pl.* **hens and chickens**) (*sing. or pl. in constr.*) any of several plants, such as the houseleek or ground ivy, that produce many offshoots or runners. **henbane** *n.* **1** a poisonous plant, *Hyoscyamus niger*, having sticky hairy leaves and an unpleasant smell. **2** a narcotic drug obtained from this. **henbit** *n.* a dead nettle, *Lamium amplexicaule.* **hen-coop** *n.* a coop or cage for fowls. **hen harrier, †hen-driver** *n.* the common harrier, *Circus cyaneus.* **hen house** *n.* a small shed for fowls to roost in. **hennery** *n.* (*pl.* **henneries**) an enclosed place or run for fowls. **hen night** *n.* (*coll.*) a party for women only, esp. held for a woman shortly before she is married. **hen-party** *n.* (*sometimes derog., coll.*) a gathering for women only. **henpeck** *v.t.* (of a woman) to harass (a man, esp. her husband) by constant nagging. ~*n.* a woman who domineers over or nags at her husband or partner. **henpecked** *a.* **henpeckery** *n.* **hen-roost** *n.* a place for fowls to roost in. **hen-run** *n.* an enclosure for fowls, esp. one made of chicken wire. **hen-toed** *a.* having the toes turned in. [OE *henn*, from *hana*, cock (cp. Dut. *hen*, Icel. *haena*, G *Henne*), cogn. with L *canere*, to sing]

hence (hens) *adv.* **1** from this time. **2** in consequence of this, consequently, therefore. **3** †from here, from this place. ~†*int.* away! begone! **henceforth, henceforward, henceforwards** *adv.* from this time on. [ME *hennes, henne*, OE *heonan, heonane*, from *hi-*, root of HE, HIS etc.]

henchman (hench´mən) *n.* (*pl.* **henchmen**) **1** (*often. derog.*) a faithful follower or supporter. **2** †a squire, a page. **3** a political worker, esp. in the US. **4** (*Sc.*) the principal attendant of a Highland chief. [ME *henxtman, henxman* (OE *hengest*, horse, MAN)]

hendeca- (hen´dekə, hendek´ə) *comb. form* eleven. [Gr. *hendeka*, eleven]

hendecagon (hendek´əgon) *n.* a plane figure of 11 sides and angles. [Gr. *hendeka*, eleven, *gōnia*, angle]

hendecasyllable (hendekəsil´əbəl) *n.* a verse or line of 11 syllables. **hendecasyllabic** (-lab´-) *a.* containing 11 syllables. ~*n.* a hendecasyllabic verse. [L *hendecasyllabus*, Gr. *hendekasullabos* (*hendeka*, eleven)]

hendiadys (hendī´ədis) *n.* a rhetorical figure representing one idea by two words connected by a conjunction rather than with subordination, e.g. go and find rather than 'go to find'. [late L, from Gr. *hen dia duoin*, one by two]

henequen (hen´ikin), **heniquen** *n.* **1** an agave plant, *Agave fourcroydes*, from Mexico. **2** the sisal fibre obtained from this plant, used in making rope etc. [Sp. *jeniquén*, from N Am. Ind.]

henge (henj) *n.* a circle of stones or staves of prehistoric date. [back-formation from *Stonehenge*]

henna (hen´ə) *n.* **1** a tropical shrub, *Lawsonia inermis*, having white or red fragrant flowers. **2** a dye from this plant used for dyeing hair and, in the East, parts of the body. ~*v.t.* (*3rd pers. sing. pres.* **hennas,** *pres.p.* **hennaing,** *past, p.p.* **hennaed**) to dye with henna. [Arab. *hinnā*]

hennery HEN.

henotheism (hen´ōthēizm) *n.* worship of or ascription of supreme power to one out of several gods. **henotheist** (-thē´-) *n.* **henotheistic** (-is´-) *a.* [Gr. *heis henos*, one, THEISM]

henry (hen´ri) *n.* (*pl.* **henries, henrys**) a unit of inductance of a circuit in which a change of current of 1 ampere per second induces an emf of 1 volt. [J. *Henry*, 1797–1878, US physicist]

hep[1] (hep) *a.* (*comp.* **hepper,** *superl.* **heppest**) (*sl.*) HIP[4]. **hepcat** *n.* a stylish or fashionable person, esp. as regards jazz.

hep[2] HIP[2].

heparin (hep´ərin) *n.* a polysaccharide, containing sulphate groups, present in most body tissues; an anticoagulant used in the treatment of thrombosis. **heparinize, heparinise** *v.t.* **heparinoid** *a.* [from Gr. *hēpar*, the liver]

hepatic (hipat´ik) *a.* **1** of or relating to the liver. **2** resembling the liver in colour or form. **3** (*Bot.*) of or relating to the liverworts. ~*n.* a drug for use in treating diseases of the liver. **hepatica** (-kə) *n.* any plant of the genus *Hepatica*, the members of which have lobed leaves. [as HEPARIN]

hepatitis (hepətī´tis) *n.* inflammation or congestion of the liver. **hepatitis A** *n.* a form of viral hepatitis transmitted in contaminated food or drink. **hepatitis B** *n.* a form of viral hepatitis transmitted by infected blood transfusions or contaminated hypodermic needles.

Hepplewhite (hep´əlwīt) *a.* belonging to a school of light and graceful furniture design characterized by the use of curves esp. in shield-shaped chair-backs. [George *Hepplewhite*, 1727–86, English cabinetmaker]

hepta- (hep´tə) *comb. form* consisting of seven. [Gr. *hepta*, seven]

heptachord (hep´təkawd) *n.* (*Mus.*) **1** a series of seven notes. **2** the interval of a seventh. **3** an instrument with seven strings. [Gr. *heptachordos* (*chordē*, CHORD[1])]

heptad (hep´tad) *n.* **1** a sum or group of seven. **2** a week. **3** (*Chem.*) an atom with a valency of seven. [Gr. *heptas -tados*, as HEPTA-]

heptagon (hep´təgən) *n.* a plane figure having seven sides and seven angles. **heptagonal** (-tag´ənəl) *a.* [Gr. *gōnia*, angle]

heptahedron (heptəhē´drən) *n.* (*pl.* **heptahedra** (-drə), **heptahedrons**) a solid figure having seven sides. **heptahedral** *a.* [Gr. *hedra*, seat, base]

heptamerous (heptam´ərəs) *a.* having seven parts or members. [Gr. *meros*, part]

heptameter (heptam´itə) *n.* a line or verse of seven metrical feet.

heptane (hep´tān) *n.* (*Chem.*) a liquid hydrocarbon of the alkane series, obtained from petroleum.

heptarchy (hep´tahki) *n.* (*pl.* **heptarchies**) **1** government by seven rulers. **2** a government made up of seven rulers. **3** a country under seven rulers. **4** the seven kingdoms thought to have been established in Britain by the Angles and Saxons, i.e. Kent, Sussex, Wessex, Essex, Mercia, Northumbria and East Anglia, and to have flourished for various periods from the 7th to the 9th cents. **5** the period when this grouping existed. **heptarchal, heptarchic, heptarchical** *a.* [Gr. *-archia*, government, from *archein*, to rule]

heptastich (hep´təstik) *n.* a poem or stanza of seven lines. [Gr. *stichos*, a row]

Heptateuch (hep´tətūk) *n.* the first seven books of the Bible. [Gr. *heptateuchos* (HEPTA-, seven, *teukhos*, book)]

heptathlon (heptath´lon) *n.* an athletic contest in which competitors take part in seven events. **heptathlete** *n.*

heptavalent (heptəvā´lənt) *a.* (*Chem.*) having a valency of seven.

her (hœ) *pron.* **1** objective (accusative and dative) of SHE. **2** (*dial.*) HERSELF. *~a.* possessive of SHE. **her indoors** *n.* (*coll.*) one's wife. [OE *hire*, gen. and dat. of *hēo*, she]

Usage note Use of *her* in a subject, as in *Her and her brother were late*, is best avoided. See also notes under AS[1], BE, THAN.

her. *abbr.* **1** heraldic. **2** heraldry.

Heraclean (heraklē´ən), **Heracleian** *a.* of or relating to Heracles. **Heracleid** (her´əklīd, -klid) *n.* a descendant of Heracles (which members of the Dorian aristocracy claimed to be). **Heracleidan** (heraklī´dən) *a.* [L *Hēraclēus*, Gr. *Hērakleios*, from *Hēraklēs*]

herald (her´əld) *n.* **1** a messenger. **2** a harbinger, a precursor. **3** (*Hist.*) (in ancient times) a person who made public proclamations and arranged ceremonies. **4** (*Hist.*) a person who had charge of the etiquette of chivalry and whose duties included blazoning the arms of the nobility etc.; an official at a tournament. **5** a member of the College of Arms. *~v.t.* **1** to announce publicly. **2** to introduce, to usher in. **herald moth** *n.* a noctuid moth, *Scoliopteryx libatrix*, which appears in the autumn and is supposed to be a forerunner of winter. **heraldry** (-ri) *n.* **1** the art and study of armorial bearings etc. **2** pomp, ceremony etc. **3** armorial bearings, emblazonment. **4** (*Hist.*) the office or functions of a herald. **heraldic** (-ral´-) *a.* of or relating to heraldry or heralds. **heraldically** *adv.* **heraldist** *n.* a student of heraldry. **Heralds' College** *n.* COLLEGE OF ARMS (under COLLEGE). [OF *heralt*, *heraut*, prob. from Gmc.]

herb (hœb) *n.* **1** a plant producing shoots of only annual duration. **2** herbage, grass and other green food for cattle. **3** a plant having medicinal, culinary or aromatic properties. **herbaceous** (-bā´shəs) *a.* **1** of or relating to herbs. **2** that is a herb. **3** (of petals etc.) green and leaflike. **herbaceous border** *n.* a flower border with mainly perennial plants. **herbaceous perennial** *n.* a plant producing shoots of only annual duration but whose roots survive. **herbage** (-ij) *n.* **1** herbs collectively. **2** grass, pasture. **3** (*Law*) the right of pasture on another's land. **herbal** *a.* of or relating to herbs in medicine, cooking or perfumery. *~n.* a book containing the names of plants, with a description of their properties, medicinal and other virtues etc. **herbalist** *n.* **1** a person skilled in the knowledge of herbs and their qualities. **2** a dealer in medicinal herbs. **3** a collector of plants. **4** an early botanist. **herbarium** (-beə´riəm) *n.* (*pl.* **herbaria** (-riə), **herbariums**) **1** a systematic collection of dried plants. **2** a case, room or building for these. **herb beer** *n.* a soft drink made from herbs. **herb bennet** *n.* a common yellow-flowered plant, *Geum urbanum*. **herb Christopher** *n.* (*pl.* **herbs Christopher**) a baneberry, *Actaea spicata*, with white flowers. **herb Gerard** *n.* (*pl.* **herbs Gerard**) ground elder. **herbicide** (-sīd) *n.* a chemical that destroys vegetation, used to control weeds. **herbicidal** (-sī´-) *a.* **herbiferous** (-bif´ərəs) *a.* producing vegetation. **herblike** *a.* **herbous** *a.* HERBY (under HERB). **herb Paris** *n.* (*pl.* **herbs Paris**) a herb, *Paris quadrifolia*, growing in woods, with four leaves in the form of a cross and a terminal green flower. **herb Robert** *n.* (*pl.* **herbs Robert**) a cranesbill, *Geranium robertianum*. **herb tea** *n.* a drink made by infusing herbs. **herb tobacco** *n.* a mixture of herbs prepared for smoking. **herby** *a.* (*comp.* **herbier**, *superl.* **herbiest**) **1** of the nature of or like herbs. **2** abounding in herbs. [ME and OF *erbe*, L *herba*, grass]

herbivore (hœ´bivaw) *n.* an animal, esp. a mammal, that feeds on grass or plants. **herbivorous** (-biv´-) *a.* [L *herbivorus*, herb-eating]

Hercules (hœ´kūlēz) *n.* a man of enormous strength. **Herculean** (-lē´ən) *a.* **1** exceedingly great, difficult or dangerous (as the labours of Hercules). **2** exceedingly strong or powerful. **3** of or relating to Hercules. **Hercules beetle** *n.* a Brazilian arboreal beetle, *Dynastes hercules*, 5–6 in. (12–15 cm) long, with hornlike projections on the head and thorax. **Hercules' club** *n.* **1** any of various N American prickly shrubs or trees. **2** a big cudgel. [L, from Gr. *Hēraklēs*, a hero celebrated for his prodigious bodily strength, which enabled him to perform twelve labours of superhuman magnitude]

Hercynian (hœsin´iən) *a.* **1** denoting a period of mountain building in Europe in the late Palaeozoic age. **2** denoting an extensive forest in Germany, the remains of which still exist in Swabia, the Harz Mountains etc. [L *Hercynia* (*silva*), Gr. *Herkunios* (*drumos*)]

herd (hœd) *n.* **1** a number of beasts or cattle feeding, kept or driven together. **2** a crowd of people, a rabble. **3** (*usu. in comb.*) a keeper of a herd (*cowherd*; *goatherd*). *~v.i.* **1** to go in herds or companies. **2** to associate. **3** to act as a herd or shepherd. *~v.t.* **1** to tend or watch (cattle etc.). **2** to form or bring into a herd. **3** to drive in a herd. **the herd** (*derog.*) the masses. **to ride herd on** (*N Am.*) to guard, to watch over. **herd book** *n.* a book containing the pedigrees of high-bred cattle or pigs. **herd instinct** *n.* the impulse that urges people and animals to associate and act together and do what others do. **herdsman, †herdman** *n.* (*pl.* **herdsmen, †herdmen**) a person who tends domestic animals, esp. cattle. [OE *heord* (cp. Icel. *hjörd*, G *Herde*)]

herdic (hœ´dik) *n.* a small horse-drawn carriage, with a low-hung body, back entrance and side seats. [Peter *Herdic* of Pennsylvania, 1824–88, the inventor]

Herdwick (hœd´wik) *n.* a hardy breed of sheep orig. raised in the mountainous parts of Cumbria. [from obs. *herdwick*, pasture ground]

here (hiə) *adv.* **1** in or at this place or position. **2** to this place or position, hither, in this direction. **3** in the present life or state. **4** at this point. **5** on this occasion. *~n.* this place, point or time. **here and now** right now, the present. **here and there 1** in this place and that. **2** hither and thither. **here goes!** said by a speaker who is about to do something. **here's how!** I drink to your good health. **here's to** let us drink a toast to. **here we are** said on arrival after a journey. **here we go again!** said when the same unpleasant, predictable etc. thing seems to be about to happen again. **here you are** said on giving something to somebody by hand. **neither here nor there** unimportant, irrelevant. **hereabouts,**

hereabout *adv.* somewhere about or near this place. **hereafter** *adv.* **1** for the future. **2** in a future state. *~n.* **1** a future state. **2** the future life. †**hereat** *adv.* at this, as a result of this. **hereby** *adv.* by this means, by virtue of this. **herein** *adv.* (*formal*) in this document etc. **hereinafter** *adv.* (*formal*) **1** from this point or time onwards. **2** later or below in this document etc. **hereinbefore** *adv.* (*formal*) earlier or above in this document etc. **hereof** *adv.* (*formal*) of this; concerning this. **hereto** *adv.* (*formal*) **1** (attached) to this. **2** up to this place, point or time. **3** †hitherto. **heretofore** *adv.* (*formal*) **1** below in this (document etc.). **2** before this time. **hereunder** *adv.* (*formal*) below in this document etc. **hereunto** *adv.* (*formal*) **1** up to this. **2** †thereto. **hereupon** *adv.* upon this, after this, at this, in consequence of this. **herewith** *adv.* with this (esp. of an enclosure in a letter etc.). [OE *hēr* (Dut. and G *hier*, Icel. *hēr*)]

hereditable (hired´itəbəl) *a.* that may be inherited. **hereditability** (-bil´-) *n.* **hereditably** *adv.* [F *héréditable*, from L *hērēditāre*, from *hērēs hērēdis*, an HEIR]

hereditament (herədit´əmənt) *n.* (*Law*) **1** any property that may be inherited. **2** inheritance. [med. L *hērēditāmentum*, as HEREDITABLE]

hereditary (hired´itəri) *a.* **1** descending or passing by inheritance. **2** transmitted by descent from generation to generation. **3** holding or deriving by inheritance. **4** of or relating to inheritance. **hereditarily** *adv.* **hereditariness** *n.* [L *hērēditārius*, as HEREDITY]

heredity (hired´iti) *n.* **1** the tendency to transmit individual characteristics to one's offspring. **2** genetically transmitted characteristics. **3** genetic constitution. [F *hérédité*, L *hērēditātem* nom. *-tas*, from *hērēs hērēdis*, HEIR]

Hereford (her´ifəd) *n.* a breed of red and white beef cattle. [a city and county in England]

heresiarch (hirē´ziahk) *n.* **1** a leader of a sect of heretics. **2** a prominent or leading heretic. [as HERESY]

heresiographer (herəsiog´rəfə) *n.* a writer on heresies. **heresiography** *n.*

heresiology (herəsiol´əji) *n.* (*pl.* **heresiologies**) **1** the study of the history of heresy. **2** a treatise on this. **heresiologist** (-ol´-) *n.*

heresy (her´əsi) *n.* (*pl.* **heresies**) **1** departure from what is held to be true doctrine, esp. when such opinions lead to division in the Christian Church. **2** opinion that is contrary to what is normally accepted. **3** an instance of heresy; an unacceptable doctrine or opinion. [OF *heresie*, L *haeresis*, Gr. *hairesis*, from *haireisthai*, to choose]

heretic (her´ətik) *n.* a person who holds unorthodox opinions, esp. in religious matters. **heretical** (-ret´-) *a.* **heretically** *adv.* [F *hérétique*, L *haereticus*, Gr. *hairetikos*, as HERESY]

heriot (her´iət) *n.* (*Hist.*) a tribute, such as a live animal, paid to a lord on the decease of a tenant. **heriotable** *a.* subject to heriot. [corr. of OE *heregeatwe*, military apparel (*here*, army, *geatwe*, equipment)]

heritable (her´itəbəl) *a.* **1** capable of being inherited. **2** (*Law*) passing by inheritance, esp. of lands and appurtenances as distinct from movable property. **3** capable of inheriting. **heritability** (-bil´-) *n.* **heritably** *adv.* by inheritance. [F *héritable*, from *hériter*, L *hērēditāre*, see HEREDITABLE]

heritage (her´itij) *n.* **1** land or other property that passes by descent or course of law to an heir. **2** a share, portion, lot. **3** anything passed from one generation to another. **4** (*Bible*) the people of God, the Israelites, the Church. **5** (*Sc. Law*) heritable estate, realty. **heritage centre** *n.* a local museum focusing on the cultural heritage of a specific area. **heritor** *n.* **1** a person who inherits. **2** (*Sc. Law*) a landholder in a parish. **heritress** (-tris) *n.* an heiress. [OF, as HERITABLE]

herl HARL[1].

herm (hœm), **herma** (-mə) *n.* (*pl.* **herms, hermae** (hœ´mē), **hermai** (hœ´mī)) in ancient Greece, a statue of a head, usu. of Hermes, placed on a square pillar and set as a boundary etc. [L *Herma*, from Gr. *Hermēs*]

hermaphrodite (hœmaf´rədīt) *n.* **1** a human being or an animal abnormally combining in itself both male and female reproductive organs. **2** an animal in which the organs of both sexes are normally combined in the same individual. **3** a plant having the stamens and pistils in the same flower. **4** a person or thing in which opposite qualities are embodied. *~a.* having the characteristics of a hermaphrodite. **hermaphrodite brig** *n.* a sailing vessel square-rigged on the foremast and schooner-rigged on the mainmast. **hermaphroditic** (-dit´-), **hermaphroditical** *a.* **hermaphroditism** (-dit-) *n.* [L *hermaphrodītus*, Gr. *-ditos* (*Hermēs, Aphroditē*), son of Hermes and Aphrodite, who grew together with the nymph Salmacis]

hermeneutic (hœmənū´tik), **hermeneutical** *a.* interpreting, explaining, explanatory. **hermeneutically** *adv.* **hermeneutics** *n.* **1** the art or science of interpretation, esp. of Scripture. **2** discussion of the purpose of life (in existentialist thought). **hermeneutist** *n.* [Gr. *hermēneutikos*, from *hermēneutēs*, *hermēneus*, interpreter]

hermetic (hœmet´ik), **hermetical** (-ikəl) *a.* **1** having an airtight closure. **2** protected from outside forces. **3** of or belonging to alchemy. **4** esoteric, abstruse. **hermetically** *adv.* **hermetics** *n.* alchemy, chemistry. **hermetic seal** *n.* an airtight seal. [low L *hermēticus*, from *Hermes Trismegistus*]

hermit (hœ´mit) *n.* **1** an early Christian recluse. **2** any person living in solitary contemplation. **3** †a beadsman. **hermitage** (-ij) *n.* **1** the cell or habitation of a hermit. **2** a monastery. **hermit crab, hermit lobster** *n.* a crab of the family Paguridae (so called because they live in abandoned mollusc shells). †**hermitess** *n.* a female hermit. **hermitic** (-mit´-), **hermitical** *a.* **hermit thrush** *n.* a migratory N American thrush *Catharus guttatus*. [F *hermite*, L *her-*, *erēmīta*, Gr. *erēmitēs*, from *erēmos*, deserted]

hernia (hœ´niə) *n.* (*pl.* **hernias, herniae** (-niē)) the protrusion of any organ, or part of an organ, from its natural place; a rupture. **hernial, herniary, herniated** *a.* [L]

hero (hiə´rō) *n.* (*pl.* **heroes**) **1** a person of extraordinary valour, fortitude or enterprise. **2** the principal male character in a novel, play, poem etc. **3** in Greek mythology, a man of superhuman powers, often deified or regarded as a demigod after death. **heroi-comic** (hirōikom´-), **heroi-comical** *a.* **1** combining the heroic and the comic. **2** mock-heroic, burlesque. **heroify** (hirō´-) *v.t.* (*3rd pers. sing. pres.* **heroifies,** *pres.p.* **heroifying,** *past, p.p.* **heroified**) to make into a hero. **heroine** (her´ōin) *n.* **1** a heroic woman. **2** the principal female character in a novel, play, poem etc. **3** in Greek mythology, a demigoddess. **heroism** (her´-) *n.* **1** the quality, character or conduct of a hero. **2** extreme bravery. **heroize** (her´-), **heroise** *v.t.* to regard or treat as a hero, to make heroic. *~v.i.* to show oneself off as a hero. **hero's welcome** *n.* a rapturous welcome, as given to a successful warrior. **hero-worship** *n.* **1** the deification of a hero. **2** excessive devotion shown to a person who is regarded as a hero. *~v.t.* (*pres.p.* **hero-worshipping,** (*N Am.*) **hero-worshiping,** *past, p.p.* **hero-worshipped,** (*N Am.*) **hero-worshiped**) to worship as a hero. **hero-worshipper** *n.* [MF *heroē* (F *héros*), L *hērōem* nom. *hērōs*, Gr. *hērōs*]

heroic (hirō´ik) *a.* **1** of, relating to or becoming a hero. **2** having the qualities or attributes of a hero. **3** producing heroes. **4** relating to or describing the deeds of heroes. **5** bold, vigorous, attempting extreme deeds or methods. **6** (of art) large in scale or subject. **7** (of language) high-flown or bombastic. **heroic age** *n.* the age in which heroes or demigods were supposed to have lived, esp. the age of Greece closing with the deeds celebrated in the *Iliad* and *Odyssey*. **heroical** *a.* **heroically** *adv.* **heroic couplet** *n.* a rhyming couplet in iambic pentameters. **heroics** *n.pl.* **1** heroic verses. **2** high-flown or bombastic language or sentiments. **3** heroic behaviour. **heroic size** *n.* a sculpture size between life-size and colossal. **heroic verse** *n.* the metre of heroic or epic poetry, in English, German and Italian poetry, the iambic pentameter, in French, the alexandrine, and in Latin and Greek the hexameter. [L *hērōicus*, Gr. *hērōikos*]

heroi-comic, heroi-comical HERO.

heroin (her´ōin) *n.* a derivative of morphine, used in medicine and by drug addicts. [prob. as HEROIC, from its effect on the user's personality]

heroine HERO.

heron (her´ən), †**hern** (hœn) *n.* a long-legged, long-necked wading bird of the family Ardeidae, esp. *Ardea cinerea*, the common European heron. **heronry** *n.* (*pl.* **heronries**) a place where herons breed. [OF *hairon*, through pop. L or It. from OHG *hegir* (cp. Icel. *hegri*, also OE *higora*, a magpie)]

herpes (hœ´pēz) *n.* a viral infection producing vesicles grouped on an inflamed skin surface such as the lip. **herpes simplex** (sim´pleks) *n.* infection with a herpes virus producing cold sores, genital inflammation or conjunctivitis. **herpes virus** *n.* any one of a family of viruses that cause herpes or other diseases. **herpes zoster** (zos´tə) *n.* SHINGLES. **herpetic** (-pet´-) *a.*, *n.* (a person) affected by a herpes virus. [L, from Gr. *herpēs -ētos*, from *herpein*, to creep]

herpetology (hœpitol´əji) *n.* the study of reptiles and amphibians. **herpetoid** (hœ´-) *a.* having the shape of a snake. **herpetologic** (-loj´-), **herpetological** *a.* **herpetologist** *n.* [Gr., from *herpeton*, a reptile, from *herpein*, to creep]

herptile (hœp´tīl) *n.* a reptile or amphibian. ~*a.* of or relating to both reptiles and amphibians. [as HERPETOLOGY, REPTILE]

Herr (heə) *n.* (*pl.* **Herren** (her´ən)) **1** the German title corresponding to the English Mr. **2** a German man. [G]

Herrenvolk (her´ənfolk) *n.* **1** the supposed Aryan race as conceived by Nazi ideology as a master race. **2** a group regarding itself as naturally superior. [G]

herring (her´ing) *n.* a soft-finned marine fish, *Clupea harengus*, of the N Atlantic, moving in large shoals and spawning near the coast. **herringbone** *n.* **1** a pattern used in textiles etc. resembling the spine and bones of a herring. **2** a kind of masonry in which the stones etc. are set obliquely in alternate rows. **3** in skiing, a method of ascending a slope by walking with the skis pointing outwards and with the weight of the body on the inside edges. ~*v.t.* **1** to sew or stitch with herringbone stitch. **2** to give a herringbone pattern to. ~*v.i.* in skiing, to ascend a slope by the herringbone method. **herringbone stitch** *n.* a kind of cross stitch used in mending sails and for ornamental purposes. **herring gull** *n.* a large seagull, *Larus argentatus*, which feeds on herrings. [OE *hæring* (cp. Dut. *haring*, G *Häring*), etym. uncertain]

Herrnhuter (heən´hootə) *n.* a Moravian, a member of the sect calling themselves the United Brethren. [*Herrnhut*, Saxony, their first settlement]

hers (hœz) *pron.* something which belongs to or is associated with her. **of hers** belonging or relating to her. [HER]

herself (həself´) *pron.* **1** SHE or HER (objective), used to give emphasis (usu. in apposition). **2** the reflexive form of HER. **3** her normal or usual self. **by herself** alone, unaided. **to be herself** to act in her normal manner. [OE *hire self*]

herstory (hœ´stawri) *n.* in feminist jargon, history emphasizing the role of women or told from a woman's point of view. [HISTORY with HER for HIS]

Herts. (hahts) *abbr.* Hertfordshire.

hertz (hœts) *n.* (*pl.* **hertz**) a standard unit of frequency equal to one cycle per second. [Heinrich *Hertz*, 1857–94, German physicist]

Hertzian (hœt´siən) *a.* of or relating to Hertz or the phenomena of electromagnetic vibrations discovered by him. **Hertzian wave** *n.* an electromagnetic wave suitable for radio broadcasting. [from HERTZ]

he's (hēz) *contr.* **1** he is. **2** he has.

Heshvan (hesh´vahn), **Hesvan** (hes´-) *n.* the second month of the Jewish civil year and the eighth month of the Jewish ecclesiastical year. [Heb.]

hesitate (hez´itāt) *v.i.* **1** to stop or pause in action. **2** to be doubtful or undecided. **3** to be reluctant (to). **4** to stammer. **hesitant** *a.* hesitating, dubious, vacillating, undecided. **hesitance, hesitancy** *n.* **hesitantly** *adv.* **hesitatingly** *adv.* **hesitation** (-ā´shən) *n.* **hesitative** *a.* **hesitator** *n.* [L *haesitātus*, p.p. of *haesitāre*, freq. of *haerēre*, to stick, cling]

Hesperian, Hesperides etc. HESPERUS.

hesperidium (hespərid´iəm) *n.* (*pl.* **hesperidia** (-iə)) a citrus fruit, e.g. the orange, with a tough rind and a pulp divided into sections. [Gr. *Hesperides*; see HESPERUS]

Hesperus (hes´pərəs), **Hesper** (hes´pə) *n.* the evening star, Venus. **Hesperian** (-piə´ri-) *a.* **1** (*poet.*) situated at or in the west, western. **2** of or relating to the Hesperides. ~*n.* an inhabitant of a western country. **Hesperides** (hesper´idēz) *n.pl.* in Greek mythology, the daughters of Hesperus, possessors of the garden of golden fruit watched over by a dragon at the western extremity of the earth. [L *Hesperius*, Gr. *Hesperios*, evening, the evening star, from *hesperis*, western]

Hessian (hes´iən) *n.* **1** a native or inhabitant of Hesse. **2** (**hessian**) a coarse cloth made of hemp and jute. **3** (*N Am.*) a mercenary politician, a hireling. ~*a.* **1** of or belonging to Hesse. **2** (**hessian**) made of hessian. **Hessian boot** *n.* a high boot with tassels, fashionable early in the 19th cent. **Hessian fly** *n.* (*pl.* **Hessian flies**) a small fly or midge, *Mayetiola destructor*, the larva of which attacks wheat in the US (believed to have been introduced to America by Hessian soldiers). [*Hesse* in Germany, -IAN]

hessonite (hes´ənīt) *n.* CINNAMON STONE (under CINNAMON). [Gr. *hēssōn*, inferior, less]

†**hest** (hest) *n.* a command, an injunction, a behest. [OE *hǣs*, from *hātan*, see HIGHT]

Hesvan HESHVAN.

hetaera (hitiə´rə), **hetaira** (-ī´rə) *n.* (*pl.* **hetaeras, hetaerae** (-rē), **hetairas, hetairai** (-rī)) one of a class of highly educated courtesans in ancient Greece. **hetaerism** *n.* **1** recognized concubinage. **2** communal marriage or sharing of women in a tribe. **hetaerist** *n.* **hetaeristic** (-is´-) *a.* **hetaerocracy** (-ok´rəsi) *n.* [Gr. *hetaira*, fem. of *hetairos*, companion]

hetero (het´ərō) *n.* (*pl.* **heteros**) (*coll.*) a heterosexual person.

hetero- (het´ərō) *comb. form* **1** different, dissimilar. **2** irregular, abnormal. [Gr. *heteros*, other]

heteroblastic (hetərōblas´tik) *a.* (*Biol.*) derived from unlike cells, as distinct from *homoblastic*. **heteroblasty** (het´-) *n.* [Gr. *blastos*, germ]

heterocercal (hetərōsœ´kəl) *a.* (of fishes) having the upper lobe of the tail longer than the lower. [Gr. *kerkos*, tail]

heterochromatic (hetərōkrōmat´ik), **heterochromous** (-krō´məs) *a.* of different colours. [Gr. *chrōma*, colour]

heteroclite (het´ərəklīt) *a.* **1** deviating from the ordinary rules or forms. **2** anomalous, irregular. ~*n.* **1** a word that deviates from the ordinary forms of inflection. **2** a person or thing deviating from the ordinary. **heteroclitic** (-klit´-) *a.* [Gr. *klinein*, to bend, inflect]

heterocyclic (hetərōsī´klik) *a.* (of an organic chemical compound) having a ring structure of atoms of different kinds in the molecules.

heterodactyl (hetərōdak´til) *a.* (of some birds) having the first and second toes directed backwards and the other two forwards. **heterodactylous** *a.*

heterodont (het´ərədont) *a.* having teeth of different forms. ~*n.* a heterodont animal.

heterodox (het´ərədoks) *a.* contrary to received or established doctrines, principles or standards; heretical, not orthodox. **heterodoxy** *n.* [Gr. *heterodoxos* (from *dokein*, to think)]

heterodyne (het´ərədīn) *a.* of or relating to a beat frequency caused in a radio receiver by the interplay of two alternating currents of similar frequencies. ~*v.i.* to produce a lower frequency in this way. [Gr. *dynamis*, power]

heteroecious (hetərē´shəs) *a.* (of parasitic fungi) developing at different times on different hosts. **heteroecism** (-sizm) *n.* [Gr. *oikia*, dwelling]

heterogamous (hetərog´əməs) *a.* **1** having flowers or florets sexually different, as in certain Compositae, where the disc florets are male and the ray florets neuter or female. **2** characterized by alternation of generations. **3** characterized by reproduction by fusion of gametes differing in size and form. **heterogamy** *n.* [Gr. *gamos*, marriage]

heterogeneous (hetərəjē´niəs), †**heterogenous** (-oj´i-) *a.* **1** diverse in character or structure. **2** varied in content. **3** (*Math.*) of different kinds, dimensions or degree. **heterogeneity** (-nē´-) *n.* **heterogeneously** *adv.* **heterogeneousness** *n.* [Gr. *genos*, kind]

heterogenesis (hetərəjen´əsis) *n.* **1** the production of offspring differing in kind from the parent. **2** spontaneous generation from inorganic matter. **3** alternation of generations. **heterogenetic** (-jinet´-) *a.*

†**heterogenous** HETEROGENEOUS.

heterogonous (hetərog´ənəs) *a.* (of certain flowers) having stamens and styles or pistils on different plants of the species differing in length so as to promote cross-fertilization. **heterogony** *n.* **1** the condition of being heterogonous. **2** alternation of generations, esp. sexual and hermaphroditic. [Gr. *gonos*, offspring]

heterograft (het´ərəgrahft) *n.* a tissue graft obtained from a member of one species for a member of another.

heterography (hetərog´rəfi) *n.* the employment of the same letters to represent different sounds, as *g* in *go* and *gin*.

heterologous (hetərol´əgəs) *a.* **1** (*Med.*) differing in structure from normal tissue. **2** not homologous. **heterology** (-ji) *n.*

heteromerous (hetərom´ərəs) *a.* differing in number, form or character of parts; not isomerous. [Gr. *meros*, part]

heteromorphic (hetərōmaw´fik), **heteromorphous** (-fəs) *a.* **1** differing from the normal form. **2** having dissimilar forms. **3** (of insects) having different forms at different stages of development. **heteromorphism, heteromorphy** *n.* the quality of being heteromorphic; existence in different forms. [Gr. *morphē*, form]

heteronomous (hetəron´əməs) *a.* **1** subject to the law or rule of another, not autonomous. **2** (*Biol.*) having different laws of growth, diverging from the type. **heteronomy** *n.* [Gr. *nomos*, law]

heteronym (het´ərənim) *n.* a word spelt the same way as another but differing in sound and meaning, as *gill* (gil), a breathing-organ, and *gill* (jil), a measure. **heteronymous** (-on´-) *a.* **heteronymy** (-on´-) *n.* [Gr. *heterōnumos* (*onoma*, name)]

Heteroousian (hetərōoo´siən, -ow´-) *a.* **1** of or relating to the Heteroousians. **2** (**heteroousian**) having a different nature or essence. ~*n.* a member of a Christian sect believing the Father and Son to be of a different essence. [Gr. *heteroousios* (*ousia*, essence)]

heteropathic (hetərōpath´ik) *a.* **1** allopathic. **2** having different effects. **heteropathy** (-rop´-) *n.*

heterophyllous (hetərəfil´əs) *a.* having leaves of different form on the same plant. **heterophylly** (-of´-) *n.* [Gr. *phullon*, leaf]

heteropolar (hetərōpō´lə) *a.* having dissimilar (magnetic) poles.

heteropteran (hetərop´tərən) *n.* an insect of the suborder Heteroptera, including bugs in which the wings are of dissimilar parts. ~*a.* belonging to the Heteroptera. **heteropterous** *a.* [Gr. *pteron*, wing]

heterosexual (hetərəsek´shuəl) *a.* **1** feeling sexual attraction to the opposite sex. **2** of or relating to heterosexuals or heterosexuality. ~*n.* a heterosexual person. **heterosexism** *n.* discrimination by heterosexuals against homosexuals. **heterosexist** *a., n.* **heterosexuality** (-al´-) *n.*

heterosis (hetərō´sis) *n.* abnormal vigour or strength typical of a hybrid plant or animal.

heterosporous (hetəros´pərəs, -ōspaw´-) *a.* having two kinds of spores. [Gr. *sporos*, seed]

heterostyled (het´ərəstīld) *a.* heterogonous. **heterostylism** (-stī´-), **heterostyly** *n.*

heterotaxy (het´ərətaksi) *n.* deviation of organs or parts from ordinary arrangement. **heterotaxic** (-tak´-) *a.* [Gr. *taxis*, arrangement]

heterotopy (hetərot´əpi), **heterotopism** *n.* displacement of a bodily organ etc. **heterotopic** (-top´-), **heterotopous** (-ot´-) *a.* [Gr. *-topia*, from *topos*, place]

heterotrophic (hetərōtrō´fik) *a.* obtaining nourishment from organic compounds. **heterotrophy** (-rot´-) *n.*

hetman (het´mən) *n.* (*pl.* **hetmans, hetmen**) a commander or leader of Cossacks or Poles. [Pol.]

het up (het) *a.* (*coll.*) excited, agitated, annoyed. [dial. p.p. of HEAT]

heuchera (hū´kərə) *n.* a herbaceous plant of the genus *Heuchera* of the saxifrage family, with roundish leaves and stalks of red, white or green flowers rising directly from the rootstock. [J. *Heucher*, 1677–1747, German botanist]

heulandite (hū´ləndīt) *n.* a monoclinic, transparent brittle mineral, consisting chiefly of silica, alumina and lime, occurring chiefly in amygdaloid rock. [H. *Heuland*, 1777–1856, English mineralogist]

heuristic (hūris´tik) *a.* **1** serving or tending to find out; not correct or provable, but aiding the discovery of truth. **2** (*Comput.*) proceeding by trial and error. ~*n.* **1** the science of heuristic procedure. **2** a heuristic procedure or method. **heuristically** *adv.* **heuristic method** *n.* in education, a system where pupils are trained to find out things for themselves. **heuristics** *n.* (*Comput.*) the study and use of heuristic techniques. [Gr. *heuriskein*, to find]

hevea (hē´viə) *n.* any tree of the South American genus *Hevea*, having a milky sap which provides rubber. [Quechua *hevé*]

HEW *abbr.* (*US*) Department of Health, Education and Welfare.

hew (hū) *v.t.* (*p.p.* **hewed, hewn** (hūn)) **1** to cut (down, away, off etc.) with an axe etc. **2** to hack, to chop. **3** to make or fashion with toil and exertion. ~*v.i.* **1** to strike cutting blows (at etc.). **2** (*N Am.*) to conform (to a code etc.). **to hew one's way** to make a passage etc. for oneself by hewing. **hewer** *n.* **1** a person who hews. **2** a person who cuts coal from a seam. **hewers of wood and drawers of water** labourers and other such menials. [OE *hēawan* (cp. Dut. *houwen*, Icel. *hōggva*, G *hauen*)]

hex[1] (heks) *v.i.* to practise witchcraft. ~*v.t.* **1** to cast a spell on. **2** to jinx. ~*n.* **1** a magic spell; a curse. **2** a person who practises witchcraft. [Pennsylvania Dutch, orig. from G *Hexe*, witch]

hex[2] (heks) *n.* the hexadecimal number system; hexadecimal notation.

hex. *abbr.* **1** hexachord. **2** hexagon. **3** hexagonal.

hexa- (hek´sə), **hex-** *comb. form* six. [Gr. *hex*, six]

hexachord (hek´səkawd) *n.* (*Mus.*) **1** a scale or diatonic series of six notes with a semitone between the third and the fourth. **2** an interval of four tones and a semitone.

hexad (hek´sad) *n.* a group of six. **hexadic** (-sad´-) *a.* [Gr. *hexas -ados*, from *hex*, six]

hexadecimal (heksədes´iməl) *a.* (of a number system) having 16 as its base. ~*n.* the hexadecimal number system; hexadecimal notation. **hexadecimally** *adv.*

hexaemeron (heksəē´məron) *n.* **1** a period of six days, esp. the six days of the Creation in the biblical account. **2** a history of this period. **hexaemeric** *a.* [late L, from Gr. (*hēmera*, day)]

hexagon (hek´səgən) *n.* a plane figure having six sides. **hexagonal** (-sag´-) *a.* [Gr. *gōnia*, angle]

hexagram (hek´səgram) *n.* **1** a figure formed by two equilateral triangles whose points coincide with those of a regular hexagon. **2** a six-sided figure. **3** any one of 64 figures each formed by six parallel lines on which the Chinese *I Ching* or *Book of Changes* is based.

hexahedron (heksəhē´drən) *n.* (*pl.* **hexahedrons, hexahedra** (-drə)) a solid body of six sides, esp. a regular cube. **hexahedral** *a.* [Gr. *hedra*, seat, base]

hexameter (heksam´itə) *n.* a line or verse consisting of six metrical feet. **hexametric** (-met´-), **hexametrical** *a.* **hexametrist** *n.* [L, from Gr. *hexametros* (*metron*, see METRE[2])]

hexane (hek´sān) *n.* a liquid hydrocarbon of the alkane series.

hexangular (heksang´gūlə) *a.* having six angles.

hexapla (hek´səplə) *n.* an edition of a book, esp. of the Bible, having six versions in parallel columns (orig. the title of Origen's text of the Old Testament). **hexaplar, hexaplarian** (-pleə´ri-), **hexaplaric** (-plar´ik) *a.* [Gr. neut. pl. of *hexaplous*, sixfold (*hex*, six, *-ploos*, fold)]

hexapod (hek´səpod) *n.* an animal having six legs; a member of the order Hexapoda or Insecta, an insect. ~*a.* **1** having six legs. **2** belonging to the Hexapoda or Insecta. **hexapodal** (-sap´-), **hexapodous** *a.* **hexapody** *n.* (*pl.* **hexapodies**) a verse or line of six metrical feet. [Gr. *pous podos*, foot]

hexastich (hek´səstik) *n.* a poem or poetical passage of six lines or verses. **hexastichic** (-stik´-) *a.* [Gr. *-stichos* (*stichos*, a row)]

hexastyle (hek´səstīl) *n., a.* (a portico or temple) having six columns. [Gr. *stūlos* pillar]

Hexateuch (hek´sətūk) *n.* the first six books of the Old Testament. [Gr. *teuchos*, book]

hexavalent (heksəvā´lənt) *a.* having a valency of six.

hexose (hek´sōz) *n.* a monosaccharide, such as glucose, that contains six carbon atoms per molecule.

hey[1] (hā) *int.* **1** used to express joy, surprise, interrogation, encouragement etc. **2** (*esp. N Am.*) used to attract someone's attention, often used meaninglessly. [ME *hei*]

hey[2] HAY[2].

heyday (hā´dā) *n.* the time of unexhausted spirits, vigour, prosperity etc. [archaic *heyday*, an expression of joy; cp. HEY[1]]

heyduck HAIDUK.

hey presto PRESTO[2].

HF *abbr.* high frequency.

Hf *chem. symbol* hafnium.

hf. *abbr.* half.

HG *abbr.* **1** His or Her Grace. **2** Home Guard.

Hg *chem. symbol* mercury.

hg *abbr.* hectogram(s).

HH *abbr.* **1** His or Her Highness. **2** His Holiness (the Pope). **3** extra hard (of a pencil lead).

hh. *abbr.* hands (as a unit of measurement).

hhd. *abbr.* hogshead(s).

HI *abbr.* **1** Hawaii. **2** the Hawaiian Islands.

hi (hī) *int.* **1** used as a greeting or to call attention. **2** used to express surprise, derision etc. [cp. HEY[1]]

hiatus (hīā´təs) *n.* (*pl.* **hiatuses**) **1** a gap, a break, a lacuna in a manuscript, connected series etc. **2** the coming together of two vowels in successive syllables or words. **hiatal** *a.* **hiatus hernia** *n.* a hernia in which part of the stomach protrudes through the oesophageal opening in the diaphragm. [L, from *hiāre*, to yawn]

Hib (hib) *n.* a bacterium, *Haemophilus influenzae* type B, causing meningitis in children. [acronym]

hibernaculum (hībənak´ūləm), **hibernacle** (hī´bənakəl) *n.* (*pl.* **hibernacula** (-lə), **hibernacles**) **1** the winter quarters of a hibernating animal. **2** a bud or bulb sheltering the future plant. **3** winter quarters, shelter, covering etc. [L *hībernaculum*, from *hīberna*, see HIBERNATE]

hibernate (hī´bənāt) *v.i.* **1** (of some animals) to pass the winter in sleep or torpor. **2** to live in seclusion or remain inactive at a time of stress. **hibernal** (-bœ´-) *a.* of or relating to winter. **hibernant** (-bœ´-) *a.* hibernating. **hibernation** (-ā´shən) *n.* **hibernator** *n.* [L *hībernātus*, p.p. of *hībernāre*, from *hīberna*, winter quarters, orig. neut. pl. of *hībernus*, wintry]

Hibernian (hībœ´niən) *a.* of or relating to Ireland. ~*n.* a native or inhabitant of Ireland. **Hibernicism** (-sizm), **Hibernianism** *n.* **1** a phrase or mode of speech peculiar to the Irish. **2** a contradictory or inconsistent expression. [L *Hibernia*, *Iverna*, Gr. *Iernē*, from OCelt.]

Hiberno- (hībœ´nō) *comb. form* of or relating to Ireland, Irish. **Hiberno-Celtic** *a.* of or relating to the Irish Celts. ~*n.* Irish Gaelic.

hibiscus (hibis´kəs) *n.* (*pl.* **hibiscuses**) a mallow of the mostly tropical genus *Hibiscus* with large brightly coloured flowers. [L, from Gr. *hibiskos*, marsh mallow]

hic (hik) *int.* used to represent a sound like a hiccup, denoting interruption, as in the speech of a drunken person. [imit.]

hiccup (hik´ŭp), **hiccough** *n.* **1** a short, audible catching of the breath due to spasmodic contraction of the diaphragm and the glottis. **2** (*pl.*) a spasm of hiccuping. **3** (*coll.*) a temporary or minor difficulty, problem etc. ~*v.i.* (*pres.p.* **hiccuping, hiccoughing,** *past, p.p.* **hiccuped, hiccoughed**) to have or utter a hiccup or series of hiccups. ~*v.t.* to utter with a hiccup. **hiccupy** *a.* [imit., cp. HIC (spelling *hiccough* due to confusion with COUGH)]

hic jacet (hik yak´et) *n.* an epitaph. [L, here lies]

hick (hik) *n.* (*coll.*) a country bumpkin, a farmer, a yokel; an unsophisticated person. ~*a.* rustic, rural. [after *Hick*, a familiar form of Richard]

hickey (hik´i) *n.* (*pl.* **hickeys**) (*N Am., coll.*) **1** a device, a gadget. **2** a mark on the skin, esp. one caused by a lovebite. [etym. unknown]

hickory (hik´əri) *n.* (*pl.* **hickories**) **1** any of several N American trees of the genus *Carya*, allied to the walnuts, esp. *C. alba*, the timber of which is tough and elastic. **2** the wood of a hickory. **3** a stick made from hickory wood. **hickory shirt** *n.* a shirt of striped or check cotton. [N Am. Ind. *pohickery*]

hid HIDE[1].

hidalgo (hidal´gō) *n.* (*pl.* **hidalgos**) a Spanish nobleman of the lowest class, a gentleman by birth. **hidalgoish** *a.* **hidalgoism** *n.* [Sp., earlier *hijo dalgo*, L *fīlius dē aliquō*, son of something]

hide[1] (hīd) *v.t.* (*past* **hid** (hid), *p.p.* **hidden** (hid´ən), †**hid**) **1** to put out of or withhold from sight or observation. **2** to obscure from view, to cover up. **3** to keep secret, to withhold from knowledge. **4** to suppress. ~*v.i.*

to lie concealed, to conceal oneself. ~*n.* a place of concealment for observing wildlife. **to hide one's head** to keep or remain out of sight, esp. from shame. **to hide one's light under a bushel** BUSHEL¹. **hidden** *a.* **hidden agenda** *n.* a concealed or ulterior motive behind one's actions, statements etc. **hidden economy** *n.* economic activity involving payment in cash or kind not declared for tax purposes. **hiddenly** *adv.* **hiddenmost** *a.* **hiddenness** *n.* **hidden reserves** *n.pl.* extra resources etc. kept concealed. **hide-and-seek,** (*NAm.*) **hide-and-go-seek** *n.* **1** a children's game in which players hide and others try to find them. **2** searching and evasion. **hideaway** *n.* a concealed or secluded place. **hideout** *n.* a place where someone can hide or take refuge. **hider** *n.* **hidey-hole, hidy-hole** *n.* (*coll.*) a hiding place. **hiding¹** *n.* **1** the act of concealing. **2** a state of concealment. **hiding place** *n.* **1** a place of concealment, a place where someone can hide or take refuge. **2** (*Hist.*) a secret chamber, a priest's hiding place. [OE *hȳdan*, cogn. with Gr. *keuthein*]

hide² (hīd) *n.* **1** the skin of an animal, esp. when dressed. **2** (*coll.*) the human skin. ~*v.t.* (*pres.p.* **hiding,** *past, p.p.* **hided**) (*coll.*) to flog. **neither hide nor hair of** nothing at all of (someone). **hidebound** *a.* **1** narrow-minded, bigoted, obstinate. **2** (of the law etc.) constricted by tradition. **3** (of an animal) difficult to skin because the hide adheres closely to the ribs and back, esp. because of poor feeding. **4** (of trees) having the bark so close and tight as to impede growth. **5** †penurious. **hiding²** *n.* (*coll.*) a thrashing, a flogging. **on a hiding to nothing** unable to succeed, no matter what happens. [OE *hȳd* (cp. Dut. *huid*, Icel. *hūth*, G *Haut*, also L *cutis*, Gr. *kutos*)]

hide³ (hīd) *n.* (*Hist.*) a certain portion of land variously estimated at from 60 to 120 acres (24 to 48 ha), orig. enough to support a family and its dependants. [OE *hīd higid*, from *hīw-*, family]

hideous (hid´iəs) *a.* **1** exceedingly ugly, repulsive. **2** horrible, frightful, shocking. **3** (*coll.*) nasty, unpleasant. **hideosity** (-os´-) *n.* (*pl.* **hideosities**). **hideously** *adv.* **hideousness** *n.* [ME *hidous*, OF *hidos* (F *hideux*), *hisdos* (from *hisde*, *hide*, horror, fear)]

hiding¹ HIDE¹.

hiding² HIDE².

hidrosis (hīdrō´sis) *n.* **1** (*Med.*) (esp. excessive) sweating, perspiration. **2** any skin disease affecting the sweat glands. **hidrotic** (-drot´-) *a.* causing perspiration. [late L *hidrōticus*, Gr. *hidrōtikos*, from *hidrōs -drōtos*, sweat]

†**hie** (hī) *v.i., v.refl.* (*3rd pers. sing. pres.* **hies,** *pres.p.* **hieing, hying,** *past, p.p.* **hied**) to hasten, to hurry. [OE *hīgian* (cp. Dut. *hijgen*, to haul)]

Hieland (hē´lənd) *a.* (*Sc., dial.*) Highland. **Hielander** *n.* **Hielands** *n.pl.*

hiemal (hī´əməl) *a.* HIBERNAL (under HIBERNATE). [L *hiems*, winter]

hier- HIERO-.

hierarchy (hīə´rahki) *n.* (*pl.* **hierarchies**) **1** a system of persons or things arranged in a graded order. **2** a rank or order of sacred persons. **3** the collective body of those organized in a graded order. **4** organization in grades or orders, esp. of a priesthood. **5** priestly or ecclesiastical government; government in sacred matters. **6** (*Theol.*) **a** any one of three orders of angels. **b** the angels collectively. **7** the bishops collectively of a province. **hierarch** *n.* **1** the chief of a sacred order, a person who has authority in sacred things, a chief priest. **2** a prelate or archbishop. **hierarchal** (-ah´-) *a.* of or relating to a hierarch. **hierarchic** (-ah´-), **hierarchical** *a.* of or relating to a hierarch or hierarchy. **hierarchism** *n.* hierarchical principles, power or character. [F *hierarchie*, from L, from Gr. *hierarchia* (*hieros*, sacred, *archein*, to govern)]

hieratic (hīərat´ik) *a.* **1** of or relating to the priesthood, priestly. **2** denoting, of or related to the form of hieroglyphics employed in early Egyptian records written by priests. **3** of or relating to early styles in Egyptian and Greek art. **hieratically** *adv.* [L *hierāticus*, Gr. *hierātikos*, from *hierasthai*, to be priest, from *hieros*, holy]

hiero- (hīə´rō), **hier-** *comb. form* sacred; of or relating to sacred things. [Gr. *hieros*, holy]

hierocracy (hīərok´rəsi) *n.* (*pl.* **hierocracies**) **1** government by priests, hierarchy. **2** a body of governing priests.

hieroglyph (hīə´rəglif) *n.* **1** the figure of an animate or inanimate object used in writing to represent a word, sound etc., as practised by the ancient Egyptians, the Aztecs and others. **2** a piece of writing consisting of such characters. **3** a character or symbol employed to convey a secret meaning. **4** (*usu. in pl., facet.*) illegible writing. ~*v.t.* to represent by or in hieroglyphs. **hieroglyphic** (-glif´-) *a.* **1** written in or covered with hieroglyphs. **2** written in characters difficult to decipher. **3** mysterious, emblematic, esoteric. **hieroglyphical** *a.* **hieroglyphically** *adv.* **hieroglyphics** *n.* hieroglyphic writing; hieroglyphs. **hieroglyphist** (-og´-) *n.* **1** a writer of hieroglyphs. **2** a person skilled in deciphering hieroglyphs. [late L *hieroglyphicus*, Gr. *hieroglouphicous* (HIERO-, *gluphē*, carving)]

hierogram (hīə´rəgram) *n.* a sacred writing, character or symbol. **hierograph** (-graf) *n.* a hierogram.

hierolatry (hīərol´ətri) *n.* the worship of sacred persons or things, esp. the worship of saints.

hierology (hīərol´əji) *n.* **1** religious or sacred literature or lore. **2** the study of religious or sacred literature or lore. **3** the study of hieroglyphics, esp. of the ancient writings of the Egyptians. **hierologic** (-əloj´-), **hierological** *a.* **hierologist** *n.* [late Gr. *hierologia*]

hierophant (hīə´rəfant) *n.* **1** a person who teaches or explains the mysteries of religion. **2** in ancient Greece, a priest who acted as an interpreter of sacred mysteries. **hierophantic** (-fan´-) *a.* [late L and Gr. *hierophantēs* (*phainein*, to show)]

hi-fi (hī´fī) *n.* (*pl.* **hi-fis**) (*coll.*) any equipment for high-quality sound reproduction. ~*a.* high-fidelity.

higgle (hig´əl) *v.i.* to haggle or dispute over terms when bargaining. **higgler** *n.* **1** a person who higgles. **2** a huckster, a pedlar. [prob. a form of HAGGLE]

higgledy-piggledy (higəldipig´əldi) *adv.* (*coll.*) in confusion, topsy-turvy. ~*a.* confused, jumbled about anyhow. ~*n.* a jumble. [etym. uncertain]

high (hī) *a.* **1** rising or extending upwards for or to a great extent. **2** rising or extending upwards for or to a specified extent. **3** situated at a great elevation. **4** upper, inland. **5** extending above the normal or average level (*trousers with a high waistband*). **6** involving a great elevation; taking place from a great elevation (*high diving*). **7** exalted in rank, position or office. **8** of noble character or purpose; exalted in quality (*high principles; high art*). **9** proud, lofty in tone or temper, arrogant. **10** great, extreme, intense. **11** full, complete, consummate. **12** (of a period, age etc.) far advanced (*high summer*). **13** expensive, costly (in price). **14** boisterous, violent. **15** (of a sound) of a high frequency, sharp, acute in pitch. **16** (esp. of meat) tainted, approaching putrefaction. **17** chief, principal. **18** (*coll.*) intoxicated by alcohol or drugs. **19** (*coll.*) in an animated or hysterical state. **20** (of latitude) near either of the poles. **21** (of a vowel) articulated with the tongue raised close to the palate. ~*adv.* **1** to a great altitude, aloft. **2** in or to a high degree. **3** at a high price. **4** eminently, greatly, powerfully. **5** at or to a high pitch (*She sings high*). ~*n.* **1** a high level, a high point. **2** the highest level, the highest point. **3** an anticyclone (with high barometric pressure). **4** (*sl.*) a state of euphoria, esp. one due to intoxication with drugs. **5** a motor vehicle's top gear. 6 (*N Am., coll.*) a high school. **from on high** from aloft, from heaven. **high, wide and handsome** (*coll.*) in an exuberant or flamboyant manner. **in high dudgeon** DUDGEON[1]. **in high feather** FEATHER. **on high** 1 aloft. 2 to or in heaven. **on one's high horse** (*coll.*) behaving arrogantly or affecting superiority. **riding high** in a state of good fortune or prosperity. **the High** (*coll.*) a High Street. **to play high** 1 to play or gamble for heavy amounts. 2 to play a high card. **to run high** 1 (of the sea) to have a strong current with high tide. 2 (of emotions) to be strongly felt. **with a high hand** in an arrogant or arbitrary manner. **High Admiral** *n.* a chief officer ranking as an admiral. **high altar** *n.* the principal altar of a church. **high and dry** *adv.* 1 left behind, stranded without resources. 2 (*Naut.*) out of the water, aground. **high and low** *adv.* everywhere (*They searched high and low for the mouse*). **high and mighty** *a.* 1 (*coll.*) arrogant. 2 †of exalted rank. **highball** *n.* 1 a drink of spirits and soda served in a tall glass. 2 (orig. on a railway) a signal to proceed. **highbinder** *n.* (*N Am., sl.*) 1 a thug, a hired killer. 2 a cheat, a swindler. **high-born** *a.* of noble birth. **highboy** *n.* (*N Am.*) a tall chest of drawers with legs. **high brass** *n.* brass containing 65 per cent copper and 35 per cent zinc. **high-bred** *a.* of noble breed, training or family. **highbrow** *n.* (*coll., often derog.*) an intellectual or cultural person. ~*a.* intellectual, cultural. **highbrowed** *a.* **high camp** *n., a.* (of or displaying) sophisticated camp style, behaviour, etc. **high card** *n.* a card, such as an ace or court card, which outranks others. **high-caste** *a.* belonging to a high caste. **high chair** *n.* a baby's chair with a tray, raised on long legs to table height. **High Church** *n.* one of the main traditions in the Anglican Church, distinguished by its maintenance of sacerdotal claims and assertion of the efficacy of the sacraments. ~*a.* of or relating to the High Church. **High Churchism** *n.* **High Churchman** *n.* (*pl.* **High Churchmen**). **high-class** *a.* of high quality, refinement. **high colour**, (*N Am.*) **high color** *n.* a flushed complexion. **high-coloured** *a.* 1 (of the complexion) having a strong deep colour, flushed. 2 represented in strong or forcible language. **high comedy** *n.* (*pl.* **high comedies**) (a) comedy set among cultured and articulate people and featuring witty dialogue. **high command** *n.* 1 an army commander-in-chief and senior staff. 2 the supreme headquarters of the armed forces. **High Commission** *n.* an embassy of one Commonwealth country in another. **High Commissioner** *n.* the chief representative of one Commonwealth country in another. **High Court, high court** *n.* a supreme court of justice. **High Court of Justice** *n.* in England, the supreme court of civil jurisdiction. **High Court of Justiciary** *n.* the supreme court of civil jurisdiction in Scotland. **high day** *n.* 1 a feast, a festival. 2 broad daylight, noon. **high-definition television** *n.* a television offering a picture with superior definition, using over 1000 scanning lines. **†High Dutch** *n.* 1 (*as pl.*) the southern Germans. 2 their language. **high enema** *n.* an enema administered into the colon. **high-energy** *a.* concerning elementary particles accelerated in a particle accelerator. **higher** *a.* **Higher** *n.* in Scotland, an examination leading to the SCE (Scottish Certificate of Education) Higher Grade. **higher animal** *n.* an animal manifesting relatively advanced characteristics. **higher court** *n.* a court able to overturn the decision of another court. **higher criticism** *n.* the analytical evaluation of biblical writings, esp. to establish their sources. **higher education** *n.* education after secondary schools, e.g. at a college or university. **higher mathematics** *n.* advanced mathematics taught at colleges, universities etc. **higher plant** *n.* a plant manifesting relatively advanced characteristics. **higher-up** *n.* (*pl.* **higher-ups**) (*coll.*) a person in a position of greater authority or higher rank. **highest** *a.* **highest common factor** *n.* the highest number that can be divided exactly into each of a group of numbers. **high explosive** *n.* an explosive of extreme rapidity and great destructive energy. **highfalutin** (-fəloo´tin), **highfaluting** *a.* (*coll.*) bombastic, affected. ~*n.* bombast. **high fashion** *n.* HAUTE COUTURE. **high fidelity** *n.* the reproduction of sound with very little distortion. **high-fidelity** *a.* of or relating to high fidelity. **high finance** *n.* transactions involving large amounts of money. **high-five** *n.* (*esp. N Am., sl.*) a gesture of victory, greeting etc. in which two people slap the palms of their hands together above their heads. ~*v.t.* to greet with a high-five. **high-five sign** *n.* **high-flown** *a.* (of language, style etc.) turgid, bombastic. **high-flyer, high-flier** *n.* 1 a person with high qualifications, or who aims to achieve high position. 2 a thing likely to be commercially successful. **high-flying** *a.* **high frequency** *n.* (*pl.* **high frequencies**) a radio-frequency band or radio frequency between 3–30 megahertz. **high gear** *n.* on cycles, motor vehicles etc., the apparatus for transmitting high speed to the driving-wheel relatively to the motion of pedals, engine etc. **High German** *n.* the form of German spoken in central and southern Germany, regarded as standard speech. **high-grade** *a.* of high quality. **high ground** *n.* the morally or intellectually superior position in a debate, argument etc. **high-handed** *a.* overbearing, domineering, arbitrary. **high-handedly** *adv.* **high-handedness** *n.* **high hat** *n.* 1 a tall hat, a top hat. 2 (*coll.*) a snobbish or overbearing person. 3 a pair of cymbals operated with the foot. **high-hat** *a.* snobbish, arrogant. ~*v.t.* (*pres.p.* **high-hatting**, *past, p.p.* **high-hatted**) (*N Am.*) to treat snobbishly or overbearingly. ~*v.i.* to be snobbish or overbearing. **high heels** *n.pl.* shoes with high heels, esp. for women. **high-heeled** *a.* **highjack** HIJACK. **high jinks** *n.pl.* high festivities or lively enjoyment. **high jump** *n.* an athletic event where competitors jump over a high bar. **to be for the high jump** (*coll.*) to be liable to receive some form of severe punishment etc. **high-jumper** *n.* **high-jumping** *n.* **high-key** *a.* (of a photograph etc.) having mostly light-grey tones or light colours. **high-keyed** *a.* 1 having a shrill pitch. 2 (*N Am.*) highly strung. 3 bright in colour. **high kick** *n.* a dancer's or athlete's kick high in the air. **high-kicking** *a.* **high latitudes** *n.pl.* regions near the poles. **high-level** *a.* 1 (of gatherings etc.) involving important people. 2 having a high rank. **high-level language** *n.* (*Comput.*) a language in which each word is equal to several machine instructions, making it closer to human language. **high life** *n.* the style of living or the manners of the fashionable world. **highlight** *n.* 1 the most brilliantly lit spot in a photograph or picture. 2 a moment or event of particular importance or interest. 3 (*pl.*) streaks of artificial light colour in dark hair. ~*v.t.* (*past, p.p.* **highlighted**) 1 to put emphasis on. 2 to put highlights in (hair). 3 to mark with a highlighter. **highlighter** *n.* a marker pen used to overlay colour on a document etc. to emphasize certain details etc. **high living** *n.* living in extravagance and luxury. **†high-lows** *n.pl.* laced boots reaching to the ankle. **highly** *adv.* 1 in a high degree, extremely, intensely. 2 honourably, favourably. **highly strung** *a.* of a nervous and tense disposition. **High Mass** *n.* a Mass in which the celebrant is attended by deacon and subdeacon, usu., but not necessarily, sung at the high altar. **high-mettled** *a.* full of fire, spirited. **high-minded** *a.* 1 magnanimous, having high moral principles. 2 †proud, arrogant. **high-mindedly** *adv.* **high-mindedness** *n.* **highness** *n.* 1 the quality or state of being high. 2 (**Highness**) a title of honour given to princes and others of royal rank (used with a possessive pronoun) (*Her Royal Highness*). 3 height. **high noon** *n.* the time when the sun is in the meridian. **high-octane** *a.* (of petrol) having a high octane number. **high old time** *n.* (*coll.*) an enjoyable and exciting time. **high opinion** *n.* a favourable opinion (of). **high-pitched** *a.* 1 (of sound) high. 2 (of style etc.) aspiring, haughty. 3 (of roofs) steeply sloping. **high places** *n.pl.* the upper ranks of an organization etc. **high point** *n.* a moment or occasion of great intensity, interest etc. **high polymer** *n.* a polymer having a high molecular weight. **high-powered** *a.* 1 having great power, energy etc. 2 important, dynamic or influential. **high pressure** *n.* 1 a pressure above the norm. 2 a condition of the atmosphere where the pressure is above the average. 3 great activity or effort. **high-pressure** *a.* 1 having, involving or designed to withstand pressure above the norm (*a high-pressure cylinder*). 2 (*coll.*) (of selling) persuasive in an aggressive and persistent manner. **high priest** *n.* 1 a chief priest, esp. the head of the Jewish hierarchy. 2 the head of any cult, sect etc. **high priestess** *n.* a chief priestess. **high priesthood** *n.* **high-principled** *a.* having high or noble principles. **high profile** *n.* a high degree of exposure to attention or publicity esp. in the media. **high-profile** *a.* **high-quality** *a.* of high quality. **high-ranking** *a.* of a high rank, senior. **high relief** *n.* ALTO-RELIEVO. **high-rise** *a.* (of a building) having many storeys. ~*n.* such a building. **high-risk** *a.* involving danger, exposed to danger (*high-risk categories; high-risk sports*). **high road** *n.* 1 a main road, a highway. 2 a direct route (to). **high roller** *n.* (*N Am., sl.*) a person who spends money extravagantly or gambles recklessly. **high school** *n.* a secondary school. **high sea, high seas** *n.* 1 the open sea or ocean. 2 (*Law*) the waters beyond low water mark. **high season** *n.* the most popular time of year at a holiday resort etc. **high-seasoned** *a.* 1 strongly seasoned, piquant. 2 lewd, obscene. **high-security** *a.* 1 (of a prison etc.) extremely secure. 2 (of a prisoner) kept in such a prison. **High Sheriff** *n.* the chief Crown officer of a county or shire charged with the keeping of the peace, the execution of writs, sentences etc., the conduct of elections etc. **high sign** *n.* (*N Am., coll.*) a surreptitious gesture etc. to show that all is well. **high-sounding** *a.* pompous, ostentatious. **high-speed** *a.* 1 moving or operating at a high speed. 2 (of photographic film) requiring brief exposure. 3 (of steel) suitable for tools, cutting extremely rapidly. **high spirit** *n.* courage, energy, vivacity, ardour. **high-spirited** *a.* 1 full of high spirits. 2 having a lofty or courageous spirit; bold, daring. **high spirits** *n.pl.* 1 cheerfulness, liveliness, vivacity. 2 lively enjoyment. **in high spirits** in a vivacious, cheerful or lively mood. **high spot** *n.* (*coll.*) a moment or event of particular importance or interest. **to hit the high spots** 1 to visit the key places in an area. 2 to go to excess or extremes. **high-stepper** *n.* 1 a horse that lifts its feet high when trotting. 2 a person of a dashing or showy walk or bearing. **high-stepping** *a.* **high street** *n.* the principal street of a town etc. (often used as the proper name of a street). **high-strung** *a.* HIGHLY STRUNG (under HIGH). **high table** *n.* the main table at a public dinner, raised on a platform; the table for the fellows of a college etc. **hightail** *v.i.* (*N Am., coll.*) to move quickly. **to hightail it** to run away. †**high-tasted** *a.* 1 having a strong taste. 2 piquant. **high tea** *n.* a main evening meal taken relatively early and at which tea and bread and butter may be served. **high tech** (tek) *n.* 1 advanced technology, high technology. 2 a style of interior design using features of industrial equipment. **high-tech** *a.* **high technology** *n.* highly sophisticated, often electronic, techniques used in manufacturing etc. **high-tensile** *a.* (of metal) having great tensile strength. **high tension** *n.* steady and high voltage. **high tide** *n.* 1 the tide at its highest and fullest level. 2 the time of this. **high time** *n.* (*coll.*) 1 the latest possible time, almost too late. 2 an enjoyable and exciting time. **high-toned** *a.* 1 high in pitch. 2 strong in sound. 3 morally or culturally elevated. **high treason** *n.* a violation of allegiance by a subject against the sovereign or government, esp. an overt attempt to subvert the government. **high-up** *n.* (*coll.*) a person of high rank or authority. **high-velocity** *a.* 1 (of a projectile) having a low trajectory and long range. 2 (of a gun) firing such projectiles. **high voltage** *n.* a voltage great enough to cause damage or injury. **high water** *n.* HIGH TIDE (under HIGH). **high water mark** *n.* 1 the level reached by the water at high tide. 2 the highest recorded value, the highest point of achievement. **high wire** *n.* a tightrope high above the ground. **high words** *n.pl.* angry talk. **high-wrought** *a.* 1 wrought with great skill. 2 (of feelings) inflamed to a high degree. **high yellow** *n.* (*US, derog.*) a light-skinned person of mixed black and white parentage. [OE *hēah* (cp. Dut. *hoog*, Icel. *hār*, G *hoch*)]

highland (hī´lənd) *n.* high or mountainous ground. **the Highlands** the northern mountainous parts of Scotland. **Highland** *a.* of or relating to the Highlands of Scotland. **Highland cattle** *n.* a breed of cattle with shaggy hair, usu. of a reddish-brown colour, and long horns. **Highland dress** *n.* 1 the historical costume, incl. the kilt, bonnet etc. as worn by Highlanders. 2 a modern version of this worn at formal occasions. **Highlander** *n.* 1 a native or inhabitant of the Highlands of Scotland. 2 (**highlander**) a native or inhabitant of a highland. **Highland fling** *n.* a whirling Scottish Highland dance. **Highlandman** *n.* (*pl.* **Highlandmen**).

high-muck-a-muck (hī´mŭkəmŭk), **high-mucketymuck** (-mŭkəti-) *n.* (*N Am.*) a self-important person. [prob. from Chinook jargon, plenty of food]

†**hight** (hīt) *v.i.* (*3rd pers. sing. past*) to be named or called. [the only instance in English of a passive verb; from OE *hātte*, I am or was called, from *hātan*, to call, to be called]

highway (hī´wā) *n.* 1 a public road open to all passengers. 2 a main route for any form of transport. 3 (*esp. N Am.*) a main road, esp. one that connects towns, cities. 4 a direct path or course. **Highway Code** *n.* the official guide and instructions for proper behaviour on the road in the UK. **highwayman** *n.* (*pl.* **highwaymen**) (*Hist.*) a robber, usu. on horseback, who held up travellers on the highway. **highwaywoman** *n.* (*pl.* **highwaywomen**) (*Hist.*) a female robber holding up travellers on the highway.

HIH *abbr.* His or Her Imperial Highness.

hijack (hī´jak), **highjack** *v.t.* 1 to take over (a vehicle, aircraft etc.) by force, esp. to divert it from its route. 2 to steal (goods) in transit. 3 to take over or change the direction of (a project etc.). ~*n.* an act of hijacking. **hijacker** *n.* [etym. unknown]

Hijra HEGIRA.

hike (hīk) *n.* 1 a ramble, a long country walk. 2 (*coll.*) an increase, e.g. in prices. ~*v.i.* 1 to go for a hike. 2 to become hoisted or hitched up. ~*v.t.* 1 to hoist or lift; to hitch up. 2 (*coll.*) to increase (prices etc.). **hiker** *n.*

hila, hilar HILUM.

hilarious (hileə´riəs) *a.* 1 extremely funny. 2 cheerful, mirthful, merry. **hilariously** *adv.* **hilariousness, hilarity** (-lar´-) *n.* [L *hilaris -us*, Gr. *hilaros* cheerful]

Hilary term (hil´əri) *n.* the spring term at Oxford and Dublin universities and the Inns of Court. [(L *Hilarius*) St *Hilary* of Poitiers d. 367, whose festival occurs on 13 Jan.]

hill (hil) *n.* 1 a noticeable natural elevation on the surface of the earth, less high and abrupt than a mountain. 2 a heap, a mound. 3 a sloping stretch of road, an incline. ~*v.t.* 1 to form into hills, heaps or mounds. 2 to heap (up) earth around the roots of. **over the hill** 1 (*coll.*) beyond one's prime. 2 (*coll.*) beyond the crisis. **the hills** (*Ang.-Ind.*) the low mountains in the north of the Indian subcontinent. **up**

hill and down dale strenuously and persistently. **hillbilly** *n.* (*pl.* **hillbillies**) (*N Am.*) **1** (*usu. derog.*) a person from the mountain country regarded as unsophisticated; a hick. **2** country music of a traditional variety. **hill climb** *n.* a competition in which competitors race up a hill in vehicles. **hill fort** *n.* a fort on a hill, a fortified hilltop. **hill man** *n.* (*pl.* **hill men**) a person from a hilly region. **hillock** (-ək) *n.* a little hill or mound. **hillocky** *a.* **hillside** *n.* the sloping side of a hill. **hill station** *n.* (*Ang.-Ind.*) a settlement in the low mountains in the north of the Indian subcontinent, esp. used as a retreat in the hot season. **hilltop** *n.* the summit of a hill. **hillwalking** *n.* walking over hilly countryside for recreation and exercise. **hillwalker** *n.* **hilly** *a.* (*comp.* **hillier**, *superl.* **hilliest**). **hilliness** *n.* [OE *hyll* (cp. MDut. *hil, hille*, L *collis*)]

hilt (hilt) *n.* **1** the handle of a sword, dagger etc. **2** the handle of a tool. ~*v.t.* to provide with a hilt. **up to the hilt** to the fullest extent. **hilted** *a.* [OE, perh. related to HELVE]

hilum (hīˊləm) *n.* (*pl.* **hila** (-lə)) **1** the spot on a seed where it was attached to the seed vessel. **2** a small aperture or a small depression in a bodily organ. [L, a trifle, a whit]

HIM *abbr.* His or Her Imperial Majesty.

him (him) *pron.* **1** objective (accusative and dative) of HE. **2** (*dial.*) HIMSELF. [OE *him*]

Usage note Use of *him* in a subject, as in *Him and his sister were late*, is best avoided. See also notes under AS[1], BE, THAN.

Himalayan (himəlāˊən) *a.* **1** of or relating to the Himalayas, a range of high mountains in Nepal. **2** vast, gigantic. [Sansk. *Himālaya* (*hima*, snow, *ālaya*, abode)]

himation (himatˊion) *n.* (*pl.* **himatia** (-tiə)) the ordinary outer garment in ancient Greece, an oblong piece of cloth thrown over the left shoulder. [Gr.]

himbo (himˊbō) *n.* (*pl.* **himbos**) (*sl.*) a man who looks good but lacks depth or intelligence, a male bimbo. [HIM, BIMBO]

himself (himselfˊ) *pron.* **1** HE or HIM (objective), used to give emphasis (usu. in apposition). **2** the reflexive form of HIM. **3** his normal or usual self. **4** (*esp. Ir.*) the important male person being referred to. **by himself** alone, unaided. **to be himself** to act in his normal manner.

hin (hin) *n.* a Hebrew measure for liquids, equal to 12 pints or 3.5 litres. [Heb. *hīn*]

Hinayana (hēnəyahˊnə) *n.* THERAVADA. [Sansk. *hīna*, lesser, *yāna*, vehicle]

hind[1] (hīnd), **hinder** *a.* of, relating to or situated at the back or rear. **on one's hind legs** LEG. **hind-afore, hind-first, hind-foremost** *a., adv.* back to front. **hindbrain** *n.* the lower part of the brainstem, the cerebellum, pons and medulla oblongata considered together. **hinder end** *n.* the buttocks. **hindermost, hindmost** *a.* **1** last in position, furthest back. **2** that is or comes last of all. **hindquarters** *n.pl.* the hind legs and rump of a quadruped. **hindsight** *n.* wisdom after the event, the reverse of foresight. [OE *hindan*]

hind[2] (hīnd) *n.* the female of the deer, esp. the red deer. [OE (cp. Dut. and G *hinde*, Icel., Dan. and Swed. *hind*)]

hind[3] (hīnd) *n.* **1** (*Hist., Sc., North.*) an agricultural labourer, a farm worker, esp. one in charge of two horses and allotted a house on the farm. **2** a steward on a farm. **3** a peasant, a rustic, a boor. [ME *hine*, OE *hīna*, gen. pl. of *hīwa*, a domestic]

hinder[1] (hinˊdə) *v.t.* to obstruct, to impede, to prevent from proceeding or moving. ~*v.i.* to cause a hindrance; to interpose obstacles or impediments. **hinderer** *n.* **hindrance** *n.* **1** the act of hindering. **2** that which hinders; an impediment, an obstacle. [OE *hindrian*]

hinder[2] HIND[1].

Hindi (hinˊdi) *n.* **1** the group of Indo-European languages spoken in northern India. **2** the literary or official form of this. **3** a speaker of Hindi. ~*a.* of or relating to Hindi. [Hind., from Pers. *hind*, India]

†**Hindoo** HINDU.

hindrance HINDER[1].

hindsight HIND[1].

Hindu (hindooˊ, hinˊ-), †**Hindoo** *n.* (*pl.* **Hindus,** †**Hindoos**) **1** a follower of Hinduism. **2** †an Indian. ~*a.* of or relating to Hindus or Hinduism. **Hinduism** (hinˊ-) *n.* the dominant religion of India, comprising the Hindu polytheistic system of Brahminism modified by Buddhism and other accretions. **Hinduize** (hinˊ-), **Hinduise** *v.t.* **Hindustani** (-stahˊni) *n.* **1** all spoken forms of Hindi and Urdu considered together. **2** the dialect of Hindi spoken in Delhi, used as a lingua franca throughout the Indian subcontinent. **3** †a native or inhabitant of Hindustan proper. ~*a.* of or relating to Hindustani or Hindustan. [HINDI]

hinge (hinj) *n.* **1** the joint or mechanical device on which a door or lid turns. **2** a natural articulation fulfilling similar functions. **3** the point on which anything depends or turns. **4** a piece of gummed paper for sticking a stamp in an album etc. ~*v.t.* to furnish with or as with a hinge. ~*v.i.* (*pres.p.* **hingeing, hinging**) **1** to turn on or as on a hinge. **2** to depend (upon). **off the hinges 1** in a state of mental or physical disorder. **2** out of working order. **hinged** *a.* **hingeless** *a.* **hingewise** *adv.* [ME *heng*, cogn. with HANG]

hinnie HINNY[3].

hinny[1] (hinˊi) *n.* (*pl.* **hinnies**) the offspring of a male horse and female donkey. [L *hinnus* (Gr. *hinnos, ginnos*)]

hinny[2] (hinˊi) *v.i.* (*3rd pers. sing. pres.* **hinnies**, *pres.p.* **hinnying**, *past, p.p.* **hinnied**) to neigh, to whinny. [F *hennir*, L *hinnīre*]

hinny[3] (hinˊi), **hinnie** *n.* (*pl.* **hinnies**) (*North., Sc.*) sweetheart, darling. [HONEY]

hint (hint) *n.* **1** a slight or distant allusion. **2** a small piece of helpful or practical information. **3** a small amount (of); a trace. ~*v.t.* to mention indirectly, to suggest, to allude to. ~*v.i.* to make remote allusion. **to hint at** to mention indirectly. **hinter** *n.* **hintingly** *adv.* [prob. from *hent*, from OE *hentan*, to seize]

hinterland (hinˊtəland) *n.* **1** the region situated behind something, esp. a coast or the shore of a river. **2** the remote or underdeveloped areas of a country. **3** an area located near and dependent on a large city, esp. a port. [G (*hinter-*, HINDER[2], LAND)]

hip[1] (hip) *n.* **1** the projection of the articulation of the femur and the thigh bone; the projecting fleshy part covering a hip joint. **2** the human body as seen or measured surrounding the hip joints (*usu. in pl.*). **3** the external angle formed by the meeting sides of a roof. †**on the hip** at a disadvantage. **to smite hip and thigh** to overthrow completely, slaughter without mercy. **hip bath** *n.* a bath in which the body can be immersed to the hips. **hip bone** *n.* a bone forming the hip. **hip disease** *n.* a scrofulous disease of the hip joint attacking the bones. **hip flask** *n.* a flask, usu. containing spirits, carried in a pocket at the hip. **hip hop** *n.* a dance culture and form of music originating among US black and Hispanic youths in the late 1970s. **hip-huggers** *n.pl.* (*N Am., coll.*) hipsters. **hip joint** *n.* the articulation of the femur and the thigh-bone. **hip-length** *a.* (of a garment) reaching down to the hips. **hip-lock** *n.* in wrestling, a grip in which one tries to throw one's opponent by putting a leg or hip in front of them. **hipped**[1] *a.* **1** (esp. of cattle) having the hip dislocated or sprained. **2** (*in comb.*) having hips of the specified kind (as *wide-hipped*). **hipped roof** *n.* HIP ROOF (under HIP[1]). **hippy**[1] *a.* (*coll.*) having large hips. **hip roof** *n.* a roof rising directly from the walls on every side and consequently having no gable. **hipsters**

(-stəz) *n.pl.* (*coll.*) trousers that start at the hips, not the waist. **hipster**[1] *a.* (*coll.*) (of trousers) starting at the hips, not the waist. [OE *hype* (cp. Dut. *heup*, Dan. *hofte*, G *Hüfte*)]

hip[2] (hip), **hep** (hep) *n.* the fruit of a rose plant. [OE *hēope*]

hip[3] (hip) *int.* used to introduce cheers (*hip, hip, hurrah*).

hip[4] (hip) *a.* (*comp.* **hipper**, *superl.* **hippest**) (*esp. N Am.* (*dated*) *sl.*) aware, in the know. **hipped**[2] *a.* infatuated, very keen (on). **hipster**[2] *n.* a person who knows what's what; a person in the know. **hipsterism** *n.* [var. of HEP[1]]

☒ **hipocrisy** common misspelling of HYPOCRISY.

hipp- HIPPO-.

hipped[1] HIP[1].

hipped[2] HIP[4].

hippic (hip´ik) *a.* of or relating to horses or horseracing. [Gr. *hippikos*, see HIPPO-]

hippie HIPPY[2].

hippo (hip´ō) *n.* (*pl.* **hippos**) (*coll.*) short for HIPPOPOTAMUS.

hippo- (hip´ō), **hipp-** *comb. form* of, relating to or resembling a horse. [Gr. *hippos*, a horse]

hippocampus (hipōkam´pəs) *n.* (*pl.* **hippocampi** (-pī)) **1** a sea horse of the genus *Hippocampus*. **2** either of two eminences on the floor of the lateral ventricle of the brain. [late L, from Gr. *hippokampos* (HIPPO-, *kampos*, sea monster)]

hippocras (hip´əkras) *n.* (*Hist.*) a cordial made of wine and spices. [earlier *ypocras*, OF *ipocras*, from *Hippocrătes*, Greek physician born about 460 BC, perh. from being strained through Hippocrates' sleeve, a woollen bag]

Hippocratic (hipəkrat´ik), **Hippocratian** (-krat´iən), **Hippocratical** (-kəl) *a.* of or relating to Hippocrates. **Hippocratic oath** *n.* (*esp. Hist.*) an oath taken by physicians binding them to observe the code of medical practice derived from that of Hippocrates. [*Hippocratēs*, see HIPPOCRAS]

Hippocrene (hip´əkrēn) *n.* (*poet.*) poetic inspiration. **Hippocrenian** (-krē´-) *a.* [a spring on Mount Helicon in Greece, L from Gr. *hippos*, horse, *krēnē*, a fountain]

hippodrome (hip´ədrōm) *n.* **1** a music hall, variety theatre or circus. **2** in ancient Greece and Rome, a circus for equestrian games and chariot races. **hippodromic** (-drom´-) *a.* **hippodromist** (-pod´rə-) *n.* a circus rider or horse trainer. [F, from L, from Gr. *hippodromos* (*dromos*, a course)]

hippogriff (hip´əgrif), **hippogryph** *n.* a fabulous winged creature, half horse and half griffin. [F *hippogriffe*]

hippopotamus (hipəpot´əməs) *n.* (*pl.* **hippopotamuses, hippopotami** (-mī)) **1** a massive African thick-skinned quadruped, *Hippopotamus amphibius*, of amphibious habits, with a heavy body, short, blunt muzzle and short limbs and tail. **2** a related but smaller animal, *Choeropsis liberiensis*, the pygmy hippopotamus. **hippopotamic** (-tam´-, -pot´-), **hippopotamoid** (-oid) *a.* [L, from Gr. *hippopotamos* (*potamos*, river)]

hippy[1] HIP[1].

hippy[2] (hip´i), **hippie** *n.* (*pl.* **hippies**) a member of the youth culture of the 1960s, which stressed universal love and brotherhood, rejection of middle-class values, the wearing of long hair and colourful clothes, and the use of drugs.

hipster[1] HIP[1].

hipster[2] HIP[4].

hiragana (hērəgah´nə) *n.* the cursive form of Japanese syllabic writing.

hircine (hœ´sīn) *a.* **1** of or like a goat esp. in smell. **2** †lustful. [L *hircīnus*, from *hircus*, he-goat]

hire (hīə) *n.* **1** the act of hiring or the state of being hired. **2** the price paid for labour or services or the use of things. **3** (*N Am.*) a person recently hired. *~v.t.* **1** to procure the temporary use of for an agreed payment. **2** to employ (a person) for a stipulated payment. **on/ for hire** available for service or temporary use in exchange for a fee. **to hire oneself out** to make oneself available for employment. **to hire out** to pay independent contractors for (work to be done). **hireable,** (*esp. N Am.*) **hirable** *a.* **hire car** *n.* a car hired or available for hire, usu. for a short period. **hired girl, hired man** *n.* (*N Am.*) a domestic servant, esp. on a farm. **hireless** *a.* gratuitous, unpaid. **hireling** *n.* (*usu. derog.*) a person who works for hire. **hire purchase** *n.* a method by which payments for hire are accepted as instalments of the price and the article eventually becomes the property of the hirer. **hirer** *n.* a person who hires or lets on hire. [OE *hȳr* (cp. Dut. *huur*, Dan. *hyre*, G *Heuer*)]

hirsute (hœ´sūt) *a.* **1** rough or hairy. **2** having uncut hair. **3** (*Bot.*) covered with bristles. **hirsuteness** *n.* **hirsutism** *n.* the condition of having excessive facial or bodily hair. [L *hirsūtus*]

hirudin (hiroo´din) *n.* a substance secreted by the salivary gland of the leech, preventing blood-clotting. [L *hirūdō -dinis*, a leech]

hirundine (hirŭn´dīn, -din) *n.* a bird of the swallow family Hirundinidae. *~a.* of or relating to swallows, like a swallow. [L *hirundo*, a swallow]

his (hiz) *a.* possessive of HE. *~pron.* something which belongs to or is associated with him. **his and hers** (of paired objects) for husband and wife, or a man and a woman. **his 'n' hers** his and hers. **his nibs** NIB. **of his** belonging or relating to him. [OE, gen. of *hē*, HE]

Hispanic (hispan´ik) *a.* **1** of or relating to Spain or Spain and Portugal. **2** of Spain and other Spanish-speaking countries or regions. *~n.* a Spanish-speaking person, esp. of Central or South American descent, living in the US. **Hispanicism** (-sizm) *n.* a Spanish idiom. **Hispanicist, Hispanist** (his´pə-) *n.* a student of Spain or Spanish. **Hispanicize, Hispanicise** *v.t.* **Hispano-** *comb. form* Spain and Spanish. **Hispanophile** (-fīl) *n., a.* (a person who is) fond of Spain. [L *Hispānicus*, from *Hispānia*, Spain]

hispid (his´pid) *a.* rough, bristly. [L *hispidus*]

hiss (his) *v.i.* **1** (of a person, snake, goose etc.) to make a sound like that of the letter *s*, to make a sibilant sound. **2** (esp. of a crowd or audience) to express disapprobation by making such a sound. *~v.t.* **1** to utter with a hissing sound. **2** to condemn or drive away by hissing. *~n.* **1** a hissing sound. **2** an expression of derision or disapprobation. **3** continuous audible interference in sound reproduction. **hissingly** *adv.* [imit.]

†**hist** (hist) *int.* used to attract attention or as a warning to be silent, behave etc. [imit.]

hist. *abbr.* **1** histology. **2** historian. **3** historical. **4** history.

hist- HISTO-.

histamine (his´tamēn) *n.* an amine formed from histidine and released by the body tissues in allergic reactions.

histic (his´tik) *a.* of or relating to tissue. [as HISTIDINE]

histidine (his´tidēn) *n.* an amino acid derived from proteins.

histioid (his´tioid) *a.* HISTIC.

histiology HISTOLOGY.

histo- (his´tō), **hist-** *comb. form* of or relating to organic tissues. [Gr. *histos*, web]

histochemistry (histəkem´istri) *n.* the application of chemistry to organic tissue. **histochemical** *a.*

histocompatibility (histōkəmpatibil´iti) *n.* the compatibility of tissues that allows one to be grafted successfully onto another.

histogen (his´təjən) *n.* an area of tissue on a plant from which a specific part develops.

histogenesis (histəjen´əsis) *n.* the formation of tissues and organs from undifferentiated cells. **histogenetic** (-jinet´-) *a.* **histogenic** (-jen´-) *a.* **histogeny** (-toj´-) *n.*

1 histogenesis. 2 the formation and development of organic tissues.

histogram (his´tɘgram) *n.* a pictorial method of showing the distribution of various quantities, e.g. rainfall month by month.

histology (histol´ɘji), **histiology** (-tiol´-) *n.* the (microscopic) study of the tissues of plants or animals. **histologic** (-loj´-), **histological** *a.* **histologically** *adv.* **histologist** *n.*

histolysis (histol´isis) *n.* the decay and dissolution of organic tissue. **histolytic** (-tɘlit´-) *a.*

histone (his´tōn) *n.* any of various water-soluble proteins found in cell nuclei.

histopathology (histōpɘthol´ɘji) *n.* (the study of) changes in tissue caused by disease. **histopathological** (-pathɘloj´-) *a.* **histopathologist** *n.*

historian (histaw´riɘn) *n.* 1 a writer of history, esp. one who is an authority on it. 2 a person studying or versed in history. [F *historien*, from L *historia*, HISTORY]

historiated (histaw´riātid) *a.* ornamented with figures (as illuminated capitals etc.). [med. L *historiāre*, from L *historia*, HISTORY]

historic (histor´ik) *a.* 1 celebrated in history, associated with historical events. 2 potentially important, momentous. 3 (*Gram.*) used in past narration. 4 †historical. **historical** *a.* 1 of or relating to history. 2 of the nature of history; not legendary, fictitious etc. 3 involving analysis of change over time. 4 belonging to the past; dealing with the past. **historically** *adv.* **historical novel** *n.* a novel set in the past, using actual historical events and characters as background. **historical picture** *n.* a picture representing a historical event. **historical year** *n.* the calendar year. **historic infinitive** *n.* the infinitive of a verb used for the indicative. **historicism** (-sizm) *n.* 1 the theory that all political and social events are historically determined. 2 the theory that history is governed by laws. 3 emphasis on historical development. 4 undue regard for the past. **historicist** *n.* **historicity** (-ris´-) *n.* historical existence; the historical genuineness of an event. **historic present** *n.* the present tense used in a past sense. **historic tense** *n.* any of the tenses normally employed to express past events. [L *historicus*, Gr. *historikos*, see HISTORY]

Usage note The adjectives *historic* and *historical* should not be confused: *historic* is relatively limited in scope, and means celebrated in history, important, while *historical* is used of more general connections with history.

historiographer (histawriog´rɘfɘ) *n.* 1 a writer of history, esp. an official historian. 2 a student of the writing of history. **historiographic** (-ɘgraf´-), **historiographical** *a.* **historiography** *n.* [late L *historiographus*]

history (his´tɘri) *n.* (*pl.* **histories**) 1 a systematic record of past events, esp. those of public importance. 2 the study of past events in human affairs. 3 a study of or a book dealing with the past of any country, people, science, art etc. 4 past events, esp. regarded as material for such a study. 5 an eventful past, an interesting career. 6 a historical play, a story. 7 a record, e.g. of someone's past medical treatment. **to make history** 1 to do something momentous. 2 to influence the course of history. [L and Gr. *historia*, from *histōr*, knowing, cogn. with *id-*, *eidenai*, to know]

histrionic (histrion´ik) *a.* 1 of or relating to actors or acting. 2 (of behaviour) theatrical, stagey, affected, unreal. ~*n.* 1 (*in pl.*) an ostentatious display of usu. false emotion. 2 (*in pl.*) theatricals. 3 (*in pl.*) the art of theatrical representation. 4 †an actor. **histrion** (his´trion) *n.* (*usu. derog.*) a stage player. **histrionically** *adv.* **histrionicism** (-sizm), **histrionism** (his´-) *n.* 1 stage representation. 2 feigned representation. 3 histrionics. [F *histrion* or L *histrio -ōnem*, -IC]

hit (hit) *v.t.* (*pres.p.* **hitting**, *past*, *p.p.* **hit**) 1 to strike or touch with a blow or missile, esp. after taking aim. 2 to collide with. 3 to affect suddenly or adversely, to wound. 4 to attain to, to light upon, to arrive at; to guess. 5 (*esp. N Am., sl.*) to kill. 6 (*coll.*) to encounter, meet. 7 in various sports and games, to propel (a ball etc.) with a bat etc. to score runs, points etc. 8 to score (runs etc.) in this way. 9 to strike a ball delivered by (a bowler etc.). ~*v.i.* 1 to direct a blow or missile (at, against etc.). 2 to come into collision (against). 3 to agree, to suit, to fall in with. ~*n.* 1 a blow, a stroke; a collision. 2 a touch with the sword or stick in fencing. 3 a shot etc. that hits the intended target. 4 a lucky chance. 5 a felicitous expression or turn of thought. 6 a successful effort. 7 (*coll.*) a best-selling book, record etc. 8 a stroke of sarcasm, wit etc. 9 (*sl.*) an injection of a drug. 10 (*sl.*) a murder, a violent attack etc. **to hit a blot** BLOT². **to hit a nerve** NERVE. **to hit back** to retaliate. **to hit below the belt** BELT. **to hit for six** to defeat in argument. **to hit home** to bring about a desirable realization. **to hit it off together** to get along well (with), to agree. **to hit it off with** to get along well together, to agree. **to hit off** to represent or describe rapidly or cleverly. **to hit one between the eyes** EYE¹. **to hit one in the eye** EYE¹. **to hit on/ upon** 1 to light or chance on. 2 to discover by luck. **to hit out** to strike out straight from the shoulder. **to hit skins** (*esp. N Am., sl.*) to have sexual intercourse. **to hit the bottle** BOTTLE¹. **to hit the deck** DECK. **to hit the ground running** (*N Am., coll.*) to proceed in an enthusiastic way. **to hit the hay** HAY¹. **to hit the headlines** HEADLINE (under HEAD¹). **to hit the jackpot** JACKPOT (under JACK¹). **to hit the nail on the head** NAIL. **to hit the right note** NOTE. **to hit the road** ROAD¹. **to hit the roof** ROOF. **to hit the sack** SACK¹. **to hit the skids** SKID. **to hit the spot** SPOT. **to hit the trail** TRAIL. **to hit up** in cricket, to score (runs) freely or with vigour. **to make a hit (with)** to be a sudden success, to become popular. **to score a hit (with)** to be a sudden success, to become popular. **hit-and-miss** *a.* succeeding and failing in a haphazard way. **hit-and-run** *a.* 1 (of a driver) causing an accident and not stopping to help or report the incident. 2 (of an accident) involving a hit-and-run driver. **hitlist** *n.* (*coll.*) 1 a list of people to be killed, punished etc. 2 in business, commerce etc., a list of clients, companies etc. to be contacted. **hitman** *n.* (*pl.* **hitmen**) (*sl.*) a hired professional killer. **hit-or-miss** *a.* HIT-AND-MISS (under HIT). **hit-out** *n.* (*Austral., sl.*) a brisk gallop. **hit parade** *n.* a list of the currently most popular recordings of pop music. **hitter** *n.* **hit wicket** *n.* in cricket, a striking of the wicket with the bat, for which the batsman is dismissed. **hitwoman** *n.* (*pl.* **hitwomen**) (*sl.*) a female hired professional killer. [prob. from Scand. (cp. Icel. and Swed. *hitta*, Dan. *hitte*)]

hitch (hich) *v.t.* 1 to fasten with a hook or knot, esp. temporarily. 2 to pull up with a jerk. 3 to drag (in). 4 (*coll.*) to obtain (a lift) by hitch-hiking. ~*v.i.* 1 to move with jerks. 2 to become entangled or caught. 3 (*coll.*) to work pleasantly together. 4 to interfere (as horses). 5 (*coll.*) to hitch-hike. ~*n.* 1 an impediment, a temporary difficulty. 2 an abrupt pull or jerk up. 3 a catch, noose or knot. 4 the act of catching, as on a hook. 5 any of various types of knot by which a rope is bent to a spar or to another rope. 6 (*coll.*) a free ride in a vehicle. 7 (*N Am., sl.*) a period of service. **to get hitched** (*sl.*) to get married. **to hitch one's wagon to a star** to rely on powers higher than one's own. **to hitch up** to lift (esp. clothing) with a jerk. **hitcher** *n.* **hitch-hike** *v.i.* to travel by obtaining free lifts from passing motorists. ~*n.* a journey made in this way. **hitch-hiker** *n.* **hitch-hiking** *n.* [etym. uncertain]

hi-tech (hītek´) *a.* HIGH-TECH (under HIGH).

hither (hidh´ɘ) *adv.* (*usu. formal*) 1 to this place, end or point. 2 in this direction. ~*a.* 1 situated on this side. 2 the nearer (of two objects) to the speaker. **hither and thither** 1 to this place and that. 2 here and there. **hither and yon** 1 to this place and that. 2 here and there. **hitherto** (-too´) *adv.* up to this place, limit or time. †**hitherward** *adv.* in this direction. [OE *hider* (cp. Icel. *hēthra*, L *citrā*), from Gmc. base of HE, HERE etc.]

Hitler (hit´lə) *n.* a person resembling the Nazi dictator Adolf Hitler, 1889–1945. **Hitlerism** *n.* the ideology of National Socialism as propounded by Adolf Hitler. **Hitlerite** (-īt) *n.* a supporter of Hitler and of German National Socialism.

hitter HIT.

Hittite (hit´īt) *a.* of or relating to the Hittites, a people of uncertain origin inhabiting parts of Asia Minor and Syria before 1000 BC. ~*n.* the language of the Hittites. [Heb. *Hittīm*]

HIV *abbr.* human immunodeficiency virus, the retrovirus which causes Aids. **HIV-positive** *a.* carrying the virus.

hive (hīv) *n.* 1 an artificial structure for housing bees, a beehive. 2 the bees inhabiting a hive. 3 a place swarming with busy occupants. 4 †a kind of bonnet or other hive-shaped object. ~*v.t.* 1 to put into or secure in a hive. 2 to house as in a hive. 3 to store up for future use. ~*v.i.* 1 to enter or live in a hive. 2 to take shelter or swarm together, as bees do. **to hive off** 1 to assign part of a firm's work to a subsidiary company. 2 to transfer (assets) from one concern to another such as in privatization. 3 to separate from a larger group. **to hive up** to hoard. **hiveless** *a.* **hive of activity** *n.* a place showing signs of great industry. **hiver** *n.* a person who collects bees into hives. **hiveward** *adv.* [OE *hȳf* (cp. Dut. *huif*, Icel. *hūfr*, also L *cupa*, a tub)]

hives (hīvz) *n.pl.* 1 nettle-rash or a similar inflammation of the skin. 2 laryngitis. [etym. uncertain]

hiya (hī´yə) *int.* (*coll.*) used as a greeting. [20th cent., from *how are you?*]

HK *abbr.* 1 Hong Kong. 2 House of Keys (the Manx Parliament).

HL *abbr.* House of Lords.

hl *abbr.* hectolitre(s).

HM *abbr.* 1 His or Her Majesty. 2 headmaster. 3 headmistress. 4 (*Mus.*) heavy metal. 5 Home Mission.

HMC *abbr.* His or Her Majesty's Customs.

HMG *abbr.* His or Her Majesty's Government.

HMI *abbr.* His or Her Majesty's Inspector or Inspectorate (of schools).

HMS *abbr.* His or Her Majesty's Ship or Service.

HMSO *abbr.* His or Her Majesty's Stationery Office.

HMV *abbr.* His Master's Voice.

HNC *abbr.* Higher National Certificate.

HND *abbr.* Higher National Diploma.

Ho *chem. symbol* holmium.

ho (hō) *int.* 1 used to call attention, or to express exultation, surprise etc. 2 used by teamsters to stop their teams. **eastward ho!** used to announce or encourage eastward travel. **westward ho!** used to announce or encourage westward travel. **ho! ho!** *int.* expressing amusement, derision etc. [cp. Icel. *hō*, *hōa*]

ho. *abbr.* house.

hoactzin (hōak´tsin), **hoatzin** (-at´-) *n.* a S American bird, *Opisthocomus hoazin*, with a brownish plumage and a harsh hissing cry. [Nahuatl *uatzin*]

hoar (haw) *a.* 1 grey with age. 2 ancient. 3 white, grey or greyish-white. 4 white with foam. ~*n.* 1 hoariness. 2 antiquity. 3 hoar frost. **hoar frost** *n.* frozen dew, white frost. **hoar-headed** *a.* **hoarstone** *n.* a stone marking out the boundary of an estate. [OE *hār* (cp. Icel. *hārr*, also G *hehr*, august)]

hoard (hawd) *n.* 1 an accumulated store (often of valuables) hidden away for future use. 2 an accumulation of knowledge etc. ~*v.t.* to collect and put away, to store. ~*v.i.* to amass and store up anything of value. **hoarder** *n.* [OE *hord*, whence *hordian*, to hoard (cp. Icel. *hodd*, G *Hort*)]

Usage note The spellings of the nouns *hoard* (a stock or store) and *horde* (a large group) should not be confused.

hoarding (haw´ding) *n.* 1 a large screen for posting bills on. 2 a temporary screen of boards round or in front of a building where erections or repairs are in progress. [from OF *hourd*, *hurt*, scaffold, or Dut. *horde*, hurdle]

hoarhound HOREHOUND.

hoarily, hoariness HOARY.

hoarse (haws) *a.* 1 (of the voice) harsh, rough or husky. 2 having such a voice, as from a cold. **hoarsely** *adv.* **hoarsen** *v.t.*, *v.i.* **hoarseness** *n.* **hoarse-sounding** *a.* [ME *hors*, *hos*, OE *hās* (cp. Dan. *hæs*, G *heiser*)]

hoary (haw´ri) *a.* (*comp.* **hoarier**, *superl.* **hoariest**) 1 white or whitish-grey as with age. 2 white- or grey-headed. 3 of great antiquity, venerable. 4 old and trite (*a hoary joke*). 5 covered with very short dense hairs, which give an appearance of whiteness to the surface. 6 †mouldy, musty. **hoarily** *adv.* **hoariness** *n.* **hoary-headed** *a.* grey-headed. [HOAR]

hoast (hōst) *v.i.* (*Sc.*) to cough. ~*n.* a cough. [prob. from Icel. *hōsta* (cp. OE *hwōstan*)]

hoatzin HOACTZIN.

hoax (hōks) *n.* a deception meant as a practical joke. ~*v.t.* to play a practical joke upon, to take in for sport. **hoaxer** *n.* [prob. from HOCUS]

hob[1] (hob) *n.* 1 the flat top part of a cooking stove containing hotplates or burners. 2 the projecting side of a grate, or the top of this, on which things are placed to be kept warm. 3 a peg or iron pin used as a mark in quoits and other games. 4 a hardened, threaded spindle by which a comb or chasing tool may be cut. 5 the runner of a sledge. [perh. rel. to HUB]

hob[2] (hob) *n.* 1 a hobgoblin or an elf, a sprite. 2 a rustic. 3 a male ferret. **to play hob** (*N Am.*, *coll.*) to cause mischief. **to raise hob** (*N Am.*, *coll.*) to cause mischief. **hobbish** *a.* [var. of *Rob*, short for ROBIN, *Robert*]

Hobbesian (hob´ziən) *a.* of or relating to the philosopher Hobbes or his political philosophy. **Hobbism** *n.* the system of philosophy contained in or deduced from the writings of Hobbes, esp. his teachings with regard to absolute monarchy. [Thomas *Hobbes*, 1588–1679, English philosopher]

hobbish HOB[2].

Hobbism HOBBESIAN.

hobbit (hob´it) *n.* a member of a fictional race of small people living in holes. [coined by J. R. R. Tolkien, 1892–1973, British writer]

hobble (hob´əl) *v.i.* 1 to walk lamely or awkwardly. 2 to move in a halting or irregular way. ~*v.t.* 1 to cause (a person etc.) to hobble. 2 to tie the legs of (horses etc.) to prevent straying. 3 to perplex. ~*n.* 1 a rope, shackle, clog etc. for hobbling an animal. 2 an awkward, uneven or limping gait. 3 (*dial.*) a difficulty, a perplexity. **hobbler** *n.* 1 a person who hobbles. 2 an unlicensed boatman or river pilot. 3 a casual dock labourer. **hobble skirt** *n.* a skirt fitting so closely round the legs and ankles that it impedes walking. **hobblingly** *adv.* [cp. Dut. *hobbelen*, to toss or rock about, to stammer]

†**hobbledehoy** (hob´əldihoi) *n.* (*dial.*) a clumsy, awkward youth. **hobbledehoyhood** (-hud), **hobbledehoyism** *n.* **hobbledehoyish** *a.* [etym. uncertain]

hobby[1] (hob´i) *n.* (*pl.* **hobbies**) 1 any recreation or pursuit. 2 a hobbyhorse. 3 †an early form of bicycle without pedals. 4 †a strong, active, middle-sized horse. **hobbyhorse** *n.* 1 a child's simple toy of a horse's head on a stick. 2 a preoccupation, a favourite subject of conversation. 3 a simple figure or model imitating a horse used in morris dances, pantomime etc. 4 a horse on a merry-go-round. 5 a rocking horse. 6 †a buffoon. **hobbyism** *n.* **hobbyist** *n.* **hobbyless** *a.* [OF *hobin*, perh. var. of ROBIN]

hobby[2] (hob´i) *n.* (*pl.* **hobbies**) a small species of falcon, *Falco subbuteo.* [OF *hobet*, prob. from *hober*, to move about (cp. Dut. *hobbelen*, see HOBBLE)]

hobday (hob´dā) *v.t.* to perform a surgical operation on (a horse) to improve breathing. [F. T. *Hobday*, 1869–1939, English veterinary surgeon]

hobgoblin (hobgob´lin) *n.* a kind of goblin, elf or fairy, esp. one of a frightful appearance.

hobnail (hob´nāl) *n.* **1** a short thick nail with a large head, used for heavy boots. **2** a clown, a clodhopper. ~*v.t.* **1** to set or stud (boots) with hobnails. **2** to trample. **hobnailed** *a.* **1** set with hobnails. **2** (of the liver) rough and uneven, as if studded with hobnails, due to cirrhosis. **hobnail liver** *n.* a hobnailed liver.

hobnob (hob´nob) *v.i.* (*pres.p.* **hobnobbing**, *past, p.p.* **hobnobbed**) **1** to associate familiarly (with). **2** to drink familiarly. [earlier *hab nab* (OE *habban*, to HAVE, *nabban*, not to have)]

hobo (hō´bō) *n.* (*pl.* **hobos, hoboes**) (*esp. N Am.*) a wandering worker, vagrant or tramp. [etym. unknown]

Hobson-Jobson (hobsənjob´sən) *n.* the practice of assimilating foreign words and modifying them to approximate to familiar sounds in the native language. [Anglo-Indian approximation to Arab. *Yā Hasan Yā Hosain*, a lament for the grandsons of Muhammad]

Hobson's choice (hobsənz chois´) *n.* no alternative. [*Hobson*, a Cambridge livery-stable keeper who insisted on every customer's taking the first horse inside the stable door or none at all]

hock[1] (hok), **hough** *n.* **1** the joint between the knee and the fetlock in the hind leg of quadrupeds. **2** the lower joint of ham or pork. **3** (*Sc.*) the posterior part of the knee joint in humans. ~*v.t.* to hamstring. [OE, *hoh*, cogn. with HEEL[1]]

hock[2] (hok) *n.* **1** a kind of light wine, still or sparkling, made at Hochheim in Nassau. **2** any white wine of the Rhine region. [formerly *hockamore*, G *Hochheimer*]

hock[3] (hok) *v.t.* (*N Am., sl.*) to pawn. ~*n.* **1** the state of being pawned or pledged. **2** prison. **in hock** in pawn, debt or prison.

hockey[1] (hok´i) *n.* **1** a team ball game played with a club having a curved end. **2** (*N Am.*) ICE HOCKEY (under ICE). [perh. conn. with F *hoquet*, a crook, or with HOOK]

hockey[2] (hok´i) *n.* (*dial.*) harvest home, or the feast celebrating this. [etym. unknown]

hockey[3] OCHE.

Hocktide (hok´tīd) *n.* a festival held on the second Monday and Tuesday after Easter. [etym. uncertain]

hocus (hō´kəs) *v.t.* (*3rd pers. sing. pres.* **hocusses,** (*N Am. also*) **hocuses,** *pres.p.* **hocussing,** (*N Am. also*) **hocusing,** *past, p.p.* **hocussed,** (*N Am. also*) **hocused**) **1** to take in, to hoax. **2** to stupefy (a person) with drugs. **3** to put a drug into (liquor). **hocus-pocus** (-pō´kəs) *n.* **1** trickery, fraud. **2** an expression used by jugglers in playing tricks. **3** jargon, mumbo-jumbo. **4** a juggler's trick, a fraud, a hoax. ~*v.i.* (*3rd pers. sing. pres.* **hocus-pocusses,** (*N Am. also*) **hocus-pocuses,** *pres.p.* **hocus-pocussing,** (*N Am. also*) **hocus-pocusing,** *past, p.p.* **hocus-pocussed,** (*N Am. also*) **hocus-pocused**) to juggle, to conjure. ~*v.t.* to cheat, to trick. [from the mock L *hocus pocus*]

hod (hod) *n.* **1** a wooden holder shaped like a trough and fixed on a long handle, for carrying mortar or bricks on the shoulder. **2** a coal scuttle. **hod-carrier, hodman** *n.* (*pl.* **hod-carriers, hodmen**) **1** a labourer who carries a hod for bricklayers etc. **2** a drudge, a hack. [prob. from obs. *hot*, OF *hotte*, from Gmc. (cp. MDut. *hodde*, G *Hotte*)]

hodden (hod´ən) *n.* (*Sc.*) a coarse woollen cloth such as would be produced by a handloom. ~*a.* **1** attired in this. **2** plain, homely. **hodden grey** *n.* grey hodden manufactured from undyed wool. [etym. uncertain]

Hodge (hoj) *n.* a typical member of the agricultural labouring class. [corr. of ROGER]

hodgepodge (hoj´poj) *n.* **1** a dish of mixed ingredients. **2** a mixture or medley; a confused jumble. [HOTCHPOTCH]

Hodgkin's disease (hoj´kinz) *n.* a malignant disease characterized by progressive anaemia and enlargement of the liver, lymph glands etc. [Thomas *Hodgkin*, 1798–1866, English physician]

hodiernal (hōdiœ´nəl) *a.* (*formal*) of or relating to the present day. [L *hodiernus*, from *hodiē*, today]

hodograph (hod´əgrahf) *n.* the curve traced by the end of lines, drawn from a fixed point, representing in magnitude and direction the velocity of a moving point. **hodographic** (-graf´-) *a.* **hodographically** *adv.* [Gr. *hodos*, way, -GRAPH]

hodometer ODOMETER.

hodoscope (hod´əskōp) *n.* any device for tracing the path of a charged particle. [Gr. *hodos*, way]

hoe (hō) *n.* a tool used to scrape or stir up earth around plants, cut weeds up from the ground etc. ~*v.t.* (*3rd pers. sing. pres.* **hoes,** *pres.p.* **hoeing,** *past, p.p.* **hoed**) to scrape or loosen (ground), cut (weeds), or dig (up) with a hoe. ~*v.i.* to use a hoe. **to hoe in** (*Austral., New Zeal., sl.*) to eat heartily. **to hoe into** (*Austral., New Zeal., sl.*) to attack vigorously. **hoe-cake** *n.* (*N Am.*) a maize cake, orig. cooked on a hoe. **hoedown** *n.* (*esp. N Am.*) **1** a type of energetic folk dance. **2** music for this. **3** a lively social gathering for dancing the hoedown. **hoer** *n.* [F *houe*, OHG *houwa*, to HEW]

hog (hog) *n.* **1** a swine, esp. a castrated boar meant for killing. **2** (*N Am.*) any kind of pig. **3** (*dial. also* **hogg**) a young sheep or bullock, usu. a year old. **4 a** a dirty, filthy or low person. **b** (*sl.*) a greedy person. **5** a scrub broom for cleaning a ship's bottom under water. **6** in curling, a stone that fails to pass the hog-score. ~*v.t.* (*pres.p.* **hogging,** *past, p.p.* **hogged**) **1** (*sl.*) to keep greedily to oneself. **2** to cut short like the bristles of a hog. **3** to cause (a ship, keel etc.) to rise in the middle and droop at the ends. **4** to clean (a ship's bottom) under water by scraping. ~*v.i.* **1** to droop at both ends. **2** (of animals) to carry the head down and back up. **to go the whole hog** (*coll.*) to do a job completely, making no compromise or reservations. **hogback, hog's back** *n.* **1** a long ridged hill. **2** (*Geol.*) a monocline. **3** an esker. **hog-backed** *a.* **hog cholera** *n.* swine fever. **hogfish** *n.* (*pl. in general* **hogfish,** *in particular* **hogfishes**) any of various wrasses, esp. *Lachnolaimus maximus.* **hoggish** *a.* **1** having the qualities or manners of a hog. **2** brutish, gluttonous, filthy, selfish. **hoggishly** *adv.* **hoggishness** *n.* **hoglike** *a.* **hogmane** *n.* a horse's mane cut so as to stand erect. **hogpen** *n.* a pigsty. **hog-plum** *n.* any of several species of W Indian trees and their fruit, which is used for feeding hogs. **hog's back** HOGBACK (under HOG). **hog-score** *n.* in curling, a line drawn across the rink which a stone must pass in order to count. **hogskin** *n.* tanned pig's skin. **hog's lard** *n.* the rendered fat of the hog. **hog's pudding** *n.* a pudding of various ingredients stuffed like a sausage into a hog's entrail. **hogtie** *v.t.* (*3rd pers. sing. pres.* **hogties,** *pres.p.* **hogtying,** *past, p.p.* **hogtied**) (*N Am.*) **1** to tie the feet of (an animal or person). **2** to make helpless. **hogwash** *n.* **1** the refuse of a kitchen or brewery, used for feeding hogs. **2** (*sl.*) bad liquor. **3** (*sl.*) anything worthless. **hogweed** *n.* any of numerous coarse plants, esp. the cow parsnip. [etym. uncertain]

hogget (hog´it) *n.* **1** (*esp. Austral., New Zeal.*) a yearling sheep. **2** (*dial.*) a year-old colt. **hoggerel** (-ərəl) *n.* (*dial.*) a sheep in its second year.

hoggin (hog´in), **hoggins** (-inz) *n.* screened gravel for footpaths. [etym. uncertain]

hoggish HOG.

hogmanay (hogmənā´) *n.* **1** in Scotland, the last day of the year, New Year's Eve. **2** an entertainment or a present given on that day. [perh. from OF *aguillan neuf*, the last day of the year, from the shout with which new year's gifts were given and asked (cp. Norman *hoguinané*)]

hogshead (hogz´hed) *n.* **1** a large cask. **2** a measure of capacity containing about 52 imperial gal. (238.7 l). **3** a butt. [HOG, HEAD[1] (reason unknown)]

ho-hum (hōhŭm´) *int.* used to express a feeling of tedium, lack of interest, resignation etc.

hoick (hoik) *v.t.* **1** (*coll.*) to pull up or out of something, esp. abruptly. **2** to force (an aeroplane) upwards.

hoicks YOICKS.

hoiden HOYDEN.

hoi polloi (hoi pəloi´) *n.* (*often derog.*) **1** the common herd, the masses. **2** the majority. [Gr., the many]

hoist (hoist) *v.t.* **1** to raise up. **2** to lift by means of tackle. **3** a sail or flag. *~n.* **1** the act of lifting or hoisting up. **2** an apparatus for hoisting or raising. **3** a lift or elevator. **4** (*Naut.*) the vertical height of a yard, sail or flag. **hoist with/ by one's own petard** PETARD. **to hoist one's flag** to signify that one is taking command. **to hoist the flag** to stake one's claim to discovered territory by displaying a flag. **hoister** *n.* [formerly *hysse*, perh. from MDut. *hyssen* (cp. Icel. *hisa*, Swed. and Norw. *hissa*, G *hissen*)]

hoity-toity (hoititoi´ti) *int.* used to express astonishment mixed with disapproval and contempt. *~a.* **1** haughty and petulant. **2** snobbish. **3** †flighty, frolicsome. *~n.* †a romp, a frolic, a rumpus. [prob. from obs. *hoit*, to romp]

hokey (hō´ki), **hoky** *a.* (*comp.* **hokier**, *superl.* **hokiest**) (*N Am., sl.*) sentimental, corny or phoney. **hokeyness, hokiness** *n.* [from HOKUM, -Y[1]]

hokey-cokey (hōkikō´ki) *n.* a dance in which a group forms a circle and moves and shakes arms and legs in accordance with the song to which it is danced. [refrain of a song, perh. from HOCUS-POCUS (under HOCUS)]

hokey-pokey (hōkipō´ki) *n.* (*coll.*) **1** ice cream formerly sold by street vendors. **2** trickery, fraud. [corr. of HOCUS-POCUS (under HOCUS)]

hoki (hō´ki) *n.* an edible fish of New Zealand coasts, *Macruronus novaezelandiae*, related to the hake. [Maori]

hokku (hok´oo) *n.* (*pl.* **hokku**) HAIKU. [Jap.]

hokum (hō´kəm) *n.* (*esp. N Am., coll., sl.*) **1** bunkum. **2** foolish stage or book plotting. **3** counterfeit culture. [*ho*cus-pocus, bun*kum*]

hoky HOKEY.

hol- HOLO-.

Holarctic (hōlahk´tik), **holarctic** *a.* of or relating to the entire northern region of the globe. *~n.* the Holarctic region. [HOL-, ARCTIC]

hold[1] (hōld) *v.t.* (*past, p.p.* **held** (held), *p.p.* †**holden**) **1** to grasp and retain. **2** to keep in, to confine. **3** to enclose, to contain. **4** to be able to contain, to keep from running or flowing out. **5** to set aside or reserve (tickets etc.). **6** to keep back, to restrain. **7** to keep in a certain manner or position. **8** to retain possession or control of. **9** to occupy, to possess (a house, qualifications etc.). **10** to regard, to believe (*He holds that the theory is correct*). **11** to maintain (that). **12** to judge, to lay down or decide; to assert (that). **13** to carry on (a meeting etc.). **14** to celebrate, to conduct (a festival, meeting etc.). **15** to use, to employ (a language etc.). **16** (*coll.*) to wager, to accept as a bet or wager. **17** (*Comput.*) to retain (data) in a storage device after copying it into another storage device. **18** (*Mus.*) to sustain (a note). *~v.i.* **1** to maintain a grasp or attachment. **2** to continue firm, not to break. **3** to adhere (to). **4** (of weather) to remain dry and bright. **5** to keep the attention of (an audience etc.). **6** to maintain a course. **7** to be valid or true, to stand. **8** to be fit or consistent. **9** (*usu. in imper.*) to stop, to stay, to refrain. **hold everything!** stop doing anything! **hold hard!** (*coll.*) stop! **hold it!** stop! **hold your jaw** JAW. **to hold a brief for** BRIEF. **to hold aloof** to avoid communication with others. **to hold a pistol to someone's head** PISTOL. **to hold (a thing) against someone** to be resentful towards another because of (a past action etc.), to regard (something) as discreditable to them. **to hold a wager** to bet. **to hold back 1** to restrain, to prevent (something or someone) from progressing. **2** to retain in one's possession. **3** to keep oneself in check. **to hold by** to hold to, to adhere to. **to hold cheap** not to value highly. **to hold court** to preside over one's admirers, entertaining or conversing etc. **to hold dear** to regard with affection. **to hold down 1** to repress, to restrain. **2** (*coll.*) to be good enough at (one's job etc.) to retain it. **to hold forth 1** to stretch or put forward. **2** to speak in public or for a long time. **3** to propose, to offer. **to hold from** to derive title from. **to hold good 1** to remain valid. **2** to apply, to be relevant. **to hold hands** HAND. **to hold harmless** (*Law*) to indemnify. **to hold in 1** to restrain, to restrain oneself. **2** to keep quiet, to keep silent. **to hold in esteem** to regard with esteem. **to hold it good** to think it sensible (to do). **to hold of** to derive title from. **to hold off 1** to keep (someone or something) at a distance. **2** to remain at a distance. **3** to delay. **4** to refrain from. **to hold on 1** to continue without interruption, to persist. **2** (*coll.*) to stop. **3** to wait a moment. **4** not to end a telephone connection. **to hold one's breath** BREATH. **to hold one's ground** not to yield or give way. **to hold one's head (high)** to behave proudly or arrogantly; to retain one's dignity. **to hold one's horses** HORSE. **to hold one's nose** to pinch one's nostrils so as not to be able to smell, inhale water etc. **to hold one's own** to maintain one's position. **to hold one's peace** PEACE. **to hold one's tongue** TONGUE. **to hold on one's way** to keep going steadily. **to hold out 1** to hold forward, to stretch out. **2** to offer. **3** to bear, to endure, not to yield. **4** to persist, to last. **to hold out for** to continue demanding in spite of alternative offers. **to hold out on** (*coll.*) to refuse or delay in telling etc. something to (a person). **to hold over 1** to keep back or reserve, to defer. **2** (*Law*) to keep possession of after the expiration of one's term. **3** to threaten (someone) with. **to hold someone's hand** HAND. **to hold the baby** BABY. **to hold the balance** BALANCE. **to hold the clock on** to be responsible for timing (a race etc.). **to hold the fort** to cope temporarily. **to hold the line 1** not to give in. **2** not to end a telephone connection. **to hold to 1** to bind to (bail, one's statement etc.). **2** to adhere to. **to hold to a draw** to draw with (an opponent), esp. against expectation. **to hold together 1** to cohere or cause to cohere. **2** to continue united. **to hold to ransom** RANSOM. **to hold true 1** to remain valid. **2** to apply, to be relevant. **to hold under** to derive title from. **to hold up 1** to raise or lift up. **2** to support, to encourage. **3** to sustain. **4** to show forth, to exhibit (to ridicule etc.). **5** to stop and rob by violence or threats. **6** to arrest the progress of, to obstruct. **7** (of the weather) to remain fine. **8** to continue at the same speed. **to hold water** WATER. **to hold with** to approve of, to side with. **holdable** *a.* **holdall** *n.* a bag or case for carrying clothes etc. **holdback** *n.* a restraint, a check, a hindrance. **holder** (hōl´də) *n.* **1** a device or implement for holding something. **2** a tenant, occupier or owner. **3** a person who holds a title etc. **4** the payee of a bill of exchange or promissory note. **5** a smallholder. **holdfast** *n.* **1** a means by which something is clamped to another. **2** any device used to secure an object. **3** the organ of attachment of a seaweed or related plant. **holdout** *n.* **1** an act of holding out against something. **2** a refusal to take part in some activity. **3** a person who does this. **hold-over** *n.* (*N Am.*) a relic. **hold-up** *n.* **1** a robbery, esp. an armed one. 2 a delay, stoppage. 3 (*N Am.*) an excessive charge, extortion. 4 either of a pair of stockings held up by elasticated tops. [OE *healdan, halden* (cp. MLG *holden*, Icel. *halda*, G *halten*)]

hold[2] (hōld) *n.* 1 the act of seizing or grasping in the hands. 2 a grasp, a clutch. 3 mental grasp. 4 a support, anything to hold by or support oneself by. 5 moral influence. 6 custody, possession. 7 a manner of seizing or grasping an opponent in wrestling etc. 8 a refuge, a fortified place. **no holds barred** observing no rules. **on hold** 1 (of a telephone call or caller) waiting to be connected. 2 deferred until later. **to get hold of** 1 to grasp. 2 to get in contact with. **to take hold** 1 to take a grip (of). 2 to become established. **to take hold of** to seize. [from HOLD[1]]

hold[3] (hōld) *n.* a cavity in the lower part of a ship or aircraft, in which the cargo is stowed. [HOLE]

holding (hōl'ding) *n.* 1 tenure or occupation. 2 that which is held, esp. land, property, stocks or shares. **holding company** *n.* a company formed to acquire the majority of shares in one or more subsidiary companies. **holding operation** *n.* a manoeuvre designed to maintain things as they are. **holding pattern** *n.* 1 the course an aircraft takes while waiting to land. 2 a state or period of no change.

hole (hōl) *n.* 1 a hollow place or cavity. 2 an aperture, an orifice, a perforation. 3 a wild animal's burrow. 4 a small pit or hollow into which the ball has to be driven in various games. 5 in golf, one of the points made by the player who drives the ball from one hole to another with the fewest strokes; the distance between the tee and a hole. 6 (*coll.*) an awkward situation. 7 (*coll.*) a dingy, disreputable place. 8 a vacancy due to absence of an electron, esp. one acting as a mobile positive particle in a semiconductor. ~*v.t.* 1 to make a hole or holes in. 2 to tunnel. 3 to put or drive into a hole. 4 to pierce the side of (a ship). 5 to undercut a coal-seam. ~*v.i.* 1 to go into a hole. 2 to hibernate. 3 in golf, to send one's ball into a hole. **in holes** (of materials etc.) worn so much that holes have formed. **to hole out** 1 in golf, to play the ball into the hole. 2 (of a batsman in cricket) to be caught out. **to hole up** (*N Am., coll.*) to go into hiding. **to make a hole in** to take or consume a large part of. **to pick a hole in** to pick holes in. **to pick holes in** to find fault with. **hole-and-corner** *a.* secret, clandestine. **hole-in-one** *n.* (*pl.* **holes-in-one**) (in golf) a shot entering the hole from the tee. **hole in the heart** *n.* a defect of the heart where there is an abnormal opening in any of the walls dividing the four chambers of the heart. **hole-in-the-wall** *n.* (*coll.*) 1 a small dingy place, esp. one that is hard to find. 2 an automatic cash dispenser situated in the outside wall of a bank etc. **hole-proof** *a.* (of materials etc.) resistant to wear. **holey** *a.* **holing-axe** *n.* a tool for cutting holes in posts. **holing-pick** *n.* a pick for undercutting coal. [OE *hol* (cp. Dut. and Icel. *hol*)]

holiday (hol'idā) *n.* 1 (*often in pl.*) a period away from work, school or one's usual duties; an extended period spent away from home for recreation. 2 a day of exemption from work by law or custom (a religious festival, bank holiday etc.). ~*a.* of or relating to a holiday (*holiday money*). ~*v.i.* to spend a holiday. **on holiday** 1 having a break from work. 2 during one's holidays. **on one's holidays** 1 during one's holidays. 2 having a break from work. †**to make a holiday** to have a break from work. **to take a holiday** to have a break from work. **holiday camp** *n.* an enclosed area with accommodation, entertainment facilities etc. for holidaymakers. **holiday centre,** (*N Am.*) **holiday center** *n.* a place or resort with many tourist attractions. **holidaymaker** *n.* a person taking a holiday away from home. **holiday village** *n.* a modern holiday camp. [OE *hæligdæg*, holy day]

holier-than-thou, holily etc. HOLY.

holism (hō'lizm), **wholism** *n.* 1 (*Philos.*) the tendency in nature to evolve wholes that are more than the sum of the parts. 2 (*Med.*) the treating of the whole person including mental factors etc. rather than just the symptoms of a disease. **holist** *a., n.* **holistic** (-is'-) *a.* **holistically** *adv.* [HOL-, -ISM]

holla (hol'ə) *int.* used to call attention. ~*n.* a call of 'holla!'. ~*v.i.* (*3rd pers. sing. pres.* **hollas,** *pres.p.* **hollaing,** *past, p.p.* **hollaed, holla'd**) to shout to call attention. ~*v.t.* to call to (hounds). [F *holà* (HO, *là*, there)]

holland (hol'ənd) *n.* coarse unbleached linen with a glazed surface, first made in Holland.

hollandaise sauce (holəndāz') *n.* a sauce made with butter, egg yolk and lemon juice etc. often served with fish. [F]

Hollander (hol'əndə) *n.* 1 a native of Holland. 2 a Dutch ship. **Hollandish** *a.* †**Hollands** *n.* Dutch gin, genever.

holler (hol'ə) *v.i.* (*esp. N Am., coll.*) to shout loudly, to cry out. ~*v.t.* to communicate in a shout. ~*n.* a loud shout or cry. [var. of HOLLO]

hollo (hol'ō), **holloa** (həlō') *int.* used to call attention. ~*n.* (*pl.* **hollos, holloas**) a call of 'hollo!'. ~*v.i.* (*also* **hollow**) (*3rd pers. sing. pres.* **holloes, holloas, hollows,** *pres.p.* **holloing, holloaing, hollowing,** *past, p.p.* **holloed, holloaed, holloa'd, hollowed**) to shout to call attention. ~*v.t.* to call to (hounds). [cp. HOLLA]

hollow[1] (hol'ō) *a.* 1 containing a cavity or empty space. 2 not solid. 3 excavated, sunken, concave. 4 empty, vacant. 5 without significance, meaningless. 6 (of sounds) deep, low. 7 insincere, not genuine. ~*n.* 1 a depression or unoccupied space. 2 a cavity, a hole, a basin. 3 a valley. ~*v.t.* to make hollow, to excavate. **in the hollow of one's hand** in a state of subservience to one. **to beat hollow** BEAT. **hollow-back** *n.* LORDOSIS. **hollow-cheeked** *a.* with sunken cheeks. **hollow-eyed** *a.* having sunken eyes. **hollow-hearted** *a.* insincere, false. **hollowly** *adv.* **hollowness** *n.* **hollow square** *n.* a body of troops drawn up in the form of a square with a vacant space in the middle. **hollowware** *n.* hollow vessels, such as pots, kettles etc. made of metal, china etc. [ME *holwe*, OE *holge*, dat. of *holh*, prob. a form of *hol*, HOLE]

hollow[2] HOLLO.

holly (hol'i) *n.* (*pl.* **hollies**) 1 a shrub or tree of the genus *Ilex*, esp. *I. aquifolium*, a tree with glossy, prickly leaves and scarlet or, more rarely, yellow berries. 2 branches of these trees used as Christmas decorations. **holly oak** *n.* HOLM[2]. [OE *holen* (cp. Dut. and G *Hulst*)]

hollyhock (hol'ihok) *n.* a tall garden plant, *Althaea rosea*, with red, pink and yellow flowers. [ME *holihoc* (*holi*, HOLY, *hoc*, mallow)]

Hollywood (hol'iwud) *n.* the films, styles and practices of the big US cinema studios. [*Hollywood*, a suburb of Los Angeles, where the studios are located]

holm[1] (hōm), **holme** *n.* 1 flat ground, liable to flooding, along the side of a river. 2 an island in a river or estuary. [Icel. *hōlmr*, perh. cogn. with OE *holm*, sea, and L *culmen*, mountain top]

holm[2] (hōm), **holm-oak** *n.* an evergreen oak, *Quercus ilex*. [corr. of OE *holen*, HOLLY]

holme HOLM[1].

holmium (hōl'miəm) *n.* a metallic element of the rare-earth group, chem. symbol Ho, at. no. 67. [L *Holmia*, Stockholm]

holo- (hol'ō), **hol-** *comb. form* complete or completely. [Gr. *holos*, whole]

holoblastic (holōblas'tik) *a.* (of an ovum) undergoing segmentation throughout. [Gr. *blastos*, shoot, bud]

holocaust (hol'əkawst) *n.* 1 a wholesale sacrifice of life, or general destruction, esp. by fire or nuclear weapons. 2 (**the Holocaust**) the wholesale slaughter of Jews in Europe by the Nazis in the 1940s. 3 a sacrifice entirely consumed by fire. **holocaustal** *a.* **holocaustic** *a.* [F *holocauste*, L *holocaustum*, Gr. *holokauston* (HOLO-, *kaiein* fut. *kausō*, to burn)]

Holocene (hol´əsēn) *n.* the most recent period of geological time. ~*a.* of or concerning this period. [HOLO-, Gr. *kainos*, new]

holocryptic (holəkrip´tik) *a.* wholly secret, unintelligible, or undecipherable. [CRYPTIC]

holoenzyme (holōen´zīm) *n.* the active complex of an enzyme and its coenzyme.

hologram (hol´əgram) *n.* **1** (a photographic reproduction of) a pattern produced by the interference between a beam of coherent light (e.g. from a laser) and a direct beam of such light reflected off an object. **2** a three-dimensional image produced by illuminating such a reproduction.

holograph (hol´əgrahf) *a.* wholly in the handwriting of the author or signatory. ~*n.* a document, letter etc. so written. **holographic** (-graf´-) *a.* **holographically** *adv.* **holography** (-log´rə-) *n.* the technique of making or using a hologram. [late L *holographus*, Gr. *-phos* (*graphein*, to write)]

holohedral (holəhē´drəl) *a.* (of crystals) having the full possible number of planes symmetrically arranged. **holohedrism** *n.* **holohedron** (-drən) *n.* [Gr. *hedra*, seat, base]

holometabolism (holōmitab´əlizm) *n.* complete metamorphosis (in insects). **holometabolic** (-metəbol´-), **holometabolous** *a.*

holomorphic (holəmaw´fik) *a.* **1** (*Math.*) having the properties of an entire function, being finite, continuous and one-valued for all finite values of the variable. **2** (of crystals) holohedral. [Gr. *morphē*, shape]

holophotal (holəfō´təl) *a.* utilizing the whole of the available light (applied to the illuminating apparatus in lighthouses). **holophote** (hol´-) *n.* a holophotal apparatus. [Gr. *phōs phōtos*, light]

holophrasis (holof´rəsis) *n.* the expression of a whole sentence in a single word. **holophrase** (hol´əfrāz), **holophrasm** (-frazm) *n.* **holophrastic** (-əfras´-) *a.* [Gr. *phrasis*, see PHRASE]

holophyte (hol´əfīt) *n.* a plant that obtains food like a green plant, esp. by photosynthesis. **holophytic** (-fit´-) *a.*

holothurian (holəthū´riən) *a.* belonging to the Holothuroidea, a class of echinoderms comprising the sea slugs. ~*n.* an animal of this class. [mod. L *holothūria*, Gr. *holothouria*, pl. of *-rion*, zoophytes]

holotype (hol´ətīp) *n.* the original specimen from which a new species is derived or described.

†**holp**, †**holpen** HELP.

hols (holz) *n.pl.* (*coll.*) holidays.

Holstein (hol´stīn) *n., a.* (*N Am.*) FRIESIAN. [region of Germany]

holster (hōl´stə) *n.* a leather case, usu. on a belt or attached to a saddle bow, to hold a pistol or revolver. **holstered** *a.* [Dut. (cp. Icel. *hulstr*, case, OE *heolstor*, a hiding place, a covering)]

†**holt**[1] (hōlt) *n.* **1** a wood, a grove, a copse. **2** a wooded hill. [OE (cp. Dut. *hout*, timbers, Icel. *holt*, a copse, G *Holz*)]

holt[2] (hōlt) *n.* **1** the burrow of an animal, esp. an otter. **2** a covert, a shelter. **3** †a hold, grasp. [prob. corr. of HOLD[1]]

holus-bolus (hōləsbō´ləs) *adv.* all at once, at one gulp. [mock L, from WHOLE (cp. HOCUS-POCUS (under HOCUS))]

holy (hō´li) *a.* (*comp.* **holier**, *superl.* **holiest**) **1** of high spiritual excellence. **2** associated with God or a deity. **3** sacred, consecrated. **4** morally pure, free from sin. **5** used in mild or trivial exclamations (*holy cow!*; *holy smoke!*). **holier-than-thou** *a.* (*coll.*) convinced of one's moral superiority, sanctimonious. **holily** *adv.* **holiness** *n.* **1** the state of being holy, sanctity. **2** moral purity or integrity. **3** the state of being consecrated to God. **4** that which is so consecrated. **His Holiness** a title of the Pope, given formerly to the Greek emperors and other sacred and ecclesiastical dignitaries. **Holy City** *n.* **1** any city regarded as especially sacred by a particular religion, esp. Jerusalem (*the Holy City*). **2** Heaven. **Holy Communion** *n.* the administration of the Eucharist. **Holy Cross** *n.* the cross on which Christ was put to death. **Holy Cross Day** *n.* the festival of the Exaltation of the Cross, 14 Sept. **holy day** *n.* **1** a day commemorating some religious event. **2** †a holiday. **Holy Family** *n.* the infant Jesus with Joseph and Mary. **Holy Father** *n.* the Pope. **Holy Ghost** *n.* (*Theol.*) the third person of the Trinity. **Holy Grail** *n.* GRAIL. **Holy Innocents' Day** *n.* INNOCENTS' DAY (under INNOCENT). **holy Joe** *n.* (*coll.*) **1** a member of the clergy. **2** a self-righteous or pious person. **Holy Land** *n.* **1** Palestine. **2** a region that is revered in non-Christian religions. **Holy Name** *n.* in the Roman Catholic Church, the name of Jesus as an object of formal devotion. **Holy Office** *n.* the Inquisition. **holy of holies** *n.* **1** the innermost and most sacred apartment of the Jewish Tabernacle and the Temple, where the ark was kept. **2** an innermost shrine. **3** something regarded as most sacred. **holy orders** *n.pl.* **1** the different ranks of the Christian ministry. **2** the clerical office. **holy place** *n.* **1** (*in pl.*) places to which religious pilgrimages are undertaken. **2** the outer chamber of the sanctuary in the Jewish Temple. **holy roller** *n.* (*derog.*) a member of a sect that expresses religious fervour in an ecstatic or frenzied way. **Holy Roman Empire** *n.* (*Hist.*) the empire established by Augustus, 27 BC, divided in AD 395 into the Western (or Latin) and Eastern (or Greek) Empires. **holy rood** *n.* a cross or crucifix, esp. one on the rood-beam in churches. **Holy Rood Day** *n.* **1** the festival of the Invention of the Cross, 3 May. **2** HOLY CROSS DAY (under HOLY). **Holy Sacrament** *n.* **1** the Eucharist. **2** the consecrated elements of the Eucharist, esp. the bread. **Holy Saturday** *n.* the Saturday before Easter. **Holy Scripture** *n.* the Bible. **Holy See** *n.* the bishopric of Rome, the Pope's see. **Holy Sepulchre** *n.* the tomb in which Christ's body was laid after the Crucifixion. **Holy Spirit** *n.* the third person of the Trinity. **holy terror** *n.* (*coll.*) **1** a formidable person, a troublesome person or thing. **2** the use of organized intimidation. **Holy Thursday** *n.* **1** (in the Anglican Church) Ascension Day. **2** (in the Roman Catholic Church) Maundy Thursday, the Thursday in Holy Week. **Holy Trinity** *n.* the union of three persons (the Father, the Son, and the Holy Ghost) in one godhead. **holy war** *n.* a war waged on behalf of a religion. **holy water** *n.* water blessed by a priest or used for holy purposes. **Holy Week** *n.* the week from Palm Sunday to Holy Saturday inclusive. **holy well** *n.* a well reputed to be invested with miraculous qualities. **Holy Willie** *n.* a hypocritically pious person. **Holy Writ** *n.* sacred scriptures, esp. the Bible. **Holy Year** *n.* in the Roman Catholic Church, a period of remission from sin, esp. one granted every 25 years. [OE *hālig* (cp. Dut. and G *heilig*, Icel. *heilagr*)]

holystone (hō´listōn) *n.* a soft sandstone used for scrubbing the decks of vessels. ~*v.t.* to scrub with this.

hom (hōm), **homa** (hō´mə) *n.* **1** a sacred plant of the Parsees and ancient Persians. **2** a drink made from this plant. [Pers., from Avestan *haoma*]

homage (hom´ij) *n.* **1** a public show of respect or honour to someone or something. **2** deference, obeisance, reverence, worship. **3** (in feudal society) the service paid and fealty professed to a sovereign etc. ~†*v.t.* to pay homage or respect to. **homager** *n.* **1** a person who does homage. **2** a person who holds a fee by homage. [OF, from late L *hominaticum*, from *homo*, man]

hombre (om´brā) *n.* (*N Am., sl.*) man.

Homburg (hom´bœg) *n.* a man's hat of soft felt with a

dented crown and a depression in the top. [German city]

home[1] (hōm) *n.* **1** the place where one lives. **2** the residence of one's family. **3** the members of a family collectively. **4** one's own country or that of one's ancestors. **5** one's family background. **6** the place of constant residence, of commonest occurrence, or where anything is indigenous. **7** a place or state of rest or comfort. **8** a charitable institution of rest or refuge for orphans, the destitute or the afflicted. **9** the environment or habitat of a person or animal. **10** in various games, the goal, den or finishing point. **11** in sport, one's own ground (*The match was at home*). **12** in football pools, a match won by a team playing on their own ground. **13** in lacrosse, a position of play nearest the opponent's goal. **14** the home base, the home plate. *~a.* **1** connected with, carried on or produced at home or in one's native country. **2** domestic, as opposed to foreign. **3** in sport, relating to one's own ground. **4** in the neighbourhood of home. **5** (*N Am.*) central, principal. *~adv.* **1** to one's home or country. **2** arrived at, returned home. **3** (*N Am.*) at home. **4** to the point, pointedly, closely, intimately. **5** to the fullest extent. **at home 1** in one's own house, area or country. **2** at ease, comfortable. **3** conversant (with). **4** accessible to visitors. **home and dry** safe after having successfully come through an experience. **home, James!** (*facet.*) drive home at once! **near home** concerning one deeply. **nothing/ not much to write home about** (*coll.*) not very impressive, great etc. **to bring home to** BRING. **to come home** COME. **home away from home** *n.* HOME FROM HOME (under HOME[1]). **home base, home plate** *n.* in baseball, the rubber plate on which the batter stands. **home-bird** *n.* (*coll.*) a homebody. **homebody** *n.* (*pl.* **homebodies**) a person who likes to stay at home, whose interests are in the home. **home-born** *a.* native, domestic, natural. **home-bound** *a.* **1** homeward-bound. **2** kept at home. **homeboy** *n.* (*esp. N Am., sl.*) a person from one's home town or neighbourhood. **home-bred** *a.* **1** bred at home, not foreign. **2** natural, native. **3** not polished by travel. **home-brew** *n.* an alcoholic beverage brewed at home. **home-brewed** *a.* brewed at home. **homebuyer** *n.* a person buying their own home. **home circuit** *n.* (*Law*) the circuit comprising the Home Counties. **homecoming** *n.* a return to, or arrival at home. *~a.* returning home. **homecomer** *n.* a person returning home. **Home Counties** *n.pl.* the counties nearest London: Middlesex, Surrey, Kent, Essex, Herts., Bucks., Berks. **home economics** *n.* the study of how to run a home, including cookery, childcare etc. **home economist** *n.* **home farm** *n.* a farm belonging to and providing food for the owner of a country estate. **home-felt** *a.* felt in one's heart, inward, private. **home from home** *n.* a place other than one's own home where one can be at ease. **home ground** *n.* a familiar topic or subject. **home-grown** *a.* (esp. of fruit and vegetables) grown in one's own garden, area, country etc. **Home Guard** *n.* **1** the citizen army formed in Britain in May 1940, under the title of Local Defence Volunteers. **2** a member of this. **home help** *n.* a person employed, often by a local authority, to do domestic work for persons unable to look after themselves sufficiently. **home-keeping** *a.* staying at home, untravelled. **homeland** *n.* **1** one's native land. **2** (*Hist.*) in S Africa, a semi-autonomous state reserved for a black African people. **3** any similar semi-autonomous area. **homeless** *a.* without a home. *~n.pl.* homeless people as a class. **homelessness** *n.* **homelike** *a.* **home loan** *n.* a loan made to a person to assist in buying a home. **homely** *a.* (*comp.* **homelier,** *superl.* **homeliest**) **1** plain, without affectation, unpretending. **2** unadorned, unvarnished. **3 a** (of a person) warm and domesticated in manner, looks etc. **b** (*N Am.*) (of a person) plain or ugly in manner, looks etc. **4** good at housekeeping. **homeliness** *n.* **home-made** *a.* **1** made at home. **2** not manufactured abroad. **3** plain. **homemaker** *n.* **1** a person who manages or creates a home. **2** a housewife or househusband. **home-making** *n.* **home movie** *n.* a film, usu. by an amateur, depicting home life, one's interests etc. **Home Office** *n.* **1** in British government, the national department of the Secretary of State for Home Affairs, dealing with law and order etc. **2** the building occupied by this. **homeowner** *n.* a person who owns their own home. **home perm** *n.* a permanent wave that a person does or has done at home. **home port** *n.* the port from where a ship originates. **home rule** *n.* the government of a country, esp. Ireland, by a separate parliament. **home run** *n.* in baseball, a hit that allows the batter to make a complete circuit and score a run. **Home Secretary** *n.* in British government, the Secretary of State for the Home Department who is in charge of the Home Office. **home shopping** *n.* shopping done from home through catalogues, satellite television, the Internet etc. **homesick** *a.* depressed at being away from one's home, family etc. **homesickness** *n.* **home signal** *n.* a railway signal that must not be passed if it is against a train, distinguished from distance signal. **home-sitter** *n.* HOUSE-SITTER (under HOUSE[1]). **homespun** *a.* **1** plain, unaffected, unsophisticated. **2** (of cloth or yarn) spun or wrought at home. **3** home-made. *~n.* **1** cloth spun at home. **2** anything plain or unsophisticated. **homestead** (-sted) *n.* **1** a house, esp. a farmhouse, with the buildings attached. **2** (*N Am.*) a lot granted for the residence and maintenance of a family, under the Homestead Act of 1862. **3** (*Austral., New Zeal.*) the owner's house on a sheep station. **homesteader** *n.* **homesteading** *n.* **home straight, home stretch** *n.* **1** the last section of a racecourse. **2** the last phase of any enterprise. **home-style** *a.* (*N Am.*) (usu. of food) home-made in style; homely. **home town** *n.* the town where one's home is or was. **home trade** *n.* trade conducted within a country. **home truth** *n.* an unwelcome truth expressed in a pointed way. **home unit** *n.* (*Austral., New Zeal.*) any one of a number of separate apartments in the same building, each under individual ownership. **homeward** *adv.* towards home. *~a.* being or going in the direction of home. **homeward-bound** *a.* returning home from abroad. **homewards** *adv.* **homework** *n.* **1** work to be done at home, esp. for school. **2** any preparatory work or study. **3** work done at home for pay. **to do one's homework** (*coll.*) to prepare well. **homeworker** *n.* **homy, homey** *a.* (*comp.* **homier,** *superl.* **homiest**). **hominess, homeyness** *n.* [OE *hām* (cp. Dut. *heem*, Icel. *heimr*, G *Heim*)]

home[2] (hōm) *v.i.* **1** (of birds, esp. pigeons and other animals) to reach home accurately from a distance. **2** to be directed on to a target, e.g. with a navigational device. **3** to go home. **4** to dwell. *~v.t.* **1** to send or guide (pigeons etc.) home. **2** to provide with a home. **3** to direct on to a target, e.g. with a navigational device. **homer**[1] *n.* **1** a homing pigeon. **2** in baseball, a home run. **homing** *a.* **1** (*Zool.*) having or relating to the ability to return home accurately from a great distance (*homing instinct*; *homing pigeon*). **2** (of a navigational device etc.) guiding itself on to a target etc. **3** returning home. **homing device** *n.* (*Mil.*) a mechanism for the automatic guiding of missiles. [from HOME[1]]

homelyn (hō´məlin) *n.* the spotted ray, *Raia maculata*, a European sea fish used for food. [etym. unknown]

homeo- (hom´iō), **homoeo-, homoio-** *comb.form* like or similar. [Gr. *homoios*, of the same kind, similar]

homeomorphous (homiəmaw´fəs) *a.* similar in form and structure (esp. of crystals differing in chemical composition). **homeomorphism** *n.* [Gr. *morphē*, shape]

homeopathy HOMOEOPATHY.

homeoplastic (homiəplas´tik) *a.* (of tumours etc.) similar in structure to the surrounding tissue.

homeostasis (hōmiəstā´sis, hom´-, -os´təsis), **homoeostasis** *n.* (*pl.* **homeostases** (-sēz), **homoeostases**) **1** the keeping of an even level within an animal's body by a tendency to compensate for disrupting changes. **2** the keeping of an even level within an individual, social group, etc. **homeostatic** (-stat´-) *a.* [Gr. *stasis*, standing still]

homeotherm (hō´miəthœm), **homoeotherm, homoiotherm** *n.* **1** an organism that maintains the same body temperature. **2** a warm-blooded organism. **homeothermal** (-thœ´məl), **homeothermic** (-thœ´mik) *a.* **homeothermy** *n.*

homeozoic (homiəzō´ik) *a.* (of regions of the earth) containing similar forms of life. [Gr. *zōē*, life]

homer[1] HOME[2].

homer[2] (hō´mə) *n.* **1** a Hebrew liquid measure of 75⅝ gal. (343.8 l). **2** a Hebrew dry measure of 11²⁄₉ bushels. (4 hl). [Heb. *khōmer*, heap]

Homeric (hōmer´ik) *a.* **1** of, relating to, or resembling Homer or his poems. **2** epic, large-scale or heroic. **3** of Bronze Age Greece as depicted in Homer's poems. **Homerically** *adv.* **Homeric laughter** *n.* loud immoderate laughter like that of the gods. **Homerist** (hō´-) *n.* **Homerology** (-ol´əji) *n.* **Homerologist** *n.* [L *Homericus*, Gr. *Homērikos*, from *Homēros*, Homer]

homicide (hom´isīd) *n.* **1** the act of killing a human being. **2** a person who kills another. **homicidal** (-sī´-) *a.* [F, from L *homicīdium*, manslaughter, *homīcida*, manslayer (HOMO, man)]

homiletic (homilet´ik) *a.* of or relating to homilies. **homiletics** *n.pl.* the art of preaching; the art or method of presenting religious doctrine to an audience in the most effective form. [Gr. *homilētikos*, from *homilein*, to hold converse with, from *homīlos*, assembly (*homos*, like, *eilein*, to crowd together)]

homily (hom´ili) *n.* (*pl.* **homilies**) **1** a discourse or sermon on a moral or religious topic. **2** a tedious moral exhortation. **homiliary** (hōmil´iəri) *n.* (*pl.* **homiliaries**) a book of homilies. **homilist** *n.* [OF *omelie* (F *homélie*), L *homīlia*, as HOMILETIC]

Homines HOMO.

hominess HOME[1].

homing HOME[2].

hominid (hom´inid) *n.* a creature of the family Hominidae, comprising humans and their precursors. ~*a.* of or relating to the Hominidae. [HOMO]

hominoid (hom´inoid) *a.* **1** of or like man. **2** of, relating to, or belonging to the superfamily Hominoidea, comprising humans and their ancestors. **3** hominid or pongid. ~*n.* **1** a hominid animal. **2** a human-like animal.

hominy (hom´ini) *n.* (*esp. N Am.*) maize hulled and coarsely ground, boiled with water or milk for food. [N Am. Ind.]

Homo (hō´mō) *n.* (*pl.* **Homines** (hom´ināz)) any primate of the genus *Homo*, of which man is the only living species. **Homo sapiens** (sap´ienz) *n.* man as a species. [L]

homo (hō´mō) *n.* (*pl.* **homos**) (*coll., usu. derog.*) short for HOMOSEXUAL.

homo- (hō´mō, hom´ō), **hom-** *comb. form* alike, similar, identical. [Gr. *homos*, same]

homoblastic (hōməblas´tik, hom-) *a.* (*Zool.*) derived from the same kind of cells, as distinct from *heteroblastic*. **homoblasty** (hō´-, hom´-) *n.* [Gr. *blastos*, germ]

homocentric (hōməsen´trik, hom-) *a.* concentric, having the same centre. **homocentrically** *adv.*

homocercal (hōməsœ´kəl, hom-) *a.* (of fishes) having the upper and lower lobes of the tail of the same length. [Gr. *kerkos*, a tail]

homochromy (həmok´rəmi, hōməkrō´-) *n.* the resemblance of an animal's colour to the colour of its surroundings.

homocyclic (hōməsī´klik, hom-) *a.* (of an organic compound) having a closed chain of atoms of the same kind.

homodont (hō´mədont) *a.* having teeth that are all of the same type, as opposed to heterodont.

homoeo- HOMEO-.

homoeopathy (hōmiop´əthi, hom-), (*esp. N Am.*) **homeopathy** *n.* the system which aims at curing diseases by administering in small doses medicines which would produce in healthy persons symptoms similar to those they are designed to remove. **homoeopath** (hō´-, hom´-) *n.* a homoeopathist. **homoeopathic** (-path´-) *a.* belonging to homoeopathy. **homoeopathically** *adv.* **homoeopathist** *n.* a person who practises or believes in homoeopathy. [Gr. *homoiopatheia*]

homoeostasis HOMEOSTASIS.

homoerotic (hōmōirot´ik) *a.* of or concerning sexual attraction to the same sex. **homoeroticism** (-sizm) *n.*

homogametic (homəgəmet´ik) *a.* of or relating to the sex that possesses two chromosomes of the same sex.

homogamous (həmog´əməs) *a.* (*Bot.*) **1** having all the florets of a capitulum hermaphrodite. **2** having the stamens and pistils ripe at the same time. **homogamy** *n.* [Gr. *gamos*, marriage]

homogeneous (homəjē´niəs) *a.* **1** composed of the same or similar parts or elements. **2** of the same kind or nature throughout. **3** (*Math.*) having all its terms of the same degree. **4** (*Math.*) commensurable. **homogeneity** (-jinē´iti, -ā´-) *n.* **homogeneously** *adv.* **homogeneousness** *n.* **homogenesis** (-jen´əsis) *n.* reproduction characterized by the likeness of the offspring to the parent and correspondence in the course of its development. **homogenetic** (-jənet´ik) *a.* **1** of, relating to or characterized by homogenesis. **2** corresponding in structure so as to show or suggest common ancestry; having evolved from the same structure. **homogenetical** *a.* **homogenist** (-moj´-) *n.* (*Hist.*) a person who believes that organs etc. differing in function can have evolved from the same structure. **homogenize** (-moj´-), **homogenise** *v.t.* **1** to make homogeneous. **2** to process (milk or cream) so that the fat globules are emulsified. ~*v.i.* to become homogeneous. **homogenization** (-zā´shən) *n.* **homogenizer** *n.* **homogenous** (-moj´-) *a.* **1** HOMOGENEOUS. **2** †HOMOGENETIC (under HOMOGENEOUS). **homogeny** (-moj´-) *n.* [Gr. *homogenēs* (*genos*, kind)]

Usage note The use of *homogenous* to mean *homogeneous* is sometimes disapproved of.

homograft (hom´əgrahft) *n.* a tissue graft from one organism to a member of the same species.

homograph (hom´əgrahf) *n.* a word having the same spelling as another, but differing in pronunciation, origin or meaning.

homoio- HOMEO-.

homoiotherm HOMEOTHERM.

homoiousian (homoioo´siən) *a.* having a similar nature or substance. ~*n.* a person who held the second person of the Trinity to be of a substance similar to but not the same as that of the Father. [Gr. *homoiousios* (HOMEO-, *ousiā*, essence); cp. HOMOOUSIAN]

homolog HOMOLOGUE (under HOMOLOGOUS).

homologate (həmol´əgāt) *v.t.* **1** to admit, to concede. **2** to ratify; to confirm. **3** to approve (a particular car etc.) for use in a motor race etc. **homologation** (-ā´shən) *n.* [late L *homologātus*, p.p. of *homologāre*, Gr. *homologein*]

homologous (həmol´əgəs) *a.* **1** having the same relative position, proportion, value, structure etc. **2** corresponding. **3** (of chromosomes) pairing at meiosis where one member of each pair is carried by every gamete. **4** (*Biol.*) (of organs etc.) of the same evolutionary origin but having different functions. **5** (*Chem.*) (of a series of organic compounds) having similar characteristics and structure but differing in composition by a number of atoms. **homologic** (homəloj´-), **homological** *a.* **homologically** *adv.* **homologize** (-jīz), **homologise** *v.i.* to be homologous; to correspond. ~*v.t.* to make homologous. **homologue** (hom´əlog), (*N Am.*) **homolog** *n.* **1** something that is homologous. **2** the same organ in different animals, e.g. a human's arm and a bird's wing. **homology** (-ji) *n.* **1** correspondence. **2** identity of relation between parts developed from the same embryonic structures, as the arm of a human and the foreleg of a quadruped. **3** the quality of being homologous. [Gr. *homologos* (HOMO-, *logos*, ratio)]

homologumena (homələgoo´minə) *n.pl.* those books of the New Testament the canonicity of which was accepted at once. [Gr. *homologoumena*, neut. pl. p.p. of *homologein*, see HOMOLOGATE]

homomorphic (homəmaw´fik), **homomorphous** (-fəs) *a.* analogous, identical or closely similar in form. **homomorphically** *adv.* **homomorphism** *n.* **homomorphy** *n.* [Gr. *morphē*, shape]

homonomous (həmon´əməs) *a.* subject to the same law of growth. **homonomy** *n.* [Gr. *homonomos* (*nomos*, law)]

homonym (hom´ənim) *n.* **1** a word having the same sound or spelling as another, but differing in meaning; a homograph or homophone. **2** a person with the same name as another. **homonymic** (-nim´-), **homonymous** (-mon´-) *a.* **homonymously** *adv.* **homonymy** (-mon´əmi) *n.* the state of being homonymous; a sameness of name with difference of meaning. [late L *homōnymum*, Gr. *homōnumon* (HOMO-, *onuma*, name)]

homoousian (homōoo´siən), **homousian** (homoo´siən) *a.* consubstantial, of the same substance or essence, as distinct from homoiousian. ~*n.* a person who held the second person of the Trinity to be of the same substance as the Father, an orthodox Trinitarian. [Gr. *homoousios* (*ousia*, essence)]

homophobia (homəfōb´iə, hō-) *n.* a hatred or fear of homosexuals or homosexuality. **homophobe** (hom´-, hō´-) *n.* **homophobic** *a.*

homophone (hom´əfōn) *n.* **1** a word having the same sound as another, but differing in meaning or spelling, as *heir* and *air*. **2** a symbol indicating the same sound as another. **homophonic** (-fon´-) *a.* **1** (*Mus.*) having the same pitch. **2** in unison, as opposed to polyphonic. **homophonically** *adv.* **homophonous** (həmof´-) *a.* **1** having the same sound. **2** (*Mus.*) homophonic. **homophony** (həmof-´) *n.* **1** identity of sound. **2** (*Mus.*) unison. [Gr. *homophōnos*]

homoplastic (homəplas´tik) *a.* similar in structure though not homogenetic. **homoplasmy** (-plaz´-), **homoplasy** (hō´məplāzi, həmop´lə-) *n.*

homopolar (homəpō´lə) *a.* **1** (*Chem.*) having an equal distribution of charge; covalent. **2** electrically symmetrical. **3** (of a generator) producing direct current without having commutators.

homopteran (həmop´tərən) *n.* any insect of the suborder Homoptera having wings of a uniform texture. **homopterous** *a.* [Gr. *pteron*, wing]

homosexual (hom´əsek´sūəl, hōm´-, -shəl) *a.* **1** feeling sexual attraction to one's own sex. **2** of or relating to homosexuals or homosexuality. **3** of or relating to the same sex. ~*n.* a homosexual person. **homosexuality** (-shual´-) *n.* **homosexually** *adv.*

homotaxis (homətak´sis) *n.* (*Geol.*) arrangement of strata in different localities in the same relative position in the geological series. **homotaxial, homotaxeous, homotaxic** *a.* **homotaxially** *adv.* [Gr. *taxis*, arrangement]

homotonous (həmot´ənəs) *a.* **1** of the same tenor or tone. **2** equable. **homotonously** *adv.* **homotony** *n.* [Gr. *tonos*, tone]

homotype (hom´ətīp) *n.* a part or organ having the same structure or relative position to that of another. **homotypal, homotypic** (-tip´ik) *a.* **homotypy** (hom´ətīpi, həmot´i-) *n.* [Gr. *typos*, type]

homousian HOMOOUSIAN.

homozygote (homəzī´gōt) *n.* (*Biol.*) an animal or plant that has two identical alleles for any one gene and so breeds true to type. **homozygosis** (-gō´sis) *n.* **homozygous** *a.* [Gr. *homoios*, like, similar]

homunculus (həmŭng´kūləs), **homuncule** (-kūl) *n.* (*pl.* **homunculi** (-lī), **homuncules**) **1** a little man; a dwarf; a manikin. **2** in early biological theory, a minute human being existing in the spermatozoon. **homuncular** *a.* [L *homunculus*, dim. of HOMO]

homy HOME[1].

Hon. *abbr.* **1** Honorary. **2** Honourable.

hon HONEY.

honcho (hon´chō) *n.* (*pl.* **honchos**) (*N Am., sl.*) **1** a boss, leader or manager. **2** an important or able man. ~*v.t.* (*3rd pers. sing. pres.* **honchoes,** *pres.p.* **honchoing,** *past, p.p.* **honchoed**) to be in charge of, to oversee. [Jap. *han'chō*, squad leader]

hone[1] (hōn) *n.* **1** a whetstone esp. for sharpening razors. **2** any of several stones used for this purpose. ~*v.t.* to sharpen on a hone. [OE *hān*, stone (cp. Icel. *hein*)]

hone[2] (hōn) *v.i.* (*dial.*) **1** to moan, to whine. **2** to pine, to yearn. [perh. from OF *hogner*, from *hon*, a cry, a complaint]

honest (on´ist) *a.* **1** upright, fair, truthful, trustworthy in dealings, business or conduct. **2** open, frank, candid, sincere, honourable. **3** just, equitable. **4** (of an act, feeling etc.) characterized by fairness or sincerity (often used patronizingly). **5** (of money, gain etc.) legitimate, fair (*an honest day's work*). **6** †(of a woman) chaste, virtuous. **7** worthy or respectable. **8** unimpeached, unstained. ~*adv.* (*coll.*) genuinely, truly. **to make an honest woman of** (*coll. or facet.*) to marry (esp. a pregnant woman). **to make/ earn/ turn an honest penny** (*coll.*) to earn money legitimately or fairly. **honest broker** *n.* an impartial mediator in international, industrial etc. disputes. **honest Injun** *adv.* (*coll.*) genuinely, really. **honestly** *adv.* **1** in an honest way. **2** really. ~*int.* used to express disgust, disbelief etc. **honest-to-God, honest-to-goodness** *a.* genuine, outright. ~*adv.* genuinely, really, completely. **honesty** *n.* (*pl.* **honesties**) **1** the quality or state of being honest. **2** sincerity or fairness. **3** truthfulness. **4** †chastity or respect. **5** a cruciferous garden plant, *Lunaria biennis*, bearing flat, round, semi-transparent seed pods. [OF *honeste*, L *honestus*, from *honos*, HONOUR]

honey (hŭn´i) *n.* (*pl.* **honeys**) **1** a sweet viscid product collected from plants by bees, and largely used as food. **2** the colour of this; golden brown. **3** sweetness. **4** the nectar of flowers. **5** (*esp. N Am.*) (*also* **hon**) used as a term of endearment. **6** a person, thing etc. considered to be excellent of its kind. ~*v.t.* (*3rd. pers. sing. pres.* **honeys,** *pres.p.* **honeying,** *past, p.p.* **honeyed, honied**) **1** to sweeten with honey. **2** †to speak fondly to. ~*v.i.* **1** to use endearing language. **2** to talk or behave fondly. **honey badger** *n.* a ratel. **honey-bag** *n.* the receptacle for honey in a bee. **honey bear** *n.* a S American quadruped, also called *kinkajou*, which robs or destroys the nests of bees. **honey bee** *n.* a bee that produces honey. **honeybun** *n.* honeybunch. **honeybunch** *n.* (*esp. N Am., coll.*) used as a term of endearment. **honey-buzzard** *n.* any bird of prey of the genus *Pernis* which feeds on the larvae and honey of bees and wasps. **honeycomb** *n.* **1** a waxy substance formed in hexagonal cells by the honey bee, for the reception of honey and for the eggs and larvae. **2** anything similarly structured or perforated, esp. flaws in a metal casting. **3** (*Zool.*) the reticulum. ~*v.t.* 1 to fill with holes or cavities. 2 to mark with a honeycomb-like pattern. **honeycreeper** *n.* 1 any bird of the family Drepanidiae of Hawaii. 2 any of several kinds of small S American birds, such as the tanager, which feeds on nectar. **honeydew** *n.* 1 a saccharine substance excreted by aphids and found on the leaves of plants. 2 HONEYDEW MELON (under HONEY). 3 something extremely sweet, nectar. 4 a kind of tobacco moistened with molasses and pressed into cakes. **honeydew melon** *n.* a type of melon with sweet flesh and a greenish rind. **honeyeater** *n.* any bird of the Australasian family Meliphagidae with a long tongue for extracting nectar from flowers. **honeyed, honied** *a.* 1 of, containing or resembling honey. 2 (of words etc.) ingratiating, sweet-sounding. **honey fungus** *n.* an edible fungus, *Armillaria mellea*, parasitic on the roots of woody plants. **honeyguide** *n.* 1 any small bird of the family Indicatoridae which feeds on beeswax, honey and insects and whose cry guides people to the nests of bees. 2 a marking on a flower said to guide bees to nectar. **honey-harvest** *n.* honey-collecting, the time for collecting honey. **honey-like** *a.* **honey locust** *n.* 1 a large American tree, *Gleditsia triacanthos*, of the family Leguminosae. 2 MESQUITE. **honey-mouthed** *a.* sweet and smooth in speech. **honey pot** *n.* 1 a container for honey. 2 a posture with the hands clasped under the hams. 3 (*pl.*) a children's game involving this posture. 4 something very attractive or irresistible. 5 (*N Am.*, *sl.*) the vagina. **honey-sac** *n.* HONEY-BAG (under HONEY). **honey-stalk** *n.* the stalk or flower of clover. **honeysuckle** *n.* 1 any climbing shrub of the genus *Lonicera*, with sweet-scented white, yellow or pink tubular flowers. 2 (*Austral.*) any shrub of the genus *Banksia*. **honey-sweet** *a.* 1 much loved. 2 sweet as honey. **honey-tongued** *a.* smooth in speech; honey-mouthed. [OE *hunig* (cp. Dut. and G *honig*, Icel. *hunang*)]

honeymoon (hŭn´imoon) *n.* 1 a holiday taken by a newly married couple. 2 a holiday reminiscent of a honeymoon (*a second honeymoon*). 3 HONEYMOON PERIOD (under HONEYMOON). ~*v.i.* to spend a honeymoon (in, at etc.). **honeymooner** *n.* **honeymoon period** *n.* a period of goodwill and harmony at the start of a new business appointment, relationship etc.

hong (hong) *n.* in China, a foreign factory, warehouse or other mercantile establishment. [Chin. *hang*, row, series]

honied HONEYED (under HONEY).

Honiton (hon´itən), **Honiton lace** *n.* a kind of lace with floral sprigs. [town in Devon where orig. made]

honk (hongk) *n.* 1 the cry of the wild goose. 2 any similar cry or noise, esp. that of a vehicle's horn. ~*v.i.* 1 to make a honk. 2 (*sl.*) to vomit. 3 (*sl.*) to smell unpleasantly. ~*v.t.* to cause to make a honk. **honker** *n.* **honking** *a.* [imit.]

honky (hong´ki), **honkie** *n.* (*pl.* **honkies**) (*N Am.*, *derog.*, *sl.*) 1 a white person. 2 white people collectively.

honky-tonk (hongkitongk´) *n.* 1 (*N Am.*, *sl.*) a disreputable nightclub, bar etc. 2 a type of ragtime piano-playing, esp. on a cheap upright piano.

honnête homme (onet om´) *n.* a decent, sophisticated man of the world; a gentleman. [F]

honor HONOUR.

honorable HONOURABLE.

honorand (on´ərand) *n.* a person receiving an honour such as an honorary degree.

honorarium (onəreə´riəm) *n.* (*pl.* **honorariums, honoraria** (-riə)) a fee or payment for the services of a professional person. [late L, as HONORARY]

honorary (on´ərəri) *a.* 1 done, made or conferred as a mark of honour. 2 holding a title or an office without payment or without undertaking the duties. 3 (of duties or obligations) depending on honour, not enforceable by law. **honorary degree** *n.* a degree conferred by a university without examination. [L *honōrārius*, from *honos*, HONOUR]

honorific (onərif´ik) *a.* 1 conferring or showing honour. 2 in oriental languages, applied to phrases, words etc. to imply respect. ~*n.* 1 an honorific title etc. 2 an honorific word, phrase etc. †**honorificabilitudinity** (onərifikəbilitūdin´iti) *n.* honourableness (often cited as one of the longest words in the English language). **honorifically** *adv.* [L *honorificus*, from as HONOUR]

honoris causa (onawris kow´zə), **honoris gratia** (grā´shə) *adv.* (esp. of an honorary degree) as a token of esteem. [L]

honour (on´ə), (*N Am.*) **honor** *n.* 1 respect, esteem, reverence. 2 reputation, glory, integrity. 3 conformity to the accepted code of social conduct. 4 nobleness of mind, probity, uprightness. 5 something conferred as a mark or token of distinction for bravery, achievement etc. 6 high rank; exalted position. 7 (of a woman) chastity, reputation of chastity. 8 (*pl.*) courteous attentions paid to guests etc. 9 (*pl.*) a distinction awarded for meritorious or advanced university work. 10 (*pl.*) a degree course that is above the level of an ordinary degree. 11 a person or thing that confers honour, position etc. 12 (*poet.*) an ornament or decoration. 13 a title of address given to certain officers, as a county court judge etc. 14 in golf, the right of driving off first. 15 (*pl.*) a in bridge etc., any of the top five cards in a suit (esp. of trumps) or the four aces at no trumps. b in whist, the four highest trump cards. 16 †a group of several manors held by one lord. ~*v.t.* 1 to treat with reverence or respect. 2 to confer honour upon. 3 to accept or pay (a bill or cheque) when due. 4 to acknowledge. 5 to dignify, to glorify, to exalt. **honour bright** (*dated sl.*) used by schoolchildren to pledge honour. **honours are even** there is evenness in the contest. **honours easy** in a card game, honours equally divided. **in honour bound** under a moral obligation. **in honour of** out of respect for; as a celebration of. **on/ upon one's honour** used to pledge one's honour or reputation on the accuracy or good faith of a statement. **to do the honours** 1 to perform the duties of a host or hostess to guests. 2 (*coll.*) to perform a social task, courtesy etc., such as serving food, proposing a toast etc. **honourer** *n.* **honour-point** *n.* (*Her.*) the point immediately above the centre or fess point of a shield. **honours list** *n.* a list of people awarded honours, e.g. knighthoods etc., from the sovereign. **honours of war** *n.* a distinction or privilege granted to an enemy who has surrendered on terms. **honour system** *n.* an unsupervised system of examinations relying on the candidates' honour. **honour-trick** *n.* QUICK TRICK (under QUICK). [OF *onor*, *honor*, L *honōrem*, nom. *honos*]

honourable (on´ərəbəl), (*N Am.*) **honorable** *a.* 1 worthy of honour. 2 conferring honour. 3 illustrious, of distinguished rank, noble. 4 actuated by principles of honour, upright; not base. 5 consistent with honour or reputation. 6 accompanied or performed with or as with marks of honour. 7 proceeding from a laudable cause (*honourable intentions*). 8 (**Honourable**) a title of respect or distinction borne by the children of peers below the rank of marquess, maids of honour, Justices of the High Court etc. **my honourable friend** FRIEND. **honourable mention** *n.* a distinction sometimes awarded to a competitor who has just failed to win a prize. **honourableness** *n.* **honourably** *adv.*

Hon. Sec. *abbr.* Honorary Secretary.

hooch (hooch), **hootch** *n.* (*N Am.*, *coll.*) crude alcoholic liquor. [*hooch*inoo, spirits made by the Hootchinoo people of Alaska]

hood[1] (hud) *n.* 1 a loose covering for the head and back of the neck, separate, or part of a cloak etc. 2 an appendage to an academic gown marking a degree. 3 anything hoodlike, as the blinding cap on a hawk, a carriage top, a paper cornet etc. **4** the folding roof or top of a car or pram etc. **5** (*N Am.*) the bonnet of a motor car etc. **6** an overhanging or protective canopy, cover etc. **7** (*Biol.*) a hoodlike structure or marking such as the expansion of a cobra's neck. ~*v.t.* to dress or cover in a hood. **hooded** *a.* **1** covered with a hood; blinded. **2** (*Bot.*) hood-shaped, cucullate. **hooded crow** *n.* a subspecies of the carrion crow having a grey body with black head, wings and tail. **hooded snake** *n.* a snake of the Elapidae family, having the power of dilating the loose skin of the neck into a hoodlike shape. **hoodie, hoody-crow** *n.* the hooded crow. **hoodless** *a.* **hoodlike** *a.* †**hoodman** *n.* (*pl.* **hoodmen**) the person blindfolded in blind man's buff. †**hoodman-blind** *n.* blind man's buff. **hood-mould, hood-moulding** *n.* (*Archit.*) a band or moulding over the head of a door, window or other opening, a dripstone. **hoodwink** *v.t.* **1** to deceive, to take in. **2** †to blindfold, to cover up. **hoodwinker** *n.* [OE *hōd* (cp. Dut. *hoed*, G *Hut*)]

hood[2] (hud) *n.* (*sl.*) a hoodlum, a gangster. [abbr.]

hood[3] (hud) *n.* (*N Am.*, *sl.*) a neighbourhood. [abbr.]

-hood (hud) *suf.* **1** denoting a state or quality, as in *childhood, parenthood.* **2** indicating a group etc., as in *sisterhood, brotherhood, neighbourhood.* [OE *-hād* (ME *-hod*), cogn. with Goth. *haidux*, manner, way]

hoodlum (hood´ləm) *n.* (*N Am.*, *sl.*) **1** a street rowdy, a hooligan, orig. esp. one of a gang of street ruffians who flourished in San Francisco during the 1870s and 1880s. **2** a gangster. **hoodlumism** *n.* [etym. unknown]

hoodoo (hoo´doo) *n.* (*pl.* **hoodoos**) (*esp. N Am.*, *coll.*) **1** bad luck. **2** the cause of bad luck, a Jonah. **3** voodoo. **4** (*Geol.*) a strangely shaped rock pinnacle or column. ~*v.t.* (*3rd pers. sing. pres.* **hoodoos**, *pres.p.* **hoodooing**, *past, p.p.* **hoodooed**) **1** to bring bad luck to. **2** to cast a spell on (something). **3** to bewitch. **hoodooism** *n.* [var. of VOODOO]

hoodwink HOOD[1].

hooey (hoo´i) *n.*, *int.* (*sl.*) rubbish, nonsense. [onomat.]

hoof (hoof) *n.* (*pl.* **hooves** (hoovz), **hoofs**) **1** the horny sheath covering the feet of horses, oxen etc. **2** an animal with hoofs. **3** (*facet.*) a human foot. ~*v.t.* **1** to strike or attack with the hoof. **2** (*sl.*) to kick. ~*v.i.* (*sl.*) to kick (out). **on the hoof** **1** (of livestock) alive; not yet slaughtered. **2** (*coll.*) while standing up or moving around. **to hoof it** **1** (*sl.*) to walk, to go on foot. **2** (*sl.*) to dance. **hoof-bound** *a.* (of a horse) having a painful dryness and contraction of the hoof, causing lameness. **hoofed** *a.* **hoofer** *n.* (*N Am.*, *sl.*) a dancer. [OE *hōf* (Dut. *hoef*, Icel. *hōfr*, G *Huf*)]

hooh-ha (hoo´hah), **hoo-ha** *n.* (*coll.*) fuss, noisy commotion or excitement. [onomat.]

hook (huk) *n.* **1** a curved piece of metal or other material by which an object is caught or suspended. **2** FISH-HOOK (under FISH[1]). **3** a curved instrument for cutting grass or corn, a sickle. **4** **a** a sharp bend. **b** a sharply curved spit of land. **5** a cape, a headland. **6** a trap, a snare. **7** in boxing, a short swinging blow made with the elbow bent. **8** in cricket, a shot in which the ball is hit square on the leg side with an upward stroke. **9** in golf, a shot in which the ball goes towards the player's left. **10** a curved stroke in writing, printing etc. **11** (*Mus.*) one of the lines at the end of a quaver. **12** (*sl.*) a repetitive catchy musical phrase. **13** a sickle. **14** (*pl.*, *sl.*) fingers. ~*v.t.* **1** to catch, grasp or hold with or as with a hook. **2** to fasten with a hook or hooks. **3** (*esp. passive, coll.*) to attract or cause to become addicted. **4** (*sl.*) to snatch, to steal, to pilfer. **5** in boxing, to hit (one's opponent) with a hook. **6** in cricket, to play (a ball) with a hook. **7** in golf, to drive (the ball) widely to the left. **8** in rugby, to secure and pass (the ball) backwards from a scrum using the feet. **9** in football, to pull (the ball) in with the foot in a certain manner. ~*v.i.* to fit or fasten (on) with or as with hooks. **by hook or by crook** by fair means or foul. **hooked on** (*coll.*) addicted to. **hook, line and sinker** completely. **off the hook** **1** (*coll.*) no longer in danger or difficulty. **2** (of a telephone receiver) not on its rest. **3** ready-made. **off the hooks** (*sl.*) dead. **on one's own hook** (*sl.*) on one's own account. **to hook it** **1** (*sl.*) to decamp. **2** (*sl.*) to run away. **to sling/ take one's hook** **1** (*sl.*) to decamp. **2** (*sl.*) to run away. **hook and eye** *n.* a metal hook and corresponding loop for fastening a dress. **hooked** *a.* **1** bent; hook-shaped. **2** furnished with hooks. **3** (of a rug etc.) created by pulling yarn through canvas etc. with a hook. **hookedness** (-kid-) *n.* the state of being hooked. **hookless** *a.* **hooklet** *n.* **hooklike** *a.* **hook-nose** *n.* an aquiline nose. **hook-nosed** *a.* **Hook of Holland** *n.* the corner of Holland projecting into the North Sea. **hook-pin** *n.* an iron pin with a hooked head used in building and carpentry. **hook-up** *n.* a radio network, a series of connected stations. **hookworm** *n.* **1** any of various parasitic nematode worms having hooked mouthparts for feeding, which infest humans and animals. **2** the disease caused by such worms. [OE *hōc* (cp. Dut. *hoek*, Icel. *haki*, G *Haken*)]

hookah (huk´ə), **hooka** *n.* a tobacco pipe in which the smoke passes through water. [Arab. *huqqah*, a casket, a bowl]

hooker[1] (huk´ə) *n.* **1** a person or thing that hooks. **2** (*sl.*) a prostitute. **3** in rugby, the central forward in the front row of the scrum who tries to hook the ball. **4** (*N Am.*, *sl.*) a draught of alcoholic drink.

hooker[2] (huk´ə) *n.* **1** a two-masted Dutch or Irish coasting or fishing vessel. **2** a one-masted fishing smack. **3** (*derog.*) a ship. [Dut. *hoeker*, from *hoek*, HOOK]

Hooke's law (huks) *n.* (*Physics*) the principle expressing the proportionality of strain to the stress causing it. [R. *Hooke*, 1635–1703, English scientist]

hookey (huk´i), **hooky** *n.* (*N Am.*, *coll.*) truant (*to play hookey*).

Hoolee (hoo´li) *n.* the great Hindu festival in honour of Krishna. [Hind. *hōlī*]

hooley (hoo´li) *n.* (*pl.* **hooleys**) (*chiefly Ir.*) a lively party usu. with singing and dancing. [etym. uncertain]

hooligan (hoo´ligən) *n.* any of a gang of street ruffians given to violent attacks on people. **hooliganism** *n.* [prob. from the name of a rowdy family (cp. Ir. *Houlihan*) in a comic song popular in music halls *c.* 1885]

hoop[1] (hoop) *n.* **1** a strip of wood or metal bent into a band or ring to hold the staves of casks etc. together or for forming part of a framework. **2** a large iron or wooden ring for a child to trundle or whirl around the body. **3** a large ring through which circus performers or animals jump. **4** a circular strip of whalebone etc. formerly used to expand the skirts of women's dresses. **5** in croquet, a small iron arch through which the ball is driven. **6** HOOP-PETTICOAT (under HOOP[1]). **7** in basketball, the round metal frame to which the net is attached. **8** an earring consisting of one or more circles of metal etc. **9** a colour-contrasting band on a sports shirt etc. **10** (*Austral.*, *coll.*) a jockey. ~*v.t.* **1** to bind or fasten with hoops. **2** to encircle. **to be put through hoops/ the hoop** to be put through an ordeal. **to go through hoops/ the hoop** to go through an ordeal. **hooper** *n.* **1** a person who hoops casks. **2** a cooper. **hoop-iron** *n.* flat, thin strips of iron used for hooping barrels. **hoopla** (-lah) *n.* **1** a game of winning prizes by throwing rings over them. **2** (*coll.*) a disturbance or commotion. **3** (*coll.*) gratuitous activity; nonsense. **hoop-petticoat, hoop-skirt** *n.* a woman's dress expanded by means of a hoop. [OE *hōp* (cp. Dut. *hoep*)]

hoop[2] WHOOP.

hoopoe (hoo´poo, -pō) *n.* a bird, *Upupa epops*, a rare British visitor, with large crest and fine plumage. [earlier *hoope*, F *huppe*, L *upupa*, onomat.]

hoorah (hurah´) *int.* HURRAH.

hooray (hurā´) *int.* 1 HURRAH. 2 (*Austral., New Zeal.*) goodbye. **Hooray Henry** (hoorā hen´ri) *n.* (*pl.* **Hooray Henries, Hooray Henrys**) (*coll.*) a young upper-class man, often with affected manners, who is extroverted and ostentatious.

hoosegow (hoos´gow), **hoosgow** *n.* (*N Am., sl.*) a prison. [Sp. *juzgado*, courtroom]

hoot[1] (hoot) *v.i.* 1 (of an owl) to utter its hollow cry. 2 to cry as an owl; to make a sound like this. 3 to shout or make loud cries in contempt or dissatisfaction, or in amusement. ~*v.t.* 1 to shout at in contempt or dissatisfaction. 2 to send (away, out etc.) with contemptuous hoots. 3 to express by hooting. 4 to sound (a motor horn, siren etc.). ~*n.* 1 the cry of an owl. 2 a cry like that of an owl, esp. that of a motor horn. 3 an inarticulate shout in contempt or dissatisfaction. 4 an outburst of laughter. 5 (*coll.*) an extremely funny or enjoyable person or event. 6 (*coll.*) anything at all (*I don't give a hoot; it doesn't matter two hoots*). **not to care two hoots** (*coll.*) not to care at all. **hooter** *n.* 1 a person, animal or object that hoots. 2 a steam whistle or siren, esp. one used to signal the beginning or end of work time. 3 (*sl.*) a nose. 4 (*pl., N Am., sl.*) a woman's breasts. [ME *houten*, perh. from Scand., or imit.]

hoot[2] HOOTS.

hootch HOOCH.

hootenanny (hoot´ənani) *n.* (*pl.* **hootenannies**) (*N Am.*) 1 an informal concert with folk music and sometimes dancing. 2 a person or thing the name of which one cannot or will not recall.

hoots (hoots), **hoot** *int.* (*Sc., North.*) used to express disgust, impatience etc.

Hoover® (hoo´və) *n.* a type of vacuum cleaner. **hoover** *v.t., v.i.* to clean with a vacuum cleaner. **to hoover up** to clean with or suck up etc. as if with a vacuum cleaner. [W. H. *Hoover*, d. 1932, American manufacturer]

hooves HOOF.

hop[1] (hop) *v.i.* (*pres.p.* **hopping,** *past, p.p.* **hopped**) 1 to spring, leap or skip on one foot. 2 to skip with both feet (as birds) or with all four feet (as quadrupeds). 3 to move or go quickly. 4 (*coll.*) to make a quick trip. 5 (*coll.*) to make a quick change of location etc. 6 to limp. ~*v.t.* 1 to jump lightly or skip over. 2 (*coll.*) to jump into (a bus etc.). ~*n.* 1 a jump, spring or light leap on one foot or (of animals etc.) on both or all feet. 2 (*coll.*) a dance. 3 a short trip by aircraft, a short run, a quick passage. 4 a distance easily covered in a few paces. **on the hop** 1 (*coll.*) unawares; unprepared. 2 (*coll.*) active. **to catch on the hop** to catch by surprise, esp. in the midst of a prank. **to hop in** (*coll.*) to get into a vehicle. **to hop it** (*coll.*) to go away. **to hop off** 1 (*coll.*) to get down or off lightly. 2 (*coll.*) to go away. **to hop out** (*coll.*) to get out of a vehicle. **to hop the twig/ stick** 1 to go away quickly. 2 (*sl.*) to die. **hop-o'-my-thumb** *n.* a person of restricted growth, a dwarf. **hopper**[1] *n.* 1 a person or thing that hops. 2 a hopping insect, a flea, the larva of a cheese-fly etc. 3 a funnel through which something is conveyed or fed such as fuel etc. to a furnace etc. 4 a barge with an opening in its bottom used for discharging refuse. 5 a railway truck able to discharge loose minerals etc. through underside doors. **hopping** *a.* 1 (*N Am., coll.*) very busy or active; lively. 2 (*in comb.*) (esp. of an aircraft) passing quickly from one type of place to another (*cloud-hopping; hedge-hopping*). **hopping mad** *a.* (*coll.*) very angry. **hop, skip and jump,** (*also*) **hop, step and jump** *n.* 1 the triple jump. 2 a short distance. [OE *hoppian* (cp. Dut. *hoppen*, Icel. and Swed. *hoppa*, G *hopfen*)]

hop[2] (hop) *n.* 1 a perennial climbing plant, *Humulus lupulus*, the mature cones of which are used in brewing. 2 (*pl.*) the dried flowers of this plant used to give a bitter flavour to beer. 3 (*Austral., New Zeal., coll.*) beer. 4 (*N Am., sl.*) opium or any other narcotic. ~*v.t.* (*pres.p.* **hopping,** *past, p.p.* **hopped**) to impregnate with hops. ~*v.i.* to pick hops. **hop-bind, hop-bine** *n.* the stem of the hop. **hop-fly, hop-louse** *n.* an aphis, *Phorodon humuli*, destructive of hops. **hophead** *n.* 1 (*esp. N Am., sl.*) a heroin or opium addict. 2 (*Austral., New Zeal., sl.*) a drunkard. **hopped up** *a.* (*N Am., sl.*) 1 intoxicated or drugged. 2 excited; agitated. **hopper**[2] *n.* a hop-picker. **hop-picker** *n.* 1 a person who gathers hops. 2 a machine for this purpose. **hop-pillow** *n.* a pillow stuffed with hops for inducing sleep. **hop-pocket** *n.* 1 a coarse sack for hops. 2 a half sack, or 168 lb (76 kg), a measure of capacity for hops. **hop-pole** *n.* a training pole for hops. **hoppy** *a.* tasting of hops. **hopsack** *n.* 1 a coarse fabric made from hemp etc. 2 (*also* **hopsacking**) sacking for hops made from this. 3 a rough woven fabric of wool etc. used for clothing. **hop-tree** *n.* an American shrub, *Ptelea trifoliata*, the bitter fruit of which is used as a substitute for hops. **hop-vine** *n.* HOP-BIND (under HOP[2]). **hop-yard, hop-garden** *n.* a field where hops are grown. [MDut. *hoppe* (cp. G *Hopfen*)]

hope[1] (hōp) *n.* 1 an expectant desire; confidence in a future event (*Her hopes were justified*). 2 a ground for such expectation, trust or confidence (*There is still room for hope*). 3 a person or thing that is the cause for hope. 4 that which is hoped for. 5 †a feeling of trust. ~*v.i.* 1 to feel hope (*We hope for a victory*). 2 to have confidence; to be hopeful. ~*v.t.* 1 to expect with desire. 2 to look forward to with confidence. 3 †to expect. **not a hope!** (*coll.*) that which will never happen. **not to have a hope in hell** HELL. **some hope!** (*coll.*) that will never happen. **to hope against hope** to cling to a slight chance. **hope chest** *n.* (*N Am.*) a woman's bottom drawer. **hopeful** *a.* 1 feeling hope. 2 giving rise to hope. 3 promising. ~*n.* a person poised for success (used ironically where a person is not likely to succeed). **hopefully** *adv.* 1 in a hopeful way. 2 (*coll.*) it is hoped (*Hopefully, he'll pay*). **hopefulness** *n.* **hopeless** *a.* 1 destitute of hope, despairing. 2 affording no hope, desperate. 3 incompetent or showing incompetence. **hopelessly** *adv.* **hopelessness** *n.* [OE *hopa* (cp. Dut. *hoop*, Swed. *hopp*, G *Hoffe*), whence *hopian*, to hope]

Usage note The use of *hopefully* to express a general hope (as a sentence adverb) is quite widely disapproved of, though it is very common.

hope[2] (hōp) *n.* a small enclosed valley, the upper part of a dale (often used in place names). [OE *-hop*, in *fennhop* etc.]

hoplite (hop´lit) *n.* in ancient Greece, a heavily-armed soldier. [Gr. *hoplitēs*, from *hoplon*, weapon]

hopper[1] HOP[1].

hopper[2] HOP[2].

hopple (hop´əl) *v.t.* to fetter (a horse, cattle etc.) by tying the feet together. ~*n.* a shackle or fetter used for this purpose. [etym. uncertain, cp. the later HOBBLE]

Hoppus foot (hop´əs) *n.* a unit of volume for timber equal to 1.27 cu. ft. (0.034 cu. m). [Edward *Hoppus*, 18th cent. English surveyor]

hopscotch (hop´skoch) *n.* a children's game in which a stone is driven by the foot of a player hopping from one compartment to another of a figure traced on the ground. [HOP[1]]

horal (haw´rəl) *a.* 1 of or relating to hours. 2 hourly. **horary** (-rəri) *a.* 1 of the hours. 2 occurring every hour. [late L *hōrālis, hōrārius*, from *hōra*, HOUR]

Horatian (hərā´shən) *a.* of, relating to or resembling the Latin poet Horace or his poetry. [L *Horātiānus*, from *Horātius*, Horace]

horde (hawd) *n.* 1 a gang, a multitude (usu. in contempt). 2 a nomadic tribe or clan esp. a Central Asian group. *~v.i.* **1** to live in hordes. **2** to gather together in gangs. **3** a large moving mass of animals or insects. [F, from Turk. *ordū*, camp (cp. URDU)]

Usage note See note under HOARD.

hordein (haw´dē in) *n.* a protein found in barley grains. [L *hordeum*, barley]

horehound (haw´hownd), **hoarhound** *n.* **1** a labiate herb, *Marrubium vulgare*, with woolly stem and leaves and aromatic juice, used as a tonic and a remedy for colds etc.; white horehound. **2** a labiate herb, *Ballota nigra*, with an unpleasant aroma; black horehound. **3** any of various allied herbs. [OE *hārehūne* (*hār*, HOAR, *hūne*, etym. unknown)]

horizon (hərī´zən) *n.* **1** the circular line where the sky and the earth seem to meet, the sensible horizon. **2** the great circle parallel to it, the centre of which is the centre of the earth, the celestial horizon. **3** the boundary of one's mental vision, experience etc. **4** in archaeology, the level at which a particular set of remains or artefacts is found. **5** (*Geol.*) a layer of rock within a stratum etc. that has particular characteristics. **6** in soil science, a layer in a soil profile having particular characteristics. **on the horizon 1** (of an event etc.) imminent; likely to appear or happen soon. **2** visible. **horizonless** *a.* [F, from late L *horīzontem*, nom. *-zōn*, Gr. *horizōn*, from *horizein*, to bound, from *horos*, a limit]

horizontal (horizon´təl) *a.* **1** of or relating to the horizon. **2** parallel to the plane of the horizon, at right angles to the vertical. **3** situated at or near the horizon. **4** measured or contained in a plane of the horizon. **5** applied uniformly to all members of a group. **6** in economics, relating to companies etc. engaged in identical stages of production etc. (*horizontal integration*). *~n.* **1** a horizontal line, plane, bar etc. **2** a Tasmanian shrub with horizontal branches. **horizontality** (-tal´-) *n.* **horizontally** *adv.* [as HORIZON]

hormone (haw´mōn) *n.* **1** a secretion from an internal gland having the property of stimulating vital and functional physiological activity. **2** in plants, an organically produced compound that is essential for growth. **3** any synthetic substance with similar effects or properties. **hormonal** (-mō´-) *a.* **hormonally** *adv.* **hormone replacement therapy** *n.* treatment involving replacement of deficient hormones to counteract conditions associated with the menopause. [from Gr. *hormaein*, to arouse, to stimulate]

horn (hawn) *n.* **1** a projecting bony growth, usu. pointed and in pairs on the heads of certain animals. **2** the substance, usu. keratin, of which such growths are composed. **3** an organ or growth resembling horns, as the feeler of a snail etc. **4** anything made of or like a horn in shape, as a powder flask or a drinking vessel. **5** a metal wind instrument, orig. of horn. **6** FRENCH HORN (under FRENCH). **7** a horn player. **8** a device for sounding a warning or other signal (*foghorn*). **9** an extremity of a curved object, as of the moon when on the wane or waxing. **10** the imaginary projection on the forehead of a cuckold. **11** a branch of a lake, inlet of the sea or stream. **12** (*also* **the Horn**) Cape Horn. **13** (*N Am., sl.*) the telephone. **14** (*Geol.*) a pyramid-shaped peak formed by glacial action. **15** (*taboo sl.*) an erection of the penis. **16** a wing of an army. **17** one of the alternatives of a dilemma. *~v.t.* **1** to provide with horns. **2** to cuckold. **3** to gore. **on the horns of a dilemma 1** in a situation involving a choice between two equally undesirable alternatives. **2** in an awkward situation. **to draw in one's horns** to pull in one's horns. **to horn in** (*sl.*) to push in, to intrude (on). **to pull in one's horns 1** to repress one's ardour. **2** to curtail one's expenses. **3** to draw back, to check oneself. **hornbeak** *n.* the garfish. **hornbeam** *n.* any tree of the genus *Carpinus*, having smooth bark and yielding tough timber. **hornbill** *n.* any bird of the family Bucerotidae, having a large bone-crested bill. **horn blower** *n.* a person who plays a horn. **hornbook** *n.* (*Hist.*) **1** an alphabet with the Lord's Prayer etc., formerly printed on a slip of paper, fastened to a board and covered with horn to prevent its being torn. **2** a primer. **horned** *a.* **1** having a horn or horns. **2** having projections or extremities like horns. **3** curved like a horn (*horned moon*). **horned horse** *n.* the gnu. **hornedness** (-nid-) *n.* **horned owl, horn owl** *n.* any owl of the genus *Bubo*, having large ear tufts. **horned snake, horned viper** *n.* an Indian or African viper of the genus *Cerastes*, with horns over the eyes. **horned toad** *n.* a small American toad-like lizard, *Phrynosoma cornutum*, covered with spines. **horner** *n.* **1** a person who works or deals in horns. **2** a person who blows or plays a horn. **horn-foot, horn-footed** *a.* having a hoof; hoofed. **hornful** *n.* as much as a drinking horn will hold. **hornish** *a.* **hornist** *n.* a horn player. **hornless** *a.* **hornlike** *a.* **horn-maker** *n.* a maker of horns, esp. for drinking. **hornmercury** *n.* native mercurous chloride or calomel. **horn of plenty** *n.* CORNUCOPIA. **horn owl** HORNED OWL (under HORN). **hornpipe** *n.* **1** a lively dance, usu. for one person, popular among sailors. **2** the music for such a dance. **3** an old wind instrument. **horn-rimmed** *a.* (esp. of spectacles) having rims made of (a material resembling) horn. **horn-rims** *n.pl.* horn-rimmed spectacles. **hornsilver** *n.* cerargyrite. **hornstone** *n.* chert. **hornwork** *n.* an outwork consisting of two half-bastions and a curtain. **hornwort** *n.* any aquatic plant of the genus *Ceratophyllum*, with submerged branching leaves. **hornwrack** *n.* a bryozoan. **horny** *a.* (*comp.* **hornier**, *superl.* **horniest**) **1** of or like horn. **2** callous (*horny-handed*). **3** having or abounding in horns. **4** (*sl.*) sexually excited; lustful. **hornily** *adv.* **horniness** *n.* [OE (cp. Icel., Dan., Swed., and G *Horn*; cogn. with L *cornu*, Gr. *keras*)]

hornblende (hawn´blend) *n.* a dark-coloured mineral consisting of silica, magnesia, lime and iron. [G *Horn* (HORN, BLENDE)]

hornet (haw´nit) *n.* a large social wasp, *Vespa crabro*, with a severe sting. **to stir up a hornet's nest** to stir up trouble or excite the animosity of other people. [OE *hyrnet* (cp. G *Hornisse*)]

hornfels (hawn´felz) *n.* a compact rock formed by the action of heat on clay rocks. [G, horn rock]

hornito (hawnē´tō) *n.* (*pl.* **hornitos**) a small smoking mound or fumarole produced by volcanic action. [Sp., dim. of *horno*, ult. from L *furnus*, oven, see FURNACE]

hornswoggle (hawn´swogəl) *v.t.* (*sl.*) to cheat, deceive. [etym. unknown]

horo- (hor´ō) *comb. form* of or relating to times or seasons, or to the measurement of time. [Gr. *hōra*, a season, an hour]

horography (horog´rəfi) *n.* the art of constructing clocks, watches etc. **horographer** *n.* [-GRAPHY]

†**horologe** (hor´əloj) *n.* a timepiece. **horologer** (-rol´-), **horologist** (-rol´-) *n.* **1** a person skilled in horology. **2** a person who makes horologes. **horologic** (-loj´-), **horological** *a.* **horology** (-rol´əji) *n.* **1** the art of measuring time, or of constructing instruments to indicate time. **2** the study of this. [OF, from L *horologium*, Gr. *hōrologion* (HORO-, *legein*, to tell)]

horometry (horom´ətri) *n.* the art or practice of measuring time. **horometrical** (horəmet´-) *a.*

horoscope (hor´əskōp) *n.* **1** the prediction of a person's future based on a map showing the relative position of the stars and planets at that person's birth. **2** such a map. **3** an observation of the sky and the configuration of the planets at a particular time, esp. at the moment of a person's birth, in order to foretell that person's future. **horoscopic** (-skop´-), **horoscopical** *a.* **horoscopy** (-os´-) *n.* (*pl.* **horoscopies**) **1** the casting of horoscopes. **2** a horoscope. [F, from L *horoscopus*, Gr. *hōroskopos* (*skopos*, observer)]

horrendous (həren´dəs) *a.* awful; horrifying. **horrendously** *adv.* **horrendousness** *n.* [L *horrendus*, ger. of *horrēre*, to bristle]

horrent (hor´ənt) *a.* (*poet.*) **1** bristling. **2** erect, as bristles. **3** shuddering. [L *horrens -ntem*, pres.p. of *horrēre*, to bristle, to shudder]

horrible (hor´ibəl) *a.* **1** causing or tending to cause horror; dreadful, shocking, harrowing. **2** (*coll.*) unpleasant, excessive. **horribleness** *n.* **horribly** *adv.* [OF, from L *horribilis*, from *horrēre*, to bristle, to shudder]

horrid (hor´id) *a.* **1** horrible, repellent. **2** (*coll.*) nasty, unpleasant, frightful. **3** †rough, bristly. **horridly** *adv.* **horridness** *n.* [L *horridus*, from *horrēre*, to bristle, to shudder]

horrify (hor´ifī) *v.t.* (*3rd pers. sing. pres.* **horrifies,** *pres.p.* **horrifying,** *past, p.p.* **horrified**) **1** to strike with horror. **2** to scandalize. **horrific** (-if´-) *a.* **horrifically** *adv.* **horrification** (-fikā´shən) *n.* **horrifiedly** *adv.* **horrifying** *a.* **horrifyingly** *adv.* [L *horrificāre* (*horrēre*, to bristle, to shudder, *-ficāre, facere*, to make)]

horripilation (horipilā´shən) *n.* (*formal*) goose-flesh, a sensation of a creeping or motion of the hair of the body, caused by disease, terror etc. **horripilant** (-ip´-) *a.* **horripilate** (-ip´-) *v.t., v.i.* [late L *horripilatio*, from *horripilāre* (from *horrēre*, to bristle, to shudder, *pilus*, hair)]

horrisonant (horis´ənənt) *a.* having a dreadful sound. [L *horrēre*, to bristle, to shudder, *sonāns -ntem*, pres.p. of *sonāre*, to sound]

horror (hor´ə) *n.* **1** dread or terror. **2** intense loathing; hatred. **3** (*coll.*) intense dismay. **4** that which excites terror or repulsion. **5** (*coll.*) a bad, ugly or mischievous person or thing (*He's a little horror*). **6** a shaking, shuddering or shivering. ~*a.* (of novels, films etc.) depicting gruesome, frightening, often paranormal events. **the horrors 1** a fit of horror or depression; the blues. **2** delirium tremens. **3** an exclamation of dismay. **horror-stricken, horror-struck** *a.* overwhelmed with horror; shocked. [OF *horrour*, L *horrōrem*, nom. *-or*, from *horrēre*, to bristle, to shudder]

hors (aw) *prep.* out of, beyond. **hors concours** (kō̃´kuə) *a.* **1** unrivalled. **2** not in competition. **hors de combat** (də kō̃´bah) *a.* out of the battle or the running. **hors d'oeuvre** (dœ´vrə) *n.* (*pl.* **hors d'oeuvres** (dœ´vrə, dœ´vrəz)) a dish not forming part of the main meal, served as an appetizer before or sometimes during a meal. [F, earlier *fors*, L *foris*]

horse (haws) *n.* **1** a solid-hoofed quadruped, *Equus caballus*, with mane and tail of long coarse hair, domesticated and employed as a beast of draught and burden. **2** the adult male of the species; a stallion or gelding. **3** any other quadruped of the genus *Equus*, such as asses, zebras etc. **4** (*collect.*) cavalry. **5** a frame or other device used as a support. **6** VAULTING HORSE (under VAULT[2]). **7** SAWHORSE (under SAW[1]). **8** CLOTHES HORSE (under CLOTHE). **9** (*coll.*) a unit of horsepower. **10** (*Hist.*) a wooden frame on which soldiers were made to sit as a punishment. **11** (*Mining*) a mass of rock, clay etc., forming an obstruction. **12** (*Naut.*) any of various ropes, bars etc. **13** (*sl.*) heroin. ~*v.t.* **1** to provide with a horse or horses. **2** (of a stallion) to copulate with (a mare). **3** to carry on the back. ~*v.i.* **1** to fool about. **2** to mount or ride on horseback. **dark horse** DARK. **horse and foot** cavalry and infantry. **horses for courses** the matching of tasks to talents, skills etc. **the horse's mouth** (of information etc.) the most reliable source. **to change horses in midstream** to alter plans, views etc. in the middle of a project. **to eat like a horse** (*coll.*) to eat a lot. **to get on one's high horse** (*coll.*) to be arrogant or disdainfully aloof. **to hold one's horses 1** (*coll.*) to stop. **2** (*coll.*) to hesitate; refrain from acting. **to horse!** mount your horses. **to take horse 1** to mount for the purpose of riding. **2** to travel on horseback. **horse-and-buggy** *a.* (*N Am.*) belonging or appropriate to an earlier period. **horse artillery** *n.* field artillery with the gunners mounted. **horseback** *n.* the back of a horse. **on horseback** mounted on a horse. **horsebean** *n.* a coarse variety of bean used for feeding horses. **horse-block** *n.* a block or stage to assist a person in mounting on horseback. **horsebox** *n.* a closed van, car or trailer for transporting horses. **horse brass** *n.* a brass decoration of a type originally hung on a horse's harness. **horse-breaker** *n.* a person who breaks in or trains horses. **horsecar** *n.* a tramcar drawn by a horse or horses. **horse chestnut** *n.* **1** (*also* **horse chestnut tree**) a large tree of the genus *Aesculus*, with coarse, bitter fruit. **2** the nut of this tree, a conker. **horse-cloth** *n.* a rug to cover a horse. **horse-coper** *n.* a horse-dealer. **horse-coping** *n.* **horse-dealer** *n.* a person who deals in horses. **horse-dealing** *n.* **horse-doctor** *n.* a veterinary surgeon. **horse-drawn** *a.* (of a vehicle) pulled by a horse or horses. **horse-faced** *a.* having a long horselike face. **horseflesh** *n.* **1** the flesh of a horse, used as food. **2** (*collect.*) horses. **horsefly** *n.* (*pl.* **horseflies**) any of the insects of the family Tabanidae that irritate horses. **Horse Guards** *n.pl.* **1** the brigade of cavalry of the English household troops (now primarily an armoured-car regiment), esp. the 3rd Regiment, the Royal Horse Guards. **2** their barracks or headquarters. **horsehair** *n.* the long hair of the mane and tail of horses, used for padding etc. **horse-knacker** *n.* a knacker. **horse latitudes** *n.pl.* the region of calms on the northern edge of the north-east trade winds (said to be so called because early navigators frequently threw overboard there any horses they were carrying to America and the W Indies). **horse laugh** *n.* a loud, coarse laugh. **horseleech** *n.* **1** a large freshwater leech of the genus *Haemopis*, which feeds by swallowing. **2** (*fig.*) a rapacious person, a bloodsucker (in allusion to Prov. xxx.15). **horseless** *a.* †**horseless carriage** *n.* a motor car. **horselike** *a.* **horse-litter** *n.* **1** a litter borne by horses. **2** horse bedding. **horse mackerel** *n.* any large mackerel-type fish such as the scad, tuna etc. **horseman** *n.* (*pl.* **horsemen**) **1** a rider on horseback. **2** a person skilled in riding or managing horses. **3** a mounted soldier. **4** a variety of the domestic pigeon. **horsemanship** *n.* the art of riding, managing etc. horses; skill in doing this. **horse marine** *n.* **1** a member of a mythical body of troops. **2** a person out of their element. **horse mill** *n.* a mill turned by horses. **horse mushroom** *n.* a large coarse edible mushroom, *Agaricus arvenis*. **horse opera** *n.* (*N Am., sl.*) a western film. **horse-pistol** *n.* a holstered pistol formerly used by horsemen. **horseplay** *n.* rough, boisterous play. **horse-pond** *n.* a pond for watering and washing horses, proverbially a place for ducking unpleasant persons. **horsepower** *n.* **1** an imperial unit of power equivalent to 550 foot-pounds (745.7 watts) per second. **2** mechanical power expressed in such units. **horse race** *n.* a race between horses with riders. **horse racing** *n.* **horse radish** *n.* **1** a plant, *Armoracia rusticana*, with long leaves and a pungent, acrid root, used as a condiment. **2** the root of this. **horse-rider** *n.* a person riding a horse. **horse-riding** *n.* **horse road, horse way** *n.* a road or way on which horses may travel, a bridleway. **horse sense** *n.* (*coll.*) common sense. **horseshit** *n.* (*esp. N Am., taboo, sl.*) nonsense, rubbish. **horseshoe** *n.* **1** a shoe for horses. **2** anything resembling this in shape. ~*a.* shaped like this. **horseshoe bat** *n.* any bat of the Old World family Rhinolophidae, having a horseshoe-shaped growth round the nostrils. **horseshoe crab** *n.* a large marine anthropod, *Xiphosura polyphemus*, having a heavily armoured crescent-shaped body. **horseshoeing** *n.* the act or occupation of shoeing horses. **horseshoer** *n.* **horse's neck**

n. (*sl.*) a drink of ginger ale usu. with spirits. **horse-soldier** *n.* a horse-mounted soldier. **horsetail** *n.* **1** the tail of a horse. **2** this used as a Turkish standard or token of rank. **3** a plant of the cryptogamous genus *Equisetum*, with whorls of branches like the hairs in a horse's tail. **4** PONYTAIL (under PONY). **horse-trading** *n.* **1** hard bargaining. **2** (*N Am.*) dealing in horses. **horsewhip** *n.* a whip for driving horses. ~*v.t.* (*pres.p.* **horsewhipping,** *past, p.p* **horsewhipped**) to flog with a horsewhip; to thrash. **horsewoman** *n.* (*pl.* **horse-women**) **1** a woman who rides on horseback. **2** a woman skilled in riding and managing horses. **horsey, horsy** *a.* (*comp.* **horsier,** *superl.* **horsiest**) **1** of or like a horse. **2** of, relating to or fond of horses or horse racing. **3** (esp. of a woman) affecting upper-class speech or manner. **horsily** *adv.* **horsiness** *n.* [OE *hors* (cp. Icel. *hross*, OHG *hros*, Dut. *ros*, G *Ross*)]

horst (hawst) *n.* (*Geol.*) a raised block of land separated by faults from the surrounding land. [G]

hortative (haw´tətiv), **hortatory** (haw´tətəri) *a.* giving or containing advice or encouragement. **hortation** (-ā´shən) *n.* [L *hortātīvus*, from *hortārī*, to EXHORT]

hortensia (hawten´siə) *n.* a type of hydrangea, *Hydrangea macrophylla*, having large infertile flower heads.

horticulture (haw´tikŭlchə) *n.* the art of cultivating or managing gardens. **horticultural** (-kŭl´-) *a.* **horticulturalist, horticulturist** *n.* [L *hortus*, garden, CULTURE]

hortus siccus (hawtəs sik´əs) *n.* **1** a collection of dried plants arranged systematically; a herbarium. **2** a collection of uninteresting facts. [L, dry garden]

Hos. *abbr.* Hosea (Old Testament).

hosanna (hōzan´ə) *n., int.* **1** an acclamatory prayer for blessing. **2** a shout of praise and adoration. [late L and Gr., from Heb. *hōshī ʿāh-nnā*, save, we pray]

hose (hōz) *n.* **1** (a piece of) flexible tubing for water or other fluid, as that used by firefighters. **2** (*pl.*) (*also* †**hosen**) stockings, socks etc. collectively. **3** (*Hist.*) close-fitting breeches or trousers reaching to the knees. ~*v.t.* **1** to water or drench with a hose. **2** to provide with hose. **hoseless** *a.* **hoseman** *n.* (*pl.* **hosemen**) a fire-fighter who works the hose. **hosepipe** *n.* a length of hose for water etc. **hose-reel** *n.* **1** a drum (usu. on a cart or truck) for carrying hoses. **2** a vehicle carrying a hose-reel. **hosier** (-ziə) *n.* a person who deals in hosiery. **hosiery** *n.* (*pl.* **hosieries**) **1** stockings and socks. **2** knitted or woven underclothing. **3** a factory for such goods. **4** the shop or business of a hosier. [OE *hosa* (cp. Dut. *hoos*, Icel. *hosa*, G *Hose*)]

hospice (hos´pis) *n.* **1** a nursing home or hospital for the terminally ill, needy or afflicted. **2** a convent or other place for the reception and entertainment of travellers on some difficult or dangerous road or pass, as among the Alps. [F, from L *hospitium*, from *hospes -pitis*, guest]

hospitable (hos´pitəbəl, -pit´-) *a.* entertaining or disposed to entertain strangers or guests with kindness. **hospitableness** *n.* **hospitably** *adv.* †**hospitage** (hos´pitij) *n.* **1** hospitality. **2** a place of hospitality. **hospitality** (-tal´-) *n.* liberal entertainment of strangers or guests. [F, from late L *hospitāre*, to receive as a guest, L *hospitium*, from *hospes -pitis*, guest]

hospital (hos´pitəl) *n.* **1** an institution for the reception and treatment of the sick or injured. **2** †a place of shelter or entertainment, a hospice; one of the establishments of the Knights Hospitallers. **3** (*Law*) any of certain charitable foundations. **hospital corners** *n.pl.* a way of tucking in bedclothes used by hospital staff. **hospital fever** *n.* a kind of typhus fever formerly widespread in crowded hospitals. **hospitalism** *n.* the adverse condition resulting from a prolonged stay in hospital. **hospitalize, hospitalise** *v.t.* **1** to send to hospital. **2** to admit for hospital treatment. **hospitalization** (-ā´shən) *n.* **hospital ship** *n.* a ship equipped for the specific task of treating and transporting sick etc. soldiers. **hospital social worker** *n.* a hospital-based social worker who tends to patients once they are discharged. **hospital train** *n.* a train transporting wounded soldiers from the scene of a battle or war. **hospital trust** *n.* a trust consisting of a National Health Service hospital which is run independent of the local authority. [OF, from late L *hospitāle*, from L pl. *hospitālia*, as HOSPICE]

hospitality HOSPITABLE.

hospitaller (hos´pitələ), (*N Am.*) **hospitaler** *n.* **1** (*Hist.*) one of a religious brotherhood whose office was to relieve the poor, strangers and the sick. **2** a chaplain residing in a hospital for the reception of the poor or strangers. **Knight Hospitaller** KNIGHT.

hospitium (hospish´iəm) *n.* (*pl.* **hospitia** (-shiə)) a hospice.

hospodar (hos´pədah) *n.* (*Hist.*) a prince or governor of Wallachia and Moldavia under the Ottomans. [Slav.]

host[1] (hōst) *n.* **1** a person who entertains another. **2** the landlord of an inn or hotel. **3** the compère of a TV or radio show. **4** (*Biol.*) an animal or plant on which another is parasitic. **5** an organism into which an organ or tissue is grafted or transplanted. ~*v.t.* **1** (of a person) to act as host at (a social event, occasion etc.). **2** to receive and entertain as one's guest. **3** to be the compère of (a show etc.). **4** †to lodge, to entertain. ~†*v.i.* to take up one's abode, to lodge. **hostess** (-is) *n.* **1** a woman who receives or entertains guests. **2** a woman paid to entertain customers in a bar, nightclub etc. **3** a woman employed to attend to the comfort of travellers on passenger planes, ships etc. **4** the landlady of an inn or hotel. [OF *hoste* (F *hôte*), L *hospitem* nom. *hospes*, a host, a guest]

host[2] (hōst) *n.* **1** a great number, a multitude. **2** †an army. **a host in oneself** a person of extraordinary skills, resources etc. **host of heaven** *n.* **1** the stars, planets etc. **2** the angels and archangels. [OF, from L *hostis* enemy, stranger]

host[3] (hōst) *n.* the consecrated bread or wafer used in the Eucharist. [ME *oste*, OF *oiste*, L *hostia*, sacrificial victim]

hosta (hos´tə) *n.* any plant of the genus *Hosta* having green decorative leaves and blue, lilac and white flowers. [N. T. *Host*, 1761–1834, Austrian physician]

hostage (hos´tij) *n.* **1** a person given or seized in pledge for the performance of certain conditions or for the safety of others. **2** the state of being so held. **3** any security or pledge. **hostageship** *n.* **hostage-taker** *n.* **hostage-taking** *n.* **hostage to fortune** *n.* **1** an acquisition or undertaking etc. considered as endangered by misfortune, unforeseen events etc. **2** (*pl.*) the people and things a person most values. **to give a hostage to fortune** to put oneself at a disadvantage by risking the loss of someone or something valued highly. [OF (F *ôtage*), ult. from L *obsidātus*, hostageship, from *obses obsidis*, a hostage]

hostel (hos´təl) *n.* **1** a house or extra-collegiate hall for the residence of students etc. **2** a place of residence not run commercially, esp. for the homeless. **3** a youth hostel. **4** †an inn. **hosteller,** (*N Am.*) **hosteler** *n.* **1** a student in a hostel. **2** †an innkeeper, an ostler. **hostelling,** (*N Am.*) **hosteling** *n.* the practice of staying at youth hostels when travelling. **hostelry** *n.* (*pl.* **hostelries**) (*facet.*) an inn, a pub. [OF, as HOSPITAL]

hostess HOST[1].

hostile (hos´tīl) *a.* **1** of or relating to an enemy. **2** showing enmity; unfriendly. **3** (of a place, situation etc.) inhospitable, harsh. **4** resistant (*He is hostile to change*). **hostilely** *adv.* **hostile witness** *n.* (*Law*) a witness whose evidence is unfavourable to the party which has called them. **hostility** (-til´-) *n.* (*pl.*

hostilities) 1 enmity; antagonism. 2 state of war. 3 (*pl.*) acts of war. 4 opposition (in thought etc.) or resistance (to change etc.). [L *hostilis*, from *hostis*, HOST[2]]

hostler (hos´lə) *n.* 1 (*Hist.*) OSTLER. 2 (*N Am.*) a person who services or is in charge of vehicles, esp. railway wagons or locomotives etc. when they are not in use.

hot (hot) *a.* (*comp.* **hotter,** *superl.* **hottest**) 1 having a high temperature. 2 (of food) made by heating and served before cooling. 3 producing a sensation of heat. 4 (of spices etc.) acrid, pungent. 5 ardent, impetuous; passionate, fierce. 6 (*coll.*) knowledgeable (*hot on sports cars*). 7 eager, enthusiastic. 8 (*coll.*) strict or severe. 9 angry or upset. 10 (*coll.*) exciting, excited, arduous. 11 sexually excited. 12 (of the scent in hunting) fresh and strong. 13 (of dancing) highly elaborated, florid. 14 (of a player) very skilful. 15 much favoured (*He's the hot favourite to win*). 16 (of animals) ruttish. 17 (of news) fresh, recent. 18 (*coll.*) (of Treasury bills) newly issued. 19 (*sl.*) (of stolen goods) easily identifiable. 20 (*sl.*) wanted by the police. 21 (*coll.*) very good. 22 (*sl.*) radioactive. 23 (of the ball in ball games) thrown or struck in such a way that the opponent has difficulty in returning it. 24 (of jazz) arousing excitement or emotion (by improvisation etc.). 25 (*coll.*) (of information) very reliable. ~*adv.* 1 hotly. 2 fiercely, angrily. 3 ardently, eagerly. ~*v.t.*, *v.i.* (*pres.p.* **hotting,** *past, p.p.* **hotted**) 1 to make or become hot. 2 to make or become active, intense or exciting. **hot under the collar** 1 indignant, angry. 2 embarrassed. **in hot water** WATER. **not so hot** (*coll.*) mediocre. **the hots** (*sl.*) strong sexual desire. **to give it one hot** (*sl.*) to punish, censure or abuse severely. **to go hot and cold** to feel alternately hot and cold (owing to fear etc.). **to have the hots for** (*sl.*) to be sexually attracted to. **to hot up** to become more intense, exciting etc. **to make it/ things hot for someone** to make a situation unpleasant for someone. **to sell/ go like hot cakes** to be sold (or go) quickly. **hot air** *n.* (*coll.*) boastful, empty talk. **hot-air** *a.* using hot air. **hot-air balloon** *n.* a balloon containing air which is heated by a flame causing it to rise. **hotbed** *n.* 1 a bed of earth heated by means of fermenting manure, used for raising early and tender plants. 2 any place which favours rapid growth of disease, vice etc. **hot blast** *n.* a blast of heated air introduced into a smelting furnace. **hot-blooded** *a.* excitable, irritable, passionate. †**hot-brained** *a.* violent, hot-headed. **hot cathode** *n.* a cathode heated to emit electrons. **hot-cockles** *n.* a child's game in which a person with eyes covered guesses who strikes them. **hot cross bun** *n.* a spicy yeast bun with a cross marked on the top, eaten esp. on Good Friday. **hot-desking** *n.* the practice of sharing workspace etc. or moving desks around according to need. **hot dog** *n.* 1 a hot sausage sandwiched in a roll. 2 (*N Am., sl.*) a person who performs acrobatic manoeuvres or stunts, esp. when skiing, skating or skateboarding. ~*int.* (*N Am., sl.*) used to express approval. **hotdog** *v.i.* (*pres.p.* **hotdogging,** *past, p.p.* **hotdogged**) (*N Am., sl.*) to perform acrobatic manoeuvres or stunts, esp. when skiing, skating or skateboarding. **hotdogger** *n.* **hotdogging** *n.* **hot favourite,** (*N Am.*) **hot favorite** *n.* the horse, runner etc. most likely to win in a race etc. **hot flash** *n.* (*N Am.*) HOT FLUSH (under HOT). **hot flush** *n.* a sudden feeling of warmth accompanied by blushing, esp. during the menopause. **hotfoot** *adv.* very hastily, swiftly. ~*a.* acting quickly. **to hotfoot it** (*sl.*) to run or go quickly. **hot gospeller,** (*N Am.*) **hot gospeler** *n.* 1 a revivalist preacher with a loud, enthusiastic style of addressing an audience. 2 a fanatical propagandist. **hothead** *n.* a fiery or impetuous person. **hot-headed** *a.* fiery, impetuous, passionate. **hot-headedly** *adv.* **hot-headedness** *n.* **hothouse** *n.* 1 a plant house where a relatively high artificial temperature is maintained to facilitate growth. 2 any environment encouraging the rapid growth (of skills etc.). ~*a.* (*coll.*) too sensitive, delicate. ~*v.t.* 1 to raise etc. in or as if in a hothouse. 2 to encourage or force the development of (skills etc.). **hotline** *n.* a telephone line for swift communication, esp. in emergencies. **hotly** *adv.* **hot metal** *n.* (*Print.*) (of machines, methods etc.) using type made from molten metal. **hot money** *n.* capital transferred from one financial institution to another at frequent intervals. **hotness** *n.* **hot pants** *n.pl.* very brief skin-tight women's shorts, often worn with a bib. **hotplate** *n.* 1 a round plate, electrically heated, on top of a cooker. 2 a portable heatable plate for keeping food warm. **hotpot** *n.* a dish of meat cooked with potatoes and other vegetables in a closed pot in an oven. **hot potato** *n.* (*pl.* **hot potatoes**) a controversial issue, something difficult or dangerous to deal with. **hot-press** *n.* a machine for giving a gloss to paper or linen by pressure between heated metal plates and glazed boards. ~*v.t.* to subject to this process. **hot rod** *n.* a car with an engine considerably modified to increase its performance greatly. **hot-rod** *v.t.* (*pres.p.* **hot-rodding,** *past, p.p.* **hot-rodded**) to soup up (a vehicle etc.). ~*v.i.* to drive a hot rod. **hot-rodder** *n.* **hot seat** *n.* (*sl.*) 1 an awkward, difficult or dangerous position. 2 the electric chair. **in the hot seat** in an awkward, difficult or dangerous position. **hot shoe** *n.* in photography, a socket on a camera through which electrical contact is made to an electronic flash. **hot-short** *a.* (of iron) brittle when hot. **hotshot** *n.* (*esp. N Am., coll.*) 1 an important, often ostentatious person. 2 a prolific goal-scorer or point-scorer in football, basketball etc. ~*a.* 1 important, ostentatious. 2 accurate, expert. 3 high-profile. **hot-spirited** *a.* having a fiery spirit. **hot spot** *n.* 1 a warm, sunny place, esp. a holiday resort. 2 a place of potential trouble. 3 a point in an engine etc. with an (excessively) high temperature. 4 (*coll.*) a lively night-club etc. **hot spring** *n.* a spring of mineral water which has been heated underground. **hotspur** *n.* a rash, sometimes violent person. **hot stuff** *n.* (*coll.*) 1 an impressive or excellent thing or person. 2 a very attractive person. 3 a spirited, vigorous or passionate person. 4 pornographic or erotic literature, film etc. **hot-tempered** *a.* quick to anger; irascible. **hotter** *n.* (*sl.*) a person who drives fast in a stolen vehicle. **hottie, hotty** *n.* (*pl.* **hotties**) (*coll.*) a hot-water bottle. **hotting** *n.* (*sl.*) driving fast in a stolen vehicle. **hottish** *a.* **hot tub** *n.* a bath resembling a Jacuzzi. **hot wall** *n.* a wall with built-in flues to assist in ripening the fruit of trees trained against it. **hot war** *n.* real war. **hot water** *n.* (*coll.*) a state of trouble or disgrace. **hot-water bottle,** (*N Am.*) **hot-water bag** *n.* a usu. rubber container filled with hot water, used for warming a bed. **hot well** *n.* 1 a natural warm spring. 2 the reservoir for warm water from the condenser in a condensing engine. **hot-wire** *a.* using the properties of heated wire. ~*v.t.* (*N Am., sl.*) to start the engine of (a car etc.) without the ignition key. [OE *hāt* (cp. Dut. *heet*, Icel. *heitr*, G *heiss*)]

hotchpot (hoch´pot) *n.* (*Law*) a general commixture of property in order to secure equal division (among heirs of an intestate person etc.). [F *hochepot* (*hocher*, to shake, toss together, from Gmc., cp. Flem. *hutsen*, POT[1])]

hotchpotch (hoch´poch) *n.* 1 a confused mixture, a jumble. 2 a dish composed of various ingredients, esp. thick broth made with mutton or other meat and vegetables. 3 (*Law*) HOTCHPOT. [corr. of HOTCHPOT]

hotel (hōtel´) *n.* 1 a commercial establishment providing accommodation, meals etc. 2 (*Austral., New Zeal.*) a public house. 3 (*Hist.*) in France, a town residence or mansion. **hôtel-de-ville** (-dəvēl´) *n.* (*pl.* **hôtels-de-ville** (-teldə-)) a town hall. **hôtel-dieu** (-dyœ´) *n.* (*pl.* **hôtels-dieu** (-teldyœ´)) a hospital. **hotelier** (-iə) *n.* a hotel-keeper. [F, from OF *hostel*, see HOSTEL]

Hottentot (hot´əntot) *n.* (*pl.* **Hottentot, Hottentots**) (*offensive*) NAMA. [Dut., prob. from a formula in a Nama song and dance]

Usage note The use of *Hottentot* gives offence: the preferred term is *Nama*.

hotter, hottie HOT.

houdah HOWDAH.

Houdini (hoodē´ni) *n.* **1** a clever escape. **2** a person who is skilled at escaping. [Harry *Houdini*, 1874–1926, US escapologist]

hough HOCK[1].

hoummos HUMMUS.

hound (hownd) *n.* **1** a dog used in hunting (*bloodhound, deerhound, foxhound*). **2** a runner who chases the hares in hare and hounds. **3** (*coll.*) a mean, contemptible man. *~v.t.* **1** to hunt or chase with or as with hounds. **2** to set a dog, person etc. in pursuit. **3** to urge or cheer (on), to nag. **the hounds** a pack of foxhounds. **to ride to hounds** RIDE. **houndfish** *n.* (*pl.* **houndfish, houndfishes**) a dogfish. **houndish** *a.* **hound's tongue** *n.* a coarse, hairy plant, *Cynoglossum officinale*, of the borage family, with dull red flowers. **houndstooth** *n.* a pattern in material of broken checks resembling dogs' teeth. [OE *hund* (cp. Dut. *hond*, Icel. *hundr*, G *Hund*), prob. allied to L *canis*, Gr. *kuōn*]

hour (owə) *n.* **1** the 24th part of a natural day, the space of 60 minutes. **2** the point of time indicated by a clock etc. **3** (*pl.*) a particular time after midnight in the 24-hour clock. **4** a time allocated to some purpose (*lunch hour; happy hour*). **5** 15° of longitude. **6** (*pl.*) times appointed for work, attendance at office etc. **7** in the Roman Catholic Church, certain prayers to be said at fixed times of the day. **8** the distance travelled in an hour. **after hours** after closing time. **at all hours** at all times. **from hour to hour** FROM. **on the hour** at exactly one, two etc. o'clock. **the hour 1** the present time. **2** the time to act. **hour angle** *n.* the angular distance of a heavenly body east or west of the meridian. **hour circle** *n.* **1** a great circle passing through the celestial poles, a meridian (24 of which are usu. marked on the globe). **2** a circle on an equatorial telescope indicating the hour angle of an object. **hourglass** *n.* a glass having two bulbs and a connecting opening through which the sand in one bulb runs into the other, used for measuring small periods of time. *~a.* (of a woman's figure) having a narrow waist and large bust and hips. **hour hand** *n.* that hand which shows the hour on a clock or watch, distinct from minute hand. **hour-long** *a.* lasting for an hour. *~adv.* for an hour. **hourly** *a.* **1** happening or done every hour. **2** continual. *~adv.* **1** hour by hour. **2** frequently. [OF *hure, ure*, L, Gr. *hōra*, hour]

houri (hoo´ri) *n.* (*pl.* **houris**) **1** a nymph of the Muslim paradise. **2** a beautiful woman. [F, from Pers. *hūrī*, from Arab. *haura'*, having gazelle-like eyes]

house[1] (hows) *n.* (*pl.* **houses** (how´ziz)) **1** a building for shelter or residence, a dwelling, a place of abode. **2** a building used for a specified purpose (*bakehouse, coffee house, farmhouse, hen house, public house, warehouse*). **3 a** the abode of a religious order, a monastery. **b** the order itself. **4** a household. **5** a family or stock, esp. a noble family. **6 a** an assembly, esp. one of the legislative assemblies of a country. **b** a quorum of a legislative body. **7 a** a residential section of a boarding school. **b** the pupils within that section. **c** a division of a day school comprising pupils of all ages. **8** the audience at a place of entertainment. **9** a commercial establishment. **10** the game of bingo. **11 a** the station of a planet in the heavens. **b** a twelfth part of the heavens. **12** house music. **13** (*Hist.*) manner of living, table. **like a house on fire** very quickly and successfully. **on the house** (esp. of alcoholic drinks) given for no payment. **the House 1** the House of Commons, Lords, Representatives etc. **2** Christ Church, a college of Oxford University. **3** (*coll.*) the Stock Exchange. **4** (*Hist., euphem.*) the workhouse. **to bring the house down** BRING. **to keep/ make a House** to succeed in assembling a quorum or sufficient support in the House of Commons. **to keep (to) the house** to be confined through illness. **to play house** to play at being members of a family in their home. **to put/ set one's house in order** to settle one's affairs. **to set up house** to move into a separate dwelling. **house agent** *n.* a person who sells and lets houses, collects rents etc. **house and home** *n.* (an emphatic expression for) home. **house arrest** *n.* detention in one's own home under guard. **houseboat** *n.* a boat or barge with a cabin or house for living in. **housebound** *a.* unable to leave one's house, e.g. because of a disability. **houseboy** *n.* a male servant in a house, esp. in N Africa or India. **housebreaker** *n.* **1** a person who breaks into and robs houses, esp. in the daytime. **2** a worker employed to pull down houses. **housebreaking** *n.* **house-broken** *a.* HOUSE-TRAINED (under HOUSE[1]). **housebuilding** *n.* the activity of building houses. **housebuilder** *n.* **house buyer** *n.* a person who buys a house. **house-buying** *n.* **house carl, house carle** *n.* (*Hist.*) a household bodyguard of a Danish or English king or noble. **house church** *n.* a group of Christians meeting in a house for prayer, worship etc. **housecoat** *n.* a woman's long overgarment, worn in the house. **housecraft** *n.* the skills of managing a household. **house dog** *n.* a dog kept to guard the house. **house-father** *n.* a man in charge of children in a children's home etc. **house finch** *n.* a red-breasted finch, *Carpodacus mexicanus*, found in western N America. **house-flag** *n.* (*Naut.*) the particular flag of a ship's owner. **housefly** *n.* (*pl.* **houseflies**) any fly of the family Muscidae, esp. the common fly, *Musca domestica*. **houseful** *n.* (*pl.* **housefuls**) as many or as much as a house will hold. **house guest** *n.* a guest in a private house. **house-hunting** *n.* the activity of seeking a house in which to live. **house-hunt** *v.i.* **house-hunter** *n.* **house-husband** *n.* a married man who stays at home to run a household while his wife has a paid job. **housekeeper** *n.* **1** a woman employed to manage the affairs of a household. **2** a person in charge of a house, place of business etc. **housekeep** *v.i.* (*past, p.p.* **housekept**). **housekeeping** *n.* **1** the care of a household. **2** the money allotted for this. **3** routine maintenance and organizational work in a business or computer context. **houseleek** *n.* a plant with thick, fleshy leaves, *Sempervivum tectorum*, growing on the tops of walls and houses in Britain. **houseless** *a.* having no house or shelter. **house lights** *n.pl.* the lights in the auditorium of a theatre, cinema etc. **house magazine** *n.* a magazine published by a company etc. largely concerning its own personnel, activities etc. **housemaid** *n.* a female servant employed to keep a house clean etc., esp. one in charge of reception rooms and bedrooms. **housemaid's knee** *n.* inflammation of the kneecap, often due to excessive kneeling. **houseman** *n.* (*pl.* **housemen**) a junior doctor resident at a hospital. **house martin** *n.* a black and white bird, *Delichon urbica*, with a forked tail, resembling a swallow. **housemaster, housemistress** *n.* a teacher in charge of a house of residence at a boarding school. **house-minder** *n.* HOUSE-SITTER (under HOUSE[1]). **house-mind** *v.i.* **housemistress** HOUSEMASTER (under HOUSE[1]). **house-mother** *n.* a woman in charge of children in a children's home etc. **house mouse** *n.* any greyish mouse of the genus *Mus*, esp. *M. musculus*, a household pest also bred as a pet and for experimental purposes. **house music** *n.* a type of dance music characterized by electronically synthesized effects and a heavy beat. **house of cards** *n.* **1** a structure built of playing cards. **2** any scheme or enterprise of an insecure or precarious kind. **House of Commons** *n.* the lower House of Parliament in the British and some other constitutions, the third estate of the realm. **house of correction** *n.* a prison, a penitentiary. **house of detention** *n.* a place where offenders are kept while under remand. **house officer** *n.* a junior hospital doctor. **house of God** *n.* a church, a place of worship. **house of ill repute, house of ill fame** *n.* a brothel. **House of Keys** *n.* the representative branch of the legislature in the Isle of Man. **House of Lords** *n.* **1** the chamber of peers and bishops in Parliament. **2** a committee of specially qualified peers acting as the ultimate court of appeal. **house of refuge** *n.* a charitable institution for the destitute and homeless. **House of Representatives** *n.* the lower house of the US Congress and of other legislative assemblies. **house-parent** *n.* a house-father or house-mother. **house party** *n.* (*pl.* **house parties**) a party of guests at a country house. **house-physician** *n.* the resident physician in a hospital. **house plant** *n.* a plant for growing indoors. **house-proud** *a.* taking a pride in the care and decoration of a home. **houseroom** *n.* space or accommodation in a house. **not to give houseroom to** not to own or accommodate under any circumstances. **house-sitter** *n.* a person who stays in a house to look after it while the occupier is away. **house-sit** *v.i.* (*pres.p.* **house-sitting,** *past, p.p.* **house-sat**). **Houses of Parliament** *n.pl.* **1** the House of Lords and Commons. **2** the building housing these. **house sparrow** *n.* the common sparrow, *Passer domesticus.* **house style** *n.* an individual printer's or publisher's preferred method of presentation, writing etc. **house-surgeon** *n.* the resident surgeon in a hospital. **house-to-house** *a.* (of an enquiry etc.) performed at every house. **housetop** *n.* the top or roof of a house. **to shout/ proclaim from the housetops** to announce very publicly. **house-trained** *a.* **1** (of an animal) trained not to foul places indoors. **2** (of a person) well-mannered. **house-train** *v.t.* **house-warming** *n.* a party to celebrate moving into a new house etc. **housework** *n.* physical work connected with housekeeping. [OE *hūs* (cp. Dut. *huis,* Icel. *hūs,* G *Haus*)]

house[2] (howz) *v.t.* **1** to place or store in a building. **2** to lodge, contain. **3** to shelter. **4** (*Naut.*) to put (a gun) in a secure state or position. ~*v.i.* **1** to have a lodging, to dwell. **2** to take shelter. [OE *hūsian,* as HOUSE[1]]

household (hows´hōld) *n.* **1** those who live together under the same roof and compose a domestic unit. **2** a domestic establishment. ~*a.* of or relating to the house and family, domestic. **householder** *n.* the head of a household, the occupier of a house. **household gods** *n.pl.* **1** in Roman mythology, the gods who preside over the home, the lares and penates. **2** the most valued possessions of a home. **household name, household word** *n.* a familiar name or word. **household troops** *n.pl.* troops specially employed to guard the person of the sovereign.

†**housel** (how´zəl) *n.* the Eucharist. ~*v.t.* (*pres.p.* **houselling,** (*N Am.*) **houseling,** *past, p.p.* **houselled,** (*N Am.*) **houseled**) **1** to administer the sacrament to. **2** to prepare for a journey. **houseling, housling** *n., a.* [OE *hūsel* (cp. Icel. *hūsl,* Goth. *hunsl,* a sacrifice)]

housewife (hows´wīf) *n.* (*pl.* **housewives** (-wīvz)) **1** a married woman who stays at home to run a household rather than having a full-time paid job. **2** a case for holding pins, needles etc. **housewifely** *a.* of or relating to a housewife or good domestic management, thrifty. ~*adv.* like a housewife, thriftily. **housewifery** (-wifri) *n.* female management of domestic affairs, housekeeping, housecraft.

Usage note As a case for holding pins, needles etc. pronounced (huz´if).

housey-housey (howsihow´si), **housie housie** *n.* the game of bingo.

housing[1] (how´zing) *n.* **1** lodging, shelter, accommodation. **2** a protective case for machinery. **3** a hole etc. cut in one piece of wood to receive the end of another. **housing association** *n.* a non-profit-making body which builds or renovates dwellings and lets them at a reasonable rent. **housing estate** *n.* a planned residential area.

†**housing**[2] (how´zing) *n.* **1** a cloth covering for a horse. **2** (*pl.*) trappings for horses. [OF *houce*]

houting (how´ting) *n.* a European freshwater whitefish *Coregonus lavaretus.* [Dut. *houtic*]

hove HEAVE.

hovel (hov´əl, hŭv´əl) *n.* **1** a miserable dwelling. **2** a conical building enclosing a kiln. **3** a shed or outhouse open at the sides. ~*v.t.* (*pres.p.* **hovelling,** (*N Am.*) **hoveling,** *past, p.p.* **hovelled,** (*N Am.*) **hoveled**) **1** to shelter in or as in a hovel. **2** to carry up the exposed sides of (a chimney) so as to prevent smoking. [etym. uncertain]

hover (hov´ə) *v.i.* **1** to hang or remain (over or about) fluttering in the air or on the wing. **2** to loiter (about). **3** to be irresolute, to waver. **hovercraft** *n.* (*pl.* **hovercraft**) a craft supported above land or water on a cushion of air which it generates itself. **hoverer** *n.* **hoverfly** *n.* (*pl.* **hoverflies**) any brightly coloured fly of the family Syrphidae, which hover and dart. **hoverport** *n.* a place where passengers enter and leave hovercraft. **hovertrain** *n.* a train that moves over a concrete track, supported by a cushion of air. [etym. uncertain]

how[1] (how) *adv.* **1** in what way or manner. **2** by what means. **3** to what extent, degree etc. **4** in what proportion. **5** in what condition. **6** by what name. **7** at what price. ~*n.* the way, manner, means (of becoming, happening, doing etc.). **and how!** (*sl.*) and how much more! **here's how!** HERE. **how about? 1** used to suggest a possible choice. **2** what is the news about. **how are you? 1** what is your state of health, well-being etc.? **2** how do you do? **how come?** (*coll.*) how does it, did that etc. happen? **how do?** hello, an informal greeting. **how do you do?** used as a conventional form of greeting. **how many** what number. **how much 1** what price. **2** what amount. †**how now?** what is the meaning of this, why is this so? †**how so?** how can this be so? **how's that? 1** what is your opinion, explanation etc.? **2** howzat. **howbeit** (-bē´it), †**howbe** (-bē´) *adv.* nevertheless, however it may be. **how-d'ye-do** *n.* (*pl.* **how-d'ye-dos**) (*coll.*) an awkward situation. **however,** (*poet.*) **howe'er** *adv.* **1** in whatever manner or degree. **2** nevertheless, notwithstanding. **3** †at all events. **howsoever,** (*poet.*) **howsoe'er** *adv.* **1** in whatsoever manner. **2** however. **3** to what extent or degree soever. **4** †at all events. **how's your father** *n.* (*coll., facet.*) illicit goings-on, esp. of a sexual nature. **howzat** (-zat´) *int.* used in cricket to ask for the batsman to be given out. [OE *hū* (cp. Dut. *hoe*), cogn. with WHO]

how[2] (how) *int.* used as a N American Indian greeting. [perh. from. Sioux *háo,* Omaha *hau*]

how[3] HOWE.

howdah (how´də), **houdah** *n.* a seat, usu. canopied, carried on an elephant's back. [Pers. *haudah,* Arab. *haudaj*]

howdy[1] (how´di) *int.* (*esp. N Am.*) hello. [short for HOW-D'YE-DO (under HOW[1])]

howdy[2] (how´di), **howdie** *n.* (*pl.* **howdies**) (*Sc.*) a midwife. [etym. uncertain]

howe (how), **how** *n.* (*Sc.*) a hollow, a valley, a dell. [prob. from OE *hol,* HOLE]

however HOW[1].

howff (howf), **houff** *n.* (*Sc.*) **1** a resort, a haunt. **2** a meeting place. **3** a public house. ~*v.i.* to frequent a place. [etym. uncertain]

howitzer (how´itsə) *n.* a short, light or heavy field gun with a high trajectory and low muzzle velocity.

[formerly *howitz*, G *Haublitze*, Czech *haufnice*, sling]

howk (howk) *v.t.* (*Sc.*) to dig (up or out). ~*v.i.* to burrow. [cogn. with HOLE]

howl (howl) *v.i.* **1** to utter a protracted hollow cry, as a dog or wolf. **2** to wail. **3** to make a wailing sound like the wind. ~*v.t.* to utter in wailing or mournful tones. ~*n.* **1** the cry of a wolf or dog. **2** a protracted, hollow cry, esp. one of anguish, distress or derision. **to howl down** to prevent (a speaker) from being heard by derisive shouting, laughter etc. **howler** *n.* **1** (*coll.*) a ludicrous blunder. **2** a S American monkey of the genus *Alouatta*. **3** a person who howls. **howling** *a.* **1** (*sl.*) extreme, glaring. **2** that howls. **howling dervish** *n.* a member of a Muslim ascetic order whose observances include howling or wailing. [ME *houlen*, imit. (cp. Dut. *huilen*, Icel. *ȳla*, G *heulen*, also L *ululāre*, Gr. *hulaein*)]

howlet (how´lit) *n.* (*poet.*) an owlet. [perh. from F *hulotte*, or from OWL]

howsoever, howzat HOW[1].

hoy[1] (hoi) *int.* **1** used to draw attention etc. **2** (*Naut.*) used to hail aloft. ~*n.* (*Austral.*) a game with playing cards, resembling bingo. [cp. Dut. and Dan. *hui*]

hoy[2] (hoi) *v.t.* (*dial.*) to throw. [etym. uncertain]

hoy[3] (hoi) *n.* **1** (*Hist.*) a one-masted coasting vessel. **2** a barge or lighter, as in *anchor-hoy*, *gun-hoy*. [MDut. *hoei*, etym. uncertain]

hoya (hoi´ə) *n.* any tropical climbing shrub of the genus *Hoya* with pink, white or yellow flowers, called by gardeners wax flowers. [Thomas *Hoy*, d. 1821, English gardener]

hoyden (hoi´dən) *n.* a boisterous girl, a tomboy. **hoydenish** *a.* **hoydenishness** *n.* **hoydenism** *n.* [etym. uncertain]

Hoyle (hoil) *n.* an authoritative source (only as below). **according to Hoyle** exactly according to the rules. [Sir Edmund *Hoyle*, 1672–1769, English writer on card games]

hozzle (hoz´əl) *v.i.* (*Sc., North.*) (of rain) to come down very heavily. [etym. uncertain]

HP, h.p. *abbr.* **1** high pressure. **2** hire purchase. **3** horsepower. **4** Houses of Parliament.

HQ *abbr.* headquarters.

HR *abbr.* House of Representatives.

hr. *abbr.* hour.

HRH *abbr.* His or Her Royal Highness.

hrs. *abbr.* hours.

HRT *abbr.* hormone replacement therapy.

hrw *abbr.* heated rear window (of a car).

HSH *abbr.* His or Her Serene Highness.

HT *abbr.* high tension.

hub (hŭb) *n.* **1** the central part of a wheel from which the spokes radiate. **2** a place of central importance. **hubcap** *n.* a (decorative) plate or disc covering the hub of a wheel. [etym. unknown]

hubble-bubble (hŭbəlbŭb´əl) *n.* **1** a type of pipe in which the smoke is drawn through water, making a bubbling noise, a kind of hookah. **2** a bubbling noise. **3** a jabbering or chattering. [onomat.]

Hubble's constant (hŭb´əlz) *n.* (*Astron.*) the ratio of the velocity at which a galaxy recedes to the distance of that galaxy from the observer. [E. P. *Hubble*, 1889–1953, US astronomer]

hubbub (hŭb´ŭb) *n.* **1** a confused noise. **2** a noisy disturbance. **3** a tumult, an uproar. **hubbuboo** (-boo´) *n.* **1** a howling. **2** a hubbub. [onomat., perh. suggested by an Irish word]

hubby (hŭb´i) *n.* (*pl.* **hubbies**) (*coll.*) husband.

hubris (hū´bris) *n.* insolent pride or security, arrogance. **hubristic** (-bris´-) *a.* [Gr.]

huckaback (hŭk´əbak) *n.* a coarse linen or cotton cloth, with a rough surface, used for towels. [etym. uncertain]

huckle (hŭk´əl) *n.* the hip, the haunch. **huckle-backed, huckle-shouldered** *a.* (*dial.*) round-shouldered. **huckle-bone** *n.* **1** the hip bone. **2** the knuckle-bone or astragalus in a quadruped. [prob. dim. of obs. *huck*, HOCK[1]]

huckleberry (hŭk´əlbəri) *n.* (*pl.* **huckleberries**) **1** any low shrub of the genus *Gaylussacia* of N America. **2** the edible fruit of this shrub. **3** the fruit of the blueberry and other plants of the allied genus *Vaccinium*. [prob. corr. of HURTLEBERRY]

huckster (hŭk´stə) *n.* **1** a retailer of small goods, a pedlar, a hawker. **2** a mean, crafty, mercenary person. **3** (*N Am.*) a person who produces advertising material for radio or TV. ~*v.i.* **1** to deal in petty goods. **2** to bargain, to haggle. **hucksterer** *n.* **hucksteress** *n.* **hucksterism** *n.* [etym. uncertain (perh. conn. with MDut. *hucken*, to stoop or bow, cp. Icel. *hokra* and HAWKER[2])]

huddle (hŭd´əl) *v.t.* **1** to throw or crowd (together, up etc.) closely. **2** to coil (oneself up) into a small space. **3** †to do or make hastily and carelessly. **4** †to put (on) hurriedly or anyhow. ~*v.i.* to gather or crowd (up or together) closely. ~*n.* **1** (*coll.*) a secretive discussion between a group of people. **2** a confused crowd. **3** disorder, confusion. **to go into a huddle** to have a secretive discussion. [cp. LG *hudern*, to shelter, to cover up (rel. to HIDE[1])]

Hudibrastic (hūdibras´tik) *a.* mock-heroic, resembling *Hudibras* in style or metre. [Butler's *Hudibras*, 1663–78, a satire against the Puritans]

hue (hū) *n.* **1** colour, tint. **2** a compound colour, esp. one in which a primary predominates. **-hued** *a.* (*in comb.*) having a particular shade or colour, as in *light-hued*. **hueless** *a.* [OE *hīw* (cp. Swed. *hy*, Goth. *hiwi*, form, appearance)]

hue and cry (hū ənd crī´) *n.* **1** a clamour or outcry (against). **2** a great stir or alarm. **3** (*Hist.*) a cry or general summons to pursue a felon or offender. [A-F *hu e cri*, from OF *hu* (*huer*, to shout, imit.) *e*, and, *cri*, cry]

huff (hŭf) *v.t.* **1** to blow or puff (up). **2** to bully, to hector. **3** in draughts, to remove (one's opponent's piece) from the board when they omit to capture with it. **4** (*usu. p.p.*) to offend. ~*v.i.* **1** to take offence. **2** †to be puffed up, to bluster. ~*n.* **1** a sudden fit of anger or petulance. **2** in draughts, the act of huffing. **3** †a boaster, a braggart. **in a huff** annoyed, offended, in a mood. **huffer** *n.* a blusterer. **huffish** *a.* **huffishly** *adv.* **huffishness** *n.* **huffy** *a.* (*comp.* **huffier,** *superl.* **huffiest**). **huffily** *adv.* **huffiness** *n.* [imit.]

hug (hŭg) *v.t.* (*pres.p.* **hugging,** *past, p.p.* **hugged**) **1** to embrace closely. **2** to clasp or squeeze tightly. **3** to hold fast or cling to, to cherish. **4** to congratulate (oneself). **5** to keep close to (*The cyclist hugged the kerb*). ~*v.i.* **1** to embrace each other. **2** †to huddle, to lie close. ~*n.* **1** a close embrace. **2** a grip in wrestling involving squeezing one's opponent. **huggable** *a.* **to hug oneself** to congratulate oneself complacently. [etym. uncertain]

huge (hūj) *a.* very large, enormous, immense. **hugely** *adv.* **1** in a huge manner. **2** (*coll.*) exceedingly, extremely. **hugeness** *n.* [OF *ahuge*, etym. unknown]

hugger-mugger (hŭg´əmŭgə) *n.* **1** secrecy, privacy. **2** disorder, confusion. ~*a.* **1** clandestine. **2** confused, slovenly. ~*adv.* **1** secretly, clandestinely. **2** in a confused way. ~*v.i.* **1** to act clandestinely. **2** to muddle. ~†*v.t.* to hush up. [prob. rhyming redupl. of HUG]

Huguenot (hū´gənō) *n.* (*Hist.*) a French Protestant. **Huguenotism** (-not-) *n.* [F, alt. of *eiguenot* (ult. from Swiss G *Eidgenoss*, confederate), after surname *Hugues*]

huh (hŭ, hə) *int.* used to express surprise, contempt, disbelief etc.

huia (hoo´yə) *n.* an extinct New Zealand bird, *Heteralocha acutirostris*, of the starling family. [Maori]

hula (hoo´lə), **hula-hula** *n.* a Hawaiian dance performed by women. **hula hoop** *n.* a light hoop kept in motion by swinging round the waist. **hula skirt** *n.* a grass skirt worn by hula dancers. [Hawaiian]

hulk (hŭlk) *n.* 1 the hull or body of a ship, esp. an unseaworthy one. 2 an old ship used as a store, (formerly) as a prison, or for other purposes. 3 a bulky and unwieldy ship. 4 (*coll.*) any unwieldy object or person. **the hulks** (*Hist.*) old dismasted ships formerly used as prisons. **hulking** *a.* (*coll.*) bulky, unwieldy, awkward. [OE *hulc* (cp. late L *hulka*, OF *hulke*, Dut. *hulk*), perh. from Gr. *holkos*, a ship that is towed, from *helkein*, to draw]

hull[1] (hŭl) *n.* the body of a ship. ~*v.t.* to pierce the hull of with a cannonball, gunshot etc. **hull down** (of a ship) so far off that only the superstructure is visible. [prob. the same as HULL[2], but confused with HOLE, HOLD[3]]

hull[2] (hŭl) *n.* 1 the outer covering of a nut or seed, the pod, shell or husk. 2 any outer covering. ~*v.t.* to strip the hull or husk off. [OE *hulu*, cogn. with *helan*, to cover]

hullabaloo (hŭləbəloo´) *n.* (*pl.* **hullabaloos**) an uproar. [redupl. of HULLO]

hullo HELLO.

hum[1] (hŭm) *v.i.* (*pres.p.* **humming,** *past, p.p.* **hummed**) 1 to make a prolonged murmuring sound like a bee. 2 to sing with the lips closed. 3 to make an inarticulate sound in speaking, from embarrassment or hesitation. 4 (*sl.*) to smell unpleasant. ~*v.t.* 1 to utter in a low murmuring voice. 2 to applaud, disapprove etc. by emitting such a sound. ~*n.* 1 a low droning or murmuring sound. 2 the act of humming. 3 an inarticulate expression of hesitation, disapproval etc. **to hum and haw/ ha** 1 to hesitate in speaking. 2 to refrain from giving a decisive answer. **to make things hum** to stir people etc. into productive activity. **hummable** *a.* able to be hummed (*a hummable tune*). **hummer** *n.* 1 someone who or something which hums. 2 a humming insect. 3 a hummingbird. **humming** (hŭm´ing) *a.* 1 that hums. 2 (of ale) strong. 3 (*sl.*) (of blows) vigorous, hard. **hummingbird** *n.* any small, mostly tropical bird of the family Trochilidae, of brilliant plumage and very rapid flight. **humming-top** *n.* a child's toy, being a hollow top with a hole in the side, which emits a humming noise in spinning. [imit.]

hum[2] (hŭm) *int.* used to express hesitation, disapproval etc. [var. of HEM[2]]

†**hum**[3] (hŭm) *v.t.* (*pres.p.* **humming,** *past, p.p.* **hummed**) 1 (*sl.*) to impose upon. 2 to humbug. ~*n.* a hoax, a humbug. [perh. same as HUM[2]]

human (hū´mən) *a.* 1 of or relating to people or humankind; of or relating to the genus *Homo.* 2 having the nature, qualities or characteristics of people or humankind. 3 of or relating to humankind as distinct from God or gods, animals or machines. ~*n.* a human being. **human being** *n.* a member of the species *Homo sapiens*, a person. **human bowling** *n.* a game in which a player strapped into a rolling globular cage attempts to knock down large soft skittles. **human chain** *n.* a line of people formed up to pass things along from hand to hand, esp. in an emergency. **human ecology** *n.* the study of the relations between people and their environment. **human engineering** *n.* 1 the management of labour in industry, esp. regarding the relationships between humans and machines. 2 the study of this. **human geography** *n.* the branch of geography studying the interaction between human beings and the earth's surface. **human interest** *n.* (in a newspaper article etc.) reference to issues of personal experience, emotions that most people can identify with. **humanize, humanise** *v.t.* 1 to make human. 2 to give human character or expression to. 3 to make humane. ~*v.i.* to become human or humane. **humanization** (-zā´shən) *n.* **humankind** *n.* the members of the species *Homo sapiens* collectively. **humanly** *adv.* 1 in the manner of human beings. 2 according to the knowledge or capacity of human beings. 3 from the human point of view. **human nature** *n.* all those characteristics considered typical of human beings, esp. the weaknesses. **humanness** *n.* **humanoid** (-oid) *a.* like a human in form or attributes. ~*n.* a humanoid animal or object. **human race** *n.* the species *Homo sapiens.* **human relations** *n.pl.* relations with or between one person or group of people and another. **human rights** *n.pl.* the rights of an individual to freedom of speech, freedom of movement, justice etc. **human shield** *n.* a person or group of people placed so as to protect a potential target from attack. [MF *humain*, L *hūmānus*, cogn. with HOMO]

humane (hūmān´) *a.* 1 having the feelings proper to humans. 2 tender, compassionate, kind, gentle. 3 elevating, refining. 4 polite, elegant. 5 relieving distress, aiding those in danger etc. **humane killer** *n.* an instrument for slaughtering animals painlessly. **humanely** *adv.* **humaneness** *n.* **humane society** *n.* a society that campaigns for humane behaviour, esp. in the treatment of animals. [as HUMAN, differentiated in meaning late]

humanism (hū´mənizm) *n.* 1 a moral or intellectual system that regards the interests of humankind as of supreme importance, as distinct from individualism or theism. 2 humanitarianism. 3 devotion to humanity or human interests. 4 (**Humanism**) culture derived from literature, esp. the Greek and Latin classics. **humanist** *n.* 1 an adherent of humanism. 2 a person versed in human history or the knowledge of human nature. 3 a person versed in the humanities, esp. one of the classical scholars of Renaissance times. **humanistic** (-is´-) *a.* **humanistically** *adv.*

humanitarian (hūmaniteə´riən) *a.* 1 humane. 2 of or relating to the humanitarians. ~*n.* 1 a person who attempts to improve human welfare. 2 a philanthropist. 3 a person who believes in the perfectibility of humanity. 4 a person who believes that Christ was a mere man. **humanitarianism** *n.* [HUMANITY, -ARIAN]

Usage note The adjective *humanitarian* is sometimes used as though it meant simply *human*, but this is best avoided.

humanity (hūman´iti) *n.* (*pl.* **humanities**) 1 human nature. 2 (*collect.*) humankind, people. 3 kindness, benevolence, humaneness. 4 (*Sc.*) Latin and Latin literature, as distinct from divinity. **the humanities** the study of literature, music, history etc. as distinct from social or natural sciences. [F *humanité*, L *hūmānitātem*, nom. *-tas*, from *hūmānus*, HUMAN]

humble[1] (hŭm´bəl) *a.* (*comp.* **humbler,** *superl.* **humblest**) 1 having or showing a sense of lowliness or inferiority, modest. 2 of lowly condition, kind, dimensions etc. 3 submissive, deferential. ~*v.t.* 1 to bring low, to abase. 2 to bring to a state of subjection or inferiority. 3 to lower the rank or status of (a person). **humble-mouthed** *a.* humble in speech. **humbleness** *n.* **humble pie** *n.* a pie made of the umbles or entrails of the deer. **to eat humble pie** 1 to apologize humbly (said to have arisen from the fact that at hunting-feasts humble pie was given to the menials). 2 to submit oneself to humiliation or insult. **humbly** *adv.* [OF, from L *humilem* nom. *-lis*, from *humus*, the ground]

humble[2] HUMMEL.

humble-bee (hŭm´bəlbē) *n.* a bumble-bee. [obs. *humble*, freq. of HUM[1], BEE]

humbug (hŭm´bŭg) *n.* 1 a boiled sweet highly flavoured with peppermint. 2 a hoax. 3 nonsense, rubbish. 4 a spirit of deception or trickery, sham. 5 an impostor. ~*int.* nonsense. ~*v.t.* (*pres.p.* **humbugging,** *past, p.p.* **humbugged**) 1 to hoax, to take in. 2 to cajole (into, out of etc.). ~*v.i.* to behave in a fraudulent or misleading manner. **humbugger** *n.* **humbuggery** *n.* [etym. uncertain (perh. HUM[3], BUG[1])]

humdinger (hŭmding´ə) *n.* (*coll.*) an excellent person or thing.

humdrum (hŭm´drŭm) *a.* dull, commonplace, tedious. ~*n.* **1** a dull, stupid person. **2** dull, tedious talk. **3** dullness. **humdrumness** *n.*

humectant (hūmek´tənt) *a.* moistening. ~*n.* **1** a substance, esp. a food additive, added to another substance to keep it moist. **2** a diluent. **3** a substance that increases the fluidity of the blood. **humectate** *v.t.* **humectation** (-tā´shən) *n.* a making wet or moist. **humective** *a.* [L *hūmectans -antem*, pres.p. of *hūmectāre*, from *hūmēre*, to be moist (cp. HUMID)]

humerus (hū´mərəs) *n.* (*pl.* **humeri** (-rī)) **1** the long bone of the upper arm, articulating above with the scapula and below with the radius and the ulna. **2** the corresponding bone in the foreleg of quadrupeds. **humeral** *a.* of or relating to the shoulder. ~*n.* a humeral veil. **humeral veil** *n.* in the Roman Catholic Church, an oblong scarf worn by priests and deacons at various ceremonies. [L, shoulder (cp. Gr. *ōmos*)]

humid (hū´mid) *a.* **1** moist, damp. **2** rather wet. **humidify** (-mid´-) *v.t.* (*3rd pers. sing. pres.* **humidifies,** *pres.p.* **humidifying,** *past, p.p.* **humidified**) to make humid. **humidification** (-fikā´shən) *n.* **humidifier** *n.* a device for making or keeping the air in a room moist. **humidistat** (-mid´-) *n.* a device for maintaining a constant level of moisture in the air of a room, a hygrostat. **humidity** (-mid´-) *n.* (*pl.* **humidities**) **1** the state of being humid. **2** a measure of the amount of moisture in the atmosphere. **humidly** *adv.* †**humidness** *n.* **humidor** (-daw) *n.* **1** a container constructed to keep its contents in a moist state. **2** a box for keeping cigars moist. [L *hūmidus*, from *hūmēre*, to be moist]

humification, humify HUMUS.

humiliate (hūmil´iāt) *v.t.* **1** to lower in self-esteem, to mortify. **2** to humble, to lower in condition, to abase. **humiliating** *a.* **humiliatingly** *adv.* **humiliation** (-ā´shən) *n.* **humiliator** *n.* [L *humiliātus*, p.p. of *humiliāre* (*humilis*, HUMBLE[1])]

humility (hūmil´iti) *n.* **1** the state of being humble. **2** modesty, a sense of unworthiness. **3** self-abasement. [F *humilité*, L *humilitātem* nom. *-tas*, as HUMILIATE]

Humism (hū´mizm) *n.* the philosophical doctrines of David Hume. **Humist** *n., a.* [David *Hume*, 1711–76, Scottish philosopher]

hummable HUM[1].

hummel (hŭm´əl), **humble** (hŭm´bəl) *a.* (of cattle) hornless. ~*v.t.* (*pres.p.* **hummelling,** (*N Am.*) **hummeling,** *past, p.p.* **hummelled,** (*N Am.*) **hummeled**) to separate or free (barley) from the awns. **hummeller,** (*N Am.*) **hummeler** *n.* [cp. LG *Hummel*, hornless beast]

hummer, humming etc. HUM[1].

hummock (hŭm´ək) *n.* **1** a mound or hillock, a protuberance formed by pressure in an ice field. **2** (*N Am.*) an elevation in a swamp or bog, esp. if wooded. **hummocky** *a.* [etym. uncertain; prob. of naut. orig. earlier than HUMP]

hummus (hŭm´əs, hum´əs), **hoummos** *n.* a kind of Middle Eastern hors d'oeuvre consisting of puréed chickpeas, sesame oil, garlic and lemon. [Turk.]

humongous (hūmŭng´gəs), **humungous** *a.* (*sl.*) huge, enormous. [20th. cent., etym. uncertain]

humor HUMOUR.

humoral (hū´mərəl) *a.* **1** (*Med.*) of or relating to bodily fluids, esp. with regard to a type of immune response from antibodies in the blood. **2** (*Hist.*) of or relating to the bodily humours. **humoralism** *n.* (*Hist.*) the formerly held doctrine that all diseases proceed from affections of the humours. **humoralist** *n.* **humoralistic** (-lis´-) *a.* [F, from L *humor*, HUMOUR]

humoresque (hūməresk´) *n.* (*Mus.*) a composition of a humorous or capricious character. [G *Humoreske*]

humorist (hū´mərist) *n.* **1** a person who displays humour in their conversation, writings etc. **2** a facetious person, a wag. **3** a whimsical person. **humoristic** (-ris´-) *a.* [F *humoriste*, med. L *hūmorista*]

humorous (hū´mərəs) *a.* **1** full of humour. **2** tending to excite laughter. **3** jocular. **4** †whimsical, capricious, crotchety. **humorously** *adv.* **humorousness** *n.*

humour (hū´mə), (*N Am.*) **humor** *n.* **1** the quality of being amusing, comical, witty etc. **2** the capacity of perceiving the ludicrous elements in life or art. **3** playful yet sympathetic imagination or mode of regarding things, delighting in the absurdity of incongruities. **4** mental disposition, frame of mind, mood. **5** bias, caprice, whim. **6** (*Hist.*) †each of the four bodily fluids (blood, phlegm, yellow bile, black bile) supposed to produce diversity of temperament. ~*v.t.* **1** to indulge, to give way to, to make concessions to. **2** to fall in with the humour of. **out of humour** in a bad mood, displeased. **-humoured** *a.* (*in comb.*) having a certain humour, as in *good-humoured*. **-humouredly** *adv.* **humourless** *a.* **humourlessly** *adv.* **humourlessness** *n.* **humoursome** *a.* led by caprice or fancy, whimsical. [A-F, from OF *humor* (F *humeur*), L *hūmōrem*, moisture (cp. HUMID)]

☒ **humourous** common misspelling of HUMOROUS.

humous HUMUS.

hump (hŭmp) *n.* **1** a swelling or protuberance, esp. on the back. **2** a rounded hillock. **3** (*coll.*) a fit of annoyance, ill-temper or the blues. ~*v.t.* **1** to make (the back) hump-shaped. **2** (*coll.*) to carry on the back. **3** (*sl.*) to have sexual intercourse with. ~*v.i.* (*sl.*) to have sexual intercourse. **over the hump** past the difficult or critical stage of something. **to live on one's hump** to be self-sufficient. **humpback** *n.* **1** a crooked back. **2** a person having a humpback. **3** (*also* **humpbacked whale**) an American whale, *Megaptera nodosa*. **humpback bridge** *n.* a small, narrow bridge with steep inclines on either side leading to its centre. **humpbacked** *a.* **hump bridge** *n.* a humpback bridge. **humped** *a.* having a hump. **humpless** *a.* **humpy**[1] *a.* (*comp.* **humpier,** *superl.* **humpiest**) **1** having many humps. **2** (*coll.*) irritable, sulky. [cp. Dut. *homp*, Norw. *hump*]

humph (hŭmf) *int.* used to express doubt, disapproval etc. [var. of HUM[2]]

humpty-dumpty (hŭmptidŭmp´ti) *n.* (*pl.* **humpty-dumpties**) **1** a short, squat person. **2** anyone or anything that, having fallen down, cannot be put back or mended (from the nursery rhyme in which the name stands for an egg). ~*a.* short and squat. [prob. HUMPY, DUMPY]

humpy[1] HUMP.

humpy[2] (hŭm´pi) *n.* (*pl.* **humpies**) (*Austral.*) a hut, shack, lean-to. [Austral. Abor.]

humus (hū´məs) *n.* soil or mould, esp. that largely composed of decayed vegetation. ~*a.* consisting of or relating to humus. **humic acid** *n.* an acid formed from humus by the action of an alkali. **humify** *v.i.* (*3rd pers. sing. pres.* **humifies,** *pres.p.* **humifying,** *past, p.p.* **humified**) to turn into humus. **humification** (-fikā´shən) *n.* **humous** *a.* **humusify** (-mŭs´-) *v.t., v.i.* (*3rd pers. sing. pres.* **humusifies,** *pres.p.* **humusifying,** *past, p.p.* **humusified**). [L, earth]

Hun (hŭn) *n.* **1** a member of an ancient Tartar people from Asia that overran Europe in the 4th and 5th cents. and gave their name to Hungary. **2** (*coll., derog.*) a German. **3** a barbarian, a destroyer, a savage. **Hunnish** *a.* [OE *Hūne*, med. L *Hunni*, prob. from Turkic]

hunch (hŭnch) *n.* **1** an intuitive feeling or premonition. **2** a hump. **3** a lump, a thick piece. ~*v.t.* **1** to crook, to arch (esp. the back). **2** to bend or thrust out into a hump. **hunchback** *n.* a person with a humped back.

hunchbacked *a.* [etym. uncertain, perh. var. of HUMP]

hundred (hŭn´drid) *n.* (*pl.* **hundred, hundreds**) **1** the cardinal number representing 10 times 10, the product of 10 multiplied by 10. **2** (*coll.*) a hundred pounds (money). **3** (*Hist.*) an administrative division of a county in England, supposed to have originally contained 100 families or freemen. *~a.* **1** amounting to a hundred. **2** used to express whole hours in the 24-hour clock (*three hundred hours (03:00)*). **(one) hundred per cent** entire(ly), total(ly), complete(ly). **Hundred Days** *n.* (*Hist.*) the period 20 Mar.–22 June 1815, from Napoleon's escape from Elba to his abdication. **hundredfold** *n.* **hundreds and thousands** *n.pl.* tiny strips or balls of sugar coated with different colours, used esp. for cake decoration. **hundredth** *a.* the ordinal of a hundred. *~n.* **1** one of a hundred equal parts. **2** the one after the ninety-ninth in a series. **hundredweight** *n.* (*pl.* **hundredweight, hundredweights**) a weight of 112 lbs. (50.8 kg), a long hundredweight. **long hundredweight** LONG[1]. **metric hundredweight** METRIC. **short hundredweight** SHORT. [OE *hundred* (*hund*, hundred, *-red*, a reckoning or account, cp. G *Rede*)]

hung (hŭng) *a.* **1** (of an election) not resulting in a clear majority for any party. **2** (of a Parliament) produced by such an election. **3** (of a jury) unable to reach a verdict. **hung-over** *a.* suffering from a hangover. **hung parliament** *n.* a parliament in which no party has an overall majority. **hung up** *a.* (*sl.*) nervous, tense, obsessed. **hung up on** neurotic about, obsessed by. [p.p. of HANG]

Hungarian (hŭng·geə´riən) *a.* of or relating to Hungary. *~n.* **1** a native or inhabitant of Hungary. **2** the Hungarian language. [late L *Hungaria*, Hungary (from *Hungari*, *Ugri*, Magyars), -AN]

hunger (hŭng´gə) *n.* **1** a craving for food. **2** a painful sensation or weakened condition caused by lack of food. **3** any strong desire. **4** †a famine. *~v.i.* **1** to feel the pain or sensation of hunger, to crave for food. **2** to desire or long eagerly (for). *~v.t.* to make hungry, to starve. **hunger march** *n.* (*Hist.*) a march of the unemployed to protest against their lot. **hunger marcher** *n.* **hunger strike** *n.* a refusal to take food, usu. as a protest. *~v.i.* to go on hunger strike. **hunger striker** *n.* [OE *hungor* (cp. Icel. *hungr*, Dut. *honger*, G *Hunger*), whence *hyngran*, to hunger]

hungry (hŭng´gri) *a.* (*comp.* **hungrier**, *superl.* **hungriest**) **1** feeling a sensation of hunger. **2** having a keen appetite. **3** showing hunger, emaciated, thin. **4** longing or craving eagerly. **5** (of soil) barren, poor. **hungrily** *adv.* **hungriness** *n.* [OE *hungrig*]

hunk (hŭngk) *n.* (*coll.*) **1** a large piece. **2** a big, strong, sexually attractive man. **hunky** *a.* (*comp.* **hunkier**, *superl.* **hunkiest**) (of a man) sexually attractive. [Flem. *hunke*]

hunker (hŭng´kə) *v.i.* (*Sc.*, *N Am.*) to squat on the calves or heels. *~n.pl.* the haunches. **on one's hunkers** squatting down. **to hunker down** to apply oneself, knuckle down (to work etc.). [etym. uncertain; cp. Dut. *huiken*, G *hocken*]

hunky-dory (hŭngkidaw´ri) *a.* (*esp. N Am.*, *coll.*) satisfactory, fine. [etym. uncertain]

Hunnish HUN.

hunt (hŭnt) *v.t.* **1** to search for, to seek after. **2** to pursue or chase in or over (a district etc.). **3** to chase (as wild animals) for the purpose of catching and killing. **4** to employ (horses, dogs etc.) in hunting. *~v.i.* **1** to search (after or for). **2** to pursue game or wild animals. **3** to follow the chase. **4** (of a machine etc.) to vary in speed of operation as if to stop. *~n.* **1** hunting, the chase. **2** a pack of hounds. **3** a group of people who regularly go hunting together. **4** a district hunted by a pack of hounds. **5** †the game captured or killed in the chase. **to hunt counter** COUNTER[2]. **to hunt down 1** to track, pursue and capture. **2** to destroy by persecution or violence. **to hunt out** to track out, to find by searching. **to hunt up** to search for. **huntaway** *n.* (*Austral.*) a dog trained to drive sheep. **hunt ball** *n.* a ball given by the members of a hunt. **hunted** *a.* (of a facial expression etc.) showing distress, fatigue etc. as if being hunted. **hunter** *n.* **1** a person or animal that hunts. **2** a horse trained for hunting. **3** a person who searches or seeks for anything (*usu. in comb.* as *fortune-hunter*). **4** a hunting watch. **hunter-gatherer** *n.* a member of a society who live by hunting animals and gathering plants etc. **hunter-killer** *n.* a naval craft designed to pursue and destroy enemy craft. **hunter's moon** *n.* the next full moon after the harvest moon. **hunting** *a.* **1** chasing game or wild animals. **2** pertaining or given to hunting. **3** (*N Am.*) shooting (birds etc.). *~n.* the practice of pursuing wild animals to kill them. **hunting box, hunting lodge, hunting seat** *n.* a temporary residence for the hunting season. **hunting cat** *n.* a cheetah. **hunting crop** *n.* a riding crop with a loop at the end for attaching a thong. **hunting ground** *n.* **1** a likely place for finding anything. **2** ground or region where hunting takes place. **happy hunting ground** HAPPY. **hunting horn** *n.* a bugle or horn used in hunting. **hunting knife** *n.* a knife used for killing game, or skinning it. **hunting leopard** *n.* a cheetah. **hunting pink** *n.* the scarlet coat worn by people at a hunt. **hunting watch** *n.* a watch with a metal cover over the face. **huntress** *n.* a woman who goes hunting. **hunt saboteur** *n.* a person who is opposed to hunting and who actively tries to disrupt it. **huntsman** *n.* (*pl.* **huntsmen**) **1** a person who hunts. **2** a person employed to manage hunting hounds. **huntsmanship** *n.* **†hunt's-up** *n.* **1** a tune used to rouse huntsmen in the morning. **2** a reveille. **hunt the fox, hunt the hare, hunt the slipper** *n.* various games in which a player or an object is searched for. [OE *huntian*, cogn. with *hentan*, to hent]

Huntington's chorea (hŭn´tingtənz) *n.* (*Med.*) a rare hereditary type of chorea accompanied by progressive dementia. [G. *Huntington*, 1850–1916, US neurologist]

huntress, huntsman HUNT.

Hunts. (hŭnts) *abbr.* (*Hist.*) Huntingdonshire.

Huon pine (hū´on) *n.* a large yew, *Dacrydium franklinii*, orig. from Tasmania, valued for its finely-marked wood, used in cabinetmaking, boat-building etc. [river *Huon*, Tasmania]

hurdies (hœ´diz) *n. pl.* (*Sc.*) the buttocks, the haunches. [etym. unknown]

hurdle (hœ´dəl) *n.* **1** a movable framework of withes or split timber serving for gates, enclosures etc. **2** a barrier for jumping over in racing. **3** (*Hist.*) a frame or sledge on which criminals were drawn to execution. **4** a barrier or obstacle. *~v.t.* **1** to leap over. **2** to surmount. **3** to enclose, hedge or barricade with hurdles. **hurdler** *n.* **1** a person who runs in hurdle-races. **2** a hurdle-maker. **hurdle-race** *n.* a race over hurdles or fences, esp. in horse racing. [OE *hyrdel*, dim. (cp. Dut. *horde*, Icel. *hürth*, G *Hürde*, also L *crātis*)]

hurds HARDS.

hurdy-gurdy (hœdigœ´di) *n.* (*pl.* **hurdy-gurdies**) **1** a barrel organ, or other similar instrument which is played with a handle. **2** (*Hist.*) a stringed musical instrument like a primitive violin, sounded by a rosined wheel turned by the left hand, the right playing on keys. [prob. imit.]

hurl (hœl) *v.t.* **1** to throw with violence. **2** to drive or fling with great force. **3** to utter or emit with vehemence. *~v.i.* to play the game of hurley. *~n.* the act of throwing with great force. **hurler** *n.* **1** a person who plays hurley. **2** a person who hurls something. **hurling** *n.* the game of hurley. [prob. imit., cp. HURTLE]

Hurler's syndrome (hœ´ləz) *n.* (*Med.*) a condition caused by a defect in metabolism resulting in bone deformity, an abnormally large head, a protruding abdomen and mental retardation. [G. *Hurler*, 19th-cent. German paediatrician]

hurley (hœ´li) *n.* (*pl.* **hurleys**) **1** an Irish game resembling hockey in which two teams of 15 players each equipped with sticks try to score goals. **2** a stick used in this.

hurling HURL.

hurly-burly (hœlibœ´li) *n.* commotion, uproar, boisterous activity. [perh. from HURL, or from OF *hurlee*, a howling, from *hurler*, to howl, L *ululāre*, imit.]

hurrah (hərah´), **hurray** (-ā´) *int.* used to express joy, welcome, applause etc. ~*v.i.* to shout hurrahs. ~*v.t.* to salute with hurrahs. ~*n.* a shout of hurrahs. [earlier HUZZA (cp. Swed., Dan., and G *hurra*)]

hurricane (hŭr´ikən) *n.* **1** a storm with a violent wind of force 12, i.e. having a mean velocity of over 75 mph (120 kph). **2** an extremely violent gale, orig. a W Indian cyclone. **3** anything that sweeps along violently. **hurricane-bird** *n.* a frigate bird. **hurricane deck** *n.* **1** the upper deck above the cabins of a river steamer. **2** a raised deck on an ocean-going vessel. **hurricane lamp** *n.* a lamp designed to keep alight in a strong wind. [Sp. *huracan*, from Carib]

hurry (hŭr´i) *v.i.* **1** to hasten. **2** to move or act with excessive haste. ~*v.t.* (*3rd pers. sing. pres.* **hurries,** *pres.p.* **hurrying,** *past, p.p.* **hurried**) **1** to impel to greater speed, to accelerate. **2** to push forward. **3** to drive or cause to act or do carelessly or precipitately. ~*n.* **1** the act of hurrying. **2** urgency, bustle, precipitation. **3** eagerness (to do etc.). **4** (*coll.*) need for haste. **5** (*Mus.*) a tremolo passage by the orchestra accompanying a dramatic situation. **in a hurry** hurrying, in a rush. **not in a hurry** not soon, not easily. **to hurry along** to hurry up. **to hurry up 1** to make haste. **2** to cause or cajole (someone) to make haste. **hurried** *a.* **1** done in a hurry. **2** impelled to speed. **3** hasty. **hurriedly** *adv.* **hurriedness** *n.* **hurryingly** *adv.* **hurry-scurry** *a., adv.* **1** in a hurry or bustle. **2** confusedly. ~*n.* a confused bustle. ~*v.i.* (*3rd pers. sing. pres.* **hurry-scurries,** *pres.p.* **hurry-scurrying,** *past, p.p.* **hurry-scurried**) to make haste, to act with disorderly haste. [imit.]

hurst (hœst) *n.* **1** a wood, a thicket. **2** a wooded eminence (a frequent element in place names). **3** a hillock, a knoll. **4** (*dial.*) a sandbank in a river. [OE *hyrst* (cp. MHG *Hurst*, LG and MDut. *horst*)]

hurt (hœt) *v.t.* (*past, p.p.* **hurt**) **1** to cause pain, injury, loss or detriment to. **2** to damage. **3** to grieve or distress (e.g. the feelings). ~*v.i.* (*usu. impers.*) to be painful, to cause pain. ~*n.* **1** anything that causes pain, injury or detriment. **2** an injury, damage, harm. **3** a wound. **hurter** *n.* a person who inflicts hurt. **hurtful** *a.* **1** causing hurt, esp. to the feelings. **2** mischievous, noxious. **hurtfully** *adv.* **hurtfulness** *n.* **hurtless** *a.* **1** without hurt or injury. **2** harmless. **hurtlessly** *adv.* **hurtlessness** *n.* [prob. from OF *hurter* (F *heurter*), to knock or push, etym. uncertain]

hurter (hœ´tə) *n.* **1** a concrete block, beam etc. placed to protect a building, kerb etc. from damage by vehicles. **2** the shoulder or the reinforcing piece on an axle. [F *hurteoir*, as HURT]

hurtle (hœ´təl) *v.i.* **1** to rush with great force and noise. **2** to make a crashing noise. ~*v.t.* **1** to strike or dash against with violence. **2** to move or whirl with great force. [prob. freq. of HURT]

hurtleberry (hœ´təlbəri) *n.* (*pl.* **hurtleberries**) the whortleberry.

husband (hŭz´bənd) *n.* **1** a married man in relation to his wife. **2** (*Naut.*) a ship's husband (see SHIP). ~*v.t.* **1** to manage (resources) carefully, to economize. **2** †to cultivate. **3** †to provide with a husband. **4** †to be a husband to, to marry. **husbander** *n.* **husbandless** *a.* having no husband. [OE *hūsbonda*, (*hūs*, HOUSE[1], *bonda*, from Icel. *bōndi*, from *būa*, to dwell)]

husbandry (hŭz´bəndri) *n.* **1** the business of a farmer, agriculture. **2** the products of farming. **3** economy, esp. domestic. **4** frugality, careful management. †**husbandman** *n.* (*pl.* **husbandmen**) **1** a farmer, a tiller of the soil. **2** a good economist. [as HUSBAND]

hush[1] (hŭsh) *v.t.* to make silent, to repress the noise of. ~*v.i.* to be still or silent. ~*n.* silence, stillness. ~*int.* silence! be still! ~†*a.* silent, quiet. **to hush up** to keep concealed, to suppress. **hushaby** (-əbī), **hushabye** *int.* used in lulling a child to sleep. ~*n.* (*pl.* **hushabies, hushabyes**) a lullaby. **hushed** *a.* **hush-hush** *a.* (*coll.*) very secret. **hush money** *n.* a bribe paid to secure silence (about a scandal etc.). **hush puppy** *n.* (*pl.* **hush puppies**) (*N Am.*) a ball of maize bread or dough, quickly fried. [from obs. a. *husht*, imit., cp. HIST]

hush[2] (hŭsh) *n.* a smooth, swift rush of water. ~*v.t.* (*Mining*) to let out (water) from a dam, esp. to clear away soil, stones etc. [onomat.]

husk (hŭsk) *n.* **1** the dry external covering of certain fruits or seeds. **2** a mere frame, shell or worthless part. **3** a bronchitic disease in cattle. ~*v.t.* to strip the husk from. **husked** *a.* **1** having or covered with a husk. **2** stripped of a husk. **husker** *n.* **husking** *n.* **1** the act of stripping off husks. **2** (*N Am.*) a husking-bee. **husking-bee** *n.* (*N Am.*) a gathering of friends at a farmer's house to husk maize. **husky** *a.* (*comp.* **huskier**, *superl.* **huskiest**) **1** dry, hoarse, rough and harsh in sound (*a husky voice*). **2** abounding in husks. **3** consisting of or resembling husks. **4** rough. **5** (*esp. N Am., coll.*) strong, stalwart. **huskily** *adv.* **huskiness** *n.* [perh. from OE *hūs*, HOUSE[1] (cp. EFris. *hüske*, G *Häuschen*, little house)]

husky (hŭs´ki) *n.* (*pl.* **huskies**) a powerful breed of Arctic sledge dog with a thick coat and a curled tail. [perh. corr. of ESKIMO]

huss (hŭs) *n.* the flesh of various kinds of dogfish. [ME *husk*]

hussar (huzah´) *n.* **1** a soldier of a light cavalry regiment in European armies. **2** (*Hist.*) a light horseman of the Hungarian cavalry in the 19th cent. [Hung. *huszar*, OSerb. *husar*, It. *corsaro*, or late Gr. *choursarios*, med. L *cursārius*, CORSAIR]

hussif (hŭs´if) *n.* (*Hist.*) the pocket sewing kit of a soldier or sailor, a housewife.

Hussite (hŭs´ īt) *n.* a follower of John Huss, a Bohemian religious reformer. **Hussitism** *n.* [John *Huss*, 1369–1415, -ITE[1]]

hussy (hŭs´i) *n.* (*pl.* **hussies**) **1** a pert, forward girl. **2** an immoral woman. **3** †a hussif. [corr. of HOUSEWIFE]

hustings (hŭs´tingz) *n.* **1** proceedings at a parliamentary election. **2** (*Hist.*) a platform from which, before the Ballot Act of 1872, candidates addressed the electors during parliamentary elections. [OE *hūsting*, Icel. *hūsthing* (*hūs*, HOUSE[1], *thing*, an assembly)]

hustle (hŭs´əl) *v.t.* **1** to hurry or cause to move quickly. **2** to jostle, to push violently, to shake together in confusion. **3** (*sl.*) to acquire (something) by aggressive or dishonest means. ~*v.i.* **1** to push one's way in an unceremonious or unscrupulous way. **2** (*sl.*) to make a living by aggressive or dishonest means. **3** to act with energy. **4** to give the appearance of being busy. **5** to press roughly. **6** to move (along) with difficulty. **7** (*esp. N Am., sl.*) to engage in prostitution. ~*n.* **1** hustling. **2** (*coll.*) a fraud or swindle. **hustler** *n.* [Dut. *hutselen*, freq. of *hutsen*]

hut (hŭt) *n.* **1** a small, simple house. **2** a cabin, a shelter. **3** a small temporary house for troops in a camp. ~*v.t.* (*pres.p.* **hutting,** *past, p.p.* **hutted**) to place (troops) in huts. ~*v.i.* to lodge in huts. **hut circle** *n.* a circle of stones or earth indicating the site of a prehistoric hut. **hutlike** *a.* **hutment** *n.* a camp of huts. [F *hutte*, from MHG *Hütte*]

hutch (hŭch) *n.* **1** a coop or boxlike pen for small animals. **2** (*derog.*) a small house. **3** a trough for kneading dough. **4** (*Mining*) a truck, a trough for washing ore. ~*v.t.* **1** to store, as in a hutch. **2** to wash (ore) in a hutch. [OF *huche*, low L *hūtica*, etym. uncertain]

Hutu (hoo´too) *n.* (*pl.* **Hutus, Bahutu** (bəhoo´too)) **1** a member of a people of Rwanda and Burundi. **2** their language, one of the Bantu group of languages. ~*a.* of or relating to this people or their language. [Bantu]

†**huzza** (həzah´) *int.* used to express joy, applause etc., hurray. ~*n.* a shout of 'huzza'. [imit.]

hw *abbr.* hit wicket.

HWM *abbr.* high water mark.

hwyl (hŭ´əl) *n.* passion or fervour, esp. in speech, recitation etc. [Welsh]

Hy. *abbr.* Henry.

hyacinth (hī´əsinth) *n.* **1** any plant of the genus *Hyacinthus*, esp. *H. orientalis*, a bulbous-rooted flowering plant of the order Lilaceae. **2** the grape hyacinth. **3** a brownish, orange or reddish variety of zircon. **4** a colour ranging from purplish-blue to violet. **5** a flower mentioned by the ancients, said to have sprung from the blood of the youth Hyacinth, beloved of Apollo, and to bear the letters AI (alas!) on its petals. **6** a precious stone known to the ancients, perhaps aquamarine. **hyacinthine** (-sin´thin, -thīn) *a.* resembling the hyacinth (the flower or the gem) in colour. [F *hyacinthe*, L *hyacinthus*, Gr. *huakinthos*, a flower, prob. iris or larkspur]

Hyades (hī´ədēz), **Hyads** (-adz) *n.pl.* a cluster of stars, including Aldebaran, in the constellation Taurus, supposed by the ancients to bring rain when they rose with the sun. [Gr. *Huades*, cogn. with *hus*, a sow (pop. derived from *huein*, to rain)]

hyaena HYENA.

hyal- HYALO-.

hyalin (hī´əlin) *n.* (*Anat.*) a glossy translucent nitrogenous compound, the chief constituent of hydatid cysts, similar to chitin. [Gr. *hualos*, glass]

hyaline (hī´əlīn, -lin) *a.* **1** glassy, transparent, crystalline. **2** vitreous. ~*n.* **1** (*Anat.*) the clear substance determining the fission of cells, hyaline. **2** (*poet.*) **a** the glassy surface of the sea. **b** the clear sky or atmosphere. **hyaline cartilage** *n.* a translucent cartilage found in joints and respiratory passages, containing little fibrous tissue. **hyalite** (-līt) *n.* a glassy variety of opal. [L *hyalīnus*, Gr. *hualinos*, from *hualos*, glass or crystal]

hyalo- (hī´əlō), **hyal-** *comb. form* **1** colourless, transparent, crystalline. **2** vitreous, glassy. [Gr. *hualos*, glass]

hyaloid (hī´əloid) *a.* (*Anat.*) glassy, vitriform. ~*n.* the hyaloid membrane. **hyaloid membrane** *n.* the transparent membrane enclosing the vitreous humour of the eye.

hyaloplasm (hī´əlōplazm) *n.* the clear, fluid constituent of cytoplasm.

hyaluronic acid (hīəlūəron´ik) *n.* (*Anat.*) a viscous fluid carbohydrate with important lubricating properties found in synovial fluid, the vitreous humour of the eye etc.

hybrid (hī´brid) *a.* **1** (*Biol.*) produced by the union of two distinct species, varieties etc. **2** mongrel, cross-bred. **3** heterogeneous. **4** derived from incongruous sources. ~*n.* **1** an animal or plant produced by the union of two distinct species, varieties etc. **2** anything composed of heterogeneous parts or elements. **3** a word compounded from elements from different languages. **4** (*offensive*) a person of mixed racial origin. **5** a mongrel. **hybridism** *n.* **1** hybridity. **2** the act or process of interbreeding, hybridization. **hybridity** (-brid´-) *n.* the state or quality of being hybrid. **hybridize, hybridise** *v.t.* **1** to produce by the union of different species or varieties. **2** to produce by cross-fertilization or interbreeding. ~*v.i.* to produce hybrids, to be capable of cross-fertilization or interbreeding. **hybridizable** *a.* **hybridization** (-ā´shən) *n.* **hybridizer** *n.* **hybrid vigour** *n.* (*Biol.*) the increased size, strength etc. of a hybrid in comparison with its parents, heterosis. [L *hybrida*, mongrel]

hydatid (hī´dətid) *n.* **1** (*Med.*) a watery cyst occurring in animal tissue, esp. one resulting from the development of the embryo of a tapeworm. **2** the tapeworm larva. **hydatidiform** (-tid´ifawm) *a.* resembling a hydatid. [Gr. *hudatis -tidos*, a watery vesicle, cogn. with *hudōr*, water]

hydr- HYDRO-.

hydra (hī´drə) *n.* (*pl.* **hydras, hydrae** (-drē)) **1** any freshwater polyp of the genus *Hydra*, with a slender body and tentacles round the mouth, which multiplies when divided. **2** any water snake. **3** an evil or calamity difficult to extinguish. **4** in Greek mythology, a water snake with many heads, each of which, when cut off, was succeeded by two, destroyed by Hercules. **5** (*Astron.*) one of the 15 ancient southern constellations. **hydroid** (-droid) *n.* (*Zool.*) any colonial hydrozoan coelenterate of the order Hydroida in which the polyp phase is dominant, as the hydras, sea anemones and corals. ~*a.* of or relating to the Hydroida. [L, from Gr. *hudra*, cogn. with *hudōr*, water]

hydracid (hīdras´id) *n.* (*Chem.*) an acid containing hydrogen but no oxygen. ~*a.* of or relating to a hydracid.

hydrangea (hīdrān´jə) *n.* any flowering shrub of the genus *Hydrangea*, from Asia and America. [HYDR-, Gr. *angeion*, *angos*, a vessel]

hydrant (hī´drənt) *n.* a spout or discharge pipe, usu. with a nozzle for attaching a hose, connected with a water main for drawing water, esp. in emergencies.

hydranth (hī´dranth) *n.* a polyp in a hydroid colony specialized for feeding. [HYDR-, Gr. *anthos*, flower]

†**hydrargyrum** (hīdrah´jirəm) *n.* mercury, quicksilver. **hydrargyric** (-jir´ik) *a.* [L *hydrargyrus*, Gr. *hudrarguros* (HYDR-, *arguros*, silver)]

hydrastine (hīdras´tīn) *n.* a bitter alkaloid prepared from the root of a N American plant, *Hydrastis canadensis*, used as a tonic, to reduce fever and arrest haemorrhage. [mod. L *Hydrastis*]

hydrate (hī´drāt) *n.* (*Chem.*) a compound of water with an element or another compound. ~*v.t.* to combine with water to form a hydrate. **hydratable** *a.* **hydrated** *a.* **hydration** (-drā´shən) *n.* **hydrator** *n.*

hydraulic (hīdrol´ik) *a.* **1** of or relating to fluids in motion, or to the power exerted by water conveyed through pipes or channels. **2** operating or operated by such power. **hydraulically** *adv.* **hydraulic cement, hydraulic mortar** *n.* a cement or mortar which hardens under water. **hydraulic engineer** *n.* an engineer dealing with the design and construction of waterworks, dams, docks etc. **hydraulic engineering** *n.* **hydraulicity** (-lis´iti) *n.* **hydraulic lift** *n.* a lift worked by means of water-power. **hydraulic press** *n.* a heavy pressing machine worked by water-power. **hydraulic ram** *n.* a machine by which the fall of a column of water supplies power to elevate a portion of the water to a greater height than that at the source. **hydraulics** *n.* the science of water or other liquids both at rest and in motion, esp. the conveyance of water through pipes etc., and the practical application of water-power. [L *hydraulicus*, Gr. *hudraulikos* (HYDR-, *aulos*, pipe)]

hydrazine (hī´drəzēn, -zin) *n.* (*Chem.*) a colourless corrosive liquid that is a strong reducing agent, used esp. in rocket fuel. [HYDR-, AZO-, -INE]

hydric (hī´drik) *a.* of or containing hydrogen in chemical combination. **hydride** (-drīd) *n.* a compound of hydrogen with another element or radical. **hydriodic** (-driod´-) *a.* of or containing hydrogen and iodine in chemical combination. **hydriodic acid** *n.* a colourless or pale yellow solution of the gas hydrogen iodide in water.

hydro (hī´drō) *n.* (*pl.* **hydros**) (*coll.*) an establishment such as a hotel or clinic orig. offering hydropathic treatment. [short for HYDROPATHIC (under HYDROPATHY)]

hydro- (hī´drō), **hydr-** *comb. form* **1** of, relating to or connected with water (*hydroponic*). **2** (*Chem.*) containing hydrogen in chemical combination (*hydrochloric*). **3** (of a mineral) containing water as a constituent. **4** (*Med.*) affected with an accumulation of watery fluid, oedematous (*hydrocephalic*). **5** belonging to the genus *Hydra* or the class Hydrozoa. [Gr. *hudōr hudatos*, water]

hydro-barometer (hīdrōbərom´itə) *n.* an instrument for determining the depth of the sea by its pressure.

hydrobromic (hīdrōbrō´mik) *a.* composed of hydrogen and bromine. **hydrobromic acid** *n.* a colourless or pale yellow solution of the gas hydrogen bromide in water.

hydrocarbon (hīdrōkah´bən) *n.* a compound of carbon and hydrogen.

hydrocele (hī´drəsēl) *n.* (*Med.*) an accumulation of fluid, often swollen and painful, in a saclike cavity, esp. in the scrotum.

hydrocephalus (hīdrəsef´ələs, -kef´-), **hydrocephaly** (-li) *n.* (*Med.*) an accumulation of water on the brain, resulting in an enlargement of the head and possible brain damage. **hydrocephalic** (-fal´-), **hydrocephaloid** (-loid), **hydrocephalous** *a.* of or relating to hydrocephalus. [Gr. *hudrokephalon*]

hydrochloric acid (hīdrəklaw´rik) *n.* a solution of hydrogen chloride in water, a strong corrosive acid.

hydrochloride (hīdrəklaw´rīd) *n.* a compound of hydrochloric acid, esp. with an organic base. **hydrochlorofluorocarbon** (-kah´-) *n.* a compound similar to CFC but believed to be less harmful.

hydrocortisone (hīdrōkaw´tizōn) *n.* (*Med.*) the steroid hormone naturally secreted by the adrenal cortex, synthesized to treat inflammatory conditions.

hydrocyanic acid (hīdrōsīan´ik) *n.* a poisonous volatile liquid formed by the combination of hydrogen and cyanogen in aqueous solution, having a faint odour of bitter almonds; also called *prussic acid, hydrogen cyanide.*

hydrodynamics (hīdrōdīnam´iks) *n.* the science which deals with water and other liquids in motion, hydromechanics. **hydrodynamic, hydrodynamical** *a.* **1** of or relating to hydrodynamics. **2** derived from the force of water. **hydrodynamicist** (-sist) *n.*

hydroelectric (hīdrōilek´trik) *a.* of or relating to electricity generated from water-power. **hydroelectrically** *adv.* **hydroelectricity** (-tris´-) *n.*

hydrofluoric acid (hīdrōfluə´rik) *n.* a colourless solution of hydrogen fluoride in water.

hydrofoil (hī´drəfoil) *n.* **1** a fast vessel with one or more pairs of vanes attached to its hull which lift it out of the water at speed. **2** such a vane.

hydrogel (hī´drəjel) *n.* protoplasm comprising gelatine or albumen in a jelly-like state with water filling the interstices. [HYDRO-, *gel-*, from L *gelāre*, to freeze]

hydrogen (hī´drəjən) *n.* (*Chem.*) an invisible, flammable, gaseous element, the lightest of all known elements, which in combination with oxygen produces water. **hydrogenase** (-droj´-) *n.* any enzyme serving as a catalyst for the reduction of a substrate by hydrogen, as in certain micro-organisms. **hydrogenate** (hīdroj´-, hī´drə-) *v.t.* **1** to cause to combine with hydrogen. **2** to charge with hydrogen. **hydrogenation** (-ā´shən) *n.* **hydrogen bomb** *n.* an exceedingly powerful nuclear bomb in which an immense release of energy is obtained by the conversion by fusion of hydrogen nuclei into helium nuclei. **hydrogen bond** *n.* (*Chem.*) a weak chemical bond between an electronegative atom, e.g. fluorine or oxygen, and a hydrogen atom bonded to another electronegative atom. **hydrogen chloride** *n.* a colourless pungent corrosive gas obtained from the interaction of sulphuric acid and sodium chloride. **hydrogen cyanide** *n.* hydrocyanic acid, prussic acid. **hydrogenize** (hī´-, -droj´-), **hydrogenise** *v.t.* to hydrogenate. **hydrogenization** (-ā´shən) *n.* **hydrogenous** (-droj´-) *a.* **hydrogen peroxide** *n.* a bleaching compound, used mainly for lightening the hair and as an antiseptic. **hydrogen sulphide** *n.* a colourless poisonous gas smelling of rotten eggs, formed by decaying animal matter. [F *hydrogène*]

hydrogeology (hīdrōjēol´əji) *n.* the branch of geology concerned with the geological effects of underground and surface water. **hydrogeological** (-jiəloj´-) *a.* **hydrogeologist** *n.*

hydrography (hīdrog´rəfi) *n.* the science and art of studying, surveying and mapping seas, lakes, rivers and other waters, and their physical features, tides, currents etc. **hydrograph** (hī´drəgrahf) *n.* a graph or diagram showing seasonal variations in bodies of water. **hydrographer** *n.* **hydrographic** (-graf´-), **hydrographical** *a.* **hydrographically** *adv.*

hydroid HYDRA.

hydrokinetic (hīdrōkinet´ik) *a.* (*Physics*) relating to the motion of liquids. **hydrokinetics** *n.* the kinetics of liquids.

hydrolase (hī´drəlāz) *n.* any enzyme serving as a catalyst in the hydrolysis of a substrate.

hydrology (hīdrol´əji) *n.* the science of water, its properties, phenomena, laws and distribution. **hydrologic** (-drəloj´-), **hydrological** *a.* **hydrologically** *adv.* **hydrologist** *n.*

hydrolysis (hīdrol´isis) *n.* (*Chem.*) the formation of an acid and a base from a salt by the action of water. **hydrolyse** (hī´drə-), **hydrolyze** *v.t.* to subject to hydrolysis. **hydrolytic** (-lit´-) *a.* **hydrolytically** *adv.* [Gr. *lusis*, loosening, from *luein*, to loose]

hydromagnetic (hīdrōmagnet´ik) *a.* relating to the behaviour of fluids within magnetic fields.

†**hydromancy** (hī´drəmansi) *n.* divination by means of water. **hydromantic** (-man´-) *a.*

hydromania (hīdrōmā´niə) *n.* morbid craving for water.

hydromechanics (hīdrōmikan´iks) *n.* the mechanics of liquids, hydrodynamics. **hydromechanical** *a.*

†**hydromel** (hī´drōmel) *n.* a drink consisting of honey diluted with water, mead. [L, from Gr. *hudromeli* (HYDRO-, *meli*, honey)]

hydrometallurgy (hīdrōmital´əji) *n.* extraction of metal from ore by treatment with fluid.

hydrometeor (hīdrōmē´tiə) *n.* a meteorological phenomenon produced by water vapour, such as rain, snow etc. **hydrometeoric** (-or´-) *a.* **hydrometeorology** (-ərol´-) *n.* **hydrometeorological** (-loj´-) *a.*

hydrometer (hīdrom´itə) *n.* an instrument for determining the specific gravity of liquids or solids by means of flotation. **hydrometric** (-drəmet´-), **hydrometrical** *a.* **hydrometry** *n.* the art or process of measuring the specific gravity of fluids etc.

hydronaut (hī´drənawt) *n.* a person trained to operate vessels for exploring the ocean's depths.

hydronium ion HYDROXONIUM ION.

hydropathy (hīdrop´əthi) *n.* (*Med.*) the treatment of disease by the internal and external application of water. **hydropathic** (-drəpath´-) *a.* of or relating to hydropathy. ~*n.* an establishment for the hydropathic treatment of disease. **hydropathically** *adv.* **hydropathist** *n.* a person who practises or believes in hydropathy.

hydrophane (hī´drəfān) *n.* an opal which becomes translucent when immersed in water. **hydrophanous** (-drof´ənəs) *a.* becoming more translucent or brighter when immersed in water. [Gr. *phanēs*, clear, from *phainein*, to show]

hydrophilic (hīdrōfil´ik), **hydrophil** (hī´drōfil), **hydrophile** (-fīl) *a.* **1** having a great affinity for water. **2**

(*Chem.*) readily mixed or wetted with water. **hydrophilous** (-drof´iləs) *a.* (*Bot.*) (of a plant) growing in or pollinated by water.

hydrophobia (hīdrəfō´biə) *n.* **1** an unnatural dread of water, esp. as a symptom of rabies resulting from the bite of a rabid animal. **2** rabies. **3** dread of water. **hydrophobic** *a.* **1** of or concerning hydrophobia. **2** (*Chem.*) tending not to mix, dissolve in or be wetted by water. [L, from Gr. *hudrophobia*]

hydrophone (hī´drəfōn) *n.* **1** an instrument for detecting sound by water, used to locate submarines etc. **2** an instrument for detecting the sound of running water, used to discover leaks etc. [Gr. *phōnē*, voice, sound]

hydrophyte (hī´drəfīt) *n.* (*Bot.*) an aquatic plant or one which grows in very moist conditions. **hydrophytic** (-fit´-) *a.* [Gr. *phyton*, plant]

hydroplane (hī´drəplān) *n.* **1** a light motor boat capable of rising partially above the surface of water. **2** a flat fin for governing the vertical direction of a submarine. **3** a plane for lifting a boat partially from the water, so as to diminish the resistance and increase the speed. ~*v.i.* (of a boat) to move across the water like a hydroplane.

hydroponics (hīdrōpon´iks) *n.* the cultivation of plants without soil in water containing chemicals. **hydroponic** *a.* **hydroponically** *adv.* [Gr. *ponos*, work]

hydropower (hī´drəpowə) *n.* hydroelectric power.

hydroquinone (hīdrōkwin´ōn) *n.* a compound derived from benzoquinone, employed in the development of photographs.

hydroscope (hī´drəskōp) *n.* **1** an instrument for viewing underwater. **2** a water-clock, a clepsydra. [Gr. *hudroskopos*]

hydrosome (hī´drəsōm) *n.* (*Zool.*) the colonial organism of a hydrozoan. **hydrosomal** (-sō´-), **hydrosomatous** (-sō´-) *a.* [HYDRA, Gr. *soma*, body]

hydrosphere (hī´drəsfiə) *n.* the watery part of the surface of the earth, the sea and oceans.

hydrostat (hī´drəstat) *n.* an electrical contrivance for detecting the presence of water esp. one used to prevent the explosion of steam boilers. [Gr. *statos*, standing]

hydrostatics (hīdrəstat´iks) *n.* the science concerned with the pressure and equilibrium of liquids at rest. **hydrostatic, hydrostatical** *a.* **1** relating to hydrostatics. **2** of or relating to the pressure and equilibrium of liquids at rest. **hydrostatically** *adv.* **hydrostatic balance** *n.* a balance for weighing substances in water to ascertain their specific gravities. **hydrostatic press** *n.* a hydraulic press.

hydrotherapy (hīdrōther´əpi) *n.* (*Med.*) the therapeutic application of water, usu. the use of swimming pools etc. for the treatment of muscular conditions, arthritis etc. **hydrotherapeutic** (-pū´tik) *a.* **1** of or relating to hydrotherapy. **2** hydropathic. **hydrotherapeutics** *n.* **hydrotherapist** *n.*

hydrothermal (hīdrōthœ´məl) *a.* relating to the action of heated water, esp. on the materials of the earth's crust. **hydrothermally** *adv.*

hydrothorax (hīdrōthaw´raks) *n.* (*Med.*) an abnormal accumulation of fluid in the chest.

hydrotropism (hīdrot´rəpizm) *n.* (*Bot.*) the tendency in the growing parts of plants to turn towards or away from moisture. **hydrotropic** (-trop´-) *a.* **hydrotropically** *adv.* [Gr. *-tropos*, a turning, from *trepein*, to turn]

hydrous (hī´drəs) *a.* (*Chem., Mineral.*) containing water.

hydrovane (hī´drəvān) *n.* a vane on a seaplane to aid take-off or increase stability.

hydroxide (hīdrok´sīd) *n.* (*Chem.*) a compound formed by the union of a basic oxide with the molecules of water.

hydroxonium ion (hīdroksō´niəm), **hydronium ion** (-drō´-) *n.* (*Chem.*) the hydrated hydrogen in H_3O^+.

hydroxy- (hīdrok´si) *comb. form* (*Chem.*) containing the radical hydroxyl.

hydroxyl (hīdrok´sil) *n.* the monad radical formed by the combination of one atom of hydrogen and one of water occurring in many chemical compounds.

hydrozoan (hīdrəzō´ən) *n.* any aquatic coelenterate of the class Hydrozoa, including the hydra, medusa, jellyfish etc. ~*a.* of or relating to this class. [Gr. *zōon* (pl. *zōa*), an animal]

hyena (hīē´nə), **hyaena** *n.* **1** any carnivorous quadruped of the family Hyaenidae, allied to the dog, with three modern species, the striped *Hyena striata*, the spotted *H. crocuta*, and the brown hyena, *H. brunnea* (the first is also called the laughing hyena). **2** the thylacine. **3** a ferocious or treacherous person. **hyena dog** *n.* a S African wild dog, *Lycaon pictus*, which hunts in packs. [L *hyaena*, Gr. *huaina*, sow-like, from *hus*, a sow]

hyet- HYETO-.

hyetal (hī´ətəl) *a.* **1** of or belonging to rain. **2** relating to the rainfall of different countries.

hyeto- (hī´ətō), **hyet-** *comb. form* of or relating to rain or rainfall. [Gr. *huetos*, rain]

hyetograph (hī´ətōgrahf) *n.* **1** an automatic instrument that registers rainfall. **2** a chart showing rainfall distribution in an area over time. **hyetographic** (-graf´-), **hyetographical** *a.* **hyetography** (-tog´rəfi) *n.* the branch of meteorology concerned with the distribution and mapping of the rainfall.

hyetology (hīətol´əji) *n.* the branch of meteorology concerned with the study of rainfall.

hyetometer (hīətom´itə) *n.* a rain gauge.

Hygeian (hījē´ən) *a.* **1** relating to Hygeia, the Greek goddess of health. **2** of or relating to hygiene. [Gr. *Hugeia, Hugieia*, from *hugiēs*, healthy]

hygiene (hī´jēn) *n.* **1** the science of the prevention of disease. **2** the art of preserving health, esp. of the community at large. **3** practices that promote health. **4** sanitary science. **hygienic** (-jē´-) *a.* **hygienically** *adv.* **hygienics** *n.* the study and principles of hygiene. **hygienist** (-jē´-) *n.* a specialist in the promotion and practice of hygiene. [F *hygiène*, Gr. *hugienē technē*, the art of health, as HYGEIAN]

hygr- HYGRO-.

hygristor (hīgris´tə) *n.* an electronic component whose resistance varies with humidity. [HYGR-, *resistor*]

hygro- (hī´grō), **hygr-** *comb. form* of, relating to or denoting the presence of moisture. [Gr. *hugros*, wet]

hygrograph (hī´grəgrahf) *n.* an automatic hygrometer.

hygrology (hīgrol´əji) *n.* the branch of physics relating to humidity, esp. of the atmosphere.

hygrometer (hīgrom´itə) *n.* an instrument for measuring the moisture of the air etc. **hygrometric** (-met´-), **hygrometrical** *a.* **hygrometrically** *adv.* **hygrometry** (-grom´-) *n.* the branch of physics concerned with the measurement of moisture, esp. of the air.

hygrophilous (hīgrof´iləs) *a.* (*Bot.*) (of a plant) living or growing in moist places.

hygrophyte (hī´grəfīt) *n.* a hydrophyte.

hygroscope (hī´grəskōp) *n.* an instrument for indicating the degree of moisture in the atmosphere. **hygroscopic** (-skop´-), **hygroscopical** *a.* **1** (of bodies) imbibing moisture from the atmosphere. **2** perceptible or liable to detection through moisture. **3** of, relating to or indicated by the hygroscope. **hygroscopically** *adv.* **hygroscopicity** (-skəpis´-) *n.*

hygrostat (hī´grəstat) *n.* a device for maintaining constant humidity, a humidistat.

hying HIE.

hyl- HYLO-.

hylic (hī´lik) *a.* of or relating to matter, material. [Gr. *hulikos*, as HYLO-]

hylo- (hī´lō) *comb.form* **1** of matter as, opposed to spirit. **2** of or relating to wood. [Gr. *hule*, matter]
hylomorphism (hīlōmaw´fizm) *n.* the theory that matter is the cause of the universe. **hylomorphic** *a.* **hylomorphist** *n.*
hylophagous (hīlof´əgəs) *a.* (of insects etc.) feeding on wood.
hylotheism (hīlōthē´izm) *n.* the system which regards God and matter as identical, pantheism. **hylotheist** *n.*
hylozoism (hīlōzō´izm) *n.* the doctrine that matter is necessarily endowed with life. **hylozoic** *a.* **hylozoistic** (-is´-) *a.* [Gr. *zoe*, life]
hymen (hī´mən) *n.* (*Anat.*) a membrane stretched across the vaginal entrance. **hymenal** *a.* [Gr. *humēn*, a membrane]
hymeneal (hīmənē´əl) *a.* (*poet.*) of or relating to marriage. ~*n.* a wedding hymn or poem. [L *Hymen*, the god of marriage, from Gr. *humēn*]
hymenium (hīmē´niəm) *n.* (*pl.* **hymenia** (-niə), **hymeniums**) (*Bot.*) the spore-bearing stratum or surface in fungi. **hymeniferous** (hīmənif´-) *a.* [Gr. *humenīon*, dim. of *humēn*, HYMEN]
hymeno- (hī´mənō) *comb. form* membranous. [Gr. *humēn humenos*, a membrane]
hymenopteran (hīmənop´tərən) *n.* any insect of the order Hymenoptera, having four membranous wings, such as the bee, wasp, ant etc. ~*a.* of or belonging to the Hymenoptera. **hymenopterous** *a.* [Gr. *pteron*, a wing]
hymn (him) *n.* **1** a song or ode in praise or adoration of God, esp. in Christian worship. **2** a solemn song or ode to a god or a revered person or thing. ~*v.t.* to praise or worship in hymns. ~*v.i.* to sing hymns. **hymnal** (him´nəl) *n.* a collection of hymns, esp. for public worship. **hymnary** (-nə-) *n.* (*pl.* **hymnaries**) a hymnal. **hymn book** *n.* a book of hymns. **hymnist** (-nist) *n.* a composer of hymns. **hymno-** (him´nō) *comb.form* of or relating to a hymn or hymns. **hymnody** (him´nədi) *n.* (*pl.* **hymnodies**) **1** the singing of hymns. **2** the composition of hymns. **3** hymns collectively. **4** a hymnology. †**hymnodist** *n.* **hymnographer** (-nog´-) *n.* a writer of hymns. **hymnography** *n.* **hymnology** (-nol´-) *n.* (*pl.* **hymnologies**) **1** the composition or the study of hymns. **2** hymns collectively. **hymnologic** (-nəloj´-) *a.* **hymnologist** *n.* [OF *hymne*, L *hymnus*, Gr. *humnos*]
hyoid (hī´oid) *a.* **1** U-shaped. **2** of or relating to the hyoid bone. ~*n.* the hyoid bone. **hyoid bone** *n.* the bone supporting the tongue. [F *hyoïde*, L *hyoïdes*, Gr. *huoeidēs* (letter υ -OID)]
hyoscyamine (hīəsī´əmēn, -mīn) *n.* a white crystalline alkaloid obtained from the seeds of henbane, *Hyoscyamus niger*, highly poisonous, used as a sedative. **hyoscine** (hī´əsēn, -sīn) *n.* a strong narcotic drug, scopolamine, used as an antiemetic and prior to eye examination. [Gr. *huoscuamos* (*huos*, gen. of *hus*, sow, *kuamos*, bean)]
hyp- HYPO-.
hypabyssal (hipəbis´əl) *a.* (*Geol.*) (of igneous rock) formed at a moderate distance below the surface of the earth.
hypaesthesia (hīpēsthē´ziə, -pes-), (*N Am.*) **hypesthesia** *n.* (*Med.*) reduced capacity for sensation, esp. of the skin. **hypaesthetic** (-thet´ik) *a.*
hypaethral (hipē´thrəl, hī-) *a.* (esp. of a temple or sanctuary not intended to be roofed) open to the sky, roofless. **hypaethron** (-ron) *n.* a temple with a central space open to the sky. [L *hypaethrus*, Gr. *hupaithros* (HYPO-, *aithēr*, ETHER)]
hypalgesia (hipaljē´ziə), **hypalgia** (-pal´jiə) *n.* (*Med.*) reduction of or freedom from pain. **hypalgesic, hypalgic** *a.* [Gr. *algēsis algos*, pain]
hypallage (hipal´əjē, hī-) *n.* (*Gram.*) the interchange of natural or grammatical relations between terms in a sentence, e.g. 'the clock's ticking time'. [L *hypallagē*, Gr. *hupallagē* (HYPO-, *allagē*, change, from *allassein*, to change)]
hype[1] (hīp) *n.* (*coll.*) **1** exaggerated or false publicity used to sell or promote. **2** a deception, a swindle. ~*v.t.* to sell or promote (something or someone) by using exaggerated or false publicity.
hype[2] (hīp) *n.* (*coll.*) **1** a drug addict. **2** a hypodermic needle. **hyped up** *a.* (*sl.*) full of nervous excitement.
hyper- (hī´pə) *comb.form* **1** above, beyond. **2** excessive, beyond measure. [L, from Gr. *huper*]
hyperacidity (hīpərəsid´iti) *n.* (*Med.*) excessive acidity in the digestive tract, esp. in the stomach.
hyperactive (hīpərak´tiv) *a.* abnormally active. **hyperactivity** (-tiv´-) *n.*
hyperaesthesia (hipərēsthē´ziə), (*N Am.*) **hyperesthesia** *n.* (*Med.*) excessive sensibility to stimuli, esp. of the nerves and the skin. **hyperaesthetic** (-thet´-) *a.*
hyperbaric (hīpəbar´ik) *a.* (esp. of oxygen) at higher than normal pressure. **hyperbarically** *adv.*
hyperbaton (hīpœ´bəton) *n.* (*Gram.*) a figure by which words are transposed or inverted from their natural and grammatical order (*Do I not like orange!*). **hyperbatic** (hīpəbat´-) *a.* **hyperbatically** *adv.* [L, from Gr. *huperbaton* (*bainein*, to go)]
hyperbola (hīpœ´bələ) *n.* (*pl.* **hyperbolas, hyperbolae** (-ē)) (*Geom.*) a plane curve formed by cutting a cone when the intersecting plane makes a greater angle with the base than the side of the cone makes. **hyperboliform** (-bol´ifawm) *a.* having the form of a hyperbola. **hyperboloid** *n.* a solid formed by the revolution of a hyperbola about its axis. **hyperboloidal** (-oid´əl) *a.* [Gr. *huperbolē*, see HYPERBOLE]
hyperbole (hīpœ´bəli) *n.* a figure of speech expressing much more than the truth, rhetorical exaggeration. **hyperbolic** (hīpəbol´ik) *a.* **1** of, relating to, or of the nature of a hyperbola. **2** hyperbolical. **hyperbolical** *a.* of the nature of hyperbole. **hyperbolically** *adv.* **hyperbolic function** *n.* any of a set of functions of an angle related algebraically to a rectangular hyperbola in the same way as a trigonometric function is related to a circle. **hyperbolism** *n.* **1** the use of hyperbole. **2** a hyperbolic expression. [L, from Gr. *huperbolē*, (HYPER-, *ballein*, to throw)]
hyperboliform HYPERBOLA.
hyperbolism HYPERBOLE.
hyperboloid, hyperboloidal HYPERBOLA.
hyperborean (hīpəbaw´riən) *a.* **1** belonging to or inhabiting the extreme north. **2** in Greek mythology, of or relating to the Hyperboreans. ~*n.* **1** a person living in the extreme north. **2** (**Hyperborean**) in Greek mythology, any of a people supposed to live in a land beyond the north wind, distinguished for piety and happiness. **hyperboreanism** *n.* [late L *hyperboreānus*, L *hyperboreus*, Gr. *huperboreos* (HYPER-, *Boreas*, the north wind)]
hypercatalectic (hīpəkatəlek´tik) *a.* (of a line of verse) having an extra syllable or extra syllables at the end. [late L *hypercatalēcticus*]
hypercharge (hī´pəchahj) *n.* (*Physics*) an interaction between elementary particles that is a weak force tending to oppose gravitational attraction between objects.
hypercholesterolaemia (hīpəkolestərolē´miə), (*N Am.*) **hypercholesterolemia** *n.* (*Med.*) an excess of cholesterol in the blood.
hypercolour (hī´pəkŭlə), (*N Am.*) **hypercolor** *n.* a process for dyeing fabric so that it changes colour when exposed to raised temperatures.
hyperconscious (hīpəkon´shəs) *a.* acutely or excessively aware (of).
hypercritical (hīpəkrit´ikəl) *a.* **1** unreasonably critical. **2** captiously censorious, overnice. **hypercritic** *n.* **hypercritically** *adv.* **hypercriticism** (-sizm) *n.* **hypercriticize** (-sīz), **hypercriticise** *v.t.* to criticize captiously. ~*v.i.* to be hypercritical.

hypercube (hī´pəkūb) *n.* (*Math.*) a theoretical solid in four or more dimensions, analogous to a cube in three dimensions.
hyperdulia (hīpədūlī´ə) *n.* in the Roman Catholic Church, the particular veneration made to the Virgin Mary, as distinct from that paid to the saints and from the worship paid to God.
hyperesthesia HYPERAESTHESIA.
hyperfocal distance (hīpəfō´kəl) *n.* the distance beyond which objects appear sharply defined through a lens focused at infinity.
hyperglycaemia (hīpəglīsē´miə), (*N Am.*) **hyperglycemia** *n.* (*Med.*) an excessive level of sugar in the blood. **hyperglycaemic** *a.* [HYPER-, GLYCO-, -AEMIA]
hypergolic (hīpəgol´ik) *a.* (of a rocket fuel) able to ignite spontaneously on contact with an oxidizer. [G *Hypergol*, perh. from HYPER-, ERG[1], -OL]
hypericum (hīper´ikəm) *n.* any herbaceous plant or shrub of the genus *Hypericum* typified by the St John's wort. [L, from Gr. *hupereikon* (*ereikē*, heath)]
hyperinflation (hīpərinflā´shən) *n.* a very high level of inflation in an economy.
hyperinosis (hīperinō´sis) *n.* an excess of fibrin in the blood. **hyperinotic** (-not´-) *a.* [Gr. *is inos*, fibre, -OSIS]
hyperkinesis (hīpəkīnē´sis), **hyperkinesia** (-ziə) *n.* (*Med.*) **1** excessive movement, as in a muscle spasm. **2** a disorder resulting in hyperactivity and a very short attention span. **hyperkinetic** (-et´ik) *a.*
hypermarket (hī´pəmahkit) *n.* a very large self-service store selling a wide range of household and other goods, usu. on the outskirts of a town or city.
hypermedia (hīpəmē´diə) *n.* multimedia.
hypermetrical (hīpəmet´rikəl) *a.* **1** (of a line of verse) having an extra syllable or extra syllables. **2** (of such a syllable) extra to the metre. **hypermeter** (-pœ´mitə) *n.* a hypermetrical line. [Gr. *hupermetros*]
hypermetropia (hīpəmitrō´piə), **hyperopia** (-pərō´-) *n.* (*Med.*) an abnormal state of the eye characterized by long-sightedness, as opposed to myopia. **hypermetropic** (-trop´-), **hyperopic** (-pərop´-) *a.* [Gr. *hupermetros*, as HYPERMETRICAL, *ōps ōpos*, eye]
hypernym (hī´pənim) *n.* a word representing a general class or family which is applicable to more specific related words (e.g. *tree* is a hypernym for *ash* and *beech*).
hyperon (hī´pəron) *n.* (*Physics*) an elementary particle of the baryon group with a greater mass than a proton or a neutron.
hyperopia, hyperopic HYPERMETROPIA.
hyperphysical (hīpəfiz´ikəl) *a.* supernatural. **hyperphysically** *adv.*
hyperplasia (hīpəplā´ziə) *n.* (*Med.*) excessive growth due to abnormal multiplication of cells. **hyperplastic** (-plas´-) *a.* [Gr. *plasis*, formation, from *plassein*, to mould]
hypersensitive (hīpəsen´sitiv) *a.* excessively sensitive. **hypersensitiveness** *n.* **hypersensitivity** (-tiv´-) *n.*
hypersonic (hīpəson´ik) *a.* (of speeds) higher than Mach 5. **hypersonically** *adv.*
hyperspace (hī´pəspās) *n.* space that has more than three dimensions.
hypersthene (hī´pəsthēn) *n.* (*Mineral.*) an orthorhombic, foliated, brittle mineral, magnesium iron silicate, allied to hornblende, with a beautiful pearly lustre. **hypersthenic** (-then´-) *a.* [F *hypersthène* (Gr. *sthenos*, strength)]
hypertension (hīpəten´shən) *n.* **1** abnormally high blood pressure. **2** a state of excessive emotional tension. **hypertensive** *a.* suffering from hypertension.
hypertext (hī´pətekst) *n.* (*Comput.*) a system of hardware and software that allows easy movement between related text, sound and graphics.
hyperthermia (hīpəthœ´miə) *n.* abnormally high body temperature. **hyperthermic** *a.* [Gr. *thermē*, heat]
hyperthyroidism (hīpəthī´roidizm) *n.* excessive activity of the thyroid gland, causing an accelerated metabolic rate, rapid heartbeat, nervousness etc. **hyperthyroid** *a.* **hyperthyroidic** (-roi´-) *a.*
hypertonic (hīpəton´ik) *a.* **1** (*Med.*) (of muscles) being excessively tense. **2** (*Chem.*) (of a solution) more concentrated than a surrounding medium or than another liquid. **hypertonia** (-tō´-) *n.* excessive muscle tension. **hypertonicity** (-tənis´iti) *n.*
hypertrophy (hīpœ´trəfi) *n.* (*Med.*) excessive development or enlargement of an organ or tissue. ~*v.t.* (*3rd pers. sing. pres.* **hypertrophies,** *pres.p.* **hypertrophying,** *past, p.p.* **hypertrophied**) to affect with hypertrophy. ~*v.i.* to be affected by hypertrophy. **hypertrophic** (-hīpətrof´-), **hypertrophous, hypertrophical, hypertrophied** *a.* [Gr. *-trophia*, from *trephein*, to nourish]
hyperventilation (hīpəventilā´shən) *n.* excessive breathing, causing excessive loss of carbon dioxide in the blood. **hyperventilate** *v.i.*
hypesthesia HYPAESTHESIA.
hypethral HYPAETHRAL.
hypha (hī´fə) *n.* (*pl.* **hyphae** (-fē)) any of the filaments in the mycelium of a fungus. **hyphal** *a.* [L, from Gr. *huphē*, web]
hyphen (hī´fən) *n.* a short stroke (-) joining two words or parts of words. ~*v.t.* to join by a hyphen. **hyphenate** *v.t.* **hyphenation** (-ā´shən) *n.* **hyphenic** (-fen´-) *a.* [L, from Gr. *huphen*]
hypnagogic (hipnəgoj´ik), **hypnogogic** *a.* (*Psych.*) of or concerning the state of drowsiness before sleep. [Gr. *agōgos*, leading, from *agein*, to lead]
hypno- (hip´nō) *comb. form* relating to sleep or hypnosis. [Gr. *hupnos*, sleep]
hypnogenesis (hipnəjen´əsis) *n.* inducement of hypnotic sleep. **hypnogenetic** (-net´-) *a.*
hypnogogic HYPNAGOGIC.
hypnology (hipnol´əji) *n.* the study of the phenomena of sleep. **hypnologist** *n.*
hypnopaedia (hipnōpē´diə), (*N Am.*) **hypnopedia** *n.* learning by hearing during sleep.
hypnopompic (hipnəpom´pik) *a.* (*Psych.*) of or concerning the state of drowsiness between sleep and waking. [Gr. *pompē*, sending, procession]
hypnosis (hipnō´sis) *n.* (*pl.* **hypnoses** (-sēz)) **1** a state resembling sleep in which the subconscious mind responds to external suggestions and forgotten memories are recovered. **2** the inducement of this state, hypnotism. **3** artificially induced sleep.
hypnotherapy (hipnōther´əpi) *n.* treatment by hypnotism. **hypnotherapist** *n.*
hypnotic (hipnot´ik) *a.* **1** of, relating to or inducing hypnotism. **2** causing sleep. **3** (of a drug) soporific. ~*n.* a drug that produces sleep. **hypnotically** *adv.*
hypnotism (hip´nətizm) *n.* **1** the practice of inducing hypnosis. **2** the artificial inducement of sleep. **3** artificially induced sleep. **hypnotist** *n.* **hypnotize, hypnotise** *v.t.* **1** to affect with hypnosis. **2** to capture the attention of completely. **hypnotizable** *a.* **hypnotizability** (-bil´-) *n.* **hypnotization** (-ā´shən) *n.* **hypnotizer** *n.*
hypnum (hip´nəm) *n.* (*pl.* **hypnums, hypna** (-nə)) any moss of the genus *Hypnum*. [Gr. *hupnon*]
hypo[1] (hī´pō) *n.* sodium thiosulphate, the normal fixing solution in photography. [sodium *hypo*sulphite]
hypo[2] (hī´pō) *n.* (*pl.* **hypos**) (*coll.*) a hypodermic needle.
hypo[3] (hī´pō) *n.* (*pl.* **hypos**) (*coll.*) an attack of hypoglycaemia.
hypo- (hī´pō), **hyp-** *comb. form* **1** under, below. **2** less than. **3** (*Chem.*) denoting compounds having a lower degree of oxidation in a series. [Gr. *hupo*, under]
hypo-allergenic (hīpōaləjen´ik) *a.* not likely to cause an allergic reaction.

hypoblast (hī´pəblahst) *n.* (*Biol.*) the innermost membrane of the blastoderm, the endoderm. **hypoblastic** (-blas´-) *a.* [Gr. *blastos*, sprout]

hypobole (hipob´əli) *n.* a mode of reasoning in which several things seemingly opposed to the argument are mentioned and then refuted. [Gr. *hupobolē* (ballein, to throw)]

hypocaust (hī´pəkawst) *n.* in ancient Roman buildings, a space or series of channels under the floor by which heat was conducted from a furnace to heat a building, room, bath etc. [late L *hypocaustum*, Gr. *hupokauston* (*kaiein*, fut. *kaus-*, to burn)]

hypochlorite (hīpəklaw´rīt) *n.* (*Chem.*) a salt or ester of hypochlorous acid. **hypochlorous acid** *n.* (*Chem.*) an unstable acid formed when chlorine dissolves in water, used as a bleach, disinfectant etc.

hypochondria (hīpəkon´driə) *n.* **1** a condition characterized by excessive anxiety with regard to one's health. **2** (*Med.*) chronic depression without apparent cause. **3** pl. of HYPOCHONDRIUM (under HYPOCHONDRIA). **hypochondriac** (-ak) *n.* a person affected with hypochondria. ~*a.* **1** produced or characterized by hypochondria. **2** having a disordered mind. **3** causing melancholy. **4** (*Anat.*) of or relating to the hypochondria. †**hypochondriacal** (-drī´-) *a.* **hypochondriacally** *adv.* **hypochondriasis** (-drī´əsis) *n.* hypochondria. **hypochondrium** (-driəm) *n.* (*pl.* **hypochondria** (-driə)) the part of the upper abdomen at either side of the epigastric region. [late L, pl., from Gr. *hupochondria*, pl., the soft parts below the cartilage (*chondros*, cartilage, esp. that of the breastbone)]

hypocorism (hīpok´ərizm) *n.* (*Gram.*) a pet name. **hypocoristic** (-pəkəris´-) *a.* [Gr. *hupokorizesthai*, from *korizesthai*, to caress, from *koros*, boy, *korē*, girl]

hypocotyl (hīpəkot´il) *n.* (*Bot.*) the part of the stem of an embryo plant between the cotyledons and the top of the radicle.

hypocrisy (hipok´rəsi) *n.* (*pl.* **hypocrisies**) **1** dissimulation, pretence, a feigning to be what one is not. **2** a pretence to virtue or goodness. **hypocrite** (hip´əkrit) *n.* a person who practises hypocrisy, a dissembler. **hypocritical** (hipəkrit´-) *a.* **hypocritically** *adv.* [OF *hypocrisie*, L *hypocrisis*, Gr. *hupokrisis*, acting of a part, from *hupokrinesthai* (*krinein*, to judge, decide)]

hypocycloid (hīpəsī´kloid) *n.* (*Geom.*) a curve generated by a point on the circumference of a circle rolling round the inside of the circumference of another circle. **hypocycloidal** (-kloi´-) *a.*

hypodermic (hīpədœ´mik) *a.* (*Med.*) **1** of or relating to the layers beneath the skin. **2** (of a drug etc.) injected subcutaneously by means of a hypodermic syringe etc. ~*n.* **1** a hypodermic syringe. **2** (a drug introduced into the system by) an injection beneath the skin. **hypoderm** (hī´pədœm), **hypoderma** (-dœ´mə) *n.* (*pl.* **hypodermata** (-mətə)) **1** (*Zool.*) a layer beneath the outer integument, as the inner membrane lining the elytra of beetles. **2** (*Bot.*) the cellular layer beneath the epidermis of some plants. **hypodermal** *a.* hypodermic. **hypodermically** *adv.* **hypodermic injection** *n.* an injection (of narcotics, antitoxins etc.) beneath the skin. **hypodermic needle** *n.* (the hollow needle of) a hypodermic syringe. **hypodermic syringe** *n.* a small syringe with a hollow needle for giving hypodermic injections. [Gr. *derma*, skin]

hypogastrium (hīpəgas´triəm) *n.* (*pl.* **hypogastria** (-striə)) (*Anat.*) the middle part of the lowest zone into which the abdomen is divided. **hypogastric** *a.* [Gr. *hupogastrion* (*gastēr*, belly)]

hypogeal (hīpəjē´əl), **hypogean** (-ən), **hypogeous** (-əs) *a.* **1** (*Biol.*) existing or growing underground. **2** (*Bot.*) (of seed germination) in which the cotyledons remain below ground. **3** subterranean. **hypogene** (hī´-), **hypogenic** (-jen´-) *a.* (*Geol.*) (of rocks) formed under the surface of the earth, plutonic. [L *hypogēus*, Gr. *hupogeios* (*gē*, earth)]

hypogeum (hīpəjē´əm) *n.* (*pl.* **hypogea** (-jēə)) (a part of) a building below the level of the ground.

hypoglossal (hīpəglos´əl) *a.* (*Anat.*) under the tongue. **hypoglossal nerve** *n.* the motor nerve of the tongue. [Gr. *glossa*, tongue]

hypoglycaemia (hīpōglīsē´miə), (*N Am.*) **hypoglycemia** *n.* (*Med.*) an abnormally low level of sugar in the blood. **hypoglycaemic** *a.*

hypognathous (hīpog´nəthəs) *a.* (*Anat.*) having a lower mandible longer than the upper. **hypognathism** *n.* [Gr. *gnathos*, jaw]

hypogynous (hīpoj´inəs) *a.* (*Bot.*) **1** (of stamens) growing from below the base of the ovary. **2** (of plants) having the stamens so situated.

hypoid (hī´poid) *n.* a type of bevel gear having a tooth form based on a hypocycloidal curve in which the pinion is offset from the centre line of the wheel to connect non-intersecting shafts and to withstand high surface loading. [perh. from HYPERBOLOID (under HYPERBOLA)]

hypolimnion (hīpəlim´nion) *n.* (*pl.* **hypolimnia** (-niə)) the lower, colder layer of water below the thermocline of a lake. [Gr. *limnē*, lake]

hypomania (hīpəmā´niə) *n.* (*Psych.*) the mental state of overexcitability. **hypomanic** (-man´-) *a.*

hyponasty (hī´pənasti) *n.* (*Bot.*) more active growth of a plant organ on the underside causing a tendency to upward curvature. **hyponastic** (-nas´-) *a.* [Gr. *nastos*, solid, from *nassein*, to press]

hyponym (hī´pənim) *n.* a word with a more specific meaning that is included in the scope of another word (e.g. *ash* is a hyponym of *tree*). **hyponymy** (-pon´-) *n.*

hypophosphate (hīpəfos´fāt) *n.* a salt of hypophosphoric acid. **hypophosphite** (-fīt) *n.* a salt of hypophosphorous acid. **hypophosphoric** (-for´ik), **hypophosphorous** (-fos´-) *a.* **hypophosphoric acid** *n.* an acid formed by the action of water and oxygen on phosphorus. **hypophosphorous acid** *n.* a weak acid composed of hydrogen, phosphorus and oxygen.

hypophysis (hīpof´isis) *n.* (*pl.* **hypophyses** (-sēz)) (*Anat.*) the pituitary gland. **hypophyseal** (-fiz´iəl), **hypophysial** *a.* [L, from Gr. *hupophusis*, offshoot]

hypoplasia (hīpəplā´ziə) *n.* (*Med.*) underdevelopment of an organ or part. [Gr. *plasis*, formation]

hyposensitize (hīpōsen´sitīz), **hyposensitise** *v.t.* to reduce the sensitivity of, to desensitize.

hypostasis (hīpos´təsis) *n.* (*pl.* **hypostases** (-sēz)) **1** that which forms the basis of anything. **2** in metaphysics, that by which a thing subsists, substance as distinct from attributes. **3** the essence or essential principle. **4** the personal subsistence as distinct from substance. **5** (*Theol.*) **a** one of the persons of the Trinity. **b** the person of Christ. **6** (*Med.*) the accumulation and congestion of blood in the lower parts of the body due to the effects of gravity in circumstances of poor circulation. **hypostasize, hypostasise** *v.t.* **1** to embody, to personify. **2** to treat as or make into a substance or concrete reality. **hypostasization** (-ā´shən) *n.* **hypostatic** (-pəstat´-), **hypostatical** *a.* **1** in Christian theology, relating to the three persons of the Trinity. **2** pertaining to hypostasis. **hypostatically** *adv.* **hypostatic union** *n.* the union between divinity and humanity represented in Christ. **hypostatize** *v.t.* (*N Am.*) to hypostasize. [late L, from Gr. *hupostasis* (*statis*, standing, basis)]

hypostyle (hī´pəstīl) *a.* (*Archit.*) having the roof supported by pillars. ~*n.* **1** a building with a roof or ceiling supported by pillars. **2** a covered colonnade. **3** a pillared hall. [Gr. *stulos*, pillar]

hyposulphite (hīpəsŭl´fīt), (*N Am.*) **hyposulfite** *n.* a thiosulphate, a salt of hyposulphurous acid. **hypo-**

sulphuric acid (-fū´-) *n.* an acid containing two more atoms of oxygen per molecule than sulphuric acid. **hyposulphurous acid** (-fū´-) *n.* an unstable acid containing one more sulphur atom per molecule than sulphuric acid.

hypotaxis (hīpətak´sis) *n.* (*Gram.*) subordinate construction in syntax, as opposed to *parataxis*. **hypotactic** (-tak´-) *a.*

hypotension (hīpōten´shən) *n.* abnormally low blood pressure. **hypotensive** *a.*

hypotenuse (hīpot´ənūz) *n.* the side of a right-angled triangle opposite to the right angle. [F *hypoténuse*, late L *hypotenusa*, Gr. *hupoteinousa*, fem. p.p. of *hupoteinein* (*teinein*, to stretch)]

hypothalamus (hīpōthal´əməs) *n.* (*pl.* **hypothalami** (-mī)) a region at the base of the brain controlling autonomic functions, e.g. hunger and thirst.

hypothec (hīpoth´ik) *n.* (*Law, esp. Sc.*) a security in favour of a creditor over the property of their debtor, while the property continues in the debtor's possession. **hypothecary** *a.* of or relating to a pledge or hypothecation. **hypothecate** *v.t.* to pledge or mortgage in security for some debt or liability. **hypothecation** (-ā´shən) *n.* **hypothecator** *n.* [F *hypothèque*, late L *hypothēca*, Gr. *hupothēkē* (HYPO-, *thēkē*, from *tithenai*, to place)]

hypothermia (hīpōəthœ´miə) *n.* subnormal body temperature, esp. when induced for surgical purposes. [Gr. *therme*, heat]

hypothesis (hīpoth´əsis) *n.* (*pl.* **hypotheses** (-th´əsēz)) **1** a proposition assumed for the purpose of an argument. **2** a theory assumed to account for something not understood. **3** a mere supposition or assumption. **hypothesist** *n.* **hypothesize, hypothesise** *v.i.* to form hypotheses. *~v.t.* to assume. **hypothesizer** *n.* **hypothetic** (-thet´-), **hypothetical** *a.* **1** founded on or of the nature of a hypothesis. **2** conjectural, conditional. **hypothetically** *adv.* [L, from Gr. *hupothesis* (HYPO-, THESIS)]

hypothyroidism (hīpəthī´roidizm) *n.* underactivity of the thyroid gland. **hypothyroid** *n., a.* **hypothyroidic** (-roi´-) *a.*

hypotonic (hīpəton´ik) *a.* **1** (*Med.*) (of muscles) deficient in tension. **2** (*Chem.*) (of a solution) less concentrated than a surrounding medium or than another liquid.

hypoventilation (hīpōventilā´shən) *n.* abnormally slow breathing, causing an excessive amount of carbon dioxide in the blood.

hypoxia (hīpok´siə) *n.* a deficiency of oxygen reaching the body tissues. **hypoxaemia** (-ē´miə), (*N Am.*) **hypoxemia** *n.* deficiency of oxygenation of the blood.

hypso- (hip´sō), **hyps-** *comb. form* height. [Gr. *hupsos*, height]

hypsography (hipsog´rəfi) *n.* the branch of geography concerned with the study and mapping of altitudes above sea level. **hypsographic** (-səgraf´-), **hypsographical** *a.*

hypsometer (hipsom´itə) *n.* an instrument for measuring heights above sea level by observing the boiling point of water with a delicate thermometer and so determining the relative atmospheric pressure. **hypsometric** (-səmet´-), **hypsometrical** *a.* **hypsometry** *n.* the art of measuring heights by observing differences in barometric pressures at different altitudes.

hyrax (hī´raks) *n.* (*pl.* **hyraxes, hyraces** (-rəsēz)) any small harelike quadruped of the order Hyracoidea, including the Syrian rock rabbit (the dassie) and the S African rock badger. [Gr. *hurax*]

hyssop (his´əp) *n.* **1** any small labiate aromatic herb of the genus *Hyssopus*, esp. *H. officinalis*, with blue flowers. **2** (*Bible*) an unidentified plant the twigs of which were used for sprinkling in Jewish rites of purification. [L *hyssōpus*, Gr. *hussōpos*, perh. from Heb.]

hyster- HYSTERO-.

hysterectomy (histərek´təmi) *n.* (*pl.* **hysterectomies**) the removal of the womb by surgery. **hysterectomize, hysterectomise** *v.t.* [HYSTER-, Gr. *ektomē* (*ek*, out, *temnein*, to cut)]

hysteresis (histərē´sis) *n.* (*Physics*) the tendency of a magnetic substance to remain in a certain magnetic condition, the lag of magnetic effects behind their causes. **hysteresial** *a.* [Gr. *husterēsis*, from *husteros*, late]

hysteria (histiə´riə) *n.* **1** an outbreak of frenzied uncontrollable emotion. **2** (*Psych.*) a nervous disorder, occurring in paroxysms, and often simulating other diseases. **hysteric** (-ter´-) *n.* a person subject to hysteria. *~a.* hysterical. **hysterical** *a.* **1** (*Psych.*) of, relating to or affected with hysteria. **2** neurotically emotional or excitable. **hysterical fit** *n.* an emotional paroxysm of crying, laughing etc., occurring in hysteria. **hysterically** *adv.* **hysterics** *n.pl.* **1** a hysterical fit. **2** (*coll.*) a fit of uncontrollable laughter. [mod. L, from Gr. *hustera*, the womb (from its having been attrib. formerly to disturbance of the womb)]

hystero- (his´tərō), **hyster-** *comb. form* **1** the womb. **2** hysteria. [Gr. *hustera*, womb]

hysterogenic (histərōjen´ik) *a.* producing hysteria. **hysterogeny** (-roj´-) *n.*

hysteroid (his´təroid) *a.* (*Psych.*) resembling hysteria.

hysteron proteron (histəron prot´əron) *n.* a figure of speech in which what should follow comes first, an inversion of the natural or logical order. [Gr. *husteron*, latter, *proteron*, former]

hysterotomy (histərot´əmi) *n.* (*pl.* **hysterotomies**) (*Med.*) delivery of a child through the walls of the abdomen, a Caesarean section. [HYSTERO-, -TOMY]

Hz. *abbr.* hertz.

I

I[1] (ī), **i** (*pl.* **Is, I's**) the ninth letter of the English and other versions of the Roman alphabet, corresponding to the Greek iota (Ι, ι). It has two principal sounds: (1) long and diphthongal as in *bind, find*, marked in this dictionary ī; (2) short as in *fin, bin, win*, left unmarked, i. It also has three minor sounds: (1) long, central and unrounded as in *dirk*, marked œ; (2) long and monophthongal as in *intrigue*, marked ē; (3) the consonantal sound of *y*, as in *behaviour, onion*, marked y. In conjunction with other vowels *i* also represents a variety of sounds, as in *hair, seize, boil, fruit* etc. ~*symbol* **1** one in Roman numerals. **2** (*Math.*) the square root of minus one. **3** electric current. **I-beam** *n.* a girder with an I-shaped cross-section.

I[2] (ī) *pron.* (*obj.* **me,** *poss.* **my, mine**) in speaking or writing denotes oneself. ~*n.* the self-conscious subject, the ego. [OE *ic* (cp. Dut. *ik*, Icel. *ek*, G *Ich*, L *ego*, Gr. *egō*)]

Usage note The use of *I* as an objective pronoun, quite commonly heard in *between you and I* and in objects ending *and I* after verbs and other prepositions, is best avoided.

I[3] *abbr.* **1** Institute. **2** Island(s), Isle(s). **3** Italy.

I[4] *chem. symbol* iodine.

-i[1] (ī) *suf.* forming the plural of L nouns in *-us*, as in *fungi, hippopotami.*

-i[2] (ē, i) *suf.* forming the plural of It. nouns in *-o* or *-e*, as in *banditti, timpani.*

-i[3] (i) *suf.* forming adjectives and nouns from names of Eastern countries or regions, as in *Bangladeshi, Yemeni.*

IA *abbr.* Iowa.

-ia (iə) *suf.* **1** forming abstract nouns, as in *mania, militia.* **2** forming names of countries etc., as in *Australia, Bulgaria, Helvetia.* **3** forming names of (members of) botanical genera etc., as in *begonia, Saponaria.* **4** forming names of diseases and medical conditions, as in *hysteria, malaria, neuralgia.* **5** forming names of alkaloids, as in *morphia.* **6** forming plurals of L nouns in *-ium* and Gr. nouns in *-ion*, as in *bacteria, regalia*, including zoological groups, as in *Reptilia.* [L, Gr.]

IAA *abbr.* indoleacetic acid.

IAEA *abbr.* International Atomic Energy Agency.

-ial (iəl) *suf.* forming adjectives, as in *celestial, terrestrial.* [Fr. *-iel*, L *-iālis, -iāle*]

iambus (īam´bəs), **iamb** (ī´amb) *n.* (*pl.* **iambuses, iambi** (-bī), **iambs**) a poetic foot of one short and one long, or one unaccented and one accented syllable. **iambic** *a.* **1** of or relating to the iambus. **2** composed of iambics. ~*n.* **1** an iambic foot. **2** (*usu. in pl.*) iambic verse. **iambically** *adv.* **iambist** *n.* [L, from Gr. *iambos*, an iambic verse, a lampoon, from *iaptein*, to assail]

-ian (iən) *suf.* forming nouns or adjectives, as *Athenian, Baconian, Cantabrigian.* [L *-ānus*, -AN, with euphonic or connective *-i-*]

-iasis (ī´əsis) *comb. form* indicating a disease, as *elephantiasis, psōriasis.* [L, from Gr. *-iasis*, state, condition]

IATA (īah´tə) *abbr.* International Air Transport Association.

iatric (īat´rik), **iatrical** (-əl) *a.* of or relating to physicians or medicine. **-iatrics** *comb. form* indicating medical care, as *paediatrics.* **iatrogenic** (-jen´ik) *a.* resulting unintentionally from medical treatment. **iatrogenically** *adv.* **iatrogenicity** (-nis´-) *n.* **-iatry** *comb. form* indicating healing treatment, as *psychiatry.* [Gr. *iātros*, physician]

ib. *abbr.* ibidem.

IBA *abbr.* Independent Broadcasting Authority.

Iberian (ībiə´riən) *a.* **1** of or relating to ancient Iberia in SW Europe, comprising modern Spain and Portugal. **2** of or relating to Spain and Portugal. **3** of or relating to ancient Iberia in Asia, now Transcaucasian Georgia. ~*n.* **1** a native or inhabitant of ancient Iberia in Europe. **2** a native or inhabitant of ancient Iberia in Asia. **3** a member of an ancient people that inhabited western Europe and probably entered the British Isles early in the Neolithic period. **4** the language of ancient Iberia in Europe. **Iberian Peninsula** *n.* Spain and Portugal. [L *Ibēria*, from Gr. *Ibēres*, -AN]

iberis (ībiə´ris) *n.* (*pl.* **iberises**) a plant of the genus *Iberis*, including the candytufts. [as IBERIAN]

Ibero- (ībiə´rō) *comb. form* Iberian.

ibex (ī´beks) *n.* (*pl. in general* **ibex,** *in particular* **ibexes**) a wild goat of any of several species inhabiting the mountain regions of Europe, N Africa and Asia, of which the best known is *Capra ibex.* [L]

IBF *abbr.* International Boxing Federation.

ibid. *abbr.* ibidem.

ibidem (ib´idem) *adv.* in the same place (when referring to a book, page etc. already cited). [L *ibi*, there, *-dem*, suf. as in *īdem*, the same]

I. Biol. *abbr.* Institute of Biology.

ibis (ī´bis) *n.* (*pl. in general* **ibis,** *in particular* **ibises**) any of the heron-like wading birds belonging to the family Threskiornithidae, esp. *Threskiornis aethiopica*, the sacred ibis, which was venerated by the ancient Egyptians. [L and Gr., prob. of Egyptian orig.]

-ibly (ibli) *suf.* forming adverbs from adjectives in *-ible*, as *forcibly.*

IBM *abbr.* International Business Machines.

Ibo (ē´bō), **Igbo** *n.* (*pl.* **Ibo, Ibos, Igbo, Igbos**) **1** (*as pl.*) a black African people living in SE Nigeria. **2** a member of this people. **3** their language. ~*a.* of or relating to the Ibo or their language.

IBRD *abbr.* International Bank for Reconstruction and Development (the World Bank).

ibuprofen (ībūprō´fən) *n.* a drug used esp. for relieving arthritic pain and reducing inflammation. [formed from its full name, *isobutylphenylpropionic acid*]

IC *abbr.* **1** integrated circuit. **2** internal combustion.

i/c *abbr.* in charge; in command.

-ic (ik), **†-ick, †-ique** (ēk) *suf.* **1** forming adjectives, of or relating to, like, as in *alcoholic, algebraic, domestic, Miltonic, plutonic.* **2** (*Chem.*) denoting a higher state of oxidation or valence than the suffix *-ous.* **3** forming names of sciences, arts etc., as in *arithmetic, logic, music*, some of which have alternative forms ending in -ICS, as *aesthetic, metaphysic* etc. **-ical** (ikəl) *suf.* forming adjectives, as *algebraical, comical, historical, political.* **-ically** *suf.* forming adverbs, as *historically, politically.* [F *-ique*, L *-icus*, usu. from Gr. *-ikos*]

ICA *abbr.* Institute of Chartered Accountants.

ICAO *abbr.* International Civil Aviation Organization.

ICBM *abbr.* intercontinental ballistic missile.

ICE *abbr.* **1** Institution of Civil Engineers. **2** internal-combustion engine.

ice (īs) *n.* **1** frozen water. **2** an ice cream. **3** a confection of sugar etc. used for coating cakes etc. **4** (*sl.*) diamonds. **5** (*sl.*) a very addictive synthetic form of crystallized metamphetamine. ~*v.t.* (*pres.p.* **icing,** *past, p.p.* **iced**) **1** to cool with ice (*iced lemonade*). **2** to freeze (up, over). **3** to coat (a cake) with icing. **4** (*N Am., sl.*) to kill. **5** (*N Am., sl.*) to achieve (victory) conclusively. ~*v.i.* **1** to freeze. **2** to become covered with ice. **dry ice** DRY. **on ice 1** in abeyance. **2** performed by ice-skaters. **to cut no ice** (*coll.*) to fail to make an impression, to be unimportant. **ice age** *n.* a glacial period. **ice axe,** (*N Am.*) **ice ax** *n.* an axe shaped like a pickaxe, used by mountain climbers for cutting steps on glaciers etc. **ice-bag** *n.* a bag filled with ice used to reduce swelling or ease pain. **iceblink** *n.* a luminous reflection over the horizon from snowfields or ice fields. **iceblock** *n.* (*Austral., New Zeal.*) ICE LOLLY (under ICE). **ice blue** *n.* a pale blue colour. ~*a.* of this colour. **iceboat** *n.* **1** (*also* **ice yacht**) a boat with runners for travelling on ice. **2** a heavily-built boat for breaking a passage through ice. **icebound** *a.* **1** completely surrounded with ice. **2** unable to get out because of ice. **icebox** *n.* **1** the freezing compartment of a refrigerator. **2** a portable insulated box containing ice. **3** (*chiefly N Am.*) a refrigerator. **ice-breaker** *n.* **1** a ship with a reinforced hull for forcing a channel through ice. **2** (*coll.*) something that encourages a relaxed atmosphere among a group of people meeting for the first time. **ice bucket, ice pail** *n.* a bucket containing ice, for keeping wine etc. cool. **ice cap** *n.* a mass of ice and snow permanently covering an area. **ice-cold** *a.* very cold, like ice. **ice cream** *n.* a creamy confection flavoured and frozen. **ice cube** *n.* a small block of ice for cooling drinks. **ice dancing** *n.* ice-skating based on ballroom dancing and performed in pairs. **ice diving** *n.* scuba diving beneath the surface of a frozen lake. **icefall** *n.* a shattered part of a glacier where it descends a steep slope. **ice field** *n.* a large expanse of ice, esp. such as exist in the polar regions. **ice fish** *n.* **1** CAPELIN. **2** a semi-transparent fish of the family *Chaenichthyidae*, found in the Antarctic seas. **ice floe** *n.* a sheet of floating ice. **ice foot** *n.* a hill or wall of ice along the shore in polar regions. **ice hockey** *n.* a type of hockey played on ice by teams of skaters. **ice house** *n.* a building for the storage of ice. **ice lolly, iced lolly** *n.* a flavoured piece of ice or ice cream on a stick. **iceman** *n.* (*pl.* **icemen**) **1** (*chiefly N Am.*) a man who delivers or sells ice. **2** a man who is skilled in traversing or navigating through ice. **ice milk** *n.* (*N Am.*) a frozen food similar to ice cream but with less butterfat. **ice pack** *n.* **1** floating ice packed together. **2** a bag etc. containing ice applied to a part of the body to reduce swelling or ease pain. **ice pail** ICE BUCKET (under ICE). **ice pick** *n.* a pointed tool for splitting ice. **ice plant** *n.* a creeping plant, *Mesembryanthemum crystallinum*, whose leaves have a glistening lustre somewhat like ice. **ice rink** *n.* a rink for ice-skating. **ice sheet** *n.* a thick layer of ice covering a very large area of land, as in the last ice age. **ice shelf** *n.* a floating mass of ice permanently attached to the land. **ice show** *n.* a performance on ice by skaters. **ice-skate** *n.* a boot with a blade attached for skating on ice. ~*v.i.* to skate on ice. **ice-skater** *n.* **ice-skating** *n.* **ice spar** *n.* a vitreous orthoclase. **ice station** *n.* a research centre in polar regions, where meteorological conditions are monitored. **ice storm** *n.* a storm in which rain freezes and leaves deposits of ice. **ice water** *n.* **1** water from melted ice. **2** (*also* **iced water**) water cooled by ice. **ice yacht** ICEBOAT (under ICE). **icing** *n.* **1** a coating of concreted sugar. **2** the formation of ice over a surface. **3** in ice hockey, a shot from one's own team's end of the rink but not at goal, incurring a penalty. **icing on the cake** *n.* an additional extra that is not necessary but is very pleasant or attractive. **icing sugar** *n.* powdered sugar used for icing cakes etc. **icy** *a.* (*comp.* **icier,** *superl.* **iciest**) **1** of, relating to or consisting of ice. **2** like ice, frozen. **3** (*fig.*) (of a tone, look) cold and unfriendly. **icily** *adv.* **iciness** *n.* [OE īs (cp. Dut. *ijs*, Icel. *īss*, G *Eis*)]

-ice (is) *suf.* forming nouns, as *justice, malice, novice, service.* [OF *-ice*, L *itia, -itius, -itium*]

iceberg (īs´bœg) *n.* **1** a large mass of ice floating in the sea, usu. formed by detachment from a glacier. **2** a cold and unresponsive person. **iceberg lettuce** *n.* a type of lettuce with crisp tightly-packed leaves. [prob. from Dut. *ijsberg* (*ijs*, ICE, *berg*, hill)]

Icelander (īs´ləndə) *n.* a native or inhabitant of Iceland, an island in the N Atlantic between Scandinavia and Greenland. **Icelandic** (-lan´-) *a.* of or relating to Iceland. ~*n.* the language of Iceland. **Iceland lichen, Iceland moss** *n.* an edible moss or lichen, *Cetraria islandica*, growing in the northern and mountainous parts of Europe, used as a medicine. **Iceland poppy** *n.* a yellow Arctic poppy. **Iceland spar** *n.* a transparent variety of calcite. [Icel. *Island* (*iss*, ICE, LAND)]

I.Chem.E. *abbr.* Institute of Chemical Engineers.

I Ching (ē ching´) *n.* an ancient Chinese method of divination employing a set of symbols, 8 trigrams and 64 hexagrams, together with the text known as the *I Ching* which serves to interpret them. [Chin., book of changes]

ichneumon (iknū´mən) *n.* **1** a small carnivorous animal, *Herpestes ichneumon*, related to the mongoose, found in Egypt, where it was formerly held sacred on account of its devouring crocodiles' eggs. **2** (*also* **ichneumon fly**) a hymenopterous insect of the family Ichneumonidae, which lays its eggs in or upon the larvae of other insects, upon which its larvae will feed. [L, from Gr. *ichneumōn*, from *ichneuein*, to track, from *ichnos*, a track]

ichnite ICHNOLITE.

ichnography (iknog´rəfi) *n.* (*pl.* **ichnographies**) **1** the art of drawing ground plans etc. **2** a ground plan. **ichnographic** (-graf´-), **ichnographical** *a.* **ichnographically** *adv.* [Gr. *ichnos*, a track]

ichnolite (ik´nəlīt), **ichnite** (ik´nīt) *n.* a stone with the impression of a footprint. [as ICHNOGRAPHY]

ichnology (iknol´əji), **ichnolithology** (-lithol´-) *n.* the department of palaeontology that treats of and classifies fossil footprints. **ichnological, ichnolithological** *a.* [see ICHNOGRAPHY]

ichor (ī´kaw) *n.* **1** in Greek mythology, the ethereal fluid which flowed in place of blood in the veins of the gods. **2** a thin watery liquid such as serum. **3** †a watery acrid discharge from a wound etc. **ichorous** *a.* [Gr. *ichōr*]

ichthy- ICHTHYO-.

ichthyic (ik´thiik) *a.* **1** of or relating to fish. **2** having the characteristics of a fish.

ichthyo- (ik´thiō), **ichthy-** *comb. form* **1** of or relating to fish. **2** having the characteristics of a fish. [Gr. *ichthus*, a fish]

ichthyoid (ik´thioid) *a.* resembling fish. ~*n.* a vertebrate of fishlike form.

ichthyolatry (ikthiol´ətri) *n.* the worship of fishes, or of a fish god such as Dagon. **ichthyolatrous** *a.*

ichthyolite (ik´thiəlīt) *n.* a fossil fish. **ichthyolitic** (-lit´-) *a.*

ichthyology (ikthiol´əji) *n.* the study of fishes. **ichthyologic** (-loj´-), **ichthyological** *a.* **ichthyologist** *n.*

ichthyophagy (ikthiof´əji) *n.* the practice of eating fish; the having of a fish diet. **ichthyophagous** (-gəs) *a.* [through F *ichtyophagie* or directly from Gr. *ichthuophagia* (ICHTHYO-, *-phagia*, from *phagein*, to eat)]

ichthyornis (ikthiaw´nis) *n.* (*pl.* **ichthyornises**) an extinct Cretaceous seabird of the genus *Ichthyornis*, having biconcave vertebrae and socketed teeth. [Gr. *ornis*, a bird]

ichthyosaurus (ikthiəsaw´rəs), **ichthyosaur** (ik´-) *n.* (*pl.* **ichthyosauruses, ichthyosauri** (-rī), **ichthyosaurs**) any extinct marine reptile of the order Ichthyosauria, shaped like a fish, with flippers and a long head. [Gr. *sauros*, lizard]

ichthyosis (ikthiō´sis) *n.* a hereditary skin disease, marked by thick, hard, overlapping grey scales. **ichthyotic** (-ot´-) *a.*

ichthys (ik´this) *n.* a symbol in the form of a fish, connected with Christ because the Greek letters ιχθυσ gave the initials of the Greek words meaning 'Jesus Christ, Son of God, Saviour'. [Gr. *ichthus*, a fish]

ICI *abbr.* Imperial Chemical Industries.

-ician (ish´ən) *suf.* indicating a specialist in a subject, as in *beautician.*

icicle (ī´sikəl) *n.* a hanging conical point of ice, formed when dripping water freezes. [OE *īses giecel* (*īses*, gen. of *īs*, ICE, *giecel*, cogn. with Icel. *jökull*, icicle, glacier, orig. dim. of *jaki*, a piece of ice)]

icily, icing etc. ICE.

-icist (isist) *suf.* forming nouns indicating a specialist in a subject from adjectives in *-ic* or nouns in *-ics*, as in *classicist.*

-icity (is´iti) *suf.* forming abstract nouns from adjectives in *-ic* etc., as in *publicity.*

†-ick -IC.

icky (ik´i), **ikky** *a.* (*coll.*) **1** cloying; over-sentimental. **2** unpleasant. [perh. alt. of *sticky*]

-icle (ikəl) *suf.* forming diminutive nouns, as in *particle, versicle.* [L *-iculus, -iculum, -icula*]

icon (ī´kon), **ikon** *n.* **1** (*also* **eikon**) in the Eastern Church, a sacred image, picture, mosaic, or monumental figure of a holy personage. **2** a symbol. **3** a hero figure, esp. one who represents a particular movement or belief (*a pop icon*). **4** a pictorial representation of a facility available to the user of a computer system. **5** a linguistic sign that shares something with or suggests what it signifies. **iconic** (-kon´-) *a.* **1** of, relating to or being an icon. **2** of, relating to or consisting of figures or pictures. **3** (of art) following a conventional pattern or type, such as busts, memorial effigies etc. **iconic memory** *n.* the continuation of a sense impression after the stimulus has disappeared. [late L *īcōn*, Gr. *eikon*, image, likeness]

icono- (ī´kənō, īkon´ō) *comb. form* of or relating to images or idols. [as ICON]

iconoclasm (īkon´əklazm) *n.* **1** active hostility towards or disregard of established opinions, practices etc. **2** the breaking of idols. **iconoclast** (-klast) *n.* **1** a person who attacks or despises established opinions, practices etc. **2** a breaker of images, esp. one of the religious zealots in the Eastern Empire in the 8th and 9th cents. who destroyed icons and religious images. **iconoclastic** (-klas´-) *a.* **iconoclastically** *adv.* [Gr. *klasma*, from *klaein*, to break]

iconography (īkənog´rəfi) *n.* (*pl.* **iconographies**) **1** the study of portraits, pictures, statues, symbolism etc. **2** the illustration of a subject by means of figures etc. **3** a treatise on pictures, statues, etc. **4** a book or other collection of figures, drawings etc. **5** pictorial matter relating to a subject. **iconographer** *n.* **iconographic** (-graf´-), **iconographical** *a.* **iconographically** *adv.* [Gr. *ikonographia*]

iconolatry (īkənol´ətri) *n.* the adoration of images. **iconolater** *n.*

iconology (īkənol´əji) *n.* **1** the study of images, pictures etc. **2** symbolism. **iconological** (-loj´-) *a.* **iconologist** *n.*

iconomatic (īkonəmat´ik) *a.* denoting a kind of writing in which pictures represent the sounds of the names of objects rather than the objects themselves, as in a stage of writing intermediate between picture-writing and phonetic writing. [Gr. *onoma*, name]

iconometer (īkənom´itə) *n.* **1** an instrument for measuring the size or distance of an object. **2** a direct-vision viewfinder. **iconometry** *n.*

iconophile (īkon´əfīl) *n.* a connoisseur of pictures, prints etc. **iconophilism** (-nof´-) *n.* **iconophilist** (-nof´-) *n.*

iconoscope (īkon´əskōp) *n.* a type of electron camera.

icosahedron (īkosəhē´drən) *n.* (*pl.* **icosahedra** (-drə), **icosahedrons**) a solid figure having 20 plane sides. **icosahedral** *a.* [Gr. *eikosaedron* (*eikosi*, twenty, *hedra*, seat, base)]

-ics (iks) *suf.* **1** indicating a science or art, as *linguistics.* **2** indicating specified activities, as *acrobatics.* **3** indicating matters etc. relating to, as *mechanics.* [-IC]

ictal ICTUS.

icterus (ik´tərəs) *n.* (*pl.* **icteruses**) **1** (*Med.*) jaundice. **2** a plant disease characterized by yellowness of the leaves. **3** any bird of the American genus *Icterus* belonging to the family Icteridae, and including the orioles. **icteric** (-ter´-) *a.* relating to or affected with jaundice. [L, from Gr. *ikteros*, jaundice]

ictus (ik´təs) *n.* (*pl.* **ictuses, ictus**) **1** the stress, or rhythmical accent on a syllable in a line of verse. **2** (*Med.*) a stroke; a fit. **ictal, ictic** *a.* [L, a stroke, from *icere*, to strike]

ICU *abbr.* intensive care unit.

icy ICE.

ID *abbr.* **1** Idaho. **2** identification (*an ID card*).

Id EID.

I'd (īd) *contr.* **1** I had. **2** I should; I would.

id (id) *n.* (*Psych.*) the instinctive impulses in the unconscious mind of the individual. [L *id*, it]

i.d. *abbr.* inner diameter.

id. *abbr.* idem.

-id (id) *suf.* **1** forming adjectives denoting the quality orig. expressed by a L verb, as in *acid, frigid, morbid, tepid.* **2** (*Bot.*) forming nouns denoting a member of a family in *-idaceae*, as in *amaryllid, orchid.* **3** (*Zool.*) forming nouns denoting a member of a family in *-idae* or class *-ida*, as in *arachnid.* **4** forming nouns denoting a member of a group, category, or class with a classical proper name, as in *cepheid* (a star), *Leonid* (a meteor). [F *-ide*, L *-idus, -idēs*, ult. from Gr. *-id-*, nom. *-is*, pl. *-idēs*]

IDA *abbr.* International Development Association.

IDD *abbr.* International Direct Dialling.

ide (īd) *n.* a northern European fish, *Leuciscus idus*, of the carp family. [Swed. *id*]

-ide (īd) *suf.* indicating chemical compounds of an element with another element or a radical, as *chloride, fluoride, oxide.* [-ID]

idea (īdē´ə) *n.* **1** a mental image, form, or representation of anything. **2** a conception, a plan (*I've just had an idea*). **3** a more or less vague belief, or fancy (*I had an idea you were divorced*). **4** an intention or design (*The idea is to raise public awareness*). **5** a view, a way of thinking or conceiving (something) (*She has her own ideas on how it should be done*). **6** an archetype or pattern as distinct from an instantiation or example of it. **7** (*Philos.*) **a** in Platonism, the archetype or perfect and eternal pattern of which actual things are imperfect copies. **b** the immediate object of cognition, present in consciousness as representing an actual thing. **c** a concept of pure reason transcending mere experience. **not one's idea of** not what one considers to be (*It's not my idea of fun*). **that's an idea** that is something worth considering. **the very idea!** that is ridiculous. **to get ideas 1** (*coll.*) to become overambitious. **2** (*coll.*) to develop the wrong expectations or impressions. **to have ideas** to be ambitious. **to have no idea 1** to be unaware of what is going on. **2** (*coll.*) to be innocent or stupid. **to put ideas into someone's head** to fill someone with overambitious and unrealistic thoughts, aspirations etc. **idealess** *a.* destitute of ideas. **ideate** *n.* (*Philos.*) the actual thing that correlates with an idea. ~*v.t.* to form an idea of, to imagine. **ideation** (-āˊshən) *n.* **ideational** *a.* **ideationally** *adv.* [late L, from Gr. (*idein*, to see)]

ideal (īdēˊəl) *a.* **1** reaching one's standard of perfection; perfect. **2** visionary, fanciful. **3** consisting of, existing in, or of or relating to ideas, mental. **4** (*Philos.*) of or relating to idealism or the Platonic ideas. ~*n.* **1** an imaginary standard of perfection. **2** an actual thing realizing this. **ideal gas** *n.* a hypothetical gas made up of molecules of negligible size and exerting no forces on each other, thereby obeying physical laws under all conditions. **idealism** *n.* **1** the practice of forming ideals. **2** the quest for an ideal. **3** the representation of things in conformity with an ideal standard of perfection. **4** (*Philos.*) the doctrine that in external perceptions the objects immediately known are ideas. **idealist** *n.* **idealistic** (-lisˊ-) *a.* **idealistically** *adv.* **ideality** (-alˊ-) *n.* (*pl.* **idealities**) **1** the quality of being ideal. **2** an ideal state or thing. **3** the capacity to form ideals of beauty etc. **idealize, idealise** *v.t.* **1** to make ideal. **2** to portray in conformity with an ideal. **3** to think of as ideal, to regard as perfect. ~*v.i.* to form ideals. **idealization** (-zāˊshən) *n.* the representing of an object in accordance with one's desires or ideals. **idealizer** *n.* **ideally** *adv.* **1** in an ideal state or manner. **2** intellectually, mentally. **idealness** *n.*

idée fixe (ēdā fēksˊ) *n.* (*pl.* **idées fixes** (ēdā fēksˊ)) a fixed idea, an obsession. [F]

idée reçue (ēdā rəsūˊ) *n.* (*pl.* **idées reçues** (ēdā rəsūˊ)) a generally accepted idea. [F]

idem (idˊem) *n.* the same (word, author, book etc.). ~*adv.* in the same author, book etc. [L]

identic (īdenˊtik) *a.* (of diplomatic communications etc.) identical. **identic note** *n.* a note or opinion expressed in precisely similar terms (addressed simultaneously by the representatives of several powers to another).

identical (īdenˊtikəl) *a.* **1** (of one thing viewed or found under different conditions) absolutely the same, not different. **2** (of different things) exactly alike. **3** (*Math.*) expressing identity. **identically** *adv.* **identicalness** *n.* **identical twins** *n.pl.* twins developed from the fertilization of a single ovum. [F *identique*, late L *identicus*, formed from *identitas*, IDENTITY]

identify (īdenˊtifī) *v.t.* (*3rd pers. sing. pres.* **identifies,** *pres.p.* **identifying,** *past, p.p.* **identified**) **1** to determine or prove the identity of. **2** to establish, to pinpoint (a problem). **3** to unite or associate closely (with a party, interests etc.). **4** to consider or represent as precisely the same (with). **5** to treat as identical (with). ~*v.i.* **1** to associate oneself (with). **2** to consider oneself to be at one (with). **identifiable** *a.* **identifiably** *adv.* **identification** (-fikāˊshən) *n.* **1** the act of identifying. **2** the state of being identified. **3** a proof of identity. **4** the assumption of the characteristics of another, esp. of an admired person. **identification parade** *n.* a number of persons assembled by the police, among whom a witness is invited to identify a suspect. **identifier** *n.* **1** a person who or thing that identifies. **2** (*Comput.*) a name or label used to identify a set of data. [F *identifier*, late L *identificāre*]

Identikit® (īdenˊtikit), **identikit** *n.* **1** a set of facial features on transparent slips, used to compose a likeness, esp. of a criminal suspect. **2** a portrait built up in this way. ~*a.* **1** of or relating to such portraits. **2** (*coll.*) conforming to an unimaginative pattern.

identity (īdenˊtiti) *n.* (*pl.* **identities**) **1** the condition of being a particular person or thing (*The police are unable to reveal his identity*). **2** one's individuality (*a loss of identity*). **3** the state of being identical; absolute sameness (*identity of opinion*). **4** identification. **5** (*Math.*) **a** absolute equality between two expressions. **b** an equation expressing such equality. **c** a transformation that does not change the object. **identity crisis** *n.* a state of psychological confusion resulting from a failure to reconcile discordant elements in one's personality. **identity element** *n.* a mathematical element belonging to a set and which leaves any other member of that set unchanged when combining with it. **identity parade** *n.* IDENTIFICATION PARADE (under IDENTIFY). [F *identité*, late L *identitātem*, nom. *-tas*, from L IDEM]

ideo- (idˊiō, īˊdiō) *comb. form* of, relating to or expressing ideas. [IDEA]

ideograph (idˊiəgrahf), **ideogram** (-gram) *n.* a symbol, figure etc., suggesting or conveying the idea of an object, without expressing its name. **ideographic** (-grafˊ-), **ideographical** *a.* **ideographically** *adv.* **ideography** (-ogˊ-) *n.* (*pl.* **ideographies**) a system of or a treatise on ideographic writing.

ideology (īdiolˊəji) *n.* (*pl.* **ideologies**) **1** the political or social philosophy of a nation, movement, group etc. **2** abstract or fanciful theorizing. **3** †the science of ideas. **ideological** (-lojˊ-) *a.* **ideologically** *adv.* **ideologist** *n.* **ideologize, ideologise** *v.t.* **ideologue** (īˊdiəlog) *n.* **1** a supporter of an ideology. **2** a theorist, a visionary.

ideomotor (idiōmōˊtə) *a.* denoting unconscious muscular movements due to the concentration of attention on an idea.

ides (īdz) *n.pl.* in the ancient Roman calendar, the 15th of March, May, July, October, and 13th of the other months. [F, from L *īdūs*]

idio- (idˊiō) *comb. form* individual, peculiar. [Gr. *idios*, peculiar to oneself]

idiocy IDIOT.

idiograph (idˊiəgrahf) *n.* a private mark or signature, esp. a trademark. **idiographic** (-grafˊ-) *a.* of or relating to an individual. [Gr. *ideographon*]

idiolect (idˊiəlekt) *n.* a form of speech or language peculiar to an individual. **idiolectal** (-lekˊ-), **ideolectic** *a.*

idiom (idˊiəm) *n.* **1** a phrase etc. whose meaning cannot be deduced simply from the meaning of each of its words. **2** a mode of expression peculiar to a particular language. **3** a peculiarity of expression or phraseology. **4** a dialect or language of a country. **5** the unique character of a language. **6** a mode of artistic expression characteristic of a particular person or school. **idiomatic** (-matˊ-), **idiomatical** *a.* **1** of or relating to an idiom; expressed in idioms. **2** peculiar to or characteristic of a particular language. **3** dialectal, vernacular. **idiomatically** *adv.*

idiomorphic (idiəmawˊfik) *a.* (of a mineral) having a distinctive form of its own, esp. having distinctive faces of crystallization.

idiopathy (idiopˊəthi) *n.* (*pl.* **idiopathies**) a primary disease, one not occasioned by another. **idiopathic** (-pathˊ-) *a.* **idiopathically** *adv.*

idiophone (idˊiōfōn) *n.* (*Mus.*) a percussion instrument, such as a cymbal, made out of a naturally resonant material.

idioplasm (idˊiəplazm) *n.* the portion of protoplasm derived from the parent organism and supposed to determine the character of the individual, distinct from that due to the development of the individual. **idioplasmatic** (-matˊ-) *a.*

idiosyncrasy (idiəsingˊkrəsi) *n.* (*pl.* **idiosyncrasies**) **1** a characteristic, habit or attitude peculiar to an individual. **2** anything that is highly eccentric. **3** a mode of expression that is peculiar to a particular author. **4** (*Med.*) **a** individual temperament or constitution. **b** an abnormal sensitivity to a particular food, drug etc. **idiosyncratic** (-kratˊ-) *a.* **idiosyncratically** *adv.* [Gr. *idiosunkrāsia*]

idiot (idˊiət) *n.* **1** a stupid, silly person. **2** a person of very low intelligence. ~*a.* idiotic. **idiocy** (-si) *n.* (*pl.* **idiocies**). **idiot board, idiot card** *n.* (*coll.*) an autocue. **idiot box** *n.* (*sl.*) a television set. **idiotic** (-ot´-), **idiotical** *a.* resembling or characteristic of an idiot; foolish, silly. **idiotically** *adv.* †**idiotism** *n.* 1 an idiom. 2 idiocy. **idiot tape** *n.* a computer tape containing an unbroken flow of text with no typesetting codes. [F, from L *idiōta*, Gr. *idiōtēs*, a private person, hence one who is ignorant or not an expert, from *idios*, see IDEO-]

idiot savant (ēdiō savõ´) *n.* (*pl.* **idiot savants** (ēdiō savõ´), **idiots savants**) a person who is considered to be mentally retarded but who has an outstanding ability in a specific area, such as mental arithmetic.

idle (ī´dəl) *a.* (*comp.* **idler,** *superl.* **idlest**) 1 averse to work, lazy. 2 doing nothing, inactive. 3 not occupied, free (*in an idle moment*). 4 (of a machine) not in use. 5 (of a threat) useless, vain, ineffectual. 6 (of a rumour) trifling, without foundation. ~*v.i.* 1 to spend time in idleness. 2 (of an engine) to run slowly without the transmission being engaged. ~*v.t.* 1 to pass (time) without doing anything very useful (*She idled the morning away*). 2 to cause (an engine) to idle. **idle money** *n.* money that is not being used to earn interest or dividends. **idleness** *n.* **idle pulley** *n.* a pulley able to rotate freely as a means of guiding or controlling the tension of a belt. **idler** *n.* 1 a person who spends their time in idleness. 2 IDLE WHEEL (under IDLE). 3 (*Naut.*) a person not required to keep night watch. **idle time** *n.* in commerce, a period of time when a machine could be operating but is not, e.g. the period between the completion of one job and the start of the next. **idle wheel** *n.* a cogged wheel between two others for transmitting motion. **idly** *adv.* [OE *idel*, empty, vain (cp. Dut. *ijdel*, G *eitel*, also Gr. *itharos*, pure)]

Usage note The spellings of the words *idle* (inactive) and *idol* (a false god) should not be confused.

Ido (ē´dō) *n.* an artificial international language based on Esperanto. [*Ido*, offspring, from Gr. *-idos*]

idocrase (ī´dəkrās, id´-) *n.* (*Mineral.*) vesuvianite. [F (Gr. *eidos*, form, *krāsis*, CRASIS)]

idol (ī´dəl) *n.* 1 an image, esp. one worshipped as a god. 2 (*Bible*) a false god. 3 a person or thing loved or honoured excessively. 4 (*Philos.*) a false conception, a misleading tendency, a fallacy. 5 †a phantom. **idolater** (īdol´ətə) *n.* 1 a person who worships idols. 2 an adorer, an extravagant admirer. **idolatress** (-tris) *n.* a female idolater. **idolatrize, idolatrise** *v.i.* to practise idolatry. ~*v.t.* 1 to adore. 2 to worship as an idol. **idolatrous** *a.* **idolatrously** *adv.* **idolatry** *n.* 1 the worship of idols. 2 excessive adoration of a person or thing. **idolism** *n.* 1 idolatry. 2 idolization. †**idolist** *n.* an idolater. **idolize, idolise** *v.t.* 1 to love or venerate to excess. 2 to make an idol of. **idolization** (-zā´shən) *n.* **idolizer** *n.* [OF *idole*, L *īdōlum*, Gr. *eidōlon*, from *eidos*, form]

Usage note See note under IDLE.

idolum (īdō´ləm) *n.* (*pl.* **idola** (-lə)) 1 an image. 2 (*Philos.*) a fallacy.

IDP *abbr.* (*Comput.*) integrated data processing.

idyll (id´əl), **idyl** *n.* 1 a brief, artistic, and picturesque narrative or description of rustic life, either in verse or prose. 2 a work of art, esp. a musical piece, of a similar character. 3 a scene, episode, or situation suitable for the tone of such a composition. **idyllic** (idil´-) *a.* 1 perfect, esp. because peaceful and beautiful. 2 of, relating to or suitable for an idyll. **idyllically** *adv.* **idyllist** *n.* **idyllize, idyllise** *v.t.* [L *īdyllium*, Gr. *eidullion*, dim. of *eidos*, form]

i.e. *abbr.* id est, that is to say.

Usage note See note under E.G.

-ie -Y[3].

IEE *abbr.* Institution of Electrical Engineers.

-ier (iə) *suf.* denoting occupation, profession etc., as in *bombardier, brigadier, chevalier, financier.* [F *-ier* or -EER]

IF *abbr.* intermediate frequency.

if (if) *conj.* 1 providing that; in the case that (*We'll have a picnic outside if the weather stays fine*; *If he rings, let me know*; *If I'd left any later I would have missed my train*). 2 on the supposition that (*If I were you I'd tell her the truth*). 3 although (*She was polite, if a little distant*). 4 whenever (*I always pop in to see them if I'm in the area*). 5 whether (*He asked me if I played tennis*). 6 a used to express a wish or a surprise (*If you could see him now!*; *If it isn't Bob!*). b used to introduce a request (*If you wouldn't mind signing this form*). 7 used to modify a statement (*many, if not most*; *rarely if ever*). ~*n.* 1 (*coll.*) an uncertain or doubtful factor (*It's a big if*). 2 a condition. **as if** as it would be if. **if anything** possibly even (*If anything, it's too short*). **if only** 1 if for no other reason than (*It's worth going, if only for the music*). 2 used to express a desire or wish (*If only I'd been there*). **ifs and buts** objections. **if so** if that is the case. [OE *gif* (cp. Dut. *of*, Icel. *ef*, *if*, G *ob*)]

IFC *abbr.* International Finance Corporation.

-iferous -FEROUS.

iff *conj.* (*Logic, Math.*) used to express *if and only if.*

iffy (if´i) *a.* (*comp.* **iffier,** *superl.* **iffiest**) (*coll.*) 1 doubtful, uncertain. 2 risky.

-ific -FIC.

-ification -FICATION.

-iform -FORM.

Igbo IBO.

igloo (ig´loo) *n.* an Eskimo (Inuit) hut, often built of snow. [Eskimo (Inuit)]

igneous (ig´niəs) *a.* 1 of or like fire. 2 (*Geol.*) (of rocks) produced by volcanic action. [L *igneus*, from *ignis*, fire]

ignescent (ignes´ənt) *a.* emitting sparks when struck, as with steel. ~*n.* a mineral emitting sparks when struck. [L *ignescens*, *-ntem*, pres.p. of *ignescere*, to catch fire]

ignimbrite (ig´nimbrīt) *n.* a volcanic rock formed by the consolidation of the lava fragments and dust of a nuée ardente.

ignis fatuus (ignis fat´ūəs) *n.* (*pl.* **ignes fatui** (ignēz fat´ūī)) 1 an apparent flame, probably due to the spontaneous combustion of inflammable gas, floating above the ground in marshes etc. 2 a delusive object or aim. [L, foolish fire (see FATUOUS)]

ignite (ignīt´) *v.t.* 1 to set on fire. 2 (*Chem.*) to heat to the temperature at which combustion occurs. 3 to arouse or excite (interest, controversy). ~*v.i.* to catch fire. **ignitable, ignitible** *a.* **ignitability** (-bil´-), **ignitibility** *n.* **igniter** *n.* 1 a person who, or a thing that, ignites, esp. a contrivance for igniting powder in an explosive, firing the gases in an internal-combustion engine etc. 2 an electrode used in an ignitron to cause an electric arc. **ignition** (-nish´-) *n.* 1 the act of igniting; the state of being ignited. 2 a mechanism for igniting the explosive mixture in an internal-combustion engine. **ignition key** *n.* a key that operates the ignition system in a motor vehicle. **ignitron** *n.* a type of rectifier in which an electrode, the igniter, is partially immersed in mercury and draws an arc to start the ionization. [L *ignītus*, p.p. of *ignīre*, from *ignis*, fire]

ignoble (ignō´bəl) *a.* (*comp.* **ignobler,** *superl.* **ignoblest**) 1 mean, base, dishonourable. 2 of humble or low birth. **ignobility** (-bil´-), **ignobleness** *n.* **ignobly** *adv.* [F, from *ignōbilis* (IN-[2], *gnōbilis*, *nōbilis*, NOBLE)]

ignominy (ig´nəmini) *n.* (*pl.* **ignominies**) 1 public disgrace or shame; dishonour. 2 an act deserving disgrace. 3 †dishonourable conduct. **ignominious** (-min´-) *a.* 1 disgraceful. 2 humiliating. **ignominiously** *adv.* **ignominiousness** *n.* [F *ignominie*, L *ignōminia* (IN-[2], *gnōmen*, *nōmen*, name, from *gnōscere*, to know)]

ignoramus (ignərā´məs) *n.* (*pl.* **ignoramuses**) an ignorant person. [L, we do not know, in legal use, we take no notice of it (formerly the endorsement on a bill by the grand jury when there was not enough evidence to support the charge)]

ignorance (ig´nərəns) *n.* the state of being ignorant, lack of knowledge (of). **ignorant** *a.* **1** lacking knowledge. **2** unaware (of a fact etc.). **3** (*coll.*) showing a lack of politeness and good manners. **ignorantly** *adv.* [F, from L *ignōrantia*, from *ignōrans -ntem*, ignorant]

Usage note The constructions *ignorant of* and *ignorant in* are preferred to *ignorant about.*

ignore (ignaw´) *v.t.* **1** to pass over without notice, to disregard. **2** to deliberately pay no attention to. **to ignore a bill** BILL[1]. **ignorable** *a.* **ignorer** *n.* [F *ignorer*, L *ignōrāre* (IN-[2], *gnō-*, stem of *gnoscere*, to know)]

iguana (igwah´nə) *n.* any large lizard of the American genus *Iguana*, esp. *I. tuberculata*, of S and Central America and the W Indies. [Sp., from Carib *iwana*]

iguanodon (igwah´nədon) *n.* a large, bipedal, herbivorous dinosaur of the Cretaceous period. [IGUANA, Gr. *odous odontos*, tooth]

i.h.p. *abbr.* indicated horsepower.

IHS *abbr.* Jesus (Greek *Iesous*), often used as a Christian symbol.

ikebana (ikibah´nə) *n.* the Japanese art of arranging flowers. [Jap.]

ikky ICKY.

ikon ICON.

IL *abbr.* **1** Illinois. **2** Israel (IVR).

il- (il) *pref.* variant form of IN-[1] and IN-[2] before *l.*

-il (əl, il), **-ile** (īl) *suf.* that may be, capable of being, of or relating to etc., as in *civil, fossil, docile, fragile, Gentile, puerile, senile.* [OF *-il*, F *-ile*, L *-īlis* (*-ilis* in OF became *-le*, as in *humble*, L *humilis*, HUMBLE[1], *frail*, *fragilis*, FRAIL[1])]

ilang-ilang YLANG-YLANG.

-ile -IL.

☒ **ilegal** common misspelling of ILLEGAL.

ileum (il´iəm) *n.* (*pl.* **ilea** (-iə)) the portion of the small intestine communicating with the larger intestine. **ileac** *a.* **ileitis** *n.* inflammation of the ileum. **ileostomy** *n.* (*pl.* **ileostomies**) a surgical operation in which a permanent opening is made through the abdominal wall into the ileum. [late L, from L *īlia*, pl., the flanks, the groin (modified in form by confusion with *īleus*, Gr. *eileos*, see ILIAC (under ILIUM))]

ileus (il´iəs) *n.* a painful obstruction of the intestine. [L, from Gr. *eileos*, pain in the intestines]

ilex (ī´leks) *n.* (*pl.* **ilexes**) **1** the holm-oak. **2** any tree or shrub of the genus *Ilex* with coriaceous leaves, esp. the holly. [L]

☒ **iliterate** common misspelling of ILLITERATE.

ilium (il´iəm) *n.* (*pl.* **ilia** (-iə)) the upper part of the hip bone. **iliac** (il´iak) *a.* of or relating to the ilium or hip bone. **iliac region** *n.* the part of the abdomen between the ribs and the hips. [L, a part of the abdomen (cp. ILEUM)]

ilk (ilk) *n.* **1** (*coll.*) a class, sort or kind (*people of that ilk*). **2** (*Sc.*) the same name. **of that ilk** (*Sc.*) of the same name (used when the surname of a person is the same as the name of their estate). [OE *ilca* (pron. stem *i-*, *-lic*, LIKE[1])]

ilka (il´kə) *a.* (*Sc.*) each, every. [*aelc*, EACH, A[1]]

Ill. *abbr.* Illinois.

I'll (īl) *contr.* I shall; I will.

ill (il) *a.* (*comp.* **worse**, *superl.* **worst**) **1** unwell, sick, diseased (*She's ill in hospital*). **2** malevolent, hostile, adverse (*ill feelings*). **3** noxious, mischievous, harmful (*the ill effects of alcohol*). **4** unfavourable, unlucky (*ill fortune*). **5** morally bad, evil (*ill deeds*). **6** faulty, incorrect, improper (*ill manners*). **7** unskilful (*ill discipline*). ~*adv.* (*comp.* **worse**, *superl.* **worst**) **1** not well, badly (*conduct ill befitting a man of his standing*). **2** not rightly (*Their success was ill-deserved*). **3** not easily (*We can ill afford another scandal*). **4** imperfectly (*ill-supplied*). **5** unfavourably (*He was warned that it would go ill with him if he refused*). ~*n.* **1** evil. **2** injury, harm (*I wish you no ill*). **3** (*pl.*) troubles, problems (*social ills*). **ill at ease** uncomfortable, anxious. **to be taken ill** to fall sick. **to speak ill** to speak unfavourably (of or about). **to take ill** to take offence at. **to take in ill part** to take offence at. **ill-advised** *a.* **1** imprudent. **2** (of a plan) not well thought out. **ill-advisedly** *adv.* **ill-affected** *a.* not well disposed (towards). **ill-assorted** *a.* poorly matched; not compatible. **ill-behaved** *a.* lacking good manners. **ill-bred** *a.* brought up badly; rude and lacking good manners. **ill breeding** *n.* **ill-conceived** *a.* not well planned. **ill-considered** *a.* done without careful thought. **ill-defined** *a.* poorly defined; lacking a clear outline. **ill-disposed** *a.* **1** unfavourably inclined (towards). **2** wickedly or maliciously inclined. **ill-equipped** *a.* inadequately qualified, equipped etc. (to do something). **ill fame** *n.* disrepute. **house of ill fame** HOUSE[1]. **ill-fated** *a.* destined to end badly or in failure. **ill-favoured,** (*N Am.*) **ill-favored** *a.* **1** ugly, unattractive. **2** objectionable. **ill-favouredly** *adv.* **ill-favouredness** *n.* **ill feeling** *n.* resentment, enmity. **ill-fitting** *a.* **1** not fitting well. **2** not appropriate. **ill-founded** *a.* lacking any foundation in fact, not substantiated. **ill-gotten** *a.* obtained in an improper way. **ill health** *n.* poor health. **ill humour** *n.* bad temper. **ill-humoured** *a.* **ill-informed** *a.* not very knowledgeable (about). **ill-judged** *a.* not well-judged; injudicious, unwise. **ill-mannered** *a.* rude, boorish. **ill-matched** *a.* not well-matched or suited. **ill nature** *n.* lack of kindness or good feeling; churlishness. **ill-natured** *a.* **ill-naturedly** *adv.* **ill-naturedness** *n.* **ill-omened** *a.* unlucky, inauspicious. **ill-prepared** *a.* not well or adequately prepared. **ill-starred** *a.* unlucky; ill-fated. **ill-suited** *a.* not suited (to something). **ill-tempered** *a.* having a bad temper, sour, peevish. **ill temper** *n.* **ill-timed** *a.* done or said at an unsuitable time. **ill-treat** *v.t.* to treat badly or cruelly. **ill treatment** *n.* **ill turn** *n.* an unkind act (*to do someone an ill turn*). **ill will** *n.* malevolence; enmity. **ill wind** *n.* an unfavourable situation that must bring advantage (from the proverb *It's an ill wind that blows nobody any good*). [ME, from Icel. *illr*]

illation (ilā´shən) *n.* **1** deduction. **2** something that is deduced, an inference. **illative** (il´ətiv, ilā´tiv) *a.* **1** denoting, expressing, or of the nature of an inference. **2** (in some Finno-Ugrian languages) denoting a noun case expressing motion or direction. ~*n.* **1** a word or word element that denotes inference, e.g. the word *therefore.* **2** the illative case. **illatively** *adv.* [F, from late L *illatiōnem*, nom. *-tio* (IL-, *lāt-*, p.p. stem of *ferre*, to bear)]

Illawarra shorthorn (iləwor´ə) *n.* a noted breed of Australian dairy cattle. [*Illawarra*, New South Wales]

illegal (ilē´gəl) *a.* **1** not according to law. **2** contrary to law, unlawful. **illegality** (-gal´-) *n.* (*pl.* **illegalities**). **illegalize, illegalise** *v.t.* to make illegal. **illegally** *adv.* [med. L *illegālis*]

illegible (ilej´ibəl) *a.* that cannot be read or deciphered. **illegibility** (-bil´-), **illegibleness** *n.* **illegibly** *adv.*

illegitimate[1] (iləjit´imət) *a.* **1** born of parents not married to each other. **2** contrary to law or recognized usage. **3** irregular, improper. **4** illogical, contrary to logical rules, unsound. ~*n.* **1** an illegitimate child, a bastard. **2** a person of illegitimate status. **illegitimacy** (-əsi) *n.* the state of being illegitimate. **illegitimately** *adv.*

illegitimate[2] (iləjit´imāt) *v.t.* to render or declare illegitimate.

illiberal (ilib´ərəl) *a.* **1** narrow-minded. **2** not characterized by wide views or by culture. **3** not generous; niggardly. **illiberality** (-ral´-) *n.* (*pl.* **illiberalities**). **illiberally** *adv.* [F *illibéral*]

illicit (ilis´it) *a.* **1** not allowed or permitted. **2** unlawful. **illicitly** *adv.* **illicitness** *n.* [F *illicite*, L *illicitus*]

Usage note See note under ELICIT.

illimitable (ilim´itəbəl) *a.* boundless, limitless. **illimitability** (-bil´-), **illimitableness** *n.* **illimitably** *adv.*

†**illinium** (ilin´iəm) *n.* PROMETHIUM (under PROMETHEAN). [*Illin*ois, -IUM, from its claimed discovery at the University of Illinois]

illiquid (ilik´wid) *a.* **1** (of assets) not easily convertible into cash. **2** (of a company etc.) lacking liquid assets. **illiquidity** (-kwid´-) *n.*

illiterate (ilit´ərət) *a.* **1** unable to read or write. **2** ignorant in a specific subject (*technologically illiterate*). **3** ignorant, uncultivated. ~*n.* an ignorant or uneducated person, esp. one unable to read. **illiteracy** (-əsi), **illiterateness** *n.* **illiterately** *adv.* [L *illīterātus*]

illness (il´nəs) *n.* **1** the state of being ill. **2** sickness, a disease or ailment.

illogical (iloj´ikəl) *a.* **1** contrary to reason. **2** ignorant or careless of the rules of logic. **illogicality** (-kal´-) *n.* (*pl.* **illogicalities**). **illogically** *adv.* **illogicalness** *n.*

illude (ilood´) *v.t.* to deceive, to cheat. [L *illūdere* (*lūdere*, to play)]

illume (iloom´) *v.t.* (*poet.*) **1** to illuminate, to lighten or brighten up. **2** (*fig.*) to enlighten. [shortened form of ILLUMINE]

illuminate[1] (iloo´mināt) *v.t.* **1** to light up. **2** to throw light upon (a subject, problem). **3** to decorate (buildings, streets etc.) with festive light. **4** to decorate (a manuscript etc.) with coloured pictures, letters etc. **5** to enlighten mentally or spiritually. **6** to make illustrious. ~*a.* **1** †lit up. **2** claiming enlightenment. **illuminant** *a.* illuminating. ~*n.* something which illuminates. **illuminating** *a.* **1** that lights up. **2** enlightening. **illuminatingly** *adv.* **illumination** (-ā´shən) *n.* **1** the act of lighting up or state of being lit up. **2** enlightenment. **3** a source of light. **4** (*often pl.*) a display of ornamental lights. **5** the decoration of manuscripts etc. with ornamental coloured letters and pictures. **6** clarification. **illuminative** (-ātiv, -nətiv) *a.* **illuminator** *n.* [L *illūminātus*, p.p. of *illūmināre* (*lūmināre*, from *lūmen -inis*, light)]

illuminate[2] (iloo´minət, -it) *n.* a person who claims to possess special enlightenment.

illuminati (iloominah´tē) *n.pl.* **1** a group of people claiming to possess knowledge or gifts. **2** (*Hist.*) (**Illuminati**) any of various sects and secret societies professing to have superior enlightenment. **illuminism** (-loo´-) *n.* **1** a belief in special enlightenment. **2** the principles or doctrines of the Illuminati. **illuminist** *n.* [L, pl. of *illūminātus*, or It., pl. of *illuminato*, as ILLUMINATE[1]]

illusion (iloo´zhən) *n.* **1** deception. **2** a mistaken belief or false perception. **3** a deceptive appearance or impression. **4** an unreal image presented to the vision. **5** (*Psych.*) a wrong interpretation of what is perceived through the senses. **to be under the illusion** to believe mistakenly (that). **illusional** *a.* **illusionism** *n.* **1** (*Philos.*) a theory that regards the external world as a mere illusion of the senses. **2** the artistic practice of giving an illusion of reality, e.g. through the use of perspective. **illusionist** *n.* **1** a conjurer. **2** a person who is given to illusions, a visionary. **3** a believer in illusionism. **illusionistic** *a.* **illusive** (-siv) *a.* illusory. **illusively** *adv.* **illusory** (-zəri) *a.* delusive, deceptive. **illusorily** *adv.* **illusoriness** *n.* [F, from L *illūsiōnem*, nom. *-sio*, from *illūdere*, to ILLUDE]

Usage note The nouns *illusion* and *allusion* should not be confused: an *illusion* is a deception, and an *allusion* an indirect reference. See also note under ELUDE.

illustrate (il´əstrāt) *v.t.* **1** to embellish (a book, etc.) with pictures. **2** to make clear or explain by means of examples, figures etc. **illustration** (-trā´shən) *n.* **1** an engraving or drawing illustrating a book or article in a periodical. **2** something which illustrates, an example, a typical instance. **3** the act of illustrating; the state of being illustrated. **illustrational** *a.* illustrative. **illustrative** *a.* serving as an illustration or example. **illustratively** *adv.* **illustrator** *n.* [L *illustrātus*, p.p. of *illustrāre* (*lustrāre*)]

illustrious (ilŭs´triəs) *a.* **1** distinguished, famous. **2** glorious. **3** †brilliant, luminous. **illustriously** *adv.* **illustriousness** *n.* [L *illustris* (*-lustris*, from stem of *lux*, light, *lūcidus*, bright)]

Illyrian (ilir´iən) *a.* **1** of or relating to Illyria, an ancient region on the east coast of the Adriatic, and roughly corresponding to parts of present-day Albania, Slovenia and Croatia. **2** of the language of Illyria. ~*n.* **1** a native or inhabitant of Illyria. **2** the language of Illyria from which modern Albanian is thought to have developed.

illywhacker (il´iwakə) *n.* (*Austral.*, *sl.*) a confidence trickster. [etym. unknown]

ilmenite (il´mənīt) *n.* a black mineral that is found in igneous rocks and is the principal ore of titanium. [*Ilmen* Mountains in the Urals]

ILO *abbr.* International Labour Organization.

ILR *abbr.* Independent Local Radio.

☒ **iluminate** common misspelling of ILLUMINATE.

-ily (ili) *suf.* forming adverbs from adjectives ending in *-y*, as in *happily*, *noisily*. [-LY[1], -Y[1]]

I'm (īm) *contr.* I am.

im-[1] (im) *pref.* variant form of IN-[1] before *b*, *m*, *p*, as in *imbibe*, *imbrue*.

im-[2] (im) *pref.* variant form of IN-[2] before *b*, *m*, *p*, as in *immaculate*, *impossible*.

image (im´ij) *n.* **1** a visible representation or likeness of a person or thing, esp. in sculpture. **2** the impression given to others of a person's character etc. (*Involvement in charities is good for a company's image*). **3** a copy, a counterpart. **4** the living embodiment of a particular quality (*the image of fairness and decency*). **5 a** an idea, a conception. **b** a mental picture. **6** an expanded metaphor or simile. **7** the figure of an object formed (through the medium of a mirror, lens etc.) by rays of light. **8** a mental representation of a sense impression. **9** (*Math.*) a set mapped from another set. ~*v.t.* **1** to make an image of; to portray. **2** to mirror. **3** to represent mentally; to conceive in the mind. **4** to typify, to symbolize. **imageable** *a.* **image intensifier** *n.* any of various electronic devices for intensifying an optical image. **imageless** *a.* **image-maker** *n.* a public relations expert employed to improve the impression that someone, e.g. a politician, makes on the general public. **image orthicon** *n.* a type of television camera tube. **image processing** *n.* (*Comput.*) the filtering, storing and retrieving of images. **image processor** *n.* **imagery** (-əri) *n.* **1** figurative description, esp. in poetry. **2** (*collect.*) images; statues. **3** mental pictures. **imagism** *n.* an early 20th-cent. poetic movement that aimed at clear and simple language and precise images. **imagist** *n.* **imagistic** (-jis´-) *a.* [F, from L *imāginem*, nom. *imāgo*, prob. from *im-*, root of IMITATE]

imaginable IMAGINE.

imaginal[1] IMAGINE.

imaginal[2] IMAGO.

imagine (imaj´in) *v.t.* **1** to form an image of in the mind, to conceive, to form an idea of. **2** to suppose, to think (*I imagine she'll come by car*). **3** to believe without any justification (*You're imagining things*). **4** to conjecture, to guess (*I can't imagine what he was thinking of*). **5** †to plot, to devise. ~*v.i.* to form images or ideas in the mind (*Can you imagine!*). **imaginable** *a.* that can be imagined (*the worst time imaginable*). **imaginably** *adv.* **imaginal**[1] *a.* of or relating to images. **imaginary** *a.* **1** existing only in imagination or fancy. **2** (of a mathematical quantity or value) assumed as real for the purposes of an equation etc. **imaginarily** *adv.* **imaginariness** *n.* **imaginary number** *n.* a number involving the square root of a negative number. **imagination** (-ā´shən) *n.* **1** the mental faculty that forms ideal images or combinations of images from the impressions left by sensuous experience. **2** the constructive or creative faculty of the mind. **3** the act or process of imagining. **4** fancy, fantasy. **imaginative** *a.* **1** endowed with imagination. **2** produced or characterized by imagination. **imaginatively** *adv.* **imaginativeness** *n.* **imaginer** *n.* **imaginings** *n.pl.* things that exist only in the mind. [F *imaginer*, L *imāginārī*]

imagism, imagist etc. IMAGE.

imago (imā´gō) *n.* (*pl.* **imagoes, imagines** (-jinēz)) **1** the adult, fully-developed insect after its metamorphoses. **2** (*Psych.*) an idealized image of a parent or other person that exercises a persistent influence in the unconscious. **imaginal**[2] (-maj´-) *a.* of or relating to a fully-developed insect. [L, IMAGE]

imam (imahm´) *n.* **1** a person who leads congregational prayer in a mosque. **2** the title of various Muslim rulers and founders. **imamate** (-āt), **imamship** *n.* [Arab. *imām*, from *amma*, to precede]

IMAX® (ī´maks) *n.* a system of wide-screen motion-picture presentation, that produces an image much larger than that from standard 35mm film. [IMAGE, MAXIMUM]

imbalance (imbal´əns) *n.* a lack of balance or proportion.

imbecile (im´bəsēl) *a.* **1** mentally weak, half-witted. **2** stupid, fatuous. ~*n.* **1** a person of abnormally low intelligence. **2** (*coll.*) a stupid or foolish person. **imbecilic** (-silik) *a.* **imbecility** (-sil´-) *n.* (*pl.* **imbecilities**). [F *imbécille* (now *imbécile*), L *imbecillus*, weak]

imbed EMBED.

imbibe (imbīb´) *v.t.* (*formal*) **1** to drink. **2** to absorb (liquid etc.). **3** to assimilate (ideas etc.). **4** to draw in (air). ~*v.i.* (*facet.*) to drink. **imbiber** *n.* **imbibition** (-bibish´ən) *n.* [through F *imbiber* or directly from L *imbibere* (*bibere*, to drink, to BIB)]

imbricate[1] (im´brikāt) *v.t.* to lap (leaves, scales on fish etc.) one over the other like tiles. ~*v.i.* to be arranged in this fashion. **imbrication** (-ā´shən) *n.* [L *imbricātus*, p.p. of *imbricāre*, from *imbrex -bricis*, a tile, from *imber -bris*, shower]

imbricate[2] (im´brikət) *a.* arranged in an imbricated fashion.

imbroglio (imbrō´liō), **embroglio** *n.* (*pl.* **imbroglios, embroglios**) **1** a perplexing or confused state of affairs. **2** a complicated plot, e.g. of a play or novel. **3** a disorderly heap. [It. (IM-[1], *broglio*, BROIL[1])]

imbrue (imbroo´), **embrue** *v.t.* (*3rd pers. sing. pres.* **imbrues, embrues,** *pres.p.* **imbruing, embruing,** *past, p.p.* **imbrued, embrued**) **1** to steep, to soak or moisten (in or with blood). **2** to stain, to dye (in or with). **imbruement** *n.* [OF *embruer*, *-breuver*, *-beuvrer*, causal of *bevre* (F *boire*), L *bibere*, to drink]

imbue (imbū´) *v.t.* (*3rd pers. sing. pres.* **imbues,** *pres.p.* **imbuing,** *past, p.p.* **imbued**) **1** to inspire, to impregnate (with). **2** to saturate (with). **3** to dye (with). [L *imbuere* (*buere*, rel. to *bibere*, to drink)]

imburse (imbœs´) *v.t.* **1** to provide with money. **2** to stow in a purse or one's purse. [late L *imbursāre* (IM-[1], *bursa*, PURSE)]

I.Mech.E. *abbr.* Institution of Mechanical Engineers.

☒ **imediate** common misspelling of IMMEDIATE.

☒ **imense** common misspelling of IMMENSE.

IMF *abbr.* International Monetary Fund.

imide (im´īd) *n.* a compound derived from ammonia by the replacement of two atoms of hydrogen by a metal or organic radical. [altered from AMIDE]

☒ **imigrant** common misspelling of IMMIGRANT (under IMMIGRATE).

I.Min.E. *abbr.* Institution of Mining Engineers.

imine (im´ēn) *n.* a compound derived from ammonia by the replacement of two atoms of hydrogen by other groups. [altered from AMINE]

imit. *abbr.* **1** imitation. **2** imitative.

imitate (im´itāt) *v.t.* **1** to follow the example of; to copy. **2** to mimic, to ape. **3** to produce a likeness or copy of. **4** to be like; to resemble. **imitable** *a.* **imitability** (-bil´-) *n.* **imitation** (-ā´shən) *n.* **1** the act of imitating; an instance of this. **2** a copy or likeness. **3** (*often attrib.*) something that is not genuine (*imitation jewellery*). **4** (*Mus.*) the repetition of a phrase or subject by another part. **imitative** (-tətiv) *a.* **1** given to or aiming at imitation. **2** done in imitation (of). **3** counterfeit. **4** (of words) onomatopoeic. **imitative arts** *n.pl.* sculpture and painting. **imitatively** *adv.* **imitativeness** *n.* **imitator** *n.* [L *imitātus*, p.p. of *imitārī*, see IMAGE]

immaculate (imak´ūlət) *a.* **1** spotlessly clean or tidy. **2** pure; free from blemish. **3** (of a performance etc.) absolutely faultless. **4** (*Biol.*) not spotted. **immaculacy** (-si), **immaculateness** *n.* **Immaculate Conception** *n.* **1** in the Roman Catholic Church, the doctrine (made an article of faith in 1854) that the Virgin Mary was conceived and born free from original sin. **2** the feast of the Immaculate Conception, 8 December. **immaculately** *adv.* [L *immaculātus* (*macula*, spot)]

immanent (im´ənənt) *a.* **1** remaining within, inherent; indwelling. **2** (*Theol.*) present throughout the universe as an essential sustaining spirit. **immanence, immanency** *n.* **immanentism** *n.* **immanentist** *n.* **immanently** *adv.* [late L *immanens -ntem*, pres.p. of *immanēre* (*manēre*, to remain)]

Usage note The adjectives *immanent* and *imminent* should not be confused: *immanent* means indwelling, and *imminent* impending.

immaterial (imətiə´riəl) *a.* **1** irrelevant, unimportant. **2** not consisting of matter; incorporeal. **3** spiritual. **immaterialism** *n.* the doctrine that there is no material substance, and that all being may be reduced to mind and ideas in the mind. **immaterialist** *n.* **immateriality** (-al´-) *n.* the quality of being immaterial. **immaterialize, immaterialise** *v.t.* to make immaterial. **immaterially** *adv.* [MF *immatériel*, from med. L *immateriālis* (MATERIAL)]

immature (imətūə´) *a.* **1** not fully developed. **2** lacking the appropriate maturity of character etc. **3** not ripe. **immaturely** *adv.* **immatureness, immaturity** *n.* [L *immātūrus* (MATURE)]

immeasurable (imezh´ərəbəl) *a.* **1** that cannot be measured. **2** immense. **immeasurability** (-bil´-), **immeasurableness** *n.* **immeasurably** *adv.*

immediate (imē´diət) *a.* **1** done or occurring at once, instant (*an immediate response*). **2** situated in the closest relation; nearest (*her immediate family*). **3** nearest in time (*in the immediate future*). **4** acting or acted upon by direct agency, direct (*the immediate cause of the conflict*). **5** present; of most concern (*our immediate needs*). **6** (of knowledge, concepts) that is directly known; intuitive. **immediacy** (-si), **immediateness** *n.* **immediately** *adv.* **1** without delay, at once. **2** closely or directly. **3** just close by. ~*conj.* as soon as. [MF *immédiat*, med. L *immediātus* (MEDIATE[2])]

immedicable (imed´ikəbəl) *a.* that cannot be healed; incurable. [F, from L *immedicābilis*]

immemorial (imimaw´riəl) *a.* **1** beyond memory or record. **2** ancient. **immemorially** *adv.* [MF *immémorial*, med. L *immemorālis*]

immense (imens´) *a.* **1** huge, vast, immeasurable. **2** very great, very large. **3** (*coll.*) very good, excellent. **immensely** *adv.* **immenseness, immensity** *n.* [F, from L *immensus* (*mensus*, p.p. of *metīrī*, to measure, to METE[1])]

immensurable (imen´shərəbəl) *a.* immeasurable. [late L *immensūrābilis*]

†**immerge** (imœj´) *v.t.* to immerse. [L *immergere* (*mergere*, to plunge, to sink)]

immerse (imœs´) *v.t.* **1** to plunge, to dip (into or under water or other fluid). **2** to baptize in this manner. **3** (*usu. reflex. or pass.*) to involve or absorb deeply (in difficulty, debt, study, etc.). **4** to bury (in). **immersible** *a.* **immersion** (-shən) *n.* **1** the act of immersing; the state of being immersed. **2** baptism by plunging completely under water. **3** the state of being deeply involved (in thought etc.). **4** (*Astron.*) the disappearance of a celestial body behind or into the shadow of another. **5** a language-teaching method involving the exclusive use of the language concerned in the learning situation. **immersion heater** *n.* an electric heater designed to heat liquid by being directly immersed in it, esp. as a fixture in a hot-water tank. **immersionist** *n.* a person who believes in baptism by immersion. [L *immersus*, p.p. of *immergere*, to IMMERGE]

immethodical (iməthod´ikəl) *a.* **1** not methodical. **2** confused. **immethodically** *adv.*

immigrate (im´igrāt) *v.i.* to enter a foreign country for settlement there. ~*v.t.* to bring (a person) into a foreign country for settlement. **immigrant** *n.* a person who immigrates. ~*a.* of or relating to immigrants (*the immigrant population*). **immigration** (-rā´shən) *n.* **immigratory** *a.* [L *immigrātus*, p.p. of *immigrāre* (*migrāre*, to MIGRATE)]

imminent (im´inənt) *a.* **1** impending; close at hand. **2** †overhanging. **imminence** *n.* **imminently** *adv.* [L *imminens -ntem*, pres.p. of *imminēre* (*minere*, cp. EMINENT)]

Usage note See note under IMMANENT.

immiscible (imis´ibəl) *a.* not capable of being mixed (with). **immiscibility** (-bil´-) *n.* **immiscibly** *adv.*

immitigable (imit´igəbəl) *a.* incapable of being mitigated. **immitigably** *adv.* [L *immītigābilis*]

immittance (imit´əns) *n.* electrical admittance or impedance. [*im*pedance, ad*mittance*]

†**immix** (imiks´) *v.t.* to mix or mingle together. **immixture** (imiks´chə) *n.* [obs. p.p. *immixt*, L *immixtus*, from *immiscēre* (*miscēre*, to mix)]

immobile (imō´bīl) *a.* **1** not moving. **2** not mobile, immovable. **immobility** (-bil´-) *n.* **immobilize** (-bil-), **immobilise** *v.t.* **1** to render (a vehicle, an attacker etc.) immobile. **2** to restrict the movement of (a limb etc.) for healing purposes. **3** to withdraw (coins) from circulation. **immobilization** (-zā´shən) *n.* **immobilizer** *n.* [F, from L *immōbilis*]

immoderate (imod´ərət) *a.* **1** excessive. **2** unreasonable. **immoderately** *adv.* **immoderation** (-ā´shən), **immoderateness** *n.* [L *immoderātus*]

immodest (imod´ist) *a.* **1** not modest, forward. **2** improper, indecent. **immodestly** *adv.* **immodesty** *n.* [F *immodeste*, L *immodestus*]

immolate (im´əlāt) *v.t.* **1** to kill or offer up in sacrifice. **2** to sacrifice (a highly valued thing). **immolation** (-ā´shən) *n.* **immolator** *n.* [L *immolātus*, p.p. of *immolāre* (*molāre*, to sprinkle with meal, to sacrifice, from *mola*, meal)]

immoral (imor´əl) *a.* **1** not moral. **2** inconsistent with or contrary to (esp. sexual) morality. **3** licentious, vicious. **immoralist** *n.* **immorality** (-al´-) *n.* (*pl.* **immoralities**). **immorally** *adv.*

Usage note See note under AMORAL.

immortal (imaw´təl) *a.* **1** not mortal, not subject to death. **2** imperishable. **3** relating to immortality. **4** eternally famous. ~*n.* **1** a person who is immortal, esp. one of the ancient gods. **2** a person, esp. an author, who is enduringly famous. **3** (*pl.*) the 40 members of the French Academy. **immortality** (-tal´-) *n.* **immortalize, immortalise** *v.t.* **1** to make immortal. **2** to perpetuate the memory of. **immortalization** (-zā´shən) *n.* **immortally** *adv.* [L *immortālis*]

immortelle (imawtel´) *n.* an everlasting flower, esp. a helichrysum. [F, fem. of *immortel*, IMMORTAL]

immovable (imoo´vəbəl), **immoveable** *a.* **1** that cannot be moved. **2** firmly fixed. **3** steadfast. **4** unchanging, unalterable. **5** unfeeling. **6** (*Law*) not liable to be removed. **immovability** (-bil´-), **immovableness** *n.* **immovable feast** *n.* a religious feast day that is observed on a fixed date every year. **immovables** *n.pl.* (*Law*) immovable property. **immovably** *adv.*

immune (imūn´) *a.* **1** protected against a particular disease, infection etc. owing to inoculation or the body's natural resistance (*immune to typhoid*). **2** of or relating to immunity (*the immune system*). **3** unaffected; free or exempt (from) (*immune to criticism*). ~*n.* a person who or a thing that is immune. **immune response** *n.* the response of the body to the introduction of an antigen. **immunity** *n.* (*pl.* **immunities**) **1** freedom from liability to infection. **2** freedom or exemption from an obligation, duty or penalty. **immunize** (im´-), **immunise** *v.t.* to give protection against a disease to, usu. by inoculation. **immunization** (-zā´shən) *n.* [L *immūnis* (IM-[2], *mūnis*, serving, rel. to *mūnus*, service, duty)]

immuno- (im´ūnō, imū´nō) *comb. form* **1** immunity. **2** immune.

immunoassay (imūnōas´ā) *n.* the identification of a substance, esp. a protein, through its behaviour as an antigen or antibody.

immunochemistry (imūnōkem´istri) *n.* **1** the chemical study of antigens, antibody reactions etc. **2** the study of biological molecules using particular immune reactions.

immunocompromised (imūnōkom´prəmīzd) *a.* having an impaired immune system.

immunodeficiency (imūnōdifish´ənsi) *n.* a deficiency in a person's immune response.

immunogenic (imūnōjen´ik) *a.* causing or able to produce an immune response.

immunoglobulin (imūnōglob´ūlin) *n.* any one of five classes of proteins showing antibody activity.

immunology (imūnol´əji) *n.* the scientific study of immunity. **immunologic** (-loj´-), **immunological** *a.* **immunologically** *adv.* **immunologist** *n.*

immunosuppressive (imūnōsəpres´iv) *a.* (of a drug) that minimizes the body's natural reactions to a foreign substance, e.g. a transplanted organ. ~*n.* an immunosuppressive drug. **immunosuppressant** *n., a.* **immunosuppressed** *a.* (of a person) whose immune response has been partially or completely suppressed. **immunosuppression** *n.*

immunotherapy (imūnōther´əpi) *n.* the treatment of disease through the stimulation of the patient's own natural immunity.

immure (imūə´) *v.t.* **1** to surround as with a wall; to confine. **2** to shut (oneself) away. **immurement** *n.* [F *emmurer*, med. L *immūrāre* (*mūrāre*, from *mūrus*, wall)]

immutable (imū´təbəl) *a.* **1** unchangeable. **2** not susceptible to change or variation, invariable. **immutability** (-bil´-), **immutableness** *n.* **immutably** *adv.* [F, from *immūtābilis*]

☒ **imortal** common misspelling of IMMORTAL.

imp (imp) *n.* **1** a mischievous child. **2** a little devil or malignant spirit. *~v.t.* **1** to supply (esp. the wing of a falcon) with new feathers in order to improve flight or replace broken feathers. **2** †to graft. **impish** *a.* having the characteristics of an imp; mischievous. **impishly** *adv.* **impishness** *n.* [OE *impa*, shoot, graft, *impian*, to graft, prob. from Gr. *emphuein*, to implant]

imp. *abbr.* **1** imperative. **2** imperfect. **3** imperial. **4** impersonal.

impact[1] (im´pakt) *n.* **1** a forcible striking (upon or against), a collision. **2** an effect or influence (on). [L *impactus*, p.p. of *impingere*, to IMPINGE]

impact[2] (impakt´) *v.t.* **1** to press or drive firmly together, to pack firmly in. **2** to have an effect on. *~v.i.* to have an effect (on). **impacted** (-pak´-) *a.* **1** (of a tooth) wedged in such a way as to be unable to come through the gum. **2** (of a fracture) having jagged ends that are wedged into each other. **3** (of faeces) lodged in the intestines. **impaction** (-pak´-) *n.* [IMPACT[1]]

impair (impeə´) *v.t.* to damage or weaken in quality, strength etc. (*impaired vision*). **impairment** *n.* [OF *empeirer*, late L *impējōrāre* (IM-[1], *pejor*, worse)]

impala (impah´lə) *n.* (*pl.* **impala, impalas**) an antelope, *Aepyceros melampus*, of southern and eastern Africa, that has lyre-shaped horns and is able to move with long high leaps. [Zulu]

impale (impāl´) *v.t.* **1** to transfix, esp. to put to death by transfixing with a sharp stake. **2** (*Her.*) to arrange (two coats of arms) on one shield, divided by a vertical line. **3** †to fence, to enclose. **impalement** *n.* [F *empaler* (IM-[1], *pal*, L *pālus*, a stake)]

impalpable (impal´pəbəl) *a.* **1** not able to be readily apprehended by the mind; intangible. **2** not perceptible to the touch. **3** (of powder) not coarse. **impalpability** (-bil´-) *n.* **impalpably** *adv.* [F, from L *impalpābilis*]

impaludism (impal´ūdizm) *n.* a disease carried by insects, affecting those living in marshy regions. [L *palus palūdis*, marsh]

impanate (impā´nāt, im´pən-) *a.* (*Theol.*) embodied in bread. *~v.t.* to embody in bread. **impanation** (-pənā´shən) *n.* the embodiment of Christ in the consecrated elements in the Eucharist. [med. L *impānātus*, p.p. of *impānāre* (*pānis*, bread)]

impanel EMPANEL.

imparadise (impar´ədīs) *v.t.* **1** to put in a place or state of perfect happiness. **2** to make (a place) like paradise.

imparipinnate (imparipin´ət) *a.* (*Bot.*) pinnate with an odd terminal leaflet. [L *impar*, see IMPARISYLLABIC, PINNATE]

imparisyllabic (imparisilab´ik) *a.* (of a noun or verb) not having the same number of syllables in the different inflected forms. [L *impar* (IM-[2], PAR[1], SYLLABIC (under SYLLABLE))]

imparity (impar´iti) *n.* (*pl.* **imparities**) disparity, inequality. [late L *imparitas*]

†**impark** (impahk´) *v.t.* **1** to form (land) into a park. **2** to enclose (animals) in a park. [A-F *emparker*, OF *emparquer*]

impart (impaht´) *v.t.* **1** to communicate (knowledge, information). **2** to give, to bestow (a quality, feeling). **impartation** (-tā´shən), **impartment** *n.* **imparter** *n.* [OF *impartir*, L *impartīre* (*partīre*, to PART)]

impartial (impah´shəl) *a.* not partial; not favouring one party or one side more than another. **impartiality** (-al´-), **impartialness** *n.* **impartially** *adv.*

impartible (impah´tibəl) *a.* (*chiefly Law*) not subject to or capable of partition. **impartibility** (-bil´-) *n.* [late L *impartībilis*]

impassable (impah´səbəl) *a.* that cannot be passed or travelled through. **impassability** (-bil´-), **impassableness** *n.* **impassably** *adv.*

Usage note The adjectives *impassable* and *impassible* should not be confused: *impassable* means unable to be passed, and *impassible* impassive or insensible.

---

impasse (am´pas, im´-) *n.* a blind alley; an insurmountable obstacle; deadlock. [F *passer*, to PASS)]

impassible (impas´ibəl) *a.* **1** impassive. **2** insensible to pain or suffering. **3** incapable of being injured. **4** not subject to feeling or passion. **impassibility** (-bil´-), **impassibleness** *n.* **impassibly** *adv.* [F, from L *impassibilis*]

Usage note See note under IMPASSABLE.

---

impassion (impash´ən) *v.t.* to rouse the deepest feelings of, to stir to ardour or passion. **impassioned** *a.* charged with passion. [It. *impassionare* (*passione*, PASSION)]

impassive (impas´iv) *a.* **1** not showing or affected by pain, feeling or passion. **2** unmoved, serene. **3** having no sensation. **impassively** *adv.* **impassiveness, impassivity** (-siv´-) *n.*

impaste (impāst´) *v.t.* in painting, to lay colours thickly and boldly on. **impastation** (-pastā´shən) *n.* **impasto** (-pas´tō) *n.* **1** the application of a thick layer of paint, to give relief etc. **2** paint applied in this way. [It. *impastare* (IM-[1], *pasta*, PASTE)]

impatiens (impā´shienz) *n.* (*pl.* **impatiens**) any plant of the genus *Impatiens*, including the busy Lizzie and balsam. [L, IMPATIENT]

impatient (impā´shənt) *a.* **1** not able to wait or to endure. **2** eager (for or to). **3** not patient or tolerant (of). **impatience** *n.* **impatiently** *adv.* [F, from L *impatientem*, nom. *-iens*]

impeach (impēch´) *v.t.* **1** to charge with a crime, esp. treason. **2** (*esp. N Am.*) to charge with misconduct while holding office. **3** to call in question (a person's honesty etc.). **impeachable** *a.* **impeacher** *n.* [OF *empescher* (F *empêcher*), late L *impedicāre* (*pedica*, fetter, from *pēs pedis*, foot)]

impearl (impœl´) *v.t.* (*poet.*) **1** to form into pearls or pearl-like drops. **2** to adorn with pearls.

impeccable (impek´əbəl) *a.* **1** (of manners, behaviour etc.) faultless. **2** not liable to fall into sin. **impeccability** (-bil´-) *n.* **impeccably** *adv.* †**impeccancy** *n.* **impeccant** *a.* sinless, impeccable. [L *impeccābilis*]

impecunious (impikū´niəs) *a.* **1** having no money. **2** short of money. **impecuniosity** (-os´-), **impecuniousness** *n.* **impecuniously** *adv.*

impede (impēd´) *v.t.* to hinder, to obstruct. **impedance** *n.* **1** resistance to alternating current, esp. due to inductance or capacitance together with ohmic resistance. **2** a similar resistance caused by applied forces (*mechanical impedances*). **impediment** (-ped´-) *n.* **1** something which impedes; a hindrance or obstruction. **2** a speech defect. **3** an obstacle to lawful marriage. **impedimenta** (-men´tə) *n.pl.* **1** things that impede progress. **2** baggage, esp. supplies for an army on the march. **impedimental** *a.* [L *impedīre* (*pēs pedis*, foot), to entangle the feet]

impel (impel´) *v.t.* (*pres.p.* **impelling,** *past, p.p.* **impelled**) **1** to drive or urge (to an action or to do). **2** to drive or push forward. **impellent** *a., n.* **impeller** *n.* **1** a person who or a thing which impels. **2** a rotor in a centrifugal pump or compressor. [L *impellere* (*pellere*, to drive)]

impend (impend´) *v.i.* **1** to threaten, to be imminent. **2** to hang (over), to be suspended (over). †**impendence,** †**impendency** *n.* **impending** *a.* [L *impendēre* (*pendēre*, to hang)]

impenetrable (impen´itrəbəl) *a.* **1** that cannot be penetrated or pierced. **2** inscrutable, incomprehensible. **3** impervious to ideas, influences etc. **4** (*Physics*) preventing any other substance from occupying the same place at the same time. **impenetrability** (-bil´-),

impenetrableness *n.* **impenetrably** *adv.* [F *impénétrable*, L *impenetrābilis*]
impenitent (impen´itənt) *a.* not penitent, not contrite. **impenitence, impenitency** *n.* **impenitently** *adv.* [L *impaenitentem*, nom. *-tens*]
impennate (impen´ət) *a.* **1** (of birds) wingless; having short wings adapted for swimming. **2** featherless.
imper. *abbr.* imperative.
imperative (imper´ətiv) *a.* **1** urgent. **2** obligatory. **3** authoritative, peremptory. **4** (*Gram.*) (of a mood of verbs) expressing command. *~n.* **1** the mood of the verb used to express command, entreaty or exhortation. **2** a command. **3** something absolutely essential or very urgent. **imperatival** (-tī´-) *a.* **imperatively** *adv.* **imperativeness** *n.* [late L *imperātivus*, from *imperāre*, to command (*parāre*, to make ready)]
imperator (impərah´taw) *n.* (*Hist.*) **1** a title originally bestowed upon a victorious Roman general. **2** under the Roman Empire, the title bestowed on the emperor. **imperatorial** (-perətaw´-) *a.* [L, as IMPERATIVE]
imperceptible (impəsep´tibəl) *a.* **1** not able to be perceived. **2** extremely slight, small, or gradual. **imperceptibility** (-bil´-), **imperceptibleness** *n.* **imperceptibly** *adv.* **imperceptive** *a.* not perceiving; not able to perceive.
impercipient (impəsip´iənt) *a.* not perceiving; not having power to perceive. **impercipience** *n.*
imperf. *abbr.* imperfect.
imperfect (impœ´fikt) *a.* **1** not perfect, defective. **2** incomplete, not fully made, done etc. **3** (*Gram.*) (of a tense or aspect) expressing action as continuous and not completed, usu. in the past. **4** (*Mus.*) **a** diminished. **b** less than a semitone. **c** (of a cadence) passing to a dominant chord from another, esp. a tonic, chord. *~n.* **1** the imperfect tense. **2** a verb in this tense. **imperfection** (-fek´-) *n.* **1** the condition of being imperfect. **2** a defect. **3** deficiency. **imperfective** (-fek´-) *a.* (of a verb aspect) showing that the action is in progress. *~n.* **1** the imperfective aspect of a verb. **2** a verb in this aspect. **imperfectively** *adv.* **imperfectly** *adv.* **imperfectness** *n.* **imperfect rhyme** *n.* a rhyme in which the sounds are related but do not fully rhyme, as in 'bit' and 'bed'. **imperfect tense** *n.* a tense expressing or denoting an uncompleted action or state, usu. relating to past time. [OF *imparfait*, L *imperfectus*, assim. to L]
imperforate (impœ´fərət) *a.* **1** not perforated. **2** (of a postage stamp) not having perforations. **3** (of a part of the body) having no opening or normal orifice. **imperforation** (-ā´shən) *n.*
imperial (impiə´riəl) *a.* **1** of or relating to an empire, an emperor, or other supreme ruler. **2** suitable to or like an emperor; sovereign, supreme; lordly, majestic. **3** (of weights and measures) conforming to official British non-metric standards. **4** (of commodities and products) of a superior size, quality etc. *~n.* **1 a** the top of a diligence or coach. **b** a trunk designed to be carried there. **2** a size of paper about 22 × 30 in. (56 × 76 cm). **3** a small tufted beard below the lower lip, made fashionable by Napoleon III. **4** an emperor or empress. **imperial city** *n.* the city of Rome. **imperial gallon** *n.* the British gallon for liquids. **imperialism** *n.* **1 a** the policy of extending the authority of a nation by means of colonies or dependencies. **b** the extension of influence or authority by a country, institution etc. (*dollar imperialism*). **2** government by an emperor. **3** the spirit, state, authority etc. of an empire. **imperialist** *n.* a supporter or advocate of imperialism. *~a.* of or relating to imperialism. **imperialistic** (-is´-) *a.* **imperialistically** *adv.* **imperially** *adv.* [OF, from L *imperiālis*, from IMPERIUM]
imperil (imper´il) *v.t.* (*pres.p.* **imperilling,** (*N Am.*) **imperiling,** *past, p.p.* **imperilled,** (*N Am.*) **imperiled**) to endanger.
imperious (impiə´riəs) *a.* **1** dictatorial, overbearing. **2** urgent, pressing. **imperiously** *adv.* **imperiousness** *n.* [L *imperiōsus*, from IMPERIUM]
imperishable (imper´ishəbəl) *a.* **1** enduring permanently. **2** not subject to decay. **imperishability** (-bil´-), **imperishableness** *n.* **imperishably** *adv.*
imperium (imper´iəm) *n.* absolute command, authority or rule. [L, command, supreme authority]
impermanent (impœ´mənənt) *a.* not permanent. **impermanence, impermanency** *n.* **impermanently** *adv.*
impermeable (impœ´miəbəl) *a.* not allowing passage, esp. of a fluid; impervious. **impermeability** (-bil´-), **impermeableness** *n.* **impermeably** *adv.* [F *imperméable*, late L *impermeābilis*]
impermissible (impəmis´ibəl) *a.* not permissible. **impermissibility** (-bil´-) *n.*
impers. *abbr.* impersonal.
imperscriptible (impəskrip´tibəl) *a.* not derived from written authority. [L *perscrībere* (PER-, *scribēre*, to write, p.p. *scriptus*)]
impersonal (impœ´sənəl) *a.* **1** without personality. **2** not relating to any particular person or thing. **3** lacking in human warmth. **4** (*Gram.*) (of a verb) used only in the third person singular in modern English with the neuter pronoun *it* as subject. **impersonality** (-nal´-) *n.* **impersonalize, impersonalise** *v.t.* to make impersonal. **impersonally** *adv.* [late L *impersōnālis*]
impersonate (impœ´sənāt) *v.t.* **1** to pretend to be (someone) in order to entertain or deceive. **2** to play the part of (a character). **3** to personify. **impersonation** (-ā´shən) *n.* **impersonator** *n.*
impertinent (impœ´tinənt) *a.* **1** impudent, insolent. **2** inappropriate. **3** (*Law*) not pertinent, not relating to the matter in hand. **impertinence, impertinency** *n.* **impertinently** *adv.* [F, from L *impertinentem*, nom. *-ens*]
imperturbable (impətœ´bəbəl) *a.* not easily disturbed or excited; calm, cool. **imperturbability** (-bil´-), **imperturbableness, imperturbation** (-pœtəbā´shən) *n.* **imperturbably** *adv.* [late L *īmperturbābilis*]
impervious (impœ´viəs) *a.* **1** not receptive or open (to). **2** not allowing passage of a liquid. **imperviously** *adv.* **imperviousness** *n.* [L *impervius*]
impetigo (impətī´gō) *n.* (*pl.* **impetigos, impetigines** (-tij´inēz)) a contagious bacterial skin infection marked by the formation of pustules and yellow crusty sores. **impetiginous** (-tij´-) *a.* [L, from *impetere*, to assail (*petere*, to seek)]
impetrate (im´pətrāt) *v.t.* to obtain by petition, esp. by prayer. **impetration** (-rā´shən) *n.* the act of impetrating. **impetrative, impetratory** *a.* [L *impetrātus*, p.p. of *impetrāre* (*patrāre*, to bring to pass)]
impetuous (impet´ūəs) *a.* **1** acting hastily or suddenly; impulsive. **2** moving with violence or great speed. **impetuosity** (-os´-), **impetuousness** *n.* **impetuously** *adv.* [F *impetueux -euse*, L *impetuōsus*, from IMPETUS]
impetus (im´pitəs) *n.* (*pl.* **impetuses**) **1** an impulse or driving force; stimulus. **2** the force with which a body moves or is impelled. [L (*petere*, to seek)]
impi (im´pi) *n.* (*pl.* **impis**) a group of Zulu fighters. [Zulu]
impiety (impī´əti) *n.* (*pl.* **impieties**) **1** the quality of being impious. **2** an impious act. [F *impieté*, L *impietātem*, nom. *-tas*, from *impius*, IMPIOUS]
impinge (impinj´) *v.i.* (*pres.p.* **impinging**) **1** to have an effect (on). **2** to encroach (on). **3** to come into collision, to strike (on, against etc.). **impingement** *n.* **impinger** *n.* [L *impingere* (*pangere*, to drive, fasten)]
impious (im´piəs, impī´əs) *a.* **1** lacking piety or reverence, esp. towards God. **2** irreverent, lacking respect. **impiously** *adv.* **impiousness** *n.* [L *impius*]

implacable (implak´əbəl) *a.* 1 not to be appeased. 2 inexorable, unrelenting. **implacability** (-bil´-), **implacableness** *n.* **implacably** *adv.* [F, from L *implācābilis*]
implacental (impləsen´təl) *a.* (of marsupials and monotremes) without a placenta.
implant[1] (implahnt´) *v.t.* 1 to plant for the purpose of growth. 2 to set or fix (in). 3 (*Med.*) a to insert (tissue, an electrode etc.) into the body. b (*pass.*) (of a fertilized ovum) to become attached to the lining of the uterus. 4 to inculcate, to instil (ideas etc.). **implantation** (-tā´shən) *n.* [F *implanter*, late L *implantāre*]
implant[2] (im´plahnt) *n.* something implanted, esp. something grafted or inserted into the body.
implausible (implaw´zibəl) *a.* not having an appearance of truth and credibility. **implausibility** (-bil´-), **implausibleness** *n.* **implausibly** *adv.*
implead (implēd´) *v.t.* 1 (*Law*) to prosecute or bring an action against. 2 to accuse. ~*v.i.* to bring an action against someone. **impleader** *n.* [ME *enpleden*, A-F *enpleder*, OF *empleidier*]
impledge (implej´) *v.t.* to pledge, to pawn.
implement (im´plimənt) *n.* 1 a tool, a utensil. 2 (*pl.*) things that serve for equipment, furniture, etc. 3 (*fig.*) an agent, an instrument. 4 (*Sc. Law*) the fulfilment of an obligation. ~*v.t.* 1 to carry (a policy, law etc.) into effect. 2 to fulfil. 3 to complete. 4 to supplement. **implemental** (-men´-) *a.* **implementation** (-tā´shən) *n.* **implementer** *n.* [L *implēmentum*, a filling up or accomplishing, from *implēre* (*plēre*, to fill)]
implex (im´pleks) *a.* involved, complicated. **implexion** (-plek´-) *n.* **implexuous** *a.* (*Bot.*) folded or plaited. [L *implexus*, p.p. of *implectere* (*plectere*, to plait)]
implicate (im´plikāt) *v.t.* 1 to show (a person) to be involved (in). 2 to involve. 3 to imply. 4 to enfold, to entwine. ~*n.* something which is involved or implied. **implication** (-ā´shən) *n.* 1 something that is implied or suggested. 2 the act of implicating; the state of being implicated. **by implication** by indirect suggestion. **implicative** (-plik´ətiv) *a.* **implicatively** *adv.* [L *implicātus*, p.p. of *implicāre* (*plicāre*, to fold)]
implicit (implis´it) *a.* 1 implied rather than directly stated. 2 tacitly contained (in) but not expressed. 3 unquestioning, unreserved (*implicit trust*). 4 (*Math.*) (of a function) that cannot be directly expressed in terms of independent variables. **implicitly** *adv.* **implicitness** *n.* [L *implicitus*, var. of *implicātus*, see IMPLICATE]
implied IMPLY.
implode (implōd´) *v.i.* to burst inwards. ~*v.t.* 1 to cause to burst inwards. 2 to pronounce (a consonant) by implosion. **implosion** (-zhən) *n.* 1 the act of imploding. 2 the inward release of obstructed breath involved in the articulation of certain stop consonants. **implosive** *a.* pronounced by implosion. ~*n.* an implosive consonant. [L *plodere*, to clap]
implore (implaw´) *v.t.* 1 to supplicate or beg (someone to do something). 2 to ask for earnestly. ~*v.i.* to entreat, to beg, to supplicate. **imploration** (-rā´shən) *n.* **imploratory** (-plor´ə-) *a.* earnestly imploring. **implorer** *n.* **imploring** *a.* **imploringly** *adv.* [F *implorer*, L *implōrāre* (*plōrāre*, to weep)]
implosion IMPLODE.
imply (implī´) *v.t.* (*3rd pers. sing. pres.* **implies,** *pres.p.* **implying,** *past, p.p.* **implied**) 1 to indicate strongly the truth or existence of (something) in an indirect way. 2 to mean indirectly, to hint (*Are you implying I did it on purpose?*). 3 to signify. **implied** *a.* strongly suggested, though not actually expressed. **impliedly** (-plī´əd-) *adv.* [OF *emplier*, L *implicāre*, see IMPLICATE]

Usage note See note under INFER.

impolder (impōl´də), **empolder** *v.t.* 1 to form into a polder. 2 to reclaim (land) from the sea.
impolicy (impol´isi) *n.* (*pl.* **impolicies**) an act of or the quality of being impolitic or inexpedient.
impolite (impəlīt´) *a.* not polite, ill-mannered. **impolitely** *adv.* **impoliteness** *n.* [L *impolītus*]
impolitic (impol´itik) *a.* not politic, injudicious, inexpedient. **impoliticly** *adv.*
imponderable (impon´dərəbəl) *a.* 1 incalculable. 2 very light. 3 (*Physics*) not having sensible weight. ~*n.* (*usu. pl.*) an element or factor whose importance cannot be assessed or evaluated. **imponderabilia** (-bil´iə) *n.pl.* imponderables. **imponderability** (-bil´-), **imponderableness** *n.*
imponent (impō´nənt) *a.* that imposes. ~*n.* a person who imposes a duty or obligation. [L *impōnere* (*pōnere*, to place)]
import[1] (impawt´) *v.t.* 1 to bring (goods) from a foreign country (into). 2 to introduce (ideas, words etc.) from elsewhere. 3 to imply, to signify, to mean. 4 (*Comput.*) to transfer (data) from one software package to another. **importable** *a.* **importability** (-bil´-) *n.* **importation** (-tā´shən) *n.* 1 the act or practice of importing. 2 something which is imported. **importer** *n.* a person who imports goods. [F *importer*, L *importāre* (*portāre*, to bring)]
import[2] (im´pawt) *n.* 1 something which is imported from abroad. 2 the act or process of importing. 3 something which is signified or implied. 4 importance. **import licence** *n.* a licence that must be obtained before a trader can import certain goods.
importance (impaw´təns) *n.* 1 the quality of being important. 2 weight, authority, consequence. 3 personal consideration, self-esteem. **important** (-paw´-) *a.* 1 of great moment or consequence, weighty. 2 notable, eminent. 3 pretentious. 4 significant (*She's talented, and more important, committed*). **importantly** *adv.*
importunate (impaw´tūnət) *a.* 1 unreasonably insistent or demanding. 2 urgent. 3 troublesome. **importunacy, importunateness, importunity** (-tū´-) *n.* **importunately** *adv.* [L *importūnus*, unfit, unsuitable, rel. to *portus*, PORT[1]]
importune (impaw´tūn) *v.t.* 1 to solicit insistently or urgently. 2 to solicit for immoral purposes. 3 †to mean, to signify. ~†*v.i.* to be importunate. **importunely** *adv.* 1 inopportunely. 2 importunately. **importuner** *n.* [as IMPORTUNATE]
importunity IMPORTUNATE.
impose (impōz´) *v.t.* 1 to lay (e.g. a burden, tax, toll etc.) upon. 2 to force (one's beliefs, views etc.) upon. 3 to palm off (upon). 4 to arrange (pages of type) in a form for printing. 5 †to lay or place (upon). ~*v.i.* 1 to cause inconvenience. 2 to take advantage of someone's good nature or kindness. **to impose on/ upon** 1 to act in a way that causes inconvenience to (someone). 2 to take advantage of (a person's good nature, kindness etc.). 3 to cheat, deceive. **imposer** *n.* **imposing** *a.* commanding; impressive. **imposingly** *adv.* **imposingness** *n.* **imposing-stone** *n.* a slab of stone or metal on which type is made up into formes. [F *imposer*, L *impōnere* (cp. COMPOSE)]
imposition (impəzish´ən) *n.* 1 the act of imposing or placing upon. 2 an unfair and excessive burden. 3 a duty or tax. 4 an exercise enjoined as a punishment in schools etc. 5 (*Print., esp. Hist.*) the process of assembling pages in type on the stone and then locking them into a chase, the whole then becoming a forme.
impossible (impos´ibəl) *a.* 1 not possible. 2 (*loosely*) impracticable, not feasible. 3 that cannot be done, thought, endured etc. 4 (*coll.*) outrageous. **impossibility** (-bil´-) *n.* (*pl.* **impossibilities**) 1 the state of being impossible. 2 something impossible. **impossibly** *adv.* [F, from L *impossibilis*]
impost[1] (im´pōst) *n.* 1 something which is imposed or levied as a tax, tribute or duty (esp. on imported goods).

2 a weight carried by a horse in a handicap race. [OF (F *impôt*), late L *impostum*, L *impositum*, nom. *-tus*, p.p. of *impōnere*, to IMPOSE]

impost[2] (im´pōst) *n.* the upper member of a pillar or entablature on which an arch rests. [F *imposte*, It. *imposta*, as IMPOST[1]]

impostor (impos´tə), **imposter** *n.* **1** a person who falsely assumes a character. **2** a deceiver by false pretences. **imposture** (-chə) *n.* **1** deception by the assumption of a false character, imposition. **2** a fraud, a swindle. [F *imposteur*, late L *impostor*, from *impōnere*, to IMPOSE; assim. to L]

†**impostume** (impos´tūm), †**imposthume** (-thūm) *n.* an abscess. [OF *empostume*, *apostume*, L and Gr. *apostēma* (APO-, *sta-*, base of *istanai*, to stand)]

impotent (im´pətənt) *a.* **1** powerless; helpless. **2** (of a male) unable to have sexual intercourse because of an inability to achieve an erection. *~n.* a man who is sexually impotent. **impotence, impotency** *n.* **impotently** *adv.* [F, from L *impotentem*, nom. *-tens*]

impound (impownd´) *v.t.* **1** to take possession of or confiscate (a document etc.). **2** to confine. **3** to shut up (animals) in a pound. **4** to collect and confine or retain (water) in a reservoir, dam etc. **impoundable** *a.* **impoundage** (-ij) *n.* the act of impounding. **impounder** *n.* **impoundment** *n.*

impoverish (impov´ərish), †**empoverish** *v.t.* **1** to make poor. **2** to exhaust the strength, fertility or resources of. **impoverisher** *n.* **impoverishment** *n.* [OF *empoveriss-*, part. stem of *empoverir* (*povre*, *pauvre*, POOR)]

impracticable (imprak´tikəbəl) *a.* **1** not able to be carried out in practice; not feasible. **2** unsuitable for a particular purpose. **3** (of a road) impassable. **4** intractable, stubborn. **impracticability** (-bil´-), **impracticableness** *n.* **impracticably** *adv.*

Usage note The meanings of the adjectives *impracticable* and *impractical* overlap (especially in North America), but *impracticable* usually means not possible, and *impractical* not realistic.

impractical (imprak´tikəl) *a.* **1** not practical. **2** (*esp. NAm.*) not possible in practice. **impracticality** (-kal´-), **impracticalness** *n.* **impractically** *adv.*

imprecate (im´prikāt) *v.t.* **1** to invoke (as an evil on). **2** to put a curse on. *~v.i.* to curse. **imprecation** (-ā´shən) *n.* **1** the act of imprecating. **2** a prayer for evil to fall on someone; a curse. **imprecatory** *a.* involving a curse. [L *imprecātus*, p.p. of *imprecārī* (*precārī*, to PRAY)]

imprecise (imprisīs´) *a.* not precise. **imprecisely** *adv.* **impreciseness, imprecision** (-izh´ən) *n.*

impregnable[1] (impreg´nəbəl) *a.* **1** (of a castle, defences) that cannot be stormed or taken by assault. **2** able to resist all attacks. **impregnability** (-bil´-) *n.* **impregnably** *adv.* [OF *imprenable* (*prendre*, L *prehendere*, to seize), *-g-* as in REIGN, SOVEREIGN etc.]

impregnable[2] IMPREGNATE.

impregnate (im´pregnāt) *v.t.* **1** to make pregnant. **2** to fertilize (an ovum). **3** to saturate (with). **4** to imbue, to inspire (with). **5** to make (soil etc.) fruitful or fertile. *~a.* **1** impregnated, pregnant. **2** imbued (with). **impregnable**[2] (-preg´-) *a.* able to be impregnated. **impregnation** (-nā´shən) *n.* [late L *impraegnātus*, p.p. of *impraegnāre* (*praegnāre*, to be PREGNANT)]

impresa (imprē´zə), **imprese** (imprēz´) *n.* **1** a heraldic device. **2** a motto. [It. *impresa*, undertaking, device, fem. of *impreso*, undertaken, cp. EMPRISE]

impresario (imprizah´riō) *n.* (*pl.* **impresarios**) **1** a person who organizes musical or theatrical performances. **2** a director of an opera company, a ballet company etc. [It. IMPRESA]

imprescriptible (impriskrip´tibəl) *a.* (*Law*) (of rights) that cannot be lost or impaired by usage or claims founded on prescription. **imprescriptibility** (-bil´-) *n.* [F (PRESCRIPTIBLE (under PRESCRIBE))]

imprese IMPRESA.

impress[1] (impres´) *v.t.* **1** to produce a favourable effect on (*I'm impressed with your efficiency*). **2** to affect strongly. **3** to press or stamp (a mark etc., in or upon). **4** to produce (a mark or figure) by pressure. **5** to make a mark etc. on (something) with a stamp or seal. **6** to apply (voltage) to a circuit etc. **to impress on/ upon** to emphasize to (someone) (*He impressed on us the need for discretion*). **impressible** *a.* **1** capable of being impressed. **2** yielding to pressure. **3** susceptible. **impressive** *a.* **1** adapted to make an impression on the mind; commanding; inspiring. **2** leaving a deep impression. **impressively** *adv.* **impressiveness** *n.* [L *impressāre*, freq. of *imprimere* (*premere*, to PRESS[1])]

impress[2] (im´pres) *n.* **1** the act of marking by pressure or with a stamp, seal etc. **2** a stamp, an impression. **3** a characteristic mark. **4** an effect produced by the senses, feelings etc.

impress[3] (impres´) *v.t.* (*Hist.*) **1** to compel (men) to enter government service. **2** to seize or set apart (goods, property etc.) for the public service. **impressment** *n.*

impression (impresh´ən) *n.* **1** an effect produced upon the senses, feelings etc. **2** a strong, esp. favourable, effect (*She made quite an impression on me*). **3** a vague notion or belief (*My impression is they're worried*). **4** an imitation or impersonation. **5 a** the act of impressing a mark. **b** the mark made by impressing. **6** a copy taken from type, an engraved plate etc. **7** a reprint from standing type, as distinct from an edition. **8 a** the total number of copies of a book printed at one time. **b** the act of printing these. **9** in dentistry, an imprint of the teeth and gums obtained by pressing them into a soft substance such as wax. **impressionable** *a.* easily impressed. **impressionability** (-bil´-) *n.* **impressionably** *adv.* **impressional** *a.* **impressionism** *n.* **1** an artistic movement that began in France and was based on the principle that the hand should paint what the eye sees, thus ruling out established conventions of lighting and composition. **2** a style of writing or music that seeks to suggest a mood or feeling rather than to give a precise description. **impressionist** *n.* **1** an entertainer who impersonates well-known people. **2** an exponent of impressionism. *~a.* of or relating to impressionism. **impressionistic** (-nis´-) *a.* **1** in an impressionist style. **2** not systematic. **impressionistically** *adv.*

imprest (im´prest) *n.* **1** an advance of money, esp. for carrying out some public service. **2** a cash fund, e.g. petty cash, from which incidental expenses are paid and which is topped up regularly from central funds. [PREST, prob. after obs. *iprest*, in ready money]

imprimatur (imprimā´tə, -ah´tə) *n.* **1** a licence to print a book, granted by the Roman Catholic Church. **2** official sanction or approval. [L, let it be printed, from *imprimere*, to IMPRESS[1]]

imprimatura (imprēmətūə´rə) *n.* a coloured transparent glaze used as a primer in painting. [It. *imprimitura*, from *imprimere*, to IMPRESS[1]]

imprimis (imprī´mis) *adv.* in the first place. [L *in primis*, among the first things]

imprint[1] (imprint´) *v.t.* **1** to impress, to stamp. **2** to print. **3** to establish firmly or impress (on the mind). **4** to cause (a young animal) to undergo the process of imprinting. **imprinting** *n.* the process by which young animals develop the tendency to recognize and be attracted to members of their own species. [OF *empreinter*, *empreindre*, L *imprimere*, to IMPRESS[1]]

imprint[2] (im´print) *n.* **1** a mark, stamp or impression. **2** the name of the printer or publisher of a book, periodical etc., with the place and usu. the date of publication (on the title-page or at the end of a book).

imprison (impriz´ən) *v.t.* **1** to put into prison. **2** to confine, to hold in custody or captivity. **imprisonment** *n.* [OF *emprisoner*]

impro (im´prō) *n.* (*pl.* **impros**) (*coll.*) **1** improvisation. **2** an instance of improvising. [abbr. of IMPROVISATION (under IMPROVISE)]

improbable (improb´əbəl) *a.* **1** not likely to be true. **2** not likely to happen. **improbability** (-bil´-) *n.* **improbably** *adv.* [L *improbābilis*]

improbity (imprō´biti) *n.* (*pl.* **improbities**) **1** lack of probity; wickedness. **2** dishonesty. **3** a dishonest or wicked act. [L *improbitās*, from *improbus*, wicked (*probus*, good, see PROBITY)]

impromptu (impromp´tū) *adv.* off-hand, without previous study. *~a.* done or said off-hand, extempore. *~n.* (*pl.* **impromptus**) **1** an extempore speech, performance, act etc. **2** a short piece of music, often for the piano, and sometimes having the character of an improvisation. [L *in promptū*, in readiness (*promptū*, abl. of *-tus*, from *prōmere*, to PROMPT)]

improper (improp´ə) *a.* **1** unbecoming, indecent. **2** unsuitable. **3** not accurate, wrong. **improper fraction** *n.* a fraction in which the numerator is equal to or greater than the denominator. **improperly** *adv.* [F *impropre*]

impropriate (imprō´priāt) *v.t.* **1** to convert (esp. ecclesiastical property) to one's own or to private use. **2** to place (ecclesiastical revenues, profits etc.) in the hands of a layman. *~a.* vested in a layman. **impropriation** (-ā´shən) *n.* **impropriator** *n.* a person, esp. a layman, to whom church lands or an ecclesiastical benefice are impropriated. [L *propriāre*, to appropriate, from *proprius*, one's own]

impropriety (imprəprī´əti) *n.* (*pl.* **improprieties**) **1** the quality of being improper, indecency. **2** an unbecoming act, expression etc. **3** incorrectness. **4** unfitness. [L *improprietās*]

improv (im´prov) *n.* (*coll.*) IMPRO.

improve (improov´) *v.t.* **1** to make better. **2** to increase the value of (land etc.) by cultivating or building. *~v.i.* **1** to become better. **2** to increase in value. **to improve on/ upon** to achieve something better than. **improvable** *a.* **1** capable of improvement or amelioration. **2** capable of being used to advantage. **improvability** (-bil´-), †**improvableness** *n.* **improvement** *n.* **1 a** the act of improving or the state of being improved. **b** an instance of improving or being improved. **2** something which is added or done to something in order to improve it. **3** a beneficial or valuable addition or substitute. **4** something which has been improved. **improver** *n.* **1** a person who or a thing which improves. **2** (*Hist.*) a worker who accepted low wages in order to learn a trade, esp. an apprentice in millinery or dressmaking. **improving** *a.* tending to improve and edify. **improvingly** *adv.* [ME *emprowen*, A-F *emprouwer*, from OF *prou*, profit, perh. from L *prōd-* (*prōdesse*, to be useful or profitable to)]

improvident (improv´idənt) *a.* **1** neglecting to make provision for the future. **2** thriftless. **3** careless, heedless. **improvidence** *n.* **improvidently** *adv.*

improvise (im´prəvīz) *v.t.*, *v.i.* **1** to play, sing or perform, composing as one goes along. **2** to do or make without prior preparation, using the materials to hand. **improvisation** (-zā´shən) *n.* **improvisational** *a.* **improvisator** (-prov´izātə) *n.* **improvisatore** (imprōvēzətaw´rā) *n.* (*pl.* **improvisatori** (-ē)) a person, esp. a performer, who improvises. **improvisatorial** (-vizətaw´-), **improvisatory** (-viz´ətəri) *a.* of or relating to improvisation. **improvisatrice** (imprōvēzətrē´chā) *n.* (*pl.* **improvisatrici** (-ē)) a female improvisatore. **improviser** *n.* [F *improviser*, It. *improvvisare*, from *improvviso*, L *imprōvīsus* (*prōvīsus*, p.p. of *prōvidēre*, to see ahead, to PROVIDE)]

imprudent (improo´dənt) *a.* rash, incautious, indiscreet. **imprudence** *n.* **imprudently** *adv.* [L *imprūdens -ntem*]

impudent (im´pūdənt) *a.* **1** rude and disrespectful. **2** lacking in shame or modesty. **impudence** *n.* **impudently** *adv.* **impudicity** (-dis´-) *n.* immodesty, shamelessness. [F, from L *impudentem*, nom. *-dens* (*pudens*, pres.p. of *pudēre*, to feel shame)]

impugn (impūn´) *v.t.* **1** to call in question, to contradict, to gainsay. **2** †to oppose. **impugnable** *a.* **impugner** *n.* **impugnment** *n.* [F *impugner*, L *impugnāre* (*pugnāre*, to fight)]

impuissant (impū´isənt, -pwē´sənt) *a.* powerless, impotent. **impuissance** *n.* [F]

impulse (im´pŭls) *n.* **1** a sudden desire or whim (*I bought it on impulse*). **2** an influence acting suddenly on the mind tending to produce action. **3** the application or effect of an impelling force. **4** a stimulus, an inspiration. **5** (*Physics*) **a** a large force acting for an extremely short time. **b** the momentum due to such a force. **6** a disturbance passing along a nerve or muscle. **impulse buying** *n.* the act of buying something on a sudden whim. **impulsion** (-pŭl´shən) *n.* **1** the act of impelling or the state of being impelled. **2** impetus. **3** a compulsion. **impulsive** (-pŭl´-) *a.* **1** resulting from or liable to be actuated by impulse rather than reflection. **2** communicating impulse, urging forward. **3** (*Physics*) acting momentarily, not continuous. **impulsively** *adv.* **impulsiveness** *n.* [L *impulsus*, from *impellere*, to IMPEL]

impunity (impū´niti) *n.* exemption from punishment or the unpleasant consequences of an action. **with impunity** without having to suffer unpleasant consequences. [F *impunité*, L *impūnītātem*, nom. *-tās* (*poena*, Gr. *poinē*, penalty)]

impure (impūə´) *a.* **1** not pure; mixed with other substances, adulterated. **2** defiled, unclean. **3** unchaste. **4** mixed with other colours. **impurely** *adv.* **impureness** *n.* **impurity** *n.* (*pl.* **impurities**) **1** the state or quality of being impure. **2** something that is impure. **3** a small amount of foreign matter added to a semiconductor. [L *impūrus*]

impute (impūt´) *v.t.* **1** to ascribe or attribute (esp. something dishonourable) to a person. **2** (*Theol.*) to ascribe (righteousness, guilt etc.) on account of another. **imputable** *a.* **imputation** (-tā´shən) *n.* **1** the act of imputing. **2** something which is imputed as a charge or fault. **3** reproach, censure. **4** (*Theol.*) the attributing of righteousness or personal guilt and its consequences to a person or persons, on account of another. **imputative** *a.* **imputatively** *adv.* **imputer** *n.* [F *imputer*, L *impūtāre* (*putāre*, to reckon)]

I.Mun.E. *abbr.* Institution of Municipal Engineers.

IN *abbr.* Indiana.

In *chem. symbol* indium.

in (in) *prep.* **1** denoting presence or situation within the limits of time, place, circumstance etc. (*in Europe*; *in prison*; *in my pocket*). **2** during (*in 1996*; *in the afternoon*). **3** within a certain period of time (*The cafe closes in 20 minutes*). **4** working in the field of (*in advertising*). **5** wearing (*in a suit*; *in red*). **6** taking part in (*in a play*). **7** with respect to (*cloudy in places*; *shot in the arm*). **8** as a proportion to (*one in five*). **9** arranged as (*in a line/circle*). **10** having the condition of; suffering from (*in danger*; *in poverty*). **11** as regards the content (*There's nothing in these rumours*). **12 a** using a particular way of talking (*in a loud voice*; *They spoke in Dutch*). **b** (of music) having as its key (*quartet in D major*). **13** using a particular material (*drawn in ink*). **14** within the capabilities of (*He doesn't have it in him*). **15** (of a word) having as its beginning or ending (*nouns in -um*). **16** in the person of (*You have a loyal friend in Sue*). **17** (of an animal) pregnant with (*in foal*). **18** used with verbs to express motion or change (*Divide* *it in two; Put it in the oven*). **19** used to introduce an indirect object after a verb (*believe in; confide in*). **20** forming adverbial and prepositional phrases (*in favour of; in fact*). **21** used after superlatives (*the fastest in the world*). *~adv.* **1** within or inside some place (*I went in; We were shut in*). **2** indoors, at home (*Are you in this evening?*). **3** inwards (*Massage it in*). **4** in office. **5** in favour (*Our luck is in*). **6** in fashion (*Miniskirts are in*). **7** (of fruit etc.) in season. **8** in a book, newspaper etc. (*The article is in tomorrow*). **9** (of a ball, serve etc.) within the playing area. **10** in cricket, at the wicket. **11** (of a train, boat etc.) having arrived (*Her flight's not in yet*). **12** sent in (*Applications must be in by Friday*). **13** (of a fire) burning. **14** (of the tide) at its highest point. *~a.* **1** directed inwards. **2** internal, living inside (*in-patients*). **3** fashionable (*It's the in thing at the moment*). **4** understood by a select group only. **in absentia** (*coll.*) in (his, her etc.) absence. **in as far as** in so far as. **in as much as** inasmuch as. **in at** present at (*in at the start*). **ins and outs** the intricacies or details (of). **in so far as** in such measure as. **in that 1** seeing that; since. **2** in so far as. **in the name of** NAME. **not in it** NOT. **to be in for 1** to be about to experience (esp. something unpleasant) (*You're in for a disappointment*). **2** to be committed to or involved in. **3** to be entered for (a race etc.). **to be in for it** to be certainly heading for trouble. **to be in with** to be on good terms with. **in-and-in** *a., adv.* (of breeding) carried out among members of the same species. **in-between** *a.* (*coll.*) intermediate. **in-car** *a.* happening or situated in a car. **in-depth** *a.* detailed, thorough, comprehensive. **in-flight** *a.* available or occurring during an aeroplane flight. **in-goal area** *n.* in rugby, the area between the dead-ball line and the goal line. **in-group** *n.* a small and esp. exclusive group of people bound by common interests. **in-house** *a.* of or relating to, or employed within, a particular organization, company etc. *~adv.* within a particular organization, company etc. **in-joke** *n.* a joke only understood by a select group. **in-line** *a.* **1** forming a part of a sequence of processes or operations. **2** (of an engine) having its cylinders arranged in a line. **in-line skate** *n.* a type of roller skate with a single row of small wheels fitted to the side of the boot. **in-off** *n.* a billiards or snooker shot in which the ball falls into a pocket after striking another ball. **in-patient** *n.* a person in hospital receiving regular treatment. **in-service** *a.* (of training) given to employees to improve their skills. **in-store** *a., adv.* inside a store. **in-swinger** *n.* **1** in cricket, a ball bowled so as to swerve towards the batsman. **2** in football, a ball kicked so as to curve towards the goal. **in-tray** *n.* a tray holding letters and documents still to be dealt with. **in-your-face, in your face** *a.* (*sl.*) offering a direct challenge, aggressively provocative. [OE, Dut., G, Goth., cogn. with L *in*, Gr. *en*]

in. *abbr.* inch, inches.

in-[1] (in) *pref.* in, into, within, on, against, towards, as in *indicate, induce.* [OE *in-*, or OF *in-*, *en-*, or directly from L *in-*]

in-[2] (in) *pref.* not, without, as in *incomprehensible, inequality.* [L, not]

-in[1] (in) *suf.* (*Chem.*) **1** denoting neutral compounds, and usu. distinct from alkaloids and basic compounds in -INE, e.g. *albumin, casein.* **2** denoting certain enzymes, as in *pepsin.* **3** denoting pharmaceutical products, as in *aspirin.* [-INE]

-in[2] (in) *comb. form* indicating a gathering for common activity (*sit-in; work-in*).

-ina[1] (ē´nə) *suf.* **1** denoting the feminine in titles and proper names, as in *Tsarina, Thomasina.* **2** forming names of musical instruments, as in *ocarina.* [L *-īna*, fem. of *-īnus*]

-ina[2] (ē´nə) *suf.* (*Zool.*) forming names of groups of animals, usu. from the name of a genus, as in *globigerina.* [L *-īna*, neut. pl. of *-īnus*]

inability (inəbil´iti) *n.* **1** the state of being unable (to do, understand etc.). **2** lack of power or means.

inaccessible (inəkses´ibəl) *a.* **1** that cannot be reached, attained, or approached. **2** (of a person) not affable, not encouraging advances. **inaccessibility** (-bil´-), **inaccessibleness** *n.* **inaccessibly** *adv.* [F, from late L *inaccessibilis*]

inaccurate (inak´ūrət) *a.* not accurate. **inaccuracy** *n.* (*pl.* **inaccuracies**) **1** a lack of accuracy. **2** an inaccurate statement, an error. **inaccurately** *adv.*

inaction (inak´shən) *n.* **1** inactivity; a lack of action. **2** sluggishness. **inactivate** *v.t.* to make inactive. **inactivation** (-ā´shən) *n.* **inactive** *a.* **1** not active. **2** sluggish, inert. **3** idle, indolent. **4** (of a substance) chemically or biologically lacking in reactivity. **5** (*Mil.*) not in active service. **inactively** *adv.* **inactivity** (-tiv´-) *n.*

inadequate (inad´ikwət) *a.* **1** not adequate; insufficient. **2** unable to cope. **inadequacy** *n.* (*pl.* **inadequacies**). **inadequately** *adv.*

inadmissible (inədmis´ibəl) *a.* (of evidence) that cannot be admitted, allowed or received. **inadmissibility** (-bil´-) *n.* **inadmissibly** *adv.*

inadvertent (inədvœ´tənt) *a.* **1** (of an action) unintentional, accidental. **2** not paying attention. **3** heedless, careless, negligent. **inadvertence, inadvertency** *n.* **inadvertently** *adv.*

inadvisable (inədvī´zəbəl) *a.* not advisable. **inadvisability** (-bil´-) *n.*

inalienable (inā´lienəbəl) *a.* that cannot be alienated or transferred. **inalienability** (-bil´-) *n.* **inalienably** *adv.*

inalterable (inawl´tərəbəl) *a.* incapable of alteration. **inalterability** (-bil´-) *n.* **inalterably** *adv.*

inamorato (inamərah´tō) *n.* (*pl.* **inamoratos**) a man who is in love or is beloved. **inamorata** (-tə) *n.* (*pl.* **inamoratas**) a woman who is in love or is beloved. [It. *innamorato*, p.p. of *innamorare* (*amore*, L *amor -em*, love)]

inane (inān´) *a.* **1** silly, fatuous. **2** empty, void. **inanely** *adv.* **inaneness** *n.* **inanition** (inənish´ən) *n.* **1** exhaustion from lack of food or nourishment. **2** emptiness, voidness. **inanity** (inan´-) *n.* (*pl.* **inanities**). [L *inānis*, empty]

inanga (ē´nŭngə) *n.* (*New Zeal.*) a small fish, *Galaxias maculutas*, whose young are eaten as whitebait. [Maori]

inanimate (inan´imət) *a.* **1** not living; lacking any sign of life. **2** not endowed with life; not animate. **3** void of animation, dull, lifeless. **inanimately** *adv.* **inanimation** (-ā´shən) *n.* [L *inanimātus*]

inanition, inanity INANE.

inappellable (inəpel´əbəl) *a.* beyond appeal; absolute, final.

inappetence (inap´itəns) *n.* lack of desire or appetite. **inappetent** *a.*

inapplicable (inap´likəbəl, -əplik´-) *a.* **1** not applicable. **2** irrelevant. **inapplicability** (-bil´-), **inapplicableness** *n.* **inapplicably** *adv.*

inapposite (inap´əzit) *a.* not apposite; not pertinent. **inappositely** *adv.* **inappositeness** *n.*

inappreciable (inəprē´shəbəl) *a.* **1** not perceptible; too insignificant to be considered. **2** not able to be appreciated. **inappreciably** *adv.* **inappreciation** (-shiā´shən) *n.* **1** lack of appreciation. **2** inability to appreciate properly. **inappreciative** *a.*

inapprehensible (inaprihen´sibəl) *a.* that cannot be apprehended or understood. **inapprehension** (-shən) *n.* **inapprehensive** *a.* not apprehensive; untroubled. **inapprehensiveness** *n.*

inapproachable (inəprō´chəbəl) *a.* inaccessible; unapproachable. **inapproachably** *adv.*

inappropriate (inəprō´priət) *a.* not appropriate, unsuitable. **inappropriately** *adv.* **inappropriateness** *n.*

inapt (inapt´) *a.* **1** not apt; unsuitable. **2** not skilful. **inaptitude, inaptness** *n.* **inaptly** *adv.*

Usage note See note under INEPT.

inarch (inahch´) *v.t.* to graft (a plant) by inserting a scion, without separating it from the parent tree, into a stock.
inarguable (inah´gūəbəl) *a.* that cannot be disputed. **inarguably** *adv.*
inarticulate (inahtik´ūlət) *a.* **1** unable to express oneself clearly. **2** not uttered with distinct articulation, indistinct. **3** dumb. **4** (*Biol.*) not articulated, not jointed. **inarticulacy** (-si), **inarticulateness** *n.* **inarticulately** *adv.* [L *inarticulātus*]
inartificial (inahtifish´əl) *a.* artless, simple, natural. **inartificially** *adv.* [L *inartificiālis*]
inartistic (inahtis´tik) *a.* **1** not designed, done etc., according to the principles of art. **2** not having artistic taste or ability. **inartistically** *adv.*
inasmuch (inəzmŭch´) *adv.* (*followed by as*) seeing that; since; in so far as.
inattention (inəten´shən) *n.* **1** lack of attention; heedlessness; negligence. **2** disregard of courtesy. **inattentive** *a.* **inattentively** *adv.* **inattentiveness** *n.*
inaudible (inaw´dibəl) *a.* not audible, that cannot be heard. **inaudibility** (-bil´-) *n.* **inaudibly** *adv.* [L *inaudībilis*]
inaugurate (inaw´gūrāt) *v.t.* **1** to install or induct into office solemnly or with appropriate ceremonies. **2** to commence, introduce, or celebrate the opening of with some degree of formality, solemnity, pomp or dignity. **inaugural** *a.* of, relating to or performed at an inauguration. ~*n.* an inaugural address. **inauguration** (-rā´shən) *n.* **inaugurator** *n.* **inauguratory** *a.* [L *inaugurātus*, p.p. of *inaugurāre* (*augurāre*, to take omens, from AUGUR)]
inauspicious (inawspish´əs) *a.* **1** unlucky, unfortunate. **2** ill-omened, unfavourable. **inauspiciously** *adv.* **inauspiciousness** *n.*
inauthentic (inawthen´tik) *a.* not authentic. **inauthenticity** (-tis´iti) *n.*
inbeing (in´bēing) *n.* **1** inherence; inherent existence. **2** essence, essential nature. [BEING]
inboard (in´bawd) *adv.* within the sides or towards the middle of a ship, aircraft or vehicle. ~*a.* situated thus (*inboard motor*). ~*prep.* inside, within (a ship etc.).
inborn (in´bawn) *a.* innate, naturally inherent.
inbound (in´bownd) *a.* coming in (*inbound flights*).
inbreathe (inbrēdh´) *v.t.* **1** to draw in (breath). **2** to inspire.
inbred (inbred´, in´bred) *a.* **1** innate, inborn, natural. **2** produced as a result of inbreeding.
inbreed (inbrēd´) *v.t.* (*past, p.p.* **inbred** (-bred´)) **1** to develop or produce within something. **2** to breed from closely related individuals. **inbreeding** *n.*
inbuilt (in´bilt) *a.* that is included as a part of something.
Inc. (ingk) *abbr.* Incorporated.
Inca (ing´kə) *n.* **1** a member of a South American Indian people in Peru until the Spanish conquest in 1531. **2** the ruler or king of this people or any member of his family. **3** the language of the Incas. **Incaic** (- k´āik), **Incan** *a.* [Quechua *inka*, king]
incalculable (inkal´kūləbəl) *a.* **1** that cannot be reckoned or estimated in advance. **2** too vast or numerous to be calculated. **3** not to be reckoned upon, uncertain. **incalculability** (-bil´-), **incalculableness** *n.* **incalculably** *adv.*
incalescent (inkəles´ənt) *a.* (*Chem.*) becoming warm. **incalescence** *n.* [L *incalescens -ntem*, pres.p. of *incalescere* (*calescere*, freq. of *calere*, to be hot)]
in camera CAMERA.
incandesce (inkandes´) *v.i.* to glow with heat. ~*v.t.* to cause to glow with heat. **incandescence** *n.* **incandescent** *a.* **1** glowing with heat. **2** strikingly radiant or bright. **incandescent lamp** *n.* an electric or other lamp in which a filament or mantle is made intensely luminous by heat. **incandescently** *adv.* [L *incandescere* (*candescere*, incept. of *candēre*, to be white)]
incantation (inkantā´shən) *n.* **1** a formula, said or sung, supposed to add force to magical ceremonies; a charm. **2** the recitation of such formulas. **incantational** *a.* **incantatory** (-kan´tə-) *a.* [F, from L *incantātiōnem*, nom. *-tio*, from *incantāre*, see ENCHANT]
incapable (inkā´pəbəl) *a.* **1** not physically, intellectually, or morally capable (of). **2** lacking power, ability, or fitness (of doing, committing etc.). **3** not susceptible (of). **4** unable to take care of oneself, esp. as a result of being incapacitated by drink. ~*n.* a person who is incapable. **incapability** (-bil´-), †**incapableness** *n.* **incapably** *adv.* [F, from med. L *incapabilis*]
incapacious (inkəpā´shəs) *a.* not capacious; not roomy. **incapaciousness** *n.* [L *incapax*]
incapacitate (inkəpas´itāt) *v.t.* **1** to render incapable; to disable. **2** to render unfit; to disqualify. **incapacitant** *n.* **incapacitated** *a.* **incapacitation** (-ā´shən) *n.* [from INCAPACITY]
incapacity (inkəpas´iti) *n.* (*pl.* **incapacities**) **1** a lack of power or capacity; inability. **2** legal disqualification. **3** an instance of incapacity. [F *incapacité*]
incarcerate (inkah´sərāt) *v.t.* to imprison; to shut up or confine. ~†*a.* imprisoned. **incarceration** (-ā´shən) *n.* **incarcerator** *n.* [med. L *incarcerātus*, p.p. of *incarcerāre* (*carcer*, prison)]
incardinate (inkah´dināt) *v.t.* in the Roman Catholic Church, to institute as principal priest, deacon etc., of a particular church or diocese. [med. L *incardinātus*, p.p. of *incardināre* (*cardo -dinis*, hinge, see CARDINAL)]
incarnadine (inkah´nədīn) *a.* (*poet.*) red or flesh-coloured. ~*n.* red or the colour of flesh. ~*v.t.* **1** to dye this colour. **2** to tinge with red. [F *incarnadin*, It. *incarnadino*, *-tino*, from *incarnato*, INCARNATE[1]]
incarnate[1] (inkah´nət) *a.* **1** invested or clothed with flesh, embodied in flesh, esp. in human form. **2** typified, personified. **3** (*esp. Bot.*) flesh-coloured, pink. [L *incarnātus*, p.p. of *incarnāre* (*caro carnis*, flesh)]
incarnate[2] (in´kahnāt, inkah´nāt) *v.t.* **1** to embody in flesh. **2** to embody (an idea) in a living form. **3** to be the embodiment of. **incarnation** (-nā´shən) *n.* **1** the act of assuming flesh. **2** embodiment, esp. in human form. **3** (**Incarnation**) Christ's assumption of human nature. **4** a vivid exemplification or personification (of). **5** (*Med.*) the process of healing wounds, and filling or covering the damaged part with new flesh.
incase ENCASE.
incautious (inkaw´shəs) *a.* lacking in caution; rash, unwary. **incaution** *n.* lack of caution. **incautiously** *adv.* **incautiousness** *n.*
incendiary (insen´diəri) *a.* **1** of or relating to the malicious burning of property. **2** exciting or tending to excite factions, seditions or quarrels; inflammatory. **3** (of a device, substance) capable of causing fires or igniting readily. ~*n.* (*pl.* **incendiaries**) **1** a person who maliciously sets fire to property etc. **2** an incendiary bomb. **3** a person who excites factions, seditions etc. **incendiarism** *n.* **incendiary bomb** *n.* a bomb containing incendiary materials that are scattered in flames on detonation. [L *incendiārius*, from *incendium*, a conflagration, from *incendere*, see INCENSE[2]]
incense[1] (in´sens) *n.* **1** a mixture of fragrant gums, spices etc. used for producing perfumes when burnt, esp. in religious rites. **2** the smoke of this. **3** any agreeable perfume. **4** flattery; adulation. ~*v.t.* **1** to perfume with or as with incense. **2** to offer incense to. **incensory** *n.* (*pl.* **incensories**) CENSER (under CENSE). **insensation**

(-sā´shən) *n.* [ME and OF *encens*, L *incensum*, that which is burnt, neut. p.p. of *incendere*, to burn (*-candere*, to burn, rel. to *candēre*, to glow)]

incense[2] (insens´) *v.t.* to inflame, to enrage. **incensement** *n.* [OF *incenser*, or directly from L *incensus*, p.p. of *incendere*, see INCENSE[1]]

incentive (insen´tiv) *n.* **1** something which acts as a motive, incitement or spur (to action). **2** a payment or benefit offered to workers to encourage greater output. *~a.* inciting, urging. **incentivize, incentivise** *v.t.* to stimulate to further activity by offering incentives. [L *incentīvus*, setting a tune, from *incinere* (*canere*, to sing)]

incept (insept´) *v.t.* (*Biol.*) (of an organism) to receive, to take in. *~v.i.* (*Hist.*) to be finally admitted to the degree of Master or Doctor at a university. [L *inceptus*, p.p. of *incipere*, to begin (*capere*, to take)]

inception (insep´shən) *n.* a beginning. **inceptive** *a.* **1 a** beginning, commencing. **b** initial. **2** (*Gram.*) denoting the beginning of an action. *~n.* a verb that denotes the beginning of an action.

inceptor (insep´tə) *n.* (*Hist.*) a person at the point of taking a master's or doctor's degree.

incertitude (insœ´titūd) *n.* uncertainty. [F (late L *certitūdo*, from *certus*, CERTAIN)]

incessant (inses´ənt) *a.* unceasing, continual. **incessancy** *n.* **incessantly** *adv.* **incessantness** *n.* [late L *incessans -antem* (*cessans -antem*, pres.p. of *cessāre*, to CEASE)]

incest (in´sest) *n.* sexual intercourse between persons who are considered to be too closely related to marry. **incestuous** (-tūəs) *a.* **1** guilty of or involving incest. **2** (of a group etc.) inward-looking, closed to external influences etc. **incestuously** *adv.* **incestuousness** *n.* [F *inceste*, L *incestus*, from *incestus -tum*, a. (*castus*, CHASTE)]

inch[1] (inch) *n.* **1** the 12th part of a linear foot (2.54 cm). **2** (as a unit of measurement) the quantity of rainfall that would cover the surface of the ground to the depth of one inch. **3** an amount of pressure, atmospheric or other, equivalent to the weight of a column of mercury one inch high in a barometer. **4** an inch on a map, used to represent a certain number of miles. **5** a small amount or degree (*He would not give an inch*; *Give someone an inch and they'll take a mile*). **6** (*pl.*) stature. *~v.t.* to drive by inches or small degrees. *~v.i.* to move in this way. **by inches** inch by inch. **every inch 1** entirely, from head to foot (*He was every inch a gentleman*). **2** the whole area (*She knows every inch of the city*). **inch by inch** bit by bit; gradually; by very small degrees. **within an inch of** very close to. **inchmeal** *adv.* inch by inch. **inchworm** *n.* MEASURING WORM (under MEASURE). [OE *ynce*, L *uncia*]

inch[2] (inch) *n.* (*Sc.*) an island. [Gael. *innis* (cp. Ir. *inis*, Welsh *ynys*, also L *insula*)]

-in-chief (inchēf´) *comb. form* leading, most important, as *commander-in-chief*.

inchoate (inkō´āt, in´-, -ət) *a.* **1** only begun, commenced. **2** incomplete, undeveloped, rudimentary. *~v.t.* to begin, to originate. **inchoately** *adv.* **inchoateness** *n.* **inchoation** (-ā´shən) *n.* **inchoative** *a.* incipient; indicating the beginning of an action. [L *inchoātus*, *incohātus*, p.p. of *incohāre*, to begin]

Usage note The adjectives *inchoate* and *incoherent* should not be confused: *inchoate* means just begun, and *incoherent* lacking intelligibility or consistency.

incident (in´sidənt) *n.* **1** an event or occurrence, esp. one of a picturesque or striking nature. **2** a relatively minor event that might lead to a more serious dispute between two countries (*a frontier/diplomatic incident*). **3** (a minor event causing a) public disturbance (*The demonstration passed off without incident*). **4** a distinct episode in a narrative. **5** (*Law*) a privilege, burden etc. legally attaching to property etc. *~a.* **1** likely to happen. **2 a** naturally appertaining or belonging (to). **b** (*Law*) attaching (to). **3** consequent (on). **4** falling or striking (on or upon). **incidence** *n.* **1** the fact, manner or frequency of occurrence. **2** the scope, bearing or range of influence of something. **3** the act or state of falling on or upon. **4** (*Physics*) the direction in which a body, a ray of light, heat etc. falls upon any surface. **incidental** (-den´təl) *a.* **1** happening in connection with something that is more important; casual; fortuitous. **2** concomitant, naturally connected with or related to. **3** liable to occur. **4** occasional. *~n.* **1** something that is incidental. **2** (*pl.*) casual expenses. **incidentally** *adv.* **1** by the way. **2** in an incidental way. **incidental music** *n.* music used to accompany the action of a film, play etc. **incidentalness** *n.* [F, from L *incidentem*, nom. *-dens*, pres.p. of *incidere* (*cadere*, to fall)]

incinerate (insin´ərāt) *v.t.* to burn completely; to reduce to ashes. **incineration** (-ā´shən) *n.* **incinerator** *n.* a furnace or receptacle in which refuse etc. is burned. [med. L *incinerātus*, p.p. of *incinerāre* (L *cinis cineris*, ashes)]

incipient (insip´iənt) *a.* beginning; in the first stages. **incipience, incipiency** *n.* **incipiently** *adv.* [L *incipiens -entem*, pres.p. of *incipere*, see INCEPT]

incise (insīz´) *v.t.* **1** to cut into. **2** to engrave. **incision** (-sizh´ən) *n.* **1** the act of incising. **2** a cut; a gash; a notch. **3** trenchancy. **incisive** (-siv) *a.* **1** sharp, acute. **2** trenchant, penetrating. **3** clear and direct. **4** having a sharp cutting edge. **incisively** *adv.* **incisiveness** *n.* [F *inciser*, from L *incīsus*, p.p. of *incīdere* (*caedere*, to cut)]

incisor (insī´zə) *n.* a pointed tooth at the front of the mouth, adapted for cutting or dividing food. **incisory** *a.*

incite (insīt´) *v.t.* to stir up; to prompt (to action). **incitation** (insitā´shən) *n.* **1** the act of inciting. **2** something which incites. **3** an incitement. **incitement** *n.* **1** the act of inciting. **2** a stimulus, an incentive, a motive. **inciter** *n.* **incitingly** *adv.* [F *inciter*, L *incitāre* (CITE)]

incivility (insivil´iti) *n.* (*pl.* **incivilities**) **1** rudeness, impoliteness. **2** an act of rudeness. [F, from L *incivīlis*]

incl. *abbr.* including.

inclement (inklem´ənt) *a.* **1** rough, severe, stormy. **2** without clemency, merciless. **inclemency** (-si) *n.* (*pl.* **inclemencies**). **inclemently** *adv.* [F, from L *inclemens -ntem*]

incline[1] (inklīn´) *v.i.* **1** to be disposed (to). **2** to have a tendency (to) (*I incline to agree*). **3** to deviate from any direction that is regarded as the normal one. **4** to bend down or forwards. *~v.t.* **1** (*usu. pass.*) to give an inclination, leaning or tendency to (*I'm inclined to believe her*). **2** to cause (the head or body) to bend down, to bow. **3** to cause to deviate from a line or direction. **inclinable** *a.* **1** having a tendency (to); disposed (to). **2** that can be inclined or sloped. **inclination** (-klinā´shən) *n.* **1** a disposition or tendency (to, towards). **2** a liking or preference (for). **3** the act of inclining or bending. **4** a deviation from any direction regarded as the normal one. **5** (*Geom.*) the angle that a plane makes with another, esp. a horizontal or vertical plane. **6** the angle that the earth's magnetic field makes with the horizontal. **inclinational** *a.* **inclined** *a.* **inclined plane** *n.* one of the mechanical powers, consisting of a plane set at an acute angle to the horizon. **incliner** *n.* **inclinometer** (-klinom´itə) *n.* **1** an instrument for detecting the vertical intensity of the magnetic force, a dipping compass. **2** an instrument for measuring slopes. **3** an instrument that indicates the angle an aircraft is making with the horizon. [F *incliner*, L *inclīnāre* (*clīnāre*, to bend)]

incline[2] (in´klīn) *n.* an inclined plane; a slope, a gradient.

inclose ENCLOSE.

include (inklood´) *v.t.* **1** to contain or to comprise as a part, member etc. **2** to put in or classify as part of a set etc. **3** to enclose, to confine (within). **to include out** (*coll. or facet.*) to exclude. **includable, includible** *a.* **included** *a.* **1** enclosed. **2** contained, comprised. **3** (of the style and stamens of a plant) not projecting beyond the mouth of the corolla. **inclusion** (inkloo´zhən) *n.* **1** the act of including. **2** the state of being included. **3** something included. **4** a particle, fragment etc. that is distinct from the substance that surrounds it. **inclusive** (inkloo´siv) *a.* **1** including, containing (*prices inclusive of VAT*). **2** including everything (*The rent is £400 a month inclusive*). **3** including the limits specified (*from the 1st to the 8th inclusive*). **4 a** not restricted to certain sections of society. **b** (of language) that includes rather than excludes particular members of society, esp. women, e.g. by avoiding the use of the masculine pronoun to refer to both men and women. **inclusively** *adv.* **inclusiveness** *n.* **inclusive terms** *n.pl.* terms including all subsidiary charges (at a hotel etc.). [L *inclūdere* (*claudere*, to shut), p.p. *inclūsus*]

incog (inkog´) *a., adv., n.* (*coll.*) INCOGNITO. [abbr.]

incogitable (inkoj´itəbəl) *a.* unthinkable. **incogitability** (-bil´-) *n.* [late L *incōgitābilis*]

incognisant INCOGNIZANT.

incognito (inkognē´tō, inkog´nitō) *a., adv.* with one's real name or identity disguised or kept secret. ~*n.* (*pl.* **incognitos**) **1** a person who is incognito. **2** the state of being unknown or in disguise. **3** an assumed identity. **incognita** (-tə) *n., a., adv.* (used of women). [It., from L *incognitus* (IN-[2], *cognitus*, p.p. of *cognōscere*, see COGNITION)]

incognizant (inkog´nizənt), **incognisant** *a.* unaware (of). **incognizance** *n.*

incoherent (inkəhiə´rənt) *a.* **1** inarticulate, unable to express oneself intelligibly. **2** lacking cohesion; disconnected; inconsistent. **3** (*Physics*) (of waves) not having the same phase. **incoherence** *n.* **incoherency** *n.* (*pl.* **incoherencies**). **incoherently** *adv.*

Usage note See note under INCHOATE.

incombustible (inkəmbŭs´tibəl) *a.* incapable of being burnt or consumed by fire. ~*n.* an incombustible thing, substance etc. **incombustibility** (-bil´-) *n.* **incombustibly** *adv.* [F, from med. L *incombustibilis*]

income (in´kəm) *n.* the amount of money (usu. annual) accruing as payment, profit, interest etc. from labour, business, profession or property. **income group** *n.* a section of the population receiving incomes within a certain range. **income support** *n.* in Britain, a social security payment made to the unemployed or people on low incomes, such as part-time workers. **income tax** *n.* a tax levied for state purposes on incomes above a certain amount. [IN-[1], COME]

incomer (in´kŭmə) *n.* **1** a person who comes in. **2** an immigrant. **3** an intruder. **4** a person who succeeds another. **incoming** *a.* **1** coming in. **2** entering; immigrant. **3** succeeding. **4** accruing. ~*n.* **1** an entrance or arrival. **2** (*usu. pl.*) income, gain, revenue.

-incomer (in´kŭmə) *comb. form* having an income of a specified type or level.

incommensurable (inkəmen´shərəbəl) *a.* **1** having no common standard and not able to be compared. **2** not fit or worthy to be compared (with). **3** (*Math.*) **a** having no common factor (with another integral or fractional number or quantity). **b** irrational. ~*n.* (*usu. pl.*) something that is incommensurable. **incommensurability** (-bil´-) *n.* **incommensurably** *adv.* **incommensurate** (-rət) *a.* **1** not commensurate or proportionate (to or with); inadequate. **2** incommensurable. **incommensurately** *adv.* **incommensurateness** *n.* [F, from late L *incommensūrābilis*]

incommode (inkəmōd´) *v.t.* to cause trouble or inconvenience to. **incommodious** *a.* **1** cramped, too small. **2** inconvenient. **incommodiously** *adv.* **incommodiousness** *n.* **incommodity** (-mod´-) *n.* (*pl.* **incommodities**) **1** inconvenience. **2** anything that causes this. [F *incommoder*, L *incommodāre* (*commodāre*, from *commodus*, COMMODIOUS)]

incommunicable (inkəmū´nikəbəl) *a.* **1** that cannot be communicated to or shared with another. **2** not communicative. **incommunicability** (-bil´-), **incommunicableness** *n.* **incommunicably** *adv.* **incommunicative** *a.* not communicative. **incommunicatively** *adv.* **incommunicativeness** *n.*

incommunicado (inkəmūnikah´dō) *a.* **1** with no means of communication with the outside world. **2** in solitary confinement. [Sp.]

incommutable (inkəmū´təbəl) *a.* **1** not commutable. **2** that cannot be changed. **incommutability** (-bil´-) *n.* **incommutably** *adv.* [F, from L *incommūtābilis*]

incomparable (inkom´pərəbəl) *a.* **1** not to be compared (to or with). **2** unequalled, peerless. **incomparability** (-bil´-), **incomparableness** *n.* **incomparably** *adv.* [F, from L *incomparābilis*]

Usage note Pronunciation of *incomparable* as (-par´-), with stress on the third syllable, is best avoided.

incompatible (inkəmpat´ibəl) *a.* **1** opposed in nature or quality; discordant. **2** inconsistent (with). **3** (of two people) unable to cooperate, live or work together. **4** (of drugs, blood groups) not suited for use together because of harmful effects. **5** (of machines etc.) incapable of being used together. ~*n.* (*often pl.*) an incompatible person or thing. **incompatibility** (-bil´-), **incompatibleness** *n.* **incompatible terms** *n.pl.* (*Logic*) terms which cannot both be affirmed of the same subject. **incompatibly** *adv.* [F, from L *incompatibilis*]

incompetent (inkom´pitənt) *a.* **1** lacking in ability or fitness for a task (*an incompetent manager*). **2** showing a lack of skill or ability (*incompetent handling of the dispute*). **3** (*Law*) (of a witness) lacking legal fitness or qualification. **4** (*Med.*) (of valves of the heart) not able to function properly. ~*n.* an incompetent person. **incompetence, incompetency** *n.* **incompetently** *adv.* [F *incompétent*, L *incompetentem*, nom. *-ens*]

incomplete (inkəmplēt´) *a.* not complete; not perfect. **incompletely** *adv.* **incompleteness, incompletion** *n.* [L *incomplētus*]

incompliant (inkəmplī´ənt) *a.* not yielding or flexible. **incompliance** *n.*

incomposite (inkom´pəzit) *a.* not composite; not properly composed. [L *incompositus*]

incomprehensible (inkomprihen´sibəl) *a.* **1** that cannot be conceived or understood. **2** †unlimited, boundless. **incomprehensibility** (-bil´-), **incomprehensibleness** *n.* **incomprehensibly** *adv.* **incomprehension** (-shən) *n.* a failure to understand. **incomprehensive** *a.* not comprehensive or inclusive. **incomprehensiveness** *n.* [F, from L *incomprehensibilis*]

incompressible (inkəmpres´ibəl) *a.* not compressible; strongly resisting compression. **incompressibility** (-bil´-) *n.*

incomputable (inkəmpū´təbəl) *a.* not computable; incalculable.

inconceivable (inkənsē´vəbəl) *a.* **1** not conceivable; incomprehensible. **2** (*coll.*) incredible, most extraordinary. **inconceivability** (-bil´-), **inconceivableness** *n.* **inconceivably** *adv.*

inconclusive (inkənkloo´siv) *a.* (of evidence, a discussion etc.) not conclusive or decisive. **inconclusively** *adv.* **inconclusiveness** *n.*

incondensable (inkənden´səbəl) *a.* not condensable; not reducible to a liquid or solid condition.

incondite (inkon´dit) *a.* **1** ill-composed. **2** unfinished, crude. [L *inconditus* (*conditus*, p.p. of *condere*, to put together)]

incongruous (inkong´gruəs) *a.* **1** not fitting, improper, out of place. **2** not congruous, not agreeing or harmonizing (with). **incongruent** *a.* **incongruity** (-groo´-) *n.* (*pl.* **incongruities**). **incongruously** *adv.* **incongruousness** *n.* [L *incongruus*]

inconsecutive (inkənsek´ūtiv) *a.* not consecutive, not in regular order. **inconsecutively** *adv.* **inconsecutiveness** *n.*

inconsequent (inkon´sikwənt) *a.* **1** irrelevant. **2** illogical. **3** disconnected. **inconsequence** *n.* **inconsequential** (-kwen´-) *a.* **1** of no consequence, trivial. **2** not consequential, inconsequent. **inconsequentiality** (-kwenshial´-) *n.* (*pl.* **inconsequentialities**). **inconsequentially** *adv.* **inconsequentialness** *n.* **inconsequently** *adv.* [L *inconsequens -entem*]

inconsiderable (inkənsid´ərəbəl) *a.* **1** small. **2** not deserving consideration; insignificant. **inconsiderableness** *n.* **inconsiderably** *adv.* [F *inconsidérable* (CONSIDERABLE (under CONSIDER))]

inconsiderate (inkənsid´ərət) *a.* **1** hasty, incautious. **2** having no consideration for the feelings of others. **inconsiderately** *adv.* **inconsiderateness** *n.* **inconsideration** (-ā´shən) *n.* [L *inconsiderātus*]

inconsistent (inkənsis´tənt) *a.* **1** not in keeping; incompatible (with). **2** (of behaviour etc.) not uniform, changeable. **3** self-contradictory, not agreeing with itself or oneself. **inconsistency** *n.* (*pl.* **inconsistencies**). **inconsistently** *adv.*

inconsolable (inkənsō´ləbəl) *a.* (of a person, grief etc.) not to be consoled. **inconsolability** (-bil´-), **inconsolableness** *n.* **inconsolably** *adv.* [F, from L *inconsōlābilis*]

inconsonant (inkon´sənənt) *a.* not consonant, discordant (with). **inconsonance** *n.* **inconsonantly** *adv.* [F]

inconspicuous (inkənspik´ūəs) *a.* **1** not conspicuous; not easy to see. **2** (*Bot.*) small in size, obscure in colour etc. **inconspicuously** *adv.* **inconspicuousness** *n.* [L *inconspicuus*]

inconstant (inkon´stənt) *a.* **1** not constant, changeable, fickle. **2** variable, unsteady, irregular. **inconstancy** *n.* (*pl.* **inconstancies**). **inconstantly** *adv.* [F, from L *inconstāntem*, nom. *-tāns*]

inconsumable (inkənsū´məbəl) *a.* not consumable; indestructible. **inconsumably** *adv.*

incontestable (inkəntes´təbəl) *a.* indisputable, undeniable, unquestionable. **incontestability** (-bil´-) *n.* **incontestably** *adv.*

incontinent[1] (inkon´tinənt) *a.* **1** unable to restrain one's desires, esp. sexual desires. **2** (*Med.*) not able to control the passing of waste from the body. **3** lacking control (of). **incontinence, incontinency** *n.* **incontinently** *adv.* [F, from L *incontinentem*, nom. *-ens*]

†**incontinent**[2] (inkon´tinənt), †**incontinently** *adv.* straightaway, immediately. [F, from late L *in contenti tempore*, in continuous time]

incontrollable (inkəntrō´ləbəl) *a.* not controllable. **incontrollably** *adv.*

incontrovertible (inkontrəvœ´tibəl) *a.* incontestable, indisputable. **incontrovertibility** (-bil´-), **incontrovertibleness** *n.* **incontrovertibly** *adv.*

inconvenience (inkənvēn´yəns) *n.* **1** the quality or state of being inconvenient. **2** something which inconveniences, a cause of difficulty. ~*v.t.* to put to inconvenience; to trouble. **inconvenient** *a.* **1** not convenient. **2** causing or tending to cause trouble, awkward. **inconveniently** *adv.*

inconvertible (inkənvœ´tibəl) *a.* incapable of being converted into or exchanged for something else, esp. money. **inconvertibility** (-bil´-) *n.* **inconvertibly** *adv.*

incoordinate (inkōaw´dinət) *a.* not coordinate. **incoordination** (-ā´shən) *n.* lack of coordination, esp. the inability to coordinate muscular action.

incorporate[1] (inkaw´pərāt) *v.t.* **1** to unite or combine into one body (with). **2** to combine (ingredients) into one mass. **3** to form into a legal corporation. **4** to receive into a corporation. ~*v.i.* **1** to become united or incorporated (with another substance, society etc.) so as to form one body or whole. **2** to form a limited company. **incorporated** *a.* forming a legal corporation. **incorporation** (-ā´shən) *n.* **incorporative** *a.* incorporating or tending to incorporate. **incorporator** *n.*

incorporate[2] (inkaw´pərət) *a.* **1** (of a society, company etc.) made into a corporation. **2** combined into one body or corporation, closely united. **3** embodied. [late L *incorporātus*, p.p. of *incorporāre* (*corpus -poris*, body)]

†**incorporate**[3] (inkaw´pərət) *a.* incorporeal, not embodied in matter. [CORPORATE]

incorporeal (inkawpaw´riəl) *a.* **1** not having a body or material form. **2** spiritual or metaphysical. **3** (*Law*) lacking material existence of itself but based on something material. **incorporeality** (-al´-), **incorporeity** (-rē´-, -rā´-) *n.* **incorporeally** *adv.* [L *incorporeus* (*corpus -poris*, body, see CORPOREAL)]

incorrect (inkərekt´) *a.* **1** wrong, inaccurate, inexact. **2** improper, unbecoming. **incorrectly** *adv.* **incorrectness** *n.* [L *incorrectus*]

incorrigible (inkor´ijibəl) *a.* **1** bad beyond hope of amendment. **2** not easily improved. ~*n.* a person who is incorrigible. **incorrigibility** (-bil´-), **incorrigibleness** *n.* **incorrigibly** *adv.* [F, from L *incorrigibilis*]

incorrupt (inkərŭpt´) *a.* **1** not corrupt; pure. **2** not decayed, marred or impaired. **incorruptible** *a.* **1** not to be bribed; high-principled. **2** incapable of corruption, decay or dissolution; eternal. **incorruptibility** (-bil´-) *n.* **incorruptibly** *adv.* **incorruption** *n.* **incorruptly** *adv.* **incorruptness** *n.* [L *incorruptus*]

incrassate (inkras´āt) *a.* (*Biol.*) thick, thickened (in form). ~†*v.t.* to make thick or thicker. ~†*v.i.* to become thick or thicker. **incrassation** (-ā´shən) *n.* [L *incrassātus*, p.p. of *incrassāre* (*crassāre*, to make thick, from *crassus*, CRASS)]

increase[1] (inkrēs´) *v.i.* to become greater in quantity, number, value, degree etc. ~*v.t.* **1** to make greater in number, quantity, value etc. **2** to intensify. **to increase the gaiety of nations** GAIETY. **increasable** *a.* **increasingly** *adv.* [A-F *encress-*, OF *encreis-*, stem of *encreistre* (cp. F *croître*), L *increscere* (IN-[1], *crescere*, to grow)]

increase[2] (in´krēs) *n.* **1** the act, state or process of increasing; growth, multiplication. **2** the amount by which something increases. **on the increase** increasing.

incredible (inkred´ibəl) *a.* **1** not credible; difficult to believe. **2** (*coll.*) very great, amazing. **incredibility** (-bil´-), **incredibleness** *n.* **incredibly** *adv.* [F, from L *incrēdibilis*]

incredulous (inkred´ūləs) *a.* indisposed to believe, sceptical (of). **incredulity** (-dū´-), **incredulousness** *n.* **incredulously** *adv.* [L *incrēdulus*]

increment (in´krimənt) *n.* **1** an increase, esp. one of a series. **2** the amount of increase. **3** the act or process of increasing. **4** (*Math.*) the finite increase of a variable. **incremental** (-men´-) *a.* **incrementally** *adv.* [L *incrēmentum*, from *increscere*, to INCREASE[1]]

increscent (inkres´ənt) *a.* **1** increasing, growing. **2** (*Her.*) (of the moon) waxing. [L *increscens -entem*, pres.p. of *increscere*, to INCREASE[1]]

incriminate (inkrim´ināt) *v.i.* **1** to make seem guilty (*incriminating evidence*). **2** to charge with a crime. **3** to involve (a person) in a charge. **incrimination** (-ā´shən) *n.* **incriminatory** *a.* [med. L *incrimināātus*, p.p. of *incrimināre* (CRIMINATE)]

incrustation (inkrŭstā´shən) *n.* **1** the act or process of encrusting. 2 a crust or hard coating on a surface etc. 3 a facing or lining of marble, stone etc. on masonry. 4 a deposit on a surface. **incrust** ENCRUST. [late L *incrustātio*, from *incrustāre*, to ENCRUST]

incubate (ingˈkūbāt) *v.t.* 1 to sit on or artificially heat (eggs) until the young birds etc. emerge. 2 to cause (bacteria etc.) to develop. 3 to evolve (a plan etc.) by meditation. ~*v.i.* 1 to sit on eggs for hatching, to brood. 2 to undergo incubation. 3 to evolve slowly. **incubation** (-bāˈshən) *n.* 1 the act or process of incubating or hatching. 2 brooding, as of a hen upon eggs. 3 meditation on a scheme etc.; brooding. 4 (*Med.*) a (*also* **incubation period**) the period between infection and the development of symptoms of a disease. b the series of changes that occur during this. **incubative, incubatory** *a.* **incubator** *n.* 1 an apparatus for hatching eggs by artificial heat, for developing bacteria etc., or rearing a child prematurely born. 2 a person, animal or thing that incubates, esp. a brooding hen. [L *incubātus*, p.p. of *incubāre* (*cubāre*, to lie)]

incubus (ingˈkūbəs) *n.* (*pl.* **incubi** (-bī)) 1 a demon supposed to have sexual intercourse with women at night. 2 a nightmare. 3 any person, thing or influence that oppresses or disturbs. [late L, nightmare, as INCUBATE]

incudes INCUS.

inculcate (inˈkəlkāt) *v.t.* to impress upon the mind by emphasis or frequent repetition. **inculcation** (-kāˈshən) *n.* **inculcator** *n.* [L *inculcātus*, p.p. of *inculcāre* (*calcāre*, to tread, from *calx calcis*, heel)]

inculpate (inˈkəlpāt) *v.t.* 1 to charge with participation in a crime. 2 to blame. **inculpation** (-pāˈshən) *n.* **inculpative** (-kŭlˈ-), **inculpatory** *a.* [late L *inculpātus*, p.p. of *inculpāre* (*culpa*, fault)]

incumbent (inkŭmˈbənt) *a.* 1 imposed (upon) as a duty or obligation. 2 currently holding a post or office. 3 lying or resting (on); pressing or weighing (upon). ~*n.* a person in possession of an office etc., esp. one of the clergy holding a benefice. **incumbency** (-si) *n.* (*pl.* **incumbencies**) the act, state, sphere or period of holding a benefice as incumbent. [L *incumbens -entem*, pres.p. of *incumbere* (*cumbere*, to lie)]

incunable (inkūˈnəbəl) *n.* an early printed book, an incunabulum.

incunabulum (inkūnabˈūləm) *n.* (*pl.* **incunabula** (-lə)) 1 an early printed book, esp. one printed before AD 1500. 2 (*pl.*) the beginning or origins of something. **incunabular** *a.* [L, swaddling clothes (*cūnābula*, dim. of *cūnae*, cradle)]

incur (inkœˈ) *v.t.* (*pres.p.* **incurring**, *past, p.p.* **incurred**) to render oneself liable to or bring upon oneself (risk, injury, punishment etc.). **incurrable** *a.* [L *incurrere* (IN-[1], *currere*, to run)]

incurable (inkūəˈrəbəl) *a.* that cannot be cured or healed. ~*n.* a person suffering from an incurable disease. **incurability** (-bilˈ-), **incurableness** *n.* **incurably** *adv.* [OF, from L *incūrābilis*]

incurious (inkūəˈriəs) *a.* 1 not curious or inquisitive. 2 indifferent, heedless. **incuriosity** (-osˈ-), **incuriousness** *n.* **incuriously** *adv.* [L *incūriōsus*]

incursion (inkœˈshən) *n.* 1 a sudden raid. 2 an irruption. **incursive** *a.* [F, from L *incursiōnem*, nom. *-sio*, from *incurrere*, see INCUR]

incurvate (inkœˈvāt) *v.t.* to cause to curve inwards. ~*a.* curved inward. **incurvation** (-vāˈshən) *n.* [L *incurvāre*]

incurve (inkœvˈ) *v.t.* INCURVATE.

incus (ingˈkəs) *n.* (*pl.* **incudes** (ingkūˈdēz, ingˈ-)) one of the small bones of the ear, shaped rather like an anvil and connected to the malleus and stapes. [L, anvil]

incuse (inkūzˈ) *v.t.* 1 to impress (a design etc.) on a coin by stamping. 2 to stamp (a coin) with a design etc. ~*a.* stamped or impressed (on a coin etc.). ~*n.* an impression made by stamping (on a coin etc.). [L *incūsus*, p.p. of *incūdere*, to forge, from INCUS]

Ind. *abbr.* 1 Independent. 2 India. 3 Indian. 4 Indiana.

ind. *abbr.* independent.

indaba (indahˈbə) *n.* (*S Afr.*) 1 a council; a conference. 2 a problem or matter for discussion. [Zulu, topic]

indebted (indetˈid) *a.* 1 being under a debt or obligation (to or for). 2 owing money (to). **indebtedness** *n.* [ME *endetted*, OF *endetté*, p.p. of *endetter* (EN-, *dette*, DEBT)]

☒ **indecate** common misspelling of INDICATE.

indecent (indēˈsənt) *a.* 1 unbecoming, unseemly. 2 offensive to modesty or propriety. **indecency** (-si) *n.* (*pl.* **indecencies**). **indecent assault** *n.* a sexual assault that does not involve rape. **indecent exposure** *n.* the offence of publicly exposing a part of the body, esp. the genitals, in breach of accepted standards of decency. **indecently** *adv.* [F *indécent*, L *indecentem*, nom. *-cens* (DECENT)]

indecipherable (indisīˈfərəbəl) *a.* not decipherable, illegible.

indecision (indisizhˈən) *n.* lack of decision; irresolution. **indecisive** (-sīˈ-) *a.* 1 not decisive, final, or conclusive. 2 irresolute, vacillating, hesitating. **indecisively** *adv.* **indecisiveness** *n.* [F *indécision*]

indeclinable (indiklīˈnəbəl) *a.* 1 (*Gram.*) having no inflections. 2 that cannot be declined. **indeclinably** *adv.* [F *indéclinable*, L *indēclīnābilis*]

indecorous (indekˈərəs) *a.* violating propriety, decorum or good manners; improper. **indecorously** *adv.* **indecorousness** *n.* **indecorum** (-dikawˈrəm) *n.* 1 violation of decorum or propriety. 2 improper behaviour. [L *indecōrus*]

indeed (indēdˈ) *adv.* 1 in reality, in truth (*It is, indeed, an extraordinary claim*). 2 used to express emphasis (*It's very unusual indeed*). 3 used to express concession (*There are indeed some disadvantages*). 4 in point of fact (*if indeed you can call it that*). 5 used to express disbelief, surprise, or annoyance (*'Paul said so.' - 'Did he indeed?'*). ~*int.* used to express surprise, irony, interrogation etc.

indef. *abbr.* indefinite.

indefatigable (indifatˈigəbəl) *a.* not yielding to fatigue or exertion; unwearied, unremitting. **indefatigability** (-bilˈ-), **indefatigableness** *n.* **indefatigably** *adv.* [obs. F *indéfatigable*, L *indēfatigābilis* (*defatigāre*, to wear out, from *fatigāre*, to FATIGUE)]

indefeasible (indifēˈzibəl) *a.* incapable of being annulled or forfeited. **indefeasibility** (-bilˈ-) *n.* **indefeasibly** *adv.*

indefectible (indifekˈtibəl) *a.* 1 not liable to defect, decay or failure. 2 faultless, flawless. **indefectibility** (-bilˈ-) *n.* **indefectibly** *adv.* [F *indéfectible*]

indefensible (indifenˈsibəl) *a.* incapable of being defended, excused or justified. **indefensibility** (-bilˈ-) *n.* **indefensibly** *adv.*

indefinable (indifīˈnəbəl) *a.* that cannot be defined. **indefinably** *adv.*

indefinite (indefˈinit) *a.* 1 not limited or defined, not determinate. 2 vague, uncertain. 3 (of certain adjectives, adverbs and pronouns) not defining or determining the persons, things etc. 4 (of tenses, e.g. the Greek aorist) not distinguishing between continuous or completed action. 5 (*Bot.*) (esp. of stamens) not constant in number. **indefinite article** *n.* (*Gram.*) a word (*a* or *an* in English) used before a noun and indicating lack of specificity. **indefinite integral** *n.* (*Math.*) an integral having the same derivative when any constant is added. **indefinitely** *adv.* **indefiniteness** *n.* [L *indēfīnītus*]

indehiscent (indihisˈənt) *a.* (of fruits) not opening to set free the seeds.

indelible (indelˈibəl) *a.* 1 that cannot be blotted out or effaced. 2 (of ink) that makes indelible marks. **indelibility** (-bilˈ-), **indelibleness** *n.* **indelibly** *adv.* [earlier *indeleble*, L *indēlēbilis* (*dēlēbilis*, from *dēlēre*, to DELETE)]

indelicate (indel´ikət) *a.* **1** lacking delicacy or tact. **2** coarse, unrefined. **3** offensive to modesty or propriety. **indelicacy** *n.* (*pl.* **indelicacies**). **indelicately** *adv.*

indemnify (indem´nifī) *v.t.* (*3rd pers. sing. pres.* **indemnifies,** *pres.p.* **indemnifying,** *past, p.p.* **indemnified**) **1** to secure from damage, loss, penalty or responsibility (*The insurance indemnifies the house against fire*). **2** to compensate (a person) for loss, damage etc. **indemnification** (-fikā´shən) *n.* **indemnifier** *n.* [L *indemnis* (*damnum*, loss)]

indemnity (indem´niti) *n.* (*pl.* **indemnities**) **1** security against damage, loss or penalty. **2** compensation for damage, loss or penalties incurred. **3** a sum paid as such compensation, esp. by a defeated state to the victor as a condition of peace. **4** legal exemption from liabilities or penalties incurred.

indemonstrable (indimon´strəbəl) *a.* that cannot be demonstrated; assumed as self-evident, axiomatic. **indemonstrability** (-bil´-) *n.*

indent[1] (indent´) *v.t.* **1** (*Print.*) to set (a line of text) further in from the margin than the rest of the paragraph. **2** **a** to divide by tearing or cutting (a document drawn up in duplicate) so that the edges of the two copies can be compared and used to prove authenticity. **b** to execute or draw up (a contract etc.) in exact duplicate. **3** to order (goods), esp. from abroad. **4** to notch or cut into as with teeth. **5** to make recesses in (a coastline etc.). **6** to indenture. ~*v.i.* to make an official requisition (upon). **indentation** (-tā´shən) *n.* **1** the act or process of indenting. **2** a notch, dent or incision, esp. in a margin. **3** a deep recess, esp. in a coastline. **4** a zigzag. **indented** *a.* notched, serrated, zigzag. **indenter, indentor** *n.* **indention** *n.* **1** (*Print.*) the setting in of a line of print farther from the margin; indentation. **2** an instance of this. [low L *indentāre*, to notch or cut into like teeth (*dens dentis*, tooth)]

indent[2] (in´dent) *n.* **1** an indented line of text. **2** an indentation or recess. **3** an official order for stores. **4** an order for goods, esp. one from abroad. **5** (*N Am.*) †an indented certificate for the principal or interest due on the public debt.

indent[3] (indent´) *v.t.* **1** to dent; to make a dent in. **2** to impress (a mark, dent etc.). ~*n.* a dent.

indenture (inden´chə) *n.* **1** an agreement or contract under seal, esp. one binding an apprentice to a master. **2** a deed or contract drawn up in duplicate, each copy having their edges cut or indented exactly alike so as to correspond with each other. **3** an official voucher, certificate, register etc. **4** an indentation. ~*v.t.* (*Hist.*) to bind (esp. an apprentice) by an indenture. **indentureship** *n.*

independence (indipen´dəns) *n.* **1** the quality or state of being independent (from, of). **2** income sufficient to make one independent of others, a competency. **Independence Day** *n.* a day set apart for publicly celebrating the attainment of national independence, esp. 4 July in the US. **independency** *n.* (*pl.* **independencies**) **1** independence. **2** an independent state. **3** the principles of the Independents or Congregationalists. **independent** *a.* **1** **a** not dependent upon or subject to the control, power or authority of another. **b** free to manage one's own affairs without the interference of others. **2** **a** able to support oneself financially. **b** making it possible to live comfortably without having to work (*an independent income*). **3** confident and capable of acting by oneself. **4** unwilling to accept help from others. **5** not affiliated with or part of a larger organization. **6** not depending on anything for its value, cogency etc. **7** not funded by the state (*an independent school*). **8** of or relating to the Independents or Congregationalists. ~*n.* **1** a person who exercises their judgement and choice of action without dependence on any person, party etc. **2** (**Independent**) a Congregationalist. **independently** *adv.*

indescribable (indiskrī´bəbəl) *a.* **1** too fine, bad etc. to be described. **2** vague, imprecise. **indescribability** (-bil´-) *n.* **indescribably** *adv.*

indesignate (indez´ignət) *a.* (*Logic*) indefinite in quantity.

☒ **indespensable** common misspelling of INDISPENSABLE.

indestructible (indistrŭk´tibəl) *a.* incapable of being destroyed. **indestructibility** (-bil´-) *n.* **indestructibly** *adv.*

indeterminable (inditœ´minəbəl) *a.* **1** that cannot be determined or defined. **2** (of a dispute etc.) that cannot be terminated. **indeterminably** *adv.* [L *indēterminābilis*]

indeterminate (inditœ´minət) *a.* **1** not fixed or limited in scope, nature etc. **2** indefinite, not precise. **3** (*Math.*) having no fixed value. **indeterminacy** (-si), **indeterminateness** *n.* **indeterminately** *adv.* **indeterminate sentence** *n.* a prison sentence, the length of which is determined by the conduct of the convicted person. **indeterminate vowel** *n.* a vowel with an obscure or slurred sound, such as the *a* in *advice*; a schwa. [L *indēterminātus*]

indetermination (inditœminā´shən) *n.* **1** lack of determination, vacillation. **2** the state of being indeterminate. **indetermined** *a.* **1** not determined. **2** indefinite.

indeterminism (inditœ´minizm) *n.* the theory that conduct is not solely determined by motives, esp. that the will is able to choose between motives. **indeterminist** *n.* **indeterministic** (-nis´-) *a.*

index (in´deks) *n.* (*pl.* **indexes, indices** (-disēz)) **1** a list of names, subjects, places etc. in alphabetical order, with page references, usu. at the back of a book. **2** CARD INDEX (under CARD[1]). **3** THUMB INDEX (under THUMB). **4** a numerical scale indicating variations in the cost of living, wages etc., by reference to a given base level. **5** (*Math.*) an exponent (indicating powers of multiplication). **6** a number expressing a ratio or property (*cranial, refractive index*). **7** a pointer on a dial, watch etc. **8** a sign, token or indicator. **9** (*Comput.*) a value that identifies an element in a set of data. **10** (**Index**) a list of books prohibited by the Roman Catholic Church. **11** a printed symbol in the shape of a pointing hand, used to point to a note, paragraph etc. ~*v.t.* **1** to provide (a book) with an index. **2** to enter (a word etc.) in an index. **3** to relate (interest rates, wages etc.) to an index. **indexation** (-sā´shən) *n.* the act of linking wages, rates of interest etc. to the cost of living index. **indexer** *n.* **Index Expurgatorius** (ikspœgətaw´riəs) *n.* (*Hist.*) in the Roman Catholic Church, a list of passages from books, condemned to be expunged as heretical. **index finger** *n.* the forefinger. **indexible** (in´deks-, -dek´-) *a.* **indexical** (-dek´-) *a.* **indexless** *a.* **Index Librorum Expurgandorum** (libraw´rəm ekspœgandaw´rəm) *n.* (*Hist.*) in the Roman Catholic Church, a list of books to be read in expurgated editions only. **Index Librorum Prohibitorum** (prōhibitaw´rəm) *n.* (*Hist.*) a list of books prohibited by the Roman Catholic Church. **index-linked** *a.* (of wages, pensions etc.) increasing or decreasing in direct relation to changes in an index, esp. the cost of living index. **index-linking** *n.* **index number** *n.* an indicator of the relative change in the price or value of something by reference to an earlier period, usu. given the number 100. **index of refraction** *n.* REFRACTIVE INDEX (under REFRACT). [L *index -dicis*, a forefinger, an informer (*indicāre*, to INDICATE)]

Indian *a.* **1** of or relating to India or the Indian subcontinent (India, Pakistan and Bangladesh). **2** of or relating to the aboriginal inhabitants of America. ~*n.* **1** a native or inhabitant of India. **2** an American Indian.

3 any of the languages spoken by the aboriginal peoples of America. **India ink** *n.* (*esp. NAm.*) INDIAN INK (under INDIAN). **Indiaman** *n.* (*pl.* **Indiamen**) (*Hist.*) a large ship employed in trade with India or the East Indies. **Indian berry** *n.* the dried fruit of the climbing shrub *Anamirta cocculus*. **Indian club** *n.* either of two bottle-shaped clubs used in gymnastic exercises to develop the arm muscles. **Indian corn** *n.* maize. **Indian elephant** *n.* the elephant, *Elephas maximus*, that lives in India and SE Asia and is smaller than the African elephant. **Indian file** *n.* single file. **Indian hemp** *n.* the plant *Cannabis sativa*. **Indian ink** *n.* **1** a black pigment, composed of lamp black and animal glue, orig. made in China and Japan. **2** a black liquid ink made from this. **Indian meal** *n.* meal made from maize. **Indian rope-trick** *n.* the supposed Indian feat of climbing an unsupported rope. **Indian sign** *n.* a magic spell, esp. one designed to bring bad luck to somebody. **Indian summer** *n.* **1** summer-like weather, occurring in late autumn. **2** a time of calm or of renewed success or activity towards the end of a particular period, e.g. the end of a person's life. **India paper** *n.* **1** a fine paper, originally imported from China, used by engravers for taking proofs. **2** a very thin tough opaque paper, used esp. for printing Bibles. **India rubber** *n.* a soft, elastic substance obtained from the coagulated juice of certain tropical plants; rubber.

Usage note See note on *Native American* under AMERICAN.

Indic (in´dik) *a.* **1** originating or existing in India. **2** of or relating to the Indian branch of the Indo-European languages. ~*n.* this group of languages. [L and Gr., from *Indos*, the Indus, Pers. *hind*, Sansk. *sindhu*, river]

indic. *abbr.* indicative.

indican (in´dikən) *n.* **1** the natural glucoside contained in the indigo plant and from which indigo is obtained. **2** a normal constituent of urine. [L *indicum*, INDIGO, -AN]

indicant (in´dikənt) *n.* something which indicates.

indicate (in´dikāt) *v.t.* **1** to show, to point out. **2** to be a sign or token of. **3** (*usu. pass.*) to require; to call for. **4** to state briefly, to suggest. **5** (of an instrument) to show a reading of. ~*v.i.* to show which way one is going to turn using an indicator. **indication** (-ā´shən) *n.* **1** the act of indicating. **2** something which indicates or suggests. **3** **a** something that is indicated as advisable or suitable. **b** a symptom suggesting certain treatment. **4** a reading shown by a gauge etc. **indicative** (-dik´ə-) *a.* **1** serving as a sign or indication (of); suggestive (of). **2** (*Gram.*) (of a mood of verbs) expressing fact. ~*n.* **1** the indicative mood. **2** a verb in this mood. **indicatively** *adv.* **indicator** *n.* **1** a person who or something which indicates. **2** (*Chem.*) a reagent used to indicate, by change of colour, the presence of an acid, alkali etc. **3** an instrument attached to apparatus, machinery, a vehicle etc., to indicate or record pressure, speed, number etc. **4** a device for indicating the times of departure etc. of trains. **5** a device, esp. a flashing light, on a vehicle to show an intention to change direction. **6** a statistic such as the level of industrial production that indicates the condition of a national economy. **7** (*Med.*) a tracer. **8** (*Biol.*) a species whose presence indicates particular environmental conditions. **indicatory** (indik´ətəri, in´dikātəri) *a.* [L *indicātus*, p.p. of *indicāre* (*dicāre*, to point out)]

indices INDEX.

indicia (indish´iə, -siə) *n.pl.* **1** distinguishing marks. **2** indications. **indicial** *a.* [L, pl. of *indicium* (see INDEX)]

indict (indīt´) *v.t.* to charge (a person) with a crime or misdemeanour, esp. by means of an indictment. **indictable** *a.* **1** (of a person) liable to be indicted. **2** (of an offence) forming a ground of indictment. **indictee** (-tē´) *n.* a person indicted. **indicter** *n.* **indictment** *n.* **1** the act of indicting. **2** a formal accusation of a crime or misdemeanour, presented upon oath by the grand jury to a court. **3** the document embodying this. **4** (*Sc. Law*) a process by which a criminal is brought to trial at the instance of the Lord Advocate. **5** something that provides a reason for condemnation (*a damning indictment of government policy*). [OF *enditer*, INDITE]

indiction (indik´shən) *n.* **1** a period of 15 years arbitrarily fixed by Constantine the Great as a fiscal arrangement, beginning 1 Sept. 312, adopted by the Popes as part of their chronological system. **2** a land tax imposed by the Roman emperors at the beginning of each of these periods. **3** a year bearing a number showing its place in one of these cycles. [through F or directly from L *indictio -ōnem*, from *indīcere*, to appoint (*dīcere*, to say)]

indie (in´di) *a.* (*coll.*) (of pop music) produced by a small independent record company. ~*n.* **1** an independent record company. **2** an independent film company.

Indies (in´diz) *n.pl.* **1** †India and the neighbouring regions. **2** the West Indies. **3** the East Indies. [pl. of obs. *Indie*, India]

indifferent (indif´rənt) *a.* **1** unconcerned, apathetic (*They were indifferent to our plight*). **2** having no inclination or disinclination (to); impartial. **3** neither good nor bad. **4** of no importance, of little moment (to). **5** of a barely passable quality, not good. **6** chemically neutral, not active. **indifference** *n.* **1** lack of interest or attention (to or towards). **2** impartiality, neutrality. **3** unimportance, insignificance. **indifferentism** *n.* systematic indifference, esp. with regard to religious belief. **indifferentist** *n.* **indifferently** *adv.* [F, from L *indifferentem*, nom. *-ens*]

indigenous (indij´ənəs) *a.* **1** **a** (of plants and animals) naturally existing in a region, not exotic. **b** (of people) not immigrant or descended from immigrants, native. **2** natural, innate (to). **indigene** (in´dijēn) *n.* **indigenize** (indij´ənīz), **indigenise** *v.t.* **1** to expose to native influence; to make indigenous. **2** to subject to an increase in the number of indigenous people in administration etc. **indigenization** (-zā´shən) *n.* **indigenously** *adv.* [L *indigenus* (*indi-*, *indu-*, IN-[1], *gen-*, root of *gignere*, to produce)]

indigent (in´dijənt) *a.* in want, poor, needy. **indigence** *n.* **indigently** *adv.* [F, from L *indigentem*, nom. *-gens* (*indi-*, as IN-[1], *egēre*, to be in want, to be in need)]

indigest (indijest´) *a.* shapeless. ~*n.* a shapeless mass. **indigested** *a.* **1** not well formed or ordered. **2** shapeless. **3** not digested. **indigestible** *a.* **1** not easily digested. **2** hard to understand or to follow. **indigestibility** (-bil´-) *n.* **indigestibly** *adv.* **indigestion** (-chən) *n.* **1** difficulty in digesting food, dyspepsia. **2** pain and belching caused by this. **indigestive** *a.* [L *indīgestus* (*dīgestus*, p.p. of *dīgerere*, to DIGEST[1])]

indignant (indig´nənt) *a.* feeling or showing indignation, esp. at meanness, injustice etc. **indignantly** *adv.* **indignation** (-nā´shən) *n.* a feeling of anger and scorn provoked by supposed injustice or unfairness. [L *indignans -antem*, pres.p. of *indignārī*]

indignity (indig´niti) *n.* (*pl.* **indignities**) **1** undeserved contemptuous treatment; humiliation. **2** a slight, an insult.

indigo (in´digō) *n.* (*pl.* **indigos, indigoes**) **1** **a** a violet-blue dye obtained from the indigo plant. **b** a dye of this colour produced synthetically. **2** a plant of the genus *Indigofera*, esp. *I. tinctoria*. **3** (*also* **indigo blue**) a violet-blue colour. ~*a.* (*also* **indigo blue**) of a violet-blue colour. **native indigo** NATIVE. **indigo bird** *n.* a North American finch, *Passerina cyanea*, the male of which is blue. **indigotic** (-got´-) *a.* [formerly *indico*, Sp., from L *indicum*, Gr. *indikon*, Indian]

indirect (indirekt´, -dī-) *a.* **1** not direct, deviating from a direct line. **2** not resulting directly or immediately from a cause (*an indirect consequence*). **3** avoiding direct reference to something. **4** not open or straightforward. **5** (*Gram.*) not as spoken, in reported form. **indirectly** *adv.* **indirectness** *n.* **indirect object** *n.* (*Gram.*) a person or thing indirectly affected by an action, e.g. *them* in *She bought them some flowers.* **indirect question** *n.* (*Gram.*) a question that is reported rather than expressed in direct speech, as in *She asked me where I lived.* **indirect speech** *n.* the reporting of spoken or written discourse by indicating what was meant rather than by repetition of the exact words, as in *He said he would be late.* **indirect tax** *n.* a tax levied on goods and services rather than on a person's income or a company's profits. [F, from L *indīrectus*]

indiscernible (indisœ´nibəl) *a.* not discernible, not distinguishable. **indiscernibility** (-bil´-), **indiscernibleness** *n.* **indiscernibly** *adv.*

indiscipline (indis´iplin) *n.* lack of discipline.

indiscreet (indiskrēt´) *a.* **1** not discreet. **2** injudicious, incautious, rash. **indiscreetly** *adv.* **indiscreetness** *n.* indiscretion. **indiscretion** (-kresh´ən) *n.* **1** lack of discretion. **2** imprudence, rashness. **3** an indiscreet act. [L *indiscrētus*]

Usage note The spellings of the adjectives *indiscreet* (not circumspect) and *indiscrete* (not distinct) should not be confused.

indiscrete (indiskrēt´) *a.* not discrete or separated.

Usage note See note under INDISCREET.

indiscriminate (indiskrim´inət) *a.* **1** not discriminating or making distinctions. **2** confused, promiscuous. **indiscriminately** *adv.* **indiscriminateness, indiscrimination** (-ā´shən) *n.* **indiscriminative** *a.*

indispensable (indispen´səbəl) *a.* **1** that cannot be dispensed with; absolutely necessary or requisite. **2** (of a law, duty etc.) that cannot be disregarded or set aside. **indispensability** (-bil´-), **indispensableness** *n.* **indispensably** *adv.* [med. L *indispensābilis*]

indispose (indispōz´) *v.t.* **1** to make disinclined or unfavourable (to or towards). **2** to render unfit or unable (for or to). **indisposed** *a.* **1** disinclined, unwilling. **2** slightly ill. **indisposition** (-pəzish´ən) *n.* **1** disinclination, aversion. **2** aversion. **3** a slight illness.

indisputable (indispū´təbəl) *a.* **1** that cannot be disputed or doubted. **2** not open to question. **indisputability** (-bil´-), **indisputableness** *n.* **indisputably** *adv.*

indissociable (indisō´shəbəl) *a.* not to be separated or disassociated.

indissoluble (indisol´ūbəl) *a.* **1** that cannot be dissolved or disintegrated. **2** (of a bond etc.) stable and binding. **indissolubilist** *n.* in the Church of England, a person who believes that divorcees should not be allowed to remarry in church. ~*a.* of or having this belief. **indissolubility** (-bil´-), **indissolubleness** *n.* **indissolubly** *adv.* [F, from L *indissolūbilis*]

indistinct (indistingkt´) *a.* **1** not distinct, obscure. **2** confused, faint. **indistinctive** *a.* not distinctive. **indistinctively** *adv.* **indistinctiveness** *n.* **indistinctly** *adv.* **indistinctness** *n.* [F, from L *indistinctus*]

indistinguishable (indisting´gwishəbəl) *a.* not distinguishable (from). **indistinguishableness** *n.* **indistinguishably** *adv.*

indite (indīt´) *v.t.* **1** (*formal or facet.*) to put into words, to compose. **2** (*formal or facet.*) to write. **3** to dictate. **inditement** *n.* **inditer** *n.* [OF *enditer*, late L *indictāre* (*dictāre*, to DICTATE[1])]

indium (in´diəm) *n.* a soft, silver-white metallic element, at. no. 49, chem. symbol In, occurring in minute quantities in zinc ores. [L *ind-icum*, see INDIGO]

individual (individ´ūəl) *a.* **1** subsisting as a single indivisible entity. **2** single, particular as opposed to general. **3** separate or distinct. **4** characteristic of a particular person or thing, distinctive. **5** designed for one person. **6** †indivisible. ~*n.* **1** a single person, esp. when regarded as distinct or separate from a group. **2** a single member of a species, class etc. **3** (*coll.*) a person. **individualism** *n.* **1** conduct or feeling centred in self, egoism. **2** an idiosyncrasy, a personal peculiarity. **3** an attitude, tendency or system in which each individual works for their own ends. **4** independent action as opposed to cooperation. **individualist** *n.* **individualistic** (-is´-) *a.* **individualistically** *adv.* **individuality** (-al´-) *n.* (*pl.* **individualities**) **1** separate or distinct existence. **2** distinctive character. **3** (*pl.*) individual preferences, tastes etc. **individualize, individualise** *v.t.* **1** to mark out or distinguish from other individuals. **2** to specify. **3** to package separately. **4** to make so as to suit the needs of a particular person. **individualization** (-zā´shən) *n.* **individually** *adv.* **1** separately. **2** in an individual capacity. **3** in an individual manner. **individuate** (individ´ūāt) *v.t.* **1** to give individuality to. **2** to make an individual or a distinct entity. **individuation** (-ā´shən) *n.* [med. L *indīviduālis*, from *indīviduus*, indivisible (*dīvidere*, to DIVIDE)]

indivisible (indiviz´ibəl) *a.* **1** not divisible. **2** that cannot be exactly divided. **indivisibility** (-bil´-) *n.* **indivisibly** *adv.* [F, from L *indīvisibilis*]

Indo- (in´dō) *comb. form* Indian. [INDIAN]

Indo-Aryan (indōeə´riən) *a.* of or relating to the Aryan peoples of India or the Indic languages. ~*n.* **1** a member of any of the Indo-Aryan peoples. **2** the Indic languages.

Indo-Chinese (indōchīnēz´) *a.* of or relating to Indo-China, its people or their languages. ~*n.* (*pl.* **Indo-Chinese**) **1** a native or inhabitant of Indo-China. **2** (*as pl.*) the people of Indo-China.

indocile (indō´sīl) *a.* not docile; unwilling to be instructed or disciplined. **indocility** (-sil´-) *n.* [F, from L *indocilis*]

indoctrinate (indok´trināt) *v.t.* **1** to teach (someone) to accept, esp. without questioning, a set of beliefs. **2** to instruct. **indoctrination** (-ā´shən) *n.* **indoctrinator** *n.*

Indo-European (indōūrəpē´ən), †**Indo-Germanic** *a.* **1** of or relating to the family of languages spoken over most of Europe and over Asia as far as northern India. **2** of or relating to the hypothetical language from which this family originates. ~*n.* **1** the Indo-European language family. **2** the hypothetical language from which the languages of this family originate. **3** (*usu. pl.*) a speaker of an Indo-European language.

Indo-Iranian (indōirā´niən, -rah´-) *a.* of or relating to the Indic and Iranian languages, constituting a subfamily of Indo-European. ~*n.* this subfamily of languages.

indole (in´dōl) *n.* a white or yellowish crystalline heterocyclic compound derived from coal tar. [INDIGO, -OLE]

indoleacetic acid (indōləsē´tik asid, -set´ik) *n.* a natural growth hormone in plants. [INDOLE, ACETIC]

indolent (in´dələnt) *a.* **1** habitually idle or lazy. **2** (*Med.*) causing no pain. **indolence** *n.* **indolently** *adv.* **indolent tumour** *n.* a tumour causing no pain. [late L *indolens -entem*]

Indology (indol´əji) *n.* the study of Indian history, philosophy, literature etc. **Indologist** *n.*

indomitable (indom´itəbəl) *a.* **1** untamable, unconquerable. **2** stubbornly determined. **indomitability** (-bil´-), **indomitableness** *n.* **indomitably** *adv.* [late L *indomitābilis* (*domitāre*, to tame)]

Indonesian (indənē´zhən) *a.* of or relating to Indonesia, its people or language. ~*n.* **1** a native or inhabitant of Indonesia. **2 a** BAHASA INDONESIA. **b** the western branch of the Austronesian family of languages. **3** a member of the main pre-Malay population of the Malay archipelago and surrounding islands. [Gr. *nesos*, an island]

indoor (in´daw) *a.* being or done inside a building or under cover. **indoors** (-dawz´) *adv.* into or within a house or other building.

indorse ENDORSE.

indraught (in´drahft), (*N Am.*) **indraft** *n.* **1** the act of drawing in. **2** an inward flow, draught or current.

indrawn (in´drawn) *a.* **1** drawn in. **2** detached and aloof.

indri (in´dri), **indris** (-dris) *n.* (*pl.* **indris**) a Madagascan lemur, *Indri indri.* [Malagasy *indry*, look! (mistaken for the name)]

indubitable (indū´bitəbəl) *a.* that cannot be doubted or questioned. **indubitability** (-bil´-), **indubitableness** *n.* **indubitably** *adv.* [F, from L *indubitābilis*]

induce (indūs´) *v.t.* **1** to lead by persuasion or reasoning, to prevail on (to do something). **2** to bring about, to cause. **3** (*Med.*) to bring on or speed up (labour) by artificial means, as by the use of drugs. **4** to produce (an electric current) by induction. **5** (*Physics*) to produce (radioactivity) by bombardment with neutrons or high-energy particles. **6** (*Logic*) to derive as a deduction, to infer. **inducement** *n.* **1** the act of inducing. **2** something which induces. **3** a motive, a reason, an incitement (to). **4** (*Law*) a preamble or statement of facts introducing other material facts. **inducer** *n.* **inducible** *a.* [L *indūcere* (*dūcere*, to lead), p.p. *inductus*]

induct (indŭkt´) *v.t.* **1** to put in possession of an ecclesiastical benefice or of any office, with the customary forms and ceremonies. **2** to initiate (into). **3** (*N Am.*) to enlist for military service. **4** †to lead (to a place, seat etc.). **inductance** *n.* the property of an electric circuit that causes an electromotive force to be generated by a change in the current passing through it. **inductee** (-tē´). *n.* (*N Am.*) a military conscript. **induction** (indŭk´shən) *n.* **1** (*Logic*) **a** the process of adducing facts to prove a general statement. **b** the process of inferring a law or general principle from particular instances, as distinct from *deduction.* **c** a general statement or conclusion attained by this kind of reasoning. **2** (*Math.*) the proving of the universal truth of a theorem by showing it to be true of any case in a series or of a particular case. **3 a** the production of an electric or magnetic state by the proximity or movement of an electric or magnetized body. **b** the production of an electric current in a conductor by changes in the magnetic field. **4** a formal introduction to or instalment in an office or position (*an induction course*). **5** (*N Am.*) enlistment for military training. **6** †a beginning, a prelude. **inductional** *a.* **induction coil** *n.* an apparatus for producing a high voltage from a low voltage. **induction heating** *n.* the heating of a conductive material as a result of an induced electric current passing through it. **induction loop** *n.* a sound system in which a wire looped around an area in a theatre, cinema etc. emits electromagnetic signals which can be picked up by hearing aids for the partially deaf. **induction motor** *n.* an electric motor in which an electromagnetic flux is set up by currents in a primary winding, which induces currents in a secondary winding, such that interaction of currents with flux produces rotation. **inductive** *a.* **1** (*Logic*) proceeding or characterized by induction. **2** of or relating to electric or magnetic induction. **3** serving to induce or draw on. **4** introductory, beginning. **inductively** *adv.* **inductiveness** *n.* **inductor** (indŭk´tə) *n.* **1** any part of an electrical apparatus acting inductively. **2** a person who inducts a member of the clergy into office. [L *inductus*, see INDUCE]

inductile (indŭk´tīl) *a.* not ductile. **inductility** (-til´-) *n.*

indue ENDUE.

indulge (indŭlj´) *v.t.* **1** to yield to (a desire, whim etc.). **2** to favour; to gratify the wishes, whims etc. of. *~v.i.* **1** to yield to one's desires (in). **2** (*coll.*) to take alcoholic drink, esp. in excess. **indulgence** (indŭl´jəns) *n.* **1** the act or practice of indulging, yielding or complying to a desire etc. **2** an indulgent act, a favour or privilege granted. **3** a pleasurable thing or habit indulged in. **4** in the Roman Catholic Church, a remission of the temporal punishment still due for sin after sacramental absolution. **indulgent** *a.* indulging or disposed to indulge the wishes, whims or caprices of others. **indulgently** *adv.* [L *indulgēre*]

induline (in´dūlīn), **indulin** (-lin) *a.* any one of a series of blue, blue-black and grey dyestuffs related to aniline. [*ind-icum*, see INDIGO, *-ul-*, dim. suf., -INE]

indult (indŭlt´) *n.* a license or privilege granted by the Pope, or authorizing something not normally permitted by the Church's common law. [F, from L *indultum*, p.p. of *indulgēre*, to INDULGE]

indumentum (indūmen´təm) *n.* (*pl.* **indumenta** (-tə)) a covering of hairs on a plant or leaf. [L, garment]

induna (indoo´nə) *n.* (*S Afr.*) **1** a leader or tribal councillor, esp. of an impi. **2** an African overseer or foreman. [Zulu *nduna*, a person in authority]

induplicate (indū´plikət), **induplicated** (-ā´tid) *a.* (of leaves and flowers in bud) having the edges folded in.

indurate (in´dūrāt) *v.t.* **1** to make hard, to harden. **2** to make obdurate or unfeeling. *~v.i.* **1** to become hard. **2** (of a habit etc.) to become fixed or inveterate. *~a.* **1** hardened. **2** obstinate, callous. **induration** (-rā´shən) *n.* insensibility. **indurative** *a.* [L *indurātus*, p.p. of *indūrāre* (*durāre*, to make hard)]

indusium (indū´ziəm) *n.* (*pl.* **indusia** (-ziə)) **1** a membranous covering that protects the developing spores of a fern. **2** a cluster of hairs that enclose the stigma of some flowers. **3** a larva case. **indusial** *a.* [L, tunic, from *induere*, to put on]

industry (in´dəstri) *n.* (*pl.* **industries**) **1** useful work, esp. mechanical and manufacturing pursuits as distinct from agriculture and commerce. **2** any branch of these. **3** diligence, steady application to any business or pursuit. **4** the employment of labour in production. **5** any field of activity as organized for economic gain. **industrial** (indŭs´triəl) *a.* **1** of or relating to industry. **2** (of a country) characterized by advanced and sophisticated industries. **3** used in industry (*industrial detergents*). *~n.* (*pl.*) shares in industrial enterprises. **industrial action** *n.* action, esp. a strike or go-slow, taken by employees as a protest. **industrial archaeology** *n.* the study of the remains of past industrial activity. **industrial espionage** *n.* attempting to obtain trade secrets by dishonest means. **industrial estate** *n.* an industrial area specially planned to provide employment in factories of different kinds. **industrialism** *n.* an economic or social system based on industry. **industrialist** *n.* a person engaged in management or ownership of industry. **industrialize, industrialise** *v.t.* to introduce industry to (a country or region). *~v.i.* to develop industries. **industrialization** (-zā´shən) *n.* **industrially** *adv.* **industrial park** *n.* (*N Am.*) INDUSTRIAL ESTATE (under INDUSTRY). **industrial relations** *n.pl.* the relations between employer and employees in industries. **Industrial Revolution** *n.* the changes brought about in the way of life by the rapid industrialization of a nation, esp. of Britain after about 1760. **industrial-strength** *a.* (*often facet.*) strong. **industrial tribunal** *n.* a tribunal which makes judgements on disputes between employers and employees regarding unfair dismissal, discrimination etc. **industrial union** *n.* a labour union for all workers in a particular industry. **industrious** (indŭs´triəs) *a.* diligent and assiduous. **industriously** *adv.* **industriousness** *n.* [F *industrie*, L *industria* (prob. *indu*, in, in, *struere*, see CONSTRUCT[1])]

indwell (indwel´) *v.t.* (*past, p.p.* **indwelt** (-dwelt´)) (of a spirit, principle etc.) to abide in or inhabit. *~v.i.* to dwell (in the soul etc.). **indweller** *n.* **indwelling** *a.* **1** that indwells. **2** (*Med.*) (of a catheter etc.) remaining in the body over a long period of time.

Indy (in´di) *n.* a kind of motor racing, practised chiefly in the US, in which cars race at very high speeds around oval circuits. **Indycar** *n.* a car used in Indy racing. [from *Indianapolis* in the US]

-ine (īn, in, ēn) *suf.* **1** forming adjectives meaning of or relating to or of the nature of, as *crystalline, divine, equine, hyacinthine, marine.* **2** forming feminine nouns, as *heroine, landgravine,* and abstract nouns, as *discipline, medicine.* **3** (*Chem.*) forming names of alkaloids and basic substances, as *cocaine, morphine.* [L *-īnus, īnus*; or from F *-ine*, L *īna*]

inebriate[1] (inē´briāt) *v.t.* **1** to make drunk. **2** to intoxicate or exhilarate. **inebriation** (-ā´shən) *n.* **inebriety** (-brī´-) *n.*

inebriate[2] (inē´briət) *a.* intoxicated, drunk. ~*n.* a habitual drunkard.

inedible (ined´ibəl) *a.* not edible; not suitable for eating. **inedibility** (-bil´-) *n.*

inedited (ined´itəd) *a.* **1** not edited. **2** not published.

ineducable (ined´ūkəbəl) *a.* incapable of being educated, esp. because of mental handicap. **ineducability** (-bil´-) *n.*

ineffable (inef´əbəl) *a.* **1** unutterable, beyond expression. **2** too sacred to be spoken. **ineffability** (-bil´-), **ineffableness** *n.* **ineffably** *adv.* [F, from L *ineffābilis* (*effārī*, EF-, *fārī*, to speak)]

ineffaceable (inifā´səbəl) *a.* that cannot be rubbed out or obliterated. **ineffaceability** (-bil´-) *n.* **ineffaceably** *adv.*

ineffective (inifek´tiv) *a.* **1** not having an effect. **2** (of a person) inefficient. **3** not having artistic effect. **ineffectively** *adv.* **ineffectiveness** *n.*

ineffectual (inifek´chuəl) *a.* **1** not producing any effect or the desired effect; powerless. **2** (of a person) not able to achieve results, ineffective. **ineffectuality** (-al´-), **ineffectualness** *n.* **ineffectually** *adv.*

inefficacious (inefikā´shəs) *a.* not efficacious; producing no result or effect. **inefficaciously** *adv.* **inefficaciousness** *n.* **inefficacy** (-ef´-) *n.*

inefficient (inifish´ənt) *a.* **1** not efficient. **2** (of a person) lacking in ability or capacity. **inefficiency** *n.* **inefficiently** *adv.*

inelastic (inilas´tik) *a.* **1** not elastic. **2** inflexible. **3** (*Physics*) (of a collision) in which there is an overall decrease in translational kinetic energy. **inelastically** *adv.* **inelasticity** (-ēlastis´-) *n.*

inelegant (inel´igənt) *a.* not elegant; wanting in grace, polish, refinement etc. **inelegance, inelegancy** *n.* **inelegantly** *adv.* [F *inélégant*, L *inelēgantem*, nom. *-gans*]

ineligible (inel´ijibəl) *a.* **1** not eligible. **2** not suitable. **ineligibility** (-bil´-) *n.* **ineligibly** *adv.*

ineluctable (inilŭk´təbəl) *a.* **1** that cannot be escaped. **2** that cannot be overcome by struggling. [L *inēluctābilis* (*ēluctāri*, E-, *luctārī*, to struggle)]

inept (inept´) *a.* **1** clumsy, incompetent. **2** silly, absurd. **3** not apt, fit or suitable. **ineptitude** (-titūd), **ineptness** *n.* **ineptly** *adv.* [L *ineptus* (*aptus*, APT)]

Usage note The meanings of the adjectives *inept* and *inapt* overlap: both can mean unsuitable, but the more common sense of *inept* is clumsy, and it is best to restrict it to that use.

inequable (inek´wəbəl) *n.* **1** unfair. **2** not uniform.

inequality (inikwol´iti) *n.* (*pl.* **inequalities**) **1** a lack of equality. **2** variability. **3** irregularity, unevenness. **4** (*Math.*) a formula stating that two expressions are not equal. **5** (*Astron.*) deviation from uniformity of motion in a heavenly body. [OF *inéqualité* (F *inégalité*), L *inaequālitas*]

inequitable (inek´witəbəl) *a.* not equitable, not fair or just. **inequitably** *adv.* **inequity** *n.* (*pl.* **inequities**) **1** lack of equity, unfairness; injustice. **2** an instance of this.

ineradicable (inirad´ikəbəl) *a.* that cannot be eradicated. **ineradicably** *adv.*

inerrable (iner´əbəl) *a.* infallible. **inerrability** (-bil´-), **inerrancy** *n.* **inerrably** *adv.* **inerrant** *a.* unerring. [L *inerrābilis* (*errāre*, to ERR)]

inert (inœt´) *a.* **1** lacking inherent power of motion or active resistance to motive power applied. **2** slow, sluggish. **3** (*Chem.*) not chemically reactive. **inert gas** *n.* any of a group of gaseous elements that react very little with other elements. **inertia** (-shə) *n.* **1** reluctance to move or act. **2** a tendency to continue unchanged. **3** a property of matter by which it persists in an existing state of rest or of uniform motion in a straight line, unless an external force changes that state. **inertial** *a.* **inertial guidance, inertial navigation** *n.* a system of guidance for missiles, in which instruments contained in the missile measure its acceleration and compare its calculated speed and direction with stored data. **inertialness** *n.* **inertia-reel seat belt** *n.* a type of vehicle seat belt in which the belt unwinds freely except when violent deceleration of the vehicle causes it to lock. **inertia selling** *n.* the practice of sending unsolicited goods to householders and requesting payment if the goods are not returned. **inertly** *adv.* **inertness** *n.* [L *iners -ertem* (*ars*, ART[1])]

inescapable (iniskā´pəbəl) *a.* inevitable, that cannot be escaped or avoided.

inescutcheon (iniskŭch´ən) *n.* (*Her.*) a small escutcheon borne within a shield.

inessential (inisen´shəl) *a.* **1** not essential or necessary. **2** dispensable. ~*n.* (*often pl.*) something that is inessential.

inestimable (ines´timəbəl) *a.* too valuable, great, excellent etc. to be estimated. **inestimably** *adv.* [F, from L *inaestimābilis*]

inevitable (inev´itəbəl) *a.* **1** that cannot be avoided or prevented. **2** that is sure to happen or predictable (*the inevitable car-chase scene*). **3** (*coll.*) customary. **inevitability** (-bil´-), **inevitableness** *n.* **inevitably** *adv.* [L *inēvītābilis* (*ēvītāre*, to avoid)]

inexact (inigzakt´) *a.* not exact, not precisely accurate. **inexactitude** (-titūd), **inexactness** *n.* **inexactly** *adv.*

inexcusable (inikskū´zəbəl) *a.* that cannot be excused or justified. **inexcusability** (-bil´-), **inexcusableness** *n.* **inexcusably** *adv.* [F, from L *inexcūsābilis*]

inexhaustible (inigzaws´tibəl) *a.* **1** that cannot be exhausted. **2** unfailing, unceasing. **inexhaustibility** (-bil´-), **inexhaustibleness** *n.* **inexhaustibly** *adv.*

inexistent (inigzis´tənt) *a.* not existing, non-existent. **inexistence** *n.*

inexorable (inek´sərəbəl) *a.* **1** relentless. **2** incapable of being persuaded or moved by entreaty or prayer. **inexorability** (-bil´-) *n.* **inexorably** *adv.* [F, from L *inexōrābilis* (*ōrāre*, to pray)]

inexpedient (inikspē´diənt) *a.* not expedient; inadvisable, disadvantageous. **inexpedience, inexpediency** *n.* **inexpediently** *adv.*

inexpensive (inikspen´siv) *a.* not expensive, cheap. **inexpensively** *adv.* **inexpensiveness** *n.*

inexperience (inikspiə´riəns) *n.* lack of experience or of knowledge gained by experience. **inexperienced** *a.* [F *inexpérience*, L *inexperientia*]

inexpert (inek´spœt) *a.* not expert, unskilful. **inexpertly** *adv.* **inexpertness** *n.* [OF, from L *inexpertus*]

inexpiable (inek´spiəbəl) *a.* **1** that cannot be expiated or atoned for. **2** implacable. **inexpiably** *adv.* [L *inexpiābilis*]

inexplicable (iniksplik´əbəl, -ek´-) *a.* that cannot be explained. **inexplicability** (-bil´-), **inexplicableness** *n.* **inexplicably** *adv.* [F, from L *inexplicābilis*]

inexplicit (iniksplis´it) *a.* not definitely or clearly stated. **inexplicitly** *adv.* **inexplicitness** *n.*

inexpressible (inikspres´ibəl) *a.* incapable of being expressed or described. **inexpressibly** *adv.* **inexpressive** *a.* not expressive. **inexpressively** *adv.* **inexpressiveness** *n.*

inexpugnable (inikspŭg´nəbəl) *a.* impregnable. **inexpugnably** *adv.* [F, from L *inexpugnābilis*]

inexpungible (inikspŭn´jibəl) *a.* that cannot be expunged.

in extenso (in eksten´sō) *adv.* at full length. [L]

inextinguishable (iniksting´gwishəbəl) *a.* incapable of being extinguished, quenched or repressed. **inextinguishably** *adv.*

in extremis (in ikstrē´mis) *a.* **1** in desperate circumstances, in extremity. **2** at the point of death. [L]

inextricable (inek´strikəbəl, -strik´-) *a.* **1** that cannot be disentangled or solved. **2** inescapable. **3** intricately involved. **inextricability** (-bil´-) *n.* **inextricably** *adv.* [F, from L *inextricābilis*]

INF *abbr.* intermediate-range nuclear force.

inf. *abbr.* **1** infantry. **2** inferior. **3** infinitive. **4** informal. **5** infra.

infallible (infal´ibəl) *a.* **1** exempt from liability to error or to failure. **2** (of a test, method etc.) certain not to fail. **infallibilism** *n.* the doctrine of papal infallibility. **infallibility** (-bil´-) *n.* **infallibilist** *a., n.* **infallibleness** *n.* **infallibly** *adv.* [F, from med. L *infallibilis*]

infamous (in´fəməs) *a.* **1** having a very bad reputation. **2** detestable, scandalous. **3** (*Hist.*) deprived of certain citizens' rights as a result of having committed a serious crime. **infamize, infamise** *v.t.* to make infamous; to defame. **infamously** *adv.* **infamy** *n.* (*pl.* **infamies**) **1** total loss of reputation or character. **2** an infamous act. **3** loss of character or position attaching to a convict. [OF *infameux*, med. L *infamōsus*, L *infāmis*]

infant (in´fənt) *n.* **1** a child during the earliest years of its life. **2** a schoolchild less than seven years old. **3** (*Law*) a minor. **4** an infante or infanta. ~*a.* **1** in infancy. **2** of, relating to or designed for infants. **3** at an early stage of development. **infancy** (-si) *n.* (*pl.* **infancies**) **1** babyhood or early childhood. **2** an early stage in the development of something. **3** (*Law*) the state of being a minor. **infantile** (-tīl) *a.* **1** of or relating to infants or infancy. **2** characteristic of infancy, childish. **3** in its early stages of development. **infantile paralysis** *n.* poliomyelitis. **infantilism** (-fan´til-) *n.* **1** infantile behaviour. **2** (*Psych.*) the persistence into adulthood of infantile characteristics. **infantility** (-til´-) *n.* (*pl.* **infantilities**). **infant mortality** *n.* death before the age of one. [OF *enfant*, L *infantem*, nom. *-fans* (*fans*, pres.p. of *fārī*, to speak)]

infanta (infan´tə) *n.* in Spain and (formerly) Portugal, any royal princess (usu. the eldest) except an heiress apparent. **infante** (-tā) *n.* in Spain and (formerly) Portugal, any son of the monarch except the heir apparent. [Sp. and Port., as INFANT]

infanticide (infan´tisīd) *n.* **1** murder of a newborn infant. **2** the practice of killing newborn children. **3** the murderer of an infant. **infanticidal** (-sī´-) *a.* [late L *infanticīdium*]

infantry (in´fəntri) *n.* (*pl.* **infantries**) foot-soldiers, usu. armed with small arms or rifle and bayonet; a branch of an army made up of such soldiers. **infantryman** *n.* (*pl.* **infantrymen**) a soldier in an infantry regiment. [F *infanterie*, Ital. *infanteria*, from *infante*, a youth, a foot-soldier, as INFANT]

infarct (infahkt´, in´-) *n.* an area of tissue that is dying from lack of blood supply. **infarction** *n.* [med. L, *infarctus* (*farctus*, stuffed)]

infatuate (infat´ūāt) *v.t.* **1** to inspire with an extravagant and usu. transitory passion. **2** to affect with folly or extravagance. ~†*a.* affected with folly or infatuation. **infatuated** *a.* inspired with an extravagant passion, usu. for a person. **infatuatedly** *adv.* **infatuation** (-ā´shən) *n.* [L *infatuātus*, p.p. of *infatuāre* (*fatuus*, FATUOUS)]

infauna (infawn´ə) *n.* the animal life that exists in the sediments of the ocean floor and river beds. **infaunal** *a.* [Dan. *ifauna* (as IN-[1], FAUNA)]

infeasible (infē´zibəl) *a.* not feasible.

infect (infekt´) *v.t.* **1** to contaminate (water, food etc.) with a bacterium, virus etc., and so cause disease. **2** to affect (a person) with the germs of disease. **3** (of a feeling, mood) to affect and spread to. **4** to imbue with noxious opinions etc. **5** to taint with crime or illegality. **6** (*Comput.*) to affect with a computer virus. ~†*a.* infected. **infection** *n.* **1** the act or process of infecting, esp. the communication of disease by means of water, the atmosphere etc., as distinct from *contagion*. **2** an infectious disease. **3** moral contamination. **4** the act of diffusing or instilling (esp. bad qualities) by means of example etc. **5** (*Comput.*) the act of infecting with a computer virus. **infectious** *a.* **1** infecting or capable of infecting. **2** (of a disease) liable to be communicated by the atmosphere, water etc. **3** (of feelings etc.) apt to spread, catching. **infectiously** *adv.* **infectiousness** *n.* **infective** *a.* infectious. **infectiveness** *n.* **infectivity** (-tiv´-) *n.* **infector** *n.* [L *infectus*, p.p. of *inficere*, to taint (*facere*, to make)]

infecund (infē´kənd) *a.* not fecund; barren. **infecundity** (-kŭn´-) *n.* [L *infēcundus* (FECUND)]

infelicitous (infilis´itəs) *a.* **1** not felicitous; unfortunate. **2** inappropriate, inept. **infelicitously** *adv.* **infelicity** *n.* (*pl.* **infelicities**) **1** unhappiness, misery. **2** misfortune. **3** inappropriateness, ineptness. **4** an inappropriate or inept remark, expression etc. [FELICITOUS (under FELICITY)]

infer (infœ´) *v.t.* (*pres.p.* **inferring**, *past, p.p.* **inferred**) **1** to deduce as a fact, consequence or result; to conclude. **2** to imply. **3** †to bring in, to adduce. ~*v.i.* to draw inferences. **inferable, inferrable** *a.* **inference** (in´-) *n.* **1** the act of inferring. **2** something which is inferred from premisses, a conclusion or deduction. **inferential** (-ren´-) *a.* **inferentially** *adv.* [L *inferre* (*ferre*, to bear, to bring)]

Usage note It is best to avoid the use of *infer* to mean imply or suggest: although it has a long history, it is still widely disapproved of.

inferior (infiə´riə) *a.* **1** lower in place, rank, value, ability etc. **2** of mediocre or poor quality. **3** (*Astron.*) **a** within the earth's orbit. **b** below the horizon. **4** (*Bot.*) growing below the calyx or the ovary. **5** (of a printed character) set below ordinary letters or below the line, as the figures in H_2SO_4, subscript. ~*n.* **1** a person who is inferior to another in ability, rank etc. **2** an inferior figure or letter. **inferiority** (-or´-) *n.* **inferiority complex** *n.* a suppressed sense of inferiority which is sometimes compensated for by aggressive behaviour. **inferiorly** *adv.* [L, comp. of *inferus*, low, nether]

Usage note *Inferior* does not function as a true comparative in English, and should not be followed by *than* (the correct form is *inferior to*).

infernal (infœ´nəl) *a.* **1** of or relating to hell or the lower regions. **2** worthy of hell, hellish; diabolic. **3** (*coll.*) abominable, detestable. **infernally** *adv.* †**infernal machine** *n.* a usually disguised explosive machine employed for the purposes of assassination or wilful damage. **inferno** (-nō) *n.* (*pl.* **infernos**) **1** hell, esp. as conceived by Dante. **2** any place or state of horror and confusion. **3** a blaze or conflagration. [F, from L *infernālis*, from *infernus*, *inferus*, lower]

inferrable INFERABLE (under INFER).

infertile (infœ´tīl) *a.* not fertile; unfruitful. **infertility** (-til´-) *n.* [F, from late L *infertilis*]

infest (infest´) *v.t.* (of vermin, parasites) to overrun, to swarm over in large numbers. **infestation** (-tā´shən) *n.* **infester** *n.* [F *infester*, L *infestāre*, from *infestus*, hostile]

infeudation (infūdā´shən) *n.* **1** the granting of or putting in possession of an estate in fee. **2** the deed conferring this. **3** the granting of tithes to laymen. [med. L *infeudātio*, from *infeudāre* (*feudum*, FEUD²)]

infibulate (infib´ūlāt) *v.t.* to carry out infibulation on. **infibulation** (-lā´shən) *n.* the practice in some African cultures of partially joining together the labia, e.g. by stitching, often after excision of the clitoris, to prevent sexual intercourse. [L *infībulātus*, p.p. of *infībulāre* (*fībula*, a clasp)]

infidel (in´fidel) *a.* disbelieving in religion or a particular religion. ~*n.* **1** a person who rejects religion or a particular religion. **2** (*Hist.*) a person who followed a religion other than Christianity, esp. a Muslim. **infidelity** *n.* (*pl.* **infidelities**) **1** breach of trust, disloyalty, esp. unfaithfulness to the marriage vow. **2** an instance of this. **3** disbelief in a religion such as Christianity. [OF *infidele*, from L *infidēlis* (*fidēlis*)]

infield (in´fēld) *n.* **1 a** in cricket, the part of the field close to the wicket. **b** the cricketers fielding in this area. **2 a** in baseball, the ground within the base lines. **b** the players, other than the pitcher and catcher, who play in this area. **c** the positions of these players. **3** land near a farmhouse. **4** land manured and under tillage. **infielder** *n.* any one of the players in the infield.

infighting (in´fīting) *n.* **1** behind-the-scenes squabbling or jockeying for power within a group or organization. **2** fighting or boxing at close quarters, so that blows from the shoulder are impossible. **infighter** *n.*

infill (in´fil) *v.t.* to fill in. ~*n.* **1** (*also* **infilling**) **a** closing up gaps, esp. between houses. **b** material for filling in holes etc.

infiltrate (in´filtrāt), **infilter** (-fil´-) *v.t.* **1** to secretly gain or cause to gain access or entrance to. **2 a** to cause (a fluid) to pass into the pores or interstices of a solid. **b** to permeate (a solid) in this way. ~*v.i.* **1** to secretly gain or cause someone to gain access or entrance to an enemy organization etc. **2** to permeate or cause to permeate by infiltration. **infiltration** (-trā´shən) *n.* **infiltrator** *n.*

infin. *abbr.* infinitive.

infinite (in´finit) *a.* **1** having no bounds or limits, endless. **2** very great (*infinite patience*). **3** numerous, very many. **4** (*Gram.*) (of a verb part) not limited by person or number. **5** (*Math.*) greater than any assignable quantity. **6** (*Math.*) (of a series) having an unlimited number of digits, factors etc. ~*n.* **1** (**the Infinite**) God. **2** (**the infinite**) infinite space. **3** (*Math.*) an infinite quantity. **infinitely** *adv.* **infiniteness** *n.* **infinitesimal** (-tes´iməl) *a.* **1** infinitely or extremely small. **2** (*Math.*) (of a variable) having values approaching zero. ~*n.* an infinitesimal quantity. **infinitesimal calculus** *n.* differential and integral calculus. **infinitesimally** *adv.* **infinitude** (infin´itūd) *n.* **1** boundlessness. **2** an infinite quantity or amount (of). **infinity** (infin´iti) *n.* (*pl.* **infinities**) **1** the state of being infinite. **2** an infinite amount or distance. **3** (*Math.*) an indefinite number of. [L *infīnītus*]

infinitive (infin´itiv) *a.* (*Gram.*) **1** unlimited. **2** (of a verb) which expresses action without regard to person, tense etc., as *go* in *let me go* and *it's time to go*. ~*n.* **1** the infinitive form. **2** a verb in this form. **infinitival** (-tī´-) *a.* **infinitively, infinitivally** *adv.* [L *infīnītīvus*, as INFINITE]

infinitude, infinity INFINITE.

infirm (infœm´) *a.* **1** lacking bodily strength or health, esp. through age or disease. **2** weak-minded, irresolute. **3** uncertain, unstable. **infirmarian** (-meə´ri-) *n.* (*Hist.*) a person who was in charge of an infirmary in a religious order in the Middle Ages. **infirmary** (infœ´məri) *n.* (*pl.* **infirmaries**) a hospital or place for the sick or injured. **infirmity** *n.* (*pl.* **infirmities**). **infirmly** *adv.* [L *infirmus*]

infix¹ (infiks´) *v.t.* **1** to fasten or fix in. **2** to implant firmly (in the mind). **3** (*Gram.*) to insert (an infix) in a word.

infix² (in´fiks) *n.* (*Gram.*) a modifying element in the body of a word.

in flagrante (in fləgran´ti), **in flagrante delicto** (diliktō) *adv.* whilst actually committing the misdeed. [L]

inflame (inflām´) *v.t.* **1** to excite, to stir up strong feelings in (someone). **2** (*Med.*) to cause inflammation in; to make hot by exciting excessive action in the blood vessels and tissues. **3** to intensify, to aggravate. **4** to cause to blaze, to kindle. ~*v.i.* **1** to become excited or angry. **2** (*Med.*) to become inflamed. **3** to burst into a blaze. [OF *enflamber*, L *inflammāre* (*flammāre*, from *flamma*, FLAME)]

inflammable (inflam´əbəl) *a.* **1** that may be easily set on fire. **2** easily excited. ~*n.* (*usu. pl.*) something that catches fire easily. **inflammability** (-bil´-), **inflammableness** *n.* **inflammably** *adv.*

Usage note It is safer to use *flammable*, which avoids possible misunderstanding of *inflammable* as its exact opposite, not easily set on fire. The corresponding negative is *non-flammable*.

inflammation (infləmā´shən) *n.* **1** (*Med.*) an abnormal physical condition characterized by heat, redness, swelling, pain and loss of function in the part affected. **2** the act of inflaming or the state of being inflamed. **inflammatory** (-flam´-) *a.* **1** exciting or arousing passions. **2** of or characterized by inflammation of the body. [INFLAME]

inflate (inflāt´) *v.t.* **1** to cause (a balloon, mattress etc.) to expand by filling with air. **2** to make greater than normal or appropriate. **3** to raise (prices, reputation etc.) artificially or excessively. **inflatable** *a.* that can be inflated. ~*n.* **1** an inflatable toy, esp. an imitation castle etc. for children to jump or climb on. **2** anything inflatable. **inflatant** *n.* something which inflates (a balloon etc.). **inflated** *a.* **1** distended with air. **2** bombastic, turgid. **3** greater than normal or appropriate, exaggerated (*an inflated idea of one's own importance*). **4** expanded or raised artificially. **5** (*Bot.*) hollow and distended. **inflation** *n.* **1** the act of inflating, the state of being inflated. **2** a systematic increase in prices over time. **3** an increase in the money supply, regarded as causing this. **inflationary** *a.* **inflationism** *n.* **inflationist** *n., a.* [L *inflātus*, p.p. of *inflāre* (*flāre*, to blow)]

inflect (inflekt´) *v.t.* **1** to modulate (the voice). **2** (*Gram.*) to change the form, esp. the ending of a word in order to express gender, tense, mood etc. **3** to bend, to curve. **inflectedness** *n.* **inflection** (inflek´shən), **inflexion** *n.* **1** the act of inflecting or the state of being inflected; an instance of this. **2** modulation of the voice. **3** (*Gram.*) **a** the variation of the forms of nouns etc. in declension, and of verbs in conjugation. **b** an inflected form. **c** a suffix etc. added to a word to produce an inflected form, e.g. *s* or *ing*. **4** (*Geom.*) a change in curvature from concave to convex. **inflectional** *a.* **inflectionally** *adv.* **inflectionless** *a.* **inflective** *a.* **1** (*Gram.*) inflectional. **2** capable of bending. **inflector** *n.* **inflexed** (-flekst´) *a.* (*Biol.*) bent inwards. [L *inflectere* (*flectere*, to bend), p.p. *inflexus*]

inflexible (inflek´sibəl) *a.* **1** incapable of being bent or curved. **2** firm; obstinate. **3** unalterable; inexorable. **inflexibility** (-bil´-) *n.* **inflexibly** *adv.*

inflexion INFLECTION (under INFLECT).

inflict (inflikt´) *v.t.* **1** (*sometimes facet.*) to impose (suffering, a penalty, oneself) on. **2** to deal out (defeat, a blow, wound etc.). **3** †to afflict. **inflictable** *a.* **inflicter, inflictor** *n.* **infliction** *n.* **1** the act of inflicting. **2** a punishment inflicted. **3** a trouble, an annoyance.

inflictive *a.* [L *inflictus*, p.p. of *inflīgere* (*flīgere*, to dash)]

Usage note See note under AFFLICT.

inflorescence (inflәres´әns) *n.* **1** the flower head of a plant. **2** the arrangement of flowers upon a branch or stem. **3** the act or process of flowering. [F, from L *inflōrescens*, pres.p. of *inflōrēscere*]

inflow (in´flō) *n.* **1** a flowing in; an influx. **2** something that flows in. **inflowing** *n.*, *a.*

influence (in´fluәns) *n.* **1** power to move, direct or control, ascendancy (over). **2** the effect of such power. **3** a person or thing exercising such power (on). **4** (*Astrol.*) an ethereal fluid supposed to flow from the stars and to affect character and control human destinies. **5** †energy affecting other bodies, such as electric and magnetic induction. ~*v.t.* **1** to exercise influence upon; to affect. **2** to bias, to sway. **under the influence** (*coll.*) drunk. **influencer** *n.* **influential** (-en´-) *a.* having great influence. **influentially** *adv.* [OF, from late L *influentia* (*fluere*, to flow)]

influent (in´fluәnt) *a.* flowing in. ~*n.* a tributary. [as INFLUENCE]

influential INFLUENCE.

influenza (influen´zә) *n.* a highly contagious virus infection, often occurring in epidemics, often characterized by muscular aches and pains, catarrh and fever. **influenzal** *a.* [It., as INFLUENCE]

influx (in´flŭks) *n.* **1** the arrival of a large number of people or things. **2** a flowing in of a stream, river (into). **3** the point of inflow (of a stream). [late L *influxus*, p.p. of *influere*, see INFLUENCE]

info (in´fō) *n.* (*coll.*) information. [abbr.]

infold ENFOLD.

infomercial (infәmœ´shәl), **informercial** *n.* (*esp. N Am.*) a short film advertising something. [*inf*ormation, com*mercial*]

infopreneurial (infōprәnœ´riәl) *a.* of or relating to the manufacture and sale of electronic equipment for the distribution of information. [*info*rmation, entre*preneurial*]

inform[1] (infawm´) *v.t.* **1** to communicate knowledge to, to tell (of, about). **2** to animate, to inspire (with feeling, vitality etc.). **3** to impart some essential quality to. **4** †to give form or shape to. **5** †to educate. ~*v.i.* **1** to disclose facts about someone; to make an accusation (against) (*He threatened to inform on them*). **2** †to take form or shape. **informant** *n.* **informatics** (infәmat´iks) *n.* information science. **information** (infәmā´shәn) *n.* **1** something communicated; knowledge. **2** news (on, about) (*the latest information on the hijacking*). **3** (*Law*) a complaint or accusation presented to a court or magistrate. **4** the act of informing or communicating knowledge of. **5** (*Comput.*) data. **6** in information theory, the measure of the probability that a particular sequence of symbols etc. will occur. **informational** *a.* **informationally** *adv.* **information retrieval** *n.* the storage, classification and recovery of esp. computerized information. **information science** *n.* the computerized processing and communication of data; the study of this. **information superhighway** *n.* a network of computer links, enabling users to communicate with each other internationally. **information technology** *n.* the gathering, processing and communication of information using computers, telecommunications etc. **information theory** *n.* the mathematical study of the transmission, storage, retrieval and decoding of information. **informative** (-faw´-) *a.* conveying information; instructive. **informatively** *adv.* **informativeness** *n.* **informatory** *a.* instructive. **informed** *a.* **1** having information. **2** based on knowledge of the facts (*an informed decision/judgement*). **3** educated (*an informed public*). **informedly** (-fawmd´li, -fawm´idli) *adv.* **informedness** (-fawmd´nis, -fawm´idnis) *n.* **informer** *n.* **1** a person who informs against someone else. **2** a person who provides information or advice. [OF *enformer*, L *informāre* (*formāre*, from *forma*, FORM)]

†**inform**[2] (infawm´) *a.* **1** without regular form. **2** shapeless. [L *informis* (*forma*, FORM)]

informal (infaw´mәl) *a.* **1** without formality; relaxed (*an informal get-together*). **2** ordinary; everyday (*informal clothes*). **3** (of writing, language) containing everyday conventional vocabulary. **informality** (-mal´-) *n.* (*pl.* **informalities**). **informally** *adv.* **informal vote** *n.* (*Austral., New Zeal.*) an invalid vote.

in forma pauperis (in fawmә paw´pәris) *adv.* (*Law*) allowed on account of poverty to sue without paying costs. [L, as a pauper]

infotainment (infōtān´mәnt) *n.* the presentation of news and current affairs as entertainment. [*info*rmation, enter*tainment*]

infra (in´frә) *adv.* (in a passage of a book etc.) below, further on. [L]

infra- (in´frә) *pref.* below, beneath, as *inframarginal*, *infraorbital*. [L, as INFRA]

infraclass (in´frәklahs) *n.* a taxonomic category below a subclass.

infracostal (infrәkos´tәl) *a.* situated below the ribs.

infraction (infrak´shәn) *n.* a violation, an infringement. **infract** *v.t.* to infringe. **infractor** *n.* [F, from L *infractiōnem*, nom. *-tio*, from *infringere*, to INFRINGE]

infradian (infrā´diәn) *a.* (of a biological cycle, rhythm) having a period of recurrence longer than 24 hours. [see INFRA, CIRCADIAN]

infra dig (infrә dig´) *a.* (*coll.*) beneath one's dignity. [L, from *infrā dignitātem*]

infralapsarian (infrәlapseә´riәn) *n.* a Calvinist holding that God decreed the salvation of the elect after the Fall, as opposed to *supralapsarian*. ~*a.* of or relating to infralapsarians or infralapsarianism. **infralapsarianism** *n.* [L *lapsus*, fall, see LAPSE]

infrangible (infran´jibәl) *a.* **1** that cannot be broken. **2** that cannot be infringed or violated. **infrangibility** (-bil´-) *n.* **infrangibly** *adv.*

infraorbital (infrәaw´bitәl) *a.* situated below the orbit of the eye.

infra-red (infrәred´), **infrared** *a.* of, relating to or using electromagnetic radiation having a wavelength longer than that of the red end of the visible spectrum but shorter than that of microwaves. ~*n.* infra-red radiation.

infrasonic (infrәson´ik) *a.* having a frequency below the usual limit of human audibility. **infrasound** (in´frәsownd) *n.*

infrastructure (in´frәstrŭkchә) *n.* **1** an underlying structure or basic framework. **2** roads, transport, schools etc. regarded as the basis of a country's economy. **3** a network of communications etc. essential for military operations etc. **infrastructural** *a.*

infrequent (infrē´kwәnt) *a.* rare, uncommon, unusual. **infrequency, infrequence** *n.* **infrequently** *adv.* [L *infrequens -entem*]

infringe (infrinj´) *v.t.* to break or violate (a law, contract etc.). ~*v.i.* to encroach, to intrude (on, upon). **infringement** *n.* **infringer** *n.* [L *infringere* (*frangere*, to break)]

infula (in´fūlә) *n.* (*pl.* **infulae** (-lē)) either of the two ribbons hanging from a bishop's mitre. [L]

infundibular (infŭndib´ūlә) *a.* funnel-shaped. **infundibulate** (-lәt), **infundibuliform** (-fawm) *a.* funnel-shaped. [L *infundibulum*, funnel (*infundere*, to pour in)]

infuriate[1] (infū´riāt) *v.t.* to provoke to fury. **infuriating** *a.* **infuriatingly** *adv.* [late L *infuriātus*, p.p. of *infuriāre* (*furia*, FURY)]

infuriate[2] (infū´riәt) *a.* (*poet.*) infuriated, enraged.

infuscate (infŭs´kāt) *a.* tinged with brown. [L *infuscātus*, p.p. of *infuscāre* (*fuscus*, dark-brown)]

infuse (infūz´) *v.t.* 1 to pervade or fill (with) (*infused with optimism*). 2 to inculcate, to instil (vitality, life etc. into something). 3 to steep (tea, herbs) in liquid so as to extract the flavour. 4 to pour (into). ~*v.i.* (of tea, herbs) to be steeped in liquid so that the flavour is extracted. **infusable** *a.* **infuser** *n.* **infusion** (infū´zhən) *n.* 1 the liquid extract obtained by steeping any substance. 2 something which is instilled, an admixture. 3 the act of infusing. 4 (*Med.*) the introduction into the body of a fluid, e.g. via a drip. **infusionism** *n.* (*Theol.*) the doctrine that the human soul is an emanation from the divine substance. **infusionist** *n.* **infusive** (-siv) *a.* having the power of infusing. [F *infuser*, L *infūsus*, p.p. of *infundere* (*fundere*, to pour)]

Usage note The adjectives *infusable* and *infusible* should not be confused: *infusable* means able to be infused, and *infusible* unable to be fused.

infusible (infū´zibəl) *a.* that cannot be fused or melted. **infusibility** (-bil´-) *n.*

Usage note See note on INFUSABLE (under INFUSE).

†**infusoria** (infūzaw´riə) *n.pl.* (*Zool.*) microscopic organisms of the former class Infusoria (mainly ciliate protozoa), found in infusions of decaying organic matter. **infusorial, infusory** (-fū´-) *a.* **infusorial earth** *n.* KIESELGUHR. **infusorian** *a.* of or relating to infusoria. ~*n.* any member of the former class Infusoria. [mod. L, pl. of *infūsōrium*, from *infūsus*, see INFUSE]

-ing[1] (ing) *suf.* 1 forming verbal nouns denoting an action or its result, as *cleansing, hunting, painting, washing.* 2 forming nouns denoting an occupation or event, as *bricklaying, lumbering, soldiering, wedding.* 3 forming nouns denoting the material used in making something, as *roofing, scaffolding.* [OE *-ung, -ing*]

-ing[2] (ing) *suf.* 1 forming the present participle of verbs, as *standing, talking.* 2 forming participial adjectives, as *charming, fleeting, horrifying.* 3 forming adjectives from nouns, as *hulking, whopping.* **-ingly** *suf.* forming adverbs, esp. denoting manner of action, as *fleetingly, unknowingly.* [OE *-ende*, part. ending, later *-inde*, confused with *-ing*, -ING[1]]

-ing[3] (ing) *suf.* forming nouns with the sense of belonging to or having the quality of, as *sweeting, shilling, atheling.* [OE *-ing*]

ingathering (ingadh´ering) *n.* the act of gathering or collecting, esp. of getting in the harvest. **ingather** *v.t.*

ingeminate (injem´ināt) *v.t.* to repeat, to reiterate. **to ingeminate peace** to call repeatedly for peace. **ingemination** (-ā´shən) *n.* [L *ingeminātus*, p.p. of *ingemināre*]

ingenerate[1] (injen´ərāt) *v.t.* to generate or produce within; to engender. [L from *ingenerāre*, IN-[1], GENERATE)]

ingenerate[2] (injen´ərit) *a.* inborn, innate. [L *ingenerātus*, p.p. of *ingenerāre*, IN-[1], GENERATE]

ingenious (injēn´yəs) *a.* 1 skilful, clever, esp. at inventing or contriving. 2 cleverly designed or contrived. 3 †having great intelligence or talent. **ingeniously** *adv.* **ingeniousness** *n.* **ingenuity** (-jənū´-) *n.* [L *ingeniōsus*, from *ingenium*, genius]

Usage note The adjectives *ingenious* and *ingenuous* should not be confused: *ingenious* means clever or inventive, and *ingenuous* candid or frank.

ingénue (īzhānü´) *n.* an ingenuous or naive girl, esp. such a character on the stage. [F, as INGENUOUS]

ingenuous (injen´ūəs) *a.* 1 innocent or artless. 2 open, candid, frank. **ingenuously** *adv.* **ingenuousness** *n.* [L *ingenuus*, free-born, frank (*gen-*, base of *gignere*, to produce, to beget)]

Usage note See note under INGENIOUS.

ingest (injest´) *v.t.* 1 to take (food) into the stomach. 2 to take in (facts, knowledge etc.). **ingesta** (-tə) *n.pl.* food taken into the body through the mouth. **ingestible** *a.* **ingestion** (-chən) *n.* **ingestive** *a.* [L *ingestus*, p.p. of *ingerere* (*gerere*, to carry)]

ingle (ing´gəl) *n.* 1 a fire on the hearth. 2 a fireplace. **inglenook** *n.* a chimney corner, an alcove by the side of a large fireplace. [Sc., etym. uncertain, perh. from Gael. *aingeal*, fire]

inglorious (inglaw´riəs) *a.* 1 shameful, ignominious. 2 unknown, not famous. **ingloriously** *adv.* **ingloriousness** *n.* [L *inglōriōsus*]

ingoing (in´gōing) *a.* 1 going in, entering. 2 thorough. ~*n.* an entrance.

ingot (ing´gət) *n.* a mass of metal, esp. steel, gold or silver, cast in a mould. [prob. from OE IN, *goten*, p.p. of *gēotan*, to pour, to fuse]

ingraft ENGRAFT.

ingrain[1] (ingrān´), **engrain** *v.t.* 1 to cause (a dye etc.) to permeate something. 2 †to dye in fast colours. **ingrained** *a.* 1 (of a habit, belief etc.) deeply imprinted. 2 complete, total. 3 (of dirt etc.) worked into the fibres, pores etc.

ingrain[2] (in´grān) *a.* 1 dyed in the grain or yarn before manufacture. 2 thoroughly imbued, inherent. ~*n.* a yarn or fabric dyed with fast colours before manufacture. **ingrain carpet** *n.* a carpet manufactured from wool dyed in the grain, the pattern showing on both sides. [orig. *in grain*, F *en graine*, see GRAIN]

†**ingrate** (in´grāt, ingrāt´) *a.* 1 ungrateful. 2 unpleasant. ~*n.* an ungrateful person. [L *ingrātus* (*grātus*, pleasing)]

ingratiate (ingrā´shiāt) *v.t.* to insinuate (oneself) into goodwill or favour (with) another. **ingratiating** *a.* **ingratiatingly** *adv.* **ingration** (-grā´shən) *n.* [It. *ingratiāre* (L *in grātiam*, into favour, see GRACE)]

ingratitude (ingrat´itūd) *n.* lack of gratitude. [F, from late L *ingrātitūdo*, from *ingrātus*, ingrate]

ingravescent (ingrəves´ənt) *a.* (of an illness) becoming worse. **ingravescence** *n.* [L *ingravescens -entem*, pres.p. of *ingravescere* (*gravis*, heavy)]

ingredient (ingrē´diənt) *n.* an element or a component part in a compound, recipe, mixture etc. [F, from L *ingredientem*, nom. *-ens*, pres.p. of *ingredī* (*gradī*, to walk), p.p. *ingressus*]

ingress (in´gres) *n.* 1 the act of entering, entrance. 2 power, right or permission to enter. 3 (*Astron.*) the start of an eclipse or occultation. **ingression** (-shən) *n.* **ingressive** *a.* 1 of or relating to ingress. 2 (of a speech sound) pronounced with inhalation rather than exhalation of breath. [L *ingressus*, see INGREDIENT]

ingrowing (in´grōing) *a.* 1 growing inwards. 2 (of a toenail) growing abnormally into the flesh. **ingrown** *a.* **ingrowth** *n.*

inguinal (ing´gwinəl) *a.* of, relating to or situated near the groin. [L *inguinālis*, from *inguen -guinis*, the groin]

ingulf ENGULF.

ingurgitate (ingœ´jitāt) *v.t.* 1 to swallow down greedily. 2 (*fig.*) to engulf. **ingurgitation** (-ā´shən) *n.* [L *ingurgitātus*, p.p. of *ingurgitāre* (*gurges gurgitis*, a whirlpool)]

inhabit (inhab´it) *v.t.* (*pres.p.* **inhabiting,** *past, p.p.* **inhabited**) to live or dwell in (a house, town etc.); to occupy. ~†*v.i.* to live, to dwell. **inhabitable** *a.* fit for habitation. **inhabitancy, inhabitance** *n.* domiciliation or residence for a considerable period, esp. such as confers the rights of an inhabitant. **inhabitant** *n.* **inhabitation** (-ā´shən) *n.* 1 the act of inhabiting or the state of being inhabited. 2 a dwelling. [ME *enhabiten*, OF *enhabiter*, L *inhabitāre* (*habitāre*, to dwell, see HABIT)]

inhale (inhāl´) *v.t.* to breathe in, to draw into the lungs. ~*v.i.* to breathe in. **inhalant** *n.* 1 a medicinal preparation designed to be inhaled. 2 a substance inhaled by drug-abusers. ~*a.* 1 inhaling. 2 of or relating to inhalants. **inhalation** (-həlā´shən) *n.* **inhaler** *n.* 1 a person who inhales. 2 a respirator. 3 a device for inhaling vapours etc., esp. one for relieving nasal congestion. [L *inhālāre* (*hālāre*, to breathe)]

inharmonious (inhahmō´niəs) *a.* not harmonious; unmusical. **inharmonic** (-mon´-) *a.* not harmonic. **inharmoniously** *adv.*

inhere (inhiə´) *v.i.* (*formal*) **1** to be an essential or necessary part (in). **2** to be vested (in). **inherence** (-hiə´-, -her´-), **inherency** *n.* **inherent** (inher´ənt, -hiə´-) *a.* **1** inseparable from and permanently existing (in). **2** innate, inborn. **inherently** *adv.* [L *inhaerēre* (*haerēre*, to stick)]

inherit (inher´it) *v.t.* (*pres.p.* **inheriting,** *past, p.p.* **inherited**) **1** to receive (property, a title etc.) by legal succession as the representative of a former possessor. **2** to derive (a characteristic etc.) from one's ancestors by genetic transmission. **3** to take over (a position etc.) from a predecessor. ~*v.i.* to take or come into possession as an heir. **inheritable** *a.* capable of inheriting or of being inherited. **inheritability** (-bil´-) *n.* **inheritably** *adv.* **inheritance** *n.* **1** the act of inheriting. **2** something which is inherited. **3** hereditary succession to an estate etc. **4** the right of an heir to succeed. **inheritance tax** *n.* a tax on inherited money or property, introduced in 1986 to replace capital transfer tax. **inheritor** *n.* **inheritress** (-tris), **inheritrix** (-triks) *n.* a female inheritor. [OF *enheriter* (late L *hērēditāre*, from *hēres -ēdis*, HEIR)]

inhesion (inhē´zhən) *n.* (*formal*) inherence. [late L *inhaesio*, from *inhaerēre*, to INHERE]

inhibit (inhib´it) *v.t.* (*pres.p.* **inhibiting,** *past, p.p.* **inhibited**) **1** to restrain, to hinder, to put a stop to (an action, process etc.). **2** to prohibit, to forbid (from doing something). **3** to prohibit (a priest) from exercising office. **inhibited** *a.* having inhibitions. **inhibition** (inibish´ən) *n.* **1** (*Psych.*) the unconscious restraining of an impulse or instinct. **2** (*coll.*) an inability to express a thought, action etc. because of feelings of embarrassment, shyness etc. (*He has no inhibitions about getting up on stage*). **3** the act of inhibiting; the state of being inhibited. **4** in the Church of England, an order suspending an incumbent. **5** (*Law*) a writ forbidding alteration to property rights. **6** the partial or complete stoppage of a physical process by a nervous influence. **7** †a writ preventing a judge from proceeding further in a cause. **inhibitor** *n.* **1** (*also* **inhibiter**) a person who or something which inhibits. **2** a substance that slows down or stops a chemical or biological process. **inhibitory, inhibitive** (-hib´-) *a.* [L *inhibitus*, p.p. of *inhibēre* (*habēre*, to have, to hold)]

inhospitable (inhəspit´əbəl, inhos´pit-) *a.* **1** not inclined to show hospitality to strangers. **2** (of a landscape, region etc.) affording no shelter, desolate. **inhospitableness** *n.* **inhospitably** *adv.*

inhuman (inhū´mən) *a.* **1** brutal; savage; unfeeling. **2** not human. **inhumanity** (-man´-) *n.* (*pl.* **inhumanities**) **1** brutality; savagery; barbarousness. **2** a barbarous act. **inhumanly** *adv.* [F *inhumain*, L *inhūmānus*]

inhumane (inhūmān´) *a.* lacking in humanity. **inhumanely** *adv.*

inhume (inhūm´) *v.t.* to bury, to inter. [F *inhumer*, L *inhumāre* (*humus*, the ground)]

inimical (inim´ikəl) *a.* **1** hostile. **2** adverse, unfavourable (to). **inimicality** (-kal´-), **inimicalness** *n.* **inimically** *adv.* [late L *inimīcālis*, from *inimīcus* (*amīcus*, friend)]

inimitable (inim´itəbəl) *a.* **1** that cannot be imitated; unique. **2** superb. **inimitability** (-bil´-), **inimitableness** *n.* **inimitably** *adv.* [F, from L *inimitābilis*]

inion (in´iən) *n.* (*pl.* **inia** (-iə)) (*Anat.*) the most prominent part of the occipital bone. [Gr.]

iniquity (inik´witi) *n.* (*pl.* **iniquities**) **1** a lack of equity, gross injustice. **2** unrighteousness, wickedness. **iniquitous** *a.* **iniquitously** *adv.* **iniquitousness** *n.* [OF *iniquité*, L *inīquitātem*, nom. *-tas*, from *inīquus* (*aequus*, just)]

initial (inish´əl) *a.* placed at, or of or relating to, the beginning. ~*n.* **1** the first letter of a word. **2** (*pl.*) the first letters of a forename and surname. ~*v.t.* (*pres.p.* **initialling,** (*N Am.*) **initialing,** *past, p.p.* **initialled,** (*N Am.*) **initialed**) to mark with one's initials, as a guarantee of correctness, a sign of ownership etc. **initialism** *n.* **1** an abbreviation consisting of the initial letters of a series of words, each pronounced separately, e.g. DOE. **2** (*N Am.*) an acronym. **initialize, initialise** *v.t.* (*Comput.*) **1** to run (a floppy disk) through a special program so as to make ready for use. **2** to define the various settings of (a printer) so as to make ready for use. **initial letter, initial consonant** *n.* a letter or consonant at the beginning of a word. **initially** *adv.* at the beginning. **initial teaching alphabet** *n.* a 44-character phonetic alphabet intended as an aid to those learning to read and write English. [L *initiālis*, from *initium*, beginning (*īre*, to go)]

initiate¹ (inish´iāt) *v.t.* **1** to begin or originate. **2** to instruct (a person) in the rudiments or principles of something. **3** to admit (a person) into a society, association, secret etc., usu. with ceremonial rites. **initiation** (-ā´shən) *n.* **initiative** *a.* serving to begin or initiate. ~*n.* **1** the energy and resourcefulness typical of those able to initiate new projects etc. (*We are looking for someone with flair and initiative*). **2** a first step. **3** the power or right to take the lead or originate (esp. legislation). **on one's own initiative** without being prompted by others. **to have the initiative** to have the advantage. **to take the initiative** to take action before others. **initiator** *n.* **initiatory** *a.* serving to begin or initiate. **initiatrix** (-triks) *n.* a female initiator. [L *initiare*, from *initium* (see INITIAL)]

initiate² (inish´iət) *a.* initiated. ~*n.* a person who has been newly initiated; a novice.

inject (injekt´) *v.t.* **1** (*Med.*) to introduce (a fluid) into the body by or as if by a syringe. **2** to introduce or insert (*I tried to inject some humour into the discussion*). **3** to interject (a comment etc.). **injection** *n.* **1** the act of injecting. **2** something which is injected, esp. a fluid injected into the body. **3** the spraying of oil fuel into the cylinder of a compression-ignition engine. **injection moulding** *n.* the manufacture of rubber or plastic items by the injection of heated material into a mould. **injection-moulded** *a.* **injector** *n.* **1** a person who or thing which injects. **2** a mechanical apparatus for supplying the boiler of a steam engine with water to make steam. **3** a nozzle for injecting fuel into an engine. [L *injectus*, p.p. of *injicere* (*jacere*, to throw)]

injudicious (injudish´əs) *a.* done without judgement, unwise. **injudiciously** *adv.* **injudiciousness** *n.*

Injun (in´jən) *n.* (*coll., offensive*) an American Indian. **honest Injun** HONEST.

injunction (injŭngk´shən) *n.* **1** (*Law*) a writ or process whereby a party is required to do or (more usually) to refrain from doing certain acts. **2** an admonition, direction or order. **injunctive** *a.* **injunctively** *adv.* [late L *injunctio*, from *injungere*, to ENJOIN]

injure (in´jə) *v.t.* **1** to hurt, to damage (*Two people were badly injured in the accident*). **2** to do wrong or harm to. **3** to impair or diminish (*This may have injured their chances of winning*). **injured** *a.* **1** hurt (*her injured leg*). **2** offended (*an injured look*). **injurer** *n.* **injurious** (-joo´ri-) *a.* **1** wrongful. **2** hurtful; detrimental (to). **3** insulting, abusive. **injuriously** *adv.* **injuriousness** *n.* [from INJURY]

injury (in´jəri) *n.* (*pl.* **injuries**) **1** damage, hurt, harm. **2** a wrong. **3** †an insult, an affront. **injury time** *n.* time added on to normal playing time in soccer, rugby etc. to compensate for interruptions to play on account of injuries. [A-F *injurie*, L *injūria* (*jūs jūris*, justice, right)]

injustice (injŭs´tis) *n.* **1** the quality of being unjust; unfairness. **2** a violation of justice, a wrong. **to do**

someone an injustice to judge someone unfairly. [F, from L *injustitia*]

ink (ingk) *n.* 1 a coloured liquid or viscous material used in writing or printing. 2 (*Zool.*) the dark fluid exuded by a cuttlefish or octopus to cover its escape. ~*v.t.* 1 to mark (in or over) with ink. 2 to cover (type) with ink before printing. 3 to blacken, daub or colour with ink. **to ink out** to blot out with ink. **ink bag, ink sac** *n.* the bladder of a cuttlefish etc. containing its ink. **ink-blot** *n.* (*Psych.*) a standardized blot of ink used in the Rorschach test. **ink-blot test** *n.* RORSCHACH TEST. **ink-cap** *n.* any of several fungi of the genus *Coprinus.* **inked** *a.* (*Austral., sl.*) drunk. **inker** *n.* an inking-roller. **ink-eraser** *n.* a piece of India rubber treated with fine sand, used for rubbing out ink marks. **ink-fish** *n.* the cuttlefish. **inkhorn** *n.* (*Hist.*) a small vessel made of horn for holding ink. **inking** *n.* **inking-roller** *n.* (*Print.*) a roller receiving ink from an inking-table and transferring it to type. **inking-table** *n.* a slab on which ink is spread to be taken up by an inking-roller for printing. **ink-jet printer** *n.* a computer printer that produces characters by sending tiny jets of electrically charged ink onto the paper. **ink-pad** *n.* a small pad, used for putting ink on a rubber stamp. **ink pencil** *n.* a pencil, used in printing, that makes marks similar to ink, a pencil making marks which can be duplicated when moistened. **inkpot** *n.* a bottle or pot for ink. **ink sac** INK BAG (under INK). **inkstand** *n.* a stand for one or more inkpots, usu. with a place for pens. **inkwell** *n.* a container for ink often fitted into a hole in a desk. **inky** *a.* (*comp.* **inkier,** *superl.* **inkiest**) 1 of the nature of or resembling ink. 2 discoloured with ink. 3 black as ink. **inkiness** *n.* [OF *enque* (F *encre*), late L *encaustum*, purple ink used by the Roman emperors, from Gr. *enkaustos*, burnt in, see ENCAUSTIC]

†**inkle** (ing´kəl) *n.* a broad linen tape. [etym. uncertain]

inkling (ing´kling) *n.* a hint; a slight suspicion or intimation (of). [ME *inclen*, to hint at]

inlaid INLAY[1].

inland (in´lənd, -land) *a.* 1 situated in the interior of a country away from the sea. 2 carried on within a country; domestic, not foreign. ~*adv.* in or towards the interior of a country. ~*n.* the interior of a country. **inland duty** *n.* a tax levied on domestic trade. **inlander** *n.* **inlandish** *a.* **inland navigation** *n.* the passage of boats on rivers and canals. **Inland Revenue** *n.* in Britain, the government department responsible for assessing and collecting inland duties and direct taxes. **inland revenue** *n.* revenue from inland duties and direct taxes such as income tax.

in-law (in´law) *n.* (*pl.* **in-laws**) (*coll.*) a relation by marriage.

inlay[1] (inlā´) *v.t.* (*past, p.p.* **inlaid** (-lād´)) 1 to lay or insert in. 2 to decorate by inserting different materials such as wood or metal into a groundwork, leaving the surfaces even. 3 to insert (a print, picture etc.) into a space in a page. **inlaid** *a.* (of a piece of furniture etc.) decorated by inlaying. **inlayer** (in´-) *n.*

inlay[2] (in´lā) *n.* 1 material inlaid or prepared for inlaying. 2 inlaid work. 3 a filling inserted into a tooth cavity.

inlet (in´lət) *n.* 1 a small arm of the sea; a creek. 2 something inserted, e.g. in dressmaking. 3 a passage allowing fuel etc. into a machine. 4 a means of entrance.

inlier (in´līə) *n.* (*Geol.*) an isolated portion of an underlying bed, which has become surrounded by a later formation.

in loco parentis (in lōkō pəren´tis) *adv.* in the place of a parent (used esp. of a teacher). [L]

inly (in´li) *adv.* (*poet.*) 1 inwardly, internally. 2 closely, deeply. [OE *inlīce* (IN, -LY[1])]

inlying (in´līing) *a.* situated inside or near a centre.

inmate (in´māt) *n.* 1 a resident or occupant, esp. of a prison or institution. 2 a person who dwells in the same house as another. ~†*a.* dwelling or resident under the same roof (with).

in medias res (in mēdias rāz´) *adv.* in or into the middle of things or of a story. [L]

in memoriam (in mimaw´riam) *prep.* in memory of. ~*n.* an obituary. [L]

inmost (in´mōst) *a.* 1 remotest from the surface; most inward. 2 deepest, most heartfelt, most secret. [OE *innemest*]

inn (in) *n.* 1 a public house providing alcoholic drink and sometimes food and lodging. 2 a lodging house, esp. for travellers. 3 †a place of residence or hostel for students. **innkeeper,** †**innholder** *n.* a person who keeps an inn. **Inns of Chancery** *n.pl.* 1 the buildings in London where young students formerly began their law studies, now occupied as chambers by lawyers etc. 2 the societies formerly occupying these buildings. **Inns of Court** *n.pl.* 1 the four corporate societies in London (*Inner Temple, Middle Temple, Lincoln's Inn, Gray's Inn*) which have the exclusive right of admitting persons to practise at the bar. 2 the buildings belonging to these societies. [OE, cogn. with IN]

☒ **innaccurate** common misspelling of INACCURATE.

innards (in´ədz) *n.pl.* 1 (*coll.*) entrails. 2 (*coll.*) the components of a machine etc. [INWARDS (under INWARD)]

innate (inät´, in´āt) *a.* inborn, natural. **innate ideas** *n.pl.* (*Philos.*) general notions which are inborn or developed by intuition in all humans. **innately** *adv.* **innateness** *n.* [L *innātus* (*nātus*, p.p. of *nascī*, to be born)]

inner (in´ə) *a.* 1 interior; farther inward or nearer the centre. 2 spiritual; relating to the mind, soul etc. 3 more obscure or hidden. ~*n.* 1 that part of a target immediately outside the bull's eye. 2 a shot striking that part. **inner bar** *n.* (*Law*) Queen's or King's Counsel collectively. **inner circle** *n.* an exclusive group within a larger group. **inner city** *n.* the central part of a city, esp. when associated with poor housing, social problems etc. (*inner-city schools*). **inner-directed** *a.* (*Psych.*) guided by one's own conscience and standards rather than by external influences. **inner ear** *n.* the part of the ear consisting of the vestibule, semicircular canals and cochlea. **innerly** *adv.* inwardly. **inner man, inner woman** *n.* 1 the inner or spiritual part of a person. 2 (*facet.*) the stomach. **innermost** *a.* INMOST. **innerness** *n.* **inner planet** *n.* any of the planets Mercury, Mars, Venus and Earth whose orbits fall within the asteroid belt. **inner space** *n.* 1 the region beneath the sea's surface or between the earth and outer space. 2 the part of the mind that is unconscious and unknown. **innerspring** *a.* (*N Am.*) INTERIOR-SPRUNG (under INTERIOR). **Inner Temple** *n.* the oldest of the Inns of Court. **inner tube** *n.* an inflatable tube inside a tyre. [OE *innera*, comp. of IN]

innervate (in´œvāt) *v.t.* 1 to supply (an organ) with nerves or nerve filaments. 2 to give a nerve impulse to (an organ). **innervation** (-vā´shən) *n.* **innerve** (inœv´) *v.t.* to stimulate, to invigorate, to strengthen.

innings (in´ingz) *n.* (*pl.* **innings,** (*coll.*) **inningses**) 1 a in cricket, the time or turn for batting of a player or a side. b the runs scored by a player during a turn at batting. 2 the time during which a party or person is in office, in power etc. 3 a a period during which things can be achieved. b (*coll.*) the lifespan of a person (*She had a good innings*). 4 (*as pl.*) lands recovered from the sea. **inning** (in´ing) *n.* (*N Am.*) each of the playing periods in a game of baseball during which both sides have a turn at batting.

innocent (in´əsənt) *a.* 1 free from moral guilt; blameless; sinless. 2 guiltless (of a crime etc.). 3 guileless; naive or credulous. 4 lacking, devoid (of). 5 a harmless. b (of a tumour) not malignant. 6 (*dial.*) weak in intellect. ~*n.* 1

an innocent person, esp. a child. **2** an imbecile, an idiot. **3** a person caught up by chance in a war, crime etc. **innocence, †innocency** *n.* **innocently** *adv.* **Innocents' Day** *n.* the festival (28 Dec.) commemorating the massacre of the children of Bethlehem by Herod (Matt. ii.16). [F, from L *innocens -entem* (*nocens*, pres.p. of *nocēre*, to hurt)]

☒ **innoculate** common misspelling of INOCULATE.

innocuous (inok´ūəs) *a.* having no injurious qualities, harmless. **innocuously** *adv.* **innocuousness** *n.* [L *innocuus*]

innominate (inom´inət) *a.* not named; nameless. **innominate artery** *n.* a large but short artery which rises from the arch of the aorta. **innominate bone** *n.* the hip bone. [late L *innōminātus nōminātus*, p.p. of *nōmināre*, to NOMINATE]

innovate (in´əvāt) *v.i.* **1** to introduce alterations (in). **2** to introduce new ideas or ways of doing things. ~*v.t.* to begin to introduce (methods, ideas etc.). **innovation** (-ā´shən) *n.* **innovational** *a.* **innovative, innovatory** (-ā´təri) *a.* **innovator** *n.* [L *innovātus*, p.p. of *innovāre* (*novāre*, to make new, from *novus*, new)]

innoxious (inok´shəs) *a.* harmless, innocuous. **innoxiously** *adv.* **innoxiousness** *n.* [L *innoxius*]

innuendo (inūen´dō) *n.* (*pl.* **innuendos, innuendoes**) **1** an indirect or oblique hint, esp. one that is disparaging or disapproving. **2** a suggestive remark. ~*v.t.* (*3rd pers. sing. pres.* **innuendoes**, *pres.p.* **innuendoing**, *past, p.p.* **innuendoed**) to insinuate. ~*v.i.* to make innuendoes. [L *innuendō*, by way of intimation, abl. gerund of *innuere* (*nuere*, to nod)]

Innuit INUIT.

innumerable (inū´mərəbəl) *a.* countless, numberless. **innumerability** (-bil´-), **innumerableness** *n.* **innumerably** *adv.* **†innumerous** *a.* [F, from L *innumerābilis*]

innumerate (inū´mərət) *a.* ignorant of or unskilled in mathematics or science.

innutrition (inūtrish´ən) *n.* lack of nutrition or nourishment. **innutritious** *a.*

inobservant (inəbzœ´vənt) *a.* **1** not observant. **2** heedless. **inobservance** *n.* lack of observance (of a law etc.). [L *inobservans -antem*]

inobtrusive (inəbtroo´siv) *a.* unobtrusive.

☒ **inocent** common misspelling of INNOCENT.

inoculate (inok´ūlāt) *v.t.* **1** to inject (a person or animal) with a mild form of a disease in order to induce immunity against the disease. **2** to introduce (bacteria, a virus) into an organism. **3** to introduce (organisms) into a culture medium. **4** (*fig.*) to imbue (a person) with ideas etc. ~*v.i.* to practise inoculation. **inoculable** *a.* **inoculation** (-lā´shən) *n.* **inoculative** *a.* **inoculator** *n.* **inoculum** *n.* (*pl.* **inocula**) a substance used for inoculating. [L *inoculātus*, p.p. of *inoculāre*, to engraft (*oculus*, eye)]

inodorous (inō´dərəs) *a.* without smell, odourless. [L *inodōrus*]

inoffensive (inəfen´siv) *a.* giving no offence; harmless. **inoffensively** *adv.* **inoffensiveness** *n.*

inofficious (inəfi´shəs) *a.* (*Law*) regardless of natural obligation and duty. [L *inofficiōsus*]

inoperable (inop´ərəbəl) *a.* **1** that cannot be operated on. **2** unworkable. **3** that cannot be operated. **inoperability** (-bil´-), **inoperableness** *n.* **inoperably** *adv.*

inoperative (inop´ərətiv) *a.* **1** not in operation. **2** producing no result; ineffective.

inopportune (inop´ətūn, -tūn´) *a.* not opportune; unseasonable. **inopportunely** *adv.* **inopportuneness** (-tū´-), **inopportunity** (-tūn´-) *n.* [F, from late L *inopportūnus*]

inordinate (inaw´dinət) *a.* **1** excessive, immoderate, passing all bounds. **2** unrestrained. **3** irregular, disorderly. **inordinately** *adv.* [L *inordinātus*, *ordinātus*, p.p. of *ordināre*, from *ordo -inis*, ORDER)]

inorganic (inawgan´ik) *a.* **1** not organic, not having the organs or characteristics of living organisms. **2** of or relating to chemical compounds not containing carbon. **3** not having an ordered physical structure. **4** not resulting from natural growth. **5** (of a letter or sound) not explained by the normal course of etymological development. **inorganically** *adv.* **inorganic chemistry** *n.* the branch of chemistry concerning mineral substances.

inosculate (inos´kūlāt) *v.i.* **1** (e.g. of two blood vessels) to become united by the mouth of one fitting into the mouth of the other, or by a duct. **2** to blend. ~*v.t.* to cause to inosculate. **inosculation** (-lā´shən) *n.* [L *osculātus*, furnished with a mouth, from *osculum*, dim. of *os*, mouth]

inositol (inos´itol) *n.* a member of the vitamin B complex, found in most plant and animal tissues. [Gr. *īs*, *īnos*, a muscle]

inotropic (inətrop´ik) *a.* of or controlling contraction of the heart muscles. [Gr. *īs īnos*, a muscle]

in propria persona (in prōpriə pœsō´nə) *adv.* in person. [L]

input (in´put) *n.* **1** something that is put into a machine, the body etc. **2 a** a place where energy, information etc. goes into an electrical system. **b** a signal or current fed into a system or device. **3** data fed into a computer. **4** the process of entering such data. **5** a contribution. ~*a.* of or relating to computer input. ~*v.t.* (*pres.p.* **inputting**, *past, p.p.* **inputted, input**) **1** to put in. **2** to enter (data) into a computer. **input-output, input/ output** *a.* of or relating to input and output.

inquest (in´kwest) *n.* **1** a judicial inquiry or investigation, esp. a coroner's inquest, usu. held before a jury. **2** the jury at such an inquiry. **3** any inquiry or investigation. [OF *enqueste*, med. L *inquesta*, orig. fem. of *inquistus*, L *inquīsītus*, p.p. of *inquīrere*, to INQUIRE]

inquietude (inkwī´ətūd) *n.* restlessness, uneasiness. **inquiet** *a.* unquiet. [L *inquietudo*, from *inquiētus*]

inquiline (in´kwilīn) *n.* an animal living in the abode of another, as certain beetles in ants' nests, or certain insects in the galls of other insects. **inquilinous** (-lī´-) *a.* [L *inquilīnus*, a sojourner, for *incolīnus*, from *incolere* (*colere*, to dwell)]

inquire (inkwīə´), **enquire** *v.i.* **1** to ask questions (of). **2** to seek information by asking questions (about or after). **3** to investigate (into). ~*v.t.* to ask (what, whether, how etc.) (*She inquired my date of birth*). **inquirer** *n.* **inquiring** *a.* given to inquiry; inquisitive. **inquiringly** *adv.* **inquiry** (inkwī´ri) *n.* (*pl.* **inquiries**) **1** an official investigation. **2** the act of inquiring. **3** a question. **4** a searching for truth, information or knowledge. **5** examination of facts or principles. **inquiry agent** *n.* a private detective. [ME *enquere*, OF *enquerre*, L *inquīrere* (*quaerere*, to seek)]

Usage note It is conventional to use *enquire, enquiry* of simple asking, and *inquire, inquiry* of investigating.

inquirendo (inkwiren´dō) *n.* (*Law*) authority given to inquire into something for the benefit of the Crown. [L, by inquiring, abl. gerund of *inquīrere*]

inquisition (inkwizish´ən) *n.* **1** (*esp. derog.*) a thorough search or investigation. **2** a judicial inquiry, an inquest. **3** (*Hist.*) (**Inquisition**) a tribunal in the Roman Catholic Church for inquiring into offences against the canon law, aimed especially at the suppression of heresy. **inquisitional** *a.* **inquisitive** (inkwiz´itiv) *a.* **1** unduly given to asking questions; prying, curious. **2** eager for knowledge. **inquisitively** *adv.* **inquisitiveness** *n.* **inquisitor** (inkwiz´itə) *n.* **1** a person who inquires. **2** a person who carries out an official investigation. **3** (*Hist.*) a functionary of the Inquisition. **Inquisitor-General** *n.* the head of the Inquisition in Spain. **inquisitorial** *a.* **1** of, relating to or like an inquisitor. **2** prying, searching. **3** (*Law*) (of criminal proceedings) in which the judge is also prosecutor. **inquisitorially** *adv.* [OF, from L *inquīsītiōnem*, nom. *-tio*, from *inquīrere*, to INQUIRE]

inquorate (inkwaw´rāt) *a.* not having enough people to constitute a quorum.

in re (in rē´, rā´) *prep.* RE[1]. [L, in the matter of]

INRI *abbr.* Jesus of Nazareth King of the Jews. [L *Iesus Nazarenus Rex Iudaeorum*]

inroad (in´rōd) *n.* **1** (*often pl.*) an encroachment (on). **2** a hostile incursion.

inrush (in´rŭsh) *n.* a sudden rush in; an influx.

ins. *abbr.* **1** inches. **2** insurance.

insalivate (insal´ivāt) *v.t.* to mix (food) with saliva during eating. **insalivation** (-ā´shən) *n.*

insalubrious (insəloo´briəs) *a.* not salubrious, unhealthy. **insalubriously** *adv.* **insalubrity** *n.* [L *insalūbris*]

insane (insān´) *a.* **1** deranged in mind; mad. **2** (*coll.*) exceedingly rash or foolish. **insanely** *adv.* **insanity** (-san´-) *n.* (*pl.* **insanities**). [L *insanus*]

insanitary (insan´itəri) *a.* not sanitary. **insanitation** (-ā´shən) *n.*

insatiable (insā´shəbəl) *a.* **1** that cannot be satisfied or appeased. **2** very greedy (of). **insatiability** (-bil´-), **insatiableness** *n.* **insatiably** *adv.* **insatiate** (-ət) *a.* **1** never satisfied. **2** insatiable. **insatiately** *adv.* [F, from L *insatiābilis*]

inscape (in´skāp) *n.* the unique essence of a person, object etc.

inscribe (inskrīb´) *v.t.* **1 a** to write, carve or engrave (words, a design etc.) on a stone, paper or some other surface. **b** to mark (a stone etc.) with writing or letters. **2** to address or dedicate (a book to someone). **3** to enter (a name) in or on a book, list etc. **4** to issue (stock etc.) to registered shareholders. **5** (*Geom.*) to draw (a figure) within another so that it touches the boundary surfaces of the latter. **inscribable** *a.* **inscriber** *n.* [L *inscrībere* (*scrībere*, to write), p.p. *inscriptus*]

inscription (inskrip´shən) *n.* **1** the art or act of inscribing. **2** something which is inscribed, e.g. a dedicatory address, the words on the reverse of some coins and medals, or the titular line or lines of an illustration. **inscriptional, inscriptive** *a.*

inscrutable (inskroo´təbəl) *a.* unfathomable, mysterious. **inscrutability** (-bil´-), **inscrutableness** *n.* **inscrutably** *adv.* [F, from late L *inscrūtābilis* (*scrūtābilis*, from *scrūtārī*, to search)]

insect (in´sekt) *n.* **1** a member of the Insecta, a class of articulate, usu. winged animals, with three pairs of legs, and divided into three distinct segments, the head, thorax and abdomen. **2** any other articulated animal resembling these, e.g. a spider or centipede. **3** a small or contemptible person or creature. **insectarium** (-teə´riəm) *n.* (*pl.* **insectariums, insectaria**) an insectary. **insectary** (in´sektəri) *n.* (*pl.* **insectaries**) a place for keeping or breeding insects. **insecticide** (-sek´tisīd) *n.* a preparation for killing insects. **insecticidal** (-sī´-) *a.* **insectile** (-sek´tīl) *a.* of the nature of insects. [F *insecte*, L *insectum*, neut. p.p. of *insecāre* (*secāre*, to cut)]

insectivore (insek´tivaw) *n.* **1** any mammal of the order Insectivora, including moles, shrews and hedgehogs. **2** any animal or plant that feeds on insects. **insectivorous** (-tiv´-) *a.* **1** feeding on insects. **2** belonging to the Insectivora. [L *insectivorus*, insect-eating, see -VOROUS (under -VORE)]

insecure (insikūə´) *a.* **1** lacking in self-confidence; apprehensive; uncertain. **2** not secure or safe; not strongly fixed or supported. **3** not effectually guarded. **insecurely** *adv.* **insecurity** *n.* [L *insēcūrus*]

inselberg (in´səlbœg, -zəl-) *n.* an isolated steep rocky hill in a flat plain. [G *Insel*, island, *Berg*, mountain]

inseminate (insem´ināt) *v.t.* **1** to impregnate, esp. by artificial means. **2** to sow (in the soil). **3** to implant (in the mind etc.). **insemination** (-ā´shən) *n.* [L *insēminātus*, p.p. of *insēmināre* (*sēmināre*, to sow, from *sēmen -minis*, seed)]

insensate (insen´sət, -sāt) *a.* **1** lacking sensation; inanimate or unconscious. **2** lacking in sensibility; unfeeling. **3** foolish, mad. **insensately** *adv.* [late L *insensātus*]

insensible (insen´sibəl) *a.* **1** not having the power of feeling or perceiving, unconscious. **2** unaware (of); indifferent (to). **3** not susceptible of feeling, emotion or passion; callous. **4** that cannot be perceived or felt; imperceptible. **insensibility** (-bil´-) *n.* **1** lack of feeling, emotion or passion. **2** unconsciousness. **3** insusceptibility or indifference (to). **insensibly** *adv.* imperceptibly, gradually. [F, from L *insensibilis*]

insensitive (insen´sitiv) *a.* **1** unfeeling, unsympathetic (to). **2** not sensitive (to). **insensitively** *adv.* **insensitiveness, insensitivity** (-tiv´-) *n.*

insentient (insen´shiənt) *a.* not sentient, inanimate. **insentience** *n.*

inseparable (insep´ərəbəl) *a.* **1** incapable of being separated. **2** (*Gram.*) incapable of being employed separately (as the prefixes DIS-, RE-). ~*n.* (*usu. pl.*) an inseparable companion or thing. **inseparability** (-bil´-), **inseparableness** *n.* **inseparably** *adv.* [F, from L *insēparābilis*]

insert (insœt´) *v.t.* **1** to set or place (a thing) into another. **2** to introduce (text, an article, an advertisement etc.) into something, such as a newspaper. ~*n.* **1** something inserted. **2** a printed sheet etc. placed inside the leaves of a newspaper, periodical etc. **inserted** *a.* **1** (*Anat.*) (of a muscle) attached to a bone. **2** (*Bot.*) growing from or upon a part. **inserter** *n.* **insertion** (insœ´shən) *n.* **1** the act of inserting. **2** something which is inserted, an intercalation, a passage etc. introduced (in or into). **3** a band of lace or embroidery inserted in a dress, handkerchief etc. **4** the manner or place in which one part is inserted into or adheres to another. [L *insertus*, p.p. of *inserere* (*serere*, to join)]

insessorial (insesaw´riəl) *a.* **1** (of feet, claws) adapted for perching. **2** (of a bird) having feet or claws of this type. [mod. L *insessor*, from *insidēre* (*sedēre*, to sit)]

inset[1] (in´set) *n.* **1** a piece let into a dress etc. **2** a small map or diagram set within a larger one. **3** a page or number of pages inserted in a book, newspaper etc.

inset[2] (inset´) *v.t.* (*pres.p.* **insetting,** *past, p.p.* **inset, insetted**) **1** to set or fix (in), to insert (in). **2** to decorate with an inset. **insetter** *n.*

inset[3] (in´set) *abbr.* in-service education and training (for teachers).

inshallah (inshal´ə) *int.* if Allah wills it. [Arab.]

inshore (inshaw´) *a., adv.* on, near or towards the shore. **inshore of** closer to the shore than.

inside[1] (in´sīd) *a.* **1** situated within; interior, internal, inner. **2** in hockey and football, near the centre of the field (*inside forward*). ~*n.* **1** the inner or interior part. **2** the inner side or surface (of). **3** the side of a path away from the road. **4** the lower section of a double-decker bus. **5** (*coll.*) a position from which inside information can be obtained. **6** (*Print.*) the side of a sheet containing the second page. **7** (*pl., coll.*) the bowels. **inside country** *n.* (*Austral.*) areas near the coast that have been settled. **inside information** *n.* confidential knowledge not generally accessible. **inside job** *n.* (*coll.*) a crime committed with the help of someone trusted or employed by the victim. **inside out** *adv.* having the inner side turned out and vice versa. **to know inside out** to have thorough knowledge of. **to turn inside out** **1** to turn the inner side of (something) outwards. **2** (*coll.*) to cause chaos or a mess in. **inside-out** *a.* **insider** (-sī´-) *n.* **1** a person who belongs to a society, clique etc. **2** a person who has inside information. **insider dealing, insider trading** *n.* the criminal practice of conducting share deals on the basis of inside information.

inside track *n.* 1 the inner and therefore shorter track. 2 a position of advantage.

inside[2] (insīd´) *adv.* 1 in or into the interior, within; indoors. 2 (*sl.*) in or into prison. ~*prep.* 1 within, on the inner side of, into. 2 in less than (*inside a week*). **inside of a mile/ an hour etc.** (*coll.*) within or in less than a mile/an hour etc.

insidious (insid´iəs) *a.* 1 treacherous, sly. 2 developing gradually or subtly but dangerously (*an insidious influence*). **insidiously** *adv.* **insidiousness** *n.* [L *insidiōsus*, from *insidiae*, an ambush, a snare, from *insidēre* (*sedēre*, to sit)]

insight (in´sīt) *n.* 1 the capacity to observe or discern the real character of things. 2 a clear and often sudden understanding of something. 3 awareness, esp. self-awareness. **insightful** *a.* **insightfully** *adv.*

insignia (insig´niə) *n.pl.* 1 (*often sing. in constr., N Am.*) badges of office or honour. 2 distinguishing marks or signs (of). [L, pl. of *insigne*, remarkable (*signum*, SIGN)]

Usage note *Insignia* is sometimes used as a countable noun (*an insignia, insignias*), but this is best avoided.

insignificant (insignif´ikənt) *a.* 1 unimportant, trivial. 2 (of a person) of a little distinction. 3 small. 4 without meaning. **insignificance, insignificancy** *n.* **insignificantly** *adv.*

insincere (insinsiə´) *a.* 1 not sincere; false. 2 hypocritical. **insincerely** *adv.* **insincerity** (-ser´-) *n.* (*pl.* **insincerities**). [L *insincērus*]

insinuate (insin´ūāt) *v.t.* 1 to indicate indirectly or obliquely; to hint. 2 to introduce (oneself, a person etc.) into favour, office, a place etc. by gradual and artful means. **insinuatingly** *adv.* **insinuation** (-ā´shən) *n.* 1 the art or power of insinuating. 2 a hint, an indirect suggestion. **insinuative** *a.* **insinuator** *n.* [L *insinuātus*, p.p. of *insinuāre* (*sinuāre*, to wind, from *sinus*, a curve)]

insipid (insip´id) *a.* 1 tasteless, savourless. 2 lacking in life or animation; dull; vapid. **insipidity** (-pid´-), **insipidness** *n.* **insipidly** *adv.* [F *insipide*, late L *insipidus* (*sapidus*, well-tasting)]

insist (insist´) *v.i.* to be emphatic, positive, urgent or persistent (on or upon). ~*v.t.* 1 to maintain emphatically. 2 to demand strongly or without accepting any refusal. **to insist on** 1 to demand emphatically. 2 to assert positively. **insistence, insistency** *n.* **insistent** *a.* 1 insisting; demanding strongly and continually. 2 obtrusive and hard to ignore (*the insistent creaking of the gate*). **insistently** *adv.* [F *insister*, L *insistere* (*sistere*, to set, causal of *stāre*, to stand)]

in situ (in sit´ū) *adv.* 1 in its place. 2 in the original position. [L]

insobriety (insəbrī´əti) *n.* lack of sobriety; intemperance (usu. in drinking).

insofar (insōfah´) *adv.* in so far (as).

insolate (in´səlāt) *v.t.* to expose to the sun's rays, e.g. for bleaching, or as a form of medical treatment. **insolation** (-ā´shən) *n.* 1 exposure to the sun. 2 sunstroke. 3 solar radiation falling on a given surface. [L *insolātus*, p.p. of *insōlāre* (*sol*, sun)]

insole (in´sōl) *n.* 1 the inner sole of a boot or shoe. 2 a strip of waterproof or other material placed inside a boot or shoe for warmth, comfort etc.

insolent (in´sələnt) *a.* 1 showing overbearing contempt; impudent. 2 insulting. **insolence** *n.* **insolently** *adv.* [F, from L *insolentum*, nom. *-lens* (*solens*, pres.p. of *solēre*, to be accustomed)]

insoluble (insol´ūbəl) *a.* 1 that cannot be solved. 2 that cannot be dissolved. **insolubility** (-bil´-), **insolubleness** *n.* **insolubilize, insolubilise** *v.t.* **insoluble soap** *n.* a compound of a fatty and another metallic base. **insolubly** *adv.* [F, from L *insolūbilis*]

insolvable (insol´vəbəl) *a.* 1 that cannot be solved, insoluble. 2 that cannot be dissolved. **insolvability** (-bil´-) *n.* **insolvably** *adv.*

insolvent (insol´vənt) *a.* 1 not able to discharge all debts or liabilities. 2 of or relating to insolvents. ~*n.* a debtor unable to pay their debts. **insolvency** *n.*

insomnia (insom´niə) *n.* sleeplessness; chronic inability to sleep or sleep well. **insomniac** (-ak) *n., a.* **insomnious** *a.* [L, from *insomnis*, sleepless (*somnus*, sleep)]

insomuch (insōmŭch´) *adv.* 1 to such a degree (that). 2 inasmuch (as).

insouciant (insoo´siənt) *a.* carefree or unconcerned. **insouciance** *n.* **insouciantly** *adv.* [F (*souciant*, caring, from *soucier*, L *sollicitāre*, to make anxious)]

insp. *abbr.* inspector.

inspan (inspan´) *v.t.* (*pres.p.* **inspanning,** *past, p.p.* **inspanned**) (*S Afr.*) 1 to yoke (horses, oxen etc.) to a wagon etc. 2 to harness animals to (a wagon). 3 (*fig.*) to harness into service. ~*v.i.* to harness or yoke up animals. [Dut. *inspannen* (IN, SPAN[1])]

inspect (inspekt´) *v.t.* 1 to look closely into or at; to scrutinize carefully. 2 to view and examine officially. **inspectable** *a.* **inspection** (inspek´shən) *n.* 1 the act of inspecting. 2 a careful, narrow or critical examination or survey. 3 an official examination. **inspective** *a.*

inspector (inspek´tə) *n.* 1 a person who inspects. 2 an overseer, a superintendent. 3 a police officer usu. ranking below a superintendent. **inspectoral** *a.* **inspectorate** (-ət) *n.* **inspector general** *n.* a chief inspector. **inspectorial** (-taw´ri-) *a.* **inspector of taxes** *n.* a person employed by the Inland Revenue to collect taxes. **inspectorship** *n.* [L *inspectāre*, freq. of *inspicere* (*specere*, to look)]

inspire (inspīə´) *v.t.* 1 to stimulate (a person) to some activity, esp. creative activity (*What inspired you to paint?*). 2 to imbue or animate (a person with a feeling). 3 to infuse or instil (an emotion in or into). 4 to create (a feeling) in someone. 5 to be the source of motivation for something (*a film inspired by real events*). 6 to breathe or take (air) into the lungs etc. ~*v.i.* to take air into the lungs. **inspirable** *a.* **inspiration** (inspirā´shən) *n.* 1 an act of inspiring, breathing in or infusing feelings, ideas etc. 2 a person, idea etc. that inspires others. 3 feelings, ideas, creativity etc. imparted by or as by divine agency. 4 a sudden and brilliant idea. 5 a supposed divine influence, such as that exerted on the writers of Scripture etc. 6 the act of drawing air into the lungs. **inspirational** *a.* **inspirationally** *adv.* **inspirator** (in´spirātə) *n.* a device or apparatus for drawing in or injecting air, steam etc. **inspiratory** (-spir´ətəri) *a.* 1 of or relating to inspiration. 2 aiding in the process of inspiration. **inspired** *a.* 1 (of a poem, piece of music etc.) imparted by or as by supernatural agency. 2 (of a guess) accurate but based on intuition rather than knowledge. **inspiredly** (-ridli) *adv.* **inspirer** *n.* **inspiring** *a.* **inspiringly** *adv.* [OF *enspirer*, L *inspirāre* (*spirāre*, to breathe)]

inspirit (inspir´it) *v.t.* (*pres.p.* **inspiriting,** *past, p.p.* **inspirited**) 1 to infuse spirit, life or animation into. 2 to inspire, to encourage (to action or to do). **inspiriting** *a.* **inspiritingly** *adv.*

inspissate (inspis´āt) *v.t.* to thicken by boiling or evaporation. **inspissation** (-ā´shən) *n.* **inspissator** *n.* [late L *inspissātus*, p.p. of *inspissāre* (*spissus*, thick)]

inst. (inst) *abbr.* 1 instant (this month). 2 institute. 3 institution.

instability (instəbil´iti) *n.* (*pl.* **instabilities**) 1 lack of stability or firmness. 2 (*Psych.*) lack of mental or emotional consistency. 3 an instance of this. [F *instabilité*, L *instābilitātem*, nom. *-tas*]

instable (instā´bəl) *a.* unstable.

install (instawl´), **instal** *v.t.* (*pres.p.* **installing,** *past, p.p.* **installed**) 1 to put (apparatus, equipment etc.) in position for use. 2 to settle or establish (a person, oneself) somewhere (*She installed herself by the fire*). 3 to place (a person) in an official position with customary ceremonies (*He was installed as bishop*). **installation** (-stəlā´shən) *n.* 1 the act of installing or the process of being installed. 2 a piece of machinery, equipment etc. installed for use. 3 a military base etc. 4 a large exhibit installed in an art gallery etc. [F *installer*, low L *installāre* (*stallum*, STALL[1])]

installment[1] INSTALL.

installment[2] INSTALMENT.

instalment (instawl´mənt), (*N Am.*) **installment** *n.* 1 each one of the parts into which a sum of money owed is divided, each part being paid at intervals over an agreed period of time. 2 each one of several parts of a serial story etc. shown on television, published in a magazine etc. **instalment plan** *n.* the hire-purchase system. [from obs. *estallment*, from A-F *estaler*, to arrange or fix]

instance (in´stəns) *n.* 1 an example, illustrative case or precedent (*There have been several instances of mismanagement*). 2 a particular situation or case (*The rules don't apply in this instance*). 3 (*Law*) a process or suit. 4 †a cause, a motive. ~*v.t.* to bring forward as an instance or example. **at the instance of** at the suggestion or desire of. **for instance** for example. **in the first/second etc. instance** at the first etc. stage; in the first etc. place. **instancy** *n.* 1 urgency. 2 imminence. [F, from L *instantia*, as INSTANT]

instant (in´stənt) *a.* 1 immediate (*an instant success*). 2 (esp. of food) processed so as to be quickly and easily prepared. 3 pressing; urgent. 4 of the current month (used in commercial correspondence). 5 present, current. ~*n.* 1 a particular point of time (*Do it this instant*; *I phoned the instant I knew*). 2 a moment, a very brief space of time. **instantaneous** (instəntā´niəs) *a.* 1 happening or done in an instant or immediately. 2 (*Physics*) relating to a particular instant. **instantaneity** (-nē´i-), **instantaneousness** *n.* **instantaneously** *adv.* **instantiate** (instan´shiāt) *v.t.* to represent by an instance. **instantiation** (-ā´shən) *n.* **instantly** *adv.* 1 immediately; without delay. 2 †urgently. **instant replay** *n.* the immediate replay, often in slow motion, of part of a sports event on television. [F, from L *instantem*, nom. *-stans* (*stāre*, to stand)]

instanter (instan´tə) *adv.* (*formal or facet.*) at once, immediately. [L]

instar (in´stah) *n.* a stage in the development of an insect or other arthropod between two moults. [L, resemblance, form]

instate (instāt´) *v.t.* to put in a certain place, office etc., to install.

in statu pupillari (in statū pūpilah´ri) *a.* 1 in a state of wardship, esp. as a pupil. 2 in a junior position at a university.

instauration (instawrā´shən) *n.* (*formal*) renewal, restoration. **instaurator** (in´-) *n.* [L *instaurātio*, from *instaurāre* (*-staurāre*, see RESTORE)]

instead (insted´) *adv.* 1 in the place (of) (*Could I have cheese instead of ham?*). 2 as an alternative or substitute (*We went to a restaurant instead*).

instep (in´step) *n.* 1 the arched upper side of the human foot, near the ankle. 2 the part of a shoe etc., corresponding to this. 3 anything shaped like a human instep. [IN, STEP, or perh. STOOP[1], bend]

instigate (in´stigāt) *v.t.* 1 to provoke or bring about (an action). 2 to incite, to urge on (to an action esp. of an evil kind). **instigation** (-ā´shən) *n.* **instigator** *n.* [L *instīgātus*, p.p. of *instīgāre* (*stig-*, cp. Gr. *stig-*, root of *stizein*, to prick)]

instil (instil´), (*N Am.*) **instill** *v.t.* (*pres.p.* **instilling**, *past, p.p.* **instilled**) 1 to introduce slowly and gradually (into the mind of a person). 2 to pour by drops (into). **instillation** (-ā´shən) *n.* **instilment** *n.* [F *instiller*, L *instillāre* (*stillāre*, to drop)]

instinct[1] (in´stingkt) *n.* 1 a natural impulse present in most animals, leading them without reasoning or conscious design to perform certain actions. 2 a similar innate or intuitive impulse in human beings. 3 intuition; unreasoning perception of rightness, beauty etc. **instinctive** (-stingk´-) *a.* 1 prompted by instinct. 2 spontaneous, impulsive. **instinctively** *adv.* **instinctual** (-stingk´-) *a.* of or relating to instinct. **instinctually** *adv.* [through F *instinct* or directly from L *instinctus*, from *instinguere*, as INSTIGATE]

instinct[2] (instingkt´) *a.* 1 animated or impelled from within. 2 imbued (with).

institute (in´stitūt) *v.t.* 1 to set up, to establish. 2 to start, to begin. 3 to nominate, to appoint (to or into), esp. to appoint to an ecclesiastical benefice. ~*n.* 1 a society established for the promotion or furtherance of science, literature etc. 2 the building in which such a society meets. 3 an established law, precept or principle. 4 (*pl.*) a book of elements or principles, esp. of jurisprudence or medicine. **institution** (institū´shən) *n.* 1 the act of instituting. 2 a society or association established esp. for charitable, social or educational purposes. 3 the building used by such a society. 4 an established order, law, regulation or custom. 5 (*coll.*) a familiar custom, person etc. 6 the act or ceremony of investing a member of the clergy with the spiritual part of a benefice. **institutional** *a.* 1 of or relating to an institution. 2 typical of institutions, e.g. in being routine or unimaginative. 3 (of advertising) designed to increase prestige rather than to increase sales. **institutionalism** *n.* **institutionalist** *n.* **institutionalize, institutionalise** *v.t.* 1 to make an institution of. 2 to confine to an institution. **institutionalization** (-zā´shən) *n.* **institutionalized** *a.* 1 (of a long-term patient etc.) made dependent and apathetic, bored etc. by a long stay in an institution. 2 that has become established or accepted. **institutionally** *adv.* **institutional religion** *n.* religion that expresses itself through ritual and church services. [L *institūtus*, p.p. of *instituere* (*statuere*, to place, from *status*, see STATUS)]

Inst.P. *abbr.* Institute of Physics.

instruct (instrŭkt´) *v.t.* 1 to teach, to educate (in a subject). 2 to order or direct (someone to do something). 3 to inform (someone of, that). 4 to supply (a solicitor, counsel etc.) with information relating to a case. 5 to authorize (a barrister or solicitor) to act for one. **instructible** *a.* **instruction** (-shən) *n.* 1 (*often pl.*) a direction or order. 2 the act of instructing; teaching, education. 3 (*pl.*) directions to a solicitor, counsel etc. 4 a code directing a computer to perform a certain operation. **instructional** *a.* **instructive** *a.* conveying instruction. **instructively** *adv.* **instructiveness** *n.* **instructor** *n.* 1 a person who instructs. 2 (*N Am.*) a college teacher having a rank inferior to professor. **instructorship** *n.* **instructress** *n.* a female instructor. [L *instructus*, p.p. of *instruere* (*struere*, to pile up)]

instrument (in´strəmənt) *n.* 1 a tool, a mechanical implement, esp. one for scientific or delicate operations. 2 MUSICAL INSTRUMENT (under MUSIC). 3 something by means of which work is done or any object or purpose effected. 4 an agent, a person used as a means by another. 5 a measuring device, e.g. in a car or an aircraft, for measuring pressure, speed etc. 6 (*Law*) a document giving formal expression to an act. ~*v.t.* 1 (*Mus.*) to arrange (music) for instruments. 2 to equip with instruments. **instrumental** (instrəmen´təl) *a.* 1 serving as an instrument or means (to some end or in some act). 2 (of errors, etc.) due to the instrument used. 3 (of music) for instruments, not for voices. 4 (*Gram.*) (of a case of nouns etc. in some languages) denoting the means or instrument. ~*n.* 1 (*Gram.*) the instrumental case. 2 a piece of music for instruments as opposed to voices. **instrumentalist** *n.* a person who plays an instrument. **instrumentality** (-tal´-) *n.* **instrumentally** *adv.* **instrumentation** (-tā´shən) *n.* **1** the arrangement of music for several instruments in combination. **2** the instruments used in a piece of music. **3** the art or manner of using an instrument or instruments. **4** instrumentality. **5** the use, design etc. of instruments or tools. **6** such instruments or tools collectively. **instrument panel, instrument board** *n.* a panel, esp. in a car or aircraft, containing instruments for measuring speed etc. [F, from L *instrūmentum*, from *instruere*, see INSTRUCT]

insubordinate (insəbaw´dinət) *a.* not submissive to authority; disobedient, disorderly. **insubordinately** *adv.* **insubordination** (-ā´shən) *n.*

insubstantial (insəbstan´shəl) *a.* **1** unreal. **2** flimsy or slight. **insubstantiality** (-al´-) *n.* **insubstantially** *adv.* [late L *insubstantiālis*]

insufferable (insŭf´ərəbəl) *a.* not able to be borne or endured; detestable; intolerable. **insufferableness** *n.* **insufferably** *adv.*

insufficient (insəfish´ənt) *a.* not sufficient; deficient; inadequate. **insufficiency** (-si) *n.* **1** (*also* **insufficience**) the state of being insufficient. **2** (*Med.*) the inability of an organ to function normally. **insufficiently** *adv.* [OF, from L *insufficientem*, nom. *-ens*]

insufflate (in´səflāt) *v.t.* **1** (*Med.*) to blow or breathe (air, vapour, powder etc.) into an opening, cavity etc. **2** to treat (a person, organ etc.) by insufflation. **3** (*Theol.*) to blow or breathe on (someone) to symbolize the influence of the Holy Spirit. **insufflation** (-lā´shən) *n.* **1** (*Med.*) blowing or breathing (therapeutic vapour etc.) into the lungs etc. **2** (*Theol.*) a symbolic breathing upon a person. **insufflator** *n.* **1** an instrument used for insufflating. **2** a device that makes fingerprints visible by blowing powder on to a surface. [L *insufflātus*, p.p. of *insufflāre* (*flāre*, to blow)]

insular (in´sūlə) *a.* **1** of or relating to an island. **2** of the nature of an island; remote. **3** narrow, contracted (in outlook). **4** of a kind of Latin handwriting that existed in Britain and Ireland in the Middle Ages. **insularism** *n.* **insularity** (-lar´-) *n.* **insularly** *adv.* [L *insulāris*, from *insula*, island]

insulate (in´sūlāt) *v.t.* **1** to separate from other bodies by a non-conductor, so as to prevent the passage of electricity or heat. **2** to place in a detached situation or position. **3** †to make into an island. **insulating tape** *n.* an adhesive tape used to insulate exposed electrical wires etc. **insulation** *n.* **1** a material used to insulate against heat, sound or electricity. **2** a device designed to give insulation and mechanical support to telegraph wires, transmission lines etc. **3** a device intended to block the passage of an electrical current. **insulator** *n.* [L *insulātus*, made like an island, as INSULAR]

insulin (in´sūlin) *n.* a protein hormone produced in the pancreas which regulates the metabolism of sugar and fat, and the lack of which causes diabetes. [L *insula*, an island]

insult[1] (insŭlt´) *v.t.* **1** to treat or speak to rudely or contemptuously. **2** to offend. **3** †to assail. **insulter** *n.* **insulting** *a.* **insultingly** *adv.* [F *insulter*, L *insultāre*, freq. of *insilīre* (*salīre*, to leap)]

insult[2] (in´sŭlt) *n.* **1** an insulting act or remark. **2** an affront; something that is offensive (*an insult to one's intelligence*). **3** (*Med.*) **a** something that causes injury to the body. **b** an injury.

insuperable (insoo´pərəbəl, -sū´-) *a.* insurmountable; impossible to overcome. **insuperability** (-bil´-) *n.* **insuperably** *adv.* [F, from L *superābilis*]

insupportable (insəpaw´təbəl) *a.* **1** insufferable, intolerable. **2** incapable of being sustained or defended; indefensible. **insupportableness** *n.* **insupportably** *adv.*

insuppressible (insəpres´ibəl) *a.* that cannot be suppressed. **insuppressibly** *adv.*

insure (inshuə´) *v.t.* **1** to secure compensation, whole or partial, in the event of loss or injury to (property, life etc.) by paying a periodical premium (*Our household goods are insured against theft*). **2** (of the owner or the insurance company) to secure the payment of (a specified sum) in the event of loss, injury etc. **3** to provide (a person) with an insurance policy. **4** (*N Am.*) ENSURE. ~*v.i.* **1** to take out an insurance policy. **2** to make provision for a possible contingency (*It's impossible to insure against every eventuality*). **insurable** *a.* **insurability** (-bil´-) *n.* **insurance** (inshuə´rəns, -shaw´-) *n.* **1** the act of insuring against damage or loss. **2** an insurance policy. **3** a sum insured. **4** **a** a sum of money paid regularly to an insurance company; a premium. **b** a means of providing for a possible contingency. **insurance agent** *n.* a person employed by an insurance company to collect premiums. **insurance broker** *n.* a person who arranges and sells insurance. **insurance company** *n.* a company which insures persons against loss or damage. **insurance policy** *n.* **1** a contract of insurance. **2** a document detailing such a contract. **insurance stamp** *n.* a stamp certifying that a person has paid a sum of money for National Insurance. **insured** *a.* covered by insurance. **the insured** **1** the person to whom compensation for fire, damage etc. will be paid. **2** the person whose life is insured. **insurer** *n.* **1** a person or company providing insurance policies for premiums. **2** a person who insures. [var. of ENSURE]

insurgent (insœ´jənt) *a.* **1** rising up in revolt; rebellious. **2** (of waves) surging or rushing in. ~*n.* a person who rises up against established government or authority; a rebel. **insurgence, insurgency** *n.* [L *insurgens -entem*, pres.p. of *insurgere* (*surgere*, to rise)]

insurmountable (insəmown´təbəl) *a.* that cannot be surmounted, passed over or overcome. **insurmountability** (-bil´-) *n.* **insurmountably** *adv.*

insurrection (insərek´shən) *n.* the act of rising in open opposition to established authority; an uprising. **insurrectional, insurrectionary** *a.* **insurrectionist** *n.* [F, from L *insurrectiōnem*, nom. *-tio*, from *insurgere*, see INSURGENT]

insusceptible (insəsep´tibəl) *a.* not susceptible (of, to); incapable of being moved by any feeling or impression. **insusceptibility** (-bil´-) *n.*

int. *abbr.* **1** interior. **2** interjection. **3** internal. **4** international.

intact (intakt´) *a.* **1** untouched. **2** unimpaired; uninjured. **3** entire. **intactness** *n.* [L *intactus* (*tactus*, p.p. of *tangere*, to touch)]

intaglio (intah´lyō) *n.* (*pl.* **intaglios**) **1** a figure cut or engraved in a hard substance. **2** the act or process of producing this. **3** a gem with a figure cut or engraved into it, as distinct from a *cameo*. **4** an engraved design. **5** a method of printing from an etched or engraved design. ~*v.t.* (*3rd pers. sing. pres.* **intaglioes**, *pres.p.* **intaglioing**, *past, p.p.* **intaglioed**) **1** to cut or engrave (a substance) with a sunk design. **2** to engrave (a design) in this way. **intagliated** (-ātid) *a.* engraved. [It., from *intagliare*, to cut, to engrave, late L *intaleāre*, to cut, from *talea*, a twig]

intake (in´tāk) *n.* **1** the act of taking in. **2** something which is taken in. **3** a number or amount taken in or received (*They've increased their intake of students*). **4** the people or things taken in or received. **5** a place where water is taken in, an inlet. **6** an air-shaft in a mine. **7** the point at which fuel enters an engine. **8** the point where something, e.g. a garment, narrows. **9** land, esp. a tract taken in from a moorland and cultivated.

intangible (intan´jibəl) *a.* **1** not tangible; imperceptible to the touch. **2** not able to be grasped mentally. ~*n.*

something intangible. **intangibility** (-bil´-) *n.* **intangibly** *adv.* [med. L *intangibilis*]

intarsia (intah´siə) *n.* 1 the practice or art of using wood to make decorative mosaics, as developed in 15th-cent. Italy. 2 similar work in stone, glass or metal. 3 in knitting, the working of a design using separate lengths of yarn for each coloured section. [It. *intarsio*]

integer (in´tijə) *n.* 1 a whole number as distinguished from a fraction. 2 anything that is whole. [L (*tag-*, root of *tangere*, to touch)]

integrable INTEGRATE[1].

integral (in´tigrəl, -teg´-) *a.* 1 whole, entire, complete. 2 necessary to completeness, forming an essential part of a whole. 3 forming a whole. 4 (*Math.*) of, relating to or constituting an integer. 5 of, relating to or produced by integration. ~*n.* 1 (*Math.*) the limit of the sum of a series of values of a differential $f(x)\,dx$ when x varies by indefinitely small increments from one given value to another. 2 a whole, a total, an integer. 3 †an integral part. **integral calculus** *n.* a method of summing up differential quantities. **integrality** (-ral´-) *n.* **integrally** *adv.* [INTEGER]

Usage note The pronunciation (-teg´-), with stress on the second syllable, is sometimes disapproved of.

integrand (in´tigrand) *n.* (*Math.*) an expression to be integrated.

integrant (in´tigrənt) *a.* making part of a whole; necessary to constitute an entire entity. **integrant parts** *n.pl.* parts into which a body may be reduced, each remaining of the same nature as the whole.

integrate[1] (in´tigrāt) *v.t.* 1 to make into a whole, to complete by adding parts. 2 to combine into a whole. 3 to bring (a person, group) into equal participation in and full acceptance by society, an organization etc. 4 to end the racial segregation of. 5 (*Math.*) to find the integral of. ~*v.i.* to become integrated into society, an organization etc. **integrable** (in´tigrəbəl) *a.* capable of being integrated. **integrability** (-bil´-) *n.* **integrated** *a.* indicating the whole or mean value of. **integrated circuit** *n.* a minute electronic circuit consisting of an assembly of elements made from a chip of semiconductor material. **integrated services digital network** *n.* a digital telecommunications network designed to transmit sounds, images and data. **integration** (-rā´shən) *n.* 1 the making into a whole. 2 the act of integrating people into society, an organization etc. 3 the amalgamation of a previously segregated group with an existing community. 4 (*Psych.*) the formation of different elements of the personality into a unified pattern. 5 (*Math.*) the act or process of integrating. **integrationist** *n.* **integrative** (in´tigrətiv) *a.* **integrator** *n.* 1 a person who or something which integrates. 2 a device or instrument for determining the value of an integral, as an area, rate of speed etc. [INTEGER]

integrate[2] (in´tigrət) *a.* 1 made up of integrant parts. 2 whole, entire, complete.

integrity (integ´riti) *n.* 1 probity; honesty; high principle. 2 entireness, completeness. 3 soundness. [F *intégrité*, from L *integritātem*, wholeness, nom. *-tas*, from INTEGRATE[1]]

integument (integ´ūmənt) *n.* a covering, esp. a natural one, such as a skin, husk, rind or shell. **integumentary** (-men´-), **integumental** *a.* [L *integumentum*, from *integere* (*tegere*, to cover)]

intellect (in´tilekt) *n.* 1 the faculty of understanding, thinking and reasoning, as distinguished from the faculty of feeling or wishing. 2 the understanding; intelligence (*a man of great intellect*). 3 an intelligent or clever person. 4 intellectual people collectively; the intelligentsia. **intellection** (-ek´shən) *n.* the act or process of understanding or comprehending, esp. as distinct from sensation or imagination. **intellective** *a.* 1 of, relating to or produced by the intellect. 2 having power to understand. **intellectual** (intilek´chūəl) *a.* 1 possessing intellect in a high degree. 2 of, relating to or performed by the intellect. 3 appealing to or perceived by the intellect. ~*n.* 1 an intellectual person. 2 (*pl.*) the most enlightened people (in a country etc.). **intellectualism** *n.* 1 the cultivation of the intellect, esp. at the expense of feelings. 2 (*Philos.*) the doctrine that knowledge is exclusively or principally derived from pure reason. **intellectualist** *n.* **intellectuality** (-al´-) *n.* **intellectualize, intellectualise** *v.t.* 1 to make intellectual. 2 to treat intellectually; to give an intellectual character or significance to. ~*v.i.* 1 to become intellectual. 2 to employ the intellect. **intellectualization** (-zā´shən) *n.* **intellectually** *adv.* **intellectual property** *n.* (*Law*) intangible property such as a copyright or patent. [L *intellectus*, as INTELLIGENT]

intelligence (intel´ijəns) *n.* 1 the exercise of the understanding; intellectual power. 2 acquired knowledge. 3 quickness or sharpness of intellect. 4 a department concerned with gathering secret or little-known information esp. of importance for military activity. 5 such information. 6 the activity of gathering such information. 7 †news, information. 8 an intelligent being, esp. an incorporeal or spiritual being regarded as pure intellect. **intelligence department** *n.* a department concerned with gathering information about an enemy, a spy etc. **intelligence quotient** *n.* a number denoting a person's intelligence, traditionally arrived at by dividing the mental age by the age in years and multiplying the result by 100. **†intelligencer** *n.* a messenger, a spy. **intelligence test** *n.* a psychological test to determine a person's relative mental capacity. [F, from L *intelligentia*, as INTELLIGENT]

intelligent (intel´ijənt) *a.* 1 endowed with understanding. 2 clever, quick. 3 (of a machine etc.) able to adapt in response to varying circumstances and requirements. 4 (of a computer terminal) within which a certain amount of computing can be done without contacting a central computer. **intelligential** (-jen´shəl) *a.* **intelligently** *adv.* **intelligentsia** (-jent´siə) *n.* 1 the class of people who are considered to be cultured, educated and politically aware. 2 intellectuals. [L *intelligens -entem*, pres.p. of *intelligere*, to understand (INTER-, *legere*, to gather, to choose)]

intelligible (intel´ijibəl) *a.* 1 capable of being understood, comprehensible. 2 (*Philos.*) capable of being understood only by the intellect, as distinct from *sensible*. **intelligibility** (-bil´-), **intelligibleness** *n.* **intelligibly** *adv.* [F, from L *intelligibilis*, as INTELLIGENT]

Intelpost (in´telpōst) *n.* the electronic transmission of messages internationally by fax, telex etc. [from *Int*ernational *El*ectronic *Post*]

Intelsat (in´telsat) *n.* an international body which operates a system of communications satellites. [*In*ternational *Tel*ecommunications *Sat*ellite Consortium]

intemperate (intem´pərət) *a.* 1 not exercising due moderation or self-restraint; immoderate. 2 indulging any appetite or passion in excess. 3 addicted to excessive indulgence in alcoholic drink. 4 (of a climate etc.) extreme; inclement. **intemperance** *n.* lack of moderation or self-restraint, esp. excessive indulgence in alcoholic drink. **intemperately** *adv.* **intemperateness** *n.* [L *intemperātus*]

intend (intend´) *v.t.* 1 to propose, to plan (*I intend to continue*; *We intend coming*). 2 to mean, to have in mind (*It was intended as a compliment*). 3 to design (for) (*It's intended for beginners*). 4 to destine (for) (*He was intended for a career in the army*). 5 to signify or mean to express. 6 †to direct (one's course etc.). **intendancy** *n.* (*pl.* **intendancies**) 1 superintendence. 2 a body of intendants. 3 the position or office of intendant. **intendant** *n.* 1 a superintendent or manager. 2 a person who manages an opera house or a theatre. **intended** *a.* **1** done deliberately or on purpose. **2** designed. *~n.* (*dated or facet.*) a person whom one is expecting to marry. **intendedly** *adv.* **intending** *a.* who intends to be. **intendment** *n.* **1** (*Law*) the true intent or meaning of something as determined by the law. **2** †intention, purpose. [F *entendre, intendere*, to stretch to, to direct (*tendere*, to stretch, see TEND[1])]

intense (intens´) *a.* (*comp.* **intenser**, *superl.* **intensest**) **1** extreme in degree (*intense feelings; intense heat*). **2** strongly or deeply emotional. **3** (of an activity, effort etc.) very concentrated (*intense concentration*). **intensely** *adv.* **intenseness** *n.* **intensify** (-fī) *v.t.* (*3rd pers. sing. pres.* **intensifies**, *pres.p.* **intensifying**, *past, p.p.* **intensified**) **1** to render more intense. **2** in photography, to increase the density of (a negative) so as to produce stronger contrasts. *~v.i.* to become more intense. **intensification** (-fikā´shən) *n.* **intensifier** *n.* **1** a person who or a thing which intensifies. **2** (*Gram.*) a word that gives force or emphasis to the word that it modifies. **intensity** *n.* (*pl.* **intensities**) **1** the condition or quality of being intense. **2** an extreme degree of force or strength. **3** the measurable amount of something, e.g. sound, radiation etc. [F, from L *intensus*, p.p. of *intendere*, to INTEND]

intension (inten´shən) *n.* **1** (*formal*) intense exertion or concentration (of the mind, will etc.). **2** (*formal*) intensity, high degree (of a quality), as distinct from *extension*. **3** (*Logic*) the content of a notion. **intensional** *a.* **intensionally** *adv.* [as INTEND]

intensive (inten´siv) *a.* **1** concentrated, thorough. **2** unremitting. **3** characterized by intensity. **4** (*chiefly in comb.*) utilizing one specified element of production proportionately more than others (*capital-intensive*). **5** conducive to high productivity within a narrow area (*intensive farming*). **6** (*Gram.*) serving to intensify, or to add force or emphasis. *~n.* (*Gram.*) an intensive particle, word or phrase. **intensive care** *n.* **1** continuous care and close monitoring of a person who is dangerously ill in hospital. **2** a unit in a hospital that is specially designed for this. **intensively** *adv.* **intensiveness** *n.*

intent (intent´) *n.* **1** design, purpose, intention (*with intent to inflict injury; That wasn't my intent*). **2** meaning, drift. *~a.* **1** bent or determined (on) (*intent on winning*). **2** giving complete attention to something (*She was intent on her books*). **3** fixed; earnest (*an intent stare*). **to all intents and purposes** practically, really, in reality. **intently** *adv.* **intentness** *n.* [OF *entent, entente*, intention, meaning, L *intentus*, a stretching out, late L, intention, from *intendere*, to INTEND]

intention (inten´shən) *n.* **1** purpose, design, intent (*He has no intention of giving up; It wasn't my intention to cause offence*). **2** determination to act in some particular manner. **3** (*pl., coll.*) designs with regard to marriage. **4** (*Logic*) a general concept. **5** (*Med.*) a process of healing. **intentional** *a.* done with design or purpose. **intentionality** (-al´-) *n.* **intentionally** *adv.* **intentioned** *a.* (*chiefly in comb.*, as *well-intentioned*). **intention tremor** *n.* a trembling of a part of the body on carrying out a voluntary movement, indicative of disease of the nervous system.

inter (intœ´) *v.t.* (*pres.p.* **interring**, *past, p.p.* **interred**) to bury; to place in a grave or tomb. **interment** *n.* [OF *interrer*, late L *interrāre* (*terra*, earth)]

Usage note The nouns *interment* and *internment* should not be confused: *interment* refers to burial, and *internment* to confinement.

---

inter. *abbr.* intermediate.

inter- (in´tə) *pref.* **1** among or between, as *interstate*. **2** mutually or reciprocally, as *interplay, interdepend*.

interact (intərakt´) *v.i.* to act reciprocally; to act on each other. **interactant** *a., n.* **interaction** (-rak´shən) *n.* **1** mutual or reciprocal action. **2** (*Physics*) the transfer of energy between particles. **interactional** *a.* **interactionism** *n.* the theory that mind and body act on one another. **interactive** *a.* **1** capable of mutual action. **2** (*Comput.*) permitting continuous mutual communication between computer and user (*interactive multimedia*).

interalia (intər ah´liə, ā´liə) *adv.* among other things. [L]

inter-allied (intəral´īd) *a.* among or relating to two or more allies.

interarticular (intərahtik´ūlə) *a.* between the surfaces of a joint.

interatomic (intərətom´ik) *a.* between or among atoms.

interbank (in´təbangk) *a.* operating, existing etc. between banks.

interbed (intəbed´) *v.t.* (*pres.p.* **interbedding**, *past, p.p.* **interbedded**) (*Geol.*) to interstratify.

interblend (intəblend´) *v.t.* to mingle with one another. *~v.i.* to blend together.

interbreed (intəbrēd´) *v.i.* to breed with members of a different species, race etc. *~v.t.* to cause to breed in this way.

intercalary (intœ´kələri, intəkal´-), **intercalar** (-lə) *a.* **1** (of a day, month) inserted in the calendar to make it correspond with the solar year. **2** (of a year) containing such an addition. **3** inserted, interpolated. **intercalate** (intœ´-) *v.t.* **1** to insert between or amongst others (esp. a day or month into a calendar). **2** to interpolate; to insert in an unusual or irregular way. **intercalated** *a.* interposed; inserted. **intercalation** (-ā´shən) *n.* **intercalative** *a.* [L *intercalārius*, from *intercalāre* (*calāre*, to proclaim), p.p. *intercalātus*]

intercede (intəsēd´) *v.i.* **1** to plead (with someone) in favour of another. **2** to mediate. **interceder** *n.* [F *intercéder*, L *intercēdere* (*cēdere*, to go), p.p. *intercessus*]

intercellular (intəsel´ūlə) *a.* occurring or situated between or among cells.

intercensal (intəsen´səl) *a.* of or relating to the interval between two censuses.

intercept[1] (intəsept´) *v.t.* **1** to stop, take or seize on the way from one place to another. **2** to obstruct; to stop; to shut off. **3** (*Math.*) to mark off or include (a space) between two points etc. **interception** *n.* **interceptive** *a.* **interceptor** (in´-) *n.* **1** a person who or thing which intercepts. **2** a swift aeroplane used to pursue and intercept enemy aircraft. [L *interceptus*, p.p. of *intercipere* (*capere*, to take)]

intercept[2] (in´təsept) *n.* (*Math.*) the part of a line that is intercepted.

intercession (intəsesh´ən) *n.* **1** the act of interceding. **2** a prayer offered for others. **intercessional** *a.* **intercessor** (-ses´ə) *n.* a person who intercedes. **intercessorial** (-saw´ri-), **intercessory** *a.* [L *intercessio*, see INTERCEDE]

interchange[1] (intəchānj´) *v.t.* **1** (of two people) to exchange with each other. **2** to put each (of two things) in the place of the other, to alternate. *~v.i.* to alternate. **interchangeable** *a.* **interchangeability** (-bil´-), **interchangeableness** *n.* **interchangeably** *adv.* [OF *entrechangier* (*changier*, to CHANGE)]

interchange[2] (in´təchānj) *n.* **1** reciprocal exchange. **2** alternate succession, alternation. **3** a junction of two or more roads designed to prevent traffic streams crossing one another.

intercity (intəsit´i) *a.* existing, carried on or travelling between different cities. *~n.* (*pl.* **intercities**) a fast train travelling between cities.

inter-class (intəklahs´) *a.* existing or carried on between different classes.

interclavicle (intəklav´ikəl) *n.* a median bony plate attached to the clavicles, present in many reptiles. **interclavicular** (-vik´ū-) *a.*

intercollegiate (intəkəlē´jət) *a.* existing or carried on between colleges or universities.

intercolonial (intəkəlō´niəl) *a.* existing or carried on between colonies.

intercolumnar (intəkəlŭm´nə) *a.* placed between columns. **intercolumniation** (-niā´shən) *n.* **1** the spacing of columns in a building. **2** the interval between two columns.

intercom (in´təkom) *n.* (*coll.*) **1** a system of intercommunication by telephone in aircraft, within a building etc. **2** a device used for this. [*inte*rnal *com*munication]

intercommunicate (intəkəmū´nikāt) *v.i.* **1** to hold or enjoy mutual communication. **2** (of rooms) to have free passage to and from each other. **intercommunicable** *a.* **intercommunication** (-ā´shən) *n.* **intercommunicative** *a.* **intercommunion** (-yən) *n.* **1** fellowship between members of different Christian denominations. **2** mutual action or communion.

intercommunity (intəkəmū´niti) *n.* the quality of being common to various people, groups etc. or of holding things in common.

interconnect (intəkənekt´) *v.i.*, *v.t.* to connect with each other. **interconnectedness** *n.* **interconnection** *n.*

intercontinental (intəkontinen´təl) *a.* existing or travelling between or connecting different continents.

interconvert (intəkənvœt´) *v.t.*, *v.i.* to convert into each other. **interconversion** *n.* **interconvertible** *a.*

intercooler (in´təkoolə) *n.* a heat exchanger used e.g. in a supercharged internal-combustion engine to cool gas between successive compressions. **intercool** *v.t.*

intercorrelate (intəkor´əlāt) *v.i.* to correlate with each other. ~*v.t.* to cause to intercorrelate. **intercorrelation** (-ā´shən) *n.*

intercostal (intəkos´təl) *a.* **1** situated between the ribs. **2** between the framework of the keel of a ship. **intercostally** *adv.*

intercounty (intəkown´ti) *a.* existing or carried on between counties.

intercourse (in´təkaws) *n.* **1** reciprocal dealings, association, communication etc., between people, nations etc. **2** sexual intercourse. **3** spiritual communion. [OF *entrecours*, late L *intercursus*, commerce, L, intervention (COURSE)]

intercrop (intəkrop´) *n.* a crop raised between the rows of another crop. ~*v.t.* (*pres.p.* **intercropping,** *past, p.p.* **intercropped**) to raise (a crop) in this way. ~*v.i.* to plant intercrops. **intercropping** *n.*

intercross (intəkros´) *v.t.* **1** to lay (things) across each other. **2** to cause (animals) to interbreed. ~*v.i.* **1** to cross each other. **2** to interbreed. ~*n.* an instance of cross-breeding.

intercrural (intəkrū´rəl) *a.* between the legs.

intercurrent (intəkŭr´ənt) *a.* **1** occurring between or among; intervening. **2** (*Med.*) occurring during the progress of another disease. **3** (*Med.*) occurring at different times. **intercurrence** *n.* [L *intercurrens -entem*, pres.p. of *intercurrere* (*currere*, to run)]

intercut (intəkŭt´) *v.t.* (*pres.p.* **intercutting,** *past, p.p.* **intercut**) to alternate (contrasting camera shots) by cutting.

interdenominational (intədinominā´shənəl) *a.* existing or carried on between different religious denominations. **interdenominationally** *adv.*

interdental (intəden´təl) *a.* **1** situated between the teeth. **2** (of consonants) sounded with the tip of the tongue between the upper and lower front teeth.

interdepartmental (intədēpahtmen´təl) *a.* involving more than one department. **interdepartmentally** *adv.*

interdepend (intədipend´) *v.i.* to depend upon each other. **interdependence, interdependency** *n.* **interdependent** *a.* **interdependently** *adv.*

interdict[1] (in´tədikt) *n.* **1** an official prohibition. **2** (*Sc. Law*) an order of the Court of Session equivalent to an injunction. **3** in the Roman Catholic Church, a sentence by which places or persons are debarred from ecclesiastical functions and privileges. **interdictory** (-dik´-) *a.* [L *interdictum*, a decree, from *interdictus*, p.p. of *interdīcere*, to impose, to forbid by a decree (*dīcere*, to say)]

interdict[2] (intədikt´) *v.t.* **1** to forbid; to prohibit. **2** to restrain (from). **3** to lay under an interdict. **4** (*N Am.*) to hinder (an enemy army), esp. by bombing lines of communication. **5** (*N Am.*) to stop or intercept. **interdiction** (-dik´shən) *n.*

interdigital (intədij´itəl) *a.* situated between the fingers or toes. **interdigitate** *v.i.* to interlock, as when the fingers of one hand are inserted between those of the other. ~*v.t.* to cause to interlock in this way. [L *interdigitālis* (*digitus*, finger, see DIGIT)]

interdisciplinary (intədisiplin´əri) *a.* involving two or more disciplines or fields of study.

interest[1] (in´trist) *n.* **1** lively, sympathetic or curious attention; concern (*She didn't show much interest*). **2** the power of eliciting attention or concern (*The subject holds little interest for me*). **3** something, such as a hobby or subject, in which one has a personal concern (*What are your interests?*). **4** participation in advantages, benefits or profits. **5** (*often pl.*) benefit, advantage (*It's not in your interest*). **6** proprietary right or concern; a share, a portion or stake (in). **7** (*collect.*) those having a concern in a particular business etc. (*the shipping interest*). **8** a business etc. in which a group or party has a concern. **9** payment for the use of borrowed money or on a debt. **10** selfish concern for one's own welfare. **at interest** (of money borrowed) on which interest is payable. **in the interest/ interests of** as a way of furthering or ensuring (*in the interests of hygiene*). **to declare an/ one's interest** (often of a Member of Parliament) to make known one's usu. financial interest in a company about which there is (parliamentary) discussion. **to lose interest** to stop being interested or interesting. **to take an interest in** to show curiosity about or concern for. **with interest 1** with interest added. **2** with added force etc. (*He hit him back with interest*). **interest group** *n.* a group of people concerned to defend a common interest. [earlier *interess*, altered after OF *interest* (F *intérêt*), L *interesse*, to concern (INTER-, *esse*, to be)]

interest[2] (in´trist) *v.t.* **1** to arouse or hold the attention or curiosity of (*Might this book interest you?*). **2** to cause to participate (in) (*Can I interest you in a game of tennis?*). **interested** *a.* **1** having one's interest excited. **2** having an interest, concern or share in. **3** liable to be biased through personal interest, not disinterested. **interestedly** *adv.* **interestedness** *n.* **interesting** *a.* arousing interest, attention or curiosity. **†in an interesting condition** pregnant. **interestingly** *adv.* **interestingness** *n.* [earlier *interess* (influ. by INTEREST[1] or formed from the p.p. *interess'd*), as INTEREST[1]]

interface (in´təfās) *n.* **1** a surface lying between two spaces. **2** the point at which independent systems, processes etc. meet and act on each other. **3** an electrical circuit linking two computers or other devices. ~*v.t.* to connect (a device) with another device by an interface. ~*v.i.* **1** to be connected with another device in this way. **2** to interact (with). **interfacial** (-fā´shəl) *a.* **1** included between two faces of a crystal etc. **2** of or relating to an interface. **interfacing** *n.* stiffening material inserted between layers of fabric.

interfaith (in´təfāth) *a.* of, relating to or occurring between different religious faiths or their representatives.

interfemoral (intəfem´ərəl) *a.* situated or extending between the thighs.

interfere (intəfiə´) *v.i.* **1** to hinder or obstruct a process, activity etc. **2** to meddle (with). **3** (*euphem.*) to assault sexually. **4** to intervene or get involved (in), esp. when this is unnecessary or unwanted. **5** (*Physics*) (of light or other waves) to act reciprocally, to modify each other. **6** (of a horse) to strike the hoof against the opposite fetlock. **interference** *n.* **1** the act of interfering. **2** an instance of this. **3** the spoiling of radio reception by atmospherics or by other signals. **4** (*Physics*) the effect of combining two or more waves of the same frequency. **interferential** (-fəren´shəl) *a.* **interferer** *n.* **interfering** *a., n.* **interferingly** *adv.* **interferometer** (-fərom´itə) *n.* an instrument for making accurate measurements mainly of wavelength, using interference patterns. **interferometric** (-ferəmet´rik) *a.* **interferometrically** (-rimet´-) *adv.* **interferometry** (-fərom´itri) *n.* [OF *entreferir* (*ferir*, L *ferīre*, to strike), to exchange blows]

interferon (intəfiə´ron) *n.* an antiviral protein substance produced in living cells in humans and other creatures in response to infection from a virus.

interfibrillar (intəfib´rilə) *a.* between fibrils.

interfile (intəfīl´) *v.t.* **1** to file (two sets of items) together. **2** to file (one or more items) into an existing arrangement of items.

interflow (in´təflō) *v.i.* to flow into each other; to merge. *~n.* the act or result of this.

interfluent (intœ´fluənt) *a.* flowing together or into each other. [L *interfluens -entem*, pres.p. of *interfluere* (*fluere*, to flow)]

interfuse (intəfūz´) *v.t.* **1** to intersperse (with). **2** to blend together, to cause to flow into each other. *~v.i.* to blend into each other. **interfusion** (-zhən) *n.* [L *interfūsus*, p.p. of *interfundere* (*fundere*, to pour)]

intergalactic (intəgəlak´tik) *a.* between galaxies. **intergalactically** *adv.*

interglacial (intəglā´shəl, -siəl) *a.* occurring or formed between two of the glacial periods. *~n.* a period between two of the glacial periods.

intergovernmental (intəgŭvənmen´təl) *a.* involving or concerning two or more governments. **intergovernmentally** *adv.*

intergrade (in´təgrād) *n.* an intermediate grade or stage. *~v.i.* to pass into or mingle gradually with another form. **intergradation** (-grədā´shən) *n.*

intergrowth (in´təgrōth) *n.* a growing into each other.

interim (in´tərim) *n.* the meantime; the intervening time or period (*in the interim*). *~a.* temporary, provisional (*an interim measure*). *~†adv.* meanwhile. **interim dividend** *n.* a dividend paid out before the end of a company's financial year. [L, in the meantime (*-im*, adv. suf.)]

interior (intiə´riə) *a.* **1** internal, inner. **2** inland; remote from the coast, frontier or exterior. **3** domestic, as distinct from foreign. **4** of or relating to the inner consciousness, the soul or spiritual matters. **5** within a building. **6** coming from within. *~n.* **1** the internal part of anything; the inside. **2** the central or inland part of a country. **3** the inside of a building or room, esp. as portrayed in a picture, photograph etc. **4** the domestic affairs of a country. **5** the government department dealing with these. **6** the inward nature; the soul. **interior angle** *n.* the angle between two sides of a polygon. **interior decoration, interior design** *n.* the design and decoration of the interior of a house, room etc. **interiorize, interiorise** *v.t.* **interiorly** *adv.* **interior monologue** *n.* in a novel, the representation of a character's train of thought. **interior-sprung** *a.* (of a mattress etc.) having springs. [L, compar. of *inter*, see INTER-]

interjacent (intəjā´sənt) *a.* lying between or among; intervening. [L *interjacens -entem*, pres.p. of *interjacēre* (*jacēre*, to lie)]

interject (intəjekt´) *v.t.* **1** to insert (a remark etc.) abruptly. **2** to interrupt with. **interjection** *n.* **1** the act of interjecting. **2** a word which expresses sudden feeling, and which is differentiated as a separate part of speech; an exclamation. **interjectional, interjectory, interjectural** *a.* **interjectionally** *adv.* [L *interjectus*, p.p. of *interjicere* (*jacere*, to throw)]

interknit (intənit´) *v.t., v.i.* (*pres.p.* **interknitting,** *past, p.p.* **interknit, interknitted**) to knit together.

interlace (intəlās´) *v.t.* **1** to lace or weave together; to interweave. **2** to intersperse (with). *~v.i.* to be interwoven (with each other); to intersect in a complicated fashion. **interlacement** *n.* [ME *entrelace*, F *entrelacer* (*lacer*, to LACE)]

interlanguage (in´təlang·gwij) *n.* a language having characteristics of two or more other languages, e.g. Pidgin English.

interlap (intəlap´) *v.i.* (*pres.p.* **interlapping,** *past, p.p.* **interlapped**) to overlap.

interlard (intəlahd´) *v.t.* to diversify (a conversation, passage in a book etc.) with unusual phrases etc. [F *entrelarder* (*larder*, to LARD)]

interleaf (in´təlēf) *n.* (*pl.* **interleaves** (-lēvz)) a leaf, usu. blank, inserted between the leaves of a book, e.g. in order to protect an illustration. **interleave** (-lēv´) *v.t.* to insert blank leaves between the leaves of (a book).

interleukin (intəlū´kin) *n.* any of a number of proteins that are produced by white blood cells and stimulate activity against infection.

interlibrary (intəlī´brəri) *a.* between libraries.

interline[1] (intəlīn´) *v.t.* **1** to write or print between the lines of. **2** to insert (words) between lines. **3** to write or print on alternate lines. **interlineal** (-lin´iəl), **interlinear** (-lin´iə) *a.* written between lines of text. **interlineation** (-ā´shən) *n.* **interlining**[1] (in´-) *n.* [prob. from late L *interlineāre* (after MF *entreligner*)]

interline[2] (intəlīn´) *v.t.* to insert an extra lining between the outer fabric and the lining of (a garment). **interlining**[2] *n.* the material used to interline a garment.

Interlingua (intəling´gwə) *n.* an artificial language based on Latin roots. [L *lingua*, tongue]

interlining[1] INTERLINE[1].

interlining[2] INTERLINE[2].

interlink (intəlingk´) *v.t., v.i.* to link together.

interlobular (intəlob´ūlə) *a.* situated or occurring between the lobes of a gland or other organ.

interlock[1] (intəlok´) *v.t.* to connect firmly together by reciprocal engagement of parts; to link or lock together. *~v.i.* to engage with each other by reciprocal connections.

interlock[2] (in´təlok) *a.* (of a fabric) closely knitted. *~n.* **1** the state of being interlocked. **2** a device in a logic circuit preventing the initiation of an activity in the absence of certain preceding events.

interlocution (intəlәkū´shən) *n.* conversation, dialogue, discussion. **interlocutor** (-lok´-) *n.* **1** a person who takes part in a conversation. **2** (*Sc. Law*) an interlocutory or interim decree in a case. **interlocutory** *a.* **1** consisting of dialogue. **2** (*Law*) intermediate, not final. **interlocutress** (-tris), **interlocutrice** (-trēs), **interlocutrix** (-triks) *n.* a female interlocutor. [L *interlocūtio* (*loquī*, to speak)]

interloper (in´təlōpə) *n.* **1** an intruder. **2** a person who interferes in someone else's affairs. **3** a person who trades without a licence or infringes upon another's business. **interlope** *v.i.* [prob. from *inter-* and *-loper* (cp. Dut. *loopen*, OE *hlēapen*, to LEAP)]

interlude (in´təlood) *n.* **1** a pause or a short entertainment between the acts of a play. **2** an intervening period or event that contrasts with what comes before and after. **3** an incident, esp. an amusing one, coming between graver events. **4** a piece of instrumental music played between the acts of a drama, between the verses of a hymn, portions of a church service etc. [med. L *interlūdium* (*lūdus*, play)]

interlunar (intəloo´nə) *a.* of or relating to the time when the moon, about to change from old to new, is invisible. **interlunation** (-nā´shən) *n.* the time when the moon is invisible.

intermarriage (intəmaˊrij) *n.* 1 marriage between people of different families, tribes, castes or nations. 2 marriage between people closely related. **intermarry** *v.i.* (*3rd pers. sing. pres.* **intermarries,** *pres.p.* **intermarrying,** *past, p.p.* **intermarried**) 1 (of different races, tribes etc.) to become connected by marriage. 2 to marry within one's family, group etc.

intermeddle (intəmed´əl) *v.i.* to meddle. [A-F *entremedler,* OF *entremesler*]

intermediary (intəmē´diəri) *a.* being, coming or acting between; intermediate. ~*n.* (*pl.* **intermediaries**) 1 an intermediate agent, a go-between. 2 intermediation. **intermediacy** (-si) *n.* **intermedial** *n.* an intermediate thing. [F *intermédiaire,* from L *intermedius* (as INTERMEDIATE[1])]

intermediate[1] (intəmē´diət) *a.* coming between two things, extremes, places etc. ~*n.* 1 something that is intermediate. 2 a chemical compound produced by a reaction and used as a starting point for the synthesis of some other product. **intermediate frequency** *n.* the frequency to which a radio signal is changed in a superheterodyne receiver. **intermediately** *adv.* **intermediateness** *n.* **intermediate technology** *n.* technology as adapted for the conditions and requirements of developing nations. [med. L *intermediatus* (INTER-, *medius,* middle)]

intermediate[2] (intəmē´diāt) *v.i.* to act as intermediary; to mediate (between). **intermediation** (-ā´shən) *n.* **intermediator** *n.*

interment INTER.

intermesh (intəmesh´) *v.i.* to become meshed together. ~*v.t.* to cause (things) to become intermeshed.

intermezzo (intəmet´sō) *n.* (*pl.* **intermezzi** (-si), **intermezzos**) 1 a short movement connecting the main divisions of an opera or a large musical composition. 2 a piece of this kind performed independently. 3 a short piece of music for a solo instrument. 4 a short dramatic or other entertainment between the acts of a play. [It., pop. var. of *intermedio,* L *intermedius,* INTERMEDIARY]

intermigration (intəmīgrā´shən) *n.* reciprocal migration.

interminable (intœ´minəbəl) *a.* 1 endless or seeming to have no end. 2 tediously protracted. **interminableness** *n.* **interminably** *adv.* [late L *interminābilis* (*termināre,* to TERMINATE)]

intermingle (intəming´gəl) *v.t.* to mingle together, to intermix. ~*v.i.* to be mingled (with).

intermit (intəmit´) *v.t.* (*pres.p.* **intermitting,** *past, p.p.* **intermitted**) to cause to cease for a time; to suspend. ~*v.i.* (of a fever, pain etc.) to cease or relax at intervals. **intermission** (-shən) *n.* 1 a pause or temporary cessation. 2 an interval between acts of a play, parts of a concert etc. 3 the act of intermitting or the state of being intermitted. **intermissive** *a.* **intermittence, intermittency** *n.* **intermittent** *a.* occurring at intervals. **intermittently** *adv.* [L *intermittere* (*mittere,* to send), p.p. *-missus*]

intermix (intəmiks´) *v.t., v.i.* to mix together. **intermixable** *a.* **intermixture** (-chə) *n.*

intermodal (intəmō´dəl) *a.* 1 (of a transport system) involving two or more modes of conveyance. 2 (of a container) able to be conveyed by two or more different modes of transport.

intermolecular (intəmələk´ūlə) *a.* between molecules.

intern[1] (intœn´) *v.t.* to confine (aliens, political opponents etc.), esp. during wartime. **internee** (-nē´) *n.* a person who is interned. **internment** *n.* **internment camp** *n.* a camp for the internment of aliens in time of war, or of prisoners of war. [F *interner,* from L *internus,* INTERNAL]

Usage note See note on INTERMENT (under INTER).

intern[2] (in´tœn), **interne** *n.* (*esp. N Am.*) an assistant surgeon or physician resident in a hospital. ~*v.i.* to serve as an intern. **internship** *n.*

internal (intœ´nəl) *a.* 1 of or relating to or situated in the inside. 2 domestic as opposed to foreign. 3 relating to or affecting the inside of the body. 4 (of a student) at a university and sitting its examinations. 5 occurring or applying within an organization. 6 inherent, intrinsic. 7 of or relating to the inner being, inward. ~*n.pl.* intrinsic or essential qualities. **internal-combustion engine** *n.* an engine in which mechanical energy is produced by the combustion or explosion of a mixture of air and gas in its cylinder. **internal ear** *n.* INNER EAR (under INNER). **internal energy** *n.* the energy of the constituent molecules of a system and their potential energies arising from their interactions with one another. **internal evidence** *n.* evidence derived from what the thing itself contains. **internal exile** *n.* banishment from one's city or province, but not from one's country. **internality** (-nal´-) *n.* **internalize, internalise** *v.t.* 1 to assimilate (an idea etc.) into one's outlook. 2 to contain (an emotion) within oneself instead of expressing it. 3 (of a business) to assimilate into the internal structure. **internalization** (-zā´shən) *n.* **internally** *adv.* **internal market** *n.* 1 SINGLE MARKET (under SINGLE). 2 in the National Health Service, a decentralized system of funding whereby health authorities purchase health care for their local residents through arranging contracts with hospitals. **internal rhyme** *n.* the use of rhyming words within a line of verse. [med. L *internālis,* from *internus,* inward]

internat. *abbr.* international.

international (intənash´ənəl) *a.* 1 of or relating to, subsisting or carried on between, different nations. 2 recognised or used by many countries. ~*n.* 1 a match between two national teams. 2 a person who takes part in such a match. 3 (**International**) any of the four associations set up between 1864 and 1936 to promote socialist or communist action throughout the world. 4 a member of any of these. **International Court of Justice** *n.* the principal judicial organ of the United Nations, inaugurated in 1946. **International Date Line** *n.* a line roughly along the 180th meridian, east and west of which the date is one day different. **Internationale** (-nahl) *n.* 1 the French socialist hymn adopted by the International. 2 International. **internationalism** *n.* 1 the promotion of a community of interests between nations. 2 (**Internationalism**) the principles or objects advocated by the Internationals. **internationalist** *n.* 1 an advocate of internationalism. 2 (**Internationalist**) a member of the International. 3 a person who is versed in international law. **internationality** (-nal´-) *n.* **internationalize, internationalise** *v.t.* 1 to make international. 2 to bring under the joint protection or control of different nations. **internationalization** (-zā´shən) *n.* **International Labour Organization** *n.* an independent body established at Geneva at the same time as the League of Nations, with the object of raising the level of the standard of labour conditions throughout the world. **international law** *n.* an accepted system of laws regulating intercourse between nations. **internationally** *adv.* **International Phonetic Alphabet** *n.* an internationally recognised series of phonetic symbols intended to give an accurate representation of human speech sounds. **international system of units** *n.* S I units. **international unit** *n.* an internationally recognized unit for measuring the concentration of vitamin material.

interne INTERN[2].

internecine (intənē´sīn) *a.* 1 mutually destructive. 2 deadly, destructive. [L *internecīnus* (*necāre,* to kill)]

Internet (in´tənet) *n.* an international computer network via which business, academic and private users can exchange information and communicate.
internist (intœ´nist) *n.* (*Med., esp. NAm.*) a specialist in internal medicine.
internode (in´tənōd) *n.* **1** (*Anat.*) a part between two nodes or joints. **2** (*Bot.*) a part of a stem between two nodes. **internodal** (-nō´-) *a.*
internuclear (intənū´kliə) *a.* between nuclei.
internuncio (intənŭn´shiō) *n.* (*pl.* **internuncios**) **1** a messenger between two parties. **2** an ambassador of the Pope sent to a court when there is no nuncio present or to minor states. **internuncial** *a.* **1** (of nerves, neurons) communicating between different parts. **2** of or relating to an internuncio or his functions. [It. *internunzio*, L *internuntius* (*nuntius*, see NUNCIO)]
interoceanic (intərōshian´ik) *a.* situated between or connecting two oceans.
interoceptive (intərōsep´tiv) *a.* of or relating to stimuli developing inside the viscera.
interoperable (intərop´ərəbəl) *a.* able to operate jointly. **interoperability** (-bil´-) *n.*
interorbital (intəraw´bitəl) *a.* situated between the orbits of the eyes.
interosculate (intəros´kūlāt) *v.i.* INOSCULATE.
interosseal (intəros´iəl), **interosseous** (-iəs) *a.* situated between bones.
interpage (intəpāj´) *v.t.* **1** to insert (pages) between other pages in a book. **2** to print (matter) on intermediate pages.
interparietal (intəparī´ətəl) *a.* situated between the parietal bones of the skull. **interparietally** *adv.*
interpellate (intœ´pəlāt) *v.t.* to interrogate, esp. to interrupt discussion in a parliament in order to demand a statement or explanation from (a minister). **interpellation** (-ā´shən) *n.* **interpellator** *n.* [L *interpellātus* (*pellāre*, var. of *pellere*, to drive)]
interpenetrate (intəpen´itrāt) *v.t.* **1** to penetrate thoroughly, to permeate. **2** to penetrate (each other). *~v.i.* to penetrate each other. **interpenetration** (-rā´shən) *n.* **interpenetrative** (-rətiv) *a.*
interpersonal (intəpœ´sənəl) *a.* involving communication between people (*interpersonal skills*). **interpersonally** *adv.*
interphase (in´təfāz) *n.* (*Biol.*) the period between one division of a cell and the next.
interplait (intəplat´) *v.i., v.t.* to plait together.
interplanetary (intəplan´itəri) *a.* **1** of or relating to travel between the planets. **2** between planets.
interplay (in´təplā) *n.* reciprocal action between parts or things.
interplead (intəplēd´) *v.i.* to take legal proceedings in order to discuss and determine an incidental issue. *~v.t.* to cause to interplead. **interpleader** (in´-) *n.* a suit by which the claims of two parties to money or property are determined, in order that a third party, on whom the claim is made, may know to which party payment is due. [A-F *enterpleder*]
Interpol (in´təpol) *n.* the International Police Commission, that ensures cooperation between police forces in the suppression and detection of crime.
interpolate (intœ´pəlāt) *v.t.* **1** to insert (esp. a spurious word or passage) in (a book or document). **2** to interject. **3** (*Math.*) to introduce (intermediate terms) in a series. *~v.i.* to make interpolations. **interpolation** (-ā´shən) *n.* **1** the act of interpolating. **2** something which is interpolated. **3** (*Math.*) the operation of finding terms (conformable to the law of the series) between any two consecutive terms of a series. **interpolative** *a.* **interpolator** *n.* [L *interpolātus*, p.p. of *interpolāre* (*polāre*, rel. to *polīre*, to POLISH)]
interpose (intəpōz´) *v.t.* **1** to place between or among. **2** to put forward (an objection, veto, obstruction etc.) by way of intervention or interference. *~v.i.* **1** to intervene; to intercede; to mediate between. **2** to remark by way of interruption, to interrupt. **interposal** *n.* **interposer** *n.*
interposition (intəpəzish´ən) *n.* **1** the act of interposing; intervention; mediation. **2** that which is interposed. **3** an interference. [F *interposer*]
interpret (intœ´prit) *v.t.* (*pres.p.* **interpreting,** *past, p.p.* **interpreted**) **1** to explain the meaning of. **2** to find out the meaning of, to construe or understand in a particular way. **3** to represent the meaning of or one's idea of artistically. *~v.i.* to act as an interpreter. **interpretable** *a.* **interpretability** (-bil´-) *n.* **interpretation** (-ā´shən) *n.* **interpretational** *a.* **interpretative** (-prətətiv) *a.* **interpretatively** *adv.* **interpreter** *n.* **1** a person who interprets, esp. one employed to translate orally to persons speaking a foreign language. **2** (*Comput.*) a program that translates and executes a second program line by line. **interpretership** *n.* **interpretive** *a.* **interpretively** *adv.* **interpretress** (-tris) *n.* a female interpreter. [F *interpréter*, L *interpretārī*, from *interpres -pretis* (*-pret-*, cogn. with Sansk. *prath-*, to spread abroad)]
interprovincial (intəprəvin´shəl) *a.* existing, carried on etc. between different provinces.
interracial (intərā´shəl) *a.* existing, carried on etc. between different races. **interracially** *adv.*
interradial (intərā´diəl) *a.* (*Zool.*) situated between radii or rays. **interradially** *adv.*
interregnum (intəreg´nəm) *n.* (*pl.* **interregnums, interregna** (-nə)) **1** the period between two reigns, ministries or governments. **2** a suspension or interruption of normal authority, succession etc. **3** an interval, a pause. **interregnal** *a.* [L (*regnum*, REIGN)]
interrelate (intərilāt´) *v.t.* to relate (things) to each other. *~v.i.* to be interrelated. **interrelation** (-ā´shən) *n.* **interrelationship** *n.*
interrex (in´təreks) *n.* (*pl.* **interreges** (-rējēz)) a person who governs during an interregnum; a regent. [L *rex*, king]
interrog. *abbr.* **1** interrogate. **2** interrogation. **3** interrogative.
interrogate (inter´əgāt) *v.t.* to put questions to, esp. in a formal or thorough way. *~v.i.* to ask questions. **interrogation** (-ā´shən) *n.* **1** the act of interrogating or the process of being interrogated. **2** a question. **interrogational** *a.* **interrogation mark, interrogation point** *n.* QUESTION MARK (under QUESTION). **interrogative** (-rog´-) *a.* **1** denoting a question. **2** expressed in the form or having the character of a question. *~n.* (*Gram.*) a word used in asking questions, e.g. *what?*, *who?* **interrogatively** *adv.* **interrogator** *n.* **interrogatory** (-rog´-) *a.* interrogative. *~n.* (*pl.* **interrogatories**) **1** a question; an enquiry. **2** (*Law*) a question or set of questions put formally to a defendant etc. [L *interrogātus*, p.p. of *interrogāre* (*rogāre*, to ask)]
interrupt (intərŭpt´) *v.t.* **1** to stop or obstruct by breaking in upon. **2** to break the continuity of. **3** to obstruct (a view etc.). **4** to disturb. *~v.i.* to make an interruption. **interruptedly** *adv.* **interrupter, interruptor** *n.* **1** a person who or a thing which interrupts. **2** a device for opening and closing an electric circuit. **interruptible** *a.* **interruption** *n.* **interruptive, interruptory** *a.* **interruptively** *adv.* [L *interruptus*, p.p. of *interrumpere* (*rumpere*, to break)]
intersect (intəsekt´) *v.t.* to divide by cutting or passing across. *~v.i.* to cut or cross each other. **intersection** *n.* **1** the act of intersecting. **2** a crossroads. **3** (*Geom.*) the point or line on which lines or planes cut each other. **intersectional** *a.* [L *intersectus*, p.p. of *intersecāre* (*secāre*, to cut)]
interseptal (intəsep´təl) *a.* situated between or of or relating to septa or partitions. [L *intersaeptum*, a partition, the diaphragm, -AL[1]]

intersex (in´təseks) *n.* 1 (*Zool.*) an individual developing characteristics of both sexes. 2 the condition of being intersexual. **intersexual** (-sek´-) *a.* 1 intermediate in sexual characteristics between male and female. 2 between the sexes. **intersexuality** (-al´-) *n.* **intersexually** *adv.*

interspace[1] (in´təspās) *n.* 1 intervening space. 2 an interval between two things or occurrences. **interspatial** (-spā´shəl) *a.* **interspatially** *adv.*

interspace[2] (intəspās´) *v.t.* 1 to put a space or spaces between. 2 to fill the intervals between.

interspecific (intəspisif´ik) *a.* subsisting between different species.

intersperse (intəspœs´) *v.t.* 1 to scatter here and there (among etc.). 2 to diversify or variegate (with scattered objects, colours etc.). **interspersion** (-shən) *n.* [L *interspersus*, p.p. of *interspergere* (*spargere*, to scatter)]

interspinal (intəspī´nəl), **interspinous** (-nəs) *a.* situated between spines or spinal processes.

interstadial (intəstā´diəl) *n.* a period of ice retreat during a glacial period. ~*a.* of or relating to such a period.

interstate (in´təstāt) *a.* subsisting, maintained or carried on between states, esp. the states of the US. ~*n.* (*US*) a motorway going from one state to another.

interstellar (intəstel´ə) *a.* situated between or passing through the regions between the stars.

interstice (intœ´stis) *n.* a space, opening, crevice etc. between things near together or between the component parts of a body. **interstitial** (-sti´shəl) *a.* of, relating to, occupying or forming interstices. **interstitially** *adv.* [MF, from L *interstitium*, from *intersistere* (*sistere*, to place, causal from *stāre*, to stand)]

interstratify (intəstrat´ifī) *v.t.* (*3rd pers. sing. pres.* **interstratifies**, *pres.p.* **interstratifying**, *past, p.p.* **interstratified**) (*Geol.*) to stratify between or among other strata. **interstratification** (-fikā´shən) *n.*

intertextuality (intətekstūal´iti) *n.* the relationship between literary texts.

intertidal (intətī´dəl) *a.* of or relating to the area between the low-water and high-water marks.

intertribal (intətrī´bəl) *a.* occurring or carried on between different tribes.

intertrigo (intətrī´gō) *n.* (*pl.* **intertrigos**) (an) inflammation caused by the rubbing of one part of the skin against another. [L *interterīgo* (*terere*, to rub)]

intertwine (intətwīn´) *v.t.* to entwine or twist together. ~*v.i.* to be twisted together. **intertwinement** *n.* **intertwiningly** *adv.*

intertwist (intətwist´) *v.t.* to twist together.

☒ **interupt** common misspelling of INTERRUPT.

interval (in´təvəl) *n.* 1 an intervening space, distance or time. 2 a break, gap or pause. 3 the extent of difference between two things, persons etc. 4 the difference in pitch between two sounds. 5 the break between scenes or acts of a play etc. **at intervals** 1 from time to time. 2 with spaces in between. **intervallic** (-val´-) *a.* [OF *intervalle*, *entreval*, L *intervallum*, the space between palisades or ramparts (*vallum*, rampart)]

intervale (in´təvāl) *a.* (*N Am.*) a tract of low ground between hills or along the banks of rivers. [var. of INTERVAL, assim. to VALE[1]]

intervallic INTERVAL.

interveined (intəvānd´) *a.* intersected as with veins.

intervene (intəvēn´) *v.i.* 1 to happen or break in so as to interrupt or disturb; to interfere. 2 to occur between points of time or events. 3 to come or be situated between. 4 to come in as an extraneous feature or thing. 5 (*Law*) to interpose in lawsuit to which one was not originally a party. **intervener, intervenor** *n.* a person who intervenes, esp. in a lawsuit. **intervenient** *a.* **intervention** (-ven´-) *n.* 1 the act of intervening. 2 violating a sovereign state's independence by interfering in its domestic or external affairs. 3 mediation. 4 the practice of buying and storing surplus products when the market price is low. 5 the action of a central bank in buying large quantities of a currency in order to prevent its international value from falling. **interventionism** *n.* **interventionist** *n.* a person who favours intervention, esp. in the economy or in the affairs of a foreign country. [L *intervenīre* (*venīre*, to come), p.p. *interventus*]

intervertebral (intəvœ´tibrəl) *a.* situated between vertebrae.

interview (in´təvū) *n.* 1 a meeting in which an employer questions a candidate for a job, college place etc. in order to test the candidate's suitability. 2 a meeting between a person of public interest and a press representative employed to obtain information or opinions for publication. 3 the article describing this or recording the result. 4 a meeting between two persons face to face. 5 a session of questioning by the police etc. ~*v.t.* to hold an interview with, esp. in order to obtain matter for publication or to test a candidate's suitability for a post. ~*v.i.* to take part in an interview; to perform in a particular way at interview (*She interviewed well*). **interviewee** (-ē´) *n.* **interviewer** *n.* [OF *entrevue*, from *entrevoir* (*voir*, L *vidēre*, to see)]

intervocalic (intəvōkal´ik) *a.* pronounced or occurring between vowels.

inter-war (intəwaw´) *a.* occurring in the period between two wars, esp. World Wars I and II.

interweave (intəwēv´) *v.t.* (*past* **interwove** (-wōv´), *p.p.* **interwoven** (-wō´vən)) 1 to weave together (with). 2 to blend or mingle closely together.

interwind (intəwīnd´) *v.t.*, *v.i.* (*past, p.p.* **interwound** (-wownd´)) to wind together.

interwork (intəwœk´) *v.t.* (*past, p.p.* **interwrought** (-rawt), **interworked**) to work (things) together or into each other. ~*v.i.* to work together; to interact.

interwound INTERWIND.

interwove, interwoven INTERWEAVE.

interwrought INTERWORK.

intestate (intes´tāt) *a.* 1 dying without having made a will. 2 (of property) not disposed of by will. ~*n.* an intestate person. **intestacy** *n.* [L *intestātus* (*testātus*, p.p. of *testārī*, to witness, to make a will)]

intestine (intes´tin) *n.* 1 (*usu. pl.*) the part of the alimentary canal from the stomach to the anus. 2 (*Zool.*) the whole of the alimentary canal. **intestinal** (-tī´-, -tes´-) *a.* of or relating to the intestines. **intestinal flora** *n.pl.* harmless bacteria inhabiting the intestinal tract. **intestinally** *adv.* [L *intestīnus*, from *intus*, within]

inthrall ENTHRAL.

intifada (intifah´də) *n.* the Palestinian uprising in the Israeli-occupied West Bank and Gaza strip, that began in 1987. [Arab., uprising]

intimate[1] (in´timət) *a.* 1 close in friendship; familiar (*an intimate friend*). 2 private, personal. 3 having an atmosphere conducive to close personal relationships. 4 thorough (*an intimate knowledge*). 5 of or relating to one's inner being. 6 close (*an intimate connection/link*). 7 having sexual relations (with). ~*n.* a close friend. **intimacy** (-si) *n.* (*pl.* **intimacies**) 1 closeness; close friendship. 2 sexual intercourse. 3 a warm intimate atmosphere. 4 (*often pl.*) an intimate remark. **intimately** *adv.* [late L *intimātus*, p.p. of *intimāre*, from *intimus*, within]

intimate[2] (in´timāt) *v.t.* 1 to make known, to announce. 2 to indicate, to hint. **intimation** (-ā´shən) *n.* [as INTIMATE[1]]

intimidate (intim´idāt) *v.t.* to frighten or to influence with threats or aggressive behaviour. **intimidating** *a.* **intimidation** (-ā´shən) *n.* **intimidator** *n.* **intimidatory** (-ā´təri) *a.* [med. L *intimidātus*, p.p. of *intimidāre* (*timidus*, TIMID)]

intinction (intingk´shən) *n.* the method of administering the Eucharist by dipping the bread in the wine. [late L *intinctio*, from *intingere* (*tinguere*, to moisten)]

intitule (intit´ūl) *v.t.* to entitle (esp. an Act of Parliament). [F *intitulé*, L *intitulāre*, to ENTITLE]

into (in´tu) *prep.* **1** expressing motion or direction within or against (*She got into the car, I bumped into him*). **2** expressing investigation, inquiry etc. (*I'll look into the matter*). **3** expressing a change from one state to another (*translated into French*). **4** after a particular period of time (*one week into the course*). **5** (*coll.*) very keen on or enthusiastic about (*She's really into aromatherapy*). **6** indicating the dividend in division. [OE *in to* (IN adv., TO)]

intolerable (intol´ərəbəl) *a.* not tolerable, unendurable. **intolerableness** *n.* **intolerably** *adv.* [F, from L *intolerābilis*]

intolerant (intol´ərənt) *a.* not tolerant (of); not enduring or allowing difference of opinion, teaching, worship etc. **intolerance** *n.* **intolerantly** *adv.* [F, from L *intolerantem*, nom. *-ans*]

intone (intōn´) *v.i.* **1** to recite or chant prayers etc., esp. in a monotone. **2** to speak with a particular tone. ~*v.t.* **1** to recite or chant in a monotone. **2** to utter with a particular tone. **intonate** (in´-) *v.i.*, *v.t.* to intone. **intonation** (intənā´shən) *n.* **1** modulation of the voice; accent. **2** intoning. **3** accuracy of pitch when playing an instrument or singing. **4** the opening phrase of a plainsong melody, usu. sung by a priest or chorister. **intoner** *n.* [med. L *intonāre* (*in tonum*, in tone (*tonus*, TONE))]

intorsion (intaw´shən), **intortion** *n.* **1** a winding or twisting. **2** the twisting of any part of a plant upon itself. [L *intortio*, from *intortus*, p.p. of *intorquere* (*torquere*, to twist)]

in toto (in tō´tō) *adv.* completely. [L]

intoxicate (intok´sikāt) *v.t.* **1** to make drunk. **2** to excite; to make delirious, as with joy. **3** (*Med.*) to poison. **intoxicant** *a.* that intoxicates. ~*n.* any intoxicating substance. **intoxicating** *a.* tending to intoxicate. **intoxicatingly** *adv.* **intoxication** (-ā´shən) *n.* [med. L *intoxicātus*, p.p. of *intoxicāre*, to smear with poison (*toxicāre*, from *toxicum*, Gr. *toxikon*, from *toxa*, arrows)]

intra- (in´trə) *pref.* within or inside, as *intrauterine*. [L *intrā*, within]

intra-abdominal (intrəabdom´inəl) *a.* situated inside the abdomen.

intra-arterial (intrəahtiə´riəl) *a.* occurring within an artery.

intracapsular (intrəkap´sūlə) *a.* situated or occurring inside a capsule.

intracardiac (intrəkah´diak), **intracardial** (-diəl) *a.* situated or occurring inside the heart.

intracellular (intrəsel´ūlə) *a.* (*Biol.*) in a cell or cells.

intracranial (intrəkrā´niəl) *a.* within the skull. **intracranially** *adv.*

intractable (intrak´təbəl) *a.* **1** unmanageable. **2** difficult, obstinate. **intractability** (-bil´-), **intractableness** *n.* **intractably** *adv.* [F, from L *intractābilis*]

intrados (intrā´dos) *n.* (*pl.* **intrados** (-dōz), **intradoses**) the inner surface or curve of an arch, as opposed to the *extrados*. [F (*dos*, the back)]

intramolecular (intrəmolek´ūlə) *a.* within a molecule.

intramural (intrəmū´rəl) *a.* **1** situated or happening within walls or boundaries. **2** taking place within or involving those in an institution, esp. a university or college. **3** (*Anat.*) situated or occurring within the walls of an organ etc.

intranet (in´trənet) *n.* a computer networking link restricted to a specific group of users. [after INTERNET]

intransigent (intran´sijənt) *a.* uncompromising, obdurate, inflexible. ~*n.* an intransigent person. **intransigency** *n.* **intransigently** *adv.* [F *intransigeant*, Sp. *intransigente* (L *transigens -entem*, pres.p. of *transigere*, to come to an understanding, to TRANSACT)]

intransitive (intran´sitiv) *a.* (*Gram.*) (of a verb) denoting action confined to the agent and so not requiring a direct object. **intransitively** *adv.* **intransitiveness**, **intransitivity** (-tiv´-) *n.* [L *intransitīvus* (TRANSITIVE)]

intrant (in´trənt) *n.* a person who enters, esp. a person who enters a college, society etc. [L *intrans -entem*, pres.p. of *intrāre*, to ENTER]

intranuclear (intrənū´kliə) *a.* situated or occurring within the nucleus of a cell.

intraocular (intrəok´ūlə) *a.* situated or occurring within the eyeball.

intrapreneur (intrəprənœ´) *n.* a person who initiates or manages a new business or division within an existing firm. [after ENTREPRENEUR]

intrauterine (intrəū´tərīn) *a.* situated or occurring inside the womb. **intrauterine device** *n.* a metal or plastic coil, loop or ring, placed in the womb to prevent conception.

intravenous (intrəvē´nəs) *a.* into a vein or veins. **intravenously** *adv.*

intrench ENTRENCH.

intrepid (intrep´id) *a.* fearless, brave, bold. **intrepidity** (-pid´-) *n.* **intrepidly** *adv.* [L *intrepidus* (see TREPIDATION)]

intricate (in´trikət) *a.* entangled, involved, complicated. **intricacy** (-si) *n.* (*pl.* **intricacies**). **intricately** *adv.* [L *intrīcātus*, p.p. of *intricāre* (*tricae*, hindrances, wiles)]

intrigant (in´trigənt, ītrēgā´) *n.* an intriguer. **intrigante** (-gənt, -gāt´) *n.* a female intriguer. [F *intriguant*, *-nte*, pres.p. of *intriguer*, see INTRIGUE[1]]

intrigue[1] (intrēg´) *v.i.* (*3rd pers. sing. pres.* **intriguing**, *past, p.p.* **intrigued**) **1** to carry on a plot or scheme to effect some object by underhand means. **2** to carry on a secret love affair. ~*v.t.* to make curious or to fascinate. **intriguer** *n.* **intriguing** *a.* **intriguingly** *adv.* [F *intriguer*, It. *intrigare*, L *intricāre*, see INTRICATE]

intrigue[2] (in´trēg, intrēg´) *n.* **1** the act of intriguing. **2** a plot to effect some object by underhand means. **3** a secret love affair.

intrinsic (intrin´sik), †**intrinsical** *a.* inherent, essential; belonging to the nature of a thing. **intrinsically** *adv.* [F *intrinsèque*, L *intrinsecus* (INTRA-, *secus*, following, rel. to *secundus*, SECOND[1], *sequī*, to follow)]

intro (in´trō) *n.* (*pl.* **intros**) (*coll.*) an introduction.

intro- (intrō) *comb. form* in, into, as *introspection*. [L *intrō*, to the inside]

introduce (intrədūs´) *v.t.* **1** to make (a person, oneself) known in a formal way to another. **2** to bring into use or notice. **3** to present (a programme etc.) to an audience. **4** to cause (a person) to discover. **5** to bring (a bill etc.) before Parliament. **6** to bring or lead in; to usher in. **7** to insert. **8** to bring before the public. **9** to preface. **introducer** *n.* **introducible** *a.* **introduction** (intrədŭk´shən) *n.* **1** the act of introducing. **2** a formal presentation of a person to another. **3** a preface or preliminary discourse in a book etc. **4** an opening section in a piece of music. **5** an elementary treatise. **6** something that is introduced. **introductory** *a.* serving as an introduction; preliminary. **introductorily** *adv.* [L *intrōdūcere* (*dūcere*, to lead), p.p. *introductus*]

†**introgression** (intrəgresh´ən) *n.* the introduction of the genes of one species into the gene pool of another. [L *intrōgressus*, p.p. of *intrōgredī* (*gradī*, to walk)]

introit (in´troit) *n.* a psalm or antiphon sung or recited as the priest approaches the altar to begin the Mass or Eucharist. [F *introït*, L *introitus*, from *introīre*, to enter (*īre*, to go)]

introject (intrəjekt´) *v.t.* to assimilate unconsciously into one's personality. **introjection** *n.*

intromit (intrəmit´) *v.t.* (*pres.p.* **intromitting**, *past, p.p.*

intromitted) 1 †to admit, to allow to enter. 2 to insert. **intromission** (-shən) *n.* **intromittent** *a.* [L *intrōmittere* (*mittere*, to send), p.p. *intrōmissus*]

intron (in´tron) *n.* a section of a nucleic acid that does not carry coded information for protein synthesis.

introrse (intraws´) *a.* (*Bot.*) turned towards the axis. [L *introrsus*, adv., from *introversus* (*versus*, towards)]

introspection (intrəspek´shən) *n.* the analysis and observation of the workings of one's own mind. **introspect** (-spekt´) *v.i.* to examine one's own mind and its workings. **introspectionist** *n.* **introspective** *a.* **introspectively** *adv.* **introspectiveness** *n.* [L *intrōspectus*, p.p. of *intrōspicere* (*specere*, to look)]

introvert[1] (in´trəvœt) *n.* 1 a person who is interested chiefly in their own feelings and mental processes rather than in the outside world. 2 a shy, reflective person. 3 (*Zool.*) a part or organ that is turned in upon itself. **introversive, introvertive** *a.* [L *intrōvertere* (*vertere*, to turn)]

introvert[2] (intrəvœt´) *v.t.* 1 to turn (one's mind or thoughts) inwards. 2 (*Zool.*) to turn (an organ or a part) in upon itself. **introversion** *n.* **introverted** *a.*

intrude (introod´) *v.t.* 1 to thrust or force (on to, into). 2 to force (volcanic rock etc.) into sedimentary strata. ~*v.i.* 1 to thrust oneself or force one's way (into). 2 to force oneself upon others; to enter without invitation. **intruder** *n.* [L *intrūdere* (*trūdere*, to thrust)]

intrusion (intrū´zhən) *n.* 1 the act of intruding. 2 an unwelcome visit, interruption etc. 3 (*Geol.*) the penetration of volcanic rocks into sedimentary strata. 4 (*Law*) an unlawful entry by a stranger upon lands or tenements.

intrusive (intrū´siv) *a.* 1 tending to intrude or characterized by intrusion. 2 entering without invitation or welcome. 3 (of a speech sound) inserted into a word or between words to make pronunciation easier, e.g. the *r* in *draw a picture*. **intrusively** *adv.* **intrusiveness** *n.* **intrusive rocks** *n.pl.* igneous rocks which have forced their way into sedimentary strata.

intrust ENTRUST.

intubate (in´tūbāt) *v.t.* (*Med.*) to insert a tube into (the larynx), as in a case of diphtheria. **intubation** (-bā´shən) *n.* [L *tuba*, TUBE, -ATE[3]]

intuition (intūish´ən) *n.* 1 immediate perception by the mind without reasoning. 2 the power of the mind for such perception. 3 instinctive knowledge. **intuit** (-tū´it) *v.t.* to know by intuition. ~*v.i.* to acquire knowledge by means of intuition. **intuitable** *a.* **intuitivism** *n.* the doctrine that ideas of right and wrong are intuitive. **intuitivist** *n.* **intuitional** *a.* **intuitionalism, intuitionism** *n.* (*Philos.*) the doctrine that the perception of truth, or of certain truths, is by intuition. **intuitionalist, intuitionist** *n.* **intuitive** (-tū´-) *a.* 1 perceived by intuition. 2 perceiving by intuition. 3 seeing immediately and clearly. **intuitively** *adv.* **intuitiveness** *n.* [F, from med. L *intuitiōnem*, nom. *-tio*, from *intuērī* (*tuērī*, to look)]

intumesce (intūmes´) *v.i.* to swell up. **intumescence** *n.* **intumescent** *a.* [L *intumescere* (*tumescere*, incept. of *tumēre*, to become tumid)]

intussuscept (intəsəsept´) *v.t.* (*Med.*) to turn or fold (an organ or part) within itself; to invaginate. **intussusception** *n.* 1 (*Med.*) the accidental insertion or protrusion of an upper segment of the bowels into a lower. 2 (*Biol.*) the deposition of new material on a cell wall. **intussusceptive** *a.* [L *intus*, within, *susceptus*, p.p. of *suscipere* (SUS-, *capere*, to take)]

intwine ENTWINE.

Inuit (in´ūit), **Innuit** *n.* (*pl* **Inuit, Inuits, Innuit, Innuits**) 1 a Canadian Eskimo. 2 a member of any of the Eskimo peoples inhabiting N America and Greenland. 3 any Eskimo. 4 any of the languages of the Inuit or Eskimos. ~*a.* of or relating to the Inuit or Eskimos, or any of their languages. [Eskimo (Inuit) *inuit*, people, pl. of *inuk*, person]

inulin (in´ūlin) *n.* a soluble, white starchy powder, obtained from the roots of elecampane and other composite plants. [L *inula*, elecampane]

inunction (inŭngk´shən) *n.* anointing or smearing with ointment, oil etc. [L *inunctio*, from *inunguere* (*unguere*, to ANOINT)]

inundate (in´əndāt) *v.t.* 1 to overflow, to flood. 2 to deluge; to overwhelm. **inundant** *a.* overflowing. **inundation** (-dā´shən) *n.* a flood, a deluge. [L *inundātus*, p.p. of *inundāre* (*unda*, a wave)]

Inupiaq (inū´piak), **Inupiat** (-at) *n.* (*pl.* **Inupiaq, Inupiat**) 1 a member of an Inuit people of northern Alaska. 2 the Inuit language spoken by this people. ~*a.* of or relating to the Inupiaq or their language. [Inuit (*inuk*, person, *piaq*, genuine)]

inurbane (inœbān´) *a.* discourteous, rude, unpolished. **inurbanely** *adv.* **inurbanity** (-ban´-) *n.* [L *inurbānus*]

inure (inūə´), **enure** *v.t.* to accustom, to habituate, to harden (to). ~*v.i.* (*Law*) to come into operation; to take or have effect. **inurement** *n.* [ME *enuren*, to habituate (*en-*, in, *ure*, to use, from OF *euvre*, habit, work, L *opera*, works)]

inurn (inœn´) *v.t.* 1 to place in a cinerary urn. 2 to bury.

in utero (in ū´tərō) *adv.* in the womb. [L]

inutile (inū´tīl) *a.* useless. **inutility** (-til´-) *n.* [L *inūtilis* (*ūtilis*, useful)]

in vacuo (in vak´ūō) *adv.* 1 in a vacuum. 2 in isolation; without reference to context. [L]

invade (invād´) *v.t.* 1 to enter (a country) by force, as an enemy. 2 to overrun (*Tourists invade the island every year*). 3 (of bacteria etc.) to assail (a body etc.). 4 to encroach on, to violate (someone's privacy, rights etc.). ~*v.i.* to make an invasion. **invader** *n.* [F *invader*, L *invādere* (*vādere*, to go)]

invaginate (invaj´ināt) *v.t.* 1 to put into or as into a sheath. 2 to introvert or turn (a tubular sheath) upon itself. **invaginable** *a.* **invagination** (-ā´shən) *n.* [L *vagīna*, a sheath, -ATE[1]]

invalid[1] (inval´id) *a.* having no force, weight or cogency; null. **invalidate** *v.t.* to weaken or destroy the validity of, to render not valid. **invalidation** (-ā´shən) *n.* **invalidator** *n.* **invalidly** *adv.* **invalidness** *n.* [L *invalidus*]

invalid[2] (in´vəlid, -ēd) *a.* infirm or disabled through ill health or injury. ~*n.* an infirm or disabled person. ~*v.t.* (*pres.p.* **invaliding**, *past, p.p.* **invalided**) 1 (*usu. pass.*) to disable by illness or injury. 2 to register or discharge as unfit for military or naval duty on account of illness etc. (*He was invalided out*). ~*v.i.* 1 to become an invalid. 2 to be enrolled as such. **invalidism** *n.* 1 chronic ill health. 2 the state of being obsessed with one's physical health. [as INVALID[1]]

invalidity (invəlid´iti) *n.* 1 the fact or condition of being without validity. 2 the fact or condition of being infirm or disabled.

invaluable (inval´ūəbəl) *a.* precious above estimation; priceless. **invaluableness** *n.* **invaluably** *adv.*

Invar® (in´vah) *n.* a nickel-steel alloy with a small coefficient of expansion, used in the manufacture of balance springs for clocks etc.

invariable (inveə´riəbəl) *a.* 1 not variable, uniform; not liable to change. 2 (*Math.*) fixed, constant. ~*n.* (*Math.*) a constant quantity. **invariability** (-bil´-), **invariableness** *n.* **invariably** *adv.* **invariance** *n.* **invariant** *a.* not varying or subject to variation. ~*n.* (*Math.*) a function which remains fixed and unchanged though its constituents may vary. [F]

invasion (invā´zhən) *n.* 1 the act of invading. 2 a hostile attack upon or entrance into the territory of others. 3 an infringement or violation. 4 the approach or onset of anything dangerous or harmful, esp. of a disease. **invasive** (-siv) *a.* 1 tending to spread. 2 (of surgery) involving making a relatively large incision in the body. **3** tending to infringe on another's rights, privacy etc. [F, from L *invāsiōnem*, nom. *-sio*, from *invādere*, to INVADE]

invective (invek´tiv) *n.* a violent expression of censure or abuse; vituperation. ~*a.* abusive. **invectively** *adv.* [F, from late L *invectīva*, fem. a. from *invectus*, p.p. of *invehere*, see INVEIGH]

inveigh (invā´) *v.i.* to utter or make use of invectives; to speak censoriously and abusively (against). **inveigher** *n.* [L *invehī*, to attack, to abuse, refl. of *vehere* (*vehere*, to carry)]

inveigle (invē´gəl, -vā´-), **enveigle** *v.t.* to entice, to wheedle; to entrap (into). **inveiglement** *n.* **inveigler** *n.* [prob. from F *aveugler* (altered to *enveoglir*), to blind, from *aveugle*, low L *aboculum*, nom. *-lus* (AB-[1], *oculus*, eye)]

invent (invent´) *v.t.* **1** to devise or contrive (a new means, instrument etc.). **2** to concoct, to fabricate. **inventible, inventable** *a.* **invention** *n.* **1** the act of inventing. **2** the production of something new. **3** the faculty or power of inventing, inventiveness. **4** something which is invented; a contrivance. **5** a fabrication, a fiction. **6** a short piece of music, usu. in double counterpoint. **inventive** *a.* **1** able to invent. **2** ingenious; imaginative. **3** characterized by creative skill. **inventively** *adv.* **inventiveness** *n.* **inventor** *n.* a person who invents things, esp. as an occupation. **inventress** (-tris) *n.* a female inventor. [F *inventer*, L *inventus*, p.p. of *invenīre*, to find, to invent (*venīre*, to come)]

inventory (in´vəntəri) *n.* (*pl.* **inventories**) **1** a detailed list or catalogue of goods, possessions etc. **2** the articles enumerated in such a list. **3** (*chiefly N Am.*) the quantity or value of a firm's current assets in terms of raw materials and stock. **4** these assets individually. **5** the material in a nuclear reactor. ~*v.t.* (*3rd pers. sing. pres.* **inventories,** *pres.p.* **inventorying,** *past, p.p.* **inventoried**) **1** to enter in an inventory. **2** to make a list or catalogue of. **inventorial** (-taw´ri-) *a.* **inventorially** *adv.* [med. L *inventōrium*, from *inventus*, as INVENT]

inveracity (invəras´iti) *n.* (*pl.* **inveracities**) **1** untruthfulness. **2** a lie.

Inverness (invənes´), **Inverness cape** *n.* a kind of sleeveless cloak with a cape hanging loosely over the shoulders. [town in Scotland]

inverse (invœs´, in´-) *a.* **1** opposite in order or relation; contrary. **2** inverted. ~*n.* **1** the state of being inverted. **2** the direct opposite (of). **3** (*Math.*) the result of inversion. **inversely** *adv.* **inverse proportion, inverse ratio** *n.* a relation between two quantities in which an increase in one results in a proportional decrease in the other. **inverse square law** *n.* (*Physics*) a law which states that the magnitude of a physical quantity is inversely proportional to the square of the distance from the source. [F *inverse*, L *inversus*, as INVERT[1]]

inversion (invœ´shən) *n.* **1** the act of inverting. **2** a reversal of order, place or relation. **3** the reversal of the natural order of words in a sentence, usu. for emphasis. **4** the result of inverting. **5** (*Mus.*) the process or result of altering or reversing the relative position of the elements of a chord etc. **6** TEMPERATURE INVERSION (under TEMPERATURE). **7** the reversal of the direction in which a plane of polarized light rotates. **8** homosexuality. **9** the assumption of the characteristics of the other sex. **10** (*Math.*) the operation of changing the order of the terms, so that the antecedent takes the place of the consequent and the reverse in both ratios. **inversion layer** *n.* in meteorology, a layer of air in which temperature increases with altitude. **inversive** *a.*

invert[1] (invœt´) *v.t.* **1** to turn upside down. **2** to place in a contrary position or order; to reverse. **3** (*Mus.*) to change (a chord, interval etc.) by placing the lowest note higher. **invertase** (-tāz) *n.* an enzyme able to convert sucrose into invert sugar. **inverted** *a.* **inverted comma** *n.* QUOTATION MARK (under QUOTE). **inverted snob** *n.* a person who admires those things that a snob might be expected to disapprove of. **inverter, invertor** *n.* a device that converts direct current into alternating current. **invertible** (-vœ´-) *a.* **invertibility** (-bil´-) *n.* [L *invertere* (*vertere*, to turn)]

invert[2] (in´vœt) *n.* **1** an inverted arch, esp. such as forms the bottom of a sewer etc. **2** a homosexual. **invert sugar** *n.* a mixture of sugar and fructose obtained by the hydrolysis of cane sugar.

invertase INVERT[1].

invertebrate (invœ´tibrət) *a.* **1** (of an animal) not having a backbone or vertebral column. **2** (of a person) lacking strength or firmness. ~*n.* **1** an invertebrate animal. **2** an irresolute person. **invertebral** *a.*

invest (invest´) *v.t.* **1** to employ (money) in remunerative property, business, stocks etc. **2** to devote (effort, time etc.) to a project etc. for future rewards. **3** to provide or endue (with office, authority, dignity etc.). **4** to attribute (qualities, characteristics etc.) to someone. **5** to cover (with or as with a garment). **6** to besiege. ~*v.i.* **1** to make an investment (in). **2** (*coll.*) to buy (*Isn't it time you invested in a new coat?*). **investable, investible** *a.* **investive** *a.* **investment** *n.* **1** the act of investing money. **2** money invested. **3** something in which money is invested. **4** the act of surrounding or besieging. **investment bond** *n.* a single-premium life assurance policy which is linked to a unit trust. **investment trust** *n.* a financial enterprise which invests its subscribers' capital in securities and distributes the net return among them. **investor** *n.* [F *investir*, L *investīre* (*vestīre*, to clothe)]

investigate (inves´tigāt) *v.t.* to examine or inquire into closely. ~*v.i.* to carry out a thorough search or inquiry. **investigable** *a.* **investigation** (-ā´shən) *n.* **1** the act or an instance of investigation. **2** a formal and careful examination. **investigational** *a.* **investigative, investigatory** *a.* **investigator** *n.* [L *investigātus*, p.p. of *investigāre* (*vestigāre*, to track, see VESTIGE)]

investiture (invest´ichə) *n.* **1** the act of investing, esp. the ceremony of investing with office, rank etc. **2** the state of being invested. **3** in feudal society, the formal granting of possessory right to an office, benefice etc. [F, from med. L *investītūra*, from *investīre*, to INVEST]

inveterate (invet´ərət) *a.* **1** determinedly settled in a habit (*an inveterate liar*). **2** long-established, deeply-rooted (*an inveterate dislike*). **3** habitual. **4** †hostile. **inveteracy** (-si), **inveterateness** *n.* **inveterately** *adv.* [L *inveterātus*, p.p. of *inveterāre* (*vetus veteris*, old)]

invidious (invid´iəs) *a.* **1** tending to incur or provoke envy, ill will or indignation. **2** offending through real or apparent unfairness or injustice. **invidiously** *adv.* **invidiousness** *n.* [L *invidiōsus*, from *invidia*, ENVY]

invigilate (invij´ilāt) *v.i.* to supervise students during an examination. ~*v.t.* to supervise. **invigilation** (-ā´shən) *n.* **invigilator** *n.* [L *invigilātus*, p.p. of *invigilāre* (*vigilāre*, to watch, see VIGIL)]

invigorate (invig´ərāt) *v.t.* **1** to give vigour or strength to. **2** to animate; to encourage. **invigorating** *a.* **invigoratingly** *adv.* **invigoration** (-ā´shən) *n.* **invigorative** *a.* **invigorator** *n.* [L *vigor*]

invincible (invin´sibəl) *a.* that cannot be conquered. **invincibility** (-bil´-), **invincibleness** *n.* **invincibly** *adv.* [F, from L *invincibilis*]

inviolable (invī´ələbəl) *a.* not to be violated, profaned or dishonoured. **inviolability** (-bil´-), **inviolableness** *n.* **inviolably** *adv.* **inviolate** (-lət) *a.* **1** not violated or profaned. **2** safe from violation, injury etc. **inviolacy** (-si), **inviolateness** *n.* **inviolately** *adv.* [F, from L *inviolābilis*]

invisible (inviz´ibəl) *a.* **1** not visible; imperceptible to the eye. **2** too small, distant, misty etc. to be seen. **3** not in sight; hidden. **4** cleverly hidden or concealed. **5** not recorded in published accounts. **6** of or relating to services as opposed to goods (*invisible earnings*). ~*n.* **1** an invisible person or thing. **2** (*pl.*) invisible exports and imports. **invisibility** (-bil´-), **invisibleness** *n.* **invisible exports, invisible imports** *n.pl.* invisible items of trade, esp. services. **invisible ink** *n.* ink that does not show until heated or otherwise treated. **invisibly** *adv.* [F, from L *invīsibilis*]

invitatory (invī´tətəri) *a.* containing or using invitation. ~*n.* (*pl.* **invitatories**) an invitatory psalm, antiphon etc., esp. the psalm *Venite exultemus Domino*.

invite[1] (invīt´) *v.t.* **1** to ask (someone) courteously to do something, come to an event etc. (*I've been invited to dinner*). **2** to request formally and courteously (*The speaker invited questions*). **3** to allure, to attract. **4** to draw upon one, esp. unintentionally (*You're inviting trouble*). ~*v.i.* to allure; to tempt. **invitation** (-vitā´shən) *n.* **1** the act of inviting or the fact of being invited. **2** a card, letter etc. inviting someone. **3** allurement; attraction. **invitee** (-tē´) *n.* a person invited. **inviter** *n.* **inviting** *a.* **1** attractive. **2** seductive; enticing. **invitingly** *adv.* **invitingness** *n.* [F *inviter*, L *invītāre*, to bid, rel. to *-vītus*, willing (as *invītus*, unwilling)]

invite[2] (in´vīt) *n.* (*coll.*) an invitation.

in vitro (in vēt´rō) *a.*, *adv.* (of biological processes etc.) taking place outside a living organism, e.g. in a test tube. [L, in a glass]

in vivo (in vē´vō) *a.*, *adv.* (of biological processes) occurring within a living organism. [L, in a living thing]

invocable INVOKE.

invocation (invəkā´shən) *n.* **1** the act of invoking. **2** a supplication or call to God, esp. as part of a religious service. **3** a petition addressed to a muse, saint etc., for help or inspiration. **4** the calling up of a spirit by incantation. †**invocate** (in´-) *v.t.* to invoke. **invocatory** (-vok´-) *a.* [F, from L *invocātiōnem*, nom. *-tio*, from *invocāre*, to INVOKE]

invoice (in´vois) *n.* a list of goods dispatched, with particulars of quantity and price, sent to a consignee. ~*v.t.* **1** to enter (goods) in an invoice. **2** to send an invoice to. [prob. from earlier *invoyes*, pl. from F *envoi*, see ENVOY[1]]

invoke (invōk´) *v.t.* **1** to address in prayer. **2** to solicit earnestly for (assistance, protection etc.). **3** to call upon solemnly. **4** to call on as a witness; to appeal to as an authority. **5** to summon by magical means. **6** (*Comput.*) to cause (a subroutine etc.) to be carried out. **invocable** *a.* **invoker** *n.* [F *invoquer*, L *invocāre* (*vocāre*, to call)]

involucre (in´vəlookə) *n.* **1** a whorl of bracts surrounding the flowers of certain plants. **2** (*Anat.*) a membranous envelope or cover of certain parts and organs. **3** a covering or envelope. **involucel** (-vol´ūsel), **involucellum** (-volūsel´əm) *n.* (*pl.* **involucels, involucella** (-sel´ə)) a group of bracts at the base of an inflorescence. **involucellate** (-sel´ət) *a.* **involucral** (-loo´krəl), **involucrate** (-loo´krət) *a.* [F, from L *involūcrum*, from *involvere* (*volvere*, to roll)]

involuntary (invol´əntəri) *a.* **1** done unintentionally, not from choice. **2** (of a movement) performed independently of will or volition. **involuntarily** *adv.* **involuntariness** *n.* [L *involuntārius*]

involute (in´vəloot) *a.* **1** complicated, involved. **2** (of leaves, petals) rolled inwards at the margins. **3** closely coiled. ~*n.* (*Math.*) a curve traced by the end of a string unwinding itself from another curve, which is called the *evolute*. **involuted** *a.* [L *involūtus*, p.p. of *involvere*, to INVOLVE]

involution (invəloo´shən) *n.* **1** the act of involving. **2** the state of being involved. **3** a complication; an entanglement. **4** intricacy. **5** a rolling up or curling of parts. **6** anything folding up or curling inwards. **7** a complicated grammatical construction. **8** the shrinking of a bodily organ, e.g. of the uterus after pregnancy. **9** (*Math.*) the act or process of raising a quantity to any power.

involve (involv´) *v.t.* **1** to cause to take part (in); to include (in). **2** to comprise as a logical or necessary consequence; to imply, to entail. **3** to implicate (in a crime etc.). **4** to have an effect on. **5** to enwrap, to enfold (in). **6** (*Math.*) †to raise to any power. **involved** *a.* **1** concerned or associated. **2** (of a story, explanation etc.) complicated. **3** having a romantic or sexual relationship (with). **involvement** *n.* **1** the act of involving. **2** the state of being involved, esp. financially. **3** a complicated affair. [F *involver*, from L *involvere* (*volvere*, to roll)]

invulnerable (invŭl´nərəbəl) *a.* incapable of being wounded or injured. **invulnerability** (-bil´-), **invulnerableness** *n.* **invulnerably** *adv.* [F, from L *invulnerābilis*]

invultuation (invŭltūā´shən) *n.* the practice of pricking or stabbing the wax or clay image of an enemy, in the belief that their death will thereby be magically brought about. [low L *invultuātiōnem*, nom. *-tio*, from *invultuāre* (*vultus*, face)]

inward (in´wəd) *a.* **1** internal; situated or being within. **2** towards the interior. **3** connected with the mind or soul. ~*adv.* inwards. **inward investment** *n.* investment in a country, esp. by foreign investors. **inward-looking** *a.* self-absorbed. **inwardly** *adv.* **1** internally, within. **2** in one's thoughts and feelings, secretly. **3** not aloud (*She sighed inwardly*). **4** †intimately. **inwardness** *n.* **1** inner quality or essence. **2** the quality of being inward. **3** the mental and spiritual nature. **4** †familiarity, intimacy. **inwards** *adv.* **1** towards the interior, internal parts or centre. **2** in the mind or soul. ~*n.* the viscera. [OE *innan-weard*]

inweave (inwēv´), **enweave** *v.t.* (*past* **inwove** (-wōv´), **enwove**, *p.p.* **inwoven** (-wō´vən), **enwoven**) **1** to weave in or together. **2** to interlace (with).

inwrap ENWRAP.

inwreathe ENWREATHE.

inwrought (in´rawt, -rawt´) *a.* **1** (of a pattern etc.) wrought or worked in. **2** (of a fabric) adorned with work or figures. **3** closely blended.

inyala *n.* NYALA.

IOC *abbr.* International Olympic Committee.

iodine (ī´ədēn, -dīn) *n.* **1** a non-metallic bluish-black element, at. no. 53, chem. symbol I, yielding violet fumes when heated, and resembling bromine and chlorine in chemical properties, used in medicine and photography. **2** a solution of this in alcohol used as an antiseptic. **iodate** (-dāt) *n.* a salt of iodic acid. **iodic** (īod´ik) *a.* belonging to, or containing, iodine. **iodide** (-dīd) *n.* a compound of iodine with an element or radical. **iodinate** (ī´ədināt, īod´-) *v.t.* to add iodine or to treat with iodine. **iodination** (-ā´shən) *n.* **iodism** *n.* the morbid effects of overdoses of iodine or iodic preparations. **iodize** (ī´ədīz), **iodise** *v.t.* **1** to treat with iodine. **2** to prepare with iodine. **iodization** (-zā´shən) *n.* **iodo-** (ī´ədō, īō´-), **iod-** *comb. form* of or relating to iodine, as *iodism*, *iodoform*. **iodoform** (īod´əfawm) *n.* an iodine compound resembling chloroform in its antiseptic effects. **iodopsin** (īədop´sin) *n.* a violet light-sensitive pigment in the retinal cones of the eye. [F *iode*, Gr. *iōdēs*, *ioeidēs* (*ion*, a violet, *eidos*, appearance), -INE]

iolite (ī´əlīt) *n.* a blue orthorhombic transparent or translucent silicate of aluminium, iron and magnesium. [Gr. *ion*, as ION, -LITE]

IOM *abbr.* Isle of Man.

ion (ī´ən) *n.* an electrically charged atom or group of atoms formed by the loss or gain of electrons. **ion exchange** *n.* a process by which ions are exchanged between a solution and a solid or another liquid, as used in the softening of water etc. **ion-exchanger** *n.* **ionic** (īon´-) *a.* **ionically** *adv.* **ionic bond** *n.* a bond within a chemical compound produced by the transfer of electrons, such that the resulting ions are held together by electrostatic attraction. **ionize** *v.t.* to convert into an ion or ions. **ionizable** *a.* **ionization** (-zā´shən) *n.* the process of forming ions as a result of high temperature, radiation etc. **ionization chamber** *n.* a device for detecting ionizing radiation. **ionizer** *n.* something which produces ionization. **ionizing radiation** *n.* radiation that is able to cause ionization. [Gr. *ion*, neut. pres.p. of *ienai*, to go]

-ion (ən, iən, yən) *suf.* forming nouns indicating an action, process or resulting state or product, as *distribution, celebration, aspiration.* [F *-ion*, L *iōnem*, nom. *-io* (cp. -ATION, -ITION, -TION)]

Ionian (īō´niən) *a.* of or relating to Ionia, a district of Asia Minor, or to the Ionians. ~*n.* a member of a Hellenic people living in ancient Ionia. **Ionian mode** *n.* (*Mus.*) the mode commencing on C, corresponding in tonality with the major diatonic scale in modern music. **Ionic** (īon´-) *a.* Ionian. ~*n.* the Ionic dialect. **Ionic dialect** *n.* the Greek dialect spoken in Ionia. **Ionic foot** *n.* a metrical foot of four syllables (either two long and two short, or two short and two long). **Ionic order** *n.* one of the five classical orders of architecture, the distinguishing characteristic of which is the volute on both sides of the capital. [L *Iōnius*, Gr. *Iōnios* (*Ionia*)]

ionosphere (īon´əsfiə) *n.* the region surrounding the earth at a height of from about 60 km to 1000 km, in which ionized layers of gas occur. **ionospheric** (-fer´-) *a.*

-ior[1] (iə, yə) *suf.* forming comparative adjectives, as in *junior, superior.* [L]

-ior[2] -IOUR.

iota (īō´tə) *n.* **1** the ninth letter of the Greek alphabet, Ι, ι. **2** (*usu. with neg.*) a jot, a very small quantity. [Gr.]

IOU (ī ō ū) *n.* a formal acknowledgement of debt, bearing these letters, the sum involved and the debtor's signature. [I owe you]

-iour (iə, yə), (*esp. NAm.*) **-ior** *suf.* forming nouns, as in *behaviour, saviour, warrior.* [OF *-ur, -or* (F *-eur*), L *-ātōrem*, nom. *-ātor*]

-ious (iəs, əs) *suf.* characterized by, full of, as in *ambitious, cautious, suspicious.* [L *-iōsus* (cp. F *-ieux*), *-i-*, -OUS]

IOW *abbr.* Isle of Wight.

IPA *abbr.* International Phonetic Alphabet (or Association).

ipecacuanha (ipikakūan´ə), *n.* the dried root of *Cephaelis ipecacuanha*, a cinchonaceous plant from Brazil, used in medicine as an emetic and purgative. **ipecac** (ip´-), *n., a.* **ipecacuanhic** *a.* [Port., from Tupi *ipekaaguéne*]

IPMS *abbr.* Institution of Professionals, Managers and Specialists.

ipomoea (ipəmē´ə) *n.* any twining plant of the genus *Ipomoea*, including the morning glory and jalap. [Gr. *ip-*, stem of *ips*, worm, *omoios*, like]

ips, i.p.s. *abbr.* inches per second.

ipse dixit (ipsi dik´sit) *n.* **1** a mere assertion. **2** a dogmatic statement. [L, he himself has said it]

ipsilateral (ipsilat´ərəl) *a.* on or occurring on the same side of the body. [formed irregularly from L *ipse*, self, *lateral*]

ipsissima verba (ipsisimə vœ´bə) *n.pl.* the precise words. [L]

ipso facto (ipsō fak´tō) *adv.* **1** by that very fact. **2** thereby. [L]

IQ *abbr.* Intelligence Quotient.

†-ique -IC.

IR *abbr.* **1** infra-red. **2** Inland Revenue.

Ir *chem. symbol* iridium.

Ir. *abbr.* **1** Ireland. **2** Irish.

ir-[1] (i) *pref.* before r, as in *irradiate.* [var. of IN-[1]]

ir-[2] *pref.* before r, as in *irrelevant, irreligion.* [var. of IN-[2]]

IRA *abbr.* Irish Republican Army.

iracund (īə´rəkŭnd) *a.* easily angered. [L *īracundus*, from *īra*, IRE]

irade (irah´di) *n.* (*Hist.*) a written decree of a Muslim ruler. [Turk., from Arab. *irādah*, desire]

Iranian (irā´niən) *a.* **1** of or belonging to Iran in SW Asia, formerly Persia. **2** of or relating to the inhabitants or language of Iran. **3** of or relating to the Iranian branch of Indo-European. ~*n.* **1** a native or inhabitant of Iran. **2** a branch of the Indo-European family of languages including Persian, Kurdish and Avestan. **3** the modern Persian language.

Iraqi (irah´ki) *a.* **1** of or relating to Iraq. **2** of or relating to the form of Arabic spoken in Iraq. ~*n.* (*pl.* **Iraqis**) **1** a native or inhabitant of Iraq. **2** the form of Arabic spoken in Iraq.

irascible (iras´ibəl) *a.* easily excited to anger; irritable. **irascibility** (-bil´-), **irascibleness** *n.* **irascibly** *adv.* [F, from L *īrascibilis*, from *īrasci*, to be angry, from *īra*, IRE]

irate (īrāt´) *a.* angry, enraged. **irately** *adv.* **irateness** *n.*

☒ **irational** common misspelling of IRRATIONAL.

IRBM *abbr.* intermediate-range ballistic missile.

ire (īə) *n.* (*poet.*) anger. **ireful** *a.* **irefully** *adv.* **irefulness** *n.* [OF, from L *īra*]

☒ **iregular** common misspelling of IRREGULAR.

☒ **irelevant** common misspelling of IRRELEVANT.

irenic (īrē´nik, -ren´-), **eirenic, irenical** (-əl), **eirenical** *a.* pacific; promoting peace. **irenicon** EIRENICON. [Gr. *eirēnikos*, from *eirēnē*, peace]

☒ **iresistible** common misspelling of IRRESISTIBLE.

irid- IRIDO-.

iridacious (iridā´shəs, ī-) *a.* (*Bot.*) of or relating to the Iridaceae family of plants which grow from bulbs, corms or rhizomes and include the iris. [mod. L *iridaceus* (as IRIS)]

iridescent (irides´ənt) *a.* **1** exhibiting a spectrum of luminous or shimmering colours. **2** changing colour as the observer's position changes. **iridescence** *n.* **iridescently** *adv.* [Gr. *īris īridos*, IRIS]

iridium (irid´iəm) *n.* a shining white metallic element belonging to the platinum group, at. no. 77, chem. symbol Ir. [as IRIDESCENT]

irido- (ir´idō), **irid-** *comb. form* of or relating to the iris of the eye. [Gr. *īris īridos*, IRIS]

iridology (iridol´əji) *n.* a diagnostic technique in alternative medicine involving studying the iris of the eye. **iridologist** *n.*

iridosmine (iridoz´min) *n.* a native alloy of iridium and osmium, used for the points of gold pens.

iris (īə´ris) *n.* (*pl.* **irises, irides** (ī´ridēz, ir´-)) **1** the flat circular coloured membrane surrounding the pupil of the eye. **2** any plant of the genus *Iris* of the family Iridaceae, with tuberous roots, sword-shaped leaves, and large variously-coloured flowers. **3** a rock crystal with iridescent properties. **4** IRIS DIAPHRAGM (under IRIS). **5** an appearance resembling the rainbow; iridescence. **iris diaphragm** *n.* an adjustable diaphragm regulating the entry of light into an optical instrument. [Gr. *īris īridos*, rainbow, iris]

Irish (īə´rish) *a.* **1** of or relating to Ireland or its inhabitants or Celtic language. **2** (*coll., offensive*) illogical or ludicrous. ~*n.* **1** a native or inhabitant of Ireland. **2** (*as pl.*) the people of Ireland. **3** the Celtic language of Ireland. **Irish bull** *n.* a ludicrous contradiction in terms, supposed to be characteristic of the Irish. **Irish coffee** *n.* a drink made of sweetened coffee mixed with Irish whiskey and topped with cream. **Irish elk** *n.* a large extinct deer, *Cervus megaceros.* **Irishism** *n.* a mode of expression or idiom peculiar to the Irish. **Irishman** *n.* (*pl.* **Irishmen**) a man who is a native or inhabitant of Ireland, or a man of Irish descent. **Irish moss** *n.* CARRAGEEN. **Irishness** *n.* **Irish stew** *n.* a stew of vegetables and meat boiled together. **Irish terrier** *n.* a breed of terrier with rough reddish-brown hair. **Irish wolfhound** *n.* a large breed of dog with a long, usually grey, coat. **Irishwoman** *n.* (*pl.* **Irishwomen**) a woman who is a native or inhabitant of Ireland, or a woman of Irish descent. [OE *Iras*, pl.]

☒ **iritate** common misspelling of IRRITATE.

iritis (īrī´tis) *n.* inflammation of the iris of the eye. [IRIS, -ITIS]

irk (œk) *v.t.* to bore, annoy or irritate. **irksome** (-səm) *a.* wearisome, tedious, tiring. **irksomely** *adv.* **irksomeness** *n.* [MG *irken*, etym. uncertain]

IRO *abbr.* **1** Inland Revenue Office. **2** International Refugee Organization.

iroko (irō´kō) *n.* **1** either of two African trees of the genus *Chlorophora.* **2** the hard light-coloured wood of these trees.

iron (ī´ən) *n.* **1** a malleable ductile metallic element, at. no. 26, chem. symbol Fe, widely used for tools etc. **2** an article, tool, utensil etc., made of iron (*a soldering iron*). **3** a usu. electrical implement for smoothing clothes. **4** great firmness and resolve (*a will of iron*). **5** a metal-headed golf club used for lofting. **6** (*pl.*) fetters. **7** (*usu. pl.*) a stirrup. **8** †a metal support for a malformed leg. **9** a preparation of iron for medicinal purposes. *~a.* **1** made or composed of iron. **2** robust, strong. **3** inflexible, unyielding or merciless. *~v.t.* **1** to smooth (clothes) with an iron. **2** to fetter with irons. **3** to furnish or cover with iron. **in irons** in fetters. **to have several irons in the fire 1** to be engaged in several projects at the same time. **2** to have several expedients. **to iron out 1** to correct (defects etc.). **2** to find a solution to (problems etc.). **Iron Age** *n.* the late prehistoric age, following the Bronze Age, when weapons and many implements began to be made of iron. **ironbark** *n.* any of several Australian eucalyptus trees, esp. *Eucalyptus paniculata* and *E. sideroxylon*, with a hard, firm bark. **iron-bound** *a.* **1** bound with iron. **2** (of a coast) surrounded with rocks. **3** unyielding; hard and fast. **ironclad** *n.* (*Hist.*) a warship having the parts above water plated with iron. *~a.* **1** covered or protected with iron. **2** impregnable, inflexible. **Iron Cross** *n.* a German war medal first struck in 1813 and revived in 1870. **Iron Curtain** *n.* **1** (*Hist.*) the imperceptible barrier to communication between the former USSR with its satellites and the West. **2** (**iron curtain**) any similar barrier to communication. **ironer** *n.* **1** a person who irons clothes. **2** a device for ironing. **iron-grey** *n.* a grey colour like that of iron freshly broken. *~a.* of iron-grey. **iron hand** *n.* strict control, often tyranny. **iron horse** *n.* (*dated, coll.*) a railway locomotive. **ironing** *n.* **1** the act of ironing clothes. **2** clothes that have just been ironed or that are about to be ironed. **ironing board** *n.* a board, usu. on legs of adjustable height, used for ironing clothes etc. on. **ironless** *a.* **iron-like** *a.* **iron lung** *n.* a mechanical device employed for maintaining or assisting respiration. **iron maiden** *n.* (*Hist.*) an instrument of torture that consisted of a large box lined with iron spikes. **iron man** *n.* (*pl.* **iron men**) **1** a strong man, esp. a powerful athlete. **2** a multi-event sporting contest in which the contestants' stamina and endurance is tested. **ironmaster** *n.* a manufacturer of iron. **ironmonger** *n.* a person who deals in ironware or hardware. **ironmongery** *n.* (*pl.* **ironmongeries**) **1** ironware, hardware. **2** an ironmonger's shop or business. **iron-mould,** (*N Am.*) **iron-mold** *n.* a spot on cloth etc. caused by ink or rust. **iron-on** *a.* that can be fixed to a fabric by ironing. **iron pyrites** *n.* a yellow native sulphide of iron, one of two common sulphides, also called *fool's gold.* **iron rations** *n.pl.* complete emergency rations packed in a sealed case. **Ironsides** *n.* **1** a man of stamina and bravery. **2** (*as pl.*) Cromwell's troops in the English Civil War. **ironstone** *n.* **1** an iron ore containing oxygen and silica. **2** a kind of hard durable china. **ironware** *n.* goods made of iron, hardware. **ironwood** *n.* any of several very hard and heavy woods. **ironwork** *n.* **1** things made of iron. **2** work, esp. decorative work, done in iron. *~n.pl.* (*often sing. in constr.*) an establishment where iron is manufactured. **irony**[1] (ī´əni) *a.* consisting of, containing or resembling iron. [OE *īren, īsen, īsern* (cp. Dut. *ījzer*, Icel. *jārn, īsarn*, G *Eisen*]

ironic, ironical etc. IRONY[2].

irony[1] IRON.

irony[2] (ī´rəni) *n.* (*pl.* **ironies**) **1** an expression, often humorous or slightly sarcastic, intended to convey the opposite of its usual meaning. **2** the use of such expressions. **3** incongruity between what is expected and what happens; a result showing such incongruity. **4** DRAMATIC IRONY (under DRAMA). **ironic** (īron´-), **ironical** *a.* **ironically** *adv.* **ironist** *n.* a person who uses irony. **ironize, ironise** *v.i.* **irony of fate** *n.* the apparent malice or perversity of events not under human control. [F *ironie*, L *īronīa*, Gr. *eirōneia*, from *eirōn*, a dissembler]

Iroquois (ir´əkwoi, -koi) *n.* (*pl.* **Iroquois**) **1** the American Indian confederacy of the Mohawk, Oneida, Seneca, Onnodaga, Cayuga and Tuscarora. **2** a member of any of these peoples. **3** any of the Iroquoian languages. **Iroquoian** *a.* of or relating to the Iroquois or their languages. *~n.* **1** a North American Indian family of languages including Cherokee and Seneca. **2** a member of the Iroquois.

irradiate (irā´diāt) *v.t.* **1** to subject to sunlight or ultraviolet rays. **2** to make bright or brilliant; to light up. **3** to shed light upon (a subject etc.). **4** to brighten up (a face, expression etc.). **5** to expose (food) to low levels of gamma radiation in order to sterilize and preserve it. *~†v.i.* to shine. **irradiance** *n.* **irradiant** *a.* **irradiation** (-ā´shən) *n.* **1** the act or process of irradiating. **2** the process of exposing food to low levels of gamma radiation in order to kill bacteria. **3** shining; lighting up. **4** the apparent enlargement of an illuminated object viewed against a dark background. **irradiative** *a.* [L *irradiātus*, p.p. of *irradiāre* (*radius*, RAY[1])]

irrational (irash´ənəl) *a.* **1** without reason or understanding. **2** illogical, contrary to reason, absurd. **3** (*Math.*) not expressible by a whole number or common fraction, not commensurable with a finite number. *~n.* an irrational number. **irrationalism** *n.* **irrationality** (-nal´-) *n.* **irrationalize, irrationalise** *v.t.* **irrationally** *adv.* [L *irrātiōnālis*]

irreclaimable (irəklā´məbəl) *a.* incapable of being reclaimed; obstinate; inveterate. **irreclaimability** (-bil´-) *n.* **irreclaimably** *adv.*

irreconcilable (irekənsī´ləbəl) *a.* **1** incapable of being reconciled; implacably hostile. **2** incompatible. *~n.* **1** a person who cannot be reconciled, appeased or satisfied; an intransigent. **2** (*usu. pl.*) each of two or more opinions, principles etc. that cannot be reconciled. **irreconcilability** (-bil´-), **irreconcilableness** *n.* **irreconcilably** *adv.*

irrecoverable (irikŭv´ərəbəl) *a.* that cannot be recovered; irreparable. **irrecoverableness** *n.* **irrecoverably** *adv.*

irrecusable (irikū´zəbəl) *a.* not to be refused or rejected. [F, from late L *irrecūsābilis* (*recūsāre*, to refuse)]

irredeemable (iridē´məbəl) *a.* **1** not redeemable. **2** beyond redemption, offering no scope for salvage or rectification. **3** (of an annuity) not terminable by payment of the principal. **4** (of a banknote) not convertible into cash. **5** irreclaimable. **irredeemability** (-bil´-), **irredeemableness** *n.* **irredeemably** *adv.*

irredentist (iriden´tist) *n.* **1** a person who advocates the reclaiming of territory that once belonged to their country. 2 (**Irredentist**) a member of a party formed about 1878 to bring about the inclusion of all Italian-speaking districts in the kingdom of Italy. **irredentism** *n.* [It. *irredentista*, from *Italia irredenta*, unredeemed Italy]

irreducible (iridū´sibəl) *a.* 1 not reducible; not to be lessened or lowered. 2 not to be brought to a required condition etc. 3 (*Math.*) not to be simplified. **irreducibility** (-bil´-), **irreducibleness** *n.* **irreducibly** *adv.*

irrefragable (iref´rəgəbəl) *a.* 1 incapable of being refuted; undeniable, unanswerable. 2 (of rules etc.) that cannot be broken. **irrefragability** (-bil´-), **irrefragableness** *n.* **irrefragably** *adv.* [late L *irrefrāgābilis*]

irrefrangible (irifran´jibəl) *a.* 1 not to be broken, inviolable. 2 (*Physics*) not able to be refracted.

irrefutable (irifū´təbəl) *a.* incapable of being refuted. **irrefutability** (-bil´-) *n.* **irrefutably** *adv.* [F, from L *irrefutābilis*]

irreg. *abbr.* irregular, irregularly.

irregular (ireg´ūlə) *a.* 1 not according to rule or established principles or custom. 2 not uniform or even; asymmetrical. 3 not occurring at regular times. 4 (*Gram.*) deviating from the common form in inflection. 5 lawless; disorderly. 6 not belonging to the regular army. 7 (of a flower) not having petals etc. of the same size or shape. ~*n.pl.* irregular troops. **irregularity** (-lar´-) *n.* (*pl.* **irregularities**). **irregularly** *adv.* [OF *irreguler*, late L *irrēgulāris*]

irrelative (irel´ətiv) *a.* 1 unconnected (to). 2 having no relations, absolute. 3 not relevant. **irrelatively** *adv.*

irrelevant (irel´əvənt) *a.* not applicable or pertinent; having no application (to the matter in hand). **irrelevance** *n.* **irrelevancy** *n.* (*pl.* **irrelevancies**). **irrelevantly** *adv.*

irreligion (irilij´ən) *n.* indifference or hostility to religion. **irreligionist** *n.* **irreligious** *a.* 1 hostile or indifferent to religion. 2 not having a religion. **irreligiously** *adv.* **irreligiousness** *n.* [F *irréligion*, L *irreligiōnem*, nom. *-gio*]

irremediable (irəmē´diəbəl) *a.* incapable of being remedied or corrected. **irremediableness** *n.* **irremediably** *adv.* [MF *irrémédiable*, L *irremediābilis*]

irremissible (irəmis´ibəl) *a.* 1 that cannot be remitted or pardoned. 2 obligatory. **irremissibility** (-bil´-) *n.* **irremissibly** *adv.* [F *irrémissible*, L *irremissibilis*]

irremovable (irimoo´vəbəl) *a.* that cannot be removed or displaced. **irremovability** (-bil´-) *n.* **irremovably** *adv.*

irreparable (irep´ərəbəl) *a.* incapable of being repaired, remedied or restored. **irreparableness, irreparability** (-bil´-) *n.* **irreparably** *adv.* [F, from L *irreparābilis*]

irrepealable (iripē´ləbəl) *a.* incapable of being repealed, irrevocable. **irrepealability** (-bil´-) *n.* **irrepealably** *adv.*

irreplaceable (iriplā´səbəl) *a.* 1 that cannot be replaced. 2 not to be made good in case of loss. **irreplaceably** *adv.*

irrepressible (iripres´ibəl) *a.* that cannot be repressed. **irrepressibility** (-bil´-), **irrepressibleness** *n.* **irrepressibly** *adv.*

irreproachable (iriprō´chəbəl) *a.* blameless, faultless. **irreproachability** (-bil´-), **irreproachableness** *n.* **irreproachably** *adv.* [F *irréprochable*]

irresistible (irizis´tibəl) *a.* 1 that cannot be resisted or withstood. 2 extremely attractive or alluring. **irresistibility** (-bil´-), **irresistibleness** *n.* **irresistibly** *adv.* [late L *irresistibilis*]

irresoluble (irez´əlūbəl) *a.* 1 incapable of being resolved into its elements; insoluble. 2 †incapable of being relieved.

irresolute (irez´əloot) *a.* 1 not resolute. 2 undecided, hesitating. **irresolutely** *adv.* **irresoluteness, irresolution** (-oo´shən) *n.* [L *irresolūtus*]

irresolvable (irizol´vəbəl) *a.* 1 incapable of being resolved, insoluble. 2 that cannot be analysed or separated into its parts. **irresolvability** (-bil´-) *n.*

irrespective (irispek´tiv) *a.* (*followed by of*) regardless of, without reference to. ~*adv.* irrespectively. **irrespectively** *adv.* without regard to circumstances or conditions.

irrespirable (ires´pirəbəl) *a.* (of air) not fit to be breathed.

irresponsible (irispon´sibəl) *a.* 1 performed or acting without a proper sense of responsibility. 2 lacking the capacity to bear responsibility. **irresponsibility** (-bil´-) *n.* **irresponsibly** *adv.*

irresponsive (irispon´siv) *a.* not responsive (to). **irresponsiveness** *n.*

irretentive (iriten´tiv) *a.* not retentive. **irretentiveness** *n.*

irretrievable (iritrē´vəbəl) *a.* not to be retrieved; irreparable. **irretrievability** (-bil´-) *n.* **irretrievably** *adv.*

irreverent (irev´ərənt) *a.* 1 lacking in reverence; disrespectful. 2 proceeding from irreverence. **irreverence** *n.* **irreverential** (-ren´shəl) *a.* **irreverently** *adv.* [F *irrévérent*, L *irreverentem*, nom. *-ens*]

irreversible (irivœ´sibəl) *a.* not reversible; irrevocable. **irreversibility** (-bil´-), **irreversibleness** *n.* **irreversibly** *adv.*

irrevocable (irev´əkəbəl) *a.* incapable of being revoked or altered, unalterable. **irrevocability** (-bil´-), **irrevocableness** *n.* **irrevocably** *adv.* [F, from L *irrevocābilis*]

irrigate (ir´igāt) *v.t.* 1 to water (land) by causing a stream to flow over it. 2 (of streams etc.) to supply (land) with water. 3 to moisten (a wound etc.) with a continuous jet or stream of antiseptic fluid. 4 to refresh or make fertile as with a stream. **irrigable** *a.* **irrigation** (-ā´shən) *n.* **irrigative** *a.* **irrigator** *n.* †**irriguous** (irig´ū-) *a.* watered. [L *irrigātus*, p.p. of *irrigāre* (*rigāre*, to moisten)]

irritate (ir´itāt) *v.t.* 1 to excite to impatience or ill-temper; to annoy; to exasperate. 2 to stir up, to excite. 3 to cause discomfort in (the skin, an organ etc.). 4 (*Biol.*) to stimulate (an organ) artificially. **irritable** *a.* 1 easily provoked or angered. 2 easily inflamed or made painful, highly sensitive. 3 (of nerves, muscles etc.) responsive to artificial stimulation. **irritability** (-bil´-), **irritableness** *n.* **irritable bowel syndrome** *n.* a condition which is marked by abdominal pain and constipation or diarrhoea and which is often associated with stress etc. **irritably** *adv.* **irritancy** *n.* **irritant** *n.* something that irritates. ~*a.* causing irritation. **irritatedly** *adv.* **irritating** *a.* **irritatingly** *adv.* **irritation** (-ā´shən) *n.* **irritative** *a.* **irritator** *n.* [L *irrītātus*, p.p. of *irrītāre*, prob. freq. of *irrīre*, *hirrīre*, to snarl]

irruption (irŭp´shən) *n.* 1 a bursting in. 2 a sudden invasion or incursion. 3 a sudden temporary increase in the local population of an animal or plant. **irrupt** *v.i.* **irruptive** *a.* [F, from L *irruptiōnem*, nom. *-tio*, from *irrumpere* (*rumpere*, to break), p.p. *irruptus*]

IS *abbr.* Iceland (IVR).

Is. *abbr.* 1 Isaiah. 2 Island(s). 3 Isle(s).

is BE.

is- ISO-.

Isa. *abbr.* Isaiah.

Isabel (iz´əbel), **Isabella** (-bel´ə) *a.*, *n.* greyish-yellow. **Isabelline** (-bel´īn) *a.* [female name]

isagogic (īsəgoj´ik) *a.* introductory. **isagogics** *n.* an introductory study, esp. of the literary history, authorship etc. of the Bible. [L *īsagōgicus*, Gr. *eisagōgikos*, from *eisagōgē*, introduction (*eīs*, into, *agōgē*, from *agein*, to lead)]

isatin (ī´sətin) *n.* a yellowish-red crystalline compound obtained by oxidizing indigo, used for making dyes. [L and Gr. *isatis*, -IN]

ISBN *abbr.* International Standard Book Number.

ischaemia (iskē´miə), (*esp. N Am.*) **ischemia** *n.* a shortage of blood in part of the body. **ischaemic** *a.* [Gr. *ischein*, to restrain, *haima*, blood]

ischium (is´kiəm) *n.* (*pl.* **ischia** (-ə)) either of the posterior bones of the pelvic girdle. **ischial** *a.* [Gr. *ischion*, hip joint]

ISD *abbr.* international subscriber dialling.

ISDN *abbr.* integrated services digital network.

-ise[1] (īz, ēz) *suf.* forming abstract nouns, as *franchise*, *merchandise*. [OF *-ise*, L *-ītia*, *-itia*, *-icia*, *-itium*, *-icium*, (cp. -ICE)]

-ise[2] (īz) *suf.* forming verbs, as *advertise*. [as -ISH[2]]

Usage note See note under -IZE.

-ise[3] -IZE.

isentropic (īsəntrop´ik) *a.* having equal entropy. [Gr. *isos*, equal, *entropē*, a turning about]

-ish[1] (ish) *suf.* **1** of the nature of, of or relating to, as *childish*. **2** rather, somewhat, as *reddish*. **3** of the nationality of, as *English*. **4** (*coll.*) indicating approximate age, time etc., as *thirtyish*, *twoish*. [OE *isc* (cp. Dut. and G *-isch*, Icel. *-iskr*, also Gr. *iskos*)]

-ish[2] (ish) *suf.* forming verbs, as *cherish*, *finish*, *punish*. [F *-iss-*, in pres.p. etc. of verbs in *-ir*, L incept. *-isc-*]

Ishmael (ish´māl) *n.* an outcast. **Ishmaelite** (-īt) *n.* an outcast. [son of Abraham and Hagar (Gen. xvi.12)]

isinglass (ī´zing·glahs) *n.* **1** a gelatinous substance prepared from the swimming-bladders of the sturgeon, cod, and other fish, used for making jellies, glue etc. **2** mica. [said to be a corr. of MDut. *huyzenblas* (cp. G *Hausenblase*), sturgeon's bladder]

Islam (iz´lahm) *n.* **1** the Muslim religion, that teaches that there is only one God and that Muhammad is his prophet. **2** the Muslim world. **Islamic** (-lah´mik) *a.* **Islamism** *n.* **Islamist** *n.* **Islamize, Islamise** *v.t.* to convert to Islam. **Islamization** (-zā´shən) *n.* [Arab. *islām*, submission, from *salama*, he was resigned, whence SALAAM]

island (ī´lənd) *n.* **1** a piece of land surrounded by water. **2** anything isolated or resembling an island. **3** an area in the middle of a road which divides the traffic and affords a refuge for the pedestrian. **4** a cluster of cells, mass of tissue etc., different in formation from those surrounding it. **5** the superstructure on a ship. *~v.t.* **1** to form into an island. **2** to isolate. **3** to dot as with islands. **islander** *n.* a native or inhabitant of an island. **island-hop** *v.i.* (*pres.p.* **island-hopping,** *past*, *p.p.* **island-hopped**) to travel from one island to another, esp. as a tourist. [ME *iland*, OE *īgland* (*īg*, *īeg*, LAND), cp. Icel. *eyland*, Dut. *eiland* (*s* introd. by conf. with ISLE)]

isle (īl) *n.* an island, esp. a small island. **islet** (-lit) *n.* **1** a little island. **2** (*Anat.*) a portion of tissue different in formation from tissues surrounding it. **3** an isolated place. **islets of Langerhans** *n.pl.* groups of endocrine cells in the pancreas that secrete insulin (discovered by Paul *Langerhans*, 1847–88, German anatomist). [ME *ile*, OF *ile*, *isle*, L *insula*]

ism (iz´m) *n.* (*usu. derog.*) a doctrine or system of a distinctive kind. [as -ISM]

-ism (izm) *suf.* **1** forming abstract nouns denoting a doctrine, theory or system, as *Conservatism*, *Socialism*. **2** forming nouns denoting an action, process or result, as *plagiarism*, *exorcism*. **3** forming nouns denoting a condition or quality, as *altruism*, *fanaticism*. **4** forming nouns denoting prejudice or discrimination on a particular basis, as *sexism*, *ageism*. **5** forming nouns denoting a particular linguistic feature or usage, as *Gallicism*, *regionalism*. **6** forming nouns denoting a pathological condition, as *rheumatism*. [F *-isme*, L *-ismus*, Gr. *-ismos* or *-isma*, from verbal ending *-izein*]

Ismaili (izmah´ē´li) *n.* (*pl.* **Ismailis**) a member of a sect of Shiite Muslims whose spiritual leader is the Aga Khan.

isn't (iz´ənt) *contr.* is not.

ISO *abbr.* **1** Imperial Service Order. **2** International Organization for Standardization.

iso- (ī´sō), **is-** (īs) *comb. form* **1** equal, having the same number of parts, as *isodynamic*. **2** indicating an isomeric substance, as *isocyanide*. [Gr. *isos*, equal]

isobar (ī´sōbah) *n.* **1** a line on a map connecting places having the same mean barometric pressure, or the same pressure at a given time. **2** (*Chem.*) a curve relating qualities measured at the same pressure. **3** (*Physics*) any of two or more isotopes of different elements that have the same atomic weight. **isobaric** (-bar´-) *a.* [Gr. *baros*, weight]

isocheim (ī´sōkīm) *n.* a line on a map connecting places having the same mean winter temperature. **isocheimal** (-kī´-), **isocheimenal** (īsōkī´mənəl) *a.* marking places having the same mean winter temperature. [Gr. *cheima*, winter (cp. L *heims*)]

isochor (ī´sōkaw) *n.* on a diagram representing relations between pressure and temperature, a line connecting the points denoting equal volumes. **isochoric** (-kor´-) *a.* [Gr. *chōra*, space]

isochromatic (īsōkrəmat´ik) *a.* of the same colour.

isochronal (īsok´rənəl), **isochronous** (-əs) *a.* **1** denoting or occupying equal spaces of time. **2** occurring at equal intervals of time. **isochronism** (īsok´-) *n.* **isochronously** *adv.*

isochroous (īsok´rōəs) *a.* having a uniform colour throughout. [Gr. *chroa*, colour]

isoclinal (īsōklī´nəl), **isoclinic** (-klin´-) *a.* **1** having the same inclination or dip. **2** having the same magnetic dip. **3** (*Geol.*) (of folds) in which the limbs are parallel to each other.

isodiametric (īsōdīəmet´rik) *a.* equal in diameter.

isodimorphism (īsōdīmaw´fizm) *n.* isomorphism between substances that are dimorphous. **isodimorphic** *a.*

isodynamic (īsōdīnam´ik) *a.* having equal force, esp. magnetic force.

isoelectric (īsōilek´trik) *a.* having identical electric potential. **isoelectric focusing, isoelectric focussing** *n.* (*Biol.*) a form of electrophoresis in which proteins are focused.

isoenzyme (ī´sōenzīm) *n.* (*Biol.*) any of two or more enzymes with identical activities but different structure.

isogamy (īsog´əmi) *n.* the sexual fusion of two gametes of similar size and form. **isogamous** *a.* [Gr. *gamia*, marriage]

isogeny (īsoj´əni) *n.* general similarity of origin. **isogenic** (īsōjen´-), **isogenous** (-soj´-) *a.*

isogeotherm (īsōjē´əthœm) *n.* an imaginary line below the surface of the earth connecting places having the same mean temperature. **isogeothermal** (-thœ´-), **isogeothermic** *a.*

isogloss (ī´sōglos) *n.* a line on a map separating off a region that has a specific dialectal feature. **isoglossal** (-glos´-), **isoglottic** (-glot´-) *a.* [Gr. *glossa*, tongue]

isogon (ī´sōgon) *n.* a geometrical figure in which all the angles are equal. **isogonal** (īsog´-) *a.* **1** equiangular. **2** isogonic. **isogonic** (-gon´-) *a.* connecting points (on the earth's surface) having the same magnetic declination or variation from true north. *~n.* an isogonic line.

isohel (ī´sōhel) *n.* a line on a map connecting places having equal amounts of sunshine. [Gr. *hēlios*, sun]

isohyet (īsōhī´it) *n.* a line on a map connecting places having equal amounts of rainfall. [Gr. *hȳetos*, rain]

isokinetic (īsōkinet´ik) *a.* **1** not involving any change in speed. **2** of or relating to muscle action that has a constant rate of movement.

isolate (ī´səlāt) *v.t.* **1** to place apart; to detach. **2** to quarantine (a person thought to be contagious). **3** to separate (a problem, idea etc.) in order to examine or deal with it. **4** to insulate (electrical equipment). **5**

(*Chem.*) to obtain in an uncombined form. **isolable** *a.* **isolability** (-ləbil´-) *n.* **isolation** (-ā´shən) *n.* **in isolation** considered separately and not in relation to anything else. **isolationism** *n.* a policy of holding aloof from international affairs. **isolationist** *n.* **isolator** *n.* [F *isoler*, It. *isolare*, L *insulāre*, to INSULATE]

isoleucine (īsōloo´sēn) *n.* an essential amino acid.

isomer (ī´sōmə) *n.* **1** (*Chem.*) any of two or more compounds with the same molecular composition but a different structure and different properties. **2** (*Physics*) any of two or more atomic nuclei which have the same atomic number and the same mass number, but have different energy states. **isomeric** (īsəmer´ik), **isomerical** *a.* **isomerism** (īsom´-) *n.* **isomerize, isomerise** *v.i.*, *v.t.* **isomerous** (īsom´-) *a.* (*Zool., Bot.*) having the same number of parts or segments. [Gr. *isomerēs* (ISO-, *meros*, share)]

isometric (īsōmet´rik), **isometrical** (-əl) *a.* **1** of equal measure. **2** (of muscle action) producing tension but not producing any contraction of the muscle. **3** (*Math.*) (of a transformation) with distance remaining unaltered. **isometrically** *adv.* **isometric line** *n.* a line on a graph representing variations of pressure and temperature at a constant volume. **isometric projection** *n.* (*Archit.*) a drawing in approximate perspective from which lengths can be scaled. **isometrics** *n.pl.* a system of exercises in which the muscles are strengthened as one muscle is opposed to another or to a resistant object. **isometry** (īsom´itri) *n.* (*Math.*) a transformation involving no change in distance.

isomorph (ī´sōmawf) *n.* an organism or substance exhibiting isomorphism. **isomorphic, isomorphous** *a.* **isomorphism** (-maw´-) *n.* **1** similarity of form. **2** the property of crystallizing in identical or nearly identical forms. **3** (*Math.*) identity of form and construction between two or more groups. [Gr. *morphē*, form]

-ison (isən) *suf.* forming nouns, as in *comparison*, *orison*. [F *-aison*, *-eison*, *-ison*, L *-ātiōnem*, *-etiōnem*, *-itiōnem*]

isonomy (īson´əmi) *n.* equality of political or legal rights. [Gr. *isonomia* (*nomos*, law)]

isophote (ī´sōfōt) *n.* a line where the light intensity is constant. [Gr. *phōs phōtos*, light]

isopleth (ī´sōpleth) *n.* a line on a map connecting points at which a variable such as humidity has a constant value. **isoplethic** (-pleth´-) *a.* [Gr. *plēthos*, quantity]

isopod (ī´sōpod) *n.* any of the Isopoda or sessile-eyed crustaceans characterized by seven pairs of thoracic legs almost of the same length, including woodlice and many aquatic species. ~*a.* isopodous. **isopodan** (īsop´-), **isopodous** (īsop´-) *a.* [Gr. *pous podos*, a foot]

isoprene (ī´sōprēn) *n.* a hydrocarbon of the terpene group used esp. in synthetic rubber.

isorhythmic (īsōridh´mik) *a.* (of medieval motets) consisting of the constant repetition of the same rhythm.

isosceles (īsos´əlēz) *a.* (of a triangle) having two sides equal. [late L *īsoscelēs*, Gr. *isoskelēs*, lit. equal-legged (*skelos*, leg)]

isoseismal (īsōsīz´məl), **isoseismic** (-mik) *a.* connecting points at which an earthquake has been of the same intensity. ~*n.* an isoseismal line.

isosmotic (īsəzmot´ik) *a.* equal in osmotic pressure.

isostatic (īsōstat´ik) *a.* (*Geol.*) in equilibrium owing to equality of pressure on every side, as that normally prevailing in the crust of the earth. **isostasy** (īsos´təsi) *n.*

isothere (ī´sōthiə) *n.* a line on a map connecting points having the same mean summer temperature. **isotheral** (īsoth´ərəl) *a.* connecting points having the same mean summer temperature. [Gr. *theros*, summer]

isotherm (ī´sōthœm) *n.* **1** a line on a globe or map passing over places having the same mean temperature. **2** (*Physics*) a curve on a graph relating quantities of equal temperature. **isothermal** (-thœ´-) *a.*, *n.* **isothermally** *adv.*

isotonic (īsōton´ik) *a.* **1** having equal tones. **2** (of muscles) having equal tension or tonicity. **3** (of the corpuscles of the blood), having the same osmotic pressure. **isotonically** *adv.* **isotonicity** (-nis´i-) *n.* [Gr. *isotonos*]

isotope (ī´sətōp) *n.* each of two or more atoms of a chemical element having the same atomic number but differing in atomic mass. **isotopic** (-top´-) *a.* **isotopically** *adv.* **isotopy** (īsot´-) *n.* [Gr. *topos*, place]

isotropic (īsōtrop´ik) *a.* manifesting the same physical properties in every direction. **isotropically** *adv.* **isotropous** (īsot´-) *a.* **isotropy** *n.* [Gr. *isotropos* (*tropos*, way, from *trepein*, to turn)]

I spy (ī spī´) *n.* **1** a children's game in which one player specifies the initial letter of a visible object, which the other players then try to guess. **2** hide-and-seek.

Israeli (izrā´li) *a.* of or relating to the modern state of Israel. ~*n.* (*pl.* **Israelis**) a native or inhabitant of Israel. **Israelite** (iz´rəlīt) *n.* a member of the ancient Hebrew people, esp. an inhabitant of the kingdom of Israel (922–721 BC). ~*a.* of or relating to the Israelites. [L and Gr. *Isrāēl*, Heb. *yisrāēl*, striver with God]

ISSN *abbr.* international standard serial number.

issue (ish´oo, is´ū) *n.* **1** the act of sending, giving out or putting into circulation. **2** something that is given out or put into circulation. **3** something which is published at a particular time as part of a regular series (*the March issue*). **4** the whole quantity or number of stamps, coins, copies of a newspaper etc. sent out or put on sale at one time. **5** the act of passing or flowing out. **6** an outgoing, outflow. **7** an outlet, e.g. the mouth of a river. **8** something which passes or flows out. **9** (*Law*) progeny, offspring. **10** the produce of the earth; profits from land or other property. **11** a result; a consequence. **12** an important point or subject of debate. **13** (*Law*) a matter of dispute between contending parties. **14** †a discharge, as of blood. ~*v.i.* (*3rd pers. sing. pres.* **issues**, *pres.p.* **issuing**, *past*, *p.p.* **issued**) **1** to go or come out. **2** to emerge (from). **3** to proceed, to be derived (from). **4** to end or result (in). ~*v.t.* **1** to send out; to publish; to put into circulation. **2** to provide or supply officially (with) (*We were issued with uniforms*). **3** to announce officially (a warning etc.). **at issue 1** in dispute. **2** at variance. **to join issue with** to take issue with. **to make an issue of** to make a fuss about (something that one disagrees with). **to take issue with** to argue against or disagree with. **issuable** *a.* **issuance** *n.* the act of issuing. **issuant** *a.* (*Her.*) emerging or issuing. **issueless** *a.* **issue of fact, issue of law** *n.* a dispute arising when the importance of a fact is denied or when the application of the law is contested. **issuer** *n.* [OF, from pop. L *exūtus*, L *exitus*, from *exīre* (EX-, *īre*, to go)]

-ist (ist) *suf.* **1** forming nouns and corresponding adjectives denoting an adherent or follower, as *Baptist*, *fatalist*, *Socialist*. **2** denoting a person who practises a particular profession or is involved in a particular field, as *botanist*, *herbalist*. **3** denoting a person who uses or performs something, as *flautist*, *motorist*, *exorcist*. **4** denoting a person characterized by a particular attribute, as *optimist*. **5** forming nouns and corresponding adjectives denoting a person with a particular prejudice, as *ageist*, *sexist*. [F *-iste*, L *-ista*, Gr. *-istēs*]

-ister (istə) *suf.* denoting an agent etc., as *chorister*, *sophister*. [OF *-istre*, var. of -IST]

isthmus (is´məs) *n.* **1** (*pl.* **isthmuses**) a neck of land connecting two larger portions of land. **2** (*Anat.*) (*pl.* **isthmi** (-mī)) a narrow passage or part between two larger cavities or parts. **isthmian** *a.* **1** of or relating to an isthmus. **2** (**Isthmian**) of or relating to the Isthmus of Corinth in Greece. **Isthmian games** *n.pl.* games celebrated in ancient Corinth in the first and third years of each Olympiad, forming one of the four great Panhellenic festivals. [L, from Gr. *isthmos*]

istle (ist´li) *n.* a species of Mexican agave, or the tough wiry fibre of its leaves, used for cord, nets etc. [Mex. Sp. *ixtli*]

IT *abbr.* information technology.

It. *abbr.* **1** Italy. **2** Italian.

it[1] (it) *pron.* (*poss.* **its**) **1** the thing, or sometimes the animal or small child, mentioned or referred to (*She unlocked the case and opened it*). **2** the person present, speaking etc. (*It is I*). **3** used as the subject of impersonal verbs (*It's snowing; It's half past six*). **4** used to stand in for a deferred object or subject (*It's a good thing you arrived when you did; It's a waste of time, all this hanging around*). **5** used as an indefinite object (*to rough it; to fight it out*). **6** used as the antecedent of a following clause (*It's one of the best plays (that) I've ever seen*). **7** the ultimate point or extreme limit. **8** something that corresponds exactly to what one is looking for. **9** the player in a children's game chosen to oppose the others. **10** (*coll.*) sexual intercourse; sex appeal. **that's it 1** that is what is wanted. **2** that is enough. **3** that is the difficulty or problem. **this is it 1** this is the moment when something that has been expected is about to actually happen. **2** this is the problem. [OE *hit*, neut. of *hē*, HE (cp. Dut. *het*, Icel. *hit*)]

it[2] (it) *n.* (*coll.*) Italian vermouth.

i.t.a., ITA *abbr.* initial teaching alphabet.

itacolumite (itəkol´ūmīt) *n.* a granular micaceous sandstone which in thin slabs is sometimes flexible. [*Itacolumi*, mountain in Brazil]

ital. *abbr.* italic.

Italian (ital´yən) *a.* of or relating to Italy, its people or language. ~*n.* **1** a native or inhabitant of Italy. **2** the Italian language. **Italianate** *a.* Italian in style. **Italianism, Italicism** *n.* **1** an Italian custom or idiom. **2** the cult of or an enthusiasm for Italian life etc. **Italianize, Italianise** *v.i., v.t.* **Italian pink** *n.* a yellow pigment. **Italian vermouth** *n.* sweet vermouth. [L *Italiānus*]

italic (ital´ik) *a.* **1** applied to a sloping type (*thus*), often used for emphasis or for foreign words. **2** (of handwriting) that slants to the right. **3** (**Italic**) of or relating to ancient Italy, it's peoples or their languages, esp. as distinguished from Roman. ~*n.pl.* italic letters or type. **italicize** (-sīz), **italicise** *v.t.* **1** to print in italics. **2** to emphasize. **italicization** (-zā´shən) *n.* [L *Italicus*, Gr. *Italikos*, as ITALIAN]

Italiot (ital´iət) *a.* of or relating to the Greek colonies in Italy. ~*n.* a native or inhabitant of these. [Gr. *Italiōtēs*, from *Italia*, Italy]

Italo- (ital´ō, it´əlō) *comb. form* Italian, as *Italophile*.

ITAR-Tass (ītahtas´) *n.* the official Russian news agency. [initials of Rus. *Informatsionnoe telegrafnoe agensvo Rossii*, Information Telegraph Agency of Russia, with TASS]

itch (ich) *v.i.* **1** to have an uncomfortable and irritating sensation in the skin causing a desire to scratch. **2** to feel a constant teasing desire (to do something). ~*n.* **1** a sensation of uneasiness in the skin causing a desire to scratch. **2** an impatient desire or craving. **3** a contagious skin disease caused by the itch mite; scabies. **one's fingers itch** one is impatient (to do something). **itching** *n., a.* **itching palm** *n.* greed; avarice. **itching powder** *n.* a powder that makes the skin itch, used esp. as a practical joke. **itch mite** *n.* a skin parasite, *Sarcoptes scabiei*, which causes scabies. **itchy** *a.* (*comp.* **itchier**, *superl.* **itchiest**) having or causing an itch. **to have itchy feet 1** to want to travel. **2** to be restless. **itchiness** *n.* [OE *giccan* (cp. Dut. *jeuken*, G *jucken*)]

it'd (it´əd) *contr.* (*coll.*) **1** it had. **2** it would.

-ite[1] (īt) *suf.* **1** denoting a follower of, as *Pre-Raphaelite, Hitlerite*. **2** denoting a fossil, mineral, as *belemnite, ichnite, dolomite*. **3** denoting a native or inhabitant of a country, as *Hittite*. **4** denoting a part of a body or organ, as *somite*. **5** denoting an explosive, as *gelignite*. **6** denoting a commercial product, as *vulcanite*. **7** denoting a salt of an acid ending with the suffix *-ous*, as *sulphite*. [F *-ite*, L *-ita*, Gr. *-itēs*]

-ite[2] (īt, it) *suf.* **1** forming nouns, as *infinite*. **2** forming adjectives, as *recondite*. **3** forming verbs, as *ignite*. [L *-itus*, p.p. of verbs in *-ēre, -ere*, and *-ire*]

item (ī´təm) *n.* **1** any of a series of things listed or enumerated. **2** an individual entry in an account, schedule etc. **3** a piece of news in a newspaper, television programme etc. **4** an article, esp. one of a number. **5** (*coll.*) two people who are in a romantic or sexual relationship. ~†*adv.* likewise, also. ~*v.t.* **1** to make a note of. **2** to itemize. **itemize, itemise** *v.t.* to list. **itemization** (-zā´shən) *n.* **itemizer** *n.* [L, in like manner, cp. *īta*, so, from *is*, he, with adv. suf. *-tem*]

iterate (it´ərāt) *v.t.* to repeat; to say over and over again. **iterant** *a.* **iteration** (-ā´shən) *n.* **iterative** *a.* **1** repetitious. **2** (*Gram.*) FREQUENTATIVE (under FREQUENT[1]). **iteratively** *adv.* [L *iterātus*, p.p. of *iterāre*, from *iterum*, again]

ithyphallic (ithifal´ik) *a.* **1** of or relating to the erect phallus carried in ancient bacchic processions. **2** (of a poem) in the metre of bacchic verse. **3** (of sculpture etc.) having an erect penis. **4** lewd. ~*n.* a poem in ithyphallic metre or style. [L *ithyphallicus*, Gr. *ithuphallikos* (*ithus*, straight, *phallikos*, from PHALLUS)]

-itic (it´ik) *suf.* forming adjectives from nouns ending in *-ite, -itis* etc., as *arthritic*. [F *-itique*, L *-iticus*]

itinerant (itin´ərənt) *a.* **1** passing or moving from place to place. **2** (of a judge, worker etc.) working for a short time in one place after another. ~*n.* **1** a person who journeys from place to place. **2** a travelling preacher, a strolling player etc. **itineracy, itinerancy** *n.* **itinerantly** *adv.* [L *itinerans -antem*, pres.p. of *itinerāri*, from *iter itineris*, a journey]

itinerary (ītin´ərəri) *n.* (*pl.* **itineraries**) **1** a route taken or to be taken. **2** an account of places and their distances on a road; a guidebook. **3** an account of travels. ~*a.* of or relating to roads or to travel. **itinerate** *v.i.* **1** to journey from place to place. **2** to preach within a circuit. **itineration** (-ā´shən) *n.*

-ition (ish´ən) *suf.* forming nouns, as *proposition, contrition*. [F *-ition*, L *itiōnem*, -ION]

-itious[1] (ish´əs) *suf.* forming adjectives that correspond to nouns ending in *-ition*, as *ambitious, nutritious*. [L *-itio -itionis*; L *-ōsus*, -OUS]

-itious[2] (ish´əs) *suf.* having the nature of, as *adventitious, factitious*. [L *-icius* or *-īcius*; L *-ōsus*, -OUS]

-itis (ī´tis) *suf.* **1** denoting inflammation, as *gastritis, peritonitis*. **2** (*coll., facet.*) denoting a condition that is like a disease, as *examitis*. [mod. L *-ītis*, Gr. *-itis*, orig. fem. of adjectives in *-itēs* (qualifying *nosos*, disease)]

-itive (itiv) *suf.* forming adjectives, as *negative, genitive*. [F *-itif -itive* or L *-itivus*]

it'll (it´əl) *contr.* (*coll.*) it will, it shall.

ITN *abbr.* Independent Television News.

ITO *abbr.* International Trade Organization.

-itor (itə) *suf.* forming nouns denoting an agent, as *editor*. [L *-itor* (-it-, OR[1])]

-itory (itəri) *suf.* forming adjectives involving an action, as *prohibitory*. [L *-itorius*]

-itous (itəs) *suf.* forming adjectives that correspond to nouns ending in *-ity*, as *serendipitous*. [F *-iteux*, L *-itōsus* (-it-, -OUS)]

its (its) *a.* possessive of IT[1]. ~*pron.* something which belongs to or is associated with it.

Usage note The spellings of the pronoun *its* and the contraction *it's* should not be confused: the possessive pronoun does not have an apostrophe, but there should always be an apostrophe for 'it is' or 'it has'.

it's (its) *contr.* **1** it is. **2** it has.

Usage note See note under ITS.

itself (itself´) *pron.* **1** IT[1], used to give emphasis (usu. in apposition). **2** the reflexive of IT[1]. **by itself** alone; separately. **in itself** independently of other things; in its essential qualities.

itsy-bitsy (itsibit´si), **itty-bitty** (itibit´i) *a.* (*coll.*) tiny.

ITU *abbr.* International Telecommunication Union.

ITV *abbr.* Independent Television.

-ity (iti) *suf.* **1** denoting a state or condition, as *equality, fragility.* **2** denoting an instance of this, as *calamity.* [F *-ité*, L *-itātem*, nom. *-itas*, see -TY[1]]

IU *abbr.* international unit.

IUD *abbr.* **1** intrauterine device. **2** intrauterine death (of a foetus).

-ium (iəm) *suf.* **1** (*also* **-um**) used to form names of metals, as *aluminium, lithium, sodium.* **2** used to form names of parts of the body, as *myocardium.* **3** used to form names of biological structures, as *prothallium.* [L]

IUPAC (ū´pak) *abbr.* International Union of Pure and Applied Chemistry.

IV *abbr.* intravenous.

I've (īv) *contr.* I have.

-ive (iv) *suf.* **1** disposed, serving or tending; of the nature or quality of, as *active, massive, pensive, restive, talkative.* **2** forming corresponding nouns, as *captive, detective.* **-ively** *suf.* forming adverbs. **-iveness** *suf.* forming nouns. [F *-if*, fem. *-ive*, L *-ivus*]

IVF *abbr.* in vitro fertilization.

ivied IVY.

ivory (ī´vəri) *n.* (*pl.* **ivories**) **1** the hard white substance composing the tusks of the elephant, the narwhal etc. **2** the colour of ivory. **3** an ornament etc. made of ivory. **4** (*pl., sl.*) things resembling or made of ivory, e.g. teeth, billiard balls, dice, keys of a piano. *~a.* **1** consisting of, made of or resembling ivory. **2** of the colour of ivory. **vegetable ivory** VEGETABLE. **ivoried** *a.* **ivory black** *n.* a black pigment obtained by grinding calcined ivory or bone. **ivory-nut** *n.* the seed of a tropical American palm, *Phytelephas macrocarpa.* **ivory tower** *n.* a shelter from the realities of everyday life. [A-F *ivorie*, OF *yvoire* (F *ivoire*), L *eboreus*, made of ivory, from *ebur eboris*, ivory]

IVR *abbr.* International Vehicle Registration.

ivy (ī´vi) *n.* (*pl.* **ivies**) **1** an evergreen climbing plant, *Hedera helix*, usu. having five-angled leaves, and adhering by aerial rootlets. **2** any of various other climbing plants, such as the poison ivy. **ivied** *a.* covered with ivy. **ivy geranium** *n.* the ivy-leaved pelargonium. **Ivy League** *n.* a group of eight long-established and prestigious US universities. [OE *ifig*]

†**iwis** (iwis´), **ywis** *adv.* certainly (often spelt erron. *I wis*). [OE *gewis*, certain (cp. Dut. *gewis*, G *gewiss*)]

IWW *abbr.* Industrial Workers of the World.

ixia (ik´siə) *n.* any S African bulbous flowering plant of the genus *Ixia* of the iris family. [Gr.]

Iyar (iyah´) *n.* in the Jewish calendar, the eighth month of the civil year and the second month of the religious year.

izard (iz´əd) *n.* a kind of antelope related to the chamois, inhabiting the Pyrenees. [F *isard*, etym. uncertain]

-ize (īz), **-ise** *suf.* **1** forming verbs meaning to follow or practise some principle, policy etc., as *economize.* **2** to come to resemble; to come into a specified state, as *crystallize.* **3** to cause to resemble or come into such a specified state, as *Anglicize, sterilize.* **4** to treat in a specified way, as *vulcanize.* **5** to feel a specified thing, as *empathize.* **6** to subject to, as *memorize, hypnotize.* **7** to provide with, as *motorize.* **-ization** (īzā´shən) *suf.* forming corresponding nouns. **-izer** *suf.* [F *-iser*, late L *-izāre*, Gr. *-izein*]

Usage note This dictionary uses the spelling *-ize*. The alternative *-ise*, which is common especially in Britain, is listed for the first relevant word in each entry. (The ending *-ise* is also found in words where it does not represent this suffix, as in *advertise*.) American spelling also prefers *-ize*.

†**izzard** (iz´əd) *n.* the letter *z.* [formerly *ezod*, F *ézed*, Gr. *zēta*]

J

J[1] (jā), **j** (*pl.* **Js, J's**) the tenth letter of the English and other versions of the Roman alphabet. It is pronounced as a voiced affricate, the sound of *g* in *gem*, except in a few words adopted from German etc., where it has the sound of *y*. ~*symbol* **1** current density. **2** one in Roman numerals, as a variant of *i* in final position, as in *vj*.

J[2] *abbr.* **1** Japan (IVR). **2** joule(s).

J. *abbr.* **1** jack. **2** Journal. **3** Judge. **4** Justice.

JA *abbr.* **1** Jamaica (IVR). **2** Judge Advocate. **3** Justice of Appeal.

jab (jab) *v.t.* (*pres.p.* **jabbing,** *past, p.p.* **jabbed**) **1** to poke violently. **2** to stab. **3** to thrust (something) roughly (into). ~*n.* **1** a sharp poke, a stab, a thrust. **2** (*coll.*) a vaccination or injection. [prob. imit. (cp. JOB[2])]

jabber (jab´ə) *v.i.* **1** to talk volubly and incoherently. **2** to chatter. **3** to utter nonsensical or unintelligible sounds. ~*v.t.* to utter rapidly and indistinctly. ~*n.* **1** rapid, indistinct or nonsensical talk. **2** gabble. **jabberer** *n.* [prob. onomat., cp. GABBLE]

jabberwocky (jab´əwoki) *n.* (*pl.* **jabberwockies**) nonsense, gibberish; an instance of this. [the *Jabberwock*, a fabulous monster created by Lewis Carroll in a poem in *Through the Looking Glass*]

jabble (jab´əl) *n.* **1** a splashing. **2** an agitation. [prob. onomat. (cp. DABBLE)]

jabiru (jab´iroo) *n.* a bird of the genus *Ephippiorhynchus*, esp. *E. mycteria*, S American storklike wading birds. [Tupi-Guarani]

jaborandi (jabəran´di) *n.* (*pl.* **jaborandis**) **1** any shrub of the genus *Pilocarpus*. **2** the dried leaflets of certain species of *Pilocarpus*, tropical American shrubs, used as sudorific and diuretic drugs. [Tupi-Guarani]

jabot (zhab´ō) *n.* **1** a lace frill worn at the neck of a woman's bodice. **2** a ruffle on a shirt front. [F, etym. unknown]

jacamar (jak´əmah) *n.* any bird of the tropical American family Galbulidae, resembling the kingfisher. [F, from Tupi-Guarani]

jacana (jak´ənə), **jaçana** (jasənah´) *n.* any bird of the family Jacanidae, from the warmer parts of N and S America. [Port. *jaçaná*, Tupi-Guarani *jasaná*]

jacaranda (jakəran´də) *n.* a tropical American tree, esp. of the genus *Jacaranda*, yielding fragrant and ornamental wood. [Tupi-Guarani]

jacinth (jas´inth, jā´-) *n.* a variety of zircon. [OF *jacinthe*, HYACINTH]

jack[1] (jak) *n.* **1** a contrivance for lifting heavy weights. **2** a device for lifting the axle of a vehicle off the ground so that a wheel etc. can be changed. **3** the knave of cards. **4** a small flag. **5** a socket for a jack plug, a jack socket. **6** in bowls, a small white ball at which bowlers aim. **7** a stone or small piece of metal etc. used in tossing games, a jackstone. **8** (*pl.*) a game played esp. by children, in which small pieces of metal etc. are tossed and caught, jackstones. **9** the figure of a man striking a bell on a clock. **10** (*sl.*) a detective or police officer. **11** (*N Am., coll.*) a lumberjack. **12** a steeplejack. **13** a sailor. **14** a labourer, an odd-job man. **15** (**Jack**) a fellow, one of the common people. **16** any of various perch-like fish of the family Carangidae. **17** a pike, esp. a young or small one. **18** a species or variety of animal smaller than other kinds. **19** the male of some animals. **20** a lever or other part in various machines. **21** a contrivance for turning a spit. **22** a device for plucking a string or moving a hammer in some instruments. **23** a wooden frame on which wood or timber is sawn. **24** (*Mining*) a gad, a wooden wedge. **25** (*N Am., sl.*) money. ~*v.t.* **1** to lift, hoist, or move with a jack. **2** (*sl.*) to resign, to give (up). **3** (*coll.*) to raise (prices etc.). **before one can say Jack Robinson** quite suddenly and unexpectedly or quickly. **every man jack** every individual. **on one's jack** (*sl.*) on one's own. **on one's Jack Jones** (*sl.*) on one's own. **to jack in** (*sl.*) to abandon. **to jack off** (*sl.*) to masturbate. **to jack up** to abandon. **jack-a-dandy** *n.* (*pl.* **jack-a-dandies**) a little foppish fellow. **jack bean** *n.* a climbing plant of the genus *Canavalia*. **jack-block** *n.* (*Naut.*) a block for raising and lowering the top gallant mast. **jackboot** *n.* **1** a large overall boot reaching to the thigh, worn by fishermen. **2** a large boot with a front piece coming above the knee. **3** (*fig.*) unintelligent and inhuman behaviour in dictatorial rule (from the high boots worn by German soldiers). **jackbooted** *a.* **Jack-by-the-hedge** *n.* a cruciferous plant, *Alliaria petiolata*, with white flowers. **jack-chain** *n.* in forestry, an endless spiked chain which carries logs from one point to another. **jackfish** *n.* (*pl. in general* **jackfish,** *in particular* **jackfishes**) **1** a pike or pikeperch. **2** any perch-like fish of the family Carangidae; also called *jack*. **jack-flag** *n.* a flag hoisted at the spritsail top-mast head. **Jack Frost** *n.* frost personified. **jackhammer** *n.* a hand-held compressed-air hammer used for drilling rock. **jack-high** *a., adv.* in bowls, the distance up the green to the jack. **jack-in-office** *n.* a person who assumes authority on account of holding a petty office. **jack-in-the-box** *n.* **1** a grotesque figure that springs out of a box when the lid is raised. **2** a kind of firework. **3** a large wooden male screw turning in a nut. **Jack-in-the-green** *n.* a dancer enclosed in a framework covered with leaves, in old-fashioned May Day festivities. **Jack-in-the-pulpit** *n.* any of several small woodland plants of the arum family, esp. cuckoo pint. **Jack Ketch** *n.* the public hangman. **jackknife** *n.* (*pl.* **jackknives**) **1** a large clasp-knife, esp. orig. one with a horn handle, carried by seamen. **2** a dive in which the diver doubles up and then straightens out again. ~*v.i.* (*pres.p.* **jackknifing,** *past, p.p.* **jackknifed**) **1** to double up like a jackknife. **2** (of an articulated vehicle) to turn or rise and form an angle of 90° or less when out of control. **3** to perform a jackknife dive. ~*v.t.* to double up like a jackknife. **jack of all trades** *n.* a person who can turn their hand to any business, activity etc. **jack-o'-lantern** *n.* **1** a will-o'-the wisp. **2** a lantern made from a hollowed-out pumpkin etc. **jack plane** *n.* the first and coarsest of the joiner's bench planes. **jack plug** *n.* a one-pronged plug used esp. in sound equipment. **jackpot** *n.* **1** the money pool in card games and competitions. **2** a fund of prize money. **to hit the jackpot 1** (*coll.*) to win a large prize. **2** (*coll.*) to have a big success. **jackrabbit** *n.* any of the various large prairie hares of N America, of the genus *Lepus*. **Jack Russell (terrier)** *n.* **1** a breed of small terrier introduced by John Russell in the 19th cent. **2** a dog of this breed. **jack screw** *n.* a lifting implement worked by a screw. **jack snipe** *n.* any of several waders, esp. *Lymnocryptes minimus*, a short-billed snipe. **jack socket** *n.* a socket for a jack plug; also called *jack*. **jackstaff** *n.* (*Naut.*) a flagstaff on the bowsprit cap for flying the jack. **jackstay** *n.* (*Naut.*) a rib or plate with holes, or a rod running through eye-bolts, passing along the upper side of a yard, to which the sail is bent. **jackstone** *n.* **1** a small piece of metal etc. used in tossing games; also called *jack*. **2** (*pl.*) the children's game of jacks. **jackstraw** *n.* **1** a person of no weight or substance. **2** a straw or twig used in jackstraws or spillikins, a children's game. **Jack tar** *n.* a sailor. **Jack the Lad** *n.* (*coll.*) an adventurous, stylish young man. **jack towel** *n.* a long round towel on a roller. **Jacky, Jackie** *n.* (*pl.* **Jackies**) (*Austral., coll.*) an Aboriginal man. [prob. dim. of *John* but perh. conn. with F *Jacques*, James, L *Jacōbus*, Gr. *Jakōbos*, Jacob]

jack[2] (jak) *n.* **1** (*Hist.*) a jacket, usu. of leather, formerly worn by foot soldiers. **2** a coat of mail. **3** a vessel for liquor, usu. of leather; a blackjack. [OF *jaque*, perh. ident. with *jaques*]

jack[3] (jak) *n.* **1** (*also* **jacktree**) a tropical Asian tree of the genus *Artocarpus*. **2** (*also* **jackfruit**) the fruit of this tree, like a coarser breadfruit. [Port. *jaca*, Malayalam *chukka*]

jackal (jak´əl, -awl) *n.* **1** a gregarious animal, *Canis aureus*, closely allied to the dog. **2** (*coll.*) a person who does dirty work or drudgery for another (from the belief that the jackal hunts up prey for the lion). [Turk. *chakāl*, Pers. *shaghāl*]

†**jackanapes** (jak´ənāps) *n.* **1** a pert fellow. **2** a coxcomb. **3** a mischievous child. **4** an ape. [*Jack Napes*, nickname of William de la Pole, Duke of Suffolk d. 1450, whose badge was a clog and chain such as was commonly used for a tame ape]

jackaroo (jakəroo´), **jackeroo** *n.* (*pl.* **jackaroos, jackeroos**) (*Austral., coll.*) a newcomer, a novice. [*Jack*, kangaroo]

jackass (jak´as) *n.* **1** a male ass. **2** a stupid ignorant person. **laughing jackass** LAUGHING (under LAUGH). **jackass fish** *n.* any of various edible fish of the family Cheilodactylidae, of Australia and New Zealand. **jackass rabbit** *n.* a male rabbit.

jackdaw (jak´daw) *n.* the smallest of the British crows, *Corvus monedula*.

jackeroo JACKAROO.

jacket (jak´it) *n.* **1** a short coat or sleeved outer garment for men or women. **2** something that resembles this, worn for protection or support. **3** the coat of an animal. **4** a wrapper, a cover. **5** an outer covering of paper put on a book bound in cloth or leather. **6** the skin of a potato. **7** an exterior covering or casing esp. a covering round a boiler, steam pipe, cylinder of an internal-combustion engine etc., to prevent radiation of heat. ~*v.t.* (*pres.p.* **jacketing,** *past, p.p.* **jacketed**) **1** to envelop in a jacket. **2** (*coll.*) to thrash. **jacketed** *a.* wearing a jacket. **jacketing** *n.* (*coll.*) a thrashing. **jacket potato** *n.* a baked potato in its skin. [OF *jaquette*, dim. of *jaque*, JACK[2]]

jacko JOCKO.

Jacobean (jakəbē´ən) *a.* **1** belonging to the reign of James I. **2** (of furniture) in the style of this time, esp. of dark oak. **3** of or relating to the Apostle St James the Less. ~*n.* a person of the time of James I. [late L *Jacōbaeus*, from *Jacōbus*, Jacob, whence also *James*]

Jacobin (jak´əbin) *n.* **1** (*Hist.*) a member of a revolutionary republican club, that met in the hall of the Jacobin friars, in the Rue St Jacques, Paris, 1789–94. **2** an extreme revolutionist, a violent republican. **3** (**jacobin**) a variety of hooded pigeon. **4** †a Dominican friar. **Jacobinic** (-bin´-), **Jacobinical** *a.* **Jacobinism** *n.* **Jacobinize, Jacobinise** *v.t.* [F, from low L *Jacōbinus*, from *Jacōbus*, Jacob]

Jacobite (jak´əbīt) *n.* (*Hist.*) a partisan of James II after his abdication, or of the Stuart pretenders to the throne. ~*a.* of, relating to or holding the opinions of the Jacobites. **Jacobitic** (-bit´-), **Jacobitical** *a.* **Jacobitism** *n.* [L *Jacōbus*, James, -ITE[1]]

Jacob's ladder (jā´kəbz) *n.* **1** a garden plant, *Polemonium caeruleum*, with closely pinnate leaves. **2** a rope ladder with wooden rungs. [with alln. to the patriarch Jacob's dream (Gen. xxviii.12)]

Jacob's staff (jā´kəbz) *n.* **1** a surveyor's rod. **2** (*Hist.*) a cross-staff, an instrument for measuring distances and heights. [with alln. to St James the Less, whose emblem was a pilgrim's staff and a scallop]

jacobus (jəkō´bəs) *n.* (*pl.* **jacobuses**) a gold coin struck in the reign of James I. [L, see JACOBITE]

jaconet (jak´ənit) *n.* a fine, close, white cotton cloth, rather heavier than cambric. [corr. from Hind. *Jagganāthī*, whence JUGGERNAUT]

jacquard (jak´ahd, -əd) *n.* **1** an apparatus with perforated cards used to weave intricate designs. **2** fabric so woven. **jacquard loom** *n.* a loom for weaving figured fabrics. [French inventor J.M. *Jacquard*, 1752–1834]

Jacquerie (zhakərē´) *n.* **1** a revolt of the peasants against the nobles in France, in 1357–8. **2** any peasant revolt. [F, from *Jacques*, a peasant]

jactation (jaktā´shən) *n.* **1** the act of throwing. **2** agitation of the body in exercise, as in riding. **3** jactitation. **4** boasting, bragging. **jactitation** (-ti-) *n.* **1** restlessness, a tossing or twitching of the body or limbs. **2** (*Law*) a false pretension to marriage. [L *jactātio*, from *jactāre*, freq. of *jacere*, to throw]

Jacuzzi® (jəkoo´zi) *n.* (*pl.* **Jacuzzis**) **1** a type of bath or small pool with a mechanism which makes the water swirl round. **2** this mechanism itself. **3** a bathe in such a bath.

jade[1] (jād) *n.* **1** a broken-down, worthless horse. **2** (*derog.*) an old woman; a wench, a young woman. ~*v.t.* **1** to overdrive. **2** (*usu. in p.p.*) to tire out. ~*v.i.* to become weary. **jaded** *a.* **jadedly** *adv.* **jadedness** *n.* **jadish** *a.* [etym. uncertain]

jade[2] (jād) *n.* **1** a green, massive, sometimes cryptocrystalline, silicate of lime and magnesia, used for ornamental purposes. **2** any of various other minerals of a similar appearance. **3** the green colour of jade. **jadeite** *n.* a sodium aluminium silicate form of jade. [F, from Sp. *piedra di ijada* (stone of the side), L ILIUM (because supposed to cure colic)]

j'adoube (zhadoob´) *int.* in chess, used as a notification that a piece is being adjusted rather than moved. [F]

Jaeger® (yā´gə) *n.* a woollen material used in clothes-making, orig. one containing no vegetable fibre. [Dr Gustav *Jaeger*, the manufacturer]

jaeger (yā´gə) *n.* **1** (*N Am.*) a seabird of the skua family esp. of the genus *Stercoraria*. **2** (*also* **jäger**) a German huntsman. **3** (*also* **jäger**) a German or Austrian sharpshooter. **4** (*also* **jäger**) an attendant waiting on an important person. [G from *jagen*, to hunt]

Jaffa (jaf´ə), **Jaffa orange** *n.* a type of orange from Jaffa in Israel.

jag[1] (jag) *n.* **1** a notch. **2** a ragged piece, tooth or point. **3** a stab, a prick. **4** (*esp. Sc.*) a vaccination or injection. ~*v.t.* (*pres. p.* **jagging,** *past, p.p.* **jagged**) **1** to cut or tear raggedly. **2** to cut into notches, to form denticulations in. **jagged** (jag´id) *a.* **1** having notches. **2** ragged, sharply uneven. **3** (*Bot.*) cut coarsely. **jaggedly** *adv.* **jaggedness** *n.* **jagger** *n.* **1** a person who or thing which jags. **2** a toothed chisel. **jaggy** *a.* (*comp.* **jaggier,** *superl.* **jaggiest**) **1** jagged. **2** (*Sc.*) (*also* **jaggie**) prickly. [prob. imit.]

jag[2] (jag) *n.* **1** (*sl.*) a bout of drinking or drug-taking. **2** (*coll.*) a bout of indulgence. **3** a bundle or load of hay etc. [etym. unknown]

jäger JAEGER.

jagger JAG[1].

jaggery (jag´əri) *n.* a coarse dark-brown kind of sugar made in India from the juice of certain palms. [Port. *jágara*, Canarese *sharkare*, Hind. *shakkar*, Sansk. *çarkarā*, SUGAR]

jaggy JAG[1].

jaguar (jag´ūə) *n.* a S American feline animal, *Panthera onca*, resembling the leopard. [Tupi-Guarani *yagouara*]
jaguarundi (jagwərŭn´di) *n.* (*pl.* **jaguarundis**) a wild cat, *Felis yaguarondi*, of Central and S America.
Jahveh YAHWEH.
jai alai (hīəlī´) *n.* a game played by two or four players on a court, who wear woven baskets tied to their wrists and using these hurl a ball at the walls. [Sp., from Basque *jai*, festival, *alai*, merry]
jail (jāl), **gaol** *n.* **1** a prison, a public place of confinement for persons charged with or convicted of crime. **2** confinement in a jail. ~*v.t.* to put in jail. **jailbait** *n.* (*sl.*) a girl who is below the legal age of consent. **jailbird** *n.* **1** a person who has been to prison. **2** an inveterate criminal. **jailbreak** *n.* an escape from jail. **jailer** *n.* the keeper of a prison. **jail-fever** *n.* typhus, formerly endemic in jails. **jailhouse** *n.* (*esp. N Am.*) a prison. [A-F *gaole*, OF *jaiole* (F *geôle*), late L *gabiola*, dim. of *gabia*, L *cavea*, CAGE]
Jain (jīn, jān), **Jaina** (-nə) *n.* an adherent of a non-Brahminical Indian religion. ~*a.* of or belonging to the Jains or Jainism. **Jainism** *n.* **Jainist** *n.* [Hind., from Sansk. *jaina*, pertaining to a Buddha or Saint, *jina*]
jake (jāk) *a.* (*coll.*) **1** honest. **2** correct. **3** (*Austral.*, *New Zeal.*) all right, very good. [etym. uncertain]
jalap (jal´əp, jol´əp) *n.* the dried tubercles of *Exogonium purga*, used as a purgative. **jalapin** *n.* an amorphous glucoside existing in jalap root. [F, from Sp. *jalapa*, *Xalapa*, Aztec *Xalapan*, city in Mexico]
jalapeño (haləpān´yō, -pē´nō) *n.* (*pl.* **jalapeños**) (*also* **jalapeño pepper**) a very hot green chilli pepper. [Mex. Sp.]
jalopy (jəlop´i) *n.* (*pl.* **jalopies**) (*coll.*) a much-worn motor vehicle. [etym. unknown]
jalouse (jəlooz´) *v.t.* (*Sc.*) **1** to suspect. **2** to surmise. [F *jalouser*, from *jaloux*, JEALOUS]
jalousie (zhal´uzi) *n.* a louvre blind, a Venetian shutter. **jalousied** *a.* [F, JEALOUSY (under JEALOUS)]
Jam. *abbr.* **1** Jamaica. **2** James.
jam[1] (jam) *v.t.* (*pres.p.* **jamming,** *past*, *p.p.* **jammed**) **1** to wedge or squeeze (in or into). **2** to squeeze, to compress between two surfaces. **3** to squeeze together. **4** to block up by crowding into. **5** to make (a machine etc.) immovable or unworkable by forcible handling. **6** to prevent clear radio reception of (a signal) by transmitting an interfering signal on the same wavelength. ~*v.i.* **1** to become wedged. **2** (of a machine etc.) to become immovable or unworkable by rough handling. **3** to push or crowd. **4** (*coll.*) (of a musician) to improvise freely. **5** (*coll.*) to take part in a jam session. ~*n.* **1** a crush, a squeeze. **2** a stoppage in a machine due to jamming. **3** a crowd, a press. **4** congestion (*a traffic jam*). **5** (*coll.*) a jam session. **money for jam** MONEY. **to be in a jam** to be in a predicament. **jammer** *n.* **jam-packed** *a.* **1** very crowded. **2** filled to capacity. **jam session** *n.* (*coll.*) an improvised session of playing by jazz, rock etc. musicians. [prob. imit., cp. CHAMP[1]]
jam[2] (jam) *n.* **1** a conserve of fruit made by boiling with sugar. **2** (*coll.*) something easy or desirable. ~*v.t.* (*pres.p.* **jamming,** *past*, *p.p.* **jammed**) **1** to spread jam on. **2** to make into jam. **jam tomorrow** better things promised but usu. never forthcoming. **jam jar** *n.* **jammy** *a.* (*comp.* **jammier,** *superl.* **jammiest**) (*coll.*) **1** sticky (with jam). **2** lucky. **3** desirable. **jam pot** *n.* [prob. use of JAM[1]]
Jamaica pepper (jəmā´kə) *n.* **1** allspice. **2** pimento. [*Jamaica*, W Indian island]
jamb (jam) *n.* **1** any one of the upright sides of a doorway, window, or fireplace. **2** (*Her.*) a leg. [F *jambe*, leg, late L *gamba*, a hoof, prob. from Celt. (cp. Welsh *cam*, crooked)]
jambalaya (jambəlī´ə) *n.* a Southern US dish consisting of meat, seafood, rice, onions etc. [F Prov. *jambalaia*]
jambok SJAMBOK.
jamboree (jambərē´) *n.* **1** a Scout rally. **2** a frolic.
jampan (jam´pan) *n.* a sedan chair borne on two bamboo poles by four people. **jampanee** (-nē´) *n.* each of the bearers of a jampan. [Bengali *jhāmpān*, Hind. *jhappān*]
Jan. *abbr.* January.
jane (jān) *n.* (*N Am.*, *Austral.*, *sl.*) a woman. **plain Jane** PLAIN[1]. [*Jane*, female name]
jangle (jăng´gəl) *v.i.* **1** to sound harshly or discordantly. **2** to wrangle, to bicker. **3** †to chatter. ~*v.t.* **1** to cause to sound discordantly. **2** to irritate, upset. **3** to utter harshly. ~*n.* **1** wrangling, bickering. **2** discordant sound, as of bells out of tune. **3** noisy chatter. **jangler** *n.* a wrangler. [OF *jangler*, prob. onomat.]
Janglish (jang´glish) *n.* JAPLISH. [*J*apanese, E*nglish*]
janissary JANIZARY.
janitor (jan´itə) *n.* **1** a doorkeeper. **2** a caretaker, porter. **3** (*N Am.*, *Sc.*) the caretaker of a school. **janitorial** (-taw´ri-) *a.* **janitorship** *n.* **janitress** (-tris), **janitrix** (-triks) *n.* a female janitor. [L from *jānua*, door]
janizary (jan´izəri), **janissary** (-səri) *n.* (*pl.* **janizaries, janissaries**) **1** (*Hist.*) a soldier of the old Turkish infantry forming the Sultan's bodyguard (orig. young prisoners trained to arms), disbanded in 1826. **2** a follower, supporter. †**janizarian** (-zeə´ri-) *a.* [Turk. *yeni-tsheri* (*yeni*, new, *tsheri*, soldiery)]
jankers (jang´kəz) *n.* (*Mil.*, *sl.*) **1** punishment, detention. **2** (*pl.*) defaulters. [etym. unknown]
jannock[1] (jan´ək) *n.* (*North.*) oaten bread, an oaten loaf. [etym. unknown]
jannock[2] (jan´ək) *a.*, *adv.* fair, straightforward. [etym. unknown]
January (jan´ūəri) *n.* (*pl.* **Januaries**) the first month of the year. [L *jānuārius*, from Janus]
Janus-faced (jā´nəsfāst) *a.* two-faced, deceitful, hypocritical. [L *Janus*, an ancient Italian deity presiding over doors and gates, and usually represented with two heads looking in opposite directions]
Jap (jap) *a.*, *n.* (*derog. or offensive*) JAPANESE. **Jap silk** *n.* a pure silk fabric plainly woven from net silk yarns.
Jap. *abbr.* Japanese.
japan (jəpan´) *n.* **1** an intensely hard varnish, or varnishing liquid, made from linseed oil, resin, shellac etc. **2** a hard, black varnish obtained from *Stagmaria verniciflua*. **3** work varnished and figured in the Japanese style. ~*v.t.* (*pres. p.* **japanning,** *past*, *p.p.* **japanned**) to cover with or as with japan. **Japan earth** *n.* catechu. **japanner** *n.* a person whose business is to japan goods. [Japan in E Asia]
Japanese (japənēz´) *a.* of or relating to Japan or its inhabitants. ~*n.* (*pl.* **Japanese**) **1** a native or inhabitant of Japan. **2** (*as pl.*) the people of Japan. **3** the language of Japan. **Japanese beetle** *n.* a chafer, *Popillia japonica*. **Japanese cedar** *n.* a tall Japanese conifer, *Cryptomeria japonica*. **Japanese print** *n.* a colour print from woodblocks. **Japanese quince** *n.* japonica. **Japanize, Japanise** *v.t.* **Japanization** (-zā´shən) *n.* [as JAPAN]
jape (jāp) *v.i.* to jest, to play tricks. ~*n.* a jest, a trick, a joke. **japer** *n.* **japery** *n.* [OF *japer*, to yelp]
Japlish (jap´lish) *n.* a blend of Japanese and English. [*J*apanese, Eng*lish*]
japonica (jəpon´ikə) *n.* any flowering shrub of the genus *Chaenomeles*, esp. *C. speciosa*, the Japanese quince. [mod. L, fem. of *japonicus*, Japanese]
jar[1] (jah) *v.i.* (*pres.p.* **jarring,** *past*, *p.p.* **jarred**) **1** to emit a harsh or discordant sound. **2** to vibrate harshly. **3** to be discordant, disagreeable, or offensive. **4** to disagree, to clash, to be inconsistent (with). ~*v.t.* **1** to cause to shake or tremble. **2** to give a shock to. **3** †to offend, to displease. ~*n.* **1** a harsh vibration as from a shock. **2** a harsh discordant sound. **3** a shock. **4** a disagreement, a conflict of opinions or interests. **jarringly** *adv.* [prob. imit.]
jar[2] (jah) *n.* **1** a vessel of glass or earthenware of various

shapes and sizes, used for various domestic purposes. 2 the contents of this. 3 (*coll.*) (a glass of) alcoholic drink. **jarful** *n.* (*pl.* **jarfuls**). [F *jarre*, prob. through Sp. *jarra*, from Arab. *jarrah*]

jar[3] (jah) *n.* a state of partial closure (only as below). **on the jar** partly closed, ajar.

jardinière (zhahdinyeə´) *n.* 1 an ornamental pot or stand for growing flowers in a room etc. 2 a dish of mixed cooked vegetables. [F, fem. of *jardinier*, gardener]

jargon[1] (jah´gən) *n.* 1 any professional, technical or specialized language. 2 debased or illiterate speech or language. 3 unintelligible talk, gibberish, gabble. ~*v.i.* 1 to talk unintelligibly. 2 (of birds) to twitter. **jargoner** *n.* **jargonesque** (-nesk´), **jargonic** (-gon´-), **jargonistic** (-nis´tik) *a.* **jargonist** *n.* **jargonize, jargonise** *v.i.* **jargonization** (-zā´shən) *n.* [OF *jargon*, *gargon*, etym. uncertain]

jargon[2] (jah´gən), **jargoon** (-goon´) *n.* a transparent, colourless or smoky variety of zircon found in Sri Lanka. [F, from It. *giargone*]

jargonelle (jahgənel´) *n.* a kind of early pear. [F]

jargoon JARGON[2].

jarl (yahl) *n.* (*Hist.*) a Norse or Dutch nobleman or chieftain, an earl or count. [Icel., EARL]

jarrah (jar´ə) *n.* 1 the W Australian mahogany gum tree, *Eucalyptus marginata*. 2 the timber of this. [Austral. Abor. *jerryh*]

jarringly JAR[1].

Jas. *abbr.* James.

jasmine (jaz´min), **jasmin, jessamin** (jes´əmin), **jessamine** *n.* any plant of the genus *Jasminum*, many of which are climbers with sweet-scented white or yellow flowers, esp. the common white *J. officinale*. **jasmine tea** *n.* tea perfumed with jasmine blossom. [F *jasmin*, *jassemin*, *jessemin*, Arab. *yāsmīn*]

jaspé (jas´pā) *a.* 1 (of ceramics) having an appearance like jasper. 2 (of cotton fabric) of mottled appearance. [F *jasper*, to marble]

jasper (jas´pə) *n.* 1 an impure variety of quartz, of many colours and shades, opaque even in thin splinters. 2 a greenish marble, with small red spots. 3 (*N Am., sl.*) a fellow, a man. **jasperite** (-rīt) *n.* a red variety of jasper found near Lake Superior. **jasperize, jasperise** *v.t.* **jasperous** *a.* **jaspoid** (-poid) *a.* resembling jasper. [OF *jaspre*, *jaspe*, L and Gr. *iaspis*, Oriental in origin (cp. Arab. *yasb*, Pers. *yashp*, Heb. *yāshpeh*)]

Jat (jaht) *n.* a member of an Indo-Aryan people of NW India. ~*a.* of or relating to this people. [Hind.]

jato (jā´tō) *n.* (*pl.* **jatos**) 1 jet assisted take-off. 2 a power unit which provides extra thrust at take-off. [acronym]

jaundice (jawn´dis) *n.* 1 a condition due to obstruction of the bile or absorption of the colouring matter into the blood, characterized by yellowness of the skin, diarrhoea and general debility. 2 a mental attitude or condition, such as that caused by jealousy, prejudice etc., which warps the vision. ~*v.t.* 1 to affect with or as with jaundice. 2 to poison the mind with jealousy, prejudice etc. **jaundiced** *a.* [ME *jaunys*, F *jaunisse*, from *jaune*, L *galbinus*, from *galbus*, yellow]

jaunt (jawnt) *n.* a ramble, an excursion, a short journey, a trip. ~*v.i.* 1 to ramble or rove about. 2 to take a short excursion. **jaunting car** *n.* (*Hist.*) an Irish horse-drawn vehicle having two seats, back to back, over the wheels, and a seat for the driver in front. [perh. connected with *jaunce*]

jaunty (jawn´ti) *a.* (*comp.* **jauntier**, *superl.* **jauntiest**) sprightly, airy, self-satisfied, perky. **jauntily** *adv.* **jauntiness** *n.* [earlier *janty*, F *gentil*, see GENTEEL]

Jav. *abbr.* Javanese.

Javanese (jahvənēz´) *a.* of or relating to Java. ~*n.* (*pl.* **Javanese**) 1 a native or inhabitant of Java. 2 (*as pl.*) the people of Java. 3 the language of Java. **Java man** *n.* a fossil human of the species *Homo erectus*. **Javan** *n., a.* **Java sparrow** *n.* a waxbill, *Padda oryzivora*, often kept in aviaries.

javelin (jav´əlin) *n.* 1 a light spear thrown by the hand, used as a weapon or in field events. 2 the competitive sport of javelin-throwing. ~*v.t.* to wound or pierce with or as with a javelin. **javelin-man** *n.* (*pl.* **javelin-men**) (*Hist.*) an armed member of a sheriff's retinue or the escort of a judge at assizes. [F *javeline*, It. *giavelina*, prob. from Celt. (cp. Ir. *gabhla*, spear, Gael. *gobhal*, a fork)]

Javelle water (zhəvel´), **Javel water** *n.* a solution of sodium hypochlorite used in disinfecting and bleaching. [*Javel*, a former French village]

jaw (jaw) *n.* 1 either of two bones or bony structures in which the teeth are fixed, forming the framework of the mouth. 2 (*pl.*) the mouth. 3 (*pl.*) the narrow opening of a gorge, narrow valley etc. 4 either of two opposing members of a vice or similar implement or machine. 5 (*pl., Naut.*) the concave or forked end of a boom or gaff. 6 (*pl.*) a narrow opening or entrance. 7 (*coll.*) abuse, wrangling, long-winded talk. 8 a lecture. ~*v.i.* (*coll.*) to talk lengthily. ~*v.t.* 1 to abuse. 2 to lecture. 3 to persuade by talking. **hold your jaw** (*sl.*) shut up. **jawbone** *n.* either of the pair of bones forming the lower jaw. **jaw-breaker** *n.* (*coll.*) an unpronounceable word. **jawed** *a.* having jaws (*usu. in comb.*, as *heavy-jawed*). **jaw-jaw** *n.* talking, esp. pointless discussion. ~*v.i.* to talk, esp. pointlessly or at length. **jawless** *a.* **jaw-lever** *n.* an instrument for opening the mouths of cattle for the administration of medicine. **jawline** *n.* the outline of the jaw. **jaw-tooth** *n.* (*pl.* **jaw-teeth**) a molar. [etym. uncertain, perh. rel. to CHEW]

jay[1] (jā) *n.* 1 a chattering bird, *Garrulus glandarius*, with brilliant plumage. 2 any other bird of the subfamily Garrulinae. 3 an impudent chatterer. 4 a loud, coarse woman. **jaywalker** *n.* (*coll.*) a pedestrian who crosses the street heedless of the traffic. **jaywalk** *v.i.* [OF *jay* (F *geai*), etym. uncertain]

jay[2] (jā) *n.* the letter J.

jazerant (jaz´ərənt), **jesserant** (jes´-) *n.* (*Hist.*) a light coat of armour composed of small plates of metal, usu. fastened to a flexible lining. [OF *jaserant*, prob. from Sp. *jazarino*, Algerian, from Arab. *al-jazīrah*, Algiers]

jazz (jaz) *n.* 1 syncopated music of African-American origin. 2 the form of dancing that goes to this music. 3 vividness. 4 garishness. 5 liveliness. 6 (*sl.*) rigmarole. 7 (*coll.*) insincere talk. ~*v.i.* to play or dance to jazz. **to jazz up** 1 to quicken the tempo of (a piece of music). 2 to make more attractive, livelier, colourful etc. **jazzer** *n.* **jazzman** *n.* (*pl.* **jazzmen**) a jazz musician. **jazz rock** *n.* music which is a mixture of jazz and rock. **jazzy** *a.* (*comp.* **jazzier**, *superl.* **jazziest**) 1 of or like jazz. 2 vivid or flashy. **jazzily** *adv.* **jazziness** *n.* [Creole *jazz*, to speed up, prob. of Afr. origin]

JB *abbr.* Jerusalem Bible.

JC *abbr.* 1 Jesus Christ. 2 Julius Caesar. 3 Justice Clerk.

JCB® (jāsēbē) *n.* a type of construction machine with a hydraulically operated shovel at the front and an excavator at the back. [*J*oseph *C*yril *B*amford, b. 1916, British manufacturer]

JCL *abbr.* (*Comput.*) job-control language.

J cloth® (jā´kloth), **J-cloth** *n.* a type of cloth used esp. for cleaning, wiping work surfaces etc.

JCR *abbr.* 1 junior combination room. 2 junior common room.

JCS *abbr.* Joint Chiefs of Staff.

jct., jctn *abbr.* junction.

jealous (jel´əs) *a.* 1 suspicious or apprehensive of being supplanted in the love or favour (of a wife, husband, lover or friend). 2 suspicious or apprehensive (of a rival). 3 solicitous or anxiously watchful (of one's honour, rights etc.). 4 envious (of another or another's advantages etc.). **5** (*Bible*) requiring exclusive devotion (of God). **jealously** *adv.* **jealousness** *n.* **jealousy** *n.* (*pl.* **jealousies**). [ME and OF *gelos*, late L *zēlōsus*, from *zēlus*, ZEAL]

Jeames (jēmz) *n.* a footman, a flunkey. [Thackeray's *Jeames* (James) de la Pluche]

jean (jēn) *n.* a twilled undressed cloth with cotton warp. [ME *Gene*, It. *Genova*, Genoa]

jeans (jēnz) *n.pl.* **1** close-fitting casual trousers usu. made of denim or other cotton fabric. **2** a garment or garments made of jean. [pl. of JEAN]

Jeep® (jēp) *n.* **1** (*US*) a fast, light car for military use. **2** a utility motor van. [*G.P.*, initials of General Purposes]

jeepers (jē´pəz), **jeepers creepers** (krē´pəz) *int.* (*N Am.*, *sl.*) used to express surprise etc. [abbr. of JESUS]

jeer (jiə) *v.i.* to scoff, to mock (at). ~*v.t.* to scoff at, to make a mock of, to deride. ~*n.* a scoff, a gibe, a taunt, mockery. **jeerer** *n.* **jeeringly** *adv.* [etym. doubtful]

Jeez (jēz) *int.* (*sl.*) used to express surprise etc. [abbr. of JESUS]

jeffersonite (jef´əsənīt) *n.* a greenish-black variety of pyroxene. [Thomas *Jefferson*, 1743–1826, US President]

jehad JIHAD.

Jehoshaphat (jihosh´əfat), **Jehosaphat** (-hos´-) *int.* used as a mild expletive, esp. in *jumping Jehoshaphat*. [Biblical name (2 Sam. viii.16)]

Jehovah (jihō´və) *n.* the most sacred name given in the Old Testament to God, esp. regarded as the God of the Jewish people. **Jehovah's Witness** *n.* a member of the millenarian sect, the International Bible Students' Association, founded by the American Pastor C. T. Russell, 1852–1916. **Jehovist** *n.* YAHWIST (under YAHWEH). **Jehovistic** (jēhəvis´-) *a.* [Heb. *Yahōvāh*]

Jehu (jē´hū) *n.* a coachman, a driver, esp. one who drives fast or furiously. [alln. to 2 Kings ix.20]

jejune (jijoon´) *a.* **1** bare, meagre, scanty. **2** wanting in substance. **3** devoid of interest or life. **4** poor, barren. **5** puerile, childish, naive. **jejunely** *adv.* **jejuneness** *n.* [L *jējūnus*, fasting]

Usage note Use in the sense 'puerile, childish' is sometimes disapproved of.

---

jejunum (jijoo´nəm) *n.* the second portion of the small intestine between the duodenum and the ileum. **jejuno-** (jijoo´nō) *comb. form* of or relating to the jejunum. [L *jējūnus*, fasting]

Jekyll and Hyde (jek´əl ənd hīd, jē´-) *n.* a person with a split personality, one side evil, the other good. [R. L. Stevenson's *The Strange Case of Dr Jekyll and Mr Hyde*, 1886]

jell (jel), **gell** *v.i.* (*coll.*) **1** to jelly. **2** (of ideas etc.) to come together. **3** (of people) to cooperate, to get on well. **jellify** *v.t.*, *v.i.* (*3rd pers. sing. pres.* **jellifies**, *pres.p.* **jellifying**, *past*, *p.p.* **jellified**) to make or become like jelly. **jellification** (-fikā´shən) *n.* [from JELLY]

jellaba DJELLABA.

jelly (jel´i) *n.* (*pl.* **jellies**) **1** any gelatinous substance, esp. that obtained by decoction from animal matter. **2** a conserve made of the inspissated juice of fruit boiled with sugar. **3** (*sl.*) gelignite. ~*v.i.* (*3rd pers. sing. pres.* **jellies**, *pres.p.* **jellying**, *past*, *p.p.* **jellied**) to turn into jelly. ~*v.t.* to convert into jelly. **Jell-O**® (jel´ō), **jello** *n.* (*pl.* **Jell-Os, jellos**) (*esp. N Am.*) a fruit-flavoured jelly-like dessert. **jelly baby** *n.* (*pl.* **jelly babies**) a sweet made of jelly and shaped like a baby. **jelly bag, jelly cloth** *n.* a bag or cloth used for straining jelly. **jelly bean** *n.* a sugar-coated, bean-shaped sweet filled with jelly. **jellyfish** *n.* (*pl. in general* **jellyfish,** *in particular* **jellyfishes**) **1** a marine coelenterate with a jelly-like body and stinging tentacles, of the class Scyphozoa. **2** (*coll.*) a feeble person. **jellygraph** (-grahf) *n.* an apparatus whose essential parts are a sheet of jelly and a special kind of ink, used for multiplying copies of writing. **jelly-like** *a.* **jelly roll** *n.* (*N Am.*) a Swiss roll. [F *gelée*, frost, L *gelāta*, fem. p.p. of *gelāre*, to freeze]

jemadar (jem´ədah) *n.* in the Indian subcontinent, an army officer. [Hind.]

jemima (jimī´mə) *n.* (*coll.*) **1** an elastic-sided boot. **2** a long galosh for a boot. [*Jemima*, female name]

jemmy[1] (jem´i) *n.* (*pl.* **jemmies**) **1** a short, stout crowbar, used by burglars. **2** (*sl.*) a baked sheep's head. **3** (*dial.*) a greatcoat. ~*v.t.* (*3rd pers. sing. pres.* **jemmies,** *pres.p.* **jemmying,** *past*, *p.p.* **jemmied**) to force open with a jemmy. [dim. of *James*]

jemmy[2] (jem´i) *a.* (*dial.*) spruce, neat. **jemminess** *n.*

je ne sais quoi (zhə nə sā kwa´) *n.* an indefinable something. [F, I do not know what]

jennet (jen´it) *n.* a small Spanish horse. [F *genet*, Sp. *ginete*, orig. light-armed horseman, perh. from Arab. *Zenāta*, Berber tribe famous for horsemanship]

jenneting (jen´iting) *n.* an early kind of apple. [prob. from F *jeanneton*, from *Jeannet*, *Jean* (cp. *pomme de St Jean*, St John's apple)]

jenny (jen´i) *n.* (*pl.* **jennies**) **1** a female ass, animal, bird etc. **2** (*Hist.*) a spinning jenny. **3** a travelling crane. **4** in billiards, a stroke pocketing the ball from an awkward position. **jenny-ass** *n.* a female ass. **jenny-wren** *n.* a wren. [familiar form of *Jane*, *Jennifer* or *Janet*]

jeopardy (jep´ədi) *n.* **1** exposure to danger, loss or injury. **2** risk, hazard, danger, peril. **3** (*Law*) danger faced by an accused person in a criminal case. **jeopardize, jeopardise** *v.t.* **1** to put in jeopardy. **2** to risk. [OF *jeu parti*, divided or even game (*jeu*, L *jocus*, game, *parti*, L *partītus*, p.p. of *partīrī*, to PART)]

jequirity (jikwir´iti) *n.* (*pl.* **jequirities**) a tropical twining shrub, *Abrus precatorius*, with particoloured seeds or beans which are used for ornaments and for medicinal purposes. **jequirity bean** *n.* [Tupi-Guarani, *jekiriti*]

Jer. *abbr.* Jeremiah.

jerboa (jœbō´ə) *n.* a small mouselike rodent of the family Dipodidae, with long hind legs adapted for leaping. [Arab. *yarbū'*, the flesh of the loins, from the powerful muscles of its hind leg]

jereed (jirēd´), **jerid** *n.* **1** a javelin, used in Iran and Turkey, esp. in games. **2** a game with this. [Arab. *jarīd*, orig. a stripped palm-branch]

jeremiad (jerəmī´əd) *n.* a lamentation, esp. over modern degeneracy, in the style of the prophet Jeremiah. [F *jérémiade*]

Jeremiah (jerəmī´ə) *n.* **1** a prophet of doom. **2** a pessimistic person. [the biblical prophet *Jeremiah*]

jerfalcon GYRFALCON.

jerid JEREED.

jerk[1] (jœk) *v.t.* **1** to pull, push, or thrust sharply. **2** to throw with a sharp, suddenly arrested action. **3** in weightlifting, to raise (a weight) from shoulder level to above the head. ~*v.i.* to move with jerks. ~*n.* **1** a sharp, sudden push or tug. **2** a twitch, a spasmodic movement due to involuntary contraction of a muscle. **3** (*sl.*) a stupid, ignorant or contemptible person. **4** (*pl.*) violent twitches or spasmodic movements of the face or members, often due to religious excitement. **5** (*pl., coll.*) exercises. **6** in weightlifting, the raising of a weight from shoulder level to above the head. **to jerk off** (*sl.*) to masturbate. **jerker** *n.* **jerky**[1] *a.* (*comp.* **jerkier,** *superl.* **jerkiest**). **jerkily** *adv.* **jerkiness** *n.* [prob. onomat.]

jerk[2] (jœk) *v.t.* to cure (beef) by cutting it into long pieces and drying it in the sun. **jerky**[2], **jerked beef** *n.* charqui. [corr. from Am. Sp. *cha quear*, from CHARQUI]

jerk[3] JERQUE.

jerkin (jœ´kin) *n.* **1** a short coat or jacket, formerly often made of leather. **2** a close waistcoat. [etym. unknown]

jerkinhead (jœ´kinhed) *n.* (*Archit.*) a combination of truncated gable and hipped roof. [etym. uncertain]

jerky[1] JERK[1].

jerky[2] JERK[2].

jeroboam (jerəbō´əm) *n.* **1** a wine bottle holding 10–12 quarts (about 12 l). **2** a drinking-bowl or beaker of great size. [in alln. to 1 Kings ix.28]

jerque (jœk), **jerk** *v.t.* to search (a vessel or her papers) for unentered goods. **jerquer** *n.* a custom house searcher. [etym. uncertain]

Jerry (jer´i) *n.* (*pl.* **Jerries**) (*sl., often derog.*) **1** a German soldier. **2** the Germans collectively. [perh. from GERMAN]

jerry (jer´i) *a.* cheaply and badly built, flimsy. ~*n.* (*pl.* **jerries**) (*sl.*) a chamber pot. **jerry-builder** *n.* a speculative builder of cheap and inferior houses. **jerry-building** *n.* **jerry-built** *a.* [prob. fam. form of *Jeremiah*]

jerrycan (jer´ikan), **jerrican** *n.* a can for petrol, water etc., orig. German.

jerrymander GERRYMANDER.

jersey (jœ´zi) *n.* (*pl.* **jerseys**) **1** a knitted garment, as a pullover, worn on the upper part of the body. **2** fine wool yarn, a plain-knitted (orig. woollen) fabric. **3** a close-fitting woollen knitted tunic worn in sports and athletics. **4** (**Jersey**) a Jersey cow. **Jersey cow** *n.* a breed of dairy cattle originating from Jersey. [the island of *Jersey*]

jerupigia GEROPIGA.

Jerusalem artichoke (jəroo´sələm) *n.* **1** a species of sunflower, *Helianthus tuberosus*, the tuberous roots of which are edible. **2** the tuber of it eaten as a vegetable. [perh. corr. of It. *girasole articiocco*]

jess (jes) *n.* in falconry, a short leather or silk ribbon for tying round each leg of a hawk, to which the leash may be attached. ~*v.t.* to put jesses on. **jessed** *a.* **1** (of a hawk) having jesses on. **2** (*Her.*) with jesses of a specified tincture. [OF *ges*, obj. *gel*, L *jactus -tum*, a cast, from *jacere*, to throw]

jessamin, jessamine JASMINE.

jessant (jes´ənt) *a.* (*Her.*) issuing or springing (from). [OF *iessant*, pres.p. of *issir*, to ISSUE]

Jesse (jes´i) *n.* a genealogical tree representing the genealogy of Christ, esp. in the form of a large brass candlestick with many branches. **Jesse window** *n.* a window of which the tracery and glazing represent a genealogical tree of Jesse. [the father of David (Is. xi.1)]

jesserant JAZERANT.

jest (jest) *n.* **1** a joke, something ludicrous said or done to provoke mirth. **2** a jeer, a taunt. **3** a laughing stock. **4** a prank, a frolic. ~*v.i.* **1** to joke. **2** to utter jests. **3** to provoke mirth by ludicrous actions or words. **4** to ridicule, to jeer (at). **in jest** **1** as a jest or joke. **2** not seriously or in earnest. **jestbook** *n.* a collection of jokes or jocular tales or sayings. **jester** *n.* a person who jests or jokes, a buffoon, esp. one formerly retained by persons of high rank to make sport. **jestingly** *adv.* [OF *jeste*, orig. an exploit, L *gesta*, neut. pl. p.p. of *gere*, to do]

Jesuit (jez´ūit) *n.* **1** a member of the Society of Jesus, a Roman Catholic order founded in 1534 by Ignatius Loyola. **2** (*offensive*) a crafty, insidious person, a subtle casuist or prevaricator. **Jesuitic** (-it´-), **Jesuitical** *a.* **1** of or relating to the Jesuits. **2** (*offensive*) crafty, cunning, designing. **Jesuitically** *adv.* **Jesuitism, Jesuitry** (-ri) *n.* **Jesuitize, Jesuitise** *v.t., v.i.* **Jesuits' bark** *n.* cinchona bark.

Jesus (jē´zəs) *n.* the Saviour of Christian belief. ~*int.* (*coll.*) used to express surprise, dismay etc. [L, from Gr. *Iēsous*, Heb. *yēshūa*, Joshua]

jet[1] (jet) *n.* **1** a black compact variety of lignite capable of being brilliantly polished, formerly much used for articles of personal ornament. **2** the colour of jet. ~*a.* of this colour. **jet black** *n.* a glossy black colour. ~*a.* [OF *jaiet*, L *gagātem*, nom. *-tēs*, Gr. *gagatēs*, from *Gagai*, in Lycia]

jet[2] (jet) *v.i.* (*pres.p.* **jetting**, *past, p.p.* **jetted**) **1** to spurt or shoot out, to come out in a jet or jets. **2** to travel by jet plane. ~*v.t.* **1** to send out in a jet or jets. **2** to send in a jet plane. ~*n.* **1** a sudden spurt or shooting out of water or flame, esp. from a small orifice. **2** a spout or nozzle for the discharge of water etc. **3** a channel for passing molten metal into a mould; also the piece of metal remaining in the aperture after the metal is cold, the spruce. **4** a jet-propelled plane. **5** a jet engine. **jet engine** *n.* an engine using jet propulsion, esp. one fitted to an aircraft. **jetfoil** *n.* a hydrofoil powered by a jet of water. **jet lag** *n.* the exhaustion caused by the body's inability to adjust to the time-zone changes involved in long-distance air travel. **jet-lagged** *a.* **jet plane** *n.* a jet-propelled plane. **jet-propelled** *a.* **1** (of an aircraft or vehicle) propelled by heating and expanding air which is directed in a jet from the rear of the plane. **2** very fast. **jet propulsion** *n.* **jet set** *n.* the group of fashionable people who can afford constant travel by jet plane. **jet-setter** *n.* **jet-setting** *n.* **jet ski** *n.* a small powered water vehicle with a flat keel shaped like a water-ski. **jet-ski** *v.i.* (*3rd pers. sing. pres.* **jet-skies,** *pres.p.* **jet-skiing,** *past, p.p.* **jet-skied**). **jet-skiing** *n.* **jet stream** *n.* **1** a belt of winds 12,000 m above the earth. **2** the exhaust from a jet engine. [OF *jetter* (F *jeter*), L *jactāre*, freq. of *jacere*, to throw]

jeté (zhet´ā, -tā´) *n.* a leap from one foot to another in ballet. [F, thrown]

jetsam (jet´səm) *n.* goods, cargo etc., thrown overboard in order to lighten a ship in distress, and subsequently washed ashore. **flotsam and jetsam** FLOTSAM. [var. of JETTISON]

jettison (jet´isən) *n.* the casting of goods overboard to lighten a vessel in distress. ~*v.t.* **1** to throw (goods) overboard in order to lighten a vessel. **2** to drop (anything unwanted) from an aircraft or spacecraft in flight. **3** to cast aside; to rid oneself of. [A-F *getteson*, OF *getaison*, L *jactātiōnem*, nom. *-tio*, from *jactāre*, freq. of *jacere*, to throw]

jetton (jet´ən) *n.* a stamped or engraved counter used in card-playing, or as a coin in a machine. [F *jeton*, from *jeter*, to throw]

jetty[1] (jet´i) *n.* (*pl.* **jetties**) **1** a structure of stone or timber projecting into water and serving as a mole, pier, or wharf. **2** a landing pier. **3** (*Archit.*) a part of a building which juts beyond the ground plan. [OF *getee* (F *jetée*), p.p. of *jeter*, to throw, see JET[2]]

jetty[2] (jet´i) *a.* **1** of the nature of jet. **2** of the colour of jet. **jettiness** *n.* [JET[1]]

jeu (zhœ) *n.* (*pl.* **jeux** (zhœ)) a game, a play, a jest. **jeu de mots** (də mō) *n.* (*pl.* **jeux de mots**) a pun. **jeu d'esprit** (desprē´) *n.* (*pl.* **jeux d'esprit**) a witticism, a play of wit, a witty sally. [F, from L *jocus*, see JOKE]

jeunesse dorée (zhœnes dorā´) *n.* gilded youth. [F]

Jew (joo) *n.* **1** a person of Hebrew descent or whose religion is Judaism. **2** (*offensive*) a usurer, a person who drives a hard bargain. **jew** *v.t.* (*offensive*) to drive a hard bargain, to cheat. **Jewess** *n.* (*sometimes offensive*) a female Jew. **jewfish** *n.* (*pl. in general* **jewfish,** *in particular* **jewfishes**) **1** a grouper, *Epinephelus itajara*. **2** any of several large Australian fish, esp. the mulloway. **jewing** *n.* the wattles at the base of the beak in some domestic pigeons (supposed to have some resemblance to a hooked nose). **Jewish** *a.* of or relating to Jews or Judaism. **Jewishly** *adv.* **Jewishness** *n.* **Jew's-ear** *n.* a tough edible fungus, *Auricularia auricula-judae*, growing on elder and elm trees. **jew's harp** *n.* a musical instrument held between the teeth, the sound produced by the vibrations of a metal tongue set in motion by the forefinger. **jew's-mallow** *n.* a plant, *Kerris japonica*, used in the Middle East as a potherb. [A-F *Jeu*, *Geu*, OF *giu* (F *juif*), L *Iudaeus -um*, Gr. *Ioudaios*, Heb. *y'hudah*, Judah, son of Jacob]

jewel (joo´əl) *n.* **1** a precious stone, a gem. **2** a personal ornament containing a precious stone or stones. **3** a person or thing of very great value or excellence. ~*v.t.*

(*pres.p.* **jewelling,** (*N Am.*) **jeweling,** *past, p.p.* **jewelled,** (*N Am.*) **jeweled**) **1** to adorn with or as with jewels. **2** to fit (a watch) with jewels in the pivot-holes. **jewel-block** *n.* a block at the yardarm of a ship, for the halyard of a studding-sail yard to pass through. **jewel-case** *n.* **jewel-fish** *n.* (*pl. in general* **jewel-fish,** *in particular* **jewel-fishes**) a brightly-coloured tropical fish, *Hemichromis bimaculatus.* **jewel in the crown** *n.* **1** (*Hist.*) any of the countries of the British Empire, esp. India. **2** the most highly-prized, beautiful etc. one of a collection or group. **jeweller,** (*N Am.*) **jeweler** *n.* a maker of or dealer in jewels. **jeweller's rouge** *n.* finely ground rouge used for polishing metal. **jewellery** (-əlri), **jewelry** *n.* **1** (*collect.*) jewels in general. **2** the art or trade of a jeweller. **jewel-like** *a.* **jewelly** *a.* [A-F *juel,* OF *joìel, joel,* etym. uncertain; perh. from late L *jocāle,* from L *jocāre,* to play (whence *juer, jouer*), or dim. of *joie,* L *gaudium,* joy]

Usage note Pronunciation of *jewellery* as (joo´ləri) is best avoided.

Jewry (joo´ri) *n.* (*pl.* **Jewries**) **1** (*collect.*) the Jews or the land where they dwell or dwelt. **2** (*Hist.*) Judaea. **3** (*Hist.*) the Jews' quarter in a town or country. [OF *juierie,* JEW, -ERY]

jewstone (joo´stōn) *n.* **1** a black basalt found in the Clee Hills, Shropshire. **2** the fossil spine of a sea urchin or echinus, formerly used as a medicine. [Welsh *ddu,* black]

Jezebel (jez´əbel) *n.* a wicked, bold, or vicious woman, esp. a woman who paints her face. [wife of Ahab, king of Israel (1 Kings, xvi.31)]

jib[1] (jib) *n.* **1** a large triangular sail set on a stay between the fore-topmast-head and bowsprit or jib-boom in large vessels and between the masthead and the bowsprit in smaller ones. **2** the extended arm of a crane or derrick. **the cut of one's jib** (*orig. Naut. sl.*) one's physical appearance. **jib-boom** *n.* a movable spar running out beyond the bowsprit. **jib-door** *n.* a door flush with the wall on both sides, and usu. papered or painted over so as to be concealed. [etym. uncertain; perh. abbr. of GIBBET, or from JIB[2]]

jib[2] (jib) *v.t.* (*pres.p.* **jibbing,** *past, p.p.* **jibbed**) to shift (a boom, yard or sail) from one side of a vessel to the other. ~*v.i.* to swing round (of a sail etc.). [cp. Dan. *gibbe,* Dut. *gijpen,* cp. GYBE]

jib[3] (jib) *v.i.* (*pres.p.* **jibbing,** *past, p.p.* **jibbed**) **1** (of a horse etc.) to move restively sideways or backwards. **2** to make difficulties (at some task, course, person etc.). **3** (of a horse etc.) to stop short and refuse to move forwards. **to jib at 1** (of a person) to refuse to do (something). **2** to show aversion to (a person or thing). **jibber** *n.* a horse etc. that jibs. [etym. uncertain]

jibba (jib´ə), **jibbah, djibba, djibbah** *n.* **1** a long, loose coat worn by Muslims. **2** a loose overall or pinafore. [Arab.]

jibber GIBBER[1].

jibe[1] (jīb) *v.i.* (*N Am., coll.*) to agree, accord (with). [etym. uncertain]

jibe[2] GIBE.

jibe[3] GYBE.

jiff (jif), **jiffy** (-i) *n.* (*pl.* **jiffs, jiffies**) (*coll.*) a moment, an instant, an extremely short time. [etym. unknown]

Jiffy bag® (jif´i) *n.* a padded envelope.

jig (jig) *n.* **1** a lively dance for one or more performers. **2** the music for such a dance. **3** a fish-hook with a weighted shank, used for snatching at fish. **4** a device for holding an object and guiding a cutting-tool in a machine for the manufacture of standard parts. ~*v.i.* (*pres.p.* **jigging,** *past, p.p.* **jigged**) **1** to dance a jig. **2** to skip about. **3** to move up and down rapidly or jerkily. **4** to fish (for) or catch with a jig. ~*v.t.* **1** to sing or play in jig time. **2** to jerk up and down rapidly. **3** to separate finer and coarser qualities of (ore etc.) by treatment in a jigger. **4** to work on or equip with a jig. **5** to fish for or catch with a jig. **6** to cheat, to hoax. **to jig about** to fidget. **jigging** *n.* **jigging-machine** *n.* an apparatus for sifting ore in water, a jigger. **jiggish** *a.* **1** resembling or fitted for a jig. **2** playful, frisky. **jigsaw** *n.* **1** a vertically-reciprocating saw moved by a vibrating lever or crank-rod, used for cutting scrolls, fretwork etc. **2** a jigsaw puzzle. **jigsaw puzzle** *n.* a puzzle to put together a picture cut into irregularly shaped pieces. [etym. uncertain]

jigger[1] (jig´ə) *n.* **1** (*Naut.*) a small tackle used for holding on to the cable as it is heaved in, and similar work. **2** a small sail, usu. set on a jigger-mast. **3** a small smack carrying this. **4** (*sl.*) any kind of mechanical contrivance, implement etc. **5** in golf, an iron club with a narrow face, used for lofting and for medium distance shots. **6** (*coll.*) a rest for a billiard cue. **7** a small measure of spirits. **8** a small glass for this. **9** a person who or thing which jigs. **10** a sieve shaken vertically in water to separate the contained ore. **11** the person using such a sieve. **12** a potter's wheel on which earthen vessels are shaped. **13** a machine for dyeing cloth. **jigger-mast** *n.* a small mast at the stem of a yawl, a small mizzen-mast.

jigger[2] (jig´ə) *n.* the flea *Tunga penetrans,* a chigger. [CHIGGER, CHIGOE]

jiggered (jig´əd) *a.* (*coll.*) very surprised, confounded. **I'll be jiggered** used to express surprise etc. **I'm jiggered** used to express surprise etc. [etym. uncertain]

jiggery-pokery (jigəripō´kəri) *n.* underhand goings-on. [onomat.]

jiggle (jig´əl) *v.t.* to jerk or rock lightly to and fro. ~*v.i.* to fidget. ~*n.* a jiggling movement. **jiggly** *a.* [freq. of JIG]

jig-jog (jig´jog) *n.* a jogging, jolting motion.

jihad (jihad´, -hahd´), **jehad** *n.* **1** a holy war proclaimed by Muslims against unbelievers or the enemies of Islam. **2** a war or crusade on behalf of a principle etc. [Arab. *jihād*]

jillaroo (jiləroo´) *n.* (*pl.* **jillaroos**) (*Austral., coll.*) a female newcomer or novice. [after JACKAROO]

jilt (jilt) *v.t.* to throw over or discard (one's lover). ~*v.i.* to play the jilt. ~*n.* a person, esp. a woman who jilts a lover. [prob. from a dim. (-*et*) of *Jill*]

jimcrack GIMCRACK.

Jim Crow (jim krō´) *n.* **1** (*N Am., offensive*) a black person. **2** the policy of segregating blacks. **3** an implement for bending or straightening rails. **4** a planing machine with a cutting-tool adapted for turning about and cutting both ways. **5** (*Mining*) a crowbar with an iron claw like a burglar's jemmy. **Jim Crowism** *n.* [character in a plantation song]

jiminy (jim´ini) *n.pl.* meteoric bodies radiating, usu. in early December, from the constellation Gemini. [alt. of GEMINI, euphem. for *Jesus Christ*]

jim-jams[1] (jim´jamz) *n.pl.* **1** (*sl.*) delirium tremens. **2** (*coll.*) fluster, jumpiness. **3** (*coll.*) a state of depression or nervousness.

jim-jams[2] (jim´jamz) *n.pl.* (*coll.*) pyjamas. [abbr. of *pie-jim-jams*]

Jimmy (jim´i) *n.* (*sl.*) an act of urination. [rhyming slang, *Jimmy Riddle,* piddle]

jimmy (jim´i) *n.* (*pl.* **jimmies**) (*N Am.*) a short crowbar, a jemmy.

Jimmy Woodser (jimi wud´zə) *n.* (*Austral., coll.*) **1** a drink one pays for oneself. **2** a drink taken alone. **3** a man who drinks alone.

jimson (jim´sən), **jimson weed** *n.* (*N Am.*) a poisonous weed, *Datura stramonium,* the thorn apple. [*Jamestown,* Virginia]

jingko GINKGO.

jingle (jing´gəl) *v.i.* **1** to make a clinking or tinkling sound like that of small bells, bits of metal etc. **2** to correspond tritely or annoyingly in sound, rhyme etc. ~*v.t.* to cause to make a clinking or tinkling sound. ~*n.* **1** a tinkling metallic sound. **2** a correspondence or repetition of sounds in words, esp. of a catchy inartistic kind. **3** doggerel. **4** a simply rhythmical verse, esp. one used in advertising. **5** a covered two-wheeled Irish or Australian horse-drawn vehicle. **jingle-jangle** *n.* **jingling-match** *n.* (*Hist.*) a game in which a player carrying a bell is chased by others blind-folded. **jingly** *a.* [imit.]

jingo (jing´gō) *n.* (*pl.* **jingoes**) **1** a person given to (excessive) belligerent patriotism. **2** a member of a party advocating a warlike foreign policy, esp. those who championed the cause of the Turks during and after the Russian-Turkish war of 1877–8 (in this sense derived directly from the refrain of a song then popular). ~*a.* of or relating to the jingoes. **by jingo 1** used to express surprise etc. **2** used to emphasize a statement of intention etc. **jingoish** *a.* **jingoism** *n.* **1** the (excessive) belligerent patriotism of jingoes. **2** a foreign policy based on this. **jingoist** *n.* **jingoistic** (-is´-) *a.* [prob. conjurer's nonsense]

jink (jingk) *v.i.* (*Sc.*) **1** to move nimbly. **2** to dance, to fling. **3** to dodge. ~*v.t.* **1** to dodge. **2** to cheat, to take in. **3** in football, to trick (an opponent) by sidestepping etc. ~*n.* a slip, an evasion, a dodging turn, a dodge. [prob. onomat.]

jinker (jing´kə) *n.* (*Austral.*) a sort of two-wheeled bogey for transporting heavy logs and timber. [etym. unknown]

jinnee (jinē´), **jinn** (jin), **djinn** *n.* (*pl.* **jinn, djinn**) any of a race of spirits or demons in Muslim mythology supposed to have the power of assuming human or animal forms. [Arab. *jinnī*, cp. GENIE]

jinrickshaw (jinrik´shaw), **jinrickisha** (-shə) *n.* a rickshaw.

jinx (jingks) *n.* (*coll.*) a person or thing that brings ill luck. ~*v.t.* to subject to bad luck, put a spell on. [perh. *Jynx*, WRYNECK (under WRY), bird used in magic]

JIT *abbr.* just-in-time.

jit (jit) *n.* a type of beat music that originated in Zimbabwe.

jitney (jit´ni) *n.* **1** a small bus that carries passengers for a low fare, orig. five cents. **2** a nickel, five cents. [etym. unknown]

jitter (jit´ə) *v.i.* to be nervous, behave in a nervous way. **jitterbug** *n.* **1** a person who spreads alarm. **2** (*Hist.*) a fast dance performed to swing music. **3** (*Hist.*) a dancer who greatly exaggerates swing dancing. ~*v.i.* (*pres.p.* **jitterbugging,** *past, p.p.* **jitterbugged**) to dance the jitterbug. **jitters** *n.pl.* (*sl.*) nervous apprehension. **jittery** *a.* **jitteriness** *n.* [etym. unknown]

jiu-jitsu JU-JITSU.

jive (jīv) *n.* **1** a style of lively, jazz-style music. **2** dancing to such music. **3** (*sl.*) misleading talk. **4** (*sl.*) jargon. ~*v.i.* **1** to dance to jive music. **2** to play jive music. **3** (*sl.*) to mislead. **jiver** *n.* **jiving** *n.* [etym. uncertain]

jizz (jiz) *n.* the characteristic features, appearance, behaviour etc. which distinguish a bird or other animal or plant from other species. [etym. uncertain]

Jnr *abbr.* Junior.

jo (jō) *n.* (*pl.* **joes**) (*Sc.*) **1** one's sweetheart. **2** one's delight. [JOY]

joanna (jōan´ə) *n.* (*sl.*) a piano. [rhyming slang]

Job (jōb) *n.* an uncomplaining sufferer or victim. **jobe** *v.t.* to reprove, to reprimand. **jobation** (-bā´shən) *n.* a long-winded reproof, a lecture. **Job's comforter** *n.* a false friend who lacerates one's feelings whilst pretending to sympathize. **Job's news** *n.* ill tidings. **Job's post** *n.* a bearer of ill tidings. **Job's tears** *n.pl.* the seeds of a grass, *Coix lacryma-jobi*, used as beads. [the patriarch, subject of the book of *Job* in the Bible]

job[1] (job) *n.* **1** a piece of work, esp. one done for a stated price. **2** an occupation; a situation in paid employment. **3** a responsibility or duty. **4** (*coll.*) a difficult task. **5** a piece of work or business yielding unfair profit or advantage, esp. one in which public interests are sacrificed to personal gain. **6** (*coll.*) a situation. **7** (*sl.*) a crime, esp. a robbery. **8** a specified operation, esp. one involving plastic surgery (*a nose job*). **9** (*sl.*) an example of a particular product. ~*a.* **1** applied to collections of things sold together. **2** let on hire. ~*v.t.* (*pres.p.* **jobbing,** *past, p.p.* **jobbed**) **1** to let out (as work) by the job. **2** to let out thus for hire. **3** to hire thus. **4** to buy up in miscellaneous lots and retail. **5** to deal in (stocks). **6** to deal with in an underhand way for one's private benefit. **7** (*NAm., sl.*) to swindle. ~*v.i.* **1** to buy and sell as a broker. **2** to do jobwork. **3** to let or hire by the job. **4** to make profit corruptly out of a position of trust, esp. at public expense. **just the job** (*coll.*) exactly what is wanted. **on the job** (*coll.*) **1** at work, in activity. **2** engaged in sexual activity. **out of a job** unemployed. **to do the job for one** to ruin or kill one. **to job out** to sublet a piece of work. **to make a (good) job of** to do thoroughly or successfully. **job analysis** *n.* the analysis of the contents of a job for the purpose of providing a job description etc. **job analyst** *n.* **jobber** *n.* **1** a person who deals in stocks and shares on the Stock Exchange. **2** (*NAm.*) a wholesaler. **3** a person who does small jobs. **4** a person who uses a position of trust, esp. a public office, commission etc., to private advantage. **5** a person who does dishonourable work. **6** a jobmaster. **jobber's turn** *n.* a term denoting the middle price between which a jobber is prepared to buy or sell. **jobbery** *n.* **1** jobbing. **2** corrupt dealing. **jobbie** *n.* (*sl.*) an example of a particular product. **jobbing** *n.* working by the job. ~*a.* of or relating to a person who works by the job. **jobbing house** *n.* a printing office where miscellaneous work (as distinct from newspapers or books) is done. **jobbing printer** *n.* a printer who does mainly miscellaneous work (as distinct from newspapers or books). **jobcentre** *n.* a government-run centre where information about available jobs is displayed. **job-control language** *n.* (*Comput.*) a language which allows the user to control the tasks undertaken by the operating system. **job-hunt** *v.i.* (*coll.*) to look for work. **jobless** *a.* **joblessness** *n.* **job lot** *n.* a miscellaneous lot of goods bought cheap in the expectation of random profit. **jobmaster** *n.* a person who lets out carriages or horses. **job-printer** *n.* a jobbing printer. **jobs for the boys** *n.pl.* (*coll.*) jobs given to someone's supporters or favourites. **job-sharing** *n.* the division of one job by two or more people who work hours complementary to each other. **job-share** *n.*, *v.i.* **jobsheet** *n.* a sheet on which details of a job are recorded. **jobsworth** *n.* (*coll.*) a minor functionary who is quite inflexible in their interpretation of the law and is very unhelpful to the public (from the phrase 'it's more than my *job's worth*'). **jobwork** *n.* work done or paid for by the job. [etym. unknown]

job[2] (job) *v.t.* (*pres.p.* **jobbing,** *past, p.p.* **jobbed**) **1** to stab, poke or prod with a sharp instrument. **2** to drive (a sharp instrument) in. ~*v.i.* to stab or thrust (at). ~*n.* **1** a sudden stab, poke or prod. **2** a jerk at a horse's bit. [prob. onomat. (cp. JAB)]

jobber JOB[1].

jobbernowl (job´ənōl) *n.* (*coll.*) a blockhead. [F *jobard*, a fool, from *jobe*, silly, NOLL]

jobbery, jobbie etc. JOB[1].

Jock (jok) *n.* (*coll.*) **1** a soldier of a Scottish regiment. **2** (*often offensive*) a Scotsman. [pers. name]

jock[1] (jok) *n.* (*coll.*) **1** a jockey. **2** a disc jockey. [JOCKEY]

jock[2] (jok) *n.* (*sl., orig. NAm.*) **1** an athlete. **2** a jockstrap. [JOCKSTRAP]

jockey (jok´i) *n.* (*pl.* **jockeys**) **1** a professional rider in horse races. **2** (*derog.*) a groom, a lad, an understrapper. **3** a person given to sharp practice (prob. from the bad reputation of horse-dealers); a cheat. ~*v.t.* (*3rd pers.*

sing. *pres.* **jockeys,** *pres.p.* **jockeying,** *past, p.p.* **jockeyed)** 1 to deceive in a bargain. 2 to employ sharp practices against. 3 to outwit, outmanoeuvre etc. 4 to cheat. 5 in horseracing, to jostle by riding against. ~*v.i.* 1 to be tricky. 2 to play a tricky game. **disc jockey** DISC. **to jockey for position** 1 to try by skill to get an advantageous position. 2 to gain an unfair advantage. **jockey cap** *n.* a cap with a long peak, worn by jockeys. **jockeydom, jockeyism, jockeyship** *n.* **jockey-pulley** *n.* in a motor, a pulley that rotates on a spring-loaded mounting, used to keep a belt taut on two fixed pulleys.

jocko (jok´ō), **jacko** (jak´ō) *n.* (*pl.* **jockos, jackos**) a chimpanzee. [F, from Bantu *engeco* or *ncheko*]

jockstrap (jok´strap) *n.* 1 a support for the genitals worn by men engaged in athletic or sporting activity. 2 (*N Am., coll.*) an athletic person, esp. a student. [sl. *jock*, penis, STRAP]

jocose (jəkōs´) *a.* 1 humorous, facetious. 2 given to jokes or jesting. 3 containing jokes, amusing. **jocosely** *adv.* **jocoseness** *n.* †**jocoserious** (jōkōsiə´riəs) *a.* partaking of mirth and sadness. **jocosity** (-kos´-) *n.* (*pl.* **jocosities**). [L *jocōsus*, from *jocus*, JOKE]

jocular (jok´ūlə) *a.* 1 addicted to jesting. 2 merry, facetious, amusing. 3 embodying a joke. **jocularity** (-lar´-) *n.* (*pl.* **jocularities**). **jocularly** *adv.*

jocund (jok´ənd) *a.* 1 sportive, merry. 2 inspiring mirth. **jocundity** (-kŭn´-) *n.* (*pl.* **jocundities**). **jocundly** *adv.* [OF *jocond*, L *jūcundus*, from *juvāre*, to help, to delight]

jodhpurs (jod´pəz) *n.pl.* long riding-breeches fitting closely from the knee to the ankle. [*Jodhpur*, city in India]

joe (jō), **joey** (jō´i) *n.* (*pl.* **joes, joeys**) (*Hist., sl.*) a fourpenny or threepenny bit. [*Joseph* Hume, MP 1836]

Joe Bloggs (jō blogz), (*N Am.*) **Joe Blow** (blō´) *n.* (*coll.*) a typical or ordinary person. **Joe Miller** *n.* an old joke, a chestnut (from Joseph Miller, 1684–1738, a comedian). **Joe-Millerism** *n.* **Joe Public** *n.* (*coll.*) the general public. **Joe Soap** *n.* 1 a person who does menial tasks. 2 a person who is taken advantage of.

joey[1] JOE.

joey[2] (jō´i) *n.* (*pl.* **joeys**) (*Austral.*) 1 a young kangaroo. 2 a young animal. [Austral. Abor. *joè*]

jog (jog) *v.t.* (*pres.p.* **jogging,** *past, p.p.* **jogged**) 1 to push or jerk lightly, usu. with the hand or elbow. 2 to nudge, esp. to excite attention. 3 to stimulate (one's memory or attention). ~*v.i.* 1 to run at a steady, slow pace for exercise. 2 to move with an up-and-down leisurely pace. 3 to walk or trudge idly, heavily, or slowly (on, along etc.). 4 to go, to depart, to be off. ~*n.* 1 a light push or nudge to arouse attention. 2 a leisurely trotting or jogging motion. **to be jogging** to take one's departure. **to jog on** to get along (somehow or in some specified manner). **to jog the elbow** ELBOW. **jogger** *n.* a person who jogs (for exercise). **jogger's knee, jogger's nipple** *n.* an injured or damaged knee or nipple, caused by jogging. **jogging** *n.* the act of jogging, esp. as a form of exercise. **jogging-suit** *n.* a garment like a tracksuit worn when jogging. **jogtrot** *n.* 1 a slow, easy, monotonous trot. 2 humdrum progress. 3 slow routine. ~*a.* monotonous. [prob. onomat. (cp. F. *choquer*)]

joggle (jog´əl) *v.t.* 1 to shake, push, nudge or jerk slightly. 2 in building, to unite by means of joggles, to prevent sliding. ~*v.i.* to shake slightly, to totter. ~*n.* 1 a joint in stone or other material to prevent sliding of one piece over another. 2 a notch, projection, dowel etc., used to form such joints. [prob. freq. of JOG]

Johannisberger (jəhan´isbœgə) *n.* a white Rhine wine. [G, from *Johannisberg*, a vineyard near Wiesbaden]

john (jon) *n.* (*sl.*) 1 a lavatory. 2 a prostitute's client. **John Barleycorn** *n.* 1 barley personified as the grain from which malt liquor is made. 2 malt liquor. **John Bull** *n.* 1 the English people personified. 2 an Englishman. **John Chinaman** *n.* (*offensive*) a male Chinese. **John Collins** (kol´inz) *n.* an alcoholic drink based on gin. †**John Company** *n.* the East India Company. **John Doe** *n.* (*N Am.*) 1 (*Law*) the fictitious plaintiff in an (obsolete) action for ejectment, the defendant being called Richard Roe. 2 (*coll.*) JOE BLOGGS. **John Dory** *n.* (*pl.* **John Dories**) a European marine fish, *Zeus faber*, which has spiny dorsal fins and a black spot on each side. [pers. name, cp. OF *Jehan* (F *Jean*), late L *Johannes*, L *Joannes*, Gr. *Jōannēs*, Heb. *Yōchānāni*, Jah is gracious]

johnny (jon´i) *n.* (*pl.* **johnnies**) 1 (*sl.*) a condom. 2 (*coll.*) a fellow, a chap. 3 a toff, a swell, a young man about town. **Johnny cake** *n.* 1 (*N Am.*) a maize cake baked on the hearth. 2 (*Austral.*) a similar wheatmeal cake. **johnny-come-lately** *n.* (*pl.* **johnny-come-latelies, johnnies-come-lately**) (*coll.*) a newcomer. **Johnny raw** *n.* a raw beginner, a novice.

Johnsonian (jonsō´niən) *a.* 1 of or relating to Dr Samuel Johnson. 2 characteristic of Johnson's style; pompous, inflated, abounding in words of classical origin. **Johnsonese** (-nēz´) *n.* **Johnsonism** *n.* [Dr Samuel *Johnson*, 1709–84, writer and lexicographer]

joie de vivre (zhwa də vēv´rə) *n.* joy of living; exuberance. [F]

join (join) *v.t.* 1 to connect, to fasten together, to unite. 2 to couple, to associate. 3 to unite (two persons, or a person or persons with or to) in marriage etc. 4 to begin, to engage in (battle etc.). 5 to become a member of (a club etc.). ~*v.i.* 1 to be contiguous or in contact. 2 to become associated or combined (with etc.) in views, partnership, action etc. 3 to become a member (of a society etc.). 4 †to begin battle. ~*n.* 1 a joint. 2 a point, line, or mark of junction. **to join forces** FORCE[1]. **to join hand in hand** to act in concert. **to join hands** 1 to clasp hands (with). 2 to come to an understanding or combine (with). **to join in** to take part. **to join issue** ISSUE. **to join the majority** MAJORITY (under MAJOR). **to join up** 1 to enlist. 2 to connect. **joinable** *a.* **joinant** *a.* (*Her.*) conjoined. **joinder** (-də) *n.* (*Law*) 1 the act of joining. 2 conjunction. 3 the coupling of two things in one suit or action, or two or more parties as defendants in a suit. 4 the acceptance by a party in an action of the challenge in their adversary's demurrer or last pleading. **joined-up** *a.* 1 (of handwriting) with the letters joined up rather than printed separately as by a small child; cursive. 2 (*coll.*) adult, sophisticated, characterized by intelligent and coherent thinking. **joiner** *n.* 1 a carpenter who makes articles of furniture, finishes woodwork etc. 2 (*N Am.*) a carpenter. 3 (*coll.*) a person who likes joining clubs etc. 4 a person who joins. **joinery** *n.* [OF *joign-*, stem of *joindre*, L *jungere* (p.p. *junctus*), cp. Gr. *zeugnunai*, to YOKE]

joint (joint) *n.* 1 a junction or mode of joining parts together. 2 the place where two things are joined together. 3 the union of two bones in an animal body. 4 an analogous point or mechanical device connecting parts of any structure, whether fixed or movable. 5 any of the pieces into which a butcher cuts up a carcass. 6 such a piece as served at table. 7 a node. 8 an internode. 9 a natural fissure or line of parting traversing rocks in a straight and well-determined line. 10 (*sl.*) a marijuana cigarette. 11 (*sl.*) a low and usu. illicit opium or gambling den. 12 (*sl., often derog.*) a place, building etc. 13 (*sl.*) a bar or nightclub. 14 (*N Am., sl.*) an eating house. ~*a.* 1 of, belonging to, performed or produced by different persons in conjunction. 2 sharing or participating (with others). ~*v.t.* 1 to form with joints or articulations. 2 to connect by joints. 3 to plane and prepare (boards etc.) for joining. 4 to point (masonry). 5 to divide or cut (meat) into joints, to disjoint. **out of joint** 1 dislocated. 2 out of order. **to put someone's nose out of joint** to upset, disconcert or supplant a person. **joint account** *n.* a bank account held by more than one person. **joint-action** *n.* the joining of several actions in one. **joint and several** *a.* (of an obligation etc.) undertaken by two or more people. **jointed** *a.* having joints, esp. of a specified kind. **jointedly** *adv.* **jointer** *n.* **1** a person who or thing which joints. **2** in carpentry, a long plane used to true the edges of boards to be joined. **3** a pointing tool used by masons and bricklayers. **joint heir** *n.* an heir having a joint interest with another. **jointing** *n.*, *a.* **jointing plane** *n.* **jointing rule** *n.* a straight rule used in marking the joints of brickwork. **jointless** (-lis) *a.* **jointly** *adv.* together or in conjunction with others. **jointress** (-tris), **jointuress** (-tūris) *n.* a woman who has a jointure. **joint stock** *n.* stock or capital divided into shares and held jointly by several persons. **joint-stock company** *n.* **joint tenancy** *n.* (*Law*) tenure of an estate by unity of interest, title, time, and possession. **joint tenant** *n.* **jointure** (-tūə) *n.* an estate in lands or tenements, settled upon a woman in consideration on marriage, which she is to enjoy after her husband's decease. *~v.t.* to settle a jointure upon.

jointweed *n.* **1** any plant of the genus *Equisetum*, a horsetail. **2** (*N Am.*) a herb, *Polygonella articulata*, of the buckwheat family. [OF, p.p. of *joindre*, see JOIN]

joist (joist) *n.* any of a series of parallel horizontal timbers to which floorboards or the laths of a ceiling are nailed. *~v.t.* to furnish with joists. **joisted** *a.* [ME and OF *giste* (F *gîte*), a bed, a place to lie in, from *gesir*, L *jacēre*, to lie]

jojoba (həhō´bə, hō-) *n.* a desert shrub, *Simmondsia chinensis*, native to Arizona, Mexico and California, whose edible seeds provide waxy oil similar to spermaceti, used in cosmetics, toiletries etc. [Mex. Sp.]

joke (jōk) *n.* **1** something said or done to excite laughter or merriment. **2** a jest. **3** a ridiculous incident, circumstance, person etc. *~v.i.* to make jokes, to jest. *~v.t.* **1** to crack jokes about. **2** to rally, to banter. **practical joke** PRACTICAL. **jokee** (-kē´) *n.* a person on whom a joke is played. **jokeless** (-lis) *a.* **jokelet** (-lit) *n.* **joker** *n.* **1** a person who jokes, a jester. **2** (*sl.*) a fellow. **3** an extra card (often printed with a comic device) used with various values in some card games. **4** (*N Am.*) a clause in a bill or document which looks innocent but effectively makes it inoperative. **5** an unforeseen factor. **joker in the pack** *n.* a person who or thing which is unpredictable. **jokesman, jokesmith, jokester** (-stə), **jokist** *n.* **jokesome** (-səm) *a.* **jokingly** *adv.* **joky, jokey** *a.* (*comp.* **jokier**, *superl.* **jokiest**). **jokily** *adv.* **jokiness** *n.* [L *jocus*]

jolie laide (zholē led´) *n.* (*pl.* **jolies laides** (zholē led´)) a fascinating ugly woman. [F, *jolie*, pretty, *laide*, ugly]

jolly[1] (jol´i) *a.* (*comp.* **jollier**, *superl.* **jolliest**) **1** merry, mirthful. **2** jovial, festive. **3** inspiring or expressing mirth. **4** slightly drunk. **5** (*coll.*) pleasant, agreeable, charming. **6** remarkable, extraordinary. **7** (*iron.*) nice, precious. *~adv.* (*coll.*) very, exceedingly. *~v.t.* **1** to banter, to joke, to rally. **2** (*coll.*) to treat agreeably so as to keep in good humour or secure a favour (usu. with *along*). *~n.* (*pl.* **jollies**) (*coll.*) a celebration. **jollify** (-fī) *v.i.* (*3rd pers. sing. pres.* **jollifies**, *pres.p.* **jollifying**, *past, p.p.* **jollified**) **1** to make merry. **2** to tipple. *~v.t.* to make (a person) merry, esp. with drink. **jollification** (-fikā´shən) *n.* merrymaking, a jolly party. **jollily** *adv.* **jolliness** *n.* **jollity** *n.* (*pl.* **jollities**). **Jolly Roger** *n.* a pirate's flag with skull and crossbones. [OF *jolif, joli*, gay, fine, etym. uncertain]

jolly[2] (jol´i), **jolly boat** *n.* (*pl.* **jollies, jolly boats**) a small boat for the general work of a ship. [cp. Dan. *jolle*, Dut. *jol*, YAWL[1]]

jolt (jōlt, jolt) *v.t.* **1** to shake with sharp, sudden jerks, as in a vehicle along a rough road. **2** to disturb, to shock. *~v.i.* (of a vehicle) to move with sharp, sudden jerks. *~n.* a sudden shock or jerk. **jolter** *n.* **joltingly** *adv.* **jolty** *a.* [etym. uncertain, perh. conn. with JOWL]

Jon. *abbr.* **1** Jonah. **2** Jonathan.

Jonah (jō´nə) *n.* a bringer of bad luck. [the prophet *Jonah*]

Jonathan (jon´əthən) *n.* **1** the American people collectively. **2** a typical American. **3** a kind of late-ripening American red apple. [prob. from *Jonathan* Trumbull 1710–85, Governor of Connecticut, to whom Washington frequently referred for advice]

jongleur (zhõglœ´) *n.* (*Hist.*) an itinerant minstrel or reciter of the Middle Ages, esp. in N France. [F, from OF *jogleor*, JUGGLER (under JUGGLE)]

jonquil (jong´kwil, jŭng´-) *n.* a narcissus, *Narcissus jonquilla*, with two to six yellow or white flowers on a stem. [F *jonquille*, Sp. *junquillo*, dim. of *junco*, L *juncus*, a rush]

Jordanian (jawdā´niən) *n.* **1** a native or inhabitant of Jordan. **2** a person of Jordanian descent. *~a.* of or relating to the kingdom of Jordan. [river *Jordan*]

jorum (jaw´rəm) *n.* **1** a large bowl or drinking vessel. **2** its contents. [prob. from *Joram* in the Bible (2 Sam. viii.10)]

Jos. *abbr.* Joseph.

Joseph (jō´zif) *n.* **1** a man of invincible chastity. **2** (**joseph**) an 18th-cent. caped riding dress for ladies, having buttons down to the skirts. [the patriarch *Joseph* (alln. to Gen. xxxvii.3)]

Josh. *abbr.* Joshua.

josh (josh) *v.t.* to make fun of, to ridicule. *~v.i.* to indulge in ridicule. *~n.* (*coll.*) a friendly joke. **josher** *n.* [etym. uncertain]

Joshua tree (josh´ūə) *n.* a yucca, *Yucca brevifolia*, with sword-shaped leaves and greenish-white flowers, of the south-western US. [the prophet *Joshua*, in alln. to the branches resembling a spear]

joskin (jos´kin) *n.* (*sl.*) a bumpkin, a yokel. [thieves' cant]

joss (jos) *n.* a Chinese idol. **josser** *n.* (*sl.*) **1** a fellow. **2** a fool. **3** (*Austral.*) a clergyman. **joss-house** *n.* a Chinese temple. **joss stick** *n.* a stick of perfumed material burnt as incense, orig. in China. [corr. of Port. *deos*, L *deus*, God]

jostle (jos´əl), **justle** (jŭs´əl) *v.t.* **1** to push against, to hustle. **2** to elbow. *~v.i.* **1** to push (against, along etc.). **2** to hustle, to crowd. *~n.* **1** a hustling. **2** a collision, a conflict. [formerly *justle*, freq. of *just*, JOUST]

jot (jot) *n.* a tittle, an iota. *~v.t.* (*pres.p.* **jotting**, *past, p.p.* **jotted**) to write (down a brief note or memorandum of). **jotter** *n.* a pad or exercise book for taking notes etc. **jotting** *n.* a note or memorandum. [L and Gr. *iōta*, the letter *i*]

joule (jool) *n.* **1** the SI unit of work and energy, equal to the work done when a force of 1 newton advances its point of application 1 metre. **2** (*Hist.*) the unit of electrical energy, the work done in 1 second by a current of 1 ampere against a resistance of 1 ohm. **joulemeter** *n.* [James Prescott *Joule*, 1818–89, British physicist]

jounce (jowns) *v.t., v.i.* to jolt or shake. *~n.* a jolt, a shake. [etym. uncertain]

journal (jœ´nəl) *n.* **1** a record of events or news; any newspaper or other periodical published at regular intervals. **2** a daily record of events, a diary. **3** a logbook or daily register of a ship's course and distance etc. **4** an account of daily transactions. **5** in bookkeeping, the book from which daily entries are posted up in the ledger. **6** the transactions of a learned society etc. **7** the part of a shaft that rests on the bearings. **the Journals** a record of the daily proceedings of parliament. **journal-box** *n.* the metal case in which the journal moves. **journalese** (-lēz´) *n.* (*derog.*) a superficial style of writing full of clichés etc., regarded as being typical of writing in newspapers etc. **journalist** *n.* **1** an editor of or contributor to a newspaper or other journal. **2** a reporter for radio or television. **3** a person who keeps a diary. **journalism** *n.* **journalistic** (-lis´-) *a.* **journalistically** *adv.* **journalize, journalise** *v.t.* **1** to enter in a diary. **2** in bookkeeping, to enter in a journal. ~*v.i.* **1** to follow the profession of a journalist. **2** to keep a journal or diary. **journo** *n.* (*pl.* **journos**) (*sl.*) a journalist. [OF, from L *diurnālis*, DIURNAL]

journey (jœ´ni) *n.* (*pl.* **journeys**) **1** passage or travel from one place to another, esp. by land or at a long distance. **2** the distance travelled in a given time. **3** the travelling of a vehicle along a route at a stated time. **4** a round of work, a turn, a spell. ~*v.i.* (*3rd pers. sing. pres.* **journeys,** *pres.p.* **journeying,** *past, p.p.* **journeyed)** **1** to travel. **2** to make a journey. **journeyer** *n.* **journeyman** *n.* (*pl.* **journeymen)** **1** a mechanic or artisan who has served an apprenticeship and works for an employer. **2** a mere drudge, hack or hireling. **journeywork** *n.* work performed for hire. [OF *jornée*, late L *jornāta, diurnāta*, a day's work, as JOURNAL]

journo JOURNAL.

joust (jowst), **just** (jŭst) *v.i.* (*Hist.*) to tilt, to encounter on horseback with lances. ~*n.* **1** a tilting match. **2** a combat between knights or men-at-arms on horseback. **jouster** *n.* [OF *jouster* (F *jouter*), from low L *juxtāre*, to approach, from *juxtā*, near]

Jove (jōv) *n.* Jupiter, the chief of the Roman divinities. **by Jove!** used to express surprise or approval. **jovial** *a.* **1** mirthful, merry, cheerful. **2** (*Astrol.*) **(Jovial)** under the influence of the planet Jupiter. **joviality** (-al´-), **jovialness** *n.* good humour. **jovially** *adv.* **Jovian** *a.* **1** of, relating to or like Jupiter, chief of the Roman divinities. **2** of or relating to the planet Jupiter. [L *Jovem*, acc. of OL *Jovis*, JUPITER]

jowar (jowah´) *n.* DURRA. [Hind. *jawār*]

jowl (jowl), †**jole** (jōl), **joll** *n.* **1** the (lower) jaw. **2** (*often pl.*) the cheek. **3** the throat or neck, esp. of a double-chinned person. **4** the dewlap. **5** the crop or wattle of a fowl. **6** the head and shoulder of fish. **cheek by jowl** CHEEK. **jowled** *a.* (*usu. in comb.* as *heavy-jowled*). **jowler** *n.* a dog with heavy jowls. **jowly** *a.* [ME *chowl, chavel*, OE *cēafl*, jaw, blended obscurely with ME *cholle*, OE *ceolur*, throat]

joy (joi) *n.* **1** the emotion produced by gratified desire, success, happy fortune etc.; gladness, happiness, delight. **2** a cause of joy or happiness. ~*v.i.* (*esp. poet.*) to rejoice. ~*v.t.* (*esp. poet.*) **1** to gladden. **2** to congratulate. **3** to enjoy. **to have no joy** (*coll.*) to be unsuccessful in a task etc. **to wish a person joy of** (*iron.*) to be gladly rid of (what that person has). **joy-bells** *n.pl.* peals rung on festive occasions. **joyful** *a.* **joyfully** *adv.* **joyfulness** *n.* **joyless** *a.* **joylessly** *adv.* **joylessness** *n.* **joyous** *a.* **1** joyful. **2** causing joy. **joyously** *adv.* **joyousness** *n.* **joyride** *n.* (*coll.*) a ride in a car for pleasure, esp. when unauthorized. ~*v.i.* (*past* **joyrode,** *p.p.* **joyridden)** to go for a joyride. **joyrider** *n.* **joystick** *n.* **1** (*coll.*) the control lever of an aeroplane. **2** a lever for controlling the movement of a cursor on a computer screen. [OF *joie*, L *gaudia*, orig. pl. of *gaudium*]

Joycean (joi´siən) *a.* of or characteristic of James Joyce, 1882–1941, Irish writer. ~*n.* a person who studies or imitates Joyce's work.

JP *abbr.* Justice of the Peace.

Jr., jr. *abbr.* junior.

jt. *abbr.* joint.

juba[1] (joo´bə) *n.* **1** a mane, as of a horse. **2** a loose beard or tuft of awns (as on certain grasses, maize etc.). **jubate** (-bāt) *a.* **1** maned. **2** fringed with or as with a mane. [L]

juba[2] (joo´bə) *n.* a characteristic dance developed by black people in the southern US.

jube[1] (joo´bi) *n.* a rood-loft or gallery dividing the choir from the nave. [F *jubé*, L *jubē*, imper. of *jubēre*, to command, from the formula, *jubē, domine, benedīcere*]

jube[2] (joob) *n.* (*Austral., New Zeal.*) a jujube. [abbr.]

jubilant (joo´bilənt) *a.* exultant, rejoicing, shouting for joy. **jubilance** *n.* **jubilantly** *adv.* [L *jūbilans -ntem*, pres.p. of *jūbilāre*; see JUBILATE[1]]

jubilate[1] (joo´bilāt) *v.i.* **1** to exult. **2** to express intense joy. **jubilation** (-ā´shən) *n.* [L *jūbilātus*, p.p. of *jūbilāre*, from *jūbilum*, a shout of joy]

jubilate[2] (joobilah´ti, yoo-) *n.* **1** **(Jubilate)** the 100th Psalm used as a canticle in the evening service of the Church of England, from its Latin commencing words *Jubilate Deo.* **2** a shout of joy or exultation. [L, shout ye for joy, as JUBILATE[1]]

jubilee (joo´bilē) *n.* **1** a season of great public rejoicing or festivity. **2** the anniversary of an event of public interest, esp. the 25th or 50th. **3** (*Hist.*) the most important festival among the Jews, proclaimed by the sound of a trumpet, and celebrated every 50th year to commemorate their deliverance from Egyptian slavery. **4** in the Roman Catholic Church, a year of special indulgence or remission of the guilt of sin, formerly periodical now occasional. **5** an outburst of joy. **Jubilee clip**® *n.* an adjustable metal band placed around a tube, hose etc. to form a watertight connection. [OF *jubilé*, late L *jūbilaeus* (assim. to *jūbil*, see JUBILATE[1]), Gr. *iōbēlaios*, of or relating to the jubilee, from *ibōbēlos*, Heb. *yōbēl*, orig., ram, ram's-horn trumpet]

Jud. *abbr.* Judith.

Judaeo- (judē´ō), (*N Am.*) **Judeo-** *comb. form* of or relating to the Jews or Judaism. **Judaeophobe** (judē´əfōb) *n.* a person who fears or dislikes the Jews. **Judaeophobia** (-fō´biə) *n.* [Gr. *Iudaios*; see JUDAIC]

Judaic (joodā´ik), **Judaical** *a.* of or relating to the Jews, Jewish. **Judaically** *adv.* **Judaism** (joo´-) *n.* **1** the religious doctrines and rites of the Jews, according to the law of Moses. **2** conformity to such doctrines and rites. **Judaist** *n.* **Judaize, Judaise** *v.t., v.i.* **Judaization** (-zā´shən) *n.* **Judaizer** *n.* [L *Judāicus*, Gr. *Ioudaïkos*, from *Ioudais*, JEW]

Judas (joo´dəs) *n.* **1** a traitor. **2** **(judas)** a Judas hole. **Judas-coloured** *a.* red, reddish (from a tradition that Judas had red hair). **Judas hole, Judas window** *n.* a small hole cut in a door etc. to enable a person to pry into a room. **Judas tree** *n.* the leguminous tree, *Cercis siliquastrum*, which flowers before the leaves appear (trad. the tree on which Judas hanged himself). [*Judas* Iscariot]

judder (jŭd´ə) *v.i.* **1** to wobble. **2** to vibrate. **3** in singing, to make rapid changes in intensity during the emission of a note. ~*n.* **1** a wobble. **2** the vibration of an aircraft. [prob. JAR[1], SHUDDER]

Judeo- JUDAEO-.

Judg. *abbr.* Judges.

judge (jŭj) *n.* **1** a civil officer invested with power to hear and determine causes in a court of justice. **2** a person authorized to decide a dispute or contest. **3** (*N Am.*) any person who sits in judgement, from a Supreme Court judge to a local magistrate. **4** a person skilled in deciding on relative merits, a connoisseur. **5** (*Hist.*) a chief civil and military magistrate among the Jews, from the death of Joshua to the Kings. ~*v.t.* **1** to decide (a question). **2** to hear or try (a cause). **3** to pass sentence upon. **4** to examine and form an opinion upon (an exhibition etc.). **5** to criticize. **6** (*coll.*) to consider, to estimate, to decide. **7** (*Hist.*) to act as chief magistrate over (the Jews), to rule. ~*v.i.* **1** to hear and determine a case. **2** to give sentence. **3** to form or give an opinion. **4** to come to a conclusion. **5** to criticize, to be censorious. **6** to sit in judgement. **judge advocate** *n.* (*pl.* **judge advocates)** an officer in charge of proceedings at a court martial. **Judge Advocate General** *n.* (*pl.* **Judge Advocates General)** an officer who advises the crown on military law and courts martial. **judgement, judgment** *n.* **1** the act of judging. **2** a judicial decision, a sentence of a court of justice. 3 discernment, discrimination. 4 the capacity for arriving at reasonable conclusions leading to well-adapted behaviour, esp. as indicated by conduct in the practical affairs of life. 5 criticism. 6 the critical faculty. 7 opinion, estimate. 8 a misfortune regarded as sent by God. **against one's better judgement** contrary to one's preferred course of action. **to reserve judgement** RESERVE. **judgemental** (-men´-) *a.* 1 involving judgement. 2 (over-) critical. **judgementally** *adv.* **judgement by default** *n.* (*Law*) a decree against a defendant who does not appear. **Judgement Day** *n.* the end of the world. **judgement debt** *n.* a debt secured by a judge's order, under which an execution can be levied at any time. **judgement of Solomon** *n.* any judgement designed to reveal the false claimant (after Solomon in 1 Kings iii.16–28). **judgement-seat** *n.* 1 the seat or bench on which judges sit. 2 a court, a tribunal. **judger** *n.* **Judges** *n.* the seventh book of the Old Testament. **Judges' Rules** *n.* (*pl.*) in English law, a set of rules governing the behaviour of the police towards suspects. **judgeship** *n.* **judge's marshal** *n.* an official who accompanies a judge on circuit. **judgingly** *adv.* [ME and OF *juge*, L *iūdex -icem*, (*jūs*, law, *dic-*, root of *dicāre*, to point out, cp. INDICATE)]

judicature (joo´dikəchə) *n.* 1 the administration of justice by trial and judgement. 2 the authority of a judge. 3 a court of justice. 4 the jurisdiction of a court. 5 judges collectively. **judicable** *a.* **judicative** *a.* **judicatory** *a.* of or relating to the administration of justice. ~*n.* (*pl.* **judicatories**) 1 a court of justice. 2 the administration of justice. [F, from med. L *jūdicātura*, from *judicāre*, to JUDGE]

judicial (joodish´əl) *a.* 1 of, relating to or proper to courts of law or the administration of justice. 2 proceeding from a court of justice. 3 showing judgement. 4 critical, discriminating. 5 impartial. 6 regarded as a divine judgement. **judicial factor** *n.* (*Sc. Law*) an administrator appointed by the Court of Session to manage estates. **judicially** *adv.* **judicial murder** *n.* capital punishment inflicted as the result of a legal but unjust sentence. **judicial separation** *n.* separation of married persons by court decree. **judiciary** *a.* 1 judicial. 2 passing judgement. ~*n.* (*pl.* **judiciaries**) a judicature. **judicious** *a.* 1 sagacious, clear-headed, discerning. 2 wise, prudent. 3 done with reason or judgement. **judiciously** *adv.* **judiciousness** *n.* [L *jūdiciālis*, from *jūdicium*, a trial, judgement, from *jūdex*, JUDGE]

Usage note The adjectives *judicial* and *judicious* should not be confused: *judicial* relates to law and legal judgements, and *judicious* to discernment or intellectual judgement.

judicium Dei (joodisiəm dā´ē) *n.* the judgement of God. [L]

judo (joo´dō) *n.* a modern sport derived from a form of ju-jitsu. **judoist** *n.* **judoka** (joo´dōkə) *n.* a person who is an expert in, or practises judo. [Jap. *jū*, gentle, *dō*, way]

Judy (joo´di) *n.* (*pl.* **Judies**) 1 Punch's wife in the Punch and Judy show. 2 (*sl.*) (*also* **judy**) a woman, a girl, a sweetheart. [short for *Judith*]

jug[1] (jŭg) *n.* 1 a vessel, usu. with a swelling body, narrow neck, and handle, for holding liquids. 2 the contents of this. 3 (*sl.*) a prison, a lock-up. 4 (*pl.*, *sl.*) a woman's breasts. ~*v.t.* (*pres.p.* **jugging**, *past*, *p.p.* **jugged**) 1 (*usu. p.p.*) to stew (a hare) in a covered vessel, orig. in a jug or jar. 2 (*sl.*) to imprison. **jugful** *n.* (*pl.* **jugfuls**). [etym. uncertain]

jug[2] (jŭg) *v.i.* (*pres.p.* **jugging**, *past*, *p.p.* **jugged**) (of the nightingale etc.) to make a sound like 'jug'. **jug-jug** *n.* [imit.]

jugal (joo´gəl) *a.* of or relating to the cheekbone. [L *jugālis*, from *jugum*, yoke]

jugate (joo´gət) *a.* (*Bot.*) having leaflets in pairs. [L *jugātus*, p.p. of *jugāre*, to couple, as JUGAL]

Jugendstil (yoo´gəntshtēl) *n.* art nouveau in Germany, Austria etc. [G, *Jugend*, youth, *Stil*, style]

juggernaut (jŭg´ənawt) *n.* 1 a very large articulated lorry (causing damage to the environment). 2 a relentless destroying force or object. 3 (**Juggernaut**) a belief, institution etc., to which one is ruthlessly sacrificed or by which one is ruthlessly destroyed. [Hind. *Jagganāth*, Sansk. *Jagganātha*, lord of the world (*jugat*, world, *nātha*, lord): Vishnu in his eighth avatar, whose idol at Krishna or Puri in Orissa is annually dragged in a procession on a huge car, under the wheels of which fanatics are said to have thrown themselves]

juggins (jŭg´inz) *n.* (*sl.*) a blockhead, a dolt. [perh. from proper name]

juggle (jŭg´əl) *v.i.* 1 to play tricks by sleight of hand, to conjure. 2 to throw in the air and catch several objects, such as balls, continuously so that some are in the air all the time. 3 to practise artifice or imposture (with). ~*v.t.* 1 to deceive by trickery. 2 to obtain, convey etc. (away, out of etc.) by trickery. 3 to manipulate (facts, figures etc.) in order to deceive. 4 to try to keep several things (such as jobs etc.) going at the same time. ~*n.* 1 a trick by sleight of hand. 2 an imposture. **juggler** *n.* **jugglery** *n.* [from OF *jogleor*, juggler, late L *joculator -torem* from *joculāre*, L *joculārī*, to jest, from *joculus*, dim. of *jocus*, JOKE]

Jugoslav YUGOSLAV.

jugular (jŭg´ūlə) *a.* 1 belonging to the neck or throat. 2 (of fish) having the ventral fins anterior to the pectoral. ~*n.* a jugular vein. **to go for the jugular** to attack someone where they are most vulnerable or most likely to be harmed. **jugular vein** *n.* any of several large veins of the neck which return the blood from the head. **jugulate** (-lāt) *v.t.* 1 to kill by cutting the throat. 2 (*Med.*) to put an end to (a disease etc.) by drastic measures. [L *jugūlum*, the collarbone, -AR[1]]

juice (joos) *n.* 1 the watery part of fruits etc. or the fluid part of animal bodies. 2 a bodily secretion. 3 (*coll.*) electricity, electric current, petrol. 4 the essence or characteristic element of anything. **to juice up** (*sl.*) to make more lively. **to step on the juice** (*sl.*) to accelerate a vehicle. **juiceless** *a.* **juicy** *a.* (*comp.* **juicier**, *superl.* **juiciest**) 1 abounding in juice, succulent. 2 (*coll.*) interesting esp. in a titillating or scandalous way. 3 (*coll.*) profitable. **juicily** *adv.* **juiciness** *n.* [OF *jus*, L *jūs*, soup, sauce]

ju-jitsu (joojit´soo), **jiu-jitsu, ju-jutsu** *n.* the Japanese art of wrestling, based on the principle of making one's opponent exert their strength to their own disadvantage. [Jap. *jūjutsu* (*jū*, gentle, *jutsu*, skill)]

ju-ju (joo´joo) *n.* 1 a fetish, an idol credited with supernatural power. 2 the ban or taboo worked by this. [Hausa, perh. from F *joujou*, a toy]

jujube (joo´joob) *n.* 1 the berry-like fruit of *Zizyphus vulgaris* or Z. *jujuba*, spiny shrubs of the buckthorn family, dried as a sweetmeat. 2 a lozenge of sweetened gum arabic or gelatin flavoured with or imitating this. 3 any plant of the genus *Zizyphus*. [F, from late L *jujuba*, L *zizyphum*, Gr. *zizuphon*]

ju-jutsu JU-JITSU.

jukebox (jook´boks) *n.* an automatic record or disc player, usu. in a public place, in which coins are inserted and buttons pressed to select the relevant tunes. [Gullah *juke*, disorderly, of W Afr. origin]

Jul. *abbr.* July.

julep (joo´ləp) *n.* 1 a sweet drink, esp. a preparation with some liquid used as a vehicle for medicine, a stimulant composed of spirit, usu. flavoured with mint. 2 (*NAm.*) a drink of spirits, sugar, ice and mint. [F, from Sp. *julepe*, Arab. *julāb*, Pers. *gulāb* (*gul*, rose, *āb*, water)]

Julian (joo´liən) *a.* of, relating to or originated by Julius

Caesar. **Julian calendar** *n.* the calendar instituted by him in 46 BC. **Julian year** *n.* the year of this, containing 365¼ days.

julienne (joolien´) *n.* **1** a clear soup made from meat with chopped or shredded vegetables. **2** any foodstuff, esp. vegetables, cut into short thin strips. **3** a variety of pear. [F, from *Jules* or *Julien*]

Juliet cap (joo´liet) *n.* a small close-fitting cap worn esp. by brides. [*Juliet* in Shakespeare's *Romeo and Juliet*]

July (jəlī´) *n.* (*pl.* **Julys**) the seventh month of the year. [A-F *julie*, L *Jūlius*, after *Jūlius* Caesar]

jumble (jŭm´bəl) *v.t.* **1** to mix confusedly. **2** to throw or put together without order. ~*v.i.* **1** to be mixed in a confused way. **2** to move (about, along etc.) confusedly. ~*n.* **1** a confused mixture. **2** a muddle, disorder, confusion. **3** articles donated to, or suitable for, a jumble sale. **jumble sale** *n.* a sale of miscellaneous articles at a bazaar etc. **jumble shop** *n.* **jumbly** *a.* [prob. onomat.]

jumbo (jŭm´bō) *n.* (*pl.* **jumbos**) **1** a huge, unwieldy person, animal or thing, esp. a large elephant. **2** a jumbo jet. **3** an oversized object. ~*a.* huge, unwieldy or oversized. **jumboesque** (-esk´) *a.* **jumboism** *n.* **jumbo jet** *n.* a very large jet-propelled aircraft. **jumbo-size, jumbo-sized** *a.* of much larger than usual size. [etym. uncertain, used as the proper name of a famous elephant (sold from the Zoological Gardens, London, to Barnum and killed by accident in 1885)]

jumbuck (jŭm´bŭk) *n.* (*Austral., coll.*) a sheep. [Austral. Abor. pidgin English]

jumelle (joomel´, zhoo-) *a.* twin, paired. [F, from L *gemellus*]

jump (jŭmp) *v.i.* **1** to throw oneself from the ground by a sudden movement of the muscles of the legs and feet. **2** to spring, to leap, to bound. **3** to move suddenly (along, up, out) with such springs or bounds. **4** to start or rise (up) abruptly. **5** to change or move suddenly from one topic to another. **6** to agree, to tally (with or together). ~*v.t.* **1** to pass over or cross by leaping. **2** to cause to leap over. **3** to skip (a chapter, pages etc.). **4** to get on or off (a train etc.) illegally. **5** to pounce on or attack. **6** to take or appropriate (land etc.). **7** to start (a car) using jump leads. **8** (of a train) to come off (a track). **9** to pass through (a red traffic light). **10** (*sl.*) (of a man) to have sexual intercourse with. ~*n.* **1** the act of jumping. **2** a leap, a spring, a bound. **3** a start, an involuntary nervous movement. **4** (*pl.*) convulsive twitching as in delirium tremens. **5** (*pl.*) nervousness or anxiety. **6** a sudden rise (in price, value etc.). **7** an obstacle to be jumped. **8** a break, a gap. **9** (*Geol.*) a fault. **one jump ahead** one stage further than someone else. **on the jump** (*coll.*) in a hurry. **to get/ have the jump on** (*coll.*) to get or have an advantage over (a person). **to jump a claim** to seize upon a mining claim by force or fraud. **to jump at 1** to accept eagerly. **2** to reach hastily (as a conclusion). **to jump bail** BAIL[1]. **to jump down someone's throat** (*coll.*) to answer or interrupt violently. **to jump on/ upon 1** to reprimand, abuse, or assail violently. **2** to pounce upon. **to jump out of one's skin** (*coll.*) to be startled. **to jump ship** (of a sailor etc.) to leave a ship without permission, to desert. **to jump the gun** GUN. **to jump the queue** to get ahead of one's turn. **to jump to it** (*coll.*) to act swiftly. **jumpable** *a.* **jumped-up** *a.* (*coll.*) upstart. **jumping** *n., a.* **jumping bean, jumping seed** *n.* the seed of various plants belonging to the Euphorbiaceae, which jump about through the movements of larvae inside them. **jumping deer** *n.* the black-tailed deer found west of the Mississippi. **jumping jack** *n.* **1** a toy figure whose limbs move when a string is pulled. **2** a small firework which jumps along the ground with small explosions. **jumping Jehoshaphat** *int.* used as a mild expletive. **jumping-off place, jumping-off point** *n.* a starting point. **jump jet** *n.* a jet aircraft that can take off and land vertically. **jump lead** *n.* each of a pair of cables for supplying power to start a vehicle from another battery. **jump-off** *n.* an extra, deciding round in a showjumping contest. **jump rope** *n.* (*N Am.*) a skipping rope. **jump seat** *n.* **1** a movable seat. **2** an open buggy with a shifting seat or seats. **jump-start** *v.t.* to start (a car) by pushing it and then engaging gear. ~*n.* the act of jump-starting (a car). **jumpsuit** *n.* a one-piece garment consisting of combined trousers and top. **jumpy** *a.* (*comp.* **jumpier,** *superl.* **jumpiest**) **1** moving or proceeding with jumps and jerks. **2** (*coll.*) nervous, easily startled. **jumpily** *adv.* **jumpiness** *n.* [prob. onomat. (cp. G dial. *gumpen*, Dan. *gumpe*, Swed. dial. *gumpa*)]

jumper[1] (jŭm´pə) *n.* **1** a knitted or crocheted woollen upper garment. **2** a loose, coarse outer jacket worn by sailors, labourers etc. **3** (*N Am.*) a pinafore dress. **jumper-suit** *n.* a woman's jacket and skirt made of a stockingette material. [perh. ult. from OF *juppe*, jacket, tunic, from Arab. *jubbah*]

jumper[2] (jŭm´pə) *n.* **1** a person who, or animal or thing which jumps or leaps. **2** (*pl., Hist.*) certain Welsh Methodists in the 18th cent. and other religious sects who danced or jumped during worship. **3** a hopper, a jumping insect. **4** a tool or implement worked with a jumping motion. **5** a short wire used to shorten a circuit, bypass a component etc. **6** a rope made fast to stop a yard, mast, etc. jumping. **7** a quarryman's boring-tool. **jumper cable** *n.* (*esp. N Am.*) a jump lead. [JUMP]

Jun. *abbr.* **1** June. **2** Junior.

juncaceous (jŭngkā´shəs) *a.* **1** of or resembling rushes. **2** belonging to the family Juncaceae. **juncal** (jŭng´-) *a.* [L *juncus*, rush, -ACEOUS]

junco (jŭng´kō) *n.* (*pl.* **juncos, juncoes**) any small American bunting of the genus *Junco*, which has a greyish plumage. [Sp., from L *juncus*, rush]

junction (jŭnk´shən) *n.* **1** the act of joining or the state of being joined, a combination. **2** a joint, a point or place of union, esp. the point where lines of railways meet. **3** in electronics, a region between regions of differing electrical properties in a semiconductor. **junction box** *n.* an earthed box in which wires and cables can be safely connected. [L *junctio*, from *jungere*, to JOIN]

Usage note The meanings of the nouns *junction* and *juncture* overlap, but in general *junction* refers to a place, and *juncture* to a point in time.

juncture (jŭnk´chə) *n.* **1** a junction, a union. **2** the place, line, or point at which two things are joined, a joint, an articulation. **3** a point of time marked by the occurrence of critical events or circumstances. [L *junctūra*, cp. JUNCTION]

Usage note See note under JUNCTION.

June (joon) *n.* the sixth month of the year. **June bug** *n.* (*esp. N Am.*) an insect or beetle that appears about June. [L *Jūnius*]

Jungian (yoong´iən) *a.* of or relating to the psychoanalytical system of Carl Jung, 1875–1961. ~*n.* an adherent of Jungian psychoanalysis.

jungle (jŭng´gəl) *n.* **1** land covered with forest trees or dense, matted vegetation. **2** a place of ruthless competition. **3** anything difficult to negotiate, understand etc. **4** a confusing mass. **5** (*also* **jungle music**) a type of fast dance music influenced by reggae and soul. **jungle bear** *n.* the Indian sloth bear, *Melursus ursinus.* **jungle cat** *n.* a small wild cat, *Felis chaus*, of Indochina. **jungle cock** *n.* a male jungle fowl. **jungled** *a.* **jungle fever** *n.* a remittent tropical fever, a form of malaria. **jungle fowl** *n.* **1** any of various Far Eastern birds, of the genus *Gallus*, related to pheasants. **2** MEGAPODE. **jungle hen** *n.* a female jungle fowl. **jungle juice** *n.* (*sl.*) alcoholic liquor, esp. of poor quality or home-made. **jungli** (-gli) *a.* uncouth, unrefined. **jungly** *a.* [Hind. *jangal*, from Sansk. *jangala*, desert]

junior (joon´yə) *a.* **1** the younger (esp. as distinguishing a son from his father of the same name, or two of the same surname). **2** lower in standing. ~*n.* **1** a person younger or of lower standing than another. **2** (*N Am.*) a son. **juniorate** *n.* in the Society of Jesus, a two years' course of higher studies for juniors before they enter the priesthood. **junior college** *n.* (*N Am.*) a college providing a two-year course esp. as the first part of a four-year course. **junior common room, junior combination room** *n.* (in some colleges and universities) a common room for the use of undergraduates. **junior high school** *n.* (*N Am.*) a school between elementary school and high school. **juniority** (-nio´-) *n.* **junior lightweight** *n.* **1** a professional boxer in the lower weight range of the lightweight category. **2** this weight category. **junior management** *n.* **1** the lowest level of management in an organization. **2** the managers at this level. **junior middleweight** *n.* **1** a professional boxer in the lower weight range of the middleweight category. **2** this weight category. **junior school** *n.* (in England and Wales), a school for pupils aged about 7 to 11. **junior service** *n.* the Army. **juniorship** *n.* **junior technician** *n.* a person next above senior aircraftman or aircraftwoman in the RAF. **junior welterweight** *n.* **1** a professional boxer in the lower weight range of the welterweight category. **2** this weight category. [L *jūnior*, comp. of *juvenis*, young]

Usage note An implicit double comparative *more junior* is occasionally encountered, but it is best avoided: *junior* already includes the notion of 'more'. However *junior* does not function as a true comparative in English, and should not be followed by *than* (the correct form is *junior to*).

juniper (joo´nipə) *n.* any evergreen shrub or tree of the genus *Juniperus*, esp. *J. communis*, the berries of which are used to flavour gin. [L *jūniperus*, etym. uncertain]

junk[1] (jŭngk) *n.* **1** rubbish, valueless odds and ends. **2** (*sl.*) narcotic drugs, esp. heroin. **3** pieces of old cable and rope cut into lengths for making mats, swabs, gaskets, fenders, oakum etc. **4** salt beef supplied to ships bound on long voyages, from its being as tough as old rope. **5** (*sl.*) drugs. **6** a lump of fibrous tissue in a sperm whale's head, containing spermaceti. ~*v.t.* **1** to discard, abandon. **2** to cut into junks. **junk bond** *n.* a bond giving a high yield but low security. **junk call** *n.* an unsolicited telephone call, usu. trying to sell some commodity or service. **junk-dealer** *n.* a marine-store dealer. **junk fax** *n.* an unsolicited fax, usu. of advertising material. **junk food** *n.* food of little nutritional value, quick to prepare. **junkie, junky** *n.* (*pl.* **junkies**) (*sl.*) a drug addict. **junk mail** *n.* unsolicited mail, usu. advertising material. **junk-ring** *n.* a steam-tight packing round a piston. **junk shop** *n.* a shop where second-hand goods of all kinds are sold. **junk-wad** *n.* an oakum wad for a muzzle-loading gun, placed between the charge and the ball. **junkyard** *n.* a scrapyard. [etym. doubtful]

junk[2] (jŭngk) *n.* a flat-bottomed vessel with lugsails, used in the Chinese seas. [Port. and Sp. *junco*, Javanese *djong*]

junk[3] (jŭngk) *n.* a lump or chunk of anything. **junk-bottle** *n.* (*N Am.*) a stout bottle of green or black glass. [prob. corr. of CHUNK]

junker (yung´kə) *n.* (*Hist.*) **1** a young German noble. **2** a member of the German reactionary aristocratic party. **junkerdom** (-dəm), **junkerism** *n.* [G (*jung*, YOUNG, HERR)]

junket (jŭng´kit) *n.* **1** a dish of curds sweetened and flavoured, and served with cream. **2** a sweetmeat, delicacy, a confection. **3** a feast, a banquet, an entertainment. **4** a supposed business trip (at public expense) which is really for pleasure. ~*v.i.* (*pres.p.* **junketing**, *past, p.p.* **junketed**) to feast, to picnic, to make good cheer. ~*v.t.* to regale at a feast. **junketer** *n.* **junketing** *n.* [MF *juncade* (cp. Norm. patois *jonquette*), Prov. *joncada*, It. *giuncata*, p.p. of *giuncare*, from *giunco*, L *juncus*, rush]

junkie, junky JUNK[1].

Juno (joo´nō) *n.* (*pl.* **Junos**) a beautiful queenly woman. **Junoesque** (-esk´) *a.* [L, the wife of Jupiter, identified with the Greek Hera]

Junr. *abbr.* Junior.

junta (jŭn´tə, hun´-) *n.* **1** a group, esp. of military officers who take control of a country e.g. after a coup. **2** a cabal. **3** a legislative or administrative council, esp. in Spain, Portugal, and S America. [Sp., from L *juncta*, fem. p.p. of *jungere*, to JOIN]

junto (jŭn´tō) *n.* (*pl.* **juntos**) **1** a secret political or other council. **2** a cabal, clique, a faction. [erron. from JUNTA]

jupati palm (joopətē´) *n.* a S American palm, *Raphia taedigera*, yielding a fibre resembling raffia. [Tupi *jupati*, PALM[1]]

Jupiter (joo´pitə) *n.* the largest planet of the solar system. [L (*Jupiter*, king of the gods, from OL *Jovis*, JOVE, L *pater*, father)]

jupon (joo´pən, zhoo´-) *n.* a skirt or petticoat. [F *jupe*, a skirt]

jural (joo´rəl) *a.* of or relating to law or jurisprudence, esp. with regard to rights and obligations. [L *jūs jūris*, law, -AL[1]]

Jurassic (jooras´ik) *a.* **1** belonging to the oolitic limestone formation well developed in the Jura Mts. **2** belonging to the second period of the Mesozoic era. ~*n.* the Jurassic system or period, coming between the Triassic and the Cretaceous. [F *jurassique*, from *Jura* (cp. LIASSIC (under LIAS))]

jurat[1] (joo´rat) *n.* **1** a person under oath. **2** a member of a corporation corresponding to an alderman, esp. of the Cinque Ports. **3** a magistrate in the Channel Islands. **jurant** *a.* taking an oath. ~*n.* a person who takes an oath. **juratory** *a.* containing an oath. [F, from med. L *jurātus*, one who is sworn, orig. p.p. of L *jurāre*, to swear]

jurat[2] (joo´rat) *n.* an official statement of the circumstances in which an affidavit is made. [L *juratum*, neut. p.p. of *jurare*, as JURAT[1]]

juridical (joorid´ikəl) *a.* of or relating to the administration of justice, to courts of justice, or to jurisprudence. **juridically** *adv.* [L *jūridicus* (*jūs jūris*, law, *dic-*, stem of *dicāre*, to proclaim)]

juried JURY.

jurisconsult (jooriskənsŭlt´) *n.* **1** a person learned in law, esp. civil or international law. **2** a jurist. [L *jūrisconsultus* (*jūris*, as JURIDICAL, *consultus*, see CONSULT)]

jurisdiction (joorisdik´shən) *n.* **1** the legal power or right of administering justice, making and enforcing laws, or exercising other authority. **2** the district or extent within which such power may be exercised. **jurisdictional** *a.* **jurisdictive** *a.* having jurisdiction. [F, from L *jūrisdictiōnem*, nom. *-tio* (*jūris*, see JURIDICAL, *dictio*, DICTION)]

jurisprudence (joorisproo´dəns) *n.* **1** the science or philosophy of law. **2** the science of human laws, constitutions, and rights. **3** the legal system of a particular country. **4** skill in law. **jurisprudent** *n., a.* **jurisprudential** (-den´-) *a.* [L *jūrisprudentia* (*jūris*, see JURIDICAL, *prudentia*, knowledge)]

jurist (joo´rist) *n.* **1** a person learned in the law. **2** a writer on legal subjects. **3** a student of law. **4** (*N Am.*) a lawyer. **5** (*N Am.*) a judge. **juristic** (-ris´-), **juristical** (-ris´tikəl) *a.* **juristically** *adv.* [F *juriste*, med. L *jūrista*, from *jūs jūris*, law]

juror (joo´rə) *n.* **1** a person who serves on a jury. **2** a person who takes an oath. [A-F *jurour*, OF *jureor*, L *jūrātōrem*, nom. *-tor*, from *jūrāre*, to swear]

jury (joo´ri) *n.* (*pl.* **juries**) **1** a body of persons selected according to law and sworn to try, and give a true verdict upon, questions put before them. **2** a body of persons selected to award prizes at public shows, exhibitions etc. **common jury** COMMON. **grand jury** GRAND. **petty jury** PETTY. **special jury** SPECIAL. **the jury is (still) out** a decision has not yet been reached. **juried** *a.* (*NAm.*) judged or selected by a jury. **jury box** *n.* the enclosure in a court where the jury sit. **juryman** *n.* (*pl.* **jurymen**). **jurywoman** *n.* (*pl.* **jurywomen**). [A-F *juree*, OF *jurée*, an oath, an inquest, a body of sworn men, p.p. of *jurer*, L *jūrāre*, to swear]

jury- (joo´ri) *comb.form* makeshift, temporary. **jurymast** (joo´rimahst) *n.* (*Naut.*) a temporary mast erected in place of one carried away. **jury-rigged** *a.* **1** (*Naut.*) having makeshift rigging. **2** makeshift. [perh. ult. from OF *ajurie*, aid, succour, from L *adjūtare*, to AID]

jussive (jŭs´iv) *a.* (*Gram.*) expressing command. ~*n.* a form or construction expressing command. [L *jussus*, p.p. of *jubēre*, to command]

just[1] (jŭst) *a.* **1** acting according to what is right and fair. **2** fair, equitable, impartial, upright, honest. **3** exact, accurate, precise. **4** fit, proper, suitable. **5** merited, deserved. **6** righteous. ~*adv.* **1** exactly, precisely. **2** barely, only, with nothing to spare. **3** precisely at the moment. **4** only a moment ago, a very little time ago. **5** (*coll.*) perfectly, quite. **6** (*coll.*) simply, merely. **7** (*coll.*) really, indeed. **just about 1** (*coll.*) nearly. **2** (*coll.*) more or less. **just in case** as a precaution. **just now 1** a very little time since, but a moment ago. **2** at this instant. **just so 1** exactly. **2** that is right. **3** with great precision. **to get one's just deserts** DESERT[3]. **to sleep the sleep of the just** SLEEP. **just-in-time** *a.* of or relating to an industrial method in which components etc. are produced as needed, eliminating waste and the need for storage. **justly** *adv.* **justness** *n.* [F *juste*, L *justus*, from *jūs*, right]

just[2] JOUST.

justice (jŭs´tis) *n.* **1** the quality of being just. **2** fairness in dealing with others. **3** uprightness, rectitude, honesty. **4** just requital of deserts. **5** the authoritative administration or maintenance of law and right. **6** a person legally commissioned to hold courts, hear causes, and administer justice between individuals. **7** a magistrate. **8** a judge, esp. of the Supreme Court of Judicature in England or of the US Supreme Court or a state Supreme Court. **9** judicial proceedings. **in justice to** out of fairness to. **Mr Justice** MR. **Mrs Justice** MRS. **to do justice to 1** to treat fairly. **2** to treat appreciatively. **to do oneself justice** to acquit oneself worthily of one's ability. **with justice** with good reason. **Justice-Clerk** *n.* (*Sc. Law*) the President of the Outer House or Second Division of the Court of Session, and Vice-President of the High Court of Justiciary. **Justice-General** *n.* the highest judge in Scotland, Lord President of the Court of Session. **Justice of the Peace** *n.* a local magistrate commissioned to keep the peace and try cases of felony and other misdemeanours. **justicer** *n.* a justiciary. **justiceship** *n.* **justices in eyre** *n.pl.* (*Hist.*) **1** judges who travelled in circuit to hold courts in the different counties. **2** judges of assize. **justiciable** (-tish´i-) *a.* liable to be tried in a court of justice. **justiciar** (-tish´iah) *n.* (*Hist.*) a chief officer or deputy of the Crown (under the Norman and Plantagenet kings) who exercised both judicial and administrative powers. **justiciary** (-əri) *n.* (*pl.* **justiciaries**) an administrator of justice. ~*a.* of or relating to the administration of justice. [OF, from L *justitia*, from *justus*, just]

justify (jŭs´tifī) *v.t.* (*3rd pers. sing. pres.* **justifies**, *pres.p.* **justifying**, *past, p.p.* **justified**) **1** to prove or show to be just or right. **2** to vindicate, to make good, to show grounds for. **3** to exonerate. **4** (*Theol.*) to declare free from the penalty of sin. **5** to adjust and make (lines of type) even in length. ~*v.i.* (of lines of type) to coincide or range uniformly. **justifiable** *a.* **justifiability** (-bil´-), **justifiableness** *n.* **justifiable homicide** *n.* the killing of a person in a lawful fashion, esp. in self-defence or in carrying out a death sentence. **justifiably** *adv.* **justification** (-fikā´shən) *n.* **justificative** (jŭs´-), **justificatory** *a.* **justificator, justifier** *n.* [F *justifier*, L *justificāre* (*jūs*, JUSTICE, *facere*, to make)]

justle JOSTLE.

jut (jŭt) *v.i.* (*pres.p.* **jutting**, *past, p.p.* **jutted**) to project, to protrude, to stick (out). ~*n.* a projection, a protruding point or part. **jut-window** *n.* a projecting window. [var. of JET[2]]

Jute (joot) *n.* a member of a Germanic people orig. from Jutland, who settled in Britain in the 5th–6th cents. **Jutish** *a.* [med. L *Jutae*, *Juti*, OE, *Eotas*, *Iotas*, people of Jutland]

jute (joot) *n.* the fibre from the inner bark of two Asian plants, *Corchorus capsularis* and *C. olitorius*, from which fabrics, paper and cordage are prepared. [Bengali *jhōto* (pop. *jhūto*), Sansk. *jūta*, *jatā*, a braid of hair]

juvenescent (joovənes´ənt) *a.* growing or being young. **juvenescence** *n.* [L *juvenescere*, from *juvenis*, young]

juvenile (joo´vənīl) *a.* **1** young, youthful. **2** befitting or characteristic of youth. **3** immature. ~*n.* **1** a young person. **2** a book for children. **3** an actor who usu. performs the part of a young person. **juvenile court** *n.* a court for young people under 17 or (in the US) 18 years of age. **juvenile delinquent** *n.* an offender under 17 years of age. **juvenile deliquency** *n.* **juvenilely** *adv.* **juvenileness** *n.* **juvenile offender** *n.* a criminal under 17 years of age. **juvenilia** (-nil´iə) *n.pl.* writings etc., produced in youth. **juvenility** (-nil´-) *n.* [L *juvenīlis*, from *juvenis*]

juxtapose (jŭkstəpōz´) *v.t.* **1** to place (things) side by side. **2** to place (a thing) next to another. **juxtaposition** (-zish´ən) *n.* **juxtapositional** *a.* [F *juxtaposer* (L *juxtā*, next, F *poser*, to put)]

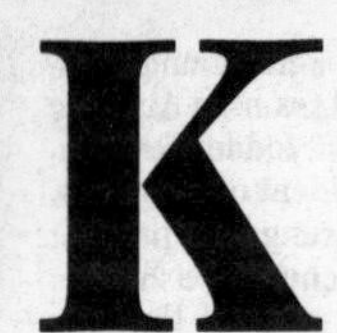

K[1] (kā), **k** (*pl.* **Ks, K's**) the 11th letter of the English and other versions of the Roman alphabet, corresponding to the Greek kappa (Κ, κ). It is pronounced as a voiceless velar plosive. ~*symbol* **1** the solar constant. **2** an unstable type of meson. **K-meson** *n.* a kaon.

K[2] *abbr.* **1** Kelvin(s). **2** King, King's. **3** Knight. **4** Köchel (catalogue of Mozart's work). **5** 1024 words, bytes or bits (from *kilo-*). **6** one thousand (from *kilo-*).

K[3] *chem. symbol* potassium.

k *abbr.* **1** karat. **2** kilo, kilo-. **3** knot, knots. **4** (*Math.*) a constant.

ka (kah) *n.* (*pl.* **kas**) the spirit of a person or statue in ancient Egyptian mythology, born with but surviving the individual. [Egypt]

Kaaba (kah´bə, -əbə), **Caaba** *n.* a sacred building in Mecca, containing the black stone, which Muslims face when they pray. [Arab. *Qa'ba*]

kaama (kah´mə) *n.* the hartebeest. [Bantu]

kaava KAVA.

kabbala, kabala CABBALA.

kabuki (kəboo´ki) *n.* a highly-stylized, traditional and popular form of Japanese drama, based on legend and acted only by men, in elaborate costumes. [Jap. *kabu*, music, *ki*, art]

Kabyle (kəbīl´) *n.* **1** a member of an agricultural branch of the Berber people inhabiting the highlands of Algeria and Tunisia. **2** the Berber dialect spoken by the Kabyles. [F, from Arab. *Qabāil*, pl. of *qabīla*, tribe]

kachina (kəchē´nə) *n.* **1** any of the spirits of the ancestors of the Pueblo Indians. **2** a dancer representing a kachina in a ceremony. **kachina doll** *n.* a doll representing a kachina. [Hopi *qačina*, supernatural]

kadaitcha KURDAITCHA.

Kaddish (kad´ish), **Qaddish** *n.* a form of thanksgiving and prayer used by the Jews, esp. in mourning. [Aram. *qaddīsh*, holy]

kadi CADI.

Kaffir (kaf´ə), **Kafir** *n.* (*offensive*) **1** a member of the S African Xhosa-speaking people. **2** their language, Xhosa. **3** (*S Afr.*) any black African. **4** (*pl.*) S African mining shares. ~*a.* of or relating to these people or their language. **kaffir beer** *n.* a S African beer made from kaffir corn or millet. **kaffirboom** *n.* a S African tree, *Erythrena caffra*, with orange or red flowers. **kaffir corn** *n.* a variety of sorghum cultivated in S Africa. [Arab. *qāfir*, infidel]

kaffiyeh KEFFIYEH.

Kafir[1] (kaf´ə) *n.* **1** a native of Kafiristan in E Afghanistan. **2** (*offensive*) an infidel. [as KAFFIR]

Kafir[2] KAFFIR.

Kafkaesque (kafkəesk´) *a.* of or like the ideas and work of the Czech novelist Franz Kafka 1883–1924, esp. his ideas on the alienation of man.

kaftan (kaf´tan, -tən), **caftan** *n.* **1** a long belted tunic worn in the East. **2** a woman's long loose dress with wide sleeves. [Turk. *qaftān*]

kagoule CAGOULE.

kahawai (kah´həwī) *n.* a large marine perch, *Arripis trutta*, that resembles a salmon, found in Australian and New Zealand coastal waters. [Maori]

☒ **kahki** common misspelling of KHAKI.

kai (kī) *n.* (*New Zeal.*) food. [Maori]

kaiak KAYAK.

kail KALE.

kaim KAME.

kain CAIN.

kainite (kī´nīt) *n.* hydrous chlorosulphate of magnesium and potassium, used as a fertilizer. [G *Kainit* from Gr. *kainos*, new]

kaiser (kī´zə) *n.* **1** an emperor. **2** (*Hist.*) the Emperor of Germany or Austria. **3** (*Hist.*) the head of the Holy Roman Empire. **kaiserdom** *n.* **kaiserism** *n.* **kaisership** *n.* **Kaiser's war** *n.* the 1914–18 war. [G, from L *Caesar*]

kaizen (kīzen´) *n.* the concept of constant improvement in Japanese business and industry. [Jap., improvement]

kajawah (kəjah´wə) *n.* a pannier or frame carried in pairs on a camel, horse or mule, used as a litter by women and children in some Eastern countries. [Hind. and Pers.]

kaka (kah´kə) *n.* (*pl.* **kakas**) a New Zealand parrot of the genus *Nestor*. **kaka beak** *n.* a shrub with beak-shaped flowers, *Clianthus puniceus*, found in New Zealand. **kakapo** (-pō) *n.* (*pl.* **kakapos**) a flightless parrot of New Zealand, *Strigops habroptilus*, resembling an owl. [Maori]

kakemono (kakimō´nō) *n.* (*pl.* **kakemonos**) a Japanese wall-picture mounted on rollers for putting away. [Jap.]

kaki (kah´ki) *n.* (*pl.* **kakis**) an Asian persimmon, *Diospyros kaki*. [Jap.]

kakistocracy (kakistok´rə´si) *n.* government by the worst citizens. **kakistocrat** (-kis´təkrat) *n.* [Gr. *kakistos*, superl. of *kakos*, bad, -CRACY]

kala-azar (kahləəzah´) *n.* a chronic tropical disease with a high mortality, caused by a protozoan *Leishmania donovani*. [Assamese]

kalanchoe (kalənkō´i) *n.* a succulent plant of the genus *Kalanchoe*, often grown indoors or in a greenhouse, with pink, red or yellow flowers. [Chin.]

Kalashnikov (kalash´nikof) *n.* a type of sub-machine gun made in Russia. [Rus.]

kale (kāl), **kail** *n.* **1** a variety of cabbage with crinkled leaves. **2** (*Sc., North.*) cabbage. **3** (*N Am., sl.*) money. **kaleyard** *n.* (*Sc.*) a kitchen garden. **kaleyard school** *n.* a group of novelists and writers depicting the homely life of Scottish lowlanders, with liberal use of broad dialect. [var. of COLE]

kaleidophone (kəlī´dəfōn) *n.* an instrument for exhibiting the character of sound waves by means of a vibrating bar or plate armed with a reflector. [as KALEIDOSCOPE, with -PHONE]

kaleidoscope (kəlī´dəskōp) *n.* **1** an instrument showing by means of bits of coloured glass, paper etc. and a series of reflecting surfaces, an endless variety of symmetrical forms. **2** any complex, changing pattern. **kaleidoscopic** (-skop´-), **kaleidoscopical** *a.* **kaleidoscopically** *adv.* [Gr. *kalos*, beautiful, *eidos*, appearance, -SCOPE]

kalends CALENDS.

kali (kal´i, kā´-) *n.* a glasswort, *Salsola kali*, from which soda ash was obtained. **kaligenous** (kəlij´-) *a.* **kalinite** (kal´inīt) *n.* (*Mineral.*) native potash alum. [Arab. *qalī*, see ALKALI]

kalian (kahlyahn´) *n.* an Iranian form of hookah. [Pers., from Arab. *qalyan*]

kalif CALIPH.

kalmia (kal´miə) *n.* an evergreen N American flowering

shrub of the genus *Kalmia*. [Peter *Kalm*, 1715–79, Swed. naturalist, professor at Abo]

Kalmuck (kal´mŭk), **Kalmyk** (-mik) *n.* (*pl.* **Kalmuck, Kalmucks, Kalmyk, Kalmyks**) **1** a member of a Mongolian people living in a region extending from W China to the Volga. **2** the language of this people. ~*a.* of or relating to the Kalmuck or their language. [Rus. *Kalmyk*]

kalong (kah´long) *n.* a flying fox, *Pteropus edulis*. [Malay]

kalpa (kal´pə) *n.* a day of Brahma, or a period of 4,320,000 years, constituting the age or cycle of a world. [Sansk.]

kalpak CALPAC.

Kama (kah´mə) *n.* **1** the god of love in the puranas. **2** impure or sensual desire. **Kama Sutra** (soo´trə) *n.* an ancient Hindu book on erotic love. [Sansk.]

kamala (kam´ələ) *n.* **1** an Indian and SE Asian tree, *Mallotus philippinensis*, of the the spurge family. **2** an orange dye obtained from the down on the fruit capsules of this tree. [Sansk.]

kame (kām), **kaim** *n.* a long mound of glacial detritus, an esker. [Sc. and North., var. of COMB]

kameez (kəmēz´) *n.* a type of loose tunic with tight sleeves worn esp. by Muslim women in the Indian subcontinent and S Asia. [Urdu *kamis*]

kamerad (kamərahd´) *int.* comrade, a German form of surrender or appeal for quarter. [G]

kami (kah´mi) *n.* (*pl.* **kami**) **1** a Japanese title, equivalent to lord, given to nobles, ministers, governors etc. **2** in Shinto, a divinity, a god. [Jap.]

kamikaze (kamikah´zi) *n.* a Japanese airman or plane performing a suicidal mission in World War II. ~*a.* **1** of or relating to a kamikaze. **2** (*coll.*) suicidal, self-destructive. [Jap. *kami*, divine, *kaze*, wind]

kampong (kam´pong, kampong´) *n.* a Malay village. [Malay]

Kampuchean (kampuchē´ən) *n.* a native or inhabitant of Kampuchea, a Cambodian. ~*a.* of or relating to Kampuchea, Cambodian. [*Kampuchea*, the official name for Cambodia from 1976–89]

Kan. *abbr.* Kansas.

kana (kah´nə) *n.* a Japanese syllabic system of writing. [Jap.]

kanaka (kənak´ə, kan´-) *n.* **1** an indigenous Hawaiian. **2** a South Sea Islander. **3** (*Hist.*) a Hawaiian or South Sea Islander employed as an indentured labourer on the Queensland sugar plantations. [Hawaiian, a man]

Kanarese (kanərēz´), **Canarese** *n.* (*pl.* **Kanarese, Canarese**) **1** a member of the Dravidian people living largely in Kanara in southern India. **2** the language of this people. ~*a.* of or relating to Kanara or the Kanarese.

kanban (kan´ban) *n.* **1** (*also* **kanban system**) the Japanese system of printing orders on cards during manufacturing processes. **2** a card used in the kanban system. [Jap.]

kanga (kang´gə), **khanga** *n.* a piece of brightly coloured cotton worn as a woman's dress in E Africa. [Swahili]

kangaroo (kang·gəroo´) *n.* **1** any of several marsupial quadrupeds of the genus *Macropus*, native to Australia, Tasmania, New Guinea and adjacent islands, distinguished by their large hind limbs, used for leaping, and short front limbs. **2** (*pl.*) Australian mining shares. ~*v.i.* (*3rd pers. sing. pres.* **kangaroos**, *pres.p.* **kangarooing**, *past, p.p.* **kangarooed**) (*coll.*) (of a car) to move forward jerkily. **kangaroo apple** *n.* **1** any of various Australian shrubs of the genus *Solanum* with fruit like an apple. **2** the edible fruit of such a shrub. **kangaroo closure** *n.* the parliamentary procedure whereby the chairman or speaker decides what shall be discussed (e.g. which amendments to a bill) and what passed over. **kangaroo court** *n.* **1** an irregular court, set up by e.g. the mob, prisoners, or strikers. **2** a court where a fair trial is impossible. **kangaroo dog** *n.* a kind of greyhound used in Australia for hunting. **kangaroo grass** *n.* an Australian grass, *Themeda australis*, used for fodder. **kangaroo mouse** *n.* any small American rodent of the genus *Microdipodops*, inhabiting deserts. **kangaroo paw** *n.* any of several Australian plants of the genus *Anigozanthus* or *Macropidia* with green and red flowers. **kangaroo rat** *n.* **1** any small rodent of the genus *Dipodamys*. **2** any of several rat-like kangaroos. **kangaroo vine** *n.* an evergreen climbing plant, *Cissus antarctica*, grown as a house plant. [Austral. Abor.]

kanji (kan´ji) *n.* (*pl.* **kanjis**) a script for representing Japanese syllables derived from Chinese orthography. [Chin. *han*, Chinese, *tsû*, word]

Kannada (kan´ədə) *n.* the Kanarese language. [Kanarese *Kannada*]

kanoon (kənoon´) *n.* a kind of dulcimer or zither with 50 or 60 strings. [Pers. and Arab. *qānūn*]

Kans. *abbr.* Kansas.

kantar (kan´tə), **cantar** *n.* an Oriental measure of weight, varying from 100 to 130 lb. (45.4–59.0 kg). [Arab. *qintār*, QUINTAL]

Kantian (kan´tiən) *a.* of or relating to the philosophy of Kant. ~*n.* a Kantist. **Kantianism, Kantism** *n.* **Kantist** *n.* a follower of the philosophy of Kant. [Immanuel *Kant*, 1724–1804]

kantikoy (kan´tikoi) *n.* **1** a N American Indian ceremonial dance. **2** a meeting for dancing, a dancing match. [Algonquian]

KANU (kah´noo) *abbr.* Kenya African National Union.

kaolin (kā´əlin) *n.* a porcelain clay (also used medicinally as a poultice or internally) derived principally from the decomposition of feldspar, China clay. **kaolinic** (-lin´-) *a.* **kaolinize, kaolinise** *v.t.* to convert into kaolin. **koalinization** (-zā´shən) *n.* [F, from Chin. *kaoling*, name of a mountain whence orig. obtained (*kao*, high, *ling*, ridge or hill)]

kaon (kā´on) *n.* an unstable type of meson, a K-meson. [K[1], -ON]

kapellmeister (kəpel´mī´stə), **capellmeister** *n.* (*pl.* **kapellmeister, capellmeister**) the musical director of a choir, band or orchestra, esp. a German one. [G from *Kapelle*, med. L *capella*, CHAPEL, *Meister*, MASTER]

kapok (kā´pok) *n.* a fine woolly or silky fibre enveloping the seeds of a tropical tree, *Ceiba pentandra*, used for stuffing cushions etc. [Malay *kāpoq*]

Kaposi's sarcoma (kəpō´siz) *n.* a type of skin cancer often found in people with Aids. [Moritz Kohn *Kaposi*, 1837–1902, Hungarian dermatologist]

kappa (kap´ə) *n.* the tenth letter of the Greek alphabet (Κ, κ).

kaput (kəput´) *a.* (*coll.*) finished, done for, smashed up. [G slang]

karabiner (karəbē´nə) *n.* a metal clip with a spring inside it, for attaching to a piton, used in mountaineering. [G *Karabinerhaken*, carbine hook]

Karaite (keə´rəīt) *n.* a member of a Jewish sect who hold by the literal inspiration of the Scriptures, rejecting rabbinical tradition. **Karaism** *n.* [Heb. *q'rāīm*, readers, -ITE[1]]

karakul (kar´əkul), **caracul** *n.* **1** a breed of sheep from the Bukhara district of Central Asia. **2** the fleece prepared as fur from the lambs of these sheep. [*Karakul*, a village in Bukhara]

karaoke (karə·ōki, kari-) *n.* a leisure activity in which members of an audience can sing solo with prerecorded backing music. **karaoke bar** *n.* [Jap. *kara*, empty, *ōkesutora*, orchestra]

karat CARAT.

karate (kərah´ti) *n.* a traditional Japanese martial art, based on blows and kicks. **karate chop** *n.* a downward blow with the side of the hand. [Jap., empty hand]

Karen (kəren´) *n.* **1** a member of a Thai people living in eastern and southern Burma (Myanmar). **2** the language of this people.

karma (kah´mə) *n.* **1** in Buddhism and Hinduism, the results of action, ethical causation as determining future existence, esp. the cumulative consequence of a person's acts in one stage of existence as controlling their destiny in the next. **2** destiny. **karmic** *a.* [Sansk.]

Karoo (kəroo´), **Karroo** *n.* (*pl.* **Karoos, Karroos**) any of the waterless S African tablelands, esp. the Great and the Little Karoo in S Cape Province. [Nama]

kaross (kəros´) *n.* a traditional S African garment made of skins with the hair left on. [Afrikaans *karos*]

karri (ka´ri) *n.* (*pl.* **karris**) a W Australian timber tree, *Eucalyptus diversicolor.* [Austral. Abor.]

karsey CARZEY.

karst (kahst) *n.* the characteristic scenery of a limestone region with underground streams, caverns and potholes forming a drainage system. [*Karst*, limestone plateau east of the Adriatic]

kart (kaht) *n.* a go-kart. **karting** *n.* go-kart racing.

karyo- (kar´iō), **caryo-** *comb. form* (*Biol.*) relating to the nucleus of an animal or vegetable cell. [Gr. *karuon*, nut]

karyogamy (kariog´əmi) *n.* the fusion of cell nuclei in fertilization.

karyokinesis (kariəkinē´sis) *n.* the series of changes that take place in indirect or mitotic cell division. **karyokinetic** (-net´-) *a.* [Gr. *kinēsis*, motion, from *kinein*, to move]

karyolymph (kar´iōlimf) *n.* the liquid part of a cell nucleus.

karyoplasm (kar´iəplazm) *n.* the protoplasm in the nucleus of a cell.

karyosome (kar´iəsōm) *n.* **1** an aggregate of chromatin in a cell nucleus. **2** the nucleus of a cell.

karyotype (kar´iətīp) *n.* the chromosomes of a cell. **karyotypic** (-tip´-) *a.*

karzy CARZEY.

kasbah (kaz´bah), **casbah** *n.* **1** the castle or fortress in a N African city. **2** the area around this. [Arab.]

kashmir CASHMERE.

Kashmiri (kashmiə´ri) *n.* (*pl.* **Kashmiris**) **1** a native or inhabitant of Kashmir. **2** the language of Kashmir. *~a.* of or relating to Kashmir. [*Kashmir* in the W Himalayas]

kashruth (kashroot´), **kashrut** *n.* **1** the state of being kosher. **2** the Jewish dietary rules. [Heb]

kat KHAT.

kata (kat´ə) *n.* a martial arts exercise consisting of a sequence of movements. [Jap.]

kata- CATA-.

katabasis (katab´əsis) *n.* a military retreat. [Gr. *katabainō*, to go down, inland]

katabatic (katəbat´ik) *a.* (of wind) blowing downhill.

katabolism CATABOLISM.

katakana (katəkah´nə) *n.* an angular form of Japanese syllabary. [Jap.]

kathak (kath´ək, kəthahk´) *n.* a type of Indian classical dance involving mime. [Sansk.]

kathakali (kathəkah´li) *n.* a type of S Indian drama consisting of dance and mime. [Malayalam]

katharevusa (kathərev´əsə), **katharevousa** *n.* a literary form of modern Greek, based on ancient Greek. [Gr.]

kathode CATHODE.

kation CATION.

katipo (kətē´pō) *n.* (*pl.* **katipos**) a venomous spider found in New Zealand and Australia. [Maori]

katydid (kā´tidid) *n.* any of various large green grasshoppers of the genus *Microcentrum* and related genera, common in N America. [imit. of its stridulating sound]

katzenjammer (kat´zənjamə) *n.* **1** a hangover. **2** emotional distress. [G, cat's misery]

kauri (kow´ri) *n.* (*pl.* **kauris**) a New Zealand coniferous forest tree, *Agathis australis.* **kauri gum** *n.* a resinous gum from the kauri. [Maori]

kava (kah´və), **kaava** *n.* **1** a Polynesian shrub, *Piper methysticum.* **2** a beverage prepared from the chewed or pounded roots of this. [Polynesian]

kawakawa (kah´wəkahwə) *n.* an aromatic New Zealand shrub, *Macropiper excelsum.* [Maori]

kayak (kī´ak), **kaiak** *n.* **1** the Eskimo (Inuit) and Alaskan canoe, made of sealskins stretched on a light wooden framework. **2** a small covered canoe resembling this. *~v.i.* (*pres.p.* **kayaking**, *past, p.p.* **kayaked**) to travel in a kayak, to paddle a kayak. [Eskimo (Inuit)]

kayo (kāō´) *n.* (*pl.* **kayos**) a knockout. *~v.t.* (*3rd pers. sing. pres.* **kayoes**, *pres.p.* **kayoing**, *past, p.p.* **kayoed**) to knock someone out. [*KO*]

Kazakh (kəzahk´) *n.* **1** a member of a Turkic people inhabiting Kazakhstan. **2** the language of this people. *~a.* of or relating to the Kazakhs or their language.

kazi CARZEY.

kazoo (kəzoo´) *n.* (*pl.* **kazoos**) a tube of metal or plastic with a membrane covering a hole in the side, through which a player sings or hums to produce sound. [perh. imit. of sound]

KB *abbr.* **1** kilobyte(s). **2** King's Bench. **3** king's bishop. **4** Knight Bachelor. **5** Knight of the Bath.

KBE *abbr.* Knight Commander of the Order of the British Empire.

kbyte *abbr.* kilobyte(s).

KC *abbr.* **1** Kennel Club. **2** King's College. **3** King's Counsel.

kc *abbr.* kilocycle(s).

kcal *abbr.* kilocalorie(s).

KCB *abbr.* Knight Commander of the Order of the Bath.

KCMG *abbr.* Knight Commander of the Order of St Michael and St George.

kc/s *abbr.* kilocycles per second.

KCVO *abbr.* Knight Commander of the Royal Victorian Order.

KD, k.d. *abbr.* knocked down (in price etc.).

KE *abbr.* kinetic energy.

kea (kā´ə) *n.* a brownish green mountain parrot, *Nestor notabilis*, of New Zealand whose diet includes carrion. [Maori, imit. of cry]

keb (keb) *n.* (*Sc., North.*) a ewe that has given birth to a premature or stillborn lamb. [etym. uncertain]

kebab (kibab´), **cabob** (kəbob´) *n.* small pieces of meat, vegetables etc. cooked on skewers. [Arab. *qabāb*, roast meat]

keck[1] (kek) *v.i.* **1** to retch, to heave. **2** to make a retching sound. [imit.]

keck[2] KEX.

ked (ked), **kade** (kād) *n.* a tick infesting sheep, esp. *Melophagus ovinus.* [etym. uncertain]

kedge (kej) *n.* (*Naut.*) a small portable anchor, used in warping. *~v.t.* to move (a ship) by a light cable attached to a kedge. *~v.i.* (of a ship) to move in this way. **kedge anchor, kedger** *n.* a kedge. [cp. CADGE]

kedgeree (kej´ərē) *n.* **1** a stew of rice, pulse, onions, eggs etc., a common Indian dish. **2** a dish of fish, rice, hard-boiled eggs etc. [Hind. *khichrī*, Sansk. *k'rsara*]

keek (kēk) *v.i.* (*Sc., North.*) to peep, to pry. *~n.* a peep. [ME *kyken* (cp. Dut. *kijken*, LG *kîken*)]

keel[1] (kēl) *n.* **1** the principal timber or steel structure of a ship, extending from bow to stern and supporting the whole structure. **2** (*poet.*) a ship. **3** a projecting ridge or longitudinal process. **4** the two lower petals of a papilionaceous corolla. *~v.i.* **1** (of a ship) to roll on its keel. **2** to turn (over), to careen. *~v.t.* to turn up the keel of, to turn over or keel upwards. **to keel over 1** to capsize, to turn over. **2** (*coll.*) to fall over. **keelage** (-ij) *n.* a toll paid by vessels entering certain harbours. **keelboat** *n.* **1** a yacht with a permanent keel. **2** (*N Am.*) a large covered riverboat without sails. **keelhaul** *v.t.* **1** to punish by dragging under water on one side of the ship and up again on the other. 2 to berate. **keelless** *a.* [prob. from Icel. *kjölr*]

keel[2] (kēl) *n.* 1 (*Hist.*) a lighter or flat-bottomed barge, esp. one of those used for loading colliers in the Tyne. 2 a quantity of coal carried on a keel. **keeler** *n.* a worker on a lighter or barge. **keelman** *n.* (*pl.* **keelmen**). [prob. from MDut. *kiel* (cp. OE *cēol*, ship)]

keelie (kē´li) *n.* (*Sc.*) 1 a kestrel. 2 a city-bred hooligan, particularly one from Glasgow or surrounding area. [etym. uncertain]

keelson (kēl´sən), **kelson** (kel´-) *n.* a longitudinal piece placed along the floor-timbers of a ship binding them to the keel. [KEEL[1], *-son*, etym. uncertain (cp. Swed. *kölsvin*, Dut. *kolzwijn*, G *Kielschwein*)]

keen[1] (kēn) *a.* 1 enthusiastic, eager, ardent. 2 sensitive, acute, penetrating. 3 having a sharp edge or point. 4 (of an edge) sharp. 5 (of cold etc.) biting, piercing, intense. 6 bitter, acrimonious. 7 (of a price) low, competitive. 8 (*coll.*) excellent. **keen as mustard** (*coll.*) very keen. **keen on** enthusiastic about, interested in. **keenly** *adv.* **keenness** *n.* [OE *cēne* (cp. Dut. *koen*, Icel. *koenn*, *koenn*, G *kühn*, bold, daring)]

keen[2] (kēn) *n.* a wailing lamentation over the body of a dead person. ~*v.i.* to wail for the dead. ~*v.t.* 1 to mourn by keening. 2 to utter with keening. **keener** *n.* a professional mourner. [Ir. *caoine*, from *caoinim*, to weep]

keep[1] (kēp) *v.t.* (*past*, *p.p.* **kept** (kept)) 1 to hold for a significant length of time, to retain. 2 to have in one's continuous charge. 3 to guard, preserve, protect. 4 to maintain in a given state, position etc. 5 to place or store regularly. 6 to conduct as a business on one's own account. 7 to supply with the necessaries of life. 8 to own and tend, to look after out of interest or for profit. 9 to have in one's pay. 10 to observe, to pay proper regard to. 11 to fulfil, to celebrate. 12 to have regularly on sale; to stock. 13 to write regular entries in. 14 to restrain (from), to cause to abstain (from). 15 to detain (in custody etc.), to cause to wait or be late. 16 to reserve (for). 17 to refrain from divulging. 18 to preserve. 19 to adhere to, to continue to follow. 20 to remain in. 21 to reside in college etc. during (a term). 22 to associate with. ~*v.i.* 1 to continue or retain one's place (in, on etc.), to remain. 2 to continue to be (in a specified condition etc.). 3 to continue (doing). 4 to remain unspoiled, untainted etc. 5 to be able to be withheld without loss of significance etc. 6 to adhere (to). 7 to restrict oneself (to). 8 to lodge, to reside. **how are you keeping?** how are you? **keep her full** FULL[1]. **keep your hair on!** HAIR. **to keep a secret** SECRET. **to keep at** 1 to persist with. 2 to cause to persist with. **to keep away** to prevent from approaching. **to keep away from** not to approach, to avoid contact with. **to keep back** 1 to restrain, to hold back. 2 to reserve, to withhold. 3 to keep secret. 4 to remain at a distance. **to keep count** COUNT[1]. **to keep down** 1 to repress, to subdue. 2 to keep (expenses etc.) low. 3 to digest (food) without vomiting. **to keep for** 1 to reserve until (a future occasion). 2 to retain on behalf of. **to keep from** 1 to abstain or refrain from. 2 not to tell (someone about something). **to keep in** 1 to repress, to restrain. 2 to confine, esp. after school hours. 3 to maintain the combustion of (a fire). 4 to remain indoors. **to keep in countenance** COUNTENANCE. **to keep in with** to remain on friendly terms with. **to keep off** 1 to hinder from approach. 2 to avert. 3 to remain at a distance. 4 to abstain from. 5 to avoid mentioning or discussing. **to keep on** 1 to continue to employ etc. 2 to continue (doing etc.), to persist. **to keep on at** to nag at, to pester. **to keep one's countenance** COUNTENANCE. **to keep oneself to oneself** to avoid other people. **to keep one's word** WORD. **to keep out** to hinder from entering or taking possession (of). **to keep someone going in** to keep someone supplied with. **to keep step** STEP. **to keep (the) score** SCORE. **to keep to** to adhere strictly to. **to keep together** to remain or cause to remain together or in harmony. **to keep to oneself** 1 to avoid other people. 2 to tell no one else about. **to keep under** to hold down, to repress. **to keep up** 1 to maintain. 2 to keep in repair or good condition. 3 to prevent from falling or diminishing. 4 to carry on. 5 to cause to stay up at night. 6 to bear up. 7 to go on at the same pace (with). **to keep up with the Joneses** (*coll.*) to keep on the same social level as one's friends and neighbours. **keeper** (kē´pə) *n.* 1 a person who keeps something. 2 a person who has the charge, care or superintendence of anything, esp. of a park, art gallery etc. 3 a person who retains others in custody or charge. 4 a gamekeeper. 5 a position in some games, a wicketkeeper or goalkeeper. 6 a perishable article that keeps well. 7 a ring worn to protect another, esp. a wedding ring. 8 an earring worn to keep the hole in a pierced ear open, a sleeper. 9 a bar of soft iron used to prevent permanent magnets from losing magnetism. **Keeper of the Great Seal** *n.* the officer of State who holds the Great Seal, the Lord Chancellor. **keepership** *n.* **keep fit** *n.* physical exercises to keep one fit and healthy. **keeping** (kē´ping) *n.* 1 the action of holding, guarding, preserving etc. 2 charge, custody, guardianship. 3 harmony, accord. 4 consistency, congruity. ~*a.* (of fruit etc.) that can be kept. **in keeping** in harmony (with). **out of keeping** not in harmony (with). **keepnet** *n.* a net kept in the water by anglers, where they put the fish they have caught to keep them alive. **keepsake** (kēp´sāk) *n.* anything kept or given to be kept for the sake of or as a reminder of the giver. **kept**[1] *a.* **kept man** *n.* a man supported financially by the woman whose lover he is. **kept woman** *n.* a woman supported financially by the man whose mistress she is. [OE *cēpan*, etym. uncertain]

keep[2] (kēp) *n.* 1 subsistence, maintenance. 2 food required for subsistence. 3 control, charge. 4 a donjon, the main tower or stronghold of a medieval castle. 5 †care, heed. **for keeps** permanently. [see KEEP[1]]

keeshond (kās´hond, kēs´-) *n.* a Dutch breed of dog, with a heavy coat, pointed muzzle, and erect ears. [Dut. *Kees*, Cornelius, *hond*, dog]

kef (kēf, kef), **kief** (kēf), **kif** (kif) *n.* 1 the drowsy, dreamy, trance-like condition produced by the use of marijuana etc. 2 dreamy repose, happy idleness. 3 Indian hemp, smoked to produce this condition. [Arab. *qaif*]

keffiyeh (kefē´yə), **kaffiyeh** (kafē´yə) *n.* a Bedouin Arab's kerchief headdress. [Arab. *qaffiyah*]

keg (keg) *n.* a small cask or barrel. **keg beer** *n.* any beer kept in pressurized kegs. [formerly *cag* (cp. Icel. *kaggi*, Swed. *kagge*)]

keister (kē´stə, kī´stə) *n.* (*N Am.*, *sl.*) 1 the buttocks. 2 a suitcase or bag.

keloid (kē´loid) *n.* a hard, pinkish growth of scar tissue, usu. occurring in dark-skinned people. [Gr. *chēlē*, claw]

kelp (kelp) *n.* 1 any large, coarse seaweed. 2 the calcined ashes of seaweed, from which carbonate of soda was obtained for glass and soap making, now chiefly used for obtaining iodine. [ME *culp*, etym. unknown]

kelpie (kel´pi) *n.* 1 (*Sc.*) a water-spirit usu. in the form of a horse, supposed to haunt fords, and to rejoice in the drowning of wayfarers. 2 (*Austral.*) a smooth-haired variety of sheepdog. [etym. uncertain]

kelson KEELSON.

Kelt CELT.

kelt (kelt) *n.* (*Sc.*) a salmon or sea trout after spawning. [etym. unknown]

kelter KILTER.

kelvin (kel´vin) *n.* the basic SI unit of temperature. **Kelvin scale** *n.* a thermometer scale in which zero is absolute zero. [Lord *Kelvin*, 1824–1907, British physicist]

kemp (kemp) *n.* **1** the coarse rough hairs of wool. **2** (*pl.*) knotty hairs that will not felt. **kempy** *a.* [prob. from Icel. *kampr*, beard, whisker]

kempt (kempt) *a.* (of hair) combed, neat. [Eng. dial. *kemb*, comb]

Ken. *abbr.* Kentucky.

ken (ken) *n.* **1** range of sight or knowledge, apprehension. **2** view, sight. *~v.t.* (*pres.p.* **kenning,** *past, p.p.* **kenned, kent** (kent)) (*esp. Sc.*) **1** to be acquainted with. **2** to know. **3** to understand. **4** to see at or from a distance. **beyond one's ken** beyond the limits of one's knowledge or experience. **in one's ken** within the limits of one's knowledge. **kenning** *n.* a metaphorical name or phrase for something, in Old English and Old Norse poetry. [cp. OE *cennan*, to make known, to declare, Goth. *kannjan*, Dut. and G *kennen*, Icel. *kenna*, to know]

kenaf (kənaf´) *n.* the fibre from an Asian hibiscus, used in ropes. [Pers.]

Kendal green (ken´dəl) *n.* **1** green cloth, orig. made at Kendal for foresters. **2** the colour of this cloth. [*Kendal*, Cumbria]

kendo (ken´dō) *n.* the Japanese martial art of fencing, usu. with pliable bamboo staves, occasionally with swords. [Jap.]

kennel[1] (ken´əl) *n.* **1** a house or shelter for a dog or hounds. **2** (*as pl.*) a place where dogs are bred or boarded. **3** a hovel, a wretched haunt or den. **4** a pack of hounds. **5** the hole of a fox or other animal. *~v.i.* (*pres.p.* **kennelling,** (*N Am.*) **kenneling,** *past, p.p.* **kennelled,** (*N Am.*) **kenneled**) to lie or lodge in or as in a kennel. *~v.t.* to confine in or as in a kennel. **kennelmaid** *n.* a woman or girl who works in kennels looking after the dogs. **kennelman** *n.* (*pl.* **kennelmen**) a man who works in kennels looking after the dogs. [ONF *kenil*, OF *chenil*, low L *canīle*, from L *canis*, dog]

kennel[2] (ken´əl) *n.* **1** a gutter, the watercourse at the side of a street. **2** a puddle. [ME and OF *canel*, CHANNEL[1]]

kenning KEN.

kenosis (kənō´sis) *n.* (*Theol.*) Christ's relinquishment of the divine nature at the Incarnation. **kenotic** (-not´-) *a.* [Gr. *kenōsis*, from *kenoein*, to empty]

kenspeckle (ken´spekəl) *a.* (*Sc.*) conspicuous, easily recognized. [ON *kennispeki*, power of recognition]

kent KEN.

Kentish (ken´tish) *a.* of or relating to the English county of Kent. **Kentish fire** *n.* rhythmical volleys of applause showing disapproval. [OE *Centisc* (*Cent*, Kent, -ISH[1])]

kentledge (kent´lij) *n.* (*Naut.*) pig-iron used for permanent ballast. [F *quintelage*, ballast]

Kenyan (ken´yən) *n.* a native or inhabitant of Kenya in E Africa. *~a.* of or relating to Kenya.

kep (kep) *v.t.* (*pres.p.* **kepping,** *past, p.p.* **kept** (kept)) (*Sc., North.*) **1** to catch. **2** to intercept, to stop. *~n.* a catch. [var. of KEEP[1]]

kepi (kā´pē, kep´ē) *n.* (*pl.* **kepis**) a French flat-topped military hat with a horizontal peak. [F, from G Swiss *käppi*, dim. of *kappe*, CAP]

Kepler's laws (kep´ləz) *n.pl.* three laws formulated by Kepler concerning the revolution of planets round the sun. **Keplerian** (-liə´ri-) *a.* of or relating to the astronomer Kepler or his laws. [Johann *Kepler*, 1517–1630, German astronomer]

kept[1] KEEP[1].

kept[2] KEP.

keramic CERAMIC.

kerat- CERATO-.

keratin (ker´ətin) *n.* a nitrogenous substance, the chief constituent of hair, feathers, claws and horns. **keratinize, keratinise** *v.i., v.t.* to become covered or to cover with keratin. **keratinization** (-zā´shən) *n.* **1** the formation of keratin. **2** the state of becoming covered with keratin. **keratinous** *a.* **keratitis** (kerətī´tis) *n.* (*Med.*) inflammation of the cornea of the eye. **kerato-** CERATO-. **keratogenous** (-toj´inəs) *a.* that develops horny matter. **keratoid** (-oid) *a.* horny. **keratoplasty** (-plasti) *n.* (*Med.*) plastic surgery of the cornea. **keratoplastic** *a.* **keratose** (ker´ətōs, -tōz) *n.* the substance of the skeleton of horny sponges. *~a.* (of sponge) horny. **keratosis** (-tō´sis) *n.* (*pl.* **keratoses** (-sēz)) (*Med.*) **1** a horny growth on the skin, e.g. a wart. **2** any skin condition causing this symptom. **keratotomy** (-tot´əmi) *n.* (*pl.* **keratotomies**) a surgical incision into the cornea. [Gr. *keras keratos*, horn, -IN[1]]

kerb (kœb) *n.* a row of stones set as edging to a pavement etc. **kerb-crawling** *n.* the act of driving along slowly with the intention of enticing someone into the car for sexual purposes. **kerb-crawler** *n.* **kerb-drill** *n.* a pedestrian's procedure, such as looking to the left and right, for crossing a road in safety, esp. as taught to and used by children. **kerbside** *n.* the side of a pavement etc., nearer the kerb. *~a.* situated or taking place on this side. **kerbstone** *n.* each of the stones edging a pavement etc. **kerbstone broker** *n.* a stockbroker who is not a member of the Stock Exchange. [var. of CURB]

kerchief (kœ´chif) *n.* (*pl.* **kerchiefs**) **1** a cloth to cover the head. **2** (*poet.*) a handkerchief, a napkin. **kerchiefed** *a.* [ME *curchef, coverchef*, OF *couvrechief* (*couvrir*, to COVER, *chief*, L *caput*, head)]

kerf (kœf) *n.* **1** the slit, notch or channel made by a saw or axe in cutting. **2** the spot where something has been cut or lopped off. **3** a cutting or lopping. [OE *cyrf*, cogn. with CARVE]

kerfuffle (kəfŭf´əl), **carfuffle** *n.* a commotion, a fuss. [Sc. *curfuffle, carfuffle*]

kermes (kœ´mēz) *n.* **1** the dried bodies of the females of an insect, *Kermes ilicis*, yielding a red or scarlet dye. **2** dye from this source. **kermes mineral** *n.* a bright red mineral, hydrous trisulphide of antimony. **kermes oak** *n.* a shrubby, dwarf Mediterranean oak, *Quercus coccifera*. [F *kermès*, Arab. and Pers. *qirmiz*, CRIMSON]

kermis (kœ´mis), **kirmess** *n.* **1** in the Netherlands, a fair or outdoor festival or merrymaking, orig. a church festival. **2** (*N Am.*) a charity fair. [Dut. *kirk*, CHURCH, *mis*, MASS]

kern[1] (kœn) *n.* **1** the part of a letter which overhangs the main body of type. **2** (*Print.*) the projecting part of a piece of metal type. *~v.t.* **1** to provide with kerns. **2** to place so as to overlap. **3** to adjust the spacing between. **kerned** *a.* **kerning** *n.* [F *carne*, L *cardinem*, nom. *cardo*, hinge]

kern[2] (kœn), **kerne** *n.* **1** (*Hist.*) a light-armed Irish foot soldier. **2** †a country lout. **3** †a vagabond. **kernish** *a.* [Ir. *ceatharn*]

kernel (kœ´nəl) *n.* **1** the substance, usu. edible, contained in the shell of a nut or the stone of a fruit. **2** that which is enclosed in a shell, husk, integument etc. **3** the nucleus, core, gist or essence. *~v.i.* (*pres.p.* **kernelling,** (*N Am.*) **kerneling,** *past, p.p.* **kernelled,** (*N Am.*) **kerneled**) to ripen or harden into kernels. **kernelled,** *a.* (*N Am.*) **kerneled** having a kernel. **kernel-less** *a.* **kernelly** *a.* [OE *cyrnel*, dim. of CORN[1]]

kerosene (ker´əsēn), **kerosine** *n.* an oil distilled from petroleum, coal or bituminous shale, used for burning in jet engines and oil lamps. [Gr. *kēros*, wax]

Kerry (ker´i) *n.* (*pl.* **Kerries**) any of a breed of small black dairy cattle, from Ireland. **Kerry blue** *n.* a large, grey-blue, long-haired breed of terrier. [County Kerry]

kersey (kœ´zi) *n.* (*pl.* **kerseys**) a coarse woollen cloth, usu. ribbed. *~a.* made of kersey. [*Kersey* in Suffolk]

kerseymere (kœs´imiə), **cassimere** (kas´-) *n.* a fine twilled woollen cloth used esp. for suits. [CASHMERE]

kerygma (kərig´mə) *n.* in the early Christian Church, the teaching of the Gospel. **kerygmatic** (-mat´-) *a.* [Gk. *kerygma*, proclamation]

keskidee KISKADEE.

kestrel (kes´trəl) *n.* a small species of hawk, *Falco tinnunculus*. [prob. from OF *cresserelle*, etym. uncertain]

ketamine (ket´əmēn) *n.* an anaesthetic drug, also used as a hallucinogenic recreational drug. [KETONE, AMINE]

ketch (kech) *n.* a fore-and-aft rigged two-masted sailing boat. [formerly CATCH]

ketchup (kech´ŭp), **catchup** (kach´-), (*N Am.*) **catsup** (kat´səp) *n.* **1** a sauce, usu. prepared from mushrooms, tomatoes etc., used as a condiment. **2** tomato sauce. [perh. from Cantonese *k'ē chap*, tomato juice]

ketone (kē´tōn) *n.* any of a class of organic compounds, usu. formed by oxidation of a secondary alcohol. **ketogenic** *a.* that stimulates the production of ketone bodies. **ketonaemia** (-nē´miə), (*esp. N Am.*) **ketonemia** *n.* (*Med.*) an excess of ketone bodies in the blood. **ketone body** *n.* a compound produced in the liver from fatty acids, found in the blood and urine in abnormal amounts in people unable to use glucose, such as diabetics. **ketonic** (kiton´-) *a.* **ketonuria** (-uə´riə) *n.* the presence of large amounts of ketone bodies in the urine. **ketosis** (-tō´sis) *n.* (*Med.*) the excessive formation of ketone bodies, as in diabetes. [G *Keton*, ACETONE]

kettle (ket´əl) *n.* a vessel, usu. of metal and with a lid, handle and spout, for heating water or other liquid. **a different kettle of fish** a matter to be considered separately. **a fine kettle of fish** a pretty kettle of fish. **a pretty kettle of fish** a mess, a muddle, a troublesome state of affairs. **kettledrum** *n.* a drum made of a thin hemispherical shell of copper or brass etc., with a parchment or plastic head. **kettledrummer** *n.* **kettle-holder** *n.* a thick piece of cloth for protecting the hand in holding a hot kettle. **kettle hole** *n.* a hollow on the ground caused by the melting of trapped glacial ice. [OE *cetel* or Icel. *ketill* (cp. Dut. *ketel*, G *Kessel*)]

keV *abbr.* kilo-electronvolt.

kevel (kev´əl) *n.* (*Naut.*) a belaying cleat, usu. fixed in pairs. [ONF *keville* (F *cheville*), L *clāvicula*, dim. of *clāvis*, key]

Kevlar® (kev´lah) *n.* a strong synthetic fibre, used in the manufacture of tyres.

Kewpie doll® (kū´pi), **kewpie** *n.* a plump baby doll with hair in a topknot. [*Cupid*]

kex (keks), **keck** (kek) *n.* **1** any of various umbelliferous plants, such as the hemlock, the hogweed or the angelica. **2** the dry hollow stem of such a plant. **kexy** *a.* [etym. unknown]

key[1] (kē) *n.* **1** a portable instrument, usu. of metal, for working the bolt of a lock to and fro. **2** a tool or instrument by which something is screwed up or turned. **3** a small lever actuated by the fingers in playing certain musical instruments, operating certain machines etc. **4** any of the buttons depressed by the fingers in operating a typewriter, entering data at a computer terminal etc. **5** a means of access to or opportunity for something. **6** that which explains anything difficult, a solution, an explanation. **7** a translation. **8** a series of solutions of problems etc. **9** the first move in the solution to a chess problem. **10** one of several systems of musical notes having definite tonic relations among themselves and to one fundamental note called the keynote. **11** the general tone or style (of a picture, literary composition, speech etc.). **12** a place whose military occupation gives control over a region of land or sea. **13** a piece of wood or metal let transversely into the back of a board to prevent warping. **14** a keystone. **15** the roughness of a surface for plastering. **16** the first coat of plaster on a wall or ceiling. **17** the winged seed of a sycamore etc. *~a.* (*attrib.*) leading, essential. *~v.t.* **1** to fasten (on, in etc.) with a key, bolt, wedge etc. **2** to enter (data) into a computer using a keyboard. **3** (*Mus.*) to tune, to regulate. **4** to align or link (to). **5** to vary the wording (of an advertisement) so that the source prompting each response can be identified. **6** to roughen (a surface) for plastering. **7** to stir (up) to an action etc. **to key in** to enter (data) into a computer using a keyboard. **to key up** to brace up, to incite, to encourage. **keyboard** *n.* **1** the range of keys on a piano, organ, typewriter, computer etc. **2** an electronic instrument with keys resembling those on a piano. *~v.t.* to set (text) in type using a keyboard, to key in. **keyboarder** *n.* a person who enters data into a computer using a keyboard. **keyboardist** *n.* a player of a keyboard. **keyed** *a.* having keys. **keyer** *n.* **key fruit** *n.* a winged fruit, like that of the sycamore (from its hanging like bunches of keys). **key grip** *n.* the person in a television studio or on a film set responsible for setting up scenery and camera tracks. **keyholder** *n.* a person who keeps a key to give access to an office etc. **keyhole** *n.* the hole in a lock, door, cover etc., by which a key is inserted. **keyhole surgery** *n.* surgery performed through very small incisions. **key industry** *n.* an industry upon which the other interests and the economic welfare of a country depend. **keyless** *a.* **1** not having a key. **2** wound without a key (as a clock or watch). **key map** *n.* a simple map with plain outlines. **key money** *n.* a premium demanded, in addition to rent, for the granting or renewal of a tenancy. **keynote** *n.* **1** (*Mus.*) the fundamental note of a key. **2** the general tone or spirit (of a picture, poem etc.). *~a.* (*attrib.*) setting the tone or agenda (*a keynote speech*). **keypad** *n.* a small device with a push-button keyboard for operating, for example, a television or teletext system. **keypunch** *n.* a keyboard operated manually and used to put data onto punched cards. *~v.t.* to transfer (data) in this way. **keypuncher** *n.* **keyring** *n.* a ring for carrying keys on. **key signature** *n.* the sharps and flats on a musical staff, showing the key of a piece of music. **keystone** *n.* **1** the central stone of an arch locking the others together. **2** the fundamental element, principle etc. **keystroke** *n.* the operation of a key on a keyboard-operated machine. **keyway** *n.* a slot into which a machined key is inserted. **keyword** *n.* **1** the key to a code. **2** an important word, e.g. describing the contents of a document. [OE *cæg*, etym. uncertain]

key[2] (kē) *n.* a low island, esp. of coral, such as off the coast of Florida. [var. of CAY]

Keynesian (kā´nziən) *a.* of or relating to the philosophy that governments should control the economy through monetary and fiscal policies. *~n.* a believer in Keynesian economics. **Keynesianism** *n.* [John Maynard *Keynes*, 1883–1946, British economist]

KG *abbr.* Knight of the Order of the Garter.

kg *abbr.* kilogram(s).

KGB *abbr.* the former Soviet secret police. [Rus. *komitet gosudarstvennoi bezpasnosti*, State Security Committee]

Kgs *abbr.* (*Bible*) Kings.

khaddar (kah´də), **khadi** (-di) *n.* Indian hand-woven cloth. [Hind.]

khaki (kah´ki) *a.* dust-coloured, dull brownish yellow. *~n.* (*pl.* **khakis**) **1** a dull brownish yellow colour. **2** a twilled cloth of this colour, used for army uniforms. [Hind., dusty, from *khāk*, dust]

khalasi (kəlas´i) *n.* (*pl.* **khalasis**) a labourer or servant in the Indian subcontinent. [Hind.]

khalif CALIPH.

Khalka (kal´kə) *n.* the official language of the Mongolian People's Republic.

khamsin (kam´sin), **hamsin** (hamsin) *n.* a hot southerly wind blowing in Egypt for some 50 days in March to May. [Arab., fifty]

khan[1] (kahn, kan) *n.* **1** a title given to officials and rulers in Central Asia etc., equivalent to 'esquire'. **2** (*Hist.*) a king or emperor, esp. the chief ruler of a Tartar,

Turkish, and Mongol tribe, or the Chinese emperor in the Middle Ages. **khanate** (-āt) *n.* [Turk. *khān*, perh. orig. *khāqan*]

khan[2] (kahn, kan) *n.* a caravanserai. [Arab. *khān*]

khanga KANGA.

khat (kat, kaht), **kat** *n.* **1** an evergreen shrub, *Catha edulis*, grown in Africa and Arabia. **2** the leaves of this shrub, chewed as a narcotic. [Arab. *qāt*]

kheda (ked´ə) *n.* an enclosure used in India etc. for catching elephants. [Hind.]

Khedive (kidēv´) *n.* (*Hist.*) the official title of the governor of Egypt under the Turks, 1867–1914. **khedivate** (-vāt) *n.* [F *khédive*, Turk. (Pers.) *khedīv*]

Khmer (kmeə, kmœ) *n.* **1** a member of a people inhabiting Cambodia. **2** the language of this people. ~*a.* of or relating to this people or their language. **Khmerian** *a.*

Khoisan (koi´sahn, -sahn´) *n.* a family of African languages which includes the Nama and Bushman languages. ~*a.* of or relating to this language family.

khus-khus (kŭs´kŭs), **cuscus** *n.* the fibrous, aromatic root of an Indian grass, used for making fans, baskets etc. [Hind. *khas khas*]

kHz *abbr.* kilohertz.

kiang (kiang´) *n.* an Asian wild ass, *Equus hemionis.* [Tibetan]

kia ora (kēə aw´rə) *int.* (*New Zeal.*) greetings!, your health! [Maori]

kibble[1] (kib´əl) *n.* a strong iron (formerly wooden) bucket for raising ore from a mine. [cp. G *Kübel*]

kibble[2] (kib´əl) *v.t.* to grind (grain, beans etc.) coarsely. ~*n.* (*N Am.*) ground meal made into pellets. [etym. unknown]

kibbutz (kibuts´) *n.* (*pl.* **kibbutzim** (-im)) a communal agricultural settlement in Israel. **kibbutznik** (-nik) *n.* a person who lives and works on a kibbutz. [Heb.]

kibe (kib) *n.* a chap occasioned by cold, an ulcerated chilblain. [perh. from Welsh *cibi* (*cib*, a cup, a husk)]

kibitka (kibit´kə) *n.* **1** a Russian wheeled vehicle with a tentlike covering, used as a sledge in snowy weather. **2** a Tartar circular tent, usu. made of lattice-work and felt. **3** a Tartar family. [Rus.]

kibitzer (kib´itsə) *n.* (*N Am., coll.*) **1** an interfering looker-on, esp. at a card game. **2** a meddler, an offerer of unwanted advice. **kibitz** *v.i.* [Yiddish, fr. G, a looker-on]

kiblah (kib´lə), **qibla** *n.* **1** the direction of the Kaaba at Mecca, to which Muslims turn during prayer. **2** a mihrab. [Arab. *qiblah*]

kibosh (kībosh), **kybosh** *n.* (*sl.*) bosh, humbug. **to put the kibosh on 1** to checkmate, to do for. **2** to put an end to. [etym. unknown]

kick[1] (kik) *v.t.* **1** to strike with the foot or hoof etc. **2** to push, move, or drive, by or as by kicking. **3** to strike in recoil. **4** in football, to score (a goal) with a kick. **5** to overcome (an addiction). ~*v.i.* **1** to strike out with the foot or feet, or with the hoof etc. **2** to recoil, as a gun. **3** to show opposition, dislike etc. (against, at etc.). **4** to be alive and well. **5** to make a sudden violent movement. **6** (of a ball in cricket etc.) to rise sharply from the pitch. ~*n.* **1** the act of kicking. **2** a blow with the foot or hoof etc. **3** a recoil (of a gun). **4** a stimulating reaction to alcohol or pungent seasoning. **5** a sudden thrill of excitement. **6** an enthusiastic, short-lived interest. **7** energy, resilience. **8** a kicker of a ball (of a given ability). **9** the erratic course of an arrow owing to wrong handling of the bow. **10** a transient high-voltage discharge in an inductive electric current. **alive and kicking** ALIVE. **for kicks** for pleasure. **to get a kick out of** to get enjoyment from. **to kick about/ around 1** (*coll.*) to go from place to place aimlessly. **2** to be discarded and left lying about or forgotten. **3** to treat harshly. **4** to discuss informally, to raise but not consider seriously. **to kick against the pricks** PRICK. **to kick in 1** to break open (a door) by kicking. **2** to begin to function, to be activated. **3** (*N Am., Austral., sl.*) to pay one's share. **to kick off 1** to remove or discard by kicking. **2** in football, to give the ball the first kick, to start play. **3** to begin. **to kick oneself** to be angry with oneself. **to kick one's heels** to stand idly waiting. **to kick out** to eject or dismiss unceremoniously or with violence. **to kick over the traces** to throw off any means of restraint or control. **to kick (some) ass** (*N Am., sl.*) to behave forcefully or aggressively. **to kick the bucket** BUCKET. **to kick up a dust** DUST. **to kick up a fuss** FUSS. **to kick up one's heels** to enjoy oneself with no inhibitions. **to kick upstairs** (*coll.*) to promote, often to a less active or less powerful post. **kickable** *a.* **kickabout** *n.* an informal football game. **kick-ass** *a.* (*N Am., sl.*) forceful, aggressive. **kickback** *n.* **1** a strong reaction to something. **2** a sum paid to another person, confidentially, for favours past or future. **kickball** *n.* (*N Am.*) **1** an informal game where the ball is kicked rather than being thrown or hit with a bat. **2** a ball used in such a game. **kick-boxing** *n.* a martial art that allows punching and kicking. **kickdown** *n.* a way of changing gear in an automatic car, by pressing the accelerator pedal right down. **kicker** *n.* **1** something who or something which kicks. **2** a horse given to kicking. **kick in the teeth, kick in the pants** *n.* (*coll.*) a humiliating rejection, an unexpected personal attack. **kick-off** *n.* in football, the first kick to start play. **for a kick-off** (*coll.*) for a start. **kick-pleat** *n.* a pleat at the back of a tight skirt. **kicksorter** *n.* a device for sorting and counting electrical pulses according to amplitude. **kickstand** *n.* a bicycle or motorcycle stand that can be kicked into position. **kick-start** *n.* **1** an act of starting an engine by kicking down a pedal. **2** an act of giving extra impetus at the beginning of a project etc. **3** a kick-starter. ~*v.t.* to start (an engine) by kicking down a pedal. **kick-starter** *n.* a pedal for kick-starting e.g. a motorcycle. **kick-turn** *n.* in skiing, a standing turn. [ME *kiken*, etym. uncertain]

kick[2] (kik) *n.* the pushed-in base of a glass bottle. [etym. unknown]

kickshaw (kik´shaw) *n.* **1** something fantastical, a trifle, a trinket. **2** †a light, insubstantial dish. [corr. of F *quelque chose*, something]

kid[1] (kid) *n.* **1 a** the young of the goat. **b** leather from the skin of this. **c** (*pl.*) gloves of this leather. **2** (*coll.*) a child, a young person. ~*v.i.* (*pres.p.* **kidding,** *past, p.p.* **kidded**) to give birth to a kid or kids. **kid brother** *n.* (*coll.*) a younger brother. **kiddie, kiddy** *n.* (*pl.* **kiddies**) (*coll.*) a little child. **kiddo** *n.* (*pl.* **kiddos**) (*coll.*) (used as a form of address) a child or young person. **kiddywink, kiddiewink** *n.* (*coll.*) a child, a kiddy. **kid glove** *n.* a glove made of kid. **with kid gloves** very carefully or tactfully. **kid-glove** *a.* **1** characterized by care and tact. **2** too fastidious for common tasks etc. **kid sister** *n.* (*coll.*) a younger sister. **kidskin** *n.* a smooth, soft leather from a young goat. **kids' stuff** *n.* (*coll.*) **1** something suitable for children. **2** something childish or very easy. **kidvid** *n.* (*sl.*) **1** children's television. **2** a children's television programme or video. [ME *kid*, *kide* (cp. Norw., Swed. and Dan. *kid*, Icel. *kith*, G *Kitze*)]

kid[2] (kid) *v.t.* (*pres.p.* **kidding,** *past, p.p.* **kidded**) (*coll.*) **1** to humbug, to hoax, to pretend. **2** to deceive for fun, to tease. **no kid** (*sl.*) no kidding, honestly. **no kidding** (*sl.*) really, honestly. **kiddingly** *adv.* **kidology** (-ol´-) *n.* (*coll.*) the art or practice of kidding, bluffing. [perh. from KID[1]]

kid[3] (kid) *n.* (*Hist.*) a small wooden tub, esp. one used at mess by sailors. [prob. var. of KIT[1]]

†**kidder** (kid´ə) *n.* a dealer in corn, esp. an engrosser of corn to enhance its price. [etym. unknown]

Kidderminster (kid´əminstə), **Kidderminster carpet**

n. a reversible two-ply ingrain carpet of a type originally made at Kidderminster in Hereford and Worcester.

kiddie KID[1].

kiddle (kid´əl) *n.* **1** a weir or dam in a river with traps or nets for catching fish. **2** a set of stake-nets for the same purpose on a beach. [OE *kidel*, OF *quidel*, later *quideau*, etym. uncertain]

kiddo, kiddy KID[1].

kidnap (kid´nap) *v.t.* (*pres.p.* **kidnapping,** (*N Am.*) **kidnaping,** *past, p.p.* **kidnapped,** (*N Am.*) **kidnaped**) to carry off (a person) by force or illegally, to abduct. **kidnapper,** (*N Am.*) **kidnaper** *n.* [KID[1], *nap*, NAB]

kidney (kid´ni) *n.* (*pl.* **kidneys**) **1** (*Anat.*) an oblong flattened glandular organ embedded in fatty tissue in the lumbar region on each side of the spine, and serving to secrete urine and remove nitrogenous matter from the blood. **2** an animal's kidney used as food. **3** anything resembling a kidney. **4** temperament, kind, fashion. **kidney bean** *n.* a kidney-shaped bean, esp. the dwarf French bean and the scarlet runner. **kidney dish** *n.* a kidney-shaped container used in surgery. **kidney machine** *n.* a machine used to carry out blood dialysis in cases of kidney failure. **kidney-shaped, kidney-form** *a.* shaped like a kidney, having one concave and one convex side. **kidney stone** *n.* (*Med.*) a hard mass in the kidney. **kidney vetch** *n.* a leguminous plant, *Anthyllis vulneraria*, lady's finger.

kidology KID[2].

kief KEF.

kiekie (kē´kē) *n.* a New Zealand climber, *Freycinetia banksii*, the berries of which are eaten and the leaves used for baskets etc. [Maori]

kieselguhr (kē´zəlguə) *n.* a type of diatomite. [G *Kiesel*, flint, *Gur*, loose earth]

kif KEF.

kike (kīk) *n.* (*offensive*) a Jew. ~*a.* (*offensive*) Jewish. [possibly from *-ki* ending of many Jewish immigrants' names in the US at the end of the 19th cent.]

Kikuyu (kikoo´ū) *n.* (*pl.* **Kikuyu, Kikuyus**) **1** a member of a Bantu-speaking people of Kenya. **2** their language. ~*a.* of or relating to the Kikuyu or their language. [Bantu]

kilderkin (kil´dəkin) *n.* **1** a small barrel, usu. of 18 gals. (81.8 l). **2** a liquid measure of this capacity. [corr. of MDut. *kindeken*, dim. of *kintal*, OF QUINTAL]

kilerg (kil´œg) *n.* a unit of measurement of work, 1000 ergs. [*kil-*, KILO-, ERG[1]]

kiley KYLIE.

kilim (kil´im, kē´lim) *n.* a pileless woven carpet made in the Middle East. [Turk. from Pers. *qilīm*]

kill (kil) *v.t.* **1** to deprive of life, to put to death. **2** to put an end to, to destroy, to quell. **3** to deaden, to still (pain etc.). **4** to neutralize (effects of colour etc.). **5** (*coll.*) to cause pain or discomfort to. **6** (*coll.*) to cause great amusement to. **7** (*coll.*) to overwhelm with admiration, astonishment, personal charms etc. **8** to pass or consume (time) idly. **9** to discard, to cancel. **10** to mark a paragraph or article not to be used. **11** (*coll.*) to delete (text) from a computer file. **12** to prevent the passing of (a bill) in Parliament. **13** in tennis etc., to strike (the ball) so forcibly that it cannot be returned. **14** in football etc., to stop the momentum of (the ball). **15** (*coll.*) to switch off (an engine, light etc.). **16** (*coll.*) to drink or eat the whole of. ~*v.i.* **1** to cause death. **2** to engage in slaughter, esp. in sport. ~*n.* **1** the act of killing. **2** an animal or number of animals killed, esp. in sport. **3** (*coll.*) the destruction of an enemy aircraft, tank etc. **4** in tennis etc., the hitting of a ball so forcibly that it cannot be returned. **dressed to kill** dressed to be as attractive as possible. **in at the kill** present at the end or conclusion of something. **to kill off 1** to get rid of by killing. **2** to destroy completely. **3** to remove from a story by writing in the death of (a fictional character). **to kill oneself 1** to commit suicide. **2** (*coll.*) to overexert oneself. **3** (*coll.*) to laugh uncontrollably. **to kill the fatted calf** CALF[1]. **to kill two birds with one stone** to achieve two things with a single action. **to kill with kindness** to be too gentle or indulgent. **killer** *n.* **1** a person or animal that kills. **2** (*coll.*) a very impressive or difficult person, thing or action. **3** (*coll.*) a very funny joke. **killer bee** *n.* an Africanized honey bee which is very aggressive when disturbed. **killer cell** *n.* a white blood cell that destroys other cells. **killer instinct** *n.* **1** a tendency to kill. **2** in business, sport etc., the ability to be merciless. **killer whale** *n.* a black-and-white toothed whale, *Orcinus orca*, found in most seas. **killing** *a.* **1** that kills. **2** fascinating, irresistibly charming. **3** (*coll.*) excruciatingly funny. ~*n.* **1** the act of causing death or a death, slaughter. **2** (*coll.*) a spectacular gain or success. **3** the number of animals killed by sportsmen. **4** the precaution against the evolution of gas in steel during the process of manufacture. **5** in bridge, the heavy defeat of a contract. **to make a killing** to make a large profit. **killing bottle** *n.* a bottle containing poisonous gas, used for killing insects. **killingly** *adv.* **killjoy** *n.* a person who sheds a general depression on company, a wet blanket. **kill or cure** *a.* drastic in its effects. [etym. unknown, prob. not rel. to QUELL]

killdeer (kil´diə) *n.* (*pl.* **killdeer, killdeers**) a N American plover, *Charadrius vociferus*. [imit. of the cry]

killick (kil´ik) *n.* **1** a stone or small anchor used for mooring a fishing boat. **2** (*Naut., sl.*) a leading seaman. [etym. unknown]

killifish (kil´ifish) *n.* (*pl. in general* **killifish,** *in particular* **killifishes**) any minnow-like fish of the genus *Fundulus* and related genera, used as bait and to control mosquitoes. [Dut. *kille*, river]

kiln (kiln) *n.* a furnace, oven or stove for calcining, drying, hardening etc., esp. one for calcining lime or firing pottery etc. ~*v.t.* to dry or bake in a kiln. [OE *cyln*, *cyline*, L *culīna*, kitchen]

kilo (kē´lō) *n.* (*pl.* **kilos**) **1** a kilogram. **2** a kilometre. [F, abbr.]

kilo- (kil´ō, kē´lō) *comb. form* denoting a factor of one thousand, esp. in the metric system. [F, from Gr. *chilioi*, a thousand]

kilobit (kil´əbit) *n.* a unit of computer information equal to 1024 bits.

kilobyte (kil´əbīt) *n.* a unit of computer storage equal to 1024 bytes.

kilocalorie *n.* a unit of heat equalling 1000 (small) calories, used in measuring the energy content of food.

kilocycle (kil´əsīkəl) *n.* (*Hist.*) a unit for measuring the frequency of alternating current, equal to 1000 cycles per second.

kilogram (kil´əgram), **kilogramme** *n.* a measure of weight, 1000 grams or 2.2046 lb. av., the SI base unit of mass.

kilohertz (kil´əhœts) *n.* a unit used to measure the frequency of radio waves, equal to 1000 hertz.

kilojoule (kil´əjool) *n.* a unit of energy equal to 1000 joules.

kilolitre (kil´əlētə), (*N Am.*) **kiloliter** *n.* a liquid measure, 1000 litres.

kilometre (kil´əmētə, kilom´itə) *n.* a measure of distance, equal to 1000 metres or 0.621 miles. **kilometrical** (-met´-) *a.*

Usage note The pronunciation of *kilometre* as (kilom´-), with stress on the second syllable, is sometimes disapproved of (other similar metric units have initial stress), though it is very common.

kiloton (kil´ətŭn), **kilotonne** *n.* a measure of explosive power, equal to 1000 tons of TNT.

kilovolt (kil´əvolt) *n.* a unit of electromotive force equal to 1000 volts.

kilowatt (kil´əwot) *n.* a unit of measurement of electrical energy, equal to 1000 watts. **kilowatt-hour** *n.* a unit of energy or work equal to that performed by 1 kilowatt acting for 1 hour.

kilt (kilt) *n.* a kind of short skirt usu. of tartan cloth gathered in vertical pleats, worn as part of male dress by the highlanders of Scotland. *~v.t.* **1** to tuck up (the skirts of a dress). **2** to gather together (the material of a dress) into vertical pleats. **kilted** *a.* **1** wearing a kilt. **2** gathered into vertical pleats. **kiltie** (-ti) *n.* (*coll.*) a person wearing a kilt, esp. a soldier of a Highland regiment. [cp. Dan. *kilte*, Icel. *kilting*, a skirt)]

kilter (kil´tə), **kelter** (kel´-) *n.* (*coll.*) good condition, fitness, form. [etym. unknown]

kimberlite (kim´bəlīt) *n.* a diamond-bearing claylike bluish rock, found in S Africa and Siberia. [*Kimberley*, S Afr.]

kimono (kimō´nō) *n.* (*pl.* **kimonos**) **1** a loose robe fastened with a sash, the principal outer garment of Japanese costume. **2** a dressing gown resembling this. [Jap.]

kin (kin) *n.* **1** one's blood relations or family connections collectively, kindred. **2** a relation, a family connection. *~a.* of the same family, nature or kind, akin. **kith and kin** KITH. **near of kin** NEAR. **next of kin** NEXT. **kinless** *a.* **kinsfolk,** (*N Am.*) **kinfolk** *n.pl.* family relations, kindred. **kinship** *n.* **1** relationship by blood. **2** affinity. **kinsman** *n.* (*pl.* **kinsmen**). **kinswoman** *n.* (*pl.* **kinswomen**). [OE *cynn* (cp. Dut. *kunne*, Icel. *kyn*), cogn. with L *genus*, Gr. *genos*]

-kin (kin) *suf.* forming diminutive nouns (*manikin*). [cog. with MDut. *-kijn*]

kina (kē´nə) *n.* the standard monetary unit of Papua New Guinea. [Papuan]

kinaesthesia (kinəsthē´ziə, kī-), (*esp. N Am.*) **kinesthesia, kinaesthesis** (-thē´sis), (*esp. N Am.*) **kinesthesis** *n.* (*Med.*) the brain's sense of the body's positioning, the perception of muscular movement. **kinaesthetic** (-thet´-) *a.* [Gr. *kinein*, to move, *aesthēsis*, perception]

kinase (kī´nāz, kin´-) *n.* **1** a chemical in the body which converts a zymogen into an enzyme. **2** an enzyme that facilitates the transfer of phosphates from ATP. [*kin*etic, -ASE]

kincob (king´kob) *n.* a rich Indian fabric interwoven with gold or silver thread. [Hind. *kimkhāb*]

kind (kīnd) *n.* **1** a genus, a species, a natural group. **2** sort, class, variety. **3** manner, fashion, way. **4** each Eucharistic element. **5** essential nature. **6** †gender, sex. **7** †natural way, natural propensity or inclination. *~a.* **1** disposed to do good to others. **2** sympathetic, benevolent, tender. **3** proceeding from or characterized by goodness of heart. **4** †affectionate. **after its kind** according to its nature. **a kind of 1** a sort of. **2** roughly or approximately of the description or class expressed. **in kind 1** (of payment, wages etc.) in produce or commodities. **2** in the same way or manner. **nothing of the kind 1** something quite different. **2** not at all (as a rejoinder). **of a kind 1** (*derog.*) that is not a good example of its type. **2** of the same type (*two of a kind*). **of one's kind** of the type or class of person to which one belongs. **something of the kind** something similar. **to differ in kind** to differ in nature, not merely in degree. **with kind regards** REGARD. **kinda** (-də) *adv.* (*coll.*) kind of, rather. **kind-hearted** *a.* of a sympathetic or generous disposition. **kind-heartedly** *adv.* **kind-heartedness** *n.* **kindly** *a.* (*comp.* **kindlier**, *superl.* **kindliest**) **1** kind, good-natured, benevolent. **2** favourable, auspicious, genial, beneficial. **3** †native, akin, natural. *~adv.* **1** in a considerate or tolerant way. **2** (*iron.*) as an act of kindness. **to take kindly to** to react favourably to. **to take something kindly** to react favourably to (something). **kindlily** *adv.* **kindliness** *n.* **kindness** *n.* **1** the fact or condition of being kind, kind behaviour. **2** a kind act. **kind of** *adv.* (*coll.*) rather. [OE *cynd*, *gecynd*, cogn. with KIN]

Usage note *Kind of* should not be used as a plural (as in *those kind of dictionaries*), or followed by the indefinite article *a*, *an* (as in *this kind of a dictionary*).

kindergarten (kin´dəgahtən) *n.* a school for infants and children below official school age, in which knowledge is imparted chiefly by simple object lessons, by toys, games, singing and work. [G, children's garden]

kindle (kin´dəl) *v.t.* **1** to set fire to, to light. **2** to inflame, to inspire (the passions etc.). **3** to excite, to stir up (to action or feeling). **4** to light up or illumine. *~v.i.* **1** to catch fire, to begin to burn or flame. **2** to become inflamed or excited. **3** to react or respond (to). **4** to become illumined. **kindler** *n.* **kindling** *n.* wood, shavings etc., for lighting fires, firewood. [prob. from Icel. *kynda*, -LE[1]]

kindred (kin´drid) *n.* **1** (*collect.*) relatives, kin. **2** relationship by blood or marriage. **3** affinity or likeness of character. *~a.* **1** related by blood or marriage. **2** of like nature or qualities, congenial, sympathetic. **kindred spirit** *n.* a person with the same interests and attitudes as one's own. [KIN, *-red*, OE *-raeden*, condition]

kine COW[1].

kinematics (kīnəmat´iks, kin-) *n.* the science of pure motion, admitting conceptions of time and velocity but excluding that of force. **kinematic** *a.* of or relating to movement or to kinematics. **kinematical** *a.* **kinematically** *adv.* **kinematic viscosity** *n.* a measure of the viscosity of a fluid equal to its absolute viscosity divided by its density. [Gr. *kinēma -matos*, movement, from *kinein*, to move]

kinematograph CINEMATOGRAPH.

kinesi- (kinē´si) *comb. form* movement. [Gr. *kinēsis*, motion, from *kinein*, to move]

kinesiology (kinēsiol´əji) *n.* the study of human movement and anatomy. **kinesiologist** *n.*

kinesis (kinē´sis) *n.* **1** movement. **2** movement under stimulus. **3** (*Zool.*) movement of the bones of the skull. **kinesics** *n.* **1** the study of body movements as non-verbal communication. **2** (*as pl.*) body movements as communicating information.

kinesthesia, kinesthesis KINAESTHESIA.

kinetic (kinet´ik) *a.* **1** of or producing motion. **2** due to or depending upon motion. **kinetically** *adv.* **kinetic art** *n.* art, e.g. sculpture, which has moving parts. **kinetic energy** *n.* the energy of a body in actual motion (measured by the product of half the mass and the square of the velocity). **kinetic pressure** *n.* the increase in pressure when a stream of fluid meets an obstruction. **kinetics** *n.* **1** the branch of dynamics which deals with forces imparting motion to or influencing motion already imparted to bodies. **2** the study and measuring of the rates of chemical or biochemical reactions. **kinetic theory** *n.* (*Chem.*) a theory which accounts for the behaviour of gases, vapours, liquids etc. in terms of the motions of molecules or atoms comprising them. [Gr. *kinētikos*, as KINESI-]

kinetin (kī´nitin) *n.* a synthetic kinin used to promote cell division in plants.

king (king) *n.* **1** the male sovereign of a nation, esp. a hereditary sovereign of an independent state. **2** a person who or thing which is pre-eminent in any sphere. **3** a playing card bearing a representation of a king, usu. ranking next to the ace and before the queen. **4** in chess, a piece which has to be protected from checkmate. **5** in draughts, a piece which has been crowned and is entitled to move in any direction. *~v.t.* **1** to make a king of. **2** to raise to a throne. *~v.i.* to act as king, to govern. **king high** in a card game, having the king as the top-ranking card. **the King** the British national anthem when there is a male sovereign. **to king it** (*coll.*) to behave as if one is superior to others. **king bird** *n.* any American flycatcher of the genus *Tyrannus.* **king bird of paradise** *n.* a bird of paradise, *Cicinnurus regius.* **kingbolt** *n.* a main or central pin, bolt or pivot. **King Charles spaniel** *n.* a small breed of spaniel. **king cobra** *n.* a large, venomous cobra, *Ophiophagus hannah.* **king consort** *n.* the husband of a queen. **king crab** *n.* **1** a horseshoe crab. **2** (*N Am.*) a large edible spider crab. †**kingcraft** *n.* the art of governing, as a king, kingly statesmanship. **kingcup** *n.* **1** the marsh marigold, *Caltha palustris.* **2** any of various other yellow-flowered plants of the buttercup family. **kingdom** *n.* **1** the territory under the rule of a king or queen. **2** a people ruled by a king (or queen). **3** a domain, a territory. **4** each of the three highest and most comprehensive of the divisions into which natural objects may be arranged. **5** (*Biol.*) the highest taxonomic classification. **6** (*Theol.*) the spiritual reign or realm of God. **7** sovereign power or authority. **8** †the position or attributes of a king. **to come into/ to one's kingdom** to reach one's desired status. **kingdom come** *n.* (*coll.*) the world to come, eternity. **till kingdom come** for ever. **kingfish** *n.* any of several types of large food and game fish. **kingfisher** *n.* any bird of the family Alcedinidae which dive for fish in rivers etc., esp. *Alcedo atthis,* a small European bird with brilliant blue and green plumage. **kinghood** *n.* **King in Council** *n.* the Privy Council acting in the same manner as the Queen in Council during the reign of a king. **King James Bible, King James Version** *n.* the Authorized Version of the Bible. **kingklip** (-klip) *n.* a South African edible eel-like fish. **kingless** *a.* **kinglet** (-lit) *n.* **1** a petty king. **2** any of several small warblers of the genus *Regulus.* **kinglike** *a.* **kingly** *a.* characteristic of or befitting a king. *~adv.* in a kingly manner. **kinglihood** (-hud) *n.* **kingliness** *n.* **kingmaker** *n.* (*Hist.*) a person who sets up kings, esp. Richard Neville, Earl of Warwick, who supported the Houses of York and Lancaster alternately in the Wars of the Roses. **King of Arms** *n.* a senior herald. **king of beasts** *n.* the lion. **king of birds** *n.* the eagle. **King of Kings** *n.* **1** God. **2** the title of various oriental monarchs. **king of metals** *n.* gold. **King of Terrors** *n.* death. **King of the Castle** *n.* **1** a children's game in which a player stands on a mound and others try to displace him or her. **2** the most important person in a group. **king of the forest** *n.* the oak. **king penguin** *n.* the largest of the penguins, *Aptenodytes forsteri,* the emperor penguin. **kingpin** *n.* **1** a main or central pin, bolt or pivot. **2 a** the centre pin in skittles. **b** the front pin in tenpin bowling. **3** (*coll.*) the most important person or thing in an organization or structure. **king post** *n.* the middle post of a roof, reaching from the ridge to the tie-beam. **king prawn** *n.* a large prawn of the genus *Penaeus.* **Kings** *n.* either of two books of the Old Testament, dealing with the histories of Judah and Israel. **King's Bench** *n.* a division of the High Court of Justice during the reign of a king (formerly a court presided over by the sovereign). **king's bishop** *n.* in chess, the bishop on the king's side of the board at the start of play. **King's Bounty** *n.* (*Hist.*) a grant made to the mother of three or more children at a birth. **King's Champion** *n.* CHAMPION OF ENGLAND (under CHAMPION). **King's colour** *n.* a flag carried by a regiment during the reign of a king. **King's Counsel** *n.* counsel to the Crown, an honorary title which gives precedence over ordinary barristers, during the reign of a king. **King's English** *n.* correct English as spoken by educated people, during the reign of a king. **King's evidence** *n.* evidence given against one's accomplice in return for a free pardon, during the reign of a king. **king's evil** *n.* (*Hist.*) scrofula, formerly believed to be cured by the royal touch. **King's Guide** *n.* a Guide who has reached the highest level of proficiency, during the reign of a king. **King's highway** *n.* a public road, a right-of-way. **kingship** *n.* **king-size, king-sized** *a.* (of beds etc.) larger than is usual. **king's knight** *n.* in chess, the knight on the king's side of the board at the start of play. **King's Messenger** *n.* a courier in the diplomatic service during the reign of a king. **king's pawn** *n.* in chess, the pawn in front of the king at the start of play. **King's peace** *n.* (*Hist.*) the state of tranquillity, order and absence of hostilities throughout the country, for which the king was responsible. **King's Proctor** *n.* an officer of the Crown during the reign of a king who intervenes in probate, divorce or nullity cases when collusion or other irregularity is alleged. **king's ransom** *n.* a large sum of money. **King's Remembrancer** *n.* (*Hist.*) an officer of the Exchequer whose business was to collect debts due to the king. **king's rook** *n.* in chess, the rook on the king's side of the board at the start of play. **King's Scout** *n.* a Scout who has reached the highest level of proficiency, during the reign of a king. **king's spear** *n.* any of several tall lilies, esp. *Asphodeline lutea.* **King's Speech** *n.* during the reign of a king, an address by the sovereign to Parliament at the beginning of every session, outlining the government's proposed legislation. **king's yellow** *n.* orpiment or yellow arsenic used as a pigment. **kingwood** *n.* **1** a Brazilian leguminous tree, *Dalbergia cearensis.* **2** the fine, hard wood from this tree, used for turning and cabinet work. [OE *cyning* (*cyn,* KIN, -ING[1]), cp. Dut. *koning,* Icel. *konungr,* G *könig*]

kinin (kī´nin) *n.* **1** any of a group of polyptetides formed in the body which cause dilation of the blood vessels. **2** a plant hormone which promotes cell division and slows down the ageing process in plants. [Gr. *kinema,* movement, -IN]

kink (kingk) *n.* **1** a twist or abrupt bend in a rope, thread, wire etc. **2** a prejudice, a whim. *~v.i.* to twist or run into kinks. *~v.t.* to cause to kink. **kinky** *a.* (*comp.* **kinkier,** *superl.* **kinkiest**) **1** (*coll.*) given to abnormal sexual practices. **2** (*coll.*) (sexually) provocative. **3** eccentric, odd. **4** twisted, curly. **kinkily** *adv.* **kinkiness** *n.* [prob. from Dut. *kink* (cp. Dan., Swed., Norse and G *Kink*)]

kinkajou (king´kəjoo) *n.* (*pl.* **kinkajous**) an arboreal fruit-eating quadruped, *Potos flavus,* of S and Central America, allied to the raccoon, with long body and prehensile tail. [F *quincajou,* from Algonquian]

kino (kē´nō) *n.* (*pl.* **kinos**) an astringent gum used for tanning or dyeing and in medicine, obtained from certain Indian, African and Australian trees. [prob. W Afr.]

-kins (kinz) *suf.* added to nouns to show affection, as in *mummykins, daddykins* etc. [cp. -KIN]

kinsfolk, kinsman etc. KIN.

kiosk (kē´osk) *n.* **1** an open-fronted structure for the sale of newspapers etc. **2** a public telephone booth. **3** an open pavilion or summerhouse in Turkey, Iran etc. **4** (*Austral.*) a café in the grounds of a park, zoo etc. **5** a band-stand. [F *kiosque,* Turk. *qiushk,* Pers. *qūshk,* palace, villa]

kip[1] (kip) *n.* (*sl.*) **1** a sleep. **2** a cheap lodging-house. **3** a bed. **4** a brothel. *~v.i.* (*pres.p.* **kipping,** *past, p.p.* **kipped**) to go to sleep. **to kip down** to lie down and go to sleep. **kip-house** *n.* [cp. Dan. *kippe*]

kip[2] (kip) *n.* **1** the hide of a calf or of small cattle, used for leather. **2** leather made from such skins. **kip-leather** *n.* **kipskin** *n.* [etym. uncertain]

kip[3] (kip) *n.* (*pl.* **kip, kips**) the standard monetary unit of Laos. [Thai]

kip[4] (kip) *n.* (*Austral., sl.*) a wooden bat for tossing coins in the game of two-up. [etym. uncertain]

kipper (kip´ə) *n.* **1** a salmon or herring split open, salted and dried in smoke or the open air. **2** a male salmon during the spawning season. *~v.t.* to cure and preserve (salmon, herrings etc.) by rubbing with salt and drying in smoke or in the open air. **kipperer** *n.* **kipper tie** *n.* a very wide tie. [etym. uncertain; identity with OE *cypera*, a kind of salmon, uncertain]

kipsie (kip´si), **kipsy** *n.* (*pl.* **kipsies**) (*Austral.*, *sl.*) a home, house or shelter. [prob. from KIP[1]]

Kir® (kiə), **kir** *n.* a drink made from white wine and cassis. [Felix *Kir*, 1876–1968, mayor of Dijon, France, said to have invented it]

kirbygrip (kœ´bigrip), **Kirbigrip®** *n.* a type of hairgrip.

Kirghiz, Kirgiz KYRGYZ.

kirk (kœk) *n.* (*Sc.*, *North.*) **1** a church. **2** (**Kirk**) the established (Presbyterian) Church of Scotland, esp. in contradistinction to the Church of England or the Scottish Episcopal Church. **kirkman** *n.* (*pl.* **kirkmen**) a member of the Church of Scotland. **Kirk-session** *n.* **1** the lowest court in the Church of Scotland. **2** (*Hist.*) the lowest court in other Presbyterian Churches consisting of the minister and elders. [var. of CHURCH]

kirmess KERMIS.

kirn (kœn) *n.* (*Sc.*) **1** a harvest home. **2** the last sheaf of the harvest. **to win/ get the kirn 1** to cut the last armful of corn. **2** to finish the harvest. **kirn-baby, kirn-dolly** *n.* a corn dolly. [etym. uncertain]

kirsch (kiəsh), **kirschwasser** (kiəsh´vasə) *n.* an alcoholic liqueur distilled from the fermented juice of the black cherry. [G (*Kirsche*, cherry, *Wasser*, water)]

†**kirtle** (kœ´təl) *n.* **1** a woman's gown or petticoat. **2** a man's short jacket, tunic or coat. [OE *cyrtel* (cp. Icel. *kyrtill*, Dan. and Swed. *kjortel*), perh. from L *curtus*]

kiskadee (kiskədē´), **keskidee** (kes-) *n.* a South and Central American flycatcher, *Pitangus sulphuratus*. [imit.]

Kislev (kis´lef, -lef´) *n.* the third month of the civil, and the ninth of the ecclesiastical Jewish year, corresponding roughly to December. [Heb.]

kismet (kiz´mət, kis´-) *n.* fate, destiny. [Turk. *qismet*, Pers. *qismat*, Arab. *qisma(t)*, from *qasama*, to divide]

kiss (kis) *n.* **1** a touch with the lips, esp. in affection or as a salutation. **2** in snooker, billiards etc., a mere touch of the moving balls. **3** a confection of sugar, white of eggs etc. *~v.t.* **1** to press or touch with the lips, esp. in affection or as a salutation. **2** (of a ball or balls) in snooker, billiards etc., to touch lightly in passing. *~v.i.* **1** to join lips in affection or respect. **2** (of moving balls) in snooker, billiards etc. to come in contact. **to kiss away** to wipe away by kissing. **to kiss goodbye to 1** to give a kiss to on parting. **2** (*coll.*) to accept the loss of. **to kiss hands** to kiss one's sovereign's hands when one accepts office. **to kiss off 1** (*N Am.*, *sl.*) to get rid of (someone) rudely. **2** (*N Am.*, *sl.*) to die, to go away. **to kiss someone's arse** (*sl.*) to be obsequious. **to kiss the book** to touch the Bible with the lips in taking an oath. **to kiss the dust 1** to be conquered, to yield. **2** to die, to be slain. **to kiss the earth** to kiss the ground. **to kiss the ground 1** to bow down, to prostrate oneself. **2** to be conquered. **to kiss the rod** to submit tamely to punishment. **kissable** *a.* **Kissagram®** (-əgram), **kissogram** *n.* a congratulatory message delivered by an agency with a kiss. **kiss and tell** *n.* the practice of selling stories of one's sexual relationships to the press. **kiss-curl** *n.* a curl hanging over the forehead, in front of the ear or at the nape of the neck. **kisser** *n.* **1** a person who kisses. **2** (*sl.*) the mouth, the face. **kissing** *n.*, *a.* **kissing cousin, kissing kin, kissing kind** *n.* a relation familiar enough to be kissed on meeting. **kissing gate** *n.* a gate hung in a U or V-shaped enclosure. **kiss of death** *n.* something which will inevitably lead to failure. **kiss-off** *n.* (*N Am.*, *sl.*) a dismissal, the sack. **kiss of life** *n.* mouth-to-mouth resuscitation. **kiss of peace** *n.* a ceremonial kiss among Christians, esp. during the Eucharist. **kissy** *a.* (*coll.*) affectionate, liking to kiss. [OE *coss*, whence the v. *cyssan* (cp. Dut. *kus* and *kussen*, Icel. *koss* and *kyssa*, G *Kuss* and *küssen*)]

kist CIST[1].

Kiswahili (kēswəhē´li) *n.* a widely-spoken Bantu language, Swahili. [Bantu, *ki-* language pref., SWAHILI]

kit[1] (kit) *n.* **1** the equipment, clothing etc. needed for a particular job, sport etc. **2** pieces of equipment, sold as a set, and ready for assembly. **3** a container for the necessaries, tools etc. for a particular job. **4** a kitbag. **5** (*Hist.*) a wooden tub, a milk pail, a tub for pickled fish, butter etc. **6** a chest, a box. *~v.t.* (*pres.p.* **kitting**, *past*, *p.p.* **kitted**) (*usu. with out, up*) to fit out with the necessary clothes or equipment. **the whole kit (and caboodle)** (*coll.*) the whole lot. **kitbag** *n.* a strong bag for holding a person's clothes and equipment, esp. that of a member of the service. **kit-car, kit-boat** *n.* a car or boat assembled from a set of pieces by an amateur. [MDut. *kitte*, a wooden bowl or tub]

kit[2] (kit) *n.* (*Hist.*) a type of small violin esp. used by dancing masters. [etym. uncertain]

kit[3] (kit) *n.* **1** a kitten. **2** a young fox or badger. **kit-fox** *n.* either of two North American foxes, *Vulpes velox* and *Vulpes macrotis*. [short for KITTEN]

kit-cat (kit´kat) *n.* **1** (*also* **kit-cat portrait**) a portrait of a particular size, rather less than half-length but showing one hand. **2** a size of canvas 28 by 36 in. (about 70 by 90 cm), used for portraits, that size being adopted by Kneller for the portraits he painted of the Kit-Cat Club. **Kit-Cat Club** *n.* (*Hist.*) a club founded by Whig politicians. [*Kit* (or Christopher) *Cat* or *Catling*, who kept a pie-house near Temple Bar where the Kit-Cat Club (founded 1688) met]

kitchen (kich´ən) *n.* **1** a room or area in a house etc. where food is cooked. **2** a set of units and fitments for a kitchen. **3** (*sl.*) the percussion section of an orchestra. **kitchen cabinet** *n.* a political leader's unofficial advisers esp. when considered too influential. **kitchen dresser** *n.* a kitchen sideboard with a set of drawers, for displaying plates etc. †**kitchen Dutch** *n.* a form of Afrikaans with an admixture of English and Xhosa etc., used by or to S Africans not of Dutch descent. **kitchenette** (-net´) *n.* a small kitchen. **kitchen garden** *n.* a garden in which herbs and vegetables etc. are cultivated for the table. **kitchen-maid** *n.* a female servant employed to assist a cook. **kitchen-midden** *n.* a prehistoric refuse heap or shell-mound indicating an ancient settlement (first noticed on the coast of Denmark, and since found in the British Isles etc.). **kitchen police** *n.pl.* (*US*, *sl.*) soldiers working in the kitchen, esp. for committing some offence. **kitchen roll** *n.* a roll of absorbent paper used for wiping, cleaning etc. **kitchen-sink** *a.* (of drama etc.) depicting the reality and often the sordid quality of everyday life. **kitchen tea** *n.* (*Austral.*, *New Zeal.*) a party held before a wedding to which the guests bring gifts of kitchenware. **kitchen unit** *n.* any of a set of units for a fitted kitchen. **kitchenware** *n.* the pots, pans, china and other utensils used in the kitchen. [OE *cycene*, late L *cucīna*, L *coquīna*, from *coquere*, to cook]

kite (kīt) *n.* **1** a device consisting of a light frame of wood covered with fabric or paper, constructed to fly in the air by means of a string. **2** any of various medium-sized birds of prey of the genus *Milvus*, esp. the European kite, *M. milvus*. **3** (*sl.*) an aircraft. **4** (*sl.*) an accommodation bill. **5** (*pl.*) light sails, set only in very light winds, above the other sails. **6** (*Geom.*) a four-sided figure that is symmetrical on each side of one diagonal. **7** †a greedy or rapacious person, a sharper. *~v.i.* **1** to fly like a kite. **2** (*sl.*) to fly a kite. *~v.t.* (*sl.*) to issue or convert into an accommodation bill. **to fly a kite 1** to try out an idea, to find out about a situation, public opinion etc. **2** (*sl.*) to raise money on an accommodation bill. **kite balloon** *n.* a captive balloon for scientific or military observations etc. **kite-flyer** *n.* **kite-flying** *n.* **1** flying and controlling a kite. **2** the circulation of rumours to test public opinion. **Kitemark** *n.* a kite-shaped mark indicating that goods conform in all particulars with the specifications of the British Standards Institution. [OE *cӯta*]

kith (kith) *n.* kindred. **kith and kin** close friends and relations. [OE *cythth*, knowledge, native country, from *cūth*, known (*cunnan*, to know)]

kitsch (kich) *n.* art or literature that is inferior or in bad taste, esp. that designed to appeal to popular sentimentality. **kitschy** *a.* (*comp.* **kitschier**, *superl.* **kitschiest**). **kitschiness** *n.* [G]

kitten (kit´ən) *n.* **1** the young of the cat. **2** a young ferret, fox etc. **3** a playful girl. *~v.i., v.t.* to give birth to (kittens). **to have kittens** (*coll.*) to be overexcited, very annoyed etc. **kittenish** *a.* **1** like a kitten. **2** (of a girl) playful in a sexy way. **kittenishly** *adv.* **kittenishness** *n.* **kitty**[1] *n.* (*pl.* **kitties**) (*coll.*) (a pet name for) a kitten. [ME *kitoun*, OF *chitoun* (F *chaton*), from *chat*, cat]

kittiwake (kit´iwāk) *n.* a seagull of the genus *Rissa*, esp. *R. tridactyla*, common on the British coasts. [imit. of its cry]

kittle (kit´əl) *a.* (*also* **kittle-cattle** (-kat´əl)) ticklish, awkward to deal with, intractable. *~v.t.* (*esp. Sc.*) **1** to tickle. **2** to excite a pleasant sensation in, to rouse. [prob. from Icel. *kitla*]

kitty[1] KITTEN.

kitty[2] (kit´i) *n.* (*pl.* **kitties**) **1** the pool into which each player puts a stake in poker, and other games. **2** a common fund of money. **3** the jack in bowls.

kitty-cornered CATER-CORNERED (under CATER[2]).

kiwi (kē´wē) *n.* (*pl.* **kiwis**) **1** a New Zealand wingless bird of the genus *Apteryx*. **2** (*coll.*) (**Kiwi**) a New Zealander. **kiwi fruit** *n.* the edible green fruit of a climbing plant, *Actinidia chinensis*, also called *Chinese gooseberry*. [Maori]

kJ *abbr.* kilojoule(s).

KJV *abbr.* King James Version (of the Bible).

KKK *abbr.* Ku Klux Klan.

kl. *abbr.* kilolitre(s).

Klan (klan) *n.* the Ku Klux Klan. **Klansman, Klanswoman** *n.* (*pl.* **Klansmen, Klanswomen**) a member of the Ku Klux Klan.

Klaxon® (klak´sən), **klaxon** *n.* a loud horn or hooter, formerly used on cars.

Kleenex® (klē´neks) *n.* (*pl.* **Kleenex, Kleenexes**) a soft paper tissue used as a handkerchief etc.

Klein bottle (klīn) *n.* (*Math.*) a one-sided surface surrounding a three-dimensional space, formed by putting the narrow end of tapered tube through the surface of the tube, then stretching it to fit into the other end. [Felix *Klein*, 1849–1925, German mathematician]

klepht (kleft) *n.* **1** any of the Greeks who refused to submit to the Turks after the conquest (15th cent.), and took refuge in the mountains. **2** any of their descendants, many of whom lived as bandits. **3** a bandit, a brigand. [mod. Gr. *klephtēs*, Gr. *kleptēs*, thief]

kleptomania (kleptōmā´niə) *n.* a form of mental illness displaying itself in an irresistible urge to steal. **kleptomaniac** (-ak) *n., a.* [Gr. *kleptēs*, thief, as KLEPHT, -MANIA]

klieg (klēg), **klieg light** *n.* a powerful arc lamp used as floodlighting in a film studio. [John *Kliegl*, 1869–1959, and Anton *Kliegl*, 1872–1927, American inventors]

klipspringer (klip´springə) *n.* a small S African antelope, *Oreotragus oreotragus*. [Afrikaans *klip*, rock, SPRINGER (under SPRING)]

Klondike (klon´dīk), **Klondyke** *n.* a source of wealth. [*Klondike* goldrush, NW Canada, 1896]

klong (klong) *n.* a canal in Thailand. [Thai]

kloof (kloof) *n.* (*S Afr.*) a ravine, gully or mountain gorge. [Dut., cleft]

kludge (klŭj) *n.* **1** (*sl.*) an untidy mixture of things. **2** (*Comput.*) an unreliable system or program. [invented, cp. *bodge*, *fudge*]

klutz (klŭts) *n.* (*N Am., sl.*) a clumsy or foolish person. **klutzy** *a.* [Yiddish, from Gr *Klotz*, wooden block]

klystron (klīs´tron) *n.* an electron tube used to amplify or generate microwaves. [Gr. *kluzō*, *klus-*, wash over]

km *abbr.* kilometre(s).

kn. *abbr.* (*Naut.*) knot(s).

knack (nak) *n.* **1** a trick or adroit way of doing a thing. **2** dexterity, adroitness. **3** a habit, a mannerism. **knacky** *a.* **knackiness** *n.* [prob. onomat.]

knacker (nak´ə) *n.* **1** a buyer of worn-out horses, cattle etc. for slaughter; a horse-slaughterer. **2** a dealer in second-hand goods, houses, ships etc. **3** (*usu. pl., sl.*) a testicle. *~v.t.* **1** (*coll.*) to break, ruin or kill. **2** to wear out, exhaust. **knackered** *a.* (*coll.*) exhausted, tired out. **knackery** *n.* (*pl.* **knackeries**) a knacker's business, a knacker's yard. [perh. from *nacker*, saddler, cp. ON *hnakkur*, saddle]

knackwurst (nak´wœst) *n.* a type of short fat spicy German sausage. [G *knacken*, to crackle, *Wurst*, sausage]

knag (nag) *n.* **1** a knot in wood. **2** a knob, a peg. **3** the shoot of a deer's horn. **4** the rough or rugged top of a hill or rock. [cp. G *knagge*, Norw. and Swed. *knagg*]

knap[1] (nap) *n.* (*dial.*) **1** a hill crest, rising ground. **2** a protuberance, a knob. [OE *cnæpp*, prob. cogn. with Icel. *knappr*, Dan. *knap*, a KNOB]

knap[2] (nap) *v.t.* (*pres.p.* **knapping**, *past, p.p.* **knapped**) **1** to break into pieces, esp. with a sharp snapping noise, to break, flake, or chip (flint). **2** to strike smartly. **knapper** *n.* **1** a person who breaks flints. **2** a person who shapes gun flints, flint implements etc. [imit., cp. Dut. *knappen*]

knapsack (nap´sak) *n.* a case or bag for clothes, food etc., carried on the back by soldiers on a march or by hikers etc. [cp. Dut. *knapzak* (*knappen*, to snap, to bite, to eat, *zak*, SACK[1])]

knapweed (nap´wēd) *n.* any of various composite plants with purple globular flowers, of the genus *Centaurea*, esp. *C. nigra*, and *C. scabiosa*. [formerly *knopweed* (KNOP, WEED)]

knar (nah), **gnar** *n.* a knot in wood, a protuberance on the trunk or branch of a tree. [cp. LG *knarre*, *knorre*, Dut. *knar*, *knar*]

knave (nāv) *n.* **1** a deceitful, cunning person, a rogue. **2** a court card with a representation of a soldier or servant, the jack. **3** †a male servant. **knavery** (-vəri) *n.* (*pl.* **knaveries**) **1** dishonesty. **2** a dishonest act. **knavish** *a.* **knavishly** *adv.* **knavishness** *n.* [OE *cnafa*, a boy (cp. Dut. *knaap*, Icel. *knapi*, G *Knabe*)]

knawel (naw´əl) *n.* any of several short plants of the genus *Scleranthus*. [G]

knead (nēd) *v.t.* **1** to work up (flour, clay etc.) into a plastic mass by pressing and folding it with the hands. **2** to shape, make, mingle or blend by this method. **3** to blend together. **4** to pummel and press with the heel of the hand in massage. **kneadable** *a.* **kneader** *n.* [OE *cnedan* (cp. Dut. *kneden*, G *kneten*)]

knee (nē) *n.* (*pl.* **knees**) **1** the joint of the thigh or femur with the lower leg. **2** a joint roughly corresponding to this in other animals. **3** the upper part of a person's thighs, when sitting. **4** the part of a garment covering the knee. **5** a piece of timber or metal cut or cast with an angle like that of the knee to connect beams etc. **6** anything resembling a knee in shape or function. *~v.t.* (*3rd pers. sing. pres.* **knees**, *pres.p.* **kneeing**, *past, p.p.* **kneed**) **1** to touch or strike with the knee. **2** to fasten or strengthen (beams etc.) with knees. **3** (*coll.*) to cause (trousers) to bag at the knees. **to bend/ bow the knee 1** to kneel in submission. **2** to submit. **to bring to one's knees** to reduce to submission. **to give a knee to 1** to support on one's knee during a pause in a fight or contest. **2** to act as second to. **knee-breeches** *n.pl.* breeches reaching just below the knee. **kneecap** *n.* **1** the heart-shaped sesamoid bone in front of the knee joint, the patella. 2 a padded cover for the knee. ~*v.t.* (*pres.p.* **kneecapping,** *past, p.p.* **kneecapped**) to shoot or injure (esp. an informer) in the knees. **kneecapping** *n.* **kneed** *a.* (*usu. in comb.*, as *loose-kneed*). **knee-deep** *a.* 1 (of a person or animal) sunk in as far as the knees. 2 (of liquid) deep enough to reach the knees. 3 deeply involved. **knee-high** *a.* coming up to the knee. **knee-high to a grasshopper** GRASSHOPPER. **kneehole** *n.* a space for the knees between the pedestals of a writing table or desk. **kneehole desk, kneehole table** *n.* **knee-jerk** *n.* 1 a reflex kick of the lower part of the leg. 2 (*coll.*) a reflex, an automatic reaction. **knee joint** *n.* 1 (*Anat.*) the articulation of the femur with the tibia. 2 a joint between two pieces hinged together. **knee-length** *a.* reaching down to, or up to, the knee. **knee-pan** *n.* the kneecap or socket of the knee. **knees-up** *n.* (*coll.*) a party, a celebration. **knee-swell** *n.* a lever for working the swell of an organ, operated by the knee. **knee-trembler** *n.* (*sl.*) an act of sexual intercourse standing up. [OE *cnēo, cnēow* (cp. Dut. and G *knie*, Icel. *knē*, also L *genu*, Gr. *gonu*)]

kneel (nēl) *v.i.* (*past, p.p.* **knelt** (nelt), (*N Am.*) **kneeled** (nēld)) 1 to bend or incline the knees. 2 to fall on the knees. 3 to support the body on the knees. **kneeler** *n.* 1 a stool or cushion for kneeling on. 2 a person who kneels. [OE *cnēowlian*, from *cnēow*, KNEE]

knell (nel) *v.i.* 1 to ring, to toll, as for a death or funeral. 2 to sound in a mournful or ominous manner. ~*v.t.* to proclaim or summon by or as by a knell. ~*n.* 1 the sound of a bell when struck, esp. for a death or funeral. 2 an evil omen, a death blow. [OE *cnyllan*, from Gmc. *knel-* (cp. Dut. and G *knallen*, Swed. *knalla*), imit. in orig.]

knelt KNEEL.

Knesset (knes´it) *n.* the single-chamber parliament of the modern state of Israel. [Heb., assembly]

knew KNOW.

knickerbocker (nik´əbokə) *n.* 1 (*pl.*) loose breeches gathered in below the knee. 2 (**Knickerbocker**) a New Yorker esp. one of original Dutch descent. **Knickerbocker Glory** *n.* a large ice cream sundae, with fruit and jelly. [imaginary author of Washington Irving's *History of New York*]

knickers (nik´əz) *n.pl.* 1 women's underpants; also called *pair of knickers.* 2 (*N Am.*) knickerbockers. 3 (*N Am.*) short trousers. ~*int.* (*sl.*) used to express disagreement or contempt. **to get one's knickers in a twist** (*coll.*) to be overanxious, upset etc.

knick-knack (nik´nak), **nick-nack** *n.* 1 any little ornamental article. 2 a showy trifle. **knick-knackery** *n.* **knick-knackish** *a.* [redupl. of KNACK]

knife (nīf) *n.* (*pl.* **knives**) 1 a blade with one edge sharpened, usu. set in a handle. 2 a cutting blade forming part of a machine. 3 †a sword or dagger. ~*v.t.* 1 to stab or cut with a knife. 2 (*coll.*) to betray, to defeat or injure deceitfully. ~*v.i.* to cut (through) like a knife. **before you can say knife** (*coll.*) very soon, very quickly. **that one could cut like a knife** 1 (*coll.*) (of an accent) thick, very marked. 2 (*coll.*) (of an atmosphere etc.) very tense, oppressive. **the knife** (*coll.*) surgical operations. **to get/ have one's knife in someone** to be vindictive towards someone. **under the knife** (*coll.*) undergoing a surgical operation. **knife-board** *n.* a board to clean knives on. **knife-edge** *n.* 1 the edge of a knife. 2 a hard steel edge used as fulcrum for a balance, pendulum etc. 3 a difficult situation where things could go either right or wrong. 4 a sharp mountain ridge. **knife-grinder** *n.* 1 a person who sharpens knives, esp. an itinerant knife-sharpener. 2 a person who grinds knives during manufacturing. **knifelike** *a.* **knife machine** *n.* a machine for cleaning knives. **knife-pleat** *n.* a narrow flat pleat turned in a single direction. **knifepoint** *n.* the pointed end of a knife. **at knifepoint** threatened by someone with a knife. **knifer** *n.* **knife rest** *n.* a support for a carving knife or fork at table. **knife switch** *n.* an electric switch consisting of knife-like pieces hinged at one end, and having contact at the other with springs. **knife-throwing** *n.* a form of entertainment in which knives are thrown at targets. **knife-thrower** *n.* [OE *cnīf* (cp. Dut. *knijf*, Icel. *knīfr, hnīfr*, G *Kneif*)]

knight (nīt) *n.* 1 a man who holds a non-hereditary dignity conferred by the sovereign or their representative, and entitling the possessor to the title of 'Sir' prefixed to his name. 2 (*Hist.*) a man of gentle birth, usu. one who had served as page and esquire, admitted to an honourable degree of military rank, with ceremonies or religious rites. 3 (*Hist.*) a champion to a lady in war or at a tournament. 4 a chivalrous or quixotic person. 5 a chess piece, usu. shaped like a horse's head, entitled to move two squares straight and one at right-angles. 6 (*Hist.*) a member of the class of Equites in ancient Rome. 7 (*Hist.*) an Athenian citizen of the middle class in ancient Greece, as constituted by Solon. ~*v.t.* to create or dub (a person) a knight. **knightage** (-ij) *n.* 1 knights collectively. 2 a list of knights. **knight bachelor** *n.* (*pl.* **knights bachelor**) 1 a knight of the oldest order of knighthood. 2 one knighted but not belonging to any of the special orders. **knight-banneret** *n.* (*pl.* **knights-banneret**) a knight holding the rank of banneret. **knight commander** *n.* a member of one of the higher grades in some orders of knighthood. **knight errant** *n.* 1 a medieval knight who wandered about in quest of adventures to show his prowess and generosity. 2 a chivalrous or quixotic person. **knight-errantry** *n.* **knighthead** *n.* (*Naut.*) either of a pair of vertical posts supporting the bowsprit (the tops formerly being ornamented with figures resembling human heads). **knighthood** *n.* **Knight Hospitaller** *n.* (*pl.* **Knights Hospitallers**) a member of a military order of monks founded in the crusades. **knight in shining armour** *n.* (*coll.*) a man who helps a woman in difficulty. **knight-like** *a.* **knightly** *a., adv.* (*poet.*) **knightliness** *n.* **knight marshal** *n.* (*Hist.*) an official in the household of the British sovereign having a judicial role. †**knight of the pad** *n.* a footpad, a highwaymen. **knight of the road** *n.* 1 (*coll.*) **a** a footpad, a highwayman. **b** a tramp. 2 a commercial traveller. 3 a lorry driver or taxi driver. **knight of the shire** *n.* (*Hist.*) a gentleman representing an English county in Parliament. **knight service** *n.* in feudal law, tenure of land on condition of military service. **knight's fee** *n.* (*Hist.*) the amount of land for which the services of a knight were accorded. **knight's progress** *n.* in chess, a combination of moves which allows a knight to visit every square on the board. **Knight Templar** *n.* (*pl.* **Knights Templars**) (*Hist.*) a member of a religious and military order founded in the 12th cent., for the protection of pilgrims to the Holy Land. [OE *cniht*, a boy, a servant (cp. Dut. and G *knecht*, Swed. *knekt*, soldier)]

kniphofia (nifō´fiə) *n.* any of various tall plants of the genus *Kniphofia*, native to S and E Africa and having spikes of red, orange or yellow flowers, esp. the red-hot poker. [J. H. *Kniphof*, 1704–63, German professor of medicine]

knish (kənish´) *n.* a filled dumpling that is baked or fried. [Yiddish, from Rus. *knysh* cake]

knit (nit) *v.t.* (*pres.p.* **knitting,** *past, p.p.* **knit, knitted**) 1 to form into a fabric or form (a fabric, garment etc.) by looping or knotting a continuous yarn or thread, by hand with knitting needles or on a knitting machine. 2 to join closely together, to unite. 3 to make close or compact. 4 to contract into folds or wrinkles. 5 to make (a plain stitch) by the simplest form of loop in knitting. ~*v.i.* 1 to make a textile fabric by interweaving yarn or thread. 2 to grow together in healing etc. 3 to become closely united. **4** (of the brows) to contract into a frowning or puzzled expression. *~n.* **1** style of knitting, knitted texture. **2** a knitted garment, knitted fabric. **to knit one's brows** BROW. **to knit up 1** to repair by knitting. **2** to conclude, to wind up (a speech, argument etc.). **knitter** *n.* **1** a person who knits. **2** a knitting machine. **knitting** *n.* **1** a piece of knitted work in the process of being made. **2** the making of a textile fabric by interweaving yarn or thread. **3** contracting, growing together etc. **knitting machine** *n.* an apparatus for mechanically knitting jerseys etc. **knitting needle** *n.* a long eyeless rod of metal, wood, plastic etc., used to hold and make stitches in knitting. **knitwear** *n.* knitted clothes, usu. sweaters. [OE *cnyttan* (cp. MDut. *knutten*, Icel. *knytja*, G *kntten*), rel. to KNOT[1]]

knives KNIFE.

knob (nob) *n.* **1** a rounded protuberance, usu. at the end of something. **2** a rounded handle of a door, lock, drawer etc. **3** (*N Am.*) a rounded hill, a knoll. **4** an ornamental terminal boss. **5** a small lump (of coal, sugar etc.). **6** (*sl.*) a penis. *~v.t.* (*pres.* **knobbing,** *past, p.p.* **knobbed**) to furnish with a knob or knobs. *~v.i.* **1** to become knobby. **2** to bulge or bunch (out). **with knobs on** (*sl.*) even more so. **knobbed** *a.* **knobble** (nob´əl) *n.* a small knob. **knobbly** *a.* (*comp.* **knobblier,** *superl.* **knobbliest**). **knobby** *a.* **knobbiness** *n.* **knoblike** *a.* **knobstick** *n.* **1** a knobbed stick used as a weapon. **2** (*sl.*) †a worker who refuses to join a strike. [cogn. with KNOP (cp. G *Knobbe*, Dut. *knobbel*)]

knobkerrie (nob´keri), **knopkierie** (knop´kiəri) *n.* the round-headed club used as a weapon by S African tribesmen. [Afrikaans *knopkirie*]

knock (nok) *v.t.* **1** to strike so as to make a sound, to hit, to give a hard blow to. **2** to drive or force by striking. **3** to make by knocking. **4** to cause to strike together. **5** (*coll.*) to criticize. **6** (*sl.*) to amaze. **7** (*sl.*) to have sex with. *~v.i.* **1** to strike hard or smartly (at, against, together etc.). **2** to rap on a door for admitting or attention. **3** to collide. **4** (of an engine) to make knocking sounds. *~n.* **1** a blow. **2** a rap, esp. on a door for admittance or attention. **3** the sound of knocking in an engine. **4** an act of knocking. **5** (*coll.*) an innings at cricket. **to knock about/ around 1** to strike with repeated blows. **2** to handle violently. **3** (*coll.*) to wander about, to lead an irregular life. **4** to keep company (with). **5** to be somewhere for no particular reason. **to knock against 1** to collide with. **2** to encounter casually. **to knock back 1** (*coll.*) to drink quickly, to eat up. **2** (*coll.*) to cost (a person). **3** (*coll.*) to shock. **4** (*Austral., New Zeal., coll.*) to reject, to rebuff. **to knock cold 1** to knock unconscious. **2** to shock. **to knock down 1** to fell with a blow. **2** to demolish. **3** to prostrate (with astonishment etc.). **4** to sell (with a blow of the hammer) to a bidder at an auction. **5** (*coll.*) to lower in price, quality etc. **6** to dismantle (furniture etc.). **7** (*N Am., sl.*) to earn. **8** (*Austral., New Zeal.*) to spend (wages etc.) freely. **to knock into a cocked hat** COCK[1]. **to knock into shape** SHAPE. **to knock into the middle of next week** (*coll.*) to butt or strike (a person) very hard, to send flying. **to knock off 1** to strike off, with a blow. **2** to dispatch, to do or finish quickly. **3** to cease work. **4** to leave off (work). **5** to deduct (from a price etc.). **6** (*sl.*) to steal. **7** (*sl.*) to kill. **8** (*sl.*) to have sex with. **to knock on** in rugby, to play (the ball) with the hand or arm and in the direction of the opponents' goal line. **to knock oneself out** (*coll.*) to exhaust oneself. **to knock one's head against** to come into collision with (awkward facts etc.). **to knock one's head against a brick wall** BRICK. **to knock on the head 1** to stun or kill with a blow on the head. **2** to frustrate, to spoil, to defeat. **to knock on wood** (*N Am.*) to touch wood (for luck etc.). **to knock out 1** to make unconscious by a blow to the head. **2** to force out with a blow. **3** to defeat (a boxer) by knocking down for a count of ten. **4** to eliminate from a contest by defeating. **5** (*coll.*) to astonish or impress. **6** (*coll.*) to do or make quickly. **7** (*sl.*) to earn. **8** to empty tobacco from (a pipe) by tapping. **to knock sideways** to knock off course, to destroy the composure of. **to knock spots off** SPOT. **to knock the bottom out of** BOTTOM. **to knock the socks off** SOCK[1]. **to knock the stuffing out of** STUFF. **to knock together** to put hastily or roughly into shape. **to knock up 1** to strike or force upwards. **2** to arouse by knocking. **3** to fatigue, to wear out, to exhaust. **4** to put together or make up hastily. **5** to score (runs) quickly at cricket. **6** (*sl.*) to make (someone) pregnant. **7** to practise before starting to play a ball game. **to knock wood** (*N Am.*) to touch wood (for luck etc.). **knockabout** *a.* **1** noisy, rough, violent, slapstick. **2** (of clothes etc.) suitable for rough usage. **3** irregular, bohemian. *~n.* **1** a knockabout performance or performer. **2** (*Austral.*) a farm or station handyman. **3** a light, partly-decked yacht or sailing boat. **knock-back** *n.* (*Austral., New Zeal., coll.*) a rejection, a setback. **knock-down** *a.* **1** (of a blow) that knocks an opponent down. **2** (of an event etc.) overwhelmingly bad, decisive. **3 a** (of a price at auction) reserve or minimum. **b** (of a sale price) very low. **4** (of furniture) easy to dismantle and reassemble. **5** (of insecticide) that acts quickly. *~n.* **1** a knock-down blow. **2** a free fight. **3** (*Austral., New Zeal., sl.*) an introduction to someone. **knocker** *n.* **1** a hammer-like attachment to an outer door to give notice that someone desires admittance or attention. **2** a person or thing that knocks. **3** (*pl.*) a woman's breasts. **4** an itinerant salesperson. **on the knocker 1** (*coll.*) door-to-door. **2** on credit. **3** (*Austral., New Zeal.*) promptly, at once. **up to the knocker 1** (*sl.*) in excellent condition. **2** (*sl.*) to the highest standard. **knocker-up** *n.* (*Hist.*) a person employed to get workers up for an early start by knocking on their doors etc. **knock-for-knock** *a.* denoting an agreement between vehicle insurance companies by which each company pays for the damage sustained to a vehicle insured by them irrespective of legal liability. **knocking** *n.* explosions in the cylinder of an internal combustion engine due to over-compression of the mixture of air and petrol vapour before sparking. **knocking copy** *n.* publicity aimed at undermining a competing product. **knocking shop** *n.* (*sl.*) a brothel. **knock knees** *n.pl.* knees that touch when the feet are still apart. **knock-kneed** *a.* **knock-off** *n.* (*coll.*) an imitation of a competitor's idea. **knock-on** *n.* in rugby, an act of playing the ball with the hand or arm in the direction of the opponents' goal line. **knock-on effect** *n.* an indirect result of an action. **knockout** *a.* **1** (of a blow etc.) disabling, causing unconsciousness. **2** (of a competition) in which the loser is eliminated in each round. *~n.* **1** the act of knocking a person out with a blow. **2** a blow that knocks the opponent out. **3** (*sl.*) a marvel, a wonder. **4** a knockout competition. **knockout drops** *n.pl.* (*sl.*) a drug put into someone's drink secretly. **knock-up** *n.* a practice session before the start of a racket game. [OE *cnocian, cnucian* (cp. Icel. *knoka*), prob. imit.]

knoll[1] (nōl) *n.* a rounded hill, a mound, a hillock. **knolly** *a.* [OE *cnoll* (cp. Dut. *knol*, a turnip, Swed. *knöl*, G *Knolle*)]

knoll[2] (nōl) *v.t.* **1** to ring or toll (a bell). **2** to toll or sound out (hours). **3** to proclaim or summon by ringing. **4** to ring a bell or knell for. *~v.i.* to sound (as a bell). *~n.* a knell. **knoller** *n.* [var. of KNELL]

knop (nop) *n.* **1** a knob, a button. **2** a bunch of leaves, flowers or similar ornaments. **3** †a bud. **knopped** *a.* adorned with knops. [perh. rel. to KNAP[1] (cp. Dut. and Dan. *knop*, G *Knopf*)]

knopkierie KNOBKERRIE.

knot[1] (not) *n.* **1** the interlacement or intertwining of a rope or ropes, cords etc., so as to fasten one part to another part of the rope etc. or to another object. **2** a particular method of tying a knot, a type of knot. **3** an ornamental bow or interlacement of a ribbon etc. on a dress. **4** an irregular or twisted portion in a tree caused by branches, buds etc. **5** a hard cross-grained part in a piece of wood, caused by interlacing fibres. **6** a tangle in hair etc. **7** anything resembling a knot. **8** a union or bond, esp. marriage. **9** a group, a cluster. **10** a difficulty, a perplexity, a problem. **11** the gist or kernel of a matter. **12** a nautical mile per hour as a unit of speed. **13** (*coll.*) a nautical mile. **14** a division of the log-line marked off by knots, used as a unit for measuring speed. **15** a node or joint in a stem. **16** a hard hump in the body of a person or animal. **17** a protuberance or excrescence. **18** a flower bud. **19** PORTER'S KNOT (under PORTER[1]). ~*v.t.* (*pres.p.* **knotting,** *past, p.p.* **knotted**) **1** to tie in a knot or knots. **2** to fasten with a knot. **3** to intertwine. **4** to make (a fringe) by means of knots. **5** to knit (the brows). **6** to join together closely or intricately. **7** to entangle, to perplex. ~*v.i.* **1** (of plants) to form knots. **2** to make knots for fringing. **at a rate of knots** (*coll.*) very quickly. **get knotted!** (*sl.*) an expression of anger, exasperation etc. **to tie in knots** (*coll.*) to baffle (a person) completely, to confuse. **knot-garden** *n.* an intricate formal garden. **knotgrass** *n.* a creeping plant, *Polygonum aviculare,* with internodes and white, pink, crimson or green inconspicuous flowers. **knot-hole** *n.* a hole in wood where a knot used to be. **knotless** *a.* **knotter** *n.* **knotting** *n.* **1** fancy knotted work. **2** the removal of knots from textile fabrics. **knotty** *a.* (*comp.* **knottier,** *superl.* **knottiest**) **1** full of knots. **2** rugged, rough. **3** intricate. **4** perplexing, difficult of solution. **knottily** *adv.* **knottiness** *n.* **knotweed** *n.* any of several plants of the genus *Polygonum*, esp. *Fallopia japonica.* **knotwork** *n.* **1** an ornamental fringe made by knotting cords together. **2** a representation of this in painting or carving. **3** a kind of ornamental needlework. [OE *cnotta* (cp. Dut. *knot*, G *Knoten*)]

knot[2] (not) *n.* a small sandpiper, *Calidris canutus.* [etym. unknown]

knotter, knotty etc. KNOT[1].

knout (nowt) *n.* (*Hist.*) a whip or scourge formerly used as an instrument of punishment in Russia. ~*v.t.* to punish with the knout. [F, from Rus. *knutu*]

know (nō) *v.t.* (*past* **knew** (nū), *p.p.* **known** (nōn)) **1** to have a clear and certain perception of. **2** to recognize from memory or description, to identify. **3** to be convinced of the truth or reality of. **4** to be acquainted with. **5** to have personal experience of. **6** to be subject to. **7** to be familiar with. **8** to be on intimate terms with. **9** to be aware of. **10** to understand from learning or study. **11** to be informed of. **12** †to have sexual intercourse with. ~*v.i.* **1** to have knowledge. **2** †to be assured (of). **3** †to be acquainted. ~*n.* knowledge, knowing. **all one knows (how) 1** all one is able. **2** as much as one can. **before one knows where one is** surprisingly quickly. **don't I know it!** (*coll.*) used to express ironic agreement. **don't you know** (*coll.*) used to express emphasis. **for all I know** as far as I am aware. **for aught I know** for all I know. **I knew it!** I imagined that this would happen. **I know what...** I have an idea. **in the know 1** in the secret. **2** acquainted with what is going on. **not to be in the know 1** to have no way of finding out. **2** not to be informed or told. **not to know someone from Adam** to have no idea at all who someone is. **not to know the half of it** HALF. **not to know what hit one** to be suddenly taken by surprise. **not to want to know** to prefer to ignore. **to have been known to** to have done in the past. **to know a hawk from a handsaw** HAWK[1]. **to know a thing or two** (*coll.*) to have considerable experience, to be worldly-wise. **to know best** to be the most informed person, in the best position for making decisions etc. **to know better than to/ that** to have enough the intelligence, common sense or courtesy not to. **to know by name 1** to have heard mentioned. **2** to be able to provide the name of. **to know by sight** to be familiar enough to recognize (but not to speak to). **to know how** to know the way to accomplish something. **to know inside out** INSIDE[1]. **to know like the back of one's hand** BACK[1]. **to know of** to be informed of, to have heard of. **to know one's onions** ONION. **to know one's own mind** to be decisive. **to know one's stuff** (*coll.*) to be competent in one's chosen field, to know what one needs to know. **to know the ropes** (*coll.*) to be acquainted with the particular conditions of any affair or proceeding. **to know the score** (*coll.*) to know the facts of the situation. **to know what's what 1** (*coll.*) to be experienced, to know the ways of the world. **2** to appreciate a good thing. **to know which side one's bread is buttered (on)** to appreciate what is in one's best interests. **to know who's who** (*coll.*) to be able to name or identify everybody. **what do you know (about that)?** an expression of incredulity. **you know 1** (*coll.*) used as a meaningless filler in conversation. **2** used as a reminder that the person addressed is familiar with who or what is mentioned. **you know something?/ what?** (*coll.*) used to introduce information regarded as new. **you never know** things are never certain. **knowable** *a.* **knowability** (-bil´-), **knowableness** *n.* **know-all** *n.* (*derog.*) someone who thinks they know everything. **knower** *n.* **know-how** *n.* **1** (*coll.*) specialized skill, expertise. **2** natural skill. **knowing** *a.* **1** conscious, deliberate. **2** skilful, experienced. **3** sharp, cunning, sly. ~*n.* awareness, possession of information. **there is no knowing** one can never tell. **knowingly** *adv.* **1** consciously, deliberately. **2** in a knowing manner. **knowingness** *n.* **know-it-all** *n.* (*esp. N Am., derog.*) a know-all. **known** *a.* **1** publicly acknowledged. **2** (*Math.*) having value that can be specified. **know-nothing** *n.* **1** an ignorant person. **2** an agnostic. [OE *cnāwan* (cp. Icel. *knā*, OHG *chnāan*, cogn. with L *gnōscere*, Gr. *gignōskein*, Sansk. *jnā*-)]

knowledge (nol´ij) *n.* **1** familiarity or understanding gained by experience or study or from instruction; an instance of this. **2** a person's range or scope of information. **3** learning, science, the sum of what is known. **4** (*Philos.*) certain or clear apprehension of truth or fact. **5** information, notice. **6** cognition, the process of knowing. **7** †sexual intercourse. **to the best of one's knowledge** BEST. **knowledgeable, knowledgable** *a.* sharp, intelligent; well informed. **knowledgeability** (-bil´-), **knowledgeableness** *n.* **knowledgeably** *adv.* [ME *knowledge* (KNOW, *-lege*, etym. uncertain)]

known KNOW.

Knt. *abbr.* knight.

knuckle (nŭk´əl) *n.* **1** the bone at each one of the joints of a finger, esp. at the base. **2** the middle or tarsal joint of a quadruped. **3** a joint of meat comprising this and adjoining parts. **4** a knuckle-shaped joint or part in a structure, machinery etc. ~*v.t.* to hit with the knuckles. ~*v.i.* **1** (*with down or under*) to submit, to yield. **2** to keep the knuckles on the ground in a game of marbles. **near the knuckle** verging on the indecent. **to go the knuckle** (*Austral., sl.*) to get into a fight. **to knuckle down** to get down to some hard work. **to knuckle under** to bow to the pressure of authority. **to rap on/ over the knuckles** RAP[1]. **knuckle-bone** *n.* **1** a bone forming a knuckle. **2 a** a bone forming the knuckle of a sheep or other animal. **b** a joint of meat including this. **3** (*pl.*) the game of jacks played with animal knucklebones. **knuckleduster** *n.* a metal guard worn to protect the knuckles, and to add force to a blow. **knucklehead** *n.* (*coll.*) an idiot. **knuckleheaded** *a.* **knuckle joint** *n.* a joint in which a projection on one part lies between two projections in the other, and is held in place by a screw or pin. **knuckle sandwich** *n.* (*sl.*) a punch. **knuckly** *adv.* [ME *knokil* (cp. MDut. *knökkel*, LG *knukkel*, G *Knochel*, rel. to G *Knochen*, bone)]

knur (nœ), **knurr** (nœ) *n.* **1** a hard swelling on the trunk of a tree, a knot. **2** a hard concretion. **3** the hard ball used in knur and spell. **knur and spell** *n.* a northern ball game, in some respects resembling trap-ball and in others somewhat like golf. [ME *knor* (cp. Dut. *knor*, Dan. *knort*, G *Knorren*)]

knurl (nœl) *n.* **1** a knot, a lump, an excrescence. **2** a bead or ridge produced on a metal surface as a kind of ornamentation. *~v.t.* to make knurls, beadings or ridges. **knurled** *a.* **knurled work** *n.* woodwork shaped on the lathe into a series of knots or knurls. **knurly** *a.* [prob. from KNUR]

KO *abbr.* **1** kick-off. **2** knockout.

koa (kō´ə) *n.* **1** a Hawaiian acacia, *Acacia koa*. **2** the wood of this, used for cabinet work and building. [Hawaiian]

koala (kōah´lə) *n.* an Australian marsupial, *Phascolarctos cinereus*, not unlike a small bear, with dense fur, which feeds on eucalyptus leaves. **koala bear** *n.* [Austral. Abor. *kūlā*]

koan (kō´an) *n.* a problem with no logical answer, used for meditation by Zen Buddhists. [Jap.]

kob (kob) *n.* (*pl.* **kob**) an African antelope, *Kobus kob*. **kob antelope** *n.* [Wolof *kooba*]

kobold (kō´bōld) *n.* in Germanic folklore, an elf or sprite frequenting houses; also a gnome or goblin haunting mines and hidden lodes. [G, etym. unknown]

Köchel number (kœ´khəl) *n.* a number given to the works of Mozart in the Köchel catalogue of his compositions. [Ludwig von *Köchel*, d. 1877, Austrian cataloguer of Mozart's work]

kochia (kō´kiə) *n.* any annual, ornamental plant of the genus *Kochia*, with purple-red foliage in the late summer. [N. D. J. *Koch*, 19th cent. German botanist]

KO'd (kāōd´) *a.* knocked out.

Kodiak (kō´diak), **Kodiak bear** *n.* a brown bear, *Ursus arctos*, found in Alaska and the neighbouring Aleutian Islands, esp. Kodiak Island.

koeksister (kuk´sistə) *n.* (*S Afr.*) a cake made with sweetened dough. [Afrikaans *koek*, cake, *sissen*, to sizzle]

koel (kō´əl) *n.* any of several SE Asian and Australasian cuckoos of the genus *Eudynamys*, esp. *E. scolopacea*. [Hind. *kóīl*, from Sansk. *kokila*]

kofta (kof´tə, kō´-) *n.* in Indian cookery, a spiced ball of meat, vegetables etc. [Urdu, Pers. *qoftah*, pounded meat]

kohl (kōl) *n.* fine black powder, usu. of antimony or lead sulphide used to darken the eyelids. [Arab. *quh'l*, *qoh'l*]

kohlrabi (kōlrah´bi) *n.* (*pl.* **kohlrabies**) a variety of cabbage, *Brassica oleracea caulorapa*, with an edible swollen stem resembling a turnip. [G, from It. *cavoli rapa*, cole, rape]

koi (koi), **koi carp** *n.* (*pl.* **koi, koi carp**) a large Japanese variety of carp. [Jap.]

koine (koi´nē) *n.* **1** a Greek dialect used as a common language in the E Mediterranean during the Hellenistic and Roman periods. **2** a lingua franca. [Gr. *koine dialektos*, common dialect]

kokanee (kokan´i) *n.* a salmon, *Oncorhynchus nerka kennerlyi*, from one of the land-locked lakes in NW America. [*Kokanee* creek, in British Columbia]

kola COLA.

kolinsky (kəlin´ski) *n.* (*pl.* **kolinskies**) **1** a type of Asian mink, *Mustela sibirica*. **2** the fur from this mink. [Rus. *kolinski*, from the Kola peninsula]

kolkhoz (kolkhoz´, kŭlk´hawz) *n.* (*pl.* **kolkhozy** (-zi)) a cooperative or collective farm in the former USSR. [Rus. abbr. for *kollektivnoe khozyaistvo*, collective farm]

Kol Nidre (kol nid´ri) *n.* **1** the service marking the beginning of Yom Kippur. **2** the opening prayer of this service. [Aram. *kol nidre*, all the vows]

komitadji, komitaji COMITADJI.

Komodo dragon (kəmō´dō), **Komodo monitor** *n.* the largest known lizard, *Veranus komodoensis*, from Indonesia. [*Komodo* Island, Indonesia]

Komsomol (kom´səmol) *n.* **1** the Young Communist League of the former USSR. **2** a member of this. [Rus.]

Kongo (kon´gō) *n.* (*pl.* **Kongo, Kongos**) **1** a member of a Bantu-speaking Central African people. **2** the language of this people. *~a.* of or relating to this people or their language.

konimeter (konimē´tə), **koniscope** (kon´iskōp) *n.* an instrument for indicating the amount of dust in the atmosphere. [Gr. *konis*, dust]

koodoo KUDU.

kook (kook) *n.* (*esp. N Am., coll.*) an eccentric, mad or foolish person. *~a.* eccentric, mad, foolish. **kooky** (-i), **kookie** *a.* (*comp.* **kookier**, *superl.* **kookiest**). [prob. from *cuckoo*]

kookaburra (kuk´əburə) *n.* any large Australian kingfisher of the genus *Dacelo*, also called the laughing jackass. [Austral. Abor.]

koomis KUMISS.

kop (kop) *n.* **1** (*S Afr.*) a prominent hill. **2** (*Hist.*) a high terrace for standing spectators at a football stadium. [Dut., head; *Spioen Kop*, Boer War battle site]

kopeck, kopek COPECK.

kopi (kō´pi) *n.* (*Austral.*) powdered gypsum. [Austral. Abor.]

kopje (kop´i), **koppie** *n.* (*S Afr.*) a small hill. [Dut., dim. of *kop*, head (cp. COP[2])]

koradji (kor´əji, kəraj´i) *n.* (*Austral.*) an Aboriginal medicine man. [Austral. Abor. *garraaji*]

Koran (kərahn´), **Quran, Qur'an** *n.* the Muslim sacred scriptures consisting of the revelations delivered orally by Muhammad and collected after his death. **Koranic** *a.* [Arab. *qurān*, from *qara'a*, to read]

Korean (kərē´ən) *a.* of or relating to Korea, its people or its language. *~n.* **1** a native or inhabitant of Korea. **2** the language spoken in N or S Korea.

korfball (kawf´bawl) *n.* a game not unlike basketball, with teams each consisting of six men and six women. [Dut. *korfball*, basketball]

korma (kaw´mə) *n.* an Indian dish composed of braised meat or vegetables cooked in spices and a yoghurt or cream sauce. [Urdu *korma*, from Turk. *kanuma*]

koruna (koroo´nə) *n.* the standard monetary unit of the Czech Republic and Slovakia, equal to 100 haleru. [Czech, crown]

kosher (kō´shə) *a.* **1** (of food or a shop where it is sold) fulfilling the requirements of the Jewish law. **2** (*coll.*) genuine, above board. **3** permitted, right. *~n.* **1** kosher food. **2** a kosher shop. [Heb. *kāshēr*, right]

koto (kō´tō) *n.* (*pl.* **kotos**) a Japanese stringed instrument with a wooden body and 13 silk strings. [Jap.]

kotow KOWTOW.

kotuku (kō´tukoo) *n.* (*pl.* **kotuku**) a white heron found in New Zealand, *Egretta alba*. [Maori]

koumiss KUMISS.

kouprey (koo´prā) *n.* a rare Indo-Chinese ox, *Bos sauveli*. [Cambodian]

kourbash (kuə´bash), **kurbash** *n.* a hide whip used as an instrument of punishment in Turkey and Egypt. [Arab.]

kowhai (kō´wī, kaw´fī) *n.* (*pl.* **kowhais**) a small shrub with clusters of golden flowers, *Sophora tetraptera*, found in Australasia and Chile. [Maori]

kowtow (kowtow´), **kotow** (kōtow´) *n.* the ancient Chinese method of obeisance by kneeling or prostrating oneself, and touching the ground with the forehead.

~*v.i.* 1 to act obsequiously. 2 (*Hist.*) to perform the kowtow. [Chin. *k'o-t'ou* (*k'o*, knock, *t'ou*, the head)]

KP (kāpē´) *n.* 1 (*pl.*) enlisted soldiers detailed to help in the kitchen. 2 kitchen duty. [abbr. of *kitchen police*]

k.p.h. *abbr.* kilometres per hour.

KR *abbr.* king's rook.

Kr[1] *chem. symbol* krypton.

Kr[2] *abbr.* 1 kreutzer. 2 krona. 3 krone.

kraal (krahl) *n.* (*S Afr.*) 1 a S African village or group of huts enclosed by a palisade. 2 an enclosure for cattle or sheep. [Afrikaans, from Port. CORRAL]

kraft (krahft), **kraft paper** *n.* strong, brown, wrapping paper. [G *Kraft*, strength]

krait (krīt) *n.* any poisonous Asian rock snake of the genus *Bungarus*. [Hind., *karait*]

kraken (krah´kən) *a.* a fabulous sea monster, said to have been seen at different times off the coast of Norway. [Norw.]

krans (krahns), **krantz** (krahnts), **kranz** *n.* (*S Afr.*) a precipitous upward slope, esp. of crags walling in a valley. [Afrikaans, from Dut. *krans*, coronet, chaplet (cp. G *Kranz*)]

Kraut (krowt) *n.* (*sl., offensive*) a German. [from *Sauerkraut*]

Krebs cycle (krebz) *n.* a sequence of biochemical reactions in living organisms in which acetate is broken down to provide energy. [H. A. *Krebs*, 1900–81, British biochemist]

kremlin (krem´lin) *n.* the citadel of a Russian town. **the Kremlin** 1 the citadel of Moscow enclosing the old imperial palace, now government buildings etc. 2 the Russian Government. **Kremlinology** (-ol´-) *n.* the study of the Russian or former Soviet government and its politics. **Kremlinologist** *n.* [F, from Rus. *kreml*, citadel]

kreuzer (kroit´sə) *n.* (*Hist.*) a copper coin (earlier silver), formerly current in Germany and Austria. [G, from *Kreuz*, cross]

kriegspiel (krēg´spēl) *n.* 1 a war game played on maps. 2 a form of chess in which each player has their own board, and does not see that of the opponent with whom they communicate through an umpire. [G *Krieg*, war, *Spiel*, game]

krill (kril) *n.* (*collect.*) tiny shrimplike crustaceans, the main food of whales. [Norw. *krill*, young fish]

krimmer (krim´ə) *n.* the tightly curled black or grey fleece from a type of lamb found in the Crimea. [G *Krim*, Crimea]

kris (krēs), **crease, creese, cris** *n.* a Malaysian or Indonesian dagger with a wavy edge. [Malay]

Krishnaism (krish´nəizm) *n.* the worship of Krishna. **Krishnaist, Krishnaite** (-īt) *n.* [*Krishna*, a Hindu hero or divinity, an avatar of Vishnu]

kromesky (krəmes´ki) *n.* (*pl.* **kromeskies**) a roll or ball of minced meat or fish wrapped in bacon, then fried. [Rus.]

krona (krō´nə) *n.* 1 (*pl.* **kronor**) the basic monetary unit of Sweden. 2 (*pl.* **kronur**) the basic monetary unit of Iceland. [Swed., Icel., crown]

krone (krō´nə) *n.* 1 (*Hist.*) (*pl.* **kroner**) the monetary unit of Denmark and Norway. 2 (*Hist.*) (*pl.* **kronen**) a German gold coin. 3 (*Hist.*) (*pl.* **kronen**) an Austrian silver coin and monetary unit. [G, Dan., Norw., crown]

kronor, kronur KRONA.

Kru (kroo), **Kroo** *n.* 1 a member of a West African people on the coast of Liberia, famous for their skill as seamen. 2 the language of this people. ~*a.* of or relating to the Kru or their language. [W Afr.]

krugerrand (kroo´gərand) *n.* a coin minted in S Africa containing 1 troy oz. of gold. [President *Kruger* 1825–1904, RAND[1]]

krummhorn (krum´hawn, krŭm´-), **crumhorn** *n.* 1 a medieval wind instrument with a curved tube and a tone like that of a clarinet. 2 an organ stop consisting of reed pipes, with a similar tone. [G (*krumm*, crooked)]

krypton (krip´tən) *n.* an inert gaseous element, at no. 38, chem. symbol Kr, discovered by Ramsay in 1898 as a constituent of the atmosphere. [Gr. *krupton*, neut. of *kruptos*, concealed (cp. CRYPT)]

Ks *abbr.* 1 Kansas. 2 King's Scholar.

Kshatriya (kshat´riyə) *n.* a member of the warrior caste in the Hindu caste system. [Sansk., from *kshatra*, rule]

KStJ *abbr.* Knight of the Order of St John.

KT *abbr.* 1 Knight of the Order of the Thistle. 2 Knight Templar.

Kt. *abbr.* Knight.

kt *abbr.* 1 karat. 2 (*also* **kt.**) knot.

K/T boundary (kātē´) *n.* (*Geol.*) the boundary between the Cretaceous and Tertiary periods. [from the symbols for those periods]

Ku *chem. symbol* kurchatovium.

kudos (kū´dos) *n.* 1 glory, fame, credit. 2 (*N Am.*) praise, acclaim. [Gr.]

Usage note *Kudos* is an uncountable noun. A singular *kudo* is sometimes encountered, as is *kudos* treated or pronounced as a plural, but both uses are best avoided.

kudu (koo´doo), **koodoo** *n.* (*pl.* **kudu, kudus, koodoo, koodoos**) either of two southern African antelopes, *Tragelaphus stepsericos* or *T. imberbis*, with white stripes. [Afrikaans *koedoe*, from Xhosa]

kudzu (kud´zoo), **kudzu vine** *n.* an ornamental plant with edible tubers, *Pueraria lobata*, native to China and Japan. [Jap.]

Kufic (koo´fik, kū´-), **Cufic** *n.* an early form of the Arabic alphabet. ~*a.* of or relating to this script. [*Kufa*, in Iraq]

Ku Klux Klan (koo klŭks klan´) *n.* a secret society in the Southern States of the US, aiming to repress the black population, orig. formed after the American Civil War of 1861–65 and though suppressed by the US government in 1871 since revived with the aim of preserving white supremacy. **Ku Klux Klanner** *n.* [perh. Gr. *kuklos*, circle, CLAN]

kukri (kuk´ri) *n.* (*pl.* **kukris**) a curved knife broadening at the end, used by the Gurkhas. [Hind.]

kulak (koo´lak) *n.* (*Hist.*) a prosperous Russian peasant of the class owning their own farms. [Rus.]

kulan (koo´lən) *n.* a SW Asian wild ass, related to the kiang. [Tartar]

Kultur (kul´tuə) *n.* (*often derog.*) German culture, esp. in its authoritarian and militaristic aspects. **Kulturkampf** (kultuə´kampf) *n.* 1 (*Hist.*) a conflict between the German government and the Catholic Church at the end of the 19th cent. 2 a conflict between secular and religious authorities over e.g. education. [G, from L *cultūra*, CULTURE]

kumara (koo´mərə), **kumera** *n.* (*New Zeal.*) the sweet potato. [Maori]

kumiss (koo´mis), **koomis, koumiss, kumis, kumiss** *n.* a spirituous liquor made by Tartars from fermented mare's milk. [Tartar *kumiz*]

kümmel (kum´əl) *n.* a liqueur flavoured with caraway seeds made in Germany and Russia. [G, from as CUMIN]

kumquat (kŭm´kwot), **cumquat** *n.* 1 a small orangelike fruit with acid pulp and a sweet rind. 2 a shrub or tree of the genus *Fortunella* yielding this fruit. [Chin. *kin keu*, golden orange]

kung fu (kŭng foo´, kung-) *n.* a Chinese martial art resembling karate. [Chin. *ch'ŭan fa*, boxing principles]

Kuomintang (kwō´mintang´) *n.* (*Hist.*) the Chinese Nationalist party founded by Sun Yat Sen and holding power from 1928 until replaced by the Communist Party in 1949.

Kuo-yü (kwōyü´, gwaw-) *n.* a form of Mandarin taught all over China. [Chin. *kuo-yü*, lit. national language]

kurbash KOURBASH.

kurchatovium (koechətō´viəm) *n.* an artificial chemical element, at. no. 104, chem. symbol Ku, whose discovery was claimed by the Soviets in 1966; also called Rutherfordium. [I. V. *Kurchatov*, 1903–1960, Russian physicist]

Kurd (kœd) *n.* a native or inhabitant of Kurdistan. **Kurdish** *a.* of or relating to the Kurds or Kurdistan. ~*n.* the language of the Kurds. [Kurdish]

kurdaitcha (kədī´tshə), **kadaitcha** *n.* **1** in some Australian Aboriginal tribes, the practice of using a bone to cast spells. **2** a man who does this. [Austral. Abor.]

kuri (koo´ri) *n.* (*pl.* **kuris**) (*New Zeal.*) a mongrel dog. [Maori]

kurrajong (kŭr´əjong), **currajong** *n.* (*Austral.*) any of several trees and shrubs with fibrous bark, esp. *Brachychitou populeum*. [Abor.]

kursaal (kuə´zahl) *n.* **1** a public room for the use of visitors, esp. at German health resorts. **2** a casino. [G (*Kur*, CURE, *Saal*, room)]

kurta (kuə´tə), **kurtha** *n.* a loose tunic worn by Hindus. [Hind.]

kurtosis (kœtō´sis) *n.* in statistics, the distribution and density of points around the mean. [Gr. *kurtos*, arched]

kuru (koo´roo) *n.* a disease, usu. fatal, of the nervous system occurring in the inhabitants of eastern New Guinea. [New Guinean, trembling]

kV *abbr.* kilovolt(s).

kvass (kvahs) *n.* beer made from rye, esp. in Russia. [Rus.]

kvetch (kvech) *v.i.* (*N Am., sl.*) to whine, to complain. **kvetcher** *n.* [Yiddish]

kW *abbr.* kilowatt(s).

Kwa (kwah) *n.* (*pl.* **Kwa**) **1** a group of languages spoken in West Africa from the Ivory Coast to Nigeria. **2** a member of a Kwa-speaking people. ~*a.* of or relating to this group of languages.

KWAC (kwak) *abbr.* (*Comput.*) keyword and context.

kwacha (kwah´chə) *n.* the standard monetary unit in Zambia and Malawi. [Afr. name, dawn]

kwanza (kwan´zə) *n.* (*pl.* **kwanza, kwanzas**) the standard monetary unit of Angola. [perh. Swahili, first]

kwashiorkor (kwashiaw´kə) *n.* a nutritional disease caused by lack of protein. [Ghanaian]

kwela (kwā´lə) *n.* a type of jazzlike pop music of central and southern Africa. [Bantu]

kWh *abbr.* kilowatt-hour(s).

KWIC (kwik) *abbr.* (*Comput.*) keyword in context.

KWOC (kwok) *abbr.* (*Comput.*) keyword out of context.

KY, Ky *abbr.* Kentucky.

kyanite (sī´ənīt), **cyanite** *n.* (*Geol.*) a hard, translucent mineral, often blue, occurring in flattened prisms in gneiss and mica-schist. **kyanitic** (-nit´-) *a.*

kyanize (kī´ənīz), **kyanise** *v.t.* to impregnate (wood) with a solution of mercuric chloride (corrosive sublimate) to prevent dry rot. **kyanization** (-zā´shən) *n.* [J. H. *Kyan*, 1774–1830, British inventor]

kyat (kyaht) *n.* (*pl.* **kyat, kyats**) the basic monetary unit of Burma (Myanmar).

kybosh KIBOSH.

kyle (kīl) *n.* a narrow channel in Scotland, between an island and another island or the mainland. [Gael. *caol*, narrow]

kylie (kī´li), **kiley** *n.* (*Austral.*) a boomerang. [W Austral. Abor.]

kylin (kē´lin) *n.* a mythical animal of composite form, shown on Chinese and Japanese pottery. [Chin. *qi*, male, *lin*, female]

kyloe (kī´lō) *n.* a small highland breed of cattle. [Gael. *gaidhealach*, Gaelic, Highland]

kymograph (kī´məgrahf) *n.* an instrument for recording wavelike oscillations, as of the pulsation of the blood in a living body. **kymographic** (-graf´-) *a.* [Gr. *kuma*, a wave]

kyphosis (kīfō´sis) *n.* a condition of the spine resulting in a hunched back. **kyphotic** (-fot´-) *a.* [Gr, *kyphos*, hump]

Kyrgyz (kœ´giz), **Kirghiz, Kirgiz** *n.* **1** a member of a Mongolian people inhabiting central Asia, mainly Kyrgyzstan. **2** the language of this people. ~*a.* of or relating to this people or their language.

Kyrie (kir´iā, kiə´ria), **Kyrie eleison** *n.* **1** this phrase used as a short petition in the liturgies of the Eastern and Western Churches, esp. at the beginning of the Eucharist or Mass. **2** a musical setting of this. [Gr. *Kurie eleēson*, Lord have mercy]

kyu (kyoo) *n.* (*pl.* **kyus**) each of the grades for beginners in judo, karate etc. [Jap.]

L[1] (el), **l** (*pl.* **Ls, L's**) the 12th letter of the English and other versions of the Roman alphabet, corresponding to the Greek lambda (Λ, λ). It is pronounced as a voiced alveolar continuant, a lateral or liquid. *~symbol* **1** (*Chem.*) Avogadro's constant. **2** 50 in Roman numerals. *~n.* **1** an L-shaped thing, part or building. **2** a rectangular joint.

L[2], **L.** *abbr.* **1** laevorotatory. **2** Lake. **3** Large. **4** Latin. **5** Learner (driver). **6** Liberal. **7** Libra (pound). **8** Licentiate. **9** (*Biol.*) Linnaeus. **10** Lire. **11** Loch. **12** Lough. **13** Luxembourg (IVR). **L-dopa** *n.* the laevorotatory form of dopa which is used in the treatment of Parkinson's disease. **L-driver** *n.* a learner driver. **L-plate** *n.* a sign, in the form of a red L on a white background, which must by law in the UK be attached to the front and rear of any vehicle driven by a learner driver.

l, l. *abbr.* **1** left. **2** length. **3** line. **4** liquid. **5** litre(s).

LA *abbr.* **1** Legislative Assembly. **2** Library Association. **3** Los Angeles. **4** Louisiana.

La *chem. symbol* lanthanum.

La. *abbr.* Louisiana.

†**la**[1] (lah) *int.* lo! see! behold! (*derisively etc.*) really! [OE *lā*]

la[2] LAH.

laager (lah´gə) *n.* **1** (*Hist.*) in S Africa, a defensive encampment, esp. one formed by wagons drawn into a circle. **2** a park for armoured vehicles etc. **3** (the mental attitude of) a group of people who draw together in defence of established ideas and institutions and to resist change. *~v.t.* **1** to form into a laager. **2** to encamp (a body of people) in a laager. *~v.i.* to encamp. **laager mentality** *n.* an attitude of embattled defiance and resistance to change. [Afrikaans *lager* (cp. G *Lager*, Dut. *leger*, LEAGUER[2])]

Lab. (lab) *abbr.* **1** Labour. **2** Labrador.

lab (lab) *n.* (*coll.*) short for LABORATORY.

labarum (lab´ərəm) *n.* **1** the imperial standard of Constantine the Great (bearing the cross and a monogram of the Greek name of Christ), adopted by him after his conversion to Christianity. **2** a banner resembling this used in religious processions. [L, from Gr. *labaron*, etym. unknown]

labdanum LADANUM.

labefaction (labifak´shən), **labefactation** (-tā´shən) *n.* **1** weakening, decay. **2** downfall, ruin. [L *labefactātio*, from *labefactāre* (*labāre*, to totter, *facere*, to make)]

label (lā´bəl) *n.* **1** a piece of cloth, paper, plastic or other material attached to an object to indicate contents, destination, ownership or other particulars. **2** a descriptive phrase associated with a person, group etc. **3** a firm's tradename or logo (esp. that of a fashion designer or of a record company). **4** a piece of paper attached to the centre of a gramophone record giving information about its contents. **5** a recording company or a section of one with its own trademark. **6** an adhesive stamp. **7** (*Archit.*) a moulding over a doorway or window, a dripstone. **8** (*Her.*) a fillet, with pendants or points, used as marks of an eldest son's cadency. **9** a character or set of characters which indicates the start of an instruction in a computer program. **10** in dictionaries, a word or abbreviation, usu. preceding a definition, that indicates its geographical provenance or area of usage, its register, the subject area to which it applies etc. **11** a radioactive isotope or fluorescent dye used to make a substance traceable. **12** an addition to a document, as a codicil. *~v.t.* (*pres.p.* **labelling,** (*N Am.*) **labeling,** *past, p.p.* **labelled,** (*N Am.*) **labeled**) **1** to affix a label to. **2** to describe, to categorize. **3** to render (a substance) traceable by replacing an atom in its molecule with a radioactive isotope by marking it with fluorescent dye. **labeller,** (*N Am.*) **labeler** *n.* [OF, a ribbon, a fillet (etym. uncertain)]

labellum (ləbel´əm) *n.* (*pl.* **labella** (-lə)) **1** the lower lip-shaped part of the corolla in an orchidaceous flower. **2** a lobe at the top of the proboscis of certain insects. [L, dim. of LABRUM]

labia LABIUM.

labial (lā´biəl) *a.* **1** of or relating to the lips or the labium. **2** serving as or resembling a lip. **3** (of the surface of a tooth) adjacent to the lips. **4** formed or modified in sound by the lips. **5** having lips or liplike edges (as an organ fluepipe). *~n.* a sound, or a letter representing a sound, formed with the lips, such as *b, f, v, p, m*, or *w*. **labialism** *n.* **labialize, labialise** *v.t.* to pronounce with rounded lips like the sound *oo*. **labialization** (-zā´shən) *n.* **labially** *adv.* by means of the lips. **labial pipe** *n.* a fluepipe of an organ. **labiate** (-ət) *a.* **1** (*Bot.*) having lips or parts like lips, esp. having a corolla with an upper and lower part like a pair of lips. **2** belonging to the order Labiatae, the mint family. *~n.* any plant of the Labiatae family, e.g. mint, rosemary. [late L *labiālis*, from L LABIUM]

labile (lā´bīl) *a.* unstable, liable to chemical or other change. **lability** (ləbil´iti) *n.* [L *lābilis*, from *lābī*, to fall]

labio- (lā´biō) *comb. form* labial. [LABIUM]

labiodental (lābiōden´təl) *a.* produced by the agency of the lips and teeth. *~n.* a sound so produced, as *f* or *v*.

labium (lā´biəm) *n.* (*pl.* **labia** (-biə)) **1** a lip or liplike structure or part. **2** each of the four liplike folds enclosing the vulva. **3** the lower surface of the mouth in insects, crustaceans etc. **4** the lower lip of a labiate corolla. **labia majora** (məjaw´rə) *n.pl.* the outer and larger pair of folds enclosing the vulva. **labia minora** (minaw´rə) *n.pl.* the inner and smaller pair of folds enclosing the vulva. [L, lip]

labor LABOUR.

laboratory (ləbor´ətri, lab´rətəri) *n.* (*pl.* **laboratories**) **1** a room or building in which scientific experiments and research are conducted. **2** a place where drugs, medicines and other chemical products etc. are manufactured. [med. L *labōrātōrium*, from *labōrāre*, to LABOUR]

labour (lā´bə), (*N Am., Austral.*) **labor** *n.* **1** physical or mental exertion, esp. to obtain the means of subsistence, the performance of work, toil. **2** workers, esp. manual workers, considered as a class or category, usu. as opposed to *capital, management*. **3** the element contributed by workers to production, esp. as opposed to *capital*. **4** a task, esp. a task requiring great effort. **5** the process of childbirth from the start of frequent uterine contractions to delivery. **6** (**Labour**) the Labour Party. *~a.* of or relating to labour or to the Labour Party. *~v.i.* **1** to work hard, to exert oneself. **2** to strive, to work (for, to do). **3** to move or proceed with difficulty. **4** to be burdened or handicapped (*labour under a delusion*). **5** (of ships) to move heavily and slowly or to pitch or roll heavily. **6** to be in travail or the pains of childbirth.

~*v.t.* 1 to overelaborate, to deal with in too much detail or at too great length. 2 †to till. **laborious** (ləbaw´riəs) *a.* 1 difficult, hard, arduous, fatiguing. 2 betraying marks of labour, laboured. 3 industrious, assiduous. **laboriously** *adv.* **laboriousness** *n.* **labour camp** *n.* a penal establishment where prisoners are forced to labour. **Labour Day** *n.* a public holiday honouring working people, esp. 1 May or (in the USA and Canada) the first Monday in September. **laboured** *a.* 1 showing signs of strain, effort or contrivance, not spontaneous or fluent. 2 (of breathing) performed with difficulty. **labourer** *n.* a person who labours, esp. someone who performs work requiring manual labour but little skill. **Labour Exchange** *n.* (*Hist.*) an employment office or jobcentre. **labour force** *n.* the workers collectively, esp. those employed at a single plant. **labour-intensive** *a.* (of a production process) requiring a large labour force or a great deal of work in relation to output. **labourism** *n.* support for working people and their rights. **labourist** *n.* **Labourite** *n.* a follower or member of the Labour Party. **labour market** *n.* the supply of unemployed labour in relation to the demand. **labour of Hercules** *n.* a task requiring an enormous effort. **labour of love** *n.* work done without expectation of payment. **Labour Party** *n.* 1 a British political party established to represent workers. 2 a similarly constituted party in another country. **labour-saving** *a.* intended to reduce or eliminate the work involved in performing a task. †**laboursome** (-səm) *a.* **labour theory of value** *n.* the Marxist theory that the amount of labour required to produce a thing should determine its value. **labour union** *n.* (*N Am.*) a trade union. [OF, from L *labōrem*, acc. of *labor*, whence *labōrāre*, F *labourer*, to labour]

labra LABRUM.

Labrador (lab´rədaw) *n.* a Labrador retriever. **labradorite** (-rīt) *n.* a feldspar from Labrador and other places, exhibiting a brilliant display of colour. **Labrador retriever, Labrador dog** *n.* 1 a breed of large, short-haired retriever dog with a coat of either a golden or black colour. 2 a dog of this breed.

labrum (lā´brəm) *n.* (*pl.* **labra** (-brə)) a lip or liplike part, as in insects, crustaceans etc. **labret** (-brit) *n.* a plug of stone, shell etc., inserted into the lip as an ornament, e.g. among the peoples of Alaska. **labrose** (-brōs) *a.* having thick lips. [L cogn. with LABIUM]

laburnum (ləbœ´nəm) *n.* a poisonous tree or shrub of the genus *Laburnum*, that has racemes of yellow flowers. [L]

labyrinth (lab´irinth) *n.* 1 a structure composed of intricate winding passages, paths, tunnels etc. rendering it difficult to penetrate to the interior and equally difficult to return, a maze. 2 an intricate combination, arrangement etc. 3 the internal portion of the ear. **labyrinth fish** *n.* a tropical fish with bright coloration and spiny fins, also called *gourami*. **labyrinthine** (-rin´thīn), †**labyrinthian** (-rin´-), **labyrinthic** (-rin´-) *a.* **labyrinthitis** (-thī´tis) *n.* an inflammation of the inner ear causing loss of balance and vomiting. **labyrinthodont** (-rin´thədont) *n.* a fossil amphibian, so called from the labyrinthine structure seen in a cross-section of a tooth. [F *labyrinthe*, L *labyrinthus*, Gr. *laburinthos*, etym. uncertain]

LAC *abbr.* Leading Aircraftman.

lac[1] (lak) *n.* a resinous incrustation secreted, chiefly on the banyan tree, by parasitic lac insects and used in the making of shellac. **lac insect** *n.* any of various insects of the family Lacciferidae, esp. *Laccifer lacca* that secretes lac. [Hind. *lākh*, from Sansk. *lākshā*]

lac[2] LAKH.

Lacanian (ləkā´niən) *a.* of or relating to Jacques Lacan, 1901–1981, a French psychoanalyst and structuralist who reinterpreted Freud. ~*n.* a follower of Lacan or his writings. **Lacanianism** *n.*

laccolith (lak´əlith), **laccolite** (-līt) *n.* an intrusive mass of lava penetrating between strata and raising the surface into domes. [Gr. *lakkos*, reservoir, -LITE]

lace (lās) *n.* 1 a kind of ornamental network of threads of linen, cotton, silk, gold or silver wire or other suitable material, forming a fabric of open texture. 2 a cord or string used to bind or fasten, esp. by interweaving between eyelets or hooks as a shoelace etc. 3 an ornamental braid or edging for uniforms etc. ~*v.t.* 1 to fasten by means of a lace or string through eyelet-holes etc. 2 to compress or tighten by lacing. 3 to add a small quantity of spirits, a drug, poison to. 4 to introduce into or intermingle with. 5 to embellish with or as with stripes. 6 to intertwist or interweave (with thread etc.). 7 to trim or adorn with lace. 8 (*coll.*) to beat, to thrash. ~*v.i.* 1 (of boots etc.) to fasten with laces. 2 to compress the waist by tightening laces. **to lace into** to attack vigorously. **lace-bark** *n.* 1 the inner bark of a W Indian shrub, *Lagetta lintearia*, which resembles coarse lace. 2 (*Austral.*) the ribbonwood tree. **laced** *a.* having laces; fastened with a lace or laces. **lace-glass** *n.* Venetian glass decorated with lacelike patterns. **lacelike** *a.* **lacemaker** *n.* **lacemaking** *n.* **lace-pillow** *n.* a cushion on which various kinds of lace are made. **lace-up** *a.* (of shoes) fastened with a lace or laces. ~*n.* a shoe or boot fastened by a lace or laces. **lacewing, lacewing fly** *n.* any of various flying insects with veiny wings, esp. any of the families Chrysopidae and Hemerobiidae. **lace-winged** *a.* **lacewood** *n.* timber from the plane tree. **lacework** *n.* articles made of lace. **lacing** *n.* 1 a fastening by a cord passing through holes etc. 2 a lace or cord for fastening. 3 lace trimming, esp. on a uniform. 4 anything added to or intermingled with something else, esp. a dose of spirit added to a liquor to strengthen or flavour it. 5 (*coll.*) a thrashing. 6 (*also* **lacing course**) a strengthening course of brick, stone etc. built into an arch or wall. **lacy** *a.* (*comp.* **lacier**, *superl.* **laciest**) made of or like lace. **lacily** *adv.* **laciness** *n.* [OF *las* (L *laqueus*, a noose), whence OF *lacier* (F *lacer*), to ensnare]

lacerate[1] (las´ərāt) *v.t.* 1 to tear, to mangle. 2 to distress or afflict severely, to harrow, to wound. **lacerable** *a.* **lacerant** *a.* agonizing, traumatic. **lacerated** *a.* LACERATE[2]. **laceration** (-ā´shən) *n.* 1 a jagged rent or wound. 2 the act of lacerating. **lacerative** *a.* [L *lacerātus*, p.p. of *lacerāre*, from *lacer*, torn (cp. Gr. *lakeros*)]

lacerate[2] (las´ərət) *a.* (*Bot.*) having the edge in irregular segments, as if torn.

lacertian (ləsœ´shən), **lacertillian** (lasətil´iən), **lacertine** (las´ətīn) *n.* any reptile of the suborder Lacertilia that includes lizards. ~*a.* of or relating to the Lacertilia; lizard-like. [L, lizard]

laches (lach´iz) *n.* (*Law*) remissness or unreasonable delay in performing a legal duty, seeking a legal remedy, asserting a right etc. [OF *laschesse*, from *lasche*, L *laxus*, LAX (with transposition of *cs* (*x*) to *sc*)]

lachryma Christi (lakrima kris´tē) *n.* a wine from S Italy, orig. a sweet white wine made from grapes grown on the slopes of Mt. Vesuvius. [L, Christ's tears]

lachrymal (lak´riməl), **lacrimal, lacrymal** *a.* 1 (*formal*) of or relating to tears. 2 (of glands, ducts etc.) secreting or conveying tears. ~*n.* 1 a lachrymatory. 2 (*pl.*) the lachrymal organs. 3 (*pl.*) outbursts of weeping. **lachrymal duct** *n.* a duct that conveys tears from the inner corner of the eye into the nose. **lachrymal gland** *n.* the gland at the outer corner of the eye that secretes tears. **lachrymal vase** *n.* a lachrymatory. **lachrymation** (-ā´shən) *n.* **lachrymator** *n.* a substance that causes or increases the flowing of tears. **lachrymatory** *a.* of, relating to or causing tears. ~*n.* (*pl.* **lachrymatories**) a small glass vessel found in ancient tombs, said to be intended for holding mourners' tears, but prob. for perfumes or ointments. **lachrymose** (-mōs) *a.* 1

excessively doleful; characterized by much shedding of tears. 2 (*formal*) given to shedding tears, weepy. 3 (*formal*) sad, mournful, tearful. **lachrymosely** *adv.* **lachrymosity** (-mos´-) *n.* [med. L *lacrymālis*, from L *lacryma*, tear (cp. Gr. *dakru*)]

Usage note The adjectives *lachrymal* and *lachrymose* should not be confused: *lachrymal* means relating to tears, and *lachrymose* tearful.

lacing LACE.

laciniate (ləsin´iət), **laciniated** (-ātid) *a.* (*Biol.*) divided into long, narrow lobes; fringed. **laciniation** (-ā´shən) *n.* [L *lacinia*, flap]

lack (lak) *n.* 1 deficiency, want, need (of). 2 something that is absent or that is needed. ~*v.t.* 1 to be in need of, to be deficient in. 2 to be without. **for lack of** because of an absence or insufficiency of. **to be lacking** 1 to be absent; to be in short supply. 2 to be deficient (in). 3 (*coll.*) (of a person) to be mentally deficient. **to lack for** (*usu. neg.*) to be without, to lack. **lackland** *a.* having no property or estate. ~*n.* 1 a person who owns no land. 2 (**Lackland**) a nickname for King John of England. **lacklustre** (lak´lŭstə), (*N Am.*) **lackluster** *a.* 1 dull, without brightness or vivacity. 2 mediocre. [cp. Dut. and LG *lak*]

lackadaisical (lakədā´zikəl) *a.* 1 careless, slipshod, inattentive. 2 listless, absent-minded. 3 affectedly pensive, languishing or sentimental. **lackadaisically** *adv.* **lackadaisicalness** *n.* [obs. *lackadaisy* from LACKADAY]

†**lackaday** (lak´ədā) *int.* alas. [from *alack the day*]

lacker LACQUER.

lackey (lak´i), **lacquey** *n.* (*pl.* **lackeys, lacqueys**) 1 a servile political follower or hanger-on. 2 a footman; a menial attendant. ~*v.t., v.i.* (*3rd pers. sing. pres.* **lackeys,** *pres.p.* **lackeying,** *past, p.p.* **lackeyed**) 1 to act or attend servilely. 2 to follow or attend as a servant. **lackey moth** *n.* a moth, *Malacosoma neustria*, whose caterpillars are brightly striped in a manner reminiscent of a footman's livery. [F *laquais*, etym. uncertain]

Laconian (ləkō´niən) *a.* of or relating to Laconia or Sparta in ancient Greece, its inhabitants or their dialect. ~*n.* 1 a native or inhabitant of Laconia. 2 the Laconian dialect. [from L *Laconia*, Sparta, from Gr. *Lakōn*, Spartan]

laconic (ləkon´ik), **laconical** *a.* using few words, brief, pithy, concise. **laconically** *adv.* **laconicism** (-sizm), **laconism** (lak´-) *n.* 1 a concise, pithy or sententious style. 2 a laconic saying. [L *lacōnicus*, Gr. *Lakōnikos*, from *Lakōn*, Spartan]

lacquer (lak´ə), **lacker** *n.* 1 a varnish composed of shellac dissolved in alcohol and often coloured with gold, gamboge, saffron etc., that dries hard and is used to coat articles of metal or wood. 2 a similar substance used to keep a hairstyle in place, hair lacquer. 3 a hard glossy varnish made from black resin. 4 decorative objects coated with such varnish and often inlaid. **hair lacquer** HAIR. **lacquerer** *n.* **lacquer tree** *n.* an E Asian tree, *Rhus verniciflua*, which produces the resin used to make black lacquer varnish. **lacquerware** *n.* decorative articles coated with lacquer. [MF *lacre*, Port. *lacre*, var. of *lacca*, from LAC[1]]

lacquey LACKEY.

lacrimal LACHRYMAL.

lacrosse (ləkros´) *n.* a ball game of N American Indian origin resembling hockey, but played with a crosse or stringed bat with which the players throw and catch the ball. **lacrosse stick** *n.* [F, the CROSSE]

lacrymal LACHRYMAL.

lact- LACTO-.

lactase (lak´tāz) *n.* an enzyme that acts on lactose to produce glucose and galactose.

lactate[1] (laktāt´) *v.i.* to secrete or produce milk. **lactation** (-tā´shən) *n.* 1 the secretion and excretion of milk from the mammary glands. 2 the period during which milk is secreted. 3 the act or process of breastfeeding an infant.

lactate[2] (lak´tāt) *n.* a salt of lactic acid.

lacteal (lak´tiəl) *a.* 1 of or relating to milk; milky. 2 conveying chyle. **lacteals** *n.pl.* the lymphatic vessels which convey chyle from the lymphatic small intestine to the thoracic duct.

lactescent (laktes´ənt) *a.* 1 having a milky appearance or consistency. 2 yielding milky juice. 3 turning to milk. **lactescence** *n.*

lactic (lak´tik) *a.* of, relating to or derived from milk. **lactic acid** *n.* a colourless liquid acid produced in tissue by the anaerobic breakdown of carbohydrates and also formed during the souring of milk.

lactiferous (laktif´ərəs) *a.* carrying or producing milk or milky juice.

lacto- (laktō), **lact-** *comb. form* of or relating to milk. [from L *lactis*, gen. of *lac*, milk]

lactobacillus (laktōbəsil´əs) *n.* (*pl.* **lactobacilli** (-lī)) any rod-shaped bacterium of the family Lactobacillaceae which ferments carbohydrates to produce lactic acid.

lactoflavin (laktōflā´vin) *n.* an earlier name for riboflavin.

lactogenic (laktōjen´ik) *a.* inducing lactation.

lactometer (laktom´itə) *n.* a kind of hydrometer for showing the specific gravity and consequent value of different samples of milk.

lactone (lak´tōn) *n.* any cyclic ester formed from a hydroxycarboxylic acid by the elimination of water.

lactoprotein (laktōprō´tēn) *n.* any protein that is present in milk.

lactoscope (lak´təskōp) *n.* an instrument for determining the quality of milk by ascertaining its relative opacity.

lactose (lak´tōs) *n.* the form in which sugar occurs in milk, a glucose and a galactose monomer.

lacuna (ləkū´nə) *n.* (*pl.* **lacunas, lacunae** (-nē)) 1 a gap, blank or hiatus, esp. in a manuscript or text. 2 a cavity, small pit or depression, e.g. in a bone. **lacunal, lacunary, lacunose** *a.* of, relating to or containing lacunae. **lacunar** *a.* lacunal. ~*n.* (*pl.* **lacunars, lacunaria** (-eə´riə)) 1 a ceiling that has sunken or hollowed compartments over its surface, a coffered ceiling. 2 any of these panels or compartments. [L, from *lacus*, LAKE[1]]

lacustrine (ləkŭs´trīn) *a.* of, relating to or living on or in a lake. **lacustral** *a.* [from L *lacus*, LAKE[1], onomat. of *palustrine*, from *palus*, marsh]

LACW *abbr.* Leading Aircraftwoman.

lacy LACE.

lad (lad) *n.* 1 a boy, a youth. 2 a (young) son. 3 (*coll.*) a man; a fellow, a companion, a mate. 4 (*coll.*) an extrovert, audacious or roguish man (*a bit of a lad*). 5 a person (of either sex) who looks after horses. **laddie** (-i) *n.* (*coll.*) a boy, a lad. **laddish** *a.* exuberant, hearty or rumbustious, esp. as a result of being one of a group of (young) men out to have a good time. **laddishness** *n.* **lad's love** *n.* (*dial.*) the southernwood. [ME *ladde*, perh. rel. to *lad*, *led*, p.p. of *leden*, to LEAD[1]]

ladanum (lad´ənəm), **labdanum** (lab´-) *n.* an odorous, resinous substance, which exudes from the leaves and twigs of various kinds of cistus. [L *lādanum*, Gr. *ladanon*, *lēdanon*, from *lēdon*, mastic]

ladder (lad´ə) *n.* 1 a device of wood, iron, rope etc. for going up or down by, often portable and consisting of two long uprights, connected by rungs or cross-pieces, which form steps. 2 a vertical rent in a stocking or tights. 3 anything serving as a means of ascent. 4 a hierarchical structure. ~*v.t.* to cause a ladder in (stockings). ~*v.i.* (of stockings, tights, knitted fabrics etc.) to form a rent through the snapping of a longitudinal thread. **ladder-back** *n.* (a chair with) a back consisting of several horizontal struts between two uprights. **laddered, laddery** *a.* **ladder-stitch** *n.* a crossbar stitch used in embroidery and fancy-work. **ladder tournament** *n.* a competition in which the contestants' names are listed in descending order and the aim is to ascend the list by defeating and replacing the contestant ranked above one. [OE *hlœder* (cp. Dut. *ladder*, G *Leiter*)]

laddie, laddish LAD.

lade (lād) *v.t.* (*p.p.* **laden** (-dən)) **1** to put a cargo or freight on board. **2** to ship (goods) as cargo. **3** (*esp. in p.p.*) to load, to weigh down. **4** to put in or take out (as water) with a ladle, bowl etc. ~*v.i.* (of a ship) to take on cargo. **laden** *a.* **1** weighed down, loaded; encumbered. **2** burdened, painfully aware of. **lading** *n.* **1** cargo. **2** the act or process of loading cargo. [OE *hladan* (cp. Dut. and G *laden*, Icel. *hlather*)]

la-di-da (lahdidah´), **lah-di-dah** *a.* (*coll.*) affectedly genteel, pretentious and precious in speech or manners. ~*n.* **1** a la-di-da person. **2** la-di-da speech or manner. [imit. of affected speech]

ladies, ladify LADY.

Ladin (lədēn´) *n.* **1** the Rhaeto-Romanic language spoken in the Engadine and part of the Tyrol. **2** a person who speaks this. [L *Latīnus*, Latin]

lading LADE.

Ladino (lədē´nō) *n.* (*pl.* **Ladinos**) **1** a dialect based on Spanish with an admixture of Hebrew, written in Hebrew characters, spoken by Sephardic Jews. **2** a Spanish American of mixed (white and Indian) descent. [Sp. and It., from L *Latinus*, LATIN]

ladino (lədē´nō) *n.* (*pl.* **ladinos**) a white clover, *Trifolium repens*, used as fodder. [It.]

ladle (lā´dəl) *n.* **1** a large spoon, usu. with a deep bowl at right angles to a long handle, with which liquids are lifted out or served from a vessel. **2** a bucket-shaped container or pan with a long handle to hold molten metal. **3** the float-board of a mill-wheel. ~*v.t.* to serve out or transfer with a ladle. **to ladle out** to give or hand out freely; to distribute liberally. **ladleful** *n.* **ladler** *n.* [OE *hlœdel*, from *hladan*, to LADE]

lady (lā´di) *n.* (*pl.* **ladies**) **1** a woman regarded as being of refinement or social standing. **2** a polite term for a woman (*often used attrib.*, as *lady doctor*). **3** (*coll.*) a wife; a girlfriend. **4** (*Hist.*) an object of romantic love, a mistress, sweetheart. **5** a woman who has authority or control, esp. the mistress of a house or family. **6** (**Lady**) a title prefixed to the surname or territorial title of a peeress or the wife of a knight or peer, or to the Christian name of the daughter of an earl, marquess or duke, or to the Christian name of a woman's husband if he is the son of a marquess or duke. **7** a respectful addition to the title of an office or position held by a woman (*lady wife*; *lady mayor*). **8** (*pl.*) the ladies' room, a public lavatory for women. **9** a euphemistic term for a female animal. **my lady** a form of address for a person holding the title of 'lady'. **Our Lady of Dolours** OUR. **painted lady** PAINT. **ladies' chain** *n.* a figure in quadrille or similar dances executed by the women dancers. **ladies' fingers** *n.* LADY'S FINGER (under LADY). **Ladies' Gallery** *n.* a gallery in the House of Commons, formerly screened off by a grille and the only place where women were admitted. **ladies' man, lady's man** *n.* a man who enjoys the company of women or is particularly attentive to them or successful in attracting or seducing them. **ladies' night** *n.* an evening function at a men's club or institution to which women are invited. **ladies' room** *n.* a women's lavatory in a large building such as a store, office etc. **ladify** LADYFY (under LADY). **Lady altar** *n.* the altar of a chapel (usu. in a cathedral or large church) dedicated to the Virgin Mary. **ladybird,** (*esp. N Am.*) **ladybug** *n.* a small coleopterous insect, of the family Coccinellidae, with red or reddish-brown wing cases with black spots. **Lady Bountiful** *n.* a wealthy woman charitable in her neighbourhood. **lady-chair** *n.* a seat made by interlacing two people's arms for carrying an injured person. **Lady chapel** *n.* a chapel dedicated to the Virgin Mary (usu. in a cathedral or large church). **Lady Day** *n.* the Feast of the Annunciation of the Virgin Mary, 25 Mar. **lady-fern** *n.* a tall slender fern, *Athyrium filix-femina*. **ladyfinger** *n.* (*N Am.*) a small finger-shaped sponge cake. **ladyfy** (-fī), **ladify** *v.t.* **1** to make a lady of. **2** to treat as a lady; to give the title 'lady' to. **ladified** *a.* affecting the manners and air of a fine lady. **ladyhood** (-hud) *n.* **lady-in-waiting** *n.* a lady attending on a queen or princess. **ladyish** *a.* having the manners and air of a fine lady. **lady-killer** *n.* **1** a man who devotes himself to seducing women. **2** a man who is irresistibly fascinating to women. **ladylike** *a.* refined, graceful. **lady-love** *n.* a female sweetheart. **lady mayoress** *n.* the wife of a lord mayor. **Lady Muck** *n.* (*sl., derog.*) a woman with social pretensions. **lady of easy virtue** *n.* a woman who is sexually promiscuous; a prostitute. **lady of the bedchamber** *n.* (*pl.* **ladies of the bedchamber**) a lady-in-waiting. **lady of the night** *n.* a prostitute. **lady's bedstraw** *n.* a herbaceous plant, *Galium verum*. **lady's companion** *n.* a small bag or case containing items required for needlework. **lady's finger** *n.* **1** the kidney vetch. **2** okra. **3** LADYFINGER (under LADY). **ladyship** *n.* the position or status of a lady. **her ladyship** the equivalent of 'your ladyship' in speaking of someone. **your ladyship** **1** a formula used in speaking deferentially to a lady. **2** (*facet.*) a formula used in speaking to a woman or girl who adopts an arrogant manner. **lady's maid** *n.* a female attendant on a lady. **lady's man** LADIES' MAN (under LADY). **lady's mantle** *n.* any of various rosaceous herbs of the genus *Alchemilla*, having clustered yellowish-green leaves and flowers resembling drapery. **lady's slipper** *n.* an orchid of the genus *Cypripedium*. **lady's smock** *n.* the cuckoo flower, *Cardamine pratensis*. **lady's-tresses** *n.pl.* orchidaceous plants of the genus *Spiranthes*. **Lady Superior** *n.* the head of a convent or nunnery in certain orders. [OE *hlœfdīge* (*hlāf*, LOAF[1], *-dīge*, prob. kneader, cp. DOUGH)]

laevo- (lē´vō), **levo-** *comb. form* **1** left, as opposed to right. **2** noting the turning of a ray of polarized light to the left, as opposed to *dextro-*. [L *laevus*, left]

laevogyrate (lēvōjī´rət), (*N Am.*) **levogyrate** *a.* laevorotatory.

laevorotatory (lēvōrō´tətəri), (*N Am.*) **levorotatory** *a.* turning the plane of polarization to the left. **laevorotation** (-tā´shən) *n.*

laevulose (lē´vūlōs), (*N Am.*) **levulose** *n.* a sugar or glucose distinguished from dextrose by its turning the plane of polarization to the left, fructose.

lag[1] (lag) *v.i.* (*pres.p.* **lagging,** *past, p.p.* **lagged**) **1** to fall behind. **2** (*esp. N Am.*) in billiards, to string. ~*n.* **1** a delay in response. **2** the interval between two events, esp. between an action and the reaction. **3** retardation of current or movement. **laggard** (-əd) *a.* slow, sluggish, lagging behind. ~*n.* **1** a slow, sluggish person. **2** a loiterer. **laggardly** *a., adv.* **laggardness** *n.* **lagger**[1] *n.* **lag of the tide** *n.* the interval by which the tide lags behind the mean time during the first and third quarters of the moon. [etym. uncertain, perh. from LAST[1] or LACK]

lag[2] (lag) *n.* **1** a convict. **2** a long-term prisoner. **3** a term of imprisonment or (formerly) transportation. ~*v.t.* (*pres.p.* **lagging,** *past, p.p.* **lagged**) **1** to send to prison. **2** (*sl.*) to arrest. [etym. uncertain]

lag[3] (lag) *n.* **1** the non-heat-conducting jacket of a boiler or cylinder. **2** a stave, lath or strip of wood, felt etc. ~*v.t.* (*pres.p.* **lagging,** *past, p.p.* **lagged**) to cover or encase with a lag or lagging, esp. to preserve against freezing. **lagger**[2] *n.* a person who insulates with lagging. **lagging** *n.* insulating material wrapped esp. around water pipes or tanks to prevent freezing or heat loss. [Icel. *lögg*, the end of a cask]

lagan (lag´ən) *n.* wreckage or goods lying at the bottom of the sea, usu. marked by a float or buoy. [A-F (cp. Icel. *lögn*, pl. *lagnir*, nets laid in the sea, cogn. with LIE[2])]

lager (lah´gə) *n.* a light beer, blond in colour and effervescent, the ordinary beer of Germany. **lager lout** *n.* (*sl.*) a youth who behaves like a hooligan, esp. when having drunk too much alcohol, esp. lager or beer. [G *Lagerbier* (*Lager*, a store, *bier*, beer)]

laggard LAG[1].

lagger[1] LAG[1].

lagger[2] LAG[3].

lagging LAG[3].

lagniappe (lan´yap), **lagnappe** *n.* (*NAm.*) **1** a small gift, esp. to a customer. **2** a gratuity, a bonus. [Louisiana F, from S Amer. Sp. *la ñapa*, from Quechua, *yápa*, addition]

lagomorph (lag´ōmawf) *n.* any gnawing mammal with two pairs of upper incisors (e.g. hares, rabbits). **lagomorphic** (-maw´-), **lagomorphous** *a.* [Gr. *lagōs*, hare, *morphē*, form]

lagoon (ləgoon´) *n.* **1** a shallow lake near a river or the sea, due to the infiltration or overflow of water from the larger body. **2** the water enclosed by an atoll or coral island. **3** an artificial pool for the storage or treatment of effluent, slurry etc. or of the overflow from surface drains after heavy rainfall. **lagoonal** *a.* [F *lagune*, It. and Sp. *laguna*, L LACUNA]

Lagrangian point (ləgrān´jiən) *n.* any one of the five points in the plane of orbit of one body around another where the combined gravitational forces of the two bodies are zero and a third body, of negligible mass, can remain at rest. [J. L. *Lagrange*, 1736–1813, French mathematician and astronomer]

lah (lah), **la** *n.* **1** the sixth note of a major scale in the tonic sol-fa system of notation. **2** the note A in the fixed-doh system. [It., orig. first syl. of L *labii*, one of the words of the gamut]

lahar (lah´hah) *n.* a landslide or mudflow consisting mainly of volcanic debris and usu. occurring after heavy rain. [Javanese]

lah-di-dah LA-DI-DA.

laic, laical etc. LAY[2].

laid (lād) *a.* **1** lying down. **2** placed or pressed down. **3** set out. **4** flattened by wind and rain. **laid-back** *a.* (*coll.*) relaxed, casual. **laid paper** *n.* paper made with a ribbed surface, marked by the wires on which the pulp is laid, as opposed to *wove paper.* **laid up** *a.* ill; confined to bed or the house. [p.p. of LAY[1]]

lain LIE[2].

lair[1] (leə) *n.* **1** the den or retreat of a wild animal. **2** (*usu. facet.*) a person's private room or place, a den. **3** a pen or shed for cattle on the way to slaughter or the market. **4** (*Sc.*) the area of ground required for a single grave. ~*v.i.* **1** to go to or lie in a lair. **2** to make one's lair (in). ~*v.t.* to place in a lair. **lairage** (-rij) *n.* [OE *leger*, a bed (cp. Dut. *leger*, G *Lager*, LAAGER), cogn. with LIE[1]]

lair[2] (leə) *n.* (*Sc.*) mire, mud. [Icel. *leir*]

lair[3] (leə) *n.* (*Austral., coll.*) an over-dressed man; a show-off. **laired up** *a.* dressed in a flashy manner. **lairy** *a.* flashy.

laird (leəd) *n.* (*Sc.*) the owner of a landed estate. **lairdship** *n.* [var. of LORD]

laissez-aller (lesāal´ā), **laisser-aller** *n.* **1** absence of restraint. **2** absence of conventionality, unconstrainedness. [F, let (them or things) go (*laissez*, imper. of *laisser*, to let, *aller*, to go)]

laissez-faire (lesāfeə´), **laisser-faire** *n.* the principle of non-interference, esp. by the Government in industrial and commercial affairs. ~*a.* operating on this principle. [F, let (them) do (as they like); cp. LAISSEZ-ALLER]

laissez-passer (lesāpas´ā), **laisser-passer** *n.* a pass or permit allowing one unrestricted access or movement. [F, let (someone) pass; cp. LAISSEZ-ALLER]

laity LAY[2].

lake[1] (lāk) *n.* **1** a large sheet of water entirely surrounded by land. **2** a large amount of wine, milk etc., a commodity surplus. **the Lakes** the Lake District. **Lake District** *n.* the mountainous district occupied by the English lakes in Cumbria. **Lakeland** *n.* the Lake District. **Lakeland terrier** *n.* a small, wirehaired breed of terrier originating from the Lake District. **lakeless** (-lis) *a.* **lakelet** (-lit) *n.* **lakelike** *a.* **Lake Poets** *n.pl.* Coleridge, Southey and Wordsworth, who lived in the Lake District. **laker** *n.* **1** any of the Lake Poets. **2** a lake fish. **3** a boat for lakes. **Lake School** *n.* the Lake Poets. **lakeside** *a.* situated, growing etc. beside a lake. **laky** *a.* [OF *lac*, L *lacum*, nom. *lacus*]

lake[2] (lāk) *n.* **1** a crimson pigment, orig. derived from lac or cochineal. **2** an insoluble coloured pigment formed by a soluble dye mixed with a mordant. **3** the colour of these, carmine. [var. of LAC[1]]

lakh (lahk), **lac** *n.* in the Indian subcontinent, the number 100,000 (usu. of a sum of rupees). [Hind., from Sansk. *lākshā*]

laky LAKE[1].

lalapalooza LOLLAPALOOZA.

Lallans (lal´ənz), **Lallan** *n.* the Lowland Scots dialect, esp. in its modern literary use. **Lallan** *a.* of or relating to the Lowlands of Scotland. [Sc.]

lallation (ləlā´shən) *n.* **1** pronunciation of *r* as *l.* **2** the continuous repetition of a single sound, as in infants. [F, from L *lallāre*, to sing (a lullaby)]

lallygag (lal´igag), **lollygag** (lol´-) *v.i.* (*pres.p.* **lallygagging, lollygagging,** *past, p.p.* **lallygagged, lollygagged**) (*N Am.*) **1** to loiter aimlessly. **2** to kiss and cuddle. [etym. unknown]

Lam. Lamentations.

lam[1] (lam) *v.t.* (*pres.p.* **lamming,** *past, p.p.* **lammed**) (*coll.*) to thrash, to wallop. **to lam into** to hit hard; to thrash. **lamming** *n.* a beating. [cp. Icel. *lemja*, OE *lemian*, to LAME[1]]

lam[2] (lam) *n.* (*N Am., sl.*) a quick escape, a hasty flight, esp. from the law. ~*v.i.* (*pres.p.* **lamming,** *past, p.p.* **lammed**) to depart quickly, to escape. **on the lam** escaping, on the run, esp. from the police. **to take it on the lam** to make a quick escape, to flee. [perh. from LAW[1]]

lama (lah´mə) *n.* a Tibetan or Mongolian Buddhist priest or monk. **lamaism** *n.* **lamaist** *a., n.* **lamaistic** (-ist´-) *a.* **lamasery** *n.* (*pl.* **lamaseries**) a lamaist monastery. [Tibetan *blama* (*b* silent)]

lamantin (ləman´tin) *n.* the manatee. [F]

Lamarckian (ləmah´kiən) *a.* of or relating to Lamarck. ~*n.* an adherent of the theory of Lamarck that all the evolution of organisms and the development of species have been due to inheritable modifications caused by habits, efforts at adaptation to environment etc. **Lamarckism, Lamarckianism** *n.* [Jean-Baptiste *Lamarck*, 1744–1829, French naturalist]

lamb (lam) *n.* **1** the young of a sheep. **2** the flesh of this used for food. **3** a person, esp. a child, who is as innocent and gentle as a lamb. **4** used as a term of endearment. **5** a gullible person, a dupe. ~*v.i.* to bring forth lambs. ~*v.t.* to tend (ewes) at lambing. **like a lamb** without fuss or protest. **like a lamb to the slaughter** defenceless, innocent, unresisting. **the Lamb** Christ. **the Lamb of God** Christ. **lamb-ale** *n.* a rural festivity at sheep-shearing. **lambhood** *n.* **lambing** *n.* **1** the birth of lambs; the time when this takes place. **2** the shepherd's work of caring for ewes about to give birth and newborn lambs. **lambkin** *n.* **1** a young or small lamb. **2** (a term of endearment to) a sweet-natured young child. **lamblike** *a.* **lamb's ears** *n.* a perennial herb, *Stachys byzantina*, grown as a garden plant for its white downy foliage. **lamb's fry** *n.* **1** the offal, esp. the testicles, of a lamb as food. **2** (*Austral., New Zeal.*) lamb's liver as food. **lambskin** *n.* the skin of a lamb dressed as a leather with the fleece on. **lamb's lettuce** *n.* a plant, *Valerianella locusta*, used in salads. **lamb's-tails** *n.pl.* catkins of hazel and filbert. **lambswool, lamb's-wool** *n.* fine wool from lambs, esp. at the first shearing, used for knitted garments. ~*a.* made of lambswool. [OE (cp. Dut. *lam*, Icel. *lamb*, G *Lamm*)]

lambada (lambah´də) *n.* **1** an erotic Brazilian dance performed by couples in close contact with one another who gyrate their hips in synchronized movements. **2** the music to accompany this dance. [Port., a whip-crack]

lambast (lambast´), **lambaste** (-bāst´) *v.t.* **1** to beat. **2** to give a verbal thrashing to.

lambda (lam´də) *n.* **1** the 11th letter of the Greek alphabet (Λ, λ) transliterated as Roman *l*. **2** a symbol denoting wavelength. **3** a symbol denoting celestial longitude. **lambdacism** *n.* **1** the too frequent repetition or improper pronunciation of the letter *l*. **2** lallation. **lambdoid** (-doid), **lambdoidal** *a.* resembling the Greek letter lambda (λ) in form, as the suture between the parietal and the occipital bones of the skull. [Gr., rel. to Heb. *lāmedh*]

lambent (lam´bənt) *a.* **1** (of flame or light) playing or moving about, touching slightly without burning. **2** softly radiant. **3** (of wit) light, sparkling. **lambency** *n.* **lambently** *a.* [L *lambens -entis*, pres.p. of *lambere*, to lick]

lambert (lam´bət) *n.* a former measure of the luminous intensity or brightness of a surface, one lumen for every square centimetre. [J. H. *Lambert*, 1728–77, German scientist]

Lambeth Walk (lam´bəth) *n.* a line dance popular in Britain in the 1930s. [*Lambeth*, a S London borough]

lambrequin (lam´brikin, -bəkin) *n.* **1** (*esp. N Am.*) an ornamental strip of drapery over a door, window, mantelshelf etc. **2** a strip of cloth or other material worn as covering over a helmet for protection from heat. **3** (*Her.*) the floating wreath of a helmet. [F, etym. uncertain]

LAMDA *abbr.* London Academy of Music and Dramatic Art.

lame[1] (lām) *a.* **1** disabled in one or more of the limbs, esp. the foot or leg. **2** limping, halting. **3** (of an excuse, argument, ending) unsatisfactory, implausible, unconvincing. **4** (of verse) not running smoothly or evenly. **5** (*N Am., sl.*) conventional, square. ~*v.t.* **1** to make lame. **2** to cripple, to disable. **lamebrain** *n.* (*N Am., coll.*) a stupid person. **lame duck** *n.* **1** a weak, ineffective or disabled person. **2** a defaulter on the Stock Exchange. **3** a company in financial difficulties, esp. one requiring government assistance. **4** (*N Am.*) an elected official (esp. the President) whose term of office is about to expire and whose successor has already been chosen. **lamely** *adv.* **lameness** *n.* **lamish** *a.* [OE *lama* (cp. Dut. *lam*, Icel. *lami*, G *lahm*)]

lame[2] (lām) *n.* a thin plate, overlapping with others, esp. in a suit of armour. [F, from L *lamina*, thin plate]

lamé (lah´mā) *n.* a fabric containing metallic, usu. gold or silver threads. ~*a.* made of such a fabric. [F, from L *lāmina*, a thin plate]

lamella (ləmel´ə) *n.* (*pl.* **lamellae** (-lē)) **1** a thin plate, layer, scale or membrane, esp. in bone tissue. **2** (*Bot.*) **a** a spore-bearing gill in a mushroom. **b** a membranous fold in a chloroplast. **lamellar, lamellate** (-ət), **lamellose** (-ōs) *a.* **lamellarly** *adv.* [L, dim. of LAMINA]

lamelli- (ləmel´i) *comb.form* of or relating to thin layers, scales etc.

lamellibranch (ləmel´ibrangk) *n.* any of the Lamellibranchiata, a class of molluscs breathing by two pairs of platelike gills. **lamellibranchiate** (-brang´kiət) *a.* of or relating to the Lamellibranchiata. ~*n.* any individual of the Lamellibranchiata. [Gr. *branchia*, gills]

lamellicorn (ləmel´ikawn) *a.* of or relating to the superfamily Scarabaeoidia (formerly Lamellicornia) a group of beetles, including the stag beetle and cockchafer, having short antennae terminated by a short lamellated club. ~*n.* a lamellicorn beetle. **lamelliferous** (laməlif´-) *a.* **lamelliform** (-fawm) *a.* shaped like a lamella, plate-like. [L *cornu*, a horn]

lamellirostral (ləmeliros´trəl) *a.* of or relating to the Lamellirostres, a group of birds, including ducks and geese, having bills with a fringe of thin plates along the inside edge. [L *rōstrum*, a beak]

lament (ləment´) *v.i.* **1** to mourn, to wail. **2** to feel or express sorrow. ~*v.t.* **1** to bewail, to mourn over. **2** to deplore, to express regret or remorse for. ~*n.* **1** a passionate expression of sorrow in cries or complaints. **2** an elegy, a dirge. **3** a mournful song or melody. **lamentable** (lam´-) *a.* **1** very unfortunate, deplorable. **2** wretched. **3** †mournful, sad. **lamentably** *adv.* **lamentation** (lamәntā´shən) *n.* **1** the act of lamenting. **2** an audible expression of grief. **3** a wail. **Lamentations** *n.* the book of the Old Testament containing the lamentations of Jeremiah. **lamented** *a.* **1** mourned for. **2** deceased, late. †**lamentedly** *adv.* **lamenter** *n.* **lamenting** *n., a.* **lamentingly** *adv.* [F *lamenter*, L *lāmentārī*, from *lāmentum*, a wail]

lamia (lā´miə) *n.* **1** in classical mythology, a lascivious evil spirit in the form of a serpent with a woman's head. **2** a sorceress, a witch. [L, from Gr.]

lamina (lam´inə) *n.* (*pl.* **laminae** (-nē)) **1** a thin layer, plate, flake esp. of mineral or bone. **2** the flat blade of a petal or leaf. **3** a plate of sensitive tissue within a hoof. **laminable** *a.* **laminar, laminose** *a.* made up of laminae. **laminar flow** *n.* a smooth liquid flow following the shape of a streamlined surface. **laminaria** (-neə´riə) *n.* algae of the genus *Laminaria* with a flat ribless expansion in place of leaves. **laminarian** (-neə´riən) *a.* of or relating to these algae or the sea-depths where they occur. **laminate**[1] (-nāt) *v.t.* **1** to beat, press or roll (metal) into thin plates. **2** to overlay or cover with a thin sheet of material, e.g. plastic. **3** to produce by bonding successive layers or sheets. **4** to cut or split into thin layers or sheets. ~*v.i.* to split into thin sheets. **laminate**[2] (-nət) *a.* consisting of laminae, laminated. ~*n.* a laminated material. **laminated** *a.* **1** produced by bonding thin sheets one on top of the other. **2** covered with a thin layer of plastic or resin. **3** laminate. **lamination** (-ā´shən) *n.* **1** the process of laminating. **2** a layer in a laminated material. **3** a thin protective covering layer. **laminator** *n.* a person who produces laminates. **laminiferous** (-nif´-), **laminose** (-nōs) *a.* **laminitis** (-ī´tis) *n.* inflammation of the lamina of the hoof. [L]

lamish *a.* LAME[1].

Lammas (lam´əs), **Lammas Day** *n.* **1** 1 Aug., the day on which first-fruits were offered in Anglo-Saxon times. **2** the Roman Catholic feast of St Peter celebrated on the same day. **Lammastide** *n.* the season around Lammas, harvest time. [OE *hlāfmœsse* (LOAF[1], MASS)]

lammergeier (lam´əgīə), **lammergeyer** *n.* the great bearded vulture, *Gypaetus barbatus*, an inhabitant of the high mountains of S Europe, Asia and N Africa. [G *Lämmergeier* (*Lämmer*, lambs, *Geier*, vulture)]

lamp (lamp) *n.* **1** a device for the production of artificial light, which may be fixed or portable and usu. has a glassed container enclosing the light source which may be an electric bulb, gas-jet or wick. **2** any of various usu. movable holders with fittings for one or more electric light bulbs, such as a *table lamp, standard lamp*. **3** an electric device which emits esp. infrared or ultraviolet light waves, such as a *sun lamp*. **4** (*poet.*) any source of light, such as the sun, moon etc. **to smell of the lamp** (of a speech, sermon etc.) to show signs of laborious preparation. **lampblack** *n.* amorphous carbon, obtained by the imperfect combustion of oil or resin, used as a pigment or filler. **lamp-chimney, lamp-glass** *n.* the upright chimney surrounding the wick and flame of an oil lamp. **lamplight** *n.* the light from a lamp or lamps. **lamplighter** *n.* 1 (*Hist.*) a person employed to light the public lamps. 2 (*N Am.*) a spill for lighting lamps. **lamplit** *a.* illuminated by lamps. **lamp-post** *n.* a post or column supporting a street lamp. **lampshade** *n.* a cover for a lamp which softens or directs the light emitted by the electric bulb. **lamp shell** *n.* a brachiopod (so called from its resemblance to an ancient Roman oil lamp). **lamp standard** *n.* a lamp-post, esp. a tall one made of concrete or metal. [OF *lampe*, L and Gr. *lampas*, from *lampein*, to shine]

lampas[1] (lam´pəs), **lampers** *n.* a swelling of the roof of the mouth in horses. [F, etym. uncertain]

lampas[2] (lam´pəs) *n.* a flowered silk or woollen cloth used in upholstery. [F, etym. uncertain]

lampern (lam´pən) *n.* the river lamprey, *Lampetra fluviatilis.* [OF *lamproyon*, dim. of *lampreie*]

lampers LAMPAS[1].

lampion (lam´piən) *n.* an oil lamp with a small coloured globe or cup, used in illuminations. [F, from It. *lampione*, from *lampa*, LAMP]

lampoon (lampoon´) *n.* a satire, often a scurrilous personal one. ~*v.t.* to write lampoons about; to satirize. †**lampooner, lampoonist** *n.* **lampoonery** *n.* [F *lampon*, from *lampons*, let us drink (*lamper*, to booze, perh. a var. of *lapper*, to lap up)]

lamprey (lam´pri) *n.* (*pl.* **lampreys**) a blood-sucking eel-like fish belonging to the family Petromyzonidae, with a suctorial mouth with which it clings to its prey or to rocks. [OF *lampreie* (F *lamproie*), It. *lampreda*, late L *lampetra* (*lambere*, to lick, *petra*, rock)]

LAN *abbr.* (*Comput.*) local area network.

lanate (lā´nāt), **lanose** (-nōs) *a.* woolly, covered with curly hairs. [L *lānātus*, from *lāna*, wool]

Lancastrian (langkas´triən) *a.* 1 of or relating to Lancashire or Lancaster. 2 of or relating to the family descended from John of Gaunt, Duke of Lancaster. ~*n.* 1 a native or inhabitant of Lancashire. 2 an adherent of the House of Lancaster, one of the Red Rose party in the Wars of the Roses.

lance (lahns) *n.* 1 a thrusting weapon consisting of a long shaft with a sharp point, formerly the weapon of knights, later used by some regiments of cavalry. 2 a similar weapon used for killing a harpooned whale, for spearing fish etc. 3 a lancet. 4 a metal-cutting tool that uses a very hot flame. ~*v.t.* 1 (*Med.*) to pierce or open with a lancet. 2 to pierce with or as with a lance. 3 (*poet.*) to hurl or fling. **lance bombardier** *n.* a rank in the Royal Artillery equivalent to lance corporal. **lance corporal** *n.* the lowest rank for a non-commissioned officer in the British army. **lance-jack** *n.* (*sl.*) a lance corporal. **lancer** *n.* 1 a cavalry soldier armed with a lance. 2 (*pl.*) a set of quadrilles for eight or sixteen couples; the music for this. 3 the music for this. **lance rest** *n.* a bracket on the breastplate of a knight or on his horse's saddle on which his lance rested in a charge. **lance-sergeant** *n.* a corporal acting as a sergeant. **lance-snake** *n.* the fer-de-lance. **lancewood** *n.* the tough, elastic wood of *Oxandra lanceolata* and other W Indian, Australian and New Zealand trees, used in making carriage shafts, fishing rods etc. [F, from L *lancea*]

lancelet (lahn´silit) *n.* a small transparent fishlike non-vertebrate of the family Branchiostomidae, esp. *Amphioxus lanceolatus*, that burrows in the sand.

lanceolate (lahn´siələt, -āt) *a.* tapering to a point at each end. [L *lanceolātus*, from *lanceola*, dim. of *lancea*, LANCE]

lancet (lahn´sit) *n.* 1 a sharp surgical instrument with a two-edged blade, used in making incisions, opening abscesses etc. 2 a lancet window or arch. ~*a.* lancet-shaped. **lancet arch** *n.* an arch with a sharply pointed top. **lanceted** *a.* having lancet arches or windows. **lancet fish** *n.* either of two deep-sea fish with a long body and long dorsal fin, *Alepisaurus ferox* or *A. borealis.* **lancet window** *n.* a high narrow window with a sharply pointed arch. [OF *lancette*, dim. of LANCE]

lancinate (lahn´sināt) *v.t.* to tear, to lacerate. **lancinating** *a.* (of a pain) piercing, cutting. **lancination** (-ā´shən) *n.* [L *lancinātus*, p.p. of *lancināre*, to rend]

Lancs. *abbr.* Lancashire.

Land (lant, land) *n.* (*pl.* **Länder** (len´də)) a federal state in Germany; a province in Austria. [G]

land (land) *n.* 1 the solid portion of the earth's surface, as distinct from the oceans and seas. 2 this solid surface considered as a usable commodity, ground. 3 a country, nation or state. 4 a district, a region. 5 landed property, real estate. 6 (*pl.*) estates. 7 the remaining raised part of a grooved surface, esp. in a rifled gun barrel. 8 (*Sc.*) a building containing several dwellings under one roof. 9 (*S Afr.*) ground fenced off for tillage. 10 a strip of land divided from others by drainage furrows. ~*v.t.* 1 to bring to or set on shore. 2 to bring (an aircraft) back to the ground after a flight. 3 to set down from a vehicle. 4 to bring (a fish) to land. 5 to bring to or place in a certain location, position, predicament etc. 6 to hit something or somebody with (a blow). 7 (*coll.*) to win, attain, capture or secure (a prize, business deal). ~*v.i.* 1 to come or go on shore. 2 to disembark from a ship. 3 to return to the ground after a flight, leap etc. 4 to find oneself in a certain location, position, predicament etc. ~*a.* 1 belonging to the land. 2 terrestrial. **how the land lies** how matters stand, the state of play in a situation. **the land** 1 agricultural or rural areas as opposed to towns. 2 agriculture as a profession or way of life. **to land on one's feet** to end up, by chance, in an advantageous situation. **to land up** to end up. **to land with** to burden with. **to make (the) land** to come in sight of land as one's ship approaches it from the sea. **land agent** *n.* 1 a person employed to manage land for the proprietor, a steward. 2 an agent for the sale of land. **Land Army** *n.* a British national organization of volunteer farm-workers during the two World Wars. **land bank** *n.* a bank lending money on the security of land. **land breeze** *n.* a wind blowing seawards off the land. **land bridge** *n.* a connecting piece of land between two large land masses, esp. one that allowed the migration of humans and animal species from one continent to the other in prehistoric times. **land-crab** *n.* a crab of the family Gecarcinidae, which lives mainly on land, visiting the sea chiefly for breeding. **land drain** *n.* a drain for subsoil drainage consisting of porous or perforated pipe laid in a gravel-filled trench. **land drainage** *n.* **landed** *a.* 1 having an estate in land. 2 consisting of real estate. **lander** *n.* a spacecraft designed to land on the surface of the moon or a planet. **landfall** *n.* 1 an approach to land after a voyage. 2 the first land sighted after a voyage. **landfill** *n.* 1 the practice of burying rubbish under layers of earth. 2 a rubbish dump where refuse is buried. 3 the rubbish so buried. **landfilling** *n.* **land force** *n.* a military force employed on land. **landform** *n.* a natural feature of the earth's surface. **land girl** *n.* (*Hist.*) a girl or woman employed in farm work during the two World Wars. **landholder** *n.* a person who owns or (usu.) rents land. **landholding** *n., a.* **landing** *n.* 1 the act or an instance of returning to earth after a flight, leap etc. 2 the act or an instance of going or setting on land from a vessel. 3 a pier, wharf, jetty or other place for disembarking or alighting. 4 a level space at the top of a flight of stairs or between flights. 5 a passage leading to rooms on an upper floor. **landing beacon** *n.* a transmitter that emits a landing beam. **landing beam** *n.* a radio beam that guides an aircraft to ground. **landing craft** *n.* a small naval vessel for making shore landings (with troops, equipment etc.). **landing field** *n.* an area for the landing or take-off of aircraft. **landing gear** *n.* the undercarriage of an aircraft. **landing net** *n.* a bag-net used to take fish from the water when hooked. **landing pad** *n.* a small area designed for helicopters to land on. **landing speed** *n.* the minimum speed at which an aircraft can land safely. **landing stage** *n.* a platform, fixed or floating, on which passengers and goods are disembarked. **landing strip** *n.* a strip of ground for aircraft landings and take-offs; an airstrip. **landlady** *n.* (*pl.* **landladies**) **1** a woman who lets land, a building, lodgings etc. to a tenant. **2** a woman who keeps a public house or a boarding or lodging house. **landless** *a.* **landline** *n.* an overland telecommunications cable or wire. **landlocked** *a.* **1** enclosed by land. **2** isolated from the sea. **landloper** (-lōpə) *n.* (*Sc.*) a vagabond or vagrant. **landlord** *n.* **1** a man who lets land, a building, lodgings etc. to a tenant. **2** a man who keeps a public house or a boarding or lodging house. **landlordism** *n.* **1** the system under which land is owned by individuals to whom tenants pay a fixed rent. **2** the proceedings or authority of landowners as a body or class. **landlubber** *n.* (*derog.*) a landsman, a person unused to the sea or ships. †**landman** *n.* (*pl.* **landmen**) a person who lives on the land, a countryman, a peasant. **landmark** *n.* **1** a prominent object on land serving as a guide. **2** a conspicuous object in a place or district. **3** an important event in history etc. **4** anything set up to mark the boundaries of land. ~*a.* constituting or manifesting an important change or development. **landmass** *n.* a large area of land uninterrupted by the sea. **land-measuring** *n.* **landmine** *n.* **1** a mine set in the ground to explode under advancing troops etc. **2** (in World War II) a large bomb dropped by parachute. ~*v.t.* to place landmines. **land of cakes** *n.* Scotland. **land office** *n.* (*N Am.*) an office that administers and registers the sale of public land. **land-office business** *n.* (*N Am.*) extensive and rapid business; a roaring trade. **land of milk and honey** *n.* **1** the fertile land promised by God to the Israelites. **2** any extremely fertile land. **3** a place, country offering wealth and ease. **land of Nod** *n.* **1** the land to which Cain was exiled after killing Abel (Gen. iv.16). **2** the state of being asleep. **land of promise** *n.* the promised land. **land of the Covenant** *n.* Canaan. **land of the living** *n.* the state of being alive or being awake. **land of the midnight sun** *n.* **1** the land within the Arctic Circle, esp. N Norway, Sweden and Finland. **2** (*coll.*) Lapland. **landowner** *n.* a person who owns land. **landownership** *n.* **landowning** *a.* **land-poor** *a.* owning a large area of unproductive land and lacking the capital to improve it. **landrace** *n.* a breed of pork pig with a very long body and lop ears. **landrail** *n.* the corncrake. **land reform** *n.* a redistribution of land or adjustment of land-rent. **landshark** *n.* **1** a person who makes vast profits from buying and selling land. **2** a land-grabber. **landside** *n.* the part of an airport complex to which the non-travelling public has access (cp. AIRSIDE (under AIR)). **landslide** *n.* **1** a landslip. **2** an overwhelming victory or overwhelming majority in an election. **landslip** *n.* **1** the sliding down of a considerable portion of ground from a higher to a lower level. **2** the ground thus slipping. **landsman** *n.* (*pl.* **landsmen**) **1** a person who lives on land. **2** a person unused to the sea and its ways. **land-spring** *n.* a spring of water appearing only after a heavy rain. **land tax** *n.* (*Hist.*) a tax assessed upon land and property. **land-tie** *n.* a structural member, such as a beam, buttress etc. that supports a wall or structure by connecting it to the ground. **landwaiter** *n.* a custom officer who watches the landing of dutiable goods. **landward** (-wəd) *a., adv.* **landwards** *adv.* **land-wind** *n.* a wind blowing off the land. **land yacht** *n.* a wheeled vehicle with a sail, usu. for recreational use on a beach. [OE (cp. Dut., Icel., G etc., *Land*)]

landammann (lan´dəmən) *n.* the chairman of the governing body in some of the Swiss cantons. [Swiss G]

landau (lan´daw, -dow) *n.* a four-wheeled horse-drawn carriage with folding hoods at the front and back which can be raised to cover the occupants. **landaulet** (-let´), **landaulette** *n.* **1** a small landau. **2** an early motor car with a covering or hood over the rear seats. [*Landau*, Germany, where the landau was orig. made]

landdros (land´ros), **landdrost** (-rost) *n.* (*Hist.*) a district magistrate, civil commissioner, fiscal agent etc., in S Africa. [Afrikaans]

Länder LAND.

landgrave (land´grāv) *n.* a German title, dating from the 12th cent., orig. used to distinguish a governor of a province from inferior counts. **landgraviate** (-viət), **landgravate** (-vāt) *n.* the territory ruled by, or the position of, a landgrave or landgravine. **landgravine** (-grəvēn) *n.* **1** a woman holding the rank of a landgrave. **2** the wife of a landgrave. [MHG *lantgrave* (G *Landgraf*), cp. Dut. *landgraaf*]

ländler (lend´lə) *n.* **1** an Austrian or S German dance, similar to a slow waltz, in which the couples spin and clap. **2** a piece of music in the rhythm or style of this dance. [G from *Ländl*, coll. name for Upper Austria]

landscape (land´skāp) *n.* **1** an extensive area of ground, esp. in the country, regarded as a setting or scenery, as a visual whole, or in relation to its particular topography. **2** a picture representing country scenery. **3** the genre to which such pictures belong. **4** a graphic format in which the width of the illustration is greater than its height (cp. *portrait*). ~*a.* **1** of, relating to or producing landscapes or landscaping. **2** (*Print.*) **a** (of a format, illustration) having the width greater than the height. **b** (of a page) containing an illustration or table printed at right angles to the text on the standard pages. ~*v.t.* to develop the natural beauty of (an area) by landscape gardening. ~*v.i.* to work as a landscape gardener. **landscape architecture** *n.* the art or practice of designing and constructing buildings, roads etc. so that they form a pleasant environment or harmonize with the existing landscape. **landscape architect** *n.* **landscape gardening** *n.* the art of laying out grounds in such a way as to create a natural-seeming but particularly harmonious and interesting landscape. **landscape gardener** *n.* **landscape-marble** *n.* a variety of marble with dendriform markings. **landscape painter** *n.* a painter of landscapes. **landscapist** *n.* **1** a landscape painter. **2** a landscape gardener. [MDut. *landscap*, region, (LAND, -SHIP)]

landsknecht (lants´knekht) *n.* (*Hist.*) a mercenary foot soldier, esp. a German pikeman, in the late 15th, 16th and 17th cents. [G (*Lands*, gen. of *Land*, country, *Knecht*, servant, soldier)]

Landsturm (lant´shtooəm) *n.* **1** the legislative assembly in a German-speaking country. **2** general conscription in time of war. [G from *Land*, land, *Sturm*, alarm]

Landtag (lant´tahk) *n.* **1** the legislative assembly of a German or Austrian Land. **2** (*Hist.*) the diet of the Holy Roman Empire or the German Federation. [G from *Land*, country, *Tag*, assembly]

Landwehr (lant´veər) *n.* the army reserve in German-speaking countries. [G from *Land*, country, *Wehr*, defence]

lane[1] (lān) *n.* **1** a narrow road, way or passage, esp. between hedges. **2** a narrow street. **3** a division of a road for a single stream of traffic. **4** a prescribed route, as for sea or air traffic. **5** a marked out strip of a track, swimming pool etc. for an individual competitor in a race. **6** a passage through a crowd of people or objects. **it's a**

long lane that has no turning things are bound to change (for the better). [OE (cp. OFris. *lana*, Dut. *laan*)]

lane[2] (lān) *a.* (*Sc.*) lone. **(on) one's lane** alone.

lang (lang) *a.* (*Sc.*) long. **langsyne** (-sīn´) *adv.* (*Sc.*) long since, long ago. ~*n.* time long ago.

lang. *abbr.* language.

langlauf (lang´lowf) *n.* cross-country skiing; a cross-country skiing race. **langlaufer** *n.* [G *lang*, long, *Lauf*, run, race]

Langobard (lang´gōbahd), **Longobard** (long´-) *n.* (*Hist.*) a member of one of the founding tribes or an early inhabitant of Lombardy. **Langobardic** (-bah´dik) *n.* the language of the ancient Lombards, a form of Old High German. ~*a.* of or relating to the Langobards.

langouste (lāgoost´) *n.* the spiny lobster. **langoustine** (-tēn´) *n.* the smaller Norway lobster. [F]

†**langrage** (lang´grij), **langridge** *n.* canister or case-shot loaded with bolts, nails and pieces of iron, formerly used against rigging. [etym. unknown]

language (lang´gwij) *n.* **1** the communication of ideas by articulate sounds or words of agreed meaning. **2** the human faculty which permits the creation and use of such systems of communication. **3** the vocabulary peculiar to a nation, tribe or people. **4** the vocabulary appropriate to a particular science, profession etc. **5** the phrases and manner of expression peculiar to an individual. **6** literary style. **7** the phraseology or wording (of a book, passage, speech etc.). **8** any formal or informal method of communicating information by symbols, gestures etc. **to speak the same language** to have a similar background, outlook, habits of mind, tastes etc. **language laboratory** *n.* a place where foreign languages are taught with the aid of tape recorders, headphones etc. **languageless** *a.* **language-teacher** *n.* [F *langage*, from *langue*, L *lingua*, tongue]

langue (lāg) *n.* (in linguistics) language regarded as an abstract system tacitly shared by a speech community. **langue de chat** (də sha´) *n.* a thin finger-shaped biscuit or piece of chocolate. **langue d'oc** (dok´) *n.* the medieval Southern French dialects collectively, esp. the Provençal language (so called from the use of the word *oc*, yes, instead of *oïl* or *oui*). **languedocian** (-dō´shən) *a.* **langue d'oïl** (doi), **langue d'oui** (dwē) *n.* Northern French, that spoken north of the Loire in the Middle Ages, the original of modern French. [F, see LANGUAGE]

languet (lang´gwet), **languette** *n.* a tongue-shaped part. [F *languette*, dim. of *langue*, as LANGUAGE]

languid (lang´gwid) *a.* **1** lacking energy; indisposed to exertion. **2** limp, slack; weak. **3** lacking animation, slow-moving; dull. **4** (of trade) sluggish. **languidly** *adv.* **languidness** *n.* [L *languidus*, as LANGUISH]

languish (lang´gwish) *v.i.* **1** to become weak, feeble or sluggish; to lose vitality, energy or animation. **2** to suffer hardship or deprivation. **3** to fall off, to fade, to grow slack. **4** to droop, to pine (for). **5** to put on a languid expression, to affect a tender, wistful or sentimental air. **languisher** *n.* **languishingly** *adv.* **languishment** *n.* [F *languiss-*, stem. of *languir*, L *languēre*, rel. to *laxus*, LAX]

languor (lang´gə) *n.* **1** languidness, lassitude, faintness, lack of energy. **2** debility, faintness, weakness. **3** a pleasantly relaxed or sleepy state. **4** oppressive stillness (of the air etc.). **5** softness, tenderness of mood or expression. **languorous** *a.* **languorously** *adv.* **languorousness** *n.* [OF, from L *languor -ōrem*, as LANGUISH]

langur (lŭng·guə´) *n.* any of several Asian monkeys, esp. of the genus *Presbytis*, having long tails and a circle of long hair around the face. [Hind. *lāgūr*]

laniard LANYARD.

laniary (lan´iəri) *a.* (of a tooth) adapted for tearing. ~*n.* (*pl.* **laniaries**) a canine tooth in the Carnivora. [L *laniārius*, pertaining to a butcher, *lanius*, from *laniāre*, to tear]

laniferous (lənif´ərəs), **lanigerous** (-nij´-) *a.* bearing wool. [L *lāna*, wool]

lank (langk) *a.* **1** lean, long and thin, shrunken-looking. **2** (of hair) long, straight and falling limply. **lankly** *adv.* **lankness** *n.* **lanky** *a.* (*comp.* **lankier**, *superl.* **lankiest**) (of a person, limb) tall or long, thin, loose-joined and rather ungainly. **lankily** *a.* **lankiness** *n.* [OE *hlanc*]

lanner (lan´ə) *n.* (the female of) a large falcon, *Falco biarmicus.* **lanneret** (-ret) *n.* the male *Falco biarmicus*, which is smaller than the female. [OF *lanier*, prob. ident. with *lanier*, cowardly]

lanolin (lan´əlin), **lanoline** *n.* an oily, viscous substance forming the basis of ointments etc., extracted from wool. [L *lāna*, wool, *oleum*, oil]

lansquenet (lans´kənet) *n.* **1** a landsknecht. **2** a card game of German origin, consisting largely of betting. [F, from G *Landsknecht* (LAND, *knetcht*, servant, cp. KNIGHT)]

lantana (lantah´nə) *n.* an evergreen shrub of the tropical American genus *Lantana* of the Verbena family, able to bloom continuously with spikes of yellow or orange flowers.

lantern (lan´tən) *n.* **1** a light enclosed in a case with transparent sides or panes. **2** such a case. **3** a glazed structure on the top of a dome or roof, for the admission of light and air. **4** the upper chamber of a lighthouse containing the light. **5** MAGIC LANTERN (under MAGIC). **lantern fish** *n.* any small deep-sea fish of the family Myctophidae with light organs on its head and body. **lantern-fly** *n.* an insect of the tropical family Fulgoridae, formerly believed to produce light. **lantern-jawed** *a.* having a long, thin, hollow-looking face. **lantern jaws** *n.pl.* **lantern slide** *n.* the glass slide holding the image projected by a magic lantern. **lantern-wheel** *n.* a form of cogwheel acting as a pinion to a spur-wheel. [F *lanterne*, L *lanterna*, prob. from Gr. *lamptēr*, from *lampein*, to shine (see LAMP)]

lanthanum (lan´thənəm) *n.* a metallic divalent element, at. no. 57, chem. symbol La, usu. occurring with didymium and cerium in cerite and used in the making of alloys and electronic devices. **lanthanide** (-nīd), **lanthanoid** (-noid), **lanthanon** (-non) *n.* any of a group of rare metallic elements, at. nos. 58–71, a rare earth. [from Gr. *lanthanein*, to lurk, to escape detection (from the lateness of its discovery in 1839)]

lanugo (lənū´gō) *n.* **1** pre-natal hair. **2** a fine down. [L *lānūginōsus*, from *lānūgo -ginis*, down, from *lāna*, wool]

lanyard (lan´yəd), **laniard** *n.* **1** cord, esp. one worn round the neck, to which a whistle or knife is attached. **2** cord for firing a large gun. **3** (*Naut.*) a short cord, line or gasket for seizing or lashing. [earlier *lannier*, F *lanière* (assim. to YARD[1])]

Lao (low) *n.* (*pl.* **Laos, Lao**) **1** a member of a Buddhist people of Laos and NE Thailand. **2** the language of this people, which is closely related to Thai. ~*a.* of or relating to this people, their language or Laos. **Laotian** (lāō´shən, low´-) *n.* a native or inhabitant of Laos. ~*a.* of or relating to Laos or its people.

Laodicean (lāōdisē´ən) *a.* lukewarm or half-hearted in religion, politics etc. ~*n.* a person of this character. [ref. to the Christians of the ancient city of Laodicea (Rev. iii.15–16)]

lap[1] (lap) *n.* **1** the part of the body from the waist to the knees in a sitting position, esp. as a place for holding an object, a child etc. **2** the part of a skirt, dress or other garment that covers this; the front part of a dress or skirt held out to catch or carry something. **3** a place where anything rests or lies securely. **4** a loose hanging part of a garment or other object. **5** a hollow or sunken area, esp. among hills. **in the lap of the gods** outside human control, up to chance. **to drop in someone's lap** to give someone responsibility for something, a situation etc. **lapboard** *n.* a board that can be held on the lap to serve as a table or desk. **lapdog** *n.* a small pet dog. **lapful** *n.* **lapheld** *a., n.* LAPTOP (under LAP[1]). **lap of luxury** *n.* a state of wealth and ease. **lap robe** *n.* (*N Am.*) a travelling rug. **lapstone** *n.* a stone held in the lap by a shoemaker for hammering leather on. **laptop** *a.* (of a portable computer etc.) small enough to be held and operated on a person's lap. ~*n.* a laptop computer. [OE *læppa* (cp. Dut. and Dan. *lap*, G *Lappen*)]

lap[2] (lap) *n.* **1** one circuit of a racecourse, running track etc. **2** a stage of a journey or similar undertaking. **3** the part of anything that extends over something else, the overlap. **4** the amount of overlap. **5** the length of rope, cord, thread etc. making one turn round a wheel, roller etc. **6** a continuous band or sheet of cotton or other fibres wound on a roller ready for further processing. **7** a wheel, disc or piece of leather made to rotate, for polishing gems, metal articles etc. ~*v.t.* (*pres.p.* **lapping,** *past, p.p.* **lapped**) **1** to overtake a competitor in a race so as to lead them by one or more laps. **2** to wrap, to twist, to roll (around, about etc.). **3** to enfold, to enwrap, to swathe. **4** to surround or envelop protectively or luxuriously. **5** to lay (one thing) partly over another. **6** to cause to overlap. **7** to polish with a lap. ~*v.i.* **1** to be turned over. **2** to lie partly over something else, to overlap. **lap-chart** *n.* (for a motor race) a lap-by-lap log of position of each car in the race. **lap dissolve** *n.* a technique for allowing two consecutive scenes in a film to overlap, the second scene being faded in as the first is faded out. **lap joint** *n.* a joint in which one part laps over the other. **lap-jointed** *a.* **lap of honour** *n.* a victory circuit made by a winning contestant (e.g. around a racing track). **lapper** *n., a.* **lap-streak** *a.* clinker-built. ~*n.* a clinker-built boat. **lap-weld** *v.t.* to weld along overlapping edges. ~*n.* a weld made in this way. [ME, prob. from LAP[1]]

lap[3] (lap) *v.i.* (*pres.p.* **lapped,** *past, p.p.* **lapped**) **1** to drink by lifting with the tongue. **2** to beat gently (as waves on the shore) with a sound as of lapping. ~*v.t.* **1** to lick or take up with the tongue. **2** to drink or consume by lapping. **3** (of water) to strike against (the shore, the side of a boat) with a rippling or gently slapping sound. ~*n.* **1** the act of lapping; the sound of water lapping. **2** a lick. **3** the amount taken up by this. **4** food or drink that can be lapped up, esp. liquid food for animals. **5** a weak kind of drink. **to lap up 1** to eat or drink, esp. eagerly or greedily. **2** to take great and often vain or self-indulgent delight in. **3** to accept or believe uncritically. [OE *lapian* (cp. Icel. *lepja*, OHG *laffan*, L *lambere*, Gr. *laptein*)]

laparoscope (lap´ərəskōp) *n.* a fibre-optical instrument for the internal examination of the abdominal organs after insertion in the wall of the abdomen. **laparoscopy** (-ros´kəpi) *n.* (*pl.* **laparoscopies**) an internal examination using a laparoscope. [Gr. *lapara*, the flank, from *laparos*, soft, -SCOPE]

laparotomy (lapərot´əmi) *n.* (*pl.* **laparotomies**) incision into the cavity of the abdomen for examination or diagnosis. [Gr *lapara*, flank, -TOMY]

lapel (ləpel´) *n.* that part of a garment made to lap or fold over, esp. the fold on the front of a coat or jacket below the collar. **lapelled** *a.* [LAP[1], -EL[1]]

lapidary (lap´idəri) *n.* (*pl.* **lapidaries**) **1** a person who cuts, polishes or engraves gems. **2** a dealer in or connoisseur of gems. ~*a.* **1** of or relating to the art of cutting, engraving or polishing gems. **2** inscribed on or suitable for inscription on stones. **3** formal or monumental in style. **lapidarian** (-deə´ri-) *a.* **lapidate** *v.t.* to stone, esp. to kill by stoning. **lapidation** (-ā´shən) *n.* **lapidicolous** (-dik´ələs) *a.* living under or among stones. **lapidify** (-pid´ifī) *v.t.* (*3rd pers. sing. pres.* **lapidifies,** *pres.p.* **lapidifying,** *past, p.p.* **lapidified**) to form or convert into stone. ~*v.i.* to become petrified. **lapidification** (-fikā´shən) *n.* [L *lapidarius*, from *lapidis*, gen. of *lapis*, stone]

lapilli (ləpil´ī) *n.pl.* volcanic ashes, consisting of small, angular, stony or slaggy fragments. **lapilliform** (-ifawm) *a.* [L, pl. of *lapillus*, dim. of *lapis*, stone]

lapis lazuli (lapis laz´ūlī) *n.* **1** a rich blue mineral, used as a gemstone, containing sodium aluminium silicate and sulphur. **2** a pigment made from this. **3** its colour. [med. L, stone of azure (*lapis*, stone, *lazulum*, azure)]

Lapp (lap) *n.* **1** a member of a nomadic tribe inhabiting the region of Lapland in the far north of Europe. **2** the Finno-Ugric language spoken by this people. ~*a.* of or relating to this people or their language. **Laplander** (lap´landə) *n.* a Lapp. **Lappish** *a., n.* [Swed. *Lappland*]

lapper LAP[2].

lappet (lap´it) *n.* **1** a little lap, fold or loose part of a garment or headdress; a flap. **2** a loose, fleshy process, a lobe, a wattle. **lappeted** *a.* **lappet-moth** *n.* a large brown velvety Eurasian moth, *Gastropacha quercifilia*, which has grey furry caterpillars with lappets on their sides. [LAP[1], -ET[1]]

lapsang souchong (lapsang soo´chong) *n.* a smoky type of souchong tea. [invented word, SOUCHONG]

lapse (laps) *v.i.* **1** to slide, to glide, to pass insensibly or by degrees. **2** to decline into or revert to a worse or inferior state. **3** to fall into disuse, usu. through negligence. **4** to discontinue one's adherence to, membership of or support for an organization. **5** to make a slip or fault. **6** to become void. ~†*v.t.* **1** to allow to slide or slip away. **2** to catch, to seize. ~*n.* **1** a mistake, a slip, an error, a fault, deviation from what is right. **2** a falling into disuse, neglect, decay or ruin. **3** an interval of time, esp. a break in the occurrence of something; the imperceptible passage of time. **4** the termination of a right or privilege through desuetude. **5** the act of lapsing, gliding, slipping or gradually falling (away, from etc.). **6** easy, smooth and almost imperceptible movement, gentle flow etc. **lapsable, lapsible** *a.* **lapsed** *a.* (of a person) no longer maintaining a former belief, adherence, membership etc. **lapser** *n.* **lapse rate** *n.* the rate of change of atmospheric factors (e.g. temperature, humidity) with changing altitude. [L *lapsāre*, freq. of *lābī* (p.p. *lapsus*), to glide]

lapsus (lap´səs) *n.* (*pl.* **lapsus**) (*formal*) a lapse, a slip. **lapsus calami** (kal´əmī) *n.* a slip of the pen. **lapsus linguae** (ling´wī, -gwē) *n.* a slip of the tongue. **lapsus memoriae** (mimaw´riī, -riē) *n.* a slip of the memory. [L, see LAPSE]

lapwing (lap´wing) *n.* a bird of the genus *Vanellus*, of the plover family, esp. *V. vanellus*, a British bird with black and white plumage, a backward-pointing crest and a shrill cry; the peewit. [OE *hlēapewince* (*hlēapan*, to LEAP), WING]

lar (lah) *n.* (*pl.* **lares** (lah´rēz)) an ancient Roman tutelary god, usu. a deified ancestor or hero. **lares and penates** *n.pl.* **1** the home, the household or the valued possessions contained in a home. **2** in ancient Rome, the household gods. **3** the statues representing these gods kept in a Roman home. [L]

larboard (lah´bəd) *n.* (*Hist.*) the port or left side of a vessel to a person standing on deck and facing the bow. ~*a.* of or relating to the left side of a vessel. [ME *ladeborde* (etym. uncertain), assim. to STARBOARD]

larceny (lah´səni) *n.* (*pl.* **larcenies**) the unlawful taking away of another's personal goods with intent to convert them for one's own use; theft. **grand larceny** GRAND. **petit larceny** PETIT. **larcener, larcenist** *n.* **larcenous** *a.* **larcenously** *adv.* [A-F *larcin*, OF *larrecin*, L *latrōcinium*, from *latro*, robber]

larch (lahch) *n.* **1** a tree of the coniferous genus

Larix, having deciduous bright-green foliage and tough, durable timber and yielding Venetian turpentine. 2 (*also* **larchwood**) the wood of this. [G *lärche*, L *laricem*, nom. *larix*]

lard (lahd) *n.* the rendered fat of pigs, esp. in solid white form for use in cooking. ~*v.t.* 1 to insert strips of fat or bacon in (meat) before roasting. 2 to cover or smear with lard. 3 to intermix or garnish (writing, talk etc.) with foreign phrases, flowery speech etc. **lardon** (-dən), **lardoon** (-doon´) *n.* a strip of bacon or fat for larding meat. **lardy** *a.* **lardy-cake** *n.* a rich cake made from yeast, lard, flour, dried fruits etc. [OF, from L *lardum*, rel. to Gr. *laros*, pleasant to the taste, *larinos*, fat]

larder (lah´də) *n.* 1 a room where meat and other provisions are kept, a pantry. 2 a store of food kept by a wild animal, esp. for consumption in winter. **larderer** *n.* [A-F, from OF *lardier*, med. L *lardārium*, as LARD]

lares LAR.

large (lahj) *a.* 1 great in size, number, quantity, extent or capacity. 2 big, bulky. 3 wide, extensive. 4 abundant, ample, copious. 5 (of two or more similar objects) the bigger or biggest. 6 wide in range or scope, comprehensive, far-reaching. 7 operating on a large scale. 8 having breadth of understanding or sympathy. 9 (*Naut.*) (of a wind) blowing from a favourable quarter. 10 liberal, generous, lavish, prodigal. 11 †free, unrestrained, licentious. ~*adv.* 1 prominently, importantly (*loom large*). 2 (*Naut.*) with the wind blowing from a favourable direction. **at large** 1 (esp. of a criminal) at liberty, free; roaming without constraint. 2 as a whole, in general. 3 diffusely, with ample detail. 4 freely, without restraint; without a particular target. 5 (of a political representative in the US) representing a whole area, not a subdivision of it. **by and large** BY. **large as life** unmistakably present or real. **larger than life** remarkably vivid or eye-catching. **of large dimensions** very large. **large calorie** *n.* a unit of heat equalling 1000 (small) calories, used in measuring the energy content of food. **large-handed** *a.* profuse; liberal. **large-hearted** *a.* having a kind, sympathetic heart or disposition. **large-heartedness** *n.* **large intestine** *n.* in the digestive system, that part of the intestine comprising the caecum, colon and rectum. **largely** *adv.* to a large extent. **large-minded** *a.* having liberal and tolerant views. **large-mindedness** *n.* **largen** *v.t., v.i.* (*poet.*) to enlarge. **largeness** *n.* **large order** *n.* a tall order. **large-paper** *a.* applied to books, prints etc., having wider margins than the ordinary. **large-print** *a.* printed in especially large type for the benefit of readers with deficient eyesight. **large-scale** *a.* 1 extensive. 2 detailed. **largish** *a.* [F, from L *larga*, fem. of *largus*]

largesse (lahjes´), **largess** *n.* 1 a present, a reward, a generous bounty (usu. from a superior to inferiors). 2 liberality, esp. in giving. [F *largesse*, as LARGE]

largo (lah´gō) *adv.* (*Mus.*) slowly, broadly, in an ample, dignified style. ~*n.* (*pl.* **largos**) a piece of music played in this manner. **larghetto** (-get´ō) *adv.* somewhat slow. **larghissimo** (-gis´imō) *adv.* very slowly. [It., from L *largus*, LARGE]

lariat (lar´iət) *n.* 1 a lasso. 2 a rope for picketing horses in camp. ~*v.t.* to secure or catch with a lariat. [Sp. *la reata*, the rope or tie (see REATA)]

larine (lar´īn, -in) *a.* 1 of, relating to or like a gull. 2 of or relating to the suborder Lari, to which gulls, terns, skuas and skimmers belong. [from Gr. *laros*, a kind of gull]

lark[1] (lahk) *n.* 1 any bird of the family Alaudidae, with five British species, esp. the skylark, *Alauda arvensis*. 2 any of various similar birds such as a meadowlark. **to rise/ get up with the lark** to rise very early in the morning. **larkspur** *n.* 1 a plant with spur-shaped calyx belonging to the genus *Consolida*, the buttercup family. 2 a plant of the genus *Delphinium*, esp. *D. ajacis*. [OE *laferce*, *lāwerce* (cp. Dut. *leeuwerik*, G *Lerche*, Icel. *laeverki*, Swed. *lärka*)]

lark[2] (lahk) *n.* 1 a prank, a frolic, a spree. 2 (*coll.*) any activity or undertaking (*don't fancy this mind-reading lark*). ~*v.i.* to behave in a carefree or mischievous way, to frolic. **larker** *n.* **larkish, larky** *a.* [etym. uncertain]

larn (lahn) *v.i.* (*dial., facet.*) to learn. ~*v.t.* to teach.

larrigan (lar´igən) *n.* a high leather boot worn by woodsmen etc. [etym. unknown]

larrikin (lar´ikin) *n.* (*chiefly Austral.*) a rowdy youngster, a young hooligan. **larrikinism** *n.* [perh. dim. of pers. name *Larry*]

larrup (lar´əp) *v.t.* (*coll.*) to thrash, to flog, to lash. **larruper** *n.* **larruping** *n.* [dial., etym. unknown]

†**larum** (lar´əm) *n.* an alarm. [ALARM]

larva (lah´və) *n.* (*pl.* **larvae** (-vē)) 1 the first condition of an insect on its issuing from the egg, when it is usu. in the form of a grub, caterpillar or maggot. 2 the half-developed state of other invertebrates that undergo metamorphosis. **larval** *a.* **larvicidal** (-sī´-) *a.* killing larvae. **larvicide** (lah´-) *n.* a preparation for this purpose. **larviform** (-ifawm) *a.* [L, a ghost, a mask]

laryng- LARYNGO-.

laryngeal (larin´jiəl), **laryngal** (-gəl) *a.* 1 of or relating to the larynx. 2 in phonetics, produced in the larynx by partial closure and vibration of the vocal cords. [see LARYNX]

larynges LARYNX.

laryngitis (larinjī´tis) *n.* inflammation of the larynx. **laryngitic** (-rinjit´-) *a.*

laryngo- (laring´go), **laryng-** *comb. form* of or relating to the larynx. [Gr. *larunx -ngos*]

laryngology (laring·gol´əji) *n.* the branch of medical science dealing with the larynx and its diseases. **laryngological** (-gəloj´-) *a.* **laryngologist** *n.*

laryngoscope (ləring´gəskōp) *n.* an instrument with a reflecting mirror for obtaining a view of the larynx; any instrument for examining, or inserting a tube through the larynx. **laryngoscopic** (-skop´-) *a.* **laryngoscopist** (-gos´-) *n.* **laryngoscopy** (-gos´-) *n.*

laryngotomy (laring·got´əmi) *n.* (*pl.* **laryngotomies**) the operation of making an incision into the larynx in order to provide an artificial channel for breathing.

larynx (lar´ingks) *n.* (*pl.* **larynges** (lərin´jēz), **larynxes**) a hollow muscular organ, situated in the upper part of the windpipe and containing the vocal cords in humans and higher vertebrates, the voice box. [Gr. *larunx -ngos*]

lasagne (ləsan´yə, -zan´-, -sahn´-), **lasagna** *n.* 1 pasta in the form of wide flat strips. 2 a baked dish consisting of this pasta, esp. layered with bolognese and béchamel sauces. [It.]

Lascar (las´kə) *n.* a sailor from SE Asia or India. [prob. from Pers. *lashkarī*, a soldier, from *lashkar*, army]

lascivious (ləsiv´iəs) *a.* 1 lewd, wanton, lustful. 2 exciting or provoking lust. **lasciviously** *adv.* **lasciviousness** *n.* [late L *lascīviōsus*, from L *lascīvia*, from *lascīvus*, sportive, lustful]

laser (lā´zə) *n.* 1 an instrument which amplifies light waves by stimulation to produce a powerful, coherent beam of monochromatic light, an optical maser. 2 a similar instrument for producing other forms of electromagnetic radiation (e.g. infrared). **lase** *v.i.* 1 to function or be capable of functioning as a laser. 2 to undergo the physical processes employed in a laser. **laser card** *n.* a plastic card with information stored on it in the form of microscopic pits that can be scanned by a laser beam. **laserdisc** *n.* a disc on which signals and data are recorded for reproduction by a laser beam directed on to its surface. **laser printer** *n.* a high-performance computer printer incorporating a laser which forms a pattern of dots on a photosensitive drum corresponding to the matter to be printed. **laser ring gyro** *n.* a system of aerial navigation employing the frequency shift of laser light in a closed circuit in a horizontal plane. **LaserVision®** *n.* a video disc system, incorporating a laser, for reproducing digitally recorded audio-visual material via a television set or hi-fi. [acronym for *l*ight *a*mplification by *s*timulated *e*mission of *r*adiation]

lash (lash) *n.* **1** a stroke with a whip. **2** the thong or flexible part of a whip. **3** a whip, a scourge. **4** an eyelash. **5** sarcasm, satire, vituperation. **6** †a leash, a snare. ~*v.t.* **1** to whisk or flick (e.g. a tail) suddenly or with a jerk in a menacing fashion. **2** to strike or flog with anything pliant and tough, to whip. **3** to drive with or as with a whip. **4** to assail fiercely with satire, reproach etc. **5** (of wind, rain, waves) to beat or dash against. **6** to fasten or bind with a rope or cord. ~*v.i.* **1** to make a whiplike movement. **2** (of rain, wind) to fall, blow, strike with great force. **3** to strike or kick violently (at, out etc.). **4** to make satirical, sarcastic etc. attacks. **5** to use a whip. **the lash** punishment by flogging. **to lash out 1** to make a strong, usu. sudden physical or verbal attack. **2** to be extravagant with money. **lasher** *n.* **1** a person who lashes or flogs. **2** a rope or binding material for securing or fastening. **lashing** *n.* **1** a rope or gasket by which anything is secured. **2** a whipping, a flogging. **lashings** *n.pl.* (*coll.*) plenty, lots, an abundance. **lashless** *a.* **lash-up** *n.* something improvised or makeshift, esp. an improvised or temporary connection. [etym. obscure, perh. from OF *lache*, whence *lachier*, var. of *lacier*, to LACE, or imit. in orig. through the verb]

lasket (las´kit) *n.* a loop of line at the foot of a sail by which an additional piece of sail is attached. [perh. from F *lacet*, LATCHET]

lass (las) *n.* (*esp. Sc., North.*) a young woman, a girl. **lassie** (-i) *n.* [ME *lasce*, cogn. with Icel. *löskr*, weak]

Lassa fever (las´ə) *n.* an often fatal tropical viral disease symptomized by fever and muscle pain and transmitted by rats etc. [*Lassa*, a village in N Nigeria]

lassitude (las´itūd) *n.* **1** weariness. **2** lack of energy or animation, languor. [F, from L *lassitūdo*, from *lassus*, weary]

lasso (lasoo´) *n.* (*pl.* **lassoes, lassos**) a rope, esp. of untanned hide, with a running noose, used for catching cattle, horses etc. ~*v.t.* (*3rd pers. sing. pres.* **lassoes, lassos**, *pres.p.* **lassoing**, *past, p.p.* **lassoed**) to catch with a lasso. **lassoer** *n.* [OSp. *laso* (Sp. *lazo*)]

last[1] (lahst) *a.* **1** coming after all others or at the end, closing, final. **2** conclusive, definitive. **3** utmost, extreme. **4** next before the present, most recent. **5** only remaining. **6** lowest, in rank or position. **7** furthest from the thoughts, least suitable, least likely etc. **8** of or relating to the end, esp. of life or of the world. ~*n.* **1** (*ellipt.*) the thing most recently done, mentioned etc., or the most recent doing, mention etc. of something. **2** the end, the conclusion. **3** the last moment, hour, day etc. **4** death. ~*adv.* **1** after all the others. **2** most recently, on the last time or occasion. **3** for the last time. **4** †lastly. **at last** after a long time or interval, esp. after a long period of waiting; after too long a time. **at long last** after a very long delay or period of waiting. **in the last analysis** ANALYSIS. **on its last legs** (of a machine, utensil etc.) near the end of its useful life, nearly worn-out. **on one's last legs 1** in an extreme stage of exhaustion. **2** near to death, ruin etc. **the last lap** the beginning of the end, the closing stages. **to breathe one's last** BREATHE. **to the last 1** to the end. **2** till death. **last agony** *n.* the pains immediately preceding death. **last bastion** *n.* any one of a small set of people or things left defending a principle, way of life etc. **Last Day** *n.* the Day of Judgement. **last ditch** *n.* a last resort; the place for a final desperate struggle or defence. **last-ditch** *a.* (of an attempt, effort etc.) done or made at the final moment or as a last resort. **last home** *n.* the grave. **last honours** *n.pl.* marks of respect paid to the deceased at a funeral. **Last Judgement** *n.* the judgement of humankind by God at the end of the world. **lastly** *adv.* finally, to conclude. **last man** *n.* the person who goes in to bat last for a cricket team. **last minute, last moment** *n.* the latest possible time. **last-minute** *a.* made or done at the latest possible time. **last name** *n.* a surname. **last offices** *n.pl.* rites due to the dead. **last post** *n.* **1** (*Mil.*) the bugle-call signalling the time of going to bed. **2** a bugle-salute at military funerals. **last resort** *n.* **1** something to which one comes for aid or relief when all else has failed. **2** a final attempt. **last rites** *n.* (*pl.*) religious rites for the dying. **last sleep** *n.* death. **last straw** *n.* the thing that finally takes one past the limit of endurance or patience. **Last Supper** *n.* the supper shared by Christ and his disciples the evening before his crucifixion. **last thing** *n.* late in the evening; just before going to bed. **last trump** *n.* the end of the world. **last word** *n.* **1** a concluding statement. **2** a final decision. **3** the latest improvement, most up-to-date model. [OE *latost*, *lætest*, superl. of *læt*, LATE]

last[2] (lahst) *v.i.* **1** to continue in existence, to go on. **2** to hold out, to continue unexhausted or unimpaired, to endure. **3** to be enough for (a person over a specified period of time). **to last out 1** to endure to the end, to persevere, to survive. **2** to be enough to meet one's requirements till the end of (a period of time). **laster** *n.* a person or thing which lasts (out). **lasting** *a.* **1** continuing in existence. **2** enduring, permanent, durable. ~*n.* a durable woollen fabric used in making the uppers of women's shoes. **lastingly** *adv.* **lastingness** *n.* [OE *læstan*, from *lāst*, see LAST[3]]

last[3] (lahst) *n.* a shaped wooden block on which boots and shoes are fashioned or repaired. **to stick to one's last** to concern oneself with what one knows about and is skilled in (and not meddle with other matters). [OE *lāst*, foot-track, *lœste*, fem., shoemaker's last (cp. Dut. *leest*, Icel. *leistr*, G *Leisten*)]

last[4] (lahst) *n.* a certain weight or quantity, varying for different commodities (commonly 2 tons, 80 bushels or 640 gallons). [OE *hlæst*, rel. to *hladan*, to LADE (cp. Dut., G, Swed., and Dan. *last*)]

Lat. *abbr.* Latin.

lat. *abbr.* latitude.

latch (lach) *n.* **1** a fastening for a door, gate etc., consisting of a bolt and catch. **2** a spring-lock that fastens with the shutting of a door and is opened with a key. ~*v.t., v.i.* to fasten with a latch. **on the latch** fastened by the latch only, not locked. **to latch on to 1** to understand the meaning of. **2** to attach oneself to. **latchkey** *n.* a key to the latch on a front door. **latchkey child** *n.* a child who lets themselves into the house after school, usu. one with working parents. [ME *lacche*, from *lacchen*, OE *læccan*, to catch (prob. blended with OF *lache*, LACE)]

†**latchet** (lach´it) *n.* a string for a shoe or sandal. [OF *lachet*, *lacet*]

late (lāt) *a.* **1** coming after the proper, usual or agreed time. **2** slow, tardy, backward, long delayed. **3** far on into the evening or night. **4** far on in any period. **5** far advanced, far on in development. **6** existing at a previous time but now gone or ceased. **7** deceased, departed (esp. recently). **8** former; recently in office etc. **9** recent in date. ~*adv.* **1** after the proper or usual time. **2** at or till a late hour, season, stage etc. **3** (*poet.*) a short time ago, lately, recently. **4** †formerly, of old. **at the latest** no later than. **late in the day 1** at an advanced stage in proceedings. **2** too late. **later on** at some unspecified later or future time. **of late 1** a short time ago, lately, recently. **2** latterly, formerly. **the late 1** the recently deceased, resigned etc. **2** the recent. **the latest** (*coll.*) the most recent news. **latecomer** *n.* a person or thing that arrives late. **Late Greek** *n.* the Greek language as spoken and written from 3rd–7th cents. AD.

Late Latin *n.* the Latin language as spoken and written *c.* AD 175–600. **lately** *adv.* a short time ago, recently; in recent times. **laten** *v.t.*, *v.i.* **lateness** *n.* **latish** *a.*, *adv.* [OE *læt* (cp. Dut. *laat*, Icel. *latr*, G *lass*, cogn. with L *lassus*, weary)]

lateen (lətēn´) *a.* a term applied to a triangular sail, inclined at an angle of about 45°, used principally in the Mediterranean. ~*n.* **1** (*also* **lateen sail**) such a sail. **2** a vessel so rigged. **lateen-rigged** *a.* [F *latine*, fem. of *latin*, LATIN]

La Tène (la ten´) *a.* of the later European Iron Age from the 5th cent. to 1st cents. BC. [*La Tène*, near Neuchâtel, Switzerland]

latent (lā´tənt) *a.* **1** hidden or concealed. **2** not seen, not apparent. **3** dormant, not active, potential. **latency** *n.* **latent energy** *n.* potential energy. **latent heat** *n.* the heat required to turn a solid into a liquid, or a liquid into a gas, at constant temperature. **latent image** *n.* a photographic image not yet made visible by developing. **latently** *adv.* **latent period** *n.* **1** the time between infection with a disease and the appearance of the first symptoms. **2** (*also* **latent time**) the length of time between stimulation and reaction. **latescent** (-tes´ənt) *a.* becoming latent or obscure. **latescence** *n.* [L *latens* -*ntem*, pres.p. of *latēre*, to lie hid]

-later (lətə) *comb. form* a person who worships a particular thing, as *idolater*. [see -LATRY]

lateral (lat´ərəl) *a.* **1** of or relating to, at, from or towards the side. **2** descended from a brother or sister of a person in the direct line. **3** (of a speech sound) pronounced with the tip of the tongue touching the alveolar ridge so that air can pass to one or both sides of it. ~*n.* **1** a part, member, process, shoot etc., situated or developing at the side. **2** a lateral consonant. **lateral axis** *n.* the crosswise axis of an aircraft. **laterality** (-ral´-) *n.* physical one-sidedness. **lateral line** *n.* a sensory organ on the side of fish for detecting movement or changes in water pressure through vibrations. **laterally** *adv.* **lateral thinking** *n.* a way of thinking which seeks to solve problems by finding new perspectives rather than following conventional or strictly logical lines of thought. **lateri-**, **latero-** *comb. form* [L *laterālis*, from *latus lateris*, side]

Lateran (lat´ərən) *n.* a cathedral church at Rome, dedicated to St John the Baptist. ~*a.* of or relating to this. **Lateran Council** *n.* each of five general ecumenical councils held in the church of St John Lateran between 1123 and 1512. **Lateran Treaty** *n.* a treaty concluded between the Italian State and the Papacy (1929) establishing the sovereign status of the Vatican City. [after the Roman *familia* of the Plautii *Laterani*, on the site of whose palace the church is built]

laterigrade (lat´ərigrād) *a.* walking sideways (like a crab). [L *latus laters*, side, *gradī*, to go]

laterite (lat´ərīt) *n.* a red porous rock, composed of silicate of alumina and oxide of iron, found in extensive beds in India and SW Asia. **lateritic** (-rit´-) *a.* [L *later*, brick, -ITE[1]]

lateroversion (laterōvœ´shən) *n.* sideways displacement of an organ or part, esp. the uterus. [*latero-*, see LATERAL, L *versio*, *-onis*, a turning]

latescent LATENT.

latex (lā´teks) *n.* (*pl.* **latexes, latices** (-tisēz)) **1** the juice of milky plants, esp. rubber trees. **2** a similar emulsion of a polymer in a watery liquid. **laticifer** (latis´ifə) *n.* a cell or group of cells containing latex. **laticiferous** (latisif´-) *a.* conveying or producing latex. [L, liquid, fluid]

lath (lahth, lath) *n.* (*pl.* **laths** (lahdhz, lahths, laths)) **1** a thin strip of wood, esp. one nailed to rafters to support tiles or to the studs of partitions to support plastering. **2** anything of similar dimensions or used for the same purposes. ~*v.t.* to cover or line with laths. **lathen** *a.* **lathing** *n.* **lath-work** *n.* a lining of laths to receive plaster. **lathy** *a.* **1** thin as a lath. **2** made of lath or laths. [cp. OE *lœth*, Dut. *lat*, G *Latte*]

lathe[1] (lādh) *n.* a machine for cutting, shaping and polishing wood, ivory, metal etc. by rotating it against a fixed tool. ~*v.t.* to work an object on a lathe. [cp. Dan. *lad* in *dreie-lad*, turning wheel (perh. however from OE *hlœd-whēogl*, lade-wheel, a wheel for drawing water)]

lathe[2] (lādh) *n.* a former division of Kent. [OE *lœth*, cp. Icel. *lāth*]

lather (lah´dhə, ladh´ə) *n.* **1** froth or foam made by soap moistened with water or caused by profuse sweating. **2** (*coll.*) a flustered or excited state. ~*v.i.* **1** to form a lather, e.g. by using soap and water. **2** (of soap) to form lather. **3** (of a horse) to become covered with lather. ~*v.t.* **1** to cover with lather. **2** (*coll.*) to thrash, to flog. **lathering** *n.* a beating. **lathery** *a.* [OE *lēathor* (cp. Icel. *lauthr*, *löthr*, also Gr. *loutron*, bath, L *lavare*, to wash)]

lathi (lah´ti) *n.* a long, heavy stick used as a weapon in India, esp. by police. [Hind.]

latices, laticifer etc. LATEX.

laticlave (lat´iklāv) *n.* a broad purple stripe worn on the front of the tunic, as a mark of senatorial rank in ancient Rome. [late L *lāticlāvium*, *lāticlāvus lātus*, broad, *clāvus*, stripe)]

latifundium (latifŭn´diəm) *n.* (*pl.* **latifundia** (-diə)) a large landed or agricultural estate, esp. in ancient Rome. [L (*lātus*, broad, *fundus*, an estate)]

Latin (lat´in) *a.* **1** of, relating to or expressed in the language of the ancient Romans. **2** of or relating to one or any of the (Romance) languages derived from this or the peoples who speak them. **3** of or relating to ancient Latium, its inhabitants or their language. **4** of or relating to the Roman Catholic Church. ~*n.* **1** the language of ancient Rome, originally the language of Latium. **2** an inhabitant of ancient Latium. **3** a person belonging to a people whose language derives from Latin. **4** (*N Am.*) a Latin American. **5** a Roman Catholic. **Latina** (lətē´nə) *n.* a female inhabitant of the United States, of Latin American origin. **Latin America** *n.* the parts of America where the official language is derived from Latin (e.g. Spanish, Portuguese). **Latin American** *a.* of or relating to the states of Latin America. ~*n.* a native or inhabitant of Latin America. **Latinate** (-nāt) *a.* imitating or derived from Latin. **Latin Church** *n.* the Church of the West, the Roman Catholic Church. **Latin cross** *n.* a cross with a long upright below the crosspiece. **Latinism** *n.* **Latinist** *n.* **Latinity** (latin´iti) *n.* quality of Latin style or idiom, or of Latin scholarship. **Latinize, Latinise** *v.t.* **1** to give a Latin form to (a word, phrase etc.). **2** to translate into Latin. **3** to bring into conformity with the ideas, customs, forms etc., of the Romans, the Latin peoples or the Roman Catholic Church. ~*v.i.* to use Latin words, idioms or phrases. **Latinization** (-zā´shən) *n.* **Latinizer** *n.* **Latino** (lətē´nō) *n.* (*pl.* **Latinos**) an inhabitant of the United States, of Latin American origin. ~*a.* of or relating to the Latinos. **Latin peoples** *n.pl.* those whose language is of Latin origin, the French, Spanish, Portuguese and Italians. **Latin Quarter** *n.* a left-bank district of Paris surrounding the Sorbonne, famous for students, artists etc. and bohemianism. **Latin square** *n.* a square array of rows and columns containing *n* different elements occurring *n* times, but never more than once in the same column or row. [F, from L *Latīnus*, from *Latium*, a region in Italy]

latish LATE.

latitude (lat´itūd) *n.* **1** angular distance on a meridian, angular distance of a place north or south of the equator. **2** (*pl.*) regions, climates, esp. with reference to distance from the equator or the tropics. **3** freedom of action; freedom to deviate from a standard or rule. **4** absence of strictness, tolerance, breadth; laxity. **5**

looseness of application or meaning. **6** the angular distance of a celestial body from the ecliptic. **latitudinal** (-tū´-) *a.* **latitudinally** *adv.* **latitudinarian** (-neə´ri-) *n.* **1** a person who does not attach great importance to dogmas. **2** a member of a party in the Church of England (mid-17th cent.) who aimed at a comprehensive system which should embrace those points on which Christians are agreed. *~a.* **1** liberal, tolerant of diversity of opinion, esp. in religion. **2** not confined within narrow or dogmatic limits. **latitudinarianism** *n.* **latitudinous** (-tū´-) *a.* [F, from L *lātitūdo*, from *lātus*, broad]

latria (lat´riə, lətrī´ə) *n.* in the Roman Catholic Church, that supreme worship which can lawfully be offered to God alone. [late L, see -LATRY, cp. DULIA, HYPERDULIA]

latrine (lətrēn´) *n.* a lavatory, a toilet, esp. in a camp or barracks. [F, from L *lātrīna* (*lavātrīna*), from *lavāre*, to wash]

-latry (lətri) *comb. form* worship or excessive devotion, as in *bibliolatry*, *idolatry*, *zoolatry*. [Gr. *-latreia* (*-later*, Gr. *-latrēs*, worshipper)]

latten (lat´ən) *n.* a finer kind of brass, of which the incised plates for sepulchral monuments, crosses etc., were made. *~a.* made of latten. [OF *laton* (F *laiton*), prob. cogn. with *latte*, LATH, from Gmc.]

latter (lat´ə) *a.* **1** (of two) second, second-mentioned. **2** (*coll.*) (of more than two) last-mentioned. **3** coming or happening after something else, later. **4** recent, modern, present. **5** of or relating to the end of a period, life, the world etc. **latter-day** *a.* modern, recent. **Latter-day Saints** *n.pl.* the Mormons. **latterly** *adv.* **1** recently. **2** towards the end of a period. [OE *lœtra*, compar. of *lœt*, LATE]

Usage note The use of *the latter* to mean the last-mentioned of more than two (*the last*) is often disapproved of.

lattice (lat´is) *n.* **1** a structure of laths or strips of metal or wood crossing and forming openwork. **2** in a crystal, the geometric pattern of molecules, atoms or ions, or of the points around which they vibrate. **3** in a nuclear reactor, the structural arrangement of fissile and non-fissile material in a geometric pattern. *~a.* consisting of or furnished with lattice-work. *~v.t.* **1** to furnish with a lattice or lattice-work. **2** to intertwine. **lattice bridge** *n.* a bridge built of lattice girders. **latticed** *a.* **lattice energy** *n.* the energy, usu. expressed in joules per mole, needed to separate the ions of a crystal to an infinite distance. **lattice girder, lattice frame** *n.* a beam or girder consisting of bars connected together by iron lattice-work. **lattice window** *n.* a window consisting of small (usu. diamond-shaped) panes set in strips of lead. **lattice-work** *n.* the arrangement of laths etc., forming a lattice. **latticing** *n.* [ME *latis*, OF *lattis*, from *latte*, see LATTEN]

Latvian (lat´viən) *n.* **1** a native or inhabitant of Latvia, a Lett. **2** the language of Latvians, Lettish. *~a.* of or relating to Latvia, its people or its language, Lettish. [*Latvia*, a republic bordering on the Baltic Sea]

laud (lawd) *v.t.* to praise, to celebrate, to extol. *~n.* **1** (*poet.*) praise; thankful adoration; worship consisting of praise. **2** a song of praise, a hymn. **3** (*pl.*) the office of the first canonical hour of prayer in the Western Church, now usu. said with matins. **laudable** *a.* praiseworthy, commendable. **laudableness, laudability** (-bil´-) *n.* **laudably** *adv.* **laudation** (-dā´shən) *n.* (*formal*) **1** the act of praising. **2** praise. **laudatory** (law´dətəri), **laudative** (-dətiv) *a.* expressing praise. **lauder** *n.* [L *laudāre*, from *laus laudis*, praise]

laudanum (law´dənəm) *n.* opium prepared in alcohol, tincture of opium, formerly used as a painkiller. [New L, a term coined by Paracelsus for a precious medicament, prob. var. of LADANUM or LABDANUM]

laugh (lahf) *v.i.* **1** to express amusement, scorn or exultation by inarticulate sounds and the convulsive movements of the face and body which are the involuntary effects of such emotions. **2** to deride, jeer or scoff (at). **3** (*poet.*) (of a non-human subject) to appear to laugh or be happy, sparkling or playful. *~v.t.* **1** to express by laughing. **2** to utter with laughter. **3** to move or influence by ridicule or laughter. *~n.* **1** the action of laughing. **2** an act or explosion of laughter. **3** a person's manner of laughing. **4** (*coll.*) something or someone that causes laughter; a bit of fun. **a laugh a minute 1** very funny or amusing. **2** (*iron.*) very unfunny. **don't make me laugh** an expression of scornful disbelief. **to be laughing** (*coll.*) to have no further problems; to be in an advantageous position. **to have the last laugh** to be ultimately triumphant after a former setback. **to laugh at** to mock, to deride, to ridicule. **to laugh away 1** to dismiss with a laugh. **2** to pass (time) in a happy or merry way. **to laugh down** to suppress or silence with derisive laughter. **to laugh in someone's face** to show someone open contempt or ridicule. **to laugh like a drain** to laugh in a loud and unrestrained way. **to laugh off** to treat as of trifling importance. **to laugh on the other side of one's face** to feel vexation or disappointment after amusement or satisfaction. **to laugh on the wrong side of one's mouth** to laugh on the other side of one's face. **to laugh out of court** to treat as not worth considering or listening to. **to laugh over** to talk about or recall to mind with amusement. **to laugh to scorn** to treat with the utmost contempt. **to laugh up/in one's sleeve** to be inwardly amused while one's expression remains serious or demure. **laughable** *a.* **1** ludicrous, ridiculous; derisory. **2** exciting laughter, comical. **laughableness** *n.* **laughably** *adv.* **laugher** *n.* **laughing** *n., a.* **no laughing matter** something serious, not a proper subject for levity. **laughing gas** *n.* nitrous oxide, used as an anaesthetic (so-called because when inhaled it produces violent exhilaration). **laughing hyena** *n.* a striped dog of the species *Hyena striata.* **laughing jackass** *n.* a kookaburra. **laughingly** *adv.* **laughing stock** *n.* **1** an object of ridicule. **2** a butt. **laughter** *n.* the act or sound of laughing. †**laughterless** *a.* [OE *hlehhan* (cp. Dut. and G *lachen*, Icel. *hlœja*), prob. from an Indo-Eur. imit. base *klak-* (cp. Gr. *klōssein*, to cluck)]

launce (lans) *n.* a sand eel. [perh. var. of LANCE (cp. LANCELET)]

launch[1] (lawnch) *v.t.* **1** to cause to glide into the water (e.g. a vessel), or take off from land (e.g. a space rocket). **2** to put (a vessel) into the water for the first time. **3** to throw, to hurl, to propel. **4** to start or set (a person etc.) going. **5** to introduce a new product or publication onto the market, usu. with a publicity campaign. *~v.i.* (of a ship, rocket etc.) to be launched; to put to sea. *~n.* the act or occasion of launching a ship, rocket, product etc. **to launch into 1** to propel oneself into a new activity, career etc. with vigour and enthusiasm. **2** to embark on a long speech, story or explanation. **to launch out 1** to enter on a new and usu. more ambitious sphere of activity. **2** (*coll.*) to spend money freely. **launcher** *n.* the apparatus for launching a rocket, vessel etc. **launch pad, launching pad** *n.* **1** a platform from which a rocket is launched. **2** the initiating event or starting place or point which propels a new activity or from which it gets underway. **launch shoe, launching shoe** *n.* a device fitted to an aircraft from which missiles are launched. **launch site, launching site** *n.* the place from which a rocket or spacecraft is launched. **launch vehicle, launching vehicle** *n.* **1** a rocket used to launch a spacecraft, satellite etc. **2** the first stage of a multistage rocket. **launch window** *n.* the period during which a spacecraft can be launched for a particular mission. [ONF *lanchier*, var. of *lancier* (F *lancer*), to LANCE]

launch[2] (lawnch) *n.* **1** a large open pleasure-boat propelled by steam, electricity or internal-combustion engine. **2** (*Hist.*) the largest boat belonging to a man-of-war. [Sp. and Port. *lancha*, perh. from Malay *lanchār*, swift]

launder (lawn´də) *v.t.* **1** to wash and iron (clothing, linen etc.). **2** (*coll.*) to legitimize illegally acquired money by transferring it through banks, foreign institutions etc. *~v.i.* **1** to wash and iron clothing, linen etc. **2** to become clean and ready for use by washing and ironing. *~n.* a trough or gutter for carrying water. **launderer** *n.* **launderette** (-dəret´, -dret´), **laundrette** *n.* an establishment containing coin-operated washing-machines etc., for public use. **laundress** (-dris) *n.* a woman who washes and irons (clothes, linen etc.). **Laundromat®** (-drəmat) *n.* a launderette. **laundry** (-dri) *n.* (*pl.* **laundries**) **1** a room or establishment where clothes are washed and ironed. **2** the batch of clothes sent to or received from a laundry. **3** washing. **4** the act of laundering. **laundryman, laundrywoman** *n.* (*pl.* **laundrymen, laundrywomen**) a person who is employed in a laundry or who collects and delivers washing. [ME *lavender*, a launder, OF *lavandier*, fem. *-diere*, late L *lavandārius*, from *lavanda*, things to be washed, from *lavāre*, to wash]

lauraceous (lawrā´shəs) *a.* of or relating to the family Lauraceae which includes the laurels and avocado. [L *laurus*, the laurel]

Laurasia (lawrā´zhə, -shə) *n.* the supercontinent thought to have existed in the northern hemisphere after the first division of Pangaea 200 million years ago, comprising what is now N America, Greenland, Europe and Asia apart from the Indian subcontinent. [New L, from *Laur*entia (referring to the ancient N American landmass), Eur*asia*]

laureate (law´riət, lor´-) *a.* **1** crowned or decked with laurel. **2** worthy of laurels, eminent, distinguished, esp. as a poet. **3** consisting or made of laurels. *~n.* **1** a person who has received a particular award or honour. **2** a Poet Laureate. **3** a person who has been crowned with laurel. **Poet Laureate** POET. **laureateship** *n.* [L *laureātus*, from *laurea*, a laurel-wreath, fem. of *laureus*, a., from *laurus*]

laurel (lor´əl) *n.* **1** a glossy-leaved evergreen shrub, *Laurus nobilis*, also called the *bay tree*. **2** (*sing. or pl.*) the foliage of this, esp. in the form of a wreath, conferred as a distinction on victorious competitors in the ancient classical games, on heroes, poets etc. **3** (*sing. or pl.*) the honours conferred by this. **4** any of various trees and shrubs resembling the laurel, e.g. the cherry laurel, spurge laurel. **to look to one's laurels** to guard against rivalry, to take care not to lose one's pre-eminence. **to rest on one's laurels** to be satisfied with what one has achieved and not to strive for further success. **laurelled,** (*N Am.*) **laureled** *a.* crowned with laurel. **lauric acid** *n.* an insoluble crystalline substance used in the manufacture of soaps and synthetic resins. [ME *laurer*, F *laurier*, prob. through a L *laurārius*, from *laurus*]

Laurentian (lawren´shiən) *a.* **1** (*also* **Lawrentian**) of, relating to or in the style of D. H. Lawrence or T. E. Lawrence. **2** a term designating a vast series of rocks north of the St Lawrence River, older than the Cambrian. **3** relating to the St Lawrence River.

lauric acid LAUREL.

laurustinus (lawrəstī´nəs) *n.* an ornamental evergreen shrub, *Viburnum tinus*, with pinkish-white winter flowers and dark-blue berries. [L *laurus*, laurel, *tīnus*, a plant, prob. laurus-tinus]

lav (lav) *n.* (*coll.*) short for LAVATORY.

lava (lah´və) *n.* (*pl.* **lavas**) **1** molten matter flowing in streams from volcanic vents. **2** the solidified rock formed from the same matter by cooling. **lava-cone** *n.* a volcanic cone formed by successive outflows of lava. **lava-flow, lava-stream** *n.* **lavaform** (-fawm) *a.* having the form of lava. **lava-like** *a.* [It., from *lavare*, to wash, see LAVE]

lavabo (ləvah´bō, -vā´-) *n.* (*pl.* **lavabos**) **1** the washing of the celebrant's hands, in the Roman Catholic and other Churches, after the offertory and before the Eucharist. **2** the towel used in this ceremony, also the basin. **3** a washing-trough or basin, often with running water, in monasteries. [L, I shall wash, from Psalm 26:6]

lavage LAVE.

lava-lava (lahvəlah´və) *n.* a rectangular piece of printed cloth worn as a shirtlike garment by both sexes in Polynesia. [Samoan, clothing]

lavatera (lavətiə´rə) *n.* a plant of the genus *Lavatera*, closely related to the mallows, grown usu. for its large white, pink or purple flowers. [the *Lavater* brothers, 18th-cent. Swiss doctors and naturalists]

lavation LAVE.

lavatory (lav´ətri) *n.* (*pl.* **lavatories**) **1** a receptacle for urinating or defecating into, usu. connected by pipes to a sewer and flushed with water; a toilet. **2** a room with a toilet and usu. a washhand basin. **3** a room or place for washing, esp. in a monastery. **lavatorial** (-taw´-) *a.* **1** of, relating to or resembling a lavatory, esp. a public lavatory. **2** (of humour) heavily reliant on references to faeces, excretion, lavatories etc. **lavatory paper** *n.* toilet paper. [Late L *lavātōrium*, from *lavāre*, to wash]

lave (lāv) *v.t.* (*poet.*) **1** to wash; to bathe. **2** (of the sea, streams) to wash or flow against. **lavage** (lā´vij, lavahj´) *n.* (*Med.*) the flushing out of a hollow organ with water or a medicated solution. **lavation** (-ā´shən) *n.* (*formal*) the act of washing. **lavement** *n.* **laver**[1] *n.* **1** a brazen vessel, containing water for the Jewish priests to wash when they offered sacrifices. **2** †a font. **3** †a vessel in which to wash, a piscina. [prob. from OE *lafian* (cp. Dut. *laven*, G *laben*), or from F *laver*, L *lavāre* (cp. Gr. *louein*)]

lavender (lav´əndə) *n.* **1** a sweet-scented flowering shrub, *Lavandula vera*, cultivated for its scent, its mauve or blue flowers, and its oil which is used in perfumery. **2** the flower and stalks or the oil used for perfuming linen etc. **3** the colour of the flowers, a pale lilac. *~a.* of the colour of lavender blossoms, pale lilac. *~v.t.* to perfume or sprinkle with lavender. **lavender bag** *n.* a small fabric bag filled with dried lavender stalks or flowers for scenting linen. **lavender-water** *n.* a liquid perfume, consisting of essential oil of lavender, ambergris, and alcohol. [A-F *lavendre* (F *lavande*), med. L *lavendula*, perh. from L *lividus*, LIVID (cp. var. *livendula*)]

laver[1] LAVE.

laver[2] (lā´və, lah´-) *n.* any of various types of seaweed, esp. *Porphyra umbilicaulis*, *P. vulgaris* and other edible species. **laver bread** *n.* a Welsh dish of boiled laver coated in oatmeal and fried. [L]

lavish (lav´ish) *a.* **1** spending or giving with profusion. **2** prodigal, spendthrift, unrestrained. **3** existing or produced in profusion. **4** excessive, superabundant. *~v.t.* **1** to expend or bestow profusely. **2** to be excessively free or liberal with, to squander. **lavisher** *n.* **lavishly** *adv.* **lavishment** *n.* **lavishness** *n.* [orig. a noun, lavishness, from OF *lavache*, *lavasse*, a deluge of rain, from *laver*, L *lavāre*, see LAVE]

lavolta (ləvol´tə) *n.* (*Hist.*) an old Italian dance for two persons, with much high leaping, popular in the 16th cent. [It. *la*, the, *volta*, turn]

law[1] (law) *n.* **1** a rule of conduct imposed by authority or accepted by the community as binding. **2** a system of such rules regulating the intercourse of mankind, of individuals within a state, or of states with one another. **3** the controlling influence of this. **4** the condition of order and stability it secures. **5** the practical application of these rules, esp. by trial in courts of justice; litigation, judicial process. **6** the interpretation of these rules, the science of legal principles and enactments, jurisprudence. **7** legal knowledge. **8** common and statute law (as opposed to *equity*). **9** one of a set of rules governing the conduct of a profession, art, association, sport, game or other activity or department of life. **10** the orderly recurrence of natural phenomena as the uniform results of corresponding conditions. **11** a generalized statement of such conditions and their consequences. **12** a theoretical principle drawn from experience or observation. **at law** according to the law. **canon law** CANON. **civil law** CIVIL. **criminal law** CRIMINAL. **in law** according to the law. **international law** INTERNATIONAL. **the Law** the Pentateuch or Torah. **the law 1** the legal profession. **2** (*coll.*) the police; a police officer. **to be a law unto oneself** to act in accordance with one's principles, wishes etc. in defiance of customs, rules etc. **to go to law** to take legal proceedings. **to have the law of/ on 1** to take legal proceedings against. **2** to report to the police. **to lay down the law** to talk or direct in a dictatorial manner. **to take the law into one's own hands** to try to secure satisfaction or retaliation by one's own methods or actions. **law-abiding** *a.* obedient to the law. **law-abidingness** *n.* **law agent** *n.* (*Sc.*) a solicitor. **law-and-order** *a.* advocating tough action against crime and violence. **law-book** *n.* a treatise on law. **lawbreaker** *n.* a person who violates the law. **lawbreaking** *n.*, *a.* **law centre** *n.* a publicly-funded office where free legal advice can be obtained. **law court** *n.* a court of law. **Law French** *n.* Anglo-Norman terms and phrases used in law. **lawful** *a.* **1** conformable with law. **2** allowed by law. **3** legitimate, valid, rightful. **lawfully** *adv.* **lawfulness** *n.* **lawgiver** *n.* a person who makes or enacts laws, a legislator. **lawgiving** *a.* **lawing** *n.* (*Sc.*) a bill or reckoning. **law Latin** *n.* the form of Latin used in legal documents. **lawless** *a.* **1** not subject to or governed by law. **2** regardless of or unrestrained by the law. **3** unbridled, licentious. **lawlessly** *adv.* **lawlessness** *n.* **Law Lord** *n.* a member of the House of Lords qualified to deal with the judicial business of the House. **lawmaker** *n.* a legislator. **law-making** *n.*, *a.* **lawman** *n.* (*pl.* **lawmen**) (*N Am.*) a law enforcement officer. **law merchant** *n.* mercantile law. **lawmonger** *n.* a pettifogging lawyer. **law of averages** *n.* the principle that extremes cancel one another out thereby reaching a balance. **law of continuity** *n.* the principle that nothing passes from one state into another without passing through all the intermediate states. **law officer** *n.* a public legal functionary, esp. the Attorney-General and Solicitor-General. **†law of kind** *n.* the natural order. **law of large numbers** *n.* a fundamental principle of statistics whereby it is posited that as the size of a sample approaches infinity, the difference between the mean of the sample and the mean of the proportion as a whole will approach zero. **law of mass action** *n.* the principle that the rate of reaction of chemical substances varies in proportion to the masses of the substances involved in the reaction. **Law of Moses** *n.* the Pentateuch. **law of nations** *n.* international law. **law of nature** *n.* **1** NATURAL LAW (under NATURAL). **2** (*coll.*) a fact of life. **law of parsimony** *n.* OCCAM'S RAZOR (under OCCAMISM). **law of succession** *n.* the law or laws governing inheritance. **law of supply and demand** *n.* the principle that the price of a commodity or service is governed by the relationship between the amount of demand for it and the quantity which can be supplied. **law of the jungle** *n.* a state of merciless competitiveness. **law of thermodynamics** *n.* any of three principles governing the relationships between different forms of energy. **law reports** *n.pl.* written records of previous cases tried which are referred to during court proceedings in order to assert legal precedents or principles. **laws of motion** *n.pl.* the three axioms laid down by Sir Isaac Newton: (1) every body remains in a state of rest or of uniform motion in the same direction, unless it is compelled to change that state; (2) change of motion is proportional to the force applied, and takes place in the direction of the straight line in which the force acts; (3) to every action there is always an equal and opposite reaction. **lawsuit** *n.* an action in a court of law. **law term** *n.* **1** a word or phrase used in law. **2** any one of the periods appointed for the sitting of the Law Courts. **lawyer** (-yə) *n.* a person who practises law, esp. an attorney or solicitor. **lawyer-like, lawyerly** *a.* [OE *lagu*, from old Icel., cogn. with LAID, LAY[1]]

†law[2] (law) *n.* (*Sc., North.*) a hill, esp. a rounded or conical hill of moderate size. [OE *hlæw*]

lawks (lawks) *int.* (*dial.*) an old exclamation of surprise or wonder. [corr. of ALACK or LORD]

lawn[1] (lawn) *n.* **1** a grassy space kept smooth and closely mown in a garden, park etc. **2** †an open space between woods, a glade in a forest. **lawnmower** *n.* a machine for mowing a lawn. **lawn-sprinkler** *n.* a device with a perforated revolving collar for watering lawns. **lawn tennis** *n.* the former name for the game of tennis, orig. played on a lawn but now frequently on a hard court. **lawny**[1] *a.* [ME *laund*, OF *launde*, from Celt. (cp. Bret. *lann*, Welsh *llan*)]

lawn[2] (lawn) *n.* a cotton or linen fabric, finer than cambric (e.g. used for the sleeves of an Anglican bishop's rochet). **lawny**[2] *a.* [OF *Lan*, now *Laon*, a town NW of Rheims]

lawny[1] LAWN[1].

lawny[2] LAWN[2].

lawrencium (lawren´siəm) *n.* a radioactive element, at. no. 103, chem. symbol Lr, with a short half-life, orig. produced in America. [after Ernest O. *Lawrence*, 1901–58, US physicist]

Lawrentian LAURENTIAN.

lawyer LAW[1].

lax (laks) *a.* **1** not exact, not strict; negligent, careless. **2** porous. **3** equivocal, ambiguous, vague. **4** slack, loose, not tight, firm or compact. **5** (of a speech sound) pronounced with relaxed vocal muscles and therefore not precisely articulated and short in duration. **laxation** (-sā´shən) *n.* **1** the act of making lax. **2** (*formal*) defecation. **laxative** *a.* opening or loosening the bowels. ~*n.* a laxative medicine. **laxity, laxness** *n.* **laxly** *adv.* [L *laxus*, cogn. with *languēre*, to LANGUISH]

lay[1] (lā) *v.t.* (*past, p.p.* **laid** (lād)) **1** to cause to lie, to place in a horizontal, prostrate or recumbent position. **2** to put or bring into a certain state or position (*laid my hand on his arm*). **3** to dispose regularly, to put in proper position (*lay a carpet*). **4** to put down, to place, to deposit; to establish as a base or basis (*lay the foundations*). **5** (of a bird) to produce (eggs). **6** to spread on a surface, to apply. **7** to cause to lie flat or smooth. **8** to cause to settle (as dust). **9** to cause to be still, to allay, to calm. **10** to exorcize. **11** to put forward, to present. **12** to attribute, to impute. **13** to impose, to enjoin, to inflict. **14** to stake, to wager. **15** to think out, to devise, to plan, to prepare. **16** to bring down (a weapon, blows etc., on). **17** to beat down, to prostrate. **18** to locate (a scene, story etc.). **19** (*Mil.*) to aim and set (a gun) prior to firing. **20** in horticulture, to propagate by layers. **21** (*taboo sl.*) to have sexual intercourse with. **22** to bury. ~*v.i.* **1** to drop or deposit eggs. **2** (*Naut., coll.*) to lie. **3** to make a bet. ~*n.* **1** the way, direction or position in which a region or object is situated. **2** (*taboo sl.*) an act of sexual intercourse. **3** (*taboo sl.*) a sexual partner. **4** the direction the strands of a rope are twisted. **5** a share of profits, esp. a portion of the catch from a whaling expedition. **in lay** (of hens) laying eggs. **to lay about one 1** to hit out on all sides; to fight vigorously. **2** to issue criticism, reprimands etc. indiscriminately. **to lay a cable** 1 to bury or sink an electric cable. 2 to twist the strands of a cable. **to lay a charge** to make an accusation. **to lay aside** 1 to put to one side. 2 to give up, to abandon; to reject. 3 to store for future use. **to lay at the door of** DOOR. **to lay away** 1 to reserve for future use. 2 to reserve (a purchase) while payments are being made. **to lay back** to place or construct sloping back from the vertical. **to lay bare** 1 to reveal. 2 to strip. **to lay before** 1 to exhibit to. 2 to bring to the notice of. **to lay by** 1 to save. 2 to reserve for a future occasion. **to lay claim to** CLAIM. **to lay down** 1 to put down. 2 to resign, to surrender. 3 to declare, to affirm, to assert; to stipulate. 4 to formulate, to draw up. 5 to put down the main structural parts of. 6 to record on paper. 7 to sacrifice. 8 to store (wine etc.). 9 (*coll.*) to wager. 10 to pay. 11 to convert (land) to pasture. 12 to record (tracks of an album). **to lay down the law** LAW[1]. **to lay eyes on** EYE[1]. **to lay fast** to seize and keep fast, to prevent from escaping. †**to lay for** (*coll.*) to lie in wait for. **to lay hands on** HAND. **to lay hold of** to grasp or seize. **to lay in** to acquire a store of, to stock up with. **to lay into** to assault physically or verbally. **to lay it on** 1 to speak or flatter extravagantly. 2 to charge exorbitantly. 3 to strike or beat hard. 4 to criticize severely. **to lay it on the line** LINE[1]. **to lay it on thick** to speak or flatter extravagantly. **to lay it on with a trowel** TROWEL. **to lay low** 1 to fell or destroy. 2 to cause to become weak or ill. **to lay odds** ODDS (under ODD). **to lay off** 1 to suspend from employment. 2 to discharge (workers) permanently, to make redundant. 3 to desist. 4 to avoid. **to lay on** 1 (*coll.*) to provide (facility, entertainment). 2 to install and supply (water, gas). 3 to impose, to inflict. 4 to deal (blows etc.). 5 to apply, to spread on. **to lay oneself open to** to expose oneself to (criticism, attack etc.). **to lay oneself out** (*coll.*) to busy or exert oneself to do something. **to lay one's hands on** HAND. **to lay on the table** TABLE. **to lay open** 1 to cut so as to expose the interior of. 2 to expose, to reveal. 3 to explain. **to lay out** 1 to arrange according to a plan. 2 to spread out. 3 to expound, to explain. 4 to expend. 5 to dress in grave-clothes and prepare for burial. 6 (*coll.*) to knock to the ground or render unconscious. **to lay over** 1 to spread over, to overlay. 2 (*N Am.*) to stop over during a journey. 3 (*N Am.*) to postpone. **to lay siege to** 1 to besiege. 2 to importune. **to lay the table** to set a table with cutlery, crockery etc. for a forthcoming meal. **to lay to** 1 (*Naut.*) to check the motion of a ship; to heave to. 2 (*Naut.*) to bring (a ship) into harbour. **to lay to rest** 1 to bury. 2 to prevent from causing further trouble or dispute. 3 to calm, to assuage. **to lay under** to subject to. **to lay up** 1 to store, to treasure, to save. 2 (of illness) to confine (someone) to their bed or room. 3 to decommission a ship or take out of service. **to lay waste** WASTE. **layabout** *n.* an idle person, a lounger. **lay-by** *n.* (*pl.* **lay-bys**) 1 a widening of a road to enable vehicles to stop without holding up traffic. 2 a similar passing point on a railway or canal. 3 (*Austral., New Zeal.*) a system whereby payment of a deposit reserves an article for future purchase; an article reserved in this way. **lay-days** *n.pl.* (*Naut.*) 1 a certain number of days allowed for loading or unloading a ship. 2 the days on which a ship is prevented from sailing because of loading, bad weather etc. **laying** *n.* 1 the act or period of setting, placing or depositing. 2 the act or period of depositing eggs. 3 the eggs laid. 4 the twisting of yarns into a strand or of strands into a rope. **laying on of hands** *n.* sacramental imposition of hands for healing or other purposes. **lay-off** *n.* 1 an act of suspending workers from employment. 2 a period when workers are suspended from employment. 3 redundancy. **layout** *n.* 1 a planned arrangement of buildings etc. 2 the way in which text, illustrations, drawings etc. are arranged on a printed page. 3 something which is set out or displayed in a particular way. [OE *lecgan* (cp. Dut. *leggen*, Icel. *leggja*, G *legen*), casual of LIE[2]]

Usage note *Lay* should not be used instead of *lie* as an intransitive verb.

lay[2] (lā) *a.* 1 of or relating to the people as distinct from the clergy. 2 non-professional, lacking specialized knowledge. **laic** (lā´ik), **laical** *a.* lay, not clerical, secular. ~*n.* a layman. **laically** *adv.* **laicity** (lāˊisiti) *n.* the status or influence of the laity. **laicize** (lā´isīz), **laicise** *v.t.* 1 to render lay or secular. 2 to throw open or hand over to the laity. **laicization** (-zā´shən) *n.* **laity** (lā´iti) *n.* 1 (*collect.*) the people, as distinct from the clergy. 2 laymen and laywomen, those not belonging to a particular profession. **lay brother, lay sister** *n.* a brother or sister in a monastery, under vows and wearing the habit of the order but not ordained, engaged chiefly in manual labour and exempt from other duties. **lay communion** *n.* 1 communicating of the laity at the Eucharist. 2 membership of the church as a layman. **layman, laywoman** *n.* (*pl.* **laymen, laywomen**) 1 a member of the people, as distinct from the clergy. 2 a non-professional, a person who is not an expert. **lay reader** *n.* 1 a member of the Church of England laity authorized to conduct certain religious services. 2 a layman in the Roman Catholic Church who reads the epistle at Mass. **lay sister** LAY BROTHER (under LAY[2]). **lay vicar** *n.* in the Church of England, a lay person acting as vicar choral. **laywoman** LAYMAN (under LAY[2]). [F *lai*, L *lāicus*, Gr. *laikos*, from *laos*, the people]

lay[3] (lā) *n.* 1 a lyric song or ballad. 2 a short narrative poem for singing or recitation. 3 song, singing (of birds etc.). [OF *lai*, prob. from OHG *leth, leich* (not rel. to G *Lied*)]

lay[4] LIE[2].

layer (lā´ə) *n.* 1 a thickness or anything spread out (usu. one of several), a stratum, a bed. 2 a person who or something which lays, esp. a hen. 3 a shoot laid with part of its length on or beneath the surface of the ground in order that it may take root. 4 in ecological studies, one of four levels of vegetation, the ground or moss, field or herb, shrub and tree layers. ~*v.t.* 1 to place, cut or form in layers. 2 to propagate by layers. ~*v.i.* (of growing corn etc.) to be laid flat by weather, weak growth etc. **layer cake** *n.* a cake made in layers with a filling in between. **layering** *n.* 1 a method of propagation in which shoots and stems are pegged to the ground and left until they root, when they can be separated. 2 any method employing layers. **layer-out** *n.* a person who prepares a body for burial. [ME from LAY[1], -ER[1]]

layette (lāet´) *n.* the outfit for a newborn infant. [F, dim. of OF *laye* (cp. OHG *lada*)]

lay figure (lā) *n.* 1 a jointed figure of the human body used by artists for hanging drapery on etc. 2 a puppet, a nonentity. 3 an unreal character in a story etc. [*lay*, from obs. *layman*, Dut. *leeman*, joint-man (*lid*, joint, *lith*, limb, MAN) FIGURE]

†**lazar** (laz´ə) *n.* a person infected with a loathsome disease, esp. a leper. **lazar house** *n.* a lazaretto. [F *lazare*, from name *Lazarus* (Luke xvi.20)]

lazaretto (lazəret´ō), **lazaret** (-ret´) *n.* (*pl.* **lazarettos, lazarets**) 1 a hospital (chiefly abroad) for persons suffering from some contagious disease, esp. leprosy. 2 a ship or other place of quarantine. 3 a storeroom or locker for provisions in ships or boats. [F *lazaret*, It. *lazzaretto*, as LAZAR]

laze LAZY.

lazulite (laz´ūlīt) *n.* an azure-blue to pale greenish-blue mineral, composed of phosphate of aluminium and magnesium. [med. L *lazulum*, LAPIS LAZULI, -ITE[1]]

lazurite (laz´ūrīt) *n.* a rare blue mineral composed of sodium aluminium silicate and sulphide, used as the gemstone lapis lazuli. [med. L *lazur*, LAPIS LAZULI, -ITE[1]]

lazy (lā'zi) *a.* (*comp.* **lazier**, *superl.* **laziest**) **1** idle, indolent, slothful, disinclined to labour or exertion. **2** conducive to or characterized by idleness or sloth. **3** (of movement) slow; languorous. **4** (of a letter) shown as lying on its side. **laze** *v.i.* **1** to be lazy. **2** to live in idleness. ~*v.t.* to waste or spend in idleness. ~*n.* a time or spell of idleness. **lazily** *adv.* **laziness** *n.* **lazy-bed** *n.* a bed in which seed potatoes are placed on the surface of the ground and covered with soil from trenches dug on each side. **lazybones** *n.* (*pl.* **lazybones**) (*coll.*) a lazy person, an idler. **lazy daisy** *n.* a type of embroidery stitch. **lazy eye** *n.* an eye which is apparently healthy but nevertheless causes impaired vision. **lazy Susan** *n.* a revolving tray for a dining table with compartments for various condiments. **lazy-tongs** *n.pl.* tongs consisting of levers, in pairs, crossing one another and turning on a pin like scissors, for picking up distant objects. [etym. uncertain]

lb *abbr.* **1** (*also* **l.b.**) in cricket, leg bye. **2** (*also* **lb.**) pound(s).

LBC *abbr.* London Broadcasting Company.

L/Bdr *abbr.* Lance Bombardier.

lbf *abbr.* pound force.

LBJ *abbr.* Lyndon Baines Johnson (President of the USA, 1963–69).

LBO *abbr.* leveraged buy-out.

LBS *abbr.* London Business School.

LBV *abbr.* Late Bottled Vintage (of port wine that has been matured in casks for six years before bottling).

l.b.w. *abbr.* in cricket, leg before wicket.

LC *abbr.* (*US*) Library of Congress.

lc *abbr.* **1** left centre. **2** letter of credit. **3** *loco citato*, in the place cited. **4** lower case (type).

LCC *abbr.* (*Hist.*) London County Council.

lcd, LCD *abbr.* **1** Liquid Crystal Display. **2** lowest common denominator.

L.Ch. *abbr.* Licentiate in Surgery.

l'chaim LECHAIM.

LCJ *abbr.* Lord Chief Justice.

lcm, LCM *abbr.* least or lowest common multiple.

L/Cpl *abbr.* Lance Corporal.

LD *abbr.* **1** lethal dosage (usu. with a subscript number appended to show the percentage of animals or organisms killed by the dose). **2** Low Dutch.

Ld. *abbr.* Lord.

Ldg. *abbr.* Leading (Seaman etc.).

LDL *abbr.* low-density lipoprotein.

LDS *abbr.* **1** Latter-day Saints. **2** *laus Deo semper*, praise be to God for ever. **3** Licentiate in Dental Surgery.

-le[1] (əl) *suf.* forming nouns esp. denoting appliances or instruments, as *handle*, *thimble* or animals and plants, *beetle*, *thistle*. [OE *-el*, from Gmc.]

-le[2] (əl), **-el** *suf.* forming nouns which orig. had a diminutive sense, as *angle*, *castle*, *puddle*, *novel*, *tunnel*. [ME *-el*, *-elle*, via OF from L *-ellus*, *-ella*, *-alis* (cp. -AL[2])]

-le[3] (əl) *suf.* forming adjectives, often with, or orig. with, the sense 'likely or liable to', e.g. *brittle*, *fickle*, *little*. [ME from OE *-el* etc., from Gmc., corresp. to L *-ulus*]

-le[4] (əl) *suf.* forming verbs, esp. expressing repeated action or having a diminutive sense, e.g. *crackle*, *tickle*, *wriggle*. [OE *-lian* from Gmc.]

LEA *abbr.* Local Education Authority.

lea[1] (lē) *n.* (*poet.*) **1** a meadow. **2** grassland. **3** open country. [OE *lēah* (cp. OHG *lôh*, also L *lūcus*, grove, glade)]

lea[2] (lē) *n.* land left untilled, fallow land, land under grass. ~*a.* fallow, unploughed. [OE *loecige* in *læghrycg*, lea-rig (*læg-*, *liegan*, to LIE[2])]

lea[3] (lē) *n.* a length of yarn which varies for different materials, usu. 80 yards for wool, 120 for cotton and silk, 300 for linen. [etym. uncertain]

leach (lēch) *v.t.* **1** to wash out or separate (a soluble constituent) by percolation. **2** to strain or drain (liquid) from some material (*usu.* out or away). **3** to wash or wet by letting liquid percolate through. ~*v.i.* (of liquid in any material) to drain out. ~*n.* **1** the solution obtained by leaching, a leachate; the substance which is leached. **2** a tub, vat or other vessel used for leaching. **3** the act of leaching. **leachate** (-āt) *n.* **1** the liquid that percolates through or out of something in leaching. **2** polluted or toxic water or other liquid that has leached from a rubbish dump. **3** the substance or solution obtained by leaching. [prob. from OE *leccan*, to water]

lead[1] (lēd) *v.t.* (*past*, *p.p.* **led** (led)) **1** to conduct, to guide by taking by the hand or halter or by showing the way. **2** to direct the actions, movements, opinions etc. of. **3** to be in command of. **4** to direct or induce by persuasion, instruction or advice. **5** to be at the head of (a procession, march etc.). **6** to be ahead in a race, competition etc. **7** to take first place or be pre-eminent among. **8** (of a path, road, route) to provide a means of reaching a place; (of a door, room) to give access to. **9** to live or cause to live (a certain kind of life). **10** to be the person who initiates and oversees (a discussion). **11** to direct by example (*lead the fashion*). **12** to be the principal player in (an orchestra) or the conductor of (a band). **13** to begin a round of cards with. **14** to conduct (a wire, rope etc.) along a particular course, esp. along a channel of some kind. **15** to phrase a question to (a witness) in such a way as to suggest the answer desired. **16** to be the main feature of (a newspaper or part of a newspaper). **17** to aim in front of (a moving target). ~*v.i.* **1** to go ahead, esp. to act as conductor or guide. **2** to be ahead of all the other competitors. **3** to be the commander, head or foremost person in any undertaking etc. **4** to go towards, to extend, to reach (to). **5** to tend (to) as a result. **6** (of a newspaper, news report) to have as its principal item. **7** in boxing, to make an attack (with); to use as one's habitual attacking hand. **8** to guide the movements of one's partner in a dance. **9** to be the first player in a game of cards to put down a card. ~*n.* **1** guidance, direction, esp. by going in front. **2** precedence, command, leadership. **3** a position ahead of all the others. **4** the distance or amount by which one is ahead. **5** a cord or strap for leading a dog. **6** an example for others to follow. **7** a clue. **8** the principal role in a play, film etc.; the person playing this role. **9** a principal conductor for distribution of current in an electrical installation. **10** in cards, the first play or the right to this. **11** the main story in a newspaper or news broadcast. **12** a way, passage, channel, esp. through ice. **13** an artificial watercourse, esp. a mill-race. **14** the direction in which a rope runs. **15** the distance advanced by a screw in one turn. **16** a boxer's habitual attacking punch. **17** a deposit of metal or ore. **18** the aiming or firing of a gun ahead of a moving target to allow for time taken by a projectile to reach it. ~*a.* principal, chief, main, leading. **to lead astray** to lead into error, misbehaviour, crime or sin. **to lead by the nose** to cause to follow unthinkingly; to deceive. **to lead captive** to take captive. **to lead off 1** to make a start. **2** (*coll.*) to lose one's temper. **to lead on 1** to entice, to draw further towards some end. **2** to fool or trick. **to lead someone a (merry) dance** DANCE. **to lead the way 1** to go first so as to point the way. **2** to take the precedence. **to lead to the altar** ALTAR. **to lead up the garden path** (*coll.*) to mislead; to trick, to deceive. **to lead up to 1** to conduct conversation towards (some particular subject). **2** to conduct towards. **3** to pave the way for. **4** in cards, to play so as to induce an opponent to play (a certain card). **leadable** *a.* **lead-in** *n.* **1** an introduction to a topic. **2** the electric conductor connecting a radio transmitter or receiver with an outside aerial or transmission cable.

lead-off *n.* **1** a start, a beginning. **2** a leading motion. **lead time** *n.* the interval between the design and manufacture of a product. **led** *a.* under another's influence or leading. [OE *lædant*, causal of *līthan*, to go (cp. Dut. *leiden*, G *leitan*, to lead, OHG *līdan*, to go)]

Usage note The past tense *led* should not be spelt like the chemical element *lead* (pronounced the same).

lead[2] (led) *n.* **1** a soft malleable and ductile, bluish-grey, toxic heavy metal, at. no. 82, chem. symbol Pb, occurring naturally in galena and used in building, in alloys and paints and as a shield against radiation. **2** graphite, as used in lead pencils; a thin stick of this as the core of a pencil. **3** a plummet, usu. consisting of a mass of lead, used for sounding. **4** (*pl.*) strips of lead used for covering a roof. **5** (*pl.*) a roof, esp. a flat roof, or part of a roof, covered with lead. **6** (*pl.*) the metal strips or cames holding the glass in diamond-paned windows. **7** (*Print.*) a thin plate of type-metal used to separate lines; a space made by this means. **8** lead bullets or (fishing) weights. ~*a.* **1** of, relating to or containing lead. **2** consisting more or less of lead. ~*v.t.* **1** to cover, fasten, weight, frame or fit with lead. **2** to space out (as lines of type) by inserting leads. **3** to add a lead compound to. **like a lead balloon** utterly useless, a complete failure. **to swing the lead** SWING. **lead-arming** *n.* a piece of tallow etc., pressed into the lower part of the sounding-lead, to ascertain the nature of the sea-bottom. **leaded** *a.* **1** set in or fitted with lead. **2** separated by leads, as lines of printing. **leaden** *a.* **1** made of lead. **2** of the colour of lead, dark. **3** heavy as lead. **4** heavy, slow, burdensome. **5** inert, indisposed to action or exertion. ~*v.t.*, *v.i.* to make or become leaden. **leadenly** *adv.* **leadenness** *n.* **leaden seal** *n.* a stamped piece of lead. **lead-free** *a.* (of petrol) unleaded; not containing tetraethyl lead. **leadglass** *n.* glass containing lead oxide. **leading**[1] *n.* **1** strips of lead inserted between lines of print, leads. **2** the space introduced between lines of type by inserting leads. **3** the lead strips framing panes of glass or covering a roof. **leadless** *a.* **lead line** *n.* a sounding-line. **lead paint** *n.* paint with a lead base. **lead pencil** *n.* a pencil containing a strip of graphite. **lead poisoning** *n.* poisoning caused by the prolonged absorption of lead into the system. **lead shot** *n.* small pellets of lead used in quantity in the cartridge of a shotgun. **leadsman** *n.* (*pl.* **leadsmen**) the sailor who heaves the lead in sounding. **lead tetraethyl** *n.* TETRAETHYL LEAD (under TETRAETHYL). **lead wool** *n.* a fibrous form of lead used in jointing water pipes. **leady** *a.* [OE *lēad* (cp. Dut. *lood*, Dan. *lod*, G *Lot*)]

leader (lē´də) *n.* **1** a person who or something which leads. **2** a chief, a commander. **3** (*Mus.*) the principal player or conductor of a band or group; the principal first violin of an orchestra; a conductor of an orchestra. **4** a chief editorial article in a newspaper. **5** a blank strip of film or tape preceding or following the recorded material. **6** (*pl.*, *Print.*) a row of dots to lead the eye across a page or column. **7** the terminal bud or shoot at the apex of a stem or branch. **8** the foremost horse, or one of the foremost horses abreast, in a team. **9** the first person on a climbing rope. **10** the leading counsel in a case. **11** (**Leader**) the Leader of the House. **12** (*esp. N Am.*) an item offered at a specially low price in order to attract customers. **13** a trace on a fishing line. **leader board** *n.* a scoreboard, esp. at a golf course, showing the names, positions etc. of the leading players in a tournament. **leaderene** (-rēn´) *n.* a female leader, esp. an autocratic one. **leaderless** *a.* **Leader of the House** *n.* in the House of Commons or House of Lords, a member of the government who has the responsibility for initiating legislative business. **leadership** *n.* **1** the position or office of leader. **2** the period during which a person is leader. **3** the authority, firmness etc. expected of a leader; the ability to lead. **4** the leaders of an organization as a group.

leading[1] LEAD[2].

leading[2] (lē´ding) *a.* **1** chief, main, principal. **2** in first position. **3** guiding, influential. ~*n.* guidance, influence. **leading aircraftman** *n.* a rank in the British Air Force below senior aircraftman. **leading aircraftwoman** *n.* a rank in the British Air Force below senior aircraftwoman. **leading article** *n.* a leader in a newspaper. **leading counsel** *n.* the senior of two or more barristers conducting a case. **leading dog** *n.* (*New Zeal.*) a dog trained to lead a flock of sheep. **leading edge** *n.* **1** on an aircraft, the foremost edge of an aerofoil (e.g. of a wing, propeller blade). **2** the forefront of something, esp. of technological advance. **3** the part of a pulse signal in which the amplitude increases. **leading-edge** *a.* very advanced. **leading lady** *n.* the actress taking the chief role in a play, film etc. **leading light** *n.* **1** an expert in a particular field. **2** an influential or prominent member of a movement, group etc. **leadingly** *adv.* **leading man** *n.* (*pl.* **leading men**) the actor taking the chief role in a play, film etc. **leading note** *n.* the seventh note of the major and minor scales. **leading question** *n.* a question (esp. in cross-examination) that suggests a certain answer. **leading-rein** *n.* **1** a rein for leading a horse by. **2** (*pl.*) LEADING-STRINGS (under LEADING[2]). **leading seaman** *n.* the most senior rank below that of a non-commissioned officer in the British navy. **leading-strings** *n.pl.* (*Hist.*) strings by which children were supported when learning to walk or by which they were restrained when walking. **to be in leading-strings** to be in a state of dependence on others. **leading tone** *n.* (*N Am.*) LEADING NOTE (under LEADING[2]).

leaf (lēf) *n.* (*pl.* **leaves** (lēvz)) **1** any of the usu. flat, green, lateral organs of plants which aid in the assimilation of food-materials and the transpiration and absorption of carbon dioxide from the atmosphere. **2** anything resembling this, esp. any similar plant structure, a petal, scale or sepal. **3** foliage. **4** a sheet of paper in a book or manuscript, usu. comprising two pages. **5** a thin sheet of metal or other material. **6** a hinged, sliding or detachable part of a bridge, door, table, shutter, screen etc. **7** the inner or outer surface of a cavity wall. **8** a crop that is harvested in the form of leaves, esp. the leaves of tea or tobacco. **9** a foil or strip of metal forming part of a laminated material or structure. ~*v.i.* to shoot out or produce leaves or foliage. **in leaf** with its leaves out. **to leaf through** to turn the pages of a book, magazine etc., in a casual way, to browse through. **to take a leaf out of someone's book** to follow the example of, to imitate. **to turn over a new leaf 1** to change one's mode of life or conduct for the better. **2** to make a new start. **leafage** (-ij) *n.* foliage. **leafbud** *n.* a bud developing into a leaf. **leafcutter** *n.* any of various insects (such as a bee or ant) which cut out sections of leaves. **leafed, leaved** *a.* (usu. *in comb.*, as *thick-leafed*). **leaf fat** *n.* dense fat accumulating in layers around the kidneys of certain animals, esp. pigs. **leaf green** *n.* the colour of green leaves, a light bright green. **leaf-green** *a.* **leafhopper** *n.* any of various jumping insects belonging to the superfamily Cicadelloidea that suck plant juices. **leaf insect** *n.* an insect having camouflaged wing covers resembling leaves. **leafless** *a.* **leaflessness** *n.* **leaflike** *a.* **leaf miner** *n.* any of various insects that as larvae bore into and eat leaf tissue. **leaf monkey** *n.* the langur. **leaf mould,** (*N Am.*) **leaf mold** *n.* decayed leaves reduced to mould, forming a constituent of soil or used as compost. **leaf sheath** *n.* a sheath enclosing the base of a grass stem. **leaf sight** *n.* a folding rear sight on a rifle. **leaf spot** *n.* any of various usu. fungal plant diseases that cause dark spots on leaves. **leaf spring** *n.* a spring consisting of several broad, flat pieces of metal. **leaf-stalk** *n.* a petiole supporting a leaf. **leafy** *a.* **1** having, or covered with, leaves. 2 (of a place) pleasantly covered or shaded with or abounding in foliage. 3 like a leaf. **leafiness** *n.* [OE *lēaf* (cp. Dut. *loof*, Icel. *lauf*, G *Laub*)]

leaflet (lēf´lit) *n.* 1 a one-page handbill, circular etc.; a pamphlet. 2 a small leaf. 3 any of the primary divisions of a compound leaf. ~*v.i.* (*pres.p.* **leafleting,** *past, p.p.* **leafleted**) to distribute leaflets. **leafleter** *n.*

league[1] (lēg) *n.* 1 a combination or union for mutual help or protection or the pursuit of common interests. 2 a treaty or compact of alliance or confederation. 3 a category, class or group. 4 an association of clubs that play matches against one another. ~*v.i.* (*3rd pers. sing. pres.* **leagues,** *pres.p.* **leaguing,** *past, p.p.* **leagued**) to join in a league, to confederate, to combine together (with). **in league with** having formed an alliance with, usu. for a dubious purpose. **not in the same league** not in the same class, not on the same level of excellence etc. **league football** *n.* (*Austral.*) Rugby League or Australian Rules football played in leagues. **league match** *n.* a match between clubs in the same league. **League of Nations** *n.* an international organization formed in 1920 pledged to cooperate in securing peace and the rigorous observance of treaties by its member states (coming to an end in 1946 when the United Nations was founded). **leaguer**[1] *n.* (*N Am.*) a league member. **league table** *n.* 1 a table of competitors in a league listed in order of performance. 2 a list showing the order of achievement, merit, performance etc. [F *ligue*, It. *liga*, L *ligāre* to tie, to bind]

league[2] (lēg) *n.* an old measure of distance, varying in different countries (in England usu. about three land or nautical miles, about 4.8 km). [perh. through Prov. *legua*, from late L *leuga*, prob. from Gaulish]

leaguer[1] LEAGUE[1].

†**leaguer**[2] (lē´gə) *n.* 1 a siege. 2 the camp of a besieging army. [Dut. *leger*, cp. LAIR[1], LAAGER]

leak (lēk) *v.i.* 1 to let liquid, gas etc. pass in or out through a hole, crevice or fissure. 2 (of a liquid, gas etc.) to pass in or out through a hole, crevice or fissure. 3 (of confidential information) to become known. 4 (*sl.*) to urinate. ~*v.t.* 1 to cause or allow to enter or pass out. 2 to divulge (confidential information). ~*n.* 1 a crack, hole, puncture etc. which accidentally lets water, fluid, gas etc. in or out. 2 the oozing of water, fluid, gas etc. through such an opening. 3 a disclosure of confidential information. 4 a loss of electric current from a conductor; the current lost. 5 (*sl.*) an act of urinating. **to leak out** to become gradually known or public, esp. in an underhand manner. **to spring a leak** to open or crack so as to admit or let out water. **leakage** (-ij) *n.* 1 a leak. 2 the substance or quantity that escapes or enters by a leak. 3 an allowance at a certain rate per cent for loss by leaking etc. **leaker** *n.* **leaky** *a.* (*comp.* **leakier,** *superl.* **leakiest**) 1 having a leak or leaks. 2 apt to divulge confidential information. **leakiness** *n.* [cp. Icel. *leka*, Dut. *lekken*, G *lecken*, also OE *leccan*, to wet]

leal (lēl) *a.* (*Sc.*) loyal, true. **leally** *adv.* **lealty** (lē´əl-) *n.* [A-F, from OF *leel*, as LOYAL]

lean[1] (lēn) *v.i.* (*past, p.p.* **leaned, leant** (lent)) 1 to incline one's body from an erect attitude. 2 to incline one's body so as to rest (against or upon). 3 to deviate from a straight or perpendicular line or direction. 4 to depend (upon) as for support. 5 to have a tendency or propensity (to or towards). ~*v.t.* 1 to cause to incline. 2 to support, to rest (upon or against). ~*n.* a leaning, inclination, slope or deviation. **to lean on** (*coll.*) to coerce, threaten (someone). **to lean over backwards** BACKWARDS. **leaning** *n.* inclination, partiality, propensity (towards or to). **lean-to** *n.* (*pl.* **lean-tos**) a building with a roof supported by another building or wall. [OE *hlinian, hleonian*, whence *hlǣnan*, to cause to lean (cogn. with L *inclīnāre*, Gr. *klinein*)]

lean[2] (lēn) *a.* 1 thin, without surplus fat or flesh, sinewy. 2 (of meat) not fat, consisting of muscular tissue. 3 (of foodstuffs) non-fattening, low in calories or fat. 4 meagre, of poor quality. 5 unproductive, unrewarding, unremunerative. 6 (of a fuel mixture) having a high or too high air content. 7 (of a mixture, compound) containing less of a major constituent than usual. ~*n.* the part of meat that consists of muscular tissue without fat. **lean-burn** *a.* (of an internal-combustion engine) designed to run on a lean mixture so as to reduce fuel consumption and exhaust emissions. **lean cuisine** *n.* cooking that uses light, non-fattening ingredients. **leanly** *adv.* **leanness** *n.* [OE *hlǣne*, etym. uncertain]

leap (lēp) *v.i.* (*past, p.p.* **leapt** (lept), **leaped** (lept, lēpt)) 1 to jump, to spring upwards or forwards. 2 to act or react swiftly; to rush, to fly, to dart. 3 (of prices) to increase suddenly by a large amount. 4 to make a sudden transition. 5 to pass over an interval, esp. in music. ~*v.t.* 1 to jump or spring over or across. 2 to cause to jump or spring. 3 (*Mus.*) to pass from one note to another by an interval which is greater than a degree of the scale. 4 (of male animals) to copulate with. ~*n.* 1 the act of leaping, a jump, a spring, a bound. 2 the space passed over by leaping. 3 a space or interval. 4 a sudden transition. 5 an increase. 6 (usu. in place names) a place, usu. a high place, from which a leap has been or might be made. **by leaps and bounds** BOUND[1]. **to leap to the eye** to be very prominent or noticeable. **leaper** *n.* **leapfrog** *n.* 1 a game in which one person stoops down and another vaults over their back. 2 a form of movement or progression in which two or more people or things overtake each other in turns. ~*v.i.* (*pres.p.* **leapfrogging,** *past, p.p.* **leapfrogged**) 1 to vault in this way. 2 to progress. **leaping** *n.* **leapingly** *adv.* **leap in the dark** *n.* a hazardous step or action, one whose consequences cannot be foreseen. **leap second** *n.* a second added to or subtracted from one scale of time when necessary to synchronize it with another. **leap year** *n.* an intercalary year of 366 days, which adds one day to February every four years (leap year is every year the number of which is a multiple of four, except those divisible by 100 and not by 400). [OE *hlēapan* (cp. Dut. *loopen*, Icel. *hlaupa*, G *laufen*, to run)]

learn (lœn) *v.t.* (*past, p.p.* **learnt** (lœnt), **learned** (lœnt, lœnd)) 1 to acquire knowledge of or skill in by study, experience or instruction. 2 to fix in the memory. 3 to find out, to be informed of, to ascertain. 4 †to teach, to tell. ~*v.i.* 1 to acquire knowledge or skill. 2 to receive instruction. **to learn by heart** HEART. **to learn of** to find out, to ascertain, to be informed of. **learnable** *a.* **learned** (-nid) *a.* 1 having acquired learning by study, erudite. 2 skilled, skilful (in). 3 characterized by great learning or scholarship. 4 (of a word, journal etc.) chiefly used, read etc. by learned people. 5 used in courteous references to lawyers (*my learned friend*; *the learned judge*). **my learned friend** FRIEND. **learnedly** *adv.* **learnedness** *n.* **learner** *n.* †**learner-like** *a.* **learning** *n.* 1 the act of learning. 2 knowledge acquired by study, erudition, scholarship. **learning curve** *n.* 1 a person's rate of progress in acquiring knowledge or skill. 2 a graphic representation of this. **learning disability** *n.* (*euphem.*) a mental handicap. [OE *leornian* (cp. G *lernen*), cogn. with LORE[1], cp. OE *læran*, to teach]

lease (lēs) *n.* 1 a letting or renting of land, houses, offices etc. for a specified period. 2 the written contract for, the term of or the rights of tenure under such letting. ~*v.t.* to grant or to take or hold under lease. **new lease of life** NEW. **leasable** *a.* **leaseback** *n.* an arrangement whereby the seller of a property leases it back from the buyer. **leasehold** *n.* 1 tenure by lease. 2 property held by lease. ~*a.* held thus. **leaseholder** *n.* [A-F *lesser* (F *laisser*), L *laxāre*, to loose, from *laxus*, LAX]

leash (lēsh) *n.* 1 a lead for a dog or other animal. 2 a thong by which a hawk is held. 3 something which controls or restrains as if by a leash. **4** in hunting, a set of three animals. *~v.t.* to bind, hold or fasten (as) by a leash. **straining at the leash** anxious or impatient to begin. [OF *lesse* (F *laisse*), late L *laxa*, orig. fem. of *laxus*, LAX]

least (lēst) *a.* **1** smallest, slightest. **2** less than all others in size, amount, degree, quantity, value, importance etc. *~adv.* in the smallest or slightest degree. *~n.* the smallest amount, degree etc. **at least 1** at any rate, whatever else may be said on the subject. **2** if nothing else. **3** at the minimum. **at the least** at the minimum. **in the least** in the slightest degree, at all. **not least** NOT. **to say the least** not to put in stronger terms; without any exaggeration. **leastaways** *adv.* **1** at least. **2** or rather. **least common denominator** *n.* LOWEST COMMON DENOMINATOR (under LOW[1]). **least common multiple** *n.* LOWEST COMMON MULTIPLE (under LOW[1]). **least squares** *n.pl.* a method of estimating a statistical quantity or fitting a curve to a set of points representing statistical data, based on the principle that the sum of the squares of the distances by which estimated values deviate from observed values should be kept to a minimum. [OE *læst*, *lœsast*, superl. of *lǣs*, LESS]

Usage note *The least* should not be used in comparisons of two: the correct form for two is *the less.*

leat (lēt) *n.* (*dial.*) a watercourse conveying water to a mill etc. [OE *gelæt*, crossroads, *wæter-gelæt*, water-conduit, from *lætan*, see LET[1]]

leather (ledh´ə) *n.* **1** the tanned or dressed skin or hide of an animal. **2** dressed hides collectively. **3** an article or part made of leather (*often in comb.*, as *stirrup-leather*); a piece of leather used for polishing. **4** (*pl.*) leather clothes, esp. for wearing on a motorcycle, or a pair of leather breeches or leggings. **5** (*sl.*) a cricket ball or football. *~a.* made of leather. *~v.t.* **1** to cover or furnish with leather. **2** to polish with a leather. **3** to thrash, as with a leather strap. **leatherback** *n.* a leathery, soft-shelled turtle, *Dermochelys coriacea.* **leather-bound** *a.* having a leather binding. **leathercloth** *n.* a fabric covered with a waterproof composition to resemble leather. **leatherette** (-ret´) *n.* a kind of imitation leather. **leatherhead** *n.* an Australian bird without head feathers, also called the *friarbird.* **leathering** *n.* a beating. **leatherjacket** *n.* **1** the tough-skinned larva of a crane-fly. **2** any of various marine fishes of the families Carangidae and Balistidae which have tough skins. †**leathern** (-ən) *a.* made of or like leather. **leatherneck** *n.* (*sl.*) a US marine. **leatherwear** *n.* clothing made of leather. **leather-wood** *n.* a N American shrub, *Dirca palustris*, the tough bark of which was used by the Indians for thongs. **leathery** *a.* **1** like leather. **2** (esp. of meat) tough. **leatheriness** *n.* [OE *lether* (cp. Dut. and G *Leder*, Icel. *lethr*)]

leave[1] (lēv) *v.t.* (*past, p.p.* **left** (left)) **1** to go or depart from, to quit. **2** to allow to remain when one departs, to go without taking, often accidentally. **3** to cease to live or work at or belong to. **4** to withdraw from, to forsake, to abandon. **5** to bequeath. **6** to be survived by. **7** to refrain from removing, consuming or interfering with. **8** to desist from, to cease, to discontinue. **9** to commit, to entrust, to refer for consideration, approval etc. **10** to depute (a person) to carry out a task. **11** to deposit (an object, message) to be collected, delivered, dealt with. **12** to deposit or allow to remain in a particular state (*left a trail of mud*). **13** to cause to be or remain in a particular state (*left the door ajar*). **14** to move on beyond (a landmark) in a particular direction relative to its position (*leave the town hall on your right*). **15** to have as a remainder (after subtraction, division). *~v.i.* **1** to depart, to go away. **2** (esp. as a command to a dog) to cease, to discontinue. **to leave alone 1** not to interfere with. **2** to have no dealings with. **to leave a lot to be desired** to be distinctly unsatisfactory. **to leave be** to avoid disturbing or interfering with. **to leave behind 1** to go away without. **2** to outstrip. **3** to leave as a record, mark, consequence etc. **to leave cold** COLD. **to leave go** to let go. **to leave hold of** to stop holding, to let go. **to leave it at that** not to do or say any more. **to leave much to be desired** to be distinctly unsatisfactory. **to leave no stone unturned** STONE. **to leave off 1** to stop, to cease. **2** to desist from, to discontinue. **3** to cease to wear. **to leave out** to omit. **to leave over** to leave for future consideration etc. **to leave someone to themselves** to refrain strictly from interfering with, approaching, becoming involved with etc. **to leave unsaid** to refrain from stating. **to leave well alone** to refrain strictly from interfering with, approaching, becoming involved with etc. **leaver** *n.* **leaving** *n.* **1** the act of departing. **2** (*pl.*) residue, remnant, refuse, offal. [OE *læfan* (cp. Icel. *leifa*, Goth. *-laibjan*), cogn. with *lāf*, lave]

leave[2] (lēv) *n.* **1** permission. **2** (*also* **leave of absence**) permission to be absent from duty. **3** the period of this. **4** the act of departing, a formal parting, a farewell, an adieu. **5** a holiday. **by/ with your leave** with your permission. **on leave 1** absent from duty by permission. **2** on holiday. **to take leave of one's senses** to think or act contrary to reason. **to take leave to** (*formal*) to venture to, to be so bold as to. **to take (one's) leave 1** to say goodbye. **2** to depart. **leave-taking** *n.* **1** a parting. **2** a farewell. [OE *lēaf*, cogn. with *lēof*, pleasing, LIEF]

leave[3] (lēv) *v.i.* (*past, p.p.* **leaved**) to produce leaves. **leaved** *a.* (*esp. in comb.*) having a leaf or leaves of the specified kind (*four-leaved clover*).

leaven (lev´ən) *n.* **1** fermenting dough or any other substance (e.g. yeast) mixed with other dough, a batter etc. in order to cause fermentation and make it lighter. **2** any influence tending to cause a general change. **3** a tincture or admixture (of). *~v.t.* **1** to raise and make light (as) with leaven. **2** to imbue, to pervade with an influence causing change. **3** to temper (with). **leavening** *n.* leaven. [F *levain*, L *levāmen*, from *levāre*, to lift]

leaves LEAF.

Lebanese (lebənēz´) *a.* (*as pl.*) of, relating or belonging to the Mediterranean country of Lebanon. *~n.* (*pl.* **Lebanese**) **1** a native or inhabitant of Lebanon. **2** (*pl.*) the people of the Lebanon.

Lebensraum (lā´bənzrowm) *n.* territory considered necessary for a country's expanding population in terms of trade and settlement. [G, living space]

lech LECHER.

lechaim (ləkhay´im), **lehaim, l'chaim** *int.* a drinking toast. *~n.* a small drink for toasting. [Heb., to life]

lecher (lech´ə) *n.* a man who continually lusts after or seduces women. **lech, letch** *v.i.* (*sl.*) **1** to lust (after). **2** to act lecherously. *~n.* **1** a lecher. **2** a strong desire, esp. a sexual one. **lecherous** *a.* feeling or motivated by strong sexual desire. **lecherously** *adv.* **lecherousness** *n.* **lechery** *n.* promiscuous and unrestrained sexual desire or activity. [OF *lecheor*, from *lechier*, to lick, to live in gluttony, OHG *leccôn*, to LICK]

lecithin (les´ithin) *n.* a nitrogenous fatty substance containing phosphorus found in the cellular tissue of animal and vegetable bodies. [Gr. *lekithos*, egg yolk]

Leclanché cell (liklã´shā) *n.* a primary electric cell consisting of a carbon cathode covered with manganese dioxide, all in a porous pot, and a zinc anode dipping into ammonium chloride solution. [G. *Leclanché*, 1839–82, French engineer]

lectern (lek´tən) *n.* **1** a reading desk or stand for a book from which parts of a church service, esp. the lessons, are said or sung. **2** any similar reading desk. [OF *letrun*, late L *lectrum*, from *lect-*, p.p. stem of *legere*, to read]

lectin (lek´tin) *n.* any of various usu. plant-derived

proteins that bind to specific carbohydrate groups and cause agglutination of specific cell types. [L *lect-*, from *legere*, to choose, select, -IN[1]]

lection (lek´shən) *n.* **1** a reading or variation in a text. **2** a portion of Scripture to be read in a church service, a lesson. **lectionary** *n.* **1** a collection of passages of Scripture for daily services. **2** a book containing these. [OF, from L *lectiōnem*, nom. *lectio*, from *legere*, to read]

lector (lek´tə) *n.* **1** a person whose duty it is to read the lessons in church services. **2** a university teacher, esp. one employed in a foreign university to give tuition in their native language. **lectorate** (-rət), **lectorship** *n.* **lectrice** (-trēs´) *n.* a female lector at a university. [L from *lect-*, *legere*, to read]

lecture (lek´chə) *n.* **1** a formal expository or instructive discourse on any subject, before an audience or a class. **2** a reproof, a reprimand. *~v.i.* **1** to deliver a lecture or lectures. **2** to give instruction by means of lectures. *~v.t.* **1** to reprimand, to talk seriously to. **2** to instruct by lectures. **lecturer** *n.* a person who gives lectures, esp. at a university. **lectureship** *n.* the academic office of a lecturer. [F, from late Latin *lectūra*, from *lectus*, p.p. of *legere*, to read]

lecythus (les´ithəs) *n.* (*pl.* **lecythi** (-thī)) in ancient Greece, a narrow-necked vase or flask for oil, unguents etc. [late L *lēcythus*, Gr. *lēkuthos*]

LED *abbr.* light-emitting diode. **LED display** *n.* a flat screen display, as in pocket calculators, digital clocks and watches etc., that uses light-emitting diodes.

led LEAD[1].

lederhosen (lā´dəhōzən) *n.pl.* leather shorts with braces, the traditional male dress of Austria and Bavaria. [G, leather trousers]

ledge (lej) *n.* **1** a shelf or shelflike projection. **2** a shelf-like ridge or outcrop of rock on a cliff or mountain. **3** a ridge of rock beneath the surface of water. **4** a metal-bearing stratum of rock. **ledged** *a.* **ledgeless** (-lis) *a.* **ledgy** *a.* [prob. from ME *leggen*, to LAY[1]]

ledger (lej´ə) *n.* **1** the principal book in a set of account-books, in which a record of all trade transactions is entered. **2** a large flat stone as for an altar-table or grave. **3** a horizontal pole parallel to the walls in scaffolding, to support the putlogs. **4** in angling, a ledger line or tackle. *~v.i.* to fish with a ledger tackle. **ledger line** *n.* **1** (*also* **leger line**) in musical notation, an additional short line above or below the stave to express ascending or descending notes. **2** a fishing line with ledger tackle. **ledger tackle** *n.* a type of fishing tackle in which a lead weight keeps the bait on the bottom. [prob. from ME *leggen*, as LEDGE, after MDut. *ligger* (Dut. *legger*), that which lies in a place]

lee (lē) *n.* **1** shelter, protection. **2** the side or quarter opposite to that against which the wind blows. **3** the sheltered side (cp. *windward side*, *weather side*). *~a.* **1** of or relating to the side or quarter away from the wind. **2** sheltered. **under the lee of 1** on the sheltered side of. **2** protected from the wind by. **lee-board** *n.* a board let down on the lee side of a flat-bottomed vessel to prevent a leeward drift. **lee gauge** *n.* the position of a ship on the sheltered (leeward) side of another vessel etc., relative to the wind. **lee shore** *n.* **1** the shore on the lee side of a vessel. **2** the shore towards which the wind blows. **lee side** *n.* the lee of a vessel. **lee tide** *n.* a tide running in the same direction as the wind blows. **leeward** (-wəd, loo´əd) *a.* relating to, in or facing the lee side. *~adv.* towards the lee side. *~n.* the lee side or direction. **leewardly** (-wədli, loo´ədli) *a.* (of a ship) with a tendency to drift to leeward. **leeway** *n.* **1** the leeward drift of a vessel. **2** allowable scope, toleration inside defined limits. **3** a safety margin. **to make up leeway** to recover lost ground or time. [OE *hlēo*, *hlēow*, a covering, shelter (cp. Icel. *hlē*, lee, *hly*, warmth, shelter)]

leech[1] (lēch) *n.* **1** an aquatic annelid worm of the suctorial order Hirudinea, employed for the local extraction of blood. **2** someone who clings tenaciously to someone else. **3** someone who abstracts or absorbs the gains of others. **4** †a physician, a healer. *~v.t.* **1** to apply leeches to, as in phlebotomy. **2** †to cure or heal. **like a leech** persistently, tenaciously. †**leechcraft** *n.* **1** the art of healing. **2** medicine. [OE *læce*, rel. to *lācnian*, to heal (cp. Icel. *laeknir*, Dan. *laege*, a physician)]

leech[2] (lēch) *n.* **1** the perpendicular edge of a square sail. **2** the after edge of a fore-and-aft sail. [cp. Icel. *līk*, Dut. *ijk*, G *Liek*]

leek (lēk) *n.* a culinary vegetable, *Allium porrum*, allied to the onion, with a straight green stem that unfurls as overlapping leaves and a small, white cylindrical bulb, the national emblem of Wales. [OE *lēac* (cp. Dut. *look*, Icel. *laukr*, G *Lauch*)]

leer[1] (liə) *n.* **1** an oblique, sly or arch look. **2** a look expressing a feeling of malice, lasciviousness or triumph. *~v.i.* to look with a leer. **leering** *n.*, *a.* **leeringly** *adv.* **leery** *a.* (*comp.* **leerier,** *superl.* **leeriest**) knowing, sly. **to be leery of** to be wary of. **leeriness** *n.* [OE *hlēor*, the cheek, the face, the look]

leer[2] LEHR.

lees (lēz) *n.pl.* **1** the sediment of liquor which settles to the bottom. **2** dregs, refuse. [formerly *lee*, OF *lie*, Gaulish L *lia*, perh. from Celt.]

†**leet**[1] (lēt) *n.* **1** a court leet; a court of record. **2** the jurisdiction of a court leet. [prob. from A-F *lete*, OE *læth*, LATHE[2]]

leet[2] (lēt) *n.* (*Sc.*) a list of candidates for any office. **short leet** SHORTLIST (under SHORT). [perh. from ELITE]

leeward, leeway LEE.

left[1] (left) *a.* **1** of, relating to or situated on the side that is to the west when a person faces south, as opposed to right. **2** correspondingly situated in relation to the front or the direction of anything. **3** (*also* **Left**) radical, politically innovative. **4** (*also* **Left**) of or relating to socialism or communism. *~adv.* on or towards the left. *~n.* **1** the side opposite to the right. **2** the left hand. **3** a left-handed blow. **4** the left foot. **5** the left wing of an army. **6** (*also* **Left**) the progressive, democratic or socialist party, wing or faction (which originally sat on the left of the president in a legislative assembly). **left face** FACE. **left-back** *n.* in football, hockey etc., a defender who plays primarily on the left side of the pitch. **Left Bank** *n.* a district in Paris on the south bank of the Seine, famous for artists. **left bank** *n.* the bank of a river that is on one's left side when facing downstream. **left bower** *n.* the knave of the same colour as the knave of trumps. **left field** *n.* **1** in baseball, the third of the outfield to the left and in front of a batter facing the pitcher; the position of a fielder defending this area. **2** (*N Am.*, *coll.*) a position that is at odds with the mainstream opinion and considered unusual, unorthodox or simply bizarre. **left-footed** *a.* **1** using the left foot by preference (e.g. for kicking). **2** made with the left foot. **left hand** *n.* the left side, direction or region. **left-hand** *a.* **1** situated on or relating to the left side. **2** executed by the left hand. **3** twisted or turning anticlockwise. **left-handed** *a.* **1** using the left hand more readily than the right. **2** designed or made for the left hand. **3** performed with the left hand; (of a blow) delivered with the left hand. **4** turning from right to left; turning anticlockwise. **5** awkward, clumsy, stupid. **6** insincere, malicious, sinister. **7** ambiguous, equivocal. **8** (of marriages) morganatic, fictitious. **left-handed compliment** *n.* a compliment which contains a (sometimes accidental) gibe or reproach. **left-handedly** *adv.* **left-handedness** *n.* **left-hander** *n.* a left-handed person or a left-handed blow. **leftie** LEFTY (under LEFT[1]). **leftism** *n.* the policies and principles of the political left. **leftist** *n.*, *a.* **leftmost** *a.* situated furthest to the left. **left-of-centre** *a.* (in politics) moderately progressive. **leftward** (-wəd) *adv.*, *a.* **leftwards** *adv.* **left wing** *n.* **1** the more radical or liberal wing of a political party. **2** the left side of a sports pitch; (the position of) an attacking player. **3** the part of an army massed on the left side of a battle position. **left-wing** *a.* **1** of, relating to, active in or sympathetic to the political left (of a party). **2** playing on the left-wing. **left-winger** *n.* a person belonging to the left-wing (of a political party) or sympathetic to left-wing policies. **lefty, leftie** *n.* (*derog.*) a left-winger, a leftist. ~*a.* left-wing. [OE *left*, *lyft*, weak, worthless]

left[2] (left) *a.* that has been discarded or laid aside. **to be left at the post** to be left far behind at the beginning of a race, contest; to be beaten by a wide margin. **to be left for dead** to be assumed to be dead and consequently abandoned. **to be left with 1** to retain (an impression, feeling) as a result of usu. lengthy exposure to something. **2** to have to deal with after an event. **to be well left** to have ample provision made for one in a will etc. **to get left** (*coll.*) to be abandoned or beaten. **to have left** to have remaining. **left luggage** *n.* **1** luggage deposited temporarily, esp. at a railway station etc. **2** a left-luggage office. **left-luggage office** *n.* a place where luggage can be temporarily deposited for a small charge. **left-off** *a.* discarded as no longer serviceable, laid aside. **leftover** *n.* (*usu. pl.*) a remainder, esp. of uneaten food. ~*a.* surplus, unused. [p.p. of LEAVE[1]]

left[3] LEAVE[1].

leg (leg) *n.* **1** each of the limbs by which humans and other mammals walk, esp. the part from the knee to the ankle. **2** the analogous member in other species. **3** an animal's hind leg (esp. the upper portion) which is eaten as meat. **4** the part of a garment that covers the leg. **5** anything resembling a leg in form or function. **6** each of a set of posts or rods supporting a table, bed, chair etc. **7** a branch of a forked object, a limb of a pair of compasses etc. **8** a stage in a long-distance flight, journey, race etc. **9** in a contest, one of two or more events, games, rounds etc. **10** the distance run by any one of the runners in a relay race. **11** a single game in darts. **12** the course and distance run by a vessel on one tack. **13** in cricket, the leg side, esp. the part on a level with and behind the batsman's stumps. **14** †a bow made by keeping the front leg straight and bending the back one. ~*a.* in cricket, fielding on or struck towards the leg side. ~*v.t.* (*pres.p.* **legging**, *past*, *p.p.* **legged**) to propel (a canal boat) through a tunnel by pushing against the tunnel roof with one's legs. **leg before** (*coll.*) leg before wicket. **leg before wicket** a grounds for dismissal in cricket, stoppage by the batsman's leg of a ball when it would have hit the wicket. **not to have a leg to stand on** to have no support or basis for one's position (e.g. in a controversy). **on one's (hind) legs 1** standing up, esp. in order to make a speech. **2** able to stand or walk about again after illness. **to be on one's last legs** LAST[1]. **to feel one's legs** to begin to support oneself on one's legs. **to find one's legs** to attain ease or mastery. **to get one's leg over** GET[1]. **to have no legs** (of a golf ball etc.) not to have enough impetus to reach the point aimed at. **to have the legs of** to be able to go further or faster than. **to leg it 1** (*coll.*) to run away. **2** (*coll.*) to run, hurry. **3** (*coll.*) to go on foot. **to pull someone's leg 1** to hoax, to make a fool of. **2** to tease. **to shake a leg** (*often int.*) to hurry up. **to show a leg 1** to get out of bed. **2** to make an appearance. **to stretch a leg/ one's legs** to take exercise, esp. after inactivity. **leg-break** *n.* in cricket, a ball which breaks from the leg side towards the off. **leg-bye** *n.* in cricket, a run scored for a ball that touches the batsman anywhere on the body except the hand and does not touch the bat. **leg-cutter** *n.* in cricket, a fast leg-break. **legged** *a.* (usu. *in comb.*, as *four-legged*). **legging** *n.* **1** (*pl.*) thick footless tights or close-fitting trousers for women and children. **2** an additional outer covering, often of leather, for the legs. **leg-guard** *n.* in cricket, baseball etc., a pad to protect the leg from knee to ankle. **leggy** *a.* (*comp.* **leggier**, *superl.* **leggiest**) **1** (*coll.*) having long legs. **2** (of a woman) having long, shapely legs. **3** (of plants) spindly. **legginess** *n.* **leg-iron** *n.* a fetter for the leg. **legless** (-lis) *a.* **1** without legs. **2** (*coll.*) very drunk. **legman, legwoman** *n.* (*pl.* **legmen, legwomen**) **1** (*NAm.*) a reporter who visits the scene of a news story, interviews people involved etc. **2** a person who is employed to do jobs such as running errands and gathering information, away from their employer's offices. **leg-of-mutton** *a.* (of a sleeve etc.) shaped like a leg of mutton, wider or fuller at the top and narrow or close-fitting at the bottom. **leg-of-mutton sail** *n.* a triangular mainsail. **leg-over** *n.* (*taboo sl.*) an act of sexual intercourse (of a man, with a woman). **leg-pull** *n.* a hoax. **leg-pulling** *n.* **leg-rest** *n.* a support for an injured leg. **legroom** *n.* space for the legs (e.g. in a car). **leg rope** *n.* a rope to fasten an animal by the leg. **leg-rope** *v.t.* to fasten (an animal) with a leg rope. **leg-show** *n.* an entertainment involving scantily clad women, usu. dancing and showing their legs. **leg side** *n.* in cricket, that half of the field, divided by a line running between the wickets, which a batsman's body is facing away from in the usual sideways-on stance. **leg slip** *n.* in cricket, (the position of) a fielder who is stationed on the leg side close behind the batsman. **leg spin** *n.* **1** in cricket, spin applied by the bowler to make the ball turn from the leg side towards the off. **2** bowling characterized by leg spin. **leg-spinner** *n.* **1** in cricket, a bowler who uses leg spin. **2** a ball bowled with leg spin. **leg stump** *n.* in cricket, the stump on the leg side. **leg theory** *n.* in cricket, a plan of attack which involves bowling at the batsman's legs and massing fielders on the leg side. **leg trap** *n.* in cricket, a group of fielders in a close arc around the wicket on the leg side. **leg-up** *n.* **1** assistance, usu. a hand under the foot, in mounting a horse, climbing onto something etc. **2** a boost; a piece of practical assistance. **legwarmers** *n.pl.* long footless stockings usu. worn to cover the lower leg, rolled down over other garments. **legwork** *n.* **1** work involving much travel on foot. **2** groundwork. [Icel. *leggr*]

leg. *abbr.* **1** legal. **2** legate. **3** legato. **4** legislation. **5** legislative. **6** legislature.

☒ **legable** common misspelling of LEGIBLE.

legacy (leg´əsi) *n.* (*pl.* **legacies**) **1** a bequest, money or property bequeathed by will. **2** anything left or handed on by a predecessor. **3** †a legateship. **legacy-hunter** *n.* a person who ingratiates themself with someone in the hope of receiving a legacy. **legatee** (-te´) *n.* a person to whom a legacy is bequeathed. **legator** (-gā´-) *n.* a person who leaves a legacy. [OF *legacie*, legateship, med. L *lēgātia*, L *lēgātus*, LEGATE]

legal (lē´gəl) *a.* **1** of, relating to, or according to law. **2** lawful, legitimate, recognized or sanctioned by the law. **3** appointed or laid down by the law. **4** concerned with the law; characteristic of lawyers. **5** recognized, enforceable or having a remedy in law rather than equity. **6** belonging or conformable to the Mosaic law, or the principle of salvation by works, not by grace. **legal aid** *n.* financial assistance for legal proceedings granted by the state to those with low incomes. **legal eagle** *n.* (*facet.*) an astute, capable and ambitious young lawyer. **legalese** (-ēz´) *n.* the (obscure or convoluted) language of legal documents. **legal fiction** *n.* a fact or point of law that is probably no longer true or valid but is assumed to be so to serve some useful, esp. legal purpose. **legal holiday** *n.* in the US, a weekday observed as a public holiday. **legalism** *n.* **1** strict adherence to law and formulas. **2** (*Theol.*) adherence to the Mosaic law; the doctrine of justification by works. **3** respect for the letter rather than the spirit of religious or ethical laws. **legalist** *n.* **legalistic** (-lis´-) *a.* **legalistically** *adv.* **legality** (ligal´-) *n.* (*pl.* **legalities**) **1** lawfulness. **2** legalism. **3** (*pl.*) obligations under the law. **legalize, legalise** *v.t.* **1** to make lawful. **2** to bring into harmony with the law. **legalization** (-zā´shən) *n.* **legally** *adv.* **legal proceedings** *n.* steps in the prosecution of an action at law. **legal tender** *n.* money which a creditor is bound to accept in discharge of a debt. [F *légal*, L *lēgālis*, from *lex lēgis*]

legate (leg´ət) *n.* **1** a papal emissary. **2** a lieutenant or deputy attached to a Roman general or governor. **3** †an ambassador, an envoy. **legateship** *n.* **legatine** (-tīn) *a.* **legation** (ligā´shən) *n.* **1** a diplomatic mission headed by a minister. **2** the official residence or office of a diplomatic minister. **3** a body of delegates. **4** the act of sending someone as legate or deputy. **5** a legateship. [OF *legat*, L *lēgātus*, orig. p.p. of *lēgāre*, to appoint, to commission]

legatee LEGACY.

legato (ligah´tō) *adv., a.* (*Mus.*) in an even gliding manner without a break. ~*n.* (*pl.* **legatos**) **1** this style of playing. **2** a legato passage. **legatissimo** (legətis´imō) *adv.* as smoothly as possible. [It., bound, p.p. of *legare*, L *ligāre*, see LIGATE]

legator LEGACY.

legend (lej´ənd) *n.* **1** a traditional story, esp. one popularly accepted as true. **2** a myth, a fable. **3** traditional or non-historical storytelling or literature. **4** a person who is renowned for outstanding deeds or qualities, whether real or fictitious etc. **5** an inscription on a coat of arms or round the field of a medal or coin. **6** a caption to an illustration; a key to a map, table etc. **7** †a chronicle, biography or series of selections from the lives of saints or sacred history, formerly read in the refectories of religious houses, and as lessons at matins. **legendary** *a.* **1** of or relating to legend. **2** celebrated in legend. **3** famous or notorious enough to be a subject of legend. **legendry** *n.* [OF *legende*, med. L *legenda*, that which is to be read, from L *legere*, to read]

legerdemain (lejədimān´) *n.* **1** sleight of hand, a trick in which the eye is deceived by the quickness of the hand, conjuring. **2** jugglery, sophistry. [OF *legier de main* (F *léger*), light of hand]

leger line LEDGER LINE (under LEDGER).

leges LEX.

legging, leggy LEG.

leghorn (leg´hawn, ligawn´) *n.* **1** a plait of the straw of bearded Italian wheat cut green and bleached, used for bonnets and hats. **2** a hat made of this plait. **3** (**Leghorn**) a breed of domestic fowl. [*Leghorn* (*Livorno*), Italy]

legible (lej´ibəl) *a.* **1** clear enough to be read. **2** easily decipherable. **3** clear, plain, evident. **legibleness** (-bil´-), **legibility** *n.* **legibly** *adv.* [OF, from late L *legibilis*, from *legere*, to choose, to read]

legion (lē´jən) *n.* **1** a division of the ancient Roman army, varying, at different periods, from 3000 to 6000 men. **2** a military force, esp. in France and other foreign countries. **3** a host, a vast army or multitude. **legionary** *a.* **1** of or relating to a legion or legions. **2** consisting of one or more legions. ~*n.* (*pl.* **legionaries**) a soldier of a legion. **legionella** (-nel´ə) *n.* the bacterium, *Legionella pneumophila*, which causes legionnaire's disease. **legionnaire** (-neə´) *n.* **1** a member of a foreign legion. **2** a member of the British or American Legions. **legionnaire's disease** *n.* a serious, sometimes fatal, bacterial disease resembling pneumonia, caused by *Legionella pneumophila* (so named because of its occurrence at an American Legion convention in 1976). **Legion of Honour** *n.* a French order of merit founded by Napoleon I as a reward for services or merit, civil or military. [OF, from L *legiōnem*, nom. *legio*, from *legere*, to choose]

legislate (lej´islāt) *v.i.* **1** to make or enact a law or laws. **2** to make allowance or provision (for). **3** to issue instructions. **legislation** (-lā´shən) *n.* **1** the act or process of making laws. **2** laws or prospective laws. **legislative** (lej´islətiv, -lātiv) *a.* **1** enacting laws. **2** having power to legislate. **3** enacted by or relating to legislation. ~*n.* **1** the legislative power or function. **2** the legislature. **legislatively** *adv.* **legislator** *n.* **1** a lawgiver. **2** a member of a legislative assembly. **legislatorial** (-taw´ri-) *a.* **legislatorship** *n.* **legislatress** (-tris) *n.* a female legislator. **legislature** (-ləchə) *n.* a body of people in which is vested the power or right to enact, alter, repeal or suspend laws. [L *lex lēgis*, law, *latum* serving as a verbal noun of *ferre*, to bear]

legist (lē´jist) *n.* a person learned in the law. [OF *legiste*, med. L *lēgista*, from *lex lēgis*, law]

legit (lijit´) *a.* (*coll.*) short for LEGITIMATE[1]. ~*n.* **1** the legitimate theatre. **2** an actor in the legitimate theatre.

legitimate[1] (lijit´imət) *a.* **1** lawful, legal, properly authorized. **2** born to parents who are lawfully married. **3** (of descent) through a legitimate person. **4** (of a title to sovereignty) derived from strict hereditary right. **5** proper, regular, natural. **6** conformable to accepted standards or usage. **7** following by logical sequence. **8** of or relating to formal or serious theatre rather than television, cinema, variety etc. **legitimacy** *n.* **legitimate drama** *n.* **1** plays belonging to the recognized, long-established theatrical genres, not opera, musicals, happenings etc. **2** the body of plays of recognized merit. **legitimately** *adv.* **legitimateness** *n.* **legitimation** (-ā´shən) *n.* **legitimatize, legitimatise** *v.t.* to legitimize. **legitimatization** (-zā´shən) *n.* **legitimism** *n.* **1** support for the principle of hereditary monarchical government. **2** support for a monarch or pretender (esp. formerly in France and Spain) whose claim is based on hereditary descent or primogeniture. **legitimist** *n., a.* **legitimize, legitimise** *v.t.* to render legitimate. **legitimization** (-zā´shən) *n.* [med. L *lēgitimātus*, p.p. of *lēgitimāre*, from L *lēgitimus*, legal]

legitimate[2] (lijit´imāt) *v.t.* **1** to make, pronounce or prove legitimate or legitimately born. **2** to justify, to serve as justification for.

Lego® (leg´ō) *n.* a building toy mainly consisting of connecting plastic bricks.

legume (leg´ūm) *n.* **1** the fruit or pod of a leguminous plant, usu. dehiscent along its face and back, and bearing its seeds on either margin of the ventral suture (as the pod of the pea). **2** any of various vegetables used as food, esp. pulses. **3** a leguminous plant. **legumin** (-gū´min) *n.* a protein resembling casein, contained in leguminous and other seeds. **leguminous** (-gū´-) *a.* **1** producing legumes. **2** of or relating to the Leguminosae, an order of herbs, shrubs and trees, including the peas and beans, that produce seed in pods. [F *légume*, L *legūmen*, pulse, from *legere*, to gather]

lehaim LECHAIM.

lehr (liə), **leer** *n.* a tunnel-shaped furnace for annealing glass. [G, pattern, model]

lei[1] (lā´i) *n.* a garland or necklace of flowers. [Hawaiian]

lei[2] LEU.

Leicester (les´tə) *n.* **1** a type of usu. orange-coloured cheese resembling cheddar. **2** a breed of sheep with a long fleece. [English county]

leishmania (līshmā´niə) *n.* (*pl.* **leishmania, leishmanias, leishmaniae** (-niē)) any of a genus, *Leishmania*, of parasitic flagellate protozoans that cause skin diseases in humans and animals. **leishmaniasis** (-mənī´əsis), **leishmaniosis** (-māniō´sis) *n.* any of several diseases, e.g. kala-azar, caused by leishmania. [W. B. *Leishman*, 1865–1926, British physician]

leister (lēs´tə) *n.* (*Sc.*) a pronged fishing-spear, esp. for salmon. ~*v.t.* to spear with a leister. [Icel. *ljóstr*, from *ljósta*, to strike]

leisure (lezh´ə) *n.* **1** freedom from business, occupation or hurry. **2** time at one's own disposal, unoccupied time. **3** opportunity, convenience. *~a.* unoccupied, free, idle. **at leisure 1** not busy or occupied. **2** without hurry. **3** deliberately. **at one's leisure** when one has the time, at one's convenience. **leisure centre,** (*N Am.*) **leisure center** *n.* a complex containing facilities for sports, entertainments, meetings etc. **leisured** *a.* **1** having a great deal of leisure. **2** leisurely. **leisureless** *n.* **leisurely** *a.* done at a slow, unhurried pace; relaxed. *~adv.* without haste. **leisureliness** *n.* **leisurewear** *n.* casual clothing. [OF *leisir*, orig. inf. verb, L *licēre*, to be allowed]

leitmotiv (līt´mōtēf), **leitmotif** *n.* a leading, representative or recurring theme in a composition, orig. a musical theme invariably associated with a certain person, situation or idea throughout an opera etc. [G (*leit*, leading, MOTIVE)]

lek[1] (lek) *n.* the chief currency of Albania.

lek[2] (lek) *n.* an area where certain species of birds (esp. black grouse) assemble for sexual display and courtship. [etym. uncertain, perh. from Swed. *leka*, to play]

LEM *abbr.* lunar excursion module.

†**leman** (lem´ən, lē´-) *n.* **1** a sweetheart of either sex. **2** a gallant, a mistress. **3** a concubine, a paramour. [ME *lemman*, *leofman* (OE *lēof*, dear)]

lemma (lem´ə) *n.* (*pl.* **lemmas, lemmata** (-mətə)) **1** an auxiliary proposition taken to be valid in order to demonstrate some other proposition. **2** a theme, a subject, esp. when prefixed as a heading. **3** a dictionary headword. **4** in linguistics, the principal form of a word together with its variants and inflections. **5** a motto appended to a picture. **lemmatize, lemmatise** *v.t.* in linguistics, to group inflected and variant forms of a word together for analysis. **lemmatization** (-zā´shən) *n.* [L and Gr. *lēmma*, from *lambanein*, to take]

lemme (lem´i) *contr.* (*coll.*) let me.

lemming (lem´ing) *n.* **1** a small Arctic volelike rodent of the genus *Lemmus* and related genera, esp. the Scandinavian variety *L. lemmus* which migrates in very large numbers when its population reaches a peak, often attempts to cross large areas of water and is popularly supposed to be prone to mass suicide. **2** someone who joins a mass movement or dashes headlong into situations without forethought. [Norw.]

Lemnian (lem´niən) *a.* of or relating to Lemnos, an island in the Aegean Sea. *~n.* an inhabitant of Lemnos.

lemniscate (lemnis´kət) *n.* a curve of the general form of a figure 8, ¥. **lemniscate function** *n.* an elliptic function used in mathematical formulae expressing the properties of such curves. [L *lēmniscātus*, from *lēmniscus*, Gr. *lēmniskos*, ribbon]

lemniscus (lemnis´kəs) *n.* (*pl.* **lemnisci** (-nis´ī, -nis´kī)) (*Anat., Zool.*) a bundle of fibres or ribbon-like appendages in the brain connected to the thalamus. [see LEMNISCATE]

lemon (lem´ən) *n.* **1** the oval, acid, yellow-skinned fruit of the lemon tree. **2** (*also* **lemon tree**) the small Asian evergreen tree, *Citrus limon*, bearing this. **3** the pale yellow colour of a lemon. **4** (*sl.*) a person who or something which is disappointing, unpleasant, useless. *~a.* **1** of or relating to the lemon. **2** of the colour of a lemon. **3** lemon-flavoured. **salt of lemon** SALT. **lemonade** (-nād´) *n.* lemon juice or flavouring mixed with still or aerated water and sweetened. **lemon balm** *n.* a common bushy plant, *Melissa officinalis*, whose leaves smell and taste of lemon. **lemon cheese, lemon curd** *n.* a spread made from lemon, butter, eggs and sugar. **lemon drop** *n.* a lemon-flavoured hard sweet. **lemon geranium** *n.* a pelargonium, *Pelargonium crispum*, with lemon-scented leaves. **lemon grass** *n.* a lemon-scented hardy grass of the tropical genus *Cymbopogon* which yields an essential oil. **lemon law** *n.* in the US, a law designed to protect the buyers of defective or substandard cars. **lemon peel** *n.* the peel or rind of the lemon (either fresh or dried, preserved and candied) used as a flavouring material. **lemon plant** *n.* LEMON VERBENA (under LEMON). **lemon squash** *n.* a sweet concentrated lemon drink. **lemon squeezer** *n.* a device for extracting juice from lemons. **lemon thyme** *n.* *Thymus citriodorus* which has lemon-scented leaves. **lemon verbena** *n.* a S American shrub, *Aloysia triphylla*, cultivated for its lemon-scented foliage. **lemonwood** *n.* a small New Zealand tree, *Pittosporum eugenoides*, with white bark and lemon-scented flowers. **lemony** *a.* [F *limon*, med. L *limōnem*, nom. *limo*, Oriental in orig. (cp. Arab. *laimūn*, Pers. *līmū*)]

lemon sole (lem´ən), **lemon dab** *n.* a flatfish, *Microstomus kitt*, with brown markings, valued as a food. [prob. from F *limande*, a mudfish]

lempira (lempiə´rə) *n.* the standard monetary unit of Honduras, equivalent to 100 centavos. [*Lempira*, 16th-cent. chief who opposed the Spaniards]

lemur (lē´mə) *n.* (*pl.* **lemurs**) any member of a genus of arboreal nocturnal animals allied to the monkeys, having pointed snouts, long tails and occurring naturally only in Madagascar. **lemures** (lem´ūrēz) *n.pl.* among the ancient Romans, spectres or spirits of the dead. **lemuroid** (lem´ūroid) *a.* **1** of or relating to the superfamily Lemuroidae containing the lemurs and indris. **2** resembling a lemur. *~n.* an animal resembling or related to a lemur. [L *lemures*, ghosts]

lend (lend) *v.t.* (*past, p.p.* **lent** (lent)) **1** to grant for temporary use. **2** to grant the use of on condition of repayment or compensation. **3** to let out (money) at interest. **4** to furnish, to contribute, esp. for temporary service. *~v.i.* to make loans. **to lend a hand** HAND. **to lend an ear** EAR[1]. **to lend itself to** to have the right qualities for, to be appropriate for using as. **to lend oneself to** to give support to. **to lend wings to** WING. **lendable** *a.* **lender** *n.* a person who lends, esp. money at interest. **lending** *n.* **lending library** *n.* a library from which books can be borrowed freely or for a subscription. **Lend-Lease** *n.* (*Hist.*) the provision of military and other equipment by the US to the allied countries of Europe during World War II. *~v.t.* to provide an ally with military equipment during wartime. [ME *lenen*, OE *lǣnan* (cp. Dut. *leenen*, Icel. *lāna*, G *lehnen*)]

lenes LENIS.

length (length) *n.* **1** measure or extent from end to end, as distinct from breadth or thickness. **2** the longest line that can be drawn from one extremity of anything to the other. **3** extent of time, duration, long continuance. **4** the extent from beginning to end of something, such as a book. **5** the distance anything extends. **6** a definite portion of the linear extent of anything, such as a piece of cloth, pipe or timber. **7** (*usu. pl.*) extent or degree of action, thoroughness etc. **8** in prosody, the quantity of a vowel or syllable. **9** in cricket, the distance traversed by a bowled ball before it strikes the ground; the most desirable or effective distance for this. **10** in racing, the linear measure of the body of a horse, boat etc. **11** the length of a swimming pool as a distance swum. **12** the extent of a piece of clothing measured vertically. **13** the full extent of a person's body. **at full length 1** lying stretched to the fullest extent. **2** of the standard length, not condensed or abridged. **at length 1** to the full extent, in full detail. **2** at last. **to go to any length/lengths 1** to stop at no obstacle. **2** to be restrained by no scruples. **to go to great lengths** to take great care, to go to a great deal of trouble. **lengthen** *v.t.* **1** to make long or longer. **2** to draw out, to extend. **3** to protract. *~v.i.* to grow longer. **lengthener** *n.* **lengthways, lengthwise** *adv., a.* along or in the direction of its length. **lengthy** *a.* (*comp.* **lengthier,** *superl.* **lengthiest**) **1** long and usu.

tedious. 2 prolix. **lengthily** *adv.* **lengthiness** *n.* [OE *lengthu*, from *lang*, LONG[1] (cp. Dut. *lengte*, Icel. *lengd*)]

Usage note Pronunciation as (lenth) is best avoided.

lenient (lē´niənt) *a.* 1 merciful, tending not to be strict or punish severely. 2 (of a punishment) mild, gentle. 3 †soothing, emollient, mitigating. ~†*n.* an emollient preparation or application. **lenience, leniency** *n.* **leniently** *adv.* **lenitive** (len´-) *a.* 1 soothing, palliative. 2 having the power or quality of softening or mitigating. ~*n.* a lenitive medicine or application. **lenity** (len´-) *n.* (*pl.* **lenities**) 1 the fact of being lenient. 2 (*formal*) a merciful act. [L *lēniens -ientem*, pres.p. of *lēnīre*, to soothe, from *lēnis*, soft, gentle]

Leninism (len´inizm) *n.* the political and economic theories of Lenin; Marxism as modified by Lenin. **Leninist, Leninite** *a., n.* [*Lenin*, name adopted by V. I. Ulyanov, 1870–1924, Russian revolutionary and leader]

lenis (lē´nis) *n.* (*pl.* **lenes** (lē´nēz)) a consonant, such as English *b* or *v*, articulated without muscular tension or force of breath. ~*a.* articulated in this way. **lenition** (linish´ən) *n.* in Celtic languages, a softening of the articulation of consonants. [L, soft]

lenitive LENIENT.

leno (lē´nō) *n.* (*pl.* **lenos**) an open cotton fabric resembling fine muslin. [perh. corr. of F *linon*]

lens (lenz) *n.* (*pl.* **lenses**) 1 a piece of transparent substance, usu. glass, with one or both surfaces curved so as to change the direction of rays of light, and diminish or increase the apparent size of objects viewed through it. 2 a combination of lenses used to focus a beam of light or form an image. 3 a contact lens. 4 the crystalline body in the eye through which rays of light are focused on the retina. 5 a device for converging beams of electrons and other charged particles. 6 a device for directing sound waves. **lensed** *a.* **lens hood** *n.* a projecting device that shields the lens of a camera from direct sunlight. **lensless** *a.* **lensman** *n.* (*pl.* **lensmen**) a cameraman. [L *lens lentis*, seed of lentil]

Lent (lent) *n.* a period of 40 days (excluding Sundays) from Ash Wednesday to Easter Eve, observed in the Christian Church as a season of penitence and fasting in commemoration of Christ's fasting in the wilderness. **lenten** *a.* 1 of, relating to or used in Lent. 2 sparing, meagre. **Lenten fare** *n.* a meatless diet. **Lent lily** *n.* the daffodil. **Lent term** *n.* the school and university term in which Lent falls. [ME *lenten*, OE *lencten*, spring (cp. Dut. *lente*, G *Lenz*, prob. cogn. with LONG[1], because the days lengthen in spring)]

lent LEND.

-lent (lənt) *suf.* forming adjectives, such as *violent, redolent.* [L *-lentus*, -FUL]

lentamente, lentando LENTO.

lenten LENT.

lenti LENTO.

lenticel (len´tisel) *n.* a lens-shaped mass of cells in the bark of a plant, through which respiration takes place. **lenticellate** (-sel´ət) *a.* **lenticle** (-tikəl) *n.* a lenticular mass of rock embedded in a differing matrix. [F *lenticelle*, dim. from L *lentēm*, nom. *lens*]

lenticular (lentik´ūlə) *a.* 1 resembling in shape a lentil or doubly convex lens. 2 of or relating to the lens of the eye. **lenticularly** *adv.* [L *lenticularis*, see LENS]

lentiform (len´tifawm) *a.* shaped like a lens.

lentigo (lentī´gō) *n.* (*pl.* **lentigines** (-tij´inēs)) a freckle, freckly eruption. **lentiginous, lentiginose** (-nōs) *a.* [L, from *lens lentis*, LENS]

lentil (len´təl) *n.* 1 a small branching leguminous plant, *Lens culinaris.* 2 any of the seeds of this plant, largely used for food. [OF *lentille*, L *lenticula*, dim. of *lens*]

lentissimo LENTO.

lentivirus (len´tiviərəs) *n.* (*pl.* **lentiviruses**) any of a family of viruses that includes the Aids virus and others which affect cattle, goats and sheep. [L *lentus*, slow, VIRUS]

lento (len´tō) *a., adv.* (*Mus.*) (to be played) slowly. ~*n.* (*pl.* **lentos, lenti** (-tē)) a piece of music played in this way. **lentamente** (-əmen´tā) *adv.* 1 (*Mus.*) slowly. 2 in slow time. **lentando** (-tan´dō) *adv.* (*Mus.*) with increasing slowness. **lentissimo** (-tis´imō) *adv., a.* (to be played) very slowly. [It., from L *lentus*, slow]

Leo (lē´ō) *n.* 1 one of the 12 zodiacal constellations, the Lion. 2 the fifth sign of the zodiac, which the sun passes through between approx. 23 July and 22 August. 3 a person born under this sign. **Leonid** (-nid) *n.* any of the meteors that appear in numbers radiating from the constellation Leo. **leonine** (-nīn) *a.* 1 of, relating to or like a lion. 2 majestic, undaunted. 3 (*also* **Leonine**) of or relating to one of the Popes Leo, esp. Leo I. 4 (*also* **Leonine**) describing pentameter or hexameter Latin verse, the last word of which rhymes with that preceding the caesura; describing English verse, having internal rhyme. **Leonine City** *n.* the portion of Rome comprising the Vatican, which was walled by Leo IV. [L *leo leōnis*]

leone (lēō´ni) *n.* the standard monetary unit of Sierra Leone, equivalent to 100 cents. [from Sierra *Leone*]

Leonid, leonine LEO.

leontiasis (lēonti´əsis) *n.* a form of leprosy in which the victim's face takes on a lionlike appearance. [Gr. *leontiāsis*, from *leōn, -ontos*, lion]

leontopodium (liontōpō´diəm) *n.* a plant of the Eurasian alpine genus *Leontopodium* that includes the edelweiss. [New L from Gr. *leōn, -ontos*, lion, *podion*, dim. of *pous*, foot]

leopard (lep´əd) *n.* 1 a large mammal, *Panthera pardus*, of the cat family from Africa and S Asia, having a pale fawn to tan coat with dark spots; the panther. 2 a leopard-like animal, such as the jaguar, the cheetah, or the ounce. 3 (*Her.*) a lion passant guardant, as in the English royal arms. **leopardess** (-dis) *n.* a female leopard. **leopard lily** *n.* a large N American lily, *Lilium pardalinum*, that has large orange-red flowers and brown-spotted leaves. **leopard moth** *n.* a white moth, *Zeuzera pyrina*, that has black spots on its wings and body. **leopard's bane** *n.* a plant of the composite genus *Doronicum* with large yellow flowers. [OF, from late L *leopardus*, late Gr. *leopardos* (LION, PARD[2])]

leotard (lē´ətahd) *n.* a close-fitting garment resembling a swimsuit, though sometimes having legs and sleeves, worn during exercise, dance practice etc. [Jules *Léotard*, 1830–70, French trapeze artist]

leper (lep´ə) *n.* 1 a person affected with leprosy. 2 a person who is deliberately avoided by others. **leprosarium** (-prəseə´riəm) *n.* (*pl.* **leprosaria** (-riə)) a leper hospital. **leprose** (-rōs) *a.* having a white scurfy surface; scaly. **leprosity** (-pros´-) *n.* scaliness. **leprosy** (-rəsi) *n.* 1 a chronic contagious bacterial disease, usu. characterized by the formation of tubercles or of painful inflamed nodules beneath the skin, thickening of the skin, loss of feeling, and ulceration and necrosis of the affected parts. 2 moral corruption. **leprous** *a.* 1 suffering from leprosy. 2 resembling leprosy. 3 leprose. [OF *lepre*, leprosy, L and Gr. *lepra*, fem. of *lepros*, from *lepos*, scale]

lepido- (lep´idō), **lepid-** *comb. form* 1 having scales. 2 resembling scales. [Gr. *lepis lepidos*, a scale]

lepidolite (lipid´əlīt) *n.* a pinky-violet mica containing lithium.

lepidopteran (lepidop´tərən) *n.* any member of an order of insects, Lepidoptera, characterized by having four wings clothed with minute powder-like scales, containing the butterflies and moths. ~*a.* of, relating or belonging to this order. **lepidopterist** *n.* a person who studies moths or butterflies. **lepidopterology** (-rol´-) *n.* **lepidopterous** *a.* [Gr. *pteron*, wing]

lepidosiren (lepidōsī´rən) *n.* a dipnoan fish of a genus, *Lepidosiren*, with one species, *L. paradoxa*, the S American mudfish from the river Amazon. [SIREN]

lepidote (lep´idōt) *a.* scaly; covered with scaly spots or leaves.

leporine (lep´ərīn) *a.* of or relating to hares, having the nature or form of a hare. [L *leporīnus*, from *lepus leporis*, hare]

leprechaun (lep´rəkawn) *n.* in Irish folklore, a brownie or dwarfish sprite who performs domestic tasks, mends shoes etc. [Ir.]

leprose, leprosy etc. LEPER.

-lepsy (lep´si), **-lepsia** (-siə) *comb. form* forming nouns denoting a seizure or sudden attack. **-leptic** *comb. form* forming adjectives. [Gr. *lēpsis*, a seizure, from *lambanein*, to seize]

lept- LEPTO-.

lepta LEPTON[1].

-leptic -LEPSY.

lepto- (lep´tō), **lept-** *comb. form* fine, thin, delicate, slender. [Gr. *leptos*, thin]

leptocephalic (leptōsifal´ik, -kef-), **leptocephalous** (-sef´ələs, -kef´-) *a.* having a long and narrow skull. **leptocephalus** (-sef´-) *n.* the oceanic larva of eels of the genus *Anguilla*, that migrates from W Indian waters to European freshwater habitats.

leptocercal (leptōsœ´kəl) *a.* slender-tailed. [Gr. *kerkos*, tail]

leptodactyl (leptōdak´til) *a.* having long, slender toes. *~n.* a bird having such toes. **leptodactylous** *a.* [Gr. *daktulos*, digit]

lepton[1] (lep´ton) *n.* (*pl.* **lepta** (-tə)) **1** a modern Greek coin and monetary unit worth one-hundredth of a drachma. **2** the smallest ancient Greek coin, the mite of the New Testament parable. [Gr., neut. of *leptos*, LEPTO-]

lepton[2] (lep´ton) *n.* (*pl.* **leptons**) any of various elementary particles (e.g. electron, muon) that participate only in weak interaction. [LEPTO-, -ON]

leptorrhine (lep´tərin) *a.* having a long, narrow nose. [Gr. *rhis rhinos*, nose]

leptosome (lep´təsōm) *n.* a person who is of slender build, narrow-chested etc. **leptosomic** (-som´-), **leptosomatic** (-səmat´-) *a.* [Gr. *soma*, body]

leptospirosis (leptōspīrō´sis) *n.* any of various infectious diseases that can be transmitted by animals to humans and are caused by spirochaete bacteria of the genus *Leptospira*. [Gr. *speira*, a coil]

leptotene (lep´tōtēn) *n.* (*Biol.*) the first stage of the prophase of meiosis in which long, single-stranded chromosomes develop. [Gr. *-tene*, from *tainia*, band]

lesbian (lez´biən) *n.* a female homosexual. *~a.* **1** of or relating to lesbians or homosexuality in women. **2** (**Lesbian**) of or relating to Lesbos. **lesbianism** *n.* [Gr. island of *Lesbos*, home of Sappho]

lese-majesty (lēzmaj´əsti), **lèse-majesté** (lāzmazh´əstā) *n.* **1** an offence against the sovereign power or its representative, high treason. **2** an insult to a ruler or authority. **3** presumption. [F *lèse-majesté*, L *laesa mājestās* (*laesa*, hurt, violated, fem. p.p. of *laedere*, see LESION)]

lesion (lē´zhən) *n.* **1** (*Med.*) physical change in a tissue or organ due to injury. **2** a hurt, an injury. **3** damage. [F *lésion*, L *laesiōnem*, nom. *-sio*, from *laedere*, to injure]

less (les) *a.* **1** not so much. **2** of smaller size, extent, amount, degree, importance, rank etc. **3** (*coll.*) fewer. *~prep.* minus, with deduction of. *~adv.* **1** in a smaller or lower degree. **2** not so much. *~n.* **1** a smaller part, quantity or number. **2** the smaller, the inferior, the junior etc., of things compared. **3** (*coll.*) enough. **in less than no time** very quickly; very soon. **less and less** gradually diminishing. **much less** used to introduce an alternative which is even less the case (*I've never met him, much less gone out with him*). **no less** NO[1]. **nothing less than** NOTHING. **still less** used to introduce an alternative, much less. **lessen** *v.t.* **1** to make less in size, extent, number, quantity or degree. **2** to reduce, to depreciate, to degrade. *~v.i.* **1** to become less in size, extent, number, degree or quantity. **2** to decrease, to shrink. **lesser** *a.* **1** less, smaller. **2** inferior. **Lesser Bairam** *n.* the three-day Muslim festival which falls at the end of Ramadan. **lesser celandine** *n.* a yellow-flowered plant related to the buttercup, *Ranunculus ficaria*. **lesser-known** *a.* not so well-known as others of the type. **lesser litany** *n.* the Kyrie Eleison, or the response 'Lord have mercy upon us'. [OE (*læssa*, a. *lǣs* adv.)]

Usage note The use of *less* rather than *fewer* with countable nouns is sometimes disapproved of. Strictly you should have *less trouble* or *fewer troubles*, and buy *six items or fewer*, rather than *six items or less*.

-less (lis) *suf.* devoid of, free from, as in *fearless*, *godless*, *sinless*, *tireless*. [OE *lēas*, loose, free from, cogn. with LOOSE]

lessee (lesē´) *n.* a person to whom a lease is granted. **lesseeship** *n.* [A-F, from OF *lessé*, p.p. of *lesser*, to LEASE]

lessen, lesser LESS.

lesson (les´ən) *n.* **1** the amount or duration of instruction given to a pupil or pupils at one time. **2** the time allocated for a period of instruction in a timetable. **3** (*pl.*) a course of instruction (in any subject). **4** an assignment or exercise set for a pupil by a teacher, esp. a portion of a book to be read or studied. **5** an occurrence or example taken as a warning or caution. **6** knowledge gained from such examples or from experience. **7** a reprimand, admonition or lecture. **8** a portion of Scripture read in divine service. *~v.t.* **1** to teach, to instruct. **2** to discipline. **3** to admonish, to lecture. **to learn one's lesson** to gain wisdom or learn prudence as a result of usu. bitter experience. **to teach someone a lesson** to show someone, esp. by punishing them, that something is unwise, wrong etc. [OF *lecon*, L *lectiōnem*, nom. *-tio*, from *legere*, to read, p.p. *lectus*]

lessor (les´ə) *n.* a person who grants a lease. [A-F, from *lesser*, to LEASE]

lest (lest) *conj.* **1** for fear that, in case, so that (one may) not. **2** (after words expressing alarm, anxiety etc.) that. [ME *leste*, *lesthe*, OE *thȳ lǣsthe*, the (instrumental) less that]

let[1] (let) *v.t.* (*pres.p.* **letting**, *past, p.p.* **let**) **1** to permit, to allow, to suffer (to be or do). **2** to give leave to. **3** to cause to. **4** to grant the use, occupation or possession of for a stipulated sum, to lease. **5** to give out on contract. **6** to allow or cause (gas or liquid) to escape from. *~v.aux.* used in the imperative mood, with the force of prayer, exhortation, assumption, permission or command. *~v.i.* to be let or leased for rent. *~n.* a letting. **let alone 1** not to mention. **2** much less. **let me see** SEE[1]. **to let** available for renting. **to let alone 1** not to interfere with. **2** not to do or deal with. **3** not to mention. **to let be** not to interfere with. **to let blood** to bleed a patient. **to let down 1** to allow to sink or fall. **2** to fail or disappoint (someone). **3** to make (a garment) longer by lowering the hem. **4** to deflate. **5** to untie (hair) and allow to hang loose. **to let down gently** to avoid humiliating or causing too great distress or disappointment to. **to let drive** DRIVE. **to let drop/ fall 1** to drop. **2** to mention by accident, or as if by accident. **3** (*Geom.*) to draw (a perpendicular) from an outside point to a line. **to let fly** FLY[2]. **to let go 1** to release. **2** to relinquish hold of. **3** to cease to retain. **4** to dismiss from the mind. **5** to drop anchor. **to let in 1** to allow to enter. **2** to insert. **3** to inlay. **to let in for** to involve (someone) in something unpleasant, difficult etc. **to let in on** to allow to be involved in or to profit from. **to let into** 1 to allow to enter. 2 to allow to have knowledge of. 3 to set within another surface. **to let it all hang out** HANG. **to let loose** 1 to free from restraint, to release. 2 to utter abruptly and violently. 3 to discharge, to fire off, to unleash abruptly. **to let off** 1 to refrain from punishing or to punish lightly. 2 to excuse or dispense from. 3 to discharge, to fire off (an arrow, gun etc.); to detonate (a bomb, firework). 4 to allow to alight or disembark. 5 to allow or cause (air, liquid) to escape from. 6 to rent out (part of a building). **to let off steam** STEAM. **to let on** 1 to divulge, to let out. 2 to pretend. **to let oneself go** 1 to give way to any impulse. 2 to lose interest in maintaining one's appearance. **to let oneself in** to use one's own key to enter a building. **to let one's hair down** HAIR. **to let out** 1 to open the door for. 2 to allow to go out. 3 to free from restraint. 4 to divulge. 5 to utter, emit, give vent to. 6 to enlarge or make less tight-fitting. 7 to lease or let on hire. 8 to allow (air, liquid) to escape. 9 to disqualify, rule out, dispense from. 10 to exculpate. **to let rip** RIP[1]. **to let slip** 1 to allow to escape. 2 to lose, to miss. 3 to reveal inadvertently. **to let through** 1 to allow to pass. 2 to overlook, to fail to correct, emend etc. **to let up** to become less (severe), to abate. **to let up on** to treat less harshly; to stop harassing, pressing etc. **let-down** *n.* 1 a disappointment. 2 the release of milk from a cow's udder or a mammary gland. 3 an aircraft's gliding descent prior to landing. **let-off** *n.* (*coll.*) an instance of escaping from a threatening danger or punishment. **let-out** *n.* (*coll.*) an opportunity to escape or avoid something. **letting** *n.* a property that is to let or that has been let. **let-up** *n.* (*coll.*) 1 an abatement, a lessening of intensity. 2 a reduction in effort. [OE *lǣtan* (cp. Dut. *laten*, Icel. *lāta*, G *lassen*)]

let[2] (let) *n.* 1 in tennis etc., a stoppage, hindrance etc., requiring the ball to be served again. 2 a rally or service affected by this. 3 †a hindrance, an obstacle. ~†*v.t.* (*pres.p.* **letting,** *past, p.p.* **letted, let**) to hinder, to impede, to obstruct, to prevent. ~†*v.i.* to cause obstruction. [OE *lettan* (cp. Dut. *letten*, Icel. *letja*), rel. to LATE]

-let (lit) *suf.* forming nouns, usu. diminutives, as *cutlet*, *tartlet*, or items of dress or ornament, as *anklet*. [OF *-let, -lete, -et* (L *-ellus, -ella, -ellum*, -ET[1])]

letch LECH (under LECHER).

lethal (lē´thəl) *a.* deadly, fatal, mortal. **lethal chamber** *n.* a chamber in which animals are killed painlessly with gas. **lethal dose** *n.* the amount of any toxic agent that will cause death if administered to a human, animal or any other organism. **lethality** (-thal´-) *n.* **lethally** *a.* [F, from L *lēthālis, lētālis*, from *lētum*, death]

lethargy (leth´əji) *n.* 1 a state of torpor, apathy, dullness or inactivity. 2 (*Med.*) morbid drowsiness, unnatural sleepiness. ~†*v.t.* to affect with lethargy. **lethargic** (-thah´-), **lethargical** *a.* **lethargically** *adv.* **lethargied** *a.* **lethargize, lethargise** *v.t.* [L and Gr. *lēthargia*, from *lēthargos*, forgetting, from LETHE]

Lethe (lē´thē) *n.* 1 in Greek mythology, a river of Hades whose waters produced forgetfulness in those who drank them. 2 forgetfulness, oblivion. **Lethean** (-thē´-) *a.* [L, from Gr. *lēthē*, forgetfulness, *lēth-*, *lath-*, root of *lanthanesthai* to forget]

let's (lets) *contr.* let us.

†**Lett** (let) *n.* a member of a people largely inhabiting Latvia (Lettland), a Latvian. **Lettic** *a.* 1 Latvian. 2 of the group of languages to which Latvian (Lettish) belongs (also containing Lithuanian and Old Prussian). **Lettish** *a.*, *n.* Latvian. [G *Lette*, Latvian *Latvi*]

letter (let´ə) *n.* 1 a mark or character employed to represent a sound in speech. 2 any of the characters in the alphabet. 3 a written, typed or printed message or communication usually sent by post. 4 the literal or precise meaning of a term or terms, as distinct from the spirit. 5 characters used in printing, type; font of type. 6 (*pl.*) literature; literary culture. 7 (*pl.*) learning, erudition. 8 (*pl.*) a university degree, membership, title etc. abbreviated after a surname. 9 (*pl.*) a formal or legal document for any of a variety of purposes addressed to a particular recipient. 10 (*pl.*, *N Am.*) the initials of a school or university as a mark of proficiency in sport. ~*v.t.* 1 to impress, mark or stamp with letters. 2 to classify by means of letters. **the letter of the law** literal or precise definition of the law. **letter bomb** *n.* an explosive device contained in an envelope, which detonates when opened. **letter box** *n.* a box or slot for the reception of letters. **letter-card** *n.* a folded card with gummed edges for sending by post as a letter. **letter-carrier** *n.* (*N Am.*) a postman or postwoman. **lettered** *a.* 1 learned, erudite. 2 marked or impressed with letters. 3 of, relating to or suited for literature or learning. 4 literate. **letterhead** *n.* 1 notepaper with a printed heading. 2 (*also* **letter-heading**) the heading on such notepaper. **lettering** *n.* 1 the act or technique of impressing or marking with letters. 2 an inscription, a title. **letter missive** *n.* (*pl.* **letters missive**) 1 a letter or letters sent by an authority, esp. from the sovereign to a dean and chapter nominating someone for the office of bishop. 2 (*Sc. Law*) a document given by the parties to a contract etc. **letter of advice** *n.* a commercial letter giving specific notification of something, e.g. the consignment of goods. **letter of attorney** *n.* a written authority by which one person authorizes another to act in their stead. **letter of comfort** *n.* an assurance given by a third party to a bank in respect of a debt, not amounting to a legal guarantee. **letter of credit** *n.* an order authorizing a person to draw money from an agent. **letter of introduction** *n.* a letter introducing a friend to a third person. **letter of marque, letter of marque and reprisal** *n.* 1 a privateer's licence to seize and plunder merchant ships of a hostile state. 2 a privateer with such a licence. **letter-perfect** *a.* (of actors etc.) having learnt one's part thoroughly, word-perfect. **letterpress** *n.* 1 printing from raised type with ink; matter printed by this method. 2 printed matter other than illustrations. **letter-quality** *a.* 1 (of the output of a computer printer) of sufficient sharpness, neatness etc. to be used for communications. 2 (of a computer printer) producing output of this quality. **letters of administration** *n.pl.* a document issued by a court authorizing a person to administer an intestate estate. **letters of credence** *n.pl.* a document held by a diplomat presenting their credentials to a foreign government. **letters of intercommuning** *n.pl.* writs issued by the Scottish Privy Council forbidding anyone to harbour or communicate with those people named. **letters patent** *n.pl.* an open document from the sovereign or an officer of the Crown conferring a title, right, privilege etc., esp. the exclusive right to make or sell a new invention. **letter-writer** *n.* a person who (commonly) writes letters. [OF *lettre*, L *littera*]

Lettic LETT.

letting LET[1].

Lettish LETT.

lettre de cachet (letrə də kash´ā) *n.* (*pl.* **lettres de cachet** (letrə)) a royal warrant for the imprisonment or exile of a person without trial, in France before the Revolution. [F]

lettuce (let´is) *n.* 1 a crisp-leaved garden plant of the genus *Lactuca*, esp. *L. sativa*, much used for salad. 2 the leaves of this plant used as food. 3 any of various plants resembling lettuce. [ME *letuce*, ult. from L *lactūca*, cogn. with *lac lactis*, milk]

leu (lā´oo) *n.* (*pl.* **lei** (lā)) the basic monetary unit of Romania, equal to 100 bani. [Romanian, lion]

leuc- LEUCO-.

leucin (loo´sin), **leucine** *n.* an essential amino acid present in many proteins.

leucite (loo´sīt) *n.* a dull, glassy silicate of aluminium and potassium, occurring at Mt. Vesuvius and Monte Somma. **leucitic** (-sit´-) *a.*

leuco- (loo´kō), **leuc-**, **leuko-**, **leuk-** *comb. form* white, pale. [Gr. *leukos*]

leucocyte (loo´kōsīt), **leukocyte** *n.* a white corpuscle or blood cell. **leucocytic** (-sit´-) *a.* **leucocytosis** (lookōsītō´sis) *n.* a condition characterized by an increase in the number of white corpuscles in the blood.

leucoma (lookō´mə) *n.* a white opaque spot in the cornea, due to a wound, inflammation etc. [Gr. *leukōma*, from *leukos*, white]

leucorrhoea (lookərē´ə), (*N Am.*) **leucorrhea** *n.* a mucous discharge from the vagina, commonly called whites. **leucorrhoeal** *a.* [Gr. *rhoia*, a flow]

leucotomy (lookot´əmi) *n.* (*pl.* **leucotomies**) a surgical operation to cut white nerve fibres within the brain, esp. a prefrontal lobotomy.

leuk- LEUCO-.

leukaemia (lookē´miə), (*N Am.*) **leukemia** *n.* any of various acute and often fatal diseases of the bone marrow in which leucocytes multiply inordinately causing loss of red corpuscles, hypertrophy of the spleen etc. [Gr. LEUCO-, *haemia*, blood]

leuko- LEUCO-.

leukocyte LEUCOCYTE.

☒ **leutenant** common misspelling of LIEUTENANT.

Lev. *abbr.* Leviticus.

lev (lef) *n.* (*pl.* **leva** (lev´ə)) the basic monetary unit of Bulgaria, equal to 100 stotinki. [Bulg., lion]

Levant (livant´) *n.* the eastern part of the Mediterranean with its adjoining countries. **levanter**[1] *n.* **1** (**Levanter**) a native or inhabitant of the Levant. **2** an easterly wind in the Mediterranean. **Levantine** (lev´əntīn) *a.* of or relating to the Levant. ~*n.* **1** a native or inhabitant of the Levant. **2** (**levantine**) a cloth of twilled silk. **Levant storax** *n.* a balsam obtained from *Liquidambar orientalis*, also called LIQUID STORAX (under LIQUID). [F, from It. *levante*, L *levantem*, nom. *-vans*, pres.p. of *levāre*, to raise]

levant (livant´) *v.i.* to abscond, to run away, esp. with gambling liabilities undischarged. **levanter**[2] *n.* [Sp. *levantar*, to break up (camp, house etc.), from *levar*, to raise, as LEVANT]

levanter[1] LEVANT.

levanter[2] LEVANT.

levator (livā´tə) *n.* a muscle that raises some part of the body. [late L, from *levāre*, to raise]

levee[1] (lev´i, lev´ā) *n.* **1** (*N Am.*) a general reception or assembly of visitors. **2** (*Hist.*) in Britain, an early afternoon reception held by a sovereign or person of high rank for men only. **3** (*Hist.*) a reception held on getting out of bed. [F *levé* or *lever*, rising]

levee[2] (lev´i) *n.* **1** an artificial bank to prevent overflow and flooding. **2** the natural bank of a river formed by the deposition of silt. **3** a quay, a landing place on a river. [F *levée*, p.p. of *lever*, to raise]

level (lev´əl) *n.* **1** a horizontal line or plane or plane surface; a line or plane at all points at right angles to the vertical. **2** the altitude of any point or surface. **3** a position on a scale of values. **4** a stage or degree of progress or rank. **5** an instrument for determining whether a surface or a series of objects is horizontal. **6** a surveying instrument incorporating a telescope for measuring relative heights of land. **7** level country. **8** a surface that is more or less level. **9** a horizontal gallery or passage in a mine. ~*a.* **1** horizontal. **2** even, not higher or lower at any part, flat. **3** at the same height as or horizontal with something else. **4** (of runners, competitors) equal in position, score etc. having no advantage or disadvantage relative to one another. **5** equal in rank or degree. **6** equable, uniform, well-balanced. **7** (of a spoonful) filled so that the contents are even with the rim. ~*v.t.* (*pres.p.* **levelling**, (*N Am.*) **leveling**, *past, p.p.* **levelled**, (*N Am.*) **leveled**) **1** to make horizontal. **2** to make smooth or even. **3** to bring (up or down) to the same level. **4** to raze, to overthrow, to make level (with the ground etc.), to knock down. **5** to point (a gun) in taking aim. **6** to aim, to direct (an attack, satire etc.). **7** to bring to an equality of state, rank, condition or degree. **8** in surveying, to use a level to ascertain the elevation of a piece of land. ~*v.i.* to aim or point a gun (at). **on a level with** on the same horizontal plane as. **on the level** honest, genuine. **to do one's level best** to do the best one can. **to find its (own) level** **1** (of liquids) to reach the same height in a number of interconnecting vessels or chambers. **2** to reach a stable level, usu. with respect to something else. **to find one's level** to settle in a position, office, rank etc. suitable for one's abilities, qualities, powers. **to level down** to bring down to the level or standard of something or someone else. **to level off** **1** to make flat. **2** to reach and stay in a state of equilibrium. **3** (of an aircraft) to return to horizontal flight after a dive. **to level out** **1** to make level. **2** to remove differences between. **3** (of an aircraft) to return to the horizontal flight after a dive. **to level up** to bring up to the level or standard of something or someone else. **to level with** (*sl.*) to be honest with, to come clean. **level crossing** *n.* a level place where a road crosses a railway line. **level-headed** *a.* sensible, shrewd, untemperamental. **level-headedly** *adv.* **level-headedness** *n.* **leveller**, (*N Am.*) **leveler** *n.* **1** a person who or something which levels. **2** a person who wishes to destroy all social distinctions. **3** (**Leveller**) a member of a radical republican and egalitarian group during the English Civil War. **levelling** *n.* **levelling screw** *n.* a screw that adjusts the level of an instrument. **levelly** *adv.* **levelness** *n.* **level of attainment** *n.* in British education, any of ten groupings within which pupils are assessed in accordance with criteria based on age and attainment. **level pegging** *a.* equal. ~*n.* (of contestants etc.) the state of being at the same level or at the same place in a race etc. **level playing field** *n.* a situation in which no participant or contestant starts with an unfair advantage over the others. [OF *livel* (F *niveau*), L *lībella*, dim. of *lībra*, balance, a level]

lever (lē´və) *n.* **1** a bar of wood, metal, or other rigid substance resting on a fixed point of support (or fulcrum), used to overcome a certain resistance or lift a certain weight. **2** a part of a machine, instrument etc., acting on the same principle. **3** a projecting handle that can be moved to operate a machine. **4** anything that brings power or influence to bear. ~*v.t.* to move or lift with or as with a lever. ~*v.i.* to use a lever. **leverage** (-rij) *n.* **1** the action of a lever. **2** the mechanical power or advantage gained by the use of a lever. **3** means of accomplishing, influencing etc. **4** an arrangement of levers. **5** (*N Am.*) the ratio between the amount of a company's borrowings and that of its share capital. **leveraged buyout** *n.* a buyout made with the assistance of third-party capital. **lever arch file** *n.* a loose-leaf binder in which the sheets are inserted onto arch-shaped metal rods which part when a lever is operated. **lever escapement** *n.* an escapement in which two levers connect the pallet and balance. **lever watch** *n.* a watch with a lever escapement. [OF *leveor*, from *lever*, to raise]

leveret (lev´ərit) *n.* a young hare, esp. one in its first year. [A-F, from OF *levrete*, dim. of *levre* (F *lièvre*), L *leporem*, nom. *lepus*, hare]

leviable LEVY.

leviathan (livī´əthən) *n.* **1** a huge aquatic monster (perh. the Nilotic crocodile) described in the Book of Job; a huge sea monster. **2** anything huge or monstrous, esp. a huge ship, a whale, the state. [late L, from Heb. *livyāthān*, etym. uncertain]

levigate (lev´igāt) *v.t.* **1** to grind or rub down to a fine powder. **2** to make into a smooth paste. *~a.* (*Bot.*) having a smooth polished surface. **levigable** *a.* **levigation** (-ā´shən) *n.* [L *lēvigātus*, p.p. of *lēvigāre*, from *lēvis*, smooth]

†**levin** (lev´in) *n.* **1** lightning. **2** a flash of lightning. [ME *levene*, etym. uncertain]

levirate (lē´virət) *n.* an ancient law of the Hebrews and others binding a man to marry the widow of his dead brother if the orig. marriage was childless. [L, *levir*, brother-in-law (cp. Sansk. *dēvar*, Gr. *daēr*)]

Levis® (lē´vīz) *n.pl.* a type of (blue) denim jeans.

Levit. *abbr.* Leviticus.

levitate (lev´itāt) *v.t., v.i.* to (cause to) rise or float in the air, esp. a body through supernatural causes. **levitation** (-ā´shən) *n.* **levitational** *a.* **levitator** *n.* [L *levis*, light, after GRAVITATE]

Levite (lē´vīt) *n.* a member of the tribe or family of Levi, esp. one of those who acted as assistants to the priests in the Jewish temple. **Levitic** (-vit´-), **Levitical** *a.* **1** of or relating to the Levites. **2** of or relating to the book of Leviticus or the laws contained in it. **3** †priestly. **Levitically** *adv.* **Leviticus** (-vit´ikəs) *n.* the third book of the Pentateuch, containing the Levitical law and ritual. [L *Levīta*, Gr. *Leuitēs*, from *Leui*, Heb. *Lēvī*, son of Jacob]

levity (lev´iti) *n.* **1** lack of seriousness or earnestness, inappropriate humour, frivolity. **2** fickleness, inconstancy. **3** †lightness of weight. [OF *levité*, L *levitātem*, nom. *-tas*, from *levis*, light]

levo- LAEVO-.

levodopa (lēvōdō´pə) *n.* L-dopa, the laevorotatory form of dopa.

levogyrate LAEVOGYRATE.

levorotatory LAEVOROTATORY.

levulose LAEVULOSE.

levy (lev´i) *n.* (*pl.* **levies**) **1** the act of raising or collecting (e.g. a tax, a fine, a fee). **2** something which is so raised or collected. **3** the calling out of troops for military service. **4** a body of troops called out for military service. **5** the number of troops called out. *~v.t.* (*3rd pers. sing. pres.* **levies**, *pres.p.* **levying**, *past, p.p.* **levied**) **1** to impose and collect (as a tax or forced contribution). **2** to raise, to collect together, to enlist (as an army). **3** to seize (property) by a judicial writ etc.; to raise (money) by such seizure. **4** to begin to wage (war). **leviable** *a.* **levy en masse, levy in mass** *n.* the conscription of large numbers of the civilian population, usu. in the face of a foreign invasion. [F *levée*, fem. p.p. of *lever*, L *levāre*, to raise]

lewd (lood, lūd) *a.* **1** lascivious, unchaste; indecent. **2** †depraved, wicked, worthless. **3** †ignorant. **lewdly** *adv.* **lewdness** *n.* [OE *lǣwede*, lay, belonging to the laity]

lewis (loo´is), **lewisson** (-sən) *n.* a hoisting device for heavy stone blocks employing metal, usu. curved pieces which fit into and grasp the stone. [perh. from the inventor]

Lewis gun (loo´is) *n.* a portable gas-operated machine-gun invented by Col. Isaac Newton Lewis, 1858–1931.

lewisite (loo´isīt) *n.* a poisonous liquid used in chemical warfare obtained from arsenic and acetylene. [W. I. *Lewis*, 1878–1943, US chemist]

lex (leks) *n.* (*pl.* **leges** (lē´jēz)) **1** a body of law. **2** a law. **lex domicilii** (domisil´iī) *n.* the law of the country in which a person is domiciled. **lex fori** (faw´rī) *n.* the law of the country in which an action is brought. **lex loci** (lō´sī) *n.* the law of the country in which the tort or transaction took place, a property is situated etc. **lex non scripta** (non skrip´tə) *n.* the unwritten or common law. **lex scripta** (skrip´tə) *n.* the written or statute law. **lex talionis** (taliō´nis) *n.* the principle of like for like, an eye for an eye etc. in relation to crime and punishment. [L, law]

lexeme (lek´sēm) *n.* in linguistics, an irreducible unit of meaning in a language; a particle, word or phrase whose meaning cannot be deduced from the sum of its separate constituents. [*lex*icon, -EME]

lexicon (lek´sikən) *n.* **1** a dictionary (usu. applied to Greek, Hebrew, Arabic or Syriac). **2** the vocabulary of a language, an individual, an area of study etc. **lexical** (-kəl) *a.* **1** of or relating to the words of a language, as opposed to grammar. **2** of or relating to a lexicon or lexicography. **lexicalize, lexicalise** *v.t., v.i.* to (cause to) be formed from constituent morphemes, words, lexemes etc. **lexicalization** (-zā´shən) *n.* **lexically** *adv.* **lexicography** (leksikog´rəfi) *n.* the art or process of compiling lexicons or dictionaries. **lexicographer** *n.* **lexicographic** (-graf´-), **lexicographical** *a.* **lexicographically** (-graf´-) *adv.* **lexicology** (-kol´-) *n.* that branch of learning concerned with the derivation, signification and application of words. **lexicologist** *n.* **lexigram** (-gram) *n.* a sign representing a word. **lexigraphy** (-sig´rəfi) *n.* a system of writing in which each word is represented by a distinct character. **lexigraphic** (-graf´-), **lexigraphical** *a.* **lexis** *n.* the complete vocabulary of a language, individual or subject. [Gr. *lexikon*, orig. neut. of *lexikos*, of or relating to words, from *lexis*, a saying, a word, from *legein*, to speak]

ley (lā) *n.* **1** arable land laid down (temporarily) to grass. **2** a ley line. **ley farming** *n.* a type of farming in which land is alternately tilled and used for pasture over periods of several years. **ley line** *n.* a straight line across the landscape joining two landmarks, supposed to be of prehistoric origin. [LEA[2]]

Leyden jar (lī´dən) *n.* a glass bottle or jar coated inside and out with tinfoil used as an electrical condenser. [invented in *Leyden*, Holland, in 1745]

LF *abbr.* low frequency.

lf *abbr.* light face (type).

LG *abbr.* Low German.

lg., lge *abbr.* large.

lgth *abbr.* length.

LH *abbr.* **1** (*also* **l.h.**) left hand. **2** luteinizing hormone.

lhaso apso (lahsə ap´sō) *n.* (*pl.* **lhaso apsos**) a breed of small Tibetan terrier with a thick, long, straight coat and a feathered tail that curls up over its back. [Tibetan]

LI *abbr.* **1** Light Infantry. **2** Long Island.

Li *chem. symbol* lithium.

li (lē) *n.* a Chinese measure of distance, rather more than one-third of a mile (0.5 km). [Chin.]

liable (lī´əbəl) *a.* **1** tending, apt or likely (to). **2** bound or obliged in law or equity. **3** responsible (for). **4** subject (to). **5** exposed or open (to). **liability** (-bil´-) *n.* (*pl.* **liabilities**) **1** the state of being liable. **2** something for which one is liable. **3** (*pl.*) debts, pecuniary obligations. **4** a person or thing that hinders, disadvantages or causes trouble. **limited liability** LIMIT. [perh. from non-extant A-F *liable*, or med. L *ligābilis* (F *lier*, L *ligāre*, to bind)]

liaison (liā´zon) *n.* **1** communication and contact between units, groups etc., esp. between military units. **2** an illicit intimacy between a man and woman. **3** in cooking, a thickening for a sauce or soup usu. made of yolk of egg. **4** the carrying on of the sound of a final consonant to a succeeding word beginning with a vowel or *h* mute. **5** a bond, a connection. **liaise** *v.i.* **1** to maintain communication and contact. **2** to form a liaison. **liaison officer** *n.* **1** an officer acting as go-between for forces or bodies of men under different commands. **2** a person in charge of communication between units, groups etc. [F, from L *ligātiōnem*, nom. *-tio*, from *ligāre*, to bind]

liana (liah´nə), **liane** (-ahn´) *n.* any of the climbing and twining plants common in the forests of tropical America. **lianoid** *a.* [F *liane*, prob. from *lier*, L *ligāre*, to bind]

liang (lyang) *n.* **1** a Chinese weight, equal to about 1⁄13 oz. av. (38 g). **2** this weight of silver as money of account. [Chin.]

liar (līˈə) *n.* a person who knowingly utters a falsehood, esp. someone addicted to lying. **liar dice** *n.* a game played using poker dice in which the result of a throw may be announced falsely. [OE *lēogere*, from *lēogan*, to LIE[1]]

Lias (līˈəs) *n.* **1** the lowest series of rock strata of the Jurassic system. **2** (**lias**) a blue limestone rock found in SW England. **Liassic** (-asˈ-) *a.* [F *liais*, etym. doubtful]

☒ **liason** common misspelling of LIAISON.

Lib. *abbr.* Liberal.

lib (lib) *n.* (*coll.*) short for LIBERATION (under LIBERATE).

lib. *abbr.* **1** *liber* (L, book). **2** librarian. **3** library.

libation (lībāˈshən) *n.* **1** a sacrificial offering to a deity involving the pouring of oil or wine. **2** the liquid poured. **3** (*usu. facet.*) an (alcoholic) drink. **4** the act of drinking this. **libational** *a.* **libatory** (līˈbə-) *a.* [L *lībātio*, from *lībāre*, to sip, to pour out (cp. Gr. *leibein*)]

libber (libˈə) *n.* (*coll.*) short for LIBERATIONIST (under LIBERATE).

Lib. Dem. *abbr.* Liberal Democrat.

libeccio (libechˈō), **libbecchio** (-ekˈiō) *n.* (*pl.* **libeccios, libecchios**) the south-west wind, esp. blowing on to the W coast of Corsica. [It., from L *libs*, Gr. *lips*]

libel (līˈbəl) *n.* **1** a publication of any kind containing false statements or representations tending to bring any person into ridicule, contempt or disrepute. **2** the act or crime of publishing a libel. **3** an unfair representation or defamatory statement. **4** in civil and ecclesiastical law, the written statement containing a plaintiff's allegations. **5** (*Sc. Law*) the statement of the grounds of the charge. ~*v.t.* (*pres.p.* **libelling,** (*N Am.*) **libeling,** *past, p.p.* **libelled,** (*N Am.*) **libeled**) **1** to make or publish a defamatory statement about. **2** to defame, to misrepresent. **3** to bring a suit against by means of a written complaint. ~*v.i.* to spread libels or defamatory statements. **libellant** *n.* in ecclesiastical law, a person who brings a libel suit. **libellee** (-lēˈ) *n.* a person against whom a libel suit is brought. **libeller, libelist** *n.* a person who commits libel or makes defamatory statements. **libellous** *a.* being or containing a libel. **libellously** *adv.* [OF, from L *libellum*, nom. *-lus*, dim. of *liber*, book]

liber (līˈbə) *n.* (*Bot.*) the bast or phloem. [L, bark]

liberal (libˈərəl) *a.* **1** favourable to individual freedom, democratic government, progress and moderate reform. **2** ample, abundant, profuse. **3** generous, open-handed, bountiful, munificent. **4** broad-minded, unprejudiced. **5** not strict, narrow or literal. **6** (**Liberal**) of or relating to a Liberal Party. **7** (esp. of education) not technical, tending to free mental development. **8** in religion and theology, progressive, re-evaluating or discarding traditional beliefs and dogmas in the light of modern thought. **9** free, open, candid. ~*n.* **1** a person who advocates progress and reform, esp. in the direction of conferring greater power upon the people. **2** (**Liberal**) a member or supporter of a Liberal Party. **liberal arts** *n.pl.* **1** non-technical or non-professional studies including the fine arts, history, languages, literature, philosophy etc., the arts. **2** in the Middle Ages, the studies comprising the *trivium* and *quadrivium*. **Liberal Democrat** *n.* in the UK, a member of a political party founded in 1988 by the merging of the Liberal Party and the bulk of the Social Democratic Party. **liberalism** *n.* **liberalist** *n.* **liberalistic** (-lisˈ-) *a.* **liberality** (-ralˈ-) *n.* **1** the quality of being liberal. **2** bounty, munificence, generosity. **3** largeness or breadth of views, catholicity. **4** freedom from prejudice. **liberalize, liberalise** *v.t.* to make more liberal. **liberalization** (-zāˈshən) *n.* **liberally** *adv.* **liberalness** *n.* **Liberal Party** *n.* **1** (*Hist.*) one of the principal political parties in Britain until 1988, being the successor of the Whig Party. **2** (*Austral.*) a major political party supporting conservative policies. **3** a party having liberal policies. **Liberal Unionist** *n.* (*Hist.*) a member of the Liberal Party who seceded in 1886 and supported the Conservatives in opposing the adoption of the Home Rule Bill. [OF, from L *līberālis*, from *līber*, free]

liberate (libˈərāt) *v.t.* **1** to set at liberty. **2** to release from domination, injustice, restraint or confinement. **3** to release from occupation by or subjugation to a foreign power. **4** to set free from chemical combination. **5** (*euphem. or facet.*) to steal. **liberated** *a.* **1** freed, having liberty. **2** freed from foreign occupation or domination. **3** no longer subject to traditional constraints, sexual and social roles etc. **liberation** (-āˈshən) *n.* **1** the act of setting free. **2** the process of becoming liberated. **liberationism** *n.* **liberationist** *n.* a person who supports the cause of equality, freedom or liberty (e.g. *women's liberationist, gay liberationist*). **liberation theology** *n.* the theory (orig. amongst the Roman Catholic clergy of Latin America) that political involvement to effect social equality and justice is a necessary part of Christianity. **liberator** *n.* **liberatory** *a.* [L *līberātus*, from *līberāre*, as LIBERAL]

libero (lēˈbərō) *n.* (*pl.* **liberos**) in football, a sweeper. [It., free, a free man]

libertarian LIBERTY.

libertine (libˈətēn) *n.* **1** a licentious or dissolute person, a debauchee, a profligate. **2** (*Hist.*) a freethinker in religious matters. **3** a person who is free from restraint and able to follow their own inclinations. ~*a.* **1** loose, licentious, dissolute. **2** free from restraint. **libertinage** (-nij), **libertinism** *n.* licentiousness. [L *lībertīnus*, a freedman, from *lībertus* (*līber*, free)]

liberty (libˈəti) *n.* (*pl.* **liberties**) **1** the quality or state of being free from captivity, bondage, subjection or despotic control. **2** freedom of choice, opinion or action. **3** an action which seems socially presumptuous or improper, a breach of decorum. **4** any instance of a person treating someone or something with too little respect. **5** (*pl.*) rights, privileges or exemptions, enjoyed by grant or prescription. **6** a place or district within which certain privileges or immunities are enjoyed. **7** †a district beyond a debtors' prison where prisoners were sometimes allowed to reside. **8** (*Naut.*) leave of absence for sailors. **at liberty 1** free. **2** having the right (to do etc.). **3** disengaged, not occupied. **to set at liberty** to free from confinement or restraint. **to take liberties (with) 1** to be unduly familiar or presumptuous (with). **2** to transgress rules or usages. **3** to falsify. **to take the liberty 1** to venture. **2** to do something without permission. **libertarian** (-teəˈri-) *a.* **1** advocating the widest possible extension of liberty. **2** believing in free will. ~*n.* **1** an advocate of liberty. **2** a believer in the doctrine of free will. **libertarianism** *n.* **liberticide** (-bœˈtisīd) *n.* **1** destruction of liberty. **2** a person who destroys liberty. ~*a.* destroying liberty. **Liberty Bell** *n.* a bell in Philadelphia that was rung at the adoption of the Declaration of Independence. **liberty boat** *n.* a boat taking sailors ashore on leave. **liberty bodice** *n.* a sleeveless bodice worn as an undergarment, esp. by children. **liberty hall** *n.* a place where one may do as one pleases. **liberty horse** *n.* a riderless circus horse. **liberty man** *n.* (*pl.* **liberty men**) a sailor having permission to go ashore. **liberty of the subject** *n.* the rights of a citizen under a constitution. **Liberty ship** *n.* a prefabricated, mass-produced cargo ship built in the US during World War II. [F *liberté*, L *lībertātem*, nom. *-tas*, from *līber*, free]

libidinous (libidˈinəs) *a.* **1** characterized by lewdness or lust, lustful. **2** lascivious. **libidinously** *adv.* **libidinousness** *n.* [L *libīdinōsus*, from *libīdo -dinis*, lust]

libido (libēˈdō) *n.* (*pl.* **libidos**) **1** the sexual drive. **2** in psychoanalysis, the life force deriving from biological impulses. **libidinal** (-bid´inəl) *a.* [L, desire]

Lib-Lab (liblab´) *a.* in the UK, involving or uniting the Liberal or Liberal Democrat and Labour Parties.

Libra (lē´brə) *n.* **1** one of the 12 zodiacal constellations, the Scales and Balance. **2** the seventh sign of the zodiac which the sun passes through between approx. 23 September and 22 October. **3** a person born under this sign. **Libran** *a., n.* [L]

libra (lī´brə) *n.* (*pl.* **librae** (-brē)) **1** an ancient Roman pound, equal to about 12 oz. (240 gr). **2** a pound weight (*lb*), a pound sterling (£). [L]

library (lī´brəri) *n.* (*pl.* **libraries**) **1** a collection of books, esp. one that is classified and catalogued, or otherwise organized, to facilitate its use either by the public or by private persons. **2** a building, room, or series of rooms containing such a collection. **3** an institution established for the formation or maintenance of such a collection. **4** a series of books similar in subject, literary form etc., issued (usu. in similar format) by a publisher. **5** a collection of computer software, films, records, tapes etc. **librarian** (-breə´ri-) *n.* a person who has charge of a library or one of their assistants. **librarianship** *n.* the professional care, organization and administration of a collection of books. **library edition** *n.* an edition with a strong binding. **library school** *n.* an institution or department where librarianship is taught. **library science** *n.* librarianship. [F *librarie*, L *librārius*, of or relating to books, from *liber*, book, orig. bark]

librate (lī´brāt) *v.i.* **1** to move like a balance, to oscillate, to swing or sway. **2** to be poised. **libration** (-brā´shən) *n.* oscillation. **librational** *a.* **libration of the moon** *n.* a real or apparent oscillation by which parts near the edges of the moon's disc are alternately visible and invisible. **libratory** *a.* [L *lībrātus*, p.p. of *lībrāre*, to poise, from *lībra*, balance]

libretto (libret´ō) *n.* (*pl.* **libretti** (-ti), **librettos**) **1** the words of an opera, oratorio etc. **2** a book containing such words. **librettist** *n.* a person who writes a libretto. [It., dim. of *libro*, L *liber*, book]

Librium® (lib´riəm) *n.* a tranquillizing drug containing chlordiazepoxide.

Libyan (lib´iən) *a.* of or relating to the N African country of Libya, its language or its people. ~*n.* **1** a native or inhabitant of Libya. **2** the Hamitic language of ancient Libya, now extinct.

lice LOUSE.

licence¹ (lī´səns), (*NAm.*) **license** *n.* **1** a document certifying consent or permission granted by a constituted authority (to marry, drive a motor vehicle, possess a firearm, carry on a business etc.). **2** authority, leave, permission. **3** permitted freedom of thought or action. **4** unrestrained liberty of action, disregard of law or propriety. **5** abuse of freedom, licentiousness. **6** in literature or art, deviation from the ordinary rules or mode of treatment. **7** a certificate of competence in a university faculty. [F, from L *licentia*, from *licēre*, to be allowed or lawful]

licence² LICENSE¹.

license¹ (lī´səns), **licence** *v.t.* **1** to authorize by a legal permit. **2** to allow, to permit, esp. to allow entire freedom of action, comment etc. **licensable** *a.* **licensed** *a.* **licensed victualler** *n.* a person who holds a licence to sell spirits, wines, beer etc. **licensee** (-sē´) *n.* a person who holds a licence (esp. a publican). **license plate** *n.* (*chiefly NAm.*) the number plate on a vehicle. **licenser, licensor** *n.* a person who grants a licence or has the authority to do so. **licentiate** (-sen´shiət) *n.* **1** a person who holds a certificate of competence in some profession from a university or other collegiate body. **2** in the Presbyterian Church, a person who has a licence to preach. **3** a higher degree conferred by some European universities. **4** the holder of such a degree.

license² LICENCE¹.

licentiate LICENSE¹.

licentious (līsen´shəs) *a.* **1** lascivious, dissolute, profligate, loose. **2** †unrestrained by rule or accepted laws of style etc. **licentiously** *adv.* **licentiousness** *n.* [L *licentiōsus*, from *licentia* (see LICENCE¹)]

lichee LYCHEE.

lichen (lī´kən) *n.* **1** a cryptogamic thallophytic plant of the order Lichenaceae, parasitic fungi on algal cells covering rocks, tree trunks etc., with variously coloured crusts. **2** a papular inflammatory eruption of the skin. **lichened** *a.* **lichenin** (-in) *n.* a kind of starch occurring in Iceland moss and other lichens. **lichenism** *n.* **lichenist** *n.* **lichenoid** (-oid), **lichenose** (-ōs), **lichenous** *a.* **lichenology** (-ol´-) *n.* that branch of botany which deals with lichens. **lichenologist** *n.* [L *līchēn*, Gr. *leichēn*, prob. rel. to *leichein*, to lick]

lich-gate (lich´gāt), **lych-gate** *n.* a churchyard gate with a roof, under which a coffin used to be placed while the introductory portion of the burial service was read. [OE *līc*, body, orig. form (cp. Dut. *lijk*, Icel. *līk*, G *Leiche*)]

licit (lis´it) *a.* lawful, allowed. **licitly** *adv.* [L *licitus*, p.p. of *licēre*, to be allowed]

lick (lik) *v.t.* **1** to draw or pass the tongue over. **2** to take in or lap (up) with the tongue. **3** (of flames etc.) to stroke or pass lightly over. **4** (*coll.*) to overcome, to defeat; to be beyond, to surpass. **5** (*coll.*) to thrash. ~*v.i.* (of flames etc.) to flicker or move with a lapping or stroking motion. ~*n.* **1** the act of licking. **2** a slight smear or coat (as of paint); a small amount. **3** SALT LICK (under SALT). **4** (*coll.*) a smart blow or slap. **5** (*coll.*) great exertion, effort or pace. **a lick and a promise** (*coll.*) something done very quickly, esp. a quick or superficial wash. **to lick into shape** to bring into a satisfactory condition or shape (from the notion that young bears are born shapeless, and are licked into shape by their dam). **to lick one's lips/ chops** to anticipate or remember something with pleasure. **to lick one's wounds** to withdraw after a defeat to recuperate physically or mentally. **to lick someone's boots/ shoes** to be servile towards. **to lick the dust** **1** to be beaten, to be killed. **2** †to act in a servile manner. **to lick up** to consume, to devour. **licker** *n.* **licking** *n.* (*coll.*) a beating, a defeat. **to take a licking** to take a beating. **lickspittle** *n.* an abject parasite or toady. [OE *liccian* (cp. Dut. *likken*, G *lecken*, also Gr. *leichein*, L *lingere*)]

lickerish (lik´ərish), **liquorish** *a.* **1** lecherous. **2** greedy. **3** pleasing to the taste, dainty, tempting. **lickerishly** *adv.* **lickerishness** *n.* [North. var. of OF *lecheros*, LECHEROUS (under LECHER)]

lickety-split (likətisplit´) *adv.* (*chiefly NAm., coll.*) very quickly. [LICK, SPLIT]

licorice LIQUORICE.

lictor (lik´tə) *n.* in ancient Rome, a civil officer who attended the chief magistrates, and bore the fasces as a sign of authority. [L, rel. to *ligāre*, to bind]

lid (lid) *n.* **1** a hinged or detachable cover or cap, usu. for shutting a vessel, container or aperture. **2** an eyelid. **3** (*Bot.*) an operculum. **4** a curb, a restraint. **5** (*sl.*) a hat. **to blow/ lift/ take the lid off** (*coll.*) to reveal, uncover (esp. something clandestine or corrupt). **to flip one's lid** (*sl.*) to go berserk, to become mad. **to put the (tin) lid on it** **1** (*coll.*) to be a final blow, misfortune etc. **2** (*coll.*) to curb, to put an end to. **lidded** *a.* **lidless** *a.* uncovered, bare. [OE *hlid* (cp. Dut. *lid*, Icel. *hlith*, G *-lid*, in *Augenlid*)]

lido (lē´dō) *n.* (*pl.* **lidos**) a bathing beach, an outdoor swimming pool. [resort near Venice]

lidocaine (lid´əkān) *n.* LIGNOCAINE.

lie¹ (lī) *v.i.* (*3rd pers. sing. pres.* **lies,** *pres.p.* **lying,** *past, p.p.* **lied**) **1** to say or write anything with the deliberate intention of deceiving. **2** to convey a false impression, to deceive. ~*v.t.* to take (away) or get (oneself into or out of) by lying. ~*n.* 1 a false statement deliberately made for the purpose of deception. 2 an intentional violation of the truth. 3 a deception, an imposture. **to give someone the lie** to accuse of deliberate falsehood. **to give the lie to** 1 to show to be false; to disprove. 2 to accuse of lying. **lie detector** *n.* a device for monitoring physiological changes taken as evidence of mental stress accompanying the telling of lies; a polygraph. **lying**[1] *a.* telling lies; false, deceitful. **lyingly** *adv.* [OE *lēogan* (cp. Dut. *liegen*, G *lügen*), whence *lyge*, a lie, *lēogere*, LIAR]

lie[2] (lī) *v.i.* (*3rd pers. sing. pres.* **lies,** *pres.p.* **lying,** *past* **lay** (lā), *p.p.* **lain** (lān)) 1 to rest or place oneself in a reclining or horizontal posture. 2 to rest on or over a horizontal surface. 3 to be situated in a specified location or direction. 4 to stretch or extend. 5 to exist, to be, to reside, in a specified state, position, relation etc. 6 to remain undisturbed (*let things lie*). 7 to be buried. 8 to seem to weigh heavily on (*the food lies on my stomach*). 9 (*Law*) (of an action, objection etc.) to be sustainable. 10 †to sleep, to lodge, to encamp (usu. at a specified place). 11 (of a game bird) not to rise. ~*n.* 1 position, arrangement, direction, manner of lying. 2 the retiring-place or lair (of an animal). 3 in golf, the position of the ball when about to be struck. **as far as in me lies** to the best of my ability. **to let lie** not to bring forward for discussion (because likely to cause controversy). **to lie about/ around** to be left scattered randomly over an area. **to lie ahead** to be in prospect or in store. **to lie at the door of** DOOR. **to lie back** to rest in a comfortable reclining position. **to lie behind** to be the cause of or explanation for. **to lie down** 1 to take up a lying position. 2 to take a short rest. 3 to submit tamely. **to lie hard/ heavy on** to oppress, to be a weight upon. **to lie in** 1 to remain in bed later than normal. 2 to be in bed to give birth to a child. **to lie in one** to be in one's power or capacity. **to lie in state** STATE. **to lie in the way** to be an obstacle or impediment. **to lie in wait (for)** 1 to wait in ambush or concealment (in order to waylay). 2 to be in store (for). **to lie low** 1 to remain in hiding. 2 to conceal one's knowledge or intentions in order to outwit, forestall etc. **to lie off** (of a ship) to stay at a distance from the shore or another ship. **to lie on the table** TABLE. **to lie over** 1 to be deferred. 2 to remain unpaid. **to lie to** (of a ship) to be checked or stopped with its head to the wind. **to lie under** to be subject to or oppressed by. **to lie up** 1 to rest, to stay in bed or in one's room to recuperate. 2 (of a ship) to go into dock. **to lie with** 1 to be the responsibility or duty of. 2 †to have sexual intercourse with. 3 †to lodge or sleep with. **to take lying down** to accept (an insult, rebuff) without retaliation, resistance or complaint. **lie-down** *n.* a short rest. **lie-in** *n.* a longer than normal stay in bed. **lie of the land** *n.* 1 the topography of a place. 2 the nature of the situation as it stands and as it is likely to develop. **lying**[2] *n.* a place to lie in. **lying-in** *n.* (*pl.* **lyings-in**) confinement in childbirth. [OE *licgan* (cp. Dut. *liggen*, Icel. *liggja*, G *liegen*, cogn. with Gr. *lechos*, L *lectus*, bed)]

Usage note *Lie* should not be instead of *lay* as a transitive verb: *Lay your head on my shoulder*, not *lie your head*.

Liebfraumilch (lēb´frowmilkh) *n.* a light white wine from the Rhine region of Germany. [G *Liebfrau*, the Virgin Mary (from the name of the convent where it was first produced), *Milch*, milk]

lied (lēd, -t) *n.* (*pl.* **lieder** (-də)) a type of German song, often a poem set to music and usu. for solo voice with piano accompaniment. [G]

†**lief** (lēf) *adv.* willingly, gladly, freely. ~*a.* 1 willing, ready. 2 dear, beloved. **had/ would as lief** would as willingly. [OE *lēof* (cp. Dut. *lief*, G *lieb*), cogn. with LOVE]

liege (lēj) *a.* 1 bound by some feudal tenure, either as a vassal or as a lord. 2 of or relating to such tenure. ~*n.* 1 a feudal superior, a lord, a sovereign. 2 a vassal bound to do service to his lord. **liegeman** *n.* (*pl.* **liegemen**) 1 a liege vassal. 2 a faithful supporter or follower. [OF *lige*, prob. from OHG *ledig*, free]

lien (lē´ən) *n.* (*Law*) a right to detain the goods of another until some claim has been satisfied. [F, from L *ligāmen*, a band, from *ligāre*, to bind]

lientery (lī´əntəri) *n.* diarrhoea in which the food passes rapidly through the bowels undigested. **lienteric** (-ter´-) *a.* [F *lienterie*, Gr. *leienteria* (*leios*, smooth, *entera*, bowels)]

lierne (liœn´) *n.* (*Archit.*) a cross-rib connecting the main ribs in Gothic vaulting, introduced about the middle of the 14th cent. [F, etym. uncertain]

☒ **liesure** common misspelling of LEISURE.

lieu (lū, loo) *n.* place, stead. **in lieu** instead, as a substitute. **in lieu of** instead of. [F, from L *locum*, nom. *locus*, place]

lieutenant (leften´ənt) *n.* 1 an officer acting as deputy or substitute to a superior. 2 an army officer ranking next below a captain. 3 a naval officer ranking next below a lieutenant-commander. 4 in the US, a police officer ranking next below a captain. 5 (*coll.*) an assistant adult leader of a Guide company. **Lord Lieutenant** LORD. **lieutenancy** *n.* (*pl.* **lieutenancies**) the post or commission of a lieutenant. **lieutenant colonel** *n.* an officer next in rank below a colonel, in actual command of a battalion. **lieutenant commander** *n.* a naval officer ranking between a lieutenant and a commander. **lieutenant general** *n.* an army officer next in rank below a general and above a major general. **lieutenant-governor** *n.* 1 a deputy governor. 2 the acting governor in subordination to a governor general. 3 (*N Am.*) the deputy to a state governor. 4 in Canada, the representative of the Crown in a province. [F (LIEU, TENANT), cp. LOCUM-TENENCY (under LOCUM)]

Usage note The usual N Am. pronunciation is (looten´ənt).

life (līf) *n.* (*pl.* **lives** (līvz)) 1 the state or condition which distinguishes animate beings from dead ones and from inorganic matter and involves the ability to grow, change, respond to stimuli, reproduce etc. 2 the period from birth to death. 3 the period from birth to the present time. 4 the period from the present to death. 5 any other specified period of a person's existence. 6 the period of time for which an object functions or operates. 7 living things collectively, animated existence. 8 human presence or activity. 9 a person's individual existence (*saved her life*). 10 a person's mode, manner or course of living; any particular aspect of this, such as one's professional or sex life. 11 human affairs. 12 a particular area of human activity or affairs. 13 animation, vivacity, spirit. 14 a person who or something which imparts spirit or animation. 15 the animating principle, the essential or inspiring idea (of a movement etc.). 16 someone or something that one devotes all or most of one's energy, attention or devotion to. 17 in art, the living form, esp. a nude model. 18 a person considered as the object of a policy of assurance. 19 the average period which a person of a given age may expect to live. 20 a narrative of one's existence, a biography. 21 (*coll.*) a life sentence. 22 each one of the points or chances to which each player is entitled in a game that are lost in certain contingencies. ~*a.* 1 for the duration or remainder of one's life. 2 in drawing, sculpture etc., taken from life. **a matter of life and death** a matter of utmost urgency. **for dear life** with extreme vigour, in order to escape death. **for one's life** for dear life. **for the life of me** even if my life depended upon it (used to indicate one's utter inability to do something). **large as life** LARGE. **larger than life** LARGE. **not on your life** under no circumstances. **the life and soul of** a person who is the chief source of amusement or interest, esp. at a party. **the life of Riley** (*coll.*) an easy, carefree existence. **the time of one's life** an experience of unequalled pleasure. **to bring to life** to give animation to, to enliven, to make interesting or exciting. **to come to life** **1** to emerge from unconsciousness, inactivity, torpor etc. **2** (of an inanimate object) to become animate. **3** (of a machine, engine) to start operating. **to give one's life** **1** to die in a self-sacrificial way. **2** to devote all one's time, energy and care. **to save one's life** under any circumstances at all (used to indicate one's utter inability to do something) (*can't speak a word of French to save his life*). **to save someone's life** **1** to prevent someone from dying. **2** (*coll.*) to help someone who is in serious difficulty. **to the life** **1** (of the way in which a likeness has been made) with great fidelity to the original. **2** (of a likeness) as if the original stood before one. **upon my life** a mild oath. **with life and limb** without serious injury. **life assurance, life insurance** *n.* insurance providing for the payment of a specified sum to a beneficiary on the policyholder's death, or to the policyholder on reaching a certain age. **lifebelt** *n.* a belt of buoyant or inflated material for supporting a person in the water. **lifeblood** *n.* **1** the blood necessary to life. **2** something which is essential to existence, success or strength. **lifeboat** *n.* **1** a boat specially constructed for saving life in storms and heavy seas. **2** a small boat carried by a ship for use in an emergency, esp. if the ship has to be abandoned. **lifeboatman** *n.* (*pl.* **lifeboatmen**) a member of the crew of a lifeboat. **lifebuoy** *n.* a buoyant device to support a person in the water. **life cycle** *n.* the series of changes in the form and function of an organism etc. during its lifetime. **life estate** *n.* a property that is held only until one's death, and then reverts to a specified heir. **life expectancy** *n.* the average number of years that a person of a certain age or in a certain category can expect to live. **life-force** *n.* **1** animating principle, driving force. **2** a vital urge supposed to be inherent in living organisms. **life form** *n.* **1** any living creature. **2** in science fiction, an alien being. **life-giving** *a.* uplifting, invigorating, animating. **lifeguard** *n.* a trained attendant at a bathing beach or pool who helps swimmers in difficulties. **Life Guards** *n.pl.* a regiment of cavalry forming part of the bodyguard of the British sovereign. **life history** *n.* (*pl.* **life histories**) **1** the events, achievements etc. that make up a person's life. **2** an account of these, often a tediously long one. **3** the series of changes undergone by an organism between conception and death. **life imprisonment** *n.* in the UK, imprisonment for an indefinite length of time, usu. about 15 years, the mandatory sentence after a conviction for murder. **life insurance** LIFE ASSURANCE (under LIFE). **life interest** *n.* an interest or estate terminating with the life of a person. **life jacket** *n.* a sleeveless inflatable or buoyant jacket used as a lifebelt. **lifeless** *a.* **1** destitute or deprived of life; dead, inanimate, inorganic, inert. **2** unconscious. **3** lacking vitality or interest, dull, heavy, spiritless, vapid. **4** deprived of physical energy. **lifelessly** *adv.* **lifelessness** *n.* **lifelike** *a.* **1** (of a portrait) like the original. **2** like a living being. **lifelikeness** *n.* **lifeline** *n.* **1** a rope used for saving life, esp. at sea. **2** a rope used as an additional safeguard. **3** a vital line of communication. **4** the line by which a deep-sea diver is raised and lowered or communicates with the surface. **5** in palmistry, a linear crease in the palm of the hand supposed to indicate the length of one's life. **6** an emergency telephone counselling service. **lifelong** *a.* (lasting) for the whole of one's life. **life mask** *n.* a cast taken from the face of a living person usu. with plaster of Paris. **life member** *n.* a person who is entitled to membership of an organization for the rest of their life. **life membership** *n.* **life peer** *n.* a peer whose title lapses at death. **life peerage** *n.* **life-preserver** *n.* **1** (*N Am.*) a lifebelt, life jacket etc. **2** a loaded stick or cane for defending one's life. **lifer** *n.* a person sentenced to imprisonment for life. **life raft** *n.* a raft kept on board ships etc. for use in emergencies. **life-saver** *n.* **1** a person who saves a person's life. **2** a person trained to rescue swimmers or bathers from drowning. **3** (*coll.*) a person who or something which provides help in distress. **life-saving** *a.* **life science** *n.* a science that deals with the structure and function of living organisms, such as biology, medicine, anthropology or zoology. **life sentence** *n.* **1** a sentence of life imprisonment. **2** something that will affect, confine or threaten one for the whole of one's life. **life-size, life-sized** *a.* representing the actual size of an object. **life-span** *n.* the length of time during which an organism lives or a machine etc. remains functional. **lifestyle** *n.* the attitudes, behaviour, surroundings etc. characteristic of an individual or group. **life-support** *a.* of or relating to a device or system which maintains a person's life, e.g. during a serious illness. **life-support machine** *n.* a respirator or ventilator. **life's work** *n.* the work to which one devotes the best part of one's life. **life-table** *n.* a table of statistics showing the average expectation of life at different ages. **life-threatening** *a.* that may cause death. **lifetime** *n.* **1** the duration of one's life. **2** the length of time something functions. [OE *līf* (cp. Icel. *līf*, OFris. *līf*, Dut. *lijf*, G *Leib*, cogn. with LIVE[1], LEAVE[1], from Indo-Eur. root *leip-*), cp. Gr. *aleiphein*, to anoint, *liparēs*, persistent]

lift[1] (lift) *v.t.* **1** to raise to a higher position, to elevate, to hold or support on high. **2** to raise or take up from the ground, to pick up. **3** to take hold of in order to move or remove, e.g. from a hook or shelf. **4** to move or direct upwards. **5** to raise, rescind or remove (a restriction, ban). **6** to give one's confidence or spirits a boost. **7** to raise to a higher spiritual, intellectual etc. plane. **8** to improve the quality of, esp. to make more interesting and lively. **9** to make audible; to make louder; to raise the pitch of. **10** (*coll.*) to carry off, to steal, to appropriate, to plagiarize. **11** to transport, esp. by air. **12** to dig up (root vegetables) to harvest them. **13** to hit, kick etc. (a ball) into the air. **14** (*poet.*) to support on high. **15** to perform cosmetic surgery to prevent wrinkling, sagging etc. *~v.i.* **1** to rise, to move upwards. **2** to perform or attempt to perform the act of raising something. **3** to rise and disperse, as a mist. **4** (of a floor) to swell and bulge upwards. *~n.* **1** an act of lifting. **2** a compartment or platform for people or goods travelling up and down a shaft between different floors of a building, levels in a mine etc. **3** any of various devices for transporting up mountain slopes. **4** a ride in a vehicle as a passenger for part or all of a journey. **5** the component of the aerodynamic force on an aircraft or aerofoil acting upwards at right angles to the airflow and opposing the pull of gravity. **6** a rise in spirits, morale. **7** a rise in condition, status etc. **8** a helping hand. **9** a layer of material inserted in the heel of a shoe, esp. to increase the height of the wearer. **10** a rise in the height of the ground. **11** the height to which anything is lifted; e.g. the distance water rises in a canal lock. **not to lift a finger** FINGER. **to lift down** to pick up and move to a lower position. **to lift off** **1** (of a spacecraft, rocket) to take off vertically from a launching pad. **2** to remove or detach by raising slightly. **3** to be removable by lifting; to come away easily from a surface to which it adheres. **to lift the elbow** ELBOW. **to lift up one's head** to hold one's head with pride. **to lift up one's voice** (to begin) to sing out loud. **lift-lock** *n.* a canal lock. **lift-off** *n.* **1** the take-off of a rocket or missile. **2** the instant at which this occurs. **lift pump** *n.* a pump that lifts to its own level, as distinct from a *force-pump*. [Icel. *lypta*, rel. to *lopt*, the air, and LIFT[2]]

lift[2] (lift) *n.* (*Sc.*) the sky, the upper regions of the air. [OE *lyft*, cogn. with LIFT[1] and with LOFT]

ligament (lig´əmənt) *n.* **1** a short band of fibrous tissue by which bones are bound together. **2** any tough bands or tissues holding parts together. **3** †anything which binds, a bond, a tie. **ligamental** (-men´-), **ligamentary**, **ligamentous** *a.* [F, from L *ligāmentum*, from *ligāre*, see LIGATE]

ligand (lī´gənd, lig´-) *n.* a single atom, molecule, radical or ion attached to a central atom to form a coordination complex. [L *ligandus*, from *ligāre*, see LIGATE]

ligate (lī´gāt) *v.t.* to tie with a ligature. **ligation** (-ā´shən) *n.* **ligative** (lig´ətiv) *a.* **ligature** (lig´əchə) *n.* **1** something which binds, esp. a thread or cord to tie arteries or veins to stop bleeding or a wire used in removing tumours. **2** (*Mus.*) a tie connecting notes, a slur. **3** (*Print.*) two or more letters cast on one shank, as *ff*, *ffi*. **4** anything that unites, a bond. **5** the act of binding or tying. *~v.t.* to bind with a ligature. [L *ligātus*, p.p. of *ligāre*, to tie]

liger (lī´gə) *n.* a cross between a lion and a tigress.

light[1] (līt) *n.* **1** electromagnetic radiation which, by acting on the retina, stimulates the sense of sight. **2** the sensation produced by the stimulation of the visual organs. **3** the state or condition in which things are visible, opposed to *darkness*. **4** the amount of illumination in a place or required by a person. **5** a source of light, a lamp, a candle, the sun etc. **6** daylight. **7** a traffic light. **8** (*pl.*) illuminations. **9** something by which light is admitted into a place, a window, a division of a window, esp. a perpendicular division in a mullioned window, a pane or glazed compartment in a greenhouse. **10** something that kindles or ignites, e.g. a spark or flame; a device which produces this. **11** exposure, publicity, general knowledge. **12** point of view, aspect. **13** mental illumination, elucidation, enlightenment. **14** brightness on the face or in the eyes. **15** (*pl.*) one's intellectual powers or capacity. **16** a person who or something which enlightens, a model, an example. **17** the manner in which the light appears to fall on the objects in a picture. **18** a part of a picture which is illuminated or highlighted. **19** the answer to a clue in a crossword. **20** (*often pl.*, *Law*) the light falling on a window which a neighbour is prohibited from obstructing. **21** (*pl.*, *sl.*) †eyes. *~a.* **1** (of a room, space) well provided with (natural) light, bright. **2** (of colours) reflecting a lot of light, pale. **3** (of hair, complexion) pale-coloured, fair. *~v.t.* (*past*, *p.p.* **lit** (lit), **lighted**) **1** to kindle, to set fire to. **2** to give light to. **3** to fill (up) with light. **4** to conduct with a light. **5** to brighten. *~v.i.* **1** to take fire, to begin to burn. **2** to be illuminated. **3** to brighten (up). **according to one's lights** according to one's information or knowledge of a situation. **in a bad/ poor light** in such a way as to reflect discredit on. **in a good/ favourable light** in such a way as to reflect credit on. **in the light of** considering, allowing for. **out like a light** deeply asleep or unconscious. **the light of one's life** (*usu. facet.*) a much loved person or thing. **to bring to light** to discover, to detect, to disclose. **to come to light** to become known. **to hide one's light under a bushel** BUSHEL[1]. **to light up 1** (*coll.*) to light a cigarette, pipe etc. **2** to illuminate. **3** to switch on (car) lights. **4** to become cheerful or animated suddenly. **to see the light** SEE[1]. **to shed/ throw light on/ upon** to elucidate, to explain. **to stand in one' s own light** to frustrate one's own purposes or wishes. **light bulb** *n.* a glass bulb filled with a low density gas and containing a metal filament which glows when an electric current is passed through it. **light-emitting diode** *n.* a semiconductor junction which emits light when an electric current passes through it, used in indicators and the displays of calculators, watches etc. **lightfast** *a.* (of dye, pigments) not affected by exposure to light. **lightfastness** *n.* **light-gun** *n.* a light-pen. **lighthouse** *n.* a tower or other structure which supports a powerful light for the warning and guidance of ships at sea. **lighting** *n.* **1** the act of providing light or illumination to something. **2** the equipment used to provide artificial light to an area, esp. to a stage, film set, photographic studio etc. **3** the effect or effects produced by the use of such equipment or by natural light. **lighting cameraman** *n.* (*pl.* **lighting cameramen**) the person who designs the lighting of scenes on a film set and supervises its execution. **lighting man** *n.* (*pl.* **lighting men**) a person in charge of the lighting equipment and lighting effects in a theatre. **lighting-up time** *n.* the time of day when vehicles are required by law to show their lights. **lightish**[1] *a.* **lightless** *a.* **light meter** *n.* EXPOSURE METER (under EXPOSE). **lightness**[1] *n.* **light of day** *n.* **1** daylight. **2** public awareness, general notice. **light-pen** *n.* **1** a pen-shaped photoelectric device which when pointed at a visual display unit senses whether a spot is illuminated, used for creating or entering information on a computer esp. in graphics and design. **2** a pen-shaped light-emitting device used to read bar codes. **light pollution** *n.* excessive brightness in the night sky caused by street lamps etc. **lightproof** *a.* able to resist any harmful effects caused by exposure to (strong) light. **light-sensitive** *a.* that reacts photoelectrically, e.g. by generating an electric current when exposed to light. **lightship** *n.* a moored vessel carrying a light to give warning or guidance to ships. **light show** *n.* a display of multicoloured lights or visual effects using laser beams etc., esp. at a pop concert. **lights out** *n.* **1** the time when residents in an institution (e.g. a boarding school) are expected to retire for the night. **2** a signal indicating when lights are to be put out. **light table** *n.* (a table with) a ground-glass surface illuminated from below used in working on layouts with translucent materials. **light year** *n.* **1** the distance (about 6,000,000,000,000 miles or 9460 × 10^9 km) travelled by light in one year. **2** (*pl.*, *coll.*) a long way away from. **lit-up** *a.* (*coll.*) slightly drunk. [OE *lēoht* (cp. Dut.and G *Licht*, Icel. *ljos*, *logi*, L *lux*, Gr. *leukos*, white)]

light[2] (līt) *a.* **1** of small weight, not heavy; easy to be lifted, carried, moved, handled etc. **2** having relatively low density (*light metal*). **3** short in weight, below the standard weight. **4** not great in degree, number, intensity etc. (*light traffic*). **5** (of a task, duties etc.) easy to perform, not requiring great effort. **6** (of equipment) employed in or adapted for easy work. **7** (of a type of vehicle) adapted for small loads. **8** (of a ship or vehicle) unladen or not heavily laden. **9** (of troops) lightly armed and equipped (*light infantry*). **10** (of a meal) small in quantity and consisting of easily digestible food. **11** (of food) not rich, low in fat, sugar etc. easily digested. **12** (of wine, beer) not strong, low in alcohol and easily digested. **13** (of bread, sponge) not dense, well risen and aerated. **14** (of reading, entertainment) intended for amusement, not serious, profound or deeply moving. **15** (of a remark) of little consequence, unimportant, trivial. **16** (of movement) nimble, active, quick. **17** (of a building or structure) not massive, not heavy in construction or appearance. **18** (of fabrics) thin, delicate. **19** (of a blow, impact) not forcible, gentle, slight. **20** (of a mood) cheerful, merry. **21** dizzy, giddy; delirious. **22** (of soil) loose, porous, sandy. **23** (of type) not bold, thick or heavy. **24** †(esp. of a woman) wanton, unchaste; flighty, frivolous, fickle. *~adv.* **1** lightly. **2** with little baggage or a small load. **light on** (*coll.*) short of, having insufficient. **light on hand** HAND. **to make light of 1** to treat as insignificant. **2** to treat as pardonable or excusable. **light air** *n.* a very gentle movement of the air, force one on the Beaufort scale. **light bob** *n.* (*sl.*) a light infantryman. **light breeze** *n.* a gentle breeze, force two on the Beaufort scale. **light engine** *n.* a locomotive running light, that is, with no train attached. **lighter-than-air** *a.* (of an aircraft) buoyant in air, weighing less than the air it displaces. **light-fingered** *a.* **1** given to thieving. **2** having nimble fingers. **light flyweight** *n.* **1** an amateur boxer in the lower part of the flyweight category, weighing not more than 106 lb. (48 kg). **2** this weight category. **light-handed** *a.* **1** light of touch, light in handling. **2** short of the proper complement of workers. **light-handedly** *adv.* **light-handedness** *n.* **light-headed** *a.* **1** delirious. **2** giddy. **3** frivolous, thoughtless. **light-headedness** *n.* **light-hearted** *a.* **1** free from care or anxiety, merry, cheerful. **2** casual, not or insufficiently serious. **light-heartedly** *adv.* **light-heartedness** *n.* **light heavy-weight** *n.* **1** a boxer or wrestler in the weight category intermediate between middleweight and heavyweight. **2** this weight category. **light horse** *n.* lightly armed and very mobile cavalry. **light industry** *n.* industry that produces smaller and lighter goods. **lightish²** *a.* **lightly** *adv.* in a light manner. **light middleweight** *n.* **1** an amateur boxer weighing 148–157 lb. (67–71 kg). **2** this weight category. **light-minded** *a.* fickle, unsteady, volatile. **light-mindedly** *adv.* **light-mindedness** *n.* **lightness²** *n.* **light opera** *n.* **1** an operetta or opera with a light, comic theme. **2** the genre to which such works belong. **light railway** *n.* a railway, usu. less than the standard gauge, adapted for light traffic. **light touch** *n.* the ability to handle people or affairs delicately or tactfully. **lightweight** *n.* **1** an animal or person below average weight. **2** a boxer, wrestler, weightlifter etc. in the weight category intermediate between featherweight and welterweight. **3** this weight category. **4** (*coll.*) a person of small importance or ability. ~*a.* **1** light in weight. **2** trivial. **light welterweight** *n.* **1** an amateur boxer weighing 132–140 lb. (60–63.5 kg). **2** this weight category. [OE *lēoht* (cp. Icel. *lēttr*, G *leicht*, Sansk. *laghu*, Gr. *elachus*)]

light³ (līt) *v.i.* (*past, p.p.* **lit** (lit), **lighted**) **1** (of a bird) to descend as from flight, to settle. **2** †to alight, to dismount. ~*v.t.* (*Naut.*) to lift or help to move (along etc.). **to light into** (*sl.*) to attack physically or verbally. **to light on/ upon** to happen on, to find by chance. **to light out** (*sl.*) to leave in a hurry. [*OE lihtan*, orig. to lighten or relieve of a burden, as LIGHT²]

lighten¹ (lī´tən) *v.i.* **1** to become light, to brighten. **2** to emit lightning, to flash. **3** to shine out. ~*v.t.* to illuminate, to enlighten. [OE *lēohtan*]

Usage note See note under LIGHTNING.

lighten² (lī´tən) *v.t.* **1** to reduce in weight. **2** to reduce the weight or load of. **3** to relieve, to mitigate, to alleviate. **4** to cheer. ~*v.i.* **1** to be lightened, to grow lighter. **2** to become less burdensome. **lightening** *n.* a feature of late pregnancy when the head of the foetus engages with the pelvis and the sensation of pressure on the diaphragm is reduced. [LIGHT², -EN]

Usage note See note under LIGHTNING.

lighter¹ (lī´tə) *n.* **1** a pocket appliance for lighting cigarettes, a pipe etc. **2** a person who or something which ignites.

lighter² (lī´tə) *n.* a large, open, usu. flat-bottomed boat, used in loading and unloading ships. **lighterage** (-rij) *n.* **1** the transportation of cargo in lighters. **2** the charge for this. **lighterman** *n.* (*pl.* **lightermen**) a person who works on a lighter. [perh. from Dut. *lichter* or LIGHT², -ER]

lightish¹ LIGHT¹.

lightish² LIGHT².

lightness¹ LIGHT¹.

lightness² LIGHT².

lightning (līt´ning) *n.* the dazzling flash caused by the discharge of electricity between clouds or from a cloud to the earth. ~*a.* very fast or sudden. **lightning-arrester** *n.* a contrivance for deflecting the electrical discharge in thunderstorms and protecting electrical instruments. **lightning bug** *n.* (*N Am.*) a firefly. **lightning conductor,** (*N Am.*) **lightning rod** *n.* a wire or rod for carrying the electric discharge to earth and protecting a building, mast etc., against damage. **lightning strike** *n.* a strike by workers at very short notice, often without official union authorization.

Usage note The spellings of the nouns *lightning* and *lightening* should not be confused: *lightning* is a flash of light, and *lightening* means making or becoming light (part of the verbs LIGHTEN¹ and LIGHTEN²).

lights (līts) *n.pl.* the lungs of animals, esp. as food for cats etc. [LIGHT²]

lightsome¹ (līt´səm) *a.* **1** light-hearted, playful. **2** airy, graceful, nimble. **lightsomely** *adv.* **lightsomeness** *n.* [LIGHT²]

†**lightsome²** (līt´səm) *a.* **1** luminous, light-giving. **2** bright, lighted up. [LIGHT¹]

lign- LIGNI-.

lignaloes (līnal´ōz) *n.* the fragrant wood of an Asian tree *Aquilaria agallocha*, also called *eaglewood*. [late L *lignum aloēs*, trans. of Gr. *xulaloē*, wood of the aloe]

ligneous (lig´niəs) *a.* **1** made or consisting of wood. **2** resembling wood, woody. [L *ligneus*, from *lignum*, wood]

ligni- (lig´ni), **ligno-** (-nō), **lign-** *comb. form* of or relating to wood. **lignicolous** (-nikələs), **lignicole** (-nicōl) *a.* growing or living in or on wood. **ligniform** (-nifawm) *a.* having the appearance of wood. **lignify** (-fī) *v.t., v.i.* (*3rd pers. sing. pres.* **lignifies,** *pres.p.* **lignifying,** *past, p.p.* **lignified**) to (cause to) become woody through the deposition of lignin. **lignification** (-fikā´shən) *n.* [L *lignum*, wood]

lignin (lig´nin) *n.* a complex organic material which forms the woody cell walls of certain plants.

ligniperdous (lignipœ´dəs) *a.* destructive of wood, as certain insects. [L *perdere*, to destroy]

lignite (lig´nīt) *n.* a partially carbonized coal showing fibrous woody structure, usu. of Cretaceous or Tertiary age. **lignitic** (-nit´-) *a.*

lignivorous (ligniv´ərəs) *a.* feeding on wood.

ligno- LIGNI-.

lignocaine (lig´nōkān) *n.* a local anaesthetic, usu. administered by injection.

lignum vitae (lignəm vī´tē, vē´tī) *n.* the very hard and heavy wood of various tropical American trees, esp. *Guaiacum officinale.* [L, wood of life]

ligroin (lig´rōin) *n.* a volatile fraction of petroleum used as a solvent. [etym. uncertain]

ligule (lig´ūl) *n.* **1** a membranous process at the top of the sheath beneath the blade of a grass. **2** any of the rays of a composite plant. **ligula** (-lə) *n.* (*pl.* **ligulae** (-lē), **ligulas**) **1** the terminal part of the labium of an insect. **2** a tongue-like organ or part. **ligular** *a.* **ligulate** (-lət), **ligulated** (-lā´tid) *a.* (*Bot.*) **1** strap-shaped. **2** having a ligule or ligula. [L, dim. of *lingua*, tongue]

likable LIKEABLE (under LIKE²).

like¹ (līk) *prep.* **1** similar to, resembling (*a voice like a foghorn*). **2** characteristic of (*it's not like her to forget*). **3** in the manner of, to the same extent or degree as. **4** such as, for example. ~*a.* similar, alike, having all or many of the same qualities as. ~*adv.* **1** (*coll., dial.*) likely (*as like as not*). **2** (*coll.*) as it were, so to speak. **3** †in the same manner as. ~*conj.* (*coll.*) **1** in the same manner as. **2** as if. ~*n.* **1** a counterpart. **2** a similar or equal thing, person or event. **and the like** and other similar things, etcetera. **as like as not** very probably. **like anything**

ANYTHING (under ANY). **like as not** very probably. **like a ton of bricks** BRICK. **like hell** HELL. **like so** in this way, thus. **more like it** nearer or more closely resembling what is desired. **nothing like 1** in no way similar to or comparable with. **2** far short of (what is required). **of like mind** holding a similar or identical opinion. **the likes of** (*coll., usu. derog.*) people such as. **to feel like** FEEL. **to look like 1** to resemble in appearance. **2** to have the appearance of. **3** to seem likely. **to make like** MAKE[1]. **what is he/ she/ it like?** what are his/ her/its main characteristics? **likely** *a.* (*comp.* **likelier,** *superl.* **likeliest**) **1** probable, credible, plausible. **2** liable, to be expected (to). **3** promising, suitable, well-adapted. *~adv.* probably. **likelihood, likeliness** *n.* **like-minded** *a.* having similar disposition, opinions, purpose etc. **liken** *v.t.* to compare, to represent as similar (to). **likeness** *n.* **1** similarity, resemblance. **2** a picture or other representation of a person or thing. **3** form, appearance, guise. **likewise** *adv.* **1** also, moreover, too. **2** in like manner. [OE *līc* in *gelīc* (cp. Dut. *gelijk*, Icel. *līkr, glīkr*, G *gleich*, also lich)]

Usage note (1) The use of *like* as a conjunction is sometimes disapproved of, though it is common. In formal contexts it is safer to use *as* or *as if* instead. (2) In standard British English, *likely* as an adverb is always preceded by *very, more* or *most.*

like[2] (līk) *v.t.* **1** to find pleasure or satisfaction in, to enjoy. **2** to be pleased with. **3** to be inclined towards or attracted by. **4** to be fond of. **5** wish, prefer (*would like her to be there*). **6** to feel about (*How do you like your new job?*). **7** (*usu. impers.*) †to be pleasing to, to suit. *~n.* (*pl.*) things that one likes. **I like that!** (*iron.*) a reaction to a piece of brazen effrontery. **like it or lump it** LUMP[2]. **like it or not** (*coll.*) whether one is pleased or not. **likeable, likable** *a.* pleasant, amiable, easy to like. **likeability** (-bil´-), **likeableness** *n.* **liking** *n.* **1** inclination, fondness, fancy (for). **2** taste, satisfaction. **to one's liking** to one's taste. [OE *līcian* (cp. Dut. *lijken*, Icel. *līka*) as LIKE[1]]

-like (līk) *suf.* **1** forming adjectives, as in *saintlike, warlike.* **2** forming adverbs, as in *childlike* (*she replied*). [LIKE[1]]

likely, liken etc. LIKE[1].

lilac (lī´lək) *n.* **1** a shrub of the genus *Syringa*, esp. *S. vulgaris*, with very fragrant pale violet or purple flowers, white in cultivated varieties. **2** a pale violet or purple colour. *~a.* of the colour of lilac. [F and Sp., from Arab. and Pers. *līlăk*, var. of *nīlak*, dim. of *nīl*, blue, indigo]

liliaceous LILY.

Lilliputian (lilipū´shən) *a.* **1** of or relating to Lilliput, an imaginary country in Swift's *Gulliver's Travels*, the inhabitants of which were minute. **2** tiny, diminutive. *~n.* **1** a native of Lilliput. **2** a very small person or thing.

LILO *abbr.* last in, last out.

Lilo® (lī´lō), **Li-lo** *n.* (*pl.* **Lilos, Li-los**) a type of inflatable mattress used in camping, on the beach etc.

lilt (lilt) *n.* **1** a jaunty, springing rhythm or movement. **2** a lively song or tune. **3** the cadence or accent of an individual voice, esp. a pleasant and musical one. *~v.i.* **1** to sing, speak, sound out with a lilt. **2** to walk or move jauntily. [ME *lulte*, etym. uncertain]

lily (lil´i) *n.* (*pl.* **lilies**) **1** a flower or plant of the bulbous genus *Lilium*, producing white or coloured trumpet-shaped flowers of great beauty, esp. the Madonna lily, *L. candidum.* **2** any of various similar plants, such as the Lent lily or daffodil, the water lily etc. **3** (*Her.*) the fleur-de-lis. **4** a person or thing of unsullied whiteness or purity. *~a.* **1** pure white. **2** pale. **to gild/ paint the lily** to try to improve what is already perfect. **liliaceous** (-ā´shəs) *a.* of or relating to lilies, or the Liliaceae, a family of plants with elongated leaves growing from bulbs, corms or rhizomes. **lily iron** *n.* the detachable barbed head of a harpoon. **lily-livered** *a.* cowardly. **lily of the valley** *n.* (*pl.* **lilies of the valley**) a fragrant spring-flowering plant of the genus *Canvallaria*, with a scape of white hanging cuplike flowers. **lily pad** *n.* the broad floating leaf of the water lily. **lily-trotter** *n.* a jacana, esp. an African one. **lily white** *n.* a pure white colour. **lily-white** *a.* **1** pure white. **2** (*coll.*) irreproachable. [OE *lilie*, L *līlium*, Gr. *leirion*]

lima bean (lē´mə) *n.* **1** a tropical American climbing bean plant, *Phaseolus lunatus.* **2** the flat white edible seed of this; a butter bean. [*Lima*, capital of Peru]

limaceous (līmā´shəs), **limacine** (lī´məsīn, lim´-, -sin) *a.* of or relating to the genus *Limax* or the family Limacidae which contains the slugs. **limaciform** (-mas´ifawm) *a.* **limaçon** (lim´əson, lēmasõ´) *n.* (*Math.*) a particular curve based on the union of two ovals. [L *līmax -ācis*, slug or snail, -ACEOUS]

limb[1] (lim) *n.* **1** each of the articulated extremities of an animal, an arm, leg or wing. **2** a main branch of a tree. **3** a projecting part. **4** a member, branch or arm of a larger group or institution. **5** (*coll.*) (*also* **limb of Satan**) an impish child or urchin. *~v.t.* to tear the limbs from, to dismember. **out on a limb 1** in a precarious or exposed position. **2** isolated. **to tear limb from limb** to dismember savagely. **with life and limb** LIFE. **limbed** *a.* (*usu. in comb.*) having limbs, as *large-limbed.* **limbless** *a.* [OE *lim* (cp. Icel. *limr*)]

limb[2] (lim) *n.* **1** the outermost edge of the sun, moon etc. **2** the graduated arc of a sextant etc. **3** the expanded portion of a gamosepalous corolla, petal etc. **limbate** (lim´bət) *a.* bordered, having a differently-coloured border. [L *limbus*, border, edging]

limber[1] (lim´bə) *a.* **1** lithe, agile. **2** flexible. **to limber up 1** to stretch and flex the muscles in preparation for physical exercise. **2** to make (something) flexible, to loosen up. [etym. uncertain]

limber[2] (lim´bə) *n.* the detachable part of a gun carriage consisting of two wheels and ammunition box. *~v.t.* to attach the limber to the gun (usu. with *up*). *~v.i.* to fasten (up) the limber and gun. [formerly *limmer, lymor*, perh. from F *limonière*, from *limon*, shaft]

limber[3] (lim´bə) *n.* (*Naut.*) **1** a gutter on each side of the keelson for draining. **2** (*pl.*) the gutters and holes in the floor timbers. [perh. a corr. of F *lumière*, light, hole]

limbo[1] (lim´bō) *n.* (*pl.* **limbos**) **1** the edge or uttermost limit of hell, the abode of those who died unbaptized through no fault of their own, such as the just before Christ and infants. **2** an uncertain or transitional state. **3** a place of neglect or oblivion. **4** prison, confinement. [L, abl. of *limbus*, see LIMB[2]]

limbo[2] (lim´bō) *n.* (*pl.* **limbos**) a West Indian dance in which the participants bend backwards and pass under a bar. [etym. uncertain]

Limburger (lim´bœgə) *n.* a white cheese with a strong taste and smell. [*Limburg*, a province of Belgium]

lime[1] (līm) *n.* **1** a white caustic alkaline substance, calcium oxide, obtained by burning calcium carbonate (usu. in limestone form), used in building and agriculture; quicklime. **2** calcium hydroxide, a white powder obtained by the action of water on quicklime; slaked lime. **3** any of various calcium compounds used to improve lime-deficient soil. *~v.t.* **1** to manure with lime; to spread lime over (land). **2** to dress (hides) in lime and water. **3** to smear with birdlime. **4** †to ensnare. **lime burner** *n.* a person who burns limestone to make lime. **limekiln** *n.* a kiln in which limestone is calcined and reduced to lime. **limelight** *n.* **1** a form of lighting, formerly used in theatres, produced by projecting a jet of ignited hydrogen and oxygen upon a ball of lime, making it incandescent. **2** the glare of publicity. **lime-pit** *n.* a pit for liming hides. **limestone** *n.* any rock the basis of which is calcium carbonate, esp. mountain limestone, the principal rock of the Carboniferous series, used as building material and in the manufacture of cement. **limestone pavement** *n.* (*Geol.*) a horizontal surface of exposed limestone intersected with deep fissures and resembling a pavement. **limewash** *n.* whitewash. ~*v.t.* to whitewash. **lime water** *n.* a solution of lime in water used medicinally and to detect the presence of carbon dioxide. **limy** *a.* **1** of the nature of, resembling or containing lime. **2** smeared with birdlime; viscous, tenacious. **liminess** *n.* [OE *līm* (cp. Dut. *lijm*, Icel. *līm*, G *Leim*, also L *līmus*, mud, LOAM)]

lime[2] (līm) *n.* (*also* **lime tree**) any tree of the genus *Tilia*, esp. *T. europaea*, with soft timber, heart-shaped leaves, and small clusters of delicately-scented flowers. [perh. var. of OE *lind*, LINDEN]

lime[3] (līm) *n.* **1** (*also* **lime tree**) a small tropical citrus tree, *Citrus aurantifolia*. **2** the greenish-yellow fruit of this tree with acid flesh. **3** lime juice or a squash or cordial made from it. **limeade** (-ād´) *n.* a drink made from sweetened lime juice and carbonated water. **lime green** *n.* a bright yellowish-green colour. ~*a.* (*also* **lime-green**) of this colour. **lime juice** *n.* the juice of the lime used as a beverage. **Limey** *n.* (*pl.* **Limeys**) (*N Am.*, *sl.*) **1** a British sailor (from the former use of lime juice on British ships to prevent scurvy). **2** any British person. [F, from Sp. *lima*, Arab. *līmah* (cp. LEMON)]

limelight LIME[1].

limen (lī´mən) *n.* (*Psych.*) the stage of consciousness at which a given stimulus begins to produce sensation and below which it is imperceptible. **liminal** (lim´i-) *a.* **1** (*Psych.*) of or relating to a limen. **2** marginal, insignificant. **3** positioned adjacent to or straddling a border or threshold. [L, threshold]

limerick (lim´ərik) *n.* a nonsense verse, usu. of five lines, the first, second and fifth having three feet and rhyming together, and the third and fourth having two feet and a different rhyme. [said to be from the chorus 'Will you come up to *Limerick*?' sung at the end of impromptu verses at convivial parties in Ireland]

limes (lī´mēz) *n.* (*pl.* **limites** (lim´itēz)) the fortified boundary of the Roman Empire. [L]

limit (lim´it) *n.* **1** a boundary, a line, point or edge marking termination or utmost extent. **2** (*pl.*) the boundary of an area, district. **3** the maximum or minimum amount permissible or possible. **4** a restraint, a check. **5** (*Math.*) a value, position, quantity etc. which a function or the sum of a series can approach indefinitely. ~*v.t.* (*pres.p.* **limiting**, *past*, *p.p.* **limited**) **1** to set a limit or boundary to. **2** to confine within certain bounds. **3** to restrict (to). **4** to serve as boundary or restriction to. **off limits** out of bounds, esp. to military personnel. **to be the limit** to be unacceptable, intolerable or extremely annoying. **within limits** to a certain degree or extent. **without limit** unrestrictedly; indefinitely. **limitable** *a.* **limitarian** (-teə´ri-) *n.* a person who believes in redemption for only a limited number of mankind. **limitary** *a.* **1** limited, circumscribed. **2** limiting, confining. **limitation** (-ā´shən) *n.* **1** the act of limiting; the state of being limited. **2** (*usu. pl.*) something which limits a person's achievements, competence etc. **3** a restriction. **4** (*Law*) the period within which an action must be brought and beyond which it may not lie. **limitative** (-ətiv) *a.* **limited** *a.* **1** not universal or general, confined within limits. **2** restricted, narrow. **3** few, sparse, scanty. **4** (*coll.*) not very clever or well-read. **5** (after the name of a company) whose shareholders have limited liability. ~*n.* a limited company. **limited company** *n.* a company whose shareholders have limited liability. **limited edition** *n.* an edition of a book, print etc. of which only a small number is issued. **limited liability** *n.* responsibility for the debts of a company only to a specified amount, which is proportionate to the amount of stock held. **limited liability company** *n.* a limited company. **limitedly** *adv.* **limited monarchy** *n.* a monarchy in which the power of the sovereign is limited by a constitution. **limitedness** *n.* **limited redemption** *n.* (*Theol.*) the doctrine that only a portion of the human race can be saved. **limiter** *n.* **1** a person who or something which limits. **2** an electronic circuit or device which produces an output in a range between certain predetermined values whatever the scale of the input. **limitless** *a.* [F *limite*, L *līmitem*, nom. *līmes*, rel. to LIMEN]

limites LIMES.

limitrophe (lim´itrōf) *a.* on the border, adjacent (to). [F, from late L *līmi trophus*, L *līmes līmitis*, LIMIT, Gr. *-trophos*, feeding, from *trephein*, to feed]

limivorous (limiv´ərəs) *a.* (*Zool.*) mud-eating. [L *līmus*, mud-, -VOROUS (under -VORE)]

limn (lim) *v.t.* **1** †to paint or draw, to depict, to portray, esp. in watercolour. **2** (*Hist.*) to illuminate (a book, manuscript etc.). **limner** (lim´nə) *n.* [ME *limnen*, contr. from *luminen*, OF *luminer*]

limnology (limnol´əji) *n.* the study of the physical, biological, geographical etc. features of lakes, ponds and other freshwater bodies. **limnological** (-loj´-) *a.* **limnologist** *n.* [Gr. *limnē*, lake, -LOGY]

limo (lim´ō) *n.* (*pl.* **limos**) (*coll.*) short for LIMOUSINE.

limonite (lī´mənīt) *n.* a common mineral consisting of hydrated ferric oxides, a source of iron. [Gr. *leimōn*, meadow]

limousine (lim´əzēn) *n.* a large opulent car (orig. having a closed body with a separate driver's seat), esp. one with a glass partition dividing the driver from the passengers. [F, orig. a coarse cape or cloak of wool or goat's hair]

limp[1] (limp) *v.i.* **1** to walk lamely, esp. dragging one injured leg. **2** to proceed slowly and with difficulty. **3** (of verse, logic etc.) to be irregular. ~*n.* a limping step or walk. **limpingly** *adv.* [etym. uncertain, perh. from obs. *limphalt*, lame, OE *lemp-healt*]

limp[2] (limp) *a.* **1** wanting in stiffness, flaccid, flexible, pliable. **2** lacking in energy or impact. **3** (of book covers) not stiffened by boards. **limply** *adv.* **limpness** *n.* **limp-wristed** *a.* **1** (of a man) effeminate. **2** effete, ineffectual. [etym. uncertain]

limpet (lim´pit) *n.* **1** any individual of the genus of gastropods *Patella*, having an open conical shell, found adhering firmly to rocks. **2** a tenacious person or thing. **limpet mine** *n.* an explosive device which clings to a ship's hull, tank etc. by magnetic or adhesive means. [ME *lempet*, OE *lempedu*, late L *lampēdra*, limpet, LAMPREY]

limpid (lim´pid) *a.* **1** clear, pellucid, transparent. **2** lucid, perspicuous. **limpidity** (-pid´-) *n.* **limpidly** *adv.* [F *limpide*, L *limpidus*, rel. to *lympha*, LYMPH]

limpkin (limp´kin) *n.* a tropical American wading bird, *Aramus guarauna*, similar to a rail, with dark brown plumage and white markings. [LIMP[1], -KIN, so named because of its awkward gait]

limulus (lim´ūləs) *n.* (*pl.* **limuli** (-lī)) a horseshoe crab of the genus *Limulus*. [New L from *līmus*, looking sideways]

limy LIME[1].

linage (lī´nij) *n.* **1** amount of printed matter reckoned by lines. **2** payment by the line.

Usage note The nouns *linage* and *lineage* should not be confused: *linage* refers to printed matter, and *lineage* to ancestry.

linchpin (linch´pin), **lynchpin** *n.* **1** a pin serving to hold a wheel on the axle. **2** a person or thing essential to an organization etc. [OE *lynis*, an axle-tree (cp. Dut. *luns*, G *Lünse*) PIN]

Lincoln green (ling´kən) *n.* **1** bright green cloth formerly made at Lincoln. **2** its colour.

lincrusta (linkrŭs´tə) *n.* a type of thick wallpaper with designs embossed in bold relief. [L *linum*, thread, *crusta*, skin, crust]

Lincs. (lingks) *abbr.* Lincolnshire.

linctus (lingk´təs) *n.* (*pl.* **linctuses**) a syrupy cough medicine. [L, a licking, from *lingere*, to lick]

linden (lin´dən) *n.* a tree of the genus *Tilia*, a lime tree. [OE *lind* (cp. Dut. and G *Linde*, Gr. *elatē*, fir)]

line[1] (līn) *n.* **1** a threadlike mark; such a mark drawn by a pencil, pen, graver or other instrument. **2** a streak, narrow band, seam, furrow, wrinkle etc. resembling this. **3** (*Math.*) something which has length without breadth or thickness. **4** the track of a moving point. **5** the curve connecting a series of points. **6** the edge or contour of a shape, outline, lineament. **7** such outlines collectively as a feature of art or of an artist's style. **8** (*pl.*) the general appearance or outline of a thing. **9** a limit, a boundary. **10** in sport, a line delimiting the playing area or part of it; the starting or finishing point for a race. **11** a row or continuous series of letters, words, people or other objects. **12** a short letter, a note. **13** a single verse of poetry. **14** (*pl.*) a piece of poetry. **15** (*pl.*) the words of an actor's part. **16** (*pl.*) a specified quantity of verse or prose for a school student to copy out as an imposition. **17** (*pl.*) a certificate of marriage. **18** a length of rope, cord, wire or string. **19** a rope, cord, string, wire etc. used for a specific purpose, such as a fishing line, a plumb line, a clothes line etc. **20** a wire or cable for telegraph or telephone. **21** a connection by means of this. **22** a course or channel for communication of any kind. **23** the course or direction taken by a moving object. **24** a railway track. **25** a particular railway route or link. **26** a railway system under one management. **27** a series of ships or public conveyances plying between certain places or under one management. **28** a company operating these. **29** a series of persons related in direct descent or succession, family, lineage. **30** a branch of business, field of activity, particular interest. **31** a certain class of goods. **32** mode of procedure, conduct, thought. **33** policy. **34** a series of trenches, ramparts etc. **35** a row of men, ships etc. ranged as in order of battle. **36** the aggregate of troops in an army apart from support units etc. **37** any one of the horizontal lines on a television screen, traced by a scanning electron beam, which creates the picture. **38** a narrow band in a spectrum that appears noticeably lighter or darker than adjacent areas. **39** (*Mus.*) each one of the five horizontal marks forming a stave; a series of notes or tones forming a part or melody. **40** (*coll.*) pertinent facts; a useful hint or tip. **41** (*sl.*) a piece of smooth talk; a false or exaggerated account. **42** the base of most letters in printing or writing. **43** the twelfth part of an inch. *~v.t.* **1** to draw lines upon, to cover with lines. **2** to mark (in, off etc.) with lines. **3** to spread out, extend or post (troops etc.) in line. **above the line 1** in accounting, above a horizontal line on a profit and loss account dividing entries that establish a profit or loss from those that show how profit is distributed. **2** in marketing, relating to or denoting advertising through the media and by posters, for which a commission is paid to an agency. **3** in bridge, denoting bonus points entered above a horizontal line on the scoresheet that do not count towards game. **all along the line** at every point, throughout. **below the line 1** in accounting, below a horizontal line on a profit and loss account dividing entries that establish a profit and loss from those that show how profit is distributed. **2** in marketing, relating to or denoting advertising by such means as free gifts or samples, mailshots etc. that are organized internally. **3** in bridge, denoting points that count towards game or rubber. **in line for** likely to receive; a candidate for. **in line with 1** in accordance with. **2** in alignment with. **in the line of** during or as part of the normal course of (esp. duty). **on the line 1** available to be communicated with, esp. by telephone. **2** (*esp. N Am.*) at risk. **out of line** (*esp. N Am.*) (of a person) acting in an inappropriate, improper or unruly manner. **out of line with 1** not in accordance with. **2** out of alignment with. **the line/ Line** the equator. **to bring into line** to cause to conform (with). **to come into line** to conform. **to draw the line at** DRAW. **to get a line on** (*coll.*) to learn or discover useful information about. **to get one's lines crossed** CROSS. **to hold the line** HOLD[1]. **to lay it on the line** to speak out frankly or uncompromisingly. **to lay/ put on the line** to put at risk. **to line up 1** to arrange in a line or lines. **2** to align. **3** to queue. **4** to secure or arrange for the appearance of (a speaker, celebrity). **5** to prepare. **6** to take a stand for or against. **to read between the lines** to detect the hidden or unexpressed meaning of a letter, speech etc. **linebacker** *n.* in American football, a defensive player whose position is just behind the line of scrimmage. **line block** *n.* a printing block on which the black and white parts only of a subject are reproduced. **line call** *n.* in tennis, a judgement as to whether a ball was in or out. **line dance** *n.* a dance in which the dancers perform synchronized movements while standing in a line. **line dancing** *n.* **line drawing** *n.* a drawing with pen or pencil using lines only. **line-engraving** *n.* **1** an engraving with incised lines. **2** the process of engraving in this way. **linefeed** *n.* **1** on a printer, the ability to advance the paper by the space of one line at a time. **2** a similar facility on a VDU screen. **line judge** *n.* in tennis, an official who notes and judges which side of a line the ball falls. **lineman** *n.* (*pl.* **linemen**) **1** a person employed in the maintenance and repair of a line of railway, telegraph etc. **2** in surveying, a person who carries the line or chain. **line management** *n.* the managers within an organization whose responsibilities relate to its main activity or production process, as opposed to those, e.g. advertising or transport managers, who provide services to line managers. **line manager** *n.* **line of battle** *n.* the formation adopted by a military or naval force when about to go into action. **line of cleavage** *n.* the line of weakness along which a mineral or a rock tends to split. **line of country** *n.* one's special field of interest. **line of credit** *n.* the maximum amount of credit allowed to a borrower. **line of defence** *n.* a succession of fortified places forming a continuous line. **line of fire** *n.* the expected path of a bullet, shell etc. fired from a gun aimed in a particular direction. **line of least resistance** *n.* the easiest course of action. **line of march** *n.* the route or direction taken by a marching body. **line of scrimmage** *n.* in American football, the imaginary line, parallel to the goal lines, along which both teams line up at the start of a scrimmage. **line of sight** *n.* a straight line along which an observer's vision is unobstructed. **line of vision** *n.* the straight line along which an observer looks. **line-out** *n.* a method of restarting a match in Rugby Union when the ball has gone out of play, by throwing it in between the forwards of each team lined up facing the touchline. **line printer** *n.* a high-speed output device, used esp. in conjunction with a computer, which prints copy a whole line at a time. **-liner** (līnə) *comb. form* (usu. preceded by a numeral) a thing with (the specified number of) lines. **lineside** *a.* situated beside a railway line. **linesman** *n.* (*pl.* **linesmen**) **1** in tennis etc., an official who has to note when and where a ball crosses a line. **2** a lineman. **line-up** *n.* **1** a row or group of persons assembled for a particular purpose, such as the members of a team, the people appearing in a show. **2** (*esp. N Am.*) a queue. **3** an identification parade. **liny** *a.* (*comp.* **linier**, *superl.* **liniest**) **1** marked with lines. **2** wrinkly. [ult. from L *līnea*, fem. of *līneus*, flaxen, from *līnum*, flax, through OE *line*, and in later senses F *ligne*]

line[2] (līn) *v.t.* **1** to put a covering of different material on the inside of (a garment, box etc.). **2** to serve as such a covering for. **3** to fill the inside of. **to line one's pockets** POCKET. **liner**[1] *n.* **1** a removable thing that fits inside something else. **2** material used as lining. **3** a person who makes or fits linings. **4** a sleeve of wear-resistant metal fitted inside or outside a cylinder. **5** (*N Am.*) a sleeve for a gramophone record. **liner note** *n.pl.* (*N Am.*) a sleeve note. **lining** *n.* **1** a covering for the inside of anything; the act of fitting such a covering. **2** an interior surface or layer (e.g. of an organ). [OE *līn*, flax (cp. Dut. *lijn*, OHG *lin*, Icel. *līn*) perh. from or cogn. with L *līnum*, see LINE[1]]

lineage (lin´iij) *n.* descendants in a direct line from a common progenitor, ancestry, pedigree. [OF *lignage* (LINE[1], -AGE)]

Usage note See note under LINAGE.

lineal (lin´iəl) *a.* **1** ascending or descending in the direct line of ancestry, as opposed to *collateral*. **2** linear. **lineality** (-al´-) *n.* **lineally** *adv.* [F *linéament*, late L *līneālis*, from *līnea*, LINE[1]]

lineament (lin´iəmənt) *n.* **1** (*usu. pl.*) characteristic lines or features. **2** outline, contour. [F *linéal*, L *līneāmentum*, from *lineāre*, from *līnea*, LINE[1]]

Usage note The nouns *lineament* and *liniment* should not be confused: a *lineament* is an outline or feature, and *liniment* an embrocation.

linear (lin´iə) *a.* **1** composed of or having the form of lines. **2** having a straight or lengthwise direction. **3** narrow, slender with parallel sides. **4** of one dimension. **5** (of mathematical functions, expressions etc.) containing only first degree terms, and able to be represented on a graph as a straight line. **Linear A** *n.* a hitherto undeciphered script found on pottery and tablets in Crete and dating from around 1500 BC. **linear accelerator** *n.* an apparatus for accelerating charged particles along a straight line by applying high-frequency potential between electrodes placed at intervals along their path. **Linear B** *n.* an ancient script from the 2nd millennium BC found in Crete and the Greek mainland, apparently a form of Mycenaean Greek modified from the earlier Linear A. **linear equation** *n.* an equation between two variables which produces a straight line when plotted on a graph. **linearly** *adv.* **linear measure** *n.* a system of units for measuring length. **linear motor** *n.* an electric motor in which the stator and rotor are linear, producing direct thrust without the use of gears. **linear perspective** *n.* perspective dealing with the apparent positions, magnitudes and forms of objects with respect to the horizon, as opposed to *aerial perspective*. **linear programming** *n.* a method of solving practical problems in economics etc., using mathematical models involving complex interactions of linear equations. [L *līneāris*, as LINEAMENT]

lineate (lin´iət, -āt) *a.* (of leaves) marked with lines, esp. long straight lines. **lineation** (-ā´shən) *n.* **1** the act of marking with lines. **2** arrangement in or division into lines. [L *lineātus*, drawn with lines]

linen (lin´in) *n.* **1** a cloth made of flax. **2** (*collect.*) articles chiefly made of linen, esp. underclothing, sheets, table cloths etc. ~*a.* made of linen or flax. **to wash one's dirty linen in public** to expose one's private scandals, quarrels etc. to public attention. **linen basket** *n.* a basket for dirty laundry. **linenfold** *n.* a form of carved decoration representing a fold or scroll of linen. ~*a.* decorated with these. **linen paper** *n.* paper made from flax fibres. [OE *līnen*, a. (*līn*, LINE[2], -EN)]

lineolate (lin´iəlāt), **lineolated** (-lātid) *a.* marked with minute lines. [from L *lineōla*, dim. of *linea*, line]

liner[1] LINE[2].

liner[2] (lī´nə) *n.* **1** each of a regular line of passenger ships or aircraft. **2** colouring material for pencilling the eyebrows. **liner train** *n.* a fast goods train with permanently-coupled wagons for transporting containers.

linesman LINE[1].

ling[1] (ling) *n.* a long slender food fish, *Molva molva*, found in the northern seas. [cp. EFris. and Dut. *leng*, G *Länge*, Icel. *langa*, cogn. with LONG[1]]

ling[2] (ling) *n.* heather or heath, *Calluna vulgaris*. [Icel. *lyng*]

-ling[1] (ling) *suf.* forming nouns denoting a person or thing, as in *grayling*, *sibling*. [OE]

-ling[2] (ling) *suf.* forming adverbs and adjectives, as in *darkling*. [OE]

lingam (ling´gəm), **linga** *n.* the phallus, representative of the god Siva in Hindu mythology. [Sansk., a mark, a penis]

linger (ling´gə) *v.i.* **1** to delay going, to be slow or reluctant to leave. **2** to remain in or around a place. **3** not to dissipate or disappear, to persist. **4** to remain alive, though slowly dying. **5** to loiter; to be slow in doing something. **lingerer** *n.* **lingering** *a.* **lingeringly** *adv.* [ME *lengen*, OE *lengan*, to protract (cp. Icel. *lengja*, G *längen*), from *lang*, LONG[1]]

lingerie (lã´zhəri) *n.* women's underwear and night-clothes. [F, from *linge*, linen]

lingo (ling´gō) *n.* (*pl.* **lingos, lingoes**) (*coll.*) a foreign language, peculiar dialect or technical phraseology. [prob. corr. of *lingua*, see LINGUA FRANCA]

lingua (ling´gwə) *n.* (*pl.* **linguae** (-gwē)) the tongue. [L]

lingua franca (ling·gwə frang´kə) *n.* (*pl.* **lingua francas**) **1** a language serving as a medium of communication between different peoples. **2** any means of communication with this function. **3** (*Hist.*) a mixture of Italian with French, Greek, Arabic etc., used in Mediterranean ports. [It., Frankish tongue]

lingual (ling´gwəl) *a.* **1** of or relating to the tongue. **2** in phonetics, formed by the tongue. **3** (*formal*) of or relating to languages. ~*n.* a consonant produced by the tongue, such as Scots *r*. **lingualize, lingualise** *v.t.* **lingually** *adv.* **linguiform** (-gwifawm) *a.* having the shape of a tongue. [med. L *linguālis*, from *lingua*, tongue]

linguine (lingwē´ni) *n.pl.* pasta in the form of long flat ribbons. [It., pl. of *linguina*, dim. of *lingua*, tongue]

linguist (ling´gwist) *n.* **1** a person who is skilled in languages. **2** a person who studies languages. **linguistic** (-gwis´-) *a.* of or relating to languages or the study of languages. **linguistically** *adv.* **linguistics** *n.* the scientific study of languages.

lingula (ling´gūlə) *n.* (*pl.* **lingulae** (-lē)) **1** a tongue-shaped part. **2** any of a genus, *Lingula*, of brachiopods, largely fossil. **lingular** *a.* **lingulate** (-lət), **lingulated** (-lātid) *a.* tongue-shaped. [L, dim. of *lingua*, tongue]

liniment (lin´imənt) *n.* a liquid preparation, usu. with oil, for rubbing on bruised or inflamed parts, an embrocation. [F, from L *linīmentum*, from *linīre*, to anoint]

Usage note See note under LINEAMENT.

lining LINE[2].

link[1] (lingk) *n.* **1** a ring or loop of a chain. **2** a connecting part in machinery etc. or in a series, sequence, argument etc. **3** a means of contact between two points in a communications system. **4** a means of transport between two places. **5** a cuff link. **6** one-hundredth of a surveyor's chain equal to 7.92 in. (about 20 cm). ~*v.t.* **1** to connect or attach (to, together, up etc.) by or as by a link or links. **2** to connect by association. **3** to clasp (hands) or intertwine (arms). ~*v.i.* to be connected. **linkage** (-ij) *n.* **1** the act or manner of linking or being linked. **2** a system of links. **3** the linking of two separate political issues in a negotiation, such that agreement on the one is unacceptable without agreement on the other. 4 the occurrence of two genes on the same chromosome so that they tend to be inherited together. 5 the product of magnetic flux and the total number of turns in a coil. **linker** *n.* (*Comput.*) a program which joins separately assembled or compiled modules into a single executable program. **linkman**[1] *n.* (*pl.* **linkmen**) 1 a television or radio presenter who provides continuity between separate items (e.g. of news, sport) in a broadcast. 2 in football, a player with an intermediate role between two main groups, as between the midfield and the strikers. **link motion** *n.* a mechanism controlling the valves of a steam engine. **link-up** *n.* 1 a connection. 2 an association or union. 3 the act of linking. [Icel. *hlekkr* (OIcel. *hlenkr*), cp. Swed. *länk*, OE *hlence* (cogn. with G *Gelenk*, joint)]

link[2] (lingk) *n.* (*Hist.*) a torch made of tow and pitch, used for lighting people in the streets. **linkboy** *n.* a boy carrying a link. **linkman**[2] *n.* (*pl.* **linkmen**) a man carrying a link. [etym. uncertain, perh. a use of LINK[1]]

linkman[1] LINK[1].

linkman[2] LINK[2].

links (lingks) *n.pl.* 1 (*sometimes treated as sing.*) a golf course. 2 (*Sc.*) flattish or undulating sandy ground near the seashore, covered with coarse grass etc. [from OE *hlincas*, pl. of *hlinc*, ridge]

linn (lin) *n.* 1 a waterfall, a torrent. 2 a pool, esp. one below a fall. 3 a precipice or precipitous ravine. [OE *hlynn*, torrent, confused with Gael. *linne*, Ir. *linn*, Welsh *llyn*, a pool]

Linnaean (linē´ən, -nā´-), **Linnean** *a.* of or relating to Linnaeus or his system of classification and naming of plants and animals. ~*n.* a follower of Linnaeus. [*Linnaeus*, Latinized name of Carl von *Linné*, 1707–78, Swedish naturalist]

linnet (lin´it) *n.* a finch, *Acanthis cannabina*, with brownish plumage. [OF *linette* (F *linotte*), from *lin*, flax (see LINEN), on which it feeds]

lino (lī´nō) *n.* (*pl.* **linos**) short for LINOLEUM. **linocut** *n.* an engraving on linoleum in the manner of a woodcut.

linoleic acid (linōlē´ik) *n.* a colourless oily polyunsaturated fatty acid occurring as a glyceride in linseed and other natural oils, used in making soaps and emulsifiers and essential to the human diet. [from L *linum*, flax, OLEIC]

linolenic acid (linōlen´ik) *n.* a fatty acid similar in its properties and provenance to linoleic acid but with one more double bond. [G *Linolensäure*]

linoleum (linō´liəm) *n.* a preparation of oxidized linseed oil mixed with ground cork and laid upon fabric, used as a floor covering. [L *līnum*, flax, *oleum*, OIL]

Linotype® (lī´nətīp) *n.* 1 a typesetting machine for producing castings or slugs of whole lines of words. 2 type produced by such a method. [LINE[1], OF, TYPE]

linsang (lin´sang) *n.* 1 a kind of civet cat common in Borneo and Java. 2 a related African species. [Javanese]

linseed (lin´sēd) *n.* the seed of the flax plant. **linseed cake** *n.* the solid mass left after the oil has been pressed out of flax seed. **linseed meal** *n.* ground linseed. **linseed oil** *n.* the oil expressed from linseed, used in paints, printer's ink, linoleum etc. [ME *lin-seed* (OE *līn*, LINE[2], SEED)]

linsey-woolsey (linziwul´zi) *n.* 1 a coarse fabric of linen or cotton warp with wool filling. 2 a motley composition, a jargon. [prob. formed from LINE[2] and WOOL, with a jingling suf., or perh. from a place name as *Lindsey*]

linstock (lin´stok) *n.* (*Hist.*) a forked staff to hold a lighted match for firing a gun. [formerly *lintstock*, Dut. *lontstok* (*lont*, match, *stok*, stick)]

lint (lint) *n.* 1 absorbent cotton cloth with the nap raised on one side, used for dressing wounds etc. 2 fluff or down from cloth. 3 (*Sc.*) flax. **linter** *n.* 1 a machine for removing short cotton fibres from ginned seeds. 2 the fibres removed by this process. [rel. to LINE[2], perh. through F *linette* or *lin*, linen]

lintel (lin´təl) *n.* the horizontal beam or stone over a door or window. **lintelled,** (*N Am.*) **linteled** *a.* [OF, from med. L *lintellus*, prob. for *līmitellus*, dim. of *līmes*, LIMIT]

lintie (lin´ti), **lintwhite** (-wīt) *n.* (*Sc.*) a linnet. [OE *līnetwige*]

liny LINE[1].

lion (lī´ən) *n.* 1 a large and powerful carnivorous quadruped, *Panthera leo*, usu. brown or tawny, with tufted tail and (in the adult male) a long mane, inhabiting southern Asia and Africa. 2 a principal emblem in heraldry; the British national emblem. 3 a courageous person. 4 an eminent celebrity, an object of general attention. **the Lion** 1 the sign of the zodiac and constellation Leo. 2 Great Britain. **the lion's mouth** a dangerous place. **the lion's share** the largest part or the whole. **lioness** (-nis) *n.* a female lion. **lion-heart** *n.* a very courageous person. **lion-hearted** *a.* having great courage. **lionize, lionise** *v.t.* to treat as an object of interest or curiosity. **lionization** (-zā´shən) *n.* **lionizer** *n.* **lionlike** *a.* **lion tamer** *n.* a circus performer who trains lions and performs tricks with them in the ring. [A-F *liun* (OF *leon*), L *leōnem*, nom. *leo*, Gr. *leōn leontos*]

lip (lip) *n.* 1 either of the two fleshy parts enclosing the opening of the mouth. 2 anything resembling a lip, such as the projecting lobe of a bilabiate corolla; a labium. 3 the edge or rim of an orifice, chasm, container etc. 4 (*sl.*) impudence, cheek. 5 (*pl.*) the mouth, as organ of speech. ~*v.t.* (*pres.p.* **lipping,** *past, p.p.* **lipped**) 1 to touch with the lips. 2 to kiss. 3 to touch gently; (of water) to lap against. 4 in golf, to hit a ball to the very edge of (a hole); (of a golf ball) to reach the edge of (a hole) but not drop in. 5 to breathe, whisper, murmur. ~*v.i.* (*Mus.*) to use the lips in playing a wind instrument. **one's lips are sealed** SEAL[2]. **to bite one's lip** to express vexation, to repress anger, laughter or other emotion. **to button one's lip** BUTTON. **to curl one's lip** to express scorn or contempt. **to hang on someone's lips** to listen eagerly for every word spoken. **to keep a stiff upper lip** to be self-reliant, inflexible, unflinching. **to lick one's lips** LICK. **to pass one's lips** to be eaten, drunk or spoken. **to smack one's lips** to part one's lips making a loud smacking noise as a sign of appetite, gleeful anticipation etc. **lip-gloss** *n.* a cosmetic which makes the lips glossy. **lipless** *a.* **lipped** *a.* (*usu. in comb.*, as *thick-lipped*). **lippy** *a.* (*comp.* **lippier,** *superl.* **lippiest**) cheeky, insolent. **lip-read** *v.t., v.i.* (*past, p.p.* **lip-read**) to follow what a person says by observing the movement of their lips. **lip-reader** *n.* **lip-reading** *n.* **lipsalve** *n.* 1 ointment for the lips. 2 compliments, flattery. **lip-service** *n.* flattery, servile agreement with a sentiment etc. expressed but not put into practice. **lipstick** *n.* a stick of cosmetic for colouring the lips. **lip-sync, lip-synch** *v.t.* to synchronize the movement of the lips with a prerecorded soundtrack (of words, music etc.) on film or television. [OE *lippa* (cp. Dut. *lip*, Dan. *laebe*, G *Lippe*, also L *labium*, *labrum*)]

lip- LIPO-.

lipase (lip´āz) *n.* any enzyme which decomposes fats.

lipid (lip´id) *n.* any of various organic compounds which are esters of fatty acids, insoluble in water but soluble in other substances, and important structural components of living cells. **lipidic** *a.* **lipidosis** (lipidō´sis) *n.* (*pl.* **lipidoses** (-sēz)) any lipidic disorder.

Lipizzaner (lipitsah´nə), **Lippizaner** *n.* a breed of horses (usu. white or grey in colour) used esp. by the Spanish Riding School in Vienna for dressage displays. [G, after *Lippiza*, Slovenia where orig. bred]

lipo- (lip´ō), **lip-** *comb. form* fat, fatty. [Gr. *lipos*, fat]

lipogenesis (lipōjen´əsis) *n.* the formation of fat from the synthesis of fatty substances. **lipogenic** *a.*

lipography (lipog´rəfi) *n.* the accidental omission of a letter or letters in writing.
lipohaemia (lipōhē´miə), (*N Am.*) **lipohemia** *n.* prevalence of fatty matter in the blood.
lipoid (lip´oid) *a.* fatlike. ~*n.* a fatlike substance, a lipid. **lipoidosis** (-dō´sis) *n.* (*pl.* **lipoidoses** (-sēz)) LIPIDOSIS (under LIPID).
lipoma (lipō´mə) *n.* (*pl.* **lipomas, lipomata** (-mətə)) a fatty tumour. **lipomatous** *a.*
lipoprotein (lipōprō´tēn) *n.* a soluble protein which carries lipids in the bloodstream.
liposome (lip´əsōm) *n.* **1** a minute synthetic sac made of a lipid substance containing an aqueous droplet, used to convey drugs to specific tissues. **2** a naturally-occurring lipid globule, also with an aqueous core, in the cytoplasm of a cell.
liposuction (lipōsŭk´shən) *n.* a surgical process for the cosmetic removal of excess fat from beneath the skin by suction.
Lippizaner LIPIZZANER.
lippy LIP.
liq. *abbr.* **1** liquid. **2** liquor.
liquate (likwāt´, lī´kwāt) *v.t.* to liquefy (metals) in order to purify. **liquable** *a.* **liquation** (-kwā´shən) *n.* [L *liquātus*, p.p. of *liquāre*, to melt, cogn. with LIQUOR]
liquefy (lik´wifī), **liquify** *v.t.* (*3rd pers. sing. pres.* **liquefies, liquifies,** *pres.p.* **liquefying, liquifying,** *past, p.p.* **liquefied, liquified**) to convert from a solid (or gaseous) to a liquid form. ~*v.i.* to become liquid. **liquefacient** (-fā´shənt) *n.* a substance which liquefies or causes liquefaction. ~*a.* serving to liquefy. **liquefaction** (-fak´-) *n.* **liquefactive** (-fak´-) *a.* **liquefiable** *a.* **liquefied** *n.* **liquefied natural gas** *n.* natural gas under pressure used as an engine fuel. **liquefied petroleum gas** *n.* a mixture of gases, esp. butane and propane, stored under pressure in liquid form and used as engine fuel. **liquefier** *n.* **liquescence** (-kwes´-), **liquescency** *n.* the process of becoming or tending to become liquid. **liquescent** (-kwes´-) *a.* [F *liquéfier*, L *liquefacere* (*liquāre*, to become fluid, *facere*, to make)]
liqueur (likūə´) *n.* **1** an alcoholic cordial sweetened or flavoured with an aromatic substance and drunk in small quantities, usu. after a meal. **2** (*in full* **liqueur chocolate**) a hollow chocolate sweet containing a small quantity of liqueur as its centre. ~*v.t.* to treat or flavour with this. **liqueur brandy** *n.* brandy of special quality drunk as a liqueur. **liqueur glass** *n.* a small glass for drinking liqueurs. [F, LIQUOR]
liquid (lik´wid) *a.* **1** flowing or capable of flowing, like water or oil. **2** (of a gas) able to flow after being subject to intense cold. **3** transparent, limpid, clear. **4** (of sounds) not guttural, fluent, smooth, easily pronounced. **5** (of assets) readily convertible into cash; (of a person, company) having cash or liquid assets. **6** (of principles etc.) unstable, changeable. ~*n.* **1** a substance that is able to flow; a substance whose molecules are incompressible and inelastic, but, though moving freely among themselves, cannot escape as in a gaseous state. **2** a letter pronounced with a slight contact of the organs of articulation, as *l*, *r*, and sometimes *m*. **liquidate** *v.t.* **1** to pay off (a debt etc.). **2** to wind up (a bankrupt estate etc.). **3** to convert (assets) into cash. **4** to assassinate; to destroy. ~*v.i.* (of a company) to have its debts, liabilities and assets liquidated. **liquidation** (-ā´shən) *n.* **1** the process of liquidating, esp. the termination of the affairs of a bankrupt company. **2** killing; destruction. **to go into liquidation** (of a company) to have its affairs terminated and its assets apportioned among creditors. **liquidator** *n.* the person officially appointed to effect a liquidation. **liquid crystal** *n.* a liquid with physical, esp. optical, properties analogous to crystals. **liquid crystal display** *n.* a display, esp. in electronic calculators, using liquid crystal cells which change their reflectivity in an electric field. **liquidity** (-kwid´-) *n.* (*pl.* **liquidities**) **1** the state of being liquid. **2** the possession of sufficient liquid assets to discharge current liabilities. **3** liquid assets. **4** the ability (of an asset) to be converted into cash. **liquidize, liquidise** *v.t.* **1** to reduce to liquid, to liquefy. **2** to purée (food) into a liquid. **3** to convert into cash. **liquidizer** *n.* a kitchen appliance with blades and various attachments for chopping or puréeing vegetables, blending soup etc. **liquidly** *adv.* **liquid measure** *n.* a unit or system of units used to measure liquids. **liquidness** *n.* **liquid paraffin** *n.* an oily liquid obtained from petroleum distillation and used as a laxative. **liquid storax** *n.* a balsam obtained from *Liquidambar orientalis*, also called LEVANT STORAX (under LEVANT). [OF *liquide*, L *liquidus*, from *liquēre*, cp. LIQUEFY, LIQUATE]
liquidambar (likwidam´bə) *n.* **1** any tropical tree of the genus *Liquidambar*, several species of which yield a fragrant resin or balsam called storax. **2** the resin so produced. [LIQUID, med. L *ambar*, AMBER]
liquify LIQUEFY.
liquor (lik´ə) *n.* **1** an alcoholic drink, usu. not including wine or beer; such drinks collectively. **2** a liquid or fluid substance, esp. the liquid part of anything, e.g. a solution, a secretion, food or the water used for cooking. **3** the water used in brewing beer. **4** an aqueous solution of a drug. ~*v.t.* **1** to moisten, to wet, to steep. **2** to grease, to dress (leather etc.). **in liquor** drunk. **to liquor up 1** (*N Am.*) to take a lot of drink. **2** (*N Am.*) to cause to become drunk. **liquorish**[1] *a.* fond of liquor. **liquorishly** *adv.* **liquorishness** *n.* [A-F *licur* (F LIQUEUR), L *liquor*, from *liquēre*, see LIQUID]
liquorice (lik´əris), (*N Am.*) **licorice** *n.* **1** a black extract from the root of the leguminous plant *Glycyrrhiza glabra*, used in medicine and confectionery. **2** this plant. **3** liquorice-flavoured sweets. **liquorice allsorts** *n.pl.* an assortment of sweets, all made of or containing liquorice. [A-F *lycorys* (F *liquerice*), late L *liquiritia*, Gr. *glukurrhiza* (*glukus*, sweet, *rhiza*, root)]
liquorish[1] LIQUOR.
liquorish[2] LICKERISH.
lira (liə´rə) *n.* (*pl.* **lire** (liə´rə, -rā, -ri), **liras**) **1** the standard monetary unit of Italy. **2** the standard monetary unit of Turkey. [It., from L *libra*, a pound]
liriodendron (liriōden´drən) *n.* (*pl.* **liriodendrons, liriodendra** (-drə)) a N American tree of the genus *Liriodendron* of the Magnoliaceae and containing the tulip tree. [Gr. *leirion*, LILY, *dendron*, tree]
liripipe (lir´ipīp), **liripoop** (-poop) *n.* the long tail attached to a graduate's hood. [med. L *liripipium*, etym. uncertain]
lisle (līl) *n.* a fine, strong cotton thread, esp. for stockings. [*Lisle*, an old name for *Lille* in France]
LISP (lisp) *n.* a high-level computer programming language used in artificial intelligence research. [*list processing*]
lisp (lisp) *v.i.* **1** to pronounce *s* and *z* with the sound of *th* or *dh*. **2** to speak affectedly; to speak imperfectly, as a child. ~*v.t.* to pronounce with a lisp. ~*n.* **1** the act or habit of lisping. **2** the speech defect which causes one to lisp. **3** (*poet.*) a rustling or rippling sound. **lisper** *n.* **lispingly** *adv.* [OE *wlispian*, extant only in *āwlispian*, from *wlisp*, lisping (cp. Dut. *lispen*, Gmc. *laespe*, G *lispeln*)]
lissom (lis´əm), **lissome** *a.* lithe, supple, nimble. **lissomly** *adv.* **lissomness** *n.* [var. of LITHESOME (under LITHE)]
list[1] (list) *n.* **1** a record or catalogue of items, names etc. which are related in some way or to be used for some specific purpose, usu. entered one below the other. **2** (*Comput.*) a data structure in linear order. ~*v.t.* **1** to make a list of. **2** to enter (an item, name) on a list. **3** to approve for dealings on the Stock Exchange. **4** in the

UK, to declare to be a listed building. **5** †to enlist. ~†*v.i.* to enlist. **listed** *a.* **listed building** *n.* in the UK, a building officially listed as being of particular architectural or historical interest which may not be altered or demolished without special consent. **listed company** *n.* a company whose shares are quoted on the main market of the London Stock Exchange. **listed security** *n.* a security quoted on the main market and appearing in the Official List of Securities of the London Stock Exchange. **listing** *n.* **1** a list. **2** an entry on a list. **3** the act of making a list. **4** placement on a list, esp. on the official List of Securities of the London Stock Exchange. **5** (*pl.*) lists printed in newspapers, magazines etc. showing the dates and times of concerts, plays, films and similar events. **list price** *n.* the price of an article as given in the manufacturer's catalogue or advertisement. [OF *liste*, as LIST²]

list² (list) *n.* **1** the border, edge or selvage of cloth. **2** a strip of this used as material. **3** (*pl., Hist.*) the palisades enclosing a piece of ground for a tournament; the ground so enclosed. **4** a scene of contest, an arena. **5** a ridge in ploughed land thrown up between two furrows. ~*v.t.* **1** to border with or as if with a list. **2** to cover or line with list (as the edge of a door). **3** (*N Am.*) to prepare (land) for corn or cotton by making alternate beds and furrows. **to enter the lists** to enter into a contest. **lister** *n.* (*N Am.*) a plough with a double mould specially designed for throwing up ridges. [OE *līste* (cp. Dut. *lijst*, G *Leiste*, OHG *lista*, whence It. *lista*, F *liste*, whence the sense of roll or catalogue)]

list³ (list) *n.* the fact of leaning over to one side (of a ship, building etc.). ~*v.i.* to lean over, to careen. ~*v.t.* to careen or heel (a ship) over. [etym. uncertain]

†list⁴ (list) *v.t.* (*3rd pers. sing. pres.* **lists, list, listeth** (-əth), *past, p.p.* **list, listed**) **1** to please, to be pleasing to. **2** to desire, to choose. ~*v.i.* to please, to choose, to be disposed. ~*n.* desire, pleasure, inclination. [OE *lystan* (cp. Dut. *lusten*, Icel. *lysta*, G *lüsten*), from *lust*, see LUST]

†list⁵ (list) *v.i.* to listen. ~*v.t.* to listen to. [OE *hlystan*, from *hlyst*, hearing (cp. Icel. *hlust*, ear), cogn. with L *cluere*, Gr. *kluein*]

listen (lis´ən) *v.i.* **1** to make an effort to hear. **2** to pay attention (to). **3** to heed, to obey, to follow. **4** to wait in the hope or expectation of hearing. ~*n.* an act of listening. **to listen in 1** to be present at, but not contribute to, a conversation, discussion etc. **2** to eavesdrop; to intercept and listen to a telephone or radio communication. **3** to listen to a radio broadcast. **to listen out** to wait in the hope or expectation of hearing. **to listen up** (*N Am., coll.*) to pay attention. **listenable** *a.* pleasant to listen to. **listener** *n.* a person who listens, esp. to radio broadcasting. **listener-in** *n.* (*pl.* **listeners-in**) a person who listens in. **listenership** *n.* the audience, or estimated audience, for a radio programme. **listening** *a.* **listening post** *n.* **1** a position where people are posted to overhear what the enemy is saying or planning. **2** a place where electronic communications are intercepted. **3** any place for gathering useful information about the affairs of another country, area, organization etc. [ONorthum. *lysna* (cp. OE *hlosnian*), cogn with LIST⁵]

listeria (listiə´riə) *n.* any bacterium of a genus, *Listeria*, found in certain foods, esp. poultry and soft cheese, and capable of affecting the central nervous system and causing meningitis, encephalitis or miscarriage if not killed by cooking. **listeriosis** (-ō´sis) *n.* serious food-poisoning caused by the presence of *Listeria monocytogenes*. [Lord *Lister*, 1827–1912, British surgeon]

listless (list´lis) *a.* lacking the will or energy to do anything; bored and languid but uneasy or querulous at the same time. **listlessly** *adv.* **listlessness** *n.* [LIST⁴]

lit¹ LIGHT¹.

lit² LIGHT³.

lit. *abbr.* **1** literal(ly). **2** literature. **3** litre.

litany (lit´əni) *n.* (*pl.* **litanies**) **1** a solemn form of supplicatory prayer, used in public worship, consisting of a series of short invocations followed by fixed responses. **2** a long, usu. boring, list or catalogue. **the Litany** the supplicatory prayer in this form found in the Book of Common Prayer. [ME and OF *letanie* (F *litanie*), med. L *litanīa*, Gr. *litaneia*, from *litaneuein*, to pray, from *litanos*, a suppliant, from *litē*, prayer]

Lit.B LITT. B.

litchi LYCHEE.

lit crit *abbr.* literary criticism.

Lit. D. LITT. D.

lite (līt) *a.* **1** low in fat, calories or alcoholic content. **2** (*N Am., coll.*) insubstantial, superficial. ~*n.* **1** a light beer with relatively few calories. **2** a light, esp. a courtesy light in a vehicle. [var. of *light*, usu. a deliberate respelling]

-lite (līt) *suf.* forming names of minerals and fossils such as *aerolite, coprolite, radiolite.* [F, from Gr. *lithos*, stone]

liter LITRE.

literacy LITERATE.

literae humaniores (litərī hūmaniaw´rēz) *n.* at Oxford University, a faculty and honours course concerned with Greek and Latin literature, ancient history and philosophy. [L, the more civilized studies]

literal (lit´ərəl) *a.* **1** according or limited to the primary or explicit meaning, not figurative or metaphorical. **2** following the exact words (as a translation). **3** unimaginative, prosaic, matter-of-fact. **4** without exaggeration; so called without exaggeration. **5** used with the meaning 'without exaggeration' but applied to an often exaggerated metaphor as in *a literal deluge of offers.* **6** consisting of or expressed by letters. ~*n.* a misprint or misspelling of a word. **literalism** *n.* **1** the interpretation or understanding of words and statements in a literal sense. **2** realistic or unimaginative portrayal in art or literature. **literalist** *n.* **literalistic** *a.* **literality** (-ral´-), **literalize, literalise** *v.t.* **literally** *adv.* **1** in a literal manner. **2** without exaggeration (often used with considerable exaggeration to reinforce a metaphor as in *I literally jumped out of my skin*). **literalness** *n.* [OF, from L *litterālis*, from *littera*, letter]

Usage note *Literal* and *literally* as emphasizers (implying some figurative use or exaggeration) reverse the usual meanings of the words, and so are often disapproved of.

literary (lit´ərəri) *a.* **1** of or relating to literature or writing. **2** versed or engaged in literature. **3** well-read. **4** consisting of written or printed compositions. **5** (of language) derived from or used in literature, formal not colloquial in style. **literary agent** *n.* a person who manages the business affairs of an author. **literary criticism** *n.* (the art of making) evaluative and interpretative judgements on literary works. **literary critic** *n.* **literary executor** *n.* a person appointed to deal with the copyrights and unpublished works of a deceased author. **literary history** *n.* **1** the treatment of a subject in literary works of various periods. **2** the history of literature. [L *litterārius*, as LITERAL]

literate (lit´ərət) *a.* **1** able to read and write. **2** educated. **3** (*as comb. form*) having knowledge or competence in (*computer-literate*). ~*n.* **1** a person who is able to read and write. **2** an educated person. **literacy** *n.* **literati** (-rah´ti) *n.pl.* **1** men and women of letters. **2** the learned. **literation** (-ā´shən) *n.* representation (of a language etc.) by means of letters. **literator** *n.* a literary person, a littérateur. **literature** (lit´rəchə) *n.* **1** (*collect.*) the written or printed productions of a country or period or those relating to a particular subject. **2** the class of writings distinguished for beauty of form or expression, as poetry, novels, essays etc. **3** printed matter, usu. of an informative kind. **4** the production of literary works. **5** the literary profession. **6** †literary culture. [L *litterātus*, as LITERARY]

literatim (litərah´tim) *adv.* letter for letter, literally. [L]

lith. *abbr.* **1** lithograph. **2** lithography.

lith- LITHO-.

-lith (lith) *suf.* denoting a type of stone, as in *monolith*.

litharge (lith´ahj) *n.* a red or yellow mineral form of lead monoxide. [OF *litarge*, L *lithargyrus*, Gr. *litharguros* (LITHO- *aguros*, silver)]

lithe (līdh) *a.* flexible, limber, supple. **lithely** *adv.* **litheness** *n.* **lithesome** (-səm) *a.* lissome. **lithesomeness** *n.* [OE *līthe*, cogn. with L *lentus*]

lithia (lith´iə) *n.* oxide of lithium. **lithia water** *n.* mineral water containing lithium salts. [formerly *lithion*, Gr. *litheion*, neut. a. stony, from *lithos*, stone]

lithic (lith´ik) *a.* **1** of, relating to or composed of stone or calculi. **2** of or containing lithium. [Gr. *lithikos*, from *lithos*, stone]

lithium (lith´iəm) *n.* a soft, silver-white element, the lightest metallic element, at. no. 3, chem. symbol Li, a member of the alkali series, used, esp. in alloys and batteries. [LITHIA, -IUM]

litho (lī´thō, lith´ō) *n.* (*pl.* **lithos**) **1** short for LITHOGRAPH. **2** short for LITHOGRAPHY (under LITHOGRAPH). *~a.* short for LITHOGRAPHIC (under LITHOGRAPH). *~adv.* short for LITHOGRAPHICALLY (under LITHOGRAPH). *~v.t.* (*3rd pers. sing. pres.* **lithoes**, *pres.p.* **lithoing**, *past, p.p* **lithoed**) to produce by lithography.

litho- (lith´ō), **lith-** *comb. form* of or relating to stone. [Gr. *lithos*, a stone]

lithogenous (lithoj´inəs) *a.* **1** stone-producing. **2** forming coral.

lithograph (lith´əgrahf) *v.t.* to print by lithography. *~n.* **1** a print made by lithography. **2** an impression from a drawing on stone or metal. **lithographer** (-thog´-) *n.* **lithographic** (-graf´-), **lithographical** *a.* **lithographically** *adv.* **lithographic stone** *n.* a slaty limestone from the upper bed of the Jurassic formation, used in lithography. **lithography** (-thog´-) *n.* the art or process of printing from a stone or plate which is treated so that it is ink-receptive in some parts and ink-repellent in others.

lithoid (lith´oid), **lithoidal** (-thoi´-) *a.* resembling a stone in nature or structure.

lithology (lithol´əji) *n.* **1** the science of the composition, structure and classification of rocks, petrology. **2** the characteristics of a rock or rocks. **lithologic** (-loj´-), **lithological** *a.* **lithologist** *n.*

lithomarge (lith´əmahj) *n.* a hydrated silicate of alumina related to or identical with kaolin.

lithophyte (lith´əfīt) *n.* **1** a plant that grows on stone. **2** a calcareous polyp, such as some corals.

lithopone (lith´ōpōn) *n.* a white pigment made from a mixture of zinc sulphide, barium sulphate and zinc oxide. [LITHO-, Gr. *ponos*, work]

lithosphere (lith´əsfiə) *n.* the outer, rocky shell of the earth, the crust of the earth. **lithospheric** (-sfer´ik) *a.*

lithotomy (lithot´əmi) *n.* (*pl.* **lithotomies**) the surgical removal of a stone in the bladder. **lithotomic** (-tom´-) *a.* **lithotomist** *n.* [Gr. *lithotomos*, stone-cutting (LITHO-, *tomos*, cutting, from *temnein*, to cut)]

lithotripsy (lith´ətripsi) *n.* (*pl.* **lithotripsies**) the use of ultrasound to pulverize stones in the bladder, kidney or gall bladder so that they can be passed out through the urethra. **lithotripter** (-trip´tə) *n.* a device which uses ultrasound to crush kidney etc. stones without the need for surgery. **lithotriptic** (-trip´-) *a., n.* (a medicine that) crushes stones in the bladder etc. **lithotritic** (-trit´-) *a., n.* LITHOTRIPTIC (under LITHOTRIPSY). **lithotrity** (lithot´riti) *n.* (*pl.* **lithotrities**) the operation of crushing stones in the bladder, kidney or gall bladder to small fragments by means of instruments. [Gr. *tripsis*, rubbing, from *tribein*, to rub]

lithotype (lith´ətīp) *n.* **1** a stereotype made with shellac, sand, tar and linseed oil, pressed hot on a plaster mould taken from type. **2** an etched stone surface for printing. **3** a machine for preparing a lithographic transfer-sheet. *~v.t.* to prepare for printing by lithotypes. **lithotypy** (-pi) *n.* [LITHO-, TYPE]

Lithuanian (lithūā´niən) *a.* of or relating to Lithuania, an independent republic (formerly part of the USSR) on the Baltic Sea. *~n.* **1** a native or inhabitant of Lithuania. **2** the language of Lithuania.

litigate (lit´igāt) *v.t.* to contest in a court of law. *~v.i.* **1** to go to law. **2** to carry on a lawsuit. **litigable** *a.* **litigant** *a.* engaged in a lawsuit. *~n.* a party to a lawsuit. **litigation** (-ā´shən) *n.* **1** the process of bringing or contesting a lawsuit. **2** judicial proceedings. **litigious** (-tij´əs) *a.* **1** fond of litigation. **2** quarrelsome, contentious. **3** subject or open to legal dispute. **4** of or relating to litigation. **litigiosity** (-ios´-), **litigiousness** *n.* **litigiously** *adv.* [L *lītigātus*, p.p. of *lītigāre*, from *līs*, *lītis*, lawsuit]

litmus (lit´məs) *n.* a substance obtained from *Roccella tinctoria* or other lichens, that is turned red by acids or blue by alkalis. **litmus paper** *n.* unsized paper stained with litmus, used to test the acidity or the alkaline nature of a solution. **litmus test** *n.* **1** a test using litmus paper. **2** any test that indicates the fundamental nature of something. [of Scand. orig., rel. to ON *litmosi*, herbs used in dyeing, *litr*, colour, *musi*, moss]

litotes (lītō´tēz) *a.* an understatement by which an affirmative is expressed by negation of its contrary, as in 'not a little' for 'very' or a weaker expression used to suggest a stronger one. [Gr., from *lītos*, smooth, meagre]

☒ **litrature** common misspelling of LITERATURE (under LITERATE).

litre (lē´tə), (*esp. N Am.*) **liter** *n.* the unit of capacity in the metric system, equal to a cubic decimetre, or about 1.75 pints. [F, late L *lītra*, from Gr. *litra*, a pound]

Litt. B, Lit. B *abbr.* Bachelor of Letters, Bachelor of Literature.

Litt. D., Lit. D. *abbr.* Doctor of Letters, Doctor of Literature.

litter (lit´ə) *n.* **1** refuse, rubbish, esp. waste paper, scattered about in a public place. **2** a scattered, disorderly collection of odds and ends. **3** a state of disorder or untidiness. **4** the young brought forth by a sow, bitch, cat etc. at one birth. **5** a couch in which a person may be carried by animals or on people's shoulders. **6** a stretcher used for transporting the sick or wounded. **7** straw, hay or other soft material used as a bed for horses, cattle etc. or as a covering for plants. **8** cat litter. **9** a layer of twigs, leaves etc. on the floor of a forest. *~v.t.* **1** to scatter (things) about carelessly. **2** to make (a place) untidy with articles scattered about. **3** to bring forth (said esp. of the sow, dog, cat etc., applied derogatively to human beings). **4** to supply (beasts) with litter. **5** to spread bedding for. *~v.i.* to bring forth a litter of young. **litter basket, litter bin** *n.* a receptacle for litter. **litterbug, litter lout** *n.* (*coll.*) a person who drops rubbish in public places. **littery** *a.* **1** covered in litter; in disorder. **2** apt to drop litter. [A-F *littere*, OF *litiere*, med. L *lectāria*, from *lectus*, bed]

littérateur (litərətœ´) *n.* an author, a professional writer. [F, from L *litterator -orem*, from *littera*, LETTER]

little (lit´əl) *a.* (*comp.* **less, lesser,** (*coll.*) **littler,** *superl.* **least,** (*coll.*) **littlest**) **1** small, not great in size, amount or quantity. **2** not tall, short in stature. **3** short in duration or distance. **4** slight, inconsiderable, trifling, petty. **5** young or younger. **6** small in comparison to others of the same name or description. **7** resembling something else, but on a small scale. **8** used to reinforce a sense of the endearing qualities of something (*a sweet little house*). **9** used to reinforce an expression of contempt (*you rotten little liar*). ~*adv.* (*comp.* **less**, *superl.* **least**) **1** to only a small extent, not much (*has improved little since my last visit*). **2** not at all (*they little expected*). ~*n.* **1** a small amount, quantity, space, distance, time etc. **2** not much. **a little** to a small extent, slightly (*feeling a little better*). **in little** in miniature. **little by little** by small degrees, (very) gradually. **little or nothing** scarcely anything. **no little** considerable; a fair amount of. **not a little 1** very, greatly, extremely. **2** a great deal. **to make little of** MAKE[1]. **to think little of** THINK. **to twist/ wind/ wrap around one's little finger** FINGER. **little auk** *n.* a small Arctic auk, *Plautus alle.* **Little Bear** *n.* the constellation Ursa Minor. **little bird** *n.* an unknown or undisclosed person. **Little Dipper** *n.* (*N Am.*) LITTLE BEAR (under LITTLE). **Little Dog** *n.* the constellation Canis Minor. **little end** *n.* the smaller end of a connecting rod in an internal-combustion engine. **little Englander** *n.* **1** an opponent of British expansion overseas in the 19th cent. **2** an opponent of British integration into Europe in the 20th cent. **little finger** *n.* the smallest of the fingers. **little go** *n.* (*Hist.*) in some UK universities, the preliminary examinations for degrees. **little grebe** *n.* a small brownish European diving bird, *Podiceps ruficolis*, of the grebe family. **little green men** *n.pl.* (*coll.*) beings from outer space. **little magazine** *n.* a magazine with a small, often highbrow readership. **little man** *n.* **1** the ordinary man in the street without special power or status. **2** (as a form of address) a boy. **littleness** *n.* **little ones** *n.pl.* children or young animals. **little owl** *n.* a small owl, *Athene noctua*, of Eurasia and Africa, which has speckled brown plumage and a flattish head. **little people** *n.pl.* the fairies. **Little Russian** *a.* (*Hist.*) Ukrainian. **little slam** *n.* SMALL SLAM (under SMALL). **little theatre,** (*N Am.*) **little theater** *n.* a small theatre, usu. presenting contemporary, experimental, avant-garde or uncommercial plays. **little woman** *n.* (*facet.*) one's wife. [OE *lȳtel, lytel*, cogn. the *lūtan*, to LOUT[2]]

littoral (lit´ərəl) *a.* of or relating to the shore, esp. the zone between high- and low-water marks. ~*n.* a coastal region. [L *littorālis, lītorālis*, from *lītus -toris*, shore]

liturgy (lit´əji) *n.* (*pl.* **liturgies**) **1** a form of public worship laid down by a Church. **2** a Church's entire ritual for public worship or the set of formularies in which this is set forth. **3** (**Liturgy**) the Communion office of the Orthodox Church. **4** in ancient Greece, a public duty discharged at his own cost by a wealthy Athenian citizen in rotation, such as the building of a warship, production of a play etc. **the Liturgy** (in the Anglican Church) the Book of Common Prayer. **liturgic** (-tœ´-), **liturgical** *a.* of or relating to a liturgy or liturgies. **liturgically** *adv.* **liturgics** *n.* the study or doctrine of liturgies. **liturgiology** (-tœjiol´-) *n.* the study of liturgical forms. **liturgiologist** *n.* **liturgist** *n.* a student or composer of liturgical forms. [through F *liturgie* or directly from med. L *lītūrgia*, Gr. *leitourgia*, a public service, from *leitourgos* (*leitos*, public, *ergon*, work)]

live[1] (liv) *v.i.* **1** to have life, to be alive, to be capable of performing animal or vegetable functions. **2** to reside, to dwell (at, in etc.). **3** to be nourished, to subsist (upon). **4** to depend for subsistence (upon). **5** to receive or gain a livelihood (by). **6** to pass or conduct one's life in a particular condition, manner etc. **7** to live strenuously, to enjoy life intensely. **8** to continue alive, to survive. **9** to remain in operation or as an active principle. ~*v.t.* **1** to pass, to spend (a specified kind of life). **2** to manifest, express or effect, by living. **long live** an expression of loyal good wishes to a particular person, institution etc. **to live and breathe** to be utterly devoted to or obsessed with (an activity, pastime). **to live and learn** to continue to learn new things. **to live and let live** to be tolerant of the deficiencies of others in return for indulgence of one's own. **to live by** to order one's life in accordance with (a principle, creed). **to live by one's wits** WIT[1]. **to live down** to efface the recollection of (former mistakes, scandal etc.) by one's conduct. **to live in 1** (of an employee) to reside at one's place of work. **2** (of a student) to reside on the campus. **to live in sin** SIN[1]. **to live it up** (*coll.*) to enjoy oneself without restraint, to go on the spree. **to live off 1** to be dependent on financially, for one's livelihood. **2** to feed oneself (exclusively) on. **to live on 1** to continue to exist, to endure, to survive. **2** to support oneself on (a specific amount of money). **3** to feed oneself (exclusively) on. **to live on one's hump** HUMP. **to live out 1** to spend the whole or the remainder of (one's life, days). **2** to express, manifest or fulfil in one's life and conduct. **3** (of an employee) to reside away from one's place of work. **4** (of a student) not to reside on campus. **to live out of a suitcase** to be restricted to and dependent on the things, usu. clothes, that one has with one in a suitcase. **to live through** to experience and survive (an unpleasant experience). **to live to** to live long enough to reach (a particular age). **to live together** to cohabit. **to live to oneself** to live in isolation. **to live up to** to be worthy of, to conform to a prescribed standard. **to live with 1** to cohabit. **2** to accept or tolerate. **liveable, livable** *a.* **1** (of life) worth living. **2** (of a house, accommodation) fit to live in. **3** (*also* **liveable with**) (of a person) fit to live with. **liveableness, liveability** (-bil´-) *n.* **lived** *a.* (*usu. in comb.*, as *long-lived*). **lived-in** *a.* **1** (of a room) showing signs of habitation; homely, comfortable, reassuring. **2** (of a face) bearing the marks of experience. **3** (*facet.*) untidy; (of clothes etc.) in need of washing, mending. **live-in** *a.* **1** (of a lover) cohabiting. **2** (of an employee) resident on the premises. **liver**[1] *n.* **1** a person who lives. **2** a resident, a dweller. **3** a person who spends their life in a specified way (as a *good liver*). [OE *lifian, libban* (cp. Dut. *leven*, Icel. *lifa*, G *leben*), cogn. with LIFE]

live[2] (līv) *a.* **1** alive, living. **2** charged with energy, esp. with electrical energy; having the potential to function or discharge immediately; not exhausted or spent. **3** (of coals) burning, ignited. **4** (of a shell, bomb) unexploded. **5** (of a volcano) still active. **6** (of a radio, television broadcast) transmitted or transmitting at the actual time of an event, not a recording. **7** (of a performance of a play, concert etc.) given in front of an audience which sees or hears the event taking place. **8** (of a recording) made at a live performance; recorded at a single take without subsequent overdubbing. **9** (of an issue) of current interest and concern. **10** (of a rock) unquarried, unmined. **11** (of a wheel, axle etc.) able to transmit power; moving with a driving member. **12** (of the ball in games) still in play. **13** (*coll.*) lively, energetic. ~*adv.* at the actual time of the event; before an actual audience. **to go live** (*Comput.*) (of a system) to become operational. **live axle** *n.* an axle that rotates with and drives a wheel. **live bait** *n.* live fish, worms etc., used as bait in fishing. **live birth** *n.* the birth of a living child. **live-box** *n.* a case in which living microscopic objects are confined for observation. **live cartridge** *n.* a cartridge containing a bullet. **live centre** *n.* a rotating rod with a conical point in the headstock of a lathe that turns with the workpiece. **live feathers, live hair** *n.* feathers or hair plucked from a living fowl or animal. **live load** *n.* a moving or variable weight on a structure such as a bridge or floor. **liven** *v.t.* to make lively, to enliven. ~*v.i.* to cheer (up). **live oak** *n.* a N American evergreen tree, esp. *Quercus virginianus*, valuable for shipbuilding. **live rail** *n.* a rail charged with an electric current. **livestock** *n.* animals kept for farming or domestic purposes. **liveware** *n.* (*Comput.*) the staff operating and working with computer systems. **live wire** *n.* **1** a wire through which an electric current is flowing. **2** (*coll.*) an energetic person. [ALIVE]

livelihood (līv´lihud) *n.* means of subsistence; occupation. [OE *līflād,* (LIFE, *lād,* course, cogn. with LOAD and LODE)]
livelong[1] (liv´long) *a.* 1 long-lasting. 2 the whole, entire, the whole length of. [orig. *lief-long* (LIEF, LONG[1])]
livelong[2] (liv´long) *n.* ORPINE. [LIVE[1], LONG[1]]
lively (līv´li) *a.* (*comp.* **livelier,** *superl.* **liveliest**) 1 full of life, brisk, active, vigorous. 2 vivacious, cheerful, sociable. 3 animated, stimulating. 4 (of a description) lifelike, actual, vivid. 5 (of an impression) striking, forcible. 6 (of a colour) bright, vivid. 7 (of pace) brisk, fast. 8 (of a bouncing ball, boat etc.) moving in a springy, jerky or unpredictable fashion. 9 (*facet.*) exciting, dangerous. **look lively** hurry up, make haste. **livelily** *adv.* **liveliness** *n.* [OE *līflīc*]
liven LIVE[2].
liver[1] LIVE[1].
liver[2] (liv´ə) *n.* 1 a glandular organ in the abdominal cavity of vertebrates which secretes bile and purifies the blood. 2 the flesh of this from a sheep, calf etc., used as food. 3 applied to certain liver-coloured sulphides or other compounds of specified elements. ~*a.* liver-coloured. **liver chestnut** *n.* a horse of a dark chestnut colour. **liver colour,** (*N Am.*) **liver color** *n.* the colour of the liver, a reddish-brown. **liver-coloured** *a.* **liver complaint** *n.* a disordered state of the liver. **livered** *a.* (*usu. in comb.*, as *white-livered*, cowardly). **liver fluke** *n.* any of various parasitic worms, esp. *Fasciola hepatica*, that infect the bile ducts of sheep, cattle etc. **liverish** *a.* 1 having a disordered liver. 2 irritable. **liverishly** *adv.* **liverishness** *n.* **liver of sulphur** *n.* a liver-coloured mixture of potassium sulphide etc. used as a lotion for the treatment of skin diseases. **liver salts** *n.pl.* a preparation of mineral salts used to relieve indigestion. **liver sausage, liverwurst** *n.* sausage made from liver. **liver spot** *n.* a liver-coloured spot which appears on the skin in old age. **liverwort** *n.* any plant of the Hepaticae family, cryptogamic plants similar to mosses, that grow in damp places and some of which have liver-shaped leaves. **livery**[1] *a.* 1 resembling liver. 2 (of soil) heavy, tenacious. 3 (*coll.*) liverish. [OE *lifer* (cp. Dut. *lever,* Icel. *lifr,* G *Leber*)]
liver[3] (lī´və) *n.* a fabulous bird, supposed to have given its name to Liverpool, and still commemorated in the arms of that town. [from *Liverpool*]
Liverpudlian (livəpŭd´liən) *n.* a native or inhabitant of Liverpool. [*Liverpool* (with PUDDLE, for POOL[1]), -IAN]
livery[1] LIVER[2].
livery[2] (liv´əri) *n.* (*pl.* **liveries**) 1 a distinctive dress worn by the servants of a particular person or the members of a city company. 2 a distinctive colour scheme used on the vehicles, trains, aircraft etc. of a particular company or line. 3 any distinctive dress, guise or outward appearance. 4 the privileges of a city company or guild. 5 (*Hist.*) a ration or allowance of clothing, food etc. to retainers of a baron or knight. 6 (*Law*) delivery of property. 7 a writ granting possession. 8 (*N Am.*) a livery stable. ~†*v.t.* to dress or clothe in or as in livery. **at livery** kept at a stable for the owner at a fixed charge. **liveried** *a.* wearing a livery. **livery company** *n.* any of the guilds or companies of the City of London that formerly had a distinctive costume. **liveryman** *n.* (*pl.* **liverymen**) 1 a freeman of the City of London, who is entitled to wear the livery of the company to which he belongs and to vote in the election of Lord Mayor, sheriffs, chamberlain etc. 2 a person who keeps or works in a livery stable. [A-F *liveré,* OF *livrée,* fem. p.p. of *livrer,* late L *līberāre,* to give, to DELIVER]
lives LIFE.
livid (liv´id) *a.* 1 (*coll.*) furious, very angry. 2 of a leaden colour. 3 black and blue, discoloured (as by a bruise). **lividity** (-vid´-), **lividness** *n.* **lividly** *adv.* [L *līvidus*]
living (liv´ing) *a.* 1 alive, having life. 2 alive now, existing, contemporary. 3 (of a language) in current use. 4 (of a portrait) true to life, exact. 5 flowing, running. ~*n.* 1 the state of being alive, existence. 2 livelihood, means of subsistence; occupation. 3 the benefice of a clergyman. 4 manner of life. 5 (of an area, room) for everyday general use. **to beat/ knock the living daylights out of** DAYLIGHT. **to scare the living daylights out of** DAYLIGHT. **within living memory** within the memory of people still alive. **living death** *n.* a life of unmitigated suffering. **living rock** *n.* rock in its native state or location (prob. from the obs. idea that rock grows). **living room** *n.* a family sitting room. **living wage** *n.* the wage on which it is possible to maintain oneself and one's family adequately. **living will** *n.* a document without legal force, stating a person's desire not to be kept alive by artificial means in case of terminal illness, serious accident etc. [LIVE[1], -ING[1]]
livre (lēv´rə) *n.* an old French coin, replaced by the franc in 1795. [F, from L LIBRA]
lixiviate (liksiv´iāt) *v.t.* to leach, to dissolve out by lixiviation. **lixivial** *a.* **lixiviation** (-ā´shən) *n.* the process of separating a soluble from an insoluble material by a washing or filtering action, leaching. **lixivium** (-əm) *n.* (*pl.* **lixiviums, lixivia** (-viə)) 1 water impregnated with alkaline salts from wood-ash. 2 any solution obtained by leaching. [from mod. L *lixīviāre,* from *lixīvium,* neut. a., from *lix,* ashes, lye]
lizard (liz´əd) *n.* any member of the reptilian order Lacertilia, esp. of the typical genus *Lacerta,* having a long, scaly body and tail, and four limbs, each with five toes of unequal length. [OF *lesard,* L *lacerta -tus*]
LJ *abbr.* Lord Justice.
LL *abbr.* 1 Late Latin. 2 Low Latin. 3 Lord-Lieutenant.
ll. *abbr.* lines (of written matter).
'll (əl) *contr.* (*coll.*) will, shall.
llama (lah´mə) *n.* 1 a domesticated Peruvian wool-bearing animal, *Lama glama,* resembling a camel, but humpless and smaller, used as a beast of burden. 2 its wool, material made from this. [Sp., from Quechua]
llano (lah´nō) *n.* (*pl.* **llanos**) a level, treeless steppe or plain in the northern part of S America. **llanero** (-neə´rō) *n.* (*pl.* **llaneros**) a person who lives on the llanos of S America. [Sp., from L *plānum,* PLAIN[1]]
LLB *abbr.* Bachelor of Laws. [L *Legum Baccalaureus*]
LLD *abbr.* Doctor of Laws. [L *Legum Doctor*]
LLM *abbr.* Master of Laws. [L *Legum Magister*]
Lloyd's (loidz) *n.* a corporation, with offices in the City of London, esp. dealing with marine insurance, the classification and registration of vessels etc. **Lloyd's List** *n.* a newspaper, orig. started by Edward Lloyd in 1696 as Lloyd's News, devoted to shipping news and data. **Lloyd's Register** *n.* an annual alphabetical list of shipping belonging to all nations, classified according to seaworthiness. [Edward *Lloyd,* who kept a coffee house frequented by shippers in the 17th cent.]
LM *abbr.* 1 long metre. 2 lunar module.
lm *abbr.* lumen.
LMS *abbr.* 1 local management of schools. 2 (*Hist.*) London Midland and Scottish (Railway).
ln *abbr.* natural logarithm.
LNB *abbr.* low noise blocker (on a satellite dish).
LNER *abbr.* (*Hist.*) London and North-Eastern Railway.
lo (lō) *int.* see! behold! look! **lo and behold** used to introduce a startling fact or revelation. [OE *lā,* perh. blended with ME *lo,* short for loke, OE *lōca,* LOOK]
loach (lōch) *n.* any of the Cobitidae, a group of the carp family, esp. *Nemachilus barbatulus,* a small British river fish. [F *loche,* etym. unknown]
load (lōd) *n.* 1 a burden. 2 something which is laid on or put in anything for conveyance. 3 as much as can be carried at a time. 4 a measure of weight varying according to the material carried. 5 something which is borne with difficulty; a mental burden, a commitment.

6 (*pl., coll.*) heaps, lots, any amount. 7 something which presses upon, obstructs or resists. 8 the downward pressure of a superstructure. 9 the resistance to an engine or motor apart from friction. 10 the power output of a machine, circuit etc. 11 a device which receives power. ~*v.t.* 1 to put a load upon or in. 2 to put (a load or cargo) on or in a ship, vehicle etc. 3 to add weight to, to make heavy or heavier, to weight. 4 to weigh down, to encumber, to oppress. 5 to charge (a gun etc.). 6 to put a film, cartridge, cassette etc. in a camera, video machine etc. 7 (*Comput.*) to transfer a program into the memory, usu. from tape or disk. 8 to fill to overflowing. 9 to cover, to heap or overwhelm (with abuse, honours etc.). 10 to bias, esp. with something to increase strength or weight. 11 to make (a question, statement) biased or tendentious. 12 to add charges to (an insurance premium). 13 to draw power from (an electrical device or circuit). ~*v.i.* 1 to take in a load or cargo (usu. with *up*). 2 to charge a firearm. **a load of** (*coll.*) used for emphasis when dismissing something as merely or completely rubbish, nonsense etc. **a load off one's mind** a great relief (from anxiety). **to get a load of** (*sl.*) to listen to, pay attention to. **to have a load on** (*sl.*) to be drunk. **to load the dice against someone** to prejudice someone's chances of success. **load-bearing** *a.* (of a wall, arch etc.) supporting another part of the structure. **load-displacement, load draught** *n.* a ship's displacement when fully loaded. **loaded** *a.* 1 carrying a (heavy) load. 2 (of a gun) charged with ammunition. 3 (*coll.*) wealthy. 4 (*sl.*) drunk or drugged. 5 biased, weighted in a certain direction. 6 likely to cause argument. **loaded dice** *n.pl.* dice so weighted that they fall with a required face up. **loaded question** *n.* a question with hidden implications designed to trap the answerer. **loader** *n.* 1 a person who or something which loads; a loading-machine. 2 (*in comb.*) a gun that is loaded in a particular way, as *breech-* or *muzzle-loader.* 3 a person employed to load a sportsman's gun. **load factor** *n.* 1 the ratio of an external load to the weight of an aircraft. 2 the percentage of the maximum permissible payload carried by an aircraft on a particular flight. 3 the ratio of an average load to peak load over a period of time. **loading** *n.* 1 a load, a burden. 2 *in comb.*, as *breech-loading.* 3 the maximum amount of current or power taken by an appliance. 4 an addition to an insurance premium to cover increased risk. 5 (*Austral., New Zeal.*) an addition to a basic wage for special skills etc. **loading coil** *n.* an extra coil inserted in an electrical circuit to increase the inductance. **loading gauge** *n.* a gauge indicating the height to which railway trucks can be loaded so that they can pass bridges and tunnels safely. **load line** *n.* a Plimsoll line. [OE *lād*, way, course, cogn. with LEAD[1] and LODE]

loadsa (lōd´zə) *a.* (*sl.*) 1 short for *loads of.* 2 denoting a person or thing that has loads of something specified. **loadsamoney** *n.* a very vulgarly wealthy person.

loadstar LODESTAR (under LODE).

loadstone LODESTONE (under LODE).

loaf[1] (lōf) *n.* (*pl.* **loaves** (lōvz)) 1 a shaped mass of bread, esp. of a standard size or weight. 2 a moulded mass of any material, esp. a conical mass of refined sugar. 3 (*sl.*) the head or brains. **loaf sugar** *n.* sugar in the form of a loaf or in sections, cubes etc. from a loaf. [OE *hlāf* (cp. Icel. *hleifr*, G *Leib*)]

loaf[2] (lōf) *v.i.* 1 to lounge or idle about. 2 to saunter. ~*v.t.* to spend or pass (time away) idly. ~*n.* a saunter, an idle time, a loafing. **loafer** *n.* 1 a person who loafs, an idler. 2 a low leather shoe similar to a moccasin. [etym. uncertain]

loam (lōm) *n.* 1 soil consisting of sand and clay loosely coherent, with admixture of organic matter or humus. 2 in brickmaking etc., a mixture of sand and clay with chopped straw, used for making moulds. ~*v.t.* to cover with loam. **loamy** *a.* **loaminess** *n.* [OE *lām* (cp. Dut. *leem*, G *Lehm*) cogn. with *līm*, LIME[1]]

loan (lōn) *n.* 1 something which is lent, esp. a sum of money lent at interest. 2 the act of lending; the state of being lent. 3 permission to make use of. 4 funds acquired by the state from individuals and regarded as a debt. 5 a word, myth, custom etc., adopted from another people. ~*v.t.* to grant the loan of. **on loan** 1 given or taken as a loan. 2 (of staff) temporarily transferred. **loanable** *a.* **loanback** *n.* a facility made available by some life-insurance companies enabling policy-holders to borrow from their pension funds. **loan collection** *n.* a set of pictures etc. lent by the owners for public exhibition. **loanee** (-nē´) *n.* **loaner** *n.* **loan holder** *n.* 1 a person who holds securities for a loan. 2 a mortgage. **loan shark** *n.* (*coll.*) a person who lends money at excessive or illegal interest rates. **loan sharking** *n.* **loan-translation** *n.* a compound word or phrase which is a literal translation of the corresponding elements of a foreign expression (e.g. *Superman* from G *Übermensch*), also called a *calque.* **loanword** *n.* a word borrowed from another language. [OE *lān*, (cp. Dut. *leen*, Icel. *lān*, G *Lehn*), cogn. with *leōn*, to lend, also with Gr. *leipein*, L *linquere*, to leave]

loath (lōth), **loth** *a.* unwilling, averse, reluctant. **nothing loath** 1 quite willing. 2 willingly. **loathness** *n.* unwillingness, reluctance. [OE *lāth* (cp. Dut. *leed*, Icel. *leithr*), cogn. with G *Leid*, sorrow]

Usage note The spellings and pronunciations of the adjective *loath* and the verb *loathe* should not be confused: *loath* (-th) means averse, and *loathe* (-dh) to detest.

loathe (lōdh) *v.t.* 1 to feel disgust at. 2 to abhor, to detest. **loather** *n.* **loathing** *n.* disgust, aversion, abhorrence. **loathingly** *adv.* †**loathly** *a.* creating loathing, loathsome. ~†*adv.* unwillingly. †**loathliness** *n.* **loathsome** (-səm) *a.* causing loathing or disgust, odious, detestable. **loathsomely** *adv.* **loathsomeness** *n.* [OE *lathian*, from LOATH]

Usage note See note under LOATH.

loaves LOAF[1].

lob (lob) *n.* 1 in tennis, a ball struck in a high arc, usu. over one's opponent's head; a stroke that sends the ball on this trajectory. 2 in cricket, a slow underarm ball. ~*v.t.* (*pres.p.* **lobbing**, *past, p.p.* **lobbed**) 1 to hit or throw (a ball) in a high arc. 2 to send (an opponent) a lobbed ball. 3 †to hang or allow to droop heavily. ~*v.i.* to make a lob. [etym. uncertain, perh. onomat.]

lobar, lobate LOBE.

lobby (lob´i) *n.* (*pl.* **lobbies**) 1 a passage, corridor or vestibule, usu. opening into several apartments. 2 a small hall or ante-room. 3 that part of a hall of a legislative assembly to which the public are admitted. 4 DIVISION LOBBY (under DIVISION). 5 a group of people who try to influence legislators on behalf of special interests. 6 an organized attempt by members of the public to influence legislators. 7 the lobby system; journalists who work in the lobby system. ~*v.i.* (*3rd pers. sing. pres.* **lobbies**, *pres.p.* **lobbying**, *past, p.p.* **lobbied**) 1 to seek to gain support, esp. from legislators, (for). 2 to frequent a parliamentary lobby, to act as a lobbyist. ~*v.t.* 1 to attempt to influence or persuade (legislators) to support something. 2 to attempt to gain (support), to attempt to gain the support of (a person). 3 to secure the passage of (a Bill) by lobbying. **lobby correspondent** *n.* a reporter who covers parliamentary affairs. **lobbyist** *n.* a person employed to lobby for a particular interest. **lobby system** *n.* the system which allows correspondents access to political information on condition that the source remains anonymous. [low L *lobia*, LODGE]

lobe (lōb) *n.* 1 any rounded and projecting or hanging

part. **2** a division of a bodily organ. **3** the soft lower part of the ear. **4** a rounded division of a leaf. **lobar** *a.* of or relating to a lobe. **lobate** (-āt), **lobated** (-ā´tid) *a.* **1** having or resembling lobes. **2** (of birds) having separate toes, each fringed with a weblike lobe. **lobectomy** (ləbek´təmi) *n.* (*pl.* **lobectomies**) the surgical removal of a lobe from an organ or gland. **lobed** *a.* **lobelet** (-lit) *n.* [F, from late L *lobus*, Gr. *lobos*, lobe or pod, cogn. with L *legūmen*, LEGUME, cp. *legula*, lobe of ear]

lobelia (ləbē´lyə) *n.* any of a genus, *Lobelia*, of herbaceous and brilliant flowering plants. [Matthias de *Lobel*, 1538–1616, Flemish botanist]

loblolly (lob´loli) *n.* (*pl.* **loblollies**) **1** any of various US pine trees. **2** †thick gruel. **loblolly man, loblolly boy** *n.* (*Hist.*) a man or boy who attends on the ship's surgeon. [etym. uncertain]

lobola (ləbō´lə, lawbaw´lə) *n.* a Southern African custom whereby the bridegroom's family makes a payment of cash or cattle to the bride's family shortly before a marriage. [Zulu]

lobotomy (ləbot´əmi) *n.* (*pl.* **lobotomies**) **1** a surgical incision into the lobe of an organ or gland. **2** an operation in which the fibres connecting the frontal lobes of the brain to the rest of the brain are cut, formerly used in the treatment of severe depression. **lobotomize, lobotomise** *v.t.* **1** to perform a lobotomy on. **2** (*coll.*) to render dull or harmless.

lobscouse (lob´skows) *n.* (*Naut.*) a hash of meat with vegetables of various kinds and ship's biscuit. [etym. uncertain]

lobster (lob´stə) *n.* **1** a large marine long-tailed and stalk-eyed decapod crustacean with large pincers, of the genus *Homarus*. **2** the flesh of this as food. **lobster pot** *n.* a wickerwork trap for lobsters. **lobster thermidor** *n.* a dish of lobster meat, mushrooms, cream, egg yolks and sherry, served in a lobster shell. [OE *loppestre*, corr. of L *locusta*, LOCUST]

lobule (lob´ūl) *n.* (a subdivision of) a small lobe. **lobular, lobulated** (-lātid) *a.*

lobworm (lob´wœm) *n.* **1** a large earthworm, used as bait by anglers. **2** a lugworm. [from obs. *lob*, a heavy object]

local (lō´kəl) *a.* **1** existing in or peculiar to a particular place or places. **2** of or relating to a neighbourhood. **3** of or relating to a part, not the whole (as a disease etc.). **4** (of a bus, train) serving a particular area; stopping at all stations or stops. **5** of or relating to place. ~*n.* **1** an inhabitant of a particular place. **2** a train or bus serving a particular district. **3** a public house in one's neighbourhood. **4** a local anaesthetic. **5** (*N Am.*) a local branch of a trade union. **6** locale. **local anaesthesia,** (*N Am.*) **local anesthesia** *n.* anaesthesia affecting only a particular area of the body and not involving general unconsciousness. **local anaesthetic** *n.* **local area network** *n.* a network of computers in close proximity to one another so that a high rate of data transfer is possible. **local authority** *n.* the elected body which administers a particular district. **local bus** *n.* **1** a bus or bus service operating in a particular district. **2** (*Comput.*) a connection from a microprocessor to an adjacent peripheral device allowing rapid transfer of data. **local call** *n.* a telephone call to a number on the same or a neighbouring exchange, usu. charged at a cheaper rate. **local colour,** (*N Am.*) **local color** *n.* **1** features characteristic of a place or district emphasized in a literary work in order to promote actuality. **2** in painting, the colour of individual objects considered apart from the general colour scheme. **local derby** *n.* (*pl.* **local derbies**) a game between two teams from the same district. **local government** *n.* **1** administration of towns, districts etc. by elective councils. **2** (*N Am.*) a local authority. **localism** *n.* **1** preference for what is local. **2** affection for a place. **3** limitations due to confinement to a place, provincialism. **4** a local idiom, custom etc. **locality** (-kal´-) *n.* (*pl.* **localities**) **1** a particular place, area or neighbourhood. **2** the site or scene of something. **3** existence in a certain portion of space. **localize** (lō´kəlīz), **localise** *v.t.* **1** to make local; to identify with a place. **2** to ascertain or indicate the exact place or locality of. **3** to restrict to a particular place. **4** to decentralize. **localizable** *a.* **localization** (-zā´shən) *n.* **locally** *adv.* **local management of schools** *n.* a system in which the governors and head teacher of a state school are responsible for managing a budget allocated to it by a local authority. **local option** *n.* the power of a particular district, region etc. to decide whether a piece of national legislation shall apply to it. **local preacher** *n.* a Methodist lay preacher authorized to conduct services on a particular circuit. **local time** *n.* time calculated on the noon of the meridian of a place, as distinct from standard time. **local veto** *n.* (*N Am.*) LOCAL OPTION (under LOCAL). [F, from L *locālis*, from *locus*, place]

locale (lōkahl´) *n.* a place, site, esp. with reference to an event taking place there. [F *local*, n., respelt to show stress]

locate (ləkāt´) *v.t.* **1** to discover or determine the site of. **2** to set or place in a particular locality. **3** to state the location of. **4** (*in p.p.*) to situate. ~*v.i.* to settle, to take up residence. **location** *n.* **1** situation or position. **2** the act of locating. **3** a site outside the studio grounds where a scene for a film is shot. **4** (*Comput.*) a specific area in memory capable of holding a unit of information, e.g. a word. **5** in South Africa, a township for black or coloured people usu. on the outskirts of a town or city. **on location** (of filming etc.) outside the studio. **locative** (lok´ətiv) *a.* (*Gram.*) denoting place. ~*n.* a case denoting place. [from L *locus*, place]

Usage note *Locate* should not be used as though it meant simply to find.

loc. cit. (lok sit´) *adv.* in the place cited. [L *loco citato*]

loch (lokh) *n.* a lake or a narrow or land-locked arm of the sea in Scotland. **lochan** (-ən) *n.* (*Sc.*) a small lake, a tarn. [Gael.]

lochia (lok´iə) *n.pl.* the uterine evacuations which follow childbirth. **lochial** *a.* [Gr., from *lochos*, a childbed]

loci LOCUS.

lock[1] (lok) *n.* **1** a device for fastening doors etc., usu. having a bolt moved by a key of a particular shape. **2** a mechanical device for checking or preventing movement, as of a wheel. **3** an enclosure in a canal, between gates, for raising and lowering vessels by letting water in or out. **4** a degree of turn imparted to the front wheels of a vehicle; the full extent to which the front wheels will turn. **5** a fastening together or interlocking. **6** a hug or grapple in wrestling that prevents an opponent from moving a limb. **7** in rugby, a lock forward. **8** the firing apparatus of a gun. **9** an airtight antechamber to a caisson or tunnel. **10** an air bubble blocking the flow of gas or liquid through a pipe. ~*v.t.* **1** to fasten (a door, window etc.) by means of a lock. **2** to secure (a building, car etc.) by locking its doors etc. **3** to fix together (a coupling, interlocking parts) so as to make secure or immovable. **4** to cause (a mechanism) to jam. **5** to hold closely and firmly (in an embrace). **6** (*usu. in pass.*) to engage in a contest, struggle, state etc. **7** (*usu. in pass.*) (of land, hills) to hem, to enclose. **8** to furnish (a canal) with locks. **9** to take (a boat) through a lock. ~*v.i.* **1** to be able to be fastened by a lock. **2** (of a coupling, interlocking parts) to become fixed together securely or immovably. **3** to become jammed. **4** to pass through a lock on a river or canal. **lock, stock and barrel** the whole lot. **to lock away 1** to hide, keep in a secure place. **2** to imprison. **3** to make unavailable or inaccessible. **4** to invest (money) so that it cannot be readily realized. **to lock horns** to become engaged in an argument or combat. **to lock in** to keep in, confine or imprison by locking doors etc. **to lock on (to)** to track automatically (an object) by means of a radar beam or sensor. **to lock out 1** to prevent from entering by locking doors etc. **2** to prevent (workers) from working during an industrial dispute usu. by closing premises. **to lock up 1** to close, fasten or secure with lock and key. **2** to close and lock all the doors and windows of (a building). **3** to hide, keep in a secure place. **4** to imprison. **5** to make unavailable or inaccessible. **6** to invest (money) so that it cannot be readily realized. **under lock and key** securely locked up. **lockage** (-ij) *n.* **1** the rise and fall in a canal through the working of locks. **2** a toll for passing through locks. **3** the construction or use of locks. **4** canal locks collectively. **lockfast** *a.* secured by a lock. **lock forward** *n.* in rugby, either of the two inside players in the second row of the scrum. **lock gate** *n.* the gate of a canal lock. **lockjaw** *n.* **1** a symptom of tetanus in which the muscles of the jaw are violently contracted and its motion suspended; trismus. **2** tetanus. **lock-keeper** *n.* a person who attends to a lock on a river or canal. **lock-knit** *a., n.* (a fabric) knitted with an interlocking stitch. **locknut** *n.* **1** a nut screwed down on top of another nut to prevent its working loose. **2** a nut specially designed so that it cannot work loose. **lockout** *n.* the temporary exclusion of workers from their workplace by an employer as a means of bringing pressure to bear on them during an industrial dispute. **locksman** *n.* (*pl.* **locksmen**) a lock-keeper. **locksmith** *n.* a maker and repairer of locks. **lock stitch** *n.* a sewing-machine stitch which locks two threads together. **lock-up** *n.* **1** a place where prisoners are temporarily confined. **2** the act of or time for locking up premises for the night. **3** a small garage. **4** a lock-up shop. **5** the investing of capital in such a way that it cannot be realized. **6** the amount so invested. *~a.* that may be locked. **lock-up shop** *n.* a small shop having access only from the street, with no connection with the rest of the building. [OE *loc* (cp. Icel. *loka*, lock, *lok*, lid, G *Loch*)]

lock[2] (lok) *n.* **1** a number of strands of hair curled or hanging together, a tress, a ringlet. **2** (*pl.*) a person's hair. **3** a tuft of wool or similar substance. **4** a lovelock. [OE *locc* (cp. Dut. *lok*, Icel. *lokkr*, G *Locke*), cogn. with Gr. *lugos*, a withy, and *lugizein*, to bend]

locker (lok´ə) *n.* **1** a cupboard, chest or other closed receptacle, with lock and key, esp. one of a number for public use e.g. at a swimming pool or railway station. **2** a chest or compartment on a ship for locking up stores etc. **3** a person who or something which locks. **not a shot in one's locker** (having) no money in one's pocket. **locker room** *n.* a room with lockers for storing clothes and other belongings, also usu. used for changing for sport etc.

locket (lok´it) *n.* **1** a small gold or silver case, worn as an ornament and adapted to contain hair, a miniature etc. **2** a plate or band on a scabbard to which the hook is fastened. [F *loquet*, dim. of OF *loc*, latch, from Gmc. (cp. Icel. *loka*, LOCK[1])]

lockjaw LOCK[1].

loco[1] (lō´kō) *n.* (*pl.* **locos**) short for LOCOMOTIVE (under LOCOMOTION).

loco[2] (lō´kō) *a.* **1** (*esp N Am., sl.*) insane, mad. **2** affected with loco disease. *~n.* (*pl.* **locos, locoes**) (*also* **loco-plant, loco-weed**) any of several leguminous plants of the genus *Astragalus* of NW America which cause loco disease in livestock when ingested. **loco disease** *n.* a disease of cattle, sheep and horses characterized by paralysis of the limbs and impaired vision and caused by the ingestion of loco. [Sp., insane]

locomotion (lōkəmō´shən) *n.* **1** the act or power of moving from place to place. **2** moving about, travel, travelling. **locomotive** *a.* **1** of or relating to locomotion. **2** moving from place to place, not stationary. **3** having the power of locomotion, or causing locomotion. **4** of or relating to travel. *~n.* **1** (*also* **locomotive engine**) an engine powered by electricity, diesel fuel or steam that runs on railway tracks and is used for hauling trains. **2** any machine capable of locomotion. **locomotively** *adv.* **locomotivity** (-tiv´-), **locomotiveness** *n.* **locomotor** *a.* of or relating to locomotion. **locomotor ataxy** *n.* tabes dorsalis, inability to coordinate the movements of the limbs, due to degeneration of the nerve fibres in the late stages of syphilis. **locomotory** *a.* [L *locō*, abl. of *locus*, place, MOTION]

loculus (lok´ūləs) *n.* (*pl.* **loculi** (-lī)) (*Anat., Biol.*) **1** a small cavity, a cell, esp. any one of a large number of such. **2** any of the chambers of an ovary or anther. **loculament** (-ləmənt) *n.* any of the cells of a seed vessel. **locular, loculate** (-lət) *a.* [L, dim. of LOCUS]

locum (lō´kəm), **locum tenens** (tē´nenz, ten´-) *n.* (*pl.* **locums, locum tenentes** (tinen´tēz)) a deputy or substitute, esp. one acting in the place of a doctor or member of the clergy. **locum tenency** (ten´ənsi) *n.* [L, holding place (see LOCUS)]

locus (lō´kəs) *n.* (*pl.* **loci** (lō´sī, -kī, -kē)) **1** the exact place, the locality (of). **2** (*Math.*) the line generated by a point, or the surface generated by a line, moving according to specified conditions. **3** the location of a particular gene on a chromosome. **locus classicus** (klas´ikəs) *n.* (*pl.* **loci classici** (lōsī klas´isī, lōkē klas´ikē)) the best or most authoritative passage that can be quoted as an instance or illustration. **locus standi** (stan´dī) *n.* (*pl.* **loci standi** (lōsī stan´dī, lōkē stan´dē)) a recognized position or status authorizing intervention, application to a court etc. [L, place]

locust (lō´kəst) *n.* **1** a winged insect of various species allied to the grasshopper, which migrates in vast swarms and is very destructive to vegetation. **2** applied to certain US and Australian grasshoppers. **3** a locust tree. **locust bean** *n.* the sweet pod of the carob. **locust-bird, locust-eater** *n.* any of various species of birds that feed on locusts. **locust tree** *n.* **1** the carob. **2** the N American false acacia, *Robinia pseudacacia*. **3** the kowhai. [L *locusta*, lobster, locust]

locution (ləkū´shən) *n.* **1** a phrase or expression considered with regard to style or idiom. **2** style of speech, mode of delivery. [L *locūtio*, from *loquī*, to speak]

locutory (lok´ūtəri) *n.* (*pl.* **locutories**) **1** a conversation room or parlour in a monastery. **2** a grille at which inmates and visitors might converse. [med. L *locūtōrium*, from L *locūtor*, speaker]

lode (lōd) *n.* a vein in rock bearing precious ore. **lodestar, loadstar** *n.* **1** a guiding star or one that a ship is steered by, usu. the pole star. **2** one's aim, ambition or guiding principle. **lodestone, loadstone** *n.* **1** magnetic oxide of iron; a natural magnet. **2** something that attracts. [OE *lād*, see LOAD]

loden (lō´dən) *n.* **1** a thick soft waterproof woollen cloth used for making coats. **2** a greyish-green colour typical of this cloth. [G, from OHG *liodo*, thick cloth]

lodge (loj) *n.* **1** a small house at the entrance to or in a park, esp. for a gatekeeper or gardener. **2** a cottage, a hut, a cabin for seasonal use; a hunting lodge. **3** a large house or hotel (esp. in the name of such). **4** (*N Am.*) a central building in a resort, camp etc. **5** a room or apartment for a porter in a college, chambers etc. **6** a local branch or place of meeting of certain societies, such as the Freemasons. **7** the local branch of a trade union. **8** a N American Indian wigwam; the family that lives in it. **9** a beaver's or otter's lair. **10** the residence of the head of a Cambridge college. *~v.t.* **1** to supply with temporary quarters, esp. for sleeping. **2** to receive as an inmate, usu. for a fixed charge. **3** to find accommodation for. **4** to deposit (a complaint, information) in court or with a prosecuting officer. **5** to deposit, to leave for security (in, with etc.). **6** to implant, to fix. **7** to place (power, authority) in the hands of. **8** (of wind) to beat down (crops). ~*v.i.* **1** to reside temporarily, esp. to have sleeping quarters. **2** to reside as an inmate at a fixed charge. **3** to stay or become fixed (in). **4** (of crops) to be laid flat. **lodgement, lodgment** *n.* **1** the act of lodging, the state of being lodged. **2** the depositing or a deposit of money. **3** an accumulation of matter that remains at rest, a deposit. **lodger** *n.* a person who rents and occupies furnished rooms. **lodging** *n.* **1** a temporary residence. **2** (*usu. in pl.*) a room or rooms hired in another's house. **3** (*formal*) a dwelling place. **4** (*often pl.*) the residence of the head of an Oxford college. **lodging house** *n.* a private home that provides accommodation for rent. [OF *loge*, low L *lobia*, LOBBY, from Gmc. (cp. OHG *louba*, G *Laube*, cogn. with *laub*, LEAF)]

lodicule (lod´ikūl) *n.* (*Bot.*) any of two or three minute green or white scales below the ovary of a grass flower. [L *lodicula*, dim. of *lodix*, coverlet]

loess (lō´is, lœs) *n.* a wind-borne deposit of clay, loam, sand etc., in the Rhine, Mississippi and other river valleys. [G *Löss*, from Swiss G *lösch*, loose]

loft (loft) *n.* **1** the room or air space under a roof. **2** an elevated gallery in a church or hall. **3** a room over a barn or stable. **4** a pigeon-house; a flock of pigeons. **5** in golf, a backward inclination of the face of a club; a lofting stroke. ~*v.t.* **1** to strike (the ball) so that it rises high in the air. **2** to slant the face of (a golf club). **lofter** *n.* a golf club for lofting. **lofty** *a.* (*comp.* **loftier**, *superl.* **loftiest**) **1** (*poet.*) very high, towering, of imposing height. **2** elevated in character, sentiment, style etc., sublime. **3** high-flown, grandiose. **4** haughty, arrogant. **loftily** *adv.* **loftiness** *n.* [Icel. *lopt* (pronounced as loft), orig. the sky (cp. LIFT[1])]

log[1] (log) *n.* **1** a bulky piece of unhewn timber. **2** a block. **3** a device (orig. a piece of wood with a line attached) used for ascertaining the rate of a ship's motion. **4** a detailed record of the voyage of a ship or flight of an aircraft. **5** a logbook. **6** any record of events, performance, transmissions made etc. or of the work done by a computer. ~*v.t.* (*pres.p.* **logging**, *past, p.p.* **logged**) **1** to enter in the logbook or other regular record. **2** (of a ship) to make (a specified distance) by the log. **3** to log up. **4** to fell (trees) for timber. **5** to cut into logs. ~*v.i.* to fell trees. **to heave the log** to determine a ship's speed with a float and line. **to log in/ on** **1** to begin to use a computer system. **2** to gain access to a computer system (by means of a code, password). **to log off/ out** to exit from or conclude the use of a computer system. **to log up** to spend (a specified amount of time) working, flying etc. as recorded in a logbook or other record. **to sleep like a log** to be in a deep sleep. **logbook** *n.* **1** a book in which an official diary of events occurring in a ship's voyage or aircraft's flight is kept. **2** any book containing a detailed record of work done, performance etc. **3** the registration document of a motor vehicle. **log cabin** *n.* a cabin built of logs. **log canoe** *n.* a canoe made from a hollowed-out tree trunk. **logger** *n.* a lumberjack. **logging** *n.* the work of felling, cutting up and preparing forest timber. **logjam** *n.* **1** a blockage in a river caused by floating logs. **2** a deadlock, a standstill. **log-line** *n.* a knotted line, fastened to the ship's log for finding the speed of the vessel. **log-man** *n.* (*pl.* **log-men**) a man employed to carry logs. **logrolling** *n.* **1** (*N Am.*) mutual political assistance in carrying legislative measures. **2** a sport in which two opponents attempt to spin each other off a floating log on which both are standing. **logroll** *v.i.* **logroller** *n.* **logwood** *n.* **1** the wood of a tropical American and W Indian tree, *Haematoxylon campechianum*, used as the source of a dark-red dyestuff. **2** this tree. [ME *logge*, etym. uncertain]

log[2] (log) *n.* short for LOGARITHM.

-log -LOGUE.

logan (log´ən), **logan-stone** *n.* a rocking-stone. [obs. *logging*, pres.p. of *log* (prob. onomat.), to rock]

loganberry (lō´gənbəri) *n.* (*pl.* **loganberries**) **1** a permanent hybrid plant obtained by crossing the raspberry and a species of blackberry. **2** the fruit of this. [J. H. *Logan*, 1841–1928, US horticulturalist]

logaoedic (logəē´dik) *a.* in ancient prosody, applied to lines consisting of a mixture of dactyls and trochees to give the effect of prose. ~*n.* a line of this character. [late L *logaoedicus*, Gr. *logaoidikos* (*logos*, speech, *aoidē*, song)]

logarithm (log´əridhm) *n.* the exponent of the power to which a fixed number, called the base, must be raised to produce a given number (tabulated and used as a means of simplifying arithmetical processes by enabling addition and subtraction to be substituted for multiplication and division). **logarithmic** (-ridh´-) *a.* **logarithmically** *adv.* [Gr. *logos*, word, ratio, *arithmos*, number]

loge (lōzh) *n.* a box in the theatre. [F; see LODGE]

-loger -LOGIST.

loggerhead (log´əhed) *n.* **1** (*also* **loggerhead turtle**) a large marine turtle, *Caretta caretta*. **2** (*also* **loggerhead shrike**) a shrike, *Lanius ludovicianus*, of Mexico and the southern US, that has black and white wings and a grey head and body with a black facial stripe. **3** a tool consisting of a long handle with a bulbous iron head for heating liquids, melting tar etc. **4** †an idiot. **at loggerheads** in conflict, locked in dispute. [dial. *logger*, from LOG[1], HEAD[1]]

loggia (loj´iə) *n.* (*pl.* **loggias, loggie** (loj´e)) **1** an open corridor, gallery or arcade along the front of a large building. **2** an open balcony in a theatre or concert hall. [It., LODGE]

logia LOGION.

logic (loj´ik) *n.* **1** the science of reasoning, correct thinking, proving and deducing. **2** a treatise on this. **3** a particular mode, system or chain of reasoning. **4** reasoning, argument etc. considered with regard to correctness or incorrectness. **5** reasoned argument. **6** the necessary consequences of an argument, a situation etc. **7** force of circumstances, situation etc. **8** (*Comput.*) the elementary principles for performing arithmetical and logical operations in a computer; logical operations collectively. **logical** *a.* **1** of or relating to, used in or according to the rules of logic, consistent or accurate in reasoning. **2** reasonable. **3** versed or skilled in accurate reasoning. **4** (*Comput.*) of, performed by or used in logic circuits. **logical atomism** *n.* the theory that all propositions can be analysed into simple independent elements. **logicality** (-kal´-), **logicalness** *n.* **logically** *adv.* **logical necessity** *n.* the necessity of believing a thing whose opposite is inconceivable. **logical positivism, logical empiricism** *n.* a philosophical school based on linguistic analysis which demands that meaningful statements must be empirically verifiable, so rejecting metaphysics etc. as nonsense. **logic bomb** *n.* an instruction programmed (usu. secretly) into a computer that will trigger a breakdown if a specified set of circumstances occurs. **logic circuit** *n.* an electronic circuit used in computers which performs logical operations on its two or more inputs. **logician** (-jish´ən) *n.* a person skilled in logic. [OF *logique*, L *logica*, Gr. *logikē* (*technē*), the art of reasoning (*logikos*, pertaining to reasoning, from LOGOS)]

-logic (loj´ik), **-logical** (-kəl) *comb. form* forming adjectives from nouns ending in *-logy*. [Gr. *-logikos*]

logion (log´iən) *n.* (*pl.* **logia** (-giə)) a traditional saying, revelation or truth, esp. one of those ascribed to Christ but not recorded in the Gospels. [Gr., oracle, dim. of LOGOS]

-logist (ləjist), **-loger** (ləjə) *comb. form* forming nouns

meaning a person versed in or working in, as *anthropologist, astrologer.* [-LOGY, -IST]
logistics (ləjis´tiks) *n.pl.* **1** the branch of strategy concerned with the moving and supply of troops. **2** the planning and organization of any complex enterprise. **logistic, logistical** *a.* of or relating to logistics. [LOGIC]
loglog (log´log) *n.* the logarithm of a logarithm.
logo (log´ō, lō´-) *n.* (*pl.* **logos**) a symbol or simple design used to identify a company, organization etc. [abbr. of *logotype*]
logo- (log´ō) *comb. form* **1** of or relating to words. **2** wordy. [LOGOS]
logogram (log´əgram) *n.* a sign representing a word, esp. in shorthand.
logography (logog´rəfi) *n.* a method of printing in which a type represents a word instead of a letter. **logographic** (-graf´-), **logographical** *a.*
logogriph (log´əgrif) *n.* a word puzzle, esp. one based on transposing the letters of a word. [F *logogriphe*, Gr. *griphos*, basket, riddle]
logomachy (ləgom´əki) *n.* (*pl.* **logomachies**) contention about words, a controversy hingeing on verbal matters. **logomachist** *n.* [Gr. *logomachia* (*-machia*, battle, from *machesthai*, to fight)]
logorrhoea (logərē´ə), (*N Am.*) **logorrhea** *n.* excessive or uncontrollable talkativeness.
Logos (log´os) *n.* **1** in Greek philosophy, the divine reason implicit in and governing the cosmos. **2** in Christian theology, the Divine Word, the Son of God, the Second Person of the Trinity. [Gr., word, speech, reason, cogn. with *legein*, to speak]
logotype (log´ətīp) *n.* **1** (*Print.*) a type having two or more letters cast in one piece, but not as a ligature, as *are, was* etc. **2** a logo. **3** a piece of type that prints a logo.
-logue (log), (*N Am.*) **-log** *comb. form* **1** forming nouns relating to discourse, as in *epilogue, prologue.* **2** equivalent to *-logist*, as in *ideologue.* [F *-logue*, from Gr. *-logos -on*, see LOGOS]
-logy (ləji), **-ology** (ol´əji) *comb. form* forming names of sciences and departments of knowledge, and nouns denoting modes of speaking or discourses, as *astrology, eulogy, tautology.* [Gr. *-logia, -logos*, see LOGOS (older examples through F *-logie*, med. L *-logia*)]
†**loimic** (loi´mik) *a.* of or relating to the plague or to contagious diseases. [Gr. *loimikos*, from *loimos*, plague]
loin (loin) *n.* **1** the part of the body of a human being or quadruped lying between the lower ribs and the hip joint. **2** a joint of meat from this part. **3** (*pl.*) the genitals and the surrounding area. **4** (*pl.*) this part as representing strength and generative power. **to gird up one's loins** GIRD[1]. **loincloth** *n.* a cloth worn round the loins as an elementary kind of garment. [OF *loigne*, ult. from L *lumbus*, cogn. with OE *lendenu*, and Dut. *lende*]
loiter (loi´tə) *v.i.* **1** to linger, to dawdle. **2** to move or travel with frequent halts. *~v.t.* to waste or consume (time) in trifles, to idle (time) away. **loiterer** *n.* **loiteringly** *adv.* [perh. from MDut. *loteren* (Dut. *lenteren*), cp. WFlem. *lutteren*, Norw. *lutra*]
Lok Sabha (lōk sŭb´ə) *n.* the lower chamber of the Indian parliament. [Hind. *lok*, people, *sabha*, house]
loll (lol) *v.i.* **1** to stand, sit or lie in a lazy attitude, to lounge. **2** (of the tongue) to hang from the mouth. *~v.t.* to let (one's head or limbs) hang or recline lazily (on or against). **loller** *n.* **lollingly** *adv.* [prob. imit. (cp. MDut. *lollen*, Icel. *lolla*, also LULL)]
lollapalooza (loləpəloo´zə), **lalapalooza** (lal-) *n.* (*N Am., sl.*) something first-rate, excellent etc. [etym. unknown]
Lollard (lol´əd) *n.* any of one of a sect of English religious reformers in the 14th and 15th cents., followers of John Wyclif (?1330–84). **Lollardism, Lollardy** *n.* [MDut. *lollaerd*, from *lollen*, to hum (conf. with LOLLER (under LOLL))]
lollipop (lol´ipop) *n.* **1** a flat or round boiled sweet on the end of a stick. **2** an ice lollipop. **3** a piece of popular classical music. **lollipop man, lollipop lady, lollipop woman** *n.* (*pl.* **lollipop men, lollipop ladies, lollipop women**) (*coll.*) a person who conducts children safely across roads by controlling traffic using a pole with a disc on the top. [etym. uncertain]
lollop (lol´əp) *v.i.* (*pres.p.* **lolloping**, *past, p.p.* **lolloped**) **1** to move with an ungainly bouncing gait. **2** to roll or flop about heavily. [from LOLL]
lolly (lol´i) *n.* (*pl.* **lollies**) **1** a lollipop, a sweet on a stick. **2** an ice lolly. **3** (*sl.*) money.
lollygag LALLYGAG.
Lombard (lom´bəd, -bahd) *n.* **1** any of a Germanic people, the Longobardi, who conquered Italy in the 6th cent. **2** a native or inhabitant of Lombardy. **3** the dialect of Lombardy. *~a.* of or relating to the Lombards or to Lombardy. **Lombardic** (-bah´-) *a.* Lombard, applied esp. to a style of architecture flourishing in Italy, 7th–13th cents., a school of Italian painters of the 15th and 16th cents., and a style of handwriting used in medieval manuscripts. **Lombardy poplar** (-bədi) *n.* a variety of poplar tree with erect branches. [F, from It. *Lombardo*, late L *Longo-, Langobardus* (Gmc. *lang-*, LONG[1], *Bardi*, L, name of the people)]
loment (lō´mənt), **lomentum** (-men´təm) *n.* (*pl.* **loments, lomenta** (-men´tə)) an indehiscent legume, that separates when ripe by means of a transverse articulation between each seed. **lomentaceous** (-tā´shəs) *a.* [L *lōmentum*, bean meal, used as a cosmetic, from *lavāre* (p.p. *lōtum*), to wash]
London clay (lŭn´dən) *n.* a formation of a lower Eocene age in SE England. **Londoner** *n.* a native or inhabitant of London. **London plane** *n.* a hybrid plane tree, *Platanus* × *hispanica*, widely grown in London streets and parks because of its tolerance of smoke. **London pride** *n.* a hybrid saxifrage, *Saxifraga urbium*, cultivated in gardens for its pink flowers. [the capital of the United Kingdom and of England, L *Londinium*, perh. of Celt. orig.]
lone (lōn) *a.* **1** single, solitary, without company or a comrade. **2** unmarried, widowed. **3** (*chiefly poet. or formal*) solitary, retired, uninhabited, lonely, deserted. **lone hand** *n.* **1** in euchre, quadrille, a hand played without help from one's partner's cards. **2** any action taken by a person without assistance or allies. **loneness** *n.* **lone pair** *n.* a pair of valency electrons unshared by other atoms. **loner** *n.* a person or animal that avoids the company of others. **lonesome** (-səm) *a.* **1** lonely, companionless. **2** (of a place) unfrequented; arousing feelings of loneliness. **on one's lonesome** alone. **lonesomely** *adv.* **lonesomeness** *n.* **lone wolf** *n.* a person who prefers to be or to operate alone. [ME, from *alone*]
lonely (lōn´li) *a.* (*comp.* **lonelier**, *superl.* **loneliest**) **1** sad through lacking company or companionship. **2** solitary, companionless. **3** (of a place) unfrequented, sequestered; causing feelings of loneliness. **4** (of an object) single, solitary, standing alone. **loneliness** *n.* **lonely heart** *n.* a lonely person, esp. one seeking friendship or marriage.
long[1] (long) *a.* (*comp.* **longer**, *superl.* **longest**) **1** of considerable or relatively great linear extent. **2** of great or relatively great extent in time. **3** of a specified linear extent or duration in time. **4** having or consisting of a large number of items or parts. **5** turning more than the average or usual quantity, extent or duration. **6** seeming to be of greater duration than it actually is. **7** lengthy, verbose, tedious. **8** far-reaching; involving a long interval. **9** (of a person's memory) retaining things over a long period of time. **10** protracted in sound, not short. **11** stressed (of vowels of syllables). **12** (of odds) representing only a small chance of success. **13** on the Stock Exchange, buying, or involving the purchase of, large

quantities of stock in expectation of a rise in prices. **14** (of a bill of exchange) maturing at a distant date. **15** (of a garment) ankle-length. **16** (of a drink) large; containing a large quantity of non-alcoholic beverage. **17** (of a suit in cards) containing more than the average number. **18** (*coll.*) (of a person) tall. ~*adv.* **1** over a great extent in distance or time. **2** for a long time. **3** by a long time. **4** throughout a specified period. **5** on the Stock Exchange, into a position where one is dependent on prices rising to make a profit. ~*n.* **1** anything that is long, esp. a period, interval etc. **2** a long syllable. **3** on the Stock Exchange, a person who takes a long position in anticipation of a rise in prices. **4** a long-dated stock. **5** (*Mus.*) a note equal in common time to two breves. **as long as 1** provided that, only if. **2** for the whole of the time that. **at long last** LAST[1]. **before long** soon, shortly. **by a long chalk** CHALK. **by a long sight** SIGHT. **for a long while** WHILE. **in the long run 1** in the end, eventually. **2** over a long period of time. **long in the tooth** TOOTH. **long on** well supplied with, strong in. **no longer** formerly but not now. **not any longer** no longer. **so long!** SO[1]. **so long as** as long as. **the long and the short of it 1** the whole matter in a few words. **2** the eventual outcome. **to be long** to take a long time. **to draw the long bow** DRAW. **to go a long way 1** to make a substantial contribution (towards). **2** (of food, money etc.) to last for a long time, to provide material or the means to do many things. **3** to be successful. **long ago** *adv.* in the distant past. ~*n.* the distant past. **long-ago** *a.* of the distant past. **long-awaited** *a.* waited for (usu. with pleasant anticipation) for a long time. **longboard** *n.* a type of surfboard. **longboat** *n.* the largest boat on a sailing vessel. **longbow** *n.* a long powerful bow drawn by hand, used as a weapon in medieval England. **long-case clock** *n.* a grandfather clock. **long-chain** *a.* (of a molecule) made up of a long chain of carbon atoms. **longcloth** *n.* a type of fine, soft cotton cloth made in strips. **long-dated** *a.* (of securities) not due for redemption in less than 15 years. **long-day** *a.* (of a plant) needing long hours of daylight in order to flower. **long-dead** *a.* who or which died a long time ago. **long-distance** *a.* **1** covering, extending over a long distance or long distances. **2** (of a telephone call) between places that are far apart. **3** (of a race) over a distance of 6 miles (or 10,000 metres) or further; (of a runner) competing at such distances. ~*adv.* using a long-distance telephone line or service. **long division** *n.* (*Math.*) the process of dividing a number by another number greater than 12, the stages being fully set out. **long dozen** *n.* thirteen. **long-drawn-out** *a.* prolonged, extended to great length. **long face** *n.* a gloomy or dejected expression. **long field** *n.* in cricket, the part of the outfield behind the wicket at the bowler's end. **long figure** *n.* a high price. **long firm** *n.* a gang of swindlers who get hold of goods for which they do not pay. **longhair** *n.* **1** a person with the characteristics popularly associated with long hair, a highbrow, an intellectual or a hippie. **2** an animal of a long-haired breed. **long-haired** *a.* (of an animal) with a long coat. **longhand** *a.* ordinary writing, as opposed to *shorthand*. **long haul** *n.* **1** a journey (esp. the transport of goods) over a great distance. **2** a difficult or extended period of time. **long-haul** *a.* for transportation over long distances. **long-headed** *a.* **1** shrewd, sensible, far-sighted. **2** dolichocephalous. **long home** *n.* the grave. **long hop** *n.* a short-pitched cricket ball making a long bounce. **longhorn** *n.* **1** any of several breeds of cattle with long horns. **2** a beetle with long antennae. **longhouse** *n.* **1** in Britain, a house with accommodation for a family and for animals under one roof. **2** a traditional communal dwelling of the Iroquois and other N American Indians and for villagers in parts of SE Asia. **3** a building on an Iroquois reservation used as a church and meeting hall. **4** in archaeology, a Viking hall. **long hundred** *n.* one hundred and twenty. **long hundredweight** *n.* the standard British hundredweight of 112 lb. (about 50.8 kg). **longish** *a.* **long johns** *n.pl.* underpants with long legs. **long jump** *n.* an athletic event involving a horizontal jump for distance from a running start. **long-lasting** *a.* that lasts or has lasted for a long time; durable. **long leg** *n.* in cricket, a fielder or fielding position close to the boundary on the leg side behind the batsman. **long-legged** *a.* having long legs. **long-life** *a.* (of foodstuffs) specially treated to resist decay and preserve freshness. **long-lived** *a.* living or having lived, existed, been current etc. for a long time. **long-lost** *a.* that has been lost or not seen or heard from for a long time. **long measure** *n.* linear measure. **long metre,** (*N Am.*) **long meter** *n.* **1** a hymn stanza consisting of four 8-syllable lines. **2** a quatrain in iambic tetrameter with alternate lines rhyming. **long odds** *n.* unequal or unfavourable odds (in betting). **long off** *n.* in cricket, a fielder or fielding position close to the boundary on the offside behind the bowler. **long on** *n.* in cricket, a fielder or fielding position close to the boundary on the onside behind the bowler. **long pig** *n.* human flesh (as food for cannibals). **long-playing** *a.* (of a gramophone record) fine-grooved and with a playing time of approx. 30 minutes per side. **long-player** *n.* a long-playing record. **long purse** *n.* a state of wealth, riches. **long-range** *a.* **1** designed to operate at long distances from a base; often without refuelling. **2** (of a missile) intended for a distant target. **3** (of a forecast) covering a period of time into the relatively distant future. **long-running** *a.* **1** (of a play) that has been continuously in performance over a long period of time. **2** (of a dispute etc.) that has been going on for a long time. **longship** *n.* a long open sturdy vessel with oars and a square sail used esp. by the Vikings for carrying warriors. **long shot** *n.* **1** a camera shot from a long distance. **2** a random guess, a remote possibility. **3** a bet at long odds. **(not) by a long shot** (not) by any means. **long sight** *n.* a condition in which one can see distant objects clearly but not those close to. **long-sighted** *a.* **1** having long sight. **2** shrewd, far-sighted. **long-sleeved** *a.* having sleeves that reach the whole length of the arm. **longspur** *n.* any of various N American buntings with a long claw on the hind toe. **long-standing** *a.* of long duration. **long staple** *n.* a type of long-fibred cotton. **long-stay** *a.* staying, or for people who are staying, a long time. **long stop** *n.* **1** in cricket, a fielder positioned to stop balls which pass the wicket-keeper. **2** any person or thing that acts as a final safeguard. **long-suffering** *a.* patient, enduring. **long suit** *n.* **1** the most numerous suit in a hand of cards. **2** a person's strong point or special interest or skill. **long-tailed** *a.* **long-tailed duck** *n.* a marine duck of the Arctic, *Clangula hymalis*, with elongated tail feathers in the male. **long-tailed tit** *n.* a European songbird of the tit family, *Aegithalos caudatus*, which has black, white and pink plumage and a very long tail. **long-term** *a.* (of a policy) looking to the future rather than the immediate present; extending over a long period of time. **long-time** *a.* of long standing. **long tom** *n.* (*Hist.*) **1** a long gun of large bore. **2** a long swivel-gun formerly carried amidships on navy ships. **long ton** *n.* an imperial ton of 2,240 lb (1016.05 kg). **long tongue** *n.* talkativeness. **long vacation** *n.* the long summer holidays of universities, schools etc. **long view** *n.* a consideration of events, consequences etc. extending relatively far into the future. **long waist** *n.* **1** (of a garment) a deep or dropped waist. **2** (of a person) a greater than average distance from armpits to hips. **long-waisted** *a.* **long wave** *a.* a radio wave with a wavelength of 1000 m or more. **longways, longwise** *adv.* lengthways. **long weekend** *n.* a holiday which extends over several days including a weekend. **long-winded** *a.* wordy, tiresome.

long-windedly *adv.* **long-windedness** *n.* [OE *lang* (cp. Dut., G and Dan. *lang*, Icel. *langr*, also L *longus*)]

long² (long) *v.i.* **1** to have an earnest desire (for). **2** to yearn (to or for). **longing** *n.* an intense desire (for). **longingly** *adv.* [OE *longian*, perh. rel. to LONG¹]

long. *abbr.* longitude.

longanimity (long·gənim´iti) *n.* long-suffering, forbearance. **longanimous** (-gan´-) *a.* [late L *longa- nimitās*, from *long animus* (*longus*, LONG¹, ANIMUS)]

longe LUNGE².

longeron (lon´jəron) *n.* a longitudinal spar of an aeroplane's fuselage. [F, girder]

longevity (lonjev´iti) *n.* great length of life. **longevous** (lonjē´-) *a.* long-lived. [L *longaevus* (*longus*, LONG¹, *aevum*, age)]

longi- (lon´ji) *comb. form* long. [L *longus*, LONG¹]

longicorn (lon´jikawn) *a.* of or relating to the Longicornes, a division of beetles with large filiform antennae. ~*n.* a beetle of this division.

longipennate (lonjipen´ət) *a.* having long wings or feathers.

longitude (long´gitūd, lon´ji-) *n.* **1** angular distance of a place E or W of a given meridian, usu. that of Greenwich. **2** (*Astron.*) distance in degrees on the ecliptic from the vernal equinox to the foot of a perpendicular from, or circle of latitude of, a heavenly body. **3** †length. **longitudinal** (-tū´-) *a.* **1** of or relating to longitude or length. **2** running lengthwise. **longitudinally** *adv.* **longitudinal wave** *n.* a wave in which the particles of the medium vibrate in the same direction as the advance of the wave. [F, from L *longitūdinem*, nom. *-tūdo*, from *longus*, LONG¹]

Usage note Pronunciation as (long´titūd), as though the word were *longtitude* (after *latitude*), is best avoided.

Longobard LANGOBARD.

longshore (long´shaw) *a.* **1** of or belonging to, existing or working on the shore. **2** directed along the shore. **longshoreman** *n.* (*pl.* **longshoremen**) **1** a person who works in or about boats along the shore or in fishing from the shore. **2** (*N Am.*) a docker. [shortened from ALONGSHORE (under ALONG)]

lonicera (lonis´ərə) *n.* **1** a dense evergreen shrub of the genus, *Lonicera*, used for hedging. **2** honeysuckle. [A. *Lonicerus*, d. 1586, German botanist]

Lonsdale belt (lonz´dāl) *n.* a broad ornamental metal belt, awarded as a trophy to British professional boxing champions who retain it as a personal possession if they win it three times. [5th Earl of *Lonsdale*, 1857–1944, who presented the first one]

loo¹ (loo) *n.* (*pl.* **loos**) (*coll.*) a lavatory. [etym. uncertain]

loo² (loo) *n.* **1** a round game at cards. **2** the pool in this game into which penalties are paid. **3** the penalty. [short for obs. *lanterloo*, F *lanturelu*, orig. nonsense, the refrain of a 17th-cent. song]

looby (loo´bi) *n.* (*pl.* **loobies**) **1** an awkward, clumsy person, a lubber. **2** a fool. [rel. to LUBBER]

loof LUFF.

loofah (loo´fə), (*N Am. also*) **luffa** (luf´ə) *n.* **1** a tropical gourdlike climbing plant, *Luffa cylindrica*, with an edible fruit. **2** the fibrous interior of the fruit of this plant used as a bath sponge, back-scrubber etc. [Arab. *lūfa*, plant]

look (luk) *v.i.* **1** to direct the eyes (towards, at etc.) in order to see an object. **2** to watch. **3** to gaze, to stare. **4** to stare in astonishment, wonder etc. **5** to direct the mind or understanding, to give consideration. **6** to face, to front, to be turned or have a particular direction (towards, to, into etc.). **7** to seem, to appear. **8** to make a physical or mental search. **9** to take care. ~*v.t.* **1** to view, to inspect, to examine. **2** to express or show by one's expression. **3** to ascertain, to determine. **4** to expect, to hope (to do something). ~*n.* **1** the act of looking or seeing, a glance. **2** (*pl.*) personal appearance, esp. of the face, attractiveness, beauty. **3** facial expression. **4** (*often pl.*) general appearance. **5** style, line, fashion (for clothes or general design). ~*int.* **1** a request or demand for someone to turn their eyes in a particular direction. **2** (*also* **look here**) used to demand attention at the beginning of a statement or to express mild annoyance or protest. **look alive** ALIVE. **look before you leap** be cautious before acting. **look lively** LIVELY. **not much to look at** unattractive, plain; unprepossessing. **not to like the look/ looks of** to find alarming or threatening. **to be looking at** (*coll.*) to have at a rough estimate, to expect to pay, spend etc. **to look after 1** to take care of. **2** to attend to. **3** to follow (a departing person, thing) with one's eyes. **to look a gift horse in the mouth** GIFT. **to look around** to look round. **to look as if** to seem or suggest from the available evidence that. **to look back 1** to turn and look in the direction from which one has come. **2** to refer back (to). **3** to review or return to (a period, event, experience in the past) in one's mind. **4** (*usu. neg.*) to cease to make progress (*never looked back after that*). **5** to pay another short visit. **to look daggers** DAGGER². **to look down one's nose at** to look down on. **to look down on/ upon 1** to despise. **2** to assume superiority over. **to look for 1** to seek. **2** to hope for. **3** to expect, anticipate, be on the watch for. **to look for trouble** TROUBLE. **to look forward to** to anticipate or hope for with pleasure. **to look in** to call, to pay a brief visit. **to look into 1** to inspect carefully, to investigate. **2** to examine the inside of. **to look kindly on** KINDLY (under KIND). **to look like 1** to resemble; to have the appearance of. **2** to seem to be going to. **3** to threaten or promise (e.g. rain). **4** to suggest the presence of. **to look on 1** to be a mere spectator. **2** to regard, to consider (as, with etc.). **to look oneself** to look healthy; to have one's customary air and appearance. **to look on the bright side** BRIGHT. **to look out 1** to be on the watch, to be prepared (for). **2** to put one's head out of a window etc. **3** to search for or select and give to. **4** to have a view or outlook (over). **to look over 1** to inspect by making a tour of. **2** to read or examine cursorily. **to look round 1** to look behind one, or in another direction than in front. **2** to make a tour of and inspect. **3** to examine various options, possible purchases etc. before coming to a decision. **to look sharp** to be quick, make haste. **to look small** SMALL. **to look someone in the eye/ eyes/ face** to look at someone steadily, unflinchingly and without shame. **to look the other way** WAY. **to look through 1** to see or direct the eyes through. **2** to penetrate with one's sight or insight. **3** to examine the contents of. **4** to ignore, or seem to ignore, the presence of (another person). **to look to/ unto 1** to direct one's eyes or thoughts towards. **2** to take heed for, to be careful about, to keep a watch over. **3** to rely upon (for). **to look up 1** to search for, esp. in a book. **2** to pay a visit to. **3** to improve, to become more prosperous. **to look up and down** to examine (a person) from head to foot attentively or with disdain or contempt. **to look upon** to regard (as or with). **to look up to** to admire and respect. **lookalike** *n.* a person or thing that closely resembles another; a double. **looker** *n.* **1** an observer. **2** (*coll.*) an attractive person, esp. a woman. **looker-on** *n.* a (mere) spectator. **look-in** *n.* (*coll.*) **1** a call, a short visit. **2** a chance, as of winning in a game. **looking-glass** *n.* a mirror. ~*a.* in which ordinary reality is reversed or distorted in some way. **lookism** *n.* prejudice in favour of people of attractive appearance. **lookout** *n.* **1** a watch. **2** a person engaged in watching or looking out. **3** a place from which watch or observation is kept. **4** a view, a prospect. **5** future prospect. **6** (*coll.*) a person's personal affair or concern. **on the lookout**

on the watch. **look-see** *n.* (*coll.*) an inspection. [OE *lōcian* (cp. G dial. *lugen*)]

loom[1] (loom) *n.* **1** a machine in which yarn or thread is woven into a fabric. **2** the handle or inboard part of an oar. [OE *gelōma*, orig. a tool or implement (cp. *andlōma*)]

loom[2] (loom) *v.i.* **1** to appear indistinctly or faintly in the distance. **2** to appear larger than the real size, as in a mist, and often threatening. **3** (of an event) to be imminent, esp. ominously so. *~n.* the first indistinct appearance, as of land at sea. **to loom over** to overhang, overshadow or stand tall beside to seem to threaten. [cp. EFris. *lōmen*, Swed. dial. *loma*, to move slowly, OHG *luomen*, to be weary]

†**loom**[3] (loom) *n.* **1** a diver (the bird). **2** a guillemot. [Icel. *lōmr*]

loon[1] (loon) *n.* **1** (*coll.*) a daft or eccentric person. **2** (*Sc., North.*) a rogue, a scamp, a worthless person. [etym. uncertain]

loon[2] (loon) *n.* (*N Am.*) a diver, any bird of the Gaviidae family. [corr. of LOOM[3]]

loony (loo´ni) *n.* (*pl.* **loonies**) (*sl.*) a lunatic; a foolish person. *~a.* (*comp.* **loonier,** *superl.* **looniest**) crazy; foolish. **loony-bin** *n.* (*sl.*) a mental hospital. **loony left** *n.* the extreme left wing of a political party. [short for LUNATIC]

loop[1] (loop) *n.* **1** a folding or doubling of a string, rope, thread etc. across itself to form a curve or eye; a noose, a bight. **2** anything resembling this, e.g. a pattern in a finger print. **3** a ring, eye or curved piece by which anything is hung up, fastened, held etc. **4** a loop-shaped intrauterine contraceptive device. **5** a loop line. **6** a flight manoeuvre comprising a complete revolution in flight in a vertical plane, the upper surface of the aircraft being on the inside of the circle. **7** in skating, a curve performed on one edge and crossing itself. **8** a length of film or tape joined end to end to form a continuous strip. **9** (*Comput.*) a set of instructions repeated in a program until a specific condition is met. **10** a closed circuit around which a signal can pass. *~v.t.* **1** to form into a loop or loops. **2** to encircle with a loop. **3** to fasten or secure with loops. *~v.t.* **1** to form a loop. **2** to follow a looplike path; to loop the loop. **3** to travel by curling itself in loops and uncurling again. **to loop the loop** to travel round in a vertical loop in an aeroplane etc. **loop aerial** *n.* an aerial consisting of one or more coils of wire on a frame. **looped** *a.* **looper** *n.* **1** the larva of the geometer moth, which moves by drawing up the hinder part of its body to the head, forming a loop. **2** a person who or something which loops. **loop line** *n.* a railway, telegraph line etc. diverging from the main line and joining it again. **loop-the-loop** *n.* the manoeuvre of looping the loop in an aircraft. **loopy** *a.* (*comp.* **loopier,** *superl.* **loopiest**) (*coll.*) slightly mad. [prob. from Celt. (cp. Gael. and Ir. *lub*)]

†**loop**[2] (loop) *n.* a loophole in a wall.

loophole (loop´hōl) *n.* **1** an aperture in a wall for shooting or looking through or for admission of light. **2** an outlet, a means of evasion or escape, esp. a means of evading the consequences or penalties of a law or regulation. *~v.t.* to make loopholes in. [prob. rel. to MDut. *lūpen* (Dut. *luipen*), to watch, to peer (cp. Dut. *gluip*, a narrow opening)]

loose (loos) *a.* **1** not tied, fastened or confined. **2** unfastened; detachable; hanging partly free. **3** not fixed or tight. **4** not specially packaged or in units or a container. **5** not crowded together, not compact or dense. **6** relaxed, slack. **7** careless, slovenly. **8** not strict; vague, indefinite. **9** incorrect; ungrammatical. **10** dissolute, wanton. **11** lax in the bowels, as opposed to *costive.* **12** (of the ball in ball games) not in any player's possession. **13** (of play) not involving a set formation or strategy. **14** (of bowling in cricket) inaccurate. **15** (of a cough) accompanied by phlegm. *~v.t.* **1** to release, to set at liberty, to unbind. **2** to undo, to untie, to unfasten. **3** to free from obligation or burden. **4** to relax. **5** to discharge (a projectile, volley etc.). **at a loose end** END. **at loose ends** END. **on the loose 1** no longer in captivity. **2** on the spree. **the loose** in rugby, play when the ball is loose and the forwards close round it or try to obtain and keep possession of it. **to break loose** to escape from captivity. **to cut loose 1** to escape or get away (from). **2** to begin to act without restraint. **to give loose to** to give free vent to (one's tongue, feelings etc.). **to hang loose** (*N Am., coll.*) to behave in a relaxed and informal manner. **to let loose** LET[1]. **to set loose** to set at liberty. **loose box** BOX[1]. **loose cannon** *n.* a person or thing that causes danger or damage because they are uncontrolled. **loose change** *n.* coins kept for small items of expenditure. **loose cover** *n.* an easily removable cloth cover for a chair, sofa etc. **loose head** *n.* in rugby, the prop forward on the hooker's left. **loose-jointed** *a.* **1** loose-limbed. **2** having ill-fitting joints. **loose-leaf** *a.* bound so that pages may be inserted or removed. *~n.* a folder, notebook etc. bound in this way. **loose-limbed** *a.* having flexible or supple limbs. **loosely** *adv.* **loosen** *v.t.* **1** to make less tight, firm, fixed etc. **2** to make less strict or severe. **3** to free, to set loose. **4** to release (the bowels) from constipation. **5** to relieve the dryness of (a cough). *~v.i.* to become loose, to become less tight, firm, fixed etc. **to loosen a person's tongue** to make a person talk more freely, often indiscreetly. **to loosen up 1** to limber up. **2** to relax, to become less shy or restrained. **looseness** *n.* **loosener** *n.* **loose order** *n.* (*Mil.*) a formation in which soldiers, vehicles, units are widely separated from one another. **loose-tongued** *a.* indiscreet. **loosish** *a.* [Icel. *lauss* (cogn. with OE *lēas*, G *los*), cp. Gr. *leuin*]

loosestrife (loos´strīf) *n.* **1** any of a genus of plants of the primrose family, esp. *Lysimachia vulgaris* with yellow flowers; yellow loosestrife. **2** a waterside plant, *Lythrum salicaria*, with red or purple flowers; purple loosestrife. [(LOOSE, STRIFE), erron. translation of late L *lysimachia*, Gr. *lusimachion*, from *Lusimachos*, a pers. name (*lusi-*, from *luein*, to loose, *machē*, strife)]

loot (loot) *n.* **1** booty, plunder, esp. from a conquered city. **2** stolen money, jewellery etc. **3** (*coll.*) money. *~v.t.* **1** to rob, or to steal from, unprotected premises e.g. during a riot. **2** to plunder, to pillage, esp. a city. **3** to carry off as plunder. *~v.i.* to plunder. **looter** *n.* a person who loots, a pillager. [Hind. *lut*]

lop[1] (lop) *v.t.* (*pres.p.* **lopping,** *past, p.p.* **lopped**) **1** to cut off the top or extremities of (a tree, body etc.). **2** to trim (trees, shrubs etc.) by cutting. **3** to omit or remove as superfluous. *~v.i.* to cut (at) as if to lop. *~n.* (*usu. in pl.*) something which is lopped. **lop and top, lop and crop** *n.* trimmings of trees. **lopper** *n.* [OE *loppian*, etym. uncertain]

lop[2] (lop) *v.i.* (*pres.p.* **lopping,** *past, p.p.* **lopped**) **1** to hang down limply, to flop, to droop. **2** to hang or idle (about). **3** to lope. *~v.t.* **1** to allow to hang down. **2** to let fall. **lop-ear** *n.* a lop-eared rabbit. **lop-eared** *a.* having hanging ears. **lop-ears** *n.pl.* hanging ears. **lopsided** *a.* **1** heavier on one side than the other. **2** not symmetrical. **3** ill-balanced. **lopsidedly** *adv.* **lopsidedness** *n.* [etym. uncertain, prob. onomat.]

lope (lōp) *v.i.* to gallop, swing or move (along) with long strides or leaps. *~n.* motion of this kind. **loper** *n.* [ON *hlaupa*, var. of LEAP, LOUP]

lopho- (lō´fō, lof´ō) *comb. form* having a crest, crested. [Gr. *lophos*, crest]

lophobranch (lō´fəbrangk, lof´-) *n.* a teleost fish of the suborder Lophobranchii, comprising the seahorses or pipefishes, that have their gills in tufts. **lophobranchiate** (-brang´kiət) *a.* of or relating to this suborder. *~n.* a fish in this suborder.

lophodont (lō´fədont, lof´-) *a.* having ridges on the crowns of the crowns of the molar teeth. ~*n.* an animal with such teeth. [Gr. *odous odontos*, tooth]

lophophore (lō´fəfaw, lof´-) *n.* a ring or horseshoe or ciliated tentacles round the mouth of some minute sessile sea creatures. **lophophorate** (-faw´rāt) *a., n.* [Gr. *lopas*, dish, -LITH]

lopolith (lop´əlith) *n.* a saucer-shaped body of igneous rock formed by the intrusion of magma into existing rock layers.

loquacious (lokwā´shəs) *a.* **1** talkative, garrulous, chattering. **2** apt to disclose secrets. **loquaciously** *adv.* **loquacity** (-kwas´-), **loquaciousness** *n.* [L *loquax -ācis*, from *loquī*, to talk, -ACIOUS]

loquat (lō´kwot) *n.* **1** a Chinese and Japanese tree, *Eriobotrya japonica*. **2** its yellow edible fruit. [Chin. *luh kwat*, lit. rush orange]

lor (law) *int.* (*coll.*) Lord.

loral LORE[2].

loran (lō´rən, lor´-) *n.* a system of navigation in which position is determined by the intervals between pulses received from widely spaced radio transmitters. [*lo*ng, *ra*nge, *n*avigation]

lorate LORE[2].

lord (lawd) *n.* **1** a ruler, a master; a man possessing supreme power, a sovereign. **2** (**Lord**) God. **3** (**Lord**) Jesus Christ. **4** a nobleman, a peer of the realm. **5** a courtesy title given to the son of a duke or marquis, or the son of an earl holding a barony. **6** a title of honour conferred on certain official personages, as Lord Chief Justice, Lord Commissioner, Lord Mayor, Lord Rector etc. **7** (*Hist.*) a feudal superior, the holder of a manor. **8** †husband. **9** (*Astrol.*) the ruling planet (of a sign, house, chart). ~†*v.t.* to raise to the peerage. ~*int.* (*coll.*) (*also* **Lord, lordy**) an exclamation of surprise or dismay. **my lord** a formula for addressing a nobleman (not a duke), bishop, lord mayor or judge of the Supreme Court. **the Lords 1** the House of Lords. **2** the members of the House of Lords. **to live like a lord** to live affluently. **Lord Advocate** *n.* the chief law officer of the Crown in Scotland, in charge of the administration of criminal justice. **Lord Bishop** *n.* the full title of any bishop. **Lord Chamberlain (of the Household)** *n.* a British officer of state having control of the royal household and formerly licensing plays for performance. **Lord Chancellor, Lord High Chancellor** *n.* the highest officer of the British Crown, keeper of the Great Seal, speaker of the House of Lords, head of the judiciary in England and Wales. **Lord Chief Justice** *n.* in the UK, the president of the Queen's Bench of the High Court of Justice. **Lord Commissioner, Lord High Commissioner** *n.* the sovereign's representative in the Church of Scotland. **Lord God of Hosts** LORD OF HOSTS (under LORD). **Lord Great Chamberlain of England** *n.* a hereditary officer of state in Britain in charge of the Palace of Westminster and performing various ceremonial functions. **Lord High Chancellor** LORD CHANCELLOR (under LORD). **Lord High Commissioner** LORD COMMISSIONER (under LORD). **Lord High Steward** *n.* an officer of state regulating precedence at coronations etc. †**lording** *n.* a lord (used as a respectful mode of address). **lordless** *a.* **Lord Lieutenant** *n.* **1** an official representing the sovereign, and the chief executive authority and head of the magistracy in a county. **2** (*Hist.*) the British viceroy in Ireland. **lordlike** *a., adv.* **lordling** (-ling) *n.* **1** a young lord. **2** a minor lord. **lordly** *a.* (*comp.* **lordlier**, *superl.* **lordliest**) **1** lofty, proud, haughty, insolent. **2** becoming or befitting a lord, noble, grand, magnificent. ~*adv.* **1** proudly. **2** imperiously. **3** arrogantly. **lordliness** *n.* **Lord Lyon** *n.* LYON. **Lord Marcher** *n.* (*Hist.*) a lord who formerly held jurisdiction and privileges on the Welsh border. **Lord Mayor** *n.* the chief magistrate of London, York and certain other large towns. **Lord Muck** *n.* (*sl., derog.*) a man with social pretensions. **Lord of Appeal** *n.* a judge appointed to assist the House of Lords in hearing an appeal. **Lord of Hosts, Lord God of Hosts** *n.* (*Hist.*) God as commander of heavenly or earthly armies. †**lord of misrule** *n.* (*Hist.*) a person who superintended the games and revels at Christmas. **lord of the ascendant** *n.* the heavenly body that rules in the ascendant or when the latter is just rising above the horizon. **lord of the bedchamber** *n.* (*pl.* **lords of the bedchamber**) an officer of the Royal Household who waits upon a male sovereign. **Lord of the flies** *n.* Beelzebub, the Devil. **lord of the manor** *n.* a person or corporation holding the rights of a manor. **lordolatry** (-dol´ətri) *n.* **Lord Ordinary** *n.* (*Sc. Law*) a judge of the Court of Session. **Lord President of the Council** *n.* a member of the House of Lords who acts as president of the Privy Council. **Lord Privy Seal** *n.* the officer of State entrusted with the Privy Seal. **Lord Protector of the Commonwealth** *n.* (*Hist.*) a title borne by Oliver Cromwell (1653–8) and his son Richard Cromwell (1658–9) as head of state. **Lord Provost** *n.* the head of the municipal corporation of Edinburgh, Glasgow, Aberdeen, Perth or Dundee. **Lord Rector** *n.* the elected head officer of certain Scottish universities. **lords and ladies** *n.* the wild arum lily, *Arum maculatum*. **Lords Commissioners** *n.pl.* the members of a board performing the duties of a high office of state that has been put to commission. **Lord's day** *n.* Sunday. **lordship** *n.* **1** control, rule (over). **2** the position or status of a lord. **his lordship** the equivalent of 'your lordship' in speaking of someone. **your lordship 1** a formula used in speaking deferentially to a lord. **2** (*facet.*) a formula used in speaking to someone who adopts a lordly or arrogant manner. **Lord's Prayer** *n.* the prayer taught by Jesus Christ to his disciples (Math. vi.9–13, Luke xi. 2–4). **Lords spiritual** *n.pl.* the archbishops and bishops who have seats in the House of Lords. **Lord's Supper** *n.* the Eucharist. **Lord's table** *n.* **1** the altar in a Christian church. **2** the Eucharist. **Lords temporal** *n.pl.* lay peers who have seats in the House of Lords. [OE *hlāford* (*hlāf*, LOAF[1], WARD)]

lordosis (lawdō´sis) *n.* curvature of a bone, esp. of the spine, forward. **lordotic** (-dot´-) *a.* [Gr., from *lordos*, bent backwards]

lore[1] (law) *n.* **1** the collective traditions and knowledge relating to a given subject. **2** learning. **3** †teaching or something that is taught. [OE *lār* (cogn. with LEARN)]

lore[2] (law) *n.* **1** a straplike part, the surface between the eye and the beak in birds. **2** the corresponding part in snakes. **loral** *a.* of or relating to the lore. **lorate** (-rət) *a.* strap-shaped. [F, from L *lōrum*, a strap]

lorgnette (lawnyet´) *n.* a pair of eyeglasses or opera glasses with a long handle. [F, from *lorgner*, squint]

lorica (lərī´kə) *n.* (*pl.* **loricae** (-sē, -kē)) **1** the carapace of a crustacean, the sheath of certain infusoria and rotifers. **2** (*Hist.*) a cuirass. **loricate** (lor´ikət) *a.* covered with defensive plates, scales or other natural armour. [L *lōrīca*, from *lōrium*, strap]

lorikeet (lor´ikēt) *n.* any of various brightly-coloured parrots of the subfamily Lorunae, belonging to Australasia and SE Asia. [dim. of LORY (*-keet*, as PARAKEET)]

†**lorimer** (lor´imə), **loriner** (-nə) *n.* **1** a maker of bits and spurs, a spurrier. **2** a maker of small ironwork. [OF *loremier*, *lorenier* (F *lorimer*), from *lorain*, med. L *loranum*, a bridle, from L *lōrum*, thong]

loris (law´ris) *n.* **1** a slow-moving, nocturnal primate with small ears and a short tail, of S India and Sri Lanka, *Nycitebus coucang*. **2** a similar creature of SE Asia, *Loris tardigradus*. [F, prob. from MDut. *loeris*, a clown]

†**lorn** (lawn) *a.* lost, abandoned, forlorn. [p.p. of obs. *leese* (OE *loren*, p.p. of *lēosan*, to LOSE)]

lorry (lor´i) *n.* (*pl.* **lorries**) **1** a large motor vehicle for carrying heavy loads. **2** †a long flat railway wagon or similar transport vehicle. **off the back of a lorry** stolen or acquired by dubious means. [etym. uncertain]

lory (law´ri) *n.* (*pl.* **lories**) a brilliantly coloured parrot-like bird of various genera of Loriinae, found in SE Asia and Australia. [Malay *lūri*]

lose (looz) *v.t.* (*past, p.p.* **lost** (lost)) **1** to be deprived of. **2** to mislay, to be unable to find; to miss, to stray from. **3** to fail to gain, win, obtain or enjoy. **4** to fail to keep possession of, to fail to hold or grasp. **5** to be freed from. **6** to part with accidentally or as a forfeit, penalty etc. **7** to fail to hear or understand. **8** to spend uselessly, to waste. **9** to be deprived of (a parent, friend) by death. **10** to fail to give birth to, esp. by miscarriage. **11** (of a doctor) to be unable to keep (a patient) alive. **12** to cause someone the loss of. **13** (of a watch, clock) to become slow (by a specified amount of time). **14** (*in pass.*) to disappear, to die, to perish. **15** (*coll.*) to get rid of, to discard. **16** (*coll.*) to elude, to outdistance (a pursuer). *~v.i.* **1** to fail to be successful, to be beaten. **2** to suffer loss. **3** to be worse off (by). **4** to decrease or depreciate in value or effectiveness. **5** (of a clock etc.) to run slow. **to lose count** COUNT[1]. **to lose countenance** COUNTENANCE. **to lose face** FACE. **to lose ground** GROUND[1]. **to lose heart** HEART. **to lose no time** TIME. **to lose one's balance** BALANCE. **to lose one's bearings** BEAR[2]. **to lose one's cool** COOL. **to lose oneself 1** to lose one's way. **2** to become bewildered. **3** to become rapt or engrossed (in). **to lose one's head** HEAD[1]. **to lose one's heart to** HEART. **to lose one's nerve** NERVE. **to lose one's temper** TEMPER. **to lose one's/ the way** to become lost, to take a false direction, to go astray. **to lose one's tongue** TONGUE. **to lose out 1** (*coll.*) to make a loss, to be at a disadvantage. **2** to fail to obtain or take advantage of. **to lose out to** to be defeated by (a competitor). **to lose time** TIME. **to lose touch** TOUCH. **to lose track of** TRACK. **to lose weight** WEIGHT. **losable** *a.* **loser** *n.* **1** a person who loses, esp. a person, horse, boat etc. failing to win a race. **2** (*pl.*) the beaten party in a game, battle etc. **3** (*coll.*) a failure, a person who seems destined to be unfortunate or to lose. **losing** *a.* **losing battle** *n.* a struggle, contest etc. in which one seems doomed to failure. **losing hazard** *n.* a billiard stroke in which a player's own ball runs into a pocket off the object ball. **losingly** *adv.* **lost** *a.* **1** unable to find the way or determine one's position or whereabouts. **2** missing, unable to be found. **3** confused, bewildered. **4** ruined, destroyed. **5** no longer possessed or known. **6** engrossed. **7** morally fallen or corrupted. **8** damned. **get lost!** GET[1]. **to be lost in 1** to be engrossed in. **2** to merge or be obscured in. **to be lost on** to make no impression on, to be wasted on. **to be lost to 1** (of a valuable thing or person) to be no longer available or accessible to. **2** (of a person) to be impervious or unresponsive to. **to be lost without** to be dependent on. **lost cause** *n.* **1** a futile endeavour. **2** a person whom one can no longer influence or help. **lost generation** *n.* **1** the generation decimated during World War I. **2** the generation, esp. of US writers, of the years immediately following World War I. **lost labour** *n.* a futile endeavour, fruitless effort. **lost soul** *n.* **1** a person who is damned or beyond redemption. **2** a person who seems bewildered by, and unable to cope with, the demands of everyday life. **lost tribes** *n.pl.* the ten tribes of Israel deported in 721 BC who are believed never to have found their way back to Palestine. **lost wax** *n.* CIRE PERDUE. [OE *losian*, to escape (from), becoming transitive by gradually superseding the obs. *leese*, OE *lēosan*]

†**losel** (lō´zəl) *n.* a worthless person, a scamp, a ne'er-do-well. *~a.* worthless, lazy. [rel. to OE *-lēosan*, see LOSE]

loss (los) *n.* **1** the act of losing or the state of being deprived of. **2** failure to win or gain. **3** something which is lost or the amount of this. **4** (*pl.*) casualties and those taken prisoner in war. **5** detriment, disadvantage. **6** wasted expenditure, effort etc. **at a loss** for less than the buying price; with costs, expenditure etc. exceeding income. **to be at a loss 1** to be embarrassed or puzzled. **2** to be rendered helpless for lack of. **to cut a loss** to cut one's losses. **to cut one's losses** to write off as lost, to abandon a speculation. **loss adjuster** *n.* a person who assesses losses through fire, theft etc. for an insurance company. **loss-leader** *n.* an article sold at a loss to attract customers. **loss-making** *a.* that makes or causes a financial loss. **loss-maker** *n.* **loss of face** *n.* humiliation, loss of personal prestige. **lossy** *a.* (of insulating material, a transmission line) designed to have high attenuation. [OE *los*, dissolution, rout, dispersion, from *-lēosan*, see LOSE (cp. Icel. *los*)]

lost LOSE.

lot (lot) *n.* **1** (*often in pl.*) a considerable quantity or amount, a great deal. **2** anything, such as a dice, paper or other object, used in reaching a decision by random selection. **3** choice or decision by this method. **4** the chance, share or fortune falling to anyone. **5** one's fortune, destiny or condition in life. **6** a distinct portion, collection or parcel of things offered for sale, esp. at auction. **7** a number or quantity of things or persons. **8** (*esp. N Am.*) a plot of land. **9** a plot of land in the vicinity of a film studio on which special exterior sets are built. *~v.t.* (*pres.p.* **lotting,** *past, p.p.* **lotted**) **1** to divide into lots. **2** to apportion. **a lot** (*coll.*) much. **a whole lot** (*coll.*) very much. **the lot** the whole quantity. **the whole lot** all, everything. **to cast lots** to determine by the throw of a dice or other contrivance. **to draw lots** to determine by drawing one name etc. from a number. **to throw/ cast in one's lot with** to join with or make common cause with and share the fortunes of. **lots** *n.* (*coll.*) a large number, a great deal (of). *~adv.* very much. **lotsa** *a.* (*sl.*) short for *lots of*; also in comb., as in *lotsalolly*. **lotta** *a.* (*sl.*) short for *a lot of*. [OE *hlot* (cp. Dut. *lot*, Icel. *hluti*, G *loos*)]

loth LOATH.

Lothario (lothah´riō, -eə´-) *n.* (*pl.* **Lotharios**) a libertine, a seducer. [character in Nicholas Rowe's tragedy *Fair Penitent*]

lotic (lō´tic) *a.* associated with or living in fast-flowing water. [L *lotus*, a p.p. of *lavāre*, to wash]

lotion (lō´shən) *n.* a medicinal or cosmetic liquid application for external use. [L *lōtio*, from *lavāre* (p.p. *lōtus*), to wash]

lottery (lot´əri) *n.* (*pl.* **lotteries**) **1** a method of allotting valuable prizes by chance or lot among purchasers of tickets. **2** an activity in which success is dependent on mere chance. **lotto** (-ō) *n.* (*pl.* **lottos**) **1** a game of chance, played with discs placed on cards divided into numbered squares. **2** (*N Am.*) a lottery. [It., from Gmc. (cp. HG *Hlōz*, LOT)]

lotus (lō´təs) *n.* (*pl.* **lotuses**) **1** in Greek legend, any of several plants the fruit of which was said to induce a dreamy languor in those who ate it. **2** the Indian water lily, *Nelumbo nucifera*, with large pink flowers. **3** this used as a sacred symbol, an architectural ornament etc. **4** the Egyptian water lily, *Nymphaea lotus*, with white flowers. **5** any of a genus, *Lotus*, of leguminous plants containing the bird's-foot trefoil. **lotus-eater** *n.* **1** any of the Lotophagi, mentioned in Homer's *Odyssey*, who lived on the fruit of the lotus. **2** a person who wants nothing more from life than dreamy ease. **lotus-eating** *a., n.* **lotus-land** *n.* a place or condition of indolence and forgetfulness. **lotus position** *n.* a position used in yoga in which one sits cross-legged with each foot nestled against or on top of the opposite thigh. [L, from Gr. *lōtos*]

louche (loosh) *a.* **1** morally suspect. **2** seedy. **3** sinister. [F, lit., cross-eyed, from L *luscus*, one-eyed]

loud (lowd) *a.* **1** powerful in sound, sonorous. **2** noisy, clamorous. **3** (of attire, manners etc.) conspicuous, ostentatious, flashy. **4** (of behaviour) bumptious, aggressive. **out loud 1** aloud. **2** loudly. **louden** *v.t., v.i.* to make or become louder. **loud hailer** *n.* a megaphone with a built-in amplifier and microphone. **loudish** *a.* **loudly** *adv.* **loudmouth** *n.* (*coll.*) someone who brags or talks offensively in a loud voice. **loudmouthed** *a.* **loudness** *n.* **loudspeaker** *n.* an electromechanical device which converts electrical signals into audible sound. [OE *hlūd* (cp. Dut. *luid*, G *laut*), cogn. with Gr. *kluein*, hear, L *cluēre*]

lough (lokh) *n.* a lake, an arm of the sea in Ireland. [Ir. *loch*]

louis (loo´i), **louis d'or** (daw´) *n.* (*pl.* **louis** (-iz), **louis d'or** (-i)) an old French gold coin issued from Louis XIII to Louis XVI, worth at different times 20 or 23 francs, superseded by the 20-franc piece. **Louis Quatorze** (katawz´) *a.* of or relating to the style of furniture, architecture etc. fashionable in the reign of Louis XIV, 1643–1715. **Louis Quinze** (kãz) *a.* of or relating to the prevailing style of the reign of Louis XV, 1715–74. **Louis Seize** (sez) *a.* of or relating to the prevailing style of the reign of Louis XVI, 1774–92. **Louis Treize** (trez) *a.* of or relating to the prevailing style of the reign of Louis XIII, 1610–43. [F *Louis*, name of many French kings, *d'or*, of gold]

lounge (lownj) *v.i.* **1** to loll or recline. **2** to move lazily, to saunter. **3** to idle about. ~*v.t.* to idle (time) away. ~*n.* **1** a place for lounging. **2** the sitting room in a house. **3** a public room with comfortable seating for waiting or relaxing in. **4** (*also* **lounge bar**) a more comfortable and expensive section of a public house or hotel. **5** a sofa with a back and one raised end. **6** the act of lounging. **lounge lizard** *n.* a person who spends a lot of time idly at social gatherings, esp. in the company of rich or famous people. **lounger** *n.* **1** a person who lounges. **2** a comfortable sofa or extending chair for relaxing on. **3** a loose-fitting garment. **lounge suit** *n.* a man's suit for daily wear. **loungingly** *adv.* [etym. unknown]

loup (lowp) *v.t., v.i.* (*Sc.*) to leap. [Icel. *hlaupa*, to LEAP]

loupe (loop) *n.* a small magnifying glass used by jewellers, watchmakers etc. [F]

lour (lowə), **lower** *v.i.* **1** (of clouds, weather etc.) to look threatening, to appear dark or gloomy. **2** to frown, to scowl. ~*n.* **1** a scowl. **2** sullenness. **3** gloominess (of weather etc.). **louring, loury** *a.* **louringly** *adv.* [ME *louren* (cp. LG *lūren*, M.Dut. *loeren*, G *lauern*, to lie in wait)]

louse (lows) *n.* (*pl.* **lice** (līs)) **1** a blood-sucking insect of the genus *Pediculus*, three species of which are parasitic on man. **2** any of various other parasites infesting animals, birds, fish and plants. **3** (*coll.*) (*pl.* **louses**) a mean, contemptible person. ~*v.t.* to remove lice from. **to louse up** to spoil, to make a mess of. **lousewort** *n.* a marsh-growing plant of the genus *Pedicularis* with spikes of white, yellow or mauve flowers. **lousy** (-´zi) *a.* (*comp.* **lousier**, *superl.* **lousiest**) **1** infested with lice. **2** (*coll.*) bad, inferior, disgusting. **lousy with** swarming with, excessively supplied with. **lousily** *adv.* **lousiness** *n.* [OE *lūs* (cp. Dut. *luis*, Icel. *lūs*, G *Laus*)]

lout[1] (lowt) *n.* a rough, crude, ill-mannered person, an oaf. **loutish** *a.* **loutishly** *adv.* **loutishness** *n.* [etym. uncertain]

lout[2] (lowt) *v.i.* to bend, to bow, to stoop. [OE *lūtan* (cp. Icel. *lūta*)]

louvre (loo´və), (*N Am.*) **louver** *n.* **1** a louvre-board. **2** (*also pl.*) a set of louvre boards and the frame in which they are set. **3** a turret on the roof of a medieval hall, with openings for the escape of smoke. **4** an opening in a chimney pot etc. to let out smoke. **louvre-board** *n.* each of a set of sloping overlapping boards across a window, door etc. to exclude rain but allow the passage of air. **louvred** *a.* **louvre-door, louvre-window** *n.* a door, window covered by louvre-boards. [ME and OF *lover*, med. L *lōdium*, etym. uncertain]

lovable LOVE.

lovage (lŭv´ij) *n.* **1** a European umbelliferous herb, used in salads and for flavouring food, *Levisticum officinale*. **2** a related white-flowered plant of N Europe, *Ligusticum scoticum*. [ME *loveache*, OF *levesche*, ult. from L *ligusticum*, Ligurian]

lovat (lŭv´ət), **lovat green** *n.* a muted blueish-grey green colour, usu. found in tweed or woollen cloth. ~*a.* of this colour. [*Lovat*, place in Highland, Scotland]

love (lŭv) *n.* **1** a feeling of deep regard, fondness and devotion (for, towards etc.). **2** deep affection, usu. accompanied by yearning or desire for. **3** sexual desire or passion. **4** (*also* **Love**) a personification of this or of Cupid, usu. in the form of a naked winged boy. **5** sexual relations. **6** a beloved one, a sweetheart (as a term of endearment). **7** (*coll.*) a delightful person; a charming thing. **8** affectionate greetings, a formula for ending an affectionate letter. **9** in games, no points scored, nil. ~*v.t.* **1** to have strong affection for, to be fond of. **2** to desire passionately, to be in love with. **3** to like greatly, to delight in, to have a strong partiality or predilection for. ~*v.i.* to be in love. **for love** for pleasure or out of benevolence, affection etc., not for payment. **for the love of** for the sake of (esp. in adjuration). **in love** feeling a strong desire and attachment (for another person, for each other). **love all** in tennis etc., nothing scored in a game on either side. **(not) for love or money** by no means, in no circumstances. **out of love** no longer in love. **there's no love lost between them** they feel great mutual dislike or hostility. **to fall in love** to begin to feel love. **to give/ send one's love** to give, send an affectionate message. **to make love to 1** to have sexual intercourse with. **2** †to woo, to pay court or attentions to. **lovable, loveable** *a.* **1** worthy of love. **2** amiable. **lovableness** *n.* **lovably** *adv.* **love affair** *n.* **1** a romantic or sexual attachment between two people, often temporary in nature. **2** an enthusiasm for or fascination with (an object, activity etc.). †**love-apple** *n.* the tomato. **lovebird** *n.* **1** a short-tailed parrot of the African genus *Agapornis*, from the attachment they show to their mates. **2** (*pl., coll.*) a very fond or demonstratively affectionate couple. **lovebite** *n.* a temporary red or purple mark on the skin caused by a partner biting or sucking it during lovemaking. **love child** *n.* an illegitimate child. **love-feast** *n.* **1** a meal among the early Christians eaten together as a sign of mutual love and fellowship. **2** a religious meeting such as the agape held by Methodists etc. **love game** *n.* a game in tennis etc., in which the loser has not scored. **love-god** *n.* Cupid. **love handles** *n.pl.* (*coll.*) excess fat at the waist. **love-hate relationship** *n.* a relationship characterized by powerful but contradictory feelings of attraction and repulsion. **love-in-a-mist** *n.* a plant, *Nigella damascena*, with blue flowers and many green bracts. **love-in-idleness** *n.* the pansy or heartsease, *Viola tricolor*. **love knot** *n.* an intricate bow or knot (a token of love). **loveless** *a.* **1** destitute of love. **2** not loving. **3** not loved. **lovelessly** *adv.* **lovelessness** *n.* **love letter** *n.* a letter between lovers or professing love. **love-lies-bleeding** *n.* a species of amaranth, esp. *Amaranthus caudatus*, which has drooping spikes of dark red flowers. **love life** *n.* a person's romantic or sexual experiences and attachments. **lovelock** *n.* a curl or tress hanging at the ear or on the forehead. **lovelorn** *a.* **1** forsaken by one's love. **2** pining away for love. **lovely** *a.* (*comp.* **lovelier**, *superl.* **loveliest**) **1** beautiful and attractive. **2** delightful, pleasant, enjoyable. **3** lovable, amiable. ~*adv.* (*coll.*) very well, delightfully. ~*n.* (*pl.* **lovelies**) (*coll.*) a beautiful woman. **lovelily** *adv.* **loveliness** *n.* **lovemaking** *n.* **1** sexual play or intercourse between partners.

2 †courtship, amorous attentions. **love match** *n.* a marriage for love, not for other considerations. **love nest** *n.* a secret place where lovers meet, esp. for illicit sexual relations. **lover** *n.* 1 a person with whom one is having a sexual relationship. 2 (*pl.*) a couple who are having a love affair. 3 a person, esp. a man, who is in love. 4 a person who is fond of anything. **loverless** *a.* **love seat** *n.* a small sofa or double chair for two people. **lovesick** *a.* 1 languishing with love. 2 expressive of languishing love. **lovesickness** *n.* **lovesome** (-səm) *a.* (*poet.*) lovely. **love song** *n.* a song expressing love. **love story** *n.* (*pl.* **love stories**) a story dealing mainly with romantic love. **love token** *n.* a present in token of love. **lovey** (-i) *n.* (*pl.* **loveys**) (*coll.*) a person who is loved, a term of endearment. **lovey-dovey** (-dŭv´i) *a.* (*coll.*) demonstratively loving, affectionate. **loving** *a.* feeling or showing affection. ~*n.* affection, love. **loving cup** *n.* a large two- or three-handled drinking-vessel passed round with wine at a banquet. **loving kindness** *n.* gentleness, consideration; mercifulness. **lovingly** *adv.* **lovingness** *n.* [OE *lufu*, whence *lufigan*, *lufian*, to love (cp. Dut. *lieven*, G *lieben*), rel. to LIEF]

low[1] (lō) *a.* (*comp.* **lower**, *superl.* **lowest**) 1 not reaching or situated far up. 2 not high or tall, below the usual or normal height. 3 below or little above a given surface or level, not elevated. 4 (of the sun, moon etc.) near the horizon. 5 (of latitude) near the equator. 6 small or below the norm in amount, extent, intensity etc. 7 reduced in amount, scanty, nearly exhausted. 8 humble in rank or position. 9 dejected, depressed. 10 lacking in vigour, weak, feeble. 11 badly nourished. 12 affording poor nourishment. 13 (of sounds) not raised in pitch, deep, produced by slow vibrations, not loud or intense, soft. 14 not sublime, not exalted, commonplace. 15 coarse, vulgar. 16 base, dishonourable. 17 not advanced in civilization. 18 not high in organization. 19 (of a vowel sound) open. 20 in the Church of England, inclined to evangelical doctrine, not favouring sacerdotal pretensions, not characterized by elaborate ritual. ~*adv.* 1 in or to a low position. 2 at a low price. 3 in a humble rank or position. 4 with a subdued voice, in low tones; softly, quietly. 5 at a deep pitch. 6 of humble birth. ~*n.* 1 a low position or level. 2 an area of low atmospheric pressure. **at a low ebb** EBB. **at lowest** to mention or judge by the least possible amount etc. **to bring low** to reduce in wealth, position, health etc. **to lay low** LAY[1]. **to lie low** LIE[1]. **to run low** RUN. **low birth** *n.* humble parentage. **low-born** *a.* **lowboy** *n.* (*N Am.*) a short-legged chest or table with drawers. **lowbrow** *n.* a person making no claims to culture or intellectuality. ~*a.* 1 unintellectual. 2 assuming no airs of intellectual superiority. **lowbrowed** *a.* lowbrow. **Low Church** *n.* the evangelical party in the Church of England. **Low Churchman** *n.* (*pl.* **Low Churchmen**). **low-class** *a.* of poor quality or of low social class. **low comedy** *n.* comedy in which the humour is very broad and verges on farce. **Low Countries** *n.pl.* a collective name for Belgium, Luxembourg and the Netherlands. **low-cut** *a.* (of a dress etc.) cut low at the neck, exposing part of the shoulders and breasts. **low-density lipoprotein** *n.* the form of lipoprotein in which cholesterol is transported in the bloodstream. **low-down** *a.* degraded, mean, abject. ~*n.* (*coll.*) the inner history, real facts. **Low Dutch** *n.* 1 (*as pl.*) the Germanic peoples of the coast, esp. of the Netherlands. 2 their language. **lowest** *a.* (the) most low. **lowest common denominator** *n.* 1 (*Math.*) the smallest number or quantity that is exactly divisible by each denominator of a set of fractions. 2 the least desirable or edifying feature common to all members of a group. **lowest common multiple** *n.* the smallest number or quantity that is exactly divisible by each of the set of numbers or quantities. **low frequency** *n.* a radio frequency lying between 30 and 300 kHz. **low gear** *n.* on cycles, motor vehicles etc., apparatus for transmitting low speed to the driving-wheel relatively to the motion of pedals, engine etc. **Low German** *n.* the dialect of German, closely related to Dutch, spoken esp. in the rural areas of N Germany. **low-grade** *a.* of low quality or strength. **low-income** *a.* 1 of or relating to people who earn low wages or have a low income. 2 having a low national income. **lowish** *a.* **low-key, low-keyed** *a.* 1 of low intensity. 2 undramatic. 3 restrained. **lowland** *n.* low-lying or level country. ~*a.* of or relating to a lowland or the Lowlands. **Lowland bonnet** *n.* SCOTCH BONNET (under SCOTCH). **Lowlander** *n.* **Lowlands** *n.pl.* the eastern and southern or less mountainous parts of Scotland. **Low Latin** *n.* medieval Latin, esp. of a debased or semi-popular kind. **low latitudes** *n.pl.* latitudes near the equator. **low-level language** *a.* computer programming language that corresponds more to machine code than to human language. **low life** *n.* life in the criminal underworld or in the lowest social strata. **lowlife** *n.* (*pl.* **lowlifes**) 1 a member of the criminal underworld. 2 criminals and the degenerate members of a society collectively. **lowlight** *n.* 1 (*facet.*) a particularly dull, inglorious or unsuccessful moment or period in the course or history of something. 2 (*usu. pl.*) a portion of hair dyed to a colour darker than the natural one. **low-loader** *n.* a road or rail vehicle with a low platform for heavy loads. **lowly** *a.* (*comp.* **lowlier**, *superl.* **lowliest**) 1 humble, modest, unpretentious. 2 low in size, rank or condition. 3 low, mean, inferior. 4 comparatively undeveloped or unevolved. ~*adv.* 1 humbly, modestly. 2 †in a low or inferior way. **lowlily** *adv.* **lowliness** *n.* **low-lying** *a.* situated at a low level with respect to the surrounding countryside and to rivers or bodies of water. **low Mass** *n.* Mass said without music and without elaborate ritual. **low-minded** *a.* having a crude mind and character. **low-neck, low-necked** *a.* (of a woman's dress) having a low-cut neck. **lowness** *n.* **low-pitched** *a.* 1 having a low tone or key. 2 (of a roof) having a low angular elevation. **low-pressure** *a.* 1 having, using or exerting a lower pressure than the norm. 2 having low barometric pressure. 3 relaxed, calm; undemanding. **low profile** *n.* a reserved or inconspicuous attitude or manner to avoid attention or publicity. **low-profile** *a.* 1 deliberately avoiding prominence or publicity. 2 (of a motor vehicle tyre) having greater than usual width in relation to its height. **low relief** *n.* bas-relief. **low-rise** *a.* (of buildings) having only one or two storeys. **low season** *n.* the season during which there is least demand, traffic etc. **low-slung** *a.* 1 (of a vehicle) with the body close to the ground. 2 hanging or carried low. **low-spirited** *a.* dejected, depressed. **Low Sunday** *n.* the Sunday next after Easter. **low technology, low tech** *n.* simple unsophisticated machinery, implements and techniques as used for centuries for the production of basic necessities. **low-technology, low-tech** *a.* **low-tension** *a.* having, generating or operating at a low voltage. **low tide** *n.* 1 the lowest point of the ebb tide; the level of the sea at ebb tide. 2 the time of this. **low-velocity** *a.* applied to projectiles propelled at a comparatively low velocity and having a high trajectory. **low visibility** *n.* indistinct visibility. **low-voiced** *a.* having a soft, gentle voice. **low water** *n.* low tide. **low-water mark** *n.* 1 the point reached by the sea at low tide or something marking this. 2 the lowest level or value; the nadir. **Low Week** *n.* the week beginning on Low Sunday. **low wine** *n.* a liquor produced by the first distillation of alcohol. [late OE *lāh*, Icel. *lāgr* (cp. Dut. *laag*), cogn. with LIE[1]]

low[2] (lō) *v.i.* to utter the moo of cow. ~*v.t.* to utter with such a sound. ~*n.* the moo of a cow. **lowing** *n.* [OE *hlōwan* (cp. Dut. *lōeien*, OHG *hlōjan*), cogn. with L *clāmāre*, Gr. *kalein*, to call]

lower[1] (lō´ə) *a.* **1** situated at a less high level than, or below, another thing. **2** smaller in quantity, number etc. **3** (*often* **Lower**) **a** situated on a lower terrain. **b** situated to the south. **4** (*Geol.*) (*often* **Lower**) relating to an older period and therefore usu. to deeper strata. ~*adv.* in or to a lower position, status etc. ~*v.t.* **1** to bring down in height, force, pitch, intensity, amount, price, estimation etc. **2** to haul or let down. **3** to degrade, to demean. **4** to diminish. ~*v.i.* **1** to become lower or less. **2** to sink, to fall. **to lower one's eyes** EYE[1]. **to lower one's sights** SIGHT. **to lower the flag** FLAG[1]. **to lower the tone** to make a conversation, social gathering etc., less refined, prestigious or edifying. **lower case** *n.* (*Print.*) small letters; a case containing the small letters. **lower-case** *a.* **lower class** *n.* (*often pl.*) the working classes. **lower-class** *a.* **lower criticism** *n.* textual criticism of the Bible. **lower deck** *n.* **1** the deck just above the hold of a ship. **2** the petty officers and men of a ship or of the Royal Navy. **Lower House** *n.* **1** the larger, usu. popularly elected house of a bicameral legislative assembly. **2** in the UK, the House of Commons. **lowermost** *a.* **lower regions** *n.pl.* hell; the realm of the dead. **lower world** *n.* **1** the earth, as opposed to heaven. **2** the lower regions. [comp. of LOW[1]]

lower[2] LOUR.

lox[1] (loks) *n.* a kind of smoked salmon. [Yiddish *laks*, from MG *lans*, salmon]

lox[2] (loks) *n.* liquid oxygen, used in rocket fuels. [*l*iquid *ox*ygen]

loxodromic (loksədrom´ik) *a.* of or relating to the rhumb lines or to map projections, such as Mercator's, in which rhumb lines appear straight. **loxodromics** *n.* navigation using rhumb lines. [Gr. *loxos*, oblique, *dromos*, course, from *dramein*, to run]

loyal (loi´əl) *a.* **1** faithful, true, constant, in a trust or obligation (to). **2** faithful to one's sovereign, government or country. ~†*n.* a loyal subject, esp. in a time of disaffection. **loyalism** *n.* **loyalist** *n.* **1** a patriotic supporter of sovereign or government. **2** (**Loyalist**) in Northern Ireland, a Protestant who supports Ulster's union with Britain. **3** (**Loyalist**) in the American War of Independence, a colonial supporter of Britain. **4** (**Loyalist**) a republican supporter in the Spanish Civil War. **loyalize, loyalise** *v.t.* **loyally** *adv.* **loyal toast** *n.* a toast to the sovereign. **loyalty** *n.* (*pl.* **loyalties**). **loyalty card** *n.* a card issued to customers by a supermarket chain etc., through which points are accumulated according to money spent and discounts or other benefits are offered. [F, from L *lēgālis*, LEGAL]

lozenge (loz´inj) *n.* **1** a rhombus or oblique-angled parallelogram. **2** a confection or medicated sweet etc. in a tablet of this shape. **3** a small rhombus-shaped pane of glass. **4** (*Her.*) a diamond-shaped bearing, appropriated to the arms of spinsters and widows. **5** a rhombus-shaped facet in a cut gem. **lozenged** *a.* **1** shaped like a rhombus or diamond. **2** arranged in a series of lozenges in alternate colours. **3** having diamond panes. **lozenge moulding** *n.* (*Archit.*) an ornament enclosing diamond-shaped panels. **lozenge-shaped** *a.* **lozengewise** *adv.* **lozengy** *a.* (*Her.*) divided into lozenge-shaped compartments. [OF *losenge*, Prov. *lauza*, tombstone, prob. from L *lapis -idem*, stone]

LP[1] (elpē´) *n.* a long-playing record, usu. 12 in. (30 cm) in diameter and designed to rotate at 33.3 revolutions per minute.

LP[2] *abbr.* **1** Lord Provost. **2** low pressure.

LPG *abbr.* liquefied petroleum gas.

lpm *abbr.* lines per minute.

LPO *abbr.* London Philharmonic Orchestra.

Lr *chem. symbol* lawrencium.

LS *abbr.* Lesotho (IVR).

LSD (elesdē´) *n.* lysergic acid diethylamide, a hallucinogenic drug.

L.S.D., l.s.d, £.s.d *abbr.* librae, solidi, denarii, pounds, shillings and pence. [L]

LSE *abbr.* London School of Economics.

LSO *abbr.* London Symphony Orchestra.

Lt. *abbr.* **1** Lieutenant. **2** light.

LTA *abbr.* Lawn Tennis Association.

Ltd. *abbr.* limited liability.

Lu *chem. symbol* lutetium.

lubber (lŭb´ə) *n.* **1** a lazy, clumsy person, an awkward lout. **2** a bad seaman. **lubberlike** *a.* **lubberly** *a.* like a lubber. ~*adv.* clumsily. **lubberliness** *n.* **lubber's hole** *n.* a hole in the top through which sailors can reach the masthead without climbing the futtock-shrouds. **lubber's line** *n.* the mark inside a compass-case which shows the direction of the ship's head. [etym. uncertain, prob. rel. to LOB]

lubra (loo´brə) *n.* an Aboriginal woman. [Austral. Abor.]

lubricate (loo´brikāt) *v.t.* **1** to cover or treat with grease, oil or similar substance, in order to reduce friction. **2** to make smooth or slippery. **3** (*coll.*) to bribe. **4** (*sl.*) to drink. **lubricant** (-brikənt) *n.* a substance used to lubricate. ~*a.* that lubricates. **lubrication** (-ā´shən) *n.* **lubricator** *n.* a person who or something which lubricates. [L *lūbricātus*, p.p. of *lūbricāre*, from *lūbricus*, slippery, cogn. with SLIP[1]]

lubricious (loobrish´əs), **lubricous** (loo´brikəs) *a.* **1** (*formal*) lewd, lascivious. **2** †slipperiness. **lubricity** (loobris´iti) *n.* **1** lewdness, lasciviousness. **2** smoothness. **3** slipperiness. **4** capacity to lubricate. [L *lubricus*, slippery]

Lucan (loo´kən) *a.* of or relating to the evangelist St Luke. [L *Lūcas*, Luke, -AN]

lucarne (lookahn´) *n.* a dormer or garret window, a light in a spire. [F, etym. uncertain]

luce (loos) *n.* **1** a pike (the fish), esp. when full-grown. **2** a figure of a pike used as an armorial bearing. [OF *lus*, L *lūcius*]

lucent (loo´sənt) *a.* (*poet.*) **1** shining, bright, luminous, resplendent. **2** translucent. **lucency** *n.* [L *lūcens -ntis*, pres.p. of *lūcēre*, to shine (*lux lūcis*, light, cogn. with Gr. *leukos*, white)]

lucerne (loosœn´), **lucern** *n.* alfalfa. [F *luzerne*, etym. unknown]

lucid (loo´sid) *a.* **1** clear, transparent, perspicuous, easily understood. **2** sane; denoting an interval of sanity occurring during insanity or dementia. **3** (*Bot.*) having a smooth, shiny surface. **4** (*poet.*) bright, shining, radiant. **lucidity** (-sid´-) *n.* **lucidly** *adv.* **lucidness** *n.* [L *lūcidus*, from *lūcēre*, see LUCENT]

Lucifer (loo´sifə) *n.* **1** the morning star. **2** Satan, the chief of the rebel angels. **3** †(**lucifer**) a match tipped with combustible substance and ignited by friction. **Luciferian** (-fiə´ri-) *a.* **luciferin** (-sif´ərin) *n.* a substance that emits light as it oxidizes and decays, found in the luminous organs of glow-worms and fireflies. †**luciferous** (-sif´-) *a.* **1** bearing or giving light. **2** making plain or clear. **3** Satanic, devilish. [L, light-bringing (*lūci-*, see LUCENT, *-fer*, from *ferre*, to bring)]

lucifugous (loosif´ūgəs) *a.* (of certain animals) shunning the light.

luck (lŭk) *n.* **1** chance, accident, as bringer of fortune, whether good or bad. **2** what happens to one, fortune, hap. **3** good fortune, success. **4** a person or thing that is supposed to bring good fortune. **down on one's luck** not having much luck. **for luck** in the hope of gaining good fortune. **no such luck** unfortunately not. **to luck into** (*sl.*) to acquire or achieve by good fortune or chance. **to luck out** (*N Am., sl.*) to be successful or fortunate, esp. by chance. **to push one's luck** PUSH. **to try one's luck** to attempt something. **with luck** if everything goes well. **worse luck** unfortunately. **luckless** *a.* unfortunate. **lucklessly** *adv.* **luckpenny** *n.* a small sum returned to the buyer 'for luck' by the person who receives money on a sale or contract. **lucky** *a.* (*comp.* **luckier,** *superl.* **luckiest**) **1** characterized or usu. attended by good luck, favoured by fortune. **2** successful, esp. by a fluke or more than is deserved. **3** bringing luck, auspicious. **luckily** *adv.* fortunately (for). **luckiness** *n.* **lucky dip** *n.* a receptacle containing an assortment of articles, for one of which people dip blindly. **lucky dog** *n.* (*coll.*) a lucky fellow. [Dut. *luk, geluk* (cp. G *Glück*), etym. uncertain]

lucrative (loo´krətiv) *a.* producing gain, profitable, bringing in money. **lucratively** *adv.*

lucre (loo´kə) *n.* (*derog. or facet.*) pecuniary gain or advantage, usu. as an object of greed. [F, from L *lucrum* (cp. Gr. *leia*, booty, *apolauein*, to enjoy, G *Lohn*, reward)]

lucubrate (loo´kūbrāt) *v.i.* (*formal*) **1** to study by lamplight. **2** to produce lucubrations. **lucubration** (-brā´shən) *n.* **1** (*usu. pl.*) composition of a learned or too elaborate and pedantic character. **2** night work, night study. [L *lūcubrātus*, p.p. of *lūcubrāre*, from *lux lūcis*, light]

luculent (loo´kūlənt) *a.* (*formal*) clear, lucid, plain. **luculently** *adv.* [L *lūculentus*, from *lux lūcis*, light]

Lucullan (lukŭl´ən) *a.* lavish, sumptuous. [Licinius *Lucullus*, ?110–56 BC, Roman general famous for his lavish banquets]

lud (lud) *n.* lord, as in *m'lud, my lud*, phrases used to address a judge in court. [corr. of LORD]

Luddite (lŭd´īt) *n.* **1** a member of a band of workmen who organized riots, 1811–16, for the destruction of machinery as a protest against unemployment. **2** any opponent of technological change. **Luddism** *n.* [supposedly after Ned *Ludd*, fl. 1779, a Leicestershire workman who destroyed machinery]

ludicrous (loo´dikrəs) *a.* liable to excite laughter or derision; comical, ridiculous. **ludicrously** *adv.* **ludicrousness** *n.* [L *lūdicrus*, from *lūdi-*, stem of *lūdus*, play]

ludo (loo´dō) *n.* a game played with counters on a specially chequered board. [L *ludo*, I play]

lues (loo´ēz) *n.* plague, contagious disease, infection, contagion, now used only for syphilis. **lues venerea** (viniə´riə) *n.* syphilis. **luetic** (-et´-) *a.* [L]

luff (lŭf), **loof** (loof) *n.* (*Naut.*) **1** the weather edge of a fore-and-aft sail. **2** the part of a ship facing into, towards the wind. **3** the act of sailing close to the wind. **4** that part of a ship's bows where the timbers begin to curve in towards the stem. *~v.i.* to bring a ship's head or to steer nearer the wind. *~v.t.* **1** to bring (a ship's head) or the head of (a ship) nearer the wind. **2** to turn (the helm) so as to do this. **3** to obstruct (an opponent) in yacht racing by sailing closer to the wind. **4** to raise or lower (the jib of a crane or derrick). [ME *luff, lof(f)* from OF *lof*; perh. derived from MDut. *loef*, peg of a tiller]

luffa LOOFAH.

Luftwaffe (looft´vahfə) *n.* the German Air Force before and during World War II. [G *Luft*, air, *Waffe*, weapon]

lug[1] (lŭg) *v.t.* (*pres.p.* **lugging,** *past, p.p.* **lugged**) **1** to drag, to pull, esp. roughly or with exertion. **2** to carry with effort and difficulty. **3** to drag in, to insert unnecessarily. **4** (of a sailing ship) to carry too much (sail). *~v.i.* to drag or pull (at). *~n.* a drag or tug. [prob. from Scand. (cp. Swed. and Norw. *lugga*, to pull by the hair, *lugg*, the forelock)]

lug[2] (lŭg) *n.* **1** a projecting part, esp. a projecting part of a machine made to hold or grip another part. **2** (*coll. or Sc.*) the ear. **3** (*N Am.*) a stupid or awkward person; an oaf. **4** a leather loop used in harness. **5** a basket-box for vegetables or fruit, having a capacity of 28 to 40 lb. (approx 13.1 to 18.1 kg). **lughole** *n.* (*coll.*) earhole. [etym. uncertain]

lug[3] LUGWORM.

lug[4] LUGSAIL.

luge (loozh) *n.* a small toboggan for one or two people. *~v.i.* to toboggan in one of these. [Swiss F]

Luger (loo´gə) *n.* a type of German automatic pistol.

luggage (lŭg´ij) *n.* a traveller's suitcases, trunks etc. **luggage van** *n.* a railway carriage for luggage, bicycles etc.

lugger (lŭg´ə) *n.* a small vessel with two or three masts, a running bowsprit and lugsails.

lugsail (lŭg´səl), **lug** *n.* a four-cornered sail bent to a yard lashed obliquely to the mast. [etym. uncertain, perh. from LUG[2]]

lugubrious (lugoo´briəs) *a.* mournful, dismal, funereal. **lugubriously** *adv.* **lugubriousness** *n.* [L *lūgubris*, from *lūgēre*, to mourn]

lugworm (lŭg´wœm), **lug** *n.* any large marine worm of the genus *Arenicola*, burrowing in the sand, used for bait. [etym. unknown]

lukewarm (look´wawm, -wawm´) *a.* **1** moderately warm. **2** tepid. **3** indifferent, cool, lacking enthusiasm or conviction. **lukewarmly** *adv.* **lukewarmness** *n.* [ME *luke*, tepid, prob. cogn. with OE *hleow*, LEE, WARM]

lull (lŭl) *v.t.* **1** to soothe to sleep, to calm, to quiet. **2** to allay someone's fears, anxieties etc. usu. in order to deceive. *~v.i.* to subside, to become quiet. *~n.* **1** a temporary calm. **2** an intermission or abatement. **lullaby** (-əbī) *n.* (*pl.* **lullabies**) a refrain or song for lulling a child to sleep. *~v.t.* (*3rd pers. sing. pres.* **lullabies,** *pres.p.* **lullabying,** *past, p.p.* **lullabied**) to sing to sleep. **lullingly** *adv.* [imit. (cp. Swed. *lulla*, MDut. *lullen*, G *lallen*, Gr. *lalein*)]

lulu (loo´loo) *n.* (*pl.* **lulus**) (*coll.*) an extremely good or bad person or thing. [perh. from *Lulu*, pet form of the name *Louise*]

lum (lŭm) *n.* (*Sc.*) a chimney. **lum hat** *n.* a top hat. [etym. uncertain]

lumbago (lŭmbā´gō) *n.* rheumatism in the lumbar region. [L *lumbus*, loin]

lumbar (lŭm´bə) *a.* of or relating to the portion of the body between the lower ribs and the upper part of the hip bone. *~n.* a lumbar nerve, vertebra, artery etc. **lumbar puncture** *n.* the insertion of a needle between two lumbar vertebrae to withdraw cerebrospinal fluid. [med. L *lumbaris*, from *lumbus*, loin]

lumber[1] (lŭm´bə) *v.i.* **1** to move heavily, cumbrously or clumsily. **2** †to make a heavy rumbling noise. **lumbering** *a.* **lumberingly** *adv.* **lumbersome** (-səm) *a.* [etym. uncertain, perh. imit. (cp. Swed. dial. *lomra*, to roar, Icel. *hljōmr*, a sound) or freq. of LAME[1]]

lumber[2] (lŭm´bə) *n.* **1** discarded articles of furniture and other rubbish taking up room. **2** useless and cumbersome things. **3** rubbish, refuse. **4** (*N Am.*) timber sawn into marketable shape. *~v.t.* **1** to burden (with), to leave to deal with (something unwanted or unpleasant). **2** to fill with lumber. **3** to encumber, to obstruct. **4** to heap up in a disorderly way. **5** (*N Am.*) to cut and prepare (timber) for the market. *~v.i.* to fell and prepare timber, to work as a lumberjack. **lumber camp** *n.* a lumberman's camp. **lumber-dealer** *n.* a timber merchant. **lumberjack, lumberman** *n.* (*pl.* **lumberjacks, lumbermen**) a person who is employed in felling, preparing and transporting forest timber. **lumber-jacket** *n.* **1** a man's loose-fitting jacket in a heavy, usu. chequered material that fastens up to the neck. **2** a woman's cardigan similarly fastened. **lumber-mill** *n.* a sawmill. **lumber-room** *n.* a room for the storage of lumber, trunks etc. **lumberyard** *n.* (*N Am.*) a timber yard. [etym. uncertain, perh. var. of *lombard*, the room where the Lombard bankers stored their unredeemed pledges, or from LUMBER[1]]

lumbrical (lŭm´brikəl) *a.* of, relating to or resembling a worm. **lumbricals, lumbrical muscles** *n.pl.* four vermiform muscles, two of the foot and two of the hand, which help to flex the digits. **lumbriciform** (-bris´ifawm) *a.* resembling a worm, vermiform. [L *lumbrīcus*, worm, -AL[1]]

lumen (loo´mən) *n.* (*pl.* **lumens, lumina** (-minə)) **1** the

SI unit of luminous flux, being the quantity of light emitted per second in a solid angle of one steradian by a uniform point-source having an intensity of one candela. 2 (*Anat.*) the cavity of a tubular organ. 3 a cavity within a plant cell wall. **lumenal, luminal** *a.* **luminance** *n.* a measure, in candela/cm², of the luminous intensity of any surface in a given direction per unit of projected area. **luminant** *n., a.* [L, light]

luminaire (loomineə´) *n.* a light fitting. [F]

Luminal® (loo´minəl) *n.* phenobarbitone. [LUMEN, -AL²]

luminary (loo´minəri) *n.* (*pl.* **luminaries**) 1 a famous person. 2 a person who enlightens mankind or is a brilliant exponent of a subject. 3 (*formal*) any body yielding light, esp. a heavenly body. [OF *luminarie*, med. L *lūminārium*, L *lūmināre*, from *lūmen -inis*, light]

luminesce (loomines´) *v.i.* to exhibit luminescence. **luminescence** *n.* the emission of light at low temperatures by processes other than incandescence, e.g. by chemical action. **luminescent** *a.* [LUMEN, -ESCE]

luminiferous (loominif´ərəs) *a.* giving, yielding or transmitting light.

luminous (loo´minəs) *a.* 1 emitting light. 2 shining brightly, brilliant. 3 visible in darkness; phosphorescent. 4 lucid, perspicuous; shedding light (on a subject etc.). 5 relating to visible radiation. **luminosity** (-nos´-) *n.* (*pl.* **luminosities**) 1 the fact of being luminous. 2 the measure of the amount of light emitted by a star irrespective of its distance from the earth. **luminous flux** *n.* a measure of the rate of flow of luminous energy. **luminous intensity** *n.* a measure of the amount of light radiated in a given direction from a point source. **luminously** *adv.* **luminousness** *n.* **luminous paint** *n.* a paint containing phosphorescent compounds which cause it to glow in the dark after exposure to light.

lumme (lŭm´i), **lummy** *int.* used to express surprise. [contr. of *Lord love me*]

lummox (lŭm´əks) *n.* (*coll.*) a clumsy person. [etym. unknown]

lummy LUMME.

lump¹ (lŭmp) *n.* 1 a small mass of matter of no definite shape. 2 a mass, a quantity, a heap, a lot. 3 a swelling, a protuberance; a tumour. 4 a heavy, stupid person. ~*v.t.* 1 to put together in a lump, to form into a mass. 2 to take collectively, to treat as all alike. ~*v.i.* 1 to form or collect into lumps. 2 to move (about) heavily or clumsily. **in the lump** 1 the whole taken together. 2 altogether, in gross. **the lump** the collective group of self-employed workers in the building trade. **to take one's lumps** (*sl.*) to put up with hard knocks, assaults, defeats. **lumpectomy** (-ek´təmi) *n.* (*pl.* **lumpectomies**) the removal by surgery of a cancerous lump in the breast. **lumper** *n.* (*N Am.*) a labourer who loads or unloads ships. **lumping** *a.* 1 large, heavy. 2 big, bulky, plentiful. **lump in the throat** *n.* a feeling of constriction in the throat caused by emotion. **lumpish** *a.* 1 like a lump. 2 heavy. 3 lazy, inert. 4 stupid. **lumpishly** *adv.* **lumpishness** *n.* **lump sugar** *n.* cube sugar; loaf sugar broken into small lumps. **lump sum** *n.* the whole amount of money taken together, as opposed to instalments. **lumpy** *a.* (*comp.* **lumpier**, *superl.* **lumpiest**) 1 full of lumps. 2 (*Naut.*) running in short waves that do not break. **lumpily** *adv.* **lumpiness** *n.* [etym. uncertain, prob. from Scand. (cp. Swed. dial. and Norw. *lump*, block, stump, Dan. *lumpe*)]

lump² (lŭmp) *v.t.* (*coll.*) to put up with. **like it or lump it** put up with it as there is no alternative. [etym. uncertain, prob. imit.]

lumpen (lŭm´pən) *a.* 1 (*coll.*) stupid, oafish. 2 denoting a degraded section of a particular social and economic grouping. **lumpenproletariat** *n.* the very poorest section of the urban population, made up of criminals, vagabonds etc. [G *Lumpen*, rags]

lumpfish (lŭmp´fish) *n.* (*pl. in general* **lumpfish**, *in particular* **lumpfishes**) 1 a suctorial fish, *Cyclopterus lumpus*, of northern seas, with a globular body covered in tubercles and pelvic fins modified as a sucker. 2 any other fish of the family Cyclopteridae. **lumpsucker** *n.* a lumpfish. [obs. *lump*, lumpfish cp. MDut. *lompe*, G *lump*, F *lompe*]

lunacy (loo´nəsi) *n.* (*pl.* **lunacies**) 1 unsoundness of mind, insanity, formerly supposed to be caused by the moon. 2 gross folly, senseless conduct; a senseless action. [see LUNATIC]

luna moth (loo´nə) *n.* a large N American moth, *Actias luna*, with crescent-shaped markings on its forewings.

lunar (loo´nə) *a.* 1 of or relating to, caused or influenced by the moon. 2 of or relating to travel to or landings on the moon. 3 resembling the moon, crescent-shaped. 4 (of light) pale, weak. 5 of or containing silver. ~*n.* a lunar distance or observation. **lunar caustic** *n.* nitrate of silver fused at a low heat. **lunar cycle** *n.* a Metonic cycle. **lunar distance** *n.* the angular distance of the moon from the sun, a planet or a star, used at sea in finding longitude. **lunarian** (-neə´ri-) *n.* 1 an inhabitant of the moon. 2 †a selenographer. 3 someone using the lunar method of finding longitude. **lunar module, lunar excursion module** *n.* a small spacecraft used in the Apollo missions to transfer astronauts from an orbiting spacecraft to the moon's surface. **lunar month** *n.* 1 the period of a complete revolution of the moon, 29½ days. 2 (in general use) four weeks. **lunar node** *n.* either of the two points at which the moon's orbit intersects the ecliptic. **lunar observation** *n.* observation of the moon's distance from the sun or a star to find the longitude. **lunar orbit** *n.* 1 the moon's orbit around the earth. 2 an orbit around the moon. **lunar year** *n.* a period of twelve lunar months. **lunate** (-nāt), **lunated** (-nātid) *n.* 1 a crescent-shaped prehistoric implement. 2 (*also* **lunate bone**) a crescent-shaped bone in the wrist. ~*a.* crescent-shaped. **lunation** (-nā´shən) *n.* the period between two returns of the moon, a lunar month. [L *Lūnārus*, from *lūna*, the moon]

lunatic (loo´nətik) *a.* 1 insane. 2 mad, frantic, crazy, extremely foolish. ~*n.* an insane person. **lunatic asylum** *n.* (*offensive*) formerly the name for a hospital for the care and treatment of the mentally ill. **lunatic fringe** *n.* members of society or of a group regarded as holding extreme or fanatical views. [F *lunatique*, late L *lūnāticus*, as LUNAR]

lunation LUNAR.

lunch (lŭnch) *n.* 1 a midday meal. 2 the food eaten at such a meal. 3 lunch hour. 4 a light meal or snack eaten at any time. ~*v.i.* to take lunch. ~*v.t.* to provide lunch for. **to do lunch** 1 to have lunch together, esp. for a business discussion. 2 to make or serve lunch. **lunch box** *n.* a container for carrrying food to eat. **lunch break** *n.* lunch hour. **luncheon** (-chən) *n.* (*formal*) lunch. **luncheonette** (-chənet) *n.* (*esp. N Am.*) a restaurant serving light lunches. **luncheon meat** *n.* a type of pre-cooked meat, usu. pork minced with cereal, served cold. **luncheon voucher** *n.* a voucher given to employees which can be used to pay for take-away food or a meal in a restaurant. **lunch hour** *n.* time allowed off work to eat lunch. **lunchtime** *n.* the time at which lunch is usually eaten. [etym. uncertain, prob. a var. of LUMP¹, a lump or slice, as of bread]

lune (loon) *n.* 1 (*Geom.*) a figure enclosed by two intersecting arcs. 2 anything in the shape of a half-moon. 3 a lunette in a monstrance. 4 (*pl.*) †fits of lunacy, crotchets, freaks. [F, from L *lūna*, moon]

lunette (loonet´) *n.* 1 a semicircular aperture in a concave ceiling. 2 a crescent-shaped or semicircular space or panel for a picture or decorative painting. 3 a flattened watch-glass. 4 a ring on a vehicle to enable it to be towed by a towing hook. 5 a temporary fortification which has two faces and two flanks. 6 a crescent-shaped holder for the consecrated host in a monstrance. [F]

lung (lŭng) *n.* **1** either of the two organs of respiration in vertebrates, situated on each side of the chest. **2** an analogous organ in invertebrates. **3** an open space in or near a city. **lunged** *a.* **lungfish** *n.* (*pl. in general* **lungfish,** *in particular* **lungfishes**) a dipnoan, having lungs as well as gills. **lungless** *a.* **lung-power** *n.* strength of voice. **lungworm** *n.* a parasitic nematode worm infecting the lungs of mammals, esp. pigs. **lungwort** *n.* **1** any plant of the genus *Pulmonaria,* of the borage family, formerly held to be good for pulmonary diseases. **2** a lichen, *Lobaria pulmonacea,* growing on the trunks of trees, also used as a domestic remedy for lung disease. [OE *lungen* (cp. Dut. *long,* Icel. *lunga,* G *Lunge*), cogn. with LIGHT[2], cp. LIGHTS]

lunge[1] (lŭnj) *n.* **1** a sudden thrust with a sword etc., esp. an attacking move in fencing in which the front foot is thrust forward and the back leg straightened as the sword arm is extended. **2** a sudden forward movement, a plunge. *~v.i.* **1** to make a lunge. **2** to plunge or rush forward suddenly. **3** in boxing, to deliver a blow from the shoulder. *~v.t.* to thrust (a weapon) forward. [earlier *allonge,* a lengthening]

lunge[2] (lŭnj), **longe** *n.* a long rope or rein used in training horses. *~v.t.* to drive (a horse) round in a circle at the end of a lunge. [F *longe,* var. of *loigne,* lune]

lungi (lung´gi) *n.* (*pl.* **lungis**) a long cloth used as a loin-cloth or sash, sometimes as a turban. [Hind.]

lunisolar (loonisō´lə) *a.* of, relating to, or compounded of the revolutions of, the sun and the moon. **lunisolar period** *n.* a period of 532 years found by multiplying the cycle of the sun by that of the moon. **lunisolar year** *n.* a year divided in accordance with the changes of the moon, but agreeing in length with the solar year. [L *lūna,* moon, *sōl,* sun]

lunitidal (loonitī´dəl) *a.* of or relating to the tidal phenomena governed by the moon. **lunitidal interval** *n.* the interval, at a particular meridian, between the moon's crossing it and the next high tide. [L *lūna,* moon, TIDAL]

lunula (loo´nūlə), **lunule** *n.* (*pl.* **lunulae** (-lē), **lunules**) **1** a crescent-shaped mark, spot or part, esp. at the base of a fingernail. **2** a crescent-shaped Bronze Age ornament forming part of a necklace. **lunular** *a.* crescent-shaped. **lunulate** (-lət), **lunulated** (-lātid) *a.* **1** having markings in the shape of crescents. **2** crescent-shaped. [L, dim. of *lūna,* moon]

Lupercal (loo´pəkəl) *n.* (*pl.* **Lupercalia** (-kā´liə)) a Roman fertility festival in honour of Lupercus, celebrated on 15 Feb. *~a.* Lupercalian. **Lupercalian** (-kā´liən) *a.* of or relating to this festival. [L, pertaining to *Lupercus,* a deity identified with Pan]

lupin (loo´pin), (*N Am.*) **lupine** *n.* **1** a leguminous plant of the genus *Lupinus,* with spikes of white or coloured flowers, grown in flower-gardens and for fodder. **2** (*pl.*) the seeds of this plant. [L *lupīnus*]

lupine[1] (loo´pīn) *a.* **1** of or relating to wolves. **2** like a wolf. [L *lupīnus,* from *lupus,* wolf]

lupine[2] LUPIN.

lupoid, lupous LUPUS.

lupulin (loo´pūlin) *n.* **1** the bitter essence of hops. **2** a yellow granular aromatic powder containing that essence, used as a sedative. [mod. L *lupulus,* hop, -IN]

lupus (loo´pəs) *n.* a spreading tuberculous or ulcerous inflammation of the skin, esp. lupus vulgaris. **lupoid** (-poid), **lupous** *a.* **lupus vulgaris** (vŭlgah´ris) *n.* tuberculosis of the skin, esp. of the face, causing dark red patches. [L, wolf]

lur (luə), **lure** *n.* a trumpet with long, curved tube, of prehistoric origin and used in Scandinavia for calling cattle home. [Icel. *lūthr*]

lurch[1] (lœch) *v.i.* **1** (of a ship) to roll suddenly to one side. **2** to stagger. *~n.* **1** a sudden roll sideways, as of a ship. **2** a stagger. [etym. uncertain]

lurch[2] (lœch) *n.* a losing position in the game of cribbage and some other games. **to leave in the lurch** to leave in difficulties. [F *lourche,* a 16th-cent. game like backgammon, etym. uncertain]

†**lurch**[3] (lœch) *v.i.* to lie in wait; to prowl about suspiciously. [var. of LURK]

lurcher (lœ´chə) *n.* **1** a dog, usu. a cross between a retriever or collie and a greyhound. **2** †a person who lurks about to steal or entrap. [LURCH[3]]

†**lurdan** (lœ´dən) *a.* stupid, lazy, useless. *~n.* a blockhead. [OF *lourdin,* from *lourd,* heavy]

lure[1] (luə) *n.* **1** an enticement, an allurement. **2** the alluring qualities of. **3** an object resembling a fowl, used to recall a hawk. *~v.t.* **1** to attract or bring back by a lure. **2** to entice. *~v.i.* to call or tempt an animal, esp. a hawk. [OF *leurre,* prob. from Gmc. (cp. G *Luder,* bait)]

lure[2] LUR.

Lurex® (lū´reks, loo´-) *n.* (a fabric made from) a thin plastic-coated metallic thread.

lurgy (lœ´gi) *n.* (*pl.* **lurgies**) (*facet.*) an unspecified (horrible) illness, usu. in *the dreaded lurgy.* [popularized or invented by *The Goon Show,* BBC Radio series 1949–60]

lurid (lū´rid, luə´-) *a.* **1** shockingly or glaringly bright. **2** gaudy, showy, in bright colours. **3** (of a story etc.) sensational, shocking, horrifying. **4** ghastly, unearthly. **5** of a pale yellow colour, wan. **to cast a lurid light on** to describe or explain in a sensational or horrifying way. **luridly** *adv.* **luridness** *n.* [L *lūridus,* perh. cogn. with Gr. *chlōros,* green]

lurk (lœk) *v.i.* **1** to move about furtively. **2** to wait concealed, esp. with a sinister purpose. **3** to lie in wait. **4** to be latent, to exist unperceived. *~n.* (*Austral.*) a dodge, a racket. **lurker** *n.* **lurking** *a.* [etym. uncertain, perh. cogn. with LOUR (cp. Norw. and Swed. dial. *lurka,* G *lauern*)]

luscious (lŭsh´əs) *a.* **1** very sweet, delicious. **2** extremely attractive, voluptuous. **3** (of music, poetry etc.) cloying, fulsome, over-rich in imagery, sensuousness etc. **lusciously** *adv.* **lusciousness** *n.* [etym. uncertain]

lush[1] (lŭsh) *a.* **1** luxuriant in growth. **2** succulent, juicy. **3** (of sound, colour) rich and voluptuous. **4** luxurious. **lushness** *n.* [var. of obs. *lash,* OF *lasche* (F *lâche*), L *laxus,* LAX]

lush[2] (lŭsh) *n.* (*sl.*) **1** a heavy drinker, an alcoholic. **2** (*N Am.*) alcohol. *~v.i.* to drink. *~v.t.* to ply with liquor. **lushy** *a.* drunk. [etym. uncertain]

lush[3] (lŭsh) *a.* (*sl.*) short for LUSCIOUS.

lust (lŭst) *n.* **1** a powerful desire for sexual pleasure, concupiscence, lasciviousness. **2** sensual appetite. **3** passionate desire (for). **4** passionate enjoyment, relish. *~v.i.* to have powerful or inordinate desire (for or after). **luster**[1] *n.* **lustful** *a.* **lustfully** *adv.* **lustfulness** *n.* **lusty** *a.* (*comp.* **lustier,** *superl.* **lustiest**) full of health and vigour. **lustily** *adv.* **lustiness** *n.* [OE (cp. Dut., Swed. and G *Lust*), cogn. with LIST[4]]

luster[1] LUST.

luster[2] LUSTRE[1].

lustral, lustrate etc. LUSTRE[2].

lustre[1] (lŭs´tə), (*N Am.*) **luster** *n.* **1** gloss, sheen, bright light, reflected light. **2** a shiny or reflective surface. **3** radiant or brilliant light. **4** splendour, illustriousness, glory (of an achievement etc.). **5** a chandelier ornamented with pendants of cut glass. **6** a glass pendant on such a chandelier. **7** a cotton, woollen or other fabric with a glossy surface. **8** a glossy enamel on pottery etc. **9** lustreware. *~v.t.* to put lustre on (pottery, cloth). **lustreless** *a.* **lustreware** *n.* ceramics with an iridescent glaze. **lustrous** (-trəs) *a.* **lustrously** *adv.* [F, from L *lūstrāre,* to lighten, illumine (cogn. with *lux lūcis,* light)]

lustre[2] (lŭs´tə), **lustrum** (-trəm) *n.* (*pl.* **lustres, lustrums, lustra** (-trə)) **1** a period of five years. **2** an expiatory offering made by the ancient Roman censors every five years. **lustral** *a.* **1** of, relating to or used in purification. **2** of or relating to a lustrum. **lustrate** *v.t.* to purify by a sacrifice or other ritual. **lustration** (-trā´shən) *n.* cleansing, esp. ceremonial cleansing. **lustrative** (-trətiv) *a.* [L *lustrum*, prob. from *luere*, to wash (cogn. with *lavāre*, to wash, see LAVE)]

†**lustring** (lŭs´tring), **lutestring** (lūt´string) *n.* a glossy silk fabric. [F *lustrine*, from LUSTRE[1]]

lustrum LUSTRE[2].

lusty LUST.

lusus (loo´səs, lū´-), **lusus naturae** (natū´rē, -rī) *n.* (*pl.* **lusus, lususes, lusus naturae**) a freak of nature. [L]

lutation LUTE[2].

lute[1] (lūt, loot) *n.* a stringed instrument with a pear-shaped body and a long fretted fingerboard. ~*v.t.* to play on or as on the lute. ~*v.i.* to sound sweetly, like a lute. **lutenist** (-tənist), **lutanist** *n.* a lute-player. **lutist** *n.* (*N Am.*) a lute-player, a lutenist. [F *lut* (now *luth*), Prov. *laut*, Sp. *laud*, Arab. *al-'ūd*, the lute, orig. wood]

lute[2] (lūt, loot) *n.* **1** (*also* **luting**) a composition of clay or cement used to secure the joints of vessels and tubes, or as a covering to protect crucibles etc. from fire. **2** a rubber washer. ~*v.t.* to seal up or coat with lute. **lutation** (-tā´shən) *n.* the act or process of luting. [OF *lut*, from L *lutum*, mud]

luteal (lū´tiəl, loo´-) *a.* of or relating to the corpus luteum. **lutein** (lū´tiin) *n.* a deep yellow pigment found in egg yolk etc. **luteinize** (-tiə-), **luteinise** *v.t., v.i.* to produce or form corpora lutea. **luteinization** (-zā´shən) *n.* **luteinizing hormone** *n.* a hormone secreted from the front lobe of the pituitary gland which stimulates, in females, ovulation and the development of corpora lutea and, in males, maturation of the interstitial cells of the testes and androgen production. [L *lūteus*, yellow, *lūteum*, egg yolk]

lutecium LUTETIUM.

luteo- (lū´tiō, loo´-) *comb. form* orange-coloured. **luteofulvous** (-fŭl´vəs) *a.* orange-tawny. **luteous** *a.* of a yellow colour, usu. a greenish yellow. [L *lūteus*, yellow]

lutestring LUSTRING.

lutetium (lootē´shiəm), **lutecium** (-si-) *n.* an extremely rare metallic element, at. no. 71, chem. symbol Lu, one of the lanthanides, discovered in 1907 by Georges Urbain, 1872–1938, a French chemist. [L *Lutetia*, Paris]

Lutheran (loo´thərən) *a.* of or belonging to Luther or his doctrines. ~*n.* **1** a follower of Luther. **2** a member of the Church based on Luther's religious doctrines. **Lutheranism, Lutherism** *n.* [Martin *Luther*, 1483–1546, German Protestant reformer]

luthier (lū´tiə, loo´-) *n.* a maker of lutes, guitars and other stringed instruments. [F, from *luth*, lute]

Lutine bell (loo´tēn) *n.* a bell recovered from the ship HMS *Lutine* and rung at Lloyd's in London before important announcements, such as the loss of a vessel.

luting LUTE[2].

lutist LUTE[1].

lutz (luts) *n.* in figure-skating, a jump from one skate with one, two or three rotations and a return to the other skate. [etym. uncertain, perh. from Gustave *Lussi*, b.1898, Swiss skater who invented it]

luvvy (lŭv´i), **luvvie** *n.* (*pl.* **luvvies**) (*coll.*) **1** a member of the acting profession, esp. one given to sentiment, effusiveness or camp. **2** lovey.

lux (lŭks) *n.* (*pl.* **lux, luxes**) the SI unit of illumination equal to one lumen per square metre. [L *lūx*, light]

luxate (lŭk´sāt) *v.t.* to put out of joint, to dislocate. **luxation** (-sā´shən) *n.* [L *luxātus*, p.p. of *luxāre*, to put out of joint, from *luxus*, Gr. *loxos*, oblique]

luxe (luks) *n.* luxury, sumptuousness, superfine elegance. [F, from L *luxus*]

Luxembourger (luks´əmbœgə) *n.* a native or inhabitant of Luxembourg.

luxury (lŭk´shəri) *n.* (*pl.* **luxuries**) **1** great comfort with abundant provision of pleasant and delightful things. **2** something which is not a necessity, esp. something particularly delightful and expensive that one indulges in only occasionally. **3** luxuriousness. ~*a.* **1** designed to provide luxury, extremely comfortable. **2** non-essential, constituting an expensive indulgence. **3** providing a high level of comfort, service etc. **luxuriant** (lŭgzū´riənt) *a.* **1** (of vegetation) abundant in growth, lush, rank. **2** fertile, prolific, profuse, exuberant. **3** (of style) ornate, florid, extravagant, sumptuous. **luxuriance, luxuriancy** *n.* **luxuriantly** *adv.* **luxuriate** *v.i.* **1** to revel, to indulge oneself voluptuously. **2** to grow abundantly or profusely. **3** to live luxuriously. **luxuriation** (-ā´shən) *n.* **luxurious** *a.* **1** characterized by luxury, provided with an ample supply of comforts and pleasures. **2** extremely comfortable. **3** self-indulgent. **4** †lecherous. **luxuriously** *adv.* **luxuriousness** *n.* [L *luxurians -iantem*, pres.p. of *luxuriāre*, from *luxuria*, *luxus*, extravagance, sumptuousness]

LV *abbr.* luncheon voucher.

LW *abbr.* **1** long wave. **2** low water.

Lw *chem. symbol* (*Hist.*) lawrencium (now *Lr*).

LWM *abbr.* low water mark.

lx *abbr.* lux.

LXX *abbr.* Septuagint. [Roman numeral for seventy]

-ly[1] (li) *suf.* forming adjectives, esp. meaning having the qualities of, e.g. *godly*, *manly* or at intervals of, e.g. *hourly*, *weekly*. [OE *līc*, LIKE[1]]

-ly[2] (li) *suf.* forming adverbs from adjectives, e.g. *badly*, *heavily*, *mightily*. [OE, *-līce*, cp. -LY[1]]

lycanthropy (līkan´thrəpi) *n.* **1** insanity in which patients believe themselves to be a wolf or some other animal, whose instincts and habits they assume. **2** a form of witchcraft by which men or women transform themselves into wolves. **lycanthrope** (lī´kənthrōp) *n.* **1** a werewolf. **2** a person suffering from lycanthropy. **lycanthropic** (-throp´-) *a.* **lycanthropist** *n.* [Gr. *lukanthrōpos* (*lukos*, wolf, *anthrōpos*, man)]

lycée (lē´sā) *n.* a French state secondary school. [F]

lyceum (līsē´əm) *n.* **1** (**Lyceum**) the garden at Athens in which Aristotle taught. **2** (**Lyceum**) the Aristotelian philosophy or philosophic school. **3** (*N Am.*) an institution for literary instruction or mutual improvement by means of lectures, libraries etc. **4** a place or building devoted to literary studies, lectures etc. [L *lycēum*, Gr. *Lukeion*, nom. *-os*, pertaining to Apollo, whose temple was adjoining]

lychee (lī´chē, lich´-), **lichee, litchi** *n.* **1** the fruit of the Chinese tree, *Nephelium litchi*, which has a hard, scaly skin and a soft white pulp. **2** this tree. [Chin. *li-chi*]

lych-gate LICH-GATE.

lychnis (lik´nis) *n.* any of a genus of plants, *Lychnis*, belonging to the family Silenaceae, comprising the campions. [L, from Gr. *luchnis*, from *luchnos*, lamp]

lycopod (lī´kəpod) *n.* a clubmoss, a member of the genus *Lycopodium*, or the order Lycopodiaceae. **lycopodiaceous** (-pōdiā´shəs) *a.* **lycopodium** (-pō´diəm) *n.* **1** a clubmoss of the genus *Lycopodium*. **2** an inflammable yellow powder in the spore-cases of some species, used for making fireworks and as an absorbent in surgery. [mod. L *lycopodium* (Gr. *lukos*, wolf, *pous podos*, foot, from the clawlike shape of the root)]

Lycra® (lī´krə) *n.* a synthetic elastic fibre and material used in swimwear and other tight-fitting garments.

lyddite (lid´īt) *n.* a powerful explosive composed mainly of picric acid, used in shells. [*Lydd*, in Kent]

Lydian (lid´iən) *a.* **1** of or relating to Lydia, in Asia

Minor, whose inhabitants were noted for effeminacy and voluptuousness. **2** (*Mus.*) applied to one of the modes in Greek music, and to the third ecclesiastical mode, corresponding to the natural diatonic scale F to F. ~*n.* a native, inhabitant or the language of Lydia.

lye (lī) *n.* **1** an alkaline solution leached from wood ashes or other alkaline substance. **2** any strong alkaline solution used for washing or cleansing, esp. potassium hydroxide. [OE *lēag* (cp. Dut. *loog*, G *Lauge*), prob. cogn. with LAVE and LATHER]

lying[1] LIE[1].

lying[2] LIE[2].

lykewake (līk´wāk) *n.* a night watch over a dead body. [ME, perh. from Icel., cp. LICH-GATE, WAKE[1]]

Lyme disease (līm) *n.* a form of arthritis caused by spirochaetes of the genus *Borrelia* and transmitted by ticks. [town in Connecticut, USA, where an outbreak affecting humans occurred]

lyme grass (līm) *n.* a coarse grass of the genus *Elymus*, planted in sand in order to bind it. [etym. uncertain, perh. from LIME[1]]

lymph (limf) *n.* **1** the comparatively transparent, colourless, alkaline fluid in the tissues and organs of the body, consisting mainly of white blood corpuscles. **2** lymphatic fluid containing the virus of a disease, obtained from a diseased body or by culture, and used in vaccination. **3** exudation from a sore etc. **4** (*poet.*) water or any clear transparent fluid. **lymphatic** (-fat´-) *a.* **1** of or relating to, containing, secreting or conveying lymph. **2** pale, flabby. **3** (of temperament) sluggish, lacking vigour. ~*n.* a vessel that conveys lymph. **lymphatic system** *n.* the network of capillary vessels that conveys lymph to the venous system. **lymph gland, lymph node** *n.* any of the small localized masses of tissue distributed along the lymphatic vessels that produce lymphocytes. **lymphocyte** (-fəsīt) *n.* a type of white blood cell formed in the lymph nodes, which forms part of the body's immunological defence against infection. **lymphoid** (-foid) *a.* containing or resembling lymph. **lymphoma** (-fō´mə) *n.* (*pl.* **lymphomas, lymphomata** (-mətə)) a tumour of lymphoid tissue. **lymphomatoid** (-toid) *a.* **lymphomatous** *a.* [L *lympha*, prob. cogn. with *limpidus*, LIMPID]

lyncean LYNX.

lynch (linch) *v.t.* (of a mob) to execute, esp. by hanging, without a trial or after mock trial. **lynch law** *n.* summary punishment without trial or upon trial by a self-appointed court. [Charles *Lynch*, 1742–1820, a Virginian farmer who inflicted summary punishment on lawless persons during the American War of Independence]

lynchet (-it) *n.* a ridge formed by ploughing or a cultivation terrace on the side of a steep hill. [OE *hlinc*, cp. LINKS]

lynchpin LINCHPIN.

lynx (lingks) *n.* (*pl.* **lynx, lynxes**) **1** a feline mammal of Europe and North America, *Felis lynx*, characterized by tufted ear-tips, short tail and extremely sharp sight. **2** its fur. **lyncean** (linsē´ən) *a.* **1** of or relating to the lynx. **2** lynx-eyed, sharp-sighted. **lynx-eyed** *n.* having sharp sight. [L, from Gr. *lunx*, rel. to *lussein*, to see (cp. with G *Luchs*, OE *lox*)]

Lyon (lī´ən), **Lyon King of Arms** *n.* the chief of the Scottish heralds. **Lyon Court** *n.* the court over which the Scottish chief herald presides. [LION]

lyophilic (līəfil´ik) *a.* (of a colloid) easily dispersed in a solvent. **lyophilize** (-of´-), **lyophilise** *v.t.* to freeze-dry. **lyophilization** (-zā´shən) *n.* **lyophobic** (-fō´-) *a.* (of a colloid) not easily dispersed in a solvent. [Gr. *lȳē*, separation, *phileein*, to love, *phobeein*, to fear]

lyre (līə) *n.* **1** an ancient Greek stringed instrument like a small harp, consisting of a resonating box with a pair of curved arms above it connected by a crossbar. **2** a medieval instrument of the violin family. **lyrate** (-rət), **lyrated** (-rātid) *a.* shaped like a lyre. **lyre-bird** *n.* an insectivorous Australian bird, *Menura superba*, having the 16 tail feathers of the male disposed in the form of a lyre. **lyre-flower** *n.* the bleeding heart. **lyrist**[1] (līə´rist) *n.* a person who plays the lyre. [F, from L *lyra*, Gr. *lura*]

lyric (lir´ik) *a.* **1** (of a poem) expressing the individual emotions of the poet. **2** (of a poet) writing poetry of this kind. **3** intended to be sung or fitted for expression in song. **4** relating to or suited for the lyre. **5** (of singing) having a light quality and tone. ~*n.* **1** a lyric poem. **2** (*often pl.*) the words of a popular song. **3** a song. **4** (*pl.*) verses used in lyric poetry. **lyrical** *a.* **1** lyric. **2** using language suitable for lyric poetry. **3** extremely enthusiastic and effusive (*wax lyrical*). **lyrically** *adv.* **lyricism** (-sizm) *n.* **1** a lyrical quality or style. **2** a lyrical expression. **3** emotional or enthusiastic effusions. **lyricist** *n.* a writer of song lyrics. **lyrist**[2] (lir´ist) *n.* a lyricist. [LYRE, -IC]

lyrist[1] LYRE.

lyrist[2] LYRIC.

lysergic acid (līsœ´jik) *n.* a crystalline compound derived from ergot. **lysergic acid diethylamide** (dīəthī´ləmīd, dīēthīlam´īd) *n.* a powerful hallucinogenic drug better known as *LSD*.

lysis (lī´sis) *n.* (*pl.* **lyses** (lī´sēz)) **1** the destruction of cells by the action of a lysin. **2** the gradual decline in the symptoms of a disease, as opposed to *crisis*. **lyse** (līz) *v.t., v.i.* (to cause) to undergo lysis. **lysimeter** (-sim´itə) *n.* an instrument for measuring the rate of percolation of rain through soil. **lysin** (-sin) *n.* a substance, esp. an antibody, which causes the disintegration of cells. **lysine** (-sīn, -sēn) *n.* an amino acid obtained from dietary sources which is essential to nutrition in humans. **-lysis** (lisis) *comb. form* denoting a breaking down, loosening or disintegration. **Lysol** (-sol) *n.* a mildly astringent solution of cresol and soap, used as a disinfectant. **lysosome** (-səsōm) *n.* any of numerous small particles, present in the cytoplasm of most cells, that contain degradative enzymes. **lysozyme** (-səzīm) *n.* an enzyme found in tears and egg white that destroys certain bacteria by hydrolysing polysaccharides in their cell walls. **-lyte** (līt) *comb. form* denoting a substance capable of being broken down. **lytic** (lit´ik) *a.* of, relating to or causing lysis. **-lytic** (lit´ik), **-lytical** *comb. form* of or producing decomposition. **-lyze** (līz), **-lyse** *comb. form* to cause or undergo loosening or decomposition through lysis. [L, from Gr. *lusos*, loosening]

M[1] (em), **m** (*pl.* **Ms, M's**) the 13th letter of the English and other versions of the Roman alphabet. It is pronounced as a bilabial nasal continuant. ~*symbol* 100 in Roman numerals. **M roof** *n.* a roof formed by the junction of two parallel ridges with a cross section like a broad M.

M[2] *abbr.* **1** Majesty. **2** Malta (IVR). **3** mark (German currency). **4** Master. **5** mega. **6** (*Chem.*) molar. **7** Monsieur. **8** Motorway (*M4*).

m *abbr.* **1** maiden over. **2** male. **3** mare. **4** married. **5** masculine. **6** mass. **7** meridian. **8** metre(s). **9** mile(s). **10** milli-. **11** minute(s). **12** month(s). **13** moon.

m' (m) *a.* my (*m'lud*).

'm (m) *contr.* (*coll.*) **1** am (*I'm*). **2** madam (*Yes'm*).

MA *abbr.* **1** Massachusetts. **2** Master of Arts. **3** Morocco (IVR).

ma (mah) *n.* (*coll.*) mother. [shortening of MAMMA[1]]

ma'am (mam, mahm, məm) *n.* madam (used esp. in addressing a queen or a royal princess). [MADAM]

maar (mah) *n.* a volcanic crater without a cone of lava, caused by a single explosion. [G]

Mac (mak) *n.* (*coll.*) **1** a Scotsman. **2** (*N Am.*) used in addressing a stranger (*You got a light, Mac?*).

mac (mak), **mack** *n.* a mackintosh, a raincoat.

macabre (məkah´brə) *a.* gruesome. **macaberesque** (-bərəsk´) *a.* **macabrely** *adv.* [F]

macaco[1] (məkā´kō) *n.* (*pl.* **macacos**) any of various kinds of lemur, esp. *Lemur macaco*. [F]

macaco[2] (məkā´kō) *n.* (*pl.* **macacos**) MACAQUE.

macadam (məkad´əm) *n.* **1** broken stone for road-making. **2** †a road made by tarmacking. ~†*v.t.* to tarmac. **tar macadam** TAR[1]. **macadamize, macadamise** *v.t.* to make, cover or pave (a road) with layers of broken stone so as to form a smooth hard surface, to tarmac. **macadamization** (-zā´shən) *n.* **macadamizer** *n.* [J. L. *McAdam*, 1756–1836, road engineer]

macadamia (makədā´miə) *n.* any evergreen tree of the genus *Macadamia* of Australia, esp. *M. integrifolia* and *M. tetraphylla*. **macadamia nut** *n.* the edible nutlike seed of macadamia. [J. *Macadam*, d. 1865, Austral. chemist]

macaque (məkahk´) *n.* any monkey of the genus *Macaca*, including the rhesus monkey and the Barbary ape. [Port., monkey]

macaroni (makərō´ni) *n.* (*pl.* **macaronies, macaronis**) **1** an Italian pasta made of fine wheat flour formed into long slender tubes. **2** (*Hist.*) a fop, a dandy. **3** a crested variety of penguin. **4** (*pl.*) a medley. ~†*a.* foppish, fashionable, affected. **macaroni cheese** *n.* a dish of macaroni in a cheese sauce. [It. *maccaroni* (now *maccheroni*, pl.), prob. from Gr. *malcaria*, food from barley]

macaronic (makəron´ik) *a.* consisting of a jumble of incongruous words, as of different languages, or of modern words Latinized or Latin words modernized, in burlesque poetry. ~*n.* **1** a confused medley or jumble. **2** (*pl.*) macaronic verse. [MACARONI]

macaroon (makəroon´) *n.* a small sweet cake or biscuit made of flour, almonds, sugar etc. [F *macaron*, It. *maccarone*, sing. of *maccaroni*, as MACARONI]

Macassar (məkas´ə), **Macassar oil** *n.* an oil formerly used on the hair to make it shiny, orig. brought from Macassar in Indonesia.

macaw (məkaw´) *n.* any S and Central American parrot, of the genus *Ara* or *Anodorhynchus*, distinguished by their large size and bright, beautiful plumage. [Port. *macao*, prob. from Tupi-Guarani]

macaw tree (məkaw) *n.* a palm of the genus *Acrocomia*, esp. *A. aculeata*. [prob. Carib, TREE]

Macc. *abbr.* Maccabees (Apocrypha).

Maccabees (mak´əbēz) *a.* **1** four books of Jewish history and theology, two of which are in the Apocrypha. **2** a patriotic Jewish family led by Judas Maccabeus, who successfully resisted the attempts of Antiochus Epiphanes (175–164 BC) to substitute Hellenism for Judaism in Judaea. **Maccabean** (-ē´ən) *a.*

maccoboy (mak´əboi) *n.* a rose-scented snuff, orig. grown at Macouba, in Martinique.

Mace® (mās) *n.* a liquid causing the eyes to run and a feeling of nausea, used in self-defence, riot control etc. ~*v.t.* (*also* **mace**) to spray Mace at.

mace[1] (mās) *n.* **1** an ornamented staff of office. **2** a medieval weapon shaped like a club with a heavy metal head, usu. spiked. **3** a mace-bearer. **4** a flat-headed stick formerly used in billiards. **5** a similar stick used in bagatelle. **mace-bearer** *n.* a person who carries the mace before a judge etc. **macer** *n.* **1** a mace-bearer. **2** (*Sc.*) an officer who keeps order in courts of law. [OF (F *masse*), from L *matea*, known from its dim. *mateola*, a mallet]

mace[2] (mās) *n.* a spice made from the dried covering of the nutmeg. [F *macis*]

macédoine (masədwan´) *n.* **1** a dish of mixed vegetables. **2** a medley. [F, Macedonian, from the mixture of nationalities in Macedonia]

macerate (mas´ərāt) *v.t.* **1** to soften by steeping. **2** to separate the parts of (food) by a digestive process. **3** to make lean, to cause to waste away. ~*v.i.* to undergo maceration. **maceration** (-ā´shən) *n.* **macerator** *n.* [L *mācerātus*, p.p. of *mācerāre* perh. cogn. with Gr. *massein*, to knead]

Mach (mak, mahkh, mahk), **Mach number** *n.* a number representing the ratio of the velocity of a body in a certain medium to the velocity of sound in the same medium, used as an indicator of air speed (*Mach 1, 2* etc.). **Machmeter** *n.* an instrument showing air speed as a Mach number. [Ernst *Mach*, 1838–1916, Austrian physicist]

machair (makh´ə) *n.* a strip of land just above the high-water mark along a sandy shore, used for pasturage. [Gael.]

machan (məchahn´) *n.* an elevated platform for hunting or watching game. [Hind.]

machete (məshet´i, -shā´ti), **matchet** (mach´it) *n.* a broad knife or cutlass used in tropical America as a weapon, to cut down sugar canes etc. [Sp.]

machiavellian (makiəvel´iən) *a.* unscrupulous, scheming, cunning. ~*n.* **1** an unscrupulous intriguer. **2** an intriguing and unscrupulous statesman or politician. **machiavel** (mak´-) *n.* **Machiavellianism, Machiavellism** *n.* [Niccolo *Machiavelli*, 1469–1527, Florentine statesman and author of *Il Principe*, an exposition of unscrupulous statecraft]

machicolation (məchikəlā´shən) *n.* an opening (on a parapet etc.) between corbels for dropping stones etc. on attackers below. **machicolate** (-āt) *v.t.* **machic-**

olated *a.* [OF *machicoler* from Provençal *machacol* from *macar*, crush, *col*, neck]
machinable MACHINE.
machinate (mək´ināt, mash´-) *v.i.* to contrive, to plot, to intrigue. **machination** (-ā´shən) *n.* **machinator** *n.* [L *māchinātus*, p.p. of *māchinārī*, to contrive, see MACHINE]
machine (məshēn´) *n.* **1** a mechanical apparatus by which motive power is applied. **2** any mechanism, simple (as a lever or tool) or compound, for applying or directing force. **3** any organization of a complex character designed to apply power of any kind. **4** any vehicle, esp. a bicycle or motorcycle, or aircraft. **5** a person who acts mechanically and without intelligence. **6** any intricate structure or system of control (*the party machine*). **7** in classical Greek theatre, a contrivance for effecting change of scenery or introducing a supernatural being. **8** supernatural agency in a poem etc. *~v.t.* **1** to produce by means of machinery. **2** to sew with a sewing machine. **3** to print by machinery. *~v.i.* to be employed in or upon machinery. **machinable** *a.* **machinability** (-bil´-) *n.* **machine code, machine language** *n.* a set of instructions for coding information in a form usable by a computer. **machine-gun** *n.* a light gun loaded and fired automatically. *~v.t.* (*pres.p.* **machine-gunning**, *past, p.p.* **machine-gunned**) to fire a machine-gun at. **machine-gunner** *n.* **machine head** *n.* (*Mus.*) a simple worm and toothed wheel mechanism fitted to the head of a guitar or other stringed instrument for stretching the strings to the required pitch. **machine-made** *a.* made by machinery, as distinct from *hand made*. **machine-minder** *n.* a person whose job is to look after a machine, usu. in a factory. **machine-readable** *a.* (of data) in a form usable by a computer. **machinery** (-nəri) *n.* (*pl.* **machineries**) **1** machines collectively. **2** the parts or mechanism of a machine. **3** any combination to keep anything in action or to effect a purpose. **4** the means and combinations, esp. supernatural, employed to develop a plot in a play etc. **machine shop** *n.* a large workshop where machines are made or repaired. **machine tool** *n.* a power-driven machine such as a lathe, router etc. for working on wood, metal etc. **machine translation** *n.* translation done by a computer. **machine-washable** *a.* able to be washed in a washing machine without damage. **machinist** *n.* **1** a person who works or tends a machine, esp. a sewing machine. **2** a person who constructs machines. **3** an expert in the principles of machinery. [F, from L *māchina*, Gr. *mēchanē*, from *mēchos*, means, contrivance, cogn. with MAY[1]]
machismo MACHO.
macho (mach´ō) *a.* masculine, virile, esp. in an ostentatious or exaggerated way. *~n.* (*pl.* **machos**) **1** a macho man. **2** machismo. **machismo** (məkiz´mo, -chiz´-) *n.* aggressive arrogant assertiveness, often associated with masculinity. [Mex. Sp., male]
Machtpolitik (makht´politēk) *n.* power politics, esp. the advocacy of force by a state to attain its ends. [G]
macintosh MACKINTOSH.
mack MAC.
mackerel (mak´ərəl) *n.* (*pl. in general* **mackerel,** *in particular* **mackerels**) a marine fish, *Scomber scombrus*, moving in shoals in the N Atlantic and coming inshore in summer to spawn, valuable as a food. **mackerel breeze** *n.* a strong fresh breeze good for mackerel fishing. **mackerel shark** *n.* the porbeagle. **mackerel sky** *n.* a sky with small roundish masses of cirrocumulus, frequent in summer. [OF *makerel* (F *maquereau*)]
mackinaw (mak´inaw) *n.* (*NAm.*) a short heavy woollen jacket, usu. of plaid. [Michilli-*mackinac*, island in Lake Michigan]
mackintosh (mak´intosh), **macintosh** *n.* **1** a raincoat. **2** a waterproof material made of rubber and cloth. [Charles *Mackintosh*, 1766–1843, inventor]
mackle (mak´əl) *n.* in printing, a blurred impression, causing printed matter to appear double. *~v.t.* to spot, stain, blur. [see MACULE (under MACULA)]
macle (mak´əl) *n.* **1** a twin crystal. **2** a dark inclusion in a mineral. **macled** *a.* [F, from MACULA]
macr- MACRO-.
macramé (məkrah´mā) *n.* **1** a fringe or trimming of knotted thread or cord. **2** knotted work. **3** the art of making knotted work. [Turk. *marqrama*]
macro (mak´rō) *n.* (*pl.* **macros**) a single computer instruction that represents a sequence of instructions in performing a task. **macro instruction** *n.* a macro.
macro- (mak´rō), **macr-** *comb. form* great, large (as distinct from small). [Gr. *makros*, long]
macrobiotic (makrōbīot´ik) *a.* **1** (of a diet) consisting chiefly of whole grains or of vegetables grown without chemical additives. **2** of or relating to such a diet. **macrobiote** (-ī´ōt) *n.* an organism that lives for a long time. **macrobiotics** *n.* the principles of such a macrobiotic diet.
macrocarpa (makrōkah´pə) *n.* a large coniferous tree, *Cupressus macrocarpa*, often cultivated for hedges, shelter belts etc.
macrocephalic (makrōsifal´ik, -kef´), **macrocephalous** (-sef´-, -kef´-) *a.* large-headed. **macrocephaly** (-sef´-, -kef´-) *n.*
macrocosm (mak´rəkozm) *n.* **1** the world, the universe, as distinct from *microcosm*. **2** the whole of any body etc., esp. as imagined on a small scale by a part. **macrocosmic** (-koz´-) *a.* **macrocosmically** *adv.*
macrocyte (mak´rəsīt) *n.* an abnormally large red blood cell.
macrodactylic (makrōdaktil´ik), **macrodactylous** (-dak´tiləs) *a.* having long fingers or toes.
macrodiagonal (makrōdīag´ənəl) *n.* the longer diagonal of a rhombic prism.
macroeconomics (makrōēkənom´iks, -ek-) *n.* the study of economics on a large scale, e.g. of national economies. **macroeconomic** *a.*
macroevolution (makrōēvəloo´shən, -ev-) *n.* (*Biol.*) major evolutionary development, usu. over a long period of time.
macrolepidoptera (makrōlepidop´tərə) *n.* butterflies and larger moths.
macromolecule (mak´rōmolikūl) *n.* a large complex molecule formed from a number of simple molecules. **macromolecular** (-lek´-) *a.*
macron (mak´ron) *n.* a short horizontal line put over a vowel (as ē) to show that it is pronounced with a long sound or with stress. [Gr. neut. a. of *makros*, long]
macronutrient (makrōnū´triənt) *n.* any substance that is required in large amounts for the growth and development of organisms, such as carbon, hydrogen, oxygen.
macrophage (mak´rəfāj) *n.* a large phagocytic white blood cell found in connective tissue. [Gr. *phagein*, to eat]
macrophotography (makrōfōtog´rəfi) *n.* close-up photography producing an image as large as or larger than the object.
macropod (mak´rəpod) *n.* any marsupial mammal of the family Macropodidae of Australia and New Guinea, including kangaroos and related animals. [Gr. *pous podos*, foot]
macropterous (makrop´tərəs) *a.* long-winged. [Gr. *pteron*, a wing]
macroscopic (makrəskop´ik) *a.* large enough to be visible with the naked eye, as distinct from *microscopic*. **macroscopical** *a.* **macroscopically** *adv.*
macrosporangium (makrōspəran´jiəm) *n.* a sporangium or capsule containing megaspores.

macrospore (mak´rəspaw) *n.* MEGASPORE.

macrurus (məkroor´əs) *a.* **1** long-tailed. **2** of or belonging to the *Macrura*, a division of decapod crustaceans comprising the lobsters and shrimps. **macruran** (-ən) *n.* [Gr. *oura*, tail]

macula (mak´ūlə) *n.* (*pl.* **maculae** (-lē)) a spot, as on the skin, the surface of the sun etc. **macula lutea** (loo´tiə) *n.* a small yellowish spot near the centre of the retina of the eye, where vision is especially acute. **macular** *a.* **maculate**[1] (-lāt) *v.t.* to spot, to stain. **maculate**[2] (-lət) *a.* spotted, impure. **maculation** (-lā´shən) *n.* **macule** (mak´ūl) *n.* **1** a spot, a stain. **2** a mackle. [L]

MAD *abbr.* mutual assured destruction, a theory of nuclear deterrence based on the ability of each side to inflict an unacceptable level of damage on the other.

mad (mad) *a.* (*comp.* **madder,** *superl.* **maddest**) **1** disordered in mind, lunatic, insane, crazy. **2** furious, frantic, wildly excited. **3** (of an animal) rabid. **4** extravagant, infatuated, inflamed, wild, frolicsome. **5** exceedingly foolish, very unwise. **6** (*coll.*) enraged, annoyed, vexed. ~†*v.i.* (*pres.p.* **madding,** *past, p.p.* **madded**) **1** to be or go mad. **2** to act madly. ~†*v.t.* to make mad. **like mad** (*coll.*) violently, wildly, excitedly. **madbrain, madbrained** *a.* hot-headed, eccentric. **madcap** *a.* mad, eccentric. ~*n.* a person of wild and eccentric habits. **mad cow disease** *n.* (*coll.*) bovine spongiform encephalopathy, BSE. **madden** *v.t., v.i.* **maddening** *a.* **maddeningly** *adv.* †**madding** *a.* furious, raging, acting madly. †**mad-doctor** *n.* (*coll.*) a doctor attending the mentally ill. **madhouse** *n.* **1** a scene of confusion or uproar. **2** (*Hist.*) a mental hospital. **mad keen** *a.* (*coll.*) very enthusiastic, eager. **madly** *adv.* **1** in an insane manner. **2** (*coll.*) extremely (*madly in love*). **madman** *n.* (*pl.* **madmen**). **madness** *n.* **madwoman** *n.* (*pl.* **madwomen**). **madwort** *n.* **1** the catchweed, *Asperugo procumbens.* **2** alyssum. [OE *gemædd, gemæded*, p.p. of *gemædan* (cp. Icel. *meiddr*, OHG *gameit*, cogn. with L *mūtāre*, to change)]

madam (mad´əm) *n.* **1** a polite form of address to a woman. **2** (*coll.*) a female brothel-keeper. **3** (*coll.*) an impertinent girl (*You little madam!*). [OF *ma dame*, my lady (see DAME)]

Madame (mədahm´) *n.* (*pl.* **Mesdames** (mādahmz´)) **1** the French title for married women and polite form of address to a woman. **2** †the title of a French princess, esp. the eldest daughter of the king or the dauphin. [MADAM]

madarosis (madərō´sis) *n.* (*Med.*) loss of the hair, esp. of the eyebrows. [Gr. (*madaros*, bald, -OSIS)]

madden MAD.

madder[1] MAD.

madder[2] (mad´ə) *n.* **1** a shrubby climbing-plant, *Rubia tinctorum*, the root of which is used in dyeing. **2** the dye obtained from this plant. **madder-print** *n.* cloth or cotton treated by madder-printing. [OE *maedere* (cp. Icel. *mathra*, Swed. *madra*)]

made (mād) *a.* that has been made. **made for** perfectly suited to. **made dish** *n.* a dish made up of various ingredients. **made ground, made earth** *n.* ground that has been formed artificially. **made man, made woman** *n.* (*pl.* **made men, made women**) a person whose success is assured. **made of money** *a.* (*coll.*) very wealthy. **made road** *n.* a road surfaced with tarmac, concrete etc. **made-to-measure** *a.* made according to the customer's measurements. **made-to-order** *a.* **1** manufactured according to a customer's individual requirements. **2** just as wanted. **made-up** *a.* **1** (of complexion etc.) artificial; wearing make-up. **2** (of a story etc.) invented, coined. **3** ready prepared. **4** surfaced with tarmac, concrete etc. [MAKE[1]]

Madeira (mədiə´rə) *n.* a fortified white wine made in Madeira. **madeira cake** *n.* a light, spongy cake without fruit. **Madeiran** *a., n.* [Port., wood, timber (the island being well wooded), L *matēria*, MATTER]

madeleine (mad´əlin) *n.* a small sponge cake, often coated with jam and coconut. [F]

Mademoiselle (madəmwəzel´) *n.* (*pl.* **Mesdemoiselles** (mādəmwəzel´)) **1** the French title for unmarried women or girls and polite form of address to an unmarried woman or a girl. **2** (**mademoiselle**) a young Frenchwoman. **3** (**mademoiselle**) a French governess or teacher.

maderize (mad´ərīz), **maderise** *v.i.* (of white wine) to go reddish and flat-tasting through oxidation. [*Madeira*, which has a reddish colour]

madge (maj) *n.* **1** the barn owl. **2** the magpie. [fam. form of *Margaret*]

Madonna (mədon´ə) *n.* **1** the Virgin Mary. **2** (*usu.* **madonna**) a picture or statue of the Virgin Mary. **madonna lily** *n.* the white lily, *Lilium candidum.* [It. (*ma, mia*, MY, *donna*, L *domina*, lady)]

madras (mədras´) *n.* **1** a fine cotton or silk fabric. **2** a large bright-coloured handkerchief worn on the head by Afro-Caribbeans. **3** (**Madras**) a style of curry, medium hot and usu. with chicken or meat. [city in India]

madrepore (mad´ripaw) *n.* **1** a perforated coral of the genus *Madrepora.* **2** the animal producing this. **madreporic** (-por´-), **madreporiform** (-por´-) *a.* **madreporite** *n.* **1** a fossil madrepore. **2** a calcareous rock of columnar structure. **3** the madreporic tubercle in echinoderms. [F *madrépore*, It. *madrepora* (*madre*, matter, *poro*, L *porus*, PORE[1], or late L *pōrus*, Gr. *pōros*, calcareous stone)]

madrigal (mad´rigəl) *n.* **1** an unaccompanied vocal composition in five or six parts. **2** a part-song, a glee. **3** a short amorous poem. **madrigalian** (-āl´iən) *a.* **madrigalist** *n.* [It. *madrigale*, perh. from *mandria*, herd, flock, fold, L and Gr. *mandra*, fold etc.]

madroño (mədrō´nyō), **madroña** (-nyə) *n.* (*pl.* **madroños, madroñas**) a large evergreen tree, *Arbutus menziesii*, of N California, with hard wood, and edible berries. [Sp.]

maduro (mədoo´rō) *n.* (*pl.* **maduros**) a type of dark, strong cigar. [Sp. *maduro*, ripe; cf. MATURE]

Maecenas (mēsē´nəs, mī-) *n.* a munificent patron of literature or art. [a Roman knight, *c.* 70–8 BC, patron of Horace and Virgil]

maelstrom (māl´strəm, -om) *n.* **1** a dangerous whirlpool, dangerously swirling water. **2** a turmoil, an overwhelming situation. [Dut. (now *maalstroom* (*malen*, to grind, to whirl, *stroom*, stream))]

maenad (mē´nəd) *n.* **1** a woman who took part in the orgies of Bacchus, a bacchante. **2** a frenzied woman. **maenadic** (-nad´-) *a.* [L *Maenas -adis*, Gr. *Mainas -ados*, from *mainesthai*, to rave]

maestoso (mīstō´sō) *a., adv.* (*Mus.*) with dignity, grandeur and strength. ~*n.* (*pl.* **maestosos**) a piece of music to be played this way. [It., majestic]

maestro (mīs´trō) *n.* (*pl.* **maestros, maestri** (-ē)) **1** a master in any art, esp. in music. **2** a great composer or conductor. [It.]

Mae West (mā west´) *n.* an inflatable life jacket. [named thus because, when inflated, it resembles the bosom of the US actress Mae West, 1892–1980]

MAFF (maf) *abbr.* Ministry of Agriculture, Fisheries and Food.

Mafia (maf´iə) *n.* **1** a secret criminal society based on active hostility to the law and its agents, engaged in international organized crime, esp. in Sicily and the US. **2** any group of people considered to be using power for their own ends. **Mafioso** (-ō´so, -zō) *n.* (*pl.* **Mafiosi** (-sē, -zē)) **1** a member of the Mafia. **2** a member of a group who in some way resemble the Mafia. [Sicilian It.]

mag[1] (mag) *n.* (*coll.*) **1** short for MAGAZINE. **2** short for

MAGNESIUM. **3** short for MAGNETO. **4** short for MAGNITUDE.

mag² (mag) *n.* **1** the magpie. **2** the long-tailed titmouse. **3** †a chatterbox. ~*v.i.* (*pres.p.* **magging,** *past, p.p.* **magged**) to chatter. [short for *Margaret*]

magalog (mag´əlog) *n.* a mail-order catalogue designed to look like a magazine. [*maga*zine, cata*log*ue]

magazine (magəzēn´, mag´-) *n.* **1** a periodical publication or broadcast containing miscellaneous articles by different people. **2** a storeroom for explosives etc. aboard ship. **3** the chamber holding cartridges in certain types of automatic gun. **4** a building or apartment for military stores, esp. ammunition. **5** a light-tight receptacle or enclosure for holding exposed or unexposed films or plates. **6** a place for storage, a depot, a warehouse. [F *magasin*, It. *magazzino*, Arab. *makhāzīn*, pl. of *makhzan*, storehouse, from *khazn*, a laying up]

magdalen (mag´dəlin) *n.* **1** a reformed prostitute. **2** a home for such women. [Mary *Magdalene*, or of *Magdala* (Luke viii.2), identified with the woman mentioned in Luke vii.37–50]

Magdalenian (magdəlē´niən) *a.* of or relating to the period of Upper Palaeolithic culture, succeeding the Solutrian period, typified by the implements and weapons of bone, horn, ivory and stone, and carvings and engravings found at La Madeleine. ~*n.* the Magdalenian culture. [rock-shelter of *La Madeleine*, Dordogne, France]

†mage (māj) *n.* a magician. [L MAGUS]

Magellanic cloud (majilan´ik) *n.* either of two galaxies in the southern hemisphere, similar to portions of the Milky Way. [F. *Magellan*, d. 1521, Portuguese explorer]

magenta (məjen´tə) *n.* **1** a brilliant crimson colour. **2** an aniline dye of this colour. [*Magenta*, a city in Italy near which the Austrians were defeated in a bloody battle by the French and Sardinians in 1859]

maggot (mag´ət) *n.* **1** a grub, a worm, esp. the larva of the cheese-fly or flesh-fly. **2** a whimsical fancy. **3** †a whimsical person. **maggoty** *a.* [perh. corr. of ME *maddock*, *mathek* (cp. Icel. *mathkr*, OE *mathu*)]

magi, magian MAGUS.

magic (maj´ik) *n.* **1** the supposed art of employing supernatural power to influence or control events. **2** sorcery, witchcraft. **3** any agency, power or action that has astonishing results. ~*a.* **1** of or relating to or used in magic. **2** using magic. **3** exercising supernatural powers. **4** produced by magic. **5** (*coll.*) excellent, wonderful. ~*v.t.* (*pres.p.* **magicking,** *past, p.p.* **magicked**) to affect or move (away) by magic. **black magic** BLACK. **white magic** WHITE. **magical** *a.* **magically** *adv.* **magic bullet** *n.* (*coll.*) a drug etc. that is very specific in its effect on a tumour, disease etc. **magic carpet** *n.* a carpet in fairy stories capable of transporting people through the air. **magic circle** *n.* **1** a circle possessing properties analogous to those of the magic square. **2** (**Magic Circle**) an organization of magicians. **magic eye** *n.* **1** a photoelectric cell operating a door, security camera etc. **2** a small cathode ray tube that indicates when a radio etc. is correctly tuned. **magician** (-jish´ən) *n.* **1** a person supposedly employing magic. **2** a conjuror. **3** a person who produces astonishing results. **magic lantern** *n.* an apparatus with a lens through which a magnified image from a glass slide is projected on a screen by a powerful light. **Magic Marker®** *n.* a type of fibre-tipped pen. **magic mushroom** *n.* a type of fungus containing a hallucinogenic substance. **magic square** *n.* a series of numbers so disposed in a square that the totals, taken perpendicularly, horizontally or diagonally, are equal. [F *magique*, L *magicus*, Gr. *magikos*, from *magos*, MAGUS]

magilp MEGILP.

Maginot Line (mazh´inō) *n.* **1** a line of defensive fortifications in NE France built in 1929 against a German invasion. **2** any line of defence in which unrealistic confidence is placed. [after A. *Maginot*, 1877–1932, French Minister of War]

magisterial (majistē´riəl) *a.* **1** authoritative, commanding. **2** of or relating to a magistrate or master. **3** dictatorial, domineering. **magisterially** *adv.* **magisterium** *n.* the teaching authority of the Roman Catholic Church. **†magistery** *n.* **1** in alchemy, a master-principle of nature, esp. the principle of transmuting substances or a substance, such as the philosopher's stone, possessing this. **2** mastership, authority. **magistral** (maj´istrəl, məjis´trəl) *a.* **1** of or like a master, magisterial. **2** (of a medicine) specially prescribed or devised, not in the ordinary pharmacopoeia. **3** †acting as a sovereign remedy. ~†*n.* **1** a magistral preparation. **2** a sovereign remedy. [med. L *magisteriālis*, L *magisterius*, from *magister*, MASTER]

magistrate (maj´istrāt, -strət) *n.* a public officer commissioned to administer the law, a Justice of the Peace. **magistracy, magistrateship, magistrature** *n.* **magistrates' court** *n.* a court of summary jurisdiction for minor offences and preliminary hearings. **†magistratic** (-strat´ik), **magistratical** (-ikəl) *a.* [F *magistrat*, L *magistrātus*, as MASTER]

Maglemosian (maglimō´ziən) *a.* of or relating to a Mesolithic culture, represented by finds at Maglemose in Denmark. ~*n.* the Maglemosian culture.

maglev (mag´lev) *n.* a rapid transport system in which trains glide along a continuous magnetic field, supported by magnetic repulsion. [abbr. for *mag*netic *lev*itation]

magma (mag´mə) *n.* (*pl.* **magmas, magmata** (-tə)) **1** the molten semi-fluid matter below the earth's crust. **2** a crude mixture of mineral or organic matter in a thin paste. [L, from Gr., from *massein*, to knead]

Magna Carta (magnə kah´tə), **Magna Charta** (chah´tə) *n.* **1** the Great Charter of English liberties sealed by King John on 15 June 1215. **2** any fundamental constitution guaranteeing rights and privileges. [med. L, great CHARTER]

magna cum laude (magnə kum law´di, low´dā) *adv.* with great distinction. [L]

magnanimous (magnan´iməs) *a.* great-minded, not petty in conduct or feelings, generous. **magnanimity** (-nim´-) *n.* **magnanimously** *adv.* [L *magnanimus* (*magnus*, great, *animus*, soul)]

magna opera MAGNUM OPUS.

magnate (mag´nāt) *n.* a person of great wealth and influence, esp. in business. [late L *magnas -nātem*, from *magnus*, great]

magnesia (magnē´shə, -zhə) *n.* **1** magnesium oxide, a white alkaline antacid earth. **2** hydrated magnesium carbonate, used as an antacid and laxative. **magnesian** *a.* **magnesite** (mag´nəsīt) *n.* naturally occurring magnesium carbonate. [med. L, from Gr., fem. of *Magnēsios*, of or pertaining to Magnesia in Thessaly (applied to two minerals, the lodestone and a silver-like stone, perh. talc)]

magnesium (magnē´ziəm, -zhəm, -shəm) *n.* a divalent metallic element, at. no.12, chem. symbol Mg, the base of magnesia, used in alloys and burned as a source of bright light. **magnesium flare, magnesium light** *n.* an extremely bright light created by burning magnesium ribbon. **magnesium ribbon, magnesium wire** *n.* magnesium prepared for burning as a light source.

magnet (mag´nit) *n.* **1** a piece of iron or steel etc. having the properties of attracting iron and pointing to the poles. **2** a lodestone. **3** a thing or person exercising a powerful attractive influence. **magnetic** (-net´-) *a.* **1** of or relating to a magnet or magnetism. **2** having the properties of a magnet. **3** attractive, mesmeric. ~*n.* any metal capable of receiving the properties of the lodestone. **magnetic azimuth** *n.* the arc intercepted between the true azimuth and the magnetic meridian. **magnetic battery** *n.* a combination of magnets with their poles similarly arranged. **magnetic compass** *n.* a compass showing the direction of magnetic north and bearings in relation to it. **magnetic declination** *n.* the angle between the geographical and the magnetic meridians. **magnetic dip** *n.* the angle between the earth's magnetic field and the horizontal. **magnetic disk** *n.* (*Comput.*) a small, circular piece of plastic in a rigid case, coated with a magnetic oxide substance, used for storing information and software. **magnetic equator** *n.* an imaginary line round the globe where the magnetic needle has no dip. **magnetic field** *n.* the area within which the force of a magnet etc. is effective. **magnetic flux** *n.* a measure of the strength of a magnetic field over a given area. **magnetic inclination** *n.* dip of the needle. **magnetic mine** *n.* a mine detonated by the passing over it of a metal ship. **magnetic moment** *n.* a measure of the strength of a magnet etc. when interacting with an applied field to produce a mechanical moment. **magnetic needle** *n.* a slender poised bar of magnetized steel, as in the mariner's compass, pointing north and south. **magnetic north** *n.* the direction indicated by the north end of a compass needle. **magnetic pole** *n.* **1** either of the two points on the earth's surface towards which a compass needle points, and where a magnetic needle dips vertically. **2** either of the regions in a magnet from which its magnetic force appears to originate. **magnetic resonance** *n.* the vibration of electrons, atoms, molecules or nuclei in a magnetic field in response to various radiation frequencies. **magnetic resonance imaging** *n.* a medical scanning technique using the magnetic resonance of protons in the body. **magnetics** *n.* the science or principles of magnetism. **magnetic storm** *n.* a disturbance of the earth's magnetism setting up an oscillation of the magnetic needle, caused by charged particles from the sun. **magnetic tape** *n.* a tape coated or impregnated with a magnetic powder used for the recording and reproduction of sound, video pictures and computer data. **magnetism** (mag´nitizm) *n.* **1** the property whereby certain bodies, esp. iron and its compounds, attract or repel each other according to certain laws. **2** the science treating of this property, its conditions or laws. **3** the attractive power itself. **4** personal attractiveness, charm. **animal magnetism** ANIMAL. **magnetist** *n.* a person who is skilled in the science of magnetism or in animal magnetism. **magnetite** (mag´nitīt) *n.* magnetic iron oxide. **magnetize, magnetise** *v.t.* **1** to communicate magnetic properties to. **2** to attract as with a magnet. **3** to mesmerize. ~*v.i.* to become magnetic. **magnetizable** *a.* **magnetization** (-zā´shən) *n.* **magnetizer** *n.* [OF *magnete*, L *magnēs -nētis*, Gr. *magnēs -nētos*, (stone) of magnetite]

magneto (magnē´tō) *n.* (*pl.* **magnetos**) a magneto-electric machine (esp. the igniting apparatus of an internal-combustion engine).

magneto- (magnē´tō) *comb.form* of a magnet or magnetism. [MAGNET]

magneto-electricity (magnētōeliktris´iti) *n.* **1** electricity generated by the inductive action of magnets. **2** the science treating of such electricity. **magneto-electric** *a.*

magnetograph (magnē´təgrahf) *n.* an instrument for measuring magnetic forces, esp. terrestrial magnetism.

magnetometer (magnitom´itə) *n.* a device for measuring the intensity or direction of a magnetic field, esp. of the earth. **magnetometry** *n.*

magnetomotive (magnēt´ōmōtiv) *a.* (of a force) being the sum of magnetic forces along an electric circuit.

magneton (mag´niton, magnē´ton) *n.* (*Physics*) the unit of magnetic moment.

magnetosphere (magnē´təsfiə) *n.* the region surrounding the earth or other planet, star etc. in which its magnetic field has effect.

magnetron (mag´nitron) *n.* a thermionic tube for generating very high frequency microwave oscillations.

†**magnific** (magnif´ik), **magnifical** (-fikəl) *a.* magnificent, grand, sublime. **magnifically** *adv.* [F *magnifique*, L *magnificus* (*magnus*, -FIC)]

Magnificat (magnif´ikat) *n.* **1** the song of the Virgin Mary (Luke i.46–55), so called from the first word in the Latin version. **2** a setting of this to music. **3** (**magnificat**) a song of praise. [L, 3rd sing. pres. of *magnificāre*, to MAGNIFY]

magnification MAGNIFY.

magnificent (magnif´isənt) *a.* **1** grand in appearance, majestic, splendid. **2** characterized by sumptuousness, luxury, splendour or generous profusion. **3** (*coll.*) first-rate, excellent. **magnificence** *n.* **magnificently** *adv.* [OF, from L *magnificent-*, stem of *magnificentior*, compar. of *magnificus*, MAGNIFIC]

magnifico (magnif´ikō) *n.* (*pl.* **magnificoes**) a magnate, a grandee, orig. of Venice. [It.]

magnify (mag´nifī) *v.t.* (*3rd pers. sing. pres.* **magnifies,** *pres.p.* **magnifying,** *past, p.p.* **magnified**) **1** to increase the apparent size of (an object) with an optical instrument. **2** to make greater, to increase. **3** to exaggerate. **4** †to extol, to glorify. ~*v.i.* to increase the apparent size of objects. **magnifiable** *a.* **magnification** (-fikā´shən) *n.* **magnifier** *n.* **magnifying glass** *n.* an optical lens for magnifying objects. [F *magnifier*, L *magnificāre* (*magnus*, great, *-ficāre*, *facere*, to make)]

magniloquent (magnil´əkwənt) *a.* using high-flown, pompous or bombastic language. **magniloquence** *n.* **magniloquently** *adv.* [L *magniloquus* (*magnus*, great, *-loquus*, assim. to *loquens -entem*, pres.p. of *loquī*, to speak)]

magnitude (mag´nitūd) *n.* **1** size, bulk, extent, quantity, amount. **2** anything that can be measured. **3** importance. **4** the degree of brightness of a star etc. **5** a class of stars arranged according to their brightness. **absolute magnitude** ABSOLUTE. **apparent magnitude** APPARENT. [L *magnitūdo*, from *magnus*, great, -TUDE]

magnolia (magnō´liə) *n.* **1** any flowering tree or shrub of the genus *Magnolia*, chiefly N American. **2** a pale pinkish-white or pinkish-cream colour. [P. *Magnol*, 1638–1715, French botanist]

magnox (mag´noks) *n.* any one of several magnesium-based alloys containing aluminium, used in nuclear reactors to enclose the uranium fuel elements. [*mag*nesium *no ox*idation]

magnum (mag´nəm) *n.* (*pl.* **magnums**) **1** a wine bottle containing the equivalent of two normal bottles (about 1½ litres). **2** a bottle containing two quarts (about 2.3 litres). **3** two quarts. **4** a large-calibre pistol. **5** a particularly powerful cartridge or shell. [L, orig. neut. sing. of *magnus*, great]

magnum opus (magnəm ō´pəs, op´-) *n.* (*pl.* **magnum opuses, magna opera** (magnə ō´pərə, op´-)) the greatest work of a writer, painter etc. [L, great work]

magot (mag´ət, məgō´) *n.* the tailless Barbary ape, *Macaca sylvana*, of Gibraltar and N Africa. [F]

magpie (mag´pī) *n.* **1** a chattering bird of the crow family, *Pica pica*, with black and white plumage. **2** a chatterer. **3** a person who collects and hoards small objects. **4** a variety of domestic pigeon resembling a magpie. **5** any of several Australian black and white birds, esp. *Gymnorhina tibicen*. **6** in rifle-shooting, the outermost division but one of the target. **7** a shot that hits this. **magpie lark** *n.* any of several Australian birds of the family Grallinidae, esp. *Grallinidae cyanoleuca*, the Australian peewee. **magpie moth** *n.* a white geometrid moth, *Abraxas grossulariata*, patterned with black and yellow spots. [MAG[2], PIE[2]]

maguey (mag´wā) *n.* a type of agave plant whose leaves yield fibre used to make an alcoholic drink. [Sp., from Taino]

magus (mā´gəs) *n.* (*pl.* **magi** (-jī)) **1** a member of the priestly caste among the Medes and Persians. **2** a magician, a sorcerer. **the Magi** the three 'wise men' of the East who brought presents to the infant Christ. **magian** (-jiən) *n., a.* **magianism** *n.* [L, from Gr. *magos*, OPers. *magus*]

Magyar (mag´yah) *n.* **1** a member of the Ural-Altaic people (entering Europe in 884), predominant in Hungary. **2** the language of this people, Hungarian. **3** a Magyar blouse or bodice. *~a.* of or relating to a type of blouse in which the sleeves and the rest of the garment are all one piece. **Magyarize, Magyarise** *v.t.* [Hung.]

maharaja (mah·hərah´jə), **maharajah** *n.* a title assumed by some Indian princes. **maharani** (-ni), **maharanee** *n.* **1** the wife or widow of a maharaja. **2** an Indian princess. [Sansk. *mahā-rājā* (*mahā*, great, RAJA)]

maharishi (mah·hərish´i, -rē´shi) *n.* a Hindu religious teacher. [Sansk. *mahā*, great, *rishi*, sage]

mahatma (məhat´mə) *n.* **1** in the Indian subcontinent, a much revered person. **2** an adept or sage of the highest order in some Indian and Tibetan religious thinking. **3** such a person supposed to have supernatural powers. [Sansk. *mahātman* (*mahā*, great, *ātman*, soul)]

Mahayana (mah·əyāuh´nə) *n.* the most widespread tradition of Buddhism, practised esp. in China, Japan and Tibet. [Sansk. *mahā*, great, *yāna*, vehicle]

Mahdi (mah´di) *n.* (*pl.* **Mahdis**) the Muslim messiah, a title once assumed by leaders of insurrection in Sudan. **Mahdism** *n.* **Mahdist** *n., a.* [Arab. *mahdīy*, he who is divinely guided]

mah-jong (mahjong´), **mah-jongg** *n.* a Chinese table game played with 136 or 144 pieces called tiles. [Chin., sparrow]

mahlstick MAULSTICK.

mahoe (məhō´i) *n.* a small bushy New Zealand tree, *Melicytus ramiflorus.* [Maori]

mahogany (məhog´əni) *n.* **1** the hard, fine-grained wood of *Swietenia mahagoni*, a tree of tropical America, largely used in making furniture. **2** the tree itself. **3** any other tree of the genus *Swietenia* yielding similar wood. *~a.* of the colour of mahogany, reddish-brown. [etym. unknown]

Mahommedan, †Mahometan MUHAMMADAN.

mahonia (məhō´niə) *n.* any evergreen shrub of the genus *Mahonia*, with small yellow flowers and spiny leaves.

mahout (məhowt´) *n.* an elephant driver or keeper. [Hind. *mahāwat*]

Mahratta MARATHA.

mahseer (mah´siə) *n.* either of two large and powerful, edible Indian freshwater fish, *Barbus tor* or *B. putitora*, both somewhat like the barbel. [Hind. *mahāsir*, perh. from Sansk. *mahāçirəs*, big-head]

maid (mād) *n.* **1** a female servant. **2** †a girl, a young unmarried woman, a virgin. **maidhood** *n.* MAIDENHEAD (under MAIDEN). **maidish** *a.* **maidishness** *n.* **maid of all work** *n.* a general servant. **maid of honour** *n.* **1** an unmarried lady attending a royal person. **2** (*esp. NAm.*) an unmarried attendant of a bride. **3** a variety of custard tart. **maidservant** *n.* a female servant. **maid's sickness** *n.* the illness chlorosis. [shortened from MAIDEN]

maidan (mīdahn´) *n.* an open space used as a sports or parade ground in India, Pakistan etc. [Pers.]

maiden (mā´dən) *n.* **1** †a girl, an unmarried woman. **2** in cricket, a maiden over. **3** a racehorse that has never won a prize. **4** (*North.*) a folding framework for drying or airing washing, a clothes horse. *~a.* **1** of or relating to a maid. **2** unmarried (*a maiden aunt*). **3** (of a female animal) unmated. **4** (of a racehorse) never having won a prize. **5** (of a race) open to such horses. **6** first, new; unused, untried (*maiden flight*). **7** of a city or fortress, never captured. **†maiden garnish** *n.* a fee, bribe etc. among workmen paid by a man getting a job. **maidenhead** *n.* **1** the state of being a virgin, virginity. **2** the hymen. **3** †newness, freshness. **maidenhood** *n.* the state of being a virgin. **maidenish** *a.* **maidenlike** *a.* **maidenly** *a., adv.* **maidenliness** *n.* **maiden name** *n.* the surname of a woman before marriage. **maiden over** *n.* in cricket, an over in which no runs are scored. **maiden speech** *n.* the first speech made by a Member of Parliament in the House. **maiden voyage** *n.* a first voyage (of a ship). [OE *mægden*, dim. of *mægth* (cp. Dut. *maagd*, G *Magd*) cogn. with MAY[1]]

maidenhair (mā´dənheə), **maidenhair fern** *n.* a fern with delicate fronds, esp. *Adiantum capillus-veneris.* **maidenhair tree** *n.* a ginkgo.

maieutic (māū´tik) *a.* helping to bring out or develop (applied to the system pursued by Socrates, in which he endeavoured to bring out latent ideas by persistent questioning). **maieutics** *n.* [Gr. *maieutikos*, from *maieuesthai*, to act as a midwife, from *maia*, midwife]

maigre (mā´gə) *a.* **1** (of a day) that is designated a fast day in the Roman Catholic Church. **2** (of food, esp. soup) suitable for fast days, not made from meat or containing gravy. [F *maigre*, lean]

mail[1] (māl) *n.* **1** the letters etc. conveyed by the post. **2** the system of conveying letters etc., the postal system. **3** a delivery or collection of letters etc. **4** electronic mail, e-mail. **5** a train, ship etc. carrying mail. **6** (*Hist.*) a bag for the conveyance of letters etc. *~v.t.* to send by mail, to post. **mailable** *a.* **mailbag** *n.* a bag or sack for carrying letters etc. **mailboat** *n.* **mailbox** *n.* a letter box. **mail carrier** *n.* (*NAm.*) a postman or postwoman. **mail cart** *n.* (*Hist.*) **1** a cart for carrying the mail. **2** a light vehicle for carrying children. **mail coach** *n.* **mail drop** *n.* (*NAm.*) a box etc. for receiving mail. **mailing** *n.* **1** the process of sending something by mail. **2** a batch of letters etc. sent by mail. **mailing list** *n.* a list of names and addresses of people to whom letters, advertising material etc. are to be posted. **mailman** *n.* (*pl.* **mailmen**) (*NAm.*) a postman. **mailmerge** *n.* the automatic merging of names and addresses from a computer file with the text of a letter etc. **mail order** *n.* the ordering of goods to be sent by post. **mailshot** *n.* **1** a batch of advertising material etc. sent by mail to a number of addresses. **2** an item of unsolicited mail, usu. an advertisement. **mail train** *n.* [OF *male* (F *malle*), from Gmc. (cp. Dut. *maal*, OHG *malha*)]

mail[2] (māl) *n.* **1** defensive armour for the body, formed of rings, chains or scales. **2** any defensive covering. *~v.t.* to clothe with or as with mail. **mailed** *a.* clad in mail. **mailed fist** *n.* the application of physical force. [OF *maille*, L *macula*, spot, mesh]

†mail[3] (māl) *n.* rent, tribute, tax. [late OE and Icel. *māl* (cp. OE *mæl*, speech)]

maillot (mī´ō) *n.* (*pl.* **maillots** (mī´ō)) **1** tights for dancing, exercising etc. **2** a tight-fitting swimsuit for women. **3** a jersey. [F, swaddling-clothes, a swimsuit]

maim (mām) *v.t.* **1** to deprive of the use of a limb. **2** to cripple, to mutilate. **3** to damage emotionally etc. *~n.* **1** †a serious, esp. a disabling mutilation or injury. **2** †an essential defect. **maimedness** *n.* [ME *mahaym*, from OF *mahaignier*, etym. uncertain]

main[1] (mān) *a.* **1** principal, chief, most important. **2** (of force) concentrated or fully exerted. **3** †mighty, powerful. **main boom** *n.* (*Naut.*) the lower spar of a small sailing boat on which the mainsail is extended. **main brace** *n.* (*Naut.*) a brace attached to the main yard of a sailing ship. **to splice the main brace** to serve an extra rum ration (on a ship). **main chance** *n.* **1** the most important issue. **2** an opportunity for personal gain. **3**

self-interest. **main clause** *n.* (*Gram.*) a clause that is able to stand on its own as a complete sentence, as distinct from *subordinate clause.* **main course** *n.* **1** the most substantial course of a meal. **2** (*Naut.*) †the mainsail of a square-rigged ship. **maincrop** *a.* (of a vegetable) from the main crop of the season. **main deck** *n.* (*Naut.*) **1** the deck below the spar-deck in a man-of-war. **2** the portion of the upper deck between poop and forecastle on a merchantman. **main drag** *n.* (*N Am., coll.*) the main street of a town. **mainframe** *n.* **1** a large, powerful computer. **2** the central processing and storage unit of a computer. **mainland** *n.* the principal body of land as opposed to islands etc. **mainlander** *n.* a resident on the mainland, esp. on the Australian continent as opposed to Tasmania. **main line** *n.* **1** a primary railway route. **2** (*sl.*) a principal vein, when used as a site for injecting drugs. **mainline** *v.t., v.i.* (*sl.*) to inject (a narcotic drug etc.) into a vein. **mainliner** *n.* **mainly** *adv.* **1** principally, chiefly, in the main. **2** greatly, strongly. **mainmast** *n.* (*Naut.*) the principal mast of a ship. **mainplane** *n.* any one of the principal supporting surfaces of an aircraft, esp. either or both of the wings. **mainsail** (-sāl, -səl) *n.* (*Naut.*) **1** a sail bent to the mainyard of a square-rigged ship. **2** the sail set on the after part of the mainmast of a fore-and-aft rigged vessel. **mainsheet** *n.* (*Naut.*) the rope that extends and fastens the mainsail. **mainspring** *n.* **1** the chief spring of a watch etc. **2** the chief driving force. **mainstay** *n.* **1** the chief support. **2** (*Naut.*) the stay from the maintop to the foot of the foremast. **main store** *n.* the central storage facility of a computer, the memory. **Main Street** *n., a.* (*N Am.*) (of) the materialism and mediocrity of small-town or city life (from the title of a novel by Sinclair Lewis (1920)). **main street** *n.* the principal street of a town or city. **maintop** *n.* a platform above the head of the lower mainmast. **maintopmast** *n.* (*Naut.*) a mast above the head of the lower main mast. **main yard** *n.* the yard on which the mainsail is extended. [from Icel. *megn*, strong, or MAIN[2], or from both]

main[2] (mān) *n.* **1** a chief sewer, conduit, conductor, electric cable etc. **2** †the main or high sea, the ocean. **3** †the mainland. **4** †strength, force, violent effort. **in the main** for the most part. **the mains 1** the electricity supply from a central distributor. **2** the distribution of electricity, water etc. from a central source. **with might and main** with all one's strength. [OE *mægen*, cogn. with MAY[1]]

main[3] (mān) *n.* **1** a throw at dice, or a number (5–9) called by the caster before throwing. **2** a match at cock-fighting. **3** a match in various sports. [etym. uncertain]

mainstream (mān´strēm) *n.* **1** the most prevalent or widely accepted aspects of a culture, society etc. **2** mainstream jazz. **3** the main current of a river. ~*a.* **1** of or relating to the mainstream of society. **2** (of jazz music) of the type prevalent between early and modern jazz, based on swing.

maintain (māntān´) *v.t.* **1** to keep in order, proper condition or repair. **2** to support, to provide with the means of living. **3** to sustain, to keep up. **4** to hold, preserve or carry on in any state. **5** to assert, to affirm, to support by reasoning, argument etc. **6** †to represent. **maintainable** *a.* **maintainability** (-bil´-) *n.* **maintained school** *n.* a school receiving financial support from the state or from a local authority. **maintainer** *n.* **1** a person who maintains someone or something. **2** †MAINTAINOR (under MAINTAIN). †**maintainor** *n.* (*Law*) a person guilty of maintenance. **maintenance** (mān´tənəns) *n.* **1** the act of maintaining or the state of being maintained. **2** means of support. **3** (*Law*) †an officious intermeddling in a suit in which the person has no interest. **maintenance man** *n.* (*pl.* **maintenance men**) a workman employed to keep machines etc. in working order. [F *maintenir*, L *manūtenēre* (*manū*, with the hand, abl. of *manus, tenēre*, to hold)]

maiolica (məyol´ikə), **majolica** (-jol´-) *n.* tin-glazed earthenware having metallic colours on a white ground (orig. from Italy). [It. *maiolica*, prob. from *Majorca*]

maisonette (māzənet´, -sə-), **maisonnette** *n.* **1** part of a house or block of flats let separately, usu. having two floors and with a separate entrance. **2** a small house. [F *maison*, house]

maitre d'hôtel (metrə dōtel´) *n.* (*pl.* **maitres d'hôtel** (metrə dōtel´)) **1** the manager, chief steward etc. of a hotel. **2** a head waiter. [F, master of house]

maize (māz) *n.* **1** a cereal plant from N America, *Zea mays*, also called Indian corn. **2** the cobs or grains yielded by this. [Sp. *maiz*, Cuban Sp. *mahiz*]

Maj. *abbr.* Major.

majesty (maj´əsti) *n.* (*pl.* **majesties**) **1** the quality of inspiring awe or reverence. **2** impressive dignity, grandeur, stateliness. **3** sovereign power and dignity. **4** (**Majesty**) used as part of a title or formula for addressing or referring to a king, queen or emperor (*His Majesty*). **5** in religious art, a representation of God or Christ in glory. **majestic** (-jes´-), **majestical** *a.* **majestically** *adv.* †**majesticalness** *n.* [F *majesté*, L *majestas, majestātem*, cogn. with MAJOR]

Maj. Gen. *abbr.* Major General.

Majlis (majlis´, maj´-) *n.* **1** the Iranian legislative assembly. **2** the legislative assembly of various other N African and Middle Eastern countries. [Pers., assembly]

majolica MAIOLICA.

major (mā´jə) *a.* **1** of considerable importance. **2** serious. **3** main, principal. **4 a** (*Mus.*) (of a scale) having the intervals tone, tone, semitone, tone, tone, tone, tone, semitone. **b** (of a key) based on a major scale. **c** (of an interval) that is a semitone greater than the minor interval of the same denomination. **5** greater in number, quantity, extent or importance. **6** of full legal age (in the UK now 18 years). ~*n.* **1** an army officer next above captain and below lieutenant colonel. **2** (*N Am.*) **a** a subject of specialization at a college or university. **b** a person specializing in a particular subject. **3** a person of full legal age. **4** an officer in charge of a section of a military band. **5** (*Mus.*) a major scale, key or interval. **6** (*Logic*) the first premise of a regular syllogism containing the major term. **majorat** *n.* in continental law, the right of primogeniture. **majorate** (-rət) *n.* the rank or office of a major. **major axis** *n.* the axis passing through the foci (in a conic section). **major-domo** (-dō´mō) *n.* (*pl.* **major-domos**) **1** the chief officer of a royal or princely household, in Italy or Spain. **2** a person who takes charge of a household, a butler or steward. **majorette** (-ret´) *n.* a member of a group of girls, who march in parades twirling batons, playing instruments etc., a drum majorette. **major-general** *n.* an officer ranking next below lieutenant general. **majority** (-jor´-) *n.* (*pl.* **majorities**) **1** the greater part, more than half. **2** the amount of the difference between the greater and the lesser number, esp. of votes in an election. **3** the greater number. **4** full legal age. **5** the rank or position of a major. **6** a party with an electoral majority. **7** †superiority. **8** †ancestry. **in the majority** belonging to the party etc. that has the greatest number of members. **to join the majority** to die. **majority rule** *n.* the principle that those who are greater in number should exercise greater power. **majority verdict** *n.* a verdict reached by a majority of a jury as distinct from a unanimous one. **major league** *n.* a league of the highest classification in US sport, esp. baseball. **major mode** *n.* (*Mus.*) the mode in which the third and sixth tones of the scale form major intervals with the keynote. **major part** *n.* the majority (of). **major piece** *n.* in chess, a rook or queen. **major planet** *n.* each of the largest planets in our solar system, Jupiter, Saturn, Uranus or Neptune. **major premise** *n.* (*Logic*) the premise containing the major term. **major prophets** *n.pl.* Jeremiah, Isaiah and Ezekiel. **majorship** *n.* **major suit** *n.* in contract bridge, spades or hearts, which have a higher value than clubs and diamonds. **major term** *n.* (*Logic*) that term which forms the predicate of the conclusion. [L, comp. of *magnus*, great]

Usage note *Majority* should not be used with uncountable nouns (so not *the majority of the time*).

Majorcan (məjaw´kən, -yaw´-) *n.* a native or inhabitant of Majorca. ~*a.* of or relating to Majorca.

majuscule (maj´əskūl) *n.* **1** a capital or large letter, as in Latin manuscripts, before the introduction of minuscules. **2** large lettering. ~*a.* of or relating to majuscules; written in majuscules. **majuscular** (məjŭs´-) *a.* [F, from L *mājuscula*, fem. of *-ulus*, dim. of *mājor*, see MAJOR]

make[1] (māk) *v.t.* (*pres.p.* **making,** *past, p.p.* **made** (mād)) **1** to frame, construct, produce. **2** to bring into existence, to create. **3** to give rise to, to effect, to bring about. **4** to execute, to perform, to accomplish (with nouns expressing action). **5** to result in, to cause to be or become. **6** to compose (a book, verses etc.). **7** to prepare for use. **8** to prepare for consumption; to infuse (tea). **9** to establish, to enact. **10** to raise or appoint to a rank or dignity. **11** to constitute, to form, to become, to turn out to be. **12** to gain, to acquire, to achieve. **13** to move or proceed (towards etc.). **14** in a card game, to win (a trick) or cause (a card) to win; to shuffle. **15** to score. **16** to cause, to compel (to do). **17** to cause to appear, to represent to be. **18** to reckon, to calculate or decide to be. **19** to conclude, to think. **20** to reach the end of. **21** to amount to, to serve for. **22** to travel over (a distance etc.). **23** to be sold for, to fetch, as a price. **24** (*Naut.*) to come near. **25** to arrive at. **26** to arrive in time for. **27** (*sl.*) to succeed in seducing. ~*v.i.* **1** to go, move, tend or lie (in a specified direction). **2** to contribute, to have effect (for or to). **3** (of the tide) to ebb or flow. **4** (*usu. with adjective*) to do, to act in a specified way (*make so bold as to*). ~*n.* **1** the brand, type etc. of manufacture. **2** form, shape. **3** arrangement of parts. **4** making. **5** style. **6** disposition, mental or moral constitution. **7** making of electrical contact, completion of a circuit. **on the make 1** (*coll.*) intent on personal profit, after the main chance. **2** (*coll.*) seeking sexual partners. **to make a day of it** to spend a day in enjoyment or festivity. †**to make after** to pursue. **to make against** to be unfavourable to, to tend to injure. **to make a night of it** to spend an evening or night in enjoyment or festivity. **to make as if** to pretend (to), to feint. **to make as though** to make as if. **to make at** to attack. **to make away** to hurry away. **to make away with 1** to get rid of, to kill. **2** to waste, to squander. **to make believe** BELIEVE. **to make conversation** to engage in polite talk. **to make do** to cope or be satisfied (with) though the resources etc. are not completely adequate. **to make for 1** to conduce to. **2** to corroborate. **3** to move toward. **4** to attack. **to make free** to venture (to). **to make free with** to treat without ceremony. **to make good** GOOD. **to make it 1** (*coll.*) to reach an objective. **2** (*coll.*) to succeed. **3** (*sl.*) to have sexual intercourse (with). **to make it up 1** to be reconciled, to stop quarrelling. **2** to compensate for something missing. **to make it up to** to compensate for an insult or injury to. **to make light of** LIGHT[2]. **to make like 1** (*esp. N Am.*) to pretend. **2** (*esp. N Am.*) to imitate. **to make little of 1** to have a low opinion of. **2** to have little benefit from. **to make merry** to feast, to be jovial. **to make merry over** to make a laughing matter of. **to make money** to obtain an income, to acquire wealth. **to make much of 1** (*usu. with neg.*) to treat with fondness or favour. **2** to treat as of great importance. **3** to derive much benefit from. **to make no doubt** to be sure. **to make of 1** to understand, interpret. **2** to attach a specified degree of importance to. **3** to construct from. **to make off 1** to hurry away. **2** to abscond. **to make off with** to take away wrongfully. **to make one's way** to proceed. **to make or break** to be crucial to the success or failure of. **to make or mar** to make or break. **to make out 1** to identify or distinguish with the eyes or ears. **2** to understand, to decipher. **3** to prove, to establish. **4** to claim or allege. **5** to draw up, to write out. **6** (*coll.*) to be successful, to get on. **7** (*N Am., coll.*) **a** to engage in necking or petting. **b** to have sexual intercourse. **to make over 1** to transfer. **2** to redesign, reshape etc., to give a new look to. **to make place** to move so as to leave space (for). **to make room** to move so as to leave space (for). **to make shift** SHIFT. **to make so bold** BOLD. **to make sure** SURE. **to make up 1** to compose. **2** to compound. **3** to collect together. **4** to compile. **5** to fabricate, to concoct. **6** to complete, to supply (what is wanting). **7** to compensate. **8** to be reconciled, to stop quarrelling. **9** to settle, to adjust, to arrange. **10** (of an actor) to dress up, to prepare the face to represent a character. **11** to prepare (a bed etc.) for use. **12** to repair. **13** to apply cosmetics to the face. **14** to apply cosmetics to the face of. **15** to arrange (type etc.) in columns or pages. **to make up one's mind** to decide, to resolve. **to make up to** to make advances to. **to make water 1** to urinate. **2** (*Naut.*) to leak. **to make way 1** to make room, to open a passage. **2** to progress. **to make with 1** (*N Am., coll.*) to happen or proceed with. **2** (*N Am., coll.*) to show, to produce. **makable** *a.* **1** able to be made. **2** able to be achieved (*a makable putt*). **make-believe, make-belief** *n.* pretending, a pretence, a sham. ~*a.* **1** unreal. **2** counterfeit. ~*v.t., v.i.* to pretend (that). **make-or-break** *a.* crucial to success or failure. **make-over** *n.* a complete redesign or reshaping, a transformation in look. **maker** *n.* **1** a person who makes something. **2** †a poet. **one's Maker** God. **the Maker** God. **to meet one's Maker** to die. **makeshift** *n.* a temporary expedient. ~*a.* used as a makeshift. **make-up** *n.* **1** cosmetics for use on the face. **2** the manner in which a person's face is made up, esp. how an actor's face is made to represent a character. **3** a person's character or temperament. **4** a thing's composition or constitution. **5** (*dated*) the arrangement of type into columns or pages; the type so arranged. **6** a made-up story, a fiction. **makeweight** *n.* **1** something, usu. small, that is added to make up the weight of a product, commodity etc. **2** an unimportant additional element. **3** a stopgap. **4** anything that counterbalances, a counterpoise. **making** *n.* **1** the act of constructing, producing, causing etc. **2** possibility or opportunity of success or full development. **3** (*pl.*) composition, essential qualities. **4** (*pl.*) profits, earnings. **5** (*pl.*) materials for rolling a cigarette. **in the making** gradually developing or being made. **to be the making of** to play a crucial part in the successful development, outcome etc. of. **making-up** *n.* balancing of accounts. [OE *macian* (cp. Dut. *maken*, G *machen*), cogn. with MATCH[1]]

†**make**[2] (māk) *n.* **1** a person's equal, like or match. **2** a mate, a husband or wife. **makeless** *a.* matchless, unequalled. [OE *gemaca* (*gamaec*, equal, well-matched, cp. Dut. *gemac*, G *Gemach*, OHG *gimah*)]

mako (mah´kō) *n.* (*pl.* **makos**) **1** a small New Zealand tree, *Aristotelia racemosa*. **2** a large shark of the genus *Isurus*. [Maori]

MAL *abbr.* Malaysia (IVR).

Mal. *abbr.* **1** Malachi. **2** Malaysia.

mal- (mal), **male-** (mal´i) *comb. form* **1** bad(ly). **2** evil. **3** faulty. **4** abnormal. [L *male*, ill, badly]

malabsorption (maləbsawp´shən) *n.* (*Med.*) imperfect absorption of food into the small intestine caused by disease.

malacca (məlak´ə), **malacca cane** *n.* the stem of a palm

tree used as a walking stick. [town and district in Malay peninsula]
malachite (mal´əkīt) *n.* a bright green monoclinic carbonate of copper, often polished for ornamental use. [OF *melochite* (Gr. *malachē*, mallow)]
malaco- (mal´əkō) *comb. form* soft. [Gr. *malakos*]
malacology (maləkol´əji) *n.* the natural history of molluscs. **malacological** (-kəloj´-) *a.* **malacologist** *n.*
malacopterygian (maləkoptərij´iən) *a.* belonging to the Malacopyterygii, a group of soft-finned fishes, including salmon and herring. *~n.* any individual of this group. **malacopyterygious** *a.* [Gr. *pteryx*, a wing]
malacostracan (maləkos´trəkən) *n.* any crustacean of the class Malacostraca, a division containing crabs, lobsters etc. *~a.* of or relating to this class. **malacostracological** (loj´-) *a.* **malacostracologist** (-kol´-) *n.* **malacostracology** (-kol´-) *n.* crustaceology. **malacostracous** *a.* [Gr. *ostrakon*, a shell]
maladaptation (maladəptā´shən) *n.* imperfect adaptation to the prevailing environment. **maladaptative** (-ədap´-) *a.*
maladjusted (maləjŭs´tid) *a.* **1** imperfectly adjusted. **2** unable to adjust oneself to the physical or social environment. **maladjustment** *n.*
maladministration (malədministrā´shən) *n.* defective or dishonest management, esp. of public affairs. **maladminister** (-min´-) *v.t.*
maladroit (malədroit´) *a.* awkward, clumsy. **maladroitly** *adv.* **maladroitness** *n.*
malady (mal´ədi) *n.* (*pl.* **maladies**) **1** a disease, an ailment, esp. a lingering or deep-seated disorder. **2** a moral defect or disorder. [F *maladie*, from *malade*, sick, late L *male habitus* (MAL-, *habitus*, p.p. of *habēre*, to have, hold, keep)]
mala fide (malə fī´di, mālə fē´dā) *a.*, *adv.* (acting or done) in bad faith. [L]
Malaga (mal´əgə) *n.* sweet, fortified white wine imported from Malaga. [seaport and province in S Spain]
Malagasy (maləgas´i) *a.* of or relating to Madagascar or its inhabitants or language. *~n.* (*pl.* **Malagasy**) **1** a native or inhabitant of Madagascar. **2** the language of Madagascar.
malagueña (maləgā´nyə) *n.* a Spanish dance or folk tune similar to the fandango.
malaise (malāz´) *n.* **1** a feeling of uneasiness, esp. as premonition of a serious malady. **2** a mild feeling of sickness or depression. [F (OF *mal*, as MAL-, *aise*, EASE)]
malamute (mal´əmūt), **malemute** *n.* a powerful dog used to pull sledges in Arctic regions. [name of an Innuit people of Alaska]
malanders MALLENDERS.
†**malapert** (mal´əpœt) *a.* pert, impudent, saucy, forward. *~n.* a pert, saucy person. †**malapertly** *adv.* †**malapertness** *n.* [OF *mal appert* (MAL-, *espert*, EXPERT)]
malapropism (mal´əpropizm), **malaprop** *n.* **1** grotesque misapplication of words. **2** a misapplied word. **malapropian** (-prop´-, -prō´-) *a.* [Mrs *Malaprop* in Sheridan's *The Rivals*, see MALAPROPOS]
malapropos (malaprəpō´) *adv.* unseasonably, unsuitably, out of place. *~a.* unseasonable etc. *~n.* an unseasonable or inopportune thing, remark, event etc. [F *mal à propos* (MAL-, APROPOS)]
malar (mā´lə) *a.* of or relating to the cheek or cheekbone. *~n.* the bone which forms the prominence of the cheek. [L *māla* (prob. rel. to MAXILLA), cheek, -AR[1]]
malaria (məleə´riə) *n.* **1** a fever of an intermittent and remittent nature caused by a parasite of the genus *Plasmodium* introduced by the bite of mosquitoes. **2** †the unpleasant, harmful air arising from marshy districts, formerly believed to produce fevers etc. **malarial, malarian, malarious** *a.* [It. *mal'aria* (MAL-, AIR)]
malarkey (məlah´ki), **malarky** *n.* (*coll.*) foolish or insincere talk, nonsense.
malassimilation (maləsimilā´shən) *n.* (*Med.*) imperfect assimilation, esp. of nutriment.
malate MALIC ACID.
malathion (maləthī´ən) *n.* an insecticide used for houseflies and garden pests.
Malay (məlā´) *a.* of or relating to a people of Malaysia and Indonesia. *~n.* **1** a member of this people. **2** their language, the official language of Malaysia. **Malayan** *n., a.* **Malayo-** *comb. form* Malayan and, as in *Malayo-Polynesian.* [Malay *Malayu*]
Malayalam (maləyah´ləm, məlī´ələm) *n.* the Dravidian language of Kerala in S India, related to Tamil. [from Tamil *malai*, mountain, *āl*, man]
Malaysian (məlā´ziən, -zhən) *n.* a native or inhabitant of Malaysia in SE Asia. *~a.* of or relating to Malaysia.
malcontent (mal´kəntent) *n.* a person who is discontented, esp. with the government, a rebel. *~a.* discontented, esp. with the government or its administration. **malcontented** (-tent´-) *a.* **malcontentedly** *adv.* **malcontentedness** *n.* [OF (MAL-, CONTENT[1])]
mal de mer (mal də meə´) *n.* seasickness. [F]
maldistribution (maldistribū´shən) *n.* imperfect, unequal or unfair distribution.
male (māl) *a.* **1** of or relating to the sex that begets young or has organs for impregnating ova. **2** (of organs) adapted for fertilization. **3** (*Bot.*) having stamens but no pistil. **4** of, relating to or characteristic of men or manhood or male animals or plants; masculine, virile. **5** designed for entering a correlative mechanical part designated female (*a male bolt*). *~n.* **1** an individual of the male sex. **2** a plant, or part of a plant, that bears the fertilizing organs. **male chauvinist (pig)** *n.* a man with an arrogant belief in the superiority of the male sex. **male die** *n.* the convex die, which is struck into the female or concave die. **male fern** *n.* a fern, *Dryopleris filixmas*, with the fronds clustered in a crown. **male menopause** *n.* a (supposed) period in a man's middle life when he experiences an emotional crisis focused on diminishing sexual prowess. **maleness** *n.* **male prostitute** *n.* a boy or man who engages in sexual activity with other men for money. **male screw** *n.* a screw whose threads enter the spiral-threaded cavity of another (female) screw. [OF, from L *masculum*, nom. *-lus*, from *mās*, male]
male- MAL-.
malediction (malədik´shən) *n.* a curse, an imprecation. **maledictive** *a.* **maledictory** *a.* [F, from L *maledictio -ōnem*, from *maledīcere* (*dīcere*, to speak)]
malefactor (mal´əfaktə) *n.* an evildoer, a criminal. **malefaction** (-fak´shən) *n.* [L *factor*, from *facere*, to do)]
malefic (məlef´ik) *a.* mischief-making, harmful, hateful.
maleficent (məlef´isənt) *a.* hurtful, mischievous, causing evil (to). **maleficence** *n.* [L *maleficus*]
maleic acid (məlē´ik) *n.* a colourless, crystalline acid used in making synthetic compounds. [F *maléique*, from *malique*, as MALIC ACID]
malemute MALAMUTE.
malevolent (məlev´ələnt) *a.* **1** ill-disposed, envious, malicious, spiteful. **2** wishing evil or injury to others. **malevolence** *n.* **malevolently** *adv.* [L *malevolens -entem* (*volens*, pres.p. of *velle*, to wish)]
malfeasance (malfē´zəns) *n.* evildoing, esp. illegal conduct by a public official. **malfeasant** *n., a.* [from OF *malfaisant* (*faisant*, pres.p. of *faire*, to do)]
malformation (malfəmā´shən) *n.* **1** faulty formation. **2** a faulty structure or irregularity of form. **malformed** (-fawmd´) *a.*
malfunction (malfŭngk´shən) *n.* **1** a failure to function. **2** defective function or operation. *~v.i.* to operate defectively.
malgré (mal´grā) *prep.* in spite of. **malgré lui** (lwē´) *adv.* in spite of himself. [F, see MAUGRE]

mali (mālē) *n.* (*pl.* **malis**) a member of the gardener caste in the Indian subcontinent. [Hind.]

malic acid (mā´lik) *n.* an organic acid derived from unripe apples and other fruit. **malate** (mal´āt) *n.* a salt or ester of malic acid. [F *malique*, from L *mālum*, apple]

malice (mal´is) *n.* **1** a disposition to injure others, active malevolence. **2** (*Law*) a premeditated design to do evil or injure another. ~†*v.t.* to bear malice towards. **malice aforethought, malice prepense** *n.* (*Law*) a premeditated desire to commit an illegal act, esp. murder. **malicious** (məlish´əs) *a.* characterized by malice, full of malice. **maliciously** *adv.* **maliciousness** *n.* [F, from L *malitia*, from *malus*, bad]

malign (məlīn´) *a.* **1** unfavourable, pernicious, malignant, hurtful. **2** malevolent. ~*v.t.* to speak evil of, to slander. ~†*v.i.* to be malicious. **maligner** *n.* **malignly** *adv.* [OF *maligne*, L *malignus* (*mali-*, MALE-, *genus*, cp. BENIGN)]

malignant (məlig´nənt) *a.* **1** (of a disease, tumour etc.) resisting treatment and threatening life. **2** exercising a pernicious influence, virulent. **3** motivated by extreme enmity or malice. ~*n.* (*Hist.*) a malevolent person, esp. applied by the Puritans to a Royalist in the time of the Civil War. **malignancy** *n.* **malignantly** *adv.* **malignant pustule** *n.* a form of anthrax. **malignity** *n.* (*pl.* **malignities**).

malinger (məling´gə) *v.i.* to exaggerate or pretend illness in order to avoid work or other responsibility. **malingerer** *n.* [F *malingre*, sickly, etym. uncertain]

malism (mā´lizm) *n.* the doctrine that on the whole this is a bad world. [L *malus*, bad]

†**malison** (mal´isən, -z-) *n.* a curse, a malediction. [OF *maleison*, MALEDICTION]

†**malkin** (maw´kin), **mawkin** *n.* **1** a female servant who works in a kitchen. **2** a slattern. **3** a cat. **4** a scarecrow, esp. one representing a woman. [dim. of *Matilda* or *Maud*]

mall (mawl, mal) *n.* **1** an enclosed street or area of shops reserved for pedestrians. **2** a sheltered public walk, promenade. **3** †the game of pall-mall. **4** †an alley for the playing of pall-mall. **5** †the mallet used in pall-mall. [MAUL]

mallanders MALLENDERS.

mallard (mal´əd, -lahd) *n.* (*pl.* **mallard, mallards**) **1** a wild duck or drake. **2** the flesh of this. [OF *malart*, perh. from OHG proper name *Madehart*]

malleable (mal´iəbəl) *a.* **1** capable of being rolled out or shaped by hammering without being broken. **2** easily influenced by outside forces, pliant. **malleability** (-bil´-), **malleableness** *n.* **malleably** *adv.* [OF, prob. from L *malleābilis*, from *malleāre*, from *malleus*, hammer]

mallee (mal´i) *n.* **1** any of various dwarf species of eucalyptus growing in the deserts of Victoria and S Australia. **2** an area of scrub dominated by these trees. **mallee bird, mallee fowl, mallee hen** *n.* an Australian megapode, *Leipoa ocellata*, similar to a turkey. [Austral. Abor.]

mallei, malleiform MALLEUS.

mallemuck MOLLYMAWK.

mallenders (mal´əndəz), **malanders, mallanders** *n.pl.* a scaly eruption at the back of the knee in horses. [F *malandre*]

malleolus (məlē´ələs) *n.* (*pl.* **malleoli** (-lī)) either of two hammer-shaped bony projections extending either side of the ankle. **malleolar** (-lē´-, mal´-) *a.* [L, dim. of MALLEUS]

mallet (mal´it) *n.* **1** a light hammer, usu. of wood. **2** a long-handled wooden hammer for striking the ball in croquet or polo. [F *maillet*, dim. of *mail*, MAUL]

malleus (mal´iəs) *n.* (*pl.* **mallei** (-iī)) one of the small bones of the middle ear or tympanum. **malleiform** (mal´iəfawm) *a.* [L, hammer]

mallow (mal´ō) *n.* **1** a plant of various species belonging to the genus *Malva*, usu. with pink or mauve flowers and hairy stems and foliage, and having emollient properties (from which perh. it derives its name). **2** any of various other plants of the same family (Malvaceae). [OE *mealwe*, L *malva* (cp. Gr. *malachē*, perh. rel. to *malakos*, soft)]

malm (mahm) *n.* **1** a soft, friable chalky rock or loam, used with clay and sand for brick-making. **2** a brick of a type originally made from this. ~*v.t.* **1** to mix (clay, chalk etc.) to make malm for bricks. **2** to cover (brick-earth) with this. [OE *mealm* (cp. Icel. *mālmr*, Goth. *malma*, from Gmc. *mal-*, to grind)]

malmsey (mahm´zi) *n.* a strong sweet white wine now chiefly made in Madeira. [ult. from med. L *malmasia*, corr. of Gr. *Monemvasia*, Napoli di Monemvasia, town in Morea, Greece (cp. MALVOISIE)]

malnourished (malnŭr´isht) *a.* suffering from malnutrition. **malnourishment** *n.*

malnutrition (malnūtrish´ən) *n.* insufficient or defective nutrition.

malocclusion (maləkloo´shən) *n.* (*Med.*) a defect in the position of the teeth in the lower jaw relative to those of the upper jaw.

malodorous (malō´dərəs) *a.* having an unpleasant smell. **malodour** *n.* an offensive odour.

Malpighian (malpig´iən) *a.* (*Anat.*) applied to certain corpuscles, layers and other structures, in the spleen and kidneys. **Malpighian layer** *n.* (*Anat.*) the innermost layer of cells in the epidermis. [Marcello *Malpighi*, 1628–94, Italian anatomist]

malpractice (malprak´tis) *n.* illegal or immoral conduct, esp. improper treatment of a case by a physician, lawyer etc.

malpresentation (malprezəntā´shən) *n.* (*Med.*) an abnormal position of the foetus at birth.

malt (mawlt) *n.* **1** grain, usu. barley, steeped in water and fermented, then dried in a kiln, usu. used for brewing and distilling. **2** (*coll.*) (a) malt whisky, malt liquor. **3** (*N Am.*) malted milk. ~*a.* of or relating to, containing or made of malt. ~*v.t.* **1** to convert into malt. **2** to treat with malt. ~*v.i.* to be converted into malt. **malted** *a.* mixed with malt or malt extract. ~*n.* (*N Am.*) malted milk. **malted milk** *n.* a hot drink made from dried milk and a powdered preparation of malt. **malt extract** *n.* a thick, sticky liquid made from malt, taken as a health food. **malt floor** *n.* the floor in a malthouse on which the grain is spread to germinate. **malthouse** *n.* a building where malt is prepared and stored. **malting** *n.* **1** brewing or distilling with malt. **2** (*also pl.*) MALTHOUSE (under MALT). **malt liquor** *n.* liquor made from malt by fermentation, such as beer, stout etc. **maltster** *n.* a person whose occupation is to make malt. **malt whisky** *n.* whisky distilled from malted barley as distinct from grain whisky or blended whisky. **malty** *a.* (*comp.* **maltier**, *superl.* **maltiest**). **maltiness** *n.* [OE *mealt* (cp. Dut. *mout*, Icel. *malt*, G *Malz*), cogn. with OHG *malz*, soft, and MELT]

Malta fever (mawl´tə) *n.* brucellosis, a fever formerly common in Malta and other places in the Mediterranean, said to be conveyed by goat's milk. [*Malta*, an island in the Mediterranean]

Maltese (mawltēz´) *a.* of or relating to Malta or its inhabitants. ~*n.* (*pl.* **Maltese**) **1** a native or inhabitant of Malta. **2** (*as pl.*) the Maltese people. **3** the Maltese language. **4** a Maltese dog. **Maltese cross** *n.* a cross with arms of equal size widening from the point of junction towards the extremities, and usu. with each arm split so as to form two points. **Maltese dog, Maltese terrier** *n.* a small variety of spaniel or terrier with long silky hair.

maltha (mal´thə) *n.* an ancient form of bituminous cement, mineral tar. [L, from Gr.]

Malthusian (malthū´ziən) *a.* of or relating to or supporting the teachings of Malthus. ~*n.* a follower of Malthus, i.e. a person who believes that some check is necessary to prevent overpopulation. **Malthusianism** *n.* [T. R. *Malthus*, 1766–1834, political economist and advocate of restraint in the propagation of children]

maltose (mawl´tōs) *n.* (*Chem.*) a sugar obtained by the action of malt or diastase on starch paste. [F (MALT, -OSE[1])]

maltreat (maltrēt´) *v.t.* to ill-treat, to abuse. **maltreater** *n.* **maltreatment** *n.* [F *maltraiter*, L *male tractāre* (MAL-, TREAT)]

malvaceous (malvā´shəs) *a.* (*Bot.*) belonging to or resembling the genus *Malva* or the family Malvaceae, including the mallows. [late L *malvaceus*, from *malva*, MALLOW]

malversation (malvəsā´shən) *n.* (*formal*) fraudulent conduct or corruption in a position of trust, esp. corrupt administration of public funds. [F *malverser* (L *male*, badly, *versārī*, to behave, freq. of *vertere*, to turn), -ATION]

malvoisie (mal´voizi, -zē´) *n.* malmsey. [ME from OF *malvesie*, corr. of Gr. *Monemvasia* (cp. MALMSEY)]

mam (mam) *n.* (*coll.*) mother.

mama MAMMA[1].

mamba (mam´bə) *n.* any of various African poisonous snakes of the genus *Dendroaspis*. [Zulu *imamba*, large snake]

mambo (mam´bō) *n.* (*pl.* **mambos**) a W Indian syncopated dance or dance tune, like the rumba. ~*v.i.* (*3rd pers. sing. pres.* **mamboes**, *pres.p.* **mamboing**, *past*, *p.p.* **mamboed**) to dance the mambo.

mamelon (mam´ələn) *n.* a small rounded hill or mound (from its resemblance to a woman's breast). [F, a teat, from *mamelle*, L MAMILLA]

Mameluke (mam´əlook) *n.* (*Hist.*) any of the mounted soldiers of Egypt (orig. Circassian slaves) who formed the ruling class in that country, destroyed by Mehmet Ali in 1811. [Arab. *mamlūk*, slave, from *malaka*, to possess]

mamilla (məmil´ə), (*N Am.*) **mammilla** *n.* (*pl.* **mamillae, mammillae** (-ē)) **1** a nipple or teat. **2** a nipple-shaped organ or part. **mamillary** (mam´-), **mamillate** (mam´ilət), **mamillated** (mam´-), **mamilliform** *a.* [L, dim. of MAMMA[2]]

mamma[1] (məmah´, mam´ə), **mama** *n.* mother (used by or to children). **mammy** (mam´i) *n.* (*pl.* **mammies**) **1** mother (used by or to children). **2** (*N Am.*, *offensive*) a black woman working as a children's nurse in a white family. [reduplication of instinctive sound made by infants]

mamma[2] (mam´ə) *n.* (*pl.* **mammae** (-ē)) the milk-secreting organ in female mammals. **mammary** *a.* of or concerning the mammae. **mammary gland** *n.* a mamma. **mammifer** *n.* a mammal. **mammiferous** (-mif´-) *a.* **1** (*Zool.*) mammalian. **2** (*Anat.*) having breasts. **mammiform** *a.* like a breast in shape. **mammogram** *n.* an image obtained by the process of mammography. **mammography** (-mog´-) *n.* examination of the breasts by X-ray. [L]

mammal (mam´əl) *n.* (*Zool.*) any vertebrate of the class Mammalia, having milk-secreting organs for suckling their young, the highest division of vertebrates. **mammalian** (-mā´-) *a.* **mammaliferous** (-lif´-) *a.* (of rocks) containing mammalian remains. **mammalogy** (-mal´-) *n.* the study of mammals. **mammalogist** *n.* [sing. from mod. L *mammālia*, neut. pl. of late L *mammālis*, from L MAMMA[2]]

mammary MAMMA[2].

mammee (məmē´) *n.* a tropical American tree, *Mammea americana*, bearing edible pulpy fruit. [through F *mammée* or Sp. *mamei*, from Haitian]

mammifer, mammiferous etc. MAMMA[2].

mammilla MAMILLA.

†**mammock** (mam´ək) *n.* a shapeless piece. [etym. unknown]

mammogram, mammography MAMMA[2].

Mammon (mam´ən) *n.* riches personified as an idol or an evil influence. **Mammonish** *a.* **Mammonism** *n.* **Mammonist, Mammonite** *n.* **Mammonize, Mammonise** *v.t.* [L *mammōna*, Gr. *mamōnas*, Aram. *māmōnā*, riches]

mammoth (mam´əth) *n.* a large extinct species of elephant of the genus *Mammuthus*. ~*a.* gigantic, huge. [Rus. *mammat* (now *mamont*)]

mammy MAMMA[1].

Man. *abbr.* Manitoba.

man (man) *n.* (*pl.* **men** (men)) **1** an adult male of the human race. **2** a human being, a person. **3** anyone. **4** (*collect.*) humankind, the human race. **5** a person with manly qualities. **6** (*dial.*, *coll.*) a husband, a male lover. **7** a manservant, a valet, a workman. **8** (*pl.*) soldiers, esp. privates. **9** a person under one's control. **10** †a vassal, a tenant. **11** (*in comb.*) a prehistoric human (*Neanderthal man*). **12** (*pl.*) pieces used in playing chess or draughts. **13** (*in comb.*) a ship, as *man-of-war*, *merchantman* etc. ~*v.t.* (*pres.p.* **manning**, *past*, *p.p.* **manned**) **1** to furnish with (a person or persons), esp. for defence, a period of duty etc. **2** to fortify the courage of (esp. oneself). **3** to accustom (a hawk) to being handled. **as one man** all together, in unison. **every man jack** JACK[1]. **inner man** INNER. **man alive!** an expression of remonstration, often sarcastic. **man and boy** from boyhood upwards. **man to man 1** as between individual people, one with or against the other. **2** with complete frankness. **my (good) man** used as a patronizing form of address to a man. **one's man** the person needed or suitable (for). **the Man** (*N Am.*, *sl.*, *derog.*) the white people in authority, e.g. the police. **the man for** the person needed or suitable for. **to a man** without exception. **to be man enough** to be sufficiently manly. **to be one's own man** to be of independent mind. **to play the man** PLAY. **to separate/ sort out the men from the boys** (*coll.*) to reveal those who are really tough or capable. **man about town** *n.* a fashionable man of leisure. **man-at-arms** *n.* (*pl.* **men-at-arms**) a heavily-armed mounted soldier, esp. in the Middle Ages. **man-day** *n.* the amount of work done by one person in one day. **man-eater** *n.* **1** a tiger, shark etc., that devours human beings. **2** (*coll.*) a promiscuous woman. **3** a cannibal. **4** a horse that bites. **man-eating** *a.* **Man Friday** *n.* a personal servant, factotum. **manful** *a.* brave, courageous, resolute, manly. **manfully** *adv.* **manfulness** *n.* **manhandle** *v.t.* **1** to move by manpower alone. **2** (*coll.*) to handle roughly, to maltreat. **man-hater** *n.* a person (esp. a woman) who hates men. **manhole** *n.* a hole in a floor, drain or parts of machinery etc., to allow entrance for cleansing and repairs. **manhood** *n.* **1** the state of being a man. **2** the state of being a male person of full age. **3** manliness, courage, resolution. **4** (*euphem.*) the penis. **5** the men of a country or place collectively. **6** the state of being a human. **manhood suffrage** *n.* the right of voting granted to every male citizen of full age not disqualified by crime etc. **man-hour** *n.* the amount of work done by one person in one hour. **manhunt** *n.* a large-scale search for a person, e.g. an escaped prisoner. **man in the moon** *n.* the personage attributed to the semblance of a face on the surface of the moon as seen from earth. **man in the street**, (*N Am.*) **man on the street** *n.* an ordinary person. **mankind** *n.* **1** the human species. **2** male people as distinct from females. **manless** *a.* **manlike** *a.* **1** manly. **2** mannish. **3** resembling a man or a human. **manly** *a.* (*comp.* **manlier**, *superl.* **manliest**) **1** befitting a man. **2** having qualities such as courage, resoluteness, magnanimity. **3** mannish. **manliness** *n.* **man-made** *a.* made by humans, not natural, artificial. **manned** *a.* **1** having a crew, workers etc. **2** (of a spacecraft) having a human pilot or crew. **mannish** *a.* (esp. of a woman) masculine, characteristic of a man. **mannishly** *adv.* **mannishness** *n.* **man of Belial** *n.* a worthless, wicked man. **man of business** *n.* a businessman, an agent, an attorney. **man of God** *n.* **1** a clergyman. **2** a male saint. **man of honour** *n.* a man who can be trusted. **man of letters** *n.* a writer, literary critic etc. **man of mark** *n.* a distinguished or famous man. **man of means** *n.* a wealthy man. **man of sense** *n.* a person with wisdom, common sense etc. **man of straw** *n.* **1** a man of no substance. **2** a false argument or adversary put forward for the sake of being refuted. **man of the cloth** *n.* a clergyman. **man of the house** *n.* the male head of a household. **man of the match** *n.* the outstanding player in a sports match. **man of the moment** *n.* a man who is important, in the news etc. at a particular time. **man of the world** *n.* an experienced person, sophisticated and urbane. **man-of-war, man-o'-war** *n.* (*pl.* **men-of-war, men-o'-war**) (*Hist.*) a warship belonging to a navy. **manpower** *n.* the amount of workpeople etc. available for any purpose. **manrope** *n.* a rope at the side of a gangway etc. acting as a railing. **manservant** *n.* (*pl.* **menservants**) a male servant. **man-size, man-sized** *a.* **1** (*coll.*) large. **2** of a suitable size for a man. **manslaughter** *n.* **1** (*Law*) the killing of a person unlawfully but without prior intent. **2** the killing of a human being or beings. **man-slayer** *n.* a person who kills a human being or commits manslaughter. **man-to-man** *a.* **1** personal, as between individuals. **2** completely frank. **mantrap** *n.* a trap set for poachers etc. **men in buckram** *n.pl.* non-existent persons, imaginary opponents. **men's (room)** *n.* a lavatory for men. [OE *mann* (cp. Dut. and Swed. *man*, G *Mann*)]

Usage note The word *humankind* is sometimes preferred to *man* or *mankind* to refer to the human species, to avoid charges of sexism.

---

mana (mah´nə) *n.* **1** spiritual power exerted through man or inanimate objects. **2** power, authority. [Maori from Polynesian]

manacle (man´əkəl) *n.* (*usu. pl.*) a handcuff, fetter, shackle. ~*v.t.* to put manacles on, to fetter. [OF *manicle*, L *manicula*, dim. of *manus*, hand]

manage (man´ij) *v.t.* **1** to direct, to carry on, to control, to conduct. **2** to conduct the affairs of. **3** to handle, to wield. **4** to bring or keep under control. **5** to lead or guide by flattery etc. **6** to break in, to train (as a horse). **7** to deal with, to make use of. **8** to make or keep an appointment for (a certain time etc.). **9** †to husband, to use cautiously. ~*v.i.* **1** to direct affairs. **2** to contrive (to do etc.). **3** to get on (with or without). **4** to succeed (with). ~†*n.* MANÈGE. **manageable** *a.* **manageability** (-bil´-), **manageableness** *n.* **manageably** *adv.* **management** *n.* **1** the act of managing. **2** conduct, administration. **3** those who manage, a board of directors etc. **4** skilful employment of means. **5** †skill, ingenuity. **management buyout** *n.* the purchase of the control of a company by its directors. **management consultant** *n.* a person who advises on the efficient management of a business, company or institution. **manager** *n.* **1** a person who manages, esp. a business, institution etc. **2** (*Law*) a person appointed to administer a business in chancery etc. **3** (*usu. with good, bad etc.*) a person skilled in economical management. **4** (*pl.*) a committee appointed by either House of Parliament to perform a duty concerning both Houses. **manageress** (-es´) *n.* a female manager, esp. of a retail shop, canteen, restaurant etc. **managerial** (-jē´-) *a.* **managerially** *adv.* **managership** *n.* **managing** *a.* **1** having the management or control of a business, department etc. **2** †careful, economical. [It. *maneggiare*, from L *manus*, hand]

manakin (man´əkin) *n.* any small bird of the family Pipridae of tropical Central and S America. [var. of MANIKIN]

mañana (mənyah´nə) *n., adv.* **1** tomorrow. **2** presently, later on, in the indefinite future. [Sp., from L *māne*]

manatee (man´ətē) *n.* a large herbivorous aquatic mammal of the genus *Trichechus*, a sea cow. [Sp. *manati*, Carib *manatoui*]

manche (mahnsh) *n.* **1** a sleeve, with long hanging ends. **2** (*Her.*) a bearing representing such a sleeve. **3** the neck of a violin etc. [F, from L *manica*, from *manus*, hand]

†**Manchester goods** (man´chəstə) *n.pl.* cotton textiles. **Manchesterism** *n.* (*Hist.*) the doctrines of the school of thought of Cobden and Bright advocating Free Trade and the principle of laissez-faire. [*Manchester*, a city within Lancashire]

manchineel (manchinēl´) *n.* **1** a W Indian tree, *Hippomane mancinella*, with a poisonous sap and apple-like fruit. **2** its timber, used for cabinet work. [F *mancenille*, Sp. *manzanilla*, dim. of *manzana*, L *matiāna*, a certain kind of apple, from *Matius*, name of a Roman gens]

Manchu (manchoo´) *n.* (*pl.* **Manchus**) **1** a member of a Chinese people which governed China, 1644–1912. **2** the language of the Manchus. ~*a.* of or relating to this people or language. [Manchu, pure]

mancipate (man´sipāt) *v.t.* (*Hist.*) under Roman law, to hand over (property), to deliver possession of, by the formal method of mancipation. **mancipable** *a.* **mancipation** (-ā´shən) *n.* the formal method of transferring property required by Roman law. **mancipative, mancipatory** *a.* [L *manipātus*, p.p. of *mancipāre*, as MANCIPLE]

manciple (man´sipəl) *n.* a steward, a buyer of stores, esp. for a college, Inn of Court etc. [OF *manciple*, L *mancipium*, from *manceps*, a buyer, a manager (*manus*, hand, *capere*, to take)]

Mancunian (mankū´niən, mang-) *n.* a native or inhabitant of Manchester. ~*a.* of or relating to Manchester. [mod. L *Mancunium*, Manchester]

-mancy (mansi) *comb. form* divination by, as in *necromancy, pyromancy*. **-mantic** *comb. form* forming adjectives. [Gr. *manteia*, divination, from *manteuesthai*, to prophesy, from *mantis*, prophet]

Mandaean (mandē´ən) *n.* **1** a member of a Gnostic sect of Iraq. **2** the language of this sect. ~*a.* of or relating to the Mandaeans or their language.

mandala (man´dələ, -dah´-) *n.* **1** any of various symbols used to represent the universe in Buddhism or Hinduism, used as an aid to meditation. **2** a circular symbol seen in dreams, supposed to represent personal wholeness. [Sansk., circle]

mandamus (mandā´məs) *n.* (*pl.* **mandamuses**) (*Law*) a writ or (now) order issued from a higher court directed to a person, corporation or inferior court, requiring them to do a particular thing relating to their office or duty. [L, we command (cp. MANDATE)]

mandarin (man´dərin) *n.* **1** (*also* **mandarine**) a mandarin orange. **2** a dark-yellow dye the colour of a mandarin orange. **3** a high-ranking public servant. **4** a Chinese official. **5** an influential, esp. reactionary (literary) figure. **6** a mandarin duck. **7** a liqueur flavoured with juice of the mandarin orange. **8** a grotesque ornament or statuette in Chinese costume. **9** (**Mandarin**) the chief dialect of the Chinese language. **mandarinate** *n.* **1** the office of a mandarin. **2** mandarins collectively. **mandarin collar** *n.* a stiff, narrow stand-up collar. **mandarin duck** *n.* a brightly-coloured Asiatic duck, *Aix galericulata*. **mandarin orange** *n.* **1** a small flattish sweet Chinese orange of a dark-yellow colour, a tangerine. **2** the tree bearing mandarins, *Citrus reticulata*. **mandarin sleeve** *n.* a wide loose sleeve. [Port. *mandarim*, from Malay and Hind. *mantrī*, Sansk., *mantrin*, counsellor, from *man*, to think, cogn. with MIND]

mandate (man´dāt) *n.* **1** an authoritative charge, order or command. **2** a direction from electors to a representative or a representative body to undertake certain legislation etc. **3** (*Law*) a judicial command to an officer or a subordinate court. **4** a contract of bailment by which a mandatary undertakes to perform gratuitously a duty regarding property committed to them. **5** a doctrinal or legal rescript of the Pope. **6** the authority given (esp. formerly by the League of Nations) to a larger power to govern another country in trust for its inhabitants. **7** a country ruled in this way. **mandatary** *n.* (*pl.* **mandataries**) a person or state etc. receiving a mandate. **mandator** (-dā´-) *n.* a person, body etc. issuing a mandate. **mandatory** *a.* **1** obligatory, compulsory. **2** containing, or of the nature of a mandate. **3** bestowing a mandate. ~*n.* (*pl.* **mandatories**) MANDATARY (under MANDATE). **mandatorily** *adv.* [L *mandātum*, neut. p.p. of *mandāre*, to command (*manus*, hand, *dare*, to give)]

Usage note The spellings of the noun *mandatary* (a person or state mandated) and the adjective *mandatory* (compulsory) should not be confused.

Mandelbrot set (man´dəlbrot) *n.* (*Math.*) a set of complex numbers which, when plotted, has a convoluted fractal boundary. [after B. B. *Mandelbrot*, Polish-American mathematician]

mandible (man´dibəl) *n.* the jaw, the lower jaw in vertebrates, the upper or lower in birds, and the pair in insects. **mandibular** (-dib´-), **mandibulate** (-lət), **mandibulated** (-lātid) *a.* [L *mandibula*, from *mandere*, to chew]

mandolin (man´dəlin), **mandoline** *n.* **1** a musical instrument with a deep almond-shaped body and two or three pairs of metal strings. **2** a kitchen utensil with metal strings or blades, for slicing vegetables. **mandolinist** *n.* [F *mandoline*, It. *mandolino*, dim. of *mandola*, *mandora*, var. of *pandora* (cp. BANDORE)]

mandorla (mandaw´lə) *n.* an area of light, oval but pointed in shape, surrounding a painting or sculpture of the risen Christ or of the Virgin at the Assumption. [It., almond]

†**mandragora** (mandrag´ərə) *n.* the mandrake. [OE and late L, from Gr. *mandragoras*]

mandrake (man´drāk) *n.* the poisonous plant *Mandragora officinarum*, having emetic and narcotic properties, the root of which was anciently believed to be like the human form and to shriek when pulled up. [ME *mandrage*, from MANDRAGORA (cp. Dut. *mandrage*)]

mandrel (man´drəl) *n.* **1** an arbor or axis of a lathe on which work is fixed for turning. **2** a cylindrical rod or core round which metal or other material is forged or shaped. **3** the revolving spindle of a circular saw. **4** a miner's pick. [perh. corr. of F *mandrin*]

mandrill (man´dril) *n.* a W African baboon, *Mandrillus sphinx*, which has a brightly-coloured face and blue hindquarters. [MAN, DRILL[1]]

manducate (man´dūkāt) *v.t.* to chew, to eat. **manducable** *a.* **manducation** (-kā´shən) *n.* **manducatory** *a.* [L *mandūcātus*, p.p. of *mandūcāre*, to chew]

mane (mān) *n.* **1** the long hair on the neck of some animals, such as the horse or (male) lion. **2** long, thick hair on a person's head. **maned** *a.* (*usu. in comb.*) having a mane, as *thick-maned*. **maneless** *a.* **manesheet** *n.* a covering for the upper part of a horse's head. [OE *manu* (cp. Dut. *mane*, Icel. *mōn*, pl. *manar*, G *Mähne*), cogn. with Sansk. *manyā*, nape of the neck, L *monīle*, necklace]

manège (manāzh´, -nezh´), **manege** *n.* **1** a school for training horses or teaching horsemanship. **2** the training of horses. **3** the movements of a trained horse. **4** horsemanship. [F]

manes (mā´nēz, mah´nāz) *n.pl.* **1** the spirits of the dead, esp. of ancestors worshipped as guardian divinities. **2** (*as sing.*) the shade of a deceased person regarded as an object of reverence. [L]

maneuver MANOEUVRE.

mangabey (mang´gəbā) *n.* a small long-tailed African monkey of the genus *Cercocebus*. [part of Madagascar]

manganese (mang´gənēz, -nēz´) *n.* a metallic element, at. no. 25, chem. symbol Mn, of a greyish-white colour. **manganate** (mang´-) *n.* a salt of manganic acid. **manganese oxide** *n.* the oxide of manganese, a black mineral used in glass-making. **manganesian** (-ē´-), **manganesic, manganic** (-gan´-), **manganous** *a.* **manganiferous** (-nif´-) *a.* **manganite** (mang´-) *n.* grey manganese ore. [F *manganèse*, corr. of MAGNESIA]

mange (mānj) *n.* a skin disease caused by a mite, occurring in cattle, dogs etc. **mangy** *a.* (*comp.* **mangier**, *superl.* **mangiest**) **1** infected with mange. **2** shabby, squalid. **mangily** *adv.* **manginess** *n.* [ME *manjewe*, OF *manjue*, from *manjuer* (F *manger*, to eat), L *mandūcāre*, to MANDUCATE]

mangel-wurzel (mang·gəlwœ´zəl), **mangold-wurzel** (-gəld-), **mangel** (mang´-), **mangold** *n.* a large-rooted variety of the common beet, *Beta vulgaris*, cultivated as fodder for cattle. [G *Mangoldwurzel* (*Mangold*, beet, *Wurzel*, root)]

manger (mān´jə) *n.* a trough for horses or cattle to eat out of. [OF *mangeure*, from *manger*, to eat, see MANGE]

mangetout (māzh´too, māzhtoo´) *n.* (*pl.* **mangetout, mangetouts** (māzh´too, māzhtoo´)) a type of pea which is eaten complete with the pod. [F, eat all]

mangle[1] (mang´gəl) *v.t.* **1** to lacerate, to mutilate, to disfigure by hacking. **2** to mar, to ruin, to destroy the symmetry or completeness of, by blundering etc. **mangler** *n.* [A-F *mangler*, *mahangler*, freq. of OF *mahaignier*, to MAIM]

mangle[2] (mang´gəl) *n.* **1** (*Hist.*) a rolling machine for pressing water out of washing, damp sheets etc. **2** (*N Am.*) a large rolling machine for ironing. ~*v.t.* to press or smooth in a mangle. [Dut. *mangel* (whence *mangelen*, to mangle), late L *manganum*, Gr. *manganon*, see MANGONEL]

mango (mang´gō) *n.* (*pl.* **mangoes**) **1** the fruit of an Indian tree, *Mangifera indica*. **2** (*also* **mango tree**) the tree bearing this. [Port. *manga*, Malay *mañggā*, Tamil *mānkāy* (*mān*, mango-tree, *kay*, fruit)]

mangold-wurzel MANGEL-WURZEL.

mangonel (mang´gənel) *n.* a medieval engine for throwing missiles. [OF, from late L *mangona*, *mango -ōnem*, Gr. *manganon*]

mangosteen (mang´gəstēn) *n.* **1** a Malaysian tree, *Garcinia mangostana*. **2** its orange-like fruit, with a sweet, juicy pulp. [Malay *manggustan*]

mangrove (mang´grōv) *n.* any tropical tree of the genus *Rhizophora*, growing in muddy places by the coast, the bark of which is used for medicine and in tanning. [etym. uncertain]

mangy MANGE.

manhattan (manhat´ən) *n.* a cocktail containing whisky, vermouth and sometimes a dash of bitters. [*Manhattan*, borough of New York City]

mania (mā´niə) *n.* **1** a form of mental disorder characterized by hallucination, emotional excitement and violence. **2** (*coll.*) an infatuation, a craze. **maniac** (-ak) *n.* **1** (*coll.*) a person exhibiting symptoms of wild, uncontrolled behaviour. **2** a person who suffers from mania. **3** (*coll.*) a person with an obsessive enthusiasm for a hobby, craze etc. ~*a.* affected with mania, insane, raving. **maniacal** (mənī´əkəl) *a.* **maniacally** *adv.* **manic** (man´ik) *a.* **1** of or affected by mania. **2** (*coll.*) overexcited, wildly energetic. **manic-depressive** *a.* suffering from or characterized by alternating bouts of mania and depression. ~*n.* a person with a manic-depressive illness. **manic depression** *n.* [L and Gr., cogn. with *mainesthai*, to be mad]

-mania (mā´niə) *comb. form* denoting special kinds of derangement, hallucination, infatuation or excessive enthusiasm, as in *erotomania, kleptomania, megalomania, monomania.* **-maniac** *comb. form* forming nouns and adjectives. [as MANIA]

Manichaean (manikē´ən), **Manichean** *a.* of or relating to Manichaeism. ~*n.* a believer in Manichaeism. **Manichaeism** (man´ikēizm) *n.* a religious doctrine, widely prevailing in the 3rd–5th cents., that the universe is controlled by two antagonistic powers, light or goodness, identified with God, and darkness, chaos or evil. **Manichee** *n.* [L *Manichaeus*, late Gr. *Manichaios*, from name of founder]

manicure (man´ikūə) *n.* **1** the care of the hands, fingernails etc. **2** a cosmetic treatment of the hands and fingernails. ~*v.t.* to give a manicure to. **manicurist** *n.* a person who undertakes the treatment of the hands and fingernails as a business. [F (L *manus*, hand, *cura*, care)]

manifest[1] (man´ifest) *a.* **1** not concealed, plainly apparent, clear, obvious. **2** †detected. ~*v.t.* **1** to make manifest, to show clearly. **2** to display, to exhibit, to evince. **3** to be evidence of. **4** to reveal or exhibit (itself). **5** to record in a ship's manifest. ~*v.i.* **1** (of a spirit) to reveal its presence. **2** to make a public demonstration of opinion. **manifestable** *a.* **manifestation** (-tā´shən) *n.* **1** manifesting or being manifested. **2** a public demonstration. **manifestative** (-fes´-) *a.* **manifestly** *adv.* **manifestness** *n.* [through F *manifeste* or directly from L *manifestus* (prob. *mani-*, *manu*, *manus*, hand, *festus*, struck, cogn. with DEFEND)]

manifest[2] (man´ifest) *n.* **1** a list of a ship's cargo for the use of customs officers. **2** a list of passengers on an aircraft. **3** a list of railway trucks, containers etc. or their cargo. **4** †a manifesto. [MANIFESTO]

manifesto (manifes´tō) *n.* (*pl.* **manifestos**) a public declaration, esp. by a political party, government, sovereign or other authoritative body, of opinions, motives or intentions. [It.]

manifold (man´ifōld) *a.* **1** of various forms or kinds. **2** many and various, abundant. **3** shown, applied or acting in various ways. ~*n.* **1** something which has many forms, parts etc. **2** a tube or system of tubes for conveying exhaust gases etc., in an engine, motor etc. **3** (*Math.*) a set, a collection of objects, a manifoldness. **4** (*Hist.*) a copy of a page, book etc. **manifoldly** *adv.* **manifoldness** *n.* **1** the state of being manifold. **2** (*Math.*) a conception of space or magnitude comprehending several particular concepts. **manifold writer** *n.* (*Hist.*) an apparatus for making several copies of a document at once. [OE *manigfeald*]

manikin (man´ikin), **mannikin** *n.* **1** a little man or a dwarf. **2** an anatomical model exhibiting the parts, organs and structure of the human body. **3** an artist's lay figure. **4** (*usu.* **mannikin**) an African and Australian bird of the genus *Lonchura*. **5** MANAKIN. [Dut. *manneken*, dim. of *man* (cp. F *mannequin*)]

Manila (mənil´ə), **Manilla** *n.* **1** a kind of cigar or cheroot made in Manila. **2** Manila hemp. **3** a rope of this. **4** (*also* **manila**) Manila paper. **Manila hemp** *n.* hemp made from the fibre of *Musa textilis*, used for making rope. **Manila paper** *n.* a strong brown paper, orig. made from Manila hemp. [capital of Philippine Islands]

manilla (manil´ə) *n.* **1** a metal ring worn by some Africans on the legs or arms. **2** a piece of metal shaped like a ring or horseshoe formerly used as a medium of exchange among the indigenous peoples of the W African coast. [Sp., from It. *maniglia* (perh. dim. of L *manus*, hand or from *monīlia*, pl. of *monīle*, necklace)]

manille (mənil´) *n.* in ombre or quadrille, the highest but one trump or honour. [corr. of Sp. *malilla*, dim. of *mala*, L *malus*, bad]

manioc (man´iok) *n.* **1** the cassava, *Manihot esculenta*, *M. dulcis* etc.. **2** flour made from the root of this. [Port., from Tupi-Guarani]

maniple (man´ipəl) *n.* **1** a strip worn as a Eucharistic vestment on a priest's left arm. **2** a subdivision of a Roman legion consisting of 60 to 120 men with their officers. **3** †a handful. **manipular**[1] (-nip´-) *a.* [OF, from L *manipulus*, handful (*mani-*, *manus-*, hand, *-pulus*, form of root *plē-*, to fill, as in *plēnus*, full)]

manipular[1] MANIPLE.

manipular[2] MANIPULATE.

manipulate (mənip´ūlāt) *v.t.* **1** to operate on with the hands, to handle. **2** to treat manually, esp. skilfully or dexterously. **3** to manage, influence or tamper with by artful or sly means. **4** (*Comput.*) to edit or move (data etc.). **5** to stimulate sexually by hand. ~*v.i.* to use the hands skilfully, as in scientific experiments etc. **manipulable** *a.* **manipulability** (-bil´-) *n.* **manipular**[2] *a.* **manipulatable** *a.* **manipulation** (-lā´shən) *n.* **manipulative, manipulatory** *a.* **1** of or relating to manipulation. **2** given to artful or sly managing or influencing for one's own ends. **manipulatively** *adv.* **manipulativeness** *n.* **manipulator** *n.* [prob. a back formation from *manipulation*, from F *manipuler*, from L *manipulus*, see MANIPLE]

Manit. *abbr.* Manitoba.

manitou (man´itoo) *n.* **1** among certain N American Indians, a spirit or being endowed with supernatural power. **2** an amulet, a fetish. [Algonquian *manitu*]

manky (man´ki) *a.* (*comp.* **mankier**, *superl.* **mankiest**) (*coll.*) **1** dirty, unpleasant, bad. **2** inferior, worthless.

manna (man´ə) *n.* **1** the food miraculously supplied to the Israelites in the wilderness. **2** divine food, spiritual nourishment, esp. the Eucharist. **3** a sweetish exudation, of a slightly laxative nature, from certain species of ash, esp. the manna-ash. **manna-ash** *n.* a S European ash tree, *Fraxinus ornus*. **manna-croup** *n.* coarse-ground granular wheatmeal, separated by bolting. **manna from heaven** *n.* anything very advantageous and unexpected. [late L and Gr., from Heb. *mān* (said to be from Heb. *mān hu*, what is this?; but more prob. the same as Arab. *mann*, applied to Hebrew or Persian manna)]

mannequin (man´ikin, -kwin) *n.* **1** a woman employed to wear and display clothes. **2** a window dummy. [F, a lay figure]

manner (man´ə) *n.* **1** the mode in which anything is done or happens. **2** method, style, mannerism. **3** practice, habit, use, custom. **4** demeanour, bearing, address. **5** (*pl.*) conduct in social interaction, behaviour, deportment. **6** (*pl.*) politeness, habits showing good breeding. **7** (*pl.*) general modes of life, social conditions. **8** †sort, kind. **all manner of** all kinds of. **by all manner of means** MEANS. **by no manner of means** MEANS. **in a manner of speaking** in a certain way, somewhat, so to speak. **to the manner born** **1** (as if) accustomed to something from birth. **2** (*Shak.*) born to follow a certain practice or custom. **mannered** *a.* **1** betraying mannerisms, affected. **2** (*usu. in comb.*) having a certain type of manners (*ill-mannered*). **mannerism** *n.* **1** an idiosyncrasy, the excessive adherence to the same manner or peculiarity. **2** peculiarity of style in art and architecture. **3** a style of Italian art of the later 16th cent., characterized by lengthened figures, distorted perspective etc. **mannerist** *n.* **manneristic** (-is´-), **manneristical** *a.* **manneristically** *adv.* **mannerless** *a.* devoid of manners or breeding. **mannerly** *a.* well-mannered, polite. ~*adv.* politely. **mannerliness** *n.* [OF *maniere*, from L *manuārius*, pertaining to the hand, from *manus*, hand]

mannikin MANIKIN.

mannish MAN.

mannite (man´īt), **mannitol** (-itol), **mannitose** (-itōs) *n.* a sweetish substance obtained from manna.

manoeuvre (mənoo´və), (*N Am.*) **maneuver** *n.* **1** a tactical movement or change of position by troops or warships. **2** (*pl.*) tactical exercises in imitation of war. **3** a contrived plan or action, a trick, a stratagem. ~*v.i.* **1** to perform manoeuvres. **2** to manage with skill. **3** to employ stratagem. ~*v.t.* **1** to move, drive or effect by means of strategy or skilful management. **2** to cause (troops) to perform manoeuvres. **3** to manipulate. **manoeuvrable** *a.* **manoeuvrability** (-bil´-) *n.* **manoeuvrer** *n.* [F, from late L *manopera*, from *manoperāre*, L *manū operārī* (*manū*, abl. of *manus*, hand, *operārī*, to work)]

manometer (mənom´itə) *n.* an instrument for measuring the pressure of a gas or liquid. **manometric** (manəmet´-) *a.* **manometry** (-nom´-) *n.* [F *manomètre* (Gr. *manos*, thin, rare, -METER[1])]

ma non troppo (mah non trop´ō) *adv.* (*Mus.*) but not too much. [It. TROPPO[1]]

manor (man´ə) *n.* **1** a large country house, usu. with an estate. **2** a landed estate consisting of a demesne and certain rights over lands held by freehold tenants etc., orig. a barony held by a lord and subject to the jurisdiction of his court-baron. **3** (*N Am.*) a tract of land occupied in perpetuity or for long terms by tenants who pay a fee-farm rent to the proprietor. **4** (*sl.*) a police district. **manor house** *n.* **manorial** (-naw´riəl) *a.* of or relating to a manor. [OF *manoir*, mansion, from L *manēre*, to remain, dwell]

manqué (mã´kā) *a.* having the potential to be, but not actually being, something specified (*actor manqué*). [F, having failed]

mansard roof (man´sahd) *n.* a roof with four sloping sides, the lower sections of which slope more steeply, giving space for attics. [F *mansarde* after F. *Mansard*, 1598–1666, French architect]

manse (mans) *n.* the residence of a clergyman, esp. a Presbyterian minister. [med. L *mansa*, a house, a farm, from *manēre*, to dwell, p.p. *mansus*]

-manship (mənship´) *comb. form* used to form nouns indicating skill, expertise or daring in a particular field, as in *penmanship*, *brinkmanship*.

mansion (man´shən) *n.* **1** a residence of considerable size and pretensions. **2** a manor house. **3** (*pl.*) a large building or set of buildings divided into residential flats. **4** (*poet.*) a place of abode. **mansion house** *n.* **1** a manor house. **2** (**Mansion House**) an official residence, esp. of the Lord Mayors in London and Dublin. [OF, from L *mansio*, *-ōnem*, as MANSE]

†**mansuete** (man´swēt) *a.* tame, gentle, meek. †**mansuetude** (-switūd) *n.* [L *mansuētus*, p.p. of *mansuescere*, to tame (*manus*, hand, *suescere*, to accustom)]

manta (man´tə), **manta ray** *n.* any of various very large fish of the family Mobulidae, esp. *Manta birostris*, with wide, winglike fins and feeding on plankton. [Sp., cloak, see MANTLE]

mantel (man´təl) *n.* **1** the ornamental facing round a fireplace with the shelf above it. **2** a mantelpiece. **3** a mantelshelf. **mantelpiece** *n.* a structure above and sometimes around a fireplace. **mantelshelf** *n.* (*pl.* **mantelshelves**) a shelf above a fireplace. **manteltree** *n.* a beam forming the lintel of a fireplace. [var. of MANTLE]

mantelet (mant´lət), **mantlet** *n.* **1** (*Hist.*) a short sleeveless cloak worn by women. **2** a bulletproof shield, enclosure or shelter for gunners. [OF, dim. of MANTLE]

mantic (man´tik) *a.* (*formal*) of or relating to prophecy or divination. [Gr. *mantikos*, from *mantis*, prophet]

-mantic -MANCY.

manticore (man´tikaw) *n.* a fabulous monster with a human head, a lion's body and the tail of a scorpion. [L *manticora*, Gr. *matichōras*, *mantichoras*, prob. from OPers.]

mantid (man´tid) *n.* MANTIS.

mantilla (mantil´ə) *n.* **1** a veil for the head and shoulders, worn in Spain and Italy. **2** a woman's light cloak or cape. [Sp., dim. of *manta*, MANTLE]

mantis (man´tis) *n.* (*pl.* **mantis, mantises**) any carnivorous orthopterous insect of the family Mantidae, esp. *Mantis religiosa*, which holds its forelegs as if in prayer lying in wait for other insects as prey. [Gr., prophet]

mantissa (mantis´ə) *n.* the decimal or fractional part of a logarithm. [L, makeweight]

mantle (man´təl) *n.* **1** a sleeveless cloak or loose outer garment. **2** a covering. **3** a conical or tubular network coated with refractory earth placed round a gas jet to give an incandescent light. **4** a covering or concealing skin, part or organ, such as the fold enclosing the viscera in molluscs. **5** the back and scapular feathers and coverts of a bird. **6** the layer of the earth between the crust and the core. **7** leadership, power or authority, esp. as handed on. ~*v.t.* **1** to clothe in or as a mantle. **2** to cover, to envelop, to conceal. ~*v.i.* **1** to be overspread or suffused (as with a blush). **2** (of a blush) to suffuse the cheeks. **3** (of liquids) to become covered or coated. **4** to stretch the wings (as a hawk on its perch). **mantle rock** *n.* unconsolidated rock at the earth's surface. **mantling** *a.* foaming, creamy, suffusing. ~*n.* (*Her.*) drapery or scrollwork round or behind a shield. [OF *mantel* (F *manteau*), L *mantellum*, from which also OE *mentel*]

mantlet MANTELET.

mantling MANTLE.

Mantoux test (mantoo´) *n.* (*Med.*) a test for past or present tuberculosis carried out by injecting tuberculin beneath the skin. [C. *Mantoux*, 1877–1956, French physician]

mantra (man´trə) *n.* **1** a word or phrase chanted inwardly in meditation, orig. a Hindu formula or charm. **2** a Vedic hymn of praise. [Sansk., from *man*, to think]

mantua (man´tūə) *n.* (*Hist.*) a woman's loose gown worn in the 17th and 18th cents. [corr. of F *manteau*, MANTLE, confused with *Mantua* in Italy]

manual (man´ūəl) *a.* **1** of or performed with the hands. **2** involving physical exertion (*manual labour*). **3** not mechanical or automatic (*manual gearbox*). ~*n.* **1** a book of instructions, a handbook. **2** any small book. **3** an organ keyboard played by the hands. **4** (*coll.*) a motor vehicle with a manual gearbox. **5** (*Mil.*) a manual exercise. **6** (*Hist.*) a service book, esp. that used by priests in the medieval church. **manual alphabet** *n.* FINGER ALPHABET (under FINGER). **manual exercise** *n.* the drill by which soldiers are taught to handle their rifles etc. properly. **manually** *adv.* [F *manuel*, L *manuālis*, from *manus*, hand]

manubrium (mənū´briəm) *n.* (*pl.* **manubria** (-ə), **manubriums**) **1** (*Zool.*) any handle-shaped part or process, such as the presternum in mammals or the peduncle hanging down from medusae such as the jellyfish. **2** the handle of an organ stop. **manubrial** *a.* [L, a haft, a handle from *manus*, hand]

manufacture (manūfak´chə) *n.* **1** the making of articles by means of labour or machinery, esp. on a large scale, industrial production. **2** any particular branch of this. **3** (*pl.*) the products of industry or any particular industry. **4** (*derog.*) the production of anything without much thought or imagination. ~*v.t.* **1** to produce or fashion by labour or machinery, esp. on a large scale. **2** to make or work up into suitable forms for use. **3** to fabricate, to invent (a story, evidence etc.). **4** to produce (pictures, literature etc.) in a mechanical way. ~*v.i.* to be occupied in manufacture. **manufactory** *n.* (*pl.* **manufactories**) a factory. **manufacturable** *a.* **manufacturability** (-bil´-) *n.* **manufacturer** *n.* **manufacturing** *n.* [F, from L *manū*, by hand, abl. of *manus*, hand, *factūra*, from *facere*, to make]

manuka (mah´nukə, manoo´kə) *n.* a New Zealand tea-tree, *Leptospernum scoparium*. [Maori]

manumit (manūmit´) *v.t.* (*pres.p.* **manumitting,** *past, p.p.* **manumitted**) (*Hist.*) to release from slavery. **manumission** *n.* [L *manūmittere* (*manū*, abl. of *manus*, hand, *mittere*, to send)]

manure (mənūə´) *n.* **1** animal dung, esp. that of horses, used to fertilize land for cultivation. **2** any substance, including compost or chemical preparations, used to fertilize land. ~*v.t.* to enrich (a soil) with fertilizing substances. †**manurance** *n.* **1** manuring. **2** cultivation or tillage. **3** (*Law*) tenure or occupation. **manurer** *n.* **manurial** *a.* [corr. of MANOEUVRE]

manus (mā´nəs) *n.* (*pl.* **manus**) the hand or a corresponding part in an animal. [L]

manuscript (man´ūskript) *n.* **1** a book or document written by hand, not printed. **2** an author's text in its original state, as submitted for publication. **3** handwritten copy or form. ~*a.* written by hand. **manuscript paper** *n.* paper for writing music on, printed with staves. [med. L *manuscriptus* (*manū*, abl. of *manus*, hand, *scriptus*, p.p. of *scrībere*, to write)]

☒ **manuver** common misspelling of MANOEUVRE.

Manx (mangks) *a.* of or relating to the Isle of Man, its inhabitants or its language. ~*n.* **1** (*pl.*) the people of the Isle of Man. **2** the Celtic language formerly spoken by natives of the Isle of Man. **Manx cat** *n.* a tailless variety of domestic cat. **Manxman** *n.* (*pl.* **Manxmen**). **Manx shearwater** *n.* a long-winged black and white shearwater, *Puffinus puffinus*, of the N Atlantic. **Manxwoman** *n.* (*pl.* **Manxwomen**). [earlier *Maniske*, Icel. *manskr*]

many (men´i) *a.* numerous, comprising a great number. ~*n.* **1** a multitude. **2** a great number. **a good many** a large number. **a great many** a very great number. **as many** the same number of (*six ambulances and as many police cars*). **as many again** the same number in addition (*ten there and as many again here*). **many a one** many individuals. **many a time** often, many times. **many's the time** often. **the many 1** the majority. **2** the multitude, the common crowd. **to have one too many** to become drunk. **too many 1** superfluous, not wanted, in the way. **2** (*coll.*) too clever, too able or skilful (for). **manyfold** *adv.* by many times (*The investment increased manyfold in value*). **many-headed** *a.* (of a mob etc.) fickle. **many-headedness** *n.* **many-sided** *a.* **1** having many sides, aspects etc. **2** widely sympathetic, versatile, liberal. **many-sidedness** *n.* [OE *manig* (cp. Dut. *menig*, Dan. *mange*, G *manch*)]

manyplies (men´iplīz) *n.* the third stomach of a ruminant, the omasum. [MANY, *plies*, pl. of PLY[1]]

manzanilla (manzənil´ə, -thənē´lyə) *n.* a very dry sherry. [Sp., camomile]

manzanita (manzənē´tə) *n.* any of several evergreen shrubs of the genus *Arctostaphylos*, esp. *A. manzanita* of California. [Sp., dim. of *manzana*, apple]

Maoism (mow´izm) *n.* (*Hist.*) the political thought expounded by the Chinese communist leader Mao Zedong, 1893–1976. **Maoist** *n.*, *a.* (an adherent) of Maoism.

Maori (mow´ri) *n.* (*pl.* **Maori, Maoris**) **1** any of the Polynesian original inhabitants of New Zealand. **2** their language. ~*a.* of or relating to the Maoris or their language. **Maori hen** *n.* the flightless woodhen of New Zealand, the weka. †**Maoriland** *n.* New Zealand. †**Maorilander** *n.* a white inhabitant of New Zealand. **Maoritanga** (-tahng´ə) *n.* Maori culture.

map (map) *n.* **1** a representation of a portion of the earth's surface or the heavens or the surface of a planet etc. on a two-dimensional surface. **2** any delineation or diagram of a route etc. **3** (*Biol.*) a diagram of the genes on a chromosome or the bases in a molecule. **4** a mathematical function. **5** (*sl.*) the face. ~*v.t.* (*pres.p.* **mapping,** *past, p.p.* **mapped**) **1** to represent or set down in a map. **2** to plan (out) in exact detail. **3** (*Math.*) to assign (each of the elements of a set) to each of the elements in a different set. **off the map 1** (*coll.*) of no account, not worth consideration, remote. **2** out of the way. **on the map** important, well-known. **to map out** to plan in detail, to lay out a plan of. **to wipe off the map** WIPE. **mapless** *a.* **maplike** *a.* **map-maker** *n.* a person who makes maps. **map-making** *n.* **mappable** *a.* **mapper** *n.* **map-read** *v.i.* to look at and interpret a map. **map-reader** *n.* **map-reading** *n.* **map reference** *n.* a set of co-ordinates giving a location on a particular map. [L *mappa*, orig. napkin]

maple (mā´pəl) *n.* **1** (*also* **maple tree**) a tree or shrub of the genus *Acer*. **2** the wood of this. **maple leaf** *n.* the leaf of the maple, used as an emblem of Canada. **maple sugar** *n.* a coarse sugar obtained from the sugar maple *Acer saccharum* and other maples. **maple syrup** *n.* a syrup produced from the sap of the sugar maple and other maples. [OE in *mapulder* and *mapeltrēow*]

maquette (maket´) *n.* **1** a sculptor's preliminary model in clay, wax etc. **2** a preliminary sketch. [F, from It. *machietta*, little spot]

maqui (makē´) *n.* a Chilean evergreen shrub, *Aristotelia chilensis*, the berries of which produce a medicinal wine. [Chilean Sp.]

maquillage (makēyahzh´) *n.* **1** make-up, cosmetics. **2** the technique of applying cosmetics. [F]

Maquis (makē´) *n.* (*pl.* **Maquis**) **1** those surreptitiously resisting the German invaders of France etc., in 1940–45. **2** a member of the French resistance. **3** (**maquis**) scrub or bush in Corsica and other Mediterranean coastal regions. [F, brushwood, from Corsican It. *macchia*, thicket]

Mar. *abbr.* March.

mar (mah) *v.t.* (*pres.p.* **marring,** *past, p.p.* **marred**) **1** to spoil, to impair; to disfigure. **2** †to ruin. ~*n.* a blemish, a drawback. †**marplot** *n.* a person who spoils a plot or undertaking by interference. [OE *merran* (cp. MDut. *merren*, to hinder, Dut. *marren*, to tarry)]

marabou (mar´əboo), **marabout** *n.* **1** a W African stork, *Leptoptilos crumeniferus*, the downy feathers from under the wings and tail of which are used for trimming hats etc. **2** a tuft of feathers used in this way. [from MARABOUT[2], because of Islamic belief that the stork is a holy bird]

marabout[1] MARABOU.

marabout[2] (mar´əboot, -boo) *n.* **1** a Muslim hermit or saint, esp. one of a priestly caste in N Africa. **2** the tomb or dwelling of such a saint. [F, from Port. *marabuto*, Arab. *murābit*]

maraca (mərak´ə) *n.* a hollow gourd or shell containing beads, shot etc. shaken, usu. in a pair, as a percussive accompaniment to music, esp. in Latin America. [Port. *maracá*, from Tupi]

maraschino (marəskē´nō, -shē´-) *n.* (*pl.* **maraschinos**) a cordial or liqueur distilled from bitter cherries grown in Dalmatia. **maraschino cherry** *n.* a cherry preserved in maraschino etc., used in cocktails. [It., a. from *marasca, amarasca*, a sharp black cherry, from *amaro*, L *amārus*, bitter]

marasmus (məraz´məs) *n.* wasting away of the body. **marasmic** *a.* [Gr. *marasmos*, from *marainein*, to wither away]

Maratha (mərah´tə), **Mahratta** (-rat´ə) *n.* a member of a people of SW India, esp. the state of Maharashtra. **Marathi** *n.* their Sanskritic language.

marathon (mar´əthən) *n.* **1** a long-distance race, usu. a running race, of 26 miles 385 yards (42.195 km). **2** any task or contest requiring great endurance. **marathoner** *n.* [*Marathon* in Greece, from where a messenger is said to have run to Athens with news of a victory over the Persians in 490 BC]

maraud (mərawd´) *v.i.* **1** to make a plundering raid (on). **2** to rove in quest of plunder. ~*v.t.* to plunder. ~†*n.* a raid, a foray. **marauder** *n.* [F *marauder*, from *maraud*, rogue, etym. uncertain]

maravedi (marəvā´di) *n.* (*pl.* **maravedis**) (*Hist.*) **1** a former Spanish copper coin of low value. **2** a former Spanish gold coin. [Sp. from Arab. *Murābitīn*, pl. of *murābit*, MARABOUT², the name of a Moorish dynasty at Córdoba, 1087–1147]

marble (mah´bəl) *n.* **1** a fine-grained or crystalline limestone often polished for decorative use in sculpture or building. **2** (*usu. pl.*) a piece of sculpture in this material. **3** a type of smoothness, hardness or inflexibility. **4** a small ball of marble, glass or other hard substance used in a game, played esp. by children. **5** (*pl.*) a game which involves rolling a marble along the ground in order to hit another and so win it. **6** (*pl., coll.*) sanity, wits (*to lose one's marbles*). ~*v.t.* to stain or vein (end-papers of books etc.) to look like marble. ~*a.* **1** composed of marble. **2** veined like marble. **3** hard, unfeeling. **4** †pure, clear. **marble cake** *n.* a cake made with light and dark sponge to have a mottled appearance. **marbled** *a.* **1** (of a book, soap etc.) stained to look like marble. **2** (of meat) streaked with veins of fat amongst lean. **marbled white** *n.* a butterfly, *Melanargia galathea*, with whitish wings and black markings. **marble-hearted** *a.* hard-hearted. **marbleize, marbleise** *v.t.* **marbler** *n.* **marbling** *n.* **1** the veined or speckled appearance of marble. **2** the presence of veins of fat amongst lean meat. **marbly** *a.* [OF *marbre*, L *marmor*, cogn. with Gr. *marmaros*, sparkling, *marmairein*, to sparkle, to glisten]

marc (mahk) *n.* **1** the compressed residue of grapes left after pressing, in the making of wine or oil. **2** brandy made from this. [F *marcher*, to tread]

Marcan (mah´kən) *a.* of or relating to St Mark. [L *Marcus*, Mark]

marcasite (mah´kəsīt) *n.* pyrites, esp. a white orthorhombic form of iron pyrites, used for making ornaments. [med. L *marcasīta*, etym. uncertain]

marcato (mahkah´tō) *a.* (*Mus.*) (of notes) heavily accented. ~*adv.* (played) with a heavy accent. [It. *marcare*, to mark]

marcel (mahsel´) *n.* (*Hist.*) a style of permanent wave in hairdressing. ~*v.t.* (*pres.p.* **marcelling**, *past, p.p.* **marcelled**) to style (hair) with a deep permanent wave. **marcel wave** *n.* a permanent wave. ~*v.t.* to perm. [*Marcel* Grateau, 1852–1936, a French hairdresser]

marcescent (mahses´ənt) *a.* (of blooms, leaves etc.) withering without falling. **marcescence** *n.* [L *marcescēns -entem*, pres.p. of *marcescere*, freq. of *marcēre*, to wither]

March (mahch) *n.* the third month of the year. **March hare** *n.* a hare during its breeding season in March, characterized by leaping, gambolling and otherwise strange behaviour. [A-F *marche* (F *mars*), from L *Martius*, pertaining to Mars]

march¹ (mahch) *v.i.* **1** to move with regular steps like a soldier. **2** to walk in a grave, deliberate or determined manner. **3** to continue steadily (*The years marched by*). **4** to participate in a protest march. ~*v.t.* to cause to move (on, off etc.) in a military order or manner. ~*n.* **1** the act of marching. **2** a stately, deliberate or measured movement, esp. of soldiers. **3** the distance marched or walked in a particular period of time. **4** progress, advance. **5** (*Mus.*) a composition for accompanying a march or one in a similar style. **on the march 1** advancing steadily. **2** making progress. **to march past** to carry out a march past. **to steal a march on 1** to get to an objective before, to start in advance of. **2** to gain an advantage over. **marcher¹** *n.* **marching order** *n.* (*Mil.*) the formation or equipment for a march. **marching orders** *n.pl.* **1** (*Mil.*) instructions for service personnel to proceed to war. **2** (*coll.*) instructions by which a worker, lodger etc. is required to leave their job, lodging etc., a dismissal. **march past** *n.* a marching of troops in a review past a superior officer etc. [F *marcher*, etym. uncertain]

march² (mahch) *n.* **1** (*pl.*) the frontier or boundary of a territory. **2** (*often pl.*) a borderland or debatable land between two countries, as the border country of England and Wales (*the Welsh Marches*). ~*v.i.* to border (upon) or have a common frontier (with). **marcher²** *n.* **1** an inhabitant of a march. **2** an officer or warden having jurisdiction over marches. [F *marche*, MARK¹]

marcher¹ MARCH¹.

marcher² MARCH².

marchioness (mah´shənes) *n.* **1** the wife or widow of a marquess. **2** a woman holding this rank in her own right. [low L *marchiōnissa*, from *marchio -ōnem*, MARQUESS; see MARQUIS]

†**marchpane** MARZIPAN.

Mardi Gras (mahdi grah´) *n.* **1** Shrove Tuesday. **2** the carnival celebrated at this time. [F, fat Tuesday]

mardy (mah´di) *a.* (*coll.*) spoilt, sulky, lacking in toughness. [*marred*, MAR]

mare¹ (meə) *n.* **1** the female of the horse or other equine animal. **2** (*sl., offensive*) a woman. **mare's-nest** *n.* **1** a discovery that turns out a hoax or a delusion. **2** a complex state of affairs. **mare's-tail** *n.* **1** an aquatic plant, *Hippuris vulgaris*. **2** (*pl.*) long fibrous cirrus clouds, similar in appearance to horses' tails. [OE *mere* (cp. Dut. *merrie*, Icel. *merr*, G *Mähre*)]

mare² (mah´rā, -ri) *n.* (*pl.* **maria** (mah´riə), **mares**) **1** any of the darkish areas on the moon or other planets etc. **2** (*Law*) the sea. **mare clausum** (klow´zum) *n.* (*Law*) the sea area under the jurisdiction of a country. **mare liberum** (lē´bərum) *n.* (*Law*) the open sea, not under the jurisdiction of any one country. [L, sea]

maremma (mərem´ə) *n.* (*pl.* **maremme** (-mā)) a marshy and usu. unhealthy region by the seashore. [It.]

margaric (mahgar´ik) *a.* **1** resembling pearl, pearly. **2** of or relating to pearl. [Gr. *margar*, in *margaritēs*, pearl]

margarine (mahjərēn´, -gər-, mah´-) *n.* an emulsion of edible oils and fat with water, skimmed milk or other substances with or without the addition of colouring matter, used for the same purposes as butter. [F *margarin*]

margarita (mahgərē´tə) *n.* a cocktail made from tequila and lemon (or other fruit) juice. [from the woman's name]

margarite (mah´gərīt) *n.* **1** pearl mica, a hydrous silicate. **2** †a pearl. [OF, from L *margarīta*, as MARGARIC]

margay (mah´gā) *n.* a Brazilian wildcat, *Felis wiedi*. [F, from Tupi *mbaracaïa*]

marge¹ (mahj) *n.* (*coll.*) short for MARGARINE.

marge² (mahj) *n.* (*poet.*) MARGIN.

margin (mah´jin) *n.* **1** an edge, a border, a brink. **2** the blank space round the printed matter on a page. **3** a line drawn in an exercise book etc. to mark off a margin. **4** the space of time or the range of conditions within which a thing is just possible. **5** an allowance of time, money, space etc. for contingencies, growth etc. **6** the difference between cost and selling price. **7** a sum deposited with a broker as protection against loss. **8** the lowest amount of profit allowing an industry etc. to continue. **9** (*Austral.*) a differential paid for skill etc. ~*v.t.* (*pres.p.* **margining**, *past, p.p.* **margined**) **1** to furnish with a margin. **2** to enter on the margin. ~*v.i.* to deposit margin on stock. **marginate¹** (-nət), **marginated** (-nātid) *a.* **1** having a margin. **2** edged. **marginate²** (-nāt) *v.t.* **1** to provide with a margin. **2** to marginalize. **margination** (-ā´shən) *n.* **margin of error** *n.* in assessing the feasibility, time, cost etc. of an action, project etc., the amount of latitude allowed for possible miscalculation, changing circumstances etc. **margin release** *n.* a facility on a typewriter allowing a word to be typed beyond the normal margin. [L *margo -ginis*]

marginal (mah´jinəl) *a.* **1** of or relating to or at the margin. **2** near the limit. **3** written or printed on the margin. **4** (*coll.*) small, slight (*a marginal chance*). **5** (of land) difficult to cultivate. **6** (of the sea) next to the shore in territorial waters. *~n.* a marginal constituency or parliamentary seat. **marginal constituency** *n.* a parliamentary constituency where there is only a small difference between the totals of votes cast for the parties of the leading candidates. **marginal cost** *n.* the additional cost of making one more of a particular product. **marginalia** (-ā´liə) *n.pl.* marginal notes. **marginality** (-nal´-) *n.* **marginalize, marginalise** *v.t.* **1** to reduce in influence, power, importance etc. **2** to cause to seem irrelevant. **marginalization** (-zā´shən) *n.* **marginally** *adv.*

margrave (mah´grāv) *n.* (*Hist.*) a German title of nobility, orig. a lord or governor of a march or border province. **margravate** (-grəvət), **margraviate** (-grā´viət) *n.* **margravine** (-grəvēn) *n.* the wife or widow of a margrave. [Dut. *markgrave* (now *markgraaf*)]

marguerite (mahgərēt´) *n.* the ox-eye daisy and other wild or cultivated varieties of chrysanthemum. [F, from L *margarīta*, L, Gr. *margarītēs*, from *margaron*, pearl]

maria MARE[2].

mariage de convenance (mariahzh´ de kõvənãs) *n.* (*pl.* **mariages de convenance** (mariahzh´)) a marriage of convenience.

Marian (meə´riən) *a.* **1** of or relating to the Virgin Mary. **2** of or relating to Mary I of England or Mary Queen of Scots. [L *Marīa*, -AN]

mariculture (mar´ikŭlchə) *n.* the cultivation of marine organisms in their own natural environment. [L *mare*, the sea, CULTURE]

marigold (mar´igōld) *n.* any plant of the genus *Calendula* or *Tagetes*, usu. bearing bright yellow or orange flowers. **marsh marigold** MARSH. [*Mary*, the Virgin Mary, GOLD]

marijuana (mariwah´nə), **marihuana** *n.* **1** dried leaves, flowering tops and stems of Indian hemp, usu. used to make cigarettes smoked as a narcotic. **2** Indian hemp. [Sp.]

marimba (mərim´bə) *n.* a musical instrument similar to a xylophone. [Congolese]

marina (mərē´nə) *n.* a system of sheltered moorings designed mainly for pleasure boats. [It. and Sp., fem. of *marino*, from L *marinus*, marine]

marinade (marinād´) *n.* **1** a mixture of vinegar, oil etc. flavoured with wine, spices etc. for soaking fish or meat prior to cooking. **2** fish or meat soaked in this. *~v.t.* to marinate. **marinate** (mar´ināt) *v.t.* to soak (meat, fish etc.) in a marinade. **marination** (-ā´shən) *n.* [F, from Sp. *marinada*, from *marinar*, to pickle in brine, from *marino*, as MARINE]

marine (mərēn´) *a.* **1** of or relating to, found in or produced by the sea. **2** used at sea or in navigation, nautical, naval. **3** serving on board ship. *~n.* **1** the shipping, fleet or navy of a country (*merchant marine*). **2** a member of a body of troops for service on board warships. **3** a member of the Royal Marines, the US Marine Corps etc., a specialist in amphibious military operations. **4** a seascape. **horse marine** HORSE. **mercantile marine** MERCANTILE. **tell that to the marines** an expression of incredulity and derision (from the sailor's contempt for landsmen). **marine glue** *n.* an adhesive made of rubber, shellac and oil which resists the action of water. **marine stores** *n.pl.* **1** a place where old ship's stores are bought and sold. **2** old ship's materials as articles of merchandise. **marine trumpet** *n.* a large viol with a single string making a trumpet-like sound. [F *marin*, fem. *-ine*, L *marīnus*, from *mare*, the sea]

mariner (mar´inə) *n.* a seaman, a sailor. **mariner's compass** *n.* a magnetic compass indicating bearings from true or magnetic north. [MARINE]

Mariolatry (meəriol´ətri) *n.* (*derog.*) idolatrous worship of the Virgin Mary. **Mariolater** *n.* [Gr. *Maria*, Mary, -LATRY]

marionette (máriənet´) *n.* a puppet moved by strings. [F *marionnette*, dim. of *Marion*, dim. of *Marie*, Mary]

†**marish** (mar´ish) *a.* marshy. [OF *mareis*, *maresche*, med. L *mariscus*, MARSH]

Marist (meə´rist) *n.* a member of the Roman Catholic order of Mary for teaching and foreign missions. *~a.* **1** of or relating to this order. **2** devoted to the Virgin Mary.

marital (mar´itəl) *a.* **1** of or relating to marriage. **2** of or relating to a husband. **maritally** *adv.* [F, from L *marītālis*, from *marītus*, husband]

maritime (mar´itīm) *a.* **1** of or relating to, connected with or bordering on the sea. **2** (of countries, cities etc.) having a navy or commerce by sea. [F, from L *maritimus* (*mare*, the sea, *-timus*, cp. *ultimus*)]

marjoram (mah´jərəm) *n.* an aromatic herb of the mint family, esp. wild or sweet marjoram. **sweet marjoram** SWEET. **wild marjoram** WILD. [OF *marjorane*, med. L *majorāna*, etym. uncertain]

mark[1] (mahk) *n.* **1** a visible sign or impression, such as a stroke, cut, dot etc. **2** an indication, symbol, character, device or token. **3** a model, brand or type (*Jaguar Mark X*). **4** a number or sign indicating merit in an examination. **5** a distinguishing feature, a characteristic, a symptom. **6** a limit, a standard. **7** a starting line in a race. **8** the point to be reached. **9** a distinguishing sign, a seal etc. **10** a character made by a person who cannot write, a signature. **11** a target, an object to aim at. **12** (*coll.*) a victim, esp. of fraud. **13 a** in rugby, an indentation made in the ground by the heel of a player who has secured a fair catch. **b** in Australian Rules football, a fair catch of a ball kicked at least ten metres; the place from which the next kick is taken. **14** a boundary, frontier or limit. **15** in boxing, the pit of the stomach. **16** †a tract of land held in common by the ancient Teutonic community. *~v.t.* **1** to make a mark on. **2** to distinguish or designate or indicate, by a mark or marks. **3** to award marks to (a student's work etc.). **4** to indicate or serve as a mark to. **5** to characterize, to be a feature of. **6** to express or produce by marks. **7** to record as a score (points in games). **8** to select, to single out. **9** to pay heed to. **10** in football, hockey etc., to keep close to (an opponent) so as to make it difficult for them to receive the ball. **11** in Australian Rules football, to catch (the ball). **12** (*Austral.*, *New Zeal.*) to castrate (a lamb). *~v.i.* to observe something critically, to take note. **below the mark** not of the desired standard, unsatisfactory. **beside the mark** wide of the mark. **dead on the mark** absolutely straight. **mark you** (*coll.*) please note (*Mark you, it will soon be raining*). **not up to the mark** below the mark. **off the mark 1** making a start. **2** wide of the mark. **of mark** noteworthy. **on the mark** accurate, straight. **on your marks** an order from the starter in a race for runners to take their position on the starting line. **to make one's mark** to do something that brings fame, recognition etc. **to mark down 1** to lower the price of. **2** to make a note of. **3** to decide to victimize. **4** to award a lower mark to. **to mark off** to separate (one thing from another), to set boundaries. **to mark out 1** to set out (boundaries and levels) for a proposed building. **2** to set out (lines and marks) on material as a guide for cutting, drilling or other operations. **3** to set out plans for. **4** to destine. **to mark time 1** (*Mil.*) to move the feet alternately as in marching, without changing position. **2** to pause until further progress can be made. **3** to do something just to pass time. **to mark up 1** to raise the price of. **2** to write alterations or instructions on for keying etc. **to toe the mark 1** to do one's duty, to perform one's obligations. **2** (*Mil.*) to touch a chalk line with the toes so as to be in rank abreast with others. **up**

to the mark up to standard, satisfactory. **wide of the mark 1** not hitting the target. **2** not to the point, irrelevant. **markdown** *n.* the amount by which a price is reduced. **marked** *a.* **1** noticeable, definite (*a marked improvement*). **2** (of a person) destined to suffer misfortune, attack, suspicion etc. **3** having a visible or distinctive mark. **4** having natural markings of a specified kind. **markedly** (-kid-) *adv.* **marked man** *n.* **1** a person whose conduct is being scrutinized, esp. with suspicion or hostility. **2** a person apparently destined to succeed, because of recognition by superiors. **markedness** (-kid-) *n.* **marker** *n.* **1** a person who marks. **2** an object placed to mark a position, distance etc. **3** a felt-tipped pen used for labelling etc. **4** a person who notes the score at billiards, snooker etc. **5** a counter used in card-playing. **6** a bookmark. **7** a source of light identifying the target of a bomb etc. **8** (*N Am.*) an IOU. **marking** *n.* **1** (*often in pl.*) a mark or pattern of colouring, esp. on an animal or natural object. **2** the activity of assessing the work of pupils, students etc. **3** the making of a mark or marks. **marking-ink** *n.* an indelible ink for marking linen etc. **mark-up** *n.* the amount by which a cost price is increased to cover overheads, profit etc. [OE *mearc* (cp. Dut. *mark*, neut. *merk*, Icel. *mark*, G *Mark*, neut. *Marke*, Gmc. *markā*), from which *mearcian*, to mark]

mark² (mahk) *n.* **1** a German unit of currency, the Deutschmark or (formerly) Ostmark. **2** any of various German coins of differing values. **3** (*Hist.*) English money of account valued at two thirds of a pound sterling. **4** (*Hist.*) a unit of weight (about ½ or ⅔lb) (227 or 300g) formerly used for gold and silver. [OE *marc* (Icel. *mörk*, Dan., Swed., Dut. *mark*, G *Mark*)]

market (mah´kit) *n.* **1** an open space or large building in which cattle, provisions or other commodities are offered for sale. **2** demand for a commodity; value as determined by this. **3** a geographical or commercial area regarded as suitable for buying and selling commodities in general or a particular form of merchandise. **4** a meeting for buying and selling. **5** a stock market. ~*v.i.* (*pres.p.* **marketing,** *past, p.p.* **marketed**) to buy or sell in a market. ~*v.t.* **1** to sell or attempt to sell (a product). **2** to sell in a market. **to be in the market for** to be ready to purchase or acquire (a particular item, commodity etc.). **to come into the market** to be offered for sale. **to make a market** to cause active dealing in a stock or shares. **to play the market** PLAY. **to put on the market** to offer for sale. **marketable** *a.* **marketability** (-bil´-), **marketableness** *n.* **marketably** *adv.* **market cross** *n.* a cross or other stone structure set up in a market place. **market day** *n.* a certain day or days of the week on which a market is regularly held in a town. **marketeer** (-iə´) *n.* a supporter of Britain's membership of the EU. **marketer** *n.* **market garden** *n.* a plot of land on which vegetables and fruit are raised for market. **market gardener** *n.* **marketing** *n.* the processes involved in selling goods, e.g. promotion, distribution etc. **market maker** *n.* a dealer in securities on the Stock Exchange who combines the roles of stockbroker and stockjobber. **market place** *n.* **1** an open space where a public market is held. **2** the sphere of commercial trading. **market price, market rate** *n.* the current price or rate in dealings. **market research** *n.* research into public demand, need etc. for particular commercial goods. **market researcher** *n.* **market square** *n.* a square in a town where a public market is held. **market town** *n.* a town which holds a regular public market. **market value** *n.* the price that something would fetch if it were offered for sale. [late OE and ONF (F *marché*), from L *mercātus*, p.p. of *mercārī*, to trade (cp. MERCANTILE)]

markhor (mah´kaw) *n.* a wild Himalayan mountain goat, *Capra falconeri*. [Pers. *mārkhōr*, serpent-eater]

markka (mah´kə) *n.* the standard unit of currency in Finland. [MARK²]

Markov chain (mah´kov, -kof) *n.* a sequence of events in which the probability of each event is dependent on the event immediately preceding it. [Andrei *Markov*, 1856–1922, Russian mathematician]

marksman (mahks´mən) *n.* (*pl.* **marksmen**) a person who shoots well. **marksmanship** *n.* **markswoman** *n.* (*pl.* **markswomen**) a female marksman.

marl¹ (mahl) *n.* soil containing clay and lime, much used as a fertilizer. ~*v.t.* to manure with marl. **marlite** (mah´līt) *n.* a variety of marl that remains solid after exposure to the air. **marlitic** (-lit´-) *a.* **marlpit** *n.* **marlstone** *n.* strata of sandy limestone with ironstone etc. dividing the upper from the lower Lias clays. **marly** *a.* [OF *marle*, late L *margila*, dim. of *marga*, perh. from Gaulish]

marl² (mahl) *n.* a yarn with different coloured threads, used to make a mottled fabric. [abbr. of *marbled*, see MARBLE]

marlin (mah´lin) *n.* any of various large oceanic fishes of the genera *Makaira* and *Tetrapterus*, with a long upper jaw. **marline** (mah´lin) *n.* (*Naut.*) a small two-stranded line, used for lashing etc. **marlinspike, marline-spike** *n.* a pointed iron pin for opening the strands of rope in splicing. [Dut. *marlijn* (*marren*, to tie, LINE¹)]

marmalade (mah´məlād) *n.* a jam or preserve prepared from fruit, esp. oranges or lemons, boiled with the sliced rind. **marmalade cat** *n.* a cat having streaks of orange and brown in its fur. [F *marmelade*, Port. *marmelada* (*marmelo*, quince, L *melimēlum*, Gr. *melimēlon*, from *meli*, honey, and *mēlon*, apple)]

Marmite® (mah´mīt) *n.* a savoury yeast extract used as a spread or for flavouring.

marmite (mah´mīt, -mēt´) *n.* an earthenware cooking pot. [F]

marmoreal (mahmaw´riəl), **marmorean** (-ən) *a.* **1** made of marble. **2** (*poet.*) like marble, esp. cold, smooth or polished, pure white. **marmoreally** *adv.* [L *marmoreus*, from *marmor*, MARBLE]

marmoset (mah´məzet) *n.* a small tropical American monkey of various species belonging to the family Callithricidae, called squirrel-monkeys from their bushy tails. [OF, a grotesque image (etym. uncertain, prob. conn. with *marmot*, a little child)]

marmot (mah´mət) *n.* any burrowing squirrel-like rodent of the genus *Marmota*, in N America the woodchuck. [F *marmotte*, Romansch *murmont* (L *mūrem*, nom. *mūs*, MOUSE¹, *montis*, gen. of *mons*, MOUNTAIN)]

marocain (mar´əkān) *n.* a cloth similar in structure to crêpe de Chine, but made from coarser yarns. [F *maroquin*, from *Maroc*, Morocco]

Maronite (mar´ənīt) *n.* a member of a Christian sect whose home is the Lebanon region. [late L *Marōnīta*, from *Marōn*, a 5th-cent. Syrian monk, the founder, or the 7th-cent. patriarch of the same name]

maroon¹ (məroon´) *a.* of a brownish-crimson colour. ~*n.* **1** this colour. **2** a detonating explosive device, often used as a warning signal. [F *marron*, It. *marrone*, chestnut, etym. unknown]

maroon² (məroon´) *v.t.* **1** to put ashore and abandon on a desolate island. **2** to leave isolated or unable to leave. ~*n.* **1** a descendant of fugitive slaves in the W Indies and Guyana. **2** a person who has been marooned. [F *marron*, fugitive, corr. of Sp. *cimarron*, savage, etym. uncertain (perh. from *cima*, mountain-top, L *cȳma*, Gr. *kūma*, wave)]

maroquin (mar´əkin, -kēn´) *n.* morocco leather. [F, a., from *Maroc*, Morocco]

marplot MAR.

marque¹ (mahk) *n.* a brand, esp. a make of motor car as distinct from a specific model of car. [OF, from Prov. *marca*, from *marcar*, to seize, perh. rel. to MARK[1]]

marque[2] (mahk) *n.* (*Hist.*) reprisals. **letter of marque (and reprisal)** LETTER.

marquee (mahkē´) *n.* **1** a large tent used for social or commercial purposes. **2** (*N Am.*) an awning over the entrance to a hotel, theatre etc. [from MARQUISE (under MARQUIS), regarded as pl.]

marquess (mah´kwis) *n.* a title or rank of nobility in England, ranking next below a duke and above an earl. **marquessate** (-sət) *n.* [MARQUIS]

marquetry (mah´kətri), **marqueterie** *n.* work inlaid with different pieces of fine wood, ivory, plates of metal, steel etc. [F *marqueterie*, from *marqueter*, to inlay, to spot, from *marquer*, to MARK[1]]

marquis (mah´kwis) *n.* a foreign title or rank of nobility between a duke and a count. **marquisate** (-sət) *n.* **marquise** (mahkēz´) *n.* **1** the wife or widow of a marquis. **2** a woman holding this rank in her own right. **3** a marquise ring. **4** †a large tent, a marquee. **marquise ring** *n.* a finger ring set with gems in a pointed oval cluster. [OF *marchis* (F *marquis*), low L *marchensis*, warden or prefect of the marches, from *marcha*, MARCH[2], MARK[1]]

marquisette (mahkizet´) *n.* a finely-woven mesh fabric used for clothing, net curtains and mosquito nets.

marram (mar´əm) *n.* a seaside grass, *Ammophilia arenaria*, frequently used to stabilize sand dunes. [ON *marr*, sea; *halmr*, haulm]

marriage (mar´ij) *n.* **1** the legal union of a man and woman, wedlock. **2** the act or ceremony of marrying, a wedding, a nuptial celebration. **3** one particular such union (*her fifth marriage*). **4** close conjunction or union (*a marriage of interests*). **5** in cards, the union of a king and queen of the same suit. **by marriage** as a result of a marriage (*nephew by marriage*). **in marriage** as a husband or wife (*given in marriage*; *taken in marriage*). **marriageable** *a.* **1** fit or of age for marriage. **2** desirable as a partner in marriage. **marriageability** (-bil´-) *n.* **marriage articles** *n.pl.* the articles of a marriage contract. **marriage bureau** *n.* an agency arranging introductions between single people with a view to marriage. **marriage certificate** *n.* an official document certifying that a marriage ceremony has been conducted. **marriage contract** *n.* a contract embodying the marriage settlement made before marriage. **marriage favour** *n.* a knot of ribbon or a rosette worn at a wedding. **marriage guidance** *n.* counselling and advice given to couples with marital problems. **marriage licence** *n.* a licence for the solemnization of a marriage without the proclamation of banns. **marriage lines** *n.pl.* (*coll.*) a marriage certificate. **marriage of convenience** *n.* **1** a marriage contracted for practical advantage rather than for love. **2** any union that is made to secure an advantage. **marriage partner** *n.* a spouse. **marriage settlement** *n.* an arrangement about property made before marriage, usu. securing a provision for the wifeand sometimes for future children. [F *mariage*, low L *marītāticum*, from *marītus*, husband, see MARITAL]

married MARRY[1].

marron glacé (marõ glas´ā) *n.* (*pl.* **marrons glacés** (marõ glas´ā)) a preserved chestnut coated with sugar. [F]

marrow[1] (ma´rō) *n.* **1** a large edible gourd with white flesh from the plant *Cucurbita pepo*. **2** a fatty substance contained in the cavities of bones. **3** the essence, the pith. **4** the pulpy interior of a fruit etc. **to the marrow** right through, completely (*chilled to the marrow*). **marrowbone** *n.* **1** a bone containing marrow. **2** (*pl., facet.*) the knees. **marrowfat** *n.* a large variety of pea. **marrowless** *a.* **marrowy** *a.* [OE *mearg* (cp. Dut. *merg*, Icel. *mergr*, G *Mark*)]

†**marrow**[2] (mar´ō) *n.* (*dial.*) **1** a match, a mate, a partner. **2** a husband or wife. **3** a person's equal or peer. **4** either of a pair. [etym. uncertain]

marry[1] (mar´i) *v.t.* (*3rd pers. sing. pres.* **marries,** *pres.p.* **marrying,** *past, p.p.* **married**) **1** to take for one's husband or wife. **2** to officiate at the marriage of, to unite as man and wife. **3** to join closely together, to unite intimately. **4** (*Naut.*) to splice together. **5** to give in marriage. ~*v.i.* to enter into the state of wedlock. **to marry into 1** to gain (esp. money) by marrying. **2** to join (a family) by marrying. **to marry off** to find a husband or wife for (a daughter or son). **to marry up** to link or join (with). **married** *a.* **1** united in marriage. **2** of or relating to married persons, conjugal. ~*n.* a married person. [F *marier*, L *marītāre*, from L *marītus*, husband, see MARITAL]

†**marry**[2] (mar´i) *int.* indeed, forsooth. [corr. of *Mary*, the Virgin]

Mars (mahz) *n.* **1** the fourth planet in order of distance from the sun. **2** the Roman god of war. [L]

Marsala (mahsah´lə) *n.* a sweet white fortified dessert wine. [*Marsala* in Sicily]

Marseillaise (mahsāez´, -səlāz´) *n.* the national anthem of the French Republic (introduced into Paris by the Marseilles contingent in 1792). [F, as MARSEILLE]

marseille (mahsā´) *n.* a stiff and heavy cotton fabric quilted in the loom. [*Marseilles*, a seaport in France]

marsh (mahsh) *n.* a tract of low land covered wholly or partially with water. **marsh fever** *n.* malaria. **marsh gas** *n.* methane, evolved from stagnant water. **marsh harrier** *n.* a European harrier hawk, *Circus aeruginosus*. **marsh hawk** *n.* HEN HARRIER (under HEN). **marshland** *n.* **marsh mallow** *n.* a shrubby herb, *Althaea officinalis*, growing near salt marshes. **marshmallow** *n.* a spongy sweet made of sugar, egg white, gelatin etc. **marsh marigold** *n.* a plant, *Caltha palustris*, of the buttercup family with bright yellow flowers, growing in marshy places, a kingcup. **marsh pennywort** *n.* a type of pennywort, *Hydrocotyle vulgaris*, which grows in marshy places. **marsh tit** *n.* a greyish-brown songbird, *Parus palustris*. **marsh trefoil** *n.* the buckbean. **marshy** *a.* (*comp.* **marshier,** *superl.* **marshiest**). **marshiness** *n.* [OE *mersc*, *merisc*, from Gmc. *mari-* MERE[1] (cp. MARISH)]

marshal (mah´shəl) *n.* **1** an officer regulating ceremonies and directing processions, races etc. **2** an officer of state with functions varying by country and period. **3** a military officer of the highest rank in some countries. **4** a field marshal. **5** a provost marshal. **6** an Earl Marshal. **7** (*N Am.*) a civil officer responsible for keeping the peace. **8** (*N Am.*) the head of a fire department. ~*v.t.* (*pres.p.* **marshalling,** (*N Am.*) **marshaling,** *past, p.p.* **marshalled,** (*N Am.*) **marshaled**) **1** to arrange or rank in order. **2** to conduct in a ceremonious manner. **3** (*Her.*) to combine (coats of arms). ~*v.i.* (of armies, processions etc.) to assemble, to take up a position. **marshaller,** (*N Am.*) **marshaler** *n.* **marshalling yard,** (*N am.*) **marshaling yard** *n.* a place where goods trucks, containers etc. are sorted according to their destination, and goods trains etc. made up. **Marshal of the Royal Air Force** *n.* the highest rank in the RAF, corresponding in rank to Field Marshal in the Army. **marshalship** *n.* [OF *mareschal*, OHG *marahschalh*, *marah*, horse, cogn. with MARE[1], *scalh*, cogn. with OE *sceale*, servant]

marsipobranch (mah´sipəbrangk) *n.* a vertebrate with sacciform gills, a cyclostome. **marsipobranchiate** (-kiət) *n., a.* [Gr. *marsipos*, purse, bag, *branchia*, gills]

marsupial (mahsū´piəl, -soo´-) *n.* any individual of the order Marsupialia, mammals carrying the young in a pouch, such as the kangaroos and opossums. ~*a.* **1** belonging to the order Marsupialia. **2** of or resembling a pouch. **marsupium** *n.* (*pl.* **marsupia**) **1** a marsupial's pouch for carrying its imperfectly developed young. **2** a pouch-like part or organ in other animals. [L *marsūpium*, Gr. *marsupion*, dim. of *marsipos*, purse, bag, -AL[1]]

mart (maht) *n.* **1** a trade centre, market, market place etc. **2** a saleroom. [prob. from Dut. *markt*, MARKET]

martagon (mah´təgən) *n.* the Turk's-cap lily, *Lilium martagon*. [F, from Turk. *martagān*, a kind of turban]

Martello (mahtel´ō), **Martello tower** *n.* (*pl.* **Martellos, Martello towers**) a circular, isolated tower of masonry, erected on the coast to oppose the landing of invaders. [corr. of *Mortella*, from a tower at Cape Mortella in Corsica captured by the British in 1793–94]

marten (mah´tin) *n.* a small carnivorous mammal, of the genus *Martes*, allied to the weasel, with a valuable fur. [ME *martren*, OF *matrine*, marten's fur, fem. of *matrin*, a., from *martre*, from Gmc. *marthuz* (cp. Dut. *marter*, G *Marder*, OE *mearth*)]

martensite (mah´tinzīt) *n.* a constituent of steel that has been rapidly cooled, a solid solution of carbon in iron. [Adolf *Martens*, d. 1914, German metallurgist]

martial (mah´shəl) *a.* **1** of or suited to war, military. **2** warlike, courageous, bellicose. **3** under the influence of the planet Mars. **martial arts** *n.pl.* the various forms of single combat pursued as a sport, e.g. judo, karate. **martialism** *n.* **martialist** *n.* **martialize, martialise** *v.t.* **martial law** *n.* military law abrogating ordinary law for the time being, proclaimed in time of war, insurrection or similar emergency. **martially** *adv.* [F, from L *Martiālis*, from MARS]

Martian (mah´shən) *n.* a supposed inhabitant of the planet Mars. ~*a.* of the planet or god Mars. [L *Martius*]

martin (mah´tin) *n.* any swallow of the family Hirundinidae, esp. the house martin or sand martin. [F, St *Martin*, Bishop of Tours, 4th cent.]

martinet (mahtinet´) *n.* a strict disciplinarian. **martinettish, martinetish** *a.* [Gen. *Martinet*, a very strict officer under Louis XIV]

martingale (mah´ting·gāl) *n.* **1** a strap or straps fastened to a horse's girth to keep the head down. **2** (*Naut.*) a lower rope for the jib-boom or flying jib-boom. **3** the system of doubling stakes after every loss in gambling. [F, etym. uncertain]

Martini® (mahtē´ni) *n.* **1** a type of Italian vermouth. **2** a cocktail made of gin and French vermouth. [name of It. firm]

Martinmas (mah´tinməs) *n.* the feast of St Martin, 11 Nov.

martlet (maht´lit) *n.* **1** (*Her.*) a swallow-like bird without feet. **2** †a swift. **3** †a house martin. [F *martelet*, prob. corr. of *martinet*, dim. of MARTIN]

martyr (mah´tə) *n.* **1** a person who suffers death or persecution in defence of their faith or principles, esp. one of the early Christians who suffered death for their religion. **2** a person who feigns or advertises their suffering in order to gain sympathy. ~*v.t.* **1** to put (someone) to death for their adherence to religion or principles. **2** to persecute, to torture. **a martyr to** a continual sufferer from. **to make a martyr of oneself** to feign or advertise suffering in order to gain sympathy. **martyrdom** *n.* **martyric** (-tir´ik) *a.* **martyrium** (mahtir´iəm) *n.* (*pl.* **martyria**) a martyry. **martyrize, martyrise** *v.t.* **martyrization** (-zā´shən) *n.* **martyrolatry** (-ol´-) *n.* worship of martyrs. **martyrology** (-ol´-) *n.* (*pl.* **martyrologies**) a list or history of martyrs. **martyrological** (-oj´-) *a.* **martyrologist** *n.* **martyry** *n.* (*pl.* **martyries**) a chapel or shrine built in honour of a martyr. [OE and L, from Gr. *martur*, *martus*, a witness]

marvel (mah´vəl) *n.* **1** a wonderful or astonishing thing. **2** a prodigy. **3** †wonder, astonishment. ~*v.i.* (*pres.p.* **marvelling,** (*N Am.*) **marveling,** *past, p.p.* **marvelled,** (*N Am.*) **marveled**) **1** to be astonished (at or that). **2** to be curious to know (why etc.). **marvellous,** (*N Am.*) **marvelous** *a.* **1** astonishing, prodigious. **2** excellent. **3** very unlikely. ~*adv.* (*coll.*) marvellously. **marvellously** *adv.* **marvellousness** *n.* **marvel of Peru** *n.* FOUR O'CLOCK (under FOUR). [OF *merveille*, L *mīrābilia*, pl. of *mīrābilis*, wonderful, from *mīrārī*, to wonder, from *mīrus*, wonderful]

Marxism (mahk´sizm) *n.* **1** the theory that human and political motives are at root economic, and that class struggle explains the events of history and will inevitably lead to the overthrow of capitalism. **2** state socialism as taught by followers of Karl Marx. **Marxism-Leninism** *n.* the political ideology developed by Lenin from the theories of Marx. **Marxist-Leninist** *n.*, *a.* **Marxist, Marxian** *a.* of or relating to Karl Marx or his theories. ~*n.* a believer in Marxism. [Karl *Marx*, 1818–83, German socialist]

marzipan (mah´zipan, -pan´), †**marchpane** (mahch´pān) *n.* a confection of ground almonds, sugar and white of egg. ~*v.t.* (*pres.p.* **marzipanning,** *past, p.p.* **marzipanned**) to cover with marzipan. [F *marcepain* (now *massepain*), etym. uncertain, cp. It. *marciapane*, G *Marzipan*]

Masai (masī´, mas´ī) *n.* (*pl.* **Masai, Masais**) **1** a member of a mainly Hamitic people inhabiting Kenya and Tanzania. **2** their language. ~*a.* of or relating to the Masai or their language. [Bantu]

masala (məsah´lə) *n.* **1** any of several spice mixtures used in Indian cookery. **2** a dish prepared with such a mixture. [Urdu]

masc. *abbr.* masculine.

mascara (maskah´rə) *n.* a dark cosmetic for eyelashes. [Sp., mask]

mascarpone (maskəpō´ni) *n.* a soft mild cream cheese made in Italy. [It.]

mascle (mas´kəl) *n.* **1** (*Her.*) a lozenge with a lozenge-shaped hole in the middle. **2** a lozenge-shaped plate or scale used in 13th-cent. armour. **mascled, masculy** (-kū-) *a.* [F, etym. uncertain, perh. corr. of MACLE]

mascon (mas´kon) *n.* (*Astron.*) any of the concentrations of dense material just beneath the moon's surface. [*mass con*centration]

mascot (mas´kot) *n.* an object or person that acts as a talisman and is thought to bring luck. [F dial. *mascotte*, perh. rel. to Prov. *masco*, witch]

masculine (mas´kūlin) *a.* **1** belonging to or having the characteristic qualities of the male sex. **2** strong, robust, vigorous. **3** manly, spirited. **4** mannish. **5** (*Gram.*) denoting or relating to the gender based on words classed as male. ~*n.* **1** the masculine gender. **2** a masculine word. **masculinely** *adv.* **masculine rhyme** *n.* a rhyme on a word ending with a stressed syllable, e.g. true/new, contend/defend. **masculinist** (-ist), **masculist** *n.* a person advocating the rights of men. ~*a.* advocating the rights of men. **masculinity** (-lin´-) *n.* **masculinize, masculinise** *v.t.* [F *masculin*, L *masculīnus*, see MALE]

maser (mā´zə) *n.* a device similar to a laser used for amplifying microwave radiation. [acronym for *m*icro-wave *a*mplification by *s*timulated *e*mission of *r*adiation]

MASH *abbr.* mobile army surgical hospital.

mash[1] (mash) *n.* **1** a mass of ingredients crushed and mixed into a pulp. **2** a mixture of bran and hot water for horses etc. **3** crushed or ground grain or malt steeped in hot water to form wort. **4** (*coll.*) mashed potatoes. **5** †a confused mixture, a mess. ~*v.t.* **1** to crush into a pulpy mass. **2** to make an infusion of (malt) in hot water. **3** to infuse (tea). ~*v.i.* (of tea) to be in the process of infusion. **masher**[1] *n.* **mash-tub, mash tun, mash-vat** *n.* a brewer's or distiller's tub or vat in which malt is mashed. †**mashy** *a.* [OE *masc-*, *max-*, in *maxwyrt*, mash-wort (cp. Dan. and Swed. dial. *mask*, G *Maische*), prob. cogn. with MIX]

†**mash**[2] (mash) *v.t.* (*sl.*) to ogle, to flirt with. ~*n.* the object of ogling or flirtation. **to be mashed on** to be in

love with. **masher**[2] *n.* 1 a man who dresses in flashy clothes. 2 a ladykiller. [etym. uncertain]

masher[1] MASH[1].

masher[2] MASH[2].

mashie (mash´i) *n.* (*Hist.*) in golf, an iron club with a deep short blade for lofted shots, a number five iron. [perh. corr. of F *massue*, a club]

masjid (mŭs´jid) *n.* a mosque. [Arab.]

mask (mahsk) *n.* 1 a covering for the face, for protection or to conceal one's identity. 2 a disguise, a pretence, a subterfuge. 3 an impression of a face in plastic material. 4 a reproduction of a face used as a gargoyle or part of a moulding. 5 a model of a human head worn in ancient classical drama. 6 a face pack. 7 in photography, a shield of paper etc. used in printing to cover part of the unexposed film. 8 the head of a fox. 9 †a person wearing a mask. 10 †a masque. ~*v.t.* 1 to cover with a mask. 2 to hide, conceal or disguise. 3 to screen during a process. 4 (*Mil.*) to hinder the effective action of (a force) by watching or by standing in the line of fire. ~*v.i.* to go in disguise. **masked** *a.* 1 that has been covered with a mask. 2 disguised with a mask. **masked ball** *n.* a ball attended by guests wearing masks. **masked battery** *n.* a battery concealed from the enemy's observation. †**masker** *n.* 1 a person wearing a mask. 2 a masquer. **masking tape** *n.* adhesive tape used in painting, car spraying etc. to protect areas where paint is not required. [F *masque*, from Sp. *máscara* (see MASQUERADE) or med. L *mascus*, *masca*, etym. uncertain]

maskinonge *n.* MUSKELLUNGE.

maslin (maz´lin) *n.* (*dial.*) a mixture of grain, esp. wheat and rye. [acc. to OED, from OF *mesteillon*, late L *mistiliō -ōnem*, from L *mistus*, p.p. of *miscēre*, to MIX]

masochism (mas´əkizm) *n.* 1 a variety of sexual perversion in which a person takes delight in being dominated or cruelly maltreated by another. 2 (*coll.*) enjoyment of something unpleasant or boring. **masochist** *n.* **masochistic** (-kis´-) *a.* **masochistically** *adv.* [L. von Sacher-*Masoch*, 1836–95, Austrian novelist, who described it]

mason (mā´sən) *n.* 1 a craftsman who works in stone. 2 (**Mason**) a Freemason. ~*v.t.* (*pres.p.* **masoning,** *past, p.p.* **masoned**) to build with masonry. **Masonic** (məson´-) *a.* of or relating to Freemasonry. **masonry** *n.* 1 stonework. 2 the art or occupation of a mason. 3 (**Masonry**) Freemasonry. **mason's mark** *n.* a mark cut in the stone of a building to identify the mason who dressed it. [OF *maçon*, med. L *maciō -ōnem*]

Mason–Dixon line (māsəndik´sən) *n.* the boundary drawn between Pennsylvania and Maryland in 1763–67 by Charles Mason and Jeremiah Dixon, regarded as the dividing line between the Northern states and the Southern slave states prior to the American Civil War.

Masorah (məsaw´rə), **Massorah** *n.* a mass of traditional information and illustrative matter on the text of the Hebrew Bible, compiled before the 10th cent. **Masorete** (mas´ərēt) *n.* any of the scholars who contributed to this. **Masoretic** (-ret´-) *a.* [Heb. *māsōreth*]

masque (mahsk) *n.* (*Hist.*) a play or dramatic entertainment, usu. presented by amateurs at court or in noblemen's houses, the performers wearing masks, orig. in dumb show, later with dialogue, poetical and musical accompaniments. **masquer** *n.* [F, see MASK]

masquerade (maskərād´, mahs-) *n.* 1 a ball or assembly at which people wear masks. 2 a disguise, a pretence. ~*v.i.* to wear a mask or disguise, to pass oneself off in a false guise. **masquerader** *n.* [Sp. *mascarada*, from *máscara*, perh. from Arab. *maskhara*, a buffoon]

Mass (mas), **mass** *n.* 1 (the celebration of) the Eucharist, esp. in the Roman Catholic Church. 2 the liturgy for this. 3 a setting of certain portions of this to music. **black mass** BLACK. **mass bell** *n.* the sanctus bell. **mass book** *n.* a missal. [OE *mæsse*, eccles. L *missa*, fem. p.p. of *mittere*, to send]

Mass. *abbr.* Massachusetts.

mass[1] MASS.

mass[2] (mas) *n.* 1 a body of matter collected, concreted or formed into a coherent whole of indefinite shape. 2 a compact aggregation of things. 3 a great quantity or amount. 4 the greater proportion, the principal part or the majority (of). 5 volume, bulk, magnitude. 6 (*Physics*) the quantity of matter which a body contains. ~*v.t.* 1 to form or gather into a mass. 2 to concentrate (as troops). ~*v.i.* to gather into a mass. **in the mass** in the aggregate. **the great mass** the great majority, the bulk. **the masses** the ordinary people, the populace. **to be a mass of** to be covered with, to have many. **mass defect** *n.* the difference in mass between a nucleus and its constituent particles. **mass energy** *n.* the ability of a body to do work in direct proportion to its mass, as indicated by the theory of relativity. **massless** *a.* **mass market** *n.* a very wide area of sales for a mass-produced product. **mass-market** *v.t.* **mass media** *n.pl.* the means of communication with large numbers of people, the media. **mass meeting** *n.* a large meeting for some specific purpose. **mass noun** *n.* (*Gram.*) a noun referring to something that cannot be counted and usu. has no plural or accompanying indefinite article, e.g. woodwork, sadness, artistry. **mass number** *n.* (*Physics*) the atomic weight of an isotope, the total number of protons and neutrons in a nucleus. **mass observation** *n.* a method of obtaining public opinion and sociological information by observing and interviewing people of various modes of life. **mass production** *n.* the production of standardized articles in large quantities in which the processes are reduced to simple, usually mechanical, operations performed along a conveyor belt, production line etc. **mass-produce** *v.t.* **mass-producer** *n.* **mass radiography** *n.* the X-ray screening of large numbers of people by mobile units. **mass spectrograph** *n.* an instrument for separating charged particles into a ray spectrum according to their mass and for detecting them photographically. **mass spectrometer** *n.* an instrument like a mass spectrograph which detects particles photographically or electrically. **mass spectrum** *n.* a record produced by a mass spectrometer of the types and amounts of ions present in a sample. **massy** *a.* (*poet.*) massive. **massiness** *n.* [F *masse*, L *massa*, prob. from Gr. *maza*, a barley-cake, rel. to *massein*, to knead]

massacre (mas´əkə) *n.* 1 indiscriminate slaughter, carnage, wholesale murder. 2 (*coll.*) an emphatic defeat in a competition, match etc. ~*v.t.* 1 to kill or slaughter indiscriminately. 2 (*coll.*) to defeat emphatically. [F, from OF *maçacre*, etym. uncertain]

massage (mas´ahzh, -ahj, -sahzh´) *n.* 1 treatment by rubbing or kneading the muscles and body, usu. with the hands. 2 an instance of this. ~*v.t.* 1 to subject to massage. 2 to manipulate or misrepresent (esp. statistics). 3 to flatter. **massage parlour,** (*N Am.*) **massage parlor** *n.* 1 a place where massages are administered. 2 (*euphem., coll.*) a kind of brothel. **massager** *n.* **masseur** (masœ´), **massagist** (-jist) *n.* a person skilled in massage. **masseuse** (masœz´) *n.* a female masseur. [F, from *masser*, to apply massage, perh. from Port. *amassar*, to knead, from *massa*, dough, MASS[2]]

massé (mas´ā) *n.* in billiards, a stroke with the cue held almost vertically. [F, p.p. of *masser*, to make such a stroke, from *masse*, MACE[1]]

masseter (məsē´tə), **masseter muscle** *n.* either of the two muscles which raise the lower jaw. [Gr. *masētēr*, from *masāsthai*, to chew]

masseur, masseuse MASSAGE.

massicot (mas´ikot) *n.* yellow lead monoxide, used as a pigment. [F, etym. uncertain]

massif (mas´ēf, masēf´) *n.* the main or central mass of a mountain or range. [F]

massive (mas´iv) *a.* 1 heavy, weighty, ponderous, bulky. 2 (*coll.*) very large. 3 substantial, solid. 4 serious in effect, of large magnitude (*a massive heart attack*). 5 (*Geol.*) without defined strata. 6 (*Mineral.*) without definite crystalline form. **massively** *adv.* **massiveness** *n.* [MASS[2]]

Massorah MASORAH.

mast[1] (mahst) *n.* 1 a long pole of timber, or a metal tube, placed upright in a ship to support the yards, sails etc. 2 a tall, slender structure carrying telecommunications aerials, dishes etc. 3 a flagpole. 4 MOORING-MAST (under MOOR[1]). **before the mast** BEFORE. **masted** *a.* furnished with a mast or masts. **-master** *comb. form* a ship with the specified number or kind or masts. **masthead** *n.* 1 the top of a mast, usu. of the lower mast as a place for a lookout etc., or of the topmast. 2 the name of a newspaper or periodical as printed at the top of the front page. 3 (*N Am.*) a list of details about a newspaper printed in its pages. ~*v.t.* 1 to send to the masthead as a punishment. 2 to raise (a sail) to its position on the mast. **mastless** *a.* [OE *mæst* (cp. Dut., Swed., Dan. *mast*, G *Mast*)]

mast[2] (mahst) *n.* the fruit of the oak, beech or other forest trees. **mast cell** *n.* a cell in connective tissue that releases histamine, serotonin etc. during inflammations and allergic reactions. [OE *mæst* (cp. G *Mast*), prob. cogn. with Sansk. *mēda*, fat]

mastaba (mas´təbə) *n.* 1 an ancient Egyptian tomb or chapel covering a sepulchral pit, used for the deposit of offerings. 2 a stone bench attached to an Eastern house. [Arab.]

mastectomy (məstek´təmi) *n.* (*pl.* **mastectomies**) surgical removal of the breast. [Gr. *mastos*, breast; *ektomē*, a cutting-out]

master (mahs´tə) *n.* 1 a person thoroughly acquainted with or skilled in an art, craft etc., an expert, a great artist. 2 a person who has secured the control or upper hand (*master of the situation*). 3 a person who has control or authority over others. 4 the owner of a dog, horse, slave etc. 5 a schoolmaster, a teacher, a tutor. 6 a holder of a degree ranking next above bachelor. 7 a the captain of a merchant vessel. b an officer who navigates a ship of war under the direction of the captain. 8 a chess player of international standard. 9 the person in charge of a pack of hounds. 10 an original or definitive version of a recording, typescript etc. from which copies can be taken. 11 a machine, device etc. which controls subsidiary machines or devices, cp. SLAVE. 12 a title of certain judicial officers. 13 (*formal*) a title prefixed to the names of boys. 14 (*Sc.*) the courtesy title of a viscount's or baron's eldest son. 15 the head of a household. 16 the head of certain colleges, corporations etc. 17 (*dated*) an employer. 18 †a respectful form of address to a man. ~*a.* 1 having control or authority. 2 overall, subsuming others. 3 principal, largest. 4 †employing workmen. 5 †in charge of work or of workmen. ~*v.t.* 1 to become thoroughly conversant with or skilled in using. 2 to become the master of. 3 to overpower, to defeat. 4 to subdue, to bring under control. 5 to be the master of, to rule as a master. **to be one's own master** to be free to do as one likes. **to make oneself (a) master** to acquire a thorough knowledge (of) or competence in. **Master Aircrew** *n.* an RAF warrant rank, equal to but before a warrant officer. **master-at-arms** *n.* (*pl.* **masters-at-arms**) a first-class petty officer acting as head of the ship's police. **master bedroom** *n.* the principal bedroom in a house. **master builder** *n.* 1 (*Hist.*) the chief builder, the architect. 2 a self-employed builder who employs workmen. **master carpenter** *n.* a highly-skilled and qualified carpenter. **masterclass** *n.* a lesson, esp. in music, given by a leading expert to gifted students. **masterdom** *n.* **masterful** *a.* 1 expressing mastery, masterly. 2 domineering, self-willed. **masterfully** *adv.* **masterfulness** *n.* **master hand** *n.* 1 an expert. 2 the performance or skill of an expert. **masterhood** *n.* **master key** *n.* a key which opens all the locks of a set, normally each opened by a separate key. **masterless** *a.* **masterly** *a.* (of a performance, display etc.) showing the skill of a master. ~†*adv.* in a masterly manner. **masterliness** *n.* **master mariner** *n.* 1 the captain of a merchant ship. 2 a person qualified to be captain of a ship. **master mason** *n.* 1 a highly-skilled and qualified mason. 2 a Freemason who has attained the third degree. **mastermind** *n.* 1 a person who has conceived and is in charge of a project etc. 2 a person of great intellect. 3 the ruling mind or intellect. ~*v.t.* to conceive and direct, to plan. **Master of Arts** *n.* (a holder of) a degree ranking next above Bachelor of Arts. **Master of Ceremonies** *n.* 1 a person who introduces speakers, announces toasts etc. on formal occasions. 2 a person in charge of procedure at ceremonies, state occasions etc. 3 the MC of a rap-music group. **master of fence** *n.* a skilled fencer or swordsman; an expert debater or dialectician. **master of foxhounds** *n.* a person elected to take charge of a hunt. **master of the horse** *n.* 1 †an officer of the royal household, formerly in charge of the horses. 2 (*Hist.*) in ancient Rome, an officer appointed by a dictator to command the cavalry. **master of the revels** *n.* (*Hist.*) a court official who had charge of entertainments etc. **Master of the Rolls** *n.* a judge who presides over the Court of Appeal in England and Wales. **masterpiece** *n.* 1 a performance superior to anything of the same kind. 2 an achievement showing surpassing skill. **master race** *n.* any race of people regarded as superior, esp. the supposed Aryan race in Nazi ideology. **master sergeant** *n.* a senior non-commissioned officer in the US armed services. **mastership** *n.* **mastersinger** *n.* MEISTERSINGER. **master stroke** *n.* an instance of great skill, mastery etc. **master switch** *n.* a single switch controlling the supply of electricity to an entire system. **master touch** *n.* outstanding skill in dealing with something. **masterwork** *n.* a masterpiece. **mastery** *n.* 1 control, authority. 2 the skill of a master. 3 complete competence, thorough knowledge (of). [ME *meister*, through OE *mægester* or OF *maistre*, *meistre* (or both), from L *magister* (cogn. with *magis*, more, Gr. *megas*, great)]

mastic (mas´tik) *n.* 1 a putty-like preparation used for bedding window frames etc. in buildings. 2 a gum or resin exuding from a Mediterranean evergreen tree, *Pistacia lentiscus*, chiefly used for varnish. 3 a liquor flavoured with mastic gum used in Greece, Syria, Lebanon etc. **mastic tree** *n.* the tree that exudes mastic. [F, from late L *mastichum*, earlier *masticha*, Gr. *mastichē*, etym. uncertain]

masticate (mas´tikāt) *v.t.* to grind and crush with the jaw, to chew. **masticable** *a.* **masticability** (-bil´-) *n.* **mastication** (-ā´shən) *n.* **masticator** *n.* **masticatory** *a.* [late L *masticātus*, p.p. of *masticāre*, perh. as MASTIC or rel. to Gr. *mastax -akos*, the jaw]

mastiff (mas´tif) *n.* a breed of large dog of great strength and courage, characterized by drooping ears, often used as a watchdog. [A-F and OF *mastin* (F *mâtin*), through a late L *mansuētīnus*, from *mansuētus*, MANSUETE]

mastitis (mastī´tis) *n.* inflammation of the breast or udder. [Gr. *mastos*, breast, rel. to *madaein* and L *madēre*, to be moist, -ITIS]

mastodon (mas´tədon) *n.* an extinct mammal of the genus *Mammut*, closely allied to the elephant, with nipple-shaped crests on the molar teeth. **mastodontic** (-don´-) *a.* [Gr. *odous odontos*, tooth]

mastodynia (mastədī´niə) *n.* (*Med.*) pain in the breast. [Gr. *odunē*, pain]

mastoid (mas´toid) *n.* 1 a conical prominence of bone behind the ear. 2 (*coll.*) mastoiditis. ~*a.* shaped like a woman's breast. **mastoiditis** (-dī´tis) *n.* inflammation of the mastoid. **mastoid process** *n.* (*Med.*) a mastoid.

masturbate (mas´təbāt) *v.i.* to excite one's genitals, usu. with the hand, to obtain sexual pleasure. ~*v.t.* to do this for (oneself or another). **masturbation** (-ā´shən) *n.* **masturbator** *n.* **masturbatory** *a.* [L *masturbātus*, p.p. of *masturbārī*, etym. uncertain]

mat[1] (mat) *n.* 1 a piece of coarse fabric of fibre, rushes, hemp, wire etc. or of perforated rubber etc., used as a carpet, to wipe shoes on, for packing etc. 2 a flat piece of cork, wood, plastic etc. placed under a dish or similar object to protect a surface from heat or moisture etc. 3 a piece of padded material to cushion landings in gymnastics. wrestling etc. 4 a small rug. 5 (*Naut.*) a mass of old rope etc. to prevent chafing. 6 a tangled mass of anything. ~*v.t.* (*pres.p.* **matting,** *past, p.p.* **matted**) 1 to cover or lay with mats. 2 to twist or twine together, to tangle. ~*v.i.* (of hair etc.) to become twisted into a tangled mass. **on the mat** on the carpet, being reprimanded. **matting** *n.* 1 mats collectively. 2 material for mats. 3 the making of mats. 4 a coarse fabric of rushes, bast, hemp etc. esp. for packing and covering. [OE *meatte, matte*, late L *matta*, perh. from Semitic (cp. Heb. *mattāh* a bed, a thing spread out)]

mat[2] (mat) *n.* (*coll.*) a matrix, a mould. [abbr. of MATRIX]

mat[3] MATT.

matador (mat´ədaw) *n.* 1 in Spanish bullfights, the person who has to kill the bull. 2 one of the three principal cards at ombre and quadrille. 3 a game played with dominoes in which each played must give a total of seven. [Sp.]

Mata Hari (mahtə hah´ri) *n.* a beautiful female spy. [after Gertrude M. Zelle, 1876–1917, a Dutch spy for Germany, from Malay *mata*, eye, *hari*, day]

match[1] (mach) *n.* 1 a person or thing, equal, like, or corresponding to another. 2 a counterpart, a facsimile. 3 a person able to cope with another. 4 a contest of skill, strength etc. 5 a pairing or alliance by marriage. 6 a person eligible for marrying. 7 †a bargain, an agreement. ~*v.t.* 1 to be a match for, to compare as equal. 2 to find a match for. 3 to oppose as equal. 4 to oppose (against or with) as a rival, opponent etc. 5 to be the equal of, to correspond to. 6 in electronics, to adjust for maximum power. 7 †to join in marriage. ~*v.i.* 1 (of different things or persons) to agree, to be equal, to tally, to correspond. 2 †to be married. **hatches, matches and dispatches** HATCH[2]. **to make a match** to encourage and bring about a marriage. **to match** matching, appropriate (*a shirt with tie to match*). **to match up** to form a whole (with). **to match up to** to be equal to or as good as. **to meet one's match** to encounter someone who is equal to or better than one in combat, skill, argument etc. **matchable** *a.* **matchboard** *n.* a board having a tongue along one edge and a corresponding groove on the other for fitting into similar boards. **matcher** *n.* **matchless** *a.* without equal, incomparable. **matchlessly** *adv.* **matchlessness** *n.* **matchmaker** *n.* 1 a person fond of planning and bringing about marriages. 2 a person who arranges introductions with a view to marriage. **matchmaking** *n., a.* **matchplay** *n.* in golf, a match or competition decided by the number of holes won as distinct from *stroke play.* **match point** *n.* 1 the point that needs to be won in order for a match to be won in tennis, squash etc. 2 a unit of scoring in bridge competitions. [OE *mæcca* (cp. Icel. *maki*, a mate, *makr*, suitable), cogn. with MAKE[1]]

match[2] (mach) *n.* 1 a small strip of wood or taper tipped with combustible material for producing or communicating fire. 2 a fuse burning at a uniform rate for firing charges. **matchbox** *n.* a box for holding matches. **matchlock** *n.* 1 a musket fired by means of a lighted match placed in its lock. 2 the lock of such a musket. **matchstick** *n.* the wooden part of a match. **matchwood** *n.* 1 wood reduced to small splinters. 2 wood suitable for making matches. **to make matchwood of** to smash to tiny pieces. [OF *mesche* (F *mèche*), wick, etym. uncertain]

matchet MACHETE.

mate[1] (māt) *n.* 1 a companion, a comrade, a fellow-worker, an equal, a match. 2 either of a pair of the lower animals, esp. birds, associated for breeding. 3 a suitable partner, esp. in marriage, a spouse. 4 (*Naut.*) **a** an officer in a merchant ship ranking below the captain. **b** an assistant to the surgeon, cook etc. 5 an assistant to a plumber etc. ~*v.t.* 1 to pair (birds, animals etc.) for breeding. 2 to match, to couple. 3 to join together in marriage. ~*v.i.* 1 to pair for breeding. 2 (of mechanical parts) to fit well. **mateless** *a.* **mateship** *n.* **matey, maty** *a.* (*comp.* **matier,** *superl.* **matiest**) (*coll.*) friendly. ~*n.* (*pl.* **mateys**) friend, companion (used as a form of address). **mateyness, matiness** *n.* **matily** *adv.* [prob. MLG (cp. LG *maat*, MDut. *maet*), cogn. with MEAT]

mate[2] (māt) *v.t.* 1 to checkmate. 2 to confound, to paralyse. ~*a.* confounded, paralysed. ~*n.* a checkmate. [from CHECKMATE]

mate[3] MATÉ.

maté (mat´ā), **mate** *n.* 1 an infusion of the leaves of *Ilex paraguayensis*, a Brazilian holly. 2 this shrub. 3 the leaves of this shrub. 4 the vessel in which the infusion is made. [Sp. *mate*, from Quechua *mati*]

matelassé (matəlas´ā) *a.* having a raised pattern as in quilting. [F, from *matelas*, MATTRESS]

matelot (mat´lō), **matlo, matlow** *n.* (*coll.*) a sailor. [F, etym. unknown]

matelote (mat´əlōt) *n.* a dish of fish with wine, onions etc. [F, from MATELOT]

mater (mā´tə) *n.* (*pl.* **matres** (-trēz)) (*sl.*) a mother (See also DURA MATER, PIA MATER). [L]

materfamilias (mahtəfəmil´ias) *n.* (*pl.* **matresfamilias** (mahtrāz-)) the mother of a family, the female head of a household. [L]

material (mətiə´riəl) *n.* 1 the substance or matter from which anything is made. 2 stuff, fabric. 3 elements or component parts (of). 4 notes, ideas etc. for a written or oral composition. 5 a person or persons suitable to fulfil a specified function after training etc. ~*a.* 1 of, relating to or consisting of matter. 2 corporeal, substantial. 3 of, relating to or concerning the human physical nature or needs (*material well-being*). 4 sensual, unspiritual, of or relating to the matter or essence of a thing, not to the form. 5 important, momentous, essential (*a material witness*). **materialism** *n.* 1 regard for the secular which neglects spiritual interests. 2 (excessive) devotion to the pursuit of material wealth and physical well-being. 3 (*Philos.*) the doctrine that there is nothing in the universe but matter, that mind is a phenomenon of matter, and that there is no ground for assuming a spiritual First Cause. 4 emphasis on the material aspects of art objects. **materialist** *n.* **materialistic** (-lis´-) *a.* **materialistically** *adv.* **materiality** (-al´-) *n.* **materialize, materialise** *v.i.* 1 to become actual fact. 2 (of a spirit) to appear. 3 (*coll.*) to arrive on the scene. ~*v.t.* 1 to make material, to invest with matter or corporeity. 2 to cause (a spirit) to become material or to appear. 3 to make materialistic. **materialization** (-zā´shən) *n.* **materially** *adv.* 1 in a material way. 2 to a significant extent. [OF *materiel*, late L *māteriālis*, from *māteria*, MATTER]

materia medica (mətiəriə med´ikə) *n.* 1 the different substances employed in medicine. 2 the scientific study of such substances. [L]

materiel (mətiəriel´) *n.* the material, supplies, machinery or instruments, as distinct from the personnel, employed in an art, business, military or naval activity etc. [F, see MATERIAL]

maternal (mətœ´nəl) *a.* **1** motherly. **2** of or relating to a mother or to maternity. **3** connected or related on the mother's side. **maternally** *adv.* **maternity** *n.* **1** motherhood. **2** motherliness. **maternity leave** *n.* paid leave granted to a woman having a baby. [F *maternel*, late L *māternālis*, L *māternus*, from MATER]

matey MATE[1].

math (math) *n.* (*N Am., coll.*) short for MATHEMATICS.

mathematical (mathəmat´ikəl) *a.* **1** of or relating to mathematics. **2** rigidly precise or accurate. **mathematical geography** *n.* those parts of geographical science involving mathematics, such as astronomical geography, geodesy and cartography. **mathematical induction** INDUCTION (under INDUCT). **mathematically** *adv.* **mathematical tables** *n.pl.* tables of logarithms, trigonometrical values etc. **mathematician** (-tish´-) *n.* [OF *mathematique*, L *mathēmaticus*, Gr. *mathēmatikos*, from *mathē-*, stem of *manthanein*, to learn]

mathematics (mathəmat´iks) *n.* **1** the science of quantity or magnitude as expressed by numbers. **2** the mathematical calculations involved in a particular problem, area of study etc. **applied mathematics** APPLIED (under APPLY). **pure mathematics** PURE.

maths (maths) *n.* (*coll.*) short for MATHEMATICS.

Matilda (mətil´də) *n.* (*Austral., coll.*) a bushman's bag of belongings, a swag. **to walk Matilda** to carry a swag. **to waltz Matilda** to carry a swag.

matily MATEY (under MATE[1]).

matinal (mat´inəl) *a.* of, relating to or occurring in the morning. [see MATINS]

matinée (mat´inā), **matinee** *n.* an afternoon performance of a play, film etc. **matinée coat, matinée jacket** *n.* an infant's top short coat of wool etc. **matinée idol** *n.* a handsome film star etc., esp. popular with women. [F, morning]

matins (mat´inz), **mattins** *n.pl.* **1** the daily office of morning prayer in the Anglican Church. **2** one of the canonical hours of prayer, properly recited at midnight but also at daybreak. **3** (*poet.*) a morning song as of birds. **4** †morning, dawn. [F *matines*, fem. pl., eccles. L *mātūtinas*, acc. fem. pl. of *mātūtinus*, of the morning]

matlow, matlo MATELOT.

matrass (mat´rəs) *n.* (*Chem.*) a round or oval glass vessel with a long neck, used for distilling etc. [F *matras*, etym. uncertain]

matresfamilias MATERFAMILIAS.

☒ **matress** common misspelling of MATTRESS.

matri- (mā´tri), **matro-** (-trō) *comb. form* mother. [L *māter*]

matriarch (mā´triahk) *n.* **1** the female head of a family, tribe etc. **2** a venerable or imposing lady. **matriarchal** (-ah´-) *a.* **matriarchalism** *n.* **matriarchalist** *n.* **matriarchate** (-ah´kāt) *n.* **matriarchy** *n.* (*pl.* **matriarchies**) **1** a social system in which the mother is head of the family, or in which descent is reckoned through the female line. **2** a society having such a system. [MATRI-, *-arch*, as in PATRIARCH]

matric (mətrik´) *n.* (*Hist., coll.*) short for MATRICULATION (under MATRICULATE[1]).

matrices MATRIX.

matricide (mā´trisīd, mat´-) *n.* **1** the murder of one's mother. **2** a person who murders their mother. **matricidal** (-sī´-) *a.* [F, from L *mātricīda* (MATRI-, -CIDE)]

matriculate[1] (mətrik´ūlāt) *v.i.* **1** to be admitted as a member or student at a university, college etc. **2** (*Hist.*) to pass the examination required to ensure such admission. *~v.t.* to admit to membership of a body or society, esp. a university, college etc. **matriculant** *n.* a person who has matriculated. **matricular** *n., a.* **matriculation** (-lā´shən) *n.* **1** the act of matriculating at a university, college etc. **2** (*Hist.*) an examination that must be passed to matriculate. **3** (*Hist.*) a former school examination in England and Wales equivalent to the highest grades of the General Certificate of Secondary Education. **matriculatory** *a.* [med. L *mātriculātus*, p.p. of *mātriculāre*, from *mātricula*, register, dim. of MATRIX]

matriculate[2] (mətrik´ūlət) *n.* a person who has matriculated.

matriculation MATRICULATE[1].

matrilineal (matrilin´iəl) *a.* of, relating to, or based on succession through the mother. **matrilineally** *adv.*

matrilocal (matrilō´kəl) *a.* of or relating to a pattern in marriage in which the man moves to live in the woman's community.

matrimony (mat´riməni) *n.* (*pl.* **matrimonies**) **1** the act of marrying. **2** the state of being married, marriage, wedlock. **3** a card game, in which the combination of king and queen of one suit wins. **4** this combination in this and other games. **matrimonial** (-mō´niəl) *a.* **matrimonially** *adv.* [OF *matrimonie*, L *mātrimōnium*, from *māter mātris*, mother]

matrix (mā´triks) *n.* (*pl.* **matrices** (-sēz), **matrixes**) **1** a mould in which anything is cast or shaped. **2** a place where anything is generated or developed. **3** the womb. **4** (*Biol.*) the formative part from which a structure is produced, intercellular substance. **5** the concave bed into which a stamp or die fits. **6** a mass of rock in which a mineral or fossil is embedded. **7** the impression left by a fossil, crystal etc. after its removal from rock. **8** (*Math.*) a rectangular table of elements in rows and columns, used to simplify problem solving, communication of information etc. **matrix printer** *n.* DOT MATRIX PRINTER (under DOT[1]). [L; see MATRI-]

matro- MATRI-.

matron (mā´trən) *n.* **1** a married woman, esp. an elderly one. **2** the head of the nursing staff in a hospital. **3** a female superintendent within an institution (*a school matron*). **matronage** *n.* **matronal** *a.* **matronhood, matronship** *n.* **matronize, matronise** *v.t.* **1** to render matronlike. **2** to chaperone. **3** (*facet.*) to patronize. **matronlike** *a.* **matronly** *a., adv.* **matron of honour** *n.* a bride's principal married attendant at a wedding. [F *matrone*, L *mātrōna*]

Matt. *abbr.* Matthew (esp. in the Bible).

matt (mat), **mat, matte** *a.* dull, lustreless, not glossy. *~n.* **1** a dull, lustreless surface, groundwork, border etc., esp. in unburnished gold or in roughened metal or frosted glass. **2** matt paint. *~v.t.* **1** to dull. **2** to give a wet surface or appearance to. **3** to frost (glass). **matt paint** *n.* paint that produces a matt finish when dry. [F, prob. from OF *mat*, mated at chess, see CHECKMATE]

mattamore (mat´əmaw) *n.* an underground storage place for grain. [F *matamore*, Arab. *matmūrah*, from *tamara*, to store up]

matte[1] (mat) *n.* an impure metallic product containing sulphur, from the smelting of ore, esp. copper. [F, from G, MAT[1]]

matte[2] (mat) *n.* in film-making etc., a mask used to obscure part of an image to allow the superimposition of another image.

matte[3] MATT.

matter (mat´ə) *n.* **1** that which constitutes the substance of physical things, as distinguished from thought, mind, spirit etc. **2** that which has weight or mass, occupies space and is perceptible by the senses. **3** a physical substance. **4** a subject for thought or feeling. **5** an object of or for attention. **6** meaning, sense or substance (of a book, discourse etc.). **7** an affair, a business. **8** the cause or occasion of or for difficulty, regret etc. **9** importance, moment. **10** (*Logic*) content as opposed to form. **11** an indefinite amount, quantity or portion. **12** (*Law*) a statement or fact forming the ground of an action etc. **13** purulent substance in an abscess, pus. **14** (*Hist.*) type set up for printing. *~v.i.* **1** to be of moment, to signify. **2** to discharge pus. **a matter of** approximately (*a matter of £500*). **as a matter of fact** in reality, in fact. **for that matter** 1 so far as that is concerned. 2 as an additional point. **for the matter of that** for that matter. **in the matter of** as regards. **no matter** 1 it does not matter. 2 regardless of. **what is the matter?** what is wrong (with)? **what matter?** used to indicate that something is of no relevance, importance etc. **†matterful** *a.* **†matterless** *a.* unimportant. **matter of course** *n.* what may be expected in the natural course of events. **matter of fact** *n.* (*Law*) the part of a judicial inquiry concerned with establishing the truth or otherwise of allegations. **matter-of-fact** *a.* 1 treating of or adhering to facts or realities. 2 not fanciful or imaginary. 3 commonplace, prosaic, plain, ordinary. **matter-of-factly** *adv.* **matter-of-factness** *n.* **matter of form** *n.* 1 an issue of etiquette or convention. 2 a purely routine matter. **matter of law** *n.* (*Law*) in a judicial inquiry, an issue which must be determined by law, as distinct from factual evidence or opinion. **matter of life and death** *n.* something of vital importance. **matter of opinion** *n.* a matter open to debate or question. **matter of record** *n.* something established as a fact by being recorded. **mattery** *a.* full of matter or pus, purulent. [ME and OF *matere*, F *matière*, L *māteria*, stuff, esp. for building]

matting MAT[1].

mattins MATINS.

mattock (mat´ək) *n.* a kind of pick with one broad adze-edged end, for loosening ground, severing roots etc. [OE *mattuc*, etym. uncertain]

mattoid (mat´oid) *a.* semi-insane. ~*n.* a semi-insane person. [It. (*matto*, foolish)]

mattress (mat´ris) *n.* 1 a case, usu. of padding, springs etc., used for the bottom of a bed. 2 any case of coarse material used to lie on. [OF *materas* (F *matelas*), It. *materasso*, Arab. *matrah*, a place where anything is thrown, from *taraha*, to throw]

maturate (mat´ūrāt) *v.t.* 1 to bring to maturity. 2 (*Med.*) to promote suppuration in. ~*v.i.* (*Med.*) to begin to suppurate. **maturative** (-tū´-) *n.*, *a.* [L *mātūrātus*, p.p. of *mātūrāre*, to MATURE]

maturation (matūrā´shən) *n.* 1 the attainment of maturity or ripeness, the completion of growth. 2 (*Med.*) the formation of pus, the bringing about of suppuration. **maturational** *a.*

mature (mətūə´) *a.* 1 ripe, ripened. 2 completely developed, fully grown. 3 fully elaborated, considered etc. 4 (of a bill etc.) become payable. 5 (*Med.*) beginning to suppurate. ~*v.t.* 1 to bring to a state of ripeness or complete development. 2 (*Med.*) to bring to a state of suppuration. ~*v.i.* 1 to become ripened or fully developed. 2 (of a bill, insurance policy etc.) to become payable. **maturely** *adv.* **mature student** *n.* an adult student, i.e. one beyond the normal age of formal education. **maturity, matureness** *n.* [L *mātūrus*, ripe, whence *mātūrāre*, to ripen]

matutinal (matūtī´nəl), **matutine** (mat´ūtīn) *a.* 1 of, relating to or occurring in the morning. 2 early. [L *mātūtīnālis*, from *mātūtīnus*, pertaining to *Mātūta*, goddess of dawn (rel. to *mātūrus*, early)]

maty MATE[1].

matzo (mat´sō) *n.* (*pl.* **matzoth** (-ōt), **matzos**) (a thin wafer of) unleavened bread, eaten esp. at the Passover. [Heb. *matsāh*]

maud (mawd) *n.* (*Sc.*) a grey-striped plaid worn by shepherds etc., or used as a travelling rug. [etym. unknown]

maudlin (mawd´lin) *a.* 1 characterized by sickly sentimentality, mawkish. 2 tearfully or pathetically sentimental, esp. when drunk. 3 †weeping. ~*n.* mawkish sentimentality. [OF *mawdeleine*, L *Magdalēnē*, MAGDALEN]

†maugre (maw´gə) *prep.* in spite of. [OF *maugré*, *malgré* (*mal*, L *malus* -*um*, bad, *gré*, L *gratus* -*um*, pleasing)]

maul (mawl) *v.t.* 1 to handle roughly. 2 to beat, to bruise (as with a maul). 3 to damage. 4 (of an animal) to paw and mutilate. ~*n.* 1 a tussle, a struggle. 2 a loose scrum in rugby. 3 a heavy wooden hammer, a beetle. **mauler** *n.* [ME *malle*, OF *mail*, L *malleus* -*um*, hammer]

maulstick (mawl´stik), **mahlstick** *n.* a light stick with a round pad at the end used as a rest for the right hand by painters, signwriters etc. [Dut. *maalstok* (*malen*, to paint, STICK[1])]

maund (mawnd) *n.* a measure of weight of western Asia and the Indian subcontinent, varying from place to place. [Hind. *man*]

maunder (mawn´də) *v.i.* 1 to grumble, to mutter. 2 to talk incoherently, to ramble. 3 to act or move about aimlessly. ~*v.t.* to utter in a grumbling or incoherent manner. **maunderer** *n.* [perh. imit.]

Maundy (mawn´di) *n.* 1 the ceremony of washing the feet of poor people on the Thursday before Easter, in commemoration of Christ's performing this office for his disciples. 2 a distribution of alms following this. **Maundy money** *n.* silver money specially struck and distributed by the sovereign on Maundy Thursday. **Maundy Thursday** *n.* the Thursday before Easter. [OF *mandé*, L *mandātum*, MANDATE]

Mauser® (mow´zə) *n.* a variety of German magazine rifle. **Mauser pistol** *n.* [Paul *Mauser*, 1838–1914, German inventor]

mausoleum (mawsəlē´əm) *n.* (*pl.* **mausolea** (-ə), **mausoleums**) a sepulchral monument of considerable size or architectural pretensions. **mausolean** *a.* [L, from Gr. *Mausōleion*, from *Mausōlos*, king of Caria, whose stately tomb was reckoned to be one of the seven wonders of the world]

mauvais quart d'heure (mōvā kah dœ´) *n.* a brief unpleasant experience. [F, bad quarter of an hour]

mauve (mōv) *n.* 1 a pale purple colour. 2 a purple or lilac-coloured aniline dye. ~*a.* of this colour. **mauvish** *a.* of a similar colour to mauve. [F, from L *malva*, MALLOW]

maven (mā´vən) *n.* (*N Am.*, *coll.*) an expert, a connoisseur. [Yiddish]

maverick (mav´ərik) *n.* 1 an individualist, a determined non-conformer. 2 (*N Am.*) an unbranded beast. 3 anything got hold of dishonestly. ~*v.t.* 1 to brand (a stray beast). 2 to seize or appropriate illegally. [Samuel *Maverick*, Texan cattle-raiser, who refrained from branding his stock, *c.* 1840]

mavis (mā´vis) *n.* (*pl.* **mavises**) (*poet. or dial.*) the song-thrush. [F *mauvis* (cp. Sp. *malvis*), etym. uncertain]

mavourneen (məvuə´nēn) *n.* (*Ir.*) my dear one, darling. [Ir. *mo mhurnin*]

maw (maw) *n.* 1 the stomach of lower animals, esp. the fourth stomach of ruminants. 2 the crop of birds. 3 (*facet.*) the human stomach, esp. that of a greedy person. 4 the mouth. [OE *maga* (cp. Dut. *maag*, Icel. *mage*, G *Magen*)]

mawkin MALKIN.

mawkish (maw´kish) *a.* 1 falsely or feebly sentimental. 2 nauseating or insipid in flavour, smell etc. **mawkishly** *adv.* **mawkishness** *n.*

max (maks) *n.* (*N Am.*, *coll.*) maximum (*pushed it to the max*). ~*a.* maximum, maximal (*max revs*). ~*adv.* to the utmost degree, maximally. ~*v.i.* to perform to the limit of one's ability (*The car maxed out at 130 m.p.h.*). **maxed out** *a.* completely exhausted after total exertion.

max. *abbr.* maximum.

maxi (mak´si) *a.* very large, long etc. for its type. ~*n.* (*pl.* **maxis**) something which is large or long esp. an ankle-length skirt, a coat etc.

maxi- (mak´si) *comb. form* very large or long.

maxilla (maksil´ə) *n.* (*pl.* **maxillae** (-ē)) 1 a jaw-bone, esp. the upper jaw in mammals. 2 the mouthpart for chewing in some arthropods. **maxillary** *a.* of or relating to a jaw or maxilla. ~*n.* the part of the skull that forms the upper jaw. **maxilliped** *n.* in crustaceans, a limb modified into a maxillary organ. **maxillo-** *comb. form* of or relating to the jaw. [L]

Maxim (mak´sim), **Maxim gun** *n.* (*Hist.*) an automatic single-barrelled quick-firing machine-gun, invented in 1884. [Sir Hiram S. *Maxim*, 1840–1916, inventor]

maxim (mak´sim) *n.* **1** a general principle of a practical kind. **2** a rule derived from experience. **3** (*Law*) an established or accepted principle. [F *maxime*, L *maxima*, fem. superl. of *magnus*, great]

maxima MAXIMUM.

maximal (mak´siməl) *a.* **1** of the greatest, largest etc. size, rate etc. **2** of an upper limit. **maximalist** *n.* **1** a person who refuses to compromise, expecting a full accedance to (esp. political) demands. **2** (*Hist.*) an adherent of the extremist section of the former Social Revolutionary Party in Russia. **maximally** *adv.*

maximin (mak´simin) *n.* the highest value of a set of minima, esp. of minimum gains in game theory. [*maxi*mum, *min*imum]

maximum (mak´siməm) *n.* (*pl.* **maximums, maxima** (-mə)) the greatest quantity or degree attainable in any given case. ~*a.* **1** greatest. **2** at the greatest or highest degree. **maxima and minima** the greatest and least values of a variable quantity. **maximize, maximise** *v.t.* to raise to a maximum, to increase to the utmost extent. **maximization** (-zā´shən) *n.* **maximizer** *n.* **maximum and minimum thermometer** *n.* a thermometer automatically recording the highest and lowest temperatures reached during a given period. [L, neut. superl. of *magnus*, great]

maxwell (maks´wəl) *n.* a unit of magnetic flux in the cgs system. [J. C. *Maxwell*, 1831–79]

May (mā) *n.* **1** the fifth month of the year. **2** (**may**) hawthorn or hawthorn blossom (from its appearing in May). **3** (*poet.*) the springtime of life, youth. **4** May-Day festivities. ~†*v.i.* to engage in the festivities of May Day. **Queen of the May** QUEEN. **rose of May** ROSE[1]. **may apple** *n.* a N American herb, *Podophyllum peltatum*, with a single white flower and an edible egg-shaped fruit. **may blossom** *n.* the bloom of the hawthorn. **May-bug** *n.* the cockchafer. **May Day** *n.* the first of May as a spring festival or, in some countries, as a public holiday in honour of workers. **may-duke** *n.* a variety of cherry said to have been introduced from Médoc. **mayflower** *n.* any of several flowers blooming in May, such as the cowslip, lady's smock or hawthorn, but esp. the trailing arbutus, *Epigaea repens.* **mayfly** *n.* (*pl.* **mayflies**) **1** any insect of the order Ephemeroptera. **2** an angler's fly made in imitation of this. **maying** *n.*, *a.* taking part in May Day festivities. **maypole** *n.* a pole decorated with garlands etc., round which people dance, esp. on May Day. **May queen** *n.* a young girl chosen to act as queen of the festivities on May Day. [F *mai*, L *Māius*, perh. pertaining to *Māia*]

may[1] (mā) *v.aux.* (*2nd pers. sing. pres.* **†mayest** (mā´əst), **†mayst,** *3rd pers. sing. pres.* **may,** *past* **might** (mīt)) expressing possibility, ability, permission, desire, obligation, contingency or uncertainty. **be that as it may** BE. **may as well** might as well. **might as well** would be as desirable or sensible as not to (*I might as well go home*). **that is as may be** that may or may not be the case (implying that there are further factors to consider). **maybe** *adv.* perhaps, possibly. **†mayhap** (-hap) *adv.* perhaps. **mayn't** (mānt) *contr.* may not. **might-have-been** *n.* (*coll.*) **1** a state of affairs that could once have obtained but is no longer possible. **2** a person who could have been more successful than they are. **mightn't** (mī´tənt) *contr.* might not. [OE *mæg*, 1st sing. of *magan*, to be able, past *mihte, meahte* (cp. Dut. *mag, mocht, mogen*, Icel. *mā, megom, mātte*, G *mag, mochte, mögen*)]

Usage note It is best to use *may* rather than *can* to express permission in very formal contexts or where *can* could be misunderstood as meaning 'to be able to'.

†may[2] (mā) *n.* a maiden, a girl. [OE *mæg*, kinswoman (see MAIDEN)]

may[3] MAY.

Maya (mī´ə) *n.* (*pl.* **Maya, Mayas**) **1** a member of an ancient Indian people of Yucatan, Honduras and other parts of central America. **2** the language of this people. ~*a.* of or relating to the Maya or their language. **Mayan** *a.*, *n.*

maya (mī´ə) *n.* in Hinduism, the world as perceived by the senses, regarded as illusory. [Sansk.]

Mayan MAYA.

maybe MAY[1].

mayday (mā´dā) *n.* an international distress signal used by ships and aircraft. [F *m'aidez*, help me]

†mayest MAY[1].

mayhap MAY[1].

mayhem (mā´hem) *n.* **1** a state of disorder or confusion. **2** wilful damage. **3** (*Hist.*) the offence of maiming a person.

mayonnaise (māənāz´) *n.* **1** a thick sauce or salad dressing made of egg yolk, vinegar etc. **2** a dish with this as a dressing (*egg mayonnaise*). [F, etym. uncertain]

mayor (meə) *n.* the chief officer of a city or borough, or a district council with the same status. **mayoral** *a.* **mayoralty** *n.* (*pl.* **mayoralties**) **1** the office of mayor. **2** the period of office of a mayor. **mayoress** *n.* **1** a female mayor. **2** the wife of a mayor, or a woman who accompanies a mayor on ceremonial duties. **mayorship** *n.* [F *maire*]

†mayst MAY[1].

mayweed (mā´wēd) *n.* a wild camomile of Eurasia, often found as a weed. **scentless mayweed** SCENT. **stinking mayweed** STINK. [obs. *maythe*, OE *magothe*, WEED]

mazard (maz´əd), **mazzard** *n.* **1** a small kind of European black cherry, *Prunus avium.* **2** †the head, the skull. **3** †the face. [etym. uncertain, perh. var. of MAZER]

mazarine (maz´ərēn) *n.*, *a.* (of) a deep rich blue. **Mazarine Bible** *n.* a Bible printed by Gutenberg in 1450, the first book printed from movable types (of which Cardinal Mazarin owned many copies). [perh. from Cardinal *Mazarin*, 1602–61]

maze (māz) *n.* **1** a network of paths and hedges etc. designed as a puzzle or challenge. **2** a labyrinth, a confusing network of winding and turning passages. **3** a state of bewilderment, uncertainty, perplexity. ~*v.t.* to bewilder, to confuse. ~†*v.i.* **1** to be bewildered. **2** to wind about perplexedly. **mazed** *a.* bewildered, confused, giddy, dizzy. **mazeful** *a.* **mazy** *a.* (*comp.* **mazier,** *superl.* **maziest**) involved, winding, perplexing, intricate. **mazily** *adv.* **maziness** *n.* [ME, rel. to AMAZE]

mazer (mā´zə) *n.* (*Hist.*) a large cup or drinking vessel, orig. made of maple wood. [OF *masere*, prob. from OHG *masar*, a knot in wood, maple wood (cp. G *Maser*, Icel. *mösurr*)]

mazuma (məzoo´mə) *n.* (*sl.*) money, cash. [Yiddish]

mazurka (məzœ´kə) *n.* **1** a lively Polish dance like the polka. **2** the music for this. [Pol., a woman of the province Mazovia (cp. POLONAISE)]

mazy MAZE.

mazzard MAZARD.

MB *abbr.* Bachelor of Medicine. [L *Medicinae Baccalaureus*]

Mb *abbr.* (*Comput.*) megabyte.

MBA *abbr.* Master of Business Administration.

MBE *abbr.* Member of the Order of the British Empire.

MBO *abbr.* management buyout.

MC[1] *abbr.* **1** Master of Ceremonies. **2** Member of Congress. **3** Military Cross. **4** Monaco (IVR). **5** music cassette.

MC[2] (emsē´) *n.* the lead vocalist in a rap-music group. [Master of Ceremonies]

Mc *abbr.* megacycle(s).

MCC *abbr.* Marylebone Cricket Club.

McCarthyism (məkah´thiizm) *n.* **1** the hunting down of suspected Communists and their dismissal from public employment. **2** intolerance of liberalism. [J. *McCarthy*, 1909–57, US politician]

McCoy REAL[1].

M.Ch., M.Chir. *abbr.* Master of Surgery. [Magister Chirurgiae]

mCi *abbr.* millicurie(s).

McNaughten rules (məknaw´tən), **M'naghten rules, McNaghten rules** *n.pl.* (*Law*) rules governing the degree of criminal responsibility of a mentally disturbed defendant. [defendant in a lawsuit of 1843]

M.Com. *abbr.* Master of Commerce.

MCP *abbr.* (*coll.*) male chauvinist pig.

MCR *abbr.* Middle Common Room.

Mc/s *abbr.* megacycles per second.

MD *abbr.* **1** Managing Director. **2** Maryland. **3** Doctor of Medicine. **4** mentally deficient. **5** Musical Director.

Md *chem. symbol* mendelevium.

Md. *abbr.* Maryland.

MDMA *abbr.* methylenedioxymethamphetamine, the hallucinatory drug Ecstasy.

MDT *abbr.* Mountain Daylight Time.

ME *abbr.* **1** Maine. **2** Mechanical Engineer. **3** Middle English. **4** Military Engineer. **5** myalgic encephalomyelitis.

Me. *abbr.* **1** Maine. **2** Maître (French advocates' title).

me[1] (mē, mi) *pron.* **1** objective (accusative and dative) of I[2]. **2** (*dial.*) MYSELF. **me and mine** me and my family. [OE *mē, mec*, acc. (cp. Dut. *mij*, Swed. and Dan. *mig*, G *mich*, dat. *mir*, L *mē*, dat. *mihi*, Gr. *me, eme, moi, emoi*)]

Usage note Use of *me* in a subject, as in *Me and Joe will come*, is best avoided. See also notes under AS[1], BE, THAN.

me[2] (mē), **mi** *n.* **1** the third note of a major scale in the tonic sol-fa system of notation. **2** the note E in the fixed-doh system.

mea culpa (māə kŭl´pə, kul´-) *int.* used to acknowledge responsibility for a mistake. ~*n.* an acknowledgement that one has made a mistake. [L, by my fault]

mead[1] (mēd) *n.* a fermented liquor made from honey, water and spices. [OE *medu* (cp. Dut. *mede*, Dan. *miöd*, G *Met*, also Sansk. *madhu*, honey, Gr. *methu*, wine, mead)]

mead[2] (mēd) *n.* (*poet.*) a meadow. [see MEADOW]

meadow (med´ō) *n.* **1** a tract of land under grass, esp. if grown for hay. **2** low, rich, moist ground, esp. near a river. **meadow brown** *n.* the common brown butterfly, *Maniola jurtina*. **meadow grass** *n.* the creeping grass, *Poa pratensis* of temperate northern regions. **meadowland** *n.* land used for grass cultivation. **meadowlark** *n.* any bird of the genus *Sturnella*, esp. the American songbird, *S. magna*. **meadow pipit** *n.* a brown and white European songbird, *Anthus pratensis*. **meadow rue** *n.* any ranunculaceous plant of the genus *Thalictrum* (buttercup family), esp. *T. flavum*. **meadow saffron** *n.* a plant of the genus *Colchicum*, esp. *C. autumnale*, the autumn crocus. **meadowsweet** *n.* **1** a rosaceous plant, *Alipendula ulmaria*, with white, plumy, fragrant flowers. **2** any N American rosaceous plant of the genus *Spiraea*. **meadowy** *a.* [OE *mǣdwe*, dat. of *mǣd*, cogn. with MOW[1]]

meagre (mē´gə), (*N Am.*) **meager** *a.* **1** lean, thin, lacking flesh. **2** destitute of richness, fertility or productiveness. **3** poor, scanty. ~†*v.t.* to make meagre. **meagrely** *adv.* **meagreness** *n.* [ME and OF *megre, maigre*, L *macer macrum*, cogn. with Gr. *makros*, long]

meal[1] (mēl) *n.* **1** food taken at one of the customary times of eating, a repast. **2** the occasion or usual time of this. **to make a meal of 1** to exaggerate the importance, difficulty etc. of. **2** to eat as a meal. **meals on wheels** *n.* a scheme by which pre-cooked meals are delivered by vehicles to the housebound, needy etc. **meal ticket** *n.* **1** a ticket given in exchange for a meal, often at a subsidized price. **2** (*coll., often derog.*) a person upon whom one can depend for financial support. **mealtime** *n.* [OE *mǣl* (cp. Dut. *maal*, Icel. *māl*, G *Mal*, time, *Mahl*, meal), cogn. with METE[1]]

meal[2] (mēl) *n.* **1** the edible portion of grain or pulse ground into flour. **2** (*Sc.*) oatmeal. **3** (*N Am.*) cornflour. **4** any powder produced by grinding. **meal-beetle** *n.* a beetle of the genus *Tenebrio*, esp. *T. molitor*, feeding on meal, flour etc. **mealworm** *n.* the larva of the meal-beetle. **mealy** *a.* (*comp.* **mealier**, *superl.* **mealiest**) **1** of, containing or resembling meal. **2** powdery, friable, floury, farinaceous. **3** besprinkled with or as with meal, spotty. **4** (of the complexion) pale. **5** mealy-mouthed. **mealiness** *n.* **mealy bug** *n.* an insect of the genus *Pseudococcus*, infesting vines and hothouse plants. **mealy-mouthed** *a.* unwilling to speak plainly and honestly, hypocritical. [OE *melu* (cp. Dut. and Dan. *meel*, G *Mehl*), cogn. with L *molere*, to grind]

mealie (mē´li), **mielie** *n.* (*S Afr.*) **1** (*usu. pl.*) maize. **2** a cob of corn. [Afrikaans *milje*, Port. *milho*, MILLET]

mean[1] (mēn) *v.t.* (*past, p.p.* **meant** (ment)) **1** to intend, to purpose, to have in the mind. **2** to denote, to signify. **3** to entail, to involve. **4** (of a word) to have as an explanation or equivalent. **5** to intend to convey or to indicate. **6** to design, to destine (for). ~*v.i.* **1** to have a specified intention or disposition. **2** to have a specified degree of importance (to). **to mean it** to be serious, not joking about something. **to mean to say** to admit reluctantly (*Do you mean to say you have crashed my car!*). **to mean well** to have good intentions. **meaning** *n.* that which is meant, significance, import. ~*a.* significant, expressive (*a meaning look*). **meaningful** *a.* **1** significant. **2** (*Logic*) able to be interpreted. **meaningfully** *adv.* **meaningfulness** *n.* **meaningless** *a.* **meaninglessly** *adv.* **meaninglessness** *n.* **meaningly** *adv.* [OE *mænan* (cp. Dut. *meenen*, Dan. *mene*, G *meinen*)]

mean[2] (mēn) *a.* **1** occupying a middle position. **2** equidistant from two extremes. **3** not extreme, moderate, not excessive. **4** intervening. **5** (*Math.*) **a** intermediate in value between the first and last quantities of a progression. **b** average. ~*n.* **1** the middle point, state, course, quality or degree between two extremes. **2** (*Math.*) **a** a quantity intermediate between the first and last quantities of a progression. **b** an average. **mean free path** *n.* the average distance travelled by a gas particle, atom etc. between collisions. **mean sea level** *n.* the sea level at the midpoint between high and low water. **mean sun** *n.* an imaginary sun moving along the celestial equator at a constant speed, used in calculating solar time, as distinct from the real sun whose speed varies. **meantime, meanwhile** *adv.* **1** in the intervening time. **2** while this was happening etc. ~*n.* the interval between two given times (*in the meantime, in the meanwhile*). **mean time** *n.* the time calculated from the movement of the mean sun. [OF *meien, moien* (F *moyen*), late L *mediānus*, L *medius*, middle]

mean[3] (mēn) *a.* **1** low in quality, capacity, value, rank etc. **2** inferior, poor, inefficient. **3** low-minded, petty, stingy, miserly. **4** shabby, lowly. **5** ignoble, disreputable, despicable. **6** (*esp. N Am.*) bad-tempered, vicious, aggressive. **7** (*coll.*) having or showing great skill, excellent. **no mean** good, not to be underestimated (*no mean cricketer*). **mean-born** *a.* of humble birth. **meanie, meany** *n.* (*pl.* **meanies**) (*coll.*) a petty-minded or miserly person. **meanly** *adv.* **meanness** *n.* **mean-spirited** *a.* **mean-spiritedly** *adv.* **mean white** *n.* POOR

WHITE (under POOR). [OE *mǣne*, *gemǣne* (cp. Dut. *gemeen*, Icel. *meinn*, G *gemein*), cogn. with L *commūnis*, COMMON]

meander (mian´də) *v.i.* to wander, wind or flow in a tortuous course. ~*n.* **1** (*usu. pl.*) a tortuous or intricate course or bend. **2** (*usu. pl.*) a winding, a circuitous path or movement, a deviation. **3** a decorative pattern, fretwork etc. composed of intricately interlacing lines. **4** †a maze, a labyrinth. **meandering** *a.* [L *Meander*, Gr. *Maiandros*, a winding river in Phrygia]

means (mēnz) *n.pl.* **1** (*also as sing.*) that by which anything is done or a result attained. **2** available resources, income, wealth. **by all manner of means** certainly, by all means. **by all means** certainly, undoubtedly. **by any means 1** in any way possible, somehow. **2** at all. **by fair means or foul** by any means whatsoever. **by means of** by the agency or instrumentality of. **by no manner of means** certainly not, by no means. **by no means** certainly not, on no account whatever. **means test** *n.* the official investigation into the means of a person applying for pension, unemployment benefit etc. **means-test** *v.t.* [MEAN[2]]

meant MEAN[1].

meantime, meanwhile MEAN[2].

measles (mē´zəlz) *n.pl.* **1** a contagious viral disease, indicated by red spots on the skin, usu. attacking children. **2** the spots of this disease. **3** a disease caused by the larvae of a tapeworm in pigs, cattle etc. **measled** *a.* **measly** *a.* **1** (*coll.*) worthless, paltry, meagre. **2** infected with measles. **3** (of pork etc.) infected with tapeworm larvae. [ME *maseles* (cp. Dut. *mazelen*), from Gmc. *mas- mæs*, whence MAZER]

measure (mezh´ə) *n.* **1** the extent or dimensions of a thing as determined by measuring. **2** an instrument for measuring, as a rod, tape etc., or a vessel of standard capacity. **3** a standard of measurement. **4** a definite unit of capacity or extent. **5** the measurements necessary to make an article of dress. **6** a system of measuring. **7** the act of measuring, measurement. **8** a quantity measured out, taken as a rule or standard. **9** a prescribed or allotted extent, length or quantity. **10** limit, moderation, just degree or amount. **11** metre, poetical rhythm. **12** an action to achieve a purpose (*emergency measures*). **13** a law, a statute, an Act of Parliament. **14** (*pl.*) a series of beds, strata. **15** (*Mus.*) time, pace, the contents of a bar. **16** †a slow and stately dance. ~*v.t.* **1** to determine the extent or quantity of by comparison with a definite unit or standard. **2** to take the dimensions of. **3** to weigh, to judge, to value or estimate by comparison with a rule or standard. **4** to serve as the measure of. **5** to allot or apportion by measure. **6** to travel over, to cover. **7** to survey, look up and down. **8** to bring into competition (with). **9** †to regulate, to keep within bounds. **10** †to set to metre. ~*v.i.* **1** to take measurements. **2** to be in extent, to show by measurement. **beyond measure** exceedingly, excessively. **for good measure** as an additional amount, over and above that required. **in a measure** in some measure. **in some measure** to some extent, to a certain degree. **to measure one's length** to fall flat on one's face. **to measure up 1** to measure with a view to fitting something. **2** to take complete measurements. **3** to be good enough. **to measure up to** to be adequate for. **to take measures** to adopt means, to take steps (to). **to take someone's measure 1** to find out what kind of a person someone is. **2** to measure someone for clothes. **within measure** in moderation. **without measure** immoderately. **measurable** *a.* that can be measured. **within a measurable distance of** almost at (a point of something undesirable etc.). **measurability** (-bil´-) *n.* **measurably** *adv.* **measured** *a.* **1** well-considered, carefully weighed. **2** of definite measure. **3** deliberate and uniform. **4** rhythmical. **measuredly** *adv.* **measureless** *a.* **measurelessly** *adv.* **measurement** *n.* **1** the act of measuring. **2** an extent or dimension determined by measurement. **3** (*pl.*) detailed dimensions; vital statistics. **measure of capacity** *n.* a measure for vessels, liquids, grain etc. **measurer** *n.* **measuring** *n.*, *a.* **measuring jug, measuring cup** *n.* a graduated jug or cup used for measuring ingredients in cooking. **measuring tape** *n.* a marked tape used to measure length. **measuring worm** *n.* the caterpillar of a geometrid moth. [OF *mesure*, L *mensūra*, from *mens-*, p.p. stem of *mētīrī*, to measure]

meat (mēt) *n.* **1** the flesh of animals, usu. excluding fish and fowl, used as food. **2** the substance of something, the pith. **3** the edible part of a nut, egg, shellfish etc. **4** †solid food of any kind. **5** †the partaking of food, a meal. **after meat** immediately after a meal. **before meat** immediately before a meal. **meat and drink** something readily acceptable (to), a source of pleasure (to). **to sit at meat** to sit at table. **meat-axe** *n.* a butcher's cleaver. **meatball** *n.* a ball of minced meat, eaten e.g. with a sauce and spaghetti. **meat-eater** *n.* **1** a person who eats meat. **2** a carnivore. **meat-fly** *n.* (*pl.* **meat-flies**) a fly that breeds in meat, a blowfly. **meat-free** *a.* (of food) vegetarian, containing, or prepared using, no animal products. **meatless** *a.* **meat loaf** *n.* a loaf-shaped mass of minced or chopped meat, cooked and often eaten cold. **meat safe** *n.* a cupboard, usu. of wire gauze or perforated zinc, for storing meat. **meaty** *a.* (*comp.* **meatier,** *superl.* **meatiest**) **1** containing much meat. **2** of or like meat. **3** substantial, pithy. **meatily** *adv.* **meatiness** *n.* [OE *mete* (cp. Icel. *matr*, Swed. *mat*, OHG *maz*)]

meatus (miā´təs) *n.* (*pl.* **meatus, meatuses**) (*Anat.*) a passage, channel or tubular canal. [L, from *meāre*, to flow]

Mecca (mek´ə) *n.* **1** a place frequently visited (*a tourist Mecca*). **2** a holy place. **3** the object of a person's aspirations. [city in Saudi Arabia, birthplace of Muhammad]

Meccano® (mikah´nō) *n.* a set of toy engineering parts that can be built up into various mechanical models.

mechanic (mikan´ik) *n.* **1** a person who is employed or skilled in repairing or maintaining machines. **2** a skilled workman. **3** (*pl.*) the practical details of an operation, project etc. **mechanician** (mekənish´ən) *n.* a person skilled in contructing machines, tools etc. **mechanico-** *comb. form.* **mechanics** *n.* **1** the branch of physics treating of the motion and equilibrium of material bodies. **2** the science of machinery. **Newtonian mechanics** NEWTONIAN. **quantum mechanics** QUANTUM. [L *mēchanicus*, Gr. *mēchanikos*, from *mēchanē*, MACHINE]

mechanical (mikan´ikəl) *a.* **1** of or relating to machinery or mechanisms. **2** working with tools or machinery. **3** of or relating to mechanics. **4 a** machine-like, automatic, done from force of habit. **b** slavish, unoriginal. **5** in accordance with physical laws. **6** acting or affected by physical power without chemical change. **7** produced by machinery. **8** of or relating to handicraft. **9** †vulgar, rude, base. ~*n.* **1** (*pl.*) the mechanical parts of something. **2** †a manual worker (*a rude mechanical*). **mechanical advantage** *n.* the ratio of personal force exerted to the force actually applied by a machine. **mechanical arts** *n.pl.* those in which the hands and body are chiefly concerned. **mechanical drawing** *n.* a precise scale drawing of a piece of machinery etc. from which measurements can be taken. **mechanical engineer** *n.* an engineer dealing with the design and construction of machinery. **mechanical engineering** *n.* **mechanical equivalent of heat** *n.* (*Physics*) the factor for converting units of mechanical energy into units of heat. **mechanical excavator** *n.* a machine to excavate soil by means of a scoop suspended from a crane jib and dragged along the ground. **mechanicalism** *n.* **mechanicalist** *n.* **1** a mechanician. **2** a believer in

philosophical mechanism. **mechanically** *adv.* **mechanicalness** *n.* **mechanical powers** *n.pl.* the simple machines, the wedge, the inclined plane, the screw, the lever, the wheel and axle and the pulley.
mechanician MECHANIC.
mechanism (mek´ənizm) *n.* **1** the structure or correlation of parts of a machine. **2** a piece of machinery. **3** a system of correlated parts working reciprocally together, as a machine. **4** a means. **5** in art, mechanical execution as distinguished from style etc., technique. **6** (*Philos.*) the doctrine that phenomena can be explained purely in terms of mechanical or biological interactions. **mechanist** *n.* **1** a mechanician. **2** a person skilled in mechanics. **3** a believer in mechanism. **mechanistic** (-nis´-) *a.* **mechanistically** *adv.*
mechanize (mek´ənīz), **mechanise** *v.t.* **1** to make mechanical. **2** to introduce machines in or to do. **3** to equip (troops) with mechanical transport. **mechanization** (-zā´shən) *n.* **mechanizer** *n.*
mechano- (mek´ənō) *comb. form* of or relating to mechanics or machinery.
mechanoreceptor (mekənōrisep´tə) *n.* (*Anat.*) a sensory receptor, as in the skin, that responds to mechanical stimuli such as pressure, sound etc.
mechanotherapy (mikanōther´əpi) *n.* the treatment of disease through the agency of mechanical appliances.
mechanotropism (mikanōtrō´pizm) *n.* the bending of tendrils or other plant organs through reaction to contact or other mechanical stimulus.
mechatronics (mekətron´iks) *n.* technology that combines electronics with mechanical engineering in design and manufacture.
Mechlin (mek´lin), **Mechlin lace** *n.* a light lace made at Mechlin (Malines), near Brussels.
M.Econ *abbr.* Master of Economics.
meconic (mikon´ik) *a.* contained in or derived from the poppy. **meconin** (mek´ənin, mē´-) *n.* a neutral substance existing in opium. **meconium** (mikō´niəm) *n.* **1** thickened poppy juice. **2** (*Med.*) the first faeces of infants consisting of excretions from the liver etc. **meconopsis** (mēkənop´sis) *n.* any flowering plant of the genus *Meconopsis*, related to and resembling the poppy. [Gr. *mēkōn*, poppy]
Med (med) *n.* (*coll.*) the Mediterranean Sea.
M.Ed. *abbr.* Master of Education.
med. *abbr.* **1** medical, medicine. **2** medieval. **3** medium.
medal (med´əl) *n.* a piece of metal, often in the form of a coin, stamped with a figure and inscription to commemorate some illustrious person, event or achievement. †**medalet** *n.* a small medal, esp. one bearing the image of a saint. **medalled,** (*N Am.*) **medaled** *a.* **medallic** (midal´-) *a.* **medallion** (midal´yən) *n.* **1** a large medal. **2** (*Archit.*) a tablet or panel, usually round or oval, containing painted or sculptured figures, decorations etc. **medallist,** (*N Am.*) **medalist** *n.* **1** a person who has gained a medal. **2** a person who designs or engraves medals. **3** a collector or dealer in medals. **medal play** *n.* in golf, scoring by strokes, not by holes, stroke play. [F *médaille*, It. *medaglia*, pop. L *metallea*, L *metallum*, METAL]
meddle (med´əl) *v.i.* **1** to interfere (in) officiously. **2** to concern or busy oneself (with) unnecessarily. **3** †to mix. **meddler** *n.* **meddlesome** *a.* **meddlesomely** *adv.* **meddlesomeness** *n.* [A-F *medler*, OF *mesler* (F *mêler*), med. L *misculāre*, L *miscēre*, to mix]
Mede (mēd) *n.* (*Hist.*) a member of an Indo-European people who established an empire in Media, now NW Iran, in the 7th and 6th cents. BC. **Median** *a.* [ME from L *medi* from Gr. *Mēdoi*]
☒ **medecine** common misspelling of MEDICINE.
media[1] (mē´diə) *n.pl.* the means of communication with large numbers of people, i.e. radio, TV, Internet, newspapers etc. **media event** *n.* an event arranged primarily to gain publicity, rather than being of intrinsic interest.

Usage note *Media* is sometimes used as a singular noun (*a media*), and a plural *medias* may also be encountered, but both these uses are best avoided.

media[2] (mē´diə) *n.* (*pl.* **mediae** (-iē)) **1** (*Anat.*) the middle coat or tunic of a vessel. **2** in phonetics, a consonant intermediate between a plosive and a fricative. [L, fem. of *medius*, middle]
media[3] MEDIUM.
mediacy MEDIATE[2].
mediae MEDIA[2].
mediaeval MEDIEVAL.
medial (mē´diəl) *a.* **1** of, relating to or situated in the middle, intermediate. **2** mean or average. ~*n.* **1** a medial letter. **2** †in phonetics, a media. **medially** *adv.* [late L *mediālis*, see MEDIA[2]]
Median MEDE.
median (mē´diən) *a.* **1** (*Anat.*) situated in the middle, esp. in the plane dividing the body longitudinally into two equal halves. **2** intermediate, as a line or zone between the extreme limits of winds, calm belts etc. ~*n.* **1** a straight line joining the vertex of a triangle to the midpoint of the opposite side. **2** in statistics, a number in the middle position within a series of numbers. **3** (*Anat.*) a median artery etc. **medianly** *adv.*
mediant (mē´diənt) *n.* (*Mus.*) the third tone of any scale. [It. *mediante*, late L *medians -antem*, pres.p. of *mediāre*, to MEDIATE[1]]
mediastinum (mēdiəstī´nəm) *n.* (*pl.* **mediastina** (-nə)) (*Anat.*) a membranous septum or cavity between the two main parts of an organ etc., esp. the folds of the pleura between the right and left lung. **mediastinal** *a.* [L, neut. of *mediastīnus*, orig. a common servant, a drudge]
mediate[1] (mē´diāt) *v.t.* **1** to interpose between (parties) in order to reconcile them. **2** to effect by means of intervention. **3** to serve as a connecting link or medium between. ~*v.i.* **1** to interpose (between) in order to reconcile parties etc. **2** to serve as a connecting link or medium (between). **mediation** (-ā´shən) *n.* **mediator** *n.* **mediatorial** (-taw´-) *a.* **mediatorially** (-taw´-) *adv.* **mediatory** (mē´-) *a.*, *n.* [late L *mediātus*, p.p. of *mediāre*, from *medius*, middle]
mediate[2] (mē´diət) *a.* **1** situated in the middle or between two extremes. **2** intervening, indirect, secondary. **3** serving or acting as an intervening or indirect means or agency. **4** effected or connected by such means. **mediacy** *n.* **mediately** *adv.* **mediateness** *n.*
mediatize (mē´diətīz), **mediatise** *v.t.* **1** to make dependent. **2** to annex (a state), disestablish politically and subject to a larger state, leaving the ruler a nominal sovereignty. **mediatization** (-zā´shən) *n.* [F *médiatiser*, from *médiat*, MEDIATE[1]]
medic[1] (med´ik) *n.* (*coll.*) **1** a medical student. **2** a physician, a doctor.
medic[2] MEDICK.
Medicaid (med´ikād) *n.* in the US, government-sponsored health insurance for the needy. [*medic*al, *aid*]
medical (med´ikəl) *a.* **1** of or relating to medicine. **2** curative, healing, medicinal. **3** of or relating to medicine as opposed to surgery etc. (*a medical ward*). ~*n.* **1** an examination to ascertain a person's state of physical fitness. **2** (*coll.*) a medical student. **medicable** *a.* able to be treated or cured. **medical certificate** *n.* a document issued by a doctor stating that a person is unfit for work etc. **medical examination** *n.* an examination by a doctor to ascertain a person's physical fitness. **medical examiner** *n.* (*N Am.*) a public official, usu. a physician, appointed to inquire into cases of sudden or suspicious death. **medical jurisprudence** *n.* FORENSIC MEDICINE (under FORENSIC). **medically** *adv.* **medical officer** *n.* a

doctor in charge of health services in a local authority, institution etc. **medical practitioner** *n.* a physician or surgeon, a doctor. **medicament** (medik´ə-, med´-) *n.* a healing substance or application. **medicamental** (-men´-) *a.* **medicamentally** *adv.* **medicate** *v.t.* **1** to treat medically. **2** to impregnate with anything medicinal. **medication** (-ā´shən) *n.* **1** treatment with medicine or drugs. **2** a medicine or drug. **medicative** (-kə-) *a.* [F *médical*, late L *medicālis*, from *medicus*, a physician, cognate with *medēre*, to heal]

Medicare (med´ikeə) *n.* **1** in the US, government-sponsored health insurance for the elderly. **2** in Canada and Australia, a government-funded health care scheme. [*medi*cal *care*]

medicate, medication etc. MEDICAL.

Medicean (medichē´ən, -sē´-) *a.* of or relating to the wealthy Medici family who were rulers of Florence in the 15th and 16th cents.

medicine (med´sin, -isin) *n.* **1** a substance, usu. taken internally, used for the alleviation or removal of disease. **2** the art or science of preserving health and curing or alleviating disease, esp. as distinct from surgery and obstetrics. **3** among N American Indians, anything supposed to possess supernatural powers or influence, a charm, a fetish. *~v.t.* to treat or cure with medicine. **a dose of one's own medicine** unpleasant treatment in retaliation for the same. **a taste of one's own medicine** unpleasant treatment in retaliation for the same. **to take one's medicine** to accept stoically an unpleasant ordeal, duty, undertaking etc. **medicinal** (-dis´-) *a.* **medicinally** *adv.* **medicine ball** *n.* a very heavy ball thrown from one person to another as physical exercise. **medicine chest** *n.* a box, cupboard etc. containing medicine, bandages etc. **medicine man** *n.* **1** a witch doctor. **2** a person believed to have magical powers of healing, esp. among N American Indians. [OF *medecine*, L *medicīna*, from *medicus*, see MEDICAL]

medick (med´ik), **medic** *n.* any plant of the genus *Medicago*, allied to the clover, esp. *M. sativa*, alfalfa. [L *mēdica*, Gr. *Mēdikē*, fem. of *-kos*, (grass) of Media]

medico (med´ikō) *n.* (*pl.* **medicos**) (*coll.*) **1** a physician, a doctor. **2** a medical student. [It.]

medico- (med´ikō) *comb. form* medical.

medieval (mediē´vəl), **mediaeval** *a.* of or relating to, or characteristic of the Middle Ages. *~n.* a person who lived in the Middle Ages. **medieval history** *n.* history from the fall of Rome (AD 476) until the Renaissance (15th cent.). **medievalism** *n.* **medievalist** *n.* **medievalize, medievalise** *v.t., v.i.* **Medieval Latin** *n.* the Latin language as used in Europe in the Middle Ages AD 600–1500. **medievally** *adv.* [L *medius*, middle, *aevum*, age]

medina (midē´nə), **Medina** *n.* the ancient Arab quarter of N African cities.

medio- (mē´diō) *comb. form* situated in, of or relating to the middle. [L *medius*, middle]

mediocre (mēdiō´kə) *a.* **1** of middling quality. **2** indifferently good or bad, average, commonplace. **mediocrity** (-ok´-) *n.* (*pl.* **mediocrities**) **1** the state of being mediocre. **2** a mediocre person. [F *médiocre*, L *mediocris -crem*, from *medius*, as MEDIO-]

meditate (med´itāt) *v.i.* **1** to engage in contemplation, esp. on religious or spiritual matters. **2** to enter into a state of relaxation and unconscious thought by means of mental exercise. **3** to ponder, to engage in thought (upon), to muse, to cogitate. *~v.t.* **1** to dwell upon mentally. **2** to plan, to design, to intend. **meditation** (-ā´shən) *n.* **meditative** (-tə-) *a.* **meditatively** *adv.* **meditativeness** *n.* **meditator** *n.* [L *meditātus*, p.p. of *meditārī*, cogn. with Gr. *medesthai*, to think about]

Mediterranean (meditərā´niən) *a.* **1** denoting, of or relating to the sea between Europe and Africa or the countries surrounding it. **2** having a warm climate similar to that of the Mediterranean countries. **3** †surrounded by or lying between lands. *~n.* the sea between Europe and Africa. [L *mediterrāneus* (*medi-*, MEDIO-, *terra*, land)]

medium (mē´diəm, mēd´yəm) *n.* (*pl.* **media** (-diə), **mediums**) **1** anything serving as an intermediary, agent or instrument. **2** a means of communication (see also MEDIA[1]). **3** an intervening substance or element, such as the air or ether, through which forces act, impressions are conveyed etc. **4** a substance in which germs are developed. **5** an instrument of exchange, such as money. **6** a middle or intermediate object, quality, degree etc. **7** a size of paper, 23½ × 18½ in. (59.5 × 47 cm), between demy and royal. **8** any material used in a work of art. **9** the middle term of a syllogism. **10** (*pl.* **mediums**) a person claiming to receive communications from the spirit world. *~a.* **1** intermediate in quantity, quality or degree. **2** average, moderate, middling, mediocre. **medium bowler** *n.* in cricket, a bowler who bowls at medium pace. **medium dry, medium sweet** *a.* (of a wine etc.) having a flavour between dry and sweet. **medium frequency** *n.* the frequency of radio waves between 300 kHz and 3 MHz. **mediumism** *n.* the beliefs or practices of spiritualistic mediums. **mediumistic** (-mis´-) *a.* of or relating to a spiritualistic medium. **mediumize, mediumise** *v.t.* to act as a spiritualistic medium. **medium of circulation** *n.* anything, such as coin, acceptable as a standard instrument of commercial transaction. **medium-range** *a.* (of a missile) having a range between 300 and 3100 miles (about 500 to 5000 km). *~n.* a medium-frequency radio wave. **mediumship** *n.* the fact of supposedly being a spiritualistic medium. **medium-sized** *a.* of average size. **medium sweet** MEDIUM DRY (under MEDIUM). **medium wave** *n.* the medium frequency; a radio wave in the medium frequency. [L, neut. of *medius*, middle]

Medjidie (məjē´diə) *n.* **1** a Turkish order of knighthood established by Sultan Abdul-Medjid in 1851. **2** a Turkish coin first minted by Sultan Abdul-Medjid. [Turk. *mejīdie*]

medlar (med´lə) *n.* **1** a rosaceous tree, *Mespilus germanica*. **2** the fruit of this tree, which is eaten when beginning to decay. [A-F *medler*, OF *meslier*, L *mespila*, Gr. *mespilē*]

medley (med´li) *n.* (*pl.* **medleys**) **1** a musical or literary miscellany. **2** a mixed or confused mass, esp. of incongruous objects, persons, materials etc. *~†a.* mixed, multifarious, motley. *~†v.t.* (*3rd pers. sing. pres.* **medleys**, *pres.p.* **medleying**, *past, p.p.* **medleyed**) to make a medley of. **medley relay** *n.* a relay race in which each swimmer uses a different stroke. [A-F *medlee*, OF *meslee* (F *mêlée*), as MEDDLE]

Medoc (mādok´) *n.* a red claret wine. [from *Médoc*, a district in Gironde, SW France]

medulla (midŭl´ə) *n.* (*pl.* **medullas, medullae** (-lē)) **1** the inner part of certain organs, as the kidneys. **2** the marrow of bones, esp. that of the spine. **3** the spinal cord. **4** the pith of hair. **5** the internal tissue or pith of plants. **medulla oblongata** (oblong·gah´tə) *n.* the elongated medulla or continuation of the spinal cord forming the hindmost segment of the brain. **medullary, medullar** *a.* **medullin** (-in) *n.* cellulose or lignin from the pith of certain plants. **medullose** (med´-) *a.* [L, prob. rel. to *medius*, middle]

medusa (midū´zə, -sə) *n.* (*pl.* **medusae** (-zē, -sē), **medusas**) **1** a jellyfish. **2** a coelenterate in its jelly-like form. **medusal, medusiform** *a.* **medusan, medusoid** *n., a.* [L, from Gr. *Medousa*, one of the three Gorgons whose head (which turned beholders to stone) was cut off by Perseus and placed by Athene on her shield]

meed (mēd) *n.* **1** (*poet.*) reward, recompense, esp. for merit. **2** †merit, worth. **meedless** *a.* [OE *mēd* (cp. G *Miete*, also Gr. *misthos*, Sansk. *mīdha*, reward)]

meek (mēk) *a.* mild, submissive, humble, tame, gentle, forbearing. **meeken** *v.t.* **meekly** *adv.* **meekness** *n.* [MG *meoc*, Icel. *mjūkr* (cp. Swed. *mjūk*, Dan. *myg*)]

meerkat (miə´kat) *n.* a small, carnivorous mongoose of southern Africa, esp. the grey meerkat. [Dut., sea-cat]

meerschaum (miə´shəm) *n.* **1** a white compact hydrous magnesium silicate, used for tobacco pipes. **2** a pipe made of this. [G, sea-foam (*Meer*, sea, *Schaum*, foam)]

meet[1] (mēt) *v.t.* (*past, p.p.* **met** (met)) **1** to come face to face with. **2** to go to a place in order to join or receive (someone). **3** to be introduced to (another person). **4** (of a road, railway, etc.) to reach and touch or unite with. **5** to encounter, to confront, to oppose. **6** to experience. **7** to refute. **8** to answer, to satisfy. **9** to pay, to discharge. *~v.i.* **1** to come face to face. **2** to assemble. **3** to be introduced, to become acquainted. **4** to come into contact. **5** to be united. *~n.* **1** a meeting of people, usu. for a hunt or sports activities involving cyclists, athletes etc. **2** the persons assembled or the place appointed for a meet. **3** (*Austral.*) an appointment. **more than meets the eye** complexities or problems that are not apparent at first. **to meet halfway** to compromise with. **to meet one's maker** MAKER (under MAKE[1]). **to meet one's match** MATCH[1]. **to meet someone's eye** to exchange glances, usu. in a knowing way. **to meet the ear** to be heard. **to meet the eye** to be seen. **to meet up** to make contact (with), esp. by chance. **to meet with 1** to come across. **2** to have a meeting with. **3** to experience, to encounter, to engage, to receive (*to meet with problems*; *to meet with approval*). †**well met** welcome (a greeting). **meeting** *n.* **1** an assembly. **2** the persons assembled. **3** a coming together, a union (*a meeting of minds*). **4** a race meeting. **5** a confluence, intersection. **6** a contest, duel etc. **meeting house** *n.* a place of worship, esp. of Quakers. [OE *mētan* (cp. Dut. *mœten*, Icel. *mœta*, Swed. *möta*), cogn. with *mōt*, *gemōt*, MOOT]

†**meet**[2] (mēt) *a.* fit, proper, suitable. **meetly** *adv.* **meetness** *n.* [MG *mēte*, OE *gemǣte*, fitting well, cogn. with METE[1]]

mega (meg´ə) *a.* (*coll.*) **1** very large in number. **2** excellent, brilliant. [as MEGA-]

mega- (meg´ə) *comb. form* **1** great, large. **2** one million. **3** (*coll.*) great in number, significance, impressiveness etc. [Gr. *megas*, fem. *megalē*, great]

megabit (meg´əbit) *n.* (*Comput.*) **1** one million bits. **2** 2^{20} bits.

megabuck (meg´əbŭk) *n.* (*coll.*) **1** a million dollars. **2** (*pl.*) a large amount of money.

megabyte (meg´əbīt) *n.* (*Comput.*) **1** one million bytes. **2** 2^{20} bytes.

megacephalic (megəsifal´ik, -kef-), **megacephalous** (-sef´ələs, -kef-) *a.* large-headed. **megacephaly** *n.*

megadeath (meg´ədeth) *n.* one million deaths, esp. in nuclear war.

megaflop (meg´əflop) *n.* **1** (*Comput.*) a measure of processing speed equal to one million floating-point operations per second. **2** (*sl.*) a huge failure.

megahertz (meg´əhœts) *n.* (*pl.* **megahertz**) a unit of frequency equal to one million hertz.

megal- MEGALO-.

megalith (meg´əlith) *n.* **1** a great stone. **2** a monument made of large stones, such as a cromlech, stone circle etc. **megalithic** (-lith´-) *a.*

megalo- (meg´əlō), **megal-** *comb. form* great. [as MEGA-]

megalomania (megələmā´niə) *n.* **1** a form of mental disorder characterized by delusions of grandeur or power. **2** a craze for overstatement etc. **megalomaniac** (-ak) *n., a.* **megalomaniacal** (-mənī´əkəl) *a.* **megalomanic** (-man´-) *a.*

megalopolis (megəlop´əlis) *n.* (*pl.* **megalopolises**) a large, densely-populated urban area. **megalopolitan** (-ləpol´itən) *a.*

megalosaurus (megələsaw´rəs), **megalosaur** *n.* an extinct carnivorous lizard of the genus *Megalosaurus.*

Megan's Law (mē´gənz) *n.* (*US*) a law requiring that a community be notified of paedophiles and other sex offenders living in the area. [*Megan* Kanka, a child murdered by neighbours who were convicted paedophiles, whose mother campaigned for the law]

megaphone (meg´əfōn) *n.* **1** a hand-held apparatus for amplifying the voice. **2** a large speaking-trumpet.

megapode (meg´əpōd), **megapod** (-pod) *n.* an Australian or Malaysian bird of the family Megapolidae, which builds mounds to incubate its eggs in.

megaron (meg´əron) *n.* (*pl.* **megara** (-rə)) the central room of a large Mycenaean house. [Gr., hall]

megaspore (meg´əspaw) *n.* **1** any one of the larger kind of spores in some cryptogams, from which female gametophytes develop. **2** an immature embryo sac in seed plants.

megass (migas´) *n.* fibrous residue after sugar has been extracted from the cane, bagasse. [etym. unknown]

megastar (meg´əstah) *n.* a very popular, internationally-known star of the cinema, theatre etc. **megastardom** *n.*

megastore (meg´əstaw) *n.* a large usu. out-of-town store selling many different products.

megathere (meg´əthiə) *n.* an extinct gigantic sloth-like edentate of the genus *Megatherium*, from S America. **megatherial** (-thiə´-) *a.*

megaton (meg´ətŭn), **megatonne** *n.* **1** one million tons. **2** a unit of explosive power in nuclear weapons, equal to a million tons of TNT.

megavolt (meg´əvōlt) *n.* one million volts.

megawatt (meg´əwot) *n.* one million watts.

Megger® (meg´ə) *n.* an instrument for measuring high electrical resistances.

megilp (məgilp´), **magilp** *n.* a mixture of linseed oil and mastic varnish added to oil paints. [etym. uncertain]

megohm (meg´ōm) *n.* one million ohms.

megrim[1] (mē´grim) *n.* **1** †a migraine. **2** a sudden attack due to congestion of the brain causing a horse at work to reel or fall, staggers. **3** (*pl.*) low spirits, depression. **4** a whim, a fad. [corr. of *migrane*, F *migraine*, L *hēmicrania*, Gr. *hēmikrania* (HEMI-, *kranion*, skull)]

megrim[2] (mē´grim) *n.* either of two deep-water flatfishes *Lepidorhombus whiffiagonis* and *Arnoglossus laterna*, the sail-fluke. [19th cent., etym. uncertain]

†**meinie** (mā´ni) *n.* **1** a household. **2** a body of household attendants, a retinue. [OF *meyné*, *mesnie*, ult. from L *mansio -ōnem*, MANSION]

meiosis (mīō´sis, mi-) *n.* (*pl.* **meioses** (-sēz)) **1** (*Biol.*) the diminution of the number of chromosomes in the cell nucleus. **2** (*Gram.*) litotes, depreciative hyperbole. **meiotic** (-ot´ik) *a.* **meiotically** *adv.* [Gr., from *meioun*, to lessen, from *meiōn*, less]

Meissen (mī´sən) *n.* a type of fine German porcelain. [produced at *Meissen* near Dresden in the 18th cent.]

meistersinger (mī´stəsingə) *n.* (*pl.* **meistersinger**) a German burgher poet and musician of the 14th–16th cents., one of the successors of the minnesingers. [G, mastersinger]

melamine (mel´əmēn) *n.* **1** a white crystalline compound used for making synthetic resins. **2** (*also* **melamine resin**) a resin made from this, used in moulded products, adhesives, coatings etc. [G *Melamin*]

melan- (mel´ən), **melano-** (-ō) *comb. form* dark, black.

melanaemia (melənē´miə), (*esp. N Am.*) **melanemia** *n.* (*Med.*) a condition in which the blood contains an excessive proportion of melanin. **melanaemic** *a.* [MELAN-, Gr. *haima*, blood]

melancholia (melənkō´liə) *n.* a mental disorder, often preceding mania, characterized by depression, frequently with suicidal tendencies (formerly supposed to be due to excess of black bile). [MELANCHOLY]

melancholy (mel´ənkəli) *n.* (*pl.* **melancholies**) **1** a gloomy, dejected state of mind, sadness, gloom, depression, despondency, melancholia. 2 (*poet.*) pensive contemplation. ~*a.* 1 sad, gloomy, depressed in spirits. 2 mournful, saddening. 3 pensive. **melancholic** (-kol´-) *a.* **melancholically** *adv.* [OF *melancolie,* L and Gr. *melancholia* (MELAN-, *cholōs,* bile)]

melanemia MELANAEMIA.

Melanesian (melənē´zhən) *a.* 1 of or relating to Melanesia, the group of islands in the Pacific Ocean lying to the east of New Guinea. 2 of or relating to the language of Melanesia. ~*n.* 1 a native or inhabitant of Melanesia, esp. one of the dominant ethnic group. 2 the group of languages spoken by the dominant Melanesians. [Gr. *melas -anos,* black, *nēsos,* an island]

mélange (mālãzh´) *n.* a mixture, medley or miscellany. [F, from *mêler,* to mix, see MEDDLE]

melanin (mel´ənin) *n.* a black or dark brown pigment occurring in the hair, skin and iris of the eye. **melanic** (milan´ik) *a.* 1 black, dark-complexioned. 2 of or relating to melanosis. **melanoma** (-nō´mə) *n.* a malignant tumour with dark pigmentation, esp. on the skin. **melanosis** (-ō´sis), **melanism** *n.* 1 (*Med.*) excess of colouring-matter in the skin, hair and tissues. 2 (*Bot.*) a disease producing blackness in plants. **melanotic** (-ot´ik), **melanistic** (-is´tik) *a.* **melanous** (mel´-) *a.* having a dark or sallow complexion and black hair. **melanuria** (-nū´-) *n.* (*Med.*) a disorder characterized by blackness of the urine. **melanuric** (-nū´-) *a.* [MELAN-, -IN[1]]

melanite (mel´ənīt) *n.* a black variety of garnet.

melano- MELAN-.

melanochroi (melənok´rōī) *n.pl.* a postulated subdivision of the Caucasian race comprising those with dark hair and pale complexion. **melanochroic** (milanəkrō´ik), **melanochrous** (-nok´-) *a.* [pl. of Gr. *melanochroos* (*chroa,* skin, or *ōchros,* pale)]

melanoma, melanosis etc. MELANIN.

melatonin (mel´ətōnin) *n.* a hormone produced by the pineal gland. [Gr. *melas,* black]

Melba toast (mel´bə) *n.* very thin crisp toast. **to do a Melba** 1 (*Austral.*) to come out of retirement. 2 (*Austral.*) to make several farewell appearances. **Melba sauce** *n.* a sauce for puddings made from raspberries and icing sugar. [Dame Nellie *Melba,* 1861–1931, Austral. operatic soprano]

meld[1] (meld) *v.t., v.i.* in the card games, rummy, canasta etc., to declare (one's cards) for a score. ~*n.* a set or run of cards in the same games. [G *melden,* to announce]

meld[2] (meld) *v.t., v.i.* to mix, blend, combine. [*melt, weld*[2]]

mêlée (mel´ā), (*N Am.*) **melee** *n.* 1 a confused hand-to-hand fight, an affray. 2 a muddle. [F]

melic (mel´ik) *a.* (esp. of certain Greek lyric poetry) intended to be sung. [Gr. *melikos,* from *melos,* song]

melilot (mel´ilot) *n.* a plant of the leguminous genus *Melilotus.* [OF, from late L and Gr. *melilōtos* (*meli,* honey, LOTUS)]

melinite (mel´inīt) *n.* a French explosive containing picric acid. [F *mélinite* (Gr. *mēlinos,* from *mēlon,* apple)]

meliorate (mē´liərāt) *v.t.* (*formal*) to make better. ~*v.i.* to grow better. **melioration** (-ā´shən) *n.* **meliorative** *a.* **meliorism** *n.* the doctrine that society etc. may be improved by persistent practical effort. **meliorist** *n.* [late L *meliōrātus,* p.p. of *meliōrāre,* from L *melior,* better]

meliphagous (milif´əgəs) *a.* (*Zool.*) eating honey. [Gr. *meli,* honey, *-phagos,* eating, from *phagein,* to eat]

melisma (miliz´mə) *n.* (*pl.* **melismata** (-mətə), **melismas**) a melodic embellishment, consisting of a group of notes sung to a single syllable. **melismatic** (melizmat´-) *a.* [Gr., a song tune]

melliferous (melif´ərəs) *a.* producing or yielding honey. **mellific** *a.* **mellification** (melifikā´shən) *n.* **mellivorous** (-liv´-) *a.* eating honey. [L *mellifer* (*mel mellis,* honey, -FEROUS)]

mellifluous (melif´luəs) *a.* flowing smoothly and sweetly, pleasant, musical (usu. of a voice, words etc.). **mellifluence** *n.* **mellifluent** *a.* **mellifluously** *adv.* **mellifluousness** *n.* [L *mellifluus* (*mel mellis,* honey, *fluere,* to flow)]

mellophone (mel´əfōn) *n.* a brass musical instrument similar in tone to a French horn. [*mellow,* -PHONE]

mellow (mel´ō) *a.* 1 fully ripe, pulpy, sweet. 2 ripened or softened by age and experience, genial, kindly. 3 (*coll.*) jolly, half tipsy. 4 (of earth) rich, friable. 5 (of tones and colours) soft and rich. ~*v.i.* to become ripe, mature or softened, by age etc. ~*v.t.* to ripen, mature, soften. **mellowly** *adv.* **mellowness** *n.* [perh. from OE *melo,* MEAL[2], perh. conf. with *mearu,* tender]

melodeon (məlō´diən), **melodion** *n.* 1 a small German accordion. 2 an instrument similar to a harmonium with a row of reeds and a keyboard. [earlier *melodium,* Latinized from MELODY]

melodic, melodious etc. MELODY.

melodrama (mel´ədrahmə) *n.* 1 a sensational play, film, novel etc. with a plot characterized by startling situations, crude sentimentality and a happy ending. 2 (*Hist.*) a dramatic composition with songs intermixed. 3 sensational and extravagant events, behaviour or speech. **melodramatic** (-drəmat´-) *a.* **melodramatically** *adv.* **melodramatics** *n.* melodramatic behaviour. **melodramatist** (-dram´-) *n.* **melodramatize** (-dram´-), **melodramatise** *v.t.* to make (a situation etc.) melodramatic. [earlier *melodrame,* F *mélodrame* (Gr. *melos,* song, DRAMA)]

melody (mel´ədi) *n.* (*pl.* **melodies**) 1 an agreeable succession of sounds, esp. of simple tones in the same key, a tune. 2 a simple setting of words to music. 3 the chief part in harmonic music, the air. 4 music. **melodic** (-lod´-) *a.* 1 of, characterized by or producing melody. 2 musical, sounding sweetly. **melodically** *adv.* **melodic minor** *n.* a minor scale with a sharpened sixth or seventh when ascending which are played at the original pitch when descending. **melodious** (-lō´-) *a.* agreeably tuneful, melodic. **melodiously** *adv.* **melodiousness** *n.* **melodist** (mel´ədist) *n.* a composer of melodies. **melodize, melodise** *v.t.* to make a musical phrase, song etc. melodious. ~*v.i.* to compose or play sweet music. **melodizer** *n.* [OF *melodie,* late L and Gr. *melōdia,* from *melōdos,* singing, musical (*melos,* song, *ōdē,* see ODE)]

melon (mel´ən) *n.* 1 the edible fruit of various plants of the gourd family, usu. large and round with pulpy flesh and many seeds. 2 the plant that produces this. 3 a waxy mass in the head of some whales. [OF, from late L *mēlo -ōnem,* for *mēlopepo,* Gr. *mēlopepōn* (*mēlon,* apple, fruit, *pepōn,* a kind of gourd)]

melt (melt) *v.i.* (*p.p.* **melted,** †**molten** (mōl´tən)) 1 to pass from a solid to a liquid state by heat. 2 to dissolve. 3 to be dissipated, to disappear, to vanish (away). 4 to be softened to kindly influences, to give way. 5 to dissolve in tears. 6 to merge or blend (into). 7 (*coll.*) to perspire with heat, to be uncomfortably hot. ~*v.t.* 1 to make liquid by heat. 2 to dissolve. 3 to soften to tenderness. 4 to dissipate. ~*n.* 1 molten material. 2 a period of melting, a thaw. 3 a quantity melted together. **to melt away** to (make) disappear, esp. by liquefaction. **to melt down** 1 to reduce (esp. metal articles) to a molten state by heat. 2 to become liquid or molten. **to melt in the mouth** (of food) to be light and tasty. **meltable** *a.* **meltdown** *n.* 1 the melting of fuel rods in a nuclear reactor, often causing the escape of radiation into the environment. 2 an economic collapse. **melter** *n.* **melting** *a.* 1 that melts. 2 (of sound etc.) gentle and moving, tender. **meltingly** *adv.* **meltingness** *n.* **melting point** *n.* the temperature at which a solid begins to melt. **melting pot** *n.* **1** a crucible. **2** a situation or place where there is a mixture of ethnic groups, cultures, ideas etc. **in the melting pot** with an undecided future. **melt water** *n.* water produced by melting snow or ice, esp. from a glacier. [OE *meltan*, intr., and *mieltan*, tr. (cp. Icel. *melta*), cogn. with Gr. *meldein*, to melt, and L *mollis*, soft]

melton (mel´tən) *n.* a stout make of cloth without nap, used largely for overcoats. [*Melton* Mowbray, in Leicestershire]

member (mem´bə) *n.* **1** a person belonging to a society or body. **2** (**Member**) a member of Parliament or a similar body. **3** a branch or division of a society or organization. **4** a component part or element of an organism or complex whole. **5** a limb, a part or organ of the body. **6** the penis. **7** a set of figures or symbols forming part of a mathematical expression. **8** (in titles) a person admitted to a particular grade of honour. *~a.* (*attrib.*) that is a member (*a member state*). **membered** *a.* **memberless** *a.* **Member of Parliament** *n.* a person elected to represent a constituency in the House of Commons. **membership** *n.* **1** the state of being a member. **2** (a number of) members. **3** the whole body of members. **membral** *a.* (of the body) relating to the limbs rather than the trunk. [F *membre*, L *membrum*]

membrane (mem´brān) *n.* **1** a thin sheet of tissue lining or covering parts of an organism. **2** a thin sheet of plastic, rubber etc. acting as a lining, barrier etc. (*damp-proof membrane*). **3** a morbid tissue produced in certain diseases. **4** a skin of parchment or vellum. **membranaceous** (-brənā´-), **membraneous** (-brā´-), **membraniform** (-brā´-), **membranous** (-brə-) *a.* **1** of or like a membrane. **2** very thin, translucent. [L *membrāna*, as MEMBER]

†membrum virile (membrəm virī´li, -ē´li) *n.* the penis. [L, male member]

memento (mimen´tō) *n.* (*pl.* **mementos, mementoes**) a memorial, a souvenir, a reminder. **memento mori** (maw´ri) *n.* an emblem of mortality, esp. a skull. [L, imper. of *meminisse*, to remember]

memo (mem´ō) *n.* (*pl.* **memos**) short for MEMORANDUM.

memoir (mem´wah) *n.* **1** (*usu. pl.*) an account of events or transactions in which the narrator took part. **2** an autobiography or a biography. **3** a communication to some learned society on a special subject. **4** (*pl.*) the published proceedings of a learned society. **memoirist** *n.* [F *mémoire*, L *memoria*, MEMORY]

memorabilia (memərəbil´iə) *n.pl.* **1** souvenirs of past events, people etc. **2** †things worthy to be remembered. [L, memorable things, as MEMORABLE]

memorable (mem´ərəbəl) *a.* **1** worthy to be remembered. **2** notable, remarkable. **memorability** (-bil´-) *n.* **memorably** *adv.* [L *memorābilis*, from *memorāre*, to call to remembrance, from *memor*, see MEMORY]

memorandum (meməran´dəm) *n.* (*pl.* **memorandums, memoranda** (-də)) **1** a note to help the memory. **2** a short informal letter, usu. unsigned, with the sender's name etc. printed at the head, often sent internally within a company etc. **3** a brief record or note. **4** (*Law*) a summary, outline or draft of an agreement etc. [L, neut. ger. of *memorāre*, see MEMORABLE]

Usage note *Memoranda* is sometimes used as a singular noun (*a memoranda*), and a plural *memorandas* may also be encountered, but both these uses are best avoided.

memorial (məmaw´riəl) *a.* intended to preserve the memory of a past event, person etc., commemorative. *~n.* **1** a monument, festival etc. commemorating a person, event etc. **2** (*Hist.*) a written statement of facts, esp. of the nature of a petition, remonstrance etc. **3** an informal diplomatic paper. **4** (*usu. pl.*) a chronicle or record. **Memorial Day** *n.* DECORATION DAY (under DECORATE). **memorialist** *n.* a person who writes or presents a memorial. **memorialize, memorialise** *v.t.* to honour, commemorate etc. **memoria technica** (tek´nikə) *n.* a system, mnemonic etc. to assist the memory. [OF, L *memoriālis*]

memorize (mem´ərīz), **memorise** *v.t.* to commit to memory, to learn by heart. **memorizable** *a.* **memorization** (-zā´shən) *n.* **memorizer** *n.*

memory (mem´əri) *n.* (*pl.* **memories**) **1** the mental faculty that retains and recalls previous ideas and impressions. **2** the exercise of this faculty, remembrance, recollection. **3** something that is remembered. **4** the state of being remembered. **5** posthumous reputation. **6** the period during which anything is remembered. **7** (*Comput.*) **a** a device for storing data in a computer. **b** the storage capacity of a computer. **8** the capacity of a material to return to its former condition after distortion. **9** †a memorial, a memento. **from memory** as far as one can remember without proper verification. **in memory of** commemorating. **memory bank** *n.* **1** the memory of a computer etc. **2** the collective memories of a group or individual. **memory board, memory card** *n.* a detachable piece of electronics providing a computer with additional memory. **memory lane** *n.* an imaginary route to nostalgic remembrance of the past (*a stroll down memory lane*). **memory mapping** *n.* (*Comput.*) a technique whereby peripheral devices may be used as if located in the main memory of a computer. [A-F *memorie*, OF *memoire*, L *memoria*, from *memor*, mindful, redupl. of *mer*-, to remember (cp. Gr. *merimna*, care, thought)]

memsahib (mem´sahb) *n.* (*Hist.*) a term of address formerly applied by Indians in speaking to or of European married women living in the Indian subcontinent. [MA'AM, SAHIB]

men MAN.

menace (men´əs) *n.* **1** a threat. **2** (*coll.*) a nuisance (*Dennis the Menace*). *~v.t.* to threaten. **menacer** *n.* **menacing** *a.* **menacingly** *adv.* [OF, from L *minācia*, from *minax -ācis* threatening, from *minae*, threats]

ménage (mānahzh´) *n.* **1** a household. **2** housekeeping, household management. **ménage à trois** (a trwah´) *n.* (*pl.* **ménages à trois** (mānahzh a trwah´)) a household of three adults living together, usu. a married couple and the lover of one of them. [OF, earlier *mesnage*, *maisnage*, pop. L *mansiōnāticum* from *mansio*, MANSION]

menagerie (mənaj´əri) *n.* **1** a collection of wild animals. **2** a place or enclosure where wild animals are kept. [F *ménagerie*, as MÉNAGE]

menaquinone (menəkwin´ōn) *n.* one of the K vitamins, produced by bacteria of the intestine and essential for blood-clotting, vitamin K_2. [*me*thyl-*na*phtho*quinone*]

menarche (mənah´ki) *n.* the first onset of menstruation. **menarcheal** *a.* [L, from Gr. *mēn*, month, *archē*, beginning]

mend (mend) *v.t.* **1** to repair, to restore, to make good. **2** to improve, to make better. **3** to correct, to amend. **4** to add fuel to (a fire). *~v.i.* **1** to grow better, to improve. **2** to recover health. *~n.* **1** the act or process of mending. **2** improvement. **3** a repaired part (in a garment etc.). **on the mend** improving, recuperating. **on the mending hand** (*N Am.*) in a fair way of recovery. **to mend one's fences** FENCE. **to mend one's manners** to improve one's behaviour. **to mend one's pace 1** to go faster. **2** to adjust one's pace to that of someone else. **to mend one's ways** to reform, to improve one's behaviour, habits etc. **mendable** *a.* **mender** *n.* **mending** *n.* **1** the act of repairing, improving etc. **2** articles, esp. clothes, to be mended. [from AMEND]

mendacious (mendā´shəs) *a.* given to lying, untruthful. **mendaciously** *adv.* **mendacity** (-das´-) *n.* [L *mendax*

-*ācis*, lying, cogn. with *mentīrī*, to lie, -OUS]

Usage note The nouns *mendacity* and *mendicity* should not be confused: *mendacity* means lying or deceiving, and *mendicity* begging.

mendelevium (mendəlē´viəm) *n.* an artificially-produced transuranic element, at. no. 101, chem. symbol Md. [Russian chemist D. I. *Mendeleyev*, 1834–1907, who devised the periodic table of elements]

Mendelism (men´dəlizm) *n.* a theory of heredity based on the observation that the characters of the parents of cross-bred offspring reappear by certain proportions in successive generations according to definite laws. **Mendelian** (-dē´-) *a.*, *n.* [G. J. *Mendel*, 1822–84, Austrian botanist]

mendicant (men´dikənt) *n.* **1** a beggar. **2** (*Hist.*) a member of a mendicant order. ~*a.* begging, reduced to beggary. **mendicancy** *n.* **mendicant order** *n.* (*Hist.*) a monastic order of friars subsisting on alms. **mendicity** (-dis´-) *n.* [L *mendīcans -antem*, pres.p. of *mendīcāre*, from *mendīcus*, beggar]

Usage note See note on *mendicity* under MENDACIOUS.

menfolk (men´fōk) *n.pl.* the men, esp. of a particular family or community.

menhaden (menhā´dən) *n.* a N American sea fish of the genus *Brevoortia*, allied to the herring. [Am. Ind. *munnawhattsang*]

menhir (men´hiə) *n.* a prehistoric monument consisting of a tall upright stone. [Bret. *men*, stone, *hir*, long]

menial (mē´niəl) *a.* **1** servile, low, degrading (*a menial task*). **2** (*derog.*) of or relating to a servant. ~*n.* a person doing servile work. **menially** *adv.* [A-F, as MEINIE]

meninges MENINX.

meningitis (meninjī´tis) *n.* (*Med.*) inflammation of the meninges owing to infection.

meninx (me´ninghzks) *n.* (*pl.* **meninges** (-in´jēs)) (*Anat.*) each of the three membranes that envelop the brain and spinal cord. **meningeal** (-in´jiəl) *a.* **meningocele** (-jəsēl) *n.* protrusion of the meninges through the skull. **meningococcus** (-kok´əs) *n.* (*pl.* **meningococci** (-kok´ī, -kok´sī)) a bacterium causing some forms of meningitis and cerebrospinal infection. [Gr., membrane]

meniscus (mənis´kəs) *n.* (*pl.* **menisci** (-is´ī), **meniscuses**) **1** (*Physics*) the top of a liquid column made convex or concave by capillarity (as mercury in a barometer). **2** a lens convex on one side and concave on the other. **3** (*Anat.*) a thin crescent-shaped cartilage between the surfaces of some joints such as the knee. **4** (*Math.*) a crescent-shaped figure. **meniscoid** *a.* [Gr. *mēniskos*, a crescent, dim. of *mēnē*, moon]

menisperm (men´ispœm) *n.* any tropical or sub-tropical plant of the family Menispermaceae, most of which are woody climbers. **menispermaceous** (-ā´shəs) *a.* [Gr. *mēnē*, moon, SPERM]

Mennonite (men´ənīt) *n.* a member of a Protestant sect originating in Friesland in the 16th cent., with principles similar to those of the Anabaptists. [*Menno* Simons, 1496–1561, its first leader]

meno- (men´ō) *comb. form* of or relating to menstruation.

menology (minol´əji) *n.* (*pl.* **menologies**) a calendar of months, esp. the martyrology of the Greek Church. [late Gr. *mēnologion* (*mēn mēnos*, month, -LOGY)]

menopause (men´əpawz) *n.* **1** final cessation of menstruation, the change of life. **2** the period of a woman's life when this occurs. **male menopause** MALE. **menopausal** (-paw´) *a.* [Gr. *mēn mēnos*, month]

menorah (minaw´rə) *n.* a candelabrum with several branches, used in Jewish worship. [Heb., candlestick]

menorrhagia (menərā´jiə) *n.* excessively heavy bleeding at menstruation. [Gr. -*ragia*, from *rhēgnunai* to break forth]

menorrhoea (menərē´ə), (*N Am.*) **menorrhea** *n.* the bleeding at menstruation. [Gr. *rhoia*, flow]

mensal[1] (men´səl) *a.* of, relating to or used at the table. [L *mensa*, table]

mensal[2] (men´səl) *a.* monthly. [as MENSES]

menses (men´sēz) *n.pl.* **1** the flow of blood etc. from the uterus of women at menstruation, the period. **2** the time of this. **3** the blood etc. discharged at menstruation. **menstrual, menstruous** *a.* **1** monthly. **2** of or relating to menstruation. **menstrual cycle** *n.* the continuing process of ovulation and menstruation in females. **menstruate** *v.i.* to undergo menstruation. **menstruation** (-ā´shən) *n.* the process of discharging blood and other uterine material, usu. occurring once every lunar month in non-pregnant adult females before the menopause. [L, pl. of *mensis*, month]

Menshevik (men´shəvik) *n.* (*Hist.*) a member of the moderate party in the Russian Revolution, as distinct from *Bolshevik*. [Rus., member of a minority, from *men'she*, fewer]

mens rea (menz rē´ə) *n.* criminal intent, the knowledge that an act is wrong. [L, guilty mind]

menstrua MENSTRUUM.

menstrual, menstruate etc. MENSES.

menstruum (men´struəm) *n.* (*pl.* **menstrua** (-struə)) any fluid that dissolves a solid, a solvent. [L, neut. of *menstruus*, monthly, from *mensis*, month (from the alchemistic analogy with the menstrual flow)]

mensurable (men´sūrəbəl, -shər-) *a.* **1** measurable, having defined limits. **2** (*Mus.*) mensural. **mensurability** (-bil´-) *n.* **mensural** *a.* **1** of or involving measure. **2** having rhythm and measure. [late L *mensūrābilis*, from *mensūrāre* to measure, from *mensūra*, MEASURE]

mensuration (mensūrā´shən) *n.* **1** the act or practice of measuring. **2** the branch of mathematics concerned with the determination of lengths, areas and volumes. [late L *mensūrātio*, as MENSURABLE]

menswear (menz´weər) *n.* clothing for men.

-ment (mənt) *suf.* forming nouns denoting result, state, action etc., as in *agreement*, *bereavement*, *enticement*, *impediment*, *ornament*. [OF, from L -*mentum*]

mental[1] (men´təl) *a.* **1** of or relating to the mind. **2** due to or done by the mind. **3** of or concerning psychiatric illness. **4** (*coll.*) slightly deranged in mind. **5** (*coll.*) very enthusiastic, fanatical. **mental age** *n.* the intellectual maturity of an individual expressed in terms of the age of the average person attaining a similar level of intellectual maturity. **mental arithmetic** *n.* arithmetic done in the head, without writing it down or using a calculator. **mental block** *n.* a temporary interruption to the thought processes due to subconscious emotional factors. **mental cruelty** *n.* behaviour that causes suffering to another, without involving physical assault, esp. as grounds for divorce. **mental defective** *n.* (*now offensive*) a mentally-handicapped person. **mental deficiency** *n.* (*now offensive*) the condition of being mentally handicapped. **mentally deficient** *a.* **mental handicap** *n.* a state of permanent intellectual disability such as to prevent normal functioning in society. **mentally handicapped** *a.* **mental illness** *n.* a disorder of the mind causing abnormality in a person's behaviour or affecting their ability to think. **mentalism** *n.* **1** the theory that nothing exists outside the mind. **2** the tendency to attribute mind to forces of nature or inanimate objects. **mentalist** *n.* **mentalistic** (-is´-) *a.* **mentality** (-tal´-) *n.* (*pl.* **mentalities**) **1** mental attitude or disposition. **2** intelligence. **3** the contents or functioning of the mind. **mentally** *adv.* **mental nurse** *n.* PSYCHIATRIC NURSE (under PSYCHIATRY). **mental patient** *n.* PSYCHIATRIC PATIENT (under PSYCHIATRY). **mental reservation** *n.* an unspoken note of caution or qualification within the mind of a speaker or listener. **mental science** *n.* psychology, mental philosophy. **mentation**

(-tā´shən) *n.* the process or result of mental action. [F, from late L *mentālis*, from *mens mentis* mind]

Usage note In the context of illness or disability, *mental* is now often felt to be derogatory or dismissive, and compounds such as *psychiatric hospital* and *psychiatric patient* are preferred to *mental hospital* and *mental patient*.

mental[2] (men´təl) *a.* (*Anat.*) of or relating to the chin. [F, from L *mentum*, chin]

mentation MENTAL[1].

menthol (men´thol) *n.* a waxy crystalline substance obtained from oil of peppermint, used as a flavouring and as a local anaesthetic for neuralgia etc. **mentholated** *a.* (esp. of cigarettes) treated with menthol. [G (L *mentha*, MINT[2], -OL)]

mention (men´shən) *n.* **1** a concise notice (of), an allusion. **2** a referring to by name. **3** the military honour of being mentioned in dispatches. *~v.t.* **1** to refer to, to allude to. **2** to indicate by naming without describing. **3** to reveal by speaking of. **don't mention it** used to indicate that apologies or thanks are unnecessary. **mentioned in dispatches** DISPATCH. **not to mention** to say nothing of. **to make mention** to talk (of a subject). **to make no mention** not to talk (of a subject). **mentionable** *a.* [F, from L *mentio -ōnem*, rel. to *mens mentis* see MENTAL[1]]

mentor (men´taw) *n.* an experienced adviser. **mentorial** (-taw´-) *a.* **mentorship** *n.* [F, from Gr. *Mentōr*, counsellor to Telemachus]

menu (men´ū) *n.* (*pl.* **menus**) **1** a list of dishes available at a restaurant etc. **2** a list of dishes to be served at a meal. **3** (*Comput.*) a list of alternative operations, topics etc., usu. displayed on-screen, which the user can choose from. **menu-driven** *a.* (*Comput.*) presenting a menu, operated through a menu. [F, orig. small, L *minūtus*, MINUTE[2]]

meow MIAOW.

MEP *abbr.* Member of the European Parliament.

mepacrine (mep´əkrēn) *n.* the drug quinacrine. [*me*thyl, *pa*ludism, *acri*dine]

meperidine (meper´idēn) *n.* the drug pethidine. [*me*thyl pi*peridine*]

Mephistopheles (mefistof´əlēz) *n.* **1** a tempter. **2** a diabolical person. **Mephistophelean** (-fē´liən), **Mephistophelian** *a.* sardonical, cynically sceptical, scoffing. [the spirit in ancient legend to whom Faust sells his soul, etym. uncertain]

mephitis (məfī´tis) *n.* **1** a foul, offensive or poisonous stench. **2** an offensive or poisonous gas emanating from the earth. **mephitic** (-fit´-), **mephitical** *a.* **mephitism** (mef´i-) *n.* [L]

-mer (mə) *comb. form* (*Chem.*) a substance of a specified type as in *polymer, elastomer*.

☒ **merangue** common misspelling of MERINGUE.

meranti (məran´ti) *n.* hardwood timber from a tree of the genus *Shorea*, found in Malaysia and Indonesia. [Malay]

mercantile (mœ´kəntīl) *a.* **1** commercial, of or relating to buying and selling. **2** mercenary. **mercantile marine** *n.* MERCHANT SERVICE (under MERCHANT). **mercantilism** (-til-) *n.* (*Hist.*) an economic theory of the 17th and 18th cents. that money is the only form of wealth. **mercantilist** *n.* [F, from It. *mercantile*, from *mercante*, MERCHANT]

Mercator projection (mœkā´tə), **Mercator's projection** *n.* a projection of a map of the surface of the earth on to a plane so that the lines of latitude are represented by horizontal lines and the meridians by parallel lines at right angles to them. [Latinized name of G. *Kremer*, 1512–94]

mercenary (mœ´sənəri, -sənri) *a.* **1** done from or actuated by motives of gain. **2** hired or serving for money. **3** venal. *~n.* (*pl.* **mercenaries**) a person who is hired, esp. a soldier hired in foreign service. **mercenarily** *adv.* **mercenariness** *n.* [L *mercēnārius*, from *merces -cēdis* reward, from *merx -cis*, see MERCHANDISE]

mercer (mœ´sə) *n.* a person who deals in silk, cotton, woollen and linen goods. **mercery** *n.* (*pl.* **merceries**). [F *mercier*, through pop. L *merciarius*, from L *merx mercis*, MERCHANDISE]

mercerize (mœ´sərīz), **mercerise** *v.t.* to treat (cotton fabrics) with an alkaline solution before dyeing, to impart strength and lustre. **mercerization** (-zā´shən) *n.* [J. *Mercer*, 1791–1866, patentee of process]

merchandise (mœ´chəndīz) *n.* goods for sale and purchase. *~v.i.* to trade, to barter. *~v.t.* **1** to trade in (a commodity). **2** to put (a product) on the market. **3** to promote, advertise etc. **merchandisable** *a.* **merchandiser** *n.* **merchandising** *n.* promotion and advertising of goods for sale. [F *marchandise*, as MERCHANT.]

merchant (mœ´chənt) *n.* **1** a person who carries on trade on a large scale, esp. with foreign countries. **2** (*esp. N Am., Sc.*) a retailer, a shopkeeper, a tradesman. **3** (*coll.*) a person with a particular inclination, habit etc. (*speed merchant*). **merchantable** *a.* saleable, of a quality to be marketed. **merchant bank** *n.* a private bank whose business chiefly involves dealing in bills of exchange and underwriting new security issues for commercial and financial institutions. **merchant banker** *n.* **merchantlike** *a.* **merchantman** *n.* (*pl.* **merchantmen**) a merchant ship. **merchant navy, merchant marine** *n.* a nation's commercial ships collectively. **merchant prince** *n.* a wealthy merchant. **merchant service** *n.* personnel etc. of shipping employed in commerce. **merchant ship** *n.* a ship for conveying merchandise, a merchantman. [OF *marchand, marchant*, from L *mercans -antem*, pres.p. of *mercārī*, to trade, from *merx mercis*, MERCHANDISE]

merciful, merciless etc. MERCY.

Mercury (mœ´kūri) *n.* **1** the planet nearest the sun. **2** the Roman god of commerce, identified with Greek Hermes, the messenger of the gods. **Mercurial** *a.* of the planet Mercury. [L *Mercurius*]

mercury (mœ´kūri) *n.* **1** a liquid, silvery, toxic, metallic element, at. no. 80, chem. symbol Hg. **2** any plant of the genus *Mercurialis*, esp. *M. perenne* or dog's mercury. **3** †a messenger. **mercurial** (mœkū´riəl) *a.* **1** flighty, volatile, fickle. **2** of, relating to, consisting of or caused by mercury. *~n.* a preparation containing mercury, used as a drug. **mercurialism** *n.* a morbid condition due to mercury poisoning. **mercuriality** (-al´-) *n.* **mercurialize, mercurialise** *v.t.* **mercurially** *adv.* **mercuric** *a.* containing mercury in the divalent state. **mercurous** (-kū´rəs) *a.* containing mercury in the monovalent state. **mercury vapour lamp** *n.* a lamp containing mercury vapour through which electricity is discharged to produce light. [A-F *Mercurie*, OF *Mercure*, L *Mercurius*]

mercy (mœ´si) *n.* (*pl.* **mercies**) **1** a disposition to temper justice with mildness. **2** forbearance, clemency, compassion. **3** an act of clemency, pity or compassion. **4** pardon, forgiveness. **5** control, discretion, liberty to punish or spare. **6** (*coll.*) something to be thankful for. **at the mercy of** wholly in the power of. **for mercy's sake** SAKE[1]. **to have mercy on/ upon** to show mercy to. **merciful** *a.* **mercifully** *adv.* **mercifulness** *n.* **merciless** *a.* **mercilessly** *adv.* **mercilessness** *n.* **mercy dash, mercy flight** *n.* a trip, flight etc. to bring help to a sick or injured person. **mercy killing** *n.* **1** euthanasia. **2** an instance of this. **mercy-seat** *n.* (*Bible*) **1** the covering of the Ark of the Covenant. **2** the throne of God as dispenser of mercy. [F *merci*, L *merces -cēdem*, reward, late L, pity, from *merx -cis*, MERCHANDISE]

mere[1] (miə) *n.* a lake, a pool. [OE (cp. Dut. *meer*, G *Meer*, Icel. *marr*, L *mare*, sea)]

mere[2] (miə) *a.* such and no more (*a mere youth*; *a mere* *trifle; no mere fluke*). **merely** *adv.* purely, only, solely. **mere right** *n.* (*Law*) a right in theory. **merest** *a.* [L *merus*, pure, unadulterated]

mere[3] (miə) *n.* **1** a boundary. **2** a boundary stone. **3** a landmark. ~†*v.t.* to limit, to mark off. **mere-stone** *n.* [OE *mǣre, gemǣre* (cp. MDut. *mere, meer*, Icel. *landa-mæri*, also L *mūrus*, wall)]

mere[4] (mer´i), **meri** *n.* a short flat Maori war club, esp. one made of greenstone. [Maori]

-mere (miə) *comb. form* part, segment as in *blastomere*. [Gr. *meros*, part]

meretricious (meritrish´əs) *a.* **1** alluring by false or empty show, unreal, tawdry. **2** of or relating to or befitting a prostitute. **meretriciously** *adv.* **meretriciousness** *n.* [L *meretrīcius*, from *meretrix -trīcis*, prostitute, from *merērī*, to earn, see MERIT]

Usage note The adjectives *meretricious* and *meritorious* should not be confused: *meretricious* means tawdry, and *meritorious* praiseworthy.

merganser (mœgan´sə) *n.* any diving or fish-eating duck belonging to the genus *Mergus*, the sawbill. [L *mergus*, a diving bird, *anser*, goose]

merge (mœj) *v.i.* **1** to be absorbed or swallowed up (with). **2** to lose individuality or identity (in). ~*v.t.* to cause to be swallowed up or absorbed, to sink (in a larger estate, title etc.). **mergence** *n.* **merger** *n.* **1** the merging of an estate, limited company etc. into another. **2** absorption. [L *mergere*, to dip (partly through low F *merger*)]

meri MERE[4].

mericarp (mer´ikahp) *n.* one of the two carpels forming the fruit of umbelliferous plants. [F *méricarpe* (Gr. *meros*, part, *karpos*, fruit)]

meridian (mərid´iən) *a.* **1** of or relating to midday. **2** of or relating to a geographical or astronomical meridian. **3** of or relating to the point or period of highest splendour or vigour. ~*n.* **1** a great circle drawn through the poles and the zenith of any given place on the earth's surface. **2** the line in which the plane of this circle intersects the earth's surface. **3** the time when the sun or other heavenly body crosses this. **4** midday, noon. **5** culmination, zenith, point of highest splendour or vigour. **meridian circle** *n.* (*Astron.*) a telescope fixed to move only on a north-south line for measuring the transit of celestial objects across the meridian. **meridional** *a.* **1** of or relating to a meridian. **2** highest, culminating. **3** of or relating to the south, esp. of Europe. **4** running north and south, as a mountain range. ~*n.* an inhabitant of the south, usu. of the south of France. **meridionality** (-nal´-) *n.* **meridionally** *adv.* [OF *meridien*, L *merīdiānus*, from *merīdiēs*, midday (*medius*, middle, *diēs*, day)]

meringue (mərang´) *n.* **1** a baked confection of white of eggs, sugar etc. **2** a cake made of this, usu. filled with cream etc. [F, etym. uncertain]

merino (mərē´nō) *n.* (*pl.* **merinos**) **1** a breed of sheep valuable for their fine wool. **2** a fine woollen dress fabric, orig. of this wool. **3** a fine woollen yarn used for hosiery. ~*a.* **1** of or relating to this breed of sheep. **2** made of merino. **pure merino** PURE. [Sp., prob. from L *mājōrīnus* (perh. overseer or major-domo), from *mājor*, greater]

meristem (mer´istem) *n.* (*Bot.*) vegetable tissue or cells in process of growth. **meristematic** (-təmat´-) *a.* [from Gr. *meristos*, from *merizein*, to divide (ending assim. to PHLOEM, XYLEM)]

merit (mer´it) *n.* **1** the quality of deserving, desert. **2** excellence deserving honour or reward, worth, worthiness. **3** a reward or recompense, a mark or award of merit. **4** (*pl.*) the essential rights and wrongs of a case. ~*v.t.* (*pres.p.* **meriting,** *past, p.p.* **merited**) **1** to deserve, to earn. **2** to be entitled to receive as a reward. **3** to have a just title to. ~*v.i.* to acquire merit. **on its merits** on its intrinsic qualities, virtues etc. **to make a merit of** to think or try to show that (one's conduct, action etc.) deserves praise. **merited** *a.* **meritocracy** (-tok´-) *n.* (*pl.* **meritocracies**) **1** (a society ruled by) those who have gained their positions through talent, intellect or industriousness, not through their family background, inherited wealth etc. **2** the rule of such people. **meritocrat** *n.* **meritocratic** (-krat´-) *a.* **meritorious** (-taw´riəs) *a.* **1** deserving reward. **2** praiseworthy. **meritoriously** *adv.* **meritoriousness** *n.* [OF *merite*, L *meritum*, neut. p.p. of *merērī*, to earn, perh. cogn. with Gr. *meros*, a share, whence *meiresthai*, to receive a portion]

Usage note See note on *meritorious* under MERETRICIOUS.

merle (mœl) *n.* (*Sc., poet.*) the blackbird. [OF, from L *merula*]

merlin (mœ´lin) *n.* the smallest of the European falcons, *Falco columbarius*. [A-F *merilun*, OF *esmerillon*, prob. from Gmc.]

merlon (mœ´lən) *n.* the solid part of an embattled parapet between two embrasures. [F, from It. *merlone*, from *merlo, merla*, battlement, prob. from *mergola*, dim. of L *mergae*, pl., a pitchfork]

Merlot (mœ´lō, -lot) *n.* **1** a black grape used in winemaking. **2** the red wine made from this grape. [Fr.]

mermaid (mœ´mād) *n.* an imaginary marine creature, having the upper half like a woman and the lower like a fish. **mermaiden** *n.* **mermaid's purse** *n.* SEA PURSE (under SEA). **merman** *n.* (*pl.* **mermen**) an imaginary creature like a mermaid but male. [MERE[1], MAID (cp. OE *mere-wīf*, mere-woman)]

mero- (mer´ō) *comb. form* partly, partial. [Gr. *meros*, part, portion]

meroblast (mer´əblahst) *n.* an ovum only a part or portion of which is directly germinal. **meroblastic** (-blas´-) *a.* undergoing or involving cleavage in part of the ovum only.

meroistic (merōis´tik) *a.* (of the ovaries of certain insects) secreting yolk-forming cells as well as ova.

-merous (mərəs) *comb. form* (*Biol., Bot.*) having so many parts, as in *dimerous*.

Merovingian (merəvin´jiən) *a.* of or relating to the Frankish dynasty reigning in Gaul and Germany, founded by Clovis in AD 486. ~*n.* a sovereign of this dynasty. [F *Merovingien*, med. L *Merovingī*, from Gmc.]

merry (mer´i) *a.* (*comp.* **merrier,** *superl.* **merriest**) **1** cheerful, happy, jovial, mirthful. **2** causing merriment. **3** (*coll.*) slightly tipsy. **the more the merrier** the pleasure will be greater, the more people are involved. **to make merry** MAKE[1]. **to make merry over** MAKE[1]. **to play merry hell with** HELL. **merrily** *adv.* **merriment, merriness** *n.* **merry andrew** *n.* (*Hist.*) a buffoon, a jester, esp. one assisting a mountebank or quack. **merry-go-round** *n.* **1** a revolving frame with seats or wooden horses on which people ride at fairs etc. **2** an endless round of activity. †**merryman** *n.* (*pl.* **merrymen**) a jester. **merry thought** *n.* the wishbone, the furcula or forked bone in the breast of a bird. [OE *myrige*, whence MIRTH, prob. from Gmc. *murgjo-*, lasting a short time, cogn. with Gr. *brachus*, short]

merycism (mer´isizm) *n.* (*Med.*) a disorder in which food is brought back from the stomach and chewed again. [Gr. *mērukismos*, from *mērukizein*, to ruminate]

mes- MESO-.

mesa (mā´sə) *n.* a plateau with steep sides, a tableland. [Sp., table]

mesail (mes´āl) *n.* the visor of a helmet, esp. if made in two parts. [F *mésail*, prob. from OF *muçaille*, from *mucier*, to hide]

mésalliance (māzaliãs´, -zal´-) *n.* marriage with a person of inferior social position. [F (*més-*, MIS-[1], ALLIANCE)]

mesaraic (mesərā´ik) *a.* mesenteric. [med. L *mesaraïcus*, Gr. *mesaraïkos*, from *mesaraion* (*meson*, middle, *araia*, the belly)]

mescal (meskal´) *n.* **1** a small globular cactus, *Lophophora williamsii*, the peyote, of the southern US and Mexico, the tubercles of which are chewed for their hallucinogenic effects. **2** an alcoholic liquor distilled from this. **mescal button** *n.* the tubercle of the mescal cactus. **mescaline** (mes´kalin), **mescalin** *n.* a hallucinogenic substance derived from mescal buttons. [Mex. Sp., from Nahuatl *mexcalli*]

Mesdames MADAME.

Mesdemoiselles MADEMOISELLE.

mesembryanthemum (mizembrian´thiməm) *n.* any succulent plant of the genus *Mesembryanthemum*, with thick, fleshy leaves and brilliant flowers, including the ice plant. [Gr. *mesēmbria*, noon, *anthemon*, flower]

mesencephalon (mesensef´əlon, -kef´-) *n.* the midbrain. **mesencephalic** (-fal´-) *a.* [Gr. *mesos*, middle, ENCEPHALON]

mesentery (mes´əntəri, mez´-) *n.* (*pl.* **mesenteries**) (*Anat.*) a fold of the peritoneum supporting the small intestines and connecting them with the wall of the abdomen. **mesenteric** (-ter´-) *a.* **mesenteritis** (-ī´tis) *n.* inflammation of the mesentery. [med. L *mesenterium*, Gr. *mesenterion* (*mesos*, middle, *enteron*, entrail)]

mesh (mesh) *n.* **1** a fabric or structure of network. **2** (*pl.*) a network. **3** the space or interstice between the threads of a net. **4** an interlacing structure. **5** the engagement of gear teeth etc. **6** (*pl.*) a trap, a snare. ~*v.t.* **1** to cause to engage (gear teeth etc.). **2** to catch in a net, to ensnare. ~*v.i.* **1** to coordinate (with). **2** (of gear teeth etc.) to engage (with). **in mesh** (of cogs) engaged. **mesh-work** *n.* **meshy** *a.* [perh. from OE *max* (cp. Dut. *maas*, G *Masche*), or from MDut. *maesche*]

mesial (mē´ziəl) *a.* **1** (*Anat.*) of or relating to, situated or directed towards the middle, esp. the middle line of the body. **2** medial. **mesially** *adv.* [Gr. *mesos*, middle, -IAL]

mesmerism (mez´mərizm) *n.* **1** the art or power of inducing an abnormal state of the nervous system, in which the will of the patient is controlled by that of the agent. **2** the hypnotic state so induced. **3** fascination. **mesmeric** (-mer´-) *a.* **mesmerically** *adv.* **mesmerist** *n.* **mesmerize, mesmerise** *v.t.* **1** to hypnotize. **2** to occupy (someone's attention) totally. **mesmerization** (-zā´shən) *n.* **mesmerizee** (-zē´) *n.* **mesmerizer** *n.* [F. A. *Mesmer*, 1733–1815, Swiss-German physician, -ISM]

mesne (mēn) *a.* (*Law*) middle, intermediate. **mesne lord** *n.* in feudal law, a lord holding an estate belonging to a superior lord. **mesne process** *n.* (*Law*) intermediate proceedings between a primary and a final process. **mesne profits** *n.pl.* the profits of an estate received by a person wrongfully in possession. [F, legal var. of A-F *meen*, MEAN[1]]

meso- (mē´sō), **mes-** *comb. form* **1** intermediate, in the middle. **2** of or relating to the middle. [Gr. *mesos*, middle]

mesoblast (mē´səblahst, -z-) *n.* (*Biol.*) the intermediate germ layer of an embryo. **mesoblastic** (-blas´-) *a.* [-BLAST]

mesocarp (mē´səkahp, -z-) *n.* the middle layer of the pericarp of a fruit. [Gr. *karpos*, fruit]

mesocephalic (mēsōsifal´ik, -z-, -kef-) *a.* having a medium-sized head, intermediate between dolichocephalic and brachycephalic. **mesocephalism** (-sef´-, -kef´-), **mesocephaly** (-sef´-, -kef´-) *n.* **mesocephalous** (-sef´-, -kef´-) *a.*

mesoderm (mēs´ədœm, -z-) *n.* **1** (*Zool.*) the middle germ layer of an animal embryo. **2** (*Bot.*) the middle layer of the bark, the wall of a sporecase etc. **mesodermal** (-dœ´-), **mesodermic** *a.*

mesolithic (mēsōlith´ik, -z-) *a.* of or relating to the phase of the Stone Age between the Neolithic and Palaeolithic phases. ~*n.* this period. [Gr. *lithos*, stone]

mesomorphic (mēsōmaw´fik, -z-) *a.* having a compact muscular physique. **mesomorph** (mē´-) *n.* **mesomorphy** (mē´-) *n.* [-MORPHIC (under -MORPH)]

meson (mē´zon) *n.* (*Physics*) a particle intermediate in mass between a proton and an electron. **mesic** *a.* **mesonic** (-zon´-) *a.*

mesopause (mē´səpawz, -z-) *n.* the zone between the mesosphere and the thermosphere, at which the temperature has fallen to its lowest and begins to rise again.

mesophyll (mē´səfil, -z-) *n.* (*Bot.*) the inner spongy tissue of a leaf. [Gr. *phullon*, leaf]

mesophyte (mē´səfīt, -z-) *n.* a plant that grows in conditions where there is a moderate supply of water. [-PHYTE]

mesosphere (mē´səsfiə, -z-) *n.* the region of the earth's atmosphere extending for about 80 km above the stratosphere.

mesothelioma (mēsōthēliō´mə, -z-) *n.* (*pl.* **mesotheliomas, mesotheliomata** (-mətə)) (*Med.*) a tumour of the lining of the lungs, heart or stomach, often caused by blue asbestos dust.

mesothorax (mēsōthaw´raks, -z-) *n.* (*pl.* **mesothoraces** (-rəsēz), **mesothoraxes**) (*Zool.*) in insects, the middle segment of the thorax bearing the anterior legs and the middle wings.

Mesozoic (mēsōzō´ik, -z-) *a.* belonging to the second great geological epoch, Secondary. ~*n.* this epoch.

mesquite (meskēt´, mes´kēt), **mesquit** *n.* (*Bot.*) any leguminous shrub or tree of the genus *Prosopis* growing in the SW United States and as far south as Peru, yielding the pods used for fodder. **mesquite-bean** *n.* **mesquite-grass** *n.* [Mex. Sp. *mezquite*]

mess (mes) *n.* **1** a state of dirt and disorder. **2** a muddle, a difficulty. **3** officers' living quarters. **4** a number of persons who sit down to table together (used esp. of soldiers and sailors). **5** a communal meal. **6** a dish or a portion of food sent to table at one time. **7** liquid or semi-liquid food, esp. for animals. **8** a quantity of such food. **9** (*coll.*) the excreta of a pet animal. **10** †a set or party of four, orig. one of the parties into which a company was divided at a banquet etc. ~*v.i.* **1** to muddle or potter (about). **2** (esp. of soldiers etc.) to take a meal or meals in company. **3** (*coll.*) to defecate. ~*v.t.* **1** to mix together, to muddle, to jumble. **2** to dirty, to soil. **to make a mess** to make a bad job (of), to bungle. **to mess about** **1** to tumble or fool about. **2** to treat roughly. **3** to treat improperly or inconsiderately. **4** to potter about. **to mess around** to mess about. **to mess up** to ruin, spoil. **to mess with** to interfere with. **mess hall** *n.* (*Mil.*) a dining area for service personnel. **mess jacket** *n.* (*Mil.*) a short tightly-fitting jacket worn on formal occasions. **mess kit** *n.* (*Mil.*) a soldier's eating utensils for use in the field. **messmate** *n.* **1** (*Mil.*) a member of the same mess. **2** an associate. **3** a parasite which does not actually feed on the body of its host, a commensal. **mess of pottage** *n.* a material gain for which something of a higher value is sacrificed. **mess tin** *n.* (*Mil.*) a small tin for cooking or eating in the field, part of the mess kit. **messy** *a.* (*comp.* **messier**, *superl.* **messiest**) **1** dirty, muddled. **2** complicated and difficult to handle. **messily** *adv.* **messiness** *n.* a state of dirt or disorder. [OF *mes*, late L *missum*, neut. p.p. of *mittere*, to send]

message (mes´ij) *n.* **1** a communication, oral or written, from one person to another. **2** the chief theme of a play, novel etc. **3** the truths, ideas or opinions of a writer or inspired person. **4** an errand, a mission. **5** (*Sc., North.*) goods purchased, shopping. ~*v.t.* to send as a message, to signal. **to get the message** to understand what another person is trying to communicate. **message stick** *n.* a stick bearing carved symbols, carried by an

Australian Aborigine as a means of identification. [F, from pop. L *missāticum*, as MESS]

Messeigneurs MONSEIGNEUR.

messenger (mes´injə) *n.* **1** a person who carries a message or messages or goes on an errand or errands. **2** (*Naut.*) a rope from the capstan to the cable for lifting the anchor. **messenger RNA** *n.* a type of RNA that carries genetic information from DNA to the ribosomes for the synthesis of protein, mRNA. [F *messager*, see MESSAGE]

Messiah (misī´ə) *n.* **1** an expected saviour or deliverer. **2** the anointed one, Christ, as the promised deliverer of the Jews. **Messiahship** *n.* **Messianic** (mesian´ik) *a.* **1** of, or inspired by the hope of, a Messiah. **2** marked by great zeal in support of a cause. **Messianism** (mes´iənizm) *n.* [F *Messie*, L and Gr. *Messīās*, Heb. *māshīah*, from *māshah*, to anoint]

Messieurs (mesyœ´), **Messrs** (mes´əz) *n.pl.* sirs, gentlemen. [see MONSIEUR]

messuage (mes´wij) *n.* (*Law*) a dwelling house with the adjacent buildings and land for the use of the household. [A-F *mesuage*, perh. from OF *masuage*, med. L *mansuāgium*, from *mansa*, see MANSE]

mestee (mestē´), **mustee** (mŭstē´) *n.* the offspring of a white person and a quadroon, an octoroon. [MESTIZO]

mestizo (mestē´zō) *n.* (*pl.* **mestizos**) **1** a person of mixed Spanish or Portuguese and American Indian blood. **2** a person of mixed Chinese and Philippine blood. **mestiza** (-zə) *n.* a female mestizo. [Sp., mongrel, from pop. L *mixtīcius*, *mixtus*, p.p. of *miscēre*, to mix]

met[1] (met) *a.* **1** meteorological. **2** metropolitan. ~*n.* **1** (*coll.*) (**Met**) the (London) Metropolitan Police. **2** (**Met**) the Metropolitan Opera, New York. **Met Office** *n.* the Meteorological Office.

met[2] MEET[1].

met- (met), **meta-** (met´ə), **meth-** (meth) *comb. form* **1** beyond, above, as in *metamathematics*. **2** behind, between, as in *metacarpus*. **3** after (implying change or transposition), as in *metabolism*. **4** derivative, as in *metaldehyde*. [Gr.]

metabolism (mitab´əlizm) *n.* the continuous chemical change going on in living matter. **constructive metabolism** CONSTRUCTIVE (under CONSTRUCTION). **destructive metabolism** DESTRUCTIVE (under DESTRUCTION). **metabolic** (metəbol´-) *a.* **metabolically** *adv.* **metabolite** *n.* a substance involved in or produced by metabolism. **metabolize, metabolise** *v.t.* **metabolizable** *a.* [Gr. *metabolē*, change, rel. to *metaballein*, to change (MET-, *ballein*, to throw), -ISM]

metacarpus (metəkah´pəs) *n.* (*pl.* **metacarpi** (-pī)) **1** the part of the hand between the wrist and the fingers. **2** the set of bones connecting the wrist and the fingers. **metacarpal** *a.*

metacentre (met´əsentə), (*N Am.*) **metacenter** *n.* the point in a floating body slightly out of equilibrium where the vertical drawn through the centre of gravity when it is in equilibrium intersects the vertical passing through the centre of buoyancy. **metacentric** (-sen´-) *a.*

metachrosis (metəkrō´sis) *n.* (*Zool.*) change of colour, as in certain lizards.

metagalaxy (metəgal´əksi) *n.* (*pl.* **metagalaxies**) the universe beyond our galaxy. **metagalactic** (-gəlak´-) *a.*

metage (mē´tij) *n.* **1** official measurement, esp. of coal. **2** a toll charged for measuring.

metagenesis (metəjen´əsis) *n.* alternation of like and unlike generations. **metagenetic** (-jinet´-), **metagenic** *a.*

metal (met´əl) *n.* **1** any of a class of elementary substances which usu. present in various degrees certain physical characters, such as lustre, malleability and ductility, possessed by the six metals known to the ancients, viz. gold, silver, copper, iron, lead and tin. **2** material of this kind. **3** a compound of the elementary metals, an alloy. **4** broken stone for road-making etc. **5** molten glass ready for blowing or casting. **6** (*pl.*) the rails of a railway etc. **7** the effective power of the guns of a warship. ~*v.t.* (*pres.p.* **metalling,** (*N Am.*) **metaling,** *past, p.p.* **metalled,** (*N Am.*) **metaled**) **1** to furnish or fit with metal. **2** to cover or repair (a road) with metal. **metal detector** *n.* an electronic instrument which gives an audible signal when metal is present. **metal fatigue** *n.* a weakening in metals due to prolonged stress or repeated blows. **metallic** (mital´-) *a.* **1** having the characteristics or properties of a metal. **2** made or consisting of metal. **3** (of a sound) sharp and reverberant, like a metal when struck. **4** lustrous like a metal. **metallically** *adv.* **metallic currency** *n.* money composed of gold, silver etc., as opposed to paper. **metalliferous** (-lif´-) *a.* bearing or yielding metal. **metalline** (met´əlīn) *a.* **metalling** *n.* broken stones etc. used in making or mending roads. **metallist,** (*N Am.*) **metalist** *n.* a person who works with metals. **metallize** (met´əlīz), **metallise** *v.t.* **1** to coat with a metal. **2** to give metallic properties to. **metallization** (-zā´shən) *n.* **metalloid** *a.* resembling a metal in form or appearance. ~*n.* an element having some of the properties of metals and some of non-metals. **metalloidal** (-loi´-) *a.* **metalwork** *n.* **1** the craft of working in metal. **2** metal objects collectively. **metalworker** *n.* **metalworking** *n.* [OF, from L *metallum*, Gr. *metallon*, mine, mineral, perh. rel. to *metallan*, to search after]

Usage note The spellings of the nouns *metal* (a substance) and *mettle* (spirit, courage) should not be confused.

metalanguage (met´əlang·gwij) *n.* **1** a language or system of symbols used to speak about another language. **2** a system of propositions used to speak about other propositions.

metalepsis (metəlep´sis) *n.* (*Gram.*) a form of metonymy, the substitution of one word for another that is itself figurative, or the union of two or more tropes of a different kind in one word. **metaleptic, metaleptical** *a.* **metaleptically** *adv.* [L and Gr. *metalēpsis*, from *metalambanein*, to substitute (MET-, *lambanein*, to take)]

metalinguistics (metəling·gwis´tiks) *n.* the branch of linguistics dealing with metalanguages. **metalinguistic** *a.*

metallic, metalliferous etc. METAL.

metallo- (metal´ō) *comb. form* metal.

metallography (metəlog´rəfi) *n.* the science of metals, esp. the microscopic study of their internal structure. **metallographic** (-lōgraf´ik), **metallographical** *a.* **metallographically** *adv.*

metalloid METAL.

metallophone (mital´əfōn) *n.* **1** any musical instrument like the xylophone with metal bars, such as the vibraphone and glockenspiel. **2** a piano with metal bars instead of wires.

metallurgy (mital´əji, met´əlœji) *n.* **1** the science of metals. **2** the art of separating metals from ores. **3** the art of working in metal. **metallurgic** (metəlœ´-), **metallurgical** *a.* **metallurgically** *adv.* **metallurgist** *n.* [Gr. *metallourgos* (*metallon*, mineral, *-ergos*, working)]

metamere (met´əmiə) *n.* (*Zool.*) each of a series of similar parts of a body. **metameric** (-mer´-) *a.* **1** having the same composition and molecular weight, isomeric but different in chemical properties. **2** (*Zool.*) of or relating to metameres. **metamerism** (-tam´ə-) *n.* [Gr. *meros*, part]

metamorphose (metəmaw´fōz) *v.t.* **1** to change into a different form. **2** to transmute (into, to). ~*v.i.* to undergo change into a different form. **metamorphic** (-maw´fik) *a.* **1** causing or showing the results of metamorphosis, transforming or transformed. **2** (*Geol.*) changed in structure by a natural agency, such as heat or pressure.

metamorphism *n.* change in the structure of rocks caused by a natural agency such as heat or pressure. **metamorphology** (-fol´-) *n.* the science of the metamorphoses of organisms. **metamorphosis** (-fəsis, -mawfō´sis) *n.* (*pl.* **metamorphoses** (-sēz)) **1** a change of form. **2** the result of such a change. **3** transformation, such as that of a chrysalis into a winged insect. **4** a complete change of character, purpose etc. [F *métamorphoser*, from L and Gr. *metamorphōsis*, transformation, from *metamorphoun* (MET-, *morphē*, form)]

metaphase (met´əfāz) *n.* (*Biol.*) the second stage of meiotic cell division at which the chromosomes become attached to the spindle fibres, forming the equatorial plate.

metaphor (met´əfə, -faw) *n.* **1** a figure of speech by which a word is transferred in application from one object to another, so as to imply comparison. **2** an instance of this. **3** a symbol (for). **metaphoric** (-for´-), **metaphorical** *a.* **metaphorically** *adv.* †**metaphorist** *n.* [F *métaphore*, L and Gr. *metaphora* (MET-, *pherein*, to bear)]

metaphrase (met´əfrāz) *v.t.* **1** to translate literally. **2** to express in other words. ~*n.* a literal translation. **metaphrasis** (-taf´rə-) *n.* **metaphrast** *n.* **metaphrastic** (-fras´-) *a.* [Gr. *metaphrasis* (MET-, *phrazein*, to speak)]

metaphysics (metəfiz´iks) *n.* **1** the philosophy of being and knowing. **2** the theoretical principles forming the basis of any particular science. **3** the philosophy of mind. **4** anything vague, abstract and abstruse. **metaphysic** *n.* a system of metaphysics. **metaphysical** *a.* **1** of or relating to metaphysics. **2** transcendental, dealing with abstractions. **3** abstruse, oversubtle. **4** imaginary, fantastic. **5** (*also* **Metaphysical**) belonging to the group of 17th-cent. poets noted for their intellectual tone and ingenious imagery. ~*n.* (*also* **Metaphysical**) a metaphysical poet. **metaphysically** *adv.* **metaphysician** (-zish´-) *n.* **metaphysicize** (-sīz), **metaphysicise** *v.t.*, *v.i.* [formerly *metaphysic*, med. L *metaphysica*, Gr. *metaphusika* (*meta ta phusika*, after physics, or coming next after the study of natural science)]

metaplasia (metəplā´ziə) *n.* (*Med.*) change of one form of tissue into another. **metaplasm** (met´əplazm) *n.* **1** the formative material of protoplasm. **2** change in a word by alteration of a letter or syllable. **metaplastic** (-plas´-) *a.* **1** of or relating to metaplasia. **2** of or relating to metaplasm. [Gr.]

metapsychology (metəsīkol´əji) *n.* **1** the body of theory on psychological matters. **2** studies, theories etc. of psychology that are beyond the limits of experimentation. **metapsychological** (-kəloj´-) *a.*

metastable (metəstā´bəl) *a.* **1** seeming stable because passing slowly from one state to another. **2** stable under small disturbances only. **metastability** (-stəbil´-) *n.*

metastasis (mitas´təsis) *n.* (*pl.* **metastases** (-sēz)) **1** a change in the seat of a disease, esp. cancer, from one organ to another. **2** a secondary tumour. **3** †metabolism. **metastasize, metastasise** *v.i.* **metastatic** (metəstat´ik) *a.*

metatarsus (metətah´səs) *n.* (*pl.* **metatarsi** (-sī)) **1** that part of the foot between the tarsus and the toes, in humans consisting of five long bones. **2** the set of bones linking the tarsus and the toes. **metatarsal** *a.*

metatheory (met´əthiəri) *n.* (*pl.* **metatheories**) a theory used to discuss the nature of another theory or theories.

metathesis (mitath´əsis) *n.* (*pl.* **metatheses** (-əsēz)) **1** (*Gram.*) the transposition of sounds or letters in a word. **2** interchange of radicals or groups of atoms in a compound with others. **metathetic** (metəthet´ik), **metathetical** *a.*

metathorax (metəthaw´raks) *n.* (*pl.* **metathoraces** (-rəsēz), **metathoraxes**) the posterior segment of the thorax in an insect.

metazoan (metəzō´ən) *n.* any animal of the subkingdom Metazoa, which includes all animals that have many-celled bodies and differentiated tissues, as distinct from *protozoan*. ~*a.* of or relating to the Metazoa. **metazoic** *a.* [Gr. *zōa*, pl. of *zōon*, animal]

mete[1] (mēt) *v.t.* **1** to allot, to apportion (out). **2** (*poet.*, *dial.*) to measure. **3** †to appraise. **4** †to be the measure of. ~†*v.i.* **1** to measure. **2** to aim. [OE *metan* (cp. Dut. *meten*, G *messen*)]

mete[2] (mēt) *n.* a limit, a boundary, a boundary stone. [OF, from L *meta*, a goal]

metempirics (metempir´iks) *n.* the philosophy of things lying beyond the bounds of experience. **metempiric, metempirical** *a.* of or relating to metempirics. ~*n.* a person who believes in metempirics. **metempiricism** *n.* **metempiricist** *n.*

metempsychosis (metempsīkō´sis) *n.* (*pl.* **metempsychoses** (-sēz)) **1** the supposed passage of the soul after death from one animal body to another. **2** an instance of this. **metempsychosist** *n.* [late L, from Gr. *metempsuchōsis*]

meteor (mē´tiə) *n.* **1** a luminous body appearing for a few moments in the sky and then disappearing, a shooting star. **2** anything which transiently dazzles or strikes with wonder. **3** †any atmospheric phenomenon, such as rain, hail etc. **meteoric** (-or´-) *a.* **1** of or relating to meteors. **2** rapid, like a meteor (*meteoric rise to fame*). **3** brilliant but fading quickly, dazzling. **4** of or relating to the atmosphere or its phenomena. **5** (of a plant) affected by atmospheric conditions. **meteorically** *adv.* **meteoric stone** *n.* a meteorite. **meteorite** *n.* a fallen meteor, a stone, metal or a compound of earth and metal, that has fallen upon the earth from space. **meteoritic** (-it´ik) *a.* **meteorograph** *n.* an instrument for recording meteorological phenomena. **meteorography** (-og´-) *n.* **meteoroid** *n.* a body that becomes visible as a meteor. **meteoroidal** (-oi´-) *a.* **meteorolite** (-līt) *n.* a meteorite. **meteor shower** *n.* a group of meteors appearing simultaneously esp. at regular intervals and from a particular place. [Gr. *meteōron*, n. from a. *meteōros*, raised (MET-, *eōra*, var. of *aiōra*, from *aeirein*, to raise)]

meteorology (mētiərol´əji) *n.* **1** the science of the atmosphere and its phenomena, esp. for the purpose of forecasting the weather. **2** the general character of the weather in a particular place. **meteorologic** (-loj´-) *a.* **meteorological** *a.* **meteorologically** *adv.* **meteorologist** *n.*

meter[1] (mē´tə) *n.* **1** a person who or something which measures, esp. an instrument for registering the quantity of gas, water, electric energy etc. supplied. **2** a parking meter. ~*v.t.* to measure by means of a meter. **meterage** *n.*

Usage note The British spellings of the nouns *meter* (an instrument) and *metre* (of verse, or as a metric unit) should not be confused.

meter[2] METRE[1].

meter[3] METRE[2].

-meter (mitə) *comb. form* **1** a measuring instrument, as in *barometer, thermometer*. **2** a verse metre with a specified number of feet, as in *pentameter*. [Gr. *metron*, measure]

meth- MET-.

methadone (meth´ədōn) *n.* a synthetic drug similar to morphine, often used in the treatment of addiction.

methamphetamine (methamfet´əmēn, -min) *n.* a variety of amphetamine used as a stimulant.

methanal (meth´ənal) *n.* (*Chem.*) formaldehyde.

methane (mē´thān) *n.* (*Chem.*) a light, colourless gas produced by the decomposition or dry distillation of vegetable matter, one of the chief constituents of coal gas, and also of firedamp and marsh gas. **methanometer** (-nom´itə) *n.* [METHYL, -ANE]

methanoic acid (methənō´ik) *n.* (*Chem.*) formic acid.

methanol (meth´ənol) *n.* a colourless, volatile liquid used as a solvent or as fuel, methyl alcohol.

Methedrine® (meth´ədrēn) *n.* METHAMPHETAMINE.

metheglin (mitheg´lin) *n.* a variety of mead, orig. Welsh. [Welsh *meddyglyn* (*meddyg*, L *medicus*, healing, *llyn*, liquor)]

methinks (mithingks´) *v.i.* (*past* **methought** (-thawt´)) it seems to me, I think.

methionine (mithī´ənēn) *n.* (*Biol.*) an amino acid containing sulphur, occurring in many proteins.

metho (meth´ō) *n.* (*pl.* **methos**) (*Austral.*, *sl.*) **1** methylated spirits. **2** a person addicted to drinking methylated spirits.

method (meth´əd) *n.* **1** a mode of procedure, way or order of doing. **2** an orderly, systematic or logical arrangement. **3** orderliness, system. **4** a system or the basis of a system of classification. **method in one's madness** careful thought underlying a seemingly careless action. **method acting** *n.* an acting technique based on the actor's identification of themselves with the part. **méthode champenoise** (mātōd shāpənwahz´) *n.* a method of producing sparkling wine by allowing the final stage of fermentation to take place in the bottle. **methodical** (mithod´-), **methodic** *a.* **1** done according to a method. **2** habitually proceeding in a systematic way. **methodically** *adv.* **methodize, methodise** *v.t.* **1** to arrange systematically. **2** to reduce to order. **methodizer** *n.* **methodology** (-dol´-) *n.* **1** the branch of logic dealing with the methods of accurate thinking. **2** the methods used in a particular project, discipline etc. **methodological** (-loj´-) *a.* **methodologically** *adv.* **methodologist** (-dol´-) *n.* [F *méthode*, L *methodus*, Gr. *methodos* (MET-, *hodos*, way)]

Methodist (meth´ədist) *n.* **1** a member of any of the religious bodies that have grown out of the evangelical movement begun in the middle of the 18th cent. by John Wesley, 1703–91, his brother Charles, and George Whitefield, 1714–70. **2** (**methodist**) a strict observer of method in philosophical inquiry or medical practice. **Methodism** *n.* the doctrines, practices or Church system of the Methodists. **Methodistic** (-dis´-), **Methodistical** *a.* **Methodistically** *adv.*

methought METHINKS.

meths (meths) *n.pl.* (*coll.*) methylated spirits.

Methuselah (mithū´zələ, -oo´-) *n.* **1** a very old person; a very old thing. **2** (*also* **methuselah**) a large wine bottle, about 8 times the usual size. [biblical patriarch said to have lived 969 years (Gen. v.27)]

methyl (meth´əl, mē´thīl) *n.* the hypothetical radical of wood spirit, formic acid and many other organic compounds. **methyl alcohol** *n.* methanol. **methylate** (meth´ilāt) *v.t.* **1** to mix or saturate with methyl alcohol. **2** to introduce a methyl group into. **methylated spirit, methylated spirits** *n.* spirit of wine, mixed with 10% of methyl alcohol so as to be rendered unfit to drink and accordingly not subject to duty. **methylation** (-ā´shən) *n.* **methyl benzene** *n.* toluene. **methylene** (meth´əlēn) *n.* a hypothetical organic radical in which two atoms of hydrogen are in chemical combination with one atom of carbon, occurring in numerous compounds. **methylic** (mithil´ik) *a.* [F *méthyle*, from *methylène* (Gr. *methu*, wine, *hulē*, wood)]

metic (met´ik) *n.* in ancient Greece, an immigrant, a resident alien. [Gr. *metoikos*, resident alien]

meticulous (mitik´ūləs) *a.* **1** very careful. **2** cautious or overscrupulous about trivial details, finicky. **meticulously** *adv.* **meticulousness** *n.* [L *meticulōsus*, from *metus*, fear]

métier (met´iā, mā´-) *n.* **1** trade, profession. **2** an area of activity in which one is skilled, feels comfortable etc., one's forte. [F, earlier *mestier*, pop. L *misterium*, L *ministerium*, MINISTRY (under MINISTER)]

Metis (mā´tēs, mātēs´), **Métis** *n.* (*pl.* **Metis, Métis**) a person of mixed blood, esp. (in Canada) the offspring of a person of European descent and an American Indian. [F, MESTIZO]

metol (met´ol) *n.* a white soluble organic substance derived from phenol, used as photographic developer. [G (arbitrary name)]

Metonic cycle (miton´ik) *n.* the cycle of 19 Julian years at the end of which the new and full moons recur on the same dates. [*Meton*, Athenian astronomer of the 5th cent.]

metonymy (miton´imi) *n.* (*pl.* **metonymies**) a figure of speech in which one word is used for another with which it is associated, as the effect for the cause, the material for the thing made etc., e.g. 'bench' for 'magistrates'. **metonym** (met´ənim) *n.* a word used metonymically. **metonymic** (-nim´-), **metonymical** *a.* **metonymically** *adv.* [late L *metōnymia*, Gr. *metōnumia* (MET-, *onoma*, Aeolic *onuma*, name)]

metope[1] (met´əpi, -ōp) *n.* (*Archit.*) the space between the triglyphs in a Doric frieze. [Gr. *metopē* (MET-, *opē*, hole for a beam)]

metope[2] (met´ōp) *n.* (*Zool.*, *Anat.*) the face or front. **metopic** (-top´-) *a.* frontal, of or relating to the forehead. [Gr. *metōpon*, forehead]

metre[1] (mē´tə), (*esp. N Am.*) **meter** *n.* the standard measure of length in the metric system, orig. the ten-millionth part of the quadrant of a meridian, 39.37 in., now defined as the distance travelled by light in a vacuum in 1/299,792,458 of a second. **metreage** (-tərij) *n.* the distance in metres. **metre-kilogram-second** *a.* denoting the metric system of units based on the metre, the kilogram and the second as units of length, mass and time. [F *mètre*, as METER[2]]

Usage note See note under METER[1].

metre[2] (mē´tə), (*esp. N Am.*) **meter** *n.* **1** the rhythmical arrangement of syllables in verse. **2** verse. **3** any particular form of poetic rhythm. **4** the basic rhythm of a piece of music. **metrify** (met´-) *v.t.* (*3rd pers. sing. pres.* **metrifies,** *pres.p.* **metrifying,** *past, p.p.* **metrified**) to compose in metre, to put into verse. **metrist** (met´-) *n.* **1** a person skilled in metres. **2** a versifier. [OF, from L *metrum*, Gr. *metron*, measure]

Usage note See note under METER[1].

metric (met´rik) *a.* **1** of or relating to the metre as a unit of measurement or the metric system. **2** metrical. *~n.* **1** a system or basis of measurement. **2** (*Math.*) a function based on distances. **3** (*usu. pl.*) the science or art of metre, prosody. **metrical** *a.* **1** of or relating to or composed in metre. **2** of or relating to measurement. **metrically** *adv.* **metricate** *v.t.* to convert to the metric system. **metrication** (-ā´shən) *n.* **metric hundredweight** *n.* a unit of weight equal to 50 kg. **metrician** (metrish´ən) *n.* METRIST (under METRE[2]). **metricize** (-isīz), **metricise** *v.t.* **metric system** *n.* a system of weights and measures in which units are multiples of ten times the basic units and in which ascending units carry Greek prefixes and descending units Latin prefixes. **metric ton, metric tonne** *n.* a unit of weight equal to 1,000 kg (2,205 lb.).

-metric (met´rik), **-metrical** (-əl) *comb. form* forming adjectives denoting measurement, as in *geometric*. **-metrically** *comb. form* forming adverbs denoting measurement, as in *isometrically*. [METRE[1]]

metrify, metrist METRE[2].

metritis (mitrī´tis) *n.* (*Med.*) inflammation of the womb. [Gr. *metra*, womb, -ITIS]

metro (met´rō) *n.* (*pl.* **metros**) an underground railway network in a city. [F *métro*, abbr. of *chemin de fer métropolitain*, metropolitan railway]

metro- (met´rō) *comb. form* measuring. [Gr. *metron*, measure]

metrology (mitrol´əji) *n.* the study of measurement. **metrological** (metrəloj´-), **metrologic** *a.* **metrologically** *adv.*

metromania (metrōmā´niə) *n.* a passion for writing verses.

metronome (met´rənōm) *n.* an instrument for indicating and marking time in music by means of a pendulum. **metronomic** (-nom´-) *a.* **metronomically** *adv.* **metronomy** (mitron´-) *n.* [F *métronome* (Gr. *nomos*, law, rule)]

metronymic (metrənim´ik) *a.* (of names) derived from the name of a mother or maternal ancestor. ~*n.* a name derived in this way. **metronymy** (mitron´-) *n.* [Gr. *mētrōnumikos* (*mētēr -tros*, mother, *onoma*, *onuma*, name)]

metropolis (mitrop´əlis) *n.* (*pl.* **metropolises**) **1** the chief town or capital of a country. **2** the seat or see of a metropolitan bishop. **3** a centre or focus of activity etc. **4** a large town or city. [L and Gr. *mētropolis*, mother-state (*mētēr -tros*, mother, *polis*, city)]

metropolitan (metrəpol´itən) *a.* **1** of or relating to a capital or large city. **2** of or relating to an archbishopric or (ecclesiastical) metropolis. **3** forming part of a sovereign state as distinct from its colonies. ~*n.* **1** a metropolitan bishop. **2** an inhabitant of a metropolis. **3** a bishop having authority over other bishops in a province, in the Western Church an archbishop, in the ancient and the modern Greek Church ranking above an archbishop and next to a patriarch. **metropolitan bishop** *n.* **metropolitan county** *n.* (*Hist.*) a large urban area acting as a unit of local government. **metropolitanism** *n.* **metropolitan magistrate** *n.* a stipendiary magistrate in London.

metrorrhagia (mētrərā´jiə) *n.* excessive bleeding from the womb. [L, from Gr. *metra*, womb, *rhegnumi*, burst]

-metry (mitri) *comb. form* science of measuring, as in *geometry*, *trigonometry*. [Gr. *metria*, measurement, from *metrēs*, measurer, see -METER]

mettle (met´əl) *n.* **1** quality of temperament or disposition. **2** constitutional ardour. **3** spirit, courage. **4** †stuff, material one is made of. **to put on one's mettle** to test one's courage, determination etc. **mettled, mettlesome** *a.* high-spirited, fiery, ardent. **mettlesomeness** *n.* [var. of METAL]

Usage note See note under METAL.

---

meu (myoo), **meum** (mē´əm) *n.* the plant spignel. [L *meum*, from Gr. *mēon*]

meunière (mœnyeə´) *a.* (of fish) cooked or served in butter with lemon juice and herbs, esp. parsley. [F]

MeV *abbr.* mega-electronvolt.

mew[1] (mū) *v.i.* to make a characteristic high-pitched cry, as a cat or seagull. ~*n.* the cry of the cat or seagull. [imit.]

mew[2] (mū), **mew gull** *n.* a kind of seagull, esp. *Larus canus*. [OE *mǣw* (cp. Dut. *meeuw*, Icel. *mar*, G *Möwe*)]

mew[3] (mū) *n.* **1** a cage for hawks, esp. whilst moulting. **2** a place of confinement. **3** a den. ~*v.t.* **1** to put (a hawk) in a mew or cage. **2** †to moult, to shed (the feathers). **3** to shut (up), to confine. ~†*v.i.* to shed the feathers. [OF *mue*, from *muer*, L *mūtāre*, to change]

mewl (mūl), **mule** *v.i.* **1** to cry, whine or whimper, as a child. **2** to mew, as a cat. **mewler** *n.*

mews (mūz) *n.* **1** stabling, orig. for carriage-horses etc. **2** a row of dwellings, garages etc. converted from such stables; a row of houses built in a similar style. [royal stables in London originally built on the spot where the royal hawks were mewed]

MEX *abbr.* Mexico (IVR).

Mexican (mek´sikən) *a.* of or relating to Mexico. ~*n.* **1** a native or inhabitant of Mexico. **2** Nahuatl, or any other indigenous language of Mexico. **Mexican wave** *n.* an apparent rippling effect passing round a crowd at a sports event etc. caused by people standing up and sitting down in sequence (first observed as a phenomenon at the soccer World Cup finals of 1986 at Mexico City).

mezereon (məziə´riən) *n.* a small ornamental shrub, *Daphne mezereum*. [med. L, from Arab. *māzaryūn*]

mezuzah (məzoo´zə), **mezuza** *n.* (*pl.* **mezuzoth** (-zōt)) a small case containing extracts from religious texts fixed to the doorpost by Jews as a sign of their piety. [Heb., doorpost]

mezzanine (mez´ənēn, met´sə-) *n.* **1** a storey intermediate in level between two main storeys, usu. between the ground and first floors. **2** a window in such a storey. **3** a floor beneath the stage of a theatre from which the traps etc. are worked. **4** (*N Am.*) the dress circle in a theatre. ~*a.* of or relating to unsecured high-interest loans of intermediate status between secured loans and equities. **mezzanine floor, mezzanine window** *n.* [F, from It. *mezzanino*, dim. of *mezzano*, L *mediānus*, MEDIAN]

mezza voce (metsə vō´chi) *a.*, *adv.* (*Mus.*) **1** (singing or sung) softly. **2** quiet(ly). [It., half voice]

mezzo (met´sō) *a.* half or medium. ~*n.* (*pl.* **mezzos**) a mezzo-soprano. **mezzo forte** *a.*, *adv.* (*Mus.*) moderately loud(ly). **mezzo piano** *a.*, *adv.* (*Mus.*) moderately soft(ly). **mezzo-relievo** (metsōrəlyā´vō), **mezzo-rilievo** *n.* (*pl.* **mezzo-relievos, mezzo-rilievos**) half-relief; a sculpture in which the figures stand out from the background to a half of their proportions. **mezzo-soprano** *n.* **1** a female singing voice lower than a soprano and higher than a contralto. **2** a singer with such a voice. **3** a part written for such a voice. [It., from L *medius*, middle]

mezzotint (met´sōtint) *n.* **1** a process of engraving in which a copper plate is uniformly roughened so as to print a deep black, tones and half-tones being then produced by scraping away the burr. **2** a print from this. ~*v.t.* to engrave in mezzotint. **mezzotinter** *n.* [It. *mezzotinto*]

MF *abbr.* medium frequency.

mf *abbr.* mezzo forte.

MFH *abbr.* Master of Foxhounds.

MG *abbr.* **1** machine gun. **2** Morris Garages (as a make of car).

Mg *chem. symbol* magnesium.

mg *abbr.* milligrams.

Mgr. *abbr.* **1** manager. **2** Monseigneur. **3** Monsignor.

mho (mō) *n.* (*pl.* **mhos**) (*Hist.*) a unit of electrical conductivity, now the *siemens*. [*ohm* reversed]

MHR *abbr.* (*N Am.*, *Austral.*) Member of the House of Representatives.

MHz *abbr.* megahertz.

MI *abbr.* **1** Michigan. **2** Military Intelligence. **MI5** *abbr.* the MI department concerned with state security. **MI6** *abbr.* the MI department concerned with espionage.

mi ME[2].

mi. *abbr.* mile(s).

MIA *abbr.* missing in action.

miaow (miow´), **meow** *n.* the cry of a cat. ~*v.i.* (of a cat) to cry 'miaow'.

miasma (miaz´mə) *n.* (*pl.* **miasmata** (-tə), **miasmas**) **1** an infectious or poisonous vapour. **2** an unwholesome atmosphere. **miasmal, miasmatic** (miəzmat´-), **miasmatical, miasmic** *a.* **miasmically** *adv.* [Gr., from *miainein*, to pollute]

miaul (miowl´) *v.i.* (of a cat) to cry 'miaow'. ~*v.t.* to sing or utter with the voice of a cat. **miauler** *n.* a cat.

Mic. *abbr.* (*Bible*) Micah.

mica (mī´kə) *n.* any of a group of silicates having a perfect basal cleavage into thin, tough and shining plates, formerly used instead of glass. **micaceous** (-kā´-) *a.* **mica-schist, mica-slate** *n.* a rock containing mica and quartz. [L, a crumb]

mice MOUSE[1].

micelle (misel´, mī-) *n.* an aggregate of molecules of colloidal size in a solution such as detergent. [L *micella*, dim. of L *mica*, a crumb]

Mich. *abbr.* 1 Michaelmas. 2 Michigan.

Michaelmas (mik´əlməs) *n.* the feast of St Michael the Archangel, 29 Sept. **Michaelmas daisy** *n.* any plant of the genus *Aster*, which flowers in the autumn. **Michaelmas term** *n.* the autumn term in some universities. [L *Michael*, Heb. *Mīkhāel*, who is like God, MASS]

mick (mik) *n.* (*sl., often offensive*) 1 an Irishman. 2 a Roman Catholic. **to take the mick** (*coll.*) to tease, to take the mickey out of someone. [as MICKEY]

mickey (mik´i), **micky** *n.* (*pl.* **mickeys, mickies**) 1 (*N Am., sl.*) an Irish lad. 2 (*Austral., sl.*) a young wild bull. **to take the mickey out of** to tease, mock, debunk. **mickey-taking** *n.* [fam. form of *Michael*, see MICHAELMAS]

Mickey Finn (miki fin´) *n.* (*esp. N Am.*) 1 a doped drink. 2 a narcotic or laxative used in this.

Mickey Mouse (mik´i) *a.* (*coll.*) 1 of poor quality, suitable for play only, as distinct from the real thing. 2 trivial, ridiculous. [20th-cent. cartoon character]

mickle (mik´əl), **muckle** (mŭk´əl) *a.* (*chiefly Sc.*) much, great. ~*n.* a large amount. **many a little/ mickle makes a muckle** many small amounts accumulate to become a large amount. [OE *micel, mycel*]

micky MICKEY.

micr- MICRO-.

micro (mī´krō) *n.* (*pl.* **micros**) 1 (*coll.*) short for MICROCOMPUTER. 2 (*coll.*) short for MICROPROCESSOR.

micro- (mī´krō), **micr-** *comb. form* 1 of or relating to small things (as opposed to large ones). 2 indicating smallness. [Gr. *mikros*, small]

microanalysis (mīkrōənal´isis) *n.* (*pl.* **microanalyses** (-sēz)) the chemical analysis of substances using a very small sample.

microbe (mī´krōb) *n.* any minute organism, esp. a bacterium or microzyme causing disease or fermentation. **microbial** (mīkrō´biəl), **micobian** (-biən), **microbic** (-bik) *a.* **microbiology** (-bīol´-) *n.* **microbiological** (-əloj´-) *a.* **microbiologically** *adv.* **microbiologist** *n.* [F (MICRO-, Gr. *bios*, life)]

microburst (mī´krəbœst) *n.* a particularly strong downward movement of turbulent air, esp. during a thunderstorm.

microcephalic (mīkrōsifal´ik, -kef-) *a.* having an unusually small skull in relation to the rest of the body. ~*n.* a microcephalic person. **microcephalous** (-sef´-, -kef´-) *a.* **microcephaly** (-sef´-, -kef´-) *n.*

microchip (mī´krəchip) *n.* a chip of silicon etc. bearing many integrated circuits.

microcircuit (mī´krəsœkit) *n.* a very small integrated circuit on a semiconductor. **microcircuitry** *n.*

microclimate (mī´krəklīmət) *n.* the climate of a very small area, as distinct from that of the area around. **microclimatic** (-mat´-) *a.*

micrococcus (mīkrəkok´əs) *n.* (*pl.* **micrococci** (-kok´sī)) any minute spherical bacterium of the genus *Micrococcus*.

microcode (mī´krəkōd) *n.* 1 a microinstruction. 2 a sequence of microinstructions.

microcomputer (mī´krəkəmpūtə) *n.* a small computer with one or more microprocessors.

microcopy (mī´krəkopi) *n.* (*pl.* **microcopies**) a very small copy of printed matter on micofilm or microfiche. ~*v.t.* (*3rd pers. sing. pres.* **microcopies,** *pres.p.* **microcopying,** *past, p.p.* **microcopied**) to make a copy of in this way.

microcosm (mī´krəkozm) *n.* 1 a representation (of) in miniature form. 2 the universe on a small scale. 3 humankind as an epitome of the macrocosm or universe. 4 a little community. **microcosmic** (-koz´-) *a.* **microcosmically** *adv.* **microcosmography** (-mog´-) *n.* **microcosmology** (-mol´-) *n.* [F *microcosme*, med. L *microcosmus*, Gr. *mikrokosmos* (MICRO-, COSMOS[1])]

microcyte (mī´krəsīt) *n.* (*Med.*) an abnormally small red blood corpuscle, such as appear in cases of anaemia.

microdot (mī´krədot) *n.* a photographic image reduced to the size of a dot, e.g. for espionage purposes.

microeconomics (mīkrōēkənom´iks, -ek-) *n.* the branch of economics concerned with individual commodities, firms etc. and the economic relationships between them. **microeconomic** *a.*

microelectronics (mīkrōilektron´iks) *n.* electronics as applied to microcircuits. **microelectronic** *a.*

microevolution (mīkroēvəloo´shən, -ev-) *n.* (*Biol.*) evolution taking place within a species or small group of organisms, esp. over a short period of time. **microevolutionary** *a.*

microfarad (mī´krəfarəd) *n.* a unit of electrical capacitance, one-millionth of a farad.

microfiche (mī´krəfēsh) *n.* (*pl.* **microfiche, microfiches**) a sheet of film bearing miniature photographs of documents etc. [F *fiche*, sheet of paper]

microfilm (mī´krəfilm) *n.* a strip of film on which successive pages of a document or book are photographed for purposes of record. ~*v.t.* to photograph using microfilm.

microfloppy (mī´krəflopi) *n.* (*pl.* **microfloppies**) (*Comput.*) a small floppy disk, usu. 3.5 inches in diameter. **microfloppy disk** *n.*

microform (mī´krəfawm) *n.* a method of storing symbolic information using microphotographic techniques.

microgeology (mī´krōjioləji) *n.* the department of geology dealing with microscopic structures.

microgram (mī´krəgram) *n.* one-millionth of a gram.

micrograph (mī´krəgrahf) *n.* 1 a very small picture, photograph etc. taken by using a microscope. 2 a kind of pantograph for extremely minute engraving. **micrographer** (-krog´-) *n.* **micrographic** (-graf´-) *a.* **micrography** (-krog´-) *n.* a description of microscopic objects.

microgravity (mī´krəgraviti) *n.* 1 a state of weak or no gravity. 2 gravitational effects operating in a localized area, e.g. a spacecraft in orbit.

microgroove (mī´krəgroov) *n.* the groove of a long-playing gramophone record.

microinstruction (mī´krōinstrŭkshən) *n.* a computer instruction that activates a particular circuit to execute part of an operation specified by a machine instruction.

microlepidoptera (mīkrōlepidop´tərə) *n.pl.* small moths.

microlight (mī´krəlīt) *n.* a very small light aircraft, usu. for one person.

microlite (mī´krəlīt) *n.* 1 a native salt of calcium found in small crystals. 2 a microlith (sense 1).

microlith (mī´krəlith) *n.* 1 a small mesolithic flint tool, forming part of a composite tool. 2 any of the microscopic bodies found in vitreous feldspar, hornblende etc. **microlithic** (-lith´-) *a.*

micrology (mīkrol´əji) *n.* 1 the branch of science dealing with microscopic objects. 2 excessive concern with petty matters, hair-splitting. **micrological** (-krəloj´-) *a.* **micrologically** *adv.* **micrologist** *n.*

micromesh (mī´krəmesh) *n., a.* (material) made of a fine mesh, esp. nylon.

micrometer[1] (mīkrom´itə) *n.* an instrument used to measure small distances or objects. **micrometric** (-krəmet´-), **micrometrical** *a.* **micrometry** *n.*

micrometer[2] MICROMETRE.

micrometre (mī´krəmētə), (*N Am.*) **micrometer** *n.* one-millionth of a metre, a micron.

microminiaturization (mīkrōminəchərīzā´shən), **microminiaturisation** *n.* the production of very small electronic components and circuitry by using integrated circuits.
micron (mī´kron) *n.* one-millionth of a metre, the unit of length in microscopic research. [Gr. *mikron*, neut. of *mikros*, small]
Micronesian (mīkrənē´ziən) *a.* of or relating to Micronesia, a group of small islands in the W Pacific. ~*n.* **1** a native or inhabitant of Micronesia. **2** the languages spoken in Micronesia.
micronutrient (mīkrōnū´triənt) *n.* a substance, chemical element etc. required in very small amounts for the survival and development of living organisms.
micro-organism (mīkrōaw´gənizm) *n.* an organism of microscopic size.
microphone (mī´krəfōn) *n.* an instrument for converting sound into electrical waves. **microphonic** (-fon´-) *a.* **1** of or relating to the microphone. **2** behaving in a manner similar to a microphone.
microphotography (mīkrōfətog´rəfi) *n.* **1** the production of microscopic photographs. **2** the photography of microscopic objects on a magnified scale. **microphotograph** (-fō´təgrahf) *n.*
microphyte (mī´krəfīt) *n.* a microscopic vegetable organism, esp. a bacterium.
microprocessor (mīkrōprō´sesə) *n.* an integrated circuit operating as the central processing unit of a microcomputer.
microprogram (mī´krōprōgram) *n.* (*Comput.*) a sequence of microinstructions controlling the central processing unit of a computer.
micropsia (mīkrop´siə) *n.* (*Med.*) a state of vision in which objects appear unnaturally small. [Gr. *-opsia*, vision]
micropterous (mīkrop´tərəs) *a.* (*Zool.*) having small wings or fins. [Gr. *pteron*, wing]
micropyle (mī´krəpīl) *n.* **1** (*Anat.*) a minute opening in the external membrane of the ovum by which spermatozoa may enter. **2** (*Bot.*) the small opening in an ovule by which the pollen reaches the apex of the nucleus. **3** (*Bot.*) the aperture representing this in the ripe seed. [Gr. *pulē*, gate]
microscope (mī´krəskōp) *n.* an optical instrument by which objects are so magnified that details invisible to the naked eye are clearly seen. **microscopic** (-skop´-) *a.* **1** too small to be visible except by the aid of a microscope. **2** very small. **3** viewed in terms of very small units. **4** microscopical. **microscopical** *a.* of or relating to the microscope. **microscopically** *adv.* **microscopist** *n.* **microscopy** (-kros´-) *n.* the use of the microscope.
microsecond (mī´krəsekənd) *n.* one-millionth of a second.
microseism (mī´krəsīzm) *n.* a slight tremor or vibration of the earth's crust. **microseismic** (-sīz´-) *a.* **microseismograph** (-sīz´-) *n.* an instrument for recording microseisms. **microseismology** (-mol´-) *n.* **microseismometry** (-mom´-) *n.* [Gr. *seismos*, earthquake]
microsome (mī´krəsōm), **microsoma** (mīkrōsō´mə) *n.* (*pl.* **microsomes, microsomata** (-tə)) any of the minute granules in the endoplasm of protoplasmic cells. **microsomatous** *a.*
microsporangium (mīkrōspəran´jiəm) *n.* (*pl.* **microsporangia** (-jiə)) a sporangium containing microspores.
microspore (mī´krəspaw) *n.* **1** any one of the smaller kind of spores in some cryptogams, from which male gametophytes develop. **2** an immature pollen grain in seed plants. **microsporous** (-spaw´-) *a.*
microstructure (mīkrōstrŭk´chə) *n.* the arrangement of crystals etc. esp. within metals and alloys, as made visible by a microscope.
microsurgery (mī´krəsœjəri) *n.* surgery performed using a microscope and special small instruments. **microsurgical** *a.*
microswitch (mī´krəswich) *n.* a very small electronic switch, operated by very slight movement or pressure.
microtome (mī´krətōm) *n.* an instrument for cutting thin sections of tissue etc. for microscopic examination. **microtomic** (-tom´-), **microtomical** *a.* **microtomist** *n.* **microtomy** (-krot´-) *n.* (*pl.* **microtomies**).
microtone (mī´krətōn) *n.* (*Mus.*) any interval smaller than a semitone.
microtubule (mīkrōtū´būl) *n.* (*Biol.*) a very small rigid structure of protein occurring in the cytoplasm of many plants and animal cells.
microwave (mī´krəwāv) *n.* **1** (*coll.*) a microwave oven. **2** an electromagnetic wave with a wavelength between 30 cm and 1 mm. ~*v.t.* to cook in a microwave oven. **microwaveable** (-wā´-), **microwavable** *a.* **microwave oven** *n.* an oven that cooks food with microwaves.
micrurgy (mī´krœji) *n.* the manipulation, examination etc. of single cells under a microscope. [MICRO-, Gr. *-ourgia*, work]
micturition (miktūrish´ən) *n.* **1** (*Med.*) a frequent desire to urinate. **2** the act of urinating. **micturate** (mik´-) *v.i.* (*Med.*) to urinate. [L *micturīre*, desiderative of *mingere*, to make water, -ITION]
mid[1] (mid) *prep.* (*poet.*) amid. [abbr.]
mid[2] (mid) *a.* (*superl.* **midmost**) middle. [as MID-]
mid- (mid) *comb.form* **1** middle, medium. **2** that is in the middle of, as in *mid-June*, *mid-calf.* **midbrain** (mid´-) *n.* (*Anat.*) the central part of the brainstem, the mesencephalon. **midday** *n.* noon, the middle of the day. ~*a.* of or relating to noon. **Mideast** *n.* (*N Am.*) the Middle East. **midfield** (mid´fēld, midfēld´) *n.* **1** the central area of a sports pitch, esp. a football pitch. **2** the players with positions between the attackers and defenders, esp. in football. **midfielder** *n.* **midgut** (mid´-) *n.* (*Zool., Anat.*) in vertebrates, the middle part of the digestive tract, including the small intestine. **mid-heaven** *n.* the middle of the sky, as viewed. **midiron** (mid´-) *n.* an iron golf club with a moderate amount of loft. **mid-life** *n.* middle age. **mid-life crisis** *n.* a feeling of panic, loss of self-confidence etc. often experienced at the onset of middle age. **midline** (mid´-) *n.* (*Geom.*) a median line forming the axis of bilateral symmetry. **mid-off** *n.* in cricket, the fieldsman to the left of the bowler (when the batsman is right-handed). **mid-on** *n.* in cricket, the fieldsman to the right of the bowler (when the batsman is right-handed). **midpoint** *n.* **1** (*Geom.*) a point on a line equidistant from either end. **2** a point in time halfway between beginning and end. **midrib** (mid´-) *n.* the central vein of a leaf. **midship** (mid´-) *n.* the middle part of a ship or boat. ~*a.* situated in or belonging to this. **midshipman** *n.* (*pl.* **midshipmen**) (*Hist.*) a naval officer ranking between a cadet and a sub lieutenant, a young officer under instruction on a ship. **midships** *adv.* AMIDSHIPS (under AMID). **midstream** *adv.* **1** in the middle of a stream. **2** in the middle of an action or process. ~*n.* the middle of a stream. **to change horses in midstream** HORSE. **midsummer** *n.* the middle of summer, esp. the period of the summer solstice, about 21 June. **Midsummer Day, Midsummer's Day** *n.* 24 June. **midsummer madness** *n.* foolish behaviour, esp. associated with summer. **midtown** (mid´-) *n.* (*N Am.*) the centre of a city, large town etc. **midway** (mid´wā, midwā´) *a.* situated in the middle or the middle of the way. ~*adv.* **1** in the middle. **2** halfway. ~*n.* (*N Am.*) a fair, a place in a carnival etc. where sideshows are located. **midweek** *n., a., adv.* (occurring in) the middle of the week, i.e. Tuesday, Wednesday, Thursday. **Midwest** *n.* the N central part of the USA, from Ohio west to the Rocky Mountains. **Midwestern** *a.* **midwicket** *n.* **1** in cricket, a fielding position on the leg side opposite the middle of the

playing strip. 2 a person at that position. **midwinter** *n.* the middle of winter, esp. the winter solstice, 21 Dec. [OE *mid*, *midd* (cp. Dut., Swed. and Dan. *mid-*, OHG *mitti*, L *medius*, Gr. *messos*)]

Midas (mī´dəs) *n.* a fabulously rich man. **Midas touch** *n.* the facility for making money or achieving success. [legendary king of Phrygia to whom Dionysus granted the power of turning all he touched into gold]

midbrain, midday MID-.

midden (mid´ən) *n.* 1 a dunghill. 2 a refuse tip near a house. 3 KITCHEN-MIDDEN (under KITCHEN). [ME *midding*, from Scand. (cp. Dan. *mödding*, cogn. with MUCK, *dynge*, heap)]

middle (mid´əl) *a.* (*superl.* **middlemost**) 1 placed equally distant from the extremes. 2 intervening, intermediate. 3 average. 4 (of a language) of the period between old and modern. 5 (*Gram.*) (esp. of verbs in Greek) between active and passive, reflexive. ~*n.* 1 the point or place equally distant from the extremes. 2 the waist. 3 the midst, the centre. 4 (*Gram.*) the middle voice, a middle verb. 5 (*Logic*) the middle term. ~*v.t.* 1 to place in the middle. 2 (*Naut.*) to fold or double in the middle. 3 in football, to pass or return (the ball) to midfield from one of the wings. 4 in cricket, to hit (the ball) with the middle of the bat. **in the middle of** during, while. **in the middle of nowhere** NOWHERE. **middle age** *n.* the period of life between youth and old age (about 45–60), or about the middle of the ordinary human life. **middle-aged** *a.* **middle-age spread, middle-aged spread** *n.* the increased amount of fat at the waist often associated with middle age. **Middle Ages** *n.pl.* the period from the 5th to the 15th cent. inclusive in Europe. **Middle America** *n.* 1 the midwestern region of the US. 2 the middle class of the US. 3 Mexico and Central America. **middlebrow** *a.* (*coll.*, *derog.*) of moderate intellect and conventional tastes. ~*n.* a person with these characteristics. **middle C** *n.* (*Mus.*) on a keyboard, the note C at the centre, between the treble and bass staves. **middle class** *n.* the class between the upper and lower classes, largely consisting of business and professional people and their families. **middle-class** *a.* **middle common room** *n.* in a university, college etc., a common room for graduates who are not fellows, teaching staff etc. **middle course** *n.* an action or decision that represents a compromise between possible extremes. **middle deck** *n.* the deck of a ship between the main deck and the lower deck. **middle distance** *n.* 1 the central portion of a picture between the foreground and the distance. 2 in athletics, a race measuring 800m or 1,500m. **middle ear** *n.* the cavity of the ear behind the drum, containing the malleus, incus and stapes. **Middle East** *n.* the geographical area including SW Asia as far as Afghanistan and parts of N Africa. **Middle Eastern** *a.* **Middle English** *n.* the English language in use from about 1150 to 1500. **middle finger** *n.* the second finger (third from the little finger inclusive). **middle game** *n.* in chess, the central phase of the game when strategies are developed, as distinct from the opening and the end game. **middle ground** *n.* 1 in a given issue, the point of view tending to moderation and compromise as opposed to extreme opinions. 2 the people holding this point of view. **middle-income** *a.* 1 of or relating to those people earning average salaries. 2 of or relating to countries with an average national income. **Middle Kingdom** *n.* (*Hist.*) China. **middleman** *n.* (*pl.* **middlemen**) 1 a person through whose hands a commodity passes between the producer and the consumer. 2 an agent, an intermediary. **middle management** *n.* 1 those people responsible for the day-to-day running of a company, organization etc. 2 this level of responsibility. **middle manager** *n.* **middle name** *n.* 1 any name between a person's first given name and their family name. 2 (*coll.*) a person's most typical quality (*Punctuality is his middle name!*). **middle-of-the-road** *a.* 1 moderate, not extreme in political views, tastes etc. 2 (of music) intended to appeal to the widest range of tastes, undemanding to listen to. **middle passage** *n.* (*Hist.*) the sea voyage between W Africa and the W Indies, the middle section of a triangular route taken by ships in the slave trade. **middle school** *n.* a school for children between 8 or 9 years of age and 12 or 13 years of age. **middle-sized** *a.* of medium size. **Middle Temple** *n.* one of the four law societies which form the Inns of Court in London. **middle term** *n.* (*Logic*) the term of a syllogism that appears in both major and minor premisses. **middle watch** *n.* (*Naut.*) the watch between midnight and 4 a.m. **middle way** *n.* 1 a middle course. 2 in Buddhism, the eightfold path through life between asceticism and indulgence. **middleweight** *n.* 1 a boxer, wrestler, weightlifter etc. in the weight category intermediate between welterweight and (light) heavyweight. 2 this weight category. **Middle West** *n.* the Midwest. **middling** *a.* 1 of middle size, quality or condition. 2 moderately good. 3 mediocre, second-rate. 4 (*coll.*) in moderately good health. 5 of the second of three grades. ~*adv.* moderately, tolerably. **fair to middling** FAIR[1]. **middlingly** *adv.* **middlings** *n.pl.* 1 the coarser part of flour. 2 the middling grade of other commodities. [OE *middel*, from *midd*, MID[2] (cp. Dut. *middle*, G *Mittel*)]

Middx. *abbr.* Middlesex.

middy[1] (mid´i) *n.* (*pl.* **middies**) (*coll.*) 1 a midshipman. 2 a middy blouse. **middy blouse** *n.* a loose blouse with a collar similar to that traditionally worn by sailors. [etym. uncertain]

middy[2] (mid´i) *n.* (*pl.* **middies**) (*Austral.*, *coll.*) 1 a glass of beer. 2 a 10 oz. (approx. 300 ml.) pot or container.

Mideast, midfield MID-.

midge (mij) *n.* 1 a gnat or other minute fly, esp. of the families Chironomidae and Ceratopogonidae. 2 a tiny person. **midget** (-it) *n.* a very small person. ~*a.* very small. [OE *mycg* (cp. Dut. *mug*, G *Mücke*, Dan. *myg*)]

midgut, mid-heaven MID-.

MIDI (mid´i) *n.* an electronic system to link musical instruments with computer technology for composition and performance. [*m*usical *i*nstrument *d*igital *i*nterface]

midi- (mid´i) *comb. form* 1 of middle size. 2 (of a skirt etc.) reaching to the mid-calf. **midi** (mid´i) *n.* (*pl.* **midis**) a midi-skirt, midi-dress etc. **midi-bus** *n.* a bus larger than a minibus, but smaller than a standard bus. **midi system** *n.* a compact stacking set of hi-fi equipment.

midinette (midinet´) *n.* a shop girl in Paris, esp. in a milliner's shop. [F, from *midi*, midday, *dinette*, light dinner]

midiron MID-.

midland (mid´lənd) *a.* 1 situated in the middle or interior of a country. 2 surrounded by land. 3 (**Midland**) of or relating to the central counties of England. ~*n.* 1 the interior of a country. 2 (**Midlands**) the midland counties of England.

mid-life, midline MID-.

midmost MID[2].

midnight (mid´nīt) *n.* 1 the middle of the night, twelve o'clock at night. 2 intense darkness. ~*a.* 1 of, relating to or occurring in the middle of the night. 2 very dark. **to burn the midnight oil** OIL. **midnight blue** *a.* very dark blue. ~*n.* this colour. **midnight sun** *n.* the sun visible around midnight in summer in the polar regions.

mid-off, mid-on etc. MID-.

Midrash (mid´rash, -ŭsh) *n.* (*pl.* **Midrashim** (-im)) a commentary on part of the Hebrew scriptures. [Heb.]

midrib MID-.

midriff (mid´rif) *n.* **1** the middle part of the front of the body, between waist and chest. **2** the diaphragm. **3** the part of a garment covering the abdomen. [OE *midrif, -hrif* (*mid, hrif,* belly)]
midship, midships MID-.
midst (midst) *n.* the middle (now only in idioms below). ~*prep.* (*poet.*) in the middle of, amidst. **in our/ your/ their midst** among us, you etc. **in the midst of** among, surrounded by or involved in. [earlier *middest* (OE *middes,* gen. of MID[2] used adverbially, prob. confused or blended with superl. of MID[2])]
midstream, midsummer etc. MID-.
midwife (mid´wīf) *n.* (*pl.* **midwives** (-wīvz)) **1** (*pl.*) a person who assists at childbirth. **2** any person who helps to bring about a significant development. **midwifery** (-wifəri) *n.* **midwife toad** *n.* the toad *Alytes obstetricans,* the male of which carries the developing eggs on his hind legs until they hatch. [OE *mid,* with (cp. G *mit,* also Gr. *meta*), WIFE]
midwinter MID-.
mielie MEALIE.
mien (mēn) *n.* air or manner, appearance, deportment, demeanour, bearing, carriage. [F *mine,* or shortened from DEMEAN[1]]
miff (mif) *n.* **1** a petty quarrel. **2** a huff. ~*v.i.* to be vexed (with or at). ~*v.t.* (*usu. in pass.*) to vex, to annoy slightly, to offend (*I was miffed that she ignored me*). **miffy** (-i) *a.* easily upset or annoyed. [prob. imit. of instinctive expression of annoyance]
might[1] (mīt) *n.* **1** strength, force. **2** power, esp. to enforce will or arbitrary authority. **with all one's might** using all one's strength, influence etc. **with might and main** MAIN[2]. **mighty** *a.* (*comp.* **mightier,** *superl.* **mightiest**) **1** strong, powerful. **2** very great, huge, immense. **3** (*coll.*) great, considerable. ~*adv.* (*coll.*) exceedingly, very (*mighty glad to see you*). **mightily** *adv.* **mightiness** *n.* [OE *miht,* cogn. with *megan,* MAY[1] (cp. G *Macht,* Dan. *magt*)]
might[2] MAY[1].
mignon (mēn´yon) *a.* delicate and small, dainty. [F]
mignonette (minyənet´) *n.* **1** any annual plant of the genus *Reseda,* esp. *R. odorata,* which has fragrant greenish flowers. **2** the greenish colour of its flowers. **3** a type of fine narrow pillowlace. [F, dim. of MIGNON]
migraine (mē´grān, mī´-) *n.* a recurrent severe headache, esp. on one side of the head only, often accompanied by nausea and visual disturbances. **migrainous** *a.* [F *migraine,* see MEGRIM[1]]
migrate (mīgrāt´) *v.i.* **1** to move permanently from one country, place or habitation to another. **2** (of birds, fishes etc.) to pass from one region to another according to the season. **3** to pass from one part of the body to another. **migrant** (mī´-) *n., a.* **migration** (-grā´shən) *n.* **migrational** *a.* **migrator** *n.* **migratory** (mī´grətəri) *a.* [L *migrātus,* p.p. of *migrāre,* to wander]
mihrab (mē´rahb) *n.* a niche etc. in a mosque indicating the direction of Mecca. [Arab., praying place]
mikado (mikah´dō) *n.* (*pl.* **mikados**) (*Hist.*) the emperor of Japan. [Jap. (*mi,* august, *kado,* gate, door)]
Mike (mīk) *n.* (*sl.*) a person's name, only as below. **for the love of Mike** used to express frustration, pleading etc. [abbr. of *Michael*]
mike[1] (mīk) *n.* (*coll.*) short for MICROPHONE.
mike[2] (mīk) *v.i.* (*sl.*) to shirk, to be idle. ~*n.* the act of shirking. [etym. unknown]
mil (mil) *n.* **1** a unit of length, a thousandth part of an inch (0.0254 mm), in measuring wire. **2** in pharmacy, a millilitre. [L *mille,* a thousand]
mil. *abbr.* military.
miladi (milā´di), **milady** *n.* (*pl.* **miladies**) (*Hist.*) **1** an English gentlewoman or noblewoman. **2** (in France) my lady (used as a form of address or reference).
milage MILEAGE (under MILE).
Milanese (milənēz´) *a.* of or relating to Milan. ~*n.* (*pl.* **Milanese**) a native or inhabitant of Milan. **Milanese silk** *n.* a finely woven silk, rayon etc. [*Milan,* a city of N Italy]
milch (milch) *a.* (of a farm animal) giving milk. **milch cow** *n.* **1** a cow kept for milk. **2** a person from whom money is easily obtained. [OE *meolc, melc,* cogn. with MILK]
mild (mīld) *a.* **1** gentle in manners or disposition. **2** tender, pacific, clement, placid, bland, pleasant. **3** (of fruit, liquor etc.) soft, not harsh, sharp or strong. **4** (of beer) not bitter, not strongly flavoured with hops. **5** moderate, not extreme, tame. **6** moderate in degree. **7** (of medicines) operating gently. ~*n.* mild beer. **to draw it mild** DRAW. **milden** *v.t., v.i.* **mildish** *a.* **mildly** *adv.* **to put it mildly** with understatement. **mild-mannered** *a.* of a gentle disposition. **mildness** *n.* **mild steel** *n.* a tough steel containing a low proportion of carbon. [OE *milde* (cp. Dut., G, Dan. and Swed. *mild,* Icel. *mildr*), cogn. with Gr. *malthakos*]
mildew (mil´dū) *n.* a harmful fungoid growth on plants, cloth, paper, food etc. after exposure to damp. ~*v.t.* to taint with mildew. ~*v.i.* to be tainted with mildew. **mildewy** *a.* [OE *meledēaw,* honeydew, cp. OHG *militou* (*milith,* cp. Gr. *meli,* honey, DEW)]
mile (mīl) *n.* **1** a measure of length or distance, 1760 yds. (1.609 km). **2** a Roman measure of 1000 paces, about 1620 yds. (1.481 km). **3** (*pl., coll.*) a great distance, a large amount. **4** a race over a course one mile long. **nautical mile** NAUTICAL. **mileage** (mī´lij), **milage** *n.* **1** the number of miles concerned. **2** an allowance paid for the number of miles travelled. **3** the distance travelled by a vehicle on one gallon or litre of petrol. **4** the benefit to be derived from something. **milepost** *n.* **1** in a race, a post set one mile from the finish. **2** (*N Am., Austral.*) a milestone. **miler** *n.* a person, animal or thing qualified to run or travel a mile, or (*in comb.*) a specified number of miles (as *ten-miler*). **miles** *adv.* (*coll.*) considerably, very much. **miles away** *adv.* lost in thought, daydreaming, preoccupied. **milestone** *n.* **1** a stone set up by a road marking the distance to relevant places. **2** an important point in the life or development of a person, historical phenomenon, project etc. **milometer** (-lom´-), **mileometer** *n.* a device for recording the number of miles travelled by a vehicle. [OE *mīl,* L *mīlia,* pl. of *mille,* a thousand (paces)]
☒ **milennium** common misspelling of MILLENNIUM.
Milesian (mīlē´ziən) *a.* (*facet.*) Irish. ~*n.* an Irishman. [*Milesius,* legendary king of Spain, whose sons are said to have conquered Ireland about 1300 BC, -AN]
milfoil (mil´foil) *n.* **1** the yarrow, *Achillea millefolium,* named because the leaves are finely divided. **2** any aquatic plant of the genus *Myriophyllum,* water milfoil. [OF, from L *millefolium* (*mille,* thousand, *folium,* leaf)]
miliary (mil´iəri) *a.* **1** like millet seed. **2** (of a medical condition) having a rash with lesions like millet seeds. [L *miliārius,* from *milium,* MILLET]
milieu (mēlyœ´, mēl´-) *n.* (*pl.* **milieux, milieus** (-yœz)) environment, surroundings, setting. [F, middle, from *mi,* middle, *lieu,* place]
militant (mil´itənt) *a.* **1** combative, warlike, aggressive. **2** actively engaged in fighting. ~*n.* a militant person. **militancy** *n.* **militantly** *adv.* [L *mīlitans, -antem,* pres.p. of *mīlitāre,* to MILITATE]
military (mil´itəri) *a.* **1** of or relating to soldiers, arms or warfare. **2** soldierly, warlike, martial. **3** engaged in war. ~*n.* **1** (*collect.*) soldiers generally. **2** the army. **militaria** (-teə´riə) *n.pl.* military uniforms, medals etc. of the past that are of interest to collectors. **militarily** *adv.* **militariness** *n.* **militarism** *n.* **1** domination by the spirit of aggression. **2** military or warlike policy. **3** military spirit. **militarist** *n.* **1** a person dominated by militarism.

2 a student of military history and the conduct of war. **militaristic** (-is´tik) *a.* **militaristically** *adv.* **militarize, militarise** *v.t.* 1 to provide with military equipment. 2 to make military or militaristic. **militarization** (-zā´shən) *n.* **Military Cross, Military Medal** *n.* a British army decoration awarded for conspicuous courage under fire. **military engineer** *n.* an engineer dealing with the design and construction of fortifications and of roads, bridges, airstrips etc. used for military purposes. **military engineering** *n.* **military honours** *n.pl.* courtesies paid to a soldier or person of high rank at their funeral, wedding etc. **military police** *n.pl.* a police force for enforcing discipline in the army. **military policeman** *n.* (*pl.* **military policemen**). **military service** *n.* 1 service (esp. when compulsory) in the armed forces. 2 (*Hist.*) the service due in time of war from a feudal vassal to his superior. **military tenure** *n.* (*Hist.*) feudal tenure on the basis of providing military service in time of war. **military tribune** *n.* a senior military officer in ancient Rome. [F *militaire*, L *mīlitāris*, from *mīles mīlitis*, soldier]

militate (mil´itāt) *v.i.* 1 to have weight or influence, to tell (against). 2 to be or stand opposed. [L *mīlitātus*, p.p. of *mīlitāre*, from *mīles mīlitis*, soldier]

Usage note The verbs *militate* and *mitigate* should not be confused: *militate* means to have weight or influence, and *mitigate* to moderate or alleviate. You cannot *mitigate against* anything.

militia (milish´ə) *n.* 1 a supplementary military force consisting of the body of citizens not enrolled in the regular army. 2 (*Hist.*) the former constitutional force of England, consisting usu. of volunteers enrolled and disciplined, but called out only in case of emergency, superseded by the Territorial Army in 1907. **militiaman** *n.* (*pl.* **militiamen**). [L, as MILITATE]

milk (milk) *n.* 1 the whitish fluid secreted by female mammals for the nourishment of their young. 2 that of the cow, goat or sheep, used as food for humans. 3 the white juice of certain plants or fruits. 4 an emulsion made from herbs, drugs etc. (*milk of magnesia*). ~*v.t.* 1 to draw milk from. 2 to exploit or get money out of (a person) in an underhand or disreputable way. 3 to exploit to the full. 4 to extract venom from. 5 (*sl.*) to tap (a telegraph wire or message). ~*v.i.* to yield milk. **to cry over spilt milk** CRY. **milk and honey** *n.* prosperity, abundance. **milk and water** *n.* namby-pamby or mawkish talk, sentiment etc. **milk-and-water** *a.* namby-pamby, weak, twaddling. **milk bar** *n.* a snack bar selling milk drinks etc. **milk chocolate** *n.* chocolate made with milk. **milker** *n.* **milk fever** *n.* 1 an illness of female farm animals etc. that have just given birth to young, caused by calcium deficiency. 2 a fever of women caused by infection after childbirth (formerly thought to be connected with the first secretion of milk). **milk float** *n.* a usu. electrically-propelled vehicle for delivering milk to houses. **milk-leg** *n.* painful inflammation, esp. of the leg, after childbirth. **milk-loaf** *n.* a loaf of bread made using milk. **milkmaid** *n.* a woman employed in dairy work. **milkman** *n.* (*pl.* **milkmen**) 1 a man who sells milk, usu. by delivering door-to-door. 2 a dairy worker. **milk of human kindness** *n.* the gentle nature considered natural to humanity. **Milk of Magnesia®** *n.* an antacid stomach medicine consisting of a suspension of hydrated magnesium carbonate. **milk of sulphur** *n.* precipitated sulphur in powder form. **milk powder** *n.* dehydrated milk in powder form. **milk pudding** *n.* a pudding made by boiling or baking milk with rice, semolina etc. **milk punch** *n.* spirits mixed with milk and sweetened. **milk round** *n.* 1 the route and the delivery points along it for a milkman etc. delivering door-to-door. 2 a regular trip from place to place for selling etc. **milk run** *n.* 1 a routine trip, flight etc. 2 a regular journey to deliver milk. **milk shake** *n.* a drink of milk, flavouring and ice cream, shaken up in a machine. **milk sickness** *n.* a fatal spasmodic cattle disease, sometimes communicated to man, peculiar to the Western States of the US, trembles. **milksop** *n.* a feeble, spiritless person, usu. a man or youth. **milk sugar** *n.* lactose. **milk-thistle** *n.* 1 a thistle-like herb of the aster family, *Silbyum marianum.* 2 the sowthistle. **milk tooth** *n.* 1 any of the temporary teeth in young mammals. 2 the foretooth of a foal. **milk train** *n.* an early morning train for transporting milk. **milk-vetch** *n.* a plant of the leguminous genus *Astragalus*, supposed to increase milk-bearing in goats. **milkweed** *n.* a plant, of various species, with milky juice. **milk white** *n.* a white colour similar to that of milk. **milk-white** *a.* **milkwort** *n.* any plant of the genus *Polygala*, formerly believed to promote the secretion of milk, esp. *P. vulgaris*, a small plant with blue, white or pink flowers. **milky** *a.* (*comp.* **milkier**, *superl.* **milkiest**) 1 consisting of, mixed with or resembling milk. 2 (of liquids) white, opaque, clouded. 3 (of cattle) yielding milk. 4 mild, effeminate. 5 timid. **milkily** *adv.* **milkiness** *n.* **Milky Way** *n.* a luminous zone of innumerable stars, stretching across the heavens, being the galaxy of which our solar system is a part. [OE *meolc* (cp. Dut. and Dan. *melk*, G *Milch*, Icel. *mjōlk*, cogn. with Gr. *amelgein*, L *mulgēre*, to milk)]

mill[1] (mil) *n.* 1 a machine for grinding corn to a fine powder. 2 a building with machinery for this purpose. 3 a machine for reducing solid substances of any kind to a finer consistency. 4 a building fitted up with machinery for any industrial purpose, a factory. 5 (*sl.*) †a fight with fists; a boxing match. ~*v.t.* 1 to grind (as corn) in a mill. 2 to produce (flour) by grinding. 3 to serrate the edge of (a coin). 4 to cut with a rotating tool. 5 to full (cloth). 6 to beat to a froth. 7 (*sl.*) †to thrash, to pummel. ~*v.i.* to move slowly (around). **to go through the mill** to undergo a harrowing, exhausting etc. experience. **to put through the mill** to subject to a harrowing, exhausting etc. experience. **millable** *a.* **millboard** *n.* thick pasteboard used by bookbinders for book covers. **mill-dam** *n.* 1 a wall or dam built across a stream to divert it to a mill. 2 a millpond. **milled** *a.* 1 passed through a mill. 2 (of coins) having the edges serrated. 3 (of cloth) fulled. **miller** *n.* 1 a person who keeps or works in a flour mill. 2 a person who mills anything. 3 any of various moths and other insects with white or powdery wings etc., esp. *Apatele leporina.* **miller's thumb** *n.* a small freshwater fish, *Cottus gobio*, the bullhead. **millhand** *n.* a factory worker. **milling** *n.* 1 the act or process of working a mill or mills. 2 the serrated edging of a coin. **millpond** *n.* a pool of water behind a mill-dam. **like a millpond** (of water) very smooth and still. **mill-race** *n.* 1 the current of water for driving a mill-wheel. 2 the channel that provides this water. **mill-rind** *n.* an iron fitting for fixing an upper millstone to the spindle. **millstone** *n.* 1 either of a pair of circular stones for grinding corn. 2 a very burdensome person or thing. **millstone grit** *n.* a coarse quartzose sandstone used for making millstones. **millstream** *n.* MILL-RACE (under MILL[1]). **mill-wheel** *n.* a large wheel moved by water, flowing over or under it, for driving the machinery in a mill. **millworker** *n.* a factory worker. **millwright** *n.* a person who constructs or repairs the machinery of mills. [OE *myln*, from late L *mulīna*, *molīna*, L *mola*, a mill (*molere*, to grind)]

mill[2] (mil) *n.* a money of account in the US, the thousandth part of a dollar or tenth of a cent. [short for L *millēsimum*, thousandth, from *mille*, a thousand]

millefeuille (mēlfœy´) *n.* a cake of puff pastry filled with jam and cream. [F, thousand-leaf]

millennium (milen´iəm) *n.* (*pl.* **millenniums,**

millennia (-iə)) 1 a period of 1000 years. 2 (*Theol.*) the 1000-year reign of Christ (prophesied in Rev. xx.1–5). 3 a period of general happiness and prosperity. 4 the festival of a thousandth anniversary. **millenarian** (milənea´riən) *a.* 1 consisting of 1000 years. 2 of or relating to the millennium. 3 believing in the millennium. ~*n.* a person who believes in the millennium. **millenarianism** *n.* **millenary** *n.* (*pl.* **millenaries**) 1 a period of 1000 years. 2 a festival of a thousandth anniversary. 3 a millenarian. ~*a.* of or relating to a millenary. **millennial** *a.* of or relating to the millennium. ~*n.* a thousandth anniversary. **millennialism** *n.* **millennialist** *n.* [L *mille*, thousand, *annus*, year]

millepede MILLIPEDE.

millepore (mil´ipaw) *n.* any coral of the order *Milleporina*, the surface of which is full of minute pores. **milleporite** *n.* a fossil millepore. [L *mille*, thousand, *porus*, PORE[1]]

miller MILL[1].

millesimal (miles´iməl) *a.* 1 consisting of thousandth parts. 2 of or relating to thousandths. ~*n.* one-thousandth. **millesimally** *adv.* [L *millēsimus*, thousandth, from *mille*, thousand]

millet (mil´it) *n.* 1 the cereal plant *Panicum miliaceum*. 2 the nutritive seeds of this plant. 3 any of various other similar species of grasses bearing edible seeds. **millet-grass** *n.* a tall N American grass, *Milium effusum*. [F, dim. of *mil*, L *milium* (cp. Gr. *melinē*)]

milli- (mil´i) *comb. form* one-thousandth. [L *mille*, a thousand]

milliammeter (miliam´itə) *n.* an instrument for measuring electrical current in milliamperes.

milliampere (miliam´peə), **milliamp** (mil´-) *n.* a unit of electrical current equal to one-thousandth of an ampere.

milliard (mil´iahd) *n.* one thousand million. [F, from L *mille*, a thousand]

†**milliary** (mil´iəri) *a.* 1 of, relating to or denoting a mile, esp. a Roman mile. 2 of or relating to a millennium. ~*n.* a milestone. [L *milliārius*, from *mille*, a thousand (paces)]

millibar (mil´ibah) *n.* a unit of atmospheric pressure, one-thousandth of a bar, equivalent to 100 pascals, the pressure exerted by a column of mercury about 0.03 in. (0.762 mm) high. [L *mille*, a thousand; BAR[2]]

milligram (mil´igram), **milligramme** *n.* one-thousandth of a gram, 0.0154 of an English grain.

millilitre (mil´ilētə), (*N Am.*) **milliliter** *n.* one-thousandth of a litre, 0.06103 cu. in.

millimetre (mil´imētə), (*N Am.*) **millimeter** *n.* one-thousandth of a metre, 0.03937 in.

milliner (mil´inə) *n.* 1 a person who makes and sells hats for women. 2 †a haberdasher. **millinery** *n.* [prob. *Milaner*, a dealer in Milan wares, such as silk and ribbons]

million (mil´yən) *n.* (*pl.* **million, millions**) 1 one thousand thousand. 2 (*pl.* **millions**) an indefinitely great number. 3 a million pounds, dollars etc. ~*a.* amounting to a million. **gone a million** (*Austral.*) completely beaten. **the million** the multitude, the masses. **millionaire** (-neə´) *n.* 1 a person who has a million pounds, francs or dollars. 2 a very rich person. **millionairess** (-neə´res) *n.* a female millionaire. **millionfold** *a., adv.* **millionth** *n., a.* [F, from It. *millione*, from L *mille*, thousand]

millipede (mil´ipēd), **millepede** *n.* 1 any arthropod of the class Diplopoda, having a cylindrical body made up of many segments, each with two pairs of legs. 2 any similar animal with numerous feet. [L *millipeda*, wood-louse (*mille*, thousand, *pes pedis*, foot)]

millisecond (mil´isekənd) *n.* one-thousandth of a second.

millivolt (mil´ivōlt) *n.* one-thousandth of a volt.

Mills bomb (milz) *n.* a type of hand grenade. [Sir W. *Mills*, 1856–1932, its inventor]

milometer MILE.

milord (milawd´) *n.* (*Hist.*) my lord (formerly applied to rich Englishmen).

milt (milt) *n.* 1 the spleen in mammals. 2 the spermatic organ of a male fish. 3 the soft roe of fishes. ~*v.t.* to impregnate with milt (as fish ova). **milter** *n.* a male fish that is ready to breed. [OE *milte* (cp. Dut. and Dan. *milt*, G *Milz*), prob. cogn. with MELT]

Miltonic (milton´ik), **Miltonian** (-tō´niən) *a.* 1 of or resembling the style of the poet Milton. 2 elevated, stately and sonorous, sublime. **Miltonism** (mil´tə-) *n.* [John *Milton* (1608–74)]

mim (mim) *a.* (*Sc.*) prim, demure, quiet, precise. [prob. imit.]

mimbar (mim´bah), **minbar** (min´-) *n.* the pulpit of a mosque. [Arab.]

mime (mīm) *n.* 1 communication through facial expression, gesture etc. and without words. 2 a theatrical performance involving this. 3 a simple kind of farce characterized by mimicry and gesture, popular among the ancient Greeks and Romans. 4 an actor in mime. 5 a mimic, a clown or buffoon. ~*v.i.* 1 to communicate through facial expression, gesture etc. and without words. 2 to act in mime. ~*v.t.* to mimic. **mime artist** *n.* **mimer** *n.* [L *mīmus*, Gr. *mīmos*]

MIMechE *abbr.* Member of the Institute of Mechanical Engineers.

mimeograph (mim´iəgrahf) *n.* a duplicating apparatus in which a paraffin-coated sheet is used as a stencil for reproducing written or typewritten matter. ~*v.t.* to reproduce by means of this. [Gr. *mīmeesthai*, to imitate, -GRAPH]

mimesis (mimē´sis) *n.* 1 (*Biol.*) mimicry, imitation of or close natural resemblance to the appearance of another animal or of a natural object. 2 the imitation of nature in art. **mimetic** (-met´-) *a.* **mimetically** *adv.* [Gr., from *mīmos*, MIME]

mimetite (mim´ətīt, mī´-) *n.* a native arsenate of lead. [G *Mimetit*, Gr. *mīmētēs*, imitator, as MIME, -ITE[1]]

mimic (mim´ik) *n.* 1 a person who mimics. 2 †an actor, a mime artist. ~*a.* 1 having an aptitude for imitation. 2 imitative. 3 counterfeit. ~*v.t.* (*pres.p.* **mimicking,** *past, p.p.* **mimicked**) 1 to imitate, esp. in order to ridicule. 2 to ape, to copy. 3 (of animals, plants etc.) to resemble closely. **mimicker** *n.* **mimicry** *n.* (*pl.* **mimicries**) 1 mimicking. 2 a thing that mimics another. 3 close resemblance (in animals, plants etc.). [L *mīmicus*, Gr. *mīmikos*, from *mīmos*, MIME]

miminy-piminy (mimənipim´əni) *a.* 1 too fastidious, finicky. 2 affectedly nice or delicate. ~*n.* writing or diction of this character. [imit., cp. MIM]

mimosa (mimō´sə) *n.* 1 any leguminous shrub of the genus *Mimosa*, including the sensitive plant, *M. pudica*. 2 any of various acacias with yellow flowers. [L *mīmus*, MIME, *-ōsa*, -OSE[1]]

mimulus (mim´ūləs) *n.* any flowering plant of the genus *Mimulus* having a mask-like corolla, including the monkey flower. [dim. of L *mīmus*, MIME]

Min (min) *n.* any of several Chinese dialects or forms of Chinese spoken in the Fukien province.

Min. *abbr.* 1 Minister. 2 Ministry.

min. *abbr.* 1 minim (liquid measure). 2 minimum. 3 minute(s).

mina[1] (mī´nə) *n.* (*pl.* **minas, minae** (-ē)) 1 an ancient Greek weight of 100 drachmae, or about 1 lb. avoirdupois (0.454 kg). 2 an ancient coin worth 100 drachmae. [L, from Gr. *minā*, prob. Eastern in orig.]

mina[2] MYNAH.

minacious (minā´shəs) *a.* threatening. **minaciously** *adv.* **minacity** (-nas´-) *n.* [L *minax -ācis*]

minaret (minəret´, min´-) *n.* a lofty slender turret on a mosque, from which the muezzin summons the people to prayers. **minareted** *a.* [F *minaret* or Sp. *minarete*, from Arab. *manārat*, rel. to *nār*, fire]

minatory (min´ətəri) *a.* threatening, menacing. [late L *minātōrius*, from *minārī*, to threaten]

minbar MIMBAR.

mince (mins) *v.t.* **1** to cut or chop into very small pieces. **2** to restrain (one's words) for politeness' sake. **3** to utter or pronounce with affected delicacy. **4** to minimize, to palliate, to gloss over. *~v.i.* **1** to walk in a prim and affected manner. **2** to talk with affected elegance. *~n.* **1** minced meat. **2** mincemeat. **not to mince matters** to speak plainly. **mincemeat** *n.* **1** a filling for pies etc. composed of suet, raisins, currants, candied peel etc. chopped fine. **2** meat chopped into very small pieces. **3** very fine or small pieces or fragments. **to make mincemeat of** to crush or destroy completely. **mince pie** *n.* a small pie filled with mincemeat. **mincer** *n.* **mincing** *a.* affectedly elegant. **mincingly** *adv.* [OF *mincier*, pop. L *minūtiāre*, from MINUTIA]

mind (mīnd) *n.* **1** the intellectual powers of a human being, the understanding, the intellect. **2** one's candid opinion (*to speak one's mind*). **3** the soul. **4** recollection, memory (*always on my mind*). **5** sanity (*to lose one's mind*). **6** disposition, liking, way of feeling or thinking. **7** intention, purpose, desire, inclination. **8** mental concentration. **9** a person regarded as an intellect. *~v.t.* **1** to heed, to regard. **2** to pay attention to, to apply oneself to. **3** to object to (*Do you mind if I smoke?*). **4** to look after (*to mind the shop*). **5** (*Sc., dial.*) to remember. **6** (*N Am., Ir.*) to obey. *~v.i.* to take care, to be on the watch. **don't mind me** (*usu. iron.*) do as you please, irrespective of my feelings, opinions etc. **do you mind?** used to express irritation at a person's inconsiderate behaviour. **in one's mind's eye** EYE[1]. **in two minds** unable to choose between alternatives, undecided. **mind out** watch out (for), be careful. **mind over matter** the power of the mind successfully exerted over the physical world. **mind you** (*coll.*) used to qualify a previous statement (*I finished work early; mind you, I had done twice the usual amount*). **mind your back/ backs** used to indicate that one wants to get past. **mind your eye** EYE[1]. **never mind** used to console someone. **never you mind** used to rebut a prying question. **to close one's mind** to refuse to consider something, often unreasonably. **to come into someone's mind 1** to be remembered. **2** to form as an idea. **to come to mind** to occur to one, to suggest itself. **to have a good mind** to be inclined (to). **to have a great mind** to be inclined (to). **to have (half) a mind** to be inclined (to). **to have in mind** to intend. **to mind one's own business** BUSINESS. **to mind one's Ps and Qs** P[1]. **to mind one's step** STEP. **to mind the shop** to take charge temporarily. **to one's mind** in one's opinion. **to open one's mind** to give thought (to something previously unconsidered or rejected). **to put in mind** to remind (of). **to put out of one's mind** to stop thinking about. **to put/ set someone's mind at rest** to reassure (someone). **to set one's mind on** to be determined to have or do. **to shut one's mind to** to refuse to or pretend not to think about. **to spring to mind** to come suddenly to mind. **mind-bending** *a.* altering one's state of mind (esp. of drugs). **mind-blowing** *a.* **1** confusing, amazing. **2** of or inducing a state like that produced by psychedelic drugs. **mind-boggling** *a.* (*coll.*) amazing, astonishing. **minded** *a.* (*usu. in comb.*) of a certain disposition or way of thinking (*evil-minded*). **minder** *n.* **1** a person whose job is to look after something or somebody. **2** (*coll.*) a bodyguard. **mind-expanding** *a.* producing a sense of heightened or broader perception, psychedelic. **mindful** *a.* attentive, heedful (of). **mindfully** *adv.* **mindfulness** *n.* **mindless** *a.* **1** done for no reason. **2** done without need for thought. **3** heedless, regardless, stupid. **mindlessly** *adv.* **mindlessness** *n.* **mind-numbing** *a.* (*coll.*) causing extreme boredom. **mind-numbingly** *adv.* **mind of one's own** *n.* an ability to think independently, an inclination to take a different course from the usual. **mind-reader** *n.* a person who claims to know what others are thinking. **mind-read** *v.t.* **mind-reading** *n.* **mindset** *n.* a fixed attitude of mind. [OE *gemynd*, cogn. with *munan*, to think, to remember (cp. OHG *gimunt*, Goth. *gamunds*, memory), from root *men-*, *mun-*, cp. L *mens*, mind]

mine[1] (mīn) *pron.* something which belongs to or is associated with me. *~†a.* my (used before vowels and sometimes *h*) (*mine host*). **of mine** belonging or relating to me. [OE *mīn* (cp. Dut. *mijn*, G *mein*)]

mine[2] (mīn) *v.t.* **1** to dig into or burrow in. **2** to obtain by excavating in the earth. **3** to make by digging. **4** to undermine, to sap. **5** to set with (explosive) mines. *~v.i.* **1** to dig a mine, to engage in digging for ore etc. **2** to burrow. **3** to practise secret methods of inquiry. *~n.* **1** an excavation in the earth for the purpose of obtaining minerals. **2** a receptacle filled with explosive, floating in the sea or buried in the ground, which is exploded by contact. **3** a rich source of wealth, or of information etc. **4** an excavation under an enemy's works for blowing them up, formerly to form a means of entering or to cause a collapse of the wall etc. **5** a rich deposit of minerals suitable for mining. **6** crude ironstone. **mine-detector** *n.* an instrument for detecting explosive mines. **minefield** *n.* **1** an area of ground in which large quantities of landmines are set. **2** an area of concern where mistakes are easily made, a potentially dangerous situation. **minehunter** *n.* MINESWEEPER (under MINE[2]). **minelayer** *n.* a ship or aircraft employed to lay mines. **miner** *n.* **1** a person who digs for minerals. **2** a person who works in mines. **3** a soldier employed to lay mines. **4** a burrowing larva or insect. **5** (*Austral.*) any of various honey-eaters of the genus *Manorina*. **miner's right** *n.* (*Austral.*) a licence to prospect for gold, minerals etc. **mine shaft** *n.* a shaft (usu. vertical) giving access to a mine. **minesweeper** *n.* a vessel employed to clear mines laid by the enemy. **mineworker** *n.* a person who works in a mine, esp. a coal miner. **mining** *n.* [F *miner* (cp. It. *minare*, Sp. *minar*), etym. uncertain]

mineral (min´ərəl) *n.* **1** an inorganic body, homogeneous in structure, with a definite chemical composition, found in the earth. **2** any inorganic substance found in the ground. **3** mineral water, lemonade etc. *~a.* **1** of, relating to or consisting of minerals. **2** impregnated with mineral matter. **mineralize, mineralise** *v.t.* **1** to convert into a mineral. **2** to give mineral qualities to. **3** to impregnate with mineral matter. *~v.i.* **1** to become mineralized. **2** to study mineralogy. **mineralization** (-ā´shən) *n.* **mineralizer** *n.* **mineral jelly** *n.* a soft, soaplike substance obtained from the residue of petroleum. **mineral kingdom** *n.* the inorganic kingdom of nature, i.e. all non-living material, as distinct from *plant kingdom, animal kingdom.* **mineralogy** (-al´əji) *n.* the science of minerals, their nature and properties. **mineralogical** (-əloj´-) *a.* **mineralogically** *adv.* **mineralogist** *n.* **mineral oil** *n.* **1** any oil derived from minerals. **2** (*N Am.*) liquid paraffin. **mineral water** *n.* **1** water naturally impregnated with mineral matter. **2** an artificial imitation of this, esp. soda water. **3** any effervescent soft drink. **mineral wax** *n.* ozocerite. **mineral wool** *n.* a fibrous packing material made from inorganic substances. [F *minéral*, med. L *minerāle*, neut. of *minerālis*, from *minera*, from MINE[2]]

minestrone (ministrō´ni) *n.* a thick soup of mixed vegetables with pasta or rice. [It.]

minever MINIVER.

Ming (ming) *n.* **1** the imperial dynasty of China

1368–1644. 2 porcelain made in China during the Ming dynasty. [Chin.]

minge (minj) *n.* (*taboo sl.*) the female genitals.

mingle (ming´gəl) *v.t.* 1 to mix up together. 2 to come into close association (with). *~v.i.* to be mixed, blended or united (with). **to mingle their tears** (*poet.*) to share grief, to cry together. **to mingle with** to go among (a group of people). **mingler** *n.* **minglingly** *adv.* [freq. of ME *mengen*, OE *mengan* (cp. Dut. *mengelen, mengen*, Icel. *menga*)]

mingy (min´ji) *a.* (*comp.* **mingier**, *superl.* **mingiest**) (*coll.*) mean, stingy. **mingily** *adv.* **minginess** *n.* [onomat.]

mini (min´i) *n.* (*pl.* **minis**) 1 (*coll.*) a miniskirt. 2 (**Mini**) a small car. [abbr. of MINIATURE]

mini- (min´i) *comb. form* smaller than the usual size.

miniature (min´əchə) *n.* 1 a small-sized painting, esp. a portrait on ivory, vellum etc., orig. a small picture in an illuminated manuscript. 2 a reproduction, image or copy. 3 anything smaller than the normal size. 4 the art of painting on a small scale. *~a.* 1 smaller than the norm. 2 represented on a very small scale. *~v.t.* to portray in miniature. **in miniature** on a small scale. **miniature camera** *n.* a camera using film negative material usu. of 35 mm. **miniaturist** *n.* **miniaturize, miniaturise** *v.t.* 1 to make or construct on a smaller scale. 2 to reduce the size of. **miniaturization** (-zā´shən) *n.* [med. L *miniātūra*, from L *miniāre*, to rubricate, from *minium* native red lead]

minibar (min´ibah) *n.* a selection of drinks placed in a hotel room for guests' possible use.

minibus (min´ibŭs) *n.* (*pl.* **minibuses,** (*N Am.*) **minibusses**) a small bus for 12 passengers.

minicab (min´ikab) *n.* a taxi that can be ordered by telephone, but may not cruise in search of passengers.

minicomputer (min´ikəmpūtə) *n.* a computer of medium capacity and power.

minify (min´ifī) *v.t.* (*3rd pers. sing. pres.* **minifies,** *pres.p.* **minifying,** *past, p.p.* **minified**) 1 to make little or less. 2 to represent (a thing) as of less size or importance than it is. [L *minor*, less]

minigolf (min´igolf) *n.* a small version of the game of golf, played on a lawn etc.

minikin (min´ikin) *a.* 1 tiny, delicate. 2 affected, mincing. *~n.* 1 a little darling, pet etc. 2 a diminutive thing. [Dut. *minnekyn*, a cupid, dim. of *minne*, love, see -KIN]

minim (min´im) *n.* 1 (*Mus.*) a note of the value of two crotchets or half a semibreve. 2 a fluid measure, one sixtieth of a drachm (0.059 g), about equal to one drop. 3 a downstroke in writing. 4 a thing of the smallest size. [OF *minime*, L *minimus*, very small]

minima MINIMUM.

minimal (min´iməl) *a.* 1 least possible. 2 smallest, very small. 3 of, relating to or being a minimum. **minimal art** *n.* abstract art showing simple geometric forms and ordinary objects in an inexpressive style. **minimalism** *n.* 1 minimal art. 2 music, art, design etc. using a few simple elements to achieve maximum effect. **minimalist** *n.* 1 a person who practises minimalism. 2 a person ready to accept the minimal course of action, policy etc. *~a.* of or relating to minimalism or minimalists. **minimally** *adv.*

minimax (min´imaks) *n.* 1 (*Math.*) the lowest of a set of maximum values. 2 (in game theory etc.) a strategy minimizing the greatest risk. 3 a choice of strategy offering the least benefit to the most advantaged member of a group. [*mini*mum, *max*imum]

minimize (min´imīz), **minimise** *v.t.* 1 to reduce to the smallest possible amount or degree. 2 to belittle, to underestimate, to downplay. *~v.i.* to reach a minimum value. **minimization** (-zā´shən) *n.* **minimizer** *n.*

minimum (min´iməm) *n.* (*pl.* **minimums, minima** (-mə)) the smallest amount or degree possible or usual. *~a.* least possible. **minimum lending rate** *n.* (*Hist.*) the minimum rate at which the Bank of England would discount bills. **minimum thermometer** *n.* a thermometer automatically recording the lowest temperature reached in a given period. **minimum wage** *n.* the rate of wages established by law or collective bargaining below which workers cannot be employed.

minimus (min´iməs) *a.* denoting the youngest of several boys of the same name in a (public) school (*Bulstrode minimus*).

minion (min´yən) *n.* 1 a servile dependant. 2 a size of printing type between nonpareil and brevier. 3 a darling, a favourite. [F *mignon*, etym. uncertain]

minipill (min´ipil) *n.* a low-dose oral contraceptive pill without oestrogen.

miniscule MINUSCULE.

miniseries (min´isiəriz) *n.* (*pl.* **miniseries**) a short series of television programmes.

miniskirt (min´iskœt) *n.* a skirt with the hem far above the knees.

minister (min´istə) *n.* 1 (*also* **Minister**) a person entrusted with the direction of a state department. 2 the pastor of a church, esp. a Nonconformist one. 3 a person representing their government with another state, an ambassador. 4 a person charged with the performance of a duty, or the execution of a will etc. 5 a person who acts under the authority of another, a subordinate, an instrument. 6 a servant. *~v.i.* 1 to render aid, service or attendance. 2 to contribute, to be conducive (to). 3 to serve as minister. *~†v.t.* to furnish, to supply. **minister general** *n.* the superior of certain religious orders. **ministerial** (-tiə´-) *a.* 1 of or relating to a minister of state or of religion. 2 of or relating to a ministry. 3 of or relating to the government in office, as distinct from the opposition. 4 subsidiary, instrumental. 5 of or relating to the execution of a legal mandate etc. **ministerialist** *n.* **ministerially** *adv.* **ministering angel** *n.* a person, esp. a woman, who brings care and comfort to others. **minister of religion** *n.* a member of the clergy. **Minister of State** *n.* a junior minister in a government department. **Minister of the Crown** *n.* a government minister of Cabinet status. **ministership** *n.* **Minister without Portfolio** *n.* a government minister of Cabinet status, but without specific departmental responsibilities. **ministrable** *a.* **ministrant** *n., a.* **ministration** (-trā´shən) *n.* 1 (*usu. in pl.*) an act of assistance or service. 2 the action of ministering. **ministrative** (min´istrətiv) *a.* **ministry** *n.* (*pl.* **ministries**) 1 (*also* **Ministry**) a a government department. b the building or offices of a government department. 2 the ministers of state or of religion collectively. 3 the occupation or calling of a minister of religion. 4 the period of tenure of a minister. 5 the act of ministering, administration. [F *minister*, L *minister*, from *minus*, less (cp. *magister*, from *magis*)]

☒ **miniture** common misspelling of MINIATURE.

†minium (min´iəm) *n.* red oxide of lead vermilion, red lead. [L]

miniver (min´ivə), **minever** *n.* a white fur used for ceremonial robes. [A-F *meniver*, F *menu vair* (*menu*, little, small, *vair*, a kind of fur, from L *varius*, VARIOUS)]

mink (mingk) *n.* 1 either of two amphibious stoatlike animals of the genus *Mustela*, esteemed for their fur. 2 their fur. 3 a coat or jacket made of this. *~a.* of this fur. [cp. LG *mink*, Swed. *menk*]

minke (ming´kə, -ki) *n.* a small whale, *Balaenoptera acutorostrata*. [prob. from *Meincke*, a Norwegian whaler]

Minn. *abbr.* Minnesota.

minnesinger (min´isingə) *n.* any of a body of German lyric poets and singers, 1138–1347, whose chief theme was love. [G (*Minne*, love, *Singer*, singer]

minnow (min´ō) *n.* 1 a small fish of the carp family common all over Europe, *Phoxinus phoxinus*. 2 any tiny fish. 3 an insignificant person or thing. [cp. OHG *minewa* and OE *myne*]

Minoan (minō´ən) *a.* of or relating to ancient Crete or its people or the Bronze Age civilization of which it was the centre. *~n.* 1 an inhabitant of ancient Crete or the Minoan world. 2 the language of the Minoans. **Minoan period** *n.* the period during which Crete was the centre of a Bronze Age civilization, loosely 3000–1100 BC. [*Minos*, king of Crete, -AN]

minor (mī´nə) *a.* 1 less, smaller (not used with *than*). 2 petty, comparatively unimportant. 3 (*Mus.*) **a** less by a semitone than the major. **b** (of a scale) having a semitone above the second, fifth and seventh note. **c** (of a key) based on a minor scale. 4 denoting the younger of two brothers in a (public) school. 5 under age. *~n.* 1 a person under legal age. 2 (*Mus.*) a minor key or a composition or strain in this. 3 a minor term or premiss in logic. 4 (*N Am.*) a subsidiary subject or course of study. 5 a Minorite. *~v.i.* (*N Am.*) to pursue study (in) as a subsidiary subject. **in a minor key** conducted or passed quietly or uneventfully. **minor axis** *n.* (*Geom.*) the axis perpendicular to the major axis of a conic. **minor canon** *n.* a cleric, not a member of the chapter, assisting in the daily service at a cathedral. **Minorite** *n.* a Franciscan friar. **minority** (-nor´-) *n.* (*pl.* **minorities**) 1 the smaller number, esp. the smaller of a group or party voting together in an election, on a bill etc. 2 the number of votes constituting this. 3 a distinct cultural etc. group within a larger society. 4 the state of being under legal age. 5 the period of this. **in the minority** in the state of being outnumbered. **minor league** *n.* (*N Am.*) a league of professional baseball or football clubs other than a major league. **minor orders** *n.pl.* (*Hist.*) the four lowest degrees of clergy in the Roman Catholic Church, those below the status of deacon. **minor piece** *n.* in chess, a bishop or a knight. **minor planet** *n.* an asteroid. **minor premiss** *n.* (*Logic*) the premiss containing the minor term of a syllogism. **minor prophets** *n.pl.* the prophets from Hosea to Malachi in the Old Testament, i.e. those whose extant writings are not lengthy. **minor suit** *n.* (*Logic*) in bridge, clubs or diamonds. **minor tenace** *n.* the second and fourth best cards thus held. **minor term** *n.* (*Logic*) the subject of the conclusion of a categorical syllogism. [L]

Minorcan (minaw´kən) *a.* of or relating to Minorca. *~n.* a black variety of domestic fowl from Spain, the Minorcan fowl. [*Minorca*, one of the Balearic Isles]

Minotaur (min´ətaw, mī´-) *n.* in Greek mythology, a monster having the head of a bull and the rest of the body human, devouring human flesh. [Gr. *Minōtauros* (*Minōs*, the legendary king of Crete, *tauros*, bull)]

minster (min´stə) *n.* 1 a cathedral or other large and important church. 2 the church of a monastery. [OE *mynster*, L *monastērium*, MONASTERY]

minstrel (min´strəl) *n.* 1 any of a class of men in the Middle Ages who lived by singing and reciting, a travelling gleeman, musician, performer or entertainer. 2 a poet. 3 a musician. 4 any of a troupe of entertainers with blackened faces. **minstrelsy** *n.* (*pl.* **minstrelsies**) 1 the art or occupation of minstrels. 2 minstrels collectively. 3 a collection of ballad poetry. [OF *menestral*, late L *ministeriālis -lem*, MINISTERIAL (under MINISTER)]

mint[1] (mint) *n.* 1 a place where money is coined, usu. under state authority. 2 a source of invention or fabrication. 3 a great quantity, supply or amount. *~v.t.* 1 to make (coin by stamping metal). 2 to invent, to coin (a phrase etc.). *~a.* (of a book, coin etc.) in its unused state, as new. **in mint condition** as perfect as when first produced. **in mint state** in mint condition. **mintage** *n.* 1 coining. 2 coinage. 3 a fee paid for minting a coin. **minter** *n.* †**mintman** *n.* (*pl.* **mintmen**) a person skilled in coins or coining. **mint mark** *n.* 1 a mark distinguishing the coins struck at a particular mint. 2 a distinctive mark of origin. **mint master** *n.* the person in charge of coinage at a mint. **mint par, mint parity** *n.* 1 the ratio between the gold equivalents of the currency of two countries. 2 the rate of exchange that corresponds to this. [OE *mynet*, L *monēta*, MONEY]

mint[2] (mint) *n.* 1 any plant of the aromatic genus *Mentha*, many of which are used for flavouring, esp. spearmint, *M. spicata*. 2 a sweet or lozenge with a peppermint flavour. **mint julep** *n.* a sweet alcoholic drink of bourbon, sugar and pounded ice flavoured with mint. **mint sauce** *n.* mint chopped up with vinegar and sugar, used as a sauce with roast lamb. **minty** *a.* (*comp.* **mintier**, *superl.* **mintiest**). [OE *minte* (L *menta*, *mentha*, Gr. *mintha*)]

minuend (min´ūend) *n.* (*Math.*) the quantity from which another is to be subtracted. [L *minuendus*, ger. of *minuere*, to DIMINISH]

minuet (minūet´) *n.* 1 a slow stately dance in triple time. 2 music for this or in the same time or style. *~v.i.* (*pres.p.* **minueting**, *past*, *p.p.* **minueted**) to dance a minuet. [F *menuet*, dim. of *menu*, MINUTE[2]]

minus (mī´nəs) *a.*, *prep.* 1 less by, with the deduction of. 2 (*coll.*) short of, lacking. 3 negative. 4 having a negative electrical charge. *~n.* (*pl.* **minuses**) 1 a minus sign. 2 a negative quantity. 3 a deficit, a disadvantage. **minus sign** *n.* the sign of subtraction (-). [L, neut. of MINOR]

minuscule (min´əskūl), **miniscule** *a.* 1 very small. 2 of or relating to a cursive script of the 7th–9th cents. 3 lower case. *~n.* 1 a cursive script of the 7th–9th cents. 2 a small or lower-case letter. 3 anything very small. **minuscular** (minŭs´-) *a.* [F, from L *minuscula*, fem. dim. of MINOR]

minute[1] (min´it) *n.* 1 the 60th part of an hour. 2 a very small portion of time, an instant (*I will only be a minute*). 3 an exact point of time (*timed to the minute*). 4 (*coll.*) the present time. 5 the 60th part of a degree of angular distance. 6 (*pl.*) official records of proceedings of a committee etc. 7 an official memorandum of a court or other authority. *~v.t.* 1 to take a note of. 2 to write minutes of. 3 to send minutes to. 4 to time to the exact minute. **just a minute** 1 (*coll.*) used to ask someone to wait for a short time. 2 (*coll.*) used as a prelude to a query or objection. **the minute (that)** (*coll.*) as soon as. **up to the minute** very modern. **wait a minute** (*coll.*) just a minute. **minute-book** *n.* a book in which the minutes of meetings are recorded. **minute-gun** *n.* a gun fired at intervals of one minute as a signal of distress or mourning. **minute hand** *n.* the hand pointing to minutes on a clock or watch. **minutely**[1] *a.*, *adv.* every minute. **minuteman** *n.* (*pl.* **minutemen**) 1 (*Hist.*) in the US, an enrolled militiaman of the Revolutionary period who held himself ready for service at a minute's notice. 2 (**Minuteman**) a type of US three-stage intercontinental ballistic missile. **minute steak** *n.* a thin steak that can be cooked quickly. **minute-watch** *n.* a watch on which the minutes are marked. [F, from late L *minūta*, as MINUTE[2]]

minute[2] (mīnūt´) *a.* (*superl.* **minutest**) 1 very small. 2 petty, trifling. 3 particular, exact, precise. **minutely**[2] *adv.* **minuteness** *n.* [L *minūtus*, p.p. of *minuere*, to DIMINISH]

minutely[1] MINUTE[1].

minutely[2] MINUTE[2].

minutia (minū´shiə, mī-) *n.* (*pl.* **minutiae** (-iē)) (*usu. in pl.*) a small and precise or trivial particular. [L, smallness, as MINUTE[2]]

minx (mingks) *n.* a flirtatious, pert or scheming young woman. [perh. corr. of LG *minsk*, a man, a pert female (cp. G *Mensch*)]

Miocene (mī´əsēn) *a.* (*Geol.*) denoting the middle division of the Tertiary strata or period. *~n.* this division. [Gr. *meiōn*, less, *kainos*, new]

miosis (mīō´sis), **myosis** *n.* abnormal constriction of the pupil of the eye. **miotic** (-ot´-) *a.* [Gr. *muein*, to shut]
MIPS (mips) *n.* a unit of computing speed, equal to a million instructions per second. [acronym]
mirabelle (mirəbel´) *n.* **1** a European plum tree, *Prunus institia*, bearing small firm yellow fruit. **2** the fruit of this tree. **3** a liqueur made from this fruit. [F]
miracidium (mīrəsid´iəm) *n.* (*pl.* **miracidia** (-iə)) (*Zool.*) the flat cilial first-stage larva of a trematode. [Gr. *meirakidion*, dim. of *meirakion*, boy]
miracle (mir´əkəl) *n.* **1** a marvellous event or act attributed to a supernatural agency. **2** an extraordinary occurrence. **3** an extraordinary example (of). **4** a miracle play. **miracle drug** *n.* a drug that represents a significant breakthrough in medical science, having apparently very beneficial effects. **miracle play** *n.* a medieval dramatic representation, usu. dealing with historical or traditional events in the life of Christ or of the Saints. **miraculous** (-rak´ū-) *a.* **1** of the nature of a miracle. **2** supernatural. **miraculously** *adv.* **miraculousness** *n.* [OF, from L *mīrāculum*, as MIRAGE]
mirador (mirədaw´) *n.* a belvedere turret or gallery, commanding an extensive view. [Sp., from *mirar*, to look, L *mīrārī*, as MIRAGE]
mirage (mirahzh´) *n.* **1** an optical illusion by which images of distant objects are seen as if inverted, esp. in a desert where the inverted sky appears as a sheet of water. **2** an illusory thing, a delusion. [F, from *se mirer*, to see oneself in a mirror, L *mīrārī*, to wonder at, to gaze]
MIRAS (mī´rəs), **Miras** *abbr.* mortgage interest relief at source.
mire (mīə) *n.* **1** an extent of wet, clayey soil, swampy ground, a bog. **2** mud, dirt. ~*v.t.* **1** to plunge in a mire. **2** to soil with mire. **3** to involve in difficulties. ~*v.i.* to sink in a mire. **in the mire** in difficulties. **miry** *a.* (*comp.* **mirier**, *superl.* **miriest**). **miriness** *n.* [ME, from Icel. *mýrr* (cp. Swed. *myra* and OE *mēos*, MOSS)]
mirepoix (miəpwah´, miə´-) *n.* (*pl.* **mirepoix**) a sauce of sautéd chopped vegetables. [prob. named after Duc de *Mirepoix*, 18th-cent. French general]
mirid (mir´id, mīə´rid) *n.* (*Zool.*) a heteropteran bug of the family Miridae, including various plant pests. ~*a.* (*Zool.*) of or relating to this family.
mirific (mirif´ik) *a.* **1** wonderful, marvellous. **2** wonder-working. [L *mirificus*, wonder-working]
mirk MURK.
mirror (mir´ə) *n.* **1** an appliance with a polished surface for reflecting images. **2** a looking-glass. **3** anything that reflects objects. **4** an exemplar, a pattern, a model. ~*v.t.* to reflect in or as in a mirror. **mirror carp** *n.* a variety of common carp with a smooth shiny body. **mirror finish** *n.* a shiny, reflective surface. **mirror image** *n.* **1** an image as observed in a mirror. **2** an object that corresponds to another in this way. **mirror symmetry** *n.* symmetry about a plane dividing an object etc. into two images, itself and its reflection. **mirror writing** *n.* handwriting from right to left, as if reflected in a mirror. [OF *mirour* (F *miroir*), prob. through a non-extant pop. L *mīrātōrium*, from *mīrārī*, see MIRAGE]
mirth (mœth) *n.* merriment, jollity, gaiety, hilarity. **mirthful** *a.* **mirthfully** *adv.* **mirthfulness** *n.* **mirthless** *a.* **mirthlessly** *adv.* **mirthlessness** *n.* [OE *myrgth*, cogn. with MERRY]
MIRV (mœv) *n.* a missile with two or more warheads designed to strike separate targets. [*m*ultiple *i*ndependently-targetable *r*e-entry *v*ehicle]
miry MIRE.
mirza (mœ´zə) *n.* **1** an Iranian title for a doctor, scholar or other learned person. **2** a Persian (Iranian) prince. [Pers.]
MIS *abbr.* (*Comput.*) management information systems.
mis-[1] (mis) *pref.* wrongly, badly, amiss, unfavourably. [partly OE *mis-* (cp. Dut., Dan. and Icel. *mis-*, G *miss-*), partly OF *mes-*, from L *minus*, less]
mis-[2] (mis), **miso-** (mi´sō, mī´-) *comb. form* dislike, hatred. [Gr. *mīseein*, to hate]
misaddress (misədres´) *v.t.* **1** to direct (a letter etc.) to the wrong address. **2** to address (a person) incorrectly.
misadventure (misədven´chə) *n.* **1** an unlucky chance or accident. **2** bad luck. **3** ill fortune. [OF *mesaventure*]
misadvise (misədvīz´) *v.t.* **1** to advise wrongly. **2** to give bad advice to. **misadvice** (-vīs´) *n.* **misadvised** *a.* ill-advised, ill-directed. †**misadvisedly** (-zid-) *adv.* **misadvisedness** (-zid-) *n.*
misalign (misəlīn´) *v.t.* to align wrongly. **misalignment** *n.*
misalliance (misəlī´əns) *n.* an improper alliance, esp. by marriage. **misallied** *a.* **misally** *v.t.* (*3rd pers. sing. pres.* **misallies**, *pres.p.* **misallying**, *past*, *p.p.* **misallied**).
misandry (mis´əndri) *n.* a hatred of men. [MIS-[2], Gr. *anēr andros*, a man]
misanthrope (mis´ənthrōp, miz´-) *n.* **1** a hater of humankind. **2** a person who avoids fellow human beings. **misanthropic** (-throp´-), **misanthropical** *a.* **misanthropist** (-an´-) *n.* **misanthropize** (-an´-), **misanthropise** *v.i.* **misanthropy** (-an´-) *n.* [Gr. *misanthrōpos* (*miseein*, to hate, *anthrōpos*, man)]
misapply (misəplī´) *v.t.* (*3rd pers. sing. pres.* **misapplies**, *pres.p.* **misapplying**, *past*, *p.p.* **misapplied**) to apply wrongly. **misapplication** (-aplikā´shən) *n.*
misappreciate (misəprē´shiāt) *v.t.* to fail to appreciate rightly or fully. **misappreciation** (-ā´shən) *n.* **misappreciative** (-shə-) *a.*
misapprehend (misaprihend´) *v.t.* to misunderstand. **misapprehension** *n.* **misapprehensive** *a.* **misapprehensively** *adv.*
misappropriate (misəprō´priāt) *v.t.* to apply to a wrong use or purpose (esp. funds to one's own use). **misappropriation** (-ā´shən) *n.*
misbegotten (misbigot´ən) *a.* **1** illegitimate. **2** badly planned, designed etc. **3** disreputable.
misbehave (misbihāv´) *v.i.* to behave badly or improperly. **misbehaviour** (-yə) *n.*
misbelief (misbilēf´) *n.* false or erroneous belief. **misbelieve** (-lēv´) *v.t.* **misbeliever** *n.*
misc. *abbr.* **1** miscellaneous. **2** miscellany.
miscalculate (miskal´kūlāt) *v.t.* to calculate wrongly. **miscalculation** (-lā´shən) *n.*
miscall (miskawl´) *v.t.* **1** to call by a wrong or unsuitable name. **2** to abuse, to call (someone) names.
miscarry (miskar´i) *v.i.* (*3rd pers. sing. pres.* **miscarries**, *pres.p.* **miscarrying**, *past*, *p.p.* **miscarried**) **1** to have a miscarriage. **2** to fail, to be unsuccessful. **3** to be carried to the wrong place. **miscarriage** (miskar´ij, mis´-) *n.* **1** the spontaneous premature expulsion of a foetus before it can survive outside the womb. **2** an act or instance of miscarrying. **3** failure. **miscarriage of justice** *n.* a mistake or wrong committed by a court of justice.
miscast (miskahst´) *v.t.* (*past*, *p.p.* **miscast**) **1** to cast (a play or an actor) inappropriately. **2** to cast or add up wrongly.
miscegenation (misijinā´shən) *n.* intermarriage or interbreeding between people of different races. [L *miscēre*, to mix, *genus*, race, -ATION]
miscellaneous (misəlā´niəs) *a.* **1** consisting of several kinds, mixed, multifarious, diversified. **2** various, many-sided. **miscellanea** (-niə) *n.pl.* **1** a collection of miscellaneous literary compositions. **2** a collection of miscellaneous items. **miscellaneously** *adv.* **miscellaneousness** *n.* **miscellany** (-sel´əni) *n.* (*pl.* **miscellanies**) a mixture of various kinds, a medley, a number of compositions on various subjects in one volume. **miscellanist** *n.* a writer of miscellanies. [L *miscellāneus*, from *miscellus*, mixed, from *miscēre*, to mix]

mischance (mischahns´) *n.* misfortune, bad luck. ~†*v.i.* to happen unfortunately. **mischancy** *a.* [OF *meschance*]

mischief (mis´chif) *n.* **1** irritating action or conduct that is non-malicious, esp. pranks, practical jokes etc. **2** harm, injury, damage. **3** a person who is mischievous. **to do someone a mischief** to wound or kill a person. **to get up to mischief** to make mischief. **to make mischief** to cause trouble or ill-feeling. **mischief-maker** *n.* a person who stirs up trouble, ill-feeling etc. esp. by gossip. **mischief-making** *n., a.* **mischievous** (mis´chivəs) *a.* **1** (of a child) full of pranks, continually in mischief. **2** making mischief, causing or intending to cause harm. **3** slightly malicious. **mischievously** *adv.* **mischievousness** *n.* [OF *meschief* (MIS-¹, *chief*, aim, result)]

Usage note *Mischievous* should not be spelt or pronounced as *mischievious.*

misch metal (mish´ metəl) *n.* an alloy of cerium with other rare earth metals, used for cigarette-lighter flints. [G *mischen*, to mix]

miscible (mis´ibəl) *a.* capable of being mixed (with). **miscibility** (-bil´-) *n.* [F, from L *miscēre*, to mix, -BLE]

miscompute (miskəmpūt´) *v.t.* to calculate wrongly, to miscalculate. ~†*n.* a miscalculation. **miscomputation** (-kompūtā´shən) *n.*

misconceive (miskənsēv´) *v.t.* to have a wrong idea of, to misapprehend. **misconceived** *a.* **misconceiver** *n.* **misconception** (-sep´-) *n.*

misconduct[1] (miskon´dŭkt) *n.* **1** improper conduct, esp. adultery. **2** mismanagement.

misconduct[2] (miskəndŭkt´) *v.t.* to mismanage. **to misconduct oneself** to misbehave.

misconstrue (miskənstroo´) *v.t.* (*3rd pers. sing. pres.* **misconstrues,** *pres.p.* **misconstruing,** *past, p.p.* **misconstrued)** **1** to put a wrong interpretation or construction upon. **2** to mistake the meaning of. **misconstruction** (-strŭk´-) *n.*

miscopy (miskop´i) *v.t.* (*3rd pers. sing. pres.* **miscopies,** *pres.p.* **miscopying,** *past, p.p.* **miscopied**) to copy incorrectly.

miscount[1] (miskownt´) *v.t.* **1** to count wrongly. **2** to estimate or regard wrongly. ~*v.i.* to make a false account.

miscount[2] (mis´kownt) *n.* a mistake in counting, esp. of votes.

miscreant (mis´kriənt) *n.* **1** a vile wretch, a scoundrel. **2** †an unbeliever, infidel or heretic. ~*a.* **1** depraved, vile, villainous. **2** †infidel, heretic. **miscreance, †miscreancy** *n.* [OF *mescreant* (*creant*, L *crēdens -entem*, pres.p. of *crēdere*, to believe)]

miscreate[1] (miskriāt´) *v.t.* to create wrongly or badly. **miscreation** *n.* **miscreative** *a.*

†miscreate[2] (mis´kriāt, mis´kriət), **†miscreated** *a.* deformed, shapeless.

miscue (miskū´) *n.* **1** in billiards, snooker etc., failure to strike a ball properly with the cue. **2** a mistake, esp. in reading. ~*v.i.* (*3rd pers. sing. pres.* **miscues,** *pres.p.* **miscuing,** *past, p.p.* **miscued**) to make a miscue. **miscue analysis** *n.* in the teaching of reading, an analysis of errors made.

misdate (misdāt´) *v.t.* to date wrongly. ~*n.* a wrong date.

misdeal (misdēl´) *v.t.* (*past, p.p.* **misdealt** (-delt´)) to deal wrongly (as cards). ~*v.i.* to make a misdeal. ~*n.* a wrong or false deal.

misdeed (misdēd´) *n.* an evil deed, a crime. [OE *misdǣd*]

misdemeanour (misdimē´nə), (*N Am.*) **misdemeanor** *n.* **1** misbehaviour, misconduct. **2** (*Law*) an indictable offence of less gravity than a felony. **misdemean** *v.t.* to misconduct (oneself), to misbehave. **misdemeanant** *n.*

misdescribe (misdiskrīb´) *v.t.* to describe wrongly. **misdescription** (-skrip´shən) *n.*

misdiagnose (misdī´əgnōz) *v.t.* to diagnose incorrectly. **misdiagnosis** (-nō´sis) *n.*

misdial (misdī´əl) *v.t., v.i.* (*pres.p.* **misdialling,** (*N Am.*) **misdialing,** *past, p.p.* **misdialled,** (*N Am.*) **misdialed**) to dial (a telephone number) incorrectly.

misdirect (misdirekt´, -dī-) *v.t.* **1** to direct (a person, letter etc.) wrongly. **2** to instruct wrongly (as a judge etc.). **misdirection** *n.*

misdivision (misdivizh´ən) *n.* wrong or erroneous division.

misdoing (misdoo´ing) *n.* a misdeed, a wrong action. **misdo** *v.t., v.i.* (*3rd pers. sing. pres.* **misdoes** (-dŭz´), *pres.p.* **misdoing,** *past, p.p.* **misdone** (-dŭn´)). **misdoer** *n.*

†misdoubt (misdowt´) *v.t.* **1** to have doubts or misgivings as to the truth or fact of. **2** to suspect, surmise or apprehend. ~*v.i.* to have suspicions or misgivings. ~*n.* **1** doubt, hesitation. **2** suspicion.

†mise (mēz, mīz) *n.* **1** a treaty, esp. a settlement by arbitration or compromise. **2** (*Law*) the issue in a writ of right. **3** (*usu. pl.*) cost, expense. [OF, from p.p. of *mettre*, to put, L *mittere*, to send]

miseducate (mised´ūkāt) *v.t.* to educate wrongly. **miseducation** (-kā´shən) *n.*

mise en scene (mēz ã sen´) *n.* **1** the settings, properties etc. of a play, film etc. **2** the art of achieving this. **3** the environment of an event. [F, putting on stage]

misemploy (misimploi´) *v.t.* to misapply, to misuse. **misemployment** *n.*

miser (mī´zə) *n.* **1** a person who denies themselves the comforts of life for the sake of hoarding. **2** an avaricious person. **3** a wretched person. **miserly** *a.* **miserliness** *n.* [L, wretched]

miserable (miz´ərəbəl) *a.* **1** very wretched or unhappy, distressed. **2** causing misery, distressing. **3** sorry, despicable, worthless. **4** very poor or mean. **5** (*Sc., Austral., New Zeal.*) stingy, mean. ~*n.* a miserable person, a wretch. **miserableness** *n.* **miserably** *adv.* [F *misérable*, L *miserābilis*, from *miserērī*, to pity, from *miser*, wretched]

misère (mizeə´) *n.* a declaration in solo whist etc. by which a player undertakes not to take a single trick. [F]

miserere (mizəreə´ri) *n.* **1** a prayer or cry for mercy. **2** the 51st Psalm (beginning with this word in the Vulgate). **3** a musical setting of this psalm. **4** a misericord. [L, have mercy, imper. of *miserērī*, see MISERABLE]

misericord (mizer´ikawd) *n.* **1** a bracketed projection on the underside of the seat of a choir stall, to allow a person standing to rest. **2** (*Hist.*) an apartment in a monastery for monks to whom special indulgences were granted. **3** a small, straight dagger for giving the final death blow. [OF, from L *misericordia*, from *misericors -cordis* (*miseri-*, stem of *miserērī*, see MISERABLE, *cor cordis*, heart)]

miserly MISER.

misery (miz´əri) *n.* (*pl.* **miseries**) **1** great unhappiness or wretchedness of mind or body. **2** affliction, poverty. **3** (*coll.*) an ill-tempered, gloomy person. **4** a cause of misery. **5** misère. **6** †miserliness, avarice. **to put out of one's misery 1** to release (an animal etc.) from suffering, esp. by killing. **2** to release (someone) from the suspense of waiting. [OF, from L *miseria*, from *miser*, wretched]

misfeasance (misfē´zəns) *n.* (*Law*) a trespass, a wrong, esp. negligent or improper performance of a lawful act. [OF *mesfaisance*, from *mesfaire* (*faire*, L *facere*, to do)]

misfield[1] (misfēld´) *v.t.* to field (a cricket ball, baseball etc.) badly.

misfield[2] (mis´fēld) *n.* an act of misfielding a cricket ball, baseball etc.

misfire (misfīə´) *n.* **1** failure to go off or explode (of a gun, charge etc.). **2** in a motor vehicle engine, failure to fire in the correct ignition sequence. ~*v.i.* **1** to fail to go off. **2** to fail to achieve the intended effect. **3** (of a motor vehicle engine) to fail to fire correctly.

misfit[1] (mis´fit) *n.* **1** a bad fit. **2** a garment that does not fit properly. **3** an awkward person. **misfit stream** *n.* a stream whose size does not correspond to that of its valley.

misfit[2] (misfit´) *v.t.*, *v.i.* (*pres.p.* **misfitting,** *past, p.p.* **misfitted**) to fail to fit.

misfortune (misfaw´chən) *n.* **1** bad luck, calamity. **2** a mishap, a disaster. **misfortuned** *a.*

misgive (misgiv´) *v.t.* (*past* **misgave** (-gāv´), *p.p.* **misgiven** (-giv´ən)) (*impers.*) to fill (one's mind) with doubt or suspicion. **misgiving** *n.* a doubt, a suspicion.

misgovern (misgŭv´ən) *v.t.* **1** to govern badly. **2** to administer unfaithfully. **misgoverned** *a.* badly governed. **misgovernment** *n.*

misguided (misgī´did) *a.* mistaken in thought, foolish. **misguidance** *n.* **misguide** *v.t.* **1** to guide wrongly. **2** to lead astray. **misguidedly** *adv.* **misguidedness** *n.*

mishandle (mis·han´dəl) *v.t.* **1** to deal with (a matter etc.) ineffectively or incorrectly. **2** to handle roughly, to ill-treat.

mishap (mis´hap) *n.* **1** an unfortunate accident, a mischance. **2** bad luck. **mishappen** (-hap´-) *v.i.*

☒ **mishape** common misspelling of MISSHAPE.

mishear (mis·hiə´) *v.t.* (*past, p.p.* **misheard** (-hœd´)) to hear incorrectly.

mishit[1] (mis·hit´) *v.t.* (*pres.p.* **mishitting,** *past, p.p.* **mishit**) to hit wrongly.

mishit[2] (mis´hit) *n.* an instance of hitting wrongly.

mishmash (mish´mash) *n.* a hotchpotch, a jumble. [redupl. of MASH[1]]

Mishnah (mish´nə), **Mishna** *n.* the second or oral Jewish law, the collection of traditions etc. forming the text of the Talmud. **Mishnaic** (-nā´ik), **Mishnic** *a.* [Heb. *mishnah*, a repetition, instruction, from *shānāh*, to repeat]

misidentify (misīden´tifī) *v.t.* (*3rd pers. sing. pres.* **misidentifies,** *pres.p.* **misidentifying,** *past, p.p.* **misidentified**) to identify wrongly. **misidentification** (-fikā´shən) *n.*

misinform (misinfawm´) *v.t.* to give erroneous information to. **misinformant, misinformer** *n.* **misinformation** (-ā´shən) *n.*

misinterpret (misintœ´prit) *v.t.* (*pres.p.* **misinterpreting,** *past, p.p.* **misinterpreted**) **1** to interpret wrongly. **2** to draw a wrong conclusion from. **misinterpretation** (-ā´shən) *n.* **misinterpreter** *n.*

misjoin (misjoin´) *v.t.* to join or connect badly or improperly. **misjoinder** *n.* (*Law*) the improper uniting of parties or things in a lawsuit etc.

misjudge (misjŭj´) *v.t.* **1** to form an erroneous opinion of. **2** to judge erroneously. **misjudgement, misjudgment** *n.*

miskey (miskē´) *v.t.* (*3rd pers. sing. pres.* **miskeys,** *pres.p.* **miskeying,** *past, p.p.* **miskeyed**) to enter (data) wrongly from a keyboard.

miskick[1] (miskik´) *v.t.* to kick (a ball) badly.

miskick[2] (mis´kik) *n.* an instance of miskicking a ball.

Miskito (miskee´tō) *n.* (*pl.* **Miskito, Miskitos**) **1** a member of a people of the Atlantic coast of Honduras and Nicaragua. **2** their language. ~*a.* of or relating to this people or their language. [N Am. Indian]

mislay (mislā´) *v.t.* (*past, p.p.* **mislaid**) **1** to put in a wrong place or in a place that cannot be remembered. **2** to lose.

mislead (mislēd´) *v.t.* (*past, p.p.* **misled** (-led´)) **1** to deceive, to delude. **2** to cause to go wrong, esp. in conduct. **misleader** *n.* **misleading** *a.* **misleadingly** *adv.* **misleadingness** *n.*

†**mislike** (mislīk´) *v.t.* to dislike. ~*v.i.* to feel dislike or aversion. ~*n.* dislike, aversion. [OE *mislīcian*]

mismanage (misman´ij) *v.t.*, *v.i.* to manage badly or wrongly. **mismanagement** *n.* **mismanager** *n.*

mismarriage (mismar´ij) *n.* an unsuitable, incongruous or unfortunate marriage.

mismatch[1] (mismach´) *v.t.* to match unsuitably.

mismatch[2] (mis´mach) *n.* an unsuitable match.

mismated (mismā´tid) *a.* mated or matched unsuitably. **mismate** *v.t.*, *v.i.*

mismeasure (mismezh´ə) *v.t.* **1** to measure wrongly. **2** to estimate wrongly. **mismeasurement** *n.*

misname (misnām´) *v.t.* to call by a wrong or unsuitable name.

misnomer (misnō´mə) *n.* **1** a mistaken or misapplied name or designation. **2** an incorrect term. [OF *mesnommer* (*nommer*, L *nōmināre*, to name)]

miso (mē´sō) *n.* a food paste made from soya beans fermented in brine, used for flavouring. [Jap.]

miso- MIS-[2].

misogamy (misog´əmi, mī-) *n.* hatred of marriage. **misogamist** *n.* [Gr. *gamos*, marriage]

misogyny (misoj´əni, mī-) *n.* hatred of women. **misogynist** *n.* **misogynistic** (-is´tik) *a.* **misogynous** *a.* [Gr. *mīsogunēs* (*gunē*, woman)]

misology (misol´əji, mī-) *n.* hatred of reason or knowledge. [Gr. *mīsologia* (-LOGY)]

misoneism (mīsōnē´izm, mis-) *n.* hatred of what is new. **misoneist** *n.* [It. *misoneismo* (Gr. *neos*, new), -ISM]

☒ **mispell** common misspelling of MISSPELL.

mispickel (mis´pikəl) *n.* a mineral composed of iron, arsenic and sulphur, arsenical pyrites. [G]

misplace (misplās´) *v.t.* **1** to mislay. **2** to set on or devote to an undeserving object (*misplaced affection*). ~*v.i.* to misapply terms. **misplacement** *n.*

misplay (misplā´) *v.t.* to play (a card, ball etc.) wrongly or ineffectively. ~*n.* wrong or foul play.

misplead (misplēd´) *v.t.*, *v.i.* (*past, p.p.* **mispleaded, mispled** (-pled´)) to plead wrongly. **mispleading** *n.* an error in pleading.

misprint[1] (misprint´) *v.t.* to print incorrectly.

misprint[2] (mis´print) *n.* a mistake in printing.

misprision[1] (misprizh´ən) *n.* **1** (*Law*) an offence involving the concealment or neglect of one's knowledge of a crime. **2** a wrong act. **3** †mistake, misconception. **misprision of treason, misprision of a felony** *n.* concealment of treason or felony without actual participation. [OF *mesprision* (MIS-[1], L *prensio -ōnem*, see PRISON)]

misprision[2] (misprizh´ən) *n.* **1** undervaluing. **2** a failure to appreciate. **3** †scorn, contempt. [from MISPRIZE]

misprize (misprīz´) *v.t.* (*poet.*) to undervalue, to slight, to despise. [OF *mespriser*]

mispronounce (misprənowns´) *v.t.* to pronounce wrongly. **mispronunciation** (-nŭnsiā´shən) *n.*

mispunctuate (mispŭngk´chuāt) *v.t.*, *v.i.* to punctuate wrongly. **mispunctuation** (-ā´shən) *n.*

misquote (miskwōt´) *v.t.* to quote erroneously. **misquotation** (-tā´shən) *n.*

misread (misrēd´) *v.t.* (*past, p.p.* **misread** (-red´)) **1** to read incorrectly. **2** to misinterpret. **misreading** *n.*

misrelate (misrilāt´) *v.t.* to relate inaccurately. **misrelation** *n.*

misremember (misrimem´bə) *v.t.* **1** to remember imperfectly. **2** (*dial.*) to forget. **misremembrance** *n.*

misreport (misripawt´) *v.t.* **1** to report wrongly. **2** †to slander. ~*n.* a false report.

misrepresent (misreprizent´) *v.t.* to represent falsely or incorrectly. **misrepresentation** (-tā´shən) *n.* **misrepresentative** *n.*, *a.* **misrepresenter** *n.*

misrule (misrool´) *n.* **1** bad government. **2** disorder, confusion, tumult, riot. ~*v.t.* to rule incompetently, misgovern.

Miss. *abbr.* Mississippi.

miss[1] (mis) *v.t.* **1** to fail to reach, hit, meet, perceive, find, or obtain. **2** to fall short of, to let slip, to overlook. **3** to fail to understand. **4** to omit. **5** to escape, to dispense with. **6** to feel or perceive the lack or absence of. *~v.i.* **1** to fail to hit the mark. **2** to misfire. **3** to be unsuccessful. **4** †to go astray, to err. *~n.* **1** a failure to hit, reach, obtain etc. **2** (*coll.*) a miscarriage (of a foetus). **3** †loss, want, feeling of loss. **4** †error, mistake. **a miss is as good as a mile** failure or escape, no matter how narrow the margin, is the point of importance. **not to miss a trick** to be alert, esp. to any possible opportunity, advantage etc. **not to miss much** to be alert and astute. **to be missing** to lack (something, esp. an integral part). **to give a miss 1** not to take an opportunity to see, visit, enjoy etc. (something). **2** in billiards, to avoid hitting (the object ball) in order to leave one's own in a safe position. **to go missing** to disappear or be lost. **to miss fire** to fail to go off (of a gun, explosive etc.). **to miss out 1** to omit. **2** to fail to receive or enjoy. **to miss the boat** to miss an opportunity, to be too late. **to miss the bus** (*coll.*) to miss an opportunity, to be too late. **missable** *a.* capable of being missed (*a missable kick*). **missing** *a.* **1** absent, not in its place, lost. **2** lacking. **3** in the act of missing. **missing link** *n.* **1** something required to complete a series. **2** a hypothetical form connecting types that are probably related, as humans and the anthropoid apes. [OE *missan* (cp. Dut. and G *missen*, Icel. *missa*), cogn. with OE *mis-*, see MIS-[1]]

miss[2] (mis) *n.* (*pl.* **misses**) **1** a title of address for an unmarried woman or girl. **2** (*coll.*) a girl. **3** used before the name of a place, activity etc. to refer to a young woman who represents that place, activity etc., often in beauty contests. **missish** *a.* **1** like a self-conscious young girl. **2** prim, affected. **missishness** *n.* **missy** *n.* (*coll.*) a form of address to a young woman or little girl, usu. affectionately or scathingly. [contr. of MISTRESS]

missal (mis´əl) *n.* **1** in the Roman Catholic Church, the book containing the service of the Mass for the whole year. **2** a medieval illuminated manuscript book of prayers. [late L *missāle*, orig. neut. a. from *missa*, MASS]

missel thrush MISTLE THRUSH.

misshape (mis·shāp´) *v.t.* (*p.p.* **misshapen** (-shā´pən)) **1** to give a bad shape to. **2** to deform. *~n.* deformity. **misshapen** *a.* **misshapenly** *adv.* **misshapenness** *n.*

missile (mis´īl) *n.* a weapon or other object projected or propelled through the air, esp. a rocket-propelled weapon, often with a nuclear warhead. **missilery** (-ri), **missilry** *n.* **1** missiles collectively. **2** the design, use or study of missiles. [L *missilis*, from *miss-*, p.p. stem of *mittere*, to send]

mission (mish´ən) *n.* **1** the commission, charge or office of a messenger, agent etc. **2** a person's appointed or chosen end, a vocation. **3** a body of persons sent on a diplomatic errand, an embassy or legation. **4** a task, goal etc. assigned to a person, group etc. **5** a body of missionaries established in a district at home or sent to a foreign country to spread religious teaching. **6** their field of work. **7** a missionary station. **8** a religious organization in the Roman Catholic Church ranking below that of a regular parish. **9** a series of special services for rousing spiritual interest. **missionary** (-əri) *a.* **1** of or relating to missions, esp. those of a religious nature. **2** of or relating to the propagation of religion or other moral, social or political influence. *~n.* (*pl.* **missionaries**) a person sent to carry on such work. **missionary box** *n.* a box for contributions to missionary work. **missionary position** *n.* (*coll.*) the conventional position for sexual intercourse, lying down with the woman on her back and the man on top of her. **missioner** *n.* **1** a missionary. **2** a person in charge of a parochial mission. **mission statement** *n.* a concise statement of the aims and principles of a company, corporation etc. distributed or otherwise made known to all connected with that organization. [L *missio -ōnem*, as MISSILE]

missis (mis´iz), **missus** *n.* (*coll.*) **1** a wife. **2** used as a form of address to a woman. **3** the mistress of a household. **the missis** used by men to refer to their own or someone else's wife. [corr. of MISTRESS]

missive (mis´iv) *n.* a message, a letter. *~a.* sent or for sending. **letter missive** LETTER. [F, from med. L *missīvus*, as MISSILE]

misspell (mis·spel´) *v.t.* (*past, p.p.* **misspelt** (-spelt´), **misspelled**) to spell incorrectly. **misspelling** *n.*

misspend (mis·spend´) *v.t.* (*past, p.p.* **misspent** (-spent´)) **1** to spend wastefully or inadvisedly. **2** to waste. **misspent** *a.*

misstate (mis·stāt´) *v.t.* to state wrongly. **misstatement** *n.*

misstep (mis·step´) *n.* a wrong step, action, speech etc.

missuit (mis·soot´, -sūt´) *v.t.* to be ill-suited or unbecoming to.

missus MISSIS.

missy MISS[2].

mist (mist) *n.* **1** visible water vapour in the atmosphere at or near the surface of the earth. **2** a watery condensation dimming a surface. **3** a suspension of a liquid in a gas. **4** a watery film before the eyes. **5** anything which dims, obscures or darkens. *~v.t.* to cover as with mist. *~v.i.* to be misty. **mistful** *a.* **mistlike** *a., adv.* **misty** *a.* (*comp.* **mistier**, *superl.* **mistiest**) **1** characterized by or overspread with mist. **2** vague, dim, indistinct, obscure. **mistily** *adv.* **mistiness** *n.* [OE, cp. Icel. *mistr*, Swed. and Dut. *mist*, cogn. with Gr. *omichlē*]

mistake (mistāk´) *v.t.* (*past* **mistook** (-tuk´), *p.p.* **mistaken** (-tā´kən)) **1** to understand wrongly, to take in a wrong sense. **2** to take (one person or thing) for another. *~v.i.* **1** to be in error. **2** to err in judgement or opinion. *~n.* **1** an error of judgement or opinion. **2** a misunderstanding. **3** a thing done incorrectly, a blunder. **by mistake** accidentally, due to error. **make no mistake** without doubt, certainly. **there is no mistaking** one is certain to recognize (someone or something). **mistakable** *a.* **mistakably** *adv.* **mistaken** *a.* wrong in judgement, opinion etc. **mistakenly** *adv.* **mistakenness** *n.* **mistaker** *n.* [Icel. *mistaka*]

misteach (mistēch´) *v.t.* (*past, p.p.* **mistaught** (-tawt´)) to teach wrongly or incorrectly.

mister (mis´tə) *n.* **1** (**Mister**) the common form of address prefixed to untitled men's names or certain official titles (abbr. in writing to Mr). **2** an untitled man. **3** (*coll.*) used as a form of address to a man. *~v.t.* to speak of or address (someone) as 'Mister'. [var. of MASTER]

misterm (mistœm´) *v.t.* **1** to misname. **2** to apply a wrong term to.

mistico (mis´tikō) *n.* (*pl.* **misticos**) a small coasting vessel used in the Mediterranean. [Sp. *mistico*, prob. from Arab. *misteh*, from *sataha*, to flatten]

mistigris (mis´tigris) *n.* **1** the joker or a blank card used as a wild card in a form of draw poker. **2** the game using this.

mistime (mistīm´) *v.t.* to say or do at an inappropriate time.

mistitle (mistī´təl) *v.t.* to call (someone) by a wrong title.

mistle thrush (mis´əl thrŭsh), **missel thrush** *n.* the largest of the European thrushes, *Turdus viscivorus*, that feeds on mistletoe berries. [OE *mistel*, basil, mistletoe (cp. G *Misteldrossel*)]

mistletoe (mis´əltō) *n.* **1** a plant, *Viscum album*, parasitic on the apple and other trees, bearing white glutinous berries. **2** a related N American plant of the genus *Phoradendron*. [OE *misteltān* (*mistel*, basil, mistletoe, *tān*, twig)]

mistook MISTAKE.

mistral (mistrahl´) *n.* a cold dry NW wind of S France. [F and Prov., from L *magistrālis*, MAGISTRAL (under MAGISTERIAL)]

mistranslate (mistranslāt´, -tranz-) *v.t.* to translate wrongly. **mistranslation** (-lā´shən) *n.*

mistreat (mistrēt´) *v.t.* to ill-treat. **mistreatment** *n.*

mistress (mis´tris) *n.* **1** a woman with whom a man has a long-term extramarital relationship. **2** a female teacher. **3** a woman who has authority or control. **4** the female head of a family, school etc. **5** the female owner of a pet animal. **6** a woman having the control or disposal (of). **7** a woman who has mastery (of a subject etc.). **8** †a woman beloved and courted, a sweetheart. **9** †a form of address prefixed to untitled married women's names (now usu. abbr. to Mrs). **Mistress of the Robes** *n.* a lady of the royal household nominally in charge of the Queen's wardrobe. [ME and OF *maistresse* (MASTER, -ESS)]

mistrial (mistrī´əl, mis´-) *n.* an abortive or inconclusive trial.

mistrust (mistrŭst´) *v.t.* to regard with doubt or suspicion. ~*n.* distrust, suspicion. **mistrusted** *a.* **mistrustful** *a.* **mistrustfully** *adv.* **mistrustfulness** *n.*

mistype (mistīp´) *v.t.* to type (a character, number etc.) incorrectly.

misunderstand (misŭndəstand´) *v.t.* (*past, p.p.* **misunderstood** (-stud´)) to mistake the meaning or sense of, to misconceive, to misapprehend. **misunderstanding** *n.* **1** a failure of understanding. **2** a slight disagreement or argument. **misunderstood** *a.*

misuse[1] (misūz´) *v.t.* **1** to use or treat improperly. **2** to apply to a wrong purpose. **3** to ill-treat. **misusage** (-´ūsij) *n.* **misuser** *n.*

misuse[2] (misūs´) *n.* **1** improper use. **2** abuse.

misword (miswœd´) *v.t.* to word incorrectly. **miswording** *n.*

miswrite (misrīt´) *v.t.* (*past* **miswrote** (-rōt´), *p.p.* **miswritten** (-rit´ən)) to write incorrectly.

MIT *abbr.* Massachusetts Institute of Technology.

mite[1] (mīt) *n.* any minute arachnid of the order Acarida occurring in terrestrial or aquatic habitats. **mity** *a.* infested with mites. [OF *mite*, prob. cogn. with MITE[2]]

mite[2] (mīt) *n.* **1** a very small coin, orig. Flemish. **2** any very small coin. **3** a small contribution, a minute amount. **4** a tiny thing, esp. a child. [OE (cp. LG *mite*, Dut. *mijt*, OHG *mīza*, gnat)]

miter MITRE.

Mithraism (mith´rāizm, -rə-) *n.* the worship of the ancient Persian god Mithra, the god of light and the sun. **Mithraic** (-rā´-) *a.* **Mithraist** (-rā-) *n.* [L and Gr. *Mithrās*, OPers. *Mithra*]

mithridatism (mithrid´ətizm, mith´ridātizm) *n.* immunity to poison brought about by the administering of gradually increasing doses of it. †**mithridate** (mith´ridāt) *n.* an antidote against poison. **mithridatic** (-dat´-) *a.* **mithridatize** (-thrid´-), **mithridatise** *v.t.* to produce mithridatism in. [*Mithridates* VI, king of Pontus, said to have made himself poison-proof]

mitigate (mit´igāt) *v.t.* **1** to make less rigorous or harsh, to relax (severity). **2** to alleviate (pain, violence etc.). **3** to soften, to diminish, to moderate. ~*v.i.* to become assuaged, relaxed or moderated. **mitigable** *a.* **mitigating circumstances** *n.pl.* (*Law*) in a trial, circumstances which are conducive to greater leniency in verdict, sentence etc. **mitigation** (-ā´shən) *n.* **mitigator** *n.* **mitigatory** *a.* [L *mītigātus*, p.p. of *mītigāre*, from *mītis*, gentle]

Usage note See note under MILITATE.

mitochondrion (mītōkon´driən) *n.* (*pl.* **mitochondria**) (-driə) (*Biol.*) a spherical or rodlike organism, found in cytoplasm, whose function is energy production. [L, from Gr. *mitos*, thread, *chondrion*, small granule]

mitokinetic (mītōkinet´ik) *a.* productive of mitosis. [MITOSIS, KINETIC]

mitosis (mītō´sis) *n.* (*pl.* **mitoses** (-sēz)) **1** indirect cell division. **2** the appearance of the nucleus during karyokinesis. **mitotic** (-tot´-) *a.* [Gr. *mitos*, a thread, -OSIS]

mitrailleuse (mitrahyœz´) *n.* a breech-loading machine-gun consisting of several barrels united, for firing simultaneously or in succession. **mitraille** (-trahy´) *n.* small shot sent in a shower from this. **mitrailleur** (-yœ´) *n.* a machine-gunner. [F, from *mitrailler*, to fire small missiles, from *mitraille*, from MITE[2]]

mitral (mī´trəl) *a.* of or resembling a mitre. **mitral valve** *n.* the valve between the left auricle and ventricle of the heart, which prevents the blood flowing back into the auricle.

mitre (mī´tə), (*N Am.*) **miter** *n.* **1** a tall ornamental cap shaped like a cleft cone rising into two peaks, worn as a symbol of office by bishops and abbots. **2** the dignity of a bishop or abbot. **3** a joint at an angle (usu. of 90°), as the corner of a picture frame, each jointing surface being cut at an angle of 45° to the piece on which it is formed. **4** a diagonal join where two edges of a folded piece of fabric meet at a corner. ~*v.t.* **1** to join with a mitre. **2** to shape off at an angle of 45°. **3** to confer a mitre upon. ~*v.i.* to join with a mitre. **mitre block, mitre bound, mitre box** *n.* a block or box used to guide the saw in cutting mitres. **mitred** *a.* **1** joined or cut at an angle of 45°. **2** wearing a mitre, of episcopal rank. **mitre joint** *n.* **mitre wheel** *n.* a bevelled cogwheel engaged with another at an angle of 45°. **mitrewort** *n.* any of various plants of the genus *Mitella*. [OF *mitre*, L and Gr. *mitra*]

mitt (mit) *n.* **1** a mitten. **2** a kind of glove or covering for the wrist and palm (but not the fingers and thumb). **3** a thick glove worn by the catcher in baseball. **4** (*sl.*) a hand, a fist. **frozen mitt** FROZEN. [shortened from MITTEN]

mitten (mit´ən) *n.* **1** a glove with a thumb but no fingers. **2** (*sl.*) a boxing glove. **to get the mitten** (*sl.*) to be rejected or dismissed. **to give the mitten** (*sl.*) to reject (a lover) or dismiss (from office etc.). **mittened** *a.* [OF *mitaine*, etym. uncertain]

mittimus (mit´iməs) *n.* (*pl.* **mittimuses**) **1** (*Law*) a warrant of commitment to prison. **2** †a writ to remove records from one court to another. [L, we send, from *mittere*, see MISSION]

mity MITE[1].

mitzvah (mits´və) *n.* **1** in Judaism, a commandment or rule. **2** a good deed done by a Jew for religious reasons.

mix (miks) *v.t.* **1** to put together or blend into one mass or compound. **2** to mingle or incorporate (several substances, quantities or groups) so that the particles of each are indiscriminately associated. **3** to compound by mingling various ingredients. **4** to combine in a single action or on a single occasion. **5** to combine into a single sound signal. **6** to produce by combining different recordings or soundtracks. **7** to cross in breeding. ~*v.i.* **1** to become united. **2** to be mingled (with or together). **3** to be compatible. **4** to be sociable. **5** to be associated or be regularly sociable (with). **6** †to copulate. **7** †to join (in battle etc.). ~*n.* **1** mixed ingredients for a cake, mortar etc. **2** a mixture, a combination. **3** an act or process of mixing. **4** the merging of sound or pictures by means of a mixer. **to be mixed up in** to be involved in (esp. something dubious). **to be mixed up with** to be involved with (esp. someone undesirable). **to mix and match** to choose from a range of combinations, e.g. of fabrics, wallpaper etc. **to mix in** to be sociable, to get on well with others. **to mix it** to start a fight. **to mix it up** (*N Am.*) to mix it. **to mix up 1** to mix thoroughly. **2** to confuse, to bewilder. **3** to involve (in an (esp. dubious) undertaking or with an (esp. undesirable) person). **mixable** *a.* **mixed** (mikst) *a.* **1** consisting of various kinds or constituents. **2** consisting of various different types of people. **3** for or involving both sexes. **4** not wholly good or bad, not of consistent quality. **mixed-ability** *a.* (of school classes etc.) made up of pupils of different levels of ability. **mixed bag, mixed bunch** *n.* a diverse mixture of people or things, often in terms of quality. **mixed bathing** *n.* bathing by both sexes together. **mixed blessing** *n.* something that has advantages and disadvantages. **mixed company** *n.* people of both sexes. **mixed crystal** *n.* a crystal made of more than one substance. **mixed doubles** *n.pl.* in tennis, badminton etc., matches with a man and woman player as partners on each side. **mixed economy** *n.* an economy containing both private enterprise and state-controlled industries etc. **mixed farm** *n.* a farm combining arable and livestock production. **mixed feelings** *n.* (*pl.*) a mixture of pleasure and sadness with regard to a single event etc. **mixed grill** *n.* a dish of various grilled meats, often served with fried egg, mushrooms and tomatoes. **mixedly** (-sid-) *adv.* **mixed marriage** *n.* a marriage in which the contracting parties are of different creeds or races. **mixed media** *n.* the use of different media in a work of art, presentation, entertainment etc. **mixed-media** *a.* **mixed metaphor** *n.* a metaphor that brings together incongruous concepts. **mixedness** *n.* **mixed number** *n.* an integer in combination with a proper fraction. **mixed school** *n.* a school at which boys and girls are educated together. **mixed train** *n.* a train composed of both passenger and goods wagons. **mixed-up** *a.* **1** confused, chaotic, muddled. **2** in emotional turmoil. **mixer** *n.* **1** a person or thing that causes mixing, that mixes. **2** a kitchen appliance for mixing food ingredients. **3** a non-alcoholic drink suitable for mixing with alcoholic drinks. **4** a person with social tact, a person who gets on well with all sorts of people. **5** (*coll.*) a person who stirs up trouble. **6** a device for combining sound or pictures into a single output. **7** a person who uses this. **mixer tap** *n.* a tap that combines hot and cold water in a single outlet. [back-formation from obs. *mixt*, F *mixte*, L *mixtus*, p.p. of *miscēre*, to mix]

mixen (mik´sən) *n.* a dunghill. [OE, from *meox*, dung]

mixture (miks´chə) *n.* **1** something which is being or has been mixed. **2** (*Chem.*) a combination of substances without any chemical reaction between them. **3** a combination of different qualities and characteristics. **4** gas or vaporized oil mixed with air to form the explosive charge in an internal-combustion engine. **5** the process of mixing. **the mixture as before** the same treatment repeated.

mizzen (miz´ən), **mizzen-sail** *n.* (*Naut.*) a fore-and-aft sail set on the mizzen-mast of a sailing ship. **mizzen-mast** *n.* the aftermost mast of a three-masted sailing ship. **mizzen-rigging, mizzen yard, mizzen-top** *n.* [F *misaine*, It. *mezzana*, fem. of *mezzano*, see MEZZANINE]

mizzle[1] (miz´əl) *v.i.* to rain in very fine drops, to drizzle. ~*n.* very fine rain. **mizzly** *a.* [cp. Dut. dial. *miezelen*]

mizzle[2] (miz´əl) *v.i.* (*sl.*) to run away, decamp. [etym. uncertain]

Mk. *abbr.* **1** Mark (in the New Testament). **2** mark (the German currency). **3** markka.

mks *abbr.* metre-kilogram-second.

Mkt. *abbr.* Market.

ml *abbr.* **1** mile(s). **2** millilitre(s).

MLA *abbr.* **1** Member of the Legislative Assembly. **2** Modern Language Association (of America).

MLC *abbr.* Member of the Legislative Council.

MLD *abbr.* minimum lethal dose.

MLF *abbr.* multilateral (nuclear) force.

M.Litt. *abbr.* Master of Letters. [L *Magister Litterarum*]

Mlle *abbr.* Mademoiselle.

Mlles *abbr.* Mesdemoiselles.

MLR *abbr.* minimum lending rate.

m'lud LUD.

MM *abbr.* **1** (*Mus.*) Maelzel's metronome (indicating tempo). **2** Messieurs. **3** Military Medal.

mm *abbr.* millimetre(s).

Mme *abbr.* Madame.

Mmes *abbr.* Mesdames.

m.m.f. *abbr.* magnetomotive force.

M.Mus. *abbr.* Master of Music.

MN *abbr.* Merchant Navy.

Mn *chem. symbol* manganese.

M'Naghten rules MCNAUGHTEN RULES.

mnemonic (nimon´ik) *n.* **1** an aid to memory. **2** (*pl.*) the art of or a system for aiding or strengthening memory. ~*a.* of, relating to or aiding the memory. **mnemonically** *adv.* **mnemonist** (nē´-) *n.* **mnemotechny** (-tekni) *n.* the art of developing the memory. **mnemotechnic** (-tek´-) *a.* [Gr. *mnēmonikos*, from *mnēmōn*, mindful (*mnāsthai*, to remember)]

MO *abbr.* **1** Medical Officer. **2** modus operandi. **3** money order.

Mo *chem. symbol* molybdenum.

Mo. *abbr.* Missouri.

mo[1] (mō) *n.* (*pl.* **mos**) (*coll.*) moment (*just a mo; half a mo*).

†**mo**[2] (mō) *n., a., adv.* more. [OE *mā*, MORE]

mo. *abbr.* month(s).

-mo (mō) *suf.* used to form nouns denoting book size (*decimo, duodecimo*).

moa (mō´ə) *n.* (*pl.* **moas**) an extinct, flightless bird of the genus *Dinornis*. [Maori]

moan (mōn) *n.* **1** a low prolonged sound expressing pain or sorrow. **2** a complaint. ~*v.i.* **1** to utter a moan or moans. **2** to complain, grumble. **moaner** *n.* **moanful** *a.* **moaningly** *adv.* [cogn. with OE *mǣnan*, to moan]

moat (mōt) *n.* a ditch round a castle, fort etc., usu. filled with water. ~*v.t.* to surround with or as with a moat. [OF *mote*, a dike, a mound (cp. F *motte*, a mound, a clod), prob. from Gmc.]

mob (mob) *n.* **1** a gang of criminals engaged in organized crime. **2** a disorderly or riotous crowd, a rabble. **3** (*coll., derog.*) a group or class (of people of a specified kind). **4** (*derog.*) the masses. ~*v.t.* (*pres.p.* **mobbing,** *past, p.p.* **mobbed**) **1** to attack in a mob. **2** to crowd roughly round and annoy. ~*v.i.* to gather together in a mob. **the Mob 1** (*esp. N Am.*) the Mafia. **2** organized crime. **mobber** *n.* **mobbish** *a.* **mobbism** *n.* **mobocracy** (-ok´-) *n.* (*pl.* **mobocracies**) **1** rule by a mob. **2** a ruling mob. **mob rule, mob law** *n.* **1** the rule of the mob. **2** lynch law. **mobsman** *n.* **mobster** *n.* a member of a criminal mob. [contr. from L *mōbile* (*vulgus*), the fickle (crowd)]

mob cap (mob) *n.* (*Hist.*) a plain indoor cap or head-dress for women, usu. tied under the chin. [cp. Dut. *mopmuts*, woman's nightcap]

mobile (mō´bīl) *a.* **1** movable, free to move. **2** easily moved. **3** easily changing (as an expression). **4** able to be moved from place to place. **5** able to move in social status. **6** †fickle, excitable. ~*n.* **1** an artistic concoction of items suspended in balance from wires etc. **2** something which moves or causes motion. **mobile home** *n.* a caravan or larger movable building used as a permanent dwelling. **mobile phone, mobile telephone** *n.* a small portable radio telephone. **mobile sculpture** *n.* a sculpture with moving parts. **mobility** (-bil´-) *n.* **mobilize** (-bil-), **mobilise** *v.t.* **1** to make mobile. **2** to put into circulation. **3** to put (troops, a fleet etc.) in a state of readiness for active service. **4** to put into action. ~*v.i.* to be put in a state of readiness for active service. **mobilizable** *a.* **mobilization** (-zā´shən) *n.* [L *mōbilis*, from *movēre*, to MOVE]

Möbius strip (mœ´biəs) *n.* (*Math.*) a long, rectangular strip of paper twisted through 180° and joined at the ends, to form a one-sided surface bounded by one continuous curve. [A. F. *Möbius*, 1790–1868, German mathematician]

mobocracy MOB.

moccasin (mok´əsin) *n.* 1 a bedroom slipper of soft leather made of one piece. 2 a foot-covering, usu. of deerskin or soft leather in one piece, worn by N American Indians. 3 the water moccasin and other snakes of the genus *Agkistrodon*. **water moccasin** WATER. [Powhatan *mockasin*]

mocha (mok´ə) *n.* 1 a choice quality of coffee, orig. from Mocha. 2 a drink made with this and often also chocolate. 3 a soft sheepskin leather. [*Mocha*, fortified seaport on the Red Sea]

mock (mok) *v.t.* 1 to deride, to laugh at. 2 to mimic, esp. in derision. 3 to defy contemptuously. 4 to delude, to take in. ~*v.i.* to express ridicule, derision or contempt. ~*a.* 1 sham, false, counterfeit. 2 imitating reality. ~*n.* 1 something which is derided or deserves derision. 2 (*usu. in pl.*) an examination taken as practice prior to an official one. 3 an imitation. 4 a derisive action, a sneer. **to make (a) mock of** to ridicule, to sneer at. **mockable** *a.* **mocker** *n.* **to put the mockers on** 1 (*sl.*) to cause to fail. 2 (*sl.*) to make impossible. **mockery** *n.* (*pl.* **mockeries**) 1 the act of mocking, ridicule, derision. 2 a delusive imitation. 3 a futile effort. 4 a subject of ridicule. **mock-heroic** *a.* (in writing) burlesquing the heroic style. ~*n.* a burlesque of the heroic style. **mocking** *n.*, *a.* **mockingbird** *n.* any American songbird of the family Mimidae, esp. *Mimus polyglottos*, with great powers of mimicry. **mockingly** *adv.* **mock moon** *n.* (*Astron.*) paraselene. **mock orange** *n.* the common syringa, *Philadelphus coronarius*, the flowers of which smell like orange blossoms. **mock sun** *n.* (*Astron.*) a parhelion. **mock turtle soup** *n.* a soup prepared from calf's head, veal etc. to imitate turtle soup. **mock-up** *n.* 1 an experimental dummy model or replica, usu. full-size. 2 an unprinted model of a book. [OF *mocquer* (F *moquer*), perh. from pop. L *muccāre*, to wipe the nose, L *muccus*, see MUCUS]

MOD *abbr.* Ministry of Defence.

mod[1] (mod) *a.* modern. ~*n.* a member of a youth subculture of the 1960s, who wore smart casual clothes, rode motor scooters and were often involved in fights with gangs of rockers, a rival subculture. [*mod*ern]

mod[2] *prep.*, *adv.* (*Math.*) modulo.

mod[3] (mod) *n.* a Highland gathering analogous to a Welsh eisteddfod. [Gael. *mōd*, cogn. with MOOT]

modal (mō´dəl) *a.* 1 of or relating to mode, form or manner, as opposed to substance. 2 (*Gram.*) (of a verb) of or relating to mood or denoting manner. 3 in statistics, of or relating to a mode. 4 (*Mus.*) using a particular mode. 5 (*Logic*) affirming with or expressing qualification. ~*n.* a modal proposition or verb. **modalism** *n.* the doctrine that the three persons of the Holy Trinity are merely different modes of the same being. **modalist** *n.* **modality** (-dal´-) *n.* (*pl.* **modalities**) 1 the fact or condition of being modal. 2 a prescribed manner of proceeding. **modally** *adv.* **modal proposition** *n.* (*Logic*) a proposition that affirms or denies with some qualification. [med. L *modālis*, from L *modus*, MODE]

mod cons (mod konz´) *n.pl.* (*coll.*) modern devices or appliances that give comfort, convenience etc. [*mod*ern *con*veniences]

mode (mōd) *n.* 1 manner, method, way of doing, existing etc. 2 style. 3 common fashion, prevailing custom. 4 in statistics, the value occurring most frequently in a set of data. 5 an operational state. 6 any of the systems of dividing the octave, the form of the scale. 7 (*Logic*) the character of the connection in or the modality of a proposition. 8 an open-work filling in lace. 9 (*Gram.*, *N Am.*) mood. 10 a kind of silk, alamode. [F, from L *modus*, *-um*, rel. to Gr. *mēdos* plan, and Eng. METE[2]]

model (mod´əl) *n.* 1 a representation or pattern in miniature, in three dimensions, of something made on a larger scale. 2 a person employed to wear clothes, make-up etc. to display their effect. 3 a particular style or type, e.g. of a car or a garment. 4 a person employed to pose as subject to an artist. 5 a standard, an example to be imitated or emulated. 6 a description or representation of something that cannot be observed directly (*computer model*). 7 a figure in clay, plaster etc. for execution in durable material. 8 a set of postulates, mathematical equations etc. used e.g. to predict developments in the economy. 9 a garment etc. made by a well-known designer. 10 (*euphem.*) a prostitute. ~*a.* 1 serving as a model or example. 2 worthy of imitation, perfect. ~*v.t.* (*pres.p.* **modelling**, (*N Am.*) **modeling**, *past*, *p.p.* **modelled**, (*N Am.*) **modeled**) 1 to display (clothes) by wearing them. 2 to shape, mould or fashion in clay etc. 3 to form after or upon a model. 4 to give a plan or shape to (a document, book etc.). 5 to give a three-dimensional appearance to. ~*v.i.* 1 to act as a mannequin. 2 to make a model or models. **modeller**, (*N Am.*) **modeler** *n.* a person who makes models. [OF *modelle*, It. *modello*, dim. of *modo*, as MODE]

modem (mō´dem) *n.* a device used to transmit and receive data, esp. between computers over a telephone line. [*mo*dulator *dem*odulator]

modena (mod´inə) *n.* a deep crimson or purple. [Italian city of *Modena*]

moderate[1] (mod´ərət) *a.* 1 temperate, reasonable, mild, keeping within bounds. 2 not extreme or excessive. 3 of medium quantity or quality. ~*n.* a person of moderate views in politics, religion etc. **moderately** *adv.* 1 with moderation. 2 not excessively, fairly. **moderateness** *n.* **moderatism** *n.* **moderato** (-rah´tō) *a.*, *adv.* (*Mus.*) in moderate time. ~*n.* (*pl.* **moderatos**) a piece of music in moderate time. [L *moderātus*, p.p. of *moderārī*, from *moder-*, stem of *modestus*, MODEST, cogn. with *modus*, MODE]

moderate[2] (mod´ərāt) *v.t.* 1 to reduce to a calmer, less violent, energetic or intense condition. 2 to restrain from excess. 3 to temper, to mitigate. 4 to assess (examination papers etc.) in order to achieve consistency in marking. ~*v.i.* 1 to become less violent. 2 to quieten or settle down. 3 to preside as a moderator. 4 to act as a moderator of examinations. 5 (*Physics*) to retard with a moderator. **moderation** (-ā´shən) *n.* 1 the act of moderating. 2 the quality or state of being moderate. 3 temperance, self-restraint. 4 (*Physics*) the retarding of neutrons with a moderator. **in moderation** not to excess, in a moderate manner or degree. **Moderations** *n.pl.* the first public examination for a degree at Oxford. **moderator** *n.* 1 a person who or something that moderates. 2 a person who presides at a meeting, esp. the presiding officer at a court of the Presbyterian Church. 3 a person whose task is to ensure fairness and consistency in the way examination papers are set and marked. 4 a person who superintends certain examinations for degrees and honours at Oxford and Cambridge Universities. 5 (*Physics*) a substance used to retard neutrons. 6 †an umpire, an arbitrator. **moderatorship** *n.* **moderatrix** *n.* a female moderator. [as MODERATE[1]]

moderato MODERATE[1].

moderator, moderatrix MODERATE[2].

modern (mod´ən) *a.* 1 of or relating to the present or recent time. 2 not ancient, old-fashioned or obsolete. 3 being or concerning the present or most recent form of a language. ~*n.* 1 a person of modern times. 2 an exponent of modernism (as artist, writer etc.). **modern English** *n.* the English language as used since *c.* 1500. **modern history** *n.* history from AD 1517 to the present day. **modernism** *n.* 1 a modern mode of expression or thought. 2 a modern term or idiom. 3 in art and literature, the conscious rejection of traditional forms and use of new forms of expression. 4 a tendency towards freedom of thought and the acceptance of the results of modern criticism and research in religious matters. **modernist** *n.* **modernistic** (-nis´-) *a.* **modernistically** *adv.* **modernity** (-dœ´-) *n.* **modernize, modernise** *v.t., v.i.* **modernization** (-zā´shən) *n.* **modernizer** *n.* **modern languages** *n.pl.* languages that are still in current use, esp. as a subject of study. **modern Latin** *n.* Latin as used since *c.* 1500. **modernly** *adv.* **modernness** *n.* **modern pentathlon** *n.* a sports contest involving swimming, cross-country running, fencing, equestrian steeplechasing and shooting. [F *moderne*, late L *modernus*, from *modo*, just now]

modest (mod´ist) *a.* **1** humble, unassuming or diffident in regard to one's merits or importance. **2** not presumptuous, forward or arrogant. **3** bashful, retiring. **4** restrained by a sense of propriety. **5** decorous, chaste. **6** moderate, not extreme or excessive. **modestly** *adv.* **modesty** *n.* **1** the quality of being modest. **2** a sense of propriety. **3** delicacy. **4** chastity. [F *modeste*, L *modestus*, as MODERATE[1]]

modi MODUS.

modicum (mod´ikəm) *n.* a little, a small amount, a scanty allowance. [L, neut. of *modicus*, moderate, as MODE]

modify (mod´ifī) *v.t.* (*3rd pers. sing. pres.* **modifies,** *pres.p.* **modifying,** *past, p.p.* **modified**) **1** to alter, to make different. **2** to change to a moderate extent the form, character or other qualities of. **3** to reduce in degree or extent, to moderate, to tone down. **4** (*Chem.*) to change the constituent radicals of (a polymer). **5** (*Gram.*) to qualify the sense of. **6** (*Gram.*) to alter (a vowel) by umlaut. **modifiable** *a.* **modifiability** (-bil´-) *n.* **modification** (-fikā´shən) *n.* **modificatory** (-fi-) *a.* **modifier** *n.* **1** (*Gram.*) a word or phrase that modifies another. **2** any person or thing that modifies. [F *modifier*, L *modificāre* (*modus*, MODE, -FY)]

modillion (mədil´yən) *n.* (*Archit.*) an ornamental bracket beneath a cornice, esp. in the Corinthian order. [It. *modiglione*, etym. uncertain]

modiolus (mədī´ələs) *n.* (*pl.* **modioli** (-lī)) the central column round which the cochlea of the ear winds. **modiolar** *a.* [L, bucket on waterwheel, dim. of *modius*, a corn measure]

modish (mō´dish) *a.* fashionable, stylish. **modishly** *adv.* **modishness** *n.* **modist** *n.* a follower of the fashion. [MODE, -ISH[1]]

modiste (modēst´) *n.* **1** a milliner. **2** a dressmaker. [F]

Mods (modz) *n.pl.* (*coll.*) Moderations.

modular (mod´ūlə) *a.* **1** of or relating to a module, consisting of modules. **2** of or relating to a modulus, consisting of moduli. **modularity** (-lar´-) *n.*

modulate (mod´ūlāt) *v.t.* **1** to adjust, to regulate. **2** to vary or inflect the sound or tone of. **3** (*Mus.*) to change the key of. ~*v.i.* (*Mus.*) to pass from one key to another. **modulation** (-lā´shən) *n.* **1** the act of modulating or being modulated. **2** alterations in the amplitude or frequency of an electrical wave at a different frequency, usually at a lower one. **modulative** *a.* **modulator** *n.* **1** a person who or something that modulates. **2** (*Mus.*) a chart of the modulations in the tonic sol-fa system. [L *modulātus*, p.p. of *modulārī*, to measure, from MODULUS]

module (mod´ūl) *n.* **1** any element or unit that forms part of a larger system, e.g. of a spacecraft, an educational course. **2** a measure or unit of proportion. **3** (*Archit.*) the semidiameter or other unit taken as a standard for regulating the proportions of a column. [F, as MODULUS]

modulus (mod´ūləs) *n.* (*pl.* **moduli** (-lī)) **1** a constant number or coefficient expressing a force, effect, function, etc. **2** a constant multiplier in a function of a variable. **3** the absolute value of a complex number. **modulo** *prep., adv.* (*Math.*) using or with respect to a (specified) modulus. [L, dim. of MODUS]

modus (mō´dəs) *n.* (*pl.* **modi** (-dī)) **1** mode, manner, way. **2** (*Hist.*) money compensation in lieu of tithe. [L, MODE]

modus operandi (mōdəs operan´dī) *n.* (*pl.* **modi operandi** (mōdī)) **1** a method of working. **2** the way something operates. [L, method of operating]

modus vivendi (mōdəs viven´dī) *n.* (*pl.* **modi vivendi** (mōdī)) **1** a way of living, or life. **2** an arrangement by means of which people who are in dispute carry on in a situation pending a settlement. [L, way of living]

mofette (mofet´) *n.* **1** a fissure in the earth giving vent to noxious gas, a fumarole. **2** an exhalation of noxious gas from this. [F, from It. *mofetta*]

mog (mog), **moggie** (-i) *n.* (*coll.*) a cat.

Mogadon® (mog´ədon) *n.* a drug used to treat insomnia.

moggie MOG.

mogul[1] (mō´gəl) *n.* **1** a powerful and influential entrepreneur. **2** (**Mogul**) **a** a Mongolian, a Mughal. **b** a follower of Baber, descendant of Tamerlane, or of Genghis Khan. [Pers. *mugul*, Mongol]

mogul[2] (mō´gəl) *n.* a mound of packed snow on a ski slope. [prob. G dial.]

MOH *abbr.* Medical Officer of Health.

mohair (mō´heə) *n.* **1** the hair of the angora goat. **2** a fabric made from it. **3** an imitation of this fabric in cotton and wool. [Arab. *mukhayyar* (assim. to HAIR)]

Mohammedan MUHAMMADAN.

Moharram MUHARRAM.

Mohawk (mō´hawk) *n.* (*pl.* **Mohawks, Mohawk**) **1** a member of a N American Indian people. **2** their language. **3** in skating, a stroke from either edge to the same edge on the other foot, but in the opposite direction. ~*a.* of or relating to the Mohawks or their language. [from an Algonquian name]

Mohican (mōhē´kən) *n.* **1** a member of a N American Indian people living in the Hudson river valley. **2** the language of the Mohicans. **3** (*also* **mohican**) a hairstyle in which the head is shaved apart from a narrow central strip of erect hair from front to rear, often brightly coloured. ~*a.* **1** of or relating to the Mohicans or their language. **2** (of a hairstyle) cut into a Mohican. [from an Algonquian name]

Moho (mō´hō) *n.* (*Geol.*) the boundary between the earth's crust and mantle, the Mohorovičić discontinuity. [A. *Moho*rovičić, 1857–1936, Croatian seismologist]

Mohock (mō´hok) *n.* (*Hist.*) any set of aristocratic ruffians who roamed the streets of London at night early in the 18th cent. [corr. of MOHAWK]

Mohs scale (mōz) *n.* a scale of 1–10 by which the hardness of minerals is measured. [Friedrich *Mohs*, 1773–1839, German mineralogist]

moidore (moi´daw) *n.* (*Hist.*) a Portuguese gold coin. [Port. *moeda d'ouro* (*moeda*, L *monēta*, MONEY, *de*, of, *ouro*, L *aurum*, gold)]

moiety (moi´əti) *n.* (*pl.* **moieties**) **1** (*Law*) a half. **2** a part or share. [OF *moitié*, L *medietas -tātem*, middle point, half, from *medius*, see MEDIUM]

†**moil** (moil) *v.i.* to toil, to drudge, to work hard. ~*v.t.* **1** to weary, to fatigue. **2** to moisten, to bedaub, to defile. [OF *moiller* (F *mouiller*), to wet, to paddle through mud, from L *mollis*, soft]

moire (mwah´), **moire antique** *n.* **1** watered silk. **2** a watered appearance on textile fabrics or metals. **moiré** (-rā) *a.* watered (of silk, surfaces of metal etc.). ~*n.* a surface or finish like watered silk. [F, prob. a form of MOHAIR]

moist (moist) *a.* **1** moderately wet, damp, humid. **2** rainy. **3** discharging pus etc. **4** †fresh, new. **moisten** (-sən) *v.t., v.i.* **moistener** *n.* **moistify** *v.t.* (*3rd pers. sing. pres.* **moistifies,** *pres.p.* **moistifying,** *past, p.p.* **moistified**). **moistly** *adv.* **moistness** *n.* **moisture** *n.* liquid throughout or on the surface of something, or in a vapour. **moistureless** *a.* **moisturize, moisturise** *v.t.* to add moisture to. **moisturizer** *n.* anything which moisturizes, esp. a cosmetic cream or lotion. **moisty** *a.* (*comp.* **moistier,** *superl.* **moistiest**). [OF *moiste* (F *moite*), perh. from late L *muccidus*, L *mūcidus*, from *mūcēre*, to be mouldy, as MUCUS]

moke (mōk) *n.* (*sl.*) **1** a donkey. **2** (*Austral.*) an inferior horse. [etym. unknown]

moki (mō´ki) *n.* (*pl.* **mokis, moki**) a New Zealand sea fish, either *Latridopsis ciliaris* or *Chinonemus spectabilis.* [Maori]

moko (mō´kō) *n.* (*pl.* **mokos**) **1** the Maori method of tattooing. **2** a pattern in this. [Maori]

moksha (mok´shə) *n.* in Hindu and Jain religions, release from the cycle of rebirth. [Sansk.]

mol *abbr.* MOLE[4].

mol. *abbr.* **1** molecular. **2** molecule.

molal MOLE[4].

molar[1] (mō´lə) *n.* any of the back or grinding teeth. ~*a.* **1** having power to grind. **2** grinding. **molary** *a.* [L *molāris*, from *mola*, mill]

molar[2] (mō´lə) *a.* **1** of or relating to mass. **2** acted on or exerted by a large mass or masses. [MOLE[3], -AR[1]]

molar[3] MOLE[4].

molasses (məlas´iz) *n.* **1** the sticky, dark-brown uncrystallizable syrup drained from sugar during the refining process. **2** treacle. [Port. *melaço*, late L *mellāceum*, must, from *mel*, honey]

mold[1] MOULD[1].

mold[2] MOULD[2].

mold[3] MOULD[3].

molder MOULDER[2].

mole[1] (mōl) *n.* a spot on the human skin, usu. dark-coloured and sometimes covered with hair. [OE *māl*]

mole[2] (mōl) *n.* **1** a small soft-furred burrowing mammal of the family Talpidae, esp. *Talpa europaea.* **2** a spy or subversive person working within an organization on behalf of a rival organization, enemy etc. ~*v.t.* to burrow or ferret (something) out. **mole cricket** *n.* a burrowing cricket of the family Gryllotalpidae. **mole-eyed** *a.* having very small eyes or imperfect vision. **molehill** *n.* **1** a hillock thrown up by a mole burrowing underground. **2** an unimportant or very small matter, problem etc. **mole-rat** *n.* any of various mouselike burrowing rodents, esp. of the family Bathyergidae of Africa. **moleskin** *n.* **1** the skin of the mole used as fur. **2** a kind of fustian, dyed after the surface has been shaved. **3** (*pl.*) clothes, esp. trousers, of this material. [cp. MDut. and LG *mol*]

mole[3] (mōl) *n.* **1** a pile of masonry, such as a breakwater, pier or jetty before a port. **2** an artificial harbour. [F *môle*, L *mōles*, mass, etym. uncertain]

mole[4] (mōl) *n.* the basic SI unit of substance, being the amount of substance of a system which contains as many specified elementary entities as there are atoms in 0.012 kg of carbon-12. **molal** *a.* (*Chem.*) (of a solution) containing one mole of solute per thousand grams of solvent. **molar**[3] *a.* (*Chem.*) **1** of or relating to one mole of a substance. **2** (of a solution) containing one mole of solute per litre of solvent.

mole[5] (mōl) *n.* (*Med.*) an abnormal fleshy growth in the uterus.

molecule (mol´ikūl) *n.* **1** (*Chem.*) any of the structural units of which matter is built up, the smallest quantity of substance capable of separate existence without losing its chemical identity with that substance. **2** a particle. **molecular** (məlek´-) *a.* **molecular attraction** *n.* **1** (*Chem.*) the force by which molecules of bodies act upon each other. **2** cohesion. **molecular biology** *n.* the study of the structure and chemical organization of living matter, esp. of nucleic acids and protein synthesis. **molecularity** (-lar´-) *n.* **molecular sieve** *n.* (*Chem.*) a material that can absorb certain compounds but not others, because of the size of its pores relative to the molecules of the compounds concerned. **molecular weight** *n.* (*Chem.*) RELATIVE MOLECULAR MASS (under RELATIVE). [F *molécule*, dim. from L *mōles*, see MOLE[3]]

molest (məlest´) *v.t.* **1** to trouble, to disturb, to harm. **2** to assault or attack, esp. for sexual purposes. **molestation** (molestā´shən, mō-) *n.* **molester** *n.* †**molestful** *a.* [OF *molester*, L *molestāre*, from *molestus*, troublesome]

moline (məlīn´) *a.* (*Her.*) (of the arms of a cross) shaped like the support for a millstone, with broad backward-curving extremities. ~*n.* a moline cross. [cp. F *moulin*, late L *molīna*, MILL[1]]

Molinism (mol´inizm, mō´-) *n.* the doctrine that the efficacy of divine grace depends on free acceptance by the human will. **Molinist** *n.* [Luis *Molina*, 1535–1600, Spanish Jesuit]

moll (mol) *n.* (*sl.*) **1** a gangster's girlfriend. **2** a wench, a prostitute. [fam. form of *Mary*]

mollah MULLAH.

mollify (mol´ifī) *v.t.* (*3rd pers. sing. pres.* **mollifies,** *pres.p.* **mollifying,** *past, p.p.* **mollified**) **1** to soften, to assuage. **2** to pacify, to appease. **mollient** *a.* **mollifiable** *a.* **mollification** (-fikā´shən) *n.* **mollifier** *n.* [F *mollifier*, L *mollificāre* (*mollis*, soft, -*ficāre*, from *facere*, to make)]

mollusc (mol´əsk), (*N Am.*) **mollusk** *n.* any invertebrate of the Mollusca. **molluscan** (-lŭs´-), **molluscoid** (-lŭs´-) *n., a.* **molluscous** (-lŭs´-) *a.* [L *molluscus*, softish, from *mollis*, soft]

molly[1] (mol´i) *n.* (*pl.* **mollies**) **1** an effeminate man or boy, a person who likes to be coddled, a milksop. **2** (*dated sl.*) a wench, a prostitute. **mollycoddle** *v.t.* to coddle. ~*n.* a milksop. [form of *Mary*]

molly[2] (mol´i), **mollie** *n.* any brightly-coloured freshwater fish of the genus *Poecilia*, esp. *P. sphenops.* [from L *Mollienisia* (former name of genus), from Count *Mollen*, 1758–1850, French statesman]

mollymawk (mol´imawk), **mallemuck** (mal´imŭk) *n.* **1** any fulmar, petrel or albatross of the genus *Diomedea.* **2** (*Hist.*) a convivial meeting on board one of a company of whalers. [Dut. *mallemok*, from *mal*, foolish, *mok*, gull]

Moloch (mō´lok) *n.* **1** an idol of the Phoenicians to which human sacrifices were offered. **2** a devouring influence such as overbearing wealth, tyranny etc. **3** (**moloch**) an Australian spiny lizard, *Moloch horridus.* [Heb. *molek*]

Molotov cocktail (mol´ətof) *n.* a home-made incendiary device consisting of a bottle containing an inflammable liquid, with a rag for a wick. [V. M. *Molotov*, 1890–1986, Russian statesman]

molt MOULT.

molten (mōl´tən) *a.* **1** made of melted metal. **2** melted by heat. **moltenly** *adv.* [p.p. of MELT]

molto (mol´tō) *adv.* (*Mus.*) much, very. [It.]

moly (mō´li) *n.* (*pl.* **molies**) **1** wild garlic, *Allium moly*, with small yellow flowers. **2** a mythical herb with white flower and black root, given to Ulysses to counteract the spells of Circe. [L, from Gr. *mōlu*]

molybdenum (məlib´dənəm) *n.* (*Chem.*) a rare metallic element, at. no. 42, chem. symbol Mo, found in combination as molybdenite. **molybdate** (-dāt) *n.* **molybdenite** *n.* a sulphide or molybdenum disulphide. **molybdenous** *a.* **molybdic, molybdous** *a.* [L *molybdaena*, Gr. *molubdaina*, from *molubdos*, lead]

mom (mom) *n.* (*N Am., coll.*) mother.

moment (mō´mənt) *n.* **1** a minute portion of time, an instant. **2** a short period of time. **3** a particular point in time. **4** importance, consequence. **5** the measure of a force by its power to cause rotation. **6** †momentum. **at a moment's notice** NOTICE. **at the moment** at the present, just now. **in a moment 1** in a short while (*I'll* *do it in a moment*). 2 instantly (*In a moment, she was gone*). **not for a moment** never, emphatically not. **the moment** the right time for anything, the opportunity. **this moment** at once. **to have one's moments** to be successful, impressive, happy etc. on occasions. **momentary** *a.* 1 lasting only for a moment. 2 done or past in a moment. 3 transient, ephemeral. **momentarily** *adv.* 1 for a moment. 2 (*N Am.*) immediately. **momentariness** *n.* **momently** *adv.* 1 from moment to moment. 2 at any moment. 3 for a moment. **moment of inertia** *n.* (*Physics*) the degree of resistance to angular acceleration in a body expressed as the quantity by which that acceleration should be multiplied. **momentous** (-men´-) *a.* weighty, important. **momentously** *adv.* **momentousness** *n.* [F, from L MOMENTUM]

momentum (məmen´təm) *n.* (*pl.* **momenta** (-tə)) 1 impetus, power of overcoming resistance to motion. 2 the quantity of motion in a body, the product of the mass and the velocity. [L, for *movimentum* (*movēre*, to MOVE, -MENT)]

momma (mom´ə) *n.* (*N Am., coll.*) mother.

mommy (mom´i) *n.* (*pl.* **mommies**) (*N Am., coll.*) mummy, mother.

Momus (mō´məs) *n.* (*pl.* **Momuses, Momi** (-mī)) a fault-finding or querulous person. [Gr. *Mōmos*, a Greek divinity, the son of Night, the god of blame and ridicule]

Mon. *abbr.* Monday.

mon- MONO-.

monachal (mon´əkəl) *a.* monastic. **monachism** *n.* 1 monasticism. 2 monkery, monkishness. **monachist** *n.* [med. L *monachālis*, from *monachus*, MONK]

monacid MONOACID.

monactinal (monak´tinəl) *a.* (of a sponge) having single-rayed, rod-shaped spicules. **monactine** (-tīn) *a.* [Gr. *aktis aktinos*, ray]

monad (mon´ad, mō´-) *n.* 1 a simple, indivisible unit. 2 (*Philos.*) one of the primary elements of being, esp. according to the philosophy of Leibnitz. 3 a univalent atom, radical or element. 4 (*Biol.*) an elementary, single-celled organism. **monadic** (-nad´-) *a.* **monadism** *n.* **monadology** (-dol´-) *n.* the theory or doctrine of monads. [late L and Gr. *monad-*, nom. *monas*, from *monos*, sole]

monadelphous (monədel´fəs) *a.* (*Bot.*) 1 having the stamens united by their filaments. 2 (of stamens) having the filaments united. [MON-, Gr. *adelphos*, brother]

monadnock (mədad´nok) *n.* a steep, isolated hill of hard rock rising from a plain of softer rock. [Mt *Monadnock*, New Hampshire, US]

monandry (monan´dri) *n.* 1 the form of marriage in which one woman has only one husband at a time. 2 (*Bot.*) the quality of having only one stamen. **monandrous** (monan´drəs) *a.* [Gr. *anēr andros*, male]

monanthous (monan´thəs) *a.* (*Bot.*) bearing only one flower (on each stalk).

monarch (mon´ək) *n.* 1 a sole ruler. 2 a hereditary sovereign, such as emperor, empress, king or queen. 3 the chief of its class. **monarchal** (-ah´-) *a.* †**monarchally** *adv.* **monarch butterfly** *n.* a large orange and black butterfly, *Danais plexippus*. **monarch flycatcher** *n.* a flycatcher of the Old World family Monarchidae. **monarchic** (-ah´-), **monarchical** (-ah´-) *a.* **monarchically** *adv.* **monarchism** *n.* 1 belief in or advocacy of monarchy. 2 the monarchic principle. **monarchist** *n.* **monarchize, monarchise** *v.t.* **monarchy** *n.* (*pl.* **monarchies**) 1 government in which the supreme power is vested in a monarch. 2 a state under this system, a kingdom. 3 supreme control. **monarchial** *a.* [F *monarque*, L *monarche*, Gr. *monarchēs* (MON-, *archein*, to rule)]

monastery (mon´əstəri) *n.* (*pl.* **monasteries**) a residence for a community, esp. of monks, living under religious vows of seclusion. **monasterial** (-stiə´-) *a.* **monastic** (-nas´-) *a.* 1 of or relating to monks or monasteries. 2 resembling the way of life of a monastic community, reclusive, austere, celibate. 3 in bookbinding, applied to an antique style of tooling without gold. **monastical** *a.* **monastically** *adv.* **monasticism** (-nas´tisizm) *n.* the theory and system of the monastic life. **monasticize** (-nas´-), **monasticise** *v.t.* [med. L *monastērium*, Gr. *monastērion*, from *monazein*, to live alone, from *monos*, see MONAD]

monatomic (monətom´ik) *a.* (*Chem.*) having one atom in the molecule, monovalent.

monaural (monaw´rəl) *a.* 1 (of recorded sound) monophonic as distinct from stereophonic. 2 having or using one ear. **monaurally** *adv.*

monazite (mon´əzīt) *n.* a mineral consisting of a phosphate of thorium, cerium and lanthanum. [G *Monazit* from Gr. *monazō*, live alone]

mondaine (mõden´) *a.* 1 of fashionable society. 2 worldly. ~*n.* a person of fashionable society. [F, MUNDANE]

Monday (mŭn´dā, -di) *n.* the second day of the week, following Sunday. ~*adv.* (*coll.*) on Monday. **Mondayish** *a.* miserable, reluctant to start the week's work. **Mondays** *adv.* (*coll.*) on Mondays, each Monday. [OE *Mōnandæg* (*Mōnan*, gen. of *Mōna*, moon, DAY)]

Monegasque (monegask´) *a.* of or relating to the principality of Monaco. ~*n.* a native or inhabitant of Monaco. [F]

Monel (mō´nəl), **Monel metal** *n.* an alloy of nickel and copper with high tensile strength and resistance to corrosion. [A. *Monell*, d. 1921, president of a metal company]

monergism (mon´əjizm) *n.* (*Theol.*) the Lutheran doctrine that regeneration is entirely the work of the Holy Spirit, as distinct from *synergism*. [Gr. *ergon*, work, -ISM]

monetary (mŭn´itəri) *a.* of or relating to money or coinage. **monetarily** *adv.* **monetarism** *n.* the economic theory that advocates strict control of the money supply as the best method of regulating the economy. **monetarist** *n., a.* **monetize, monetise** *v.t.* 1 to give a standard value to (a metal) as currency. 2 to form into coin. **monetization** (-zā´shən) *n.* [L *monētārius*, from *monēta*, see MONEY]

money (mŭn´i) *n.* (*pl.* **moneys, monies**) 1 coin or other material used as medium of exchange. 2 banknotes, bills, notes of hand and other documents representing coin. 3 wealth, property, regarded as convertible into coin. 4 (*with pl.*) coins of a particular country or denomination. 5 (*pl.*) sums of money, receipts or payments. **for my money** in my opinion. **in the money** having or having won a lot of money. **money for jam** (*coll.*) money made with little effort. **money for old rope** (*coll.*) money made with little effort. **money to burn** more money than one needs. **to make money** MAKE[1]. **to put money into** to invest in. **to throw good money after bad** THROW. **moneybags** *n.* a rich or miserly person. **money box** *n.* a box with a slit through which savings or contributions are put in. **money broker** *n.* a person who carries out transactions in money for others, i.e. banking, loans, exchange etc. **money changer** *n.* a person who changes foreign money at a fixed rate. **moneyed** *a.* 1 rich. 2 consisting of money. **moneyer** *n.* 1 a banker. 2 an authorized coiner of money. **money-grubber** *n.* a person who greedily saves or amasses money. **money-grubbing** *n.* **moneylender** *n.* a person whose business is to lend money at interest. **moneylending** *n., a.* **moneyless** *a.* **moneymaking** *n., a.* highly profitable (business). **moneymaker** *n.* 1 a person who earns a lot of money. 2 a project, idea etc. that makes a lot of money. **money market** *n.* the field of operation of dealers in stocks etc., the financial world. **money matter** *n.* an affair involving money. **money of account** *n.* a denomination not actually coined, but used for convenience in keeping accounts, e.g. the guinea. **money order** *n.* an order for money, granted at one post office and payable at another. **money spider** *n.* a small spider, esp. of the family Linyphiidae, supposed to bring financial luck. **money-spinner** *n.* a thing that makes a good profit. **money supply** *n.* the total amount of money in a country's economy at a given time. **money's-worth** *n.* full value, an equivalent for money paid. **money to burn** *n.* more money than one needs. **moneywort** *n.* a trailing plant, *Lysimachia nummularia*, with round glossy leaves. [ME and OF *moneie* (F *monnaie*), L *monēta*, mint, money, orig. name of Juno in whose temple money was coined]

monger (mŭng´gə) *n.* a trader, a dealer (now only in comb., as *ironmonger, scandalmonger*). [OE *mangere*, from *mangian*, to traffic, from L *mango*, a dealer]

Mongol (mong´gəl) *n.* **1** a member of an Asian people now inhabiting Mongolia. **2** (*offensive*) (**mongol**) a person with Down's syndrome. ~*a.* **1** of or relating to the Mongols. **2** (*offensive*) (**mongol**) of, relating to or having Down's syndrome. **Mongolian** (-gō´-) *a.* **1** of or relating to Mongolia or the Mongols. **2** †Mongoloid. ~*n.* **1** a native or inhabitant of Mongolia. **2** the language of the Mongols or of Mongolia. **3** †a Mongoloid person. **mongolism** *n.* (*offensive*) Down's syndrome. **Mongoloid, mongoloid** *a.* **1** characteristic of or resembling the Mongolians, esp. in broad facial features and yellowish complexion. **2** (*offensive*) (**mongoloid**) having Down's syndrome. ~*n.* **1** a Mongoloid person. **2** (*offensive*) (**mongoloid**) a person with Down's syndrome. [Mongolian]

Usage note The use of *mongol, mongolism* etc. with reference to Down's syndrome gives offence, and is best avoided.

mongoose (mong´goos) *n.* (*pl.* **mongooses**) any of various small civet-like mammals of the family Viverridae, esp. of the genus *Herpestes*, found in Africa, S Europe and SE Asia, which feed on venomous snakes. [Marathi *mangūs*]

mongrel (mŭng´grəl) *n.* **1** anything, esp. a dog, of mixed breed. **2** (*offensive*) a person of mixed racial origin. ~*a.* **1** of mixed breed, arising from the crossing of two varieties. **2** of mixed nature or character. **mongrelism** *n.* **mongrelize, mongrelise** *v.t.* **mongrelization** (-zā´shən) *n.* **mongrelly** *adv.* [prob. cogn. with OE *mang*, a mixture]

'mongst (mŭngst) *prep.* (*poet.*) among. [shortening of *amongst*]

monial (mō´niəl) *n.* (*Archit.*) a mullion. [OF, etym. unknown]

monies MONEY.

moniker (mon´ikə), **monicker, monniker** *n.* (*sl.*) a name. [etym. unknown]

moniliform (mənil´ifawm) *a.* (*Anat., Zool.*) shaped like a necklace or string of beads. [L *monīle*, necklace]

monism (mon´izm) *n.* (*Philos.*) **1** the doctrine that all existing things and activities are forms or manifestations of one ultimate principle or substance. **2** any philosophic theory such as idealism, pantheism or materialism, opposed to dualism. **monist** *n.* **monistic** (-nis´-) *a.* [Gr. *monos*, one]

monition (mənish´ən) *n.* **1** (*poet.*) a warning (of). **2** an intimation or notice. **3** (*Law*) a summons or citation in a civil action. **4** a formal letter from a bishop or court warning a member of the clergy to abstain from certain practices. **monitive** (mon´-) *a.* [F, from L *monitio -ōnem*, from *monēre*, to warn]

monitor (mon´itə) *n.* **1** a television screen used e.g. in a studio or with a computer for displaying and checking pictures or information. **2 a** (*Hist.*) a senior pupil appointed to keep order in a school or to look after junior classes. **b** a pupil given a particular area of responsibility within a class. **3** a person who warns or admonishes. **4** a person whose duty it is to listen to foreign or other broadcasts. **5** any large tropical lizard of the genus *Varanus* found in Asia, Africa and Australia. **6** a detector for radioactivity. **7** (*Hist.*) an ironclad ship of low draught having revolving turrets. ~*v.t., v.i.* **1** to maintain regular surveillance on (a situation). **2** to listen to (radio broadcasts) in order to glean information. **monitorial** (-taw´-) *a.* **monitorially** *adv.* **monitorship** *n.* **monitory** *a.* giving warning or admonition. ~*n.* (*pl.* **monitories**) a warning or admonition from a bishop, Pope etc. **monitress** *n.* a female monitor.

monk (mŭngk) *n.* a member of a religious community of men, living apart under vows of poverty, chastity and obedience. **monkdom** *n.* **monkery** *n.* (*pl.* **monkeries**) (*derog.*) **1** monasticism. **2** a monkish practice. **3** monks collectively. **monkfish** *n.* **1** any of various angler fish of the genus *Lophius*, esp. *L. piscatorius*. **2** the angel-shark, *Squatina squatina*. **monkhood, monkship** *n.* **monkshood** *n.* a plant of the genus *Aconitum*, esp. *A. napellus* (from its hooded sepals). [OE *munec, munuc*, L and Gr. *monachos*, from *monos*, alone]

monkey (mŭng´ki) *n.* (*pl.* **monkeys**) **1** a long-tailed quadrumanous mammal of various species and families ranging from the anthropoid apes to the lemurs. **2** (*coll.*) a rogue, an imp, a mischievous child. **3** an ape, a mimic. **4** a monkey engine. **5** a monkey-jar. **6** (*sl.*) a sum of £500 or $500. ~*v.i.* (*3rd pers. sing. pres.* **monkeys,** *pres.p.* **monkeying,** *past, p.p.* **monkeyed**) **1** to meddle or interfere (with). **2** to play foolish or mischievous tricks. ~*v.t.* to mimic, to ape. **to get/ put someone's monkey up** (*coll.*) to make angry, to enrage. **to have a monkey on one's back** to be a drug addict. **to make a monkey of** to cause to seem foolish. **monkey bars** *n.pl.* a children's climbing frame. **monkey block** *n.* a single block strapped to a swivel. **monkey bread** *n.* the fruit of the baobab tree, *Adansonia digitata*. **monkey business** *n.* (*coll.*) **1** devious or underhand behaviour. **2** mischievous behaviour. **monkey engine** *n.* a pile-driving machine. **monkey flower** *n.* a plant of the genus *Mimulus*, esp. *M. cardinalis*. **monkeyish** *a.* **monkeyishness** *n.* **monkeyism** *n.* behaviour like that of a monkey. **monkey-jacket** *n.* a short, close-fitting jacket worn by sailors etc. **monkey-jar** *n.* a globular earthenware vessel used in tropical countries for cooling water. **monkey-nut** *n.* a peanut. **monkey-puzzle, monkey-puzzle tree** *n.* the Chile pine, *Araucaria araucana*, having spiny leaves and branches. **monkey-rail** *n.* a light rail running above the quarter-rail of a ship. **monkeyshines** *n.pl.* (*N Am.*) monkey tricks. **monkey suit** *n.* a dinner suit, evening dress. **monkey tricks** *n.pl.* mischievous pranks etc. **monkey wrench** *n.* a spanner with a movable jaw. **monkeywrench** *v.t.* to sabotage, esp. as a protest. **monkeywrenching** *n.* [prob. from LG]

monniker MONIKER.

mono (mon´ō) *n., a.* monophonic (sound).

mono- (mon´ō), **mon-** (mon) *comb.form* alone, single, as in *monograph, monosyllable*. [Gr. *monos*]

monoacid (monōas´id), **monacid** (monas´id) *a.* (*Chem.*) capable of saturating one molecule of monobasic acid, having only one hydroxide ion per molecule.

monobasic (monōbā´sik) *a.* (*Chem.*) (of an acid) with one base or replaceable atom.

monocardian (monōkah´diən) *a.* having a single undivided heart.

monocarpic (monōkah´pik), **monocarpous** (-pəs) *a.* (*Bot.*) bearing fruit only once, and dying after fructification. **monocarp** (mon´-) *n.* a monocarpic plant.

monocausal (monōkaw´zəl) *a.* attributing or assuming a single cause.
monocephalous (monōsef´ələs, -kef´-) *a.* **1** having one head. **2** (*Bot.*) having a single head of flowers.
monoceros (mənos´ərəs) *n.* (*pl.* **monoceroses**) a one-horned creature, the unicorn. **monocerous** *a.* [Gr. *keras*, a horn]
monochlamydeous (monōkləmid´iəs) *a.* (*Bot.*) (of a flower) having a single floral envelope, as a calyx, but no corolla. [see CHLAMYDIA]
monochord (mon´əkawd) *n.* a musical instrument with one string for determining the ratios of musical intervals.
monochromatic (monōkrəmat´ik) *a.* **1** (*Physics*) (of light) presenting rays of one colour only. **2** painted etc. in monochrome. **monochromatically** *a.* **monochromatism** *n.* **monochromator** (-krō´-) *n.* (*Physics*) a spectroscope capable of segregating for use a narrow portion of spectrum. **monochrome** (mon´əkrōm) *n.* **1** a painting in tints of one colour only. **2** any representation in one colour. ~*a.* monochromic. **monochromic** *a.* executed in one colour. **monochromy** (mon´-) *n.*
monocle (mon´əkəl) *n.* an eyeglass for one eye.
monoclinal (monōklī´nəl) *a.* (*Geol.*) (of strata) dipping continuously in one direction. **monocline** *n.* a monoclinal fold, a hogback. **monoclinic** (-klin´-), **monoclinate** (-nət) *a.* (of a crystal) having two oblique axes and a third at right angles to these. [Gr. *klinein*, to bend]
monoclinous (monōklī´nəs) *a.* **1** (*Bot.*) having male and female reproductive organs on the same flower, as distinct from *diclinous*. **2** (*Geol.*) monoclinal. [Gr. *klinē*, couch]
monoclonal (monōklō´nəl) *a.* forming a single clone, deriving from a single cell. **monoclonal antibody** *n.* an antibody composed of cells derived from a single cell.
monocoque (mon´əkok) *n.* **1** in an aircraft, a form of streamlined fuselage shaped like an elongated egg. **2** an aeroplane with such a fuselage. **3** a car or vehicle with a body and chassis manufactured as an integrated structure. **4** a boat with a hull all made of one piece.
monocotyledon (monōkotilē´dən), **monocot** (mon´-) *n.* (*Bot.*) a plant having a single cotyledon. **monocotyledonous** *a.*
monocracy (monok´rəsi) *n.* government by a single person. **monocrat** (mon´əkrat) *n.* **monocratic** (-krat´-) *a.*
monocular (monok´ūlə) *a.* **1** one-eyed. **2** for use with one eye only. **monocularly** *adv.* [late L *monoculus*, see MONOCLE]
monoculture (mon´əkŭlchə) *n.* **1** the cultivation of a single type of crop. **2** an area where a single type of crop is grown.
monocycle (mon´əsīkəl) *n.* a unicycle.
monocyte (mon´əsīt) *n.* the largest white blood cell in vertebrate blood.
monodactylous (monōdak´tiləs) *a.* having one finger, toe or claw. [Gr. *monodaktulos* (*daktulos*, finger)]
monodrama (mon´ədrahmə) *n.* a dramatic piece for one performer only. **monodramatic** (-drəmat´-) *a.*
monody (mon´ədi) *n.* (*pl.* **monodies**) **1** in Greek tragedy, an ode, usu. of a mournful character, for a single actor. **2** a song for one voice, or a musical composition in which one voice predominates. **3** a mournful or plaintive song or poetical composition, a threnody. **monodic** (mənod´-) *a.* **monodist** *n.*
monoecious (mənē´shəs) *a.* **1** (*Bot.*) belonging to the Monoecia, a class comprising plants in which the stamens and pistils are in distinct flowers. **2** having separate male and female flowers on the same plant. **3** (*Zool.*) hermaphrodite. [mod. L (Gr. *oikos*, house)]
monofil (mon´əfil), **monofilament** (-fil´əmənt) *n.* **1** a single strand of synthetic fibre. **2** a type of fishing line using this.
monogamy (mənog´əmi) *n.* **1** marriage to one wife or husband only at a time. **2** (*Zool.*) the habit of pairing with a single mate. **monogamist** *n.* **monogamous** *a.* **monogamously** *adv.* [F *monogamie*, L and Gr. *monogamia* (Gr. *gamos*, marriage)]
monogenesis (monōjen´əsis) *n.* **1** generation from one parent, asexual reproduction. **2** development of an organism from a parent resembling itself. **monogenetic** (-jinet´-) *n.* **monogenism** (mənoji´-), **monogeny** *n.* the doctrine that all human beings are descended from a single pair. **monogenist** *n.*
monoglot (mon´əglot) *a.* speaking only one language. ~*n.* a monoglot person. [Gr. *monoglōttos* (*glōtta*, tongue)]
monogony (mənog´əni) *n.* asexual propagation. [Gr. *-gonia*, begetting, from *gon-*, *gen-*, to beget]
monogram (mon´əgram) *n.* **1** a character composed of two or more letters interwoven. **2** a single character representing a word etc. **monogrammatic** (-mat´-) *a.* **monogrammed** *a.* [late L *monogramma*, Gr. *monogrammon*]
monograph (mon´əgrahf) *n.* a treatise on a single thing or class of things. ~*v.t.* to write a monograph (on). **monographer** (-nog´-), **monographist** *n.* **monographic** (-graf´-) *a.* **monographically** *adv.*
monogynous (monoj´inəs), **monogynian** (-ōjin´iən) *a.* **1** having only one wife at a time. **2** (*Bot.*) (of plants) having flowers with one pistil. **monogyn** (mon´-) *n.* (*Bot.*) a plant of this kind. **monogyny** (-noj´-) *n.* **1** the custom of having only one wife at a time. **2** the practice of mating with only one female. [mod. L, from *monogynus* (Gr. *gunē*, woman)]
monohull (mon´əhŭl) *n.* (*Naut.*) a vessel with a single hull as distinct from a catamaran, trimaran etc.
monohybrid (monōhī´brid) *n.* (*Biol.*) the offspring of two parents that differs with respect to the alleles of one gene.
monohydric (monōhī´drik) *a.* (*Chem.*) containing one hydroxyl group per molecule. [MONO, HYDROGEN, -IC]
monokini (mon´əkēni) *n.* a one-piece beach garment for a woman, usu. similar to the bottom half of a bikini. [MONO-, bi*kini*]
monolatry (mənol´ətri) *n.* worship of one god, esp. among many. **monolater, monolatrist** *n.* **monolatrous** *a.*
monolayer (mon´əleə) *n.* **1** (*Chem.*) a single layer of atoms or molecules adsorbed on a surface. **2** (*Biol.*, *Med.*) a tissue culture in a layer one cell thick.
monolingual (monōling´gwəl) *a.* using or expressed in only one language. **monolingualism** *n.*
monolith (mon´əlith) *n.* a monument or other structure formed of a single stone. **monolithic** (-lith´-) *a.* **1** of or like a monolith. **2** consisting of a large and undifferentiated whole, often entailing inflexibility. [F *monolithe* or L *monolithus*, Gr. *monolithos*, made of a single stone]
monologue (mon´əlog) *n.* **1** a dramatic scene in which a person speaks by themselves, a soliloquy. **2** a dramatic piece for one actor. **3** a long speech in conversation. **monologic** (-loj´-), **monological** *a.* **monologist** (-nol´əjist), **monologuist** (-gist) *n.* **monologize** (-nol´əjīz, -gīz), **monologise** *v.i.* †**monology** (-nol´-) *n.* (*pl.* **monologies**). [F, a person who likes to hear themselves talk, Gr. *monologos*]
monomania (monōmā´niə) *n.* an obsession of the mind on one subject only. **monomaniac** (-ak) *n.*, *a.* **monomaniacal** (-mənī´əkəl) *a.*
monomark (mon´əmahk) *n.* any of a system of combinations of numbers serving to identify property or manufactured goods.
monomer (mon´əmə) *n.* (*Chem.*) a compound that can undergo polymerization. **monomeric** (-mer´-) *a.* **monomerous** (-nom´-) *a.* (*Bot.*) (of flowers) having

one member in each whorl. [Gr. *monomerēs* (*meros*, part)]
monometallism (monōmet´əlizm) *n.* a one-metal standard of value for coinage. **monometallic** (-tal´-) *a.* **monometallist** *n.*
monometer (mənom´itə) *n.* **1** a verse consisting of one foot. **2** metre of this kind. **monometric** (-met´-) *a.* **1** in this metre. **2** (of crystals) having the axes equal or similar, isometric. [L, from Gr. *monometros*]
monomial (mənō´miəl) *n.* a mathematical expression consisting of a single term. *~a.* consisting of a single term.
monomolecular (monōməlek´ūlə) *a.* (*Chem.*) only one molecule in thickness.
monomorphic (monōmaw´fik), **monomorphous** (-fəs) *a.* having the same structure or morphological character, esp. throughout successive stages of development. **monomorphism** *n.*
mononuclear (monōnū´kliə) *a.* having only one nucleus.
mononucleosis (monōnūkliō´sis) *n.* (*Biol.*) the presence of an abnormally large number of monocytes in the blood. [MONO-, NUCLEO-, -OSIS]
monopetalous (monōpet´ələs) *a.* (*Bot.*) having the petals coherent in a single corolla.
monophagous (mənof´əgəs) *a.* (*Zool.*) feeding on only one type of food.
monophobia (monōfō´biə) *n.* morbid dread of being alone.
monophonic (monōfon´ik) *a.* (of sound) reproduced through only one electronic channel, monaural. **monophonically** *adv.*
monophthong (mo´nəfthong) *n.* **1** a simple or single vowel sound. **2** two written vowels pronounced as one. **monophthongal** (-thong´gəl) *a.* [Gr. *monophthongos* (*phthongos*, sound)]
monophyletic (monōfīlet´ik) *a.* of or relating to a single family or race or descended from one parental form. [Gr. *phuletikos*, from *phulē*, tribe]
monophyllous (monōfil´əs) *a.* having or formed of one leaf. [Gr. *phullon*, leaf]
Monophysite (mənof´isīt) *n.* a member of an Eastern 5th-cent. sect affirming that there is only one nature in the person of Christ. **monophysitic** (-sit´-) *a.* **monophysitism** *n.* [eccles. L *Monophysīta*, eccles. Gr. *Monophysītēs* (*phusis*, nature, from *phuein*, to generate, -ITE[1])]
monoplane (mon´əplān) *n.* an aircraft with one set of wings.
monoplegia (monōplē´jiə) *n.* (*Med.*) paralysis of a single part or limb. [Gr. *plēgē*, stroke]
monopod (mon´əpod) *n.* a structure with only one foot, e.g. a shooting stick. **monopode** (-pōd) *n.* **1** an animal having one foot. **2** a monopod. **3** any of a fabulous race of people having one foot with which they shaded themselves against the heat of the sun. [Gr. *pous podos*, foot]
monopole[1] (mon´əpōl) *n.* **1** (*Physics*) a single electrical charge or a magnetic pole considered in isolation. **2** a radio aerial consisting of one, usu. straight, element.
monopole[2] (mon´əpōl), **Monopole** *n.* champagne supplied exclusively to or by one shipper.
monopoly (mənop´əli) *n.* (*pl.* **monopolies**) **1** an exclusive trading right in a certain commodity or class of commerce or business. **2** this as conferred by government. **3** a company or combination enjoying this. **4** the subject of such a right. **5** exclusive possession, control or enjoyment (of). **6** (**Monopoly®**) a board game for two or more people, who throw dice to move their pieces round a board marked with the names of streets etc., the object being to accumulate capital through buying the property on which the pieces land. **monopolism** *n.* **monopolist** *n.* **monopolistic** (-lis´-) *a.* **monopolize**, **monopolise** *v.t.* **1** to obtain or possess a monopoly of. **2** to engross the whole of (attention, conversation etc.). **monopolization** (-zā´shən) *n.* [late L *monopōlium*, Gr. *monopōlion* (*pōleein*, to sell)]
monopteros (mənop´tərəs) *n.* (*pl.* **monopteroi** (-oi)) a circular temple composed of columns supporting a roof. **monopteral** *n.*, *a.* [late L *monopteros* (Gr. *pteron*, wing)]
monorail (mon´ərāl) *n.* a railway, usu. elevated, with a track consisting of a single rail.
monorchid (monaw´kid) *a.* (*Zool.*, *Med.*) having only one testicle. **monorchism** *n.* [Gr. *monorchis* (*orchis*, testicle)]
monorhyme (mon´ərīm) *n.* a composition in which all the lines end in the same rhyme. *~a.* having only one rhyme. [F *monorime*]
monosaccharide (monōsak´ərīd) *n.* (*Chem.*) a sugar that cannot be hydrolysed to form simpler sugars.
monosepalous (monōsep´ələs) *a.* (*Bot.*) having one sepal.
monoski (mon´əskē) *n.* a single ski on which both the skier's feet are placed. *~v.i.* to use a monoski. **monoskier** *n.* **monoskiing** *n.*
monosodium glutamate (monōsōdiəm gloo´təmāt) *n.* a salt of glutamic acid used as a flavour-enhancing food additive.
monospermous (monōspœ´məs) *a.* (*Bot.*) having only one seed. **monospermal** *a.* [Gr. *sperma*, seed]
monostich (mon´əstik) *n.* a single metrical line forming a complete composition, such as an epigram. *~a.* consisting of a single metrical line. **monostichous** (-nos´-) *a.* (of part of an animal or plant body etc.) having, arranged in or consisting of a single row or layer. [late L *monostichum*, Gr. *monostichon* (*stichos*, row)]
monostrophic (monōstrof´ik) *a.* in prosody, having only one form of strophe. [Gr. *monostrophikos*]
monostyle[1] (mon´əstīl) *a.* (*Archit.*) consisting of a single shaft. [Gr. *stulos*, pillar]
monostyle[2] (mon´əstīl) *a.* built in the same style throughout. **monostylar** (-stī´-) *a.* [STYLE]
monosyllable (mon´əsiləbəl) *n.* a word of one syllable. **in monosyllables** in simple direct words. **monosyllabic** (-lab´-) *a.* **1** (of a word) having one syllable. **2** speaking in words of a single syllable. **monosyllabically** *adv.* **monosyllabism** (-sil´-) *n.* **monosyllabize** (-sil´-), **monosyllabise** *v.t.*
monosymmetric (monōsimet´rik) *a.* (of a crystal) monoclinic. **monosymmetrical** *a.* (*Bot.*) divisible into symmetrical halves in only one plane. **monosymmetry** *n.*
monothalamous (monōthal´əməs) *a.* possessing a single chamber, as some shells. **monothalamic** (-lam´-) *a.* **1** monothalamous. **2** (*Bot.*) (of certain fruits) developed from a single pistil.
monotheism (mon´əthēizm) *n.* the doctrine that there is only one God. **monotheist** *n.* **monotheistic** (-is´-) *a.* **monotheistically** *adv.*
monotint (mon´ətint) *n.* a picture or other representation in one colour.
monotone (mon´ətōn) *n.* **1** continuance of or repetition in the same tone. **2** a succession of sounds of the same pitch. **3** intoning of words on a single note. *~a.* monotonous. *~v.t.*, *v.i.* to chant, recite or speak in the same tone or note. **monotonic** (-ton´-) *a.* **monotonically** *adv.* **monotonize** (-not´-), **monotonise** *v.t.* **monotonous** (mənot´-) *a.* **1** wearisome through sameness, tedious. **2** unvarying in pitch. **monotonously** *adv.* **monotony**, **monotonousness** *n.* [late Gr. *monotonos*, monotonous]
monotreme (mon´ətrēm) *n.* any mammal of the sub-class Monotremata, having only one aperture or vent for the genital organs and the excretions. *~a.* of the sub-class Monotremata. **monotrematous** *a.* [Gr. *trēma -atos*, perforation, hole]

monotype (mon´ətīp) *n.* an impression on paper produced by inking glass or metal. **Monotype®** *n.* a typesetting machine that casts and sets single printing-types.
monotypic (monōtip´ik) *a.* (of a genus etc.) having only one type of animal or plant.
monounsaturated (monōŭnsach´ərātid) *a.* (*Chem.*) (of a compound, esp. oils, fats etc.) saturated except for one multiple bond.
monovalent (monōvā´lənt) *a.* UNIVALENT.
monoxide (mənok´sīd) *n.* (*Chem.*) an oxide containing one atom of oxygen in combination with a radical. **monox-, monoxy-** *comb. form*
monozygotic (monəzīgot´ik) *a.* (*Biol.*) from a single zygote.
Monroe doctrine (mŭnrō´) *n.* the principle that non-American powers should not intervene in affairs in either of the American continents, formulated by Monroe in 1823. [James *Monroe*, 1758–1831, US President, 1816–25]
Monseigneur (monse´nyœ, mō-) *n.* (*pl.* **Messeigneurs** (māsenyœ´)) a French title of honour given to high dignitaries, esp. in the Church. [F *mon*, my, SEIGNEUR]
Monsieur (məsyœ´, mis-) *n.* (*pl.* **Messieurs**) **1** the French title of address, Mr or Sir. **2** a Frenchman. [F *mon*, my, *sieur*, lord]
Monsignor (monsē´nyə) *n.* (*pl.* **Monsignori** (-yaw´ri)) a title given to Roman Catholic prelates, officers of the Pope's court and others. [It.]
monsoon (monsoon´) *n.* **1** a wind in SW Asia and the Indian Ocean. **2** any of various other periodical winds. **dry monsoon** DRY. **wet monsoon** WET. **monsoonal** *a.* [MDut. *monssoen*, Port. *monção*, Arab. *mausim*, time, season]
mons pubis (monz pū´bis) *n.* (*Anat.*) the mound of subcutaneous fatty tissue lying over the joint of the pubic bones. [L, hill of the pubis]
monster (mon´stə) *n.* **1** something misshapen, abnormal, out of the ordinary course of nature, a deformed creature. **2** an imaginary animal, usually compounded of incongruous parts, such as a centaur, griffin, mermaid, gorgon etc. **3** an abominably cruel or depraved person. **4** a person, animal or thing of extraordinary size. *~a.* of extraordinary size, huge. **monsterful** *a.* [OF *monstre*, L *monstrum*, a portent or omen, from *monēre*, to warn]
monstera (monstē´rə) *n.* any climbing plant of the genus *Monstera*, esp. *M. deliciosa*, the Swiss cheese plant. [perh. from L *monstrum*, monster]
monstrance (mon´strəns) *n.* an open or transparent vessel in which the Host is carried in procession or exposed for adoration, esp. in a Roman Catholic church. [OF, from med. L *monstrantia*, from *monstrāre*, to show]
monstrous (mon´strəs) *a.* **1** unnatural in form. **2** out of the ordinary course of nature. **3** enormous, huge. **4** shocking, atrocious, outrageous. **5** absurd, incredible. *~†adv.* extraordinarily, very, exceedingly. **monstrosity** (-stros´-) *n.* (*pl.* **monstrosities**) **1** a monster. **2** a deformity, a distortion. **3** the quality of being monstrous. **monstrously** *adv.* **monstrousness** *n.* [OF *monstreux*, late L *monstrōsus*, from *monstrum*, MONSTER]
mons Veneris (monz ven´əris) *n.* (*pl.* **montes Veneris** (mon´tēz)) the pad of fatty tissue over the pubic bone of the human female. [L, mount of Venus]
Mont. *abbr.* Montana.
montage (montahzh´) *n.* **1** the cutting and assembling of shots taken when making a film, video etc. **2** a sequence of such shots. **3** an artistic, literary or musical work consisting of heterogeneous elements in juxtaposition.
montagnard (mōtanyah´) *n.* (*pl.* **montagnard, montagnards**) **1** an inhabitant of mountain country. **2** (*Hist.*) a member of the 'Mountain' or extreme democratic wing in the French Revolutionary Legislative Assembly (1791–92). [F, from *montagne*, MOUNTAIN]
Montagu's harrier (mon´təgūz) *n.* a migratory Eurasian bird of prey, *Circus pygarguas*, having long wings and tail. [G. *Montagu*, 1751–1815, British naturalist]
montane (mon´tān) *a.* of or relating to mountainous regions. [L *montānus*, from *mons montis*, MOUNT²]
montbretia (montbrē´shiə) *n.* a bulbous-rooted plant with orange flowers of the genus *Crocosmia*. [A. F. E. Coquebert de *Montbret*, 1780–1801, French botanist]
monte (mon´ti) *n.* **1** a Spanish game of chance with 45 cards, resembling faro. **2** in Latin America, a tract of wooded country. **three-card monte** THREE. [Sp., mountain, as MOUNT²]
Monte Carlo method (monti kah´lō) *n.* in statistics, the use of random sampling of numbers to estimate the solution to mathematical problems. [*Monte Carlo* in Monaco, noted for its casino]
montero (monteə´rō) *n.* (*pl.* **monteros**) a Spanish huntsman's cap with flaps and a round crown. [Sp., a huntsman, a mountaineer, from *monte*, MOUNT²]
Montessori method (montisaw´ri) *n.* a system of teaching the very young, in which physical activity, individual tuition and early attention to writing are main features. [Dr Maria *Montessori*, 1870–1952]
montes Veneris MONS VENERIS.
Montezuma's revenge (montizū´məz) *n.* (*sl., facet.*) acute diarrhoea, esp. as suffered by travellers in Mexico. [*Montezuma* II, 1466–1520, Aztec emperor]
month (mŭnth) *n.* **1** each of the twelve parts into which the year is divided, orig. the period of one revolution of the moon round the earth, a calendar month. **2** a period of four weeks. **monthly** *a.* **1** done in or continuing for a month. **2** happening or payable once a month. *~adv.* once a month. *~n.* (*pl.* **monthlies**) **1** a periodical published every month. **2** (*pl.*) menstruation. **month of Sundays** *n.* an indefinitely long period. [OE *mōnath* (cp. Dut. *maand*, G *Monat*, Icel. *mānuthr*, also L *mensis*), cogn. with MOON]
monticule (mon´tikūl), **monticle** (-kəl) *n.* a little hill, a mound, a hillock, esp. a small volcanic cone. [F *monticule*, late L *monticulus*, dim. of *mons -tem*, MOUNT²]
montmorillonite (montməril´ənīt) *n.* (*Geol.*) a soft clayey mineral, a hydrated aluminium silicate, the chief constituent of bentonite and fuller's earth. [*Montmorillon* in France]
monument (mon´ūmənt) *n.* **1** anything by which the memory of persons or things is preserved, esp. a building or permanent structure. **2** anything that serves as a memorial of a person, event or of past times. **3** a document, a record. **4** a distinctive mark. **5** (*N Am.*) a natural or artificial landmark. **6** †a tomb. **7** †a statue, an effigy. **monumental** (-men´-) *a.* **1** of or serving as a monument. **2** stupendous, colossal. **3** lasting. **monumentalism** *n.* **1** the style of monuments. **2** building on a massive scale. **monumentality** (-tal´-) *n.* **monumentalize** (-men´-), **monumentalise** *v.t.* to commemorate with a monument. **monumentally** *adv.* **monumental mason** *n.* a stonemason who engraves and erects tombstones etc. [L *monumentum*, from *monēre*, to remind]
-mony (məni) *suf.* forming nouns, esp. denoting abstract concepts, as in *ceremony*, *matrimony*, *parsimony*. [L *-monium*, *-monia*]
moo (moo) *v.i.* (*3rd pers. sing. pres.* **moos,** *pres.p.* **mooing,** *past, p.p.* **mooed**) to make the vocal noise of cattle, to make a noise like a cow. *~n.* the sound 'moo'. **moo cow** *n.* a cow (used by or to children). [imit.]
mooch (mooch) *v.i.* (*coll.*) **1** to wander aimlessly, amble. **2** to beg. *~v.t.* **1** to cadge. **2** to steal. **moocher** *n.* [prob. from F *muchier*, to lurk, hide]
mood¹ (mood) *n.* **1** a state of mind, disposition, humour.

2 the expression of mood in art, literature etc. ~*a.* expressing a mood. **in a mood** experiencing a period of sulkiness, gloom, withdrawal etc. **in the mood** inclined (to or for), in a positive state of mind. **moody** *a.* (*comp.* **moodier,** *superl.* **moodiest**) 1 indulging in unpredictable moods, temperamental. 2 peevish, sullen, out of temper. ~*n.* (*pl., coll.*) a bad mood, temper tantrum etc. **moodily** *adv.* **moodiness** *n.* [OE *mōd* (cp. Dut. *moed*, Icel. *mōthr*, Dan. and Swed. *mod*, G *Mut*)]

mood[2] (mood) *n.* 1 (*Gram.*) a verb form expressing the manner in which the act, event or fact is conceived, whether as actual, contingent, possible, desirable etc. 2 (*Logic*) the nature of the connection between antecedent and consequent in a proposition, modality. 3 (*Logic*) the form of a syllogism with regard to the quantity and quality of the propositions. 4 (*Mus.*) a mode. [var. of MODE, assim. to MOOD[1]]

Moog® (moog, mōg), **Moog synthesizer, Moog synthesiser** *n.* an electronic keyboard instrument producing a variety of sounds. [Robert *Moog*, born 1934, US engineer]

moolah (moo´lə) *n.* (*sl.*) money. [etym. unknown]

mooli (moo´li) *n.* (*pl.* **moolis**) a large white root vegetable like a radish. [Hind. *mūlī*, from Sansk. *mūla*, root]

moolvi (mool´vi), **moolvie** *n.* (*pl.* **moolvis, moolvies**) 1 a Muslim doctor of law. 2 a learned or respected person, a teacher. [Urdu]

moon (moon) *n.* 1 the earth's satellite revolving round it monthly. 2 the satellite of any planet. 3 anything shaped like a moon or crescent. 4 (*poet.*) a lunar month. ~*v.i.* 1 to wander (about) or stare in a listless manner. 2 (*sl.*) to expose one's buttocks to others. ~*v.t.* to pass (time) in a listless manner. **man in the moon** MAN. **many moons ago** a long time ago. **over the moon** very pleased or happy. **to cry for the moon** CRY. **moonbeam** *n.* a ray of light reflected from the moon. **moon-blind** *a.* 1 suffering from nyctalopia. 2 blinded by the moon. **moon blindness** *n.* nyctalopia, mooneye. **moon boot** *n.* a tall thickly-padded boot for wearing in low temperatures. **mooncalf** *n.* (*pl.* **mooncalves**) 1 a blockhead, a born fool. 2 a monstrosity. 3 a false conception. **moon daisy, moon-flower** *n.* the ox-eye daisy. **mooned** *a.* 1 shaped like the moon, crescent-shaped. 2 moonlit. **mooneye** *n.* 1 nyctalopia. 2 any of several N American freshwater fish of the family Hiodontidae. **moon-eyed** *a.* 1 round-eyed, as in awe. 2 suffering from moon blindness. **moon-faced** *a.* having a round face. **moonfish** *n.* (*pl.* **moonfish**) any fish that is silvery and disc-shaped, e.g. the opah or the platy. **moon-glade** *n.* the track of moonlight on water. **moonless** *a.* **moonlight** *n.* the light of the moon. ~*a.* moonlit. ~*v.i.* (*past, p.p.* **moonlighted**) to have a part-time job in the evening as well as full-time work during the day. **moonlighter** *n.* 1 a person in full-time work who has a second, part-time job (in the evening). 2 (*Hist.*) a member of gangs of ruffians who committed violent nocturnal outrages on tenants in Ireland who had transgressed the mandates of the Land League. **moonlight flit** *n.* a removal of household furniture after dark to escape paying rent etc. **moonlighting** *n.* **moonlit** *a.* **moonquake** *n.* a light tremor detected on the surface of the moon. **moonraker** *n.* a foolish person (from the Wiltshire legend that some rustics mistook the reflection of the moon in the water for a cheese). **moonrise** *n.* 1 the rising of the moon. 2 the time of this. **moonscape** *n.* 1 the surface or landscape of the moon. 2 a desolate landscape similar to this. **moonseed** *n.* a plant of the genus *Menispermum*. **moonset** *n.* 1 the setting of the moon. 2 the time of this. **moonshine** *n.* 1 moonlight. 2 unreality, visionary ideas, nonsense. 3 smuggled or illicitly-distilled spirits. **moonshiner** *n.* 1 an illicit distiller. 2 a smuggler, esp. of spirits. **moonshiny** *a.* **moonshot** *n.* the launching of a spacecraft to the moon. **moonstone** *n.* a variety of feldspar with whitish or opalescent reflections. **moonstruck, moon-stricken** *a.* 1 mentally deranged. 2 fanciful, sentimental. 3 affected by the moon. **moonwort** *n.* 1 any fern of the genus *Botrychium*, esp. *B. lunaria*, grape fern. 2 the honesty, *Lunaria annua.* **moony** *a.* (*comp.* **moonier,** *superl.* **mooniest**) 1 like the moon. 2 crescent-shaped. 3 like moonlight. 4 moonstruck, listless, dreamy, silly. 5 (*sl.*) tipsy. **moonily** *adv.* **mooniness** *n.* [OE *mōna* (cp. Dut. *maan*, Icel. *māni*, Goth. *mēna*, G *Mond*), cogn. with Gr. *mēnē*, L *mensis*, MONTH]

Moonie (moo´ni) *n.* (*coll.*) a member of the Unification Church, whose followers give all their possessions to it and live in communes. [Sun Myung *Moon*, Korean industrialist, who founded the Church in 1954]

moonshee (moon´shi), **munshi** *n.* a secretary, teacher of languages or interpreter in the Indian subcontinent. [Hind.]

Moor (maw, muə) *n.* a member of a mixed Berber and Arab people inhabiting Morocco and the adjoining parts of NW Africa. **Moorish** *a.* **Moorish idol** *n.* a brightly-coloured tropical fish, *Zanclus canescens*, common in the Pacific esp. around coral reefs. [F *More*, L and Gr. *Maurus*, etym. uncertain]

moor[1] (maw, muə) *v.t.* to secure (a ship, boat etc.) with chains, ropes or cable and anchor. ~*v.i.* 1 to secure a ship in this way, to anchor. 2 to lie at anchor or secured by cables etc. **moorage** *n.* **mooring** *n.* 1 (*usu. pl.*) the place where a ship is moored. 2 anchors, chains etc. by which a ship is moored. **mooring-mast** *n.* a tower for mooring an airship to. [prob. from an unrecorded OE *mārian* (cp. *mǣrels*, mooring-rope, and MDut. *maren*, to tie)]

moor[2] (maw, muə) *n.* a tract of wild open land, esp. if overgrown with heather. **moorcock** *n.* the male of the red grouse. **moorfowl** *n.* the red grouse *Lagopus scoticus.* **moor game** *n.* the red grouse. **moorhen** *n.* 1 a small water bird, *Gallinula chloropus*, with black plumage and a red bill. 2 the female of the moorfowl. **moorish** *a.* **moorland** *n.* an expanse of moor. ~*a.* of or relating to moorland, living on moorland. **moorman, moorsman** *n.* (*pl.* **moormen, moorsmen**) a native or inhabitant of a moor. **moorswoman** *n.* (*pl.* **moorswomen**) a female native or inhabitant of a moor. **moory** *a.* (*comp.* **moorier,** *superl.* **mooriest**). [OE *mōr* (cp. Dut. *moer*, G *Moor*)]

moose (moos) *n.* (*pl.* **moose**) the elk, *Alces alces*, inhabiting the colder parts of N America. [Algonquian *musu*]

moot (moot) *v.t.* 1 to raise for discussion, to suggest. 2 †to debate. ~*v.i.* to argue or plead on a supposed case. ~*a.* open to discussion or argument. ~*n.* 1 (*Hist.*) an assembly of freemen in a township, tithing etc. 2 a law students' debate on a supposed case. **moot court** *n.* a meeting in an inn of court for discussing points of law. **mooter** *n.* **moot hall** *n.* 1 a hall of meeting. 2 a town hall. 3 a hall for courts. **moot point, moot case** *n.* 1 a debatable point or case. 2 an open question. [OE *mōtian*, rel. to *gemōt*, an assembly (cp. Dut. *gemoet*)]

mop[1] (mop) *n.* 1 a bundle of rags, yarn etc. or a pad of synthetic material fastened to a long handle, and used for cleaning floors etc. 2 a thick mass, as of hair. 3 (*Hist.*) a mop-fair. ~*v.t.* (*pres.p.* **mopping,** *past, p.p.* **mopped**) to wipe or soak up moisture from with a mop etc. **to mop the floor with someone** FLOOR. **to mop up** 1 to wipe up with or as with a mop. 2 to clear (a place) of enemy troops etc. 3 (*sl.*) to seize, to appropriate, to get hold of. 4 to dispatch, to finish off. **mopboard** *n.* (*N Am.*) a skirting board. **mop-fair** *n.* (*Hist.*) an annual fair at which servants were hired. **mophead** *n.* 1 a thick head of hair. 2 a person with such a head. 3 the head of a mop. **moppy** *a.* (*comp.* **moppier,** *superl.* **moppiest**). [15th cent. *mappe*, L *mappa*, see NAPKIN]

†**mop**[2] (mop) *v.i.* (*pres.p.* **mopping,** *past, p.p.* **mopped**) to make wry faces or grimaces. ~*n.* a grimace, a wry face. **mops and mows** grimaces. [prob. imit. of pouting]

mope (mōp) *v.i.* to be dull or dispirited. ~*v.t.* (*usu. refl., p.p.*) to make dull or dispirited. ~*n.* **1** a person who mopes. **2** (*pl.*) ennui, the blues. **moper** *n.* **mopy** *a.* (*comp.* **mopier,** *superl.* **mopiest**). **mopily** *adv.* **mopiness** *n.* [etym. uncertain]

moped (mō´ped) *n.* a motorized pedal cycle, of less than 50cc.

mopoke (mō´pōk), **morepork** (maw´pawk) *n.* **1** a small brown spotted owl, *Ninox novaseelandiae*, the boobook, native to Australia and New Zealand. **2** (*Austral.*) an insect-eating bird, *Podargus strigoides*, the frogmouth. [imit. of cry]

moppet (mop´it) *n.* **1** a pet, a darling (applied to children, young girls etc.). **2** a small shaggy type of dog. [perh. dim. of MOP[2]]

moquette (moket´) *n.* a woven fabric of wool and hemp or linen with a velvety pile, used for carpets and upholstery. [F, etym. uncertain]

MOR *abbr.* middle-of-the-road (of music).

mor (maw) *n.* (*Geol.*) acidic humus formed where decomposition is slow. [Dan.]

mora (maw´rə) *n.* (*pl.* **morae** (-rē), **moras**) in prosody, a unit of time equal to a short syllable. [L]

moraine (mərān´) *n.* the debris of rocks brought down by glaciers. **morainal, morainic** *a.* [F]

moral (mor´əl) *a.* **1** of or relating to character and conduct in terms of the distinction between right and wrong. **2** conforming to or regulated by what is right, good, virtuous, esp. in sexual relations. **3** subject to the rules of morality, distinguishing between right and wrong. **4** based on morality. **5** concerned with or treating of conduct or morality. **6** conveying a moral. **7** practical, virtual, in spirit (*a moral victory*). **8** (esp. of support) psychological rather than practical. ~*n.* **1** the moral lesson taught by a story, incident etc. **2** (*pl.*) moral habits, conduct, behaviour, esp. in sexual relations. **3** (*pl.*) ethics, moral science. **moral certainty** *n.* probability that leaves little doubt. **moral courage** *n.* fortitude in matters of life and conduct, esp. in resisting unjust or iniquitous opposition, ill-feeling, abuse etc., as opposed to physical courage. **moral defeat** *n.* an indecisive result or a partial success the moral effects of which are equivalent to defeat. **moral faculty** *n.* the capacity to distinguish between right and wrong. **moral high ground** *n.* in a discussion, dispute etc., the position which appears to be morally correct. **moralism** *n.* **1** morality distinguished from religion or divested of religious teaching. **2** †a moral maxim. **moralist** *n.* **1** a person who teaches morality. **2** a person who behaves in accordance with moral rules. **moralistic** (-lis´-) *a.* **moralistically** *adv.* **morality** (-ral´-) *n.* (*pl.* **moralities**) **1** the doctrine, principles or practice of moral duties, moral science, ethics. **2** morals, moral conduct, esp. in sexual relations. **3** moralizing. **4** a morality play. **morality play** *n.* (*Hist.*) a kind of drama (popular in the 16th cent.) in which the characters represent virtues, vices etc. **moralize, moralise** *v.i.* to make moral reflections (on). ~*v.t.* **1** to provide with moral lessons. **2** to interpret or apply in a moral sense. **3** to render moral. **moralization** (-zā´shən) *n.* **moralizer** *n.* **moralizingly** *adv.* **moral judgement** *n.* judgement as to the rightness or wrongness of an act. **moral law** *n.* the rules of right and wrong which any right course of action must satisfy. **morally** *adv.* **1** according to morality. **2** practically, virtually. **moral majority** *n.* (*esp. N Am.*) the majority of the country's population, regarded as acting on and favouring adherence to strict moral principles. **moral philosophy** *n.* ethics. **moral pressure** *n.* an attempt to persuade by appealing to a person's sense of morality. **Moral Rearmament** *n.* **1** the principles of the Oxford Group. **2** the movement to promote these. **moral science** *n.* a systematic study and knowledge of moral issues. **moral sense** *n.* the ability to judge what is right and wrong in one's conduct. **moral victory** *n.* an indecisive result or a partial success the moral effects of which are equivalent to victory. [F, from L *mōrālis*, from *mōs mōris*, custom]

morale (mərahl´) *n.* **1** mental or moral condition. **2** courage and endurance in supporting fatigue, danger or other threats to one's mental well-being. [as MORAL, to show F pronunc.]

morass (məras´) *n.* **1** anything that is confused or complicated, esp. when it impedes progress. **2** a swamp, a bog. [Dut. *moeras*, earlier *moerasch*, OF *maresche*, MARISH]

moratorium (morətaw´riəm) *n.* (*pl.* **moratoriums, moratoria** (-riə)) **1** a deferment, delay or temporary suspension. **2** a legal act authorizing a debtor or bank to defer or suspend payment for a time. **3** the period of such a suspension. [L, from *morārī*, to delay, from MORA]

Moravian (mərā´viən) *a.* of or relating to Moravia, the Moravians or their dialect of Czech. ~*n.* **1** a member of a Protestant sect founded in Saxony in the 18th cent. by emigrants from Moravia adhering to the doctrines taught by John Hus, 1369–1415. **2** a native or inhabitant of Moravia. [*Moravia*, in the Czech Republic]

moray (mor´ā) *n.* any brightly-patterned coastal eel of the family Muraenidae, esp. *Muraena helena*. [Port. *moreia*, L *mūraena*, Gr. *muraina*]

morbid (maw´bid) *a.* **1** unhealthily preoccupied with unpleasant matters, esp. with death. **2** (*Med.*) sickly, unhealthy, diseased. **3** pathological. **morbid anatomy** *n.* the anatomy of diseased organs, tissues etc. **morbidity** (-bid´-) *n.* **1** (*Med.*) unhealthiness, prevalence of morbid conditions. **2** morbidness. **morbidly** *adv.* **morbidness** *n.* **morbific** (-bif´-) *a.* producing disease. [L *morbidus*, from *morbus*, disease]

morbilli (mawbil´ī) *n.pl.* **1** (*Med.*) measles. **2** the spots associated with measles. **morbilliform, morbillous** *a.* **1** like morbilli. **2** like measles. [L, pustules, from *morbus*, disease]

morceau (mawsō´) *n.* (*pl.* **morceaux** (-sō´)) **1** a small piece. **2** a short literary or musical composition. [F]

mordant (maw´dənt) *a.* **1** biting, caustic, pungent. **2** causing pain or smarting. **3** serving to fix colours etc. ~*n.* **1** a substance for fixing colouring matter in dyeing. **2** an adhesive substance used in applying gold leaf. **3** acid or other corrosive used by etchers. **mordacious** (-dā´shəs) *a.* **1** biting, acrid. **2** sarcastic. **mordaciously** *adv.* **mordancy** *n.* **mordantly** *adv.* †**mordication** (-ā´shən) *n.* [F, pres.p. of *mordre*, L *mordēre*, to bite]

mordent (maw´dənt) *n.* **1** (*Mus.*) a rapid alternation of a note with the one immediately below it, a kind of trill. **2** the character indicating this. [G, from It. *mordente*, as MORDANT]

more (maw) *a.* **1** greater in quantity, extent, degree, number, importance etc. **2** additional, extra. ~*adv.* **1** in or to a greater degree, extent, or quantity (used to form comp. of most adjectives and adverbs of more than one syllable). **2** further, besides, again. ~*n.* **1** a greater quantity, amount, number or degree. **2** an additional quantity. **more and more** with continual increase. **more by token** as further proof. **more of** to a greater extent (*more of a director than an actor*). **more or less** **1** about. **2** thereabouts. **3** to a greater or less extent. **more so** to a greater extent or degree. **more's the pity** PITY. **more than** very. **more than meets the eye** MEET[1]. **no more** NO[2]. **the more the merrier** MERRY. **to be more like it** LIKE[1]. **moreish, morish** *a.* (*coll.*) (of food) causing one to want more, delicious. [OE *māra* (cp. MDut.

mêre, Icel. *meire*, Goth. *maiza*), from an adverbial form *maiz*, whence MO[2]]

moreen (mərēn´) *n.* a stout woollen or wool and cotton fabric for hangings etc. [etym. uncertain]

morel[1] (mərel´) *n.* an edible fungus, *Morchella esculenta*, and other species of *Morchella*. [F *morille*, prob. from Gmc.]

morel[2] (mərel´) *n.* the black nightshade, *Solanum nigrum*, and other nightshades of the family Solanaceae. [OF *morele*, It. *morello*, perh. from L *mōrum*, mulberry]

morello (mərel´ō) *n.* (*pl.* **morellos**) a bitter dark-red cherry. [prob. from It. *amarella*, dim. of L *amarus*, bitter, and It. *morello*, blackish]

moreover (mawrō´və) *adv.* besides, in addition, further.

morepork MOPOKE.

mores (maw´rāz) *n.pl.* the customs and conduct which embody the fundamental values of a social group. [L, pl. of *mōs*, custom]

†**Moresco** MORISCO.

Moresque (məresk´) *a.* Moorish in style and decoration. ~*n.* Moorish decoration, as the profusely ornamented work in the Alhambra. [F, from It. *Moresco*]

☒ **morgage** common misspelling of MORTGAGE.

morganatic (mawgənat´ik) *a.* of or relating to a marriage between a person of high rank and one of lower rank, by virtue of which the latter does not acquire the spouse's rank and, along with any children of the marriage, is not entitled to inherit the spouse's title or possessions. **morganatically** *adv.* [low L *morganātica*, MHG *morgengabe*, morning gift]

morgen (maw´gən) *n.* in SE Africa, the Netherlands and parts of the US, a unit of land measurement based on the area that can be ploughed by one team in one morning, about 0.8 ha (just over 2 acres). [G, morning]

morgue (mawg) *n.* **1** a mortuary. **2** a building or room where the bodies of unknown persons found dead are exposed for identification. **3** a stock of files, clippings etc., esp. future obituaries, kept by a newspaper for reference. [F, etym. unknown]

MORI (maw´ri) *abbr.* Market and Opinion Research Institute.

moribund (mor´ibŭnd) *a.* **1** in a dying state. **2** lacking vitality and energy. **moribundity** (-bŭn´-) *n.* [L *moribundus*, from *morī*, to die]

morion (mor´iən, maw´-) *n.* (*Hist.*) a helmet having no beaver or visor. [F, from Sp. *morrion*, perh. from *morra*, crown of the head]

Moriori (moriaw´ri) *n.pl.* (*Hist.*) the original inhabitants of New Zealand before the arrival of the Maoris. [Maori]

†**Morisco** (məris´kō), **Moresco** (-es´-) *n.* (*pl.* **Moriscos, Morescos, Moriscoes, Morescoes**) **1** a Moor, esp. one of the Moors remaining in Spain after the conquest of Granada. **2** the language of the Moors. **3** a morris dance. ~*a.* Moorish. [Sp. *morisco*, from *Moro*, MOOR]

morish MORE.

Mormon (maw´mən) *n.* a member of an American religious body, founded by Joseph Smith in 1830, now calling themselves the Latter-Day Saints, who claim continuous divine revelation through their priesthood, and formerly practised polygamy. **Mormonism** *n.* [from a reputed prophet *Mormon*, author of the *Book of Mormon*, containing the revelations on which their creed was based]

morn (mawn) *n.* (*poet.*) morning. **the morn** (*Sc.*) tomorrow. [OE *morgen* (cp. Dut., Dan. *morgen*, G *Morgen*, Icel. *morginn*, perh. from root *mergh-*, to blink or twinkle)]

mornay (maw´nā) *a.* served with a cheese sauce (*salmon mornay*). [perh. Philippe de *Mornay*, 1549–1623, French Huguenot leader]

morning (maw´ning) *n.* **1** the first part of the day, beginning at twelve o'clock at night and extending to twelve noon, or from dawn to midday. **2** the early part of a period or epoch. **3** (*poet.*) dawn. ~*int.* (*coll.*) good morning. ~*a.* of, relating to or meant to be taken or worn in the morning. **in the morning** tomorrow morning. **morning after** *n.* **1** a time of physical and mental discomfort following the activity of the previous night. **2** a hangover. **morning-after pill** *n.* a contraceptive pill effective when taken within a specified time after intercourse. **morning call** *n.* an early-morning alarm call. **morning coat** *n.* a coat with tails and a cutaway front. **morning dress** *n.* men's clothes worn on formal occasions during the day, esp. for weddings etc. **morning glory** *n.* (*pl.* **morning glories**) any of various climbing or twining plants of the genus *Ipomoea*. **morning prayer** *n.* in the Anglican Church, the service of matins. **morning room** *n.* a sitting room used in the morning. **mornings** *adv.* (*coll.*) during most mornings. **morning sickness** *n.* nausea and vomiting frequently accompanying early pregnancy. **morning star** *n.* **1** the planet Venus when visible in the east at dawn. **2** (*Hist.*) †a weapon consisting of a ball with spikes, united by a chain to a staff. **morning watch** *n.* (*Naut.*) the watch from 4 to 8 a.m. [ME *morwening*, dawning (*morwen*, MORN, -ING[1])]

Moro (maw´rō) *n.* (*pl.* **Moros**) **1** a member of a Muslim people of the S Philippines. **2** the language of this people. ~*a.* of this people or its language. [Sp., Moor, L *maurus*]

Moroccan (mərok´ən) *a.* of or relating to Morocco or its inhabitants. ~*n.* a native or inhabitant of Morocco. **morocco** (-ō) *n.* (*pl.* **moroccos**) a fine leather from goatskin, tanned with sumach and dyed (formerly made in Morocco). [It. *Marocco*, ult. from Arab. *Marrākesh*, Marrakesh]

moron (maw´ron) *n.* **1** (*coll.*) a very stupid or foolish person. **2** (*Psych.*) an adult with the mental age of between eight and twelve years. **moronic** (məron´-) *a.* **moronically** *adv.* **moronism** *n.* [Gr. *mōros*, stupid]

morose (mərōs´) *a.* peevish, sullen, gloomy, churlish, given to morbid brooding. **morosely** *adv.* **moroseness** *n.* [L *mōrōsus*, from *mōs mōris*, manner, self-will]

morph (mawf) *n.* **1** the phonological representation of a morpheme, an allomorph. **2** a variant form of animal or plant. [Gr. *morphē*, form]

morph- MORPHO-.

-morph (mawf) *comb. form* denoting shape or structure (*endomorph, ectomorph*). **-morphic, -morphous** *comb. form* forming adjectives. **-morphism, -morphy** *comb. form* forming nouns.

morpheme (maw´fēm) *n.* a linguistic element that can carry meaning and cannot be divided into smaller elements of this kind. **morphemic** (-fēm´-) *a.* **morphemically** *adv.* **morphemics** *n.* the study of the composition of words.

morphia MORPHINE.

morphic (maw´fik) *a.* morphological. [Gr. *morphē*, form]

morphine (maw´fēn), **morphia** (-fiə) *n.* the alkaloid derived from opium, used in medicine as a sedative and analgesic. **morphinism** (-fin-) *n.* addiction to the abuse of morphine. [G *Morphin*, L *morphia*, from *Morpheus*, the god of dreams]

morphing (maw´fing) *n.* in a film, video etc. the transformation of one image to another by means of computer technology. [meta*morphosing*]

morpho- (maw´fō), **morph-** *comb. form* of or relating to form.

morphogenesis (mawfōjen´əsis) *n.* (*Biol.*) the development of the form of an organism during its growth to maturity. **morphogenetic** (-net´-) *a.* **morphogenic** *a.*

morphology (mawfol´əji) *n.* **1** the branch of biology dealing with the form of organisms. **2** the study of the forms of words. **morphologic** (-fəloj´-), **morphological** *a.* **morphologically** *adv.* **morphologist** *n.*

morphosis (mawfō´sis) *n.* (*pl.* **morphoses** (-sēz)) the mode or order of development of an organ or organism. **morphotic** (-fot´-) *a.*

Morris chair (mor´is) *n.* an armchair with an adjustable back. [William *Morris* (1834–96), British painter, writer and craftsman]

morris dance (mor´is) *n.* a style of folk dance performed by groups in colourful rustic costume, often using bells, sticks, handkerchiefs etc. and accompanied by the concertina or fiddle. **morris dancer** *n.* **morris dancing** *n.* [var. of MORISCO, Moorish]

Morrison shelter (mor´isən) *n.* (*Hist.*) an indoor air-raid shelter in the form of a steel table. [Herbert *Morrison*, 1888–1965, British minister responsible for its introduction in 1941]

morrow (mor´ō) *n.* **1** (*poet.*) the day next after the present, the following day. **2** (*poet.*) the succeeding period. **3** †morning, morn. [ME *morwe, morwen*, MORNING]

Morse (maws), **Morse code** *n.* a system of sending messages by telegraph in which letters are represented by combinations of dots and dashes. [S. F. B. *Morse*, 1791–1872, US inventor]

morsel (maw´səl) *n.* **1** a mouthful, a bite, a small piece of food. **2** a small quantity, a piece. [OF, dim. of *mors*, from L *morsus*, bite, from *mordēre*, to bite]

mort (mawt) *n.* a note sounded on a hunting horn at the death of the deer. [F, from L *mors mortis*, death]

mortadella (mawtədel´ə) *n.* (*pl.* **mortadelle** (-i)) a type of large spicy pork sausage, sold ready to eat. [It., dim. of L *murtatum*, seasoned with myrtle berries]

mortal (maw´təl) *a.* **1** liable to death; human. **2** causing death, deadly, fatal. **3** inveterate, implacable (*mortal foe*). **4** involving physical or spiritual death. **5** of or relating to death. **6** (*coll.*) extreme, excessive. **7** (*coll.*) long and tedious. **8** (*coll.*) imaginable. ~*n.* **1** a being subject to death; a human being. **2** (*facet.*) a person. ~*adv.* (*coll.*) exceedingly, extremely. **this mortal coil** COIL[2]. **mortal battle** *n.* a battle fought to the death. **mortality** (-tal´-) *n.* (*pl.* **mortalities**) **1** the quality of being mortal. **2** human nature. **3** (*collect.*) human beings. **4** loss of life, esp. on a large scale. **5** (*in full* **mortality rate**) the number of deaths in a given period, the death rate. **mortally** *adv.* **1** so as to cause death. **2** (*coll.*) exceedingly, greatly. **mortal sin** *n.* (*Theol.*) a grave sin regarded as involving the total loss of grace. [OF, from L *mortālis*, from *mors mortis*, death]

mortar (maw´tə) *n.* **1** a cement, made of lime, sand and water, for joining bricks etc. in building. **2** a short large-bore cannon used for throwing missiles at a high angle. **3** a vessel in which substances are pounded with a pestle. **4** a device for firing fireworks, lifelines etc. ~*v.t.* **1** to join, plaster or close up with mortar. **2** to fire mortars at. **mortarboard** *n.* **1** a square-topped academic cap. **2** a square board for holding mortar. **mortarless** *a.* **mortary** *a.* [OE *mortere*, or F *mortier*, L *mortārium*, etym. uncertain]

mortgage (maw´gij) *n.* **1** the conditional conveyance of a house, estate or other property into the ownership of a building society etc. as security for the repayment of a loan, to be voided on the discharge of the debt or loan. **2** the loan thus made; the debt thus secured. **3** a deed effecting this. ~*v.t.* **1** to grant or make over (property) by mortgage. **2** to pledge, to plight (oneself etc. to or for). **mortgageable** *a.* **mortgagee** (-jē´) *n.* the party who makes the loan in a mortgage arrangement. **mortgager** (-jə), **mortgagor** (-jaw´) *n.* a person who mortgages their property. **mortgage rate** *n.* the rate of interest charged by building societies, banks etc. for mortgage loans. [OF (*mort*, L *mortuus*, dead, from *mors mortis*, death, GAGE[1])]

Usage note *MortgagEr* is the form of the agent noun in everyday use; *mortgagOr* is usual in legal contexts.

mortice MORTISE.

mortician (mawtish´ən) *n.* (*N Am.*) an undertaker. [L *mors mortis*, death]

mortify (maw´tifī) *v.t.* (*3rd pers. sing. pres.* **mortifies,** *pres.p.* **mortifying,** *past, p.p.* **mortified**) **1** to humiliate, to wound. **2** to subdue (the passions etc.) by abstinence or self-discipline. ~*v.i.* to lose vitality, to decay, to go gangrenous. **mortification** (-fikā´shən) *n.* **mortifier** *n.* **mortifying** *a.* **mortifyingly** *adv.* [F *mortifier*, L *mortificāre* (*mors mortis*, death, *-ficāre, facere*, to make)]

mortise (maw´tis), **mortice** *n.* a hole cut in timber etc. to receive the end of another part, esp. a tenon. ~*v.t.* **1** to cut a mortise in. **2** to join by means of mortise and tenon. **mortise lock** *n.* a lock set into a mortise in the edge of a door, so that the lock mechanism is enclosed by the door. [F *mortaise*, etym. unknown]

mortmain (mawt´mān) *n.* (*Law*) **1** inalienable possession or tenure of lands or tenements by an ecclesiastical or other corporation. **2** lands or tenements so held. **in mortmain** in inalienable possession, unable to be sold, transferred etc. [A-F *morte mayn*, OF *mortemain*, med. L *mortua manus*, dead hand]

mortuary (maw´chuəri, -chəri) *n.* (*pl.* **mortuaries**) a building for the temporary reception of the dead. ~*a.* of or relating to death or the burial of the dead. [A-F *mortuarie*, L *mortuārius*, from *mortuus*, dead]

morula (maw´rūlə, mor´ələ) *n.* (*pl.* **morulae** (-lē), **morulas**) **1** the stage of development in which an ovum has become completely segmented. **2** an ovum at this stage. [mod. L, dim. of *mōrum*, mulberry]

morwong (maw´wong) *n.* an edible fish of the family Cheilodactylidae, found off the coasts of Australia and New Zealand. [Austral. Abor.]

Mosaic (məzā´ik) *a.* of or relating to Moses or to the law given through him. **Mosaic law** *n.* the laws of the Hebrews attributed to Moses and contained in the Pentateuch. **Mosaism** (mō´-), **Mosaist** *n.* [*Moses*, -IC]

mosaic (məzā´ik) *n.* **1** a pattern, picture etc. produced by the arrangement of small pieces of coloured marble, glass or stone. **2** the art of producing such patterns etc. **3** a diverse or composite thing. **4** (*Biol.*) an organism, or part of one, consisting of tissues with different genetic constitutions, a chimera. **5** a composite photosensitive surface in a television camera tube. ~*a.* **1** of, relating to or resembling a mosaic. **2** tessellated, inlaid. ~*v.t.* (*pres.p.* **mosaicking,** *past, p.p.* **mosaicked**) **1** to decorate with mosaic. **2** to combine into a mosaic. **mosaically** *adv.* **mosaic disease** *n.* a viral disease of plants in which the leaves display a mottled yellowing. **mosaic gold** *n.* **1** tin disulphide. **2** an alloy of copper and zinc used in gilding cheap jewellery etc. **mosaicist** (-sist) *n.* [F *mosaique*, med. L *mōsāicus, mūsāicus*, as from a late Gr. *mousaikos, mouseios*, of the Muses]

mosasaurus (mōsəsaw´rəs) *n.* (*pl.* **mosasauruses, mosasauri** (-ī)) a large fossil marine reptile of the Cretaceous period esp. of the genus *Mosasaurus*, first found near Maastricht on the Meuse. [L *Mosa*, Meuse or Maas, Gr. *sauros*, lizard]

moschatel (moskətel´) *n.* a small perennial herb, *Adoxa moschatellina*, with yellowish-green flowers and a musky scent. [F *moscatelle*, It. *moscatella*, dim. of *moscato*, MUSK]

Moselle (məzel´), **Mosel** *n.* a white wine made in the valley of the river Moselle. [F, *Moselle*, G, *Mosel*]

mosey (mō´zi) *v.i.* (*3rd pers. sing. pres.* **moseys,** *pres.p.* **moseying,** *past, p.p.* **moseyed**) (*esp. N Am., coll.*) to walk, amble. [etym. unknown]

moshav (mō´shav, -shav´) *n.* (*pl.* **moshavim** (-im)) a co-operative association of small farms in Israel.

Moslem MUSLIM.

mosque (mosk) *n.* a Muslim place of worship. [F *mosquée* (later *mosque*), It. *moschea*, Arab. *masgid*, MASJID]

mosquito (məskē´tō) *n.* (*pl.* **mosquitoes**) an insect of the family Culicidae, esp. of the genera *Culex*, *Anopheles* or *Aedes*, with a proboscis for piercing the skin of animals and sucking their blood. **mosquito-boat** *n.* (*N Am.*) a motor torpedo boat. **mosquito net** *n.* a fine-mesh netting round a bed, over windows etc. to ward off mosquitoes. [Sp., dim. of *mosca*, L *musca*, fly]

moss (mos) *n.* **1** a low, tufted, herbaceous plant of the cryptogamous class Musci, usually growing on damp soil or the surface of stones, trees etc. **2** a bog, a peat-bog, wet spongy land. **moss agate** *n.* agate with dendritic markings similar to moss. **mossback** *n.* (*N Am.*, *coll.*) an old-fashioned or conservative person. **moss-backed** *a.* **mossbunker** *n.* the menhaden. **moss-grown** *a.* overgrown with moss. **moss-hag** *n.* (*Sc.*) **1** a pit or cutting in a bog from which peat has been taken. **2** a mass of firm heathery ground in a peatbog. **mosslike** *a.* **moss-rose** *n.* a variety of *Rosa centifolia muscosa*, with mosslike calyx. **moss stitch** *n.* a stitch in knitting consisting of alternating plain and purl stitches. **moss-trooper** *n.* (*Hist.*) any of the marauders who formerly roamed the borders of England and Scotland. **mossy** *a.* (*comp.* **mossier**, *superl.* **mossiest**) **1** overgrown with moss. **2** mosslike. **3** (*N Am.*, *coll.*) old-fashioned, conservative. **mossiness** *n.* [OE *mos*, bog (cp. Dut. *mos*, Icel. *mosi*, G *Moos*, also OE *mēos*, moss, G *Mies*, lichen)]

mosso (mos´ō) *adv.* (*Mus.*) with liveliness and speed. [It.]

most[1] (mōst) *a.* greatest in amount, number, extent, quality, degree etc. ~*adv.* **1** in the greatest or highest degree (forming the superl. of most adjectives and adverbs of more than one syllable). **2** (*coll.*) very. ~*n.* **1** the greatest number, quantity, amount etc. **2** the best, the worst etc. **3** the majority. **at most 1** at the utmost extent. **2** no more than. **at the most 1** as the greatest amount. **2** not more than. **for the most part** in the main, usually. **to make the most of** to use to the best advantage. **Most High** *n.* the Supreme Being, God. **Most Honourable** *n.* a courtesy title given to marquesses and members of the Privy Council and the Order of the Bath. **mostly** *adv.* **1** chiefly, mainly. **2** on most occasions, usually. **Most Reverend** *n.* a title given to an Archbishop or an Irish Roman Catholic bishop. **Most Reverend Father in God** *n.* the formal title of a bishop or archbishop. [OE *mǣst* (cp. Dut. *meest*, Icel. *mestr*, G *meist*), cogn. with MORE]

Usage note The use of *most* (rather than *more*) when comparing only two is best avoided.

most[2] (mōst) *adv.* (*N Am.*, *coll.*) short for ALMOST.

-most (mōst) *suf.* forming superlatives of adjectives and adverbs denoting position, order etc., as in *hindmost*, *inmost*, *utmost*. [OE *-mest*, double superl. suf. (*-ma*, Gmc. *-mo-*, -EST[1], Gmc. *-isto*), conn. with MOST[1]]

MOT (emōtē´) *abbr.* (*Hist.*) Ministry of Transport. ~*n.* (*pl.* **MOTs**) (*coll.*) an MOT test. **MOT test** *n.* a test of the roadworthiness of a motor vehicle more than three years old.

mot (mō) *n.* (*pl.* **mots** (mō)) **1** a witty or pithy saying. **2** †a motto. **mot juste** (zhoost´) *n.* the appropriate or felicitous word or phrase. [F, a word, It. *motto*, L *muttum*, from *muttīre*, to murmur]

mote[1] (mōt) *n.* **1** a particle of dust, a speck, a spot. **2** anything proverbially small. [OE *mot* (cp. Dut. *mot*, sawdust, dirt, LG *mut*, dust)]

†**mote**[2] (mōt) *v.t.* may, must.

motel (mōtel´) *n.* a roadside hotel or furnished cabins providing accommodation for motorists. [*mo*tor ho*tel*]

motet (mōtet´) *n.* (*Mus.*) a vocal composition in harmony, of a sacred character. [F, dim. of MOT]

moth (moth) *n.* **1** any of a group of nocturnal or crepuscular insects of the order Lepidoptera, distinct from butterflies by not having knotted antennae and folding the wings flat when at rest. **2** something which gradually eats, consumes or wears away anything. **mothball** *n.* a ball of naphthalene or similar substance that keeps away clothes-moths. ~*v.t.* **1** to lay up in mothballs. **2** to lay up for later use. **in mothballs** in long-term storage pending possible future use. **to put into mothballs** to defer execution of (a plan, project etc.). **moth-eaten** *a.* **1** eaten into holes by moths. **2** ragged, decayed, time-worn, outdated. **mothproof** *a.* (of clothes etc.) treated so as to repel moths. ~*v.t.* to treat in this way. **mothy** *a.* (*comp.* **mothier**, *superl.* **mothiest**) **1** full of moths. **2** moth-eaten. [F, dim. of MOT]

mother[1] (mŭdh´ə) *n.* **1** a female parent. **2** a woman performing the function of a mother in continuously caring for a child. **3** the source or origin of anything. **4** the head of a religious community, a Mother Superior. **5** (*N Am.*, *taboo sl.*) short for MOTHERFUCKER (under MOTHER[1]). **6** †a motherly or elderly woman. ~*v.t.* **1** to act as mother towards. **2** to give birth to. **3** to give rise to. **4** to acknowledge that one is or claim to be mother or originator of. ~*a.* **1** holding the place of a mother. **2** giving birth or origin. **3** native, natural, inborn, vernacular. **adoptive mother** ADOPTIVE (under ADOPT). **to be mother** to pour out a drink, esp. tea. **motherboard** *n.* (*Comput.*) the principal printed circuit in a microcomputer etc. through which all other systems are routed. **Mother Carey's chicken** *n.* the storm petrel. **mother-cell** *n.* (*Biol.*) a cell that produces other cells by division. **Mother Church** *n.* **1** the Church regarded as having the status and authority of a parent. **2** a church from which others have sprung. **3** the principal church of a district. **mother country** *n.* **1** one's native country. **2** a country in relation to its colonies. **mothercraft** *n.* expertise, knowledge etc. in rearing children as a mother. **mother figure** *n.* an older woman whom one looks to for advice and support. **motherfucker** *n.* (*N Am.*, *taboo sl.*) an offensive or unpleasant person or thing. **motherfucking** *a.* **Mother Goose rhyme** *n.* (*N Am.*) a nursery rhyme. **motherhood** *n.* **Mother Hubbard** *n.* a woman's flowing gown or cloak. **Mothering Sunday** *n.* the fourth Sunday in Lent, when mothers traditionally receive presents from their children. **mother-in-law** *n.* (*pl.* **mothers-in-law**) the mother of a person's wife or husband. **mother-in-law's tongue** *n.* a herbaceous perennial plant, *Sansevieria trifasciata*, with long pointed leaves. **motherland** *n.* a person's native country. **mother language** *n.* MOTHER TONGUE (under MOTHER[1]). **motherless** *a.* **motherlike** *a.*, *adv.* **mother-liquor, mother-water** *n.* (*Chem.*) the portion of a mixed solution which remains after the less soluble salts or other bodies have crystallized out. **mother lode** *n.* (*Mining*) the main vein of a system. **motherly** *a.* **1** like a mother; nurturing, loving. **2** proper to or becoming a mother. ~*adv.* in the manner of a mother. **motherliness** *n.* **mother-naked** *a.* completely naked. **mother-of-pearl** *n.* the iridescent pearly substance forming the internal layer of many shells. ~*a.* made of this. **mother of (the) chapel** *n.* the president of a branch of a printers' or journalists' trade union. **mother-of-thousands** *n.* a perennial herb of the genus *Linaria*, having ivy-shaped leaves, and usu. with yellow or bluish flowers. **Mother's Day** *n.* **1** Mothering Sunday. **2** (*N Am.*) the second Sunday in May, similarly set apart for the honouring of one's mother. **mother's help** *n.* a person whose job is to help look after children. **mother ship** *n.* a ship which supplies a number of other ships with stores, ammunition etc. **mother's ruin** *n.* (*coll.*) gin. **mother's son** *n.* (*coll.*) a man. **every**

mother's son all without exception. **Mother Superior** *n.* a woman having charge of a community of women in religious orders. **mother-to-be** *n.* (*pl.* **mothers-to-be**) a pregnant woman. **mother tongue** *n.* **1** a person's native language. **2** a language from which others have sprung. **mother wit** *n.* natural sagacity, common sense. **motherwort** *n.* any plant of the genus *Leonurus*, esp. *L. cardiaca*, orig. supposed to be beneficial for diseases of the womb. [OE *mōder, mōdor* (cp. Dut. *moeder*, Icel. *mōthur*, G *Mutter*), cogn. with L *māter*, Gr. *mētēr*]

mother[2] (mŭdh´ə) *n.* a thick slimy substance forming in various liquids during fermentation. ~*v.i.* to develop mother (as vinegar). **mothery** *a.* [prob. same as MOTHER[1] (cp. MDut. *moeder*, Dut. *maer*, G *Mutter*)]

motif (mōtēf´) *n.* **1** the dominant feature or idea in a literary, musical or other artistic composition. **2** an ornamental piece of lace etc. sewn on a dress. **3** a theme in music. [F, MOTIVE]

motile (mō´tīl) *a.* (*Zool., Bot.*) capable of motion. **motility** (-til´-) *n.* [L *mōt-*, stem, *movēre*, to move, -ILE]

motion (mō´shən) *n.* **1** the act, process or state of moving. **2** passage of a body from place to place. **3** change of posture. **4** a gesture. **5** an evacuation of the bowels. **6** a combination of moving parts in a machine etc. **7** a proposal, esp. in a deliberative assembly. **8** (*Law*) an application to a court for a rule or order. **9** impulse, instigation. ~*v.t.* **1** to direct by a gesture. **2** †to propose. ~*v.i.* **1** to make significant gestures. **2** †to make proposals. **in motion** moving; not at rest. **to go through the motions** to do something without enthusiasm or conviction. **to put/ set in motion** to set going or in operation. **motional** *a.* **motionless** *a.* **motionlessly** *adv.* **motion picture** *n.* a cinematograph film. **motion sickness** *n.* nausea induced by travelling in a car, ship, aircraft etc. **motion study** *n.* time and motion study. [F, from L *motio -ōnem*, as MOTILE]

motive (mō´tiv) *n.* **1** that which incites to action, or determines the will; a cause, ground, incentive. **2** in art, the predominant idea, feeling etc., motif. ~*a.* **1** causing or initiating motion. **2** of or relating to movement. **3** of or relating to a motive or motives. ~*v.t.* **1** to motivate. **2** (*usu. p.p.*) to furnish with an adequate motive (as a story, play etc.). **motivate** *v.t.* **1** to provide an incentive or motive to. **2** to instigate. **3** to rouse to interest or effort. **motivation** (-ā´shən) *n.* **motivational** *a.* **motivationally** *adv.* **motive energy** *n.* kinetic energy. **motiveless** *a.* **motivelessly** *adv.* **motivelessness** *n.* **motive power** *n.* **1** the power by which mechanical motion is imparted. **2** any impelling force. **motivity** (-tiv´-) *n.* the power of moving or of causing motion. [OF *motif*, med. L *mōtīvus -vum*, from *mot-*, stem of *movēre*, to MOVE]

motley (mot´li) *a.* (*comp.* **motlier**, *superl.* **motliest**) **1** of varied character, heterogeneous. **2** variegated in colour. **3** dressed in multicoloured clothes. ~*n.* **1** a heterogeneous mixture. **2** the multicoloured quartered dress of fools or jesters. **3** †a fool, a jester. **to wear motley** to play the fool. [etym. uncertain, perh. rel. to MOTE[1]]

motmot (mot´mot) *n.* a S American and Mexican bird of the family Momotidae allied to the kingfishers. [imit.]

motocross (mō´təkros) *n.* the sport of racing on motorcycles over rough ground. [*moto*r, *cross*-country]

moto perpetuo (mōtō pœpet´ūō) *n.* (*Mus.*) a short fast-moving instrumental piece.

motor (mō´tə) *n.* **1** something that imparts motive power, esp. a machine imparting motion to a vehicle or vessel (usu. excluding steam engines). **2** a device that converts electrical energy into mechanical energy. **3** (*coll.*) a car. **4** (*Anat.*) **a** a muscle for moving some part of the body. **b** a nerve exciting muscular action. ~*a.* causing or imparting motion. ~*v.i.* to drive or ride in a car. ~*v.t.* to convey in a car. **motorable** *a.* (of a road) able to be used by motor vehicles. **motor area** *n.* part of the frontal lobe of the brain which initiates the action of muscles. **motor bicycle, motor bus, motor car, motor coach, motor lorry, motor truck** *n.* various kinds of vehicle propelled by their own motor. **motorbike** *n.* (*coll.*) a motorcycle. **motor boat** *n.* a boat propelled by a motor. **motorcade** (-kād) *n.* a procession of motor vehicles. **motor caravan** *n.* a motor vehicle fitted with sleeping accommodation, cooking facilities etc. **motorcycle** *n.* a two-wheeled motor vehicle without any form of pedal propulsion. **motorcycling** *n.* **motorcyclist** *n.* **motorhome** *n.* a large motor caravan. **motorist** *n.* a driver of a car. **motorize, motorise** *v.t.* **1** to convert to being motor-driven. **2** to equip (troops) with motor vehicles. **motorization** (-zā´shən) *n.* **motor launch** *n.* a motor-driven small boat, for plying between vessels and the shore. **motorman** *n.* (*pl.* **motormen**) a man in charge of a motor, esp. of an electric tram or train. **motormouth** *n.* (*sl.*) someone who talks incessantly and trivially. **motor nerve** *n.* an efferent nerve that excites muscular activity. **motor neurone disease** *n.* (*Med.*) a disease involving progressive degeneration of the motor neurones leading to wasting of the muscles. **motor racing** *n.* the sport of racing in motor vehicles, usu. on a track. **motor scooter** *n.* a small motorcycle, usu. with a fairing reaching from below the handlebars in a curve to under the rider's feet. **motor sport** *n.* a sport involving racing in motor vehicles. **motor torpedo boat** *n.* (*Hist.*) a light, fast naval vessel equipped chiefly with torpedoes. **motor vehicle** *n.* a road vehicle driven by a motor or engine, esp. by an internal-combustion engine. **motorway** *n.* a road for fast motor traffic, usu. with a relatively high speed limit. **motory** *a.* **motor yacht** *n.* a motor-driven yacht. [L, from *movēre*, to MOVE]

Motown (mō´town) *n.* (*Hist.*) a form of music associated with Detroit, Michigan, containing elements of rhythm and blues and pop, often combined with the rhythm of gospel music. [*mo*tor *town*, the nickname of Detroit]

motte (mot) *n.* a mound on which a castle, camp etc. is situated. [ME, from OF, *mote*, mound]

mottle (mot´əl) *v.t.* to blotch, to variegate with spots of different colours or shades of colour. ~*n.* **1** a blotch or patch of colour. **2** a spotted, blotched or variegated appearance on a surface. **mottled** *a.* [prob. from MOTLEY]

motto (mot´ō) *n.* (*pl.* **mottoes**) **1** (*pl.*) a short pithy sentence or phrase expressing a sentiment or maxim. **2** a principle or maxim adopted as a rule of conduct. **3** a joke, verse or maxim contained in a paper cracker. **4** (*Her.*) a word or sentence used with a crest or coat of arms. **mottoed** *a.* [It., as MOT]

moue (moo) *n.* a small pouting grimace. [F, cp. MOW[3]]

mouflon (moo´flon), **moufflon** *n.* a wild sheep, *Ovis orientalis*, of Sardinia and Corsica. [F, from late L *mufron*]

mouillé (moo´yā) *a.* (of a consonant) palatalized (as *gn* in *lasagne*, *ñ* in *señor*). [F, wetted]

moujik MUZHIK.

moulage (moolahzh´) *n.* **1** the taking of plaster casts of footprints etc. **2** a plaster cast made in this way. **3** in the US, a section of a police force that specializes in this. [F, cast from a mould]

mould[1] (mōld), (*N Am.*) **mold** *n.* **1** a hollow shape into which molten metal etc. is poured in a fluid state to cool into a permanent shape. **2** a template used by plasterers for shaping cornices etc. **3** any of various analogous appliances used in trades and manufactures. **4** a hollow vessel for shaping puddings etc. **5** (*Archit.*) a moulding or group of mouldings. **6** a pudding etc. shaped in a mould. **7** physical form, shape, build. **8** character, nature. ~*v.t.* **1** to form into a particular shape. **2** to fashion, to make, to produce. **3** to give a particular character to. **4** to fit closely to. **5** to shape (bread) into loaves. **moulder**[1] *n.* **moulding** *n.* **1** an ornamental part of a cornice, capital, arch, woodwork etc., usu. in the form of continuous grooves and projections, showing in profile a complex series of curves. **2** a strip of wood, stone etc. for use as a moulding. **3** anything formed in or as in a mould. **4** the act or process of shaping anything in or as in a mould. [ONF *molde*, OF *modle*, L MODULUS]

mould[2] (mōld), (*N Am.*) **mold** *n.* a minute fungoid growth forming a woolly or furry coating on matter left in the damp. **mouldy** *a.* (*comp.* **mouldier,** *superl.* **mouldiest**) **1** covered with mould. **2** (*coll.*) bad, poor, nasty. **3** (*coll.*) mean, shabby. **mouldiness** *n.* [prob. from *mould*, *mouled*, p.p. of ME *moulen*, to become mouldy (cp. Swed. *mögla*, Dan. *muggeh*, also Eng. MUGGY)]

mould[3] (mōld), (*N Am.*) **mold** *n.* **1** fine soft earth, easily pulverized, suitable for cultivation. **2** the earth, the ground. **3** the grave. **mould-board** *n.* the curved plate in a plough which turns the furrow-slice over. **†mouldwarp** *n.* the mole. [OE *molde* (cp. Dut. *moude*, Icel. *mold*, Dan. *muld*), cogn. with L *molere*, to grind, Eng. MEAL[1]]

moulder[1], **moulding** MOULD[1].

moulder[2] (mōl´də), (*N Am.*) **molder** *v.i.* **1** to turn to dust by natural decay. **2** to crumble. **3** to waste away gradually. [prob. from MOULD[3]]

mouldy MOULD[2].

moulin (moo´lĩ) *n.* a vertical pit in a glacier created and maintained by a constant stream of water from the surface. [F, a mill]

moult (mōlt), (*N Am.*) **molt** *v.i.* to shed the feathers, hair, skin, horns etc. (of certain birds and animals). ~*v.t.* to shed or cast. ~*n.* the act of moulting. [ME *mouten*, OE *bemūtian*, L *mūtāre*, to change]

mound[1] (mownd) *n.* **1** an artificial elevation of earth, stones etc. **2** a hillock, a knoll. **3** a barrow, a tumulus. **4** in baseball, a slight elevation on which the pitcher stands to pitch. ~*v.t.* **1** to heap up in a mound or mounds. **2** to furnish, enclose or protect with a mound. **mound bird** *n.* MEGAPODE. [etym. uncertain]

mound[2] (mownd) *n.* (*Her.*) a ball or globe representing the earth, usu. of gold and surmounted by a cross, used as part of regalia, an orb. [F *monde*, L *mundus*, the world]

mount[1] (mownt) *v.t.* **1** to ascend, to climb. **2** to ascend upon, to get up on to. **3** to form a path up. **4** to copulate with. **5** to place on a raised support, to raise. **6** to prepare for use. **7** to put (a picture etc.) on a mount. **8** to affix (a stamp, photograph etc.) with mounts. **9** to place for microscopic examination on. **10** to stage (a play etc.); to present (an exhibition etc.) for public view. **11** to put (someone) on a horse. **12** to provide with a horse or horses. ~*v.i.* **1** to rise, to ascend. **2** to get on horseback. **3** to rise in amount. **4** to soar. **5** (of blood) to flush the cheeks. ~*n.* **1** something on which anything is mounted. **2** an adhesive hinge for affixing stamps, photographs etc. to a page. **3** a piece of cardboard etc. upon which a drawing is placed. **4** a slide on which something is placed for microscopic examination. **5** the margin around a picture. **6** the parts by which various objects are prepared for use, strengthened or ornamented. **7** a horse with the appurtenances necessary for riding. **8** a horse-block or other means of mounting on horseback. **to mount guard** GUARD. **mountable** *a.* **mounted** *a.* **1** on horseback. **2** placed on a mount. **mounter** *n.* **Mountie, Mounty** *n.* (*pl.* **Mounties**) (*coll.*) a member of the Royal Canadian Mounted Police. **mounting** *n.* **mounting block** *n.* a horse-block. [OF *munter*, *monter*, ult. from L *mons montis* MOUNT[2]]

mount[2] (mownt) *n.* **1** a high hill, a mountain (in poetry, or as first part of a proper name). **2** in palmistry, each of the fleshy protuberances on the palm of the hand. **3** (*Her.*) a figure of a green hill occupying the base of a shield. [OE *munt*, L *mons montis*, influ. by MOUNT[1]]

mountain (mown´tin) *n.* **1** a natural elevation of the earth's surface rising high above the surrounding land. **2** a large heap or pile. **3** something of very great bulk. **4** a commodity surplus, esp. of an agricultural product. **the Mountain** (*Hist.*) the extreme democratic party in the first French Revolution, from their occupying the highest seats in the National Convention. **to make a mountain out of a molehill** to make far more of an issue, task etc. than is justified or reasonable. **to move mountains** to achieve what was seemingly impossible by effort, persistence etc. **mountain ash** *n.* **1** the rowan, *Sorbus aucuparia*. **2** (*Austral.*) any of various kinds of eucalyptus. **mountain avens** *n.* a trailing evergreen alpine plant, *Dryas octopetala*, of the rose family, having white flowers. **mountain bike** *n.* a sturdy bicycle with many gears and thick tyres for use on steep or rugged terrain. **mountain chain** *n.* a range or series of mountains. **mountain dew** *n.* whisky, formerly often secretly distilled in the mountains. **mountaineer** (-niə´) *n.* **1** a person who climbs mountains as a hobby or occupation. **2** a person who lives among mountains. **mountaineering** *n.* **†mountainet** (-net´) *n.* **mountain goat** *n.* **1** any wild goat living in mountainous areas, often associated with being agile. **2** the Rocky Mountain goat, *Oreamnos americanus*, of western N America. **mountain-high, mountains-high** *a.*, *adv.* (esp. of waves) high as mountains. **mountain laurel** *n.* an ericaceous shrub, *Kalmia latifolia*, of N America. **mountain limestone** *n.* carboniferous limestone. **mountain lion** *n.* a puma. **mountainous** *a.* **1** full of mountains. **2** exceedingly large. **mountainously** *adv.* **mountainousness** *n.* **mountain panther** *n.* the Asian wild cat, the ounce. **mountain range** *n.* an area or line of mountains of similar origin. **mountain sickness** *n.* a feeling of indisposition, varying in different people, brought on by ascending into rarefied mountain air. **mountainside** *n.* **mountain soap** *n.* a soft, earthy, brownish-black mineral, used in crayon painting. **Mountain Standard Time, Mountain Time** *n.* the standard time in a zone of US and Canada in or near the Rocky Mountains, seven hours behind GMT. **mountainy** *a.* [OF *montaigne* (F *montagne*), pop. L *montānea*, L *montāna*, pertaining to a mountain, from *mons montis*, mountain]

mountant (mown´tənt) *n.* an adhesive for mounting photographs etc.

mountebank (mown´tibangk) *n.* **1** a swindler, a boastful pretender, a charlatan. **2** (*Hist.*) a quack doctor, orig. one who proclaimed his nostrums from a platform. ~*v.t.* to cheat by false boasts or pretences. **mountebankery, mountebankism** *n.* [It. *montambanco* (*monta in banco*, mount on a bench)]

Mountie MOUNT[1].

mourn (mawn) *v.i.* **1** to express or feel sorrow or grief. **2** to observe the mourning customs, dress etc. ~*v.t.* to grieve or sorrow for. **mourner** *n.* **mournful** *a.* **mournfully** *adv.* **mournfulness** *n.* **mourning** *a.* **1** grieving, sorrowing. **2** expressive of grief or sorrow. ~*n.* **1** grief, sorrow, lamentation. **2** the customary dress, usu. black, worn by mourners. **in mourning** wearing mourning. **mourning-band** *n.* a band of black material worn esp. round the sleeve to show that one is in mourning. **mourning cloak** *n.* a large butterfly, the Camberwell Beauty. **mourning dove** *n.* an American dove, *Zenaida macroura*, so called from its plaintive note. **mourningly** *adv.* **mourning-paper** *n.* notepaper edged with black, used during a period of mourning. **mourning ring** *n.* a black ring worn as a memorial of a deceased person. [OE *murnan* (cp. Icel. *morna*, OHG *mornēn*), cogn. with Gr. *merimna*, sorrow]

mousaka MOUSSAKA.

mouse[1] (mows) *n.* (*pl.* **mice** (mīs)) **1** a small rodent quadruped of various species belonging to the family Muridae. **2** any of various similar animals, such as the shrews, voles etc. **3** (*Comput.*) (*pl.* **mouses**) a device that allows manual control of the cursor and selection of computer functions without use of the keyboard. **4** (*coll.*) a shy or inconspicuous person. **5** (*sl.*) a black eye. **mouse-colour, mouse-coloured,** (*N Am.*) **mouse-color, mouse-colored** *a.* darkish grey with a tinge of brown. **mouse deer** *n.* a chevrotain. **mouse-ear** *n.* any of several plants with velvety leaves resembling a mouse's ear (usu. attrib. as *mouse-ear chickweed, mouse-ear hawkweed*). **mouse hare** *n.* a pika. **mouse-like** *a.* **mousetail** *n.* a plant of the ranunculaceous genus, *Myosurus.* **mousetrap** *n.* **1** a trap for catching mice. **2** (*coll.*) low-quality cheese. **mousy, mousey** *a.* (*comp.* **mousier,** *superl.* **mousiest**) **1** of a drab grey or brown colour. **2** (*coll.*) shy, timid or inconspicuous. **mousily** *adv.* **mousiness** *n.* [OE *mūs* (cp. Dut. *muis,* Icel. *mūs,* pl. *mȳss,* G *Maus,* L and Gr. *mūs*)]

mouse[2] (mows, mowz) *v.i.* **1** to hunt for or catch mice. **2** to hunt, to watch craftily, to prowl (about). ~*v.t.* **1** to hunt for persistently. **2** to tear or pull about as a cat does a mouse. **mouser** *n.* a cat good at catching mice. [from MOUSE[1]]

mousquetaire (mooskətea´) *n.* (*Hist.*) MUSKETEER (under MUSKET). [F]

moussaka (moo´səkə, -sah´kə), **mousaka** *n.* a Greek dish of minced meat, aubergines and tomatoes, topped with a cheese sauce.

mousse (moos) *n.* **1** a dish of flavoured cream whipped and frozen. **2** any of various light, stiff liquid preparations, e.g. used for hairstyling or cosmetic purposes. **3** oil and sea water forming a froth after a spillage of oil. [F, froth]

mousseline (mooslēn´) *n.* **1** fine French muslin. **2** a light sauce made by whipping cream with hollandaise sauce. **mousseline de laine** (də len´) *n.* an untwilled woollen dress fabric resembling muslin. **mousseline de soie** (də swah´) *n.* a thin silk fabric resembling muslin in texture, usu. patterned. [F, as MUSLIN]

moustache (məstahsh´), (*N Am.*) **mustache** *n.* **1** the hair on the upper lip, esp. the hair of men when left to grow. **2** a growth of hair round the mouth on various animals. **moustache cup** *n.* a drinking-cup with a guard to keep liquid from wetting the moustache. **moustached** *a.* [F, from It. *mostaccio,* Gr. *mustax -takos*]

Mousterian (moostiə´riən) *n.* the main culture of the palaeolithic period, from *c.* 80,000–35,000 BC, characterized by flint flake tools and associated with Neanderthal man. ~*a.* of or relating to this culture. [F *moustiérien,* from *Le Moustier,* Dordogne region, where remains were found]

mousy MOUSE[1].

mouth[1] (mowth) *n.* (*pl.* **mouths** (mowdhz)) **1** the opening through which food is taken into the body. **2** the cavity behind this, containing the organs of mastication, salivation and vocalization. **3** anything analogous to a mouth, the opening of a vessel, pit, cave or the like. **4** a person regarded as needing to be fed. **5** the outfall of a river. **6** (*coll.*) **a** talkativeness. **b** impudent talk, cheek. **7** a horse's responsiveness to the bit. **to give mouth** (of a dog) to bark or bay. **to keep one's mouth shut** (*coll.*) not to speak, esp. not to reveal secrets. **to make a wry mouth** to make grimaces. **to make mouths** to make grimaces. **to make one's mouth water** WATER. **to put words into a person's mouth** to represent, perh. incorrectly, what one assumes another person means. **to shoot one's mouth off** SHOOT. **to stop the mouth of** to put to silence. **to take words out of a person's mouth** to say what another person was about to say. **mouthbreather** *n.* a person who usually breathes through the mouth. **mouthbrooder** *n.* any fish that carries its eggs and young around in the mouth. **mouthed** (-dhd) *a.* (*usu. in comb.*) having a mouth, as *big-mouthed.* **mouth-filling** *a.* **1** filling the mouth. **2** inflated. **3** sonorous. **mouthful** *n.* (*pl.* **mouthfuls**) **1** an amount that fills the mouth. **2** a small quantity of food etc. **3** (*coll.*) a word or phrase that is pompous or difficult to say. **4** (*coll.*) an abusive tirade. **5** (*N Am.*) an important statement. **mouthless** *a.* **mouth organ** *n.* a small musical instrument, played by blowing on metallic reeds, a harmonica. **mouthpart** *n.* any of the usu. paired appendages around the mouth of an insect, arthropod etc. and adapted for feeling. **mouthpiece** *n.* **1** that part of a musical instrument put between the lips. **2** that party of a telephone spoken into. **3** a tube by which a cigar or cigarette is held in the mouth. **4** a spokesman for others. **5** (*coll.*) a lawyer. **6** an attached outlet. **mouth-to-mouth** *a.* (of resuscitation) carried out by breathing air into someone's mouth directly. **mouthwash** *n.* **1** an antiseptic liquid used to cleanse the mouth. **2** (*coll.*) nonsense. **mouth-watering** *a.* (appearing to be) delicious. **mouth-wateringly** *adv.* **mouthy** (-dhi) *a.* (*comp.* **mouthier,** *superl.* **mouthiest**) **1** (*coll.*) impudent, cheeky. **2** ranting, bombastic, aggressively loud. [OE *mūth* (cp. Dut. *mond,* G *Mund,* Icel. *munnr*), cogn. with L *mentum,* chin]

mouth[2] (mowdh) *v.t.* **1** to utter pompously or in an elaborate or constrained manner, to declaim. **2** to utter in exaggerated manner to help communication. **3** to say (words) silently moving the lips. **4** to take up or seize with the mouth. **5** to chew or roll with the mouth. **6** to train (a horse) to the use of the bit. **7** †to insult. ~*v.i.* **1** to talk pompously or affectedly. **2** to communicate by forming words silently with the lips. **3** to make grimaces. †**mouther** *n.* [MOUTH[1]]

move (moov) *v.t.* **1** to cause to change position or posture. **2** to carry, lift, draw or push from one place to another. **3** to put in motion, to stir. **4** to cause (the bowels) to act. **5** to incite, to incline, to prompt, to rouse (to action). **6** to excite, to provoke (laughter etc.). **7** to prevail upon. **8** to affect with feelings, usu. of tenderness, to touch. **9** to propose, to submit for discussion. **10** †to apply to. ~*v.i.* **1** to change place or posture. **2** to go from one place to another. **3** to advance, to progress. **4** to change one's place of residence. **5** to change the position of a piece at chess etc. **6** to make an application, appeal etc. **7** to begin to act. **8** to take action, to proceed. **9** to be moved, to have an evacuation (of the bowels). **10** to live, to exercise one's activities (in or among). ~*n.* **1** the act of moving. **2** the right to move (in chess etc.). **3** proceeding, action, line of conduct. **4** a step, a device to obtain an object. **5** a change of abode. **on the move 1** stirring. **2** moving from place to place, travelling about. **to get a move on** (*coll.*) to hurry. **to make a move 1** to go, to leave the table etc. **2** to start. **3** to begin to go. **4** to move a piece at chess etc. **to move away** to go to live elsewhere, esp. at some distance. **to move heaven and earth** to make every effort, to leave no stone unturned (to secure an object). **to move in 1** to move into a new house etc. **2** to take up a position of power, influence, advantage etc. **to move in with** to start to share accommodation with (an established resident). **to move mountains** MOUNTAIN. **to move on/ along** to change one's position, esp. to avoid crowding or to accommodate others. **to move out 1** to go to live elsewhere. **2** to leave a job, position etc. **to move over/ up** to adjust one's position to accommodate others. **to move the goalposts** GOAL. **movable, moveable** *a.* **1** capable of being moved. **2** occurring at varying times (as a festival). **3** †changeable, inconstant. ~*n.* **1** anything that can be moved or removed, esp. a movable or portable piece of furniture etc. that is not a fixture. **2** (*pl.*) goods, furniture, chattels etc., as distinct from houses and lands, personal as distinct from real property. **3** (*Sc. Law*) property not able to be inherited, as distinct from heritable property. **movability** (-bil´-), **movableness** *n.* **movable-doh** *a.* (*Mus.*) denoting a notation used in sight-singing in which 'doh' is adjusted to become the key note of the scale being used, as distinct from *fixed-doh.* **movable feast** *n.* **1** a festival the date of which varies. **2** (*facet.*) a meal taken at irregular times. †**movably** *adv.* **movement** *n.* **1** the act or process of changing position, place or posture. **2** manner or style of moving. **3** the working mechanism of a watch, clock, machine etc., or a connected group of parts of this. **4** a connected series of impulses, efforts and actions, directed to a special end. **5** a tendency in art, politics, literature etc., either actively promoted or occurring spontaneously. **6** the people involved in this. **7** an activity in a market, esp. change of value. **8** the mode or rate of a piece of music, also a section of a large work having the same general measure or time. **9** change in temper, disposition, feeling etc. **10** action, incident or process of development in a story etc. **11** a military evolution. **mover** *n.* **1** someone who or something which moves. **2** a cause or source of motive power. **3** a proposer (of a resolution etc.). **4** a person who originates or instigates. **mover and shaker** *n.* (*usu. in pl., coll.*) a person with power and influence in politics, business etc. **moving** *a.* **1** causing motion. **2** in motion. **3** impelling, persuading. **4** pathetic, affecting. **moving-coil** *a.* (of an electromechanical device) containing a coil of wire hanging in a magnetic field so that the coil produces a current when it is made to move (as in a microphone) or moves in response to a current (as in a loudspeaker). **movingly** *adv.* **moving pavement** *n.* a type of conveyor belt for pedestrians, a travolator. **moving picture** *n.* the photographic record of a series of events in the form of shots taken at very short intervals and projected in sequence. **moving staircase** *n.* an escalator. [OF *movoir* (F *mouvoir*), L *movēre*]

movie (moo´vi) *n.* (*coll.*) **1** (*esp. N Am.*) a cinema film. **2** (*US*) a cinema. **movie-goer** *n.* a person who goes to see films, esp. regularly. **movie-maker** *n.* a film producer, director etc. **movie-making** *n.* **movie theatre, movie house** *n.* a cinema. [*mov*ing picture, -IE]

moving MOVE.

mow[1] (mō) *v.t.* (*past* **mowed,** *p.p.* **mown** (mōn), **mowed**) **1** to cut down (grass, corn etc.) with a mower, scythe etc. **2** to cut the grass off (a lawn etc.). *~v.i.* to cut grass by mowing. **to mow down 1** to kill in great numbers. **2** to destroy indiscriminately. **mower** *n.* **mowing** *n.* **1** the act of cutting with a mower, scythe etc. **2** land from which grass is cut. *~a.* (of land, crops etc.) intended to be mown. [OE *māwan* (cp. Dut. *maaien*, G *mahen*, also Gr. *amaein* and L *mētere*, to reap)]

mow[2] (mō) *n.* (*dial. or N Am.*) **1** a heap or pile of hay, corn or other field produce, a stack. **2** a place in a barn etc. for storing heaps of hay etc. *~*†*v.t.* to put in a mow or mows. [OE *mūga* (cp. Icel. *mūge*, a swathe, Swed. and Norw. *muga*)]

†**mow**[3] (mow) *n.* a wry face, a grimace. *~v.i.* to make grimaces. **mops and mows** MOP[2]. [OF *moue, moe*, mouth, pout, perh. from MDut. *mouwe*, etym. uncertain]

moxa (mok´sə) *n.* a downy material obtained from the dried leaves of *Crossostrephium artemisioides*, burnt on the skin in oriental medical treatments such as acupuncture, or as a counterirritant. **moxibustion** (-bŭs´-) *n.* the burning of moxa on or near the skin. [Jap. *mokusa* (*moe kusa*, burning herb)]

moxie (mok´si) *n.* (*N Am., sl.*) vigour, courage, force of character, wit. [*Moxie*, proprietary name of a soft drink]

Mozarab (mōzar´əb) *n.* (*Hist.*) any of those Christians in Spain after the Moorish conquest who were allowed the exercise of their religion in return for allegiance to the Moors. **Mozarabic** *a.* [Sp. *Mozárabe*, Arab. *musta 'rib*, desiderative from *arab*, ARAB]

mozzarella (motsərel´ə) *n.* a soft white unsalted Italian curd cheese. [It.]

mozzetta (məzet´ə, motset´ə), **mozetta** *n.* a short cape with a small hood worn by cardinals, bishops, abbots etc. in the Roman Catholic Church. [It. *mozzetta*, dim. of *mozza*, see AMICE[1]]

MP *abbr.* **1** Member of Parliament. **2** Military Police.

mp *abbr.* **1** melting point. **2** (*Mus.*) mezzo piano.

m.p.g. *abbr.* miles per gallon.

m.p.h. *abbr.* miles per hour.

M.Phil. *abbr.* Master of Philosophy.

mpingo (əmping´gō) *n.* (*pl.* **mpingos**) **1** a leguminous tree, *Dalbergia melanoxylon* native to E Africa. **2** the black wood of this tree.

MR *abbr.* Master of the Rolls.

Mr (mis´tə) (*pl.* **Messrs**) mister. **Mr Justice** *n.* a form of address used when speaking or referring to a Supreme Court Judge. **Mr Right** *n.* (*facet.*) the ideal marriage partner for a woman.

MRA *abbr.* Moral Rearmament.

MRBM *abbr.* medium-range ballistic missile.

MRC *abbr.* Medical Research Council.

MRCA *abbr.* multi-role combat aircraft.

MRCP *abbr.* Member of the Royal College of Physicians.

MRCS *abbr.* Member of the Royal College of Surgeons.

MRCVS *abbr.* Member of the Royal College of Veterinary Surgeons.

MRE *abbr.* (*Mil.*) meals ready to eat.

MRI *abbr.* magnetic resonance imaging.

MRIA *abbr.* Member of the Royal Irish Academy.

MRM *abbr.* mechanically recovered meat.

mRNA *abbr.* (*Biol.*) messenger RNA.

MRPhS *abbr.* Member of the Royal Pharmaceutical Society.

Mrs (mis´iz) *n.* (*pl.* **Mrs**) the title of a married woman. **Mrs Grundy** GRUNDY (under GRUNDYISM). **Mrs Justice** *n.* a form of address used when speaking or referring to a Supreme Court Judge.

MS *abbr.* **1** manuscript. **2** Mauritius (IVR). **3** motor ship. **4** multiple sclerosis.

Ms (miz) *n.* the title of a woman of unknown or undisclosed marital status.

MSC *abbr.* Manpower Services Commission.

M.Sc *abbr.* Master of Science.

MS-DOS® (emesdos´) *abbr.* (*Comput.*) Microsoft disk operating system.

MSF *abbr.* Manufacturing, Science and Finance Union.

MSG *abbr.* monosodium glutamate.

Msgr *abbr.* (*N Am.*) **1** Monseigneur. **2** Monsignor.

MSM *abbr.* men having sex with men.

MSS *abbr.* manuscripts.

MST *abbr.* Mountain Standard Time.

MT *abbr.* mechanical transport.

Mt *abbr.* Mount.

MTB *abbr.* motor torpedo boat.

M.Tech. *abbr.* Master of Technology.

mu (mū) *n.* (*pl.* **mus**) the twelfth letter of the Greek alphabet, Μ, μ. **mu-meson** *n.* MUON.

mucedinous (mūsed´inəs, -sē´-) *a.* **1** mouldy, mildewy. **2** of or like mould or mildew. [L *mūcēdo -dinis*, from *mūcēre*, to be mouldy, from MUCUS]

much (mŭch) *a.* (*comp.* **more,** *superl.* **most**) **1** great in quantity or amount. **2** long in duration. **3** †numerous, many. *~adv.* **1** in or to a great degree or extent. **2** almost, nearly, about. *~n.* **1** a great quantity, a great deal. **2** something uncommon. **a bit much** (*coll.*) rather excessive, unreasonable etc. **as much** an equal quantity. **much as** even though (*Much as I had hoped to...*). **much less** LESS. **much obliged** OBLIGE. **not much** (*sl.*)

certainly not, not likely. **not much cop** COP[1]. **not much in it** little difference between things being compared. **not up to much** (*coll.*) not very good, of poor quality. **to make much of** MAKE[1]. **too much** more than enough. **too much for 1** superior in a contest etc., more than a match for. **2** beyond what is acceptable, endurable etc. **muchly** *adv.* (*sl., facet.*) very much. **muchness** *n.* **much of a muchness** practically the same, very nearly alike. [ME *moche, miche, michel,* OE *micel,* MICKLE]

mucic (mū´sik) *a.* denoting an acid formed by the oxidation of milk, sugar and various gums. [F *mucique,* from L MUCUS]

mucilage (mū´silij) *n.* **1** a sticky or viscous substance from the seeds, bark or roots of various plants. **2** adhesive prepared for use. **3** a viscous lubricating secretion in animal bodies. **mucilaginous** (-laj´-) *a.* [F, from L *mūcilāgo -ginis,* as MUCUS]

muck (mŭk) *n.* **1** dung or manure. **2** refuse, filth. **3** anything filthy, disgusting or nasty. **4** (*coll.*) untidiness. **5** (*coll.*) mortar. ~*v.t.* **1** to make dirty or untidy. **2** to bungle, to make a mess of. **3** to manure. **Lady Muck** LADY. **Lord Muck** LORD. **to make a muck of** to bungle, to make a mess of. **to muck about/ around 1** to fool around, to mess around. **2** to potter, to mess about. **to muck in** (*coll.*) to help others to do something. **to muck out** to clean muck from (esp. a stable). **to muck up 1** to make dirty or untidy. **2** to bungle, to make a mess of. **mucker** *n.* **1** (*coll.*) a friend. **2** (*sl.*) a bad fall, esp. in the mud. **muckheap** *n.* **muckrake** *v.i.* to stir up scandal. **muckraker** *n.* **muckraking** *n.* **muck-spreader** *n.* a machine for spreading manure. **muck-spreading** *n.* **muck sweat** *n.* (*coll.*) a state of profuse sweating. **in a muck sweat** (*sl.*) sweating, esp. with fear or confusion. **mucky** *a.* (*comp.* **muckier,** *superl.* **muckiest**). **muckiness** *n.* [prob. from Scand. (cp. Icel. *myki,* dung, Norw. *myk,* Dan. *mög*)]

muckle MICKLE.

muco- (mū´kō) *comb. form* mucus, mucous.

mucopolysaccharide (mūkōpolisak´ərīd) *n.* any of a group of polysaccharides whose molecules contain two sugars, often found as components of connective tissue.

mucosa, mucosity MUCUS.

mucro (mū´krō) *n.* (*pl.* **mucrones** (mūkrō´nēz), **mucros**) (*Bot., Zool.*) a sharp point, process, or organ. **mucronate** (-nət), **mucronated** (-nātid) *a.* terminating abruptly in a point. **mucronately** (-nət-) *adv.* [L]

mucus (mū´kəs) *n.* **1** the slimy secretion of the mucous membrane. **2** applied to other slimy secretions in animals and fishes. **3** gummy matter found in all plants, soluble in water but not in alcohol. **mucoid** *a.* **mucosa** (-kō´-) *n.* (*pl.* **mucosae** (-sē)) a mucous membrane. **mucous** (-kəs) *a.* **1** of or relating to, like or covered with mucus. **2** secreting mucus. **3** slimy, sticky. **mucosity** (-kos´-) *n.* **mucous membrane** *n.* the membraneous lining of the cavities and canals of the body. **muculent** (-kū-) *a.* [L *mūcus, muccus,* cogn. with Gr. *mussesthai,* L *ēmungere,* to blow the nose]

Usage note The spellings of the adjective *mucous* and the noun *mucus* (pronounced the same) should not be confused.

mud (mŭd) *n.* **1** moist, soft earth, or earthy matter. **2** mire. **3** anything that is worthless or defiling. ~*v.t.* **1** to bury in or bedaub with mud. **2** to make turbid or foul. **mud in your eye!** used as a drinking toast. **one's name is mud** one is in disgrace, unpopular etc. **to drag through the mud** to disgrace publicly, to denigrate. **to sling/ fling/ throw mud** to make disgraceful imputations. **mudbank** *n.* a bank of mud on the bed of a river, the floor of the sea. **mudbath** *n.* **1** (*coll.*) a very muddy area, sports pitch, event etc. **2** a bath of mineral water and mud in which patients are immersed for medicinal purposes. **mudbrick** *n.* a brick made of baked mud. **muddy** *a.* (*comp.* **muddier,** *superl.* **muddiest**) **1** covered with mud. **2** of the colour of mud. **3** resembling mud. **4** turbid, cloudy. **5** confused, muddled, obscure. ~*v.t.* (*3rd pers. sing. pres.* **muddies,** *pres.p.* **muddying,** *past, p.p.* **muddied**) **1** to make muddy or foul. **2** to confuse. **muddily** *adv.* **muddiness** *n.* **mudfish** *n.* a New Zealand fish that burrows in the mud at a distance from water. **mudflap** *n.* a flap hanging behind the road-wheel of a vehicle to prevent mud etc. being thrown behind. **mudflat** *n.* a flat expanse of mud revealed by the ebb tide. **mudflow** *n.* a flow of soil mixed with water down a slope. **mudguard** *n.* a board or strip of metal fastened over a wheel of a bicycle, motorcycle etc. to protect persons riding from mud. **mudhole** *n.* **1** a place full of mud. **2** an opening in a boiler for discharging sediment. **mudlark** *n.* **1** (*Hist.*) a person who cleans out sewers, or fishes up pieces of coal, metal etc. from the mud of tidal rivers. **2** (*Hist.*) a street urchin. **mud pack** *n.* a cosmetic containing fuller's earth, applied in paste form to the face. **mud pie** *n.* a heap of mud shaped by a child to resemble a pie. **mud puppy** *n.* (*N Am.*) any aquatic salamander of the genus *Necturus,* esp. *N. maculosus* of the eastern US. **mud-scow** *n.* (*N Am.*) a heavy boat for carrying mud, esp. that from dredging. **mudskipper** *n.* any small goby of the family Periophthalmidae, able to move over mud by means of its strong pectoral fins. **mud-slinger** *n.* a person given to making malicious remarks about others. **mud-slinging** *n.* **mudstone** *n.* a dark grey clay rock. **mud volcano** *n.* (*pl.* **mud volcanoes**) a cone-shaped mound formed from mud discharge from hot springs, geysers etc. [cp. LG *mudde, mōde,* Dut. *modder,* G dial. *Mott*]

muddle (mŭd´əl) *v.t.* **1** to confuse, to bewilder. **2** to mix (up), to jumble (together) confusedly. **3** to make a mess of, to bungle, to waste, to squander. **4** to make muddy or turbid. ~*v.i.* **1** to act or proceed in a confused or bungling way. **2** to become confused. ~*n.* **1** a mess. **2** a state of confusion or bewilderment. **to make a muddle of 1** to reduce to disorder. **2** to bungle. **to muddle along** to get along somehow. **to muddle on** to keep going somehow. **to muddle through** to attain a desired result without any efficiency or organization. **to muddle up** to confuse (two or more things). **muddle-headed** *a.* **muddle-headedly** *adv.* **muddle-headedness** *n.* **muddler** *n.* **muddlingly** *adv.* [perh. from MDut. *moddelen,* to make muddy]

mudir (moodiə´) *n.* **1** a governor of a village or canton in Turkey. **2** a governor of a province in Egypt. [Turk. and Arab., from *adāra,* to administer]

muesli (mūz´li) *n.* (*pl.* **mueslis**) a dish of crushed cereals, dried fruit and nuts, usu. eaten as a breakfast cereal. [Swiss G]

muezzin (mooez´in) *n.* a Muslim crier of the hour of prayer. [Arab. *mu'azzin, mu'aththin,* from *azana, athana,* to call, to proclaim]

muff[1] (mŭf) *n.* a covering, usu. cylindrical, of fur or other material, in which the hands are placed to keep them warm. [prob. from Dut. *mof,* F *moufler,* to MUFFLE[1]]

muff[2] (mŭf) *v.t.* **1** to bungle or fail in. **2** to miss (a catch) or to fail to catch (the ball) at cricket etc. ~*v.i.* to fail, to bungle badly. ~*n.* **1** a bungling action, esp. failure to catch the ball at cricket etc. **2** an awkward or stupid fellow. [etym. uncertain]

muffin (mŭf´in) *n.* **1** a plain, round cake made with yeast dough, usu. toasted and eaten hot with butter. **2** (*N Am.*) a small sponge cake. **muffin man** *n.* (*Hist.*) a person who sells muffins. [perh. rel. to OF *moufflet,* soft bread]

muffle[1] (mŭf´əl) *v.t.* **1** to wrap or cover (up) closely and warmly. **2** to wrap up the head of so as to silence. **3** to wrap up (oars, bells etc.) so as to deaden the sound. **4** to dull, to deaden. ~*n.* **1** anything employed to deaden sound. **2** an oven or receptacle placed in a furnace used in operations in which the pottery etc. is not in direct contact with the products of combustion. **muffled** *a.* **muffler** *n.* **1** a wrapper or scarf for the throat. **2** a pad or other contrivance for deadening sound, as in a piano. **3** (*N Am.*) the silencer on a motor vehicle. [perh. from OF *mofle, moufle*, med. L *muffula*, a winter glove, a mitten, etym. unknown]

muffle[2] (mŭf´əl) *n.* the thick, naked upper lip and nose of ruminants and rodents. [F *mufle*, etym. uncertain]

mufti (mŭf´ti) *n.* **1** an official interpreter or expounder of the Koran and Muslim law. **2** civilian dress worn by members of the armed service off duty. **3** ordinary dress as distinct from that worn on state or ceremonial occasions. [Arab.]

mug[1] (mŭg) *n.* **1** a drinking vessel, usu. cylindrical without a lip, used without a saucer. **2** the contents of this. **3** (*coll.*) a dupe, a gullible person. **4** (*sl.*) the face or mouth. **5** a beerglass with a handle. ~*v.i.* (*pres.p.* **mugging,** *past, p.p.* **mugged**) to make faces, to grimace. **mugful** *n.* (*pl.* **mugfuls**). **mug's game** *n.* an unwise or unprofitable activity. **mugshot** *n.* (*sl.*) a photograph of the face, esp. for official purposes. [cp. LG *mokke, mukke*, Norw. *mugga, mugge*, Swed. *mugg*]

mug[2] (mŭg) *v.t.* (*pres.p.* **mugging,** *past, p.p.* **mugged**) to rob (someone) violently or by threatening violence, esp. in the street. **mugger**[1] *n.* **mugging** *n.* [prob. from MUG[1]]

mug[3] (mŭg) *v.i.* (*pres.p.* **mugging,** *past, p.p.* **mugged**) (*coll.*) to study hard, to grind. ~*v.t.* to work or get up (a subject). **to mug up** to work hard (on) learning a subject, esp. in a rapid, superficial way. [etym. uncertain]

mugger[1] MUG[2].

mugger[2] (mŭg´ə) *n.* an Indian crocodile, *Crocodylus palustris*, with a broad snout. [Hind. *magar*]

muggins (mŭg´inz) *n.* (*pl.* **muggins, mugginses**) **1** (*sl.*) a fool, a simpleton, used esp. of oneself (*I suppose muggins will have to do it*). **2** a children's card game resembling snap. **3** a game of dominoes. [etym. uncertain, perh. from the surname *Muggins*]

muggy (mŭg´i) *a.* (*comp.* **muggier,** *superl.* **muggiest**) damp and close, sultry. **mugginess** *n.* [cp. Icel. *mugga*, Norw. *mugg*, drizzle]

Mughal (moo´gahl) *n.* **1** a Mongolian. **2** used to refer to the Muslim dynasty in India in the 16th–19th cents. [Pers., as MONGOL]

mugwort (mŭg´wœt) *n.* any of several herbs of the genus *Artemisia*, esp. *A. vulgaris*, the motherwort. [OE *mucg-wyrt* (cp. LG *mugge*, Dut. *mug*, MIDGE, WORT)]

mugwump (mŭg´wŭmp) *n.* (*N Am.*) **1** a person of importance, a leader, a consequential person. **2** a person who abstains from voting or otherwise declines to be led by party politics. [Algonquian *mugquomp*, a chief]

Muhammadan (mŭham´ədən), **Mohammedan** *a.* of or relating to Muhammad or Islam. ~*n.* a follower of Muhammad, a Muslim; an adherent of Islam. **Muhammadanism, †Muhammadism** *n.* the Muslim religion founded by Muhammad (*c.* 570–632). **Muhammadanize, Muhammadanise, †Muhammadize, †Muhammadise** *v.t.* [Arab., praiseworthy, from *hamada*, to praise]

Usage note This series of words can give offence to Muslims: it is best to use *Muslim* or *Islam* or some associated word or phrase instead.

Muharram (mŭhŭr´əm), **Moharram** (mō-) *n.* **1** the first month (30 days) of the Muslim year. **2** the first 10 days of this observed as a fast in memory of the martyrdom of Husain, the son of Ali. [Arab., sacred]

mujahedin (mŭjah·hidēn´), **mujahideen, mujahidin** *n.pl.* fundamentalist Muslim guerrilla fighters. [Arab. *mujahidin*, fighters]

mulatto (mūlat´ō) *n.* (*pl.* **mulattos, mulattoes**) the offspring of a white person and a black person. ~*a.* of the skin colour of a mulatto, tawny, esp. when intermediate in colour between the parents. [Sp. *mulato*, from *mulo*, MULE[1]]

mulberry (mŭl´bəri) *n.* (*pl.* **mulberries**) **1** any tree of the genus *Morus*, bearing a collective fruit like a large blackberry. **2** its fruit. **3** the colour of this. **black mulberry** BLACK. **white mulberry** WHITE. **Mulberry harbour** *n.* (*Hist.*) the prefabricated port towed across to France for the invasion of 1944. **mulberry tree, mulberry bush** *n.* [prob. from OHG *mūlberi, mūrberi* (*mūr*, L *morus, beri*, BERRY), cp. G *Maulbeere*, and OE *mōrbēam*]

mulch (mŭlch) *n.* a surface layer of dead vegetable matter, manure etc. to keep the ground or the roots of plants moist. ~*v.t.* to cover with mulch. [prob. from the obs. a. *mulch*, soft (cp. OE *melse* and G dial. *Molsch*)]

mulct (mŭlkt) *n.* a fine, esp. for an offence or misdemeanour. ~*v.t.* **1** to deprive (a person) (of). **2** to swindle. **3** to punish with a fine or forfeiture. [L *mulcta*, a fine, whence *mulctāre*, to fine]

mule[1] (mūl) *n.* **1** the offspring of a male donkey and a female horse. **2** a hinny, the offspring of a male horse and a female donkey. **3** a stupidly stubborn or obstinate person. **4** a hybrid between different animals or plants. **5** a spinning mule. **mule deer** *n.* the N American black-tailed deer, *Odocoileus hemionus.* **muleteer** (-litiə´) *n.* a mule driver. **mulish** *a.* **1** like a mule. **2** obstinate, sullen. **mulishly** *adv.* **mulishness** *n.* [OE *mūl*, or OF *mul, mule*, L *mūlus*]

mule[2] (mūl) *n.* a backless shoe or slipper. [OF, from L *mulleus*, a magistrate's shoe]

mule[3] MEWL.

muley (mū´li) *n.* **1** a hornless cow. **2** any cow. ~*a.* hornless. [var. of Sc. and Ang.-Ir. *moiley*, from *moil*, Ir. *maol* (cp. Welsh *moll*, bald)]

mulga (mŭl´gə) *n.* **1** (*Austral.*) the tree *Acacia aneura.* **2** the wood of this tree. **3** the outback, the bush. **mulga grass** *n.* a fodder grass. [Austral. Abor.]

muliebrity (mūlieb´riti) *n.* (*poet.*) **1** womanhood. **2** the characteristics of womanhood. [L *muliebritas*, from *muliebris*, pertaining to women, from *mulier*, woman]

mulish MULE[1].

mull[1] (mŭl) *v.t.* (*usu. followed by* over) to ponder, consider. [etym. uncertain]

mull[2] (mŭl) *v.t.* to warm (wine, beer etc.), sweeten and flavour with spices. **mulled** *a.* [etym. uncertain]

mull[3] (mŭl) *n.* a layer of humus formed rapidly in non-acid conditions. [G, from Dan. *muld*]

mull[4] (mŭl) *n.* (*Sc.*) a promontory. [ME from Gael. *maol*, from Icel. *muli*]

mull[5] (mŭl) *n.* a thin soft muslin. [earlier *mulmull*, Hind. *malmal*]

mullah (mŭl´ə), **mollah** (mol´ə) *n.* an honorary title among Muslims for persons learned in theology and sacred law, and for Muslim ecclesiastical and civil dignitaries. [Arab. *maulā*, a judge (in Pers., Turk. and Hind. *mullā*)]

mullein (mŭl´in) *n.* any herbaceous plant of the genus *Verbascum*, such as *V. thapsus*, having woolly leaves and tall spikes of yellow flowers, sometimes called Aaron's rod. [A-F *moleyne* (F *molène*), perh. from *mol*, L *mollis*, soft]

muller (mŭl´ə) *n.* a stone with a flat surface, used to grind and mix pigment etc. on a slab. [perh. from *moloir*, grinding, from OF *moldre* (F *moudre*), L *molere*, to grind]

Müllerian mimicry (muliə´riən) *n.* (*Zool.*) a form of mimicry in which two harmful or inedible creatures develop similar appearance etc. as a protection from predators. [U. F. T. *Müller*, German zoologist, 1821–97]

mullet[1] (mŭl´it) *n.* a fish living near coasts and

ascending rivers, belonging either to the genus *Mullus* and family Mullidae (red mullet) or the genus *Mugil* and the family Mugilidae (grey mullet). [ME and OF *mulet*, dim. of L *mullus* (cp. Gr. *mullos*)]

mullet[2] (mŭl´it) *n.* (*Her.*) the figure of a five-pointed star, supposed to resemble the rowel of a spur, the mark of cadency indicating a third son. [OF *molette*, rowel, etym. uncertain]

mulligatawny (mŭligətaw´ni) *n.* a highly-flavoured curry soup. [Tamil *milagutannīr*, pepper-water]

mullion (mŭl´yən), **munnion** (mŭn´-) *n.* a vertical bar separating the compartments of a window. ~*v.t.* to divide or separate by mullions. **mullioned** *a.* [formerly *muniall*, prob. var. of MONIAL]

mullock (mŭl´ək) *n.* **1** (*Austral.*) rock containing no gold. **2** (*Austral.*) mining refuse from which the gold has been extracted. **3** (*dial.*) rubbish. **4** a muddle. [from obs. or dial. *mull*, dust, powder, from the root *mul*, to grind, cogn. with MEAL[2]]

mulloway (mŭl´əwā) *n.* a large edible Australian seafish, *Argyrosomos hololepidotus.* [Austral. Abor. *malowe*]

mult- MULTI-.

multangular (mŭltang´gūlə) *a.* having many angles. **multangularly** *adv.*

multarticulate (mŭltahtik´ūlit) *a.* many-jointed.

multi- (mŭl´ti), **mult-** *comb. form* many, several. [L *multus*, many, much]

multi-access (mŭltiak´ses) *n.* (*Comput.*) a system in which several users have simultaneous connection to the same computer.

multiaxial (mŭltiak´siəl) *a.* having many axes or lines of growth.

multicellular (mŭltisel´ūlə) *a.* (*Biol.*) many-celled.

multichannel (mŭltichan´əl) *a.* having or using many communication or television channels.

multicipital (mŭltisip´itəl) *a.* (*Bot.*) having many heads. [as BICIPITAL (under BICEPS)]

multicolour (mŭl´tikŭlə), (*NAm.*) **multicolor** *a.* of or in many colours, many-coloured. **multicoloured** *a.*

multicultural (mŭltikŭl´chərəl) *a.* **1** (of a society) made up of many cultural and ethnic groups. **2** relating to, or designed for, such a society. **multiculturalism** *n.* **multiculturalist** *n.* **multiculturally** *adv.*

multidimensional (mŭltidimen´shənəl, -dī-) *a.* having more than three dimensions. **multidimensionality** *n.* **multidimensionally** *adv.*

multidirectional (mŭltidirek´shənəl, -dī-) *a.* extending in several directions.

multi-ethnic (mŭltieth´nik) *a.* composed of, or relating to several ethnic groups.

multifaced (mŭltifāst´) *a.* (of some crystals) having many faces.

multifaceted (mŭltifas´itid) *a.* **1** (of a gem) having many facets. **2** having many aspects or factors.

multifarious (mŭltifeə´riəs) *a.* having great multiplicity, variety or diversity (*multifarious interests*). **multifariously** *adv.* **multifariousness** *n.* [L *multifārius* (MULTI-, *-fārius*, perh. rel. to *fārī*, to speak), cp. *multifāriam*, adv.]

multifid (mŭl´tifid), **multifidous** (mŭltif´idəs) *a.* having many divisions, cleft into parts, lobes, segments etc. [L *fid-*, stem of *findere*, to cleave]

multifoil (mŭl´tifoil) *a.* (*Archit.*) having more than five foils. ~*n.* an ornament having more than five foils.

multiform (mŭl´tifawm) *a.* having many forms. **multiformity** (-fawm´-) *n.*

multifunctional (mŭltifŭngk´shənəl), **multifunction** *a.* having many functions.

multigrade (mŭl´tigrād) *a.*, *n.* (of) an engine oil with a viscosity that matches several standard grades.

multigym (mŭl´tijim) *n.* **1** a single piece of apparatus with weights, levers etc. for improving muscular fitness in a variety of ways. **2** a room containing similar apparatus.

multihull (mŭl´tihŭl) *n.* a vessel with more than one hull.

multilateral (mŭltilat´ərəl) *a.* **1** of an agreement or treaty in which more than two states participate. **2** many-sided. **multilateralism** *n.* favouring multilateral action, esp. in the reduction of nuclear armament, as distinct from *unilateral.* **multilateralist** *n.* **multilaterally** *adv.*

multilingual (mŭltiling´gwəl) *a.* **1** able to speak, or speaking, several languages. **2** in many languages. **multilingualism** *n.* **multilingually** *adv.*

multimedia (mŭl´timēdiə) *a.* using different media. ~*n.pl.* systems of access by computer to text, sound and graphics for information, education, entertainment etc.

multimillionaire (mŭltimilyəneə´) *n.* a person who possesses several million pounds, dollars etc. **multimillion** (mŭl´-) *a.* costing or involving several million pounds, dollars etc.

multinational (mŭltinash´ənəl) *n.*, *a.* (a company) operating in several countries. **multinationally** *adv.*

multinomial (mŭltinō´miəl) *a.* (*Math.*) having many terms, polynomial. ~*n.* a quantity of more than two terms, connected by the plus or minus sign.

multinucleate (mŭltinū´kliət), **multinuclear** (-kliə), **multinucleated** (-ātid) *a.* (of cells) having several nuclei. **multinucleolate** (-ōlət) *a.*

multipack (mŭl´tipak) *n.* a pack containing a number of items of a foodstuff etc., sold at less than the price of that number of individual items.

multiparous (mŭltip´ərəs) *a.* **1** giving birth to many at one time. **2** bearing or having borne more than one child. **multipara** (-rə) *n.* (*pl.* **multiparae** (-rē)) a woman who has borne more than one child. **multiparity** (-par´-) *n.* [L *multiparus*]

multipartite (mŭltipah´tīt) *a.* divided into many parts.

multi-party (mŭl´tipahti) *a.* (of a state etc.) having several political parties.

multiped (mŭl´tiped) *a.* having many feet. ~*n.* an animal having many feet. [L *pēs pedis*, foot]

multiphase (mŭl´tifāz) *a.* (of an electrical device etc.) polyphase.

multiplane (mŭl´tiplān) *n.* an aeroplane having more than one pair of wings.

multiple (mŭl´tipəl) *a.* **1** having many parts, components or relations. **2** numerous and multifarious, manifold. ~*n.* **1** a quantity that contains another a number of times without a remainder. **2** (*coll.*) a multiple store. **multiple-choice** *a.* (of an examination question etc.) giving a number of different answers, from which the candidate must choose the correct one. **multiple fruit** *n.* (*Bot.*) a single fruit formed by the aggregation of numerous flowers, as in the mulberry, pineapple etc. **multiple personality** *n.* (*Psych.*) a condition occasioned by the splitting of the normal organization of mental life into a number of distinct parts, each of which is comparable with an individual personality. **multiple-poinding** *n.* (*Sc. Law*) an action in which several claimants to a fund or property are compelled to come into court and settle their claims together. **multiple sclerosis** *n.* a progressive disease causing paralysis, speech and visual defects etc., caused by the loss of myelin sheath from nerve tissue in the brain and spinal cord. **multiple standard** *n.* a standard of value obtained from the average price of several products. **multiple star** *n.* three or more stars in close proximity to each other due to their gravitational force. **multiple store, multiple shop** *n.* a number of retail stores under the same ownership. **multiplicity** (-plis´-) *n.* (*pl.* **multiplicities**) **1** many of the same kind. **2** the quality of being many or manifold. [F, from late L *multiplus* (MULTI-, *-plus*, see DUPLE)]

multiplex (mŭl´tipleks) *a.* **1** multiple, manifold. **2** (of a channel, cable etc.) allowing more than one signal to be transmitted simultaneously. **3** (of a cinema) having several screens within one building. *~n.* **1** a multiplex system or electronic signal. **2** a cinema having several screens. *~v.t.* to incorporate into a multiplex system or signal. **multiplexer, multiplexor** *n.* **multiplexing** *n.* [L MULTI-, *plex* -fold]

multiply (mŭl´tiplī) *v.t.* (*3rd pers. sing. pres.* **multiplies,** *pres.p.* **multiplying,** *past, p.p.* **multiplied**) **1** to add (a quantity called the multiplicand) to itself a certain number of times (called the multiplier) so as to produce a quantity called the product. **2** to make more numerous, to increase in number or quantity. *~v.i.* **1** to increase in number or extent. **2** to increase by propagation. **multiplicable** (-plik-), **multipliable** (-plī-) *a.* **multiplicand** (-plikand´) *n.* the quantity to be multiplied. †**multiplicate** (-plikət, -tip´-) *a.* **multiplication** (-plikā´shən) *n.* **multiplication sign** *n.* the sign × indicating multiplication. **multiplication table** *n.* a table exhibiting the products of quantities taken in pairs, usually to 12 times 12. **multiplicative** (-plikə-, -tip´-) *a.* †**multiplicator** (-pli-) *n.* **1** a person who or something that multiplies or increases. **2** the number by which the multiplicand is multiplied. **3** an instrument for intensifying an electric current. **multiplier** *n.* **1** a quantity by which a number is multiplied. **2** the ratio of an increase in income to the resulting increase in savings and investment. **3** (*Physics*) an instrument for increasing the intensity of a current, force etc. **multiplying** *n., a.* **multiplying lens, multiplying glass** *n.* a lens with a number of facets giving many reflections of an object. [OF *multiplier*, L *multiplicāre* (MULTI-, *plicāre*, to fold)]

multipolar (mŭltipō´lə) *a.* having more than two poles. *~n.* a machine having several magnetic poles.

multiprocessing (multiprō´sesing) *n.* (*Comput.*) processing by a number of central processing units working together in parallel. **multiprocessor** *n.* a computer capable of this.

multiprogramming (mŭltiprō´graming) *n.* (*Comput.*) the handling of several computer programs simultaneously by interleaving them in a single system.

multi-purpose (mŭltipœ´pəs) *a.* serving several purposes.

multiracial (mŭltirā´shəl) *a.* relating to or incorporating several racial groups. **multiracially** *adv.*

multiramified (mŭltiram´ifīd) *a.* having many ramifications or branches.

multi-role (mŭl´tirōl), **multi-rôle** *a.* having several different roles or uses.

multiserial (mŭltisiə´riəl), **multiseriate** (-riət) *a.* (*Bot.*) having many series or rows.

multiskill (mŭl´tiskil) *v.t.* to train in a range of skills, esp. relating to the same manufacturing process. **multiskilling** *n.*

multi-stage (mŭl´tistāj) *a.* **1** (of a rocket) having several sections which fall off in series at set points during flight. **2** having many stages.

multi-storey (mŭltistaw´ri), (*N Am.*) **multi-story** *a.* (esp. of a car park) having several storeys. *~n.* (*pl.* **multi-storeys,** (*N Am.*) **multi-stories**) a multi-storey car park.

multitasking (mūltitahs´king) *n.* (*Comput.*) the carrying out by a computer or system of several tasks simultaneously.

multi-track (mŭl´titrak) *a.* (of a sound recording) using several different tracks blended to produce the final sound. **multi-tracked** *a.* **multi-tracking** *n.*

multitude (mŭl´titūd) *n.* **1** the state of being numerous. **2** a great number. **3** a very large crowd or throng of people. **the multitude** the common people. **multitudinous** (-tū´-) *a.* **1** very numerous. **2** made up of many constituent parts. **3** vast. **multitudinously** *adv.* **multitudinousness** *n.* [F, from L *multitūdo -dinem* (MULTI-, -TUDE)]

multi-user (mŭltiū´zə) *a.* (*Comput.*) (of a computer system) designed for use by several people simultaneously.

multivalent (mŭltivā´lənt) *a.* (*Chem.*) **1** having several degrees of valency. **2** having a valency greater than two. **multivalence, multivalency** *n.*

multivalve (mŭl´tivalv) *a.* (of a shell) having many valves. *~n.* **1** an animal having a shell of many valves or pieces. **2** a multivalve shell. **multivalvular** (-val´-) *a.*

multivariate (mŭltiveə´riət) *a.* having two or more variable quantities.

multiversity (multivœ´siti) *n.* (*pl.* **multiversities**) (*N Am.*) a university with many departments and affiliated institutions.

multivitamin (mŭltivit´əmin) *n.* a pill etc. containing doses of several vitamins.

multivocal (mŭltiv´əkəl) *a.* having several possible interpretations, ambiguous. *~n.* an ambiguous word. [cp. EQUIVOCAL]

multi-way (mul´tiwā) *a.* having several paths of communication etc.

multum in parvo (multəm in pah´vō) *n.* much in little, a lot in a small space. [L]

multungulate (mŭltŭng´gūlət) *a.* (of an ungulate) having more than two separate toes on each foot. *~n.* a multungulate mammal, such as an elephant or tapir.

mum[1] (mŭm) *n.* (*coll.*) MOTHER[1].

mum[2] (mŭm) *a.* silent. *~int.* silence, hush! *~v.i.* (*pres.p.* **mumming,** *past, p.p.* **mummed**) **1** to play as a mummer. **2** (*Hist.*) to act in a masked mime. **mum's the word** a phrase used to ask for silence or discretion. [onomat. (cp. G *mumm*, Dut. *mommen*, to mum)]

mumble (mŭm´bəl) *v.i.* to speak indistinctly, to mutter. *~v.t.* **1** to mutter indistinctly or inarticulately. **2** to chew or mouth gently. *~n.* **1** an indistinct utterance. **2** a mutter. **mumbler** *n.* **mumbling** *a., n.* **mumblingly** *adv.* [ME *momelen*, from MUM[2]]

mumbo-jumbo (mŭmbōjŭm´bō) *n.* (*pl.* **mumbo-jumbos**) **1** (*coll.*) incomprehensible or nonsensical language. **2** an absurd object of popular veneration. [etym. uncertain]

mummer (mŭm´ə) *n.* **1** an actor in a mime, esp. one of a number of people who formerly went from house to house at Christmas in fantastic disguises performing a folk play. **2** (*derog. or facet.*) †an actor. **mummery** *n.* (*pl.* **mummeries**) **1** the act or performance of mumming. **2** tomfoolery, hypocritical parade of ritual etc. [OF *momeur*, from *momer*, to mum, perh. from Gmc. (cp. MUM[2])]

mummy[1] (mŭm´i) *n.* (*pl.* **mummies**) **1** a body of a person or animal preserved from decay by embalming, esp. after the manner of the ancient Egyptians. **2** †the dried flesh of such a body used medicinally. **3** a bituminous pigment giving a rich brown tint. **4** a pulpy mass. *~v.t.* (*3rd pers. sing. pres.* **mummies,** *pres.p.* **mummying,** *past, p.p.* **mummied**) to mummify. **mummiform** *a.* **mummify** *v.t.* (*3rd pers. sing. pres.* **mummifies,** *pres.p.* **mummifying,** *past, p.p.* **mummified**). **mummification** (-fikā´shən) *n.* **mummy case** *n.* a wooden or papier-mâché case, usu. semi-human in shape, and decorated with hieroglyphics, in which Egyptian mummies were preserved. [F *momie*, med. L *mumia*, Arab. *mūmiyā*, from *mūm*, wax used in embalming]

mummy[2] (mŭm´i) *n.* (*pl.* **mummies**) (*coll.*) MOTHER[1].

mump (mŭmp) *v.i.* (*dial.*) **1** to sulk, to mope. **2** to mumble, to munch. **3** to grimace. *~v.t.* to munch. [perh. imit.]

mumps (mŭmps) *n.* **1** a contagious disease characterized by a swelling and inflammation in the parotid and salivary glands. **2** the sulks. **mumpish** *a.* sulky. †**mumpishly** *adv.* [MUMP]

mumsy (mŭm´zi) *a.* (*comp.* **mumsier**, *superl.* **mumsiest**) maternal, drab, homely, unfashionable. ~*n.* (*facet.*) mummy.

munch (mŭnsh, mŭnch) *v.t.* to chew audibly, to eat with much movement of the jaws. ~*v.i.* to chew audibly or with much movement of the jaws. **muncher** *n.* [prob. onomat.]

Münchausen's syndrome (munsh´howzənz, münsh-) *n.* a syndrome in which the patient repeatedly simulates illness in order to obtain hospital treatment. **Münchausen's syndrome by proxy** *n.* a syndrome in which a person seeks attention by inducing illness in someone else, esp. a child. [Baron *Münchausen*, mendacious hero of tales by R. E. Raspe, 1737–94]

mundane (mŭndān´) *a.* **1** prosaic, everyday, banal. **2** belonging to this world, earthly, worldly. **3** matter-of-fact. **4** (*Astrol.*) of or relating to the horizon. **mundanely** *adv.* **mundaneness** *n.* **mundanity** (-dan´-) *n.* (*pl.* **mundanities**). [F *mondain*, L *mundānus*, from *mundus*, the world]

mung (mŭng), **mung bean** *n.* (the seed of) an E Asian bean plant of the genus *Vigna*, used as a forage plant and as the main source of beansprouts.

mungo (mŭng´gō) *n.* woollen cloth made of second-hand material (of rather higher grade than shoddy). [etym. uncertain]

municipal (mūnis´ipəl) *a.* of or relating to the government of a town or city or to local government in general. **municipalism** *n.* **municipalist** *n.* **municipality** (-pal´-) *n.* (*pl.* **municipalities**) **1** a town, city or district having a charter of incorporation or enjoying local self-government. **2** the local government of such an area. **municipalize, municipalise** *v.t.* **municipalization** (-zā´shən) *n.* **municipally** *adv.* [F, from L *mūnicipālis*, from *mūniceps -cipis*, a citizen of a town having the rights of Roman citizenship (*mūnia*, civic offices, pl. of *mūnus*, duty, *capere*, to take)]

munificent (mūnif´isənt) *a.* liberal, generous, bountiful, characterized by splendid liberality. **munificence** *n.* **munificently** *adv.* [L *mūnificus* (*mūnus*, duty, -FIC), after MAGNIFICENT]

muniment (mū´nimənt) *n.* **1** a title deed, charter or record kept as evidence or defence of a title. **2** an archive. **3** a means of help, support, defence. **4** †a fortification, a stronghold. [OF, from L *mūnīmentum*, from *mūnīre*, to fortify]

munition (mūnish´ən) *n.* **1** (*usu. pl.*) military ammunition and stores of all kinds. **2** anything required for an undertaking. **3** †a stronghold. ~*v.t.* to supply with munitions. **munitioner** *n.* [F, from L *mūnitio -ōnem*, as MUNIMENT]

munnion MULLION.

munshi MOONSHEE.

munt (mŭnt) *n.* (*sl.*, *offensive*) a black African. [Bantu *umuntu*, person]

muntin (mŭn´tin) *n.* a vertical strip dividing panels in a door or panes in a sash window, a glazing bar. [altern. of F *mountant*, pres.p. of *monter*, to MOUNT[1]]

muntjac (mŭnt´jak), **muntjak** *n.* a small SE Asian deer of the genus *Muntiacus*. [Javanese]

Muntz metal (mŭnts) *n.* a type of brass alloy (60% copper, 40% zinc) used for casting, extrusion, sheathing ships etc. [G. F. *Muntz*, 1794–1857, British metallurgist]

muon (mū´on) *n.* a subatomic particle, an unstable lepton with a mass approx. 207 times that of the electron. [contr. of MU-MESON (under MU)]

muraena (mūrē´nə) *n.* the moray, an edible marine eel-like fish of the genus *Muraena*. [L, from Gr. *muraina*, fem. of (*s*)*mūros*, sea-eel]

murage (mū´rij) *n.* (*Hist.*) a toll for the repair or maintenance of the walls of a town. [OF, from *mur*, L *mūrus -um*, wall]

mural (mū´rəl) *n.* a large painting, mosaic etc. on a wall. ~*a.* of or relating to, on or like a wall. **mural arc, mural circle, mural quadrant** *n.* a graduated arc, circle or quadrant, formerly fixed to a wall in the plane of the meridian, for determining altitudes and zenith distances. **mural crown** *n.* a crown, indented and embattled, given to the Roman soldier who first mounted a breach in storming a town. **muralist** *n.* a painter of murals. [F, from L *mūrālis*, as MURAGE]

murder (mœ´də), †**murther** (-dhə) *n.* **1** homicide with malice aforethought, a premeditated killing of another person. **2** (*coll.*) an extremely unpleasant or dangerous experience. ~*v.t.* **1** to kill (a human being) with malice aforethought. **2** to slay barbarously. **3** to spoil, to mar, by blundering or clumsiness. **4** to mangle, to ruin. **murder will out** a hidden matter will certainly come to light. **to cry/ scream bloody murder** (*N Am.*, *sl.*) to cry blue murder. **to cry/ scream blue murder** (*sl.*) to make a terrible din or commotion. **to get away with murder** (*coll.*) to do something criminal, outrageous etc. without being punished. **murderer** *n.* **murderess** *n.* **murderous** *a.* **1** of or relating to murder. **2** (apparently) intent on murder. **3** (*coll.*) extremely unpleasant or difficult. **murderously** *adv.* **murderousness** *n.* [OE *morthor* (cp. Goth. *maurthr*, Dut. *moord*, Icel. *morth*, L *mors mortis*, death), whence *myrthrian*, to murder (cp. Goth. *maurthrjan*)]

†**mure** (mūə) *v.t.* **1** to immure, to shut up. **2** to wall in. [F *murer*, L *mūrāre*, from *mūrus*, wall]

murex (mūə´reks) *n.* (*pl.* **murices** (-risēz), **murexes**) any marine gastropod mollusc of the genus *Murex*, used as a source of a purple dye. [L]

muriatic acid (mūriat´ik) *n.* hydrochloric acid. †**muriate** (-riət, -āt) *n.* chloride. [L *muriāticus*, pickled in brine, from *muria*, brine]

muricate (mūə´rikāt) *a.* (*Bot.*) having sharp points or prickles. [L *mūricātus*, shaped like the *mūrex*, see MUREX]

murices MUREX.

muriform (mūə´rifawm) *a.* (*Bot.*) arranged like bricks in a wall. [L *mūrus*, wall]

murine (mū´rīn, -rin) *a.* of or related to, or similar to a mouse. [L *murinus*, from *mus*, *muris* mouse]

murk (mœk), **mirk** *n.* **1** darkness. **2** fog, mist, poor seeing conditions. ~†*a.* **1** murky. **2** thick, obscure. **murky** *a.* (*comp.* **murkier**, *superl.* **murkiest**) **1** dark, gloomy. **2** unclear, hazy. **3** turbid, muddy. **4** dubiously respectable. **murkily** *adv.* **murkiness** *n.* [OE *mirce* (cp. Icel. *myrkr*, Dan. and Swed. *mörk*)]

murmur (mœ´mə) *n.* **1** a low, confused, continuous or repeated sound, as of running water. **2** a half-suppressed protest or complaint, a grumble. **3** a subdued speech. **4** an abnormal sound heard on listening with a stethoscope to the heart, lungs or arteries. ~*v.i.* **1** to make a low continued noise, like that of running water. **2** to mutter in discontent. **3** to find fault. ~*v.t.* to utter in a low voice. **murmurer** *n.* a grumbler, a complainer. **murmuringly** *adv.* **murmurous** *a.* [F *murmure*, L *murmur*, whence *murmurāre* (cp. Gr. *mormurein*, to boil up (as waves))]

murphy (mœ´fi) *n.* (*pl.* **murphies**) (*sl.*) a potato. [Ir. surname]

Murphy's Law (mœ´fiz) *n.* (*facet.*) the maxim that if something can go wrong, it *will* go wrong.

murrain (mŭr´ən) *n.* **1** an infectious disease among cattle. **2** †a plague, a blight. ~*a.* affected with murrain. [OF *morine*, perh. rel. to L *morī*, to die]

murre (mœ) *n.* (*N Am.*) an awk or guillemot. **murrelet** (-lit) *n.* any of several N Pacific diving birds of the genera *Brachyramphus* and *Synthliboramphus*, similar to and related to the awks. [etym. uncertain]

†**murrey** (mŭr´i) *a.* of a dark-red colour. ~*n.* this colour. [OF *moré*, *morée*, L *mōrātus*, *-ta*, from *mōrum*, mulberry]

murrhine (mŭr´īn, -in) *a.* denoting a delicate kind of Eastern ware made of fluorspar. [L *murrhinus*, from *murra*, late Gr. *morria*, a material of which costly vases were made]

†**murther** MURDER.

Mus.B., Mus.Bac. *abbr.* Bachelor of Music. [L *Musicae Baccalaureus*]

musca (mŭs´kə) *n.* (*pl.* **muscae** (mŭs´kē)) (*pl.*) any dipterous insect of the genus *Musca*, which includes the houseflies. **muscae volitantes** (volitan´tēz) *n.pl.* black specks apparently moving before the eyes. [L]

muscadel MUSCATEL.

Muscadet (mŭs´kədā) *n.* **1** a light dry white wine from the Loire region of France. **2** the grape from which this wine is made. [F, from *muscade*, nutmeg, from MUSK, -ET[1]]

muscardine (mŭs´kədin) *n.* a disease fatal to silkworms, caused by a fungoid or parasitic growth. [F *muscardine*, *muscadin*, It. *moscardino*, nutmeg, musk-lozenge, as MUSCADET]

muscarine (mŭs´kərēn, -in) *n.* an alkaloid poison from the fungus *Amanita muscaria*. [L *muscarius*, from *musca* fly]

muscatel (mŭskətel´), **muscadel** (-del´), **muscat** (mŭs´kat) *n.* **1** a kind of rich wine made from muscadine grapes. **2** the grapes from which such wine is made. **3** a sweet fragrant pear. **muscadine** (mŭs´kədīn, -din) *n.* **1** any of several varieties of grape with a musky flavour or odour. **2** †the wine muscatel. [OF, from It. *moscadello*, *-tello*, dim. of *moscato*, from *musco*, MUSK]

muscle (mŭs´əl) *n.* **1** an organ consisting of a band or bundle of contractile fibrous tissue serving to move or hold in place some part of an animal body. **2** the tissue of which this is composed. **3** muscular strength. **4** power or influence. **not to move a muscle** to keep absolutely still. **to muscle in 1** to force one's way in. **2** to interfere. **muscle-bound** *a.* stiff and inflexible as a result of over-developed muscles. **muscled** *a.* (*usu. in comb.*) having muscles, as *brawny-muscled*. **muscleless** *a.* **muscle-man** *n.* (*pl.* **muscle-men**) a man with very developed muscles, often used to intimidate. **muscly** *a.* [F, from L *musculus*, *-um*, dim. of *mus*, MOUSE[1]]

muscoid (mŭs´koid) *a.* resembling moss. ~*n.* a moss-like plant. **muscology** (-kol´-) *n.* the science of mosses, bryology. **muscologist** *n.* **muscose** *a.* †**muscosity** (-kos´-) *n.* [L *muscus*, moss, -OID]

muscovado (mŭskəvah´dō) *n.* (*pl.* **muscovados**) a moist, dark-coloured, unrefined sugar left after evaporation from the juice of sugar cane and the draining off from the molasses. [Sp. *mascabado*, unrefined]

Muscovite (mŭs´kəvīt) *n.* **1** a native or inhabitant of Moscow. **2** †a native of Muscovy (Russia). ~*a.* of Muscovy or Moscow. †**Muscovy** *n.* Russia. **Muscovy duck** (-vi) *n.* the tropical American duck, *Cairina moschata*. †**Muscovy glass** *n.* muscovite. [from F *Muscovie*, Rus. *Moskva*, Moscow]

muscovite (mŭs´kəvīt) *n.* a silver-grey form of mica, used for electrical insulation. [MUSCOVITE]

muscular (mŭs´kūlə) *a.* **1** of or relating to the muscles. **2** having well-developed muscles, strong, brawny. **muscular Christianity** *n.* the combination of full physical, moral and religious development advocated in the 19th cent. by Charles Kingsley, Thomas Hughes etc. **muscular dystrophy** *n.* a genetic disease causing progressive deterioration of the muscles. **muscularity** (-lar´-) *n.* **muscularly** *adv.* **muscular rheumatism** *n.* myalgia. **muscular stomach** *n.* any organ using muscles to digest food by grinding or squeezing. **musculature** (-ləchə) *n.* the arrangement or disposition of the muscles in the body or an organ. **musculo-** *comb. form* **musculoskeletal** *a.* of or relating to the musculature and skeleton together. †**musculous** *a.* [L *musculus*, MUSCLE]

Mus.D., Mus.Doc. *abbr.* Doctor of Music. [L *Musicae Doctor*]

muse[1] (mūz) *n.* **1** (**Muse**) in Greek mythology, each of nine goddesses, daughters of Zeus and Mnemosyne, who presided over the liberal arts. **2** the inspiring power of poetry, poetical genius. **3** a person, esp. a woman, who inspires or influences a poet or poem. [F, from L *Mūsa*, Gr. *Mousa*]

muse[2] (mūz) *v.i.* **1** to ponder, to meditate (upon). **2** to study or reflect (upon) in silence. **3** to dream, to engage in reverie. ~*v.t.* **1** to meditate on. **2** to think or say meditatively. ~*n.* †abstraction of mind, reverie. **museful** *a.* †**musefully** *adv.* **muser** *n.* **musingly** *adv.* [F *muser*, prob. from OF *muse*, mouth, snout, whence *musel*, *museau*, MUZZLE]

museology MUSEUM.

musette (mūzet´) *n.* **1** (*Hist.*) a small bagpipe formerly used in France. **2** (*Hist.*) a soft pastoral melody imitating the sound of the bagpipe. **3** (*Hist.*) a French instrument resembling the oboe. **4** †a French rustic dance. **5** (*N Am.*) a small knapsack. [F, dim. of OF *muse*, bagpipe]

museum (mūzē´əm) *n.* a room or building for the preservation or exhibition of objects illustrating antiquities, art, natural science etc. **museology** (-ol´-) *n.* the study or practice of organizing and managing museums. **museologist** *n.* **museum-piece** *n.* an object so splendid or old-fashioned that it should be on display in a museum. [L, from Gr. *mouseion*, a temple of the Muses (see MUSE[1])]

mush[1] (mŭsh) *n.* **1** a mash, a soft pulp, pulpy mass. **2** (*sl.*) sentimental nonsense. **3** (*N Am.*) porridge made of maize meal boiled. **mushy** *a.* (*comp.* **mushier**, *superl.* **mushiest**). **mushily** *adv.* **mushiness** *n.* [prob. var. of MASH[1]]

mush[2] (mŭsh) *v.i.* **1** (*in imper.*) a command to a team of sled dogs to move forward. **2** to go on a journey by dog sled. ~*n.* a journey by dog sled. [prob. from F *marchons*, advance!]

mushroom (mŭsh´room, -rum) *n.* **1** a quick-growing edible fungus, esp. *Agaricus campestris*, the field mushroom. **2** the pale brownish colour of this. **3** an object shaped like a mushroom. **4** an upstart. ~*a.* **1** of, relating to or made from mushrooms. **2** similar to a mushroom in colour. **3** ephemeral, upstart. ~*v.i.* **1** to grow or increase quickly. **2** to gather mushrooms. **3** (of bullets) to expand and flatten out. **mushroom cloud** *n.* a cloud shaped like a mushroom produced by a nuclear explosion. **mushroom growth** *n.* **1** a sudden large increase, development, expansion etc. **2** anything undergoing this. **mushroomy** *a.* [F *mousseron*, prob. from OF *mousse*, moss]

music (mū´zik) *n.* **1** the art of combining vocal and instrumental tones in a rhythmic form for the expression of emotion and pleasing of the aesthetic sense. **2** such an artistic combination of tones, musical compositions. **3** any pleasant combination of sounds. **4** melody, harmony. **5** musical taste. **6** a musical score. **7** †a band, an orchestra. **musical** *a.* **1** of or relating to music. **2** fond of or skilled in music. **3** harmonious, melodious. **4** set to or accompanied by music. ~*n.* a stage show, film etc. with much singing and dancing. **musical box,** (*N Am.*) **music box** *n.* a box with a barrel-organ mechanism for playing different tunes. **musical bumps** *n.* a party game similar to musical chairs where players sit on the floor when the music stops. **musical chairs** *n.* **1** a party game in which players strive to sit on a decreasing number of chairs when music stops playing. **2** (*derog.*) any series of changes, manoeuvres etc. taking place within politics, organizations etc. **musical comedy** *n.* (*pl.* **musical comedies**) **1** a light, romantic play or film with singing and dancing. **2** such plays or films collectively. **musical director** *n.* the person in charge of music within a stage or film production. **musicale** (-kahl´) *n.* (*N Am.*) a musical party. **musical film** *n.* a film in which singing and dancing play an important part. **musical glasses** *n.pl.* a musical instrument consisting of a series of glass vessels or tubes of varying pitch. **musical instrument** *n.* a device for producing music by vibrations, air, percussion etc. **musicality** (-kal´-), **musicalness** *n.* **musicalize, musicalise** *v.t.* **musically** *adv.* **musical saw** *n.* a bent saw played with a violin bow. **music case, music folio, music holder** *n.* a cover for sheet music. **music centre,** (*N Am.*) **music center** *n.* a unit incorporating several devices for sound reproduction, e.g. a turntable, tape deck. **music drama** *n.* an opera where music and drama are of equal importance, having no formal arias. **music hall** *n.* **1** (*Hist.*) a theatre devoted to variety entertainments. **2** a variety entertainment in the style of the old music halls. **musician** (-zish´ən) *n.* a person skilled in music, esp. in playing an instrument. **musicianly** *a.* **musicianship** *n.* **music master, music mistress** *n.* a person who teaches music in a school. **music of the spheres** *n.* in Pythagorean theory, the natural harmonies said to be produced by the movement of the celestial spheres or of the heavenly bodies set in them. **musicology** (-kol´-) *n.* the science of musical lore and history. **musicological** (-loj´-) *a.* **musicologist** *n.* a writer on this. **music paper** *n.* manuscript paper. **music stand** *n.* a light frame for supporting a sheet of music. **music stool** *n.* a stool with a revolving adjustable seat, usu. for a pianist. **music theatre,** (*N Am.*) **music theater** *n.* music and drama combined in forms different from conventional opera etc., esp. designed for small groups of performers. **music to one's ears** *n.* something that one is pleased to hear. [F *musique*, L *mūsica*, Gr. *mousikē technē*, the art of the Muses (see MUSE[1])]

musique concrète (mūzēk konkret´) *n.* CONCRETE MUSIC (under CONCRETE[1]). [F]

musk (mŭsk) *n.* **1** an odoriferous, resinous substance obtained from a sac in the male musk deer. **2** the odour of this. **3** any similar perfume. **4** the plant *Mimulus moschatus* (which originally had the smell of musk). **musk-bag** *n.* the bag or sac containing musk in various animals, esp. the musk deer. **musk deer** *n.* a small hornless deer, *Moschus moschiferus*, of Central Asia, from which musk is obtained. **musk duck** *n.* an Australian duck, *Biziura lobata*, having a musky smell. **musk melon** *n.* the melon, *Cucumis melo*. **musk ox** *n.* an Arctic-American bovine ruminant, *Ovibos moschatus*, the male of which emits a strong smell during rutting. **muskrat** *n.* **1** any of several rodents emitting a musky odour, esp. *Ondatra zibethicus*. **2** the fur of this. **musk-rose** *n.* a rambling rose, *Rosa moschata*, with large white flowers and a musky odour. **musk thistle** *n.* the thistle *Carduus nutans*, whose drooping heads have a musky fragrance. **musk tree** *n.* an Australian tree with a musky odour, esp. *Olearia argyrophylla*. **muskwood** *n.* a wood giving off a musky odour, esp. that of a musk tree or of certain W Indian trees. **musky** *a.* (*comp.* **muskier**, *superl.* **muskiest**). **muskiness** *n.* [F *musc*, late L *muscus -cum*, late Gr. *moschos*, Pers. *musk*, perh. from Sansk. *muska*, testicle]

muskeg (mus´keg) *n.* an undrained level area of mossy bog or swamp in Canada. [Cree]

muskellunge (mŭs´kəlŭnj), **maskinonge** (mas´kinonj) *n.* a large N American pike, *Esox masquinongy*, found esp. in the Great Lakes. [Algonquian]

musket (mŭs´kit) *n.* (*Hist.*) **1** the old firearm of the infantry superseded by the rifle. **2** any old-fashioned smooth-bore gun. **musketeer** (-tiə´) *n.* a soldier armed with a musket. **musketry** *n.* **1** muskets or musketeers collectively. **2** the art of using the musket. **3** fire from small arms. **musket shot** *n.* **1** the distance a musket will carry. **2** a ball or shot from a musket. [F *mousquet*, It. *mosquetto*, orig. a sparrowhawk, perh. from L MUSCA]

Muslim (muz´lim, mŭz´-), **Moslem** (moz´ləm) *n.* a person of the Islamic faith. ~*a.* of or relating to the Islamic faith, culture etc. **Muslimism** *n.* **Muslimize, Muzlimise** *v.t.* [Arab. *muslim*, pres.p. of *aslama*, to be safe or at rest, whence ISLAM]

muslin (mŭz´lin) *n.* **1** a fine, thin, cotton fabric used for dresses, curtains etc. **2** a dress made of this. **3** (*N Am.*) calico. ~*a.* made of muslin. **bit of muslin** BIT[1]. **muslin-de-laine** (-dəlen´) *n.* MOUSSELINE DE LAINE (under MOUSSELINE). **muslined** *a.* [F *mousseline*, It. *mussolina*, *-ino*, dim. of *Mussolo*, Mosul in Iraq where it was formerly made]

musmon (mŭs´mon) *n.* (*Zool.*) the mouflon. [L *mūsimon*, late Gr. *mousmōn*]

muso (mū´zō) *n.* (*pl.* **musos**) (*sl.*) a musician. [abbr.]

musquash (mŭs´kwosh) *n.* MUSKRAT (under MUSK). [Algonquian]

muss (mŭs) *n.* (*N Am.*) a state of confusion or disorder, a mess. ~*v.t.* to disarrange, to throw into disorder. **mussy** *a.* untidy, disordered. **mussiness** *n.* [var. of MESS]

mussel (mŭs´əl) *n.* **1** any mollusc of the bivalve genus *Mytilus*, esp. the edible *M. edulis*. **2** any similar freshwater, pearl-forming mollusc of the genera *Margaritifer* and *Anodonta*. [OE *mūscelle*, *muxle*, late L *muscula*, as MUSCLE]

†**Mussulman** (mŭs´əlmən) *n.* (*pl.* **Mussulmans, Mussulmen**) a Muslim. ~*a.* Muslim. [Pers. *musulmān*, that is a true believer, from Arab. MUSLIM]

must[1] (mŭst) *v.aux.* (*3rd pers. sing. pres.* **must,** *past in indirect speech* **must**) **1** to be obliged to, to be under a necessity to. **2** to be required or recommended to. **3** to be requisite to. **4** to be virtually or logically necessary to, to be certain to. **5** (as a sort of historic present) to be fated to (*What must they go and do but invade the pitch*). ~*n.* a thing that must not be missed, an essential thing. **must not 1** to be forbidden to. **2** ought not, need not. **3** to be essential that not. **must-have** *a.*, *n.* (a product) that is considered essential to have to keep up with fashion. [OE *mōste*, past of *mōt*, may, be free to (infin. *mōtan*, not found)]

Usage note In direct speech the past is expressed by *had to*.

must[2] (mŭst) *n.* mustiness, mould. [prob. from MUSTY]

must[3] (mŭst) *n.* new wine, the expressed juice of the grape before fermentation. [OE, from L *mustum*, neut. of *mustus*, fresh, new]

must[4] (mŭst), **musth** *a.* (of male elephants and camels) in a dangerous state of frenzy, connected with the mating season. ~*n.* this state. [Hind. and Pers. *mast*, intoxicated]

mustache MOUSTACHE.

mustachio (məstah´shiō) *n.* (*pl.* **mustachios**) a moustache, esp. a large one. **mustachioed** *a.* [MOUSTACHE]

mustang (mŭs´tang) *n.* the wild horse of the American prairies. **mustang grape** *n.* a small red Texan grape from a wild vine, *Vitis candicans*. [Sp. *mestengo* (now *mesteño*), prob. from *mesta* (rel. to L *mixta*, see MIX), a company of graziers, confused with *mostrenco*, astray, rel. to L *monstrāre*, to show, to point out]

mustard (mŭs´təd) *n.* **1** the seeds of *Sinapis alba* ground and used esp. as a condiment. **2** any plant of the genus *Brassica*, with yellow flowers and slender pods, esp. *B. nigra*. **3** a brownish-yellow colour. **4** (*coll.*) zest. ~*a.* brownish-yellow. **to cut the mustard** (*N Am.*, *sl.*) to be up to the required standard. **mustard and cress** *n.* white mustard and cress used in the seed-leaf as salad herbs. **mustard gas** *n.* an irritant poison gas. **mustard oil** *n.* an oil obtained from black mustard seeds. **mustard plaster** *n.* a mixture of powdered mustard seeds applied to the skin as a stimulant, counter-irritant etc. **mustard seed** *n.* **1** the seed of the mustard plant. **2** a small thing from which something bigger may develop. [OF *mostarde* (F *moutarde*), as MUST[3]]

mustee MESTEE.

mustelid (mŭs´təlid, mŭstel´id) *n.* a small mammal of the family Mustelidae which contains the weasels, martens, skunks, badgers etc. ~*a.* of or relating to this family. **musteline** (mŭs´təlin) *n., a.* [L, weasel, from *mūs*, MOUSE[1]]

muster (mŭs´tə) *v.t.* **1** to summon (up) (strength, courage etc.). **2** to bring together. **3** to collect or assemble for review, roll-call etc. **4** (*N Am.*) to enrol in the army. **5** (*Austral.*) to round up (livestock). ~*v.i.* to meet in one place. ~*n.* **1** the assembling of troops for parade or review. **2** a register of forces mustered. **3** a collection, a gathering. **4** (*Austral.*) a round-up of livestock. **5** a collection of peacocks. **6** †a pattern, a show. **to muster in** (*N Am.*) to enrol (a recruit) in the forces. **to muster out** (*N Am.*) to discharge (a soldier) from the army. **to pass muster 1** to be accepted as satisfactory. **2** to pass inspection without censure. **muster-book** *n.* a book in which military forces are registered. **musterer** *n.* **†muster-master** *n.* (*Hist.*) a person who takes account of troops and their equipment. **muster-roll** *n.* a roll or register of troops, a ship's company etc. **muster station** *n.* a place, esp. on board ship, where people have to assemble in emergency. [OF *mostre*, It. *mostra*, a show, a display, from L *monstrāre*, to show (see MONSTER)]

musth MUST[4].

mustn't MUST[1].

musty (mŭs´ti) *a.* (*comp.* **mustier,** *superl.* **mustiest**) **1** mouldy. **2** sour, stale. **3** vapid, antiquated, spiritless. **mustily** *adv.* **mustiness** *n.* [etym. uncertain]

mutable (mū´təbəl) *a.* **1** liable to change. **2** inconstant, fickle, unstable. **mutability** (-bil´-), **†mutableness** *n.* **mutably** *adv.* [L *mūtābilis*, from *mūtāre*, to change]

mutagen (mū´təjən) *n.* something that causes or assists genetic mutation. **mutagenesis** (-jen´ə-) *n.* **mutagenic** *a.* [*muta*te, -GEN]

mutant (mū´tənt) *n.* an organism that has undergone mutation. ~*a.* resulting from mutation.

mutate (mūtāt´) *v.i.* **1** to change. **2** to be transmuted. **3** (*Biol.*) to develop into a new species, to sport. ~*v.t.* to change or modify (a sound), esp. by umlaut. **mutation** *n.* **1** the act or process of changing. **2** a permanent variation in organisms giving rise to a new species. **3** a species so produced. **4** umlaut. **5** the change of an initial consonant in Celtic languages. **mutational** *a.* **mutationally** *adv.* **mutative** (-tə-), **mutatory** *a.*

mutatis mutandis (mūtahtis mūtan´dis) *adv.* the necessary alterations having been made. [L]

mutch (mŭch) *n.* (*Sc.*) a close-fitting woman's cap. [MDut. *mutse* (Dut. *muts*), prob. from *amutse* or *almutse*, cp. AMICE[2] and MOZZETTA]

mutchkin (mŭch´kin) *n.* (*Hist.*) a Scottish measure of about three-quarters of a pint (426 ml). [MDut. *mudseken*, dim. of *mudde*, *mud*, L *modius*, a corn measure]

mute[1] (mūt) *a.* **1** silent, uttering no sound, speechless. **2** not having the power of speech, dumb. **3** (of hounds) not giving tongue. **4** not spoken. **5** not sounded, unpronounced. **6** (of a consonant) plosive. ~*n.* **1** a dumb person. **2** a contrivance for deadening sound (as in a trumpet). **3** a person who is silent or speechless. **4** an actor in mime or whose part is speechless. **5** a letter of a word which is not pronounced. **6** a plosive consonant. **7** a hired attendant at a funeral. **8** a dumb porter or janitor in Eastern countries. ~*v.t.* **1** to deaden or muffle the sound of. **2** to make more subdued. **to stand mute 1** to refuse or be unable to speak. **2** (*Law*) to refuse to plead (usu. from malice). **mute button** *n.* a device on a telephone which, when depressed, renders any speech etc. inaudible at the receiver's end. **muted** *a.* unassertive, subdued. **mutely** *adv.* **muteness** *n.* **mute swan** *n.* a Eurasian swan, *Cygnus olor*, with white plumage and an orange bill. **mutism** *n.* muteness; silence; inability to hear and speak, dumbness. [ME and OF *muet*, pop. L *mūtettus*, dim. of *mūtus*, assim. later to L]

†mute[2] (mūt) *v.i.* (of birds) to excrete. ~*v.t.* to void (as excrement). ~*n.* birds' faeces. [OF *mutir*, *muetir*, *esmeutir*, *esmaltir*, perh. from Gmc.]

mutilate (mū´tilāt) *v.t.* **1** to maim, to mangle. **2** to disfigure. **3** to cut off a limb or an essential part of. **4** to damage (literary and other work) by excision. **mutilation** (-ā´shən) *n.* **mutilator** *n.* [L *mutilātus*, p.p. of *mutilāre*, from *mutilus*, maimed (perh. rel. to Gr. *mutilos*, *mutulos*, hornless)]

mutineer (mūtiniə´) *n.* a person who mutinies. ~*v.t.* to mutiny. **mutinous** (mū´-) *a.* ready or inclined to mutiny; rebellious. **mutinously** *adv.* **mutinousness** *n.* **mutiny** (mū´tini) *n.* (*pl.* **mutinies**) (an instance of) open resistance to or a revolt against constituted authority, esp. by sailors or soldiers against their officers. ~*v.i.* (*3rd pers. sing. pres.* **mutinies,** *pres.p.* **mutinying,** *past, p.p.* **mutinied**) to rise or rebel against authority (esp. in the army or navy). [F *mutinier*, from *mutin*, mutinous, pop. L *movita*, a movement, commotion, from L *movēre*, to MOVE]

mutism MUTE[1].

muton (mū´ton) *n.* (*Biol.*) the smallest element of genetic material capable of giving rise to a new form by mutation.

mutt (mŭt) *n.* **1** (*sl.*) a fool, a stupid or inept person. **2** (*derog.*) a dog, esp. a mongrel. [etym. uncertain]

mutter (mŭt´ə) *v.i.* **1** to speak, in a low voice or with compressed lips. **2** to grumble, to murmur (at or against). **3** to make a low rumbling noise. ~*v.t.* **1** to utter in a low or indistinct voice. **2** to say in secret. ~*n.* **1** a low or indistinct utterance. **2** a low rumbling sound. **3** a murmur, a grumble. **mutterer** *n.* **mutteringly** *adv.* [prob. imit.]

mutton (mŭt´ən) *n.* **1** the flesh of sheep used as food. **2** (*facet.*) a sheep. **3** (*sl.*) †a loose woman. **mutton-bird** *n.* **1** any Pacific bird of the genus *Puffinus*, esp. the sooty shearwater, *P. griseus* of New Zealand, and the short-tailed shearwater, *P. tenuirostris* of Australia. **2** any of various petrels. **mutton chop** *n.* **1** a rib or other small piece of mutton for broiling. **2** a mutton chop whisker. **mutton chop whiskers** *n.pl.* a man's long side whiskers shaped like mutton chops. **mutton dressed as lamb** *n.* (*coll.*) an older woman dressed or made up to look younger. **mutton-head** *n.* (*coll.*) a stupid person. **mutton-headed** *a.* [OF *moton* (F *mouton*), med. L *multo-ōnem*, prob. from Celt. (cp. OIr. *molt*, Gael. *mult*, Welsh *mollt*)]

mutual (mū´chuəl) *a.* **1** reciprocal, reciprocally given and received. **2** possessed, done, felt etc. by each of two persons, parties etc., to or towards the other. **3** shared by or common to two or more persons (*mutual friend*). **mutual fund** *n.* (*N Am.*) a unit trust. **mutual inductance** *n.* the coupling of two electrical circuits in such a way that an alteration of current in one effects an electromotive force in the other. **mutual induction** *n.* the production of an electromotive force in a circuit by a current change in an adjacent circuit that is magnetically linked. **mutual insurance** *n.* **1** insurance under a company granting a certain share of the profits to policyholders. **2** a system of insurance in which parties agree to indemnify each other for specified losses. **mutualism** *n.* **1** the doctrine that true welfare is based on mutual dependence. **2** symbiosis in which organisms are associated without detriment to either. **mutualist** *n.* **mutualistic** *a.* **mutualistically** *adv.* **mutuality** (-al´-) *n.* **mutualize, mutualise** *v.t., v.i.* **mutually** *adv.* [F *mutuel*, L *mūtuus*, reciprocal, from *mūtāre*, to change]

Usage note The use of *mutual* to mean shared or common is still sometimes disapproved of, though it has been recorded for 400 years.

mutuel (mū´tūəl) *n.* PARI-MUTUEL.
mutule (mū´tūl) *n.* (*Archit.*) one of the projecting blocks under the corona of a Doric cornice, a modillion. [F, from L *mūtulus*]
†mutuum (mū´tūəm) *n.* (*Hist.*) a contract under which goods are lent for consumption, to be repaid in property of the same kind and quantity. [L, neut. of *mūtuus*, borrowed]
muu-muu (moo´moo) *n.* a loose brightly-coloured dress worn by women in Hawaii. [Hawaiian]
Muzak® (mū´zak), **muzak** *n.* **1** recorded background music played in shops, restaurants etc. **2** a system for this.
muzhik (moo´zhik), **moujik** *n.* (*Hist.*) a Russian peasant, a serf. [Rus.]
muzzle (mŭz´əl) *n.* **1** the projecting mouth and nose of an animal, as of a horse, dog etc., the snout. **2** a guard put over an animal's muzzle to prevent biting or feeding. **3** the mouth of a gun or cannon. *~v.t.* **1** to put a muzzle on. **2** to silence. **muzzle-loader** *n.* a gun loaded at the muzzle, as distinct from *breech-loader*. **muzzle velocity** *n.* the velocity of a projectile as it leaves the muzzle of a gun etc. [OF *musel* (F *museau*), prob. from med. L *mūsellum*, dim. of *mūsus -um*, etym. uncertain]
muzzy (mŭz´i) *a.* (*comp.* **muzzier**, *superl.* **muzziest**) **1** muddled, dazed. **2** fuddled, tipsy. **3** blurred. **muzzily** *adv.* **muzziness** *n.* [etym. uncertain]
MV *abbr.* **1** megavolt. **2** motor vessel.
MVO *abbr.* Member of the Royal Victorian Order.
MVP *abbr.* (in sport) most valuable player.
MW *abbr.* **1** Malawi (IVR). **2** medium wave. **3** megawatt.
mW *abbr.* milliwatt(s).
Mx *chem. symbol* maxwell.
MY *abbr.* motor yacht.
my (mī) *a.* **1** possessive of I[2]. **2** used in some forms of address, as *my boy, my dear.* **3** used in some expressions of surprise, admiration etc., as *my goodness!, my word!* *~int.* used to express mild surprise. **my Lady** a form of address to certain titled women. **my Lord** a form of address to certain titled men. [ME *mī*, *mīn*, MINE[1]]
my- MYO-.
myalgia (mīal´jiə) *n.* (*Med.*) a morbid state of the muscles characterized by pain and cramp, muscular rheumatism. **myalgic** *a.* **myalgic encephalomyelitis** *n.* (*Med.*) a condition of excessive fatigue, general malaise, lack of coordination, depression etc., often following a viral infection. [Gr. *mūs*, MUSCLE, *-algia*, *algos*, pain]
myalism (mī´əlizm) *n.* a kind of witchcraft practised in the W Indies. [*myal*, prob. from W Afr., -ISM]
myall (mī´əl) *n.* **1** any tree of the genus *Acacia*, esp. *A. pendula*, yielding scented wood used in making tobacco pipes. **2** an Australian Aborigine leading a traditional way of life. [Austral. Abor. *maiāl*]
Myanman (mī´anman) *a.* of or relating to Myanmar (Burma) in SE Asia. *~n.* a native or inhabitant of Myanmar.
myasthenia (mīəsthē´niə) *n.* (*Med.*) a condition causing loss of muscle power. **myasthenia gravis** (grah´vis, grav´is) *n.* a chronic progressive disease of the autoimmune system causing muscular weakness without atrophy. **myasthenic** (-then´-) *a.*
mycelium (mīsē´liəm) *n.* (*pl.* **mycelia** (-liə)) (*Bot.*) the vegetative parts of fungi, mushroom spawn. **mycelial** *a.* [Gr. *mukēs*, mushroom, *-l*, -IUM]
Mycenaean (mīsinē´ən) *a.* of or relating to the late Bronze Age civilization of Mycenae, an ancient city of Argolis, Greece. *~n.* an inhabitant of Mycenae or the area influenced by its culture.
-mycete (mī´sēt) *comb. form* used to form the names of fungi, as in *myxomycete.*
myceto- (mīsē´tō), **myco-** (mī´kō) *comb. form* used to form words denoting a connection with fungi, as in *mycetophagous, mycobacterium.* [Gr. *mukētes*, pl. of *mukēs*, mushroom]
mycetoma (mīsitō´mə) *n.* (*pl.* **mycetomas, mycetomata** (-mətə)) (*Med.*) a fungoid disease affecting the bones of the feet or hand. **mycetomatous** *a.*
-mycin (mī´sin) *comb. form* used to form the names of antibiotic compounds developed from fungi, as in *streptomycin.*
myco- MYCETO-.
mycology (mīkol´əji) *n.* **1** the study of fungi. **2** the fungi of a particular area. **3** a treatise on fungi. **mycological** (-loj´-) *a.* **mycologically** *adv.* **mycologist** *n.*
mycophagy (mīkof´əji) *n.* the eating of fungi. **mycophagist** *n.* **mycophagous** (-gəs) *a.*
mycoplasma (mīkōplaz´mə) *n.* (*pl.* **mycoplasmas, mycoplasmata** (-mətə)) any of a group of prokaryotic mainly parasitic micro-organisms of the genus *Mycoplasma.*
mycoprotein (mī´kəprōtēn) *n.* protein obtained from fungi, esp. that produced for human consumption.
mycorrhiza (mīkōrī´zə) *n.* (*pl.* **mycorrhizae** (-zē)) a fungoid growth supplying the roots of a plant with material from humus. **mycorrhizal** *a.* [Gr. *rhiza*, a root]
mycosis (mīkō´sis) *n.* **1** (*Med.*) the presence of parasitic fungi in the body. **2** any disease caused by these. **mycotic** (-kot´-) *a.*
mycotoxin (mīkōtok´sin) *n.* (*Bot.*) a poisonous substance produced by a fungus.
mycotrophy (mīkot´rəfi) *n.* (*Bot.*) the condition of a plant in a symbiotic association with its mycorrhizae. [Gr. *trophe*, nourishment]
mydriasis (midrī´əsis, mī-) *n.* (*Med.*) an abnormal dilation of the pupil of the eye. **mydriatic** (-driat´-) *n.* a drug that causes the pupils to dilate. [late L, from Gr. *mudriāsis*]
myel- MYELO-.
myelin (mī´əlin) *n.* (*Anat.*) a soft, white, fatty tissue forming a sheath round certain nerve fibres. **myelinated** *a.* having a myelin sheath. **myelination** (-ā´shən) *n.*
myelitis (mīəlī´tis) *n.* (*Med.*) inflammation of the spinal cord. **myelitic** (-lit´-) *a.* [Gr. *muelon*, var. of *muelos*, marrow]
myelo- (mī´əlō), **myel-** *comb. form* of or relating to the spinal cord. [Gr. *muelos*, marrow]
myeloid (mī´əloid) *a.* of or relating to the spinal cord.
myeloma (mīəlō´mə) *n.* (*pl.* **myelomas, myelomata** (-mətə)) a usu. malignant tumour of the bone marrow.
mylodon (mī´lədon) *n.* a gigantic Pleistocene slothlike edentate of the genus *Mylodon.* **mylodont** *n., a.* [Gr. *mulē*, mill, *odous odontos*, tooth]
mylohyoid (mīlōhī´oid) *a.* (*Anat.*) of or relating to the molar teeth and the hyoid bone. **mylohyoidean** (-oi´-) *n., a.* [as MYLODON, HYOID]
mynah (mī´nə), **mina, myna** *n.* any of various SE Asian passerine birds, esp. *Gracula religiosa*, known particularly for its ability to imitate the human voice. [Hind. *maina*]
mynheer (mīnhiə´) *n.* **1** the Dutch title of address equivalent to Mr or Sir. **2** a Dutchman. [Dut. *mijnheer*, Mr, Sir (*mijn*, my, *heer*, lord, master, cp. HERR)]
myo- (mī´ō), **my-** *comb. form* of or relating to muscles. [Gr. *mūs muos*, muscle]

myocardium (mīōkah´diəm) *n.* (*pl.* **myocardia** (-diə)) the muscular substance of the heart. **myocardial** *a.* **myocardial infarction** *n.* destruction of an area of the heart muscle, a heart attack. **myocarditis** (-dī´tis) *n.* inflammation of the myocardium.

myofibril (mīōfī´bril) *n.* (*Anat.*) any of the elongated contractile threads that make up striated muscle cells.

myogenic (mīōjen´ik) *a.* (*Med.*) originating in the muscles.

myoglobin (mīōglō´bin) *n.* (*Anat.*) a protein containing iron that stores oxygen in muscle.

myography (mīog´rəfi) *n.* the recording of muscular contractions. **myographic, myographical** (-graf´-) *a.* **myographist** *n.*

myology (mīol´əji) *n.* **1** the study of the muscles. **2** a treatise on the muscles. **myologic** (-loj´-), **myological** *a.* **myologist** *n.*

myopia (mīō´piə) *n.* **1** short-sightedness. **2** lack of imagination, foresight etc. **myope** (mī´ōp) *n.* a short-sighted person. **myopic** (-op´-) *a.* **myopically** *adv.* [F, from late L *myōps myōpis*, Gr. *muōps muōpos* (*muein*, to shut, *ōps*, eye)]

myosin (mī´əsin) *n.* (*Anat.*) a protein in the contractile muscular tissue.

myosis MIOSIS.

myositis (mīəsī´tis) *n.* (*Med.*) inflammation of a muscle.

myosotis (mīəsō´tis), **myosote** (mī´əsōt) *n.* any hardy plant of the genus *Myosotis*, esp. the forget-me-not. [L, from Gr. *muosōtis* (*mūs muos*, MOUSE[1], *ous ōtos*, ear)]

myotic MIOTIC (under MIOSIS).

myotonia (mīətō´niə) *n.* (*Med.*) the inability to relax muscles after vigorous effort, muscle stiffness or spasm. **myotonic** (-ton´ik) *a.*

myriad (mir´iəd) *a.* innumerable, countless. ~*n.* (*poet.*) **1** ten thousand. **2** a very great number. [med. L *myrias -adis*, Gr. *mūrias -ados* (from *mūrios*, countless, *mūrioi*, ten thousand)]

myriapod (mir´iəpod) *n.* any terrestrial arthropod of the class Myriapoda, including the centipedes and millipedes and characterized by a very large indeterminate number of jointed feet. ~*a.* having numerous legs. [Gr. *pous podos*, foot]

myrica (mirī´kə) *n.* **1** the tamarisk. **2** any of various plants of the genus *Myrica*, esp. the bog myrtle or sweet gale. [L, from Gr. *murikē*]

myrmeco- (mœ´miko), **myrmec-** *comb. form* of or relating to ants. [Gr. *myrmēx*, ant]

myrmecology (mœmikol´əji) *n.* the study of ants. **myrmecological** (-loj´-) *a.* **myrmecologist** *n.*

myrmecophile (mœ´mikəfīl) *n.* an organism living in a symbiotic relationship with ants.

myrmidon (mœ´midən) *n.* a faithful follower, esp. an unscrupulous underling, a hired ruffian. [L, from Gr. *Murmidones*, a warlike people of Thessaly, ruled over by Achilles, and led by him to the siege of Troy]

myrobalan (mīrob´ələn), **myrobalan plum** *n.* the cherry plum. **myrobalan nut** *n.* the dried plumlike fruit of an Asian tree *Terminalia chebula*, used in medicines and for dyeing and tanning. [F, from L *myrobalanum*, Gr. *murobalanos* (*muron*, unguent, *balanos*, acorn)]

myrrh[1] (mœ) *n.* a gum resin from trees of the genus *Commiphora* or other trees growing in the Near East, used in the manufacture of incense, perfumes etc. **myrrhic** (mœ´rik-, mir´-), **myrrhy** *a.* [OE *myrre* or OF *mirre*, L *myrrha*, Gr. *murra*, from Semitic (cp. Arab. *murr*, Heb. *mōr*)]

myrrh[2] (mœ) *n.* an umbelliferous plant, *Myrrhis odorata*, also called *sweet cicely*. [late L *myrrhis*, Gr. *murris*]

myrrhine MURRHINE.

myrtle (mœ´təl) *n.* **1** a tree or shrub of the genus *Myrtus*, esp. *M. communis*, a tall shrub with glossy evergreen leaves and sweet-scented white or rose-coloured flowers, anciently sacred to Venus. **2** (*N Am.*) the periwinkle. **myrtaceous** (-tā´-) *a.* of or relating to the plant family Myrtaceae. **myrtle wax** *n.* a vegetable wax from the bayberry or wax myrtle, *Myrica cerifera*. [OF *myrtille*, L *myrtus*, Gr. *murtos*]

myself (mīself´) *pron.* **1** I[2] or ME[1] (objective) used to give emphasis (usu. in apposition). **2** the reflexive form of ME[1]. **3** my normal or usual self. **by myself** alone, unaided. **I myself** I, for my part. **to be myself** to act in my normal manner.

mystagogue (mis´təgog) *n.* a person who interprets or initiates into divine mysteries, esp. an initiator into the Eleusinian and other ancient Greek mysteries. **mystagogic** (-goj´-), **mystagogical** *a.* **mystagogy** (-ji) *n.* [L *mystagōgus*, Gr. *mustagōgos* (*mustēs*, from *muein*, to close the eyes or lips, *agein*, to lead)]

mystery[1] (mis´təri) *n.* (*pl.* **mysteries**) **1** a secret or obscure matter. **2** something beyond human comprehension. **3** secrecy, obscurity. **4** a divine truth partially revealed. **5** (*pl.*) secret rites and ceremonies known to and practised only by the initiated. **6** the esoteric rites practised by the ancient Greeks, Romans etc. **7** the Eucharist. **8** a mystery story. **to make a mystery of** to treat something with exaggerated secrecy. **mysterious** (-tiə´ri-) *a.* **1** secret, incomprehensible, not easily understood. **2** obscure, mystic, occult. **3** fond of mystery. **mysteriously** *adv.* **mysteriousness** *n.* **mystery play** *n.* a form of medieval drama the characters and events of which are drawn from sacred history. **mystery story** *n.* (*pl.* **mystery stories**) a fictional work that involves the reader in a puzzling event. **mystery tour** *n.* an excursion to a destination that is kept secret until it is reached. [prob. through an A-F *misterie*, OF *mistere* (F *mystère*), L *mystērium*, Gr. *mustērion*, as MYSTAGOGUE]

†**mystery**[2] (mis´təri) *n.* (*pl.* **mysteries**) a handicraft, trade or occupation. [ME *mistere*, med. L *misterium*, *ministerium*, MINISTRY (under MINISTER)]

mystic (mis´tik) *a.* **1** of or relating to mystery or mysticism. **2** occult, esoteric. **3** allegorical, emblematical. ~*n.* **1** a person who practises mysticism. **2** a supporter of the doctrine of mysticism. **mystical** *a.* **mystically** *adv.* **mysticalness** *n.* **mysticism** (-sizm) *n.* **1** the doctrine that self-surrender and spiritual understanding can lead to direct communion with and absorption in God, or that truth may be apprehended directly by the soul without the intervention of the senses and intellect. **2** the pursuit of these ends. **mysticize** (-sīz), **mysticise** *v.t.* [OF *mystique*, L *mysticus*, Gr. *mustikos*, as MYSTERY[1]]

mystify (mis´tifī) *v.t.* (*3rd pers. sing. pres.* **mystifies**, *pres.p.* **mystifying**, *past, p.p.* **mystified**) **1** to bewilder, to puzzle, to hoax. **2** to involve in mystery. **mystification** (-fikā´shən) *n.* **mystifying** *a.* **mystifyingly** *adv.* [F *mystifier* (as MYSTICISM (under MYSTIC), -FY]

mystique (mistēk´) *n.* **1** professional skill or technique that impresses the layperson. **2** the mystery surrounding some creeds, professions etc. **3** any mysterious aura surrounding a person or thing. [MYSTICISM (under MYSTIC)]

myth (mith) *n.* **1** a fictitious legend or tradition, accepted as historical, usu. embodying the beliefs of a people on the creation, the gods, the universe etc. **2** the body of such legends or traditions. **3** a parable, an allegorical story. **4** a fictitious event, person, thing etc. **5** a thing widely believed in but not true. **mythic, mythical** *a.* **1** of or relating to myths. **2** legendary. **3** imaginary, untrue. **mythically** *adv.* **mythicism** (-sizm) *n.* **mythicist** *n.* **mythicize** (-sīz), **mythicise** *v.t.* **1** to make into myth. **2** to interpret as a myth. **mythicizer** *n.* [Gr. *muthos*, fable]

mythi MYTHUS.

mytho- (mith´ō) *comb. form* **1** of or relating to myth. **2** mythical.

mythogenesis (mithōjen´əsis) *n.* the creation or production of myths.
mythography (mithog´rəfi) *n.* the writing or narration of myths, fables etc. **mythographer** *n.*
mythology (mithol´əji) *n.* (*pl.* **mythologies**) **1** a system of myths in which are embodied the beliefs of a people concerning their origin, deities, heroes etc. **2** the study of myths. **3** a treatise on myths. **mythologer, mythologist** *n.* **mythologic** (-loj´-), **mythological** *a.* **mythologically** *adv.* **mythologize, mythologise** *v.i.* **1** to invent myths. **2** to study or interpret myths. ~*v.t.* to make (an event, person, story etc.) the basis of a myth. **mythologizer** *n.* [F *mythologie*, late L *mythologia*, Gr. *mūthologia* (MYTHO-, -LOGY)]
mythomania (mithōmā´niə) *n.* an abnormal tendency to lie or exaggerate. **mythomaniac** *n.*
mythopoeia (mithəpē´ə) *n.* the making of myths. **mythopoeic** (-pē´ik), **mythopoetic** (-pōet´-) *a.* **1** myth-making. **2** of or relating to a stage of culture when myths were developed. [Gr. *mūthopoios* (*poiein*, to make)]
mythos (mī´thos, mith´-) *n.* (*pl.* **mythoi** (-oi)) **1** (*poet.*) myth. **2** the mythology, beliefs, attitudes etc. of a society. **3** a narrative theme, a scheme of events.
mythus (mī´thəs) *n.* (*pl.* **mythi** (-thī)) (*poet.*) a myth.
myxedema MYXOEDEMA.
myxo- (mik´sō), **myx-** *comb. form* **1** of, relating to or living in slime. **2** of, relating to or consisting of mucus. [Gr. *muxa*, slime, mucus]
myxoedema (miksədē´mə), (*N Am.*) **myxedema** *n.* (*Med.*) a condition characterized by underactivity of the thyroid gland and consequent weight gain, mental sluggishness, thickening of the skin, listlessness and sensitivity to cold. **myxoedematous, myxoedemic** *a.*
myxoma (miksō´mə) *n.* (*pl.* **myxomas, myxomata** (-mətə)) a benign tumour composed of mucous or gelatinous tissue. **myxomatous** *a.*
myxomatosis (miksəmətō´sis) *n.* a contagious and fatal virus disease in rabbits.
myxomycete (miksəmī´sēt) *n.* a slime mould of the class Myxomycetes.
myxovirus (mik´səvīrəs) *n.* (*pl.* **myxoviruses**) any of a group of viruses causing such illnesses as influenza, mumps etc.

N[1] (en), **n** (*pl.* **Ns, N's**) the 14th letter of the English and other versions of the Roman alphabet, corresponding to the Greek nu (N, ν). It is pronounced as a dentilingual or alveolar nasal continuant. *~symbol* **1** (*Math.*) an indefinite number. **2** a printed dash the width of a letter n, an en. **to the nth (degree) 1** (*Math.*) to any power. **2** to the utmost.

N[2], **N.** *abbr.* **1** knight (in chess). **2** New. **3** newton(s). **4** North; Northern. **5** nuclear.

N[3] *chem. symbol* nitrogen.

n, n. *abbr.* **1** name. **2** nano-. **3** neuter. **4** noon. **5** note.

'n (ən), **'n'** *conj.* (*coll.*) and.

NA *abbr.* **1** Netherlands Antilles (IVR). **2** North America.

Na *chem. symbol* sodium.

na (nə) *adv.* (*usu. in comb.*) not (*dinna*).

n/a *abbr.* **1** no account. **2** non-acceptance. **3** not applicable. **4** not available.

NAAFI (naf´i), **Naffy** *n.* **1** an organization running canteens for the Services. **2** a canteen run by this organization. [acronym for the *N*avy, *A*rmy and *A*ir *F*orce *I*nstitutes]

naan NAN[2].

nab (nab) *v.t.* (*pres.p.* **nabbing,** *past, p.p.* **nabbed**) (*sl.*) to catch, to seize, to apprehend. [cp. Norw. and Swed. *nappa*, Dan. *nappe*]

nabob (nā´bob) *n.* **1** (*Hist.*) a deputy-governor or prince under the Mughal empire in India. **2** a very rich person, esp. one who amassed wealth in India. [NAWAB]

nacarat (nak´ərat) *n.* **1** a pale-red colour tinged with orange. **2** a fine linen or crêpe dyed this colour. [F, from Sp. and Port. *nacarado*, from *nacar*, NACRE]

nacelle (nəsel´) *n.* **1** the basket suspended from a balloon. **2** a small, streamlined body on an aircraft, distinct from the fuselage, housing engines, crew etc. [F, from late L *nāvicella*, dim. of *nāvis*, ship]

nache NATCH[2].

nacho (nah´chō) *n.* (*pl.* **nachos**) a crisp corn chip used as an appetizer in Mexican cuisine, often served with melted cheese, a chilli dip etc.

NACODS (nā´kodz) *abbr.* National Association of Colliery Overmen, Deputies and Shotfirers.

nacre (nā´kə) *n.* **1** mother-of-pearl. **2** a fish yielding mother-of-pearl. **nacreous** (nā´kriəs), **nacrous** (nā´krəs) *a.* **nacrite** (-rīt) *n.* a pearly variety of mica. [F, from Sp. and Port. *nacar* (cp. Arab. *naqrah*, a cavity)]

NAD *abbr.* nicotinamide adenine dinucleotide, a coenzyme which is important in metabolic reactions.

nadir (nā´diə) *n.* **1** the point of the heavens directly opposite to the zenith or directly under our feet. **2** the lowest point or stage (of decline, degradation etc.). [Arab., opposite (to the zenith)]

naevus (nē´vəs), (*N Am.*) **nevus** *n.* (*pl.* **naevi** (-vī), (*N Am.*) **nevi**) a congenital discoloration of the skin, a birthmark or mole. **naevoid** (-void) *a.* [L]

naff[1] (naf) *a.* (*sl.*) unfashionable, lacking in taste, style or credibility. [etym. unknown]

naff[2] (naf) *v.i.* (*sl.*) to go away (*Naff off!*). **naffing** *a.* (*sl., euphem.*) bloody. [prob. euphemism for FUCK, cp. EFF]

Naffy NAAFI.

nag[1] (nag) *v.i.* (*pres.p.* **nagging,** *past, p.p.* **nagged**) **1** to be continually finding fault. **2** to scold (at). **3** to cause pain or discomfort. **4** to worry (at). *~v.t.* **1** to find fault with or scold continually. **2** to be continually pestering with complaints or fault-finding. **3** to cause pain, discomfort or worry to. *~n.* a person who continually nags. **nagger** *n.* **naggingly** *adv.* [perh. from Scand. (cp. Norw. and Swed. *nagga*, Dan. *nage*, Icel. *gnaga*, to gnaw)]

nag[2] (nag) *n.* **1** a small horse or pony for riding. **2** (*coll.*) a horse. [ME *nagge*, akin to Dut. *negge*, a small horse]

Nagari (nah´gəri) *n.* Devanagari.

nagger, naggingly NAG[1].

nagor (nā´gaw) *n.* the reedbuck. [arbitrary name]

Nah. *abbr.* (*Bible*) Nahum.

Nahuatl (nahwah´təl) *n.* (*pl.* **Nahuatl, Nahuatls**) **1** a member of any of various peoples native to Central America and Mexico. **2** the language of the Nahuatl. *~a.* of or relating to the Nahuatl. **Nahuatlan** *a.* [Sp., from Nahuatl]

naiad (nī´ad) *n.* (*pl.* **naiads, naiades** (-ədēz)) **1** a water nymph. **2** the larva of a dragonfly. **3** any aquatic plant of the genus *Najas*, having narrow leaves and small flowers. **4** any of various freshwater shellfish of the genus *Unio*. [L and Gr. *naiad-*, nom. *naias*, from *naiein*, to flow]

naiant (nā´ənt) *a.* (*Her.*) swimming, natant. [prob. through an A-F *naiant* (OF *noiant*, pres.p. of *noier*), L *natāre*, to swim]

naïf (nīēf´) *a.* NAIVE. *~n.* a naive person.

nail (nāl) *n.* **1** a small, pointed spike, usu. of metal, with a head, for hammering into wood or other material to fasten things together, or for use as a peg etc. **2** the horny substance at the tip of human fingers and toes. **3** a claw, a talon. **4** a horny plate on the soft bill of certain birds. **5** (*Hist.*) a measure of 2¼ in. (5.7 cm). *~v.t.* **1** to fasten or secure with nails. **2** to stud with nails. **3** to hold, to fix. **4** to seize, to catch. **5** to engage (attention). **6** to expose (a lie). **nail in the coffin of** something likely to cause the ruin of. **on the nail** on the spot; at once. **to hit the nail on the head 1** to hit upon the true facts of a case. **2** to do exactly the right thing. **to nail down 1** to extract a promise from. **2** to determine, to find out the identity or meaning of. **3** to fix with nails. **to nail one's colours to the mast** to persist in one's support of something. **to nail to the counter** to expose, to brand as spurious. **to nail up 1** to close or fasten up by nailing. **2** to fix at a height with nails. **nail-biting** *n.* chewing off the ends of one's fingernails. *~a.* (of an event or experience) creating tension. **nail brush** *n.* a small brush for cleaning the fingernails. **nailed** *a.* (*usu. in comb.*) as in *long-nailed, nailed-on.* **nail enamel** *n.* (*N Am.*) nail polish. **nailer** *n.* a maker of nails. **nailery** *n.* **nail file** *n.* a small file for trimming fingernails. **nail head** *n.* **1** the head of a nail. **2** (*Archit.*) an ornament on late Norman and Early English mouldings, shaped like the head of a nail. **nail-headed** *a.* **nailless** *a.* **nail polish** *n.* a type of varnish, often coloured, for putting on fingernails or toenails. **nail punch** *n.* a punch for driving a nail down so that the head is flush with the surface. **nail scissors** *n.pl.* small scissors for cutting the fingernails and toenails. **nail set** *n.* a nail punch. **nail varnish** *n.* nail polish. [OE *nægel*, cogn. with L *unguis*, Gr. *onux*]

nainsook (nān´suk) *n.* a thick muslin, formerly made in India. [Hind. *nainsukh* (*nain*, eye, *sukh*, pleasure)]

naira (nī´rə) *n.* the standard monetary unit of Nigeria. [contr. of *Nigeria*]

naissant (nā´sənt) *a.* (*Her.*) rising or coming forth, from a fesse or other ordinary. [F, pres.p. of *naître*, ult. from L *nascī*, to be born]

naive (nīēv´), **naïve** *a.* **1** artless, ingenuous, simple, unaffected. **2** gullible, credulous. **3** (of art) deliberately unsophisticated and childlike. **naively** *adv.* **naiveness** *n.* **naivety, naïvety, naïveté** (-tā) *n.* (*pl.* **naiveties, naïveties, naïvetés**) **1** the state of being naive. **2** a naive act or deed. [F, fem. of *naïf*, L *nātīvus*, NATIVE]

naked (nā´kid) *a.* **1** without clothing, uncovered, nude. **2** without natural covering, as leaves, hair, shell etc. **3** not sheathed. **4** exposed, unsheltered, defenceless, unarmed. **5** stripped, destitute or devoid (of). **6** having no trees. **7** unfurnished; not ornamented. **8** bare, plain, undisguised (*naked greed*). **9** unsupported, uncorroborated, unconfirmed. **the naked ape** modern man. **the naked eye** the eye unassisted by any optical instrument. **naked ladies, naked boys** *n.pl.* the meadow saffron. **nakedly** *adv.* **nakedness** *n.* [OE *nacod* (cp. Dut. *naakt*, G *nackt*, Swed. *naken*, Dan. *nögen*), cogn. with L *nūdus*]

†**naker** (nā´kə) *n.* a kind of kettledrum. [OF *nacre*, *nacaire*, Arab. *nakāra*]

NALGO (nal´gō) *abbr.* (*Hist.*) National and Local Government Officers' Association.

Nama (nah´mə) *n.* (*pl.* **Nama, Namas**) **1** a member of a people of South Africa and Namibia. **2** the language of the Nama. ~*a.* of or relating to the Nama. [Nama]

namby-pamby (nambipam´bi) *a.* **1** weakly and insipidly sentimental. **2** affectedly pretty or simple. ~*n.* (*pl.* **namby-pambies**) **1** namby-pamby talk or writing. **2** a namby-pamby person. **namby-pambyism** *n.* [from *Ambrose* Philips, 1671–1749, a sentimental pastoral poet]

name (nām) *n.* **1** a word denoting any object of thought, esp. one by which a person, animal, place or thing is known, spoken of or addressed. **2** a mere term, as distinct from substance; sound or appearance, as opposed to reality. **3** a famous person. **4** reputation, honourable character, fame, glory. **5** a race, a family. **6** an underwriter of a Lloyd's syndicate. ~*v.t.* **1** to give a name to, to call, to style. **2** to call by name. **3** to nominate, to appoint. **4** to mention, to specify, to cite. **5** (of the Speaker) to mention (an MP) as being guilty of disorderly conduct. ~*a.* well-known. **a name to conjure with** CONJURE[1]. **by name** called (*Mary Smith by name*). **by the name of** called (*a writer by the name of John Truten*). **in all but name** virtually, practically. **in name only** officially but not genuinely (*a marriage in name only*). **in one's own name** by one's own authority. **in the name of** for the sake of. **no names, no pack-drill** (*coll.*) mention no names and no one gets into trouble. **of the name of** by the name of. **one's name is mud** MUD. **the name of the game** (*coll.*) the central or important thing; what something is all about. **to call names** to abuse verbally. **to have to one's name** to own, to possess. **to make a name for oneself** to become well known. **to name after** to call (a child) by the same name as (*I am named after my grandmother*). **to name for** (*N Am.*) to name after. **to name names** to mention people by name usu. in order to accuse or blame them. **to name the day** DAY. **to put one's name down for** **1** to apply for. **2** to promise to give. **to take someone's name in vain** VAIN. **what's in a name?** the name is less important than the essence. **you name it** (*coll.*) whatever you want or think of (*There was smoked salmon, caviar, you name it*). **nameable** *a.* **name-calling** *n.* verbal abuse. **name-child** *n.* a child or person named after one. **name-day** *n.* **1** the day sacred to a saint after whom one is named. **2** ticket-day. **name-dropper** *n.* a person who tries to impress by mentioning the names of important or famous people as if they were close friends. **name-drop** *v.i.* (*pres.p.* **name-dropping**, *past, p.p.* **name-dropped**). **nameless** *a.* **1** having no name. **2** anonymous. **3** illegitimate. **4** unknown, obscure, inglorious. **5** inexpressible, indefinable. **6** unfit to be named, abominable, detestable. **namelessly** *adv.* **namelessness** *n.* **namely** *adv.* that is to say. **name part** *n.* a title role. **nameplate** *n.* a sign showing the name of the occupant of a room or building. **namesake** *n.* a person or thing having the same name as or named after another. **name-tape** *n.* a tape attached to a garment or other object showing the owner's name. [OE *nama* (cp. Dut. *naam*, G *Name*, Icel. *nafn*, Sansk. *nāman*, L *nōmen*, Gr. *onoma*), whence OE *genamian*, *nemnan*]

Namibian (nəmib´iən) *n.* a native or inhabitant of Namibia. ~*a.* of or relating to Namibia.

namma GNAMMA.

nan[1] (nan) *n.* (*dial.*) a grandmother.

nan[2] (nahn), **naan** *n.* in Indian cookery, a type of slightly leavened bread. [Hind.]

nana[1] (nah´nə) *n.* (*sl.*) a fool. [perh. from BANANA[1]]

nana[2] (nan´ə), **nanna** *n.* (*coll.*) a grandmother.

nancy (nan´si), **nance** (nans) *n.* (*pl.* **nancies, nances**) (*offensive, sl.*) **1** an effeminate young man. **2** a homosexual. ~*a.* effeminate. **nancy boy** *n.* a nancy. [from the female forename]

nanism (nā´nizm) *n.* dwarfishness; being stunted. **nanization** (-zā´shən), **nanisation** *n.* [F *nanisme* (L *nānus*, Gr. *nānos*, dwarf)]

nankeen (nangkēn´) *n.* **1** a cotton fabric, usu. of a buff or yellow colour, exported from Nanjing. **2** a fabric made in imitation of this. **3** a yellowish-buff colour. **4** (*pl.*) clothes, esp. trousers, made of nankeen. [*Nanjing*, capital of province of Jiangsu, China]

nanna NANA[2].

nanny (nan´i) *n.* (*pl.* **nannies**) **1** a children's nurse. **2** an overprotective person, government etc. **3** NAN[1]. ~*v.t.* (*3rd pers. sing. pres.* **nannies**, *pres.p.* **nannying**, *past, p.p.* **nannied**) to treat in an overprotective manner. **nanny goat** *n.* a female goat. [dim. of *Anne*]

nannygai (nan´igī) *n.* (*pl.* **nannygais**) an edible red fish, *Centroberyx affinis*, found in Australian rivers. [Austral. Abor.]

nano- (nan´ō) *comb. form* one thousand-millionth. [Gr. *nānos*, a dwarf]

nanogram (nan´ōgram), **nanogramme** *n.* one thousand-millionth of a gram.

nanometre (nan´ōmētə), (*N Am.*) **nanometer** *n.* one thousand-millionth of a metre.

nanosecond (nan´ōsekənd) *n.* one thousand-millionth of a second.

nanotechnology (nanōteknol´əji) *n.* the branch of technology which deals with measuring, making or manipulating extremely small objects. **nanotechnological** (-loj´-) *a.* **nanotechnologist** *n.*

naos (nā´os) *n.* (*pl.* **naoi** (nā´oi)) in ancient Greece, the inner part of a temple. [Gr., a temple]

nap[1] (nap) *v.i.* (*pres.p.* **napping**, *past, p.p.* **napped**) **1** to sleep lightly or briefly, to doze. **2** to be careless or unprepared. ~*n.* a short sleep, a doze, esp. in the daytime. **to catch napping** **1** to find asleep. **2** to take unawares; to catch unprepared or at a disadvantage. [OE *hnæppian* (cp. OHG *hnaffezan*)]

nap[2] (nap) *n.* **1** the smooth and even surface produced on cloth or other fabric by cutting and smoothing the fibre or pile. **2** a smooth, woolly, downy or hairy growth on a surface. **3** (*Austral., coll.*) bedding, blankets. ~*v.t.* (*pres.p.* **napping**, *past, p.p.* **napped**) to put a nap on. **napless** *a.* [prob. from MDut. or MLG *noppe* (cp. Dut. *nop*, Dan. *noppe*, Norw. *napp*)]

nap[3] (nap) *n.* **1** **a** a card-game in which five cards are dealt to each player, the one engaging to take the highest number of tricks playing against the others. **b** a call of five in nap. **2 a** the act of betting all one's money on one horse etc. **b** a tip claimed to be a certainty. *~v.t.* (*pres.p.* **napping,** *past, p.p.* **napped**) to name as a likely winner. **not to go nap on** (*Austral., coll.*) not to like much. **to go nap 1** in nap, to offer to take all five tricks. **2** to risk everything on one venture. **3** to win all the games or matches in a series. **nap hand** *n.* a position in which there is a good chance of succeeding in a risky venture. [short for NAPOLEON]

napa NAPPA.

napalm (nā´pahm) *n.* **1** a thickening agent which is produced from naphthenic acid, other acids and aluminium. **2** a highly inflammable petroleum jelly which is produced from naphthalene and coconut-palm oil, largely used for bombs. *~v.t.* to attack with napalm bombs. [*na*phthene *palm*itic]

nape (nāp) *n.* the back of the neck. [etym. uncertain]

Naperian NAPIERIAN (under NAPIER'S BONES).

napery (nā´pəri) *n.* (*esp. Sc.*) linen, esp. table linen. [OF *naperie, napperie,* from *nape, nappe,* L *mappa,* NAPKIN]

naphtha (naf´thə) *n.* an inflammable oil produced by dry distillation of organic substances, such as bituminous shale or coal. **naphthalene** (-lēn) *n.* a white crystalline product of the dry distillation of coal tar, used as a disinfectant and in the manufacture of dyes and explosives. **naphthalic** (-thal´-) *a.* **naphthalize, naphthalise** *v.t.* to treat with naphtha. **naphthene** (-thēn) *n.* a liquid hydrocarbon obtained from Caucasian naphtha. **naphthenic** (-thē´nik) *a.* **naphthenic acid** *n.* any carboxylic acid produced in the refining of petroleum. **naphthol** (-thol) *n.* either of two phenols derived from naphthalene. [L and Gr.]

Napier's bones (nā´piəz), **Napier's rods** *n.pl.* a contrivance invented by John Napier for facilitating the multiplication and division of high numbers by means of slips of bone or other material divided into compartments. **Napierian** (-piə´ri-), **Naperian** *a.* **Napierian logarithm** *n.* a natural logarithm. [John *Napier,* 1550–1617, Scottish mathematician]

napiform (nā´pifawm) *a.* (*Bot.*) turnip-shaped. [L *nāpus,* turnip, -FORM]

napkin (nap´kin) *n.* **1** a small square of linen or paper, esp. one used at table to wipe the hands, protect the clothes, or serve fish etc., on; a serviette. **2** a baby's nappy. **3** a small towel. **4** a handkerchief. **5** (*N Am.*) a sanitary towel. **table napkin** TABLE. **napkin ring** *n.* a ring used to hold a table napkin and indicate the owner. [ME *nappekyn* (F *nappe,* see NAPERY)]

Naples yellow (nā´pəlz) *n.* **1** a yellow pigment made from antimony. **2** the colour of this. [*Naples,* city in S Italy]

napoleon (nəpō´liən) *n.* **1** (*Hist.*) a French gold coin of 20 francs issued by Napoleon I. **2** (*Hist.*) a kind of top-boot. **3** the card game, nap. **4** (*N Am.*) a millefeuille. [F *napoléon* from *Napoléon* Bonaparte, 1769–1821, Emperor of the French]

Napoleonic (nəpōlion´ik) *a.* **1** of or relating to Napoleon I or his times. **2** resembling Napoleon I; dominating, masterful; spectacular. **Napoleonism** (-pō´-) *n.* **1** belief in the hereditary claims of the Napoleonic dynasty. **2** belief in autocracy. **Napoleonist** *n., a.*

nappa (nap´ə), **napa** *n.* a soft leather made from sheepskin or goatskin. [*Napa,* California]

nappe (nap) *n.* (*Geol.*) a large sheet of rock which has been moved from its original position by thrusting. [F, a tablecloth]

napper (nap´ə) *n.* (*sl.*) the head. [etym. uncertain]

nappy¹ (nap´i) *n.* (*pl.* **nappies**) a piece of soft absorbent material fastened round a baby's bottom to absorb urine and faeces. **nappy rash** *n.* a rash on a baby's body caused by prolonged contact with a wet nappy. [NAPKIN]

nappy² (nap´i) *a.* (*comp.* **nappier,** *superl.* **nappiest**) (of ale or beer) foaming, strong, heady. *~n.* ale, liquor. [prob. from NAP¹]

narc (nahk) *n.* (*N Am., sl.*) a narcotics agent.

narceine (nah´sēn) *n.* a bitter crystalline alkaloid contained in opium after the extraction of morphine. [F *narcéine,* Gr. *narkē,* numbness, torpor, -INE]

narcissi NARCISSUS.

narcissism (nah´sisizm) *n.* (*Psychol.*) a state of self-love present at an early stage of development when one's own body rather than an outside love object furnishes sensual gratification. **narcissist** *n.* **narcissistic** (-sis´tik) *a.* **narcissistically** *adv.* [*Narcissus,* in Gr. myth., a beautiful youth who fell in love with his own reflection]

narcissus (nahsis´əs) *n.* (*pl.* **narcissi** (-ī), **narcissuses**) any bulbous plant of the genus *Narcissus,* containing the daffodils and jonquils, esp. the white *N. poeticus.* [L, from Gr. *narkissos,* perh. rel. to *narkē,* numbness, from its supposed narcotic effect]

narco- (nah´kō) *comb. form* of or relating to torpor or narcotics. [Gr. *narkē,* torpor]

narcolepsy (nah´kəlepsi) *n.* (*Med.*) a nervous disease characterized by fits of irresistible drowsiness. **narcoleptic** (-lep´tik) *a., n.* [Gr. *-lepsy* (see EPILEPSY)]

narcosis (nahkō´sis) *n.* **1** narcotic poisoning, the effect of continuous use of narcotics. **2** a state of stupor.

narcoterrorism (nahkōter´ərizm) *n.* terrorism involving illegal drugs. **narcoterrorist** *n.*

narco-therapy (nahkōther´əpi) *n.* the treatment of mental disorder by drug-induced sleep.

narcotic (nahkot´ik) *a.* **1** producing torpor or coma. **2** soporific. **3** causing sleep or dullness. *~n.* **1** a substance that allays pain by inducing sleep or torpor. **2** any of a group of addictive drugs, such as opium and morphine, which induce numbness and stupor. **narcotically** *adv.* **narcotism** (nah´kə-) *n.* **narcotist** (nah´-) *n.* **narcotize** (nah´kə-), **narcotise** *v.t.* **narcotization** (-zā´shən) *n.*

nard (nahd) *n.* **1** any of various plants of the valerian family, esp. *Valeriana celtica.* **2** an unguent or balsam used by the ancients, prepared from an aromatic plant; spikenard. [F, from L *nardus,* Gr. *nardos,* of Oriental orig. (cp. Heb. *nēr'd,* Sansk. *narada, nalada*)]

nardoo (nah´doo) *n.* (*pl.* **nardoos**) an Australian plant, *Marsilea quadrifolia,* the spore case of which is pounded and eaten by the Aborigines. [Austral. Abor.]

nares (neə´rēz) *n.pl.* (*Anat.*) the nostrils. **narial** *a.* [L]

narghile (nah´gilā, -li) *n.* a hookah or tobacco pipe in which the smoke is drawn through water. [Pers. *nārgīleh,* from *nārgīl,* coconut]

narial NARES.

nark (nahk) *n.* (*sl.*) **1** a police spy, a decoy. **2** (*Austral.*) an annoying person or thing. **nark it!** (*sl.*) stop it! **narked** *a.* (*sl.*) annoyed. **narky** *a.* (*comp.* **narkier,** *superl.* **narkiest**) (*sl.*) irritable, complaining. [Romany *nak,* nose]

Narragansett (narəgan´sət) *n.* an almost extinct Algonquian language of Rhode Island. [Algonquian, people of the small point]

narrate (nərāt´) *v.t.* to tell, to relate, to give an account of the successive particulars of in speech or writing. **narratable** *a.* **narration** (-ā´shən) *n.* **narrative** (nar´ə-) *n.* **1** a recital of a series of events; a tale, a story. **2** the art of narrating. *~a.* **1** in the form of narration. **2** relating to an event or story. **narratively** *adv.* **narratology** (-rətol´-) *n.* the study of the form and function of narrative. **narratological** (-loj´-) *a.* **narratologist** (-rətol´-) *n.* **narrator** *n.* [L *narrātus,* p.p. of *narrāre* (prob. cogn. with *gnārus,* aware, and Eng. KNOW)]

narrow (na´rō) *a.* (*comp.* **narrower,** *superl.* **narrowest**)

1 of little breadth or extent from side to side. 2 constricted, limited. 3 restricted, of limited scope. 4 illiberal in views or sentiments; prejudiced, bigoted. 5 (*dial.*) selfish, niggardly. 6 close, near, within a small distance, with little margin. 7 precise, accurate. 8 (of a vowel) tense. ~*v.i.* to become narrow or narrower. ~*v.t.* 1 to make narrow or narrower. 2 to contract in range, views or sentiments. 3 to confine, to limit, to restrict. ~*n.* (*usu. pl.*) 1 a strait. 2 a narrow mountain pass. **narrow boat** *n.* a long, narrow canal boat. **narrowcast** *v.t., v.i.* (*past, p.p.* **narrowcast, narrowcasted**) (*esp. N Am.*) to transmit (television programmes) by cable to a small area. ~*n.* 1 the practice of narrowcasting. 2 a narrowcast programme or transmission. **narrowcaster** *n.* **narrowcasting** *n.* **narrow circumstances** *n.pl.* poverty. **narrow escape** *n.* an escape only just managed. **narrow gauge** *n.* a railway gauge of less than 4 ft. 8½ in. (1.43 m). **narrowish** *a.* **narrowly** *adv.* **narrow-minded** *a.* illiberal, bigoted. **narrow-mindedly** *adv.* **narrow-mindedness** *n.* **narrowness** *n.* **narrow seas** *n.pl.* the English Channel and the Irish Sea. **narrow squeak** *n.* (*coll.*) a narrow escape. [OE *nearu* (cp. Dut. *naar*, dismal)]

narthex (nah´theks) *n.* (*pl.* **narthexes**) 1 a vestibule or porch across the west end in early Christian churches, to which catechumens, women and penitents were admitted. 2 a similar vestibule in a modern church. [Gr. *narthēx*, a plant]

nartjie (nah´chi) *n.* (*S Afr.*) a small sweet orange like a mandarin. [Afrikaans]

narwhal (nah´wəl) *n.* an Arctic delphinoid cetacean, *Monodon monoceros*, with a long tusk or tusks developed from one or both of its teeth. [Dan. or Swed. *narhval* (cp. Icel. *nāhvalr*)]

nary (neə´ri) *a.* (*coll., dial.*) not one single (*nary a one*). [alt. of *ne'er a*]

NAS *abbr.* Noise Abatement Society.

NASA (nah´sə) *abbr.* (*US*) National Aeronautics and Space Administration.

nasal (nā´zəl) *a.* 1 of or relating to the nose. 2 sounded or produced with the nasal passage open. 3 pronounced through or as if through the nose. ~*n.* 1 a letter or sound produced with the nasal passage open. 2 (*Hist.*) a noseguard. **nasality** (-zal´-) *n.* **nasalize, nasalise** *v.i., v.t.* **nasalization** (-zā´shən) *n.* **nasally** *adv.* [F, from med. L *nāsālis* (*nāsus*, nose)]

nascent (nas´ənt, nā´-) *a.* 1 coming into being. 2 beginning to develop; immature. 3 (*Chem.*) having a higher reactivity than usual because just being formed. **nascency** *n.* [L *nascens -ntis*, pres.p. of *nascī*, to be born]

naseberry (nāz´bəri) *n.* (*pl.* **naseberries**) a sapodilla. [Sp. or Port. *nespera*, L *mespila*, Gr. *mespilē*, MEDLAR]

naso- (nā´zō) *comb. form* of or relating to the nose. [L *nāsus*, nose]

nasofrontal (nāzōfrŭn´təl) *a.* of or relating to the nose and frontal bone.

nasogastric (nāzōgas´trik) *a.* of or relating to the nose and stomach.

nasolacrymal (nāzōlak´riməl), **nasolachrymal, nasolacrimal** *a.* of or relating to the nose and tears.

nastic (nas´tik) *a.* (*Bot.*) (of movement) not related to the direction of the stimulus. [Gr. *nastos*, close-pressed]

nasturtium (nəstœ´shəm) *n.* (*pl.* **nasturtiums**) 1 a trailing plant, *Tropaeolum majus*, with vivid orange flowers. 2 any cruciferous plant of the genus *Nasturtium*, containing the watercress. [L (*nāsus, tort-*, stem of *torquēre*, to TORMENT[1])]

nasty (nahs´ti) *a.* (*comp.* **nastier**, *superl.* **nastiest**) 1 extremely unpleasant. 2 objectionable, annoying, vexatious. 3 awkward, trying. 4 spiteful, odious, vicious. 5 dirty, foul, filthy to a repulsive degree. 6 indecent, obscene. 7 repellent to taste, smell etc., nauseous. ~*n.* (*pl.* **nasties**) 1 a nasty person. 2 a video nasty. **something nasty in the woodshed** WOODSHED (under WOOD). **nastily** *adv.* **nastiness** *n.* **nasty one** *n.* 1 a rejection. 2 a difficult or awkward question. 3 a bad injury. **nasty piece of work** *n.* (*coll.*) a nasty person. [cp. Dut. *nestig*, Swed. dial. *naskug*]

NASUWT *abbr.* National Association of Schoolmasters and Union of Women Teachers.

Nat. *abbr.* 1 National. 2 Nationalist. 3 Natural.

natal[1] (nā´təl) *a.* of, from or relating to one's birth. **natality** (-tal´-) *n.* (*pl.* **natalities**) birth rate. [F, from L *nātālis*, from *nātus*, p.p. of *nascī*, to be born]

natal[2] (nā´təl) *a.* (*Anat.*) of or relating to the buttocks. [NATES]

natant (nā´tənt) *a.* 1 (*formal*) swimming. 2 (*Bot.*) floating. **natation** (nətā´shən) *n.* **natatorial** (-taw´ri-), **natatory** (-təri) *a.* **natatorium** (-taw´riəm) *n.* (*pl.* **natatoriums, natatoria** (-riə)) (*N Am.*) an indoor swimming pool. [L *natans -ntem*, pres.p. of *natāre*, freq. of *nāre*, to swim]

natch[1] (nach) *int.* (*sl.*) of course. [short for *naturally*]

natch[2] (nach), **nache** (nāch) *n.* (*dial.*) the part of an ox between the loins, the rump. [var. of *nache*, see AITCHBONE]

nates (nā´tēz) *n.pl.* (*Anat.*) the buttocks. **natiform** (-ifawm) *a.* having the form of buttocks. [L]

†**nathless** (nath´lis), †**natheless** *adv.* nevertheless.

natiform NATES.

nation (nā´shən) *n.* 1 a people under the same government and inhabiting the same country. 2 a people belonging to the same ethnological family and speaking the same language. 3 a federation of N American Indian tribes. **nationhood** (-hud) *n.* **nation state** *n.* a state which is entirely inhabited by a single nation. **nationwide** *a., adv.* covering the whole nation. [F, from L *nātiōnem*, nom. *-tio*, from *nāt-*, see NATAL[1]]

national (nash´ənəl) *a.* 1 of or relating to the nation, esp. to the whole nation. 2 peculiar to a nation. 3 public, general, as distinct from *local*. 4 attached to one's country, nationalistic. ~*n.* 1 a member or subject of a particular nation. 2 one's fellow countryman. **the National** the Grand National. **national anthem** *n.* a hymn or song embodying the patriotic sentiments of a nation, such as the British 'God Save the Queen' or the French 'La Marseillaise'. **National Assistance** *n.* (*Hist.*) a government benefit paid to people with low income or no income. **national bank** *n.* (*US*) a commercial bank chartered under the federal government. **national convention** *n.* (*US*) a convention of either of the main political parties held to nominate presidential candidates etc. **National Covenant** *n.* the Scottish Presbyterian compact of 1638. **national curriculum** *n.* a standardized curriculum for all schools in England and Wales, specifying the subjects which all pupils must study and the required levels of attainment at various stages. **national debt** *n.* the debt of a nation in its corporate capacity. **national epic** *n.* a heroic poem embodying a nation's traditional history. **national football** *n.* (*Austral.*) Australian Rules Football. **National Front** *n.* an extreme right-wing political party in the UK. **national grid** *n.* 1 a country-wide network of high-voltage electric power lines linking major power stations. 2 the coordinate system in Ordnance Survey maps. **National Guard** *n.* 1 organized militia of individual states in the US. 2 a force which took part in the French Revolution, first formed in 1789. **National Health (Service)** *n.* in Britain, the system of state-provided medical service, established in 1948. **national income** *n.* the total income of a nation. **National Insurance** *n.* a system of compulsory insurance paid for by employers and employees and yielding benefits to the sick, retired and unemployed. **nationalism** *n.* 1 patriotic effort, sentiment etc. 2 extreme devotion to the nation. **3** the policy of national independence. **4** nationalization of industry. **nationalist** *n., a.* **nationalistic** (-lis´tik) *a.* **nationalistically** *adv.* **nationality** (-nal´-) *n.* (*pl.* **nationalities**). **nationalize, nationalise** *v.t.* **1** to make national. **2** to naturalize. **3** to bring (an industry etc.) under State control. **nationalization** (-zā´shən) *n.* **nationalizer** *n.* **nationally** *adv.* **national park** *n.* an area owned by the nation and set aside to preserve beauty, wildlife etc. **national service** *n.* (*Hist.*) compulsory service in the armed forces. **National Socialism** *n.* (*Hist.*) the political doctrine of the National Socialist German Workers' Party, which came into power in Germany under Adolf Hitler in 1933, with prominent among its teachings the superiority of the German race, hatred of Jews and a need for world expansion. **National Socialist** *n.* **National Trust** *n.* an organization in the UK etc. concerned with the preservation of historic buildings and areas of countryside of great beauty. **National Vocational Qualification** *n.* a qualification in any of a variety of vocational subjects, set at various levels.

native (nā´tiv) *n.* **1** a person born in a specified place. **2** a local resident. **3** a plant or animal indigenous to a district or country. **4** (*offensive*) a member of a non-white indigenous people of a country. **5** (*Austral.*) a white person born in Australia. **6** (*offensive*) any non-white person. **7** an oyster raised in British waters, esp. in an artificial bed. *~a.* **1** of or relating to a place or country by birth, indigenous, not exotic. **2** belonging to a person, animal or thing, by nature; inborn, innate, natural, not acquired. **3** of or relating to the time or place of one's birth. **4** rightful, hereditary. **5** natural (to). **6** plain, simple, unaffected. **7** (of metals) occurring in a pure or uncombined state. **8** (of an oyster) raised in British waters. **9** of or relating to the natives of a place or region. **10** (*Austral.*) resembling an animal or plant from another country (*native bear*). **to go native** (of a settler) to live and dress like local inhabitants. **Native American** *n.* an American Indian from the US. **native bear** *n.* (*Austral.*) a koala. **native heath** *n.* one's home country or area. **native indigo** *n.* (*Austral.*) the poisonous Darling pea. **natively** *adv.* **nativeness** *n.* **native rock** *n.* a rock found in its original place. **native speaker** *n.* a person who speaks a particular language as their first language. **nativism** *n.* **1** (*Philos.*) the doctrine of innate ideas. **2** (*US*) advocacy of the rights of natives as opposed to naturalized Americans. **nativist** *n.* [L *nātīvus*, NATION]

Usage note Because of associations with racism and imperialist domination, the use of *native* of the original inhabitants of formerly (or still) colonized countries has come to be considered offensive, and is best avoided. See also, however, the note on *Native American* under AMERICAN.

nativity (nətiv´iti) *n.* (*pl.* **nativities**) **1** birth, esp. that of Jesus Christ, the Virgin Mary or St John the Baptist. **2** a festival in commemoration of this. **3** a picture of the birth of Jesus Christ. **4** a horoscope. **nativity play** *n.* a play about the birth of Jesus Christ performed by children at Christmas. [as NATIVE]

NATO (nā´tō), **Nato** *abbr.* North Atlantic Treaty Organization.

natron (nā´trən) *n.* a mineral consisting of hydrated sodium carbonate. **natrolite** (nat´rəlīt, nā´trə) *n.* a hydrated silicate of aluminium with a high soda content. [F and Sp., from Arab. *natrūn, nitrūn*, Gr. *nitron*, NITRE]

natter (nat´ə) *v.i.* **1** to chatter idly; to chat, exchange gossip. **2** to find fault, to be peevish. *~n.* **1** idle chatter. **2** a chat, gossip. **3** grumbling. **nattered** *a.* peevish. **natterer** *n.* [etym. uncertain]

natterjack (nat´əjak) *n.* a European toad, *Bufo calamita*, with a yellow stripe down the back. [etym. uncertain]

nattier blue (nat´yā) *n.* a soft blue. *~a.* of this colour. [J. M. *Nattier*, d.1766, French painter]

natty (nat´i) *a.* (*comp.* **nattier**, *superl.* **nattiest**) (*coll.*) neat, tidy, spruce. **nattily** *adv.* **nattiness** *n.* [etym. uncertain]

natural (nach´ərəl) *a.* **1** of, relating to, produced by or constituted by nature. **2** innate, inherent, uncultivated, not artificial. **3** inborn, instinctive. **4** in conformity with the ordinary course of nature, normal, not irregular, exceptional or supernatural. **5** of or relating to physical things, animal, not spiritual. **6** true to life. **7** unaffected, not forced or exaggerated. **8** undisguised. **9** ordinary, to be expected, not surprising. **10** coming by nature, easy (to). **11** related by nature only. **12** illegitimate. **13** (*Mus.*) **a** (of a note) not sharp or flat. **b** denoting the diatonic scale of C. **c** (of a key) having no sharps or flats. **14** (*Theol.*) in a natural state, unregenerate. **15** (of a fabric) unbleached; cream or beige. *~n.* **1** a certainty, something by its very nature certain, esp. a person who is naturally good at something. **2** †a mentally deficient person. **3** (*Mus.*) **a** a sign cancelling the effect of a preceding sharp or flat. **b** a natural note. **4** in pontoon, a hand which makes 21 when first dealt. **5** in craps, a throw of seven or eleven. **6** cream, beige, or fawn. **natural-born** *a.* having a quality or position by birth (*a natural-born winner*). **natural childbirth** *n.* (*Med.*) a method of childbirth involving breathing and relaxation exercise with no anaesthetic. **natural classification** *n.* classification according to natural features. **natural day** *n.* a sidereal day. **natural death** *n.* death owing to disease or old age, not violence or accident. **natural food** *n.* food with no added preservatives. **natural gas** *n.* gas from the earth's crust, specifically a combination of methane and other hydrocarbons, used mainly as a fuel and as raw material in industry. **natural history** *n.* **1** the science or study of animal life, zoology. **2** the study or description of the earth and its productions, loosely applied to botany, zoology, geology and mineralogy. **3** a description of all the flora and fauna of a particular place. **natural historian** *n.* **naturalism** *n.* **1** strict adherence to nature in literature and art, realism. **2** a philosophical or theological system that explains the universe as being produced and governed entirely by physical laws. **3** condition or action based on natural instincts. **4** non-adherence to convention. **naturalist** (nach´ərəlist) *n.* **1** a person who is versed in natural history. **2** a believer in naturalism. **3** a realist, as distinct from an idealist. *~a.* naturalistic. **naturalistic** (-lis´-) *a.* **1** in accordance with nature. **2** realistic, not conventional or ideal. **3** of or relating to natural history. **naturalistically** *adv.* **naturalize, naturalise** *v.t.* **1** to make natural. **2** to adopt (a foreign expression or custom). **3** to acclimatize. **4** to confer the rights and privileges of a natural-born subject on. **5** to explain by natural laws, to free from the miraculous. **6** to cause to look natural. *~v.i.* **1** to become naturalized. **2** to study natural history. **naturalization** (-zā´shən) *n.* **natural language** *n.* a language which has evolved naturally. **natural law** *n.* **1** the sense of right and wrong implanted by nature. **2** a law governing the operations of physical life etc. **natural life** *n.* one's lifetime. **natural logarithm** *n.* a logarithm to the base *e* (2.71828.....). **naturally** *adv.* **1** according to nature. **2** spontaneously. **3** as might be expected, of course. **natural magic** *n.* magic based on a superior knowledge of the powers of nature. **naturalness** *n.* **natural note** *n.* (*Mus.*) a note which is not sharp or flat. **natural numbers** *n.pl.* the whole numbers starting from one upwards. **natural order** *n.* (*Bot.*) an order of plants in a system of classification based on the nature of their sexual organs or their natural affinities. **natural philosophy** *n.* (*Hist.*) the study of natural phenomena; physics. **natural philosopher** *n.* **natural religion** *n.*

religion not depending upon revelation. **natural resources** *n.pl.* features or properties of the land, such as minerals, water, timber etc., which occur naturally and can be exploited by people. **natural scale** *n.* (*Mus.*) a scale without sharps or flats. **natural science** *n.* the science of physical things, as distinguished from mental and moral science; natural history. **natural selection** *n.* the process by which plants and animals best fitted for the conditions in which they are placed survive and reproduce, while the less fitted leave fewer or no descendants. **natural theology** *n.* theology based on principles established by reason, not derived from revelation. **natural uranium** *n.* unenriched uranium. **natural wastage** *n.* the reduction of staff through retirements and resignations, rather than sackings or redundancies. **natural year** *n.* the time it takes for the earth to revolve round the sun, 365 days, 5 hours and 48 minutes. [L *nātūrālis* (NATURE, -AL[1])]

Usage note The nouns *naturalist* and *naturist* should not be confused: a *naturalist* studies natural history, a *naturist* is a nudist.

nature (nā´chə) *n.* **1** the essential qualities of anything. **2** the physical or psychical constitution of a person or animal. **3** natural character or disposition. **4** kind, sort, class. **5** the inherent energy or impulse determining character or disposition. **6** vital or animal force. **7** the whole sum of things, forces, activities and laws constituting the physical universe. **8** the physical power that produces the phenomena of the material world. **9** this personified. **10** the sum of physical things and forces regarded as distinct from human beings. **11** the material universe regarded as distinct from the supernatural or from a creator. **12** the natural condition of human beings preceding social organization. **13** the undomesticated condition of animals or plants. **14** picturesque countryside. **15** nakedness. **against nature 1** unnatural. **2** miraculous; miraculously. **by nature** innately. **contrary to nature** miraculous; miraculously. **from nature** in art, directly from the living model or natural landscape. **in a state of nature 1** in an uncultivated state. **2** completely naked. **3** in an unregenerate state. **in nature 1** in actual existence. **2** anywhere; at all. **in the nature of** rather like, more or less. **in the nature of things** to be expected. **to get back to nature** to return to a simple way of life. **nature cure** *n.* naturopathy. **natured** *a.* **nature-myth** *n.* a myth symbolizing some natural phenomenon. **nature printing** *n.* a process by which impressions are produced from natural objects such as leaves, feathers etc. on a metal plate from which prints may then be made. **nature reserve** *n.* an area of land which is protected in order to preserve its flora, fauna and other natural features. **nature study** *n.* the study of plant and animal life at a basic level. **nature trail** *n.* a route through the countryside which is signposted to highlight the natural features. **nature-worship** *n.* the worship of natural objects or phenomena or of the powers of nature. **naturism** *n.* **1** nature-worship. **2** naturalism in religion. **3** nudism. **naturist** *n., a.* **naturistic** (-ris´-) *a.* **naturopathy** (-rop´əthi) *n.* a method of treating or preventing disease without drugs, but with diet, exercise, fresh air etc. **naturopath** (-path) *n.* **naturopathic** (-path´ik) *a.* [F, from L *nātūra*, from *nāt-*, p.p. stem of *nascī*, to be born]

Usage note See note on *naturist* under NATURALIST (under NATURAL).

naught (nawt) *n.* **1** †nothing. **2** (*N Am.*) zero, nought. ~†*a.* worthless. ~*adv.* not at all. **to bring to naught** to thwart, frustrate, defeat; to ruin. **to come to naught** to be unsuccessful. **to set at naught** to disregard. [OE *nāwiht* (*nā*, NO[1], *wiht*, WHIT)]

naughty (naw´ti) *a.* (*comp.* **naughtier**, *superl.* **naughtiest**) **1** perverse, mischievous; disobedient, badly behaved. **2** (*coll.*) mildly indecent. **naughtily** *adv.* **naughtiness** *n.* [NAUGHT]

naumachia (nawmā´kiə), **naumachy** (naw´məki) *n.* (*pl.* **naumachiae** (-kiē), **naumachies**) **1** in ancient Rome, a naval combat, esp. a mock battle shown as a spectacle. **2** an artificial basin for the production of a mock naval combat in ancient Rome. [L and Gr. *naumachia* (*naus*, ship, *machē*, a battle)]

nauplius (naw´pliəs) *n.* (*pl.* **nauplii** (-pliī)) a larval stage of development in some of the lower crustaceans. **naupliiform** (-iifawm), **nauplioid** (-ioid), **nauplial** *a.* [L, from Gr. *Nauplios*, son of Poseidon]

Nauruan (nahū´rooən) *n.* a native or inhabitant of Nauru, in the S Pacific. ~*a.* of or relating to Nauru.

nausea (naw´ziə) *n.* **1** a feeling of sickness, with a propensity to vomit. **2** loathing. **nauseant** *a., n.* **nauseate** *v.t.* **1** to cause to feel nausea. **2** to fill with loathing. ~*v.i.* **1** to feel nausea. **2** to turn away in disgust (at). **nauseating** *a.* causing nausea. **nauseatingly** *adv.* **nauseation** (-ā´shən) *n.* **nauseous** *a.* **1** feeling sick. **2** causing nausea. **3** disgusting, distasteful. **nauseously** *adv.* **nauseousness** *n.* [L, from Gr. *naus*, ship]

nautch (nawch) *n.* an Indian exhibition of dancing by girls. **nautch girl** *n.* [Hind. *nach*]

nautical (naw´tikəl) *a.* of or relating to ships, navigation or sailors; naval. **nautical almanac** *n.* a book of astronomical tables published in advance, for use by navigators and astronomers. **nautically** *adv.* **nautical mile** *n.* a unit of measurement equal to 6080 ft., or 2026⅔ yards (1.853 km). [L *nauticus*, Gr. *nautikos*, from *nautēs*, sailor, from *naus*, ship]

nautilus (naw´tiləs) *n.* (*pl.* **nautiluses, nautili** (-lī)) **1** any cephalopod of the genus *Nautilus*, esp. the pearly nautilus. **2** the paper nautilus or argonaut. **nautiloid** (-loid) *n.* [L, from Gr. *nautilos*, a seaman, as NAUTICAL]

NAV *abbr.* net asset value.

Navajo (nav´əhō), **Navaho** *n.* (*pl.* **Navajo, Navaho, Navajos, Navahos**) **1** a member of an American Indian people of New Mexico and Arizona. **2** the language of the Navajo. ~*a.* of or relating to the Navajo. [Sp., a pueblo]

naval (nā´vəl) *a.* **1** consisting of or relating to ships or a navy. **2** fought or won by warships or navies. **naval academy** *n.* a training college for naval officers. **naval architecture** *n.* the process of designing ships. **naval architect** *n.* **naval ensign** *n.* a flag with a field of white, blue or red, with the union in the upper corner next to the staff (white ensign carried by Royal Navy and Royal Yacht Squadron, blue by naval reserve and red by merchant service). **navally** *a.* **naval officer** *n.* an officer in a navy. **naval stores** *n.pl.* materials used in shipping. [F, from L *nāvālis*, from *nāvis*, a ship]

navarin (nav´ərin) *n.* a lamb casserole with vegetables. [F]

nave[1] (nāv) *n.* the body of a church, extending from the main doorway to the choir or chancel, distinct, and usually separated by pillars, from the aisles. [L *nāvis*, ship (cp. Gr. *naus*)]

nave[2] (nāv) *n.* the central block of a wheel in which the axle and spokes are inserted, the hub. [OE *nafu* (cp. Dut. *naaf*, G *Nabe*, Icel. *nöf*, Dan. *nav*, Swed. *naf*), cp. NAVEL]

navel (nā´vəl) *n.* **1** the scar of the umbilical cord, forming a depression on the surface of the abdomen. **2** a central point. **navel-gazing** *n.* vague, introspective meditation. **navel orange** *n.* a variety of orange with a navel-like depression and a smaller orange enclosed. **navel-string** *n.* the umbilical cord. **navelwort** (-wœt) *n.* a pennywort. [OE *nafela* (cp. Dut. *navel*, G *Nabel*, Icel. *nafli*, Dan. *navle*), cogn. with NAVE[2], cp. Sansk. *nābhīla*, Gr. *omphalos*, L *umbilicus*]

navew (nā´vū) *n.* a turnip. [MF *naveau*, L *nāpellum*, *-lus*, dim. of *nāpus*, turnip]

navicert (nā´visœt) *n.* a certificate authorizing the passage in wartime of approved seaborne merchandise to neutral ports.

navicular (nəvik´ūlə) *a.* **1** shaped like a boat. **2** of or relating to the navicular bone. *~n.* the navicular bone. **navicular bone** *n.* the scaphoid bone of the foot or hand. **navicular disease** *n.* inflammation of the navicular bone in horses. [late L *nāviculāris*, from *nāvicula*, dim. of *nāvis*, ship]

navigate (nav´igāt) *v.i.* **1** to sail, to pass from place to place by water or air. **2** to direct and plot the route or position of a ship, aircraft etc. **3** to manage a ship. **4** to be in charge of plotting and pointing out a route to the driver of a car. *~v.t.* **1** to pass over or up or down, in a ship etc. **2** to manage the course, to conduct (a ship, aircraft etc.). **3** (*coll.*) to make (one's way) through a crowd. **navigable** *a.* **navigability** (-bil´-) *n.* **navigableness** *n.* **navigably** *adv.* **navigation** (-ā´shən) *n.* **1** the act, art or science of navigating. **2** a voyage. **3** (*dial.*) a canal or waterway. **navigational** *a.* **navigation light** *n.* a light used to indicate a ship's or an aircraft's position at night. **navigator** *n.* **1** a person who navigates. **2** a person who is skilled in navigation. **3** an explorer by sea. **4** a navvy. [L *nāvigātus*, p.p. of *nāvigāre* (*nāvis*, a ship, *agere*, to drive)]

navvy (nav´i) *n.* (*pl.* **navvies**) a labourer in any kind of excavating work, such as the construction of railways etc. (orig. of canals). [short for NAVIGATOR (under NAVIGATE)]

navy (nā´vi) *n.* (*pl.* **navies**) **1** the warships of a nation. **2** their officers, men, dockyards etc. **3** navy blue. **4** (*poet.*) a fleet. *~a.* navy-blue. **navy bean** *n.* a haricot bean. **navy blue** *n.* the dark-blue colour used for naval uniforms. **navy-blue** *a.* **Navy Department** *n.* (*US*) the government department in charge of the navy. **Navy List** *n.* an official list of naval officers. **navy yard** *n.* (*N Am.*) a naval dockyard. [OF *navie*, L *nāvis*, a ship]

nawab (nəwahb´) *n.* **1** in Pakistan, a distinguished Muslim. **2** (*Hist.*) an Indian governor or nobleman; a nabob. [Hind. *nawwāb*]

nay (nā) *adv.* **1** not only so, not this alone, more than that, and even. **2** no; a word expressing negation or refusal. *~n.* **1** the word 'nay'; a denial, a refusal. **2** a vote against. **naysay** (nā´sā) *v.i.* (*past, p.p.* **naysaid**) (*esp. N Am.*) to make a refusal or denial. *~v.t.* to refuse, to contradict. **naysayer** *n.* [Icel. *nei* (*ne*, not, *ei*, AYE[1]), cp. Swed. and Dan. *nei*]

Nazarene (naz´ərēn) *n.* **1** a native or inhabitant of Nazareth. **2** (*derog.*) an early Christian. **3** an early Judaizing sect of Christians. **4** a member of the Church of the Nazarene, a Protestant sect. *~a.* **1** of or belonging to either of these sects. **2** of or relating to Nazareth. [L *Nazarēnus*, Gr. *Nazarēnos*, from *Nazaret*, Nazareth]

Nazarite (naz´ərīt), **Nazirite** *n.* (*Hist.*) a Hebrew who had taken certain vows of abstinence (specified in Numbers vi). **Nazaritism** *n.* [Heb. *nāzar*, to separate oneself, -ITE[1]]

naze (nāz) *n.* (*dial.*) a promontory, a headland. [OE *næs*, NESS]

Nazi (naht´si) *n.* (*pl.* **Nazis**) **1** (*Hist.*) a member of the German National Socialist Party. **2** (*derog.*) a racist, extremist or authoritarian person. **3** a person who belongs to any extreme right-wing organization. *~a.* of or relating to the Nazis. **Nazidom** (-dəm) *n.* **Nazify** (-fī) *v.t.* (*3rd pers. sing. pres.* **Nazifies**, *pres.p.* **Nazifying**, *past, p.p.* **Nazified**). **Naziism, Nazism** *n.* [abbr. of G *National Sozialist*]

nazir (nah´ziə) *n.* **1** (*Hist.*) a non-European official formerly employed in Anglo-Indian courts. **2** a title of various Muslim officials. [Hind.]

Nazirite NAZARITE.

NB *abbr.* note well. [L *nota bene*]

Nb *chem. symbol* niobium.

NBC *abbr.* (*US*) National Broadcasting Company.

N. by E. *abbr.* North by East.

N. by W. *abbr.* North by West.

NC *abbr.* North Carolina.

NCB *abbr.* (*Hist.*) National Coal Board.

NCO *abbr.* non-commissioned officer.

NCP *abbr.* National Car Parks.

NCU *abbr.* National Communications Union.

ND *abbr.* North Dakota.

Nd *chem. symbol* neodymium.

n.d. *abbr.* no date.

-nd[1] (nd) *suf.* used to form nouns, as *friend*. [OE, orig. participial ending]

-nd[2] -AND, -END.

N. Dak. *abbr.* North Dakota.

Ndebele (əndəbē´li) *n.* (*pl.* **Ndebele, Ndebeles**) **1** a member of a Nguni people. **2** the Bantu language of the Ndebele. *~a.* of or relating to the Ndebele. [Bantu, from Ndebele, sing. pref. *n-* and Sesotho *(lè)tèbèlè*, Nguni]

NE *abbr.* **1** Nebraska. **2** north-east. **3** north-eastern.

Ne *chem. symbol* neon.

né (nā) *a.* born (used with a man's original name), as *Elton John, né Reginald Dwight.*

Neanderthal (nian´dətahl) *a.* **1** of or relating to a Palaeolithic species of man whose remains were first found in the Neanderthal valley. **2** (*coll.*) extremely old-fashioned, reactionary. **3** (*coll.*) boorish. **Neanderthal man** *n.* **Neanderthaloid** (-oid) *a.*

neap (nēp) *a.* low or lowest (applied to the tides which happen in the middle of the second and fourth quarters of the moon, when the rise and fall are least). *~n.* a neap tide. *~v.i.* **1** (of a tide) to diminish towards the neap. **2** (of a neap tide) to reach the flood. **3** (of a ship) to be left aground by a neap tide. *~v.t.* (of a neap tide) to leave (a ship) aground. [OE *nēp*, in *nēp flōd*, etym. uncertain]

Neapolitan (nēəpol´itən) *a.* of or relating to Naples. *~n.* a native or inhabitant of Naples, Italy. **Neapolitan ice cream** ice cream made of different ices in distinct layers. **Neapolitan violet** *n.* a double, sweet-scented viola. [L *Neāpolitānus*, from *Neāpolītēs*, from L and Gr. *Neāpolis*, Naples]

near (niə) *adv.* **1** at or to a short distance, at hand; not far off, not remote in place, time or degree. **2** closely. **3** †nearly, almost. **4** †carefully, sparingly, parsimoniously. *~prep.* close to in place, time, condition etc. *~a.* **1** nigh, close at hand, not distant in place, time or degree. **2** closely resembling, almost. **3** closely related. **4** familiar, intimate. **5** close, narrow. **6** (of a road etc.) direct, short, straight. **7** (of a horse, part or side of a vehicle etc.) on the left, as distinct from *off*. **8** (*coll.*) parsimonious, niggardly. *~v.t.* to approach, to draw near to. *~v.i.* to draw near. **near as dammit** (*coll.*) very nearly. **near at hand** close in distance or time. **near by** NEARBY[2]. **near home** HOME[1]. **near one's heart** HEART. **near the knuckle** KNUCKLE. **†near upon** close in time from. **to come near** almost to (do something) (*I came near to losing my temper*). **to go near** to only just fail (to do something). **near-beer** *n.* any of several malt liquors permitted in the US in the era of Prohibition. **near-death experience** *n.* an experience of being outside one's body and observing the scene, reported by some people who have come very close to death. **Near East** *n.* **1** the Middle East. **2** eastern Europe. **Near Eastern** *a.* **nearest and dearest** *n.pl.* one's close relatives and friends. **near go** *n.* (*coll.*) a narrow squeak, a close shave. **nearish** *a.* **nearly** *adv.* **1** almost. **2** intimately, closely. **3** in a parsimonious manner. **not nearly** nowhere near, far from (*not nearly as good*). **near miss** *n.* a miss that is almost a hit, such as a bomb which narrowly misses its target. **nearness** *n.*

near rhyme *n.* a rhyme in which the vowel sounds are not identical. **nearside** *n., a.* 1 (of) the left side of a horse etc., as distinct from *offside.* 2 (of) the side of a vehicle nearer the kerb, as distinct from *offside.* **near sight** *n.* (*N Am.*) short sight. **near-sighted** *a.* **near-sightedly** *adv.* **near-sightedness** *n.* **near thing** *n.* a narrow escape. [OE *nēar* (comp. of *nēah*, NIGH), blended with Icel. *nær* (comp. of *nā*, nigh, also used as positive)]

near- (niə) *comb. form* 1 almost, as *near-fatal.* 2 being a substitute for, as *near-beer.*

nearby[1] (niə´bī) *a.* situated close at hand.

nearby[2] (niəbī´), **near by** *adv.* close at hand.

Nearctic (niahk´tik) *a.* of or relating to the northern (Arctic and temperate) part of North America. ~*n.* the Nearctic region. [Gr. *neos*, new]

neat[1] (nēt) *a.* 1 tidy, trim. 2 simply but becomingly ordered. 3 nicely proportioned, well made. 4 elegantly and concisely phrased. 5 adroit, dexterous, clever. 6 (of an alcoholic drink) undiluted, pure. 7 †net. 8 (*N Am., sl.*) excellent, admirable. **neaten** *v.t.* to make neat or tidy. **neat-handed** *a.* clever, dexterous, deft. **neatly** *adv.* **neatness** *n.* [A-F *neit*, F *net*, L *nitidum*, nom. *-dus*, from *nitēre*, to shine]

†**neat**[2] (nēt) *n.* 1 cattle of the bovine kind. 2 an animal of this kind. **neat-herd** *n.* **neat-house** *n.* **neat's-foot oil** *n.* [OE *nēat* (cp. Icel. *naut*, Swed. *nöt*, Dan. *nōd*), cogn. with *nēotan*, to use, to enjoy]

neath (nēth) *prep.* (*poet.*) beneath. [BENEATH]

NEB *abbr.* 1 National Enterprise Board. 2 New English Bible.

Neb *abbr.* Nebraska.

neb (neb) *n.* (*Sc., North.*) 1 a beak, a bill. 2 a nose, a snout. 3 the tip or point of anything. 4 a spout. 5 a nib. 6 the face, the mouth. [OE *nebb*, cp. Dut. *nebbe*, *neb*, Icel. *nef*, Dan. *næb*]

nebbish (neb´ish) *n.* (*coll.*) a timid person. ~*a.* timid, submissive. [Yiddish *nebach*, poor thing!]

nebbuk (neb´ək) *n.* a thorny shrub, *Ziziphus spina-christi*, supposed to have supplied the thorns for Christ's crown. [Arab. *nebq*]

Nebr. *abbr.* Nebraska.

Nebuchadnezzar (nebūkədnez´ə) *n.* a large wine bottle which holds 20 times as much as a standard bottle. [King of Babylon, 6th cent. BC]

nebula (neb´ūlə) *n.* (*pl.* **nebulae** (-lē), **nebulas**) 1 (*Astron.*) a cloudy patch of light in the heavens produced by groups of stars or by a mass of gaseous or stellar matter. 2 (*Med.*) a speck on the cornea causing defective vision. **nebular** *a.* **nebular theory, nebular hypothesis** *n.* the theory that the bodies composing the solar and stellar systems once existed in the form of nebulae. **nebulizer, nebuliser** *n.* a device which produces a fine spray. **nebulize** *v.t.* **nebulosity** (-los´-) *n.* **nebulous** *a.* 1 cloudy. 2 turbid; hazy, vague, indistinct, obscure, uncertain. 3 muddled, bewildered. 4 (*Astron.*) belonging to or resembling a nebula. **nebulously** *adv.* **nebulousness** *n.* **nebulous star** *n.* (*Astron.*) a hazy single star or a cluster of small indistinct stars appearing as a cloudy patch of light. [L, mist (cp. Gr. *nephelē*, G *Nebel*, Dut. *nevel*, Icel. *nifl*)]

nebuly (neb´ūli), **nebulé** (neb´ūlā) *a.* (*Her.*) represented by, shaped in or ornamented with wavy lines. [F *nebulé*, med. L *nebulātus*, p.p. of *nebulāre*, to cloud, as NEBULA]

NEC *abbr.* National Executive Committee.

necessary (nes´isəri) *a.* 1 needful, requisite, indispensable, requiring to be done. 2 such as cannot be avoided, inevitable. 3 happening or existing by necessity. 4 resulting from external causes or determinism. 5 determined by natural laws. 6 not voluntary, not of free will, compulsory. ~*n.* (*pl.* **necessaries**) 1 what is indispensably requisite. 2 (*pl.*) things that are essentially requisite, esp. to life. 3 †a toilet. **the necessary** 1 (*coll.*) money. 2 (*coll.*) anything which is essential for some purpose. **necessarian** (-seə´ri-) *n.* a necessitarian. **necessarianism** *n.* **necessarily** (nes´-, -ser´ə-) *adv.* of necessity; inevitably. **necessitarian** (nisesiteə´ri-) *n.* (*Philos.*) a person who believes in the doctrine that the human will is not free, but that actions and volitions are determined by antecedent causes. ~*a.* of or relating to necessitarianism. **necessitarianism** *n.* **necessitate** (nises´itāt) *v.t.* 1 to make necessary or unavoidable. 2 to constrain, to compel. 3 to entail as an unavoidable condition, result etc. **necessitation** (-ā´shən) *n.* **necessitous** (nises´-) *a.* needy, destitute, in poverty. **necessitously** *adv.* **necessity** (nises´-) *n.* (*pl.* **necessities**) 1 (*often in pl.*) something which is necessary, an essential requisite. 2 the quality of being necessary; inevitableness. 3 absolute need, indispensability. 4 constraint, compulsion. 5 the compelling force of circumstances, the external conditions that compel one to act in a certain way. 6 want, poverty. **of necessity** unavoidably, necessarily. [L *necessārius*, from *necesse*, unavoidable]

Usage note (1) The pronunciation of *necessarily* with stress on the third syllable is sometimes disapproved of. (2) The uses of *necessaries* and *necessities* overlap, though *necessities* is now more usual for the essentials of life.

neck (nek) *n.* 1 the narrow portion of the body connecting the trunk with the head. 2 this part of an animal, used for food. 3 anything resembling this, such as an isthmus, a narrow passage or strait. 4 the slender part of a bottle near the mouth. 5 the long, slender part of a guitar, violin etc. 6 the length of a horse's head and neck, used to measure its lead in a race. 7 (*Geol.*) a solid block of lava in an old volcano crater. 8 (*Archit.*) the lower part of a capital. 9 the part of a garment that is close to the neck. 10 (*coll.*) impudence, cheek. ~*v.i.* 1 (*coll.*) to kiss and hug passionately. 2 to become narrow. ~*v.t.* to make narrow. **neck and crop** altogether, completely. **neck and neck** equal, very close (in a race or contest). **neck or nothing** at all risks; desperately. **one's neck of the woods** the part of the country to which one belongs. **pain in the neck** PAIN. **to get it in the neck** 1 (*coll.*) to be reprimanded severely. 2 (*coll.*) to be hit hard. **to risk one's neck** RISK. **to save one's neck** to escape injury. **up to one's neck** deeply involved (in). **neckband** *n.* a part of a garment fitting round the neck. **neckcloth** *n.* (*Hist.*) a cravat or necktie. **necked** *a.* (*usu. in comb.* as *low-necked*). **neckerchief** (-əchif) *n.* (*pl.* **neckerchiefs**) a kerchief worn round the neck. **necking** *n.* 1 (*Archit.*) the hollow part of a column between the shaft and the capital. 2 (*coll.*) passionate kissing and hugging. **neckless** *a.* **necklet** (-lit) *n.* 1 a small necklace. 2 a small fur boa for the neck. **neckline** *n.* the edge of a garment which goes round the neck. **neck-moulding** *n.* a moulding surrounding a column at the junction of the shaft and capital. **necktie** *n.* (*esp. N Am.*) a tie for wearing round the neck. **necktie party** *n.* (*sl.*) a lynching, a hanging. **neckwear** *n.* garments worn round the neck, such as ties and scarves. [OE *hnecca* (cp. Dut. *nek*, G *Nacken*, Icel. *nakki*]

necklace (nek´ləs) *n.* 1 a string of beads or gems worn round the neck. 2 (*S Afr.*) a tyre soaked in petrol, put round a person's neck and set alight, in order to kill by burning. ~*v.t.* (*S Afr.*) to kill (a person) by means of a burning necklace. **necklacing** *n.*

necro- (nek´rō) *comb. form* of or relating to dead bodies or the dead. [Gr. *nekros*, a dead body]

necrobiosis (nekrōbīō´sis) *n.* decay of living tissue, as in old age. **necrobiotic** (-ot´-) *a.* [Gr. *bios*, life]

necrolatry (nekrol´ətri) *n.* worship of the dead, esp. ancestors.

necrology (nekrol´əji) *n.* (*pl.* **necrologies**) **1** a register of deaths. **2** an obituary. **necrological** (-loj´-) *a.* **necrologist** *n.*

necromancy (nek´rəmansi) *n.* **1** the supposed art of revealing future events by communication with the dead. **2** enchantment, magic. *~n.* **necromancer** *n.* **necromantic** (-man´-) *a.* [ME and OF *nigromancie*, med. L *nigromantia*, L *necromantia*, Gr. *nekromanteia*, -MANCY]

necrophagous (nikrof´əgəs) *a.* eating or feeding on carrion.

necrophilia (nekrəfil´iə) *n.* an obsession with, and usu. an erotic interest in, corpses. **necrophile** (nek´rəfīl) *n.* **necrophiliac** (-ak) *n.* **necrophilic** (-fil´-) *a.* **necrophilism** (-krof´-) *n.* **necrophilist** (-krof´-) *n.*

necrophobia (nekrəfō´biə) *n.* revulsion from or fear of anything to do with the dead. **necrophobic** *a.*

necropolis (nekrop´əlis) *n.* (*pl.* **necropolises**) a cemetery, esp. one on a large scale. [Gr.]

necropsy (nek´ropsi) *n.* (*pl.* **necropsies**) an autopsy, a post-mortem examination. [Gr. *opsis*, sight]

necroscopy (nekros´kəpi) *n.* (*pl.* **necroscopies**) a post-mortem examination.

necrosis (nekrō´sis) *n.* (*Med.*) the mortification of part of the body, esp. of bone. **necrotic** (-krot´-) *a.* **necrotize** (nek´rə-), **necrotise** *v.i.* **necrotizing fasciitis** (fashiī´tis) *n.* (*Med.*) severe fasciitis resulting in necrosis.

nectar (nek´tə) *n.* **1** in Greek and Roman mythology, the drink of the gods. **2** any delicious drink. **3** the honey or sweet fluid secretion of plants. **nectarean** (-teə´ri-) *a.* **nectareous** (-teə´ri-), **nectarous** *a.* **nectariferous** (-rif´-) *a.* **nectary** *n.* (*pl.* **nectaries**) the organ or part of a plant or flower secreting honey. **nectarial** (-teə´ri-) *a.* [L, from Gr. *nektar*, etym. uncertain]

nectarine (nek´tərēn) *n.* **1** a smooth-skinned, firm variety of peach. **2** a tree on which nectarines grow.

nectocalyx (nektōkā´liks) *n.* (*pl.* **nectocalyces** (-lisēz)) the bell-shaped swimming organ in the Hydrozoa. [Gr. *nēktos*, swimming, from *nēchein*, to swim]

NEDC *abbr.* (*Hist.*) National Economic Development Council.

Neddy *n.* (*Hist.*, *coll.*) the NEDC.

neddy (ned´i) *n.* (*pl.* **neddies**) **1** a donkey (used by or to children). **2** (*coll.*) a fool. [fam. form of *Edward*]

née (nā), (*N Am.*) **nee** *a.* born (used with the maiden name of a married woman), as in *Joan Murphy née Smith*. [F, fem. p.p. of *naître*, to be born]

need (nēd) *v.t.* (*3rd pers. sing. pres.* **needs, need**) **1** to be in want of, to require. **2** to be necessary, to require, to be bound, to be under necessity or obligation (to do something). *~v.i.* †to be necessary. *~n.* **1** a state of urgently requiring something; lack of something. **2** something which is wanted, a requirement. **3** a state requiring relief, urgent want. **4** indigence, destitution. **5** a difficult, critical or perilous situation; an emergency. **at need** at a time of need. **had need** †ought to, should. **in need** poor or in distress. **in need of** requiring, needing. **need not have** did not need to (*I need not have worried*). **to have need of** to require, to need. **to have need to** to require to, to need to. **needful** *a.* **the needful** (*coll.*) something which is required, esp. money. **needfully** *adv.* **needfulness** *n.* **needless** *a.* **1** unnecessary, not required. **2** useless, superfluous. **needless to say** obviously, of course. **needlessly** *adv.* **needlessness** *n.* †**needs** *adv.* of necessity, necessarily, indispensably (*usu. with* must). **needy** *a.* (*comp.* **needier**, *superl.* **neediest**) **1** in need. **2** necessitous, indigent. **needily** *adv.* [OE *nied*, *nēad*, *nēod* (cp. Dut. *nood*, G *noth*, Icel. *nauth*), whence *nēadian*, to need]

needle (nē´dəl) *n.* **1** a small, thin, rod-shaped, pointed steel instrument with an eye for carrying a thread, used in sewing. **2** any of various analogous instruments of plastic, metal, bone, wood etc., used in knitting, crocheting etc. **3** a piece of magnetized steel used as an indicator in a mariner's compass, a telegraphic receiver etc. **4** any of various pointed instruments used in surgery, assaying, etching etc., and in machinery, firearms etc. **5** a beam, esp. one used as a temporary support in underpinning. **6** a pointed peak or pinnacle of rock. **7** an obelisk. **8** a needle-like leaf of a pine tree. **9** a needle-shaped crystal. **10** a pointed piece of metal, fibre etc., used to receive or transmit the vibrations in the groove of a revolving gramophone record. *~v.t.* **1** (*coll.*) to irritate; to force into action. **2** to make or sew with a needle. **3** to work upon with a needle. **4** to penetrate. **5** to thread (one's way) through or between. *~v.i.* **1** to form needle-like crystals. **2** to thread one's way. **3** to work with a needle. **to get the needle** (*sl.*) to become irritated or bad-tempered. **to look for a needle in a haystack** to engage in a hopeless search. **needle-bath** *n.* a kind of shower bath in which the water is emitted in thin needle-like jets. **needle-book**, **needle-case** *n.* a case for holding needles. **needlecord** *n.* a cotton material with closer ribs and flatter pile than corduroy. **needlecraft** *n.* the art of needlework. **needle exchange** *n.* a place where drug addicts may exchange their used hypodermic needles for new ones. **needlefish** *n.* (*pl. in general* **needlefish**, *in particular* **needlefishes**) a garfish. **needleful** *n.* (*pl.* **needlefuls**). **needle game** *n.* a game which is intensified because it involves a personal grudge. **needle-gun** *n.* a breech-loading gun in which a cartridge is exploded by the prick of a needle. **needle-lace** *n.* lace made with needles, not with bobbins. **needle match** *n.* a needle game. **needlepoint** *n.* **1** any fine sharp point. **2** needle-lace. **3** gros point or petit point. **needle's eye** *n.* the smallest opening possible. **needle time** *n.* the time allocated by a radio station for the playing of music. **needle valve** *n.* a valve which is closed by a needle-like part. **needlewoman** *n.* (*pl.* **needlewomen**) a seamstress. **needlework** *n.* sewing, embroidery etc. **needly** *a.* (*comp.* **needlier**, *superl.* **needliest**). [OE *nædl* (cp. Dut. *neald*, G *Nadel*, Icel. *nāl*, Dan. *naal*), prob. cogn. with Gr. *neein*, L *nēre*, to spin]

needn't (nē´dənt) *contr.* need not.

neem (nēm) *n.* a tree, *Azadirachta indica*, found in India, whose leaves and bark are used for medicinal purposes.

neep (nēp) *n.* (*Sc.*) a turnip, a swede. [OE *næp*, L *nāpus*]

ne'er (neə) *adv.* (*poet.*) never. **ne'er-do-well** *n.*, *a.* (a) good-for-nothing. [contr. of NEVER]

†**neeze** (nēz) *v.i.* to sneeze. *~n.* a sneeze. [prob. from Icel. *hnōjsa* (cp. Dan. *nyse*, Dut. *niezen*, G *niesen*)]

nef (nef) *n.* **1** an ornamental piece of plate shaped like a boat or ship, formerly used for holding the salt cellars, table napkins etc. of people of great distinction. **2** †the nave of a church. [F, ship]

nefandous (nifan´dəs) *a.* unspeakable, atrocious. [L *nefandus* (*ne*, not, *fandus*, ger. of *fārī*, to speak)]

nefarious (nifeə´riəs) *a.* wicked, abominable, infamous. **nefariously** *adv.* **nefariousness** *n.* [L *nefārius*, from *nefas* (*ne*, not, *fas*, right, divine justice)]

neg (neg) *n.* (*coll.*) a photographic negative.

neg. *abbr.* negative.

negate (nigāt´) *v.t.* **1** to render negative, to nullify. **2** to be the negation of. **3** to deny, to affirm the non-existence of. **negation** (-ā´shən) *n.* **1** denial. **2** a declaration of falsity. **3** refusal, contradiction. **4** the absence or the opposite of certain qualities, nullity, voidness. **5** (*Logic*) negative statement, affirmation of absence or exclusion. **negationist** *n.* a person who denies something, esp. one who holds merely negative views in religion. **negative** (neg´ə-) *a.* **1** containing, declaring or implying negation. **2** denying, contradicting, prohibiting, refusing. **3** lacking positive qualities such as optimism or enthusiasm. 4 characterized by the absence of a quality (*negative results*). 5 (of a word etc.) indicating negation. 6 (*Logic*) denoting difference or discrepancy. 7 denoting the opposite to positive, denoting what is to be subtracted (expressed by the minus sign -). 8 denoting the kind of electricity produced by friction on resin, as opposed to positive, produced on glass. 9 showing the lights dark and the shadows light. ~*n.* 1 a proposition, reply, word etc., expressing negation. 2 an image or plate bearing an image in which the lights and shades of the object are reversed. 3 (*Gram.*) a negator. 4 the side of a question that denies. 5 a negative quality, lack or absence of something. 6 (*Logic*) a negation. 7 negative electricity, or the negative plates in a voltaic cell. 8 a negative or minus sign or quantity. 9 †the right of veto. ~*v.t.* 1 to veto, to reject, to refuse to accept, sanction or enact. 2 to disprove. 3 to contradict. 4 to neutralize. **in the negative** indicating dissent or refusal. **negative equity** *n.* the state of owing more in mortgage repayments on a property than the market value of the property. **negative evidence** *n.* evidence that something is not the case. **negative feedback** *n.* 1 the interconnection of input and output terminals of an amplifier in such a manner that the output opposes the input, thereby decreasing the gain but increasing the stability and the fidelity of the amplifier. 2 the lessening of an effect by its own influence on the process from which it originated. 3 a negative result or response. **negative geotropism** *n.* the tendency of plant stems to grow upwards irrespective of the position in which they are placed. **negative income tax** *n.* a tax-free allowance paid as a benefit by the State to people with an income below a certain level. **negative instance** *n.* negative evidence. **negatively** *adv.* **negativeness** *n.* **negative pole** *n.* the pole of a freely swinging magnet that swings to the south. **negative prescription** *n.* the time limit for making a claim. **negative proposition** *n.* (*Logic*) a negative. **negative quantity** *n.* (*facet.*) a minus quantity, nothing. **negative sign** *n.* a symbol (-) used to indicate subtraction or a negative number. **negative virtue** *n.* avoidance of vice. **negativism** *n.* 1 the quality of being negative. 2 the doctrine of a negationist. **negativist** *n.* **negativistic** (-is´tik) *a.* **negativity** (-tiv´-) *n.* **negator** *n.* 1 a person who denies something. 2 (*Gram.*) a word or suffix used to express the negative, such as *not.* **negatory** (neg´ətəri) *a.* [from L *negāre*, to deny]

neglect (niglekt´) *v.t.* 1 to treat carelessly. 2 to slight, to disregard. 3 to pass over. 4 to leave undone. 5 to omit (to do or doing). ~*n.* 1 disregard (of). 2 omission to do anything that should be done. 3 carelessness, negligence. 4 the state of being neglected. **neglectedness** *n.* **neglecter, neglector** *n.* **neglectful** *a.* **neglectfully** *adv.* **neglectfulness** *n.* [L *neglectus*, p.p. of *negligere* (*neg-*, not, *legere*, to pick up)]

negligée (neg´lizhā), **negligee, négligé** *n.* 1 a woman's loose dressing gown of flimsy material. 2 a lady's loose gown worn in the 18th cent. 3 a state of undress or free-and-easy attire. 4 a long necklace of irregular beads or coral. [F]

negligence (neg´lijəns) *n.* 1 disregard of appearances, conventions etc., in conduct, literature etc. 2 a negligent act or deed. 3 (*Law*) contributory negligence. **negligent** *a.* careless, neglectful. **negligently** *adv.* **negligible** *a.* able to be ignored, not worth considering. **negligible quantity** *n.* someone or something not worth considering. [OF, from L *negligentia*, as NEGLECT]

negotiate (nigō´shiāt) *v.i.* 1 to discuss a matter with other people in order to make a bargain, agreement, compromise etc. 2 to traffic. ~*v.t.* 1 to arrange, bring about or procure by negotiating. 2 to carry on negotiations concerning. 3 to transfer (a bill, note etc.) for value received. 4 to obtain or give value for. 5 to accomplish, to get over successfully. **negotiable** (-shəbəl) *a.* **negotiability** (-bil´-) *n.* **negotiant** *n.* **negotiation** (-ā´shən) *n.* **negotiator** *n.* [L *negōtiātus*, p.p. of *negōtiārī*, from *negōtium*, business (*neg-*, not, *ōtium*, leisure)]

Negress NEGRO.

Negrillo (nigril´ō) *n.* (*pl.* **Negrillos**) a member of a black people of small stature in central and southern Africa. [Sp., dim. of NEGRO]

Negrito (nigrē´tō) *n.* (*pl.* **Negritos**) a member of a black people in some islands of the Malay Archipelago etc. [as NEGRILLO]

Negritude (neg´ritūd) *n.* 1 the state of belonging to a black race. 2 awareness and promotion of black culture. [F *négritude*, NIGRITUDE]

Negro (nē´grō) *n.* (*pl.* **Negroes**) (*offensive*) a person belonging to, or descended from, one of the dark-skinned African peoples. ~*a.* of or relating to these peoples. **Negress** (-gris) *n.* (*offensive*) a female black. **negro-corn** *n.* Indian millet, durra. **negrohead** *n.* strong, black, plug tobacco soaked in molasses. **Negroid** (-groid) *a.* 1 of or relating to blacks. 2 having the physical characteristics associated with black peoples of or originating in Africa. ~*n.* a Negroid person. **negroidal** (-groi´-) *a.* Negroid. **Negro spiritual** *n.* a type of religious song which originated among the black slaves in the southern US. [Sp. from L *nigrum*, nom. *niger*, black]

Usage note The terms *Negro* and *Negress* give offence: it is better to use *black* instead.

negro (nē´grō) *a.* (*Zool.*) black, dark. [NEGRO]

Negus (nē´gəs) *n.* (*Hist.*) the sovereign of Ethiopia. [Amharic *n'gus*, a king]

negus (nē´gəs) *n.* (*Hist.*) a beverage of wine, hot water, sugar and spices. [Col. Francis *Negus*, d. 1732, its English inventor]

Neh. *abbr.* (*Bible*) Nehemiah.

☒ **neice** common misspelling of NIECE.

neigh (nā) *v.i.* to utter the cry of a horse; to whinny. ~*v.t.* to utter with a neighlike sound. ~*n.* 1 the cry of a horse. 2 a neighlike laugh or other sound. **neighlike** *a.* [OE *hnægan* (cp. LG *neigen*, MHG *nêgen*), imit. in orig.]

neighbour (nā´bə), (*N Am.*) **neighbor** *n.* 1 a person who lives near, a person living in the same street, village, community etc. 2 a person or thing standing or happening to be next to or near another. 3 a person having the claims of a fellow man etc., such as friendship. ~*a.* near, adjoining, neighbouring. ~*v.t.* 1 to adjoin. 2 to lie near to. ~*v.i.* to border (upon). **neighbourhood** (-hud) *n.* 1 the locality round or near; the vicinity. 2 (*collect.*) those who live near, neighbours. 3 neighbourliness. 4 the state of being neighbours. 5 nearness. **in the neighbourhood of** approximately. **neighbourhood watch** *n.* a crime-prevention scheme organized by the residents of a street or area, who keep watch on each other's property. **neighbouring** *a.* situated or living near. **neighbourless** *a.* **neighbourly** *a.* friendly and helpful. **neighbourliness** *n.* **neighbourship** *n.* [OE *nēahgebūr* (NIGH, BOOR)]

neither (nī´dhə, nē´-) *a.* not either. ~*pron.* not the one nor the other. ~*conj.* 1 not either, not on the one hand (usu. preceding one of two alternatives and correlative with *nor* preceding the other). 2 nor, nor yet. ~*adv.* (*at end of sentence, coll.*) either, any more than another person or thing. **neither here nor there** HERE. [OE *nawther*, *nāhwæther* (*nā*, not, WHETHER), assim. to EITHER]

Usage note A following verb should be in the singular (as also after *neither...nor*), though the plural is common.

nek (nek) *n.* (*S Afr.*) a mountain pass. [Dut., a neck]

nekton (nek´ton) *n.* (*Zool.*) all forms of organic life found in various depths of salt and fresh water. [Gr. *nēchein*, to swim]

nelly (nel´i), **nellie** *n.* (*pl.* **nellies**) a foolish or weak person. **not on your nelly** (*sl.*) certainly not. [perh. from *not on your Nelly Duff*, with Duff, being rhyming slang for puff, meaning life]

nelson (nel´sən) *n.* a wrestling hold in which one or both arms are passed under the opponent's arm or arms from behind, and the hands joined so that pressure can be exerted with the palms on the back of the opponent's neck. **full nelson** FULL[1]. **half nelson** HALF. [from the name, Nelson]

Nelson touch (nel´sən) *n.* a skilful approach to a problem. [Horatio *Nelson*, 1758–1805, British admiral]

nelumbo (nilŭm´bō), **nelumbium** (-biəm) *n.* (*pl.* **nelumbos, nelumbiums**) any water lily of the genus *Nelumbo*, esp. the sacred lotus, *N. nucifera*. [Sinhalese *nelumbu*]

nemathelminth (nemәthel´minth) *n.* (*Zool.*) a threadworm or nematode. **nemathelminthic** (-min´thik) *a.* [*nēma -matos*, as NEMATO-, *helmins -nthos*, worm]

nematic (nimat´ik) *a.* denoting a liquid crystal state in which the molecules are parallel but not arranged in distinct planes. ~*n.* a nematic substance. [as NEMATO-]

nemato- (nem´ətō) *comb. form* threadlike; filamentous. [Gr. *nēma nēmatos*, thread]

nematocyst (nimat´əsist, nem´ətəsist) *n.* a thread cell in jellyfish and other coelenterates from which the stinging thread is projected.

nematode (nem´ətōd) *n.* a worm of the phylum Nematoda, which includes the parasitic roundworm and the threadworm. ~*a.* of or relating to nematodes. **nematoid** (-toid) *a.*

Nembutal® (nem´būtal) *n.* sodium ethyl methylbutyl barbiturate, used as a sedative, hypnotic and antispasmodic.

nem. con. (nem kon´) *adv.* with no one dissenting. [L, *nemine contradicente*]

Nemean (nimē´ən) *a.* in ancient Greece, of or relating to Nemea. **Nemean games** *n.pl.* one of the great Hellenic festivals held at Nemea in the second and fourth years of each Olympiad. [L *Nemeæus, Nemæus, Nemeus*, Gr. *Nemeæos, Nemeios, Nemeos*, from *Nemea*, in Argolis]

nemertean (nimœ´tiən), **nemertine** (-tīn) *a.* belonging to the phylum Nemertea, comprising flatworms and ribbonworms, chiefly marine. ~*n.* any worm of this phylum. [Gr. *Nēmertēs*, a sea nymph]

nemesia (nimē´zhə) *n.* any plant of the S African genus *Nemesia*, grown for their brightly coloured flowers. [mod. L, from Gr. *nemesion*, the name of a similar plant]

nemesis (nem´əsis) *n.* (*pl.* **nemeses** (-sēz)) **1** retributive justice. **2** an instance or agent of this. [*Nemesis*, the Greek goddess of retribution, from Gr. *nemein*, to allot]

nemophila (nimof´ilə) *n.* (*pl.* **nemophilas**) an annual trailing plant with blue-and-white flowers. [Gr. *nemos*, a glade, wooded pasture, *phileein*, to love]

nenuphar (nen´ūfah) *n.* the white water lily, *Nymphaea alba*. [F, from Pers. *nīnūfar*, Sansk. *nīlōtpala* (*nīla*, blue, *utpala*, lotus)]

neo- (nē´ō) *comb. form* new, recent, modern, later, revived. [Gr. *neos*]

neo-Catholic (nēōkath´əlik) *a.* of or relating to the Puseyite school in the Church of England, or to the school of Liberal Catholicism headed by Lamennais and Lacordaire in the Church of France.

neo-Christian (nēōkris´chən) *a.* of or relating to rationalized Christianity.

neoclassical (nēōklas´ikəl), **neoclassic** *a.* of or relating to the 18th-cent. revival of classicism. **neoclassicism** (-sizm) *n.* **neo-classicist** (-sist) *n.*

neocolonialism (nēōkəlō´niəlizm) *n.* the policy of a strong nation gaining control over a weaker one through economic pressure etc. **neocolonialist** *n., a.*

Neocomian (nēōkō´miən) *a.* (*Geol.*) of or relating to the lower division of the Cretaceous strata typically exhibited near Neuchâtel in Switzerland. [F *Néocomien*, from *Neocomium* (NEO-, Gr. *kōmē*, village), Latinized from *Neuchâtel*]

Neo-Darwinism (nēōdah´winizm) *n.* Darwinism as modified by later investigators, esp. to take account of the findings of genetics. **Neo-Darwinian** (-win´-) *a., n.* **Neo-Darwinist** *n.*

neodymium (nēōdim´iəm) *n.* a silver-grey metallic element, at. no. 60, chem. symbol Nd, of the cerium group of rare earth elements. [Gr. *neos*, new, *didymos*, twins]

neo-fascism (nēōfash´izm) *n.* a movement attempting to reinstate the policies of fascism. **neo-fascist** *n., a.*

neo-Georgian (nēōjaw´jən) *a.* (*Archit.*) of or relating to a revival of the Georgian style.

neogothic (nēōgoth´ik) *n.* the Gothic revival of the mid-19th cent. ~*a.* of or relating to the neogothic.

neogrammarian (nēōgrəmeə´riən) *n.* any one of a modern school of grammarians insisting upon the invariability of the laws governing phonetic change. **neogrammatical** (-mat´-) *a.*

Neohellenism (nēōhel´ənizm) *n.* the revival of Greek ideals in art and literature, as in the Italian Renaissance.

Neo-Kantian (nēōkan´tiən) *a.* of or relating to the teaching of Kant as modified by later interpreters. ~*n.* an adherent of Neo-Kantianism. **neo-Kantianism** *n.* the philosophy of Kant as modified by later interpreters.

Neo-Lamarckian (nēōləmah´kiən) *a.* of or relating to the teaching of Lamarck on organic evolution as revived in a modified form by those who believe in the inheritance of acquired characters.

neolithic (nēəlith´ik) *a.* of or relating to the later Stone Age, characterized by ground and polished implements and the introduction of agriculture. ~*n.* the neolithic period. **neolith** (nē´-) *n.* a weapon, implement or person belonging to this period. [Gr. *lithos*, stone]

neologism (niol´əjizm) *n.* **1** a new word or phrase, or a new sense for an old one. **2** the use of new words. **3** neology. **neology** *n.* (*pl.* **neologies**) **1** the introduction or use of new words. **2** a neologism. **3** the adoption of or the tendency towards rationalistic views in theology. **neologian** (nēəlō´jən) *a., n.* **neological** (nēəloj´-) *a.* **neologically** *adv.* **neologist** *n.* **neologistic** (-jis´-) *a.* **neologize, neologise** *v.i.* [F *néologisme*]

neomycin (nēōmī´sin) *n.* an antibiotic effective against some infections that resist ordinary antibiotics. [Gr. *mykes*, fungus]

neon (nē´on) *n.* a colourless gaseous element, at. no. 10, chem. symbol Ne, existing in minute quantities in the air, isolated from argon in 1898. **neon lamp** *n.* a lamp possessing two electrodes and containing an atmosphere of rarefied neon gas. [neut. of Gr. *neos*, new]

neonatal (nēōnā´təl) *a.* of or relating to the first few weeks after birth in human babies. **neonate** (nē´-) *n.* a baby at this stage in its development.

neo-Nazi (nēōnaht´si) *n.* (*pl.* **neo-Nazis**) a person belonging to an organization attempting to reinstate the policies of Naziism. ~*a.* of or relating to neo-Nazis. **neo-Nazism** *n.*

neopaganism (nēōpā´gənizm) *n.* a revived form of paganism. **neopagan** *a., n.* **neopaganize, neopaganise** *v.t., v.i.* [Gr.]

neophobia (nēōfō´biə) *n.* a fear of anything new.

neophyte (nē´əfīt) *n.* **1** a person who is newly converted or newly baptized. **2** a person who is newly admitted to a monastery or to the priesthood. **3** a beginner, a novice. **neophytic** (-fit´-) *a.* [late L *neophytus*, Gr. *neophutos* (*phutos*, grown, from *phuein*, to plant)]

neoplasm (nē´əplazm) *n.* an abnormal growth of new tissue in some part of the body, a cancer. **neoplastic** (-plas´-) *a.* [Gr. *plasma*, from *plassein*, to form]
neoplasty (nē´əplasti) *n.* restoration of a part by granulation, adhesive inflammation etc.
Neoplatonism (nēōplā´tənizm) *n.* a system of philosophy combining the Platonic ideas with the theosophy of the East, originating in Alexandria in the 3rd cent. AD. **Neoplatonic** (-pləton´-) *a.* **Neoplatonist** *n.*
neoprene (nē´əprēn) *n.* a synthetic rubber-like polymer, used in waterproof products.
neoteny (nēot´əni) *n.* (*Zool.*) **1** the retention of juvenile characteristics in the adult. **2** sexual maturity while still in a larval stage. **neotenic** (nēəten´ik) *a.* **neotenous** *a.* [G *Neotenie* (NEO-, Gr. *teinō*, to extend)]
neoteric (nēəter´ik) *a.* new; of recent origin. ~*n.* a writer or philosopher of modern times. **neoterically** *adv.* **neoterism** (-ot´-) *n.* **neoterist** (-ot´-) *n.* **neoterize** (-ot´-), **neoterise** *v.t.* [Gr. *neoteros*, newer]
neotropical (nēōtrop´ikəl) *a.* of, relating to or characteristic of tropical and S America.
Neozoic (nēōzō´ik) *a.* belonging to the later or post-Palaeozoic period, including both Mesozoic and Cenozoic, or corresponding to Cenozoic.
Nepali (nipaw´li), **Nepalese** (nepəlēz´) *n.* (*pl.* **Nepali, Nepalis, Nepalese**) **1** a native or inhabitant of Nepal, or a descendant of one. **2** the language of Nepal. ~*a.* of or relating to Nepal.
nepenthes (nipen´thēz) *n.* (*pl.* **nepenthes**) **1** (*poet.*) (*also* **nepenthe** (-thi)) a drug or potion that drives away sorrow or grief. **2** any pitcher plant of the genus *Nepenthes.* [L and Gr. *nēpenthes* (*nē-*, not, *penthos*, grief)]
nephalism (nef´əlizm) *n.* total abstinence from intoxicants, teetotalism. [late Gr. *nēphalismos*, from *nēphalios*, sober]
nepheline (nef´əlin), **nephelite** (-līt) *n.* a vitreous silicate of aluminium and sodium found in volcanic rocks. [F *néphéline*, from Gr. *nephelē*, cloud]
nephelometer (nefəlom´itə) *n.* an instrument for measuring cloudiness esp. in liquids.
nephew (nef´ū) *n.* **1** the son of a brother or sister. **2** the son of a brother-in-law or sister-in-law. **3** †a descendant, a cousin. [OF *neveu*, L *nepōtem*, nom. *-pos*, grandson, nephew (cp. OE *nefa*, Dut. *neef*, G *Neffe*)]
nephology (nefol´əji) *n.* the scientific study of clouds.
nephoscope (nef´əskōp) *n.* an instrument for observing the elevation, direction and velocity of clouds.
nephr- NEPHRO-.
nephralgia (nifral´jə) *n.* pain or disease in the kidneys. [NEPHRO-, *-algia*, from *algos*, pain]
nephrectomy (nifrek´təmi) *n.* (*pl.* **nephrectomies**) removal of a kidney by surgical means.
nephric (nef´rik) *a.* of or relating to the kidney.
nephrite (nef´rīt) *n.* jade, formerly believed to cure kidney disease. [G *Nephrit*, from Gr. *nephros*, a kidney]
nephritic (nefrit´ik) *a.* **1** of or relating to the kidneys. **2** suffering from kidney disease. ~†*n.* a medicine for relieving kidney diseases. **nephritis** (nifrī´tis) *n.* a disease or disorder of the kidneys.
nephro- (nef´rō), **nephr-** *comb. form* of or relating to the kidneys. [Gr. *nephros*, kidney]
nephroid (nef´roid) *a.* of or relating to the kidneys.
nephrology (nifrol´əji) *n.* the scientific study of the kidneys.
nephrotomy (nifrot´əmi) *n.* (*pl.* **nephrotomies**) surgical incision of the kidney. [-TOMY]
ne plus ultra (nā plus ul´trə) *n.* the most perfect or uttermost point. [L]
nepotism (nep´ətizm) *n.* favouritism towards one's relations, for example in business (originally applied to the patronage of a Pope's illegitimate sons, euphemistically called 'nephews'). **nepotic** (nipot´-) *a.* **nepotist** *n.* **nepotistic** (-tis´-) *a.* [It. *nepotismo* (*nepote*, see NEPHEW, -ISM)]
Neptune (nep´tūn) *n.* one of the sun's planets, the eighth from the sun. **Neptunian** (-tū´-) *a.* **1** of or relating to Neptune or the sea. **2** deposited by the sea or produced by water. ~*n.* a Neptunist. **Neptunist** *n.* a person who asserts the aqueous origin of certain rocks. [L *Neptūnus*, the Roman god of the sea]
neptunium (neptū´niəm) *n.* a radioactive metallic element, at. no. 93, chem. symbol Np, obtained by the bombardment of uranium with neutrons.
NERC *abbr.* Natural Environment Research Council.
nerd (nœd), **nurd** *n.* (*sl.*) an ineffectual or socially awkward person, a fool. **nerdish** *a.* **nerdy** *a.* (*comp.* **nerdier,** *superl.* **nerdiest**). [etym. uncertain]
nereid (niə´riid) *n.* (*pl.* **nereids**) **1** a sea nymph. **2** a sea worm or marine centipede of the family Nereidae. **nereidian** (-id´-), **nereidous** (nirē´i-) *a.* [L and Gr. *Nēreid-*, stem of *Nēreis*, daughter of Nereus, a sea god]
nerine (nirī´nē) *n.* any S African plant of the genus *Nerine*, with scarlet or rose-coloured flowers, including the Guernsey lily. [L *nērinē*, a nereid]
neroli (niə´rəli), **neroli oil** *n.* an essential oil distilled from the flowers of the bitter or Seville orange, used as a perfume. [F *néroli*, from It. *neroli*, perhaps from the name of the Italian princess said to have discovered it]
Neronian (nirō´niən) *a.* **1** of, relating to or like the Emperor Nero. **2** cruel, tyrannical, debauched. [L *Nerōniānus* from C. Claudius *Nero*, Roman emperor]
nerve (nœv) *n.* **1** any of the fibres or bundles of fibres conveying sensations and impulses to and from the brain or other organs. **2** the tissue constituting these fibres. **3** strength, coolness, resolution, pluck. **4** any of the ribs or fibrovascular bundles in a leaf. **5** (*pl.*) the nervous system, esp. as regards its state of health or the state of interaction between it and the other parts of the organism. **6** (*pl.*) an excited or disordered condition of the nerves, nervousness. **7** (*coll.*) impudence, cheek, audacity. **8** †a tendon or sinew. ~*v.t.* **1** to prepare (oneself) for something which requires courage. **2** to give strength or firmness to. **to get on someone's nerves** (*coll.*) to irritate someone. **to have nerves of iron** to be strong and courageous and not easily frightened. **to have nerves of steel** to have nerves of iron, not to be easily frightened. **to hit a nerve** to touch a nerve. **to lose one's nerve** to lose confidence; to become afraid. **to touch a nerve** to upset someone by mentioning a sensitive subject. **nervate** (-vāt) *a.* having nerves or ribs. **nervation** (-vā´shən) *n.* **nerve cell** *n.* any cell forming part of the nervous system. **nerve centre,** (*N Am.*) **nerve center** *n.* **1** an aggregation of nerve cells from which nerves branch out. **2** the central or most important part of a business, organization etc. **nerved** *a.* (*usu. in comb.*, as *strong-nerved*). **nerve gas** *n.* any one of a number of gases which have a paralysing and potentially fatal effect on the nervous system, used in warfare etc. **nerveless** (-lis) *a.* **1** destitute of strength, energy or vigour. **2** calm and confident. **3** without nerves. **4** without nervures. **5** diffuse. **6** feeble, flabby. **nervelessly** *adv.* **nervelessness** *n.* **nervelet** (-lit) *n.* **nerve-racking** *a.* tense, frightening, worrying. **nervine** (nœ´vīn) *a.* (of a medicine) capable of acting upon the nerves. ~*n.* a medicine that acts on the nerves. **nervo-** (nœ´vō), **nerv-** *comb. form* a nerve or nerves. **nervous** *a.* **1** having weak or sensitive nerves, excitable, highly strung, timid. **2** abounding in nervous energy. **3** affecting the nerves. **4** apprehensive (of). **5** of, relating to or composed of nerves. **6** sinewy, muscular. **7** †vigorous in sentiment or style. **nervous breakdown** *n.* an attack or period of mental illness which prevents a person from functioning normally, often characterized by depression, agitation or excessive anxiety. **nervously**

adv. **nervousness** *n.* **nervous system** *n.* a network of nerve cells, including the spinal cord and brain, which collectively controls the body. **nervous wreck** *n.* (*coll.*) an extremely nervous or worried person. **nervule** (-vūl) *n.* a small nerve or nervure. **nervular, nervulose** (-lōs) *a.* **nervure** (-vūə) *n.* 1 the principal vein of a leaf. 2 any of the ribs supporting the membranous wings of insects. **nervuration** (-ā´shən) *n.* **nervy** *a.* (*comp.* **nervier**, *superl.* **nerviest**) 1 nervous, jerky, jumpy. 2 (*N Am.*) full of nerve, cool, confident. 3 †strong, muscular, sinewy. **nervily** *adv.* **nerviness** *n.* [L *nervus* (cp. Gr. *neuron*)]

nescient (nes´iənt) *a.* (*formal*) 1 ignorant, having no knowledge (of). 2 agnostic. **nescience** *n.* [L *nesciens -ntem*, pres.p. of *nescīre* (*ne-*, not, *scīre*, to know)]

nesh (nesh) *a.* (*dial.*) 1 soft, friable. 2 tender, succulent. 3 delicate, poor-spirited. 4 sensitive to the cold. **neshness** *n.* [OE *hnesce* (cp. Dut. *nesch*, *nisch*, Goth. *hnasqus*), etym. unknown]

ness (nes) *n.* a promontory, a cape. [OE *næs* (cp. Icel. *nes*), rel. to *nasu*, NOSE]

-ness (nəs, nis) *suf.* forming nouns denoting state, condition, as *happiness*. [OE *-nes*, *-ness*, *-nis*, *-niss* (cp. Dut. *-nis*, G *-niss*, OHG *-nessi*, *-nassi*, *-nissi*, Goth. *-nassus*, orig. *-assus*)]

nest (nest) *n.* 1 the bed or shelter constructed or prepared by a bird for laying its eggs and rearing its young. 2 any place used by animals or insects for similar purposes. 3 a snug place of abode, shelter or retreat. 4 a haunt (of robbers etc.). 5 a brood, a swarm. 6 a series or set, esp. a number of small tables each fitting inside the next larger. *~v.t.* to put, lodge or establish in or as if in a nest. *~v.i.* 1 to build and occupy a nest. 2 to hunt for or take birds' nests or eggs. 3 to pack one inside another. **nest box** *n.* a box provided for a domestic chicken or other bird to lay eggs in. **nest egg** *n.* 1 a sum of money laid by as savings for the future. 2 a real or artificial egg left in a nest to encourage hens to lay eggs there. **nestful** *n.* (*pl.* **nestfuls**). **nesting** *n.* **nesting box** *n.* a nest box. **nestlike** *a.* **nestling** (-ling) *n.* 1 a bird too young to leave the nest. 2 a young child. [OE (cp. Dut. and G *nest*, and OIr. *net*, Welsh *nyth*, also L *nīdus*, from *ni-*, down, and the root *sed-*, to sit)]

nestle (nes´əl) *v.i.* 1 to settle oneself (down, in etc.). 2 to press closely up to someone. 3 to lie half concealed. 4 to be close or snug. 5 †to nest. *~v.t.* 1 to put or shelter in or as if in a nest. 2 to settle down snugly. **nestler** *n.* [OE *nestlian*, from NEST]

Nestor (nes´tə) *n.* a wise counsellor; a sage; a venerable senior. [Gr. *Nestōr*, king of Pylus, a character in Homer]

Nestorian (nestaw´riən) *a.* of or relating to Nestorius or his doctrines. *~n.* a follower of Nestorius, patriarch of Constantinople (5th cent.), who held that there were two distinct persons and two natures, divine and human, in Christ. **Nestorianism** *n.* [L *Nestoriānus* (*Nestorius*, -AN[1])]

net[1] (net) *n.* 1 a fabric of twine, cord etc., knotted into meshes, for catching fish, birds, or other animals, or for covering, protecting, carrying etc. 2 a snare. 3 a piece of netting used in various sports, often as a goal. 4 a network of spies, interconnected computers etc. *~v.t.* (*pres.p.* **netting**, *past*, *p.p.* **netted**) 1 to make or form in a network. 2 to make network of, to reticulate. 3 to cover, hold or confine with a net. 4 to catch in a net. 5 to fish with nets or set nets in (a stream, pond etc.). 6 to catch as if in a net, to ensnare. 7 to score (a goal). 8 to make into a net or netting. *~v.i.* to make netting or network. **the net** the Internet. **netball** *n.* a team game in which a ball has to be thrown into a suspended net. **netful** *n.* (*pl.* **netfuls**). **netting** *n.* **netting-needle** *n.* **net-veined** *a.* (of an insect's wing, a leaf etc.) having a reticulated series of veins or nervules. **net-winged** *a.* having net-veined wings. **network** *n.* 1 an open-work fabric, netting. 2 a system of intersecting lines, a reticulation. 3 a system of stations for simultaneous broadcasting. 4 any system of lines, roads etc., resembling network. 5 (*Comput.*) a system of communication between different computers, terminals, circuits etc. 6 a system of interconnected electrical conductors. 7 a system of units related in some way, e.g. part of a business organization. 8 a group of people who are useful to each other because of the similarity of their aims, background etc., as in *old boy network*. *~v.t.* 1 to connect. 2 to broadcast (a television or radio programme) throughout the country rather than in one region. 3 (*Comput.*) to create or use a system of communication between computers, circuits etc. *~v.i.* 1 to form or be part of a network, e.g. through business contacts. 2 to establish professional contacts through social meetings. **networker** *n.* **networking** *n.* [OE (cp. Dut., Icel. and Dan. *net*, G *Netz*), cogn. with L *nassa*, creel]

net[2] (net), **nett** *a.* 1 free from all deductions. 2 obtained or left after all deductions. 3 not subject to discount. 4 (of a weight) minus packaging. 5 (of a result etc.) final, ultimate. *~v.t.* (*pres.p.* **netting**, *past*, *p.p.* **netted**) to yield or realize as clear profit. **Net Book Agreement** *n.* (*Hist.*) an agreement between UK booksellers and publishers that booksellers would not sell books at less than the marked price. **net profit** *n.* profit after expenses have been deducted. **net ton** *n.* a unit measuring net internal capacity, equivalent to 100 cu. ft. (2.83 m^3). [F, NEAT[1]]

†nether (nedh´ə) *a.* 1 lower. 2 belonging to the region below the heavens or the earth. **nethermost** *a.* **nether regions** *n.pl.* hell. **nether world** *n.* the nether regions. [OE *neothera* (cp. Dut. *neder*, G *nieder*, Icel. *nethri*)]

Netherlander (nedh´ələndə) *n.* a native or inhabitant of the Netherlands, or a descendant of one. **Netherlandish** *a.* **Netherlands** *n.* 1 Holland. 2 (*Hist.*) the Low Countries. [Dut. *Nederlander*, from *Nederland*, Netherlands]

netsuke (net´suki) *n.* (*pl.* **netsuke, netsukes**) a small piece of carved wood or ivory worn or attached to various articles, as a toggle or button, by the Japanese. [Jap.]

nett NET[2].

netted, netting etc. NET[1].

nettle (net´əl) *n.* 1 any plant of the genus *Urtica*, with two European species, the great or common and the small nettle, with inconspicuous flowers and minute stinging hairs. 2 any of various plants bearing some resemblance to these. *~v.t.* 1 to irritate, to provoke. 2 to sting. **to grasp the nettle** to take decisive or bold action. **nettle-rash** *n.* an eruption on the skin resembling the sting of a nettle. **nettle-tree** *n.* the hackberry. [OE *netele* (cp. Dut. *netel*, G *Nessel*, Dan. *nelde*, Swed. *nässla*)]

network NET[1].

Neufchâtel (nœshatel´) *n.* a soft white cheese, similar to cream cheese but with less fat. [town in France]

neume (nūm), **neum** *n.* (*Mus.*) a sequence of notes to be sung to one syllable in plainsong. [F, from med. L *neuma*, Gr. *pneuma*, breath]

☒ **neumonia** common misspelling of PNEUMONIA.

neur- NEURO-.

neural (nū´rəl) *a.* of or relating to the nerves or the nervous system. **neurally** *adv.* **neural network, neural net** *n.* (*Comput.*) a system with interconnected processors working simultaneously and sharing information, and capable of learning from experience. [NEURO-]

neuralgia (nūral´jə) *n.* an acute pain in a nerve or series of nerves, esp. in the head or face. **neuralgic** *a.* [Gr. *algos*, pain]

neurasthenia (nūrəsthē´niə) *n.* weakness of the nervous system, nervous debility. **neurasthenic** (-then´-) *a.*, *n.*

neuration (nūrā´shən) *n.* the arrangement of the nervures, as in an insect's wings.
neurectomy (nūrek´təmi) *n.* (*pl.* **neurectomies**) excision of a nerve, or part of it.
neurilemma (nūrilem´ə) *n.* the membranous sheath encasing a nerve. [Gr. *eilema*, covering]
neurility (nūril´iti) *n.* the power of a nerve to convey stimuli.
neurine (nū´rēn) *n.* a poisonous ptomaine derived from putrefying organic matter.
neuritis (nūrī´tis) *n.* inflammation of a nerve. **neuritic** (-rit´-) *a.*
neuro- (nū´rō), **neur-** *comb. form* **1** of or relating to a nerve cell. **2** of or relating to nerves. **3** of or relating to the nervous system. [Gr. *neuron*, a nerve]
neuroanatomy (nūrōənat´əmi) *n.* the anatomy of the nervous system. **neuroanatomical** (-anətom´-) *a.* **neuroanatomist** *n.*
neurobiology (nūrōbīol´əji) *n.* the biology of the nervous system. **neurobiological** (-bīəloj´-) *a.* **neurobiologist** *n.*
neurocomputer (nūrōkəmpū´tə) *n.* a computer using a neural network.
neurogenesis (nūrōjen´əsis) *n.* the development of nervous tissue.
neurogenic (nūrōjen´ik) *a.* originating in nervous tissue.
neuroglia (nūrog´liə) *n.* the supporting tissue of the central nervous system. [Gr. *glia*, glue]
neurohormone (nūrōhaw´mōn) *n.* a hormone produced by nerve cells.
neurolinguistics (nūrōling·gwis´tiks) *n.* the branch of linguistics which deals with the relationship between language and the functioning of the brain. **neurolinguistic** *a.*
neurology (nūrol´əji) *n.* the scientific study of the anatomy, physiology and pathology of nerves. **neurological** (-loj´-) *a.* **neurologically** *adv.* **neurologist** *n.*
neuroma (nūrō´mə) *n.* (*pl.* **neuromas, neuromata** (-tə)) a tumour consisting of nerve tissue.
neuromuscular (nūrōmŭs´kūlə) *a.* of or relating to nerves and muscles.
neurone (nū´rōn), **neuron** (-ron) *n.* a nerve cell with its processes and ramifications, one of the structural units of the nervous system. **neuronal** (-rō´nəl) *a.* **neuronic** (-ron´ik) *a.*
neuropath (nū´rəpath) *n.* a person suffering from a nervous disorder or having abnormal nervous sensibility. **neuropathic** (-path´-) *a.* **neuropathist** (-rop´-) *n.* **neuropathology** (-thol´-) *n.* the pathology of the nervous system. **neuropathologist** *n.* **neuropathy** (-rop´əthi) *n.* any nervous disease.
neurophysiology (nūrōfiziol´əji) *n.* the physiology of the nervous system. **neurophysiological** (-loj´-) *a.* **neurophysiologist** *n.*
neuropsychology (nūrōsīkol´əji) *n.* psychology based upon the study of the nervous system. **neuropsychological** (-loj´-) *a.* **neuropsychologist** *n.*
neuropteran (nūrop´tərən) *n.* any insect of the order Neuroptera, having four reticulated membranous wings. **neuropterous, neuropteral, neuropteroid** *a.* [NEURO-, Gr. *pteron*, wing]
neuroradiology (nūrōrādiol´əji) *n.* a method of diagnosis of such conditions as cerebral tumours, aneurysms etc. by X-ray examination.
neuroscience (nū´rōisīəns) *n.* the study of the structure and function of the brain and the nervous system. **neuroscientist** (-sī´-) *n.*
neurosis (nūrō´sis) *n.* (*pl.* **neuroses** (-sēz)) **1** functional disorder of the nervous system. **2** a mild mental disorder, usu. with symptoms of anxiety. **3** the change in the nerve cells or neurones, or the discharge of nerve energy, forming the physical basis of psychic activity.
neurotic (-rot´-) *a.* **1** of or relating to neurosis. **2** suffering from neurosis. **3** (*coll.*) unreasonably anxious, oversensitive. ~*n.* **1** a neurotic person. **2** †a substance acting upon the nerves. **neurotically** *adv.* **neuroticism** (-sizm) *n.*
neurosurgery (nūrōsœ´jəri) *n.* the branch of surgery dealing with the nervous system. **neurosurgeon** *n.* **neurosurgical** *a.*
neurotic NEUROSIS.
neurotomy (nūrot´əmi) *n.* (*pl.* **neurotomies**) an incision in a nerve, usu. to produce sensory paralysis. **neurotomist** *a.*
neurotoxin (nūrōtok´sin) *n.* any poison which acts on the nervous system.
neurotransmitter (nūrōtranzmit´ə) *n.* a chemical substance by means of which nerve cells communicate with each other.
neuter (nū´tə) *a.* **1** (*Gram.*) **a** neither masculine nor feminine. **b** †intransitive. **2** (of a plant) neither male nor female, without pistil or stamen. **3** (of an animal, esp. an insect) undeveloped sexually, sterile. ~*n.* **1** a neuter word. **2** a flower having neither stamens nor pistils. **3** a sterile female insect, such as a working bee. **4** a castrated animal. ~*v.t.* to remove the reproductive organs of (an animal). [L, neither (*ne-*, not, *uter*, either)]
neutral (nū´trəl) *a.* **1** taking no part with either side, esp. not assisting either of two belligerents. **2** belonging to a state that takes no part in hostilities. **3** indifferent, impartial. **4** having no distinct or determinate character, colour etc. **5** neither good nor bad, indefinite, indeterminate. **6** denoting the position of parts in a gear mechanism when no power is transmitted. **7** (*Chem.*) neither acid nor alkaline. **8** (*Physics*) neither positive nor negative. **9** (*Biol.*) neuter, asexual. ~*n.* **1** a neutral state. **2** a subject of a neutral state. **3** a neutral gear. **neutralism** *n.* the policy of remaining neutral. **neutralist** *n.* **neutrality** (-tral´-) *n.* **neutralize, neutralise** *v.t.* **1** to render neutral. **2** to render inoperative or ineffective, to counteract. **3** to declare (a state or territory) neutral, either permanently or during hostilities. **4** (*euphem.*) to make harmless, to kill. **neutralization** (-zā´shən) *n.* **neutralizer** *n.* **neutrally** *adv.* [L *neutrālis*, as NEUTER]
neutrino (nūtrē´nō) *n.* (*pl.* **neutrinos**) any of a class of subatomic particles with almost zero mass and zero charge but specified spin.
neutron (nū´tron) *n.* (*Physics*) a particle that is neutral electrically with approximately the same mass as a proton. **neutron bomb** *n.* a bomb which produces neutrons without a huge blast, designed to destroy all life in the area hit without causing much damage to property. **neutron star** *n.* a very dense star composed of neutrons.
Nev. *abbr.* Nevada.
névé (nev´ā) *n.* consolidated snow above the glaciers, in the process of being converted into ice. [F, ult. from L *nivem*, nom. *nix*, snow]
never (nev´ə) *adv.* **1** not ever, at no time. **2** on no occasion. **3** not at all. ~*int.* surely not! **never a one** not a single person etc., none. **never mind** MIND. **never say die** DIE[1]. **never you mind** MIND. **well I never!** (*coll.*) used to express surprise. **never-ending, never-failing** *a.* **nevermore** (-maw´) *adv.* at no future time; never again. **never-never** *n.* **1** (*coll.*) the hire-purchase system. **2** (*Austral.*) the uninhabited areas in N and W Queensland. **never-never land** *n.* an imaginary place with conditions too ideal to exist in real life. **nevertheless** *conj.* but for all that; notwithstanding; all the same. [OE *næfre* (*ne*, not, *æfre*, ever)]
nevus NAEVUS.
new (nū) *a.* **1** not formerly in existence. **2** lately made, invented or introduced. **3** not before known. **4** recently

entered upon or begun. **5** never before used, not worn or exhausted. **6** renewed; reinvigorated. **7** replacing something (*a new job*). **8** in addition to others of the same kind (*a new cinema*). **9** fresh, unfamiliar, unaccustomed. **10** fresh (from), not yet accustomed (to). **11** modern, newfangled. **12** advanced. *~adv.* **1** newly, recently (*usu. in comb.*, as *new-born*). **2** anew, afresh. **that's a new one on me** (*coll.*) I have never heard of that before. **to put a new face on** FACE. **New Age** *n.* a cultural movement which emphasizes the spiritual and mystical aspects of western society, incorporating elements of eastern religion, astrology, alternative medicine and ecology. *~a.* of or relating to the New Age movement or New Age music. **New Age music** *n.* a type of gentle, melodic popular music played mainly on synthesizer and acoustic instruments. **new arrival** *n.* (*coll.*) a newborn baby. **New Australian** *n.* a non-British immigrant to Australia. **new birth** *n.* (*Theol.*) spiritual regeneration. **new blood** *n.* a person with fresh talent or a refreshing influence. **new-blown** *a.* having just come into bloom. **newborn** *a.* **1** just born. **2** reborn, regenerated. **new broom** *n.* a recently appointed person who is expected to make many changes. **newcomer** *n.* a person who has recently arrived in a place or who has just begun to take part in something. **New Covenant** *n.* the Christian relation to God. **New Deal** *n.* economic and social measures introduced by President Roosevelt in the US in 1933, after the economic crisis of 1929. **new deal** *n.* new arrangements, new conditions. **new departure** *n.* **1** a new course of thought or ideas. **2** a new enterprise. **new dimension** *n.* a new aspect. **new-fashioned** *a.* **new-fledged** *a.* **newish** *a.* **new-laid** *a.* (of an egg) freshly laid. **New Latin** *n.* Latin of periods after AD 1500. **New Learning** *n.* the Renaissance. **new lease of life** *n.* an anticipated spell of life or enjoyment (e.g. after recovery from illness or release from trouble). **New Look** *n.* a post-World War II women's fashion featuring long, full skirts. **new look** *n.* an up-to-date appearance. **new-look** *a.* having a new, different appearance. **newly** *adv.* **1** recently. **2** anew. **3** differently. **newly-wed** *n.* a recently married person. **new man** *n.* (*pl.* **new men**) a man who supports women's liberation and who undertakes tasks traditionally associated with women, such as housework. **new mathematics, new maths** *n.* a system of teaching mathematics with a strong emphasis on investigation and set theory. **new-model** *v.t.* (*pres.p.* **new-modelling,** (*N Am.*) **new-modeling,** *past, p.p.* **new-modelled,** (*N Am.*) **new-modeled**) to give a fresh form to. **new moon** *n.* the moon at the beginning of its course with its face invisible or partially illuminated. **newness** *n.* **new potatoes** *n.pl.* potatoes which have been harvested early. **Newspeak** *n.* a form of language, often used by officials and bureaucrats, which is ambiguous, misleading and verbose (coined by George Orwell in his novel *Nineteen Eighty-Four*). **new star** *n.* a nova. **New Style** *n.* the method of reckoning dates which is currently used, based on the Gregorian calendar. **new-style** *a.* in a new style (*a new-style passport*). **New Testament** *n.* the part of the Christian Bible dealing with the Christian dispensation composed after the birth of Christ. **new town** *n.* a town planned by the government to relieve housing problems in nearby large cities, stimulate development etc. **new wave** *n.* **1** the nouvelle vague. **2** a style of rock music of the late 1970s, developing from punk. **new woman** *n.* (*pl.* **new women**) (*Hist.*) a woman of advanced ideas, esp. one who claimed equality with men in the social, economic and political spheres. **New World** *n.* the American continent. **new year** *n.* **1** the beginning of a new calendar year. **2** the first few days or weeks of a year. **New Year's Day** *n.* the first day of the year. **New Year's Eve** *n.* the last day of the year. [OE *nīve* (cp. Dut. *nieuw*, G *neu*, Icel. *nȳr*, Gr. *neos*, L *novus*)]

Newcastle disease (nū´kahsəl) *n.* an acute, highly contagious disease of chickens and other birds (first recorded in Newcastle upon Tyne in 1926).

newel (nū´əl) *n.* **1** the central column from which the steps of a winding stair radiate. **2** an upright post at the top or bottom of a stair supporting the handrail. [OF *nuel* (F *noyau*), kernel, from late L *nucāle*, from *nux nucis*, nut]

newfangled (nūfang´əld) *a.* **1** (*derog.*) new-fashioned; different from the accepted fashion. **2** fond of novelties, inconstant. **newfangledly** *adv.* **newfangledness** *n.* [ME *fangel*, from OE *fang-*, p.p, *fōn*, to take (see FANG)]

Newfoundland (nū´fəndlənd, -fownd´-), **Newfoundland dog** *n.* a large breed of dog, famous for swimming powers, orig. from Newfoundland. [island in Gulf of St Lawrence]

Newfoundlander (nū´fəndləndə, nūfəndlan´də) *n.* a native or inhabitant of Newfoundland, Canada.

Newmarket (nū´mahkit) *n.* a gambling card game in which players try to match cards with cards laid out. **Newmarket coat** *n.* a close-fitting overcoat, orig. for riding, worn by men or women. [Newmarket, town in Cambridgeshire]

news (nūz) *n.* **1** recent or fresh information. **2** a regular radio or television broadcast of up-to-date information on current affairs. **3** (*coll.*) information previously unknown (to) (*that's news to me*). **news agency** *n.* an organization for supplying information to newspapers etc. **newsagent** *n.* a dealer in newspapers, magazines etc. **newsboy** *n.* a boy who delivers or sells newspapers in the street. **newsbrief** *n.* a newsflash. **news bulletin** *n.* a collection of news items for broadcasting. **newscast** *n.* a radio or television news programme. **newscaster** *n.* a newsreader. **news conference** *n.* a press conference. **newsflash** *n.* a short important news item, esp. one which interrupts a television or radio programme. **news-gatherer** *n.* a person who researches news items for broadcast or publication. **newsgirl** *n.* a girl who delivers or sells newspapers in the street. **news hound** *n.* (*coll.*) a reporter in search of news. **newsless** *a.* **newsletter** *n.* a printed report of news sent out regularly to a particular group. **newsman** *n.* (*pl.* **newsmen**) a news reporter. **newsmonger** *n.* a person who makes it their business to spread news, usu. false; a busybody in news. **newspaper** *n.* a printed publication, usu. issued daily or weekly, containing news, usu. with leaders expressing opinions on questions of the hour, articles on special topics, advertisements etc. **newspaperman, newspaperwoman** *n.* (*pl.* **newspapermen, newspaperwomen**) a journalist working for a newspaper. **newsprint** *n.* the cheap-quality paper upon which newspapers are printed. **newsreader** *n.* a person who reads the news on radio or television. **newsreel** *n.* a short film giving the day's news. **newsroom** *n.* **1** a room where news is edited for broadcasting or publication. **2** a room in a library for reading newspapers etc. **news-sheet** *n.* a printed sheet of news, an early form of newspaper. **news-stand** *n.* a newspaper kiosk. **news-vendor** *n.* a seller of newspapers. **newsworthy** *a.* interesting enough to be reported as news. **newsworthiness** *n.* **newsy** *a.* (*comp.* **newsier,** *superl.* **newsiest**). **newsiness** *n.* [pl. of NEW (cp. F *novelles*, L *nova*, pl. of *novus*, new)]

newt (nūt) *n.* a small, tailed amphibian of the genus *Tritunus*, like the salamander. [ME *ewte* (*a newt*, from *an ewt*), A-S *efeta*, EFT]

newton (nū´tən) *n.* (*Physics*) a unit of force equal to 100,000 dynes.

Newtonian (nūtō´niən) *a.* **1** of or relating to Sir Isaac Newton or his theories. **2** discovered or invented by Newton. **Newtonian mechanics** *n.* the system of mechanics based on Newton's laws of motion. **Newtonian telescope** *n.* a type of reflecting telescope. [Sir Isaac *Newton*, 1642–1727, British mathematician]

New Yorker (nū yaw´kə) *n.* a native or inhabitant of New York, USA.

New Zealander (nū zē´ləndə) *n.* a native or inhabitant of New Zealand, or a descendant of one.

next (nekst) *a.* 1 nearest in place, time or degree. 2 nearest in order or succession, immediately following. ~*adv.* 1 nearest or immediately after. 2 in the next place or degree. ~*n.* the next person or thing. ~*prep.* (*coll.*) nearest to. **next, please** let the next person come. **next to** almost; all but. **next to nothing** scarcely anything. **next-best** *a.* second best. **next but one** *n.* the one immediately after the one following. **next door** *adv.*, *n.* (in, at or to) the adjoining house or room. **next door to** 1 in or at the house adjoining. 2 almost, near to. **next-door** *a.* of or relating to the adjoining house or room, living next door. **next of kin** *n.* the nearest blood relation. **next world** *n.* life after death. [OE *nēahst* (NIGH, -EST[1])]

nexus (nek´səs) *n.* (*pl.* **nexuses**) 1 a connected group. 2 a link, a connection. [L, from *nec-*, stem of *nectere*, to bind]

NF *abbr.* 1 National Front. 2 Newfoundland.

NFL *abbr.* (*N Am.*) National Football League.

Nfld. *abbr.* Newfoundland.

NFU *abbr.* National Farmers' Union.

n.g. *abbr.* no good.

NGA *abbr.* (*Hist.*) National Graphical Association.

ngaio (nī´ō) *n.* (*pl.* **ngaios**) a New Zealand tree, *Myoporum laetum*, noted for its fine white wood. [Maori]

NGO *abbr.* non-governmental organization.

ngultrum *n.* (*pl.* **ngultrums**) the chief monetary unit of Bhutan, central Asia.

Nguni *n.* (*pl.* **Nguni**) 1 a member of a group of peoples of southern Africa. 2 the group of Bantu languages spoken by the Nguni. ~*a.* of or relating to the Nguni. [Zulu]

NH *abbr.* New Hampshire.

NHI *abbr.* National Health Insurance.

NHS *abbr.* National Health Service.

NI *abbr.* 1 National Insurance. 2 Northern Ireland.

Ni *chem. symbol* nickel.

niacin (nī´əsin) *n.* nicotinic acid.

nib (nib) *n.* 1 the point of a pen. 2 the point of a tool etc. 3 the beak of a bird. 4 (*dial.*) one of the handles projecting from the shaft of a scythe. 5 (*pl.*) crushed cocoa beans. ~*v.t.* (*pres.p.* **nibbing**, *past, p.p.* **nibbed**) 1 to put a nib into (a pen). 2 to sharpen the nib of (a quill pen). 3 to nibble. ~*v.i.* to nibble. **his nibs** (*coll.*) an important or self-important person. [prob. var. of NEB]

nibble (nib´əl) *v.t.* 1 to bite little by little. 2 to bite little bits off. 3 to bite at cautiously. ~*v.i.* 1 to take small bites or to bite cautiously (at). 2 to take a cautious interest (in). 3 to criticize carpingly, to cavil. ~*n.* 1 the act of nibbling. 2 (*pl.*) party snacks, such as crisps, nuts and biscuits. 3 a little bite. 4 a bit which is nibbled off. 5 (*Comput.*) half a byte. **nibbler** *n.* **nibblingly** *adv.* [etym. uncertain, cp. LG *nibbelen*, Dut. *knibbelen*]

niblet (nib´lit) *n.* a small piece (of food). [prob. NIBBLE, -LET]

niblick (nib´lik) *n.* a golf club with a small cup-shaped iron head. [etym. uncertain]

NIC *abbr.* 1 newly industrializing country. 2 Nicaragua (IVR).

nicad (nī´kad), **nicad battery** *n.* a battery which has a nickel anode and a cadmium cathode. [NICKEL, CADMIUM]

Nicam (nī´kam) *n.* a sound system in which audio signals are converted into digital form and transmitted along with a standard television signal. [*n*ear-*i*nstantaneous *c*ompanded *a*udio *m*ultiplexing]

Nicaraguan (nikərag´ūən, -wən) *n.* a native or inhabitant of Nicaragua, Central America. ~*a.* of or relating to Nicaragua.

niccolite (nik´əlīt) *n.* arsenide of nickel.

nice (nīs) *a.* 1 pleasing or agreeable. 2 delightful, attractive, friendly, kind. 3 (*iron.*) terrible (*a nice mess*). 4 fastidious, over-particular, hard to please, dainty, punctilious, scrupulous. 5 acute, discerning, discriminating, sensitive to minute differences. 6 requiring delicate discrimination or tact, delicate, subtle, minute. **nice and** pleasantly satisfactory (*nice and cool*). **nicely** *adv.* **niceness** *n.* **nice one** *int.* (*coll.*) used to express approval or pleasure. **nicety** (nī´siti) *n.* (*pl.* **niceties**) 1 exactness, precision. 2 a minute point, a delicate distinction. 3 a small detail. 4 (*pl.*) refinements, delicacy. **to a nicety** exactly, with precision. **nice work** *int.* used to express approval. **nicish** (nī´sish), **niceish** *a.* rather nice, rather pleasant. [OF, from L *nescium*, nom. *-us*, ignorant (see NESCIENT)]

Nicene (nī´sēn) *a.* of or relating to Nicaea, Bithynia, Asia Minor. **Nicene Councils** *n.pl.* two councils held at Nicaea (the first in AD 325 to settle the Arian controversy, the second in 787 on the question of images and the iconoclasts). **Nicene Creed** *n.* a statement of Christian belief formulated by the first council of Nicaea. [late L *Nicēnus*, from *Nīcæa*, Gr. *Nikaia*, a town in Asia Minor]

nicety NICE.

niche (nich, nēsh) *n.* 1 a recess in a wall for a statue, vase etc. 2 one's proper place or natural position. 3 in business, a small, specialized, but profitable area of the market. ~*v.t.* 1 to put in a niche. 2 to settle (oneself) in a comfortable place. [F, from It. *nicchia*, etym. uncertain]

Nichrome® (nī´krōm) *n.* a nickel-chromium alloy with high electrical resistance and an ability to withstand high temperature.

nicish NICE.

Nick (nik) *n.* OLD NICK (under OLD). [short for *Nicholas*]

nick[1] (nik) *n.* 1 a small notch, cut or dent, esp. used as a guide or a tally or score for keeping account. 2 the critical moment. 3 a winning throw at dice. 4 the exact point or moment. 5 (*sl.*) a prison, a police station. 6 (*coll.*) condition (of a given description) (*in good nick*). 7 in a squash court, the junction between the floor and the walls. ~*v.t.* 1 to cut or make a nick or nicks in. 2 to snip, to cut. 3 to catch at the exact moment. 4 (*sl.*) to steal. 5 (*sl.*) to arrest. ~*v.i.* (of breeding animals) to mingle well, to produce offspring of good quality. **in the nick of time** only just in time. **to nick a horse** to make an incision at the root of a horse's tail, in order to make the horse carry its tail higher. [etym. uncertain]

nick[2] (nik) *v.i.* (*Austral., sl.*) to go quickly or furtively. [etym. uncertain; cp. NIP[1]]

nickel (nik´əl) *n.* 1 a lustrous silvery-white ductile metallic element, at. no. 28, chem. symbol Ni, usu. found in association with cobalt, used in the manufacture of German silver and in other alloys. 2 (*N Am.*) a 5-cent piece. ~*v.t.* (*pres.p.* **nickelling**, (*N Am.*) **nickeling**, *past, p.p.* **nickelled**, (*N Am.*) **nickeled**) to coat with nickel. **nickel brass** *n.* an alloy of copper, zinc and nickel. **nickelic** *a.* **nickeliferous** (-lif´-) *a.* **nickelize, nickelise** *v.t.* **nickelous** *a.* **nickel-plate** *v.t.* to cover with nickel. **nickel-plating** *n.* **nickel silver** *n.* German silver. **nickel steel** *n.* an alloy of nickel and steel. [Swed., abbrev. from G *Kupfernickel* (*Kupfer*, copper, *Nickel*, a demon, cp. OE *nicol*), so called from disgust at its not yielding copper]

nickelodeon (nikəlō´diən) *n.* (*pl.* **nickelodeons**) (*N Am.*) 1 (*coll.*) an early form of jukebox, esp. one operated by a 5-cent piece. 2 (*Hist.*) a cinema whose admission fee was one nickel. [NICKEL, mel*odeon*]

nicker[1] (nik´ə) *n.* (*pl.* **nicker**) (*sl.*) a pound (money).

nicker[2] (nik´ə) *v.i.* **1** to neigh. **2** to guffaw. ~*n.* **1** a neigh. **2** a guffaw. [Sc., North., imit.]

nick-nack KNICK-KNACK.

nickname (nik´nām) *n.* a name given in derision or familiarity. ~*v.t.* **1** to give a nickname to. **2** to call by a nickname. [ME *nekename*, corr. of *ekename*, from *an ekename* (EKE, NAME)]

nicol (nik´əl), **nicol prism** *n.* a crystal of calcium carbonate so cut and cemented as to transmit only the extraordinary ray, used for polarizing light. [William *Nicol*, *c.* 1768–1851, Scottish inventor]

nicotine (nik´ətēn) *n.* an acrid, poisonous alkaloid contained in tobacco. **nicotian** (-kō´shiən) *a.* of or relating to tobacco. ~*n.* a person who smokes tobacco. **nicotiana** (nikotiah´nə, -kōshi-) *n.* a tobacco plant. **nicotinamide** (-tin´əmīd) *n.* the amide of nicotinic acid, essential for the prevention of pellagra. **nicotinamide adenine dinucleotide** *n.* NAD. **nicotinic acid** (-tin´ik) *n.* a vitamin of the B complex, a deficiency of which causes pellagra. **nicotinism** *n.* (*Med.*) a morbid condition caused by overindulgence in tobacco. **nicotinize, nicotinise** *v.t.* [F, Jean *Nicot*, 1530–1600, who introduced tobacco into France]

nictitate (nik´titāt), **nictate** (nik´tāt) *v.i.* to wink, esp. to open and shut the eyes rapidly. **nictitating membrane** *n.* a third or inner eyelid possessed by birds, fishes and many animals. **nictitation** (-ā´shən) *n.* [L *nictātus*, p.p. of *nictāre*, to wink (freq. *nictitāre*)]

niddle-noddle (nid´əlnodəl) *v.i.* to wag the head. ~*v.t.* to wag (the head). ~*a.* nodding.

†**nide** (nīd), †**nye** (nī) *n.* **1** a collection of pheasants. **2** a nest of young pheasants. [L *nidus*, a nest]

nidi NIDUS.

nidify (nid´ifī) *v.i.* (*3rd pers. sing. pres.* **nidifies**, *pres.p.* **nidifying**, *past, p.p.* **nidified**) to build a nest or nests. **nidification** (-ā´shən) *n.* **nidificate** *v.t.* [L *nīdificātus*, p.p. of *nīdificāre* (*nīdus*, nest, *-ficāre*, *facere*, to make)]

nid-nod (nid´nod) *v.i.* (*pres.p.* **nid-nodding**, *past, p.p.* **nid-nodded**) to keep nodding, as if sleepy. [redupl. from NOD]

nidus (nī´dəs) *n.* (*pl.* **nidi** (-dī), **niduses**) **1** a nest, a place for the deposit of eggs laid by birds, insects etc. **2** a place in which spores develop. **3** (*Med.*) a place in an organism where germs develop, a centre of infection. **4** a source or origin, a place of development. [L]

niece (nēs) *n.* the daughter of one's brother or sister, or one's brother-in-law or sister-in-law. [OF *nièce*, pop. L *neptia*, L *neptis*, rel. to *nepos*, NEPHEW]

niello (niel´ō) *n.* (*pl.* **nielli** (-lē), **niellos**) **1** a black alloy used to fill the lines of incised designs on metal plates. **2** an example of this work. **niellist** *n.* **nielloed** *a.* [It., from L *nigellum*, neut. of *nigellus*, dim. of *niger*, black]

Niersteiner (niə´shtīnə) *n.* a white Rhenish wine. [*Nierstein*, near Hesse, Germany]

Nietzschean (nē´chiən) *a.* of or relating to Friedrich Nietzsche, 1844–1900, or his philosophy. ~*n.* a follower of Nietzsche.

niff (nif) *n.* (*coll.*) a stink, a bad smell. ~*v.i.* to stink, to smell bad. **niffy** *a.* (*comp.* **niffier**, *superl.* **niffiest**). [perh. from SNIFF]

nifty (nif´ti) *a.* (*comp.* **niftier**, *superl.* **niftiest**) (*coll.*) **1** quick, slick. **2** smart, stylish. **niftily** *adv.* **niftiness** *n.* [etym. uncertain]

NIG *abbr.* Niger (IVR).

nigella (nījel´ə) *n.* a plant of the genus *Nigella*, of ranunculaceous plants comprising love-in-a-mist. [L fem. of *nīgellus*, dim. of *niger*, black]

Nigerian (nījiə´riən) *n.* a native or inhabitant of Nigeria, Africa. ~*a.* of or relating to Nigeria.

Nigerien (nī´jəriən, nījərien´) *n.* a native or inhabitant of Niger, Africa. ~*a.* of or relating to Niger.

niggard (nig´əd) *n.* a stingy person, a miser; a person who is grudging. ~†*a.* niggardly. **niggardly** *a.* miserly, mean, parsimonious. ~*adv.* in a miserly manner. **niggardliness** *n.* [etym. obscure (cp. Icel. *hnöggr*, Swed. *nugg*, Swed. dial. *nugger*, also OE *hnēaw*, sparing)]

nigger (nig´ə) *n.* **1** (*offensive*) a black person. **2** (*offensive*) any dark-skinned person. **3** the black caterpillar of the turnip sawfly. **to work like a nigger** (*offensive*) to work hard. **nigger in the woodpile** *n.* (*offensive*) a person who or something which spoils something good. [F *nègre*, Sp. NEGRO]

niggle (nig´əl) *v.i.* **1** to busy oneself with petty details. **2** to find fault constantly. **3** to fiddle, to trifle. ~*v.t.* **1** to worry, to annoy. **2** to trick. ~*n.* **1** a minor criticism or worry. **2** small, cramped handwriting. **niggler** *n.* **niggling** *a.*, *n.* **nigglingly** *adv.* [cp. Norw. *nigla*]

†**nigh** (nī) *adv.* **1** near. **2** almost. ~*a.* near. ~*prep.* near, close to. [OE *nēah* (cp. Dut. *na*, G *nah*, Icel. *na-*), cp. NEAR, NEXT]

night (nīt) *a.* **1** the time of darkness from sunset to sunrise. **2** the darkness of this period. **3** the end of daylight, nightfall. **4** a period or state of darkness. **5** an evening set aside for a particular activity. **6** ignorance. **7** intellectual and moral darkness. **8** (*euphem.*) death. **9** a period of grief or mourning. ~*int.* (*coll.*) goodnight. **to make a night of it** MAKE[1]. **night-bell** *n.* a doorbell for use at night. **nightbird** *n.* **1** (*coll.*) a person who habitually stays up late. **2** the owl or nightingale. **night-blindness** *n.* nyctalopia. **nightcap** *n.* **1** (*Hist.*) a cap worn in bed. **2** a hot drink or an alcoholic drink taken at bedtime. **night-chair** *n.* a night-stool. **nightclothes** *n.* clothes worn in bed. **nightclub** *n.* a club open late at night, providing refreshments, dancing and entertainment. **night-commode** *n.* a table or chair containing a chamber pot. **nightdress** *n.* a woman's or child's loose dress-shaped garment worn in bed. **nightfall** *n.* the beginning of night, the coming of darkness; dusk. **nightfaring** *a.* travelling by night. **night fighter** *n.* an aircraft used for intercepting at night. **nightfire** *n.* **1** a fire burning at night. **2** a will-o'-the-wisp. **night-flower** *n.* a flower which opens at night and shuts in the day. **night-fly** *n.* (*pl.* **night-flies**) a moth or other insect that flies by night. **nightgear** *n.* nightclothes. **night-glass** *n.* a telescope enabling one to see objects at night. **nightgown** *n.* **1** nightdress. **2** (*Hist.*) a dressing gown. **nighthawk** *n.* **1** a person, esp. a thief, who prowls about at night. **2** an American nightjar of the genus *Chordeiles*. **nightie** *n.* (*coll.*) a nightdress. **nightjar** *n.* any nocturnal bird of the family Caprimulgidae, having grey-brown plumage. **nightless** *a.* **nightlife** *n.* late evening entertainment or social life. **night light** *n.* **1** a low light kept alight at night. **2** the light of the moon or stars. **night-line** *n.* a line with baited hooks left in the water at night to catch fish. **night-long** *a.* lasting through a night. ~*adv.* all night. **nightly** *a.*, *adv.* **nightmare** (-meə) *n.* **1** a terrifying dream. **2** a haunting sense of dread. **3** (*coll.*) anything inspiring such a feeling; a terrifying experience. **4** (*Hist.*) a monster supposed to sit upon a sleeper, an incubus. **nightmarish** *a.* **nightmarishly** *adv.* **night monkey** *n.* a douroucouli. **night nurse** *n.* a nurse who is on duty during the night. **night out** *n.* **1** an evening spent in festivity. **2** the evening on which a servant is allowed out. **night owl** *n.* **1** (*coll.*) a person who habitually stays up late. **2** an exclusively nocturnal owl. **nightpiece** *n.* **1** a picture or description representing a night scene. **2** a picture best seen by artificial light. **night raven** *n.* a bird of ill omen supposed to cry at night. **night safe** *n.* a safe built into the outer wall of a bank where customers can deposit money when the bank is closed. **night school** *n.* an evening school for those at work during the day. **night-season** *n.* nighttime. **night shift** *n.* **1** work during the night, as distinct from *day shift* and *back shift*. **2** the group of workers undertaking such work. **nightshirt** *n.* a long shirt worn in bed. **night-soil** *n.* (*Hist.*) the contents of lavatories and cesspools removed at night. **nightspot** *n.* (*coll.*) a nightclub. **nightstick** *n.* (*N Am.*) a truncheon. **night-stool** *n.* a bedroom commode. **night terrors** *n.pl.* great fear felt esp. by children on waking suddenly during the night, not remembered next morning. **night-time** *n.* **nightward** (-wəd) *a.* **night-watch** *n.* a watch or guard on duty at night. **nightwatchman** *n.* (*pl.* **nightwatchmen**) **1** a person who keeps watch on a public building, factory etc. at night, a night security guard. **2** in cricket, a batsman sent in towards the close of a day's play, esp. in place of a higher order batsman. **nightwear** *n.* clothes worn in bed. **night-work** *n.* **nighty** *a.* (*pl.* **nighties**) (*coll.*) a nightdress. [OE *niht* (cp. Dut. *nacht* and G *Nacht*, Icel. *nātt*, *nōtt*, L *nox*, Gr. *nux*, Sansk. *nekta*)]

nightingale[1] (nīˊting·gāl) *n.* a small, brownish migratory bird, *Luscinia megarhynchos*, singing at night as well as by day. [OE *nihtegale* (NIGHT, *galan*, to sing)]

nightingale[2] (nīˊting·gāl) *n.* a jacket or wrap worn by invalids sitting up in bed. [Florence *Nightingale*, 1820–1910, British hospital reformer]

nightmare NIGHT.

nightshade (nītˊshād) *n.* **1** any of several plants of the genus *Solanum*, esp. the black nightshade or woody nightshade. **2** DEADLY NIGHTSHADE (under DEADLY).

nigrescent (nīgresˊənt) *a.* **1** blackish. **2** growing black. **nigrescence** *n.* [L *nigrere*, to grow black, from *niger*, black]

nigrify (nigˊrifī) *v.t.* (*3rd pers. sing. pres.* **nigrifies**, *pres.p.* **nigrifying**, *past*, *p.p.* **nigrified**) to blacken.

nigritude (nigˊritūd) *n.* blackness. [L *nigritudo* (as NIGRESCENT)]

nigrosine (nigˊrəsēn, -sin) *n.* a blue-black dyestuff obtained from aniline hydrochlorates.

nihil (nīˊhil) *n.* nothing. **nihilism** (nīˊilizm) *n.* **1** any theological, philosophical or political doctrine of a negative kind. **2** (*Philos.*) denial of all existence, or of the knowledge of all existence. **nihilist** *n.* **nihilistic** (-lisˊ-) *a.* **nihility** (nihilˊ-) *n.* (*pl.* **nihilities**) **1** the state of being nothing or of nothingness. **2** a mere nothing. **nihil obstat** (obˊstat) *n.* **1** in the Roman Catholic Church, a certificate stating that there is no objection to a publication. **2** an official authorization. [L, nothing]

-nik (nik) *comb.form* a person who practises something, e.g. *beatnik*, *kibbutznik*, *peacenik*. [from Rus. suffix, from Yiddish suffix, denoting an agent]

nikau (nēˊkow) *n.* the New Zealand palm, *Rhopalostylis sapida*. [Maori]

Nikkei index (nikˊā) *n.* an index of the relative prices of stocks and shares on the Tokyo Stock Exchange. [*Ni*hon *Kei*zai Shimbun, a Japanese financial newspaper which publishes the index]

nil (nil) *n.* nothing; zero.

nil desperandum (nil desperanˊdəm) *int.* do not despair. [L, no need to despair]

Nile (nīl) *n.* (*also* **Nile blue, Nile green**) a pale greenish-blue or pale green. ~*a.* (*also* **Nile-blue, Nile-green**) pale greenish-blue or pale green.

nilgai (nilˊgī), **nilghau** (nilˊgaw), **nylghau** *n.* (*pl.* **nilgais, nilghaus, nylghaus**) a large Indian antelope, *Boselaphus tragocamelus*. [Pers. and Hind. *nil*, blue, Hind. *gai*, Pers. *gaw*, cow]

Nilometer (nīlomˊitə) *n.* an instrument for measuring the rise of the River Nile during its floods.

Nilotic (nīlotˊik) *a.* **1** of or relating to the Nile etc. **2** of or relating to a group of Negroid peoples of E Africa or their languages.

nim (nim) *n.* an ancient game for two players in which a number of counters are used. [perh. OE *niman*, to take]

nimbi NIMBUS.

nimble (nimˊbəl) *a.* **1** light and quick in motion; agile, swift, dexterous. **2** alert, clever, brisk, lively, versatile. **nimble-fingered** *a.* **nimble-footed** *a.* **nimbleness** *n.* **nimbly** *adv.* [OE *numol* (root of *niman*, to take, -LE[1])]

nimbostratus (nimbōstrahˊtəs) *n.* (*pl.* **nimbostrati** (-tī)) a dense, grey, rain- or snow-bearing cloud. [mod. L, NIMBUS, STRATUS]

nimbus (nimˊbəs) *n.* (*pl.* **nimbi** (-bī), **nimbuses**) **1** a halo or glory surrounding the heads of divine or sacred personages in paintings etc. **2** a rain cloud, a dark mass of cloud, usu. with ragged edges, from which rain is falling or likely to fall. **nimbused** *a.* [L, cloud]

Nimby (nimˊbi) *a.* supporting the dumping of nuclear waste, the construction of ugly buildings etc., as long as one's own property is not affected. ~*n.* (*pl.* **Nimbies**) a person who takes this attitude. **nimbyism** *n.* [*n*ot *i*n *m*y *b*ack *y*ard]

niminy-piminy (niminipimˊini) *a.* affecting niceness or delicacy; mincing; affected. [imit. of affected pronun.]

Nimrod (nimˊrod) *n.* a great hunter. [the mighty hunter of Gen. x.8–9]

nincompoop (ningˊkəmpoop) *n.* an idiot, a fool. [etym. unknown]

nine (nīn) *n.* **1** the number or figure 9 or IX. **2** the age of 9. **3** a set of nine things; a team of nine players. **4** the ninth hour after midnight or midday. **5** a card, counter etc. with nine pips. **6** a size measuring nine. ~*a.* nine in number. **dressed (up) to the nines** (*coll.*) very smartly or glamorously dressed. **nine times out of ten** usually, generally. **nine to five** normal office working hours. **the Nine** the Muses. **nine days' wonder** *n.* an event, person or thing that is a novelty for the moment but is soon forgotten. **ninefold** *a.*, *adv.* **1** nine times as much or as many. **2** consisting of nine parts. **ninepin** *n.* **1** a skittle. **2** (*pl.*) a game with nine skittles set up to be bowled at. **to fall like ninepins** to go down like ninepins. **to go down like ninepins** to become ill or fail in large numbers. **nineteen** (-tēnˊ) *n.* **1** the number or figure 19 or XIX. **2** the age of 19. **3** a set of 19 things; a group of 19 people. ~*a.* **1** 19 in number. **2** aged 19. **to talk nineteen to the dozen** DOZEN. **nineteenth** (-th) *n.* any one of 19 equal parts. ~*n.*, *a.* **1** (the) last of nineteen (people, things etc.). **2** (the) next after the 18th. **nineteenth hole** *n.* (*sl.*) the clubhouse bar at a golf club. **nine-tenths** *n.* (*coll.*) nearly all (of). **ninetieth** (-tiəth) *n.* any one of 90 equal parts. ~*n.*, *a.* **1** (the) last of ninety (people, things etc.). **2** (the) next after the 89th. **ninety** *n.* (*pl.* **nineties**) **1** the number or figure 90 or XC. **2** the age of 90. **nineties** *n.pl.* **1** the period of time between one's 90th and 100th birthdays. **2** the range of temperature between 90 and 100 degrees. **3** the period of time between the 90th and final year of a century. **ninety-first, ninety-second etc.** *n.*, *a.* the ordinal numbers corresponding to ninety-one etc. **ninetyfold** *a.*, *adv.* **1** ninety times as much or as many. **2** made up of ninety parts. **ninety-one, ninety-two etc.** *n.* the cardinal numbers between 90 and 100. [OE *nigon* (cp. Dut. *negen*, G *neun*, Icel. *nīu*, L *novem*, Gr. *ennea*, Sansk. *navan*)]

ninja (ninˊjə) *n.* (*pl.* **ninjas**) a person who is skilled in ninjutsu. [Jap.]

ninjutsu (ninjŭtˊsoo) *n.* a Japanese martial art involving stealth and camouflage. [Jap., *nin*, stealth, *jutsu*, art, science]

ninny (ninˊi) *n.* (*pl.* **ninnies**) (*coll.*) a fool, a simpleton. [perh. imit., cp. Sp. *niño*, It. *ninno*, child]

ninon (nēˊnon) *n.* a lightweight silk material. [F]

ninth (nīnth) *n.* **1** any one of nine equal parts. **2** (*Mus.*) **a** a diatonic interval of an octave and a second. **b** two notes separated by this interval sounded together. ~*n.*, *a.* **1** (the) last of nine (people, things etc.). **2** (the) next after the eighth. **ninthly** *adv.* [NINE, -TH[1]]

niobium (nīōˊbiəm) *n.* a grey-blue metallic element, at. no. 41, chem. symbol Nb, occurring in tantalite etc.

niobic *a.* **niobite** (nī´əbīt) *n.* columbite. **niobous** *a.* [*Niobe*, daughter of Tantalus, -IUM]

Nip (nip) *n.* (*sl., offensive*) a Japanese person. [abbr. of NIPPONESE]

nip[1] (nip) *v.t.* (*pres.p.* **nipping,** *past, p.p.* **nipped**) **1** to pinch, to squeeze or compress sharply. **2** to cut or pinch off the end or point of. **3** to bite. **4** to sting, to pain. **5** (of cold or frost) to check the growth of. **6** (*N Am., sl.*) to steal. ~*v.i.* **1** (*coll.*) to move, go, or step quickly (in, out, etc.). **2** to cause pain. ~*n.* **1** a pinch, a sharp squeeze or compression. **2** a bite. **3** bitter cold. **4** a check to vegetation, esp. by frost. **to nip in the bud** BUD[1]. **nip and tuck** *n.* (*coll.*) a surgical operation performed for cosmetic reasons. ~*adv.* (*N Am.*) neck and neck. **nipcheese** *n.* (*Naut., sl.*) a purser. **nipper** *n.* **1** a person who or something which nips. **2** a horse's incisor. **3** the claw of a crab or other crustacean. **4** (*sl.*) a boy, a lad. **5** (*pl.*) a pair of pincers, forceps or pliers. **6** (*Austral.*) a prawn of the order Thalassinidea, used as fishing bait. **7** a device for seizing and holding. **8** a fish of various kinds. **9** a pince-nez. **nipping** *a.* **nippingly** *adv.* **nippy** *a.* (*comp.* **nippier,** *superl.* **nippiest**) (*coll.*) **1** cold. **2** active; agile. **3** quick, alert. **nippily** *adv.* [cp. Dut. *nўpen*, G *kneifen*]

nip[2] (nip) *n.* a small drink of spirits. ~*v.i.* (*pres.p.* **nipping,** *past, p.p.* **nipped**) to take a nip or nips. ~*v.t.* to take a nip of. [etym. uncertain]

nipa (nē´pə, nī´-) *n.* **1** a palm tree of tropical SE Asia and the islands of the Indian Ocean, *Nipa fruticans*, with feathery leaves used in thatching, basket-weaving etc., and for packing bunches of fruit. **2** an alcoholic drink made from the sap of the nipa. [Sp. and Port., from Malay *nīpah*]

nipper NIP[1].

nipple (nip´əl) *n.* **1** the small prominence in the breast of female mammals, by which milk is sucked or drawn. **2** a similar structure in male mammals. **3** a similar contrivance attached to a baby's feeding bottle. **4** a nipple-shaped perforated projection, as on a gun-breach for holding a percussion-cap. **5** a nipple-shaped prominence on the surface of metal or glass. **6** (*N Am.*) a section of pipe with a screw-thread at each end. **nipple-shield** *n.* a protection worn over the nipple by nursing mothers. **nipplewort** *n.* a slender weed, *Lapsana communis*, with small yellow flowers. [a dim. of NEB or NIB]

Nipponese (nipənēz´) *n.* (*pl.* **Nipponese**) a Japanese person. ~*a.* Japanese. [*Nippon*, Jap. name for Japan]

nippy NIP[1].

NIREX (nī´reks) *abbr.* Nuclear Industry Radioactive Waste Executive, a government body which oversees the disposal of nuclear waste in the UK.

nirvana (niəvah´nə) *n.* **1** absorption of individuality into the divine spirit with extinction of personal desires and passions, the Buddhist state of beatitude. **2** (*coll.*) bliss, heaven. [Sansk., from *nirvā*, to blow]

†**nis** (nis) *v.i.* is not. [ne, IS]

nisei (nē´sā, -sā´), **Nisei** *n.* a person of Japanese descent born in the US. [Jap.]

nisi (nī´sī) *a.* (*Law*) taking effect on certain conditions. **decree nisi** DECREE. **nisi prius** (prī´əs) *n.* (*Hist.*) **1** a writ commanding a sheriff to empanel a jury. **2** an authority to judges of assize to try causes. **3** trial of civil causes before judges of assize. [L, unless]

Nissen hut (nis´ən) *n.* a long hut of corrugated iron with a semicircular roof. [Col. P. N. *Nissen*, 1871–1930, British engineer]

nisus (nī´səs) *n.* (*pl.* **nisus**) (*formal*) an effort, striving. [L, from *nītī*, to endeavour]

nit[1] (nit) *n.* the egg of a louse or other small, esp. parasitic, insect. **nit-picking** *n.* (*coll.*) petty criticism of minor details. ~*a.* criticizing minor details. **nit-pick** *v.i.* **nit-picker** *n.* **nitty** *a.* (*comp.* **nittier,** *superl.* **nittiest**). [OE *hnitu* (cp. Dut. *neet*, G *Niss*, Icel. *nitr*)]

nit[2] (nit) *int.* (*Austral., sl.*) used to express warning of someone's approach. **to keep nit** to keep a lookout. [etym. unknown; cp. NIX[2]]

nit[3] (nit) *n.* (*coll.*) a fool. [perh. from NITWIT]

nit[4] (nit) *n.* the unit of luminance, one candela per square metre. [L *nitor*, brightness]

nit[5] (nit) *n.* a unit of information in computing (1.44 bits). [*N*apierian dig*it*]

niter NITRE.

nitid (nit´id) *a.* (*poet.*) shining; bright, gay. [L *nitidus*, from *nitēre*, to shine]

nitinol (nit´inol) *n.* an alloy of nickel and titanium. [*ni*ckel, *ti*tanium, *N*aval *O*rdnance *L*aboratory]

niton (nī´ton) *n.* radon. [L *nitere*, to shine]

nitrate[1] (nī´trāt) *n.* **1** a salt of nitric acid. **2** sodium or potassium nitrate.

nitrate[2] (nītrāt´) *v.t.* to treat or combine with nitric acid. **nitration** (-ā´shən) *n.*

nitre (nī´tə), (*N Am.*) **niter** *n.* saltpetre, potassium nitrate, occurring as an orthorhombic mineral. **nitriferous** (-trif´-) *a.* **nitrify** (-fī) *v.t.* (*3rd pers. sing. pres.* **nitrifies,** *pres.p.* **nitrifying,** *past, p.p.* **nitrified**) **1** to turn into nitre. **2** to make nitrous. ~*v.i.* to become nitrous. **nitrifiable** *a.* **nitrification** (-ā´shən) *n.* **nitrite** (-trīt) *n.* any salt or ester of nitrous acid. [F, from L *nitrum*, Gr. *nitron*, perh. of Oriental orig. (cp. Heb. *nether*)]

nitric (nī´trik) *a.* of or relating to nitre. **nitric acid** *n.* a colourless, corrosive acid liquid based on the ingredients of nitre. **nitric oxide** *n.* a colourless gas, nitrogen monoxide, involved in physiological processes in minute quantities.

nitride (nī´trīd) *n.* a compound of nitrogen with phosphorus, boron, silicon etc.

nitriferous, nitrify NITRE.

nitrile (nī´trīl) *n.* any organic compound consisting of an alkyl radical bound to a cyanide radical.

nitrite NITRE.

nitro- (nī´trō) *comb. form* nitric.

nitrobenzene (nītrōben´zēn) *n.* an oily compound of benzene with nitric acid, having an odour of oil of bitter almonds, used for flavouring perfumes and confectionery.

nitrocellulose (nītrōsel´ūlōz, -lōs) *n.* an extremely flammable material made by treating cellulose with nitric acid, used to make explosives and celluloid.

nitro compound (nī´trō kompownd) *n.* a compound obtained by treatment with nitric acid.

nitrogen (nī´trəjən) *n.* a colourless, tasteless, gaseous element, at. no. 7, chem. symbol N, forming 80% of the atmosphere, the basis of nitre and nitric acid. **nitrogen cycle** *n.* the cycle of processes by which nitrogen is absorbed from the atmosphere and returned to it by biological systems. **nitrogen dioxide** *n.* a reddish-brown poisonous gas. **nitrogen fixation** *n.* a chemical process in which nitrogen in the atmosphere is converted into organic compounds, used for the manufacture of fertilizers. **nitrogenize** (-troj´-), **nitrogenise** *v.t.* **nitrogenous** (-troj´-), **nitrogenic** (-trōjen´-) *a.* [F *nitrogène*]

nitroglycerine (nītrōglis´ərēn, -rin), **nitroglycerin** *n.* a highly explosive colourless oil, obtained by adding glycerine to a mixture of nitric and sulphuric acids.

nitrometer (nītrom´itə) *n.* an instrument for determining nitrogen in some of its combinations.

nitrosamine (nitrō´səmēn) *n.* any carcinogenic substance containing the chemical group: N-N:O.

nitrous (nī´trəs) *a.* obtained from, impregnated with, or resembling nitre. **nitrous acid** *n.* a weak acid which exists only in solution and in the gaseous state. **nitrous oxide** *n.* dinitrogen oxide used as an anaesthetic, laughing gas.

nitroxyl (nītrok´sil) *n.* a radical composed of one atom of nitrogen in chemical combination with two of oxygen.

nitter, nitty NIT[1].

nitty-gritty (nitigrit´i) *n.* the basic facts, the realities of a situation. [etym. uncertain]

nitwit (nit´wit) *n.* (*coll.*) a foolish or stupid person. **nit-witted** *a.* stupid. **nitwittedness** *n.* **nitwittery** (-wit´əri) *n.*

NIV *abbr.* New International Version (of the Bible).

nival (nī´vəl) *a.* **1** growing in or under snow. **2** niveous. **nivation** (-ā´shən) *n.* erosion due to the action of snow. **niveous** (niv´iəs) *a.* resembling snow; snowy. [L *nivālis*, from *nivem*, nom. *nix*, snow]

nix[1] (niks) *n.* (*sl.*) **1** nothing, nobody. **2** a rejection, a denial. ~*v.t.* (*sl.*) **1** to cancel. **2** to reject. [G, colloq. for *nichts*]

nix[2] (niks), **nixie** *n.* a water sprite. [G *Nix*, fem. *Nixe* (cogn. with OE *nicor*, Icel. *nykr*, prob. rel. to Gr. *nizein*, *niptein*, to wash)]

nix[3] (niks) *int.* look out! **to keep nix** to keep watch. [etym. uncertain; perh. from NIX[1]]

nizam (nīzam´) *n.* (*pl.* **nizam**) **1** a soldier in the Turkish regular army. **2** (**Nizam**) the title of the ruler of Hyderabad. [Hind. from Arab. *nidhām*, order, government]

NJ *abbr.* New Jersey.

NM *abbr.* New Mexico.

nm *abbr.* **1** nanometre(s). **2** nautical mile(s).

N.Mex. *abbr.* New Mexico.

NMR, nmr *abbr.* nuclear magnetic resonance.

NNE *abbr.* north-north-east.

NNW *abbr.* north-north-west.

No[1] *chem. symbol* nobelium.

No[2] NOH.

No. *abbr.* **1** (*N Am.*) North. **2** (*also* **no.**) number.

no[1] (nō) *a.* **1** not any. **2** not one, not a. **3** quite other than, quite the opposite or reverse of. **4** hardly any. **5** expressing opposition, objection, or rejection (as *no popery*). **by no means** MEANS. **no comment** COMMENT. **no cop** COP[1]. **no dice** DICE. **no end** END. **no fear** FEAR. **no fool** FOOL[1]. **no holds barred** HOLD[2]. **no little** LITTLE. **no man** no one, no person, nobody. **no small** SMALL. **no sweat** SWEAT. **no time** TIME. **no way** (*coll.*) definitely not, under no circumstances. **no wonder** WONDER. **...or no...** in spite of, regardless of (*Husband or no husband, you must turn him in*). **there is no ...ing** it is impossible to... (*There is no getting out of this visit*). **to have no joy** JOY. **no-account** *a.* good-for-nothing, worthless. **no-ball** *n.* in cricket, a ball not delivered according to the rules, counting for one to the other side. ~*v.t.* to declare (a bowler) to have bowled this. **no-claims bonus, no-claim bonus** *n.* a reduction in the price of an insurance policy because no claims have been made on it. **no-claims discount, no-claim discount** *n.* no-claims bonus. **no-fault compensation** *n.* a system of compensation for accidental injury which does not depend on proving someone guilty of misconduct, negligence etc. **no-fly zone** *n.* a zone in which aircraft are not permitted to fly. **no-frills** *a.* basic, having no unnecessary extra features. **no go** *n.* a complete failure. **no-go** *a.* **1** of no use. **2** not to be done. **no-go area** *n.* an area which unauthorized people are not permitted to enter. **no good** *n.* mischief, trouble (*up to no good*). ~*a.* useless, vain, pointless. **no-good** *a.* (*coll.*) worthless. ~*n.* (*coll.*) a bad or worthless person or thing. **no-hitter** *n.* in baseball, a match in which a team concedes no hits. **no-hoper** *n.* (*sl.*) an ineffectual or worthless person. **nohow** *adv.* **1** (*N Am.*) in no way, not by any means. **2** (*dial.*) out of order. **no joke** *n.* (*coll.*) a serious matter. **no man's land** *n.* **1** (*Mil.*) the contested land between two opposing forces. **2** waste or unclaimed land. **no-nonsense** *n.* efficient and sensible. **no object** *n.* **1** no obstacle. **2** no deterrent. **no one** *pron.* nobody, no person. †**no other** *pron.* nothing else. **no place** *adv.*, *pron.* nowhere. **no-score draw** *n.* in football, a draw in which no goals are scored. **no-see-em** (nōsē´əm), **no-see-um** *n.* (*N Am.*) a small, bloodsucking insect. **no-show** *n.* a person who does not take up something reserved and does not cancel in advance. **no side** *n.* in rugby, the end of a game, as announced by the referee. **no thoroughfare** *n.* a notice that a road is closed or has no exit or through way. **no through road** *n.* no thoroughfare. **no trump** *n.* no-trumps. **no-trumper** *n.* a hand on which a no-trump bid can be made. **no trumps** *n.* in bridge, a call for the playing of a hand without any trump suit. **no-vote** *n.* a vote against a motion. **noway,** (*N Am.*, *dial.*) **noways** *adv.* nowise. **no whit** WHIT. **no-win situation** *n.* a situation in which it is impossible to succeed. **nowise** *adv.* in no way, not at all. [NONE[1]]

no[2] (nō) *adv.* **1** a word of denial or refusal, the categorical negative. **2** not. **3** (*with comp.*) not at all, by no amount. ~*n.* (*pl.* **noes**) **1** the word 'no'. **2** a negative reply, a denial, a refusal. **3** (*pl.*) voters against a motion. **no better than one should be** having dubious morals. **no can do** (*coll.*) I cannot do that. **no less 1** as much. **2** as important or special. **3** no fewer. **no longer** LONG[1]. **no, no** (*emphat.*) no. **no sooner...than** SOON. **not to take no for an answer** not to be deterred by refusal or rejection. **the noes have it** the voters against the motion are in the majority. **no more** *n.* nothing more. ~*a.* not any more. ~*adv.* **1** not any more. **2** nothing further. **3** no longer. **4** dead, gone. **5** never again. **6** just as little. **no-no** *n.* (*pl.* **no-nos**) (*coll.*) something which is forbidden or unacceptable. [OE *nā* (*ne*, ever)]

n.o. *abbr.* in cricket, not out.

no. No.

Noachian (nōā´kiən), **Noachic** (nōak´ik) *a.* of or relating to Noah or his times. [*Noah*, Hebrew patriarch (Genesis vi–ix)]

Noah's ark (Nō´əz) *n.* **1** the vessel in which Noah and his family were saved from the Deluge. **2** a toy model of this with toy animals. **3** a very large, old or cumbersome conveyance or container. **4** a small bivalve mollusc, *Arca noae*, that has a boat-shaped shell.

nob[1] (nob) *n.* (*sl.*) a person of rank or distinction. **nobby** *a.* (*comp.* **nobbier**, *superl.* **nobbiest**) smart, elegant. [etym. uncertain]

nob[2] (nob) *n.* **1** (*sl.*) the head. **2** in cribbage, a point scored for holding the knave of the same suit as the turn-up. [prob. var. of KNOB]

nobble (nob´əl) *v.t.* (*sl.*) **1** to dose, lame or otherwise tamper with (a horse) to prevent its winning a race. **2** to persuade or win over by dishonest means, to influence (a member of a jury etc.) esp. by bribery or threats. **3** to catch, to nab. **4** to steal. **nobbler** *n.* [perh. *nab*]

nobby NOB[1].

Nobelist (nōbel´ist) *n.* (*N Am.*) a Nobel prizewinner.

nobelium (nōbē´liəm) *n.* an artificially produced, radioactive element, at. no. 102, chem. symbol No. [*Nobel* Institute, Stockholm]

Nobel Prize (nōbel´) *n.* any of six prizes awarded annually by the will of Alfred Nobel for excellence in various branches of learning and the furtherance of universal peace. **Nobel prizewinner** *n.* [Alfred *Nobel*, 1833–96, Swedish chemist]

nobility (nōbil´iti) *n.* (*pl.* **nobilities**) **1** the quality of being noble. **2** magnanimity, greatness, dignity. **3** nobleness of birth or family. **4** nobles, the peerage. **nobiliary** (nōbil´yəri) *a.* **nobiliary particle** *n.* a preposition, such as *de* or *von*, which forms part of a title of nobility. [F *nobilité*, L *nōbilitātem*, nom. *-tas*, as NOBLE]

noble (nō´bəl) *a.* (*comp.* **nobler**, *superl.* **noblest**) **1** lofty or illustrious in character, worth or dignity; magnanimous, high-minded, morally elevated. **2** of high rank, of ancient or illustrious lineage; belonging to the nobility.

3 magnificent, grand, stately, splendid, imposing. 4 excellent, fine, admirable. 5 (*Chem.*) (of a metal) valuable, pure. ~*n.* 1 a nobleman or noblewoman, a peer. 2 an obsolete gold coin. **my noble friend** FRIEND. **noble art of self-defence** *n.* boxing. **noble gas** *n.* any member of a group of gaseous elements which do not combine with other elements. **nobleman** *n.* (*pl.* **noblemen**) a peer. **noble metal** *n.* a metal such as gold, silver or platinum, which is not affected by air or water, and not easily attacked by acids. **noble-minded** *a.* **noble-mindedness** *n.* **nobleness** *n.* **noble rot** *n.* a type of fungi which causes over-ripe grapes to rot, producing the characteristic richness of wines such as Sauterne and Tornay. **noble savage** *n.* in Romantic literature, an idealized view of primitive man. **noble science** *n.* boxing. **noblewoman** *n.* (*pl.* **noblewomen**) a peeress. **nobly** *adv.* [F, from L *nōbilis*, from base of *noscere*, to KNOW]

noblesse (nōbles´) *n.* the nobility (of a foreign country). **noblesse oblige** (əblēzh´) *n.* the idea that privileged people are obliged to behave honourably and to help less privileged people. [ME, nobility, from OF, as NOBLE]

nobody (nō´bədi) *pron.* no one, no person. ~*n.* (*pl.* **nobodies**) a person of no importance. **like nobody's business** (*coll.*) very energetically or intensively. **nobody's fool** *n.* a sensible or wise person.

nock (nok) *n.* 1 the notched tip at each end of a bow. 2 a notched tip of horn etc. at the butt-end of an arrow. 3 the notch in this. 4 the upper fore corner of a sail. ~*v.t.* to fit (an arrow) to the bowstring. [ME *nokke*, prob. from Dut. or LG *nokk*]

noct- NOCTI-.

noctambulism (noktam´būlizm) *n.* somnambulism. **noctambulation** (ā´shən) *n.* **noctambulist** *n.* [L *ambulare*, to walk]

nocti- (nok´ti), **noct-** *comb. form* nocturnal, by night. [L *nox*, *noctis*, night]

noctiluca (noktiloo´kə) *n.* (*pl.* **noctilucae** (-sē)) a phosphorescent marine animalcule.

noctilucent (noktiloo´sənt) *a.* shining by night.

noctivagant (noktiv´əgənt) *a.* wandering by night. **noctivagation** (-ā´shən) *n.* **noctivagous** *a.*

noctuid (nok´tūid) *n.* any nocturnal moth of the family Noctuidae. ~*a.* of or relating to the Noctuidae. [L, night owl]

noctule (nok´tūl) *n.* a large European bat, *Nyctalus noctula.*

nocturn (nok´tœn) *n.* in the Roman Catholic Church, one of the divisions of matins, usually said at night.

nocturnal (noktœ´nəl) *a.* relating to or occurring in the night, performed, or active by night. **nocturnal emission** *n.* an involuntary emission of semen while asleep. **nocturnally** *adv.*

nocturne (nok´tœn) *n.* 1 a dreamy piece of music suited to the night or evening. 2 a painting or drawing of a night scene.

nocuous (nok´ūəs) *a.* (*formal*) hurtful, noxious. **nocuously** *adv.* [L *nocuus*, from *nocēre*, to injure]

nod (nod) *v.i.* (*pres.p.* **nodding**, *past, p.p.* **nodded**) 1 to incline the head with a slight, quick motion in token of assent, command, indication, or salutation. 2 to let the head fall forward; to be drowsy, to sleep. 3 (of a flower) to bend over and sway. 4 to make a careless mistake. 5 (of a building) to incline, to totter. ~*v.t.* 1 to bend or incline (the head). 2 to signify by a nod. ~*n.* 1 a quick bend of the head. 2 a bending downwards. **land of Nod** LAND. **on the nod** 1 (*coll.*) without question or argument. 2 (*coll.*) on credit. **to get the nod** (*N Am.*) to be given approval or permission. **to nod off** (*coll.*) to fall asleep. **to nod through** 1 to pass (a motion etc.) without formal discussion, voting etc. 2 in Parliament, to allow to vote by proxy. **nodder** *n.* **nodding** *n., a.* **nodding acquaintance** *n.* a slight acquaintance. [ME *nidde*, not known in OE]

nodal NODE.

noddle[1] (nod´əl) *n.* (*coll.*) the head. [etym. uncertain]

noddle[2] (nod´əl) *v.t.* to nod, to wag.

noddy (nod´i) *n.* (*pl.* **noddies**) 1 a simpleton, a fool. 2 any tropical seabird of the genus *Anous stolida* or *Procelsterna.* [prob. rel. to NOD]

node (nōd) *n.* 1 a knot, a knob. 2 (*Bot.*) the point of a stem from which leaves arise. 3 (*Anat.*) **a** a thickening or swelling e.g. of a joint of the body. **b** an interruption of the myelin sheath of a nerve. 4 the point at which the orbit of a planet intersects the ecliptic, or in which two great circles of the celestial sphere intersect. 5 (*Math.*) **a** the point at which a curve crosses itself and at which more than one tangent can be drawn or a similar point on a surface. **b** a vertex in a graph. 6 (*Physics*) a point of rest in a vibrating body. 7 (*Comput.*) a network component. 8 the plot of a story, play or poem. **nodal** *a.* **nodical** *a.* **nodose** (-dōs) *a.* knotty; having nodes. **nodosity** (-dos´-) *n.* **nodule** (nod´ūl) *n.* 1 a small knot, node or lump; a rounded lump or mass of irregularly rounded shape. 2 a small tumour. **nodular, nodulated, noduled, nodulose** (-lōs), **nodulous** *a.* **nodulation** (-ā´shən) *n.* **nodus** (nō´dəs) *n.* (*pl.* **nodi** (-dī)) 1 a knotty point, a complication, a difficulty. 2 a node. [L *nodus*, a knot]

Noel (nōel´), **Noël, †Nowel, †Nowell** *n.* Christmas. [F, from L]

noetic (nōet´ik), **noetical** *a.* 1 of or relating to the intellect. 2 performed by or originating in the intellect. 3 habitually indulging in intellectual speculation. ~*n.* (*often pl.*) the science of the intellect. **noesis** (nōē´sis) *n.* 1 pure thought. 2 an intellectual view of the world. [Gr. *noētikos*, mental perception, from *noein*, to perceive (*noos*, mind, thought)]

nog[1] (nog) *n.* 1 a pin, treenail or peg. 2 a wooden block shaped like a brick, built into a wall to take nails. 3 a snag or stump. 4 nogging. ~*v.t.* (*pres.p.* **nogging**, *past, p.p.* **nogged**) 1 to fix or secure with a nog or nogs. 2 to build with nogging. [etym. uncertain]

†nog[2] (nog) *n.* 1 a strong ale brewed in East Anglia. 2 an egg-nog. [etym. uncertain]

noggin (nog´in) *n.* 1 a small mug. 2 a measure of spirits, usu. a gill (125 ml). 3 the contents of such a measure. 4 (*coll.*) the head. [etym. uncertain]

nogging (nog´ing) *n.* a timber frame filled with bricks. [NOG[1], -ING[1]]

Noh (nō), **No** *n.* the Japanese drama developed out of religious dance. [Jap.]

nohow NO[1].

noil (noil) *n.* (*often pl.*) tangles and knots of wool removed by a comb. [etym. uncertain]

noise (noiz) *n.* 1 a sound of any kind, esp. a loud, discordant, harsh or disagreeable one. 2 clamour, din, loud or continuous talk. 3 any unwanted electrical disturbance in a circuit. 4 (*pl.*) vague remarks of an appropriate kind (*She made encouraging noises*). ~*v.t.* to make public, to spread about. ~†*v.i.* to make a noise. **to make a noise** to become well known or notorious. **to make a noise about** to complain about. **noiseless** *a.* **noiselessly** *adv.* **noiselessness** *n.* **noisemaker** *n.* something used to make a loud noise at a celebration. **noises off** *n.pl.* offstage sounds intended to be heard by the audience of a play. **noisy** *a.* (*comp.* **noisier**, *superl.* **noisiest**) 1 causing noise. 2 making a lot of noise. 3 full of loud noise. 4 (of a colour, dress, style etc.) glaring, violent, loud. **noisily** *adv.* **noisiness** *n.* [F, quarrel]

noisette[1] (nwazet´) *n.* 1 a small round piece of mutton, veal, etc. 2 a chocolate made with chopped hazelnuts. [F, hazelnut, dim. of *noix*]

noisette[2] (nwazet´) *n.* a variety of rose, a cross between the China rose and the musk-rose. [Philippe *Noisette*, US horticulturalist]

noisome (noi´səm) *a.* (*formal*) **1** hurtful, noxious. **2** (esp. of a smell) unwholesome, offensive, disgusting. **noisomely** *adv.* **noisomeness** *n.* [ME *noy*, ANNOY, -SOME[1]]

noisy NOISE.

nolens volens (nōlenz vō´lenz) *adv.* willingly or unwillingly, willy-nilly. [*nōlens*, pres.p. of *nolle*, to be unwilling, *volens*, pres.p. of *velle*, to be willing]

noli-me-tangere (nō´limātang´gəri) *n.* **1** the touch-me-not. **2** an ulcerous disease of the skin, lupus. [L, touch me not]

noll (nōl) *n.* the head. [OE *hnol* (cp. OHG *hnol*, top)]

nolle prosequi (noli pros´ikwī) *n.* (*Law*) **1** the act by a plaintiff discontinuing a suit. **2** the recording of a nolle prosequi. [L, to refuse to pursue]

nolo contendere (nō´lō konten´dəri) *n.* I will not contest it, a plea which accepts conviction without pleading guilt. [L]

nom. *abbr.* **1** nominal. **2** nominative.

noma (nō´mə) *n.* (*pl.* **nomas**) a destructive ulceration of the cheek, esp. affecting debilitated children. [L *nomē*, ulcer, Gr. *nemein*, to consume]

nomad (nō´mad) *n.* **1** a member of a people that wanders about seeking pasture for their flocks. **2** a wanderer. ~*a.* **1** being a nomad. **2** wandering. **nomadic** (-mad´-) *a.* **nomadically** *adv.* **nomadism** *n.* **nomadize, nomadise** *v.i.* [L and Gr. *nomad-*, nom. *nomas*, from *nemein*, to allot, to pasture]

nomarch (nom´ahk) *n.* a ruler or governor of an Egyptian nome or Greek nomarchy. **nomarchy** *n.* (*pl.* **nomarchies**) a province of modern Greece. [Gr. *nomarchēs* or *nomarchos* (*nomos*, NOME, *archein*, to govern)]

nombril (nom´bril) *n.* (*Her.*) the point of an escutcheon between the fess point and the base point. [F, the navel]

nom de guerre (nom də geə´) *n.* (*pl.* **noms de guerre** (nom)) an assumed name, a pseudonym. [F, war name]

nom de plume (nom də ploom´) *n.* (*pl.* **noms de plume** (nom)) a pen-name.

nome (nōm) *n.* a province of a country, esp. modern Greece or Egypt. [Gr. *nomos*, from *nemein*, to divide]

nomen (nō´men) *n.* in ancient Rome, a person's second name, designating the gens.

nomenclator (nō´mənklātə) *n.* a person who gives names to things, esp. in classification of natural history etc. **nomenclative** (-men´klə-) *a.* [L (*nōmen*, name, *calāre*, to call)]

nomenclature (nōmeng´kləchə) *n.* **1** a system of names for the objects of study in any branch of science. **2** a system of terminology. **3** a vocabulary, a glossary. **4** a catalogue, a register. **nomenclatural** (-klach´-) *a.* [L *nomenclatura*, list of names, see NOMENCLATOR]

nomic (nom´ik) *a.* (of spelling) ordinary, customary. [Gr. *nomikos*, from *nomos*, law]

nominal (nom´inəl) *a.* **1** existing in name only, as distinct from *real*. **2** trivial, inconsiderable. **3** of, relating to or consisting of a name or names. **4** containing names. **5** of or relating to a noun. **nominal definition** *n.* a statement of all the connotations of the name of a concept. **nominalism** *n.* (*Philos.*) the doctrine that general or abstract concepts have no existence but as names or words, as distinct from *realism*. **nominalist** *n.* **nominalistic** (-lis´tik) *a.* **nominalize, nominalise** *v.t.* to form a noun from (a verb, adjective etc.). **nominalization** (-ā´shən) *n.* **nominally** *adv.* in name only. **nominal value** *n.* the face value of coins, shares etc. [L *nōminālis*, from *nōmen -inis*, name]

nominate (nom´ināt) *v.t.* **1** to propose as a candidate. **2** to appoint to an office or duty. **3** to name, to designate. **4** to mention by name. **5** to call, to denominate. **nominately** *adv.* **nomination** (-ā´shən) *n.* **nominator** *n.* **nominee** (-nē´) *n.* **1** a person named or appointed by name. **2** a person in whose name a stock is registered. [L *nōminātus*, p.p. of *nōmināre*, as NOMINAL]

nominative[1] (nom´inətiv) *n.* (*Gram.*) **1** the case of the subject of a verb. **2** a word in this case. ~*a.* of or relating to this case. **nominatival** (-tī´-) *a.*

nominative[2] (nom´inātiv) *a.* appointed by nomination, rather than by election.

nominator, nominee NOMINATE.

nomistic (nəmis´tik) *a.* of or based on law.

nomo- (nom´ō) *comb. form* of or relating to law. [Gr. *nomos*, law]

nomocracy (nomok´rəsi) *n.* (*pl.* **nomocracies**) a system of government according to a code of laws.

nomogeny (nomoj´əni) *n.* origination of life according to natural law, rather than by miracle.

nomogram (nom´əgram), **nomograph** (-grahf) *n.* a chart with scales of quantities arranged side by side, which can be used to carry out rapid calculations. **nomographer** (-mog´) *n.* **nomographic** (-graf´-) *a.* **nomographically** *adv.* **nomography** (-mog´-) *n.*

nomology (nōmol´əji) *n.* the science of law. **nomologist** *n.*

nomothetical (noməthet´ikəl), **nomothetic** *a.* legislative. [Gr. *nomothetikos*, from *nomothetēs*, a lawgiver (*tithenai*, to put or set)]

noms de guerre NOM DE GUERRE.

noms de plume NOM DE PLUME.

-nomy (nəmi) *comb. form* an area of knowledge (*astronomy*).

non- (non) *pref.* not. [L]

non- (+ a– words) non-ability *n.* lack of ability. **non-abstainer** *n.* a person who is not a total abstainer from alcoholic drink. **non-academic** *a.* **non-acceptance** *n.* **non-access** *n.* a lack of access. **non-addictive** *a.* not causing addiction. **non-aggression** *n.* restraint from aggression. **non-aggression pact** *n.* an agreement between two states to settle differences by negotiation rather than by force. **non-agricultural** *a.* **non-alcoholic** *a.* not containing alcohol. **non-aligned** *a.* not taking any side in international politics, esp. (formerly) not belonging to the Warsaw Pact or NATO. **non-alignment** *n.* **non-allergic** *a.* not causing or suffering from allergy. **non-ambiguous** *a.* **non-appearance** *n.* default of appearance, esp. in court. **non-art** *n.* something which does not conform to the accepted forms of art. **non-Aryan** *a.* not Aryan or of Aryan descent. ~*n.* a non-Aryan person. **non-attached** *a.* not being attached. **non-attendance** *n.* **non-attributable** *a.* not able to be attributed to any particular source. **non-attributably** *adv.* **non-authoritative** *a.* **non-automated** *a.* **non-automatic** *a.* **non-availability** *n.* the state of not being available.

nona- (non´ə, nō´nə) *comb. form* nine. [L, from *nonus*, ninth]

nonage (nō´nij) *n.* **1** (*Hist.*) the state of being under age; minority. **2** a period of immaturity. [OF (NON-, AGE)]

nonagenarian (nonəjineə´riən) *n.* a person aged between 90 and 100. ~*a.* a person aged between 90 and 100. [L *nōnāgēnārius*, from *nōnāgēnī*, ninety each]

nonagesimal (nōnəjes´iməl) *a.* **1** of or relating to 90. **2** (*Astron.*) of or relating to a nonagesimal. ~*n.* (*Astron.*) the point of the ecliptic highest above the horizon. [L *nōnāgēsimus*, from *nōnāginta*, ninety]

nonagon (non´əgon) *n.* a figure having nine sides and nine angles. [from L *nōnus*, ninth, after DECAGON, etc.]

nonary (nō´nəri) *a.* (*Math.*) (of a scale of notation) based on the number nine. ~*n.* (*pl.* **nonaries**) a group of nine. [L *nōnārius*, from *nōnus*, ninth]

non- (+ b– words) non-basic *a.* **non-believer** *n.* a person who does not believe, esp. in God. **non-belligerent** *a.* not involved in hostilities. ~*n.* **1** a neutral. **2** a country that remains neutral in name only, supporting a belligerent country with everything except armed force. **non-belligerency** *n.* **non-biological** *a.* 1 not relating to biology. 2 (of washing powder etc.) containing no enzymes. **non-black** *a.* 1 not belonging to a dark-skinned race. 2 of or relating to non-blacks. ~*n.* a non-black person. **non-breakable** *a.*

non- (+ c– words) non-capital *a.* not punishable by death. **non-carbonated** *a.* **non-carnivorous** *a.* **non-Catholic** *a.* not Roman Catholic. ~*n.* a non-Catholic person. **non-Caucasian** *a., n.* **non-causal** *a.* **non-celestial** *a.* not celestial. **non-cellular** *a.* **non-central** *a.* **non-cerebral** *a.* **non-chargeable** *a.* not chargeable. **non-Christian** *a., n.* **non-citizen** *n.* a person who is not a citizen of a particular town etc. **non-claim** *n.* failure to make a claim within the legal time. **non-classic, non-classical** *a.* **non-classified** *a.* (of information) not classified. **non-clerical** *a.* not involving clerical work. **non-coagulating** *a.* **non-collegiate** *a.* 1 (of a student) not belonging to a college. 2 (of a university) not having colleges. **non-com** (non´kom) *n.* (*sl.*) a non-commissioned officer. **non-combatant** *n.* a civilian, esp. a surgeon, chaplain etc. attached to troops. **non-combining** *a.* **non-commercial** *a.* **non-commissioned** *a.* (of a military officer) not holding a commission. **non-committal** *a.* not committing oneself, impartial. ~*n.* 1 refusal to commit or pledge oneself. 2 the state of not being committed to either side. **non-committally** *adv.* **non-communicant** *n.* a person who does not attend Holy Communion. **non-communicating** *a.* **non-communicative** *a.* **non-communist, non-Communist** *a.* not practising communism. ~*n.* a non-communist person. **non-competitive** *a.* **non-compliance** *n.* (*Law*) failure to comply. **non-conciliatory** *a.* **non-conclusive** *a.* **non-concurrence** *n.* **non-concurrent** *a.* **non-conducting** *a.* not conducting heat or electricity. **non-conductive** *a.* **non-conductor** *n.* a substance or medium that offers resistance to heat or electricity. **non-confidential** *a.* **non-conflicting** *a.* **nonconformist** *n.* a person who does not conform, esp. a member of a Protestant Church or sect dissenting from the Church of England. ~*a.* of or relating to nonconformists or nonconformism. **nonconformism** *n.* **nonconformity** *n.* **non-congenital** *a.* **non-connective** *a.* **non-consecutive** *a.* **non-consenting** *a.* **non-constitutional** *a.* **non-constraining** *a.* **non-constructive** *a.* **non-contagious** *a.* not contagious. **non-contemporary** *a.* **non-content** *n.* in the House of Lords, a person who votes in the negative. **non-contentious** *a.* **non-contributing** *a.* **non-contributory** *a.* (of a pension scheme etc.) not requiring employees to pay contributions. **non-controllable** *a.* **non-controlling** *a.* **non-controversial** *a.* **non-controvertible** *a.* **non-conventional** *a.* **non-convergent** *a.* **non-conversant** *a.* **non-convertible** *a.* **non-cooperation** *n.* 1 refusal to cooperate. 2 refusal, by non-payment of taxes, to cooperate with the government of a country. **non-corroborative** *a.* **non-corroding** *a.* **non-creative** *a.* **non-criminal** *a.* **non-critical** *a.* **non-cultivated** *a.* **non-current** *a.*

nonce (nons) *n.* the present time, occasion, purpose etc. **for the nonce** for the time being. **nonce-word** *n.* a word coined for the occasion. [*for then once*, read as *for the nonce* (ONCE)]

nonchalant (non´shələnt) *a.* careless, cool, unmoved, indifferent. **nonchalance** *n.* **nonchalantly** *adv.* [F pres.p. of OF *nonchaloir* (L *calere*, to glow)]

Usage note Pronunciation with (ch) rather than (sh) is best avoided.

non compos mentis (non kompos men´tis), **non compos** (non kom´pos) *a.* not in one's right mind. [L, *non*, not, COMPOS MENTIS]

non- (+ d– words) non-deciduous *a.* **non-deductible** *a.* **non-delivery** *n.* **non-democratic** *a.* **non-demonstrable** *a.* **non-denominational** *a.* not restricted to a particular religious denomination. **non-departmental** *a.* **non-dependence** *a.* **non-destructive** *a.* not causing destruction. **non-detachable** *a.* **non-detonating** *a.* **non-development** *n.* **non-dictatorial** *a.* **non-diffusing** *a.* **non-diplomatic** *a.* **non-directorial** *a.* **non-disciplinary** *a.* **non-discovery** *n.* **non-discriminating** *a.* **non-distinctive** *a.* **non-divisible** *a.* **non-doctrinal** *a.* **non-dogmatic** *a.* **non-domesticated** *a.* **non-dramatic** *a.* **non-drinker** *n.* a person who does not drink alcohol. **non-driver** *n.* a person who does not drive a car. **non-durable** *a.*

nondescript (non´diskript) *a.* not easily described or classified; neither one thing nor another; hybrid. ~*n.* a nondescript person or thing. **nondescriptly** *adv.* **nondescriptness** *n.* [L *descriptus*, p.p. of *descrībere*, to DESCRIBE]

none[1] (nŭn) *pron.* 1 no one, no person. 2 (*coll.*) no persons. 3 not any, not any portion. ~*a.* 1 no, not any. 2 not to be included in a specified category. ~*adv.* 1 by no amount. 2 in no respect; not at all (*none too clever*). **none other than** exactly, precisely (the person or thing specified). **none the less** nonetheless. **none too** TOO. **none-so-pretty** *n.* London Pride. **nonetheless** *adv.* nevertheless. [OE *nān* (*ne*, ONE)]

none[2] (nōn) *n.* in the Roman Catholic Church, the nones.

non- (+ e– words) non-earning *a.* not earning. **non-economic** *a.* **non-edible** *a.* **non-effective** *a.* not having an effect. **non-ego** *n.* (*Philos.*) the external or objective in perception or thought. **non-egoistical** *a.* **non-elastic** *a.* **non-eligible** *a.* **non-emotional** *a.* **non-equal** *a.* **non-equivalent** *a.* **non-essential** *a.* not essential. ~*n.* something non-essential. **non-establishment** *n.* **non-ethical** *a.* not ethical. **non-Euclidean** *a.* (*Geom.*) denying Euclidean principles. **non-European** *a.* not European. ~*n.* a non-European person. **non-event** *n.* a disappointing or unexciting occurrence. **non-exchangeable** *a.* **non-exclusive** *a.* **non-executive** *a.* **non-existence** *n.* **non-existent** *a.* **non-explosive** *a.* **non-exportation** *n.*

nonentity (nonen´titi) *n.* (*pl.* **nonentities**) 1 an unimportant person or thing. 2 non-existence. 3 a thing not existing, a mere figment, an imaginary thing.

nones (nōnz) *n.pl.* 1 in ancient Rome, the ninth day before the ides of a month. 2 in the Roman Catholic Church, the office for the ninth hour after sunrise, or 3 p.m. [F, from L *nōnas*, nom. *nōnæ*, fem. pl. of *nōnus*, ninth (or pl. of obs. *none*, L *nōna*, NOON)]

nonesuch NONSUCH.

nonet (nōnet´) *n.* 1 a musical composition for nine players or singers. 2 the performers of a nonet. 3 any group of nine. [It. *nonetto*, ninth]

nonetheless NONE[1].

non- (+ f– words) non-factual *a.* **non-fatal** *a.* **non-fattening** *a.* **non-fatty** *a.* **nonfeasance** (nonfē´zəns) *n.* failure to perform an act that is legally incumbent on one. **non-federal** *a.* **non-ferrous** *a.* containing no iron. **non-fiction** *n.* literary work, containing no deliberate fictitious element. **non-fictional** *a.* **non-finite** *a.* **non-flam** *a.* non-flammable. **non-flammable** *a.* not capable of supporting flame, though combustible, difficult or impossible to set alight. **non-flexible** *a.* **non-fluid** *n.* **non-forfeiting** *a.* denoting an insurance policy which is not forfeited upon non-payment of premiums. **non-formation** *n.* **non-freezing** *a.* **non-fulfilment** *n.* **non-functional** *a.* not having a function. **non-fusible** *a.*

nong (nong) *n.* (*Austral., sl.*) a stupid person, a fool. [etym. unknown]

non- (+ g–h words) non-gaseous *a.* **non-governmental** *a.* not belonging to or associated with a government. **non-greasy** *a.* **non-habitable** *a.* **non-hazardous** *a.* **non-heritable** *a.* **non-historical** *a.* **non-human** *a.* not belonging to the human race. ~*n.* a non-human being.

non-(+i–k words) non-identical *a.* not identical. **non-idiomatic** *a.* **non-importation** *n.* the state of not importing. **non-importing** *a.* **non-inclusion** *n.* **non-independent** *a.* **non-indictable** *a.* **non-industrial** *a.* **non-infectious** *a.* **non-inflammable** *a.* **non-inflected** *a.* (of a language) without inflections. **non-informative** *a.* **non-inherent** *a.* **non-inheritable** *a.* **non-injurious** *a.* **non-instinctive** *a.* **non-institutional** *a.* **non-intellectual** *a.* **non-interchangeable** *a.* **non-interference** *n.* a lack of interference. **non-intersecting** *a.* **non-intervention** *n.* the principle or policy of not becoming involved in the disputes of other nations. **non-interventionist** *a., n.* **non-intoxicating** *a.* **non-intuitive** *a.* **non-invasive** *a.* (*Med.*) **1** not involving surgery. **2** not tending to spread. **non-involvement** *n.* **non-iron** *a.* (of a fabric) not requiring ironing. **non-irritant** *a., n.* **nonjoinder** *n.* (*Law*) failure to join with another as party to a suit. **nonjuring** *a.* **nonjuror** *n.* a person who refuses to take an oath. **non-jury** *a.* without a jury. **non-kosher** *a.*

nonillion (nənil´yən) *n.* **1** a million raised to the ninth power, denoted by a unit with 54 zeros annexed. **2** (*esp. N Am.*) the tenth power of a thousand, denoted by a unit with 30 zeroes. **nonillionth** *a., n.* [from L *nōnus*, ninth, after BILLION]

non- (+ l–n words) non-laminated *a.* **non-lethal** *a.* **non-linear** *a.* not progressing smoothly from one stage to the next. **non-literary** *a.* **non-liturgical** *a.* **non-local** *a.* **non-logical** *a.* **non-logically** *adv.* **non-luminous** *a.* **non-magnetic** *a.* **non-malignant** *a.* **non-maritime** *a.* **non-married** *a.* **non-materialistic** *a.* **non-maternal** *a.* **non-mathematical** *a.* **non-measurable** *a.* **non-mechanical** *a.* **non-medical** *a.* **non-medicinal** *a.* **non-melodic** *a.* **non-member** *n.* a person who is not a member of a club etc. **non-membership** *n.* **non-metal** *a.* not made of metal. **non-metallic** *a.* **non-metric** *a.* **non-migratory** *a.* **non-militant** *a.* **non-military** *a.* **non-ministerial** *a.* **non-moral** *a.* not involving ethical considerations. **non-morally** *adv.* **non-mountainous** *a.* **non-mystical** *a.* **non-mythical** *a.* **non-national** *a.* **non-native** *a.* **non-natural** *a.* not natural (in a simply descriptive sense). **non-navigable** *a.* **non-negotiable** *a.* **non-nervous** *a.* **non-net** *a.* (of a book) not restricted to a minimum selling price. **non-nuclear** *a.* not having, or using, nuclear power or weapons.

non-(+o–p words) non-obedience *n.* **non-objective** *a.* in art, abstract, non-representational. **non-obligatory** *a.* **non-observance** *n.* **non-occurrence** *n.* **non-official** *a.* **non-operable** *a.* **non-operational** *a.* **1** not operating. **2** out of order. **non-operative** *a.* **non-organic** *a.* **non-orthodox** *a.* **non-ostensible** *a.* **non-parallel** *a.* **non-parasitic** *a.* **non-parental** *a.* not parental. **non-parliamentary** *a.* **non-parochial** *a.* **non-participating** *a.* **non-partisan** *a.* **non-party** *a.* not concerned with questions of political party. **non-paternal** *a.* **non-paying** *a.* **non-payment** *n.* **non-penetrative** *a.* (of sexual activity) not involving penetration. **non-performance** *n.* **non-permanent** *a.* **non-permeable** *a.* **non-person** *n.* an insignificant person. **non-personal** *a.* **non-philosophical** *a.* **non-phonemic** *a.* **non-physical** *a.* **non-physically** *adv.* **non-physiological** *a.* **non-playing** *a.* not playing, not taking part in a game. **non-poisonous** *a.* not poisonous. **non-political** *a.* **non-polluting** *a.* **non-porous** *a.* **non-possession** *n.* **non-practical** *a.* **non-practising** *a.* **non-precious** *a.* **non-predatory** *a.* **non-predictable** *a.* **non-prejudicial** *a.* **non-prescriptive** *a.* **non-preservable** *a.* **non-preservation** *n.* **non-production** *n.* **non-productive** *a.* **non-productively** *adv.* **non-professional** *a.* **1** not professional, amateur. **2** unskilled. **non-proficient** *a.* **non-profit, non-profit-making** *a.* **non-progressive** *a.* **non-proliferation** *n.* the limiting of the production of nuclear or chemical weapons etc. **non-proportional** *a.* **non-protective** *a.* **non-provided** *a.* denoting a school which is not provided by the Education Authority, e.g. a Church School. **non-punishable** *a.*

nonpareil (nonpərā´) *a.* having no equal; peerless, unrivalled, unique. ~*n.* **1** a paragon or a thing of unequalled excellence. **2** (*Hist., Print.*) a size of type equal to 6 point. **3** a fine variety of apple. [F *pareil*, med. L *pariculus*, dim. of *par*, equal]

non placet (non plā´set) *n.* the formula used in university and ecclesiastical assemblies in giving a negative vote. [L, it does not please]

nonplus (nonplŭs´) *v.t.* (*3rd pers. sing. pres.* **nonplusses,** (*N Am.*) **nonpluses,** *pres.p.* **nonplussing,** (*N Am.*) **nonplusing,** *past, p.p.* **nonplussed,** (*N Am.*) **nonplused**) to puzzle, to confound, to bewilder. ~*n.* a state of perplexity; a puzzle, a quandary. [L *nōn plūs*, no more]

non possumus (non pos´ūməs) *n.* a plea of inability. [L, we cannot]

non- (+ r– words) non-racial *a.* **non-radical** *a.* **non-reader** *n.* a person who cannot read. **non-realistic** *a.* **non-recognition** *n.* **non-recoverable** *a.* **non-reflective** *a.* **non-regimented** *a.* **non-registered** *a.* **non-religious** *a.* **non-renewable** *a.* **non-representative** *a.* **non-residence** *n.* **non-resident** *a.* **1** not residing in a place. **2** (of a post) not requiring the holder to reside at the place of work. ~*n.* a non-resident person. **non-residential** *a.* **non-resistance** *n.* passive obedience or submission, even to power unjustly exercised. **non-resistant** *a.* **non-resisting** *a.* **non-restricted** *a.* **non-returnable** *a.* **non-rigid** *a.* **non-routine** *a.* **non-rural** *a.*

non- (+ s– words) non-scientific *a.* **non-scientist** *n.* **non-sectarian** *a.* **non-secular** *a.* **non-segregated** *a.* **non-selective** *a.* **non-sensitive** *a.* not sensitive. **non-sexist** *a.* not sexist. **non-sexual** *a.* not involving sex. **non-sexually** *adv.* **non-shrinkable** *a.* **non-significant** *a.* **non-sinkable** *a.* **non-skid** *a.* (of a tyre) designed to prevent skidding. **non-skilled** *a.* **non-slip** *a.* designed to prevent slipping. **non-smoker** *n.* **1** someone who does not smoke. **2** a part of a train etc. in which it is not permitted to smoke. **non-smoking** *a., n.* **non-social** *a.* **non-society** *a.* not connected with a society. **non-soluble** *a.* **non-speaking** *a.* **non-specialist** *n.* **non-specific** *a.* **non-specific urethritis** *n.* (*Med.*) inflammation of the urethra caused by an unspecified infection. **non-speculative** *a.* **non-spiritual** *a.* **non-sporting** *a.* **non-stainable** *a.* **non-staining** *a.* **non-standard** *a.* **non-starter** *n.* **1** in a race, a person or animal that is entered but does not start. **2** (*coll.*) an idea or person with no chance whatsoever of success. **non-statistical** *a.* **non-stick** *a.* (of a cooking pan) treated so that food will not stick to it. **non-stop** *a.* **1** not stopping at intermediate stations. **2** without a pause. ~*adv.* without a pause. ~*n.* a non-stop train etc. **non-strategic** *a.* **non-structural** *a.* **non-submissive** *a.* **non-subscriber** *n.* **non-suggestive** *a.* not suggestive. **non-sulphurous** *a.* not sulphurous. **non-suppression** *n.* **non-surgical** *a.* **non-sustaining** *a.* **non-swimmer** *n.* a person who cannot swim. **non-symbolic** *a.* **non-systematic** *a.*

nonsense (non´səns) *n.* **1** unmeaning words, ideas etc. **2** foolish or extravagant talk, conduct etc. **3** foolery, absurdity. **4** rubbish, worthless stuff, trifles. **5** a form of literature which is intentionally absurd, written to amuse. **nonsense verse** *n.* **1** verse which is intentionally absurd, written to amuse. **2** verse which has no meaning, used for mnemonic purposes. **nonsensical** (-sen´sikəl) *a.* **nonsensicality** (-kal´-), **nonsensicalness** *n.* **nonsensically** *adv.*

non sequitur (non sek´witə) *n.* an inference not warrantable from the premisses. [L, it does not follow]

nonsuch (non´sŭch), **nonesuch** (nŭn´-) *n.* **1** a person who or something which is without an equal, a paragon, a nonpareil. **2** a leguminous plant, *Mendicago lupilina*, which has black pods.

nonsuit (nonsoot´) *n.* the stoppage of a suit during trial through insufficient evidence or non-appearance of the plaintiff. *~v.t.* to subject to a nonsuit.

non- (+ t–u words) non-taxable *a.* **non-teaching** *a.* **non-technical** *a.* **1** not technical. **2** having no technical knowledge or skill. **non-temporal** *a.* **non-territorial** *a.* **non-theatrical** *a.* **non-toxic** *a.* **non-traditional** *a.* **non-transferable** *a.* **non-tropical** *a.* **non-typical** *a.* **non-U** *a.* (*coll.*) not characteristic of the upper class. **non-uniform** *a.* **non-union** *a.* not connected with a trade union. **non-unionist** *n., a.* **non-usage** *n.* non-use. **non-use** *n.* failure to use something. **non-user** *n.*

non- (+ v–w words) non-venomous *a.* **non-verbal** *a.* without using words or speech. **non-verbally** *adv.* **non-verifiable** *a.* **non-vintage** *a.* **non-violence** *n.* the practice of refraining from violence on principle. **non-violent** *a.* **non-vocal** *a.* **non-volatile** *a.* **non-voter** *n.* **non-voting** *a.* **non-white** *a.* **1** not belonging to a light-skinned race. **2** of or relating to non-whites. *~n.* a non-white person. **non-word** *n.* a word which has never been recorded. **non-working** *a.*

noodle[1] (noo´dəl) *n.* a strip or ring of pasta. [G *Nudel*, etym. uncertain]

noodle[2] (noo´dəl) *n.* **1** a simpleton, a fool. **2** (*sl.*) the head. **noodledom** (-dəm) *n.* [etym. uncertain]

nook (nuk) *n.* **1** a corner. **2** a cosy place, as in an angle. **3** a secluded retreat. [ME *nōk*, prob. Scand.]

nooky (nu´ki), **nookie** *n.* (*sl.*) sexual intercourse. [perh. from NOOK]

noology (nōol´əji) *n.* the science of the understanding. [Gr. *noos*, mind]

noon (noon) *n.* **1** the middle of the day, twelve o'clock. **2** (*fig.*) the culmination or height. *~a.* of or relating to noon. **noonday** *n., a.* **nooning** *n.* (*dial., esp. N Am.*) a rest or a meal at noon. **noontide, noontime** *n.* [OE *nōn* (in *nōn-tīd*), from L *nōna hōra*, ninth hour]

noose (noos) *n.* **1** a loop with a running knot binding the closer the more it is pulled, as in a snare or a hangman's halter. **2** a tie, a bond, a snare. **3** (*facet.*) the marriage tie. *~v.t.* **1** to catch in a noose; to entrap. **2** to tie a noose on. **3** to tie in a noose. **to put one's head in a noose** to put oneself into a dangerous or exposed situation. [perh. from OF or Prov. *nous*, L *nodus*]

Nootka (noot´kə) *n.* the language of an Indian people of Vancouver, Canada.

nopal (nō´pəl) *n.* any American cactus of the genus *Nopalea*, esp. *N. cochinellifera*, grown for the support of the cochineal insect. [Sp.]

nope (nōp) *adv.* (*coll.*) no.

nor (naw) *conj.* and not (a word marking the second or subsequent part of a negative proposition; occasionally used without the correlative). *~†adv.* neither. [prob. short for ME *nother*, OE *nāwaether* (*nā*, NO[2], WHETHER)]

Usage note See note under NEITHER.

---

nor' (naw) *n., a., adv.* north. **nor'-wester** (-wes´tə) *n.* **1** a north-wester. **2** a glass of strong liquor. **3** a sou'-wester hat.

noradrenalin (norədren´əlin), **noradrenaline** *n.* an amine related to adrenalin, used as a heart resuscitant. [*normal*, *adrenalin*]

Nordic (naw´dik) *a.* **1** of or relating to a tall, blond, dolichocephalic physical type inhabiting Scandinavia, parts of Scotland and other parts of N Europe. **2** of or relating to Scandinavia. **3** (of skiing) involving cross-country racing and jumping. *~n.* a Nordic person. [F *nordique*, from *nord*, north]

norepinephrine (nawrepinef´rin) *n.* noradrenalin.

Norfolk jacket (naw´fək), **Norfolk** *n.* a man's loose jacket with vertical pleats in the back and front, and a waistband. [*Norfolk*, an English county]

noria (naw´riə) *n.* an endless chain of buckets on a wheel for raising water from a stream or similar. [Sp., from Arab. *nā´ūrah*]

nork (nawk) *n.* (*Austral., sl.*) a woman's breast. [etym. uncertain]

norland (naw´lənd) *n.* northland.

norm (nawm) *n.* **1** a standard, model, pattern or type. **2** a standard structure, behaviour etc. [L *norma*, a carpenter's square]

normal (naw´məl) *a.* **1** according to rule, standard, or established law; regular, typical, usual. **2** mentally and physically healthy. **3** (*Geom.*) perpendicular. **4** (*Chem.*) (of a solution) containing the equivalent of one gram of solute per litre. *~n.* **1** the mean temperature, volume etc. **2** the usual state, quality, quantity etc. **3** (*Geom.*) a perpendicular line. **4** the average or mean value of observed quantities. **normalcy** *n.* **normal distribution** *n.* in statistics, the distribution of many random variables represented in a bell-shaped graph. **normality** (-mal´-) *n.* **normalize, normalise** *v.t.* **1** to make normal. **2** to cause to conform to normal standards etc. *~v.i.* to become normal. **normalization** (-zā´shən) *n.* **normally** *adv.* **1** usually. **2** in the conventional way. **normally aspirated** *a.* not turbocharged or supercharged. **normal school** *n.* (in the US, France etc.) a school where teachers are trained. [as NORM]

Norman (naw´mən) *n.* **1** a native or inhabitant of Normandy. **2** a member of a mixed people of Northmen and Franks established there in the 10th cent. **3** Norman French. **4** (*Archit.*) Norman architecture. **5** any of the kings of England from William I to Stephen. *~a.* of or relating to Normandy or the Normans. **Norman architecture** *n.* a massive Romanesque style of architecture prevalent in Normandy (10th–11th cents.) and England (11th–12th cents.). **Norman Conquest** *n.* the conquest of England by Duke William of Normandy in 1066. **Norman English** *n.* English mixed with Norman-French forms, as spoken in England after the Norman Conquest. **Normanesque** (-nesk´) *a.* **Norman French** *n.* **1** French as spoken by the Normans. **2** the form of this that continued in use in the English law courts. **Normanism** *n.* **Normanize, Normanise** *v.t.* **Normanization** (-zā´shən) *n.* [OF *Normans*, pl. of *Normant* (F *Normand*), from Gmc., as NORTH, MAN]

norman (naw´mən) *n.* (*Naut.*) a bar inserted in a capstan or bitt for fastening the cable. [perh. ident. with NORMAN (cp. Dut. *noorman*, G *Normann*, Dan. *normand*)]

normative (naw´mətiv) *a.* of, relating to or establishing a norm. **normatively** *adv.* **normativeness** *n.* [F, *normatif, -ive*, from L *norma* (see NORM)]

Norn (nawn), **Norna** (-nə) *n.* any one of the Norse Fates. [Icel.]

Norroy (nor´oi), **Norroy and Ulster** *n.* (*Her.*) the third King of Arms, having jurisdiction north of the Trent. [A-F *nor*, NORTH, *roy*, king]

Norse (naws) *n.* (*pl.* **Norse**) **1** the Norwegian language. **2** the Scandinavian languages, including early Swedish and Danish. **3** (*as pl.*) the Norwegians. **4** (*as pl.*) the Vikings. *~a.* of or relating to Norway or ancient Scandinavia. **Norseman** *n.* (*pl.* **Norsemen**). [prob. from Dut. *noorsch*, *noordsch* (*noord*, NORTH, -ISH[1])]

north (nawth) *n.* **1** one of the four cardinal points, the one to the right of a person facing the setting sun at the equinox. **2** a region or part north of any given point. **3** the northern part of any country. **4** the portion of the US to the north of the former slave-holding States. **5** the Arctic. **6** the industrialized nations. **7** in bridge, the player occupying the position at the table corresponding to north on the compass. **8** (*poet.*) the north wind. *~a.* **1** situated in or towards the north. **2** (of the wind) blowing from the north. *~adv.* towards or in the north. **north and south** along a line running to and from north and south. **north by east** one point east of north. **north by west** one point west of north. **north of** farther north than. **to the north** in a northerly direction. **North American** *a.* of or relating to North America. ~*n.* a native or inhabitant of North America. **northbound** *a.* heading towards the north. **North Country** *n.* the part of a country to the north, esp. northern England or the northern part of Great Britain. ~*a.* relating to or characteristic of this. **north-countryman** *n.* (*pl.* **north-countrymen**). **north-east** *n.* **1** the point midway between north and east. **2** a region lying in this quarter. ~*a.* of, relating to or coming from the north-east. ~*adv.* towards, at or in the north-east. **northeaster** *n.* a north-east wind. **northeasterly** *a., adv.* north-east. **north-eastern** *a.* **north-east passage** *n.* a shipping route along the northern coast of Europe and Asia. **north-eastward** *a., adv.* towards the north-east. **north-eastwardly** *a., adv.* **north-eastwards** *a., adv.* north-eastward. **norther** *n.* (*N Am.*) a cold north wind which blows in autumn and winter. **northerly** (-dhə-) *a., adv.* **1** towards or in the north. **2** (of the wind) blowing from the north. ~*n.* (*pl.* **northerlies**) a north wind. **northerliness** *n.* **northern** (-dhən) *a.* **1** of, relating to, situated, living in or proceeding from the north. **2** towards the north. **3** of the northern States of the US. ~*n.* a northerner. **northerner** *n.* a native or inhabitant of the north. **northern hemisphere** *n.* the half of the earth which lies north of the equator. **northern lights** *n.pl.* the aurora borealis. **northernmost** *a.* **Northern States** *n.pl.* the states in the north of the US. **North Germanic** *n., a.* (of) the Scandinavian group of languages. **northing** *n.* (*Naut.*) distance or progress in a northward direction. **North Korean** *a.* of or relating to North Korea. ~*n.* a native or inhabitant of North Korea. **northland** (-lənd) *n.* (*poet.*) **1** countries in the north. **2** the northern part of a country. **north light** *n.* good natural light, without direct sun. **Northman** *n.* (*pl.* **Northmen**) an inhabitant of the north of Europe, esp. of Scandinavia. **north-north-east** *n.* the point midway between north and north-east. **north-north-west** *n.* the point midway between north and north-west. **North Pole** *n.* **1** the northernmost extremity of the axis on which the earth revolves. **2** the point in the northern sky round which the stars appear to revolve. **north-south divide** *n.* the contrast between the north and the south (of the UK). **North Star** *n.* the pole star. **northward** (-wəd) *a., adv.* towards the north. ~*n.* a northward direction. **northwardly** *a., adv.* **northwards** *a., adv.* **north-west** *n.* **1** the point midway between north and west. **2** a region lying in this quarter. ~*a.* of, relating to or coming from the north-west. ~*adv.* towards, at or in the north-west. **northwester** *n.* a north-west wind. **north-westerly** *a., adv.* north-west. **north-western** *a.* **north-west passage** *n.* a shipping route along the northern coast of America. **north-westward** *a., adv.* towards the north-west. **north westwardly** *a., adv.* **north-westwards** *a., adv.* north-westward. [OE (cp. Dut. *noord*, G, Dan. and Swed. *nord*, Icel. *northr*)]

Northants (nawthants´) *abbr.* Northamptonshire.

Northumb. *abbr.* Northumberland.

Northumbrian (nawthŭm´briən) *n.* **1** a native or inhabitant of ancient Northumbria (England north of the Humber) or of Northumberland. **2** the old English dialect of ancient Northumbria; the dialect of Northumberland. ~*a.* of or relating to either of these districts. [OE *Northhymbre* (NORTH, *Humber*)]

Norway lobster (naw´wā) *n.* a small European lobster, *Nephrops norvegicus.*

Norway rat *n.* the brown rat, *Rattus norvegicus.*

Norwegian (nawwē´jən) *n.* **1** a native or inhabitant of Norway. **2** the language of Norway. ~*a.* of or relating to Norway. [med. L *Norvegia*]

Nos. *abbr.* numbers.

nose (nōz) *n.* **1** the projecting part or the face between the forehead and mouth, containing the nostrils and the organ of smell. **2** the power of smelling. **3** odour, scent; aroma, esp. the bouquet of wine. **4** a part of a thing resembling a nose, such as the nozzle of a pipe, tube or bellows, a beak, point, prow etc. **5** a nosing. **6** (*sl.*) a police informer. **7** (*fig.*) an instinctive ability to find something (*a nose for trouble*). ~*v.t.* **1** to perceive, trace or detect by smelling. **2** (*fig.*) to find out. **3** to rub or push with the nose. **4** to push (one's way). ~*v.i.* **1** to smell, to sniff. **2** (*fig.*) to search, to pry. **3** to push one's way, to push ahead. **as plain as the nose on your face** clearly to be seen. **by a nose** by the smallest possible margin. **to count noses 1** to reckon the number of persons present. **2** to count votes, supporters etc. **to cut off one's nose to spite one's face** to harm oneself in the course of trying to harm someone else. **to follow one's nose** to act according to one's instincts. **to get up someone's nose** (*sl.*) to annoy someone. **to keep one's nose clean** (*sl.*) to behave well, to stay out of trouble. **to keep one's nose to the grindstone** GRINDSTONE (under GRIND). **to lead by the nose** LEAD[1]. **to look down one's nose at** LOOK. **to pay through the nose** PAY[1]. **to poke one's nose into** to stick one's nose into. **to put someone's nose out of joint** JOINT. **to rub noses** RUB[1]. **to rub someone's nose in it** RUB[1]. **to see no further than one's nose** to be short-sighted or lacking in insight. **to speak through one's nose** to have a nasal quality to one's voice. **to stick one's nose into** to meddle officiously in. **to turn up one's nose at** to show contempt for. **under someone's nose** in someone's actual presence or sight. **with one's nose in the air** in a haughty manner. **nosebag** *n.* **1** a bag containing fodder for hanging over a horse's head. **2** (*sl.*) a bag of provisions. **noseband** *n.* the part of a bridle passing over the nose and attached to the cheek-straps. **nosebleed** *n.* a bleeding from the nose. **nose-cone** *n.* the cone-shaped forward section of a rocket etc. **nosed** *a.* (*usu. in comb.*, as *red-nosed*). **nosedive** *n.* **1** a sudden plunge towards the earth made by an aircraft. **2** any sudden plunge. ~*v.i.* to make a nosedive. **nose flute** *n.* a type of flute blown through the nose. **nose leaf** *n.* a membraneous appendage on the nose of certain bats, constituting an organ of touch. **noseless** *a.* **nose of wax** *n.* a person who or something which is easily influenced or moulded. **nose-piece** *n.* **1** a noseband. **2** the part of a helmet which protects the nose. **3** the endpiece of a microscope to which the object-glass is fastened. **4** a nozzle. **nosepipe** *n.* a piece of pipe used as a nozzle. **noser** *n.* (*coll.*) **1** a fall on the nose. **2** a wind in one's face, a headwind. **nose-rag** *n.* (*sl.*) a handkerchief. **nosering** *n.* **1** a ring worn in the nose as ornament. **2** a leading ring for a bull etc. **nose tackle** *n.* in American football, the defensive player in the centre of the linemen in formation. **nose-to-tail** *a., adv.* with the front of one vehicle close behind the back of another. **nose wheel** *n.* a landing wheel under the nose of an aircraft. **nosing** *n.* the prominent edge of a moulding, step etc. **nosy, nosey** *a.* (*comp.* **nosier**, *superl.* **nosiest**) **1** (*coll.*) very inquisitive. **2** having a large or prominent nose. **3** strong- or evil-smelling. **4** fragrant. **5** sensitive to bad odours. ~*n.* (*pl.* **nosies**) a person with a large nose. **Nosy Parker** *n.* (*coll.*) a nosy person. [OE *nosu* (cp. Dut. *neus*, Icel. *nōs*)]

nosegay (nōz´gā) *n.* a bunch of flowers, esp. fragrant flowers. [GAY in obs. sense, an ornament]

nosey NOSE.

nosh (nosh) *n.* (*sl.*) **1** food. **2** a meal. **3** (*N Am.*) a snack. ~*v.t., v.i.* **1** to eat. **2** (*N Am.*) to eat between meals. **noshery** *n.* (*pl.* **nosheries**) (*sl.*) a restaurant or café. **nosh-up** *n.* (*sl.*) a large meal, a feast. [Yiddish]

noso- (nos´ō) *comb. form* of or relating to diseases. [Gr. *nosos*, disease]

nosocomial (nosəkō´miəl) *a.* (*Med.*) of or relating to hospitals. [Gr. *nosokomeion*, a hospital]

nosography (nosog´rəfi) *n.* the scientific description of diseases.

nosology (nosol´əji) *n.* **1** a systematic classification of diseases. **2** the branch of medical science dealing with such a classification. **nosological** (-loj´-) *a.* **nosologist** *n.*

nosophobia (nosəfō´biə) *n.* morbid fear of disease.

nostalgia (nostal´jə) *n.* **1** a yearning for the past. **2** the evocation of a time in the past. **3** an acute longing for home, homesickness. **nostalgic** *a.* **nostalgically** *adv.* [Gr. *nostos*, return, *-algia* from *algos*, pain]

nosto- (nos´tō) *comb. form* of or relating to a return. [Gr. *nostos*, return]

nostoc (nos´tok) *n.* any gelatinous freshwater alga of the genus *Nostoc*. [G *Nostoch*, a term invented by Paracelsus]

nostology (nostol´əji) *n.* (*Med.*) gerontology. [Gr. *nostos*, return, -LOGY]

nostomania (nostəmā´nia) *n.* an abnormal anxiety to go back to a familiar place.

nostophobia (nostəfō´biə) *n.* an abnormal fear of going back to a familiar place.

Nostradamus (nostrədah´məs) *n.* (*pl.* **Nostradamuses**) a person who predicts or professes to predict. [Michel de *Nostredame*, 1503–66, French physician, astrologer and professional prophet]

nostril (nos´tril) *n.* either of the two apertures of the nose. **nostrilled** *a.* [OE *nosthyrl* (NOSE, *thyrel*, hole, cogn. with THRILL)]

nostrum (nos´trəm) *n.* (*pl.* **nostrums**) **1** a medicine based on a secret formula; a quack remedy. **2** a scheme for political or social reform. [L, neut. of *noster*, our]

nosy NOSE.

not (not) *adv.* a particle expressing negation, denial, prohibition or refusal. **not a few** FEW. **not at all** a polite way of acknowledging thanks. **not a thing** nothing at all. †**not but what** nevertheless. **not half** HALF. **not in the slightest** not at all. **not least** particularly, especially. **not much** MUCH. **not on 1** (*sl.*) not possible. **2** (*sl.*) not morally, socially etc. acceptable. **not out** having reached the end of a cricket innings or of play for the day without being dismissed. **not quite 1** almost. **2** definitely not. **not that** it is not meant however that. **not (too) well** feeling rather unwell. **not very 1** to a minor extent. **2** far from being. [NAUGHT]

nota NOTUM.

nota bene (nōtə ben´ā) *v.t.* (*imper.*) note well, take note. [L]

notable (nō´təbəl) *a.* **1** worthy of note; remarkable, memorable, distinguished. **2** excellent, capable. *~n.* a notable person. **notabilia** (-bil´iə) *n.pl.* notable things. **notability** (-bil´) *n.* (*pl.* **notabilities**) **1** the state of being notable. **2** a notable person. **notableness** *n.* **notably** *adv.* [F, from L *notābilis*, from *notāre*, to note]

notandum (nōtan´dəm) *n.* (*pl.* **notanda** (-də)) something to be noted, a memorandum. [L ger. of *notāre*, to NOTE]

notary (nō´təri) *n.* (*pl.* **notaries**) a public official appointed to attest deeds, contracts etc., and administer oaths etc. **notarial** (-teə´ri-) *a.* **notarially** *adv.* **notarize, notarise** *v.t.* (*N Am.*) to certify as a notary. **notary public** *n.* (*pl.* **notaries public**) a notary. [A-F *notarie* (F *notaire*), L *notārium*, nom. *-us*, from *notāre*, to NOTE]

notation (nōtā´shən) *n.* **1** the act or process of representing by signs, figures etc. **2** a system of signs, figures etc., employed in any science or art. **3** (*N Am.*) a note, an annotation; a record. **4** scale of notation. **notate** (nōtāt´) *v.t.* to write in notation. **notational** *a.* [L *notātio*, as NOTARY]

notch (noch) *n.* **1** a nick, a cut, a V-shaped indentation. **2** a tally point. **3** (*coll.*) a step, a degree. **4** (*N Am.*) an opening, narrow pass or short defile. *~v.t.* **1** to cut a notch or notches in. **2** to score by notches. **3** to fix (stairs etc.) by means of notches. **to notch up** to score, to achieve. **notched** *a.* **notcher** *n.* **notchy** *a.* (*comp.* **notchier**, *superl.* **notchiest**). [F *oche* (now *hoche*) through *an oche* (cp. NEWT)]

note (nōt) *n.* **1** a brief record, a memorandum. **2** a short or informal letter. **3** a diplomatic communication. **4** a bank note or piece of paper money. **5** a written promise to pay a certain sum of money. **6** an annotation, a comment, explanation, or gloss, appended to a passage in a book etc. **7** notice, attention, observation. **8** distinction, repute, importance. **9** a sign representing the pitch and duration of a sound. **10** a musical sound. **11** a significant sound, tone or mode of expression. **12** a key in a musical instrument. **13** a bird's call. **14** a sign, mark or token. **15** a distinctive feature, a characteristic, a mark of identity, genuineness, quality etc. **16** a mark of interrogation, exclamation etc. **17** a stigma. *~v.t.* **1** to observe, to take notice of; to show respect to; to pay attention to. **2** to make a memorandum of; to set down or record as worth remembering. **3** to annotate. **4** (*chiefly pass.*) to make famous. **of note** important, distinguished. **to hit the right note** to behave in an appropriate or suitable manner. **to strike the right note** to hit the right note. **to take note** to pay attention. **notebook** *n.* **1** a book for writing notes in. **2** a small, portable, battery-operated computer, about the size of an exercise book. *~a.* denoting a notebook computer. **notecase** *n.* a wallet for holding paper money. **noted** *a.* eminent, remarkable. **noteless** *a.* **notelet** *n.* a folded piece of paper with a decorative design on the front, for a short, informal letter. **note of hand** *n.* a promissory note. **notepad** *n.* a pad of paper for writing letters or notes on. **notepaper** *n.* paper for letters, esp. private correspondence. **noter** *n.* **noteworthy** *a.* **1** worth attention. **2** outstanding, famous. **noteworthiness** *n.* [OF, from L *nota*, a mark (whence *notāre*, to mark, OF *noter*)]

nothing (nŭth´ing) *n.* **1** no thing. **2** not anything, nought. **3** no amount, zero, a nought. **4** nothingness, nonexistence. **5** an insignificant or unimportant thing, a trifle. *~a.* (*coll.*) insignificant, unimportant. *~adv.* in no degree, in no way, not at all. **for nothing 1** free, without paying. **2** to no purpose. **next to nothing** NEXT. **no nothing** (*coll.*) (at the end of a list of negatives) not at all. **nothing doing 1** (*coll.*) there is no chance of success. **2** (*coll.*) nothing is happening. **3** (*coll.*) I refuse (to do something). **nothing else for it** no alternative. **nothing for it but** no alternative. **nothing in it 1** untrue. **2** extremely easy. **3** very little difference between two alternatives. **nothing less than 1** positively, downright, absolutely. **2** (*dated*) anything rather than. **nothing loath** LOATH. **nothing of the kind** KIND. **nothing to it** nothing in it. **nothing to write home about** HOME[1]. **sweet nothings** SWEET. **think nothing of it** there is no need for apology or thanks. **to be nothing to 1** not to concern. **2** not to compare with. **to be nothing to do with** not to be connected or involved with. **to come to nothing 1** to turn out a failure. **2** to result in no amount. **to have nothing on someone** HAVE. **to have nothing to do with** to be nothing to do with. **to make nothing of** to fail to understand or deal with. **to say nothing of** SAY. **to stop at nothing** STOP. **nothingarian** (-eə´ri-) *a.* a person who has no religious beliefs. **nothingarianism** *n.* **nothingism** *n.* **nothingness** *n.*

notice (nō´tis) *n.* **1** observation, regard, attention. **2** intelligence, information, warning. **3** a written or printed paper giving information or directions. **4** an intimation or instruction. **5** intimation of the termination of an agreement, contract of employment etc., at a specified date. **6** an account of something in a newspaper etc., esp. a review of a book, play etc. **7** the act of noting. *~v.t.* **1** to take notice of, to perceive. **2** to remark upon. **3** to pay respect to. **4** to serve a notice upon. **5** to give notice to. **at a moment's notice** with hardly any advance warning. **at short notice** with little advance warning. **to give notice** to intimate the termination of an agreement, particularly a contract of employment. **to take no notice of** to pay no attention to; to ignore. **to take notice 1** to observe. **2** to show alertness. **to take notice of** to pay attention to, to heed. **under notice** served with a formal notice. **noticeable** *a.* easy to see, hear or recognize. **noticeably** *adv.* **noticeboard** *n.* a board exposed to public view on which notices are posted. [F, from L *nōtitia*, from *nōtus*, p.p. of *noscere*, to know]

notify (nō´tifi) *v.t.* (*3rd pers. sing. pres.* **notifies,** *pres.p.* **notifying,** *past, p.p.* **notified**) **1** to give notice to, to inform (of or that). **2** to make known, to announce, to declare, to publish. **notifiable** *a.* (esp. of cases of disease that must be reported to the sanitary authorities) to be notified. **notification** (-fikā´shən) *n.* [F *notifier*, L *nōtificāre* (*nōtus*, known, *-ficāre*, *facere*, to make)]

notion (nō´shən) *n.* **1** an idea, a conception. **2** an opinion, a view. **3** (*coll.*) an inclination, desire, intention or whim. **4** (*N Am.*) a small ingenious device or useful article, knick-knack. **5** (*pl., N Am.*) fancy goods, haberdashery, novelties etc. **6** a general concept or idea. **notional** *a.* **1** of or relating to notions or concepts. **2** abstract, imaginary, hypothetical. **3** speculative, ideal. **4** (*Gram.*) (of a verb) having a full meaning of its own. **5** given to notions or whims, fanciful. **notionally** *adv.* **notionist** *n.* [F, from L *notio*, *nōtiōnem*, acc., as NOTIFY]

notitia (nōtish´iə) *n.* (*pl.* **notitias**) a list, register, or catalogue. [L]

noto- (nō´tō) *comb. form* of or relating to the back. [Gr. *notos*, back]

notochord (nō´təkawd) *n.* the elastic cartilaginous band constituting a rudimentary form of the spinal column in the embryo and some primitive fishes.

notonectal (nōtonek´təl) *a.* of or relating the genus *Notonecta* of hemipterous insects. [Gr. *nektōs*, swimmer]

notorious (nōtaw´riəs) *a.* widely or publicly or commonly known (now used only in a bad sense). **notoriety** (nōtərī´ə-) *n.* **notoriously** *adv.* **notoriousness** *n.* [med. L *nōtōrius*, from *nōtus*, known]

notornis (nətaw´nis) *n.* (*pl.* **notornises**) a gigantic flightless New Zealand bird, *Porphyrio mantelli*, now very rare. [Gr. *ornis*, bird]

nototherium (nōtəthiə´riəm) *n.* (*pl.* **nototheriums**) an extinct Australian gigantic marsupial of the genus *Nototherium*. [Gr. *thērion*, beast]

Notts. (nots) *abbr.* Nottinghamshire.

notum (nō´təm) *n.* (*pl.* **nota** (-tə)) the back of the thorax in insects. [mod. L, from Gr. *noton*, *notos*, back]

notwithstanding (notwidhstan´ding) *prep.* in spite of, despite. *~adv.* nevertheless; in spite of this. *~conj.* although, in spite of the fact that.

nougat (noo´gah, nŭg´ət) *n.* a confection made of nuts and sugar. [F, from Sp. *nogado*, from L *nucem*, nom. *nux*]

nought (nawt) *n.* **1** zero. **2** †nothing. **noughts and crosses** *n.pl.* a game, the object of which is to complete a row of three noughts or three crosses in a grid of nine squares. [NAUGHT]

noumenon (noo´minən, now´-) *n.* (*pl.* **noumena** (-nə)) **1** the substance underlying a phenomenon. **2** an object or the conception of an object as it is in itself, or as it appears to pure thought. **noumenal** *a.* **noumenally** *adv.* [Gr. *nooumenon*, neut. pres.p. of *noein*, to apprehend]

noun (nown) *n.* (*Gram.*) a word used as the name of anything. **nounal** *a.* [A-F, from OF *nun*, *num*, L *nōmen*, NAME, rel. to *noscere*, to KNOW]

nourish (nŭr´ish) *v.t.* **1** to feed, to sustain, to support. **2** to maintain, to educate. **3** to foster, to cherish, to nurse. **nourisher** *n.* **nourishing** *a.* **nourishingly** *adv.* **nourishment** *n.* **1** food, sustenance. **2** the act of nourishing. **3** the state of being nourished. **nouriture** (nŭr´ichə) *n.* **1** nourishment, sustenance. **2** nurture, education. [OF *noris-*, stem of *norir* (F *nourrir*), from L *nutrīre*]

nous (nows) *n.* **1** (*coll.*) sense, wit, intelligence. **2** (*Philos.*) mind, intellect. [Gr.]

nouveau (noo´vō), (*fem.*) **nouvelle** (-vel) *a.* new. **nouveau riche** (rēsh) *n.* (*pl.* **nouveaux riches** (-rēsh)) a person who has recently acquired wealth but who has not acquired good taste or manners. **nouvelle cuisine** (kwizēn´) *n.* a style of simple French cooking which does not involve rich food, creamy sauces etc. and relies largely on artistic presentation. **nouvelle vague** (vahg) *n.* a movement in the French cinema, dating from just before 1960, which aimed at imaginative quality in films. [F]

Nov. *abbr.* November.

nova (nō´və) *n.* (*pl.* **novae** (-ē), **novas**) a star which flares up to great brightness and subsides after a time. [L *novus*, new]

novaculite (nōvak´ūlīt) *n.* **1** a fine-grained slate used for hones. **2** a hone, a whetstone. [L *novacula*, razor, -ITE[1]]

novae NOVA.

novalia (nōvā´liə) *n.pl.* (*Sc. Law*) waste lands newly brought into cultivation. [L, pl. of *novāle*, neut. sing., from *novus*, new]

Novatian (nōvā´shən) *n.* a follower of Novatianus (3rd cent.), who taught that the Church had no power to absolve the lapsed or to admit them to the Eucharist. **Novatianism** *n.* **Novatianist** *n.*

novation (nōvā´shən) *n.* the substitution of a new obligation or debt for an old one. [L *novātio*, from *novāre*, to make new, from *novus*, new]

novel (nov´əl) *n.* **1** a fictitious narrative in prose, usu. of sufficient length to fill a volume. **2** this type of literature. **3** in Roman law, a new or supplementary decree or constitution. *~a.* **1** new, recent, fresh. **2** unusual, strange. **novelese** (-lēz´) *n.* (*derog.*) the language or style considered appropriate for inferior novels. **novelette** (-let´) *n.* **1** a short novel, usu. of a sentimental nature. **2** (*Mus.*) a kind of romance dealing freely with several themes. **novelettish** *a.* (*derog.*) cheaply sentimental. **novelish** *a.* **novelism** *n.* **novelist** *n.* a writer of novels. **novelistic** (novəlis´-) *a.* **novelize, novelise** *v.t.* to make (a play, facts etc.) into a novel. **novelization** (-zā´shən) *n.* **novella** (nōvel´ə) *n.* (*pl.* **novellas**) **1** a tale, a short story. **2** a short novel. **novelly** *adv.* **novelty** *n.* (*pl.* **novelties**) **1** newness, freshness, originality. **2** something new. **3** a cheap, unusual object, sold as a gift or souvenir. *~a.* having novelty value. [OF *novelle* (F *nouvelle*) or It. *novella*, L *novella*, neut. pl. of *novellus*, dim. of *novus*, new]

November (nōvem´bə) *n.* the 11th month of the year, the ninth of the Roman year. [L, from *novem*, nine (cp. DECEMBER)]

novena (nōvē´nə) *n.* (*pl.* **novenas**) in the Roman Catholic Church, a devotion consisting of a prayer or service repeated on nine successive days. [med. L, from *novem*, nine]

novenary (nov´ənəri) *n.* (*pl.* **novenaries**) a group or set of nine. **novennial** (nōven´iəl) *a.* happening every ninth year. [L *novēnārius*, as NOVENA]

novercal (nōvœ´kəl) *a.* of, relating to or suitable to a stepmother. [L *novercālis*, from *noverca*, a stepmother]

novice (nov´is) *n.* **1** a person entering a religious house on probation before taking the vows. **2** a new convert. **3** a person who is new to any business, an inexperienced person, a beginner. **4** a person or an animal that has not won a specified prize in a race or competition. **noviciate** (nōvish´iət), **novitiate** *n.* **1** the term of probation passed by a novice. **2** a religious novice. **3** the part of a religious house allotted to novices. **4** any period of probation or apprenticeship. [OF, from L *novīcius*, from *novus*, new]

Novocaine® (nō´vəkān), **novocaine** *n.* a synthetic produce derived from coal tar, used as a local anaesthetic. [L *novus*, new, COCAINE]

now (now) *adv.* **1** at the present time. **2** at once, immediately. **3** very recently. **4** (in narrative) at this point or time, then. **5** in these circumstances. **6** on this further occasion. **7** used as an expletive in explaining, remonstrating, conciliating, threatening etc. ~*conj.* since, seeing that, this being the case. ~*n.* the present time. ~*a.* (*coll.*) present, existing. **as of now** from this time. **for now** until later. **from now on** FROM. **just now** JUST[1]. **now and again** from time to time, now and then. **now and then** from time to time; occasionally. **now or never** at this moment or the chance is gone for ever. **nowadays** *adv.* at the present time; in these days. ~*n.* the present time. [OE *nu* (cp. Dut. *nu*, G *nun*, Icel. *nū*, Dan. and Swed. *nu*, Gr. *nūn*, L *nunc*, Sansk. *nu*)]

noway, †noways NO[1].

†Nowel, †Nowell NOEL.

nowhere (nō´weə) *adv.* not in, at, or to any place or state. ~*pron.* no place. **in the middle of nowhere** (*coll.*) in a remote location. **nowhere near** not nearly. **to be nowhere** (*coll.*) to come in nowhere. **to come from nowhere** **1** to appear suddenly or unexpectedly. **2** to achieve sudden or unexpected success. **to come in nowhere** (*coll.*) to be badly defeated in a race or other contest. **to get nowhere** to make or cause to make little or no progress.

nowise NO[1].

nowt[1] (nowt) *n.* (*dial.*) nothing. [from *naught*]

†nowt[2] (nowt) *n.* (*dial.*) cattle or a bullock. [from Icel. *naut* (cp. OE *nēat*, NEAT[1])]

nowy (nō´i) *a.* (*Hist.*) having a convex projection in the middle. [OF *noé* (F *noué*), p.p. of *noer*, L *nōdāre*, to tie, from *nōdus*, a knot]

noxious (nok´shəs) *a.* **1** hurtful, harmful, unwholesome. **2** pernicious, destructive. **noxiously** *adv.* **noxiousness** *n.* [L *noxius*, from *noxa*, harm, rel. to *nocēre*, to injure]

noyade (nwah·yahd´) *n.* a mode of executing political prisoners by drowning, esp. during the Reign of Terror in France in 1794. [F, from *noyer*, to drown, L *necāre*, to kill]

noyau (nwah·yō´) *n.* (*pl.* **noyaux** (-yōz´)) brandy cordial flavoured with bitter almonds etc. [F, from L *nucāle*, from *nucem*, nom. *nux*, a nut]

nozzle (noz´əl) *n.* a spout, a projecting mouthpiece, or end of pipe or hose. [NOSE]

NP *abbr.* Notary Public.

Np *chem. symbol* neptunium.

n.p. *abbr.* **1** new paragraph. **2** no place of publication.

NPA *abbr.* Newspaper Publishers' Association.

NPL *abbr.* National Physical Laboratory.

NPV *abbr.* net present value.

nr. *abbr.* near.

NRA *abbr.* National Rivers Authority.

NRSV *abbr.* New Revised Standard Version (of the Bible).

NS *abbr.* **1** new series. **2** new style. **3** Nova Scotia.

ns *abbr.* nanosecond.

NSA *abbr.* National Security Agency.

NSB *abbr.* National Savings Bank.

NSC *abbr.* National Security Council.

NSF *abbr.* National Science Foundation.

NSPCC *abbr.* National Society for the Prevention of Cruelty to Children.

NSU *abbr.* (*Med.*) non-specific urethritis.

NSW *abbr.* New South Wales.

NT *abbr.* **1** National Trust. **2** New Testament. **3** Northern Territory (of Australia). **4** no trumps.

-n't (ənt) *contr.* not (*in comb.*, as in *isn't, doesn't*).

Nth *abbr.* North.

nth N[1].

NTP *abbr.* normal temperature and pressure.

NTS *abbr.* National Trust for Scotland.

nu (nu) *n.* the thirteenth letter of the Greek alphabet (Ν, ν). [Gr. *ny*]

nuance (nū´ahns) *n.* **1** a delicate gradation in colour or tone. **2** a fine distinction between things, feelings, opinions etc. ~*v.t.* to give a nuance to. [F, from *nuer*, to shade, from *nue*, L *nūbes*, cloud]

nub (nŭb) *n.* **1** the pith or gist (of). **2** a small lump, as of coal. **3** a stub, something left over. **4** a tangle, a knot, a snarl. **nubble** (nŭb´əl) *n.* a small lump. **nubbly, nubby** *a.* (*comp.* **nubblier, nubbier**, *superl.* **nubbliest, nubbiest**). [var. of KNOB]

nubecula (nūbek´ūlə) *n.* (*pl.* **nubeculae** (-lē)) **1** one of the two southern nebulae called the Magellanic clouds. **2** a cloudy appearance in the urine. **3** a film on the eye. [L, dim. of *nūbes*, cloud]

nubiferous (nūbif´ərəs) *a.* producing or bringing clouds. [L *nūbifer* (*nūbes*, see NUBECULA, -FEROUS)]

nubile (nū´bīl) *a.* **1** (of a woman) marriageable. **2** sexually mature. **3** sexually attractive. **nubility** (-bil´-) *n.* [L *nūbilis*, from *nūbere*, to marry]

nucellus (nūsel´əs) *n.* (*pl.* **nucelli** (-lī)) the nucleus of an ovule. [mod. L, dim. of NUCLEUS]

nuchal (nū´kəl) *a.* of or relating to the nape of the neck. [med. L *nucha*, Arab. *nukhā'*, spinal cord, -AL[1]]

nuci- (nū´si) *comb. form* of or relating to nuts. [L *nux*, nut]

nuciferous (nūsif´ərəs) *a.* (*Bot.*) bearing nuts.

nucivorous (nūsiv´ərəs) *a.* eating or feeding on nuts.

nucleal NUCLEUS.

nuclear (nū´kliə) *a.* **1** of or relating to atomic nuclei. **2** of or relating to the nucleus of a biological cell. **3** of or using nuclear power or weapons. **nuclear bomb** *n.* a bomb which explodes by using the energy released by nuclear fission or nuclear fusion. **nuclear charge** *n.* the positive electric charge in the nucleus of an atom. **nuclear disarmament** *n.* the reduction or giving up of a country's nuclear weapons. **nuclear energy** *n.* energy released during a nuclear reaction, whether by nuclear fission or nuclear fusion. **nuclear family** *n.* the basic family unit consisting of a mother and father and their children. **nuclear fission** *n.* the breaking up of a heavy atom, as of uranium, into atoms of smaller mass, causing a great release of energy. **nuclear force** *n.* the attractive force between nucleons in the atomic nucleus which holds the nucleus together. **nuclear-free** *a.* containing no nuclear weapons, nuclear installations or nuclear-waste dumps. **nuclear fuel** *n.* uranium, plutonium and other metals consumed to produce nuclear energy. **nuclear fusion** *n.* the creation of a new nucleus by merging two lighter ones, with release of energy. **nuclear magnetic resonance** *n.* resonance which can be produced in nuclei or in isotopes of the elements, used as an analytic technique and in diagnosis. **nuclear physics** *n.* the study of atomic nuclei. **nuclear power** *n.* power obtained from a controlled nuclear reaction. **nuclear-powered** *a.* **nuclear reaction** *n.* a reaction in which the nuclei of atoms are transformed into isotopes of the element itself, or atoms of a different element. **nuclear reactor** *n.* a structure of fissile material such as uranium, with a moderator such as carbon or heavy water, so arranged that nuclear energy is continuously released under control. **nuclear**

umbrella *n.* the protection provided by being allied with a nuclear power. **nuclear warfare** *n.* the use of nuclear weapons in warfare. **nuclear waste** *n.* radioactive waste material. **nuclear weapon** *n.* a missile or bomb which explodes by using the energy released by nuclear fission or nuclear fusion. **nuclear winter** *n.* a period of coldness and darkness predicted as likely to follow a nuclear war. [NUCLEUS]

Usage note Pronunciation of *nuclear* as (nū´kūlə), as though the word were *nucular*, is best avoided.

nuclease (nū´kliāz) *n.* any of a group of enzymes which catalyse the breakdown of nucleic acids.
nucleate[1] (nū´kliət) *a.* having a nucleus, nucleated.
nucleate[2] (nū´kliāt) *v.t.* to form into a nucleus. *~v.i.* to form a nucleus. **nucleation** (-ā´shən) *n.*
nuclei NUCLEUS.
nucleic acid (nūklē´ik) *n.* either of two complex organic acids forming part of nucleoproteins.
nuclein (nū´kliin) *n.* the protein forming the chief constituent of cell nuclei.
nucleo- (nū´kliō) *comb. form* of or relating to a nucleus. [L, from *nucula*, dim. of *nux nucis*, a nut]
nucleolus (nūkliō´ləs) *n.* (*pl.* **nucleoli** (-lī)) (*Biol.*) a nucleus of or within another nucleus. **nucleolar, nucleolated** (-əlātid) *a.*
nucleon (nū´klion) *n.* (*Physics*) a proton or neutron. **nucleonic** *a.*
nucleonics (nūklion´iks) *n.* the science of the nucleus of the atom.
nucleoprotein (nūkliōprō´tēn) *n.* a complex of nucleic acid and protein.
nucleoside (nū´kliəsīd) *n.* an organic compound containing a purine or pyrimidine base linked to a sugar.
nucleosynthesis (nūkliōsin´thisis) *n.* (*Astron.*) the cosmic formation of heavier elements from lighter by nuclear fusion.
nucleotide (nū´kliətīd) *n.* an organic compound containing a nucleoside linked to a phosphate group.
nucleus (nū´kliəs) *n.* (*pl.* **nuclei** (-ī)) **1** a central part about which aggregation, accretion or growth goes on. **2** a kernel. **3** (*Physics*) the charged centre of an atom consisting of protons and neutrons. **4** (*Biol.*) the central body in an ovule, seed, cell etc., constituting the organ of vitality, growth, or other functions. **5** a mass of grey matter in the central nervous system. **6** (*fig.*) a centre of growth, development, activity etc. **7** (*Astron.*) the brightest part of the head of a comet. **nucleal** *a.* [L, from *nucula*, dim. of *nux nucis*, a nut]
nuclide (nū´klīd) *n.* (*Physics*) a kind of atom characterized by a specific number of protons and neutrons. **nuclidic** (-klid´-) *a.*
nucule (nū´kūl) *n.* a small nut or nutlike fruit or seed. [F, from L *nucula*, see NUCLEUS]
nuddy (nŭd´i) *n.* (*coll.*) a state of nudity. **in the nuddy** naked. [jocular alteration of NUDE]
nude (nūd) *a.* **1** bare, naked, uncovered, unclothed. **2** (*Law*) made without any consideration and consequently void. *~n.* **1** an undraped figure in painting or sculpture. **2** a naked person. **the nude** the undraped human figure or the state of being undraped. **nudely** *adv.* **nudeness** *n.* **nudism** *n.* the practice of going naked on beaches and other specially designated areas. **nudist** *n.* **nudity** *n.* [L *nūdus*]
nudge (nŭj) *v.t.* **1** to push gently, esp. with the elbow. **2** to draw attention or give a hint with, or as if with, such a push. *~n.* such a push. **nudge-nudge** *int.* (*coll.*) used to suggest some secret or underhand behaviour, esp. sexual. **nudger** *n.* [etym. uncertain]
nudi- (nū´di) *comb. form* bare, naked. [L *nudus*, nude]
nudibranch (nū´dibrangk) *n.* a mollusc of the order Nudibranchia, characterized by naked gills or the absence of a shell. *~a.* of or relating to the Nudibranchia. **nudibranchiate** (-brang´kiət) *a., n.* [Gr. *branchia*, gills]
nudism, nudist etc. NUDE.
nuée ardente (nūā ahdont´) *n.* (*Geol.*) a hot cloud of ash, gas and lava fragments ejected from a volcano. [F, lit., a burning cloud]
nuevo sol (nwāvō sol´) *n.* the standard unit of currency of Peru. [Sp., a new sol]
nugae (nū´gē, -jē) *n.pl.* trifles, esp. literary compositions of a trifling kind. [L]
nugatory (nū´gətəri) *a.* **1** trifling, insignificant, futile. **2** ineffective, inoperative. [L *nugatorius*, via *nugari*, to trifle, from *nugae*, trifles]
nuggar (nŭg´ə) *n.* a broad, strongly built boat used on the upper Nile. [Arab. *nuggar*]
nugget (nŭg´it) *n.* **1** a lump of native metal, esp. of gold. **2** a lump of anything. **3** something small but valuable. [etym. uncertain]
nuisance (nū´səns) *n.* **1** anything that annoys, irritates or troubles. **2** an offensive or disagreeable person, action, experience etc. **3** (*Law*) anything causing annoyance, inconvenience or injury to another. **nuisance value** *n.* the capacity to cause irritation, obstruction etc. [OF, from *nuire*, L *nocēre*, to injure]
NUJ *abbr.* National Union of Journalists.
nuke (nūk) *n.* (*coll.*) a nuclear weapon. *~v.t.* to attack with nuclear weapons. [from *nuclear*]
null (nŭl) *a.* **1** having no legal force or validity. **2** non-existent. **3** (*fig.*) without character, expression, or individuality. **4** (*Math., Logic*) amounting to nothing, equal to zero, nil. **5** (*Comput.*) having no elements or only elements which are zeros. *~n.* a dummy letter in a cipher. **null and void** having no legal force or validity. **null character** *n.* (*Comput.*) a character, usu. a zero, which represents nothing. **null hypothesis** *n.* in statistics, a hypothesis which suggests that the difference between samples does not mean that there is a difference between populations. **null instrument, null indicator** *n.* an instrument for measuring an electrical quantity by making adjustments until a reading of zero is obtained. **null link** *n.* (*Comput.*) a reference indicating that an item is the last item in a list. [OF *nul, nulle*, L *nullum*, nom. *-lus* (*ne*, not, *ullus*, any)]
nullah (nŭl´ə) *n.* (*Ang.-Ind.*) a ravine, gully or watercourse. [Hind. *nālā*]
nulla-nulla (nŭl´ənŭl´ə), **nulla** *n.* (*pl.* **nulla-nullas, nullas**) a club-shaped weapon of hard wood used by the Australian Aborigines. [Dharuk *ngalla-ngalla*]
nullifidian (nŭlifid´iən) *n.* a person who has no religion. *~a.* having no religion. [L *nulli-*, *nullus*, (see NULL) *fidēs*, faith]
nullify (nŭl´ifī) *v.t.* (*3rd pers. sing. pres.* **nullifies,** *pres.p.* **nullifying,** *past, p.p.* **nullified**) **1** to make void. **2** to cancel. **3** to annul, to invalidate. **nullification** (-fikā´shən) *n.* **nullifier** *n.* [late L *nullificāre* (L *nulli-*, *nullus*, *-ficāre*, *facere*, to make)]
nullipara (nŭlip´ərə) *n.* a woman who has never given birth to a child. **nulliparous** *a.* [L *parēre*, to bring forth]
nullipore (nŭl´ipaw) *n.* a seaweed with calcareous fronds. [L *nullus* (see NULL), PORE[1]]
nullity (nŭl´iti) *n.* (*pl.* **nullities**) **1** invalidity. **2** an invalid act, instrument, etc. **3** nothingness, non-existence. **4** a nonentity, a mere cipher.
NUM *abbr.* National Union of Mineworkers.
Num. *abbr.* (*Bible*) Numbers.
numb (nŭm) *a.* **1** deprived of sensation and motion. **2** torpid, stupefied, dulled. *~v.t.* to benumb, to paralyse. **numb-fish** *n.* (*pl. in general* **numb-fish,** *in particular* **numb-fishes**) the electric ray. **numbly** *adv.* **numbness** *n.* [earlier, *num*, OE *numen*, p.p. of *niman*, to take (*b* excrescent, cp. NIMBLE)]
numbat (nŭm´bat) *n.* a small marsupial, *Myrmecobius*

fasciatus, of Australia, with a bushy tail. [Nyungar *numbad*]

number (nŭm´bə) *n.* **1** a measure of discrete quantity. **2** a name or symbol representing any such quantity, a numeral. **3** a sum or aggregate of people, things or abstract units. **4** one of a numbered series, for example a single issue of a periodical, one of the parts of a literary or other work so issued, a division of an opera etc. **5** numerical reckoning. **6** arithmetic. **7** (*often pl.*) poetical measure, verse, rhythm. **8** (*usu. pl.*) plurality, multitude, numerical preponderance. **9** (*Gram.*) the distinctive form of a word used to denote unity or plurality. **10** a song or piece of music forming part of a popular musician's act or repertoire. **11** a group of friends or associates (*one of our number*). **12** (*coll.*) a person or thing as specified (*a nifty little number*). **13** (*sl.*) a position or job, esp. an advantageous or lucrative one. *~v.t.* **1** to count, to reckon; to ascertain the number of. **2** to amount to. **3** to assign a number to, to distinguish with a number. **4** to include, to comprise (among etc.). **5** to have lived (a specified number of years). **a number of** several. **any number of 1** any particular number of. **2** (*coll.*) a large quantity of. **by numbers** performed in simple stages, esp. with each one numbered. **in round numbers** ROUND. **one's days are numbered** one will not live much longer. **one's number is up** (*coll.*) one is going to die. **to have someone's number** (*coll.*) to understand someone's intentions, motives or character. **to have someone's number on it** (of a bullet or bomb) to be destined to hit someone. **without number** too many to be counted. **number cruncher** *n.* (*sl.*) a computer capable of large-scale processing of numbered information. **number crunching** *n.* **numberer** *n.* **numberless** *a.* too many to be counted. **number one** *n.* **1** the first in a series. **2** (*coll.*) oneself. **3** (*coll.*) the most senior person in an organization. **4** (*coll.*) the product which is at the top of a sales chart, esp. a pop record. *~a.* most important. **number plate** *n.* the plate on a motor vehicle showing its registration number. **Numbers** *n.* the fourth book of the Old Testament, giving an account of the two censuses of the Israelites. **numbers game** *n.* **1** (*derog.*) the act or practice of considering only the numerical aspects of a situation. **2** (*N Am.*) a type of lottery based on a certain combination of numbers occurring in race results. **Number Ten** *n.* 10 Downing Street, the British Prime Minister's residence. **number two** *n.* a deputy. [OF *nombre, numbre*, L *numerum*, nom. *-rus*, cogn. with Gr. *nemein*, to distribute]

Usage note Although singular in form, *number* is usually treated as a plural in uses such as *A number (of them) are staying.*

---

numbles (nŭm´bəlz) *n.pl.* certain inner parts of a deer used as food. [OF *nombles*, prob. var. of *lombles*, L *lumbulus*, dim. of *lumbus*, loin]

numbskull NUMSKULL.

numdah (nŭm´də) *n.* an embroidered felt rug from India etc. [Hind. *namdā*]

numen (nū´mən) *n.* (*pl.* **numina** (-minə)) a deity or spirit presiding over a place. [L *numen, -minis*, divinity]

numeral (nū´mərəl) *n.* a word, symbol or group of symbols denoting number. *~a.* of, relating to, consisting of or denoting number. **numerable** *a.* **numerably** *adv.* **numerally** *adv.* **numerary** *a.* of or relating to numbers. **numerical** (-mer´i-), **numeric** *a.* of or relating to numbers. **numerical analysis** *n.* the branch of mathematics dealing with developing numerical methods for problem-solving. **numerically** *adv.* [late L *numerālis*]

numerate[1] (nū´mərət) *a.* able to count; competent in mathematics. **numeracy** (-əsi) *n.*

numerate[2] (nū´mərāt) *v.t.* to reckon, to number. **numeration** (-ā´shən) *n.* **numerator** *n.* **1** the part of a vulgar fraction written above the line indicating how many fractional parts are taken. **2** a person who numbers.

numeric NUMERAL.

numerology (nūmərol´əji) *n.* the study of the alleged significance of numbers. **numerological** (-loj´-) *a.* **numerologist** *n.*

numerous (nū´mərəs) *a.* **1** many in number. **2** consisting of a great number of individuals. **3** rhythmical, musical, harmonious. **numerously** *adv.* **numerousness** *n.*

numina NUMEN.

numinous (nū´minəs) *a.* **1** of or relating to divinity. **2** feeling awe of the divine. [L *numen*, divinity]

numismatic (nūmizmat´ik) *a.* of or relating to coins or medals. **numismatically** *adv.* **numismatics, numismatology** (-mətol´-) *n.* the science or study of coins and medals. **numismatist** (-miz´-), **numismatologist** (-mətol´-) *n.* [F *numismatique*, L *numismat-*, stem of *numisma*, Gr. *nomisma*, from *nomizein*, to practise, to have in current use]

nummary (nŭm´əri) *a.* of or relating to coins. **nummular** (-ū-), **nummulary** *a.* of, relating to or resembling coins. **nummulated** *a.* coin-shaped. **nummulation** (-ā´shən) *n.* the arrangement of the blood corpuscles like piles of coins. [L *nummārius*, from *nummus*, a coin]

nummulite (nŭm´ūlīt) *n.* a fossil foraminifer resembling a coin. **nummuline** (-līn), **nummulitic** (-lit´-) *a.*

numnah (nŭm´nə) *n.* a fabric or sheepskin pad placed under a saddle to prevent chafing. [Urdu *namdā*, see NUMDAH]

numskull (nŭm´skŭl), **numbskull** *n.* a stupid person. **numskulled** *a.*

nun (nŭn) *n.* **1** a woman devoted to a religious life and living in a convent under certain vows, usu. of poverty, chastity and obedience. **2** a variety of pigeon with a black-and-white plumage. **3** a male smew. **4** the blue titmouse. **nunhood** (-hud), **nunship** *n.* **nunlike** *a.* **nunnery** *n.* (*pl.* **nunneries**) a religious home for nuns. **nunnish** *a.* **nun's cloth** *n.* a variety of bunting used as material for dresses etc. **Nuns of the Visitation** *n.pl.* in the Roman Catholic Church, the order of Visitants. **nun's veiling** *n.* nun's cloth. [OE *nunne*, late L *nonna*, fem. of *nonnus*, a monk, orig. a title of address to old people]

nunatak (nŭn´ətak) *n.* a mountain peak which projects through an ice sheet. [Eskimo (Inuit)]

nun-buoy (nŭn´boi) *n.* a buoy shaped like two cones united at the base. [obs. *nun* (perh. from NUNATAK), a spinning top, BUOY]

Nunc Dimittis (nŭngk dimit´is) *n.* the canticle 'Lord, now lettest thou thy servant depart in peace' (Luke ii.29). [L, now lettest thou depart]

nuncio (nŭn´siō, -shiō) *n.* (*pl.* **nuncios**) a papal envoy or ambassador to a foreign power. **nunciature** (-shətūə) *n.* [It., from L *nuncius*, a messenger]

nuncupate (nŭng´kūpāt) *v.t.* to declare (a will, vow etc.) orally, rather than in writing. **nuncupation** (-ā´shən) *n.* **nuncupative** (nung´kūpətiv) *a.* oral, not written. [L *nuncupātus*, p.p. of *nuncupāre* (*nōmen*, a name, *capere*, to take)]

nundinal (nŭn´dinəl) *a.* of or relating to fairs or markets. [L *nundinālis*, from *nundinae*, pl., a market day (*novem*, nine, *dies*, a day)]

nunnation (nŭnā´shən) *n.* the addition of final *n* to words, in the declension of Arabic nouns etc. [Arab. *nun*, the letter *n*, -ATION]

nunnery, nunnish NUN.

NUPE (nū´pi) *abbr.* (*Hist.*) National Union of Public Employees.

Nupe (noo´pā) *n.* (*pl.* **Nupe, Nupes**) **1** a member of a

Negroid people of West Central Nigeria. 2 the language of the Nupe. ~*a.* of or relating to the Nupe or their language.

nuphar (nū´fah) *n.* the yellow water lily, of the genus *Nuphar.* [NENUPHAR]

nuptial (nŭp´shəl) *a.* of or relating to a wedding. **nuptial flight** *n.* (*Zool.*) the flight of a virgin queen bee, during which she is impregnated. **nuptial plumage** *n.* (*Zool.*) the brightly coloured plumage developed by many male birds prior to the start of the breeding season. **nuptials** *n.pl.* a wedding. [F, from L *nuptiālis*, from *nuptiæ*, a wedding, from *nubere* (p.p. *nuptus*), to marry]

NUR *abbr.* National Union of Railwaymen.

nurd NERD.

nurdle (nœ´dəl) *v.i.* to score runs in cricket by gently pushing the ball with the bat.

nurl KNURL.

nurr KNUR.

nurse (nœs) *n.* 1 a person who tends to the sick, wounded or infirm. 2 (*Hist.*) a person employed to look after young children. 3 a wet-nurse. 4 a tree planted to protect another or others during growth. 5 (*Zool.*) a sexually imperfect bee, ant etc., which tends the young brood. 6 a person who or something which fosters or promotes. 7 the condition of being nursed (*at nurse*). 8 any of various sharks or dogfishes. ~*v.t.* 1 to look after (a sick person). 2 to treat (an illness or injury). 3 to suckle; to give suck to or feed (an infant). 4 to rear, to nurture. 5 to hold or clasp, esp. on one's knees or lap. 6 to foster, to tend, to promote growth in. 7 to cherish, to brood over. 8 to manage with care. 9 to be economical with. 10 in billiards, to keep (the balls) in a good position for cannons. ~*v.i.* 1 to be a nurse. 2 to suckle a baby. 3 (of a baby) to suck milk from the breast. **nurse hound** *n.* a large NE Atlantic dogfish, *Scyliorhinus stellaris.* **nursemaid** *n.* 1 a woman in charge of young children. 2 a person who is very nurturing or protective of another. **nurser** *n.* **nurse shark** *n.* a slow-moving, brownish, Atlantic shark, *Ginglymostoma cirratum.* **nursing** *n.* the act of nursing or the profession of being a nurse. ~*a.* of or relating to nursing (*nursing staff*). **nursing-chair** *n.* a low chair without arms, used when feeding a baby. **nursing home** *n.* a private hospital or home where care is provided for the elderly or chronically ill. **nursing officer** *n.* any of several grades of nurse having administrative duties. **nursling** (-ling), **nurseling** *n.* an infant that is being breast-fed. [ME and OF *norice*, late L *nūtricia*, fem. of *nūtricius*, from *nūtrix -īcis*, from *nūtrīre*, to nourish]

nursery (nœ´səri) *n.* (*pl.* **nurseries**) 1 a room set apart for young children. 2 a day nursery or nursery school. 3 a place or garden for rearing plants. 4 the place, sphere or condition in which persons, qualities etc. are bred or fostered. 5 in billiards, grouped balls. 6 a place where animal life is developed. 7 nursery stakes. **nursery cannon** *n.* in billiards, a cannon on three close balls. **nursery-governess** *n.* a woman or girl in charge of young children, usu. combining the duties of a nurse and a teacher. **nurserymaid** *n.* a servant who looks after a children's nursery. **nurseryman** *n.* (*pl.* **nurserymen**) a man who raises plants in a nursery. **nursery rhyme** *n.* a traditional rhyme for children. **nursery school** *n.* a school for young children aged three to five. **nursery slopes** *n.pl.* gentle ski slopes set apart for novices. **nursery stakes** *n.pl.* a race for two-year-old horses.

nursing, nursling NURSE.

nurture (nœ´chə) *n.* 1 the act of bringing up, training, fostering. 2 nourishment. 3 education, breeding. ~*v.t.* 1 to nourish. 2 to rear, to train, to educate. **nurturer** *n.* [A-F, from OF *nourture, nourriture*, L *nūtrītūra*, from *nūtrīre*, to NOURISH]

NUS *abbr.* 1 (*Hist.*) National Union of Seamen. 2 National Union of Students.

☒ **nusance** common misspelling of NUISANCE.

NUT *abbr.* National Union of Teachers.

nut (nŭt) *n.* 1 the indehiscent fruit of certain trees, containing a kernel in a hard shell. 2 the kernel itself. 3 a pod containing hard seeds. 4 a metal block with a hole for screwing on and securing a bolt, screw etc. 5 a screw fitted to a violin bow, for adjusting tension. 6 the ridge on the neck of stringed instruments over which the strings pass to the tuning pegs. 7 any of various parts of machinery, usu. one in which a screw works. 8 (*sl.*) the head. 9 (*sl.*) **a** a crazy or eccentric person. **b** a fanatic (*a martial-arts nut*). 10 a small lump of coal. 11 (*pl., taboo, sl.*) testicles. ~*v.i.* (*pres.p.* **nutting,** *past, p.p.* **nutted**) to gather nuts. ~*v.t.* (*sl.*) to head-butt. **can't do something for nuts** (*coll.*) am/are/is very bad at doing something (*he can't dance for nuts*). **nuts and bolts** (*coll.*) the basic essential facts. **off one's nut** 1 (*sl.*) mad. 2 (*sl.*) drunk. **to do one's nut** (*sl.*) to become very angry. **nut brown** *n., a.* (of) a dark reddish-brown colour. **nut-brown** *a.* dark reddish-brown. **nut butter** *n.* a substitute for butter, extracted from the oil of nuts. **nutcase** *n.* (*sl.*) a crazy or eccentric person. **nutcracker** *n.* 1 (*usu. pl.*) an instrument for cracking nuts. 2 a crow of the genus *Nucifraga.* ~*a.* denoting a nose and chin that tend to meet. **nut cutlet** *n.* a preparation of crushed nuts etc., eaten by vegetarians as a substitute for meat. **nutgall** *n.* an oak gall, used in dyeing. **nuthatch** *n.* any small bird of the genus *Sitta*, allied to the woodpecker, esp. *S. europaea.* **nuthouse** *n.* (*sl.*) a psychiatric hospital. **nutlet** (-lit) *n.* **nutlike** *a.* **nut oil** *n.* oil obtained from hazelnuts, walnuts or other nuts. **nut pine** *n.* either of two varieties of pine of the genus *Pinus*, bearing nutlike edible seeds. **nuts** *a.* (*sl.*) crazy, eccentric. ~*int.* (*sl.*) used to express contempt or defiance. **to be nuts about** (*coll.*) to delight in; to be very fond of. **to be nuts on** to be nuts about. **nutshell** *n.* the hard shell enclosing the kernel of a nut. **in a nutshell** expressed in a very concise statement. **nutter** *n.* (*sl.*) a crazy or eccentric person. **nut tree** *n.* a tree bearing nuts, esp. a hazel. **nutty** *a.* (*comp.* **nuttier,** *superl.* **nuttiest**) 1 full of nuts. 2 tasting like nuts. 3 (*sl.*) crazy, eccentric. **nutty about** very fond of or enthusiastic about. **nutty on** nutty about. **nuttiness** *n.* **nut-weevil** *n.* a beetle infesting nuts, esp. *Curculio nucum*, which lays eggs in green hazelnuts etc. **nut-wrench** *n.* a spanner. [OE *hnutu* (cp. Dut. *noot*, G *Nuss*, Icel. *hnot*)]

nutate (nūtāt´) *v.i.* to nod, to bend forward, to droop. **nutant** (nū´-) *a.* (*Bot.*) drooping, hanging with the apex downwards. **nutation** (-ā´shən) *n.* 1 a nodding or oscillation. 2 a movement of the tips of growing plants, usu. towards the sun. 3 (*Astron.*) a periodical oscillation of the earth's axis due to the attractive influence of the sun and moon on the greater mass round the equator. 4 (*Med.*) morbid oscillation of the head. [L *nūtātus*, p.p. of *nūtāre*, freq. of *nuere* (in *abnuere*), to nod]

nutmeg (nŭt´meg) *n.* 1 an evergreen tree, *Myristica fragrans*, whose hard aromatic seed is used for flavouring and in medicine. 2 the seed of the nutmeg, often used grated in cookery. **nutmeg-apple** *n.* the pear-shaped fruit of the nutmeg tree. **nutmeggy** *a.* [ME *notemuge* (NUT, OF *muge, mugue*, in *noix mugue* or *muguede*, med. L *nux muscāta*, a musklike nut)]

nutria (nū´triə) *n.* 1 the coypu. 2 its skin or fur, formerly frequently used in hat-making. [Sp., from L *lutra*, otter]

nutrient (nū´triənt) *n.* a nutritious substance. ~*a.* nourishing; serving as or conveying nourishment. **nutriment** *n.* 1 any substance which nourishes or promotes growth, esp. food. 2 an intellectual stimulus. **nutrimental** (-men´-) *a.* **nutrition** (-trish´-) *n.* 1 the function or process of promoting the growth of organic bodies. **2** nourishment, food. **3** the study of nutrition. **nutritional** *a.* **nutritionally** *adv.* **nutritionist** *n.* **nutritious** *a.* affording nourishment, efficient as food. **nutritiously** *adv.* **nutritiousness** *n.* **nutritive** *a., n.* **nutritively** *adv.* [L *nūtriens -ntem*, pres.p. of *nūtrīre*, to nourish]

nuts, nutter etc. NUT.

nux vomica (nŭks vom´ikə) *n.* **1** a S Asian tree, *Strychnos nux-vomica.* **2** the seed of the nux vomica, which yields strychnine. [med. L *nux*, a nut, *vomere*, to VOMIT]

nuzzle (nŭz´əl) *v.t.* **1** to rub or press the nose against. **2** to fondle. **3** to root up with the nose. ~*v.i.* **1** to root about with the nose. **2** to nestle, to hide the head, as a child in its mother's bosom. [NOSE, -LE[1]]

NV *abbr.* Nevada.

NVQ *abbr.* National Vocational Qualification.

NW *abbr.* **1** north-west. **2** north-western.

NY *abbr.* New York.

nyala (nyah´lə), **inyala** (inyah´) *n.* (*pl.* **nyala, inyala**) a large S African antelope, *Tragelaphus angasi*, with spiral horns. [Zulu]

NYC *abbr.* New York City.

nyctalopia (niktəlō´piə), **nyctalopy** (nik´təlōpi) *n.* (*Med.*) a disease of the eyes in which vision is worse in shade or twilight than in daylight, night-blindness. [late L *nyctalopia*, from Gr. *nuktalōps* (*nukti-*, *nux*, night, *alaos*, blind, *ōps*, eye)]

nyctitropic (niktitrōp´ik) *a.* (*Bot.*) (of leaves) changing position or direction at night. **nyctitropism** (-tit´-) *n.* [Gr. *tropos*, a turn]

nyctophobia (niktəfō´biə) *n.* a morbid fear of darkness.

†nye NIDE.

nylghau NILGAI.

nylon (nī´lən) *n.* **1** any of various thermoplastics, used largely for tights, shirts, dress fabrics, imitation furs, ropes, brushes etc. **2** a nylon fabric. **3** (*pl.*) nylon stockings. ~*a.* made of nylon. [arbitrary, after *cotton* etc.]

nymph (nimf) *n.* **1** any one of a class of mythological youthful female divinities inhabiting groves, springs, mountains, the sea etc. **2** (*poet.*) a beautiful or attractive young woman. **3** a pupa or chrysalis. **nymphae** (-ē) *n.pl.* (*Anat.*) LABIA MINORA (under LABIUM). **nymphean** (-fē´ən), **nymphal** *a.* **nymphet** (nim´fet) *n.* a young girl who is very sexually attractive and precocious. **nymphish, nymphlike** *a.* [F *nymphe*, L *nympha*, Gr. *numphē*, a bride]

nymphalid (nimfal´id) *a.* of or relating to the family Nymphalidae of butterflies. ~*n.* a butterfly of the family Nymphalidae. [mod. L genus name *Nymphalis*, from L *nympha*, a NYMPH]

nympho (nim´fō) *n.* (*pl.* **nymphos**) (*coll.*) a nymphomaniac.

nympholepsy (nim´fəlepsi) *n.* **1** a state of ecstasy or frenzy supposed to affect someone who has gazed on a nymph. **2** (*fig.*) a wild desire for the unattainable. **nympholept** *n.* **nympholeptic** (-lep´-) *a.*

nymphomania (nimfəmā´niə) *n.* excessive sexual desire in a woman. **nymphomaniac** (-ak) *n., a.* **nymphomaniacal** (-mənī´ə-) *a.*

nystagmus (nistag´məs) *n.* a spasmodic movement of the eyeballs, a condition affecting miners and others working in a dim light. **nystagmic** *a.* [Gr. *nustagmos*, a nodding, from *nustazein*, to nod, to be sleepy]

nystatin (nī´stətin) *n.* an antibiotic used for fungal infections. [*New York State* (where it originated), -IN[1]]

Nyungar (nyung´ə) *n.* an extinct Aboriginal language of SW Australia.

NZ *abbr.* New Zealand.

O[1] (ō), **o** (*pl.* **Os, O's**) the 15th letter of the English and other versions of the Roman alphabet, corresponding to the Greek omicron (O, o). It has four principal sounds: (1) low, back and short, as in *pot*, unmarked in this dictionary, o; (2) this raised and lengthened historically by a following *r*, as in *or*, marked aw; (3) as a rising diphthong, as in *go*, marked ō; (4) mid, central and short, as in *glove*, marked ŭ. In unstressed ~syllables *o* is often obscured, as in *bacon, tailor*, marked ə. In conjunction with other vowels *o* also represents a variety of sounds, as in *boat, foetus, join, pour* etc. ~*symbol* a blood type in the ABO system. ~*n.* **1** an O-shaped thing or mark. **2** a circle, oval, or any round or nearly round shape. **3** a nought, nothing, zero. **O-ring** *n.* a rubber ring used as a seal.

O[2] *chem. symbol* oxygen. [prob. from L]

O[3], **o** *abbr.* **1** ocean. **2** octavo. **3** (**O**) Ohio. **4** ohm. **5** old. **6** only. **7** order. **8** ordinary. **O grade** *n.* ORDINARY GRADE (under ORDINARY). **O level** *n.* ORDINARY LEVEL (under ORDINARY).

O[4] (ō), **oh** *int.* an exclamation of earnest or solemn address, entreaty, invocation, pain, surprise, wonder etc. **oh boy!** BOY. **oh well** used to express resignation. **o/ oh for** FOR. [prob. from L]

O' (ō) *pref.* descendant of, in Irish surnames. [Ir. *ó, ua*, descendant]

o' (ō, ə) *prep.* (*coll. or dial.*) of, on.

o- (ō) *pref.* (*Chem.*) ortho-.

-o (ō) *suf.* (*coll.*) **1** serving as a diminutive, as in *cheapo, wino.* **2** forming an interjection, as in *cheerio, righto.*

-o- (ō) *suf.* used as the terminal vowel in combining forms, as in *Russo-, petro-.*

oaf (ōf) *n.* (*pl.* **oafs**) **1** a silly, stupid person, a lout. **2** †a silly child supposedly left by fairies in place of one taken by them. **oafish** *a.* **oafishly** *adv.* **oafishness** *n.* [var. of obs. *auf*, Icel. *ālfr*, ELF]

oak (ōk) *n.* **1** (*also* **oak tree**) any tree or shrub of the genus *Quercus*, esp. *Q. robur*, a forest tree much valued for its timber. **2** the wood of this. **3** any tree of the Australian genus *Casuarina.* **4** any of various trees and plants bearing a real or fancied resemblance to the oak. ~*a.* made of oak. **the Oaks** a race for three-year-old fillies, named after an estate at Epsom. **oak-apple** *n.* a gall or excrescence of various kinds produced on oaks by various gall-flies. **Oak-apple Day** *n.* 29 May, the anniversary of the escape of Charles II at Boscobel in 1651. **oaken** *a.* of the wood of the oak. **oak-fern** *n.* a slender, three-branched polypody, *Thelypteris dryopteris.* **oak-gall** *n.* OAK-APPLE (under OAK). **oak-leather** *n.* a tough fungus growing on old oaks. **oakling** *n.* a young oak. **oak-nut** *n.* OAK-APPLE (under OAK). **oaky** *a.* **1** full of oaks. **2** like oak. [OE *āc* (cp. Dut. and Icel. *eik*, G *Eiche*)]

oakum (ō´kəm) *n.* old rope, untwisted and pulled into loose fibres, used for caulking seams, stopping leaks etc. in ships. [OE *ācumba*, tow, lit. combings (*ā-*, *æ-*, off, *cemban*, to comb)]

O. & M. *abbr.* organization and method(s).

OAP *abbr.* old age pensioner, old age pension.

oar (aw) *n.* **1** a long pole with a flattened blade, for rowing, sculling or steering a boat. **2** a rower. **3** anything resembling an oar in form or function, such as a fin, wing or arm used in swimming etc. ~*v.i.* to row. ~*v.t.* to propel by or as by rowing. **to lay on one's oars** (*NAm.*) to rest on one's oars. **to lie on one's oars** to rest on one's oars. **to put one's oar in** **1** to intrude into a conversation. **2** to interfere, esp. with unasked-for advice. **to rest on one's oars** **1** to cease rowing without shipping the oars. **2** to stop for rest, to cease working. **to stick one's oar in** to put one's oar in. **oarage** (-rij) *n.* **1** oars collectively. **2** rowing movement. **oared** *a.* having oars. **oarfish** *n.* (*pl. in general* **oarfish**, *in particular* **oarfishes**) a ribbonfish, *Regalecus glesne.* **oarless** *a.* **oarlike** *a.* **oarlock** *n.* (*NAm.*) a rowlock. **oarsman, oarswoman** *n.* (*pl.* **oarsmen, oarswomen**) a (skilled) rower. **oarsmanship** *n.* **oarweed, oreweed** *n.* any large marine alga, esp. of the genus *Laminaria.* **oary** *a.* having the form or use of oars. [OE *ār*, (cp. Icel. *-ār*, Dan. *aare*), perh. rel. to Gr. *eretēs*, rower]

OAS *abbr.* **1** on active service. **2** *Organisation de l'Armée Secrète* (violently opposed to Algerian independence, 1961–3). **3** Organization of American States.

oasis (ōā´sis) *n.* (*pl.* **oases** (-sēz)) **1** a fertile spot in a waste or desert. **2** a thing or place offering peace, pleasure, refuge etc. **Oasis®** *n.* in flower arranging, a soft, porous material into which cut flowers, foliage etc. are inserted. [L and Gr., prob. from Egypt. (cp. Copt. *ouahe*, from *ouīh*, to dwell)]

oast (ōst) *n.* a kiln for drying hops. **oast house** *n.* [OE *āst* (cp. Dut. *eest*), rel. to L *aestus*, heat, *aedes*, house, Gr. *aithos*, heat]

oat (ōt) *n.* **1** (*usu. in pl.*) a cereal plant of the genus *Avena*, esp. *A. sativa.* **2** (*pl.*) the grain of this, used for food. **3** any related grass, esp. the wild oat, *A. fatua.* **4** (*poet.*) a musical pipe made from an oat-stem. **5** pastoral, bucolic poetry or song. **6** (*pl., sl.*) sexual gratification. **off one's oats** (*coll.*) off one's food; without appetite. **to feel one's oats** (*coll.*) to feel vitality or be full of self-esteem. **to get one's oats** (*sl.*) to have regular sexual intercourse. **to sow one's (wild) oats** to indulge in youthful (esp. sexual) excess. **oatcake** *n.* a flat cake or biscuit made from oatmeal. **oaten** *a.* **oat-grass** *n.* any of various grasses, esp. of the genus *Arrhenatherum* or *Helictotrichon.* **oatmeal** *n.* **1** oats ground into meal, used chiefly for making porridge or oatcakes. **2** a fawny-grey colour (as of porridge). ~*a.* of this colour. **oaty** *a.* [OE *āte*]

oath (ōth) *n.* (*pl.* **oaths** (ōdhz)) **1** a solemn appeal to God or some holy or revered person or thing, in witness of the truth of a statement or of the binding nature of a promise, esp. in a court of law. **2** the form of an oath. **3** a profane imprecation or expletive, a curse. **4** a swear word. **on/ under/ upon oath** **1** sworn to attesting the truth. **2** pledged or attested by oath. **3** having taken an oath. **to swear an oath** to take an oath. **to take an oath** to swear formally to the truth of one's attestations. **oathable** *a.* (*Shak.*) capable of taking an oath. **oath-breaking** *n.* (*Shak.*) perjury. [OE *āth* (cp. Dut. *eed*, G *Eid*, Icel. *eithr*, OHG *Eit*)]

OAU *abbr.* Organization of African Unity.

OB *abbr.* **1** old boy. **2** outside broadcast.

ob. *abbr.* **1** *obiit*, he/she died. **2** *obiter*, incidentally, in passing. **3** oboe.

ob- (ob) *pref.* **1** toward, to, meeting, in, facing, as in *obvious.* **2** against, opposing, hindering, resisting, hostile, as in *obstinate*. **3** reversely, obversely, contrary to the normal, as in *obovate*. [L, in the way of, against]

Obad. *abbr.* Obadiah.

obang (ō´bang) *n.* an oblong gold coin formerly current in Japan. [Jap. *ōban*, great sheet]

obbligato (obligah´tō), **obligato** *a.* (*Mus.*) **1** not to be omitted. **2** indispensable to the whole. ~*n.* (*pl.* **obbligatos, obligatos, obbligati** (-tē), **obligati**) an instrumental part or accompaniment that forms an integral part of the composition or is independently important (usu. by a single instrument). [It., from L *obligātus*, p.p. of *obligāre*, to OBLIGE]

obconic (obkon´ik), **obconical** (-ikəl) *a.* (*Bot.*) inversely conical.

obcordate (obkaw´dāt) *a.* inversely heart-shaped.

obdurate (ob´dūrət) *a.* **1** stubborn. **2** hardened in heart, esp. against moral influence. **3** impenitent. ~*v.t.* to make obdurate. **obduracy, obdurateness** *n.* **obdurately** *adv.* **obduration** (-rā´shən) *n.* [L *obdūrātus*, p.p. of *obdūrāre* (OB-, *dūrāre*, to harden, from *dūrus*, hard)]

OBE *abbr.* Officer of (the Order of) the British Empire.

obeah (ō´biə), **obi** (ō´bi) *n.* **1** a form of sorcery practised by blacks, esp. in the W Indies. **2** a magical charm. **obiman, obiwoman** *n.* (*pl.* **obimen, obiwomen**) an expert practitioner in obeah. [W Afr.]

obedience (əbēd´yəns) *n.* **1** the act or practice of obeying. **2** dutiful submission to authority. **3** compliance with law, command or direction. **4** the authority of a Church or other body. **5** (*collect.*) those subject to such authority (e.g. a monastic order). **6** a written command or instruction from a religious superior. **in obedience to** in accordance with. **obedient** *a.* **obediential** (-ien´shəl) *a.* of or relating to obedience. **obedientiary** (-ien´shəri) *n.* (*pl.* **obedientiaries**) a member of, esp. a holder of office in, a monastery or convent, subject to obedience to the superior. **obediently** *adv.* [OF, from L *obēdientia*, from *obēdīre*, to OBEY]

obeisance (əbā´səns) *n.* **1** a bow, a curtsy, or any gesture signifying deference, submission, respect or salutation. **2** homage. **obeisant** *a.* **obeisantly** *adv.* [F *obéissance*, orig. obedience]

obeli OBELUS.

obelion (əbē´liən) *n.* the part of the skull between the two parietal foramina where the sagittal suture becomes simple.

obelisk (ob´əlisk) *n.* **1** a quadrangular stone shaft, usually monolithic and tapering, with a pyramidal apex. **2** an obelus. **obeliscal** (-lis´-), **obeliscoid** (-lis´koid) *a.* [L *obeliscus* from Gr. *obeliskos*, dim. of *obelos*, a spit]

obelus (ob´ələs) *n.* (*pl.* **obeli** (-lī)) **1** a mark (-, ÷, or †), used to mark spurious or doubtful passages in ancient manuscripts. **2** in printing, a dagger symbol (†) indicating a cross-reference, footnote or death date. **double obelus** DOUBLE[1]. **obelize, obelise** *v.t.* [L, from Gr. *obelos*, a spit; dim. *obeliskos*]

obese (əbēs´) *a.* excessively fat, fleshy, corpulent. **obeseness, obesity** *n.* [L *obēsus*, p.p. of *obedere* (OB-, *edere*, to eat)]

obex (ō´beks) *n.* **1** (*Anat.*) a band of white matter in the medulla oblongata. **2** an obstacle, an impediment. [L, cogn. with *obicere* (OB-, *jacere*, to cast)]

obey (ōbā´) *v.t.* **1** to perform or carry out (a command, instruction or direction). **2** to be obedient to. **3** to yield to the direction or control of. **4** to act according to. ~*v.i.* to do as one is directed or commanded. **obeyer** *n.* **obeyingly** *adv.* [F *obéir*, L *obēdīre* (OB-, *audīre*, to hear)]

obfuscate (ob´fəskāt) *v.t.* **1** to darken, to obscure. **2** to bewilder, to confuse. **obfuscation** (-kā´shən) *n.* **obfuscatory** *a.* [L *obfuscātus*, p.p. of *obfuscāre* (OB-, *fuscāre*, from *fuscus*, dark)]

obi[1] (ō´bi) *n.* (*pl.* **obi, obis**) a coloured sash worn around a Japanese kimono. [Jap. *obi*, belt]

obi[2] OBEAH.

obit (ob´it) *n.* **1** a memorial service or commemoration of a death. **2** (*coll.*) an obituary. **obitual** (əbit´-) *a.*

obiter (ob´itə) *adv.* incidentally, by the way. **obiter dictum** (dik´təm) *n.* (*pl.* **obiter dicta** (-tə)) **1** a passing remark. **2** a judge's personal opinion on a point of law, as distinct from the decision of a court. [L]

obituary (əbit´ūəri) *a.* relating to or recording a death or deaths. ~*n.* (*pl.* **obituaries**) **1** a notice of a death, usu. in the form of a short biography of the deceased. **2** a register or list of deaths. **obituarial** (-eə´riəl) *a.* **obituarily** *adv.* **obituarist** *n.* [OF, from L *obitus*, p.p. of *obīre*, to set, to die]

obj. *abbr.* objective.

object[1] (əbjekt´) *v.t.* **1** to oppose. **2** to offer or adduce in opposition. **3** to allege (a fact, usu. with *that*) in criticism, disapproval, or condemnation. ~*v.i.* **1** to make objections. **2** to be averse, to disapprove. [L *objectāre*, freq. of *objicere* (OB-, *jacere*, to throw)]

object[2] (ob´jikt) *n.* **1** anything presented to the senses or the mind, esp. anything visible or tangible. **2** a material thing. **3** that to which an action or feeling is directed; an aim, end, ultimate purpose. **4** a person or thing of pitiable or ridiculous appearance. **5** (*Gram.*) a noun, or word, phrase or sentence equivalent to a noun, governed by a transitive verb or preposition. **6** a thing or idea regarded as external to, distinct from, or independent of the subjective consciousness. **7** (*Comput.*) a package of information. **object-ball** *n.* in billiards etc., the ball at which a player aims with their cue ball. **object code, object program** *n.* a computer program which has been translated from a high-level language (source code) into machine code by an assembler or compiler program. **object-finder** *n.* **1** an eyepiece on a microscope for enabling one to locate the object on a slide. **2** an analogous instrument on a large telescope. **object-glass** *n.* the lens or combination of lenses at the end of an optical instrument nearest the object. **objectify** (-jek´tifī) *v.t.* (*3rd pers. sing. pres.* **objectifies,** *pres. p.* **objectifying,** *past, p.p.* **objectified**) **1** to render objective. **2** to present to the mind as a concrete or sensible reality. **objectification** (-fikā´shən) *n.* **objection** (-jek´-) *n.* **1** the act of objecting. **2** an adverse argument, reason or statement. **3** disapproval, dislike, or the expression of this. **objectionable** *a.* **1** liable to objection, reprehensible. **2** offensive, unpleasant. **objectionability** (-bil´-) *n.* **objectionableness** *n.* **objectionably** *adv.* **object language** *n.* **1** a language which is described by another language. **2** (*Comput.*) a language into which a program is translated. **objectless** *a.* **object lesson** *n.* **1** a practical illustration. **2** a lesson in which the actual object described or a representation of it is used for illustration. **object of the exercise** *n.* the purpose of a particular action or activity. **object of virtu** *n.* an object that is rare, old or beautiful. **objector** *n.* a person who objects. **object-soul** *n.* a primitive belief in the presence of a soul in inanimate objects. [med. L *objectum*, from L *objicere* (OB-, *jacere*, to throw)]

objective (objek´tiv) *a.* **1** proceeding from the object of knowledge or thought as opposed to the perceiving or thinking subject. **2** external, actual, real, self-existent, substantive. **3** of, relating to or concerned with outward things as distinct from the subjective. **4** uninfluenced by emotion, impulse, prejudice etc. **5** (*Gram.*) denoting the case of the object of a transitive verb or preposition; accusative. ~*n.* **1** an objective point, e.g. of military operations. **2** an aim, goal or target. **3** (*Gram.*) the objective case. **4** (*also* **objective lens**) an object-glass. **objectival** (objiktī´vəl) *a.* **objectively** *adv.* **objectiveness** *n.* **objectivism** *n.* **1** the tendency to give priority to what is objective. **2** the theory that stresses objective reality. **objectivist** *n.* **objectivistic** (-vis´-) *a.* **objectivity** (objiktiv´-) *n.* **objectivize, objectivise** *v.t., v.i.* **objectivization** (-zā´shən) *n.*

objet (ob´zhā) *n.* (*pl.* **objets** (-zhā)) an object. **objet d'art** (dah´) *n.* (*pl.* **objets d'art**) an art object. **objet trouvé** (troo´vā) *n.* (*pl.* **objets trouvés** (-vā)) a found object. [F]

objurgate (ob´jəgāt) *v.t., v.i.* to chide, to reprove. **objurgation** (-ā´shən) *n.* **objurgator** *n.* **objurgatory** *a.* [L *objurgātus*, p.p. of *objurgāre* (OB-, *jurgāre*, to chide)]

oblanceolate (oblan´siəlāt) *a.* (*Bot.*) inversely lanceolate.

oblast (ob´lahst) *n.* (*pl.* **oblasts, oblasti** (-sti)) an administrative district or province in the former Soviet Union. [Rus.]

oblate[1] (ob´lāt) *a.* (*Geom.*) flattened at the poles, as opposed to *prolate*. **oblately** *adv.* **oblateness** *n.* **oblate spheroid** *n.* such a sphere as is produced by the revolution of an ellipse about its shorter axis. [L *oblātus* (OB-, *lātus*, p.p. of *ferre*, to carry)]

oblate[2] (ob´lāt) *n.* a person not under vows but dedicated to monastic or religious life or work. **oblation** (-lā´shən) *n.* **1** the act of offering or anything offered in worship. **2** a sacrifice. **3** the presentation of the elements in the Eucharist. **4** a gift or donation to the Church. **oblational, oblatory** *a.* [as OBLATE[1]]

obligation (obligā´shən) *n.* **1** the binding power of a promise, contract, vow, duty, law etc. **2** a duty, responsibility, commitment. **3** (*Law*) a binding agreement, esp. one with a penal condition annexed. **of obligation** obligatory. **under an obligation** indebted for some benefit, favour or kindness. **obligant** (ob´-) *n.* **obligate**[1] (ob´ligāt) *v.t.* **1** to place under an obligation, legal or moral. **2** to compel. **3** (*N Am.*) to commit (assets) as security. **obligate**[2] (-gət) *a.* (*Biol.*) limited to a single mode of life. **obligator** *n.* **obligatory** (əblig´ə-) *a.* mandatory. **obligatorily** *adv.* [OF, from L *obligātiōnem*, nom. *-tio*, from *obligāre*, to oblige]

Usage note The meanings of the verbs *obligate* and *oblige* overlap, but *obligate* is usual for legal and moral binding, and *oblige* for other more general kinds of constraint or compulsion.

obligato OBBLIGATO.

oblige (əblīj´) *v.t.* **1** to bind or constrain by legal, moral or physical force. **2** to be binding on. **3** to place under a debt of gratitude by a favour or kindness. **4** to do a favour to, to gratify. **5** (*pass.*) to be under an obligation (to). *~v.i.* to perform a favour or task. **much obliged** used to express thanks. **obligee** (-jē´) *n.* **1** (*Law*) a person to whom another is obligated. **2** a person who is under an obligation for a favour. **obligement** *n.* a favour conferred. **obliger** *n.* **obliging** *a.* **1** kind, complaisant. **2** helpful, accommodating. **obligingly** *adv.* **obligingness** *n.* **obligor** (ob´ligaw) *n.* (*Law*) a person who is legally bound to another.

Usage note See note on obligate under OBLIGATION.

oblique (əblēk´) *a.* **1** slanting, deviating from the vertical or horizontal. **2** deviating from the straight or direct line, indirect, roundabout. **3** evasive, not to the point. **4** inclined at an angle other than a right angle. **5** (of an angle) acute or obtuse. **6** (*Anat.*) (of muscles etc.) slanting, neither parallel nor vertical to the longer axis of the body or limb. **7** (*Bot.*) (of leaves) unequal-sided. **8** of or relating to any grammatical cases other than the nominative or vocative. *~n.* **1** something that is at an angle or slanting, esp. a geometric figure, military advance, solidus etc. **2** an oblique muscle. *~v.i.* (*pres.p.* **obliquing,** *past, p.p.* **obliqued**) **1** (*Mil.*) to move forwards obliquely. **2** to slant. **oblique case** *n.* (*Gram.*) any case other than the nominative or vocative. **obliquely** *adv.* **oblique narration, oblique oration, oblique speech** *n.* indirect speech. **obliqueness** *n.* **obliquity** (əblik´wi-) *n.* (*pl.* **obliquities**) **1** obliqueness. **2** (an instance of) mental or moral deviation. [L *obliquus* (OB-, *liquis*, slanting]

obliterate (əblit´ərāt) *v.t.* **1** to efface, to erase. **2** to wear out, to destroy. **3** to reduce to an illegible or imperceptible state. **obliteration** (-ā´shən) *n.* **obliterative** *a.* **obliterator** *n.* [L *obliterātus*, p.p. of *obliterāre* (OB-, *litera*, LETTER]

oblivion (əbliv´iən) *n.* **1** forgetfulness, unawareness. **2** the state of having forgotten. **3** the state of being forgotten. **4** an amnesty or pardon. **to fall into oblivion** to be forgotten. **oblivious** *a.* **1** forgetful (of). **2** unaware (of), paying no heed (to). **3** lost in thought or abstraction. **4** (*poet.*) causing forgetfulness. **obliviously** *adv.* **obliviousness** *n.* [OF, from L *oblīviōnem*, nom. *-vio*, from *oblīviscī* (OB-, *līviscī*, to forget, perh. rel. to *līvēre*, to be livid or black and blue)]

Usage note The use of *oblivious* to mean unaware is still sometimes disapproved of, though it is very common.

oblong (ob´long) *a.* **1** longer than broad, of greater breadth than height esp. of rectangles with adjoining sides unequal. **2** (of leaves) elliptical. *~n.* an oblong figure or object. [L *oblongus* (OB-, *longus*, LONG[1])]

obloquy (ob´ləkwi) *n.* (*pl.* **obloquies**) **1** censorious language. **2** discredit, disgrace, infamy. [late L *obloquium*, from *obloquī*, to speak against (OB-, *loquī*, to speak)]

obmutescence (obmūtes´əns) *n.* **1** loss of speech. **2** obstinate silence or taciturnity. **obmutescent** *a.* [L *obmūtescere* (*mūtescere*, incept., from *mūtus*, MUTE[1])]

obnoxious (obnok´shəs) *a.* offensive, objectionable, hateful, odious. **obnoxiously** *adv.* **obnoxiousness** *n.* [L *obnoxius* (*noxa*, harm)]

obo *abbr.* (*N Am.*) or best offer.

oboe (ō´bō) *n.* **1** a woodwind instrument with a double reed, usu. of soprano pitch. **2** a person who plays this instrument in an orchestra. **3** a reed organ stop of similar tone. **oboe d'amore** (damaw´rā) *n.* an oboe pitched a minor third below a normal oboe, used in baroque music. **oboist** *n.* an oboe-player. [It., from F *hautbois*, HAUTBOY]

obol (ob´ol), **obolus** (-ləs) *n.* (*pl.* **obols, oboli** (-lī)) a small coin of ancient Greece weighing and worth one-sixth of a drachma. **obole** (ob´ōl) *n.* a small French coin (10th–15th cents.), worth half a denier. [L *obolus*, from Gr. *obolos*, var. of *obelos*, OBELUS]

obovate (obō´vət) *a.* (*Bot.*) inversely ovate. **obovately** *adv.* **obovoid** (-void) *a.*

obreption (obrep´shən) *n.* acquisition or attempted acquisition of gifts etc. by falsehood. **obreptitious** (-tish´əs) *a.* [F, from L *obreptiōnem*, nom. *-tio* (*repere*, to creep)]

obs. *abbr.* obsolete.

obscene (əbsēn´) *a.* **1** repulsive, disgusting, indecent, lewd. **2** (*Law*) (of publications etc.) liable to corrupt or deprave. **obscenely** *adv.* **obsceneness** *n.* **obscenity** (-sen´-) *n.* (*pl.* **obscenities**) **1** the state or fact of being obscene. **2** an obscene word, gesture etc. [L *obscēnus* (*scēnus*, etym. uncertain)]

obscurant (əbskū´rənt) *n.* an opponent of intellectual progress. **obscurantism** (-rant´-) *n.* **obscurantist** *n., a.* [OBSCURE]

obscure (əbskūə´) *a.* **1** dark, dim. **2** not clear, indefinite, indistinct. **3** abstruse. **4** difficult to understand. **5** unexplained, doubtful. **6** hidden, secluded, remote from public observation. **7** unknown, lowly, humble. **8** dull, dingy. *~v.t.* **1** to make dark, to cloud. **2** to make less intelligible, visible or legible. **3** to dim, to throw into the shade, to outshine. **4** to conceal. *~v.i.* to darken, to conceal. *~n.* **1** obscurity. **2** indistinctness. **obscuration** (obskūərā´shən) *n.* **obscurely** *adv.* **obscurement, obscureness** *n.* **obscurer** *n.* **obscure vowel** *n.* an indeterminate vowel. **obscurity** *n.* (*pl.* **obscurities**) **1** the quality or state of being obscure. **2** an obscure person or thing. [OF *obscur*, L *obscurus* (*scurus*, from *scu*-, Sansk. *sku*-, to cover, cp. *scūtum*, shield)]

obsecration (obsikrā´shən) *n.* **1** the act of imploring, entreaty. **2** a clause in the Litany beginning with 'by'. **obsecrate** (ob´-) *v.t.* to implore, to supplicate. [L *obsecrātio*, from *obsecrāre*, to beseech (*sacrāre*, to make sacred, from *sacer*, SACRED)]

☒ **obsene** common misspelling of OBSCENE.

obsequent (ob´sikwənt) *a.* (of a stream) flowing in the opposite direction to the original slope of the land. [L *sequi*, to follow]

obsequies (ob´sikwiz) *n.pl.* **1** funeral rites. **2** a funeral. **obsequial** (-sē´-) *a.* [pl. of obs. *obsequy*, A-F *obsequie*, OF *obsèque*, med. L *obsequiae* (L *exsequiae*, perh. conf. with *obsequium*, see OBSEQUIOUS)]

obsequious (əbsē´kwiəs) *a.* servile, cringing, fawning, over-ready to comply with the desires of others. **obsequiously** *adv.* **obsequiousness** *n.* [L *obsequiōsus*, from *obsequium*, from *obsequī*, to comply (*sequī*, to follow)]

observe (əbzœv´) *v.t.* **1** to regard attentively, to note, to take notice of, to perceive. **2** to watch, to scrutinize. **3** to examine and note scientifically. **4** to follow attentively, to heed. **5** to perform duly. **6** to comply with. **7** to celebrate. **8** to remark, to express as an opinion. ~*v.i.* to make a remark or remarks (upon). **observable** *a., n.* **observableness** *n.* **observably** *adv.* **observance** *n.* **1** the act of observing, complying with, keeping, following, performing etc. **2** a customary rite, form or ceremony. **3** a rule or practice, esp. in a religious order. **4** †respectful attention, compliance or submission, deference. **observancy** *n.* **observant** *a.* **1** watchful, attentive. **2** quick or strict in observing, esp. rules etc. ~*n.* **1** an Observantine. **2** †a person who observes carefully. **observantly** *adv.* **Observantine** (-tin, -tēn) *n.* a member of a branch of the Franciscan order observing the stricter rule, also called *Observants*. **observation** (obzəvā´shən) *n.* **1** the act, habit or faculty of observing. **2** scientific watching and noting of phenomena as they occur, as distinct from experiment. **3** the result of such a scrutiny, a fact scientifically noted or taken from an instrument. **4** experience and knowledge gained by systematic observing. **5** a remark, an incidental comment or expression of opinion or reflection. **under observation** in a state of being watched carefully, undergoing scrutiny. **observational** *a.* **1** deriving from observation (rather than experiment). **2** containing or consisting of comment or observation. **observationally** *adv.* **observation car** *n.* (*esp. N Am.*) a railway carriage designed so that one can view passing scenery. **observation post** *n.* **1** (*Mil.*) a post from which an observer can watch the effect of artillery fire. **2** a position from which one observes. **observatorial** (-taw´ri-) *a.* **observatory** *n.* (*pl.* **observatories**) an institution, building, room etc. for observation of astronomical or meteorological phenomena. **observedly** (-vid-) *adv.* **observer** *n.* **1** a person who observes. **2** an official looker-on at a proceeding. **3** (*Hist.*) the member of an aircraft's crew employed on reconnaissance, the flying officer. **observing** *a.* **observingly** *adv.* [OF *observer*, L *observāre* (*servāre*, to keep, to heed)]

obsess (əbses´) *v.t.* **1** to haunt, to beset, to trouble (as an evil spirit). **2** to preoccupy the mind of (as a fixed idea). ~*v.i.* (*N Am.*) to be continually preoccupied with (with *on, over*). **obsession** (-sesh´ən) *n.* (the condition of having) an unhealthily deep-rooted or persistent fixation. **obsessional** *a.* **obsessionalism** *n.* **obsessionally** *adv.* **obsessionist** *n.* an obsessive (person). **obsessive** *a., n.* **obsessively** *adv.* **obsessiveness** *n.* [L *obsessus*, p.p. of *obsidēre*, to besiege (*sedēre*, to sit)]

obsidian (obsid´iən) *n.* a black or dark-coloured vitreous lava. [L *Obsidiānus*, from *Obsidius*, erron. for *Obsius*, pers. name]

obsidional (obsid´iənəl) *a.* of or relating to a siege. [L *obsidiōnālis*, from *obsidio -ōnis*, siege]

obsign (obsīn´), **obsignate** (-sig´nāt) *v.t.* to seal, to ratify. **obsignation** (-nā´shən) *n.* [L *obsignātus*, p.p. of *obsignāre*, *signāre*, to SIGN]

obsolescent (obsəles´ənt) *a.* **1** becoming obsolete. **2** gradually disappearing, going out of use. **3** outmoded. **obsolescence** *n.* **obsolete** (ob´səlēt) *a.* **1** passed out of use, no longer practised, current or accepted. **2** discarded, bygone, out of date. **3** imperfectly developed, atrophied. **obsoletely** *adv.* **obsoleteness, obsoletism** *n.* [L *obsolescens -ntem*, pres.p. of *obsolescere*, incept. of *obsolēre* (*solēre*, to be accustomed)]

obstacle (ob´stəkəl) *n.* an impediment, an obstruction. **obstacle race** *n.* a race in which the competitors have to surmount or avoid a series of natural or artificial obstacles. [OF, from L *obstāculum* (*stāre*, to stand)]

obstetric (əbstet´rik), **obstetrical** (-əl) *a.* of or relating to childbirth or obstetrics. **obstetrically** *adv.* **obstetrician** (obstətrish´-) *n.* **obstetrics** *n.* the branch of medical science dealing with childbirth and ante- and postnatal care of women. [L *obstetrīcius*, from *obstetrix*, midwife (*stāre*, to stand)]

obstinate (ob´stinət) *a.* **1** pertinaciously adhering to one's opinion or purpose, stubborn, refractory. **2** not easily remedied, persistent. **obstinacy** *n.* (*pl.* **obstinacies**). **obstinately** *adv.* **obstinateness** *n.* [L *obstinātus*, p.p. of *obstināre* (*stanāre*, from *stāre*, to stand)]

obstipation (obstipā´shən) *n.* extreme constipation. [L *stīpāre*, to cram, to pack]

obstreperous (əbstrep´ərəs) *a.* **1** noisy, clamorous. **2** boisterous, unruly. **obstreperously** *adv.* **obstreperousness** *n.* [L *obstreperus* (*strepere*, to make a noise)]

obstriction (obstrik´shən) *n.* **1** the state of being legally constrained. **2** an obligation. [med. L *obstrictio*, from *stringere*, to tie]

obstruct (əbstrŭkt´) *v.t.* **1** to block up, to close by means of obstacles. **2** to hinder, to impede. **3** to hamper, to check, to retard, to stop. ~*v.i.* to practise obstruction, esp. in Parliament. **obstructer** *n.* **obstruction** *n.* **obstructional** *a.* **obstructionism** *n.* deliberate obstruction of (legislative) business, procedure etc. **obstructionist** *n.* **obstructionistic** *a.* **obstructive** *a.* **1** causing or tending to cause obstruction. **2** intended to retard progress, esp. of parliamentary business. ~*n.* **1** a person who causes obstruction, esp. in Parliament. **2** a hindrance. **obstructively** *adv.* **obstructiveness** *n.* **obstructor** *n.* [L *obstructus*, p.p. of *obstruere* (*struere*, to build)]

obtain (əbtān´) *v.t.* **1** to gain, to acquire, to secure. **2** to procure, to get. **3** to attain, to reach. ~*v.i.* **1** to be prevalent or accepted. **2** to be in common use. **obtainable** *a.* **obtainability** (-bil´-) *n.* **obtainer** *n.* **obtainment** *n.* **obtention** (-ten´shən) *n.* [F *obtenir*, L *obtinēre* (*tenēre*, to hold)]

obtect (obtekt´), **obtected** (-id) *a.* (of the pupae of some insects) protected, encased by a chitinous covering. [L *obtectus*, p.p. of *obtegere* (*tegere*, to cover)]

obtention OBTAIN.

obtest (obtest´) *v.t.* **1** to beseech, to supplicate, to adjure. **2** to beg for. ~*v.i.* to protest. **obtestation** (-tā´shən) *n.* [L *obtestārī* (*testārī*, to bear witness)]

obtrude (əbtrood´) *v.t.* **1** (*usu. with on, upon*) to thrust out, forward or upon. **2** to introduce or thrust in without warrant or invitation. ~*v.i.* to enter without right, to thrust oneself forward. **obtruder** *n.* **obtrusion** (-zhən) *n.* **obtrusive** *a.* **obtrusively** *adv.* **obtrusiveness** *n.* **1** a thrusting forward, a desire to be noticed. **2** undue prominence. [L *obtrūdere* (*trūdere*, to thrust, p.p. *trūsus*)]

obtund (obtŭnd´) *v.t.* to blunt, to deaden. **obtundent** *a., n.* [L *obtundere* (OB-, *tundere*, to beat)]

obturate (ob´tūrāt) *v.t.* to stop up or close (esp. the breech of a gun). **obturation** (-rā´shən) *n.* **obturator** *n.*

1 something which closes an aperture, cavity etc. 2 (*Anat.*) either of two muscles of the gluteal region. 3 in gunnery, a device for closing the aperture of the breech and preventing the escape of gas. [L *obturātus*, p.p. of *obturāre*, to close]

obtuse (əbtūs´) *a.* 1 blunt or rounded, not pointed or acute. 2 denoting an angle greater than a right angle. 3 dull, stupid, slow of apprehension. **obtuse-angular, obtuse-angled** *a.* **obtusely** *adv.* **obtuseness** *n.* **obtusity** *n.* [L *obtūsus*, p.p. of *obtundere*, to OBTUND]

obverse (ob´vœs) *a.* 1 turned towards one. 2 (of leaves) having a base narrower than the apex. 3 forming a counterstatement, complementary. ~*n.* 1 the face or front. 2 the side of a coin or medal bearing the main device. 3 the counterpart or complementary side or aspect of a statement, fact etc. **obversely** *adv.* **obversion** (-voe´shən) *n.* (*Logic*) a method of immediate inference by reversing the predicate and changing the quality of a proposition. **obvert** (obvœt´) *v.t.* 1 to turn the front of towards one. 2 (*Logic*) to infer the obverse of (a proposition). [L *obversus*, p.p. of *obvertere* (*vertere*, to turn)]

obviate (ob´viāt) *v.t.* 1 to clear away, to remove, to overcome, counteract or neutralize (dangers, difficulties etc.). 2 to anticipate, to forestall. **obviation** (-ā´shən) *n.* [L *obviātus*, p.p. of *obviāre* (*via*, way)]

obvious (ob´viəs) *a.* 1 plain to the eye, perfectly manifest, immediately evident. 2 unsubtle. ~*n.* what is obvious or needing no explanation. **obviously** *adv.* **obviousness** *n.* [L *obvius* (*ob viam*, in the way)]

obvolute (ob´vəlūt), **obvoluted** (-tid) *a.* folded together so that the alternate margins are respectively exposed or covered. **obvolution** (-ū´shən) *n.* **obvolutive** *a.* **obvolvent** (-vol´-) *a.* [L *obvolūtus*, p.p. of *obvolvere* (*volvere*, to roll)]

OC *abbr.* Officer Commanding.

Oc. *abbr.* Ocean.

oc- (ok) *pref.* var. of OB- (before *c*).

oca (ō´kə) *n.* any of various S. American herbaceous plants of the genus *Oxalis*, which have edible tubers. [Sp., from Quechua]

ocarina (okərē´nə) *n.* a musical instrument of terracotta with finger-notes and a mouthpiece, giving a mellow whistling sound. [It. *oca*, goose]

☒ **ocasion** common misspelling of OCCASION.

Occamism (ok´əmizm), **Ockhamism** *n.* the doctrines of William of Occam or Ockham, *c.* 1270–*c.* 1349, the English scholastic philosopher and teacher of nominalism. **Occamist** *n.* **Occam's razor** *n.* the philosophic principle that interpretations should include as few assumptions as possible.

occas. *abbr.* occasional(ly).

occasion (əkā´zhən) *n.* 1 an event, circumstance or position of affairs, giving an opportunity, reason, or motive for doing something. 2 motive, ground, reason, need. 3 an opportunity. 4 an incidental or immediate cause or condition. 5 a time or occurrence, esp. of special interest or importance. 6 (*Sc.*) †a communion service. ~*v.t.* 1 to cause directly or indirectly. 2 to be the occasion of. 3 to induce, to influence. **as the occasion arises** when needful, when circumstances demand. **on occasion** now and then. **to rise to the occasion** to be equal to a demanding event or situation. **to take the occasion to** to take the opportunity of. **occasional** *a.* 1 happening, made, employed or done as opportunity arises. 2 irregular, infrequent, incidental, casual. 3 of or made for a special occasion. **occasional cause** *n.* a secondary cause. **occasionalism** *n.* the doctrine of certain Cartesians that body and mind form a dualism of heterogeneous entities, and that there is no real interaction, the corresponding phenomena of sensation and volition being due to the simultaneous action of God. **occasionalist** *n.* **occasionality** (-nal´-) *n.* **occasionally** *adv.* **occasional table** *n.* a small movable table (used as occasion demands). [F, from L *occāsiōnem*, nom. *-sio*, from *occidere* (*cadere*, to fall)]

Occident (ok´sidənt), **occident** *n.* 1 (*poet.*) the West. 2 western Europe, Europe and America. 3 the western hemisphere. 4 sunset. **Occidental** (-den´-) *a.* 1 western. 2 characteristic of Western culture, thoughts etc. 3 applied to gems of inferior quality or worth, the best supposedly coming from the East. ~*n.* a westerner. **occidentalism** *n.* **occidentalist** *n.* **occidentalize, occidentalise** *v.t.* **occidentally** *adv.* [F, from L *occidentem*, nom. *-dens*, pres.p. of *occidere* (OC-, *cadere*, to fall)]

occiput (ok´sipət) *n.* the back part of the head. **occipital** (-sip´i-) *a.* of or relating to the back part of the head. ~*n.* the occipital bone. **occipital bone** *n.* the bone forming the back and part of the base of the skull. **occipitally** *adv.* **occipito-** (ok´sipitō) *comb. form* the back of the head. [L *occiput* (OC-, *caput*, head)]

Occitan (ok´sitən) *n.* the Provençal language. **Occitanian** (-tā´niən) *n., a.* [F]

occlude (əklood´) *v.t.* 1 to shut or stop up. 2 to close, to bring together (the eyelids, the teeth). 3 to form or cause to form an occlusion. 4 (of metals etc.) to absorb (a gas). **occluded front** *n.* an occlusion. **occludent** *a., n.* **occlusal** (-zəl) *a.* relating to dental occlusion. **occlusion** (-zhən) *n.* 1 a shutting or stopping up. 2 in meteorology, the closing of a cold front upon a warm one, which is narrowed and raised up, an occluded front. 3 absorption. 4 the manner in which teeth come together, the bite. 5 in phonetics, closure of the breath passage prior to articulating a sound. **occlusive** (-siv) *a.* in phonetics, denoting a sound made when the breath passage is completely closed. ~*n.* an occlusive sound. **occlusor** (-zə) *n.* [L *occlūdere* (OC-, *claudere*, to shut), p.p. *occlūsus*]

occult (əkŭlt´, ok-) *a.* 1 supernatural, magical, mystical. 2 concealed, kept secret, esoteric. 3 mysterious, recondite, beyond the range of ordinary knowledge or perception. ~*v.t.* (*Astron.*) to hide, to conceal, to cover or cut off from view (esp. during a planetary eclipse). ~*v.i.* (*Astron.*) to become temporarily hidden or eclipsed. ~*n.* 1 that which is hidden, mysterious or magical. 2 the supernatural. **occultation** (-tā´shən) *n.* **occulted, occulting** *a.* (of a lighthouse beacon) temporarily shut off, becoming invisible at regular intervals. **occultism** *n.* **occultist** *n.* **occultly** *adv.* **occultness** *n.* [L *occultus*, p.p. of *occulere* (OC-, *-celere*, rel. to *celāre*, to hide)]

occupant (ok´ūpənt) *n.* 1 a person who occupies. 2 a person who resides or is in a place. 3 a tenant in possession as distinct from an owner. 4 a person who establishes a claim by taking possession. **occupancy** *n.* (*pl.* **occupancies**). **occupation** (okūpā´shən) *n.* 1 the act of occupying or taking possession (e.g. of a country by a foreign army). 2 the state of being occupied. 3 occupancy, tenure. 4 the state of being employed or engaged in some way. 5 pursuit, employment, business, trade, calling, job. **occupational** *a.* caused by or related to employment. **occupational disease, occupational hazard** *n.* a disease, injury, risk etc. resulting directly from or common to an occupation. **occupationally** *adv.* **occupational therapy** *n.* treatment of various illnesses by providing a creative occupation or hobby. **occupational therapist** *n.* **occupative** *a.* held by tenure based on occupation.

occupy (ok´ūpī) *v.t.* (*3rd pers. sing. pres.* **occupies,** *pres.p.* **occupying,** *past, p.p.* **occupied**) 1 to take possession of. 2 to hold in possession, to be the tenant of. 3 to reside in, to be in. 4 to take up, to fill. 5 to give occupation to. 6 to employ, to engage (oneself, or in p.p.). **occupier** *n.* an occupant of a house etc. [F *occuper*, L *occupāre* (OC-, *capere*, to take)]

occur (əkœ´) *v.i.* (*pres.p.* **occurring,** *past, p.p.* **occurred**) 1 to happen, to take place. 2 to be met with, to be found, to exist. **3** to present itself to the mind. **occurrence** (əkŭr´əns) *n.* **1** an event, an incident. **2** the happening or taking place of anything. **occurrent** *a.* [MF *occurrer*, L *occurrere* (OC-, *currere*, to run)]

ocean (ō´shən) *n.* **1** the vast body of water covering about two-thirds of the surface of the globe. **2** any one of its principal divisions, the Antarctic, Atlantic, Arctic, Indian and Pacific Oceans. **3** the sea. **4** an immense expanse or quantity. ~*a.* of or relating to the ocean. **oceanarium** (-eə´riəm) *n.* (*pl.* **oceanariums, oceanaria** (-riə)) an aquarium for specimens of deep-sea animal life. **ocean basin** *n.* the depression of the earth's surface containing an ocean. **ocean-going** *a.* (suitable for) travelling on the ocean. **ocean greyhound** *n.* a fast steamer or liner. **Oceania** (ōshiah´niə, ōsi-) *n.* the islands of the Pacific and adjoining seas. **Oceanian** *a., n.* **oceanic** (ōshian´-, ōsi-) *a.* **1** of, relating to, occurring in or (expansive) like the ocean. **2** (of a climate) governed by the ocean. **3** (**Oceanic**) of or relating to Oceania. **Oceanid** (ōsē´ənid, ōshē´-) *n.* (*pl.* **Oceanids, Oceanides** (-an´idēz)) an ocean nymph of Greek mythology. **oceano-** *comb. form* ocean. **oceanography** (-og´-) *n.* the branch of science concerned with oceans and their biological, geographical and chemical features etc. **oceanographer** *n.* **oceanographic** (-graf´-), **oceanographical** *a.* **oceanology** (-ol´-) *n.* **1** the study of the sea esp. concerned with the distribution of its economic resources. **2** oceanography. **ocean tramp** *n.* a merchant ship with no regular route. **oceanward, oceanwards** *adv.* [OF, from L *ōceanu*, Gr. *ōkeanos*]

ocellus (əsel´əs) *n.* (*pl.* **ocelli** (-lī)) **1** a simple eye, as opposed to the compound eye of insects. **2** a part or facet of a compound eye. **3** an eye-spot or spot of colour surrounded by a ring or rings of other colour, as on feathers, wings etc. **ocellar, ocellate** (-lāt), **ocellated** *a.* **ocellation** (-ā´shən) *n.* **ocelli-** (-li) *comb. form.* [L, dim. of *oculus*, eye]

ocelot (os´əlot, ō´-) *n.* **1** a small American feline, *Felis pardalis*, which has a yellow or orange coat marked with black stripes and spots. **2** its fur. [F, from Nahuatl *ocelotl*, jaguar]

och (okh) *int.* (*Ir., Sc.*) used to express impatience, contempt, regret, surprise etc. [Gael. and Ir.]

oche (ok´i), **hockey** (ok´i, hok´i) *n.* in darts, the line or mark behind which a player must stand when throwing at the dartboard. [etym. uncertain, prob. from ME *oche*, groove, notch, from MF]

ocher OCHRE.

ochlocracy (oklok´rəsi) *n.* (*pl.* **ochlocracies**) **1** mob rule. **2** an instance of this. **ochlocrat** (ok´ləkrat) *n.* **ochlocratic** (-krat´-), **ochlocratical** *a.* **ochlocratically** *adv.* **ochlophobia** (okləfō´biə) *n.* fear of crowds. [F *ochlocratie*, Gr. *ochlokratia* (*ochlos*, crowd, -CRACY)]

ochone OHONE.

ochre (ō´kə), (*N Am.*) **ocher** *n.* **1** a native earth consisting of hydrated peroxide of iron with clay in various proportions, used as a red or yellow pigment. **2** a yellow colour. **3** (*sl.*) money (from the yellow colour of gold). ~*a.* of or relating to this pigment or colour. **ochraceous** (ōkrā´shəs), **ochreish** (ōk´ərish), **ochreous** (ōk´riəs), **ochroid** (ō´kroid), **ochrous, ochry** *a.* **ochreo-** (ōk´riō) *comb. form* [OF *ocre*, L and Gr. *ōchra*, from *ōchros*, yellow]

ochrea OCREA.

-ock (ək) *suf.* indicating smallness or youngness, as in *bullock, hillock.* [OE *-oc, -uc*]

ocker (ok´ə) *n.* (*Austral., sl.*) a boorish, chauvinistic Australian. ~*a.* characteristic of such a person. [form of *Oscar*, an Australian television character]

Ockhamism OCCAMISM.

o'clock (əklok´) *adv.* of the clock.

ocotillo (ōkōtē´yō) *n.* (*pl.* **ocotillos**) a cactus-like shrub, *Fouquiera splendens*, of Mexico and the south-western US. [Am. Sp., dim. of *ocote*, a type of tree, from Nahuatl *ocotl*, torch]

OCR *abbr.* optical character reader, recognition.

ocrea (ok´riə), **ochrea** *n.* (*pl.* **ocreae** (-iē), **ochreae**) **1** (*Bot.*) a sheath formed by the union of two stipules round a stem. **2** a sheath round the foot or leg of a bird. **ocreaceous** (-ā´shəs), **ocreate** (-ət) *a.* [L *ocrea*, a legging]

Oct. *abbr.* October.

oct. *abbr.* octavo.

octa- (ok´tə), **oct-, octo-** (-tō) *comb. form* **1** having eight. **2** consisting of eight. [Gr. *oktō*, eight]

octachord (ok´təkawd) *n.* **1** a musical instrument with eight strings. **2** a system of eight sounds, such as the diatonic scale.

octad (ok´tad) *n.* a group or series of eight. **octadic** (-tad´-) *a.* [Gr. *oktas*, *oktō*, eight]

octagon (ok´təgən) *n.* **1** a plane figure of eight sides and angles. **2** any object or building of this shape. **octagonal** (-tag´-) *a.* **octagonally** *adv.* [L *octā-*, *octōgōnos*, Gr. *oktagōnos*, *gōnia*, corner]

octahedron (oktəhē´drən), **octohedron** *n.* (*pl.* **octahedra** (-drə), **octahedrons, octohedra, octohedrons**) a solid figure contained by eight plane faces. **octahedral** *a.* **octahedrite** (-rīt) *n.* native titanic dioxide. [Gr. *hedra*, seat, base]

octal (ok´təl) *a.* referring to or based on the number eight. [Gr. *oktō*, eight]

octamerous (oktam´ərəs) *a.* having parts in eights or in series of eight.

octameter (oktam´itə) *n.* in verse, a line of eight metrical feet.

octandrous (oktan´drəs) *a.* (*Bot.*) having eight stamens. [Gr. *anēr andros*, male]

octane (ok´tān) *n.* a colourless liquid hydrocarbon of the alkane series that occurs in petroleum. **octane number, octane rating** *n.* a percentage measure of the antiknock quality of a liquid motor fuel.

octangular (oktang´gūlə) *a.* having eight angles.

octant (ok´tənt) *n.* **1** an arc comprising the eighth part of a circle's circumference. **2** an eighth of the area of a circle contained within two radii and an arc. **3** each of the eight parts into which a space is divided by three planes (usu. at right angles) intersecting at one point. **4** the position of a celestial body when it is 45° distant from another or from a particular point. **5** an instrument similar to a sextant for measuring angles, having a graduated arc of 45°.

octapodic (oktəpod´ik) *a.* containing eight metrical feet. **octapody** (-tap´ədi) *n.*

octaroon OCTOROON.

octastich (ok´təstik) *n.* a strophe, stanza or series of eight lines of verse. **octastichous** (-tas´-) *a.* [Gr. *stichos*, a row]

octastrophic (oktəstrof´ik) *a.* consisting of eight strophes.

octastyle (ok´təstīl), **octostyle** *n.* a building having eight columns in front. ~*a.* having eight columns in front. [Gr. *stylos*, a pillar]

octateuch (ok´tətūk) *n.* the first eight books of the Old Testament. [Gr. *teuchos*, book]

octavalent (oktəvā´lənt) *a.* (*Chem.*) having a valency of eight.

octave (ok´tiv, -tāv) *n.* **1** the interval between any musical note and that produced by twice or half as many vibrations per second (lying eight notes away inclusively). **2** a note at this interval above or below another. **3** two notes separated by this interval. **4** the scale of notes filling this interval. **5** any group of eight, such as the first eight lines of a sonnet or a stanza of eight lines. **6** the eighth day after a church festival. **7** a festival day and the seven days following it. **8** a cask containing one-eighth of a pipe of wine or 13½ gallons (about 60 l). 9 this volume. 10 in fencing, a low thrust towards the right side of the opponent. **octave coupler** *n.* a mechanism on an organ or harpsichord that allows keys or pedals that are an octave apart to be played simultaneously. [F, from L *octāvus*, eighth]

octavo (oktā´vō) *n.* (*pl.* **octavos**) 1 a book in which a sheet is folded into 8 leaves or 16 pages. 2 the size of such a book or paper (written 8vo). ~*a.* of this size, having this number of leaves per sheet.

octennial (okten´iəl) *a.* 1 recurring every eighth year. 2 lasting eight years. **octennially** *adv.* [L *octennium* (*oct-*, eight, *annus*, year), -AL[1]]

octet (oktet´), **octette** *n.* 1 a musical composition of eight parts or for eight instruments or singers. 2 a group of eight, esp. musicians or singers. 3 an octave (of verse). 4 (*Chem.*) a stable group of eight electrons. [It. *ottetto*, G *Oktett*, on analogy of DUET]

octile (ok´tīl) *n.* an eighth part.

octillion (oktil´yən) *n.* 1 the number produced by raising a million to the eighth power of a thousand, represented by 1 followed by 48 zeros. 2 (*esp. N Am.*) the eighth power of a thousand, 1 followed by 27 zeros. **octillionth** *a., n.*

octingenary (oktinjē´nəri), **octingentenary** (oktinjəntē´nəri) *n.* (*pl.* **octingenaries, octingentenaries**) an 800th anniversary, an octocentenary.

octo- OCTA-.

October (oktō´bə) *n.* 1 the tenth month of the year (the eighth of the Roman year). 2 ale or cider brewed in October, good ale. **Octobrist** *n.* (*Hist.*) a member of a moderate reforming party in Tsarist Russia (after the Tsar's liberal manifesto published in Oct. 1905). [L, *octōber*, from *octo*, eight]

octobrachiate (oktōbrak´iət) *a.* having eight limbs, arms or rays.

octocentenary (oktōsentē´nəri, -ten´-) *n.* (*pl.* **octocentenaries**) an 800th anniversary. ~*a.* of or relating to an ocotocentenary. **octocentennial** (-ten´iəl) *n.*

octodecimo (oktōdes´imō) *n.* (*pl.* **octodecimos**) 1 a book having 18 leaves to the sheet. 2 the size of such a book (written 18mo). ~*a.* having 18 leaves to the sheet. [L *octodecimus*, eighteenth (*decimus*, tenth), after OCTAVO]

octodentate (oktōden´tət) *a.* having eight teeth.

octofid (ok´tōfid) *a.* having eight segments.

octogenarian (oktōjəneə´riən) *n.* a person who is 80, or between 80 and 90 years old. ~*a.* of, relating to or being an octogenarian. **octogenary** (-jē´-) *a.* [L *octogēnārius* (*octōgēni*, eighty each)]

octogynous (oktoj´inəs) *a.* (*Bot.*) having eight pistils. [Gr. *gunē*, woman]

octohedron OCTAHEDRON.

octonary (ok´tənəri) *a.* relating to, computing or proceeding by the number eight. ~*n.* (*pl.* **octonaries**) 1 a group of eight. 2 a stanza or group of eight lines. **octonarian** (-neə´ri-) *a.* consisting of eight metrical feet. ~*n.* a line of eight metrical feet. [L *octōni*, eight each]

octonocular (oktōnok´ūlə) *a.* having eight eyes.

octoped (ok´təped) *n.* an eight-footed animal. [L *pes pedis*, foot]

octopetalous (oktōpet´ələs) *a.* having eight petals.

octopod (ok´təpod) *a.* having eight feet. ~*n.* any cephalopod of the order Octopoda, with eight arms and usually suckers. **octopodous** (-top´-) *a.* [Gr. *oktōpod-*, stem of *oktōpous* (*pous podos*, foot)]

octopus (ok´təpəs) *n.* (*pl.* **octopuses**) 1 any cephalopod mollusc of the genus *Octopus*, having eight arms with suckers. 2 an organization or influence having far-extending powers (for harm). [Gr. *oktōpous* (*pous podos*, foot)]

octoroon (oktəroon´), **octaroon** *n.* the offspring of a quadroon and a white person (having one-eighth black ancestry).

octosepalous (oktōsep´ələs) *a.* (*Bot.*) having eight sepals.

octospermous (oktōspœ´məs) *a.* having eight seeds.

octosporous (oktōspaw´rəs) *a.* eight-spored.

octostyle OCTASTYLE.

octosyllabic (oktōsilab´ik) *a.* having eight syllables. ~*n.* a line of eight syllables. **octosyllable** (ok´-) *n.* a word of eight syllables.

octroi (ok´trwah) *n.* 1 a tax levied at the gates of some European, esp. French, towns on goods brought in. 2 the barrier or place where this is levied. 3 the body of officials collecting it. 4 a road toll for cars. [F, from *octroyer*, from late L *auctorizāre*, to AUTHORIZE]

octuple (ok´tūpəl) *a.* eightfold. ~*n.* the product of multiplication by eight. ~*v.t., v.i.* to multiply by eight. **octuplet** (-plit) *n.* each of eight offspring produced at one birth. [L *octuplus*]

octyl (ok´til) *n.* the hypothetical organic radical of a hydrocarbon series. **octylene** (-lēn) *n.* an oily hydrocarbon obtained by heating octylic alcohol with sulphuric acid. **octylic** (-til´-) *a.*

ocular (ok´ūlə) *a.* 1 of, relating to, by or with the eye or eyes, visual. 2 known from actual sight. ~*n.* an eyepiece. **ocularist** *n.* a maker of artificial eyes. **ocularly** *adv.* **ocular spectrum** *n.* an image persisting on the retina after the eyes are removed, an after-image. **oculate** (-lət), **oculated** (-lātid) *a.* 1 having eyelike spots. 2 having eyes or sight. **oculist** *n.* an ophthalmologist or optician. **oculistic** (-lis´-) *a.* **oculo-** (ok´ūlō) *comb. form* eye. [L *oculus*, eye]

☒ **ocult** common misspelling of OCCULT.

☒ **ocupy** common misspelling of OCCUPY.

☒ **ocur** common misspelling of OCCUR.

OD[1] *abbr.* 1 Officer of the Day. 2 Old Dutch. 3 ordnance data, datum. 4 (*also* **od**) outside diameter.

OD[2] (ōdē´) *n.* (*sl.*) an overdose of a drug. ~*v.i.* (*3rd pers. sing. pres.* **OD's**, *pres.p.* **ODing**, *past, p.p.* **OD'd**) to take an overdose of a drug. [*over dose*]

O/D, o/d *abbr.* 1 on demand. 2 overdrawn.

†**od**[1] (od) *int., n.* a minced form of 'God' used as an expletive or asseveration. †**od's bodikins** *n.* by God's dear body.

od[2] (od, ōd), **odyl** (-il), **odyle** *n.* a natural force once thought to pervade the universe and to produce the phenomena of magnetism, crystallization, hypnotism etc. **odic**[1] *a.* **odism** *n.* [arbitrary coinage by Baron von Reichenbach, 1788–1869, German scientist]

od[3] OD[1].

odal UDAL.

odalisque (ō´dəlisk), **odalisk** *n.* (*Hist.*) an Oriental female slave or concubine, esp. in a harem. [F, from Turk. *ōdalīq*, chambermaid, from *ōdah*, chamber]

odd (od) *a.* 1 remaining after a number or quantity has been divided into pairs. 2 not even, not divisible by two. 3 bearing such a number. 4 lacking a match or pair. 5 singular, strange, eccentric, queer. 6 occasional, casual. 7 indefinite, incalculable. 8 (*ellipt.*) and more, with others thrown in (added to a round number in enumeration, as *two hundred odd*). ~*n.* 1 a handicap stroke in golf. 2 a stroke more than one's opponent's score. 3 in whist, one trick above book. **odd or even** a game of chance. **oddball** *n.* a person who is eccentric or peculiar. ~*a.* eccentric, peculiar. **odd bod** *n.* (*sl.*) a person who is strange or eccentric. **Oddfellow** *n.* a member of a Friendly Society founded in the 18th cent. known as the Order of Oddfellows. **oddish** *a.* **oddity** *n.* (*pl.* **oddities**) 1 oddness. 2 a peculiar feature or trait. 3 an odd person or thing. **odd job** *n.* a casual, irregular or occasional piece of work, esp. a domestic repair. **odd jobber, odd-job man, odd-job woman** *n.* **odd-looking** *a.* **oddly** *adv.* **odd man out** *n.* 1 a person who is left when a number pair off. 2 a person who is at variance with, excluded from, or stands out as dissimilar to a group etc. **oddment** *n.* **1** a remnant. **2** (*pl.*) odds and ends. **3** (*pl.*, *Print.*) matter other than the main part of a book, such as the preface. **oddness** *n.* **odd pricing** *n.* the practice of pricing commodities in such a way as to suggest a bargain (e.g. £9.99 instead of £10). **odds** *n.pl.* (*usu. as sing.*) **1** the ratio by which the amount staked by one party to a bet exceeds that by the other. **2** the chances in favour of a given event. **3** the balance of superiority, advantage. **4** an allowance to the weaker of two competitors. **5** inequality, difference. **6** variance, strife, dispute. **at odds** at variance. **by all odds** certainly. **over the odds** higher, more than is acceptable, necessary, usual etc. **to give odds** to lay odds. **to lay odds** to offer a bet with favourable odds. **to make no odds** to make no difference, not to matter. **to shout the odds** (*coll.*) to talk loudly, stridently, vehemently etc. **to take odds** to accept a bet with favourable odds. **what's the odds?** (*coll.*) what difference does it make? **odds and ends** *n.pl.* miscellaneous remnants, trifles, scraps etc. **odds and sods** *n.pl.* (*coll.*) odds and ends. **odds-on** *a.* having a better than even chance of happening, winning, succeeding etc. ~*n.* a state when success is more likely than failure. **odd trick** *n.* in bridge, every trick after six won by the declarer's side. [Icel. *odda-* (in *oddamathr*, odd man, *oddalala*, odd number), cogn. with OE *ord*, point, tip]

ode (ōd) *n.* **1** a lyric poem in an elevated style, rhymed or unrhymed, of varied and often irregular metre, usu. in the form of an address or invocation. **2** (*Hist.*) a lyric poem meant to be sung. **odic**[2] *a.* **odist** *n.* a writer of odes. [F, from late L *ōda*, Gr. *ōdē*, *aoidē*, from *aeidein*, to sing]

-ode[1] (ōd) *suf.* denoting a thing resembling or of the nature of, as *geode*, *sarcode*. [Gr. *-ōdēs* (*-o-*, *eidēs*, like, cogn. with *eidos*, form)]

-ode[2] (ōd) *suf.* denoting a path or way, as *anode*, *cathode*. [Gr. *hodos*, way]

odeon (ō´diən), **odeum** (-əm) *n.* (*pl.* **odea** (-ə), **odeums**) **1** in ancient Greece or Rome, a theatre in which poets and musicians contended for prizes. **2** a concert hall, a theatre used for musical performances. **3** a cinema. [Gr. *odeion*, as ODE]

odic[1] OD[2].

odic[2] ODE.

odious (ō´diəs) *a.* **1** hateful, repulsive. **2** offensive. **odiously** *adv.* **odiousness** *n.* **odium** (-əm) *n.* **1** general dislike, reprobation. **2** repulsion. [L *odiōsus*, from *odium*, hatred, cogn. with *ōdī*, I hate]

Usage note The adjectives *odious* and *odorous* should not be confused: *odious* means hateful, and *odorous* fragrant.

---

odism OD[2].

odist ODE.

odium ODIOUS.

odometer (ōdom´itə), **hodometer** (hod-) *n.* an instrument attached to a vehicle for measuring and recording the distance travelled. **odometry** *n.* [Gr. *hodos*, way, -METER[1]]

odont- ODONTO-.

-odont (ədont´) *comb. form* -toothed. [as ODONTO-]

odontalgia (odontal´jiə), **odontalgy** (-ji) *n.* toothache. **odontalgic** *a.*, *n.* [Gr. *algos*, pain]

odontiasis (odontī´əsis) *n.* the cutting of teeth, dentition.

odontic (odon´tik) *a.* dental.

odonto- (odont´ō), **odont-** *comb. form* having teeth or processes resembling teeth. [Gr. *odous odontos*, tooth]

odontoblast (odon´təblahst) *n.* a cell producing dentine.

odontocete (odon´təsēt) *n.* a toothed whale.

odontogeny (odontoj´əni) *n.* the origin and development of teeth. **odontogenic** (-jen´-) *a.*

odontoglossum (odontəglos´əm) *n.* any of various orchids of the tropical American genus *Odontoglossum*, with finely coloured flowers which have jagged edges. [Gr. *glōssa*, a tongue]

odontography (odontog´rəfi) *n.* the description of teeth.

odontoid (odon´toid) *a.* **1** toothlike. **2** of or relating to an odontoid process. **odontoid process** *n.* a toothlike projection from the axis or second cervical vertebra in certain mammals and birds.

odontology (odontol´əji) *n.* the science dealing with the structure and development of teeth. **odontologic** (-loj´-), **odontological** *a.* **odontologist** (-tol´-) *n.*

odontoma (odontō´mə) *n.* (*pl.* **odontomas, odontomata** (-mətə)) a small tumour or excrescence composed of dentine. **odontomatous** *a.*

odontophore (odon´təfaw) *n.* a ribbon-like organ covered with teeth, used for mastication by certain molluscs. **odontophoral** (-tof´-) *a.* **odontophorous** (-tof´-) *a.*

odontorhyncus (odontəring´kəs) *a.* having toothlike serrations in the bill or beak.

odontotherapia (odontōtherəpī´ə) *n.* the treatment and care of the teeth; dental hygiene or therapeutics.

odontotoxia (odontōtok´siə) *n.* unevenness of the teeth.

odontotrypy (odontot´ripi) *n.* (*pl.* **odontotrypies**) the operation of perforating a tooth to draw off pus from an abscess in the internal cavity.

odour (ō´də), (*N Am.*) **odor** *n.* **1** a smell, whether pleasant or unpleasant. **2** scent, fragrance. **3** (*coll.*) a bad smell. **4** repute, esteem. **in bad odour 1** in bad repute. **2** out of favour. **in good odour** in favour. **odorant** *a.* odoriferous. **odoriferous** (-rif´-) *a.* **1** diffusing fragrance. **2** (*coll.*) smelly. **odoriferously** *adv.* **odoriferousness** *n.* **odorizer, odoriser** *n.* **odorous** *a.* having a sweet scent, fragrant. **odorously** *adv.* **odorousness** *n.* **odourless** *a.* **odour of sanctity** *n.* **1** a reputation for holiness. **2** (*facet.*) the odour of an unwashed body. **3** sanctimoniousness. [OF *odor*, L *odōrem*, nom. *odor*]

Usage note See note on *odorous* under ODIOUS.

---

odyl, odyle OD[2].

odyssey (od´isi) *n.* (*pl.* **odysseys**) (a story of) a long journey containing a series of adventures and vicissitudes. **Odyssean** (-sē´ən) *a.* [L *Odyssēa*, Gr. *Odusseia*, from *Odusseus*, Ulysses, from an epic poem by Homer describing the wanderings of Ulysses after the fall of Troy]

OE *abbr.* Old English.

Oe *abbr.* oersted.

OECD *abbr.* Organization for Economic Cooperation and Development.

oecology ECOLOGY.

oecumenical ECUMENICAL.

OED *abbr.* Oxford English Dictionary.

oedema (idē´mə), (*esp. N Am.*) **edema** *n.* **1** swelling due to accumulation of serous fluid in the cellular tissue; dropsy. **2** in plants, swelling due to water accumulation in the tissues. **oedematose** (-tōs), **oedematous** *a.* **oedematously** *adv.* [Gr. *oidēma -matos*, from *oideein*, to swell]

Oedipus complex (ē´dipəs) *n.* a psychical impulse in offspring characterized by excessive love or sexual desire for the parent of the opposite sex and hatred for the parent of the same sex. **Oedipal, Oedipean** (-pē´ən) *a.* [*Oedipus*, king of Thebes, COMPLEX]

oenanthic (ēnan´thik), **enanthic** *a.* possessing a vinous odour. [L *oenanthē*, Gr. *oinanthē* (*oinē*, vine, *anthē*, bloom), -IC]

oeno- (ē´nō), **oino-**, (*esp. N Am.*) **eno-**, **oen-** (ēn), **oin-**, (*esp. N Am.*) **en-** *comb. form* wine. **oenology** (ēnol´əji) *n.* the science or study of wines. **oenological** (-loj´-) *a.* **oenologist** *n.* **oenomancy** (ē´nōmansi) *n.* divination from the appearance of wine poured out in libations.

oenomania (ēnōmā´niə) *n.* 1 dipsomania. 2 mania due to intoxication. **oenomaniac** (-ak) *n.* **oenomel** (ē´nəmel) *n.* wine mingled with honey, a beverage drunk by the ancient Greeks. **oenometer** (ēnom´itə) *n.* an instrument for testing the alcoholic strength of wines. **oenophile** (ē´nəfīl), **oenophil** (-fil), **oenophilist** (-nof´i-) *n.* a wine connoisseur. **oenophily** (-nof´ili) *n.* love or knowledge of wines. [Gr. *oinos*, wine]

oenothera (ēnəthiə´rə) *n.* any plant of the genus *Oenothera*, which includes the evening primrose. [L, from Gr. *oinothēras* (*oinos*, wine, *-thēras*, catcher, from *thēraein*, to hunt)]

o'er (aw) *prep., adv.* (*poet.*) over. [contr.]

oersted (œ´sted) *n.* a unit of magnetic field or magnetizing force. [H. C. *Oersted*, 1777–1851, Danish physicist]

oesophag- (ēsof´əg), (*esp. N Am.*) **esophag-**, **oesophago-** (-gō), (*esp. N Am.*) **esophago-** *comb. form* oesophagous. **oesophagalgia** (ēsofəgal´jiə) *n.* pain, esp. neuralgia, in the oesophagus. **oesophageal** (-jē´əl) *a.* **oesophagectomy** (ēsofəjek´təmi) *n.* (*pl.* **oesophagectomies**) excision of part of the oesophagus. **oesophagitis** (ēsofəjī´tis) *n.* inflammation of the oesophagus. **oesophagocele** (ēsof´əgəsēl) *n.* hernia of the mucous membrane of the oesophagus. **oesophagopathy** (-op´əthi) *n.* disease of the oesophagus. **oesophagoplegia** (-plē´jiə) *n.* paralysis of the oesophagus. **oesophagorrhagia** (-rā´jiə) *n.* haemorrhage of the oesophagus. **oesophagospasmus** (-spaz´məs) *n.* spasm of the oesophagus. **oesophagotomy** (-got´əmi) *n.* (*pl.* **oesophagotomies**) the surgical operation of opening the oesophagus. **oesophagotome** (ēsof´əgətōm) *n.* a cutting instrument for use in oesophagotomy.

oesophagus (ēsof´əgəs), (*esp. N Am.*) **esophagus** *n.* (*pl.* **oesophagi** (-jī), **oesophaguses,** (*esp. N Am.*) **esophagi, esophaguses**) the gullet, the canal by which food passes to the stomach. [late L, from Gr. *oisophagos*, etym. unknown]

oestrogen (ēs´trəjən, es´-), (*esp. N Am.*) **estrogen** *n.* 1 any of the female sex hormones which induce oestrus and encourage the growth of female secondary sexual characteristics. 2 a substance produced artificially that has these effects. **oestradiol** (-dī´ol) *n.* the major oestrogenic hormone in human females (used to treat breast cancer and oestrogen deficiency). **oestriol** (-triol) *n.* an oestrogenic hormone often used to treat menopausal symptoms. **oestrogenic** (-jen´ik) *a.* **oestrogenically** *adv.* **oestrone** (-trōn) *n.* an oestrogenic hormone derived from oestradiol. [L *oestrus*, gadfly; -GEN]

oestrus (ēs´trəs, es´-), **oestrum** (-trəm), (*esp. N Am.*) **estrus, estrum** *n.* 1 the cyclical period of sexual receptivity in some female mammals, heat. 2 a violent impulse, a raging desire or passion. **oestral** *a.* **oestrous** *a.* **oestrous cycle, oestrus cycle** *n.* the hormonal changes occurring in a female mammal from one oestrus to the next. [L *oestrus*, Gr. *oistros*, gadfly, hence frenzy]

oeuvre (œv´rə) *n.* the works of an author, painter etc. [F, from L *opera*, pl. of *opus*, work]

OF *abbr.* Old French.

of (ov, əv) *prep.* 1 denoting connection with or relation to in situation, origin or point of departure. 2 denoting connection with or relation to in motive, cause or agency. 3 denoting connection with or relation to in removal, separation or privation. 4 denoting connection with or relation to in substance. 5 denoting possession or inclusion. 6 denoting identity or equivalence. 7 denoting connection with or relation to in direction or distance. 8 denoting reference or respect to. 9 denoting connection with or relation to in quality or condition. 10 denoting the object of an action, feeling etc. 11 (*N Am.*) denoting time in relation to the next hour on the clock. **of an evening/ morning/ etc.** 1 (*coll.*) usually in the evening etc. 2 (*coll.*) at some point during most evenings etc. **of late** LATE. **of old** OLD. [OE (cp. Dut. *af*, G *ab*, Icel., Swed. and Dan. *af*, L *ab*, Gr. *apo*)]

of- (ov) *pref.* var. of OB- (before *f*, as *offence*).

ofay (ō´fā, ōfā´) *n.* (*N Am., sl.*) a white person. *~a.* (of a person) white. [etym. uncertain, prob. of Afr. origin]

off (of) *adv.* 1 away, at a distance or to a distance in space or time (expressing removal, separation, suspension, discontinuance, decay or termination). 2 to the end, utterly, completely. 3 (*Naut.*) away from the wind. *~prep.* from (denoting deviation, separation, distance, disjunction, removal etc.). *~a.* 1 more distant, further, opp. to *near*. 2 right, as opposed to left. 3 removed or aside from the main street etc., divergent, subsidiary. 4 (*coll.*) unacceptable, unfair. 5 contingent, possible. 6 not occupied, disengaged, on bad form (*an off day*). 7 denoting that part of a cricket field to the left side of the bowler when the batsman is right-handed. *~n.* 1 the off side of a cricket field. 2 the beginning, start. *~v.i.* 1 (*coll.*) to go off, to put off, to withdraw. 2 (*Naut.*) to go away from the land. *~int.* away, begone. **badly off** BAD. **off and on** intermittently, now and again. **off form** FORM. **off guard** GUARD. **off one's feet** FOOT. **off one's hands** HAND. **off one's head** HEAD[1]. **off the cuff** CUFF[1]. **off the peg** PEG. **off the point** POINT. **off the record** RECORD[2]. **off the wall** WALL. **to be off** to leave. **to take off** (of a plane) to leave the ground. **well off** WELL[1]. **off-air** *a., adv.* 1 of or relating to the transmission of programmes by broadcasting. 2 connected with a radio or television programme but not broadcast. **offbeat** (of´bēt, ofbēt´) *a.* 1 in music, not coinciding with the beat. 2 (*coll.*) unconventional, unusual. *~n.* any of the normally unaccented beats in a bar. **off-break** *n.* 1 in cricket, a ball which deviates inwards from the off side. 2 spin given to a ball to cause such deviation. 3 such deviation. **off Broadway** *n., a.* 1 situated outside the Broadway theatrical area of New York (of a theatre). 2 relating to New York fringe theatre, experimental, low-cost, non-commercial etc. **off-off Broadway** *n., a.* **off-centre,** (*N Am.*) **off-center** *a.* not quite central. *~adv.* **off chance** *n.* a remote possibility. **on the off chance** in the slim hope (that), just in case. **off-colour,** (*N Am.*) **off-color** *a.* 1 faulty in colour, as a gem. 2 faulty. 3 out of sorts. 4 slightly obscene. **offcut** *n.* a section cut off the main piece of a material (of fabric, meat, paper, wood etc.). **off day** *n.* a day when one is on bad form. **off-drive** *v.t.* in cricket, to drive (the ball) off. *~n.* a drive to the off side. **offhand** *adv.* 1 without consideration, preparation or warning. 2 casually, summarily, curtly or brusquely. *~a.* 1 impromptu. 2 casual. 3 summary, curt or brusque. **offhanded** *a.* **offhandedly** *adv.* **offhandedness** *n.* **offing** *n.* that portion of the sea beyond the halfway line between the coast and the horizon. **in the offing** likely to occur soon. **offish** *a.* (*coll.*) inclined to be distant, reserved or stiff in manner. **offishly** *adv.* **offishness** *n.* **off-key** *a., adv.* 1 out of tune. 2 out of keeping. **off-licence** *n.* 1 a licence to sell intoxicating liquors to be consumed off the premises. 2 premises operating under such a licence. **off-limits** *a.* out of bounds. **off-line** *a.* (of a computer peripheral) switched off, not under the control of a central processor. *~adv.* with a delay between the production and processing of data. **offload** *v.i., v.t.* 1 to unload. 2 to get rid of (something on to someone else). **off of** *prep.* (*sl.*) off (*Get off of the floor*). **off-peak** *a.* (of a service) during a period of low demand. *~adv.* at times of low demand. **off-piste** *a., adv.* away from regular ski runs. **off-price** *a.* (*N Am.*) (of goods) sold at lower than the manufacturer's recommended price. **offprint** *n.* a reprint of an article or separate part of a periodical etc. **off-putting** *a.* 1 disconcerting. 2 causing aversion, repellent. **off-puttingly** *adv.* **off-road** *a.* 1 on rough ground away from the road. 2 (of a vehicle etc.) designed for driving or riding on rough ground.

off-roader *n.* **off-roading** *n.* **offscourings** *n.pl.* scum; dregs. **off-screen** *adv., a.* (appearing or happening) out of sight of the viewer of a film, television programme etc. **off-season** *a., adv.* out of season. ~*n.* a period of low (business) activity. **offset** *n.* **1** a lateral shoot or branch that takes root or is caused to take root and is used for propagation; an offshoot, a scion. **2** a spur or branch of a mountain range. **3** anything allowed as a counterbalance, equivalent, or compensation. **4** an amount set off (against). **5** in surveying, a short course measured perpendicularly to the main line. **6** a part where the thickness of a wall is diminished, usu. towards the top. **7** a bend or fitting bringing a pipe past an obstacle. ~*v.t.* (*pres.p.* **offsetting,** *past, p.p.* **offset**) **1** to balance by an equivalent. **2** to counterbalance, to compensate. **3** to print using the offset process. **offset printing** *n.* a (lithographic) printing process in which the image is first transferred from a plate on to a cylinder before it is printed on to paper. **offshoot** *n.* **1** a branch or shoot from a main stem. **2** a subsidiary matter. **offshore** *a., adv.* **1** blowing off the land. **2** situated a short way from the land. **3** (made or registered) abroad. **offside** *n.* **1** in football etc., the field between the ball and the opponents' goal. **2** the right side of a horse etc. **3** the side of a vehicle away from the kerb. ~*a.* (of a player in football etc.) illegally ahead of the ball etc. when it is played. **offsider** *n.* (*Austral., coll.*) a friend, partner. **offspring** *n.* (*pl.* **offspring**) **1** issue, progeny. **2** (*collect.*) children, descendants. **3** a child. **4** a production or result of any kind. **off-stage** *a., adv.* out of sight of the theatre audience. **off-street** *a.* (of parking) in a car park; away from the street. **off-the-shelf** *a.* (of goods) available from stock; ready-made. **off the shelf** *adv.* **off-the-shoulder** *a.* (of a dress etc.) cut so as to reveal the shoulders. **off-time** *n.* a time when little is happening. **off-white** *n.* a white colour with a tinge of grey, yellow etc. ~*a.* not quite white. [stressed form of OF]

offal (of´əl) *n.* **1** parts of the carcass of an animal, including the head, tail, kidneys, heart, liver etc. (used as food). **2** refuse, rubbish, waste. **3** carrion. [OFF, FALL]

offcut, offbeat OFF.

offend (əfend´) *v.t.* **1** to wound the feelings of, to hurt. **2** to make angry, to cause displeasure or disgust in, to outrage, to annoy, to transgress. ~*v.i.* **1** to transgress or violate a law. **2** to cause anger, disgust etc., to scandalize. **offence** (əfens´), (*N Am.*) **offense** *n.* **1** the act of offending, an aggressive act. **2** an affront, an insult. **3** the state or a sense of being hurt, annoyed, or affronted; umbrage. **4** a breach of custom, a transgression, a sin. **5** a misdeed. **6** an illegal act. **to give offence** to cause umbrage, to affront or insult. **to take offence** to be offended, to feel a grievance. **offenceless** *a.* **offendedly** *adv.* **offender** *n.* **offending** *a.* **offensive** *a.* **1** of, relating to or used for attack, aggressive. **2** causing or meant to cause offence. **3** irritating, vexing, annoying. **4** disgusting. **5** disagreeable, repulsive. **6** (*esp. N Am.*) of or relating to the team in possession of the ball etc. at a particular point during a game. ~*n.* **1** the attitude, method or act of attacking. **2** (*Mil.*) a strategic attack. **offensively** *adv.* **offensiveness** *n.* [OF *offendre*, L *offendere* (OF -, *fendere*, to strike), p.p. *offensus*]

OFFER (of´ə) *abbr.* Office of Electricity Regulation.

offer (of´ə) *v.t.* **1** to present, to put forward, to tender for acceptance or refusal. **2** to present as an act of worship. **3** to sacrifice, to immolate. **4** to propose. **5** to bid (as a price). **6** to evince readiness (to do something). **7** to essay, to attempt. **8** to proffer, to make available for sale. **9** to show an intention (to). ~*v.i.* **1** to present or show itself, to appear, to occur. **2** to make an attempt (at). ~*n.* **1** an act of offering. **2** an expression of willingness or readiness (to). **3** a tender, proffer or proposal, to be accepted or refused. **4** a price or sum bid. **5** an attempt, an essay. **on offer** presented for sale, consumption etc., esp. at a bargain price. **under offer** provisionally sold prior to and subject to the signing of a contract. **offerable** *a.* **offerer** *n.* **offering** *n.* **offeror** *n.* **offertory** (-təri) *n.* (*pl.* **offertories**) **1** that part of the Mass or liturgical service during which offerings or oblations are made. **2** in the Church of England, an anthem sung or the text spoken while these are being made. **3** the offering of these oblations. **4** the gifts offered. **5** any collection made at a religious service. [OE *offrian*, to bring an offering, to sacrifice; in later senses from F *offrir*; both from L *offerre* (OF -, *ferre*, to bring)]

offhand OFF.

office (of´is) *n.* **1** a room, building or other place where business is carried on. **2** (*collect.*) the persons charged with business at a particular place, the official staff or organization as a whole. **3** a duty, charge, function; the task or service attached to a particular post or station. **4** a post of service, trust or authority, esp. under a public body. **5** a particular task, service or duty. **6** a government department or agency. **7** (*N Am.*) a consulting room. **8** an act of worship of prescribed form, an act of help, kindness or duty. **9** (*often in pl.*) a service. **10** (*pl.*) the rooms or places in which the domestic duties of a house are discharged. **11** (*coll.*) a lavatory. **12** (*sl.*) a hint or signal. **office-bearer** *n.* **1** a person who holds office. **2** a person who performs an appointed duty. **office block** *n.* a large building containing offices. **office boy, office girl** *n.* a person employed to perform minor tasks in an office. **office hours** *n.pl.* the time during which an office is open for business. **office of arms** *n.* the College of Arms. **officer** *n.* **1** a person holding a post or position of authority, esp. a government functionary. **2** a person elected to perform certain duties by a society, committee etc., or appointed to a command in the armed services or merchant navy. **3** a police officer. ~*v.t.* **1** to provide with officers. **2** to act as commander of. **officer of arms** *n.* an officer of the College of Arms responsible for creating and granting heraldic arms. **officer of the day** *n.* an army officer responsible for security on a particular day. **office worker** *n.* an employee in an office. **official** (əfish´əl) *a.* **1** of or relating to an office or public duty. **2** holding an office, employed in public duties. **3** derived from or executed under proper authority. **4** duly authorized. **5** characteristic of persons in office. **6** authorized by the pharmacopoeia, officinal. ~*n.* **1** a person who holds a public office. **2** (*also* **official principal**) a judge or presiding officer in an ecclesiastical court. **official birthday** *n.* the day in June when the British sovereign's birthday is observed. **officialdom, officialism** *n.* **officialese** (-ēz´) *n.* official jargon. **officially** *adv.* **official receiver** *n.* an officer appointed by a receiving order to administer a bankrupt's estate. **official secrets** *n.pl.* confidential information relating to national security. **officiate** (əfish´-) *v.i.* **1** to perform official duties, to act in an official capacity. **2** to perform a prescribed function or duty. **3** to conduct public worship. **officiant** *n.* **officiation** (-ā´shən) *n.* **officiator** *n.* [OF, from L *officium* (OF -, *facere*, to make or do)]

Usage note See note on *official* under OFFICIOUS.

---

officinal (əfis´inəl, ofisī´-) *a.* **1** (of a pharmaceutical product) ready-prepared. **2** authorized by the pharmacopoeia. **3** used in medicine. **4** medicinal. **5** used in, of or relating to a shop. ~*n.* an officinal preparation or plant. **officinally** *adv.*

officious (əfish´əs) *a.* **1** aggressively interfering. **2** forward in doing or offering unwanted kindness, meddling, intrusive. **3** in diplomacy, informally related to official concerns or objects, not official. **officiously**

adv. **officiousness** *n.* [L *officiōsus*, obliging]

Usage note The adjectives *officious* and *official* should not be confused: *officious* means meddlesome, and *official* relating to office or duty.

offing, offish etc. OFF.
Ofgas (of´gas) *abbr.* Office of Gas Supply.
OFris *abbr.* Old Frisian.
OFSTED (of´sted) *abbr.* Office for Standards in Education.
OFT *abbr.* Office of Fair Trading.
oft OFTEN.
Oftel (of´tel) *abbr.* Office of Telecommunications.
often (of´ən, -tən) *adv.* **1** frequently, many times. **2** in many instances. ~*a.* (*Bible*) frequent, repeated. **as often as not** in roughly half of the instances. **more often than not** (quite) frequently. **oft** (oft) *adv.* (*poet.*) often (*esp. in comb.*). **oft-recurring** *a.* frequently recurring. **oftenness** *n.* †**oftentimes, oft-times** *adv.* frequently. [OE, cp. Icel. and G *oft*, Dan. *ofte*, Swed. *ofta*]
Ofwat (of´wot) *abbr.* Office of Water Services.
ogam OGHAM.
ogdoad (og´dōad) *n.* a set of eight. [Gr. *ogdoas -ados*, from *oktō*, eight]
ogee (ō´jē) *n.* **1** a wavelike moulding having an inner and outer curve like the letter S, a talon. **2** an ogee arch. ~*a.* having such a double curve. **ogee arch** *n.* a pointed arch each side of which is formed of a concave and a convex curve. **ogee'd** *a.* [prob. from F OGIVE, this moulding being commonly used for ribs in groining]
Ogen melon (ō´gən) *n.* a variety of small sweet melon resembling a cantaloupe. [the kibbutz in Israel where it was developed]
ogham (og´əm), **ogam** *n.* **1** an ancient Celtic system of writing consisting of an alphabet of twenty characters derived from the runes. **2** any character in this. **3** an inscription in this. **oghamic** (-am´-, og´-) *a.* [OIr. *ogam*, *ogum*, said to be from the inventor *Ogma*]
ogive (ō´jīv, ōjiv´) *n.* **1** a diagonal rib of a vault. **2** a pointed or Gothic arch. **3** an S-shaped line. **4** a cumulative frequency graph. **ogival** (ōjī´-) *a.* [F, earlier *augive*, perh. from Sp. *auge*, Arab. *āwf*, the summit]
ogle (ō´gəl) *v.t.* to look or stare at with admiration, wonder etc., esp. amorously. ~*v.i.* to cast amorous or lewd glances. ~*n.* **1** an amorous glance or look. **2** a lewd stare. **ogler** *n.* [cp. LG *äegeln*, G *hugeln*, freq. of *augen*, to look, from *Auge*, eye]
ogre (ō´gə) *n.* **1** a fairy-tale giant living on human flesh. **2** a monster, a barbarously cruel person. **ogreish, ogrish** *a.* **ogress** (ōg´ris) *n.* a female ogre. [F, first used by Charles Perrault in his *Contes*, 1697]
Ogygian (ōjij´iən) *a.* **1** of great or obscure antiquity, primeval. **2** of or relating to Ogyges, a legendary king of Attica or Boeotia. [L *Ogygius*, Gr. *Ogugios*, from *Ogugos* or *Ogugēs*]
OH *abbr.* Ohio.
oh O[4].
o.h.c. *abbr.* overhead camshaft.
OHG *abbr.* Old High German.
ohm (ōm) *n.* the unit of electrical resistance, that between two points on a conductor when a potential difference of one volt produces a current of one amp. **ohmage** (-ij) *n.* **ohmic** *a.* **ohmically** *adv.* **ohmmeter** *n.* **Ohm's law** *n.* the law that current is proportional to voltage and inversely proportional to resistance. [Georg Simon *Ohm*, 1787–1854, German physicist]
OHMS *abbr.* On Her/His Majesty's Service.
oho (əhō´) *int.* used to express surprise, irony or exultation. [O[4], HO]
-oholic -AHOLIC.
ohone (ōhōn´), **ochone** (ōkhōn´) *int., n.* a Scottish and Irish cry of lamentation. [Gael. and Ir. *ochōin*]
OHP *abbr.* overhead projector.
o.h.v. *abbr.* overhead valve.
oi (oi) *int.* used to give warning, attract attention etc. ~*n.* an aggressive type of early 1980s music which often expressed racist sentiments. ~*a.* of or relating to oi.
-oid (oid) *comb. form* forming adjectives and nouns denoting resemblance, as in *colloid, cycloid, rhomboid*. **-oidal** *comb. form* forming adjectives. **-oidally** *comb. form* forming adverbs. [mod. L *-oïdes*, Gr. *-oeidēs* (*-eidēs*, like, rel. to *eidos*, form)]
-oidea (oi´dēə) *comb. form* denoting zoological classes or families. [L *-oīdēs*, -oid]
oidium (oi´diəm) *n.* (*pl.* **oidia** (-ə)) **1** any of various fungal spores. **2** a powdery mildew. [mod. L, from Gr. *ōon*, egg, *-idion*, dim. suf.]
OIEO *abbr.* offers in excess of.
oik (oik) *n.* (*coll.*) **1** a stupid or uncouth person. **2** a fool, a cad. [etym. uncertain]
oil (oil) *n.* **1** an unctuous liquid, insoluble in water, soluble in ether and usually in alcohol, obtained from various animal and vegetable substances. **2** (*pl.*) oil colours, paints. **3** (*pl.*) oilskins. ~*v.t.* **1** to smear, anoint, rub, soak, treat or impregnate with oil. **2** to lubricate with or as with oil. ~*v.i.* **1** to turn into oil. **2** to take oil aboard as fuel. **3** to become oily. **to burn the midnight oil** to study or work far into the night. **to oil someone's palm** to bribe someone. **to oil the wheels** to facilitate matters, to help things go smoothly. **oil-bird** *n.* a nocturnal S American bird, *Steatornis caripensis*, the fat of whose young yields edible oil. **oilcake** *n.* the refuse after oil is pressed or extracted from linseed etc., used as fodder. **oil can** *n.* a can for holding oil, esp. one used for oiling machinery. **oilcloth** *n.* **1** a fabric coated with white lead ground in oil. **2** an oilskin. **oil colour,** (*N Am.*) **oil color** *n.* (an) oil paint. **oil drum** *n.* a metal drum in which oil is transported. **oiled** *a.* **1** greased with, lubricated by, saturated or preserved in oil. **2** (*coll.*) drunk. **on oiled wheels** very smoothly. **oiled silk** *n.* silk treated with oil so that it is waterproof. **oil engine** *n.* an internal-combustion engine which burns vaporized oil. **oiler** *n.* **1** a person who or something which oils. **2** an oil can for lubricating machinery etc. **3** (*N Am.*) an oil well. **4** (*pl.*) oilskins. **5** an oil tanker. **oilfield** *n.* a region where mineral oil is obtained. **oil-fired** *a.* burning oil as fuel. **oilgas** *n.* gas obtained from oil by distillation. **oil gauge** *n.* an instrument showing the level of oil in a tank etc. **oil-gland** *n.* a gland secreting oil. **oil hole** *n.* a hole through which lubricating oil is applied to parts of machinery. **oil lamp** *n.* a lamp that uses oil as fuel. **oilless** *a.* **oilman** *n.* (*pl.* **oilmen**) **1** a person whose business is oils. **2** a person who works in the oil industry. **3** a person who owns an oil well. **oil-meal** *n.* oilcake ground into meal. **oil-mill** *n.* **1** an oil-press. **2** a factory where oil is expressed. **oilnut** *n.* any of various oil-yielding nuts including the butternut and buffalo nut. **oil of juniper** *n.* oil from juniper cones, used in medicine and in gin etc. **oil of rhodium** *n.* an oil obtained from the rhodium. **oil of turpentine** *n.* a volatile oil distilled from turpentine, for mixing paint, varnishes etc. and in medicine. **oil of vitriol** *n.* sulphuric acid. **oil of wintergreen** *n.* an aromatic oil orig. made from the leaves of the checkerberry, *Gaultheria procumbens*. **oil paint** *n.* (a) paint made by grinding a pigment in oil. **oil painting** *n.* **1** the art of painting with oil paints. **2** a painting in oil paints. **no oil painting** physically unattractive. **oil-palm** *n.* a palm tree bearing fruits yielding palm oil, esp. *Elaeis guineensis* of W Africa. **oil pan** *n.* an engine sump. **oil platform** *n.* a floating or fixed offshore structure which supports an oil rig. **oil-press** *n.* a machine for pressing the oil from seeds, nuts etc. **oil rig** *n.* an installation for drilling and extracting oil and natural gas. **oil-sand** *n.* a stratum of porous rock impregnated with petroleum. **oilseed** *n.* any of various

oil-yielding seeds including sesame and sunflower seeds. **oil-shale** *n.* a shale from which mineral oils can be distilled. **oil-shark** *n.* a species of shark that yields oil. **oilskin** *n.* 1 cloth rendered waterproof by treatment with oil. 2 a garment of this cloth. 3 (*pl.*) a suit of such garments. **oil slick** *n.* a patch of floating oil, usu. pollutant. **oilstock** *n.* a vessel for holding holy oil. **oilstone** *n.* a fine-grained whetstone lubricated with oil before use. **oil tanker** *n.* a large vessel for transporting oil. **oil tree** *n.* any bush or tree which yields oil, e.g. the castor oil plant. **oil well** *n.* a boring made for petroleum. **oily** *a.* (*comp.* **oilier**, *superl.* **oiliest**) 1 consisting of, containing, covered with or like oil. 2 unctuous, smooth, insinuating. **oilily** *adv.* **oiliness** *n.* [ME, OF *oile*, L *oleum*, from *olea*, olive]

oin- OENO-.

oink (oingk) *n.* the grunt of a pig. ~*v.i.* to make such a sound. [imit.]

oino- OENO-.

ointment (oint´mənt) *n.* a soft unctuous preparation applied to diseased or injured parts or used as a cosmetic; an unguent. [ME *oinement*, OF *oignement*, L *unguentum*, UNGUENT]

Oireachtas (er´əkhtəs) *n.* the legislature of the Republic of Ireland. [Ir., assembly, convocation]

OIRO *abbr.* offers in the region of.

Ojibwa (ōjib´wā), **Ojibway** *n.* (*pl.* **Ojibwa, Ojibwas, Ojibway, Ojibways**) 1 a member of a N American people living in the westerly region of the Great Lakes. 2 their language. ~*a.* of or relating to the Ojibwa or their language. [Algonquian *ojib-ubway*, a type of moccasin]

OK[1] (ōkā´), **okay** *a., int., adv.* (*coll.*) quite correct, all right. ~*v.t.* (*3rd pers. sing. pres.* **OK's, okays,** *pres.p.* **OK'ing, okaying,** *past, p.p.* **OK'd, OKed, okayed**) to authorize, to endorse, to approve. ~*n.* (*pl.* **OKs, okays**) approval, sanction, agreement. **okey-doke** (ōkidōk´), **okey-dokey** (-dō´ki) *int.* (*coll.*) used as a casual or amiable form of assent or agreement. [said to be short for *orl korrect*]

OK[2] *abbr.* Oklahoma.

okapi (ōkah´pi) *n.* (*pl. in general* **okapi,** *in particular* **okapis**) a ruminant mammal, *Okapia johnstoni*, with a dark chestnut coat and stripes on the hindquarters. [W Afr.]

okay, okey-doke OK[1].

Okla. *abbr.* Oklahoma.

okra (ō´krə, ok´-) *n.* an African plant, *Abelmoschus esculentus*, cultivated for its green pods used in curries, soups, stews etc.; also called *gumbo* and *ladies' fingers.* [W Afr.]

-ol (ol) *suf.* denoting a chemical compound containing an alcohol, or (loosely) an oil, as *benzol, menthol, phenol.* [L *oleum*, oil]

old (ōld) *a.* (*comp.* **older, elder,** *superl.* **oldest, eldest**) 1 advanced in years or long in existence. 2 not young, fresh, new or recent. 3 like an old person, experienced, thoughtful. 4 crafty, cunning, practised (at), confirmed (in). 5 decayed by process of time, worn, dilapidated. 6 stale, trite. 7 customary, wonted. 8 obsolete, effete, out of date, antiquated, matured. 9 of any specified duration. 10 belonging to a former period, made or established long ago, ancient, bygone, long cultivated or worked. 11 early, previous, former, quondam. 12 (of a language) denoting the earliest known form. 13 (*coll.*) used to express familiarity or endearment. 14 (*coll.*) used to emphasize (*high old time*). **any old** ANY. **for old sake's sake** SAKE[1]. **for old time's sake** SAKE[1]. **money for old rope** MONEY. **of old** 1 in or from ancient times. 2 long ago, formerly. **of old standing** long established. **old as the hills** (*coll.*) very old, ancient. **one's old self** SELF. **the oldest profession** PROFESSION. **the (same) old story** a familiar sequence of events, the usual thing. **old age** *n.* the latter part of life. **old-age pension** *n.* RETIREMENT PENSION (under RETIRE). **old-age pensioner** *n.* **Old Bailey** *n.* the Central Criminal Court of the City of London. **old bean** *n.* (*dated sl.*) old fellow, old chap. **Old Bill** *n.* (*sl.*) the police. **old bird** *n.* (*sl.*) a wary person. **Old Blazes** *n.* (*sl.*) the Devil. **old blue** *n.* a former University athlete. **old boy** *n.* 1 (*also* **Old Boy**) a former pupil of a school. 2 (*coll.*) used as a friendly form of address to a man or boy. 3 (*coll.*) an elderly man. **old boy network** *n.* (*coll.*) a network of former pupils of public schools and universities, who can use their contacts for employment opportunities etc. **old buffer** *n.* a doddering old man. **Old Church Slavonic** *n.* the earliest written Slavonic language. **old cock** *n.* (*coll.*) used as a familiar form of address to a man. **old country** *n.* the country of origin of an immigrant or their ancestors. **Old Covenant** *n.* the Jewish dispensation. **Old Dart** *n.* (*Austral., sl.*) 1 Britain. 2 England. **old dear** *n.* (*coll.*) 1 an elderly person, esp. a woman. 2 one's mother. **Old Dragon** *n.* the Devil. **olden** *a.* old, ancient, bygone. **Old English** *n.* 1 the English language in use before about 1150, also called *Anglo-Saxon.* 2 (*Print.*) BLACK LETTER (under BLACK). **Old English Sheepdog** *n.* a large English breed of sheepdog with a shaggy coat. **olde worlde** (ōldi wœ´ldi) *a.* (emphatically) old-fashioned and quaint. **old-fashioned** *a.* 1 out of date, outmoded. 2 quaint. **old fogy** *n.* (*pl.* **old fogies**) (*derog.*) an older person with conservative, eccentric or old-fashioned ideas or ways. **Old French** *n.* the French language of the period before *c.* 1400. **old fruit** *n.* (*coll.*) a form of address to a man. **old fustic** *n.* 1 a tropical American tree, *Chlorophora tinctoria.* 2 the wood of this. **Old Gentleman** *n.* (*coll.*) the Devil. **old girl** *n.* 1 (*also* **Old Girl**) a former pupil of a school. 2 (*coll.*) used as a friendly form of address to a woman or girl. 3 (*coll.*) an elderly woman. **Old Glory** *n.* (*N Am.*) the US flag. **old gold** *n.* a dull brownish-gold colour. **old-gold** *a.* **old guard** *n.* the old or conservative members of a party etc. **old hand** *n.* 1 a person who is skilled or practised at a trade or craft of any kind. 2 any of the early convicts in Australia etc. **old hat** *a.* (*coll.*) 1 outdated, old-fashioned. 2 familiar and dull. **Old High German** *n.* High German before *c.* 1200. **Old Icelandic** *n.* the Icelandic language up to the 16th cent. **old identity** *n.* (*Austral., New Zeal., coll.*) an old inhabitant. **oldie** *n.* (*coll.*) an old thing or person (e.g. an old song or film). **oldish** *a.* **old lady** *n.* (*coll.*) 1 a female sexual partner, a wife. 2 a mother. 3 used as a friendly form of address to a woman. 4 an elderly woman. **old lag** *n.* a habitual convict. **old leaven** *n.* the elements of original sin in human nature. **old maid** *n.* 1 (*derog.*) an unmarried woman of advanced years or unlikely ever to marry. 2 a card game in which an unpaired queen at the end of a hand scores against one. 3 a precise, prudish, fidgety person of either sex. **old-maidish** *a.* **old man** *n.* (*coll.*) 1 a male sexual partner, a husband. 2 a father. 3 used as a friendly form of address to a man. 4 an elderly man. 5 an employer. **old man's beard** *n.* traveller's joy. **old master** *n.* a masterly painter or painting of former times, esp. of the 16th–18th cents. **old moon** *n.* the moon at the end of its course, before the new moon. **oldness** *n.* **Old Nick** *n.* (*coll.*) the Devil. **Old Norse** *n.* the language of Norway and its territories until the 14th cent. **Old One** *n.* (*coll.*) the Devil. **old one** *n.* a familiar joke. **Old Pals Act** *n.* (*coll.*) the principle that friends should help one another. **old penny** *n.* a former unit of British money of which there were 240 to the pound. **Old Prussian** *n.* an extinct Baltic language spoken in Prussia until the 17th cent. **old retainer** *n.* an old and faithful servant. **old salt** *n.* a sailor. **Old Saxon** *n.* the dialect of the period *c.* 1200 from which Low German developed. **old school** *n.* those who adhere to past traditions or principles. ~*a.* of or relating to past traditions or principles.

of the old school belonging to past ways, traditions etc. **old school tie** *n.* **1** a tie sporting a public school's colours worn by its former pupils. **2** a symbol of the mutual allegiance of a group of (esp. privileged or upper class) people. **Old Scratch** *n.* the Devil. **old soldier** *n.* **1** a former soldier or veteran. **2** a person with experience. **old squaw** *n.* (*N Am.*) the long-tailed northern sea duck, *Clangula hyemalis.* **old stager** *n.* an old hand. **oldster** *n.* an old or elderly person. **Old Style** *n.* (*Hist.*) the Julian method of reckoning dates, used till 1582. **Old Testament** *n.* the part of the Christian Bible that covers the old or Mosaic dispensation. **old-time** *a.* **1** old, ancient. **2** old-fashioned. **old-timer** *n.* (*coll.*) **1** an old man. **2** a veteran. **3** a person who has remained in a situation for a long time. **old wives' tale** *n.* a legend, a foolish story. **old woman** *n.* (*coll.*) **1** a wife or mother. **2** a timid, fidgety or fussy man. **old-womanish** *a.* **old-womanishness** *n.* **Old World** *n.* the eastern hemisphere. **old-world** *a.* **1** old-fashioned, quaint. **2** belonging to old times. **old year** *n.* the year just ended or on the point of ending. [OE *eald, ald* (cp. Dut. *oud,* G *alt,* L *ultus,* in *adultus*), from the root *al-,* to nourish, as in L *alere,* to feed]

olé (ōlā´) *int.* used to express approval or victory at a bullfight. [Sp., Arab. *wa,* and, *allah,* God]

ole- OLEO-.

-ole (ōl) *comb. form* (*Chem.*) forming names of organic compounds, esp. heterocyclic ones. [L *oleum,* oil]

oleaceous (ōliā´shəs) *a.* of the plant family Oleaceae, which includes ash, privet, olive, jasmine and lilac. [L *Oleaceae,* from *olea,* olive tree]

oleaginous (ōliaj´inəs) *a.* oily, greasy, unctuous. **oleaginously** *adv.* **oleaginousness** *n.* [through F *oléagineux* or directly from L *oleāginus,* from *oleum,* oil]

oleander (ōlian´də) *n.* a poisonous evergreen shrub, *Nerium oleander,* with lanceolate leaves and pink or white flowers. [med. L, perh. var. of *lōrandrum,* corr. of *rhododendrum,* RHODODENDRON, or *lauridendrum* (L *laurus,* LAUREL, Gr. *dendron,* tree)]

oleaster (ōlias´tə) *n.* **1** any shrub or tree of the genus *Elaeagnus,* esp. *E. angustifolia,* also called *Russian olive.* **2** the true wild olive, *Olea oleaster.* [L (*olea,* olive, -ASTER)]

oleate (ō´liət) *n.* a salt or ester of oleic acid.

olecranon (ōlikrā´non) *n.* the bony projection of the ulna at the elbow. [Gr. *ōlekrānon,* from *ōlenē,* elbow, *krānion,* head]

olefin (ō´lifin), **olefine** (-fēn) *n.* any one of a group of hydrocarbons containing two atoms of hydrogen to one of carbon. **olefinic** (-fin´-) *a.*

oleic (ōlē´ik) *a.* of, relating to or derived from oil. **oleic acid** *n.* an unsaturated liquid fatty acid that occurs as a glyceride in many fats and oils. **oleiferous** (-if´-) *a.*

olein (ō´liin) *n.* **1** an oily compound, chief constituent of fatty oils, triolene. **2** a liquid oil occurring in most natural oils or fats.

olent (ō´lənt) *a.* smelling, yielding fragrance. [L *olens -ntem,* pres.p. of *olēre,* to smell]

oleo (ō´liō) *n.* (*pl.* **oleos**) **1** short for OLEOMARGARINE. **2** short for OLEOGRAPH.

oleo- (ō´liō), **ole-** *comb. form* oil. [L *oleum,* oil]

oleograph (ō´liəgrahf) *n.* a picture printed in oil colours to resemble a painting. **oleographic** (-graf´-) *a.* **oleography** (-og´-) *n.*

oleomargarine (ōliōmah´jərēn) *n.* **1** a yellow fatty substance from beef tallow, used in margarine. **2** (*chiefly N Am.*) margarine.

oleometer (ōliom´itə) *n.* an instrument for determining the relative densities of oils.

oleon (ō´lion) *n.* an oily liquid obtained by the dry distillation of oleic acid with lime.

oleoresin (ōliōrez´in) *n.* a mixture of an essential oil and a resin.

oleraceous (olərā´shəs) *a.* **1** of the nature of a pot-herb. **2** edible. [L *oleraceus* (*olus oleris,* pot-herb, -ACEOUS)]

oleum (ō´liəm) *n.* fuming sulphuric acid.

olfactory (olfak´təri) *a.* of, relating to or used in smelling. ~*n.* (*pl.* **olfactories**) (*usu. pl.*) an organ of smell. **olfaction** *n.* the sense or process of smelling. **olfactive** *a.* [L *olfacere* (*olēre,* to smell, *facere,* to make)]

OLG *abbr.* Old Low German.

olibanum (olib´ənəm) *n.* a gum resin from certain species of *Boswellia,* formerly used in medicine, now as incense; frankincense. [med. L, from late L and Gr. *libanos,* incense]

olid (ol´id) *a.* rank, stinking. [L *olidus,* from *olēre,* to smell]

olig- OLIGO-.

oligarch (ol´igahk) *n.* a member of an oligarchy. **oligarchal** (-gah´-) *a.* **oligarchic** (-gah´-), **oligarchical** *a.* **oligarchically** *adv.* **oligarchist** *n.* **oligarchy** *n.* (*pl.* **oligarchies**) **1** a form of government in which power is vested in the hands of a small exclusive class. **2** the members of such a class. **3** a state so governed. [Gr. *oligarchēs* (OLIGO-, *archein,* to govern)]

oligo- (ol´igō), **olig-** *comb. form* denoting few, small. [Gr. *oligos,* small, *oligoi,* few]

oligocarpous (oligōkah´pəs) *a.* having few fruits.

Oligocene (ol´igəsēn) *a.* of or relating to the age or strata between the Eocene and Miocene. ~*n.* this epoch or system.

oligochaete (ol´igōkēt) *n.* an annelid worm of the division Oligochaeta having bristles along its length to aid locomotion. ~*a.* of or relating to the Oligochaeta.

oligochrome (ol´igōkrōm) *a.* painted or decorated in few colours.

oligoclase (ol´igōklās) *n.* a soda-lime feldspar resembling albite.

oligopod (olig´əpod) *a.* (*Zool.*) having few legs or feet.

oligopoly (oligop´əli) *n.* (*pl.* **oligopolies**) a situation in the market in which a few producers control the supply of a product. **oligopolist** *n.* **oligopolistic** (-lis´-) *a.*

oligopsony (oligop´səni) *n.* (*pl.* **oligopsonies**) a situation in the market in which purchase is in the hands of a small number of buyers. **oligopsonist** *n.* **oligopsonistic** (-nis´-) *a.*

oligosaccharide (oligōsak´ərīd) *n.* any carbohydrate consisting of a few monosaccharide units linked together.

oligotrophic (oligōtrof´ik) *a.* (of lakes etc. in rocky terrain) being nutritionally poor, sparsely vegetated, but rich in oxygen.

olio (ō´liō) *n.* (*pl.* **olios**) **1** a mixed dish. **2** a mixture, a medley, a variety, a pot-pourri. [Sp. *olla,* stew, L, a pot]

olive (ol´iv) *n.* **1** an evergreen tree of the genus *Olea,* with narrow leathery leaves and clusters of oval drupes yielding oil when ripe and eaten unripe as a relish, esp. *O. europaea* and *O. africana.* **2** the fruit of this tree. **3** its wood. **4** the colour of the unripe olive, a dull yellowish green or brown. **5** either of a pair of olive-shaped swellings in the medulla oblongata. **6** any olive-shaped gastropod of the genus *Oliva,* or its shell. **7** an oval bar or button fitting into a loop, for fastening a garment. **8** (*usu. in pl.*) a slice of beef or veal rolled with onions etc., stewed. **9** a metal ring or fitting such as that in a compression joint. ~*a.* of an olive colour. **olivaceous** (-vā´shəs) *a.* olive-coloured. **olivary** *a.* olive-shaped, oval. **olive branch** *n.* **1** a branch of the olive tree as an emblem of peace. **2** something which indicates a desire for peace (e.g. a goodwill gesture, an offer of reconciliation). **olive crown** *n.* a garland of olive leaves as a symbol of victory. **olive drab** *n.* (*N Am.*) **1** a dull olive-green colour. **2** a fabric or garment of this colour, esp. a US army uniform. **olive-drab** *a.* **olive green** *a.*, *n.* (of) a dull yellowish green or brown colour. **olive oil** *n.* an oil extracted from olives. **olivet** (-vet) *n.* **1** an olive-shaped button. **2** a kind of mock pearl, used as a trading bead. **olive yard** *n.* a piece of ground on which olives are cultivated. **olivine** (ol´ivēn, -vēn´) *n.* a mineral silicate of magnesium and iron. **olivinic** (-vin´-), **olivinitic** *a.* [F, from L *olīva*]

oliver (ol´ivə) *n.* a small trip-hammer worked by the foot, used in making nails etc. [etym. uncertain, prob. from the proper name]

Oliverian (oliviə´riən) *n.* a partisan or adherent of Oliver Cromwell in the English Civil War.

olivet, olivine OLIVE.

olla (ol´ə) *n.* **1** an olio. **2** an olla podrida. **olla podrida** (pədrē´də) *n.* **1** a Spanish dish consisting of meat chopped fine, stewed with vegetables. **2** a multifarious or incongruous mixture. [Sp.]

ollamh (ol´əv), **ollav** *n.* among the ancient Irish, a learned man, a doctor, a scholar. [Ir.]

olm (olm) *n.* a blind, cave-dwelling type of European salamander, *Proteus anguinus.* [G]

ology (ol´əji) *n.* (*pl.* **ologies**) **1** a science. **2** any of the sciences whose names end in *-ology.*

-ology -LOGY.

oloroso (olərō´sō) *n.* (*pl.* **olorosos**) a medium-sweet golden sherry. [Sp., fragrant]

Olympiad (əlim´piad) *n.* **1** a period of four years, being the interval between the celebrations of the Olympic Games, a method of chronology used from 776 BC to AD 394. **2** (a staging of) an international contest, esp. the modern Olympic Games. **Olympian** *a.* **1** of or relating to Mount Olympus, the home of the Greek gods; celestial. **2** magnificent, lofty, superb. **3** Olympic. ~*n.* **1** any one of the twelve Greek gods regarded as living on Olympus. **2** a godlike person. **3** (*chiefly N Am.*) a contestant in the Olympic Games. **Olympic** *a.* of or relating to Olympia or the Olympic Games. **Olympic flame** *n.* the flame which burns throughout the Olympic Games, lit by the Olympic torch. **Olympic Games** *n.pl.* **1** the greatest of the Greek national games, held every four years at Olympia, in honour of Zeus. **2** a revival (since 1896) of this festival, an international four-yearly sports meeting. **Olympics** *n.pl.* the modern Olympic Games. **Olympic torch** *n.* the lighted torch brought by a runner from Olympia to light the Olympic flame. [F *olympiade*, L *olympias -adis*, Gr. *olumpias -ados*, from *Olumpios*, relating to *Olumpos*]

OM *abbr.* Order of Merit.

-oma (ō´mə) *comb. form* (*pl.* **-omas, -omata** (-tə)) denoting a tumour or growth. [Gr. *oma*, tumour]

omadhaun (om´ədawn) *n.* (*Ir.*) a fool, a simpleton. [Ir. *amedan*]

omasum (ōmā´səm) *n.* (*pl.* **omasa** (-sə)) (*Zool.*) the third stomach of a ruminant. [L]

-omata -OMA.

ombre (om´bə) *n.* a game of cards, for two, three or five players, popular in the 17th and 18th cents. [Sp. *hombre*, L *homo hominem*, man]

ombré (om´brā) *a.* (of a fabric etc.) with colours shading into each other from light to dark. [F, p.p. of *ombrer*, to shade]

ombro- (om´brō) *comb. form* denoting rain. [Gr. *ombros*]

ombrology (ombrol´əji) *n.* the branch of meteorology concerned with rainfall.

ombrometer (ombrom´itə) *n.* a rain gauge.

ombudsman (om´budzmən) *n.* (*pl.* **ombudsmen**) an official investigator of complaints against government bodies or employees; in the UK, the Parliamentary Commissioner for Administration. **ombudswoman** *n.* (*pl.* **ombudswomen**) a female ombudsman. [Swed.]

-ome (ōm) *comb. form* denoting a mass or part. [var. of -OMA]

omega (ō´migə, om´-) *n.* **1** the last letter of the Greek alphabet, Ω, ω. **2** the last of a series. **3** the conclusion, the end, the last stage or phase. [Gr. *ō mega*, the great]

omelette (om´lit), **omelet** *n.* a flat dish made with beaten eggs cooked in fat, eaten plain or seasoned and filled with herbs, cheese etc. [F *omelette*, earlier *amelette*, corr. of *alemette*, var. of *alemelle*, a thin plate, prob. from L LAMELLA]

omen (ō´mən) *n.* **1** an incident, object or appearance taken as indicating a good or evil event or outcome; a portent etc. **2** prognostication or prophetic signification. ~*v.t.* to prognosticate, to portend. **omened** *a.* (*usu. in comb.*). [L, earlier *osmen*, perh. for *ausmen* (cogn. with *audīre*, to hear)]

omentum (əmen´təm) *n.* (*pl.* **omenta** (-tə)) a fold of the peritoneum connecting the viscera with each other. **omental** *a.* [L]

omer (ō´mə) *n.* a Hebrew measure of capacity, 5¹⁄₁₆ pts (about 2.8 l). [Heb.]

omertà (omœtah´) *n.* a conspiracy of silence, part of the Mafia code of honour. [It.]

omicron (ōmī´kron, om´i-) *n.* the 15th letter of the Greek alphabet, O, o, the short o. [Gr. *o mikron*, the small o]

ominous (om´inəs) *a.* **1** threatening, portending evil. **2** of evil omen, inauspicious. **3** relating to or containing an omen. **ominously** *adv.* **ominousness** *n.* [L *ōminōsus* (OMEN, -OUS)]

omit (əmit´) *v.t.* (*pres.p.* **omitting,** *past, p.p.* **omitted**) **1** to leave out, not to include, insert or mention. **2** to neglect, to leave undone. **omissible** *a.* **omission** (-shən) *n.* **1** the act of omitting or fact of being omitted. **2** something omitted. **omissive** *a.* **omitter** *n.* [L *omittere* (*o-*, OB-, *mittere*, to send), p.p. *omissus*]

ommateum (omətē´əm) *n.* (*pl.* **ommatea** (-ə)) a compound eye. **ommatidium** (-tid´iəm) *n.* (*pl.* **ommatidia** (-ə)) any of the elements of a compound eye. [Gr. *omma -atos*, an eye]

omni- (om´ni) *comb. form* universally, in all ways, of all things. [L *omnis*, all]

omnibus (om´nibəs) *n.* **1** (*formal*) a bus. **2** a volume containing reprints of a number of works, usually by the same author. ~*a.* inclusive, embracing several or various items, objects etc. **omnibus bill** *n.* a legislative bill dealing with several subjects. **omnibus clause** *n.* a clause dealing with several subjects. **omnibus resolution** *n.* a resolution dealing with several subjects. [L, dat. pl. of *omnis*, for all]

omnicompetence (omnikom´pitəns) *n.* competence in all areas or matters. **omnicompetent** *a.*

omnidirectional (omnidirek´shənəl) *a.* (capable of) moving, sending or receiving in every direction (of radio waves, a radio transmitter or receiver).

omnifarious (omnifeə´riəs) *a.* of all kinds. **omnifariously** *adv.* **omnifariousness** *n.* [L *omnifarius*]

OMNIMAX® (om´nimaks) *a.* (of a film) shot for showing on a special screen that produces a hemispherical effect.

omnipotent (omnip´ətənt) *a.* **1** almighty. **2** having unlimited power. **the Omnipotent** God. **omnipotence, omnipotency** *n.* **omnipotently** *adv.*

omnipresent (omniprez´ənt) *a.* present in every place at the same time. **omnipresence** *n.*

omniscience (omnis´iəns) *n.* infinite knowledge. **omniscient** *a.* **omnisciently** *adv.*

omnium (om´niəm) *n.* in the Stock Exchange, the aggregate value of the different stocks in which a loan is funded. **omnium gatherum** (gah´dhərəm) *n.* (*coll.*) a miscellaneous collection or assemblage, a medley. [L, of all (things, kinds etc.)]

omnivore (om´nivaw) *n.* a creature that eats any type of available food (i.e. vegetable matter and meat). **omnivorous** (-niv´ərəs) *a.* **1** all-devouring. **2** feeding on anything available. **3** reading or making use of anything and everything. **omnivorously** *adv.* **omnivorousness** *n.*

omo- (ō´mō) *comb. form* of or relating to the shoulder. [Gr. *ōmos*, shoulder]

omohyoid (ōmōhī´oid) *a.* of or relating to the shoulder blade and the hyoid bone. ~*n.* the muscle between these.

omophagic (ōmōfaj´ik), **omophagous** (ōmof´əgəs) *a.* eating raw flesh. [Gr. *ōmophagos* (*ōmos*, raw, *phagein*, to eat)]

omoplate (ō´məplāt) *n.* the shoulder blade.

omosternum (ōmōstœ´nəm) *n.* an ossified process at the anterior extremity of the sternum, in certain animals.

omphacite (om´fəsīt) *n.* a green variety of pyroxene. [G *Omphazit* (Gr. *omphax*, unripe, -ITE[1])]

omphalo- (om´fəlō) *comb. form* relating to the navel. **omphalos** (-os) *n.* **1** the boss of an ancient Greek shield. **2** a stone in the temple of Apollo at Delphi, believed to be the middle point or navel of the earth. **3** a central point, a hub. **omphalic** (omfal´ik), **omphaloid** (om´fəloid) *a.* of, relating to or resembling the navel. [Gr. *omphalos*, navel]

ON *abbr.* Old Norse.

on (on) *prep.* **1** in or as in contact with, esp. as supported by, covering, encircling or suspended from the upper surface or level of. **2** into contact with the upper surface of, or in contact with from above. **3** in the direction of, tending toward, arrived at, against. **4** exactly at, next in order to, beside, immediately after, close to. **5** about, concerning, in the act of, in the making, performance, support, interest, process etc., of. **6** attached to. **7** present on. **8** carried with. **9** taking regularly (e.g. a drug). **10** at the expense of. **11** at the date, time or occasion of. **12** in a condition or state of. **13** sustained by. **14** by means of. **15** on the basis of. **16** in the manner of. ~*adv.* **1** so as to be in contact and supported, covering, environing, suspended from or adhering to something. **2** in advance, forward, in operation, action, movement, progress, persistence, or continuance of action or movement. **3** (*coll.*) drunk, nearly drunk. **4** taking place. **5** arranged. ~*a.* **1** denoting the side of a cricket field to the left of the batsman. **2** operating. **3** (*coll.*) wagered. **4** performing, broadcasting, playing (e.g. of a batsman). **5** definitely happening as arranged. **6** acceptable, possible, tolerable. ~*n.* in cricket, the on side. **off and on** intermittently. **on and off** intermittently. **on and on** ceaselessly, continuously. **to be on about** to talk about, esp. tediously. **to be on at** (*coll.*) to nag or grumble at. **to be on to 1** to be aware of, to have twigged on to or tumbled to. **2** to get in touch with. **to go on at someone** to nag someone. **to go on to** to advance, progress, move or travel to (a further level, position or place). **on-board** *a.* on, installed in or carried on a vehicle, ship etc. **oncoming** *n.* the coming on, advance or approach (of). ~*a.* approaching. **oncost** *n.* a supplementary or additional expense, an overhead. **onfall** *n.* an attack, an onset. **onflow** *n.* an onward flow. **onglaze** *a.* (of painting etc.) done on a glazed surface. **ongoing** *n.* **1** procedure, progress. **2** (*pl.*) goings-on, misbehaviour. **3** proceedings. ~*a.* **1** unceasing, continuous. **2** in progress. **ongoingness** *n.* **on-licence** *n.* a licence to sell intoxicating liquor for consumption on the premises. **on-line** *a.*, *adv.* (of a computer peripheral) under the control of the central processor. **onlooker** *n.* a spectator, a person who looks on. **onlooking** *a.* **on-off** *a.* **1** (of a switch) having two positions, 'on' or 'off'. **2** intermittent. **onrush** *n.* a rushing on, an attack, an onset. **on-screen** *a.* appearing on a cinema, television or VDU screen. ~*adv.* **1** on or by means of a screen. **2** within the view shown on a film scene. **onset** *n.* **1** an attack, an assault, an onslaught. **2** the outset, beginning. **on-set** *a.* taking place on the set of a play or film. **onsetter, onsetting** *n.* **onshore** *a.*, *adv.* towards the land. **onside** *a.*, *adv.* (of a player) in football etc., in a legal position, not offside. **on-site** *a.* taking place or available on a site. **onslaught** *n.* a furious attack or onset. **on-stage** *a.* on a part of the stage that the audience can see. **on-stream** *a.*, *adv.* (of a manufacturing plant, industrial installation etc.) in operation. **on-street** *a.* (of parking) at the side of the street. **on time** *adv.* punctually. **on to, onto** *prep.* to and upon, to a position on or upon. **onward** *adv.* towards the front or a point in advance, forward, on. ~*a.* **1** moving, tending or directed forward. **2** advancing, progressive. **onwards** *adv.* [OE *on*, *an*, cp. Dut. *aan*, G *an*, Icel. *ā*, Dan. *an*, Gr. *ana*]

Usage note The written form *onto* is still often disapproved of, though it parallels *into* and is very common.

-on (on) *suf.* **1** denoting a chemical compound, as in *interferon*. **2** denoting an elementary particle, as in *electron*, *neutron*. **3** denoting a quantum, as in *photon*. **4** denoting an inert gas, as in *neon*. [Gr. *ion*, going, from *ienai*, to go]

onager (on´əjə) *n.* **1** a wild ass, esp. *Equus hemionus* of Asian deserts. **2** (*Hist.*) an ancient and medieval war machine resembling a large catapult for hurling rocks at the enemy. [L, from Gr. *onagros* (*onos*, ass, *agrios*, wild)]

onanism (ō´nənizm) *n.* **1** masturbation. **2** the withdrawal of the penis from the vagina prior to ejaculation. **onanist** *n.* **onanistic** (-nis´-) *a.* [*Onan* (Gen. xxxviii.9), -ISM]

ONC *abbr.* (*Hist.*) Ordinary National Certificate.

once (wŭns) *adv.* **1** one time. **2** one time only. **3** at one time, formerly, at some past time. **4** at any time, ever, at all. **5** at some future time, some time or other. ~*n.* one time. ~*a.* former. ~*conj.* as soon as. **all at once** all together, simultaneously, suddenly. **at once 1** immediately, without delay. **2** simultaneously. **for once** for one time or occasion only. **not once or twice** NOT. **once again** another time. **once (and) for all 1** finally. **2** definitively. **once bitten twice shy** BITTEN (under BITE). **once in a way** occasionally. **once in a while** occasionally. **once more** another time. **once or twice** a few times. **once removed** REMOVED (under REMOVE). **once upon a time** at some past date or period (usu. beginning a fairytale). **once-over** *n.* (*coll.*) a look of appraisal. **oncer** *n.* **1** (*Hist.*, *sl.*) a £1 note. **2** (*coll.*) something that only happens once. **3** (*Austral.*, *coll.*) (an election of) an MP likely to serve only one term.

onchocerciasis (ongkōsəkī´əsis) *n.* (*pl.* **onchocerciases** (-sēz)) a disease caused by infestation with parasitic threadworms of the genus *Onchocerca*, esp. river blindness. [Gr. *onkos*, a hook, *kerkos*, a tail]

onco- (ong´kō) *comb. form* denoting a tumour. [Gr. *onkos*]

oncogene (ong´kəjēn) *n.* any of several genes capable of causing cancer. **oncogenic** (-jen´-), **oncogenous** (-koj´-) *a.* causing tumours. **oncogenicity** (-nis´-), **oncogenesis** *n.*

oncology (ongkol´əji) *n.* the study of tumours and cancers. **oncological** (-loj´-), **oncologic** *a.* **oncologist** *n.*

oncoming, oncost ON.

oncotomy (ongkot´əmi) *n.* (*pl.* **oncotomies**) the opening of an abscess or the excision of a tumour.

OND *abbr.* (*Hist.*) Ordinary National Diploma.

ondes martenot (ōd mah´tənō) *n.* (*pl.* **ondes martenot**) an electronic keyboard instrument producing one note of variable pitch. [F *ondes*, waves, M *Martenot*, French inventor, 1898–1980]

on dit (ō dē´) *n.* (*pl.* **on dits** (dē´)) **1** hearsay, gossip. **2** a bit of gossip. [F, they say]

one (wŭn) *a.* 1 single, undivided. 2 being a unit and integral. 3 a or an. 4 single in kind, the only, the same. 5 this, some, any, a certain. ~*pron.* 1 a person or thing of the kind implied, someone or something, anyone or anything. 2 a person unspecified. 3 (*coll.*) any person, esp. the speaker. 4 I. ~*n.* 1 a single unit, unity. 2 the number 1, a thing or person so numbered. 3 one o'clock. 4 a single thing or person. 5 (*coll.*) a drink. 6 (*coll.*) a joke or story. 7 a blow, a setback. **all in one** combined. **all one** ALL. **at one** in accord or agreement. **for one** being one; even if the only one. **for one thing** as a single consideration. **in one piece** PIECE. **many a one** MANY. **one and all** jointly and severally. **one and only** 1 unique. 2 unequalled. **one day** DAY. **one jump ahead** JUMP. **one of these days** DAY. **one of those days** DAY. **one or two** a few. **one over the eight** EIGHT. **one to eight bells** BELL[1]. **one way and another** altogether, on balance. **one with** in harmony or unity with, synonymous with, part of the same whole as. **one with another** on the average, in general. **on one side** SIDE. **to be one flesh** FLESH. **to be one for** to be an enthusiast for. **to be one's own man** MAN. **to be one's own woman** WOMAN. **under one roof** ROOF. **one another** *pron.* each other. **one-armed** *a.* having or executed by one arm. **one-armed bandit** *n.* (*coll.*) a fruit machine operated by a single lever. **one by one** *n.* singly, individually, successively. **one-day event** *n.* an equestrian competition taking place over one day and including dressage, show-jumping and cross-country riding. **one-dimensional** *a.* superficial, shallow, flat. **one-eyed** *a.* **onefold** *a.* 1 having only one member or constituent. 2 single. 3 (coll.) single-minded, simple in character. **one for the road** *n.* (*coll.*) a last drink before leaving. **one-handed** *a.* 1 single-handed, done with one hand. 2 having only one hand. **one-horse** *a.* 1 drawn by a single horse. 2 (*coll.*) of meagre capacity, resources or efficiency. 3 (*coll.*) insignificant, petty. **one-horse race** *n.* a race or competition which one particular person is certain to win. **one in the eye** *n.* a disappointment or rebuff (for). **one-legged** (-legid) *a.* **one-liner** *n.* (*coll.*) a short punchy joke or witticism. **one-man** *a.* employing, worked by or consisting of one person. **one-man-band, one-man-show** *n.* 1 a sole musician playing a variety of instruments simultaneously. 2 a company, enterprise etc., consisting of, or run by, a single person. **oneness** *n.* 1 singleness. 2 singularity, uniqueness. 3 unity, union, agreement, harmony. 4 sameness. **one-night stand** *n.* 1 a single performance at one venue. 2 (*coll.*) a sexual encounter or relationship lasting one evening or night. 3 a person engaging in such an encounter. **one-off** *a.* (*coll.*) unique, unrepeated. ~*n.* a unique object, product, event etc. **one-parent family** *n.* a family living together having only one parent present to tend the child or children. **one-piece** *n.* a garment consisting of one piece of material (e.g. a swimsuit). ~*a.* made in one piece. **oner** (wŭn´ər) *n.* (*sl.*) 1 £1. 2 a striking, extraordinary or pre-eminent person or thing. 3 an expert, an adept. 4 a heavy blow. 5 a big lie. 6 in cricket, a hit for one run. **one-sided** *a.* 1 having or happening on one side only. 2 partial, unfair, favouring one side of an argument, topic etc. 3 more developed on one side than another. **one-sidedly** *adv.* **one-sidedness** *n.* **one-step** *n.* a quick-stepping type of ballroom dancing. **one-time** *a.* 1 former. 2 at some time in the past. **one-to-one** *a.* 1 corresponding, esp. in mathematics, pairing each element of a set with only one of another. 2 of one person to or with another (*a one-to-one relationship*). ~*adv.* **one-track** *a.* 1 single-track. 2 (*coll.*) capable of, or obsessed by, only one idea at a time. **one-track mind** *n.* a mind preoccupied with one thing. **one-two** *n.* (*coll.*) 1 in boxing, two successive blows rapidly delivered. 2 a type of football pass from and then immediately back to a player. **one-up** *a.* (*coll.*) having, or in, a position of advantage. **one-upmanship** *n.* (*coll.*) the art of gaining or keeping an advantage over someone. **one-way** *a.* 1 denoting a traffic system which allows vehicles to go in one direction only through certain streets. 2 unilateral. 3 valid for travel in one direction only. [OE *ān* (cp. Dut. *een*, G *ein*, Icel. *einn*), cogn. with L *ūnus*, Gr. *oinē*, ace]

Usage note The pronoun *one* is formal: in generalizations, *you* is considered less stilted and can often be used instead (as in *You should always be careful*, meaning everyone should take care); in speaking of oneself, simple *I* is preferable.

-one (ōn) *suf.* denoting certain chemical compounds, esp. hydrocarbons, as in *acetone*, *ketone*, *ozone*. [Gr. *-ōnē*, fem. patronymic]

oneiric (ōnī´rik), **oniric** *a.* of or relating to dreams. [as ONEIRO-]

oneiro- (ōnī´rō) *comb. form* of or relating to dreams. [Gr. *oneiros*, dream]

oneirodynia (ōnīrədin´iə) *n.* nightmare, disturbed sleep. [Gr. *odunē*, pain]

oneirology (ōnīrol´əji) *n.* the science of dreams. **oneirologist** *n.*

oneiromancy (ōnī´rəmansi) *n.* divination by dreams. **oneiromancer** *n.*

oner ONE.

onerous (ō´nərəs) *a.* 1 burdensome, heavy, weighty, troublesome. 2 (*Law*) involving heavy obligations. **onerously** *adv.* **onerousness** *n.* [OF *onereus*, L *onerōsus*, from *onus oneris*, burden]

oneself (wŭnself´) *pron.* 1 the reflexive and emphatic form *one*. 2 one's normal or usual self. **by oneself** alone, unaided. **to be oneself** to act in one's normal manner.

ONF *abbr.* Old Norman French.

onfall, ongoing etc. ON.

onion (ŭn´yən) *n.* 1 a plant, *Allium cepa*, with an underground bulb of several coats and a pungent smell and flavour, much used in cookery. 2 other species of the genus *Allium*. **to know one's onions** (*coll.*) to be knowledgeable in one's subject or competent in one's job. **onion dome** *n.* a bulb-shaped dome characteristic of Russian church architecture. **onion-skin** *n.* a thin glazed paper. **oniony** *a.* [F *oignon*, L *ūniōnem*, nom. *ūnio*, a large pearl, a kind of onion]

oniric ONEIRIC.

onkus (ong´kəs) *a.* (*Austral.*, *sl.*) bad, no good. [etym. uncertain]

onlooking, onlooker ON.

only (ōn´li) *a.* 1 solitary, single or alone in its or their kind. 2 the single, the sole. ~*adv.* 1 solely, merely, exclusively, alone. 2 with no other, singly. 3 wholly. 4 not otherwise. 5 not earlier. ~*conj.* 1 except that. 2 but. 3 were it not (that). **if only** IF. **only too true** regrettably true. **only too willing** more than willing. **onliness** *n.* **only-begotten** *a.* begotten as the sole issue. **only child** *n.* a child without brothers or sisters. [OE *ānlic* (ONE, -LY[1])]

o.n.o. *abbr.* or near(est) offer.

onomastic (onəmas´tik) *a.* of or relating to a name. **onomasticon** (-kon) *n.* a dictionary of proper names. **onomastics** *n.* the study of proper names. [Gr. *onoma*, name]

onomat. *abbr.* onomatopoeic.

onomato- (on´ōmatō) *comb. form* of or relating to a name or word. [Gr. *onoma -matos*, name]

onomatopoeia (onəmatəpē´ə) *n.* 1 the formation of words in imitation of the sounds associated with or suggested by the things signified. 2 the rhetorical use of a word so formed. **onomatopoeic, onomatopoetic** (-pōet´-) *a.* **onomatopoeically, onomatopoetically**

adv. **onomatopoesis** (-pōē´sis), **onomatopoiesis** (-poi´-) *n.* [L, from Gr. *onomatopoiia* (ONOMATO-, *-poios*, making, from *poieein*, to make)]

onrush, onset etc. ON.

Ont. *abbr.* Ontario.

-ont (ont) *comb. form* denoting an individual of a specified type, as in *symbiont.* [Gr. *ōn ont-*, being]

onto ON.

onto- (on´tō) *comb. form* being. [Gr. *ōn ontos*, being]

ontogenesis (ontōjen´əsis) *n.* the origin and development of the individual organism. **ontogenetic** (-net´-), **ontogenic** *a.* **ontogenetically, ontogenically** *adv.* **ontogeny** (ontoj´əni) *n.* **1** ontogenesis. **2** the history or science of this, embryology.

ontology (ontol´əji) *n.* the branch of metaphysics dealing with the theory of pure being or reality. **ontologic** (-loj´-), **ontological** *a.* **ontologically** *adv.* **ontologist** *n.*

onus (ō´nəs) *n.* (*pl.* **onuses**) **1** a duty, obligation or responsibility. **2** a burden. [L]

onward, onwards ON.

onychia (ənik´iə) *n.* inflammation of or near the nail, a whitlow. **onychitis** (onikī´tis) *n.* [mod. L, from Gr. *onux onuchos*, nail]

onychophoran (onikof´ərən) *n.* a soft-bodied arthropod of the class Onychophora, which have segmented bodies and are intermediate in evolution between annelids and arthropods. ~*a.* of or relating to this class. [Gr. *onux onukh-* nail, claw, *-phoros*, -PHORE]

-onym (ənim´) *comb. form* denoting a name or word, as in *pseudonym, antonym.* **onymous** (on´iməs) *a.* having or bearing a name or signature, opp. to anonymous. [from Doric variant *onuma* of Gr. *onoma -atos*, name]

onyx (on´iks) *n.* a variety of quartz resembling agate, with variously-coloured layers. **onyx marble** *n.* a calcium carbonate mineral resembling marble. [Gr. *onux*, a nail, onyx]

oo- (ō´ə, ō´ō) *comb. form* of or relating to ova or an egg. [Gr. *ōion*, egg]

oocyte (ō´əsīt) *n.* the unfertilized ovum or egg cell.

oodles (oo´dəlz) *n.pl.* (*coll.*) a great quantity, superabundance. [etym. uncertain]

oof (oof) *n.* (*sl.*) money. **oofy** *a.* rich. **oofiness** *n.* [Yiddish *ooftisch*, cp. G *auf dem Tische*, on the table]

oogamous (ōog´əməs) *a.* reproducing by the union of male and female cells. **oogamete** (-mēt) *n.* any one of such cells. **oogamy** (-mi) *n.* [Gr. *gamos*, marriage]

oogenesis (ōəjen´əsis), **oogeny** (ōoj´əni) *n.* the origin and development of an ovum. **oogenetic** (-net´-) *a.*

ooh (oo) *int.* used to express delight, surprise, pain, admiration etc. ~*v.i.* to say 'ooh'.

oolite (ō´əlīt) *n.* **1** a limestone composed of grains or particles of sand like the roe of a fish. **2** the upper portion of the Jurassic strata in England, composed in great part of oolitic limestone. **3** an oolith. **oolith** *n.* any of the rounded grains of which oolite is composed. **oolitic** (-lit´-) *a.*

oology (ōol´əji) *n.* **1** the study of birds' eggs. **2** the collecting of birds' eggs. **oological** (-loj´-) *a.* **oologically** *adv.* **oologist** *n.*

oolong (oo´long) *n.* a kind of China tea. [Chin. *wu*, black, *lung*, dragon]

oomiak, oomiac UMIAK.

oompah (oom´pah) *n.* (*coll.*) an imitation or representation of the sound of a large brass musical instrument. ~*v.i.* to make such a sound.

oomph (umf), **oomf** *n.* (*sl.*) **1** vigour, energy. **2** sexual attractiveness, magnetism. [etym. uncertain]

-oon (oon) *suff.* forming nouns, as in *balloon, poltroon.* [F, *-on* (stressed)]

oopak (oo´pak) *n.* a variety of black tea. [Chin. *u-pak*, *Hu-peh*, province in central China]

oophorectomy (ōəfərek´təmi) *n.* (*pl.* **oophorectomies**) a surgical operation to remove an ovary.

oops (oops, ups) *int.* (*coll.*) used to express surprise, dismay, apology, esp. on having dropped something. **oops-a-daisy** UPSYDAISY.

Oort cloud (awt) *n.* a cloud of small frozen bodies orbiting the solar system. [Jan Hendrick *Oort*, 1900–92, Dutch astronomer]

oosperm (ō´əspœm) *n.* a fertilized egg.

oospore (ōə´spaw) *n.* a fertilized ovum.

ooze (ooz) *n.* **1** wet mud, slime. **2** a slimy deposit consisting of foraminiferal remains, found on ocean beds. **3** the liquor of a tanning vat, consisting of an infusion of bark etc. **4** a gentle, sluggish flow, an exudation. ~*v.i.* **1** to flow or pass gently. **2** to percolate (through the pores of a body etc.). ~*v.t.* to emit or exude. **oozy** *a.* (*comp.* **oozier**, *superl.* **ooziest**). **oozily** *adv.* **ooziness** *n.* [OE *wōs*, juice, and also *wāse*, mud]

OP *abbr.* **1** observation post. **2** opposite prompt. **3** *Ordinis Praedicatorum*, Order of Preachers.

op (op) *n.* (*coll.*) (an) operation. [abbr.]

o.p. *abbr.* **1** out of print. **2** overproof.

op. *abbr.* **1** opera. **2** operation. **3** operator. **4** opposite. **5** optical. **6** opus.

op- (op) *pref.* var. of OB- (before *p*).

opacify, opacity OPAQUE.

opah (ō´pə) *n.* a rare Atlantic fish, *Lampris guttatus*, of the mackerel family, having brilliant colours. [Ibo *ùbá*]

opal (ō´pəl) *n.* **1** an amorphous, transparent, vitreous form of hydrous silica, several kinds of which are characterized by a play of iridescent colours and used as gems. **2** the colour of opal. ~*a.* opal-like, of opal. **opaled** *a.* **opalescent** (-les´ənt) *a.* characterized by a play of iridescent colours. **opalesce** *v.i.* **opalescence** *n.* **opal glass** *n.* a semi-translucent white glass. **opaline** (-līn) *a.* of, relating to or like opal. ~*n.* **1** a translucent variety of glass. **2** a yellow chalcedony. [F *opale*, L *opalus*, Sansk. *upala*]

opaque (əpāk´) *a.* (*comp.* **opaquer**, *superl.* **opaquest**) **1** impervious to rays of light, not transparent or translucent. **2** impenetrable to sight. **3** obscure, unintelligible. **4** obtuse, unintelligent. ~*n.* **1** opacity. **2** darkness. **3** an opaque thing or substance, esp. a pigment used in photography. **opacify** (ōpas´ifī) *v.t., v.i.* (*3rd pers. sing. pres.* **opacifies**, *pres.p.* **opacifying**, *past, p.p.* **opacified**) to make or become opaque. **opacifier** *n.* **opacity** (ōpas´-) *n.* **opaquely** *adv.* **opaqueness** *n.* [F, from L *opācum*, nom. *-cus*, shady]

op art (op) *n.* a type of abstract art employing shapes arranged to produce an optical illusion, esp. that of movement. [optical]

op. cit. (op sit´) *abbr. opere citato*, in the work cited. [L]

ope (ōp) *a., v.t., v.i.* (*poet.*) (to) open. [OPEN]

OPEC (ō´pek) *abbr.* Organization of Petroleum-Exporting Countries.

opeidoscope (əpī´dəskōp) *n.* an instrument for exhibiting sound vibrations by means of reflections of light. [Gr. *ōps*, voice, *eidos*, form, -SCOPE]

open (ō´pən) *a.* **1** not closed, obstructed or enclosed. **2** affording entrance, passage, or access. **3** unclosed, unshut, having any barrier, gate, cover etc. removed, withdrawn or unfastened. **4** uncovered, bare, unsheltered, exposed. **5** unconcealed, undisguised, manifest. **6** unrestricted, not exclusive or limited. **7** ready to admit, receive or be affected. **8** liable, subject (to). **9** unoccupied, vacant. **10** disengaged, free. **11** affording wide views. **12** widely spaced. **13** loosely woven, latticed, having frequent gaps or spaces. **14** generous, liberal. **15** frank, candid. **16** spread out, unfolded. **17** not closed or decided, debatable, moot. **18** (of weather) not frosty. **19** (*Mus.*) not stopped, or produced from an unstopped pipe, string etc. **20** enunciated with the vocal organs comparatively unclosed. **21** (of a syllable) not ended by a consonant. ~*n.* **1** unenclosed space or ground. 2 public view. 3 (**Open**) in sport, a tournament open to any class of player. ~*v.t.* 1 to make open. 2 to unclose. 3 to unfasten, unlock. 4 to remove the covering from. 5 to unfold, spread out, expand. 6 to free from obstruction or restriction, to make free of access. 7 to reveal, to make manifest or public. 8 to announce open. 9 to widen, to enlarge, to develop. 10 to make a start in, to begin. 11 to set going. 12 (*Law*) to state (a case) before calling evidence. ~*v.i.* 1 to become unclosed or unfastened. 2 to crack, to fissure, to gape. 3 to unfold, to expand. 4 to develop. 5 to make a start, to begin. **to be open with** to speak frankly to. **to bring into the open** to disclose (what was hitherto hidden or secret). **to open fire** to begin firing ammunition. **to open out** 1 to unfold, to expand. 2 to develop. 3 to reveal, to disclose. 4 to become communicative. 5 (*Naut.*) to bring into full view. 6 to accelerate. 7 to begin firing. **to open someone's eyes** to astonish or enlighten someone. **to open the door to** DOOR. **to open up** 1 to make accessible. 2 to reveal. 3 to discover, to explore, to colonize, to make ready for trade. 4 to accelerate. 5 to begin firing. 6 to talk openly. **under the open sky** SKY. **with open arms** enthusiastically. **openable** *a.* **open air** *n.* an unenclosed space outdoors. **open-air** *a.* outdoor. **open-and-shut** *a.* needing little deliberation, easily solved, simple. **open-armed** *a.* ready to receive with cordiality. **open book** *n.* someone or something easily understood. **opencast** *a.* in mining, of a surface excavation. **open cheque** *n.* an uncrossed cheque. **open circuit** *n.* an electrical circuit that has been broken so that no current can flow. **open college** *n.* an adult-education college. **open court** *n.* a court to which the public are admitted. **open day** *n.* a day when an institution (e.g. a school or university) is open to the public. **open door** *n.* 1 free admission or unrestricted access. 2 a policy of equal trading with all nations. **open-door** *a.* **open-ended** *a.* having no set limit or restriction on duration, time, amount etc. **opener** *n.* 1 a person who opens something. 2 an implement for opening bottles, tins etc. 3 (*coll.*) the first of a series of performances, events etc. **for openers** (*coll.*) to start with. **open-eyed** *a.* 1 watchful, vigilant, aware. 2 astonished, surprised. **open-faced** *a.* innocent-looking, having a candid expression. **open field** *n.* undivided arable land. **open goal** *n.* a goalmouth unprotected or inadequately protected by the goalkeeper or other defenders. **open government** *n.* government conducted in an unsecretive manner open to public scrutiny etc. **open-handed** *a.* generous, liberal. **open-handedly** *adv.* **open-handedness** *n.* **open-hearted** *a.* frank, ingenuous, sincere, candid, unsuspicious. **open-heartedly** *adv.* **open-heartedness** *n.* **open-hearth** *a.* of, made by or used in an open-hearth furnace or process. **open-hearth furnace** *n.* a reverberatory furnace for producing steel from pig iron. **open-hearth process** *n.* the process of making steel in such a furnace. **open-heart surgery** *n.* surgery performed on a heart while its functions are temporarily performed by a heart-lung machine. **open house** *n.* 1 hospitality proffered to all comers. 2 (*N Am.*) an open day. **open ice** *n.* ice through which ships can navigate. **opening** *a.* 1 that opens. 2 beginning, first in order, initial. ~*n.* 1 the act of making or becoming open. 2 a gap, a breach, an aperture. 3 a beginning, a commencement, the first part or stage, a prelude. 4 (*Law*) a counsel's statement of a case before evidence is called. 5 in chess etc., a series of moves beginning a game. 6 a vacancy, an opportunity. 7 the two facing pages of an open book. **opening time** *n.* the time at which bars and public houses can legally begin selling alcohol. **open-jaw** *a.* of or relating to return air travel involving arrival at one airport and return from another. ~*v.i.* to travel under such an arrangement. **open letter** *n.* a letter addressed to an individual but published in a newspaper. **openly** *adv.* **open market** *n.* a market situation of unrestricted commerce and free competition. **open marriage** *n.* a marriage in which the partners are free to be socially and sexually independent. **open mind** *n.* **open-minded** *a.* accessible to ideas, unprejudiced, candid, unreserved. **open-mindedly** *adv.* **open-mindedness** *n.* **open-mouthed** *a.* 1 gaping with stupidity, surprise etc. 2 greedy, ravenous. 3 clamorous. ~*adv.* with the mouth open in surprise etc. **openness** *n.* **open-plan** *a.* having no, or few, dividing partitions or walls. **open prison** *n.* a prison allowing greater than usual freedom of movement. **open question** *n.* a question that is undecided. **open-reel** *a.* (of a tape recorder) reel-to-reel. **open sandwich** *n.* a sandwich without an upper slice of bread, exposing its filling. **open sea** *n.* sea not enclosed or obstructed by land. **open season** *n.* 1 a period during which it is legal to hunt or angle for various species of game or fish. 2 an unrestricted period for an attack or attempt (on). **open secret** *n.* an apparently undivulged secret which is however generally known. **open sesame** *int.* a magic formula for opening a door, mentioned in the *Arabian Nights*. ~*n.* 1 a key to a mystery etc. 2 an easy means of entry to a profession etc. **open shop** *n.* an establishment where union membership is not a condition of employment. **open-side** *a.* in rugby, of the side of the field between the scrum and the further touchline. **open side** *n.* **open society** *n.* a free society. **open-top, open-topped** *a.* (of a vehicle) not having a fixed roof. **Open University** *n.* a British university established (1971) in Milton Keynes to teach those not usu. able to attend a university through broadcasts and by correspondence. **open verdict** *n.* a verdict which names no criminal or records no cause of death. **openwork** *n.* ornamental work showing openings. [OE (cp. Dut. *open*, G *offen*, Icel. *opinn*), rel. to UP]

opera[1] (op´ərə) *n.* 1 a dramatic entertainment in which music forms an essential part. 2 a composition comprising words and music for this. 3 the branch of the musical and dramatic arts concerned with this. 4 a company which performs opera. 5 an opera house. 6 a libretto, a score. **opera bouffe** (boof´), **opera buffa** (boo´fə) *n.* a farcical variety of opera. **opéra comique** (komēk´) *n.* 1 a type of opera having some spoken dialogue. 2 comic opera. **opera glasses** *n.pl.* small binoculars for use in theatres. **opera hat** *n.* a collapsible tall hat for men. **opera house** *n.* a theatre in which opera is performed. **opera seria** (seə´riə) *n.* a serious type of opera having a heroic or mythical plot. **operatic** (-rat´-) *a.* **operatically** *adv.* **operatics** *n.pl.* 1 (*usu. sing. in constr.*) the producing or study of operas. 2 a display of exaggerated behaviour. **operetta** (-ret´ə) *n.* a short opera of a light character. **operettist** *n.* [It., from L, work]

opera[2] OPUS.

operate (op´ərāt) *v.t.* 1 to work or control the working of. 2 to control, manage, run (a business, an organization etc.). ~*v.i.* 1 to work, to act. 2 to produce an effect. 3 to exert power, force, strength, influence etc. 4 (*Med.*) to produce a certain effect on the human system. 5 to perform a surgical operation (on). 6 (*Mil.*) to carry out strategic movements. 7 to deal in stocks. 8 to trade, to carry on a business. **operable** *a.* 1 suitable for or capable of being operated (on). 2 practicable. **operability** (-bil´-) *n.* **operand** (-rənd) *n.* that which is operated on, esp. a quantity in mathematics. **operant** *a., n.* **operating** *n.* **operating system** *n.* a program that controls the running of a computer system. **operating table** *n.* a table on which a patient lies during a surgical operation. **operating theatre,** (*N Am.*) **operating room** *n.* a specially-fitted room where surgery is performed. **operation** (-ā´shən) *n.* 1 the act or process of operating.

2 working, action, mode of working. 3 activity, performance of a function. 4 effect. 5 a planned campaign or series of military or naval movements. 6 a surgical act performed with or without instruments upon the body, to remove diseased parts, extract foreign matter, remedy infirmities etc. 7 (*Math.*) the act of altering the value or form of a number or quantity by such a process as multiplication or division. 8 a commercial or financial transaction. 9 a procedure, a process. **operational** *a.* 1 ready for or capable of action or use. 2 working, in operation. 3 of or relating to military operations. **operationalize, operationalise** *v.t.* to express in operational terms. **operationally** *adv.* **operational research, operations research** *n.* the application of mathematical techniques to problems of military or naval strategy, industrial planning, economic organization etc. **operations room** *n.* a room from where (esp. military) operations are controlled or directed. **operative** *a.* 1 acting, exerting force. 2 producing the proper result. 3 efficacious, effective. 4 relevant, significant. 5 of or relating to a surgical operation. 6 practical, as distinguished from theoretical or contemplative. ~*n.* 1 a (skilled) worker, an operator. 2 (*NAm.*) a private detective or secret agent. **operatively** *adv.* **operativeness** *n.* **operator** *n.* 1 a person who runs or operates a machine, a telephone switchboard, a business etc. 2 (*Math., Logic*) a symbol etc. representing a function to be performed. 3 a financial speculator. 4 (*coll.*) a skilled manipulator. **operon** (op´əron) *n.* a group of genes controlled by another gene. [L *operātus*, p.p. of *operārī*, from *opus*, work]

operculi- (əpœ´kūli) *comb. form* denoting an operculum.

operculum (əpœ´kūləm) *n.* (*pl.* **opercula** (-lə)) 1 a lid or cover as of the leaf of the pitcher plant, *Nepenthes*, or of the spore vessel in mosses. 2 the gill cover in fishes. 3 the plate closing the mouth of many univalve shells. 4 any of various similar parts. **opercular, operculate** (-lət), **operculated** (-lātid) *a.* **operculiferous** (-lif´-) *a.* [L, from *operīre*, to cover, rel. to *aperīre*, see APERIENT]

opere citato (opere kitah´tō, sī-) *adv.* in the work cited. [L]

operetta, operettist OPERA[1].

operon OPERATE.

operose (op´ərōs) *a.* done with or requiring much labour, laborious, wearisome. **operosely** *adv.* **operoseness** *n.* [L *operōsus*, from *opus operis*, work]

OPers. *abbr.* Old Persian.

ophi- OPHIO-.

ophicleide (of´iklīd) *n.* 1 a musical wind instrument, consisting of a wide conical tube with usu. eleven finger-levers and a bass or alto pitch. 2 an organ reed-stop with a similar tone.

ophidian (ofid´iən) *n.* a reptile of the suborder Serpentes (formerly Ophidia). ~*a.* 1 of or relating to this suborder. 2 snakelike. **ophidiarium** (-eə´riəm) *n.* (*pl.* **ophidiariums, ophidiaria**) a place where snakes are kept. [L *Ophidia* from Gr. *ophis*, snake]

ophio- (of´iō), **ophi-** *comb. form* of or relating to a snake. [Gr. *ophis*, snake]

ophiolatry (ofiol´ətri) *n.* worship of snakes. **ophiolater** *n.*

ophiology (ofiol´əji) *n.* the study of snakes. **ophiologic** (-loj´-), **ophiological** *a.* **ophiologist** *n.*

ophiophagous (ofiof´əgəs) *a.* feeding on snakes.

ophite (of´īt) *n.* 1 serpentine, serpentine marble. 2 (**Ophite**) a member of a gnostic sect who regarded the snake as an embodiment of divine wisdom. **ophitic** (-fit´ik) *a.*

ophthalm- OPHTHALMO-.

ophthalmia (ofthal´miə) *n.* inflammation of the eye.

ophthalmic (ofthal´mik) *a.* of or relating to the eye. **ophthalmic optician** *n.* an optician qualified to test eyesight and prescribe and dispense glasses or lenses.

ophthalmitis (ofthalmī´tis) *n.* ophthalmia, esp. inflammation involving all the structures of the eye.

ophthalmo- (ofthal´mō), **ophthalm-** *comb. form* of or relating to the eye. [Gr. *ophthalmos*, eye]

ophthalmology (ofthalmol´əji) *n.* the science of the eye, its structure, functions and diseases. **ophthalmologic** (-loj´-), **ophthalmological** *a.* **ophthalmologically** *adv.* **ophthalmologist** *n.*

ophthalmoscope (ofthal´məskōp) *n.* an instrument for examining the inner structure of the eye. **ophthalmoscopic** (-skop´ik), **ophthalmoscopical** *a.* **ophthalmoscopy** (-mos´kəpi) *n.*

-opia (ō´piə) *comb. form* denoting a condition or defect of the eye, as in *myopia*, *diplopia*. [Gr. *ōps*, eye]

opiate[1] (ō´piət) *n.* 1 a medicine compounded with opium. 2 a narcotic. 3 anything serving to dull sensation, relieve uneasiness or induce sleep. ~*a.* 1 soporific, narcotic, soothing. 2 consisting of or containing opium. [med. L *opiātus*, from L OPIUM]

opiate[2] (ō´piāt) *v.t.* 1 to treat with opium. 2 to dull the sensibility of. **opiated** *a.*

opine (əpīn´) *v.i., v.t.* 1 to think, to suppose (that). 2 to express an opinion (that). [L *opīnārī*]

opinion (əpin´yən) *n.* 1 a judgement, conviction or belief falling short of positive knowledge. 2 a view regarded as probable. 3 views, sentiments, esp. those generally prevailing. 4 one's judgement, belief or conviction with regard to a particular subject. 5 the formal statement of a judge, counsel, physician or other expert on a question submitted to them. 6 estimation, reputation. **in one's opinion** according to one's view or belief. **to be of the opinion that** to believe or think that. **opinionated** (-ātid), **opinionative** *a.* 1 obstinate in one's opinions. 2 dogmatic, stubborn. **opinionatedly, opinionatively** *adv.* **opinionatedness, opinionativeness** *n.* **opinionless** *a.* **opinion poll** *n.* a Gallup poll. [F, from L *opīniōnem*, nom. *-nio*, as OPINE]

opioid OPIUM.

opistho- (əpis´thō) *comb. form* behind. [Gr. *opisthen*, behind]

opisthobranchiate (əpisthōbrang´kiət) *a.* belonging to the Opisthobranchiata, an order of gastropods having the gills behind the heart. **opisthobranch** (əpis´-) *n.* a gastropod of this order. **opisthobranchism** *n.* [Gr. *branchia*, gills]

opisthognathous (opisthog´nəthəs) *a.* having receding jaws or teeth.

opisthograph (əpis´thəgrahf) *n.* a manuscript or tablet having writing on the back as well as the front. **opisthographic** (-graf´-) *a.*

opium (ō´piəm) *n.* 1 an addictive narcotic drug prepared from the dried exudation of the unripe capsules of the poppy, esp. the opium poppy. 2 anything considered to be stupefying or tranquillizing. **opioid** (-oid) *n.* a compound resembling an opiate in effects. ~*a.* of or relating to such compounds. **opium den** *n.* a place where opium is sold or used as a narcotic. **opium-eater** *n.* a person who habitually uses opium as a narcotic. **opium poppy** *n.* a poppy, *Papaver somniferum*, with red, white, pink or purple flowers. **opium-smoker** *n.* a person who habitually smokes opium. [L, from Gr. *opion*, dim. of *opos*, juice]

☒ **oponent** common misspelling of OPPONENT.

opoponax (əpop´ənaks) *n.* 1 the resinous juice from the root of *Opoponax chironium*, formerly used as a stimulant and in medicine. 2 a gum resin from the tree *Commiphora kataf*, used in perfumery. 3 SPONGE TREE (under SPONGE). [L and Gr. (*opos*, juice, *panax*, all-heal, cp. PANACEA)]

☒ **oposite** common misspelling of OPPOSITE.

opossum (əpos´əm) *n.* (*pl. in general* **opossum,** *in* *particular* **opossums**) 1 an American marsupial quadruped of the family Didelphidae, with a prehensile tail and a thumb on the hind foot, most species of which are arboreal and one aquatic. 2 a similar marsupial of Australia and New Zealand, esp. the phalanger. [Virginian Ind. *āpassūm*]

opotherapy (opōther´əpi) *n.* the treatment of diseases with prepared extracts of glands or organs. [Gr. *opokos*, juice, *therapeia*, medical treatment]

opp. *abbr.* 1 opera (pl. of opus). 2 opposed. 3 opposite. 4 opposition.

☒ **opperation** common misspelling of OPERATION (under OPERATE).

oppilate (op´ilāt) *v.t.* (*Med.*) to block up, to obstruct. **oppilation** (-ā´shən) *n.* [L *oppīlātus*, p.p. of *oppīlāre* (OP-, *pīlāre*, to ram, from *pīlum*, pestle)]

oppo (op´ō) *n.* (*pl.* **oppos**) (*coll.*) a colleague or friend. [*oppo*site number]

opponent (əpō´nənt) *n.* 1 a person who opposes, esp. in a debate, argument or contest. 2 an adversary, an antagonist. ~*a.* opposing, opposed, antagonistic, adverse. **opponency** *n.* **opponent muscle** *n.* a muscle that brings two parts, such as a finger and thumb, into opposition. [L *oppōnens -ntem*, pres.p. of *oppōnere* (OP-, *pōnere*, to put)]

opportune (op´ətūn, -tūn´) *a.* 1 situated, occurring, done etc. at a favourable moment. 2 seasonable, timely, well-timed. 3 fit, suitable. **opportunely** *adv.* **opportuneness** *n.* 1 utilizing circumstances or opportunities to gain one's ends, esp. the act or practice of shaping policy according to the needs or circumstances of the moment. 2 acceptance of what may be realized as a partial advance towards an ideal. 3 adaptation to circumstances, compromise. 4 sacrifice of principle to expediency. 5 political time-serving. **opportunist** *n.* 1 of, relating to or characterized by opportunism. 2 able to adapt to or take over a new habitat. 3 occurring only when the suitable circumstances arise. **opportunism** *n.* **opportunistic** (-nis´tik) *a.* **opportunistically** *adv.* **opportunity** (-tū´-) *n.* (*pl.* **opportunities**) 1 a chance, an opening. 2 a favourable circumstance. 3 an opportune or convenient time or occasion. **opportunity knocks** an opportunity occurs. **opportunity cost** *n.* in economics, the cost of an investment in terms of its best alternative use. [ME from L *opportunus*]

oppose (əpōz´) *v.t.* 1 to set against, to place or bring forward as an obstacle, adverse force, counterpoise, contrast or refutation (to). 2 to set oneself against or act against, to resist, withstand, obstruct. 3 to object to, to dispute. 4 (*in p.p.*) opposite, contrasted. ~*v.i.* to offer resistance or objection. **as opposed to** in contrast with. **opposable** *a.* 1 able to be opposed. 2 (of the thumb) capable of facing the fingers on the same hand. **opposability** (-bil´-) *n.* **opposer** *n.* [F *opposer* (OP-, *poser*, to POSE[1])]

opposite (op´əzit) *a.* 1 situated in front of or contrary in position (to). 2 fronting, facing. 3 antagonistic, adverse, contrary, diametrically different (to or from). 4 (*Bot.*) (of leaves on a stem) placed in pairs on contrary sides on the same horizontal plane. ~*n.* 1 a person who or something which is opposite. 2 an opponent, an adversary. 3 a contrary thing or term. 4 (*Logic*) a contradictory proposition. 5 (*coll.*) a person facing one. ~*adv.* in an opposite place or direction. ~*prep.* 1 opposite to. 2 as a co-star with (in a play, film etc.). **opposite angles** *n.pl.* the angles between the opposite sides of the intersection of two lines. **oppositely** *adv.* **oppositeness** *n.* **opposite number** *n.* 1 a person in the corresponding position on another side. 2 a counterpart. **opposite prompt** *n.* the side of a theatre stage to an actor's right; stage right. **opposite sex** *n.* women in relation to men, or vice versa. [L *oppositus*, p.p. of *opponere* (OP-, *pōnere*, to put)]

opposition (opəzish´ən) *n.* 1 the act or state of opposing. 2 antagonism, resistance, hostility. 3 the state of being opposite. 4 antithesis, contrast, contrariety. 5 an obstacle, a hindrance. 6 (**Opposition**) the chief parliamentary party opposed to the party in office. 7 (*Astron.*) the situation of two heavenly bodies when their longitudes differ by 180°. 8 (*Logic*) difference of quantity or quality, or of both, in propositions having the same subject and predicate. **oppositional** *a.* **oppositionist** *a., n.* [L *oppositio* (OP-, POSITION)]

oppress (əpres´) *v.t.* 1 to tyrannize over, to keep subservient. 2 to inflict hardships, cruelties, or exactions upon, to govern cruelly or unjustly. 3 to lie heavy on the mind of, to weigh down. 4 to overburden. **oppression** (-shən) *n.* **oppressive** *a.* 1 overbearing, exacting, tyrannous. 2 hard to tolerate. 3 (of the weather) close, muggy, sultry. **oppressively** *adv.* **oppressiveness** *n.* **oppressor** *n.* [OF *oppresser*, med. L *oppressāre* (OP-, *pressāre*, to PRESS[1])]

opprobrium (əprō´briəm) *n.* 1 disgrace, infamy, ignominy, obloquy. 2 a cause of this. **opprobrious** *a.* abusive, vituperative, scornful. **opprobriously** *adv.* **opprobriousness** *n.* [through OF *opprobrieux* or directly from late L *opprobriōsus*, from *opprobrium* (OP-, *probrum*, infamous act)]

oppugn (əpūn´) *v.t.* (*formal*) 1 to oppose, to dispute, to call in question. 2 to fight against, to oppose, to resist. **oppugnancy** (əpŭg´nən-) *n.* **oppugnant** (əpŭg´nənt) *a.* **oppugnation** (opŭgnā´shən) *n.* **oppugner** *n.* [F *oppugner*, L *oppugnāre* (OP-, *pugnāre*, to fight)]

OPRA (op´rə) *abbr.* Occupational Pensions Regulation Authority.

☒ **opress** common misspelling of OPPRESS.

opsimath (op´simath) *n.* a person who acquires education late in life. **opsimathy** (-sim´əthi) *n.* [Gr. *opsimathēs* (*opse*, late, *manthanein*, to learn)]

opsomania (opsəmā´niə) *n.* 1 an abnormal craving for some special kind of food. 2 abnormal daintiness of the appetite. [Gr. *opson*, food; MANIA]

opsonin (op´sənin) *n.* an antibody in the blood which renders germs more vulnerable to destruction by phagocytes. **opsonic** (-son´-) *a.* [Gr. *opsōnion*, victuals]

Opt. *abbr.* Optics.

opt (opt) *v.i.* to choose, to make a choice (for, between). **to opt out** 1 to choose not to be involved in something. 2 (of a school, hospital etc.) to choose no longer to be under the control or management of a local authority. **opt-out** *n.* 1 the action of opting out. 2 an instance of this. [OPTION]

opt. *abbr.* 1 optative. 2 optical. 3 optician. 4 optimum. 5 optional.

opt- OPTO-.

optative (op´tətiv, optā´-) *a.* (*Gram.*) expressing a wish or desire. ~*n.* 1 the optative mood. 2 a verbal form in this mood. **optatively** *adv.* **optative mood** *n.* a set of verb forms expressing a wish. [F *optatif*, late L *optātivus*, from *optāre*, to choose, opt]

optic (op´tik) *a.* of or relating to vision or the eye. ~*n.* 1 a lens. 2 a glass device fixed to the neck of a bottle to measure out spirits. 3 (*facet.*) an eye. **optical** *a.* 1 of or relating to sight, vision or the eye. 2 of or relating to optics. **optical activity** *n.* the ability (of some substances and their solutions) to rotate the plane of vibration of polarized light. **optical art** *n.* (*formal*) OP ART. **optical brightener** *n.* any fluorescent substance used to make laundry whiter. **optical character reader** *n.* a device which scans and reads printed characters optically, translating them into binary code which can then be processed by a computer. **optical character recognition** *n.* the scanning and identification of printed characters using photoelectric means. **optical disk** *n.* (*Comput.*) an inflexible non-magnetic disk on which information is stored digitally by laser. **optical fibre,**

(*N Am.*) **optical fiber** *n.* a thin glass fibre which can transmit light, used in communications and in fibre optics. **optical glass** *n.* a high-quality glass used for making lenses. **optical illusion** *n.* **1** an object which has an appearance so like something else that the eye is deceived. **2** an instance of such deception. **optical isomer** *n.* each of two or more forms of a chemical substance which differ in optical activity due to the spatial arrangement of the atoms. **optical isomerism** *n.* **optically** *adv.* **optical microscope** *n.* a microscope used to view objects by the light it emits, as opposed to an electron microscope. **optical telescope** *n.* a telescope used to view objects by the light it emits, as opposed to a radio telescope. **optic angle** *n.* the angle between the eyes and a given point, or between the extremities of an object and the eye. **optic axis** *n.* **1** the axis of the eye. **2** in a doubly refracting crystal, a direction for which no double refraction occurs. **optician** (-tish´ən) *n.* a person who prescribes or dispenses spectacles and contact lenses to correct eye defects. **optic lobe** *n.* the dorsal lobe in the brain, concerned with sight. **optic nerve** *n.* a nerve of sight connecting the retina with the brain. **optics** *n.* the science of the nature, propagation, behaviour and function of light. [F *optique*, med. L *opticus*, Gr. *optikos*, from *optos*, seen, from *op-*, stem of *opsomai*, I shall see]

optima, optimal OPTIMUM.

optimism (op´timizm) *n.* **1** a sanguine temperament, disposition to take a hopeful view of things. **2** the view that the existing state of things is the best possible, orig. expounded by Leibnitz from the postulate of the omnipotence of God. **3** the view that the universe is tending towards a better state and that good must ultimately prevail. **optimist** *n.* **optimistic** (-mis´-) *a.* **optimistically** *adv.* [F *optimisme* (L *optimus*, best)]

optimum (op´timəm) *n.* (*pl.* **optima** (-mə), **optimums**) **1** the most favourable condition. **2** the best compromise. *~a.* (of conditions, circumstances etc.) best or most favourable. **optimal** *a.* optimum. **optimally** *adv.* **optimize, optimise** *v.t.* **1** to make the most of. **2** to organize or execute with maximum efficiency. **3** to write or restructure (a computer program) to achieve maximum efficiency. *~v.i.* to be an optimist. **optimization** (-zā´shən) *n.* [L, neut of *optimus*, best]

option (op´shən) *n.* **1** the right, power or liberty of choosing. **2** a choice, a preference. **3** the thing chosen or preferred. **4** the right to deliver or call for the delivery of securities, land, commodities etc. at a specified rate within a specified time. **to have no option but to** to have to. **to keep/ leave one's options open** to refrain from committing oneself. **optional** *a.* open to choice; not compulsory. **optional extra** *n.* an additional item which can be bought as part of another purchase. **optionality** (-nal´-) *n.* **optionally** *adv.* [F, from L *optiōnem*, nom. *-tio*, rel. to *optāre*, to choose]

opto- (op´tō), **opt-** *comb. form* of or relating to sight or optics. [Gr. *optos*, seen]

optoelectronics (optōeliktron´iks) *n.* the branch of technology concerned with visual and electronic signals. **optoelectronic** *a.*

optometer (optom´itə) *n.* an instrument for ascertaining the range of vision and other powers of the eye. **optometric** (-met´-) *a.* **optometrist** *n.* a person who practises optometry. **optometry** *n.* the occupation of an optician.

optophone (op´təfōn) *n.* a device for enabling the blind to read by sound.

opulent (op´ūlənt) *a.* **1** rich, wealthy, affluent. **2** abounding (in). **3** abundant, profuse, copious. **opulence** *n.* **opulently** *adv.* [L *opulentus*, from *ops opem*, pl. *opēs*, power, wealth]

opuntia (əpŭn´shiə, op-, ō-) *n.* a cactus of the genus *Opuntia*, the prickly pear. [L, from *Opus*, a city of Locris, an ancient region of Greece]

opus (ō´pəs, op´-) *n.* (*pl.* **opera** (op´ərə), **opuses**) **1** a work, esp. a musical composition. **2** a work numbered in order of publication. **opuscule** (əpŭs´kūl), **opusculum** (-ləm) *n.* (*pl.* **opuscules, opuscula** (-lə)) a minor literary or musical work. **opus Dei** (dā´ē) *n.* **1** liturgical worship; the duty of prayer. **2** (**Opus Dei**) a Roman Catholic organization which aims to re-establish Christian ideals and principles. [L, work]

OR *abbr.* **1** operational research. **2** Oregon. **3** other ranks.

or[1] (aw) *conj.* **1** a disjunctive introducing an alternative. **2** used to connect synonyms, words explaining, correcting etc. [contr. of obs. *other*, prob. from OE *oththe*, or]

†**or**[2] (aw) *prep.* ere, before, sooner than. [OE *ār*, early, with sense of the comp. *ær*, ERE]

or[3] (aw) *n.* (*Her.*) gold. *~a.* golden or yellow. [F, from L *aurum*]

-or (ə) *suf.* denoting agency or condition, as *actor*, *author*, *creator*, *equator*. [(1) through OF *-or*, *-ur*, or F *-eur*, or directly from L *-or*, *-ōrem*, denoting agency; (2) through OF *-eor*, *-eur*, from L *-ātor*, *-ētor*, *-itor*, or *-ītor*, denoting agency; (3) A–F *-our*, OF *-or*, *-ur* (F *-eur*), L *-or -ōrem*, denoting conditions (in Eng. usu. *-our*, N Am. always *-or*)]

orache (or´ich), **orach** *n.* a plant, *Atriplex hortensis*, sometimes used as a vegetable; also called *saltbush*. [previously *arache*, F *arroche*, L *atriplicem*, nom. *atriplex*, Gr. *atraphaxus*]

Oracle® (or´əkəl) *abbr.* the teletext service of British Independent Television. [*O*ptional *R*eception of *A*nnouncements by *C*oded *L*ine *E*lectronics]

oracle (or´əkəl) *n.* **1** the answer of a god or inspired priest to a request for advice or prophecy. **2** the agency or medium giving such responses. **3** the seat of the worship of a deity where these were sought. **4** the sanctuary or holy of holies in the Jewish Temple. **5** a person of profound wisdom, knowledge or infallible judgement. **6** an utterance regarded as profoundly wise, authoritative or infallible. **7** a mysterious, ambiguous or obscure utterance. **8** a divine messenger, a prophet. *~v.i.* to speak as an oracle. *~v.t.* to utter as an oracle. **to work the oracle** **1** to secure by craft a desired answer from the mouthpiece of an oracle. **2** to obtain some object by secret influence. **3** to gain one's point by stratagem. **oracular** (orak´ū-) *a.* **oracularity** (-lar´-) *n.* **oracularly** *adv.* [F, from L *ōrāculum*, from *ōrāre*, to speak, to pray]

oracy (aw´rəsi) *n.* skill in spoken communication and self-expression. [L *ōs ōris*, mouth]

oral (aw´rəl) *a.* **1** spoken, not written, by word of mouth. **2** of, at or near the mouth. **3** taken by mouth. **4** of or relating to the early stage of infantile sexual development when gratification is obtained from eating and sucking. *~n.* (*coll.*) an oral examination. **oral contraceptive** *n.* a contraceptive pill. **oral history** *n.* interviews with living people about past events, recorded and written down as historical evidence. **oralism** *n.* the principle that deaf people should use speech and lip-reading rather than sign language. **oralist** *a.*, *n.* **orally** *adv.* **oral sex** *n.* sex involving contact between one person's mouth and another's genitals. **oral society** *n.* a society that has not developed literacy. [L *ōs ōris*, mouth, -AL[1]]

Usage note In standard English *oral* is pronounced the same as *aural*, and the two are easily confused or liable to misinterpretation. Some people try to distinguish them by giving *aural* the pronunciation (ow´-), but this is not a generally accepted practice. In some dialects they are in fact differentiated, with *oral* pronounced (or´-).

Orange (or´ənj) *a.* of or relating to the Orangemen.

Orangeism *n.* the practices or principles of Orangemen. **Orangeman** *n.* (*pl.* **Orangemen**) a member of a society formed in 1795 to uphold the Protestant ascendancy in Ireland. [town in department of Vaucluse, France, formerly seat of a principality, whence the Princes of Orange, including William III, King of England, took their title]

orange (or´ənj) *n.* **1** the large roundish cellular pulpy fruit of *Citrus aurantium* or *C. sinensis.* **2** (*also* **orange tree**) any of various trees or shrubs of the genus *Citrus* yielding this fruit. **3** a fruit or plant resembling this. **4** the colour of the fruit, reddish-yellow. *~a.* of the colour of an orange. **orangeade** (-jād´) *n.* a fizzy drink flavoured with orange. **orange blossom** *n.* the blossom of the orange tree (commonly worn in wreaths by brides). **orange flower water** *n.* a solution of oil of neroli. **orange lily** *n.* a cultivated lily, *Lilium bulbiferum*, var. *croceum*, with large reddish or orange flowers. **orange marmalade** *n.* marmalade made from oranges. **orange peel** *n.* **1** the rind of an orange. **2** a pitted effect on porcelain. **orange pekoe** *n.* a type of black tea made from the leaves at the tips of the plant stems. **orangery** (-jəri) *n.* (*pl.* **orangeries**) a building designed for the cultivation of orange trees in a cool climate. **orange squash** *n.* a concentrated orange drink. **orange stick** *n.* a thin piece of orange-tree wood used for manicure purposes. **orange-tip** *n.* a variety of butterfly, *Anthocharis cardamines*, with orange-tipped forewings. **orange-wood** *n.* the wood of the orange tree. [ME and OF *orenge*, *orange*, It. *narancia* (now *arancia*), Arab. *nāranj*]

orang-utan (orangutan´), **orang-outang** (-tang´), **orangutan, ourang-outang** *n.* a large, red-haired, arboreal anthropoid ape, *Pongo pygmaeus*, of Borneo and Sumatra. [Malay *ōrang hūtan*, wild man of the woods]

orarium (əreə´riəm) *n.* (*pl.* **oraria** (-riə), **orariums**) **1** a scarf sometimes wound round the handle of the medieval crozier. **2** an ecclesiastical stole. **orarion** (-ən) *n.* in the Greek Church, a deacon's stole, wider than the orarium. [L, from *ōs ōris*, mouth, face]

oration (ərā´shən) *n.* **1** a formal speech, dealing with some important subject in elevated language. **2** (*Gram.*) language, discourse. **orate** *v.i.* (*esp. facet.*) **1** to make an oration. **2** to talk at length. **orator** (or´ə-) *n.* **1** a person who delivers an oration. **2** an eloquent speaker. **3** PUBLIC ORATOR (under PUBLIC). **oratorial**[1] (orətaw´ri-), **oratorical** (-tor´i-) *a.* of, relating to or characterized by oratory. **oratorically** *adv.* **oratorize** (or´ə-), **oratorise** *v.i.* **oratory** (or´ə-) *n.* **1** the art of public speaking, rhetoric. **2** eloquence. **3** rhetorical language. [L *ōrātio*, from *ōrāre*, to speak]

oratorial[1] ORATION.

oratorial[2] ORATORIO.

oratorio (orətaw´riō) *n.* (*pl.* **oratorios**) a musical composition for voices and instruments, usually semi-dramatic in character, having a scriptural theme. **oratorial**[2] *a.* of or relating to an oratorio. [It., from L *ōrātōrium*, ORATORY[2]]

oratory[1] ORATION.

oratory[2] (or´ətəri) *n.* (*pl.* **oratories**) **1** a small chapel, esp. one for private devotions. **2** (*usu.* **Oratory**) any of several congregations of Roman Catholic priests living in a community without vows, the first of which was established at Rome by St Philip Neri in 1564 to preach and hold services among the people. **oratorian** (-taw´ri-) *a.* **1** of an oratory. **2** (**Oratorian**) belonging to any congregation of the Oratory. *~n.* **1** a priest of an oratory. **2** (**Oratorian**) a member of any congregation of the Oratory. [L *ōrātōrium*, neut. of *ōrātōrius*, from *ōrāre*, to pray]

orb (awb) *n.* **1** a sphere, a globe. **2** (*poet.*) a heavenly body. **3** (*poet.*) an eye or eyeball. **4** a circle, ring or orbit. **5** anything circular. **6** the globe forming part of the regalia. **7** a round or complete whole. *~v.t.* (*esp. poet.*) **1** to form into a circle. **2** to surround, encircle or enclose in an orb. *~v.i.* to become round or like an orb. **orbed** *a.* in the form of an orb. **orbicular** (-bik´ū-) *a.* **orbicularity** (-lar´-) *n.* **orbicularly** *adv.* **orbiculate** (-lət) *a.* (of a leaf etc.) circular. **orbless** *a.* **orblet** *n.* **orby** *a.* orbed. [L *orbis*, ring]

orbit (aw´bit) *n.* **1** the path of a celestial body around another. **2** the path of an electron around the nucleus of an atom. **3** a course or sphere of action, a career. **4** the bony cavity of the eye. **5** the ring or border round the eye in insects, birds etc. *~v.t.* (*pres.p.* **orbiting**, *past, p.p.* **orbited**) **1** to move in a curved path around. **2** to circle (a planet etc.) in space. **3** to send into an orbit. *~v.i.* to revolve in an orbit. **orbital** *a.* **1** of an orbit or orbits. **2** (of a road) going around a town. *~n.* a region surrounding an atomic nucleus, in which the electrons are shown by a wave function. **orbital sander** *n.* a sander with a circular motion. **orbiter** *n.* a spacecraft designed to orbit a planet etc. [L *orbita*, a track, from *orbis*, ring]

orc (awk) *n.* **1** a whale of the genus *Orca*, esp. *O. gladiator*, a grampus. **2** a marine animal, a sea monster, an ogre. **orca** (aw´kə) *n.* the killer whale. [F *orque*, L *orca*]

Orcadian (awkā´diən) *a.* of or relating to the Orkney Islands. *~n.* a native or inhabitant of the Orkney Islands. [L *Orcades*, Orkney Islands]

orcein ORCIN.

orch. *abbr.* **1** orchestra. **2** orchestrated by.

orchard (aw´chəd) *n.* an enclosure containing fruit trees, or a plantation of these. **orchard-house** *n.* a glasshouse for fruit trees. **orcharding** *n.* **orchardist** *n.* **orchardman** *n.* (*pl.* **orchardmen**) a fruit-grower. [OE *orceard*, *ortgeard* (L *hortus*, garden)]

orchestra (aw´kistrə) *n.* **1** a body of musicians playing a variety of instruments, performing in a theatre, concert room etc. **2** (*also* **orchestra pit**) the place for the band, or band and chorus, in a theatre, concert room etc. **3** (*N Am.*) the stalls in a theatre. **4** in an ancient Greek theatre, the semicircular space between the stage and the seats for the spectators, where the chorus danced and sang. **orchesis** (-kē´sis) *n.* the art of dancing. **orchestic** (-kes´-) *a.* **orchestics** *n.* orchesis. **orchestral** (-kes´-) *a.* **orchestrally** *adv.* **orchestra stalls** *n.pl.* seats just behind the orchestra in a theatre. **orchestrate** *v.t.* **1** to compose or arrange (music) for an orchestra. **2** to arrange, organize etc. to achieve the best effect. **orchestration** (-trā´shən) *n.* **orchestrator** *n.* **orchestrina** (-trē´nə), **orchestrion** (-kes´triən), **orchestrionette** (-net´) *n.* a mechanical musical instrument designed on the principle of the barrel organ to give the effect of an orchestra. [L and Gr. *orchēstra*, from *orcheesthai*, to dance]

orchid (aw´kid) *n.* **1** any of a large order of monocotyledonous plants, the Orchidaceae, of which the genus *Orchis* is the type, characterized by tuberous roots and flowers usually of a fantastic shape and brilliant colours in which the pistils and stamens are united with the floral axis. **2** a flower of such a plant. **orchidaceous** (-dā´shəs), **orchidean** (-kid´i-), **orchideous** *a.* **orchidist** *n.* **orchidology** (-dol´-) *n.* the knowledge of orchids. **orchidomania** (-ōmā´niə) *n.* a craze for orchids. **orchis** (-kis) *n.* (*pl.* **orchises**) **1** any orchid of the genus *Orchis*, usu. having pink, red or purple flowers and fleshy tubers. **2** any of various wild orchids. [from L and Gr. *orchisios*, testicle, an orchid, from the shape of the tubers]

orchid- ORCHIDO-.

orchidectomy (awkidek´təmi), **orchiectomy** *n.* (*pl.* **orchidectomies, orchiectomies**) the surgical removal of one or both testicles.

orchido- (aw´kidō), **orchid-** *comb. form* denoting a testicle or testicles.

orchil (aw´chil, -kil), **archil** (ah´chil, -kil), **orchilla** (-chil´ə, -kil´ə) *n.* **1** a violet, purple or red dye obtained from various lichens, esp. *Roccella tinctoria.* **2** this and other species of lichen yielding such dye. [OF *orchel*, etym. uncertain]

orchis ORCHID.

orchitis (awkī´tis) *n.* inflammation of the testicles. **orchitic** (-kit´-) *a.* [Gr. *orchis*, a testicle; -ITIS]

orcin (aw´sin), **orcine, orcinol** (aw´sinol) *n.* a colourless crystalline compound obtained from several species of lichen, yielding colours used for dyeing on treatment with various reagents. **orcein** (aw´siin) *n.* a purple dye-stuff present in orchil. [mod. L *orcina*, from It. *orcello*, orchil]

ord. *abbr.* **1** ordained. **2** ordinal. **3** ordinance. **4** ordinary.

ordain (awdān´) *v.t.* **1** to set apart for an office or duty, to appoint and consecrate, to confer holy orders on. **2** to decree, to establish, to destine. **ordainable** *a.* **ordainer** *n.* **ordainment** *n.* [OF *ordener* (F *ordonner*), L *ordināre*, from *ordo -dinis*, ORDER]

ordeal (awdēl´) *n.* **1** an experience testing endurance, patience, courage etc. **2** (*Hist.*) the ancient practice of referring disputed questions of criminality to supernatural decision, by subjecting a suspected person to physical tests by fire, boiling water, battle etc. [OE *ordēl, ordāl* (cp. Dut. *oordeel*, G *Urteil*), rel. to *dǣlan*, to DEAL[1], *adǣlan*, to divide, to allot, to judge]

order (aw´də) *n.* **1** regular or methodical disposition or arrangement. **2** sequence, succession, esp. as regulated by a system or principle. **3** normal, proper or right condition. **4** a state of efficiency, a condition suitable for working. **5** tidiness, absence of confusion or disturbance. **6** established state of things, general constitution of the world. **7** customary mode of procedure, esp. the rules and regulations governing an assembly or meeting. **8** a rule, regulation. **9** a mandate, an injunction, an authoritative direction. **10** a direction to supply specified commodities or to carry out specified work. **11** a signed document instructing a person or persons to pay money or deliver property. **12** a tier. **13** a social class, rank or degree. **14** kind, sort, quality. **15** a class or body of persons united by some common purpose. **16** (*also* **Order**) a fraternity of monks or friars, or formerly of knights, bound by the same rule of life. **17** a grade of the Christian ministry. **18** (*pl.*) the clerical office or status. **19** (*also* **Order**) a body usu. instituted by a sovereign, graded like the medieval orders of knights, to which distinguished persons may be admitted as an honour. **20** the insignia worn by members of this. **21** any of the nine grades of angels and archangels. **22** a system of parts, ornaments and proportions of columns etc. distinguishing styles of architecture, esp. classical, as the Doric, Ionic, Corinthian, Tuscan and Composite. **23** in the Roman Catholic Church, a sacrament bestowing grace for the performance of sacred duties conferred on those entering any of the seven grades or orders of priestly office. **24** (*Math.*) degree of complexity. **25** (*Biol.*) a division below that of class and above that of family and genus. **26** (*Mil.*) the dress, equipment etc. for a particular purpose. **27** a pass giving cheap or free entry to a theatre, museum etc. **28** (*esp. N Am.*) a portion or helping in a restaurant etc. *~v.t.* **1** to direct, to command. **2** to instruct (a person, firm etc.) to supply goods or perform work. **3** to regulate. **4** to ordain. **5** to manage. **6** to arrange beforehand. **7** to direct the supplying, doing or making of. **8** to put in order. *~v.i.* to give orders. **by order** according to direction by proper authority. **in bad order** not working properly. **in good order** working properly. **in/ on the order of** approximately the size or quantity specified. **in order 1** properly or systematically arranged. **2** in due sequence. **3** ready and fit for use. **in order that** so that. **in order to 1** to the end that. **2** so as to. **not in order** not working. **on order** having been ordered but not yet arrived. **Order! Order!** used to call for silence, esp. by the Speaker of the House of Commons. **out of order 1** disarranged. **2** untidy. **3** not consecutive. **4** not systematically arranged. **5** not fit for working or using. **6** (*coll.*) (of behaviour) not acceptable. **to keep order** to enforce or maintain order. **to order** according to, or in compliance with, an order. **to order about 1** to send from one place to another. **2** to domineer over. **to order arms** (*Mil.*) to bring rifles vertically against the right side with the butts resting on the ground. **to take holy orders** to be ordained. **to take orders 1** to accept commissions, commands etc. **2** to be ordained. **order book** *n.* **1** a book, usu. with counterfoils and detachable leaves, on which orders for goods, work etc. are written. **2** a book in which motions to be submitted to the House of Commons must be entered. **order clerk** *n.* a clerk appointed to enter orders. **orderer** *n.* **order form** *n.* a printed paper with blanks for a customer to enter goods to be supplied. **Order in Council** *n.* a sovereign's order on the advice of the Privy Council. **ordering** *n.* **1** arrangement, disposition. **2** ordination of priests etc. **orderless** *a.* **orderly**[1] *a.* **1** in order. **2** methodical, regular. **3** keeping or disposed to keep order, free from disorder or confusion. **4** of or relating to orders and their execution. *~adv.* duly, regularly. **orderliness** *n.* **orderly bin** *n.* a box for street refuse. **order of battle** *n.* the disposition of troops for attack or defence. **order of magnitude** *n.* the approximate size of something, esp. measured in powers of ten. **Order of Merit** *n.* an order conferred on British servicemen or -women or civilians for eminence in any field. **Order of the Bath** *n.* a British order of knighthood, so called because the candidates formerly bathed before installation. **order of the day** *n.* **1** business arranged beforehand, esp. the programme of business in a legislative assembly. **2** the prevailing state of things. **Order of the Garter** *n.* the highest order of British knighthood, instituted by Edward III. **Order of the Thistle** *n.* a Scottish order of knighthood instituted in 1687 and revived in 1703. **order paper** *n.* a paper on which the order of business, esp. in Parliament, is written or printed. **order to view** *n.* a request by a house agent to allow a client to inspect premises. [ME and OF *ordre*, L *ordinem*, nom. *ordo*]

orderly[1] ORDER.

orderly[2] *n.* **1** a soldier who attends on an officer to carry orders, messages etc. **2** a male hospital attendant. **orderly book** *n.* a book for regimental orders. **orderly officer** *n.* the officer of the day. **orderly room** *n.* a room in barracks used as the office for company or regimental business.

ordinaire (awdineə´) *n.* everyday drinking wine, *vin ordinaire.* [F, ordinary]

ordinal (aw´dinəl) *a.* **1** denoting order or position in a series. **2** (*Biol.*) of or relating to an order. *~n.* **1** an ordinal number. **2** a book containing orders, rules, rubrics etc., esp. forms for ordination in the Church of England. **ordinal number** *n.* a number denoting order or position in a series, e.g. first, second. [late L *ordinālis*, as ORDER]

ordinance (aw´dinəns) *n.* **1** an order, decree or regulation laid down by a constituted authority. **2** an established rule, rite or ceremony etc. **ordinand** (-nənd) *n.* a person preparing for holy orders. **ordinant** *a.* ordaining, regulating, directing. *~n.* a person who confers orders. [OF *ordenance* (F *ordonnance*), med. L *ordinantia*, from *ordināre*, to ORDAIN]

Usage note The nouns *ordinance, ordnance* and *ordonnance* should not be confused: an *ordinance* is an order or decree, *ordnance* heavy artillery or military stores, and *ordonnance* systematic arrangement.

ordinary (aw´dinəri) *a.* **1** usual, habitual, customary, regular, normal, not exceptional or unusual. **2** commonplace. **3** mediocre. **4** having immediate or ex officio jurisdiction. **5** not good-looking, plain. ~*n.* (*pl.* **ordinaries**) **1** a rule or order, as of the Mass. **2** a bishop or a bishop's deputy, esp. sitting as an ecclesiastical judge. **3** (*Her.*) any of the simplest and commonest charges, esp. the chief, pale, fesse, bend, bar, chevron, cross and saltire. **4** (*Sc. Law*) (*usu.* **Ordinary**) a judge of the Court of Session. **5** (*Hist., esp. N Am.*) an early type of bicycle, a penny-farthing. **6** (*Hist.*) a tavern or inn meal prepared at a fixed rate for all comers. **7** (*Hist.*) an eating house. **8** the ordinary run of humanity, course of life, procedure etc. **in ordinary** in actual and constant service. **in the ordinary way** in normal circumstances. **out of the ordinary** exceptional. **ordinarily** *adv.* **ordinariness** *n.* **ordinary grade** *n.* (a pass in) an examination at the lower of the two main levels of the Scottish Certificate of Education. **ordinary level** *n.* (*Hist.*) (a pass in) an examination at the lower of the two main levels of the General Certificate of Education in England and Wales. **ordinary scale** *n.* DECIMAL SCALE (under DECIMAL). **ordinary seaman** *n.* a sailor not fully qualified as able seaman. **ordinary share** *n.* a share (in a company) which pays dividends according to profit only after the claims of preference shares have been met. [L *ordinārius*, from *ordo -dinis*, ORDER]

ordinate (aw´dinət) *a.* **1** arranged in a row or rows. **2** ordinary, regular, proper. ~*n.* a line drawn from a point parallel to one of a pair of reference lines, called the coordinate axes, and meeting the other. **ordination** (-ā´shən) *n.* **1** the act of ordaining. **2** the state of being ordained or appointed. **3** arrangement in order, classification. **4** appointment, ordainment. **ordinee** (-nē´) *n.* a person who is newly ordained. [L *ordinātus*, p.p. of *ordināre*, to ORDAIN]

ordnance (awd´nəns) *n.* **1** heavy guns, cannon, artillery. **2** the department of public service dealing with military stores and equipment, except those of or relating to the quartermaster's department. **ordnance datum** *n.* the level taken as the basis for the Ordnance Survey, since 1921 the mean sea level at Newlyn, Cornwall. **Ordnance Survey** *n.* the (Government mapmaking body responsible for the) survey of Great Britain and Northern Ireland. **Ordnance Survey map, Ordnance map** *n.* a map produced by the Ordnance Survey. [var. of ORDINANCE]

Usage note See note under ORDINANCE.

ordonnance (aw´dənəns) *n.* the arrangement of the elements of a picture, building, literary composition etc. [OF *ordenance*, arrangement, see ORDINANCE]

Usage note See note under ORDINANCE.

Ordovician (awdōvish´iən) *n.* the middle period of the lower Palaeozoic era, which followed the Cambrian period. ~*a.* of or relating to this era. [*Ordovices*, an ancient British people]

ordure (aw´dyə) *n.* excrement, dung, filth. [F, from OF *ord*, foul, L *horridus*, see HORRID]

Ore. *abbr.* Oregon.

ore (aw) *n.* a natural mineral substance from which metal may be profitably extracted. [OE *ār*, brass (cp. Icel. *eir*, Goth. *aiz*, L *aes aeris*), confused with *ōra*, unwrought metal (cp. Dut. *oer*)]

öre (œ´rə) *n.* (*pl.* **öre**) a monetary unit in Sweden.

øre (œ´rə) *n.* (*pl.* **øre**) a monetary unit in Norway and Denmark.

oread (aw´riad) *n.* a mountain nymph. [L *orēas -ados*, Gr. *oreias*, from *oros*, mountain]

orectic (ərek´tik) *a.* of or relating to appetite or desire. **orexis** (ərek´sis) *n.* appetite. [Gr. *orektikos*, from *orektos*, stretched out, from *oregein*, to stretch out, to grasp after, to desire]

Oreg. *abbr.* Oregon.

oregano (origah´nō, oreg´ənō) *n.* (*pl.* **oreganos**) the (usu. dried) leaves of wild marjoram, *Origanum vulgare*, used as a culinary herb. [N Am. Sp. *orégano*, wild marjoram, from L *origanum*, Gr. *origanon*]

oreography OROGRAPHY.

oreology OROGRAPHY.

oreweed OARWEED (under OAR).

orexis ORECTIC.

orfe (awf) *n.* a small yellow or golden-coloured fish, *Leuciscus idus*, of the carp family. [Gr. *orphos*, a sea perch]

organ (aw´gən) *n.* **1** a musical wind instrument composed of an assemblage of pipes sounded by means of a bellows and played by keys. **2** a wind instrument having some resemblance to this, played by keys or other mechanism. **3** an instrument. **4** a barrel organ. **5** a part of an animal or vegetable body performing some definite vital function. **6** a medium or agent of communication etc., such as a newspaper or other periodical. **7** †the human voice with regard to its musical quality, power etc. **8** †a mental faculty regarded as an instrument. **mouth organ** MOUTH[1]. **organ-blower** *n.* a person or mechanism working an organ's bellows. **organ-builder** *n.* **organ-grinder** *n.* a player on a barrel organ. **organist** *n.* a person who plays a church or other organ. **organ loft** *n.* **organ of Corti** (kaw´ti) *n.* a part of the cochlea which converts sounds into nerve impulses. **organ-piano** *n.* a piano with a series of small hammers for striking the strings repeatedly and giving a sustained organ-like sound. **organ pipe** *n.* any one of the sounding-pipes of a pipe organ. **organ-screen** *n.* a screen or partition, usu. between the nave and the choir, on which the organ is placed in a large church. **organ stop** *n.* **1** the handle by which a set of pipes in an organ is put in or out of action. **2** the set of pipes or reeds of a certain quality controlled by this. [ME and OF *organe* (F *orgue*), L *organa*, pl. treated as sing. of *organum*, Gr. *organon*, rel. to *ergon*, work]

organa ORGANUM.

organdie (aw´gəndi), (*N Am.*) **organdy** *n.* (*pl.* **organdies**) a stiff, light transparent muslin. [F *organdi*, etym. uncertain]

organelle (awgənel´) *n.* a unit in a cell having a particular structure and function.

organic (awgan´ik) *a.* **1** of or relating to a bodily organ or organs. **2** of, relating to or of the nature of organisms or plants or animals. **3** having organs. **4** (of diseases etc.) of, relating to or affecting an organ or organs. **5** (*Chem.*) (of a compound etc.) of, relating to or belonging to the class formed from carbons. **6** (of vegetables etc.) grown without artificial fertilizers, pesticides etc. **7** structural, fundamental, inherent, not accidental. **8** organized, systematic, coordinated. **9** of or relating to an organized system. **10** vital, not mechanical. **11** formed or developed using natural factors, rather than to a plan. **organical** *a.* **1** organic. **2** (of music) instrumental. **3** performed on an organ. **organically** *adv.* **organic architecture** *n.* architecture that blends into the landscape. **organic chemistry** *n.* the study of the compounds of carbon. **organic compound** *n.* a chemical compound containing carbon combined with oxygen and other elements. **organicism** (-sizm) *n.* (*Biol.*) the theory that all things in nature have an organic basis. **organic law** *n.* a law stating a country's constitution. [L *organicus*, Gr. *organikos* (ORGAN, -IC)]

organise ORGANIZE.

organism (aw´gənizm) *n.* **1** an organized body consisting of mutually dependent parts fulfilling functions necessary to the life of the whole. **2** an animal or a plant. **3** organic structure. **4** a whole having mutually related parts analogous to those of a living body.

organize (aw´gənīz), **organise** *v.t.* **1** to put into proper working order. **2** to arrange or dispose (things or a body of people) in order to carry out some purpose effectively. **3** to enlist (workers etc.) in a trade union. **4** to correlate the parts of and make into an organic whole. **5** to make organic, to make into an organism, to make into a living part, structure or being. **6** to form or provide with organs. **7** (*Mus.*) to render or sing in parts. *~v.i.* **1** to become organic. **2** to unite into an organic whole. **organizable** *a.* **organization** (-zāʹshən) *n.* **1** the act of organizing. **2** the state of being organized. **3** an organized system, body or society. **4** tidiness, method. **organizational** *a.* **organizationally** *adv.* **organization man** *n.* a person who subordinates their personal life to the organization which employs them. **organizer** *n.* **1** a person who organizes. **2** a thing used for organizing, esp. a personal organizer. **3** a part of an embryo that affects the development of specialized cells.

organo- (awʹgənō, -ganʹ-) *comb. form* **1** organ. **2** organic.

organogenesis (awgənōjenʹəsis), **organogeny** (-nojʹəni) *n.* the development of organs in animals and plants. **organogenetic** (-netʹ-) *a.* **organogenetically** *adv.*

organography (awgənogʹrəfi) *n.* (*pl.* **organographies**) a description of the organs of plants and animals. **organographist** *n.*

organoleptic (awgənōlepʹtik) *a.* **1** affecting the bodily or sense organs. **2** relating to substances that stimulate the senses (e.g. taste). [Gr. *organon*, see ORGAN]

organology (awgənolʹəji) *n.* the branch of biology or physiology concerned with the organs of the body. **organological** (-lojʹ-) *a.* **organologist** *n.*

organometallic (awganōmitalʹik) *a.* of, being or relating to a compound containing linked carbon and metal atoms.

organon (awʹgənon) *n.* a system of principles and rules of investigation, deduction and demonstration regarded as an instrument of knowledge. [Gr. *organon* and L *organum*, see ORGAN]

organophosphate (awganōfosʹfāt) *n.* an organic compound that contains phosphate.

organotherapy (awgənōtherʹəpi) *n.* the treatment of disease by the administration of one or more hormones in which the body is deficient. **organotherapeutic** (-pūʹ-) *a.*

organum (awʹgənəm) *n.* (*pl.* **organums, organa** (-nə)) in medieval music, a part sung a fourth or fifth below or above a plainsong melody.

organza (awganʹzə) *n.* a thin transparent fabric of silk, rayon or nylon.

organzine (awʹgənzēn) *n.* **1** silk thread made of several threads twisted together in a direction contrary to that of the strands; thrown silk. **2** a fabric made from this. [F *organsin*, It. *organzino*, etym. unknown]

orgasm (awʹgazm) *n.* **1** the culminating excitement in the sexual act. **2** violent excitation and turgescence of an organ, as in sexual coition. **3** a paroxysm of excitement or passion. **4** immoderate excitement. *~v.i.* to experience an orgasm. **orgasmic** (-gazʹ-) *a.* **orgasmically** *adv.* **orgastic** (-gasʹ-) *a.* **orgastically** *adv.* [Gr. *orgaein*, to swell (for *-sm* cp. SPASM)]

orgeat (awʹzhah, -jiət) *n.* a liquor made from barley or sweet almonds and orange flower water. [F, from *orge*, L *hordeum*, barley]

orgiastic ORGY.

†**orgulous** (awʹgūləs) *a.* proud, haughty. [OF *orguillus* (F *orgueilleux*), from *orgueil*, pride, prob. from Gmc.]

orgy (awʹji) *n.* (*pl.* **orgies**) **1** a wild revel, a drunken carouse, esp. involving indiscriminate sexual activity. **2** a bout of indulgence. **3** (*Hist.*) secret and licentious rites, the worship of Dionysus or Bacchus etc. **4** (*pl.*) revelry, debauchery. **orgiastic** (-asʹ-) *a.* [orig. in pl. only, F *orgeis*, L and Gr. *orgia*]

-orial -ORY[1].

oribi (orʹibi) *n.* (*pl. in general* **oribi**, *in particular* **oribis**) a small fawn-coloured antelope, *Ourebia ourebi*, of S and E Africa. [Afrikaans, from an Afr. language]

oriel (awʹriəl) *n.* **1** a projecting polygonal recess with a window or windows, usu. built out from an upper storey and supported on corbels or a pier. **2** (*also* **oriel window**) the window of such a structure. [OF *oriol*, etym. uncertain]

orient (awʹriənt) *n.* **1** (**Orient**) the East, the countries east of S Europe and the Mediterranean. **2** (*poet.*) (**Orient**) the eastern sky. **3** the peculiar lustre of a pearl of the finest quality. **4** an orient pearl. *~a.* **1** (*poet.*) eastern, Oriental. **2** lustrous, perfect, without a flaw (of pearls). **3** bright, shining. **4** (*poet.*) †rising, ascending, as the sun. *~v.t.* **1** to adjust, align or bring into position. **2** to determine the position of, with reference to the east and accordingly to all points of the compass. **3** to place (a church) so that the chancel points due east. **4** to bury (a body) with feet towards the east. **5** to find the bearings of. **6** to find or correct one's mental relations and principles. *~v.i.* to turn or face towards the east. **to orient oneself** to check one's position according to one's surroundings. **oriency** *n.* orient quality. **oriental** (-enʹ-) *a.* **1** (*also* **Oriental**) situated in, of or relating to the East or the (esp. Asian) countries east of S Europe and the Mediterranean. **2** (*also* **Oriental**) derived from or characteristic of the civilization etc. of the East. **3** (*poet.*) easterly, orient. **4** (of pearls) excellent, precious. *~n.* (*also* **Oriental**) a native or inhabitant of the East. **oriental alabaster** *n.* ONYX MARBLE (under ONYX). **oriental amethyst** *n.* a violet or purple variety of corundum resembling amethyst. **oriental emerald** *n.* a green variety of corundum resembling emerald. **orientalism** *n.* **1** an idiom or custom peculiar to the East. **2** knowledge of Oriental languages and literature. **orientalist** *n.* **orientality** (-talʹ-) *n.* **orientalize, orientalise** *v.t., v.i.* **orientalization** (-zāʹshən) *n.* **orientally** *adv.* **oriental ruby** *n.* the true ruby, a variety of corundum. **oriental topaz** *n.* a yellow variety of corundum resembling topaz. **oriental turquoise** *n.* true turquoise. **oriented** *a.* directed (towards) (*esp. in comb.*, as *profits-oriented*). [F, from L *orientem*, nom. *-ens*, pres.p. of *orīrī*, to rise]

Usage note Using *Oriental* of people can give offence, and is best avoided.

---

orientate (awʹriəntāt) *v.t., v.i.* ORIENT. **orientation** (-tāʹshən) *n.* **1** the act of orienting oneself. **2** the state of being oriented. **3** the determination of one's position, mental or physical, with regard to the surroundings. **4** (*Psych.*) awareness of one's temporal, social and physical situation. **5** an introduction or briefing. **orientational** *a.* **orientational course** *n.* (*esp. N Am.*) a course giving an introduction. **orientator** *n.* an instrument for orientating.

orienteering (awrientiəʹring) *n.* a sport in which the contestants race cross-country following checkpoints located by a map and compass. **orienteer** *v.i.* to take part in orienteering. *~n.* a person who orienteers. [Swed. *orientering*]

orifice (orʹifis) *n.* **1** an opening or aperture, as of a tube etc. **2** a perforation, a mouth, a vent. [F, from late L *orificium* (*ōs ōris*, mouth, *facere*, to make)]

oriflamme (orʹiflam) *n.* **1** (*Hist.*) the ancient royal banner of France, orig. the red silk banderole of the Abbey of St Denis handed to the early kings in setting out for war. **2** a symbol of lofty endeavour. **3** a bright or glorious object. [F (*or*, L *aurum*, gold, *flamme*, FLAME)]

orig. *abbr.* **1** origin. **2** original(ly).

origami (origahʹmi) *n.* the (traditionally Japanese) art of paper folding. [Jap. *ori*, a fold, *kami*, paper]

origanum (ərigʹənəm) *n.* any plant of the genus *Origanum*, esp. wild marjoram. **origan** (orʹigən), **origane** *n.*

marjoram, esp. wild marjoram. [L *origanum*, from Gr. *origanon*]

origin (or´ijin) *n.* **1** the beginning, commencement or rise (of anything). **2** derivation, a source. **3** extraction, a person's ancestry. **4** ground, foundation, occasion. **5** (*Math.*) the point where coordinate axes intersect. **6** (*Anat.*) the point of attachment of a muscle, opposite to its insertion. **original** (ərij´-) *a.* **1** of or relating to the origin, beginning or first stage. **2** first, primary, primitive; initial, innate. **3** not copied or imitated, not produced by translation; fresh, novel. **4** able to devise, produce, think or act for oneself; inventive, creative. *~n.* **1** the pattern, the archetype, the first copy. **2** that from which a work is copied or translated. **3** the language in which a work is written. **4** an eccentric person. **5** origin, derivation, cause, primitive stock, ancestry. **original instrument** *n.* a musical instrument, or a copy of this, that dates from the time of the music played on it. **originality** (-nal´-) *n.* **originally** *adv.* **original print** *n.* a print made directly from a woodcut, etching etc. **original sin** *n.* (*Theol.*) **1** the innate depravity of humankind. **2** the sin of Adam in eating the forbidden fruit. **originate** (ərij´-) *v.t.* **1** to cause to begin, to bring into existence. **2** to be the origin of. *~v.i.* **1** to have origin (in, from or with). **2** to rise, to begin. **origination** (-ā´shən) *n.* **originative** *a.* **originator** *n.* [F *origine*, L *orīginem*, nom. *orīgo*; rel. to *orīrī*, to rise]

Orimulsion®, orimulsion (or´imulshən) *n.* a mixture of bitumen, water and detergents, used in fossil-fuelled power stations.

orinasal (awrinā´zəl) *a.* of, relating to or sounded by the mouth and nose. *~n.* a vowel sounded by the mouth and nose, such as the nasal vowels in French. [L *ōri-*, *ōs*, mouth, NASAL]

oriole (aw´riōl, -riəl) *n.* **1** any bird of the genus *Oriolus*, esp. *O. oriolus*, the golden oriole. **2** any bird of the genus *Icterus*, such as the Baltimore oriole, *I. galbula*. [med. L *oriolus*, L *aureolus*, from *aureus*, golden, from *aurum*, gold]

Orion (ərī´ən) *n.* one of the best-known constellations, a group of stars seen as representing a hunter with belt and sword. **Orion's belt** *n.* a row of three bright stars across the middle of this constellation. **Orion's hound** *n.* the star Sirius. [L and Gr., a giant hunter in Greek mythology]

orismology (orizmol´əji) *n.* the branch of science concerned with definitions and the explanation of technical terms. **orismologic** (-loj´-), **orismological** *a.* [Gr. *horismos*, definition, from *horizein*, to define, from *horos*, boundary]

orison (or´izən) *n.* (*usu. pl.*, *formal*) a prayer, a supplication. [OF (F *oraison*), from L *ōrātiōnem*, nom. *-tio*, from *ōrāre*, to pray]

-orium (aw´riəm) *suff.* denoting a place where something specific is done, as *sanatorium*. [L, see -ORY[1]]

Oriya (orē´yə) *n.* **1** a member of a people living in Orissa in India. **2** the language of Orissa. [Hind.]

ORL *abbr.* otorhinolaryngology.

orle (awl) *n.* (*Her.*) a bearing in the form of a narrow band round the edge of a shield. [F, from med. L *orla*, dim. of *ora*, border]

orleans (aw´liənz) *n.* **1** a cloth of cotton and wool used for women's dresses. **2** a kind of plum. [city in France]

Orlon® (aw´lon) *n.* (a fabric made from) acrylic fibre.

orlop (aw´lop), **orlop deck** *n.* the lowest deck of a vessel having three or more decks. [Dut. *overloop*, a covering, rel. to *overloopen* (OVER, *loopen*, to run, see LEAP)]

ormer (aw´mə) *n.* an edible mollusc, esp. *Haliotis tuberculata*; also called *sea-ear*. [Channel Islands var. of F *ormier* (*oreille-de-mer*, sea-ear), from L *auris maris*]

ormolu (aw´məloo) *n.* **1** a gold-coloured alloy of copper, zinc and tin, used for cheap jewellery. **2** gold leaf ground and used as a pigment for decorating furniture etc. **3** metallic ware, furniture etc. decorated with this. [F *ormoulu* (*or*, gold, *moulu*, p.p. of *moudre*, to grind)]

ornament[1] (aw´nəmənt) *n.* **1** a thing or part that adorns. **2** an embellishment, a decoration. **3** ornamentation. **4** a person, possession or quality that reflects honour or credit. **5** a mark of distinction, a badge. **6** (*usu. pl.*) furniture or accessories, esp. such as pertain to a church or worship. **7** (*pl.*, *Mus.*) decorations such as trills, mordents etc. to be improvised. **ornamental** (-men´-) *a.* *~n.* an ornamental thing, esp. a plant cultivated for show. **ornamentalism** *n.* **ornamentalist** *n.* **ornamentally** *adv.* **ornaments rubric** *n.* the short rubric respecting the ornaments to be used in church immediately preceding the order for Morning and Evening Prayer in the Prayer Book. [OF *ornement*, L *ornāmentum*, from *ornāre*, to adorn]

ornament[2] (aw´nəment) *v.t.* to adorn, to decorate, to embellish. **ornamentation** (-tā´shən) *n.* **ornamenter** *n.* [as ORNAMENT[1]]

ornate (awnāt´) *a.* **1** adorned, ornamented, richly embellished. **2** (of literary style etc.) florid, elaborately finished. **ornately** *adv.* **ornateness** *n.* [L *ornātus*, p.p. of *ornāre*, to adorn]

ornery (aw´nəri) *a.* (*N Am.*, *coll.*) mean, low. **orneriness** *n.* [corr. of ORDINARY]

Ornith. *abbr.* Ornithology.

ornith- ORNITHO-.

ornithic (awnith´ik) *a.* relating to birds.

ornithischian (awnithis´kiən, -thish´-) *a.* of or relating to the order Ornithischia, an order of dinosaurs. *~n.* any dinosaur of this order, such as the stegosaurus or triceratops. [L from Gr. *ornis ornithos*, bird, *iskhion*, hip joint]

ornitho- (aw´nithō), **ornith-** *comb. form* of or relating to birds. [Gr *ornis -ithos*, bird]

ornithodelphian (awnithōdel´fiən), **ornithodelphic** (-fik), **ornithodelphid** (-fid), **ornithodelphous** (-fəs) *a.* of the order Ornithodelphia, comprising monotremes and prototherians. [Gr. *delphus*, womb]

ornithology (awnithol´əji) *n.* the branch of zoology dealing with birds. **ornithological** (-loj´-) *a.* **ornithologically** *adv.* **ornithologist** *n.*

ornithopod (aw´nithəpod) *n.* any bipedal herbivorous dinosaur of the suborder Ornithopoda, including the iguanodon. *~a.* of or relating to this suborder.

ornithopter (awnithop´tə) *n.* an aeroplane driven by power supplied by the aviator and not by an engine.

ornithorhyncus (awnithōring´kəs) *n.* the duck-billed platypus, *Ornithorhyncus anatinus*, an Australian aquatic oviparous mammal. [Gr. *rhunchos*, a bill]

ornithoscopy (awnithos´kəpi) *n.* observation of birds for purposes of divination.

ornithosis (awnithō´sis) *n.* a disease similar to psittacosis that occurs in birds other than parrots.

oro- (or´ō) *comb. form* of or relating to mountains. [Gr. *oros*, a mountain]

orogenesis (orōjen´əsis), **orogeny** (oroj´əni) *n.* the process of forming mountains. **orogenetic** (-net´-), **orogenic** (-jen´-) *a.*

orography (orog´rəfi), **oreography** (oriog´-) *n.* the branch of physical geography concerned with mountains and mountain systems. **orographic** (-graf´-) *a.* **orographical** *adv.*

orohippus (orōhip´əs) *n.* a fossil quadruped considered to be the ancestor of the horse. [Gr. *hippos*, a horse]

oroide (aw´rōīd) *n.* an alloy of copper and zinc, resembling gold in appearance, used for cheap jewellery. [F or L *aurum*, gold, -OID]

orology (orol´əji), **oreology** (oriol´-) *n.* the scientific study of mountains. **orological** *a.* **orologist** *n.*

OROM *abbr.* optical read-only memory.

orometer (orom´itə) *n.* an instrument for measuring the height of mountains.

oropesa float (orōpē´zə) *n.* a float used in minesweeping to support the sweeping wire between two trawlers.
orotund (or´ətŭnd) *a.* **1** characterized by fullness and resonance. **2** (of the voice and utterance) rich and musical. **3** pompous, magniloquent, inflated. **orotundity** (-tŭn´-) *n.* orotund quality of voice. [L *ore rotundo*, lit. with round mouth]

Usage note The uses of the adjectives *orotund* and *rotund* overlap, but *orotund* is usual of the voice, and of spoken and written words, and *rotund* of objects and people.

orphan (aw´fən) *n.* **1** a child bereft of one parent, or of both. **2** a person bereft of previous advantages. **3** (*Print.*) the first line of a paragraph at the foot of a page or column. *~a.* bereft of one parent, or of both. *~v.t.* to make an orphan of. **orphanage** (-ij) *n.* **1** an institution for bringing up orphans. **2** orphan condition. **orphaned** *a.* **orphanhood, orphanism** *n.* **orphanize, orphanise** *v.t.* [late L *orphanus*, Gr. *orphanos*, destitute, bereaved, from *orphus* (cp. L *orbus*)]
Orphean (aw´fiən) *a.* **1** of or relating to Orpheus, a celebrated mythical musician of Thrace, or his music. **2** melodious, enchanting. **Orphic** *a.* **1** of or relating to Orpheus or the mysteries supposed to be founded by him. **2** oracular, mysterious. **Orphism** *n.* [L *Orphēus*, Gr. *Orpheios*]
orphrey (aw´fri) *n.* (*pl.* **orphreys**) a band of gold and silver embroidery decorating an ecclesiastical vestment. [ME and OF *orfreis*, med. L *aurifrisium*, L *auriphrygium* (*aurum*, gold, *Phrygium*, Phrygian)]
orpiment (aw´pimənt) *n.* **1** native yellow trisulphide of arsenic, used as a pigment and a dyestuff. **2** REALGAR. [OF, from L *auripigmentum* (*aurum*, gold, PIGMENT)]
orpine (aw´pīn), **orpin** (-pin) *n.* a fleshy-leaved plant, *Sedum telephium*, of the stonecrop family, with purple flowers. [F *orpin*, corr. of ORPIMENT]
Orpington (aw´pingtən) *n.* a variety of domestic fowl. [village in W Kent]
orra (or´ə) *a.* (*Sc.*) **1** odd, extra, left over. **2** incidental. **3** disreputable, low. [etym. unknown]
orrery (or´əri) *n.* (*pl.* **orreries**) a mechanical model for illustrating the motions, magnitudes and positions of the planetary system. [4th Earl of *Orrery*, 1676–1731, for whom one of the first was made]
orris[1] (or´is) *n.* **1** any plant of the genus *Iris*, esp. *I. florentina*. **2** orris root. **orris-powder** *n.* **orris root** *n.* the root of the orris, used as a perfume and in medicine. [prob. corr. of IRIS]
orris[2] (or´is) *n.* a kind of gold or silver lace. [contr. of ORPHREY]
ort (awt) *n.* (*usu. in pl.*) refuse, fragments, odds and ends, leavings. [late ME *ortes*, pl., cp. Dut. *oor-aete* (*oor-*, not, *etan*, to eat, cogn. with EAT)]
ortanique (awtənēk´) *n.* a citrus fruit, a cross between an orange and a tangerine. [*or*ange, *tan*gerine, uni*que*]
ortho- (aw´thō) *comb. form* **1** straight. **2** upright; perpendicular. **3** correct. **4** (*Chem.*) denoting an organic compound having substituted atoms attached to two adjacent carbon atoms in a benzene ring. **5** (*Chem.*) denoting an oxyacid derived from an acid anhydride by combination with the largest number of water molecules. [Gr. *orthos*, straight]
orthocentre (aw´thōsentə), (*N Am.*) **orthocenter** *n.* the point of intersection of two altitudes of a triangle.
orthocephalic (awthōsifal´ik, -kefal´-) *a.* having a breadth of skull from 70 to 75 per cent of the length, between brachycephalic and dolichocephalic.
orthochromatic (awthōkrəmat´ik) *a.* giving the correct values of colours in relations of light and shade.
orthoclase (aw´thəklās, -klāz) *n.* common or potash feldspar having a rectangular cleavage. [Gr. *klasis*, cleavage]
orthodontics (awthədon´tiks), **orthodontia** (-tiə) *n.* dentistry dealing with the correction of irregularities of the teeth. **orthodontic** *a.* **orthodontist** *n.* [Gr. *odous odontos*, tooth]
orthodox (aw´thədoks) *a.* **1** holding right or accepted views, esp. in matters of faith and religious doctrine. **2** in accordance with sound or accepted doctrine. **3** approved, accepted, conventional, not heretical, heterodox or original. **4** (**Orthodox**) of or relating to the Orthodox Church. **5** (**Orthodox**) adhering to the traditional doctrines and rituals of Judaism. **Orthodox Church** *n.* the Eastern Church, which has the patriarch of Constantinople as its head. **orthodoxy** *n.* (*pl.* **orthodoxies**) **1** the state of being orthodox. **2** orthodox belief or practice. **3** an instance of this. **4** the members of the Orthodox Church collectively. **5** Orthodox Jews collectively. [Gr. *doxa*, opinion]
orthodromic (awthədrom´ik) *a.* of or relating to orthodromics. **orthodromics, orthodromy** (-thod´rəmi) *n.* the art of sailing in the arc of some great circle (the shortest distance between any two points on the surface of the globe). [Gr. *dromos*, course]
orthoepy (awthō´əpi) *n.* **1** the branch of grammar dealing with the pronunciation of words. **2** the study of correct speech or pronunciation. **orthoepic** (-ep´-), **orthoepical** *a.* **orthoepically** *adv.* **orthoepist** *n.* [Gr. *epos*, a word]
orthogenesis (awthəjen´əsis) *n.* a theory of evolution that postulates that variation is determined by the action of environment. **orthogenetic** (-net´-) *a.* **orthogenetically** *adv.*
orthognathous (awthog´nəthəs, awthəgnā´thəs) *a.* straight-jawed, having little forward projection of the jaws. **orthognathic** (-nath´-) *a.* **orthognathism** *n.*
orthogon (aw´thəgon) *n.* **1** a rectangular figure. **2** a right-angled triangle. **orthogonal** (-thog´-) *a.* **orthogonally** *adv.* **orthogonal projection** *n.* projection by lines perpendicular to the plane of projection. [Gr. *gōnia*, corner, angle]
orthography (awthog´rəfi) *n.* (*pl.* **orthographies**) **1** correct spelling. **2** that part of grammar which deals with letters and spelling. **3** mode of spelling as regards correctness and incorrectness. **4** the art of drawing plans, elevations etc. in accurate projection, as if the object were seen from an infinite distance. **orthographer, orthographist** *n.* **orthographic** (-graf´-), **orthographical** *a.* **orthographically** *adv.* **orthographic projection** *n.* projection in which the point of sight is supposed to be at an infinite distance, so that the rays are parallel. [OF *ortographie*, L and Gr. *orthographia* (ORTHO-, -GRAPHY)]
orthometry (awthom´itri) *n.* the art of correct versification. **orthometric** (-met´-) *a.*
orthopaedics (awthəpē´diks), (*esp. N Am.*) **orthopedics** *n.* the branch of medicine concerned with bones and joints; the act or art of curing muscular or skeletal deformities by surgery, esp. in children. **orthopaedic, orthopaedical** *a.* **orthopaedist** *n.* [Gr. *pais paidos*, child]
orthophosphate (awthōfos´fāt) *n.* any salt or ester of orthophosphoric acid. **orthophosphoric acid** (-fosfor´ik) *n.* a colourless soluble solid tribasic acid; also called *phosphoric acid*.
orthopnoea (awthopnē´ə), (*N Am.*) **orthopnea** *n.* difficulty of breathing except in an upright posture, a form of asthma. **orthopnoic** (-nō´-) *a.* [L, from Gr. *orthopnoia* (*pnoē*, breathing)]
orthopraxy (aw´thəpraksi) *n.* orthodox procedure or behaviour, correct practice. [Gr. *praxis*, doing]
orthopsychiatry (awthōsīkī´ətri) *n.* the study and treatment of mental disorders, esp. the prevention of mental illness in childhood. **orthopsychiatric** (-at´rik) *a.* **orthopsychiatrist** *n.*

orthopteran (awthop´tərən) *n.* (*pl.* **othoptera**) any insect of the order *Orthoptera*, with two pairs of wings, the hind wings membranous and those in front coriaceous and usually straight; any orthopterous insect. **orthopteral, orthopterous** *a.* [Gr. *pteron*, wing]
orthoptic (awthop´tik) *a.* **1** relating to correct vision with both eyes. **2** (*Math.*) referring to tangents that intersect at right angles. ~*n.* a perforated disc on the backsight of a firearm, used in aiming. **orthoptics** *n.* the correction of defective eyesight, e.g. by exercising weak eye muscles. **orthoptist** *n.*
orthorhombic (awthōrom´bik) *a.* (of a crystal) having three planes of dissimilar symmetry at right angles to each other.
orthoscope (aw´thəskōp) *n.* (*Hist.*) an instrument for examining the interior of the eye, the refraction of the cornea being corrected by a body of water. **orthoscopic** (-skop´-) *a.* having or giving correct vision, normal proportions, or a flat field of view.
orthostichy (awthos´tiki) *n.* (*pl.* **orthostichies**) (*Bot.*) **1** an imaginary straight line connecting a row of leaves on a stem. **2** an arrangement of leaves connected in this way. **orthostichous** (-thos´tikəs) *a.* [Gr. *stichos*, a row]
orthotics (awthot´iks) *n.* the provision and use of aids to assist the movement of weak joints and muscles. **orthotic** *a.* **orthotist** (aw´thətist) *n.* a person who is skilled in orthotics.
orthotone (aw´thətōn) *a.* (*Gram.*) (of a Greek word) having its own accent, independently accented. ~*n.* an orthotone word. **orthotonic** (-ton´-) *a.*
orthotropal (awthot´rəpəl), **orthotropous** (-pəs) *a.* (of ovules, embryos etc.) turned or growing straight. **orthotropic** (-trop´-) *a.* growing vertically upwards or downwards. **orthotropism** (-thot´-) *n.* [Gr. *tropos*, turning]
ortolan (aw´tələn) *n.* **1** (*also* **ortolan bunting**) a small bunting, *Emberiza hortulana*, formerly esteemed as a delicacy. **2** any of several W Indian and American birds, esp. the bobolink. [F, from It. *ortolano*, earlier *hortolano*, gardener, L *hortulānus*, from *hortulus*, dim. of *hortus*, garden]
Orwellian (awwel´iən) *a.* relating to or in the style of George Orwell, English writer, 1903–50. ~*n.* a student of Orwell or his ideas.
-ory[1] (əri) *suf.* denoting place where or instrument, as *dormitory, lavatory, refectory*. **-orial** (awriəl) *suf.* forming adjectives, as *lavatorial*. [A-F *-orie*, L *-ōrium*, from adjectives in *-ōrius*]
-ory[2] (əri) *suf.* forming adjectives, as *amatory, admonitory, illusory*. [ONF *-ori, -orie*, L *-ōrius, -ōria, -ōrium*]
oryx (or´iks) *n.* (*pl. in general* **oryx**, *in particular* **oryxes**) any straight-horned antelope of the genus *Oryx*, of Africa and Arabia. [L, from Gr. *orux*]
oryza (orī´zə) *n.* a grass of the genus *Oryza*, esp. *O. sativa*, rice. [Gr. *oruza*, rice]
OS *abbr.* **1** Old Saxon. **2** (*also* **o.s.**) Old Style. **3** operating system. **4** Ordinary Seaman. **5** Ordnance Survey. **6** out of stock. **7** outsize.
Os *chem. symbol* osmium.
os (os) *n.* (*pl.* **ossa** (-ə)) a bone. [L]
Osage orange (ō´sāj, osāj´) *n.* **1** a thorny N American tree, *Maclura pomifera*. **2** the orange-like fruit of this. **3** the timber from this. [N American Indian tribe]
Oscan (os´kən) *n.* **1** a member of an ancient Italian people. **2** their language. ~*a.* of or relating to this people or their language. [L *Oscī*, -AN]
Oscar (os´kə) *n.* a gold-plated statuette awarded by the American Academy of Motion Picture Arts and Sciences to the actor, director, film-writer etc. whose work is adjudged the best of the year. [etym. uncertain, poss. from an employee of the Academy, who claimed that it resembled his Uncle *Oscar*]
oscillate (os´ilāt) *v.i.* **1** to swing, to move like a pendulum. **2** to vibrate. **3** to fluctuate, to vacillate, to vary. ~*v.t.* to cause to swing or vibrate. **oscillation** (-ā´shən) *n.* **1** the movement of oscillating. **2** the regular variation in an alternating current. **3** a single cycle (of something oscillating) from one extreme to the other. **oscillative, oscillatory** *a.* **oscillator** *n.* **1** someone or something that oscillates. **2** a device for producing alternating current. **oscillo-** (os´ilō) *comb.form.* **oscillogram** (osil´əgram) *n.* **oscillograph** (os´iləgrahf) *n.* a device for giving a visible representation of the oscillations of an electric current. **oscillographic** (-graf´-) *a.* **oscillography** (-log´-) *n.* **oscillometer** (-lom´itə) *n.* an instrument for measuring the roll of a ship at sea. **oscilloscope** (osil´əskōp) *n.* **1** an instrument which registers the oscillations of an alternating current or the fluorescent screen of a cathode ray tube. **2** an instrument to facilitate the detection of vibrations and other faults in machinery. **oscilloscopic** (-skop´-) *a.* [L *oscillātus*, p.p. of *oscillāre*, from *oscillum*, a swing, orig. a little mask of Bacchus suspended from a tree, dim. of *osculum*, dim. of *ōs*, mouth]
oscine (os´īn, -sin), **oscinine** (os´inīn, -nēn) *a.* of or relating to the suborder Oscines of passerine birds that includes most of the songbirds. [L *oscen*, singing bird]
oscitation (ositā´shən) *n.* (*formal*) **1** yawning, sleepiness. **2** negligence, dullness. **oscitant** (os´itənt) *a.* **1** yawning, sleepy. **2** dull, negligent. **oscitancy** *n.* (*pl.* **oscitancies**). **oscitantly** *adv.* **oscitate** (os´-) *v.i.* [L *oscitatio* from *oscitāre*, to gape (*ōs*, mouth, *citāre*, to move)]
oscula OSCULUM (under OSCULATE).
osculate (os´kūlāt) *v.t.* **1** to kiss. **2** (*Geom.*) (of a curve) to have two branches with a common tangent with (another curve), where each branch extends in both directions of the tangent. ~*v.i.* **1** to kiss. **2** (*Geom.*) to osculate each other. **3** (*Biol.*) to come into contact with through having characters in common or through an intermediate species etc. **osculant** *a.* **oscular** *a.* **1** of or relating to the mouth. **2** of or relating to kissing. **osculation** (-lā´shən) *n.* **osculatory** (os´-) *a.* **1** kissing. **2** (*Geom.*) osculating. ~*n.* (*pl.* **osculatories**) a tablet or board on which a sacred picture is painted, to be kissed by the priest and people during Mass. **oscule** (os´-) *n.* a small mouth or bilabiate opening. **osculum** (os´kūləm) *n.* (*pl.* **oscula** (-lə)) a pore or orifice, esp. an opening in a sponge, out of which water passes. [L *osculātus*, p.p. of *osculāri*, to kiss, from *osculum*, dim. of *ōs*, mouth]
-ose[1] (ōs, ōz) *suf.* forming adjectives denoting fullness, abundance, as *grandiose, jocose, verbose*. **-osely** *suf.* forming adverbs. **-oseness** *suf.* forming nouns. [L *-ōsus*]
-ose[2] (ōs) *suf.* forming nouns denoting carbohydrates and isomeric compounds. [after GLUCOSE]
osier (ō´ziə) *n.* any of various willows, esp. *Salix viminalis*, the pliable shoots of which are used for basketmaking. **osier bed** *n.* **osiered** *a.* [F, from L *ausāria*, *ōsāria*, willow bed]
-osis (ō´sis) *comb.form* (*pl.* **-oses** (ō´sēz)) denoting condition, esp. morbid states, as *chlorosis, necrosis*. [Gr. *-ōsis*, suf. forming nouns from verbs in *-oein*]
-osity (os´iti) *suf.* forming nouns from adjectives in -OSE[1] or -OUS, as *grandiosity, luminosity*. [F *-osité*, L *-ōsitātem*, nom. *-ōsitas* (-OSE[1], -OUS, -TY[1])]
OSlav. *abbr.* Old Slavonic.
Osmanli (ozman´li) *a.* of or relating to the Ottoman Empire, the W branch of the Turkish peoples or their language. ~*n.* (*pl.* **Osmanli, Osmanlis**) **1** a member of the Ottoman dynasty. **2** a Turk. [Turk. *osmānli*, from *Osman* or Othman I, 1259–1326, founder of the Turkish empire]
osmazome (os´məzōm) *n.* (*Chem.*) the portion of the aqueous product of meat in which are found those constituents of the flesh which decide its taste and smell. [Gr. *osmē*, a smell, *zomos*, broth]

osmic[1] (oz´mik) *a.* of or relating to odours or the sense of smell. **osmically** *adv.* [Gr. *osmē*, a smell]
osmic[2] OSMIUM.
osmiridium (ozmirid´iəm) *n.* a very hard natural alloy of osmium and iridium used esp. in pen nibs. [*osmium, iridium*]
osmium (oz´miəm) *n.* the heaviest known metallic element, at. no. 76, chem. symbol Os, usu. found in association with platinum. **osmic**[2] *a.* containing osmium. [Gr. *osmē*, smell (from the disagreeable smell of the oxide), -IUM]
osmograph (oz´məgrahf), **osmometer** (-mom´itə) *n.* an instrument for measuring osmotic pressures.
osmoregulation (ozmōregūlā´shən) *n.* the adjustment of osmotic pressure in a cell in relation to the surrounding fluid.
osmosis (osmō´sis, oz-) *n.* **1** the diffusion of a solvent through a semipermeable membrane into a more concentrated solution. **2** diffusion through any membrane or porous barrier. **3** gradual absorption or adoption of ideas etc. **osmose** *v.t.* to cause to diffuse by osmosis. ~*v.i.* to diffuse by osmosis. **osmotic** (-mot´-) *a.* **osmotically** *adv.* **osmotic pressure** *n.* the pressure required to prevent osmosis into a solution through a semipermeable membrane separating the solution and the pure solvent. [Gr. *ōsmos*, push, thrust, from *ōthein*, to push]
osmund (oz´mənd), **osmunda** (-mun´də) *n.* the flowering fern, *Osmunda regalis*; also called *royal fern*. [A-F *osmunde*, OF *osmonde*, etym. unknown]
osnaburg (oz´nəbœg) *n.* a coarse kind of linen. [*Osnabrück*, in Germany]
OSp. *abbr.* Old Spanish.
osprey (os´prā) *n.* (*pl.* **ospreys**) **1** a large bird, *Pandion haliaetus*, preying on fish; also known as the *sea eagle* or *fish-hawk*. **2** an egret plume used for trimming hats and bonnets. [ult. from L *ossifraga* (*os ossis*, bone, *frag-*, stem of *frangere*, to break)]
ossa OS.
ossein (os´iin) *n.* the gelatinous tissue left when mineral matter is eliminated from a bone.
osselet (os´əlit) *n.* **1** an ossicle. **2** the cuttle-bone of cephalopods.
osseous (os´iəs) *a.* **1** of the nature of or like bone, bony. **2** consisting of bone, ossified. **3** containing or abounding in fossil bones. [L *osseus*, from *os ossis*, bone]
ossicle (os´ikəl) *n.* **1** a small bone. **2** a bony calcareous or chitinous part or process in various animals.
Ossie AUSSIE.
ossiferous (osif´ərəs) *a.* (of cave deposits etc.) containing or yielding bones.
ossify (os´ifī) *v.t.* (*3rd pers. sing. pres.* **ossifies**, *pres.p.* **ossifying**, *past, p.p.* **ossified**) to turn into bone. ~*v.i.* **1** to become bone. **2** to become inflexible in attitudes, habits etc. **ossific** (-sif´-) *a.* **ossification** (-kā´shən) *n.*
osso bucco (osō boo´kō) *n.* a stew made from knuckle of veal and marrowbone. [It., marrowbone]
ossuary (os´ūəri) *n.* (*pl.* **ossuaries**) **1** a charnel house. **2** an urn for bones. **3** a deposit of bones (as in a cave).
oste- OSTEO-.
osteal (os´tiəl) *a.* **1** osseous, bony. **2** sounding like bone (of sounds made by percussion of bones).
ostealgia (ostial´jə) *n.* pain in a bone.
osteitis (ostiī´tis) *n.* inflammation of bone. **osteitic** (-it´-), **ostitic** *a.*
ostensible (osten´sibəl) *a.* **1** put forward for show or to hide the reality. **2** professed, pretended, seeming. **ostensibly** *adv.* **ostension** *n.* in the Roman Catholic Church, the uplifting or holding forth of the Host for public adoration. **ostensive** *a.* **1** exhibiting, showing. **2** ostensible. **3** (*Logic*) setting forth a general principle obviously including the proposition to be proved. **ostensively** *adv.* **ostensiveness** *n.* **ostensory** *n.* (*pl.* **ostensories**) in the Roman Catholic Church, a monstrance. **ostentation** (ostəntā´shən) *n.* **1** pretentious or ambitious display. **2** parade, pomp. **ostentatious** *a.* **ostentatiously** *adv.* **ostentatiousness** *n.* [F, from L *ostens-*, p.p. stem of *ostendere*, to show (*os-*, OB-, *tendere*, to stretch)]
osteo- (os´tiō), **oste-** (os´ti) *comb. form* bone. [Gr. *osteon*, bone]
osteoarthritis (ostiōahthrī´tis) *n.* degenerative arthritis, esp. of the weight-bearing joints of the spine, hips and knees. **osteoarthritic** (-thrit´-) *a.*
osteoblast (os´tiəblast) *n.* a cell concerned in the development of bone. [Gr. *blastos*, bud]
osteoclasis (ostiōklā´sis) *n.* the operation of breaking a bone to remedy a deformity etc. **osteoclast** (os´tiōklast) *n.* **1** a surgical instrument for breaking bone. **2** a cell formed in bone marrow that is associated with the normal absorption of bone.
osteocolla (ostiōkol´ə) *n.* **1** an incrustation of carbonate of lime on the roots and stems of plants growing in sandy ground. **2** an inferior kind of glue obtained from bones. [Gr. *kolla*, glue]
osteogenesis (ostiōjen´əsis) *n.* the formation of bone. **osteogenetic** (-net´-) *a.* **osteogenic** *a.*
osteoid (os´tioid) *a.* like bone.
osteology (ostiol´əji) *n.* the branch of anatomy treating of bones, osseous tissue etc. **osteologic** (-loj´-), **osteological** *a.* **osteologically** *adv.* **osteologist** (-ol´-) *n.*
osteomalacia (ostiōməlā´shiə) *n.* softening of the bones. **osteomalacic** (-ā´sik) *a.* [Gr. *malakia*, softness]
osteomyelitis (ostiōmīəlī´tis) *n.* inflammation of the marrow of the bones.
osteopathy (ostiop´əthi) *n.* a method of treating diseases by eliminating structural derangement by manipulation, mainly of the spinal column. **osteopath** (os´tiəpath), **osteopathist** (-op´-) *n.* a practitioner of osteopathy.
osteoplasty (os´tiəplasti) *n.* (*pl.* **osteoplasties**) transplantation of bone with its periosteum. **osteoplastic** (-plas´-) *a.*
osteoporosis (ostiōpawrō´sis) *n.* development of porous or brittle bones due to lack of calcium in the bone matrix.
osteosarcoma (ostiōsahkō´mə) *n.* a disease of the bones due to the growth of medullary or cartilaginous matter within them.
osteotome (os´tiətōm) *n.* an instrument used in the dissection of bones. **osteotomy** (-ot´əmi) *n.* (*pl.* **osteotomies**) the surgical cutting of a bone to remedy a deformity etc.
ostia, ostial OSTIUM.
ostinato (ostinah´tō) *n.* (*pl.* **ostinatos, ostinati** (-ti)) a musical figure continuously reiterated throughout a composition. [It., from L *obstinatus*, OBSTINATE]
ostiole OSTIUM.
ostitik OSTEITIC (under OSTEITIS).
ostium (os´tiəm) *n.* (*pl.* **ostia**) **1** (*Anat.*) the mouth or opening of a passage. **2** the mouth of a river. **ostial** *a.* **ostiole** (-ōl) *n.* a small opening in the perithecia of fungi etc. [L]
ostler (os´lə), **hostler** (hos´lə) *n.* (*Hist.*) a man who looks after horses at an inn, a stableman. [orig. *hostler* (HOSTEL, -ER)]
Ostmark (ost´mahk) *n.* (*Hist.*) the standard unit of currency in the Democratic Republic of Germany. [G, lit. east mark]
Ostpolitik (ost´politēk) *n.* (*Hist.*) the foreign policy of establishing normal relations with the Communist bloc. [G, *Ost*, east, *Politik*, politics]
ostracize (os´trəsīz), **ostracise** *v.t.* **1** to exclude from society, to ban, to send to Coventry. **2** (*Hist.*) in ancient Greece, to banish by a popular vote recorded on a

potsherd or shell. **ostracism** *n.* [Gr. *ostrakizein*, from *ostrakon*, shell, potsherd]

ostre- (os´trē), **ostreo-** (os´trēō) *comb. form* oyster. [L *ostrea, ostreum*, Gr. *ostreon*, oyster]

ostreiculture (os´trēikŭlchə) *n.* the artificial breeding of oysters.

ostreo- OSTRE-.

ostreophagous (ostriof´əgəs) *a.* eating or feeding on oysters.

ostrich (os´trich) *n.* (*pl. in general* **ostrich,** *in particular* **ostriches**) **1** a large African bird, *Struthio camelus*, having rudimentary wings, but capable of running with great speed, and valued for its feathers, which are used as plumes, and for its meat. **2** a person who refuses to recognize unpleasant facts. **ostrich farm** *n.* **ostrich plume** *n.* **ostrich-tip** *n.* the end of an ostrich feather. [ME *ostrice*, OF *ostruce*, pop. L *avis strūthio* (*avis*, bird, late L *strūthio*, Gr. *strouthiōn*, from *strouthos*)]

Ostrogoth (os´trəgoth) *n.* (*Hist.*) an eastern Goth, a member of the division of the Gothic peoples who conquered Italy in the 5th cent. **Ostrogothic** (-goth´-) *a.* [late L *Ostrogothī*, pl. (cp. OS *ōstar*, eastward, GOTH)]

OT *abbr.* **1** occupational therapy. **2** Old Testament. **3** operating theatre. **4** overtime.

ot- (ōt), **oto-** (ō´tō) *comb. form* of or relating to the ear. [Gr. *ous ōtos*, ear]

-ot[1] (ət) *suf.* forming nouns, originally diminutives, as *parrot*. [F]

-ot[2] (ət) *suf.* forming nouns denoting persons, as *patriot*. [F *-ote*, L *-ota*, Gr. *-otēs*]

otalgia (ōtal´jiə) *n.* earache. [Gr. *algos*, pain]

otarian (ōteə´riən) *a.* of or relating to the Otariidae, a family of pinnipeds with external ears, including the fur seals and sea lions. **otariid** (-riid) *n.* **otarioid** (-iroid), **otarine** (-rīn) *a.* [Gr. *ōtaros*, large-eared]

OTB *abbr.* off-track betting.

OTC *abbr.* **1** Officers' Training Corps. **2** over-the-counter (of medicines).

OTE *abbr.* on-target earnings.

other (ŭdh´ə) *a.* **1** not the same as one specified or implied. **2** different, distinct in kind. **3** alternative, additional. **4** extra. **5** second, only remaining (of two alternatives). **6** opposite, contrary. *~n., pron.* **1** an or the other person, thing, example, instance etc. **2** (*pl.*) the ones remaining. **3** (*sl.*) sexual intercourse. **4** (*Philos.*) (*usu.* **Other**) that which is distinct or different. *~adv.* otherwise. **every other** every alternate (day, week etc.). **of all others** out of the many possible or likely. **on the other hand** HAND. **other things being equal** conditions being unchanged. **someone/ something or other** SOMEONE (under SOME). **the other day** on a day recently. **the other night** on a night recently. **the other thing** an unexpressed alternative. **the other way round** in the opposite direction; in a reversed, inverted etc. position. **the other week** during a week recently. **other-directed** *a.* influenced in thought and action by values derived from external sources. **other fish to fry** *n.pl.* other more important matters to attend to. **other half** *n.* one's spouse or partner. **other man** *n.* the lover of a married or attached woman. **otherness** *n.* **other place** *n.* **1** hell (as opposed to heaven). **2** Oxford University as regarded by Cambridge, and vice versa. **3** the House of Lords as regarded by the House of Commons, and vice versa. **other ranks** *n.pl.* soldiers not holding a commissioned rank. **otherwhere** *adv.* (*poet.*) elsewhere. **otherwhile, otherwhiles** *adv.* (*poet.*) on other occasions, sometimes. **otherwise** *adv.* **1** in a different way or manner. **2** in other respects. **3** by or from other causes. **4** in quite a different state. *~conj.* **1** else, or. **2** but for this. **and/ or otherwise** the negation or opposite (of a specified thing). **other woman** *n.* the lover of a married or attached man. **other world** *n.* **1** the future life. **2** a world existing outside of or in a different mode from this. **3** fairyland. **other-world** *a.* of or relating to an imaginary or future world. **other-worldly** *a.* **other-worldliness** *n.* [OE *ōther* (cp. Dut. and G *ander*, Icel. *annarr*, Swed. *andra*, Sansk. *anatras*, L *alter*)]

Usage note The use of *other* as an adverb (rather than *otherwise*) is sometimes disapproved of, though it is quite common, especially in North America.

otic (ō´tik) *a.* of or relating to the ear. [Gr. *ōtikos*, from *ous ōtos*, ear]

-otic (ot´ik) *suf.* forming adjectives corresponding to nouns ending in -OSIS, as *neurotic, osmotic*. **-otically** *suf.* forming adverbs. [Gr. *-ōtikos*, formed on the same stems as -OSIS]

otiose (ō´tiōs) *a.* **1** not wanted, useless, superfluous. **2** futile, sterile. **3** †at leisure, unemployed, lazy. **otiosely** *adv.* **otioseness** *n.* [L *ōtiōsus*, from *ōtium*, leisure]

otitis (ōtī´tis) *n.* inflammation of the ear. **otitis media** *n.* inflammation of the middle ear.

oto- OT-.

otolaryngology (ōtōlaring·gol´əji) *n.* the study of diseases of the ear and throat. **otolaryngological** (-gəloj´-) *a.* **otolaryngologist** *n.*

otolith (ō´tōlith) *n.* a calcareous concretion found in the inner ear of vertebrates and some invertebrates. **otolithic** (-lith´ik) *a.*

otology (ōtol´əji) *n.* **1** the science of the ear or of diseases of the ear. **2** the anatomy of the ear. **3** a treatise on the ear. **otological** (-loj´-) *a.* **otologist** *n.*

otorhinolaryngology (ōtōrīnōlaring·gol´əji) *n.* ear, nose and throat medicine.

otorrhoea (ōtərē´ə), (*N Am.*) **otorrhea** *n.* purulent discharge from the ear.

otoscope (ō´təskōp) *n.* an instrument for inspecting the ear and eardrum. **otoscopic** (-skop´-) *a.*

OTS *abbr.* officer training school.

OTT *abbr.* (*coll.*) over the top.

ottava rima (otahvə rē´mə) *n.* a form of versification consisting of stanzas of eight lines, of which the first six rhyme alternately, and the last two form a couplet (as in Byron's *Don Juan*). [It., octave rhyme]

otter (ot´ə) *n.* (*pl. in general* **otter,** *in particular* **otters**) **1** any of several semiaquatic mammals of the genus *Lutra* with dense fur and webbed feet. **2** the fur of this. **3** the sea otter. **4** a device for catching fish consisting usu. of a float armed with hooks. **5** a type of paravane. **otter-board** *n.* a device for keeping the mouth of a trawl net open. **otter-dog, otter-hound** *n.* a variety of dog used for hunting otters. [OE *oter, ottor* (cp. Dut. and G *Otter*, Icel. *otr*), cogn. with Gr. *hudra*, water-snake, *hudōr*, water]

otto ATTAR.

Ottoman (ot´əmən) *a.* (*Hist.*) **1** of or relating to the dynasty of Othman or Osman I. **2** of or relating to the Turks. *~n.* (*pl.* **Ottomans**) a Turk. **Ottoman Porte** *n.* (*Hist.*) PORTE. [F, ult. from Arab. *Othmān*, Turk. *Osmān*, see OSMANLI]

ottoman (ot´əmən) *n.* (*pl.* **ottomans**) **1** a cushioned seat or sofa without back or arms, introduced from Turkey. **2** a heavy silk fabric. [F, *ottomane*, as OTTOMAN]

OTU *abbr.* operational training unit.

OU *abbr.* **1** Open University. **2** Oxford University.

ouabain (wahbah´in) *n.* a poisonous white crystalline glycoside extracted from certain trees. [F *ouabaïo*, from Somali *waba yo*, name of tree]

oubit (oo´bit), **woobut** (woo´bət) *n.* a hairy caterpillar. [perh. from OE *wibba*, beetle, or *wull*, WOOL]

oubliette (oobliet´) *n.* an underground dungeon in which persons condemned to perpetual imprisonment or secret death were confined. [F, from *oublier*, to forget]

ouch[1] (owch) *int.* used to express sudden pain. [etym. uncertain]

†**ouch**[2] (owch) *n.* the setting of a gem. [OF *nouche* (cp. ADDER[2], APRON), late L *nusca*, OHG *nusche*, prob. of Celtic orig.]

ought[1] (awt) *v.aux.* **1** to comply with duty or rightness (*You ought to be kind to animals*). **2** to comply with common sense or prudence (*I ought to save more money*). **3** to comply with expectation or probability (*The weather ought to be fine tomorrow*). **4** to comply with unfulfilled expectation or desire (*It ought to be finished by now*). **ought not** the negative form of ought. [OE *āhte*, past of *āgan*, to possess, to OWE]

ought[2] (awt), **aught** *n.* (*coll.*) a figure denoting nothing; nought. [perh. from *an ought* from a *nought*, (cp. ADDER[2])]

ought[3] AUGHT[2].

oughtn't (awt´ənt) *contr.* ought not.

Ouija® (wē´jə), **Ouija board** *n.* a board inscribed with the letters of the alphabet, used for receiving messages etc. in spiritualistic manifestations. [F *oui*, yes; G *ja*, yes]

ounce[1] (owns) *n.* **1** a unit of weight, of one-sixteenth of a pound avoirdupois (about 28 g). **2** a unit of one-twelfth of a pound troy, equal to 480 grains (about 31 g). **3** a small quantity. [OF *unce* (F *once*), L *uncia* (cp. INCH[1])]

ounce[2] (owns) *n.* a wild cat, *Panthera uncia*, of Asia; also called *mountain panther* and *snow leopard*. [OF *once* (*l'once*), *lonce*, It. *lonza*, L *lyncea*, LYNX (cp. ADDER[2], APRON)]

OUP *abbr.* Oxford University Press.

our (owə) *a.* possessive of WE. **Our Father** *n.* **1** the Lord's Prayer. **2** God. **Our Lady** *n.* the Virgin Mary. **Our Lady of Dolours** *n.* in the Roman Catholic Church, a title given to the Virgin Mary on account of her sorrows at the Passion. **Our Lady's bedstraw** *n.* LADY'S BEDSTRAW (under LADY). **Our Lord** *n.* **1** Jesus Christ. **2** God. [OE *ūre*, orig. gen. pl. of *ūs*, US (cp. G *unser*, Goth. *unsar*)]

-our (ə) *suf.* forming nouns, as *ardour, clamour, favour.* [-OR]

ourang-outang ORANG-UTAN.

ourie (oo´ri) *a.* (*Sc.*) **1** shivering, chilly. **2** dreary, depressed, dejected. [cp. Icel. *ūrig*, from *ūr*, drizzle]

ours (owəz) *pron.* something which belongs to or is associated with us. **of ours** belonging or related to us.

Usage note (1) The pronoun *ours* does not have an apostrophe (it is not spelt *our's*). (2) *Ourselves* is preferred to *ourself* even where *we* refers to a singular collective noun (so *We regard ourselves as a team*).

ourselves (owəselvz´) *pron.* **1** WE or US (objective), used to give emphasis. **2** the reflexive form of *us*. **3** our normal or usual selves. **by ourselves** alone, unaided. **to be ourselves** to act in our normal manner. **ourself** (-self´) *pron.* **1** †MYSELF (used by a sovereign, newspaper editor etc.) (usu. in apposition). **2** OURSELVES.

-ous (əs) *suf.* **1** full of, abounding in, as *dubious, glorious*. **2** (*Chem.*) denoting a compound having more of the element indicated in the stem than those whose names end in -IC, as *nitrous, sulphurous*. **-ously** *suf.* forming adverbs. **-ousness** *suf.* forming nouns. [OF *-ous, -os, -us* (F *-eux*), L *-ōsus* (cp. -OSE[1])]

ousel OUZEL.

oust (owst) *v.t.* **1** to eject, to expel, to turn out (from). **2** to dispossess, to deprive (of). **ouster** *n.* **1** (*Law*) ejection, dispossession. **2** a person who ousts. **3** (*esp. N Am.*) dismissal, expulsion. [OF *oster* (F *ôter*), to take away, etym. uncertain]

out (owt) *adv.* **1** from the inside or within. **2** not in, not within. **3** from among. **4** forth or away. **5** not at home, not in office. **6** no longer in prison. **7** not engaged or employed. **8** on strike. **9** not batting. **10** dismissed from the wicket. **11** in boxing, denoting defeat through inability to rise within the ten seconds allowed after being knocked down. **12** not in fashion. **13** not in practice. **14** in error, wrong. **15** at a loss. **16** at odds, not in agreement. **17** not to be thought of. **18** so as to be visible, audible, revealed, published etc. **19** introduced to society. **20** exhausted or extinguished. **21** clearly. **22** forcibly. **23** at full extent. **24** (*coll.*) no longer conscious. **25** (*esp. N Am.*) (of a homosexual man or woman) having declared publicly their sexual orientation. **26** to an end or conclusion, completely, thoroughly. **27** (of a tooth) extracted. **28** (of a bone etc.) dislocated. **29** (of a jury) considering its verdict. **30** (of a flower) open. **31** (of time) not spent working. **32** (of the tide) at the lowest point. *~prep.* (*coll.*) from inside of. *~n.* **1** (*usu. pl.*) those out of office, the opposition. **2** an outing. **3** (*Print.*) an omission, matter omitted. **4** (*coll.*) a way of escape. **5** in baseball, the action or an act of putting a player out. *~a.* **1** external. **2** outlying, remote, distant. **3** played away from the home ground. *~int.* (*ellipt.*) begone! away! an expression of impatience, anger or abhorrence. *~v.t.* **1** to put out or eject. **2** to knock out, to disable. **3** (*coll.*) to publicize, without permission, the supposed homosexuality of (esp. a person in public life). *~v.i.* to come out or emerge. **all out** striving to the uttermost. **at outs** at variance, at odds. **from out** out of. **murder will out** MURDER. **not out** (of a side or batsman in cricket) not having been caught, bowled etc. **out and about** able to get up and go outside. **out and away** beyond comparison. **out at elbows** ELBOW. **out of bounds** BOUND[2]. **out of breath** BREATH. **out of hand** HAND. **out of it** **1** not included, neglected. **2** at a loss. **3** in error, mistaken. **4** (*coll.*) unaware of one's surroundings due to drink, drugs etc. **out of one's head** delirious. **out of one's time** having served one's apprenticeship. **out of one's way** away from one's intended or desired route. **out of order** ORDER. **out of pocket** POCKET. **out of print** PRINT. **out of sorts** SORT. **out of stock** STOCK. **out of temper** TEMPER. **out of the blue** BLUE. **out of the question** QUESTION. **out of the way** **1** unusual. **2** remote. **out of this world** WORLD. **out of trim** not in good order. **out to** aiming to, working to. **out with** **1** away with. **2** not friendly with. **out with it** say what you are thinking. **out and out** *a.* complete, thorough. *~adv.* completely, unreservedly. **out-and-outer** *n.* **1** (*sl.*) a thorough-going person. **2** an extremist. **outer** *a.* **1** being on the exterior side, external. **2** farther from the centre or the inside. **3** objective, material, not subjective or psychical. *~n.* **1 a** the part of a target outside the rings round the bull's-eye. **b** a shot striking this. **2** (*coll.*) a person who makes public a claim that another person is homosexual. **3** an outer garment. **4** (*Austral., sl.*) the part of the spectator area at a sports ground that is unsheltered. **5** an outer container. **outer Bar** *n.* the barristers who are not Queen's Counsels. **outer garments** *n.pl.* clothes worn over other clothes. **Outer House** *n.* (*Law*) in Scotland, the hall where judges of the Court of Session sit. **outer man** *n.* external appearance, attire (of a man). **outermost, outmost** *a.* **1** most or farthest out. **2** most distant. **outer planet** *n.* any of the planets whose orbit lies outside the asteroid belt (i.e. Jupiter, Saturn, Uranus, Neptune and Pluto). **outer space** *n.* the vast, immeasurable region beyond the earth. **outer wear** *n.* outergarments. **outer woman** *n.* external appearance, attire (of a woman). **outer world** *n.* the world beyond one's familiar sphere, people in general. **out for** *a.* striving for. **outing** *n.* **1** an excursion, a pleasure-trip, an airing. **2** an appearance in a match, race etc. **3** (*coll.*) the practice or policy of publicizing the supposed homosexuality of a man or woman in public life. **outness** *n.* externality, objectivity, separateness from the perceiving mind. **out of** *adv.* **1** from the inside of. **2** from among. **3** beyond the reach of. **4** from (material, source, condition etc.). **5** born of. **6** without. **7** deprived of, having used up.

out-of-body experience *n.* a sensation of being outside one's body. **out-of-court** *a.* (of a settlement) made or done without using a court. **out of date** *a.* no longer in fashion or use. **out of doors** *a.* in the open air. *~adv.* into the open air. **out-of-pocket expenses** *n.pl.* the actual outlay of cash incurred. **out-of-town** *a.* situated or taking place outside a town. **out to lunch** *a.* (*coll.*) crazy. [OE *ūt*, whence *ūte*, away, abroad, *ūtan*, from outside (cp. Dut. *uit*, Icel. *ūt*, G *aus*)]

out- (owt) *pref.* **1** out, towards the outside, external. **2** from within, forth. **3** separate, detached, at a distance. **4** denoting issue or result. **5** expressing excess, exaggeration, superiority, surpassing, defeating, enduring, getting through or beyond.

out- (+ a–e words) outact *v.t.* to exceed in action, to excel, to outdo. **outage** (owt´) *n.* a period of time during which a power supply, machine etc. is not operating. **outask** *v.t.* to publish the banns of for the last time. **outate** OUTEAT (under OUT- (+ A–E WORDS)). **outback** (owt´-) *n.*, *a.*, *adv.* (*esp. Austral.*) the hinterland, the bush, the interior. **outbacker** *n.* **outbalance** *v.t.* to outweigh, to exceed. **outbargain** *v.t.* to get the better of in a bargain. **outbid** *v.t.* (*pres.p.* **outbidding,** *past* **outbad, outbade,** *p.p.* **outbidden**) **1** to bid more than. **2** to outdo by offering more. **outblaze** *v.i.* to blaze out or outwards. *~v.t.* to blaze more brightly than. **outbluster** *v.t.* to silence, worst or get the better of by blustering. **outboard** (owt´-) *a.* **1** situated on or directed towards the outside of a ship. **2** having an engine and propeller outside the boat. *~adv.* out from a ship's side or away from the centre. **outbound**[1] *v.t.* to leap farther than, to overleap. **outbound**[2] (owt´-) *a.* outward bound. **outbox** *v.t.* to box better than. **outbrag** *v.t.* (*pres.p.* **outbragging,** *past, p.p.* **outbragged**) to outdo in bragging. **outbrave** *v.t.* **1** to surpass in bravery, beauty, splendour etc. **2** to stand up against defiantly. **outbreak** (owt´-), **outbreaking** *n.* **1** a sudden bursting forth, an eruption. **2** a riot or insurrection. **3** an outcrop. **outbreaker** (owt´-) *n.* a breaker far from the shore. **outbreathe** *v.t.* **1** to breathe out. **2** to exhaust, to wear out. *~v.i.* to be exhaled. **outbreeding** *n.* interbreeding of unrelated plants or animals. **outbreed** *v.i.*, *v.t.* (*past, p.p.* **outbred**). **outbudding** (owt´-) *n.* a budding out, a bursting forth. **outbuilding** (owt´-) *n.* a detached building, an outhouse. **outburn** *v.i.* (*past, p.p.* **outburned, outburnt**) to burn out, to be consumed. *~v.t.* to burn longer than. **outburst** (owt´-) *n.* **1** an outbreak, an explosion. **2** an outcry. **3** an outcrop. **outcast** (owt´-) *n.* **1** a castaway, a vagabond. **2** an exile. *~a.* **1** rejected, cast out. **2** exiled. **outcaste**[1] (owt´-) *n.* **1** a person who has been expelled from a caste. **2** a person with no caste. **outcaste**[2] (-kahst´) *v.t.* to cause (someone) to lose their caste. **outclass** *v.t.* **1** to be of a superior class, kind or qualifications than. **2** to surpass as a competitor. **outclearing** (owt´-) *n.* **1** the sending out of cheques, bills etc., drawn on other banks to the clearing house. **2** the total amount thus standing to the account of a bank. **outcome** (owt´-) *n.* issue, result, consequence, effect. **outcraft** *v.t.* to excel in cunning. **outcrop** (owt´-) *n.* **1** (*Geol.*) the exposure of a stratum at the surface. **2** a noticeable manifestation or occurrence. *~v.i.* (*pres.p.* **outcropping,** *past, p.p.* **outcropped**) to crop out at the surface. **outcry** (owt´-) *n.* (*pl.* **outcries**) **1** a vehement or loud cry. **2** noise, clamour. *~v.t.* (*3rd pers. sing. pres.* **outcries,** *pres.p.* **outcrying,** *past, p.p.* **outcried**) to cry louder than. **outdance** *v.t.* to surpass in dancing. **outdare** *v.t.* **1** to exceed in daring. **2** to defy. **outdated** *a.* obsolete, out of date. **outdistance** *v.t.* to outstrip. **outdo** *v.t.* (*3rd pers. sing. pres.* **outdoes,** *pres.p.* **outdoing,** *past* **outdid,** *p.p.* **outdone**) to excel, to surpass. **outdoor** (owt´-) *a.* **1** living, existing, being, happening etc. out of doors or in the open air. **2** fond of the open air. **outdoor pursuits** *n.pl.* sports or leisure activities undertaken out of doors. **outdoors** *adv.* in the open air, out of the house. *~n.* the open air. **outdoorsy** *a.* **outdrink** *v.t.* (*pres.p.* **outdrinking,** *past* **outdrank,** *p.p.* **outdrunk**) to drink more than (someone). **outeat** *v.t.* (*pres.p.* **outeating,** *past* **outate,** *p.p.* **outeaten**) to eat more than (someone).

outer OUT.

out- (+ f– words) outface *v.t.* **1** to brave. **2** to confront boldly. **3** to stare down. **outfall** (owt´-) *n.* **1** the point of discharge of a river, drain etc. **2** an outlet. **outfield** (owt´-) *n.* **1** in cricket, baseball etc., the part of the field at a distance from the batsman. **2** the players occupying this. **3** (*Sc.*) the outlying land of a farm formerly cropped but not manured. **outfielder** *n.* **outfight** *v.t.* (*past, p.p.* **outfought**) **1** to fight better than. **2** to beat in a fight. **outfit** (owt´-) *n.* **1** the act of equipping for a journey, expedition etc. **2** the tools and equipment required for a trade, profession etc. **3** a set of (esp. selected) clothes. **4** (*coll.*) a set or group of people who work as a team. *~v.t.* (*pres.p.* **outfitting,** *past, p.p.* **outfitted**) to fit out, to provide with an outfit. **outfitter** *n.* a person who deals in outfits for journeys, athletic sports, ceremonies, schools etc. **outflank** *v.t.* **1** to extend beyond or turn the flank of. **2** to get the better of. **outflow** (owt´-) *n.* **1** the process of flowing out. **2** that which flows out. **3** a place of flowing out, an outlet. **outflung** *a.* flung out to one side. **outfly** *v.t.* (*3rd pers. sing. pres.* **outflies,** *pres.p.* **outflying,** *past* **outflew,** *p.p.* **outflown**) **1** to fly faster than. **2** to outstrip. **outfoot** *v.t.* to outstrip, to outrun, outpace etc. **outfox** *v.t.* (*coll.*) **1** to outwit. **2** to surpass in cunning. **outfrown** *v.t.* to frown down.

†outfangthief (owt´fangthēf) *n.* (*Hist., Law*) the right of a lord to try a thief who was his own man in his own court. [OE *ūtfangenne thēof* (OUT, *fangen*, p.p. of *fōn*, to seize, THIEF)]

out- (+ g–l words) outgas *v.i.* (*3rd pers. sing. pres.* **outgases,** *pres.p.* **outgassing,** *past, p.p.* **outgassed**) to release or give off an adsorbed or occluded gas or vapour. *~v.t.* **1** to release or give off as a gas or vapour. **2** to drive off a gas or vapour from. **outgassing** *n.* **outgeneral** *v.t.* (*pres.p.* **outgeneralling,** (*N Am.*) **outgeneraling,** *past, p.p.* **outgeneralled,** (*N Am.*) **outgeneraled**) **1** to surpass in generalship. **2** to manoeuvre so as to get the better of. **outgive** *v.t.* (*pres.p.* **outgiving,** *past, p.p.* **outgiven**) **1** to give more than. **2** to surpass in giving. *~v.i.* (*poet.*) to give out, to come to an end. **outgo**[1] (owt´-) *n.* (*pl.* **outgoes**) **1** that which goes out. **2** expenditure, outlay, cost, outflow, issue. **†outgo**[2] (-gō´) *v.t.* (*3rd pers. sing. pres.* **outgoes,** *pres.p.* **outgoing,** *past* **outwent,** *p.p.* **outgone**) to surpass, to go beyond, to excel. **outgoer** *n.* **outgoing** (owt´-) *a.* **1** leaving. **2** friendly and sociable; extrovert. *~n.* **1** a going out, departure, termination. **2** (*usu. in pl.*) outlay, expenditure. **outgrow** *v.t.* (*pres.p.* **outgrowing,** *past* **outgrew,** *p.p.* **outgrown**) **1** to surpass in growth. **2** to grow too much or too great for. **3** to grow out of. **to outgrow one's strength** to become thin and weak through too rapid growth. **outgrowth** (owt´-) *n.* **1** something, or the process of, growing out from a main body. **2** a result or byproduct. **outguard** (owt´-) *n.* **1** a guard at a distance from the main body. **2** an outpost. **outguess** *v.t.* to guess what someone else intends. **outgun** *v.t.* (*pres.p.* **outgunning,** *past, p.p.* **outgunned**) **1** to defeat with superior weaponry. **2** to surpass. **out-Herod** *v.t.* **1** to outdo, to exaggerate, to overact. **2** to surpass any kind of excess. **outhit** *v.t.* (*pres.p.* **outhitting,** *past, p.p.* **outhit**) to hit better than. **outhouse** (owt´-) *n.* **1** a smaller building away from the main building. **2** (*N Am.*) an outdoor lavatory. *~v.t.* to store (books etc.) away from the main collection. **outjest** *v.t.* to jest or laugh away. **outjet** (owt´-) *n.* a projection. **outjockey** *v.t.* (*3rd pers. sing. pres.* **outjockeys,** *pres.p.* **outjockeying,** *past, p.p.* **outjockeyed**) to outwit. **outjump** *v.t.* to surpass in jumping. **outjut, outjutting** *n.* **outland**

(owt´-) *n.* **1** a foreign land. **2** land beyond the domain lands, let to tenants. **outlander** *n.* **1** a foreigner, a stranger. **2** an alien settler. **outlast** *v.t.* **1** to last longer than. **2** to surpass in duration, endurance etc. **outlay** (owt´-) *n.* expenditure. ~*v.t.* (*pres.p.* **outlaying,** *past, p.p.* **outlaid**) to expend, to lay out. **outleap**[1] *v.t.* (*pres.p.* **outleaping,** *past, p.p.* **outleaped, outleapt**) to surpass in leaping, to leap farther than. **outleap**[2] (owt'-) *n.* a leaping out. **outlet** (owt´lit) *n.* **1** a passage outwards. **2** a vent. **3** a means of egress. **4** an agency or market for goods. **5** (*N Am.*) a power point. **outlier** (owt´-) *n.* **1** a person who lodges or resides away from their office or business. **2** (*Geol.*) a portion of a bed detached from the main mass by denudation of the intervening parts. **3** in statistics, a result differing greatly from others in the sample. **outline** (owt´-) *n.* **1** the line or lines enclosing and defining a figure. **2** a drawing of such lines without shading. **3** the first general sketch, rough draft or summary. **4** (*pl.*) general features, facts, principles etc. **5** the representation of a word in shorthand. ~*v.t.* **1** to draw the outline of. **2** to sketch. **in outline** sketched or represented as an outline. **outlive** *v.t.* **1** to survive. **2** to outlast. **3** to live through. ~*v.i.* to survive. **outliver** *n.* **outlook**[1] (owt´-) *n.* **1** the prospect, general appearance of things, esp. as regards the future. **2** a view, a prospect. **3** looking out, watch, vigilance. **outlook**[2] (-luk´) *v.t.* to stare down. **outlying** (owt´-) *a.* situated at a distance, or on the exterior frontier.

outlandish (owtlan´dish) *a.* **1** foreign-looking, strange, extraordinary. **2** foreign, alien. **3** bizarre, unconventional. **outlandishly** *adv.* **outlandishness** *n.* [OE *ūtlendisc*, from *ūtland*, foreign country, from OUT, LAND]

outlaw (owt´law) *n.* **1** a lawless person. **2** (*Hist.*) a person deprived of the protection of the law. **3** †an exile, a fugitive. **4** (*Austral.*) an untameable horse. ~*v.t.* **1** to deprive of the protection of the law. **2** to make illegal. **outlawry** *n.* [OE *ūtlaga, ūtlagian*, from ON *útlagi*, from *útlagr*, outlawed, OUT, LAW[1]]

out- (+ m–p words) outmanoeuvre, (*N Am.*) **outmaneuver** *v.t.* **1** to get the better of by manoeuvring. **2** to outdo in manoeuvring. **outmarch** *v.t.* to march faster than, to outstrip by marching. **outmatch** *v.t.* to be more than a match for. **outmeasure** *v.t.* to exceed in quantity or extent. **outmoded** *a.* **1** out of fashion. **2** obsolete. **outmodedly** *adv.* **outmodedness** *n.* **outnumber** *v.t.* to exceed in number. **outpace** *v.t.* **1** to walk faster than. **2** to outdo. **outpart** (owt´-) *n.* an outer or exterior part. **outpatient** (owt´-) *n.* a patient receiving treatment at a hospital without being a resident. **outperform** *v.t.* to do much better than. **outperformance** *n.* **outplacement** (owt´-) *n.* professional relocation of redundant employees arranged by their former employer. **outplace** *v.t.* **outplacer** *n.* a person or agency providing this service. **outplay** *v.t.* to play better than or defeat an opponent in a game. **outpoint** *v.t.* to score more points than. **outport** (owt´-) *n.* **1** a seaport outside a chief town or chief seat of trade. **2** (*Can.*) a small remote fishing village. **outpost** (owt´-) *n.* a post or station at a distance from the main body. **outpour**[1] *v.t.* to pour out, to discharge. ~*v.i.* to flow forth. **outpour**[2] (owt´-) *n.* **1** a pouring out. **2** an overflow. **outpouring** *n.* **outpsych** *v.t.* (*esp. N Am. coll.*) to defeat using psychology.

outmost OUTERMOST (under OUT).

output (owt´put) *n.* **1** the produce of a factory, mine etc. **2** the aggregate amount produced. **3** the data produced by a computer. **4** the signal delivered by an electronic system or device. **5** the terminal for the output of a computer etc. ~*v.t.* (*pres.p.* **outputting,** *past, p.p.* **output, outputted**) **1** to produce output. **2** (of a computer) to supply (results etc.).

out- (+ r– words) outrace *v.t.* to race faster than. **outran** OUTRUN[1] (under OUT- (+ R– WORDS)). **outrange** *v.t.* (of artillery) to have a longer range than. **outrank** *v.t.* to exceed in rank. **outreach**[1] *v.t.* **1** to exceed in reach, to surpass. **2** to overreach, to reach out. ~*v.i.* to extend. **outreach**[2] (owt´-) *n.* **1** a reaching out. **2** the extent or distance of this. **3** the involvement of an organization with the community, esp. a church or a charity's involvement for welfare purposes. **outreign** *v.t.* **1** to reign longer than. **2** to reign throughout (a long period). **out-relief** (owt´-) *n.* (*Hist.*) aid given out of the rates to the poor who are not inmates of an institution. **outride** *v.t.* (*pres.p.* **outriding,** *past* **outrode,** *p.p.* **outridden**) **1** to ride faster than. **2** (of a ship) to come safely through (a storm). **outrider** (owt´-) *n.* **1** an escort who rides ahead of or beside a carriage or other vehicle. **2** a person sent in advance as a scout, or to discover a safe route etc. **3** (*N Am.*) a cowboy keeping cattle within bounds. **outriding** *n.* **outrigger** (owt´-) *n.* **1** a projecting spar, boom, beam or framework extended from the sides of a ship for various purposes. **2** a bracket carrying a rowlock projecting from the sides of a boat to give increased leverage in rowing. **3** a boat with these. **4** a projecting beam or framework used in building etc. **5** a projection from the shafts for attaching an extra horse to a vehicle. **6** the horse so attached. **7** a chassis extension supporting the body of a motor vehicle. **outrigged** *a.* (of a boat etc.) having outriggers. **outright**[1] *adv.* **1** completely, entirely. **2** at once, once for all. **3** openly. **outright**[2] (owt´-) *a.* **1** downright, positive. **2** unrestrained, thorough. **outrightness** *n.* **outrival** *v.t.* (*pres.p.* **outrivalling,** (*N Am.*) **outrivaling,** *past, p.p.* **outrivalled,** (*N Am.*) **outrivaled**) to surpass as a rival. **outro** (owt´rō) *n.* (*pl.* **outros**) (*coll.*) a concluding section of a piece of music etc. **outroar** *v.t.* to roar louder than. **outrode** OUTRIDE (under OUT- (+ R– WORDS)). **outroot** *v.t.* to root out, eradicate. **outrun**[1] *v.t.* (*pres.p.* **outrunning,** *past* **outran,** *p.p.* **outrun**) **1** to run faster or farther than, to outstrip. **2** to escape by running. **3** to go beyond (a specified point). **outrun**[2] (owt´-) *n.* (*Austral.*) a distant sheep-run. **out-runner** (owt´-) *n.* **outrush** (owt´-) *n.* **1** a rushing out. **2** a violent overflow.

outrage (owt´rāj) *n.* **1** wanton injury to or violation of the rights of others. **2** a gross offence against order or decency. **3** a flagrant insult. **4** fierce anger or indignation. ~*v.t.* **1** to commit an outrage on. **2** to injure or insult in a flagrant manner. **3** to violate, to commit a rape upon. **4** to shock and anger. **5** to transgress, flagrantly. **outrageous** (-rā´-) *a.* **1** flagrant, heinous, atrocious, extravagant. **2** excessive, shocking. **3** violent, furious. **4** grossly offensive or abusive. **outrageously** *adv.* **outrageousness** *n.* [OF *ultrage, oultrage* (L *ultrā*, beyond, -AGE)]

outré (oo´trā) *a.* **1** extravagant, exaggerated, eccentric. **2** outraging convention or decorum. [F, p.p. of *outrer* (from L *ultrā*, beyond)]

out- (+ s– words) outsail *v.t.* to sail better or faster than. **outsat** OUTSIT (under OUT- (+ S– WORDS)). **outscold** *v.t.* to scold louder than. **outscorn** *v.t.* to bear down with contempt. **outscouring** *n.* (*usu. in pl.*) anything scoured or washed out, refuse. **outsell** *v.t.* (*pres.p.* **outselling,** *past, p.p.* **outsold**) **1** to exceed in price or value. **2** to sell more or faster than. **outset** (owt´-) *n.* commencement, beginning, start. **at/ from the outset** at or from the beginning. **outshine** *v.i.* (*pres.p.* **outshining,** *past, p.p.* **outshone**) to shine forth. ~*v.t.* **1** to excel in lustre. **2** to surpass in splendour. **3** to surpass in ability, excellence etc. **outshoot** *v.t.* (*pres.p.* **outshooting,** *past, p.p.* **outshot**) **1** to shoot better or farther than. **2** (*esp. N Am.*) to attempt or score more goals etc. than. **outsight** (owt´-) *n.* perception of external things, observation. **outsit** *v.t.* (*pres.p.* **outsitting,** *past, p.p.* **outsat**) **1** to sit beyond the time of. **2** to sit longer than. **outsize** (owt´-) *a.* **1** abnormally large. **2** larger than the standard size. ~*n.* an exceptionally large person or thing, such as a garment. **outsized** *a.* **outsizeness** *n.* **outskirt** (owt´-) *n.* (*usu. in pl.*) the outer border. **outsleep** *v.t.* (*past, p.p.* **outslept**) **1** to sleep beyond (a particular time). **2** to sleep longer than. **outsmart** *v.t.* **1** (*coll.*) to outwit. **2** to get the better of. **outsoar** *v.t.* to soar beyond or higher than. **outsold** OUTSELL (under OUT- (+ S– WORDS)). **outsole** (owt´-) *n.* the outside or lower sole, which comes in contact with the ground. **outsource** (owt´-) *v.t.* (*esp. N Am.*) to subcontract work to another company, esp. as a means of reducing costs. **outsourcing** *n.* **outspan**[1] *v.t.* (*pres.p.* **outspanning,** *past, p.p.* **outspanned**) (*S Afr.*) to unyoke or unharness. *~v.i.* **1** to unyoke or unharness animals. **2** to break a wagon journey. **outspan**[2] (owt´-) *n.* the act or place of unyoking animals or allowing them to graze. **outspeak** *v.t.* (*pres.p.* **outspeaking,** *past* **outspoke,** *p.p.* **outspoken**) **1** to outdo in speaking. **2** to speak (something) out. **outspend** *v.t.* (*pres.p.* **outspending,** *past, p.p.* **outspent**) to spend more than. **outspoken** *a.* open, candid, frank in speech. **outspokenly** *adv.* **outspokenness** *n.* **outsport** *v.t.* to outdo in sport. **outspread**[1] *v.t.* (*past, p.p.* **outspread**) to spread out. **outspread**[2] (owt´-) *a.* spread out. **outstand** *v.t.* (*past, p.p.* **outstood**) to stand out against, to withstand. *~v.i.* to stand out, to sea. **outstanding** *a.* **1** remaining unpaid. **2** projecting outward. **3** salient, conspicuous, prominent. **4** superior, excellent. **outstandingly** *adv.* **outstare** *v.t.* to outface, to abash by staring. **outstation** (owt´-) *n.* **1** (*Austral.*) a distant station. **2** a branch of an organization, business etc. which is remote from headquarters. **outstay** *v.t.* to stay longer than (a specified time or another person). **to outstay one's welcome** WELCOME. **outstep** *v.t.* (*pres.p.* **outstepping,** *past, p.p.* **outstepped**) to overstep. **outstood** OUTSTAND (under OUT- (+ S– WORDS)). **outstretch** *v.t.* **1** to extend, to expand. **2** to stretch out. **3** to stretch or strain to the utmost. **4** to reach further than. **outstrike** *v.t.* (*pres.p.* **outstriking,** *past, p.p.* **outstruck**) to strike faster or heavier blows than. **outstrip** *v.t.* (*pres.p.* **outstripping,** *past, p.p.* **outstripped**) **1** to outrun, to leave behind. **2** to escape by running. **3** to surpass in progress. **outswear** *v.t.* (*pres.p.* **outswearing,** *past* **outswore,** *p.p.* **outsworn**) to overwhelm by swearing. **out-swinger** (owt´-) *n.* in cricket, a ball that swings away from the batsman.

outside (owtsīd´, owt´-) *n.* **1** the external part or surface, the exterior. **2** the external appearance, superficial aspect. **3** that which is without. **4** external space, region, position etc. **5** the utmost limit, the extreme. **6** the side of a path away from a wall or next to a road. **7** an outside player in football etc. **8** (*Hist.*) an outside passenger on a horse-drawn coach etc. **9** (*pl.*) the outer sheets of a ream of paper. *~a.* **1** of or relating to, situated on, near, or nearer to the outside, outer. **2** external, superficial. **3** highest or greatest possible, extreme. **4** remote, most unlikely. **5** not of or belonging to an institution etc. **6** not a member of the Stock Exchange. *~adv.* **1** to or on the outside. **2** without, not within. **3** (*sl.*) not in prison. *~prep.* **1** at, on, to, or of the exterior of. **2** without, out from, forth from. **3** beyond the limits of. **at the outside** at the most. **outside and in** outside and inside. **outside in** having the outer side turned in, and vice versa. **to get outside of** (*sl.*) to eat or drink. **outside broadcast** *n.* a radio or television broadcast from outside the studio. **outside edge** *n.* in skating, a stroke on the outer edge of the skate. **outside interest** *n.* a hobby. **outside-left, outside-right** *n.* in football, hockey etc., an attacking player on the extreme left or right. **outside of** *prep.* **1** outside. **2** (*N Am., coll.*) apart from. **outsider** (-sī´-) *n.* **1** a person who is not a member of a profession, party, circle, coterie etc. **2** a person not acquainted with or interested in something that is going on. **3** a person not admissible to decent society. **4** in racing etc., a horse or competitor not included among the favourites. **outside seat** *n.* a seat at the end of a row. **outside track** *n.* the outside lane of a sports track.

Usage note The use of *outside of* as a preposition (rather than simple *outside*) is sometimes disapproved of.

out- (+ t–w words) out-take (owt´-) *n.* an unreleased piece of recorded music, film or television. **out-talk** *v.t.* **1** to outdo in talking. **2** to talk down. **out-think** *v.t.* (*past, p.p.* **out-thought**) **1** to outwit. **2** to outdo in thinking. **out-thrust**[1] (owt´-) *n.* **1** outward thrust or pressure. **2** the act or an instance of becoming noticeable. *~a.* thrust or projected forward. **out-thrust**[2] *v.t.* (*past, p.p.* **out-thrust**) to thrust forth or forward. **out-top** *v.t.* to surmount or surpass in height etc. **out-tray** (owt´-) *n.* a tray in an office for outgoing documents, correspondence etc. **out-turn** (owt´-) *n.* **1** the quantity produced. **2** the result of a process, an outcome. **outvalue** *v.t.* (*3rd pers. sing. pres.* **outvalues,** *pres.p.* **outvaluing,** *past, p.p.* **outvalued**) to exceed in value. **outvote** *v.t.* **1** to outnumber in voting. **2** to cast more votes than. **outwalk** *v.t.* **1** to outdo or outstrip in walking. **2** the walk beyond. **outwash** (owt´-) *n.* a mass of gravel, sand etc. carried by melted water from a glacier and deposited. **outwatch** *v.t.* **1** to watch longer than. **2** to watch throughout (a specified time). **outwear**[1] *v.t.* (*pres.p.* **outwearing,** *past* **outwore,** *p.p.* **outworn**) **1** to wear out. **2** to exhaust, to weary out. **3** to last longer than. **outwear**[2] (owt´-) *n.* outer garments. **outweigh** *v.t.* **1** to weigh more than. **2** to be too heavy for. **3** to be of more value, importance etc. than. **outwell** *v.i.* to pour or flow forth. **outwent** OUTGO. **outwick** (owt´-) *n.* in curling, a shot striking another stone so as to drive it nearer the tee. **outwit** *v.t.* (*pres.p.* **outwitting,** *past, p.p.* **outwitted**) **1** to defeat by superior ingenuity and cunning. **2** to overreach, to cheat. **outwith** *prep.* (*Sc.*) outside, beyond. **outwore** OUTWEAR[1] (under OUT- (+ T–W WORDS)). **outwork**[1] (owt´-) *n.* **1** a work included in the defence of a place, but outside the parapet. **2** work done outside the shop, factory etc. **outwork**[2] (-wœk´) *v.t.* (*pres.p.* **outworking,** *past, p.p.* **outworked, outwrought**) **1** to work out, to complete. **2** to work faster than. **outworker** (owt´-) *n.* a person who works outside (a factory, shop etc.). **outworking** (owt´-) *n.* the action or process of working out. **outworn**[1] OUTWEAR[1] (under OUT- (+ T–W WORDS)). **outworn**[2] *a.* **1** worn out. **2** obsolete. **outworth** *v.t.* to exceed in value.

outward (owt´wəd) *a.* **1** exterior, outer. **2** tending or directed toward the outside. **3** (of a ship, voyage etc.) leaving for a particular destination. **4** external, visible, apparent, superficial. **5** material, worldly, corporeal, not spiritual. **6** extraneous, extrinsic. *~adv.* (*also* **outwards**) in an outward direction. *~n.* **1** outward or external appearance. **2** (*pl.*) externals. **to outward seeming** apparently. **outward bound** *a.* going away from home. **Outward Bound®** *n.* a movement that provides adventure training for young people. **outward form** *n.* appearance. **outwardly** *adv.* **outward man** *n.* the carnal person as opposed to the spiritual or the soul. **outwardness** *n.* **outwards** OUTWARD. **outward things** *n.pl.* **1** visible or sensible things. **2** things of this world. [OE *ūteweard* (OUT, -WARD)]

ouzel (oo´zəl), **ousel** *n.* **1** a thrush, *Turdus torquatus,* the ring ouzel. **2** the dipper, *Cinclus cinclus,* the water ouzel. [OE *ōsle* (cp. G *Amsel,* OHG *amsala*)]

ouzo (oo´zō) *n.* (*pl.* **ouzos**) an aniseed-flavoured spirit from Greece. [mod. Gr. *ouzon*]

ov-[1] (ov), **ovi-** (ō´vi), **ovo-** (ō´vō) *comb. form* of or relating to an egg or ovum. [L *ovum,* egg]

ov-[2] (ov), **ovi-** (ō´vi) *comb. form* of or relating to sheep. [L *ovis,* sheep]

ova OVUM.

oval (ō´vəl) *a.* egg-shaped, roughly elliptical. ~*n.* **1** a closed convex curve with one axis longer than the other. **2** an egg-shaped figure or thing, e.g. a sports field. **ovality** (-val´-) *n.* **ovally** *adv.* **ovalness** *n.* **Oval Office** *n.* the office of the US President. [med. L *ovalis*, from L *ovum*, egg]

ovary (ō´vəri) *n.* (*pl.* **ovaries**) **1** each of the organs (two in number in the higher vertebrates) in a female in which the ova are produced. **2** (*Bot.*) the portion of the pistil in which the ovules are contained. **ovarian** (-veə´ri-) *a.* **ovariectomy** (-ekt´əmi) *n.* (*pl.* **ovariectomies**) the removal of the ovary by excision, or of a tumour from the ovary. **ovariotomy** (-ot´əmi) *n.* (*pl.* **ovariotomies**). **ovaritis** (-rī´tis) *n.* inflammation of the ovary. **ovate** (ō´vāt) *a.* egg-shaped. [OVUM, -ARY[1]]

ovation (ōvā´shən) *n.* **1** a display of popular favour, an enthusiastic reception. **2** (*Hist.*) in ancient Rome, a minor triumph. **ovational** *a.* [L *ovātio*, from *ovāre*, to rejoice]

oven (ŭv´ən) *n.* **1** a close chamber in which substances are baked etc. **2** a furnace or kiln for assaying, annealing etc. **ovenbird, ovenbuilder** *n.* any Central or S American bird of the family Furnariidae, which make domed nests. **oven glove** *n.* a thick glove for handling hot dishes. **ovenproof** *a.* suitable for use in an oven. **oven-ready** *a.* (of food) already prepared for immediate cooking in an oven. **ovenware** *n.* heat-resistant dishes used for cooking and serving food. [OE *ofn* (cp. Dut. *oven*, G *Ofen*, Icel. *ofn*) cogn. with Gr. *ipnos*]

over (ō´və) *prep.* **1** above, in a higher position than. **2** above or superior to in excellence, dignity or value. **3** more than, in excess of. **4** in charge of, concerned or engaged with. **5** across from side to side of. **6** through the extent or duration of. **7** having recovered from the effect of. **8** (*Math.*) divided by. **9** transmitted by. **10** in comparison with. **11** so as to cover. ~*adv.* **1** so as to pass from side to side or across some space, barrier etc. **2** in width, in distance across. **3** on the opposite side. **4** from one side to another. **5** so as to be turned down or upside down from an erect position. **6** so as to be across or down from a brink, brim etc. **7** so as to traverse a space etc. **8** from end to end, throughout. **9** at an end. **10** in excess, in addition. **11** excessively, with repetition, again. **12** for or until a later time. ~*a.* **1** upper, outer. **2** superior. **3** extra. ~*int.* (*also* **over to you**) in radio signalling etc., indicating that a reply is expected. ~*n.* **1** in cricket, the interval between the times when the umpire calls 'over'. **2** the number of balls (6 or 8) delivered by one bowler during this. **all over** ALL. **not over** not very. **over all** taken as a whole. **over and above** **1** in addition to. **2** besides. **over and over** **1** so as to turn completely round several times. **2** repeatedly. **over head and ears** HEAD[1]. **over one's head** HEAD[1]. **over the fence** FENCE. **over the hill** HILL. **over the moon** MOON. **over the way** across the street. **to begin over** (*N Am.*) to start over. **to get it over with** to do something unpleasant that has to be done. **to start over** (*N Am.*) to start again. **over again** *adv.* afresh, anew. **over against** *prep.* **1** opposite. **2** in front of. **3** in contrast with. **over-the-counter** *a.* obtainable without a prescription. **over-the-top** *a.* extreme, outrageous. [OE *ofer* (cp. Dut. *over*, G *über*, *ober*, Icel. *yfir*, *ofr*), cogn. with Gr. *huper*, Sansk. *upari*]

over- (ōvə´) *pref.* **1** above. **2** across. **3** outer, upper. **4** as a covering. **5** past, beyond. **6** extra. **7** excessively, too much, too great. **8** completely, utterly.

over- (+ a–t words) **overabound** *v.i.* **1** to be superabundant. **2** to abound too much (with or on). **overabundant** *a.* in excessive quantity. **over-abundance** *n.* **over-abundantly** *adv.* **overaccentuate** *v.t.* **overaccumulation** *n.* **overachieve** *v.i.* to do more than might be expected. ~*v.t.* to achieve more than (a goal). **overachievement** *n.* **overachiever** *n.* **overact** *v.t.* **1** to act (a part) in an exaggerated way. **2** to overdo. ~*v.i.* to act more than is necessary. **overactivity** *n.* **overactive** *a.* excessively active. **overadorned** *a.* **overadvance** *v.t.* **overaffect** *v.t.* **overage** (ō´vərij) *n.* a surplus or excess. **over-age** *a.* over a certain age limit. **overaggressive** *a.* **overall**[1] (ō´-) *a.* from end to end, total. ~*n.* **1** an outer garment worn as a protection against dirt etc. **2** (*pl.*) trousers or other garments worn over others as a protection against dirt etc. **3** (*pl.*) close-fitting trousers worn as part of army uniform. **overall**[2] (-awl´) *adv.* everywhere, in all parts or directions. **overalled** *a.* **overambitious** *a.* too ambitious. **overambition** *n.* **overambitiously** *adv.* **overambitiousness** *n.* **overanalyse,** (*N Am.*) **overanalyze** *v.t.* **overangry** *a.* **overanimated** *a.* **overanimatedly** *adv.* **overanimation** *n.* **over-anxious** *a.* excessively anxious. **over-anxiety** *n.* **over-anxiously** *adv.* **overappreciation** *n.* **overappreciative** *a.* **overapprehensive** *a.* **overapprehensively** *adv.* **overapprehensiveness** *n.* **overarch** *v.t.* to form an arch over. ~*v.i.* to form an arch overhead. **overarching** *a.* **overargumentative** *a.* **overarm** (ō´-) *a.* **1** in sports, esp. cricket, bowled or thrown with the arm raised above the shoulder. **2** in swimming, with the arm or arms lifted out of the water. ~*adv.* the arm raised above the shoulder. **overassert** *v.t.* **overassertion** *n.* **overassertive** *a.* **overassertively** *adv.* **overassertiveness** *n.* **overassessment** *n.* **overassured** *a.* **overate** OVEREAT (under OVER- (+ A–T WORDS)). **overattached** *a.* **overattentive** *a.* **overattentively** *adv.* **overattentiveness** *n.* **overawe** *v.t.* **1** to keep in awe. **2** to control or restrain by awe. **overbalance** *v.t.* **1** to outweigh. **2** to destroy the equilibrium. **3** to upset. ~*v.i.* **1** to lose one's equilibrium. **2** to topple over. ~*n.* **1** excess of value or amount. **2** that which exceeds an equivalent. **overbear** *v.t.* (*pres.p.* **overbearing,** *past* **overbore,** *p.p.* **overborne**) **1** to bear down, to overpower. **2** to surpass in importance etc. **overbearing** *a.* arrogant, haughty, imperious. **overbearingly** *adv.* **overbearingness** *n.* **overbid** *v.t.*, *v.i.* (*pres.p.* **overbidding,** *past, p.p.* **overbid**) **1** to outbid. **2** to bid more than the value of (one's hand of cards). ~*n.* a higher bid. **overbidder** *n.* **overbite** (ō´-) *n.* in dentistry, the overlapping of the lower teeth by the upper. **overblouse** (ō´-) *n.* a garment worn like a blouse, worn outside other clothing. **overblow** *v.i.*, *v.t.* (*past* **overblew,** *p.p.* **overblown**) to blow over. **overblown**[1] *a.* inflated, pretentious. **overblown**[2] (ō´-) *a.* more than full blown. **overboard** (ō´-) *adv.* **1** over the side of a ship. **2** out of a ship. **to go overboard** **1** (*coll.*) to go to extremes of enthusiasm. **2** to go too far. **to throw overboard** to abandon, discard. **overbold** *a.* bold to excess. **overboldly** *adv.* **overboldness** *n.* **overbook** *v.t.*, *v.i.* to make bookings for more places than are available (e.g. in a hotel, plane, ship etc.). **overboot** (ō´-) *n.* a boot worn over another boot or shoe. **overbore, overborne** OVERBEAR (under OVER- (+ A–T WORDS)). **overbrave** *a.* **overbrim** *v.t.* (*pres.p.* **overbrimming,** *past, p.p.* **overbrimmed**) to flow over the brim of. ~*v.i.* (of a vessel or liquid) to overflow at the brim. **overbuild** *v.t.* (*past, p.p.* **overbuilt**) **1** to build more than is required. **2** to build too much upon (land etc.). **3** to build over or upon. **overburden**[1] (ō´-) *n.* **1** rock etc. that must be removed before mining can take place. **2** an excessive burden. **overburden**[2] (-bœ´-) *v.t.* to overload, to overweigh. **overburdensome** *a.* **overbusy** *a.* excessively busy. **overbuy** *v.i.* to buy more than is required. ~*v.i.* (*past, p.p.* **overbought**) to pay too much for. **overby** (ō´-) *adv.* (*Sc.*) **1** a little way across. **2** over the way. **overcall**[1] *v.t.* to bid higher than a previous bid or player at bridge. **overcall**[2] (ō´-) *n.* a higher bid than the preceding one. **overcame** OVERCOME (under OVER- (+ A–T WORDS)). **overcanopy** *v.t.* (*3rd pres. sing. pres.* **overcanopies,** *pres.p.* **overcanopying,** *past, p.p.* **overcanopied**) to cover with or as with a canopy.

overcapacity *n.* a state of saturation or an excess of productive capacity. **overcapitalize, overcapitalise** *v.t.* to rate or fix the nominal value of the capital of (a company etc.) at too high a figure. **overcareful** *a.* careful to excess. **overcarefully** *adv.* **overcast** *v.t.* (*pres.p.* **overcasting,** *past, p.p.* **overcast**) **1** to darken, to cloud. **2** to render gloomy or depressed. **3** to sew (an edge etc.) with long stitches to prevent unravelling etc., or as embroidering. **4** to cast off (an illness etc.). **5** to rate too high. ~*a.* **1** clouded all over (of the sky). **2** sewn or embroidered by overcasting. **3** in excess of the proper amount. ~*n.* **1** something thrown over. **2** a cloud covering the sky. **3** overcast needlework. **overcasting** *n.* **overcasual** *a.* **overcaution** *n.* excess of caution. **overcautious** *a.* **overcautiously** *adv.* **overcautiousness** *n.* **overcentralization, overcentralisation** *n.* **overcerebral** *a.* **overcharge**[1] *v.t.* **1** to charge with more than is properly due. **2** to overburden, to overload. **3** to load (a firearm) with an excessive charge. **4** to saturate. **5** to exaggerate. **overcharge**[2] (ō´-) *n.* an excessive charge, load or burden. **overcheck** (ō´-) *n.* **1** a combination of two different-sized check patterns. **2** a cloth having this pattern. **overcivil** *a.* **overcivilize, overcivilise** *v.t.* **overcloud** *v.t.* **1** to cloud over. **2** to depress, to deject. ~*v.i.* to become overcast (of the sky). **overcloy** *v.t.* to surfeit, to satiate. **overcoat** (ō´-) *n.* **1** a heavy coat. **2** a protective coat of paint etc. **overcoated** *a.* **overcoating** *n.* material for overcoats. **overcome** *v.t.* (*pres.p.* **overcoming,** *past* **overcame,** *p.p.* **overcome**) to overpower, to vanquish, to conquer. ~*v.i.* to be victorious. ~*a.* exhausted, helpless, affected by emotion etc. **overcomer** *n.* **overcommit** *v.t.* (*pres.p.* **overcommitting,** *past, p.p.* **overcommitted**) (*usu. reflex.*) to commit to an excessive degree. **overcommitment** *n.* **overcommon** *a.* **overcompensate** *v.t.* **1** to provide too much in compensation. **2** to react excessively to feelings of inferiority or inadequacy etc. **overcompensation** *n.* **overcompensatory** *a.* **overcompetitive** *a.* **overcomplacency** *n.* **overcomplacent** *a.* **overcomplex** *a.* **overcomplicate** *v.t.* **overconcern** *n.* **overconfidence** *n.* excessive confidence. **overconfident** *a.* **overconfidently** *adv.* **overconscientious** *a.* **overconservative** *a.* **overconsiderate** *a.* **overconsume** *v.t.* **overconsumption** *n.* **overcook** *v.t.* to cook too much or for too long. **overcooked** *a.* **overcool** *v.t., a.* **overcorrect** *v.t., a.* **overcorrection** *n.* **overcostly** *a.* **overcount** *v.t.* to rate above the true value. **overcredulous** *a.* too credulous. **overcredulity** *n.* **overcredulously** *adv.* **overcritical** *a.* excessively critical. **overcriticize, overcriticise** *v.t.* **overcrop** *v.t.* (*pres.p.* **overcropping,** *past, p.p.* **overcropped**) **1** to crop (land) to excess. **2** to exhaust by continual cropping. **overcrow** *v.t.* to crow or triumph over. **overcrowd** *v.t., v.i.* to crowd to excess. **overcrowding** *n.* **overcrust** *v.t.* to cover with a crust. **overcultivate** *v.t.* **overcunning** *a.* too cunning. **overcurious** *a.* too curious. **overcuriosity** *n.* **overdecorate** *v.t.* **overdefensive** *a.* **overdeferential** *a.* **overdeliberate** *a.* **overdelicate** *a.* excessively delicate. **overdelicacy** *n.* **overdependence** *n.* **overdependent** *a.* **overdesirous** *a.* **overdetailed** *a.* **overdetermination** *n.* **overdetermine** *v.t.* to determine in more than one way, or with more conditions than are necessary. **overdetermined** *a.* **overdevelop** *v.t.* (*pres.p.* **overdeveloping,** *past, p.p.* **overdeveloped**) **1** to develop a photographic negative too much so that the image is too dense. **2** to develop too much. **overdid** OVERDO (under OVER- (+ A–T WORDS)). **overdiligent** *a.* **overdiligently** *adv.* **overdilute** *v.t.* **overdistant** *a.* **overdiversify** *v.t., v.i.* (*3rd pers. sing. pres.* **overdiversifies,** *pres.p.* **overdiversifying,** *past, p.p.* **overdiversified**). **overdiversification** *n.* **overdiversity** *n.* **overdo** *v.t.* (*3rd pers. sing. pres.* **overdoes,** *pres.p.* **overdoing,** *past* **overdid,** *p.p.* **overdone**) **1** to do to excess. **2** to exaggerate. **3** to overact. **4** to excel. **5** to cook to excess. **6** to fatigue, to wear out. **to overdo it** to exhaust oneself, do too much. **to overdo things** to overdo it. **overdose**[1] (ō´-) *n.* an excessive dose. **overdose**[2] (-dōs´) *v.t.* to give too large a dose to. ~*v.i.* to take an overdose. **overdosage** *n.* **overdraft** (ō´-) *n.* **1** a withdrawal of money from a bank in excess of the amount to one's credit. **2** the amount of this. **overdramatic** *a.* excessively dramatic. **overdramatize, overdramatise** *v.t.* to be excessively dramatic in one's reaction, behaviour etc. **overdrank** OVERDRINK (under OVER- (+ A–T WORDS)). **overdraw** *v.t.* (*past* **overdrew,** *p.p.* **overdrawn**) **1** to draw upon for a larger sum than stands to one's credit. **2** to exaggerate. ~*v.i.* to overdraw one's account. **overdrawer** *n.* **overdrawn**[1] *a.* having overdrawn one's account. **overdrawn**[2] OVERDRAW (under OVER- (+ A–T WORDS)). **overdress**[1] *v.t., v.i.* to dress too formally or ostentatiously. **overdress**[2] (ō´-) *n.* a dress worn over other clothes. **overdrew** OVERDRAW (under OVER- (+ A–T WORDS)). **overdrink** *v.i.* (*past* **overdrank,** *p.p.* **overdrunk**) to drink too much. **overdrive**[1] *v.t.* (*pres.p.* **overdriving,** *past.* **overdrove,** *p, p.* **overdriven**) to drive too far or too hard. **overdrive**[2] (ō´-) *n.* **1** an extra high gear in a motor car which drives the propeller shaft at a higher speed than the engine crankshaft. **2** a state of great activity. **overdrove** OVERDRIVE. **overdrunk** OVERDRINK (under OVER- (+ A–T WORDS)). **overdub** *v.t.* (*pres.p.* **overdubbing,** *past, p.p.* **overdubbed**) to add additional sounds to a recording. ~*n.* an act or instance of overdubbing. **overdue** *a.* **1** remaining unpaid after the date on which it is due. **2** not arrived at the time it was due. **3** (of a library book etc.) kept longer than the period allowed. ~*n.* a debt or account that is overdue. **overdye** *v.t.* to dye too deeply or with a second colour. **overeager** *a.* excessively eager. **overeagerly** *adv.* **overeagerness** *n.* **overearnest** *a.* too earnest. **overearnestly** *adv.* **overearnestness** *n.* **overeat** *v.i.* (*past* **overate,** *p.p.* **overeaten**) **1** to eat to excess. **2** (*reflex.*) to injure (oneself) by eating to excess. ~*v.t.* to eat or nibble all over. **overeducate** *v.t.* **overeffusive** *a.* **over-elaborate** *a.* excessively elaborate. ~*v.t.* to explain in too much detail. **over-elaborately** *adv.* **over-elaboration** *n.* **overembelllish** *v.t.* **overembroider** *v.t.* **over-emotional** *a.* excessively emotional. **over-emotionally** *adv.* **over-emphasis** *n.* excessive emphasis. **overemphasize, overemphasise** *v.t., v.i.* **overemphatic** *a.* **overemulation** *n.* **overenthusiasm** *n.* excessive enthusiasm. **overenthusiastic** *a.* **overenthusiastically** *adv.* **overestimate** *v.t.* to give too high a value to. ~*n.* too high an estimate. **overestimation** *n.* **overexacting** *a.* **overexcitable** *a.* **overexcitably** *adv.* **overexcite** *v.t.* to excite excessively. **overexcitement** *n.* **over-exercise** *v.t.* to use too much. ~*v.i.* to take too much exercise. ~*n.* excessive exercise. **overexert** *v.t.* to exert too much. **overexertion** *n.* **overexpand** *v.t., v.i.* **overexpansion** *n.* **overexpectant** *a.* **overexpenditure** *n.* **overexplicit** *a.* **overexpose** *v.t.* **1** to expose too much. **2** to expose (a film) to light too long so as to make the negative defective. **overexposure** *n.* **overexpressive** *a.* **overextend** *v.t.* **1** to extend too far. **2** (*reflex.*) to take on too much work etc. **3** to impose too much work on. **overfacile** *a.* **overfall** *n.* **1** a turbulent race or current with choppy waves caused by shoals, the meeting of cross-currents etc. **2** a structure for the overflow of water from a canal etc. **overfamiliar** *a.* too familiar. **overfamiliarity** *n.* **overfanciful** *a.* **overfar** *a., adv.* **overfastidious** *a.* **overfatigue** *n.* excessive fatigue. **overfearful** *a.* **overfeed** *v.t.* (*past, p.p.* **overfed**) to surfeit with food. ~*v.i.* to eat to excess. **overfill** *v.t., v.i.* to fill to excess. **overfine** *a.* excessively fine or precise. **overfish** *v.t.* to deplete (a stream etc.) by too much fishing. **overflew** OVERFLY (under OVER- (+ A–T WORDS)). **overflourish** *v.t.* **1** to adorn superficially. **2** to cover with flowers and verdure. **overflow**[1] *v.t.* **1** to flow over, to flood, to inundate. **2** to cover as with a liquid. ~*v.i.* **1** to run over. **2** to abound. **3** to overflow the banks (of a stream). **4** to be full of. **overflow**[2] (ō´-) *n.* **1** a flood, an inundation. **2** a superabundance, a profusion. **3** any outlet for surplus liquid. **4** (*Comput.*) the generation of a number having more digits than the assigned location. **overflowing** *a.* **overflowingly** *adv.* **overflow meeting** *n.* an extra meeting for people unable to attend the main meeting. **overfly** *v.t.* (*3rd pers. sing. pres.* **overflies,** *pres.p.* **overflying,** *past* **overflew,** *p.p.* **overflown**) to fly over or beyond. **overflight** *n.* **overfold**[1] (ō´-) *n.* (*Geol.*) a fold of strata in which the lower part has been pushed over the upper, a reflexed or inverted fold. **overfold**[2] (-fōld´) *v.t.* (*usu. in p.p.*) to push or fold (strata) over in this manner. **overfond** *a.* **1** too fond. **2** doting. **overfondly** *adv.* **overfragile** *a.* **overfraught** *a.* overladen. **overfulfil,** (*N Am.*) **overfulfill** *v.t.* (*pres.p.* **overfulfilling,** *past, p.p.* **overfulfilled**) to fulfil beyond expectation or before the appointed time. **overfulfilment** *n.* **overfull** *a.* **1** too full. **2** surfeited. **overfurnish** *v.t.* **overgarment** *n.* a garment worn over other clothing. **overgeneralize, overgeneralise** *v.i.* **1** to draw general conclusions from inadequate data. **2** to argue more widely than is justified by the evidence etc. ~*v.t.* to draw an excessively general conclusion from (data etc.). **overgeneralization** *n.* **overgenerous** *a.* excessively generous. **overgenerously** *adv.* **overglaze** *n.* **1** a second glaze on ceramic ware. **2** decoration on a glazed surface. ~*a.* (of painting etc.) done on a glazed surface. **overgo** *v.t.* (*3rd pers. sing. pres.* **overgoes,** *pres.p.* **overgoing,** *past* **overwent,** *p.p.* **overgone**) **1** to go beyond. **2** to pass over. **3** to overcome. ~*v.i.* **1** to go by. **2** to pass away. **overgraze** *v.t.* **1** to allow (land) to be excessively grazed. **2** (of livestock) to feed on (land) too heavily so that the vegetation is damaged. **overgrazing** *n.* **overgreedy** *a.* excessively greedy. **overgrew** OVERGROW (under OVER- (+ A–T WORDS)). **overground** (ō´-) *a.* situated or running above ground, as opposed to *underground.* ~*adv.* **overgrow** *v.t.* (*past* **overgrew,** *p.p.* **overgrown**) **1** to cover with vegetation. **2** to outgrow (one's strength etc.). ~*v.i.* to grow too large. **overgrown** *a.* **overgrowth** (ō´-) *n.* **overhand** (ō´-) *a.* thrown or done with the hand raised above the level of the shoulder or elbow (of a ball, bowling etc.). ~*adv.* in this manner. **overhanded**[1] (ō´-) *a.* with the hand over the object grasped. **overhanded**[2] (-han´-) *a.* having too many hands or workers employed. **overhand knot** *n.* a simple knot made by forming a loop and passing the free end through it. **overhang**[1] *v.i.* (*past, p.p.* **overhung**) to hang over, to jut out. ~*v.t.* **1** to hang or impend over. **2** to threaten. **overhang**[2] (ō´-) *n.* **1** the act or an instance of overhanging. **2** the part or thing that overhangs. **3** the amount by which a thing overhangs. **overhappy** *a.* too happy. **overhaste** *n.* excessive haste. **overhasty** *a.* **overhastily** *adv.* **overhastiness** *n.* **overhaul**[1] *v.t.* **1** to turn over thoroughly for examination. **2** to examine thoroughly. **3** to overtake, to gain upon. **overhaul**[2] (ō´-) *n.* inspection, thorough examination. **overhead**[1] *adv.* **1** above the head, aloft. **2** in the zenith, ceiling, roof etc. ~*a.* **1** situated overhead. **2** working from above downwards. **3** all round, average, general. **overhead**[2] (ō´-) *n.* **1** a stroke in racket games made above head height. **2** (*pl., N Am. sing.*) expenses of administration etc. **overhead projector** *n.* a device that projects an enlarged image of a transparency on to a screen behind the operator. **overhear** *v.t.* (*past, p.p.* **overheard**) to hear (words not meant for one) by accident or stratagem. **overheat** *v.t.* **1** to heat to excess. **2** to stimulate or agitate. ~*v.i.* to become overheated. **overheated** *a.* **overhung** OVERHANG[1] (under OVER- (+ A–T WORDS)). **overhurried** *a.* **overidealistic** *a.* **overidealize, overidealise** *v.t.* **overimaginative** *a.* **overimpress** *v.t.* **overimpressionable** *a.* **overincline** *v.t.* **over-indulge** *v.t., v.i.* (*often reflex.*) to indulge to excess. **over-indulgence** *n.* **over-indulgent** *a.* **over-indulgently** *adv.* **overindustrialize, overindustrialise** *v.t., v.i.* **over-inflate** *v.t., v.i.* **over-inflated** *a.* exaggerated, excessively large. **overinfluence** *v.t.* **overinfluential** *a.* **overinsistence** *n.* **overinsistent** *a.* **overinsistently** *adv.* **over-insure** *v.t.* **1** to insure (property etc.) for more than its real value. **2** to insure excessively. **over-insurance** *n.* **overintellectual** *a.* **overintellectually** *adv.* **over-intense** *a.* **overintensely** *adv.* **overinterest** *n.* **overinvest** *v.t.* **overissue** *v.t.* (*3rd pers. sing. pres.* **overissues,** *pres.p.* **overissuing,** *past, p.p.* **overissued**) to issue in excess (as banknotes, etc.). ~*n.* an issue in excess. **overjoy** *v.t.* to transport with joy. **overjoyed** *a.* **overjump** *v.t.* **1** to jump over. **2** to jump beyond. **3** to injure (oneself) by too great a jump. **overkill** (ō´-) *n.* **1** destructive capability, esp. in nuclear weapons, in excess of military requirements. **2** something applied in excess of what is suitable or required. ~*v.t., v.i.* to kill or destroy to a greater extent than necessary. **overlabour** *v.t.* **1** to harass with labour. **2** to work upon excessively, to elaborate too much. **overladen** *a.* overburdened. **overlaid** OVERLAY (under OVER- (+ A–T WORDS)). **overlain** OVERLIE (under OVER- (+ A–T WORDS)). **overland** (ō´-) *a.* lying, going, made or performed by land. ~*adv.* across the land. ~*v.t.* (*Austral.*) to take livestock across country. ~*v.i.* (*Austral.*) to go a long distance overland. **overlander** *n.* (*Austral., New Zeal.*) **1** a person who takes livestock a great distance for sale to a new station. **2** (*sl.*) a tramp. **overlap**[1] *v.t.* (*pres.p.* **overlapping,** *past, p.p.* **overlapped**) **1** to lap or fold over. **2** to extend so as to lie or rest upon. ~*v.i.* to coincide. **overlap**[2] (ō´-) *n.* **1** an act, case or the extent of overlapping. **2** the part that overlaps something else. **over-large** *a.* too large. **overlavish** *a.* lavish to excess. **overlay**[1] *v.t.* (*past, p.p.* **overlaid**) **1** to cover or spread over the surface of. **2** to cover with a layer. **3** to overcast, to cloud. **4** (*Print.*) to put overlays on. **5** to weigh down. **overlay**[2] (ō´-) *n.* **1** something laid over (as a covering, layer etc.). **2** (*Print.*) paper pasted on the tympan to produce a heavier impression. **3** (*Comput.*) **a** the process of transferring data etc. to replace what is already stored. **b** a section so transferred. **overlay**[3] OVERLIE (under OVER- (+ A–T WORDS)). **overlaying** (ō´-) *n.* a covering.

Usage note See note under OVERLIE (under OVER- (+ A–T WORDS)).

overleaf *adv.* on the other side of the leaf (of a book etc.). **overleap** *v.t.* (*past, p.p.* **overleaped, overleapt**) **1** to leap over. **2** to leap beyond. **3** to leap too far. **4** to omit. **to overleap oneself** to miss one's aim by leaping too far or too high. **overlie** *v.t.* (*pres.p.* **overlying,** *past.* **overlay,** *p.p.* **overlain**) **1** to lie above or upon. **2** to smother by lying on.

Usage note The meanings of *overlie* and *overlay* overlap, but in general *overlie* is preferred for lying on top of or smothering something, and *overlay* is the appropriate term for covering or coating a surface.

overload[1] *v.t.* **1** to load too heavily. **2** to overcharge. **overload**[2] (ō´-) *n.* an excessive load. **overlong** *a., adv.* too long, excessively long. **overlook**[1] *v.t.* **1** to look over, to pass over with indulgence, to disregard, to slight. **2** to view from a high place. **3** to be situated so as to command a view of from above. **4** to superintend, to oversee. **5** to inspect or peruse, esp. in a cursory way. **6** to bewitch, to look at with an evil eye. **overlook**[2] (ō´-) *n.* (*N Am.*) a commanding position or view. **overlooker** (ō´-) *n.* **overlord** (ō´-) *n.* **1** a superior lord, one who is lord over other lords. **2** a person who is supreme over another or others. ~*v.t.* **1** to lord it over. **2** to rule as an overlord. **overlordship** *n.* **overly** (ō´-) *adv.* excessively, too. **overlying** OVERLIE (under OVER- (+ A–T WORDS)). **overmagnify** *v.t.* (*3rd pers. sing. pres.* **overmagnifies,** *pres.p.* **overmagnifying,** *past, p.p.* **overmagnified**). **overman**[1] (ō´-) *n.* (*pl.* **overmen**) **1** a superman. **2** an overseer or foreman. **overman**[2] (-man´) *v.t.* (*pres.p.* **overmanning,** *past, p.p.* **overmanned**) to furnish with too many people. **overmanage** *v.t.* **overmantel** (ō´-) *n.* ornamental woodwork placed over a mantelpiece. **over-many** *a.* too many. **overmaster** *v.t.* **1** to master completely. **2** to overcome, to subdue. **overmasterful** *a.* **overmasterfulness** *n.* **overmastering** *a.* **overmasteringly** *adv.* **overmastery** *n.* **overmatch**[1] *v.t.* to be more than a match for. **overmatch**[2] (ō´-) *n.* a person or thing that is superior in power, skill etc. **overmeasure** *n.* a measure above what is sufficient or due. ~*v.t.* to estimate too largely. **over-mighty** *a.* excessively powerful. **overmodest** *a.* **overmodestly** *adv.* **overmodify** *v.t.* (*3rd pers. sing. pres.* **overmodifies,** *pres.p.* **overmodifying,** *past, p.p.* **overmodified**). **overmount**[1] *v.t.* to rise above. ~*v.i.* to mount too high. **overmount**[2] (ō´-) *n.* a mount for a picture etc. **overmuch** *a.* too much, more than is sufficient or necessary. ~*adv.* in or to too great a degree. ~*n.* more than enough. **overnice** *a.* too nice, scrupulous, or fastidious. **overnicely** *adv.* **overniceness** *n.* **overnicety** *n.* **overnight** *a.* **1** done or happening the night before. **2** for use overnight. ~*adv.* **1** in the course of the night or evening. **2** in or on the evening before. **3** during or through the night. **4** suddenly, immediately. **overnighter** *n.* **1** a person who stays somewhere overnight. **2** an overnight bag. **overofficious** *a.* too officious. **overofficiously** *adv.* **overofficiousness** *n.* **overoptimistic** *a.* excessively or unjustifiably optimistic. **overoptimism** *n.* **over-optimist** *n.* **overpaid** OVERPAY (under OVER- (+ A–T WORDS)). **overpaint** *v.t.* to paint over. **overparted** *a.* (of an actor) given too demanding a part. **overparticular** *a.* excessively particular. **overpass**[1] *v.t.* (*past, p.p.* **overpassed, overpast**) **1** to pass or go over. **2** to overlook. **3** to pass or go beyond. **overpass**[2] (ō´-) *n.* a flyover. **overpay** *v.t., v.i.* (*past, p.p.* **overpaid**) **1** to pay more than is sufficient. **2** to pay in excess. **overpayment** *n.* **overpeer** *v.t.* **1** to look or peer over. **2** to rise above, to crow over. **overpeople** *v.t.* to overstock with people. **overpeopled** *a.* **overpersuade** *v.t.* to persuade against one's inclination or judgement. **overpessimistic** *a.* **overpicture** *v.t.* to represent in an exaggerated manner. **overpitch** *v.t.* **1** to bowl (a ball) so that it pitches too near the stumps. **2** to exaggerate. **overplay** *v.t.* **1** to exaggerate the importance of. **2** to overemphasize. **to overplay one's hand 1** to overestimate one's capabilities. **2** to spoil one's case by exaggerating. **overplus** (ō´-) *n.* **1** surplus, excess. **2** an amount left over. **overply** *v.t.* (*3rd pers. sing. pres.* **overplies,** *pres.p.* **overplying,** *past, p.p.* **overplied**) to ply or exercise to excess. **overpopulate** *v.t.* **overpopulated** *a.* having too large a population. **overpopulation** *n.* **overpower** *v.t.* **1** to be too strong or powerful for. **2** to overcome, conquer, vanquish. **3** to overcome the feelings or judgement of, to overwhelm. **overpowerful** *a.* **overpowering** *a.* **overpoweringly** *adv.* **overpraise** *v.t.* to praise too highly. **overpraising** *n.* excessive eulogy. **overprecise** *a.* **overprescribe** *v.t.* to prescribe excessively. **overprescription** *n.* **overpress** *v.t.* to overwhelm, to crush, to overpower. **overprice** *v.t.* to price too highly. **overprint**[1] (ō´-) *n.* printed matter added to a previously printed surface, esp. a postage stamp. **overprint**[2] (-print´) *v.t.* **1** to print on a previously printed surface. **2** in photography, to print (a positive) darker than was intended. **3** to print too many copies of (a work). **overprize** *v.t.* **1** to overvalue. **2** to exceed in value. **overproduction** *n.* production in excess of demand. **overproduce** *v.t., v.i.* **overprominent** *a.* **overprompt** *a.* **overpromptly** *adv.* **overproof** *a.* above proof, containing a larger proportion of alcohol than is contained in proof-spirit. **overproportion** *v.t., n.* **overprotective** *a.* excessively protective. **overproud** *a.* excessively proud. **overpublicize, overpublicise** *v.t.* **overqualified** *a.* too highly qualified. **overran** OVERRUN[1] (under OVER- (+ A–T WORDS)). **overrate** *v.t.* to rate too highly. **overrated** *a.* **overreach** *v.t.* **1** to reach or extend beyond. **2** to get the better of, to outwit, to cheat. **3** to overtake. ~*v.i.* (of horses) to bring the hind feet too far forwards so as to strike the fore foot. **to overreach oneself 1** to strain oneself by reaching too far. **2** to defeat one's object by going too far. **overreact** *v.i.* to respond excessively. **overreaction** *n.* **overread** *v.t.* (*past, p.p.* **overread**) **1** to injure (oneself) by too much reading. **2** to read over. **over-refine** *v.t.* to refine too much, to be oversubtle. **over-refinement** *n.* **overreliance** *n.* **overrestrict** *v.t.* **overrestriction** *n.* **overrich** *a.* **override**[1] *v.t.* (*pres.p.* **overriding,** *past* **overrode,** *p.p.* **overridden**) **1** to ride over. **2** to trample as if underfoot, to disregard, to set aside, to supersede. **3** to fatigue or exhaust by excessive riding. **4** to outride, to overtake. **5** to take manual control of an automatic system. **override**[2] (ō´-) *n.* **1** a device used to override automatic control. **2** the action or process of overriding. **overrider** (ō´-) *n.* either of a pair of attachments to the bumper of a motor vehicle to prevent it becoming interlocked with the bumper of another vehicle. **overriding** (-rī´-) *a.* dominant, taking precedence. **overrighteous** *a.* **overrighteously** *adv.* **overrighteousness** *n.* **overripe** *a.* ripe to excess. **overripen** *v.i., v.t.* **overroast** *v.t.* to roast too much. **overrode** OVERRIDE[1] (under OVER- (+ A–T WORDS)). **overromanticize, overromanticise** *v.t., v.i.* **overruff**[1] *v.t.* in cards, to overtrump. **overruff**[2] (ō´-) *n.* an instance of this. **overrule** *v.t.* **1** to control by superior power or authority. **2** to set aside. **3** to reject, to disallow. ~*v.i.* to bear sway. **overrun**[1] *v.t.* (*pres.p.* **overrunning,** *past* **overran,** *p.p.* **overrun**) **1** to run or spread over. **2** to grow over. **3** to invade or harass by hostile incursions. **4** to extend over. **5** to run beyond, to outrun. **6** in mechanics, to run faster than. **7** (*Print.*) to carry over and change the arrangement of (type set up). ~*v.i.* **1** to overflow. **2** to extend beyond the proper limits. **overrun**[2] (ō´-) *n.* **1** an instance of overrunning. **2** the amount of this. **3** the movement of a vehicle at a speed greater than is imparted by the engine. **overrunner** *n.* **oversailing** (ō´-) *a.* (of a part of a building) projecting beyond what is below. **oversaw** OVERSEE (under OVER- (+ A–T WORDS)). **oversceptical** *a.* **overscrupulous** *a.* excessively scrupulous. **oversea** *a.* **1** beyond the sea, foreign. **2** of or connected with movement over the sea. ~*adv.* from beyond the sea. **overseas** *adv.* **from overseas** from abroad. **oversee** *v.t.* (*pres.p.* **overseeing,** *past* **oversaw,** *p.p.* **overseen**) **1** to overlook, to superintend. **2** to overlook, to disregard, to neglect. **overseer** (ō´-) *n.* **1** a superintendent, an inspector. **2** (*Hist.*) (*also* **overseer of the poor**) a parish officer charged with the care of the poor. **overseership** *n.* **oversell** *v.t.* (*past, p.p.* **oversold**) **1** to sell more than. **2** to sell more of (stocks etc.) than one can deliver. **3** to exaggerate the merits (of a commodity). **4** to use aggressive sales methods. **oversensitive** *a.* excessively sensitive. **oversensitiveness** *n.* **oversensitivity** *n.* **overset** *v.t.* (*pres.p.* **oversetting,** *past, p.p.* **overset**) **1** to upset. **2** to overthrow. **3** (*Print.*) to set up too much type for (a page etc.). ~*v.i.* to upset, to be turned over. **oversevere** *a.* **oversew** *v.t.* (*past* **oversewed,** *p.p.* **oversewn, oversewed**) to sew (two pieces or edges) together by passing the needle through from one side only so that the thread between the stitches lies over the edges. **oversexed** *a.* **1** obsessed with sexual activity. **2** having an abnormally active sex life. **overshade** *v.t.* to cover with shade. **overshadow** *v.t.* **1** to throw shadow over, to shade over, to obscure with or as with cloud. **2** to shelter, to protect. **3** to tower high above, to exceed in importance. **oversharp** *a.* **overshine** *v.t.* to shine upon. **overshoe** (ō´-) *n.* a shoe worn over another. **overshoot**[1] *v.t.* (*past, p.p.* **overshot**) **1** to shoot over or beyond. **2** to go beyond, to overstep, to exceed. **3** to shoot more game than is good for (a moor, covert etc.). ~*v.i.* to go beyond the mark. **to overshoot oneself 1** to go too far, to overreach oneself. **2** to make assertions that cannot be substantiated. **to overshoot the mark** to go beyond what is intended. **overshoot**[2] (ō´-) *n.* **1** the act of overshooting. **2** the amount of this. **overshot** *a.* **1** driven by water sent over the top. **2** projecting, overlapping. **overshot wheel** *n.* a waterwheel driven by water flowing over the top. **overside**[1] *adv.* over the side (as of a ship). **overside**[2] (ō´-) *a.* discharging, unloaded or effected over the side. **oversight** (ō´-) *n.* **1** superintendence, supervision, care. **2** a mistake, an inadvertence, an unintentional error or omission. **oversimplify** *v.t., v.i.* (*3rd pers. sing. pres.* **oversimplifies,** *pres.p.* **oversimplifying,** *past, p.p.* **oversimplified**) to distort the perception of (a problem etc.) by making it seem too simple. **oversimplification** *n.* **oversize**[1] *v.t.* to surpass in bulk. ~*n.* a size above the ordinary. **oversize**[2] *v.t.* **1** to cover or treat with too much size. **2** to size too much. **oversized** *a.* **overskirt** (ō´-) *n.* an outer skirt. **overslaugh** (ō´vəslaw) *n.* (*Mil.*) the passing over of one's turn of duty. ~*v.t.* **1** (*Mil.*) to pass over (one's duty) in consideration of another duty that takes precedence. **2** (*N Am.*) to pass over in favour of another. **3** (*N Am.*) to omit to consider. **oversleep** *v.i., v.t.* (*past, p.p.* **overslept**) (*often reflex.*) to sleep too long. **oversleeve** (ō´-) *n.* a protective sleeve covering another sleeve. **oversmart** *a.* **oversold** OVERSELL (under OVER- (+ A–T WORDS)). **oversolicitous** *a.* excessively worried, concerned etc. **oversolicitude** *n.* **oversophisticated** *a.* **oversoul** (ō´-) *n.* God as a spirit animating the universe. **oversparing** *a.* **overspecialize, overspecialise** *v.i.* to concentrate too much on one aspect or area. **overspecialization** *n.* **overspend** *v.t.* (*past, p.p.* **overspent**) **1** to spend too much of (income etc.). **2** to wear, to exhaust. ~*v.i.* (*often reflex.*) to spend beyond one's means. **overspill** (ō´-) *n.* **1** something spilt over. **2** people who have moved from crowded cities into surrounding areas. **oversprang** OVERSPRING (under OVER- (+ A–T WORDS)). **overspread** *v.t.* (*past, p.p.* **overspread**) **1** to spread over. **2** to cover (with). **3** to be spread over. **overspring** *v.t.* (*pres.p.* **overspringing,** *past* **oversprang,** *p.p.* **oversprung**) **1** to leap over. **2** to surmount. **overstaff** *v.t.* to provide with too large a staff. **overstand** *v.t.* (*past, p.p.* **overstood**) to insist too strictly on the conditions of. **overstare** *v.t.* to outstare. **overstate** *v.t.* to state too strongly, to exaggerate. **overstatement** *n.* **overstay** *v.t.* to stay longer than or beyond the limits of. **to overstay one's welcome** WELCOME. **oversteer**[1] *v.i.* (of a motor vehicle) to have a tendency to turn too sharply. **oversteer**[2] (ō´-) *n.* (of a motor vehicle) the tendency to turn too sharply. **overstep** *v.t.* (*pres.p.* **overstepping,** *past, p.p.* **overstepped**) to exceed, to transgress. **to overstep the mark** to violate conventions of behaviour. **overstimulate** *v.t.* **overstitch** *n.* a stitch made over an edge or over another stitch. ~*v.t.* to sew with an overstitch. **overstock**[1] (ō´-) *n.* superabundance, excess. **overstock**[2] (-stok´) *v.t.* **1** to stock to excess. **2** to fill too full. **overstood** OVERSTAND (under OVER- (+ A–T WORDS)). **overstrain**[1] *v.i.* to strain or exert too much. **overstrain**[2] (ō´-) *n.* excessive strain or exertion. **overstress**[1] *v.t.* to stress too much. **overstress**[2] (ō´-) *n.* an excessive degree of stress. **overstretch** *v.t.* to stretch too much, to make too many demands on. **overstretched** *a.* **overstrict** *a.* **overstride** *v.t.* (*past* **overstrode,** *p.p.* **overstridden**) **1** to stride across. **2** to stand astride of. **overstrike** *v.t.* (*pres.p.* **overstriking,** *past, p.p.* **overstruck**) to strike beyond. **overstrung**[1] *a.* too highly strung. **overstrung**[2] (ō´-) *a.* (of a piano) with strings in sets crossing each other obliquely. **overstudied** *a.* affected; excessively deliberate. **overstudy** *v.t., v.i.* (*3rd pers. sing. pres.* **overstudies,** *pres.p.* **overstudying,** *past, p.p.* **overstudies**) to study excessively. **overstuff** *v.t.* **1** to stuff more than is necessary. **2** to cover (furniture) with thick upholstery. **oversubscribe** *v.t.* to subscribe or apply for more than is available. **oversubscribed** *a.* **oversubscription** *n.* **oversubtle** *a.* too subtle. **oversubtlety** *n.* **oversupply** *v.t.* (*3rd pers. sing. pres.* **oversupplies,** *pres.p.* **oversupplying,** *past, p.p.* **oversupplied**) to supply with too much. ~*n.* (*pl.* **oversupplies**) an excessive supply. **oversure** *a.* too confident. **oversusceptible** *a.* too susceptible or vulnerable. **oversuspicious** *a.* **oversway** *v.t.* **1** to overrule. **2** to surpass. **overswell** *v.t., v.i.* (*past* **overswelled,** *p.p.* **overswollen**) to overflow. **overswift** *a.* too swift. **overswollen** OVERSWELL (under OVER- (+ A–T WORDS)). **oversystematic** *a.* **overtake** *v.t.* (*pres.p.* **overtaking,** *past* **overtook,** *p.p.* **overtaken**) **1** to come up with, to catch. **2** to reach, to attain to. **3** to take by surprise, to come upon suddenly. **overtask** *v.t.* **1** to burden with too heavy a task. **2** to be too heavy a task for. **overtax** *v.t.* **1** to tax too heavily. **2** to overburden. **overtechnical** *a.* **overtedious** *a.* too tedious. **overthrow**[1] *v.t.* (*past* **overthrew,** *p.p.* **overthrown**) **1** to overturn, throw down, demolish. **2** to overcome, conquer, subvert. **overthrow**[2] (ō´-) *n.* **1** defeat, discomfiture. **2** ruin, destruction. **3** in cricket, a ball returned to but missed by the wicketkeeper, allowing further runs to be made. **4** such a run. **5** a panel of decorated wrought-iron work in an arch or gateway. **overthrust** (ō´-) *n.* **1** (*Geol.*) the thrust of strata over those on the other side of a fault. **2** the amount of this. ~*a.* thrust over (of strata). **overthwart** *adv.* across, over from side to side. ~*prep.* **1** from side to side of. **2** across, athwart. **overtime** (ō´-) *n.* **1** time during which one works beyond the regular hours. **2** work done during this period. **3** the rate of pay for such work. **4** (*N Am.*) in sport, extra time. ~*adv.* in addition to regular hours. **overtire** *v.t.* (*also reflex.*) to exhaust or wear out. **overtired** *a.* **overtone** (ō´-) *n.* **1** a harmonic. **2** a secondary meaning, a nuance. **overtop** *v.t.* (*pres.p.* **overtopping,** *past, p.p.* **overtopped**) **1** to tower over, to surmount, to surpass. **2** to override. **overtrade** *v.i.* to trade beyond one's capital. **overtrain** *v.t.* to subject to excessive training. ~*v.i.* **overtrick** *n.* in bridge, a trick taken in excess of one's contract. **overtrump** *v.t.* to play a higher trump than. **overturn**[1] *v.t.* to turn over, to upset. ~*v.i.* to be upset or turned over. **overturn**[2] (ō´-) *n.* **1** the act of overturning. **2** the state of being overturned. **overturner** (-tœ´-) *n.*

overt (ōvœt´) *a.* **1** open, plain, public, apparent. **2** (*Her.*) spread open (of wings). **overtly** *adv.* **overtness** *n.* [OF, p.p. of *ovrir* (F *ouvrir*), L *operīre*, to open]

overture (ō´vətūə) *n.* **1** (*Mus.*) an introductory piece for instruments, a prelude to an opera or oratorio. **2** a single-movement orchestral piece. **3** (*usu. in pl.*) a preliminary proposal, an offer to negotiate, or of suggested terms. **4** an exordium of a poem etc. ~*v.t.* to bring forward, introduce or transmit as an overture. [OF (OVERT, -URE)]

over- (+ u–z words) overuse[1] (-ūz´) *v.t.* to use too much. **overuse**[2] (-ūs´) *n.* excessive use. **overvalue** *v.t.* (*3rd pers. sing. pres.* **overvalues,** *pres.p.* **overvaluing,** *past, p.p.* **overvalued**) to value too highly. **overvaluation** *n.* **overview** (ō´-) *n.* an inspection, a survey. **overviolent** *a.* **overwater**[1] *v.t.* to water too much. **overwater**[2] (ō´-) *a.* situated above the water. **overweather** *v.t.* to damage by violence of weather. **overween** *v.i.* to think too highly (of). **overweening** *a.* arrogant, conceited, presumptuous. ~*n.* excessive conceit. **overweeningly** *adv.* **overweeningness** *n.* **overweight** *v.t.* **1** to exceed in weight. **2** to weigh down. **3** to give too much emphasis to. ~*n.* **1** excess of weight. **2**

preponderance. ~*a.* exceeding the normal or accepted weight. **overwent** OVERGO (under OVER- (+ A–T WORDS)). **overwhelm** *v.t.* **1** to cover completely, to submerge. **2** to crush, to engulf. **3** to destroy utterly. **4** to overcome, to bear down, to overpower. **overwhelming** *a.* **overwhelmingly** *adv.* **overwhelmingness** *n.* **overwilling** *a.* **overwind**[1] (-wīnd´) *v.t.* (*past, p.p.* **overwound**) to wind too much or too tight. **overwind**[2] (ō´-) *n.* an instance of overwinding. **overwinter** *v.i.* **1** to spend the winter. **2** (of insects, fungi etc.) to live through the winter. ~*v.t.* to keep (animals, plants etc.) alive through the winter. **overwise** *a.* **1** too wise. **2** wise to affectation. **overwork** *v.t.* **1** to impose too much work upon. **2** to exhaust with work. **3** to work up into a morbid state of excitement. ~*v.i.* to work to excess. ~*n.* work beyond what is required or regular. **overworked** *a.* **1** used or working excessively. **2** overdone, overwrought. **overworn** *a.* **1** worn out. **2** wearied. **3** trite, commonplace. **overwound** OVERWIND[1] (under OVER- (+ U–Z WORDS)). **overwrite** *v.t.* (*pres.p.* **overwriting,** *past* **overwrote,** *p.p.* **overwritten**) **1** to write too much about. **2** to write data into computer memory, or on to magnetic tape or disk, thereby erasing the existing contents. **3** to write in an artificial or ornate style. **4** to write on top of (other writing). ~*v.i.* **1** to write in an artificial or ornate style. **2** to write too much. **3** in shipping insurance, to accept more risk than the premium income limits allow. **overwriting** *n.* **overwrought** *a.* **1** overworked. **2** excited, agitated, nervous. **3** elaborately decorated. **overzealous** *a.* too zealous. **overzealously** *adv.*

ovi-[1] OV-[1].

ovi-[2] OV-[2].

ovibovine (ōvibō´vīn) *a.* having characteristics intermediate between those of sheep and oxen. ~*n.* such an animal, e.g. a musk-ox. [L *ovis,* sheep, *bōs bovis,* ox]

Ovidian (ovid´iən) *a.* of or in the manner of the Roman poet Ovid.

oviduct (ō´vidŭkt) *n.* a passage through which ova pass from the ovary, esp. in oviparous animals. **oviducal** (-dū´kəl), **oviductal** (-dŭk´təl) *a.*

oviferous (ōvif´ərəs) *a.* egg-bearing.

oviform (ō´vifawm) *a.* egg-shaped.

ovigerous (ōvij´ərəs) *a.* egg-bearing, carrying eggs.

ovine (ō´vīn) *a.* of, relating to, or like sheep. [L *ovis,* sheep]

oviparous (ōvip´ərəs) *a.* producing young by means of eggs that are expelled and hatched outside the body. **oviparity** (-ar´-) *n.* **oviparously** *adv.* **oviparousness** *n.*

oviposit (ōvipoz´it) *v.i.* (*pres.p.* **ovipositing,** *past, p.p.* **oviposited**) (*Zool.*) to deposit eggs, esp. with an ovipositor. **oviposition** (-ish´-) *n.* **ovipositor** *n.* a tubular organ in many insects serving to deposit the eggs.

ovisac (ō´visak) *n.* a closed receptacle in the ovary in which ova are developed.

ovo- OV-[1].

ovoid (ō´void) *a.* egg-shaped, oval with one end larger than the other, ovate. ~*n.* an ovoid body or figure. **ovoidal** (-voi´-) *a.*

ovolo (ō´vəlō) *n.* (*pl.* **ovoli** (-lē)) (*Archit.*) a convex moulding, in Roman architecture a quarter-circle in outline in Greek, elliptical with the greatest curve at the top. [It. (now *uovolo,*), dim. of *ovo,* egg, L *ōvum*]

ovotestis (ōvōtes´tis) *n.* (*pl.* **ovotestes** (-tēz)) an organ producing both ova and spermatozoa.

ovoviviparous (ōvōvīvip´ərəs) *a.* producing young by ova hatched within the body of the parent. **ovoviviparity** (-par´-) *n.*

ovule (ov´ūl) *n.* **1** the rudimentary seed. **2** the body in the ovary which develops into the seed after fertilization. **3** the ovum or germ cell in an animal, esp. before fertilization. **ovular** *a.* **ovulate** *v.i.* to produce or discharge ovaries or ovules. **ovulation** (-lā´shən) *n.* the periodical discharge of the ovum or egg cell from the ovary. [F, from mod. L *ōvulum,* dim. of *ovum*]

ovum (ō´vəm) *n.* (*pl.* **ova** (ō´və)) **1** the female egg cell, or gamete, produced within the ovary and capable, usu. after fertilization by the male, of developing into a new individual. **2** an egg. **3** (*Bot.*) an ovule. **4** (*Archit.*) an egg-shaped ornament. [L *ōvum,* an egg]

ow (ow) *int.* used to express pain. [natural exclamation]

owe (ō) *v.t.* **1** to be indebted to for a specified amount. **2** to be under obligation to pay or repay (a specified amount). **3** to be obliged or indebted for. **4** to have to thank for (a service, a grudge etc.). ~*v.i.* to be indebted or in debt. **to owe a person a grudge** to hold a grudge against a person. **to owe it to oneself** to feel the need to do something that is in one's own interests. **owing** *a.* **1** due as a debt. **2** attributable, ascribable, resulting from, on account of. [OE *āgan* (cp. Icel. *eiga,* Dan. *eie,* OHG *aigan*)]

ower (ō´ə) *prep., adv., a.* (*Sc.*) over.

owl (owl) *n.* **1** any nocturnal raptorial bird of the order Strigiformes, with large head, short neck and short hooked beak, including barn owls, tawny owls etc. **2** a fancy breed of domestic pigeons. **3** a solemn-looking person. **owlery** *n.* (*pl.* **owleries**). **owlet** (-lit) *n.* **1** a young owl. **2** a small owl. **owlish** *a.* **owlishly** *adv.* **owlishness** *n.* **owl-light** *n.* imperfect light, dusk, twilight. **owl-like** *a., adv.* **owl monkey** *n.* DOUROUCOULI. [OE *ūle* (cp. Dut. *uil,* G *Eule,* Icel. *ugla*), cp. L *ulula,* owl]

own[1] (ōn) *a.* **1** belonging or proper to, particular, individual, not anyone else's (usu. appended as an intensive to the poss. pronoun, adjective etc.). **2** (*ellipt.*) in the closest degree, by both parents (of a brother or sister). **for one's own hand** HAND. **in one's own name** NAME. **in one's own person** PERSON. **in one's own right** RIGHT. **in one's own time** TIME. **of one's own** belonging to oneself. **on one's own** without aid from other people, independently. **on one's own head** HEAD[1]. **on one's own hook** HOOK. **to call one's own** CALL. **to come into one's own 1** to gain what one is due. **2** to have one's talents or potential acknowledged. **to get one's own back** to be even with. **to hold one's own** HOLD[1]. [OE *āgen,* p.p. of *āgan,* OWE]

own[2] (ōn) *v.t.* **1** to possess. **2** to have as property by right. **3** to acknowledge as one's own. **4** to recognize the authorship, paternity etc. of. **5** to admit, to concede as true or existent. ~*v.i.* to confess (to). **to own a borough** BOROUGH. **to own up** to confess, to make a clean breast (of). **own brand** *a.* (of goods on sale) displaying the name or label of the retailer rather than the producer. ~*n.* **1** such a make of goods. **2** a kind particular to a person or group. **owned** *a.* (*in comb.,* as *part-owned*). **owner** *n.* **1** a lawful proprietor. **2** (*sl.*) a ship's captain. **ownerless** *a.* **owner-occupier** *n.* someone who owns the house they live in. **owner-occupied** *a.* **ownership** *n.* **own goal** *n.* **1** in football etc., a goal scored by a player against their own side by accident. **2** (*coll.*) any action which results in disadvantage to the person taking it. **to score an own goal** (*coll.*) to do something to one's disadvantage by mistake. **own label** *a.* own brand. [OE *āgnian,* from *āgen,* OWN[1]]

owt (owt) *n.* (*coll., dial.*) anything. [var. of AUGHT[2]]

ox (oks) *n.* (*pl.* **oxen** (ok´sən)) **1** any bovine animal, esp. of domesticated species, large cloven-hoofed ruminants, usu. horned. **2** the castrated male of the domesticated *Bos taurus.* **oxbot, oxfly** *n.* a botfly, *Oestrus bovis,* or its larva. **oxbow** (-bō) *n.* **1** the bow-shaped piece of wood in an ox-yoke. **2** a bend in a river. **3** a lake formed by this. **oxer** *n.* **1** an ox-fence. **2** a similar fence used in showjumping. **ox-eye** *n.* any of various plants of the daisy family with dark centres, esp. *Leucanthemum* *vulgare*, also called *ox-eye daisy*. **ox-eyed** *a.* having large, full eyes. **ox-fence** *n.* a strong fence for keeping in cattle. **oxgall** *n.* the gall of the ox, used as a cleansing agent in watercolour drawing. **oxhead** *n.* a dolt, a blockhead. **oxherd** *n.* a cowherd. **oxhide** *n.* **1** the skin of an ox. **2** oxskin. **oxlip** *n.* **1** a primula, *Primula elatior*, which has pale yellow flowers. **2** a similar plant that is a hybrid between a primrose and a cowslip. **ox-pecker** *n.* any African bird of the genus *Buphagus*, which feeds from the hides of cattle. **oxtail** *n.* the tail of an ox, esp. when used for making soup. **ox-tongue** *n.* **1** the tongue of an ox, esp. used as food. **2** any plant of the genus *Picris*, with oblong bristly leaves. [OE *oxa* (cp. Dut. *os*, G *Ochse*, Icel. *uxe*, *oxe*, Sansk. *ukshan*, pl.)]

ox- OXY-.

oxalis (ok´səlis, -sal´-) *n.* any plant of the genus *Oxalis*, e.g. wood sorrel. **oxalate** (ok´sələt) *n.* a salt or ester of oxalic acid. **oxalic** (-sal´-) *a.* belonging to or derived from oxalis. **oxalic acid** *n.* a sour, highly-poisonous acid found in numerous plants. [L and Gr., from *oxus*, sour]

Oxbridge (oks´brij) *n.* the Universities of Oxford and Cambridge, esp. seen as elitist educational establishments conferring social, economic and political advantages. *~a.* of or relating to Oxbridge. [*Ox*ford, Cam*bridge*]

oxen OX.

Oxf. *abbr.* Oxford.

Oxfam (oks´fam) *abbr.* Oxford Committee for Famine Relief.

Oxford (oks´fəd) *a.* of, relating to, or derived from Oxford. **Oxford bags** *n.pl.* trousers very wide at the ankles. **Oxford blue** *n.* **1** a dark shade of blue. **2** a person who has represented Oxford University in a sport. *~a.* of the colour Oxford blue. **Oxford Group** *n.* a Christian movement founded in 1921 in Oxford. **Oxford mixture** *n.* a dark-grey cloth. **Oxford Movement** *n.* a movement in the Church of England against a tendency toward liberalism, rationalism and Erastianism, originating in the University of Oxford (1833–41) under the leadership of J. H. Newman. **Oxford ragwort** *n.* a kind of ragwort, *Senecio squalidus*. **Oxford shoe** *n.* a low shoe with a toecap, laced over the instep. [university city in England]

oxide (ok´sīd) *n.* a binary compound of oxygen with another element or an organic radical. **oxidant** (-si-) *n.* a substance used as an oxidizing agent. **oxidation** (-sidā´shən) *n.* the process of oxidizing. **oxidation number, oxidation state** *n.* **1** a number indicating the number of electrons lost or gained by an atom of an element when chemically combined. **2** the state represented by a value of this. **oxidative** (ok´si-) *a.* **oxidize** (-si-), **oxidise** *v.t.* **1** to combine with oxygen. **2** to cover with a coating of oxide, to make rusty. **3** to cause to undergo a loss of electrons. *~v.i.* **1** to enter into chemical combination with oxygen. **2** to rust. **3** to undergo loss of electrons. **oxidizable** *a.* **oxidization** (-zā´shən) *n.* **oxidized** *a.* **oxidizer** *n.* **oxidizing agent** *n.* a substance that oxidizes another substance and is itself reduced. [OXYGEN, -IDE]

Oxon (ok´son) *abbr.* **1** Oxfordshire. **2** of Oxford (used for degrees etc.).

Oxonian (oksō´niən) *n.* **1** a student or graduate of Oxford University. **2** a native or inhabitant of Oxford. *~a.* belonging to Oxford or Oxford University. [mod. L *Oxonia*, Oxford, -AN]

oxter (ok´stə) *n.* (*Sc., North*) the armpit. [OE *ōxta*, cogn. with *ōxn*, cogn. with L *axilla*]

oxy- (ok´si), **ox-** (oks) *comb.form* **1** sharp, keen. **2** denoting the presence of oxygen or its acids or of an atom of hydroxyl substituted for one of hydrogen. [Gr. *oxus*, sharp, biting, acid]

oxyacetylene (oksiəset´ilēn) *a.* yielding a very hot blowpipe flame from the combustion of oxygen and acetylene, used for welding metals etc.

oxyacid (oksias´id) *n.* **1** an acid containing oxygen as distinguished from one formed with hydrogen. **2** any one of the groups of acids derived from the fatty or aromatic series by the substitution of an atom of hydroxyl for one of hydrogen.

oxycarpous (oksikah´pəs) *a.* having pointed fruit. [Gr. *karpos*, fruit]

oxygen (ok´sijən) *n.* a colourless, tasteless, odourless divalent element, at. no. 8, chem. symbol O, existing in a free state in the atmosphere, combined with hydrogen in water, and with other elements in most mineral and organic substances. **oxygenate** (-āt) *v.t.* **1** to treat or impregnate with oxygen. **2** to oxidize. **oxygenation** (-ā´shən) *n.* **oxygenator** *n.* **oxygenize, oxygenise** *v.t.* **oxygen mask** *n.* an apparatus for supplying oxygen in rarefied atmospheres to aviators etc. **oxygenous** *a.* **oxygen tent** *n.* an oxygen-filled tent placed over a patient to assist breathing. [F *oxygène* (OXY-, -GEN), from the belief that it was the essential element in all acids]

oxyhaemoglobin (oksihēməglō´bin), (*N Am.*) **oxyhemoglobin** *n.* the bright red product formed when oxygen from the lungs combines with haemoglobin.

oxyhydrogen (oksihī´drəjən) *a.* consisting of a mixture of oxygen and hydrogen (used to create an intense flame for welding).

oxymoron (oksimaw´ron) *n.* a rhetorical figure in which an epithet of a quite contrary signification is added to a word for the sake of point or emphasis, e.g. a clever fool, a cheerful pessimist. [Gr. *oxumōron* (OXY-, *mōros*, stupid)]

oxytetracycline (oksitetrəsī´klēn) *n.* a broad-spectrum antibiotic.

oxytocin (oksitō´sin) *n.* **1** a hormone secreted by the pituitary gland that stimulates uterine muscle contraction during childbirth. **2** a synthetic form of this. [Gr. *tokos*, birth]

oxytone (ok´sitōn) *a.* having an acute accent on the last syllable. *~n.* an oxytone word. [Gr. *oxutonos* (OXY-, *tonos*, TONE)]

oyer (oi´ə) *n.* (*Law, Hist.*) a hearing or trial of causes under writ of oyer and terminer. **oyer and terminer** (tœ´minə) *n.* a commission formerly issued to two or more of the judges of assize, empowering them to hear and determine specified offences. [A-F, in *oyer et terminer*, hear and determine (L *audīre*, to hear, *termināre*, to TERMINATE)]

oyez (ō´yes, ōyez´, ōyā´), **oyes** *int.* repeated three times as introduction to any proclamation made by an officer of a court of law or public crier. [OF, hear ye, pl. imper. of *oir* (F *ouïr*), L *audīre*, to hear]

oyster (oi´stə) *n.* **1** any of various bivalve molluscs of the families Ostreidae and Aviculidae, esp. *Ostrea edulis*, found in salt or brackish water, eaten as food. **2** an oyster-shaped morsel of meat in the hollow on either side of a fowl's back. **3** something regarded as a source of advantage, delight etc. **oyster bank, oyster bed** *n.* a part of a shallow sea-bottom forming a breeding-place for oysters. **oystercatcher** *n.* any wading bird of the genus *Haematopus*, feeding on shellfish. **oyster-farm, oyster-field, oyster-park** *n.* a part of the sea bottom used for breeding oysters. **oyster-knife** *n.* (*pl.* **oyster-knives**) a knife specially shaped for opening oysters. **oyster mushroom** *n.* an edible fungus, *Pleurotus ostreatus*. **oyster patty** *n.* a small pie made from oysters. **oyster-plant** *n.* **1** salsify. **2** a blue-flowered plant, *Mertensia maritima*. **oyster white** *n.* a greyish-white colour. **oyster-white** *a.* [OF *oistre* (F *huître*, L *ostrea*, Gr. *ostreon*)]

Oz (oz) *n.* (*Austral., sl.*) **1** Australia. **2** an Australian. *~a.* Australian.

oz, oz. *abbr.* ounce(s). [It. *onza*]

ozocerite (ōzō´kərīt, -siə´rīt, -zos´ə-), **ozokerite** (ōzō´kərīt, -kiə´rīt) *n.* a fossil resin like spermaceti in appearance, used for making candles, insulators etc. [G *Ozokerit* (Gr. *ozō*, I smell, *kēros*, wax, -ITE[1])]

ozone (ō´zōn) *n.* **1** an allotropic form of oxygen, having three atoms to the molecule, with a slightly pungent odour, found in the atmosphere, probably as the result of electrical action. **2** (*coll.*) fresh, invigorating air as found at the seaside. **ozone-depleting** *a.* (of atmospheric pollutants) contributing to ozone depletion. **ozone depletion** *n.* reduction in the amount of ozone in the upper atmosphere caused by atmospheric pollution, esp. by chlorofluorocarbons. **ozone-friendly** *a.* (of sprays etc.) not damaging the ozone layer, not containing chlorofluorocarbon (cfc). **ozone hole** *n.* a hole in the ozone layer, allowing ultraviolet radiation on to the earth's surface beneath it. **ozonic** (-zon´-), **ozoniferous** (-nif´-) *a.* **ozonize, ozonise** *v.t.* to charge with ozone. **ozonization** (-zā´shən) *n.* **ozonizer** *n.* **ozonosphere** (ōzō´nəsfiə, -zon´-), **ozone layer** *n.* a layer of ozone in the stratosphere which protects the earth from the sun's ultraviolet rays. [F (Gr. *ozein*, to smell, -ONE)]

Ozzie AUSSIE.

P

P[1] (pē), **p** (*pl.* **Ps, P's**) the 16th letter of the English and other versions of the Roman alphabet, corresponding to the Greek pi (Π, π). It is pronounced as a voiceless bilabial plosive. **to mind one's Ps & Qs** to be careful over details, esp. in behaviour.

P[2] *abbr.* **1** parking. **2** in chess, pawn. **3** Portugal (IVR). **4** (*also* ℗) proprietary.

P[3] *chem. symbol* phosphorus.

p *abbr.* **1** page. **2** penny, pence. **3** (*Mus.*) piano, used as an instruction to play softly. **4** pico-. **5** (*Physics*) power. **6** pressure.

PA *abbr.* **1** Panama (IVR). **2** Pennsylvania. **3** personal assistant. **4** Press Association. **5** public address (system).

Pa *chem. symbol* protactinium.

pa[1] (pah) *n.* (*pl.* **pas**) (*coll.*) father (used by or to children). [short for PAPA[1]]

pa[2] (pah), **pah** *n.* a Maori settlement. [Maori]

p.a. *abbr.* per annum.

pa'anga (pahng´gə) *n.* (*pl.* **pa'angas**) the standard unit of currency of Tonga, in the SW Pacific. [Tongan, from a type of vine with disc-shaped seeds]

pabulum (pab´ūləm) *n.* **1** food; nourishment. **2** nutriment of a physical, mental or spiritual kind. **pabular** *a.* [L from *pascere*, to feed]

PABX *abbr.* private automatic branch (telephone) exchange.

paca (pak´ə) *n.* (*pl.* **pacas**) a large Central and South American tailless rodent, of the genus *Agouti.* [Tupi-Guarani]

pace[1] (pās) *n.* **1** a step, the space between the feet in stepping (about 30 in., 76 cm). **2** in ancient Rome, the space between the point where the heel left the ground and that where the same heel descended in the next stride (about 60 in., 152 cm). **3** gait, manner of going, either in walking or running. **4** the carriage and action of a horse etc. **5** rate of speed or progress. **6** (*Mus.*) speed, tempo. ~*v.i.* **1** to walk with slow or regular steps. **2** to walk with even strides or in a slow, deliberate manner. **3** to amble. ~*v.t.* **1** to traverse in slow and measured steps. **2** to set the pace for. **3** to measure by carefully regulated steps. **to be put through one's paces** to be examined closely, to be tested. **to force the pace** to try to increase the speed or tempo of any activity. **to go the pace 1** to go very fast. **2** to lead a life of dissipation or recklessness. **to keep pace with** to go or progress at equal rate with. **to make the pace** to set the pace. **to mend one's pace** MEND. **to set the pace** to fix the rate of going in a race or any other activity. **to stand the pace** to keep up with other people. **to stay the pace** to keep up with other people. **pace bowler** *n.* in cricket, a fast bowler. **-paced** *a.* having a particular pace or gait (*in comb.*, as *fast-paced*). **pacemaker** *n.* **1** a rider or runner who sets the pace in a race. **2** a person who sets the pace in any form of activity. **3** a small device, usu. implanted in the chest, that corrects irregularities in the heartbeat. **pacemaking** *n., a.* **paceman** *n.* (*pl.* **pacemen**) a pace bowler. **pacer** *n.* **pace-setter** *n.* **1** a leader. **2** a rider or runner who sets the pace in a race. **pace-setting** *a., n.* **pacy, pacey** *a.* (*comp.* **pacier**, *superl.* **paciest**) (*coll.*) (of a story, film etc.) moving at a fast, exciting pace. [ME and OF *pas*, L *passum*, nom. *-sus*, p.p. of *pandere*, to stretch]

pace[2] (pā´si, pah´chā) *prep.* with the permission of; with due respect to (someone who disagrees). [L, abl. of PAX, peace]

pacey PACY (under PACE[1]).

pacha PASHA.

pachinko (pəching´kō) *n.* a Japanese form of pinball. [Jap.]

pachisi (pəchē´zi) *n.* an Indian game played on a board with cowries for dice, named after the highest throw. [Hind., lit. twenty-five]

pachy- (pak´i) *comb. form* denoting thickness. [Gr. *pachus*, thick, large]

pachydactyl (pakidak´til) *a.* having thick toes.

pachyderm (pak´idœm) *n.* **1** any large, thick-skinned mammal, esp. an elephant, rhinoceros or hippopotamus. **2** an insensitive person. **pachydermatous** (-dœ´mətəs), **pachydermatoid** (-dœ´mətoid) *a.* **pachydermia** (-dœ´miə) *n.* abnormal thickening of the skin.

pachymeter (pəkim´itə) *n.* an instrument for determining the thickness of glass, paper etc.

Pacific (pəsif´ik) *a.* of or relating to the Pacific Ocean. ~*n.* the Pacific Ocean. **Pacific Ocean** *n.* the ocean between America and Asia. **Pacific Rim** *n.* the regions or countries bordering the Pacific Ocean. **Pacific (Standard) Time** *n.* the standard time in a zone on the Pacific coast of Canada and the US.

pacific (pəsif´ik) *a.* **1** inclined or tending to peace, conciliatory. **2** tranquil, quiet, peaceful. **pacifical** *a.* **pacifically** *adv.* **pacification** (pasifikā´shən) *n.* the act of pacifying. **pacificator** (-sif´-) *n.* **pacificatory** (-kā´-) *a.* **pacifism** *n.* the doctrine of non-resistance to hostilities and of total non-cooperation with any form of warfare. **pacifist** *n., a.* **pacify** (-fī) *v.t.* (*3rd pers. sing. pres.* **pacifies**, *pres.p.* **pacifying**, *past, p.p.* **pacified**) **1** to appease, to calm, to quiet. **2** to restore peace to. **pacifier** (pas´i-) *n.* **1** a person who or something which pacifies. **2** (*N Am.*) a baby's dummy. [F *pacifique*, L *pacificus* (*pax pācis, -ficāre, facere*, to make)]

pack (pak) *n.* **1** a bundle of things tied or wrapped together for carrying. **2** a backpack. **3** a parcel, a burden, a load. **4** a quantity going in such a bundle or parcel taken as a measure, varying with different commodities. **5** a small packet, e.g. of cigarettes. **6** (*usu. derog.*) a set, a crew, a gang. **7** a set of playing cards. **8** a number of dogs kept together. **9** a number of wolves or other beasts or birds, esp. grouse, going together. **10** a group of Cub Scouts or Brownies. **11** a quantity of broken ice floating in the sea. **12** a quantity of fish, fruit etc. packed for the market. **13** in rugby, the forwards of a team. **14** the main group of competitors following the leader or leading group in a race. **15** a face pack. **16** a hot or cold pad for treating a wound. **17** (*Med.*) a sheet or blanket for wrapping a body or part of the body. ~*v.t.* **1** to put together into a pack or packs. **2** to stow into a bag, suitcase etc. for transporting or storing. **3** to crowd closely together, to compress. **4** to fill completely. **5** to cram (with). **6** to wrap tightly, to cover or surround with some material to prevent leakage, loss of heat etc. **7** (*coll.*) to carry (a gun). **8** to load with a pack. **9** to select or bring together (a jury etc.) so as to obtain some unfair advantage. ~*v.i.* **1** to put things in a bag, suitcase etc. for transporting or storing. **2** to crowd together. **3**

(of animals or rugby forwards) to form a pack. **4** to be suitable for packing. **5** to depart hurriedly. **to pack a punch 1** (*coll.*) to be able to punch hard. **2** (*coll.*) to be forceful or effective. **to pack in 1** (*coll.*) to stop doing (something). **2** (*coll.*) to stop going out with (someone). **to pack off** (*coll.*) to send or go away. **to pack up 1** (*coll.*) to stop functioning; to break down. **2** (*coll.*) to pack in. **to send packing** (*coll.*) to dismiss summarily. **packable** *a.* **package** (-ij) *n.* **1** a parcel, a bundle. **2** the packing of goods, the manner in which they are packed. **3** the container, wrapper etc. in which a thing is packed. **4** a number of items offered together. **5** (*Comput.*) a piece of software which can be used for various applications. **6** a package holiday. ~*v.t.* **1** to place in a pack. **2** to bring (a number of items) together as a single unit. **package deal** *n.* a deal in which a number of items are offered together. **package holiday** *n.* a holiday where travel, accommodation, meals etc. are all included in the price. **packager** *n.* **packaging** *n.* **1** the wrapping, container etc. in which something is packaged. **2** the act of packing goods. **3** the presentation of a person or thing to the public in a particular, esp. favourable, way. **pack animal** *n.* an animal used for carrying packs. **pack drill** *n.* a form of military punishment consisting of high-speed drill in full kit. **no names, no pack drill** NAME. **packed** *a.* **packed lunch** *n.* lunch packed in a container or wrapping, to be transported to work, school etc. and eaten there. **packed out** *a.* (*coll.*) full of people. **packer** *n.* **1** a person who packs, esp. one employed to pack meat, fish, fruit etc. for the market. **2** a machine for doing this. **packhorse** *n.* a horse used for carrying goods. **pack ice** *n.* large pieces of ice floating in the polar seas. **packing** *n.* **1** the act of packing. **2** something which is used for packing. **3** material closing a joint or helping to lubricate a journal. **packing case** *n.* a large box made of unplaned wood. **packing-needle** *n.* a long curved needle, used for sewing up packages. **packing-sheet** *n.* a large sheet of coarse material for packing. **packman** *n.* (*pl.* **packmen**) a pedlar. **pack rat** *n.* **1** a rat of western N America, esp. *Neotoma cinerea*, with a long furry tail. **2** a hoarder. **packsaddle** *n.* a saddle for supporting packs. **packstaff** *n.* a pedlar's staff for slinging his pack on. **packthread** *n.* strong thread for sewing or tying up parcels. [cp. Dut. *pak*, Icel. *pakki*, G *Pack*]

packet (pak´it) *n.* **1** a small package. **2** (*coll.*) a large sum of money. **3** (*Hist.*) a packet-boat. ~*v.t.* to make up in a packet. **packet-boat** *n.* (*Hist.*) a vessel conveying mail, goods and passengers at regular intervals. **packet switching** *n.* (*Comput.*) a system of communication in which a message is broken down into units and sent separately to a pre-allocated address. [PACK]

paco (pah´kō) *n.* (*pl.* **pacos**) the alpaca. [Sp., from Quechua]

pact (pakt) *n.* an agreement, a compact. [OF, from L *pactum*, an agreement, orig. neut. p.p. of *paciscere*, cogn. with PAX]

pad[1] (pad) *n.* **1** a soft cushion. **2** a bundle or mass of soft stuff of the nature of a cushion. **3** a soft saddle without a tree. **4** a cushion-like package, cap, guard etc., for stuffing, filling out, protecting parts of the body etc. **5** a sanitary towel. **6** an ink-pad. **7** a number of sheets of paper fastened together at the edge for writing upon and then detaching. **8** a rocket-launching platform. **9** an area for take-off and landing, esp. for helicopters. **10** the cushion-like sole of the foot, or the soft cushion-like paw of certain animals. **11** (*coll.*) one's home or room, esp. a flat. **12** the floating leaf of a water lily. ~*v.t.* (*pres.p.* **padding,** *past, p.p.* **padded**) **1** to stuff or line with padding. **2** to furnish with a pad or padding. **3** to fill out (a sentence, article etc.) with unnecessary words. **4** to impregnate with a mordant. **padded** *a.* **padded cell** *n.* a room with padded walls for confining violent patients in a psychiatric hospital. **padded room** *n.* a padded cell. **padding** *n.* **1** material used for stuffing a saddle, cushion etc. **2** unnecessary matter inserted to fill out an article, magazine or book. **padsaw** *n.* a small narrow saw for cutting curves. [etym. uncertain]

pad[2] (pad) *v.i.* (*pres.p.* **padding,** *past, p.p.* **padded**) **1** to trudge. **2** to travel on foot. ~*v.t.* to tramp or travel over; to tread. ~*n.* the sound of trudging. **to pad the hoof** (*sl.*) to tramp on foot. [Dut., a PATH]

padded, padding PAD[1].

paddle[1] (pad´əl) *n.* **1** a broad short oar used without a rowlock. **2** a paddle-shaped instrument. **3** a blade of a paddle wheel or water wheel. **4** a paddle wheel. **5** a spell of paddling. **6** a spadelike implement used for cleaning a ploughshare of earth, digging up weeds etc. **7** a table tennis bat. **8** (*Zool.*) a broad, flat limb for swimming, a flipper. ~*v.t.* **1** to propel by means of paddles. **2** to row gently. **3** (*N Am.*) to spank. ~*v.i.* **1** to ply a paddle; to move along by means of a paddle. **2** to row gently. **3** to swim with short, downward strokes. **to paddle one's own canoe** CANOE. **paddle-board** *n.* any one of the floats or blades of a paddle wheel. **paddle boat** *n.* a boat propelled by a paddle wheel. **paddle-box** *n.* the casing over the upper part of a paddle wheel. **paddler**[1] *n.* **paddle steamer** *n.* a steamer propelled by a paddle wheel. **paddle wheel** *n.* a wheel with floats or boards projecting from the periphery for pressing against the water and propelling a vessel. [etym. uncertain]

paddle[2] (pad´əl) *v.i.* **1** to wade in shallow water. **2** to dabble in the water with the hands or, more usually, the feet. **3** to toddle. ~*n.* the act of paddling. **paddler**[2] *n.* [etym. uncertain]

paddler[1] PADDLE[1].

paddler[2] PADDLE[2].

paddock (pad´ək) *n.* **1** a small field or enclosure, usu. under pasture and near a stable. **2** a turfed enclosure attached to a stud farm. **3** a turfed enclosure adjoining a racecourse where horses are kept before racing. **4** an area beside a motor-racing circuit where cars are parked, repaired etc. **5** (*Austral., New Zeal.*) any pasture land enclosed by a fence. ~*v.t.* to keep in a paddock. [prob. corr. of OE *pearruc*, cp. PARK]

Paddy (pad´i) *n.* (*pl.* **Paddies**) (*often offensive*) an Irishman. **paddy wagon** *n.* (*N Am., sl.*) a police van. [short for *Padraig*, St *Patrick*, the patron saint of Ireland]

paddy[1] (pad´i) *n.* (*pl.* **paddies**) **1** a paddy field. **2** rice in the straw or in the husk. **paddy field** *n.* a field planted with rice. [Malay *pādī*]

paddy[2] (pad´i) *n.* (*pl.* **paddies**) (*coll.*) a rage, a temper.

paddymelon PADEMELON.

padella (pədel´ə) *n.* a shallow dish containing oil etc. in which a wick is set, used esp. in Italy for illuminations. [It., from L PATELLA]

pademelon (pad´imelən), **paddymelon** *n.* (*Austral.*) a small bush kangaroo or wallaby of the genus *Thylogale*. [corr. of Dharuk *badimaliyan*]

Padishah (pah´dishah) *n.* (*Hist.*) the title of the Shah of Iran, also in India of the British sovereign and of the Great Mogul. [Turk., from Pers. *pādshāh* (Sansk. *pati*, master, lord, SHAH)]

padlock (pad´lok) *n.* a detachable lock with a bow or loop for fastening to a staple etc. ~*v.t.* to fasten with a padlock. [*pad*, etym. uncertain, LOCK[1]]

padouk (padowk´) *n.* **1** a leguminous tree of the genus *Pterocarpus*, of Africa and Asia. **2** the wood of the padouk. [Burmese]

padre (pah´drā) *n.* **1** father (used in addressing a priest in Italy, Spain and Spanish America). **2** a chaplain in the armed forces. [Port., Sp. and It., father, priest]

padrone (pədrō´ni) *n.* **1** a master, an Italian employer or house-owner. **2** the proprietor of an inn in Italy. [It., from med. L *patrōnem*, nom. *patro*, L *patrōnus*, a PATRON]

padsaw PAD[1].

paduasoy (pad´ūəsoi) *n.* **1** a kind of silk material, frequently used in the 18th cent. **2** a garment made of paduasoy. [F *pou-de-soie*, corr. by association with *Padua*, a city in Italy]

paean (pē´ən) *n.* **1** a choral song addressed to Apollo or some other deity. **2** a song of triumph or rejoicing. [L, from Gr. *Paian*, a name of Apollo]

paed- PAEDO-.

paederast PEDERAST.

paedeutics (pēdū´tiks), **paideutics** *n.* the science of education. [Gr. *paideutikos*, from *paideuein*, to bring up a child, from *pais paidos*, a child]

paediatrics (pēdiat´riks), (*N Am.*) **pediatrics** *n.* the branch of medicine dealing with children's diseases. **paediatric** *a.* **paediatrician** (-iətrish´ən) *n.* a specialist in paediatrics.

paedo- (pē´dō), (*N Am.*) **pedo-**, **paed-**, (*N Am.*) **ped-** *comb. form* of or relating to children. [Gr. *pais paidos*, a boy, a child]

paedobaptism (pēdōbap´tizm), (*N Am.*) **pedobaptism** *n.* infant baptism, as opposed to adult baptism. **paedobaptist** *n.* [BAPTISM (under BAPTIZE)]

paedomorphosis (pēdōmaw´fəsis) *n.* (*Biol.*) the retention of juvenile features in the adult.

paedophilia (pēdōfil´iə), (*N Am.*) **pedophilia** *n.* the condition of being sexually attracted to children. **paedophile** (pē´dəfīl) *n.* a person, usually a man, who is sexually attracted to children.

paella (pīel´ə) *n.* a Spanish dish of rice, seafood, meat and vegetables, flavoured with saffron. [Sp., lit., a pan, from L *patella*]

paeon (pē´ən) *n.* a metrical foot of four syllables, one long and the others short in different order. **paeonic** (-on´-) *a.* [L, from Gr. *paiōn*, Attic form of *paian*, a PAEAN]

paeony PEONY.

pagan (pā´gən) *n.* **1** a heathen; a barbarous or unenlightened person. **2** a person who has no religion or disregards Christian beliefs. **3** a person who finds spirituality in nature; a pantheist. *~a.* **1** heathen, heathenish; unenlightened; irreligious. **2** finding spirituality in nature. **pagandom** *n.* **paganish** *a.* **paganism** *n.* **paganize, paganise** *v.t., v.i.* [L *pāgānus* (from *pāgus*, the country), a countryman, hence a non-militant (opp. to *miles Christi*, a soldier of Christ)]

page[1] (pāj) *n.* **1** either side of a leaf of a book etc. **2** a leaf of a book etc. **3** a record, a book. **4** an episode. **5** a subdivision of a computer memory. *~v.t.* to put numbers on the pages of (a book etc.). *~v.i.* **1** to leaf through a book etc. **2** (*Comput.*) to display text one page at a time. **paginal** (paj´in-), **paginary** *a.* **paginate** (paj´-) *v.t.* **pagination** (-ā´shən) *n.* [F, from L *pāgina*, from *pāg-*, stem of *pangere*, to fasten]

page[2] (pāj) *n.* **1** a young male attendant on people of rank. **2** any of various functionaries attached to the royal household. **3** a boy acting as an attendant at a wedding. **4** a boy in livery employed to go on errands, attend to the door etc. **5** (*Hist.*) a youth in training for knighthood attached to a knight's retinue. *~v.t.* **1** to summon (a person in a hotel etc.) by calling their name aloud. **2** to summon by using a pager. **3** to attend on as a page. **page-boy** *n.* **1** a page. **2** a woman's medium-length hairstyle, with the ends curled under. **pager** *n.* a small, portable, electronic device which alerts the carrier that someone is trying to telephone them. [OF, etym. uncertain]

pageant (paj´ənt) *n.* **1** a brilliant display or spectacle, esp. a parade or procession of an elaborate kind. **2** a theatrical exhibition, usu. representing well-known historical events, and illustrating costumes, buildings, manners etc. **3** a tableau or allegorical design, usu. mounted on a car in a procession. **4** empty and specious show. **pageantry** *n.* [perh. as PAGE[1]]

pager PAGE[2].

paginate, paginal etc. PAGE[1].

pagoda (pəgō´də) *n.* **1** a sacred temple, usu. in the form of a pyramidal tower in many receding storeys, all elaborately decorated, in China, Japan and other Eastern countries. **2** a building imitating this. **3** a gold coin formerly current in India. **pagoda tree** *n.* a Chinese leguminous tree, *Sophora japonica*, shaped like a pagoda. [Port. *pagode*, prob. from Pers. *butkada*, an idol temple]

pagurian (pəgū´riən), **pagurid** (-rid) *n.* any decapod crustacean of the family Paguridae, a hermit crab. *~a.* of or relating to pagurians. [L *pagūrus*, Gr. *pagouros*]

pah[1] (pah) *int.* used to express disgust or contempt.

pah[2] *n.* PA[2].

Pahlavi (pah´ləvi), **Pehlevi** (pā´-) *n.* **1** the system of characters used for the sacred writings of the Iranians. **2** the literary language of Iran under the Sassanian kings; Old Persian. [Pers., from *Pahlav*, a district in Parthia]

pahoehoe (pəhō´ihōi) *n.* (*Geol.*) hardened lava forming smooth, undulating masses. [Hawaiian]

paid PAY[1].

paideutics PAEDEUTICS.

paigle (pā´gəl) *n.* (*dial.*) the cowslip, oxlip or buttercup. [etym. uncertain]

pail (pāl) *n.* **1** an open vessel, usu. round, of metal or plastic, for carrying liquids. **2** a pailful. **pailful** *n.* (*pl.* **pailfuls**) the quantity contained in a pail. [cp. OE *pǣgel*, Dut. *pegel*, G *Pegel*, a small measure of liquid]

paillasse PALLIASSE.

paillette (palyet´) *n.* **1** a small piece of metal or foil used in enamel painting. **2** a spangle. [F, dim. of *paille*, L *palea*, straw, chaff]

paillon (pal´yən) *n.* a bright metal backing for enamel or painting in translucent colours.

pain (pān) *n.* **1** bodily or mental suffering (*excruciating pain*). **2** an instance of bodily or mental suffering (*a sharp pain*). **3** (*pl.*) effort, trouble. **4** (*coll.*) a nuisance. *~v.t.* to inflict pain upon, to afflict or distress bodily or mentally. **in pain** feeling pain. **on pain of** subject to the penalty of. **to be at pains to** to take trouble to, to be careful to. **to take pains to** to take trouble, to labour hard or be exceedingly careful. **under pain of** on pain of. **pained** *a.* looking upset or annoyed. **painful** *a.* **1** (of a part of the body) hurting, sore. **2** causing mental or physical pain. **3** laborious, toilsome, difficult. **painfully** *adv.* **painfulness** *n.* **pain in the neck** *n.* (*coll.*) a nuisance. **painkiller** *n.* a drug that alleviates pain. **painkilling** *a.* **painless** *a.* **painlessly** *adv.* **painlessness** *n.* **painstaking** *a.* extremely thorough. **painstaker** *n.* **painstakingly** *adv.* **painstakingness** *n.* [OF *peine*, L *poena*, Gr. *poinē*, a penalty]

paint (pānt) *n.* **1** a solid colouring substance or pigment, usu. dissolved in a liquid vehicle, used to give a coloured coating to surfaces. **2** (*facet.*) colouring matter used as a cosmetic, esp. rouge. *~v.t.* **1** to cover or coat with paint. **2** to give a specified colour to with paint. **3** to tinge. **4** to portray or represent in colours. **5** to adorn. **6** to depict vividly in words. *~v.i.* **1** to practise painting. **2** (*facet.*) to apply rouge or other cosmetics. **to paint out** to efface by painting over. **to paint the town red** RED[1]. **paintable** *a.* **paintball** *n.* **1** a game in which teams shoot pellets of coloured paint at each other in simulated battle. **2** a pellet of coloured paint used in paintball. **paintballer** *n.* **paintbox** *n.* a box in which oil paint or watercolours are kept in compartments. **paintbrush** *n.* **painted lady** *n.* **1** an orange-red butterfly spotted with black and white. **2** the sweet pea. **painter**[1] *n.* **1** a person whose occupation is to colour walls, woodwork etc. with paint. **2** an artist who paints pictures. **painterly** *a.* **1** of, relating to or having the qualities of painting. **2** (of a painting) without sharp outlines. **painterliness** *n.* **painter's colic** *n.* a kind of lead poisoning to which painters are subject. **painting** *n.* **1** the act, art or occupation of laying on colours or producing representations in colours. **2** a painted picture. **paint shop** *n.* the part of a factory where goods are painted. **paintstick** *n.* a crayon-like stick of water-soluble paint. **paintwork** *n.* **1** the parts of a room or vehicle which are painted. **2** the work of painting. **painty** *a.* (*comp.* **paintier,** *superl.* **paintiest**) (*coll.*) **1** like paint in smell etc. **2** covered in paint. [OF *peint,* p.p. of *peindre,* L *pingere*]

painter[1] PAINT.

painter[2] (pān´tə) *n.* a bow-rope for fastening a boat to a ring, stake etc. [perh. from OF *pentoir,* med. L *penditōrium,* from *pendēre,* to hang; or from A-F *panter* (F *pantière*), a snare]

pair (peə) *n.* **1** two things or people of a kind, similar in form, or applied to the same purpose or use. **2** a set of two, a couple, usu. corresponding to each other. **3** an implement or article having two corresponding and mutually dependent parts, such as scissors, spectacles, trousers (*pair of knickers; pair of scales; pair of tongs*). **4** two playing cards of the same value. **5** an engaged or married couple. **6** a couple of mated animals. **7** two horses harnessed together. **8** either member of a matching pair. **9** a flight of stairs. **10** two Members of Parliament of opposite views abstaining from voting by mutual agreement. ~*v.t.* **1** to make or arrange in pairs or couples. **2** to cause to mate. **3** to join in marriage. **4** in Parliament, to make a pair with. ~*v.i.* **1** to be arranged in pairs. **2** to mate. **3** to unite in love. **4** (*coll.*) to marry. **5** in Parliament, to make a pair. **in pairs** in twos. **to pair off 1** to separate into couples. **2** to go off in pairs. **pair bond** *n.* a lasting, exclusive relationship between a male and a female. **paired** *a.* occurring in pairs. **pair-horse** *a.* (of a harness etc.) suitable for a pair of horses. **pairing** *n.* two people who work together as a pair. **pairing-time** *n.* the time when birds mate. **pair-oar** *n.* a boat rowed by two men each with one oar. **pair of bellows** *n.* a two-handled bellows for fanning fire. **pair of compasses** *n.* an instrument with two legs connected by a joint for describing circles, measuring distances etc. **pair of virginals** *n.* a keyed musical instrument, shaped like a box, used in the 16th–17th cents. **pair production** *n.* (*Physics*) conversion of a radiation quantum into an electron and a positron. **pair royal** *n.* three cards of the same denomination in certain games. [F *paire,* L *paria,* neut. pl. of *par,* equal]

paisa (pī´sah) *n.* (*pl.* **paise** (-sā)) a monetary unit of countries of the Indian subcontinent, equal to one hundredth of a rupee or taka. [Hind.]

Paisley (pāz´li) *n.* **1** (a fabric with) a colourful pattern of small intricate curves. **2** a shawl made of this fabric. ~*a.* denoting this fabric or pattern. [*Paisley,* town in Scotland]

pajamas PYJAMAS.

PAK *abbr.* Pakistan (IVR).

pakeha (pah´kihah) *n.* (*pl.* **pakehas**) (*New Zeal.*) a white person, as distinct from a Maori. ~*a.* of or relating to pakehas. **pakeha Maori** *n.* (*Hist.*) a European who lived as a Maori with them. [Maori]

Paki (pak´i) *n.* (*pl.* **Pakis**) (*sl., offensive*) a Pakistani.

Pakistani (pahkistah´ni) *n.* (*pl.* **Pakistanis**) a native or inhabitant of Pakistan, or a descendant of one. ~*a.* of or relating to Pakistan.

pakora (pəkaw´rə) *n.* an Indian dish of pieces of vegetable, chicken etc. dipped in spiced batter and deep-fried. [Hind.]

paktong (pak´tong) *n.* a Chinese alloy of zinc, nickel and copper, like silver. [Cantonese Chin. *peh t'ung* (*peh,* white, *t'ung,* copper)]

PAL (pal) *abbr.* phase alternation line, a system of colour television broadcasting used in Europe.

pal (pal) *n.* (*coll.*) a friend. ~*v.i.* (*pres.p.* **palling,** *past, p.p.* **palled**) (*coll.*) to be friends (with). **to pal up with** (*coll.*) to become friendly with. **pally** *a.* (*comp.* **pallier,** *superl.* **palliest**) (*coll.*) friendly. [Romany, a brother, a mate, from Sansk. *bhrātr,* a brother]

palace (pal´is) *n.* **1** the official residence of a monarch, emperor, bishop or other distinguished personage. **2** a splendid mansion. **3** a large building for entertainments, such as a cinema or theatre. **palace-car** *n.* a luxuriously appointed railway car. **palace revolution** *n.* the non-violent overthrow of a government or monarch by people in positions of power. [OF *palais,* L *palātium,* orig. a house built by Augustus on the Palatine Hill at Rome]

paladin (pal´ədin) *n.* (*Hist.*) **1** any one of Charlemagne's 12 peers. **2** a knight errant. [F, from L *palātīnus,* PALATINE[2]]

palae- PALAEO-.

Palaearctic (paliahk´tik), **palaearctic,** (*N Am.*) **Palearctic, palearctic** *a.* of or relating to the Arctic and northern parts of the Old World. ~*n.* the Palaearctic region.

palaeichthyology (paliikthiol´əji), (*N Am.*) **paleichthyology** *n.* the branch of palaeontology concerned with extinct fishes.

palaeo- (pal´iō), (*N Am.*) **paleo-, palae-,** (*N Am.*) **pale-** *comb. form* ancient, old, prehistoric. [Gr. *palaios,* ancient]

palaeoanthropology (paliōanthrəpol´əji), (*N Am.*) **paleoanthropology** *n.* the branch of anthropology concerned with fossil hominids. **palaeoanthropological** (-loj´-) *a.* **palaeoanthropologist** *n.*

palaeobotany (paliōbot´əni), (*N Am.*) **paleobotany** *n.* the botany of extinct or fossil plants. **palaeobotanical** (-tan´-) *a.* **palaeobotanist** *n.*

Palaeocene (pal´iəsēn), (*N Am.*) **Paleocene** *a., n.* (of or relating to) the oldest epoch of the Tertiary period.

palaeoclimatology (paliōklīmətol´əji), (*N Am.*) **paleoclimatology** *n.* the science of the climates of the geological past. **palaeoclimatological** (-loj´-) *a.* **palaeoclimatologist** *n.*

palaeoecology (paliōikol´əji), (*N Am.*) **paleoecology** *n.* the ecology of extinct and prehistoric organisms. **palaeoecological** (-loj´-) *a.* **palaeoecologist** *n.*

palaeogeography (paliōjiog´rəfi), (*N Am.*) **paleogeography** *n.* the study of geographical features of the geological past. **palaeogeographer** *n.* **palaeogeographical** (-graf´-) *a.*

palaeography (paliog´rəfi), (*N Am.*) **paleography** *n.* **1** the art or science of deciphering ancient inscriptions or manuscripts. **2** ancient inscriptions or manuscripts collectively. **palaeographer** *n.* **palaeographic** (-graf´-) *a.*

palaeolithic (paliōlith´ik), (*N Am.*) **paleolithic** *a.* of or relating to the earlier Stone Age. ~*n.* the palaeolithic period. **palaeolith** (pal´-) *n.* a stone implement of this period. [Gr. *lithos,* a stone]

palaeomagnetism (paliōmag´nətizm), (*N Am.*) **paleomagnetism** *n.* the study of the magnetic properties of rocks. **palaeomagnetic** (-net´-) *a.*

palaeontology (paliəntol´əji), (*N Am.*) **paleontology** *n.* the science or the branch of biology or geology dealing with fossil animals and plants. **palaeontological** (-loj´-) *a.* **palaeontologist** *n.*

palaeotherium (paliōthiə´riəm) *n.* a pachydermatous mammal, chiefly from the Eocene strata. [Gr. *thērion,* beast]

Palaeozoic (paliōzō´ik), (*N Am.*) **Paleozoic** *a.* of or relating to the lowest fossiliferous strata and the earliest forms of life. ~*n.* the Palaeozoic era.

palaestra (pəlēs´trə), **palestra** (-les´-) *n.* in ancient Greece, a place where athletic exercises were taught and practised; a gymnasium or wrestling school. **palaestral, palaestric** *a.* [Gr. *palaistra*, from *palaiein*, to wrestle]

palafitte (pal´əfit) *n.* a prehistoric house built on piles, a lake-dwelling. [F, from It. *palafitta* (*palo*, PALE[2], *fitto*, fixed)]

palais (pal´ā), **palais de danse** (də dās´) *n.* (*pl.* **palais** (-āz), **palais de danse** (-ā)) (*coll.*) a dance hall. [F]

palama (pal´əmə) *n.* (*pl.* **palamae** (-mē)) the webbing of the feet of aquatic birds. [Gr. *palamē*, the palm of the hand]

palampore (pal´əmpaw) *n.* a decorated chintz bed-spread, formerly made in India. [etym. uncertain]

palanquin (palənkēn´), **palankeen** *n.* a couch or litter in India and the East carried by four or six people on their shoulders. [Port. *palanquim*, Hind. *pālakī* or *palang*, Sansk. *palyanka*, *paryanka*, a couch, a bed]

palatable (pal´ətəbəl) *a.* **1** pleasing to taste. **2** agreeable, acceptable. **palatability** (-bil´-), **palatableness** *n.* **palatably** *adv.* [PALATE, -ABLE]

palate (pal´ət) *n.* **1** the roof of the mouth. **2** the sense of taste. **3** liking, fancy. **hard palate** HARD. **soft palate** SOFT. **palatal** *a.* of, relating to or uttered with the aid of the palate. ~*n.* a sound produced with the palate, esp. the hard palate, such as *k, g, ch, y, s, n.* **palatalize, palatalise** *v.t.* **palatalization** (-ā´shən) *n.* **palatally** *adv.* **palatine**[1] (-tīn) *a.* of or relating to the palate. ~*n.* a palatine bone. **palatine bone** *n.* either of the two bones forming the hard palate. [L *palātum*]

palatial (pəlā´shəl) *a.* of, relating to or befitting a palace, magnificent, splendid. **palatially** *adv.* [L *palātium*, a PALACE, -AL[1]]

palatine[1] PALATE.

palatine[2] (pal´ətīn) *a.* **1** of, relating to or connected with a palace, orig. the palace of the Caesars, later of the German Emperors. **2** palatial. **3** possessing or exercising royal privileges. **4** of or relating to a count palatine. ~*n.* **1** a person invested with royal privileges. **2** a count or earl palatine. **3** a woman's fur tippet worn over the shoulders. **the Palatine** the territory of the Count Palatine of the Rhine, an elector of the Holy Roman Empire. **palatinate** (-lat´inət) *n.* the territory of a palatine. [F *palatin*, *-tine*, L *palātīnus*, from *palātium*, PALACE]

palaver (pəlah´və) *n.* **1** (*coll.*) unnecessary fuss and bother, tedious activity. **2** talk, chatter. **3** cajolery, flattery. **4** (*Hist.*) a discussion, a conference, a parley. ~*v.i.* **1** to talk idly and profusely. **2** to confer. ~*v.t.* to talk over, to flatter. **palaverer** *n.* [Port. (Sp. *palabra*), from L *parabola*, a PARABLE]

palay (palā´) *n.* a small Indian tree with hard, close-grained wood used for turnery. [Tamil]

palberry (pal´beri) *n.* (*pl.* **palberries**) a type of currant. [Austral. Abor. *palbri*]

pale[1] (pāl) *a.* **1** whitish, ashen, lacking in colour, not ruddy. **2** (of a colour or light) dim, faint. **3** poor, feeble, inadequate. ~*v.t.* to make pale. ~*v.i.* **1** to turn pale. **2** to be pale, dim or poor in comparison. **pale ale** *n.* light-coloured ale. **paleface** *n.* (supposedly among N American Indians) a white person. **palely** *adv.* **paleness** *n.* **palish** *a.* [OF *pale*, *palle*, L *pallidus*, from *pallēre*, to be pale]

pale[2] (pāl) *n.* **1** a pointed stake. **2** a narrow board used in fencing. **3** a limit or boundary. **4** a region, a district, a territory, a sphere. **5** (*Her.*) a vertical band down the middle of a shield. ~*v.t.* to enclose with or as if with pales. **beyond the pale** unacceptable. **in pale** (*Her.*) arranged vertically. **paled** *a.* fenced in. **paling** *n.* **1** a fence made with pales. **2** material for making fences. [F *pal*, L *pālus*]

pale- PALAEO-.

palea (pā´liə) *n.* (*pl.* **paleae** (-liē)) (*Bot.*) a bract or scale resembling chaff, at the base of the florets in composite flowers, enclosing the stamens and pistil in grass flowers, or on the stems of ferns. **paleaceous** (-ā´shəs) *a.* [L, chaff]

Palearctic PALAEARCTIC.

paleo- PALAEO-.

Paleocene PALAEOCENE.

Paleozoic PALAEOZOIC.

Palestinian (paləstin´iən) *a.* of or relating to Palestine, a region on the E Mediterranean coast. ~*n.* a native or inhabitant of Palestine, or a descendant of one.

palestra PALAESTRA.

paletot (pal´tō) *n.* a loose overcoat for men or women. [F, etym. uncertain (perh. *palle*, L *palla*, a cloak, a TOQUE)]

palette (pal´it) *n.* **1** a flat board used by artists for mixing colours on. **2** the colours or arrangement of colours used for a particular picture or by a particular artist. **palette knife** *n.* **1** a thin, flexible knife for mixing and sometimes for applying colours. **2** a kitchen knife with a flat, blunt, rounded, flexible blade. [F, dim. of *pale*, L *pāla*, shovel]

palfrey (pawl´fri) *n.* (*pl.* **palfreys**) a small horse, esp. to be ridden by a woman. [OF *palefrei* (F *palefroi*), low L *palafrēdus*, *paraverēdus* (PARA-[1], *verēdus*, post-horse, prob. of Celt. orig.)]

Pali (pah´lē) *n.* the canonical language of Buddhist literature, related to Sanskrit. ~*a.* of or relating to Pali. [Hind., a line (of letters), a canon]

†**palification** (palifikā´shən) *n.* the driving of piles for a foundation etc. **paliform** (pā´lifawm) *a.* having the form of a pale. [med. L *pālificātio*, from *pālificāre* (*pālus*, PALE[2], *-ficāre*, *facere*, to make)]

palimony (pal´iməni) *n.* (*chiefly N Am., coll.*) alimony paid to an unmarried partner after the end of a long-term relationship. [*pal*, al*imony*]

palimpsest (pal´impsest) *n.* a manuscript on parchment or other material from which the original writing has been erased to make room for another record. ~*a.* written on or used as a palimpsest. [L *palimpsēstus*, Gr. *palimpsēstos* (*palin*, again, *psēstos*, scraped, from *psaein*, Ionic *pseen*, to scrape or rub)]

palindrome (pal´indrōm) *n.* a word, verse or sentence that reads the same backwards and forwards, e.g. 'Madam I'm Adam' (Adam's alleged self-introduction to Eve). **palindromic** (-drom´-) *a.* **palindromist** *n.* [Gr. *palindromos* (*dromos*, from *dromein*, to run)]

paling PALE[2].

palingenesia (palinjənē´ziə), **palingenesy** (-jen´əsi) *n.* a new birth, a regeneration.

palingenesis (palinjen´əsis) *n.* **1** (*Biol.*) the form of ontogenesis in which the development of the ancestors is exactly reproduced. **2** the repetition of historical events in the same order in an infinite number of cycles, or the theory of such repetition. **palingenetic** (-jinet´-) *a.* **palingenetically** *adv.*

palingenesy PALINGENESIA.

palingenetic PALINGENESIS.

palinode (pal´inōd) *n.* **1** a poem in which a previous poem, usu. satirical, is retracted. **2** a recantation. [from L and Gr. *palinōdia*]

palisade (palisād´) *n.* **1** a fence or fortification of stakes, timbers or iron railings. **2** (*pl., N Am.*) a row of high cliffs. ~*v.t.* to enclose or to fortify with stakes. **palisade cells** *n.pl.* a layer of cells rich in chloroplasts situated beneath the epidermis of leaves. **palisade layer** *n.* (*Bot.*) a layer of elongated cells in a leaf. [F *palissade*, from *palisser*, to enclose with poles, from *palis*, PALE[2]]

palish PALE[1].

pall[1] (pawl) *n.* **1** a large cloth, thrown over a coffin, hearse or tomb. **2** an ecclesiastical pallium. **3** anything that covers or shrouds. **4** an oppressive atmosphere. **5** (*Her.*) a Y-shaped bearing with crosses. **pall-bearer** *n.*

a person who attends the coffin at a funeral, or who holds up the funeral pall. [OE *pæll*, L *pallium*, a cloak]

pall[2] (pawl) *v.i.* to become vapid or insipid; to become boring. ~*v.t.* **1** to cloy, to dull. **2** to make vapid, insipid or spiritless. [prob. from APPAL]

palladia PALLADIUM[2].

Palladian[1] (pəlā´diən) *a.* **1** of or relating to the Italian architect Andrea Palladio, 1518–80 or his school of architecture. **2** of or relating to the free and ornate classical style modelled on the teaching of Vitruvius. **Palladianism** *n.*

Palladian[2] PALLADIUM[2].

palladium[1] (pəlā´diəm) *n.* a greyish-white metallic element of the platinum group, at. no. 46, chem. symbol Pd, used as an alloy with gold and other metals. [Gr. *Pallas -ados*, the Greek goddess of wisdom, the second asteroid]

palladium[2] (pəlā´diəm) *n.* (*pl.* **palladia** (-diə)) a defence, a safeguard. **Palladian**[2] *a.* of or relating to Pallas. [L, from Gr. *palladion*, a statue of Pallas on the preservation of which, according to tradition, the safety of Troy depended]

pallescent (pəles´ənt) *a.* (*Bot.*) growing pale. **pallescence** *n.* [L *pallescens -ntem*, pres.p. of *pallescere*, incept. of *pallēre*, to pale]

pallet[1] (pal´it) *n.* **1** a straw mattress. **2** a small crude bed. [ME and A–F *paillete*, from *paille*, L *pālea*, straw]

pallet[2] (pal´it) *n.* **1** a flat wooden structure on which boxes, crates etc. are stacked or transported. **2** a tool, usu. consisting of a flat blade and handle, used for mixing and shaping clay in pottery making, or for taking up gold leaf and for gilding or lettering in bookbinding. **3** a palette. **4** a pawl or projection on a part of a machine, for converting reciprocating into rotary motion or vice versa. **5** (*Mus.*) a valve regulating the admission of air from the wind chest to an organ pipe. **palletize, palletise** *v.t.* **palletization** (-zā´shən) *n.* [PALETTE]

pallial PALLIUM.

palliasse (pal´ias), **paillasse** *n.* a mattress of straw. [F *paillasse*, from *paille*, L *pālea*, straw]

palliate (pal´iāt) *v.t.* **1** to excuse; to extenuate. **2** to mitigate or alleviate (a disease etc.) without curing. **palliation** (-ā´shən) *n.* **palliative** *n.*, *a.* (a substance) serving to alleviate a disease etc. without curing it. **palliatively** *adv.* **palliator** *n.* [L *palliātus*, p.p. of *palliāre*, to cloak, from PALLIUM]

pallid (pal´id) *a.* **1** pale, wan. **2** feeble, insipid. **pallidity** (-lid´-) *n.* **pallidly** *adv.* **pallidness** *n.* [L *pallidus*]

pallium (pal´iəm) *n.* (*pl.* **palliums, pallia** (-iə)) **1** a scarf-like vestment of white wool with red crosses, worn by the Pope and certain metropolitans and archbishops. **2** (*Hist.*) a man's square woollen cloak, worn esp. by the ancient Greeks. **3** (*Zool.*) the mantle of a bivalve. **pallial** *a.* [L]

pall-mall (palmal´) *n.* (*Hist.*) **1** an old game in which a ball was driven with a mallet through an iron ring. **2** an alley or long space in which this was played. [MF *pallemaille*, It. *pallamaglio* (*palla*, a ball, *maglio*, L *malleus*, a MAUL)]

pallone (pahlō´nā) *n.* an Italian game like tennis, in which the ball is struck with the arm protected by a wooden guard. [It., from *palla*, a ball]

pallor (pal´ə) *n.* paleness, lack of healthy colour. [L, from *pallēre*, to be pale]

pally PAL.

palm[1] (pahm) *n.* **1** (*also* **palm tree**) a tree of the Palmae, a family of tropical or subtropical endogens, usu. with a tall branched stem and head of large fan-shaped leaves. **2** a palm branch or leaf as a symbol of victory or triumph. **3** victory, triumph, the prize, pre-eminence. **4** any of various trees, such as the sallow, or their branches carried instead of palms in northern countries on Palm Sunday. **palmaceous** (palmā´shəs) *a.* **palmary** (pal´məri) *a.* bearing or worthy of the palm; pre-eminent, chief, noblest. **palm-cabbage** *n.* the edible terminal bud of some palms. **palm-civet, palm-cat** *n.* any of various civet-like animals with a long curving tail, of Africa, S Asia and Malaysia. **palm-house** *n.* a glasshouse for palms and other tropical plants. **palm oil** *n.* an oil obtained from the fruit of certain kinds of palm. **Palm Sunday** *n.* the Sunday immediately preceding Easter, commemorating the triumphal entry of Christ into Jerusalem. **palmtop** *n.* a computer with a full keyboard, small enough to be held in one hand while being used. **palm wine** *n.* an alcoholic drink made from fermented palm sap. **palmy** *a.* (*comp.* **palmier,** *superl.* **palmiest**) **1** abounding in palms. **2** victorious, flourishing. [OE, from L *palma*]

palm[2] (pahm) *n.* **1** the inner part of the hand. **2** the part of a glove covering this. **3** a measure of breadth (3–4 ins., 7.5–10 cm) or of length (8–8½ ins., 20–21.5 cm). **4** the underpart of the foot. **5** the broad flat part of an oar, tie, strut, antler etc. **6** the fluke of an anchor. ~*v.t.* **1** to conceal in the palm. **2** to steal by concealing in the palm. **3** to pass off fraudulently. **4** to touch with the palm, to handle. **5** (*sl.*) to bribe. **in the palm of one's hand** under one's control; in one's power. **to cross someone's palm (with silver)** CROSS. **to palm off** to foist (on). **palmar** (pal´mə) *a.* of or relating to the palm. **palmate** (pal´māt), **palmated** *a.* **1** resembling a hand with the fingers spread out. **2** (of the foot of a bird) webbed. **palmately** *adv.* **palmatifid** (palmat´ifid) *a.* (*Bot.*) palmately cleft or divided. **palmed** *a.* having a palm or palms (*usu. in comb.*, as *full-palmed*). **palmful** *n.* (*pl.* **palmfuls**). **palmist** *n.* **palmistry** *n.* fortune-telling by examining the lines and marks on the palm of the hand. [ME and F *paume*, L *palma*, cp. Gr. *palamē*]

palmaceous PALM[1].

palmar PALM[2].

palmary PALM[1].

palmate, palmated etc. PALM[2].

palmer (pah´mə) *n.* **1** (*Hist.*) a pilgrim who carried a palm branch as a token of having been to the Holy Land. **2** (*Hist.*) a pilgrim, devotee, itinerant monk etc. **3** a palmer-worm. **4** an angler's imitation of this. **palmer-worm** *n.* a hairy caterpillar, *Euproctis chrysorrhea*. [A-F *palmer*, OF *palmier*, med. L *palmārius*, PALMARY (under PALM[1])]

palmette (palmet´) *n.* (*Archit.*) a carved or painted ornament in the form of a palm leaf. [F, dim. of *palme*, PALM[1]]

palmetto (palmet´ō) *n.* (*pl.* **palmettos**) **1** a small palm, esp. *Sabal palmetto*, a fan palm of the southern US. **2** the dwarf fan palm or any of various other species of *Chamaerops*. [Sp. *palmito*, dim. of *palma*, PALM[1]]

palmier (pal´miā) *n.* (*pl.* **palmiers** (-miā)) a sweet pastry shaped like a palm leaf. [F, PALM[1]]

palmification (palmifikā´shən) *n.* a method, employed by the Babylonians, of artificially fertilizing the female flowers of the date palm by suspending clusters of male flowers of the wild date above them. [cp. CAPRIFICATION]

palmiped (pal´miped), **palmipede** (-pēd) *a.* (of a bird) having palmate or webbed feet. ~*n.* a web-footed bird. [L *palmipēs* (*pes pedis*, a foot)]

palmist, palmistry PALM[2].

palmitic (palmit´ik) *a.* of or derived from palm oil. **palmitate** (pal´mitāt) *n.* a salt or ester of palmitic acid. **palmitic acid** *n.* (*Chem.*) a white, crystalline solid, which is a saturated acid, found in palm oil and other fats. **palmitin** (pal´mitin) *n.* a natural fatty compound contained in palm oil etc. [F *palmitique* (*palmite*, palm-pith, from L *palma*)]

palmy PALM[1].

palmyra (palmī´rə) *n.* an Asian palm, *Borassus*

flabellifer, with fan-shaped leaves used for mat-making. [Port. *palmeira*, as PALMARY (under PALM[1]), assim. to *Palmyra*, a city in Syria]

palomino (paləmē´nō) *n.* (*pl.* **palominos**) a cream, yellow or gold horse with a white mane and tail. [Sp., like a dove]

paloverde (palōvœ´di) *n.* any yellow-flowered American tree of the genus *Cercidium*. [Sp., a green tree]

palp (palp), **palpus** (-pəs) *n.* (*pl.* **palps, palpi** (-pī)) a jointed sense organ developed from the lower jaw of an insect etc., a feeler. **palpal** *a.* [L *palpus*]

palpable (pal´pəbəl) *a.* **1** easily perceived, plain, obvious. **2** perceptible to the touch. **palpability** (-bil´-) *n.* **palpably** *adv.* [late L *palpābilis*, from L *palpāre*, to feel]

palpate (pal´pāt) *v.t.* to feel, to handle, to examine by touch. **palpation** (-pā´shən) *n.* [see PALPABLE]

palpebral (pal´pibrəl) *a.* of or relating to the eyelid. [F *palpébral*, L *palpebrālis*, from *palpebra*, an eyelid]

palpi PALP.

palpitate (pal´pitāt) *v.i.* **1** (of the heart) to beat rapidly. **2** to throb, to pulsate, to flutter. **palpitant** *a.* **palpitation** (-ā´shən) *n.* [L *palpitātus*, p.p. of *palpitāre*, freq. of *palpāre*, to PALPATE]

palpus PALP.

palsgrave (pawlz´grāv) *n.* (*Hist.*) a Count Palatine, orig. one who had the superintendence of a prince's palace. **palsgravine** (-grəvēn) *n.* a female having the rank of palsgrave. [Dut. *paltsgrave* (now *paltsgraaf*), cp. G *Pfalzgraf*, OHG *pfalenzgrâvo* (*pfalenza*, PALACE, *grâvo*, a COUNT[2])]

palstave (pawl´stāv) *n.* a bronze chisel shaped like an axe head, made to fit into a handle instead of being socketed. [Dan. *paalstav*, from Icel. *pālstafr* (*pāll*, a hoe, a STAVE)]

palsy (pawl´zi) *n.* (*pl.* **palsies**) **1** paralysis. **2** infirmity, inefficiency, helplessness. **3** a cause of helplessness. ~*v.t.* (*3rd pers. sing. pres.* **palsies,** *pres.p.* **palsying,** *past, p.p.* **palsied**) **1** to paralyse. **2** to make helpless. **palsied** (-zid) *a.* [ME *palesy*, OF *paralisie*, PARALYSIS]

palter (pawl´tə) *v.i.* **1** to equivocate, to shuffle, to haggle. **2** to trifle. **palterer** *n.* [etym. unknown]

paltry (pawl´tri) *a.* (*comp.* **paltrier,** *superl.* **paltriest**) mean, petty, despicable; trivial. **paltrily** *adv.* **paltriness** *n.* [cp. dial. *paltry*, rubbish, trash, ME *palter*, pl., rags (cp. Swed. *paltor*, Dan. *pjalter*, rags, LG *palte*, MDut. and Fris. *palt*)]

paludal (pəlū´dəl), **paludinal** (-dinəl), **paludinous** (-dinəs) *a.* **1** of or relating to marshes or fens, marshy. **2** malarial. **paludism** (pal´-) *n.* malaria. **paludose** (pal´-), **paludous** *a.* growing or living in or among or produced by marshes. [L *palus palūdis*, a marsh]

paludament (pəlū´dəmənt) *n.* a cloak worn by an ancient Roman general and his chief officers. [L *palūdāmentum*]

paludinal, paludism etc. PALUDAL.

Paludrine® (pal´ūdrin) *n.* a synthetic quinine substitute for the treatment of malaria.

palynology (palinol´əji) *n.* the study of pollen grains and other spores. **palynological** (-loj´-) *a.* **palynologist** *n.* [Gr. *palunein*, to sprinkle]

pam (pam) *n.* in cards, the knave of clubs, esp. in the game loo, where this is the highest trump. [F *pamphile*, prob. from L *Pamphilus*, Gr. *Pamphilos*, a personal name, beloved of all]

pampas (pam´pəs) *n.pl.* the open, far-extending, treeless plains in S America, south of the Amazon. **pampas grass** *n.* a tall grass, *Cortaderia selloana*, originally from the pampas. **pampean** (-piən) *a.* [Sp., pl. of *pampa*, Quechua *bamba*, a plain, a steppe]

pamper (pam´pə) *v.t.* **1** to indulge (a person, oneself), often excessively. **2** to gratify (tastes etc.) to excess. **3** to feed (a person, oneself etc.) luxuriously. **pampered** *a.* **pamperer** *n.* [prob. freq. of obs. *pamp*, LG *pampen*, to gorge oneself]

pampero (pampeə´rō) *n.* (*pl.* **pamperos**) a violent westerly or south-westerly wind blowing over the pampas. [Sp.]

pamphlet (pam´flit) *n.* a small book of a few sheets, unbound, usu. on some subject of temporary interest. ~*v.t.* (*pres.p.* **pamphleting,** *past, p.p.* **pamphleted**) to give out pamphlets to. **pamphleteer** (-tiə´) *n.* a writer of pamphlets. ~*v.i.* to write pamphlets. **pamphleteering** *n., a.* [OF *Pamphilet*, fem. form of *Pamphile*, L *Pamphilus*, title of a Latin erotic poem of the 12th cent.]

pamplegia (pamplē´jə) *n.* general paralysis. [Gr. *pam-*, PAN-, *plēgē*, a stroke, a blow]

pan[1] (pan) *n.* **1** a broad shallow vessel of metal or earthenware, usu. for cooking. **2** a panful. **3** a vessel for boiling, evaporating etc., used in manufacturing etc. **4** a hollow in the ground for evaporating brine in salt making. **5** a sheet-iron dish used for separating gold from gravel etc., by shaking in water. **6** the part of a flintlock that holds the priming. **7** hardpan. **8** a lavatory bowl. **9** either of the two shallow receptacles of a pair of scales. **10** the act or process of panning a camera. **11** (*N Am., sl.*) the face. **12 a** a metal drum played in a steel band. **b** steel-band music. ~*v.t.* (*pres.p.* **panning,** *past, p.p.* **panned**) **1** (*coll.*) to criticize severely. **2** (*coll.*) to hit or punch. **3** (usu. with *out*) to wash (gold-bearing earth or gravel) in a pan. **4** to move (a camera) in panning. ~*v.i.* **1** to search for gold by panning earth or gravel. **2** to move the camera while taking the picture of a moving object. **to pan out 1** to yield a specified result (esp. well or badly). **2** to have a specified result (*My plan panned out well*). **3** to yield gold. **Pan Cake®** *n.* a stick or cake of face make-up. **pancake** *n.* **1** a thin flat cake of batter cooked in a frying-pan. **2** make-up resembling Pan Cake. ~*v.i., v.t.* to make or cause to make a pancake landing. **Pancake Day** *n.* Shrove Tuesday, when it is traditional to eat pancakes. **pancake landing** *n.* an emergency landing in an aircraft, involving alighting from a low altitude at a large angle of incidence, remaining on an even keel. **pan-fry** *v.t.* (*3rd pers. sing. pres.* **pan-fries,** *pres.p.* **pan-frying,** *past, p.p.* **pan-fried**) to fry in a frying pan. **panful** *n.* (*pl.* **panfuls**) the quantity contained in a pan. **panlike** *a.* shaped like or resembling a pan. [OE *panne* (cp. Dut. *pan*, G *Pfanne*, Icel. *panna*)]

pan[2] (pan) *n.* **1** a betel leaf. **2** a betel leaf wrapped around sliced betel nut mixed with spices, used for chewing. [Hind. *pan*, from Sansk. *parna*, a wing, a leaf]

pan- (pan) *comb. form* all. [Gr. *pas pantos*, all]

panacea (panəsē´ə) *n.* (*pl.* **panaceas**) a universal remedy. [L, from Gr. *panakeia* (*ak-*, root of *akeomai*, I heal)]

Usage note The phrase *universal panacea* is best avoided: a panacea is universal by definition.

panache (pənash´) *n.* **1** show, swagger, bounce; style; airs. **2** a tuft or plume, esp. on a headdress or helmet. [F, from It. *pennacchio*]

panada (pənah´də) *n.* **1** a paste made of flour, water etc. **2** bread boiled to a pulp, sweetened and flavoured. [Sp *panada* (F *panade*), ult. from L *pānis*, bread]

panaesthesia (panəsthē´ziə), (*N Am.*) **panesthesia** *n.* the whole sum of perceptions by an individual at any given time. [Gr. *panaisthēsia* (PAN-, *aisthēsis*, perception, *aisthanesthai*, to perceive)]

Pan-African (panaf´rikən) *a.* **1** of or relating to the whole of the African continent. **2** of or relating to Pan-Africanism. **Pan-Africanism** *n.* the advocacy of co-operation between or unification of all the African nations.

panama (pan´əmah) *n.* a hat made from the undeveloped leaves of a pine tree. [*Panama*, Central America]

Panamanian (panəmā´niən) *n.* a native or inhabitant of the Republic of Panama, Central America, or a descendant of one. ~*a.* of or relating to Panama.

Pan-American (panəmer´ikən) *a.* **1** of or relating to the whole of North, South and Central America. **2** of or relating to Pan-Americanism. **Pan-Americanism** *n.* the advocacy of cooperation between the nations of North, South and Central America.

Pan-Arabic (panar´əbik) *a.* of or relating to Pan-Arabism. **Pan-Arab** *a., n.* **Pan-Arabism** *n.* the advocacy of cooperation between the Arab nations.

panarthritis (panahthrī´tis) *n.* inflammation involving the whole structure of a joint.

panatella (panətel´ə) *n.* a type of long, slender cigar. [Am. Sp., a long thin biscuit, from It. *panatella*, a small loaf]

Panathenaea (panathənē´ə) *n.* (*Hist.*) in ancient Greece, the chief annual festival of the Athenians, celebrating with games and processions the union of Attica under Theseus. [Gr. *panathēnaia*]

pancake PAN[1].

panchayat (pŭnchī´yət) *n.* a village council in India. [Hind., from Sansk. *pancha*, five, *āyatta*, depending on]

Panchen Lama (panchən lah´mə) *n.* a Grand Lama of Tibet, next in rank after the Dalai Lama. [Tibetan *panchen*, great learned one]

pancheon (pan´shən) *n.* a large earthenware pan, used for standing milk in etc.

panchromatic (pankrōmat´ik) *a.* uniformly sensitive to all colours.

pancratium (pankrā´shiəm) *n.* (*pl.* **pancratia** (-iə)) in ancient Greece, an athletic contest including both boxing and wrestling. **pancratic** (-krat´-) *a.* **pancratist** (pan´krə-), **pancratiast** *n.* [L, from Gr. *pankration* (PAN-, *kratos*, strength)]

pancreas (pang´kriəs) *n.* (*pl.* **pancreases**) a gland near the stomach secreting a fluid that aids digestive action. **pancreatic** (-at´-) *a.* **pancreatic juice** *n.* the fluid secreted by the pancreas into the duodenum to aid the digestive process. **pancreatin** (-tin) *n.* a protein compound found in the pancreas and the pancreatic juice. **pancreatitis** (-tī´tis) *n.* inflammation of the pancreas. [L and Gr. (PAN-, *kreas -atos*, flesh)]

panda (pan´də) *n.* **1** a large, black-and-white, bearlike mammal, *Ailuropoda melanoleuca*, from China and Tibet, a giant panda. **2** a small raccoon-like animal, *Aelurus fulgens*, from the SE Himalayas and Tibet, a red panda. **panda car** *n.* a police patrol car, usu. painted with a dark stripe on a light background. [Nepali name]

pandanus (pandā´nəs) *n.* (*pl.* **pandanuses**) **1** a tropical tree or bush of the genus *Pandanus*, containing the screw pines. **2** pandanus fibre, used for making mats. [mod. L, from Malay *pandan*]

Pandean (pandē´ən) *a.* of or relating to the god Pan. **pandean pipes** *n.pl.* pan pipes.

pandect (pan´dekt) *n.* (*usu. pl.*) **1** (*Hist.*) the digest of the Roman civil law made by direction of the emperor Justinian in the 6th cent. **2** any complete system or body of laws. [F *pandecte*, L *pandecta*, Gr. *pandektēs* (PAN-, *dechesthai*, to receive)]

pandemic (pandem´ik) *a.* affecting a whole country or the whole world. ~*n.* a pandemic disease. [Gr. *pandēmos* (PAN-, *dēmos*, people)]

pandemonium (pandimō´niəm) *n.* **1** confusion, uproar. **2** a place or state of lawlessness, confusion or uproar. **3** the abode of all demons or evil spirits. [coined by Milton (PAN-, DEMON)]

pander (pan´də) *v.i.* to do something that someone wants (*She panders to his every whim*). ~†*v.t.* to act as pander to. ~*n.* **1** a procurer, a pimp, a go-between in an amorous intrigue. **2** a person who ministers to base or vulgar passions, prejudices etc. **panderess** (-ris) *n.* a procuress. **panderism** *n.* [*Pandare* (L *Pandarus*), who procured for Troilus the favour of Criseyde, in Chaucer's *Troilus and Criseyde*]

pandiculation (pandikūlā´shən) *n.* (*Med.*) **1** a stretching of the body and limbs in drowsiness or in certain nervous disorders. **2** yawning. [L *pandiculārī*, to stretch oneself, from *pandere*, to stretch]

pandit PUNDIT.

P. & O. *abbr.* Peninsular and Oriental (Shipping Company).

pandora PANDORE.

Pandora's box (pandaw´rəz) *n.* an action which triggers a series of problems. [in Greek mythology, a box containing all human ills and blessings, which *Pandora*, the first woman, brought with her from heaven; when she opened it, out of curiousity, all escaped into the world, except Hope]

pandore (pandaw´), **pandora** (pandaw´rə) *n.* a lutelike musical instrument, a bandore. [It. *pandora*, *pandura* (F *pandore*), L *pandūra*, Gr. *pandoura*, etym. unknown]

pandour (pan´dooə), **pandoor** *n.* (*Hist.*) any one of a body of Croatian foot soldiers, noted for their ferocity, who were enrolled in the Austrian army. [F *Pandour*, Serbo-Croatian *pàndūr*, *bàndūr*, med. L *bandērius*, from *bandum*, see BANNER]

pandowdy (pandow´di) *n.* (*pl.* **pandowdies**) (*N Am.*) a deep-dish dessert of sweetened apple slices topped with a cake crust. [etym. unknown]

p.& p. *abbr.* postage and packing.

panduriform (pandū´rifawm) *a.* fiddle-shaped. [L *pandūra*, PANDORE]

pane (pān) *n.* **1** a sheet of glass in a window. **2** any square of the pattern in a plaid etc. ~*v.t.* **1** to put panes in (a window). **2** to make up (a garment etc.) with panes or strips of different colours. **paned** *a.* [F *pan*, L *pannum*, nom. *-nus*, a piece of cloth]

panegyric (panəjir´ik) *n.* a eulogy written or spoken in praise of some person, act or thing. **panegyrical** *a.* **panegyrically** *adv.* **panegyrist** *n.* **panegyrize** (pan´-), **panegyrise** *v.t.* [F *panégyrique*, L *panēgyricus*, Gr. *panēgurikos* (PAN-, AGORA[1])]

panel (pan´əl) *n.* **1** a rectangular piece (orig. of cloth). **2** a rectangular piece of wood, metal or other material inserted in or as if in a frame, forming a compartment of a door, wall, car body etc. **3** a thin board on which a picture is painted. **4** a picture, photograph etc., the height of which is much greater than the width. **5** a flat section of metal, plastic etc. into which switches and instruments are set; a control panel. **6** a piece of material of a different colour let in lengthwise in a garment. **7** a crude saddle. **8** (*Law*) a list of persons summoned by the sheriff as jurors; a jury. **9** the team in a quiz game, discussion etc. **10** (*Hist.*) a list of people receiving medical treatment under the National Insurance Act or of doctors available to give such treatment. **11** (*Sc. Law*) a prisoner or the prisoners at the bar. ~*v.t.* (*pres.p.* **panelling,** (*N Am.*) **paneling,** *past, p.p.* **panelled,** (*N Am.*) **paneled**) **1** to fit or furnish (a door, wall etc.) with panels. **2** to decorate (a garment) with panels. **panel beater** *n.* a person who repairs the damaged body panels of motor vehicles. **panel game** *n.* a quiz game on television or radio in which a panel of experts etc. answers questions from an audience or a chairman. **panel heating** *n.* a system of heating rooms by wall panels containing heating pipes. **panelling,** (*N Am.*) **paneling** *n.* **1** wood panels covering the walls of a room. **2** wood for making panels. **panellist,** (*N Am.*) **panelist** *n.* a member of a team in a quiz game, discussion etc. **panel pin** *n.* a short, thin nail with a small head. **panel saw** *n.* a saw used in panel-making. **panel**

truck *n.* (*N Am.*) a delivery van. [OF, from med. L *pannellus*, dim. of *pannus*, a PANE]

panesthesia PANAESTHESIA.

pang (pang) *n.* a sudden paroxysm of extreme pain, either physical or mental; a throe, agony. [etym. uncertain]

panga (pang´gə) *n.* (*pl.* **pangas**) a broad, heavy, African knife. [local name]

pangenesis (panjen´əsis) *n.* reproduction from every unit of the organism, a theory of heredity provisionally suggested by Darwin. **pangenetic** (-net´-) *a.*

Pan-German (panjœ´mən) *a.* of or relating to Germans collectively or to Pan-Germanism. **Pan-Germanism** *n.* the movement to unite all Germanic peoples into one nation.

pangolin (pang·gō´lin) *n.* a scaly anteater, of various species belonging to the genus *Manis* or *Phataginus.* [Malay *pang-gōling*, a roller (from its habit of rolling itself up)]

panhandle (pan´handəl) *n.* (*N Am.*) a strip of territory belonging to one political division extending between two others. ~*v.t.*, *v.i.* (*N Am.*, *coll.*) to beg. **panhandler** *n.*

panharmonicon (panhahmon´ikon) *n.* (*pl.* **panharmonicons**) a mechanical musical instrument.

Panhellenic (panhəlen´ik) *a.* of, characteristic of, including or representing all Greeks. **Panhellenism** (-hel´-) *n.*

panic[1] (pan´ik) *n.* **1** sudden, overpowering, unreasoning fear, esp. when many people are affected. **2** a general alarm about financial concerns, causing ill-considered action. ~*a.* **1** sudden, extreme, unreasoning. **2** caused by panic. ~*v.t.*, *v.i.* (*pres.p.* **panicking**, *past*, *p.p.* **panicked**) to affect or be affected with panic. **panic button** *n.* a button, switch etc. operated to signal an emergency. **to press the panic button** to panic or cause others to panic. **panic buying** *n.* buying goods in panic, e.g. in anticipation of a shortage. **panicky** *a.* **panicmonger** *n.* a person who spreads panic. **panic stations** *n.pl.* a state of alarm or panic. **panic-stricken, panic-struck** *a.* struck with sudden fear. [F *panique*, Gr. *panikos*, from the god Pan, who caused sudden fear]

panic[2] (pan´ik) *n.* **1** any of several species of the genus *Panicum.* **2** a cereal grass, *Setaria italica.* **panic grass** *n.* [L *pānicum*]

panicky PANIC[1].

panicle (pan´ikəl) *n.* (*Bot.*) a loose and irregular compound flower cluster. **panicled, paniculate** (-nik´ūlət) *a.* **paniculately** *adv.* [L *pānicula*, dim. of *pānus*, a swelling, an ear of millet]

panification (panifikā´shən) *n.* the process of making or converting into bread. [F, from *panifier*, to make into bread, from L *pānis*, bread]

Pan-Islam (paniz´lahm) *n.* **1** the whole of Islam. **2** a movement for the union of the Muslim peoples. **Pan-Islamic** (-lam´-) *a.* **Pan-Islamism** *n.*

panjandrum (panjan´drəm) *n.* (*pl.* **panjandrums**) **1** a mock title for a self-important or arrogant person. **2** a high-and-mighty functionary or pompous pretender. [humorous coinage (1755) by Samuel Foote, British playwright and actor]

panlogism (pan´ləjizm) *n.* the doctrine that the universe is the outward manifestation of the inward idea or logos. [Gr. *logos*, word, reason]

panmixia (panmik´siə) *n.* (*Biol.*) fortuitous mingling of hereditary characters due to the cessation of the influence of natural selection with regard to organs that have become useless. [Gr. *-mixia*, *mixis*, mixing, from *mignunai*, to MIX]

panne (pan), **panne velvet** *n.* a soft, long-napped fabric. [F]

pannier[1] (pan´iə) *n.* **1** a large basket, esp. one of a pair slung over the back of a beast of burden. **2** each one of a pair of bags fixed on either side of the wheel of a bicycle or motorcycle. **3** a covered basket for drugs and surgical instruments for a military ambulance. **4** (*Hist.*) **a** a framework, usu. of whalebone, used for distending a woman's skirt at the hips. **b** the part of the skirt so distended. **5** (*Archit.*) a sculptured basket, a corbel. **panniered** *a.* [ME and F *panier*, L *pānārium*, bread basket, from *pānis*, bread]

pannier[2] (pan´iə) *n.* (*coll.*) any of the robed waiters in the dining hall at the Inns of Court. [etym. uncertain]

pannikin (pan´ikin) *n.* **1** a small drinking cup of metal. **2** the contents of a pannikin. **pannikin boss** *n.* (*Austral.*, *coll.*) a sub-overseer on a station. [PAN[1], -KIN]

pannose (pan´ōs) *a.* (*Bot.*) like cloth in texture. [as PANNUS]

pannus (pan´əs) *n.* (*Med.*) **1** an opaque vascular state of the cornea. **2** a tent for a wound. **3** a birthmark. [prob. L *pannus*, cloth, see PANE]

panoistic (panōis´tik) *a.* (of the ovaries of some insects) producing ova only, as distinct from *meroistic.* [Gr. *ōon*, an egg]

panophobia (panōfō´biə) *n.* excessive fear (literally of everything).

panoply (pan´əpli) *n.* (*pl.* **panoplies**) **1** a full, impressive array. **2** a complete suit of armour. **panoplied** *a.* [Gr. *panoplia* (PAN-, *hopla*, arms, pl. of *hoplon*, a tool, an implement)]

panoptic (panop´tik) *a.* **1** viewing all aspects. **2** all-embracing, comprehensive. **panopticon** (-kon) *n.* **1** a prison constructed on a circular plan with a central well for the warders so that the prisoners can always be under observation. **2** an exhibition room. [Gr. *optikon*, neut. of *optikos*, of sight, OPTIC]

panorama (panərah´mə) *n.* **1** a continuous picture of a complete scene on a sheet unrolled before the spectator or on the inside of a large cylindrical surface viewed from the centre. **2** a complete view in all directions. **3** a general survey. **panoramic** (-ram´-) *a.* **panoramically** *adv.* **panoramic sight** *n.* a gun sight that can be rotated, giving a wide field of view. [Gr. *horama*, a view, from *horaein*, to see]

panpipes (pan´pīps) *n.pl.* a musical instrument made of a number of pipes or reeds, a mouth organ, originally associated with Pan, the chief rural divinity of the Greeks.

Pan-Presbyterian (panprezbitiə´riən) *a.* of or relating to all Presbyterians.

Pan-Slavism (panslah´vizm) *n.* a movement for the union of all the Slavic peoples. **Pan-Slavic** *a.* **Pan-Slavist** *n.* **Pan-Slavistic** (-vis´-) *a.* †**Pan-Slavonic** (-vŏn´-) *a.*

pansophy (pan´səfi) *n.* universal knowledge. **pansophic** (-sof´-), **pansophical** *a.* **pansophically** *adv.* [Gr. *sophia*, wisdom]

panspermatism (panspœ´mətizm), **panspermia** (-miə), **panspermism** (-mizm), **panspermy** (-mi) *n.* the theory that the atmosphere is pervaded by invisible germs which develop on finding a suitable environment. **panspermatist** *n.* **panspermic** *a.* [Gr. *sperma*, a seed]

pansy (pan´zi) *n.* (*pl.* **pansies**) **1** any of various garden plants of the genus *Viola*, with flowers of various rich colours. **2** (*coll.*, *offensive*) **a** an effeminate man. **b** a homosexual man. **pansied** (-zid) *a.* [F *pensée*, thought, orig. fem. p.p. of *penser*, to think, L *pensāre*, freq. of *pendere*, to weigh]

pant[1] (pant) *v.i.* **1** to breathe quickly, to gasp for breath. **2** to throb, to palpitate. **3** to long, to yearn for. ~*v.t.* to utter gaspingly or convulsively. ~*n.* **1** a gasp. **2** a throb, a palpitation. **panting** *n.* the bulging in and out of the plating of a ship under the stress of heavy seas. **pantingly** *adv.* [cp. A-F *pantoiser*, OF *pantaisier* (F *panteler*), pop. L *phantasiāre*, to dream, to have a nightmare, L *phantasiārī*, see PHANTASM]

pant² (pant) *n.* (*N Am.*) pants. **pant suit** *n.* PANTS SUIT (under PANTS).

pant- PANTO-.

pantagamy (pantag´əmi) *n.* a system of communistic marriage in which all the men are married to all the women, as practised in the Oneida Community in Idaho, from 1838 onwards. [*panta-*, irreg. for PANTO-, *-gamia, gamos*, marriage]

pantagraph PANTOGRAPH.

Pantagruelism (pantəgroo´əlizm) *n.* coarse and boisterous burlesque and buffoonery, esp. with a serious purpose, like that of Pantagruel. **Pantagruelian** (-el´-) *a.* **Pantagruelist** *n.* [*Pantagruel*, character in Rabelais's *Gargantua and Pantagruel*]

pantalets (pantəlets´), **pantalettes** *n.pl.* (*Hist.*) **1** loose drawers extending below the skirts, with frills at the bottom, worn by children and women in the early 19th cent. **2** detachable frilled legs for these. **3** drawers, cycling knickerbockers etc. for women.

pantaloons (pantəloonz´) *n.pl.* **1** tight trousers fastened below the shoe, as worn in the Regency period. **2** trousers, esp. loose-fitting ones gathered at the ankles. **Pantaloon** *n.* a character in pantomime, the butt of the clowns' jokes. [F *pantalon*, It. *pantalone*, a Venetian character on the Italian stage, prob. from San *Pantaleone*, a popular saint in Venice]

pantechnicon (pantek´nikən) *n.* (*pl.* **pantechnicons**) **1** a pantechnicon van. **2** a storehouse for furniture. **3** a place where all sorts of manufactured articles are displayed for sale. **pantechnicon van** *n.* a large van for removing furniture. [Gr. *technikon* (*technē*, art)]

pantheism (pan´thēizm) *n.* **1** the doctrine that God and the universe are identical. **2** the heathen worship of all the gods. **pantheist** *n.* **pantheistic** (-is´-), **pantheistical** *a.* **pantheistically** *adv.*

pantheon (pan´thion) *n.* (*pl.* **pantheons**) **1** a building dedicated to the illustrious dead. **2** the divinities of a nation collectively. **3** a treatise on all the gods. **4** (**Pantheon**) a famous temple with a circular dome at Rome, built about 27 BC, and dedicated to all the gods. **5** any temple dedicated to all the gods. **6** a building for public entertainment. **7** a group of illustrious people. [L, from Gr. *pantheion* (PAN-, *theios*, divine, from *theos*, a god)]

panther (pan´thə) *n.* **1** a black leopard. **2** (*N Am.*) a puma. [ME and OF *pantere*, L *panthēra*, Gr. *panthēr*]

panties (pan´tiz) *n.pl.* (*coll.*) women's or girls' short knickers.

pantihose PANTYHOSE.

pantile (pan´tīl) *n.* a tile having an S-shaped cross-section. **pantiled** *a.*

pantisocracy (pantisok´rəsi) *n.* a Utopian scheme of communism in which all are equal in rank, and all are ruled by all. **pantisocrat** (-tis´-) *n.* **pantisocratic** (-krat´-) *a.* [Gr. *isokratia*]

panto (pan´tō) *n.* (*pl.* **pantos**) (*coll.*) a (Christmas) pantomime.

panto- (pan´tō), **pant-** *comb. form* all. [Gr. *pas pantos*, all]

pantograph (pan´təgrahf), **pantagraph, pentagraph** (pen´-) *n.* **1** a drawing instrument used to enlarge, copy or reduce plans etc. **2** a framework similar in appearance to this, attached to the roof of an electrically driven vehicle, for collecting electrical power from an overhead cable. **pantographic** (-graf´-), **pantographical** *a.* **pantography** (-tog´-) *n.*

pantomime (pan´təmīm) *n.* **1** a theatrical entertainment for children, usu. based on a fairy tale and produced at Christmas time. **2** representation in dumbshow. **3** (*coll.*) a muddled or farcical situation. **4** in ancient Rome, a person who performed in dumbshow. *~v.t.* to express or represent by dumbshow. *~v.i.* to express oneself by dumbshow. **pantomimic** (-mim´-), **pantomimical** *a.* **pantomimically** *adv.* **pantomimist** *n.* [L *pantomīmus*, Gr. *pantomimos*]

pantophagist (pantof´əjist) *n.* a person or animal that eats all kinds of food, an omnivore. **pantophagous** (-gəs) *a.* **pantophagy** (-ji) *n.* [Gr. *pantophagos* (PANTO-, *phagein*, to eat)]

pantoscope (pan´təskōp) *n.* **1** a panoramic camera. **2** a lens with a very wide angle. **pantoscopic** (-skop´-) *a.*

pantothenic acid (pantəthen´ik) *n.* an oily acid, a member of the vitamin B complex. [Gr. *pantothen*, from all sides]

pantry (pan´tri) *n.* (*pl.* **pantries**) **1** a room or cupboard in which dishes, cutlery etc. are kept. **2** a room or cupboard in which bread and other provisions are kept. **pantryman** *n.* (*pl.* **pantrymen**) a butler or a butler's assistant. [OF *paneterie*, med. L *pānetāria*, a place where bread is made, from L *pānis*, bread]

pants (pants) *n.pl.* **1** underpants for men and boys. **2** women's knickers. **3** (*N Am.*) trousers. **by the seat of one's pants** SEAT. **to bore the pants off someone** (*coll.*) to bore someone greatly. **to scare the pants off someone** (*coll.*) to scare someone greatly. **with one's pants down** (*coll.*) in an embarrassing or ill-prepared position. **pants suit** *n.* (*N Am.*) a trouser suit. [PANTALOONS]

Usage note Also called *pair of pants*.

panty girdle (pan´ti) *n.* a girdle shaped like pants.

pantyhose (pan´tihōz), **pantihose** *n.pl.* women's tights.

panzer (pan´zə) *n.* **1** (*pl.*) armoured troops, esp. an armoured division, in the German army. **2** a vehicle in such a division, esp. a tank. *~a.* heavily armoured. [G, armour, armour-plating]

pap¹ (pap) *n.* **1** soft or semi-liquid food for infants etc. **2** pulp. **3** trivial or insubstantial reading matter. **pappy** *a.* [prob. imit.]

pap² (pap) *n.* **1** †a teat, a nipple. **2** a conical hill or small peak. [imit., cp. PAP¹]

†papa¹ (pəpah´) *n.* (*pl.* **papas**) father (used by or to children). [F, from L *pāpa*, imit. in orig. (cp. Gr. *pappas*)]

papa² (pah´pah) *n.* (*pl.* **papas**) **1** the pope. **2** a parish priest or one of the inferior clergy of the Greek Church. [med. L, from Gr. *pappas*, see PAPA¹]

papa³ (pah´pah) *n.* a blue clay found in New Zealand. [Maori]

papabile (pəpah´bilā) *a.* suitable for high office. [It., suitable to be pope, from L *papa*, a pope]

papacy (pā´pəsi) *n.* (*pl.* **papacies**) **1** the office, dignity or tenure of office of a pope. **2** the papal system of government. **papal** *a.* of or relating to the Pope or his office, or to the Roman Catholic Church. **papal cross** *n.* a cross with three horizontal shafts. **papal infallibility** *n.* the dogma that the Pope, when he defines a doctrine regarding faith or morals to be held by the universal Church, is infallible. **papalism** *n.* **†papalize, papalise** *v.t.*, *v.i.* **papally** *adv.* **Papal States** *n.pl.* (*Hist.*) the temporal domain of the Pope, in central Italy. [med. L *pāpātia*, from PAPA²]

papain (pəpā´in) *n.* a protein compound found in the milky juice of the pawpaw, used to tenderize meat and to aid digestion. [Sp. *papaya*, a pawpaw]

papal, papalism etc. PAPACY.

paparazzo (papərat´sō) *n.* (*pl.* **paparazzi** (-sē)) a freelance professional photographer who specializes in photographing celebrities at private moments, usu. without their consent. [It.]

papaveraceous (pəpāvərā´shəs) *a.* of or relating to the poppy family Papaveraceae.

papaverous (pəpā´vərəs) *a.* resembling or allied to the poppy. [L *papāver*, a poppy, -OUS]

papaw, papaya PAWPAW.

paper (pā´pə) *n.* **1** a thin flexible substance made of wood pulp or similar material, used for writing and printing on, wrapping etc. 2 a piece, sheet or leaf of this. 3 a newspaper. 4 a written or printed document. 5 an essay, a dissertation. 6 a lecture. 7 a a set of questions for an examination. b a student's answers to these questions. 8 negotiable documents such as bills of exchange. 9 paper money. 10 wallpaper. 11 (*sl.*) free passes, or persons admitted to a theatre etc. by such passes. 12 (*pl.*) documents establishing identity etc. 13 (*pl.*) a ship's documents. ~*a.* 1 made of paper. 2 like paper. 3 stated only on paper, having no real existence. ~*v.t.* 1 to cover with or decorate with paper. 2 to wrap or fold up in paper. 3 to rub with sandpaper. 4 to furnish with paper. 5 (*sl.*) to admit a large number to (a theatre etc.) by free tickets. **on paper** 1 written down. 2 theoretically, rather than in reality. **to paper over** to disguise, cover up (a dispute, mistake etc.). **paperback** *n.* a book with a soft cover of flexible card. ~*a.* being or relating to a paperback or paperbacks. **paper blockade** *n.* a blockade that has been proclaimed but not rendered effective. **paper boy** *n.* a boy who delivers newspapers. **paperchase** *n.* a game in which one or more people (called the hares) drop pieces of paper as scent for pursuers (called the hounds) to track them by. **paper clip** *n.* a small clip of looped wire used to fasten pieces of paper together. **paper-credit** *n.* credit allowed on the score of bills, promissory notes etc., showing that money is due to the person borrowing. **paper-cutter** *n.* a paperknife. **paper girl** *n.* a girl who delivers newspapers. **paperhanger** *n.* 1 a person whose occupation is hanging wallpaper. 2 (*N Am.*, *sl.*) a person who passes false cheques. **paperhangings** *n.pl.* **paperknife** *n.* (*pl.* **paperknives**) a tool shaped like a blunt knife, used to slit open envelopes. **paperless** *a.* **papermaker** *n.* **papermaking** *n.*, *a.* **paper mill** *n.* a mill in which paper is manufactured. **paper money** *n.* banknotes or bills used as currency, as distinct from *coin.* **paper mulberry** *n.* a small tree from Asia, *Broussonetia papyrifera*, belonging to the mulberry family, which is used for making papers. **paper nautilus** *n.* (*pl.* **paper nautiluses, paper nautili** (-lī)) a cephalopod of the genus *Argonauta*, the female of which has a thin, papery shell. **paper profits** *n.pl.* hypothetical profits shown on a company's prospectus etc. **paper round,** (*N Am.*) **paper route** *n.* a job of delivering newspapers on a particular route, usually done by schoolchildren. **paper-stainer** *n.* a manufacturer of paperhangings. **paper tape** *n.* (*Comput.*) a strip of paper with holes punched in it, for conveying instructions to a computer. **paper-thin** *a.* exceedingly thin. ~*adv.* very thinly. **paper tiger** *n.* a person or thing that is apparently threatening or powerful, but is not so in reality. **paperweight** *n.* a small heavy object for keeping loose papers from being disturbed. **paperwork** *n.* 1 clerical work, e.g. writing letters. 2 documents, letters etc. **papery** *a.* **paperiness** *n.* [OF *papier*, L PAPYRUS]

papeterie (pap´ətri) *n.* an ornamental case for writing materials. [F, from *papetier*, a paper factory, a papermaker, med. L *papeterius*, as PAPER]

Paphian (pā´fiən) *a.* 1 of or relating to Paphos, a city of Cyprus sacred to Aphrodite. 2 of or relating to Aphrodite or her worship. ~*n.* 1 a native or inhabitant of Paphos. 2 a courtesan.

papier mâché (papiā mash´ā) *n.* a material made from pulped paper, moulded into trays, boxes etc. ~*a.* made of papier mâché. [F, chewed paper]

papilionaceous (pəpiliənā´shəs) *a.* (*Bot.*) resembling a butterfly (used of plants with butterfly-shaped flowers, such as the pea). [L *papilio -ōnis*, a butterfly]

papilla (pəpil´ə) *n.* (*pl.* **papillae** (-ē)) (*Anat.*, *Bot.*) a small pap, nipple or similar process; a small protuberance on an organ or part of the body or on plants. **papillary, papillate** (pap´ilāt) *a.* **papilliferous** (-lif´-) *a.* **papilliform** (-pil´ifawm) *a.* **papillitis** (papilī´tis) *n.* inflammation of the optic papilla. **papilloma** (papilō´mə) *n.* (*pl.* **papillomas, papillomata** (-tə)) a tumour formed by the growth of a papilla or group of papillae, such as a wart, corn etc. **papillomatous** (-lōm´-) *a.* **papillose** (pap´ilōs), **papillous** (-pil´-) *a.* [L, dim. of *papula*, see PAPULE]

papillon (pap´ilon, pap´iyõ) *n.* a breed of toy spaniel with large butterfly-shaped ears. [L *papilio -ōnis*, a butterfly]

papillote (pap´ilōt) *n.* a paper frill round a cutlet etc. [F, perh. from *papillon*, L *papilio -ōnis*, a butterfly]

papist (pā´pist) *n.* (*often derog.*) 1 a Roman Catholic. 2 (*Hist.*) a person advocating papal supremacy. ~*a.* of or relating to Roman Catholicism. **papism** *n.* **papistic** (-pis´-), **papistical** *a.* **papistry** *n.* [F *papiste* (PAPA[2], -IST)]

papoose (pəpoos´) *n.* a young N American Indian child. [Algonquian]

pappus (pap´əs) *n.* (*pl.* **pappi** (-ī)) 1 (*Bot.*) the calyx of composite plants, consisting of a tuft of down or fine hairs or similar agent for dispersing the seed. 2 the first hair of the chin. **pappose** (-ōs), **pappous** *a.* [mod. L, from Gr. *pappos*]

pappy PAP[1].

paprika (pap´rikə, pəprē´kə) *n.* 1 a sweet variety of red pepper. 2 a powdered condiment made from paprika. [Hung.]

Pap test (pap), **pap test** *n.* a test for the early diagnosis of cervical cancer in which cells are scraped from the cervix, and examined under a microscope. **Pap smear** *n.* a cervical smear examined in a Pap test. [George N. *Pap*anicolaou, 1883–1962, US anatomist]

Papua New Guinean (papūə nū gin´iən) *a.* of or relating to Papua New Guinea. ~*n.* a native or inhabitant of Papua New Guinea.

papule (pap´ūl), **papula** (-ūlə) *n.* (*pl.* **papules, papulae** (-lē)) 1 a pimple. 2 a small fleshy projection on a plant. **papular** *a.* **papulation** (-lā´shən) *n.* **papuliferous** (-lif´-) *a.* **papulose** (-lōs), **papulous** *a.* [L *papula*, a pustule, dim. from *pap-*, to swell]

papyraceous PAPYRUS.

papyrology (papirol´əji) *n.* the study of ancient papyri. **papyrological** (-loj´-) *a.* **papyrologist** *n.*

papyrus (pəpīə´rəs) *n.* (*pl.* **papyri** (-rī)) 1 a rushlike plant of the genus *Cyperus papyrus*, formerly common on the Nile and still found in Ethiopia, Syria etc. 2 a writing material made from this by the Egyptians and other ancient peoples. 3 a manuscript written on this material. **papyraceous** (papirā´shəs) *a.* 1 made of, or of the nature of papyrus. 2 of the consistency of paper, papery. [L, from Gr. *papuros*, of Egypt. orig.]

par[1] (pah) *n.* 1 average or normal condition, rate etc. 2 a state of equality, parity. 3 in golf, the number of shots which a good player is expected to play in order to complete a hole. 4 equal value, esp. equality between the selling value and the nominal value expressed on share certificates and other scrip. 5 par of exchange. **above par** at a price above the face value, at a premium. **at par** at face value. **below par** 1 at a discount. 2 tired, slightly unwell. **on a par with** of equal value, degree etc. to. **up to par** of the required standard. **par for the course** *n.* what is to be expected, usual. **par of exchange** *n.* the value of a given amount of the currency of one country in terms of another currency. [L, equal, equally]

par[2] (pah) *n.* (*coll.*) in journalism, a paragraph.

par[3] PARR.

par. *abbr.* 1 paragraph. 2 parallel. 3 parish.

par- PARA-[1].

para[1] (par´ə) *n.* (*coll.*) short for PARATROOPER.

para[2] (par´ə) *n.* (*sl.*) short for PARAGRAPH.

para-[1] (par´ə), **par-** *comb. form* 1 denoting closeness of position, correspondence of parts, situation on the other side, wrongness, irregularity, alteration etc. 2 (*Chem.*) denoting substitution or attachment of carbon atoms directly opposite in a benzene ring. [Gr. *para*, by the side of, beyond]

para-[2] (par´ə) *comb. form* of or relating to protection. [F, from It., from L *parāre*, to defend]

parabaptism (parəbap´tizm) *n.* irregular or uncanonical baptism. [late Gr. *parabaptisma*]

parabasis (pərab´əsis) *n.* (*pl.* **parabases** (-sēz)) a choral part in ancient Greek comedy in which the chorus addressed the audience, in the name of the poet, on personal or public topics. [Gr., from *parabainein* (*bainein*, to go)]

parabiosis (parəbīō´sis) *n.* (*Biol.*) the anatomical union of two organisms with shared physiological processes. **parabiotic** (-ot´-) *a.*

parablast (par´əblahst) *n.* (*Anat.*) the peripheral nutritive yolk of an ovum, or a germ layer supposed to be developed from this and to produce the blood etc. **parablastic** (-blas´-) *a.* [Gr. *blastos*, a sprout]

parable (par´əbəl) *n.* **1** an allegorical narrative of real or fictitious events from which a moral is drawn. **2** an allegory, esp. of a religious kind. **parabolic**[1] (-bol´-), **parabolical** *a.* of, relating to or of the nature of a parable; allegorical, figurative. **parabolist** *n.* **parabolize, parabolise** *v.t.* [OF *parabole*, as PARABOLA]

parabola (pərab´ələ) *n.* (*pl.* **parabolas, parabolae** (-lē)) (*Geom.*) a plane curve formed by the intersection of the surface of a cone with a plane parallel to one of its sides. **parabolic**[2] (parəbol´-) *a.* of, relating to or of the form of a parabola. **parabolically** *adv.* **paraboloid** (-loid) *n.* a solid of which all the plane sections parallel to a certain line are parabolas, esp. one generated by the revolution of a parabola about its axis. **paraboloidal** (-loi´-) *a.* **paraboloid of revolution** *n.* a paraboloid generated by the revolution of a parabola about its axis. [L, from Gr. *parabolē* (*ballein*, to throw)]

parabolic[1] PARABLE.

parabolic[2] PARABOLA.

Paracelsian (parəsel´siən) *a.* of, relating to or characteristic of the philosophical teaching or medical practice of Swiss physician and philosopher Paracelsus, 1493–1541.

paracentesis (parəsentē´sis) *n.* (*Med.*) the operation of perforating a cavity of the body, or tapping, for the removal of fluid etc. [L, from Gr. *parakentēsis* (*kentein*, to pierce)]

paracetamol (parəsē´təmol, -set´-) *n.* **1** a painkilling drug. **2** a tablet of this. [*para-acetam*idophen*ol*]

parachronism (pərak´rənizm) *n.* an error in chronology, esp. post-dating of an event. [Gr. *chronos*, time]

parachute (par´əshoot) *n.* **1** an umbrella-shaped contrivance by which a safe descent is made from a height, esp. from an aircraft. **2** a part of an animal or an appendage to a fruit or seed serving for descent or dispersion by the wind. ~*a.* of or relating to parachutes or parachuting. ~*v.t., v.i.* (to cause) to land by means of a parachute. **parachute flare** *n.* a pyrotechnic flare which can be dropped from an aeroplane to illuminate the ground below. **parachutist** *n.* [F (It. *para*, imper. of *parare*, to ward off, F *chute*, a fall)]

Paraclete (par´əklēt) *n.* an advocate, esp. as a title of the Holy Ghost, the Comforter. [F *paraclet*, L *paraclētus*, Gr. *paraklētos* (*kalein*, to call)]

paracme (pərak´mi) *n.* (*Biol.*) a point past the acme or highest development. [Gr. (ACME)]

paracrostic (parəkros´tik) *n.* a poetic composition in which the first verse contains, in order, all the letters which commence the remaining verses.

paracyanogen (parəsīan´əjən) *n.* a porous brown substance obtained from cyanide of mercury when heated.

parade (pərād´) *n.* **1** a muster of troops for inspection etc. **2** a parade ground. **3** show, ostentatious display. **4** a procession, esp. in celebration of an important event. **5** a public promenade. **6** a row of shops. ~*v.i.* **1** to be marshalled in military order for display or review. **2** to march in a parade. ~*v.t.* **1** to march through (streets) in a parade. **2** to display, esp. ostentatiously. **on parade 1** taking part in a parade. **2** being paraded, on display. **parade ground** *n.* an area where soldiers parade. [F, from Sp. *parada*, It. *parata*, from L *parāre*, to get ready]

paradiddle (par´ədidəl) *n.* a simple drumming pattern consisting of four beats played either *left, right, left, right* or *right, left, right, left.* [imit.]

paradigm (par´ədīm) *n.* **1** an example, a pattern. **2** an example of a word in its grammatical inflections. **paradigmatic** (-digmat´-) *a.* **paradigmatically** *adv.* **paradigm shift** *n.* a basic change in approach. [F *paradigme*, L *paradigma*, Gr. *paradeigma* (*deiknunai*, to show)]

paradise (par´ədīs) *n.* **1** heaven. **2** a place or condition of perfect bliss. **3** the garden of Eden. **4** a park or pleasure ground in which animals are kept, a preserve. **paradisaical** (-disā´ikəl) *a.* **paradisal** (-dī´səl) *a.* **paradise fish** *n.* a S Asian fish of the genus *Macropodus*, which is sometimes kept in aquariums for its brilliant colouring. **paradisiacal** (-disī´əkəl) *a.* **paradisical** (-dis´ikəl) *a.* [F *paradis*, L *paradīsus*, Gr. *paradeisos*, OPers. *paradaeza* (*pairi*, PERI-, *diz*, to mould)]

parador (par´ədaw) *n.* (*pl.* **paradors, paradores** (-daw´rez)) a Spanish state-owned hotel. [Sp.]

parados (par´ədos) *n.* (*pl.* **paradoses**) (*Mil.*) a rampart or earthwork to protect against fire from the rear. [F]

paradox (par´ədoks) *n.* **1** a statement, view or doctrine contrary to received opinion. **2** an assertion seemingly absurd but really correct. **3** a self-contradictory or essentially false and absurd statement. **4** a person, thing or phenomenon at variance with normal ideas of what is probable, natural or possible. **paradoxer** *n.* **paradoxical** (-dok´si-) *a.* **paradoxicality** (-kal´-), **paradoxicalness** *n.* **paradoxically** *adv.* **paradoxical sleep** *n.* sleep that is apparently deep but is marked by rapid eye movement, increased brain activity etc. **paradoxist** *n.* **paradoxy** *n.* [F *paradoxe*, L *paradoxum*, Gr. *paradoxon* (*doxa*, opinion)]

paradoxure (parədok´sūə) *n.* the palm-civet. **paradoxurine** (-sūə´rīn) *a., n.* [PARADOX, Gr. *oura*, a tail]

paraenesis (parē´nəsis) *n.* an exhortation. **paraenetic** (parənet´ik), **paraenetical** *a.* [med. L *paraeneticus*, Gr. *parainetikos*, from *parainein* (*ainein*, to speak of, to praise)]

paraesthesia (paristhēz´yə), (*N Am.*) **paresthesia** *n.* (*Med.*) disordered perception or hallucination. [Gr. *aisthēsis*, perception]

paraffin (par´əfin) *n.* **1** (*also* **paraffin oil**) a mixture of liquid paraffins used as a lubricant or fuel. **2** (*Chem.*) an alkane. **paraffin wax** *n.* a colourless, tasteless, odourless, fatty substance consisting primarily of a mixture of paraffins, and obtained from distillation of coal, bituminous shale, petroleum, peat etc., used for making candles, waterproofing etc. [F *paraffine*, from L *parum*, little, *affinis*, akin, so called from the small affinity with other bodies]

paragenesis (parəjen´isis) *n.* **1** the production in an organism of characteristics of two different species. **2** hybridism in which the individuals of one generation are sterile among themselves but those of the next fertile. **paragenetic** (-jinet´-), **paragenic** *a.*

paragliding (par´əglīding) *n.* the sport of gliding while attached to a device like a parachute, in which one is pulled by an aircraft etc., then allowed to drift to the ground. **paraglide** *v.i.* **paraglider** *n.*

paraglossa (parəglos´ə) *n.* (*pl.* **paraglossae** (-ē)) either of the two appendages of the ligula in insects. [Gr. *glōssa*, a tongue]

paragoge (parəgō´ji) *n.* the addition of a letter or syllable to a word. **paragogic** (-goj´-) *a.* [Gr., leading past]

paragon (par´əgən) *n.* **1** a pattern of perfection. **2** a model, an exemplar (*a paragon of virtue*). **3** a person or thing of supreme excellence. **4** a diamond of 100 carats or more. **5** (*Print.*) a size of type, two-line long primer. ~*v.t.* **1** to rival, to equal. **2** to compare. [F, from It. *paragone*, etym. uncertain]

paragraph (par´əgrahf) *n.* **1** a distinct portion of a discourse or writing marked by a break in the lines. **2** (*Print.*) a reference mark (¶). ~*v.t.* **1** to form into paragraphs. **2** to mention or write about in a paragraph. **paragrapher** *n.* **paragraphic** (-graf´-), **paragraphical** *a.* **paragraphist** *n.* [F *paragraphe*, late L *paragraphus*]

paragraphia (parəgrahf´iə) *n.* (*Psych.*) the habitual writing of words or letters other than those intended, often a sign of brain disorder. [Gr. *graphein*, to write]

Paraguayan (parəgwī´ən) *n.* a native or inhabitant of Paraguay, in S America. ~*a.* of or relating to Paraguay.

Paraguay tea (par´əgwī) *n.* an infusion of the leaves of *Ilex paraguayensis*, maté.

paraheliotropic (parahēliətrop´ik) *a.* (*Bot.*) (of leaves) turning so that the surfaces are parallel to the rays of sunlight. **paraheliotropism** (-ot´rə-) *n.*

para-influenza virus (paraïnfluen´zə) *n.* any of various viruses causing influenza-like symptoms.

parakeet (par´əkēt), **parrakeet** *n.* any one of the smaller long-tailed parrots. [OF *paroquet* (F *perroquet*), perh. from It. *parrochetto*, dim. of *parroco*, a parson, or of *parrucca*, a PERUKE]

paralanguage (par´əlang·gwij) *n.* elements such as intonation, nods and gestures, which accompany language.

paraldehyde (pəral´dihīd) *n.* a hypnotic used in asthma, respiratory and cardiac diseases and epilepsy.

paralegal (parəlē´gəl) *a.* (*N Am.*) of or relating to auxiliary aspects of the legal profession. ~*n.* a person who assists lawyers but who is not yet fully qualified.

☒ **paralel** common misspelling of PARALLEL.

paralipomena (parəlipom´inə), **paraleipomena** (-lī-) *n.pl.* **1** things omitted in a work. **2** the Books of Chronicles as giving particulars omitted in the Books of Kings. [L, from Gr. *paraleipomena*, from *paraleipō*, to omit (as PARA-[1], *leipō*, to leave)]

paralipsis (parəlip´sis), **paraleipsis** (-līp´-) *n.* (*pl.* **paralipses** (-sēz), **paraleipses**) **1** a rhetorical figure by which a speaker pretends to omit mention of what at the same time they really call attention to. **2** an instance of paralipsis. [Gr. *paraleipsis* (*leipein*, to leave)]

parallax (par´əlaks) *n.* **1** apparent change in the position of an object due to change in the position of the observer. **2** the angular amount of this. **3** (*Astron.*) angular measurement of the difference between the position of a heavenly body as viewed from different places on the earth's surface or from the earth at different positions in its orbit round the sun. **parallactic** (-lak´-) *a.* [F *parallaxe*, Gr. *parallaxis*, alternation, change (*allassein*, to change)]

parallel (par´əlel) *a.* **1** (of lines etc.) having the same direction and equidistant everywhere. **2** having the same tendency, similar, corresponding. **3** occurring or performed simultaneously. ~*n.* **1** a line which throughout its whole length is everywhere equidistant from another. **2** (*also* **parallel of latitude**) any one of the parallel circles on a map or globe marking degrees of latitude on the earth's surface. **3** a direction parallel to that of another line. **4** a trench parallel to the front of a place that is being attacked. **5** a comparison. **6** a person or thing corresponding to or analogous with another, a counterpart. **7** (*Print.*) a reference mark (||) calling attention to a note etc. ~*v.t.* (*pres.p.* **paralleling,** *past, p.p.* **paralleled**) **1** to be parallel to, to match, to rival, to equal. **2** to put in comparison with. **3** to find a match for. **4** to compare. **in parallel** (of electrical circuits) arranged across a common voltage supply. **parallel bars** *n.pl.* a pair of horizontal bars used for various exercises in gymnastics. **parallelism** *n.* **parallel parking** *n.* the act of parking a vehicle parallel to the kerb. **parallel ruler** *n.* a draughtsman's instrument consisting of two rulers movable about hinged joints, but always remaining parallel. [ME *parallele*, L *parallēlus*, Gr. *parallēlos* (*allēlos*, one another)]

parallelepiped (parəlelәpī´ped), **parallelepipedon** (-pidən) *n.* (*Geom.*) a regular solid bounded by six parallelograms, the opposite pairs of which are parallel. [Gr. *parallēlepipedon* (PARALLEL, *epipedon*, a level, a plane, from *epi*, upon, and *pedon*, the ground)]

parallelogram (parəlel´əgram) *n.* (*Geom.*) a four-sided rectilinear figure whose opposite sides are parallel and equal. **parallelogrammatic** (-grəmat´-), **parallelogrammatical, parallelogrammic** (-gram´-) *a.* **parallelogram of forces** *n.* a parallelogram constructed according to the parallelogram rule. **parallelogram rule** *n.* a rule for finding the resultant of two vectors, by constructing a parallelogram in which two sides represent the vectors, and the diagonal originating at their point of intersection represents the resultant. [F *parallèlogramme*, L *parallēlogrammum*, Gr. *parallēlogrammon* (PARALLEL, *grammē*, a line)]

paralogism (pəral´əjizm) *n.* a fallacious argument, esp. one of which the reasoner is unconscious. **paralogist** *n.* **paralogize, paralogise** *v.i.* [F *paralogisme*, L *paralogismus*, Gr. *paralogismos*, from *paralogizesthai* (*logizesthai*, to reason, from *logos*, reason)]

Paralympics (parəlim´piks) *n.pl.* an international sporting event for disabled people, modelled on the Olympic Games. **Paralympic** *a.* [PARAPLEGIC (under PARAPLEGIA), OLYMPIC (under OLYMPIAD)]

paralyse (par´əlīz), (*N Am.*) **paralyze** *v.t.* **1** to affect with paralysis. **2** to render powerless or ineffective. **3** to render immobile or unable to function. **paralysation** (-zā´shən) *n.* **paralysingly** *adv.* [F *paralyser*, as PARALYSIS]

paralysis (pəral´isis) *n.* (*pl.* **paralyses** (-sēz)) **1** total or partial loss of the power of muscular contraction or of sensation in the whole or part of the body; palsy. **2** complete helplessness or inability to act. **3** inability to move or function properly. **paralytic** (-lit´-) *a.* **1** of, relating to or characterized by paralysis. **2** afflicted with paralysis. **3** (*sl.*) very drunk. ~*n.* a paralysed or paralytic person. **paralytically** *adv.* [L, from Gr. *paralusis* (*lusis*, from *luein*, to loosen)]

paramagnetic (parəmagnet´ik) *a.* having the property of being attracted by the poles of a magnet; magnetic, as distinct from *diamagnetic*. **paramagnetism** (-mag´-) *n.*

paramastoid (parəmas´toid) *a.* (*Anat.*) situated near the mastoid process of the temporal bone. ~*n.* a paramastoid process.

paramatta PARRAMATTA.

paramecium (parəmē´siəm), **paramoecium** *n.* (*pl.* **paramecia** (-ə), **paramoecia**) any member of a genus, *Paramecium*, of protozoa. [mod. L, from Gr. *paramēkēs* (*mēkos*, length)]

paramedic (parəmed´ik) *n.* a person who is trained to help doctors, e.g. an ambulance operative. **paramedical** *a.* auxiliary to the work of medical doctors.

parameter (pəram´itə) *n.* **1** (*Math.*) a quantity remaining constant for a particular case, esp. a constant quantity entering into the equation of a curve etc. **2** (*coll.*) a limiting factor, a constraint. **parametric** (parəmet´-) *a.* **parametrize, parametrise** *v.t.*

Usage note The use of *parameter* to mean a limiting factor is sometimes disapproved of.

---

paramilitary (parəmil´itəri) *a.* having a similar nature or structure to military forces. ~*n.* (*pl.* **paramilitaries**) a member of a paramilitary organization.

paramnesia (paramnēz´yə) *n.* déjà vu.

paramo (par´əmō) *n.* (*pl.* **paramos**) a high plateau with no trees in S America. [Sp. and Port., from L *paramus*]

paramoecium PARAMECIUM.

paramorph (par´əmawf) *n.* (*Mineral.*) a pseudomorph having the same chemical composition but differing in molecular structure. **paramorphic** (-maw´-) *a.* **paramorphism** (-maw´-) *n.* **paramorphous** (-maw´-) *a.* [Gr. *morphē*, a form]

paramount (par´əmownt) *a.* **1** supreme, pre-eminent, most important. **2** having supreme authority. ~*n.* the person who is highest in rank or authority. **paramountcy** (-si) *n.* **paramountly** *adv.* [A-F *paramount*, OF *par amont*, at the top (*par*, by, AMOUNT)]

paramour (par´əmooə) *n.* (*dated or derog.*) a lover, usu. an illicit one. [OF *par amour*, L *per amōrem*, by love]

parang (pah´rang) *n.* a heavy sheath knife. [Malay]

paranoia (parənoi´ə), **paranoea** (-nē´ə) *n.* **1** mental derangement, esp. in a chronic form characterized by delusions etc. **2** (*coll.*) a sense of being persecuted. **paranoiac** (-ak) *a.*, *n.* **paranoiacally** *adv.* **paranoic** (-nō´-) *a.* **paranoid** (par´ənoid) *a.*, *n.* [Gr. *paranoia* (*nous*, the mind)]

paranormal (parənaw´məl) *a.* not rationally explicable. ~*n.* paranormal events. **paranormally** *adv.*

paranthelion (paranthē´lion) *n.* (*pl.* **paranthelia** (-liə)) a diffuse image of the sun at the same altitude and at an angular distance of 120° due to reflection from ice-spicules in the air. [Gr. *anth'*, ANTI-, *hēlios*, the sun]

parapet (par´əpit) *n.* **1** a low or breast-high wall at the edge of a roof, bridge etc. **2** a breast-high wall or rampart for covering troops from observation and attack. **parapeted** *a.* [F, from It. *parapetto* (*parare*, to defend, *petto*, L *pectus*, a breast)]

paraph (par´af) *n.* a flourish after a signature, orig. intended as a protection against forgery. ~*v.t.* **1** to sign. **2** to initial. [F *paraphe*, med. L *paraphus*, *paragraphus*, a PARAGRAPH]

paraphernalia (parəfənā´liə) *n.pl.* **1** miscellaneous belongings, ornaments, trappings, equipment. **2** (*Law*) personal property formerly allowed to a wife over and above her dowry, including her clothes, ornaments etc. [neut. pl. of L *paraphernālis*, from Gr. *parapherna*, neut. pl. (Gr. *phernē*, a dowry, from *pherein*, to bring)]

paraphimosis (parəfīmō´sis) *n.* (*Med.*) permanent retraction of the prepuce.

paraphrase (par´əfrāz) *n.* **1** a free translation or rendering of a passage. **2** a restatement of a passage in different terms. **3** any one of a series of hymns, used in the Church of Scotland etc., consisting of poetical versions of passages of Scripture. ~*v.t.* to express or interpret in other words. ~*v.i.* to make a paraphrase. **paraphrast** (-frast) *n.* a person who paraphrases. **paraphrastic** (-fras´-) *a.* [F, from L and Gr. *paraphrasis* (*phrazein*, to tell)]

paraphrenia (parəfrē´niə) *n.* a type of schizophrenia characterized by ideas of persecution, grandeur etc.

paraphysis (pəraf´isis) *n.* (*pl.* **paraphyses** (-sēz)) (*Bot.*) a sterile filament accompanying sexual organs in some cryptogams. [Gr. *phusis*, growth]

paraplegia (parəplē´jə) *n.* (*Med.*) paralysis of the lower limbs and the lower part of the body. **paraplegic** *n.*, *a.* [Gr. *paraplēgia* (*plēssein*, to strike)]

parapodium (parəpō´diəm) *n.* (*pl.* **parapodia** (-diə)) (*Zool.*) any one of the jointless lateral locomotory organs of an annelid. [Gr. *pous podos*, foot]

parapophysis (parəpof´isis) *n.* (*pl.* **parapophyses** (-sēz)) (*Anat.*) a process on the side of a vertebra, usu. serving as the point of articulation of a rib. [Gr. *apophusis*, an offshoot (APO-, *phusis*, growth)]

parapsychical (parəsī´kikəl) *a.* denoting phenomena such as hypnotism or telepathy which appear to be beyond explanation by the ascertained laws of science.

parapsychology (parəsīkol´əji) *n.* the study of mental phenomena which are beyond the sphere of ordinary psychology. **parapsychological** (-loj´-) *a.* **parapsychologist** *n.*

paraquat (par´əkwot) *n.* a very poisonous weedkiller. [PARA-[1], *quat*ernary (referring to its chemical composition)]

parasailing (par´əsāling) *n.* the sport of gliding through the air attached to the back of a motor boat while wearing an open parachute. **parasail** *v.i.*, *n.*

parasang (par´əsang) *n.* an ancient Persian measure of length, about 3¼ miles (5.25 km). [L *parasanga*, Gr. *parasangēs*, from Pers. *farsang*]

parascending (par´əsending) *n.* **1** paragliding. **2** parasailing. **parascend** *v.i.* **parascender** *n.* [*para*chute, *ascending*]

parasceve (par´əsēv) *n.* the day of preparation for the Jewish Sabbath. [L *parascēvē*, Gr. *paraskeuē* (*skeuē*, an outfit)]

paraselene (parəsilē´ni) *n.* (*pl.* **paraselenae** (-nē)) a mock moon appearing in a lunar halo. **paraselenic** *a.* [Gr. *selēnē*, the moon]

parasite (par´əsīt) *n.* **1** an animal or plant subsisting at the expense of another organism. **2** a person who lives off other people, a hanger-on, a sponger. **3** an inorganic sound or letter which develops from an adjacent one. **4** (*loosely*) a plant that lives on another without deriving its nutriment from it, a commensal. **5** (*loosely*) a plant that climbs about another. **parasitic** (-sit´-), **parasitical** *a.* **parasitically** *adv.* **parasiticide** (-sit´isīd) *n.* a preparation for destroying parasites. **parasitism** *n.* **parasitize**, **parasitise** *v.t.* **parasitization** (-zā´shən) *n.* **parasitoid** (-sitoid) *n.* (*Zool.*) an insect whose larvae live as parasites, eventually killing their hosts. ~*a.* of or relating to parasitoids. **parasitology** (-tol´-) *n.* **parasitologist** *n.* [L *parasītus*, Gr. *parasitos* (*sitos*, food)]

parasol (pa´rəsol) *n.* **1** a small umbrella used to give shelter from the sun, a sunshade. **2** any of several fungi of the genus *Lepiota*, having an umbrella-shaped cap. [F, from It. *parasole* (*para*, imper. of *parare*, to ward off, *sole*, L *sol*, the sun)]

parastatal (parəstā´təl) *a.* esp. in some African countries, having some political authority, but indirectly controlled by the State. ~*n.* a parastatal organization.

parasuicide (parəsoo´isīd) *n.* (*Psych.*) **1** an apparent attempt at suicide without any genuine intention of killing oneself. **2** a person who attempts parasuicide in this way.

parasympathetic (parəsimpəthet´ik) *a.* (*Anat.*) of or relating to the part of the autonomic nervous system which slows the heartbeat, stimulates the smooth muscles of the digestive tract, constricts the bronchi of the lungs etc. and thus counteracts the sympathetic nervous system.

parasynthesis (parəsin´thəsis) *n.* the principle or process of forming derivatives from compound words. **parasynthetic** (-thet´-) *a.* **parasyntheton** (-ton) *n.* (*pl.* **parasyntheta** (-tə)) a word so formed.

parataxis (parətak´sis) *n.* (*Gram.*) an arrangement of clauses, sentences etc., without connectives indicating subordination etc. **paratactic** (-tak´-) *a.* **paratactically** *adv.* [Gr. *parataxis* (*tassein*, to arrange)]

paratha (pərah´tə) *n.* in Indian cookery, a piece of flat, round, unleavened bread fried on a griddle. [Hind. *parāthā*]

parathesis (pərath´əsis) *n.* (*Gram.*) apposition. [Gr. *tithenai*, to place]

parathion (parəthī´ən) *n.* a highly toxic insecticide. [PARA-[1], *thio*phosphate]

parathyroid (parəthī´roid) *n.* (*Anat.*) a small endocrine gland, one of which is situated on each side of the thyroid. ~*a.* of or relating to the parathyroids.
paratonic (parəton´ik) *a.* (*Bot.*) (of a plant-movement) due to external stimuli. **paratonically** *adv.*
paratrooper (par´ətroopə) *n.* a soldier belonging to a unit transported in aircraft and dropped by parachute, with full equipment, usu. behind enemy lines. **paratroop** *a.* **paratroops** *n.pl.*
paratyphoid (parətī´foid) *n.* an infectious fever of the enteric group, similar in symptoms to typhoid but of milder character. ~*a.* of or relating to paratyphoid.
paravane (par´əvān) *n.* a mine-sweeping appliance for severing the moorings of submerged mines.
par avion (pahr avyõ´) *adv.* by airmail. [F, by aeroplane]
parazoan (parəzō´ən) *n.* a member of the subkingdom Parazoa, the multicellular invertebrates, such as sponges. [Gr. *zōon*, an animal]
parboil (pah´boil) *v.t.* to boil partially. [OF *parboillir*, from late L *perbullīre*, to boil thoroughly (PER-, *bullīre*, to BOIL[1]), conf. with PART]
parbuckle (pah´bŭkəl) *n.* a double sling usu. made by passing the two ends of a rope through a bight for hoisting or lowering a cask or gun. ~*v.t.* to hoist or lower by a parbuckle. [etym. unknown]
Parcae (pah´sē) *n.pl.* in Roman mythology, the Fates. [L, those who spare]
parcel (pah´səl) *n.* **1** a quantity of things wrapped up together. **2** a bundle, a package. **3** a distinct portion, for example of land. **4** a number or quantity of things dealt with as a separate lot. **5** †a portion or part, an item. ~*v.t.* (*pres.p.* **parcelling,** (*N Am.*) **parceling,** *past, p.p.* **parcelled,** (*N Am.*) **parceled**) **1** to make into a parcel. **2** to divide (out) into parts or lots. **3** to wrap (a rope) with strips of canvas, or cover (a seam) with strips of canvas and pitch. **parcel post** *n.* a branch of the postal service for the delivery of parcels. [F *parcelle*, late L *particella*, dim. of *particula*, a PARTICLE]
parcenary (pah´sənəri) *n.* joint heirship, coparcenary. **parcener** *n.* a person having an equal share with another person or other people. [A-F *parcenarie*, OF *parçonerie*, from *parçonier*, *parcener*, med. L *partiōnārius* (PARTITION, -ARY[1])]
parch (pahch) *v.t.* to scorch or roast partially dry, to dry up. ~*v.i.* to become hot or dry. **parched** *a.* **1** dried up. **2** (*coll.*) very thirsty. [etym. unknown]
Parcheesi® (pahchē´zi) *n.* a modern board game based on pachisi.
parchment (pahch´mənt) *n.* **1** the skin of calves, sheep, goats etc., prepared for writing upon, painting etc. **2** a manuscript written on this, esp. a deed. **3** VEGETABLE PARCHMENT (under VEGETABLE). ~*a.* made of or resembling parchment. **parchmenty** *a.* [F *parchemin*, L *pergamēna*, orig. fem. of *Pergamēnus*, pertaining to *Pergamum*, city in Asia Minor]
parclose (pah´klōz) *n.* a screen or railing enclosing an altar, tomb etc. in a church. [ME and OF *parclos*, *-close*, p.p. of *parclore* (PER-, *claudere*, to CLOSE[2])]
pard[1] (pahd), **pardner** (-nə) *n.* (*N Am., sl.*) a partner. [abbr.]
†**pard**[2] (pahd) *n.* a panther, a leopard. [OF *pard*, L *pardus*, Gr. *pardos*, earlier *pardalis*, of Eastern orig.]
pardalote (pah´dəlōt) *n.* any small, spotted Australian bird of the genus *Pardalotus*. [mod. L *Pardalotus*, from Gr. *pardalotos*, spotted like a leopard (as PARD[2])]
pardner PARD[1].
pardon (pah´dən) *n.* **1** the act of excusing or forgiving. **2** a complete or partial remission of the legal consequences of crime. **3** an official warrant of a penalty remitted. **4** a papal indulgence. **5** †a religious festival when this is granted. **6** courteous forbearance. ~*v.t.* **1** to forgive, to absolve from. **2** to remit the penalty of. **3** to refrain from exacting. **4** to excuse, to make allowance for. **I beg your pardon** excuse me, a polite apology for an action, contradiction or failure to hear or understand what is said. **pardon me** I beg your pardon. **pardon my French** FRENCH. **pardonable** *a.* **pardonableness** *n.* **pardonably** *adv.* **pardoner** *n.* **1** (*Hist.*) a person licensed to sell papal pardons or indulgences. **2** a person who pardons. [OF *pardoner*, *perduner*, late L *perdōnāre* (PER, *dōnāre*, to give, from *dōnum*, a gift)]
pare (peə) *v.t.* **1** to cut or shave (away or off). **2** to cut away or remove the rind etc. of (fruit etc.). **3** to trim by cutting the edges or irregularities of. **4** to diminish by degrees. **parer** *n.* **paring** *n.* **1** the act of cutting off, pruning or trimming. **2** the part which is pared off; a shaving, rind etc. [F *parer*, L *parāre*, to prepare]
paregoric (parigor´ik) *a.* assuaging or soothing pain. ~*n.* a camphorated tincture of opium for assuaging pain. [late L *parēgoricus*, Gr. *parēgorikos*, soothing, from *parēgoros*, addressing, exhorting (PARA-[1], AGORA[1], assembly)]
pareira (pəreə´rə) *n.* a drug used in urinary disorders, obtained from the root of *Chondrodendron tomentosum*, a Brazilian climbing plant. [Port. *parreira*]
parella (pərel´ə) *n.* a crustaceous lichen, *Lecanora parella*, from which litmus and orchil are obtained. [mod. L, from F *parelle*, med. L *paratella*]
paren (pəren´) *n.* (*usu. pl.*) a round bracket, a parenthesis.
parenchyma (pəreng´kimə) *n.* **1** (*Anat.*) the soft cellular tissue of glands and other organs, as distinct from connective tissue etc. **2** (*Bot.*) thin cellular tissue in the softer part of plants, pith, fruit pulp etc. **parenchymal, parenchymatous** (-kim´-) *a.* [Gr. *parenchuma* (PARA-[1], *enchuma*, infusion, from *encheein*, to pour in)]
parent (peə´rənt) *n.* **1** a father or mother. **2** a person who acts as a parent, e.g. an adoptive parent. **3** †a forefather. **4** an organism from which others are produced. **5** a source, origin, cause or occasion. **6** a company having control of one or more subsidiaries. ~*v.t.* to be a parent or the parent of. **parentage** (-ij) *n.* birth, extraction, lineage, origin. **parental** (pəren´-) *a.* **parentally** *adv.* **parent company** *n.* a company having control of one or more subsidiaries. **parenthood** (-hud) *n.* **parenting** *n.* the skills or activity of being a parent. **parentless** *a.* **Parents' Charter** *n.* a document drawn up by the British Government, outlining the structure and policies of school education, and parents' and children's rights. **parent-teacher association** *n.* an association formed by the parents and teachers of a school, esp. for social and fund-raising purposes. [F, from L *parentem*, nom. *-ens*, from *parēre*, to produce, to beget]
parenteral (pəren´tərəl) *a.* (*Med.*) situated or occurring outside the digestive tract, esp. being the means of administering a drug other than via the digestive tract. **parenterally** *adv.* [Gr. *enteron*, an intestine]
parenthesis (pəren´thəsis) *n.* (*pl.* **parentheses** (-sēz)) **1** (*Gram.*) a word, phrase or sentence inserted in a sentence that is grammatically complete without it, usu. marked off by brackets, dashes or commas. **2** (*pl.*) round brackets () to include such words. **3** an interval, interlude, incident etc. **in parenthesis** as an aside, by the way. **parenthesize, parenthesise** *v.t.* **1** to insert as a parenthesis. **2** to place (a clause etc.) between parentheses. ~*v.i.* to insert something as a parenthesis. **parenthetic** (-thet´-), **parenthetical** *a.* **parenthetically** *adv.* [med. L and Gr., from *parentithenai* (PARA-[1], EN-, *tithenai*, to put)]
parergon (pərœ´gon) *n.* (*pl.* **parerga** (-gə)) **1** a subsidiary work. **2** an ornamental accessory. [L and Gr. (*ergon*, work)]
paresis (parē´sis) *n.* (*pl.* **pareses** (-sēz)) (*Med.*) incomplete paralysis, affecting muscular movement but not sensation. **paretic** (-ret´-) *a.* [Gr., from *parienai* (*hienai*, to let go)]

paresthesia PARAESTHESIA.

par excellence (pahr ek´sələns) *adv.* above all others, pre-eminently. [F]

parfait (pahfā´) *n.* **1** a rich, cold dessert made with whipped cream, eggs, fruit etc. **2** a dessert made of layers of ice cream, meringue, fruit and sauce, served in a tall glass. [F, perfect]

parfleche (pahflesh´) *n.* **1** a hide, usu. of buffalo, stripped of hair and dried on a stretcher. **2** a tent, wallet or other article made of this. [Can. F, from F *parer*, to ward off, *flèche*, an arrow]

pargana (pəgŭn´ə), **pergunnah, pergana** *n.* in India, a subdivision of a district. [Urdu, a district]

pargasite (pah´gəsīt) *n.* (*Geol.*) a greenish variety of hornblende. [G *Pargasit*, from *Pargas*, Finland]

parget (pah´jit) *v.t.* (*pres.p.* **pargeting,** *past, p.p.* **pargeted**) **1** to plaster over. **2** to roughcast. ~*n.* **1** plaster. **2** pargeting. **pargeter** *n.* **pargeting** *n.* plasterwork, esp. decorative plasterwork. [OF *pargeter, porgeter*, L *prōjectāre* (PRO-[1], *jactāre*, freq. of *jacere*, to throw)]

parhelion (pah·hē´liən) *n.* (*pl.* **parhelia** (-liə)) a mock sun or bright spot in a solar halo, due to ice crystals in the atmosphere. **parheliacal** (-hilī´-), **parhelic** *a.* **parhelic circle** *n.* a circle of light parallel to the horizon at the altitude of the sun, caused by the reflection of sunlight by ice crystals in the atmosphere. [L and Gr. (PARA-[1], *hēlios*, the sun)]

pariah (pərī´ə) *n.* **1** a social outcast. **2** (*Hist.*) **a** a member of a people of very low caste in S India and Burma. **b** a person of low caste or without caste. **pariah dog** *n.* a pye-dog. [Tamil *paraiyar*, pl. of *paraiyan*, a drummer, from *parai*, a drum]

Usage note As a social classification, *pariah* has been abolished in India, and its use can give offence to Indians.

Parian (peə´riən) *a.* of or relating to the island of Paros, Greece, celebrated for its white marble. ~*n.* a white variety of porcelain, used for statuettes etc.

parietal (pərī´itəl) *a.* **1** of or relating to a wall or walls, esp. those of the body and its cavities. **2** (*Bot.*) of, relating to or attached to the wall of a structure, esp. of a placenta or ovary. **3** (*N Am.*) of or relating to residence within a college. **parietal bone** *n.* either of the two bones forming part of the top and sides of the skull. **parietal lobe** *n.* either of the two lobes of the brain at the top of the head, concerned with the perception and interpretation of sensory information. [F *pariétal*, L *parietālis*, from *paries -etis*, wall]

parieto- (pərī´itō) *comb. form* of or relating to a wall or walls. [see PARIETAL]

pari-mutuel (parimū´tūəl) *n.* **1** a system of betting in which the winners divide the losers' stakes less a percentage for management. **2** a totalizator. [F]

paring PARE.

pari passu (pari pas´oo) *adv.* (esp. in legal contexts) with equal pace, in a similar degree, equally. [L]

paripinnate (paripin´āt) *a.* (*Bot.*) equally pinnate, without a terminal leaflet. [L *pari-*, *pār*, equal, PINNATE]

Paris (par´is) *a.* of or relating to Paris, France. **plaster of Paris** PLASTER. **Paris Commune** *n.* (*Hist.*) **1** the communalistic body that took possession of Paris in 1871 after its evacuation by the Germans. **2** the revolutionary committee that replaced the municipality in 1789. **Paris green** *n.* a light green pigment obtained from arsenic oxide of copper.

parish (par´ish) *n.* **1** an ecclesiastical district with its own church and clergyman. **2** a subdivision of a county. **3** a civil district for the purposes of local government etc. **4** the people living in a parish. **5** (*N Am.*) a county in Louisiana. ~*a.* of, relating to or maintained by a parish. **on the parish** (*Hist.*) being financially supported by the parish. **parish clerk** *n.* a subordinate lay official in the church, formerly leading the congregation in the responses. **parish council** *n.* a local administrative body elected by the parishioners in rural districts. **parishioner** (-rish´ənə) *n.* a person who belongs to a parish. **parish pump** *a.* (*coll.*) of local interest only, parochial. ~*n.* a symbol of parochialism. **parish register** *n.* a register of christenings, marriages and burials, kept at a parish church. [A-F *parosse*, *paroche* (F *paroisse*), late L *parochia*, Gr. *paroikia* (PARA-[1], *oikos*, dwelling)]

Parisian (pəriz´iən) *a.* of or relating to Paris, France. ~*n.* **1** a native or inhabitant of Paris. **2** the dialect of French spoken in Paris.

parison (par´isən) *n.* a rounded mass of glass before it is shaped. [F, *paraison*, from *parer*, to prepare, from L *parare*]

parisyllabic (parisilab´ik) *a.* (of a Greek or Latin noun) having the same number of syllables, esp. in all the cases.

parity[1] (par´iti) *n.* (*pl.* **parities**) **1** equality of rank, condition, value etc. **2** parallelism, analogy. **3** the amount of a foreign currency equal to a specific sum of domestic currency. **4** equivalence of a commodity price as expressed in one currency to its price expressed in another. **5** (*Math.*) the property of being odd or even. **6** (*Physics*) (of quantity) the condition of changing or not changing under a transformation of coordinates etc. **parity check** *n.* a check of computer data which uses the state of oddness or evenness of the number of bits in a unit of information as a means of detecting errors. [F *parité*, L *paritātem*, nom. *-tas*, from *pār*, equal]

parity[2] (par´iti) *n.* (*Med.*) **1** the condition of having given birth. **2** the number of children a woman has given birth to. [see -PAROUS]

park (pahk) *n.* **1** a piece of ground, ornamentally laid out, enclosed for public recreation. **2** a piece of land, usu. for ornament, pleasure or recreation, with trees, pasture etc., surrounding or adjoining a mansion. **3** a large tract or region, usu. with interesting physical features, preserved in its natural state for public enjoyment. **4** an enclosed area of land where wild animals are kept in captivity. **5** an area where vehicles can be parked. **6** the position in automatic gear transmission in which the vehicle's gears are locked. **7** an area set aside for a specific purpose (*a science park*). **8** (*N Am.*) a sports stadium or arena. **9** (*coll.*) a soccer pitch. **10** (*Mil.*) a space occupied by the artillery, stores etc. in an encampment. ~*v.t.* **1** to leave (a vehicle) in a place allotted for the purpose. **2** (*coll.*) to leave temporarily. **3** to enclose in or as a park. **4** to mass (artillery) in a park. ~*v.i.* to leave a vehicle in a place allotted for the purpose. **to park oneself** (*coll.*) to sit down. **parking** *n.* **parking disc** *n.* a disc displayed in a parked vehicle to show the time of arrival or the latest time of departure. **parking lot** *n.* (*N Am.*) a car park. **parking meter** *n.* a coin-operated appliance on a kerb, that charges for the time cars are parked there. **parking ticket** *n.* a document issued for a parking offence, requiring payment of a fine or appearance in court. **parkish** *a.* **park keeper** *n.* **parkland** *n.* open land with grass and trees on it. **parkway** *n.* **1** (*N Am.*) a highway lined with trees and grass. **2** a railway station with a sizeable car park. [OF *parc* (cp. Dut. *perk*, Swed. and Dan. *park*, G *Pferch*), from Gmc., cp. OE *pearruc*, PADDOCK]

parka (pah´kə) *n.* a hooded jacket edged or lined with fur. [Aleutian, skin]

parkin (pah´kin) *n.* a biscuit made of gingerbread, oatmeal and treacle. [etym. unknown]

Parkinson's disease (pah´kinsənz), **Parkinsonism** (-sənizm) *n.* a chronic disorder of the central nervous system causing loss of muscle coordination and tremor. [James *Parkinson*, 1755–1824, British surgeon who first described it]

Parkinson's law (pah´kinsənz) *n.* the supposed principle in office management etc. that work expands to fill the time available for its completion. [put forward facetiously by C. Northcote *Parkinson*, 1909–88, British historian]

parky (pah´ki) *a.* (*comp.* **parkier**, *superl.* **parkiest**) (*coll.*) chilly. [etym. uncertain]

Parl. *abbr.* Parliament(ary).

parlance (pah´ləns) *n.* way of speaking, idiom. [OF, as PARLEY]

parlay (pah´lā) *v.t.* (*N Am.*) **1** to bet (one's winnings) on a further stake. **2** to increase the value of, by parlaying or as if by parlaying. *~n.* (*N Am.*) **1** the act or an instance of parlaying. **2** a bet made by parlaying. [F, *paroli*, from It., from *paro*, like, from L *par*, equal]

parley (pah´li) *n.* (*pl.* **parleys**) a conference for discussing terms, esp. between enemies. *~v.i.* (*pres.p.* **parleying**, *past, p.p.* **parleyed**) **1** to confer with an enemy with peacemaking intentions. **2** to talk, to dispute. *~v.t.* to speak (a foreign language). [F *parler* or OF *parlee*, fem. p.p. of *parler*, pop. L *parabolāre*, from *parabola*, a PARABLE]

parleyvoo (pahlivoo´) *v.i.* (*dated, sl.*) to speak French. *~n.* **1** the French language. **2** a Frenchman. [F *parlez-vous Français*, do you speak French?]

parliament (pah´ləmənt) *n.* **1** a deliberative assembly. **2** a legislative body, esp. the British legislature, consisting of the Houses of Lords and Commons, together with the sovereign. **parliamentarian** (-teə´ri-) *n.* **1** a person well-versed in parliamentary rules and usages or in parliamentary debate. **2** a Member of Parliament. **3** (*Hist.*) a person who supported the Parliament against King Charles I in the time of the English Civil War. *~a.* parliamentary. **parliamentary** (-men´-) *a.* **1** of, relating to or enacted by (a) parliament according to the rules of (a) parliament. **2** (esp. of language) admissible in (a) parliament, civil. **parliamentary agent** *n.* a person employed by a private person or persons to draft bills or manage the business of private legislation. **Parliamentary Commissioner** *n.* an ombudsman in the UK. **parliamentary private secretary** *n.* an ordinary member of the British Parliament appointed to assist a minister. [ME and OF *parlement* (PARLEY, -MENT)]

Usage note Pronunciation as (pah´liəmənt) is best avoided.

parlour (pah´lə), (*N Am.*) **parlor** *n.* **1** the family sitting-room in a private house. **2** a room in a convent, hotel etc. for conversation. **3** any of various commercial establishments (*a beauty parlour*). **4** a building used for milking cows. *~a.* (*derog.*) of or relating to a person who professes certain political views but makes no attempt to practise them. **parlour-boarder** *n.* a pupil at a boarding school living with the principal's family. **parlourcar** *n.* (*N Am.*) a luxuriously fitted railway carriage. **parlour game** *n.* an indoor game, such as charades, sometimes played at a party. **parlourmaid** *n.* (*Hist.*) a maid waiting at table. [OF *parleor*, med. L *parlātōrium*, from *parlāre*, *parabolāre*, to speak (see PARLEY)]

†**parlous** (pah´ləs) *a.* **1** perilous, awkward, trying. **2** difficult, cunning, shrewd. *~adv.* extremely. **parlously** *adv.* **parlousness** *n.* [var. of PERILOUS (under PERIL)]

Parma ham (pah´mə) *n.* a type of ham eaten uncooked. [*Parma*, city in Italy]

Parma violet (pah´mə) *n.* a variety of violet with a strong scent and lavender-coloured flowers.

Parmesan (pahmizan´) *n.* a kind of hard, dry cheese made at Parma and elsewhere in N Italy, used grated as a topping for pasta dishes.

Parnassian (pahnas´iən) *a.* **1** of or relating to Mount Parnassus. **2** poetic. **3** of or relating to the Parnassians, a group of late-19th-cent. French poets who emphasized strictness of form. *~n.* any one of the Parnassian group of poets.

Parnassus (pahnas´əs) *n.* poetry, literature. [mountain in Greece, famous in ancient times as the favourite resort of the Muses]

Parnellism (pah´nəlizm) *n.* (*Hist.*) the political views and tactics of C. S. Parnell, who aimed to force Parliament to grant Irish Home Rule, by persistent obstruction etc. **Parnellite** (-īt) *n., a.* [C. S. *Parnell*, 1846–91, leader of the Irish Home Rule party, 1880–91]

parochial (pərō´kiəl) *a.* **1** of or relating to a parish. **2** petty, narrow in outlook. **parochialism, parochiality** (-al´-) *n.* **parochialize, parochialise** *v.t.* **parochially** *adv.* [OF, from late L *parochiālis*, from *parochia*, a PARISH]

parody (par´ədi) *n.* (*pl.* **parodies**) **1** a literary composition imitating an author's work for the purpose of humour. **2** a poor imitation, a mere travesty. *~v.t.* (*3rd pers. sing. pres.* **parodies**, *pres.p.* **parodying**, *past, p.p.* **parodied**) to turn into a parody, to burlesque. **parodic** (-rod´-) *a.* **parodist** *n.* [L and Gr. *parōdia* (PARA-[1], ODE)]

parol (pərōl´) *a.* **1** given orally. **2** not given under seal. *~n.* an oral declaration. [OF *parole* (as PAROLE)]

parole (pərōl´) *n.* **1** the release of a prisoner under certain conditions, esp. good behaviour. **2** a word of honour. **3** actual speech, by contrast with language as an abstract system. **4** (*Mil.*) the daily password used by officers etc., as distinct from the *countersign*. *~v.t.* to put or release on parole. **on parole** (of a prisoner) released under certain conditions esp. good behaviour. **parolee** (-lē) *n.* [F, from late L *parabola*, a PARABLE]

paronomasia (parənəmā´ziə) *n.* a play on words, a pun. †**paronomasy** (-nom´-) *n.* **paronomasial, paronomasian** *a.* **paronomastic** (-mas´-), **paronomastical** *a.* [L and Gr. (*onomazein*, to name, from *onoma*, a name)]

paronym (par´ənim) *n.* a paronymous word. **paronymous** (-pəron´-) *a.* **1** having the same root, cognate. **2** alike in sound, but differing in origin, spelling and meaning. **paronymy** (pəron´-) *n.* [Gr. *parōnumos*, paronymous (*onoma*, a name)]

parotid (pərot´id) *a.* (*Anat.*) situated near the ear. *~n.* (*Anat.*) a parotid gland. **parotic** *a.* **parotid duct** *n.* a duct from the parotid gland by which saliva is conveyed to the mouth. **parotideal** (-dē´əl) *a.* **parotid gland** *n.* either of a pair of salivary glands situated on either side of the cheek in front of the ear, with a duct to the mouth. **parotiditis** (-dī´tis), **parotitis** (parətī´tis) *n.* (*Med.*) **1** inflammation of the parotid gland. **2** mumps. **parotis** (-rō´-) *n.* a parotid gland. [F *parotide*, from L and Gr. *parōtis -tidos* (*ous ōtos*, an ear)]

-parous (pərəs) *comb. form* producing, bringing forth, as *oviparous*. [L *-parus*, from *parere*, to bring forth]

Parousia (pəroo´ziə) *n.* (*Theol.*) Christ's second coming, to judge the world. [Gr., presence]

paroxysm (par´əksizm) *n.* **1** a sudden and violent fit. **2** the exacerbation of a disease at periodic times. **3** a fit of laughter or other emotion. **paroxysmal** (-siz´-), **paroxysmic** *a.* **paroxysmally** *adv.* [F *paroxysme*, L *paroxysmus*, Gr. *paroxusmos* (*oxunein*, to sharpen, from *oxus*, sharp)]

paroxytone (pərok´sitōn) *a.* (in classical Greek, of a word) having an acute accent on the penultimate syllable. *~n.* a word having such an accent. **paroxytonic** (-ton´-) *a.* [Gr. *paroxutonos*]

parpen (pah´pən) *n.* a stone going through a wall. [OF *parpain* (F *parpaing*), etym. uncertain]

parquet (pah´kā) *n.* **1** a flooring of parquetry. **2** (*N Am.*) the part of the floor of a theatre between the orchestra and the row immediately under the front of the gallery. *~a.* made of parquet. *~v.t.* (*pres.p.* **parqueting**, *past, p.p.* **parqueted**) to floor (a room) with parquetry. **parquetry** (-itri) *n.* inlaid woodwork for floors. [F, a floor, orig. a compartment, dim. of *parc*, a PARK]

parr (pah), **par** *n.* a young salmon. [etym. uncertain]

parrakeet PARAKEET.

parramatta (parəmat´ə), **paramatta** *n.* a light twilled dress fabric of merino wool and cotton (orig. from Parramatta in New South Wales).

parrhesia (pərē´ziə, -siə) *n.* freedom or boldness in speaking. [late L and Gr. (*rhēsis*, speech)]

parricide (par´isīd) *n.* **1** the murder of a parent or other close relative, or of a revered person. **2** a person who murders a parent or other close relative, or a revered person. **parricidal** (-sī´-) *a.* [F, from L *parricīda* or *parricīdium*]

Usage note The nouns *parricide* and *patricide* should not be confused: *parricide* refers to a parent, close relative or revered person, and *patricide* just to a father.

parrot (par´ət) *n.* **1** any of various tropical birds with brilliant plumage of the order Psittaciformes, remarkable for their faculty of imitating the human voice. **2** a person who repeats words or imitates actions mechanically or unintelligently. **3** a person who talks a lot. *~v.t.* (*pres.p.* **parroting,** *past, p.p.* **parroted**) to repeat mechanically or by rote. *~v.i.* to chatter like a parrot. **parroter** *n.* **parrot-fashion** *adv.* accurately but without understanding the meaning. **parrotfish** *n.* (*pl. in general* **parrotfish,** *in particular* **parrotfishes**) any fish of the genus *Scarus*, so called because of their brilliant colouring and the beaklike projection of their jaws. **parrotry** *n.* [etym. uncertain, perh. from *periquito*, dim. of *perico*, cp. PARAKEET]

parry (par´i) *v.t.* (*3rd pers. sing. pres.* **parries,** *pres.p.* **parrying,** *past, p.p.* **parried**) **1** to ward off (a blow or thrust). **2** to evade cleverly, to shirk. *~n.* (*pl.* **parries**) the act of parrying. [F *parer*, to parry, L *parāre*, see PARADE]

parse (pahz) *v.t.* **1** to describe or classify (a word) grammatically, its inflectional forms, relations in the sentence etc. **2** to analyse (a sentence) and describe its component words and their relations grammatically. **3** (*Comput.*) to analyse (a string) syntactically. *~v.i.* (of a word or sentence) to be conformable with grammatical rules. **parser** *n.* [L *pars*, a PART]

parsec (pah´sek) *n.* a unit of length in calculating the distance of the stars, being 1.9×10^{13} miles (3×10^{13} km) or 3.26 light years. [*par*allax *sec*ond]

Parsee (pah´sē) *n.* **1** a Zoroastrian, a descendant of the Persians who fled to India from the Muslim persecution in the 7th and 8th cents. **2** the Pahlavi language. **Parseeism, Parsiism** *n.* the Parsee religion, Zoroastrianism. [Pers. *Pārsī*, Persian, from *Pārs*, Persia]

parsimonious (pahsimō´niəs) *a.* **1** careful in the expenditure of money. **2** frugal, niggardly, stingy. **parsimoniously** *adv.* **parsimoniousness** *n.* **parsimony** (pah´-) *n.* [L *parsimōnia*, *parci-* from *parcere*, to spare]

parsley (pahs´li) *n.* an umbelliferous herb, *Petroselinum crispum*, cultivated for its aromatic leaves used for seasoning and garnishing dishes. **parsley fern** *n.* a type of fern, *Cryptogramma crispa*, which has parsley-like leaves. **parsley-piert** (-piət´) *n.* a small plant, *Aphanes arvensis*, of the rose family. [ME *percil*, OF *peresil* (F *persil*), late L *petrosillum*, L *petroselīnum*, Gr. *petroselīnon* (*petro-*, *petros*, stone, *selīnon*, parsley)]

parsnip (pah´snip) *n.* an umbelliferous plant, *Pastinaca sativa*, with an edible root used as a vegetable. [ME *pasnep*, OF *pastenaque*, L *pastināca*, from *pastinum*, a fork for digging]

parson (pah´sən) *n.* **1** a rector, vicar or other clergyman holding a benefice. **2** (*coll.*) a member of the clergy, esp. a Protestant one. **parsonage** (-ij) *n.* **1** the home of a parson. **2** the benefice of a parish. **parson bird** *n.* the tui. **parsonic** (-son´-) *a.* **parson's nose** *n.* the rump of a fowl. [ME *persone*, a PERSON]

part (paht) *n.* **1** a portion, piece or amount of a thing or number of things. **2** a portion separate from the rest or considered as separate. **3** a small component of a machine, vehicle etc. **4** a member, an organ. **5** a proportional quantity. **6** any of several equal portions, quantities or numbers into which a thing is divided, or of which it is composed. **7** (*pl.*) PRIVATE PARTS (under PRIVATE). **8** a section of a book, periodical etc., as issued at one time. **9** a share, a lot. **10** interest, concern. **11** a share of work etc., act, duty. **12** side, party. **13** the role, character, words etc. allotted to an actor. **14** a copy of the words so allotted. **15** a person's allotted duty or responsibility. **16** (*pl.*) qualities, accomplishments, talents. **17** (*pl.*) region, district, quarters. **18** (*Mus.*) one of the constituent melodies of a harmony. **19** (*Mus.*) a melody allotted to a particular voice or instrument. **20** (*N Am.*) a parting in the hair. *~v.t.* **1** to divide into portions, shares, pieces etc. **2** to separate. **3** to brush or comb (the hair) with a division along the head. *~v.i.* **1** to divide. **2** to separate from another person or other people. *~adv.* partly. *~a.* partial. **for my part** so far as I am concerned. **for the most part** MOST[1]. **in part/parts** partly. **on the part of** done by or proceeding from. **part and parcel** an essential part or element. **to look the part** to appear to be exactly right for a role. **to part company** to separate. **to part with** to relinquish, to give up. **to play a part 1** to assist or be involved. **2** to act deceitfully. **3** to act in a play or film. **to take in good part** GOOD. **to take in ill part** ILL. **to take part** to assist or participate. **to take the part of** to back up or support. **part exchange** *n.* a form of purchase in which one item is offered as partial payment for another, the balance being paid as money. **part-exchange** *v.t.* to offer in part exchange. **part of speech** *n.* a grammatical class of words of a particular character, usu. being one of noun, pronoun, adjective, verb, adverb, preposition, conjunction, interjection. **part-owner** *n.* a person who has a share in property with others. **part-song** *n.* a composition for at least three voices in harmony, usu. without accompaniment. **part-time** *a., adv.* working or done for less than the usual number of hours. **part-timer** *n.* **part-way** *adv.* **1** to some extent. **2** partially. **part-work** *n.* a publication issued in instalments, intended to be bound to form a complete book or course of study. [OE, from L *partem*, nom. *pars*, whence *partīre*, F *partir*, to divide]

part. *abbr.* participle.

partake (pahtāk´) *v.i.* (*pres.p.* **partaking,** *past* **partook** (-tuk´), *p.p.* **partaken** (-tā´kən)) **1** †to take or have a part or share (of or in, with another or others). **2** to have something of the nature (of). **3** to eat and drink (of). *~v.t.* to have or have a part or share in common with others. **partakable** *a.* **partaker** *n.*

parterre (pahteə´) *n.* **1** an ornamental arrangement of flower beds, with intervening walks. **2** (*N Am.*) the ground floor of a theatre or the part of this behind the orchestra. [F *par terre*, on the ground]

parthenogenesis (pahthinəjen´əsis) *n.* (*Biol.*) generation without sexual union. **parthenogenetic** (-net´-) *a.* **parthenogenetically** *adv.* [Gr. *parthenos*, a virgin]

Parthian (pah´thiən) *a.* of or relating to Parthia, an ancient kingdom in W Asia. **Parthian shot** *n.* a look, word etc. delivered as a parting blow (like the arrows shot by the Parthians in the act of fleeing).

parti (pahtē´) *n.* (*pl.* **partis**) a person regarded as eligible for marriage. [F]

partial (pah´shəl) *a.* **1** affecting a part only, incomplete. **2** biased in favour of one side or party, unfair. **3** having a preference for something. *~n.* (*Mus.*) any constituent of musical sound. **partial derivative** *n.* (*Math.*) a derivative obtained by varying only one of several variables. **partial differential equation** *n.* (*Math.*) an equation which contains a partial derivative. **partial eclipse** *n.* an eclipse in which the body, usually the sun, is only partially covered. **partiality** (-al´-) *n.* **partially** *adv.* **partialness** *n.* **partial pressure** *n.* (*Physics*) the pressure exerted by one of the gases in a mixture of gases. **partial verdict** *n.* a verdict in which the accused is found guilty of part of the charge. [F, from L *partiālis*, from *pars partis*, PART]

Usage note See note on *partially* under PARTLY.

participate (pahtis´ipāt) *v.i.* **1** to have or enjoy a share, to partake (in). **2** †to have something of the nature (of). **participable** *a.* **participant** *n., a.* **participating** *a.* **participation** (-ā´shən) *n.* **participative** *a.* **participator** *n.* **participatory** *a.* [L *participātus*, p.p. of *participāre* (PART, *capere*, to take)]

participle (pah´tisipəl) *n.* (*Gram.*) a word partaking of the nature of a verb and of an adjective, a verbal adjective qualifying a noun. **participial** (-sip´-) *a.* **participially** *adv.* [OF (F *participe*), L *participium*, as PARTICIPATE]

particle (pah´tikəl) *n.* **1** an atom. **2** a minute part or portion. **3** (*Gram.*) a word not inflected, or not used except in combination. **particle accelerator** *n.* a device for accelerating elementary particles, used in high-energy physics. **particle board** *n.* chipboard. **particle physics** *n.* the branch of physics concerned with fundamental particles and their properties. **particulate** (-tik´ūlət) *a.* [L *particula*, dim. of *pars*, a PART]

particoloured (pah´tikŭləd), (*N Am.*) **particolored, party-coloured,** (*N Am.*) **party-colored** *a.* partly of one colour, partly of another; variegated.

particular (pətik´ūlə) *a.* **1** of or relating to a single person or thing as distinct from others. **2** special, peculiar, characteristic. **3** single, separate, individual. **4** minute, circumstantial. **5** fastidious, exact, precise. **6** remarkable, noteworthy. **7** (*Logic*) stating something about only some members of a class. ~*n.* **1** an item, a detail, an instance. **2** (*pl.*) a detailed account. **in particular** particularly. **particular average** *n.* in marine insurance, loss borne by the shipowner and one cargo owner only. **particular intention** *n.* a special intention. **particularism** *n.* **1** devotion to private interests or those of a party, sect etc. **2** the policy of allowing political independence to the separate states of an empire, confederation etc. **3** (*Theol.*) the doctrine of the election or redemption of particular individuals of the human race. **particularist** *n.* **particularistic** (-is´-) *a.* **particularity** (-lar´-) *n.* (*pl.* **particularities**) **1** the quality of being particular. **2** (*usu. pl.*) a minute point or instance, a detail. **particularize, particularise** *v.t.* **1** to mention individually. **2** to specify, to give the particulars of. ~*v.i.* to be attentive to particulars or details. **particularization** (-zā´shən) *n.* **particularly** *adv.* **particularness** *n.* [ME and OF *particuler*, L *particulāris*, from *particula*, PARTICLE]

particulate PARTICLE.

partim (pah´tim) *adv.* partly. [L, from *pars partis*, PART]

parting (pah´ting) *n.* **1** a departure, leave-taking. **2** a dividing line, esp. between sections of hair combed or falling in opposite directions. **3** separation, division. **4** a point of separation or departure. ~*a.* **1** given or bestowed on departure or separation. **2** †departing. **3** serving to part. **parting shot** *n.* a Parthian shot.

parti pris (pahti prē´) *n.* (*pl.* **partis pris** (pahti prē´)) a preconceived view, bias, prejudice. ~*a.* biased, prejudiced. [F, side taken]

partisan[1] (pah´tizan, -zan´), **partizan** *n.* **1** an adherent of a party, faction, cause etc., esp. one showing unreasoning devotion. **2** (*Mil.*) a member of a body of irregular troops carrying out special enterprises, such as raids. ~*a.* of, relating or attached to a party. **partisanship** *n.* [It. *partigiano*]

partisan[2] (pah´tizən), **partizan** *n.* a pike or long-handled spear like a halberd. [F *partizane* (now *pertuisane*), It. *partesana, partegiana*, perh. rel. to PARTISAN[1], or from Gmc. (cp. OHG *parta*, a halberd)]

partita (pahtē´tə) *n.* (*pl.* **partitas, partite** (-tā)) (*Mus.*) **1** a suite of music. **2** an air with variations. [It., cp. PART]

partite (pah´tīt) *a.* **1** divided (*usu. in comb.* as *bipartite*). **2** (*Bot., Zool.*) divided nearly to the base. [L *partītus*]

partition (pahtish´ən) *n.* **1** division into parts, distribution. **2** something which separates into parts, esp. a wall or screen. **3** a separate part. **4** (*Law*) division of property among joint owners. ~*v.t.* **1** to divide into parts or shares. **2** to separate (off). **partitioned** *a.* **partitioner** *n.* **partitionist** *n.* **partitive** (pah´-) *a.* (*Gram.*) denoting a part. ~*n.* a word denoting partition, such as *some* or *any*. **partitive genitive** *n.* a genitive which indicates a whole divided into parts, e.g. *of* in *some of them*. **partitively** *adv.* [F, from L *partītiōnem*, nom. *-tio*, from L *partīrī*, to PART]

partizan[1] PARTISAN[1].

partizan[2] PARTISAN[2].

partly (paht´li) *adv.* **1** in part. **2** to some extent, not wholly.

Usage note The uses of the adverbs *partially* and *partly* overlap, but *partly* is more usual to introduce an explanation, and when the adverb is repeated as a correlative (*partly for this reason, and partly for that*).

partner (paht´nə) *n.* **1** a person who shares with another, esp. one associated with others in business; an associate. **2** either of two people who dance together. **3** either of two playing on the same side in a game. **4** either party in a marriage or a romantic relationship. **5** (*pl., Naut.*) timber framing round a mast, pump etc., relieving the strain on the deck timbers. ~*v.t.* to join in partnership with, to be a partner of. **partnerless** *a.* **partnership** *n.* **1** the state of being a partner or partners. **2** a contractual relationship between a number of people involved in a business enterprise. **3** a pair or group of partners. [var. of PARCENER (under PARCENARY)]

parton (pah´ton) *n.* (*Physics*) an elementary particle postulated as a constituent of neutrons and protons.

partook PARTAKE.

partridge (pah´trij) *n.* (*pl.* **partridge, partridges**) any game bird of the genus *Perdix*, esp. *P. perdix*. [ME *pertriche*, OF *perdiz, pertuz*, L *perdīcem*, nom. *perdix*, Gr. *perdix -dikos*]

parturient (pahtū´riənt) *a.* **1** about to give birth. **2** (of the mind) learned, fertile. **parturition** (-rish´ən) *n.* (*formal*) the act of giving birth. [L *parturiens -ntem*, pres.p. of *parturīre*, to be in labour, from *parere*, to produce]

party[1] (pah´ti) *n.* (*pl.* **parties**) **1** a social gathering, usually in someone's home, often to celebrate a special occasion such as a birthday. **2** a number of persons united together for a particular purpose, esp. a national political group. **3** the principle or practice of taking sides on questions of public policy. **4** each of the actual or fictitious personages on either side in a legal action, contract etc. **5** (*Law*) an accessory, a person concerned in any affair. **6** (*coll.*) a person. ~*v.i.* (*3rd pers. sing. pres.* **parties**, *pres.p.* **partying**, *past, p.p.* **partied**) to attend parties, go out drinking etc. ~*v.t.* to entertain at a party. **the party's over** (*coll.*) something enjoyable, pleasant etc. is at an end. **party-goer** *n.* a person who likes going to parties or who is at a particular party. **party line** *n.* **1** the policy laid down by a political party. **2** a telephone exchange line used by a number of subscribers. **party politics** *n.* politics relating to political parties rather than the public good. **party political** *a.* of or relating to party politics. ~*n.* (*also* **party political broadcast**) a short, promotional television or radio programme made by a political party, usually broadcast just before an election. **party-poop, party-pooper** *n.* (*esp. N Am., sl.*) a person who spoils other people's fun, a spoilsport. **party-pooping** *n.* **party-popper** *n.* a small device from which paper streamers shoot out, sometimes used at parties. **party spirit** *n.* the mood for a party or to have fun. **party-spirited** *a.* **party-verdict** *n.* a joint verdict. **party wall** *n.* a wall separating two buildings etc., the joint property of the respective owners. [F *partie*, L *partīta*, fem. p.p. of *partīrī*, to divide, from *pars partis*, PART]

party[2] (pah´ti) *a.* (*Hist.*) divided into compartments distinguished by different colours. **party-coloured, party-colored** PARTICOLOURED. [F *parti*, as PARTY[1]]

parure (pərue´) *n.* a set of jewels or other personal ornaments. [F, from *parer*, L *parāre*, to adorn]

parvanimity (pahvənim´iti) *n.* smallness of mind, mean-spiritedness. [L *parvus*, petty, *animus*, the mind, after MAGNANIMITY (under MAGNANIMOUS)]

parvenu (pah´vənoo, -nū) *n.* (*pl.* **parvenus**) **1** a person who has risen socially or financially. **2** an upstart. *~a.* of or relating to a parvenu or parvenue. **parvenue** *n.* a female parvenu. [F, p.p. of *parvenir*, L *pervenīre*, to arrive (PER, *venīre*, to come)]

parvis (pah´vis), **parvise** *n.* **1** the vacant space in front of a church. **2** a room above a church porch. [F, from L *paradīsus*, PARADISE]

parvovirus (pah´vōvīrəs) *n.* (*pl.* **parvoviruses**) any one of a group of viruses each of which affects a particular species, such as *canine parvovirus*. [L *parvus*, small]

pas (pah) *n.* (*pl.* **pas** (pah)) **1** a dance step, esp. in ballet. **2** precedence. **to have the pas of** to take precedence over. **pas de chat** (də sha´) *n.* (*pl.* **pas de chat**) in ballet, a leap in which each foot is lifted in turn to the opposite knee. **pas de deux** (dœ´) *n.* (*pl.* **pas de deux**) a dance for two people. **pas glissé** *n.* GLISSÉ. **pas seul** (sœl´) *n.* (*pl.* **pas seuls** (sœl´)) a solo dance. [F, step, from L *passus*, a PACE[1]]

Pascal (paskahl´) *n.* a computer language suitable for many applications. [Blaise *Pascal*, 1623–62, French scientist and thinker]

pascal (pas´kəl) *n.* the SI unit of pressure, 1 newton per square metre. [as PASCAL]

paschal (pas´kəl) *a.* of or relating to the Passover or to Easter. **Pasch** (pahsk) *n.* **1** the Passover. **2** Easter. **paschal lamb** *n.* **1** a lamb sacrificed at Passover. **2** Jesus Christ. **pasch-egg** *n.* an Easter egg. [F *pascal*, L *paschālis*, from L and Gr. *pascha*, Heb. *pasakh*, the Passover, from *pāskh*, to be passed over]

pash (pash) *n.* (*sl.*) a violent infatuation, a crush. [PASSION]

pasha (pah´shə), **bashaw** (bəshaw´), **pacha** *n.* (*Hist.*) a Turkish title of honour, usu. conferred on officers of high rank, governors etc. **pashalic** (-shəlik) *n.* the jurisdiction of a pasha. [Turk.]

pashm (pash´əm) *n.* the under-fur of various Tibetan animals, esp. goats, used to make cashmere shawls. [Pers. *pašm*, wool]

Pashto (pŭsh´tō), **Pushto, Pushtu** (-too) *n.* a language spoken in Afghanistan and parts of Pakistan. *~a.* of or using this language.

pasigraphy (pəsig´rəfi) *n.* a universal system of writing, by means of signs representing ideas and not words. **pasigraphic** (pasigraf´-), **pasigraphical** *a.* [Gr. *pasi*, for all, pl. dat. of *pan*, PAN-, -GRAPHY]

paskha (pahs´kə) *n.* a Russian dessert made from curd cheese and dried fruit, traditionally eaten at Easter. [Rus., Easter]

pasodoble (pasō dō´blā) *n.* **1** a Latin American ballroom dance in fast 2/4 time, based on a march step. **2** this march step. [Sp., double step]

pasque flower (pask) *n.* a plant of the buttercup family, *Pulsatilla vulgaris*, with bell-shaped purple flowers. [formerly *passe-flower*, F *passefleur* (*pasque*, Easter, FLOWER), assim. to PASCH (under PASCHAL)]

pasquinade (paskwinād´) *n.* a lampoon, a satire. *~v.t.* to lampoon, to satirize. [*Pasquino* or *Pasquillo*, popular name of a piece of ancient statuary at Rome on which in the 15th cent. Latin verses were displayed, said to be named after a satirical cobbler]

pass (pahs) *v.i.* **1** to move from one place to another, to proceed, to go (along, on, quickly etc.). **2** to get through. **3** to circulate, to be current. **4** to be changed from one state to another. **5** to change hands, to be transferred. **6** to disappear, to vanish. **7** (*euphem.*) to die. **8** to go by, to elapse. **9** to go through, to be accepted without censure or challenge. **10** (*N Am.*) (of a person of mixed race) to be accepted as white. **11** (of a bill before parliament) to be enacted. **12** to receive current recognition. **13** to be successful in a test or examination. **14** to adjudicate. **15** to take place, to happen, to occur. **16** in team games, to kick or hit the ball to a team-mate. **17** in cards, to give up one's option of playing, making trumps etc. **18** to choose not to do something, esp. to answer a question. **19** (*Law*) to be transferred or handed on. *~v.t.* **1** to go by, beyond, over or through. **2** to overtake (a vehicle). **3** to transfer, to hand round. **4** to circulate, to give currency to. **5** to spend (time etc.). **6** in team games, to kick or hit (the ball) to a team-mate. **7** to endure. **8** to admit, to approve, to enact. **9** to satisfy the requirements of (an examination etc.). **10** to outstrip, to surpass. **11** to move, to cause to move. **12** to cause to go by. **13** to allow (a bill, a candidate etc.) to go through after examination. **14** to pledge (one's word etc.). **15** to pronounce, to utter. **16** to void, to discharge. **17** not to declare. **18** to overlook, to disregard, to reject. **19** to omit. *~n.* **1** the act of passing. **2** a passage, avenue or opening, esp. a narrow or difficult way. **3** a narrow passage through mountains, a defile. **4** a navigable passage, esp. at the mouth of a river. **5** a written or printed permission to pass. **6** a ticket authorizing one to travel (on a railway etc.) or to be admitted (to a theatre etc.) free. **7** a critical state or condition of things. **8** the act of passing an examination, esp. without special merit or honours. **9** in fencing, a thrust. **10** (*coll.*) a sexual advance. **11** a passing of hands over anything (as in conjuring). **12** a juggling trick. **13** in team games, the act of passing the ball. **to bring to pass** BRING. **to come to pass** COME. **to make a pass at** (*coll.*) to attempt to seduce. **to pass around** (*N Am.*) to pass round. **to pass as** to be accepted as. **to pass away** (*euphem.*) to die, to come to an end. **to pass by 1** to go past. **2** to omit, to disregard. **to pass current** CURRENT. **to pass for** to be taken for. **to pass muster** MUSTER. **to pass off 1** to disappear gradually. **2** to proceed in a specified manner (*to pass off without a hitch*). **3** to circulate as genuine, to palm off. **to pass one's eye over** to skim over, to read quickly. **to pass out 1** to faint. **2** (of an officer cadet) to complete training at a military academy. **3** to hand out, to distribute. **to pass over 1** to go across. **2** to allow to go by without notice, to overlook. **3** to omit. **4** to die. **to pass round** to hand round, to distribute. **to pass round the hat** HAT. **to pass the hat (round)** HAT. **to pass the time of day** to exchange greetings. **to pass through** to undergo, to experience. **to pass up** (*coll.*) to renounce. **to pass water** to urinate. **to sell the pass** to betray a cause. **passable** *a.* **1** acceptable, tolerable, fairly good. **2** able to be passed. **passableness** *n.* **passably** *adv.* **passband** *n.* a frequency band in which there is very little attenuation. **passbook** *n.* **1** a book in which a record is kept of transactions relating to a building society or bank account. **2** a book that passes between a tradesman and a customer, in which purchases on credit are entered. **pass degree** *n.* a university degree without honours. **passed pawn** *n.* in chess, a pawn with no opposing pawn restricting its ability to queen. **passer** *n.* **passer-by** *n.* (*pl.* **passers-by**) a person who passes by or near, esp. casually. **pass-key** *n.* **1** a key for passing in when a gate etc. is locked. **2** a master key. **pass laws** *n.pl.* (*Hist.*) in South Africa, laws restricting black Africans' freedom of movement. **pass-mark** *n.* the lowest mark required to pass an examination. **pass-out** *n.* a ticket conferring permission to leave temporarily. **password** *n.* **1** (*Comput.*) a string of characters by which a particular user can gain access to a system. **2** a word by which to distinguish friends from strangers, a watchword. [F *passer*, from L *passus*, PACE[1]]

Usage note The past tense and participle *passed* should not be spelt *past* like the noun, adjective, preposition etc. See also note on *passable* under PASSIBLE.

pass. *abbr.* passive.

passacaglia (pasəkah´liə) *n.* (*Mus.*) an instrumental piece with a ground bass. [It., from Sp. *pasacalle*, from *pasar*, to pass, *calle*, a street]

†**passade** (pasād´) *n.* in dressage, a turn or course of a horse backwards or forwards on the same spot. [F, from Prov. *passada* or It. *passata*, p.p. of *passare*, to PASS]

passage[1] (pas´ij) *n.* **1** the act of passing. **2** movement from one place to another, transit, migration. **3** transition from one state to another. **4** a journey, a voyage, a crossing. **5** a way by which one passes, a way of entrance or exit. **6** a corridor or gallery giving admission to different rooms in a building. **7** right or liberty of passing. **8** a separate portion of a book, piece of music etc. **9** the passing of a bill etc. into law. **10** (*pl.*) events etc. that pass between people, incidents, episodes. **11** (*Anat.*) a duct in the body. **bird of passage** BIRD. **to work one's passage 1** to work as a sailor etc., receiving a free passage in lieu of wages. **2** to work one's way without help from influence etc. **passage of arms, passage at arms** *n.* **1** a fight. **2** a contest or encounter. **passageway** *n.* a corridor. [F, from *passer*, to PASS]

passage[2] (pas´ij) *v.i.* in dressage, to move sideways with diagonal pairs of legs lifted alternately. ~*v.t.* to make (a horse) passage. [F, *passager*, earlier *passéger*, via It. *passeggiare*, to walk, from L *passus*, PACE[1]]

passant (pas´ənt) *a.* (*Her.*) walking and looking towards the dexter side with the dexter forepaw raised. [F, pres.p. of *passer*, to PASS]

passé (pas´ā) *a.* **1** old-fashioned, behind the times. **2** †past one's prime, faded. [F, p.p. of *passer*, to PASS]

passementerie (pas´məntri) *n.* a trimming for dresses, esp. of gold and silver lace. [F, from *passement*, gold or silver lace]

passenger (pas´injə) *n.* **1** a person who travels on a public conveyance. **2** (*coll.*) a person, esp. a member of a team who benefits from something without contributing to it. ~*a.* of or relating to passengers. **passenger-mile** *n.* a unit of traffic equal to one mile travelled by one passenger. **passenger pigeon** *n.* an extinct N American migratory pigeon. [ME and OF *passager*]

passepartout (paspah´too) *n.* **1** a master key. **2** a simple frame for a picture, photograph etc. **3** the sticky tape or paper used for such a frame. [F, pass everywhere]

passepied (paspyā´) *n.* a Breton dance resembling a minuet, popular in the 17th cent. [F, from *passer*, to pass, *pied*, a foot]

passerine (pas´ərīn) *a.* **1** of or relating to the order Passeriformes, which contains the great mass of the smaller perching birds, such as sparrows. **2** like a sparrow, esp. in size. ~*n.* a passerine bird. [L *passer*, a sparrow]

passible (pas´ibəl) *a.* (*Theol.*) capable of feeling or suffering, susceptible to impressions from external agents. **passibility** (-bil´-) *n.* [OF, from late L *passibilis*, from *patī*, to suffer]

Usage note The adjectives *passible* and *passable* should not be confused: *passible* means capable of feeling or suffering, and *passable* able to be passed or acceptable.

passiflora (pasiflaw´rə) *n.* (*pl.* **passifloras**) any plant of the genus *Passiflora*, containing the passion flower. [L *passi-*, *passio*, PASSION, *-florus*, flowering]

passim (pas´im) *adv.* here and there, throughout (indicating the occurrence of a word, allusion etc. in a cited work). [L, from *passus*, p.p. of *pandere*, to scatter]

passimeter (pasim´itə) *n.* an automatic ticket-issuing machine.

passing (pah´sing) *a.* **1** going by, occurring. **2** incidental, casual, cursory. **3** transient, fleeting. ~*n.* **1** the act of passing. **2** passage, transit, lapse. **3** (*euphem.*) death. **in passing** casually, without making direct reference. **passing bell** *n.* a bell tolled at the hour of a person's death to invite prayers on their behalf. **passingly** *adv.* **passing note** *n.* (*Mus.*) a note forming a transition between two others, but not an essential part of the harmony. **passing shot** *n.* in tennis, a stroke that wins the point by passing an opponent beyond their reach.

passion (pash´ən) *n.* **1** intense emotion, a deep and overpowering affection of the mind, such as grief, anger, hatred etc. **2** an outburst of violent anger. **3** strong sexual love. **4 a** zeal, ardent enthusiasm (for). **b** the object of this. **5** (*also* **Passion**) **a** the last agonies of Christ. **b** an artistic representation of this. **c** a musical setting of the Gospel narrative of the Passion. ~*v.i.* (*poet.*) to be affected with passion. **passional, passionary** *a.* of or relating to passion. ~*n.* (*pl.* **passionals, passionaries**) a book describing the sufferings of saints and martyrs. **passionate** (-nət) *a.* easily moved to strong feeling, esp. love or anger; excited, vehement, warm, intense. **passionately** *adv.* **passionateness** *n.* **passioned** *a.* impassioned. **passion flower** *n.* any plant of the genus *Passiflora*, chiefly consisting of climbers, with flowers bearing a fancied resemblance to the instruments of the Passion. **passion fruit** *n.* the edible fruit of a passion flower, a grenadilla. **Passionist** *n.* a member of a religious order in the Roman Catholic Church devoted to the commemoration of Christ's passion. **passionless** *a.* **passionlessly** *adv.* **passionlessness** *n.* **passion play** *n.* a mystery play representing the Passion. **Passion Sunday** *n.* the fifth Sunday in Lent. **Passiontide** *n.* the last two weeks of Lent. **Passion Week** *n.* **1** the week following Passion Sunday. **2** Holy Week. [OF, from L *passiōnem*, nom. *-sio*, from *patī*, to suffer]

passive (pas´iv) *a.* **1** suffering, acted upon, not acting. **2** (*Gram.*) (of a verb form) expressing an action done to the subject of a sentence. **3** (esp. of a metal) not chemically reactive. **4** inactive, inert, submissive, not opposing. **5** (of a debt) yielding no interest. ~*n.* (*Gram.*) the passive voice of a verb. **passivate** *v.t.* to make passive. **passivation** (-ā´shən) *n.* **passively** *adv.* **passiveness** *n.* **passive obedience** *n.* submissiveness, unquestioning obedience. **passive resistance** *n.* inert resistance, without active opposition. **passive resister** *n.* **passive smoking** *n.* the inhalation of others' cigarette smoke by non-smokers. **passive vocabulary** *n.* all the words that a person understands. **passive voice** *n.* the form of a transitive verb representing the subject as the object of the action. **passivity** (-siv´-) *n.* [L *passīvus*, as PASSION]

Passover (pah´sōvə) *n.* **1** a Jewish feast, on the 14th day of the month Nisan, commemorating the destruction of the first-born of the Egyptians and the 'passing over' of the Israelites by the destroying angel (Exodus xii). **2** Jesus Christ, the paschal lamb.

passport (pahs´pawt) *n.* **1** an official document authorizing a person to travel in a foreign country and entitling them to legal protection. **2** anything ensuring admission (*a passport to high society*). [F *passe-port*]

past (pahst) *a.* **1** gone by, neither present nor future. **2** just elapsed. **3** (*Gram.*) denoting an action or state belonging to the past. **4** former. ~*n.* **1** past times. **2** one's past career or the history of this, esp. a disreputable one. **3** the past tense of a verb. ~*prep.* **1** beyond in time or place. **2** beyond the influence or range of. **3** more than. ~*adv.* so as to go by. **not to put it past someone to do something** not to be surprised if someone does something (*I wouldn't put it past him to lie about his age*). **past it** (*coll.*) no longer young and vigorous. **past question** QUESTION. **past definite** *n.* in French grammar, the tense corresponding to the Greek aorist and the English past. **past master** *n.* **1** a thorough master (of a subject etc.). **2** a person who has been master of a Freemasons' lodge, a guild etc. **past participle** *n.* (*Gram.*) a participle derived from the past tense of a verb, with a past or passive meaning. **past participial** *a.* **past perfect** *n.* PLUPERFECT. [p.p. of PASS]

pasta (pas´tə) *n.* **1** a flour and water dough, often shaped and eaten fresh or in processed form, e.g. spaghetti. **2** a dish made with this dough. **3** a particular type or shape of this dough. [It., paste]

paste (pāst) *n.* **1** a mixture of flour and water, usu. with butter, lard etc., kneaded and used for making pastry etc. **2** a sweet of similar consistency. **3** a spread made of ground meat or fish. **4** an adhesive compound of flour, water, starch etc. boiled. **5** any doughy or plastic mixture, esp. of solid substances with liquid. **6** a vitreous composition used for making imitations of gems. **7** a mixture of clay, water etc. used to make ceramics. ~*v.t.* **1** to fasten or stick with paste. **2** (*sl.*) to thrash, to beat. **3** to bomb heavily. **pasteboard** *n.* **1** a board made of sheets of paper pasted together or of compressed paper pulp. **2** a card, such as a visiting card, railway ticket or playing card. ~*a.* **1** made of pasteboard. **2** thin, flimsy. **3** sham. **paste-up** *n.* a sheet of paper with proofs, drawings etc. pasted on to it prior to being photographed for a printing process. **pasting** *n.* (*coll.*) a thrashing, a beating. [OF (F *pâte*), Prov., It. and Sp. *pasta*, perh. from Gr. *pastē*, fem. of *pastos*, sprinkled]

pastel (pas´təl) *n.* **1** a dry paste composed of a pigment mixed with gum water. **2** a coloured crayon made from this. **3** a picture drawn with such crayons. **4** the art of drawing with these. **5** a pale, subdued colour. **6** woad. ~*a.* of a pastel colour. **pastelist, pastellist** *n.* [F, from It. *pastello*, dim. of *pasta*, PASTE]

pastern (pas´tən) *n.* the part of a horse's leg between the fetlock and the hoof. [OF *pasturon* (F *paturon*), from *pasture*, a shackle, prob. ident. with PASTURE]

pasteurism (pas´tərizm) *n.* a method of preventing or curing certain diseases, esp. hydrophobia, by progressive inoculation. **pasteurize** (-chərīz), **pasteurise** *v.t.* **pasteurization** (-zā´shən) *n.* **pasteurized milk** *n.* milk subjected to treatment by heat in order to destroy the organisms which may be present. **pasteurizer** *n.* [Louis *Pasteur*, 1822–95, French chemist and biologist]

pastiche (pastēsh´), **pasticcio** (-tich´ō) *n.* (*pl.* **pastiches, pasticcios**) a medley, musical work, painting etc. composed of elements drawn from other works or which imitates the style of a previous work. [F *pastiche*, It. *pasticcio*, from *pasta*, PASTE]

pastille (pas´təl) *n.* **1** an aromatic lozenge. **2** a roll, cone or pellet of aromatic paste for burning as a fumigator or disinfectant. **pastille-burner** *n.* a decorative ceramic container for burning aromatic pastilles in. [F, from L *pastillum*, nom. *-lus*, etym. uncertain]

pastily PASTY[1].

pastime (pahs´tīm) *n.* something that makes time pass agreeably, a game, a recreation, sport, diversion. [PASS, TIME]

pastiness PASTY[1].

pasting PASTE.

pastis (pas´tis, pastēs´) *n.* (*pl.* **pastis**) an aniseed-flavoured alcoholic drink. [F]

pastor (pahs´tə) *n.* **1** a minister in charge of a church and congregation. **2** a person acting as a spiritual guide. **3** a pink starling, *Sturnus roseus*, of Europe and Asia. **pastorate** (-rət) *n.* **pastorship** *n.* [ME and OF *pastour*, OF *pastor*, L *pastōrem*, nom. *-or*, from *pascere*, to feed]

pastoral (pahs´tərəl) *a.* **1** of or relating to shepherds. **2** (of land) used for pasture. **3** (of poetry etc.) portraying country life, rural, rustic. **4** of or relating to the cure of souls or the duties of a pastor. **5** befitting a pastor. **6** of or relating to the personal needs, as distinct from the educational needs, of school pupils. ~*n.* **1** a pastoral poem, play, picture etc. **2** a letter or address from a pastor, esp. from a bishop to his diocese. **3** (*Mus.*) a pastorale. **pastoralist** *n.* (*Austral.*) a sheep or cattle farmer, as distinct from an agriculturalist. **pastoralism** *n.* **pastorality** (-ral´-) *n.* **pastorally** *adv.* **pastoral staff** *n.* a bishop's crosier. **pastoral theology** *n.* theology dealing with religion as it relates to spiritual needs.

pastorale (pastərahl´, -rah´li) *n.* (*pl.* **pastorales** (-ahlz´), **pastorali** (-ah´li)) **1** a simple rustic melody. **2** a cantata on a pastoral theme. **3** a symphony dealing with a pastoral subject. [It.]

pastrami (pastrah´mi) *n.* a highly seasoned smoked beef. [Yiddish, from Romanian *pastramă*, from *păstra*, to serve]

pastry (pās´tri) *n.* (*pl.* **pastries**) **1** a dough of flour, fat and water, used baked to make pies. **2** articles of food made with a crust of such dough, baked. **3** an item of pastry, a cake. **pastry-cook** *n.*

pasture (pahs´chə) *n.* **1** ground suitable for the grazing of cattle etc., grass for grazing. **2** the act of putting cattle etc. out to pasture. ~*v.t.* **1** to put (cattle etc.) on land to graze. **2** (of sheep etc.) to eat down (grassland), to feed by grazing. ~*v.i.* to graze. **pasturable** *a.* **pasturage** (-ij) *n.* **pastureland** *n.* **pastureless** *a.* [F *pâture*, from late L *pastūra*, as PASTOR]

pasty[1] (pās´ti) *a.* (*comp.* **pastier**, *superl.* **pastiest**) **1** of or like paste. **2** pale, unhealthy-looking. **pastily** *adv.* **pastiness** *n.* **pasty-faced** *a.* having a pale, dull complexion.

pasty[2] (pas´ti) *n.* (*pl.* **pasties**) a small pie, usu. of meat, baked without a dish. [ME and OF *pastee* (F *pâte*), from *pasta*, PASTE]

Pat (pat) *n.* (*sl., often offensive*) an Irishman. **on one's pat** (*Austral.*) on one's own, all alone (from rhyming sl. *Pat Malone*). [short for *Patrick*]

pat (pat) *v.t.* (*pres.p.* **patting**, *past, p.p.* **patted**) **1** to strike gently and quickly with something flat, esp. the fingers or hand. **2** to pat into a shape, esp. a flattened shape. **3** to tap, to stroke gently. ~*v.i.* **1** to strike gently. **2** to run with light steps. ~*n.* **1** a light, quick blow with the hand; a tap, a stroke. **2** the sound of a light blow with something flat. **3** a small mass or lump (of butter etc.) moulded by patting. ~*a.* **1** facile. **2** exactly suitable or fitting, opportune, apposite, apt. ~*adv.* **1** facilely. **2** aptly, opportunely. **to have down pat** to have off pat. **to have off pat** to have learned or prepared thoroughly. **to pat someone on the back** to praise or congratulate someone. **to stand pat 1** (*esp. N Am.*) to stand by one's decision or beliefs. **2** in poker, to play with the hand one has been dealt, without drawing other cards. **pat-a-cake** *n.* a child's game in which two people clap hands with each other whilst reciting a rhyme. **patball** *n.* **1** a game in which two players hit a ball back and forth between them. **2** (*derog.*) slow-paced tennis. **patly** *adv.* **patness** *n.* **pat on the back** *n.* a demonstration of approval. [prob. onomat.]

pat. *abbr.* patent(ed).

pataca (pətah´kə) *n.* (*pl.* **patacas**) the standard unit of currency of Macao. [Port.]

patagium (pətajī´əm) *n.* (*pl.* **patagia** (-jī´ə)) (*Zool.*) **1** the wing membrane of a bat, flying lemur etc. **2** a scale on the wing joint of a moth or butterfly. [L, from Gr. *patageion*, a gold border]

patch (pach) *n.* **1** a piece of cloth, metal or other material put on to mend anything. **2** a piece put on to strengthen a fabric etc. **3** a piece of cloth worn over an injured eye. **4** a dressing covering a wound etc. **5** a small piece of black silk worn (esp. in the 17th and 18th cents.) for decoration. **6** (*Mil.*) a piece of cloth worn on the shoulder of a uniform to identify the unit. **7** a differently coloured part of a surface. **8** a small piece of ground, a plot. **9** (*coll.*) the district for which a police officer, social worker etc. has responsibility. **10** a number of plants growing together. **11** a scrap, a shred. **12** a temporary electrical connection. **13** (*Comput.*) a small piece of code used to correct or improve instructions. *~v.t.* **1** to put a patch or patches on. **2** to mend with a patch or patches (usu. with *up*). **3** to mend clumsily. **4** to make with or as if with shreds or patches. **5** to put together or arrange hastily. **6** to connect by a temporary connection. **7** (*Comput.*) to correct or improve by means of a patch. **8** to serve as a patch for. *~v.i.* to be connected by a temporary connection. **not a patch on** (*coll.*) not nearly as good as. **to patch up** to mend. **to patch up a quarrel** to be reconciled, esp. temporarily. **patchboard** *n.* a board with a number of electrical sockets used for making temporary circuits. **patch cord** *n.* an insulated lead with a plug at each end, used with a patchboard. **patcher** *n.* **patch panel** *n.* a patchboard. **patch pocket** *n.* a pocket consisting of a flat piece of cloth sewn on to the outside of a garment. **patch test** *n.* an allergy test in which patches containing different allergenic substances are applied to the skin. **patchwork** *n.* **1** work composed of pieces of different colours, sizes etc., sewn together. **2** something composed of a variety of parts. **3** clumsy work. *~a.* **1** made of patchwork. **2** resembling patchwork. **3** cobbled together. **patchy** *a.* (*comp.* **patchier,** *superl.* **patchiest**) **1** of inconsistent quality, frequency etc. **2** appearing in patches. **3** covered with patches. **patchily** *adv.* **patchiness** *n.* [etym. uncertain]

patchouli (pach´uli, pəchoo´-) *n.* **1** an Indian shrub of the genus *Pogostemon*, yielding a fragrant oil. **2** a perfume prepared from this. [Tamil *pacculi*]

pate (pāt) *n.* (*facet.*) the head, esp. the top of the head. **pated** *a.* [etym. uncertain]

pâte (paht) *n.* the paste from which porcelain is made. [F, PASTE]

pâté (pat´ā) *n.* **1** a spread made of cooked, diced meat, fish or vegetables blended with herbs etc. **2** a pie, a patty. **pâté de foie gras** (də fwah grah´) *n.* pâté made of fatted goose liver. [F]

patella (pətel´ə) *n.* (*pl.* **patellae** (-lē)) **1** the kneecap. **2** a small dish or pan. **patellar, patellate** (-lət), **patelliform** (-ifawm) *a.* [L, dim. of *patina*, a PATEN]

paten (pat´ən) *n.* **1** a plate or shallow dish for receiving the Eucharistic bread. **2** a circular metal plate. [OF *patene*, L *patena, patina*]

patent (pā´tənt, pat´-) *n.* **1** a grant from the Crown by letters patent of a title of nobility, or from the Crown or a government of the exclusive right to make or sell a new invention. **2** an invention so protected. **3** anything serving as a sign or certificate (of quality etc.). *~a.* **1** plain, obvious, manifest. **2** protected or conferred by letters patent. **3** made under a patent, proprietary. **4** ingenious. **5** permitting free passage. **6** open to the perusal of all. **7** (*Biol.*) expanded, spreading. *~v.t.* to secure by patent. **letters patent** LETTER. **patency** (-si) *n.* **patentable** *a.* **patentee** (-tē´) *n.* a person granted a right or privilege by patent. **patent leather** *n.* a leather with a shiny or varnished surface. **patently** *adv.* **patent medicine** *n.* a medicine sold under a licence with a registered name and trade mark. **patent office** *n.* a government department responsible for granting patents. **Patent Roll** *n.* the register of patents granted by the Crown in a year. **patent still** *n.* a still in which distillation can be carried on continuously, as distinct from a *pot still*. [OF, from L *patentem*, nom. *-tens*, pres.p. of *patēre*, to lie open]

pater (pā´tə) *n.* (*sl., usu. facet.*) a father. [L]

patera (pat´ərə) *n.* (*pl.* **paterae** (-rē)) **1** a round dish used for wine in ancient Rome. **2** a flat, round ornament on a frieze or in bas-reliefs. [L, from *patēre*, to be open]

paterfamilias (patəfəmil´ias, pā-) *n.* (*pl.* **patresfamilias** (pahtrāz-)) the father of a family, the male head of a household. [L]

paternal (pətœ´nəl) *a.* **1** of or relating to a father. **2** fatherly. **3** connected or related through the father. **4** (of a government) restricting freedom and responsibility through overprotectiveness. **paternalism** *n.* the exercise of benign, overprotective authority, esp. in a form of government, often seen as interference with individual rights. **paternalist** *n.* **paternalistic** (-lis´-) *a.* **paternalistically** *adv.* **paternally** *adv.* **paternity** *n.* **1** fatherhood. **2** ancestry or origin on the male side, descent from a father. **3** authorship, source. **paternity leave** *n.* paid leave granted to a man when his wife has a baby. **paternity suit** *n.* a lawsuit held to establish whether a particular man is the father of a particular child. **paternity test** *n.* a blood test used to establish whether a particular man may be or cannot be the father of a particular child. [F *paternel*, late L *paternālis*, from *paternus*, fatherly, from PATER]

paternoster (patənos´tə) *n.* **1** the Lord's Prayer, esp. in Latin. **2** every 11th bead of a rosary, indicating that the Lord's Prayer is to be said. **3** a rosary. **4** a type of lift with compartments attached to a continuous, circular belt. **5** a fishing line with a weight at the end and short lines with hooks extending at intervals. [L, our Father]

path (pahth) *n.* (*pl.* **paths**) **1** a footway, esp. one beaten only by feet. **2** a course or track. **3** a course of life, action etc. **4** a sequence of operations taken by a system. **pathfinder** *n.* **1** an explorer or pioneer. **2** a radar device used for navigational purposes or for targeting missiles. **pathless** *a.* **pathway** *n.* **1** a path. **2** a sequence of reactions in a living organism. [OE *pæth* (cp. Dut. *pad*, G *Pfad*)]

-path (path) *comb. form* **1** a medical practitioner, as in *homoeopath*. **2** a person suffering from a pathological disorder, as in *psychopath*. **-pathy** (pəthi) *comb. form* **1** disease, treatment of this, as in *homoeopathy*. **2** suffering, feeling, as in *sympathy*. [Gr. *-patheia*, PATHOS, suffering]

Pathan (pətahn´) *n.* a member of a people of NW Pakistan and SE Afghanistan. [Hind.]

pathetic (pəthet´ik) *a.* **1** affecting or moving the feelings, esp. those of pity and sorrow. **2** (*coll.*) poor, weak or contemptible. **3** †passionate. *~n.* something pathetic. **pathetically** *adv.* **pathetic fallacy** *n.* in literature, the attribution of human feelings to objects associated with nature such as trees. [late L *pathēticus*, Gr. *pathētikos*, from PATHOS]

pathic (path´ik) *n.* a catamite. [Gr. *pathikos*, passive]

patho- (path´ō), **path-** *comb. form* disease. [Gr. *pathos*, suffering]

pathogen (path´əjən) *n.* any disease-producing substance or micro-organism. **pathogenic** (-jen´-) *a.* **pathogenicity** (-is´-) *n.* **pathogenous** (-thoj´-) *a.*

pathogenesis (pathəjen´əsis) *n.* the origin and development of disease. **pathogenetic** (-net´-) *a.* **pathogeny** (-thoj´-) *n.*

pathognomy (pəthog´nəmi) *n.* **1** expression of the passions. **2** the science of their signs.

pathology (pəthol´əji) *n.* **1** the science of diseases, esp. of the human body. **2** the changes which characterize disease. **pathologic** (pathəloj´-), **pathological** *a.* **1** of or relating to pathology. **2** caused by or involving disease. **3** (*coll.*) driven or motivated by compulsion rather than reason. **pathologically** *adv.* **pathologist** *n.*

pathophobia (pathəfō´biə) *n.* a morbid fear of disease.

pathos (pā´thos) *n.* a quality or element in events or expression that excites emotion, esp. pity or sorrow. [Gr., suffering, from *path-*, root of *paschein*, to suffer]

-pathy -PATH.

patience (pā´shəns) *n.* **1** the quality of being patient. **2** calm endurance of pain, provocation or other evils; fortitude. **3** a card game played by one person. **to have no patience with 1** to be unable to stand or put up with. **2** to be irritated by. [OF, from L *patientia*, from *patī*, to suffer]

patient (pā´shənt) *a.* **1** capable of bearing pain, suffering etc. without fretfulness. **2** not easily provoked, indulgent. **3** persevering, diligent. *~n.* **1** a person under medical treatment. **2** †a person who suffers. **patiently** *adv.*

patina (pat´inə) *n.* (*pl.* **patinas**) **1** the green incrustation that covers ancient bronzes. **2** a similar film on any surface. **3** a soft shine produced by age on woodwork. **patinated** (-nātid) *a.* **patination** (-ā´shən) *n.* [L *patina*, *patena*, a shallow dish, or F *patine*, perh. from this]

patio (pat´iō) *n.* (*pl.* **patios**) **1** a paved area beside a house, used for outdoor meals, sunbathing etc. **2** the open inner court of a Spanish or Spanish-American house. **patio rose** *n.* a miniature floribunda rose. [Sp.]

patisserie (pətē´səri) *n.* **1** a pastry-cook's shop. **2** pastries collectively. [F]

Patna rice (pat´nə) *n.* a variety of long-grain rice used for savoury dishes. [*Patna*, a city in NE India]

patois (pat´wah) *n.* (*pl.* **patois** (-wahz)) a non-standard dialect of a district. [F, etym. uncertain]

patonce (pətons´) *a.* (*Her.*) denoting a cross the four arms of which expand in curves from the centre and have floriated ends. [etym. uncertain]

patresfamilias PATERFAMILIAS.

patri- (pat´ri) *comb. form* father. [L *pater*, a father]

patrial (pā´triəl) *a.* (*Hist.*) legally entitled to reside in the UK. *~n.* a person legally entitled to reside in the UK. **patriality** (-al´-) *n.*

patriarch (pā´triahk) *n.* **1** the head of a family or tribe, ruling by paternal right. **2** (*Bible*) any of the founding fathers Abraham, Isaac and Jacob, their forefathers, and the sons of Jacob. **3** in the Eastern and early Churches, a bishop, esp. of Alexandria, Antioch, Constantinople, Jerusalem and some other sees. **4** the highest grade in the hierarchy of the Roman Catholic Church. **5** the founder of a religion, science etc. **6** a venerable old man. **7** the oldest living person in a group. **patriarchal** (-ah´kəl) *a.* **patriarchally** *adv.* **patriarchate** (-kət) *n.* †**patriarchical** (-ah´ki-) *a.* **patriarchism** *n.* **patriarchy** *n.* (*pl.* **patriarchies**) a patriarchal system of government or social organization, esp. as distinct from *matriarchy*. [OF *patriarche*, L *patriarcha*, Gr. *patriarchēs* (*patria*, family, *archein*, to rule)]

patrician (pətrish´ən) *n.* **1** a member of the Roman aristocracy. **2** a member of ancient or later orders established by the Western and the Byzantine emperors, esp. a chief magistrate of a Roman province in Italy or Africa. **3** a noble, an aristocrat, a member of the highest class of society. **4** (*N Am.*) a refined or sophisticated person. *~a.* **1** noble, aristocratic. **2** (*Hist.*) in ancient Rome, senatorial, not plebeian. **3** (*N Am.*) refined, sophisticated. **patriciate** (-ət) *n.* [L *patricius*, from *pater*, a father, *patrēs*, senators, nobles]

patricide (pat´risīd) *n.* **1** (the act of) killing one's father. **2** a person who commits patricide. **patricidal** (-sī´-) *a.*

Usage note See note under PARRICIDE.

patrilineal (patrilin´iəl) *a.* by descent through the father.

patrimony (pat´riməni) *n.* (*pl.* **patrimonies**) **1** an estate or right inherited from one's father or ancestors. **2** a heritage. **3** a church estate or endowment. **patrimonial** (-mō´-) *a.* **patrimonially** *adv.* [F *patrimoine*, L *patrimōnium*]

patriot (pat´riət, pā´triət) *n.* a person who loves their country and is devoted to its interests, esp. its freedom and independence. **patriotic** (-ot´ik) *a.* **patriotically** *adv.* **patriotism** *n.* [F *patriote*, late L *patriōta*, Gr. *patriōtēs*, from *patrios*, of one's fathers, from *patēr -tros*, a father]

patristic (pətris´tik), **patristical** (-kəl) *a.* of or relating to the ancient Fathers of the Christian Church or their writings. **patristics** *n.* the study of patristic writings. [F *patristique* (L *patri-*, *pater*, a father)]

patrol (pətrōl´) *n.* **1** the action of moving around an area, esp. at night, for the maintenance of order and for security. **2** the detachment of soldiers, police, firemen etc., or the soldier, officer etc., doing this. **3** a detachment of troops, sent out to reconnoitre. **4** such reconnaissance. **5** a routine operational voyage or flight. **6** a monitoring of phenomena. **7** a person who controls traffic so that children may cross the road safely. **8** a group of six to eight Scouts or Guides. *~v.i.* (*pres.p.* **patrolling,** *past, p.p.* **patrolled**) to go on a patrol. *~v.t.* to go round. **patrol car** *n.* a car in which police officers patrol an area. **patrolman** *n.* (*pl.* **patrolmen**) (*N Am.*) a low-ranking police officer. **patrol wagon** *n.* (*N Am.*) a police van for the transportation of prisoners. [F *patrouiller*, *patouiller*, to dabble in the mud (cp. OF *patouil*, a pool)]

patrology (pətrol´əji) *n.* (*pl.* **patrologies**) **1** patristics. **2** a collection of patristic writings.

patron (pā´trən) *n.* **1** a person who supports, fosters or protects a person, cause, art etc. **2** (*coll.*) a regular customer (at a shop etc.). **3** in ancient Rome, the former owner of a freed slave. **4** in ancient Rome, a guardian or protector of a client. **5** in ancient Rome, an advocate or defender in a court of law. **6** a patron saint. **7** a person who holds the gift of a benefice. **patronage** (pat´rənij) *n.* **1** support, fostering, encouragement or protection. **2** the right of presentation to a benefice or office. **3** the act of patronizing. **4** in ancient Rome, the rights, duties or position of a patron. **5** support by customers (of a shop etc.). **patronal** (pətrō´-) *a.* **patroness** *n.* a female patron. **patronize** (pat´rənīz), **patronise** *v.t.* **1** to treat in a condescending way. **2** to act as a patron towards. **3** to frequent as a customer. **patronization** (-zā´shən) *n.* **patronizer** *n.* **patronizing** *a.* **patronizingly** *adv.* **patron saint** *n.* a saint regarded as the patron of a particular group, country etc. [OF, from L *patrōnum*, nom. *-us*, from *pater patris*, father]

patronymic (patrənim´ik) *n.* a name derived from a father or ancestor; a family name. *~a.* (of a name) derived from a father or ancestor. [L *patrōnymīcus*, Gr. *patrōnumikos*, from *patrōnumos* (*onoma*, Aeolic *onuma*, a name)]

patroon (pətroon´) *n.* (*N Am.*) a proprietor of land with manorial privileges and right of entail under a Dutch grant, esp. in New York and New Jersey (abolished 1850). [var. of PATRON]

patsy (pat´si) *n.* (*pl.* **patsies**) (*N Am., sl.*) a person who is easily deceived, cheated etc., a sucker, a scapegoat. [etym. unknown]

pattée (pat´ā) *a.* (of a cross) having almost triangular arms widening outwards. [F, from *patte*, a paw]

patten (pat´ən) *n.* **1** (*Hist.*) a clog or overshoe mounted on an iron ring etc., for keeping the shoes out of the mud or wet. **2** (*Archit.*) the base of a column. [F *patin*, perh. from OF *patte*, a paw]

patter[1] (pat´ə) *v.i.* **1** (of rain) to fall with a quick succession of light, sharp sounds. **2** to move with short, quick steps. *~v.t.* to cause (water etc.) to patter. *~n.* a quick succession of sharp, light sounds or taps. [freq. of PAT]

patter[2] (pat´ə) *n.* **1** rapid speech introduced impromptu into a song, comedy etc. **2** glib talk, chattering, gossip. **3** the patois or slangy lingo of a particular class or group. *~v.t.* to say (one's prayers) in a mechanical, singsong way. ~*v.i.* **1** to talk glibly. **2** to pray in this manner. [ME *pateren*, from PATERNOSTER]

pattern (pat´ən) *n.* **1** a decorative design for a carpet, wallpaper, fabric etc. **2** a type, style. **3** a model or original to be copied or serving as a guide in making something. **4** a model, an exemplar. **5** a shape used to make a mould into which molten metal is poured to make a casting. **6** a sample or specimen (of cloth etc.). **7** the marks made by shot on a target. ~*v.t.* **1** to copy, to model (after, from or upon). **2** to decorate with a pattern. **pattern bombing** *n.* bombing over a wide area. **pattern-maker** *n.* a maker of patterns for the moulders in a foundry. **pattern-shop** *n.* a room or shop in a foundry etc., where patterns are made. [ME *patron*, as PATRON]

pattle (pat´əl) *n.* (*Sc.*) an implement used for cleaning the earth from a ploughshare.

patty (pat´i) *n.* (*pl.* **patties**) **1** a little pie. **2** a small, flat cake of minced food. **3** (*N Am.*) a small, round sweet. **pattypan** *n.* a pan for baking patties. [F PÂTÉ]

patulous (pat´ūləs) *a.* **1** (*Bot.*) (of boughs etc.) spreading, expanding. **2** (*formal*) open, having a wide aperture. **patulously** *adv.* **patulousness** *n.* [L *patulus*, cogn. with *patēre*, to be open]

patzer (paht´sə) *n.* a poor chess player. [perh. rel. to G *patzen*, to bungle]

paua (pah´wə, pow´ə) *n.* (*pl.* **pauas**) **1** a large New Zealand shellfish of the genus *Haliotis*. **2** the iridescent shell of the paua. **3** a fish-hook made from paua. [Maori]

paucity (paw´siti) *n.* an insufficient amount; scarcity. [F *paucité*, L *paucitātem*, nom. *-tas*, from *paucus*, few]

Pauli exclusion principle (pow´li) *n.* a law of quantum mechanics stating that two fermions cannot exist in identical states in the same atom. [W. *Pauli*, 1900–58, Austrian-born physicist]

Pauline (paw´līn) *a.* of or relating to St Paul or his writings. ~*n.* a scholar of St Paul's School, London. **Paulinism** *n.* the theological doctrine taught by or ascribed to the apostle Paul.

Paul Jones (pawl jōnz´) *n.* a ballroom dance in which partners are exchanged several times. [American naval officer, d. 1792]

paulo-post-future (pawlōpōstfū´chə) *n.* the future-perfect tense in classical Greek. [L *paulo post futurum*, future after a little]

paulownia (pawlō´niə) *n.* any Chinese tree of the genus *Paulownia*, having purple flowers. [Anna *Paulovna*, d.1865, Russian princess]

paunch (pawnch) *n.* **1** the belly, the abdomen. **2** a fat or protruding belly. **3** the first and largest stomach in ruminants. **4** (*Naut.*) a thick mat or wooden shield fastened on a mast etc., to prevent chafing. ~*v.t.* to rip open the belly of, to disembowel, to stab in the belly. **paunchy** *a.* (*comp.* **paunchier**, *superl.* **paunchiest**). **paunchiness** *n.* [ONF *panch*, L *panticem*, nom. *pantex*]

pauper (paw´pə) *n.* **1** a person without means of support, a destitute person, a beggar. **2** (*Hist.*) a person entitled to public assistance. **3** (*Law*) a person permitted to sue *in forma pauperis*. **pauperdom, pauperism** *n.* **pauperize, pauperise** *v.t.* **pauperization** (-zā´shən) *n.* [L, poor]

pause (pawz) *n.* **1** a cessation or intermission of action, speaking etc. **2** a break in reading, speaking, music etc., esp. for the sake of emphasis. **3** (*Mus.*) a mark (𝄐 or 𝄑) over a note etc., indicating that it is to be prolonged. **4** a control to interrupt the operation of a video recorder etc. **5** in prosody, a mark to denote a break or pause. ~*v.i.* **1** to make a pause or short stop; to wait. **2** to linger (upon or over). **to give someone pause** to cause someone to hesitate and reconsider. **pausingly** *adv.* [F, from L *pausa*, Gr. *pausis*, from *pauein*, to cease]

pavage PAVE.

pavane (pəvan´), **pavan** (pav´ən) *n.* **1** a slow and stately dance, usu. in elaborate dress, in vogue in the 16th and 17th cents. **2** music for this. [F *pavane*, It. or Sp. *pavana*, etym. uncertain]

pave (pāv) *v.t.* **1** to make a hard, level surface upon, with stone, bricks etc. **2** to cover with or as if with a pavement. **to pave the way for** to prepare for, to make possible. **pavage** (-ij) *n.* **1** paving. **2** (*Hist.*) a tax or toll to pay for paving streets. **pavement** *n.* **1** a paved footway at the side of a street or road. **2** a hard level covering, bricks, tiles, wooden blocks. **3** (*N Am.*) the paved surface of a road. **4** (*Zool.*) a close, level structure or formation (e.g. of teeth) resembling a pavement. **5** the material with which anything is paved. **pavement artist** *n.* a person drawing figures etc. on a pavement in the hope of being given money from passers-by. **paver** *n.* **paving** *n.* **paving stone** *n.* **paviour** (-yə), (*N Am.*) **pavior** *n.* **1** a person who lays pavements. **2** a machine for ramming paving stones. **3** a paving stone, block etc. [OF *paver*, L *pavīre*, to ram]

pavé (pav´ā) *n.* **1** a pavement. **2** a stone-paved road. **3** a setting of gems placed close together.

pavilion (pəvil´yən) *n.* **1** an ornamental building, usu. of light construction, for amusements etc., esp. one for spectators and players at a cricket ground etc. **2** a tent, esp. a large one, of conical shape. **3** a temporary or movable structure for entertainment, shelter etc. **4** one of the buildings which make up a hospital. **5** a belvedere, projecting turret or other portion of a building, usu. of ornamental design. **6** the part of a cut gemstone below the girdle. ~*v.t.* to furnish with or shelter in a pavilion. [F *pavillon*, L *pāpiliōnem*, nom. *-lio*, a butterfly]

paving, paviour PAVE.

pavlova (pavlō´və, pav´ləvə) *n.* a dessert consisting of a meringue base topped with fruit and whipped cream. [Anna *Pavlova*, 1885–1931, Russian ballerina]

Pavlovian (pavlō´viən) *a.* of or relating to conditioned reflexes. [I. P. *Pavlov*, 1849–1936, Russian physiologist who first described them]

pavonazzo (pavənat´sō) *n.* (*pl.* **pavonazzos**) a variety of marble with brilliant markings like the colours of a peacock. [It., from L *pāvōnāceum*, as PAVONINE]

pavonine (pav´ənīn) *a.* **1** of, relating to or resembling a peacock. **2** resembling the tail of a peacock, iridescent. **pavonian** (-vō´-) *a.* [L *pāvōnīnus*, from *pāvo -ōnis*, peacock]

paw (paw) *n.* **1** the foot of an animal having claws, as distinct from a hoof. **2** (*sl.*) one's hand. ~*v.t.* **1** to scrape or strike with the forefoot. **2** (*coll.*) to handle roughly, familiarly, sexually or clumsily. ~*v.i.* (of a horse) to strike the ground with a hoof. [OF *powe*, prob. from Frankish (cp. Dut. *poot*, G *Pfote*)]

pawky (paw´ki) *a.* (*comp.* **pawkier**, *superl.* **pawkiest**) (*chiefly Sc., North.*) **1** humorous, arch. **2** sly, shrewd. **pawkily** *adv.* **pawkiness** *n.* [obs. *pawk*, a trick]

pawl (pawl) *n.* **1** a hinged piece of metal or lever engaging with the teeth of a wheel etc., to prevent it from running back etc. **2** (*Naut.*) a bar for preventing the recoil of a windlass etc. ~*v.t.* to stop from recoiling with a pawl. [prob. from OF *paul* (F *pal*), L *pālum*, nom. *-lus*, stake, a PALE[2]]

pawn[1] (pawn) *n.* **1** a piece of the lowest value in chess. **2** an insignificant person used by a cleverer one for their advantage. [ME and A-F *poun*, OF *paon*, *peon* (F *pion*), med. L *pedōnem*, nom. *pedo*, a foot soldier, from *pes pedis*, a foot]

pawn[2] (pawn) *v.t.* **1** to deliver or deposit as a pledge for the repayment of a debt or loan, or the performance of a promise. **2** to stake, to wager, to risk. ~*n.* **1** something deposited as security for a debt or loan, a pledge. **2** the state of being held as a pledge. **at pawn** deposited as a pledge or security. **in pawn** at pawn. **pawnbroker** *n.* a person who lends money on the security of goods pawned. **pawnbroking** *n.* **pawnee** (-nē´) *n.* **pawner** *n.* **pawnshop** *n.* a place where goods can be pawned. [OF *pan*, prob. from Gmc. (cp. OFris. and Dut. *pand*, G *Pfand*)]

pawpaw (paw´paw), **papaw** (pəpaw´) *n.* 1 (*also* **papaya** (pəpī´ə)) a large, oblong, edible yellow fruit. 2 (*also* **papaya**) a tropical American tree, *Carica papaya*, which yields papain and bears the papaya fruit. 3 a N American tree, *Asimina triloba*, having purple flowers and edible fruit. [earlier *papay(a)*, from Sp. and Port. *papaya*, of Carib orig.]

PAX *abbr.* private automatic (telephone) exchange.

pax (paks) *n.* 1 the kiss of peace. 2 a tablet or plaque bearing a representation of the Crucifixion or other sacred subject which was formerly kissed by the priest and congregation at Mass; an osculatory. *~int.* (*sl.*) used to express a call for a truce (in children's games). **Pax Romana** (rōmah´nə) *n.* peace imposed by the Roman Empire. [L, PEACE]

paxwax (paks´waks) *n.* (*Anat.*) a strong, stiff tendon from the dorsal vertebrae to the occiput in many mammals and, in a modified form, in humans. [formerly *faxwax* (OE *feax*, hair, *weaxan*, to grow, to WAX[2])]

pay[1] (pā) *v.t.* (*past, p.p.* **paid** (pād)) 1 to hand over to (someone) what is due in discharge of a debt or for services or goods. 2 to discharge (a bill, claim, obligation etc.). 3 to deliver as due. 4 to deliver the amount, defray the cost or expense of. 5 to reward or punish. 6 to compensate, to recompense, to requite. 7 to be remunerative or worthwhile to. 8 to bestow, to tender (a compliment, visit etc.). *~v.i.* 1 to make payment. 2 to discharge a debt. 3 to make an adequate return (to). 4 to be remunerative or worthwhile. *~n.* 1 wages, salary. 2 payment, compensation, recompense. **he who pays the piper calls the tune** the person who finances a venture has the right to decide how it should be run. **in the pay of** employed by. **to pay a call** CALL. **to pay a compliment** COMPLIMENT[1]. **to pay away** to let (a rope) run out by slackening it. **to pay back** 1 to repay. 2 to take revenge on. 3 to return (a favour etc.). **to pay dearly for** 1 to pay with a lot of money or effort for. 2 to suffer as a result of. **to pay for** 1 to make a payment for. 2 to suffer as a result of. **to pay heed** to take notice. **to pay in** to deposit in a bank account. **to pay its way** to cover costs. **to pay off** 1 to make (an employee) redundant, with a final payment. 2 (*coll.*) to be profitable or rewarding. 3 to pay the full amount of, to pay in full and discharge. 4 (*Naut.*) to turn to leeward. **to pay off old scores** SCORE. **to pay one's dues** (*esp. N Am.*) 1 to fulfil one's obligations. 2 to achieve success after enduring a period of hardship. **to pay one's footing** FOOTING. **to pay one's last respects** RESPECT. **to pay one's respects** RESPECT. **to pay one's way** to keep out of debt. **to pay out** 1 to disburse. 2 to punish. 3 to cause (a rope) to run out. **to pay someone back in their own coin** COIN. **to pay through the nose** to pay an exorbitant price. **to pay up** to pay someone what is owed or due to them. **paid** *a.* **to put paid to** (*coll.*) to end, to destroy. **paid holidays** *n.pl.* holidays from work for which one is paid as normal. **paid-up member** *n.* 1 a member of a trade union etc. who has paid the full subscription. 2 (*coll.*) an enthusiastic or committed supporter of a cause or organization. **payable** *a.* 1 that can or must be paid. 2 profitable. *~n.* (*pl.*) debts owed by a business. **pay-as-you-earn** *n.* a method of collecting income tax by deducting it before payment of the earnings. **pay-as-you-go** *n.* a system of paying debts and expenses as they arise. **payback** *n.* profit or benefit from an investment etc. **payback period** *n.* the time allowed for the repayment of a loan. **pay bed** *n.* a bed for a private patient in a National Health Service hospital. **pay-bill** *n.* a bill stating the amounts due as wages to workers, soldiers etc. **pay claim** *n.* a demand for a pay increase, esp. by a trade union. **pay day** *n.* 1 the day on which one's wages or salary are paid. 2 on the Stock Exchange, the day on which transfers of stock are to be paid for. **pay dirt** *n.* (*N Am.*) 1 a deposit containing enough gold to make mining worthwhile. 2 anything profitable or useful. **payee** (-ē´) *n.* **pay envelope** *n.* (*N Am.*) a pay packet. **payer** *n.* **paying guest** *n.* a lodger who lives with a family. **payload** *n.* 1 the part of a transport vehicle's load that brings profit. 2 the passengers, cargo or weaponry carried by an aircraft. 3 the explosive capacity of a bomb, missile warhead etc. 4 the equipment which a spacecraft carries as the purpose of its mission, contrasted with those things necessary for its operation. **paymaster** *n.* 1 a person who pays, esp. one who regularly pays wages etc. 2 an officer in the armed services whose duty it is to pay the wages. **Paymaster-General** *n.* the officer at the head of the Treasury department concerned with the payment of civil salaries and other expenses. **payment** *n.* **pay-off** *n.* (*coll.*) 1 the final payment of a bill etc. 2 a return on an investment etc. 3 the conclusion of a story, joke etc. 4 the final result or outcome. **pay-office** *n.* a place where payment is made of wages, debts etc. **pay-out** *n.* a sum paid to someone, by an insurance company or as a prize. **pay packet** *n.* an envelope containing a person's wages. **payphone** *n.* a public telephone operated by coins. **payroll** *n.* a list of employees. **payslip** *n.* a slip of paper giving details of one's pay, income tax deductions etc. **pay station** *n.* (*N Am.*) a payphone. [OF *paier* (F *payer*), L *pācāre*, to appease, from *pax pācem*, peace]

pay[2] (pā) *v.t.* (*past, p.p.* **payed**) (*Naut.*) to coat, cover or fill with hot pitch for waterproofing. [ONF *peier*, L *picāre*, from *pix picis*, PITCH[2]]

PAYE *abbr.* pay-as-you-earn.

†**paynim** (pā´nim) *n.* 1 a pagan, a heathen. 2 a Muslim. [A-F *paienime*, late L *pāgānismus*]

payola (pāō´lə) *n.* (*esp. N Am.*) clandestine reward paid for illicit promotion of a commercial product, e.g. of a record by a disc jockey. [PAY[1], *-ola*, perh. from *Victrola*, a make of gramophone]

†**paysage** (pāzahzh´) *n.* 1 a rural scene or landscape. 2 a landscape painting. **paysagist** (pā´zəjist) *n.* [F, from *pays*, country]

Pb *chem. symbol* lead. [L *plumbum*]

PBX *abbr.* private branch exchange.

PC *abbr.* 1 Parish Council. 2 personal computer. 3 police constable. 4 political correctness. 5 politically correct. 6 Privy Counsellor.

p.c. *abbr.* 1 per cent. 2 personal computer. 3 postcard.

PCAS (pē´kas) *abbr.* (*Hist.*) Polytechnics Central Admissions System.

PCB *abbr.* 1 (*Chem.*) polychlorinated biphenyl. 2 (*Comput.*) printed circuit board.

PCM *abbr.* pulse code modulation.

PCMCIA *abbr.* (*Comput.*) Personal Computer Memory Card International Association.

PCP *abbr.* 1 phencyclidine. 2 (*Med.*) pneumocystis carinii pneumonia.

pct *abbr.* (*N Am.*) per cent.

PD *abbr.* (*N Am.*) Police Department.

Pd *chem. symbol* palladium.

pd. *abbr.* paid.

p.d.q. *abbr.* (*coll.*) pretty damn quick.

PDSA *abbr.* People's Dispensary for Sick Animals.

PDT *abbr.* Pacific Daylight Time.

PE *abbr.* 1 Peru (IVR). 2 physical education.

p/e *abbr.* market price/earnings (ratio per share).

pea (pē) *n.* 1 a leguminous plant, *Pisum sativum*, the seeds of which are used as food. 2 the seed of this. 3 any of various similar leguminous plants, e.g. the chickpea. **pea-brain** *n.* (*coll.*) a stupid person. **pea-brained** *a.* **pea crab** *n.* a small crab living in the shell of a mollusc. **pea green** *n.* a colour like that of fresh green peas. **pea-green** *a.* **peapod** *n.* the seed case of the pea. **pea-shooter** *n.* a tube through which dried peas are blown. **pea-soup** *n.* soup made with peas, esp. dried and split peas. **pea-souper** *n.* (*coll.*) a dense yellowish fog. **pea-soupy** *a.* **peastone** *n.* pisolite. [from PEASE, taken as pl.]

peace (pēs) *n.* **1** a state of quiet or tranquillity. **2** calmness of mind. **3** freedom from or cessation of war or hostilities. **4** a treaty reconciling two hostile nations. **5** absence of civil disturbance or agitation. **6** a liturgical greeting. **7** a state of friendliness. **at peace 1** in a state of harmony or tranquillity. **2** (*euphem.*) dead. **to hold one's peace** to stay silent. **to keep the peace 1** to abstain from strife. **2** to prevent a conflict. **to make one's peace with** to end one's quarrel with. **to make peace 1** to reconcile or be reconciled (with). **2** to bring about a treaty of peace. **peaceable** *a.* **1** disposed to peace. **2** peaceful, quiet. **peaceableness** *n.* **peaceably** *adv.* **peace-breaker** *n.* **Peace Corps** *n.* a US government body that sends volunteers to help developing countries with agricultural and other projects. **peace dividend** *n.* public money which, in the absence of hostilities, no longer needs to be spent on defence and therefore is available for civilian projects. **peace establishment** *n.* the reduced military and naval forces in time of peace. **peaceful** *a.* **1** quiet, peace-loving, mild. **2** free from noise or disturbance. **3** in a state of peace. **peacefully** *adv.* **peacefulness** *n.* **peacekeeper** *n.* a person or organization that preserves peace between hostile parties. **peacekeeping** *n.*, *a.* **peaceless** *a.* **peacemaker** *n.* a person who reconciles. **peace-making** *n.*, *a.* **peace-offering** *n.* **1** a gift to procure peace or reconciliation. **2** (*Bible*) an offering to God as a token of thanksgiving. **peace-officer** *n.* a civil officer whose duty it is to preserve the public peace. **peace pipe** *n.* a pipe smoked by N American Indians as a sign of peace. **peacetime** *n.* a time when there is no war. [ME and OF *pais*, L *pācem*, nom. *pax*]

Usage note The meanings of the adjectives *peaceable* and *peaceful* overlap, but in general *peaceable* is used of people, and *peaceful* of quiet or tranquil conditions.

peach[1] (pēch) *n.* **1** a fleshy, downy stone fruit with sweet yellow flesh and a pinkish-orange skin. **2** the tree, *Prunus persica*, on which peaches grow. **3** a pinkish-yellow colour. **4 a** (*coll.*) a pretty girl. **b** anything extremely good or pretty. ~*a.* pinkish-yellow. **peach-bloom** *n.* a reddish-pink porcelain glaze with green markings. **peach-blossom** *n.* a peach flower. **peach-blow** *n.* **1** a delicate purplish pink. **2** a light purple or pink glaze on porcelain. **3** a type of glass of similar colour. ~*a.* purplish-pink. **peach brandy** *n.* a spirit distilled from fermented peaches. **peach-coloured** *a.* of the colour of peach-blossom. **peaches and cream** *a.* (of a complexion) clear, smooth and creamy. **peach Melba** (mel´bə), **pêche Melba** (pesh) *n.* a dish of ice cream, peaches and sauce. **peachy** *a.* (*comp.* **peachier,** *superl.* **peachiest**). **peachiness** *n.* **peach-yellows** *n.* a disease attacking peach trees in the eastern US. [OF *pesche*, L *persicum*, Persian (apple)]

peach[2] (pēch) *v.i.* to turn informer against an accomplice, to inform (against or upon). ~†*v.t.* to inform against. [ME *apechen*, as IMPEACH]

peacock (pē´kok) *n.* **1** a male peafowl, having gorgeous plumage and a long tail capable of expanding like a fan. **2** a vain, arrogant person. ~*v.t.* to display or plume (oneself). ~*v.i.* to strut about ostentatiously. **peacock blue** *n.* a rich greenish blue. **peacock-blue** *a.* **peacock butterfly** *n.* a butterfly, *Inachis io*, having eyelike markings on the wings. **peacockery** *n.* vain, arrogant behaviour. **peacockish, peacock-like** *a.* **peafowl** *n.* a pheasant of the genus *Pavo*, of which the peacock is the male. **pea-chick** *n.* a young peafowl. **peahen** *n.* a female peafowl. [OE *pēa*, *pāwe*, L *pāvo*]

pea-jacket (pē´jakit) *n.* a coarse, thick, loose overcoat worn by seamen. [prob. after Dut. *pij-jakker* (*pij*, a pea-jacket)]

peak[1] (pēk) *n.* **1** a sharp point or top, esp. of a mountain. **2** a mountain with a peak. **3** the projecting brim in front of a cap. **4** a pointed beard. **5** (*Naut.*) **a** the upper after-corner of a sail extended by a gaff. **b** the upper end of a gaff. **6** the culminating point of an electricity load curve during a specified period, and the maximum load of electricity required. **7** the point of greatest activity, use, demand etc. ~*v.i.* to reach a peak. ~*a.* of or relating to the point of greatest activity, use, demand etc. **peaked**[1] *a.* having or forming a peak. **peak hour** *n.* the time when there is most traffic, activity etc. **peak load** *n.* the maximum load of electricity required. **peaky**[1] *a.* (*comp.* **peakier,** *superl.* **peakiest**). **peakiness** *n.* [var. of PIKE[2]]

peak[2] (pēk) *v.i.* **1** to pine away. **2** to look sickly. **peaked**[2] *a.* sharp-featured or emaciated. **peaky**[2] *a.* (*comp.* **peakier,** *superl.* **peakiest**). [etym. uncertain]

peak[3] (pēk) *v.t.* (*Naut.*) **1** to raise (a gaff or yard) until nearly vertical. **2** to raise (the oars) until nearly vertical. [from APEAK]

peaked[1] PEAK[1].

peaked[2] PEAK[2].

peaky[1] PEAK[1].

peaky[2] PEAK[2].

peal[1] (pēl) *n.* **1** a loud, esp. a prolonged or repercussive sound, as of thunder, bells etc. **2** a set of bells tuned to each other. **3** a series of changes rung on these. ~*v.i.* to sound a peal, to resound. ~*v.t.* **1** to utter or give forth sonorously. **2** to cause to give out loud and solemn sounds. [prob. from APPEAL]

peal[2] (pēl) *n.* (*dial.*) **1** a grilse or young salmon, usu. under 2 lb. (0.9 kg). **2** a young sea trout. [etym. unknown]

pean (pēn) *n.* a heraldic fur, represented by sable with or (golden) spots. [etym. uncertain]

peanut (pē´nŭt) *n.* **1** a plant, *Arachis hypogaea*, of the bean family with pods ripening underground, the seeds of which are edible and used for their oil. **2** the seed of the peanut plant. **3** (*pl.*, *coll.*) an insignificant sum of money. **peanut butter** *n.* a paste made from ground roasted peanuts.

pear (peə) *n.* **1** the fleshy yellow or greenish fruit of the pear tree. **2** (*also* **pear tree**) any of various trees of the genus *Pyrus*, on which pears grow. **pear-shaped** *a.* [OE *pere*, late L *pira*, L *pirum*]

pearl[1] (pœl) *n.* **1** a smooth, white or bluish-grey, lustrous and iridescent, calcareous concretion, found in several bivalves, the best in the pearl-oyster, prized as a gem. **2** an imitation pearl. **3** (*pl.*) a pearl necklace. **4** mother-of-pearl. **5** anything exceedingly valuable, or the finest specimen of its kind. **6** something round and clear and resembling a pearl, such as a dewdrop, tooth etc. **7** a bluish grey. **8** (*Print.*) a small size of type. **9** pearl-eye. ~*a.* **1** of, relating to, containing or made of pearls. **2** bluish-grey. ~*v.t.* **1** (*poet.*) to sprinkle with pearly drops. **2** (*poet.*) to make pearly. **3** to rub and strip (barley) into pearly grains. **4** to set or embroider with pearls. ~*v.i.* **1** to fish for pearls. **2** (*poet.*) to form pearly drops or fragments. **to cast pearls before swine** to offer something valuable or beautiful to someone who does not appreciate it. **pearl ash** *n.* crude potassium carbonate. **pearl barley** *n.* barley stripped of the husk and ground to a small white grain. **pearl bulb** *n.* a translucent light bulb. **pearl button** *n.* a button made of mother-of-pearl. **pearl-diver** *n.* a person who dives for pearl-oysters. **pearled** *a.* **1** decorated with pearls. **2** in pearl-like drops. **3** of the colour of pearls. **pearler** *n.* **pearlescent** *a.* resembling mother-of-pearl. **pearl-eye** *n.* a pearl-coloured film or speck on the eye, causing cataract.

pearl-eyed *a.* **pearl-fisher** *n.* a person who fishes for pearls. **pearl-fishing** *n.* **pearling**[1] *n.* **pearlized, pearlised** *a.* having a finish resembling mother-of-pearl. **pearl-like** *a.* **pearl millet** *n.* a tall grass, *Pennisetum typhoides*, grown esp. as fodder in Africa, India and the southern US. **pearl onion** *n.* a very small onion used for pickling. **pearl-oyster** *n.* **pearl-powder** *n.* pearl-white. **pearl-shell** *n.* mother-of-pearl in its natural state. **pearl-spar** *n.* a variety of dolomite, with a pearly lustre. **pearl-stone** *n.* perlite. **pearlware** *n.* a kind of fine, white, glazed earthenware. **pearl-white** *n.* oxychloride of bismuth, used as a cosmetic for whitening the skin. **pearlwort** *n.* any herbaceous plant of the genus *Sagina*, found in rocky and sandy areas. **pearly** *a.* (*comp.* **pearlier**, *superl.* **pearliest**). **pearlies** (-liz) *n.pl.* **1** pearly kings and queens. **2** a pearly king's or queen's ceremonial costume, covered with pearl buttons. **3** (*sl.*) teeth. **pearliness** *n.* **Pearly Gates** *n.pl.* (*coll., facet.*) the entrance to Heaven. **pearly king** *n.* a male London costermonger wearing pearlies. **pearly nautilus** *n.* (*pl.* **pearly nautiluses, pearly nautili** (-lī)) a cephalopod of the genus *Nautilus*, with a many-chambered shell with nacreous divisions. **pearly queen** *n.* a female London costermonger wearing pearlies. [F *perle*, etym. uncertain]

pearl[2] (pœl) *n.* a picot. ~*v.t.* to purl. **pearl-edge** *n.* a border or edging made of picots. **pearling**[2] *n.* [prob. var. of PURL[1]]

pearling[1] PEARL[1].

pearling[2] PEARL[2].

pearlite PERLITE.

pearmain (peə´mān) *n.* a kind of apple with firm, white flesh. [F *permain*]

peart (pœt) *a.* (*N Am., dial.*) lively and cheerful, pert. [var. of PERT]

peasant (pez´ənt) *n.* **1** a rustic labourer. **2** (*coll.*) a countryman. **3** (*derog.*) a rough, uncouth person. ~*a.* rustic, rural. **peasantry** *n.* (*pl.* **peasantries**). **peasanty** *a.* [OF *paisant* (F *paysan*), L *pāgensem*, nom. *-sis*, of or relating to a *pāgus* or village]

pease (pēz) *n.pl.* peas. **pease pudding** *n.* a pudding made of peas. [OE *pise*, pea, pl. *pisan*, late L *pisa*, L *pisum*, Gr. *pison* (cp. PEA)]

peat (pēt) *n.* **1** decayed and partly carbonized vegetable matter found in boggy places and used as fuel. **2** a piece of peat. **peatbog** *n.* a bog containing peat. **peatery** *n.* (*pl.* **peateries**) a place where peat is cut and prepared for use. **peat-hag** *n.* a moss-hag. **peatland** *n.* land which consists of peat. **peatmoss** *n.* **1** a peatbog. **2** sphagnum. **peat reek** *n.* **1** smoke from a peat fire. **2** whisky distilled over a peat fire, whisky illicitly distilled, mountain dew. **peaty** *a.* (*comp.* **peatier**, *superl.* **peatiest**). [ME *pete*, etym. uncertain]

peau-de-soie (pōdəswah´) *n.* a rich, finely ribbed fabric of silk or rayon. [F, skin of silk]

pebble (peb´əl) *n.* **1** a small stone rounded by the action of water. **2** a transparent rock crystal, used for spectacles etc. **3** a lens made of this. **4** an agate. ~*a.* (*coll.*) (of spectacle lenses) very thick and convex. ~*v.t.* **1** to pelt with pebbles. **2** to pave with pebbles. **3** to impart a rough indented surface or grain to (leather). **not the only pebble on the beach** able to be replaced easily. **pebbled** *a.* **pebble-dash** *n.* a coating for external walls consisting of small stones imbedded in mortar. **pebble-dashed** *a.* **pebble-stone** *n.* **pebble-ware** *n.* a variety of Wedgwood ware having different-coloured clays worked into the paste. **pebbly** *a.* (*comp.* **pebblier**, *superl.* **pebbliest**). [OE *papol-stān*, a pebble-stone, etym. uncertain]

pébrine (pābrēn´) *n.* an epidemic disease, characterized by black spots, attacking silkworms. [F, from Port. *pebrino*, from *pebre*, PEPPER]

p.e.c. *abbr.* photoelectric cell.

pecan (pē´kən, pikan´) *n.* a N American hickory, *Carya illinoensis*, or its fruit or nut. **pecan pie** *n.* a pie made with pecan nuts. [F *pacane*, Sp. *pacana*, of Algonquian orig.]

peccable (pek´əbəl) *a.* (*formal*) liable to sin. **peccability** (-bil´-) *n.* [med. L *peccābilis*, from *peccāre*, to sin]

peccadillo (pekədil´ō) *n.* (*pl.* **peccadilloes, peccadillos**) a minor sin or offence. [Sp., dim. of *pecado*, L *peccātum*, sin, as PECCABLE]

peccant (pek´ənt) *a.* (*formal*) **1** sinful, guilty. **2** (*coll.*) wrong. **3** morbid, inducing or indicating disease. **peccancy** (-si) *n.* [F, from L *peccantem*, nom. *-cans*, pres.p. of *peccāre*, to sin]

peccary (pek´əri) *n.* (*pl.* **peccaries**) any American pig-like mammal of the family Tayassuidae. [Carib *pakira*]

peccavi (pekah´vē) *int.* used to express contrition. ~*n.* (*pl.* **peccavis**) a confession of guilt. [L, I have sinned]

pech (pekh) *v.i.* (*Sc., North.*) to breathe hard, to pant. ~*n.* a pant, a puff. [perh. onomat.]

pêche Melba PEACH MELBA (under PEACH[1]).

peck[1] (pek) *v.t.* **1** to strike with a beak or pointed instrument. **2** to kiss lightly. **3** to pick up with or as if with a beak. **4** to break, open, eat etc. thus. **5** (*coll.*) to eat, esp. in small amounts. **6** to mark with short strokes. **7** to break (up or down) with a pointed implement. **8** to type. ~*v.i.* to strike or aim with a beak or pointed implement. ~*n.* **1** a sharp stroke with or as with a beak. **2** a mark made by this. **3** a light kiss. **4** †food. **to peck at 1** to nibble at. **2** to nag. **3** to bite at (something) with a beak. **pecker** *n.* **1** a bird which pecks. **2** (*coll.*) a woodpecker. **3** (*N Am., taboo sl.*) the penis. **4** (*sl.*) spirits, courage. **5** a kind of hoe. **to keep one's pecker up** (*coll.*) to stay cheerful. **pecking order** *n.* the hierarchical order of importance in any social group. **peckish** *a.* (*coll.*) **1** hungry. **2** (*N Am.*) irritable, bad-tempered. **peck order** *n.* pecking order. [var. of PICK[2]]

peck[2] (pek) *n.* **1** a measure of capacity for dry goods, 2 gallons (about 9 l); the fourth part of a bushel. **2** a vessel used for measuring this. **3** a large quantity. [A-F and OF *pek*, etym. uncertain]

pecorino (pekərē´nō) *n.* (*pl.* **pecorinos**) an Italian ewe's-milk cheese. [It., from *pecorino*, of ewes, from *pecora*, a sheep]

pecten (pek´ten) *n.* (*pl.* **pectens, pectines** (-tinēz)) (*Zool.*) **1** a comblike process forming a membrane in the eyes of birds and some reptiles. **2** an appendage behind the posterior legs in scorpions, and various other parts or organs. **3** any mollusc of the genus *Pecten*, containing the scallops. **pectinate** (-nət), **pectinated** (-nātid) *a.* having projections like the teeth of a comb. **pectination** (-ā´shən) *n.* **pectinato-** (pektinah´tō), **pectini-** (pektin´i) *comb.form* comblike. [L *pecten -tinis*, a comb, from *pectere*, to comb (cp. Gr. *pektein*)]

pectin (pek´tin) *n.* a white, amorphous compound found in fruits and certain fleshy roots, formed from pectose by the process of ripening. **pectic** *a.* derived from or containing pectin. **pectose** (-tōs) *n.* an insoluble compound allied to cellulose, found in unripe fruits and other vegetable tissue. [Gr. *pēktos*, from *pēg-*, stem of *pēgnuein*, to make firm or solid]

pectinate, pectines etc. PECTEN.

pectoral (pek´tərəl) *a.* (*Anat.*) of, relating to or for the breast or chest. ~*n.* **1** a pectoral muscle. **2** a pectoral fin. **3** an ornament worn on the breast, esp. the breastplate of a Jewish high priest. **4** a medicine to relieve chest complaints. **pectoral muscle** *n.* (*Anat.*) either of the two muscles at the top of the chest on each side, controlling certain arm and shoulder movements. [F, from L *pectorālis*, from *pectus -toris*, a breast]

pectose PECTIN.

peculate (pek´ūlāt) *v.t., v.i.* to appropriate (money or goods entrusted to one's care) to one's own use.

peculation (-lā´shən) *n.* **peculator** *n.* [L *pecūlātus*, p.p. of *pecūlārī*, as PECULIAR]

peculiar (pikū´lyə) *a.* **1** singular, strange, odd. **2** belonging particularly and exclusively (to). **3** of or relating to the individual. **4** particular, special. **5** one's own, private, not general. ~*n.* **1** †exclusive property, right or privilege. **2** a parish or church exempt from diocesan jurisdiction. **3** (*also* **Peculiar**) a member of the Peculiar People. **peculiarity** (-iar´iti-) *n.* (*pl.* **peculiarities**) **1** the quality of being peculiar. **2** an idiosyncrasy. **3** a characteristic. **peculiarize, peculiarise** *v.t.* **peculiarly** *adv.* **Peculiar People** *n.pl.* a Christian sect having no ministry or regular organization and believing in the cure of diseases by prayer. [L *pecūliāris*, from *pecūlium*, private property, from *pecū*, cattle]

pecuniary (pikū´niəri) *a.* **1** of, relating to or consisting of money. **2** (of an offence) entailing a financial penalty. **pecuniarily** *adv.* [L *pecūniārius*, from *pecūnia*, as PECULIAR]

ped- PAEDO-.

-ped -PEDE.

pedagogue (ped´əgog) *n.* a teacher of young children, a schoolmaster (usu. in contempt, implying conceit or pedantry). ~†*v.t.* to teach. **pedagogic** (-gog´-, -goj´-), **pedagogical** *a.* **pedagogically** *adv.* **pedagogics** (-goj´-, -gō´jiks) *n.* the science of teaching. **pedagogism, pedagoguism** *n.* the occupation, manners or character of a pedagogue. **pedagogy** (-gogi, -goji) *n.* **1** pedagogics. **2** pedagogism. [MF, from L *paedagōgus*, Gr. *paidagōgos* (*pais paidos*, a boy, *agein*, to lead)]

pedal[1] (ped´əl) *n.* **1** a lever acted on by the foot, e.g. on a bicycle or motor vehicle. **2** in an organ, a wooden key moved by the feet, or a foot-lever for working several stops at once, for opening and shutting the swell-box etc. **3** a foot-lever for lifting the damper of a piano, for muffling the notes, and other purposes. **4** (*Mus.*) a sustained note, usu. in the bass. ~*v.t.* (*pres.p.* **pedalling,** (*N Am.*) **pedaling,** *past, p.p.* **pedalled,** (*N Am.*) **pedaled**) **1** to work (a bicycle, sewing machine etc.) by pedals. **2** to play (an organ) by pedals. ~*v.i.* to play an organ or work a bicycle etc. by pedals. **pedal bin** *n.* a bin with a lid which can be opened by means of a pedal. **pedal cycle** *n.* a bicycle. **pedaller,** (*N Am.*) **pedaler** *n.* **pedalo** (-ō) *n.* (*pl.* **pedalos, pedaloes**) a small boat propelled by paddles operated with pedals. **pedal-pipe** *n.* an organ pipe acted on by a pedal. **pedal-pusher** *n.* (*coll.*) **1** a cyclist. **2** (*pl.*) women's calf-length trousers. [prob. through F *pédale*, It. *pedale*, L *pedālem*, nom. *-lis*, from *pes pedis*, a foot]

pedal[2] (ped´əl, pē´dəl) *a.* (*Zool.*) of or relating to a foot or footlike part (esp. of a mollusc). [L *pedalis*, from *pes pedis*, a foot]

pedant (ped´ənt) *n.* **1** a person who makes a pretentious show of book-learning, or lays undue stress on rules and formulas. **2** a person with more book-learning than practical experience or common sense. **3** a person obsessed by a theory. **4** †a schoolmaster. **pedantic** (pidan´-), **pedantical** *a.* **pedantically** *adv.* †**pedantize, pedantise** *v.i.* **pedantocracy** (-tok´rəsi) *n.* government by pedants. **pedantry** *n.* (*pl.* **pedantries**). [F *pédant*, It. *pedante*, a schoolmaster, prob. cogn. with PEDAGOGUE]

pedate (ped´āt) *a.* **1** (*Zool.*) having feet. **2** (*Bot.*) palmately divided with the two lateral lobes divided into smaller segments like digits or toes. **pedately** *adv.* [L *pedātus*, from *pes pedis*, a foot]

peddle (ped´əl) *v.t.* **1** to sell in small quantities, to retail as a pedlar. **2** to promote (an idea etc.). **3** to sell (illegal drugs). ~*v.i.* **1** to travel about the country selling small wares. **2** †to busy oneself about trifles. **peddler** *n.* **1** a person who sells illegal drugs. **2** (*N Am.*) PEDLAR. **peddling** *a.* trifling, insignificant. [etym. uncertain; in first sense prob. from PEDLAR]

Usage note British English generally distinguishes *peddler*, a seller of drugs, from *pedlar*, a hawker of small wares; in the US *peddler* is general.

-pede (pēd), **-ped** (ped) *comb. form* a foot, as in *centipede, quadruped*. [L *pes*, a foot]

pederast (ped´ərast), **paederast** *n.* a man who practises sodomy with a boy. **pederastic** (-as´-) *a.* **pederasty** *n.* [Gr. *paiderastēs* (*pais paidos*, a boy, *eraein*, to love)]

pedestal (ped´istəl) *n.* **1** an insulated base for a column, statue etc. **2** either of the supports of a kneehole desk. **3** a base, foundation or support. **4** the china pan of a lavatory, or its base. ~*v.t.* (*pres.p.* **pedestalling,** (*N Am.*) **pedestaling,** *past, p.p.* **pedestalled,** (*N Am.*) **pedestaled**) **1** to set on a pedestal. **2** to serve as a pedestal for. **on a pedestal** in a position of (excessive) respect or devotion. **pedestal table** *n.* a table which sits on a single central support. [G *Pedestal* or F *piédestal*, It. *piedestallo* (*piè*, L *pes pedis*, foot, *di*, of, *stallo*, STALL[1])]

pedestrian (pədes´triən) *n.* **1** a person who is walking. **2** a person who takes part in walking races. **3** an expert walker. ~*a.* **1** of or relating to walking. **2** going or performed on foot. **3** prosaic, dull, commonplace. **pedestrian crossing** *n.* a marked strip across a road where vehicles must stop to allow pedestrians to cross. **pedestrianism** *n.* **pedestrianize, pedestrianise** *v.t., v.i.* to convert (a road etc.) so that it may be used only by pedestrians. **pedestrianization** (-zā´shən) *n.* **pedestrian precinct** *n.* an area of a city or town which can be used only by pedestrians. [L *pedester -tris*, from *pes pedis*, foot]

pedi- (ped´i) *comb. form* a foot. [L *pes pedis*, a foot]

pediatrics PAEDIATRICS.

pedicab (ped´ikab) *n.* a rickshaw operated by pedals.

pedicel (ped´isel) *n.* **1** (*Bot.*) the stalk supporting a single flower etc., as distinct from *peduncle*. **2** (*Zool., Anat.*) any small, stalklike structure. **pedicellate** (-lāt) *a.* **pedicle** (-ikəl) *n.* **1** (*Med.*) part of a graft still temporarily attached to its original place. **2** (*Anat., Zool.*) a small, stalklike structure, a pedicel or peduncle. **pediculate** (-dik´ūlət) *a.* **pediculated** (-lātid) *a.* [mod. L *pedicellus*, dim. of *pedīculus*, dim. of *pes pedis*, a foot]

pedicular (pidik´ūlə), **pediculous** (-ləs) *a.* lousy, infested with lice. **pediculosis** (-lō´sis) *n.* (*Med.*) lousiness, infestation with lice. [L *pedīculāris*, *-lōsus*, from *pedīculus*, a louse]

pediculate, pediculated PEDICEL.

pediculosis PEDICULAR.

pedicure (ped´ikūə) *n.* **1** the surgical treatment of the feet. **2** cosmetic care of the feet. **3** a chiropodist. ~*v.t.* to treat (the feet). [F *pédicure* (L *pes pedis*, a foot, *curāre*, to CURE)]

pedigree (ped´igrē) *n.* **1** genealogy, lineage, esp. of a domestic or pet animal. **2** a genealogical table or tree. **3** derivation of a word, etymology. ~*a.* (of a horse, dog etc.) pure-bred, having a known ancestry. **pedigreed** *a.* [formerly *pedegru*, OF *pee de grue*, F *pié de grue* (L *pes pedis*, a foot, *de*, of, *grue*, L *gruem*, nom. *grus*, a crane)]

pediment (ped´imənt) *n.* **1** (*Archit.*) **a** the triangular part surmounting a portico, in buildings in the Grecian style. **b** a similar member crowning doorways, windows etc. in buildings in classical Renaissance styles. **2** (*Geol.*) a gently sloping rock surface at the foot of a mountain. **pedimental** (-men´-) *a.* **pedimented** *a.* [formerly *periment*, perh. corr. of L *operīmentum*, from *operīre*, to cover, or of PYRAMID]

pedipalp (ped´ipalp) *n.* an arachnid of the order Pedipalpi, characterized by pincer-like feelers, comprising the true scorpions. [L *pes pedis*, a foot, *palpus*, PALP]

pedlar (ped´lə) *n.* **1** (*Hist.*) a travelling hawker of small wares, usu. carried in a pack. **2** a person who retails gossip etc. **pedlary** *n.* [etym. uncertain, prob. cogn. with obs. *ped*, a basket]

Usage note See note under PEDDLE.

pedo- PAEDO-.
pedobaptism PAEDOBAPTISM.
pedology (pədol´əji) *n.* the science of soils. **pedological** (pedəloj´-) *a.* **pedologist** *n.* [Gr. *pedon*, ground]
pedometer (pidom´itə) *n.* an instrument for measuring the distance covered on foot by registering the number of steps taken. [F *pédomètre* (L *pes pedis*, a foot)]
pedophilia PAEDOPHILIA.
pedrail (ped´rāl) *n.* **1** a contrivance for enabling a traction engine to move over rough ground. **2** the traction engine equipped in this way.
peduncle (pidŭng´kəl) *n.* **1** (*Bot.*) a flower stalk, esp. of a solitary flower or one bearing the subsidiary stalks of a cluster, as distinct from *pedicel*. **2** (*Zool.*) a stalklike process for the attachment of an organ or an organism. **peduncular** (-kū-), **pedunculate** (-kūlət), **pedunculated** (-lātid) *a.* **pedunculate oak** *n.* an oak, *Quercus robur*, having clusters of acorns growing on long stalks. [L *pes pedis*, a foot, -UNCLE]
pedway (ped´wā) *n.* (*esp. N Am.*) a pedestrian footpath in a city. [PEDESTRIAN, WAY]
pee (pē) *v.i.* (*3rd pers. sing. pres.* **pees,** *pres.p.* **peeing,** *past, p.p.* **peed**) (*coll.*) to urinate. ~*v.t.* to pass as or with urine. ~*n.* **1** an act of urinating. **2** urine. [initial letter of taboo PISS]
peek (pēk) *v.i.* to peer, to peep, to pry. ~*n.* a peep. **peekaboo** (pēk´əboo) *a.* **1** (of a garment) revealing or almost revealing parts of the body. **2** (of a hairstyle) covering one eye. ~*n.* a game used for amusing young children, in which the face is hidden and then suddenly revealed. [etym. uncertain]
peel[1] (pēl) *v.t.* **1** to strip the skin, bark or rind off. **2** to strip (rind etc.) off a fruit etc. **3** in croquet, to send (another player's ball) through a hoop. **4** †to pillage, to plunder. ~*v.i.* **1** to lose the skin or rind, to become bare. **2** (of paint etc.) to flake off. **3** (*coll.*) to undress. ~*n.* skin, rind. **to peel off 1** to leave and move away from (e.g. a column of marchers). **2** (*coll.*) to undress. **peeler**[1] *n.* **peeling** *n.* the skin of a fruit etc. that has been peeled off. [var. of *pill*, to pillage (F *piller*, prob. from L *pilare*, from *pilus*, a hair), perh. influ. by F *peler*, to peel]
peel[2] (pēl) *n.* **1** a wooden shovel used by bakers. **2** the blade of an oar. [OF *pele* (F *pelle*), L *pāla*]
peel[3] (pēl), **pele** *n.* (*Hist.*) a square fortified tower, esp. those built about the 16th cent. in the border areas of Scotland and England for defence against raids. [ME and OF *pel*, a palisade, L *pālum*, nom. *-lus*, stake, PALE[2]]
peeler[1] PEEL[1].
peeler[2] (pē´lə) *n.* (*dated sl.*) a policeman, orig. a constable in the police organized by Sir Robert Peel in 1828.
Peelite (pēl´īt) *n.* an adherent of Sir Robert Peel, 1788–1850, esp. a Conservative supporting his measure for the repeal of the Corn Laws. [as PEELER[2]]
peen (pēn) *n.* the point of a mason's hammer, opposite to the face. ~*v.t.* **1** to hammer. **2** to strike (sheet metal) with a stream of metal shot in order to shape it. [etym. uncertain]
peep[1] (pēp) *v.i.* **1** to look through a crevice or narrow opening. **2** to look slyly or furtively. **3** to show oneself or appear partially or cautiously, to come (out) gradually into view. **4** (of a quality or characteristic) to show itself unconsciously. ~*n.* **1** a furtive look, a hasty glance, a glimpse. **2** the first appearance. **peep-bo** *n.* peekaboo. **peeper**[1] *n.* **1** a person who peeps. **2** (*coll.*) an eye. **3** (*N Am., sl.*) a private detective. **peephole** *n.* a small hole for looking through. **peeping Tom** *n.* a person who is guilty of prurient curiosity, a voyeur. **Peep-o'-day boys** *n.pl.* (*Hist.*) a secret society of Protestants in Ireland, founded in 1784 (named after their early visits to the houses of Roman Catholics in search of arms). **peep-show** *n.* **1** an exhibition of pictures etc., shown through a small aperture containing a lens. **2** a sex show seen by customers in separate compartments fitted with a small window. **peep-sight** *n.* a movable disc on the breech of a firearm pierced with a small hole through which aim can be taken with accuracy. **peep-toe** *a.* (of a shoe) cut away at the toe. [perh. rel. to PEEK]
peep[2] (pēp) *v.i.* (of a young bird, a mouse etc.) to cry, chirp or squeak. ~*n.* **1** a chirp, squeak etc. **2** (*coll.*) any spoken sound (*not a peep*). **peeper**[2] *n.* a chicken just out of the shell. [perh. from OF *pipier*, L *pīpāre*, of imit. orig., or var. of PIPE]
peeper[1] PEEP[1].
peeper[2] PEEP[2].
peeper[3] (pē´pə) *n.* (*N Am.*) a tree frog of the genus *Hyla*.
peepul (pee´pəl), **pipal** *n.* the bo tree. [Hind. *pīpal*, from Sansk. *pippala*]
peer[1] (piə) *v.i.* **1** to look very closely (at, into etc.). **2** to peep out. **3** †to appear, to come into sight. [etym. uncertain]
peer[2] (piə) *n.* **1** in the UK, a member of one of the degrees of nobility, comprising dukes, marquesses, earls, viscounts and barons. **2** a noble, esp. a member of a hereditary legislative body. **3** a person of the same rank. **4** an equal in any respect. ~*v.t.* **1** to equal, to rank with. **2** (*coll.*) to make a peer. ~*v.i.* to be equal. **peerage** (-rij) *n.* **1** the body of peers, the nobility, the aristocracy. **2** the rank of a peer or peeress. **3** a book containing particulars of the nobility. **peeress** (-ris) *n.* **1** a woman holding the rank of a peer. **2** the wife or widow of a peer. **peer group** *n.* a group of people equal in status, age etc. **peerless** *a.* without an equal. **peerlessly** *adv.* **peerlessness** *n.* **peer of the realm, peer of the United Kingdom** *n.* any of the British peers all of whom are entitled to sit in the House of Lords. **peer pressure** *n.* pressure to conform with the attitudes and behaviour of one's peers. [OF *per*, L *parem*, nom. *par*, equal]
peesweep (pēz´wēp) *n.* (*Sc.*) the peewit. [imit. of the bird's cry]
peeve, peeved PEEVISH.
peevers (pē´vəz) *n.* (*Sc.*) the game of hopscotch.
peevish (pē´vish) *a.* fretful, irritable, petulant, expressing discontent. **peeve** *v.t.* (*coll.*) to annoy, to irritate. ~*n.* (*coll.*) **1** a person who or something which annoys. **2** vexation. **peeved** *a.* (*sl.*) irritated, annoyed. **peevishly** *adv.* **peevishness** *n.* [etym. uncertain]
peewee (pē´wē) *n.* **1** (*Sc.*) a lapwing. **2** (*Austral.*) a magpie lark. [imit. (cp. PEWEE)]
peewit (pē´wit), **pewit** *n.* **1** a lapwing. **2** its cry. [imit. of the cry]
peg (peg) *n.* **1** a pin or bolt, usu. of wood, for holding parts of a structure or fastening articles together, hanging things on, supporting, holding, marking etc. **2** a clothes-peg. **3** a step, a degree. **4** an occasion, pretext, excuse or topic for discourse etc. **5** (*coll.*) a small drink of spirits or wine. **6** in a fishing competition, the area allotted to a competitor, marked by a peg in the ground. ~*v.t.* (*pres.p.* **pegging,** *past, p.p.* **pegged**) **1** to fix or fasten (down, in, out etc.) with a peg or pegs. **2** to fix (esp. prices) at an agreed level. **3** to mark (a score) with pegs on a cribbage board. **4** to mark (out) the boundaries of. **off the peg** ready-made. **peg to hang something on** an appropriate occasion for something, such as an idea, to be aired or expressed. **round peg in a square hole** a square peg in a round hole. **square peg in a round hole** a person in an unsuitable job or function. **to peg away at** to work at or struggle with persistently. **to peg**

down 1 to restrict (to rules etc.). **2** to fasten down with pegs. **to peg on** to peg away. **to peg out 1** (*sl.*) to die. **2** in cribbage, to win by attaining the final hole in the cribbage board. **3** in croquet, to go out by hitting the final peg. **4** to mark out the boundaries of. **5** (*sl.*) to fail, to be ruined. **to take (someone) down a peg (or two)** to humiliate, to deflate the ego of. **pegboard** *n.* a board with holes into which pegs can be fixed, used for scoring in games, or placed on a wall and used for hanging things. **pegged** *a.* **1** having been pegged. **2** (*N Am.*) pegtop. **peg-leg** *n.* (*coll.*) **1** an artificial leg. **2** a person who has an artificial leg. **pegtop** *n.* **1** a spinning top with a metal peg, usu. spun by means of a string which unwinds rapidly when the top is thrown from the hand. **2** (*pl.*) trousers very wide at the top and narrowing towards the ankles. *~a.* (of a garment) wide at the top and narrowing towards the bottom. [ME *pegge* (cp. Dut. dial. *peg*, Swed. dial. *pegg*)]

Pegasus (peg´əsəs) *n.* poetic inspiration. [in Greek mythology, a winged horse which, with a blow of its hoofs, produced the fountain from which poets were fabled to draw their inspiration]

pegasus (peg´əsəs) *n.* any member of the genus *Pegasus* of fishes, with broad pectoral fins. [as PEGASUS]

pegmatite (peg´mətīt) *n.* a coarse-grained variety of granite, with a little mica. **pegmatitic** (-tit´-) *a.* [L and Gr. *pēgma*, from *pēgnuein*, to fasten, -ITE[1]]

Pehlevi PAHLAVI.

PEI *abbr.* Prince Edward Island.

☒ **peice** common misspelling of PIECE.

peignoir (pān´wah) *n.* a loose robe or dressing gown worn by a woman. [F, from *peigner*, to comb]

☒ **peirce** common misspelling of PIERCE.

peishwa PESHWA.

pejorative (pijor´ətiv) *a.* depreciatory, disparaging. *~n.* a word or form expressing depreciation. **pejorate** (pē´jər-) *v.t.* **pejoration** (-ā´shən) *n.* **pejoratively** *adv.* [L *pējōrātus*, p.p. of *pējōrāre*, to make worse, from *pējor*, worse, -ATIVE]

pekan (pek´ən) *n.* a N American marten, *Martes pennanti*, of the weasel family, prized for its fur. [Can. F, from Algonquian *pékané*]

Pekinese (pēkinēz´), **Pekingese** *a.* of or relating to Beijing (formerly Peking). *~n.* (*pl.* **Pekinese, Pekingese**) **1** a rough-coated variety of Chinese pug. **2** a citizen of Beijing, China. **3** the dialect of Chinese spoken in Beijing. **peke** *n.* (*coll.*) a Pekinese dog. **Peking man** (pēking´) *n.* a fossil man of the Lower Palaeolithic age, first found SW of Beijing in 1929. [F *pékin*, Chin. *Pe-king*, lit., northern capital]

pekoe (pē´kō) *n.* a fine black tea. [Chin. *pek-ho* (*pek*, white, *ho*, down)]

pelage (pel´ij) *n.* the coat or hair of an animal, esp. of fur. [F, from OF *pel*, ult. from L *pilus*, hair]

Pelagian (pelā´jiən) *n.* a follower of Pelagius, a British monk of the 5th cent., who denied the doctrine of original sin. *~a.* of or relating to Pelagius or his doctrines. **Pelagianism** *n.*

pelagian (pilā´jiən) *a.* inhabiting the deep sea. *~n.* a pelagian animal. [L *pelagius*, Gr. *pelagios*, from *pelagos*, sea]

pelagic (pilaj´ik) *a.* of or inhabiting the deep sea. [L *pelagicus*, from Gr. *pelagikos*, as PELAGIAN]

pelargonium (peləgō´niəm) *n.* (*pl.* **pelargoniums**) an ornamental plant of the genus *Pelargonium*, popularly called the geranium. [Gr. *pelargos*, a stork]

Pelasgic (pəlaz´jik) *a.* of or relating to the Pelasgi, a widely diffused prehistoric race inhabiting the coasts and islands of the eastern Mediterranean and the Aegean.

pele PEEL[3].

pelerine (pel´ərēn) *n.* a lady's long narrow fur cape. [F *pèlerine*, fem. of *pèlerin*, L *peregrīnus*, a PILGRIM]

pelf (pelf) *n.* (*derog.* or *facet.*) money, wealth. [ME *pelfe*, OF *pelfre*, etym. uncertain]

pelham (pel´əm) *n.* a horse's bit having a curb and a snaffle. [surname *Pelham*]

pelican (pel´ikən) *n.* a large waterbird of the family Pelecanidae, with an enormous pouch beneath the mandibles for storing fish when caught. **pelican crossing** *n.* a type of pedestrian crossing controlled by pedestrian-operated traffic lights. [F, from late L *pelicānus*, Gr. *pelekan*, prob. rel. to *pelekus*, an axe]

pelisse (pilēs´) *n.* (*Hist.*) **1** a woman's long cloak or mantle. **2** a fur-lined cloak worn by a hussar. **3** a garment worn over other clothes by a child. [F, from L *pellicia*, fem. of *pellicius*, of skin, from *pellis*, skin]

pelite (pē´līt) *n.* (*Geol.*) a rock made up of a claylike sediment. [Gr. *pēlos*, clay, mud]

pellagra (pelag´rə, -lā´-) *n.* a virulent disease attacking the skin and causing nervous disorders and mania, caused by deficiency of B vitamins. **pellagrous** *a.* [prob. from It. *pelle agra*, rough skin]

pellet (pel´it) *n.* **1** a little ball, esp. of bread, paper or something easily moulded. **2** a small pill. **3** a rounded boss or prominence. **4** a small shot. *~v.t.* (*pres.p.* **pelleting**, *past*, *p.p.* **pelleted**) **1** to form into pellets. **2** to hit with pellets. **pelletize, pelletise** *v.t.* [OF *pelote*, med. L *pelōta*, dim. of L *pila*, a ball]

pellicle (pel´ikəl) *n.* a thin skin, a membrane or film. **pellicular** (-lik´ū-) *a.* [F *pellicule*, from L *pellicula*, dim. of *pellis*, skin]

pellitory (pel´itəri) *n.* **1** (*also* **pellitory of Spain**) a herb of the aster family, *Anacyclus pyrethrum*. **2** (*also* **pellitory of the wall**) a low, bushy plant, *Parietaria judaica*. [obs. *pelleter*, A-F *peletre*, L *piretārum*, Gr. *purethron*, feverfew, coalescing with obs. *parietary*, A-F *paritarie*, L *parietāria*, from *paries parietis*, a wall]

pell-mell (pelmel´) *adv.* **1** in disorderly haste. **2** in a confused or disorderly manner. *~a.* confused, disorderly. *~n.* **1** disorder, confusion. **2** a medley. [F *pêle-mêle*, prob. a redup. of *mêle*, from *mêler*, late L *misculāre*, L *miscēre*, to mix]

pellucid (piloo´sid) *a.* **1** clear, limpid, transparent. **2** clear in thought, expression or style. **pellucidity** (-sid´-) *n.* **pellucidly** *adv.* **pellucidness** *n.* [F *pellucide*, L *pellūcidus*, from *pel-*, *perlūcēre* (PER-, *lūcēre*, to shine)]

Pelmanism (pel´mənizm) *n.* **1** a system of training to improve the memory. **2** a card game based on Pelmanism. **Pelmanize, Pelmanise** *v.t.* [the *Pelman* Institute in London, where devised]

pelmet (pel´mit) *n.* a canopy, built-in or detachable, which conceals the fittings from which curtains hang; a valance. [PALMETTE]

peloria (pelaw´riə) *n.* symmetry or regularity in flowers that are normally irregular. [mod. L, from Gr. *pelōros*, monstrous, from *pelōr*, a prodigy]

pelorus (pilaw´rəs) *n.* a sighting device on a ship's compass. [*Pelorus*, supposed name of Hannibal's pilot]

pelota (pilot´ə, -lō´-) *n.* (*pl.* **pelotas**) **1** a game similar to squash played with a ball and a curved racket fitting upon the hand, popular in Spain and the Basque country. **2** the ball used in pelota. [Sp., from *pella*, L *pila*, ball]

pelotherapy (pelōther´əpi) *n.* treatment of disease by the application of mud. [Gr. *pelos*, mud, *therapeuein*, to heal]

pelt[1] (pelt) *v.t.* **1** to strike or assail by throwing missiles. **2** to throw. **3** to strike repeatedly. **4** to assail with insults or abuse. *~v.i.* **1** (of rain etc.) to beat down heavily. **2** to hurry (along). **3** to keep on throwing, firing etc. (at). *~n.* a blow from something thrown. **at full pelt** at full speed. **pelter** *n.* **pelting** *a.* [etym. uncertain]

pelt[2] (pelt) *n.* **1** a hide or skin with the hair on, esp. of a sheep or goat. **2** an undressed fur skin. **3** a raw skin stripped of hair or wool. **4** (*facet.*) the human skin. **peltmonger** *n.* **peltry** *n.* pelts. [ME, rel. to *pell*, skin, from OF *pel* (F *peau*), L *pellem*, nom. *-lis*, skin]

pelta (pel´tə) *n.* (*pl.* **peltae** (-tē)) (*Hist.*) **1** a small light shield or target used by the ancient Greeks and Romans. **2** a structure or part like a shield in form or function. **peltate** *a.* **peltati-** (peltā´ti), **peltato-** (peltā´tō) *comb. form* a shield. **peltation** (-ā´shən) *n.* [L, from Gr. *peltē*, perh. rel. to *pella*, a hide]

pelvis (pel´vis) *n.* (*pl.* **pelvises, pelves** (-vēz)) (*Anat.*) **1** the lower portion of the great abdominal cavity. **2** the bony walls of this cavity. **3** the interior cavity of the kidney. **pelvic** *a.* **pelvic girdle, pelvic arch** *n.* (*Anat.*) the arrangement of bones which supports the hind limbs of vertebrates and the lower limbs in humans. **pelviform** *a.* **pelvimeter** (-vim´itə) *n.* an instrument for measuring the diameter of the pelvis. **pelvimetry** *n.* [L, a basin]

Pembs. *abbr.* Pembrokeshire.

pemmican (pem´ikən) *n.* **1** dried meat, pounded, mixed with a large proportion of melted fat and pressed into cakes. **2** a similar preparation of beef with currants. **3** digested or condensed information. [Cree *pimecan*]

pemphigus (pem´figəs) *n.* (*Med.*) a disease characterized by the eruption of watery vesicles on the skin. **pemphigoid** *a.* **pemphigous** *a.* [Gr. *pemphix*, a bubble]

PEN *abbr.* International Association of Poets, Playwrights, Editors, Essayists and Novelists.

Pen. *abbr.* Peninsula.

pen[1] (pen) *n.* **1** an instrument for writing with ink. **2** (*Hist.*) a quill. **3** writing. **4** a style of writing. **5** a writer, a penman. **6** (*Zool.*) the long internal shell of a squid. **7** a female swan. ~*v.t.* (*pres.p.* **penning,** *past, p.p.* **penned**) to write, to compose and write. **to put pen to paper** to write something in a purposeful way. **pen and ink** *n. pl.* **1** instruments for writing. **2** writing. **pen-and-ink** *a.* written or drawn with pen and ink. **pen-case** *n.* **pencraft** *n.* penmanship, authorship. **pen-feather** *n.* **1** a quill-feather. **2** (*dial.*) a pin-feather. **pen-feathered** *a.* half-fledged. **penfriend** *n.* a person, usu. one living abroad and whom one has not met, with whom one corresponds. **penful** *n.* **pen holder** *n.* a rod of wood or other material forming a handle for a pen. **penknife** *n.* (*pl.* **penknives**) a small knife, usu. carried in the pocket. **penlight** *n.* a small torch in the shape of a fountain pen. **penman** *n.* (*pl.* **penmen**). **penmanship** *n.* **1** the art of writing. **2** style of writing. **pen-name** *n.* a literary pseudonym. **pen pal** *n.* (*coll.*) a penfriend. **pen-pusher** *n.* (*coll., derog.*) a person doing dull, routine, clerical work. **pen-pushing** *n.* **penwiper** *n.* [ME and OF *penne*, L *penna*, a feather]

pen[2] (pen) *n.* **1** a small enclosure for cattle, sheep, poultry etc. **2** a place of confinement. **3** (*N Am., sl.*) a penitentiary, a prison. **4** an enclosure for submarines. **5** (*W Ind.*) a country house, a farm etc. ~*v.t.* (*pres.p.* **penning,** *past, p.p.* **penned**) **1** to enclose, to confine, to shut or coop (up or in). **2** to confine (water) with a dam etc. [OE *penn*, whence prob. *pennian* (found only in *onpennad*, unpenned)]

penal (pē´nəl) *a.* **1** enacting, inflicting, of or relating to punishment. **2** punishable, esp. by law. **3** of the nature of punishment, very harsh. **penalize, penalise** *v.t.* **1** to subject to a penalty or handicap. **2** to put under an unfair disadvantage. **3** to make or declare penal. **penalization** (-zā´shən) *n.* **penally** *adv.* **penal servitude** *n.* (*Hist.*) imprisonment with hard labour. [F *pénal*, L *pēnālis*, from *poena*, penalty, Gr. *poinē*, a fine]

penalty (pen´əlti) *n.* (*pl.* **penalties**) **1** legal punishment for a crime, offence or misdemeanour. **2** a sum of money to be forfeited for non-performance or breach of conditions. **3** a fine, a forfeit. **4** a handicap imposed for a breach of rules or on the winner in a previous contest. **5** a penalty kick, hit etc. in a game. ~*a.* given against a side as a penalty. **on penalty of** under penalty of. **the penalty of** something unpleasant resulting from (an action or circumstance). **under penalty of** under the threat of. **penalty area** *n.* in football, a rectangular area in front of the goal, where a foul against the attacking team results in a penalty and in which the goalkeeper is allowed to handle the ball. **penalty box** *n.* **1** the penalty area. **2** an area to which penalized players are confined in ice hockey. **penalty goal** *n.* in football, hockey etc., a goal scored from a penalty. **penalty kick** *n.* in football, a kick allowed to the attacking side when a foul has been committed in the penalty area. **penalty rate** *n.* (*Austral.*) overtime rates. **penalty shoot-out** *n.* in football, a shoot-out, involving penalty shots. **penalty shot** *n.* in football, a shot on goal from the penalty spot, to break a tie etc. **penalty spot** *n.* in football, the point from which a penalty kick is taken. [F *pénalité*, med. L *pœnālitas*, as PENAL]

penance (pen´əns) *n.* **1** sorrow for sin evinced by acts of self-mortification etc. **2** in the Roman Catholic and Greek Orthodox Churches, a sacrament consisting of contrition, confession and satisfaction, with absolution by the priest. **3** an act of self-mortification undertaken as a satisfaction for sin, esp. one imposed by a priest before giving absolution. ~*v.t.* to inflict penance on. **to do penance** to do something unpleasant as a penance. [OF *penance, peneance*, L *poenitentia*, PENITENCE (under PENITENT)]

penannular (penan´ūlə) *a.* nearly annular, almost a complete ring. [L *paene*, nearly]

penates (pinah´tēz) *n.pl.* (*Hist.*) the Roman household gods, orig. of the storeroom and kitchen. **lares and penates** LAR. [L, rel. to *penes*, within]

pence PENNY.

penchant (pā´shā) *n.* a strong inclination or liking, a bias. [F, orig. pres.p. of *pencher*, to lean, ult. from L *pendēre*, to hang]

pencil (pen´səl) *n.* **1** a cylinder or slip of graphite, crayon etc., usu. enclosed in a casing of wood, used for writing, drawing etc. **2** any of various appliances in the form of a pencil, such as an eyebrow pencil. **3** anything long and slim. **4** in optics, a system of rays diverging from or converging to a point. **5** (*Geom.*) the figure formed by a series of straight lines meeting at a point. **6** skill or style in painting, the art of painting. ~*a.* **1** of or relating to pencils. **2** long and slim (*a pencil skirt*). ~*v.t.* (*pres.p.* **pencilling,** (*N Am.*) **penciling,** *past, p.p.* **pencilled,** (*N Am.*) **penciled**) **1** to paint, draw, write or mark with a pencil. **2** to mark or shade in delicate lines. **to pencil in** to agree or arrange something provisionally. **pencil box** *n.* a box for holding pencils etc. **pencil case** *n.* a case for holding pencils etc. **pencilled,** (*N Am.*) **penciled** *a.* **penciller,** (*N Am.*) **penciler** *n.* **pencilling,** (*N Am.*) **penciling** *n.* **pencil sharpener** *n.* a device for sharpening pencils with a rotating blade. [OF *pincel* (F *pinceau*), L *pēnicillum, -lus*, dim. of *pēniculus*, a brush, dim. of PENIS]

pendant (pen´dənt) *n.* **1** anything hanging down or suspended by way of ornament etc., such as an earring, a locket. **2** a pendant chandelier. **3** a carved ornament hanging from a ceiling or roof. **4** the shank and ring of a watch-case. **5** (*Naut.*) **a** a short rope hanging from a masthead etc. **b** a tapering flag or pennant. **6** a companion, a counterpart, a match. ~*a.* PENDENT. [F, orig. pres.p. of *pendre*, L *pendēre*, to hang]

pendent (pen´dənt) *a.* **1** hanging. **2** overhanging. **3** pending, undetermined. **4** (*Gram.*) incomplete in construction, having the sense suspended. **pendency** *n.* **pendentive** (-den´-) *n.* (*Archit.*) any of the triangular pieces of vaulting resting on piers or arches and forming segments of a dome. **pendently** *adv.* **pending** *a.* **1** depending, awaiting settlement, undecided. **2**

about to happen. ~*prep.* 1 during. 2 until. **pending tray** *n.* a tray for correspondence etc. waiting to be dealt with. [as PENDANT]

pendente lite (pendenti lī´ti) *adv.* (*Law*) while a suit is in progress. [L]

pendragon (pendrag´ən) *n.* (*Hist.*) a leader of the ancient Britons. [Welsh, chief war-leader, from *pen*, the head, *dragon*, standard]

pendulous (pen´dūləs) *a.* 1 hanging, suspended. 2 swinging, oscillating. **pendulate** *v.i.* to swing as a pendulum. **penduline** (-līn) *a.* 1 (of a nest) hanging. 2 (of a bird) building a hanging nest. **pendulously** *adv.* **pendulousness** *n.* [L *pendulus*, from *pendēre*, to hang]

pendulum (pen´dūləm) *n.* (*pl.* **pendulums**) a body suspended from a fixed point and oscillating freely by the force of gravity, esp. the weighted rod regulating the movement of the works in a clock. [L, neut. of *pendulus*, see PENDULOUS]

penelopize (pinel´əpīz), **penelopise** *v.t.* to undo (a piece of work) to cause delay. [*Penelope*, wife of Odysseus, who undid at night the work she had done by day as a check to the importunity of her suitors]

peneplain (pē´niplān) *n.* (*Geol.*) an area of flat land produced by erosion. [L *paene*, *pene*, almost, PLAIN[1]]

penetralia (penitrā´liə) *n.pl.* 1 the inner part of a house, palace, temple or shrine. 2 secrets, mysteries. [L, pl. of *penetrāle*, as PENETRATE]

penetrate (pen´itrāt) *v.t.* 1 to enter, to pass into or through. 2 to permeate, to saturate or imbue (with). 3 to reach or discern by the senses or intellect. 4 to move or affect the feelings of. 5 to pierce. 6 to put one's penis into the vagina of. ~*v.i.* 1 to be understood. 2 to make way, to pass (into, through, to etc.). **penetrable** (-trəbəl) *a.* **penetrability** (-bil´-) *n.* **penetrance** *n.* **penetrant** *a.*, *n.* **penetrating** *a.* 1 subtle, discerning. 2 sharp, piercing. **penetratingly** *adv.* **penetration** (-ā´shən) *n.* **penetrative** (-trətiv) *a.* **penetratively** *adv.* **penetrativeness** *n.* **penetrator** *n.* [L *penetrātus*, p.p. of *penetrāre*, rel. to *penitus*, within]

penfold PINFOLD.

penguin (peng´gwin) *n.* a black-and-white bird of the family Spheniscidae, belonging to the southern hemisphere, consisting of seabirds with rudimentary wings or paddles and scalelike feathers. **penguinery** *n.* (*pl.* **penguineries**) a place where penguins breed. [etym. uncertain]

penial PENIS.

penicillate (penisil´ət) *a.* (*Biol.*) 1 furnished with, forming or consisting of a bundle of short close hairs or fibres. 2 having delicate markings, pencilled. **penicillately** *adv.* **penicillation** (-ā´shən) *n.* **penicilliform** (-sil´-) *a.* [L *pēnicillus*, a PENCIL]

penicillin (penisil´in) *n.* an ether-soluble substance produced from the mould *Penicillium* and having an intense growth-inhibiting action against various bacteria.

penile PENIS.

peninsula (pənin´sūlə) *n.* a piece of land almost surrounded by water, poss. connected to the mainland by an isthmus. **the Peninsula** the Iberian Peninsula, Spain and Portugal. **peninsular** *a.* of or relating to a peninsula. **peninsularity** (-lar´-) *n.* **Peninsular War** *n.* the war in Spain and Portugal (1808–14) between the British, Spanish and Portuguese and the French. **peninsulate** *v.t.* to form or convert into a peninsula. [L *paeninsula* (*paene*, almost, *insula*, an island)]

Usage note The spellings of the noun *peninsula* and the adjective *peninsular* should not be confused.

penis (pē´nis) *n.* (*pl.* **penises, penes** (-nēz)) 1 the copulatory and urethral organ of a male mammal. 2 the copulatory organ of the males of lower vertebrates. **penial, penile** (-nīl) *a.* **penis envy** *n.* in Freudian theory, the female's subconscious desire to be male. [L, a tail]

penitent (pen´itənt) *a.* contrite, repentant, sorry. ~*n.* 1 a person who is penitent, a contrite sinner. 2 a person submitting to penance under the direction of a confessor. 3 a member of any of various Roman Catholic orders devoted to the practice of penance and mutual discipline. **penitence** *n.* **penitential** (-ten´-) *a.* 1 of, relating to or expressing penitence. 2 relating to or of the nature of penance. ~*n.* in the Roman Catholic Church, a book containing rules relating to penitence. **penitentially** *adv.* **penitential psalms** *n.pl.* seven psalms which express penitence. **penitentiary** (-ten´-) *n.* (*pl.* **penitentiaries**) 1 (*N Am.*) a prison. 2 in the Roman Catholic Church, a papal court granting dispensations and dealing with matters relating to confessions. 3 an asylum for prostitutes seeking reformation. 4 a reformatory prison, a house of correction. ~*a.* 1 penitential. 2 of or relating to the reformatory treatment of criminals etc. 3 (*N Am.*) (of an offence) entailing a prison sentence. **penitently** *adv.* [OF, from L *poenitentem*, nom. *-tens*, pres.p. of *poenitēre*, rel. to *punīre*, to PUNISH]

Penn. (pen), **Penna.** (pen´ə) *abbr.* Pennsylvania.

pennant (pen´ənt) *n.* 1 (*Naut.*) **a** a long narrow streamer borne at the masthead of a ship of war. **b** a pendant. 2 a pennon. 3 (*N Am.*) a flag indicating championship, e.g. in baseball. [conf. of PENNON and PENDANT]

pennate, pennated PINNATE.

penne (pen´i) *n.* pasta quills, pasta in short, thick, ridged tube shapes. [It., pl. of *penna*, a quill]

penniform (pen´ifawm) *a.* (*Biol.*) having the form of a feather. [L *penna*, a feather, -FORM]

penniless (pen´ilis) *a.* without money, destitute. **pennilessly** *adv.* **pennilessness** *n.*

pennon (pen´ən) *n.* 1 a small pointed or swallow-tailed flag, formerly carried on the spears of knights and later as the ensign of a regiment of lancers. 2 (*Naut.*) a long streamer carried by a ship. 3 a flag. **pennoned** *a.* [ME and OF *penon*, prob. from L *penna*, a feather, see PEN[1]]

penn'orth PENNYWORTH (under PENNY).

Pennsylvania Dutch (pensilvā´niə) *n.* 1 a dialect of High German spoken by Pennsylvanian descendants of 17th- and 18th-cent. German and Swiss immigrants. 2 (*as pl.*) these immigrants or their descendants.

Pennsylvanian (pensilvā´niən) *n.* 1 a native or inhabitant of Pennsylvania, USA. 2 (*Geol.*) the upper Carboniferous period or system esp. in N America. ~*a.* 1 of or relating to Pennsylvania. 2 (*Geol.*) of or relating to the upper Carboniferous period etc.

penny (pen´i) *n.* (*pl.* **pennies** (-niz), **pence** (pens)) 1 a bronze coin, a 100th part of a pound sterling. 2 (*Hist.*) a bronze coin, formerly a 12th part of a shilling. 3 (*N Am.*) a one-cent piece. 4 (*Bible*) a denarius. 5 (*coll.*) money, a small sum of money (*I haven't a penny*). **a penny for your thoughts?** what are you thinking about? **a pretty penny** considerable cost or expense. **in for a penny, in for a pound** total commitment is advisable. **like a bad penny** repeatedly returning, esp. when not wanted. **penny wise and pound foolish** saving small sums at the risk of larger ones. **the penny drops** (*coll.*) the truth is realized, something is made clear. **two a penny** having little value because very common. **without a penny to bless oneself with** penniless, very poor. **pennies from heaven** *n.* an unexpected bonus or advantage. **penny black** *n.* (*Hist.*) the first ever adhesive postage stamp, which cost one (old) penny. **penny cress** *n.* a plant, *Thlaspi arvense*, which has round, flat pods. **penny dreadful** *n.* a cheap crime story. **penny-farthing** *n.* (*Hist.*) an early type of bicycle with a large front wheel and small back wheel. **penny-in-the-slot** *a.* denoting an automatic machine for giving out small articles, tickets etc. in return for a coin inserted in a slot. **penny-pinch** *v.i.* to save money by being miserly. **penny-pincher** *n.* **penny-pinching** *n.* miserliness, niggardliness. ~*a.* miserly, niggardly. **penny post** *n.* (*Hist.*) a post for conveying letters at the ordinary rate of a penny. **pennyweight** *n.* 24 grains, or one-twentieth of an ounce troy (1.5 g). **penny whistle** *n.* a tin pipe with six holes, played as a whistle. **penny wise** *a.* saving small sums. **pennywort** *n.* any one of several plants with round peltate leaves. **marsh pennywort** MARSH. **wall pennywort** WALL. **water pennywort** WATER. **pennyworth** (pen´iwœth), **penn'orth** (pen´əth) *n.* **1** as much as can be bought for a penny. **2** a good (or bad) bargain. **3** a small amount (*not a pennyworth*). [OE *pening* (cp. Dut., Dan. and Swed. *penning*, G *Pfennig*)]

Usage note Use of *pence* as a singular (after *one* etc.) is best avoided.

-penny (pəni) *comb. form* denoting a specified number of pennies, esp. old pennies, as in *sixpenny*.

pennyroyal (peniroi´əl) *n.* **1** a kind of mint, *Mentha pulegium*, formerly and still popularly used for medicinal purposes. **2** (*N Am.*) a similar plant, *Hedeoma pulegioides*. [prob. a corr. of *puliol ryale* (OF *puliol*, *poliol*, prob. from a dim. of *pūlēgium*, thyme, ROYAL)]

penology (pēnol´əji), **poenology** *n.* the science of punishment and prison management. **penological** (-loj´-) *a.* **penologist** *n.* [Gr. *poinē*, a fine, PENALTY, -LOGY]

pensée (pã´sā) *n.* a thought, a reflection. [F]

pensile (pen´sīl) *a.* **1** hanging, suspended, pendulous. **2** (of a bird) constructing a pendent nest. **pensileness** *n.* [L *pensilis*, from *pensus*, p.p. of *pendēre*, to hang]

pension[1] (pen´shən) *n.* **1** a periodical allowance for past services paid by the government or an employer. **2** a similar allowance to a person for goodwill, to secure services when required etc., or to literary people, scientists etc., to enable them to carry on their work. ~*v.t.* **1** to grant a pension to. **2** to pay a pension to for the retention of services. **to pension off 1** to cease to employ and to give a pension to. **2** to discard as useless, worn etc. **pensionable** *a.* **pensionability** (-bil´-) *n.* **pensionary** *a.* of or relating to a pension. ~*n.* (*pl.* **pensionaries**) **1** a pensioner. **2** a hireling. **pensioner** *n.* **1** a person in receipt of a pension. **2** a dependant. **3** a hireling. **4** a Cambridge undergraduate who is not a scholar on the foundation or a sizar. **pensionless** *a.* [F, from L *pensiōnem*, nom. *-sio*, payment, from *pendere*, to pay]

pension[2] (pãsyõ´) *n.* a boarding house. [F]

pensive (pen´siv) *a.* **1** thoughtful. **2** serious, anxious, melancholy. **3** expressing sad thoughtfulness. **pensively** *adv.* **pensiveness** *n.* [F *pensif*, *-sive*, from *penser*, to think, L *pensāre*, freq. of *pendere*, to weigh]

penstemon (penstē´mən), **pentstemon** *n.* any herbaceous plant of the genus *Penstemon* with showy tubular flowers. [Gr. *stēmōn*, erron. for STAMEN]

penstock (pen´stok) *n.* **1** a floodgate. **2** (*N Am.*) a conduit, usu. in the form of a wooden trough, conveying water to a waterwheel. [PEN[2], STOCK]

pent (pent) *a.* penned in or confined, shut (up or in). **pent-up** *a.* **1** not openly expressed. **2** suppressed. [for *penned*, p.p. of PEN[2]]

penta- (pen´tə) *comb. form* five. [Gr. *pente*, five]

pentachord (pen´təkawd) *n.* (*Mus.*) **1** a musical instrument with five strings. **2** a scale of five notes.

pentacle (pen´təkəl) *n.* **1** a figure like a star with five points formed by producing the sides of a pentagon in both directions to their points of intersection. **2** such a figure, used as a symbol by the mystics and astrologers of the Middle Ages. [med. L *pentaculum* (prob. PENTA-, -CULE)]

pentad (pen´tad) *n.* **1** the number five. **2** a group of five. **3** (*Chem.*) a chemical element or radical having a valency of five. [Gr. *pentas -ados*, from *pente*, five]

pentadactyl (pentədak´til) *a.* having five fingers or toes. ~*n.* a person or animal having five digits on each limb. **pentadactylic** (-til´-) *a.* **pentadactylism** *n.* [Gr. *daktulos*, a toe]

pentadelphous (pentədel´fəs) *a.* having the stamens united in five sets. [Gr. *adelphos*, a brother]

pentagon (pen´təgən) *n.* a plane (usu. rectilineal) figure having five sides and five angles. **the Pentagon 1** the pentagonal headquarters of the US Defence Department in Washington, DC. **2** the Defence Department of the US in Washington, DC. **pentagonal** (-tag´-) *a.* [L *pentagōnus*, Gr. *pentagōnos* (*gōnia*, an angle)]

pentagram (pen´təgram) *n.* a pentacle. [Gr. *pentagrammon*]

pentagraph PANTOGRAPH.

pentagynian (pentəjin´iən), **pentagynous** (-taj´-) *a.* of or relating to the Linnaean order Pentagynia, containing plants with five pistils. [Gr. *gunē*, a woman, a female]

pentahedron (pentəhē´drən) *n.* (*pl.* **pentahedra** (-drə), **pentahedrons**) a figure having five sides, esp. equal sides. **pentahedral** *a.* [Gr. *hedra*, a base]

pentalpha (pental´fə) *n.* a pentagram or pentacle. [Gr. ALPHA, the letter *a*]

pentamerous (pentam´ərəs) *a.* **1** (*Bot.*) (of a flower-whorl) composed of five parts. **2** (*Zool.*) five-jointed. [Gr. *meros*, a part]

pentameter (pentam´itə) *n.* **1** a verse of five feet, such as the iambic verse of ten syllables. **2** a Greek or Latin dactylic verse consisting of two halves, each containing two feet (dactyls or spondees in the first half, dactyls in the second, and one long syllable), used principally with alternate hexameters in elegiacs.

pentandrian (pentan´driən), **pentandrous** (-drəs) *a.* of or relating to a Linnaean class containing plants with five stamens. [Gr. *anēr andros*, a man, a male]

pentane (pen´tān) *n.* (*Chem.*) a volatile, fluid, paraffin hydrocarbon contained in petroleum etc.

pentangle (pen´tang·gəl) *n.* a pentagram. **pentangular** (-tang´gū-) *a.* having five angles.

pentanoic acid (pentənō´ik) *n.* (*Chem.*) a colourless, liquid, carboxylic acid, used to make perfumes.

pentapody (pentap´ədi) *n.* (*pl.* **pentapodies**) a verse or sequence of five natural feet. [Gr. *pentapous* (*pous podos*, a foot)]

pentapolis (pentap´əlis) *n.* (*pl.* **pentapolises**) a group or confederacy of five towns. **pentapolitan** (-təpol´-) *a.* of or relating to a pentapolis, esp. that of Cyrenaica. [Gr. *polis*, a city]

pentaprism (pen´təprizm) *n.* a five-sided prism used in reflex cameras to invert the image by deflecting light from any direction through 90°.

pentarchy (pen´tahki) *n.* (*pl.* **pentarchies**) **1** government by five rulers. **2** a group of five kingdoms. [Gr. *archia*, from *archein*, to rule]

pentastich (pen´təstik) *n.* a stanza or group of five lines of verse. **pentastichous** (-tas´-) *a.* [Gr. *pentastichos* (*stichos*, a row)]

pentastyle (pen´təstīl) *a.* (*Archit.*) (of a building) having five columns at the front or end. ~*n.* a pentastyle building or portico. [Gr. *stulos*, a pillar]

Pentateuch (pen´tətūk) *n.* the first five books of the Old Testament, usu. ascribed to Moses. **Pentateuchal** (-tū´-) *a.* [L *Pentateuchus*, Gr. *Pentateuchos* (PENTA-, *teuchos*, a tool, a book)]

pentathlon (pentath´lon) *n.* (*pl.* **pentathlons**) **1** a modern athletics contest comprising five events for each competitor. **2** in ancient Greece, an athletic contest comprising leaping, running, wrestling, throwing the discus and hurling the spear. **pentathlete** (-lēt) *n.* [Gr. *athlon*, a contest]

pentatomic (pentətom´ik) *a.* (*Chem.*) containing five atoms in the molecule, esp. five replaceable atoms of hydrogen.
pentatonic (pentəton´ik) *a.* (*Mus.*) **1** consisting of five tones. **2** of or relating to a pentatonic scale.
pentavalent (pentəvā´lənt) *a.* (*Chem.*) having a valency of five.
Pentecost (pen´tikost) *n.* **1** Whit Sunday. **2** a festival to celebrate the descent of the Holy Spirit. **3** a solemn Jewish festival at the close of harvest, held on the 50th day from the second day of the Passover. **Pentecostal** (-kos´-) *a.* **1** of or relating to Pentecost. **2** of or relating to any of various fundamentalist Christian groups who stress the powers of the Holy Spirit, e.g. in healing. ~*n.* a follower of Pentecostalism. **Pentecostalism** *a.*, *n.* **Pentecostalist** *n.* [L *pentēcostē*, Gr. *pentēkostē*, fiftieth (day), from *pentēkonta*, fifty]
penthemimer (penthəmim´ə) *n.* in Greek prosody, a group of two and a half metrical feet, as a half of a pentameter. **penthemimeral** *a.* [Gr. *penthēmimerēs* (*hēmimerēs*, halved)]
penthouse (pent´hows) *n.* **1** a flat built on the rooftop of a tall building. **2** a roof or shed standing aslope against a main wall or building. **3** a shedlike structure against a wall, a canopy, a protection over a window or door etc. **4** (*N Am.*) a subsidiary roof construction. ~*v.t.* to furnish with a penthouse. [ME *pentice*, *pentis*, prob. from OF *apentis*, late L *appendicium*, from *appendere*, to APPEND]
pentimento (pentimen´tō) *n.* (*pl.* **pentimenti** (-tē)) (a part of) a painting that has been painted over and later becomes visible. [It., correction]
pentobarbitone (pentəbah´bitōn), (*N Am.*) **pentobarbital** (-təl) *n.* a barbiturate, formerly used as a sedative.
pentode (pen´tōd) *n.* a five-electrode thermionic valve.
pentose (pen´tōz) *n.* any of various sugars containing five carbon atoms in the molecule.
Pentothal® (pen´təthal) *n.* thiopentone.
pent roof (pent) *n.* a lean-to roof. [PENTHOUSE]
pentstemon PENSTEMON.
pentyl (pen´tīl, -til) *n.* amyl.
penuchle PINOCHLE.
penult (pinŭlt´) *n.* the last but one, esp. the last syllable but one of a word. ~*a.* last but one. **penultimate** (-mət) *a.* last but one. ~*n.* the last but one, esp. the last syllable but one of a word. [L *paenultima*, fem. a. (*paene*, almost, *ultimus*, last)]
penumbra (pinŭm´brə) *n.* (*pl.* **penumbrae** (-brē), **penumbras**) **1** the partly shaded zone around the total shadow caused by an opaque body intercepting the light from a luminous body, esp. round that of the earth or moon in an eclipse. **2** (*Astron.*) the lighter fringe of a sunspot. **3** a partial shadow. **4** something obscure or uncertain. **5** the blending or boundary of light and shade in a painting etc. **penumbral** *a.* [L *paene*, almost, *umbra*, shadow]
penury (pen´ūri) *n.* (*pl.* **penuries**) **1** extreme poverty, destitution. **2** a lack or scarcity (of). **penurious** (pinū´-) *a.* **1** poor, penniless. **2** niggardly, stingy. **penuriously** *adv.* **penuriousness** *n.* [F *pénurie*, L *pēnūria*, cogn. with Gr. *peina*, hunger, *penia*, poverty]
peon (pē´on) *n.* **1** a Spanish-American day labourer etc. **2** in India, a foot soldier, a non-European constable, an attendant. **3** an assistant to a bullfighter. **4** (*Hist.*) in SW US, a bondman serving his creditor in order to work off a debt. **5** (*N Am.*) a menial worker. **peonage** (-nij) *n.* [Sp., from L *pedōnem*, nom. *pedo*, a foot soldier, see PAWN[1]]
peony (pē´əni), **paeony** *n.* (*pl.* **peonies, paeonies**) any plant of the genus *Paeonia*, with large globular terminal flowers, usu. double in cultivated varieties. [OE *peonie*, L *paeōnia*, Gr. *paiōnia* from *Paiōn*, the god of healing]
people (pē´pəl) *n.* **1** (*usu. as pl.*) the persons composing a nation, community or race. **2** (*usu. as pl.*) any body of persons, such as those belonging to a place, a class, a congregation or company of any sort etc. **3** (*as pl.*) persons generally or indefinitely. **4** (*as pl.*) one's family, kindred or tribe. **5** (*as pl.*, *N Am.*) one's ancestors. **6** (*as pl.*) followers, retinue, servants, workpeople etc. ~*v.t.* **1** to stock with inhabitants, to populate. **2** to occupy, to inhabit. **the people 1** the commonalty, the populace, as distinct from the self-styled higher orders. **2** the electorate. **people carrier** *n.* a people mover. **peopled** *a.* inhabited. **people mover** *n.* **1** any of various methods of moving many people over short distances, e.g. moving pavements or driverless shuttles. **2** a large vanlike estate car with an extra row of seats. **people power** *n.* the power to influence the course of events exerted by the mass of the people, by mass demonstrations etc. **people's democracy** *n.* a political (esp. formerly Communist) system in which power is invested in the people. [A-F *people*, *poeple*, OF *pople* (F *peuple*), L *populum*, nom. *populus*]
PEP *abbr.* **1** personal equity plan. **2** Political and Economic Planning.
pep (pep) *n.* (*coll.*) vigour, spirit, energy. ~*v.t.* (*pres.p.* **pepping,** *past, p.p.* **pepped**) (*coll.*) to pep up. **to pep up** to give energy, vigour etc. to. **pep pill** *n.* a pill containing a stimulant. **peppy** *a.* (*comp.* **peppier,** *superl.* **peppiest**) (*coll.*) full of vitality, energetic. **pep talk** *n.* (*coll.*) a talk intended to encourage or stimulate. [PEPPER]
peperino (pepərē´nō) *n.* a porous volcanic rock, composed of sand, cinders etc. cemented together. [It., from *pepere*, PEPPER]
peperoni PEPPERONI.
peplum (pep´ləm), **peplus** (-ləs) *n.* (*pl.* **peplums, pepluses**) **1** a flared extension attached to the waist of a tight-fitting jacket or bodice. **2** an outer robe or gown worn by women in ancient Greece. **3** an overskirt supposed to resemble the ancient peplum. [L *peplum*, Gr. *peplos*]
pepo (pē´pō) *n.* (*pl.* **pepos**) any of various fruits of the gourd family, e.g. cucumber, melon, with a hard rind, watery pulp, and many seeds. [Gr. *pepōn*, ripe, from *peptein*, to ripen]
pepper (pep´ə) *n.* **1** a pungent aromatic condiment made from the dried berries of *Piper nigrum* or other species of the genus *Piper*, used whole or ground into powder. **2** the pepper plant, *P. nigrum*, or other species of the genus *Piper*. **3** rough treatment, pungent criticism or sarcasm etc. **4** a capsicum. **5** cayenne. ~*v.t.* **1** to sprinkle or season with pepper. **2** to sprinkle. **3** to attack with pungent remarks. **4** to pelt with missiles. **5** to beat severely. **pepper-and-salt** *a.* (of hair) dark mingled with grey. **pepperbox** *n.* **1** a pepper pot. **2** a gun with revolving barrels. **pepper-cake** *n.* a kind of gingerbread or spiced cake. **pepper-caster, pepper-castor** *n.* a pepper pot. **peppercorn** *n.* **1** the dried fruit of the *Piper nigrum*, used as a condiment. **2** anything of little value. **3** a peppercorn rent. **peppercorn rent** *n.* a nominal rent. **peppergrass** *n.* **1** the pepperwort. **2** the pillwort. **pepper mill** *n.* a small hand-operated device for grinding peppercorns. **pepper pot** *n.* **1** a small container with a perforated top for sprinkling pepper on food. **2** a W Indian dish of meat or fish with okra, chillies etc., flavoured with cayenne. **pepper shaker** *n.* (*N Am.*) a pepper pot. **pepper tree** *n.* any of various trees of the genus *Schinus*, having whitish flowers and red ornamental fruit. **pepperwort** *n.* any plant of the genus *Lepidium*, esp. garden cress. **peppery** *a.* **1** tasting of or like pepper. **2** hot-tempered, irascible, hasty. **3** pungent, sharp. **pepperiness** *n.* [OE *pipor*, L *piper*, Gr. *peperi*, of Oriental orig. (cp. Sansk. *pippalī*)]
peppermint (pep´əmint) *n.* **1** a pungent aromatic herb, *Mentha piperita*. **2** an essential oil distilled from this

plant. 3 a sweet flavoured with peppermint oil. 4 (*Austral.*) any of various eucalyptuses which yield an oil similar to peppermint oil. **pepperminty** *a.*

pepperoni (peparō´ni), **peperoni** *n.* a dry sausage of pork and beef that is heavily seasoned, esp. with pepper.

peppy PEP.

Pepsi-Cola® (pepsikō´lə) *n.* a cola-flavoured carbonated soft drink, dark brown in colour.

pepsin (pep´sin) *n.* a protein-digesting enzyme contained in gastric juice. **peptic** (-tik) *a.* 1 of or relating to digestion. 2 promoting digestion. 3 having good digestive powers. **peptic gland** *n.* a gland which secretes gastric juice. **pepticity** (-tis´-) *n.* **peptic ulcer** *n.* an ulcer in the stomach, duodenum etc. caused by the action of pepsin and stomach acid. **peptide** (-tīd) *n.* a group of two or more amino acids, in which the carbon of one amino acid is linked to the nitrogen of another. [F *pepsine* (Gr. *pepsis*, digestion, cogn. with *peptein*, to cook)]

peptone (pep´tōn) *n.* any of the soluble compounds into which the proteins in food are converted by the action of pepsin. **peptonize** (-tə-), **peptonise** *v.t.* **peptonization** (-zā´shən) *n.*

PER *abbr.* Professional Employment Register.

per (pœ) *prep.* 1 for each. 2 by, through, by means of. 3 according to. 4 (*Her.*) in the direction of. [L]

per- (pœ) *pref.* 1 through, completely. 2 very, exceedingly, to the extreme. 3 (*Chem.*) denoting the highest degree of combination or of valency in similar chemical compounds. [PER]

peracute (pœrəkūt´) *a.* (*Med.*) very acute or violent.

peradventure (pœrədven´chə, pər-) *adv.* (*formal or facet.*) perhaps. ~*n.* uncertainty, doubt, conjecture. [ME *peraventure*, OF *par aventure*]

perambulate (pəram´būlāt) *v.t.* 1 to walk over or through, esp. for the purpose of surveying or inspecting. 2 to walk along the boundaries of (a parish etc.) in order to survey or preserve them. ~*v.i.* to walk about. **perambulation** (-lā´shən) *n.* **perambulator** *n.* 1 (*formal*) a pram. 2 an instrument for measuring distances travelled, an odometer, a pedometer. **perambulatory** *a.* [L *perambulātus*, p.p. of *perambulāre* (*ambulāre*, to walk)]

per annum (pər an´əm) *adv.* yearly, each year. [L]

percale (pəkāl´) *n.* a closely woven cotton cambric. **percaline** (pœ´kəlēn) *n.* a glossy cotton cloth. [F, etym. uncertain]

per capita (pə kap´itə), **per caput** (kap´ut) *adv.* for each person. [L, by the head]

perceive (pəsēv´) *v.t.* 1 to observe, to see. 2 to apprehend with the mind, to discern, to understand. **perceivable** *a.* **perceiver** *n.* [OF *perceiv-*, stem of *perceivre*, *perçoivre* (F *percevoir*), L *percipere* (*capere*, to take)]

per cent (pə sent´), (*N Am.*) **percent** *adv.* in terms of 100 parts of a whole. ~*n.* 1 a percentage. 2 one part per hundred. 3 (*pl.*) securities yielding interest as specified. **percentage** (-tij) *n.* 1 a rate or proportion expressed per cent. 2 (*coll.*) advantage, profit. 3 in commerce, allowance, commission, duty. **to play the percentages** PLAY. **percentile** *n.* in statistics, one of 99 values of a variable dividing its distribution into 100 groups with equal frequencies.

perception (pəsep´shən) *n.* 1 the act or an instance of perceiving. 2 intuitive apprehension, insight or discernment. 3 an impression based on one's perception of something. 4 (*Philos.*) the mental action of knowing external things through the medium of sense presentations. 5 (*Law*) collection or receipt of rents. **percept** (pœ´sept) *n.* 1 something that is perceived. 2 the mental product of perception. **perceptible** *a.* able to be perceived by the senses or intellect. **perceptibility** (-bil´-) *n.* **perceptibly** *adv.* **perceptional** *a.* **perceptive** *a.* 1 having the faculty of perceiving. 2 discerning, astute. **perceptively** *adv.* **perceptiveness** *n.* **perceptivity** (pœseptiv´-) *n.* **perceptual** (-tūəl) *a.* **perceptually** *adv.* [L *perceptio*, n. from *percipere*, to PERCEIVE]

perch[1] (pœch) *n.* 1 a pole or bar used as a rest or roost for birds, or anything serving this purpose. 2 a high seat or position. 3 (*Hist.*) a land measure of 5½ yd. (5.03 m). 4 the centre pole connecting the front and back gear of a high carriage. ~*v.i.* 1 (of a bird) to alight or rest. 2 to alight or settle on or as if on a perch. ~*v.t.* to set or place on or as if on a perch. **to knock someone off their perch** 1 to beat or destroy someone. 2 to lower the esteem in which someone is held. **percher** *n.* 1 any of the perching birds. 2 a person who or thing which perches. [ME and OF *perche*, L *pertica*, a pole]

perch[2] (pœch) *n.* (*pl. in general* **perch**, *in particular* **perches**) a striped spiny-finned freshwater fish, *Perca fluviatilis*, or *P. flavescens*, the yellow perch of the US. **percoid** (pœ´koid) *n.*, *a.* [F *perche*, L *perca*, Gr. *perkē*]

†**perchance** (pəchahns´) *adv.* 1 by chance. 2 perhaps. [ME and OF *par chance* (*par*, by, CHANCE)]

percher PERCH[1].

percheron (pœ´shəron) *n.* a breed of heavy and powerful horses (orig. from the district of le Perche, France). [F]

perchlorate (pœklaw´rət) *n.* (*Chem.*) a salt of perchloric acid. **perchloric** *a.* (*Chem.*) of or relating to a compound of chlorine containing oxygen in the highest possible proportion. **perchloric acid** *n.* (*Chem.*) a colourless, toxic liquid containing heptavalent chlorine, used as an oxidizing agent. **perchloride** (-īd) *n.*

percipient (pəsip´iənt) *a.* 1 perceiving, apprehending, conscious. 2 discerning, perceptive. ~*n.* a person who perceives, esp. one receiving a supposed telepathic message. **percipience** *n.* **percipiently** *adv.* [L *percipiens -ntem*, pres.p. of *percipere*, to PERCEIVE]

percoct (pəkokt´) *a.* overdone, hackneyed. [L *percoctus*, p.p. of *percoquere* (*coquere*, to COOK)]

percoid PERCH[2].

percolate (pœ´kəlāt) *v.i.* 1 to pass through small interstices, to filter (through). 2 (of an idea) to spread through a group of people. ~*v.t.* 1 to make (coffee) in a percolator. 2 to ooze through, to permeate. 3 to strain, to filter. **percolation** (-ā´shən) *n.* **percolator** *n.* 1 a coffee pot in which the boiling water filters through the coffee. 2 a person who or thing which strains or filters; a filter. [L *percōlātus*, p.p. of *percōlāre* (*cōlum*, a strainer)]

per contra (pœ kon´trə) *adv.* on the opposite side. [It.]

percuss (pəkŭs´) *v.t.* (*Med.*) to strike quickly or tap forcibly in order to test or diagnose. **percussant** *a.* (*Her.*) (of the tail of a lion etc.) beating or lashing. [L *percussus*, p.p. of *percutere* (*quatere*, to shake)]

percussion (pəkŭsh´ən) *n.* 1 (*Mus.*) **a** the production of sound by striking on an instrument. **b** musical instruments played by striking. 2 (*Med.*) medical examination by gently striking some part of the body with the fingers or an instrument. 3 **a** forcible striking or collision. **b** the shock of such collision. **c** the effect of the sound of a collision on the ear. **percussion cap** *n.* a small metal or paper cap containing fulminating powder, used in toy guns and in percussion locks. **percussionist** *n.* a person who plays a percussion instrument. **percussion lock** *n.* a gunlock in which the hammer strikes a cap to explode the charge in a firearm. **percussive** *a.* **percussively** *adv.* [L *percussio*, as PERCUSS]

percutaneous (pœkūtā´niəs) *a.* acting or done through the skin. **percutaneously** *adv.* [L *per cutem*, through the skin]

per diem (pœ dē´em) *a.*, *adv.* by the day, for each day. ~*n.* a per diem payment or allowance. [L]

perdition (pədish´ən) *n.* the loss of the soul or of

happiness in a future state, damnation. [ME and OF *perdiciun*, L *perditiōnem*, nom. *-tio*, from *perdere*, to destroy (*dare*, to give)]

perdurable (pədū´rəbəl) *a.* (*formal*) very lasting or durable, permanent, everlasting. **perdurability** (-bil´-) *n.* **perdurably** *adv.* [OF, from late L *perdūrābilis*]

père (peə) *n.* father, senior, as distinct from *fils* (*Douglas père*).

Père David's deer (peə dā´vidz) *n.* a large deer, *Elaphurus davidianus*, with antlers.

peregrination (perigrinā´shən) *n.* **1** a sojourning in foreign countries. **2** a travelling about. †**peregrinate** (per´-) *v.i.* **peregrinator** (per´-) *n.* [F *pérégrination*, L *peregrinātiōnem*, nom. *-tio*, from *peregrīnārī*, from *peregrīnus*, foreign, as PEREGRINE]

peregrine (per´igrin) *n.* a peregrine falcon. ~*a.* foreign, outlandish. **peregrine falcon** *n.* a falcon, *Falco peregrinus*, used for hawking. [L *peregrīnus*, from *peregre*, abroad (PER, *ager*, a field)]

pereion (pərī´on) *n.* (*pl.* **pereia** (-rī´ə)) the thorax in crustaceans. [Gr. *peraiōn*, pres.p. of *peraioein*, to transport (in mistake for *periienai*, to walk about)]

peremptory (pəremp´təri) *a.* **1** precluding question or hesitation. **2** imperious, dogmatic, dictatorial. **3** (*Law*) final, determinate. **4** absolute, positive, decisive, determined. **peremptorily** *adv.* **peremptoriness** *n.* **peremptory challenge** *n.* (*Law*) a defendant's objection to a proposed juror without giving a reason. [A-F *peremptorie*, L *peremptōrius*, destructive, from *perimere* (*emere*, to take, to buy)]

perennial (pəren´iəl) *a.* **1** lasting throughout the year. **2** (of a plant) living for more than two years. **3** unfailing, unceasing, lasting long, never ceasing. **4** (of a stream) flowing through every season. ~*n.* a perennial plant. **perenniality** (-al´-) *n.* **perennially** *adv.* [L *perennis* (*annus*, a year)]

perennibranchiate (pərenibrang´kiət) *a.* belonging to the Perennibranchiata, a division of amphibians retaining their gills through life. [as PERENNIAL, BRANCHIATE (under BRANCHIA)]

perestroika (perəstroi´kə) *n.* in the former USSR, the policy of restructuring and reforming Soviet institutions initiated in the 1980s by Mikhail Gorbachev. [Rus.]

perf. *abbr.* **1** perfect. **2** perforated.

perfect[1] (pœ´fikt) *a.* **1** complete in all its parts, qualities etc. **2** finished, thoroughly versed, trained, skilled etc. **3** precise, exact. **4** of the best, highest and most complete kind. **5** entire, complete, unqualified. **6** (*Bot.*) (of a flower) having all the essential parts. **7** (*Bot.*) (of a fungus) in the stage in which the sexual spores are formed. **8** (*Gram.*) expressing action completed. **9** (of a lesson) thoroughly learned. **10** without defect or fault. ~*n.* (*Gram.*) the perfect tense or a perfect form of a verb. **perfect binding** *n.* a type of bookbinding in which the leaves are glued to the spine. **perfect interval** *n.* (*Mus.*) a fourth or fifth as in a major or minor scale starting on the lower note of the interval. **perfection** (pəfek´-) *n.* **1** the act of making or the state of being perfect. **2** supreme excellence. **3** complete development. **4** faultlessness. **5** a perfect person or thing. **6** the highest degree, the extreme (of). **7** an excellent quality or acquirement. **to perfection** completely, perfectly. **perfectionist** *n.* **1** a person who strives after perfection and tolerates no faults. **2** a person who believes in the possibility of attaining moral or religious perfection. **3** a member of a communistic community founded by J. H. Noyes in 1838 at Oneida Creek, in Madison County, New York State. **perfectionism** *n.* **perfective** (-fek´-) *a.* **1** (*Gram.*) expressing completed action as distinct from *imperfective*. **2** tending to make perfect. **perfectly** *adv.* **perfectness** *n.* **perfect number** *n.* (*Math.*) an integer, e.g. 6, that is equal to the sum of all its possible factors, excluding itself. **perfect pitch** *n.* (*Mus.*) absolute pitch. **perfect square** *n.* a square number. **perfect year** *n.* GREAT YEAR (under GREAT). [ME and OF *perfit*, L *perfectus* (*factus*, p.p. of *facere*, to make)]

Usage note In general the adjective *perfect* is not gradable but absolute, so the comparative *more perfect* and superlative *most perfect* are best avoided.

perfect[2] (pəfekt´) *v.t.* **1** to make perfect. **2** to finish or complete, to bring to perfection. **3** to print on the other side of (a sheet). **4** to render thoroughly versed or skilled (in). **perfecta** (-tə) *n.* (*N Am.*) a type of betting involving predicting the first two places in a race in the correct order. **perfecter** *n.* **perfectible** *a.* **perfectibilian** (-bil´-), **perfectibilist** (-fek´-) *n.* a person who believes that it is possible for humanity to attain moral and social perfection, a perfectionist. **perfectibility** (-bil´-) *n.*

perfecto (pəfek´tō) *n.* (*pl.* **perfectos**) a large cigar which tapers at both ends. [Sp., perfect]

perfervid (pəfœ´vid) *a.* (*poet.*) very fervid. **perfervidly** *adv.* **perfervidness, perfervour,** (*N Am.*) **perfervor** *n.*

perfidy (pœ´fidi) *n.* (*pl.* **perfidies**) (a) violation of faith, allegiance or confidence. **perfidious** (-fid´-) *a.* treacherous, faithless, deceitful, false. **perfidious Albion** *n.* Britain or England as viewed by some of the French etc. **perfidiously** *adv.* **perfidiousness** *n.* [F *perfidie*, L *perfidia*, from *perfidus*, treacherous (*fides*, faith)]

perfin (pœ´fin) *n.* a postage stamp perforated with an organization's initials. [*perf*orated *in*itials]

perfoliate (pəfō´liət) *a.* (of a plant) having leaves surrounding the stem so as to appear as if perforated by it. [L *folium*, a leaf]

perforate[1] (pœ´fərāt) *v.t.* **1** to bore through, to pierce. **2** to make a row of holes in. **3** to pass or reach through. ~*v.i.* to penetrate (into or through). **perforation** (-ā´shən) *n.* **perforative** (-rətiv) *a.* **perforator** *n.* [L *perforātus*, p.p. of *perforāre* (*forāre*, to bore)]

perforate[2] (pœ´fərət) *a.* **1** perforated. **2** (*Biol.*) pierced with small holes or having transparent dots like holes.

†**perforce** (pəfaws´) *adv.* of necessity, compulsorily. [earlier *parforce*, OF *par force*, by FORCE[1]]

perform (pəfawm´) *v.t.* **1** to carry through, to execute, to accomplish. **2** to discharge, fulfil. **3** to represent on the stage. **4** to play, to render (music). ~*v.i.* **1** to act a part. **2** to play a musical instrument, sing etc. **3** to do tricks. **4** to do what is to be done. **5** to function (well). **6** (of an investment) to yield a return. **7** (*sl.*) to have sexual intercourse. **performable** *a.* **performability** (-bil´-) *n.* **performance** *n.* **1** execution, carrying out, completion. **2** a thing done, an action. **3** a feat, a notable deed. **4** a piece of work. **5** the performing of a play, display of feats etc. **6** an entertainment. **7** (of a vehicle etc.) the capacity to function (well). **8** language as manifested in actual use in speech or writing. **9** (*coll.*) an elaborate or laborious action, a fuss. **10** a return on an investment. ~*a.* (of a car) capable of travelling very fast and accelerating quickly. **performance art** *n.* a theatrical presentation including various art forms. **performance artist** *n.* **performative** *a.* **1** of or relating to performance. **2** denoting a sentence or a verb which constitutes the action described, e.g. *promise* in *I promise to do my best*. ~*n.* a performative sentence or verb. **performatory** *a., n.* (*pl.* **performatories**). **performer** *n.* a person who performs, esp. an actor, musician etc. **performing** *a.* **performing art** *n.* an art form requiring performance before an audience. [ME *perfourmer*, prob. var. (assim. to FORM) of ME and OF *perfournir* (*fournir*, to FURNISH)]

perfume[1] (pœ´fūm) *n.* **1** a sweet smell. **2** a substance emitting a sweet odour, fragrance, scent. **3** the sweet-smelling fumes of something burning, cooking etc. **perfumed** *a.* having a sweet, pleasant smell. **perfume**

dynamics *n.* the use of sweet odours diffused in the air to make the working environment more pleasant for workers and clients, and to improve performance. **perfumeless** *a.* **perfumy** *a.* [F *parfumer* (*par-*, PER-, L *fūmāre*, to smoke, from *fūmus*, smoke)]

perfume² (pœ´fūm, pəfūm´) *v.t.* to fill or impregnate with a scent or sweet odour; to scent. **perfumer** (-fū´-) *n.* **1** a person who makes or sells perfumes. **2** a person who or something which perfumes. **perfumery** (-fū´-) *n.* (*pl.* **perfumeries**) **1** a place where perfumes are sold. **2** (the preparation of) perfumes. [as PERFUME¹]

perfunctory (pəfŭngk´təri) *a.* **1** done merely as a duty, or routinely; done in a half-hearted or careless manner. **2** careless, negligent, superficial, mechanical. **perfunctorily** *adv.* **perfunctoriness** *n.* [late L *perfunctōrius*, from *perfunctus*, p.p. of *perfungī* (*fungī*, to perform)]

perfuse (pəfūz´) *v.t.* **1** to besprinkle. **2** to spread over, to suffuse (with). **3** to pour (water etc.) over or through. **4** (*Med.*) to pass a fluid through. **perfusion** (-zhən) *n.* **perfusive** (-siv) *a.* [L *perfūsus*, p.p. of *perfundere* (*fundere*, to pour)]

pergameneous (pœgəmē´niəs) *a.* (of skin etc.) having the texture of parchment. **pergamentaceous** (-məntā´shəs) *a.* like parchment. [from L *pergamēna*, PARCHMENT]

pergana PARGANA.

pergola (pœ´gələ) *n.* (*pl.* **pergolas**) a covered walk or arbour with climbing plants trained over posts, trellis-work etc. [It., from L *pergula*, projecting roof, balcony etc., from *pergere*, to proceed]

pergunnah PARGANA.

perh. *abbr.* perhaps.

perhaps (pəhaps´) *adv.* **1** it may be, possibly. **2** please (*Perhaps you could take over from me?*). [PER, HAP¹]

peri (piə´ri) *n.* (*pl.* **peris**) **1** a being represented as a descendant of fallen angels, excluded from paradise until some penance is accomplished. **2** a beautiful being, a fairy. [Pers. *parī*]

peri- (per´i) *pref.* **1** around. **2** (*Astron.*) near. [Gr., around, about]

perianth (per´ianth) *n.* the outer part of a flower. [Gr. *anthos*, a flower]

periapt (per´iapt) *n.* something worn as a charm. [F *périapte*, Gr. *periapton* (*haptein*, to fasten)]

periblast (per´iblahst) *n.* (*Biol.*) the protoplasm around a cell nucleus.

pericardium (perikah´diəm) *n.* (*pl.* **pericardia** (-diə)) (*Anat.*) the membrane enveloping the heart. **pericardiac** (-ak), **pericardial** *a.* **pericarditis** (-dī´tis) *n.* (*Med.*) inflammation of the pericardium. [Gr. *perikardion* (*kardia*, the heart)]

pericarp (per´ikahp) *n.* the seed vessel or wall of the developed ovary of a plant. **pericarpial** (-kah´-) *a.* [Gr. *perikarpion* (*karpos*, a fruit)]

perichondrium (perikon´driəm) *n.* (*pl.* **perichondria** (-driə)) (*Anat.*) the membrane investing the cartilages except at joints. [Gr. *chondros*, cartilage]

periclase (per´iklāz, -klās) *n.* a greenish mineral composed of magnesia and protoxide of iron, from Vesuvius. [Gr. PERI-, very, *klasis*, a fracture]

periclinal (periklī´nəl) *a.* (of geological strata) sloping from a common centre. [Gr. *periklinēs* (*klinein*, to lean)]

pericope (pərik´əpi) *n.* an extract, a quotation, esp. a selection from the gospels or epistles read in public worship. [late L, from Gr. *perikopē* (*kopein*, to cut)]

pericranium (perikrā´niəm) *n.* (*pl.* **pericrania** (-niə)) **1** (*Anat.*) the membrane surrounding the skull. **2** (*facet.*) the skull, the brain. **pericranial** *a.*

pericycle (per´isīkəl) *n.* (*Bot.*) a thin layer of cells surrounding the vascular tissue in roots and stems. [Gr. *kuklos*, spherical]

pericynthion (perisin´thiən) *n.* the perilune.

periderm (per´idœm) *n.* **1** outer bark. **2** the whole of the tissues comprising the outer bark and the cork-cambium. **3** the hard integument of certain hydrozoons.

peridesmium (perides´miəm) *n.* (*Anat.*) the sheath of a ligament. [Gr. *desmos*, a band]

peridium (pərid´iəm) *n.* (*pl.* **peridia** (-diə)) (*Bot.*) the outer envelope of certain fungi enclosing the spores. **peridial** *a.* [Gr. *pēridion*, dim. of *pēra*, a bag, a wallet]

peridot (per´idot) *n.* a yellowish-green chrysolite, olivine. **peridotic** (-dot´-) *a.* **peridotite** (-dō´tīt) *n.* a mineral composed chiefly of olivine. [F *péridot*, etym. uncertain]

peridrome (per´idrōm) *n.* the open space between the columns and the wall in an ancient temple. [Gr. *peridromos* (*dromos*, a course)]

periegesis (periējē´sis) *n.* **1** a travelling round, a perambulation. **2** a description of this. [Gr. *periegēsis* (*agein*, to lead)]

perigastric (perigas´trik) *a.* surrounding the alimentary canal.

perigee (per´ijē) *n.* the nearest point to the earth in the orbit of the moon, one of the planets or an artificial satellite, as distinct from *apogee*. **perigeal** (-jē´-), **perigean** *a.* [F *périgée*, late L *perigēum*, *perigaeum*, Gr. *perigeion* (*gē*, earth)]

perigenesis (perijen´əsis) *n.* reproduction through rhythmic vibrations of protoplasmic molecules.

periglacial (periglā´shəl) *a.* of or relating to the region around a glacier.

perigone (per´igōn) *n.* (*Bot.*) **1** a perianth. **2** the walls of a spore-sac in a hydroid. **perigonial** (-gō´-) *a.* [F *périgone* (Gr. *gonos*, offspring, seed)]

perigynous (pərij´inəs) *a.* (*Bot.*) (of stamens) growing upon some part surrounding the ovary. [Gr. *gunē*, female]

perihelion (perihē´liən) *n.* (*pl.* **perihelia** (-liə)) the part of the orbit of a planet, comet etc. nearest the sun, as distinct from *aphelion*. [Gr. *hēlios*, the sun]

perihepatic (perihipat´ik) *a.* surrounding the liver. [Gr. *hēpas hēpatos*, a liver]

peril (per´əl) *n.* danger, risk, hazard, jeopardy, exposure to injury, loss or destruction. ~*v.t.* (*pres.p.* **perilling**, (*N Am.*) **periling**, *past*, *p.p.* **perilled**, (*N Am.*) **periled**) to risk, to endanger. **at one's peril** at risk of harm to oneself. **in peril of** with great danger to. **perilous** *a.* **perilously** *adv.* **perilousness** *n.* [OF *péril*, L *perīclum*, *perīculum*, rel. to *perīrī*, to try]

perilune (per´iloon) *n.* the point in the orbit of a body round the moon where the body is closest to the centre of the moon, as distinct from *apolune*. [F *lune*, L *luna*, the moon]

perilymph (per´ilimf) *n.* (*Anat.*) the clear fluid surrounding the labyrinth in the ear.

perimeter (pərim´itə) *n.* **1** (*Geom.*) **a** the bounding line of a plane figure. **b** the length of this. **2** the boundary of a camp etc. **3** an instrument for measuring the field of vision. **perimetric** (-met´-) *a.* [L and Gr. *perimetros* (*metron*, a measure)]

perimorph (per´imawf) *n.* a mineral enclosing another. **perimorphic** (-maw´-), **perimorphous** *a.* **perimorphism** *n.* [Gr. *morphē*, form]

perimysium (perimiz´iəm) *n.* (*pl.* **perimysia** (-ziə)) (*Anat.*) the fibrous connective tissue surrounding muscle fibres. [Gr. *mūs*, *muos*, a muscle]

perinatal (perinā´təl) *a.* of or relating to the period shortly before and after birth.

perineum (perinē´əm) *n.* (*pl.* **perinea** (-nē´ə)) (*Anat.*) the part of the body between the genital organs and the anus. **perineal** *a.* [late L *perinēum* -*naeum*, Gr. *peri-*, *pērinaion*, from *pēris* -*inos*, the scrotum]

period (piə´riəd) *n.* **1** any specified portion of time. **2** a definite or indefinite portion of time, an age, an era, a cycle. **3** a portion of time marked off by some recurring event, esp. an astronomical phenomenon. **4** the time taken up by the revolution of a planet round the sun. **5** a length of time allotted to a school lesson. **6** a complete sentence, esp. a complex one in which the predicate is not fully stated till the end. **7** (*pl.*) rhetorical language. **8** (*N Am.*) **a** a pause. **b** a full stop (.) marking this. **9** (*Chem.*) any one of the horizontal rows of elements in the periodic table. **10** an end, a limit. **11** an occurrence of menstruation. **12** the interval between the recurrences of equal values in a periodic function. ~*a.* (of a picture, object etc.) characteristic of a certain period, belonging to a historical period. **periodate** *n.* (*Chem.*) a salt or ester of periodic acid. **periodic** (-od´-) *a.* **1** happening or appearing at fixed intervals. **2** of or relating to a period or periods. **3** performed in a regular revolution. **4** constituting a complete sentence. **periodic acid** *n.* (*Chem.*) any oxyacid of iodine containing a larger proportion of oxygen than iodic acid. **periodical** *a.* **1** (of a magazine etc.) appearing at regular intervals. **2** periodic. ~*n.* a magazine or other publication published at regular intervals, e.g. monthly or quarterly. **periodically** *adv.* **periodic decimal** *n.* (*Math.*) a set of figures repeated in a recurring decimal. **periodic function** *n.* (*Math.*) a function whose value is repeated at regular intervals. **periodicity** (-dis´-) *n.* **periodic table** *n.* a table showing the chemical elements in order of their atomic number, and grouped in rows to show similar properties. **periodization** (-zā´shən), **periodisation** *n.* the act of dividing history into periods. **period piece** *n.* **1** an objet d'art, piece of furniture etc. belonging to a historical period, esp. one of value. **2** a person with outdated views, dress etc. [F *période*, L *periodus*, Gr. *periodos* (*hodos*, way)]

periodontal (periədon´təl) *a.* (of tissue) around a tooth. **periodontics** *n.* the treatment of periodontal disorders. **periodontist** *n.* **periodontology** (-tol´-) *n.* periodontics. [ODONTO-]

perioperative (periop´ərətiv) *a.* (*Med.*) occurring around the time of an operation.

periosteum (perios´tiəm) *n.* (*pl.* **periostea** (-tiə)) a dense membrane covering the bones. **periosteal** *a.* **periostitic** (-tit´-) *a.* **periostitis** (-tī´tis) *n.* (*Med.*) inflammation of the periosteum. [Gr. *periosteon* (*osteon*, bone)]

periotic (periō´tik) *a.* surrounding the inner ear. ~*n.* a periotic bone. [Gr. *ous ōtos*, an ear]

peripatetic (peripətet´ik) *a.* **1** (of a teacher) working in several schools. **2** walking about, itinerant. **3** (**Peripatetic**) of or relating to the philosophy of Aristotle (from his habit of walking about while teaching in the Lyceum). ~*n.* a peripatetic person, esp. a teacher. **peripatetically** *adv.* **peripateticism** (-sizm) *n.* [F *péripatétique*, L *peripatēticus*, Gr. *peripatētikos* (*patein*, to walk)]

peripatus (pərip´ətəs) *n.* any wormlike arthropod of the genus *Peripatus*, living in damp places in the southern hemisphere, and believed to represent an ancestral type of both insects and myriapods. [mod. L, from Gr. *peripatos*, walking about, as PERIPATETIC]

peripeteia (peripitī´ə) *n.* a reversal of circumstances or sudden change of fortune in a play or in life. [Gr. *pet-*, stem of *piptein*, to fall]

periphery (pərif´əri) *n.* (*pl.* **peripheries**) **1** the perimeter or circumference of a figure or surface. **2** the outer region. **peripheral** *a.* **1** of relatively little importance. **2** of or relating to a periphery. **3** (*Anat.*) near the surface of the body. **4** being an additional or auxiliary device, esp. in computing. ~*n.* a device, e.g. a printer, a VDU, connected to a computer for input/output, storage etc. **peripherality** (-al´-) *n.* **peripherally** *adv.* **peripheral nervous system** *n.* (*Anat.*) the nervous system outside the brain and the spinal cord. [ME and OF *periferie*, late L *peripheria*, Gr. *periphereia*, a circumference (*pherein*, to bear)]

periphrasis (pərif´rəsis) *n.* (*pl.* **periphrases** (-sēz)) **1** roundabout speaking or expression, circumlocution. **2** a roundabout phrase. **periphrastic** (-fras´-) *a.* **1** of or using periphrasis. **2** (*Gram.*) using two words instead of an inflected form of one word. **periphrastically** *adv.* [L and Gr. (*phrasis*, a speech, a PHRASE)]

periplast (per´iplast) *n.* (*Zool.*) **1** the main substance of a cell, as distinguished from the external coating of the nucleus. **2** a cell wall or cell envelope. [Gr. *plastos*, formed, moulded]

periplus (per´ipləs) *n.* (*pl.* **peripli** (-plī)) a circumnavigation. [L *periplūs*, Gr. *periplous* (-*plous*, a voyage)]

peripteral (pərip´tərəl) *a.* (*Archit.*) surrounded by a single row of columns. **periptery** *n.* (*pl.* **peripteries**) a peripteral building. [Gr. *peripteron* (*pteron*, a wing)]

perique (pərēk´) *n.* a strong, dark-coloured variety of tobacco grown and manufactured in Louisiana, used chiefly in mixtures. [etym. uncertain]

periscope (per´iskōp) *n.* an apparatus enabling people inside a submarine, trench etc. to look about above the surface of the water etc. **periscopic** (-skop´-) *a.* **periscopical** *a.* **periscopically** *adv.* **periscopic lens** *n.* a lens which allows clear vision over a wide angle.

perish (per´ish) *v.i.* **1** to be destroyed, to come to nothing. **2** to die, to lose life or vitality in any way. **3** to decay, to wither. **perish the thought** used to express horror or disapproval. **perishable** *a.* liable to perish, subject to rapid decay. ~*n.pl.* foodstuffs and other things liable to rapid decay or deterioration. **perishability** (-bil´-), **perishableness** *n.* **perishably** *adv.* **perished** *a.* (*coll.*) **1** (of a person) very cold. **2** (of rubber etc.) in poor condition due to age, damp etc. **perisher** *n.* (*sl.*) an irritating person, esp. a child. **perishing** *a.* (*coll.*) **1** infernal, damned. **2** freezing cold. **perishingly** *adv.* **perishless** *a.* [OF, stem of *perir*, L *perīre* (PER-, *īre*, to go)]

perisperm (per´ispœm) *n.* (*Bot.*) the mass of albumen outside the embryo-sac in certain seeds. [F *périsperme*]

perispomenon (perispō´mənon), **perispome** (per´ispōm) *a.* (of a Greek word) having a circumflex accent on the last syllable. ~*n.* a word with such an accent. [Gr. *perispōmenon*, neut. p.p. of *perispaein* (*spaein*, to draw)]

perissodactyl (pərisōdak´til) *a.* (*Zool.*) of or belonging to the order Perissodactyla of ungulates in which all the feet are odd-toed. ~*n.* any animal of the Perissodactyla. [Gr. *perissos*, uneven, *daktulos*, a digit]

peristalith (pəris´təlith) *n.* a group of stones standing round a burial mound etc. [Gr. *peristatos* (*statos*, standing), -LITH]

peristalsis (peristal´sis) *n.* the automatic, wavelike, contractile motion of the alimentary canal and similar organs by which the contents are propelled along. **peristaltic** *a.* **peristaltically** *adv.* [Gr. *stellein*, to send]

peristeronic (pəristəron´ik) *a.* of or relating to pigeons. [Gr. *peristerōn*, a dovecot, from *peristera*, a pigeon]

peristome (per´istōm) *n.* **1** (*Bot.*) the fringe round the mouth of the capsule in mosses. **2** (*Zool.*) the margin of the aperture of a mollusc, the oval opening in insects, crustaceans etc. **peristomal** (-stō´-), **peristomial** *a.* [F *péristome* (Gr. *stoma*, the mouth)]

peristyle (per´istīl) *n.* **1** a row of columns surrounding a building, court etc. **2** a court etc. with a colonnade around it. [F *péristyle*, L *peristylum*, Gr. *peristulon* (*stulos*, a pillar)]

peritoneum (peritənē´əm) *n.* (*pl.* **peritoneums, peritonea** (-ə)) (*Anat.*) the serous membrane lining the abdominal cavity and enveloping all the abdominal viscera. **peritoneal** *a.* **peritonitis** (-nī´tis) *n.* (*Anat.*) inflammation of the peritoneum. [L *peritonaeum*, Gr. *peritonaion* (*ton-*, stem of *teinein*, to stretch)]

perityphlitis (peritiflī´tis) *n.* (*Med.*) inflammation of the connective tissue surrounding the caecum or blind gut. [Gr. *tuphlon*, the caecum, neut. of *tuphlos*, blind]

periwig (per´iwig) *n.* (*Hist.*) a wig. **periwigged** *a.* [earlier *perwigge, perwicke*, F *perruque*, a PERUKE]

periwinkle[1] (per´iwingkəl) *n.* **1** any plant of the genus *Vinca*, comprising trailing evergreen shrubs with blue or white flowers. **2** a shrub, *Catharanthus roseus*, of Madagascar. [OE *perwince, pervince*, L *pervinca*]

periwinkle[2] (per´iwingkəl) *n.* a winkle. [etym. unknown]

☒ **perjorative** common misspelling of PEJORATIVE.

perjure (pœ´jə) *v.t.* (*Law*) (*reflex.*) to forswear (oneself), to lie under oath. **perjured** *a.* forsworn, guilty of perjury. **perjurer** *n.* **perjurious** (-joo´-) *a.* **perjury** (-jəri) *n.* (*pl.* **perjuries**) (*Law*) **1** the act of swearing falsely, the violating of an oath. **2** the act of wilfully giving false evidence. [OF *parjurer*, L *perjūrāre* (*jūrāre*, to swear)]

perk[1] (pœk) *v.t.* **1** to hold or stick up. **2** to thrust (oneself) forward. **3** to make smart or trim. *~v.i.* **1** to bear oneself saucily or jauntily. **2** to be jaunty, self-assertive or impudent. *~a.* pert, brisk, smart, trim. **to perk up** (*coll.*) (to cause) to be more cheerful, lively or smart. **perky** *a.* (*comp.* **perkier,** *superl.* **perkiest**) **1** lively. **2** cheerful, jaunty. **perkily** *adv.* **perkiness** *n.* [etym. uncertain]

perk[2] (pœk) *n.* (*coll.*) a benefit enjoyed by an employee over and above their salary. [from PERQUISITE]

perk[3] (pœk) *v.i., v.t.* (*coll.*) to percolate.

perk[4] (pœk) *v.i.* (*dial.*) to perch. *~v.t.* (*reflex.*) to perch (oneself) on an elevated spot. [var. of PERCH[1]]

perky PERK[1].

perlite (pœ´līt), **pearlite** *n.* (*Geol.*) a glassy igneous rock characterized by spheroidal cracks formed by contractile tension in cooling. **perlitic** (-lit´-) *a.* [F *perlite* (*perle*)]

perm[1] (pœm) *n.* a hairstyle in which hair is shaped and then set by chemicals, heat etc. *~v.t.* to put a perm in (hair). [short for *permanent wave*]

perm[2] (pœm) *n.* (*coll.*) a forecast of a number of football match results selected from a larger number of matches. *~v.t.* to make a perm of. [short for *permutation*]

permaculture (pœ´məkŭlchə) *n.* the development of self-sustaining agricultural ecosystems. [*perma*nent agri*culture*]

permafrost (pœ´məfrost) *n.* a layer of permanently frozen earth in very cold regions. [*perma*nent *frost*]

permalloy (pœ´məloi) *n.* an alloy with high magnetic permeability.

permanent (pœ´mənənt) *a.* lasting, remaining or intended to remain in the same state, place or condition, as distinct from *temporary*. **permanence, permanency** *n.* **permanent hardness** *n.* hardness of water which cannot be removed by boiling. **permanentize, permanentise** *v.t.* **permanently** *adv.* **permanent magnet** *n.* a magnet which retains properties after the removal of the magnetic field producing the magnetization. **permanent press** *n.* treatment with chemicals or heat to give fabric resistance to creasing and often to give permanent creases or pleats. **permanent-press** *a.* **Permanent Secretary** *n.* a senior civil servant who acts as a permanent adviser to ministers in a particular government department. **permanent set** *n.* **1** the permanent deformation of a substance after subjection to stress. **2** the extent of permanent set. **permanent tooth** *n.* (*pl.* **permanent teeth**) an adult tooth, which grows in after a milk tooth has fallen out. **Permanent Under Secretary** *n.* **1** a senior permanent adviser to a Secretary of State. **2** a senior civil servant who is usually the head of a division within the State Department. **permanent wave** *n.* PERM[1]. **permanent way** *n.* the finished roadbed of a railway. [F, from L *permanentem*, nom. *-nens*, pres.p. of *permanēre* (*manēre*, to remain)]

permanganate (pəmang´gənət) *n.* (*Chem.*) a salt of permanganic acid. **permanganic** (pœmangan´-) *a.* of or containing manganese in its highest valency. **permanganic acid** *n.* an acid containing heptavalent manganese.

permeate (pœ´miāt) *v.t.* **1** to penetrate and pass through. **2** to pervade, to saturate. **3** to pass through the pores or interstices of. *~v.i.* to be diffused (in, through etc.). **permeable** *a.* yielding passage to fluids, penetrable. **permeability** (-bil´-) *n.* **1** the state of being permeable. **2** the degree to which a magnetizable medium affects the magnetic field surrounding it. **permeably** *adv.* **permeance** *n.* **permeant** *a.* **permeation** (-ā´shən) *n.* **permeative** *a.* **permeator** *n.* [L *permeātus*, p.p. of *permeāre* (*meāre*, to run, to pass)]

permethrin (pəmēth´rin) *n.* a garden pesticide, esp. used against whitefly.

Permian (pœ´miən) *a.* (*Geol.*) of or relating to the uppermost strata of the Palaeozoic series, consisting chiefly of red sandstone and magnesian limestone, which rest on the Carboniferous strata. *~n.* the Permian period. [*Perm*, E Russia]

per mille (pœ mil´i), **per mil** (mil) *adv.* in every thousand. [L]

permit[1] (pəmit´) *v.t.* (*pres.p.* **permitting,** *past, p.p.* **permitted**) **1** to give permission to or for, to authorize. **2** to allow by consent. **3** †to resign, to leave. *~v.i.* **1** to provide an opportunity. **2** to allow, to admit (of). **permissible** (-mis´-) *a.* **permissibility** (-bil´-) *n.* **permissibly** *adv.* **permission** (-mish´ən) *n.* **1** the act of permitting. **2** consent or authorization given. **permissive** *a.* **1** allowing great licence in social and sexual conduct. **2** permitting, allowing. **3** granting liberty, leave or permission. **4** not hindering or forbidding. **permissive legislation** *n.* legislation which grants powers without imposing their use. **permissively** *adv.* **permissiveness** *n.* **permittee** (pœmitē´) *n.* **permitter** *n.* **permittivity** (-tiv´-) *n.* (*pl.* **permittivities**) a measure of a substance's ability to store potential energy in an electric field. [L *permittere* (*mittere*, to send, p.p. *missus*)]

permit[2] (pœ´mit) *n.* an order to permit, a permission or warrant, esp. a written authority to land or remove dutiable goods.

permutable PERMUTE.

permutation (pœmūtā´shən) *n.* **1** (*Math.*) **a** change of the order of a series of quantities. **b** each of the different arrangements, as regards order, that can be made in a permutation. **2** PERM[2]. **3** alteration, transmutation. **permutate** (pœ´-) *v.t.* to change the order of. **permutational** *a.* [ME and OF *permutacion*, L *permūtātiōnem*, nom. *-tio*, as PERMUTE]

permute (pəmūt´) *v.t.* **1** to change thoroughly. **2** (*Math.*) to subject to permutation. **permutable** *a.* interchangeable. **permutableness** *n.* **permutably** *adv.* [L *permūtāre* (*mūtāre*, to change)]

Permutit® (pœ´mūtit) *n.* an artificial zeolite used to soften water. [G, from L *permutare* (as PERMUTE)]

pern (pœn) *n.* a bird of the genus *Pernis*, a honey buzzard. [mod. L *pernis*, erron. from Gr. *pternis*]

pernicious (pənish´əs) *a.* **1** destructive, ruinous, deadly, noxious, hurtful. **2** malicious, wicked. **pernicious anaemia** *n.* a very severe, sometimes fatal, form of anaemia. **perniciously** *adv.* **perniciousness** *n.* [F *pernicieux*, L *perniciōsus*, from *pernicies*, destruction (*nex necis*, death)]

pernickety (pənik´əti), (*N Am.*) **persnickety** (-snik´-) *a.* (*coll.*) **1** fastidious, fussy. **2** over-particular. **3** awkward to handle, ticklish. [etym. uncertain]

pernoctation (pœnoktā´shən) *n.* (*formal*) a remaining out or watching all night. **pernoctate** (pœ´-) *v.t.* [L *pernoctātio*, from *pernoctāre* (*nox noctis*, night)]

Pernod® (pœ´nō) *n.* an aniseed-flavoured aperitif.

perone (per´onē) *n.* (*Anat.*) the fibula or small bone of the leg. **peroneal** (-nē´-) *a.* [Gr. *peronē*, pin, the fibula]

perorate (per´ərāt) *v.i.* **1** to deliver an oration. **2** (*coll.*) to speechify. ~*v.t.* to declaim. **peroration** (-ā´shən) *n.* the concluding part of an oration. [L *perōrātus*, p.p. of *perōrāre* (*ōrāre*, to speak)]

peroxide (pərok´sīd) *n.* (*Chem.*) **1** hydrogen peroxide. **2** the oxide of a given base that contains the greatest quantity of oxygen. **3** any salt or ester of hydrogen peroxide. ~*a.* of or relating to hydrogen peroxide as used to lighten the hair (*a peroxide blonde*). ~*v.t.* (*coll.*) to bleach (hair) with hydrogen peroxide. **peroxidase** (-idāz) *n.* any of a class of enzymes which catalyse the oxidation of a compound by the decomposition of hydrogen peroxide. **peroxidation** (-idā´shən) *n.* **peroxide of hydrogen** *n.* hydrogen peroxide. **peroxidize** (-si-), **peroxidise** *v.t., v.i.*

perpendicular (pœpəndik´ūlə) *a.* **1** at right angles to the plane of the horizon. **2** (*Geom.*) at right angles to a given line or surface. **3** (of a hill, road etc.) nearly vertical, extremely steep. **4** (*facet.*) perfectly upright or vertical. ~*n.* **1** a perpendicular line. **2** a plumb rule, plumb level or other instrument for determining the vertical. **3** perpendicular attitude or condition. **perpendicularity** (-lar´-) *n.* **perpendicularly** *adv.* **Perpendicular style** *n.* (*Archit.*) the style of pointed architecture in England succeeding the Decorated, characterized by the predominance of vertical, horizontal and rectangular lines, esp. in window tracery, flattish arches and profuse ornamentation. [ME and OF *perpendiculer*, L *perpendiculāris*, from *perpendiculum*, a plummet (*pendere*, to weigh)]

perpetrate (pœ´pətrāt) *v.t.* to perform, to commit, to be guilty of. **perpetrable** *a.* **perpetration** (-ā´shən) *n.* **perpetrator** *n.* [L *perpetrātus*, p.p. of *perpetrāre* (*patrāre*, to effect)]

perpetual (pəpech´ūəl) *a.* **1** unending, eternal. **2** persistent, continual, constant. **3** permanent, for a lifetime. **4** (of a plant) blooming continually throughout the season. **perpetual calendar** *n.* a calendar adjustable to any year. **perpetual check** *n.* in chess, a situation in which one player's king continually puts the other player's king in check, resulting in a draw. **perpetualism** *n.* **perpetually** *adv.* **perpetual motion** *n.* the motion of a hypothetical machine which continues to move indefinitely without any external source of energy. **perpetuity** (pœpətū´-) *n.* (*pl.* **perpetuities**) **1** the state of being perpetual. **2** a perpetual annuity. **3** a perpetual possession. **4** the number of years' purchase to be given for an annuity. **for perpetuity** in perpetuity. **in perpetuity** for ever. **to perpetuity** in perpetuity. [F *perpétuel*, L *perpetuālis*, from *perpetuus* (*pet-*, rel. to *petere*, to seek)]

perpetuate (pəpech´uāt) *v.t.* **1** to make perpetual. **2** to preserve from extinction or oblivion. **perpetuance**, **perpetuation** (-ā´shən) *n.* **perpetuator** *n.*

perpetuity PERPETUAL.

perpetuum mobile (pœpetūəm mō´bili) *n.* **1** perpetual motion. **2** (*Mus.*) moto perpetuo. [L *perpetuus*, continuous, *mobilis*, movable (cogn. with PRIMUM MOBILE)]

perplex (pəpleks´) *v.t.* **1** to puzzle, to bewilder, to embarrass, to make anxious. **2** to complicate, confuse or involve; to make difficult to understand or to unravel. **3** †to entangle. **perplexed** *a.* confused, puzzled. **perplexedly** (-plek´sid-) *adv.* **perplexedness** (-plek´sid-) *n.* **perplexing** *a.* **perplexingly** *adv.* **perplexity** *n.* (*pl.* **perplexities**). [from obs. *perplex*, perplexed, confused, L *perplexus*, p.p. of *perplectere* (*plectere*, to plait)]

per pro. (pœ prō´) *abbr.* through the agency of. [L *per procurationem*]

Usage note Most commonly used where one person signs a letter or other document on behalf of another. In *AB per pro.* (or *pp*) *CD*, the person who signs should be CD (so *per pro.* does not mean 'on behalf of', as popularly interpreted, because the signing is on behalf of the first person specified, AB).

perquisite (pœ´kwizit) *n.* **1** gain, profit or emolument, over and above regular wages or salary, a perk. **2** anything to which a servant etc. has a prescriptive right after it has served its purpose. **3** (*coll.*) a gratuity, a tip. **4** (*Law*) profit accruing to a lord of a manor over and above the ordinary revenue. [L *perquīsītum*, neut. p.p. of *perquīrere* (*quaerere*, to seek)]

Usage note The nouns *perquisite* and *prerequisite* should not be confused: a *perquisite* is an extra payment, and a *prerequisite* an advance requirement.

perradial (pœrā´diəl) *a.* (*Zool.*) (in hydrozoons etc.) of, relating to or constituting a primary ray. **perradius** (-əs) *n.* (*pl.* **perradii** (-diī)) in certain coelenterates, a perradial ray or primary ray.

Perrier® (per´iə) *n.* a sparkling mineral water. [spring at Vergèze, France]

perron (per´ən) *n.* a platform with steps in front of a large building. [F, from It. *petrone*, L *petra*, a stone]

perruque PERUKE.

perry (per´i) *n.* (*pl.* **perries**) a fermented liquor made from the juice of pears. [OF *peré*, from *peire* (F *poire*), a PEAR]

per se (pœ sā´) *adv.* by itself, in itself. [L]

persecute (pœ´sikūt) *v.t.* **1** to pursue in a hostile, envious or malicious way; to afflict with suffering or loss of life or property, esp. for adherence to a particular opinion or creed. **2** to harass, to worry, to importune. **3** to bombard with questions. **persecution** (-ū´shən) *n.* **persecution complex, persecution mania** *n.* an irrational conviction that others are conspiring against one. **persecutor** *n.* **persecutory** *a.* **persecutrix** (-triks) *n.* a female persecutor. [F *persécuter*, L *persecūtus*, p.p. of *persequī* (*sequī*, to follow)]

Perseid (pœ´siid) *n.* any one of a group of meteors appearing about 12 August, having their radiating point in Perseus. [Gr. *Persēides*, daughters of Perseus]

perseverate (pəsev´ərāt) *v.i.* **1** to persist in an action for a long time. **2** (*Psych.*) to have a tendency to continue with a response after the original stimulus has stopped. **perseveration** (-ā´shən) *n.* [L *perseverare* (as PERSEVERE)]

persevere (pœsiviə´) *v.i.* to persist in or with any undertaking, plan or course. **perseverance** *n.* **1** persistent endeavour. **2** persistence in any plan or undertaking. **3** (*Theol.*) continuance in a state of grace. **perseverant** *a.* persevering. **perseveringly** *adv.* [F *persévérer*, L *persevērāre* (*sevērus*, SEVERE)]

Persian (pœ´zhən, -shən) *a.* of or relating to Persia (now Iran). ~*n.* **1** a native or inhabitant of Persia, a person of Persian descent. **2** the Persian (or Iranian) language. **3** a Persian cat. **4** (*Archit.*) a figure in Persian dress forming a pillar or pilaster supporting an entablature etc. **Persian blind** *n.* PERSIENNE. **Persian carpet** *n.* a carpet made of knotted twine etc., finely decorated, from Persia. **Persian cat** *n.* a breed of cat with long silky hair. **Persian lamb** *n.* the curly fur of a young karakul, used for clothing. **Persian rug** *n.* a rug made of knotted twine etc., finely decorated, from Persia. **Persian wheel** *n.* a wheel with buckets on the rim used for raising water.

persicaria (pœsikeə´riə) *n.* a weed, *Polygonum persicaria*. [med. L, from L *persicum*, a peach, neut. of *Persicus*, Persian]

persicot (pœ´sikō) *n.* a cordial made from peaches, nectarines etc., macerated in spirit and flavoured with their kernels. [F *persico* (now *persicot*), It. *persico*, L *persicum*, a PEACH[1]]

persienne (pœsien´) *n.* **1** an Oriental cambric or muslin.

2 (*pl.*) window blinds or shutters like Venetian blinds. [F, Persian]

persiflage (pœ´siflahzh) *n.* banter, raillery, frivolous treatment of any subject. **persifleur** (-flœ´) *n.* [F, from *persiffler*, to jeer (*siffler*, L *sībilāre*, to whistle, to hiss)]

persimmon (pəsim´ən) *n.* 1 any evergreen tree of the genus *Diospyrus*. 2 the plumlike fruit of the persimmon. [corr. of Algonquian *pessemmins*]

persist (pəsist´) *v.i.* 1 to continue steadfastly, in the pursuit of any plan. 2 to remain, to continue, to endure. **persistence** *n.* **persistence of vision** *n.* the ability of the eye to retain perception for a brief period after the stimulus has been removed, as in the illusion of a continuous picture formed from the number of still pictures in a cinema film. **persistency** *n.* **persistent** *a.* 1 persisting, persevering. 2 lasting, enduring. 3 constantly repeated. 4 (*Biol.*) (of leaves etc.) not falling off. 5 (of a chemical) slow to break down. **persistently** *adv.* **persistent vegetative state** *n.* (*Med.*) an irreversible condition in which a person's body is kept functioning by medical intervention but there are no signs of higher brain function. **persistingly** *adv.* [F *persister*, L *persistere* (*sistere*, causal of *stāre*, to stand)]

persnickety PERNICKETY.

person (pœ´sən) *n.* 1 a human being, an individual. 2 a being possessed of personality. 3 a human being as distinct from one of the lower animals or an inanimate object. 4 the living body of a human being. 5 a human being or body corporate having legal rights and duties. 6 (*Theol.*) each of the three individualities in the Godhead, Father, Son or Holy Spirit. 7 (*Gram.*) each of the three relations of the subject or object of a verb, as speaking, spoken to or spoken of. 8 an individual in a compound organism or a hydrozoan colony. 9 the genitals. 10 a part or character (on the stage). **in one's own person** as oneself. **in person** by oneself, not by deputy. **-person** *comb. form* a person, esp. one in a particular job or position, as in *salesperson*, *chairperson*. **personable** *a.* attractive and likeable. **personableness** *n.* **personably** *adv.* **personage** (-nij) *n.* 1 a person. 2 a person of rank, distinction or importance. 3 a character in a play, story etc. **personal** *a.* 1 of or relating to a person as distinct from a thing. 2 of, relating to or affecting an individual. 3 individual, private. 4 a (of criticism etc.) reflecting on an individual, esp. disparaging, hostile. b making or prone to make such remarks. 5 of or relating to the physical person, bodily, corporeal. 6 transacted or done in person. 7 (*Gram.*) denoting or indicating any of the three persons. 8 (*Law*) of or relating to the person (applied to all property except land or heritable interests in land). ~*n.* 1 (*esp. N Am.*) a personal ad. 2 (*Law*) a movable article of property. **personal ad** *n.* (*esp. N Am.*) a notice in the personal column of a newspaper. **personal column** *n.* a newspaper column in the classified advertisement section containing personal messages, requests for donations to charity etc. **personal computer** *n.* a small computer designed for business or home use, e.g. for keeping records, word processing etc. **personal effects** *n.pl.* articles of property intimately related to the owner. **personal equation** *n.* 1 (*Astron.*) the quantity of time by which a person is in the habit of noting a phenomenon wrongly. 2 (*fig.*) aberration from strict accuracy, logical reasoning or absolute fairness, due to personal characteristics. **personal equity plan** *n.* a scheme under which individuals may invest a fixed sum each year in UK shares without paying tax on capital gains or dividend income. **personal estate** *n.* personal property. **personal identification number** *n.* a secret number allotted to a person for use as a password for an automated cash dispenser etc. **personality** (-nal´-) *n.* (*pl.* **personalities**) 1 the quality or state of being a person. 2 individual existence or identity. 3 the sum of qualities and characteristics that constitute individuality. 4 a distinctive personal character. 5 a strong or attractive character. 6 an important or famous person, a celebrity. 7 a person who has a strong or unusual character. 8 personal application of remarks etc. 9 (*pl.*) disparaging personal remarks. 10 (*Law*) †personalty. **personality cult** *n.* the excessive adulation and boosting of a person, esp. a political leader. **personality disorder** *n.* any of various psychological disorders marked by a tendency to do harm to oneself or others. **personalize, personalise** *v.t.* 1 to make personal. 2 to tailor to the needs of a particular person. 3 to take as referring to a particular person. 4 to mark (something) so that it is identifiable as belonging to a particular person. 5 to inscribe with a person's name, initials etc. 6 to personify. **personalization** (-zā´shən) *n.* **personally** *adv.* 1 in person. 2 as regards oneself. 3 particularly, individually. 4 as a person. **personal organizer** *n.* 1 a portable personal filing system, usu. in the form of a small loose-leafed book, containing details of appointments, telephone numbers, memoranda etc. 2 a hand-held microcomputer used for the same purpose. **personal pronoun** *n.* a pronoun, e.g. *I*, *you*, *we*, used to refer to a person or thing. **personal property** *n.* (*Law*) movable property, as distinct from *real property*. **personal service** *n.* individual attention given to a customer. **personal space** *n.* 1 the area immediately around a person where encroachment is unwelcome. 2 space available for a person to use. 3 freedom and time to be alone. **personal stereo** *n.* (*pl.* **personal stereos**) a very small, portable stereo set with headphones, designed to be attached to a belt or held in the hand. **personal touch** *n.* an individual approach. **personalty** (-əlti) *n.* (*pl.* **personalties**) (*Law*) movable property as distinct from *realty*. **personhood** *n.* the state of being a person. **person-to-person** *a.* 1 between individuals. 2 (of a telephone call) arranged through the operator to a particular person, with no substitutes. [ME and OF *persone*, L *persōna*, a mask, a character, a personage, perh. rel. to *personāre* (*sonāre*, to sound)]

persona (pəsō´nə) *n.* (*pl.* **personas, personae** (-nē)) 1 a person's social façade, as distinct from *anima*. 2 (*often pl.*) a character in a play, novel etc. **persona grata** (grah´tə) *n.* (*pl.* **personae gratae** (-tē)) an acceptable person, esp. in diplomatic circles. **persona non grata** (non grah´tə) *n.* an unacceptable person. [L]

personate[1] (pœ´sənāt) *v.t.* 1 to assume the character or to act the part of. 2 to impersonate, esp. for the purpose of voting without being entitled to do so, or for any other fraudulent purpose. **personation** (-ā´shən) *n.* **personator** *n.* [L *personātus*, p.p. of *personāre*, from *persōna*, mask, see PERSON]

personate[2] (pœ´sənət) *a.* (*Bot.*) masklike (applied to a two-lipped corolla in which the mouth is closed by an upward projection of the lower part, as in the snapdragon).

personation, personator PERSONATE[1].

personify (pəson´ifī) *v.t.* (*3rd pers. sing. pres.* **personifies,** *pres.p.* **personifying,** *past, p.p.* **personified**) 1 to regard or represent (an abstraction) as possessing the attributes of a living being. 2 to symbolize by a human figure. 3 to embody, to exemplify, to typify, in one's own person. **personification** (-fikā´shən) *n.* **personified** *a.* **personifier** *n.* [F *personnifier* (PERSON, -FY)]

personnel (pœsənel´) *n.* 1 the body of persons engaged in some service, esp. a public institution, military or naval enterprise etc. 2 the staff of a business firm etc. 3 a personnel department. **personnel carrier** *n.* an armoured vehicle for transporting personnel. **personnel department** *n.* the department of a business firm etc. that deals with the appointment, records and welfare of personnel. [F, orig., personal]

perspective (pəspek´tiv) *n.* **1** the art of representing solid objects on a plane surface exactly as regards position, shape and dimensions, as the objects themselves appear to the eye at a particular point. **2** the apparent relation of visible objects as regards position and distance. **3** a representation of objects in perspective. **4** the relation of facts or other matters as viewed by the mind. **5** a view, a vista, a prospect. **6** a point of view from which something is considered. *~a.* **1** of or relating to perspective. **2** in perspective. **in perspective 1** according to the laws of perspective. **2** in due proportion. **out of perspective 1** not according to the laws of perspective. **2** not in due proportion. **perspectival** (-tī´vəl) *a.* **perspectively** *adv.* [F, from med. L *perspectīva* (*ars*), perspective (art), from L *perspectus*, p.p. of *perspicere* (*specere*, to look)]

Perspex® (pœ´speks) *n.* a transparent plastic, very tough and of great clarity.

perspicacious (pœspikā´shəs) *a.* quick-sighted, mentally penetrating or discerning. **perspicaciously** *adv.* **perspicacity** (-kas´-), **perspicaciousness** *n.* [L *perspicax -cācis* (*specere*, to see)]

Usage note The adjectives *perspicacious* and *perspicuous* should not be confused: *perspicacious* means discerning, and *perspicuous* clearly expressed.

perspicuous (pəspik´ūəs) *a.* **1** free from obscurity or ambiguity, clearly expressed, lucid. **2** expressing things clearly. **perspicuity** (-ū´-) *n.* **perspicuously** *adv.* **perspicuousness** *n.* [L *perspicuus*, as PERSPICACIOUS]

Usage note See note under PERSPICACIOUS.

perspire (pəspīə´) *v.i.* to sweat. *~v.t.* to give out (the excretions of the body) through the pores of the skin, to sweat. **perspirable** *a.* **1** able to be perspired or excreted by perspiration. **2** liable to perspire. **perspiration** (pœspirā´shən) *n.* **perspiratory** (-spir´-) *a.* [L *perspīrāre* (*spīrāre*, to breathe)]

persuade (pəswād´) *v.t.* **1** to influence or convince by argument, advice, entreaty, or expostulation. **2** to induce. **3** to try to influence, to advise. **persuadable** *a.* **persuadability** (-bil´-) *n.* **persuader** *n.* **1** a person who persuades. **2** (*sl.*) a pistol, a firearm, a weapon. **persuasible** (-si-) *a.* **persuasibility** (-bil´-) *n.* **persuasion** (-zhən) *n.* **1** the act of persuading. **2** power to persuade, persuasiveness. **3** the state of being persuaded, a settled conviction. **4** creed, belief, esp. in religious matters. **5** a religious sect or denomination. **6** (*coll.*) a sort, a kind. **persuasive** (-siv) *a.* able or tending to persuade, winning. *~n.* something which persuades, a motive, an inducement. **persuasively** *adv.* **persuasiveness** *n.* [F *persuader*, L *persuādēre* (*suādēre*, to advise)]

persulphate (pəsŭl´fāt), (*esp. N Am.*) **persulfate** *n.* a sulphate containing the greatest relative quantity of acid.

PERT *abbr.* programme evaluation and review technique.

pert (pœt) *a.* **1** saucy, forward. **2** sprightly, lively. **pertly** *adv.* **pertness** *n.* [corr. of obs. *apert*, OF from L *apertus* (p.p. of *aperīre*, to open), confused with *expertus*, EXPERT]

pertain (pətān´) *v.i.* **1** to relate, to apply, to have reference (to). **2** to belong (to) as an attribute, an appendage, a part etc. **3** to be appropriate (to). [OF *partenir*, L *pertinēre* (*tenēre*, to hold)]

pertinacious (pœtinā´shəs) *a.* **1** obstinate. **2** stubborn, persistent. **pertinaciously** *adv.* **pertinaciousness, pertinacity** (-nas´-) *n.* [L *pertinax -ācis* (*tenax*, TENACIOUS)]

pertinent (pœ´tinənt) *a.* **1** relevant, apposite. **2** related to the matter in hand. **3** fit, suitable. **pertinence, pertinency** *n.* **pertinently** *adv.* [F, from L *pertinentem*, nom. *-ens*, pres.p. of *pertinēre*, to PERTAIN]

perturb (pətœb´) *v.t.* **1** to throw into confusion or physical disorder. **2** to disturb, to disquiet, to agitate. **3** to cause (a planet, electron etc.) to deviate from a regular path. **perturbable** *a.* **perturbate** (pœ´tə-) *v.t.* to perturb. **perturbation** (pœtəbā´shən) *n.* **perturbingly** *adv.* [L *perturbāre* (*turbāre*, to disturb, from *turba*, a crowd)]

pertuse (pətūz´), **pertused** *a.* (esp. of leaves) punched, pierced with holes. [L *pertūsus*, p.p. of *pertundere* (*tundere*, to beat)]

pertussis (pətŭs´is) *n.* whooping cough. **pertussal** *a.*

Peru balsam (pəroo´) *n.* balsam from a tropical American tree, *Myroxylon pereirae*.

peruke (pərook´), **perruque** *n.* (*Hist.*) a wig. [F *perruque*, It. *parrucca* (cp. Sardinian *pilucca*), prob. ult. from L *pilus*, a hair]

peruse (pərooz´) *v.t.* **1** to read. **2** to read with attention. **3** to observe or examine carefully. **perusal** *n.* **peruser** *n.* [USE[1] (earlier, to use up)]

Peruvian (pəroo´viən) *a.* of or relating to Peru. *~n.* a native or inhabitant of Peru, or a descendant of one. **Peruvian bark** *n.* the bark of several species of cinchona, used as a tonic in debility and intermittent fevers.

perv PERVE.

pervade (pəvād´) *v.t.* **1** to pass through. **2** to permeate, to saturate. **3** to be diffused throughout. **pervasion** (-zhən) *n.* **pervasive** (-siv) *a.* **pervasively** *adv.* **pervasiveness** *n.* [L *pervādere* (*vādere*, to go)]

perve (pœv), **perv** *n.* (*sl.*) **1** a sexual pervert. **2** (*Austral.*) a lecherous gaze. *~v.i.* **1** to behave like a sexual pervert. **2** (*Austral.*) to gaze lecherously (at).

perverse (pəvœs´) *a.* **1** wilfully or obstinately wrong. **2** turned against what is reasonable or fitting. **3** unreasonable, intractable, petulant, peevish. **4** perverted. **5** against the weight of evidence. **6** †unlucky, unpropitious. **perversely** *adv.* **perverseness** *n.* **perversity** *n.* (*pl.* **perversities**). [F *pervers*, L *perversus*, p.p. of *pervertere*, see PERVERT[1]]

perversion (pəvœ´shən) *n.* **1** the act of perverting. **2** a misinterpretation, misapplication or corruption. **3** abnormal sexual proclivity. **4** an act of perversion.

pervert[1] (pəvœt´) *v.t.* **1** to turn aside from the proper use, to put to improper use. **2** to misapply, to misinterpret. **3** to lead astray, to mislead, to corrupt. **perversive** *a.* **perverted** *a.* marked by (esp. sexual) perversion. **perverter** *n.* **pervertible** *a.* [F *pervertir*, L *pervertere* (*vertere*, to turn)]

pervert[2] (pœ´vœt) *n.* **1** a person who has been perverted. **2** a person with abnormal sexual proclivities.

pervicacious (pœvikā´shəs) *a.* very obstinate, wilfully perverse. **†pervicaciousness, pervicacity** (-kas´-) *n.* [L *pervicax -cācis*, -OUS]

pervious (pœ´viəs) *a.* **1** permeable. **2** allowing passage (to). **3** accessible (to facts, ideas etc.). **perviousness** *n.* [L *pervius* (*via*, way)]

Pesach (pā´sahkh) *n.* Passover. [Heb. *Pesah*]

pesade (pesahd´) *n.* in dressage, the motion of a horse when raising the forequarters without advancing. [F, earlier *posade*, It. *posata*, from *posare*, to PAUSE]

peseta (pəsā´tə) *n.* (*pl.* **pesetas**) **1** the standard unit of currency of Spain and Andorra. **2** (*Hist.*) a silver coin. [Sp., dim. of *pesa*, weight, cp. POISE[1]]

pesewa (pəsā´wah) *n.* a unit of currency of Ghana, worth 100th of a cedi. [local name]

Peshito (pəshē´tō) *n.* the Syriac version of the Holy Scriptures. [Syriac *p'shītâ*, *p'shītô*, the simple orphan]

peshwa (pāsh´wa), **peishwa** *n.* **1** the hereditary ruler of the Marathas. **2** orig. the chief minister of the Marathas. [Pers., a chief]

pesky (pes´ki) *a.* (*comp.* **peskier**, *superl.* **peskiest**) (*esp. N Am., coll.*) annoying, troublesome. **peskily** *adv.* **peskiness** *n.* [etym. uncertain, perh. from PEST]

peso (pā´sō) *n.* (*pl.* **pesos**) the standard unit of currency of several Central and S American countries and the

Philippines. [Sp., weight, L *pensus*, p.p. of *pendere*, to weigh]

pessary (pes´əri) *n.* (*pl.* **pessaries**) **1** a device inserted in the vagina to prevent or remedy prolapse of the womb or as a contraceptive. **2** a medicated plug or suppository introduced into the vagina. [med. L *pessārium*, from L *pessum*, Gr. *pessos*, an oval pebble used in games]

pessimism (pes´imizm) *n.* **1** the habit of taking a gloomy and despondent view of things. **2** (*Philos.*) the doctrine that pain and evil predominate enormously over good, or that there is a predominant tendency towards evil throughout the universe, as distinct from *optimism*. **pessimist** *n.* **pessimistic** (-mis´-) *a.* **pessimistically** *adv.* [L *pessimus*, worst, superl. of *malus*, bad]

pest (pest) *n.* **1** a person who or something which is extremely destructive, hurtful or annoying. **2** any plant or animal that harms crops, livestock or humans. **3** †plague, pestilence. **pest-house** *n.* (*Hist.*) a hospital for contagious diseases. **pesticide** (pes´tisīd) *n.* a chemical used to kill pests that damage crops etc. **pesticidal** (-sī´-) *a.* **pestology** (pestol´əji) *n.* the study of pests, esp. insects, and methods of dealing with them. **pestological** (-loj´-) *a.* **pestologist** *n.* [F *peste*, L *pestem*, nom. *-tis*, plague]

pester (pes´tə) *v.t.* to bother, to worry, to annoy. **pesterer** *n.* [prob. short for earlier *empester*, F *empestrer* (now *empêtrer*)]

pesticide PEST.

pestiferous (pestif´ərəs) *a.* **1** pestilent. **2** hurtful or noxious in any way. **3** bearing social or moral contagion. **pestiferously** *adv.* [L *pestifer*]

pestilence (pes´tiləns) *n.* any contagious disease that is epidemic and deadly, esp. bubonic plague. **pestilent** *a.* **1** noxious to health or life, deadly. **2** fatal to morality or society. **3** (*coll.*) vexatious, troublesome, mischievous. **pestilential** (-len´shəl) *a.* **1** of or relating to pestilence. **2** destructive, pestilent. **pestilentially** *adv.* **pestilently** *adv.* [F, from L *pestilentia*, from *pestis*, a PEST]

pestle (pes´əl) *n.* **1** an implement used in pounding substances in a mortar. **2** any appliance used for pounding or crushing things. *~v.t.* to pound with or as if with a pestle. *~v.i.* to use a pestle. [ME and OF *pestel*, L *pistillum*, from *pinsere*, to pound, p.p. *pistus*]

pesto (pes´tō) *n.* an Italian sauce made of basil, garlic, pine nuts etc. [It., from *pestare*, to pound]

pestology PEST.

PET *abbr.* **1** polyethylene terephthalate (used in recyclable packaging). **2** positron emission tomography (used for brain scans).

Pet. *abbr.* Peter (New Testament).

pet[1] (pet) *n.* **1** an animal kept in the house as a companion. **2** a darling, a favourite. *~a.* **1** kept as a pet. **2** of or relating to pets. **3** petted, indulged, favourite. *~v.t.* (*pres.p.* **petting**, *past, p.p.* **petted**) **1** to make a pet of, to pamper. **2** to fondle. *~v.i.* to engage in amorous fondling. **pet aversion, pet hate** *n.* a thing especially disliked. **pet name** *n.* a name used to express affection or intimacy. **petter** *n.* [etym. uncertain]

pet[2] (pet) *n.* a fit of peevishness or bad temper. **pettish** *a.* peevish, fretful, inclined to be bad-tempered. **pettishly** *adv.* **pettishness** *n.* [etym. uncertain]

peta- (pet´ə) *comb. form* a factor of 10 to the fifteenth power. [perh. from PENTA-]

petal (pet´əl) *n.* any one of the divisions of a corolla of a flower. **petaline** (-līn) *a.* **petalled, petaled** *a.* (*usu. in comb.*, as *fine-petalled*). **petal-like** *a.* **petaloid** *a.* **petalous** *a.* having petals. [Gr. *petalon*, a thin plate or leaf (of metal etc.)]

pétanque (pətangk´) *n.* a game similar to boules, played esp. in Provence.

petard (pitahd´) *n.* (*Hist.*) **1** a conical case or box of iron etc., formerly used for blowing open gates or barriers. **2** a firework in the form of a bomb or cracker. **hoist with/by one's own petard** caught in one's own trap. [F *pétard*, from *péter*, L *pēdere*, to break wind]

petasus (pet´əsəs) *n.* **1** a broad-brimmed, low-crowned hat worn by the ancient Greeks. **2** the winged cap of Hermes. [L, from Gr. *petasos*]

Pete (pēt) *n.* short for Peter. **for Pete's sake** SAKE[1]. [abbr. of the name *Peter*]

petechia (pətē´kiə) *n.* (*pl.* **petechiae** (-kiē)) (*Med.*) a spot on the skin formed by extravasated blood etc., in malignant fevers etc. **petechial** *a.* [mod. L, from It. *petecchia*, etym. uncertain]

peter[1] (pē´tə) *v.i.* in bridge, to play an echo. *~n.* in bridge, an echo. **to peter out 1** to come to an end, to die out. **2** (of a lode or vein in mining) to thin or give out. [sl., etym. unknown]

peter[2] (pē´tə) *n.* (*sl.*) **1** a prison cell. **2** a safe. **peterman** *n.* (*pl.* **petermen**) **1** (*sl.*) a safe-breaker. **2** a fisherman. [perh. from the name *Peter*]

Peter Pan (pētə pan´) *n.* a man who looks youthful or who behaves in a youthful manner. **Peter Pan collar** *n.* a collar on a round-necked garment having two rounded ends meeting at the front. [eponymous hero of a play (1904) by J. M. Barrie]

Peter Principle (pē´tə) *n.* (*facet.*) the theory that all members of a hierarchy rise to the level at which they are no longer competent. [L. J. *Peter*, b. 1919, who propounded it]

petersham (pē´təshəm) *n.* **1** a thick corded-silk ribbon used for belts, hatbands etc. **2** a heavy woollen cloth. **3** a heavy overcoat made of petersham. [Viscount *Petersham*, one of the 'dandies', d.1851]

Peter's pence (pē´təz) *n.pl.* **1** (*Hist.*) an annual tax of a penny from each householder, formerly paid to the Pope. **2** (since 1860) a voluntary contribution to the Pope from Roman Catholics. [L *Petrus*, from Gr. *Petros*, a masculine name, orig. a stone]

pethidine (peth´idēn) *n.* a synthetic analgesic drug with sedative effects similar to but less powerful than morphine, used esp. in childbirth. [perh. from *piperidine, ethyl*]

pétillant (pā´tēyā) *a.* (of wine) slightly sparkling. [F *pétiller*, to effervesce]

petiole (pet´iōl) *n.* **1** the leaf-stalk of a plant. **2** (*Zool.*) a small stalk. **petiolar, petiolate, petiolated** *a.* **petiolule** (pē´tiōlūl) *n.* a small petiole. [F *pétiole*, L *petiolus*, perh. dim. of *pes pedis*, a foot]

petit (pet´i) *a.* (*esp. Law*) small, petty, inconsiderable, inferior. **petit bourgeois** (peti buə´zhwah) *n.* (*pl.* **petits bourgeois** (peti buə´zhwah)) a member of the petite bourgeoisie. **petit four** (peti faw´) *n.* (*pl.* **petits fours** (fawz´)) a small fancy cake or biscuit. **petit jury** *n.* a petty jury. **petit larceny** *n.* (*Hist.*) theft of anything under a value fixed by statute (in England before 1827, one shilling). **petit-maître** (pətēmā´trə) *n.* a fop, a coxcomb. **petit mal** (pətē mal´) *n.* **1** a mild form of epilepsy, as distinct from *grand mal*. **2** a mild epileptic fit. **petit point** (pətē pwā) *n.* **1** a kind of fine embroidery, as distinct from *gros point*. **2** tent stitch. **petits pois** (peti pwah´) *n.pl.* small, sweet green peas. [F]

petite (pətēt´) *a.* **1** (of a woman) slight, dainty, graceful. **2** designed for a small woman. **petite bourgeoisie** *n.* the lower middle classes. [fem. of F PETIT]

petition (pitish´ən) *n.* **1** an entreaty, a request, a supplication. **2** a formal written supplication to persons in authority, esp. to the people, Parliament etc. **3** the paper containing such supplication. **4** (*Law*) a formal written application to a court, as for a writ of habeas corpus, in bankruptcy etc. *~v.t.* **1** to address a petition to. **2** to solicit, to ask humbly for etc. *~v.i.* to appeal humbly (to). **petitionable** *a.* **petitionary** *a.* **petitioner** *n.* **Petition of Right** *n.* **1** (*Hist.*) the declaration of the rights and liberties of the people made by Parliament to Charles I and assented to in 1628. **2** (*Law*) a common law redress against the Crown for recovery of property. **petitory** (pet´-) *a.* petitioning, begging, supplicating. [F *pétition*, L *petitiōnem*, nom. *-tio*, from *petere*, to seek]

petitio principii (pətishiō prinsip´iī) *n.* (*Logic*) begging the question. [L, assuming a principle (see PETITION)]

petits fours, petits pois PETIT.

Petrarchan (pitrah´kən) *a.* denoting a sonnet which has an octave rhyming *abbaabba* and a sestet rhyming *cdcdcd* or *cdecde*. [*Petrarch*, 1304–74, Italian poet]

petre (pē´tə) *n.* (*coll.*) saltpetre.

petrel (pet´rəl) *n.* any member of the family Procellariidae or Hydrobatidae, small dusky seabirds, with long wings and great power of flight. [F *pétrel* (prob. from association with St Peter)]

Usage note The spellings of the nouns *petrel* (a bird) and *petrol* (refined petroleum) should not be confused.

Petri dish (pet´ri, pē´-) *n.* a shallow, circular, flat-bottomed dish used for cultures of micro-organisms. [Julius *Petri*, 1852–1921, German bacteriologist]

petrify (pet´rifī) *v.t.* (*3rd pers. sing. pres.* **petrifies**, *pres.p.* **petrifying**, *past, p.p.* **petrified**) **1** to convert into stone or a stony substance. **2** to stupefy with fear, astonishment etc. **3** to make hard, callous, benumbed or stiffened. ~*v.i.* **1** to be converted into stone or a stony substance. **2** to become stiffened, benumbed, callous etc. †**petrescent** (pitres´ənt) *a.* **1** changing into stone. **2** petrifactive. **petrifaction** (-fak´-) *n.* **petrifactive** (-fak´-) *a.* having the power to petrify. [F *pétrifier*, It. *petrificare* (L *petra*, stone, -FY)]

Petrine (pē´trīn) *a.* of, relating to or derived from the apostle Peter. **Petrinism** (-tri-) *n.* the theological doctrine attributed to St Peter, esp. as distinct from *Paulinism*.

petro- (pet´rō) *comb. form* **1** stone. **2** petrol. [Gr. *petra*, stone, rock]

petrochemical (petrōkem´ikəl) *n.* any chemical obtained from petroleum. *a.* of or relating to petrochemicals or petrochemistry.

petrochemistry (petrōkem´istri) *n.* **1** the chemistry of rocks. **2** the chemistry of petroleum.

petrocurrency (petrōkŭr´ənsi) *n.* the currency of a country which exports significant quantities of petroleum.

petrodollar (pet´rōdolə) *n.* a dollar earned from the exporting of petroleum.

petroglyph (pet´rōglif) *n.* a rock-carving. **petroglyphic** (-glif´-) *a.* **petroglyphy** (-rog´-) *n.* [F *pétroglyphe* (Gr. *gluphē*, carving)]

petrography (petrog´rəfi) *n.* descriptive petrology. **petrographer** *n.* **petrographic** (-graf´-), **petrographical** *a.*

petrol (pet´rəl) *n.* a refined form of petroleum used in motor cars etc. ~*a.* of or relating to the supply of petrol. ~*v.t.* (*pres.p.* **petrolling**, *past, p.p.* **petrolled**) to supply with petrol. **petrolatum** (-lā´təm) *n.* (*N Am.*) a fatty compound of paraffin hydrocarbons obtained by refining the residue from petroleum after distillation, pure petroleum jelly. **petrol bomb** *n.* a bottle or other container full of petrol, used as an incendiary. **petrol lighter** *n.* a cigarette lighter with a petrol-soaked wick. **petrol station** *n.* a filling station. [F *pétrole*, med. L PETROLEUM]

Usage note See note under PETREL.

petroleum (pitrō´liəm) *n.* an inflammable, oily liquid exuding from rocks or pumped from wells, used for lighting, heating and the generation of mechanical power. **petroleum ether** *n.* a volatile mixture of hydrocarbons, distilled from petroleum. **petroleum jelly** *n.* a product of petroleum used in pharmacy as a lubricant. **petrolic** (-rol´-) *a.* of or relating to petroleum or petrol. **petroliferous** (-lif´-) *a.* [med. L *petroleum* (PETRO-, *oleum*, OIL)]

pétroleur (pātrəlœ´) *n.* an arsonist who uses petroleum. **pétroleuse** (-lœz´) *n.* a female pétroleur. [F]

petrology (pitrol´əji) *n.* the study of the origin, structure and mineralogical and chemical composition of rocks. **petrologic** (-loj´-), **petrological** *a.* **petrologically** *adv.* **petrologist** *n.*

petrosal (petrō´səl) *a.* (*Anat.*) of great hardness, like stone. ~*n.* the petrosal bone, the petrous part of the temporal bone. [L *petrōsus*, PETROUS, -AL[1]]

petrous (pet´rəs) *a.* **1** (*Anat.*) denoting the hard part of the temporal bone. **2** (*Geol.*) like stone, stony. [L *petrōsus*, from L and Gr. *petra*, rock]

petter PET[1].

pettichaps (pet´ichaps) *n.* the garden warbler, *Sylvia borin*. [PETTY, CHAP[3]]

petticoat (pet´ikōt) *n.* **1** a loose underskirt. **2** (*sl.*) a woman, a girl. ~*a.* (*coll., often derog.*) of or relating to women, feminine. **petticoated** *a.* **petticoat government** *n.* government by women, esp. in domestic affairs. **petticoatless** *a.* [PETTY, COAT]

pettifog (pet´ifog) *v.i.* (*pres.p.* **pettifogging**, *past, p.p.* **pettifogged**) **1** to do legal business in a mean or tricky way, to practise chicanery. **2** to act in a mean, quibbling or shifty way. **pettifogger** *n.* **1** a petty, second-rate lawyer, esp. one given to sharp practices. **2** a petty or second-rate practitioner in any profession. **pettifoggery** *n.* **pettifogging** *a.* petty, trivial, quibbling. [PETTY, *-fog* (perh. from *-fogger*), etym. uncertain]

pettily, pettiness PETTY.

pettish PET[2].

pettitoes (pet´itōz) *n.pl.* the feet of a pig as food, pig's trotters. [etym. uncertain, perh. from F *petite oie*, little goose, giblets]

petty (pet´i) *a.* (*comp.* **pettier**, *superl.* **pettiest**) **1** little, trifling, insignificant. **2** small-minded, mean. **3** minor, inferior, subordinate, on a small scale. **4** (*Law*) (of a crime) of minor importance. **pettily** *adv.* **pettiness** *n.* **petty average** *n.* a standard charge on goods over and above the freight. **petty bourgeois** *n.* a petit bourgeois. **petty bourgeoisie** *n.* the petite bourgeoisie. **petty cash** *n.* minor items of receipt and expenditure. **petty jury** *n.* a jury in criminal cases who try the bills found by the grand jury. **petty larceny** *n.* in the US and formerly in England, the theft of property worth less than a specified figure. **petty officer** *n.* a naval officer corresponding in rank to a non-commissioned officer. **petty sessions** *n.pl.* **1** a court of two or more justices of the peace for trying minor offences. **2** quarter sessions. **petty treason** *n.* (*Hist.*) murder of one's master or husband. [ME and F *petit*, etym. uncertain]

petulant (pet´ūlənt) *a.* given to fits of bad temper, peevish, irritable. **petulance, petulancy** *n.* **petulantly** *adv.* [F *pétulant*, L *petulantem*, nom. *-lans*, prob. from *petere*, to seek, to aim at, through a dim. form *petulāre*]

petunia (pitū´niə) *n.* any member of the genus *Petunia* of S American plants, allied to the tobacco plant, cultivated in gardens for their showy funnel-shaped flowers. [mod. L from F *petun*, Guarani *petȳ*, tobacco]

petuntse (pātŭnt´sə) *n.* (*Geol.*) a fusible substance similar to feldspar used for the manufacture of porcelain. [Chin. *pai-tun-tzu*]

pew (pū) *n.* **1** a long bench with a back, for worshippers in church. **2** a boxlike enclosed seat in a church for a family etc. **3** (*coll.*) a seat, a chair. ~*v.t.* to furnish with pews. **to take a pew** (*coll.*) to sit down. **pewage** (-ij) *n.* **pewless** *a.* **pew-rent** *n.* rent paid for a pew. [ME *puwe*, OF *puie*, a stage or platform, L *podia*, pl. of *podium*, Gr. *podion*, pedestal, from *pous podos*, a foot]

pewee (pē´wē) *n.* a N American flycatcher of the genus *Contopus*. [imit. (cp. PEEWEE)]

pewit PEEWIT.

pewter (pū´tə) *n.* **1** an alloy usu. of tin and lead, sometimes of tin with other metals. **2** dishes or utensils made of this. **3** a pewter tankard or pot. **4** (*dated sl.*) a prize tankard, prize money. ~*a.* made of pewter. **pewterer** *n.* [OF *peutre*, It. *peltro*, etym. uncertain]

peyote (pāō´ti) *n.* **1** a Mexican cactus, *Lophophora williamsii*. **2** a hallucinogenic drug made from peyote. [Nahuatl *peyotl*]

Pf *abbr.* pfennig.

Pfc *abbr.* (*N Am.*) Private First Class.

pfennig (pfen´ig) *n.* (*pl.* **pfennigs, pfennige** (-igə)) a German unit of currency, worth one-hundredth of a mark. [G, cogn. with PENNY]

PFLP *abbr.* Popular Front for the Liberation of Palestine.

PG *abbr.* **1** parental guidance (used to classify the content of cinema films). **2** paying guest.

pH (pēāch´) *n.* (*Chem.*) a measure of the acidity or alkalinity of a solution on a scale from 0 to 14, with 7 representing neutrality, figures below it denoting acidity and those above it alkalinity. [G *Potenz*, power, *H*, the symbol for hydrogen]

phaenogam (fē´nōgam) *n.* a phanerogam.

phaenomenon PHENOMENON.

phaeton (fā´tən) *n.* a light four-wheeled open carriage, usu. drawn by two horses. [F *phaéton*, L and Gr. *Phaethōn*, shining, proper name of the son of Helios and Clymene, who, having obtained permission to drive the chariot of the sun for one day, would have set the world on fire had not Jupiter transfixed him with a thunderbolt]

phag- PHAGO-.

phage (fāj) *n.* a bacteriophage.

-phage (fāj) *comb. form* eater, as *bacteriophage*. **-phagia** (fā´jiə), **-phagy** (fəji) *comb. form* eating, as *anthropophagia*. [PHAGO-]

phago- (fag´ō), **phag-** *comb. form* eating. [Gr. *phagein*, to eat]

phagocyte (fag´ōsīt) *n.* a leucocyte that absorbs microbes etc., protecting the system against infection. **phagocytic** (-sit´-) *a.* **phagocytism** *n.* **phagocytize, phagocytise** *v.t.* **phagocytose** *v.t.* **phagocytosis** (-tō´sis) *n.* the destruction of microbes etc. by phagocytes.

-phagous (fəgəs) *comb. form* eating, devouring, as *anthropophagous*. [Gr. *phagos*, from *phagein*, see PHAGO-]

-phagy -PHAGIA (under -PHAGE).

phalange (fal´anj) *n.* **1** (*Anat.*) a phalanx. **2** (**Phalange**) a Christian right-wing party in Lebanon. **phalangeal** (fəlan´jiəl) *a.* (*Anat.*) of or relating to a phalanx. **Phalangist** (fəlan´-, fal´ən-) *n.* a member of the Phalange party. ~*a.* of or relating to the Phalangists. [F, from L *phalanx* (see PHALANX)]

phalanger (fəlan´jə) *n.* any small, Australian, woolly-coated, arboreal marsupial of the family Phalangeridae, comprising the flying squirrel and flying opossum. [F, from Gr. *phalangion*, a spider's web]

phalanx (fal´angks) *n.* (*pl.* **phalanxes**, (*Anat., Bot.*) **phalanges** (fəlan´jēz)) **1** (*Hist.*) the close order in which the heavy-armed troops of a Greek army were drawn up, esp. a compact body of Macedonian infantry. **2** any compact body of troops or close organization of people. **3** (*Anat.*) any one of the small bones of the fingers. **4** (*Bot.*) any one of the bundles of stamens in polyadelphous flowers. **phalangiform** (fəlan´-) *a.* [L and Gr. *phalanx -angos*]

phalarope (fal´ərōp) *n.* any small wading bird of the subfamily Phalaropodidae, related to the snipes. [F (Gr. *phalaris*, a coot, *pous*, a foot)]

phallus (fal´əs) *n.* (*pl.* **phalli** (-lī), **phalluses**) **1** a penis. **2** a figure of a penis, venerated as a symbol of the fertilizing power in nature. **3** (*Bot.*) a genus of fungi containing the stinkhorn. **phallic** *a.* **phallically** *adv.* **phallicism** (-sizm), **phallism** *n.* **phallocentric** (falōsen´trik) *a.* centred on the phallus or on male attitudes. **phallocentricity** (-tris´-) *n.* **phallocentrism** *n.* [Gr. *phallos*]

phanariot (fənar´iət) *n.* **1** (*Hist.*) a member of the class of Greek officials under Turkey. **2** (**Phanariot**) a resident in the Greek or Fanar quarter of Istanbul. [mod. Gr. *phanariōtēs*, from *phanari*, Gr. *phanarion*, a lighthouse, dim. of *phanos*, a lamp]

phanerogam (fan´ərōgam) *n.* (*Bot.*) a plant having pistils and stamens, a flowering plant. **phanerogamic** (-gam´-), **phanerogamous** (-rog´ə-) *a.* [F *phanérogame* (Gr. *phaneros*, visible, *gamos*, marriage)]

phantasiast (fantā´ziast) *n.* (*Hist.*) any one of those among the Docetae, who believed that Christ's body was not material but mere appearance. [Gr. *Phantasiastēs*, from *phantasia*, FANTASY]

phantasize FANTASIZE (under FANTASY).

phantasm (fan´tazm), †**fantasm** *n.* **1** a phantom, an optical illusion. **2** a deception, a figment, an unreal likeness or presentation (of). **3** a vision or image of an absent or deceased person. **4** (*Psych.*) a mental representation of an object. **5** an imaginary idea of a fantastic kind, a fancy, a fantasy. **phantasmal** (-taz´-) *a.* **phantasmally** *adv.* **phantasmic** (-taz´-) *a.* [ME and OF *fantosme* (F *fantasme*), L and Gr. *phantasma*, from *phantazein*, to display, from *phan-*, stem of *phainein*, to show]

phantasmagoria (fantazməgor´riə), **phantasmagory** (-taz´məgəri) *n.* (*pl.* **phantasmagorias, phantasmagories**) **1** a series of phantasms, fantastic appearances or illusions appearing to the mind as in nightmare, frenzy etc. **2** (*Hist.*) an exhibition of dissolving views and optical illusions produced by a magic lantern. **phantasmagorial, phantasmagoric** (-gor´-), **phantasmagorical** *a.* [Gr. AGORA[1], an assembly]

phantast FANTAST.

phantasy FANTASY.

phantom (fan´təm), †**fantom** *n.* **1** an apparition, a ghost, a spectre. **2** a vision, an illusion, an imaginary appearance. **3** an empty show or mere image (of). **4** (*Med.*) a model of the human body used for demonstration or practice. ~*a.* seeming, apparent, illusory, imaginary, fictitious. **phantom circuit** *n.* an arrangement of electrical wires equivalent to an extra circuit. **phantom limb** *n.* the sensation that a limb is still present after it has been amputated. **phantom pregnancy** *n.* (*Med.*) the manifestation of symptoms of pregnancy in a woman who is not pregnant. [ME and OF *fantosme*, as PHANTASM]

Pharaoh (feə´rō) *n.* any one of the ancient Egyptian kings. **Pharaoh's ant** *n.* a small reddish-yellow ant, *Monomorium pharaonis*, of tropical regions, which has spread to other countries and infests heated buildings etc. **Pharaoh's serpent** *n.* a firework consisting of sulphocyanide of mercury, which fuses into a serpentine shape when lit. **Pharaonic** (-rāon´-) *a.* [L and Gr., from Egypt. *pr-'o*, a great house]

phare (feə) *n.* a lighthouse. [F, from L *pharus*, Gr. PHAROS]

Pharisee (far´isē) *n.* **1** a member of an ancient Jewish sect who rigidly observed the rites and ceremonies prescribed by the written law, and were marked by their exclusiveness towards the rest of the people. **2** a self-righteous person, an unctuous hypocrite. **Pharisaic** (-sā´ik) *a.* **Pharisaical** *a.* **Pharisaically** *adv.* **Pharisaism** (far´isā-) *n.* [OF, from L *pharisaeus, -sēus*, Gr. *pharisaios*, ult. from Heb. *pārūsh*, separated]

pharm. *abbr.* **1** pharmaceutical. **2** pharmacy.

pharmaceutical (fahməsū´tikəl) *a.* of, relating to or engaged in pharmacy. ~*n.* a medicinal preparation. **pharmaceutically** *adv.* **pharmaceutics** *n.* **pharmaceutist** *n.* a pharmacist. [L *pharmaceuticus*, Gr.

pharmakeutikos, from *pharmakeutēs*, *pharmakeus*, druggist, from *pharmakon*, a drug]

pharmaco- (fah´məkō) *comb. form* of or relating to chemistry or drugs. [Gr. *pharmakon*, a drug]

pharmacognosy (fahməkog´nəsi) *n.* the branch of pharmacology concerned with drugs of plant and animal origin. [Gr. *pharmakon*, a drug, *gnōsis*, knowledge]

pharmacology (fahməkol´əji) *n.* the science of drugs and medicines. **pharmacological** (-kəloj´-) *a.* **pharmacologically** *adv.* **pharmacologist** *n.*

pharmacopoeia (fahməkəpē´ə) *n.* (*pl.* **pharmacopoeias**) **1** a book, esp. an official publication, containing a list of drugs, formulas, doses etc. **2** a collection of drugs. **pharmacopoeial** *a.* [Gr. *pharmakopoiia*, from *pharmakopoios*, a preparer of drugs (*-poios*, from *poieein*, to make)]

pharmacy (fah´məsi) *n.* (*pl.* **pharmacies**) **1** the art or practice of preparing, compounding and dispensing drugs, esp. for medicinal purposes. **2** a chemist's shop, a dispensary. **pharmacist** *n.* a person who is trained in pharmacy and is legally entitled to sell drugs and poisons. [OF *farmacie*, late L *pharmacīa*, Gr. *pharmakeia*, practice of the druggist]

pharos (feə´ros) *n.* (*pl.* **pharoses**) a lighthouse, a beacon. [L and Gr., *Pharos*, name of a small island in the bay of Alexandria, on which a beacon was erected]

pharyngal, pharyngeal etc. PHARYNX.

pharyngo- (fəring´gō), **pharyng-** *comb. form* of or relating to the pharynx.

pharyngoscope (fəring´gəskōp) *n.* an instrument for inspecting the throat. **pharyngoscopy** (faring·gos´kəpi) *n.*

pharyngotomy (faring·got´əmi) *n.* (*pl.* **pharyngotomies**) the surgical operation of cutting the pharynx.

pharynx (far´ingks) *n.* (*pl.* **pharynges** (fərin´jēz)) (*Anat.*) the canal or cavity opening from the mouth into the oesophagus and communicating with the air passages of the nose. **pharyngal** (fəring´gəl), **pharyngeal** (fərin´jiəl) *a.* **pharyngitis** (-jī´-) *n.* inflammation of the pharynx. **pharyngitic** (-jit´-) *a.* [Gr. *pharunx -ngos*]

phase (fāz) *n.* **1** a stage of change or development. **2** a particular aspect of the illuminated surface of the moon or a planet, applied esp. to the successive quarters etc. of the moon. **3** (*Physics*) the relationship in time between the peaks of two alternating voltages etc. **4** a difficult period, esp. in adolescence. **5** a variation in an animal's coloration owing to seasonal changes etc. **6** (*Chem.*) a distinct, mechanically separable, homogeneous portion of matter that is part of a physical-chemical system. **7** a particular aspect or appearance. ~*v.t.* **1** to carry out in phases. **2** to organize in phases. **in phase** happening together or in harmony. **out of phase** not happening together or in harmony. **to phase in** to introduce gradually. **to phase out** to discontinue gradually. **phase-contrast microscope** *n.* a microscope used for examining colourless, transparent objects, which operates by changing differences in the phase of light transmitted, reflected or refracted by the object into differences in the intensity of the image. **phaseless** *a.* **phase rule** *n.* (*Chem.*) a rule which relates degrees of freedom, components and number of phases. **phasic** *a.* [late L and Gr. *phasis*, from the stem *pha-*, to shine]

-phasia (fā´ziə) *comb. form* speech disorder, as *dysphasia*. [Gr. *phasis*, an utterance, from *phanai*, to speak]

phasic PHASE.

†**phasis** (fā´sis) *n.* (*pl.* **phases** (-sēz)) a phase.

phasmid (faz´mid) *n.* any orthopterous insect of the family Phasmidae, comprising the stick insects etc. [L and Gr., *phasma*, a spectre]

phatic (fat´ik) *a.* (of speech) used to express feelings, sociability etc., rather than to express meaning. [Gr. *phatos*, spoken]

Ph.D. *abbr.* Doctor of Philosophy. [L *philosophiae doctor*]

pheasant (fez´ənt) *n.* any game bird of the family Phasianidae, naturalized in Britain and Europe, noted for their brilliant plumage and delicate flesh. **pheasantry** *n.* (*pl.* **pheasantries**) a place where pheasants are kept. [A-F *fesant* (F *faisan*), L *phāsiānus*, Gr. *Phasionos*, of or relating to the *Phasis*, a river of Colchis]

phellem (fel´əm) *n.* (*Bot.*) a layer of cork cells formed by phellogen.

phello- (fel´ō) *comb. form* cork. [Gr. *phellos*, cork]

phelloderm (fel´ōdœm) *n.* (*Bot.*) a layer of parenchymatous tissue containing chlorophyll, sometimes formed on the inner side of a layer of phellogen. **phellodermal** (-dœ´-) *a.*

phellogen (fel´əjən) *n.* (*Bot.*) the layer of meristematic cells in the cortex of the stems and roots of woody plants, from which cork tissue is formed; cork tissue. **phellogenetic** (felōjinet´-), **phellogenic** (felōjen´-) *a.*

phelloplastic (felōplas´tik) *n.* **1** a figure carved or modelled in cork. **2** (*pl., sing. in constr.*) the art of making phelloplastics.

phen- PHENO-.

phenacetin (finas´itin) *n.* a white crystalline compound used as an antipyretic.

phenakistoscope (fenəkis´təskōp) *n.* (*Hist.*) a scientific toy in which a disc bearing figures in successive attitudes of motion was rapidly revolved so as to convey to the observer, by means of a mirror or a series of slits, the impression of continuous movement. [Gr. *phenakistēs*, an impostor, from *phenakizein*, to cheat, -SCOPE[1]]

phencyclidine (fensī´klidēn) *n.* a hallucinogenic drug derived from piperidine.

phenix PHOENIX.

pheno- (fē´nō, fen´ō) *comb. form* **1** (*Chem.*) derived from coal tar, orig. in the production of coal gas for illuminating. **2** showing. [Gr. *phainos*, shining, from *phainein*, to show]

phenobarbitone (fēnōbah´bitōn), (*N Am.*) **phenobarbital** (-təl) *n.* a white, crystalline powder used as a sedative or hypnotic drug, esp. in cases of epilepsy.

phenocryst (fē´nōkrist) *n.* a large crystal in porphyritic rock. [F *phénocryste* (as PHENO-, CRYSTAL)]

phenol (fē´nol) *n.* (*Chem.*) **1** carbolic acid. **2** any of various weakly acidic compounds derived from benzene, and containing a hydroxyl group. **phenolic** (finol´-) *a.* **phenolphthalein** (fēnolfthal´ēn) *n.* (*Chem.*) a white, crystalline compound used as a laxative and as an acid-base indicator.

phenology (finol´əji) *n.* the study of the times of recurrence of natural phenomena, esp. of the influence of climate on plants and animals. **phenological** (fēnəloj´-) *a.* [contr. of PHENOMENOLOGY (under PHENOMENON), after G *phänologisch*]

phenom (fin´om) *n.* (*N Am., coll.*) an exceptionally gifted person.

phenomenon (finom´inən), **phaenomenon** *n.* (*pl.* **phenomena** (-nə), **phaenomena**) **1** something which appears or is perceived by observation or experiment, esp. a thing or occurrence whose cause is in question. **2** (*coll.*) a remarkable or unusual person or thing. **3** (*Philos.*) something which is apprehended by the mind, as distinguished from real existence. **phenomenal** *a.* **1** of or relating to phenomena, esp. as distinct from underlying realities or causes. **2** extraordinary, prodigious. **3** of the nature of a phenomenon, perceptible by the senses. **phenomenalism, phenomenism** *n.* (*Philos.*) the doctrine that phenomena are the sole material of knowledge, and that underlying realities and causes are unknowable. **phenomenalist, phenomenist** *n.* **phenomenalistic** (-lis´-) *a.* **phenomenalize, phenomenalise** *v.t.* **phenomenally** *adv.* **phenomenistic** (-nis´-) *a.* **phenomenize, phenomenise** *v.t.*

phenomenology (-nol´-) *n.* (*Philos.*) **1** the science of phenomena, as distinct from *ontology.* **2** the division of any inductive science concerned with the phenomena forming its basis. **phenomenological** (-loj´-) *a.* **phenomenologically** *adv.* **phenomenologist** *n.* [L *phænomenon,* Gr. *phainomenon,* neut. pres.p. of *phainein,* to show]

Usage note *Phenomena* is sometimes used as a singular noun (*a phenomena*), and a plural *phenomenas* may also be encountered, but both these uses are best avoided.

phenotype (fē´nōtīp) *n.* (*Biol.*) the observable characteristics of an organism produced by the interaction of the genotype and the environment. **phenotypic** (-tip´ik) *a.* **phenotypical** *a.* **phenotypically** *adv.* [Gr. *phainein,* to show, TYPE]
phenyl (fē´nīl, fen´il) *n.* (*Chem.*) the organic radical found in benzene, phenol, aniline etc. **phenylalanine** (-al´ənēn) *n.* an amino acid found in plant proteins and essential to the human diet. **phenylbutazone** (fenilbū´təzōn) *n.* an analgesic drug used for treating rheumatic disorders. **phenylketonuria** (-kētənuə´riə) *n.* (*Med.*) a congenital inability to metabolize phenylalanine, which can lead to mental handicap.
pheon (fē´on) *n.* (*pl.* **pheons**) (*Her.*) the barbed head of a dart, arrow or javelin, a broad arrow. [etym. uncertain]
pheromone (fer´əmōn) *n.* any chemical substance secreted by an animal that stimulates responses from others of its species. **pheromonal** (-mō´-) *a.* [Gr. *pherein,* to bear, hor*mone*]
phew (fū) *int.* used to express relief, surprise, disgust etc. [onomat.]
phi (fī) *n.* the 21st letter of the Greek alphabet (Φ, ϕ). [Gr. *phei*]
phial (fī´əl) *n.* a small glass vessel or bottle, esp. for medicine or perfume. *~v.t.* (*pres.p.* **phialling,** (*N Am.*) **phialing,** *past, p.p.* **phialled,** (*N Am.*) **phialed**) to put or keep in or as if in a phial. [ME and OF *fiole,* L *phiala,* Gr. *phialē*]
Phi Beta Kappa (fī bētə kap´ə) *n.* (*N Am.*) **1** a national honorary society for distinguished scholars. **2** a member of this society. [Gr. abbr. of *philosophia biou kubernētēs,* philosophy is the helmsman of life]
Phil. *abbr.* **1** Philadelphia. **2** Philharmonic. **3** Philippians (New Testament). **4** Philosophy.
phil- PHILO-.
-phil -PHILE.
philabeg FILIBEG.
philadelphus (filədel´fəs) *n.* a strongly-scented flowering shrub of the genus *Philadelphus.* [mod. L, from Gr. *philadelphon*]
philander (filan´də) *v.i.* (of a man) to have casual affairs with women, to flirt. **philanderer** *n.* [Gr. *philandros* (*anēr andros,* man, perh. after a character in Beaumont and Fletcher's *Laws of Candy,* or from a lover in Ariosto's *Orlando Furioso*)]
philanthropy (filan´thrəpi) *n.* **1** love of humankind. **2** active benevolence towards one's fellow humans. **philanthrope** (fil´ənthrōp) *n.* a philanthropist. **philanthropic** (-throp´-), **philanthropical** *a.* **philanthropically** *adv.* **philanthropism** *n.* **philanthropist** *n.* **philanthropize, philanthropise** *v.t., v.i.* [late L and Gr. *philanthrōpia* (*anthrōpos,* a human being)]
philately (filat´əli) *n.* the collecting of postage stamps. **philatelic** (filətel´-) *a.* **philatelically** *adv.* **philatelist** *n.* [F *philatélie* (Gr. *ateleia,* freedom from toll, from *a-,* not, *telos,* a toll, a tax)]
-phile (fīl), **-phil** (fil) *comb. form* a lover of, or loving, as *bibliophile, Anglophile.* [Gr. *philos,* loving, dear, friendly, from *philein,* to love]
Philem. *abbr.* Philemon (New Testament).
philharmonic (filəmon´ik) *a.* **1** loving music. **2** used as part of the name of an orchestra or choir. *~n.* a philharmonic orchestra or choir. [F *philharmonique*]
philhellene (fil´helēn, filhel´ēn) *n.* **1** a friend or lover of Greece and Greeks. **2** (*Hist.*) a supporter of Greek independence. *~a.* **1** friendly to Greece. **2** (*Hist.*) supporting Greek independence. **philhellenic** (-lē´-) *a.* **philhellenism** (-hel´-) *n.* **philhellenist** (-hel´-) *n.*
-philia (fil´iə), **-phily** (fili) *comb. form* **1** love of, as *necrophilia.* **2** a strong tendency towards, as *haemophilia.* **-philiac** (fil´iak) *comb. form* **-philic** (fil´ik), **-philous** (fil´əs) *comb. form* [-PHILE]
philibeg FILIBEG.
-philic -PHILIA.
philippic (filip´ik) *n.* **1** a speech or declamation full of acrimonious invective. **2** any one of three orations of Demosthenes against Philip of Macedon. [L *Philippicus,* Gr. *philippikos,* from *Philippos,* Philip]
philippina PHILOPENA.
Philippine (fil´ipēn) *a.* of or relating to the Philippines, in SE Asia.
Philistine (fil´istīn) *n.* **1** a member of an ancient warlike people in S Palestine who were hostile to the Jews. **2** (*usu.* **philistine**) a person of narrow or materialistic views or ideas; a person deficient in liberal culture. **3** among German students, a non-university person. *~a.* **1** (*usu.* **philistine**) commonplace, uncultured, prosaic. **2** of or relating to the Philistines. **philistinism** (-tin-) *n.* [F *Philistin,* late L *Philistīnus,* Gr. *Philistīnoi,* pl., Assyrian *Palastu, Pilistu*]
Phillips® (fil´ips) *a.* denoting a screw having a cross-shaped slot in the head, or a screwdriver for use with such a screw. [US manufacturer]
phillipsite (fil´ipsīt) *n.* (*Mineral.*) a monoclinic hydrous silicate of aluminium, potassium and calcium. [J. W. *Phillips,* 1800–74, British mineralogist]
phillumeny (filoo´məni) *n.* the collecting of matchboxes or matchbox labels. **phillumenist** *n.* [L *lumen,* light]
Philly (fil´i) *n.* (*N Am., sl.*) Philadelphia.
philo- (fil´ō), **phil-** *comb. form* fond of, affecting, inhabiting. [Gr. *philos,* loving, from *philein,* to love, cp. -PHILE]
philodendron (filəden´drən) *n.* (*pl.* **philodendra** (-drə), **philodendrons**) any of various plants of the genus *Philodendron* (arum family), cultivated for their showy foliage. [Gr. *dendron,* a tree]
philogyny (filoj´ini) *n.* devotion to women. **philogynist** *n.* **philogynous** *a.* [Gr. *philogunia,* love of woman (*gunē,* a woman)]
philology (filol´əji) *n.* **1** the historical or comparative study of language. **2** love of learning or literature. **philologer, philologian** (filəlō´-), **philologist** *n.* **philological** (-loj´-) *a.* **philologically** *adv.* **philologize, philologise** *v.i.* [L and Gr. *philologia* (*logos,* a word, a discourse)]
philomath (fil´əmath) *n.* a lover of learning, esp. of mathematics, a scholar. **philomathic** (-math´-), **philomathical** *a.* **philomathy** (-lom´əthi) *n.* [Gr. *philomathēs* (*math-,* stem of *manthanein,* to learn)]
Philomel (fil´əmel), **Philomela** (-mē´lə) *n.* (*poet.*) the nightingale. [F *philomèle,* L and Gr. *Philomēla,* daughter of Pandion, king of Athens, changed by the gods into a nightingale]
philopena (filəpē´nə), **philippina** (fili-) *n.* **1** a game in which two people share the double kernel of a nut, the first being entitled to a forfeit, under certain conditions, on the next meeting with the other sharer. **2** the kernel so shared. **3** the forfeit. [corr. of G *Vielliebchen,* dim. of *viellieb* (*viel,* much, *lieb,* dear)]
philoprogenitive (filōprōjen´itiv) *a.* **1** prolific. **2** characterized by love of offspring. **philoprogenitiveness** *n.* [L *progenit-,* stem of *progignere,* to beget]
philosopher (filos´əfə) *n.* **1** a person who studies philosophy. **2** a person who regulates conduct and actions

by the principles of philosophy. **3** a person of philosophical disposition. **4** a lover of wisdom. **philosophe** (fil´əsof) *n.* a philosophist or pretender to philosophy. **philosophers' stone, philosopher's stone** *n.* an imaginary stone, sought by the alchemists in the belief that it would change the baser metals into gold or silver. [A-F *philosofre*, F *philosophe*, L *philosophus*, Gr. *philosophos* (*sophos*, wise)]

philosophy (filos´əfi) *n.* (*pl.* **philosophies**) **1** the knowledge or investigation of ultimate reality or of general principles of knowledge or existence. **2** a particular system of philosophic principles. **3** the fundamental principles of a science etc. **4** practical wisdom, calmness and coolness of temper, serenity, resignation. **5** love of wisdom. **philosophical** (-əsof´-), **philosophic** *a.* **1** of, relating to or according to philosophy. **2** devoted to or skilled in philosophy. **3** wise, calm, temperate, unimpassioned. **philosophically** *adv.* **philosophism** *n.* affectation of philosophy (applied esp. to the French Encyclopedists). **philosophist** *n.* **philosophistic** (-fis´-) *a.* †**philosophistical** *a.* **philosophize, philosophise** *v.t., v.i.* **philosophizer, philosophiser** *n.* [see PHILOSOPHER]

Usage note The uses of the adjectives *philosophic* and *philosophical* overlap, but *philosophical* is more usual for the sense calm or temperate.

-philous -PHILIA.

philtre (fil´tə), (*N Am.*) **philter** *n.* a love potion. [F, from L *philtrum*, Gr. *philtron*, from *philein*, to love]

-phily -PHILIA.

phimosis (fīmō´sis) *n.* (*Med.*) constriction of the opening of the foreskin. **phimotic** (-mot´-) *a.* [Gr., from *phimoein*, to muzzle]

phiz (fiz), **phizog** (-zog´) *n.* (*coll.*) **1** the face. **2** a facial expression. [short for obs. *phisnomy*, PHYSIOGNOMY]

phleb- PHLEBO-.

phlebitis (flibī´tis) *n.* (*Med.*) inflammation of the inner membrane of a vein. **phlebitic** (-bit´-) *a.*

phlebo- (fleb´ō), **phleb-** *comb. form* a vein. [Gr. *phleps phlebos*, a vein]

phlebolite (fleb´əlīt) *n.* (*Med.*) a calculus in a vein.

phlebotomy (flibot´əmi) *n.* the opening of a vein, bloodletting. **phlebotomist** *n.* **phlebotomize, phlebotomise** *v.t.* [OF *flebothomie* (F *phlébotomie*), L and Gr. *phlebotomia*]

phlegm (flem) *n.* **1** viscid mucus secreted in the air passages or stomach, esp. as a morbid product and discharged by coughing etc. **2** self-possession, coolness, sluggishness, apathy. **3** (*Hist.*) watery matter forming one of the four humours of the body. †**phlegmagogue** (fleg´məgog) *n.* a medicine for expelling phlegm, an expectorant. **phlegmagogic** (-goj´-) *a.* **phlegmasia** (flegmā´ziə) *n.* inflammation, esp. with fever. **phlegmatic** (flegmat´-), **phlegmatical** *a.* cool, sluggish, apathetic, unemotional. **phlegmatically** *adv.* **phlegmy** (flem´i) *a.* (*comp.* **phlegmier**, *superl.* **phlegmiest**) abounding in or of the nature of phlegm. [ME and OF *fleume* (F *phlegme*), L and Gr. *phlegma*, from *phlegein*, to burn]

phlegmon (fleg´mən) *n.* (*Med.*) a tumour or inflammation of the cellular tissue. **phlegmonic** (-mon´-), **phlegmonous** (fleg´-) *a.* [ME *flegmon*, L *phlegmon*, *-mona*, Gr. *phlegmonē*, as PHLEGM]

phloem (flō´em) *n.* (*Bot.*) the softer cellular portion of fibrovascular tissue in plants, the bark and the tissues closely connected with it, as opposed to *xylem*. [Gr. *phloos*, bark]

phlogiston (fləjis´tən) *n.* (*Hist.*) the principle of inflammability formerly supposed to be a necessary constituent of combustible bodies. **phlogistic** *a.* **1** (*Med.*) inflammatory. **2** of or relating to phlogiston. **phlogisticate** *v.t.* [Gr., neut. of *phlogistos*, burnt up, from *phlogizein*, to set on fire, cogn. with *phlegein*, to burn]

phlox (floks) *n.* a plant of the genus *Phlox*, with clusters of showy flowers. [Gr., flame, name of a plant]

phlyctena (fliktē´nə) *n.* (*pl.* **phlyctenae** (-nē)) (*Med.*) a vesicle, pimple or blister, esp. on the eyeball. **phlyctenar, phlyctenoid** (-oid), **phlyctenous** *a.* [Gr. *phluktaina*, from *phluein*, to swell]

-phobe (fōb) *comb. form* a person who fears or hates, as *homophobe, Francophobe*. **-phobia** (fō´biə) *comb. form* fear, morbid dislike, as *claustrophobia, hydrophobia*. **-phobic** *comb. form* [F, as PHOBIA]

phobia (fō´biə) *n.* (*pl.* **phobias**) an irrational fear or hatred. **phobic** *a., n.* [from L and Gr. *-phobos*, from *phobos*, fear]

phoca (fō´kə) *n.* (*pl.* **phocas, phocae** (-sē)) (*Zool.*) a seal. [L, from Gr. *phōkē*, a seal]

phoebe (fē´bi) *n.* any American flycatcher of the genus *Sayornis*. [imit.]

Phoebus (fē´bəs) *n.* (*poet.*) the sun. [L, from Gr. *phoibos*, bright, shining]

Phoenician (fənish´ən) *a.* of or relating to Phoenicia, an ancient Semitic country on the coast of Syria, or to its colonies. ~*n.* a native or inhabitant of Phoenicia or its colonies.

phoenix (fē´niks), (*N Am.*) **phenix** *n.* (*pl.* **phoenixes,** (*N Am.*) **phenixes**) **1** a mythical Arabian bird, the only one of its kind, said to live for 500 or 600 years in the desert, burn itself on a funeral pyre, and rise again in renewed youth. **2** a person or thing of extreme rarity or excellence, a paragon. [L, from Gr. *phoinix*, phoenix, also purple, Carthaginian]

pholas (fō´ləs) *n.* (*pl.* **pholades** (-dēz)) a member of the genus *Pholas* of stone-boring bivalves, a piddock. [Gr.]

phon (fon) *n.* a unit of loudness. **phonmeter** *n.* an instrument for estimating the loudness of sound. [Gr. *phōnē*, voice]

phon. *abbr.* **1** phonetics. **2** phonology.

phon- PHONO-.

phonate (fō´nāt) *v.i.* to make a vocal sound. **phonation** (-nā´shən) *n.* **phonatory** (fō´nətəri) *a.*

phonautograph (fōnaw´təgrahf) *n.* an apparatus for recording the vibrations of sounds. **phonautographic** (-graf´-) *a.* **phonautographically** *adv.*

phone[1] (fōn) *v.t., v.i.* to telephone. ~*n.* a telephone. **phone book** *n.* a telephone directory. **phonecard** *n.* a plastic card inserted into a slot in a cardphone, which cancels out the prepaid units on the card as the call is made. **phone freak, phone phreak** *n.* (*sl.*) a person who makes obscene calls or otherwise misuses the telephone system. **phone-in** *n.* a radio or TV programme in which members of the audience at home telephone to make comments, ask questions etc., as part of a live broadcast. [by shortening]

phone[2] (fōn) *n.* an articulate sound, such as a simple vowel or consonant. [Gr. *phōnē*, a voice]

-phone (fōn) *comb. form* **1** sound, voice, a device producing sound, as *telephone*. **2** (a person) speaking a specified language, as *Francophone*. [Gr. *phōnē*, a sound, a voice]

phoneme (fō´nēm) *n.* any one of the smallest distinctive group of phones in a language. **phonemic** (-nē´-) *a.* **phonemically** *adv.* **phonemics** *n.* the study of phonemes. [Gr. *phōnēma*, a sound]

phonendoscope (fənen´dəskōp) *n.* (*Med.*) a variety of stethoscope for enabling small sounds, esp. within the human body, to be distinctly heard. [Gr. *endon*, within, -SCOPE]

phonetic (fənet´ik) *a.* **1** of or relating to the voice or vocal sounds. **2** representing sounds, esp. by means of a distinct letter or character for each. **3** of or relating to phonetics. **phonetically** *adv.* **phonetician**

(fōnətish´ən) *n.* **phoneticism** (-sizm) *n.* **phoneticist** (-sist) *n.* **phoneticize** (-sīz), **phoneticise** *v.t.* **phoneticization** (-zā´shən) *n.* **phonetics** *n.* **1** vocal sounds and their classification. **2** the science of articulate sounds, phonology. **phonetist** (fō´-) *n.* **1** a person who is versed in phonetics, a phonologist. **2** an advocate of phonetic writing, a phoneticist.

phoney (fō´ni), (*esp. N Am.*) **phony** *a.* (*comp.* **phonier**, *superl.* **phoniest**) (*coll.*) **1** bogus, false. **2** fraudulent, counterfeit. **3** (of a person) pretentious. *~n.* (*pl.* **phoneys, phonies**) a phoney person or thing. **phonily** *adv.* **phoniness** *n.* [etym. uncertain]

phonic (fon´ik) *a.* **1** of or relating to sounds, acoustic. **2** of or relating to vocal sounds. **phonically** *adv.* **phonics** *n.* a method of teaching people to read by associating letters with their phonetic values.

phonmeter PHON.

phono (fō´nō) *a.* denoting a type of plug, and the socket with which it is used, in which one conductor is cylindrical and the other a longer, central part. [abbr. of PHONOGRAPH (under PHONOGRAM)]

phono- (fō´nō), **phon-** *comb. form* sound. [Gr. *phōnē*, a voice, a sound]

phonogram (fō´nəgram) *n.* **1** a written character indicating a particular spoken sound. **2** a record made by a phonograph. **phonograph** (-grahf) *n.* **1** an instrument for automatically recording and reproducing sounds. **2** (*N Am.*) a gramophone. **phonographer** (-nog´-) *n.* a person who is skilled in phonography. **phonographic** (-graf´-) *a.* **phonographically** *adv.* **phonographist** (-nog´-) *n.* a phonographer. **phonography** (-nog´-) *n.* **1** a system of shorthand in which each sound is represented by a distinct character. **2** automatic recording and reproduction of sounds by phonograph. **3** the art of using the phonograph.

phonolite (fō´nəlīt) *n.* clinkstone.

phonology (fənol´əji) *n.* **1** the science of the vocal sounds. **2** the sounds and combinations of sounds in a particular language. **phonological** (fonəloj´-) *a.* **phonologically** *adv.* **phonologist** *n.*

phonometer (fənom´itə) *n.* an instrument for recording the number and intensity of vibrations, esp. of sound waves.

phonon (fō´non) *n.* (*Physics*) a quantum of vibrational energy in a crystal lattice.

phonopore (fōn´əpaw) *n.* a device attached to a telegraph wire for allowing telephonic messages to be sent over the line at the same time as telegraphic messages, without interference from the current transmitting the latter. [Gr. *poros*, passage]

phonoscope (fō´nəskōp) *n.* an instrument of various kinds for translating sound vibrations into visible figures.

phonotype (fō´nətīp) *n.* a character used in phonetic printing. **phonotypic** (-tip´-), **phonotypical** *a.* **phonotypy** (fō´-) *n.* phonetic printing.

phony PHONEY.

phooey (foo´i) *int.* (*coll.*) used to express disbelief or dismissal. [imit.]

-phore (faw) *comb. form* bearer, as *gonophore*, *semaphore*. **-phorous** (fərəs) *comb. form* bearing, as *electrophorous*, *galactophorous*. [Gr. *phoros*, bearing]

-phoresis (fərē´sis) *comb. form* transmission, as *electrophoresis*. [Gr. *phorēsis*, carrying]

phoresy (fərē´si) *n.* (*Zool.*) an association in which one organism is carried by another without feeding on it. **phoretic** (-ret´-) *a.* [as -PHORESIS]

phormium (faw´miəm) *n.* any plant of the New Zealand genus *Phormium*, having evergreen leaves and red or yellow flowers. [mod. L, from Gr. *phormion*, as species of plant]

phosgene (foz´jēn) *n.* gaseous carbon oxychloride, used as a poison gas. **phosgenite** (-jinīt) *n.* a mineral consisting of carbonate and chloride of lead in nearly equal proportions. [F *phosgène* (Gr. *phōs*, light, -GEN)]

phosph- PHOSPHO-.

phosphate (fos´fāt) *n.* **1** (*Chem.*) any salt of phosphoric acid. **2** a phosphate of calcium, iron, alumina etc., used as fertilizing agents. **3** an aerated soft drink containing a small amount of phosphate. **phosphatase** (fos´fətāz) *n.* any enzyme which catalyses the hydrolysis of an organic phosphate. **phosphatic** (-fat´-) *a.*

phosphene (fos´fēn) *n.* a luminous image produced by pressure on the eyeball, caused by irritation of the retina. [Gr. *phōs*, light, *phainein*, to show]

phosphide (fos´fīd) *n.* a combination of phosphorus with another element or radical.

phosphine (fos´fēn) *n.* (*Chem.*) a colourless, fishy-smelling gas, which is slightly soluble. **phosphinic** (-fin´-) *a.*

phosphite (fos´fīt) *n.* (*Chem.*) any salt of phosphorous acid.

phospho- (fos´fō), **phosph-** *comb. form* (*Chem.*) containing phosphorus.

phospholipid (fosfōlip´id) *n.* (*Chem.*) any lipid which consists of a phosphate group and one or more fatty acids.

phosphor (fos´fə) *n.* **1** phosphorus. **2** a substance that exhibits phosphorescence. **3** (**Phosphor**) the morning star. **phosphor bronze** *n.* a combination of phosphorus with bronze. **phosphoresce** (-res´) *v.i.* to give out a light unaccompanied by perceptible heat or without combustion. **phosphorescence** *n.* **1** the emission of or the property of emitting light unaccompanied by perceptible heat or without combustion. **2** the emission of light caused by radiation bombardment, and continuing after the radiation has ceased. **phosphorescent** *a.* [L PHOSPHORUS]

phosphorate, phosphoric etc. PHOSPHORUS.

phosphoroscope (fosfor´əskōp) *n.* an apparatus for measuring the duration of phosphorescence.

phosphorus (fos´fərəs) *n.* (*Chem.*) a non-metallic element, at. no. 15, chem. symbol P, occurring in two allotropic forms, white phosphorus, which is waxy, poisonous, spontaneously combustible at room temperature and appears luminous, and red phosphorus which is non-poisonous and ignites only when heated. **phosphorate** (-rāt) *v.t.* to combine or impregnate with phosphorus. **phosphoric** (-for´-) *a.* **1** (*Chem.*) of or relating to phosphorus in its higher valency. **2** phosphorescent. **phosphoric acid** *n.* a crystalline solid used to make fertilizer and soap, and in food processing. **phosphorism** *n.* phossy jaw. **phosphorite** (-rīt) *n.* a massive variety of phosphate of lime. **phosphorous** *a.* **1** (*Chem.*) of, relating to, of the nature of or obtained from phosphorus, esp. in its lower valency. **2** phosphorescent. [L, the morning star, from Gr. *phōsphoros*, bringing light]

phosphorylate (fosfor´ilāt) *v.t.* (*Chem.*) to introduce a phosphate group into (a compound etc.). **phosphorylation** (-ā´shən) *n.*

phossy jaw (fos´i) *n.* (*Hist.*, *coll.*) gangrene of the jaw caused by the fumes of phosphorus, esp. in the manufacture of matches.

phot (fōt) *n.* the unit of illumination, one lumen per square centimetre. [Gr. *phōs phōtos*, light]

phot. *abbr.* **1** photographic. **2** photography.

phot- PHOTO-.

photic (fō´tik) *a.* **1** of or relating to light. **2** accessible to the sun's light; denoting the upper layers of the sea, which receive the sun's light.

photism (fō´tizm) *n.* a hallucinatory sensation of colour accompanying some other sensation. [Gr. *phōtismos*, from *phōtizein*, to shine, from *phōs phōtos*, light]

photo (fō´tō) *n.* (*pl.* **photos**) a photograph. *~v.t.* (*3rd pers. sing. pres.* **photoes**, *pres.p.* **photoing**, *past*, *p.p.* **photoed**) to photograph. **photo finish** *n.* a close finish of a race or contest, in which only a photograph enables a judge to decide the winner. **photo opportunity, photo op** (op) *n.* (*N Am., coll.*) a photocall. **photo session** *n.* a session arranged for a photographer to take photographs of a person for an advertisement etc. [short for PHOTOGRAPH]

photo- (fō´tō), **phot-** *comb. form* of or relating to light or to photography. [Gr. *phōs phōtos*, light]

photobiology (fōtōbīol´əji) *n.* the study of the effect of light on living organisms.

photocall (fō´tōkawl) *n.* an occasion when someone is photographed by arrangement for publicity purposes.

photocell (fō´tōsel) *n.* a photoelectric cell.

photochemical (fōtōkem´ikəl) *a.* of, relating to or produced by the chemical action of light. **photochemically** *adv.* **photochemical smog** *n.* smog caused by the action of sunlight on pollutants, which results in haze and high levels of ozone. **photochemistry** *n.*

photochromic (fōtōkrō´mik) *a.* changing colour in response to the incidence of radiant energy. **photochromism** *n.* **photochromy** (fō´-) *n.* colour photography.

photochronograph (fōtōkrō´nəgrahf) *n.* (*Physics*) an instrument for taking a series of photographs, for example of moving objects, at regular intervals of time. **photochronography** (-nog´-) *n.*

photocomposition (fōtōkompəzish´ən) *n.* (*Print.*) filmsetting.

photoconductivity (fōtōkondŭktiv´iti) *n.* electrical conductivity that varies with the incidence of radiation, esp. light. **photoconductive** (-kəndŭk´-) *a.* **photoconductor** (-kəndŭk´-) *n.*

photocopy (fō´tōkopi) *n.* (*pl.* **photocopies**) a photographic reproduction of matter that is written, printed etc. ~*v.t.* (*3rd pers. sing. pres.* **photocopies,** *pres.p.* **photocopying,** *past, p.p.* **photocopied**) to make a photocopy of. **photocopiable** *a.* **photocopier** *n.* a machine for making photocopies.

photodegradable (fōtōdigrā´dəbəl) *a.* capable of being decomposed by the action of sunlight.

photodiode (fōtōdī´ōd) *n.* a semiconductor diode, whose conductivity is controlled by incident illumination.

photoelectric (fōtōilek´trik) *a.* of or relating to photoelectricity, or to the combined action of light and electricity. **photoelectric cell** *n.* a device for measuring light by a change of electrical resistance when light falls upon a cell, or by the generation of a voltage. **photoelectricity** (-tris´-) *n.* electricity produced or affected by light.

photoelectron (fō´tōilektron) *n.* (*pl.* **photoelectrons**) an electron emitted during photoemission.

photoemission (fō´tōimishən) *n.* the emission of electrons from a substance on which radiation falls. **photoemitter** *n.*

photoengraving (fōtōingrā´ving) *n.* any process for producing printing blocks by means of photography.

photofit (fō´tōfit) *n.* (a method of composing) a likeness of someone's face consisting of photographs of parts of faces, used for the identification of criminal suspects.

photogen (fō´tōjən) *n.* a light hydrocarbon obtained by distilling coal, shale, peat etc., used for burning in lamps.

photogenic (fōtōjen´ik) *a.* **1** looking attractive in photographs or in cinema films. **2** (*Biol.*) producing light, phosphorescent. **3** produced by the action of light. **photogenically** *adv.*

photogram (fō´tōgram) *n.* **1** an image produced with photographic material, but without a camera. **2** †a photograph.

photogrammetry (fōtōgram´ətri) *n.* the technique of taking measurements from photographs, e.g. making maps from aerial photographs. **photogrammetist** *n.*

photograph (fō´təgrahf) *n.* a picture etc. taken by means of photography. ~*v.t.* to take a photograph. ~*v.i.* **1** to practise photography. **2** to appear (well or badly) in a photograph. **photographable** *a.* **photographer** (fətog´-) *n.* **photographic** (-graf´-) *a.* **photographically** *adv.* **photographic memory** *n.* the ability to memorize facts etc. in great detail, even after a very short exposure to them. **photography** (fətog´-) *n.* the process or art of producing images or pictures of objects by the chemical action of light on certain sensitive substances.

photogravure (fōtōgravūə´) *n.* **1** the process of producing an intaglio plate for printing by the transfer of a photographic negative to the plate and subsequent etching. **2** a picture produced by photogravure. [F (GRAVURE)]

photojournalism (fōtōjœ´nəlizm) *n.* journalism featuring photographs more than or instead of text. **photojournalist** *n.*

photolithography (fōtōlithog´rəfi), **photolitho** (-lī´thō) *n.* a mode of producing by photography designs upon stones etc., from which impressions may be taken at a lithographic press. **photolithograph** (-lith´əgrahf) *n.* **photolithographer** *n.* **photolithographic** (-graf´-) *a.* **photolithographically** *adv.*

photolysis (fōtol´isis) *n.* decomposition resulting from the incidence of radiation. **photolyse** (fō´təlīz) *v.t., v.i.* **photolytic** (fōtəlit´-) *a.*

photomechanical (fōtōmikan´ikəl) *a.* of or relating to a process by which photographic images are reproduced or employed in printing by mechanical means.

photometer (fōtom´itə) *n.* an instrument for measuring the relative intensity of light. **photometric** (fōtōmet´-) *a.* **photometry** *n.*

photomicrography (fōtōmīkrog´rəfi) *n.* the process of making magnified photographs of microscopic objects. **photomicrograph** (-mī´krəgrahf) *n.* **photomicrographer** *n.* **photomicrographic** (-mīkrəgraf´-) *a.*

photomontage (fōtōmontahzh´) *n.* **1** a means of producing pictures by the montage of many photographic images. **2** the picture thus produced.

photomultiplier (fōtōmŭl´tiplīə) *n.* a photocell with a series of electrodes, used to detect and amplify light from faint sources.

photon (fō´ton) *n.* (*pl.* **photons**) **1** the unit of light intensity. **2** a quantum of radiant energy. **photonics** (-ton´-) *n.* the branch of technology concerned with the applications of photons.

photonovel (fō´tōnovəl) *n.* a novel presented as a series of photographs with speech bubbles.

photo-offset (fōtōof´set) *n.* offset printing from photolithographic plates.

photoperiod (fō´tōpiəriəd) *n.* (*Biol.*) the period of daylight in every 24 hours which an organism receives. **photoperiodic** (-od´-) *a.* **photoperiodism** (-piə´-) *n.* the response of an organism to changes in photoperiods.

photophobia (fōtōfō´biə) *n.* abnormal shrinking from or intolerance of light. **photophobic** *a.*

photophone (fō´təfōn) *n.* an instrument for transmitting sounds by the agency of light.

photophore (fō´təfaw) *n.* (*Zool.*) any organ that emits light.

photopia (fōtō´piə) *n.* vision in normal daylight. **photopic** (-top´-) *a.*

photo-process (fōtōprō´ses) *n.* any photomechanical process.

photopsia (fōtop´siə), **photopsy** (-si) *n.* a disorder of the eye causing the patient to see lines, flashes of light etc.

photorealism (fōtōriə´lizm) *n.* meticulous realism in art, esp. depicting mundane or sordid subjects. **photorealist** *n.* **photorealistic** (-lis´-) *a.*

photoreceptor (fōt´ōriseptə) *n.* a nerve ending receptive to light.

photo-relief (fō´tōrilēf) *n.* an image in relief produced by a photographic process. ~*a.* of or relating to any process of producing such reliefs.

photosensitive (fōtōsen´sitiv) *a.* sensitive to the action of light. **photosensitivity** (-tiv´-) *n.* **photosensitize, photosensitise** *v.t.* to make photosensitive. **photosensitization** (-ā´shən) *n.*

photosetting (fō´tōseting) *n.* filmsetting. **photoset** *v.t.* (*pres.p.* **photosetting,** *past, p.p.* **photoset**). **photosetter** *n.*

photosphere (fō´təsfiə) *n.* the luminous envelope of the sun or a star. **photospheric** (-sfer´-) *a.*

Photostat® (fō´təstat), **photostat** *n.* **1** a type of photocopier. **2** a type of photocopy. ~*v.t.* (*pres.p.* **photostatting,** *past, p.p.* **photostatted**) to make a photostat of. **photostatic** (-stat´-) *a.*

photosynthesis (fōtōsin´thəsis) *n.* the process by which carbohydrates are produced from carbon dioxide and water through the agency of light, esp. when it occurs in green plants. **photosynthesize, photosynthesise** *v.t., v.i.* **photosynthetic** (-thet´-) *a.* **photosynthetically** *adv.*

phototherapy (fōtəther´əpi) *n.* the treatment of skin diseases by means of certain kinds of light rays.

phototransistor (fōtōtranzis´tə) *n.* a transistor which responds to incident light by generating and amplifying an electric current.

phototropism (fōtōtrō´pizm) *n.* tropism due to the influence of light. **phototropic** (-trop´-) *a.*

phototype (fō´tōtīp) *n.* **1** a printing plate produced by photoengraving. **2** a print from this. **phototypesetting** (fōtōtīp´seting) *n.* filmsetting. **phototypeset** *a.* **phototypesetter** *n.* a filmsetting machine. **phototypography** (-pog´rəfi) *n.* a photomechanical process of engraving in relief for reproduction with type in an ordinary printing press. **phototypy** *n.*

photovoltaic (fōtōvoltā´ik) *a.* of or relating to the production of electric current caused by electromagnetic radiation.

photoxylography (fōtōzīlog´rəfi) *n.* engraving on wood from photographs printed on the block.

photozincography (fōtōzingkog´rəfi) *n.* the process of producing an engraving on zinc by photomechanical means for printing in a manner analogous to photolithography. **photozincograph** (-zing´kəgrahf) *n.*

phrase (frāz) *n.* **1** an expression denoting a single idea or forming a distinct part of a sentence. **2** a brief or concise expression. **3** a mode, manner or style of expression, diction. **4** an idiomatic expression. **5** a small group of words equivalent grammatically to a single word, esp. to an adjective, adverb or noun. **6** (*Mus.*) a short, distinct passage forming part of a melody. ~*v.t.* **1** to express in words or phrases. **2** to divide up (a sentence) when reading aloud etc., by pausing slightly at appropriate points. **3** (*Mus.*) to divide up (a piece of music) into phrases when playing or singing. **phrasal** *a.* **phrasal verb** *n.* a combination of a verb and an adverb, or a verb and a preposition. **phrase book** *n.* a tourists' handbook of phrases or idioms in a foreign language. **phrasemonger** (-mŭng·gə) *n.* **1** a person who uses mere phrases. **2** a person addicted to extravagant phrases. **phrasing** *n.* [F, from L and Gr. *phrasis*, from *phrazein*, to speak]

phraseogram (frā´ziəgram), **phraseograph** (-grahf) *n.* a character standing for a whole phrase, for example in shorthand.

phraseology (frāziol´əji) *n.* (*pl.* **phraseologies**) **1** a choice or arrangement of words. **2** a manner of expression, diction. **phraseological** (frāziəloj´-) *a.* **phraseologically** *adv.* **phraseologist** *n.*

phratry (frā´tri) *n.* (*pl.* **phratries**) **1** any tribal subdivision based on shared ancestry. **2** in ancient Greece, a division of the people for political or religious purposes. **3** each of the three subdivisions of a tribe in Athens. [F *phratrie*, Gr. *phratria*, from *phratēr*, a clansman, cogn. with L *frāter*, Eng. a BROTHER]

phreak (frēk) *n.* a phone freak.

phreatic (friat´ik) *a.* **1** (*Geol.*) of or relating to groundwater. **2** (of a volcanic eruption) caused by the heating and expansion of underground water. [Gr. *phrear phreatos*, a well]

phren- PHRENO-.

†**phrenetic** FRENETIC.

phrenic (fren´ik) *a.* (*Anat.*) of or relating to the diaphragm. ~*n.* the phrenic nerve.

phrenitis (frinī´tis) *n.* **1** encephalitis. **2** inflammation of the brain or its membranes, with delirium. **phrenitic** (-nit´-) *a.*

phreno- (fren´ō) *comb. form* **1** the mind. **2** the diaphragm. [Gr. *phrēn*, the mind, the diaphragm]

phrenology (frənol´əji) *n.* (*Hist.*) the theory that the mental faculties and affections are located in distinct parts of the brain denoted by prominences on the skull. **phrenological** (frenəloj´-) *a.* **phrenologically** *adv.* **phrenologist** *n.*

phrontistery (fron´tistəri) *n.* (*pl.* **phrontisteries**) a place for thought or study. [Gr. *phrontistērion*, from *phrontizein*, to think, from *phrontis*, thought]

Phrygian (frij´iən) *a.* of or relating to Phrygia, an ancient country in Asia Minor. ~*n.* **1** a native or inhabitant of Phrygia. **2** the language of the Phrygians. **Phrygian bonnet, Phrygian cap** *n.* a conical cap worn by the ancient Phrygians, since adopted as an emblem of liberty. **Phrygian mode** *n.* (*Mus.*) one of the four ancient Greek modes, having a warlike character.

phthalic (fthal´ik) *a.* of, relating to or derived from naphthalene. **phthalate** (-āt) *n.* **phthalein** (thā´lēn, fthal´-) *n.* any one of a series of organic compounds, largely used for dyeing, produced by the combination of phthalic anhydride with the phenols. **phthalic acid** *n.* (*Chem.*) any one of three isomeric dicarboxylic acids derived from benzene. **phthalic anhydride** *n.* a white crystalline substance used in the production of dyestuffs. **phthalin** (-lin) *n.* a colourless, crystalline substance obtained from phthalein. [short for NAPHTHALIC (under NAPHTHA)]

phthiriasis (thirī´əsis, fthir-) *n.* (*Med.*) a condition in which lice multiply on the skin. [L, from Gr. *phtheiriasis*, from *phtheiriaein*, to have lice]

phthisic (thī´sik, fthī´-) *a.* of or relating to phthisis. **phthisical** (thiz´-, fthiz´-), **phthisicky** *a.* [ME and OF *tisike*, L *phthisicus*, Gr. *phthisikos*]

phthisis (thī´sis, fthī´-) *n.* (*Med.*) a wasting disease, esp. pulmonary tuberculosis. [Gr., from *phthiein*, to decay]

phut (fŭt) *n.* a dull bang. **to go phut** (*coll.*) (of a plan) to falter, to be unsuccessful. [perh. from Hind. *phatnā*, to burst]

phycology (fīkol´əji) *n.* the botany of seaweeds or algae. **phycological** (-loj´-) *a.* **phycologist** *n.* [Gr. *phukos*, seaweed]

phycomycete (fīkōmī´sēt) *n.* any of various fungi which form a non-septate mycelium. [Gr. *phukos*, seaweed, mod. L *-mycetes*, from Gr. *mukēs mukētos*, fungus]

phyl- PHYLO-.

phyla PHYLUM.

phylactery (filak´təri) *n.* (*pl.* **phylacteries**) **1** a small leather box in which are enclosed slips of vellum inscribed with passages from the Pentateuch, worn on the head and left arm by Jews during morning prayer, except on the Sabbath. **2** a charm, spell or amulet worn as a preservative against disease or danger. **3** ostentatious religious ceremony. **4** a border, an edge, a fringe. **phylacteric** (-ter´-) *a.* [L *phylactērium*, Gr. *phulaktērion*, from *phulaktēr*, a guard, from *phulassein*, to guard]

phyletic (fīlet´ik) *a.* (*Biol.*) of or relating to a phylum,

racial. **phyletically** *adv.* [Gr. *phūletikos*, from *phūletēs*, a tribesman]
phyll- PHYLLO-.
-phyll *comb. form* a leaf, as *chlorophyll.* [Gr. *phullon*]
phyllite (fil´īt) *n.* (*Geol.*) an argillaceous schist or slate.
phyllo- (fil´ō), **phyll-** *comb. form* a leaf. [Gr. *phullon*, a leaf]
phyllobranchia (filōbrang´kiə) *n.* (*pl.* **phyllobranchiae** (-kiē)) (*Zool.*) a gill of a leaflike or lamellar structure, as in certain crustaceans. [Gr. *branchia*, gills]
phyllode (fil´ōd) *n.* (*Bot.*) a petiole having the appearance and functions of a leaf. **phylloid** (-oid) *a.* [F *phyllode*, mod. L *phyllōdium*, from Gr. *phyllōdēs*]
phyllomania (filəmā´niə) *n.* (*Bot.*) abnormal production of leaves.
phyllome (fil´ōm) *n.* (*Bot.*) a leaf or organ analogous to a leaf. **phyllomic** (-lom´-) *a.*
phyllophagous (filof´əgəs) *a.* (*Zool.*) feeding on leaves.
phyllopod (fil´əpod) *n.* (*Zool.*) any crustacean of the order Phyllopoda, having at least four pairs of leaflike feet. [Gr. *pous podos*, a foot]
phylloquinone (filōkwin´ōn) *n.* a vitamin found in leafy green vegetables, and essential for blood-clotting; vitamin K_1.
phyllotaxis (filōtak´sis), **phyllotaxy** (-tak´si) *n.* (*Bot.*) the arrangement of the leaves etc. on the stem or axis of a plant. **phyllotactic** (-ak´tik) *a.*
phylloxera (filoksiə´rə, -lok´sərə) *n.* (*pl.* **phylloxeras**) an aphid or plant-louse, *Daktulosphaira vitifoliae*, orig. from America, very destructive to grapevines. [Gr. *xēros*, dry]
phylo- (fī´lō), **phyl-** *comb. form* a tribe, a race. [Gr. *phūlon*, *phūlē*, a tribe]
phylogeny (phīloj´əni), **phylogenesis** (phīlōjen´isis) *n.* (*pl.* **phylogenies, phylogeneses** (-sēz)) (*Biol.*) **1** the evolution of a group, species or type of plant or animal life. **2** the history of this. **phylogenetic** (-jənet´-), **phylogenic** (-jen´-) *a.*
phylum (fī´ləm) *n.* (*pl.* **phyla** (-lə)) **1** (*Biol.*) a primary group consisting of related organisms descended from a common form. **2** a group of related languages.
phys. *abbr.* **1** physical. **2** physics.
phys- PHYSIO-.
physalia (fīsā´liə) *n.* any member of the genus *Physalia* of large oceanic hydrozoons, including the Portuguese man-of-war. [mod. L, from Gr. *phusaleos*, inflated]
physalis (fī´səlis, fis´-, fīsā´-) *n.* any plant of the genus *Physalis*, having fruit in lantern-like calyxes. [Gr. *physallis*, a bladder]
physic (fiz´ik) *n.* **1** a medicine, esp. a purge or cathartic. **2** the science or art of healing. **3** the medical profession. ~*v.t.* (*pres.p.* **physicking,** *past, p.p.* **physicked**) to administer physic to, to dose, to purge. **physic garden** *n.* a garden where medicinal herbs are grown. [ME *fisike*, OF *fisique*, L *physica*, Gr. *phusikē*, of nature, from *phusis*, nature, from *phuein*, to produce]
physical (fiz´ikəl) *a.* **1** bodily, corporeal, as opposed to *spiritual.* **2** of or relating to matter, material. **3** obvious to or cognizable by the senses. **4** of or relating to physics, esp. as opposed to *chemical.* ~*n.* (*also* **physical examination**) an examination to ascertain physical fitness. **physical chemistry** *n.* the branch of chemistry concerned with the ways in which the physical properties and the chemical structure of a substance affect each other. **physical education** *n.* a school subject involving physical exercises and sports. **physical geography** *n.* the branch of geography concerned with the features of the earth's surface, the distribution of land and water, climate and the distribution of plants and animals. **physicalism** *n.* (*Philos.*) the theory that all phenomena can be described in the language of physics. **physicalist** *n., a.* **physicalistic** (-is´-) *a.* **physicality** (-kal´-) *n.* **physical jerks** *n.pl.* (*coll.*) physical exercises to promote fitness. **physically** *adv.* **physically challenged** *a.* (*euphem.*) disabled. **physicalness** *n.* **physical science** *n.* any branch of science, such as physics, chemistry and geology, concerned with natural forces. **physical training** *n.* programmed physical exercise to promote fitness.
physician (fizish´ən) *n.* **1** a person versed in or practising the art of healing, including medicine and surgery. **2** a legally qualified practitioner who prescribes remedies for diseases. **3** any medical practitioner. **4** (*fig.*) a healer.
physicist (fiz´isist) *n.* **1** a person versed in physics. **2** a person who believes in the physical and chemical origin of vital phenomena, as distinct from *vitalist.*
physico- (fiz´ikō) *comb. form* physical.
physico-chemical (fizikōkem´ikəl) *a.* of or relating to physics and chemistry.
physics (fiz´iks) *n.* the science dealing with the phenomena of matter, esp. as affected by energy, and the laws governing these, excluding biology and chemistry.
physio (fiz´iō) *n.* (*pl.* **physios**) (*coll.*) short for PHYSIOTHERAPIST (under PHYSIOTHERAPY).
physio- (fiz´iō), **phys-** *comb. form* **1** of or relating to nature. **2** physical. [Gr. *phusis*, nature]
physiocracy (fiziok´rəsi) *n.* (*pl.* **physiocracies**) **1** (*Hist.*) government according to a natural order, taught by François Quesnay, 1694–1774, founder of the physiocrats, to be inherent in society. **2** a society based on physiocracy. **physiocrat** (fiz´iəkrat) *n.* **physiocratic** (-krat´-) *a.*
physiognomy (fizion´əmi) *n.* (*pl.* **physiognomies**) **1** the art of reading character from features of the face or the form of the body. **2** the face or countenance as an index of character; cast of features. **3** (*coll.*) the face. **4** the lineaments or external features of a landscape etc. **5** an aspect, appearance, look of a situation, event etc. **physiognomic** (fizienom´-), **physiognomical** *a.* **physiognomically** *adv.* **physiognomist** *n.* [ME *fisnomie*, OF *phisonomie*, med. L *phisonomia*, Gr. *phusiognōmonia* (*gnōmōn*, an interpreter)]
physiography (fiziog´rəfi) *n.* the scientific description of the physical features of the earth, and the causes by which they have been modified; physical geography. **physiographer** *n.* **physiographic** (fiziəgraf´-), **physiographical** *a.* **physiographically** *adv.*
physiol. *abbr.* physiology.
physiolatry (fiziol´ətri) *n.* nature-worship.
physiology (fiziol´əji) *n.* the science of the vital phenomena and the organic functions of animals and plants. **physiologic** (fiziəloj´-) *a.* **physiological** *a.* **physiologically** *adv.* **physiological saline** *n.* a solution of salts which is isotonic with the body fluids. **physiologist** *n.* [L and Gr. *physiologia*]
physiotherapy (fiziōther´əpi) *n.* a form of medical treatment in which physical agents such as movement of limbs, massage, electricity etc. are used in place of drugs or surgery. **physiotherapeutic** (-pū´-) *a.* **physiotherapist** *n.*
physique (fizēk´) *n.* the physical structure or constitution of a person. [F, as PHYSIC]
physitheism (fizithē´izm) *n.* deification of natural forces or phenomena.
physoclistous (fīsəklis´təs) *a.* (*Zool.*) having the air bladder closed and not connected with the intestines. [Gr. *kleistos*, shut]
physostomous (fīsos´təməs) *a.* (*Zool.*) having the air bladder connected by a duct with the intestinal canal. [Gr. *stoma*, a mouth]
-phyte (fīt) *comb. form* denoting a vegetable organism, as *zoophyte.* **-phytic** (fit´ik) *comb. form* [Gr. *phuton*, a plant]
phyto- (fī´tō) *comb. form* plant. [Gr. *phuton*, a plant]

phytochemistry (fītōkem´istri) *n.* the chemistry of plants. **phytochemical** *a.* **phytochemist** *n.*
phytochrome (fī´təkrōm) *n.* (*Bot.*) a blue-green pigment found in most plants, which regulates many light-dependent processes.
phytogenesis (fītōjen´isis), **phytogeny** (-toj´əni) *n.* the origin, generation or evolution of plants.
phytogeography (fītōjiog´rəfi) *n.* the geographical distribution of plants.
phytography (fītog´rəfi) *n.* the systematic description and naming of plants.
phyton (fī´ton) *n.* a plant unit.
phytopathology (fītōpəthol´əji) *n.* the science of the diseases of plants. **phytopathological** (-pathəloj´-) *a.* **phytopathologist** *n.*
phytophagous (fītof´əgəs) *a.* plant-eating.
phytoplankton (fī´tōplangktən) *n.* plant life as a constituent of plankton.
phytotomy (fītot´əmi) *n.* the dissection of plants.
phytotoxin (fītōtok´sin) *n.* **1** any toxin derived from a plant. **2** a substance which is poisonous to plants, esp. one produced by a parasite. **phytotoxic** *a.* poisonous to plants.
PI *abbr.* Philippine Islands (IVR).
pi[1] (pī) *n.* **1** the 16th letter of the Greek alphabet (Π, π). **2** the symbol representing the ratio of the circumference of a circle to the diameter, i.e. 3.14159265. [Gr. *pi*]
pi[2] (pī) *a.* (*sl.*) pious.
pi[3] PIE[3].
pia (pē´ə) *n.* any Polynesian herb of the genus *Tacca*, esp. *T. leontopetaloides*, yielding a variety of arrowroot. [Hawaiian]
piacular (pīak´ūlə) *a.* (*formal*) **1** expiatory. **2** requiring expiation. **3** atrociously bad. [L *piāculāris*, from *piāculum*, expiation, from *piāre*, to propitiate]
piaffe (piaf´) *v.i.* (of a horse) to move at a piaffer. ~*n.* an act of piaffing. **piaffer** *n.* a movement like a trot but slower. [F *piaffer*, etym. uncertain]
pia mater (pīə´ mā´tə) *n.* (*Anat.*) a delicate membrane, the innermost of the three meninges enveloping the brain and spinal cord. [med. L version of Arab. *umm raqīqan*, tender mother]
pianette (pēənet´) *n.* a small piano. [F, dim. of PIANO[1]]
piani PIANO[2].
pianino (pēənē´nō) *n.* (*pl.* **pianinos**) a small piano. [It., dim. of PIANO[1]]
pianissimo (piənis´imō) *adv.* (*Mus.*) very softly. ~*a.* to be played very softly. ~*n.* (*pl.* **pianissimos, pianissimi** (-mi)) a passage to be played pianissimo. [It., superl. of PIANO[2]]
pianist, pianiste etc. PIANO[1].
piano[1] (pian´ō) *n.* (*pl.* **pianos**) a musical instrument, the sounds of which are produced by blows on the wire strings from hammers acted upon by levers set in motion by keys. **pianism** (pē´ənizm) *n.* **1** piano playing. **2** the technique of this. **pianist** (pē´-) *n.* a piano player. **pianiste** (piənēst´) *n.* a female piano player. **pianistic** (-nis´-) *a.* **pianistically** *adv.* **piano accordion** *n.* an accordion with a keyboard resembling that of a piano. **pianoforte** (-faw´ti) *n.* (*formal*) a piano. **Pianola®** (piənō´lə) *n.* **1** a type of player-piano. **2** in bridge, a hand which requires no skill. **3** an easy task. **piano organ** *n.* a mechanical organ worked on similar principles to those of the barrel organ. **piano-player** *n.* **1** a pianist. **2** a device for playing a piano mechanically. **piano trio** *n.* a trio for piano, violin and cello. **piano-tuner** *n.* a person whose occupation is tuning pianos. [It., earlier *piano e forte*, L *plānus et fortis*, soft and loud]
piano[2] (pyah´nō) *adv.* **1** (*Mus.*) softly. **2** in a subdued manner. ~*a.* **1** (*Mus.*) to be played softly. **2** subdued. ~*n.* (*pl.* **pianos, piani** (-ni)) a passage to be played piano. [It., from L *plānus*, even, flat, from late L, soft, low]
pianoforte, Pianola® PIANO[1].
piano nobile (piahnō nō´bilā) *n.* (*Archit.*) the main floor of a large house. [It., a noble floor]
piassava (pēəsah´və) *n.* **1** a coarse stiff fibre obtained from Brazilian palms, used esp. to make ropes and brushes. **2** a Brazilian palm yielding piassava. [Port., from Tupi *piaçaba*]
piastre (pias´tə), (*N Am.*) **piaster** *n.* **1** a small coin of Turkey and several former dependencies. **2** the Spanish dollar or silver peso. [F, from It. *piastra*, a plate or leaf of metal, as PLASTER]
piazza (piat´sə) *n.* (*pl.* **piazzas**) **1** a square open space, public square or market place, esp. in an Italian town. **2** any open space surrounded by buildings or colonnades. **3** (*N Am.*) the veranda of a house. **4** (*loosely*) a colonnade, or an arcaded or colonnaded walk. [It., from pop. L *plattia*, L *platea*, Gr. *plateia*, broad, see PLACE]
pibroch (pē´brokh) *n.* a series of variations, chiefly martial, played on the bagpipes. [Gael. *piobaireachd* (*piobair*, a piper, from *piob*, from PIPE)]
pic (pik) *n.* (*pl.* **pix** (piks), **pics**) (*coll.*) a picture.
pica[1] (pī´kə) *n.* (*pl.* **picas**) (*Print.*) **1** a unit of type size (one sixth of an inch). **2** a size of type, the standard of measurement in printing. [med. L, an ordinal giving rules for movable feasts, perh. ident. with PICADOR]
pica[2] (pī´kə) *n.* (*Med.*) an appetite affected by illness etc. causing a person to crave for things unfit for food, such as coal and chalk. [L, a magpie]
picador (pik´ədaw) *n.* in Spanish bullfights, a horseman with a lance who goads the bull. [Sp., from *picar*, to prick]
picamar (pik´əmah) *n.* an oily compound, one of the products of the distillation of wood tar. [L *pix picis*, PITCH[2], *amarus*, bitter]
picaresque (pikəresk´) *a.* describing the exploits and adventures of rogues or vagabonds, of or relating to a style of fiction describing the episodic adventures of an errant rogue. [see PICAROON]
†**picaroon** (pikəroon´) *n.* **1** a rogue, a vagabond. **2** a cheat. **3** a thief, a robber. **4** a pirate, a corsair. **5** a pirate ship. [Sp. *picaron*, from *picaro*, perh. rel. to *picar*, to prick]
picayune (pikəyoon´) *n.* (*N Am.*) **1** a 5-cent piece or other small coin. **2** (*coll.*) something of small value. **3** a small Spanish coin, value 6¼ cents, now obsolete. ~*a.* of little value, petty, trifling. [F Louisiana, from Prov. *picaioun* (F *picaillon*), etym. uncertain]
piccalilli (pik´əlili, pikəlil´i) *n.* (*pl.* **piccalillis**) a pickle of various chopped vegetables with pungent spices. [etym. uncertain]
piccaninny (pik´ənini), (*N Am.*) **pickaninny** *n.* (*pl.* **piccaninnies,** (*N Am.*) **pickaninnies**) (*offensive*) a little black or Aboriginal child. ~†*a.* tiny, baby. [W Ind., from Sp. *pequeño* or Port. *pequeno*, small, rel. to PICCOLO]
piccolo (pik´əlō) *n.* (*pl.* **piccolos**) **1** a small flute, with the notes one octave higher than the ordinary flute. **2** a piccolo player. [It., small, a small flute]
pice (pīs) *n.* (*pl.* **pice**) (*Hist.*) an Indian copper coin worth quarter of an anna. [Hind. *paisa*]
piceous (pis´iəs) *a.* **1** pitch-black, brownish-black. **2** inflammable. [L *piceus*, from *pix picis*, PITCH[2]]
pichiciago (pichysyā´gō), **pichiciego** *n.* (*pl.* **pichiciagos, pichiciegos**) a small S American armadillo, esp. *Chlamyphorous truncatus*. [Sp. *pichiciego* (prob. Tupi-Guarani *pichey*, Sp. *ciego*, L *caecus*, blind)]
pick[1] (pik) *v.t.* **1** to choose, to select carefully. **2** to pluck, to gather. **3** to strike at with something pointed. **4** to remove extraneous matter from (the teeth etc.) by picking. **5** to clean by removing matter which adheres with the teeth, fingers etc. **6** to take up with a beak etc. **7** to eat in little bits. **8** to make (one's way) carefully on foot. **9** to find an occasion for (a quarrel etc.). **10** to steal the contents of. **11** to open (a lock) with an implement

other than the key. 12 to pluck, to pull apart. 13 to twitch the strings of, to play (a guitar, banjo etc.). 14 to remove the stalks from (soft fruit) before cooking. 15 to break, pierce or indent with a pointed instrument. 16 to make (a hole) or to open by picking. ~*v.i.* 1 to make a careful choice. 2 to eat in little bits. 3 to pick a banjo, guitar etc. 4 to strike at with a pointed implement. 5 to pilfer. ~*n.* 1 choice, selection. 2 the best (of). **to pick a hole in** HOLE. **to pick and choose** to make a fastidious selection. **to pick at** 1 to eat sparingly. 2 to criticize in a cavilling way. **to pick holes in** HOLE. **to pick off** 1 to gather or detach (fruit etc.) from a tree etc. 2 to shoot with careful aim one by one. 3 to eliminate (opposition) one by one. 4 in baseball, to put out by throwing the ball to a base. **to pick on** 1 to single out for unpleasant treatment, to bully. 2 to single out, to select. **to pick out** 1 to select. 2 to distinguish (with the eye) from surroundings. 3 to play (a tune) by ear on the piano etc. 4 to relieve or variegate with or as if with distinctive colours. 5 to gather (the meaning of a passage etc.). **to pick over** to examine carefully in order to reject unwanted items. **to pick someone's brains** to consult someone with special expertise or experience. **to pick to pieces** to analyse or criticize spitefully. **to pick up** 1 to take up with the fingers, beak etc. 2 to raise (oneself) after a fall. 3 to raise (one's feet) off the ground. 4 to gather or acquire here and there or little by little. 5 to collect and take away. 6 to accept and pay (a bill). 7 to arrest and detain (a suspect etc.). 8 to receive (an electronic signal etc.). 9 to make the acquaintance of. 10 to resume. 11 to regain or recover (health etc.). 12 to recover one's health. 13 in golf, to pick up one's ball when conceding a hole. **to take one's pick** to make a choice. **picked** *a.* 1 gathered, culled. 2 chosen, selected, choice. **picker** *n.* **pickings** *n.pl.* 1 profit or reward, esp. when obtained dishonestly. 2 gleanings, odds and ends. **picklock** *n.* 1 a person who picks locks, a thief. 2 an instrument for opening a lock without the key. **pick-me-up** *n.* 1 a drink or medicine taken to restore the nerves etc. 2 something which makes one feel better when tired or depressed. **pick of the basket** *n.* the best of the lot. **pickpocket** *n.* a person who steals from other people's pockets. **pickpocketing** *n.* **pick-up** *n.* 1 (*also* **pick-up truck**) a vehicle with a driver's cab at the front, and an open back with sides and a tailboard. 2 a device holding a needle which follows the track of a gramophone record and converts the resulting mechanical vibrations into acoustic or electrical vibrations. 3 a device on a musical instrument for converting sound vibrations into electrical signals for amplification. 4 a casual acquaintance, esp. one made for the purpose of having sexual intercourse. 5 the act of making such an acquaintance. 6 the act of picking up, esp. giving a lift. 7 a person or thing picked up. 8 an increase in trade, economy, speed etc. 9 (*Mus.*) the introductory notes to a tune. 10 in fishing, a metal semicircle for guiding the line back on to the reel. **picky** *a.* (*comp.* **pickier**, *superl.* **pickiest**) (*coll.*) excessively fastidious, choosy. **pickiness** *n.* **pick-your-own** *a.* (of commercially grown fruit etc.) available to be picked by customers. [ME *pikken*, *piken*, perh. rel. to PICK[2] and to F *piquer*, to prick]

pick[2] (pik) *n.* 1 a tool with a long iron head, usu. pointed at one end and pointed or chisel-edged at the other, fitted in the middle on a wooden shaft, used for breaking ground etc. 2 (*coll.*) a plectrum. 3 any of various implements used for picking. ~*v.t.* 1 to break with or as if with a pick. 2 to make (holes). **picked** (pik´id) *a.* having a point or spike, pointed, sharp. [prob. var. of PIKE[2]]

pickaback PIGGYBACK.

pickaninny PICCANINNY.

pickaxe (pik´aks), (*N Am.*) **pickax** *n.* an instrument for breaking ground etc., a pick. ~*v.t.* to break up with a pickaxe. ~*v.i.* to use a pickaxe. [ME *pikois*, OF *picois*, rel. to OF *pic*, see PIKE[2]]

picked PICK[1].

pickeer (pikiə´) *v.i.* 1 to skirmish. 2 to reconnoitre. [etym. uncertain]

pickelhaube (pik´əlhowbə) *n.* (*Hist.*) the spiked helmet of a German soldier. [G]

pickerel (pik´ərəl) *n.* (*pl.* **pickerel, pickerels**) a young or small pike.

picket (pik´it) *n.* 1 a person or group of people set by a trade union to watch a shop, factory etc., during labour disputes. 2 a person or group posted in a certain place as part of a protest or demonstration. 3 a pointed stake, post or peg, forming part of a palisade or paling, for tethering a horse to etc. 4 (*Mil.*, *also* **picquet, piquet**) **a** a small body of troops posted on the outskirts of a camp etc., as a guard, sent out to look for the enemy, or kept in camp for immediate service. **b** a guard sent out to bring in men who have exceeded their leave. ~*v.t.* (*pres.p.* **picketing**, *past*, *p.p.* **picketed**) 1 to set a picket or pickets at (the gates of a factory etc.). 2 to post as a picket. 3 to fortify or protect with stakes etc., to fence in. 4 to tether to a picket. ~*v.i.* to act as a picket. **picketer** *n.* **picket line** *n.* a group of people picketing a factory etc. [F *piquet*, from *piquer*, to prick]

pickle (pik´əl) *n.* 1 a liquid, such as brine, vinegar etc., for preserving fish, meat, vegetables etc. 2 (*often pl.*) vegetables or other food preserved in pickle. 3 (*N Am.*) a pickled cucumber. 4 diluted acid used for cleaning etc. 5 (*coll.*) a disagreeable or embarrassing position. 6 (*coll.*) a troublesome child. ~*v.t.* 1 to preserve in pickle. 2 to treat with pickle. **to have a rod in pickle** to have a beating or scolding in store. **pickled** *a.* (*coll.*) drunk. **pickle-herring** *n.* a pickled herring. **pickler** *n.* 1 a person who pickles vegetables etc. 2 a vegetable suitable for pickling. [cp. Dut. and LG *pekel*, etym. uncertain]

Pickwickian (pikwik´iən) *a.* 1 of, relating to or characteristic of Mr Pickwick; plump and jovial. 2 (*facet.*) (of the sense of words) merely technical or hypothetical. [Mr *Pickwick*, in Dickens's *Pickwick Papers*]

picnic (pik´nik) *n.* 1 an excursion into the country etc. with a packed lunch to be eaten outside. 2 an informal meal, eaten outside. ~*v.i.* (*pres.p.* **picnicking**, *past*, *p.p.* **picnicked**) to go on a picnic. **no picnic** (*coll.*) a difficult or unpleasant experience. **picnicker** *n.* **picnicky** *a.* [F *pique-nique*, etym. uncertain]

pico- (pē´kō, pī´kō) *comb. form* one millionth of a millionth part (10^{-12}). [Sp. *pico*, a small amount]

picot (pē´kō) *n.* a small loop of thread forming part of an ornamental edging. [F, dim. of *pic*, a peak, see PIKE[2]]

picotee (pikətē´) *n.* a hardy garden variety of the carnation, with a spotted or dark-coloured margin. [F *picoté*, p.p. of *picoter*, from *piquer*, to prick, as PICOT]

picotite (pik´ətīt) *n.* (*Mineral.*) a variety of spinel containing chromium oxide. [*Picot*, Baron de la Peyrouse, 1744–1818]

picquet PICKET.

picric (pik´rik) *a.* 1 having an intensely bitter taste. 2 (*Chem.*) an acid obtained by the action of nitric acid on phenol etc., used in dyeing and in certain explosives. **picrate** (-rāt) *n.* **picric acid** *n.* [Gr. *pikros*, bitter, -IC]

picro- (pik´rō), **picr-** *comb. form* bitter. [Gr. *pikros*]

picrotoxin (pikrətok´sin) *n.* a bitter crystalline compound constituting the bitter principle of *Anamirta cocculus*.

Pict (pikt) *n.* a member of an ancient people who once inhabited parts of Northern Britain. **Pictish** *a.* of or relating to the Picts. ~*n.* the language of the Picts. [late L *Pictī*, perh. from *pictus*, p.p. of *pingere*, to paint]

pictograph (pik´təgrahf), **pictogram** (-gram) *n.* **1** a picture standing for an idea, a pictorial character or symbol. **2** a record or primitive writing consisting of these. **3** a diagram showing statistical data in pictorial form. **pictographic** (-graf´-) *a.* **pictography** (-tog´-) *n.* [L *pictus*, p.p. of *pingere*, to paint, -GRAPH]

pictorial (piktaw´riəl) *a.* **1** of, relating to, containing, expressed in or illustrated by pictures. **2** picturesque. ~*n.* an illustrated journal etc. **pictorially** *adv.* [late L *pictōrius*, from *pictor*, a painter, as PICTOGRAPH]

picture (pik´chə) *n.* **1** a painting or drawing representing a person, natural scenery or other objects. **2** a photograph, engraving or other representation on a plane surface. **3** (*coll.*) an image, a copy. **4** a perfect example. **5** (*coll., facet.*) a striking or funny sight. **6** (*coll., esp. facet.*) a beautiful object. **7** a scene, a subject suitable for pictorial representation. **8** a motion picture, a film. **9** the image on a television screen. ~*a.* of or relating to a picture or pictures. ~*v.t.* **1** to represent by painting. **2** to form a mental likeness of, to imagine vividly. **3** to describe vividly. **in the picture** having all the relevant information. **out of the picture** not involved in a situation. **the pictures** (*coll.*) a public showing of motion pictures, the cinema. **to get the picture** to understand the situation. **picture book** *n.* an illustrated book, esp. for children. **picture card** *n.* a court card. **picture frame** *n.* a frame for displaying a picture. **picture gallery** *n.* a gallery or large room in which pictures are exhibited. **picturegoer** *n.* a person who regularly goes to the cinema. **picture hat** *n.* a lady's hat with a wide, drooping brim (as seen in Reynolds's and Gainsborough's pictures). **picture house** *n.* (*dated*) a cinema. **picture-moulding** *n.* **1** material used to make picture frames. **2** a wooden rail near the top of a wall for hanging pictures from. **†picture palace** *n.* a cinema. **picture postcard** *n.* a postcard with a picture on one side. **picture-postcard** *a.* picturesque. **picture rail** *n.* a wooden rail near the top of a wall for hanging pictures from. **picture theatre, picture theater** *n.* (*esp. N Am., Austral., New Zeal.*) a cinema. **picture window** *n.* a large window, usu. with a single pane, framing an attractive view. **picture-writing** *n.* a primitive method of recording events etc., by means of pictorial symbols, as in hieroglyphics. [L *pictūra*, from *pictus*, p.p. of *pingere*, to paint]

picturesque (pikchəresk´) *a.* **1** having those qualities that characterize a good picture. **2** (of language) graphic, vivid. **picturesquely** *adv.* **picturesqueness** *n.*

piddle (pid´əl) *v.i.* (*coll.*) **1** to urinate (used by or to children). **2** to work, act, behave etc., in a trifling way; to trifle. ~*n.* **1** an act of urinating (used by or to children). **2** urine (used by or to children). **piddler** *n.* **piddling** *a.* trifling. [etym. uncertain]

piddock (pid´ək) *n.* any bivalve mollusc of the family Pholadidae, used for bait. [etym. uncertain]

pidgin (pij´in) *n.* a language that is a combination of two or more languages, used esp. for trading between people of different native languages. **pidgin English** *n.* a pidgin in which one of the languages is English. [Chin. (corr. of BUSINESS)]

pi-dog PYE-DOG.

pie[1] (pī) *n.* a pastry case filled with meat, fruit etc. **to have a finger in every pie** FINGER. **pie chart** *n.* a pictorial representation of relative quantities, in which the quantities are represented by sectors of a circle. **piecrust** *n.* the baked pastry crust of a pie. **piecrust table** *n.* a table which has a carved edge resembling a piecrust. **pie-eater** *n.* (*Austral., sl.*) an insignificant person. **pie-eyed** *a.* (*sl.*) drunk. **pie in the sky** *n.* an unrealistic aspiration. **pieman** (-mən) *n.* (*pl.* **piemen**) a man who sells pies.

†pie[2] (pī) *n.* **1** a magpie. **2** any of various other pied birds, such as the spotted woodpecker or the oystercatcher. **3** a pied animal. [OF, from L *pīca*, a magpie]

pie[3] (pī), (*N Am.*) **pi** *n.* **1** a confused mass of printers' type. **2** a jumble, disorder, confusion. ~*v.t.* (*pres.p.* **pieing**, *past, p.p.* **pied**) to mix or confuse (type). [perh. from PIE[2], from the appearance of the black-letter type on white paper]

pie[4] *n.* (*Hist.*) an Indian copper coin worth one-twelfth of an anna. [Hind. *pa'i*, prob. cogn. with PICE]

piebald (pī´bawld) *a.* **1** (of a horse or other animal) having patches of two different colours, usu. black and white; particoloured, mottled. **2** motley, mongrel. ~*n.* a piebald horse or other animal.

piece (pēs) *n.* **1** a distinct part of anything. **2** a detached portion, a fragment (of). **3** a division, a section. **4** a plot or enclosed portion (of land). **5** a definite quantity or portion in which commercial products are made up or sold. **6** an example, an instance. **7** an artistic or literary composition or performance, usu. short. **8** a coin. **9** (*esp. N Am., sl.*) a gun, a firearm. **10** a man at chess, draughts etc. **11** (*offensive, sl.*) a woman. **12** (*coll.*) a share of something. **13** (*Sc.*) a sandwich. ~*v.t.* **1** to add pieces to, to mend, to patch. **2** to eke out. **3** to form (a theory) by putting facts together. **4** to put together so as to form a whole, to join together. **5** to join (threads) together in spinning. ~*v.i.* to come together, to fit (well or ill). **by the piece** (of wages) according to the amount of work done. **in one piece 1** not broken. **2** not damaged or hurt. **in pieces** broken. **nasty piece of work** NASTY. **of a piece** of the same sort, uniform. **to break to pieces** to break into separate fragments. **to give someone a piece of one's mind** to criticize or reprimand someone sharply. **to go to pieces** to collapse emotionally. **to piece out 1** to complete by adding one or more pieces. **2** to eke out. **to piece up** to patch up. **to say one's piece** to express one's opinion. **to take to pieces 1** to separate (something) into its various components. **2** to criticize harshly. **piece-goods** *n.pl.* fabrics woven in standard lengths. **pieceless** *a.* whole, entire. **piecemeal** *adv.* **1** piece by piece, part at a time. **2** in pieces. ~*a.* **1** fragmentary. **2** done by the piece. **piece of cake** *n.* something very easy. **piece of eight** *n.* (*Hist.*) a Spanish dollar of eight reals, worth about 22½p. **piece of goods** *n.* (*offensive, sl.*) a woman. **piece of one's mind** *n.* (giving someone) an outburst of anger or strong opinion. **piece of tail** *n.* (*sl., derog.*) a woman, esp. when thought of in sexual terms. **piece of the action** *n.* (*coll.*) active involvement. **piece of water** *n.* a small lake. **piece of work** *n.* an object produced by working. **piecer** *n.* **piece-rate** *n.* a rate of pay for piecework. **piecework** *n.* work paid for by the piece or job. [OF *pece* (cp. Prov. *peza, pessa*, It. *pezza, pezzo*, Sp. *pieza*), etym. uncertain]

pièce de résistance (pyes də rezis´tãs) *n.* (*pl.* **pièces de résistance** (pyes)) **1** an outstanding item. **2** the main dish of a meal. [F, piece of resistance]

pied (pīd) *a.* particoloured, variegated, spotted. **piedness** *n.* **Pied Piper** *n.* a person who entices people to follow them, esp. to their doom. **pied wagtail** *n.* a small, British, black-and-white wagtail *Motacilla alba.* [PIE[2]]

pied-à-terre (pyādəteə´) *n.* (*pl.* **pieds-à-terre** (pyādəteə´)) a flat or house for occasional use, e.g. a city apartment for a country dweller. [F, a foot on the ground]

piedmont (pēd´mont) *n.* a gentle slope at the foot of a mountain or mountain range. [It. *piemonte*, a mountain foot]

pie-dog PYE-DOG.

pier (piə) *n.* **1** a structure projecting into the sea, used as a landing stage, promenade etc. **2** a breakwater, mole, jetty. **3** a mass of masonry supporting an arch, the superstructure of a bridge or other building, a pillar, a column. **4** a solid portion of masonry between windows etc. **5** a covered passageway leading from an airport building to aircraft. **6** a buttress. **pierage** (-rij) *n.* a toll for using a pier or jetty. **pier glass** *n.* a large ornamental mirror, orig. placed between windows. **pier table** *n.* a low table placed between windows. [ME and A-F *pere*, OF *piere* (F *pierre*), L *petra*, stone]

pierce (piəs) *v.t.* **1** to penetrate or transfix with a pointed instrument. **2** (of a pointed instrument) to penetrate, to transfix, to prick. **3** to make a hole in. **4** to make (a hole). **5** to affect or penetrate keenly. **6** to force a way into, to explore. **7** (of light) to shine through. **8** (of sound) to break (a silence etc.). *~v.i.* to penetrate (into, through etc.). **pierceable** *a.* **piercer** *n.* **piercing** *a.* **1** penetrating. **2** affecting deeply. **piercingly** *adv.* **piercingness** *n.* [OF *percer*, *percier*, etym. uncertain]

Pierian (pīiə´riən) *a.* of or relating to Pieria, in ancient Macedonia, or to the Pierides or Muses.

pierrot (pyer´ō, piə´-) *n.* a buffoon or itinerant minstrel, orig. French and usu. dressed in loose white costume with the face whitened. **pierrette** (-ret´) *n.* a female pierrot. [F, dim. of *Pierre*, Peter]

piet (pī´ət) *n.* (*Sc.*) a magpie. [ME *piot*, from PIE[2]]

pietà (piātah´) *n.* a pictorial or sculptured representation of the Virgin Mary and the dead Christ. [It., from L *pietas*, PIETY]

pietas (pī´ətahs) *n.* respect due to an ancestor. [L (see PIETY)]

pietist (pī´ətist) *n.* **1** a person who makes a display of strong religious feelings. **2** (*Hist.*) (*usu.* **Pietist**) a member of a group of revivalists in the Lutheran Church in the 17th cent. who cultivated personal godliness to the disregard of dogma and the services of the church. **pietism** *n.* **pietistic** (-tis´-), **pietistical** *a.*

piety (pī´əti) *n.* (*pl.* **pieties**) **1** the quality of being pious. **2** reverence towards God. **3** an act of piety. [F *pieté*, L *pietas*]

piezo- (pīē´zō) *comb. form* pressure. [Gr. *piezein*, to press]

piezochemistry (pīēzōkem´istri) *n.* the study of the effect of high pressures on chemical reactions.

piezoelectricity (pīēzōilektris´iti), **piezoelectric effect** (-lek´-) *n.* a property possessed by some crystals, e.g. those used in gramophone crystal pick-ups, of generating surface electric charges when mechanically strained. **piezoelectric** *a.* **piezoelectrically** *adv.*

piezometer (pīizom´itə) *n.* an instrument for determining the compressibility of liquids or other forms of pressure. [Gr. *piezein*, to press]

piffero (pif´ərō) *n.* (*pl.* **pifferos**) a small flute like an oboe. **pifferaro** (-rah´-) *n.* (*pl.* **pifferari** (-rē)) an itinerant player on the piffero. [It., from Gmc. (cp. FIFE)]

piffle (pif´əl) *n.* (*coll.*) trash, rubbish, twaddle. *~v.i.* to talk or act in a feeble, ineffective or trifling way. **piffler** *n.* **piffling** *a.* small or unimportant. [imit.]

pig (pig) *n.* **1** any ungulate, omnivorous mammal of the family Suidae, esp. the domesticated variety, *Sus scrofa*. **2** (*N Am.*) a piglet. **3** any similar animal, such as a guinea pig. **4** the flesh of the pig, pork. **5** (*coll.*) a greedy, gluttonous, filthy, obstinate, or annoying person. **6** (*coll.*) a very difficult or unpleasant thing. **7** (*sl., offensive*) a police officer. **8** (*sl.*) an oblong mass of metal (esp. iron or lead) as run from the furnace. **9** (*Sc., dial.*) an earthenware hot-water bottle. *~v.i.* (*pres.p.* **pigging**, *past, p.p.* **pigged**) **1** to give birth to piglets. **2** to be huddled together like pigs. *~v.t.* (*past, p.p.* **pigged**) **1** to give birth to (piglets). **2** to overindulge oneself in (food). **in a pig's eye** (*coll.*) certainly not. **in pig** (of a sow) pregnant. **pigs might fly** (*iron.*) used to express disbelief. **to bleed like a (stuck) pig** to lose a large amount of blood. **to make a pig of oneself** to eat too much. **to make a pig's ear of** (*sl.*) to make a mess of, to botch. **to pig it** to live in squalor. **to pig out** (*esp. N Am., sl.*) to make a pig of oneself. **pig-eyed** *a.* having small, sunken eyes. **pigfish** *n.* (*pl. in general* **pigfish**, *in particular* **pigfishes**) any of various kinds of fish that make a grunting noise, esp. *Orthopristis chrysopterus*. **piggery** *n.* (*pl.* **piggeries**) **1** a pig farm. **2** a pigsty. **3** piggishness. **piggie** *n.* a piggy. **piggish** *a.* **1** of or relating to pigs. **2** like a pig, esp. in greed. **piggishly** *adv.* **piggishness** *n.* **piggy** *n.* (*pl.* **piggies**) (*coll.*) **1** a little pig. **2** a pig (used by or to a child). **3** a toe (used by or to children). **4** the game of tipcat. *~a.* (*comp.* **piggier**, *superl.* **piggiest**) like a pig. **piggy bank** *n.* a bank in the shape of a pig. **piggy in the middle** *n.* pig in the middle. **pig-headed** *a.* **1** stupidly obstinate or perverse. **2** having a piglike head. **pig-headedly** *adv.* **pig-headedness** *n.* **pig-ignorant** *a.* (*coll.*) very ignorant. **pig in a poke** *n.* goods purchased without being seen beforehand. **pig in the middle** *n.* a person who is unwillingly involved in a dispute between two other parties. **pig-iron** *n.* crude iron from a furnace. **Pig Island** *n.* (*Austral., New Zeal., sl.*) New Zealand. **pig-jump** *v.i.* (*Austral., sl.*) (of a horse) to jump with all four legs without bringing them together. *~n.* a jump made in this way. **pig Latin** *n.* a secret jargon made up by children. **piglet** (-lit) *n.* **piglike** *a.* **pigling** *n.* a piglet. **pig meat** *n.* pork, ham or bacon. **pignut** *n.* an earth-nut. **pigpen** *n.* (*N Am.*) a pigsty. **pig-root** *v.i.* (*New Zeal., sl.*) to pig-jump. **pigskin** *n.* **1** the skin of a pig. **2** leather made from this. **3** (*N Am.*) a football. **4** (*sl.*) a saddle. *~a.* made of pigskin. **pig's swill, pigswill** (-swil) *n.* refuse from kitchens, etc., for feeding pigs. **pigsticking** *n.* **1** the sport of hunting wild boars with a spear. **2** pig-killing. **pig-sticker** *n.* **pigsty** *n.* (*pl.* **pigsties**) **1** an enclosure where pigs are kept. **2** a dirty place, a hovel. **pigtail** *n.* **1** a plait of hair. **2** tobacco prepared in a long twist. **3** the tail of a pig. **pigtailed** *a.* **pigwash, pig's wash** *n.* pigswill. **pigweed** *n.* the goosefoot or other herb eaten by pigs. [ME *pigge*, etym. uncertain]

pigeon[1] (pij´ən) *n.* **1** any grey-and-white bird of the family Columbidae, esp. *Columbia livia*; a dove. **2** (*sl.*) a gullible person, a simpleton. *~v.t.* to fleece, to swindle, esp. by tricks in gambling. **pigeon-breast, pigeon-chest** *n.* a deformity in which the human breast is constricted and the sternum thrust forward. **pigeon-breasted, pigeon-chested** *a.* **pigeon fancier** *n.* a person who keeps pigeons as a hobby. **pigeon-fancying** *n.* **pigeon-hawk** *n.* a merlin. **pigeon-hearted** *a.* timid, easily frightened. **pigeon-hole** *n.* **1** a compartment in a cabinet etc., for papers, etc. **2** a nesting compartment for pigeons. **3** a category, esp. an over-simplified one. *~v.t.* **1** to give a definite place to in the mind, to label, to classify. **2** to defer for future consideration, to shelve. **3** to put away in a pigeon-hole. **pigeon pair** *n.* **1** twins consisting of one boy and one girl. **2** the children of a family consisting of one boy and one girl. **pigeon pea** *n.* dhal. **pigeon-post** *n.* the conveyance of letters by homing pigeons. **pigeonry** *n.* (*pl.* **pigeonries**). **pigeon's milk** *n.* **1** a milky substance consisting of half-digested food with which pigeons feed their young. **2** a sham object for which fools or children are sent. **pigeon-toed** *a.* (of a person) having the toes turned in. **pigeonwing** *n.* (*N Am.*) a fancy dance step. [ME *pyjon*, OF *pijon* (F *pigeon*), late L *pīpiōnem*, nom. *pīpio*, from *pīpīre*, to chirp]

pigeon[2] (pij´in) *n.* **1** a pidgin. **2** (*coll.*) someone's business or concern. **not my pigeon** (*coll.*) not my business, not my concern. **pigeon English** *n.* pidgin English.

piggery PIG.

piggin (pig´in) *n.* a small pail or vessel, usu. of wood, with a handle formed by one of the staves, for holding liquids. [etym. uncertain]

piggyback (pig´ibak), **pickaback** (pik´əbak) *adv.* **1** on the back or shoulders, like a pack. **2** on the back or top of something larger. *~v.i.* to ride piggyback. *~v.t.* **1** to carry (a person) piggyback. **2** to carry or mount on top of something. ~*n.* an act of carrying a person piggyback. [etym. uncertain]

pightle (pī´təl) *n.* (*chiefly dial.*) a small enclosure of land, a croft. [etym. uncertain]

pigment (pig´mənt) *n.* **1** colouring matter used as paint or dye. **2** a substance giving colour to animal or vegetable tissues. **pigmental** (-men´-), **pigmentary** (pig´-) *a.* **pigmentation** (-tā´shən) *n.* [L *pigmentum*, cogn. with *pingere*, to paint]

pigmy PYGMY.

†**pignoration** (pignərā´shən) *n.* the act of pledging or pawning. [L *pignerātio*, from *pignerāre*, from *pignus* -*neris*, a pledge]

pi jaw (pī jaw´) *n.* a long, moralizing lecture. [PI[2]]

pika (pī´kə) *n.* (*pl.* **pikas**) a small burrowing mammal of the genus *Ochotona*, related to the rabbit, a native of Asia and N America. [Tungus, *piika*]

pike[1] (pīk) *n.* **1** a large slender voracious freshwater fish of the family Esocidae, with a long pointed snout. **2** a similar fish, such as the garpike. **3** (*Hist.*) a military weapon, consisting of a narrow, elongated lance-head fixed to a pole. **4** a pickaxe, a spike. **5** a peak, a peaked or pointed hill, esp. in the English Lake District. **6** a diving position in which the legs are straight and the hips bent, and the hands clasp the feet or knees. ~*v.t.* (*Hist.*) to run through or kill with a pike. **to pike on** (*esp. Austral., coll.*) to back out of, to withdraw timidly from. **piked** *a.* pointed, peaked. **pikeman**[1] *n.* (*pl.* **pikemen**) **1** (*Hist.*) a soldier armed with a pike. **2** a miner working with a pickaxe. **pikeperch** *n.* (*pl.* **pikeperch**) any of various perches of the genus *Lucioperca* or *Stizostedion*, which resemble pike. **piker**[1] *n.* a timid gambler. **pikestaff** *n.* **1** (*Hist.*) the wooden shaft of a pike. **2** a pointed stick carried by pilgrims etc. **plain as a pikestaff** perfectly clear or obvious. [F *pique*, in first sense, cogn. with *piquer*, to pierce, *pic*, pickaxe, others prob. from cogn. OE *pīc*]

pike[2] (pīk) *n.* **1** a toll gate. **2** a turnpike road. **to come down the pike** (*N Am.*) to come to attention, to arrive. **pikeman**[2] *n.* (*pl.* **pikemen**) a turnpike keeper. **piker**[2] *n.* a tramp. [short for TURNPIKE (under TURN)]

pikelet (pīk´lit) *n.* (*North.*) a round, thin crumpet. [short for obs. *bara-piklet*, Welsh *bara-pyglyd*, pitchy bread]

pikeman[1] PIKE[1].

pikeman[2] PIKE[2].

piker[1] PIKE[1].

piker[2] PIKE[2].

pilaf (pilaf´), **pilaff, pilau** (-low´), **pilaw** (-law´), **pillau** (-low´) *n.* a Middle Eastern or Indian mixed dish consisting of rice boiled with meat, poultry, or fish, together with raisins, spices etc. [Pers. *pilāw* (cp. Hind. *pilāo*, *palāo*)]

pilaster (pilas´tə) *n.* (*Archit.*) a rectangular column projecting from a wall or pier. **pilastered** *a.* [F *pilastre*, It. *pilastro* (*pila*, L *pīla*, a pillar, -ASTER)]

pilau, pilaw PILAF.

pilchard (pil´chəd) *n.* a small sea fish, *Sardinia pilchardus*, allied to the herring, and an important food fish. [etym. uncertain]

pile[1] (pīl) *n.* **1** a heap, a mass of things heaped together. **2** a funeral pyre, a heap of combustibles for burning a dead body. **3** a very large, massive or lofty building or a group of such buildings. **4** an accumulation. **5** (*coll.*) a great quantity or sum. **6** a fortune. **7** a series of plates of different metals arranged alternately so as to produce an electrical current. **8** an atomic pile. ~*v.t.* **1** to collect or heap up or together, to accumulate. **2** to load. **3** to stack (rifles) with butts on the ground and muzzles together. ~*v.i.* to move in a crowd. **to pile it on** (*coll.*) to exaggerate. **to pile on the agony** AGONY. **to pile up 1** to accumulate. **2** to cause to be involved in a pile-up. **piler** *n.* **pile-up** *n.* (*coll.*) a crash involving several vehicles. [F, from L *pīla*, a pillar]

pile[2] (pīl) *n.* **1** a heavy timber driven into the ground, esp. under water, to form a foundation. **2** a sharp stake or post. **3** (*Her.*) a wedge-shaped device. ~*v.t.* **1** to furnish or strengthen with piles. **2** to drive piles into. **piledriver** *n.* a machine for driving piles into the ground. **piledriving** *n., a.* **pile dwelling** *n.* a dwelling built on piles. **pile-worm** *n.* a worm attacking piles. [OE *pīl*, L *pīlum*, a javelin]

pile[3] (pīl) *n.* **1** the nap of velvet, plush or other cloth, or of a carpet. **2** soft hair, fur, down, wool. **pileless** *a.* [L *pilus*, hair]

pilea PILEUM.

pileate, pilei etc. PILEUS.

piles (pīlz) *n.* (*coll.*) haemorrhoids. **pilewort** *n.* the lesser celandine or figwort, supposed to be a remedy for piles. [L *pila*, a ball]

pileum (pī´liəm) *n.* (*pl.* **pilea** (-liə)) (*Zool.*) the top of the head, from the base of the bill to the nape, in a bird. [L, var. of PILEUS]

pileus (pī´liəs) *n.* (*pl.* **pilei** (-liī)) **1** the cap of a mushroom. **2** (*pl.*) in ancient Rome, a brimless felt cap. **pileate** (-liət), **pileated** (-liātid) *a.* **pileated woodpecker** *n.* a large N American woodpecker, *Dryocopus pileatus*, having a red head. [L *pīleus*, *pilleus* (cp. Gr. *pīlos*)]

pilfer (pil´fə) *v.t., v.i.* to steal in small quantities. **pilferage** (-rij) *n.* **pilferer** *n.* **pilfering** *n.* **pilferingly** *adv.* [OF *pelfrer*, from *pelfre*, a PELF]

pilgrim (pil´grim) *n.* **1** a person who travels a distance to visit some holy place for religious reasons. **2** a person journeying through life. **3** a traveller, a wanderer. **4** (*Hist.*) a member of the Pilgrim Fathers. ~*v.i.* (*pres.p.* **pilgriming**, *past, p.p.* **pilgrimed**) to go on a pilgrimage, to wander as a pilgrim. **pilgrimage** (-mij) *n.* **1** a pilgrim's journey to some holy place. **2** the journey of human life. **3** any journey to a place of special significance. ~*v.i.* to go on a pilgrimage. **Pilgrim Fathers** *n.pl.* the English Puritan colonists who sailed to N America, and founded Plymouth, Massachusetts in 1620. **pilgrimize, pilgrimise** *v.i.* [ME *pelegrim*, prob. through an OF *pelegrin* (cp. F *pèlerin*, It. *pellegrino*), L *peregrīnus*, a stranger, see PEREGRINE]

piliferous (pīlif´ərəs) *a.* bearing hairs. **piliform** (pī´-) *a.* [L *pilus*, a hair]

Pilipino (pilipē´nō) *n.* the language of the Philippines. [Tagalog, from Sp. *Filipino*]

pill (pil) *n.* **1** a little ball of some medicinal substance to be swallowed whole. **2** something unpleasant which has to be accepted or put up with. **3** (*coll.*) a ball. **4** (*pl., facet.*) billiard balls. ~*v.i.* (*sl.*) to blackball, to reject. **the pill** (*coll.*) the contraceptive pill. **to gild/ sugar/ sweeten the pill** to make something unpleasant more acceptable. **pillbox** *n.* **1** a small box for holding pills. **2** a small round brimless hat worn by women. **3** (*Mil.*) a concrete blockhouse, used as a machine-gun emplacement or for other defensive purposes. **4** a small carriage. **pill-popper** *n.* (*coll.*) **1** a person who takes a lot of pills. **2** a drug addict. **pill-popping** *n., a.* **pillworm** *n.* a millipede which rolls up into a ball. **pillwort** *n.* an aquatic plant of the genus *Pilularia globulifera*, with spore-producing globular bracts. [L *pilula*, dim. of *pila*, a ball]

pillage (pil´ij) *n.* **1** the act of plundering. **2** plunder, esp. the property of enemies taken in war. ~*v.t.* **1** to strip of money or goods by open force. **2** to lay waste. ~*v.i.* to rob, to ravage, to plunder. **pillager** *n.* [F, from *piller* (see PEEL[2])]

pillar (pil´ə) *n.* **1** an upright structure of masonry, iron, timber etc., of considerable height in proportion to thickness, used for support, ornament or as a memorial; a column, a post, a pedestal. **2** an upright mass of anything analogous in form or function. **3** a mass of coal, stone etc., left to support the roof in a mine or quarry. **4** a person or group of people acting as chief support of an institution, movement etc. ~*v.t.* to support with or as if with pillars. **from pillar to post 1** from one place to another. **2** from one difficult situation to another. **pillar box** *n.* a short hollow pillar in which letters may be placed for collection by the post office. **pillar-box red** *n., a.* vivid red (the colour of a pillar box). **pillared** *a.* **pillaret** *n.* a small pillar. **Pillars of Hercules** *n.pl.* two rocks on either side of the Straits of Gibraltar. [ME and OF *piler*, pop. L *pīlāre*, from *pīla*]

pillau PILAF.

pillion (pil´yən) *n.* **1** a passenger seat on a motorcycle. **2** (*Hist.*) a low light saddle for a woman. **3** (*Hist.*) a cushion for a person, usu. a woman, to ride on behind a person on horseback. ~*a., adv.* (riding) on a pillion. [prob. through Celt. (cp. Gael. *pillean, pillin*), from L *pellis*, skin]

pilliwinks (pil´iwingks) *n.* (*Hist.*) an instrument of torture for squeezing the fingers and thumbs. [ME *pyrwykes, pyrewinkes*, etym. unknown]

pillock (pil´ək) *n.* (*sl.*) a stupid person. [var. of *pillicock*, the penis]

pillory (pil´əri) *n.* (*pl.* **pillories**) (*Hist.*) a wooden frame supported on a pillar and with holes through which the head and hands of a person were put, so as to expose them to public derision. ~*v.t.* (*3rd pers. sing. pres.* **pillories**, *pres.p.* **pillorying**, *past, p.p.* **pilloried**) **1** to hold up to ridicule. **2** (*Hist.*) to put in the pillory. **pillorize, pillorise** *v.t.* [ME *pillori*, OF *pellori* (F *pilori*), etym. unknown]

pillow (pil´ō) *n.* **1** a cushion filled with feathers or other soft material, used as a rest for the head of a person lying down, esp. in bed. **2** a block used as a cushion or support on a machine. **3** the block on which the inner end of the bowsprit of a ship rests. **4** anything resembling a pillow in form or function. **5** a lace-pillow. ~*v.t.* **1** to lay or rest on or as if on a pillow. **2** to prop up with a pillow. **pillow block** *n.* a metal block or case supporting the end of a revolving shaft, with a movable cover for allowing adjustment of the bearings. **pillowcase** *n.* a washable cover of linen etc., for a pillow. **pillow-fight** *n.* a game in which the participants strike each other with pillows. **pillow lace** *n.* lace made on a lace-pillow. **pillow lava** *n.* lava in pillow-shaped masses. **pillowslip** *n.* a pillowcase. **pillow talk** *n.* intimate conversation in bed. **pillowy** *a.* [OE *pyle, pylu* (cp. Dut. *peluw*, G *Pfühl*), L *pulvīnus*]

pillule PILULE.

pilocarpine (pīlōkah´pīn) *n.* a white crystalline or amorphous alkaloid from the jaborandi, a tropical American shrub of the genus *Pilocarpus*. [Gr. *pilos*, wool, *karpos*, a fruit]

pilose (pī´lōs), **pilous** (-ləs) *a.* covered with or consisting of hairs. **pilosity** (-los´-) *n.* [L *pilōsus*]

pilot (pīlət) *n.* **1** a person directing the course of an aeroplane, spacecraft etc. **2** a person qualified to conduct ships into or out of harbour or along particular coasts, channels etc. **3** a radio or TV programme made to test its suitability to be extended into a series. **4** a guide or director, esp. in difficult or dangerous circumstances. **5** †a steersman. ~*a.* serving as a preliminary test or trial. ~*v.t.* **1** to act as pilot on or direct the course of (esp. a ship, aircraft etc.). **2** to introduce or test (a new scheme etc.). **pilotage** (-tij) *n.* **pilot balloon** *n.* a small, hydrogen-filled balloon sent up to obtain the direction and velocity of the upper winds. **pilot-bird** *n.* a sweet-toned Australian scrub bird, *Pycnoptilus floccosus*. **pilot-boat** *n.* a boat in which pilots cruise off the shore to meet incoming ships. **pilot chute** *n.* a small parachute which brings the main parachute into operation. **pilot-cloth** *n.* a heavy blue woollen cloth for sailors' clothing. **pilot engine** *n.* a locomotive sent in advance to clear the line for a train. **pilot fish** *n.* a small sea fish, *Naucrates ductor*, said to act as a guide to sharks. **pilot house** *n.* a wheelhouse. **pilot-jacket** *n.* a pea-jacket. **pilotless** *a.* **pilot light** *n.* **1** a small jet of gas kept burning in order to light a boiler etc. **2** a small light on the dial of a radio etc. that goes on when the current is switched on. **pilot officer** *n.* a junior commissioned rank in the RAF corresponding to second lieutenant in the Army. **pilot whale** *n.* a small whale of the genus *Globicephalus*. [F *pillotte* (now *pilote*), It. *pilota*, perh. corr. of *pedota*, prob. from Gr. *pēdon*, a rudder]

pilous PILOSE.

Pilsner (pilz´nə), **Pilsener** *n.* a pale beer with a strong flavour of hops. [*Pilsen* in the Czech Republic, where it was first brewed]

Piltdown man (pilt´down) *n.* an early hominid postulated on the basis of fossil bones found in a gravel pit at Piltdown, E Sussex in 1912, but later found to be a hoax.

pilule (pil´ūl) *n.* a pill, esp. a small pill. **pilular, pilulous** *a.* [L *pilula*]

pimento (pimen´tō) *n.* (*pl.* **pimentos**) **1** a pimiento. **2** (*esp. W Ind.*) allspice. [Port. *pimenta* (cp. Sp. *pimienta*), L *pigmentum*, PIGMENT]

pi-meson (pīmē´zon) *n.* a pion.

pimiento (pimien´tō) *n.* (*pl.* **pimientos**) a red pepper. [Sp., from L *pigmentum*, pigment, in med. L spice]

pimp (pimp) *n.* a man who finds customers for a prostitute or lives from her earnings. ~*v.i.* to act as a pimp. [etym. uncertain, cp. F *pimpant*, spruce, attractive, seductive]

pimpernel (pim´pənel) *n.* any plant of the genus *Anagallis*, esp. the scarlet pimpernel. [OF *pimprenele* (F *pimprenelle*), med. L *pipinella*, perh. corr. of *bipinnela*, dim. of *bipennula*, dim. of *bipennis* (*penna*, a feather)]

pimping (pim´ping) *a.* **1** small, puny. **2** feeble, sickly. [etym. uncertain]

pimple (pim´pəl) *n.* **1** a small pustule, or inflamed swelling on the skin. **2** anything resembling a pimple. **pimpled** *a.* **pimply** *a.* (*comp.* **pimplier**, *superl.* **pimpliest**). [etym. uncertain]

PIN (pin), **PIN number** *n.* a personal identification number.

pin (pin) *n.* **1** a short, slender, pointed piece of metal, wood etc., used for fastening parts of clothing, papers etc., together. **2** a peg or bolt of metal or wood used for various purposes, such as the bolt of a lock, a thole, a peg to which the strings of a musical instrument are fastened, a hairpin, a ninepin etc. **3** an ornamental device with a pin used as a fastening etc., or as a decoration. **4** a badge pinned to clothing. **5** anything of slight value. **6** (*coll.*) legs. **7** (*Med.*) a metal rod for joining together the ends of fractured bones while healing. **8** in chess, a position in which a piece is pinned to another. **9** in golf, a small flagpole marking the position of the hole. **10** a keg or small cask. ~*v.t.* (*pres.p.* **pinning**, *past, p.p.* **pinned**) **1** to fasten (to, on, up etc.) with or as if with a pin. **2** to pierce, to transfix. **3** to place (the blame) (on). **4** to seize, to make fast, to secure. **5** in chess, to cause (an opposing piece) to be immobilized by attacking it with a queen, rook or bishop so that moving the piece would expose a more valuable piece. **6** to enclose. **not to care a pin** not to care in the slightest. **on pins and needles** in a state of nervousness. **to pin down 1** to bind to a promise or obligation. **2** to force (someone) to make a decision. **3** to restrict the movements of. **4** to try to discover the identity or location of. **5** to hold down by force. **to pin one's faith on** to place full reliance on. **to pin one's hopes on** to pin one's faith on. **pinball** *n.* a game played on a machine with a sloping board on which a ball moves, propelled by flippers, striking targets and thus accumulating points. **pinball machine** *n.* a machine for playing pinball. †**pincase** *n.* **pincushion** *n.* a small cushion for sticking pins into. **pin-down** *n.* the act of keeping children in care in solitary confinement for a long period of time. **pin-dust** *n.* small particles of metal rubbed off in pointing pins. **pin-feather** *n.* (*Zool.*) an incipient feather. **pin-feathered** *a.* **pinhead** *n.* **1** the head of a pin. **2** a very small object. **3** (*coll.*) a very stupid person. **pinheaded** *a.* (*coll.*) very stupid. **pinheadedness** *n.* **pin-high** *a.* (of a golf ball) at the same distance ahead as the pin. **pinhole** *n.* **1** a very small aperture. **2** a hole into which a pin or peg fits. **pinhole camera** *n.* a camera with a pinhole instead of a lens. **pin-maker** *n.* **pin money** *n.* **1** (*Hist.*) an allowance of money for dress or other private expenses. **2** money earned or saved, esp. by a woman, for personal expenditure. **pinpoint** *n.* **1** the point of a pin. **2** anything sharp or painful. ~*v.t.* to locate accurately and precisely. ~*a.* **1** very small. **2** accurate and precise. **pinprick** *n.* **1** a prick or minute puncture with or as if with a pin. **2** a petty annoyance. ~*v.t.* to prick with or as if with a pin. **pins and needles** *n.pl.* a tingling sensation when a limb has been immobile for a long time. **pinstripe** *n.* **1** (a cloth with) a very narrow stripe. **2** (*sing. or pl.*) a pinstripe suit. ~*a.* made of pinstripe. **pinstriped** *a.* **pin-table** *n.* a table for playing pinball. **pintail** *n.* **1** a duck, esp. *Anas acuta*, with a pointed tail. **2** a grouse with a pointed tail. **pin-tuck** *n.* a narrow ornamental tuck on a shirt or dress. **pin-up** *n.* **1** a poster of an attractive person, often scantily clothed. **2** an attractive person who appears on posters. **pinwheel** *n.* **1** a small Catherine wheel. **2** a wheel with pins set in the face instead of cogs in the rim. ~*v.i.* to rotate like a pinwheel. **pinworm** *n.* a small threadworm, *Enterobius vermicularis*. [OE *pinn* (cp. Dut. and G *Pin*, *Pinne*, Icel. *pinni*, Norw. and Swed. *Pinne*)]

piña (pē´nyə), **piña cloth, piña muslin** *n.* a delicate cloth made in the Philippines from the fibres of the pineapple leaf. [Sp. from L *pīnea*, a pine cone]

☒ **pinacle** common misspelling of PINNACLE.

pina colada (pēnə kəlah´də) *n.* a cocktail made from rum, pineapple juice and coconut juice. [Sp., lit., strained pineapple]

pinafore (pin´əfaw) *n.* **1** an apron or sleeveless overall worn to protect the front of clothes. **2** a pinafore dress. **pinafored** *a.* **pinafore dress** *n.* a sleeveless dress worn over a blouse or sweater. [PIN, AFORE]

pinaster (pīnas´tə) *n.* a pine, *Pinus pinaster*, indigenous to the Mediterranean regions of Europe. [L, wild pine]

pince-nez (pansnā´) *n.* (*pl.* **pince-nez**) a pair of armless eyeglasses held in place by a spring clipping the nose. [F, pinch-nose, see PINCH]

pincers (pin´səz) *n.pl.* **1** (*also* **pair of pincers**) a tool with two limbs working on a pivot as levers to a pair of jaws, for gripping, crushing, extracting nails etc. **2** a nipping or grasping organ, as in crustaceans. **pincer movement** *n.* a military manoeuvre in which one army encloses another on two sides at once. [ME *pynsors*, *pinsours*]

pincette (pinset´) *n.* a pair of small tweezers or forceps. [F dim. of *pince*, pincers, see PINCH]

pinch (pinch) *v.t.* **1** to nip or squeeze, to press so as to cause pain or inconvenience. **2** to take off or remove by nipping or squeezing. **3** to afflict, to distress, esp. with cold, hunger etc. **4** to straiten, to stint. **5** to urge (a horse). **6** to steer (a ship) close-hauled. **7** (*coll.*) to steal. **8** (*sl.*) to arrest, to take into custody. **9** †(of an animal) to grip, to bite. ~*v.i.* **1** to nip or squeeze anything. **2** to be niggardly. **3** to sail close-hauled. **4** to be straitened. **5** to cavil. ~*n.* **1** a sharp nip or squeeze, as with the ends of the fingers. **2** as much as can be taken up between the finger and thumb. **3** a pain, a pang. **4** distress, straits, a dilemma, stress, pressure. **5** (*sl.*) **a** an arrest. **b** a theft. **at a pinch** in an urgent case, if hard pressed. **in a pinch** at a pinch. **to feel the pinch** to be affected by a lack of money. **with a pinch of salt** SALT. **pinchcommons** *n.* a pinchpenny. **pinched** *a.* thin and pale, esp. because of illness. **pincher** *n.* **pinchers** *n.pl.* pincers. **pinch-hitter** *n.* **1** a baseball player who bats as a substitute for another. **2** (*N Am.*) a substitute. **3** in limited-overs cricket, a batsman who seeks to bat aggressively early in the innings to take advantage of restricted field placing. **pinch-hit** *v.i.* (*pres.p.* **pinch-hitting,** *past, p.p.* **pinch-hit**). **pinchingly** *adv.* **pinchpenny** *n.* (*pl.* **pinchpennies**) a miser. ~*a.* miserly. **pinch-run** *v.i.* (*pres.p.* **pinch-running,** *past, p.p.* **pinch-run**) in baseball, to run as a substitute for another, esp. at an important point in the game. **pinch-runner** *n.* [ONF *pinchier* (F *pincer*), etym. uncertain]

pinchbeck (pinch´bek) *n.* an alloy of copper, zinc, etc., formerly used for cheap jewellery. ~*a.* **1** specious, spurious. **2** cheap in quality. [Christopher *Pinchbeck*, *c.* 1670–1732, English inventor]

pindari (pindah´ri) *n.* (*pl.* **pindaris**) a mounted marauder employed as an irregular soldier by princes in central India during the 17th and 18th cents. [Hind.]

Pindaric (pindar´ik) *a.* of, relating to or in the style of Pindar, the Greek lyric poet. ~*n.* an ode, metre etc. of an irregular kind, more or less resembling the style of Pindar. **Pindarism** (pin´dər-) *n.*

pine[1] (pīn) *n.* **1** (*also* **pine tree**) any tree of the coniferous genus *Pinus*, consisting of evergreen trees with needle-shaped leaves. **2** the timber from a pine tree. **3** a pineapple. ~*a.* of pines or pine timber. **pineapple** *n.* **1** a tropical plant, *Ananas comosus*. **2** the large multiple fruit of the pineapple, having sweet, yellow flesh and a tough, brownish skin. **3** (*Mil., sl.*) a hand grenade. **pine-barren** *n.* a tract of sandy land producing only pines. **pine-beauty** *n.* (*pl.* **pine-beauties**) a moth destructive to pine trees. **pine-beetle** *n.* any beetle feeding on pine leaves. **pine-carpet** *n.* a moth destructive to pine trees. **pine-chafer** *n.* a beetle, *Hylurgus piniperda*, which feeds on pine leaves by boring up through the leader. **pine cone** *n.* the cone-shaped fruit of the pine tree. **pine marten** *n.* a European marten, *Martes martes*, having a dark brown coat and a yellowish throat. **pine needle** *n.* the needle-shaped leaf of the pine tree. **pine nut** *n.* the edible seed of some pine trees. **pinery** *n.* (*pl.* **pineries**). **pinetum** (-nē´təm) *n.* (*pl.* **pineta** (-tə)) a plantation of pine trees. **pine wood** *n.* a forest of pine trees. **pinewood** *n.* the timber of pine trees. **piny** (pī´ni), **piney** *a.* (*comp.* **pinier,** *superl.* **piniest**). [OE *pīn*, L *pīnus*]

pine[2] (pīn) *v.i.* **1** to languish, waste away. **2** to long or yearn (for, after or to). [OE *pīnian*, to torture, from *pīn*, torment, pain]

pineal (pin´iəl, pī´niəl) *a.* shaped like a pine cone. **pineal body** *n.* (*Anat.*) a dark grey conical structure situated behind the third ventricle of the brain which secretes melatonin into the bloodstream. **pineal eye** *n.* (*Zool.*) a rudimentary eye, perhaps orig. connected with the pineal gland, found between the brain and the parietal foramen in many lizards. **pineal gland** *n.* the pineal body. [F *pinéal* (L *pīnea*, a pine cone, -AL[1])]

pineapple, pinery etc. PINE[1].

pinfold (pin´fōld), **penfold** (pen´-) *n.* **1** (*Hist.*) a pound in which stray cattle were shut up. **2** a narrow enclosure. ~*v.t.* to shut up in a pinfold. [OE *punfald* (POUND[3], FOLD[2])]

ping (ping) *n.* a sharp ringing sound, like the sound of a bullet flying through the air. ~*v.i.* **1** to make such a sound. **2** (*N Am.*) (of an internal-combustion engine) to pink. ~*v.t.* to cause to make a pinging sound. **pinger** *n.* [imit.]

pingo (ping´gō) *n.* (*pl.* **pingos**) (*Geol.*) a mound of earth or gravel found in permanent areas. [Eskimo (Inuit)]

ping-pong (ping´pong) *n.* table tennis. [imit.]

pinguid (ping´gwid) *a.* (*formal or facet.*) fat, oily, greasy, unctuous. **pinguidity** (-gwid´-), **pinguitude** (-tūd) *n.* [L *pinguis*, fat]

pinguin (ping´gwin) *n.* a W Indian plant, *Bromelia pinguin*, of the pineapple family, with a fleshy fruit. [etym. unknown]

pinion[1] (pin´yən) *n.* **1** the joint of a bird's wing remotest from the body. **2** (*poet.*) a wing. **3** a wing feather. ~*v.t.* **1** to cut off the pinion of to prevent flight. **2** to shackle, to fetter the arms of. **3** to bind (the arms etc.). **4** to bind fast (to). [OF *pignon*, L *penna*, var. *pinna*, a feather, a wing]

pinion[2] (pin´yən) *n.* **1** the smaller of two cogwheels in gear with each other. **2** a cogged spindle engaging with a wheel. [F *pignon*, OF *pinon*, *penon*, L *pinna*, a pinnacle, a gable, cp. PINION[1]]

pink[1] (pingk) *n.* **1** a pale rose colour or pale red slightly inclining towards purple. **2** any plant or flower of the genus *Dianthus*, largely cultivated in gardens. **3** any of several allied or similar plants, such as moss pink. **4** the supreme excellence, the very height (of). **5** a fox-hunter's scarlet coat or the cloth used to make one. **6** a fox-hunter. **7** (*coll., often derog.*) a moderately left-wing person. ~*a.* **1** pale red or rose. **2** (*coll., often derog.*) moderately left-wing. **3** (of wine) rosé. **4** of or relating to homosexuals (*the pink vote*). **in the pink** in fine condition. **tickled pink** TICKLE. **pink-collar** *a.* (of an occupation) traditionally associated with women. **pink disease** *n.* a disease affecting young children in which the extremities turn pink. **pink elephants** *n.pl.* (*coll.*) hallucinations induced by intoxication with alcohol. **pink-eye** *n.* **1** a contagious influenza among horses, cattle and sheep, characterized by inflammation of the conjunctiva. **2** a form of conjunctivitis in humans. **pink gin** *n.* gin mixed with Angostura Bitters. **pinkish** *a.* **pinkly** *adv.* **pinkness** *n.* **pink noise** *n.* recordings of mid-to-low-frequency background noise, designed to be soothing to young babies. **pinko** *n.* (*pl.* **pinkos, pinkoes**) (*esp. N Am., sl., usu. derog.*) a person with (moderately) left-wing views. **pink slip** *n.* (*esp. N Am.*) a note given to an employee, terminating employment. **pinky**[1] *a.* **pinkiness** *n.* [etym. uncertain]

pink[2] (pingk) *v.t.* **1** to pierce, to stab. **2** to make a punched pattern in leather etc. for ornament. **3** to decorate in this manner. **4** †to adorn, to decorate. **pinking** *n.* **pinking shears, pinking scissors** *n.pl.* a pair of shears with zigzag cutting edges, used to cut cloth to prevent fraying. [ME *pinken* (cp. LG *pinken*, also PICK[1])]

pink[3] (pingk) *v.i.* (of an internal-combustion engine) to detonate prematurely, making a series of popping sounds. [imit.]

†**pink**[4] (pingk) *n.* (*Hist.*) a sailing ship with a very narrow stern, used chiefly in the Mediterranean. [MDut. *pinke* (now *pink*), etym. uncertain]

pink[5] (pingk) *n.* a yellow pigment obtained from quercitron bark or other vegetable sources. [etym. unknown]

pink[6] (pingk) *n.* **1** a young salmon. **2** (*dial.*) a minnow. [etym. unknown]

†**pink**[7] (pingk) *a.* small. [etym. uncertain]

pinkie (ping´ki), **pinky** *n.* (*pl.* **pinkies**) (*esp. N Am., Sc., coll.*) the little finger.

pinko PINK[1].

Pinkster (pink´stə) *n.* (*N Am., dial.*) Whitsuntide. **pinkster flower** *n.* the pink azalea, *Rhododendron periclymenoides*. [Dut., Pentecost]

pinky[1] PINK[1].

pinky[2] PINKIE.

pinna (pin´ə) *n.* (*pl.* **pinnae** (-nē), **pinnas**) **1** the projecting upper part of the external ear. **2** (*pl.*) a leaflet of a pinnate leaf. **3** a wing, a fin, or an analogous structure. [L, a feather, a wing, a fin]

pinnace (pin´is) *n.* (*Naut.*) **1** a man-of-war's boat with six or eight oars. **2** †a small schooner-rigged vessel provided with sweeps. [F *pinasse*, prob. ult. from L *pīnus*, a PINE[1]]

pinnacle (pin´əkəl) *n.* **1** the apex, the culmination (of). **2** a pointed summit. **3** a turret, usu. pointed or tapering, placed as an ornament on the top of a buttress etc., or as a termination on an angle or gable. ~*v.t.* **1** to set on or as if on a pinnacle. **2** to surmount as a pinnacle. **3** to furnish with pinnacles. [OF *pinacle*, late L *pinnāculum*, dim. of PINNA]

pinnae PINNA.

pinnate (pin´āt), **pennate** (pen´-), **pinnated** (-ātid), **pennated** *a.* **1** (*Bot.*) **a** having leaflets arranged featherwise along the stem. **b** divided into leaflets. **2** (*Zool.*) having lateral processes along an axis. **pinnately** *adv.* **pinnatifid** (-nat´ifid) *a.* (*Bot.*) divided into lobes nearly to the midrib. **pinnation** (-ā´shən) *n.* **pinnatiped** (-nat´iped) *a.* (*Zool.*) fin-footed, having the toes bordered by membranes. **pinnatisect** (-nat´isekt) *a.* (of a pinnate leaf) having the lobes cleft to the midrib. [L *pinnātus*, from PINNA]

pinner (pin´ə) *n.* **1** a person who pins. **2** (*dial.*) a pinafore. **3** a cap or coif with the lappets or laps pinned on. **4** a pin-maker. [PIN, -ER]

pinni- (pin´i) *comb. form* a wing, a fin. [L *pinna*]

pinniped (pin´iped) *a.* having feet like fins. ~*n.* any member of a group of pinniped marine carnivores containing the seals, sea lions and walruses. [L *pes pedis*, a foot]

pinnock (pin´ək) *n.* (*dial.*) **1** a hedge sparrow. **2** a titmouse. [etym. uncertain]

pinnule (pin´ūl) *n.* **1** (*Bot.*) any one of the smaller or ultimate divisions of a pinnate leaf. **2** (*Zool.*) a small fin, wing, barb of a feather etc. **pinnular** *a.* **pinnulate** (-lət), **pinnulated** (-lātid) *a.* [L *pinnula*, dim. of PINNA]

pinny (pin´i) *n.* (*pl.* **pinnies**) (*coll.*) a pinafore, an apron.

pinochle (pē´nokəl), **penuchle** (-nŭkəl), **pinocle** *n.* **1** a card game similar to bezique, played with a 48-card pack by two or four players. **2** in pinochle, the combination of queen of spades and jack of diamonds. [etym. unknown]

pinocytosis (pēnōsītō´sis) *n.* (*Biol.*) the ingestion by cells of vesicles containing fluid. [Gr. *pino*, drink, *-cytosis*, cogn. with PHAGOCYTOSIS (under PHAGOCYTE)]

pinole (pēnō´lā) *n.* (*N Am.*) meal made from maize, mesquite beans etc. [Am. Sp., from Nahuatl *pinolli*]

piñon (pinyon´), **pinyon** *n.* **1** any of various low-growing pines of the west of N America, esp. *Pinus edulis*. **2** the edible seed of the piñon. [Sp., pine nut, see PINEAL]

pint (pīnt) *n.* **1** a measure of capacity, the eighth part of a gallon (0.568 l). **2** (*coll.*) a pint of beer, milk etc. **3** the amount of shellfish contained in a pint mug. **pinta** (pīn´tə) *n.* (*dated, coll.*) a pint of milk. **pint pot** *n.* a vessel, esp. made of pewter, for holding a pint of beer. **pint-sized** *a.* (*coll.*) small. [F *pinte*, perh. through Sp. *pinta*, from late L *pincta*, *picta*, fem. p.p. of *pingere*, to paint]

pintado (pintah´dō) *n.* (*pl.* **pintados**) **1** a species of petrel. **2** a guinea fowl. [Port. or Sp., p.p. of *pintar*, ult. from L *pingere* (p.p. *pinctus*, *pictus*), to PAINT]

pintle (pin´təl) *n.* **1** a pin or bolt, esp. one used as a pivot. **2** any of the pins on which a rudder swings. [OE *pintel*, the penis, etym. uncertain]

pinto (pin´tō) *a.* (*N Am.*) piebald. ~*n.* (*pl.* **pintos**) a horse or pony with patches of white and another colour. [Am. Sp., spotted, cp. PINTADO]

pinxit (pingk´sit) *v.i.* (he or she) painted it (in the signature to a picture). [L]

piny PINE[1].

Pinyin (pinyin´) *n.* a system of romanized spelling used to transliterate Chinese characters. [Chin. *pīn-yīn*, lit., spell sound]

pinyon PIÑON.

piolet (pyōlā´) *n.* a climber's ice axe. [F Savoy dial., dim. of *pialo*, prob. rel. to *pioche*, from *pic*, see PIKE[1]]

pion (pī´on) *n.* (*pl.* **pions**) (*Physics*) a meson with positive or negative or no charge, chiefly responsible for nuclear force. **pionic** (pīon´ik) *a.* [*pi*-*meson*]

pioneer (pīəniə´) *n.* **1** an early leader or developer of an enterprise. **2** an explorer. **3** a member of a body of soldiers whose duty it is to clear and repair roads, bridges etc., for troops on the march. ~*v.t.* **1** to initiate or develop (a new enterprise). **2** to act as pioneer to. **3** to lead, to conduct. ~*v.i.* to act as a pioneer. [F *pionnier*, from *pion*, PAWN[1]]

pious (pī´əs) *a.* **1** reverencing God, religious, devout. **2** sanctimonious. **3** dutiful. **pious fraud** *n.* **1** a deception in the interests of religion or of the person deceived. **2** (*coll.*) a sanctimonious hypocrite. **piously** *adv.* [L *pius*, orig. dutiful]

pip[1] (pip) *n.* the seed of an apple, orange etc. ~*v.t.* (*pres.p.* **pipping,** *past, p.p.* **pipped**) to remove the pips from (fruit). **pipless** *a.* [prob. from PIPPIN]

pip[2] (pip) *n.* a short, high-pitched sound. ~*v.i.* (*pres.p.* **pipping,** *past, p.p.* **pipped**) (of a bird) to chirp. ~*v.t.* (of a baby bird) to break through (the shell) in hatching. [perh. var. of PEEP[2], or imit.]

pip[3] (pip) *n.* **1** a spot on a playing card, domino, dice etc. **2** a star on an army officer's uniform indicating rank. **3** a small flower in a clustered inflorescence etc. **4** any one of the segments on the rind of a pineapple. **5** an image of an object on a radar screen. [formerly *peep*, etym. uncertain]

pip[4] (pip) *n.* **1** a disease in poultry etc., causing a secretion of thick mucus in the throat. **2** (*coll.*) a fit of bad temper. **3** (*facet.*) any of various human disorders. [prob. from MDut. *pippe*, ult. from pop. L *pipita*, corr. of *pītuīta*]

pip[5] (pip) *v.t.* (*pres.p.* **pipping,** *past, p.p.* **pipped**) (*coll.*) **1** to hit with a shot. **2** to beat, to get the better of. **3** to blackball. **to pip at the post** to beat, outdo etc. at the last moment, e.g. in a race or contest. **to pip out** to die. **to pip to the post** to pip at the post. [perh. from PIP[1]]

†**pip**[6] (pip) *n.* signallers' name for letter P. **pip emma** (em´ə) *n.* p.m., afternoon.

pipa (pipah´) *n.* the Suriname toad. [prob. from Galibi]

pipal PEEPUL.

pipe (pīp) *n.* **1** a long hollow tube or line of tubes, esp. for conveying liquids, gas etc. **2** a wind instrument consisting of a tube. **3** (*Mus.*) a tube producing a note of a particular tone in an organ. **4** (*pl.*) bagpipes. **5** (*pl.*) pan pipes. **6** a boatswain's whistle. **7** a signal on a boatswain's whistle. **8** a tubular organ, vessel, passage etc., in an animal body. **9** (*usu. pl.*) the windpipe. **10** a shrill note or cry of a bird etc. **11** a tube with a bowl for smoking tobacco. **12** a pipeful (of tobacco). **13** **a** a large cask for wine. **b** this used as a measure of capacity, usu. 150 gall. (682 l). **14** a vein containing ore or extraneous matter penetrating rock. **15** a cavity in cast metal. **16** †the voice, esp. in singing. ~*v.t.* **1** to play or execute on a pipe. **2** to whistle. **3** to utter in a shrill tone. **4** to lead or bring (along or to) by playing or whistling on a pipe. **5** to call or direct by a boatswain's pipe or whistle. **6** to furnish with pipes. **7** to propagate (pinks) by slips from the parent stem. **8** to trim or decorate with piping. **9** to convey or transmit along a pipe or wire. ~*v.i.* **1** to play on a pipe. **2** to whistle, to make a shrill, high-pitched sound. **put that in your pipe and smoke it** (*coll.*) accept that unwelcome fact. **to pipe away** to signal the departure of (a boat). **to pipe down** **1** (*coll.*) to stop talking. **2** (*Naut.*) to dismiss from duty. **to pipe the eye** EYE[1]. **to pipe up** **1** to begin to sing, to sing the first notes of. **2** (*coll.*) to begin to speak. **pipe band** *n.* a band consisting of pipers, drummers and a drum major. **pipeclay** *n.* a fine, white, plastic clay used for making tobacco pipes, and for cleaning military accoutrements etc. ~*v.t.* **1** to whiten with pipeclay. **2** to put in order. **pipecleaner** *n.* a piece of twisted wire covered in fine yarn, used for cleaning tobacco pipes. **piped music** *n.* music recorded for playing in shops, restaurants etc. as background music. **pipe dream** *n.* a fantastic notion, an unrealistic hope. **pipefish** *n.* (*pl. in general* **pipefish,** *in particular* **pipefishes**) any fish of the family Syngnathidae, having an elongated snout. **pipeful** *n.* (*pl.* **pipefuls**). **pipeless** *a.* **pipe-light** *n.* a spill for lighting tobacco pipes. **pipeline** *n.* **1** a long pipe or conduit laid down from an oil well, or oil region, to convey the petroleum to a port etc. **2** a channel of communication. **in the pipeline** under preparation, soon to be supplied, produced etc. **pipe major** *n.* a non-commissioned officer in charge of pipers. **pipe of peace** *n.* a peace pipe. **pipe organ** *n.* (*Mus.*) an organ which uses pipes as well as reeds. **piper** *n.* **1** a person who plays upon a pipe, esp. a strolling player or a performer on the bagpipes. **2** a broken-winded horse. **3** a dog used to lure birds into a decoy-pipe. **he who pays the piper calls the tune** PAY[1]. **pipe-rack** *n.* a stand for tobacco pipes. **pipe roll** *n.* (*Hist.*) the great roll of the Exchequer containing the pipes or annual accounts of sheriffs and other officers. **pipe-stem** *n.* the tube of a tobacco pipe. **pipe-stone** *n.* a hard stone used by N American Indians for making tobacco pipes. †**pipe-tree** *n.* **1** the mock orange. **2** the lilac. **pipework** *n.* pipes collectively. **pipy** (pī´pi) *a.* (*comp.* **pipier,** *superl.* **pipiest**). [OE *pipe* (cp. Dut. *pijp*, G *Pfeife*, Icel. *pīpa*), late L *pīpa*, from *pīpāre*, to chirp]

piperaceous (pipərā´shəs), **piperic** (-per´-) *a.* of, relating to or derived from pepper. **piperine** (pip´ərīn) *n.* an alkaloid obtained from black pepper. [L *piper*, PEPPER, -ACEOUS]

piperidine (piper´idēn) *n.* (*Chem.*) a liquid which smells like pepper, formed by the reduction of pyridine. [L, *piper*, pepper, -IDE, -INE]

pipette (pipet´) *n.* a fine tube for removing quantities of a fluid, esp. in chemical investigations. ~*v.t.* to transfer or measure with a pipette. [F, dim. of *pipe*, a pipe]

piping (pī´ping) *n.* **1** the act of playing the pipes. **2** a shrill whistling or wailing sound, a fluting. **3** a covered cord for trimming dresses. **4** a cordlike decoration of icing, cream etc., on a cake or other dish. **5** a quantity, series or system of pipes. ~*a.* **1** shrill, whistling. **2** playing upon a pipe. **piping hot** *a.* very hot.

pipistrelle (pipistrel´) *n.* any small, reddish-brown bat of the genus *Pipistrellus*, the commonest British bat. [F, from It. *pipistrello*, ult. from L *vespertilio*, from *vesper*, evening]

pipit (pip´it) *n.* any larklike bird of the genus *Anthus*. [prob. imit. of the cry]

pipkin (pip´kin) *n.* a small earthenware pot, pan or jar. [etym. uncertain]

pippin (pip´in) *n.* **1** any of several varieties of apple. **2** (*coll.*) an outstanding person or thing. [OF *pepin*, a pip or seed, etym. uncertain]

pippy (pip´i) *a.* (*comp.* **pippier,** *superl.* **pippiest**) full of pips. [PIP[1], -Y]

pipsqueak (pip´skwēk) *n.* (*coll.*) a small, contemptible or insignificant person.

pipy PIPE.

piquant (pē´kənt) *a.* **1** having an agreeably sharp, pungent taste. **2** interesting, stimulating, lively, sparkling. **piquancy** *n.* **piquantly** *adv.* [F, as PIQUE[1]]

pique[1] (pēk) *v.t.* (*pres.p.* **piquing,** *past, p.p.* **piqued**) **1** to irritate. **2** to touch the envy, jealousy or pride of. **3** to stimulate or excite (curiosity etc.). **4** to plume or congratulate (oneself on). ~*n.* ill feeling, irritation, resentment. [F *piquer*, to prick, see PIKE[1]]

pique[2] (pēk) *n.* in the game of piquet, the scoring of 30 points before one's opponent begins to count, entitling one to 30 more points. ~*v.t.* (*pres.p.* **piquing,** *past, p.p.* **piqued**) to score a pique against. ~*v.i.* to score a pique. [F *pic,* etym. uncertain]

piqué (pē´kā) *n.* a heavy cotton fabric with a corded surface, quilting. [F, p.p. of *piquer,* see PIQUE[1]]

piquet[1] (piket´) *n.* a game of cards for two persons, with a pack of cards from which all below the seven have been withdrawn. [F, etym. uncertain]

piquet[2] PICKET.

piracy PIRATE.

piragua (pirag´wə) *n.* (*pl.* **piraguas**) a pirogue. [Sp., from Carib. dug-out]

piranha (pirah´nə), **piraya** (-yə) *n.* a small, voracious, flesh-eating S American tropical fish, of the genus *Serrasalmus* which can attack and wound people and large animals. [Port., from Tupi *pira,* a fish, *sainha,* a tooth]

pirate (pī´rət) *n.* **1** a robber on the high seas, a marauder. **2** a pirates' ship. **3** a person who infringes the copyright of another. **4** an unauthorized radio station. **5** (*coll.*) a bus that runs on the recognized routes of others or overcharges passengers. ~*a.* denoting an unauthorized radio station, video copy etc. ~*v.t.* **1** to publish (literary or other matter belonging to others) without permission or compensation. **2** to plunder. **piracy** (pī´rəsi) *n.* (*pl.* **piracies**) **1** the crime of a pirate, robbery on the high seas. **2** any similar illegal practice, such as hijacking. **3** unauthorized publication, infringement of copyright. **piratic** (-rat´-), **piratical** *a.* **piratically** *adv.* [F, from L *pīrāta,* Gr. *peiratēs,* from *peiran,* to attempt]

piraya PIRANHA.

piripiri (pir´ipiri) *n.* (*pl.* **piripiris**) (*New Zeal.*) a plant of the rose family, *Acaena anserinifolia,* having prickly burs. [Maori]

pirogue (pirōg´) *n.* **1** a large canoe made from a hollowed trunk of a tree. **2** a large, flat-bottomed boat or barge for shallow water, usu. with two masts rigged fore-and-aft. [F, as PIRAGUA]

pirouette (piruet´) *n.* a rapid whirling round on the point of one foot, in dancing. ~*v.i.* to dance or perform a pirouette. [F, a whirligig, a top (cp. It. *piruolo,* a top)]

pis aller (pēz al´ā) *n.* a makeshift, a last resort. [F *pis,* worse, *aller,* to go]

piscary (pis´kəri) *n.* (*Law*) right of fishing.

piscatory (pis´kətəri) *a.* **1** of or relating to fishers or fishing. **2** (*formal*) keen on fishing. **piscatorial** (-taw´ri-) *a.* piscatory. **piscatorially** *adv.* [L *piscātōrius,* from *piscātor,* a fisher]

Pisces (pī´sēz) *n.* (*pl.* **Pisces**) **1** (*Astron.*) a large constellation representing two fishes joined by their tails. **2** (*Astrol.*) **a** the Fishes, the 12th sign of the zodiac. **b** a person born under the sign of Pisces. **Piscean** (-siən) *a.* [L, pl. of *piscis,* a fish]

pisci- (pis´i) *comb. form* a fish. [L *piscis,* a fish]

pisciculture (pis´ikŭlchə) *n.* the artificial breeding, rearing and preserving of fish. **piscicultural** (-kŭl´-) *a.* **pisciculturist** (-kŭl´-) *n.*

pisciform (pis´ifawm) *a.* like a fish in form.

piscina (pisē´nə) *n.* (*pl.* **piscinae** (-nē), **piscinas**) **1** a stone basin with outlet beside the altar in some churches to receive the water used in purifying the chalice etc. **2** a fish pond. **3** (*Hist.*) a Roman bathing pond. **piscinal** (pis´inəl) *a.*

piscine (pis´īn) *a.* of or relating to fish.

piscivorous (pisiv´ərəs) *a.* living on fish.

pisé (pē´zā) *n.* rammed clay forming a wall. [F, p.p. of *piser,* L *pīnsāre,* to pound]

pish (pish) *int.* used to express contempt, disgust etc. ~*v.i.* to express contempt by saying 'pish'. [instinctive sound]

pishogue (pishōg´) *n.* (*Ir.*) sorcery, witchery or enchantment of a sinister kind. [Ir. *píseog*]

pisiform (pī´sifawm, piz´-) *a.* pea-shaped. **pisiform bone** *n.* a small bone in the wrist, on the ulnar side of the carpus. [L *pisum,* a pea, -FORM]

pisky (pis´ki) *n.* (*pl.* **piskies**) (*dial.*) a pixie.

pismire (pis´mīə) *n.* (*dial.*) an ant. [PISS (with alln. to smell of an anthill), obs. *mire,* an ant (cp. Dut. *mier,* E Fris. *mīre*)]

pisolite (pī´sōlit) *n.* a variety of calcite made up of pealike concretions. **pisolitic** (-lit´-) *a.* [Gr. *pisos,* a pea, -LITE]

piss (pis) *v.i.* (*taboo, sl.*) to urinate. ~*v.t.* **1** to discharge in the urine. **2** to wet with urine. ~*n.* (*taboo, sl.*) **1** urine. **2** the act of urinating. **to piss about** to waste time in foolish behaviour. **to piss down** (*sl.*) to rain heavily. **to piss in the wind** to do something futile or detrimental to oneself. **to piss off 1** to go away. **2** to annoy, to bore, to make discontented. **to piss on** to treat with deep contempt, to humiliate. **to piss oneself 1** to urinate in one's clothes. **2** to laugh uncontrollably. **3** to be frightened, nervous. **to take the piss out of** to tease, to make fun of. **piss-a-bed** *n.* (*dial.*) the dandelion. **piss artist** *n.* **1** a habitual heavy drinker, a drunk. **2** a foolish or incompetent person. **3** a person who exaggerates or is insincere. **pissed** *a.* **1** drunk. **2** (*N Am.*) annoyed. **pissed off** *a.* annoyed. **pisspot** *n.* a chamber pot. **piss-take** *n.* the act of making fun of someone. **piss-taker** *n.* **piss-taking** *n.* **piss-up** *n.* a bout of drinking. [OF *pissier* (F *pisser*), prob. imit.]

pissoir (pēs´wah) *n.* a public urinal. [F, from *pisser,* to urinate]

pistachio (pistah´shiō) *n.* **1** an Asian tree, *Pistacia vera,* having a reddish fruit with an edible pale greenish kernel. **2** (*also* **pistachio nut**) the edible pale greenish kernel of the fruit of the pistachio. **3** the flavour of the pistachio nut. **4** a pale green colour. [It. *pistacchio* or Sp. *pistacho,* L *pistācium,* Gr. *pistakion*]

pistareen (pistərēn´) *n.* (*Hist.*) a former Spanish-American silver coin. [from PESETA]

piste (pēst) *n.* **1** a slope prepared for skiing. **2** a rectangular area on which a fencing contest is held. **pisteur** *n.* a person who prepares the snow on a skiing piste. [F, from OIt. *pista* from *pistare,* to tread down]

pistil (pis´til) *n.* (*Bot.*) the female organ in flowering plants, comprising the ovary and stigma, usu. with a style supporting the latter. **pistillary** *a.* **pistillate** (-lət) *a.* **1** having pistils. **2** having pistils but no stamens. **pistilliferous** (-lif´-), **pistilline** (-līn) *a.* [L *pistillum,* a PESTLE]

pistol (pis´təl) *n.* **1** a small firearm for use with one hand. **2** something shaped like a pistol. ~*v.t.* (*pres.p.* **pistolling,** (*N Am.*) **pistoling,** *past, p.p.* **pistolled,** (*N Am.*) **pistoled**) to shoot with a pistol. **to hold a pistol to someone's head** to force someone to do something by threats. **pistoleer** (-liə´) *n.* a soldier armed with a pistol. **pistol grip** *n.* a handle shaped like the butt of a pistol. **pistol shot** *n.* **1** the range of a pistol. **2** a shot from a pistol. **pistol-whip** *v.t.* (*pres.p.* **pistol-whipping,** *past, p.p.* **pistol-whipped**) to strike with a pistol. [F *pistole,* from *pistolet,* a pistol, orig. a dagger, It. *pistolese,* a dagger, from *Pistoja,* where made]

†**pistole** (pistōl´) *n.* (*Hist.*) a foreign gold coin, esp. a 16th- and 17th-cent. Spanish coin. [F, prob. from *pistolet,* perh. as PISTOL]

piston (pis´tən) *n.* **1** a device fitted to occupy the sectional area of a tube and be driven to and fro by alternating pressure on its faces, so as to impart or receive motion, as in a steam engine or a pump. **2** a valve in a musical wind instrument. **3** in an internal-combustion engine, a plunger which passes on the working pressure of the burning gases via the connecting rod to the crankshaft. **piston engine** *n.* an engine in which motion is derived from a piston or pistons. **piston-engined** *a.* **piston ring** *n.* a split ring encircling the piston in a groove. **piston rod** *n.* a rod attaching a piston to machinery. **piston slap** *n.* a noise caused by the piston fitting too loosely in a cylinder. [F, from It. *pistone*, var. of *pestone*, a pestle, cogn. with *pestare*, from late L *pistāre*, freq. of *pinsere*, to pound, see PESTLE]

pit[1] (pit) *n.* **1** a natural or artificial hole in the ground, esp. one of considerable depth in proportion to its width. **2** a pit made in order to obtain minerals or for industrial or agricultural operations. **3** a coal mine. **4** a hole dug and covered over as a trap for wild animals or enemies. **5** hell. **6** a hollow or depression in the surface of the ground, of the body etc. **7** a hollow scar, esp. one left by smallpox. **8** an orchestra pit. **9** the ground floor of the auditorium in a theatre, esp. behind the stalls, or the part of an audience occupying this. **10** an area on a motor-racing course where cars are repaired, their tyres are changed etc. **11** a sunken area in a car workshop giving access to the underside of cars. **12** (*N Am.*) a part of the floor of an exchange, for special trading. **13** an area for cock-fighting, a cockpit. **14** (*sl.*) a bed. **15** an abyss. **16** a trap, a snare. *~v.t.* (*pres.p.* **pitting,** *past, p.p.* **pitted**) **1** to match (against) in a pit. **2** to match, to set in competition against. **3** to mark with pits or hollow scars, as with smallpox. **4** to put into a pit, esp. for storage. *~v.i.* (of the flesh) to retain the impression of a finger when touched. **the pit 1** the grave. **2** hell. **the pits** (*sl.*) a very unpleasant person, thing, place or situation. **to dig a pit for** to try to trap. **pit bull terrier, pit bull** *n.* a sturdy, very fierce variety of bull terrier, sometimes used for dogfights. **pit-coal** *n.* mineral coal. **pitfall** *n.* **1** a hidden danger. **2** a pit slightly covered so that animals may fall in, a trap. **pithead** *n.* (the area or buildings near) the top of a mine shaft. **pitman** *n.* **1** (*pl.* **pitmen**) a man who works in a pit, a coal miner. **2** (*pl.* **pitmans**) a connecting rod in machinery. **pit-mirk** *a.* (*Sc.*) as dark as a pit, very dark. **pit of the stomach** *n.* **1** the bottom of the stomach. **2** the hollow below the breastbone. **pit pony** *n.* (*pl.* **pit ponies**) (*Hist.*) a pony used for haulage in coal mines. **pit prop** *n.* a length of wood, metal etc. used to support the roof of a coal seam during and after mining. **pit-saw** *n.* (*Hist.*) a large saw worked in a saw-pit by two men. **pit-sawyer** *n.* the sawyer who works in a saw-pit, as distinct from *top-sawyer*. **pit stop** *n.* in motor racing, a stop at a pit for servicing and refuelling. **pitted** *a.* having pits or hollow scars, esp. left by smallpox. **pitting** *n.* **pit viper** *n.* a N American viper of the subfamily Crotaline with a heat-sensitive pit on each side of the head. [OE *pytt* (cp. Dut. *put*, G *Pfütze*), L *puteus*, a well]

pit[2] (pit) *n.* (*esp. N Am.*) the stone of a fruit. *~v.t.* (*pres.p.* **pitting,** *past, p.p.* **pitted**) to remove the pit from (fruit). [PITH]

pita PITTA[1].

pit-a-pat (pit´əpat), **pitter-patter** (pit´əpatə) *n.* a tapping, a flutter, a palpitation. *~adv.* **1** with this sound. **2** palpitatingly, falteringly. [imit.]

Pitcairn Islander (pitkeən´) *n.* a native or inhabitant of the Pitcairn Islands.

pitch[1] (pich) *v.t.* **1** to fix or plant in the ground. **2** to fix. **3** to set in orderly arrangement, to fix in position. **4** to throw, to fling, esp. with an upward heave or underhand swing. **5** to pave with cobbles. **6** to expose for sale. **7** to set to a particular pitch or keynote. **8** to put or relate in a particular way. **9** (*coll.*) to tell (a story). **10** in baseball, to throw (the ball) to the batter. **11** in golf, to strike (the ball) with a lofted club. **12** to toss (hay) with a fork. *~v.i.* **1** to encamp. **2** to light, to settle. **3** to plunge, to fall. **4** in cricket, (of a ball) to bounce. **5** to fall headlong. **6** (of a ship) to plunge at the bow or stern. **7** to move with a jolting motion. *~n.* **1** the act of pitching. **2** mode of pitching. **3** the delivery of the ball in various games. **4** height, degree, intensity. **5** extreme height, extreme point. **6** point or degree of elevation or depression. **7** degree of inclination or steepness. **8** degree of slope in a roof. **9** the place or position taken up by a person for buying and selling, a stall. **10** (*coll.*) an attempt at persuasion, usu. to induce someone to buy something. **11** the place in which the wickets are placed or the distance between them. **12** any area marked out for playing sports, e.g. football. **13** the lineal distance between points etc., arranged in series, as between teeth on the pitchline of a cog-wheel, between floats on a paddle-wheel, between successive convolutions of the thread of a screw etc. **14** the height to which a falcon soars before pouncing on its prey. **15** (*Mus.*) the degree of acuteness or gravity of a tone. **16** in cricket, the point at which a bowled ball bounces. **17** in golf, a pitch shot. **to pitch in 1** (*coll.*) **a** to begin or set to vigorously. **b** to participate or contribute. **to pitch into 1** (*coll.*) **a** to assail with blows, abuse, etc. **b** to attack vigorously. **to pitch on** to select, to decide upon. **to pitch up** in cricket, to bowl (the ball) to bounce near the batsman. **to pitch upon** to pitch on. **to pitch wickets** in cricket, to set up the stumps and bails. **to queer someone's pitch** QUEER. **pitch-and-toss** *n.* a game in which coins are pitched at a mark, the player getting nearest having the right to toss all the others' coins into the air and take those that come down with heads up. **pitch circle** *n.* the circle of contact of a cog-wheel in gear. **pitched** *a.* **pitched battle** *n.* **1** a fierce fight or argument. **2** (*Mil.*) a battle for which both sides have made deliberate preparations. **pitched roof** *n.* a sloping roof. **pitch-farthing** *n.* chuck-farthing. **pitchfork** *n.* a large, two-pronged fork with a long handle, used for lifting hay, sheaves of corn etc. *~v.t.* **1** to lift or throw with a pitchfork. **2** to place unexpectedly or unwillingly in a certain situation. **pitch-pipe** *n.* (*Mus.*) a small pipe which is blown to set the pitch for singing or tuning. **pitch shot** *n.* in golf, a shot in which the ball is struck with a lofted club. **pitchwheel** *n.* a gear-wheel. [ME *pichen*, *pykken*, etym. uncertain, perh. rel. to PICK[1]]

pitch[2] (pich) *n.* **1** a dark brown or black resinous substance obtained from tar, turpentine and some oils, used for caulking, paving roads etc. **2** any of various bituminous substances. *~v.t.* to cover, coat, line or smear with pitch. **pitch-black** *a.* deep black, as dark as pitch. **pitchblende** (-blend) *n.* native uranium oxide, the chief source of radium. **pitch-dark** *a.* as dark as pitch, very dark. **pitch pine** *n.* any of various highly resinous pines, esp. *Pinus rigida* or *P. palustris*, much used for woodwork. **pitchstone** *n.* (*Geol.*) a brittle, vitreous, volcanic rock almost identical to obsidian. **pitchy** *a.* (*comp.* **pitchier,** *superl.* **pitchiest**) like pitch; dark, dismal. **pitchiness** *n.* [OE *pic*, from L *pix picis* (cp. Dut. *pek*, G *Pech*, Icel. *bik*)]

pitcher[1] (pich´ə) *n.* **1** a large vessel, usu. of earthenware, with a handle and a spout, for holding liquids. **2** (*N Am.*) a jug. **3** a pitcher-shaped leaf. **4** (*pl.*) pottery which has been crushed and reused. **pitcherful** *n.* (*pl.* **pitcherfuls**). **pitcher plant** *n.* any one of various plants with pitcher-shaped leaves of the families Nepenthaceae and Sarraceniceae. [ME and OF *picher*, med. L *picārium*, *bicārium*, a BEAKER]

pitcher[2] (pich´ə) *n.* **1** a person who or something which pitches. **2** a player delivering the ball in baseball and other games. **3** a block of stone used for paving. **4** a street performer, costermonger etc., who pitches a tent or stall in a particular place.

piteous (pit´iəs) *a.* exciting or deserving pity, lamentable, sad, mournful. **piteously** *adv.* **piteousness** *n.*

pith (pith) *n.* **1** the soft, white tissue under the skin of an orange, grapefruit etc. **2** the essence, the essential part, the main substance. **3** (*Bot.*) a cellular spongy substance occupying the middle of a stem or shoot in dicotyledonous plants. **4** strength, vigour, energy. **5** cogency, point. **6** the spinal cord. **7** importance. *~v.t.* **1** to remove the pith of. **2** to sever the spinal cord of. **3** to kill by pithing. **pith hat, pith helmet** *n.* a lightweight sun-helmet made of pith. **pithless** *a.* **pithy** *a.* (*comp.* **pithier,** *superl.* **pithiest**) **1** condensed, sententious. **2** forcible, energetic. **3** consisting of, like, or containing a lot of pith. **pithily** *adv.* **pithiness** *n.* [OE *pitha* (cp. Dut. and Dan. *pit*)]

†**pithecanthropus** (pithikan´thrəpəs) *n.* (*pl.* **pithecanthropi** (-pī)) *Homo erectus,* an extinct human species of which remains have been found in Java and elsewhere. **pithecanthropoid** (-poid) *a.* [Gr. *pithekos,* ape, *anthrōpos,* man]

pithos (pith´os) *n.* (*pl.* **pithoi** (pith´oi)) in archaeology, a large storage jar. [Gr.]

pitiable, pitiful etc. PITY.

piton (pē´ton) *n.* a bar, staff or stanchion used for fixing ropes on precipitous mountainsides etc. [F, etym. unknown]

Pitot tube (pē´tō) *n.* a right-angled tube open at both ends used with a manometer to measure pressure in a flow of liquid or gas. [Henri *Pitot,* 1696–1771, French physicist]

pitpan (pit´pan) *n.* a narrow, long, flat-bottomed dugout canoe, used in Central America. [etym. uncertain]

pitta[1] (pit´ə), **pita** *n.* a flat, round, slightly leavened bread, hollow inside so that it can be filled with food. [mod. Gr., a cake]

pitta[2] (pit´ə) *n.* a brightly coloured bird of the family Pittidae. [Telugu]

pittance (pit´əns) *n.* **1** a dole, an allowance, esp. of a meagre amount. **2** a small number or quantity. **3** (*Hist.*) a gift or bequest to a religious house for food etc. [OF *pitance,* etym. uncertain, perh. from L *pietas,* PIETY]

pitted PIT[1].

pitter-patter PIT-A-PAT.

pittosporum (pitos´pərəm) *n.* any evergreen shrub of the Australasian genus *Pittosporum,* having small, sweet-scented flowers. [Gr. *pitta,* pitch, *sporos,* a seed]

pituitary (pitū´itəri) *a.* (*Anat.*) of or relating to the pituitary gland. *~n.* (*pl.* **pituitaries**) the pituitary body. **pituitary gland, pituitary body** *n.* a small structure attached by a pedicle to the base of the brain, secreting hormones which regulate growth, the production of other hormones etc. **pituitrin** *n.* a compound hormone extract from the posterior lobe of the pituitary gland. [L *pītuītārius,* from *pītuīta,* phlegm]

pituri (pich´əri) *n.* (*pl.* **pituris**) a solanaceous plant, *Duboisia hopwoodii,* the leaves of which are used medicinally and as a narcotic. [Austral. Abor.]

pity (pit´i) *n.* (*pl.* **pities**) **1** a feeling of grief or tenderness aroused by the sufferings or distress of others, compassion. **2** a subject for pity, a cause of regret, an unfortunate fact. *~v.t.* (*3rd pers. sing. pres.* **pities,** *pres.p.* **pitying,** *past, p.p.* **pitied**) to feel pity for. **for pity's sake** SAKE[1]. **more's the pity** unfortunately. **to take pity on** to feel compassionate or act compassionately towards. **what a pity!** how unfortunate! **pitiable** (pit´iəbəl) *a.* **1** deserving or calling for pity. **2** contemptible. **pitiableness** *n.* **pitiably** *adv.* **pitiful** *a.* **1** calling for pity. **2** pitiable, contemptible. **3** †full of pity, compassionate. **pitifully** *adv.* **pitifulness** *n.* **pitiless** *a.* feeling no pity, merciless, unfeeling, hard-hearted. **pitilessly** *adv.* **pitilessness** *n.* **pitying** *a.* **pityingly** *adv.* [OF *pitet,* L *pietātem,* nom. *-tas,* PIETY]

pityriasis (pitirī´əsis) *n.* (*Med.*) squamous inflammation of the skin, dandruff. [Gr. *pituriasis,* from *pituron,* bran]

più (pū) *adv.* (*Mus.*) more. [It., from L *plūs*]

pivot (piv´ət) *n.* **1** a pin, shaft or bearing on which anything turns or oscillates. **2** a thing or event on which an important issue depends. **3** (*Mil.*) a soldier at the flank about whom a company wheels. *~v.i.* (*pres.p.* **pivoting,** *past, p.p.* **pivoted**) **1** to turn on or as if on a pivot. **2** to hinge (on). *~v.t.* to place on or provide with a pivot. **pivotable** *a.* **pivotability** (-bil´-) *n.* **pivotal** *a.* **1** acting as a pivot. **2** critical, crucial. [F, perh. from It. *piva,* L *pīpa,* a PIPE]

Usage note The use of the adjective *pivotal* in the sense critical or crucial is sometimes disapproved of.

pix[1] PIC.

pix[2] PYX.

pixel (pik´səl) *n.* any one of the minute units which together form an image, e.g. on a cathode-ray tube. **pixelate** (-lāt) *v.t.* to split into pixels. **pixelation** (-ā´shən) *n.* [PIX[1], *el*ement]

pixie (pik´si), **pixy** *n.* (*pl.* **pixies**) a supernatural being akin to a fairy or an elf. **pixie hat** *n.* a child's hat with a pointed top. [etym. uncertain]

pixilated (pik´silātid), **pixillated** *a.* mentally unbalanced, eccentric. [perh. from earlier *pixy-led*]

pixy PIXIE.

pizazz (pizaz´), **pizzazz, pzazz** *n.* (*sl.*) the quality of being exciting, lively and stylish. [etym. unknown]

pizza (pēt´sə) *n.* (*pl.* **pizzas**) a flat, round piece of baked dough covered with cheese and tomatoes, and also often with anchovies, mushrooms, slices of sausage etc. **pizzeria** (-rē´ə) *n.* (*pl.* **pizzerias**) a place where pizzas are made or sold. [It., prob. from fem. of L *pinceus,* of pitch]

pizzazz PIZAZZ.

pizzicato (pitsikah´tō) *a.* (*Mus.*) played by plucking the strings of a violin etc. with the fingers. *~adv.* in this manner. *~n.* (*pl.* **pizzicatos, pizzicati** (-ti)) a passage or work so played. [It., p.p. of *pizzicare,* to twitch, to twang]

pizzle (piz´əl) *n.* (*esp. Austral.*) the penis of an animal, esp. a bull, used as a whip for flogging. [cp. Flem. *pēzel,* LG *Pesel,* Dut. *pees,* sinew]

pk *abbr.* **1** park. **2** peak. **3** peck(s).

PL *abbr.* Poland (IVR).

pl. *abbr.* **1** place. **2** plate. **3** (*esp. Mil.*) platoon. **4** plural.

PLA *abbr.* Port of London Authority.

placable (plak´əbəl) *a.* able to be appeased, ready to forgive, mild, complacent. **placability** (-bil´-), **placableness** *n.* **placably** *adv.* [F, from L *plācābilis,* from *plācāre,* to PLACATE]

placard (plak´ahd) *n.* a written or printed paper or bill posted up in a public place, a poster. *~v.t.* **1** to post placards on. **2** to announce or advertise by placards. **3** to display as a placard. [OF *placard, plaquard,* from *plaquier,* Dut. *plakken,* to paste, to glue]

placate (pləkāt´) *v.t.* to appease, to pacify, to conciliate. **placatingly** *adv.* **placation** (-ā´shən) *n.* **placatory** *a.* [L *plācātus,* p.p. of *plācāre*]

place (plās) *n.* **1** a particular portion of space. **2** a spot, a locality. **3** a city, a town, a village. **4** a residence, an abode. **5** a building, esp. one devoted to some particular purpose. **6** a residence with its surroundings, esp. in the country. **7** an open space in a town. **8** a point or passage in a book etc. **9** a particular place on a surface, esp. on the skin. **10** position in a definite order, as of a figure in relation to others in a series or group. **11** stead, lieu. **12** space, room for a person. **13** rank, station in life, official position. **14** situation, employment, appointment, esp. under government. **15** a vacancy, e.g. for a student at a university. **16** duty, sphere, province. **17** a position among the competitors that have been placed. **18** (*N Am.*) the second position in a race or competition (*win, place or show*). *~v.t.* **1** to put or set in a particular place. **2** to put, to set, to fix. **3** to arrange in proper places. **4** to identify. **5** to assign class to. **6** to put in office, to appoint to a post. 7 to find an appointment, situation or living for. 8 to put in someone's care. 9 to put out at interest, to invest, to lend. 10 to dispose of (goods) to a customer. 11 to make (an order for goods). 12 to arrange (a bet). 13 to set or fix (confidence etc., in or on). 14 to assign a definite date, position etc. to, to locate. 15 in racing, to indicate the position of (a horse etc.), usu. among the first three passing the winning-post. 16 to get a goal by a place-kick. **all over the place** in a mess, in chaos. **in place** 1 suitable, appropriate. 2 (*N Am.*) on the spot (*to run in place*). **in place of** instead of. **in places** at several points. **out of place** 1 in the wrong position. 2 unsuitable, inappropriate. **to give place to** 1 to make room for. 2 to give precedence, to give way to. 3 to be succeeded by. **to go places** (*coll.*) to be successful. **to keep someone in their place** to remind someone of their lowly status. **to make place** MAKE[1]. **to put oneself in another's place** to imagine what one would do if one was in someone else's situation. **to put someone in their place** to humiliate someone who is arrogant, presumptuous etc. **to take one's place** to go to one's rightful position. **to take place** to happen, to occur. **to take the place of** to be substituted for. **place-bet** *n.* a bet that a horse will finish among the first three, or sometimes four, places in a race. **place brick** *n.* a brick imperfectly burnt through being on the windward side of the clamp during firing. **place card** *n.* a small card with a person's name on it indicating their place at a table. **placed** *a.* 1 among the first three, or sometimes four, places in a race. 2 (*N Am.*) second in a race. **place in the sun** *n.* a favourable situation, scope for action etc. **place-kick** *n.* in football, rugby etc., a kick after the ball has been placed for the purpose. **place-kicker** *n.* **placeless** *a.* **placeman** *n.* (*pl.* **placemen**) a man holding an appointment, esp. under government. **place mat** *n.* a table mat. **placement** *n.* **place name** *n.* the name of a place, esp. as distinct from a personal name. **place of worship** *n.* a church, chapel etc., where religious services are held. **placer**[1] *n.* **place setting** *n.* the plate, knife, fork etc. set for one person at a table. **placing** *n.* 1 the fact of being placed. 2 an instance of being placed. [F, from L *platea*, Gr. *plateia*, a broad way, a street, orig. fem. of *platus*, flat, wide]

placebo (pləsēˈbō) *n.* (*pl.* **placebos**) 1 a medicine having no physiological action, given to humour the patient, to provide psychological comfort or as a control during experiments to test the efficacy of a genuine medicine. 2 something said or done to placate someone without addressing the cause of their anxiety. 3 in the Roman Catholic Church, the first antiphon in the vespers for the dead. **placebo effect** *n.* an effect produced by the administration of a placebo, not produced by any property of the placebo. [L, I shall please, 1st pers. sing. fut. of *placēre*, to please]

placenta (pləsenˈtə) *n.* (*pl.* **placentae** (-tē), **placentas**) 1 the organ by which the foetus is nourished in the higher mammals. 2 (*Bot.*) the part of the ovary to which the ovules are attached. **placental** *a.* **placentate** (-tāt) *a.* **placentation** (plasentāˈshən) *n.* (*Zool.*, *Bot.*) the formation, arrangement or mode of attachment of the placenta. [L, from Gr. *plakous plakounta*, contr. of *-oenta*, a flat cake, from *plax*, a flat plate]

placer[1] PLACE.

placer[2] (plāˈsə) *n.* 1 an alluvial or other deposit containing valuable minerals. 2 a place where deposits are washed for minerals. 3 any mineral deposit not classed as a vein. [Am. Sp., from *plaza*, a PLACE]

placet (plāˈset) *n.* permission, assent, sanction. [L, it pleases, 3rd pers. sing. pres. of *placēre*, to PLEASE]

placid (plasˈid) *a.* 1 gentle, quiet. 2 calm, peaceful, serene, unruffled. **placidity** (pləsidˈ-) *n.* **placidly** *adv.* **placidness** *n.* [F *placide*, L *placidus*, as PLACET]

†**placitum** (plasˈitəm) *n.* (*pl.* **placita** (-tə)) a decree, judgement or decision, esp. in a court of justice or a state assembly. **placitory** (-təri) *a.* [L, orig. p.p. of *placēre*, to PLEASE]

placket (plakˈit) *n.* 1 the opening or slit in a garment. 2 the flap of fabric under a placket. 3 a woman's pocket. [var. of PLACARD]

placoderm (plakˈədœm) *a.* (*Zool.*) belonging to the class Placodermi, of fishes, having the head and pectoral region covered with large bony plates. ~*n.* a fish of this division. [as PLACOID, -DERM]

placoid (plakˈoid) *a.* 1 (of fish scales) plate-shaped. 2 (of a fish) covered with placoids. ~*n.* a placoid fish. [Gr. *plax plakos*, a flat plate, -OID]

plafond (plafˈõ) *n.* 1 a ceiling, esp. one of a richly decorated kind. 2 a painting on a ceiling. 3 an early form of contract bridge. [F (*plat*, flat, *fond*, bottom)]

plagal (plāˈgəl) *a.* 1 (*Mus.*) (of the Gregorian modes) having the principal notes between the dominant and its octave. 2 denoting a plagal cadence. **plagal cadence, plagal close** *n.* (*Mus.*) a cadence formed when a subdominant chord immediately precedes the final tonic chord. [med. L *plagālis*, from *plaga*, perh. from med. Gr. *plagios*, orig. oblique, slanting, from Gr. *plagios*, side]

plage (plahzh) *n.* 1 (*Astron.*) a light or dark spot on a spectroheliogram, associated with hot or cool gas on the earth's surface. 2 a beach, a shore at a seaside resort. [F]

plagiarize (plāˈjərīz), **plagiarise** *v.t.*, *v.i.* to appropriate and give out as one's own (the writings, inventions, or ideas of another). **plagiarism** *n.* 1 the act of plagiarizing. 2 something plagiarized. **plagiarist** *n.* **plagiaristic** (-risˈ-) *a.* **plagiarizer** *n.* a person who appropriates the writings or ideas of another and passes them off as their own. **plagiary** *n.* (*pl.* **plagiaries**) literary theft, plagiarizing. [L *plagiārius*, from *plagiāre*, to kidnap]

plagio- (plāˈjiō, plagˈiō) *comb. form* slanting, oblique. [Gr. *plagios*]

plagiocephaly (plājiōsefˈəli) *n.* (*Med.*) the condition of having the skull developed more on one side than the other.

plagioclastic (plājiōklasˈtik) *a.* (*Mineral.*) having the cleavage oblique, as distinct from *orthoclastic*. **plagioclase** (plāˈjiəklāz) *n.* a plagioclastic feldspar.

plagiostome (plāˈjiōstōm) *n.* any fish with the mouth placed transversely beneath the snout, such as a shark or ray. **plagiostomatous** (-stomˈ-), **plagiostomous** (-osˈ-) *a.*

plagiotropic (plājiōtropˈik) *a.* obliquely geotropic, the two halves (of plants, organs etc.) reacting differently to external influences. **plagiotropically** *adv.* **plagiotropism** (-otˈrəpizm) *n.*

plagium (plāˈjiəm) *n.* (*Law*) kidnapping. [L, kidnapping, from *plagiāre*, see PLAGIARY (under PLAGIARIZE)]

plague (plāg) *n.* 1 a pestilence, an intensely malignant epidemic, esp. the bubonic or pneumonic plague. 2 an infestation (*a plague of locusts*). 3 a blow, a calamity, an affliction. 4 (*coll.*) a nuisance, a trouble. ~*v.t.* (*pres.p.* **plaguing**, *past*, *p.p.* **plagued**) 1 to afflict with any calamity or evil. 2 to vex, to tease, to annoy. 3 to affect with a plague. †**a plague on...!** used to express irritation. **plaguer** *n.* **plaguesome** *a.* **plague-spot** *n.* a centre of infection. [OF *plage*, *plague*, L *plāga*, a stroke, cogn. with *plangere*, to beat (cp. Gr. *plēgē*, blow, *plēssein*, to strike)]

plaice (plās) *n.* (*pl.* **plaice**) 1 a European flatfish, *Pleuronectes platessa*, much used for food. 2 AMERICAN PLAICE (under AMERICAN). [OF *pliïs*, late L *platessa*, prob. from Gr. *platus*, broad]

plaid (plad) *n.* 1 a long rectangular outer garment of tartan woollen cloth, worn by Scottish Highlanders. 2 tartan cloth. ~*a.* made of tartan. **plaided** *a.* **plaiding** *n.*

tartan cloth for making plaids. [Gael. *plaide*, cp. Ir. *ploid*]

plain[1] (plān) *a.* **1** clear, evident. **2** simple, without difficulties, easy to understand. **3** easily seen. **4** not intricate. **5** (of knitting) consisting of plain stitches, as distinct from *purl*. **6** without ornament. **7** unvariegated, uncoloured. **8** not in code. **9** not seasoned highly. **10** (of flour) having no raising agent. **11** homely, unaffected, unsophisticated. **12** straightforward, sincere, frank. **13** direct, outspoken. **14** not luxurious. **15** ugly. *~adv.* **1** plainly, clearly. **2** totally, utterly. *~n.* a tract of level country. **as plain as the nose on your face** NOSE. **plain as a pikestaff** PIKE[1]. **to be plain with** to speak candidly to. **plain card** *n.* a playing card which is neither a trump card nor a court card. **plainchant** *n.* plainsong. **plain chocolate** *n.* dark chocolate with a slightly bitter flavour. **plain clothes** *n.pl.* private clothes, as distinct from *uniform*. **plain-clothes** *a.* wearing such clothes (*plain-clothes policeman*). **plain cook** *n.* a person who is skilled at simple, traditional British cookery. **plain dealer** *n.* a person who speaks their mind plainly. **plain dealing** *n.* **plain English** *n.* plain, unambiguous terms. **plain-hearted** *a.* sincere, without hypocrisy. **plain Jane** (jān) *n.* (*coll.*) an unattractive woman or girl. **plainly** *adv.* **plainness** *n.* **plain sailing** *n.* **1** sailing a straightforward course. **2** a simple course of action. **plainsman** *n.* (*pl.* **plainsmen**) a man who lives on plains. **plainsong** *n.* a variety of vocal music according to the ecclesiastical modes of the Middle Ages, governed as to time not by metre but by word accent, and sung in unison. **plain-spoken** *a.* speaking or said plainly and without reserve. **plain stitch** *n.* a simple stitch in knitting, in which a loop is made by passing wool round the right-hand needle and pulling it through a loop on the left-hand needle. **plain suit** *n.* a suit of cards which is not trumps. **plainswoman** *n.* (*pl.* **plainswomen**) a woman who lives on plains. **plain text** *n.* a text which is not in code. **plain time** *n.* working time which is not paid at overtime rates. **plain weaving** *n.* weaving in which the weft passes alternately over and under the warp. **plainwork** *n.* functional needlework, as distinct from embroidery etc. [OF, from L *plānum*, nom. *plānus*, flat]

†**plain**[2] (plān) *v.i.* **1** to mourn, to lament, to complain. **2** to make a mournful sound. [OF *plaign-*, stem of *plaindre*, L *plangere*, to beat (the breast)]

plaint (plānt) *n.* (*Law*) **1** an accusation, a charge. **2** †a lamentation, a mournful song. **plaintless** *a.* [OF, from L *planctus*, a lamentation (with which OF *plainte*, from L *plancta*, fem. p.p. of *plangere*, see PLAIN[2], has been assim.)]

plaintiff (plān´tif) *n.* (*Law*) a person who brings a suit against another, a complainant, a prosecutor.

plaintive (plān´tiv) *a.* **1** expressive of sorrow or grief. **2** having a mournful sound. **plaintively** *adv.* **plaintiveness** *n.* [OF *plaintif*, *-tive* (as PLAINTIFF, -IVE)]

plait (plat), **plat** *n.* **1** a braid of several strands of hair, straw, twine etc. **2** a pleat. *~v.t.* (*pres.p.* **plaiting, platting**, *past, p.p.* **plaited, platted**) **1** to braid, to form into a plait or plaits. **2** to make by plaiting. **plaiter** *n.* [OF *ploit*, *pleit*, L *plicitum*, p.p. of *plicāre*, to fold]

plan (plan) *n.* **1** a drawing of a building, machine etc., by projection on a plane surface, usu. showing the relative positions of the parts on one floor or level. **2** a map of a town or estate, on a large scale. **3** a scheme, a project, a design. **4** an outline of a discourse, sermon etc. **5** method of procedure. **6** one of the ideal planes, perpendicular to the line of vision, passing through the objects in a picture, in which these appear of diminishing size according to the distance. *~v.t.* (*pres.p.* **planning**, *past, p.p.* **planned**) **1** to design, to contrive, to scheme, to devise. **2** to draw a plan of. *~v.i.* to make plans. **to plan on** (*coll.*) to intend. **planform** *n.* the outline of an object, e.g. an aircraft, seen from above. **planless** *a.* **planned** *a.* done according to a plan. **planned economy** *n.* COMMAND ECONOMY (under COMMAND). **planned obsolescence** *n.* built-in obsolescence. **planner** *n.* **planning** *n.* **planning blight** *n.* the reduction in property values caused by uncertainty with regard to possible future building development. **planning permission** *n.* official permission from a local authority etc. to erect or convert a building or change its use. [F, var. of PLAIN[1]]

planar PLANE[1].

planarian (planeə´riən) *n.* any minute, flat, aquatic worm of the division Tricladida, found in salt or fresh water and in moist places. *~a.* of or relating to planarians. [L *plānārius*, flat]

planch (plahnsh) *n.* a slab of metal, firebrick etc., used in enamelling. **planchet** (plahn´chit) *n.* a disc of metal for making into a coin. [F *planche*, a PLANK]

planchette (plahnshet´) *n.* a small, usu. heart-shaped, board resting on two castors, and a pencil which makes marks as the board moves under the hands of the person resting upon it (believed by spiritualists to be a mode of communicating with the unseen world). [F, dim. of *planche*, a PLANK]

Planck's constant (plangks), **Planck constant** *n.* a constant (*h*) which expresses the ratio of a quantum of energy to its frequency. [Max *Planck*, 1858–1947, German physicist]

plane[1] (plān) *n.* **1** a surface such that a straight line joining any two points in it lies wholly within it. **2** such a surface imagined to extend to an indefinite distance, forming the locus for certain points or lines. **3** a level surface. **4** an even surface extending uniformly in some direction. **5** a main road in a mine. **6** a level (of thought, existence etc.). *~a.* **1** level, flat, without depressions or elevations. **2** lying or extending in a plane. *~v.i.* **1** to glide, to soar. **2** to skim across water. **planar** (-nə) *a.* **plane chart** *n.* a chart used in plane sailing on which lines of latitude and longitude are represented by straight, parallel lines. **plane geometry** *n.* the branch of geometry dealing with distances and shapes in one plane, i.e. in two dimensions only. **plane of cleavage** *n.* the plane of weakness along which a mineral or rock tends to split. **plane polarization** *n.* a type of polarization in which the vibrations of electromagnetic radiation are restricted to one direction. **plane sailing** *n.* **1** the art of determining a ship's position on the supposition that it is moving on a plane. **2** plain sailing. **plane-table** *n.* a surveying instrument marked off into degrees from the centre for measuring angles in mapping. *~v.t.* to survey with a plane-table. [L *plānus*, flat, level (cp. PLAIN[1] in use in this sense till 17th cent.)]

plane[2] (plān) *n.* a tool for smoothing boards and other surfaces. *~v.t.* **1** to smooth or dress with a plane. **2** to remove (away) or pare (down) irregularities. **3** †to make flat and even. **planer** *n.* **planing-machine** *n.* a machine for planing wood or metal. [F, from late L *plāna*, as PLANE[1], whence *plānāre*, to plane, and F *planer*]

plane[3] (plān) *n.* any tree of the genus *Platanus*, having large, spreading branches with broad angular leaves palmately lobed. **plane tree** *n.* [F, from L *platanum*, nom. *-nus*, Gr. *platanos*, from *platus*, broad]

plane[4] (plān) *n.* **1** an aeroplane. **2** each of the thin horizontal structures used as wings to sustain an aeroplane in flight.

planer PLANE[2].

planet (plan´it) *n.* **1** a heavenly body revolving round the sun, either as a primary planet in a nearly circular orbit or as a secondary planet or satellite revolving round a primary. **2** in ancient astronomy, each of the major planets, Mercury, Venus, Mars, Jupiter, Saturn, together with the sun and moon, distinguished from other heavenly bodies as having an apparent motion of its own. **the planet** the earth. **planetarium** (-eə´riəm) *n.* (*pl.* **planetariums, planetaria** (-riə)) **1** an apparatus for exhibiting the motions of the planets. **2** a building in which this is exhibited on a large scale. **3** an orrery. **planetary** *a.* **1** of or relating to the planets or the planetary system. **2** terrestrial, worldly. **3** wandering. **planetary nebula** *n.* a ring-shaped nebula round a star, consisting of a shell of gas. **planetesimal** (-tes´iməl) *n.* a small body of matter in solar orbit existing at an earlier stage in the formation of the solar system. **planetesimal hypothesis** *n.* the theory that the planets were formed from the coalescing of planetesimals in a cold state. **planet gear** *n.* a system of gearing in which planet wheels are used. **planetoid** *n.* an asteroid. **planetoidal** (-oi´-) *a.* **planetology** (-ol´əji) *n.* **planet wheel** *n.* a cogged wheel revolving round a wheel with which it engages. [OF *planete*, late L *planēta*, Gr. *planētēs*, from *planan*, to lead astray, *planasthai*, to wander]

plangent (plan´jənt) *a.* **1** sounding noisily. **2** resounding sorrowfully. **plangency** (-si) *a.* **plangently** *adv.* [L *plangens -ntem*, pres.p. of *plangere*, see PLAINT]

plani- (plan´i) *comb. form* level, flat, smooth. [L *plānus*, PLANE[1]]

planigraph (plan´igrahf) *n.* an instrument for reproducing drawings on a different scale. [F *planigraphe* (-GRAPH)]

planimeter (plənim´itə) *n.* an instrument for measuring the area of an irregular plane surface. **planimetric** (planimet´-), **planimetrical** *a.* **planimetry** *n.*

planish (plan´ish) *v.t.* **1** to flatten, smooth, or toughen (metal) by hammering or similar means. **2** to reduce in thickness by rolling. **3** to polish (metal plates, photographs etc.) by rolling. **4** to polish by hammering. **planisher** *n.* [F *planiss-*, stem of *planir* (now *aplanir*), from *plan*, level, PLANE[1]]

planisphere (plan´isfiə) *n.* a plane projection of a sphere, esp. of part of the celestial sphere. **planispheric** (-sfer´-) *a.*

plank (plangk) *n.* **1** a long piece of sawn timber thicker than a board. **2** an article or principle of a political programme. ~*v.t.* **1** to cover or lay with planks. **2** (*coll., esp. NAm.*) to lay down (money, etc.) as if on a board or table. **3** (*coll., esp. NAm.*) to put down roughly. **to walk the plank** to be compelled to walk blindfold along a plank thrust over a ship's side (a pirates' mode of putting to death). **plank bed** *n.* a bed of boards without a mattress (a form of prison discipline). **planking** *n.* planks collectively, for flooring. [ONF *planke*, late L *planca*, prob. cogn. with Gr. *plax plakos*, a flat plate]

plankton (plangk´tən) *n.* minute animals and plants or those of low organization, floating in water at any level. **planktology** (-tol´əji) *n.* **planktonic** (-ton´-) *a.* [G, from Gr. *plankton*, neut. of *planktos*, wandering, from *plazesthai*, to wander]

planner, planning PLAN.

plano- (plā´nō) *comb. form* flat, level. [L *planus*, flat]

planoconcave (plānōkon´kāv) *a.* plane on one side and concave on the other.

planoconvex (plā´nōkon´veks) *a.* plane on one side and convex on the other.

planographic (plānograf´ik) *a.* of or relating to a process by which printing is done from a plane surface. **planography** (-nog´-) *n.*

planometer (plənom´itə) *n.* a plane plate used as a gauge for plane surfaces.

plant (plahnt) *n.* **1** any vegetable organism of the kingdom Plantae, usu. one of the smaller plants as distinct from shrubs and trees. **2** a sapling. **3** a shoot, a slip, a cutting. **4** an offshoot, a descendant. **5** the tools, machinery, apparatus and fixtures used in an industrial concern. **6** a factory. **7** (*coll.*) a person or thing used to entrap another, esp. an article secretly left so as to be found in a person's possession and provide incriminating evidence. **8** mobile mechanical equipment used for earth-moving, road-building etc. ~*v.t.* **1** to set in the ground for growth. **2** to put (young fish, spawn etc.) into a river etc. **3** to furnish or lay out with plants. **4** to fix firmly, to station. **5** to settle, to found, to introduce, to establish. **6** to implant (an idea etc.). **7** to aim and deliver (a blow etc.). **8** (*coll.*) to put into position secretly in order to observe, deceive or entrap. **9** to bury. ~*v.i.* **1** to sow seed. **2** to perform the act of planting. **to plant out** to plant (young plants) outdoors. **plantable** *a.* **plantation** (-tā´shən) *n.* **1** a large estate for the cultivation of sugar, cotton, coffee etc. **2** a large quantity of trees or growing plants that have been planted; a growing wood, a grove. **3** (*Hist.*) a colony or settlement, settling of colonists, colonization. **4** the act of planting. **plantation song** *n.* a type of song formerly sung by black plantation workers in America. **plant-canes** *n.pl.* the crop of sugar cane of the first growth. **planter** *n.* **1** a person who plants. **2** a person who owns or works a plantation. **3** an ornamental pot for plants. **4** an implement or machine for planting. **5** a settler in a colony. **6** (*sl.*) a well-directed blow. **plantless** *a.* **plantlet** *n.* **plantlike** *a.* **plant-louse** *n.* (*pl.* **plant-lice**) an insect infesting plants, esp. the aphis. **plantsman** (-mən) *n.* (*pl.* **plantsmen**) a gardening expert. **plantswoman** *n.* (*pl.* **plantswomen**) a female gardening expert. [OE *plante*, L *planta*, a sucker, shoot or slip, also OE *plantian*, L *plantare*]

Plantagenet (plantaj´inət) *a.* of or relating to the kings of England from Henry II to Richard III. ~*n.* any one of these Plantagenet kings. [sprig of broom (L *planta genista*), worn as a distinctive mark]

plantain[1] (plan´tin) *n.* any plant of the genus *Plantago*, with broad flat leaves and a spike of dull green flowers. **plantain lily** *n.* a hosta. [OF, from L *plantāginem*, nom. *-go*, prob. from *planta*, the sole of the foot, from the prostrate leaves]

plantain[2] (plan´tin) *n.* **1** a tropical American herbaceous tree, *Musa paradisiaca*, closely related to the banana, and bearing similar fruit. **2** the fruit of the plantain. [Sp. *plantano*, *platano*, L *platanus*, PLANE[3]]

plantar (plant´ə) *a.* of or relating to the sole of the foot. [L *plantāris*, from *planta*, the sole of the foot]

plantation, planter PLANT.

plantigrade (plan´tigrād) *a.* walking on the sole of the foot as bears, badgers etc. ~*n.* a plantigrade animal. [F (L *planta*, the sole, *-gradus*, walking)]

planula (plan´ūlə) *n.* (*pl.* **planulae** (-lē)) the locomotory embryo of coelenterates. **planular** *a.* **planulate** (-lət) *a.* **planuliform** (-nū´-) *a.* **planuloid** *a.* [dim. of L *plānus*, a PLANE[1]]

planuria (planū´riə) *n.* (*Med.*) discharge of urine through an abnormal channel. [Gr. *planos*, wandering, Gr. *ouron*, urine]

planxty (plangk´sti) *n.* (*pl.* **planxties**) (*Ir.*) a lively melody for the harp. [etym. unknown]

plap (plap) *v.i.* (*pres.p.* **plapping**, *past, p.p.* **plapped**) to fall with a flat impact. ~*n.* the sound of this. [onomat.]

plaque (plahk) *n.* **1** a plate, slab or tablet of metal, porcelain, ivory etc., usu. of an artistic or ornamental character. **2** a filmy deposit on the surface of the teeth consisting of mucus and bacteria. **3** a patch or spot on the surface of the body. **4** a small plate worn as a badge or personal ornament. **plaquette** (plaket´) *n.* [F, prob. from Flem. *placke*, a coin of the Netherlands]

plash[1] (plash) *n.* a large puddle, a marshy pool. **plashy**[1] *a.* (*comp.* **plashier**, *superl.* **plashiest**) marshy, swampy. [OE *ploesc* (cp. Dut. and LG *plas*) prob. cogn. with PLASH[2]]

plash[2] (plash) *v.t.* **1** to cause (water) to splash. **2** to dabble in. ~*v.i.* **1** to make a splash. **2** to dabble in water.

~*n.* **1** a splash, a plunge. **2** the sound made by a splash. **plashy**[2] *a.* (*comp.* **plashier,** *superl.* **plashiest**) splashy. [prob. imit., cp. Dut. *plassen*, G *platschen*, Swed. *plaska*]

plash[3] (plash) *v.t.* **1** to bend down or cut partly and intertwine (branches), to form a hedge. **2** to make or repair (a hedge) in this way. ~*n.* a branch partly cut and interwoven with other branches. [OF *plessier*, *plaissier*, to PLEACH]

plashy[1] PLASH[1].

plashy[2] PLASH[2].

-plasia (plā´ziə), **-plasy** (pləzi) *comb. form* growth, development, as *hypoplasia.* [new L *-plasia* from Gr. *plasis*, a moulding, from *plassein*, to mould]

plasma (plaz´mə), **plasm** (plaz´əm) *n.* **1** the fluid part of the blood, lymph or milk. **2** sterilized blood plasma used for transfusions. **3** the viscous living matter of a cell, protoplasm. **4** a hot, ionized gas containing approximately equal numbers of positive ions and electrons. **5** a green variety of quartz allied to chalcedony. **plasmatic** (-mat´-), **plasmic** *a.* **plasma torch** *n.* a device in which gas is converted to a plasma by being heated electrically and which is used for melting metals etc. **plasmid** (-mid) *n.* (*Biol.*) a small circle of DNA found esp. in bacteria, which exists and replicates itself independently of the main bacterial chromosome. ~*a.* **plasmin** (-min) *n.* an enzyme in blood plasma that dissolves fibrin. [late L and Gr. *plasma*, from *plassein*, to mould]

plasmo- (plaz´mō) *comb. form* plasma.

plasmodesma (plazmōdez´mə) *n.* (*pl.* **plasmodesmata** (-mətə)) a very fine thread of cytoplasm which passes through cell walls, providing communication between plant cells. [PLASMA, Gr. *desma*, a bond, a fetter]

plasmodium (plazmō´diəm) *n.* (*pl.* **plasmodia** (-diə)) **1** any parasitic protozoan of the genus *Plasmodium*, found in the blood in malaria and quartan and tertian ague. **2** a mass of mobile, naked protoplasm resulting from the fusion or aggregation of numerous amoeboid cells, as in the vegetative stage of slime moulds. **plasmodial** *a.*

plasmolysis (plazmol´isis) *n.* the contraction of the protoplasm in active cells under the influence of a reagent or of disease. **plasmolyse** (-məlīz), (*esp. N Am.*) **plasmolyze** *v.i.*, *v.t.* **plasmolytic** (-məlit´-) *a.*

-plast (plast) *comb. form* a living cell or subcellular particle, as *protoplast.* [Gr. *plastos*, moulded, from *plassein*, to mould]

plasteel (plastēl´) *n.* in science fiction, an extremely strong non-metallic material. [*plastic, steel*]

plaster (plahs´tə) *n.* **1** a mixture of lime, sand etc., for coating walls etc. **2** a sticking plaster. **3** plaster of Paris. **4** (*Hist.*) an adhesive application of some curative substance, usu. spread on linen, muslin or a similar fabric, placed on parts of the body. **5** (*Hist.*) calcined gypsum or sulphate of lime, used, when mixed with water, for coating or for moulding into ornaments, figures etc. ~*a.* made of plaster. ~*v.t.* **1** to cover with plaster or other adhesive substance. **2** to apply a sticking plaster or plaster cast to (a wound etc.). **3** to daub, to smear over, to smooth over. **4** to cause to lie flat or adhere. **5** to cover with excessive quantities of, to use excessively or tastelessly. **6** to stick (on) as if with plaster. **7** (*sl.*) to inflict heavy damage, injury, or casualties on. **plasterboard** *n.* (a thin, rigid board consisting of) a layer of plaster compressed between sheets of fibreboard, used in making partition walls, ceilings etc. **plaster cast** *n.* **1** a covering of plaster of Paris used to immobilize and protect a broken limb etc. **2** a plaster copy, made from a mould, of any object, esp. a statue. **plastered** *a.* (*sl.*) drunk. **plasterer** *n.* **plastering** *n.* a covering or coat of plaster. **plaster of Paris** *n.* gypsum, esp. calcined gypsum, used for making plaster casts. **plaster saint** *n.* (*iron.*) a person regarded as being extremely virtuous. **plaster-stone** *n.* raw gypsum. **plasterwork** *n.* **plastery** *a.* [OE, from L *emplastrum*, Gr. *emplastron, emplaston*, from *emplassein*, to daub on (EM-, *plassein*, to mould)]

plastic (plas´tik) *n.* **1** any of a group of synthetic, polymeric substances which, though stable in use at ordinary temperatures, are plastic at some stage in their manufacture and can be shaped by the application of heat and pressure. **2** (*coll.*) plastic money. ~*a.* **1** made of plastic. **2** (*sl.*) outwardly and conventionally attractive but lacking substance or reality. **3** synthetic, insincere. **4** having the power of giving form or shape. **5** capable of being modelled or moulded. **6** of, relating to or produced by modelling or moulding. **7** continuously extensible or pliable without rupturing. **8** (*Biol.*) capable of adapting to varying conditions. **9** (*Philos.*) formative, causing growth. **10** forming living tissue. **plastically** *adv.* **plastic art** *n.* **1** art which is concerned with moulding, shaping or representation in three dimensions. **2** any visual art. **plastic bomb** *n.* a bomb containing plastic explosive. **plastic bullet** *n.* a cylinder of plastic approximately 4 in. (10 cm) long, less lethal than an ordinary bullet, used mainly for riot control. **plastic explosive** *n.* an adhesive, jelly-like explosive substance. **plasticity** (-tis´-) *n.* **plasticize** (-sīz), **plasticise** *v.t.* **plasticization** (-zā´shən) *n.* **plasticizer** *n.* a substance which renders rubber, plastic, etc. more flexible. **plasticky** *a.* **plastic money** *n.* (*coll.*) credit cards, bank cards etc. **plastic surgery** *n.* the branch of surgery concerned with the restoration of missing, deformed or disfigured parts of the body or with the cosmetic improvement of any feature. **plastic wood** *n.* a malleable material which resembles wood when hardened, used for filling in cracks. [L *plasticus*, Gr. *plastikos*, as PLASTER]

Plasticine® (plas´tisēn) *n.* a soft, modelling substance used esp. by children.

plastid (plas´tid) *n.* a small particle in the cells of plants and some animals containing pigment, starch, protein etc.

plastron (plas´tron) *n.* **1** a padded leather shield worn by fencers to protect the breast. **2** an ornamental front on a woman's dress. **3** a shirt-front. **4** the under part of the buckler of a tortoise or turtle; an analogous part in other animals. **5** (*Hist.*) a breastplate, usu. worn under a coat of mail. **plastral** (-trəl) *a.* [F, from It. *piastrone*, from *piastria*, a breastplate, see PIASTRE]

-plasty (plas´ti) *comb. form* formation or replacement by plastic surgery, as *rhinoplasty.* [F *-plastie*, from Gr. *-plastia*, moulding, from *plassein*]

-plasy -PLASIA.

plat[1] (plat) *n.* **1** a small plot, patch or piece of ground. **2** a plan of a piece of ground. ~*v.t.* (*pres.p.* **platting,** *past, p.p.* **platted**) (*N Am.*) **1** to make a plan of. **2** to lay out in plats or plots. [var. of PLOT]

plat[2] PLAIT.

platan (plat´ən) *n.* a plane tree. **plataneous** (-tā´niəs) *a.* [L *platanus*, PLANE[3]]

platband (plat´band) *n.* **1** a flat, rectangular, slightly projecting moulding. **2** a square lintel. **3** a border or strip of flowers, turf etc. [F *plateband* (*plate*, flat, as PLATE, BAND[1])]

plat du jour (plah doo zhuə´) *n.* (*pl.* **plats du jour** (plah)) the dish of the day on the menu of a restaurant etc. [F]

plate (plāt) *n.* **1** a small shallow vessel, now usu. of crockery, for eating from. **2** a plateful, the contents of a plate, a portion served on a plate. **3** any shallow receptacle, esp. for taking a collection in church. **4** (*N Am.*) a main course of a meal. **5** (*Austral., New Zeal.*) a plate of cakes or sandwiches as a contribution to a party. **6** (*collect.*) domestic utensils, such as spoons, forks, knives, cups, dishes etc., of gold, silver or other metal. 7 plated ware. 8 a flat, thin piece of metal etc., usu. rigid and uniform in thickness. 9 a very thin coating of one metal upon another. 10 a flat, rigid layer of bone, horn etc. forming part of an animal's body or shell. 11 a huge platelike section of the earth's crust. 12 a piece of metal with an inscription for attaching to an object. 13 a number plate. 14 a piece of metal used for engraving. 15 a print taken from a plate. 16 a sheet of glass or other material coated with a sensitized film for photography. 17 an electrotype or stereotype cast of a page of type, to be used for printing. 18 an illustration in a book, often on different paper from the text. 19 a device for straightening teeth. 20 the plastic base of a denture, fitting the gums and holding the false teeth. 21 in baseball, a flat piece of whitened marker which marks the position of a batter and pitcher. 22 (*N Am.*) the anode of a thermionic valve. 23 a horizontal timber laid on a wall as base for framing. 24 a cup or other article of gold or silver offered as a prize in a race etc. 25 a race for such a prize. ~*v.t.* 1 to coat with a layer of metal, esp. gold, silver or tin. 2 to cover with plates of metal for defence, ornament etc. 3 to make a plate of type for printing. 4 to roll or beat into thin plates. **handed to one on a plate** (*coll.*) obtained without effort. **to clean one's plate** CLEAN. **to have on one's plate** to have waiting to be done, to be burdened with. **plate armour,** (*N Am.*) **plate armor** *n.* 1 armour composed of heavy plates of metal with which ships, forts etc., are covered to protect them against artillery fire. 2 defensive armour formerly worn by knights and men-at-arms, as distinct from chain or mail armour. **plate-basket** *n.* a receptacle for spoons, forks etc. **plate-fleet** *n.* (*Hist.*) a fleet of ships carrying bullion, esp. from America to Spain. **plateful** *n.* (*pl.* **platefuls**). **plate glass** *n.* a superior kind of glass made in thick sheets, used for mirrors, large windows etc. **platelayer** *n.* a person who fixes or repairs railway track. **plateless** *a.* **platelet** *n.* a small blood particle involved in clotting. **platemaker** *n.* a person or machine that makes plates for printing. **plate-powder** *n.* powder for cleaning silver. **plater** *n.* **plate rack** *n.* a frame for holding plates and dishes. **plate rail** *n.* a flat rail formerly used on railways. **plate-ship** *n.* (*Hist.*) a plate-fleet ship. **plate tectonics** *n.* (the study of the earth's crust based on) the theory that the lithosphere is made up of a number of continually moving and interacting plates. **plate tracery** *n.* (*Archit.*) tracery, esp. in Early English and Decorated windows, giving the appearance of solid surfaces pierced with ornamental patterns. **plating** *n.* 1 a coating of gold, silver or other metal. 2 in racing, competing for plates. 3 (*collect.*) the plates covering a ship, fort etc. [OF, fem. of *plat*, flat, perh. from Gr. *platus*, broad]

plateau (plat´ō) *n.* (*pl.* **plateaux** (-ōz), **plateaus**) 1 a tableland, an elevated plain. 2 a period of stability after or during an upward progression, a levelling-off. 3 a large ornamental centre dish. 4 an ornamental plaque. 5 a woman's flat-topped hat. ~*v.i.* (*3rd pers. sing. pres.* **plateaus,** *pres.p.* **plateauing,** *past, p.p.* **plateaued**) to level off after an upward progression. [F, dim. of *plat*, a platter, a dish, orig. flat, as PLATE]

platen (plat´ən) *n.* 1 the part of a printing press which presses the paper against the type to give the impression. 2 the roller in a typewriter serving the same purpose. [ME *plateyne*, OF *platine*, from *plat*, flat, as PLATE]

plateresque (platəresk´) *a.* (*Archit.*) in a richly ornamented style resembling silverware. [Sp. *plateresco*, from *platero*, a silversmith (*plata*, silver)]

platform (plat´fawm) *n.* 1 any flat or horizontal surface raised above some adjoining level. 2 a stage or raised flooring in a hall etc., for speaking from. 3 a raised pavement etc., beside the line at a railway station etc. 4 a vehicle or emplacement on which weapons are mounted and fired. 5 a raised metal structure moored to the seabed and used for offshore drilling, marine exploration etc. 6 the small floor by which one enters or alights from a bus. 7 (a shoe with) a thick sole. 8 platform oratory. 9 a political programme, the principles forming the basis of a party. ~*v.t.* to place on or as if on a platform. ~*v.i.* to speak from a platform. **platform ticket** *n.* a ticket allowing access to a railway-station platform to non-travellers. [F *plateforme*, a model, a ground plan (*plat*, flat, see PLATE, FORM)]

plating PLATE.

platinum (plat´inəm) *n.* (*Chem.*) a heavy, ductile and malleable metallic element of a silver colour, at. no. 78, chem. symbol Pt, fusing only at extremely high temperatures, immune to attack by most chemical reagents. **platinic** (plətin´-) *a.* of or containing (tetravalent) platinum. **platiniferous** (-nif´-) *a.* containing platinum. **platinize, platinise** *v.t.* to coat with platinum. **platinization** (-zā´shən) *n.* **platinoid** (-noid) *n.* 1 any of various metals found associated with platinum. 2 an alloy of German silver etc. ~*a.* like platinum. **platinous** *a.* of or containing (divalent) platinum. **platinum-black** *n.* finely divided platinum in the form of a black powder, obtained by the reduction of platinum salts. **platinum blond** *a.* (of a man or boy) having hair so fair as to be almost white. ~*n.* a man or boy with platinum blond hair. **platinum blonde** *a.* (of a woman or girl) having hair so fair as to be almost white. ~*n.* a woman or girl with platinum blond hair. **platinum disc** *n.* the highest award given to a recording artist, group etc. for sales of a particular record, CD etc. above a specified very high number of copies, often presented in the form of a platinum replica disc. **platinum metal** *n.* a platinoid. [formerly *platina*, from Sp., dim. of *plata*, silver, a PLATE]

platitude (plat´itūd) *n.* 1 a trite remark, esp. of a didactic kind. 2 flatness, commonplaceness, insipidity, triteness. **platitudinarian** (-neə´ri-) *n.* a person who habitually uses platitudes. **platitudinize** (-tū´dinīz), **platitudinise** *v.i.* **platitudinous** (-tū´-) *a.* [F, from *plat*, flat, see PLATE]

Platonic (plǝton´ik) *a.* 1 of or relating to Plato, the Greek philosopher, *c.* 427–347 BC, or to his philosophy or school. 2 (**platonic**) not involving sexual desire or activity (*a platonic relationship*). 3 (**platonic**) in theory, harmless. **Platonically** *adv.* **Platonic body** *n.* a Platonic solid. **Platonic solid** *n.* any one of the five regular solids: a cube, tetrahedron, octahedron, dodecahedron, and icosahedron. **Platonic year** *n.* the great or perfect year, estimated by early Greek and Hindu astronomers at about 26,000 years, at the end of which all the heavenly bodies were imagined to return to the same places as they occupied at the Creation. **Platonism** (plā´tə-) *n.* **Platonist** *n.*

platoon (plətoon´) *n.* 1 (*Mil.*) a subdivision, usu. half, of a company, formerly a tactical unit under a lieutenant. 2 a group of people. [corr. of F *peloton*, dim. of *pelote*, PELLET]

plats du jour PLAT DU JOUR.

platteland (plat´əland) *n.* (*S Afr.*) rural areas. **plattelander** *n.* [Afrikaans, flat land]

platter (plat´ə) *n.* 1 a large shallow dish or plate. 2 (*sl.*) a gramophone record. 3 the metal disc in the turntable of a record player. 4 (*Comput.*) a hard disk for storing data magnetically. **handed to one on a platter** (*coll.*) obtained without effort. [ME and A-F *plater*, from *plat*, a PLATE]

platy- (plat´i) *comb. form* broad, flat. [Gr. *platu-*, from *platus*, broad, flat]

platycephalous (platisef´ələs, -kef´), **platycephalic** (-sifal´ik, -kef´-) *a.* (of skulls) flat and broad relatively to length.

platyhelminth (platihel´minth) *n.* the flatworm. [mod. L, *Platyhelminthes* (n.pl.), from PLATY-, Gr. *helminth*, a worm]
platypus (plat´ipəs) *n.* (*pl.* **platypuses**) a small, aquatic, egg-laying mammal of E Australia having a broad bill and tail, thick fur and webbed feet; also *duck-billed platypus*. [Gr. *platus*, broad]
platyrrhine (plat´irīn) *a.* (of monkeys) broad-nosed, as distinct from *catarrhine*. ~*n.* a platyrrhine monkey. [Gr. *rhis rhinos*, a nose]
plaudit (plaw´dit) *n.* (*usu. pl.*) **1** an expression of applause. **2** praise or approval. **plauditory** *a.* [L *plaudite*, imper. of *plaudere*, to applaud (with suppression of final vowel)]
plausible (plaw´zibəl) *a.* **1** apparently right, reasonable or probable, but specious. **2** apparently trustworthy, ingratiating, but insincere. **plausibility** (-bil´-) *n.* **plausibly** *adv.* [L *plausibilis*, from *plaus-*, p.p. stem of *plaudere*, see PLAUDIT]
plaustral (plaw´strəl) *a.* (*facet.*) of or relating to a wagon. [L *plaustrum*, a wagon, -AL[1]]
play (plā) *n.* **1** a series of actions engaged in for pleasure or amusement. **2** sport, exercise, amusement, fun. **3** playing in a game. **4** the manner or style of this. **5** the period during which a game is in progress. **6** a manoeuvre, esp. in a game. **7** free, light, aimless movement or activity. **8** freedom of movement or action. **9** space or scope for freedom of movement or action. **10** a state of activity. **11** gambling. **12** a dramatic composition or performance, a drama. **13** conduct or dealing towards others (esp. as fair or unfair). ~*v.i.* **1** to sport, to frolic. **2** to do something as an amusement. **3** to toy, to trifle with. **4** to take part in a game. **5** (*coll.*) to participate, to cooperate. **6** (of a sports ground) to be likely to produce play as specified. **7** to take one's turn at performing an action specific to a game. **8** to perform in a specified position or manner in a game (*He plays in defence*). **9** to perform on a musical instrument. **10** to move about in a lively, light or aimless manner, to dance, frisk, shimmer etc. **11** to act or move freely. **12** (of a part of a machine etc.) to move loosely or irregularly. **13** (of water, light etc.) to be discharged or directed on to something. **14** to emit or reproduce sound. **15** to take part in a game of chance, to gamble. **16** to behave, to act, to conduct oneself in regard to others (*to play false*). **17** to play a part, esp. on stage. **18** (of a drama, show etc.) to be in performance. ~*v.t.* **1** to give a performance or performances of (a musical or dramatic work, the works of a specified composer or author). **2** to perform music on. **3** to cause to emit or reproduce sounds, esp. music. **4** to emit or reproduce sounds, esp. music. **5** to act the role of. **6** to act, or stage a play, in (a specified theatre or town). **7** to pretend to be. **8** to handle, to deal with, to regard (as). **9** to perform (a trick etc.) esp. in jest or mockery. **10** to engage in (a game or sport). **11** to execute (a stroke, a shot etc.). **12** to proceed through (a game, a rubber etc.). **13** to oppose, to compete against. **14** to play in (a specified position) in a game. **15** to make use of (a player or an implement) in a game. **16** to bring (a card etc.) into operation in a game. **17** to cause (a ball etc.) to move in a certain direction by striking, kicking etc. **18** to gamble on. **19** to give (a fish) freedom to exhaust itself. **20** to accompany (someone entering or leaving a room) with music. **21** to discharge (guns, a hose etc.) continuously (on or upon). **22** to cause to move lightly or aimlessly (on). **at play** engaged in playing. **in play** in fun, not seriously. **to bring into play** to make operative. **to call into play** to put into operation, to introduce as an influence or factor. **to make a play for** (*coll.*) to try to get. **to make (great) play with** to parade, to flourish ostentatiously. **to make play** to act effectively. **to play about** to act in a frivolous or irresponsible manner. **to play along (with)** to seem to agree or cooperate (with). **to play a part** PART. **to play around 1** to play about. **2** to have casual sexual relationships. **to play at 1** to engage in (a game). **2** to perform or execute in a frivolous or half-hearted way. **3** to pretend to be. **to play back** to replay (something just recorded). **to play ball** (*coll.*) to cooperate, to comply. **to play by ear 1** to play without reading the printed music. **2** to react to (a situation) by responding instinctively to events as they occur, rather than by following a plan. **to play down** to treat as unimportant, not to stress. **to play ducks and drakes with** DUCK[1]. **to play false** to betray. **to play fast and loose 1** to be fickle. **2** to act recklessly. **to play first fiddle** FIDDLE. **to play for safety** to play safe. **to play for time** to protract something deliberately to allow other events to catch up. **to play foul** FOUL. **to play God** to (seek to) control other people's destinies. **to play hard to get** (*coll.*) to act coyly, esp. as a come-on. **to play havoc with** HAVOC. **to play high** HIGH. **to play hob** HOB[2]. **to play hookey** HOOKEY. **to play house** HOUSE[1]. **to play into someone's hands** to unknowingly give the advantage to one's opponent. **to play it by ear** not to plan one's actions in advance, to improvise a response as situations develop. **to play it cool** (*coll.*) not to show emotion, to keep calm. **to play (merry) hell with** HELL. **to play off 1** to oppose (one person) against another, esp. for one's own advantage. **2** to take part in a play-off. **3** in golf, to tee off. **to play on 1** to move about lightly or unsteadily on. **2** to continue to play. **3** to exploit. **4** in cricket, to play the ball on to one's own wicket. **5** to perform upon. **to play one's ace** ACE. **to play one's cards close to one's chest** CARD[1]. **to play one's cards well/ right etc.** CARD[1]. **to play oneself in** to accustom oneself to the conditions in a game etc. **to play safe** to take no risks. **to play second fiddle** FIDDLE. **to play the field** FIELD. **to play the fool** FOOL[1]. **to play the game** GAME[1]. **to play the giddy goat** GIDDY. **to play the man** to be brave or courageous, to be a man. **to play the market** to speculate on the stock market. **to play the percentages** (*coll.*) to play cautiously as regards odds in favour of success. **to play to the gallery** GALLERY. **to play up 1** to cause trouble or suffering (to). **2** to misbehave. **3** to malfunction or function erratically. **4** to give prominence to. **5** to play more vigorously. **to play upon** to exploit (something or somebody). **to play up to** to humour, to flatter. **to play with 1** to treat with levity. **2** to amuse oneself with. **to play with fire** FIRE. **playable** *a.* **playability** (-bil´-) *n.* **play-act** *v.i.* **1** to act in a play. **2** to behave insincerely or overdramatically. ~*v.t.* to act (a part). **play-acting** *n.* **play-actor** *n.* **playback** *n.* **1** a reproduction, esp. immediately after the recording has been made, of recorded sound or vision. **2** a device for producing playback. **playbill** *n.* a bill or programme announcing or giving the cast of a play. **playbook** *n.* a book of dramatic compositions. **playboy** *n.* a wealthy man who appears to live only for pleasure. **play-day** *n.* a holiday. **play-debt** *n.* a gambling debt. **played out** *a.* tired out, worn out, used up. **player** *n.* **1** a person who plays. **2** a person engaged in a game. **3** a person skilled in a particular game. **4** an actor. **5** a performer on a musical instrument. **6** a device which plays records, tapes or compact discs. **7** an automatic device for playing a musical instrument. **player-manager** *n.* a member of a team who is also the manager of the team. **player-piano** *n.* a piano with a device by which it can be played automatically. **playfellow** *n.* a playmate. **playful** *a.* **1** frolicsome, sportive. **2** humorous, jocular, amusing. **playfully** *adv.* **playfulness** *n.* **playgirl** *n.* a wealthy woman who appears to live only for pleasure. **playgoer** *n.* a person who regularly goes to the theatre. **playgoing** *a.* **playground** *n.* **1** a piece of ground used for games, esp. one attached to a school. **2** a favourite district for

tourists, mountain climbers etc. **playgroup** *n.* a group of pre-school children who meet regularly for supervised and usu. creative play. **playhouse** *n.* 1 a theatre. 2 a toy house for playing in. **playing** *n.* **playing card** *n.* any of a pack of 52 cards used for card games. **playing field** *n.* a field or open space used for sports. **playlet** *n.* **playlist** *n.* a list of records to be played in a radio show. ~*v.t.* to put on a playlist. **playmaker** *n.* a member of a sports team who often sets up an attack. **playmate** *n.* 1 a companion one plays with. 2 a lover. **play-off** *n.* a game to decide the final winner of a competition, esp. an extra game when two competitors are tied. **play on words** *n.* a pun. **playpen** *n.* a portable framework inside which young children can play in safety. **play-reading** *n.* 1 the act of reading a play. 2 an instance of play-reading. **playroom** *n.* a room for children to play in. **play school** *n.* a nursery school or playgroup. **play-suit** *n.* a garment suitable for a young child to wear for playing. **plaything** *n.* 1 a toy. 2 a person used for one's amusement. **playtime** *n.* time in the school day which is allotted for play. **playwright** *n.* a person who writes plays. **playwriting** *n.* [OE *plega*, cogn. with *plegian*, *plagian*, *plœgian* (cp. Dut. *plegen*, G *pflegen*, to have the care of, *Pflege*, care)]

playa (plīʹə) *n.* (*pl.* **playas**) a dried-up lake in a desert basin. [Sp., a beach, from late Latin, *plagia*]

plaza (plahʹzə) *n.* (*pl.* **plazas**) 1 a public square or open paved area. 2 (*chiefly N Am.*) a shopping mall. [Sp. from L *platea*, see PLACE]

plc, PLC *abbr.* public limited company.

plea (plē) *n.* 1 an urgent entreaty. 2 (*Law*) the accused's answer to an indictment. 3 (*Law*) something alleged by a party to legal proceedings in support of a claim or defence. 4 an excuse. **plea bargaining** *n.* (*chiefly N Am.*) the practice of arranging more lenient treatment by the court in return for an admission of guilt by the accused. **plea bargain** *n.*, *v.i.* **plea tender** *n.* (*Law*) a plea that the accused is prepared to satisfy the plaintiff's claim and has brought the necessary sum of money to court. [A-F *plee*, OF *plai*, *plaid*, L PLACITUM]

pleach (plēch) *v.t.* to interlace, to intertwine, to plash. [ME *plechen*, OF *plessier*, *plaisser*, late L *plectiāre* (not extant), L *plectere*, to PLAIT (cp. PLASH[1])]

plead (plēd) *v.i.* (*past*, *p.p.* **pleaded**, (*esp. N Am.*, *Sc.*, *dial.*) **pled** (pled)) 1 to speak or argue in support of a claim or in defence against a claim. 2 to supplicate earnestly. 3 (*Law*) to put forward a plea or allegation, to address a court on behalf of someone. 4 to urge arguments for or against something. ~*v.t.* 1 to discuss, maintain or defend by arguments. 2 (*Law*) to allege in pleading or argument. 3 to offer in excuse, to allege in defence. **to plead guilty** (*Law*) to admit guilt or liability. **to plead not guilty** (*Law*) to deny guilt or liability. **to plead with** to entreat, supplicate. **pleadable** *a.* **pleader** *n.* **pleading** *n.* 1 (*Law*) a (*usu. pl.*) a written statement of a party in a suit at law. b the art or practice of drawing up such statements. c the act of making a plea. 2 entreating, imploring. ~*a.* imploring, appealing. **pleadingly** *adv.* [OF *plaidier*, from *plaid*, a PLEA]

pleasance (plezʹəns) *n.* a pleasure ground, esp. a park or garden attached to a mansion. [OF *plaisance*, as PLEASANT]

pleasant (plezʹənt) *a.* (*comp.* **pleasanter**, *superl.* **pleasantest**) 1 pleasing, agreeable, affording gratification to the mind or senses. 2 affable, friendly, good-humoured. **pleasantly** *adv.* **pleasantness** *n.* **pleasantry** (-tri) *n.* (*pl.* **pleasantries**) 1 (*usu. pl.*) an agreeable remark, made esp. for the sake of politeness. 2 (*esp. pl.*) a jest, a joke, an amusing trick. 3 jocularity, facetiousness. 4 pleasure, pleasantness. [ME and OF *plaisant* (PLEASE, -ANT)]

please (plēz) *v.t.* 1 to give pleasure to, to be agreeable to. 2 to satisfy, to win approval from. 3 to be the desire or wish of. ~*v.i.* 1 to like, to think fit, to prefer. 2 to afford gratification to someone. ~*int.* a polite formula used in making requests. **if you please** 1 if it is agreeable to you, with your permission. 2 (*iron.*) expressing sarcasm or protest. **may it please you** please. **please yourself** do as you wish. **pleased** *a.* 1 gratified, satisfied. 2 delighted, happy. **pleased as Punch** PUNCH. **pleasedly** (-zid-) *adv.* **pleaser** *n.* **pleasing** *a.* **pleasingly** *adv.* **pleasingness** *n.* [ME *plese*, plaise, OF *plesir*, *plaisir* (F *plaire*), L *placēre*]

pleasure (plezhʹə) *n.* 1 the gratification of the mind or senses. 2 enjoyment, gratification, delight. 3 sensual gratification. 4 a source of gratification. 5 (*formal*) choice, wish, desire. ~*a.* for pleasure. ~*v.t.* to give pleasure to. ~*v.i.* to take pleasure (in). **to take pleasure in** to get enjoyment from. **with pleasure** gladly, willingly. **pleasurable** *a.* giving pleasure, pleasant, gratifying. **pleasurableness** *n.* **pleasurably** *adv.* **pleasure boat** *n.* a boat for pleasure excursions. **pleasure garden** *n.* a public garden used as a meeting place and for lavish entertainments. **pleasure gardens** *n.pl.* a pleasure garden. **pleasure ground** *n.* a park or garden (usu. public) used for outdoor entertainments. **pleasure trip** *n.* [ME and OF *plesir*, *plaisir*, to PLEASE, used as noun]

pleat (plēt) *n.* a flattened fold, a crease. ~*v.t.* to fold or double over, to crease. [var. of PLAIT]

pleb (pleb) *n.* 1 (*derog.*) a common, vulgar person. 2 a plebeian in ancient Rome. **plebby** *a.* (*comp.* **plebbier**, *superl.* **plebbiest**). [short for PLEBEIAN]

plebeian (pləbēʹən) *n.* 1 a commoner in ancient Rome. 2 one of the common people. ~*a.* 1 of or relating to the ancient Roman commoners. 2 of or relating to the common people. 3 ignorant, uncultured. 4 common, vulgar. **plebeianism** *n.* **plebeianize, plebeianise** *v.t.* [F *plébéien*, L *plēbēius*, from *plebs*, earlier *plēbes*, the common people]

plebiscite (plebʹisīt, -sit) *n.* 1 a direct vote of the whole body of citizens in a state on a definite question, a referendum. 2 an expression of opinion by the whole community. 3 in ancient Rome, a law enacted by a vote of the commonalty in an assembly presided over by a tribune of the people. **plebiscitary** (-bisʹitəri) *a.* [F *plébiscite*, L *plēbiscītum* (*plebs plēbis*, *scītum*, decree, p.p. of *sciscere*, to vote, incept. of *scīre*, to know)]

plectognath (plekʹtognath) *a.* (*Zool.*) of the Plectognathi, an order of teleostean fishes having the cheekbones united with the jaws. ~*n.* a fish of this order. **plectognathic** (-nathʹ-), **plectognathous** (-togʹnəthəs) *a.* [Gr. *plektos*, plaited, *gnathos*, a jaw]

plectrum (plekʹtrəm) *n.* (*pl.* **plectrums, plectra** (-trə)) a small implement of ivory etc., with which players pluck the strings of the guitar, harp, lyre etc. [L, from Gr. *plēktron*, cogn. with *plēssein*, to strike]

pled PLEAD.

pledge (plej) *n.* 1 anything given or handed over by way or guarantee of security for the repayment of money borrowed or for the performance of some obligation. 2 a thing put in pawn. 3 a promise of a donation to a charity, or the donation itself. 4 an earnest, a token. 5 an agreement, promise or binding engagement. 6 the state of being pledged. 7 a gage of battle. 8 a health, a toast. 9 one's child. ~*v.t.* 1 to give as a pledge or security. 2 to deposit in pawn. 3 to promise solemnly. 4 to drink a toast to. **†to pledge one's troth** TROTH. **to sign the pledge** to take the pledge. **to take the pledge** to vow to abstain from alcoholic drink. **pledgeable** *a.* **pledgee** (-ēʹ) *n.* **pledger** *n.* **pledgor** *n.* [ME and OF *plege* (F *pleige*), prob. rel. to *plevir*, to warrant, to engage, from Gmc. (cp. PLIGHT[2])]

pledget (plejʹit) *n.* a compress of lint for laying over an ulcer, wound etc. [etym. uncertain]

-plegia (plēʹjə) *comb.form* paralysis, as *paraplegia*. [Gr. *plēgē*, stroke, from *plēssein*, to strike]

pleiad (plī´əd) *n.* a cluster of brilliant persons, esp. seven. **Pleiades** (-dēz) *n.pl.* a cluster of small stars in the constellation Taurus, seven of which are discernible by the naked eye. [L *Plēias -adis*, Gr. *Pleias -ados*]

plein-air (planeə´) *a.* (done) out of doors, esp. in relation to the principles and practice of the Impressionist school of painting. [F]

pleio- PLIO-.

Pleiocene PLIOCENE.

pleiotropy (plīot´rəpi) *n.* (*Biol.*) the production of two or more apparently unrelated effects by a single gene. **pleiotropic** (-trō´pik) *a.* **pleiotropism** *n.* [Gr. *pleiōn*, more, *tropē*, turning]

Pleistocene (plīs´təsēn) *a.* (*Geol.*) of or relating to the strata or epoch overlying or succeeding the Pliocene formation. *~n.* the Pleistocene epoch. [Gr. *pleistos*, most, *kainos*, new]

plenary (plē´nəri) *a.* **1** full, complete, entire, absolute. **2** attended by all members. **plenarily** *adv.* **plenary indulgence** *n.* in the Roman Catholic Church, an indulgence remitting all the temporal penalties due to sin. **plenary inspiration** *n.* full inspiration, with complete freedom from error. [late L *plēnārius*, from *plēnus*, full]

plenipotentiary (plenipəten´shəri) *n.* (*pl.* **plenipotentiaries**) an ambassador or envoy to a foreign court, with full powers. *~a.* **1** invested with full powers. **2** (of power) full, absolute. [med. L *plēnipotentiārius*, from *plēnus*, full, *potentia*, power]

plenist (plēnist) *n.* a person who maintains that all space is full of matter. [PLENUM, -IST]

plenitude (plen´itūd) *n.* completeness, abundance, fullness. [OF, from L *plēnitūdo*, from *plēnus*, full]

Usage note The form *plentitude* (after *plenty*) is best avoided.

plenty (plen´ti) *n.* **1** a large quantity or number, an ample supply, lots. **2** abundance, copiousness. **3** fruitfulness. *~a.* (*coll.*) plentiful, abundant. *~adv.* (*coll.*) very, abundantly. **plenteous** (-tiəs) *a.* **plenteously** *adv.* **plenteousness** *n.* **plentiful** *a.* **1** existing in abundance, copious. **2** yielding abundance. **plentifully** *adv.* **plentifulness** *n.* [OF *plentet*, L *plēnitātem*, nom. *-tas*, from *plēnus*, full]

plenum (plē´nəm) *n.* (*pl.* **plenums**) **1** a full meeting. **2** (*Physics*) space, as considered to be full of matter, opposed to *vacuum*. **3** an enclosure containing gas at a higher pressure than the surrounding environment. **4** the condition of being full. [L, neut of *plēnus*, full]

pleo- PLIO-.

pleochroic (plēəkrō´ik) *a.* (of a crystal etc.) showing different colours when looked at from different directions. **pleochroism** *n.*

pleomorphism (plēəmaw´fizm) *n.* the occurrence of more than one different form in the life cycle of a plant or animal; polymorphism. **pleomorphic** *a.*

pleonasm (plē´ənazm) *n.* redundancy of expression in speaking or writing. **pleonastic** (-nas´-) *a.* **pleonastically** *adv.* [L *pleonasmus*, Gr. *pleonasmos*, from *pleonazein*, to abound or be redundant, from *pleon*, full]

pleroma (plirō´mə) *n.* **1** fullness, abundance. **2** in Gnosticism, the divine being filling the universe and including all the aeons emanating from it. [Gr. *plērōma*, from *plēroun*, to make full, from *plērēs*, full]

☒ **plesant** common misspelling of PLEASANT.

plesiosaurus (plēsiəsaw´rəs), **plesiosaur** (plē´-) *n.* (*pl.* **plesiosauruses, plesiosaurs**) any member of the genus *Plesiosaurus* of extinct marine saurian creatures with long necks, small heads and four paddles. [Gr. *plēsios*, near, *sauros*, a lizard]

plessor PLEXOR.

plethora (pleth´ərə) *n.* **1** superabundance, excess. **2** (*Med.*) **a** excessive fullness of blood. **b** an excess of any body fluid. **plethoric** (-tho-) *a.* **plethorically** *adv.* [med. L, from Gr. *plēthōrē*, fullness, from *plēthein*, to become full]

pleur- PLEURO-.

pleura[1] (pluər´ə) *n.* (*pl.* **pleurae** (ploo´rē)) (*Anat., Zool.*) **1** a thin membrane covering the interior of the thorax and enveloping the lungs. **2** a part of the body wall in arthropods. **3** a part to which the secondary wings are attached in insects. **pleural** *a.* **pleurisy** (-isi) *n.* (*Med.*) inflammation of the pleurae, usu. accompanied by fever, pain in the chest or side etc. **pleuritic** (-rit´-) *a.* [med. L and Gr., side]

pleura[2] PLEURON.

pleurisy, pleuritic PLEURA[1].

pleuro- (pluə´rō), **pleur-** *comb. form* **1** of or relating to the side or ribs. **2** of or relating to the pleura. [Gr. *pleuron*, the side, a rib]

pleurodynia (pluərōdī´niə) *n.* (*Med.*) pain in the side due to chronic rheumatism of the walls of the chest.

pleuron (pluə´ron) *n.* (*pl.* **pleura** (-rə)) (*Anat.*) a pleura. [Gr., the side of the body, a rib]

pleuropneumonia (pluərōnūmō´niə) *n.* (*Med., Zool.*) inflammation of the lungs and pleurae, esp. as contagious disease among cattle.

plexiform PLEXUS.

Plexiglas® (plek´siglahs) *n.* a transparent plastic, the same as Perspex.

plexor (plek´sə), **plessor** (ples´ə) *n.* (*Med.*) an instrument used as a hammer to examine the chest by mediate percussion. **pleximeter** (-sim´) *n.* (*Med.*) a plate employed in examining the chest by mediate percussion. **pleximetric** (-met´-) *a.* **pleximetry** *n.* the art of using the pleximeter. [Gr. *plēxis*, a stroke, cogn. with *plēssein*, to strike]

plexus (plek´səs) *n.* (*pl.* **plexus, plexuses**) **1** (*Anat.*) a network of veins, fibres or nerves. **2** a network, a complication. **plexiform** *a.* [L, from *plectere*, to PLAIT, p.p. *plexus*]

pliable (plī´əbəl) *a.* **1** easily bent, flexible, pliant. **2** supple, limber. **3** yielding readily to influence or arguments. **pliability** (-bil´-), **pliableness** *n.* **pliably** *adv.* **pliancy** (-ənsi) *n.* **pliant** *a.* pliable. **pliantly** *adv.* [F, from *plier*, L *plicāre*, to bend (see PLY[1])]

plica (plī´kə) *n.* (*pl.* **plicae** (-sē)) (*Med.*) **1** a fold of membrane etc. **2** a skin disease in which the hair becomes matted and filthy. [med. L, from *plicāre*, to fold]

plicate (plī´kət, -kāt), **plicated** (-kā´tid) *a.* (*Biol., Geol.*) plaited, folded like a fan. **plication** (plikā´shən), **plicature** (plik´əchə) *n.* [L *plicātus*, p.p. of *plicāre*, to fold]

plié (plē´ā) *n.* (*pl.* **pliés**) a ballet movement in which the knees are bent outwards while the back remains straight. [F, p.p. of *plier*, to bend]

pliers (plī´əz) *n.pl.* small pincers with long jaws for bending wire etc. [obs. *ply*, F *plier*, see PLIABLE, -ER]

plight[1] (plīt) *n.* condition, state, case, esp. one of distress or disgrace. [ME and A-F *plit*, OF *ploit*, a PLAIT]

†**plight**[2] (plīt) *v.t.* to pledge, to promise, to engage (oneself, one's faith etc.). *~n.* an engagement, a promise. **to plight one's troth** TROTH. [OE *plihtan*, from *pliht*, danger (cp. Dut. *plight*, G *Pflicht*, duty, obligation, OHG *plegan*, to engage)]

plim (plim) *v.i.* (*pres.p.* **plimming**, *past, p.p.* **plimmed**) (*dial.*) to fill out, to become plump. *~v.t.* to cause to swell or expand. [perh. rel. to PLUMP[1]]

plimsoll (plim´səl), **plimsole** *n.* a rubber-soled canvas shoe worn for physical education etc. [from the resemblance of the upper edge of the sole to a Plimsoll line]

Plimsoll line (plim´səl), **Plimsoll mark** *n.* a line, required to be placed on every British ship, marking the level to which the authorized amount of cargo submerges it. [Samuel *Plimsoll*, 1824–98, promoter of Merchant Shipping Act (1876)]

plinth (plinth) *n.* 1 (*Archit.*) a square member forming the lower division of a column etc. 2 a block serving as a pedestal. 3 the plain projecting face at the bottom of a wall. [L *plinthus*, from Gr. *plinthos*, a brick]

plio- (plī´ō), **pleio-**, **pleo-** (plē´ō) *comb. form* more. [Gr. *pleiōn* or *pleōn*, more]

Pliocene (plī´əsēn), **Pleiocene** *n.* (*Geol.*) the most modern epoch of the Tertiary. *~a.* of or relating to the Pliocene period. [Gr. *pleiōn*, more, *kainos*, new]

plissé (plē´sā) *a.* (of a fabric) having a wrinkled finish. *~n.* (a fabric having) a wrinkled finish. [F, p.p. of *plisser*, to pleat]

PLO *abbr.* Palestine Liberation Organization.

plod (plod) *v.i.* (*pres.p.* **plodding**, *past, p.p.* **plodded**) 1 to walk painfully, slowly and laboriously, to trudge. 2 to toil, to drudge. 3 to study with steady diligence. *~v.t.* to make (one's way) thus. *~n.* 1 a laborious walk, a trudge. 2 a wearisome piece of work. **plodder** *n.* **plodding** *a.* **ploddingly** *adv.* [prob. onomat.]

-ploid (ploid) *comb. form* (*Biol.*) denoting the number of sets of chromosomes in a cell, as *polypoid.* [as HAPLOID]

ploidy (ploi´di) *n.* (*Biol.*) the number of sets of chromosomes in a cell. [as DIPLOIDY (under DIPLOID), POLYPLOIDY (under POLYPLOID)]

plonk[1] (plongk) *v.t., v.i.* to (be) put down or drop heavily, forcefully or with a plonk. *~n.* 1 the act of plonking. 2 a heavy, hollow sound. **plonker** *n.* (*sl.*) 1 a stupid person. 2 the penis. **plonking** *a.* (*sl.*) large, unwieldy. [imit.]

plonk[2] (plongk) *n.* (*coll.*) cheap (and inferior) wine. [perh. from F *blanc*, as in *vin blanc*, white wine]

plop (plop) *n.* 1 the sound of something falling heavily into water. 2 the act of falling with a plop. *~adv.* suddenly and heavily, with a plop. *~v.i., v.t.* (*pres.p.* **plopping**, *past, p.p.* **plopped**) to fall into water or drop with a plop. [imit.]

plosion (plō´zhən) *n.* in phonetics, the abrupt release of air in the pronunciation of a plosive.

plosive (plō´siv) *a.* in phonetics, produced by stopping and then suddenly releasing the airflow; explosive. *~n.* a plosive consonant.

plot (plot) *n.* 1 a small piece of ground. 2 a plan of a field, farm, estate etc. 3 a complicated plan, scheme or stratagem; a conspiracy. 4 the plan or skeleton of the story in a play, novel etc. 5 a graphic representation. *~v.t.* (*pres.p.* **plotting**, *past, p.p.* **plotted**) 1 to make a plan, map or diagram of. 2 to mark (e.g. the course of a ship or aircraft on a map etc.). 3 to locate and mark on a graph by means of coordinates. 4 to draw (a curve) through points so marked. 5 to lay out in plots. 6 to plan, to devise, to contrive secretly. 7 to plan the plot of (a novel etc.). *~v.i.* to form schemes or plots against another, to conspire. **plotless** *a.* **plotlessness** *n.* **plotter** *n.* [OE *plot*, a patch of ground, perhaps influ. by F *complot*, a conspiracy]

plough (plow), (*esp. N Am.*) **plow** *n.* 1 an implement for cutting, furrowing and turning over land for tillage. 2 arable land. 3 an implement or machine resembling a plough in form or function, such as a snowplough. 4 (**the Plough**) the seven brightest stars in Ursa Major, also called *Charles's Wain* and the *Big Dipper*. *~v.t.* 1 to turn up (ground) with a plough. 2 to make (a furrow) with a plough. 3 to furrow, groove or scratch, with or as if with a plough. 4 to wrinkle. 5 (*sl.*) to reject in an examination. 6 (*sl.*) to fail (an examination subject). *~v.i.* 1 to turn up ground with a plough. 2 to advance laboriously through. 3 (*sl.*) to fail an examination. **to plough back** 1 to plough (grass etc.) into the soil for enrichment. 2 to reinvest (profits). **to plough in** to bury or cover with earth by ploughing. **to plough into** to collide with violently. **to plough out** to root out or remove by ploughing. **to plough the sands** to labour in vain. **to plough through** 1 to smash a way through. 2 to work or read through laboriously. **to plough under** to bury in the soil by ploughing. **to plough up** to break up by ploughing. **to put one's hand to the plough** to begin a task or undertaking. **ploughable** *a.* **ploughboy** *n.* a boy leading the horses drawing the plough. **plougher** *n.* **ploughland** *n.* land fit for tillage, arable land. **ploughman** *n.* (*pl.* **ploughmen**) 1 a person who ploughs. 2 a farm labourer. **ploughman's lunch, ploughperson's lunch** *n.* a cold snack of bread and cheese with pickle, served esp. in a pub. **ploughman's spikenard** *n.* a European composite plant, *Inula conyzae*, having fragrant purple-and-yellow flowers. **Plough Monday** *n.* the Monday after Epiphany. **ploughshare** *n.* the blade of a plough. **ploughstaff** *n.* a spade-shaped appliance for cleaning the coulter etc., of earth, weeds etc. **ploughtail** *n.* 1 the rear part or the handle of the plough. 2 a ploughman, a farm labourer. **ploughwright** *n.* a person who makes or repairs ploughs. [late OE *plōh* (cp. Dut. *ploeg*, G *Pflug*, Icel. *plōgr*, Swed. *plog*, Dan. *plov*)]

plouter (plow´tə) *v.i.* (*Sc.*) 1 to dabble, to paddle, to flounder. 2 to potter (about). *~n.* a floundering, a splashing. [prob. onomat.]

plover (pluv´ə) *n.* any one of several short-billed birds of the family Charadriidae, esp. the golden, yellow or green plover. [OF *pluvier*, prob. from a late L *pluvārius*, from *pluvia*, rain]

plow PLOUGH.

ploy (ploi) *n.* 1 a manoeuvre, a tactic, a stratagem. 2 employment, an undertaking. 3 a game, a pastime. 4 a prank. [etym. uncertain]

PLP *abbr.* Parliamentary Labour Party.

PLR *abbr.* Public Lending Right.

pluck (plŭk) *v.t.* 1 to pull off or out, to pick. 2 to pull, to twitch. 3 to strip by pulling out feathers. 4 to pull the strings of (a guitar etc.) with the fingers or a plectrum. 5 to plunder. 6 to fleece, to swindle. *~v.i.* to pull, drag, or snatch (at). *~n.* 1 courage, spirit. 2 the act of plucking. 3 the heart, lungs and liver of an animal as food. 4 a pull, a twitch. **to pluck up courage** COURAGE. **plucked** *a.* (*usu. in comb.*) as *well-plucked.* **plucker** *n.* **pluckless** *a.* **plucky** *a.* (*comp.* **pluckier**, *superl.* **pluckiest**) having pluck, spirit or courage. **pluckily** *adv.* **pluckiness** *n.* [OE *pluccian* (cp. Dut. *plukken*, G *pflücken*, Icel. *plokke*, Dan. *plukke*)]

pluff (plŭf) *n.* (*Sc.*) a puff, a burst. *~v.t.* 1 to emit in a puff or puffs. 2 to shoot. *~v.i.* to become swollen. **pluffy** *a.* (*comp.* **pluffier**, *superl.* **pluffiest**). [imit.]

plug (plŭg) *n.* 1 a piece of wood or other substance used to stop a hole; a stopper, a peg, a wedge. 2 anything wedged in or stopping up a pipe, or used to block the outlet to a wastepipe. 3 a piece of wood etc. inserted into masonry to take a nail or screw. 4 a mass of volcanic rock stopping a vent. 5 a cake, stick or small piece of compressed tobacco. 6 a spark plug. 7 a fireplug. 8 a device with a non-conducting case, having three or two pins, which is attached to an electric cable to make an electrical connection with a suitable socket. 9 (*coll.*) an electrical socket. 10 (*coll.*) a piece of favourable publicity, esp. one inserted into other material. *~v.t.* (*pres.p.* **plugging**, *past, p.p.* **plugged**) 1 to stop with a plug. 2 to insert as a plug. 3 (*sl.*) to shoot. 4 (*sl.*) to strike with the fist. 5 (*coll.*) to give favourable publicity to (something), esp. by alluding to it repeatedly. **to plug away at** to work doggedly and persistently at. **to plug in** to establish an electrical connection (with). **to pull the plug on** (*coll.*) to bring to an (abrupt) end. **plugger** *n.* **plugging** *n.* **plughole** *n.* the outlet for waste water in a sink, bath etc., which can be closed with a plug. **plug-in** *a.* able to be connected by means of a plug. **plug-ugly** *n.* (*pl.* **plug-uglies**) (*N Am., sl.*) a hooligan, a rowdy. *~a.* looking like a hooligan. [prob. from MDut. *plugge* (Dut. *plug*, cp. G *Pflock*)]

plum (plŭm) *n.* **1** a small, sweet, fleshy fruit with reddish or purple skin. **2** (*also* **plum tree**) a tree of the genus *Prunus* bearing plums. **3** the wood of the plum tree. **4** a dried grape or raisin used in cakes, puddings etc. **5** plum colour. **6** the best part of anything, the choicest thing of a set. *~a.* **1** dark reddish-purple. **2** choice, cushy (*a plum job*). **a plum in one's mouth** a voice which is rich to the point of affectation. **plum cake** *n.* a cake containing raisins, currants etc. **plum colour,** (*N Am.*) **plum color** *n.* dark reddish purple. **plum duff** *n.* a plain boiled flour pudding with raisins etc. **plummy** *a.* (*comp.* **plummier,** *superl.* **plummiest**) **1** full of or rich in plums. **2** luscious, inviting, desirable. **3** (of the voice) rich to the point of affectation. **plum-porridge** *n.* porridge with raisins or currants. **plum pudding** *n.* a pudding containing raisins, currants, etc., esp. a rich one with spices etc., eaten at Christmas. [OE *plūme*, late L *prūna*, L *prūmum*, late Gr. *prounon*, Gr. *proumnon*]

plumage, plumassier PLUME.

plumb[1] (plŭm) *n.* **1** a weight, usu. of lead, attached to a line, used to test perpendicularity. **2** a position parallel to this, the vertical. **3** a sounding lead, a plummet. *~adv.* **1** exactly, correctly, right. **2** vertically. **3** (*N Am., sl.*) completely, very (*plumb ugly*). *~a.* **1** perpendicular, vertical. **2** downright, sheer, perfect, complete. **3** in cricket, (of a wicket) level. *~v.t.* **1** to sound with a plummet, to measure the depth of. **2** to adjust by a plumb line. **3** to make vertical or perpendicular. **4** to experience in the extreme (*to plumb the depths of despair*). **5** to fathom, to understand. **out of plumb** not exactly vertical. **plumb bob** *n.* a conical weight used in a plumb rule or on a plumb line. **plumbeous** (-biəs) *a.* **1** consisting of or resembling lead. **2** glazed with lead. **plumbic** (-bik) *a.* **1** of, relating to, derived from or combined with lead. **2** due to the presence of lead. **plumbiferous** (-bif´-) *a.* containing or yielding lead. **plumbism** (-bizm) *n.* (*Med.*) lead poisoning. **plumbless** *a.* fathomless, too deep to measure. **plumb line** *n.* **1** the cord by which a plumb is suspended for testing perpendicularity. **2** a vertical line. **plumbous** (-bəs) *a.* (*Chem.*) containing lead in its divalent form. **plumb rule** *n.* a mason's or carpenter's rule with a plumb line attached. [F *plomb*, L *plumbum*, lead]

plumb[2] (plŭm) *v.t.* **1** to provide with plumbing. **2** to plumb in. *~v.i.* to work as a plumber. **to plumb in** to connect to a water main and/or drainage system. [back formation from PLUMBER]

plumbago (plŭmbā´gō) *n.* (*pl.* **plumbagos**) **1** graphite. **2** a perennial herb of the genus *Plumbago*, with blue, rose or violet flowers. **plumbaginous** (-baj´i-) *a.* [L *plumbāgo -ginis*, from *plumbum*, lead]

plumbean, plumbeous etc. PLUMB[1].

plumber (plŭm´ə) *n.* **1** a person who fits and repairs cisterns, pipes, drains, gas fittings etc., in buildings. **2** (*Hist.*) a person who worked in lead. **plumber-block** PLUMMER-BLOCK. **plumber's snake** *n.* a long flexible wire for unblocking drains or cleaning obstacles in piping. **plumbing** *n.* **1** the arrangement of water pipes, gas installations etc. in a building. **2** the work of a plumber. **3** (*coll.*) the lavatory or lavatories. [OF *plummier* (F *plumbier*), L *plumbārius*, as PLUMBAGO]

plume (ploom) *n.* **1** a feather, esp. a large or conspicuous one. **2** a feather-bunch or tuft of feathers, or anything resembling this worn as an ornament. **3** something resembling a plume (*a plume of smoke*). **4** (*Zool.*) a feather-like part or form. **5** a feathery appendage to a seed etc. *~v.t.* **1** to adorn with or as with feathers. **2** to pride oneself (on something). **3** to trim, dress, or arrange (feathers), to preen. **4** to strip of feathers. **plumage** (-mij) *n.* a bird's entire covering of feathers. **plumaged** *a.* **plumassier** (-məsiə´) *n.* a worker or dealer in feathers for clothing. **plumeless** *a.* **plumelet** *n.* **plumelike** *a.* **plume moth** *n.* a small moth of the family Pterophoridae, having long legs and feathery wings. **plumery** *n.* **plumose** (-ōs), **plumous** *a.* resembling a feather or feathers, feathery. **plumy** *a.* (*comp.* **plumier,** *superl.* **plumiest**) **1** feathery. **2** adorned with plumes. **3** covered with feathers. [OF, from L *plūma*]

plummer-block (plŭm´ə), **plumber-block** *n.* a pillow block. [etym. uncertain]

plummet (plŭm´it) *n.* **1** a weight attached to a line used for sounding. **2** a ball of lead for a plumb line. **3** a weight attached to a fishing line, used to keep the float upright. *~v.i.* (*pres.p.* **plummeting,** *past, p.p.* **plummeted**) to fall sharply or rapidly. [OF *plommet*, dim. of *plomb*, PLUMB[1]]

plummy PLUM.

plump[1] (plŭmp) *a.* **1** well-rounded, fat, fleshy, chubby. **2** (of a purse etc.) well-filled. **3** rich, abundant. *~v.t.* to make plump; to fatten, to distend. *~v.i.* to grow plump; to swell (out or up). **to plump up** to make (pillows or cushions) rounded and soft by shaking. **plumper**[1] *n.* a dish, ball or pad carried in the mouth by actors to distend hollow cheeks. **plumpish** *a.* **plumply**[1] *adv.* **plumpness** *n.* **plumpy** *a.* (*comp.* **plumpier,** *superl.* **plumpiest**). [cp. LG and EFris. *plump*, Dut. *plomp*, rude, blunt, Swed., Dan., and G *plump*, coarse, rude]

plump[2] (plŭmp) *v.i.* **1** to plunge or fall suddenly and heavily. **2** to vote for one candidate when more might be voted for. **3** to give all one's votes to a single candidate. *~v.t.* **1** to fling or drop suddenly and heavily. **2** to say suddenly, to blurt out. *~n.* **1** a sudden plunge, a heavy fall. **2** the sound of a plump. *~adv.* (*coll.*) **1** suddenly and heavily. **2** directly, straight down. **3** flatly, bluntly. *~a.* (*coll.*) downright, plain, blunt. **to plump for** to decide in favour of, to choose. **plumper**[2] *n.* **1** a vote given to a single candidate when more than one has to be elected. **2** a voter who plumps. **3** (*sl.*) a downright lie. **4** a person who or something which plumps. **plumply**[2] *adv.* bluntly, flatly, plainly. [cp. LG *plumpen*, Dut. *plompen*]

plumper[1] PLUMP[1].

plumper[2] PLUMP[2].

plumply[1] PLUMP[1].

plumply[2] PLUMP[2].

plumularian (ploomūleə´riən) *n.* any member of the genus *Plumularia* of plumelike hydroids. *~a.* of or relating to plumularians. [as PLUMULE]

plumule (ploo´mūl) *n.* **1** the rudimentary stem in an embryo. **2** a little feather, one of the down feathers. **3** a downy scale on the wings of butterflies etc. **plumulaceous** (-lā´shəs), **plumular** *a.* [L *plūmula*, dim. of *plūma*, a PLUME]

plumy PLUME.

plunder (plŭn´də) *v.t.* **1** to pillage, to rob, to strip. **2** to steal from. *~n.* **1** forcible or systematic robbery. **2** spoil, booty. **3** (*coll.*) profit, gain. **4** (*N Am.*) luggage, personal belongings. **plunderage** (-rij) *n.* **1** pillage, esp. the embezzlement of goods on board ship. **2** the booty so obtained. **plunderer** *n.* [G *plündern*, to plunder, orig. household stuff, from *Plunder*, bedclothes etc.]

plunge (plŭnj) *v.t.* **1** to force or thrust into water or other fluid. **2** to immerse. **3** to force, to drive (into a condition, action etc.). *~v.i.* **1** to throw oneself, to dive (into). **2** to rush or enter impetuously (into a place, condition, etc.). **3** to fall or descend very steeply or suddenly. **4** to decrease quickly and suddenly. **5** (of a horse) to throw the body forward and the hind legs up. **6** (of a ship) to pitch. **7** (*coll.*) to gamble or bet recklessly, to spend money or get into debt heavily. *~n.* **1** the act of plunging, a dive. **2** a sudden and violent movement. **3** a risky or critical step. **to take the plunge** (*coll.*) to commit oneself after hesitating. **plunge neckline** *n.* a plunging neckline. **plunger** *n.* **1** a part of a machine working with a plunging motion, such as the long solid cylinder used as a piston in a force pump. 2 a rubber suction cup on a handle, used to unblock drains etc. 3 (*coll.*) a reckless gambler, speculator or spendthrift. 4 a person who plunges. **plunging** *a.*, *n.* **plunging neckline** *n.* a low-cut neckline on a woman's dress or top. [OF *plunjer* (F *plonger*), prob. from late L *plumbicāre* (not extant), from L *plumbum*, lead]

plunk (plŭngk) *n.* 1 a dull, metallic sound. 2 (*N Am.*) a heavy blow. 3 (*N Am.*) a plonk. ~*v.t.* 1 to cause to emit a plunk. 2 (*N Am.*) to hit heavily. 3 (*N Am.*) to plonk. 4 to pluck the strings of (a banjo etc.). ~*v.i.* to emit a plunk.

plup. *abbr.* pluperfect.

pluperfect (ploopœ´fikt) *a.* (*Gram.*) expressing action or time prior to some other past time. ~*n.* 1 the pluperfect tense. 2 a pluperfect form. [L *plūs quam perfectum*, more than perfect]

plural (pluə´rəl) *a.* 1 consisting of more than one. 2 (*Gram.*) denoting more than one. ~*n.* 1 (*Gram.*) **a** the form of a word which expresses more than one, or (in languages having a dual number) more than two. **b** the plural number. **pluralism** *n.* 1 the state of being plural. 2 the holding of more than one office, esp. an ecclesiastical benefice, at the same time. 3 a system of power-sharing among several political parties. 4 a system of devolution, rather than overall state control. 5 (*Philos.*) the doctrine that there is more than one ultimate principle in the universe, as distinct from *monism*. 6 a social system in which members of diverse ethnic, cultural etc. groups coexist, preserving their own customs and lifestyle but having equal access to power. **pluralist** *n.* **pluralistic** (-lis´-) *a.* **pluralistically** *adv.* **plurality** (-ral´-) *n.* (*pl.* **pluralities**) 1 pluralism. 2 a majority, or the excess of (votes etc.) over the next highest number. 3 (*Math.*) a number consisting of two or more. 4 a benefice or other office held by a pluralist. **pluralize, pluralise** *v.t.* **pluralization** (-zā´shən) *n.* **plurally** *adv.* **plural voter** *n.* an elector with a vote in more than one constituency. [OF *plurel*, L *plūrālis* from *plūs plūris*, more]

pluri- (pluə´ri) *comb. form* several, more, more than one. [L *plūs plūris*, more]

pluriliteral (pluərilit´ərəl) *a.* in Hebrew grammar, containing more than the usual number of letters, i.e. more than three.

plurilocular (pluərilok´ūlə) *a.* multilocular.

pluripara (pluərip´ərə) *n.* a woman who has given birth to more than one child.

plus (plŭs) *prep.* 1 (*Math.*) with the addition of. 2 (of temperature) above zero. 3 (*coll.*) having gained. ~*a.* 1 at least (after a number). 2 better than (after an exam grade). 3 (*Math.*) above zero, positive. 4 electrified positively. 5 additional, extra, esp. additional and advantageous. ~*n.* 1 a plus sign. 2 an addition, a positive quantity. 3 an advantage, a positive feature. 4 a surplus. ~*conj.* (*coll.*) and in addition, and what is more. **plus fours** *n.pl.* long, baggy knickerbockers for men. **plus sign** *n.* a character (+) used as the sign of addition. [L, more]

Usage note The use of *plus* as a conjunction is sometimes disapproved of.

plus ça change (plü sa shãzh´) *int.* used to express the view that superficial changes cannot alter the essential nature of something, esp. human nature. [F *plus ça change, plus c'est la même chose*, the more it changes, the more it stays the same]

plush (plŭsh) *n.* 1 a cloth of various materials with a pile or nap longer than that of velvet. 2 (*pl.*) breeches made of plush, worn by footmen. ~*a.* 1 made of plush. 2 plushy. **plushly** *adv.* **plushness** *n.* **plushy** *a.* (*comp.* **plushier**, *superl.* **plushiest**) (*coll.*) rich, luxurious, lavish. **plushiness** *n.* [F *pluche*, contr. form of *peluche* (cp. Sp. *pelusa*, It. *peluzza*), prob. from a late L *pilūceus*, hairy, from *pilus*, a hair]

plutarchy (ploo´tahki) *n.* (*pl.* **plutarchies**) (a) plutocracy. [Gr. *plutos*, wealth, *archein*, to rule]

pluteus (ploo´tiəs) *n.* (*pl.* **pluteuses**) a free-swimming larva of a sea urchin etc. [L]

Pluto (ploo´tō) *n.* the ninth planet in the solar system in order of distance from the sun. **Plutonian** (-tō´-) *a.* 1 of or relating to Pluto or the lower regions. 2 infernal, subterranean, dark. **plutonic** (-ton´-) *a.* 1 (*Geol.*) igneous. 2 (**Plutonic**) Plutonian. [L *Plūtōnius*, Gr. *Ploutōnios*, from *Ploutōn*, the god of the infernal regions]

pluto- (ploo´tō) *comb. form* of or relating to wealth. [see PLUTO]

plutocracy (plootok´rəsi) *n.* (*pl.* **plutocracies**) 1 the rule of wealth or the rich. 2 a state ruled by a plutocracy. 3 a ruling class of rich people. **plutocrat** (ploo´təkrat) *n.* (*esp. derog., facet.*) 1 a member of a plutocracy. 2 a wealthy, powerful person. **plutocratic** (-krat´-) *a.* **plutocratically** *adv.* [Gr. *ploutokratia* (*ploutos*), wealth]

pluto-democracy (plootōdimok´rəsi) *n.* (*pl.* **pluto-democracies**) (a) democracy dominated by wealth.

plutolatry (plootol´ətri) *n.* worship of wealth.

pluton (ploo´tən) *n.* (*Geol.*) a mass of plutonic rock.

plutonium (plootō´niəm) *n.* a radioactive element, at. no. 94, chem. symbol Pu, formed by the radioactive decay of neptunium.

pluvial (ploo´viəl) *a.* 1 of or relating to rain, rainy. 2 (*Geol.*) due to the action of rain. **pluviometer** (-om´itə) *n.* a rain gauge. **pluviometric** (-met´-) *a.* **pluviometrical** *a.* **pluviometrically** *adv.* **pluvious** *a.* **pluvius insurance** *n.* insurance to cover damage sustained through bad weather. [F, from L *pluviālis*, from *pluvia*, rain]

ply[1] (plī) *n.* (*pl.* **plies**) 1 a thickness, a layer. 2 a fold, a plait, a twist, a strand (of a rope, twine etc.). **plywood** *n.* board consisting of three or more thin layers of wood glued together in such a manner that the grain of each is at right-angles to that of its neighbour. [F *pli*, fold, OF *ploy*, from *ployer* (F *plier*), L *plicāre*, to bend]

ply[2] (plī) *v.t.* (*3rd pers. sing. pres.* **plies**, *pres.p.* **plying**, *past, p.p.* **plied**) 1 to use (a tool) vigorously or busily. 2 to work at, to employ oneself in. 3 to pursue, to press, to persist in questioning. 4 to supply (with) or subject (to) repeatedly. 5 to travel regularly along. ~*v.i.* 1 to go to and fro, to travel or sail regularly. 2 to be busy, to be employed. 3 to stand or wait for custom. 4 (*Naut.*) to sail to windward. [from ME *applier*, to APPLY]

Plymouth Brethren (plim´əth) *n.pl.* a strict evangelical group formed at Plymouth about 1830, having no regular ministry and formulating no creed. **Plymouthism** *n.* **Plymouthite** (-īt) *n.* [*Plymouth*, town in Devon]

PM *abbr.* 1 Prime Minister. 2 post-mortem. 3 Provost Marshal.

Pm *chem. symbol* promethium.

pm *abbr.* premium.

p.m. *abbr.* post meridiem (after noon).

PMG *abbr.* 1 Paymaster General. 2 Postmaster General.

PMS *abbr.* premenstrual syndrome.

PMT *abbr.* premenstrual tension.

PNdB *abbr.* perceived noise decibel(s).

pneuma (nū´mə) *n.* breath, spirit, soul. [Gr., wind, spirit, see PNEUMATIC]

pneumatic (nūmat´ik) *a.* 1 of, relating to or consisting of air, gaseous. 2 actuated by means of compressed air or a vacuum. 3 containing or filled with air. 4 having air-filled cavities. 5 (*Theol.*) spiritual. ~*n.* a pneumatic tyre. **pneumatically** *adv.* **pneumatic drill** *n.* a rock drill in which compressed air reciprocates a loose piston which hammers a steel bit. **pneumaticity** (-tis´-) *n.* **pneumatics** *n.* the branch of science concerned with the mechanical properties of air and other gases. **pneumatic trough** *n.* a trough containing mercury or water used for the collection of gases in inverted vessels slightly immersed. **pneumatic tyre,** (*N Am.*) **pneumatic tire** *n.* a rubber tube inflated with air under pressure, used as a tyre for cycles, motor cars etc. [L *pneumaticus*, Gr. *pneumatikos*, from *pneuma -matos*, wind, cogn. with *pneein*, to breathe]

pneumato- (nū´mətō) *comb. form* **1** air. **2** breath. **3** spirit, soul. [PNEUMA]

pneumatology (nūmətol´əji) *n.* **1** the theory of spiritual existence. **2** (*Theol.*) the doctrine of the Holy Spirit. **3** †psychology. **pneumatological** (-təloj´-) *a.* **pneumatologist** *n.*

pneumatometer (nūmətom´itə) *n.* (*Med.*) an instrument for measuring the air exhaled at one expiration.

pneumatophore (nū´mətəfaw) *n.* **1** the pneumatocyst or other air cavity of a compound hydrozoon. **2** a respiratory organ in the roots of some tropical trees growing in mud.

pneumo- (nū´mō) *comb. form* of or relating to the lungs. [Gr. *pneumōn -monos*, a lung]

pneumococcus (nūmōkok´əs) *n.* (*pl.* **pneumococci** (-kok´sī)) (*Med.*) a bacterium which causes pneumonia.

pneumoconiosis (nūmōkōniō´sis) *n.* any disease of the lungs or bronchi caused by habitually inhaling metallic or mineral dust. [Gr. *konis*, dust]

pneumocystis carinii pneumonia (nūmosistis kərī´niī) *n.* (*Med.*) a fatal lung infection common among Aids patients; PCP.

pneumogastric (nūmōgas´trik) *a.* of or relating to the lungs and the stomach.

pneumonectomy (nūmōnek´təmi) *n.* (*pl.* **pneumonectomies**) the surgical removal of a lung or part of a lung.

pneumonia (nūmō´niə) *n.* acute inflammation of a lung or the lungs. **pneumonic** (-mon´-) *a.* **pneumonic plague** *n.* a contagious bacterial disease causing fever, delirium and infection of the lungs. **pneumonitic** (-nit´-) *a.* **pneumonitis** (-nī´tis) *n.* [Gr. *pneumōn -monos*, a lung]

pneumothorax (nūmōthaw´raks) *n.* (*Med.*) accumulation of air in the pleural cavity, usu. associated with pleurisy.

PNG *abbr.* Papua New Guinea.

PO *abbr.* **1** Petty Officer. **2** Pilot Officer. **3** postal order. **4** Post Office.

Po *chem. symbol* polonium.

po (pō) *n.* (*pl.* **pos**) (*coll.*) a chamber pot. [prob. euphem. F pronunciation of *pot*]

POA *abbr.* Prison Officers' Association.

poa (pō´ə) *n.* any plant of the genus *Poa* of grasses, meadow grass. [Gr., grass]

p.o.a. *abbr.* price on application.

poach[1] (pōch) *v.t.* to cook (an egg, fish etc.) in simmering liquid. **poacher**[1] *n.* [OF *pochier* (F *pocher*), from *poche*, pocket, see POKE[2]]

poach[2] (pōch) *v.t.* **1** to take (game, fish etc.) from another's lands or by illegitimate methods. **2** to take or use dishonestly or illegally. **3** in tennis, to take (a shot) when in one's partner's part of the court. **4** to take game from (another's lands). **5** to trample, to tread into mire. ~*v.i.* **1** to encroach or trespass on another's lands, esp. to take game, fish etc. **2** to take game, fish etc. by illegal or unsportsmanlike methods. **3** to intrude or encroach upon another's rights, area of responsibility etc. **4** to take an advantage unfairly, e.g. in a race or game. **5** (of ground) to become soft, swampy or miry. **6** in tennis, to hit the ball when in one's partner's part of the court. **poacher**[2] *n.* **poachy** *a.* (*comp.* **poachier**, *superl.* **poachiest**) wet and soft; swampy; easily trodden into holes by cattle. **poachiness** *n.* [prob. from OF *pocher*, to thrust into, to encroach, prob. rel. to POKE[1]]

poacher[1] POACH[1].

poacher[2] POACH[2].

pochard (pō´chəd) *n.* (*pl.* **pochard, pochards**) any European diving sea duck of the genus *Aethya*, esp. *A. ferina*. [etym. uncertain]

pochette (poshet´) *n.* a small handbag shaped like an envelope. [F, dim. of *poche*, a pocket (see POKE[2])]

pock (pok) *n.* a pockmark. **pocked** *a.* **pockmark** *n.* **1** the pit or scar left by a pustule. **2** any similar mark or indentation. **pockmarked, pock-pitted** *a.* **pocky** *a.* (*comp.* **pockier**, *superl.* **pockiest**). [OE *poc* (cp. Dut. *pok*, G *Pocke*), whence POX]

pocket (pok´it) *n.* **1** a small bag, sack or pouch, esp. a small bag inserted in the clothing, to contain articles carried about the person. **2** a pouchlike compartment in a car door etc. **3** pecuniary means. **4** an isolated area or patch. **5** (*Geol.*) a cavity in rock, containing foreign matter. **6** (*Mining*) a cavity containing gold or other ore. **7** a small netted bag in snooker or pool to receive the balls. **8** an air pocket. **9** a measure for hops, wool, ginger etc. ~*a.* **1** for the pocket. **2** small. ~*v.t.* (*pres.p.* **pocketing,** *past, p.p.* **pocketed**) **1** to put into a pocket. **2** to keep in or as if in the pocket. **3** to appropriate, esp. illegitimately. **4** to put up with. **5** to repress or conceal (one's feelings). **6** in snooker or pool, to drive (a ball) into a pocket. **7** to hem in (a horse etc.) in a race. **8** to submit to (an insult etc.) without showing resentment. **in pocket 1** having made a profit. **2** (of money) available. **in someone's pocket 1** under someone's influence or control. **2** intimate with someone. **out of pocket** having made a loss, having less money than before. **to line one's pockets** to abuse a position of trust in order to make money for oneself. **to pocket one's pride** not to stand on one's dignity, to adopt an amenable attitude. **to put one's hand in one's pocket** to spend or give money. **pocketable** *a.* **pocket battleship** *n.* (*Hist.*) a small battleship. **pocketbook** *n.* **1** a notebook or a book or case for carrying papers etc. in the pocket. **2** (*N Am.*) a purse or handbag. **3** (*N Am.*) a paperback book or any small book. **pocket borough** *n.* (*Hist.*) a borough whose political representation was controlled by a particular individual or family. **pocketful** *n.* (*pl.* **pocketfuls**) the amount that can be held in a pocket. **pocket glass** *n.* a small portable mirror. **pocket gopher** *n.* a gopher. **pocket handkerchief** *n.* **pocket knife** *n.* a knife with blades shutting into the handle, for carrying in the pocket. **pocketless** *a.* **pocket money** *n.* **1** money for occasional expenses or amusements. **2** a small, regular allowance given to a child. **pocket piece** *n.* a coin kept in the pocket for luck. **pocket pistol** *n.* **1** a small pistol for carrying in the pocket. **2** a small spirit-flask for the pocket. **pocket-sized** *a.* small enough to fit into a pocket. **pockety** *a.* [ME *poket*, Ang.-Norman *pokete*, dim. of ONF *poque*, as F *poche*, a POKE[2]]

poco (pō´kō) *adv.* (*Mus.*) a little. [It.]

pococurante (pōkōkūran´ti) *n.* a careless or apathetic person. ~*a.* indifferent. **pococurantism** *n.* [It., little-caring]

poculiform (pok´ūlifawm) *a.* cup-shaped. [L *pōculum*, a cup]

pod[1] (pod) *n.* **1** a long capsule or seed vessel, esp. of leguminous plants. **2** any of various similar receptacles, such as the case enclosing the eggs of a locust, a silkworm cocoon, a narrow-necked eel-net etc. **3** a streamlined container, housing an engine, fuel, armaments etc., attached to the outside of an aircraft. **4** the socket into which the bit enters in a brace. **5** the channel or groove in an auger etc. **6** any protective (external) housing. **7** a detachable compartment on a spacecraft. ~*v.i.* (*pres.p.* **podding,** *past, p.p.* **podded**) **1** to produce pods. **2** to swell into pods. ~*v.t.* to shell (peas etc.). **in pod** (*coll.*) pregnant. [etym. unknown]

pod[2] (pod) *n.* a flock, bunch or small herd of whales, seals etc. ~*v.t.* (*pres.p.* **podding,** *past, p.p.* **podded**) to drive (seals etc.) into a pod. [etym. uncertain]

pod- PODO-.

-pod (pod) *comb. form* foot. [Gr. *pous podos*, foot]

podagra (pədag´rə) *n.* (*Med.*) gout, esp. in the foot. **podagral, podagric, podagrous** *a.* [L and Gr. (*pous podos*, a foot, *agra*, catching)]

poddy (pod´i) *n.* (*pl.* **poddies**) (*Austral.*) a hand-fed calf or foal. **poddy-dodger** *n.* a station-hand, a dairy-man.

podestà (podes´tə, -stah´) *n.* a subordinate municipal judge in an Italian city. [It. *podestà*, from L *potestatem*, nom. *-tas*, power, authority]

podge (poj) *n.* a short and stout person. **podgy** *a.* (*comp.* **podgier,** *superl.* **podgiest**) **1** short and stout. **2** (of a face) plump. **podginess** *n.* [var. of PUDGE]

podia PODIUM.

podiatry (pōdī´ətri) *n.* chiropody. **podiatrist** *n.* [Gr. *iatros*, physician]

podium (pō´diəm) *n.* (*pl.* **podiums, podia** (-diə)) **1** a low projecting wall or basement supporting a building etc. **2** a platform encircling the arena in an amphitheatre. **3** a continuous structural bench round a hall etc. **4** a small raised platform (for a conductor, lecturer etc.). **podial** *a.* [L, from Gr. *podion*, from *pous podos*, foot]

podo- (pod´ō), **pod-** *comb. form* foot. [Gr. *pous podos*, foot]

podophyllin (podōfil´in) *n.* a purgative resin extracted from the root of the mayapple.

podzol (pod´zol), **podsol** (-sol) *n.* an infertile soil, with a greyish-white upper layer, like ash, and a brown subsoil. **podzolic** (-zol´-) *a.* **podzolize, podzolise** *v.t.* to render podzolic. ~*v.i.* (of soil) to become podzolic. **podzolization** (-zā´shən) *n.* [Rus., from *pod*, under, *zola*, ashes]

poem (pō´im, -əm) *n.* **1** a metrical composition, esp. of an impassioned and imaginative kind. **2** an artistic and imaginative composition in verse or prose. **3** anything supremely beautiful, well-executed or satisfying. [F *poème*, L *poēma*, Gr. *poieēma*, from *poiein*, to make]

poenology PENOLOGY.

poesy (pō´izi, -si) *n.* (*pl.* **poesies**) **1** the art of poetry. **2** metrical compositions collectively. [ME and OF *poesie*, L *poēsis*, Gr. *poiēsis*, as POEM]

poet (pō´it) *n.* **1** a writer of poems or metrical compositions, esp. one possessing high powers of imagination and rhythmical expression. **2** a person possessed of high imaginative or creative power. **poetaster** (-tas´tə) *n.* an inferior or petty poet; a pitiful versifier. **poetess** (-tis) *n.* (*dated*) a woman poet. **poetic** (-et´-), **poetical** *a.* **1** of or relating to, or suitable for poetry or poets. **2** expressed in poetry, written in poetry. **3** having the finer qualities of poetry. **4** fit to be expressed in poetry. **poetically** *adv.* **Poetic Edda** *n.* ELDER EDDA (under ELDER[1]). **poeticize** (-sīz), **poeticise** *v.t.* to make poetic. **poetic justice** *n.* punishment or reward ideally (often ironically) well-deserved. **poetic licence** *n.* the latitude in grammar etc. allowed to poets. **poetics** *n.* **1** the theory or principles of writing poetry. **2** the branch of literary criticism dealing with poetry. **poetize, poetise** *v.i.* to compose verses, to write poetry. ~*v.t.* **1** to poeticize. **2** to write poetry about. **Poet Laureate** *n.* (*pl.* **Poets Laureate**) an officer of the British royal household whose nominal duty is to compose an ode every year for the sovereign's birthday, for any great national victory etc. **poetry** (-ri) *n.* **1** the art or work of a poet. **2** that one of the fine arts which expresses the imagination and feelings in sensuous and rhythmical language, usu. in metrical forms. **3** imaginative, impassioned, and rhythmical expression whether in verse or prose. **4** imaginative or creative power. **5** a quality in anything that powerfully stirs the imagination or the aesthetic sense. **6** metrical compositions collectively, verse, poems. **7** something resembling poetry in beauty, grace etc. **Poet's Corner** *n.* a part of Westminster Abbey where several poets are buried or have memorials. [OF *poete*, L *poēta*, Gr. *poiētēs*, maker, poet, see POEM]

po-faced (pōfāst´) *a.* (*coll.*) **1** deadpan. **2** humourless, stolid. **3** stupidly solemn. **4** smug. [perh. *poor-faced*, or from PO]

pogo (pō´gō), **pogo stick** *n.* (*pl.* **pogos, pogo sticks**) a toy consisting of a strong pole attached to a spring and having a handle at the top and a crossbar on which one stands to bounce along. [etym. uncertain]

pogrom (pog´rəm, pəgrom´) *n.* an organized attack, usu. with pillage and massacre, upon a class of the population, esp. Jews. [Rus., destruction]

poh (pō) *int.* used to express contempt or disgust. [instinctive sound]

pohutukawa (pōhootəkah´wə) *n.* (*New Zeal.*) an evergreen myrtle, *Metrosideros excelsa*, with bright red flowers. [Maori]

poi (pō´ē) *n.* a Hawaiian dish made of a paste of fermented taro root. [Hawaiian]

poignant (poin´yənt) *a.* **1** sharp, painful to the emotions, moving. **2** arousing sympathy. **3** stimulating to the palate, pungent. **4** keen, piercing. **5** bitter, painful. **poignance, poignancy** *n.* **poignantly** *adv.* [OF, pres.p. of *poindre*, L *pungere*, to prick]

poikilothermal (poikiləthœ´məl), **poikilothermic** (-mik) *a.* having a body temperature which varies with the surrounding temperature. **poikilotherm** (poi´-) *n.* an animal of this type. **poikilothermia, poikilothermism, poikilothermy** *n.* [Gr. *poikilos*, multi-coloured, variable]

poilu (pwa´lü) *n.* (*pl.* **poilus** (-lü)) (*Hist., coll.*) a French private soldier. [F, hairy (*poil*, a hair)]

poinciana (poinsiah´nə) *n.* any tree of the tropical genus *Caesalpinia* (formerly *Poinciana*) with bright red or orange flowers. [M. de *Poinci*, 17th-cent. governor of the French Antilles]

poind (poind, pind) *v.t.* (*Sc. Law*) **1** to distrain upon; to seize and sell (a debtor's goods). **2** to impound. ~*n.* **1** the act of poinding, distraint. **2** something poinded. [OE *pyndan*, to impound, cogn. with POUND[2], PINFOLD]

poinsettia (poinset´iə) *n.* a shrub of the S American and Mexican genus *Poinsettia*, with red leaflike bracts and small greenish-yellow flowerheads. [J. R. *Poinsett*, 1779–1853, US politician]

point (point) *n.* **1** a mark made by the end of anything sharp, a dot. **2** a dot used as a mark of punctuation, to indicate vowels (as in Hebrew) etc. **3** (*Print.*) a full stop, or decimal mark to separate integral from fractional digits in decimal numbers etc. **4** a particular item, a detail. **5** a particular place or position. **6** a specific position or stage in a development or on a scale. **7** the temperature level at which consistency changes (*freezing point*). **8** a state or condition. **9** **a** a particular moment. **b** the precise moment for an event, action etc., the instant. **10** the verge. **11** a step or stage in an argument, discourse etc. **12** a unit used in measuring or counting, in assessing superiority etc., in appraising qualities of an exhibit in a show, a racehorse etc., in reckoning odds given to an opponent in a game, in betting, or in scoring in games. **13** a success in argument. **14** a unit of weight etc. for diamonds (2 mg). **15** a salient quality, a trait, a characteristic. **16** the essential element, the exact object (of a discussion, joke etc.), the main purport, the gist. **17** the aim, the purpose; the value of an activity. **18** a conclusion. **19** a suggestion, a tip. **20** **a** the sharp end of a tool, weapon etc., the tip. **b** a nib. **21** a cape, a promontory (esp. in place names). **22** point lace. **23** a sharp-pointed tool, such as an etcher's needle, glass-cutter's diamond, various implements or parts of machinery used in the industrial arts etc. **24** **a** a tapering rail moving on a pivot for switching a train from one line to another. **b** (*pl.*) a railway switch. **25** (*pl.*) the contact-breakers in the distributor of an internal-combustion engine. **26** a power point. **27** a tine of a deer's horn. **28** pungency, effectiveness, force. **29** (*Geom.*) that which has position but not magnitude. **30** (*Print.*) the unit of measurement for type bodies, approx. 1/72 in. (0.351 mm). **31** (*Her.*) any of nine fixed positions on a shield. **32** a fielder or position on the off-side square of, and close in to, the batsman in cricket. **33** **a** a spot to which a straight run is made, in hunting. **b** such a run. **34** a musical passage or subject to which special importance is drawn. **35** the leading party of an advanced guard. **36** (*pl.*) the extremities of a horse, a dog etc. **37** in ballet, pointe. **38** a unit of increase or decrease in the price of stocks or the value of currencies. **39** **a** the act of pointing by a setter etc. **b** the position adopted by the dog. **40** in fencing, a twist. **41** **a** a point of the compass. **b** a particular place on the horizon corresponding to one of these. **42** (*Naut.*) a short cord for reefing sails. **43** a buckling-strap on a harness. **44** in boxing, the tip of the chin. **45** a patch of a different colour in the fur of some cats. **46** (*Hist.*) a tagged lace for lacing bodices, doublets etc. **47** †a signal on a musical instrument in war or the chase. **48** †the pommel of a saddle. *~v.t.* **1** to sharpen. **2** to mark with points, to punctuate; to indicate the vowels of (as Hebrew). **3** to mark off (e.g. a psalm) in groups of syllables for singing. **4** to give force or point to. **5** to fill (the joints of masonry) with mortar or cement pressed in with a trowel. **6** to indicate, to show. **7** to direct (a finger etc. at). **8** to turn in a particular direction, to aim. **9** to give effect or pungency to (a remark, jest etc.). **10** to indicate the meaning or point of by a gesture. **11** to turn in (manure etc.) with the point of a spade. *~v.i.* **1** to direct attention to. **2** (of a pointer or setter) to draw attention to game by standing rigidly and looking at it. **3** to aim (at or towards). **4** to face or be directed (towards). **5** to tend towards. **6** to hint at, or to be evidence of. **7** to sail close to the wind. **at all points** **1** in every part or direction. **2** completely, perfectly. **at/ on the point** on the verge (of). **†at point** in readiness. **beside the point** BESIDE. **case in point** CASE[1]. **in point** apposite, relevant. **in point of fact** FACT. **off the point** beside the point. **on the point of** about to do. **to carry one's point** to prevail in an argument or dispute. **to come to a point** COME. **to have a point** to have an effective or relevant argument. **to make a point** **1** to score a point. **2** to establish a point in argument. **to make a point of** **1** to attach special importance to. **2** to take special care to. **to make one's point** to establish a point in argument, to make one's opinion clear. **to point a/ the bone** BONE. **to point out** to indicate, to draw attention to. **to point the finger (at)** FINGER. **to point up** to emphasize, to highlight. **to prove one's point** to establish the truth of one's assertion. **to score points** SCORE. **to score points off** SCORE. **to take someone's point** to understand someone's argument. **to the point** appropriate, apposite, pertinent. **to win on points** in boxing, to win by scoring more points, not by a knockout. **up to a point** partially, not completely. **point after** *n.* in American football, a goal scored by kicking the ball between the posts after a touchdown. **point-blank** *a.* **1** aimed or fired horizontally directly at the mark making no allowance for the downward curve of the trajectory; hence very close (permitting such aim to be taken). **2** direct, blunt. *~adv.* **1** at very close range; horizontally, with direct aim. **2** directly, bluntly. *~n.* a point-blank shot. **point d'appui** (pwã dapwē´) *n.* (*Mil.*) any particular strong point in a line of defence. **†point-device** *a.* correct, precise, finical, neat. *~adv.* correctly, precisely, to a nicety. **point duty** *n.* the work of a police officer or traffic warden stationed at a junction of streets or other point to regulate traffic. **pointed** *a.* **1** having a sharp point. **2** having point, penetrating, cutting. **3** referring to some particular person or thing. **4** emphasized, made obvious. **pointedly** *adv.* with special meaning. **pointedness** *n.* **pointer** *n.* **1** a person or thing which points. **2** the index hand of a clock etc. **3** a rod used for pointing on a blackboard etc. **4** an indication, a hint, a tip. **5** **a** a dog of a breed trained to point at game. **b** this breed of dog. **6** (*pl.*) two stars of the Plough, a line drawn through which points nearly to the pole star. **7** (*Austral.*) a trickster, a swindler. **8** (*Austral.*) one of the bullocks next to the pole in a team. **pointing** *n.* **1** the act of indicating, directing, sharpening etc. **2** **a** the process of finishing or renewing a mortar-joint in a wall. **b** the mortar used in this process. **c** the finish produced. **3** **a** punctuation. **b** division into groups of words or syllables for singing. **point lace** *n.* lace made with the point of a needle. **pointless** *a.* **1** having no point. **2** purposeless, futile. **3** in sport, without any points scored. **pointlessly** *adv.* **pointlessness** *n.* **point of appui** *n.* point d'appui. **point of contact** *n.* the point at which two lines, planes or bodies touch each other. **point of distance** *n.* that point of a picture where the visual rays meet. **point of honour** *n.* a matter involving personal honour or reputation. **point of no return** *n.* **1** a critical point (at which one must commit oneself irrevocably to a course of action). **2** the point in a flight where shortage of fuel makes it necessary to go on as return is impossible. **point of order** *n.* a question of procedure in a debate etc. **point of sale** *n.* the place, esp. a retail shop, where the sale of an article physically takes place. **point of the compass** *n.* **1** each one of the 32 angular divisions of the compass. **2** the angle of 11° 15′ between two such points. **point of view** *n.* **1** the position from which a thing is looked at. **2** a way of regarding a matter. **pointsman** *n.* (*pl.* **pointsmen**) **1** a police officer or traffic warden on point duty. **2** a person in charge of the switches on a railway. **point source** *n.* a source of light or other radiation so small as to be considered a point. **point system** *n.* a standard system for measuring type bodies. **point-to-point** *a.* of or relating to a steeplechase or other race in a direct line from one point of a course to another. *~n.* such a race. **point-to-pointer** *n.* **point-to-pointing** *n.* **pointy** *a.* (*comp.* **pointier**, *superl.* **pointiest**) having a sharp point or points. [partly through F *point*, a dot, a point, *pointe*, a sharp end (L *punctum*, orig. neut. p.p. L *puncta*, piercing) and *pointer*, to point, med. L *punctāre*, all from L *punct-*, p.p. stem of *pungere*, to prick]

pointe (pwãt) *n.* (*pl.* **pointes** (pwãt)) **1** (in ballet) the extreme tip of the toe. **2** a position in which the dancer balances on this. [F]

pointillism (pwã´tilizm) *n.* (in painting) delineation by means of dots of various pure colours which merge into a whole in the viewer's eye. **pointillist** *n.*, *a.* **pointillistic** *a.* [F *pointiller*, to draw in points]

poise[1] (poiz) *v.t.* **1** to balance to hold or carry in equilibrium. **2** to place in a carefully balanced position. **3** to counterpoise. **4** to ponder. *~v.i.* **1** to be balanced or in equilibrium. **2** to hang (in the air) over, to hover. *~n.* **1** composure, assurance, self-possession. **2** equipoise, equilibrium. **3** a counterpoise. **4** a state of suspense, indecision etc. **5** physical balance. **poised** *a.* **1** balanced. **2** having or showing composure, self-possession etc. **3** in a state of readiness, all set (to). [ME and OF *poiser*, F *peser*, ult. from L *pensāre*, freq. of *pendere*, to weigh]

poise[2] (poiz) *n.* (*Physics*) the cgs unit of viscosity. [J. L. M. *Poiseuille*, 1799–1869, French physician]

poison (poi´zən) *n.* **1** a substance that injures or kills an organism into which it is absorbed. **2** anything destructive or corrupting. **3** a substance which retards catalytic activity or a chemical reaction, or, by absorbing neutrons, the course of a nuclear reaction. ~*v.t.* **1** to put poison in or upon; to infect with or administer poison. **2** to kill or injure by this means. **3** to embitter or turn (someone) against. **4** to taint, to corrupt, to vitiate, to pervert. **what's your poison?** (*coll.*) what would you like to drink? **poisonable** *a.* **poisoned chalice** *n.* something apparently desirable which has a hidden inconvenience or disadvantage. **poisoner** *n.* **poison gas** *n.* (*Mil.*) poisonous or stupefying gas or vapour used in warfare to disable an enemy. **poison ivy** *n.* (*pl.* **poison ivies**) any of various N American shrubs or climbing plants of the genus *Rhus*, which cause an intensely itching skin rash. **poison oak** *n.* either of two N American shrubs, *Rhus toxicodendron* and *R. diversilobia*, related to poison ivy and causing a similar rash. **poisonous** *a.* **poisonously** *adv.* **poisonousness** *n.* **poison pen letter** *n.* a letter written maliciously and usu. anonymously, to abuse or frighten the recipient. **poison pill** *n.* **1** a pill containing poison. **2** a tactic used by a company to make itself unattractive to a possible takeover bidder. [F *poison*, as POTION]

Poisson distribution (pwas´on) *n.* in statistics, a frequency distribution which gives the probability of events taking place in a fixed time. [S. D. *Poisson*, 1781–1840, French mathematician]

poke[1] (pōk) *v.t.* **1** to thrust, to push (in, out, through etc.) with the end of something. **2** to jab, to prod (with a finger, a stick etc.). **3** to stir (a fire) with a poker. **4** to cause to protrude. **5** to put, move etc. by poking. **6** to make (a hole etc.) by poking. **7** (*coll.*) to punch. **8** (*sl.*) to have sexual intercourse with. **9** to shut (up) in a confined space. ~*v.i.* **1** to thrust, to jab. **2** to protrude. **3** (*coll.*) to pry, to search. **4** to dawdle, to busy oneself without any definite object. ~*n.* **1** a poking, a push, a thrust, a prod, a nudge. **2** a collar with a drag attached to prevent animals from breaking through fences etc. **3** (*coll.*) a punch. **4** (*sl.*) an act of sexual intercourse. **to poke fun at** FUN. **to poke one's bib in** BIB. **to poke one's nose into** NOSE. **poky**[1] *a.* (*comp.* **pokier,** *superl.* **pokiest**) **1** (of a room etc.) cramped, confined, stuffy. **2** (*coll.*) shabby. **3** slow, petty, dull. **pokily** *adv.* **pokiness** *n.* [cp. Dut. and LG *poken*, to thrust, *Poke*, dagger, G *pochen*, also POACH[2]]

poke[2] (pōk) *n.* (*esp. Sc.*) a bag, a sack. **pig in a poke** PIG. [cp. ONF *poque*, F *poche*, Icel. *poki*, perh. rel. to OE *pohha*]

poke[3] (pōk) *n.* **1** a projecting front on a woman's hat or bonnet, formerly a detachable rim. **2** a bonnet having such a front. **poke-bonnet** *n.* **poke-bonneted** *n.* [perh. ident. with POKE[1], POKE[2]]

poker[1] (pō´kə) *n.* **1** an iron rod used to stir a fire. **2** a metal rod used in pokerwork. ~*v.t.* to adorn with pokerwork. ~*v.i.* to carry out (a design) in this. **red-hot poker** RED-HOT (under RED[1]). **pokerwork** *n.* the production of decorative designs on wood by burning or scorching with a heated metal rod. [POKE[1]]

poker[2] (pō´kə) *n.* a card game in which the players bet on the value in their hands. **poker dice** *n.* **1** a dice marked with designs of the playing cards from nine to ace, instead of spots. **2** a game played with such dice. **poker-face** *n.* **1** an expressionless face. **2** a person with such a face. **poker-faced** *a.* [etym. uncertain]

pokeweed (pōk´wēd) *n.* a N American herb, *Phytolacca americana*, with purple berries used medicinally. [perh. Algonquian *poke*]

poky[1] POKE[1].

poky[2] (pō´ki), **pokey** *n.* (*pl.* **pokies, pokeys**) (*sl.*) (a) prison. [perh. POKY (under POKE[1])]

POL *abbr.* petrol, oil and lubricants.

Pol. *abbr.* **1** Poland. **2** Polish.

pol. *abbr.* **1** political. **2** politics.

polacca (pəlak´ə), **polacre** (-lah´-) *n.* a three-masted sailing boat used in the Mediterranean. [F *polacre*, It. *polacca*, etym. uncertain]

Polack (pō´lak) *n.* (*sl., offensive*) a Pole or a person of Polish origin. [Pol. *Polak*]

polar (pō´lə) *a.* **1** of, relating to or situated near the poles of the earth or of the celestial sphere. **2** coming from the regions near the poles. **3** of or relating to a magnetic pole, having polarity, magnetic. **4** having two opposite elements or tendencies, esp. positive and negative electricity. **5** directly opposite in character or tendencies. **6** of or relating to the poles of a cell. **7** (*Math.*) relating to or of the nature of a polar. **8** resembling the pole star, attracting, guiding. ~*n.* **1** (*Math.*) a plane curve having a particular relation to another and to a point called the pole. **2** the line connecting the points of contact of two tangents drawn to a given curve from the pole. **polar angle** *n.* the angle formed by two meridians at a pole. **polar axis** *n.* (*Astron.*) that diameter of a sphere which passes through the poles. **polar bear** *n.* a white arctic bear, *Thalarctos maritimus.* **polar body** *n.* (*Biol.*) a small cell produced from the ovum during its formation. **polar cap** *n.* either of two white regions round the poles of the planet Mars. **polar circle** *n.* either of the Arctic and Antarctic parallels of latitude. **polar coordinate** *n.* (*Math.*) either one of a pair of coordinates which define the position of a point by means of a line from the point to the origin and the angle this makes with a fixed line through the origin. **polar curve** *n.* (*Math.*) a curve related to a given curve and to a fixed point, the pole. **polar distance** *n.* the angular distance of a point from the nearest pole. **polar equation** *n.* (*Math.*) an equation in terms of polar coordinates. **polarly** *adv.* **polar star** *n.* the pole star. **polar wandering** *n.* the movement over time of the earth's magnetic poles in relation to its geographic poles. [med. L *polāris*, from L *polus*, POLE[2]]

polari- (pō´ləri), **polaro-** (-ō) *comb. form* of or relating to poles or polarized light.

polarimeter (pōlərim´itə) *n.* an instrument for measuring the polarization of light, or the rotation of the plane of polarized light. **polarimetric** (-met´-) *a.* **polarimetry** *n.*

Polaris (pəlah´ris) *n.* **1** the pole star. **2** a type of intermediate-range ballistic missile fired from a submarine.

polariscope (pōlar´iskōp) *n.* a polarimeter. **polariscopic** (-skop´-) *a.*

polarity (pōlar´iti) *n.* (*pl.* **polarities**) **1** the state of having two opposite poles, or of having different or opposing properties in opposite parts or directions. **2** the tendency of a magnetized bar to point to the magnetic poles. **3** the quality (in electricity) of being attracted to one pole and repelled from the other. **4** the disposition in a body to place its mathematical axis in a particular direction. **5** diametric opposition in opinions etc.

polarize (pō´lərīz), **polarise** *v.t.* **1** to cause to acquire polarity or polarization. **2** to restrict the vibrations of (a light wave) to one direction. **3** to reduce the voltage of (a battery) by the collection of hydrogen on the positive electrode. **4** to cause to divide into two opposing groups or camps. ~*v.i.* **1** to acquire polarity or polarization. **2** to split up into two opposing camps or groups. **polarizable** *a.* **polarization** (-zā´shən) *n.* **1** the act of polarizing, or the state of being polarized. **2** the development of opposing poles. **polarizer** *n.*

polaro- POLARI-.

polarography (pōlərog´rəfi) *n.* (*Chem.*) the analysis of a substance by measuring the current produced by electrolysing it at different voltages. **polarograph** (pō´lərəgrahf) *n.* **polarographic** (-graf´ik) *a.*

Polaroid® (pō´ləroid) *n.* **1** a light-polarizing material used esp. in sunglasses. 2 a type of camera which produces a finished print from inside itself within seconds of the picture's being taken. 3 such a finished print.

polder (pōl´də) *n.* a tract of land below sea or river level, that has been drained and cultivated, esp. in the Netherlands. [Dut.]

Pole (pōl) *n.* 1 a native or inhabitant of Poland. 2 a person of Polish descent.

pole[1] (pōl) *n.* 1 a long slender piece of wood or metal, usu. rounded and tapering, esp. fixed upright in the ground as a flagstaff, support for a tent, telegraph wires etc. 2 the shaft of a large horse-drawn vehicle. 3 (*Hist.*) an instrument for measuring; a measure of length, a rod or perch, 5½ yd. (5 m). 4 a mast. 5 the flexible rod of wood or fibreglass used in pole-vaulting. 6 (*esp. N Am.*) a simple fishing rod. ~*v.t.* to furnish or support with, to convey or push by a pole or poles. **bare poles** BARE. **up the pole** 1 (*sl.*) crazy, mad. 2 mistaken, wrong. **pole position** *n.* the most advantageous position at the start of a race, esp. a motor or horse race. **poler** *n.* (*Austral.*) 1 the bullock next to the pole in a team. 2 (*sl.*) a sponger. **pole vault** *n.* a field event in which the competitor attempts to clear a very high bar with the aid of a long flexible pole. **pole-vault** *v.i.* **pole-vaulter** *n.* **poling** *n.* [OE *pāl*, L *pālus*, PALE[2]]

pole[2] (pōl) *n.* 1 either of the extremities, north and south, of the axis on which a sphere or spheroid, esp. the earth, revolves. 2 each of the points where the projection of the axis of the earth pierces the celestial sphere and round which the stars appear to revolve. 3 a point from which a pencil of rays radiates, a fixed point of reference. 4 either of the two points in a body where the attractive or repelling force is greatest, as in a magnet. 5 either of the two terminals, positive and negative, of an electric cell, battery etc. 6 (*Biol.*) the extremity of the axis of a cell nucleus etc. 7 either of the two polar regions. 8 either of two opposite extremes. 9 either of the two points where the axis of a circle cuts the surface of a sphere. 10 (*Geom.*) a fixed point. 11 (*poet.*) the sky, the firmament. **poles apart** 1 as far apart as possible. 2 having widely divergent views, attitudes etc. **pole star** *n.* 1 a bright star, Polaris in Ursa Minor, within a degree and a quarter of the northern celestial pole. 2 a guiding principle. 3 a lodestar, a centre of attraction. **poleward** *a.* **polewards** *a.*, *adv.* [through OF *pole*, or directly from L *polus*, Gr. *polos*, pivot, axis]

Usage note It is conventional to use capital letters (*North Pole*, *South Pole*) when referring to the polar regions.

pole-axe (pōl´aks), (*N Am.*) **poleax** *n.* 1 (*Hist.*) a form of battleaxe consisting of an axe set on a long handle. 2 such a weapon with a hook formerly used by sailors in boarding etc. 3 a long-handled butcher's axe with a hammer at the back, used for slaughtering cattle. ~*v.t.* to strike, kill or destroy (as if) with a poleaxe. [ME *pollax* (POLL[1], AXE)]

polecat (pōl´kat) *n.* (*pl. in general* **polecat,** *in particular* **polecats**) 1 a small carnivorous European weasel-like mammal, *Mustela putorius*, with two glands emitting an offensive smell. 2 (*N Am.*) a skunk. [ME *polcat* (perh. from *poule*, chicken, CAT[1])]

poleis POLIS.

polemarch (pol´əmahk) *n.* (*Hist.*) in Greece, the third archon, orig. a military commander-in-chief, later a civil magistrate with varying functions. [Gr. *polemarchos* (*polemos*, war, *archein*, to rule)]

polemic (pəlem´ik) *n.* 1 a controversy or controversial discussion. 2 a controversialist. 3 (*pl.*) the art or practice of controversial discussion, esp. in theology. 4 an aggressive attack on, or rebuttal of, another's conduct or views. ~*a.* polemical. **polemical** *a.* 1 of or relating to controversy. 2 controversial, disputatious. **polemically** *adv.* **polemicist** (-sist) *n.* **polemicize** (-sīz), **polemicise, polemize** (pol´əmīz), **polemise** *v.i.* [Gr. *polemikos*, from *polemos*, war]

polenta (pəlen´tə) *n.* a kind of porridge made of maize meal, or less commonly from barley or chestnut meal, a common food in Italy. [It.]

poler POLE[1].

poley (pō´li) *a.* (*Austral.*) (of cattle) without horns. [POLL[2]]

police (pəlēs´) *n.* 1 **a** (*usu. as pl.*) a civil force organized by a state for the maintenance of order, the detection of crime, and the apprehension of offenders. **b** a similar force enforcing regulations on behalf of an official body (*military police*). 2 (*as pl.*) constables etc. belonging to this force. 3 (*Hist.*) the executive administration concerned in the preservation and enforcement of public order. 4 the government department responsible for this. ~*v.t.* 1 to control by the use of police. 2 to provide with police. 3 to supervise, to regulate, to discipline. **police constable** *n.* a police officer of the lowest rank. **police court** *n.* a magistrates' court. **police dog** *n.* a dog, usu. an Alsatian, trained to assist police. **police force** *n.* a separately organized body of police. **police informer** *n.* a person who gives information to the police about criminals and their activities. **policeman** *n.* (*pl.* **policemen**) any male member of a police force, esp. a constable. **police office** *n.* a police station. **police officer** *n.* a policeman or policewoman. **police state** *n.* a totalitarian state maintained by the use of political police. **police station** *n.* the headquarters of a local section of the police. **police trap** *n.* an ambush by police to trap offenders against road regulations. **policewoman** *n.* (*pl.* **policewomen**) a female member of the police force. [F, from med. L *pōlīta*, L *polītia*, POLICY[1]]

policy[1] (pol´isi) *n.* (*pl.* **policies**) 1 a course of action or administration recommended or adopted by a party, government, firm, organization or individual. 2 prudent conduct. 3 prudence, foresight or sagacity in managing or conducting, esp. state affairs. 4 conduct governed by material or selfish interests. [OF *policie*, L *polītīa*, Gr. *polīteia*, from *polītēs*, citizen, from *polis*, city]

Usage note See note under POLITY.

policy[2] (pol´isi) *n.* (*pl.* **policies**) 1 **a** a contract of insurance. **b** the document containing such a contract. 2 a warrant, voucher etc. 3 (*N Am.*) a method of gambling by betting on numbers drawn in a lottery. **policyholder** *n.* a person or organization holding a contract of insurance. **policy shop** *n.* (*N Am.*) a place where draws take place in connection with policy lotteries. [F *police*, prob. from med. L *apodissa*, *-dixa*, Gr. *apodeixis*, demonstration, proof, from *apodeiknunai* (APO-, *deiknunai*, to show)]

policy[3] (pol´isi) *n.* (*pl.* **policies**) 1 (*Sc.*, *often pl.*) the pleasure grounds around a country house. 2 †the improvement or the improvements and embellishments of an estate. [prob. from L *polītus*, improved, see POLITE, confused with POLICY[1]]

poling POLE[1].

poliomyelitis (pōliōmīəlī´tis), **polio** *n.* an acute infectious viral disease affecting the central nervous system, which can cause paralysis and muscle wasting. [Gr. *polios*, grey, *muelos*, marrow]

polis (pol´is) *n.* (*pl.* **poleis** (-īs)) a Greek city state. [Gr.]

-polis (pəlis) *comb. form* city.

Polish (pō´lish) *a.* of or relating to Poland or to its inhabitants or their language. ~*n.* 1 the language of the Poles. 2 (*pl.*) the Polish people. **Polish notation** *n.* (*Math.*) a notation which does not use brackets or punctuation and places operators before their arguments, also called *prefix notation.*

polish (pol´ish) *v.t.* 1 to make smooth or glossy, usu. by friction. 2 to refine, to free from roughness or coarseness. 3 to bring to a fully finished state. ~*v.i.* to take a polish. ~*n.* 1 a smooth glossy surface, esp. produced by friction. 2 friction applied for this purpose. 3 a substance applied to impart a polish. 4 the act, or an instance, of polishing. 5 refinement, elegance of manners. **to polish off** 1 (*coll.*) to finish speedily. 2 to get rid of. **to polish up** 1 to give a polish to. 2 to improve, or refresh (one's knowledge of something) by study. **polishable** *a.* **polished** *a.* 1 accomplished. 2 impeccably executed. 3 (of rice) having had the outer husk removed. **polisher** *n.* **polishing** *n.* **polishing paste, polishing powder, polishing slate** *n.* substances applied in polishing the surface of various materials. [F *poliss-*, stem of *polir*, L *polīre*]

politburo (pol´itbūrō) *n.* (*pl.* **politburos**) the political bureau of the Central Committee of the Communist Party of the former USSR. [Rus.]

polite (pəlīt´) *a.* (*comp.* **politer**, *superl.* **politest**) 1 refined in manners. 2 courteous. 3 well-bred. 4 cultivated. 5 (of literature) elegant, refined. **politely** *adv.* **politeness** *n.* [L *polītus*, p.p. of *polīre*, to POLISH]

politesse (polites´) *n.* formal politeness. [F]

politic[1] (pol´itik) *a.* 1 prudent and sagacious. 2 prudently devised, judicious, expedient. 3 crafty, scheming, artful. 4 political. **politicly** *adv.* artfully, cunningly. [F *politique*, L *polīticus*, Gr. *politikos*, as POLICY[1]]

politic[2] POLITICKING.

political (pəlit´ikəl) *a.* 1 of or relating to civil government and its administration. 2 of or relating to politics, esp. party politics. 3 taking or belonging to a side in politics. 4 interested or involved in politics. 5 of or relating to aspects of power and status in any organization, rather than to those of principle. 6 having an established system of government. **political agent, political resident** *n.* (*Hist.*) in British India, a government official appointed to advise a local ruler. **political asylum** *n.* protection from extradition given by one country to a political refugee from another country. **political correctness** *n.* the avoidance of discrimination, in language or action, against minorities such as women, people of colour, lesbians and gays or people with disabilities. **political economy** *n.* the science of the production and distribution of wealth, the study of economics in relation to government. **political economist** *n.* a person skilled in political economy. **political geography** *n.* the branch of geography dealing with countries, states, political, social and economic conditions. **politically** *adv.* **politically correct, politically incorrect** *a.* of or relating to language, behaviour etc. associated with political correctness. **political prisoner** *n.* a person imprisoned for their political beliefs or activities. **political science** *n.* the study of government, politics and the state. **political scientist** *n.* [L *polīticus*, see POLITIC[1]]

politician (politish´ən) *n.* 1 a person experienced or skilled in politics. 2 a person engaged in or devoted to party politics, usu. as a career. 3 (*N Am.*) a person who makes use of politics for private ends.

politicize (pəlit´isīz), **politicise** *v.t.* 1 to give a political tone or scope to. 2 to make politically aware. ~*v.i.* to engage in or discuss politics. **politicization** (-zā´shən) *n.*

politicking (pol´itiking) *n.* political activity, esp. vote-getting. **politic**[2], **politick** *v.i.* (*pres.p.* **politicking**, *past, p.p.* **politicked**) to engage in political activity. **politicker** *n.*

politico (pəlit´ikō) *n.* (*pl.* **politicos, politicoes**) (*coll.*) a politician.

politico- (pəlit´ikō) *comb. form* 1 political and. 2 politically.

politics (pol´itiks) *n.* 1 the art or science of civil government. 2 the relationships, involving power and authority, between people, or between people and organizations. 3 the profession of politics. 4 (*sing. or pl. in constr.*) political affairs. 5 (*as pl.*) the political dimension to any action or activity. 6 (*as pl.*) any activities concerned with the acquisition, apportionment or exercise of power within an organization, manoeuvring, intrigue. 7 (*as pl.*) a person's political views or sympathies.

polity (pol´iti) *n.* (*pl.* **polities**) 1 the form, system or constitution of the civil government of a State. 2 the State. 3 an organized community, a body politic. 4 the form of organization of an institution etc.

Usage note The nouns *polity* and *policy* should not be confused: a *polity* is a form of civil government, and a *policy* a course of action.

---

polka (pōl´kə, pol´-) *n.* (*pl.* **polkas**) 1 a lively round dance of Bohemian origin. 2 a piece of music in duple time for this. 3 (*Hist.*) a woman's tight-fitting jacket, usu. made of knitted wool. ~*v.i.* (*3rd pers. sing. pres.* **polkas**, *pres.p.* **polkaing**, *past, p.p.* **polkaed, polka'd**) to dance a polka. **polka dot** *n.* a small dot in a regular pattern of dots, esp. as a textile design. **polka-dot** *a.* [etym. uncertain, perh. from Pol. *Polka*, fem. of *Polak*, POLACK]

poll[1] (pōl) *n.* 1 the voting at an election, the number of votes polled, or the counting of these. 2 the time or place of election. 3 an attempt to ascertain public opinion by questioning a few individuals. 4 a register or enumeration of heads or persons, esp. of persons entitled to vote at elections. 5 a human head. 6 the part of the head on which the hair grows. 7 the butt-end of an axe or other tool. ~*v.t.* 1 to remove the top of (trees etc.). 2 to crop the hair of. 3 to cut off the horns of. 4 to clip, to shear. 5 to take the votes of. 6 to receive (a specified number of votes). 7 to give (one's vote). 8 to ascertain and record the opinion of, in a poll. 9 (*Comput.*) to interrogate (computer terminals) in sequence to ascertain whether they have any data on them for use. 10 †to plunder. ~*v.i.* to give one's vote. **to poll a jury** (*N Am.*) to examine each juror as to their concurrence in a verdict. **pollable** *a.* **pollee** (-lē) *n.* a member of the public questioned in an opinion poll. **poller** *n.* **polling** *n.* 1 the casting or registering of votes. 2 (*Comput.*) the automatic interrogation of terminals by a central computer to see whether there are messages to transmit. **polling booth** *n.* a semi-enclosed structure in which a voter marks their ballot paper. **polling day** *n.* the day on which an election is held. **polling station** *n.* a building designated as a place where voters should go to cast their votes. **pollster** (-stə) *n.* a person who conducts or analyses an opinion poll. **poll tax** *n.* 1 a capitation tax or one levied on every person. 2 (*Hist.*) the community charge in Britain. [ME and MDut. *polle*, head or pate (cp. Dan. *puld*)]

poll[2] (pōl), **polled** (pōld) *a.* 1 (of cattle) having had the horns cut off. 2 hornless. **poll-beast, poll-cow, poll-ox** *n.* a polled beast, esp. one of a breed of hornless cattle. [short for dial. *pold*, for *polled*, p.p. of POLL[1]]

poll[3] (pol) *n.* (*coll.*) (used as a name for) a parrot. **poll parrot** *n.* a person given to speaking and thinking in clichés. [var. of *Moll*, see MOLL]

pollack (pol´ək), **pollock** *n.* (*pl. in general* **pollack, pollock**, *in particular* **pollacks, pollocks**) a sea fish, *Pollachius pollachius*, with a protruding lower jaw, used for food. [etym. uncertain]

pollan (pol´ən) *n.* a herring-like Irish freshwater fish, *Coregonus pollan.* [rel. to Gael. *pollag* or Ir. *pollôg*, perh. from Gael. *poll, phuill*, pool, pit]

pollard (pol´əd) *n.* 1 a tree with its branches cut off so as to have a dense head of new young branches. 2 a stag or other animal that has cast its horns. 3 a polled or hornless ox, sheep or other animal. **4** the chub. **5** a mixture of fine bran with a small quantity of flour, orig. bran sifted from flour. ~*v.t.* to lop the top of (a tree). **pollarded** *a.* **1** lopped, cropped. **2** wanting horns. [POLL[1]]

polled POLL[2].

pollen (pol´ən) *n.* a powder of fine dustlike grains discharged from the anthers of flowers and able to fertilize in the ovules. **pollen analysis** *n.* PALYNOLOGY. **pollen basket** *n.* a hollow in a bee's hind leg for carrying pollen. **pollen count** *n.* a measure of the pollen present in the air, published to assist hay fever sufferers etc. **pollenless** *a.* **pollenosis** POLLINOSIS (under POLLEN). **pollinarious** (-neə´riəs), **pollinary** (pol´-) *a.* **pollinate** *v.t.* to sprinkle (a stigma) with pollen so as to cause fertilization. **pollination** (-ā´shən) *n.* **pollinator** *n.* **pollinic** (-lin´-) *a.* of or relating to pollen. **polliniferous** (-nif´-) *a.* bearing or producing pollen. **pollinosis** (-ō´sis), **pollenosis** *n.* (*Med.*) hay fever. [L, fine flour]

pollex (pol´eks) *n.* (*pl.* **pollices** (-isēz)) in mammals, the first digit of the forelimb, in primates usu. the thumb. **pollical** *a.* [L, a thumb]

pollie POLLY[2].

pollinarious, pollinate etc. POLLEN.

polliwog (pol´iwog), **pollywog** *n.* (*N Am.*, *dial.*) a tadpole. [ME, *polwygle* (POLL[1], WIGGLE)]

pollock POLLACK.

pollster POLL[1].

pollute (pəloot´) *v.t.* **1** to make foul or unclean. **2** to contaminate (an environment), esp. with man-made waste. **3** to defile; to corrupt the moral purity of. **4** to dishonour, to ravish. **5** to profane. **pollutant** *a.*, *n.* **polluted** *a.* **pollutedly** *adv.* **pollutedness** *n.* **polluter** *n.* **pollution** (-shən) *n.* [L *pollūtus*, p.p. of *polluere* (*pol-*, earlier *por-*, *pro-*, forth, *luere*, to wash]

polly[1] (pol´i) *n.* (*pl.* **pollies**) (*dated*, *coll.*) (a drink of) Apollinaris water. [contr. of *Apollinaris*]

polly[2] (pol´i), **pollie** *n.* (*pl.* **pollies**) (*Austral.*, *coll.*) a politician. [contr. of *politician*]

Pollyanna (polian´ə) *n.* (*pl.* **Pollyannas**) an excessively or irritatingly cheerful and optimistic person. **Pollyannaish** *a.* **Pollyannaism** *n.* [character in a novel (1913) by E. H. Porter, 1868–1920, US writer]

pollywog POLLIWOG.

polo (pō´lō) *n.* (*pl.* **polos**) a game of Asian origin resembling hockey but played on horseback. **polo jumper** *n.* a knitted jumper with a fold-over collar. **polo neck** *n.* (a jumper with) a close-fitting, doubled-over collar. **polo shirt** *n.* a short-sleeved knitted cotton shirt with a collar, opening only partly down the front. **polo stick** *n.* a long-handled mallet for playing polo. [Tibetan *pulu*, ball]

polonaise (polənāz´) *n.* **1** a slow dance of Polish origin. **2** a piece of music in 3/4 time for this. **3** (*Hist.*) an article of dress for women, consisting of a bodice and short skirt in one piece. **4** a similar garment for men worn early in the 19th cent. ~*a.* cooked in a Polish style. [F, fem. of *polonais*, Polish]

polonium (pəlō´niəm) *n.* (*Chem.*) a radioactive element, at. no. 84, chem. symbol Po. [med. L *Polonia*, Poland]

polony (pəlō´ni) *n.* (*pl.* **polonies**) a sausage of partly-cooked pork. [prob. corr. of BOLOGNA]

poltergeist (pōl´təgīst, pol´-) *n.* an alleged spirit which makes its presence known by noises and moving objects. [G, noisy ghost]

poltroon (poltroon´) *n.* a contemptible coward. ~*a.* cowardly, base, contemptible. **poltroonery** *n.* [F *poltron*, It. *poltrone*, from *poltro*, sluggard, orig. bed, perh. cogn. with BOLSTER]

poly[1] (pol´i) *n.* (*pl.* **polys**) (*coll.*) short for POLYTECHNIC.

poly[2] (pol´i) *a.* (*coll.*) short for POLYTHENE, as in *poly bag*.

poly- (pol´i) *comb. form* **1** several, many. **2** excessive, abnormal. **3** (*Chem.*) denoting a polymer. [Gr. *polus*, many]

polyact (pol´iakt) *a.* having several rays, as a sponge spicule.

polyadelphous (poliədel´fəs) *a.* (*Bot.*) having many stamens arranged in three or more groups. [Gr. *adelphos*, brother]

polyamide (poliam´īd, -ā´-) *n.* (*Chem.*) a synthetic, polymeric material such as nylon.

polyandry (pol´iandri) *n.* **1** the practice of a woman having more than one husband at a time. **2** (*Bot.*) the state of a flower having many stamens. **polyandrist** *n.* a woman who has more than one husband. **polyandrous** *a.* **1** (of a woman) having more than one husband. **2** (*Bot.*) (of a flower) having many stamens. [Gr. *anēr andros*, a man, a male]

polyanthus (polian´thəs) *n.* (*pl.* **polyanthuses**) a garden variety of primula, prob. a development from the cowslip or oxlip. [Gr. *poluanthos* (*anthos*, flower)]

polyatomic (poliətom´ik) *a.* (*Chem.*) (of elements) having more than one atom in their molecules, esp. replaceable atoms of hydrogen.

polybasic (polibā´sik) *a.* (of acids etc.) having two or more replaceable hydrogen atoms per molecule.

polybasite (pəlib´əsīt, polibā´sīt) *n.* an iron-black orthorhombic mineral.

polycarbonate (polikah´bənāt) *n.* any of a class of strong thermoplastics, mostly used as moulding materials.

polycarpellary (polikah´pələri), **polycarpous** (-pəs) *a.* (*Bot.*) composed of several carpels.

polycentric (polisen´trik) *a.* having more than one centre or focus. **polycentrism** *n.*

polychaete (pol´ikēt) *a.* belonging to the Polychaeta, a class of marine worms with setae. ~*n.* a polychaete worm. **polychaetan** (-kē´-), **polychaetous** *a.*

polychlorinated biphenyl (poliklōrinātid bīfē´nīl) *n.* any of various compounds with two benzene molecules in which chlorinated atoms have replaced hydrogens.

polychromatic (polikrəmat´ik) *a.* **1** exhibiting many colours or a play of colours. **2** (of radiation) containing more than one wavelength. **polychromatism** (-krō´mətizm) *n.* **polychrome** (pol´ikrōm) *n.* **1** a work of art executed in several colours, esp. a statue. **2** varied colouring. ~*a.* having or executed in many colours. **polychromic** (-krō´-), **polychromous** *a.* **polychromy** (pol´ikrōmi) *n.* the art of decorating (pottery, statuary or buildings) in many colours.

polyclinic (poliklin´ik) *n.* a clinic dealing with various diseases; a general hospital.

polycotton (pol´ikotən) *n.* a fabric made of a mixture of polyester and cotton fabrics. ~*a.* (of a garment etc.) made of such a fabric.

polycotyledon (polikotilē´dən) *n.* (*Bot.*) a plant with seeds having more than two cotyledons. **polycotyledonous** *a.*

polycrystalline (polikris´təlīn) *a.* (of a solid substance) having constituent substances with differently-oriented crystals. **polycrystal** (pol´-) *n.* such a substance.

polycyclic (polisī´klik, -sik´lik) *a.* **1** (*Chem.*) having more than one ring of atoms in the molecule. **2** (*Biol.*) having more than one ring or whorl.

polydactyl (polidak´til) *a.* having more than the normal number of fingers or toes. ~*n.* a polydactyl animal. **polydactylism** *n.* **polydactylous** *a.*

polyester (polies´tə) *n.* **1** any of a group of synthetic polymers made up of esters, used esp. in making fibres for cloth, plastics and resins. **2** a fabric made of such fibres.

polyethene, polyethylene POLYTHENE.

polygamy (pəlig´əmi) *n.* **1** the practice or condition of having more than one wife or husband at the same time. **2** the state of having more than one mate. **3**

(*Bot.*) the state of having male, female and hermaphrodite flowers on the same plant. **polygamic** (-gam´ik) *a.* **polygamist** *n.* **polygamous** *a.* **polygamously** *adv.*

polygene (pol´ijēn) *n.* (*Biol.*) any of a group of genes that together control a single characteristic.

polygenesis (polijen´isis) *n.* the theory that a race or species descends from several independent ancestral groups. **polygenetic** (-jinet´-) *a.*

polygenism (polij´ənizm), **polygeny** (-əni) *n.* the theory that the different races of humankind are descended from different original ancestors, and therefore represent different species. **polygenic** (-jen´-) *a.* **1** (*Chem.*) forming more than one compound with hydrogen. **2** (*Geol.*) polygenous. **polygenist** *n.* **polygenistic** (-nis´-) *a.* **polygenous** (-lij´-) *a.* **1** (*Geol.*) consisting of many kinds of material. **2** (*Chem.*) polygenic.

polyglot (pol´iglot) *a.* expressed in or speaking many languages. ~*n.* **1** a polyglot person. **2** a book, esp. the Bible, written in or translated into many languages. **polyglottal** (-glot´-), **polyglottic** *a.* **polyglottism** *n.* [Gr. *poluglōttos* (*glōtta*, tongue)]

polygon (pol´igon) *n.* a closed plane figure, usu. rectilinear and of more than four angles or sides. **polygonal** (pəlig´ənəl), †**polygonous** (-lig´-) *a.* **polygonally** *adv.* **polygon of forces** *n.* a polygon which represents the various forces acting on a body by the arrangement of its sides. [L *polygōnum*, Gr. *polugōnon* (*gōnia*, corner, angle)]

polygonum (pəlig´ənəm) *n.* any plant of the genus *Polygonum*, comprising the knotgrass etc., with jointed stems. [Gr. *polugōnon* (*gonu*, knee)]

polygraph (pol´igrahf) *n.* **1** an instrument which registers several small physiological changes simultaneously, e.g. in pulse rate, body temperature, often used as a lie detector. **2** an apparatus for multiplying copies of writing, drawings etc. **polygraphic** (-graf´-) *a.* **polygraphically** *adv.* **polygraphy** (-lig´-) *n.*

polygyny (polij´ini) *n.* **1** the practice or condition of having more than one wife at a time. **2** the practice of mating with more than one female in a season. **3** (*Bot.*) the state of having several styles. **polygynous** (-lij´-) *a.* [Gr. *gunē*, woman]

polyhedron (polihē´drən) *n.* (*pl.* **polyhedrons, polyhedra** (-drə)) a solid bounded by many (usu. more than four) plane sides. **polyhedral, polyhedric, polyhedrous** *a.* [Gr. *poluedron* (*hedra*, a base)]

polyhistor (polihis´tə) *n.* a polymath. [Gr. *poluistōr* (*histōr*, learned, see HISTORY)]

polymath (pol´imath) *n.* a person of great and varied learning. **polymathic** (-math´-) *a.* **polymathist** (-lim´-) *n.* **polymathy** (-lim´-) *n.* wide and multifarious learning. [Gr. *polumathēs* (*manthanein*, to learn)]

polymer (pol´imə) *n.* (*Chem.*) a compound, formed by polymerization, which has large molecules made up of many comparatively simple repeated units. **polymerase** (pol´imərāz, pəlim´ərāz) *n.* an enzyme which catalyses the polymerization of DNA or RNA. **polymeric** (-mer´ik) *a.* of, relating to or constituting a polymer. **polymerize, polymerise** *v.t.* **1** to cause to undergo polymerization. **2** (*Biol.*) to render polymerous. ~*v.i.* to undergo polymerization. **polymerization** (-zā´shən) *n.* a chemical reaction in which two or more small molecules combine as repeating units in a much larger molecule. **polymerous** (-lim´-) *a.* **1** (*Biol.*) consisting of many parts. **2** polymeric. [Gr. *polumerēs* (*meros*, portion)]

polymorphic (polimaw´fik) *a.* having, assuming, or occurring in many forms. **polymorph** (pol´-) *n.* **polymorphism** *n.* **polymorphous** *a.* [Gr. *morphē*, form]

Polynesian (polinē´zhən) *a.* of or relating to Polynesia, a group of islands of the central and southern Pacific. ~*n.* **1** a native or inhabitant of Polynesia. **2** the group of related languages spoken in Polynesia, including Maori and Hawaiian. [Gr. *nēsos*, island]

polyneuritis (polinūrī´tis) *n.* (*Med.*) simultaneous inflammation of many nerves. **polyneuritic** (-nūrit´ik) *a.*

polynia POLYNYA.

polynomial (polinō´miəl) *a.* (*Math.*) multinomial. ~*n.* a multinomial. **polynomialism** *n.* [L *nōmen*, name]

polynya (pəlin´iə), **polynia** *n.* an open place in water that is for the most part frozen over, esp. in the Arctic. [Rus. *polynya*]

polyonymous (polion´iməs) *a.* having many different names. **polyonymic** (-nim´-) *a.* **polyonymist** *n.* **polyonymy** *n.* [Gr. *onoma*, a name]

polyp (pol´ip) *n.* **1** any one of various coelenterates, such as the hydra, the sea anemone etc., an individual in a compound organism of various kinds. **2** (*Med.*) a polypus. **polypary** *n.* (*pl.* **polyparies**) the calcareous or chitonous structure supporting a colony of polyps. [F *polype*, L POLYPUS]

polypeptide (polipep´tīd) *n.* (*Chem.*) any of a group of polymers made up of long amino-acid chains.

polypetalous (polipet´ələs) *a.* (*Bot.*) having many or separate petals.

polyphagous (pəlif´əgəs) *a.* **1** feeding on various kinds of food. **2** abnormally voracious. **polyphagia** (polifā´jiə) *n.*

polyphase (pol´ifāz) *a.* (of a circuit or system) having, producing or using two or more alternating voltages of equal frequency, the phases of which are cyclically displaced by fractions of a period.

polyphone (pol´ifōn) *n.* a symbol or letter standing for more than one sound. **polyphonic** (-fon´-), **polyphonous** (-lif´-) *a.* **1** (of a symbol or letter) representing different sounds. **2** (*Mus.*) contrapuntal. **3** having several sounds or voices, many-voiced. **polyphonically** *adv.* **polyphonism** *n.* **polyphonist** *n.* a contrapuntist. **polyphony** *n.* (*pl.* **polyphonies**) **1** the state of being polyphonic. **2** composition in parts, each part having an independent melody of its own, counterpoint. [Gr. *poluphōnos* (*phōnē*, voice, sound)]

polyphosphate (polifos´fāt) *n.* (*Chem.*) any of several complex phosphates, used as food additives.

polyphyletic (polifīlet´ik) *a.* (*Biol.*) (of a group of organisms) descended from more than one ancestral group.

polypi POLYPUS.

polyploid (pol´iploid) *a.* (*Biol.*) having more than twice the basic (haploid) number of chromosomes. ~*n.* a polyploid organism or nucleus. **polyploidy** *n.* [by analogy with *haploid*, *diploid*]

polypod (pol´ipod) *a.* having numerous feet. ~*n.* a millipede, e.g. a woodlouse. **polypodous** (pəlip´ədəs) *a.* [F *polypode* (Gr. *pous podos*, foot)]

polypody (pol´ipōdi) *n.* (*pl.* **polypodies**) a fern of the genus *Polypodium*, growing on rocks, walls, trees etc. **polypodiaceous** (-ā´shəs) *a.* [L *polypodium*, Gr. *polupodion* (*podion*, dim. of *pous podos*, foot)]

polypoid (pol´ipoid) *a.* like a polyp or polypus. **polypose, polypous** *a.*

polypropylene (poliprōp´ilēn), **polypropene** (-prō´pēn) *n.* (*Chem.*) any of various plastics or fibres that are polymers of propylene, used for laminates, pipes and various fibres.

polypus (pol´ipəs) *n.* (*pl.* **polypuses, polypi** (-pī)) (*Med.*) a usu. benign growth with ramifications growing in a mucous cavity; a polyp. [L, from Gr. *polupous* (*pous podos*, foot)]

polyrhythm (pol´iridhm) *n.* (*Mus.*) the use of two or more different rhythms in the same piece. **polyrhythmic** (-ridh´mik) *a.*

polysaccharide (polisak´ərīd) *n.* any of a class of carbohydrates, e.g. starch, insulin etc., whose molecules contain chains of monosaccharides.

polysemous (polisē´məs) *a.* having several meanings in one word. **polysemic** *a.* **polysemy** (pol´isēmi, pəlis´imi) *n.* [Gr. *sema*, a sign]

polysepalous (polisep´ələs) *a.* (*Bot.*) having the sepals distinct.

polystyrene (polistī´rēn) *n.* a thermoplastic polymer of styrene used esp. as a transparent plastic for moulded products or in expanded form, as a rigid white foam, for packaging and insulation.

polysyllabic (polisilab´ik) *a.* **1** (of a word) consisting of many syllables. **2** characterized by polysyllables. **polysyllabically** *adv.* **polysyllable** (pol´-) *n.* a polysyllabic word. [L *polysyllabus*, Gr. *polusullabos*]

polysyndeton (polisin´ditən) *n.* a rhetorical figure in which the conjunction or copulative is repeated several times. [Gr. *sundetos*, from *sundeein* (*deein*, to bind)]

polysynthetic (polisinthet´ik) *a.* **1** compounded of several elements. **2** combining several words (verbs and adverbs, complements etc.) into one. **polysynthesis** (-sin´-) *n.* **polysynthetically** *adv.* **polysynthetism** *n.*

polytechnic (politek´nik) *a.* connected with, of or relating to, or giving instruction in many subjects, esp. technical ones. ~*n.* (*Hist.*) a college where degree and other advanced courses were given in technical, vocational and academic subjects. [F *polytechnique*, Gr. *polutechnos* (*technē*, art)]

polytetrafluoroethylene (politetrəfluərōeth´ilēn) *n.* a tough, translucent plastic used esp. for moulded articles and as a non-stick coating.

polytheism (pol´ithēizm, -thē´-) *n.* the belief in or worship of a plurality of gods. **polytheist** *n.* **polytheistic, polytheistical** *a.* **polytheistically** *adv.* [F *polythéisme*, Gr. *polutheos* (*theos*, god)]

polythene (pol´ithēn), **polyethene** (-eth´ēn), **polyethylene** (polieth´ilēn) *n.* any of various thermoplastics that are polymers of ethylene, used for packaging, domestic utensils, insulation etc.

polytonality (politənal´iti) *n.* (*Mus.*) the use of two or more keys at the same time in a piece. **polytonal** (-tō´nəl) *a.* **polytonalism** *n.* **polytonally** *adv.*

polytypic (politip´ik) *a.* having or existing in many forms. **polytypical** *a.*

polyunsaturated (poliŭnsat´ūrātid) *a.* (of certain animal and vegetable fats) having long carbon chains with many double bonds. **polyunsaturate** *n.* a polyunsaturated animal or vegetable fat.

polyurethane (poliū´rəthān) *n.* any of a class of polymeric resins used esp. as foam for insulation and packing or in paints.

polyvalent (polivā´lənt) *n.* MULTIVALENT.

polyvinyl (polivī´nil, -əl) *n.*, *a.* (*Chem.*) (of, related to or being) a polymerized vinyl compound. **polyvinyl acetate** *n.* a soft colourless polymer used in paint, adhesives etc. **polyvinyl chloride** *n.* a tough transparent polymer used esp. for coating wires and cables, insulation etc.

polyzoan (polizō´ən) *n.* any member of a class of invertebrate animals, mostly marine, existing in coral-like or plantlike colonies. ~*a.* of or relating to these animals. **polyzoal** *a.* **polyzoarial** (-eə´ri-) *a.* **polyzoary** *n.* (*pl.* **polyzoaries**) the polypary of a polyzoan colony. **polyzoic** *a.* **polyzooid** (-oid) *a.* [Gr. *zōon*, animal]

polyzonal (polizō´nəl) *a.* (of lighthouse lenses) composed of many zones or annular segments.

POM *abbr.* prescription-only medicine.

Pom[1] POMMY.

Pom[2] (pom) *n.* (*coll.*) a Pomeranian dog.

pomace (pŭm´is) *n.* **1** the mashed pulp of apples crushed in a cider-mill, esp. the refuse after the juice has been pressed out. **2** any pulpy substance left after crushing, esp. of fish after oil has been extracted. [med. L *pōmācium*, cider, from L *pōmum*, apple]

pomaceous (pəmā´shəs) *a.* of the nature of a pome or of trees producing pomes, such as the apple, pear, quince etc. [from F *pomme* or L *pōmum*, apple]

pomade (pəmād´, -mahd´) *n.* a perfumed ointment for dressing the hair and the scalp. ~*v.t.* to apply this to (the hair etc.). [F *pommade*, from *pomme*, apple (perh. orig. prepared partly from the pulp of apples)]

pomander (pōman´də, pom-) *n.* **1** a perfumed ball or powder kept in a box, bag etc., used as a scent and formerly carried about the person to prevent infection. **2** the perforated box or hollow ball in which this is kept or carried. **3** a spiced orange similarly used. [altered from *pomamber*, OF *pomme d'ambre* (*pomme*, apple, *ambre*, AMBER)]

pomatum (pəmā´təm) *n.* pomade. ~*v.t.* to dress (the hair) with pomatum. [mod. L, from L *pōmum*, apple]

pome (pōm) *n.* **1** a compound fleshy fruit, composed of an enlarged receptacle enclosing carpels containing the seeds, such as the apple, pear, quince etc. **2** (*poet.*) an apple. **†pomecitron** (-sit´rən) *n.* a citron. **pomiculture** (pō´mikŭlchə) *n.* fruit-growing. **pomiferous** (-mif´-) *a.* bearing apples or pomes. **pomiform** (pō´mifawm) *a.* shaped like a pome or apple. **pomology** (pəmol´-) *n.* the art or science of the cultivation of fruit. **pomological** (pōməloj´-) *a.* **pomologist** (pəmol´-) *n.* [OF *pome* (F *pomme*), L *pōmum*]

pomegranate (pom´igranit) *n.* **1** the fruit of a N African and W Asian tree, *Punica granatum*, resembling an orange, with a thick, tough rind and acid red pulp enveloping numerous seeds. **2** the tree bearing this fruit. **3** a carving etc. representing a pomegranate. [OF *pome grenate* (POME, *grenate*, L *grānāta*, seeded, from *grānum*, seed)]

pomelo (pom´ilō, pŭm´-) *n.* (*pl.* **pomelos**) **1** a shaddock. **2** a grapefruit. [etym. uncertain]

Pomeranian (pomərā´niən) *a.* of or relating to Pomerania, a region of N Europe, now mainly in Poland. ~*n.* **1** a native or inhabitant of Pomerania, or a person of Pomeranian descent. **2** a breed of dog, small with a fox-like pointed muzzle and long, silky hair. **3** a dog of this breed.

pomfret (pom´frit) *n.* (*pl. in general* **pomfret**, *in particular* **pomfrets**) **1** any of various food-fishes of the Indian and Pacific oceans, of the family Stromateidae. **2** a food-fish of northern oceans, *Brama brama*. [perh. Port. *pampo*]

pomfret-cake (pom´frit, pŭm´-), **Pontefract-cake** (pon´tifrakt-) *n.* a flat cake of liquorice, orig. made in Pontefract. [*Pomfret*, now *Pontefract*, town in Yorkshire]

pomiculture, pomiferous etc. POME.

pommel (pom´əl, pŭm´əl) *n.* **1** a round ball or knob, esp. on the hilt of a sword. **2** the upward projection at the front of a saddle. **3** either of the two handles on top of a pommel horse. ~*v.t.* (*pres.p.* **pommelling**, (*N Am.*) **pommeling**, *past, p.p.* **pommelled**, (*N Am.*) **pommeled**) to pummel. **pommel horse** *n.* a vaulting horse with a pair of curved handles. [ME and OF *pomel* (F *pommeau*), dim. of L *pōmum*, POME]

Pommy (pom´i), **Pommie, Pom** (pom) *n.* (*pl.* **Pommies, Poms**) (*Austral., New Zeal., derog.*) a British person, esp. an immigrant to Australia or New Zealand. ~*a.* British. [etym. uncertain, perh. from *pomegranate*, rhyming with *Jimmy Grant, immigrant*]

pomology POME.

pomp (pomp) *n.* **1** a pageant. **2** ceremonial display, splendour. **3** ostentatious display or parade. [F *pompe*, L *pompa*, Gr. *pompē*, sending, procession, cogn. with *pempein*, to send]

pompadour (pom´pəduə) *n.*, *a.* (*Hist.*) a method of wearing the hair brushed up from the forehead or (in women) turned back in a roll from the forehead. [Marquise de *Pompadour*, 1721–64, mistress of Louis XV]

pompano (pom´pənō) *n.* (*pl. in general* **pompano,** *in particular* **pompanos**) a W Indian food-fish of various species belonging to the family Garangidae or Stromateidae. [Sp. *pámpano*]

Pompeian (pompā´ən, -ē´ən) *a.* of or relating to Pompeii, an Italian town buried by an eruption of Vesuvius in AD 79.

pom-pom (pom´pom) *n.* an automatic quick-firing gun, usu. mounted for anti-aircraft defence. [imit.]

pompon (pom´pon), **pompom** (-pom) *n.* **1** an ornament in the form of a tuft or ball of feathers, ribbon etc. worn on women's and children's hats, shoes etc., on the front of a soldier's shako, on a French sailor's cap etc. **2** a small compact chrysanthemum or dahlia. [F *pompon*, etym. uncertain]

pompous (pom´pəs) *a.* **1** exaggeratedly solemn or portentous, self-important. **2** ostentatious, pretentious. **3** grand, magnificent. **4** displaying pomp. **pomposity** (-pos´-) *n.* (*pl.* **pomposities**). **pomposo** (-pō´sō) *adv.* (*Mus.*) in a stately or dignified manner. **pompously** *adv.* **pompousness** *n.* [F *pompeux*, late L *pompōsus*]

†**'pon** (pon) *prep.* upon.

ponce (pons) *n.* (*sl.*) **1** a prostitute's pimp. **2** an effeminate man. ~*v.i.* to pimp. **to ponce about/ around 1** to act in an ostentatious or effeminate manner. **2** to fool about, to waste time. **poncey, poncy** *a.* (*comp.* **poncier,** *superl.* **ponciest**). [perh. from POUNCE[1]]

poncho (pon´chō) *n.* (*pl.* **ponchos**) **1** a woollen cloak, worn in S America, with a slit in the middle through which the head passes. **2** a cycling-cape of this pattern. [S Am. Sp., from Araucanian]

poncy PONCE.

pond (pond) *n.* **1** a body of still water, often artificial, smaller than a lake. **2** (*facet.*) the sea, esp. the Atlantic Ocean. ~*v.t.* **1** to dam back. **2** to make into a pond. ~*v.i.* (of water) to form a pool or pond. **pondage** (-ij) *n.* **pondlet** *n.* **pond life** *n.* all the animals living in ponds. **pond lily** *n.* a water lily. **pond-skater** *n.* any of various heteropterous insects of the family Gerridae, able to run on the surface of a pond supported by surface tension. **pond snail** *n.* a freshwater snail that lives in ponds, esp. one of the genus *Limnaea.* **pondweed** *n.* an aquatic plant growing on stagnant water, esp. species of *Potamogeton.* [prob. var. of POUND[2]]

ponder (pon´də) *v.t.* to weigh carefully in the mind; to think over, to consider deeply, to reflect upon. ~*v.i.* to think, to deliberate, to muse (on, over etc.). **ponderable** *a.* (*formal*) capable of being weighed, having appreciable weight, as distinct from *imponderable.* **ponderability** (-bil´-), **ponderableness** *n.* **ponderal** *a.* **ponderance** *n.* (*formal*) **1** weight. **2** gravity, importance. **ponderation** (-ā´shən) *n.* (*formal*) **1** the act of pondering. **2** the act of weighing. **ponderer** *n.* **ponderingly** *adv.* **ponderosity** (-os´-) *n.* **ponderous** *a.* **1** very heavy or weighty. **2** bulky, unwieldy. **3** dull, tedious. **4** pompous, self-important. **ponderously** *adv.* **ponderousness** *n.* [OF *ponderer*, L *ponderāre*, from *pondus -deris*, weight]

ponderosa (pondərō´zə, -sə) *n.* **1** a N American pine tree, *Pinus ponderosa.* **2** the wood from this tree. [mod. L, fem. of *ponderosus*, heavy, from *pondus -deris*, weight]

pone[1] (pōn) *n.* (*N Am.*) **1** a kind of bread made by N American Indians of maize meal. **2** a similar bread made with eggs, milk etc. **3** a loaf of this. [Algonquian]

pone[2] (pōn, pō´ni) *n.* **1** the player to the dealer's right who cuts the cards. **2** in a two-handed card game, the non-dealer. [from L *pone*, imper. of *ponere*, to put]

pong (pong) *n.* (*coll.*) a bad smell, a stink. ~*v.i.* to stink. **pongy** *a.* (*comp.* **pongier,** *superl.* **pongiest**) having an unpleasant smell. [prob. Romany *pan*, to stink]

pongal (pong´gəl) *n.* **1** the Tamil festival celebrating New Year, in which rice is cooked. **2** a dish of cooked rice. [Tamil]

pongee (pŭnjē´, pon-) *n.* **1** a soft unbleached kind of Chinese silk. **2** a fine cotton fabric resembling this. [perh. from N Chin. *pun-chī*, own loom]

pongid (pon´jid) *n.* any ape of the family Pongidae, incl. orang-utans, gorillas and chimpanzees. ~*a.* of or relating to this family of apes. [mod. L, see PONGO]

pongo (pong´gō) *n.* (*pl.* **pongos**) **1** a large African anthropoid ape. **2** the orang-utan. **3** (*Mil., sl.*) a soldier. **4** (*Austral., New Zeal., sl., derog.*) an Englishman. [Kongo *mpongi*]

poniard (pon´yəd) *n.* (*formal*) a small fine-bladed dagger. ~*v.t.* to stab with a poniard. [F *poignard*, from *poing*, L *pugnus*, fist]

pons (ponz) *n.* (*pl.* **pontes** (pon´tēz)) **1** a bridge. **2** (*Anat.*) a connecting part, esp. the pons Varolii. **pons asinorum** (asinaw´rəm) *n.* any severe test for a beginner. **pons Varolii** (vərō´liī) *n.* a band of fibres connecting the two hemispheres of the cerebellum. **pontine** (-tīn) *a.* [L *pons pontis*]

pont (pont) *n.* (*S Afr.*) a small ferry boat, esp. one guided across a river by a cable. [Dut.]

Pontefract-cake POMFRET-CAKE.

pontes PONS.

Pontic (pon´tik) *a.* of or relating to the Black Sea. [L *ponticus*, Gr. *Pontikos*, from *pontos*, sea, esp. the Black Sea]

pontifex (pon´tifeks) *n.* (*pl.* **pontifices** (-tif´isēz)) **1** the Pope. **2** (*Hist.*) a member of the highest of the ancient Roman colleges of priests. **Pontifex Maximus** (mak´siməs) *n.* **1** (*Hist.*) the president of the ancient Roman pontifex. **2** the Pope. [L (*pons pontis*, bridge, sacrifice, *-fex*, *-fic*, from *facere*, to make)]

pontiff (pon´tif) *n.* **1** (*also* **sovereign pontiff, supreme pontiff**) the Pope. **2** a pontifex, a high priest. **pontifical** (-tif´-), †**pontific** *a.* **1** of, relating to or befitting a pontiff, high priest or pope. **2** papal, popish. **3** with an assumption of authority, pompous, dogmatic. ~*n.* **1** a book containing the forms for rites and ceremonies to be performed by bishops. **2** (*pl.*) the vestments and insignia of a pontiff or bishop. **pontifically** *adv.* **pontifical Mass** *n.* a High Mass celebrated by a bishop, cardinal etc. **pontificate**[1] (-kət) *n.* the office, or period of office, of a bishop or pope. **pontify** (-fī) *v.i.* (*3rd pers. sing. pres.* **pontifies,** *pres.p.* **pontifying,** *past, p.p.* **pontified**) to act in the style of a pontiff, esp. to claim infallibility. [F *pontife*, *pontif*, from PONTIFEX]

pontificate[1] PONTIFF.

pontificate[2] (pontif´ikāt) *v.t.* to celebrate (Mass etc.) as a bishop. ~*v.i.* **1** to officiate as a pontiff or bishop, esp. at Mass. **2** to speak or behave in a pompous and dogmatic manner. [as PONTIFF]

pontifices PONTIFEX.

pontify PONTIFF.

pontil (pon´til) *n.* **1** an iron rod used for handling, twisting or carrying glass in process of manufacture. **2** a punty. [F, prob. from It. *pontello*, *puntello*, dim. of *punto*, POINT]

pontine PONS.

pontoon[1] (pontoon´) *n.* **1** a card game in which the object is to make the aggregate number of the pips on the cards as nearly as possible 21, without exceeding this number. **2** a hand making 21 at the first deal in this game. [as VINGT-ET-UN]

pontoon[2] (pontoon´) *n.* **1** a flat-bottomed boat, cylinder or other buoyant structure supporting a floating bridge. **2** a caisson. **3** a barge or lighter. **4** a pontoon bridge. ~*v.t.* to bridge with pontoons. **pontoon bridge** *n.* a platform or roadway laid across pontoons. [F *ponton*, L *pontōnem*, nom. *-to*, from *pons pontis*, bridge]

pony (pō´ni) *n.* (*pl.* **ponies**) **1** a horse of any small breed. **2** a small glass. **3** (*sl.*) 25 pounds sterling. **4** (*pl., sl.*)

racehorses. 5 (*N Am., sl.*) a crib or translation used in preparing lessons etc. **pony engine** *n.* a small locomotive for shunting. **pony express** *n.* (*Hist.*) a postal and delivery system across the western US, 1860–61, using relays of horses and riders. **ponytail** *n.* a hairstyle in which the hair is gathered at the back and hangs down over the nape of the neck like a tail. **pony-trekking** *n.* cross-country pony-riding in groups as a pastime. **pony-trekker** *n.* [OF *poulenet*, dim. of *poulain*, late L *pullānus*, L *pullus*, foal]

poo POOH.

pooch (pooch) *n.* (*esp. N Am., coll.*) a dog.

pood (pood) *n.* a Russian unit of weight of about 36 lb. (16 kg). [Rus. *pudu*, from LG or ON *pund*, POUND[1]]

poodle (poo´dəl) *n.* 1 a breed of pet dog with long woolly hair, often clipped in a fanciful style. 2 a dog of this breed. 3 a servile follower. ~*v.i.* (*sl.*) to travel in a lazy or leisurely way. †**poodle-faker** *n.* (*sl.*) a ladies' man. [G *Pudel*, *Pudelhund*, from *pudeln*, to waddle or to splash (cp. PUDDLE)]

poof[1] (puf, poof), **pooftah** (-tə), **poofter, poove** (poov), **pouf** *n.* (*sl., offensive*) 1 a male homosexual. 2 an effeminate man. **poofy** *a.* [perh. from F *pouffe*, puff]

poof[2] (puf) *int.* 1 used to express rejection or contempt. 2 used to announce a disappearance as if by magic. [imit.]

pooftah, poofter POOF[1].

pooh (poo), **poo** *int.* 1 used to express contempt or impatience. 2 used to express disgust, esp. at a bad smell. ~*n.* excrement (used by or to children). **pooh-pooh** (-poo´) *v.t.* 1 to laugh or sneer at. 2 to make light of. [imit. of instinctive action of blowing away]

Pooh-bah (poobah´), **pooh-bah** *n.* 1 a person holding many offices. 2 a pompous and conceited person. [character in W. S. Gilbert's *The Mikado* (1885)]

pooh-pooh POOH.

pooja PUJA.

pooka (poo´kə) *n.* (*pl.* **pookas**) a hobgoblin, sometimes represented in the form of a horse. [Ir. *púca*]

pool[1] (pool) *n.* 1 a small body of water, still or nearly still. 2 a deep, still part of a stream. 3 a puddle. 4 a pond, natural or ornamental. 5 a swimming pool. 6 an underground accumulation of oil or gas. ~*v.i.* to gather or settle in a pool or pools; to form a pool. **poolside** *n.* the area round the side of a swimming pool. ~*a., adv.* beside a pool. [OE *pōl* (cp. Dut. *poel*, G *Pfuhl*)]

pool[2] (pool) *n.* 1 a group of people, vehicles, tools etc. available for use when required. 2 a group of people who share duties or routine work. 3 a game played on a billiard table in which the players aim to drive different balls into the pockets in a certain order. 4 the collective stakes in a betting arrangement. 5 the receptacle for the stakes in certain games of cards. 6 (*pl.*) football pools. 7 a group of competitors who play against each other for the right to progress in a tournament. 8 a combination of persons, companies etc., for manipulating prices and suppressing competition. 9 a common stock or fund to be used for such manipulation. ~*v.t.* 1 to put (funds, risks etc.) into a common fund or pool. 2 to share (goods, resources) in common. 3 (*Austral., sl.*) to inform on, involve (a person in a crime). **to scoop the pool** 1 to win all the money staked in a gambling game. 2 to come away with everything, to be totally successful. **pool hall** *n.* a room, or an establishment, where pool is played. **pool room** *n.* (*N Am.*) a pool hall. **pool table** *n.* a table, like a billiard table, for playing pool. [prob. from F *poule*, hen]

poon (poon) *n.* any large Indian tree of the genus *Calophyllum*. **poon oil** *n.* a bitter oil obtained from the seeds of this, used in medicine and in lamps. **poon wood** *n.* [Sinhalese *pūna*]

poop[1] (poop) *n.* 1 the stern of a ship. 2 a high deck over the after part of a spar-deck. ~*v.t.* 1 (of waves) to break heavily over the poop of. 2 (of a ship) to take (a wave) over the stern. **poop deck** *n.* **pooped**[1] *a.* having a poop. [ME and OF *pupe* (F *poupe*), late L *puppa*, L *puppis*]

poop[2] (poop) *v.t.* (*esp. N Am., coll.*) to render breathless, to exhaust. ~*v.i.* to become exhausted. **to poop out** 1 to become exhausted. 2 to give up. **pooped**[2] *a.* [etym. uncertain]

poop[3] (poop) *v.i.* (*coll.*) 1 to defecate. 2 to break wind. ~*n.* 1 faeces. 2 the act of defecating or breaking wind. 3 a toot. **poop scoop, pooper scooper** *n.* a device for cleaning dogs' excrement from a pavement etc. [imit.]

poop[4] (poop) *n.* (*coll.*) a stupid or ineffectual person. [short for NINCOMPOOP]

poop[5] (poop) *n.* (*N Am., sl.*) information, esp. useful or up-to-date. [etym. uncertain]

pooped[1] POOP[1].

pooped[2] POOP[2].

poor (puə) *a.* 1 lacking enough money to live on, needy, indigent. 2 badly supplied, lacking (in). 3 (of land) barren, unproductive. 4 scanty, meagre, inadequate in quantity or quality, unsatisfactory. 5 lean, thin, wasted; unhealthy. 6 uncomfortable. 7 inferior, sorry, paltry, miserable, contemptible. 8 insignificant, humble, meek. 9 unfortunate, pitiable, used as a term of slight contempt, pity or endearment. **in a poor light** LIGHT[1]. **in poor taste** TASTE. **the poor** those who are needy or indigent, esp. those who depend on charity or state benefit. **to take a poor view of** to regard unfavourably or pessimistically. **poor box** *n.* a money box, esp. in a church for charitable contributions. **poorhouse** *n.* (*Hist.*) a workhouse. **poor law** *n.* (*Hist.*) the body of laws relating to the maintenance of paupers. **poorly** *adv.* 1 with poor results, with little success. 2 defectively, imperfectly. 3 meanly, despicably. ~*a.* in delicate health; unwell, indisposed. **poorliness** *n.* **poor man's** *a.* cheap, inferior (substitute for something). **poor man's weather-glass** *n.* the pimpernel. **poorness** *n.* **poor rate** *n.* (*Hist.*) a rate levied for the support of paupers. **poor relation** *n.* a person or thing looked down on, considered inferior, or shabbily treated in comparison to others. **poor show** *n.* something badly done. **poor-spirited** *a.* 1 timid, cowardly. 2 mean, base. **poor-spiritedness** *n.* **poor value** *n.* not worth the money, time, attention etc. expended on it. **poor white** *n.* (*usu. derog.*) a member of a class of poverty-stricken and socially inferior white people in the southern US or S Africa. [ME and OF *povre*, *poure* (F *pauvre*), L *pauper*]

pootle (poo´təl) *v.i.* (*coll*) to move along in a leisurely or lazy way. [var. of POODLE]

poove POOF[1].

POP *abbr.* Post Office Preferred (of size of envelopes etc.).

pop[1] (pop) *v.i.* (*pres.p.* **popping**, *past, p.p.* **popped**) 1 to make a short, sharp, explosive noise as of the drawing of a cork. 2 to burst open with such a sound. 3 (esp. of the eyes) to protrude as with amazement. 4 to enter or issue forth with a quick, sudden motion. 5 to dart. 6 to move quickly. 7 to shoot (at) with a gun, pistol etc. ~*v.t.* 1 to push or thrust (in, out, up) suddenly. 2 to put (down etc.) quickly or hastily. 3 to fire off (a gun etc.). 4 to cause (a thing) to pop by breaking etc. 5 (*sl.*) to pawn. 6 (*sl.*) to take (drugs) orally or by injection. 7 (*sl.*) to consume habitually. 8 to cause (maize kernels) to burst by heating. ~*adv.* 1 with a pop. 2 suddenly. ~*n.* 1 a short, sharp, explosive noise. 2 (*coll.*) an effervescing drink, esp. ginger beer or champagne. 3 (*sl.*) the act of pawning. **in pop** (*sl.*) in pawn. **to go pop** to make, or burst with, a popping sound. **to pop off** 1 (*coll.*) to leave hastily. 2 to die. **to pop the question** (*coll.*) to propose marriage. **to pop up** to appear suddenly. **popcorn** *n.* 1 maize kernels burst and puffed up by heating.

2 the kind of maize suitable for this. **pop-eyed** *a.* (*coll.*) 1 having bulging eyes. 2 wide-eyed with surprise or shock. **popgun** *n.* 1 a small toy gun used by children, shooting a pellet or cork with air compressed by a piston. 2 a poor or defective firearm. **popper** *n.* 1 something that pops. 2 (*coll.*) a press stud. 3 (*sl.*) a capsule of amyl nitrite which is crushed and the contents inhaled. **popping-crease** *n.* in cricket, a line four feet in front of the stumps parallel with the bowling crease. **pop-shop** *n.* (*sl.*) a pawnshop. **pop socks** *n.pl.* knee-length women's stockings. **pop-up** *a.* 1 (of books) having illustrations etc. which stand up off the page when the book is opened to give a quasi-three-dimensional effect. 2 having a device which causes the contents to spring up, such as a toaster. 3 (*Comput.*) of, relating to or being a computer facility (e.g. a menu) which can be accessed during the running of a program. [imit.]

pop[2] (pop) *n.* 1 pop music. 2 a pop record, a pop song. 3 (*coll.*) a popular piece of (usu. light) classical music. ~*a.* 1 popular or modern. 2 of or relating to pop music. **top of the pops** TOP[1]. **pop art** *n.* art incorporating everyday objects from popular culture and the mass media. **pop artist** *n.* **pop concert** *n.* a concert at which pop music is played. **pop culture** *n.* behaviour, attitudes, consumption and consumables etc., based on popular music, art etc. **pop festival** *n.* a festival at which pop music is played. **pop group** *n.* a (usu. small) group of musicians who play pop music. **pop music** *n.* modern popular music, post 1950, esp. as characterized by a simple, heavy rhythmic beat and electronic amplification. **poppy**[1] *a.* characteristic of, or sounding like, pop music. **pop record** *n.* **pop singer** *n.* **pop song** *n.* [short for POPULAR]

pop[3] (pop), **pops** (pops) *n.* (*N Am., coll.*) 1 father. 2 used as a familiar form of address to an old or elderly man. [short for POPPA]

pop. *abbr.* 1 popular(ly). 2 population.

popadum, popadam, popadom POPPADOM.

pope[1] (pōp) *n.* 1 (**Pope**) the bishop of Rome as the head of the Roman Catholic Church. 2 the patriarch of Alexandria, the head of the Coptic Church. 3 (*fig.*) a person claiming or credited with infallibility. 4 a small freshwater fish, *Gymnocephalus cernua*, akin to the perch, the ruff. **popedom** *n.* **popeless** *a.* **Popemobile** *n.* (*coll.*) an open vehicle with a raised platform in it, used by the Pope when on tour. **popery** (-pəri) *n.* (*derog.*) the religion, ecclesiastical system or ceremonial of the Roman Catholic Church. **pope's eye** *n.* 1 the gland surrounded with fat in the middle of the thigh of an ox or sheep. 2 (*Sc.*) a cut of steak. **pope's nose** *n.* PARSON'S NOSE (under PARSON). **popish** *a.* 1 (*often derog.*) of or relating to the Pope. 2 (*derog.*) of or relating to popery, papistical. **popishly** *adv.* [OE *pāpa*, as PAPA[2]]

pope[2] (pōp) *n.* a priest in the Greek or Russian Orthodox Church. [Rus. *pop*]

popinjay (pop´injā) *n.* 1 a conceited chattering fop. 2 †a parrot. 3 (*Hist.*) a mark like a parrot set up on a pole to be shot at by archers etc. [ME *popingay*, OF *papingay* (cp. It. *papagallo*, med. L *papagallus*, med. Gr. *papagallos*, *papagas*, Arab. *babaghā*, prob. of imit. orig.)]

popish POPE[1].

poplar (pop´lə) *n.* 1 a large tree of the genus *Populus*, of rapid growth, and having a soft, light wood. 2 (*N Am.*) the tulip tree. [OF *poplier* (F *peuplier*, L *pōpulus*)]

poplin (pop´lin) *n.* a fine cotton fabric with a ribbed surface. [F *popeline*, earlier *papeline*, It. *papalina*, PAPAL (under PAPACY), because made at Avignon]

popliteal (poplit´iəl, poplitē´əl), **poplitic** (-lit´ik) *a.* of or relating to the ham or hollow behind the knee joint. [L *popliteus*, from *poples poplitem*, ham, hough]

poppa (pop´ə) *n.* (*N Am., coll.*) father (used esp. by children). [var. of *papa*]

poppadom (pop´ədəm), **poppadum, popadum, popadam, popadom** *n.* a crisp, thin Indian bread, spiced and fried or roasted, often served with chutneys. [Tamil, Malayalam *poppatam*]

popper POP[1].

poppet (pop´it) *n.* 1 (*coll.*) a darling, a term of endearment. 2 a puppet, a marionette. 3 (*Naut.*) a piece of wood fitted inside the gunwale of a boat. 4 any of the timbers on which a vessel rests in launching. **poppet-head** *n.* (*Mining*) a framework bearing the hoisting-gear at a pithead. **poppet-valve** *n.* a mushroom-shaped valve that can be lifted bodily. [early form of PUPPET]

poppied POPPY[2].

popple (pop´əl) *v.i.* (of floating bodies or water) to bob up and down, to toss, to heave. ~*n.* 1 a tossing or rippling. 2 the sound of this. **popply** *a.* [prob. imit.]

poppy[1] POP[2].

poppy[2] (pop´i) *n.* (*pl.* **poppies**) 1 any of various plants or flowers of the genus *Papaver*, containing plants with large showy flowers chiefly of scarlet colour, with a milky juice having narcotic properties. 2 a poppy-head. **poppied** *a.* full of poppies. **Poppy Day** *n.* Remembrance Sunday. **poppy head** *n.* 1 the seed capsule of a poppy. 2 a finial of foliage or other ornamental top to ecclesiastical woodwork, esp. a pew-end. [OE *popig*, *popæg*, L *papāver*]

poppycock (pop´ikok) *n.* (*sl.*) nonsense, balderdash. [Dut. dial. *pappekack*, soft dung]

pops POP[3].

Popsicle® (pop´sikəl) *n.* (*N Am.*) an ice lolly.

popsy (pop´si), **popsie** *n.* (*pl.* **popsies**) (*dated sl., often derog.*) an attractive young woman. [perh. from *pop*, short for POPPET]

populace (pop´ūləs) *n.* the common people; the masses. [F, from It. *popolaccio*, *popolazzo*, from *popolo*, L *populus*, PEOPLE]

popular (pop´ūlə) *a.* 1 pleasing to or esteemed by the general public or a specific group or an individual. 2 of, relating to, carried on by or prevailing among the general public or the common people. 3 suitable to or easy to be understood by ordinary people, not expensive, not abstruse, not esoteric. 4 democratic. **popular front** *n.* a coalition of left-wing parties in a common front, often against dictatorship. **popularism** *n.* **popularity** (-lar´-) *n.* **popularize, popularise** *v.t.* 1 to make popular. 2 to treat (a subject etc.) in a popular style. 3 to spread (knowledge etc.) among the people. **popularization** (-zā´shən) *n.* **popularizer** *n.* **popularly** *adv.* **popular music** *n.* music of an undemanding kind, appealing to a wide audience. [through OF *populeir* (F *populaire*) or directly from L *populāris*, as POPULACE]

populate (pop´ūlāt) *v.t.* 1 to furnish with inhabitants, to people. 2 to form the population of, to inhabit. **population** (-lā´shən) *n.* 1 the inhabitants of a country etc., collectively. 2 the number of such inhabitants. 3 the (number of) people of a certain class and/or in a specified area. 4 in statistics, the aggregate of individuals or items from which a sample is taken. 5 the group of organisms, or of members of a particular species, in a particular area. 6 the act of populating. **population control** *n.* a policy of controlling the increase in numbers of a population, esp. by encouraging the use of contraception. **population explosion** *n.* a sudden and rapid increase in the size of a population. [late L *populātus*, p.p. of *populāre*, as POPULACE]

populist (pop´ūlist) *n.* 1 a person claiming to represent the interests of the common people. 2 a person who believes in the rights, virtues or wisdom of the common people. ~*a.* of or relating to a populist or to populism. **populism** *n.* **populistic** (-lis´-) *a.*

populous (pop´ūləs) *a.* full of people; thickly populated.

populously *adv.* **populousness** *n.* [F *populeux*, L *populōsus*, as POPULACE]

poral PORE[1].

porbeagle (paw´bēgəl) *n.* a large shark of the genus *Lamna*, a mackerel shark. [Cornish dial., etym. unknown]

porcelain (paw´səlin, -slin) *n.* **1** a fine kind of earthenware, white, thin, and semi-transparent. **2** objects made of this. ~*a.* **1** of, relating to or composed of porcelain. **2** fragile, delicate. **porcelain clay** *n.* kaolin. **porcelainous** (-lā´-), **porcellanic** (-lan´-), **porcellanous** (-sel´ə-), **porcellaneous** (-lā´niəs) *a.* [F *porcelaine*, It. *porcellana*, the sea snail, porcelain, dim. of *porco*, L *porcus*, hog, prob. from the resemblance of the shell to a hog's back]

porch (pawch) *n.* **1** a covered structure in front of, or extending from the entrance to, a building. **2** a covered approach to a doorway. **3** (*N Am.*) a veranda. **4** †a covered walk or portico. **the Porch** the school of philosophy of the Stoics (from the painted portico at Athens in which Zeno and his disciples held their discussions). **porched** *a.* **porchless** *a.* [F *porche*, L *porticum*, nom. *-cus*, PORTICO]

porcine (paw´sīn) *a.* of, relating to or resembling a pig. [F *porcin -cine*, L *porcīnus*, from *porcus*, hog]

porcupine (paw´kūpīn) *n.* **1** any individual of the families Hystricidae or Erethizontidae, rodent quadrupeds covered with erectile, quill-like spines. **2** an animal, plant etc. similarly covered with spines. **porcupine fish** *n.* a tropical fish, *Diodon hystrix*, covered with spines. **porcupine grass** *n.* spinifex. **porcupinish, porcupiny** *a.* [ME *porkepyn*, OF *porc espin*, L *porcus*, hog, *spina*, thorn, SPINE]

pore[1] (paw) *n.* **1** a minute opening, esp. a hole in the skin for absorption, perspiration etc. **2** any of the stomata or other apertures in the cuticle of a plant. **3** a minute interstice between granules, molecules etc. **poral** *a.* **poriferous** (-rif´-) *a.* **poriform** (-fawm) *a.* **porosity** (-ros´-) *n.* (*pl.* **porosities**). **porous** *a.* **1** having (many) pores. **2** permeable to liquids etc. **3** not fully secure. **porously** *adv.* **porousness** *n.* [F, from L *porus*, Gr. *poros*, passage]

pore[2] (paw) *v.i.* **1** to gaze at or study with steady, continued attention and application. **2** to meditate or study patiently and persistently (over, upon etc.). **porer** *n.* [ME *pouren*, *pūren*, etym. uncertain]

porgy (paw´ji) *n.* (*pl. in general* **porgy,** *in particular* **porgies**) any one of a number of N American sea-fishes used for food, esp. of the genus *Calamus*. [Sp. and Port. *pargo*]

poriferan (pərif´ərən) *n.* any aquatic invertebrate animal of the phylum Porifera, the sponges. ~*a.* of or relating to the Porifera or a poriferan. **poriferal** *a.* [L *porus*, PORE[1], *-fer*, bearing]

poriform PORE[1].

porism (paw´rizm) *n.* **1** a proposition dealing with the conditions rendering certain problems indeterminate or capable of innumerable solutions. **2** a corollary. **porismatic** (-mat´-), **poristic** (-ris´-), **poristical** *a.* [L and Gr. *porisma*, from *porizein*, to deduce, from *poros*, way]

pork (pawk) *n.* **1** the flesh of pigs, esp. fresh, as food. **2** (*N Am., sl.*) pork barrel. **pork barrel** *n.* **1** (*N Am.*) a project involving spending large amounts of government money in a way that will please voters. **2** the government money spent. **pork-barrelling,** (*N Am.*) **pork-barreling** *n.* **pork butcher** *n.* **1** a person who kills pigs for sale. **2** a butcher who specializes in pork. **porker** *n.* a pig raised for killing, esp. a young fattened pig. **porklet** (-lit) *n.* **porkling** (-ling) *n.* a small or a young pig. **pork pie** *n.* a pie made of minced pork, usu. round with vertical sides. **pork-pie hat** *n.* a round hat with flat crown and rolled-up brim. **pork scratchings** *n.pl.* crisp pieces of pork fat strained out of melted lard. **porky[1]** *a.* (*comp.* **porkier,** *superl.* **porkiest**) **1** like pork. **2** (*coll.*) fat, fleshy. ~*n.* (*rhyming sl.*) (*also* **porky-pie,** *pl.* **porkies, porky-pies**) a lie. **porkiness** *n.* [F *porc*, L *porcus*, hog]

porky[1] PORK.

porky[2] (paw´ki) *n.* (*pl.* **porkies**) (*N Am., coll.*) a porcupine. [short for PORCUPINE]

porn (pawn), **porno** (paw´nō) *n.* (*coll.*) pornography. ~*a.* pornographic. [Gr. *pornē*, a prostitute]

pornocracy (pawnok´rəsi) *n.* the rule or domination of prostitutes, as in the government of Rome during the 10th cent.

pornography (pawnog´rəfi) *n.* **1** the obscene and exploitative depiction of erotic acts. **2** written, graphic etc. material consisting of or containing this. **pornographer** *n.* **pornographic** (-graf´-) *a.* **pornographically** *adv.*

poro- (por´ō) *comb. form* of or relating to pores. [L *porus*]

poromeric (porəmer´ik) *a.* permeable to water vapour, as certain synthetic leathers. ~*n.* a substance having this characteristic.

porosity, porous PORE[1].

porphyria (pawfir´iə) *n.* any one of a group of inborn metabolic disorders characterized by an abnormal pigment in the urine, severe pain, photosensitivity, and periods of mental confusion. **porphyrin** *n.* any of a class of red or purple pigments found in animal and plant tissues. [Gr. *porphuros*, purple]

porphyrogenitism (pawfirōjen´itizm) *n.* succession to the throne of a younger son born while his father was actually monarch, in preference to an older son born before his father's accession. **porphyrogenite** (-roj´inīt) *n.* **1** a prince born after his father's accession to a throne. **2** a person born in the purple, orig. into the imperial family of Constantinople. **porphyrogeniture** (-chə) *n.* [med. L *porphyrogenitus*, late Gr. *porphurogennētos* (*porphuros*, purple, *gennētos*, born, from *gennaein*, to beget)]

porphyry (paw´firi) *n.* (*pl.* **porphyries**) **1** an igneous rock consisting of a felsitic or cryptocrystalline groundmass full of feldspar or quartz crystals. **2** a rock quarried in Egypt having a purple groundmass with enclosed crystals of feldspar. **porphyrite** (-rīt) *n.* porphyry. **porphyritic** (-rit´-) *a.* **porphyry shell** *n.* a shell of the genus *Murex*, esp. any species yielding a purple dye. [through OF or L from Gr. *porphuros*, purple]

porpoise (paw´pəs) *n.* (*pl. in general* **porpoise,** *in particular* **porpoises**) any small whale of the genus *Phocaena*, as an adult about 5 ft. (1.5 m) long, with a blunt snout. [ME *porpays*, OF *porpeis* (L *porcum*, nom. *-cus*, hog, *piscem*, nom. *-cis*, fish)]

porrect (pərekt´) *v.t.* **1** to stretch forward horizontally (esp. a part of the body, such as the palpi of moths). **2** in ecclesiastical law, to tender or submit. ~*a.* (*Bot.*) stretched forward horizontally. [L *porrectus*, p.p. of *porrigere* (*por-*, PRO-[1], *regere*, to stretch, direct)]

porridge (por´ij) *n.* **1** a dish made by boiling oatmeal etc. in water or milk till it thickens. **2** (*sl.*) a term of imprisonment. **porridgy** *a.* [var. of POTTAGE]

porringer (por´injə) *n.* a small basin or bowl out of which soup etc. is eaten. [corr. of earlier *potager*, as POTTAGE]

Port. *abbr.* **1** Portugal. **2** Portuguese.

port[1] (pawt) *n.* **1** a harbour, a sheltered piece of water into which vessels can enter and remain in safety. **2** a town or other place having a harbour, esp. where goods are imported or exported under the customs authorities. **3** a place of refuge. **port admiral** *n.* the admiral commanding at a naval port. **port charges, port dues** *n.pl.* HARBOUR DUES (under HARBOUR). **port of call** *n.* **1** a port at which a ship stops during a voyage. **2** any stopping place on an itinerary. **port of entry** *n.* an airport, harbour etc. having customs facilities through which goods or persons may enter or leave a country. **Port of London Authority** *n.* the body which oversees the harbour and docks of London. [OE, from L *portus*]

port[2] (pawt) *n.* **1** an opening in the side of a ship, allowing access to the holds etc. **2** a porthole. **3** an aperture in a wall or the side of an armoured vehicle for firing a gun through. **4** an opening in machinery for the passage of steam, gas, water etc. **5** a connector on a computer into which a peripheral can be plugged. **6** (*esp. Sc.*) a gate, an entrance, esp. to a walled town, fortress etc. **porthole** *n.* **1** a small window in the side of a ship or aircraft. **2** (*Naut., Hist.*) an aperture in a ship's side for light, air etc., and for firing guns through. [F *porte*, L *porta*]

port[3] (pawt) *n.* a fortified dessert wine (usu. dark-red or tawny) made in Portugal. **port wine** *n.* [*Oporto*, a city in Portugal]

port[4] (pawt) *n.* the left-hand side of a ship, aircraft etc., as one looks forward, as distinct from *starboard*. *~a.* towards or on the left. *~v.t.* to turn or put (the helm) to the left side of a ship. *~v.i.* to turn to port (of a ship). **on the port beam** BEAM. **port watch** *n.* the watch comprising the officers and crew whose living quarters are on the port side of a ship. [etym. uncertain, perh. from PORT[1]]

port[5] (pawt) *v.t.* to carry or hold (a rifle etc.) in a slanting position across the body in front. *~n.* **1** the position of a weapon carried thus. **2** (*formal*) carriage, deportment. [F *porter*, L *portāre*, to carry]

port[6] (pawt) *n.* **1** (*Austral., coll.*) a suitcase, a travelling bag. **2** a bag for carrying something specific, such as a shopping bag. [short for PORTMANTEAU]

port[7] (pawt) *v.t.* (*Comput.*) to transfer (software) from one system to another. **portable**[1] *a.* **portability**[1] (-bil´-) *n.* [prob. from PORT[2]]

porta (paw´tə) *n.* (*pl.* **portas, portae** (-ē)) the portal or aperture where veins, ducts etc. enter an organ, esp. the transverse fissure of the liver. [L, gate]

portability[1] PORT[7].

portability[2] PORTABLE[2].

portable[1] PORT[7].

portable[2] (paw´təbəl) *a.* **1** capable of being easily carried, esp. about the person. **2** not bulky or heavy. **3** (of a pension etc.) transferable as the holder changes jobs or other circumstances. **4** †endurable. *~n.* a portable version of anything. **portability**[2] (-bil´-) *n.* **†portableness** *n.* **portably** *adv.* [F, from L *portābilis*, from *portāre*, to carry]

portae PORTA.

portage (paw´tij) *n.* **1** the act or an instance of carrying, carriage. **2** the cost of carriage. **3** a break in a line of water-communication over which boats, goods etc. have to be carried. **4** transportation of boats etc. over this. *~v.t.* to carry (goods or a boat) over a portage. *~v.i.* to make a portage. [F, from *porter*, PORT[1]]

Portakabin® (paw´təkabin) *n.* a portable building delivered intact to, or speedily erected on, a site as temporary offices etc.

portal[1] (paw´təl) *n.* a door, a gate, a gateway, an entrance, esp. one of an ornamental or imposing kind. [OF, from med. L *portāle*, neut. of *portālis*, from L *porta*, gate, PORT[2]]

portal[2] (paw´təl) *a.* of, relating to or connected with, the porta. **portal vein** *n.* the large vein conveying blood to the liver from the stomach, pancreas etc. [med. L *portālis*, see PORTAL[1]]

portamento (pawtəmen´tō) *n.* (*pl.* **portamentos, portamenti** (-tē)) **1** a smooth, continuous glide from one note to another across intervening tones. **2** a style of piano-playing between legato and staccato. [It., a carrying]

portative (paw´tətiv) *a.* **1** capable of carrying or supporting. **2** (*Hist.*) (of a small pipe organ) portable. [F *portatif, -tive*, from med. L, from *portare*, to carry]

portcullis (pawtkŭl´is) *n.* **1** a strong timber or iron grating, sliding in vertical grooves over a gateway, and let down to close the passage in case of assault. **2** (**Portcullis**) one of the four pursuivants of the English College of Arms, using a portcullis as a badge. **portcullised** *a.* [ME *porte-colys*, OF *porte coleïce* (*porte*, L *porta*, door, PORT[2], COULISSE)]

Porte (pawt) *n.* (*Hist.*) the old Imperial Turkish Government in Constantinople; also *Sublime Porte, Ottoman Porte.* [F *Sublime Porte*, sublime gate (see PORT[2]), translation of Turkish name of the chief government office, the high gate, orig. the gate of the palace where justice was administered]

porte cochère (pawt koshea´) *n.* **1** a carriage-entrance leading into a courtyard. **2** (*esp. NAm.*) a roof extending from the entrance of a building over a drive to shelter people entering or alighting from vehicles. [F (PORT[2], *cochère*, from *coche*, COACH)]

portend (pawtend´) *v.t.* **1** to indicate by previous signs, to presage, to foreshadow. **2** to be an omen or a warning of. **portent** (paw´tent) *n.* **1** something which portends. **2** an omen, esp. of evil. **3** prophetic significance, ominousness. **4** a prodigy, a marvel. **portentous** (-ten´təs) *a.* **1** ominous. **2** impressive. **3** solemn. **4** self-consciously solemn or meaningful. **portentously** *adv.* **portentousness** *n.* [L *portendere* (*por-*, PRO-[1], *tendere*, to stretch]

Usage note Pronunciation of *portentous* as (pawten´tiəs), as though the word were *portentious*, is best avoided.

porter[1] (paw´tə) *n.* **1** a person employed to carry loads, esp. parcels, luggage etc. at a railway station, airport or hotel, or goods in a market. **2** a person who transports patients and does other manual labour in a hospital. **3** a dark-brown beer made from charred or chemically-coloured malt etc. (perh. so called from having been made specially for London porters). **4** (*N Am.*) a sleeping-car attendant. **porterage** (-rij) *n.* **1** the work of carrying luggage etc. **2** a charge for such work. **porterhouse** *n.* **1** a tavern at which porter etc. is sold. **2** an eating house, a chophouse. **porterhouse steak** *n.* a choice cut of beefsteak next to the sirloin, and including part of the tenderloin. **porterly** *a.* **porter's knot** *n.* a pad worn on the shoulders by porters when carrying heavy loads. [ME and OF *portour* (F *porteur*), from *porter*, to carry, see PORT[1]]

porter[2] (paw´tə) *n.* a gatekeeper, a doorkeeper esp. of a large building, who usu. regulates entry and answers enquiries. **porteress** (-tərəs), **portress** (-tris) *n.* a woman porter. **porter's lodge** *n.* a room, apartment or house beside a door or gateway for the porter's use. [OF *portier*, L *portārius*, from *porta*, PORT[2]]

portfire (pawt´fīə) *n.* a slow-burning fuse, formerly used for firing guns, now chiefly in mining etc. [F *porte-feu* (assim. to FIRE)]

portfolio (pawtfō´liō) *n.* (*pl.* **portfolios**) **1** a portable case for holding papers, drawings etc. **2** a collection of such papers, esp. samples of recent work etc. **3** the office and duties of a minister of state. **4** the investments made, or securities held, by an investor. [It. *portafogli* (*portare*, L *portāre*, to carry, *fogli*, leaves, from L *folium*)]

portico (paw´tikō) *n.* (*pl.* **porticoes, porticos**) **1** a colonnade, a roof supported by columns. **2** a porch with columns. **porticoed** *a.* [It., from L *porticus*, from *porta*, gate]

portière (pawtyeə´) *n.* **1** a door-curtain. **2** a woman porter, a concierge. [F, from L *portāria*]

portion (paw´shən) *n.* **1** a part; a share, a part assigned, an allotment. **2** a helping. **3** a wife's fortune, a dowry. **4** the part of an estate descending to an heir. **5** one's destiny in life. ~*v.t.* **1** to divide into portions, to distribute. **2** to allot, to assign. **3** to give a dowry to. **portionless** *a.* without a dowry. [F, from L *portiōnem*, nom. *-tio*, cogn. with *pars*, PART]

Portland (pawt´lənd) *a.* of or derived from Portland. **Portland cement** *n.* a cement having the colour of Portland stone. **Portland stone** *n.* a yellowish-white limestone, quarried in Portland, much used for building. [Isle of *Portland*, a peninsula in Dorset]

portly (pawt´li) *a.* (*comp.* **portlier**, *superl.* **portliest**) **1** stout, corpulent. **2** †dignified or stately in behaviour or appearance. **portliness** *n.* [PORT[1], -LY[1]]

portmanteau (pawtman´tō) *n.* (*pl.* **portmanteaus, portmanteaux** (-tōz)) a travelling bag which opens out flat, for carrying clothes. ~*a.* combining several uses or qualities. **portmanteau word** *n.* an invented word combining the sense and the sound of two distinct words, as *chortle*, from *chuckle* and *snort*, coined by Lewis Carroll. [F *portemanteau*]

portolan (paw´təlan), **portolano** (pawtəlah´nō) *n.* (*pl.* **portolans, portolanos**) (*Hist.*) a sailing manual containing charts, descriptions of ports, coastlines etc. [It., from *porto*, port]

portrait (paw´trit) *n.* **1** a likeness or representation of a person or animal, esp. from life. **2** a vivid description. **3** a type, a similitude. ~*a.* (of an illustration in a book etc.) having its height greater than its width, as distinct from *landscape*. **portrait gallery** *n.* (*pl.* **portrait galleries**) a gallery where portraits are exhibited. **portraitist** *n.* a painter or photographer who specializes in portraits. **portrait painter** *n.* a person whose occupation is to paint portraits. **portraiture** (-chə) *n.* **1** the art of painting portraits. **2** a portrait. **3** portraits collectively. **4** vivid description. **portray** (pətrā´) *v.t.* **1** to make a portrait of. **2** to describe. **3** to play the role of. **4** to present (as). **portrayable** *a.* **portrayal** *n.* **portrayer** *n.* [OF *pourtraict*, p.p. of *pourtraire*, to portray]

portress PORTER[2].

Port Salut (paw səloo´) *n.* a type of mild cheese, made in a round flat shape. [*Port du Salut*, a Trappist monastery at Bayonne, France, where it was first made]

Portuguese (pawtūgēz´) *a.* of or relating to Portugal, its people or its language. ~*n.* (*pl.* **Portuguese**) **1** a native or inhabitant of Portugal. **2** (*as pl.*) the people of Portugal. **3** the Portuguese language. **Portuguese man-of-war** *n.* a jellyfish of the genus *Physalia* with a poisonous sting.

portulaca (pawtūlā´kə) *n.* any plant of the genus *Portulaca*, low succulent herbs with flowers opening only in direct sunshine, comprising the purslane. **portulacaceous** (-kā´shəs) *a.* [L]

POS *abbr.* point of sale.

pos. *abbr.* **1** position. **2** positive.

posada (pəsah´də) *n.* (*pl.* **posadas**) an inn, in a Spanish-speaking country. [Sp., from *posar*, to lodge]

posaune (pōzow´nə) *n.* a rich and powerful reed-stop in an organ. [G, a trombone]

pose[1] (pōz) *v.t.* **1** to place, to cause (an artist's model etc.) to take a certain attitude. **2** to affirm, to lay down. **3** to put forward, to ask (a question etc.). **4** to present, to be the cause of. ~*v.i.* **1** to assume an attitude or character. **2** to attempt to impress by affecting an attitude or style, to behave affectedly. **3** to appear or set up (as). ~*n.* **1** a bodily or mental attitude or position, esp. one put on for effect. **2** in dominoes, the first play. **posé** (pō´zā) *a.* (*Her.*) (applied to a lion, horse etc.) standing still, with all its feet on the ground. **poser**[1] *n.* **1** a person who poses. **2** a poseur. **poseur** (-zœ´) *n.* an affected person. **poseuse** (-zœz´) *n.* a female poseur. **posey** *a.* affected, pretentious. [F *poser*, L *pausāre*, to PAUSE, late L, to rest, to set (conf. with *pōnere*, to put)]

pose[2] (pōz) *v.t.* to puzzle (a person), to cause to be at a loss. **poser**[2] *n.* **1** a person who or a thing which puzzles. **2** a puzzling question or proposition. **posingly** *adv.* [short for OPPOSE]

poser[1] POSE[1].

poser[2] POSE[2].

☒ **posess** common misspelling of POSSESS.

poseur, posey etc. POSE[1].

posh (posh) *a.* **1** (*coll.*) smart, elegant, fashionable. **2** (*sometimes derog.*) genteel, upper-class. ~*adv.* in a smart, or an upper-class, manner. **to posh up** to smarten up, to polish. [perh. from obs. sl. *posh*, a dandy: not an acronym for *p*ort *o*ut *s*tarboard *h*ome]

posit (poz´it) *v.t.* (*pres.p.* **positing**, *past, p.p.* **posited**) **1** to place, to set in position. **2** to lay down as a fact or principle, to assume, to postulate. ~*n.* (*Philos.*) a fact or an idea posited on the assumption that it will be proved valid. [L *positus*, p.p. of *pōnere*, to put]

position (pəzish´ən) *n.* **1** a location, the place occupied by a person or thing. **2** the place belonging or assigned to a person or thing. **3** (*Mil.*) an occupied and defended or a defensible point or area. **4** a player's place in a team formation or usual area of operation on the field of play. **5** a posture. **6** arrangement, disposition. **7** a point of view, a stance. **8** a situation, a state of affairs. **9** a situation relative to other persons or things. **10** social rank. **11** status, rank, condition. **12** an office, a post, an appointment. **13** the act of positing. **14** a principle laid down, a proposition. **15** the commitment in the market of a dealer in securities, currencies etc. **16** any one of the basic poses in ballet. **17** the relative placing of chessmen during a game. ~*v.t.* to place in position; to locate. **in a position to** able to. **positional** *a.* **positionally** *adv.* **positioned** *a.* placed. **positioner** *n.* **position paper** *n.* a report setting out a person's point of view or plans in a particular matter. **position vector** *n.* (*Math.*) a vector determining the position of a point. [L *positiōnem*, nom. *-tio*, as POSIT]

positive (poz´itiv) *a.* **1** definitely, explicitly or formally laid down or affirmed. **2** explicit, express, definite. **3** intrinsic, inherent, absolute, not relative. **4** existing, real, actual. **5** authoritatively laid down, prescribed by artificial enactment as distinct from natural. **6** incontestable, certain, undoubted. **7** fully convinced. **8** confident, cocksure, dogmatic. **9** (*coll.*) downright, thorough. **10** tending to emphasize the good or laudable aspects, constructive. **11** constructive, helpful. **12** (*Gram.*) not comparative or superlative. **13** (*Philos.*) practical, positivist. **14** (*Physics*) denoting the presence of some quality, not negative. **15** having the same polarity as the charge of a proton. **16** having relatively higher electrical potential. **17** denoting the north-seeking pole of a magnet or the south pole of the earth. **18** (*Math.*) denoting increase or progress, additive, greater than zero. **19** (*Med.*) indicating the presence of a suspected condition or organism. **20** (of a photograph) exhibiting lights and shades in the same relations as in nature. ~*n.* **1** that which may be affirmed. **2** (*Gram.*) the positive degree, a positive adjective. **3** (*Math.*) a positive quantity. **4** a photograph in which the lights and shades are shown as in nature. **positive discrimination** *n.* discrimination in favour of an individual or a group of people previously discriminated against or likely to be discriminated against in areas such as employment. **positive feedback** *n.* **1** a helpful response to a questionnaire etc. **2** the return of part of the output of an electronic system to the input, thus reinforcing the signal etc. **3** (*Biol.*) the adjusting of an effect in a cyclic process by its own influence on the process giving rise to it. **positive geotropism** *n.* (*Bot.*) the tendency of a root to grow downwards, towards the centre of the earth. **positively** *adv.* **positiveness** *n.* **positive philosophy** *n.* positivism. **positive pole** *n.* the north-seeking pole of a magnet. **positive prescription** *n.* (*Law*) long-continued or immemorial use or possession without interruption, as giving right or title. **positive ray** *n.* a canal ray. **positive sign** *n.* the sign +, denoting addition. **positive vetting** *n.* active investigation of a person's background etc. to check whether they are suitable for work involving national security.

positivism *n.* **1** the philosophical system of Auguste Comte, 1798–1857, which recognizes only observed phenomena and rejects speculation or metaphysics. **2** the religious system based on this, professing to be a synthesis of all human conceptions of the external order of the universe, and to secure the victory of social feeling over self-love. **3** logical positivism. **positivist** *n., a.* **positivistic** (-vis´-) *a.* **positivistically** *adv.* **positivity** (-tiv´-) *n.* [ME and F *positif,* L *positīvus* (see POSIT)]

positron (poz´itron) *n.* (*Physics*) a subatomic particle having the same mass as an electron, but a positive charge. **positron emission tomography** *n.* a technique for monitoring brain activity by recording the emission of positrons from a radioactive substance injected into the bloodstream. **positronium** (-trō´niəm) *n.* (*pl.* **positroniums**) a short-lived unit consisting of a positron and an electron bound together. [*posi*tive elec*tron*]

posology (pəsol´əji) *n.* the science treating of doses or the quantities of medicines to be administered. **posological** (-loj´-) *a.* [F *posologie* (Gr. *posos,* how much)]

poss. *abbr.* **1** possession. **2** possessive. **3** possible. **4** possibly.

posse (pos´i) *n.* **1** a body or force (of persons). **2** (*US*) a group of men called on by a sheriff to help with law enforcement. **3** a posse comitatus. **4** (*sl.*) a criminal gang. **5** (*sl.*) a group of people from the same area, or sharing a background or interest. **6** (*Law*) possibility. **in posse** within possibility, possible. **posse comitatus** (komitā´təs) *n.* a force which the sheriff of a county is empowered to raise in case of riot etc. [L, to be able]

possess (pəzes´) *v.t.* **1** to have the ownership of, to own as property, to have full power over, to control (oneself, one's mind etc.). **2** to occupy, to dominate the mind of. **3** to have sexual intercourse with (a woman). **4** to imbue, to impress (with). **5** to acquire. **to be possessed of** to own. **to possess oneself of** to acquire, to obtain as one's own. **what possessed you?** a rhetorical question expressing shock or disapproval of another's actions. **possessed** *a.* **1** owned. **2** owning. **3** dominated (by an idea etc.). **4** controlled (as by a devil), mad. **5** self-possessed. **possessor** *n.* **possessory** *a.* [OF *possesser,* L *possess-,* p.p. stem of *possidēre* (*potis,* able, *sedēre,* to sit)]

possession (pəzesh´ən) *n.* **1** the act or state of possessing. **2** the state of being possessed or under physical or supernatural influence. **3** a person or thing which is possessed. **4** holding or occupancy as owner. **5** the exercise of such control as attaches to ownership, actual detention, or occupancy. **6** territory, esp. a subject dependency in a foreign country. **7** (*pl.*) property, goods, wealth. **8** in ball games, esp. football, control of the ball by a particular team or player. **9** self-possession. **10** †conviction, certainty. **in possession 1** in actual occupancy. **2** holding, possessing. **in possession of** owning, possessing. **in the possession of** owned or possessed by. **to give possession** to put another in possession. **to take possession of 1** to become the possessor of. **2** to seize. **possession by entireties** *n.* joint possession by two persons, neither of whom can alienate without the other's consent. **possessionless** *a.* **possession order** *n.* a court order entitling a landlord to evict a tenant or squatter and regain possession of the property.

possessive (pəzes´iv) *a.* **1** of or relating to possession. **2** showing a strong urge to possess or dominate, unwilling to share, unwilling to allow another to be independent of oneself. **3** (*Gram.*) denoting possession, genitive. ~*n.* **1** the possessive case. **2** a word in this case. **possessive case** *n.* **possessively** *adv.* **possessiveness** *n.* **possessive pronoun** *n.* any one of the pronouns indicating possession (as Eng. *mine, yours, his* etc.).

posset (pos´it) *n.* **1** a drink made of hot milk curdled with ale, wine etc. **2** a small quantity of milk regurgitated by a baby after a feed. ~†*v.t.* to curdle. ~*v.i.* (of a baby) to regurgitate milk after a feed. [ME *possyt, poshote,* etym. uncertain]

possible (pos´ibəl) *a.* **1** that may happen, be done, or exist. **2** not contrary to the nature of things. **3** feasible, practicable. **4** having a specified potential use or quality. **5** that may be dealt with or put up with, tolerable, reasonable. ~*n.* **1** something which is possible. **2** a person who is a possible competitor, member etc. **3** the highest score that can be made in shooting etc. **possibilist** *n.* a member of a political party, esp. a Spanish constitutional republican or a French Socialist, aiming only at reforms that are actually practicable. **possibilism** *n.* **possibility** (-bil´-) *n.* (*pl.* **possibilities**) **1** the state, or the fact, of being possible. **2** a possible thing. **3** a contingency. **4** a person or thing which has an outside to moderate chance of success, selection etc. **5** (*usu. pl.*) potential. **possibly** *adv.* **1** by any possible means. **2** perhaps. **3** by remote chance. [F, from L *possibilis* (*posse,* to be able)]

possie (poz´i), **pozzy** *n.* (*pl.* **possies, pozzies**) (*Austral., coll.*) a place, position. [short for POSITION]

possum (pos´əm) *n.* (*coll.*) an opossum. **to play possum** to feign ignorance or unawareness, to dissemble (in allusion to the opossum's feigning death on the approach of danger). [short for OPOSSUM]

POST *abbr.* point of sale terminal.

post[1] (pōst) *n.* **1** a piece of timber, metal etc., set upright, and intended as a support to something, or to mark a boundary. **2** a pole for fastening notices to. **3** a starting or winning post. **4** an upright forming part of various structures, machines etc. **5** a pillar or vertical mass of coal or ore left as a support in a mine. ~*v.t.* **1** to fix (*usu.* up) on a post or in a public place. **2** to fasten bills etc., upon (a wall etc.). **3** to advertise, to make known. **4** to enter (a name) in a list posted up of defaulters etc., esp. of students failing at an examination. **5** to publish (the name of a ship) as overdue or missing. **6** (*N Am.*) to achieve (a score etc.) in a game. **post hole** *n.* in archaeology, the traces of a hole sunk in the ground to hold a wooden etc. post. **post-mill** *n.* a windmill, the whole of which can turn round a central post to catch the wind. [OE, from L *postis,* prob. rel. to *pōnere* (p.p. *positus*), to set, to fix]

post[2] (pōst) *n.* **1** a fixed place, position or station. **2** a military station. **3** the troops at such a station. **4** a fort. **5** a place established for trading purposes, esp. in a remote place. **6** a situation, an appointment. **7** (*Naut., Hist.*) an officer with a commission as a full captain. **8** (*Mil.*) a bugle call announcing the time of retiring for the night etc. ~*v.t.* **1** to station, to place (an employee, soldiers etc.) in a particular position. **2** to transfer to another unit or location. **post-captain** *n.* (*Hist.*) a full naval captain, usu. of three years' standing. **post exchange** *n.* (*US*) a general shop at a military camp, subsidized by the government. **posting** *n.* an appointment to a particular position within an organization. [F *poste,* It. and late L *posta,* from L *posita,* fem. p.p. of *pōnere,* to set, to place]

post[3] (pōst) *n.* **1** an established system of conveyance and delivery of letters and parcels; orig. one of a series of men stationed at points along a road whose duty was to ride forward to the next man with letters. **2** a post office. **3** a postbox. **4** a single collection or dispatch of letters or parcels. **5** the letters delivered at a house at one time. **6** a size of writing paper, about 18¾ in.

(47.6 cm) by 15¼ in. (38.7 cm). **7** (*Hist.*) a courier, a messenger. **8** (*Hist.*) a mail cart. **9** (*Hist.*) a relay of horses. *~adv.* **1** (*Hist.*) in relays of horses. **2** express, with speed. *~v.t.* **1** to transmit by post. **2** to put into a postbox for transmission. **3** (*Hist.*) to send by or as by post-horses. **4** to send with speed. **5** to transfer (accounts) to a ledger, to enter in this from a day-book etc. **6** to fill (a ledger) in this way. **7** †to postpone, to delay. *~v.i.* **1** (*Hist.*) to travel with post-horses. **2** to travel rapidly, to hurry. **to keep someone posted** to keep someone supplied with up-to-date information. **to post up 1** to complete (a ledger) with entries of accounts from a day-book etc. **2** to supply with full information. **to ride post** (*Hist.*) to ride with post-horses; to ride in haste. **postbag** *n.* **1** a mailbag. **2** mail received (esp. by a public figure, magazine, radio show etc.). **postboat** *n.* a boat employed in postal work, a mailboat, or one conveying passengers. **postbox** *n.* a box where letters may be put for collection and subsequent delivery. **post boy, post rider** *n.* **1** a boy who carries the post. **2** (*Hist.*) a boy who rides a post-horse, a postilion. **post bus** *n.* a small bus used in rural areas for delivering mail and conveying passengers. **postcard** *n.* a card for sending by post without an envelope. **post-chaise, †post-coach** *n.* (*Hist.*) a horse-drawn vehicle for travelling by post. **postcode** *n.* a code of letters and numbers denoting a particular subsection of a postal area, used to help in sorting mail. **post-free** *a., adv.* carried by post free of charge, or with the postage prepaid. **post-haste** *adv.* with all speed. **post-horn** *n.* (*Hist.*) a long straight horn blown to announce the arrival of a mail coach. **post-horse** *n.* (*Hist.*) a horse kept as a relay at an inn etc., for post or for travellers. **post-house** *n.* (*Hist.*) a house where post-horses were kept for relays. **postie** *n.* (*Austral., Sc., coll.*) a postman or postwoman. **postman** *n.* (*pl.* **postmen**) **1** a man who collects and delivers mail. **2** †a courier or post. **postman's knock** *n.* a children's game in which a kiss is the reward for delivering an imaginary letter. **postmark** *n.* a mark stamped by post-office officials on letters etc., usu. stating place, date, and hour of dispatch, and serving to cancel the postage stamp. *~v.t.* to stamp (an envelope etc.) with this. **postmaster** *n.* **1** a man in charge of a post office. **2** (*Hist.*) a man who let out post-horses. **postmaster general** *n.* the executive head of a national post office. **postmastership** *n.* **postmistress** *n.* a woman in charge of a post office. **post office** *n.* **1** a place for the receipt and delivery of letters etc. **2** (**Post Office**) a government department or a national corporation in charge of the dispatch and delivery of letters and packets etc. **3** (*N Am.*) postman's knock. **post office box** *n.* a private numbered box at a post office in which the holder's mail is deposited awaiting collection. **post-paid** *a., adv.* having the postage prepaid. **postperson** *n.* a postman or postwoman. **post rider** *n.* (*Hist.*) a post boy. **post-road** *n.* (*Hist.*) a road on which relays of horses were available for posting. **post room** *n.* a department in a company where incoming and outgoing mail is dealt with. **post town** *n.* **1** a town in which there is a head post office. **2** (*Hist.*) a town in which post-horses were kept for travellers. **postwoman** *n.* (*pl.* **postwomen**) a woman who collects and delivers mail. [as POST[2]]

post- (pōst) *pref.* **1** after, in time or order. **2** behind. [L *post*]

postage (pōs´tij) *n.* the fee for sending a letter etc. by post. **postage meter** *n.* (*N Am.*) a franking machine. **postage stamp** *n.* an embossed or printed stamp or an adhesive label to indicate how much postage has been paid. [POST[3]]

postal (pōs´təl) *a.* **1** of or relating to the mail service. **2** carried on by post. *~n.* (*US*) a postcard. **postal card** *n.* (*US*) a postcard. **postal code** *n.* POSTCODE (under POST[3]). **postally** *adv.* **postal meter** *n.* a franking machine. **postal note** *n.* (*Austral., New Zeal.*) a postal order. **postal order** *n.* an order for a sum of money (specified on the document) issued at one post-office for payment at another. **Postal Union** *n.* an association of the governments of various countries which regulates international postage. **postal vote** *n.* a vote submitted by post. [POST[3]]

post- (+ b–e words) post-bellum *a.* after a war, esp. after the American Civil War. **post-Cambrian** *a.* **post-Carboniferous** *a.* **postcava** *n.* (*Anat.*) the inferior vena cava. **postcaval** *a.* **post-classical** *a.* later than the classical writers, artists etc., esp. those of Greece and Rome. **post-coital** *a.* **post-coitally** *adv.* **post-communion** *n., a.* (of or relating to) that part of the eucharistic service which follows after the act of communion. **post-consonantal** *a.* **post-consumer waste** *n.* recyclable household goods or materials. **post-costal** *a.* behind a rib. **post-date**[1] *v.t.* to assign or mark with a date later than the actual one. **post-date**[2] (pōst´-) *n.* a date later than the actual one. **post-Devonian** *a.* **post-diagnostic** *a.* **post-digestive** *a.* **postdiluvial** *a.* being or happening after the Flood. **postdiluvian** *n., a.* **post-doc.** *a.* (*coll.*) post-doctoral. **post-doctoral** *a.* of or relating to studies, research etc. carried out after obtaining a doctorate. **post-election** *a.* **post-entry** *n.* (*pl.* **post-entries**) **1** an additional or subsequent entry. **2** a late entry (for a race etc.). **post-Eocene** *a.* **post-exilian, post-exilic** *a.* later than the Babylonian exile.

poster (pōs´tə) *n.* **1** a large placard or advertising bill. **2** a person who posts this. **3** a large printed picture. **poster paint, poster colour** *n.* an opaque, gum-based watercolour paint. [POST[1]]

poste restante (pōst res´tãt) *n.* **1** a department in a post office where letters are kept until called for. **2** an address on a letter to a poste restante department. [F, remaining post]

posterior (postiə´riə) *a.* **1** coming or happening after. **2** later. **3** situated behind or at the back. *~n.* the buttocks. **posteriority** (-or´-) *n.* **posteriorly** *adv.* [L, comp. of *posterus*, from *post*, after]

posterity (pəster´iti) *n.* **1** those proceeding in the future from any person, descendants. **2** succeeding generations. [F *postérité*, L *posteritātem*, nom. *-tas*, as POSTERIOR]

postern (pos´tən) *n.* **1** a small doorway or gateway at the side or back. **2** a private entrance, esp. to a castle, town etc. **3** a way of escape. *~a.* situated at the side or the back. [OF *posterne*, *posterle* (F *poterne*), late L *posterula*, dim. of *posterus*, from *post*, after, behind]

post- (+ f–h words) post-feminist *a.* later than, or developed from, the ideas or attitudes characteristic of the original feminist movement. *~n.* a person having such ideas or attitudes. **post-feminism** *n.* **postfix** *v.t.* to append (a letter etc.) at the end of a word. *~n.* a suffix. **post-Fordism** *n.* the theory that industry should no longer be based on mass production (as advocated by Henry Ford), but be smaller-scale, more flexible and responsive to markets. **post-Fordist** *n., a.* **postglacial** *a.* later than the glacial period. *~n.* a postglacial period. **postgrad** *n., a.* (*coll.*) (a) postgraduate. **postgraduate** *a.* **1** carried on or awarded after graduation. **2** working for a postgraduate qualification. *~n.* a graduate who pursues a further course of study. **posthypnotic suggestion** *n.* the giving of instructions to a hypnotic subject which the latter will act on after emerging from the trance.

post-haste POST[3].

post hoc (pōst hok´) *n.* (*Logic*) the fallacy of assuming that if something happened after something else, it must have happened because of it. [L *post hoc* (*ergo propter hoc*), after this (therefore on account of this)]

posthumous (pos´tūməs) *a.* 1 (of a child) born after the death of the father. 2 happening after decease. 3 published after the death of the author or composer. **posthumously** *adv.* [L *postumus*, superl. of *post*, after (late L *posthumus*, as if *post humum*, after the ground)]

post- (+ i–k words) post-Impressionism *n.* the doctrines and methods of a school of (esp. French) painters of the late 19th cent. who rejected the naturalism and momentary effects of Impressionism in favour of a use of pure colour for more formal or subjective ends. **post-Impressionist** *a., n.* **post-industrial** *a.* of or relating to an economy or a society no longer dependent on heavy industry. **post-Jurassic** *a.* **post-Keynesian** *a., n.*

postiche (postēsh´) *n.* 1 a hairpiece. 2 an imitation, a sham. ~*a.* artificial, superadded (of superfluous ornament). [F, from It. *posticcio*, from L *postus*, *positus*, p.p. of *pōnere*, to place]

posticous (postī´kəs) *a.* (*Bot.*) 1 posterior. 2 turned away from the axis, extrorse. [L *postīcus*, from *post*, after, behind]

postie POST[3].

†**postil** (pos´til) *n.* 1 a marginal note in a Bible. 2 any explanatory note, esp. one in the margin. 3 a commentary. 4 a homily on the Gospel or Epistle for the day. [ME and F *postille*, med. L *postilla* (prob. *post illa*, after these)]

postilion (pəstil´yən), **postillion** *n.* the rider on the near horse of the leaders or of a pair drawing a carriage. [F *postillon*, from It. *postiglione*, from *posta*, POST[2]]

Post-it Note® (pōs´tit nōt) *n.* a small sheet of paper for writing messages, with a strip of adhesive along one edge which allows the note to be stuck to a surface and removed again without damaging the surface.

postliminy (pōstlim´ini) *n.* 1 in Roman law, the right of resumption of former rights and privileges by an exile or captive returning to their own country. 2 in international law, the right of restoration of things taken in war to their former civil status or ownership on their coming back into the power of the nation to which they belonged. [L *postliminium* (*limen liminis*, threshold)]

postlude (pōst´lood) *n.* (*Mus.*) a closing piece or voluntary. [from PRELUDE]

post-(+m–words) postmenopausal *a.* **postmenstrual** *a.* **post-millennial** *a.* of or relating to a period after the millennium. **post-millennialism** *n.* the doctrine that the second advent of Christ will follow the millennium. **post-millennialist** *n.* **post-Miocene** *a.* **postmodernism** *n.* in art, architecture, literature etc., a movement which rejects the basic tenets of 20th-cent. modernism. **postmodern** *a.* **postmodernist** *a., n.* **postmodernity** *n.*

post meridiem (pōst mərid´iem) *adv.* after noon. **postmeridian** *a.* 1 of or belonging to the afternoon. 2 late. [L]

post-mortem (pōstmaw´təm) *adv.* after death. ~*a.* made or occurring after death. ~*n.* 1 an examination of a dead body to determine the cause of death. 2 an analysis or review after a game etc., esp. after defeat or failure. [L, after death]

post- (+ n–o words) post-Napoleonic *a.* **post-nasal** *a.* behind the nose. **post-natal** *a.* of, relating to or typical of the period after childbirth. **post-natal depression** *n.* depression suffered by a mother after childbirth. **post-natally** *adv.* **post-nuptial** *a.* made or happening after marriage. **post-ocular** *a.* behind the eye. **post-Oligocene** *a.* **post-op** *a.* (*coll.*) post-operative. **post-operative** *a.* of or relating to the period just after a surgical operation. **post-oral** *a.* behind the mouth. **post-orbital** *a.* behind the orbit of the eye. **post-production** *a.* of or relating to editing etc. of a film or TV programme, done after shooting.

post-obit (pōstō´bit, -ob´it) *a.* taking effect after death; post-mortem. ~*n.* a bond securing payment of a sum of money to a lender on the death of a specified person from whose estate the borrower has expectations. [L *post obitum* (*post*, after, *obitus*, decease, from *obīre*, to die)]

post- (+ p– words) post-Pliocene *a.* (*Geol.*) of or relating to the formation immediately above the Pliocene. **postprandial** *a.* (*formal or facet.*) after lunch or dinner. **post-primary** *a.*

post-partum (pōstpah´təm) *a.* of or relating to the period immediately after childbirth. [L, after childbirth]

postpone (pəspōn´) *v.t.* 1 to put off, to defer, to delay. 2 to regard as of minor importance to something else. ~*v.i.* (*Med.*) to be late in recurring. **postponable** *a.* **postponement** *n.* **postponer** *n.* [L *postpōnere* (*pōnere*, to put)]

postposition (pōstpəzish´ən) *n.* 1 the act of placing after. 2 the state of being placed after or behind. 3 a word or particle placed after a word, esp. an enclitic. **postpose** *v.t.* to place (a word or particle) after another. **postpositional** *a.* **postpositive** (-poz´itiv) *a.* (*Gram.*) placed after something else. ~*n.* a postpositive word or particle. **postpositively** *adv.* [L *postpositio -ōnem*, as POSTPONE]

post- (+ r–t words) post-Reformation *a.* **post-Revolutionary** *a.* **post-season, post-seasonal** *a.* **post-structuralism** *n.* a development of structuralism, esp. as used in textual analysis. **post-structuralist** *n., a.* **post-synch** *v.t.* (*coll.*) to post-synchronize. ~*n.* post-synchronization. **post-synchronize, post-synchronise** *v.t.* to record and edit a soundtrack after the shooting of a film. **post-synchronization** *n.* **post-tax** *a.* (of income) after taxes have been deducted. **post-Tertiary** *a.* **post-traumatic stress disorder, post-traumatic stress syndrome** *n.* (*Psych.*) a psychologically disturbed condition suffered by a person who has been through a very traumatic experience (e.g. a shipwreck or aeroplane crash), the symptoms including anxiety, guilt and depression.

postscenium (pōstsē´niəm) *n.* the back part of a theatre behind the scenes. [L *postscaenium* (*scaena*, Gr. *skēnē*, stage, SCENE)]

postscript (pōst´skript) *n.* 1 a paragraph added to a letter after the writer's signature. 2 any supplement added on to the end of a book, document, talk etc. 3 (later) additional information. [L *postscriptum* (*scriptum*, neut. p.p. of *scrībere*, to write)]

postulant (pos´tūlənt) *n.* a candidate for entry into a religious order or for an ecclesiastical office. **postulancy** *n.* [L *postlans -ntem*, see POSTULATE[1]]

postulate[1] (pos´tūlət) *n.* 1 a position assumed without proof as being self-evident. 2 a fundamental assumption. 3 a necessary condition, an indispensable preliminary. 4 a statement of the possibility of a simple operation such as a geometrical construction. [L *postulatum*, neut. p.p. of *postulāre*, to demand]

postulate[2] (pos´tūlāt) *v.t.* 1 to demand, to claim, to assume without proof, to take as self-evident. 2 to stipulate. 3 in ecclesiastical law, to nominate subject to sanction by superior authority. **postulation** (-lā´shən) *n.* **postulator** (pos´-) *n.* 1 a person who postulates. 2 a person who presents the case for beatification or canonization. [see POSTULATE[1]]

☒ **postumous** common misspelling of POSTHUMOUS.

posture (pos´chə) *n.* 1 a pose, attitude or arrangement of the parts of the body. 2 the manner of holding the body. 3 a mental attitude. 4 a situation, condition, state (of affairs etc.). ~*v.t.* to arrange the body and limbs of (a person) in a particular posture. ~*v.i.* 1 to assume a posture, to pose. 2 to endeavour to look or sound impressive. **postural** *a.* **posturer** *n.* [F, from L *positūra*, from *posit-*, p.p. stem of *pōnere*, to put]

post- (+ v–w words) **post-Victorian** *a.* **post-viral syndrome, post-viral fatigue syndrome** *n.* (*Med.*) a condition occurring after a viral infection, characterized by prolonged fatigue, depression etc. **post-vocalic** *a.* following a vowel. **post-war** *a.* existing or happening after a war, esp. the latest war.

posy (pō´zi) *n.* (*pl.* **posies**) **1** a bunch of flowers, a nosegay. **2** a motto or short inscription, esp. in a ring; orig. one in verse. **posy ring** *n.* a ring inscribed with a posy. [contr. of POESY]

pot[1] (pot) *n.* **1** a round vessel of earthenware, metal or glass, usu. deep relative to the breadth, for holding liquids etc. **2** a vessel of this kind used for cooking. **3** a large drinking-cup of earthenware, pewter etc. **4** the quantity this holds. **5** a quart (0.95 l). **6** a vessel used for various domestic or industrial purposes; a chamber pot, a coffee pot, a flower pot, a teapot etc. **7** a chimney pot. **8** a wicker trap for catching lobsters etc. **9** (*coll.*) a cup offered as a prize in a race etc. **10** (*often pl., coll.*) a large sum of money. **11** a heavy sum staked on a horse etc. **12** the money or stakes in the pool in gambling games. **13** a pot belly. ~*v.t.* (*pres.p.* **potting,** *past, p.p.* **potted**) **1** to put into a pot or pots. **2** to plant in pots. **3** to season and preserve in a sealed pot. **4** to pocket a ball (in billiards etc.). **5** (*coll.*) to shoot at or bring down, esp. with a pot-shot. **6** to bag, to secure. **7** to sit (a young child) on a potty. **8** to shape clay as a potter. **9** to abridge (*a potted history*). ~*v.i.* (*coll.*) to shoot (at). **to go to pot** (*sl.*) to be ruined or done for, to degenerate. **to keep the pot boiling** (*coll.*) to maintain progress or activity, to keep the game alive. **to pot on** to transfer (a plant) to a larger pot. **to pot up** to plant (a seedling) into a pot. **pot-ale** *n.* fermented grain as refuse from a distillery. **pot barley** *n.* barley which has had the outer husk removed. **pot belly** *n.* (*pl.* **pot bellies**) **1** a protuberant belly. **2** a pot-bellied person. **3** (*N Am.*) a small bulbous stove burning wood or coal. **pot-bellied** *a.* **potboiler** *n.* **1** a work of art or literature produced merely for money. **2** a painter or writer who produces this. **pot-bound** *a.* (of a plant) filling the pot with its roots, not having room to grow. †**potboy** *n.* a person employed in a public house to clean pots etc. **pot cheese** *n.* (*N Am.*) cottage cheese. **potful** *n.* (*pl.* **potfuls**). **pot-herb** *n.* any culinary herb. **pothole** *n.* **1** a cauldron-shaped cavity in the rocky bed of a stream. **2** a pitlike cavity or a system of caves in mountain limestone etc., usu. produced by a combination of faulting and water action. **3** a cavity in a roadway caused by wear or weathering. ~*v.i.* to explore cave systems. **potholer** *n.* a person who explores underground cave systems as a sport. **potholing** *n.* **pot-hook** *n.* **1** an S-shaped hook for suspending a pot or kettle over a fire. **2** a letter like a pot-hook, esp. in clumsy handwriting. **pot-house** *n.* a low public house. **pot-hunter** *n.* **1** a person who kills game, fish etc., for food or profit rather than sport. **2** a person who competes merely to win prizes. **pot-hunting** *n.* **pot-lid** *n.* **potluck, pot luck** *n.* **1** whatever food may be available without special preparation. **2** whatever luck or chance may offer. †**potman** *n.* (*pl.* **potmen**) a potboy. **pot-metal** *n.* **1** a cheap alloy of copper and lead used for making pots. **2** stained glass coloured throughout while in a state of fusion. **pot of gold** *n.* an imaginary treasure, or one searched for in vain (traditionally found at the end of the rainbow). **pot pie** *n.* a pie with a crust, cooked in a stewpot. **pot plant** *n.* a plant grown in a flowerpot. **pot roast** *n.* a piece of meat stewed in a closed receptacle. **pot-roast** *v.t.* to cook (meat) thus. **potsherd** *n.* a broken piece of pottery, esp. as an archaeological find. **pot-shot** *n.* **1** a shot at game etc. that happens to be within easy range. **2** a random shot. **3** a shot for filling the pot, esp. one of an unsportsmanlike kind. **pot still** *n.* a kind of still used in whisky-making, in which heat is applied directly to the pot, as distinct from a *patent still.* **potstone** *n.* **1** a granular variety of steatite. **2** a large mass of flint found in chalk. **potted** *a.* **1** put in a pot. **2** preserved in the form of a paste. **3** condensed, abridged. **4** (of music) recorded for reproduction by gramophone etc. **5** (*coll.*) drunk. **potting** *n.* **potting shed** *n.* a garden shed in which tools are kept, plants are potted etc. **pot-valiant** *a.* made courageous by drink. **pot-valour,** (*N Am.*) **pot-valor** *n.* **pot-walloper** *n.* (*Hist.*) a man having a parliamentary vote because he had boiled his pot at his own fireside, a qualification in certain English boroughs before 1832. [OE *pott* (cp. Dut. *pot,* G *Pott,* Icel. *pottr,* F *pot*), perh. cogn. with L *pōtus,* drunk, Gr. *potos,* a drinking]

pot[2] (pot) *n.* (*sl.*) marijuana. **pothead** *n.* a person who takes marijuana regularly. [perh. from Mex. Sp. *potiguaya*]

pot[3] (pot) *n.* (*Austral., New Zeal.*) a drop goal in rugby. ~*v.t.* (*pres.p.* **potting,** *past, p.p.* **potted**) to score (a drop goal). [perh. from *pot-shot,* see POT[1]]

pot. *abbr.* potential.

potable (pō´təbəl) *a.* drinkable. ~*n.* (*usu. pl.*) anything drinkable. **potability** (-bil´-) *n.* **potableness** *n.* [F, from late L *pōtābilis,* from L *pōtāre,* to drink]

potage (potahzh´) *n.* thick soup. [F]

potager (pot´əjə) *n.* a vegetable garden. [F]

potamic (pətam´ik) *a.* of or relating to rivers. **potamology** (potəmol´-) *n.* **potamological** (-loj´-) *a.* **potamologist** (-mol´-) *n.* [Gr. *potamos,* river]

potash (pot´ash) *n.* **1** a powerful alkali, consisting of potassium carbonate in a crude form, orig. obtained from the ashes of plants. **2** caustic potash. **3** potassium or a potassium compound. [POT[1], ASH[1] (perh. after Dut. *potasch*)]

potassium (pətas´iəm) *n.* a bluish or pinkish white metallic element, at. no. 19, chem. symbol K. **potassic** *a.* **potassium-argon dating** *n.* (*Geol.*) a method of dating rocks by measuring the ratio of potassium-40 to its decay product argon-40. **potassium carbonate** *n.* a white alkaline substance used in the manufacture of glass, soap etc. **potassium chlorate** *n.* a white, soluble crystalline substance used in fireworks, matches etc., and as a disinfectant. **potassium chloride** *n.* a white crystalline substance used as a fertilizer and in photographic processing. **potassium cyanide** *n.* a very poisonous soluble substance used in extracting gold and silver from their ores. **potassium hydroxide** *n.* CAUSTIC POTASH (under CAUSTIC). **potassium iodide** *n.* a white crystalline substance used as an additive to table salt. **potassium permanganate** *n.* a purple, soluble crystalline substance, used in solution as a disinfectant, bleach etc. [POTASH]

potation (pōtā´shən) *n.* (*formal or facet.*) **1** the act, or an instance, of drinking. **2** a beverage. **3** (*usu. pl.*) tippling. **potatory** (pō´-, -tā´-) *a.* [ME and OF *potacion,* L *pōtātiōnem,* nom. *-tio,* from *pōtāre,* to drink]

potato (pətā´tō) *n.* (*pl.* **potatoes**) **1** a plant, *Solanum tuberosum,* with edible farinaceous tubers. **2** a tuber of this. **3** (*coll.*) a hole in a sock or stocking. **potato beetle** *n.* the Colorado beetle. **potato blight** *n.* a disease of the potato plant caused by the fungus *Phytophthora infestans.* **potato bug** *n.* a potato beetle. **potato chip** *n.* **1** a long slice of potato fried in deep fat. **2** (*N Am., S Afr.*) a potato crisp. **potato crisp** *n.* a flake of potato fried in deep fat. **potato trap** *n.* (*sl.*) the mouth. [Sp. *patata,* Haitian *batata,* sweet potato]

potatory POTATION.

pot-au-feu (potōfœ´) *n.* (*pl.* **pot-au-feu**) **1** a traditional French stew of beef and vegetables. **2** the type of pot used for this stew. **3** the broth from this stew. [F, pot on the fire]

potch (poch) *n.* an opal of inferior quality. [etym. uncertain]

poteen (pətēn´), **potheen** (-chēn´) *n.* Irish whiskey illicitly distilled. [Ir. *poitin*, dim. of *poite*, POT[1]]

potence[1] (pō´təns) *n.* (*pl.* **potence, potencies**) **1** (*Her.*) a cross with ends resembling the head of a crutch or a T. **2** a T-shaped framework. **3** in watchmaking, a stud or support for a bearing, esp. the lower pivot of a verge. †**potent**[1] *n.* **1** a fur made up of pieces in the shape of crutch-heads. **2** a support, a crutch. ~*a.* **1** (of a fur) made up thus. **2** (*Her.*) having the arms (of a cross) terminating in cross-pieces or crutch-heads. [F, a crutch, as POTENT[2]]

potence[2], **potency** POTENT[2].

potent[1] POTENCE[1].

potent[2] (pō´tənt) *a.* **1** (*formal*) powerful, mighty. **2** having great force or influence. **3** cogent. **4** strong, intoxicating. **5** (of a male) capable of having sexual intercourse. **potence**[2], **potency** *n.* (*pl.* **potences, potencies**). **potentate** (-tāt) *n.* **1** a person who possesses great power. **2** a monarch, a ruler. **potential** (-ten´shəl) *a.* **1** (of energy) existing but not in action, latent. **2** existing in possibility, not in actuality. **3** (*Gram.*) expressing possibility. **4** †having force or power, potent. ~*n.* **1** anything that may be possible. **2** a possibility. **3** as yet undeveloped value, resources or ability. **4** (*Gram.*) the potential mood. **5** the voltage of a point above zero or earth. **6** the work done in transferring a unit (of mass, electricity etc.) from infinity to a given point. **potential barrier** *n.* (*Physics*) an area of high potential in a field of force, where the passage of particles is impeded. **potential difference** *n.* the work required to move an electrical charge between two points, measured in volts. **potential energy** *n.* the energy possessed by virtue of the relative condition of parts of a body or of bodies to each other. **potential function** *n.* (*Math.*) a quantity by the differentiation of which the value of the force at any point in space arising from any system of bodies can be obtained. **potentiality** (-shial´-) *n.* (*pl.* **potentialities**). **potentialize, potentialise** *v.t.* to transform into a potential condition. **potentially** *adv.* **potential well** *n.* (*Physics*) an area of low potential in a field of force. **potentiate** (-ten´shi-) *v.t.* **1** to make potent. **2** to make more effective. **3** to make possible. **potentiation** (-ā´shən) *n.* **potentiator** *n.* **potentiometer** (-om´itə) *n.* an instrument for measuring electromotive force or potential difference. **potentiometric** (-əmet´rik) *a.* **potentiometry** (-om´itri) *n.* **potently** *adv.* **potentness** *n.* [L *potens -ntem*, pres.p. of *posse*, to be able]

potentilla (pōtəntil´ə) *n.* any plant or shrub of the genus *Potentilla*, comprising the cinquefoil, tormentil etc. [med. L, dim. from L *potens -ntem*, POTENT[2]]

potheen POTEEN.

pother (podh´ə) *n.* **1** bustle, confusion. **2** a cloud of dust or smoke. ~*v.i.* **1** to make a bustle or stir. **2** to make a fuss. [etym. uncertain]

potiche (potēsh´) *n.* a kind of oriental pot or vase, round or polygonal, narrowing towards the top and with a detachable lid. [F, from *pot*, POT[1]]

potion (pō´shən) *n.* **1** a liquid mixture intended as a medicine, poison or a magic charm. **2** a drink, a draught. [ME and OF *pocion*, L *pōtiōnem*, nom. *-tio*, from *pōtus*, drunk]

potlatch (pot´lach) *n.* a ceremonial feast among Indians of the northwestern US involving emulation in the giving of extravagant gifts. [Chinook]

potometer (pətom´itə) *n.* an instrument which measures the rate at which a plant takes in water. [L *potare*, to drink]

potoroo (potōroo´) *n.* (*pl.* **potoroos**) the marsupial rat kangaroo. [Austral. Abor.]

pot-pourri (pōpərē´, pōpoo´ri) *n.* (*pl.* **pot-pourris**) **1** a mixture of dried flower-petals and spices, usu. kept in a bowl for perfuming a room. **2** a literary miscellany, a musical medley etc. [F, rotten pot]

potrero (potrea´rō) *n.* (*pl.* **potreros**) **1** (*US, S Am.*) a paddock or pasture for horses etc. **2** (*US*) a steep-sided, narrow plateau. [Sp., from *potro*, a colt]

pottage (pot´ij) *n.* **1** a kind of soup or stew. **2** †porridge. [F *potage* (POT[1], -AGE)]

potted POT[1].

potter[1] (pot´ə) *n.* a maker of pottery. **potter's clay** *n.* a tenacious clay containing kaolin, used for pottery. **potter's field** *n.* (*N Am.*) a public burying-place for the poor or strangers. **potter's wheel** *n.* a horizontal wheel on which pots are shaped. **pottery** *n.* (*pl.* **potteries**) **1** earthenware. **2** a place where this is manufactured, a potter's workshop. **3** the making of earthenware. **the Potteries** a region in Staffordshire which is the centre of the English pottery industry. [late OE *pottere* (POT[1], -ER[1])]

potter[2] (pot´ə), (*N Am.*) **putter** (pŭt´ə) *v.i.* **1** to busy oneself in a desultory but generally agreeable way. **2** to proceed in a leisurely and often random fashion. **3** to study or work (at) in a superficial way. ~*v.t.* to waste or pass (time away) in a desultory way. **potterer** *n.* **pottering** *n., a.* **potteringly** *adv.* [perh. freq. of obs. *pote*, OE *potian*, to prod, to push, etym. uncertain]

potting POT[1].

pottle (pot´əl) *n.* **1** a vessel or basket for holding fruit. **2** a liquid measure of 4 pt. (2.3 l). **3** a large tankard. **pottle-pot** *n.* a 4 pt. (2.3 l) pot or tankard. [ME and OF *potel*, dim. of POT[1])]

potto (pot´ō) *n.* (*pl.* **pottos**) a W African lemuroid, *Perodicticus potto*. [W Afr.]

Pott's fracture (pots) *n.* (*Med.*) a fracture of the leg, at the lower end of the fibula, usu. with dislocation of the ankle. [Percival *Pott*, 1714–88, English surgeon]

potty[1] (pot´i) *a.* (*comp.* **pottier**, *superl.* **pottiest**) **1** crazy, foolish. **2** insignificant. **pottiness** *n.* [etym. uncertain]

potty[2] (pot´i) *n.* (*pl.* **potties**) (*coll.*) a chamber pot, esp. one for use by small children. **potty-train** *v.t.* to teach (a young child) to use a potty. **potty-training** *n.*

pouch (powch) *n.* **1** a small bag. **2** a purse, a detachable pocket. **3** the baglike pocket of skin in which marsupials carry their young. **4** a similar receptacle in other animals, e.g. in a rodent's cheeks. **5** a puffy fold of skin under the eye. **6** a bag for holding mail. **7** †a leather bag for holding cartridges etc. **8** a pouchlike sac in plants. ~*v.t.* **1** to put into a pouch. **2** to put into a pocket. **3** to cause (a bodice etc.) to hang like a pouch. **4** to swallow. ~*v.i.* (of a dress) to hang like a pouch. **pouched** *a.* **pouchful** *n.* (*pl.* **pouchfuls**) as much as a pouch will hold. **pouchy** *a.* [ME and ONF *pouche*, OF *poche*, POKE[2]]

pouf[1] (poof), **pouffe** *n.* **1** a large, solid cushion used as a seat or a footstool. **2** a part of a woman's dress gathered into a kind of knot or bunch. **3** a mode of dressing women's hair fashionable in the 18th cent. [F]

pouf[2] POOF[1].

pouffe POUF[1].

Poujadism (poozhah´dizm) *n.* a reactionary political movement aiming to protect the interests of small businesses. **Poujadist** *n., a.* [Pierre *Poujade*, b. 1920, French politician]

poulard (poo´lahd) *n.* a hen that has been spayed and fattened for eating. [F *poularde*, from *poule*, a hen]

poult[1] (poolt, pult) *n.* paduasoy. **poult-de-soie** (poodəswah´) *n.* [F, etym. uncertain]

poult[2] POULTRY.

poultice (pōl´tis) *n.* a heated and medicated composition, for applying to sore or inflamed parts of the body to reduce inflammation, a cataplasm. ~*v.t.* to apply a poultice to. [L *puls pultis*, PULSE[2]]

poultry (pōl´tri) *n.* domestic fowls, including chickens, geese, ducks, turkeys etc. **poult**[2] (pōlt) *n.* a young pullet, partridge, turkey etc. **poulterer, †poulter** *n.* a dealer in poultry for the table. **poultry farm, poultry yard, poultry house** *n.* [F *poulet*, dim. of *poule*, see PULLET]

pounce[1] (powns) *n.* **1** a pouncing, an abrupt swoop, spring etc. **2** the claw of a bird of prey. ~*v.i.* **1** to sweep down or spring upon and seize prey with the claws. **2** to seize (upon), to dart or dash (upon) suddenly. **3** to speak abruptly in reply to a remark etc. **pounced** *a.* (*Her.*) furnished with claws. **pouncer**[1] *n.* [etym. uncertain, perh. rel. to PUNCH[1], and PUNCHEON[1]]

pounce[2] (powns) *n.* **1** a fine powder formerly used to dry up ink on manuscript. **2** a powder used for sprinkling over a perforated pattern in order to transfer the design. ~*v.t.* **1** to dust (paper) with pounce. **2** to smooth with pounce or pumice. **3** to mark out (a pattern) by means of pounce. **pounce-box** *n.* a box out of which pounce is sprinkled. **pouncer**[2] *n.* **†pouncet-box** (-sit-) *n.* a box with a perforated lid for holding perfumes. [F *ponce*, L *pūmicem*, nom. *pūmex*, PUMICE]

pouncer[1] POUNCE[1].

pouncer[2] POUNCE[2].

pound[1] (pownd) *n.* **1** an avoirdupois unit of weight divided into 16 ounces and equal to approx. 0.454 kg. **2** a troy unit of weight divided into 12 ounces and equal to approx. 0.373 kg. **3** (*also* **pound sterling,** *pl.* **pound, pounds**) the basic monetary unit of the UK, divided into 100 (new) pence (formerly 20 shillings). **4** the standard monetary unit of various other countries. **poundage**[1] (-dij) *n.* **1** an allowance, fee, commission etc., of so much in the pound. **2** a percentage of the aggregate earnings of an industrial concern paid as or added to wages. **3** a payment or charge per pound weight. **4** the charge on a postal order. **5** weight in pounds. **6** a person's weight, esp. if considered excessive. **poundal** *n.* (*Physics*) a unit of force, that required to give an acceleration of one foot per second to a mass of one pound. **pound cake** *n.* a rich sweet cake, so called from the ingredients being pound for pound of each. **pound coin** *n.* a UK coin with the value of one pound sterling. **pounder**[1] *n.* **1** (*usu. in comb.*) a gun firing a shot of a specified number of pounds weight. **2** a person worth or possessing a specified sum in pounds sterling. **3** something weighing a pound, or a specified number of pounds, such as a fish. **pound-foolish** *a.* neglecting the care of large sums, esp. through trying to make small economies. **pound of flesh** *n.* the exact amount owing to one, esp. when recovering it involves one's debtor in considerable suffering or trouble. **pound Scots** *n.* (*Hist.*) 1s. 8d. **pound sign** *n.* the sign £, representing a pound sterling. [OE *pund* (cp. Dut. *pond*, G *Pfund*), L *pondo*, rel. to *pendere*, to weigh, *pendēre*, to hang]

pound[2] (pownd) *n.* **1 a** an enclosure for confining stray cattle etc. **b** a yard for keeping cars removed from the street by police, or distrained goods etc. **2** an enclosure, a pen. **3** a trap, a prison. ~*v.t.* **1** to confine in or as in a pound. **2** (*usu. p.p.*) to shut in, to enclose in front and behind. **poundage**[2] (-dij) *n.* **1** confinement in a pound. **2** a charge upon cattle impounded. **pound-keeper** *n.* **pound lock** *n.* a lock with two gates and usu. a reservoir at the side to regulate the water level. **pound-net** *n.* a series of nets, set in shoal water, to form a trap. [OE *pund*, enclosure]

pound[3] (pownd) *v.t.* **1** to crush, to pulverize. **2** to beat, to strike heavily. **3** to thump, to pommel. ~*v.i.* **1** to strike heavy blows, to hammer (at, upon etc.). **2** to fire heavy shot (at). **3** to walk or go heavily (along). **4** (of the heart, a drum etc.) to beat heavily or very fast. **to pound out** to produce, as if with heavy blows (esp. on a typewriter). **pounder**[2] *n.* a person who or a thing which pounds, esp. a pestle. [OE *pūnian*]

poundage[1] POUND[1].

poundage[2] POUND[2].

poundal POUND[1].

pounder[1] POUND[1].

pounder[2] POUND[3].

pour (paw) *v.t.* **1** to cause (liquids etc.) to flow downwards. **2** to serve (a drink) by pouring. **3** to discharge, to emit copiously. **4** to send (forth or out) in a stream, or in great numbers. **5** to shed freely. **6** to utter, to give vent to. ~*v.i.* **1** to flow in a stream of rain, to fall copiously. **2** to rush in great numbers. **3** to come in a constant stream. ~*n.* **1** a heavy fall, a downpour. **2** the amount of molten material poured at one time. **it never rains but it pours** misfortunes always happen several at a time or in quick succession. **to pour cold water on** COLD. **to pour oil on troubled waters** to exercise a soothing, calming or conciliatory influence. **to pour scorn on** SCORN. **pourable** *a.* **pourer** *n.* [ME *pouren*, etym. uncertain]

pourboire (puəbwah´) *n.* a gratuity, a tip. [F, for drinking]

pour-parler (puəpah´lā) *n.* a preliminary discussion with a view to formal negotiation. [F, to discuss (*pour*, for, before, *parler*, to speak)]

pour-point (puə´point) *n.* (*Hist.*) a quilted doublet. [OF, p.p. of *pour-poundre* (*pour-*, *par*, L PER-, *pungere*, to prick)]

poussette (pooset´) *v.i.* (of partners in a country dance) to move up or down the set with hands joined. ~*n.* this figure. [F, dim. of *pousse*, PUSH]

poussin (poo´sī) *n.* a young chicken reared for eating. [F]

pout[1] (powt) *v.i.* **1** to thrust out the lips in sullenness, displeasure, or contempt. **2** (of lips) to be protruded or prominent. ~*v.t.* to thrust out (the lips). ~*n.* **1** a protrusion of the lips. **2** a fit of sullenness. **the pouts** a fit of sullenness. **pouter** *n.* **1** a person who pouts. **2** a variety of pigeon which can inflate its crop. **poutingly** *adv.* **pouty** *a.* [ME *pouten* (cp. Swed. *puta*, pad, Dan. *pude*, pillow)]

pout[2] (powt) *n.* any one of various fishes that have a pouting appearance, esp. the eelpout and the bib or whiting-pout. [OE *-pūta*, in *ælepūtan*, eelpouts (cp. Dut. *puit*, G. *-putte*), cogn. with POUT[1]]

poverty (pov´əti) *n.* **1** the state of being poor; want, destitution, indigence. **2** scarcity, meagreness, dearth (of). **3** deficiency (in). **4** inferiority. **5** renunciation (by monks etc.) of the right to hold property. **poverty line** *n.* a level of income below which one is in poverty. **poverty-stricken** *a.* very poor. **poverty trap** *n.* a situation in which any increase in one's earned income is immediately offset by a decrease in one's entitlement to state benefit, thus making it impossible to raise one's standard of living. [ME and OF *poverte*, L *paupertātem*, nom. *-tas*, from PAUPER]

POW *abbr.* prisoner of war.

pow (pow) *int.* used to express the sound of an impact, blow etc.

powan (pow´ən) *n.* a freshwater fish, *Coregonus clupeoides*, found in Loch Lomond etc. [Sc. POLLAN]

powder (pow´də) *n.* **1** any dry dustlike substance or fine particles. **2** dust. **3** a cosmetic in the form of fine dust. **4** a medicine in the form of powder. **5** gunpowder. ~*v.t.* **1** to reduce to powder. **2** to put powder on. **3** to sprinkle or cover with powder. **4** to sprinkle with fine spots or figures for decoration. ~*v.i.* **1** to become powder or like powder. **2** (*Hist.*) to powder one's hair. **to keep one's powder dry** to take precautions and wait for an opportunity to act. **to take a powder** (*N Am., coll.*) to run away, leave quickly. **powder blue** *n.* **1** a pale blue colour. **2** pulverized blue glass, esp. for use in laundry. ~*a.* having a pale blue colour. **powder box** *n.* a box for cosmetic powder etc. **powder burn** *n.* a burn on the skin caused by proximity to an explosion of gunpowder. **powder cart** *n.* (*Hist.*) a cart for conveying ammunition for artillery. **powder closet** *n.* (*Hist.*) a small room where women's hair used to be powdered. **powder compact** *n.* COMPACT[2]. **powder-down** *n.* a peculiar kind of down-feathers disintegrating into fine powder, occurring in definite patches on herons etc. **powderer** *n.* **powder flask, powder horn** *n.* (*Hist.*) a case or horn fitted to hold gunpowder. **powdering tub** *n.* a tub in which meat is salted or pickled. **powder keg** *n.* **1** a small barrel to hold gunpowder. **2** a potentially explosive place or situation. **powder magazine** *n.* a storage place for gunpowder. **powder metallurgy** *n.* the technology of making metal objects by compacting and sintering powdered metal. **powder mill** *n.* a works in which gunpowder is made. **powder monkey** *n.* (*Naut.*) a boy formerly employed to carry powder from the magazine to the guns. **powder puff** *n.* a soft pad for applying powder to the skin. **powder room** *n.* **1** (*coll.*) a women's cloakroom. **2** the apartment in a ship where gunpowder is kept. **powder snow** *n.* very fine dry snow. **powdery** *a.* **powderiness** *n.* **powdery mildew** *n.* a plant disease caused by a fungus of the family *Erysiphaceae*, whose spores appear as a white powder on the stems and leaves. [F *poudre*, OF *poldre*, *polre*, L *pulver*]

power (pow´ə) *n.* **1** the ability to do or act so as to effect something. **2** a mental or bodily faculty, or potential capacity. **3** strength, force, energy, esp. as actually exerted. **4** influence, dominion, authority (over). **5** right or ability to control. **6** legal authority or authorization. **7** political ascendancy. **8** a person, group or body invested with authority or having influence. **9** military strength. **10** a state having influence on other states. **11** (*coll.*) a great deal. **12** the product obtained by multiplication of a quantity or number into itself. **13** the index showing the number of times a factor is multiplied by itself. **14** mechanical energy as distinguished from hand labour. **15 a** electricity. **b** electrical energy or power. **16** the capacity (of a machine etc.) for performing mechanical work. **17** the rate at which energy is emitted or transferred, esp. the rate of doing work, measured in watts (joules per second), foot-pounds per second, or ergs per second. **18** the magnifying capacity of a lens etc. **19** the sixth order of angels. **20** †a naval or military force. **21** a supernatural being having sway over some part of creation, a deity. ~*a.* **1** concerned with power. **2** worked by mechanical or electrical power. **3** involving a high degree of physical strength or skill. ~*v.t.* **1** to supply with esp. motive power. **2** (*coll.*) to cause to move with great speed or force. ~*v.i.* (*coll.*) to move with great force or speed. **in power** in office. **in someone's power 1** within the limits of someone's capabilities or authority. **2** under someone's control, at someone's mercy. **more power to your elbow!** (*coll.*) used to express one's approval of someone's efforts, urging someone to continue and even intensify them. **the powers that be** (*often facet.*) established authority. **to power down** to switch off, to decrease the power supply to. **to power up** to switch on, to increase the power supply to. **power amplifier** *n.* a low-frequency amplifier for powerful loudspeakers. **power-assisted** *a.* (of the steering or brakes in a motor car) made easier to use by added mechanical power. **power base** *n.* supporters etc. from whom one draws authority or power. **power behind the throne** *n.* a person with no official position in government who exercises a strong personal influence on a ruler. **power block** *n.* a group of nations etc. who together wield political, military etc. power. **powerboat** *n.* a boat propelled by a powerful motor, esp. a speedboat. **powerboating** *n.* **power-broker** *n.* a person who acts as an intermediary in setting up political alliances etc. **power-broking** *n.*, *a.* **power component** *n.* that part of an alternating current which is in phase with the voltage. **power cut** *n.* an interruption or reduction in the supply of electricity. **power-dive** *n.* a steep dive of an aircraft under engine power. ~*v.i.* to make such a dive. **power dressing** *n.* the wearing by businesswomen of plain suits tailored in a masculine style in order to give an impression of authority and power. **power drill, power lathe, power loom** *n.* a drill, lathe or loom worked by mechanical or electrical power. **power-driven** *a.* worked by electric or mechanical power. **powered** *a.* **power factor** *n.* that fraction which is less than unity by which the produce of amperes and volts in an alternating-current circuit has to be multiplied in order to estimate the true power. **powerful** *a.* **1** having great strength or energy. **2** mighty, potent. **3** impressing the mind, forcible, efficacious. **4** producing great effects. **5** (*coll.*) great, numerous, extreme. **powerfully** *adv.* **powerfulness** *n.* **powerhouse** *n.* **1** a power station. **2** (*coll.*) a very forceful and dynamic person or thing. **powerless** *a.* **1** without strength or power. **2** unable (to). **powerlessly** *adv.* **powerlessness** *n.* **power line** *n.* a cable carrying electric power, esp. one supported on pylons or poles. **power of attorney** *n.* a written authority by which one person authorizes another to act in their stead. **power of the keys** *n.* the supreme ecclesiastical authority claimed by the Pope (Matt. xvi.19). **power pack** *n.* **1** a unit for converting a power supply to the voltage required by an electronic circuit. **2** a unit for supplying power. **power plant** *n.* **1** a power station. **2** the machinery etc. used to generate power. **3** the engine and related parts which power a car, aircraft etc. **power play** *n.* **1** in team sports, aggressive tactics, esp. concentrating players on one part of the defence. **2** similar tactics in business or politics. **3** in ice hockey, a formation used when the opposing team are one or more players down. **power point** *n.* an electrical socket by which an appliance can be connected to the mains. **power politics** *n.* (*sometimes as pl.*) diplomacy backed by armed force or the threat of it. **power set** *n.* (*Math.*) a set consisting of all the subsets of a given set. **power-sharing** *n.* the involvement of all the parties or groups in an organization in making and implementing policy. **power shovel** *n.* a mechanical excavator. **power station** *n.* an installation for the generation of power, esp. electrical power. **power steering** *n.* a system in which the torque applied to a vehicle's steering wheel is augmented by engine power. **power stroke** *n.* in an internal-combustion engine, the downward stroke of the piston. **power structure** *n.* **1** the way in which power is distributed within an organization. **2** the people, parties etc. who between them wield power. **power tool** *n.* an electrically-powered tool. **power train** *n.* the sequence of parts in a motor vehicle from the engine through the transmission to the axle and wheels. **power transmission** *n.* the transmission of electrical power from the generating system to the point of application. **power unit** *n.* a power amplifier. [ME and OF *poër* (F *pouvoir*), late L *potēre*, from L *pot-*, stem of *posse*, to be able]

powwow (pow´wow) *n.* **1** a meeting, talk or conference, orig. among N American Indians. **2** a N American Indian medicine man or wizard. **3** magic rites for the cure of diseases. ~*v.i.* to hold a powwow. [N Am. Ind.]

pox (poks) *n.* **1** any disease characterized by the formation of pustules that leave pockmarks. **2** syphilis. **3** †smallpox. **4** a plant disease which causes spots like pox pustules. **†a pox on** used to express anger or dislike of a person or thing. **poxy** *a.* (*comp.* **poxier**, *superl.* **poxiest**) **1** syphilitic. **2** (*sl.*) unpleasant, rotten. [pl. of POCK]

Pozidriv® (poz´idrīv) *n.* a type of cross-head screwdriver.

pozzolana (potsōlah´nə), **pozzuolana** (-swō-),

puzzolana (puts-) *n.* a volcanic ash used in hydraulic cements. [It., from *Pozzuoli*, near Naples]
pozzy POSSIE.
PP *abbr.* 1 parish priest. 2 past President.
pp *abbr.* 1 per pro. 2 pianissimo.

Usage note See note under PER PRO.

p.p. *abbr.* 1 past participle. 2 per pro.
pp. *abbr.* pages.
PPARC *abbr.* Particle Physics and Astronomy Research Council.
ppd *abbr.* 1 post-paid. 2 prepaid.
PPE *abbr.* philosophy, politics and economics.
p.p.m., ppm *abbr.* parts per million.
PPS *abbr.* 1 Parliamentary Private Secretary. 2 post-postscriptum, further postscript.
PQ *abbr.* 1 Parti Québecois. 2 Province of Quebec.
PR *abbr.* 1 proportional representation. 2 public relations. 3 Puerto Rico (IVR).
Pr[1] *chem. symbol* praseodymium.
Pr[2] *abbr.* 1 priest. 2 prince.
pr *abbr.* 1 pair. 2 present. 3 price.
pr. *abbr.* pair.
PRA *abbr.* President of the Royal Academy.
praam PRAM[2].
practicable (prak´tikəbəl) *a.* 1 capable of being done, feasible. 2 (of roads etc.) usable, passable. 3 (of stage properties) functioning, real, not simulated. **practicability** (-bil´-), **practicableness** *n.* **practicably** *adv.* [F *practicable*, from *practiquer*, to PRACTISE, assim. to PRACTICAL]

Usage note The meanings of the adjectives *practicable* and *practical* overlap, but *practicable* usually means possible in practice, feasible, while *practical* contrasts practice or performance with theory or speculation, with reference either to a person or an action.

practical (prak´tikəl) *a.* 1 of or relating to action not theory or speculation. 2 realistic, down-to-earth. 3 (of a person) preferring action to speculation. 4 capable of being used, available, serving or suitable for use. 5 such in effect, virtual. 6 of, relating to or governed by practice. 7 derived from practice, experienced. ~*n.* a practical examination, lesson etc. **practicality** (-kal´-) *n.* (*pl.* **practicalities**). **practical joke** *n.* a joke or trick entailing some action and intended to make the victim look foolish. **practical joker** *n.* **practically** *adv.* 1 in a practical manner. 2 virtually, in effect, as regards results. †**practicalness** *n.* [earlier *practic*, late L *practicus*, see PRACTISE]

Usage note See note under PRACTICABLE.

practice[1] (prak´tis) *n.* 1 habitual or customary action or procedure. 2 habit, custom. 3 the continued or systematic exercise of any profession, art, craft etc. 4 **a** professional work. **b** the business of a professional person. 5 actual performance, doing or execution, as opposed to theory or intention. 6 (*often pl.*) conduct, dealings. 7 **a** regular, repeated exercise in order to gain proficiency in something. **b** a session of such exercise. 8 a rule for multiplying quantities of various denominations. 9 legal procedure, the rules governing this. **in practice** 1 in the sphere of action. 2 in training, in condition for working, acting, playing etc., effectively. **out of practice** out of training. **to put into practice** to convert an idea or theory into actuality, to do something previously only thought of. **practician** (-tish´ən) *n.* a person who works or practises, a practitioner. [prob. from PRACTISE]
practice[2] PRACTISE.
practician PRACTICE[1].
practise (prak´tis), (*N Am.*) **practice** *v.t.* 1 to do or perform habitually; to carry out. 2 to exercise a profession etc. 3 to exercise oneself in or on (to improve or maintain a skill etc.). 4 to instruct, to exercise, to drill (in a subject, art etc.). 5 to accustom. 6 †to plot, to scheme. ~*v.i.* 1 to exercise oneself. 2 to exercise a profession or art. 3 to do a thing or perform an act habitually. 4 †to scheme, to plot, to use stratagems. 5 to use influence, to impose (upon). **practisant** *n.* an agent, a plotter. **practised** *a.* experienced, expert. **practiser** *n.* **practising** *a.* doing or actively engaged in now (*practising Christian*). [OF *practiser* (F *pratiquer*), med. L *practicāre*, from *practicus*, Gr. *praktikos*, from *prassein*, to do]
practitioner (praktish´ənə) *n.* a person who regularly practises any profession, esp. medicine. **general practitioner** GENERAL.
prae- (prē) *pref.* pre-. [L *prae*, before]
praecipe (prē´sipē) *n.* 1 a writ requiring something to be done, or a reason for its non-performance. 2 an order requesting a writ. [L, imper. of *praecipere*, to enjoin; *capere*, to take]
praecocial PRECOCIAL.
praecordia PRECORDIA.
praedial PREDIAL.
praemunire (prēmūnī´ri), **premunire** *n.* (*Hist.*) 1 a writ or process against a person charged with obeying or maintaining the papal authority in England. 2 an offence against the Statute of Praemunire (1393) on which this is based. 3 the penalty incurred by it. [L, to defend, conf. with *praemonēre*, to forewarn (PRAE-, *monēre*, to warn)]
praenomen PRENOMEN.
praepostor (prēpos´tə), **prepositor** (-itə), **prepostor** *n.* a prefect in some public schools. [L (*pōnere positus*, to place, to put)]
praesidium PRESIDIUM.
praetor (prē´tə), (*N Am.*) **pretor** *n.* (*Hist.*) a Roman magistrate; orig. a consul as leader of the army, later a curule magistrate elected yearly to perform various judicial and consular duties. **praetorial** (pritaw´ri-) *a.* **praetorian** *a.* 1 of or relating to a praetor. 2 of or relating to the bodyguard of a Roman general or emperor, esp. the imperial bodyguard established by Augustus. ~*n.* 1 a soldier in this bodyguard. 2 a man of praetorian rank. **praetorian gate** *n.* the gate of a Roman camp in front of the general's quarters towards the enemy. **praetorian guard** *n.* **praetorium** (-əm) *n.* (*pl.* **praetoria** (-ə)) 1 the general's tent or official quarters in a Roman camp. 2 a Roman governor's official residence or court. **praetorship** *n.* [L, for *praeitor*, from *praeīre* (PRAE-, *īre*, to go)]
pragmatic (pragmat´ik) *a.* 1 concerned with practicalities or expediency rather than principles. 2 concerned with the causes and effects and the practical lessons of history. 3 (*Hist.*) of or relating to the affairs of a state. 4 pragmatical. **pragmatical** *a.* 1 officious, given to interfering in the affairs of others. 2 dogmatic. 3 relating to pragmatism. 4 pragmatic. **pragmaticality** (-kal´-), **pragmaticalness** *n.* **pragmatically** *adv.* **pragmatics** *n.* 1 in linguistics, the study of the social etc. aspects of language. 2 the study of signs and symbols and their use. **pragmatic sanction** *n.* (*Hist.*) an ordinance made by a sovereign and constituting a fundamental law, esp. that of the Emperor Charles VI settling the succession to the throne of Austria. **pragmatism** (prag´-) *n.* 1 pragmaticalness, officiousness. 2 treatment of things, esp. in history, with regard to causes and effects. 3 a practical approach to problems and affairs. 4 (*Philos.*) the doctrine that our only test of the truth of human cognitions or philosophical principles is their practical results. **pragmatist** *n.* **pragmatistic** (-tis´-) *a.* **pragmatize, pragmatise** *v.t.* 1 to represent (an imaginary thing) as real. 2 to rationalize (a myth). [F *pragmatique*, L *pragmaticus*, Gr. *pragmatikos*, from *pragma pragmatos*, deed, from *prassein*, to do]

prahu PROA.

prairie (preəʹri) *n.* an extensive tract of level or rolling grassland, usu. destitute of trees, esp. in N America. **prairie chicken, prairie hen** *n.* a N American grouse, *Tympanuchus cupido.* **prairie dog** *n.* any small rodent of the genus *Cynomys*, living in large communities on the N American prairies. **prairie oyster** *n.* a pick-me-up made of raw egg, Worcester sauce etc. **prairie schooner** *n.* (*N Am.*) a covered wagon used in crossing the western plains. **prairie value** *n.* the value of land before labour has been expended on it. **prairie wolf** *n.* the coyote, *Canis latrans.* [F, through a pop. L *prātāria*, from L *prātum*, meadow]

praise (prāz) *v.t.* **1** to express approval and commendation of. **2** to extol, to glorify. ~*n.* **1** the act, or an instance, of praising, approbation, encomium. **2** glorifying, extolling. **3** an object of praise. **praise be!** an exclamation expressing gratitude and pleasure. **praisable** *a.* **praiseful** *a.* laudable, commendable. **praisefulness** *n.* **praiseless** *a.* **praiser** *n.* **praiseworthy** *a.* **1** deserving of praise. **2** laudable, commendable. **praiseworthily** *adv.* **praiseworthiness** *n.* [ME *preiser*, OF *preisier*, late L *pretiāre*, from L *pretium*, price, value, cp. PRICE]

Prakrit (prahʹkrit) *n.* any of a group of North and Central Indian languages or dialects no longer used, based on Sanskrit. **Prakritic** (-kritʹik) *a.* [Sansk. *prākrta*, natural, vulgar]

praline (prahʹlēn) *n.* a confection of almond or other nut with a brown coating of sugar. [F]

pralltriller (prahlʹtrilə) *n.* (*Mus.*) an ornament in which a note is preceded by itself and the note immediately above it, an inverted mordent. [G, rebound, trill]

pram[1] (pram) *n.* a four-wheeled conveyance for a baby, with a cradle-like body and pushed by a person walking. [abbr. of PERAMBULATOR (under PERAMBULATE)]

pram[2] (prahm), **praam** *n.* **1** a flat-bottomed barge or lighter used in the Netherlands and the Baltic. **2** a similar boat formerly used as a floating battery. [Dut.]

prana (prahʹnə) *n.* **1** in Hinduism, the breath of life. **2** breath, breathing. **pranayama** (-yahʹmə) *n.* in yoga, controlled breathing. [Sansk.]

prance (prahns) *v.i.* **1** to spring or caper on the hind legs, as a horse in high mettle. **2** to walk or strut in a pompous or swaggering style. ~*n.* **1** the act of prancing. **2** a prancing movement. **prancer** *n.* **prancing** *n.*, *a.* **prancingly** *adv.* [etym. uncertain, perh. rel. to PRANK[1]]

prandial (pranʹdiəl) *a.* (*formal or facet.*) relating to lunch or dinner. **prandially** *adv.* [L *prandium*, breakfast]

prang (prang) *v.t.* (*sl.*) **1** to crash. **2** to bomb heavily. **3** to strike. ~*n.* **1** a bombing raid. **2** a crash. [onomat.]

prank[1] (prangk) *n.* **1** a wild frolic. **2** a trick, a playful act, a practical joke. **3** a gambol, a capricious action. **prankful** *a.* **prankish** *a.* **prankishness** *n.* **pranksome** *a.* **prankster** *n.* a person given to playing pranks or practical jokes. **pranky** *a.* [etym. unknown]

prank[2] (prangk) *v.t.* **1** to dress up in a showy fashion; to deck (out). **2** to adorn (with). ~*v.i.* to make a show. [ME *pranken*, cp. G *prangen*, to make a show, Dut. *pronken*, G *prunken*, to make a show of; also Eng. PRINK]

prase (prāz) *n.* a dull leek-green translucent quartz. [F, from L *prasius*, Gr. *prasios*]

praseodymium (prāziōdimʹiəm) *n.* a rare metallic element, at. no. 59, chem. symbol Pr, occurring in certain rare-earth minerals. [Gr. *prasios*, leek-green]

prat (prat) *n.* (*sl.*) **1** a stupid or contemptible person. **2** the buttocks. **pratfall** *n.* **1** (*esp. N Am.*) a fall on one's buttocks. **2** a humiliating blunder or mishap. [etym. uncertain]

prate (prāt) *v.i.* **1** to chatter; to talk a lot and without purpose or reason. **2** to babble, to cackle. ~*v.t.* **1** to utter foolishly. **2** to boast idly about. ~*n.* idle or silly talk, unmeaning loquacity. **prater** *n.* **prating** *n.*, *a.* **pratingly** *adv.* [ME *praten*, cp. Dut. *praten*, Dan. *prate*, Swed. *prata*]

pratie (prāʹti) *n.* (*Ir.*) a potato. [corr. of POTATO]

pratincole (pratʹingkōl) *n.* any of a genus, *Glareola*, of birds related to the plover, living near water. [mod. L *pratincola*, from L *prātum*, a meadow, *incola*, an inhabitant]

pratique (pratʹēk, -ēkʹ) *n.* a licence to a ship to hold communication with a port after quarantine, or upon certification that the vessel has not come from an infected place. [F, PRACTICE[1]]

prattle (pratʹəl) *v.i.* to talk in a childish or foolish manner. ~*v.t.* to utter or divulge thus. ~*n.* childish or idle talk. **prattler** *n.* **prattling** *n.*, *a.* **prattlingly** *adv.* [freq. of PRATE]

prau PROA.

prawn (prawn) *n.* any of several small decapod crustaceans, like large shrimps. ~*v.t.* to fish for prawns. **prawn cracker** *n.* in Chinese cookery, a savoury puff made from rice flour flavoured with prawn. [ME *prane*, *prayne*, etym. uncertain]

praxis (prakʹsis) *n.* (*pl.* **praxises, praxes** (-ēz)) **1** use, practice, accepted practice. **2** the practice of an art; the practical as distinct from the theoretical side. **3** (*Gram.*) a collection of examples for practice. [Gr., rel. to *prassein*, to do]

pray (prā) *v.t.* **1** to ask for with earnestness or submission. **2** to beseech, to entreat, to supplicate. **3** to address devoutly and earnestly. ~*v.i.* **1** to address God with adoration or earnest entreaty. **2** to make supplication, to beg or petition (for). ~*int.* (*often iron.*) may I ask, I ask you. **prayer**[1] (prāʹə) *n.* a person who prays. **prayingly** *adv.* **praying mantis** MANTIS. [OF *preier* (F *prier*), late L *precāre*, L *precārī*, from *prex precis*, prayer]

prayer[1] PRAY.

prayer[2] (preə) *n.* **1** the act of praying. **2** a solemn petition or a thanksgiving addressed to God or any object of worship. **3** the practice of praying, a formula for praying. **4** a prescribed formula of divine worship; a liturgy. **5** (*often pl.*) a religious service. **6** an entreaty. **7** something entreated or prayed for. **8** a memorial or petition. **9** that part of a petition which specifies the thing desired. **10** a petition to the Queen to annul an Order in Council. **not to have a prayer** (*N Am., coll.*) to have not the slightest chance or hope. **prayer beads** *n.pl.* the beads on a rosary. **prayer book** *n.* a book containing prayers and forms of devotion, esp. the Anglican Book of Common Prayer. **prayerful** *a.* **1** given to prayer, devout. **2** devotional, characterized by prayer. **prayerfully** *adv.* **prayerfulness** *n.* **prayerless** *a.* **prayerlessly** *adv.* **prayer mat** *n.* a small carpet on which a Muslim kneels and prays. **prayer meeting** *n.* a meeting for divine worship in which prayer is offered by several persons. **prayer rug** *n.* a prayer mat. **prayer shawl** *n.* a tallith. **prayer wheel** *n.* a revolving wheel or cylinder on which written prayers are inscribed or fastened by Tibetan Buddhists. [ME and OF *preiere*, med. L *precāria*, as PRECARIOUS]

PRB *abbr.* Pre-Raphaelite Brotherhood.

pre (prē) *prep.* (*coll.*) before.

pre- (prē) *pref.* **1** before, earlier than; in advance. **2** in front of, anterior to. **3** surpassingly. [OF and med. L *pre-*, L PRAE-, before]

pre- (+ a– words) preabsorb *v.t.* to absorb in advance. **preaccustom** *v.t.* to accustom in advance. **preacquaint** *v.t.* to acquaint beforehand. **preacquaintance** *n.* **pre-Adamite** *n.* **1** a supposed inhabitant of the world before Adam. **2** a person who holds that there were persons in existence before Adam. ~*a.* **1** existing before Adam. **2** of or relating to the pre-Adamites. **pre-Adamic, pre-Adamitic** *a.* **preadaptation** *n.* (*Biol.*) the possession by a species of features which are not useful at present, but might be if the environment were to change. **preadapt** *v.i.* **preaddress** *v.t.* to address (an envelope) in advance. **preadjust** *v.t.* to adjust in advance. **pre-adolescent** *a.* 1 (of a child) having nearly reached adolescence. 2 of or relating to the stage between childhood and adolescence. ~*n.* a pre-adolescent child. **pre-adolescence** *n.* **preamp** (prē´amp) *n.* a preamplifier. **preamplifier** *n.* an amplifier used to boost a low-level signal and often to equalize it before feeding it to the main amplifier. **preamplified** *a.* **pre-announce** *v.t.* to announce in advance. **preappoint** *v.t.* to appoint in advance. **preapprehension** *n.* 1 a preconceived opinion. 2 a foreboding. **pre-arrange** *v.t.* to arrange in advance. **pre-arranged** *a.* **pre-arrangement** *n.* **pre-assurance** *n.* **preatomic** *a.* of or relating to the period before the use of atomic energy.

preach (prēch) *v.i.* 1 to deliver a sermon or public discourse on some religious subject. 2 to give earnest religious or moral advice, esp. in an obtrusive or persistent way. ~*v.t.* 1 to proclaim, to expound in a common or public discourse. 2 to deliver (a sermon). 3 to teach or advocate in this manner. ~*n.* (*coll.*) a preaching, a sermon. **to preach down** 1 to denounce or disparage by preaching. 2 to preach against. **to preach to the converted** to advocate an opinion etc. to people already in favour. **preachable** *a.* **preacher** *n.* **preachership** *n.* **preachify** (-ifī) *v.i.* (*3rd pers. sing. pres.* **preachifies,** *pres.p.* **preachifying,** *past, p.p.* **preachified**) to hold forth in a sermon, esp. tediously; to sermonize. **preachification** (-fikā´shən) *n.* **preachment** *n.* (*usu. derog.*) a discourse or sermon. **preachy** *a.* (*comp.* **preachier,** *superl.* **preachiest**) fond of preaching or sermonizing, disposed to preach. **preachiness** *n.* [OF *prechier*, L *praedicāre* (*dicāre*, to proclaim, rel. to *dīcere*, to say)]

preamble (prēam´bəl) *n.* 1 an introductory statement, esp. the introductory portion of a statute setting forth succinctly its reasons and intentions. 2 a preliminary event, fact etc. ~*v.i.* to make a preamble. **preambular** (-bū-), **preambulary** *a.* [OF *preambule*, med. L *praeambulum*, from L *praeambulus*, going before (*ambulāre*, to walk)]

Preb. *abbr.* Prebendary.

pre- (+ b– words) prebiotic *a.* of or relating to the time before the appearance of life on earth. **pre-book** *v.t.* to reserve, to arrange in advance. **pre-bookable** *a.*

prebend (preb´ənd) *n.* 1 (*Hist.*) the stipend or maintenance granted to a canon of a cathedral or collegiate church out of its revenue. 2 (*Hist.*) the land or tithe yielding this. 3 a prebendary. 4 a prebendaryship. **prebendal** *a.* of or relating to a prebend or a prebendary. **prebendal stall, prebendary stall** *n.* a prebendary's stall in a cathedral or his benefice. **prebendary** *n.* (*pl.* **prebendaries**) 1 an honorary canon. 2 (*Hist.*) the holder of a prebend. **prebendaryship** *n.* [OF *prebende*, med. L *praebenda*, payment, pension, orig. neut. pl. ger. of L *praebēre*, to grant (*habēre*, to have)]

prec. *abbr.* preceding.

pre- (+ c– words) Precambrian *n., a.* (of or relating to) the earliest geological era, before the appearance of early life forms. **precancel** *v.t.* (*pres.p.* **precancelling,** (*NAm.*) **precanceling,** *past, p.p.* **precancelled,** (*NAm.*) **precanceled**) to cancel (a postage stamp) before use. **precancellation** *n.* **precancerous** *a.* (*Med.*) (of cells or tissues) showing changes which may lead to the development of cancer. **pre-Carboniferous** *a.* **precast** *a.* (of concrete blocks, panels etc.) cast before being put in position. ~*v.t.* (*past, p.p.* **precast**) to cast (concrete) before putting it in position. **pre-Christian** *a.* of or relating to the times before Christ or before Christianity. **pre-Christmas** *a.* **preclassical** *a.* before the classical period, esp. in music and literature. **preclinical** *a.* (*Med.*) 1 of or relating to the early stages of a disease, before the symptoms are recognizable. 2 of or relating to the early stage of medical studies, before the student has practical experience with patients. **pre-coital** *a.* **pre-coitally** *adv.* **pre-Columbian** *a.* of or relating to the period in US history before the arrival of Columbus. **preconcert**[1] (-sœt´) *v.t.* to contrive or agree on by previous arrangement. **preconcert**[2] (-kon´sət) *n.* an arrangement previously made. **preconcertedly** *adv.* **preconcertedness** *n.* **precondition** *n.* a necessary preliminary condition. ~*v.t.* to prepare beforehand, to put into a desired condition or frame of mind beforehand. **pre-connection** *n.* **pre-Conquest** *a.* before the time of the Norman Conquest (1066). **preconscious** *a.* 1 of or relating to a state antecedent to consciousness. 2 of or relating to ideas or memories which are not conscious but which can readily be recalled. ~*n.* the part of the mind where preconscious ideas etc. exist. **preconsciousness** *n.* **preconsidered** *a.* **pre-consonantal** *a.* **pre-construct** *v.t.* **pre-construction** *n.* **precontract**[1] (-kon´-) *n.* a previous contract. **precontract**[2] (-trakt´) *v.i., v.t.* to contract beforehand. **pre-cook** *v.t.* to cook beforehand. **pre-cool** *v.t.* to cool beforehand. **precostal** *a.* in front of the ribs. **precritical** *a.* 1 of, relating to or occurring in the period before a crisis or a critical phase. 2 preceding the critical treatment of a subject, esp. preceding the critical philosophy of Kant. **pre-cut** *v.t.* (*pres.p.* **pre-cutting,** *past, p.p.* **pre-cut**) to cut beforehand.

precarious (prikeə´riəs) *a.* 1 not well-established, insecure, unstable. 2 doubtful, dependent on chance, uncertain, hazardous. 3 depending on the will or pleasure of another. 4 held by a doubtful tenure. **precariously** *adv.* **precariousness** *n.* [L *precārius*, obtained by prayer, from *precārī*, to PRAY]

precative (prek´ətiv) *a.* (*Gram.*) expressing a wish or entreaty. **precatory** *a.* of the nature of or expressing a wish or recommendation, to pray. [late L *precativus*, *precatorius*, from *precatus*, p.p. of *precārī*]

precaution (prikaw´shən) *n.* 1 a measure taken beforehand to guard against or bring about something. 2 (*pl.*) contraceptive measures. 3 previous caution, prudent foresight. ~*v.t.* to caution or warn beforehand. **precautionary, †precautional** *a.* **precautious** *a.* **precautiously** *adv.* [F *précaution*, med. L *praecautiōnem*, nom. *-tio*, from L *praecavēre* (*cavēre*, to beware)]

precede (prisēd´) *v.t.* 1 to go before in time, order, rank or importance. 2 to walk in front of. 3 to exist before. 4 to cause to come before, to preface or prelude. ~*v.i.* 1 to go or come before. 2 to have precedence. **precedence** (pres´i-), **precedency** *n.* 1 the act or state of preceding. 2 priority. 3 superiority. 4 the right to a higher position or a place in advance of others at public ceremonies, social functions etc. **to take precedence** to have a higher priority (over). **precedent**[1] (pres´idənt) *n.* 1 something done or said which may serve as an example to be followed in a similar case, esp. a legal decision, usage etc. 2 a necessary antecedent. **precedented** *a.* having or warranted by a precedent. **precedent**[2] (prisē´dənt, pres´idənt) *a.* 1 going before in time, order, rank etc. 2 antecedent. **precedently** *adv.* **preceding** *a.* 1 going before in time, order etc. 2 previous. 3 immediately before. [F *précéder*, L *praecēdere* (*cēdere*, to go)]

precentor (prisen´tə) *n.* 1 a cleric who directs choral services in a cathedral. 2 a person who leads the singing of choir or congregation. 3 a person who leads the prayers in a synagogue. 4 in Presbyterian churches, the leader of the psalmody. **precent** *v.i.* to act as precentor. ~*v.t.* to lead the singing of (psalms etc.). **precentorship** *n.* [late L *praecentor* (*cantor*, from *cantāre*, freq. of *canere*, to sing)]

precept (prē´sept) *n.* 1 a command, a mandate. 2 a rule of conduct. 3 a maxim. 4 a writ, a warrant. 5 a sheriff's order to hold an election. 6 an order for the levying or collection of a rate. **preceptive** (-sep´-), †**preceptial** (-sep´chəl) *a.* 1 of the nature of a precept. 2 containing or giving moral instruction, didactic. **preceptor** (-sep´-) *n.* 1 a teacher, an instructor. 2 (*Hist.*) the head of a preceptory among the Knights Templars. **preceptorial** (-taw´ri-) *a.* **preceptorship** *n.* **preceptory** (-sep´-) *n.* (*pl.* **preceptories**) (*Hist.*) 1 a subordinate house or community of the Knights Templars. 2 the estate, manor etc., of or relating to this. ~†*a.* preceptive. **preceptress** (-sep´tris) *n.* a woman teacher; a governess. [OF (F *précepte*), L *praeceptum*, neut. p.p. of *praecipere* (*capere*, to take)]

precession (prisesh´ən) *n.* 1 precedence in time or order. 2 the wobbling motion of the axis of a spinning body, so that it forms a cone-shape. **precessional** *a.* **precession of the equinoxes** *n.* (*Astron.*) a slow but continual shifting of the equinoctial points from east to west, occasioned by the earth's axis slowly revolving in a small circle about the pole of the ecliptic, causing an earlier occurrence of the equinoxes in successive sidereal years. [late L *praecessio*, from *praecēdere*, to PRECEDE]

precinct (prē´singkt) *n.* 1 the space enclosed by the walls or boundaries of a place, esp. a church. 2 a boundary, a limit. 3 a pedestrianized area of a town set aside for a particular activity, usu. shopping. 4 (*US*) a municipal police district. 5 (*US*) a polling district. 6 (*pl.*) the environs or immediate surroundings (of). [med. L *praecinctum*, orig. neut. p.p. of L *praecingere* (*cingere*, to gird)]

precious (presh´əs) *a.* 1 of great price or value. 2 very costly. 3 highly esteemed, dear, beloved. 4 affected, over-refined in manner, style, workmanship etc. 5 (*coll., iron.*) worthless, rascally; considerable. ~*adv.* (*coll.*) very, extremely. **preciosity** (-ios´-) *n.* (*pl.* **preciosities**) 1 overfastidiousness or affected delicacy in the use of language, in workmanship etc. 2 an instance of this. **preciously** *adv.* **precious metals** *n.pl.* gold, silver and platinum. **preciousness** *n.* **precious stone** *n.* a gem. [OF *precios* (F *précieux*), L *pretiōsus*, from *pretium*, PRICE]

precipice (pres´ipis) *n.* 1 a vertical or very steep cliff. 2 the edge of a cliff, hence a situation of extreme danger. **precipiced** *a.* [F *précipice*, L *praecipitium*, a falling headlong, precipice, from *praeceps*, headlong (*caput*, head)]

precipitate[1] (prəsip´itāt) *v.t.* 1 to throw headlong. 2 to urge on with eager haste or violence. 3 to hasten; to bring on, esp. prematurely. 4 (*Chem.*) to cause (a substance) to be deposited at the bottom of a vessel, as from a solution. 5 to cause (moisture) to condense and be deposited, as from vapour. 6 to cause to fall as rain, snow etc. 7 to cause (dust) to be deposited on a surface from the air. ~*v.i.* 1 (of a substance in solution) to fall to the bottom of a vessel. 2 (of vapour) to condense and be deposited in drops. 3 to fall as rain, snow etc. **precipitable** *a.* capable of being precipitated, as a substance in solution. **precipitability** (-bil´-) *n.* **precipitation** (-ā´shən) *n.* 1 the act of precipitating, the state of being precipitated. 2 violent speed. 3 rash haste. 4 (the amount of) rain, snow, sleet etc. falling to the ground. **precipitator** *n.* [L *praecipitātus*, p.p. of *praecipitāre*, from *praeceps*, see PRECIPICE]

precipitate[2] (prisip´itət) *a.* 1 headlong. 2 flowing or rushing with haste and violence. 3 hasty, rash, inconsiderate. 4 adopted without due deliberation. ~*n.* 1 (*Chem.*) a solid substance deposited from a state of solution. 2 moisture condensed from vapour and deposited, as rain, dew etc. **red precipitate** RED[1]. **white precipitate** WHITE. **precipitance, precipitancy, precipitateness** *n.* **precipitant** *a.* 1 falling or rushing headlong. 2 headlong, precipitate. ~*n.* (*Chem.*) any substance that, being added to a solution, causes precipitation. †**precipitantly** *adv.* **precipitately** *adv.* [as PRECIPITATE[1]]

Usage note See note under PRECIPITOUS.

precipitin (prisip´itin) *n.* (*Med.*) an antibody that produces a precipitation when mixed with its antigen.

precipitous (prisip´itəs) *a.* 1 like or of the nature of a precipice, very steep. 2 headlong, precipitate, hasty, rash. **precipitously** *adv.* **precipitousness** *n.* [MF *precipiteux*, as PRECIPICE]

Usage note The adjectives *precipitous* and *precipitate* should not be confused: *precipitous* means steep, and *precipitate* hasty or rash.

précis (prā´sē) *n.* (*pl.* **précis** (-sēz)) 1 an abstract, a summary. 2 the act or practice of drawing up such abstracts. ~*v.t.* (*3rd pers. sing. pres.* **précises** (prā´sēz), *pres.p.* **précising** (prā´sēing), *past, p.p.* **précised** (prā´sēd)) to make a précis of. [F, as PRECISE]

precise (prisīs´) *a.* 1 definite, sharply defined or stated. 2 accurate, exact. 3 strictly observant of rule, punctilious, overnice, overscrupulous. 4 particular, identical. **precisely** *adv.* 1 in a precise manner. 2 exactly, quite so. **preciseness** *n.* **precisian** (-sizh´ən) *n.* 1 a punctilious person. 2 a person rigidly observant of rules etc., a formalist, a stickler. **precisianism** *n.* **precision** (-sizh´ən) *n.* accuracy, exactness. ~*a.* 1 characterized by great accuracy in execution. 2 intended for very accurate measurement or operation. **precisionism** *n.* **precisionist** *n.* [F *précis*, *-ise*, L *praecīsus*, p.p. of *praecīdere* (*caedere*, to cut)]

preclude (priklood´) *v.t.* 1 to shut out, to exclude. 2 to hinder, to prevent. 3 to render inoperative. 4 to neutralize. **preclusion** (-zhən) *n.* **preclusive** (-siv) *a.* **preclusively** *adv.* [L *praeclūdere* (*claudere*, to shut), *p.p. praeclūsus*]

precocial (prikō´shəl), **praecocial** *a.* (having young which are) hatched with a complete covering of down and capable of leaving the nest within a very short time. ~*n.* a precocial bird. [as PRECOCIOUS]

precocious (prikō´shəs) *a.* 1 (*often derog.*) prematurely developed intellectually. 2 (*often derog.*) forward, pert. 3 characteristic of such development. 4 developing or ripe before the normal time. **precociously** *adv.* **precociousness** *n.* **precosity** (-kos´-) *n.* [L *praecox -cōcis*, from *praecoquere* (*coquere*, to COOK)]

precognition (prēkəgnish´ən) *n.* 1 foreknowledge; clairvoyance. 2 (*Sc. Law*) preliminary examination of witnesses with a view to determining whether there is ground for a prosecution. **precognitive** (-kog´nitiv) *a.* **precognosce** (-nos´) *v.t.* [late L *praecognitio*, from *praecognoscere* (*cognoscere*, to know), see COGNITION]

preconceive (prēkənsēv´) *v.t.* to conceive or form (an opinion of) beforehand. **preconception** *n.*

preconize (prē´kənīz), **preconise** *v.t.* 1 to proclaim publicly. 2 to cite or summon publicly. 3 (of the Pope) to confirm publicly (an appointment or a person nominated). **preconization** (-zā´shən) *n.* [med. L *praecōnīzāre*, from *praeco -cōnis*, herald]

precordia (prikaw´diə), **praecordia** *n.pl.* (*Med.*) the chest and the parts it contains, the region about the heart. **precordial** *a.* [L (*cor cordis*, heart)]

precursor (prikœ´sə) *n.* 1 a forerunner, a harbinger. 2 a predecessor in office etc. 3 (*Chem.*) a substance from which another is formed by chemical reaction etc. **precursive** *a.* precursory. **precursory** *a.* 1 preceding and indicating as a forerunner or harbinger. 2 preliminary, introductory. [L *praecursus*, p.p. of *praecurrere* (*currere*, to run)]

pred. *abbr.* predicate.

pre- (+ d– words) pre-Darwinian *a.* preceding the

doctrines of evolution etc. propounded by Charles Darwin in 1859. **pre-date** *v.t.* 1 to exist or happen at an earlier date than. 2 to assign a date to (an event, document etc.) earlier than the actual date. **pre-dawn** *a.* **predecease** *n.* the death of a person before some other person. ~*v.t.* to die before (a particular person). **predecimal** *a.* before the introduction of a decimal system, esp. of coinage. **predefine** *v.t.* to define, limit or settle beforehand. **predefinition** *n.* **predesign** *v.t.* **predesignate** *v.t.* 1 to designate or indicate beforehand. 2 (*Logic*) to designate by a sign or word denoting quantity, as *only, sole, some*. ~*a.* (*Logic*) having such a sign prefixed. **predesignation** *n.* **pre-develop** *v.t.* to develop in advance. **pre-development** *n.* **predigest** *v.t.* 1 to digest partially before introducing into the stomach. 2 to render (literature or any difficult reading material) easier to understand by simplifying. **predigested** *a.* **predigestion** *n.* **pre-doom** *v.t.* to doom in advance. **predorsal** *a.* in front of the dorsal region. **predynastic** *a.* of or relating to a time, esp. in ancient Egypt, before the emergence of dynasties.

predacious (pridā´shəs), **predaceous** *a.* 1 living by prey, predatory. 2 of or relating to animals living by prey. **predacean** *n.* **predaciousness** *n.* **predacity** (-das´-) *n.* [see PREDATOR]

predator (pred´ətə) *n.* 1 a predatory animal. 2 a predatory person. **predation** (-ā´shən) *n.* 1 the way of life of a predator, the relationship between a predator and its prey. 2 (*usu. pl.*) depredation. **predatory** *a.* 1 habitually hunting and killing other animals for food. 2 living by plunder. 3 of, relating to or characterized by plunder or pillage. 4 rapacious, exploitive. **predatorily** *adv.* **predatoriness** *n.* **predatory pricing** *n.* the offering of a product or service at such a low price that competitors cannot match it and are driven out of the market. [L *praeda*, booty]

predecessor (prē´disesə) *n.* 1 a person who precedes another in any position, office etc. 2 a thing preceding another thing. 3 a forefather, an ancestor. [F *prédécesseur*, late L *praedēcessor* (*dēcessor*, from *dēcēdere*, to go away, see DECEASE)]

predella (pridel´ə) *n.* (*pl.* **predelle** (-lā)) 1 the platform on which an altar stands or the highest of a series of altar steps. 2 a painting on the face of this. 3 a painting on a steplike or shelflike appendage, usu. at the back of the altar, at the foot of an altarpiece, a gradine. [It., a stool, dim. prob. from OHG *Pret*, board]

predestine (prēdes´tin) *v.t.* 1 to appoint beforehand by irreversible decree. 2 to preordain (to salvation, to do a certain deed etc.). 3 to predetermine. **predestinarian** (-neə´ri-) *a.* of or relating to predestination. ~*n.* a believer in predestination. **predestinate**[1] (-āt) *v.t.* to predestine. **predestinate**[2] (-ət) *a.* ordained or appointed beforehand. **predestination** (-ā´shən) *n.* (*Theol.*) the act of predestining, esp. the act of God in foreordaining some to salvation and some to perdition. **predestinator** (-ā´tə) *n.* [L *praedestinātus*, p.p. of *praedestināre* (*destināre*, to DESTINE)]

predetermine (prēditœ´min) *v.t.* 1 to determine or settle beforehand. 2 to foreordain, to predestine. ~*v.i.* to determine beforehand. **predeterminable** *a.* **predeterminate** (-nət) *a.* **predeterminately** *adv.* **predetermination** (-ā´shən) *n.* **predeterminative** *a.* **predeterminer** *n.* [late L *praedetermināre*]

predial (prē´diəl), **praedial** *a.* (*Hist.*) 1 consisting of lands or farms. 2 (of a tenant or slave) attached to lands or farms. 3 rural, agrarian. 4 arising from or produced by land. ~*n.* a predial slave. [F *prédial*, med. L *praediālis*, from L *praedium*, farm]

predicable (pred´ikəbəl) *a.* capable of being predicated or affirmed. ~*n.* 1 anything that may be predicated of something. 2 (*Logic*) each of Aristotle's five classes of predicates – genus, species, difference, property, accident. **predicability** (-bil´-) *n.* [F *prédicable*, L *praedicābilis*, from *praedicāre*, to PREDICATE[1]]

predicament (pridik´əmənt) *n.* 1 a particular state, condition or position, esp. a difficult or unpleasant one. 2 (*Philos.*) that which is predicted, a category. **predicamental** (predikəmen´-) *a.* [late L *praedicāmentum*, as PREDICABLE]

predicant (pred´ikənt) *n.* 1 (*Hist.*) a preaching friar, esp. a Dominican. 2 (*S Afr.*) a predikant. ~*a.* (*Hist.*) engaged in preaching. [L *praedicans -ntem*, pres.p. of *praedicāre*, see PREDICATE[1]]

predicate[1] (pred´ikāt) *v.t.* 1 to affirm, to assert as a property etc. 2 (*Logic*) to assert about the subject of a proposition. 3 to found, to base (an argument etc. on). ~*v.i.* to make an affirmation. **predication** (-ā´shən) *n.* **predicative** (-dik´-) *a.* 1 (*Gram.*) (of an adjective) occurring within the predicate, as distinct from *attributive*. 2 predicating, affirming. **predicatively** *adv.* [L *praedicātus*, p.p. of *praedicāre* (*dicāre*, to proclaim), see PREACH]

predicate[2] (pred´ikət) *n.* 1 (*Logic*) that which is predicated, that which is affirmed or denied of the subject. 2 (*Gram.*) the entire statement made about the subject, including the copula as well as the logical predicate. [as PREDICATE[1]]

predict (pridikt´) *v.t.* to forecast, to foretell, to prophesy. **predictable** *a.* 1 able to be forecast or foretold. 2 (occurring or apt to behave in a manner which is) easily foreseen. **predictability** (-bil´-), **predictableness** *n.* **predictably** *adv.* **prediction** (-dik´shən) *n.* 1 something predicted. 2 the act, or the art, of predicting. **predictive** *a.* **predictively** *adv.* **predictor** *n.* 1 a person who predicts. 2 a range-finding and radar device for anti-aircraft use. [L *praedictus*, p.p. of *praedīcere* (*dīcere*, to say)]

predikant (pred´ikənt) *n.* a minister of the Dutch Reformed Church, esp. in S Africa. [Dut., as PREDICANT]

predilection (prēdilek´shən, pred-) *n.* a prepossession in favour of something, a preference, a partiality. [F *prédilection* (L *dīlectio*, from *dīligere*, see DILIGENT)]

predispose (prēdispōz´) *v.t.* 1 to dispose or incline beforehand (to some course of action etc.). 2 to influence favourably towards. 3 to make susceptible or liable to. **predisposition** (-zish´ən) *n.* [F *prédisposer*]

prednisone (pred´nizōn) *n.* (*Med.*) a drug similar to cortisone used to treat rheumatic and allergic conditions, and leukaemia. [perh. *pre*gnant, *d*iene, corti*sone*]

predominate (pridom´ināt) *v.i.* 1 to be superior in strength, influence or authority. 2 to prevail, to have the ascendancy (over). 3 to have control (over). 4 to preponderate. ~†*v.t.* to dominate over. **predominance**, **predominancy** *n.* **predominant** *a.* 1 predominating (over). 2 superior, overruling, controlling. **predominantly** *adv.* **predominately** *adv.* **predominatingly** *adv.* †**predomination** (-ā´shən) *n.* [through F *prédominer* or a med. L *praedomināre*]

Usage note The adverb *predominantly* is preferred to *predominately*.

pre- (+ e– words) pre-echo *n.* (*pl.* **pre-echoes**) 1 a faint echo-like sound heard in a recording before the actual sound, caused by a transfer of signals between surfaces of the tape. 2 a foreshadowing; a foretaste. **pre-eclampsia** *n.* (*Med.*) a serious toxic condition occurring in late pregnancy, characterized by high blood pressure and oedema. **pre-eclamptic** *a.* **pre-elect** *v.t.* to elect beforehand. ~†*a.* chosen beforehand or in preference to others. **pre-election** *n.* an election held previously. ~*a.* occurring or done before an election. **pre-embryo** *n.* (*pl.* **pre-embryos**) (*Med.*) the structure formed after fertilization of the human ovum, which will have developed into an embryo after 14 days. **pre-emphasis** *n.*

pre-employ *v.t.* **pre-engage** *v.t.* **1** to engage by previous contract or pledge. **2** to preoccupy. **3** to engage in conflict beforehand. **pre-engagement** *n.* **pre-establish** *v.t.* to establish beforehand. **pre-establishment** *n.* **pre-estimate** *v.t.* to estimate in advance. **pre-estimation** *n.* **pre-examine** *v.t.* to examine beforehand. **pre-examination** *n.* **pre-exilian** *a.* before a period of exile, esp. of the Jewish exile in Babylon. **pre-exilic** *a.* **pre-exist** *v.i.* to exist previously. ~*v.t.* to exist earlier than. **pre-existence** *n.* **pre-existent** *a.*

preemie (prē´mi), **premie** *n.* (*N Am., coll.*) a premature baby. [short for PREMATURE]

pre-eminent (prēem´inənt) *a.* **1** eminent beyond others. **2** superior to or surpassing all others, paramount, outstanding. **pre-eminence** *n.* **pre-eminently** *adv.* [F *prééminent*, L *praeēminentem*, nom. *-ens*, pres.p. of *praeēminēre* (*ēminēre*, see EMINENT)]

pre-empt (priempt´) *v.t.* **1 a** to secure by pre-emption. **b** to acquire in advance. **2** to seize on to the exclusion of others. **3** to act before another (in order to thwart), to anticipate. **4** (*US*) to occupy (public land) so as to acquire a right to purchase. ~*v.i.* in bridge, to make a pre-emptive bid. **pre-emption** *n.* **1 a** the act or right of buying before others. **b** (*Hist.*) in the US and Australia, the right to purchase land before others. **2** a government's right to seize the property of subjects of another state while in transit, esp. in wartime. **3** anticipating, forestalling. **4** the making of a pre-emptive strike. **pre-emptive** *a.* **pre-emptive bid** *n.* in bridge, an unusually high bid intended to shut out opposition. **pre-emptive strike** *n.* an attack on enemy installations intended to forestall a suspected attack on oneself. **pre-emptor** *n.*

Usage note *Pre-empt* should not be used as though it simply meant to prevent.

preen[1] (prēn) *v.t.*, *v.i.* **1** to clean and arrange (feathers) using the beak. **2** to take great trouble with, or an excessive interest in (one's appearance). **3** to pride or congratulate oneself (on). **preener** *n.* **preen gland** *n.* in birds, a gland at the base of the tail which produces oil used in preening. [prob. var. of PRUNE[2], conf. with PREEN[2]]

preen[2] (prēn) *n.* (*Sc.*) **1** a pin, a brooch. **2** a trifle. ~*v.t.* to fasten, to pin. [OE *prēon* (cp. LG *Preen*, *Preem*, Dut. *priem*, G *Pfriem*, Icel. *prjōnn*)]

pref. *abbr.* **1** preface. **2** preference. **3** preferred. **4** prefix.

pre- (+ f- words) prefab (prē´fab) *n.* (*coll.*) a prefabricated building, esp. a small house. **prefabricate** (prēfab´rikāt) *v.t.* **1** to manufacture (the component parts of a structure) in advance for rapid on-site assembly. **2** to produce (objects) in a very standardized way. **prefabrication** *n.* **prefabricator** *n.* **pre-fade** *v.t.* to produce fading in the colour of (cloth) before it is used. **pre-flight** *a.* happening or provided before an aircraft flight. **prefloration** *n.* (*Bot.*) the way in which petals are folded in a flower bud. **prefoliation** *n.* (*Bot.*) the way in which a leaf is folded within its bud. **preform** *v.t.* to form beforehand. **preformation** *n.* the act of preforming. **preformative** *a.* **1** forming beforehand. **2** prefixed, as a formative letter etc. to a word. ~*n.* a formative letter or other element prefixed to a word. **pre-franked** *a.* (of an envelope) having the frank already printed on it. **prefrontal** *a.* **1** situated in front of the frontal bone or the frontal region of the skull. **2** in the forepart of the frontal lobe of the brain. ~*n.* a prefrontal bone, esp. in reptiles and fishes. **pre-frozen** *a.* frozen in advance.

preface (pref´əs) *n.* **1** something spoken or written as introductory to a discourse or book. **2** an introduction; an exordium, a preamble, a prelude. **3** the thanksgiving etc. forming the prelude to the consecration of the Eucharist. ~*v.t.* **1** to introduce (with preliminary remarks etc.). **2** to provide with a preface. **3** to serve as a preface or introduction to. **prefacer** *n.* **prefatorial** (-taw´ri-), **prefatory** (pref´-) *a.* **prefatorily** *adv.* [OF, med. L *praefātia*, *praefātio*, from *praefārī* (*fārī*, to speak)]

prefect (prē´fekt) *n.* **1** (*Hist.*) a Roman commander, a governor, a chief magistrate. **2** the civil governor of a department in France, or of a province in Italy. **3** in some schools, a senior pupil with limited disciplinary powers over others. **prefectoral** (-fek´-), **prefectorial** (-taw´ri-) *a.* **prefecture** (-chə) *n.* the office, jurisdiction, official residence, or the term of office of a prefect. **prefectural** (-fek´chə-) *a.* [OF (F *préfet*), L *praefectus*, an overseer, orig. p.p. of *praeficere* (*facere*, to make)]

prefer (prifœ´) *v.t.* (*pres.p.* **preferring**, *past*, *p.p.* **preferred**) **1** to set before, to hold in higher estimation, to like better. **2** to bring forward, to submit. **3** to promote; to recommend, to favour. **preferable** (pref´ə-) *a.* **1** more desirable. **2** to be preferred. **preferability** (-bil´-) *n.* †**preferableness** *n.* **preferably** *adv.* **preference** (pref´ə-) *n.* **1** the act of preferring one thing to another, or of being preferred. **2** liking for one thing more than another, predilection. **3** right or liberty of choice. **4** something which is preferred. **5** favour displayed towards a person or country before others, esp. in commercial relations. **6** (*Law*) priority of right to payment, esp. of debts. **in preference to** rather than. **preference bond, preference share, preference stock** *n.* a bond, a share or stock entitled to a dividend before ordinary shares. **preferential** (preferen´shəl) *a.* **1** giving, receiving or constituting preference. **2** favouring certain countries in the matter of tariffs etc., as in the commercial relations between Great Britain and the rest of the Commonwealth. **preferentialism** *n.* **preferentialist** *n.* **preferentially** *adv.* **preferential voting** *n.* a system of proportional representation in which the voter puts the candidates in order of preference. **preferment** *n.* **1** advancement, promotion. **2** a superior office or dignity, esp. in the church. **3** the act of preferring. **preferred** *a.* **preferred debt** *n.* a debt having priority of payment. **preferred share, preferred stock** *n.* (*N Am.*) preference share or preference stock. **preferrer** *n.* [F *préférer*, L *praeferre* (*ferre*, to bear)]

Usage note (1) After *prefer to* the contrastive clause should be introduced by *rather than*, not simply *than* (*I prefer to die rather than (to) submit*). (2) The implicit double comparative *more preferable* is best avoided. (3) Pronunciation of *preferable* as (prifœ´rəbəl), with stress on the second syllable, is best avoided.

prefigure (prēfig´ə) *v.t.* **1** to represent beforehand by figures, types or similitudes; to foreshadow. **2** to picture to oneself beforehand. **prefigurate** (-gūrāt) *v.t.* **prefiguration** (-rā´shən) *n.* **prefigurative** (-fig´-) *a.* **prefigurement** *n.* [late L *praefigurāre*]

prefix[1] (prēfiks´) *v.t.* **1** to put, place or set in front of. **2** to attach at the beginning (as an introduction, prefix etc.). **prefixation** (-ā´shən) *n.* **prefixion** (-shən), **prefixture** (-chə) *n.* [OF *prefixer*]

prefix[2] (prē´fiks) *n.* **1** a letter, syllable or word put at the beginning of a word to modify the meaning. **2** a title prefixed to a name. **prefixal** *a.* [L *praefixum* (*figere fixus*, to FIX)]

pre- (+ g- words) preglacial *a.* belonging to the period before a glacial epoch.

preggers (preg´əz) *a.* (*coll.*) pregnant.

pregnable (preg´nəbəl) *a.* capable of being taken by force. [late ME and F *prenable*, as IMPREGNABLE[1]]

pregnant (preg´nənt) *a.* **1** having a child or young developing in the womb. **2** full of meaning or suggestion, significant. **3** inventive, imaginative. **4** fruitful, big (with consequences etc.). **5** portentous, fraught. **6** implying more than is expressed. **pregnancy** *n.* (*pl.* **pregnancies**). **pregnant construction** *n.* (*Gram.*) a construction which conveys more meaning than is in the actual words. **pregnantly** *adv.* [L *praegnans -ntis* (*gna-* root of *gnāscī*, to be born)]

pre- (+ h– words) prehallux *n.* a rudimentary digit or toe found in certain mammals, reptiles etc. **preheat** *v.t.* to heat beforehand. **prehistoric** *a.* **1** of or relating to the time prior to that known to history. **2** (*coll.*) completely out of date. **prehistorian** *n.* **prehistorically** *adv.* **prehistory** *n.* (*pl.* **prehistories**) **1** the prehistoric era. **2** the study of this era. **pre-hominid** *n.* any of various extinct primates, ancestors of modern man. **pre-human** *a.* **1** existing before the appearance of human beings. **2** at an earlier stage of development than human beings.

prehensile (prihen´sīl) *a.* adapted to seizing or grasping, as the tails of monkeys. **prehensible** *a.* (*formal*) capable of being grasped. **prehensility** (prēhensil´-) *n.* **prehension** (-shən) *n.* **1** the act of taking hold of or seizing. **2** mental apprehension. [F *préhensile*, from L *prehens-*, p.p. stem of *prehendere* (*hendere*, cogn. with Gr. *chandanein*, to seize)]

pre- (+ i– words) pre-ignition *n.* premature ignition of the explosive mixture in the cylinder of an internal-combustion engine. **pre-indicate** *v.t.* to indicate in advance. **pre-industrial** *a.* of, relating to or belonging to the time before the Industrial Revolution. **pre-inform** *v.t.* to inform beforehand. **pre-instruct** *v.t.* to instruct beforehand.

prejudge (prējŭj´) *v.t.* **1** to form a premature opinion about. **2** to judge before a case has been fully heard, to condemn in advance. **prejudgement, prejudgment** *n.* **prejudger** *n.* [F *préjuger*, L *praejūdicāre*]

prejudice (prej´ədis) *n.* **1** opinion, bias or judgement formed without due consideration of facts or arguments. **2** intolerance or hostility toward a particular group, race etc. **3** mischief, damage or detriment arising from unfair judgement or action. ~*v.t.* **1** to prepossess with prejudice, to bias. **2** to affect injuriously, esp. to impair the validity of a right etc. **without prejudice** (*Law*) without impairing any pre-existing right, detracting from any subsequent claim, or admitting any liability. **prejudiced** *a.* prepossessed, biased, bigoted. **prejudicial** (-dish´əl) *a.* **1** causing prejudice or injury. **2** mischievous, detrimental. **prejudicially** *adv.* [OF, from L *praejūdicium* (*jūdicium*, from *jūdex*, JUDGE)]

pre- (+ l– words) prelapsarian *a.* **1** before the Fall of man. **2** without original sin, innocent. **prelingual, prelinguistic** *a.* preceding the acquisition or development of language, as *prelingual deafness*. **preliterate** *a.* of or relating to a society in which writing has not been developed. **preliteracy** *n.* **pre-locate** *v.t.* to locate in advance.

prelacy PRELATE.

prelate (prel´ət) *n.* an ecclesiastical dignitary of the highest order, such as an archbishop, bishop etc., formerly including abbot and prior. **prelacy** *n.* (*pl.* **prelacies**) **1** the office, dignity or see of a prelate. **2** prelates collectively. **3** episcopacy (in a hostile sense). **prelateship** *n.* **prelatic** (-lat´-), **prelatical** *a.* **prelatically** *adv.* **prelatism** *n.* **1** government of the Church by prelates. **2** adherence to or partisanship of this. **prelatist** *n.* **prelatize, prelatise** *v.i.* to support or encourage prelacy. ~*v.t.* to bring under the influence of the prelacy. **prelature** (-chə) *n.* prelacy. [OF *prelat*, L *praelātus* (*lātus*, p.p. of *ferre*, to bear)]

prelect (prilekt´) *v.i.* (*formal*) to read a lecture or discourse in public. **prelection** *n.* **prelector** *n.* [L *praelectus*, p.p. of *praelegere* (*legere*, to choose, to read)]

prelibation (prēlībā´shən) *n.* (*formal*) **1** a foretaste. **2** a libation previous to tasting. [late L *praelībātio* (*lībātio*, from *lībāre*, to taste)]

prelim. *abbr.* preliminary.

preliminary (prilim´inəri) *a.* **1** introductory. **2** previous to the main business or discourse. ~*n.* (*pl.* **preliminaries**) **1** something introductory. **2** (*pl.*) introductory or preparatory arrangements etc. **3** a preliminary trial, examination etc. **preliminary to 1** in advance of. **2** as a preparation for. **preliminarily** *adv.* **prelims** (prē´limz) *n.pl.* **1** preliminary matter of a book. **2** preliminary examinations at university or school. [L *līmen -minis*, threshold]

prelude (prel´ūd) *n.* **1** something done, happening etc., introductory or preparatory to that which follows. **2** a harbinger, a precursor. **3** (*Mus.*) **a** a short introductory strain preceding the principal movement, a piece played as introduction to a suite. **b** an independent piece of a similar type. ~*v.t.* **1** to perform or serve as a prelude to. **2** to introduce with a prelude. **3** to usher in, to foreshadow. **preluder** *n.* **preludial** *a.* **preludize, preludise** *v.i.* **prelusive** (-loo´siv) *a.* **prelusively** *adv.* **prelusory** *a.* [F *prélude*, late L *praelūdium* (*lūdere*, to play)]

prem (prem) *n.* (*coll.*) a premature baby. [short for PREMATURE]

pre- (+ m– words) premandibular *a.* (*Anat.*) situated in front of the lower jaw. **premarital** *a.* occurring before marriage. **premaritally** *adv.* **pre-Marxian** *a.* **premaxillary** *a.* situated in front of the maxilla or upper jaw. ~*n.* (*pl.* **premaxillaries**) the premaxillary bone. **pre-med** *n.* **1** pre-medication. **2** (**premed**) a premedical student, or premedical studies. ~*a.* premedical. **premedical** *a.* of or relating to a course of study undertaken before medical studies. ~*n.* **1** a premedical student. **2** premedical studies. **pre-medicate** *v.t.* **premedication** *n.* drugs administered to sedate and to prepare a patient for general anaesthesia. **premenstrual** *a.* preceding menstruation. **premenstrually** *adv.* **premenstrual syndrome, premenstrual tension** *n.* any or all of a range of symptoms, including nervous tension, fluid retention etc., caused by the hormonal changes which precede menstruation. **premillennial** *a.* existing or happening before the millennium. **premillenarian** *n.* a person who believes that the Second Advent will precede the millennium. **premillenarianism, premillennialism** *n.* **premillennialist** *n.* **pre-mix** *v.t.* to mix beforehand. **premolar** *n.* any one of the eight teeth situated in pairs in front of the molars. ~*a.* in front of a molar tooth. **pre-Mosaic** *a.* of, relating to or happening in the time before Moses (in the Hebrew Bible).

premature (preməṭūə´, prem´-) *a.* **1** ripe or mature too soon. **2** happening, arriving, existing or performed before the proper time. **3** over-hasty. **4** (of a baby) born after a gestation period of less than 37 weeks. **prematurely** *adv.* **prematureness** *n.* **prematurity** (-tūə´-) *n.* [L *praemātūrus* (*mātūrus*, ripe)]

premeditate (primed´itāt) *v.t.* **1** to meditate on beforehand. **2** to plan and contrive beforehand. ~*v.i.* to deliberate previously. **premeditatedly** *adv.* **premeditation** (-ā´shən) *n.* **premeditative** *a.* [L *praemeditātus*, p.p. of *praemeditārī* (*meditārī*)]

premie PREEMIE.

premier (prem´iə) *a.* **1** first, chief, principal. **2** the earliest created (*premier earl*). ~*n.* (*usu.* **Premier**) a prime or chief minister, or any other head of government. **premiership** *n.* [F, from L *prīmārius*, PRIMARY]

premiere (prem´ieə, -iə), **première** *n.* a first performance of a play or film. ~*v.t.* to give a first performance of (a play or film). ~*v.i.* (of a play or film) to have its first performance. [F, fem. of PREMIER]

premise[1] (prem´is) *n.* **1** (*Logic*) a premiss. **2** (*pl.*) a piece of land and the buildings upon it, esp. considered as a place of business. **3** (*pl.*, *Law*) matters previously specified (in a deed or conveyance), esp. the aforesaid house or lands etc. **on the premises** actually in the building referred to. [F *prémisse*, L *praemissa* (*propositio* or *sententia*), fem. p.p. of *praemittere* (*mittere*, to send)]

premise[2] (primīz´, prem´is) *v.t.* 1 to put forward as preparatory to what is to follow. 2 to state as an antecedent proposition or condition. 3 to assume from a premiss. ~*v.i.* to state antecedent propositions. [see PREMISE[1]]

premiss (prem´is) *n.* (*Logic*) 1 a statement from which another is inferred. 2 either of the two propositions of a syllogism from which the conclusion is drawn. [var. of PREMISE[1]]

premium (prē´miəm) *n.* (*pl.* **premiums**) 1 a payment (usu. periodical) made for insurance. 2 a sum paid in addition to interest, wages etc., a bonus. 3 the rate at which shares, money etc. are selling above their nominal value. 4 a reward, a recompense, a prize. 5 a fee for instruction in a craft, profession etc. ~*a.* (of goods etc.) the best quality, and hence more expensive. **at a premium** 1 above their nominal value, above par. 2 in great esteem or demand because scarce. **to put a premium on** 1 to render more than usually valuable or advantageous. 2 to provide, or to be, an incentive to. **Premium Bond, Premium Savings Bond** *n.* a British government bond bearing no interest but subject to a monthly draw for money prizes. [L *praemium* (*emere*, to buy, to take)]

premonition (premənish´ən) *n.* 1 a foreboding, a presentiment. 2 previous warning or notice. **premonish** (-mon´ish) *v.t.* (*formal*) to admonish beforehand. **premonitor** (-mon´-) *n.* **premonitory** *a.* [F, from late L *praemonitio*, from *praemonēre* (*monēre*, to warn)]

Premonstratensian (primonstrəten´siən) *n.* a member of an order of regular canons, founded by St Norbert, at Prémontré, near Laon, France, about 1119, or of the corresponding order of nuns. ~*a.* belonging to the Premonstratensians. [med. L *Praemonstrātensis*, from *Praemonstrātus*, Prémontré]

premorse (primaws´) *a.* (*Biol.*) ending abruptly as if bitten off. [L *praemorsus*, p.p. of *praemordere* (*mordere*, to bite)]

premunire PRAEMUNIRE.

premunition (prēmūnish´ən) *n.* 1 the act of guarding beforehand, as against objections. 2 (*Med.*) immunity acquired from a persistent latent infection. [late L *praemūnītio*, from *praemūnīre* (*mūnīre*, to defend)]

pre- (+ n– words) prenasal *a.* situated in front of the nose. **prenatal** *a.* of or relating to the period before birth. **prenatally** *adv.* **pre-negotiate** *v.t.*, *v.i.* to negotiate beforehand. **pre-negotiation** *n.* **prenominal**[1] *a.* (of esp. an adjective) placed before a noun. **prenominal**[2] PRENOMEN. †**prenominate** *v.t.* to name or mention beforehand. ~*a.* named beforehand. **pre-notify** *v.t.* (*3rd pers. sing. pres.* **pre-notifies**, *pres.p.* **pre-notifying**, *past, p.p.* **pre-notified**) to notify in advance. **pre-notification** *n.* **prenotion** *n.* a preconception. **prenuptial** *a.* existing or happening before marriage. **prenuptial agreement** *n.* a contract drawn up between a man and a woman before a marriage, setting out how the property is to be divided in the event of a divorce.

prenomen (prēnō´men), **praenomen** *n.* (*pl.* **prenomina** (-nom´inə), **prenomens, praenomina, praenomens**) (*Hist.*) a Roman personal name, first name, corresponding to the modern Christian name. **prenominal**[2] *a.* [L *nomen*, name]

†**prentice** (pren´tis) *n.* an apprentice. †**prenticed** *a.* **prentice hand** *n.* an inexperienced hand. †**prenticeship** *n.*

pre- (+ o– words) preocular *a.* situated in front of the eye. **pre-operational** *a.* **pre-operative** *a.* before, in advance of, a surgical operation. **preoral** *a.* situated in front of the mouth. **preordain** *v.t.* to ordain or decide beforehand. **preordainment** *n.* **preordination** *n.* **pre-order** *v.t.* to order beforehand. **pre-owned** *a.* (*esp. N Am.*) second-hand.

preoccupy (priok´ūpī) *v.t.* (*3rd pers. sing. pres.* **preoccupies**, *pres.p.* **preoccupying**, *past, p.p.* **preoccupied**) 1 to pre-engage, to engross (the mind etc.). 2 to occupy beforehand or before another. **preoccupancy** *n.* the act or right of taking possession before others. **preoccupation** (-ā´shən) *n.* 1 something which preoccupies, such as a business affair etc. 2 the state of being preoccupied or engrossed (with). 3 prior occupation. **preoccupied** *a.* 1 thinking about one thing to the exclusion of all others; lost in thought. 2 (*Biol.*) (of a genus or species name) not available because it is already in use. **preoccupiedly** *adv.* [L *praeoccupāre* (*occupāre*, to OCCUPY)]

prep (prep) *n.* 1 (*sl.*) preparation or private study done at home or outside lesson time. 2 (*sl.*) the time set aside for this. 3 (*N Am.*) a student at a preparatory school. ~*a.* 1 of or relating to the preparation of school work. 2 (*N Am.*) of or relating to preparatory schools. ~*v.t.* (*pres.p.* **prepping**, *past, p.p.* **prepped**) (*N Am.*) to prepare. **preppy, preppie** *a.* (*comp.* **preppier**, *superl.* **preppiest**) (*N Am.*) 1 denoting a young but classic look in clothes, clean-cut, conventionally smart. 2 holding (middle-class) values associated with students at preparatory schools. ~*n.* (*pl.* **preppies**) 1 (*N Am.*) a student at a preparatory school. 2 a person who dresses in a preppy fashion. **preppily** *adv.* **preppiness** *n.* **prep school** *n.* a preparatory school. [short for PREPARATION (under PREPARE), PREPARATORY (under PREPARE)]

prep. *abbr.* 1 preparation. 2 preparatory. 3 preposition.

pre- (+ p– words) pre-pack, pre-package *v.t.* to package (esp. food products) before they are offered for sale. **pre-packed** *a.* **pre-packing** *n.* **prepaid** *a.* paid in advance (as postage etc.). **prepalatal** *a.* situated in front of the palate. **prepay** *v.t.* (*pres.p.* **prepaying**, *past, p.p.* **prepaid**) 1 to pay beforehand. 2 to pay (postage) in advance, esp. by affixing a stamp to. **prepayable** *a.* **prepayment** *n.* **pre-plan** *v.t.* (*pres.p.* **pre-planning**, *past, p.p.* **pre-planned**) to plan in advance. **prepose** *v.t.* to place (a word) in front of another. **pre-position** *v.t.* (*Gram.*) to position (a word) in front of another. **pre-prandial** *a.* (*formal or facet.*) done, happening etc. before lunch or dinner. **pre-preference** *a.* ranking before preference shares etc. **pre-primary** *a.* **preprint** *n.* a part of a publication printed in advance of the whole. **pre-process** *v.t.* to subject to preliminary processing. **pre-processor** *n.* (*Comput.*) a program that modifies data to suit the requirements of another program. **pre-production** *a.* of or relating to work done on a film or TV programme before shooting. **preprogram** *v.t.* (*pres.p.* **pre-programming**, *past, p.p.* **pre-programmed**) to program (a computer etc.) in advance. **pre-programmed** *a.* **pre-pubertal, prepubescent** *a.* 1 existing or happening (just) before puberty. 2 of or relating to a child who has not yet reached puberty. ~*n.* such a child. **pre-publication** *a.* happening, or produced, before publication (of a book etc.). ~*n.* publication in advance of some other event.

prepare (pripeə´) *v.t.* 1 to make ready. 2 to bring into a suitable condition, to fit for a certain purpose, esp. food for eating. 3 to make ready or fit (to do, to receive etc.). 4 to produce. 5 to construct, to put together, to draw up. 6 to get (work, a speech, a part etc.) ready by practice, study etc. 7 (*Mus.*) to lead up to (a discord) by sounding the dominant note in a consonance. ~*v.i.* 1 to get everything ready. 2 to take the measures necessary (for). 3 to make oneself ready. ~†*n.* preparation. **preparation** (prepərā´shən) *n.* 1 the act, or an instance, of preparing. 2 the state of being prepared. 3 (*often pl.*) a preparatory act or measure. 4 anything prepared by a special process, such as food, a medicine, a part of a body for anatomical study etc. 5 the preparing of lessons or school work. 6 (*Mus.*) the introduction of a note to be continued in a subsequent discord. 7 †a military or naval force. 8 ceremonious introduction. 9 †accomplishment. **preparative** (-par´ə-) *a.* preparatory. ~*n.* 1 that which tends or serves to prepare; an act of preparation. 2 (*Mil.*, *Naut.*) a signal to make ready. **preparatively** *adv.* **preparatory** *a.* 1 tending or serving to prepare. 2 introductory (to). ~*adv.* in a preparatory way. **preparatorily** *adv.* **preparatory school** *n.* 1 a private school for pupils usu. aged 6–13, which prepares them for entry to a public school. 2 (*N Am.*) a private secondary school which prepares students for college. **prepared** *a.* **to be prepared** 1 to be ready (for). 2 to be willing (to). **preparedly** (-rid-) *adv.* **preparedness** (-rid-) *n.* a state of readiness, esp. for war. **preparer** *n.* [F *préparer*, L *praeparare* (*parāre*, to make ready)]

prepense (pripens´) *a.* (*usu. placed after the noun*) premeditated, deliberate. **malice prepense** MALICE. **prepensely** *adv.* [formerly *prepensed*, p.p. of *prepense*, *purpense*, OF *purpenser* (*pur-*, *pour-*, L *prō*, forth, OF *penser*, to think)]

☒ **preperation** common misspelling of PREPARATION (under PREPARE).

†**prepollent** (pripol´ənt) *a.* having superior power or influence, predominating. **prepollence, †prepollency** *n.* [L *praepollens -ntem*, pres.p. of *praepollēre* (*pollēre*, to be strong)]

preponderate (pripon´dərāt) *v.i.* 1 to be superior or to outweigh in number, power, influence etc. 2 †to sink (as the scale of a balance). 3 to be heavier. **preponderance, †preponderancy** *n.* **preponderant** *a.* **preponderantly, preponderatingly** *adv.* **preponderation** (-ā´shən) *n.* [L *praeponderātus*, p.p. of *praeponderāre* (*ponderāre*, to PONDER)]

prepone (pripōn´) *v.t.* to bring forward to an earlier date or time. [PRE-, post*pone*]

preposition (prepəzish´ən) *n.* (*Gram.*) a word or group of words, e.g. *at*, *by*, *in front of*, used to relate the noun or pronoun it is placed in front of to other constituent parts of the sentence. **prepositional** *a.* **prepositionally** *adv.* **prepositive** (pripoz´-) *a.* prefixed, intended to be placed before (a word). ~*n.* a prepositive word or particle. [L *praepositio*, from *praepōnere* (*pōnere*, to put, p.p. *positus*)]

prepositor PRAEPOSTOR.

prepossess (prēpəzes´) *v.t.* 1 to imbue (with an idea, feeling etc.). 2 to bias (esp. favourably). 3 (of an idea etc.) to preoccupy. **prepossessing** *a.* 1 tending to win favour, attractive. 2 biasing. **prepossessingly** *adv.* **prepossession** (-shən) *n.*

preposterous (pripos´tərəs) *a.* 1 contrary to nature, reason or common sense. 2 obviously wrong, foolish, absurd. **preposterously** *adv.* **preposterousness** *n.* [L *praeposterus* (*prae*, before, *posterus*, coming after)]

prepostor PRAEPOSTOR.

prepotent (pripō´tənt) *a.* 1 very powerful. 2 possessing superior force or influence. 3 overbearing. 4 (*Biol.*) possessing superior fertilizing influence, and hence able to transmit more hereditary characteristics. **prepotence, prepotency** *n.* **prepotently** *adv.* [L *praepotens -ntem*, pres.p. of *praeposse* (*posse*, to be able)]

preppy PREP.

prepuce (prē´pūs) *n.* 1 the foreskin, the loose covering of the glans penis. 2 a similar fold of skin over the clitoris. **preputial** (-pū´-) *a.* [L *praepūtium*]

pre- (+ q– words) pre-qualify *v.i.* (*3rd pers. sing. pres.* **pre-qualifies,** *pres.p.* **pre-qualifying,** *past, p.p.* **pre-qualified**) to qualify (for entry) in advance (of a sporting competition etc.).

prequel (prē´kwəl) *n.* a novel, film etc. which narrates the events leading up to those in an existing novel or film. [PRE-, se*quel*]

pre- (+ r– words) Pre-Raphaelite (prēraf´əlīt) *n.* a member of the Pre-Raphaelite Brotherhood. ~*a.* 1 having the characteristics of Pre-Raphaelitism. 2 resembling those (esp. women) painted by the Pre-Raphaelites. **Pre-Raphaelite Brotherhood** *n.* a small group of painters formed in London in 1848, including Holman Hunt, Millais and D. G. Rossetti, to cultivate the spirit and methods of the early Italian painters, esp. in respect to truth to nature and vividness of colour. **Pre-Raphaelitism** *n.* **pre-reading** *n.* a reading or measurement taken in advance. **pre-record** *v.t.* to record beforehand. **pre-recorded** *a.* **pre-recording** *n.* **pre-Reformation** *a.* existing or happening before the Reformation. **pre-register** *v.t.* **pre-registration** *n.* **pre-release** *n.* the release (of a film) before the scheduled date. **pre-remote** *a.* occurring, done etc. still more remotely in the past. **prerequisite** *a.* required beforehand. ~*n.* a requirement that must be satisfied in advance, a precondition.

Usage note See note under PERQUISITE.

pre-retirement *a.* existing or happening before retirement from work. **pre-Revolutionary** *a.* **pre-Romantic** *a.*

prerogative (prirog´ətiv) *n.* 1 an exclusive right or privilege vested in a particular person or body of persons, esp. a sovereign, in virtue of their position or relationship. 2 any peculiar right, option, privilege, natural advantage etc. 3 †precedence. ~*a.* of, relating to or having a prerogative. **prerogatived** *a.* [F *prérogative*, L *praerogatīva*, a previous choice, privilege, fem. of *praerogatīvus* (*rogātīvus*, rel. to *rogātus*, p.p. of *rogāre*, to ask)]

Pres. *abbr.* President.

pres. *abbr.* present.

pre- (+ s– words) pre-sanctify *v.t.* (*3rd pers. sing. pres.* **pre-sanctifies,** *pres.p.* **pre-sanctifying,** *past, p.p.* **pre-sanctified**) to consecrate in advance. **pre-school** *a.* (for children who are) under school age. **pre-schooler** *n.* **prescientific** *a.* of or relating to the period before the rise of science or of scientific method. **pre-season** *n.* the period before a (sporting) season begins. **pre-seasonal** *a.* **pre-select** *v.t.* to select in advance. **pre-selection** *n.* **pre-selective** *a.* that can be selected in advance. **preselector** *n.* a device which preselects an electrical or mechanical operation, e.g. a gear change. **pre-sell** *v.t.* (*past, p.p.* **pre-sold**) 1 to sell (something) in advance of its being available. 2 to promote or advertise (a product) before it is available. **pre-senile** *a.* of or relating to the period before the onset of old age. **pre-senile dementia** *n.* a form of dementia which starts before a person has reached old age. **pre-set** *v.t.* (*pres.p.* **pre-setting,** *past, p.p.* **pre-set**) to set the controls of (an electric or electronic device) in advance, so that it starts to operate at the required time in the required way. ~*n.* a control for presetting. **pre-shrink** *v.t.* (*past* **pre-shrank,** *p.p.* **pre-shrunk**) to shrink (fabric) before it is made up into garments. **pre-soak** *v.t., n.* **presocratic** *a.* (of philosophy) of the period before Socrates (5th cent. BC). **presternum** *n.* (*pl.* **presternums, presterna**) 1 (*Anat.*) the front part of the sternum. 2 the prosternum of an insect. **prestressed** *a.* (of concrete) reinforced with stretched steel wires or rods. **pre-stun** *v.t.* (*pres.p.* **pre-stunning,** *past, p.p.* **pre-stunned**) to stun (cattle) before slaughter. **presuppose** *v.t.* 1 to assume beforehand. 2 to imply as a necessary antecedent. **presupposition** *n.* 1 the act, or an instance, of presupposing. 2 a supposition adopted beforehand.

presage[1] (pres´ij) *n.* 1 something that foretells a future event, an omen, a prognostic. 2 foreboding, presentiment. **presageful** *a.* [F *présage*, L *praesāgium* (*sāgīre*, to perceive quickly)]

presage[2] (prisāj´, pres´ij) *v.t.* 1 to foreshadow, to betoken. 2 to indicate by natural signs etc. 3 (of a person) to foretell, to have a presentiment of. ~†*v.i.* to prophesy. †**presagement** *n.* **presager** *n.* [as PRESAGE[1]]
presbyopia (prezbiō´piə) *n.* a form of long-sightedness with indistinct vision of near objects, caused by alteration in the refractive power of the eyes with age. **presbyope** (prez´-) *n.* a person affected with this. **presbyopic** (-op´-) *a.* [Gr. *presbus*, old man, *ōpia*, from *ōps ōpos*, eye]
presbyter (prez´bitə) *n.* 1 an elder who had authority in the early Church. 2 in the Episcopal Church, a minister of the second order, a priest. 3 in the Presbyterian Church, a minister of a presbytery, an elder. **presbyteral** (-bit´-) *a.* **presbyterate** (-bit´ərət) *n.* **presbyterial** (-tiə´riəl) *a.* **Presbyterian** (-tiə´ri-) *n.* 1 any adherent of Presbyterianism. 2 a member of a Presbyterian Church. ~*a.* 1 of or relating to Church government by presbyters. 2 governed by presbyters. **Presbyterian Church** *n.* a Church governed by elders, including ministers, all equal in rank. **Presbyterianism** *n.* **presbytership** *n.* **presbytery** (-ri) *n.* (*pl.* **presbyteries**) 1 a court consisting of the pastors and ruling elders of the Presbyterian churches of a given district, ranking above the Kirk-session and below the synod. 2 the district represented by a presbytery. 3 in the Roman Catholic Church, a priest's residence. 4 the eastern portion of a chancel beyond the choir in a cathedral or other large church, the sanctuary. 5 a body of elders in the early Church. [late L, from Gr. *presbuteros*, elder, comp. of *presbus*, old]
prescient (pres´iənt) *a.* foreknowing, far-seeing. **prescience** *n.* **presciently** *adv.* [F, from L *praescientem*, nom. *-ens*, pres.p. of *praescīre* (*scīre*, to know)]
prescind (prisind´) *v.t.* 1 to cut off, to separate. 2 to abstract, to consider independently. ~*v.i.* to withdraw one's attention (from). [L *praescindere* (*scindere*, to cut)]
prescribe (priskrīb´) *v.t.* 1 to direct (a medicine etc.) to be used as a remedy. 2 to recommend (some course of action). 3 to lay down with authority; to appoint (a rule of conduct etc.). ~*v.i.* 1 to write directions for medical treatment. 2 (*Law*) to assert a prescriptive title (to or for). **prescriber** *n.* **prescript** (prē´skript) *n.* a direction, a command, a law. ~*a.* prescribed, directed. **prescriptible** (-skrip´-) *a.* **prescriptibility** (-bil´-) *n.* **prescription** (-skrip´-) *n.* 1 the act, or an instance, of prescribing. 2 something which is prescribed, esp. a written direction for the preparation of medical remedies, and the manner of using them. 3 the medication etc. prescribed. 4 (*Law*) POSITIVE PRESCRIPTION (under POSITIVE). 5 right or title founded on this. 6 ancient or long-continued custom, esp. when regarded as authoritative. 7 a claim based on long use. **prescriptive** (-skrip´-) *a.* 1 prescribing. 2 laying down rules; concerned with rules. 3 acquired or authorized by long use. 4 based on long use or prescription. **prescriptively** *adv.* **prescriptiveness** *n.* **prescriptivism** *n.* **prescriptivist** *n.* [L *praescrībere* (*scrībere*, to write), p.p. *praescriptus*]

Usage note The verbs *prescribe* and *proscribe* should not be confused: something prescribed is to be taken, given, used or studied, and is assumed to be useful or beneficial; something proscribed is forbidden, and so assumed to be harmful.

☒ **presede** common misspelling of PRECEDE.
presence (prez´əns) *n.* 1 the quality or state of being present. 2 a the immediate vicinity of a person. b the immediate vicinity of a person of high rank. 3 (a person with) an imposing or dignified bearing. 4 personal magnetism, the ability to grasp and hold an audience's attention. 5 a group or force representing one's interests or exercising an influence on one's behalf. 6 an influence as of a being invisibly present. 7 †a presence chamber. **in the presence of** in front of, within sight of (a person). **to make one's presence felt** FEEL. **presence chamber, presence room** *n.* the room in which a great personage receives company. **presence of mind** *n.* a calm, collected state of mind, esp. in danger or emergency. [OF, from L *praesentia*, as PRESENT[2]]
present[1] (prez´ənt) *a.* 1 being here or in a place referred to, as distinct from *absent*. 2 being in view or at hand. 3 found or existing in the thing referred to. 4 being now under discussion, consideration etc. 5 now existing, occurring, going on etc. 6 (*Law*) instant, immediate. 7 (*Gram.*) expressing what is actually going on. 8 ready at hand, assisting in emergency, attentive, propitious. ~*n.* 1 the present time. 2 the present tense. 3 (*pl.*) these writings, a term used in documents to express the document itself. **at present** at the present time, now. **by these presents** (*Law*) by this document. **for the present** 1 for the time being. 2 just now. 3 so far as the time being is concerned. **present company excepted** with the exception of the people here now. **the present day** modern times. **present-day** *a.* contemporary, of the current time. **present tense** *n.* the form of the verb expressing being or action at the present time. [OF, from L *praesentem*, nom. *-ens*, pres.p. of *praeesse* (*esse*, to be)]
present[2] (prizent´) *v.t.* 1 to introduce to the acquaintance or presence of, esp. to introduce formally. 2 to introduce to a sovereign at Court. 3 to submit (oneself) as a candidate, applicant etc. 4 to exhibit, to show, to offer to the sight. 5 to hold in position or point (a gun etc.). 6 to offer or suggest (itself) to the attention. 7 to offer for consideration, to submit. 8 to offer or deliver (a cheque or an invoice). 9 to exhibit (an actor, a play etc.) on the stage. 10 to act as the presenter of (as a television programme). 11 to portray, to depict, to represent. 12 to offer, to give, to bestow, esp. in a ceremonious way. 13 to invest or endow (with a gift). 14 to tender, to deliver. 15 (*Hist.*) to offer (a clergyman) to a bishop for institution (to a benefice). ~*v.i.* 1 (*Med.*) a to come forward as a patient (with). b (of an illness) to manifest itself. 2 (of a foetus) to be in a specified position during labour with respect to the mouth of the uterus. ~*n.* (*Mil.*) position for, or act of, aiming a firearm. **to present arms** to hold a rifle etc., in a perpendicular position in front of the body to salute a superior officer. **to present oneself** to appear, to come forward. **presentable** *a.* 1 fit to be presented. 2 of suitable appearance for company etc. 3 fit to be shown or exhibited. 4 suitable for offering as a gift. 5 (*Hist.*) suitable for presentation to a living. **presentability** (-bil´-) *n.* **presentableness** *n.* **presentably** *adv.* [OF *presenter*, L *praesentāre*, as PRESENT[1]]
present[3] (prez´ənt) *n.* something which is presented, a gift. **to make a present of** to give as a gift.
presentation (prezəntā´shən) *n.* 1 the act, or an instance, of presenting, or the process of being presented. 2 a formal offering or proffering. 3 a present, a gift. 4 an exhibition, a theatrical representation. 5 a verbal report on, or exposé of, a subject, often with illustrative material. 6 the manner of presenting, esp. the appearance, arrangement, neatness etc. of material submitted. 7 a an introduction, esp. a formal introduction to a superior personage. b a formal introduction to the sovereign at Court. 8 (*Psych.*) the process by which an object becomes present to consciousness, or the modification of consciousness involved in the perception of an object. 9 (*Med.*) the particular position of the foetus at birth. 10 (*Hist.*) the act or right of presenting to a benefice. **presentational** *a.* **presentationally** *adv.* **presentation copy** *n.* a book presented gratis by an author or publisher. **presentationism** *n.* (*Philos.*) the

doctrine that the mind has immediate cognition of objects of perception, or of elemental categories such as space, time etc. **presentationist** *n.* **presentative** (prizen´-) *a.* 1 (*Philos.*) of, relating to or of the nature of mental presentation. 2 subserving mental presentation. 3 (*Hist.*) (of a benefice) admitting of the presentation of an incumbent.

presentee (prezəntē´) *n.* 1 a person receiving a present. 2 a person recommended for office. 3 a person presented at Court. 4 (*Hist.*) a person presented to a benefice.

presenter (prizen´tə) *n.* 1 a person who presents. 2 a broadcaster who introduces and comperes, or provides a linking commentary for, a radio or television programme.

presentient (prizen´shənt, -sen´-) *a.* feeling or perceiving beforehand. [L *praesentiens -ntem*, pres.p. of *praesentīre* (*sentīre*, to feel)]

presentiment (prizen´timənt) *n.* apprehension or anticipation, more or less vague, of an impending event, esp. of evil, a foreboding.

presently (prez´əntli) *adv.* 1 soon, shortly. 2 (*chiefly N Am., Sc.*) at the present time. 3 †at once, immediately.

presentment (prizent´mənt) *n.* 1 the act of presenting (information). 2 a theatrical representation, a portrait, a likeness, a semblance. 3 a statement, an account, a description. 4 the act or mode of presentation to the mind. 5 (*esp. US*) a report by a grand jury respecting an offence, from their own knowledge. [OF *presentement*]

preserve (prizœv´) *v.t.* 1 to keep safe, to guard, to protect. 2 to save, to rescue. 3 to maintain in a good or the same condition. 4 to retain, to keep intact. 5 to keep from decay or decomposition by chemical treatment, boiling, pickling, freezing etc. 6 to keep (a stream, covert, game etc.) for private use by preventing poaching etc. ~*v.i.* 1 to make preserves. 2 to maintain protection for game in preserves. ~*n.* 1 fruit boiled with sugar or preservative substances, jam. 2 **a** a place where game is preserved. **b** water where fish are preserved. 3 a special domain, something reserved for certain people only. **preservable** *a.* **preservation** (prezəvā´shən) *n.* 1 the act, or an instance, of preserving, or the process of being preserved. 2 the state of being preserved. **preservationist** *n.* a person who is interested in preserving traditional and historic things. **preservation order** *n.* an official order to preserve a building of historic importance. **preservative** *a.* 1 having the power of preserving from injury, decay or corruption. 2 tending to preserve. ~*n.* something which preserves, esp. a chemical substance used to prevent decomposition in foodstuffs. **preserver** *n.* **preserving pan** *n.* a large pan used for making jams and preserves. [F *préserver*, late L *praeservāre* (*servāre*, to keep)]

preses (prē´sēz) *n.* (*pl.* **preses**) (*Sc.*) a chairman, a president. [L *praeses*, cogn. with PRESIDE]

preside (prizīd´) *v.i.* 1 to be set in authority over others; to sit at the head of a table; to act as director, controller, chairman or president. 2 to lead, to superintend. 3 to officiate (at the organ, piano etc.). **presidency** (prez´idənsi) *n.* (*pl.* **presidencies**) 1 the office, jurisdiction or term of office of a president. 2 the territory administered by a president. **president** (prez´idənt) *n.* 1 a person (usu. elected) presiding over a temporary or permanent body of persons. 2 the chief executive or elective head of government in a modern republic. 3 a person presiding over the meetings of a society. 4 the chief officer of certain colleges and universities, esp. in the US. 5 (*N Am.*) the permanent chairman and chief executive officer of a corporation, board of trustees, government department etc. **president-elect** *n.* (*pl.* **presidents-elect**) a president who has been elected but has not yet taken office. **presidential** (-den´-) *a.* **presidentially** *adv.* **presidentship** *n.* **presider** *n.* **presiding officer** *n.* the person in charge of a polling place. [F *présider*, L *praesidēre* (*sedēre*, to sit)]

presidia PRESIDIUM.

presidio (prisid´iō) *n.* (*pl.* **presidios**) 1 a fort or fortified settlement, in areas under Spanish control. 2 a Spanish penal colony. [Sp.]

presidium (prisid´iəm), **praesidium** *n.* (*pl.* **presidiums, presidia** (-diə), **praesidiums, praesidia** (-diə)) a permanent executive committee in a Communist country.

presignify (prēsig´nifī) *v.t.* (*3rd pers. sing. pres.* **presignifies,** *pres.p.* **presignifying,** *past, p.p.* **presignified**) to signify or intimate beforehand. [MF *presignifier*, L *praesignificāre*]

press[1] (pres) *v.t.* 1 to act steadily upon with a force or weight. 2 to push (something up, down, against etc.) with steady force. 3 to put or hold (upon etc.) with force. 4 to squeeze, to crush, to compress. 5 to make smooth by pressure (as cloth or paper). 6 **a** to extract juice from (esp. fruit). **b** to extract (juice) from fruit. 7 to make by pressing in a mould, esp. to make (a gramophone record) from a matrix. 8 to clasp, to embrace, to hug. 9 to crowd upon. 10 to urge, to ply hard, to bear heavily on. 11 to invite with persistent warmth. 12 to put forward vigorously and persistently, to urge. 13 to weigh down, to distress. 14 to straiten, to constrain. 15 to enforce strictly, to impress. 16 to insist on the acceptance of (something). ~*v.i.* 1 to exert pressure; to bear heavily, or weigh heavily (on). 2 to be urgent. 3 to make demands (for). 4 to throng, to crowd, to encroach, to intrude. 5 to strive eagerly, to hasten, to strain, to push one's way. 6 in golf etc., to try too hard and so mishit a ball. ~*n.* 1 the act, or an instance, of pressing, urging or crowding. 2 a crowd, a throng. 3 urgency, pressure, hurry. 4 (*esp. Ir., Sc.*) an upright case, cupboard or closet, for storing things, esp. linen; a bookcase. 5 **a** an instrument or machine for compressing any body or substance, forcing it into a more compact form, shaping, extracting juice etc. **b** a device for keeping the shape of a tennis racket. 6 a machine for printing. 7 (**Press**) a printing establishment, or a publishing house. 8 the process or practice of printing. 9 the reaction of newspapers etc. to a person, event etc. (*a good press*). 10 cabinet-work made by pressing successive cross-grained veneers together while hot. **at press** in press. **in (the) press** 1 being printed. 2 on the eve of publication. **the press** 1 the news media collectively, esp. newspapers and periodicals. 2 journalists. **to be pressed for** to have very little of (esp. time). **to go to press** to start printing, to begin to be printed. **to press on/ ahead/ forward** 1 to continue (determinedly) on one's way. 2 to proceed, esp. in spite of difficulties or opposition. **to press the button** 1 to start a machine etc. by pressing a button. 2 (*fig.*) to set a train of events in motion. **to press the flesh** (*sl.*) (esp. of politicians) to shake hands. **to press the panic button** PANIC[1]. **to send to press** to send for printing. **press agent** *n.* a person employed to handle relations with the press, esp. to ensure good publicity for an actor, organization etc. **press book** *n.* a book printed by a private press. **press box** *n.* an enclosure for reporters at a sports ground. **press-button** *n., a.* push-button. **press conference** *n.* a meeting with journalists to announce a policy etc., or answer their questions. **press cutting** *n.* a clipping from a newspaper. **pressed steel** *n.* steel moulded under pressure. **presser** *n.* **press fastener** *n.* a press stud. **press gallery** *n.* a gallery set aside for reporters, esp. in a legislative assembly. **pressing** *a.* urgent, importunate, insistent. ~*n.* 1 something made by pressing. 2 the gramophone records etc. made from a single matrix at one time. **pressingly** *adv.* **pression** (presh´ən) *n.* 1 the act of pressing. 2 pressure. **pressman** *n.* (*pl.* **pressmen**) 1 a journalist. 2 a person who operates a printing press. **pressmark** *n.* a number, symbol or other mark indicating the place of a book on the shelves of a library. **press office** *n.* the department (of an organization, a ministry etc.) which releases information to the press etc. **press officer** *n.* **press of sail** *n.* as much sail as the wind will let a ship carry. **press-on** *a.* (of a fabric) able to be pressed on or ironed on to something. **press release** *n.* an official statement or report given to the press. **press room** *n.* the room in a printing office where the presses are. **press stud** *n.* a fastener consisting of two small round buttons, one of which has a small raised knob which snaps into a hole in the other. **press-up** *n.* a gymnastic exercise in which the body is held rigid in a prone position and raised and lowered by bending and straightening the arms. **presswoman** *n.* (*pl.* **presswomen**) a woman journalist. **presswork** *n.* **1** the pressing of metal into a shaped die. **2** a piece of metal shaped thus. **3** the work or management of a printing press. **4** journalistic work. [F *presser*, L *pressāre*, freq. of *premere*]

press[2] (pres) *v.t.* **1** (*Hist.*) to force into naval or military service. **2** (*fig.*) to bring into service. ~*v.i.* (*Hist.*) to impress soldiers or sailors. ~*n.* (*Hist.*) **1** a compulsory enlisting of men into naval or military service. **2** a commission to force men into service. **press-gang** *n.* (*Hist.*) **1** a detachment of men employed to impress men, usu. into the navy. **2** a group of people using coercive methods. ~*v.t.* to force (a person) to do something. **press money** *n.* money paid to men who enlist. [from PREST]

pressie PREZZIE.

pressor (pres´ə) *a.* (*Med.*) causing an increase in blood pressure. ~*n.* an agent which does this. [late L, from L *premere pressus*, to PRESS[1]]

pressure (presh´ə) *n.* **1** the act of pressing. **2** the state of being pressed. **3** a force steadily exerted upon or against a body by another in contact with it. **4** the amount of this, usu. measured in units of weight upon a unit of area. **5** constraining force, compulsion. **6** moral force. **7** persistent attack. **8** stress, urgency. **9** trouble, affliction, oppression. ~*v.t.* **1** to apply pressure to. **2** to constrain, to subject to compelling moral force against one's will. **pressure cabin** *n.* a pressurized cabin in an aircraft. **pressure cooker** *n.* an apparatus for cooking at a high temperature under high pressure of steam. **pressure-cook** *v.t.* to cook in a pressure cooker. **pressure gauge** *n.* an instrument which measures pressure (of steam etc.). **pressure group** *n.* a group or small party exerting pressure on government etc. to promote a particular interest. **pressure point** *n.* **1** any of various points on the body where a blood vessel may be pressed against a bone to check bleeding. **2** a point on the skin which is sensitive to pressure. **3** a policy area etc. where political pressure may be exerted. **pressure sore** *n.* (*Med.*) a bedsore. **pressure suit** *n.* an airman's suit that inflates automatically if there is a failure in the pressure cabin. **pressurize, pressurise** *v.t.* **1** to fit an aircraft cabin with a device that maintains normal atmospheric pressure at high altitudes. **2** to increase the pressure on. **3** to (seek to) coerce. **pressurization** (-zā´shən) *n.* **pressurized-water reactor** *n.* a type of nuclear reactor that uses water under pressure as coolant and moderator. [OF, from L *pressūra*, from *pressāre*, see PRESS[1]]

†prest (prest) *n.* **1** an advance, a loan. **2** earnest money paid to a sailor or soldier on enlistment. ~*a.* ready, prepared. [OF (F *prêt*), from *prester*, L *praestāre* (*stāre*, to come forward, to stand)]

Prestel® (pres´tel) *n.* the British Telecom viewdata system.

prestidigitation (prestidijitā´shən) *n.* (*formal*) sleight of hand, conjuring. **prestidigitator** (-dij´-) *n.* [F *preste*, It. PRESTO[1], L *digitus*, finger]

prestige (prestēzh´) *n.* influence or weight derived from former fame, excellence, achievements etc. ~*a.* **1** having or conferring prestige. **2** superior, very high-quality, very stylish etc. **prestigeful** *a.* **prestigious** (-tij´əs) *a.* having, showing or conferring prestige. **prestigiously** *adv.* **prestigiousness** *n.* [F, from L *praestigium*, a trick, illusion, glamour, from *praestringere* (*stringere*, to bind)]

presto[1] (pres´tō) *adv.* (*Mus.*) quickly. ~*a.* quick. ~*n.* (*pl.* **prestos**) a quick movement or passage. ~*int.* (*also* **hey presto**) immediately (used to indicate the speed with which e.g. a conjuring trick is done). **prestissimo** (-tis´imō) *adv.* (*Mus.*) very fast indeed. ~*a.* very fast. ~*n.* (*pl.* **prestissimos**) a very fast movement or passage. [It., from late L *praestus*, from L *praesto* (*sitū*, abl. of *situs*, SITUATION (under SITUATE[1]))]

presume (prizūm´) *v.t.* **1** to take for granted or assume without previous enquiry or examination. **2** to venture. **3** to be impudent enough (to). ~*v.i.* **1** to venture without previous leave, to take liberties. **2** to form overconfident or arrogant opinions. **3** to behave with assurance or arrogance. **to presume on/ upon 1** to rely on, to depend on. **2** to take unfair advantage of. **presumable** *a.* **presumably** *adv.* as can be presumed. **presumedly** (-mid-) *adv.* **presumer** *n.* **presuming** *a.* presumptuous. **presumingly** *adv.* **presumingness** *n.* **presumption** (-zŭmp´-) *n.* **1** the act of presuming. **2** assumption of the truth or existence of something without direct proof. **3** something which is taken for granted. **4** a ground for presuming. **5** overconfidence, arrogance, impudence, effrontery. **presumption of fact** *n.* an inference as to a fact from facts actually known. **presumption of law** *n.* **1** assumption of the truth of a proposition until the contrary is proved. **2** an inference established by law as universally applicable to particular circumstances. **presumptive** *a.* giving grounds for, or based on, presumption. **heir presumptive** HEIR. **presumptive evidence** *n.* evidence derived from circumstances which necessarily or usually attend a fact. **presumptively** *adv.* **presumptiveness** *n.* **presumptuous** (-chuəs) *a.* **1** full of presumption, arrogant, forward. **2** rash, venturesome. **presumptuously** *adv.* **presumptuousness** *n.* [OF *presumer*, L *praesūmere* (*sūmere*, to take)]

Usage note (1) *Presume* usually implies less tentativeness (and more arrogance) than *assume*. (2) The form *presumptious* for *presumptuous* is best avoided.

pre-(+t–words) pre-tax *a.* (of income or profits) before taxes have been deducted. **pre-teen** *a.* of or relating to a child approaching the age of 13. ~*n.* such a child. **pre-tension** *v.t.* to stretch (the reinforcing wires or rods in prestressed concrete) before the concrete is cast. **pre-tensioned** *a.* **pre-term** *a.* born, or happening, prematurely. ~*adv.* prematurely. **pre-test** *v.t.* to test in advance. ~*n.* a test administered in advance. **pretreat** *v.t.* to treat beforehand. **pretreatment** *n.* **pretypify** (prētip´ifī) *v.t.* (*3rd pers. sing. pres.* **pretypifies**, *pres.p.* **pretypifying**, *past, p.p.* **pretypified**) to prefigure.

prêt-à-porter (pretapaw´tā) *a.* (of clothes) ready-to-wear. ~*n.* (a collection of) such clothes. [F, ready to wear]

pretend (pritend´) *v.t.* **1** to assume the appearance of; to feign to be. **2** to simulate, to counterfeit in order to deceive. **3** to make believe in play, to imagine. **4** to allege or put forward falsely. **5** to put forward, to assert, to claim. **6** †to aim at, to aspire to. ~*v.i.* **1** to feign, to make believe. **2** to put forward a claim (to). **3** †to aim, to attempt. ~*a.* make-believe. **pretence** (-tens´), (*NAm.*) **pretense** *n.* **1** (an act of) pretending or feigning. **2** an excuse, a pretext. **3** a claim (true or false) (to). **4** a false profession. **5 a** display, show, ostentation. **b** affectation. **6** (a) semblance. **pretenceless** *a.* **pretended** *a.* **pretendedly** *adv.* **pretender** *n.* **1** a person who makes a claim, esp. a claim that cannot be substantiated. 2 a claimant, esp. a claimant to a throne held by another. **pretendership** *n.* **pretendingly** *adv.* **pretension** (-shən) *n.* 1 (*often pl.*) a claim. 2 (*often pl.*) an aspiration. 3 a pretext. 4 pretentiousness, self-importance. **pretentious** (-shəs) *a.* 1 full of pretension; making specious claims to excellence etc. 2 ostentatious, arrogant, conceited. **pretentiously** *adv.* **pretentiousness** *n.* [F *prétendre*, L *praetendere* (*tendere*, to stretch), p.p. *praetensus*]

preter- (prē´tə) *comb.form* 1 beyond. 2 beyond the range of. 3 more than. [L *praeter*, past, beyond, comp. of *prae*, before]

preterhuman (prētəhū´mən) *a.* more than human, superhuman.

†**preterimperfect** (prētərimpœ´fikt) *a.* applied to the imperfect tense as expressing a past action that is described as still going on.

preterist (pret´ərist) *n.* 1 a person whose chief interest is in the past. 2 a person who holds that the prophecies in the Apocalypse have already been fulfilled. [see PRETERITE]

preterite (pret´ərit), (*esp. N Am.*) **preterit** *a.* (*Gram.*) denoting completed action or existence in past time. ~*n.* 1 the preterite tense. 2 a verb in the preterite tense. **preteriteness** *n.* **preterition** (prētərish´ən) *n.* 1 the act of passing over or omitting. 2 the state of being passed over. 3 a rhetorical figure, the summary mention of a thing while one pretends to pass it over. 4 (*Theol.*) the Calvinist doctrine of the passing over of the non-elect, as distinct from *election*. **preteritive** (priter´-) *a.* (of a verb) having only past tense forms. [OF, from L *praeteritus*, p.p. of *praeterīre* (PRETER-, *īre*, to go)]

pretermit (prētəmit´) *v.t.* (*pres.p.* **pretermitting,** *past, p.p.* **pretermitted**) (*formal*) 1 to pass by or over, to neglect, to omit (to mention, to do etc.). 2 to discontinue. **pretermission** (-shən) *n.* [L *praetermittere* (*mittere*, to send, to let go)]

preternatural (prētənach´ərəl) *a.* beyond what is natural; out of the regular course of nature. **preternaturalism** *n.* 1 the state of being preternatural. 2 a preternatural occurrence, thing etc. 3 belief in or doctrine of the preternatural. **preternaturalist** *n.* **preternaturally** *adv.* **preternaturalness** *n.*

†**preterperfect** (prētəpœ´fikt) *n.* the perfect tense. ~*a.* more than perfect. **preterpluperfect** (-ploo-) *n., a.* pluperfect.

pretext (prē´tekst) *n.* 1 an excuse. 2 an ostensible reason or motive. **on/ under the pretext** putting forward as an excuse. [F *prétexte*, L *praetextus*, p.p. of *praetexere* (*texere*, to weave)]

pretor PRAETOR.

pretty (prit´i) *a.* (*comp.* **prettier,** *superl.* **prettiest**) 1 good-looking, attractive, appealing (though without the striking qualities or perfect proportions of beauty). 2 aesthetically pleasing (with the same qualification). 3 superficially or conventionally attractive. 4 (*coll., derog.*) (of a man) effeminate-looking. 5 (*chiefly iron.*) nice, fine. 6 considerable, large. 7 †commendable. ~*adv.* 1 moderately, fairly. 2 very. ~*n.* (*pl.* **pretties**) a pretty thing or person. ~*v.t.* (*3rd pers. sing. pres.* **pretties,** *pres.p.* **prettying,** *past, p.p.* **prettied**) (*often with up*) to make pretty, to adorn. **a pretty kettle of fish** KETTLE. **a pretty penny** PENNY. **sitting pretty** SIT. **prettify** (-fī) *v.t.* (*3rd pers. sing. pres.* **prettifies,** *pres.p.* **prettifying,** *past, p.p.* **prettified**) 1 to make pretty. 2 to express or depict in a pretty way. **prettification** (-fikā´shən) *n.* **prettifier** *n.* **prettily** *adv.* 1 in a pretty manner. 2 daintily, with taste and elegance. 3 pleasingly to the eye, ear etc. **prettiness** *n.* **pretty go** *n.* (*sl.*) a startling affair. **prettyish** *a.* **prettyism** *n.* **pretty much, pretty nearly, pretty well** *adv.* (*coll.*) nearly, almost. **pretty-pretty** *a.* affectedly pretty, over-pretty. **pretty-pretties** *n.pl.* knick-knacks, gewgaws. [OE *prætig, prættig*, from *præt, prætt*, trick, trickery (cp. Dut. *part*, Norw. *pretta*)]

pretzel (pret´səl) *n.* a crisp biscuit of wheaten flour flavoured with salt, usu. in the shape of a stick or a knot. [G]

pre- (+ v– words) pre-verbal *a.* 1 of or relating to the period in childhood before the acquisition of speech. 2 (*Gram.*) coming before a verb. **pre-vernal** *a.* flowering early, before the spring. **pre-vocalic** *a.* (of a consonant) coming immediately before a vowel. **pre-vocalically** *a.*

prevail (privāl´) *v.i.* 1 to have the mastery or victory (over, against etc.). 2 to predominate. 3 to be in force, to be in general use or in vogue; to be customary. **to prevail on/ upon** to succeed in persuading, to induce. **prevailing** *a.* 1 predominant, most frequent. 2 current, generally accepted. **prevailingly** *adv.* **prevailing wind** *n.* the wind that blows most frequently in a particular place. **prevalence** (prev´ə-) *n.* 1 the act of prevailing. 2 a superiority, predominance. 3 frequency, vogue, currency. **prevalent** *a.* **prevalently** *adv.* [L *praevalēre* (*valēre*, to be strong)]

prevaricate (privar´ikāt) *v.i.* 1 to quibble. 2 to act or speak evasively. 3 to equivocate. **prevarication** (-ā´shən) *n.* **prevaricator** (-var´-) *n.* [L *praevārīcātus*, p.p. of *praevārīcārī* (*vārīcus*, straddling, from *vārus*, bent)]

Usage note The verbs *prevaricate* and *procrastinate* should not be confused: *prevaricate* means to quibble, and *procrastinate* to delay action.

prevenient (privēn´yənt) *a.* (*formal*) going before, preceding, previous. **prevenience** *n.* **prevenient grace** *n.* (*Theol.*) grace preceding repentance and predisposing to conversion. **preveniently** *adv.* [L *praeveniens -ntem*, pres.p. of *praevenīre*, to precede, to anticipate, to prevent (*venīre*, to come)]

prevent (privent´) *v.t.* 1 to keep from happening. 2 to hinder, to thwart, to stop. 3 †to anticipate. 4 †to go before, to precede, to be earlier than. **preventable, preventible** *a.* capable of prevention. **preventability** (-bil´-) *n.* **preventative** *a.* PREVENTIVE (under PREVENT). **preventatively** *adv.* **preventer** *n.* 1 a person who or thing which prevents or hinders. 2 (*Naut.*) a supplementary rope, chain, spar, stay etc., to support another. **preventingly** *adv.* **prevention** *n.* 1 the act of preventing. 2 hindrance, obstruction. **preventive** *a.* 1 tending to hinder or prevent. 2 prophylactic. 3 of or belonging to the coastguard or customs and excise service. ~*n.* 1 something which prevents. 2 a medicine or precaution to ward off disease. 3 a contraceptive. **preventive detention** *n.* a system for dealing with a habitual criminal by detention for a definite period after the completion of the sentence for a specific crime. **preventively** *adv.* **preventive service** *n.* the coastguard or customs and excise service. [L *praeventus*, p.p. of *praevenīre*, as PREVENIENT]

preview (prē´vū) *n.* 1 an advance view, a foretaste. 2 an advance showing of a play, film, art exhibition etc. before its general presentation to the public. 3 a television or cinema trailer. ~*v.t.* to view or show in advance.

previous (prē´viəs) *a.* 1 going before in time or order; antecedent, prior (to). 2 (*coll.*) premature, hasty. ~*adv.* before, previously (to). **previously** *adv.* **previousness** *n.* **previous question** *n.* 1 in the House of Commons, a motion 'that the question be not now put', which, if carried, has the effect of delaying a vote. 2 in the House of Lords and US legislature, a motion to proceed to a vote immediately. 3 in public meetings, a motion to proceed with the next business. [L *praevius* (*via*, way)]

previse (privīz´) *v.t.* (*formal*) 1 to know beforehand, to foresee. 2 to advise in advance. **prevision** (-vizh´ən) *n.*

previsional *a.* **previsionally** *adv.* [L *praevīsus*, p.p. of *praevidēre* (*vidēre*, to see)]

prevue (prēˊvū) *n.* (*esp. N Am.*) a television or cinema trailer. [PREVIEW]

pre- (+ w– words) pre-war *a.* existing or happening before a war, esp. the latest war. **pre-warm** *v.t.* to warm up in advance. **pre-warn** *v.t.* to warn in advance. **pre-wash** *n.* a preliminary wash, before the main one, in a washing machine. *~a.* of or relating to such a wash. *~v.t.* to give such a wash to.

prex (preks), **prexy** (prekˊsi) *n.* (*pl.* **prexes, prexies**) (*US, sl.*) a college president. [from abbr. of PRESIDENT (under PRESIDE)]

prey (prā) *n.* **1** an animal which is or may be seized to be devoured by carnivorous animals. **2** booty, spoil, plunder. **3** a person who becomes a victim of an unscrupulous person, or is vulnerable to unpleasant influences etc. **4** (*Bible*) something which is brought away safe (from a battle etc.). *~v.i.* **1** to take booty or plunder. **2** to take food by violence. **beast of prey** BEAST. **bird of prey** BIRD. **to prey on 1** to rob, to plunder. **2** to chase and seize as food. **3** to make a victim of, to subject to robbery, extortion etc. **4** to have a depressing or obsessive effect on. **preyer** *n.* [OF *praie, preia*, L *praeda*, booty]

prezzie (prezˊi), **pressie** *n.* (*coll.*) a present, a gift. [short for PRESENT[3]]

priapism (prīˊəpizm) *n.* **1** lasciviousness. **2** (*Med.*) continuous erection of the penis without sexual excitement. **priapean** (-pēˊən), **priapic** (-apˊ-) *a.* phallic. [L, from Gr. *Priapos*, the god of procreation]

price (prīs) *n.* **1** the amount asked for a thing or for which it is sold. **2** the cost of a thing. **3** (*coll.*) the amount needed to bribe somebody. **4** that which must be expended, sacrificed, done etc., to secure a thing. **5** the odds in betting. **6** estimation, value, preciousness. *~v.t.* **1** to fix the price of, to value, to appraise. **2** to ask the price of. **above price** beyond price. **a price on one's head** a reward offered for one's killing or capture. **at any price** no matter what the cost. **at a price** for a lot of money etc. **beyond price** priceless, invaluable. **not at any price** under no circumstances. **to price oneself out of the market** to lose trade by charging too high prices. **to set the price of** to state the price of. **what price...? 1** what are the chances of (something) happening? **2** so much for (something). **without price** priceless, invaluable. **price control** *n.* the fixing by government of maximum prices for goods and services. **priced** *a.* having a price. **-priced** *comb. form* having a specified price. **price-fixing** *n.* **1** the setting of prices by agreement between producers and distributors. **2** price control. **priceless** *a.* **1** invaluable, inestimable. **2** (*sl.*) very funny. **pricelessly** *adv.* **pricelessness** *n.* **price list** *n.* a list of the current prices of merchandise, stocks etc. **pricer** *n.* **price ring** *n.* a group of manufacturers or traders who cooperate to maintain prices at an agreed, high level. **price-sensitive** *a.* **1** (of a product) a variation in whose price might affect sales. **2** (of information) that could affect the price of something. **price tag** *n.* **1** the label attached to an object showing its price. **2** price, cost. **price war** *n.* competition among traders or manufacturers to lower prices and so increase sales. **pricey, pricy** *a.* (*comp.* **pricier**, *superl.* **priciest**) expensive. **priciness** *n.* [ME and OF *pris* (F *prix*), L *pretium*, cp. PRAISE, PRIZE[1]]

prick (prik) *n.* **1** the act, or an instance, of pricking. **2** the state or the sensation of being pricked. **3** a puncture; a dot, point or small mark made by or as by pricking. **4 a** a sharp, stinging pain. **b** a mental pain. **5** (*sl.*) the penis. **6** (*sl.*) an obnoxious or inept man. **7** †a pointed instrument, a goad, a spur. *~v.t.* **1** to pierce slightly, to puncture. **2** to make by puncturing. **3** to mark off or delineate with small holes or pricks. **4** to cause (the ears) to point upwards. **5** to goad, to rouse, to incite, to spur on. *~v.i.* **1** to make a thrusting motion, as if to prick. **2** to point upward. **3** to feel as if pricked. **4** †to ride rapidly, to spur. **to kick against the pricks** to hurt oneself in unavailing struggle against something. **to prick off** to prick out. **to prick out 1** to mark a pattern out with dots. **2** to plant seedlings more widely apart with a view to transplanting later to their permanent quarters. **to prick up one's ears** EAR[1]. **prick-eared** *a.* (of dogs etc.) having erect or pointed ears. **pricker** *n.* a sharp-pointed instrument, a bradawl. [OE *prica* (cp. Dan. *prik*, Swed. *prick*), cogn. with *prician*, to prick (cp. Dan. *prikke*, Dut. *prikken*)]

pricket (prikˊit) *n.* **1** a buck in its second year. **2** a sharp point for sticking a candle on. [from PRICK, in alln. to the straight unbranched horns]

prickle (prikˊəl) *n.* **1** a small, sharp point. **2** a thornlike growth capable of being peeled off with the skin or bark, as opposed to a thorn or spine. **3** (*loosely*) a small thorn, spine etc. **4** a prickling sensation. **5** a spine of a hedgehog etc. *~v.t.* **1** to prick slightly. **2** to give a pricking or tingling sensation to. *~v.i.* **1** to have such a sensation. **2** to take offence or react defensively. **prickle-back** *n.* the stickleback. **prickly** *a.* (*comp.* **pricklier**, *superl.* **prickliest**) **1** full of or armed with prickles. **2** tingling. **3** (of a person) oversensitive, ready to take offence. **prickliness** *n.* **prickly heat** *n.* an inflammatory skin condition characterized by itching and stinging sensations, prevalent in hot countries. **prickly pear** *n.* (the pear-shaped fruit of) any cactus of the genus *Opuntia*, usu. covered with prickles. **prickly poppy** *n.* an annual poppy, *Argemone mexicana*, of tropical America, with yellow or white flowers and prickly leaves. [OE *pricel*, cogn. with PRICK]

pricy PRICE.

pride (prīd) *n.* **1** generous elation or satisfaction arising out of some accomplishment, possession or relationship. **2** a source of such elation. **3** inordinate self-esteem, unreasonable conceit of one's own superiority; insolence, arrogance. **4** sense of dignity, self-respect, proper self-esteem. **5** the acme, the highest point, the best condition. **6** a collection of lions. **to pride oneself on** to be proud of oneself for. **to take (a) pride in 1** to be proud of. **2** to be conscientious about the maintenance of. **pride and joy** *n.* someone or something that one is very proud of. **prideful** *a.* **pridefully** *adv.* **pridefulness** *n.* **prideless** *a.* **pride of place** *n.* the highest, most prominent or most important position. **pride of the morning** *n.* a shower of rain or a mist as the sun comes up. [OE *prȳto, prȳte*, cogn. with *prūt*, PROUD]

prie-dieu (prēdyœˊ) *n.* (*pl.* **prie-dieux** (-dyœˊ)) a kneeling-desk for prayers. **prie-dieu chair** *n.* a chair with a tall sloping back, esp. for praying. [F, pray God]

prier PRYER (under PRY[1]).

priest (prēst) *n.* **1** a person who officiates in sacred rites, esp. by offering sacrifice. **2** a minister in the Roman Catholic, Orthodox or Anglican Church, below a bishop and above a deacon, esp. as having authority to administer the sacraments and pronounce absolution. **3** (*coll.*) a clergyman, a minister (esp. in a hostile sense). **4** a small mallet or club for killing fish when caught. *~v.t.* to ordain, to make (someone) a priest. **priestcraft** *n.* priestly policy based on material interests. **priestess** *n.* a woman priest, esp. pagan. **priesthood** *n.* **1** the office or position of a priest. **2** priests collectively. **priest-in-charge** *n.* (*pl.* **priests-in-charge**) a priest temporarily in charge of a parish which is without its own priest. **priest-in-the-pulpit** *n.* the wild arum, priest's hood. **priestless** *a.* **priestlike** *a.* **priestling** *n.* **priestly** *a.* (*comp.* **priestlier**, *superl.* **priestliest**) of, relating to or befitting a priest or the priesthood; sacerdotal. **priestliness** *n.* **priest-ridden** *a.* (*derog.*) dominated or swayed by priests. **priest's hole**

n. (*Hist.*) a hiding place for fugitive Catholic priests, esp. in England under the penal laws. **priest's hood** *n.* the wild arum. **priest-vicar** *n.* a minor canon in certain cathedrals. [OE *prēost*, PRESBYTER]

prig (prig) *n.* 1 a self-righteous, formal or moralistic person. 2 (*sl.*) †a thief. ~†*v.t.* (*pres.p.* **prigging,** *past, p.p.* **prigged**) (*sl.*) to filch, to steal. **priggery** *n.* **priggish** *a.* conceited, affectedly precise, formal, moralistic. **priggishly** *adv.* **priggishness** *n.* [prob. var. of PRICK]

prill (pril) *n.* a button or pellet of metal from an assay. ~*v.t.* to turn (metal) into a pellet-like form, esp. by melting and allowing to solidify while dripping. [Cornish dial.]

prim (prim) *a.* (*comp.* **primmer,** *superl.* **primmest**) formal, affectedly proper, demure, prudish. ~*v.t.* (*pres.p.* **primming,** *past, p.p.* **primmed**) 1 to put (the lips, mouth etc.) into a prim expression. 2 to deck with great nicety or preciseness. ~*v.i.* to make oneself look prim. **primly** *adv.* **primness** *n.* [prob. 17th cent. sl.]

prim. *abbr.* 1 primary. 2 primitive.

prima (prē´mə) *a.* first, chief, principal. **prima ballerina** *n.* (*pl.* **prima ballerinas**) the leading female ballet dancer in a company. **prima buffa** (buf´ə) *n.* (*pl.* **prima buffas, prime buffe** (-mā buf´ā)) a chief female comic singer or actress. **prima donna** (don´ə) *n.* (*pl.* **prima donnas, prime donne** (-mā don´ā)) 1 a chief female singer in an opera or an opera company. 2 a person who is temperamental, hard to please, and given to histrionics. **prima-donnaish** *a.* [It., fem. of *primo*, L *prīmus*, first]

primacy (prī´məsi) *n.* (*pl.* **primacies**) 1 the dignity or office of a primate. 2 pre-eminence. [OF *primacie*, med. L *prīmātia*, L *primātus*, from *prīmus*, PRIME[1]]

primaeval PRIMEVAL.

prima facie (prīmə fā´shē) *adv.* at first sight, on the first impression. ~*a.* based on first impressions. **prima facie case** *n.* (*Law*) a case apparently established by the evidence. [L, abl. of *prīma facies*, first face]

primage (prī´mij) *n.* a percentage on the freight paid to the owner of a ship for care in loading or unloading cargo. [med. L *primāgium*, etym. uncertain]

primal (prī´məl) *a.* 1 primary, original, primitive. 2 fundamental, chief. **primally** *adv.* **primal therapy, primal scream** *n.* a kind of psychotherapy in which patients are encouraged to scream as they remember the agonies of birth and the frustrations of babyhood. [L *prīmālis*, from *prīmus*, PRIME[1]]

primary (prī´məri) *a.* 1 first in time, order or origin. 2 original, radical, firsthand. 3 primitive, fundamental. 4 first in rank or importance, chief. 5 first or lowest in development, elementary. 6 (of education) for children between the ages of 5 and 11. 7 of or relating to an industry that produces raw materials. 8 of or relating to the inducing current or its circuit in an induction coil or transformer. 9 (*Geol.*) (**Primary**) of or relating to the Palaeozoic strata. 10 (*Gram.*) of or relating to one of the tenses in Latin and Greek which refer to present and future time (the present, future, perfect and future perfect tenses). ~*n.* (*pl.* **primaries**) 1 something which stands first in order, rank or importance. 2 (*Astron.*) a primary planet. 3 (*Astron.*) a celestial body round which other members of a system orbit. 4 a primary election. 5 a primary feather. 6 a primary colour. 7 a primary school. 8 (**Primary**) the Palaeozoic period. **primarily** (prī´-, -mar´i-) *adv.* **primariness** *n.* **primary cell** *n.* a battery in which an irreversible chemical action is converted into electrical energy (cp. SECONDARY CELL (under SECONDARY)). **primary coil** *n.* a coil in a transformer to which current is supplied. **primary colour,** (*N Am.*) **primary color** *n.* any of the fundamental colours from which others can be obtained by mixing (for paints red, blue and yellow; for transmitted light red, blue and green). **primary consumer** *n.* a herbivore. **primary education** *n.* the first formal and compulsory stage of education in primary, junior and infant schools. **primary election** *n.* a meeting or election for the selection of party candidates by voters of a state or region, esp. in the US. **primary feather** *n.* a large quill feather of a bird's wing. **primary planet** *n.* (*Astron.*) a planet as distinguished from its satellites. **primary school** *n.* a school providing primary education, usu. for children aged under 11 (England and Wales) or under 12 (Scotland). **primary winding** *n.* 1 the winding of a transformer which is on the input side. 2 the input winding on the stator of an induction motor. [L *prīmārius*, from *prīmus*, PRIME[1]]

primate (prī´māt, -mət) *n.* 1 a member of the Primates, the highest order of mammals, comprising humans, apes, monkeys and lemurs. 2 the chief prelate in a national episcopal church, an archbishop. **Primate of all England** *n.* the Archbishop of Canterbury. **Primate of England** *n.* the Archbishop of York. **primateship** *n.* **primatial** (-mā´shəl) *a.* **primatology** (-tol´-) *n.* the branch of zoology concerned with the study of primates. **primatological** (-loj´-) *a.* **primatologist** (-tol´-) *n.* [late L *prīmas -ātis*, from L *prīmus*, PRIME[1]]

primavera (prēməveə´rə) *n.* (*pl.* **primaveras**) 1 a tree bearing yellow flowers, *Cybistax donellsmithii*, growing in central America. 2 the wood of this tree, hard and light in colour. [Sp., spring]

prime[1] (prīm) *a.* 1 first in time, rank, excellence or importance. 2 (esp. of meat and provisions) chief, first-rate, excellent. 3 original, primary, fundamental. 4 in the vigour of maturity, blooming. 5 (of a number) divisible by no integral factors except itself and unity (e.g. 2, 3, 5, 7, 11, 13). ~*n.* 1 the period or state of highest perfection. 2 the best part (of anything). 3 the first stage, the beginning (of anything). 4 the first canonical hour of the day, beginning at 6 a.m. or at sunrise. 5 in the Roman Catholic Church, the office for this hour. 6 dawn, spring, youth. 7 a prime number. 8 the first of the eight parries in fencing, or a thrust in this position. 9 (*Print.*) a symbol (´) added to a letter etc. as a distinguishing mark, or to a number signifying minutes or feet. **prime cost** *n.* the cost of material and labour in the production of an article. **primely** *adv.* **prime meridian** *n.* 1 a meridian from which longitude is reckoned, usu. that of Greenwich. 2 a corresponding line on a map. **prime minister** *n.* 1 the chief minister of a state. 2 the head of an elected government. **prime ministership** *n.* **prime mover** *n.* 1 a person who or thing which originates a movement or an action, esp. the force putting a machine in motion. 2 the author, or the first promoter, of a project. 3 (**Prime Mover**) God. **primeness** *n.* **prime number** *n.* a number that is divisible by no integral factors except itself and unity. **prime rate** *n.* the lowest commercial rate of interest charged by a bank at a particular time. **prime time** *n.* peak viewing or listening time for television or radio audiences, for which advertising rates are highest. **prime-time** *a.* **prime vertical** *n.* a great circle of the heavens passing through the east and west points of the horizon and the zenith. [F, from L *prīmus*, first]

prime[2] (prīm) *v.t.* 1 to prepare something, esp. a gun, for use. 2 to supply (with information). 3 to coach. 4 to fill (a person) with food or drink in order to prepare them for some activity. 5 to fill (a pump) with fluid to expel the air before starting. 6 to inject fuel into (the float chamber of a carburettor). 7 to prepare (wood, metal etc.) for painting by applying primer. ~*v.i.* 1 (of a boiler) to carry over water with the steam to the cylinder. 2 (of a tide) to come before the mean time. **primer**[1] *n.* 1 a person or thing that primes. 2 (a type of) paint used as a sealant and a base for subsequent coats. 3 a priming wire. 4 a detonator. **priming** *n.* 1 the act, or an instance, of preparing a firearm for discharge. 2 the powder placed in the pan of a flint gun. **3** a train of powder connecting a blasting-charge with the fuse. **4** fluid introduced before starting a pump. **5** a first layer of paint etc. **6** a mixture used as a preparatory coat. **7** water carried from the boiler into the cylinder of a steam-engine. **8** hasty instruction, cramming. **9** the shortening of the interval between tides (from neap to spring tides), as distinct from *lagging*. **priming iron, priming wire** *n.* a wire for piercing a cartridge when home, or for clearing the vent of a gun etc. [etym. uncertain]

primer[1] PRIME[2].

primer[2] (prī´mə) *n.* **1** an elementary reading book for children. **2** a short introductory book. [OF, from med. L *prīmārius*, PRIMARY]

primer[3] (prim´ə) *n.* (*Print.*) either one of two sizes of type, great primer and long primer. [see PRIMER[2]]

primero (primeə´rō) *n.* a game of cards fashionable in the 16th and 17th cents., the original of poker. [Sp. *primera*, from *primero*, as PRIMER[2]]

primeval (prīmē´vəl), **primaeval** *a.* belonging to the earliest ages, ancient, original, primitive. **primevally** *adv.* [L *prīmaevus* (*prīmus*, PRIME[1], *aevum*, age)]

primigravida (prīmigrav´idə) *n.* (*pl.* **primigravidas, primigravidae** (-dē)) (*Med.*) a woman who is pregnant for the first time. [mod. L, from *prīmus*, first, *gravida*, pregnant]

primine (prī´min) *n.* (*Bot.*) the outer coating of an ovule. [L *prīmus*, first]

priming PRIME[2].

primipara (prīmip´ərə) *n.* (*pl.* **primiparas, primiparae** (-rē)) (*Med.*) a woman who is giving birth for the first time. **primiparous** *a.* [L *prīmus*, PRIME[1], *parere*, to bring forth]

primitive (prim´itiv) *a.* **1** of or relating to the beginning or the earliest periods, early, ancient, original, primary, primordial. **2** rude, simple, plain, old-fashioned. **3** crude, uncivilized. **4** (of a culture or society) not advanced, lacking a written language and all but basic technical skills. **5** (*Gram.*) radical, not derivative. **6** (*Math.*) (of a line etc.) from which another is derived. **7** (*Geol.*) belonging to the lowest strata or the earliest period. **8** (*Biol.*) of or relating to an early stage of development. **9** (of a colour) primary. **10** (of art) belonging to the period before the Renaissance. **11** not conforming to the traditional standards of Western painting. **12** (*Hist.*) that paints in a naive, childlike, or apparently untaught manner. *~n.* **1** a primitive painter. **2** a picture by such a painter. **3** a primitive word. **4** a Primitive Methodist. **Primitive Church** *n.* the Christian Church in its earliest form. **primitive colour,** (*NAm.*) **primitive color** *n.* a primary colour. **primitively** *adv.* **Primitive Methodism** *n.* a sect aiming at a preponderance of lay control in church government, established in 1810 by secession from the Methodist Church. **Primitive Methodist** *n.* **primitiveness** *n.* **primitive rocks** *n.pl.* primary rocks. **primitivism** *n.* **1** the state of being primitive; primitive behaviour. **2** the belief that primitive things, ways etc. are superior to modern ones. **3** primitive art, culture, religion etc. **primitivist** *n.*, *a.* **primitivistic** (-vis´tik) *a.* [F *primitif*, *-tive*, L *prīmitīvus*, the first of its kind, *prīmus*, first]

primo (prē´mō) *n.* (*pl.* **primos**) (*Mus.*) the first part (in a duet etc.). [It., as PRIME[1]]

primogeniture (prīmōjen´ichə) *n.* **1** seniority by birth amongst children of the same parents. **2** the right, system or rule under which, in cases of intestacy, the eldest son succeeds to the real estate of his father. **primogenital, primogenitary** *a.* **primogenitor** *a.* **1** the first father or ancestor. **2** an ancestor. [F *primogéniture*, med. L *prīmogenitūra* (L *prīmus*, PRIME[1], *geniture*, procreation, see GENITOR)]

primordial (prīmaw´diəl) *a.* **1** first in order, primary, original, primitive. **2** existing at or from the beginning; first-formed. *~n.* **1** an origin. **2** a first principle or element. **primordiality** (-al´-), **primordialism** *n.* **primordially** *adv.* **primordial soup** *n.* a mixture of organic compounds supposed to have covered the surface of the earth, and in which life originated. **primordium** *n.* (*pl.* **primordia** (-diə)) (*Biol.*) an organ or tissue in the earliest stage of its development. [late L *prīmordiālis*, L *prīmordium*, origin (*prīmus*, PRIME[1], *ordīrī*, to begin)]

primp (primp) *v.t.* to prink; to tidy up or smarten (oneself). *~v.i.* to prink oneself, to preen. [dial. var. of PRIM]

primrose (prim´rōz) *n.* **1** any plant of the genus *Primula*, esp. *Primula vulgaris*, a common British wild plant, flowering in early spring. **2** a pale yellow colour. *~a.* **1** like a primrose. **2** of a pale yellow colour. **Primrose League** *n.* a Conservative party league formed in memory of Benjamin Disraeli, Earl of Beaconsfield, called after his supposed favourite flower. **primrose path** *n.* the pursuit of ease and pleasure, esp. as leading to perdition. **primrose yellow** *n.*, *a.* [ME and OF *primerose* (med. L *prīma rōsa*, early rose), corr. of ME and OF *primerole*, ult. from L *prīmula*, dim. from *prīmus*, PRIME[1]]

primula (prim´ūlə) *n.* any plant of the genus of herbaceous plants *Primula*, belonging to the family Primulaceae, comprising the primrose, cowslip etc. **primulaceous** (-lā´shəs) *a.* [L]

primum mobile (prīməm mō´bili) *n.* **1** the first source of motion, the mainspring of any action. **2** in the Ptolemaic system, a sphere believed to revolve from east to west in 24 hours, carrying the heavenly bodies with it. [L, first moving thing]

Primus® (prī´məs) *n.* a portable paraffin cooking stove used esp. by campers.

primus (prī´məs) *n.* the presiding bishop in the Scottish Episcopal Church. *~a.* first, eldest (of the name, among boys in a school). **primus inter pares** (intə pah´rēz) *n.* the first among equals; the senior member of a group. [L, first]

prin. *abbr.* **1** principal. **2** principle.

prince (prins) *n.* **1** a male member of a royal family, other than a reigning king. **2** (*also* **prince of the blood**) the son or grandson of a reigning monarch. **3** a member of a foreign order of nobility usu. ranking next below a duke. **4** the ruler of a principality or small state, usu. feudatory to a king or emperor. **5** in parliamentary writs, a duke, marquess or earl. **6** a chief, leader or foremost representative. **7** †a sovereign, a monarch. **prince-bishop** *n.* a bishop whose see is a principality. **Prince Charming** *n.* an ideal young suitor. **prince consort** *n.* a prince who is also the husband of a queen. **princedom, †princehood** *n.* **princekin, princelet, princeling** *n.* a young or petty prince. **princelike** *a.* **princely** *a.* (*comp.* **princelier,** *superl.* **princeliest**) **1** of, relating to or befitting a prince. **2** belonging to a prince. **3** having the rank of a prince. **4** stately, dignified. **5** generous, lavish. *~adv.* as becomes a prince. **princeliness** *n.* **Prince of Darkness** *n.* the Devil. **Prince of Peace** *n.* the Messiah, Christ. **prince of the Church** *n.* a cardinal. **Prince of Wales** *n.* the title customarily conferred on the heir-apparent to the British throne. **Prince Regent** *n.* a prince acting as regent. **prince royal** *n.* the eldest son of a sovereign. **Prince Rupert's drop** *n.* a pear-shaped lump of glass formed by falling in a molten state into water, bursting to dust when the thin end is nipped off. **prince's feather** *n.* a Mexican plant, *Amaranthus hypochondriacus*, tall, with small red flowers. **princeship** *n.* **prince's metal** *n.* an alloy of copper and zinc. **princess** (-ses, -ses´) *n.* **1** the wife of a prince. **2** a female member of a royal family, other than a reigning queen. **3** (*also* **princess of the blood**) the daughter or granddaughter of a sovereign. **4** a woman who is pre-eminent in her field. **5** (*also* **princesse**) a style of woman's dress, flared and with a close-fitting bodice, made up of panels from bodice to hem with no waist seam. **6** †a female sovereign. **Princess Regent** *n.* **1** a princess acting as regent. **2** the wife of a Prince Regent. **Princess Royal** *n.* a title conferrable for life on the eldest daughter of a reigning sovereign. [F, from L *principem*, nom. *-ceps* (*prin-*, *prīmus*, PRIME[1], *capere*, to take)]

princeps (prin´seps) *a.* (*pl.* **principes** (-sipēz)) first. ~*n.* **1** a chief or head man. **2** the title of the Roman emperor as constitutional head of the state. [L, first, chief, see PRINCE]

princess PRINCE.

principal (prin´sipəl) *a.* **1 a** chief, leading, main. **b** first in rank, authority, importance, influence or degree. **2** (of money) constituting the capital sum invested. ~*n.* **1** a chief or head. **2** a president, a governor, the head of a college etc. **3** a leader or chief actor in any transaction, the chief party, the person ultimately liable. **4** a person employing another as agent. **5** the actual perpetrator of a crime, the principal in the first degree, or one aiding and abetting, principal in the second degree. **6** a performer who takes a leading role. **7** a capital sum invested or lent, as distinguished from income. **8 a** a main rafter, esp. one extending to the ridge pole. **b** a main girder. **9** an organ stop of the open diapason family, usu. sounding an octave above standard pitch. **10** a civil servant of the grade below secretary. **11** a person for whom another becomes surety. **12** (*Mus.*) the leading player in each section of an orchestra. **13** (*Hist.*) each of the two combatants in a duel. **principal boy** *n.* the leading male role in a pantomime, usu. taken by a woman. **principal clause** *n.* (*Gram.*) the main clause in a sentence, to which other clauses are subordinate. **principal girl** *n.* the leading actress in a theatrical production, esp. a pantomime. **principally** *adv.* chiefly, mainly, for the most part. **principal parts** *n.pl.* those inflected forms of a verb from which all other inflections can be derived. **principalship** *n.* [F, from L *principālis*, from *princeps -cipis*, see PRINCE]

Usage note The spellings of the adjective and noun *principal* (first, a head etc.) and the noun *principle* (a general rule, a moral standard etc.) should not be confused.

principality (prinsipal´iti) *n.* (*pl.* **principalities**) **1** the territory or jurisdiction of a prince. **2** the state from which a prince derives his title. **3** sovereignty, royal state or condition, superiority. **4** (*pl.*) one of the nine orders of angels. **the Principality** Wales.

principate (prin´sipāt) *n.* **1** (*Hist.*) the form of government under the early Roman emperors when some republican features were retained. **2** the period of this form of government. **3** a principality.

principes PRINCEPS.

principia (prinsip´iə) *n.pl.* beginnings, origins, elements, first principles. **principial, †principiant** *a.* [L, pl. of *principium*, see PRINCIPLE]

principle (prin´sipəl) *n.* **1** a source, an origin; a fundamental cause or element. **2** a comprehensive truth or proposition from which others are derived. **3** a general truth forming a basis for reasoning or action. **4** a fundamental doctrine or tenet. **5** a rule of action or conduct deliberately adopted, as distinct from *impulse*. **6** the habitual regulation of conduct by moral law. **7** a law of nature by virtue of which a given mechanism etc. brings about certain results. **8** the mechanical contrivance, combination of parts, or mode of operation, forming the basis of a machine, instrument, process etc. **9** (*Chem.*) the constituent that gives specific character to a substance. **10** †a beginning. **in principle** as far as the basic idea or theory is concerned. **on principle** because of the fundamental (moral) issue involved; in order to assert a principle. **principled** *a.* **1** guided by principle. **2** based on a principle. [F *principe*, L *principium*, beginning, from *princeps -cipis*, see PRINCE]

Usage note See note under PRINCIPAL: *principle* is never an adjective.

prink (pringk) *v.i.* **1** to dress for show. **2** to make oneself smart, esp. excessively so. ~*v.t.* **1** to dress or smarten (oneself) up. **2** (of a bird) to preen. **prinker** *n.* [rel. to PRANK[2]]

print (print) *n.* **1** an indentation or other mark made by pressure, an imprint, an impression. **2** an impression from type, an engraved plate etc. **3** printed lettering. **4** printed matter. **5** a printed publication, esp. a newspaper. **6** the print run of a book etc. **7** an engraving, a lithograph etc. **8** a reproduction of a work of art made by a photographic process. **9** printed cotton cloth. **10** a positive photographic image produced from a negative. **11** a fingerprint. ~*v.t.* **1** to impress, to mark by pressure. **2** to take an impression of, to stamp. **3** to impress or make copies of (a book, picture etc.) by pressure, as from inked types, plates or blocks, on paper, cloth etc. **4** to cause (a book etc.) to be so impressed or copied. **5** to reproduce a design, writing etc. by any transfer process. **6** to mark with a design etc. by stamping. **7** to mark (a textile, ceramic etc.) with a decorative design. **8** to imprint, to form (letters etc.) in imitation of printing. **9** to impress (on the memory etc.) as if by printing. **10** to produce (a positive photographic image) from a negative. ~*v.i.* **1** to practise the art of printing. **2** to publish books etc. **3** to form letters etc. in imitation of printing. **in print 1** in a printed form. **2** (of a printed book etc.) on sale. **out of print** no longer obtainable from the publisher. **to appear in print** to have one's work published. **to print out 1** to print. **2** to produce a printout (of). **to rush into print** to write to a newspaper or publish a book without adequate justification. **printable** *a.* **1** able to be printed, or to be printed on or from. **2** fit to appear in print. **printability** (-bil´-) *n.* **printed circuit** *n.* an electronic circuit consisting of conductive material printed or etched on to an insulating base. **printed circuit board** *n.* the circuit with its insulating base. **printer** *n.* **1** a person engaged in printing books, pamphlets, newspapers etc.; a typesetter, a compositor. **2** a person who carries on a printing business. **3** a person who prints textiles. **4** a machine or instrument for printing copies, designs etc. **5** a device for producing a printout. **printer's devil** *n.* (*Hist.*) a boy of all work in a printing office. **printer's ink** *n.* a viscous mixture of black pigment and oil or varnish used as ink in printing. **printer's mark** *n.* an engraved design used as a device or trademark by a printer or publisher, an imprint. **printer's pie** *n.* PIE[3]. **printer's ream** *n.* 516 sheets of paper. **printery** *n.* (*pl.* **printeries**) (*N Am.*) a printing office. **printhead** *n.* (*Comput.*) the component in a printer that forms and prints the characters. **printing** *n.* **1** the act, process or practice of impressing letters, characters or figures on paper, cloth or other material. **2** the business of a printer, the production of printed material. **3** typography. **4** a single impression of a book. **5 a** printed matter. **b** handwriting with separated letters looking like printed ones. **printing ink** *n.* printer's ink. **printing machine** *n.* a machine for taking impressions from type etc., esp. a power-operated one. **printing office** *n.* an establishment where printing is carried on. **printing paper** *n.* paper suitable for printing. **printing press** *n.* **1** a printing machine. **2** a hand-press for printing. **printless** *a.* taking, or leaving, no impression. **printmaker** *n.* a person who makes prints. **printmaking** *n.* **printout** *n.* (a) printed copy produced by a computer.

print run *n.* (the number of copies produced in) a single printing of a book etc. **print seller** *n.* a person who deals in engravings. **print shop** *n.* 1 a place where printing is carried out. 2 a place where engravings etc. are sold. **print-through** *n.* 1 the degree to which material printed on one side of the paper shows through on the other side. 2 the accidental transfer of a recording from one layer of magnetic tape to another when the tape is wound. **printworks** *n.pl.* a factory for printing fabrics. [OF *preinte*, from *preint*, p.p. of *preindre*, L *premere*, to PRESS[1]]

prion[1] (prī´on) *n.* (*pl.* **prions**) (*Biol.*) an infectious protein particle associated with diseases of the brain and nervous system in human beings and animals, such as BSE, Creutzfeldt–Jakob disease, scrapie etc. [alteration of *pro*teinaceous *in*fectious particle]

prion[2] (prī´ən) *n.* (*pl.* **prions**) any of various petrels of the genus *Pachyptila* with a serrated bill, living in the southern oceans. [Gr. *priōn*, a saw]

prior[1] (prī´ə) *a.* 1 former, preceding; earlier, antecedent. 2 taking precedence. *~adv.* previously, antecedently (to). [L, comp. of obs. *pri*, before]

prior[2] (prī´ə) *n.* 1 a superior of a monastic house or order next in rank below an abbot. 2 the deputy of an abbot. 3 (*Hist.*) a chief magistrate in certain Italian republics, a head of a guild at Florence etc. **priorate, priorship** *n.* **prioress** *n.* 1 the deputy of an abbess. 2 the superior of a priory of nuns. **priory** *n.* (*pl.* **priories**) a religious house governed by a prior or prioress. [late OE, as PRIOR[1]]

priority (prīor´iti) *n.* (*pl.* **priorities**) 1 the fact or the state of going before, antecedence. 2 precedence, a superior claim or entitlement. 3 something given or meriting special attention. 4 the right to proceed while other vehicles wait. *~a.* having or entitling to priority. **prioritize, prioritise** *v.t.* 1 to arrange (things to be done) in order of priority. 2 to give priority to. **prioritization** (-zā´shən) *n.* [med. L *prioritas -tatis*, from PRIOR[1]]

priory PRIOR[2].

†**prisage** (prī´zij) *n.* (*Hist.*) a customs duty on wine. [obs. *prise*, OF *prise*, a taking or seizure, from *pris*, *prise*, p.p. of *prendre*, to take]

prise (prīz), (*N Am.*) **prize** *v.t.* 1 to wrench. 2 to force open with or as with a lever. 3 to extract with difficulty. *~n.* 1 leverage. 2 †a lever. [PRIZE[2]]

prisere (prī´siə) *n.* a primary sere, a succession from bare ground to the community climax. [*pri*mary *sere*]

prism (priz´m) *n.* 1 a solid having similar, equal and parallel plane bases or ends, its sides forming similar parallelograms. 2 a transparent solid of this form, usu. triangular, with two refracting surfaces set at an acute angle to each other, used as an optical instrument. 3 a spectrum produced by refraction through this. 4 any medium acting on light etc. in a similar manner. **prismal** *a.* **prismatic** (-mat´-), †**prismatical** *a.* 1 of, relating to or resembling a prism. 2 formed, refracted or distributed by a prism. 3 (of crystals) orthorhombic. **prismatically** *adv.* **prismatic binoculars** *n.pl.* binoculars shortened by the insertion of prisms. **prismatic colour** *n.* any of the colours into which pure white light is resolved when dispersed, for example, in a prism or raindrop. **prismatic compass** *n.* a hand-compass with an attached prism by which the dial can be read while taking the sight. **prismatoid** (-mətoid) *n.* a solid with parallel polygonal bases connected by triangular faces. **prismatoidal** (-toi´-) *a.* **prismoid** (-moid) *n.* a solid like a prism, having similar but unequal ends. **prismoidal** *a.* **prismy** (-mi) *a.* (*comp.* **prismier**, *superl.* **prismiest**) prismatic in colour. [late L *prisma*, from Gr. *prisma -matos*, from *prizein*, to saw]

prison (priz´ən) *n.* 1 a place of confinement, esp. a public building for the confinement of criminals, persons awaiting trial etc. 2 confinement, captivity. *~v.t.* (*pres.p.* **prisoning**, *past, p.p.* **prisoned**) 1 (*poet.*) to imprison. 2 to confine, to restrain. **prison bars** *n.pl.* 1 the bars of a prison, whatever serves to confine. 2 (*as sing.*) prisoner's base. †**prison base** *n.* prisoner's base. **prison bird** *n.* a jailbird. **prison-breaker** *n.* a person who escapes from legal imprisonment. **prison-breaking** *n.* **prison camp** *n.* a camp for prisoners of war etc. **prisoner** *n.* 1 a person confined in a prison. 2 a person under arrest on a criminal charge. 3 a captive. 4 a prisoner of war. **to take prisoner** 1 to capture. 2 to arrest and hold in custody. **prisoner at the bar** *n.* a person in custody or on trial upon a criminal charge. **prisoner of conscience** *n.* a person whose political, religious etc. beliefs have led to imprisonment. **prisoner of state** *n.* a person imprisoned for political reasons. **prisoner of war** *n.* a person captured in war. **prisoner-of-war** *a.* **prisoner's base,** †**prison base,** †**prison bars** *n.* a children's game played by two sides occupying opposite goals or bases, the object being to touch and capture a player away from their base. **prison house** *n.* (*poet.*) a prison. **prison officer** *n.* a person who guards and supervises prisoners in a prison. **prison van** *n.* a strong, closed van for transporting prisoners to and from prison. **prison visitor** *n.* a person who undertakes to visit prisoners as a voluntary service. **prison visiting** *n.* [OF *prison*, *prisun*, L *prensiōnem*, nom. *prensio*, *prehensio*, from *prehendere*, to seize]

prissy (pris´i) *a.* (*comp.* **prissier**, *superl.* **prissiest**) prim, fussy, prudish. **prissily** *adv.* **prissiness** *n.* [perh. PRIM and SISSY (under SIS)]

pristine (pris´tēn, -tīn) *a.* 1 of or relating to an early or original state or time. 2 ancient, primitive. 3 pure, unadulterated, uncorrupted; as new. [L *pristinus*, former]

Usage note The use of *pristine* in the sense 'as new' is sometimes disapproved of.

†**prithee** (pridh´i) *int.* pray, please. [corr. of *pray thee*, see PRAY]

prittle-prattle (prit´əlpratəl) *n.* foolish or idle chatter; babbling. [redupl. of PRATTLE]

priv. *abbr.* private.

privacy PRIVATE.

privatdozent (privatdotsent´) *n.* in a German university, a recognized teacher or lecturer not on the regular staff. [G, private teacher (L *prīvātus*, see PRIVATE, *docens -ntem*, pres.p. of *docēre*, to teach)]

private (prī´vət) *a.* 1 not public; kept or withdrawn from publicity or observation; retired, secluded. 2 secret, confidential. 3 (of a person) not holding a public position. 4 a not administered or provided by the state. b not part of, or being treated under, the National Health Service. 5 not official. 6 personal, not of or relating to the community. 7 one's own. 8 secretive, reticent. *~n.* 1 a soldier of the lowest rank. 2 (*pl.*) the private parts. **in private** 1 privately, confidentially. 2 in private life. **privacy** (prī´vəsi, priv´-) *n.* 1 the state of being private. 2 (a person's right to) freedom from intrusion or publicity. 3 the avoidance of publicity or display. 4 secrecy. **private act, private bill** *n.* one affecting a private person or persons and not the general public. **private bar** *n.* a saloon bar. **private company** *n.* a company with a restricted number of shareholders, whose shares are not offered for sale to the general public. **private detective** *n.* a private person or an agent of a detective agency employed privately to investigate cases. **private enterprise** *n.* 1 economic activity undertaken by private individuals or organizations. 2 individual initiative. **private eye** *n.* (*coll.*) a private detective. **private first class** *n.* (*pl.* **privates first class**) (*US*) a soldier of a rank between private and corporal. **private hotel** *n.* a hotel or boarding house which is not obliged to take in chance travellers. **private house** *n.* a dwelling house belonging to a private individual, as distinct from a public building. **private income** *n.* private means. **private investigator** *n.* a private detective. **private judgement** *n.* a person's individual judgement, esp. as applied to a religious doctrine or passage of Scripture. **private law** *n.* the branch of law which deals with individuals and their rights and duties, and private property. **private life** *n.* an individual's personal and family life, as distinct from work or public life. **privately** *adv.* **private means** *n.pl.* income from investments etc., as distinct from earned income. **private member** *n.* a member of Parliament who does not hold a government office. **private member's bill** *n.* a bill introduced and sponsored by a member of Parliament, not by the government. **privateness** *n.* **private parts** *n.pl.* the genitals. **private patient** *n.* a patient who is treated privately by a doctor, not under the National Health Service. **private press** *n.* a usu. small printing establishment run as a hobby rather than for profit. **private property** *n.* land or goods owned by an individual and kept for private use. **private school** *n.* **1** a school run independently by an individual or group, esp. for profit. **2** (*US*) a school which is not supported by the state. **private secretary** *n.* (*pl.* **private secretaries**) **1** a secretary entrusted with personal and confidential matters. **2** a civil servant acting as an aide to a minister or senior government official. **private sector** *n.* the economy which is not state-owned or state-controlled. **private service** *n.* **1** a medical practice which is outside the National Health Service. **2** (*N Am.*) the practice of a self-employed doctor or lawyer. **private soldier** *n.* **1** a soldier of the lowest rank. **2** (*US*) a soldier who is not a recruit. **private treaty** *n.* a way of selling property in which the price is agreed directly between the buyer and seller. **private view** *n.* an occasion when only those invited to an exhibition are admitted. **private war** *n.* **1** a war against citizens of another state conducted by private individuals, not by government. **2** a feud between persons or groups in which even murder may be committed. **private wrong** *n.* an offence committed against an individual, not against society. **privatize, privatise** *v.t.* to denationalize, to take back into the private sector, to return to private ownership. **privatization** (-zā´shən) *n.* **privatizer** *n.* [L *prīvātus*, p.p. of *prīvāre*, to bereave, to set apart]

privateer (prīvətiə´) *n.* **1** an armed ship owned and officered by private persons commissioned by Government by letters of marque to engage in war against a hostile nation, esp. to capture merchant shipping. **2** an officer or one of the crew of such a ship. **3** a person who engages in privateering. ~*v.i.* to cruise or engage in hostilities in a privateer. **privateering** *n.* **privateersman** *n.* (*pl.* **privateersmen**). [PRIVATE]

privation (prīvā´shən) *n.* **1** deprivation or lack of what is necessary to a comfortable life; want, destitution. **2** absence, loss, negation (of). **privative** (priv´ə-) *a.* **1** causing privation. **2** consisting in the absence or loss or removal of something. **3** (*Gram.*) expressing privation or absence of a quality etc., negative. ~*n.* **1** something which depends on, or of which the essence is, the absence of something. **2** (*Gram.*) a prefix or suffix (as *un-* or *-less*) giving a negative meaning to a word. **privatively** *adv.* [L *privatio*, see PRIVATE]

privet (priv´it) *n.* any evergreen, white-flowered shrub of the genus *Ligustrum*, esp. *L. vulgare*, largely used for hedges. [etym. uncertain]

privilege (priv´ilij) *n.* **1** a benefit, right, advantage or immunity belonging to a person, class, office etc. **2** favoured status, the possession of privileges, a special advantage. **3** the rights and freedoms enjoyed by members of a legislative assembly. **4** (*Law*) a particular right or power conferred by a special law. **5** an exemption belonging to an office. **6** a right of priority or precedence in any respect. **7** a franchise, monopoly or patent granted to an individual or a company. **8** (*US*) an option to buy or sell securities on the Stock Exchange. ~*v.t.* **1** to invest with a privilege. **2** to license, to authorize (to do). **3** to exempt (from). **privileged** *a.* **privileged communication** *n.* (*Law*) a communication which there is no compulsion to disclose in evidence. **privilege of clergy** *n.* benefit of clergy. [OF, from L *prīvilēgium* (*prīvi-*, *prīvus*, private, *lex lēgis*, law), whence med. L *prīvilēgiāre* and F *privilegier*, to privilege]

privy (priv´i) *a.* **1** secluded, hidden, secret, clandestine, private. **2** cognizant of something secret with another, privately knowing (with *to*). ~*n.* (*pl.* **privies**) **1** a lavatory, esp. an outside one. **2** (*Law*) a person having an interest in any action or thing. **privily** *adv.* secretly, privately. **privity** *n.* (*pl.* **privities**) **1** the state of being privy to (certain facts, intentions etc.). **2** (*Law*) any relationship to another party involving participation in interest, reciprocal liabilities etc. **privy chamber** *n.* a private apartment in a royal residence. **Privy Council** *n.* **1** a committee of advisers to the British sovereign (the functions of which are now largely exercised by the Cabinet and committees), consisting of the princes of the blood, past and present government ministers, and members appointed by the Crown. **2** (*Hist.*) a sovereign's or Governor-General's private counsellors. **privy councillor, privy counsellor** *n.* **privy purse** *n.* **1** an allowance of money for the personal use of the sovereign. **2** the officer in charge of this. **privy seal** *n.* the seal formerly appended to grants etc. which have not to pass the Great Seal. [F *privé*, L *prīvātus*, PRIVATE]

prix fixe (prē fēks´) *n.* (*pl.* **prix fixes** (fēks)) in a restaurant, (a menu at) a fixed price. [F]

prize[1] (prīz) *n.* **1** something which is offered or won as the reward of merit or superiority in any competition, contest, exhibition etc. **2** a sum of money or other object offered for competition in a lottery etc. **3** a well-paid appointment, a fortune, or other desirable object of perseverance, enterprise etc. ~*a.* **1** offered or gained as a prize. **2** gaining or worthy of a prize, first-class, of superlative merit. ~*v.t.* to value highly, to esteem. **prizable** *a.* **prized** *a.* treasured, highly valued. **prizefight** *n.* a boxing match fought for stakes. **prizefighter** *n.* **prizefighting** *n.* **prize-giving** *n.* a formal awarding of prizes, esp. at the end of a school year. **prizeless** *a.* **prize list** *n.* a list of prizewinners. **prizeman** *n.* (*pl.* **prizemen**) the winner of a prize, esp. an academic one. **prize money**[1] *n.* money offered as a prize. †**prizer** *n.* **1** a prizefighter. **2** a valuer, an appraiser. **prize ring** *n.* **1** the roped space (now usu. square) for a prizefight. **2** prizefighting. **prizewinner** *n.* the winner of a prize. **prizewinning** *a.* **prizewoman** *n.* (*pl.* **prizewomen**) a woman who has won a prize, esp. an academic one. [ME and OF *pris*, PRICE; v. from OF *preisier* (F *priser*), to PRAISE]

prize[2] (prīz) *n.* **1** something which is taken from an enemy in war, esp. a ship or other property captured at sea. **2** a find, a windfall. ~*v.t.* to make a prize of. **prize court** *n.* a court adjudicating on cases of prizes captured at sea, in England and the US a department of the courts of Admiralty. **prize money**[2] *n.* the proceeds of the sale of a captured vessel etc. [F *prise*, a taking, a seizure, booty, orig. fem. of *pris*, p.p. of *prendre*, *prehendere*, to take]

prize[3] PRISE.

prize money[1] PRIZE[1].

prize money[2] PRIZE[2].

prn *abbr.* *pro re nata*, as the need arises.

PRO *abbr.* 1 Public Records Office. 2 public relations officer.

pro[1] (prō) *prep.* 1 for. 2 in favour of. *~adv.* in favour of. *~n.* (*pl.* **pros**) an argument or a reason in favour of. *~a.* in favour of. **pro and con** for and against; on both sides. **pros and cons** *n.pl.* reasons or arguments for and against. [L *prō*, for]

pro[2] (prō) *n.* (*pl.* **pros**) 1 (*coll.*) a professional (actor, footballer etc.), or a person who behaves professionally. 2 (*sl.*) a prostitute. *~a.* professional. [short for PROFESSIONAL (under PROFESSION)]

pro-[1] (prō) *pref.* 1 in favour of. 2 replacing, substituting for. 3 onward, forward, in front of. [L *prō*, for]

pro-[2] (prō) *pref.* 1 before in time or position; earlier than. 2 projecting forward. 3 rudimentary. [Gr. *pro*, before]

proa (prō´ə), **prahu** (prah´oo), **prau** *n.* (*pl.* **proas, prahus, praus**) a long, narrow, swift Malay canoe, usu. equipped with both sails and oars. [Malay *prāū, prāhū*]

proactive (prōak´tiv) *a.* 1 energetic, enterprising, taking the initiative. 2 (*Psych.*) of or relating to a learned habit or mental conditioning which affects a later process. **proaction** (-ak´shən) *n.* **proactively** *adv.* **proactivity** (-tiv´iti) *n.* [PRO-[1], re*active*]

pro-am (prō´am) *a.* involving both professionals and amateurs. *~n.* a pro-am tournament etc.

prob *abbr.* problem.

prob. *abbr.* probably.

probabilism (prob´əbilizm) *n.* in Roman Catholic theology, the doctrine that, in matters of conscience about which there is disagreement or doubt, it is lawful to adopt any course, at any rate if this has the support of any recognized authority. **probabilist** *n.* **probabilistic** (probəbilis´tik) *a.* 1 of or relating to probability. 2 based on probability. 3 of the nature of probabilism. **probabilistically** *adv.* [F *probabilisme*]

probability (probəbil´iti) *n.* (*pl.* **probabilities**) 1 the quality of being probable. 2 the likelihood of something happening. 3 something which is or appears probable or most probable. 4 (*Math.*) the likelihood of an event measured by the ratio of the favourable chances to the whole number of chances. **in all probability** most likely. [F *probabilité*, L *probābilitātem*, nom. *-tas*]

probable (prob´əbəl) *a.* likely to happen or prove true, having more evidence for than against, likely. *~n.* a person likely to be chosen for a team, post etc. **probably** *adv.* [F, from L *probābilem*, nom. *-lis* (*probāre*, to PROVE)]

proband (prō´bənd) *n.* a person with a distinctive characteristic who serves as the starting point for a genetic study of a family etc. [L *probandus*, ger. of *probāre*, to PROVE]

probang (prō´bang) *n.* (*Med.*) a slender flexible rod with a piece of sponge, a button or ball at the end, for removing obstructions in the throat or applying medication. [orig. *provang*, name given by the inventor]

probate (prō´bāt) *n.* 1 the official proving of a will. 2 a certified copy of a proved will. 3 (*US*) the right or jurisdiction of proving wills. *~v.t.* (*N Am.*) to establish the validity of (a will). **probate duty** *n.* (*Hist.*) a tax charged upon the personal property of deceased persons, now merged in estate duty. [L *probātum*, neut. of *-tus*, p.p. of *probāre*, to PROVE]

probation (prəbā´shən) *n.* 1 a method of dealing with criminals by allowing them to go at large under supervision during their good behaviour. 2 a proving or testing of character, ability etc., esp. of a candidate for a religious ministry etc. by employment for a fixed period. 3 a moral trial, esp. the discipline undergone in this life as a means to salvation. 4 the act of proving. 5 evidence, proof. **on probation** 1 being tested for suitability etc. 2 under the supervision of a probation officer. **probational** *a.* of, relating to or serving as probation or trial. **probationary** *a.* 1 probational. 2 undergoing probation. *~n.* (*pl.* **probationaries**) a probationer. **probationer** *n.* 1 a person on probation or trial, esp. a divinity student licensed to preach and eligible for a charge, or a newly-appointed teacher or nurse. 2 an offender under probation. **probationership** *n.* **probation officer** *n.* a court official who supervises and assists offenders who are on probation. [ME and OF *probacion*, L *probātiōnem*, nom. *-tio*, as PROBATE]

probative (prō´bətiv) *a.* 1 proving or tending to prove. 2 serving as proof, evidential. 3 probational. **probatively** *adv.* **probatory** *a.* probative. [L *probātīvus*]

probe (prōb) *n.* 1 a surgical instrument, usu. a silver rod with a blunt end, for exploring cavities of the body, wounds etc. 2 a thorough investigation, as by a newspaper of e.g. alleged corruption. 3 an electric lead containing or connected to a monitoring circuit. 4 a docking device, esp. a projecting pipe which connects with the drogue of a tanker aircraft to permit in-flight refuelling. 5 an unmanned spacecraft carrying equipment for collecting scientific measurements of conditions. 6 an exploratory survey. *~v.t.* 1 to search or examine (a wound, ulcer etc.) with, or as with, a probe. 2 to scrutinize or enquire into thoroughly. 3 to pierce with or as if with a probe. *~v.i.* to make a tentative or exploratory investigation. **probeable** *a.* **prober** *n.* **probingly** *adv.* [late L *proba*, PROOF]

probit (prob´it) *n.* a unit of probability in statistics. [*prob*ability un*it*]

probity (prō´biti, prob´-) *n.* 1 honesty, sincerity or integrity. 2 uprightness, rectitude. [F *probité*, L *probitātem*, nom. *-tas*, from *probus*, good]

problem (prob´ləm) *n.* 1 a question proposed for solution. 2 a matter, situation or person that is difficult to deal with or understand. 3 a source of perplexity or distress. 4 (*Geom.*) a proposition requiring something to be done. 5 an investigation starting from certain conditions for the determination or illustration of a physical law etc. 6 an arrangement of pieces on a chessboard or of cards on a bridge board, from which a certain result has to be attained, usu. in a specified number of moves. *~a.* causing or posing a problem; hard to deal with. **no problem** 1 it's all right. 2 it doesn't matter. **that's your problem** (*coll.*) you must deal with that yourself, it is nothing to do with me. **to have a problem/ problems** 1 to have difficulty (with). 2 to be in trouble. **problematic** (-mat´-), **problematical** *a.* 1 doubtful, questionable, uncertain. 2 (*Logic*) propounding or supporting that which is possible or probable but not necessarily true, contingent. **problematically** *adv.* **problematist** *n.* **problematize, problematise** *v.t.* to make into a problem; to regard as a problem. **problematization** (-zā´shən) *n.* **problem child** *n.* a child whose character presents parents, teachers etc. with exceptional difficulties. **problemist** *n.* a person who studies or composes (chess) problems. **problem page** *n.* a regular feature in a magazine which offers advice to people who write in with problems. **problem play, problem picture** *n.* a play or picture dealing with a social problem or with tricky moral questions. [ME and OF *probleme*, L *problēma -matis*, Gr. *problēma -matos* (*ballein*, to cast)]

pro bono (prō bō´nō) *a.* (*Law, US*) of or relating to legal work done without charge for poor clients, or to a lawyer who does such work. [L *pro bono publico*, for the public good]

proboscis (prəbos´is) *n.* (*pl.* **probosces** (-ēz), **proboscides** (-idēz), **proboscises**) 1 the trunk of an elephant or the elongated snout of a tapir etc. 2 the elongated mouth of some insects. 3 the suctorial organ of some worms etc. 4 (*facet.*) the human nose. **proboscidean** (probəsid´-) *a.* 1 having a proboscis. 2 of, relating to or like a proboscis. 3 of or relating to the Proboscidea, an order of mammals containing the elephants, the extinct mastodon etc. ~*n.* any individual of the Proboscidea. **proboscidiferous** (-dif´-) *a.* **proboscidiform** (-sid´-) *a.* **proboscis monkey** *n.* a monkey, *Nasalis larvatus*, of Borneo, the male having a long, flexible nose. [L *proboscis -cidis*, Gr. *proboskis -kidos* (*boskein*, to feed)]

proc. *abbr.* **1** procedure. **2** proceedings. **3** process.

procaine (prō´kān), **procain** *n.* a synthetic crystalline substance used as a local anaesthetic, esp. in dentistry. [co*caine*]

procaryote PROKARYOTE.

pro-cathedral (prōkəthē´drəl) *n.* a church used temporarily as a substitute for a cathedral.

proceed (prəsēd´) *v.i.* **1** to go (in a specified direction or to a specified place). **2** to go on; to go forward, to advance, to continue to progress. **3** to carry on a series of actions, to go on (with or in). **4** to take steps. **5** to act in accordance with a method or procedure. **6** (of an action) to be carried on. **7** to issue or come forth, to originate (from). **8** to advance (to) a degree. **9** to take or carry on legal proceedings (against). **procedure** (-dyə) *n.* **1** an act, or a manner, of proceeding. **2** the (customary or established) mode of conducting business etc. esp. in a court or at a meeting. **3** a course of action. **4** an action, a step in a sequence of actions. **5** a proceeding. **6** (*Comput.*) a subroutine. **procedural** *a.* **procedurally** *adv.* **proceeder** *n.* a person who proceeds, esp. to a university degree. **proceeding** *n.* **1** progress, advancement. **2** an action or line of conduct. **3** a transaction. **4** (*pl.*) events, what was going on. **5** (*pl.*) legal proceedings. **6** (*pl.*) the records of a learned society. **proceeds** (pro´-) *n.pl.* produce, material results, profits, e.g. the amount realized by the sale of goods. [F *procéder*, L *prōcēdere* (*cēdere*, to go), p.p. *prōcessus*]

pro-celebrity (prōsileb´riti) *a.* of or relating to a sporting event, esp. a golf tournament, involving professional players and showbusiness celebrities.

proceleusmatic (prosəlūsmat´ik) *a.* (in poetry) of or relating to a metrical foot of four short syllables. ~*n.* **1** a foot of four short syllables. **2** (*pl.*) verse in this metre. [late L *proceleusmaticus*, Gr. *prokeleusmatikos*, from *prokeleusma*, incitement, from *prokeleuein* (*keleuein*, to urge)]

procephalic (prōsifal´ik) *a.* of or relating to the anterior part of the head, esp. in invertebrates. [Gr. *kephalē*, head]

process[1] (prō´ses) *n.* **1** a course or method of proceeding or doing, esp. a method of operation in manufacture, scientific research etc. **2** a natural series of continuous actions, changes etc. **3** a progressive movement or state of activity, progress, course. **4** the course of proceedings in an action at law. **5** a writ or order commencing this. **6** a method of producing a printing surface by photography and mechanical or chemical means. **7** (*Anat.*, *Zool.*, *Bot.*) an outgrowth, an enlargement, a protuberance of a bone etc. ~*v.t.* **1** to subject to routine procedure, to deal with. **2** to institute legal proceedings against. **3** to serve a writ on. **4** to treat (food etc.) by a preservative or other process. **5** (*Comput.*) to perform operations on (data). **6** to reproduce by a photomechanical process. **in process of time** as time goes on. **in the process** during the carrying out (of a specified operation). **in the process of 1** engaged in. **2** undergoing. **processable** *a.* **process block** *n.* a printing block produced by photomechanical means. **process control** *n.* automatic control, by computer, of industrial processes. **processed** *a.* having undergone an industrial process, esp. a manufacturing or preserving one. **processor** *n.* **1** a person or thing that processes. **2** (*Comput.*) a device or program that processes data; a central processing unit. **3** a food processor. **process server** *n.* a sheriff's officer who serves writs or summonses. [OF *proces*, L *prōcessus*, see PROCEED]

process[2] (prəses´) *v.i.* to go in procession. [from PROCESSION]

procession (prəsesh´ən) *n.* **1** a group of persons, vehicles etc. proceeding in regular order for a ceremony, display, demonstration etc. **2** the movement of such a train. **3** (*Theol.*) the act or state of proceeding or issuing forth, emanation (as of the Holy Ghost from the Father). **4** a race in which competitors are unable to overtake each other. ~*v.i.* to go in procession. ~*v.t.* **1** to go round in procession. **2** to perambulate the bounds of. **processional** *a.* of, relating to or used in processions. ~*n.* **1** a service book giving the ritual of, or the hymns sung in, religious processions. **2** a processional hymn. **processionally** *adv.* **processionary** *a.* **processionist** *n.* a person who takes part in a procession. [F, from L *prōcessiōnem*, nom. *-sio*, from *prōcēdere*, to PROCEED]

procès-verbal (prosāvœbal´) *n.* (*pl.* **procès-verbaux** (-bō´)) **1** in French law, a written statement of particulars relating to a charge. **2** an official record of proceedings, minutes. [F, verbal process]

pro-chancellor (prōchahn´sələ) *n.* in some universities, a deputy to the vice-chancellor.

pro-choice (prōchois´) *a.* in favour of a woman's right to choose whether or not to have an abortion. **pro-choicer** *n.*

prochronism (prō´krənizm) *n.* an error in chronology dating an event before its actual occurrence. [Gr. *chronos*, time]

proclaim (prəklām´) *v.t.* **1** to announce publicly, to promulgate. **2** to declare publicly or openly, to publish. **3** to declare (war etc.). **4** to announce the accession of (a monarch). **5** to reveal or indicate. **6** to outlaw (a person) by public proclamation. **7** to put (a district etc.) under certain legal restrictions by public proclamation. **proclaimer** *n.* **proclamation** (prokləmā´shən) *n.* **proclamatory** (-klam´-) *a.* [F *proclamer*, L *prōclāmāre* (*clāmāre*, to cry out)]

proclitic (prōklit´ik) *a.* (*Gram*) (of a monosyllable) attached to and depending in accent upon a following word. ~*n.* a proclitic monosyllable. **proclitically** *adv.* [after ENCLITIC]

proclivity (prəkliv´iti) *n.* (*pl.* **proclivities**) a tendency, bent, propensity. **proclivitous** *a.* steep, abrupt. [L *prōclīvitas*, from *prōclīvus* (*clīvus*, a slope)]

proconsul (prōkon´səl) *n.* **1** (*Hist.*) a Roman magistrate, usu. an ex-consul, exercising consular power as governor of a province or commander of an army. **2** a governor or viceroy of a modern dependency etc. **3** a deputy consul. **proconsular** (-sū-) *a.* **proconsulate** (-sūlət), **proconsulship** *n.*

procrastinate (prōkras´tināt) *v.i.* **1** to put off action. **2** to be dilatory. **procrastinatingly** *adv.* **procrastination** (-ā´shən) *n.* **procrastinative, procrastinatory** *a.* **procrastinator** *n.* [L *procrastinātus*, p.p. of *procrastināre* (*crastinus*, pertaining to tomorrow)]

Usage note See note under PREVARICATE.

procreate (prō´kriāt) *v.t.* to generate, to beget. ~*v.i.* to produce offspring. **procreant** *a.* **procreation** (-ā´shən) *n.* **procreative** *a.* **procreativeness** *n.* **procreator** *n.* [L *prōcreātus*, p.p. of *prōcreāre* (*creāre*, to CREATE)]

Procrustean (prəkrŭs´tiən) *a.* reducing to strict conformity by violent measures. [Gr. *Prokroustēs* (from *prokrouein*, to hammer out), a mythical robber of Attica, who stretched or mutilated his victims till their length was exactly that of his bed]

procrypsis (prōkrip´sis) *n.* (*Biol.*) protective colouring of a plant or animal. **procryptic** *a.* **procryptically** *adv.* [Gr. *prokrupsis*, hiding, from *kruptein*, to hide]

proct- PROCTO-.

proctal (prok´təl) *a.* (*Med.*) anal, rectal.

proctalgia (proktal´jiə) *n.* pain in the anus.

proctectomy (proktek´təmi) *n.* (*pl.* **proctectomies**) excision of the rectum or anus.
proctitis (proktī´tis) *n.* inflammation of the anus or rectum.
procto- (prok´tō), **proct-** *comb.form* of or relating to the anus. [Gr. *prōktos*, anus]
proctology (proktol´eji) *n.* the branch of medicine concerned with the anus and the rectum. **proctological** (-loj´-) *a.* **proctologist** (-tol´-) *n.*
proctor (prok´tə) *n.* 1 an English University official (usu. one of two elected annually) with the duty of maintaining order and discipline. 2 (*US*) a supervisor or invigilator at examinations. 3 a person employed to manage another's cause, esp. in an ecclesiastical court. 4 in the Church of England, a representative of the clergy at a convocation. **proctorage** (-rij) *n.* management by a proctor. **proctorial** (-taw´ri-) *a.* **proctorially** *adv.* **proctorship** *n.* [a form of PROCURATOR]
proctoscope (prok´təskōp) *n.* (*Med.*) an instrument for examining the rectum. **proctoscopic** (-skop´ik) *a.* **proctoscopy** (-tos´kəpi) *n.*
procumbent (prōkŭm´bənt) *a.* 1 lying down on the face; leaning forward. 2 (*Bot.*) lying or trailing along the surface of the ground. [L *prōcumbens -ntem*, pres.p. of *prōcumbere* (*cumbere*, to lie, to lay oneself)]
procuracy PROCURATOR.
procuration (prokūrā´shən) *n.* 1 (*formal*) the act of procuring or obtaining. 2 action on behalf of another, the management of another person's affairs. 3 a document authorizing one person to act for another. 4 entertainment formerly provided, or the fee now paid in commutation of this, by the clergy for the bishop, archdeacon etc. at their visitations. 5 (*Law*) the procuring of girls for immoral purposes. [F, from L *prōcūrātiōnem*, nom. *-tio*, from *prōcūrāre*, to PROCURE]
procurator (prok´ūrātə) *n.* 1 a person who manages another's affairs, esp. those of a legal nature, an agent, a proxy, an attorney. 2 (*Hist.*) a fiscal officer in an imperial Roman province having certain administrative powers. **procuracy** (-rəsi) *n.* **procurator fiscal** *n.* (*Sc.*) the public prosecutor and coroner in a county or district. **procuratorial** (-taw´ri-) *a.* **procuratorship** *n.* **procuratory** *n.* 1 the instrument appointing a procurator. 2 a power of attorney. **procuratrix** (-triks) *n.* any of the superiors managing the temporal affairs in a nunnery. [L, as PROCURATION]
procure (prəkūə´) *v.t.* 1 to obtain, to get by some means or effort. 2 to bring about. 3 to acquire, to gain. 4 to obtain for purposes of prostitution. ~*v.i.* to act as procurer or procuress, to pimp. **procurable** *a.* **procural, procurance, procurement** *n.* **procurer** *n.* a person who procures or obtains, esp. one who procures women as prostitutes. **procuress** *n.* a woman procurer. [F *procurer*, L *prōcūrāre* (*cūrāre*, to see to, from *cūra*, care)]
Prod (prod), **Proddie** (prod´i), **Proddy** *n.* (*pl.* **Prods, Proddies**) (*sl., offensive*) a Protestant (esp. in Ireland). [short for PROTESTANT]
prod (prod) *n.* 1 a pointed instrument, a goad. 2 a poke with or as with this. 3 a stimulus to action. ~*v.t.* (*pres.p.* **prodding**, *past, p.p.* **prodded**) 1 to poke with or as with the finger or a pointed instrument. 2 to goad, to irritate, to incite. ~*v.i.* to make a prodding movement (at). **prodder** *n.* **prodnose** *n.* (*sl.*) a meddlesome person, one who pokes their nose into other people's affairs. [etym. uncertain]
prod. *abbr.* 1 produce(d). 2 product.
prod- (prod) *pref.* a form of PRO-[1] used before vowels.
Proddie, Proddy PROD.
prodigal (prod´igəl) *a.* 1 given to extravagant expenditure. 2 wasteful, lavish (of). ~*n.* a prodigal person, a spendthrift. ~†*adv.* prodigally. **prodigality** (-gal´-) *n.* 1 extravagance, profusion. 2 lavishness, waste. **prodigally** *adv.* **prodigal son** *n.* 1 a spendthrift son who repents. 2 a wanderer returned. [F (now *prodigue*), from L *prōdigus* (*agere*, to drive)]
prodigy (prod´iji) *n.* (*pl.* **prodigies**) 1 something wonderful or extraordinary. 2 a wonderful example (of). 3 a person, esp. a child, or thing with extraordinary gifts or qualities. 4 something out of the ordinary course of nature, a monstrosity. **prodigious** (-dij´-) *a.* 1 wonderful, astounding. 2 enormous in size, quality, extent etc. 3 abnormal. **prodigiously** *adv.* **prodigiousness** *n.* [L *prōdigium*, portent (*agium*, cp. ADAGE)]
prodrome (prō´drōm), **prodromus** (-drəməs) *n.* (*pl.* **prodromes, prodromi** (-drəmī)) 1 (*Med.*) a symptom of approaching disease. 2 an introductory book or treatise. **prodromal** (-drō´məl), **prodromic** (-drom´ik) *a.* [Gr. *prodromos* (*dromos*, running, from *dramein*, to run)]
produce[1] (prədūs´) *v.t.* 1 to bring into view, to bring forward. 2 to publish, to exhibit. 3 to bring into existence, to bring forth. 4 to bear, to yield. 5 to manufacture, to make. 6 to bring about, to cause. 7 (*Geom.*) to extend, to continue (a line) in the same direction. 8 to act as producer of (a play of film). **producer** *n.* 1 a person who or thing which produces. 2 a person, or an organization, that produces goods or services for sale. 3 a person who exercises general administrative and financial control over a play, film or broadcast. 4 (*esp. Hist.*) a director. 5 a furnace used for the manufacture of carbon monoxide gas. **producer gas** *n.* gas produced in a producer. **producer goods, producer's goods** *n.pl.* goods (e.g. machinery or tools) used in the production of consumer goods. **producible** *a.* **producibility** (-bil´-), †**producibleness** *n.* [L *prōdūcere* (*dūcere*, to lead)]
produce[2] (prod´ūs) *n.* 1 goods produced or yielded. 2 the result (of labour, skill etc.). 3 **a** the natural or agricultural products of a country etc. collectively. **b** the amount of this. 4 in assaying, the percentage of copper or other metal yielded by a given amount of ore. 5 materials produced from the breaking up of condemned military and naval stores. [as PRODUCE[1]]
product (prod´ŭkt) *n.* 1 that which is produced by natural processes, labour, art or mental application. 2 an effect, a result. 3 (*Math.*) the quantity obtained by multiplying two or more quantities together. 4 (*Chem.*) a compound not previously existing in a substance but produced by its decomposition. **productile** (-dŭk´tīl) *a.* capable of being extended in length. **production** (-dŭk´shən) *n.* 1 the act, or an instance, of producing, esp. as opposed to consumption. 2 the process of being manufactured. 3 a thing produced, a product. 4 the amount produced, the output. 5 in economics, the creation of goods and services with exchange value. 6 a play, film, broadcast etc., esp. in relation to its producers. 7 the work of a film etc. producer. 8 (preparation for) the public presentation of a stage work. **to make a production (out) of** (*coll.*) to make an unnecessary fuss about. **productional** *a.* **production car** *n.* a production model. **production line** *n.* a system of stage-by-stage manufacture in which a product undergoes various processes or operations as it passes along a conveyor belt. **production model** *n.* a standard mass-produced model of esp. a car. **production platform** *n.* in the offshore oil industry, a structure from which a well is drilled, which also houses production facilities. **productive** (-dŭk´-) *a.* 1 **a** producing or tending to produce. **b** giving rise to. 2 yielding in abundance, fertile. 3 in economics, producing commodities having exchangeable value. 4 (*Gram.*) of or relating to an affix which is currently much used to produce new words. **productively** *adv.* **productiveness** *n.* **productivity** (prodŭktiv´-) *n.* 1 efficiency of production. 2 the capacity to produce. 3 yield in abundance. **productivity bargaining** *n.* the negotiations which lead to a productivity deal. **productivity deal** *n.* an agreement

making wage increases dependent on increased efficiency and output. **product liability** *n.* the legal responsibility of a manufacturer if a product is faulty. **product life cycle** *n.* the four stages in the marketing of a product: introduction, growth, maturity, decline. **product placement** *n.* a form of advertising in which a product is placed very visibly in a shot in a cinema or TV film.

pro-educational (prōedūkā´shənəl) *a.* in favour of education.

proem (prō´em) *n.* a preface, a preamble, an introduction, a prelude. **proemial** (-ē´miəl) *a.* [OF *proëme* (F *proème*), L *prooemium*, Gr. *prooimion* (*oimos*, way, or *oimē*, song)]

proembryo (prōem´briō) *n.* (*pl.* **proembryos**) a cellular structure of various forms in plants from which the embryo is developed. **proembryonic** (-on´-) *a.*

proenzyme (prōen´zīm) *n.* an enzyme in its early, inactive form.

proestrus PRO-OESTRUS.

pro-European (prōūrəpē´ən) *n.* a person who is in favour of the European Union and of the UK's membership of it. ~*a.* of or relating to such people or to their opinions.

Prof. *abbr.* Professor.

prof (prof) *n.* (*coll.*) a professor at a university etc.

profane (prəfān´) *a.* **1** not sacred, not inspired, not initiated into sacred or esoteric rites or knowledge; secular. **2** (of a person) irreverent towards holy things. **3** (of language) irreverent, impious, blasphemous. **4** heathenish. **5** common, vulgar. ~*v.t.* **1** to treat with irreverence. **2** to desecrate, to violate, to pollute. **profanation** (profənā´shən) *n.* **profanely** *adv.* **profaneness** *n.* **profaner** *n.* **profanity** (-fan´-) *n.* (*pl.* **profanities**) **1** profane language, blasphemy; swearing. **2** a profane act. [F, from L *prōfānus* (*fānum*, temple, see FANE, whence *prōfānāre*, to profane]

profess (prəfes´) *v.t.* **1** to make open or public declaration of, to avow publicly. **2** to affirm one's belief in or allegiance to. **3** to affirm one's skill or proficiency in. **4** to undertake the teaching or practice of (an art, science etc.). **5** to teach (a subject) as a professor. **6** to lay claim to, to make a show of, to pretend (to be or do). **7** to receive into a religious order under vows. ~*v.i.* **1** to act as a professor. **2** to make protestations or show of. **professed** *a.* **1** avowed, declared, acknowledged. **2** pretending to be qualified (as a teacher, practitioner etc.). **3** in the Roman Catholic Church, of or relating to a religious person who has taken vows. **professedly** (-sid-) *adv.* **1** by profession. **2** avowedly. **3** pretendedly, ostensibly. **professor** *n.* **1** a public teacher of the highest rank, esp. in a university. **2** (*US*) any university or college teacher. **3** a person who makes profession, esp. of a religious faith. **professorate** (-ət) *n.* **professorial** (-saw´ri-) *a.* of, relating to or characteristic of professors. **professorially** *adv.* **professoriate** (-saw´riət) *n.* **professorship** *n.* [L *prōfessus*, p.p. of *prōfitērī* (*fatēri*, to confess)]

profession (prəfesh´ən) *n.* **1** the act of professing; a declaration, an avowal. **2** a protestation, a pretence. **3** an open acknowledgement of sentiments, religious belief etc. **4** a vow binding oneself to, or the state of being a member of, a religious order. **5** a calling, a vocation, esp. an occupation involving high educational or technical qualifications. **6** the body of persons engaged in such a vocation. **the oldest profession** (*coll.*) prostitution. **the profession** (*coll.*) actors. **professional** *a.* **1** of or relating to a profession. **2** engaging in an activity as a means of livelihood, esp. as distinct from *amateur*. **3** characterized by, or conforming to, the technical or ethical standards of a profession. **4** competent, conscientious. **5** (*derog.*) permanently or habitually undertaking some activity perceived as undesirable. ~*n.* **1** a member of a profession. **2** a person who makes a living by some art, sport etc., as distinguished from one who engages in it for pleasure. **3** a person who shows great skill and competence in any activity. **professional foul** *n.* a deliberate foul in football etc., in order to prevent the opposition from scoring. **professionalism** *n.* **1** the qualities, stamp or spirit of a professional. **2** participation by professionals, esp. in sports. **professionalize, professionalise** *v.t.* **1** to render (an activity) professional in character. **2** to allow professionals to participate in (a sport). **professionalization** (-zā´shən) *n.* **professionally** *adv.* **professionless** *a.*

professor PROFESS.

proffer (prof´ə) *v.t.* to offer or tender for acceptance. ~*n.* (*formal*) an offer, a tender. **profferer** *n.* [OF *proffrir* (*offrir*, L *offerre*, to OFFER)]

proficient (prəfish´ənt) *a.* a person well versed or skilled in any art, science etc.; expert, competent. ~*n.* a person who is proficient, an adept, an expert. **proficiency** *n.* **proficiently** *adv.* [L *proficiens -ntem*, pres.p. of *prōficere*, see PROFIT]

profile (prō´fīl) *n.* **1** an outline, a contour. **2** a side view, esp. of the human face. **3** a drawing, silhouette or other representation of this. **4** the outline of a vertical section of a building, the contour of architectural detail etc. **5** a vertical section of soil or rock showing the various layers. **6** a set of statistical data showing the salient features of some organization, e.g. a company. **7** a person's characteristic attitudes or behaviour. **8** a vertical section of a fort, rampart etc. **9** the relative thickness of a rampart etc. **10** a short biographical or character sketch. ~*v.t.* **1** to draw in profile or in vertical section. **2** to shape (stone, wood, metal etc.) to a given profile. **3** to write a profile of. **in profile** as seen from the side. **profiler** *n.* **profilist** *n.* a person who draws profiles. [It. *profilo* (now *proffilo*), from *profilare*, to draw in outline (late L *filāre*, to spin, from *fīlum*, thread)]

profit (prof´it) *n.* **1** any advantage or benefit, esp. one resulting from labour or exertion. **2** (*often pl.*) excess of receipts or returns over outlay, financial gain. **3** the portion of the gains of an industry received by the capitalist or the investors. ~*v.t.* (*pres.p.* **profiting**, *past, p.p.* **profited**) to benefit, to be of advantage to. ~*v.i.* **1** to be of advantage (to). **2** to receive benefit or advantage (by or from). **at a profit** making a financial gain. **profit and loss** income and gains credited and expenditure and losses debited in an account so as to show the net loss or profit. **profitable** *a.* **1** yielding or bringing profit or gain, lucrative. **2** advantageous, beneficial, useful. **profitability** (-bil´-) *n.* **profitableness** *n.* **profitably** *adv.* **profiteer** (-tiə´) *v.i.* to make undue profits at the expense of the public, esp. in a time of shortage or other emergency. ~*n.* a person who profiteers. **profiteering** *n.* **profitless** *a.* **profitlessly** *adv.* **profitlessness** *n.* **profit margin** *n.* the amount of profit in a business after all outgoings etc. have been deducted. **profit motive** *n.* the incentive of private profit for the production and distribution of goods. **profit-orientated** *a.* having profit as the chief motive. **profit-sharing** *n.* a system of remuneration by which the workers in an industrial concern are apportioned a percentage of the profits in order to give them an interest in the business. **profit-taking** *n.* the selling of shares etc. at a time when the selling price is expected to be at its highest. **profit-taker** *n.* [OF, from L *prōfectum*, nom. *prōfectus*, p.p. of *prōficere*, *facere*, to do]

profiterole (prəfit´ərōl) *n.* a small, hollow ball of choux pastry with a sweet filling, usu. served with chocolate sauce. [F from *profiter*, to profit]

profligate (prof´ligət) *a.* **1** licentious, dissolute. **2** wildly extravagant. ~*n.* a profligate person. **profligacy, profligateness** *n.* **profligately** *adv.* [L *prōflīgātus*, p.p. of *prōflīgāre*, to cast down (*flīgere*, to strike)]

profluent (prō´fluənt) *a.* flowing out or onwards. **profluence** *n.* [L *prōfluens -ntem*, pres.p. of *prōfluere* (*fluere*, to flow)]

pro forma (prō faw´mə) *a.*, *adv.* (done) as a matter of form, as a formality. ~*n.* a pro forma invoice. **pro forma invoice** *n.* an invoice made out in advance to show the market price of goods. [L]

profound (prəfownd´) *a.* **1** having great intellectual penetration or insight. **2** having great knowledge. **3** requiring great study or research, abstruse, recondite. **4** (of a quality etc.) deep, intense. **5** deep-seated, far below the surface. **6** reaching to or extending from a great depth. **7** coming from a great depth, deep-drawn. **8** thoroughgoing, extensive. ~*n.* **1** the depths of the earth, the abyss. **2** the deep, the ocean. **3** chaos. **profoundly** *adv.* **profoundness** *n.* **profundity** (-fŭn´di-) *n.* (*pl.* **profundities**). [OF *profund* (F *profond*), L *profundus*]

profundity PROFOUND.

profuse (prəfūs´) *a.* **1** poured out lavishly, exuberant, copious, superabundant. **2** liberal to excess, prodigal, extravagant. **profusely** *adv.* **profuseness** *n.* **profusion** (-zhən) *n.* [L *profūsus*, p.p. of *profundere* (*fundere*, to pour)]

Prog. *abbr.* Progressive.

prog[1] (prog) *n.* (*coll.*) a radio or TV programme. [short for PROGRAMME]

prog[2] (prog) *v.i.* (*pres.p.* **progging,** *past, p.p.* **progged**) **1** to poke about, esp. for food. **2** to forage, to beg. ~*n.* (*sl.*) victuals, provender, food. [etym. uncertain]

†**prog**[3] (prog) *n.* (*sl.*) a proctor at Oxford and Cambridge universities. ~*v.t.* (*pres.p.* **progging,** *past, p.p.* **progged**) to proctorize. [short for PROCTOR]

progenitor (prōjen´itə) *n.* **1** an ancestor in the direct line, a forefather, a parent. **2** a predecessor, an original. **progenitive** *a.* **1** of or relating to the bearing of offspring. **2** capable of bearing offspring. **progenitiveness** *n.* **progenitorial** (-taw´ri-) *a.* **progenitorship** *n.* **progenitress** (-tris), **progenitrix** (-triks) *n.* a female ancestor. **progeniture** (-chə) *n.* **1** the art, or an instance, of begetting, generation. **2** offspring. [MF *progeniteur*, L *prōgenitōrem*, nom. *-tor*, from *prōgignere* (*gignere*, to beget)]

progeny (proj´əni) *n.* (*pl.* **progenies**) **1** the offspring of human beings, animals or plants. **2** a child or children, descendants. **3** issue, results, consequences. [OF *progenie*, L *progeniem*, nom. *-ies*, as PROGENITOR]

progeria (prōjiə´riə) *n.* (*Med.*) a rare condition causing premature old age in children. [Gr. *gēras*, old age]

progesterone (prōjes´tərōn) *n.* a female steroid hormone that prepares and maintains the uterus for pregnancy. **progestogen** (-jən) *n.* any of a range of hormones of the progesterone type, synthetic progestogens being used in oral contraceptives. [*ge*station, *ster*ol]

proglottis (prōglot´is), **proglottid** (-id) *n.* (*pl.* **proglottides** (-dēz), **proglottids**) each of the segments making up the body of a tapeworm, forming distinct organisms with a reproductive system. **proglottic** *a.* **proglottidean** (-tid´iən) *a.* [mod. L (Gr. *glōtta*, tongue)]

prognathic (prognath´ik), **prognathous** (prog´nəthəs, -nā´thəs) *a.* **1** having the jaws projecting. **2** (of the jaws) projecting. **prognathism** (prog´-) *n.* [Gr. *gnathos*, jaw]

prognosis (prognō´sis) *n.* (*pl.* **prognoses** (-sēz)) **1** a forecast of the probable course or result of an illness. **2** a forecast, a prediction. [L and Gr. (Gr. *progignōskein*, *gignōskein*, to know)]

prognostic (prognos´tik) *n.* **1** a symptom on which a prognosis can be based. **2** a prognosis. **3** a sign or indication of a future event; an omen, a token. **4** a prediction, a forecast. ~*a.* **1** of or relating to prognosis. **2** foreshowing, indicative of something future by signs or symptoms. **prognosticable** *a.* **prognostically** *adv.* **prognosticate** *v.t.* **1** to foretell from present signs. **2** to foreshadow, to presage, to betoken. **prognostication** (-ā´shən) *n.* **prognosticative** *a.* **prognosticator** *n.* **prognosticatory** *a.* [ME and OF *pronostique*, med. L *prognōsticon*, Gr. *prognōstikon*, as PROGNOSIS]

programme (prō´gram), (*Comput.*, *N Am.*) **program** *n.* **1** (a paper, booklet etc. giving) a list of the successive items of any entertainment, public ceremony, conference, course of study etc. plus other relevant information. **2** the items on such a list. **3** a broadcast presented at a scheduled time. **4** (*Comput.*) (**program**) a sequence of instructions which, when fed into a computer, enable it to process data in specified ways. **5** a curriculum or syllabus. **6** a plan or outline of proceedings or actions to be carried out. **7** material for programmed instruction. ~*v.t.* (*pres.p.* **programming,** (*N Am. also*) **programing,** *past, p.p.* **programmed,** (*N Am. also*) **programed**) **1** to arrange a programme for. **2** to enter in a programme. **3** to cause to conform to a certain pattern, esp. of thought, behaviour. **4** (*usu.* **program**) to prepare as a program for, to feed a program into, a computer. **programmable** (-gram´-) *a.* (*Comput.*) capable of being programmed for processing by a computer. **programmability** (-bil´-) *n.* **programmatic** (-mat´-) *a.* **1** of or having a programme. **2** of, or of the nature of, programme music. **programmatically** *adv.* **programmed** *a.* **programmed instruction, programmed learning** *n.* a teaching method involving the breaking down of the subject matter into small items in a logical sequence on which students can check themselves as they proceed. **programme music** *n.* music intended to suggest a definite series of scenes, incidents etc. **programmer** *n.* (*Comput.*) a person who writes programs. **programming** *n.* **programming language** *n.* any of various code systems used in writing computer programs and giving instructions to computers. **program statement** *n.* (*Comput.*) a single instruction in a program. **program trading** *n.* a method of trading on international stock exchanges, using a computer to buy or sell stock automatically when the price reaches a predetermined level. **program trader** *n.* [F, from L and Gr. *programma* (*graphein*, to write)]

progress[1] (prō´gres) *n.* **1** a moving or going forward; movement onward, advance. **2** advance towards completion, a specified destination, fruition or a higher state. **3** increased proficiency. **4** (*Biol.*) growth, development. **5** (*Hist.*) a journey of state, esp. by royalty. **in progress** going on, developing, proceeding. **progress-chaser** *n.* a person employed to check at each stage in a manufacturing etc. process that the work is on schedule. **progress-chasing** *n.* **progressist** (prō´-, prog´-, -gres´-) *a.* advocating progress, esp. in politics. ~*n.* a progressive, a reformer. **progressively** *adv.* **progress payment** *n.* an instalment of a larger payment for a job, made when the work has reached a specified stage. **progress report** *n.* a report setting out the progress that has been made in a project. [ME, from L *prōgressus*, p.p. of *prōgredī*, to step forward, to advance (*gradī*, to step, walk)]

progress[2] (prəgres´) *v.i.* **1** to move forward, to advance; to be carried on, to proceed. **2 a** to advance, to develop. **b** to make improvement. **3** (*Hist.*) to travel in state. ~*v.t.* to cause (a project, a career etc.) to advance steadily. **progression** (-gresh´ən) *n.* **1** the act, or an instance, of progressing. **2** progress, motion onward; movement in successive stages. **3** a regular succession of notes or chords in melody or harmony. **4** regular or proportional advance by increase or decrease of numbers. **progressional** *a.* **progressionism** *n.* **progressionist** *n.* **1** a believer in, or advocate of, social and political progress. **2** a person who believes in the perfectibility of man and society. **3** a person who believes that organisms have advanced from lower to higher forms, an evolutionist. **progressive** (-gres´-) *a.* **1** moving forward or onward;

advancing. 2 improving. 3 (of a disease) increasing in extent or severity. 4 (of taxation) at a rate which increases as the taxable sum increases. 5 in a state of progression, proceeding step by step, successive. 6 continuously increasing. 7 a believing in or advocating social and political reform. b modern or efficient. 8 (of a dance or a card game) involving a change of partner every so often. 9 denoting an educational system which allows flexibility and takes the needs and abilities of the individual child as its determinant. 10 (*Gram.*) denoting a verb form which expresses action in progress. ~*n.* 1 a progressive person. 2 (*usu.* **Progressive**) an adherent of a party called progressive. 3 the progressive form of a verb. **progressiveness** *n.* **progressive whist, progressive bridge** *n.* whist or bridge played by a number of sets of players at different tables, each winning player moving to another table at the end of each hand or series of hands. **progressivism** *n.* the principles of a progressive or reformer. **progressivist** *n.* [as PROGRESS[1]]

pro hac vice (prō hak vī´sē) *adv.* for this occasion only. [L]

prohibit (prəhib´it) *v.t.* (*pres.p.* **prohibiting,** *past, p.p.* **prohibited**) 1 to forbid authoritatively, to interdict. 2 to hinder, to prevent. **prohibited degrees** *n.pl.* FORBIDDEN DEGREES (under FORBID). **prohibiter, prohibitor** *n.* **prohibition** (prōibish´-) *n.* 1 the act, or an instance, of prohibiting. 2 an order or edict prohibiting. 3 (*Law*) a writ from a superior court forbidding an inferior court from proceeding in a matter beyond its jurisdiction. 4 the forbidding by law of the manufacture and the sale of intoxicating liquors for consumption as beverages. **prohibitionary** *a.* **prohibitionist** *n.* a person in favour of prohibiting the sale of intoxicating liquors. **prohibitionism** *n.* **prohibitive** *a.* 1 tending to prohibit or preclude. 2 (of costs, prices etc.) such as to debar purchase, use etc. **prohibitively** *adv.* **prohibitiveness** *n.* **prohibitory** *a.* [L *prōhibitus,* p.p. of *prōhibēre* (*habēre,* to have)]

project[1] (proj´ekt, prō´-) *n.* 1 a plan, a scheme, a design. 2 an (esp. large-scale) planned undertaking. 3 a piece of work undertaken by a pupil or group of pupils to supplement and apply classroom studies. [MF (F *projet*), L *prōjectum,* neut. p.p. of *prōicere* (*jacere,* to throw)]

project[2] (prəjekt´) *v.t.* 1 to throw or shoot forward. 2 to cause to extend forward or jut out. 3 to cast (light, shadow, an image) on to a surface or into space. 4 to enable (one's voice) to be heard at a distance. 5 to express or present (oneself) in a way that creates a favourable image. 6 to transport (oneself) in the imagination. 7 to predict or expect (something) based on known data. 8 to impute (something in one's own mind) to another person, group or entity. 9 to contrive, to plan (a course of action etc.). 10 to make (an idea etc.) objective. 11 a (*Geom.*) to draw straight lines from a given centre through every point of (a figure) so as to form a corresponding figure on a surface. b to draw (such lines). c to produce (such a projection). 12 to make a projection of (the earth, sky etc.). ~*v.i.* 1 to jut out, to protrude. 2 to make oneself audible at a distance. 3 to communicate effectively. 4 to express one's personality so as to create a favourable impression. **projectile** (-´tīl) *n.* 1 a body (e.g. a bullet, a spear) projected or thrown forward with force. 2 a self-propelling missile, esp. one adapted for discharge from a heavy gun. ~*a.* 1 impelling forward. 2 adapted to be forcibly projected, esp. from a gun. **projection** *n.* 1 the act or state of projecting, protruding, throwing or impelling. 2 a part or thing that projects, a prominence. 3 the act of planning. 4 the process of externalizing an idea or making it objective. 5 a mental image viewed as an external object. 6 the process whereby one ascribes to others one's own mental factors and attributes. 7 the showing of films or slides by projecting images from them on to a screen. 8 a prediction based on known data. 9 the making of such a prediction. 10 the geometrical projecting of a figure. 11 the representation of the terrestrial or celestial sphere, or a part of it, on a plane surface. 12 in alchemy, the casting of a substance into a crucible. 13 the transmutation of metals. **projectional** *a.* **projectionist** *n.* a person who operates a film projector. **projection room** *n.* a small room behind the auditorium in a cinema where the projectors are operated. **projection television** *n.* the optical projecting of a TV picture on to a separate, large screen. **projective** *a.* 1 of, relating to or derived from projection. 2 (*Geom.*) such that they may be derived from one another by projection (of two plane figures). 3 (*Psych.*) externalizing or making objective. **projective geometry** *n.* the branch of geometry dealing with those properties of figures that are unchanged under projection. **projectively** *adv.* **projective property** *n.* a property that remains unchanged after projection. **projectivity** (-tiv´-) *n.* **projectment** *n.* a scheme, a design, a contrivance. **projector** *n.* 1 an apparatus for projecting rays of light, images, slides or cinema films on to a screen. 2 a person who forms schemes. 3 a promoter, esp. of speculative companies. †**projecture** *n.* 1 a projecting or jutting out. 2 a projection, a prominence. [as PROJECT[1]]

prokaryote (prōkar´iot), **procaryote** *n.* an organism whose cells have no distinct nucleus, their genetic material being carried in a single filament of DNA. **prokaryotic** (-ot´ik) *a.* [Gr. *karyon,* a kernel]

prolactin (prōlak´tin) *n.* a hormone produced by the pituitary gland, which stimulates lactation. [L *lac lactis,* milk]

prolamine (prō´ləmēn) *n.* any one of a group of simple plant proteins, which are alcohol-soluble. [*prol*ine, *am*monia]

prolapse (prō´laps, -laps´) *n.* 1 a falling down or slipping out of place of an organ or part, such as the uterus or rectum. 2 the displaced organ or part. ~*v.i.* to fall down or out. **prolapsus** (-lap´səs) *n.* a prolapse. ~*v.i.* to undergo prolapse. [late L *prōlapsus,* from L *prōlaps-,* p.p. stem of *prōlābī* (*lābī,* to slip)]

prolate (prō´lāt) *a.* 1 (*Geom.*) extended in the direction of the longer axis, elongated in the polar diameter, as distinct from *oblate.* 2 widespread; growing in width. 3 (*Gram.*) prolative. **prolately** *adv.* **prolateness** *n.* **prolative** (-lā´-, prō´-) *a.* (*Gram.*) extending or completing the predicate. [L *prōlātus* (*lātus,* p.p. of *ferre,* to bear)]

prole (prōl) *n., a.* (*coll., derog.*) PROLETARIAN.

proleg (prō´leg) *n.* any one of the soft, fleshy appendages or abdominal limbs of caterpillars etc., distinct from the true legs.

prolegomenon (prōligom´inən) *n.* (*pl.* **prolegomena** (-inə)) (*usu. pl.*) an introductory or preliminary discourse prefixed to a book etc. **prolegomenary, prolegomenous** *a.* [Gr., neut. p.p. of *prolegein* (*legein,* to say)]

prolepsis (prōlep´sis) *n.* (*pl.* **prolepses** (-sēz)) 1 anticipation. 2 a rhetorical figure by which objections are anticipated or prevented. 3 the anticipatory use of a word as attributive instead of as a predicate, as in *their murdered man* for *the man they intended to murder.* 4 prochronism. **proleptic, proleptical** *a.* **proleptically** *adv.* [L and Gr. *prolēpsis* (Gr. *lambanein,* to take)]

proletarian (prōlətea´riən) *a.* of or relating to the common people. ~*n.* a member of the proletariat. **proletarianism** *n.* **proletarianize, proletarianise** *v.t.* **proletarianization** (-zā´shən) *n.* **proletariat** (-riət, -at), **proletariate** *n.* 1 wage earners collectively, people without property who sell their labour. 2 (*derog.*) the lowest and most uncultured class. 3 (*Hist.*) the lowest class of Roman citizens. **proletary** (prō´-) *a., n.* (a) proletarian. [L *prōlētārius,* one of the lowest class of citizens, one whose only property is his children, from *prōles*, offspring]

pro-life (prōlīf´) *a.* favouring greater restrictions on the availability of legal abortions and/or a ban on the use of human embryos for experimental purposes. **pro-lifer** *n.*

proliferate (prəlif´ərāt) *v.i.* **1** to grow or reproduce itself by budding or multiplication of parts. **2** to grow or increase rapidly and abundantly. **3** to become more widespread. ~*v.t.* to produce (cells etc.) by proliferation. **proliferation** (-ā´shən) *n.* **proliferative** *a.* **proliferator** *n.* **proliferous** *a.* **1** producing buds, shoots etc. from leaves, flowers etc. **2** producing new individuals from buds, parts etc. **3** spreading by proliferation. **proliferously** *adv.* [med. L *prōlifer* (*prōles*, see PROLETARIAN, *-fer*, bearing)]

prolific (prəlif´ik) *a.* **1** producing offspring, esp. abundantly. **2** fruitful, productive, fertile. **3** abounding (in). **4** very productive (of). **5** (*Bot.*) bearing fertile seed. **prolificacy** *n.* **prolifically** *adv.* **prolificity** (prolifis´-), **prolificness** *n.* [F *prolifique*, L *prōlificus* (*prōles*, offspring)]

proline (prō´lēn) *n.* an amino acid occurring in proteins, esp. collagen. [short for *pyrrolidine*, name of a chemical]

prolix (prō´liks) *a.* **1** long and wordy. **2** tedious, tiresome, diffuse. **prolixity** (-lik´si-), **prolixness** *n.* **prolixly** *adv.* [F *prolixe*, L *prōlixus*, *-lixus*, p.p. of (*liquēre*, to flow)]

prolocutor (prōlok´ūtə) *n.* **1** a chairperson or speaker, esp. of the lower houses of convocation in the Church of England. **2** a spokesperson. **prolocutorship** *n.* [L, from *prōloquī* (*loquī*, to speak, p.p. *locūtus*)]

Prolog (prō´log), **PROLOG** *n.* (*Comput.*) a high-level programming language used esp. in artificial intelligence and expert systems. [*pro*gramming *log*ic]

prologue (prō´log), (*N Am.*) **prolog** *n.* **1** an introductory discourse, esp. lines introducing a play. **2** an act or event forming an introduction to some proceeding or occurrence. **3** the speaker of a prologue. ~*v.t.* (*3rd pers. sing. pres.* **prologues,** (*N Am.*) **prologs,** *pres.p.* **prologuing,** (*N Am.*) **prologing,** *past, p.p.* **prologued,** (*N Am.*) **prologed** (-logd)) to introduce with a prologue. **prologist** (-jist) *n.* **prologize** (-gīz), **prologise, prologuize, prologuise** *v.t.* to introduce, to preface. ~*v.i.* to write or speak a prologue. [F, from L *prologus*, Gr. *prologos*, *logos*, speech)]

prolong (prəlong´) *v.t.* **1** to extend in duration (an action or a state). **2** to lengthen, to extend in space or distance. **3** to lengthen the pronunciation of. **prolongable** *a.* †**prolongate** (-gāt) *v.t.* **prolongation** (prōlong·gā´shən) *n.* **1** the act of lengthening or extending. **2** a lengthening in time or space. **3** the part by which anything is lengthened. **prolonged** *a.* lengthy. **prolongedly** (-idli) *adv.* **prolonger** *n.* [F *prolonger*, late L *prōlongāre* (*longāre*, from *longus*, LONG[1])]

prolonge (prəlonj´) *n.* a rope in three pieces connected by rings with a hook at one end and a toggle at the other, used for moving a gun etc. [F, as PROLONG]

prolusion (prəloo´zhən) *n.* (*formal*) **1** a prelude. **2** a preliminary essay, exercise or attempt. **prolusory** (-səri) *a.* [L *prōlūsio*, from *prōlūdere* (*lūdere*, to play)]

PROM (prom) *abbr.* (*Comput.*) programmable read-only memory.

prom (prom) *n.* (*coll.*) **1** a paved promenade. **2** a promenade concert. **3** (*N Am.*) a dance at a school etc. [short for PROMENADE]

pro-marketeer (prōmahkətiə´) *n.* a person who is in favour of the Common Market (European Union) and the UK's membership of it.

promenade (promənahd´, prom´-) *n.* **1** a walk, drive, or ride for pleasure, exercise or display. **2** a place for promenading, esp. a paved terrace on a seafront. **3** any paved public walk. **4** a processional sequence in a square or country dance. **5** (*N Am.*) a dance at a college, school, unit or association. ~*v.i.* **1** to take a walk etc. for pleasure, exercise or show. **2** to perform a promenade in dancing. ~*v.t.* **1** to take a promenade along, about or through (a place). **2** to lead (a person) about, esp. for display. **promenade concert, promenade performance** *n.* a concert or performance at which part of the floor of the hall is left bare for the audience to stand and to walk about. **promenade deck** *n.* an upper deck on a ship where passengers may stroll. **promenader** *n.* **1** a standing member of the audience at a promenade concert or performance. **2** a person who regularly attends promenade concerts. [F, from *promener*, to walk, late L *prōmināre*, to drive (*mināre*, to threaten)]

promethazine (prōmeth´əzēn) *n.* an antihistamine drug used to treat allergies, travel sickness etc. [*pro*pyl, di*methy*lamine, phenothi*azine*]

Promethean (prəmē´thiən) *a.* of, relating to or like Prometheus; original, creative, daring. **promethium** (-thiəm) *n.* a radioactive metallic element, at. no. 61, chem. symbol Pm, obtained as a fission product of uranium. [Gr. *Promētheus*, son of Iapetus, said to have stolen fire from Olympus, and to have bestowed it on mortals, teaching them the use of it and the arts of civilization]

prominent (prom´inənt) *a.* **1** standing out, jutting, projecting, protuberant. **2** conspicuous. **3** distinguished. ~*n.* a prominent moth. **prominence, prominency** *n.* **1** the state of being prominent. **2** something which is prominent, such as an outcrop. **3** a cloud of incandescent gas erupting from the surface of the sun which can be seen during an eclipse. **prominently** *adv.* **prominent moth** *n.* a moth of the family Notodontidae, having tufts of scales on the forewing. [F, from L *prōminentem*, nom. *-ens*, pres.p. of *prōminēre*, to project (*minēre*, from *minae*, projections, threats)]

prominenti (prominen´tē) *n.pl.* distinguished or important people. [It., pl. of *prominente*, prominent]

promiscuous (prəmis´kūəs) *a.* **1** indulging in casual indiscriminate sexual intercourse. **2** mixed together in a disorderly manner. **3** of different kinds mingled confusedly together. **4** not restricted to a particular person, kind etc. **5** (*coll.*) fortuitous, accidental, casual, heedless. **promiscuity** (promiskū´-) *n.* **1** sexual promiscuousness. **2** indiscriminate or disorderly mingling. **promiscuously** *adv.* **promiscuousness** *n.* [L *prōmiscuus* (*miscēre*, to MIX)]

promise (prom´is) *n.* **1** a verbal or written engagement to do or forbear from doing some specific act. **2** something which is promised. **3** a ground or basis of expectation, esp. of success, improvement or excellence. ~*v.t.* **1** to engage to do or not to do (something). **2** to engage to give or procure (something). **3** to make a promise of something to. **4** to give good grounds for expecting. **5** (*usu. pass.*) to engage to marry, to betroth. ~*v.i.* **1** to bind oneself by a promise. **2** to give grounds for favourable expectations. **to promise ill** to hold out unfavourable prospects. **to promise oneself** to look forward to (something pleasant). **to promise well** to hold out favourable prospects. **promise-breaker** *n.* a person who violates their promises. **promised land** *n.* **1** any place of expected happiness or prosperity. **2** heaven. **3** the land of Canaan promised to Abraham and his seed. **promisee** (-sē´) *n.* (*Law*) a person to whom a promise is made. **promiser** *n.* **promising** *a.* **1** giving grounds for expectation or hope, likely to turn out well. **2** hopeful, favourable. **promisingly** *adv.* **promisor** *n.* (*Law*) a person who enters into a covenant. **promissory** *a.* containing, or of the nature of, a promise, esp. a promise to pay money. **promissory note** *n.* a signed engagement to pay a sum of money to a specified person or the bearer at a stated date or on demand. [L *prōmissum*, neut. p.p. of *prōmittere* (*mittere*, to send)]

prommer (prom´ə) *n.* (*coll.*) a person who attends a promenade concert, esp. regularly. [short for PROMENADER (under PROMENADE)]

promo (prō´mō) *n.* (*pl.* **promos**) (*coll.*) something used to promote a product, esp. a pop video. ~*a.* promotional. [short for PROMOTION (under PROMOTE)]

promontory (prom´əntəri) *n.* (*pl.* **promontories**) **1** a headland, a point of high land projecting into the sea. **2** (*Anat.*) a rounded protuberance. **promontoried** *a.* [L *prōmontōrium* (*mons montis*, MOUNT[2])]

promote (prəmōt´) *v.t.* **1** to raise to a higher rank or position, to exalt, to prefer. **2** to transfer (a sports team) to a higher division of a league etc. **3** to forward, to advance, to contribute to the growth, increase or advancement of. **4** to support, to foster, to encourage. **5** to bring to the notice of the public, to encourage the sale of (a product) by advertising. **6** to help to ensure the passing of (an act of parliament). **7** in chess, to raise (a pawn) to the rank of queen. **promotable** *a.* **promotability** (-bil´-) *n.* **promoter** *n.* **1** a person who or thing which promotes or furthers. **2** a person who organizes a sporting event, esp. a boxing match. **3** a company promoter. **4** (*Chem.*) a substance which increases the efficiency of a catalyst. **5** the plaintiff in an ecclesiastical suit. **promotion** *n.* **1** advancement in position. **2** furtherance, encouragement. **3** a venture, esp. in show business. **4** (an advertising campaign, special offer etc., intended as a means of) bringing a product, or a person to public notice. **on promotion 1** awaiting, expecting or preparing oneself for promotion. **2** on one's best behaviour. **promotional** *a.* **promotive** *a.* [L *prōmōtus*, p.p. of *prōmovēre*, *movēre* (to MOVE)]

prompt (prompt) *a.* **1** acting quickly or ready to act as occasion demands. **2** done, made or said with alacrity, or at once. **3** (of a payment) made without delay. ~*adv.* punctually. ~*n.* **1 a** the act of prompting, or the thing said to prompt an actor etc. **b** a person who prompts in a theatre etc. **2** time allowed for payment of a debt as stated in a prompt-note. **3** (*Comput.*) a reminder to an operator, in the form of a question or statement appearing on the VDU, that the system is ready for input. ~*v.t.* **1** to urge or incite (to action or to do); to instigate. **2** to suggest to the mind, to inspire, to excite (thoughts, feelings etc.). **3** to assist (a speaker, actor etc.) when at a loss, by suggesting the words forgotten. ~*v.i.* to supply an actor etc. with forgotten words. **prompt book** *n.* a copy of a play for the use of the prompter at a theatre. **prompt box** *n.* a box at the front of the stage below the footlights, where the prompter sits. **prompter** *n.* a person who prompts, esp. one employed at a theatre to prompt actors. **prompting** *n.* **promptitude** (-titūd), **promptness** *n.* **promptly** *adv.* **prompt-note** *n.* a note reminding a purchaser of a sum due and the date of payment. **prompt side** *n.* the side of a stage on which the prompter stands, usu. to the left of the actor in Britain and to the right in the US. [F, from L *promptum*, nom. *-tus*, p.p. of *prōmere* (*emere*, to take)]

promulgate (prom´əlgāt) *v.t.* **1** to make known to the public; to disseminate; to announce publicly. **2** to put (a law etc.) into effect by proclaiming it. **promulgation** (-gā´shən) *n.* **promulgator** (prom´-) *n.* †**promulge** (-mŭlj´) *v.t.* †**promulger** *n.* [L *prōmulgātus*, p.p. of *prōmulgāre*, etym. uncertain, perh. corr. of *prōvulgāre* (*vulgus*, the crowd)]

promycelium (prōmīsē´liəm) *n.* (*pl.* **promycelia** (-liə)) (*Bot.*) a short tubular growth from some fungal spores, which itself produces spores. **promycelial** *a.*

pron. *abbr.* **1** pronoun. **2** pronounced. **3** pronunciation.

pronaos (prōnā´os) *n.* (*pl.* **pronaoi** (-nā´oi)) **1** (*Hist.*) the area immediately before a Greek or Roman temple enclosed by the portico. **2** a vestibule. [L and Gr. (*naos*, temple)]

pronate (prō´nāt) *v.t.* to lay (a hand or forelimb) prone so as to have the palm downwards, as distinct from *supinate*. **pronation** (-nā´shən) *n.* **pronator** *n.* (*Anat.*) any muscle used to turn the palm downwards. [late L *prōnātus*, p.p. of *prōnāre*, from *prōnus*, PRONE]

prone (prōn) *a.* **1** leaning or bent forward or downward. **2** lying with the face downward, as distinct from *supine*. **3** lying flat, prostrate. **4** sloping downwards, descending steeply or vertically. **5** disposed, inclined, apt (esp. in comb., as *accident-prone*). **pronely** *adv.* **proneness** *n.* [L *prōnus*]

pronephros (prōnef´ros) *n.* (*pl.* **pronephroi** (-roi), **pronephra** (-rə)) (*Zool.*) in vertebrates, the anterior part of the embryonic kidney, nonfunctional, or absent, in the adult.

proneur (prōnœ´) *n.* a flatterer. [F *prôneur*, from *prôner*, to flatter]

prong (prong) *n.* **1** any one of the spikes of a fork. **2** a sharp-pointed instrument or spikelike projection. **3** (*dial.*) a forked instrument. ~*v.t.* **1** to pierce, stab or prick with a prong. **2** to dig (soil) with a fork. **3** to provide with prongs. **prongbuck, pronghorn, pronghorned antelope** *n.* a N American ruminant, *Antilocapra americana*. **pronged** *a.* [etym. uncertain]

pronominal (prōnom´inəl) *a.* **1** (*Gram.*) of, relating to or of the nature of a pronoun. **2** serving as a pronoun. **pronominalize, pronominalise** *v.t.* **pronominalization** (-zā´shən) *n.* **pronominally** *adv.* [late L *prōnōminālis*, from *prōnōmen -minis*, pronoun]

pronotum (prənō´təm) *n.* (*pl.* **pronota** (-tə)) the dorsal part of the prothorax of an insect. **pronotal** *a.* [mod. L (Gr. *nōton*, back)]

pronoun (prō´nown) *n.* (*Gram.*) a word used in place of a noun to denote a person or thing already mentioned or implied. [after L *prōnōmen* or F *pronom*]

pronounce (prənowns´) *v.t.* **1** to utter articulately, to say correctly. **2** to utter formally, officially or rhetorically (a judgement, a curse etc.). **3** to declare, to affirm. ~*v.i.* **1** to articulate sounds or words. **2** to declare one's opinion (on, for, against etc.). **pronounceable** *a.* **pronounceability** (-bil´-) *n.* **pronounced** *a.* **1** strongly marked, emphatic, decided. **2** conspicuous, obvious. **pronouncedly** (-sid-) *adv.* **pronouncement** *n.* a statement. **pronouncer** *n.* **pronunciation** (-nŭnsiā´shən) *n.* **1** the act, or an instance, of pronouncing words etc. **2** the correct pronouncing of words etc. **3** a person's way of pronouncing. [ME *pronunce*, OF *pronuncier*, late L *prōnuntiāre* (*nuntiāre*, to announce, from *nuntius*, messenger)]

Usage note Pronunciation of *pronunciation* as (prənown´siāshən) (after *pronounce*) and the corresponding spelling *pronounciation* are best avoided.

---

pronto (pron´tō) *adv.* (*coll.*) without delay; quickly. [Sp., from L *promptus*, quick]

pronuclear[1] (prōnū´kliə) *a.* in favour of the use of nuclear power. **pronuclearist** *n.*

pronuclear[2] PRONUCLEUS.

pronucleus (prōnū´kliəs) *n.* (*pl.* **pronuclei** (-kliī)) (*Biol.*) the nucleus of a germ cell before fertilization. **pronuclear**[2] *a.*

pronunciamento (prənŭnsiəmen´tō) *n.* (*pl.* **pronunciamentos**) a manifesto, a proclamation, esp. one issued by revolutionaries in Spanish-speaking countries. [Sp.]

pronunciation PRONOUNCE.

pro-nuncio (prōnŭn´siō, -shō) *n.* (*pl.* **pro-nuncios**) a papal ambassador of lower status than a nuncio.

pro-oestrus (prōēs´trəs), (*N Am.*) **proestrus** *n.* in mammals, the phase in the oestrus cycle immediately before oestrus.

proof (proof) *n.* 1 the act of proving, a test, a trial. 2 testing, assaying, experiment. 3 demonstration. 4 a sequence of steps establishing the correctness of a mathematical or logical proposition. 5 convincing evidence of the truth or falsity of a statement, charge etc., esp. oral or written evidence submitted in the trial of a cause. 6 (*Sc. Law*) evidence taken before a judge, or a trial before a judge instead of by jury. 7 the state or quality of having been proved or tested. 8 (*Hist.*) proved impenetrability, esp. of armour. 9 a standard degree of strength in distilled spirits. 10 (*Print.*) a trial impression from type for correction. 11 an impression of an engraving taken with special care before the ordinary issue is printed. 12 a first or early impression of a photograph, coin, medal etc. ~*a.* 1 proved or tested as to strength, firmness etc. 2 impenetrable. 3 able to resist physically or morally. 4 used in testing, verifying etc. 5 of a certain degree of alcoholic strength. ~*v.t.* 1 to make proof, esp. waterproof. 2 to make a proof of (printed matter, an engraving etc.). **above proof** (of alcoholic liquor) of a stronger than standard strength. **proof before letters** *n.* a proof taken of an engraving etc. before the inscription is appended. **proofer** *n.* **proofing** *n.* **proofless** *a.* **proof-plane** *n.* a disc-shaped conductor with an insulating handle used in measuring the electrification of a body. **proof positive** *n.* convincing proof. **proof-read** *v.t.* (*past, p.p.* **proof-read** (-red)) to read and correct (printer's proofs). **proof-reader** *n.* **proof-reading** *n.* **proof-sheet** *n.* a sheet of printer's proof. **proof spirit** *n.* a mixture of alcohol and water containing a standard amount of alcohol, in Britain 57.1% by volume. [ME *preove, preve,* OF *prueve,* late L *proba,* from *probāre,* to PROVE]

-proof (proof) *comb. form* (to make) resistant, impervious, immune to, as *rainproof, soundproof.*

pro-otic (prō´otik) *a.* (*Anat.*) in front of the ear. ~*n.* each one of three bones usually found in the skulls of lower vertebrates.

prop[1] (prop) *n.* 1 a rigid support, esp. a loose or temporary one; a buttress, a pillar, a stay. 2 a person supporting a cause etc. 3 a prop forward. ~*v.t.* (*pres.p.* **propping,** *past, p.p.* **propped**) 1 to support or hold (up) with or as with a prop. 2 to support, to hold up (of a prop). **to prop up** 1 to support in an upright position. 2 to keep going with financial etc. help. **prop forward** *n.* in rugby, either of the two forwards supporting the hooker in the front row of the scrum. [ME *proppe,* cp. Dut. *proppe,* etym. uncertain]

prop[2] (prop) *n.* a stage property. **props** *n.* (*also* **props man, props mistress**) PROPERTY MAN (under PROPERTY).

prop[3] (prop) *n.* (*coll.*) an aeroplane propeller. **prop-fan** *n.* (an aircraft with) a jet engine having turbine-driven, rear-mounted, propellers. **prop-jet** *n.* TURBOPROP (under TURBO-).

prop[4] (prop) *v.i.* (*pres.p.* **propping,** *past, p.p.* **propped**) (*Austral., coll.*) (of a horse) to come to a sudden halt, to pull up sharply. ~*n.* such an action. [prob. PROP[1]]

prop. *abbr.* 1 proper(ly). 2 property. 3 proprietor. 4 proposition.

propaedeutic (prōpēdū´tik) *a.* of, relating to or of the nature of introductory or preparatory study. **propaedeutical** *a.* **propaedeutics** *n.pl.* preliminary learning or instruction introductory to any art or science. [Gr. *propaideuein* (*paideuein,* to teach, from *pais paidos,* child)]

propagable PROPAGATE.

propaganda (propəgan´də) *n.* 1 (*often derog.*) information, ideas, opinions etc. propagated as a means of winning support for, or fomenting opposition to, a government, cause, institution etc. 2 an organization, scheme or other means of propagating such information etc. 3 (**Propaganda**) in the Roman Catholic Church, a congregation of cardinals charged with all matters connected with foreign missions. **propagandist** *n.* a person devoted to, or engaged in, propaganda. ~*a.* propagandistic. **propagandism** *n.* **propagandistic** (-dis´-) *a.* 1 consisting of propaganda. 2 spreading propaganda. **propagandistically** *adv.* **propagandize, propagandise** *v.t.* 1 to spread by propaganda. 2 to subject to propaganda. ~*v.i.* to spread propaganda. [PROPAGATE]

propagate (prop´əgāt) *v.t.* 1 to cause to multiply by natural generation or other means; to reproduce. 2 to hand down (a characteristic) to the next generation. 3 to cause to spread or extend. 4 to diffuse, to disseminate. 5 to impel forward, to transmit, to cause to extend in space. ~*v.i.* 1 to be reproduced or multiplied by natural generation or other means. 2 to have offspring. **propagable** *a.* **propagation** (-ā´shən) *n.* 1 the act, or an instance, of propagating. 2 dissemination, diffusing. 3 extension or transmission through space. **propagative** *a.* **propagator** *n.* 1 a person or thing that propagates. 2 a heated, covered box for growing plants from seed or cuttings. [L *prōpāgātus,* p.p. of *prōpāgāre,* to propagate by layers (*pāg-,* stem of *pangere,* to set, to fix)]

propagule (prop´əgūl), **propagulum** (prōpag´ūləm) *n.* a small part of a plant, esp. a bud, which becomes detached and grows into a new plant. [L, from *prōpāgāre,* see PROPAGATE]

propane (prō´pān) *n.* a flammable, gaseous hydrocarbon used as fuel. **propanoate** (-pan´ōāt) *n.* **propanoic acid** *n.* PROPIONIC ACID. **propanol** *n.* propyl alcohol. **propanone** *n.* acetone.

proparoxytone (prōpərok´sitōn) *a.* (*Gram.*) (in ancient Greek) having an acute accent on the antepenultimate syllable. ~*n.* a proparoxytone word. [Gr. *proparoxutonos*]

pro patria (prō pat´riə) *adv.* for one's country. [L]

propel (prəpel´) *v.t.* (*pres.p.* **propelling,** *past, p.p.* **propelled**) 1 to drive forward; to cause to move forward or onward. 2 to urge on, to encourage. **propellant** *a.* propellent. ~*n.* something which propels, esp. the fuel mixture used by a rocket engine, the gas in an aerosol, or the explosive charge in a gun. **propellent** *a.* propelling; capable of propelling. **propeller** *n.* 1 a person who or thing which propels. 2 a rotating device, usu. consisting of two to four blades set at an angle and twisted like the thread of a screw, at the end of a shaft driven by steam, electricity etc., for propelling a vessel through the water or an aeroplane or airship through air. **propeller shaft** *n.* the shaft which transmits from an engine to a propeller in an aircraft or ship, or from a gearbox to the driving axle in a motor vehicle. **propeller turbine** *n.* a turboprop. **propelling pencil** *n.* a pencil having a metal or plastic casing which, when turned, extends or retracts a replaceable lead. **propelment** *n.* [L *prōpellere* (*pellere,* to drive)]

†**propend** (prəpend´) *v.t.* to incline, to have a leaning or propensity. [L *prōpendēre* (*pendēre,* to hang)]

propene (prō´pēn) *n.* (*Chem.*) propylene.

propensity (prəpen´siti) *n.* (*pl.* **propensities**) bent, natural tendency, inclination. [L *prōpensus,* inclined, p.p. of *prōpendēre,* as PROPEND]

proper (prop´ə) *a.* 1 belonging or pertaining exclusively or peculiarly (to). 2 correct, just, accurate. 3 suitable, appropriate; fit, becoming. 4 decent, respectable; strictly decorous. 5 (*usu. following its noun*) real, genuine, according to strict definition. 6 own. 7 †well-made, good-looking. 8 (*coll.*) thorough, complete. 9 (of a psalm, a lesson etc.) used only on a particular day or season. 10 (*Her.*) in the natural colours. ~*n.* the part of a church service which varies according to the liturgical calendar. ~*adv.* (*coll.*) 1 completely, exceedingly. 2 correctly, genteelly. **proper fraction** *n.* a fraction less than unity. **properly** *adv.* 1 in a proper manner, fitly, suitably. 2 rightly, justly, correctly, accurately. 3 (*coll.*)

thoroughly, quite. **proper motion** *n.* (*Astron.*) part of the apparent motion of a star, responsible for the star's change of position relative to the sun over a long period of time. **proper name, proper noun** *n.* a name or noun designating an individual person, animal, place etc., as distinct from a *common noun.* **properness** *n.* **proper pride** *n.* a person's sense of dignity or self-respect. [ME and OF *propre,* L *proprium,* nom. *proprius,* one's own]

properdin (prōpœ´din) *n.* a protein found in blood serum which plays a part in the destruction of viruses, bacteria etc. [L *perdere,* to destroy]

properispomenon (prəperispom´inən) *a.* (*Gram.*) (in ancient Greek) having the circumflex accent on the penultimate syllable. ~*n.* a properispomenon word. [Gr. *properispōmenon*]

property (prop´əti) *n.* (*pl.* **properties**) **1** something which is owned; a possession, possessions, a piece of real estate. **2** a peculiar or inherent quality. **3** character, nature. **4** (*Law*) exclusive right of possession, ownership. **5** (*pl.*) articles required for the production of a play on the stage. **6** (*Logic*) an attribute which is common to a whole class, but not essential to it. **propertied** *a.* possessing property, esp. land. **property band** *n.* each of the ranges of house values on which council tax liability is calculated. **property man, property master, property mistress, property woman** *n.* the man or woman in charge of theatrical properties. **property qualification** *n.* a qualification for voting, holding an office etc. derived from the possession of property. **property tax** *n.* a direct tax on property. [ME *proprete,* OF *proprieté,* L *proprietātem,* nom. *-tas,* from *proprius,* PROPER]

prophage (prō´fāj) *n.* a virus in a bacterial cell which undergoes division with the bacterium and does not destroy it. [bacterio*phage*]

prophase (prō´fāz) *n.* (*Biol.*) the first stage of mitosis, or of meiosis.

prophecy (prof´əsi) *n.* (*pl.* **prophecies**) **1** a prediction, esp. one divinely inspired. **2** the prediction of future events. **3** the gift or faculty of prophesying. [OF *profecie* (F *prophétie*), late L *prophētīa,* Gr. *prophēteia,* as PROPHET]

prophesy (prof´əsī) *v.t.* (*3rd pers. sing. pres.* **prophesies,** *pres.p.* **prophesying,** *past, p.p.* **prophesied**) **1** to predict, to foretell. **2** to herald. ~*v.i.* **1** to utter prophecies. **2** †to interpret Scripture, to preach. **prophesiable** *a.* **prophesier** (-sīə) *n.* [OF *profecier, -phecier, -phesier,* as PROPHECY]

prophet (prof´it) *n.* **1** a person who foretells future events, esp. under divine inspiration. **2** a revealer or interpreter of the divine will. **3** a religious leader, a founder of a religion. **4** a preacher or teacher of a cause etc. **5** (*sl.*) a tipster. **major prophets** MAJOR. **minor prophets** MINOR. **the Prophet 1** Muhammad. **2** Joseph Smith, the founder of the Mormon Church. **the Prophets 1** the prophetic writers of the Old Testament. **2** the books written by them. **prophetess** *n.* a woman prophet. **prophethood, prophetship** *n.* **prophetic** (-fet´-), **prophetical** *a.* **1** of, relating to or containing prophecy. **2** predictive, anticipative. **prophetically** *adv.* **propheticism** (-fet´isizm) *n.* a prophetic quality. **prophetism** *n.* **prophet of doom** *n.* a person who is continually predicting ruin and disaster. [ME and OF *prophete,* L *prophēta,* Gr. *prophētēs* (*phē-,* stem of *phanai,* to speak)]

prophylactic (profilak´tik) *a.* **1** protecting against disease. **2** preventive. ~*n.* **1** a preventive medicine. **2** (*esp. N Am.*) a condom. **prophylaxis** (-lak´sis) *n.* preventive treatment against disease. [F *prophylactique,* Gr. *prophulaktikos,* from *prophulassein* (*phulassein,* to guard)]

propinquity (prəping´kwiti) *n.* **1** nearness in time, space or relationship. **2** similarity. [OF *propinquité,* L *propinquitas -tatem,* from *propinquus,* near, from *prope,* near]

propionic acid (prōpion´ik), **propanoic acid** (prōpanō´ik) *n.* a colourless carboxylic acid used esp. to inhibit the growth of mould in bread. **propionate** (prō´-) *n.* a salt or ester of propionic acid. [Gr. *piōn,* fat]

propitiate (prəpish´iāt) *v.t.* to appease, to conciliate; to render well-disposed. **propitiable** *a.* **propitiation** (-ā´shən) *n.* **1** the act of propitiating, appeasement. **2** (*Bible*) atonement, esp. that of Christ. **3** †a propitiatory gift. **propitiator** *n.* **propitiatory** *a.* intended or serving to propitiate. ~*n.* **1** a propitiation. **2** the covering of the Ark of the Covenant, esp. as symbolizing Christ. **propitiatorily** *adv.* **propitious** (-shəs) *a.* **1** (of an omen) favourable. **2** disposed to be kind or gracious. **3** auspicious, suitable (for etc.). **propitiously** *adv.* **propitiousness** *n.* [L *propitiātus,* p.p. of *propitiāre,* from *propitius,* propitious, perh. a term in augury (*petere,* to fly)]

propolis (prop´əlis) *n.* a resinous substance obtained by bees from buds etc. and used to cement their combs, stop up crevices etc. [Gr., a suburb, bee-glue (*polis,* city)]

propone (prəpōn´) *v.t.* (*Sc.*) to propose, put forward (esp. before a court of law). [L *prōpōnere,* see PROPONENT]

proponent (prəpō´nənt) *a.* proposing or advocating. ~*n.* **1** a person who makes a proposal or proposition. **2** a person who argues for, an advocate. [L *prōpōnens -ntem,* pres.p. of *prōpōnere,* to PROPOSE]

proportion (prəpaw´shən) *n.* **1** the comparative relation of one part or thing to another with respect to magnitude, number or degree; ratio. **2** due relation, suitable or pleasing adaptation of one part or thing to others. **3** a proportional part, a share. **4** (*pl.*) dimensions. **5** (*Math.*) **a** equality of ratios between pairs of quantities. **b** a series of such quantities. **6** the rule by which from three given quantities a fourth may be found bearing the same ratio to the third as the second bears to the first, the rule of three. ~*v.t.* **1** to adjust in suitable proportion. **2** to make proportionate (to). **3** to apportion. **in proportion 1** in due relation as to magnitude, number etc. **2** consistent with the real importance of the matter in hand. **out of proportion** not in proportion. **proportionable** *a.* **1** capable of being made proportional. **2** being in proportion, corresponding, proportional. **3** well-proportioned, symmetrical. **proportionableness** *n.* **proportionably** *adv.* **proportional** *a.* **1** having due proportion. **2** of or relating to proportion. **3** (*Math.*) having a constant ratio. ~*n.* a quantity in proportion with others, each of the terms of a ratio. **proportionalist** *n.* **1** a person who makes designs according to the laws of proportion. **2** an advocate of proportional representation. **proportionalism** *n.* **proportionality** (-nal´-) *n.* **proportionally** *adv.* **proportional representation** *n.* an electoral system in which the representation of parties in an elected body is as nearly as possible proportional to their voting strength. **proportional spacing** *n.* in some typewriters and printers, the allotting of space to a character according to the character's width. **proportionate**[1] (-nət) *a.* in due or a certain proportion (to). **proportionate**[2] (-nāt) *v.t.* to make proportional or proportionate. **proportionately** *adv.* **proportionateness** *n.* **proportioned** *a.* having proportions (*usu. in comb., as well-proportioned*). **proportionless** *a.* **1** without proportion. **2** unsymmetrical, shapeless. **proportionment** *n.* [F, from L *proportiō -tiōnem* (PORTION)]

Usage note *Proportion* should not be used as though it meant simply a part (without implicit comparison).

propose (prəpōz´) *v.t.* **1** to put forward, to offer, to present for consideration. **2** to nominate for election. **3** to put forward as a plan, to purpose, to intend. **4** to present (a person etc.) as the subject for a toast. *~v.i.* **1** to put forward a plan or intention. **2** to make an offer, esp. of marriage. **proposable** *a.* **proposal** *n.* **1** the act, or an instance, of proposing. **2** something proposed. **3** an offer of marriage. **4** an application for insurance. **proposer** *n.* [F *proposer*, from L *prōponere*, see PROPOUND]

propositi PROPOSITUS.

proposition (propəzish´ən) *n.* **1** something which is propounded. **2** a statement, an assertion. **3** (*Logic*) a sentence in which something is affirmed or denied. **4** (*Math.*) a formal statement of a theorem or problem, sometimes with the demonstration. **5** a proposal, a scheme proposed for consideration or adoption. **6** an invitation to have sexual intercourse. **7** (*coll.*) a person or thing that has to be dealt with, esp. when considered in terms of success or failure. *~v.t.* (*coll.*) to make a proposition to, esp. to invite to have sexual intercourse. **not a proposition** not likely to succeed. **propositional** *a.* [F, from L *prōposio -tiōnem*, as PROPOUND]

propositus (prəpoz´itəs) *n.* (*pl.* **propositi** (-tī)) a proband. [L, see PROPOUND]

propound (prəpownd´) *v.t.* **1** to state or set out for consideration, to propose. **2** (*Law*) to bring forward (a will etc.) for probate. **propounder** *n.* [from obs. *propone*, L *prōpōnere* (*pōnere*, to put), p.p. *prōpositus*]

propr. *abbr.* proprietor.

propraetor (prōprē´tə), (*N Am.*) **propretor** *n.* (*Hist.*) a praetor who at the expiration of his term of office was made governor of a province. **propraetorial** (-taw´-), **propraetorian** *a.* [L, orig. *pro praetore*, (acting) for a praetor]

propranolol (prōpran´əlol) *n.* (*Med.*) a drug used to treat angina, abnormal heart rhythm and high blood pressure. [*propyl*, *propanol*]

propretor PROPRAETOR.

propria PROPRIUM.

proprietor (prəprī´ətə) *n.* an owner, esp. of a business; a person who has the exclusive legal right or title to anything, whether in possession or not, a possessor in one's own right. **proprietary** *a.* **1** of or relating to a proprietor or proprietorship. **2** owned as property. **3** (of a product) made and marketed under a patent, trademark etc. *~n.* (*pl.* **proprietaries**) **1** a proprietary drug. **2** a body of proprietors collectively. **3** proprietorship; a right to property. **4** †a proprietor, esp. (in the US) a grantee of a proprietary colony, as of Maryland. **proprietary name, proprietary term** *n.* a name of a product registered as a trademark. **proprietorial** (-taw´ri-) *a.* **proprietorially** *adv.* **proprietorship** *n.* **proprietress, proprietrix** *n.* a woman proprietor. [formerly *proprietary*, late L *proprietārius*, from *proprietas*, PROPERTY]

propriety (prəprī´əti) *n.* (*pl.* **proprieties**) **1** the quality of being conformable to an acknowledged or correct standard or rule. **2** fitness, correctness, rightness; correctness of behaviour, becomingness. **3** (*pl.*) the rules of correct or polite behaviour. [F *propriété*]

proprioception (prōpriəsep´shən) *n.* reception of, or activation by, stimuli from within the organism. **proprioceptive** *a.* **proprioceptor** *n.* any receptor which receives such stimuli. [L *proprius*, own, *reception*]

proprium (prō´priəm) *n.* (*pl.* **propria** (-iə)) (*Logic*) a property. [L, neut. of *proprius*, one's own]

props PROP[2].

proptosis (proptō´sis) *n.* (*pl.* **proptoses** (-sēs)) (*Med.*) displacement or protusion, esp. of an eye. [late L, from Gr. *proptōsis* (*piptein*, to fall)]

propulsion (prəpŭl´shən) *n.* **1** the act, or an instance, of propelling, a driving forward. **2** †something which propels, a driving force. **propulsive, †propulsory** *a.* [F, from L *prōpellere*, to PROPEL]

propyl (prō´pīl, -pil) *n.* a hydrocarbon radical derived from propane. **propyl alcohol** *n.* an aliphatic alcohol, propanol. **propylene** (prop´ilēn) *n.* a colourless, gaseous alkene obtained from petroleum. [*pro*pionic acid]

propyla PROPYLON.

propylaeum (propilē´əm) *n.* (*pl.* **propylaea** (-lē´ə)) **1** the entrance, esp. one of imposing architectural character, to a temple. **2** (**Propylaeum**) the entrance to the Acropolis in Athens. [L, from Gr. *propulaion* (*pulē*, a gate)]

propylon (prop´ilon) *n.* (*pl.* **propylons, propyla** (-lə)) a propylaeum, esp. to an Egyptian temple. [Gr. *propulon* (*pulē*, a gate)]

pro rata (prō rah´tə) *a.* proportional. *~adv.* proportionally, in proportion. [L, according to the rate]

prorate (prōrāt´, prō´-) *v.t.* (*esp. N Am.*) to distribute proportionally. **prorateable, proratable** *a.* **proration** (-ā´shən) *n.* [L *pro rata*, in proportion]

prorogue (prərōg´) *v.t.* (*pres.p.* **proroguing**, *past, p.p.* **prorogued**) to put an end to the meetings of (Parliament) without dissolving it. *~v.t.* to be prorogued. **prorogation** (-ā´shən) *n.* [F *proroger*, L *prōrogāre*, to extend, to defer (*rogāre*, to ask)]

pros- (pros) *pref.* **1** to, towards. **2** before. **3** in addition. [Gr. *pros*]

prosaic (prəzā´ik) *a.* **1** of, relating to or resembling prose. **2** unpoetic, unimaginative. **3** dull, commonplace. **prosaically** *adv.* **prosaicism** (-sizm) *n.* **prosaicness** *n.* **prosaism** *n.* **prosaist** (prō´-) *n.* **1** a writer of prose. **2** a prosaic person. [med. L *prōsaicus*, from *prōsa*, PROSE]

proscenium (prəsē´niəm) *n.* (*pl.* **prosceniums, proscenia** (-niə)) **1** the part of a stage between the curtain and the orchestra. **2** (*also* **proscenium arch**) the frame through which the audience views the traditional type of stage. **3** in a Roman or Greek theatre, the space in front of the scenery, the stage. [L, from Gr. *proskēnion* (*skēnē*, SCENE)]

prosciutto (proshoo´tō) *n.* (*pl.* **prosciutti** (-tē), **prosciuttos**) cured Italian ham, usu. eaten as an hors d'oeuvre. [It., dried beforehand (*asciutto*, dried)]

proscribe (prəskrīb´) *v.t.* **1** to interdict, to forbid. **2** to denounce as dangerous. **3** (*Hist.*) to publish the name of, as condemned to death, subjected to forfeiture of property etc.; to outlaw. **4** to banish, to exile. **proscriber** *n.* **proscription** (-skrip´-) *n.* **proscriptive** (-skrip´-) *a.* [L *prōscrībere* (*scrībere*, to write)]

Usage note See note under PRESCRIBE.

---

prose (prōz) *n.* **1** ordinary written or spoken language not in metre, as distinct from *verse*. **2** a passage of prose for translation into a foreign language. **3** commonplaceness. **4** a tedious or unimaginative discourse. **5** a hymn recited or sung after the Gradual. *~a.* **1** written in or consisting of prose. **2** dull, commonplace, prosaic. *~v.i.* to write or talk in a dull, tedious manner. *~v.t.* **1** to write or utter in prose. **2** to turn into prose. **Prose Edda** *n.* YOUNGER EDDA (under YOUNG). **prose idyll** *n.* a description in prose of a picturesque or poetic scene, incident etc. **proselike** *a.* **prose poem, prose poetry** *n.* a piece of prose that has some of the characteristics of poetry. **proser** *n.* **prose writer** *n.* **prosify** (-fī) *v.t.* (*3rd pers. sing. pres.* **prosifies**, *pres.p.* **prosifying**, *past, p.p.* **prosified**) **1** to turn into prose. **2** to make prosaic. *~v.i.* to write prose. **prosification** (-fikā´shən) *n.* **prosifier** *n.* **prosing** *n.* speaking or writing in a prosy way. **prosy** *a.* (*comp.* **prosier**, *superl.* **prosiest**) dull, tedious, long-winded. **prosily** *adv.* **prosiness** *n.* [F, from L *prōsa*, from *prōsa* (*prorsa*) *orātio*, straightforward discourse, masc. *prorsus* (*prō*, forward, *versus*, p.p. of *vertere*, to turn)]

prosector (prəsek´tə) *n.* (*Hist.*) a dissector, esp. a person who dissects bodies in preparation for lectures, demonstrations etc. **prosection** *n.* **prosectorial** (prōsektaw´ri-) *a.* **prosectorium** (prōsektaw´riəm) *n.* (*pl.*

prosectoria (-riə)) a building or laboratory where prosections are performed. **prosectorship** *n.* [late L *prōsector* (SECTOR)]

prosecute (pros´ikūt) *v.t.* **1** to take legal proceedings against. **2** to seek to obtain by legal process. **3** to pursue or follow up with a view to attaining or accomplishing. **4** to carry on (work, trade etc.). ~*v.i.* **1** to act as a prosecutor. **2** to take legal proceedings against someone. **prosecutable** *a.* **prosecuting attorney** *n.* (*US*) a person appointed to conduct criminal prosecutions on behalf of the state. **prosecution** (-kū´shən) *n.* **1** the act, or an instance, of prosecuting. **2** the setting out of a charge against an accused person before a court. **3** the instituting and carrying on of a civil or criminal suit. **4** the prosecutor or prosecutors collectively. **prosecutor** *n.* a person who prosecutes, esp. in a criminal court. **prosecutorial** (-taw´riəl) *a.* **prosecutrix** (-triks) *n.* a woman prosecutor. [L *prosecūtus*, p.p. of *prosequī* (*sequī*, to follow)]

proselyte (pros´ilīt) *n.* a new convert to some religion, party or system, esp. a gentile convert to Judaism. ~*v.t.* (*NAm.*) to proselytize. **proselytism** (-li-) *n.* **proselytize** (-li-), **proselytise** *v.t.*, *v.i.* **proselytization** (-zā´shən) *n.* **proselytizer** *n.* [ME and OF *proselite*, late L *prosēlytus*, Gr. *prosēlutos*, from *prosēluth-*, aorist stem of *proserchesthai* (*erchesthai*, to come)]

prosencephalon (prosənsef´əlon, -kef´-) *n.* (*pl.* **prosencephala** (-lə)) (*Anat.*) the anterior part of the brain comprising the cerebral hemispheres etc., and sometimes including the olfactory lobes. **prosencephalic** (-sifal´ik, -kef-) *a.*

prosenchyma (prəseng´kimə) *n.* plant tissue composed of elongated thick-walled cells closely interpenetrating, esp. fibrovascular tissue. **prosenchymal** *a.* **prosenchymatous** (prosəngkim´-) *a.* [Gr. *enchuma*, infusion, after PARENCHYMA]

prosify PROSE.

prosilient (prōsil´iənt) *a.* (*formal*) outstanding. [L *prōsiliens -ntem*, pres.p. of *prōsilīre*, to leap forward (*salīre*, to leap)]

prosimian (prōsim´iən) *a.* of or relating to a primitive suborder of primates, Prosimii, which includes lemurs, lorises and tarsiers. ~*n.* any primate of the Prosimii. [L *simia*, ape]

prosit (prō´sit), **prost** (prōst) *int.* used as a (German) drinking toast. [L, may it be to your good]

prosody (pros´ədi) *n.* **1** the study of the art of versification, formerly regarded as a branch of grammar. **2** the study of the rhythms and intonation of a language. **prosodist** *n.* [L and Gr. *prosōdia*]

prosopagnosia (prosōpagnō´ziə) *n.* (*Psych.*) an inability to recognize the faces of people whom one knows well. [Gr. *prosōpon*, a face, a person, *a-*, not, *gnōsis*, knowledge]

prosopography (prosōpog´rəfi) *n.* (*pl.* **prosopographies**) **1** a biographical sketch. **2** the study of such sketches as part of Roman history. **prosopographer** *n.* **prosopographic** (-graf´ik), **prosopographical** *a.* **prosopographically** *adv.* [L, from Gr. *prosōpon*, a person, *graphein*, to write]

prosopopoeia (prosōpəpē´ə), (*esp. NAm.*) **prosopopeia** *n.* a rhetorical figure by which abstract things are represented as persons, or absent persons as speaking. [L, from Gr. *prosōpopoiia* (*prosōpon*, person, *poieein*, to make)]

prospect[1] (pros´pekt) *n.* **1** an extensive view of a landscape etc. **2** the way a house etc. fronts or looks. **3** a scene. **4** a pictorial representation of a view. **5** a mental picture of what is to come. **6** expectation, ground of expectation. **7** (*pl.*) expectation of money to come or of an advancement in career. **8** a prospective customer. **9** a place likely to yield ore. **10** an indication of the presence of ore. **11** a sample of ore for testing. **12** the mineral obtained by testing. **prospectless** *a.* [see PROSPECTUS]

prospect[2] (prəspekt´) *v.i.* **1** to search, to explore (a place), esp. for minerals. **2** to work (a mine) experimentally. **3** to promise well or ill (of a mine). ~*v.t.* **1** to search or explore (a region) for minerals. **2** to promise (a good or poor yield). **3** †to look over, to survey. **to prospect ill** (of a mine) to promise badly. **to prospect well** (of a mine) to promise well. **prospection** *n.* **prospective** *a.* **1** of or relating to the future. **2** anticipated, expected, probable. **3** looking to the future. ~*n.* prospect, view, anticipation. **prospectively** *adv.* **prospectiveness** *n.* **prospector** *n.* a person who searches for minerals or mining sites. [see PROSPECTUS]

prospectus (prəspek´təs) *n.* (*pl.* **prospectuses**) a descriptive circular announcing the main objects and plans of a commercial scheme, institution, literary work etc. [L, a lookout, a prospect, from *prōspicere*, *specere*, to look]

prosper (pros´pə) *v.i.* to succeed; to thrive. ~*v.t.* to make successful or fortunate. **prosperity** (-sper´-) *n.* the condition of being prosperous; success, wealth. **prosperous** *a.* **1** successful, thriving, making progress, or advancement. **2** favourable, fortunate, auspicious. **prosperously** *adv.* **prosperousness** *n.* [F *prospérer*, L *prosperāre*, to cause to succeed, from *prosper*, favourable, fortunate]

prost PROSIT.

prostaglandin (prostəglan´din) *n.* any of a group of hormone-like substances which have wide-ranging effects on body processes, e.g. muscle contraction. [the *prosta*te *gland*, a major source of these]

prostate (pros´tāt) *n.* the prostate gland. ~*a.* situated in front. **prostatectomy** (-stətek´təmi) *n.* (*pl.* **prostatectomies**) surgical removal of the prostate gland. **prostate gland** *n.* a gland situated round the neck of the bladder in male mammals, secreting a fluid which forms part of semen. **prostatic** (-tat´-) *a.* of or relating to the prostate gland. **prostatic body, prostatic gland** *n.* **prostatitis** (-tətī´tis) *n.* inflammation of the prostate. [med. L *prostata*, Gr. *prostatēs*, one who stands before (*sta-*, stem of *histanai*, to stand)]

Usage note The noun and adjective *prostate* and the adjective *prostrate* should not be confused: there is only one *r* in the word for the male gland; *prostrate* means lying flat, overcome.

---

prosternum (prōstœ´nəm) *n.* (*pl.* **prosternums, prosterna** (-nə)) the ventral segment of the thorax of an insect.

prosthesis (pros´thəsis, -thē´-) *n.* (*pl.* **prostheses** (-sēz)) **1** the addition of an artificial part for the body to supply a deficiency. **2** an artificial part thus supplied. **3** (*Gram.*) the addition of one or more letters to the beginning of a word. **prosthetic** (-thet´-) *a.* **prosthetically** *adv.* **prosthetics** *n.* the branch of surgery or dentistry concerned with prosthesis. **prosthetist** *n.* [L and Gr. (*thesis*, a thing laid down, from *tithenai*, to put)]

prosthodontics (prosthōdon´tiks) *n.* the branch of dentistry concerned with the provision of false teeth, bridgework etc.; dental prosthetics. **prosthodontist** *n.* [*prosth*etics, Gr. *odous odontos*, tooth]

prostitute (pros´titūt) *n.* **1** a person (esp. a woman or girl) who engages in sexual activity for money. **2** a boy or man who engages in sexual activity with other men for money. **3** a person who hires out their work, talent etc. for unworthy purposes. ~*v.t.* **1** to hire (oneself, another) out for sexual purposes. **2** to offer or sell for base or unworthy purposes. **3** to devote to unworthy uses. ~*a.* prostituted. **prostitution** (-tū´shən) *n.* **prostitutor** (pros´-) *n.* [L *prostitūtus*, p.p. of *prostituere* (*statuere*, to place, to set)]

prostomium (prōstō´miəm) *n.* (*pl.* **prostomia** (-miə)) (*Zool.*) the part of a worm's head in front of the mouth, bearing tentacles etc. **prostomial** *a.* [Gr. *stoma*, mouth]

prostrate[1] (pros´trāt) *a.* **1** lying flat or prone. **2** lying in a horizontal position, procumbent, lying in a posture of humility or at mercy. **3** overcome (by grief etc.), exhausted. **4** (*Bot.*) growing along the ground. [L *prostrātus*, p.p. of *prosternere* (*sternere*, to lay flat)]

Usage note See note under PROSTATE.

prostrate[2] (prostrāt´) *v.t.* **1** to lay (a person etc.) flat. **2** to throw (oneself) down, esp. in reverence or adoration (before). **3** to throw down, to overthrow, to overcome, to demolish. **4** to reduce to physical exhaustion. **prostration** (-ā´shən) *n.* [as PROSTRATE[1]]

prostyle (prō´stīl) *a.* (*Archit.*) having a row of columns, usu. four, entirely in front of the building. ~*n.* **1** a portico supported on columns entirely in front of the building, as opposed to those having antae at the sides. **2** a building having such a portico. [F, from L *prostylos*, Gr. *prostulos* (*stulos*, STYLE)]

prosy PROSE.

Prot. *abbr.* **1** Protectorate. **2** Protestant.

prot- PROTO-[1].

protactinium *n.* a radioactive metallic element, at. no. 91, chem. symbol Pa, yielding actinium on disintegration. [ACTINIUM]

protagonist (prətag´ənist) *n.* **1** an advocate, champion etc. (of a cause). **2** the leading character or actor in a Greek play. **3** the leading character in any play or story. **4** a leading contestant. [Gr. *prōtagōnistēs* (*agōnistēs*, actor, see AGONISTIC (under AGONIST))]

Usage note The use of *protagonist* to mean a champion of a cause etc. is sometimes disapproved of: *proponent* can often be used instead.

protamine (prō´təmēn) *n.* any of a group of simple proteins occurring in the sperm of some fish.

protandry (prōtan´dri) *n.* in plants and hermaphrodite animals, the production of male gametes before female ones. **protandrous** *a.* [Gr. *anēr andros*, a man, a male]

protanopia (prōtənō´piə) *n.* a form of colour-blindness in which the retina does not respond well to red, and red and green are confused. **protanope** (prō´-) *n.* a person who suffers from protanopia. **protanopic** (-op´ik) *a.* [Gr. *ōps*, an eye]

protasis (prot´əsis) *n.* (*pl.* **protases** (-sēz)) **1** (*pl.*) the clause containing the condition in a conditional sentence. **2** the first part of a classic drama, in which the characters are introduced and the argument explained. **protatic** (-tat´-) *a.* [late L and Gr. (*tasis*, from *teinein*, to stretch)]

protea (prō´tiə) *n.* any member of a S African genus of shrubs and small trees, *Protea*, with large cone-shaped flowers. **proteaceous** (-ā´shəs) *a.* [PROTEUS]

protean (prō´tiən, prōtē´ən) *a.* **1** readily assuming different shapes or aspects; variable, changeable. **2** (of an artist etc.) versatile. **proteiform** (-tē´ifawm) *a.* [PROTEUS]

protease (prō´tiāz) *n.* any enzyme which can hydrolyse proteins; a proteolytic enzyme. [PROTEIN]

protect (prətekt´) *v.t.* **1** to shield, defend or keep safe (from or against injury, danger etc.). **2** to support (industries) against foreign competition by imposing duties on imports. **3** to provide funds so as to guarantee payment of (bills etc.). **4** to screen (e.g. machinery) so as to minimize the risk of injury etc. **protectant** *n.* a chemical which protects against frost, rust etc. **protectingly** *adv.* **protection** *n.* **1** the act, or an instance, of protecting. **2** the state of being protected. **3** something which protects, a covering, shield or defence. **4** a passport, a safe conduct. **5** protection money. **6** (*coll.*) freedom from injury, molestation etc. purchased by protection money. **7** (*N Am.*) a certificate of citizenship of the US issued to seamen by the customs authorities. **8** protectionism. **9** †the keeping of a mistress or concubine. **protectionism** *n.* the doctrine or system of protecting home industries against foreign competition by import duties etc. **protectionist** *n., a.* **protection money** *n.* a bribe extorted by gangsters from shopkeepers etc. by threats of damage to property, personal assault etc. **protection racket** *n.* an organized system whereby gangsters extort protection money. **protective** *a.* **1** affording protection; intended to protect. **2** (of a person) desirous of shielding another from harm or distress. **3** (of food) protecting against disease, esp. deficiency diseases. ~*n.* **1** something that protects. **2** a condom. **protective clothing** *n.* clothing, esp. covering the whole body, made of materials which protect the body from heat, toxic substances etc. **protective coloration, protective colouring** *n.* colouring that enables animals to escape detection by blending with their surroundings, camouflage. **protective custody** *n.* detention before trial in order to ensure an accused's personal safety. **protective detention** *n.* (*Law*) detention of a criminal to protect society from their further activities. **protectively** *adv.* **protectiveness** *n.* **protective tariff** *n.* an import tax imposed more to protect the domestic economy than to raise revenue. [L *prōtectus*, p.p. of *prōtegere* (*tegere*, to cover)]

protector (prətek´tə) *n.* **1** a person who protects against injury or evil etc.; a guardian or patron. **2** a protective device, a guard. **3** (*Hist.*) (**Protector**) a person in charge of a kingdom during the minority, incapacity etc. of the sovereign. **4** (**Protector**) a title of Oliver Cromwell, Lord Protector of the Commonwealth, 1653–58, and his son Richard Cromwell, 1658–59. **protectoral** *a.* **protectorate** (-rət) *n.* **1** protection, usu. combined with partial control, of a weak state by a more powerful one. **2** territory under such protection. **3** (**Protectorate**) the office of protector of a kingdom. **4** (**Protectorate**) the period of this, esp. that of Oliver and Richard Cromwell. **protectorless** *a.* **protectorship** *n.* **protectory** *n.* (*pl.* **protectories**) in the Roman Catholic Church, an institution for the care of destitute or vicious children. **protectress, protectrix** *n.* a woman protector. [ME and OF *protectour* (F *protecteur*), L *prōtectōr -tōrem*]

protégé (prot´āzhā, prō´-) *n.* a person under the protection, care, or patronage of another. **protégée** *n.* a female protégé. [F, p.p. of *protéger*, to PROTECT)]

proteiform PROTEAN.

protein (prō´tēn) *n.* **1** any of a class of complex organic compounds, containing carbon, oxygen, hydrogen and nitrogen, usu. with some sulphur, found in all living organisms and forming an essential constituent of animal foods. **2** such compounds collectively, esp. considered as a component in foodstuffs. **proteinaceous** (-nā´shəs), **proteinic** (-tē´-), **proteinous** (-tē´-) *a.* [F *protéine* or G *Protein* (Gr. *prōteios*, from *prōtos*, first)]

pro tem (prō tem´), **pro tempore** (tem´pəri) *a.* temporary. ~*adv.* for the time being. [L]

proteolysis (prōtiol´isis) *n.* (*Chem.*) the resolution or splitting up of proteins or peptides by the process of digestion or the application of enzymes. **proteolytic** (-lit´-) *a.* [*protein*, Gr. *lusis*, loosening, resolving, from *luein*, to loosen]

proter- PROTERO-.

protero- (prot´ərō), **proter-** *comb. form* former, anterior. [Gr. *proteros*, comp. of *pro*, before]

Proterozoic (protərōzō´ik) *a.* (*Geol.*) of or relating to the later part of the Precambrian era, when the earliest forms of life appeared. ~*n.* this era.

protest[1] (prətest´) *v.i.* **1** to make a solemn affirmation. **2** to express dissent or objection. ~*v.t.* **1** to affirm or declare formally or earnestly. **2** to object (that). **3** (*N*

Am.) to express one's disapproval of or objection to. 4 (*Law*) to make a formal declaration, usu. by a notary public, that payment (of a bill) has been demanded and refused. **protester** *n.* **protestingly** *adv.* **protestor** *n.* [F *protester*, L *prōtestārī* (*testārī*, to declare, to witness, from *testis*, witness)]

protest[2] (prō´test) *n.* 1 the act, or an instance, of protesting. 2 a solemn or formal declaration of opinion, usu. of dissent or remonstrance. 3 an expression or demonstration of dissent, disapproval etc. 4 (*Law*) a formal declaration, by the holder, of the non-payment of a bill. 5 a written declaration by the master of a ship, usu. before a magistrate, consul etc., stating the circumstances attending an injury or loss of a ship or cargo. ~*a.* expressing or intended to express objection, dissent. **under protest** unwillingly; having expressed objections. [see PROTEST[1]]

Protestant (prot´istənt) *n.* 1 a member of a Church upholding the principles of the Reformation, or (loosely) of any western Church not within the Roman communion. 2 any one of the party adhering to Luther at the Reformation, who at the second Diet of Speyer, 1529, protested against the decree of the majority involving submission to the authority of the Roman Catholic Church. 3 (**protestant**) a person who makes a protest. ~*a.* 1 of or relating to the Protestants, or to Protestantism. 2 (**protestant**) making a protest. **Protestantism** *n.* **Protestantize, Protestantise** *v.t.*, *v.i.* (to cause) to become Protestant. **Protestant work ethic** *n.* the attitude, ascribed to Protestants, that accords more importance to hard work than to enjoyment of life. [F, pres.p. of *protester*, to PROTEST[1]]

protestation (protistā´shən) *n.* 1 a solemn affirmation or declaration. 2 a solemn declaration of dissent, a protest. 3 a vow or promise. 4 (*Law*) a declaration in pleading. [see PROTEST[1]]

Proteus (prō´tiəs) *n.* (*pl.* **Proteuses**) 1 a changeable, shifty or fickle person or thing. 2 (**proteus**) an olm. 3 (**proteus**) a member of the genus *Proteus* of bacteria, found in animal intestines. [L and Gr., a marine deity, Neptune's herdsman, who had power to change his shape at will]

prothalamion (prōthəlā´miən), **prothalamium** (-əm) *n.* (*pl.* **prothalamia** (-miə)) a song or poem celebrating a forthcoming wedding. [coined by Spenser (EPITHALAMIUM)]

prothalli PROTHALLUS.

prothallium (prōthal´iəm) *n.* (*pl.* **prothallia** (-iə)) (*Bot.*) a cellular structure bearing the sexual organs in vascular cryptogams. **prothallial, prothallic** *a.* [Gr. *thallion*, dim. of *thallos*, THALLUS]

prothallus (prōthal´əs) *n.* (*pl.* **prothalli** (-lī)) a prothallium.

prothesis (proth´isis) *n.* (*pl.* **protheses** (-sēz)) 1 the placing of the elements in readiness for use in the Eucharist, esp. in the Orthodox church. 2 a credence-table, or the part of a church in which this stands. 3 (*Gram.*) prosthesis. **prothetic** (-thet´-) *a.* [Gr. (*thesis*, a thing laid down, from *tithenai*, to put)]

prothonotary (prəthon´ətəri, prōthənō´təri), **protonotary** (prōt-) *n.* (*pl.* **prothonotaries, protonotaries**) 1 a chief clerk or notary. 2 the chief clerk or registrar of a court, now chiefly in some American and Australian courts, and formerly of the Courts of Chancery, Common Pleas and King's Bench. 3 (*also* **prothonotary Apostolic, Prothonotary Apostolic**) a member of the Roman Catholic College responsible for registering the papal acts. **prothonotarial** (-teə´riəl) *a.* **prothonotariat** (-teə´riət, -at) *n.* **prothonotaryship** *n.* **prothonotary warbler** *n.* a N American bird, the wood warbler *Protonotarius citrea*. [obs. F *prothonotaire*, late L *prōtonotārius*, Gr. *prōtonotarios* (L *notārius*, NOTARY)]

prothorax (prōthaw´raks) *n.* (*pl.* **prothoraxes, prothoraces** (-rəsēz)) the anterior segment of the thorax in insects. **prothoracic** (-thəras´-) *a.*

prothrombin (prōthrom´bin) *n.* a substance like a protein found in blood plasma, the inactive precursor of thrombin.

protist (prō´tist) *n.* any organism of the kingdom Protista, microscopic organisms whose position (as animals or plants) is doubtful, incl. protozoans, algae and fungi. **protistic** (-tis´tik) *a.* **protistology** (-tol´-) *n.* the scientific study of the Protista. **protistologist** *n.* [Gr. *prōtistos*, superl. of *prōtos*, first]

protium (prō´tiəm) *n.* (*Chem.*) the ordinary isotope of hydrogen, of atomic weight 1, as distinct from *deuterium*, *tritium*. [Gr. *prōtos*, first]

proto-[1] (prō´tō), **prot-** *comb. form* 1 chief. 2 earliest, original, primitive, ancestral. 3 denoting that chemical compound in a series in which the distinctive element or radical combines in the lowest proportion with another element. 4 denoting the earliest, reconstructed, form of a language, as *proto-Celtic*, *proto-Germanic*. [Gr. *prōtos*, first]

protochordate (prōtōkaw´dāt) *n.* any chordate animal which is not a vertebrate, marine animals having a notochord but no skull or spinal cord, the sea squirts etc.

protococcus (prōtōkok´əs) *n.* (*pl.* **protococci** (-kok´sī)) (*Bot.*) any member of a genus of unicellular algae, *Protococcus*, such as form the familiar green layers on damp stones, trees, timber etc. **protococcal** (-kok´əl) *a.* [Gr. *kokkos*, grain, seed]

protocol (prō´təkol) *n.* 1 the original draft of an official document or transaction, esp. minutes or a rough draft of a diplomatic instrument or treaty, signed by the parties to a negotiation. 2 the formal etiquette and procedure governing diplomatic and ceremonial functions. 3 the customs and rules of etiquette governing any social or official occasion. 4 the official formulas used to start and finish diplomatic instruments, charters, wills etc. 5 an official memorandum or account. 6 an annexe to a treaty which adds to its provisions or clarifies them. 7 (*N Am.*) a record of observations in scientific experiments. 8 (*Comput.*) a set of rules governing the transmission of data between two devices which are not directly connected. ~*v.i.* (*pres.p.* **protocolling,** *past, p.p.* **protocolled**) to draft protocols. ~*v.t.* to reduce to or record in a protocol. **protocolist** *n.* [OF *prothocole* (F *protocole*), med. L *prōtocollum*, Gr. *prōtokollon*, orig. the first leaf glued to a MS (*kolla*, glue)]

protogalaxy (prōtōgal´əksi) *n.* (*pl.* **protogalaxies**) (*Astron.*) a cloud of gas supposed to be slowly condensing to form the stars of a new galaxy.

protogenic (prōtōjen´ik), **protogenetic** (-net´-) *a.* (*Chem.*) (of a compound) able to donate a hydrogen ion in a chemical reaction. [Gr. *prōtogenes* (*gen-*, root of *gignesthai*, to be born)]

protogine (prō´təjin) *n.* a variety of granite forming the central mass of Mont Blanc and other mountains in the Alps, having a foliated structure due to dynamic action. [Gr. *ginesthai* (*gignesthai*), to come into being]

protogyny (prōtoj´ini) *n.* in plants and hermaphrodite animals, the production of female gametes before male ones. **protogynous** *a.* [Gr. *gunē*, a woman]

protohistoric (prōtōhistor´ik) *a.* of or relating to the period of history at the end of prehistory and immediately before the development of written records. **protohistory** (-his´təri) *n.* this period.

protohuman (prōtōhū´mən) *n.* any of various prehistoric primates, supposed ancestors of humans. ~*a.* of or relating to these primates.

protolanguage (prōtōlang´gwij) *n.* a hypothetical language, the earliest ancestor of any group of modern languages and reconstructed from them.

protolithic (prōtōlith´ik) *a.* of or relating to the very earliest Stone Age.
protomartyr (prōtōmah´tə) *n.* **1** a first martyr (applied esp. to St Stephen). **2** the first who suffers in any cause. [med. L (MARTYR)]
protomorphic (prōtōmaw´fik) *a.* primitive in form; primordial.
proton (prō´ton) *n.* (*pl.* **protons**) (*Physics*) a particle occurring in atomic nuclei and identical with the nucleus of the hydrogen atom, having an electric charge equal and opposite to that of the electron, and a mass 1840 times as great. **protonic** (-ton´-) *a.* **proton microscope** *n.* a microscope using a beam of protons for high resolution. [Gr., neut. of *prōtos*, first]
protonema (prōtənē´mə) *n.* (*pl.* **protonemata** (-mətə)) a branched threadlike structure that grows from a moss spore and develops into a moss plant. **protonemal, protonematal** *a.*
protonotary PROTHONOTARY.
protopathic (prōtōpath´ik) *a.* of or relating to a sensory nerve that only reacts to coarse stimuli like pain. **protopathy** (-top´əthi) *n.*
protopectin (prōtōpek´tin) *n.* pectose.
protophloem (prōtōflō´əm) *n.* (*Bot.*) the first part of the phloem, or food-conducting tissue, to be formed.
protophyte (prō´təfīt) *n.* **1** a unicellular plant bearing gametes. **2** any member of the Protophyta, plants of the lowest organization, usu. microscopic in size and unicellular. **protophytic** (-fit´ik) *a.* [Gr. *phuta*, plants, sing. *phuton*]
protoplasm (prō´tōplazm) *n.* (*Biol.*) the viscid semifluid substance composed of oxygen, hydrogen, carbon and nitrogen, constituting the living matter of a cell and its nucleus. **protoplasmal** (-plaz´-), **protoplasmatic** (-mat´-), **protoplasmic** (-plaz´-) *a.* [Gr. *prōtoplasma* (Gr. *plasma*, a moulded thing, from *plassein*, to mould)]
protoplast (prō´təplahst) *n.* **1** (*Biol.*) a unit of protoplasm, the nucleus and cytoplasm of a cell, but not the cell wall. **2** the first individual, esp. the first-created man. **3** an original, an archetype, the model. **protoplastic** (-plas´-) *a.* [F *protoplaste*, late L *prōtoplastus*, Gr. *prōtoplastos* (*plastos*, moulded, as PROTOPLASM)]
protostar (prō´təstah) *n.* (*Astron.*) a slowly-condensing cloud of interstellar gas or dust from which a star is thought to develop.
protostele (prō´təstēl, -stēli) *n.* (*Bot.*) a simple sort of stele with a solid core of vascular tissue. **protostelic** (-stē´lik) *a.*
prototherian (prōtəthiə´riən) *n.* any mammal of the subclass Prototheria, comprising the Monotremata and their ancestors. ~*a.* of or relating to the subclass Prototheria. **protothere** (prō´-) *n.* [Gr. *thēria*, beasts]
prototrophic (prōtōtrof´ik) *a.* (*Biol.*) (of bacteria) feeding solely on inorganic matter. **prototroph** (prō´tə-) *n.* such a bacterium.
prototype (prō´tətīp) *n.* **1** an original or primary person or thing, an exemplar, an archetype. **2** a pre-production model on which tests can be carried out to trace design faults, indicate possible improvements etc. ~*v.t.* to make a prototype of. **prototypal** (-tī´-) *a.* **prototypical** (-tip´-), **prototypic** *a.* **prototypically** *adv.* [F, from Gr. *prōtotupon*]
protoxide (prōtok´sīd) *n.* (*Chem.*) the compound of oxygen and an element containing the lowest proportion of oxygen of all such compounds. **protoxidize** (-si-), **protoxidise** *v.t.*
protoxylem (prōtōzī´ləm) *n.* (*Bot.*) the first part of the xylem, or water-conducting tissue, to be formed.
protozoan (prōtəzō´ən), **protozoon** (-zō´on) *n.* (*pl.* **protozoans, protozoa** (-zō´ə)) any member of the phylum Protozoa, consisting of microscopic unicellular organisms, amoebas, ciliates etc. ~*a.* of or relating to this phylum. **protozoal** *a.* of or relating to the Protozoa. **protozoic** *a.* protozoal. **protozoology** (-zōol´-) *n.* the branch of zoology dealing with the Protozoa. **protozoological** (-loj´-) *a.* **protozoologist** (-zōol´-) *n.* [Gr. *zōa*, animals, sing. *zōon*]
protract (prətrakt´) *v.t.* **1** to extend in duration, to prolong. **2** to draw (a map, plan etc.) to scale, esp. with a scale and protractor. **protracted** *a.* **protractedly** *adv.* **protractedness** *n.* **protracter** *n.* **protractile** (-tīl) *a.* (of the organ etc. of an animal) capable of extension. **protraction** *n.* **protractive** *a.* **protractor** *n.* **1** an instrument, usu. in the form of a graduated arc, for laying down angles on paper etc. **2** a muscle that protracts or extends a limb. **3** an instrument for drawing extraneous bodies out of a wound. [L *prōtractus*, p.p. of *prōtrahere* (*trahere*, to draw)]
protrude (prətrood´) *v.t.* **1** to thrust forward or out. **2** to cause to project or thrust out. **3** to obtrude. ~*v.i.* to project, to be thrust forward, or above a surface. **protrudent** *a.* **protrusible** (-si-) *a.* **protrusile** (-sīl) *a.* (*Zool.*) capable of being thrust forward, as a limb, jaw etc. **protrusion** (-zhən) *n.* **protrusive** *a.* **protrusively** *adv.* [L *prōtrūdere* (*trūdere*, to thrust, p.p. *trūsus*)]
protuberant (prətū´bərənt) *a.* swelling, bulging out, prominent. **protuberance** *n.* a swelling, a prominence, a knob, a bump. **protuberantly** *adv.* **protuberate** *v.i.* [L *prōtūberans -ntem*, pres.p. of *prōtūberāre*]

Usage note The forms *protruberant, protruberance* etc. (after *protrude*) are best avoided.

protyle (prō´til) *n.* a hypothetical primal matter existing before the differentiation of the chemical elements. [Gr. *hulē*, matter; introduced by Sir William Crookes (1886)]
proud (prowd) *a.* **1** having high or inordinate self-esteem; haughty, arrogant. **2** having a due sense of dignity. **3** elated, exultant, feeling honoured, pleased, gratified. **4** grand, imposing. **5** (of words, looks etc.) stately, inspired by pride. **6** (of deeds etc.) inspiring pride, noble, grand. **7** projecting, standing out above a plane surface. **8** (of a stream) swollen, in flood. **to do someone proud 1** to entertain someone lavishly. **2** to give someone cause to be proud. **proud flesh** *n.* a granular growth resembling flesh growing over a wound. **proud-hearted** *a.* proud in spirit, arrogant. **proudly** *adv.* **proudness** *n.* [OE *prūt*, perh. from OF *prud* (F *preux*), prob. ult. from L *prōdesse*, to be of use]
proustite (proos´tīt) *n.* a red mineral, sulphide of silver and arsenic. [J. L. *Proust*, 1754–1826, French chemist]
Prov. *abbr.* **1** Provençal, Provence. **2** Proverbs. **3** Province. **4** Provost.
prove (proov) *v.t.* (*past* **proved,** *p.p.* **proved, proven** (proo´vən, prō´-)) **1** to establish or demonstrate the truth of by argument, reasoning or testimony. **2** to test, to try by experiment, to make trial of. **3** to show to be true. **4** to test the accuracy of, esp. by an established procedure. **5** to have experience of, to undergo. **6** to establish the authenticity or validity of, esp. to obtain probate of (a will). **7** (*Print.*) to take a proof impression from. ~*v.i.* **1** to be found by experience or trial. **2** to turn out to be. **3** to turn out (to be). **4** to make a trial or attempt. **5** (of dough) to rise and become aerated before baking. **not proven** (*Sc. Law*) not proved (a verdict given when there is not sufficient evidence to convict). **to go to prove** to go to show. **to prove oneself** to do something which shows one's qualities, esp. courage. **to prove one's point** POINT. **provable** *a.* **provability** (-bil´-), **provableness** *n.* **provably** *adv.* **prover** *n.* **1** a person who or thing which proves or tests. **2** a person employed in printing proof impressions. **3** (*Law*) an approver. **proving** *n., a.* **proving flight** *n.* a test flight. **proving ground** *n.* **1** a place where something, esp. a vehicle, is subjected to trials and scientific tests. **2** any testing experience or situation. [OF *prover* (F

prouver), L *probāre*, to test, to approve]

Usage note The past participle *proven* is largely encountered in Scottish and American English, although it occurs in a few fixed expressions (as *of proven ability*) and, increasingly, in television and radio advertising with overtones of the technical sense 'tested'.

provenance (prov´inəns) *n.* 1 an origin or source. 2 the place of origin of a work of art. [F, from *provenant*, pres.p. of *provenir*, L *prōvenīre* (*venīre*, to come)]

Provençal (provāsahl´) *n.* 1 a native or inhabitant of Provence (France). 2 the Romance language of Provence. *~a.* of or relating to Provence, its language, or inhabitants. **provençale** *a.* (of food) cooked with garlic, oil and usu. tomatoes. [F, from L *provincia*, PROVINCE]

provender (prov´əndə) *n.* 1 dry food for beasts, fodder. 2 (*facet.*) provisions, food. [OF *provendre*, corr. of med. L *praebenda*, PREBEND]

provenience (prəvēn´yəns) *n.* (*esp. NAm.*) PROVENANCE.

proventriculus (prōventrik´ūləs) *n.* (*pl.* **proventriculi** (-lī)) (*Zool.*) 1 in birds, the thin-walled first part of the stomach in front of the gizzard, where the gastric juices are secreted. 2 in insects and crustaceans, the thick-walled muscular stomach.

proverb (prov´œb) *n.* 1 a short, pithy sentence, containing some truth or wise reflection proved by experience or observation; a maxim, a saw, an adage. 2 a typical example, a byword. *~v.t.* 1 to speak of in a proverb, to make a byword of. 2 to provide with a proverb. **Book of Proverbs** BOOK. **proverbial** (prəvœ´-) *a.* 1 like, or of the nature of, a proverb. 2 notorious. **proverbialism** *n.* **proverbialist** *n.* a writer, composer or collector of proverbs. **proverbiality** (-al´-) *n.* **proverbialize, proverbialise** *v.t., v.i.* **proverbially** *adv.* **Proverbs** *n.* the Book of Proverbs. [F *proverbe*, L *prōverbium* (*verbum*, word)]

proviant (prov´iənt) *n.* provisions, esp. for an army. [G, from It. *provianda*, provisions]

provide (prəvīd´) *v.t.* 1 to procure or prepare beforehand. 2 to furnish, to supply. 3 to equip (with). 4 to lay down as a preliminary condition, to stipulate. 5 to appoint to an ecclesiastical benefice. 6 (of the Pope) to grant the right to be appointed (to a benefice not yet vacant). *~v.i.* 1 to make preparation or provision (for or against). 2 to furnish means of subsistence (for a person). **provided** *a.* 1 supplied, furnished. 2 provided in readiness. 3 laid down, stipulated. *~conj.* on the understanding or condition (that). **provider** *n.* 1 a person or thing that provides. 2 the breadwinner of a family. **providing** *n.* the action of supplying, furnishing or preparing beforehand. *~conj.* provided (that). [L *prōvidēre* (*vidēre*, to see)]

providence (prov´idəns) *n.* 1 the beneficent care or control of God or nature. 2 (**Providence**) God or nature regarded as exercising such care. 3 a manifestation of such care. 4 foresight, timely care or preparation. 5 frugality, economy, prudence. **provident** *a.* 1 making provision for the future, thrifty. 2 showing foresight, prudent. **providential** (-den´-) *a.* 1 due to or effected by divine providence. 2 lucky, fortunate, opportune. **providentially** *adv.* **providently** *adv.* **provident society** *n.* a friendly society. [F, from L *prōvidentia*, as PROVIDE]

Provie (prō´vi, prov´i) *n.* (*coll.*) a member of the Provisional IRA. [short for PROVISIONAL (under PROVISION)]

province (prov´ins) *n.* 1 a large administrative division of a kingdom, country or state. 2 (*pl.*) all parts of a country except the metropolis. 3 a proper sphere of action, business, knowledge etc. 4 the territory under the authority of an archbishop or metropolitan. 5 (*Hist.*) a country or territory beyond the confines of Italy under a Roman governor. **the Province** Northern Ireland.

provincial (-vin´shəl) *a.* 1 of or relating to a province. 2 constituting a province. 3 of, relating to or characteristic of the provinces. 4 narrow, rustic, unpolished, uncultured. *~n.* 1 a person who belongs to a province or the provinces. 2 a narrow-minded or unsophisticated person. 3 the superior of a religious order etc., in a province. **provincialism** *n.* 1 the quality of being provincial. 2 a mode of speech, thought, behaviour etc., or a word or expression, peculiar to a province or the provinces. 3 the restricting of one's interest to local affairs, narrow-mindedness. **provincialist** *n.* **provinciality** (-shial´-) *n.* **provincialize, provincialise** *v.t.* to make provincial. **provincially** *adv.* [F, from L *prōvincia*, business or duty, province, etym. uncertain]

proving PROVE.

provirus (prōvī´rəs) *n.* (*pl.* **proviruses**) (*Med.*) an inactive form of a virus within a host cell.

provision (prəvizh´ən) *n.* 1 the act, or an instance, of providing. 2 something provided, or prepared beforehand. 3 a precautionary measure. 4 a stipulation or condition providing for something. 5 a clause in a law or a deed. 6 (*pl.*) a supply of food etc. for a household. 7 (*pl.*) food and drink prepared for an expedition. 8 (*Hist.*) an appointment to an ecclesiastical benefice not yet vacant. *~v.t.* to provide with provisions. **provisional** *a.* 1 provided for present need; temporary, not permanent. 2 requiring future confirmation. 3 (**Provisional**) denoting the militant breakaway faction of the IRA or Sinn Fein. *~n.* (**Provisional**) a member of the Provisional IRA. **provisionality** (-nal´-) *n.* **provisionally** *adv.* **provisionalness** *n.* **provisionary** *a.* provisional. **provisioner** *n.* **provisionless** *a.* **provisionment** *n.* [F, from L *prōvīsiōnem*, from *prōvidēre*, to PROVIDE]

proviso (prəvī´zō) *n.* (*pl.* **provisos, provisoes**) 1 a provisional condition, a stipulation. 2 a clause in a covenant or other document rendering its operation conditional. [L, being provided that, see PROVIDE]

provisor (prəvī´zə) *n.* 1 a bishop's or archbishop's deputy. 2 a person appointed, esp. by the Pope, to a benefice before the death of the incumbent. [ME and A-F *provisour* (F *proviseur*), L *prōvīsor -sōrem*, as PROVISION]

provisory (prəvī´zəri) *a.* 1 conditional. 2 provisional. **provisorily** *adv.*

provitamin (prōvit´əmin) *n.* a substance which can be converted into a vitamin within an organism after ingestion.

Provo (prō´vō) *n.* (*pl.* **Provos**) (*coll.*) a member of the Provisional IRA. [short for PROVISIONAL (under PROVISION)]

provocateur (prəvokatœ´) *n.* a political agitator. [F]

provoke (prəvōk´) *v.t.* 1 to rouse; to incite or stimulate to action, anger etc. 2 to irritate, to incense, to exasperate. 3 to instigate, to call forth, to cause. 4 to tempt. **provocation** (provəkā´shən) *n.* 1 the act, or an instance, of provoking. 2 something that provokes or irritates. 3 (*Law*) an action that provokes a physical attack. **provocative** (-vok´-) *a.* 1 tending to provoke, esp. sexual desire. 2 irritating, annoying, esp. with the intention to excite anger or rouse to action. *~n.* a provocative action, thing, word etc. **provocatively** *adv.* **provocativeness** *n.* **provokable** *a.* †**provokement** *n.* **provoker** *n.* **provoking** *a.* tending to provoke, annoying, exasperating. **provokingly** *adv.* [OF *provoker* (F *provoquer*) L *prōvocāre* (*vocāre*, to call)]

provolone (prōvəlō´ni) *n.* a soft, pale yellow kind of Italian cheese made from cow's milk. [It., from *provola*, from med. L *probula*, buffalo-milk cheese]

provost (prov´əst) *n.* 1 a person appointed to superintend or hold authority. 2 the head of some colleges or schools. 3 the head of a chapter, a prior, a dignitary in a cathedral corresponding to a dean. 4 (*Sc.*) the head of a municipal corporation or burgh. 5 in Germany, a

Protestant minister in charge of the principal church in a town. 6 (*Hist.*) an officer in charge of a body of men, establishment etc. a steward, a provost marshal. 7 (*US*) a senior administrative officer in a university. **provost guard** (prəvō´) *n.* (*US*) a detachment of soldiers commanded by a provost marshal. **provost marshal** (prəvō´) *n.* 1 a commissioned officer, the head of the military police in a camp or in the field. 2 a naval officer in charge of prisoners awaiting court-martial. 3 in the W Indies, a chief of police. 4 (*Hist.*) a French semi-military public officer. **provost sergeant** (prəvō´) *n.* (*US*) a sergeant of the military police. **provostship, provostry** *n.* [OE *prōfost, prāfost*, L *praepositus*]

prow (prow) *n.* 1 the fore part of a vessel, the bow. 2 the projecting front part of anything, such as the nose of an aeroplane. [F *proue*, prob. from L and Gr. *prōra*, rel. to *pro*, before]

prowar (prōwaw´) *a.* in favour of war, or of a particular war; belonging to a party or faction which favours war.

prowess (prow´is) *n.* 1 outstanding ability or skill. 2 valour, bravery, gallantry. [OF *prouesse*, from OF *prou* (F *preux*), prob. from L *prōdesse*, see PROUD]

prowl (prowl) *v.i.* to rove (about) stealthily as if in search of prey. ~*v.t.* to go through or about (a place) in this way. ~*n.* the act or an instance of prowling. **on the prowl** prowling in search of prey. **prowl car** *n.* (*US*) a police patrol car. **prowler** *n.* **prowlingly** *adv.* [ME *prollen*, etym. uncertain]

prox. *abbr.* proximo.

prox. acc. *abbr.* proxime accessit.

proxemics (proksē´miks) *n.* the study of the spatial relationships of people in ordinary conditions and activities. [PROXIMITY (under PROXIMAL)]

proximal (prok´siməl) *a.* nearest the centre of the body or the point of attachment, as distinct from *distal*. **proximally** *adv.* **proximate** (-ət) *a.* 1 nearest, next. 2 immediately preceding or following. 3 approximate. **proximate cause** *n.* something which immediately precedes, and produces, an effect. **proximately** *adv.* **proximity** (-sim´-) *n.* immediate nearness in place, time, relation etc., esp. of kinship. **proximity fuse** *n.* an electronic device which detonates a missile when it gets near its target. **proximity of blood** *n.* kinship. [L *proximus*, superl. of *prope*, near]

proxime accessit (proksimi akses´it) *n.* (*pl.* **proxime accessits**) the person who comes second in an examination, or who gains the second prize. [L, he came next]

proximo (prok´simō) *a.* in or of the month succeeding the present, next month (in old commercial use).

proxy (prok´si) *n.* (*pl.* **proxies**) 1 the agency of a substitute for a principal. 2 a person deputed to act for another, esp. in voting. 3 a document authorizing one person to act or vote for another. 4 a vote given under this authority. ~*a.* done, made etc. by proxy. **proxyship** *n.* [contr. from PROCURACY (under PROCURATOR)]

PRS *abbr.* 1 Performing Rights Society. 2 President of the Royal Society.

PRT *abbr.* petroleum revenue tax.

prude (prood) *n.* a person who affects great modesty or propriety, esp. in regard to sexual matters. **prudery** (-əri) *n.* (*pl.* **pruderies**). **prudish** *a.* **prudishly** *adv.* **prudishness** *n.* [F, from OF *prude* (fem. of *prou, prod*, worthy, or from *prudefemme*, fem. of *prud'homme*)]

prudent (proo´dənt) *a.* 1 cautious, discreet, circumspect. 2 worldly-wise, careful of consequences. 3 showing good judgement or foresight. **prudence** *n.* **prudential** (-den´shəl) *a.* 1 actuated or characterized by prudence. 2 worldly-wise. **prudentialism** *n.* **prudentialist** *n.* **prudentiality** (-shial´-) *n.* **prudentially** *adv.* **prudentials** *n.pl.* 1 prudential considerations, matters of practical wisdom. 2 (*NAm.*) administrative or financial matters, esp. minor ones. 3 prudential maxims or precepts. **prudently** *adv.* [F, from L *prūdens, prōvidens -ntem*, PROVIDENT (under PROVIDENCE)]

Usage note The meanings of the adjectives *prudent* and *prudential* overlap, but *prudent* is a term of approval, applied to people as well as actions, and *prudential* is more neutral and usually describes the conduct of business.

prudery PRUDE.

pruinose (proo´inōs) *a.* (*Bot.*) covered with a white powdery substance or bloom, frosted. **pruinescence** (-nes´əns) *n.* [L *pruīnōsus*, frosty, from *pruīna*, hoar frost]

prune[1] (proon) *n.* 1 the dried fruit of various kinds of *Prunus domestica*, the common plum. 2 (*coll.*) a stupid or uninteresting person. 3 a dark purple colour. **pruniferous** (-nif´-) *a.* [F, from L *prūnum*, Gr. *prounon*]

prune[2] (proon) *v.t.* 1 to cut or lop off the superfluous branches etc. from (a shrub or tree). 2 to cut or lop (branches etc.) from a shrub or tree. 3 to reduce (costs, administration etc.). 4 to free from anything superfluous or undesirable. ~*n.* an instance of pruning. **pruner** *n.* **pruning hook, pruning knife, pruning shears** *n.* an instrument of various forms for pruning trees etc. [OF *proignier*, etym. uncertain]

prunella[1] (prunel´ə) *n.* any plant of the labiate genus *Prunella*, with purplish, bluish or white flowers, the common self-heal. [var. of med. L *brunella*, dim. of *brūnus*, brown]

prunella[2] (prunel´ə) *n.* a smooth dark silk or woollen cloth, used for making the uppers of shoes and gaiters, and formerly for clergymen's and barristers' gowns. [etym. uncertain (cp. F *prunelle*, perh. plum-colour, rel. to PRUNE[1])]

pruniferous PRUNE[1].

prunus (proo´nəs) *n.* any member of the genus *Prunus*, fruit trees and shrubs including plum, cherry, peach, almond etc. [L, plum tree]

prurient (pruə´riənt) *a.* 1 disposed to, characterized by or arousing an unhealthy interest in sexual matters. 2 characterized by a morbid curiosity. **prurience, pruriency** *n.* **pruriently** *adv.* [L *prūriens -ntem*, pres.p. of *prūrīre*, to itch]

prurigo (proorī´gō) *n.* a papular disease of the skin producing severe itching. **pruriginous** (-rij´-) *a.* **pruritus** (-təs) *n.* (*Med.*) itching. **pruritic** (-rit´ik) *a.* [L]

prusik (prŭs´ik) *n.* in mountaineering, a type of sliding knot, which locks when weight is put on it, used to make loops in a rope. ~*v.i., v.t.* (*pres.p.* **prusiking,** *past, p.p.* **prusiked**) to climb, or to hoist, by means of prusiks. **prusik knot** *n.* **prusik sling** *n.* a kind of sling fastened to a rope by means of a prusik knot. [Karl *Prusik*, Austrian climber]

Prussian (prŭsh´ən) *a.* 1 of or relating to Prussia, a former German state. 2 overbearing. 3 militaristic. ~*n.* (*Hist.*) a native or inhabitant of Prussia. **Prussian blue** *n.* a deep-blue pigment obtained from ferrocyanide or iron. **Prussian-blue** *a.* **Prussianism** *n.* practices or policies (e.g. the imposition of rigid discipline, militaristic organization) held to be typically Prussian. **Prussianize, Prussianise** *v.t.* **Prussianizer** *n.* **prussiate** (-siət, -shi-) *n.* any cyanide, ferrocyanide or ferricyanide. **prussic** (prŭs´-) *a.* of or derived from Prussian blue. **prussic acid** *n.* hydrocyanic acid, first obtained from Prussian blue. [med. L *Prussiānus* (*Pruzzi, Borussi*)]

pry[1] (prī) *v.i.* (*3rd pers. sing. pres.* **pries,** *pres.p.* **prying,** *past, p.p.* **pried**) 1 to look closely or inquisitively; to peep, to peer. 2 to search or enquire curiously or impertinently (into). ~*v.t.* to search or find (out) inquisitively or impertinently. ~*n.* (*pl.* **pries**) the act of prying. **to pry out** to discover by prying. **pryer,**

prier *n.* **prying** *a.* **pryingly** *adv.* [ME *prien*, etym. uncertain]

pry[2] (prī) *v.t.* (*3rd pers. sing. pres.* **pries,** *pres.p.* **prying,** *past, p.p.* **pried**) (*N Am.*) to prise.

prytaneum (pritənē´əm) *n.* (*pl.* **prytanea** (-nē´ə)) (*Hist.*) the public hall, esp. in ancient Athens, in which the duties of hospitality were exercised towards ambassadors and citizens honoured with special distinction. [L, from Gr. *prutaneion*, from *prutanis*, president]

Przewalski's horse (pœzhəval´skiz) *n.* a wild horse of central Asia, having an erect mane and no forelock. [Nikolai *Przewalski*, 1839–88, Russian explorer, who discovered it]

PS *abbr.* **1** Police Sergeant. **2** postscript. **3** private secretary. **4** (in a theatre) prompt side.

Ps., Psa. *abbr.* Psalm(s).

PSA *abbr.* **1** Property Services Agency. **2** Public Services Authority.

psalm (sahm) *n.* **1** a sacred song or hymn. **2** (**Psalm**) any one of the sacred songs contained in the Book of Psalms. **Book of Psalms** BOOK. **psalm-book** *n.* a book, for use in church, containing psalms, esp. in metrical form. **psalmic** *a.* **psalmist** *n.* a composer of psalms. **the Psalmist** David or the composer of any of the Psalms. **psalmody** (sah´mədi, sal´-) *n.* (*pl.* **psalmodies**) **1** the act, art or practice of singing psalms, esp. in divine worship. **2** psalms collectively. **3** the setting to music of psalms. **psalmodic** (-mod´-) *a.* **psalmodist** (sah´-) *n.* a composer or singer of psalms. **psalmodize, psalmodise** *v.i.* **Psalms** *n.* the Book of Psalms. [L *psalmus*, Gr. *psalmos*, from *psallein*, to twang, to sing to the harp]

psalter (sawl´tə) *n.* **1** (**Psalter**) The Book of Psalms. **2** a version of this. **3** a book containing the Psalms for use in divine service, esp. the version of the Psalms in the Prayer Book or the Latin collection used in the Roman Catholic Church. [OE *saltere*, from L *psaltērium*, see PSALTERY]

psalterium (sawltiə´riəm) *n.* (*pl.* **psalteria** (-riə)) the third stomach of a ruminant, the omasum. [as PSALTERY]

psaltery (sawl´təri) *n.* (*pl.* **psalteries**) a medieval stringed instrument somewhat resembling the dulcimer, but played by plucking the strings. **psalterian** (sawltiə´riən) *a.* [OF *psalterie*, L *psaltērium*, Gr. *psaltērion*, cp. PSALM]

psammite (sam´īt) *n.* (*Mineral.*) sandstone. **psammitic** (-mit´-) *a.* [F, from Gr. *psammos*, sand]

PSBR *abbr.* public sector borrowing requirement.

pschent (pskhent, skent) *n.* the double crown of ancient Egypt, combining the white pointed mitre of Upper Egypt and the red crown with square front of Lower Egypt. [Gr. *pschent*, Egypt. *p-skhent* (*p*, the, *skhent*, *sekhent*)]

PSDR *abbr.* public sector debt repayment.

psephite (sē´fīt) *n.* a coarse rock containing pebbles or other fragments. **psephitic** (-fit´ik) *a.* [Gr. *psēphos*, a pebble]

psephology (sefol´əji) *n.* the statistical and sociological study of elections, voting patterns etc. **psephological** (-loj´-) *a.* **psephologically** *adv.* **psephologist** *n.* [Gr. *psēphos*, a pebble (as used for voting in the Athenian assembly)]

pseud (sūd) *n.* (*coll.*) an affected or pretentious person, a pretender, a sham. *~a.* pseudo. **pseudery** *n.* **1** pretentiousness. **2** falseness. **pseudish** *a.* **pseudo** (sū´dō) *a.* **1** false, sham, spurious. **2** affected, pretentious. *~n.* (*pl.* **pseudos**) an insincere or pretentious person. [as PSEUDO-]

pseud- PSEUDO-.

pseudaesthesia (sūdəsthē´ziə), (*NAm.*) **pseudesthesia** *n.* an imaginary sense of feeling in organs that have been removed. [cp. ANAESTHESIA]

pseudaxis (sūdak´sis) *n.* (*pl.* **pseudaxes** (-sēz)) (*Bot.*) a sympodium.

pseudepigrapha (sūdəpig´rəfə) *n.pl.* spurious writings, esp. uncanonical writings ascribed to Scriptural authors etc. **pseudepigraphal, pseudepigraphic** (-graf´-), **pseudepigraphical** *a.* **pseudepigraphy** *n.* the ascription of false names of authors to books. [neut. pl. of Gr. *pseudepigraphos* (*epigraphein*, to inscribe, see EPIGRAPH)]

pseudesthesia PSEUDAESTHESIA.

pseudo PSEUD.

pseudo- (sū´dō), **pseud-** *comb. form* **1** false, counterfeit, spurious. **2** closely resembling, as *pseudoclassical*, *pseudo-Gothic*, *pseudohistorical*. [Gr., from *pseudēs*, false]

pseudocarp (sū´dōkahp) *n.* a fruit composed of other parts besides the ovary. **pseudocarpous** (-kah´-) *a.* [Gr. *karpos*, fruit]

pseudocyesis (sūdōsīē´sis) *n.* (*pl.* **pseudocyeses** (-sēz)) a false pregnancy, a psychosomatic condition in which many of the physical signs of pregnancy are present. [Gr. *kuēsis*, from *kuein*, to be pregnant]

pseudograph (sū´dəgrahf) *n.* a spurious writing, a literary forgery. **pseudography** (-dog´-) *n.* [Gr. *pseudographia*]

pseudohermaphroditism (sūdōhœmaf´rədītizm) *n.* a congenital condition in which a person has the reproductive organs of one sex and the external genitalia of the other.

pseudomonas (sūdōmō´nas) *n.* (*pl.* **pseudomonades** (-nədēz)) any member of the genus *Pseudomonas* of rod-shaped bacteria which live in the soil or in decaying organic matter. **pseudomonad** *n.* (*pl.* **pseudomonads**) a pseudomonas. [Gr. *monas -ados*, a unit, from *monos*, alone]

pseudomorph (sū´dəmawf) *n.* **1** a mineral having the crystalline form of another. **2** a false form. **pseudomorphic** (-maw´-) *a.* **pseudomorphism** (-maw´-) *n.* **pseudomorphous** *a.* [Gr. *morphē*, form]

pseudonym (sū´dənim) *n.* a fictitious name, esp. a pen name. **pseudonymity** (-nim´-) *n.* **pseudonymous** (-don´-) *a.* **pseudonymously** *adv.* [Gr. *pseudōnumos* (*onoma*, Aeolic *onuma*, name)]

pseudopod (sū´dəpod) *n.* **1** a pseudopodium. **2** a protrusion from the bodywall of e.g. a caterpillar, used as a leg. [as PSEUDOPODIUM]

pseudopodium (sūdōpō´diəm) *n.* (*pl.* **pseudopodia** (-diə)) a temporary protrusion from the cell surface of a protozoan etc., used for movement or feeding. **pseudopodial** *a.* [Gr. *podion*, dim. of *pous podos*, a foot]

pseudo-random (sūdōran´dəm) *a.* (of a set of numbers) generated by a computer or a mathematical process, and thus not truly random, but sufficiently so for most purposes.

pseudo-science (sūdōsī´əns) *n.* a spurious science, an untested set of beliefs that passes as a science. **pseudoscientific** *a.*

pshaw (pshaw) *int.* used to express contempt, impatience, disdain or dislike. *~n.* this exclamation. *~v.i.* to say 'pshaw' (at). *~v.t.* to express contempt for thus. [instinctive sound]

psi (sī) *n.* **1** the twenty-third letter of the Greek alphabet (Ψ, ψ), equivalent to *ps.* **2** paranormal or psychic phenomena collectively. **psion** (sī´on) *n.* (*pl.* **psions**) a psi particle. **psi particle** *n.* an elementary particle formed by electron–positron collision. **psi phenomena** *n.pl.* paranormal phenomena.

p.s.i. *abbr.* pounds per square inch.

psilocybin (sīlōsī´bin) *n.* a hallucinogenic drug obtained from Mexican mushrooms of the genus *Psilocybe*. [Gr. *psilos*, bare, *kybe*, head]

psilomelane (sīlom´əlān) *n.* a black mineral mainly

consisting of oxide of manganese, an important source of manganese. [Gr. *psilos*, bare, *melās -lanos*, black]

psilosis (sīlō´sis) *n.* (*Med.*) sprue. **psilotic** (-lot´-) *a.* [Gr. *psilos*, bare]

psion PSI.

psittaceous (sitā´shəs), **psittacine** (sit´əsīn) *a.* **1** belonging or allied to the parrots. **2** parrot-like. **psittacism** *n.* (*formal*) the mechanical repetition of words or ideas, without understanding. **psittacosis** (sitəkō´sis) *n.* a contagious disease of parrots communicable to humans, with symptoms like those of pneumonia. [L *psittacus*, parrot]

PSL *abbr.* private sector liquidity.

psoas (sō´əs) *n.* (*pl.* **psoases**) either of the two large muscles involved in flexing and rotating the hip joint. **psoatic** (-at´-) *a.* [Gr., acc. pl. of *psoa*, mistaken for the sing.]

psoriasis (sərī´əsis) *n.* a dry, scaly skin disease. **psora** (saw´rə) *n.* (*Med.*) scabies or an analogous skin disease. **psoriatic** (-at´-) *a.* **psoriatiform** *a.* [L and Gr.]

PSS *abbr.* postscripts.

psst (pəst), **pst** *int.* used as a whispered call to attract someone's attention surreptitiously. [imit.]

PST *abbr.* Pacific Standard Time.

pst PSST.

PSV *abbr.* public service vehicle.

psych (sīk), **psyche** *v.t.* (*coll.*) **1** to psychoanalyse. **2** to psych out. *~v.i.* to make a psychic bid. **to psych out 1** (*N Am.*) to work out, to divine, to anticipate correctly (a person's motivation etc.). **2** to intimidate or defeat by psychological means. **3** (*coll.*) to have a psychological breakdown. **to psych up** to prepare or stimulate psychologically as a preliminary to action.

psych- PSYCHO-.

psyche[1] (sī´ki) *n.* **1** the soul, the spirit, the mind. **2** the principles of emotional and mental life. [Gr. *psuchē*, breath, life, soul]

psyche[2] PSYCH.

psychedelic (sīkədel´ik) *a.* **1** of or relating to new, altered or heightened states of consciousness and sensory awareness as induced by the use of certain hallucinatory drugs. **2** (of drugs) capable of producing such states. **3** having an effect on the mind similar to that of psychedelic drugs. **4** resembling the phenomena of psychedelic experience. **5** (of colours) unnaturally vivid, fluorescent. *~n.* a hallucinogenic drug. **psychedelia** (-dē´liə) *n.pl.* **1** psychedelic objects, clothing, art etc. **2** psychedelic drugs. **psychedelically** *adv.* [Gr. PSYCHE[1], *dēlos*, clear, visible]

psychiatry (sīkī´ətri) *n.* the study and treatment of mental disorders. **psychiatric** (-kiat´-) *a.* **psychiatrical** *a.* **psychiatrically** *adv.* **psychiatric nurse** *n.* a nurse who works with mentally ill people. **psychiatric patient** *n.* a person who is being treated for mental illness. **psychiatrist** (-kī´-) *n.*

psychic (sī´kik) *a.* **1** of or relating to the human soul, spirit or mind. **2** of or relating to phenomena that appear to be outside the domain of physical law, paranormal, extrasensory. **3** (of a person) believed to be sensitive to non-physical or paranormal forces and influences. *~n.* **1** a person believed to have psychic powers, a medium. **2** a psychic bid. **3** (*pl.*) psychology. **psychical** *a.* **1** of or relating to the soul or mind. **2** of or relating to paranormal phenomena. **psychically** *adv.* **psychical research** *n.* scientific research into apparently paranormal phenomena. **psychic bid** *n.* in bridge, a bid that deliberately gives the impression of a stronger hand than is the case. **psychic determinism** *n.* the theory that mental processes do not occur by chance, but always have an ascertainable cause. **psychic force** *n.* a non-physical force supposed to be the agent in spiritualistic phenomena. **psychicism** (-isizm) *n.* psychical research. **psychicist** (-isist) *n.* **psychism** *n.* [Gr. *psuchikos*]

psycho (sī´kō) *n.* (*pl.* **psychos**) a psychopath. *~a.* psychotic, psychopathic.

psycho- (sī´kō), **psych-** *comb.form* **1** mental. **2** psychical. [PSYCHE[1]]

psychoactive (sīkōak´tiv) *a.* (of drugs) capable of affecting the mind or behaviour.

psychoanalysis (sīkōənal´isis) *n.* a method devised by Sigmund Freud for exploring and bringing to light concepts, experience etc. hidden in the unconscious mind as a form of treatment for functional nervous diseases or mental illness. **psychoanalyse** (-an´əlīz), (*N Am.*) **psychoanalyze** *v.t.* to subject to, or treat by, psychoanalysis. **psychoanalyst** (-an´ə-) *n.* **psychoanalytic** (-anəlit´-), **psychoanalytical** *a.* **psychoanalytically** *adv.*

psychobabble (sī´kōbabəl) *n.* (*coll., derog.*) the excessive or inappropriate use of psychological jargon, esp. in popular psychotherapy.

psychobiography (sīkōbīog´rəfi) *n.* (*pl.* **psychobiographies**) a biography which concentrates on the psychological development of its subject. **psychobiographical** *a.*

psychobiology (sīkōbīol´əji) *n.* the study of the relationship between biology and mental and behavioural phenomena. **psychobiological** (-loj´-) *a.* **psychobiologically** *adv.* **psychobiologist** (-ol´-) *n.*

psychodrama (sī´kōdrahmə) *n.* (*pl.* **psychodramas**) **1** an improvised dramatization of events from a patient's past life, used as a form of mental therapy. **2** a film or a play which concentrates on the psychological development of the characters. **psychodramatic** (-drəmat´-) *a.*

psychodynamics (sīkōdīnam´iks) *n.* the study of mental and emotional forces and their effect on behaviour. **psychodynamic** *a.* **psychodynamically** *adv.*

psychogenesis (sīkōjen´əsis) *n.* **1** (the study of) the origin or development of the mind. **2** origination in the mind. **psychogenetic** (-net´-) *a.*

psychogenic (sīkōjen´ik) *a.* (of symptoms or illnesses) having a mental, as opposed to physical, origin.

psychogeriatrics (sīkōjeriat´riks) *n.* the study and treatment of the mental disorders associated with old age. **psychogeriatric** *n., a.* (*Med.*) (an old person) having such mental disorders. **psychogeriatrician** (-trish´ən) *n.* a doctor who specializes in such disorders.

psychographics (sīkōgraf´iks) *n.* the study of personalities, aspirations, attitudes etc., esp. in market research. **psychographic** *a.*

psychohistory (sīkōhis´təri) *n.* (*pl.* **psychohistories**) history written from a psychological point of view. **psychohistorian** (-taw´riən) *n.* **psychohistorical** (-tor´-) *a.*

psychokinesis (sīkōkinē´sis) *n.* apparent movement or alteration in physical objects produced by mental effort alone. **psychokinetic** (-net´-) *a.*

psycholinguistics (sīkōling·gwis´tiks) *n.* the study of the psychology of language, its acquisition, development, use etc. **psycholinguist** (-ling´-) *n.* **psycholinguistic** (-gwis´-) *a.*

psychology (sīkol´əji) *n.* (*pl.* **psychologies**) **1** the science of the human mind or soul. **2** a system or theory of mental laws and phenomena. **3** (characteristic) mentality or motivation. **4** (*coll.*) skill in understanding or motivating people. **5** a treatise on psychology. **psychological** (-loj´-) *a.* **1** of or relating to psychology. **2** relating to or affecting the mind. **3** existing only in the mind. **psychological block** *n.* a mental block. **psychologically** *adv.* **psychological moment** *n.* the critical moment, the exact time for action etc. **psychological warfare** *n.* the use of propaganda to reduce enemy morale. **psychologism** *n.* the belief that psychology is the basis for all other natural and social sciences. **psychologist** *n.* **psychologistic** (-jis´-) *a.* **psychologize, psychologise** *v.t., v.i.* [PSYCHO-, -LOGY]

psychometrics (sīkōmet´riks) *n.* the branch of psychology dealing with the measurement of mental capacities and attributes, esp. by the use of psychological tests and statistical methods. **psychometer** (sīkom´itə) *n.* 1 an instrument for measuring times of reactions etc. 2 a person who measures mental processes. 3 a person who has the power of psychometry. **psychometric, psychometrical** *a.* **psychometrically** *adv.* **psychometrist** *n.* **psychometry** *n.* 1 psychometrics. 2 the occult faculty of divining by touching a physical object, the character, surroundings, experiences etc. of persons who have touched it.

psychomotor (sīkōmō´tə) *a.* of or relating to muscular action proceeding from mental activity.

psychoneurosis (sīkōnūrō´sis) *n.* (*pl.* **psychoneuroses** (-sēz)) a neurosis, esp. one due to emotional conflict. **psychoneurotic** (-rot´-) *a.*

psychopath (sī´kəpath) *n.* 1 a person suffering from a severe personality disorder characterized by antisocial behaviour and a tendency to commit acts of violence. 2 (*coll.*) a mentally or emotionally unstable person. **psychopathic** (-path´-) *a.* **psychopathically** *adv.* **psychopathy** (-kop´əthi) *n.* psychologically abnormal behaviour.

psychopathology (sīkōpəthol´əji) *n.* (the branch of psychology dealing with) mental and behavioural aberrance. **psychopathological** *a.*

psychopathy PSYCHOPATH.

psychopharmacology (sīkōfahməkol´əji) *n.* the study of the effect of drugs on the mind.

psychophysics (sīkōfiz´iks) *n.* the science of the relations between mind and body, esp. between physical stimuli and psychological sensation. **psychophysical** *a.* **psychophysicist** (-sist) *n.*

psychophysiology (sīkōfiziol´əji) *n.* the branch of physiology which deals with mental phenomena. **psychophysiological** (-loj´-) *a.*

psychoprophylaxis (sīkōprōfilak´sis) *n.* a method of training women for natural childbirth by teaching breathing and relaxation techniques for the management of pain.

psychosexual (sīkōsek´shəl, -sūəl) *a.* of or relating to the psychological aspects of sex. **psychosexually** *adv.*

psychosis (sīkō´sis) *n.* (*pl.* **psychoses** (-sēz)) a severe mental disorder, not due to organic lesion, characterized by distortion of the sufferer's concept of reality. **psychotic** (-kot´-) *n., a.* (a person) suffering from psychosis. **psychotically** *adv.*

psychosocial (sīkōsō´shəl) *a.* of or relating to the interaction of social and psychological factors, esp. in illness. **psychosocially** *adv.*

psychosomatic (sīkōsəmat´ik) *a.* 1 denoting a physical disorder caused by or influenced by the patient's emotional condition. 2 of or relating to the mind and the body considered together. **psychosomatically** *adv.*

psychosurgery (sīkōsœ´jəri) *n.* the use of brain surgery in the treatment of mental disorder. **psychosurgical** *a.*

psychotherapy (sīkōther´əpi) *n.* the treatment of mental disorder by psychological or hypnotic means. **psychotherapeutic** (-therəpū´tik) *a.* treating disease by psychological methods. **psychotherapeutics** *n.* **psychotherapist** *n.*

psychotic PSYCHOSIS.

psychotropic (sīkōtrō´pik, -trop´-) *a.* psychoactive.

psychrometer (sīkrom´itə) *n.* the wet-and-dry bulb hygrometer for measuring the humidity of the atmosphere. **psychrometric** (-met´-), **psychrometrical** *a.* **psychrometry** (-krom´-) *n.*

☒ **psycology** common misspelling of PSYCHOLOGY.

PT *abbr.* 1 Pacific Time. 2 physical training.

Pt[1] *abbr.* 1 point. 2 port.

Pt[2] *chem. symbol* platinum.

pt. *abbr.* 1 part. 2 pint(s). 3 (*Math.*) point. 4 port.

PTA *abbr.* 1 parent–teacher association. 2 Passenger Transport Authority.

ptarmigan (tah´migən) *n.* (*pl. in general* **ptarmigan,** *in particular* **ptarmigans**) any of various birds of the genus *Lagopus*, allied to the grouse, having grey or brown plumage in the summer and white in the winter, esp. *Lagopus mutus*, of subarctic regions. [Gael. *tàrmachan*, etym. uncertain]

PT boat (pētē´) *n.* (*US*) a motor torpedo boat. [*p*atrol, *t*orpedo]

PTE *abbr.* Passenger Transport Executive.

Pte. *abbr.* (*Mil.*) Private.

pter- PTERO-.

-ptera (ptərə) *comb. form* organisms having a certain number or type of wings. [Gr., pl. of *pteron*, a feather, a wing]

pteri- PTERO-.

pteridology (teridol´əji) *n.* the scientific study of ferns. **pteridological** (-loj´-) *a.* **pteridologist** *n.* [Gr. *pteris -idos*, fern, from *pteron*, feather]

pteridophyte (ter´idōfīt) *n.* any member of the division Pteridophyta including ferns, clubmosses and horsetails. **pteridophytic, pteridophytous** (-dof´itəs) *a.* [Gr. *pteris -idos*, a fern, *phuton*, a plant]

pteridosperm (ter´idōspœm) *n.* a fossil plant of the group Pteridospermae, fernlike but producing seeds. [Gr. *pteris -idos*, a fern, *sperma*, seed]

pterion (ter´iən) *n.* (*pl.* **pteria** (-riə)) (*Anat.*) the H-shaped suture where the frontal, parietal and sphenoid bones of the skull meet. [dim. of Gr. *pteron*, wing]

ptero- (ter´ō), **pteri-** (-i), **pter-** *comb. form* 1 winged. 2 having processes resembling wings. [Gr. *pteron*, a feather, a wing]

pterodactyl (terədak´til) *n.* an extinct winged reptile from the Mesozoic strata with membranous wings and a long birdlike head. [Gr. *daktulos*, finger]

pteropod (ter´əpod) *n.* (*Zool.*) any individual of the Pteropoda, a subclass of Mollusca in which the foot is expanded into winglike lobes or paddles. [Gr. *pous podos*, foot]

pterosaur (ter´əsaw) *n.* any individual of the Pterosauria, an order of flying reptiles of the Mesozoic age. **pterosaurian** (-saw´-) *n., a.* [Gr. *sauros*, lizard]

pteroylglutamic acid (terōilglutam´ik) *n.* folic acid.

pterygium (tərij´iəm) *n.* (*pl.* **pterygia** (-iə)) a varicose excrescence of the conjunctiva of the eye. **pterygial** *a.* [Gr. *pterugion*, dim. as of *pterux*, see PTERYGOID]

pterygoid (ter´igoid) *a.* 1 (*Anat.*) wing-shaped. 2 of or connected with the pterygoid processes. ~*n.* a pterygoid bone or process. **pterygoid process** *n.* either of the winglike processes descending from the great wings of the sphenoid bone of the skull. [Gr. *pterugoeides* (*pterux -ugos*, wing)]

pteryla (ter´ilə) *n.* (*pl.* **pterylae** (-lē)) any of the tracts or patches of feathers on the skin of a bird. [mod. L, from Gr. *pteron*, feather]

PTFE *abbr.* polytetrafluoroethylene.

ptisan TISANE.

PTO *abbr.* please turn over.

ptochocracy (tōkok´rəsi) *n.* (*pl.* **ptochocracies**) government by the poor, as distinct from *plutocracy*. [Gr. *ptōchos*, poor]

Ptolemaic (toləmā´ik) *a.* 1 of or relating to Ptolemy, Alexandrian astronomer (2nd cent. AD) who maintained that the earth was a fixed body in the centre of the universe, the sun and moon revolving round it. 2 (*Hist.*) of or relating to the Ptolemies, kings of Egypt, 323–30

BC. **Ptolemaic system** *n.* Ptolemy's conception of the universe. **Ptolemaist** *n.*

ptomaine (tō´mān) *n.* any one of a class of sometimes poisonous amines derived from decaying animal and vegetable matter. **ptomaic** (-mā´ik) *a.* **ptomaine poisoning** *n.* food poisoning (formerly, and erroneously, thought to be due to ptomaines). [It. *ptomaina*, from Gr. *ptōma*, corpse, cogn. with *piptein*, to fall]

ptosis (tō´sis) *n.* (*pl.* **ptoses** (-sēz)) a drooping of the upper eyelid from paralysis of the muscle raising it. **ptotic** (tō´tik) *a.* [Gr., falling, see PTOMAINE]

PTSD *abbr.* post-traumatic stress disorder.

Pty. *abbr.* (*Austral.*, *New Zeal.*) proprietary (denotes a private limited company).

ptyalin (tī´əlin) *n.* an enzyme contained in saliva, which converts starch into dextrin. **ptyalism** *n.* excessive salivation. **ptyalize, ptyalise** *v.t.* to induce ptyalism in. [Gr. *ptūalon*, spittle, from *ptūein*, to spit]

Pu *chem. symbol* plutonium.

pub[1] (pŭb) *n.* **1** a public house. **2** (*Austral.*, *coll.*) a hotel. ~*v.i.* (*pres.p.* **pubbing,** *past, p.p.* **pubbed**) to visit public houses. **pub crawl** *n.* (*coll.*) a drinking tour of a number of pubs.

pub[2] *n.* (*sl.*) publication. ~*v.t.* (*pres.p.* **pubbing,** *past* **pubbed,** *p.p.* **pubbed, pub**) to publish.

pub. *abbr.* **1** public. **2** publish. **3** published. **4** publisher. **5** publishing.

puberty (pū´bəti) *n.* the period of life at which persons become capable of begetting or bearing children. **puberal** (-bərəl), **pubertal** *a.* **puberulent** (-bœ´rūlənt) *a.* pubescent, downy. **pubes**[1] (-bēz, pūbz) *n.* (*pl.* **pubes**) **1** the hypogastric region which in the adult becomes covered with hair. **2** (*coll.*) the hair of the pubic region. **pubescence** (-bes´əns) *n.* **1** the state or age of puberty. **2** †soft, hairy down on plants or parts of animals, esp. insects, downiness, hairiness. **pubescent** *a.* **1** arrived at the age of puberty. **2** covered with soft hairy down. **pubic** *a.* of or relating to the pubes or pubis. **pubis** (-bis) *n.* (*pl.* **pubises, pubes** (-bēz)) either of two bones forming the anterior part of the pelvis. [F *puberté*, L *pūbertas -tātem*, from *pūber*, youth, or *pūbes*, hair]

pubes[1] PUBERTY.

pubes[2] PUBIS (under PUBERTY).

public (pŭb´lik) *a.* **1** of, relating to or affecting the people as a whole, as distinct from *personal* or *private*. **2** open to the use or enjoyment of all, not restricted to any class. **3** done, existing or such as may be observed by all, not concealed or clandestine. **4** open, notorious. **5** **a** well-known, prominent. **b** of or relating to a person in their capacity as a public figure. **6** of or relating to the affairs or service of the people. **7** employed by, or provided by, local or central government. **8** of or for a university. ~*n.* **1** the people in general. **2** any particular section of the people. **3** (*coll.*) a public house, or a public bar. **in public** openly, publicly. **in the public eye** famous. **to go public 1** to become a public company. **2** to make publicly known. **public act** *n.* an act of parliament that affects the public as a whole. **public address system** *n.* a system of microphones, amplifiers, loudspeakers etc. used for addressing a large audience. **public analyst** *n.* a chemist who carries out independent analyses of consumer products to check for toxins etc. **public art** *n.* large works of art (e.g. statues, murals) set up in public spaces such as parks or streets. **public bar** *n.* a bar in a public house, usu. less well appointed, and serving drinks at cheaper prices than a saloon bar. **public bill** *n.* a bill before parliament that affects the public as a whole. **public company** *n.* a company whose shares can be purchased on the Stock Exchange by members of the public. **public convenience** *n.* a public lavatory. **public corporation** *n.* an organization set up by government to run a nationalized service or industry. **public credit** *n.* the faith in the honesty and financial ability of a government seeking to borrow money. **public defender** *n.* (*US*) a defence lawyer provided by the state for those who cannot afford to pay a lawyer themselves. **public domain** *n.* **1** the status in law of a published work on which the copyright has expired. **2** (*Comput.*) of or relating to software which is not copyrighted or sold commercially, but is available for a small handling charge. **3** (*US*) land owned by a state or by the federal government. **public enemy** *n.* a person, esp. a notorious criminal, considered to be a menace to the community. **public figure** *n.* a famous person. **public health** *n.* the field of responsibility for the general health of the community covering e.g. sanitation, food-handling in shops and restaurants, hygiene in public places. **public holiday** *n.* a holiday observed generally through a whole country. **public house** *n.* a house licensed for the retail of intoxicating liquors, an inn, a tavern. **public image** *n.* a person's reputation as perceived by the general public. **public law** *n.* **1** the body of law governing the relations between individuals and the state. **2** international law. **3** a public act. **public lending right** *n.* the right of authors to royalties when their books are borrowed from public libraries. **public libel** *n.* (*Law*) a published libel. **public library** *n.* (*pl.* **public libraries**) a library open to members of the public. **publicly** *adv.* **publicness** *n.* **public nuisance** *n.* **1** (*Law*) an illegal act affecting the whole community rather than an individual. **2** (*coll.*) a generally objectionable person. **public opinion** *n.* the views of the general public or the electorate on political and social issues. **public opinion poll** *n.* an assessment of public opinion on an issue based on the responses of a scientifically selected sample of the community to certain questions. **public orator** *n.* an officer at a university who acts as public speaker on ceremonial occasions. **public ownership** *n.* ownership by the state of e.g. large industries, utilities etc. **public prosecutor** *n.* an official who conducts criminal prosecutions on behalf of the state. **public purse** *n.* a national treasury. **Public Record Office** *n.* an institution in which official papers are kept, for inspection by the public. **public records** *n.pl.* official state papers to which the public has access. **public relations** *n.* **1** (*sing. or pl. in constr.*) the relationship between an organization and the public. **2** (a department entrusted with) the maintenance of goodwill towards, and a favourable image of, an organization in the mind of the public. **public relations officer** *n.* **public school** *n.* **1** a non-fee-paying school under the control of a publicly elected body. **2** an independent fee-paying school (in England and Wales) esp. for boarders. **public sector** *n.* the state-owned part of the economy. **public servant** *n.* a government employee. **public service** *n.* **1** employment by the government. **2** a service provided for the public. **public-service corporation** *n.* (*US*) a private corporation providing services to the public, such as transport. **public speaking** *n.* (the art of) making speeches to large audiences. **public speaker** *n.* **public spending** *n.* expenditure by central or local government, or their agencies. **public spirit** *n.* interest in or devotion to the community. **public-spirited** *a.* **public-spiritedly** *adv.* **public-spiritedness** *n.* **public transport** *n.* a system of buses, trains etc. run by the State for use by the public. **public trustee** *n.* an official appointed by the State to act as a trustee or executor where one is needed. **public utility** *n.* an enterprise concerned with the provision of an essential service, e.g. gas, water, electricity, to the public. **public weal** *n.* the common weal. **public works** *n.pl.* roads, buildings etc. constructed for public use by or on behalf of the government. **public wrong** *n.* an offence committed against the public as a whole. [F, from L *pūblicus*, contr. of *populus*, from *populus*, people]

publican (pŭb´likən) *n.* 1 a keeper of a public house. 2 (*Austral.*) a keeper of a hotel. 3 (*Hist.*) a collector or farmer of the revenues, taxes etc. in the Roman empire. [ME, from OF *publicain*, from L *pūblicānus*, a tax collector, from *pūblicum*, public revenue, see PUBLIC]

publication (pŭblikā´shən) *n.* 1 the act, or an instance, of making publicly known. 2 the act of publishing a book, periodical, musical composition etc. 3 a work printed and published. [L *pūblicātio -ōnem*, see PUBLISH]

publicise PUBLICIZE.

publicist (pŭb´lisist) *n.* 1 a writer on current social or political topics, esp. a journalist, a person who publicizes, esp. a press or publicity agent. 2 a public relations officer. 3 a writer or authority on international law. **publicism** *n.* **publicistic** (-sis´-) *a.* [F *publiciste*, from L (*ius*) *pūblicum*, public law]

publicity (pŭblis´iti) *n.* 1 the process of attracting public attention to a product, person etc. 2 anything calculated to arouse public interest, such as a newsworthy event or information, advertising etc. 3 public attention or interest. 4 the quality of being public. **publicity agent** *n.* a person employed to keep before the public the name of a product, film etc. **publicity stunt** *n.* an unusual or attention-grabbing event engineered specifically for purposes of publicity. [F *publicité*, from L *pūblicitās -tātem*, see PUBLIC]

publicize (pŭb´lisīz), **publicise** *v.t.* to make known to the public; to advertise.

publish (pŭb´lish) *v.t.* 1 to make public, to promulgate, to announce publicly. 2 to issue or print and offer for sale (a book, newspaper etc.) to the public. 3 to issue the works of (an author). 4 to read (the banns of marriage). 5 to communicate (a libel) to someone apart from the person libelled. *~v.i.* to print and offer for sale. **publishable** *a.* **published** *a.* (of a writer) having had one's works issued. **publisher** *n.* 1 a person or a company that publishes, esp. books and other literary productions. 2 (*N Am.*) a newspaper proprietor. 3 a person who makes anything public. **publishing** *n.* [ME *publischen*, F *publier*, L *publicāre*, as PUBLIC]

puccoon (pəkoon´) *n.* any one of various N American plants yielding a red or yellow dye. [Algonquian]

puce (pūs) *n.* a dark reddish purple colour. *~a.* of this colour. [F, from L *pūlicem*, nom. *pūlex*, flea]

puck[1] (pŭk) *n.* 1 a mischievous sprite, elf or fairy. 2 a mischievous child. **puckish** *a.* **puckishly** *adv.* **puckishness** *n.* **pucklike** *a.* [OE *pūca*, cogn. with Icel. *pūki*, Ir. *púca*, POOKA]

puck[2] (pŭk) *n.* a vulcanized rubber disc used instead of a ball in ice hockey. [etym. unknown]

pucka PUKKA.

pucker (pŭk´ə) *v.t.* to gather into small folds or wrinkles. *~v.i.* to become wrinkled or gathered into small folds etc. *~n.* a fold, a wrinkle, a bulge. **puckery** *a.* [prob. rel. to POKE[2]]

pud (pud) *n.* (*coll.*) short for PUDDING.

puddening (pud´əning) *n.* (*Naut.*) a pad of rope etc. used as a fender. [corr. of PUDDING]

pudding (pud´ing) *n.* 1 a sweet dish, usu. cooked, and usu. made with flour, eggs, milk etc. 2 a savoury dish, usu. meat with pastry or batter etc. 3 the dessert course of a meal. 4 a skin or intestine stuffed with minced meat etc., a large sausage. 5 (*N Am.*) a cold dessert, usu. creamy. 6 (*coll.*) a fat or stupid person. 7 (*Naut.*) a puddening. **in the pudding club** (*sl.*) pregnant. **pudding basin** *n.* a basin for steaming a pudding in. **pudding cloth** *n.* a cotton or muslin cloth for wrapping a pudding for boiling. **pudding face** *n.* (*coll.*) a fat, round, smooth face. **pudding-faced** *a.* **pudding-head** *n.* (*coll.*) a stupid person. **pudding-heart** *n.* (*coll.*) a spiritless person. **pudding-pie** *n.* 1 a pudding with meat baked in it. 2 a tart made with piecrust and custard. **pudding-sleeve** *n.* a full sleeve gathered at the wrist, as in a clerical gown. **pudding-stone** *n.* a conglomerate of pebbles in a siliceous matrix. **puddingy** *a.* [ME, etym. uncertain]

puddle (pŭd´əl) *n.* 1 a small pool, esp. of rainwater. 2 clay and sand worked together to form a watertight lining for a pond, canal etc. 3 the patch of rough water left by the blade of an oar. *~v.i.* 1 to dabble (in mud, water etc.). 2 to mess, to muddle (about). 3 to make puddle from clay and sand. *~v.t.* 1 to work (clay etc.) into puddle. 2 to line or render watertight with puddle. 3 to stir up (molten iron) in a furnace so as to convert it into wrought iron. 4 to make dirty or muddy. 5 to work (clay and water) so as to separate gold or opals. **puddler** *n.* a person who puddles, esp. a workman employed in puddling iron. **puddling** *n.* **puddly** *a.* [ME *podel*, dim. from OE *pudd*, a ditch]

pudency (pū´dənsi) *n.* (*formal*) modesty, shamefacedness. **pudendum** (-den´dəm) *n.* (*pl.* **pudenda** (-də)) (*often pl.*) the genitals, esp. those of a woman. *~a.* of or relating to the pudenda. **pudendal** *a.* **pudic** (pū´-) *a.* **pudicity** (-dis´-) *n.* (*formal*) modesty, chastity. [late L *pudentia*, from L *pudens -ntis*, pres.p. of *pudēre*, to make or be ashamed]

pudge (pŭj) *n.* a short, thick or fat person or figure. **pudgy** *a.* (*comp.* **pudgier**, *superl.* **pudgiest**). **pudgily** *adv.* **pudginess** *n.* [cp. PODGE]

pudic PUDENCY.

pudsy (pŭd´zi) *a.* (*comp.* **pudsier**, *superl.* **pudsiest**) (*coll., dial.*) plump. [etym. uncertain, perh. rel. to PUDGY (under PUDGE)]

pueblo (pweb´lō) *n.* (*pl.* **pueblos**) 1 a village, town or settlement, esp. of the Indians of New Mexico etc. 2 (**Pueblo**) a member of a N American Indian people who live in pueblos, in New Mexico etc. *~a.* (**Pueblo**) of or relating to the Pueblos. **pueblan** *a.* [Sp.]

puerile (pūə´rīl) *a.* childish, silly, inane. **puerilely** *adv.* **puerility** (-ril´-) *n.* (*pl.* **puerilities**) 1 the state of being childish or silly. 2 a puerile action, expression etc. [L *puerīlis*, from *puer*, boy]

puerperal (pūœ´pərəl) *a.* of, relating to or resulting from childbirth. **puerperal fever** *n.* a fever, caused by infection of the genital tract, attacking women after childbirth. **puerperalism** *n.* **puerperal psychosis** *n.* a mental disorder sometimes occurring after childbirth, characterized by depression, delusions etc. **puerperium** (-piər´iəm) *n.* the period of approx. six weeks after childbirth after which the uterus returns to its normal size. [L *puerperus* (*puer*, boy, *-parus*, bearing, from *parere*, to bear)]

Puerto Rican (pwœtō rē´kən) *n.* a native or inhabitant of Puerto Rico, in the Greater Antilles. *~a.* of or relating to Puerto Rico or its inhabitants.

puff (pŭf) *v.i.* 1 to breathe, to blow, to emit or expel air, steam etc. in short, sudden blasts. 2 to move or go while puffing. 3 to breathe hard. 4 to come (out) in a short, sudden blast. 5 to become inflated or distended. *~v.t.* 1 to emit, to blow out, with a short sudden blast or blasts. 2 to blow or drive (away) thus. 3 to draw at (a cigarette, pipe). 4 to utter pantingly. 5 to inflate, to blow (up or out). 6 to blow (away etc.). 7 to bid at an auction in order to inflate the price. 8 to cause to be out of breath. 9 to praise or advertise in an exaggerated or misleading way. *~n.* 1 a short, sudden blast of breath, smoke, steam etc., a whiff, a gust. 2 the sound made by this. 3 a small amount of breath, smoke etc., emitted at one puff. 4 a light, puffy thing or small mass of any material. 5 a cake, tart etc. of light or spongy consistency. 6 a light wad, pad or tuft for applying powder to the skin. 7 an exaggerated or misleading advertisement, review etc. 8 a rolled mass of hair pinned over a pad. 9 (*N Am.*) an eiderdown. **10** (*sl., derog.*) a male homosexual. **in all one's puff** (*coll.*) in all one's life. **puffed up 1** inflated. **2** swollen up with conceit or self-importance. **to puff and blow** to breathe hard or noisily. **puff-adder** *n.* a highly venomous African snake, *Bitis arietans*, which inflates part of its body when aroused. **puffball** *n.* **1** any of several fungi, the roundish spore case of which emits dry, dustlike spores. **2** a full skirt gathered in at the hem to make a rounded shape. **3** a powder puff. **puff-bird** *n.* a bird of the family Bucconidae, so called from their habit of puffing out their plumage. **puffed** *a.* **1** inflated. **2** (of a sleeve) short and full, gathered into a close fitting band. **3** (*coll.*) (*also* **puffed out**) out of breath. **puffer** *n.* **1** a person or thing that puffs, esp. a steamboat, steam engine etc. **2** (**puffer fish**) a globe-fish. **puffery** *n.* (*pl.* **pufferies**) **1** exaggerated praise. **2** an instance of this. **puffing** *a., n.* **puffingly** *adv.* **puff pastry,** (*N Am.*) **puff paste** *n.* (a rich dough used to make) a light, flaky pastry etc. **puff-puff** *n.* a steam locomotive (used by or to children). **puffy** *a.* (*comp.* **puffier,** *superl.* **puffiest**) **1** puffing, blowing or breathing in puffs. **2** short-winded. **3** swollen, distended. **4** tumid, turgid, bombastic. **puffily** *adv.* **puffiness** *n.* [ME *puffen*, imit.]

puffin (pŭf´in) *n.* any of various seabirds of the genus *Fratercula*, esp. the N Atlantic *F. arctica*, with black and white plumage and a brightly-coloured bill. **puffin crossing** *n.* a type of pelican crossing incorporating sensors which monitor the movements of pedestrians and keep the traffic lights red until the crossing is clear. [etym. uncertain]

pug[1] (pŭg) *n.* **1** a pug-dog. **2** a pug-moth. **3** a pug-engine. **4** a fox. **pug-dog** *n.* a small, short-haired breed of dog with wrinkled face, up-turned nose and tightly curled tail. **pug-engine** *n.* a small locomotive for shunting etc. **pug-faced** *a.* **puggish** *a.* **puggy** *a.* (*comp.* **puggier,** *superl.* **puggiest**). **pug-moth** *n.* a small geometrid moth, esp. of the genus *Eupithecia*. **pug-nose** *n.* a short squat nose. **pug-nosed** *a.* [etym. unknown]

pug[2] (pŭg) *n.* clay and other material mixed and prepared for making into bricks. ~*v.t.* (*pres.p.* **pugging,** *past, p.p.* **pugged**) **1** to grind and render plastic (clay etc.) for brick-making. **2** to puddle with clay. **3** to pack (a wall, floor etc.) with sawdust etc. to deaden sound. **pug-mill** *n.* a mill in which clay is made into pug. [etym. uncertain]

pug[3] (pŭg) *n.* (*sl.*) a boxer. [short for PUGILIST]

pugaree (pŭg´əri), **puggaree, puggree** *n.* (*Ang.-Ind.*) **1** a light turban. **2** a long piece of muslin wound round a hat or helmet in hot climates as protection against the sun. **pugareed** *a.* [Hind. *pagrī*]

pugilist (pū´jilist) *n.* a boxer, a prizefighter. **pugilism** *n.* **pugilistic** (-lis´-) *a.* [L *pugil*, boxer, from *pugillus*, a handful, from *pug-*, root of *pugnus*, fist (cp. Gr. *pugmē*)]

pugnacious (pŭgnā´shəs) *a.* inclined to fight; quarrelsome. ~*adv.* **pugnacity** (-nas´-), **pugnaciousness** *n.* [L *pugnax -ācis*, from *pugnāre*, to fight, as PUGILIST]

puisne (pū´ni) *a.* (*Law*) (of a judge) junior or inferior in rank. ~*n.* a puisne judge. [OF *puis*, L *postea*, from *post*, after, *né*, L *nātus*, born]

puissant (pū´isənt, pwis´-) *a.* (*formal*) powerful, strong, mighty. **puissance** (pū´isəns, pwē´sās) *n.* **1** a show-jumping event that tests a horse's power to jump high obstacles. **2** (*formal*) power, strength. **puissantly** *adv.* [F, cp. It. *possente*; both prob. from a low L *possens -ntem*, pres.p. of L *posse*, to be able]

puja (poo´jə), **pooja** *n.* a Hindu act of worship. [Sansk.]

puke (pūk) *v.t., v.i.* (*sl.*) to vomit. ~*n.* **1** vomit. **2** the act of vomiting. **puker** *n.* **pukey, puky** *a.* [etym. uncertain]

pukeko (poo´kikō, pŭk´-) *n.* (*pl.* **pukekos**) (*New Zeal.*) a wading bird, *Porphyrio porphyrio*, with bright plumage. [Maori]

pukka (pŭk´ə), **pucka, pukkah** *a.* (*Ang.-Ind.*) **1** genuine. **2** superior. **3** durable, substantial. **4** of full weight. [Hind., cooked, ripe]

puky PUKE.

pulchritude (pŭl´kritūd) *n.* (*formal or facet.*) beauty. **pulchritudinous** (-tū´din-) *a.* [L *pulchritūdo*, from *pulcher*, beautiful]

pule (pūl) *v.i.* to cry plaintively or querulously, to whine, to whimper. **puler** *n.* **puling** *a., n.* **pulingly** *adv.* [perh. from F *piaulir*, or imit.]

pulicide (pū´lisīd) *n.* any chemical agent used for killing fleas. [L *pulex -icis*, flea, *caedere*, to kill]

Pulitzer prize (poo´litsə, pū´-) *n.* any one of a series of prizes awarded annually in the US for literature, journalism and music. [Joseph *Pulitzer*, 1847–1911, US newspaper publisher]

pull (pul) *v.t.* **1** to draw towards one by force. **2** to drag, to haul, to tug. **3** to draw (up, along, nearer etc.). **4** to move (a vehicle) in a particular direction. **5** to pluck. **6 a** to remove by plucking (a tooth, a cork etc.). **b** to remove (a weed) by the root. **7** to draw (beer etc.) from a barrel etc. **8 a** to strip (a fowl) of feathers. **b** to draw the entrails from (a fowl). **9** to bring out (a weapon). **10** to strain (a muscle or tendon). **11 a** to row (a boat). **b** to take (a person in a boat) by rowing. **12** (*coll.*) to attract (a crowd, support etc.). **13** (*sl.*) to carry out, esp. with daring and imagination or with deceptive intent. **14** (*sl.*) to succeed in attracting sexually. **15** (*Print.*) to take (an impression), to take (a proof). **16** to strike (a cricket ball) from the off to the on side. **17** to strike a golf ball to the left. **18** to rein in (a horse), esp. so as to lose a race. ~*v.i.* **1** to give a pull. **2** to tug, to haul. **3** to move with difficulty, or effortfully. **4** to move (a vehicle) in a particular direction. **5** (of a horse) to strain against the bit. **6** to draw, to suck (at a pipe). **7** to pluck, to tear (at). ~*n.* **1 a** the act of pulling, a tug. **b** the force exerted by this. **2** something which is pulled. **3** a handle by which beer is drawn, a door opened, a bell rung etc. **4** a quantity of beer etc. drawn. **5** a draught, a swig. **6** influence or advantage. **7** (*coll.*) a hold, unfair or illegitimate influence. **8** (*coll.*) a spell of hard exertion. **9** something which draws one's attention. **10** (*Print.*) a proof. **11** in cricket, a stroke by which a ball is sent from the off to the on side. **12** in golf, a stroke sending a ball to the left. **13** the checking of a horse by its rider, esp. to secure defeat in a race. **14** a spell of rowing. **15** a draw at a cigarette. **pull the other one** (*coll.*) used as an expression of disbelief (i.e. pull the other leg). **to pull about** to pull to and fro, to handle roughly. **to pull a face** FACE. **to pull a fast one** FAST[1]. **to pull ahead** to move ahead, or into the lead. **to pull all the stops out** to make every effort. **to pull apart 1** to pull asunder or into pieces. **2** to become separated or severed. **3** to criticize severely. **to pull away** to move (further) into the lead. **to pull back** to retreat or cause to retreat; to withdraw. **to pull down 1** to demolish. **2** to degrade, to humble. **3** to weaken, to cause (prices etc.) to be reduced. **4** (*sl.*) to earn a (specified) amount of money. **to pull in 1** to retract, to make tighter. **2** (of a train) to enter a station. **3** (of a vehicle, driver) to stop (at), to pull over. **4** (*coll.*) to attract (audiences etc.). **5** (*sl.*) to arrest. **6** to earn. **to pull off 1** to remove by pulling. **2** to accomplish (something difficult or risky). **to pull oneself together** to regain one's composure or self-control. **to pull one's punches** PUNCH[1]. **to pull one's weight** WEIGHT. **to pull out 1** to remove by pulling. **2** to leave, to depart. **3** to withdraw. **4** to cease to participate in. **5** to move out from the side of the road or from behind another vehicle. **6** (of an aircraft) to level off after a dive. **to pull out all the stops** STOP. **to pull over** (of a vehicle) to draw in to the side of the road (and stop). **to pull rank** RANK[1]. **to pull round** to (cause to) recover. **to pull someone's leg** LEG. **to pull strings**

STRING. **to pull the plug on** PLUG. **to pull the wires** WIRE. **to pull the wool over someone's eyes** WOOL. **to pull through** to (cause to) survive, recover or not fail against the odds. **to pull together** to cooperate. **to pull to pieces 1** to tear (a thing) up. **2** to criticize, to abuse. **to pull up 1** to drag up forcibly. **2** to pluck out of the ground. **3** to cause to stop. **4** to come to a stop. **5** to rebuke. **6** to gain on, to draw level (with). **to pull up by the roots** ROOT[1]. **pull-back** *n.* **1** a drawback, a restraint, hindrance. **2** a retreat, a withdrawal. **pull-down** *a.* **1** that can be pulled down. **2** (*Comput.*) of or relating to a menu which can be accessed during the running of the program and which brings a list of options down over the screen. ~*n.* a thing which can pull down or be pulled down. **pulled** *a.* **1** plucked, stripped (as fowls, skins etc.). **2** depressed in health, spirits etc., dragged (down). **puller** *n.* **1** a person who or thing which pulls. **2** an implement, machine etc. for pulling. **3** a horse that pulls against the bit, a hard-mouthed or high-spirited horse. **pull-in** *n.* **1** a stopping place. **2** a transport café. **pull-off** *a.* that can be pulled off. ~*n.* **1** an act of pulling off. **2** a lay-by. **pull-on** *n., a.* (a garment) without fastenings, requiring simply to be pulled on. **pull-out** *n.* **1** a removable section of a magazine. **2** a large fold-out leaf in a book. **3** a withdrawal. **pullover** *n.* a knitted garment which is pulled on over the head. **pull-through** *n.* a cord with a rag attached, used for cleaning the barrel of a firearm. **pull-up** *n.* **1** the act, or an instance of pulling up. **2** a stop. **3** a lay-by. **4** an exercise in which one hangs by the hands from a bar and pulls oneself up until the chin is level with the bar. [OE *pullian*, etym. uncertain]

pullet (pul´it) *n.* a young fowl, esp. a hen less than a year old. [ME and OF *polete* (F *poulet*), dim. of *poule*, late L *pulla*, hen, fem. of L *pullus*, a young animal, cogn. with FOAL]

pulley (pul´i) *n.* (*pl.* **pulleys**) **1** a wheel with a grooved rim, or a combination of such wheels, mounted in a block for changing the direction or for increasing the effect of a force. **2** a wheel used to transmit power or motion by means of a belt, chain etc. passing over its rim. ~*v.t.* (*3rd pers. sing. pres.* **pulleys,** *pres.p.* **pulleying,** *past, p.p.* **pulleyed**) **1** to lift or hoist with a pulley. **2** to furnish or fit with pulleys. [OF *polie* (F *poulie*), prob. ult. from a late Gr. *polidion*, dim. of *polos*, POLE[2]]

Pullman (pul´mən) *n.* (*pl.* **Pullmans**) **1** a Pullman car. **2** a train made up of these. **3** a similarly luxurious motor coach. **Pullman car** *n.* a luxurious railway saloon or sleeping car. [George M. *Pullman*, 1831–97, US inventor and first manufacturer]

pullorum disease (pulaw´rəm) *n.* an acute bacterial disease of young chickens characterized by whitish diarrhoea, caused by *Salmonella pullorum*. [L *pullōrum*, of chickens, gen. pl. of *pullus*, a chicken]

pullulate (pŭl´ūlāt) *v.i.* **1** (of a shoot etc.) to shoot, bud. **2** (of a seed) to germinate. **3** (of animals) to breed rapidly and prolifically. **4** to swarm, to abound. **5** to develop, to spring up. **pullulant** *a.* **pullulation** (-lā´shən) *n.* [L *pullulātus*, p.p. of *pullulāre*, to sprout, from *pullulus*, dim. of *pullus*, see PULLET]

pulmo- (pŭl´mō, pul´mō) *comb. form* of or relating to the lungs. [Latin *pulmo -mōnis*, lung]

pulmonary (pŭl´mənəri) *a.* **1** of or relating to the lungs. **2** having lungs or similar organs. **3** susceptible to lung diseases. **pulmonary artery** *n.* the artery carrying blood from the heart to the lungs. **pulmonary disease** *n.* lung disease, esp. tuberculosis. **pulmonary tuberculosis** *n.* a form of tuberculosis caused by inhaling the tubercle bacillus into the lungs. **pulmonary vein** *n.* the vein carrying oxygenated blood from the lungs back to the heart. **pulmonic** (-mon´-) *a.* **1** pulmonary. **2** affected with or subject to disease of the lungs. ~*n.* **1** a person with diseased lungs. **2** a medicine for lung diseases.

pulp (pŭlp) *n.* **1** any soft, moist, coherent mass. **2** the fleshy or succulent portion of a fruit. **3** the soft tissue of an animal body or in an organ or part, as in the internal cavity of a tooth. **4** the soft mixture of rags, wood etc. from which paper is made. **5** a magazine or book printed on cheap paper and sentimental or sensational in content. **6** fiction of the type published in such books and magazines. **7** (*Mining*) pulverized ore mixed with water. ~*v.t.* **1** to convert into pulp. **2** to reduce (unsold copies of a magazine etc.) to pulp for reuse of the paper. **3** to extract the pulp from. ~*v.i.* to become pulpy. **pulper** *n.* a machine which reduces materials to pulp. **pulp fiction** *n.* **pulpless** *a.* **pulplike** *a.* **pulp novel** *n.* **pulpous** *a.* **pulpwood** *n.* softwood suitable for making into pulp. **pulpy** *a.* (*comp.* **pulpier,** *superl.* **pulpiest**) of the consistency of pulp, soft or succulent. **pulpiness** *n.* [L *pulpa*]

pulpit (pul´pit) *n.* **1** an elevated enclosed stand in a church from which a preacher delivers a sermon. **2** a medium through which one can express one's opinions, such as a radio programme or newspaper column. **3** a railed area at the bow or stern of a boat. ~*a.* of or relating to the pulpit or to preaching. ~*v.t.* to provide with a pulpit or pulpits. ~*v.i.* (*pres.p.* **pulpiting,** *past, p.p.* **pulpited**) to preach. **the pulpit 1** preachers generally. **2** preaching. **pulpiteer** (-tiə´) *n.* (*derog.*) a preacher. **pulpiteering** *n.* **pulpiter** *n.* a preacher. [L *pulpitum*]

pulque (pul´ki, -kā) *n.* a Mexican vinous beverage made by fermenting the sap of a species of agave. **pulque brandy** *n.* a liquor distilled from this. [Mex. Sp.]

pulsar (pŭl´sah) *n.* (*Astron.*) an interstellar source of regularly pulsating radio waves, prob. a swiftly rotating neutron star. [*puls*ating st*ar*]

pulsate (pŭlsāt´, pŭl´-) *v.i.* **1** to move, esp. to expand and contract, with rhythmical alternation, to beat, to throb. **2** to vibrate, to thrill. **pulsatile** (pŭl´sətīl) *a.* **1** having the property of pulsation. **2** (*Mus.*) played by beating, percussive. **pulsatility** (-til´-) *n.* **pulsating current** *n.* an electric current that varies in intensity but not in direction. **pulsation** (-ā´shən) *n.* **1** the action of pulsating. **2** the movement of the pulse. **pulsative** (pŭl´sə-) *a.* **1** of or relating to pulsation. **2** actuated by or having the property of pulsation. **pulsatively** *adv.* **pulsator** (-sā´-) *a.* **1** a machine for separating diamonds from earth, a jigging machine. **2** a part of a milking machine. **3** a pulsometer. **pulsatory** (pŭl´-) *a.* [L *pulsātus*, p.p. of *pulsāre*, freq. of *pellere*, to drive, p.p. *pulsus*]

pulsatilla (pŭlsətil´ə) *n.* (*pl.* **pulsatillas**) the pasque flower, *Pulsatilla vulgaris*. [med. L, dim. of *pulsāta*, beaten, as PULSATE]

pulse[1] (pŭls) *n.* **1** the rhythmic beating of the arteries caused by the propulsion of blood along them from the heart. **2** a single beat of the arteries or the heart. **3** a pulsation, a vibration. **4** a short-lived variation in some normally constant value in a system, as in voltage etc. **5** an electromagnetic or sound wave of brief duration. **6** a quick, regular stroke or recurrence of strokes (as of oars). **7** a throb, a thrill. **8** bustle, excitement. **9** the public mood or opinion. ~*v.i.* **1** to pulsate. **2** to be produced in pulses. ~*v.t.* to produce or transmit by or as by rhythmic beats. **to feel someone's pulse 1** to gauge the rate or regularity of a person's pulse as a sign of health etc. **2** to sound someone's intentions, views etc. **to keep one's finger on the pulse of** to keep up to date with developments in. **pulse code** *n.* the coding of information using pulses. **pulse code modulation** *n.* a form of pulse modulation in which the information is carried by a sequence of binary codes. **pulsejet** *n.* a type of jet engine using a pulsating thrust. **pulseless** *a.* **pulselessness** *n.* **pulse modulation** *n.* a type of modulation in which a series of varied pulses is used to carry a signal. **pulse rate** *n.* the number of pulse beats per minute. **pulsimeter** (-sim´itə) *n.* an instrument for measuring the rate, force, regularity etc. of a pulse. **pulsometer** (-som´itə) *n.* **1** a pumping device operated by the admission and condensation of steam in alternate chambers. **2** a pulsimeter. [ME and OF *pous*, L *pulsum*, nom. *-sus*, as PULSATE]

pulse[2] (pŭls) *n.* **1** the edible seeds of leguminous plants. **2** a plant or plants producing such seeds. [ME and OF *pols*, L *puls pultis*, pottage of meal etc.]

pulsimeter, pulsometer PULSE[1].

pulverize (pŭl´vərīz), **pulverise** *v.t.* **1** to reduce to fine powder or dust. **2** (*coll.*) to demolish, to smash, to defeat utterly. *~v.i.* to be reduced to powder. **pulverable** *a.* **pulverizable** *a.* **pulverization** (-zā´shən) *n.* **pulverizator** *n.* **pulverizer** *n.* **1** a person who or thing which pulverizes. **2** a machine for pulverizing earth. **pulverous** *a.* **pulverulent** (-vœ´ru-) *a.* **1** consisting of fine powder. **2** covered with powder, powdery. **3** liable to disintegrate into fine powder. **pulverulence** *n.* [late L *pulverīzāre*, from L *pulvus -veris*, dust]

pulvillus (pŭlvil´əs) *n.* (*pl.* **pulvilli** (-lī)) the pad or cushion of an insect's foot. **pulvillar** *a.* **pulvilliform** (-fawm) *a.* [L, contr. for *pulvīnulus*, dim. of *pulvīnus*, a cushion, pillow]

pulvinate (pŭl´vinət) *a.* (*Biol.*) cushion-shaped, padlike. **pulvinated** (-nātid) *a.* having a convex face (as a frieze). [L *pulvīnus*, a cushion, pillow]

puma (pū´mə) *n.* (*pl.* **pumas**) the cougar, *Felis concolor*, a large feline carnivore of the Americas. [Sp., from Quechua]

pumice (pŭm´is) *n.* **1** a light, porous or cellular kind of lava, used as a cleansing and polishing material. **2** a piece of this stone. *~v.t.* to rub, polish or clean with pumice. **pumiceous** (pūmish´əs) *a.* **pumice stone** *n.* pumice. [OF *pomis*, late L *pumicem*, L *pūmex -icem*]

pummel (pŭm´əl) *v.t.* (*pres.p.* **pummelling,** (*N Am.*) **pummeling,** *past, p.p.* **pummelled,** (*N Am.*) **pummeled**) to strike or pound repeatedly, esp. with the fists. *~n.* a pommel.

pump[1] (pŭmp) *n.* **1** a device or machine usu. in the form of a cylinder and piston, for raising water or other liquid. **2** a similar machine for exhausting or compressing air, an air-pump. **3** the act of pumping, a stroke of a pump. *~v.t.* **1** to raise or remove (liquid or gas) with a pump. **2** to free from water, make dry or fill with air with a pump. **3** to propel, to pour, with or as with a pump. **4** to move up and down as if working a pump-handle. **5** to elicit information from by persistent interrogation. **6** to shake (someone's hand) vigorously. *~v.i.* **1** to work a pump. **2** to raise water etc. with a pump. **3** to move up and down in the manner of a pump-handle. **to pump iron** to do weight-lifting exercises. **to pump up 1** to inflate (a pneumatic tyre). **2** to inflate the tyres of (a cycle etc.). **pump-action** *a.* (of a repeating rifle or shotgun) requiring a pumplike movement to bring a shell into the chamber. **pumpage** *n.* **pump-brake** *n.* the handle of a pump, esp. with a transverse handle. **pumped** *a.* **pumped storage** *n.* in hydroelectric generation, the use of spare electricity at times of low demand to pump water up to a high storage reservoir, to be released to generate electricity at times of high demand. **pumper** *n.* **pump gun** *n.* a pump-action gun. **pump-handle** *n.* **1** the handle by which a pump is worked. **2** (*coll.*) the hand or arm. *~v.t.* (*coll.*) to shake (someone's hand). **pump-head** *n.* the casing at the head of a chain pump for directing the water into the discharge-spout. **pump-priming** *n.* **1** the introduction of fluid into a pump to expel the air before operation. **2** the investing of money to stimulate commercial activity esp. in stagnant or depressed areas. **pump room** *n.* **1** a room where a pump is worked. **2** a room at a spa where the waters from the medicinal spring are dispensed. **pump water** *n.* water from a pump. [ME *pumpe*, Dut. *pomp*, G *Pumpe*, F *pompe*]

pump[2] (pŭmp) *n.* **1** a light low-heeled, slipperlike shoe worn with evening dress and for dancing. **2** a plimsoll. **3** (*N Am.*) a court shoe. [etym. uncertain]

pumpernickel (pŭm´pənikəl) *n.* German wholemeal rye bread. [G, etym. uncertain]

pumpkin (pŭmp´kin) *n.* **1** any plant of the genus *Cucurbita*, creeping plants with large lobed leaves. **2** the large globular edible fruit of *Cucurbita maxima*. [earlier *pumpion, pompion*, from MF *po(m)pon*, L *pepo -onis*, Gr. *pepōn*, large melon]

pun[1] (pŭn) *n.* the playful use of a word in two different senses or of words similar in sound but different in meaning. *~v.i.* (*pres.p.* **punning,** *past, p.p.* **punned**) to make a pun. **punningly** *adv.* **punster** *n.* **1** a person who makes puns. **2** a person addicted to pun-making. [etym. uncertain]

pun[2] (pŭn) *v.t.* (*pres.p.* **punning,** *past, p.p.* **punned**) **1** to pound, to crush, to consolidate by ramming. **2** to work (up clay etc.) with a punner. **punner** *n.* a tool used for ramming earth, in a hole etc. [dial. form of POUND[3]]

puna (poo´nə) *n.* (*pl.* **punas**) **1** a cold high plateau between the two ranges of the Andes. **2** the cold wind prevalent there. **3** mountain sickness. [Quechua]

Punch (pŭnch) *n.* the chief character in the popular puppet show of Punch and Judy, represented as a grotesque hump-backed man. **pleased as Punch** highly delighted. [short for PUNCHINELLO]

punch[1] (pŭnch) *n.* **1** a tool, usu. consisting of a short cylindrical piece of steel tapering to a sharp or blunt end, for making holes, indenting, forcing bolts out of holes etc. **2** a machine in which a similar tool is used, esp. one for making holes in paper or cardboard. **3** a tool or machine for stamping a die or impressing a design. **4** a blow with the fist. **5** vigour, forcefulness. **6** striking power. *~v.t.* **1** to stamp or perforate with a punch. **2** to make (a hole or indentation) thus. **3** to drive (out etc.) with a punch. **4** to strike, esp. with the fist. **5** to press in vigorously, as a key or button. **6** to record by pressing a key. **7** (*N Am.*) to drive (cattle) by pushing with or as with a stick. **to pack a punch** PACK. **to pull one's punches** (*usu. in neg.*) to strike or criticize with less than full force. **punchbag** *n.* **1** a heavy, stuffed bag struck with the fists as exercise or by boxers in training. **2** an unresisting victim. **punchball** *n.* **1** a ball usu. suspended or on an elastic stand used for punching practice. **2** (*N Am.*) a game in which a ball is punched with the fist. **punchcard, punched card** *n.* a card in which data are represented by perforations, used in computers. **punch-drunk** *a.* suffering a form of cerebral concussion from having taken repeated blows to the head; dazed. **punched** *a.* **punched tape** *n.* (*Comput.*) a paper tape. **puncher** *n.* **punching bag** *n.* (*N Am.*) a punchbag. **punchline** *n.* the conclusion of a joke or story that shows the point of it, produces the laugh or reveals an unexpected twist. **punch tape** *n.* (*Comput.*) paper tape. **punch-up** *n.* (*coll.*) a brawl, a fist fight. **punchy**[1] *a.* (*comp.* **punchier,** *superl.* **punchiest**) (*coll.*) **1** forceful, incisive. **2** punch-drunk. **punchily** *adv.* **punchiness** *n.* [prob. from PUNCHEON[1]]

punch[2] (pŭnch) *n.* a beverage made of wine or spirits, water or milk, lemons, sugar, spice etc., usu, served hot. **punchbowl** *n.* **1** a round bowl in which punch is made. **2** a round hollow in a hill. [perh. from Hind. *panch*, five, from its consisting originally of five ingredients, or from PUNCHEON[2]]

punch[3] (pŭnch) *n.* **1** a Suffolk punch, a short-legged draught horse orig. bred in Suffolk. **2** †a short, fat person. **punchy**[2] *a.* (*comp.* **punchier,** *superl.* **punchiest**). [etym. uncertain]

puncheon[1] (pŭn´chən) *n.* **1** a short upright timber, used for supporting the roof in a mine or as an upright in the framework of a roof. 2 a perforating or stamping tool, a punch. [ONF *punchon*, OF *poinçon*, L *punctiōnem*, nom. *-tio*, a pricking, from *pungere*, to prick, p.p. *punctus*]

puncheon[2] (pŭn´chən) *n.* (*Hist.*) a large cask holding from 72 to 120 gallons (324–540 l). [perh. ident. with PUNCHEON[1]]

Punchinello (pŭnchinel´ō) *n.* (*pl.* **Punchinellos**) 1 a buffoon, a Punch, a grotesque person. 2 the chief character in an Italian puppet show. [It. *polichinello*, *Pulcinello*, a character in Neapolitan low comedy]

punchy[1] PUNCH[1].

punchy[2] PUNCH[3].

puncta PUNCTUM.

punctate (pŭngk´tāt) *a.* (*Biol.*) covered with points, dots, spots etc. **punctation** (-tā´shən) *n.* **punctiform** (-tifawm) *a.* 1 like a point or dot. 2 punctate. [L *punctum*, POINT]

punctilio (pŭngktil´iō) *n.* (*pl.* **punctilios**) 1 a nice point in conduct, ceremony or honour. 2 precision in form or etiquette. 3 petty formality. **punctilious** *a.* 1 precise or exacting in punctilio. 2 strictly observant of ceremony or etiquette. **punctiliously** *adv.* **punctiliousness** *n.* [Sp. *puntillo*, or It. *puntiglio*, dim. of *punto*, POINT]

punctual (pŭngk´chuəl) *a.* 1 observant and exact in matters of time. 2 done, made or occurring exactly at the proper time. 3 (*Geom.*) of or relating to a point. 4 †exact, punctilious. **punctuality** (-al´-) *n.* **punctually** *adv.* [med. L *punctuālis*, from *punctum*, a POINT]

punctuate (pŭngk´chuāt) *v.t.* 1 to mark (written matter) with stops, to divide into sentences, clauses etc. with stops. 2 to interrupt or intersperse. 3 (*coll.*) to emphasize, to accentuate. 4 to reinforce (a speech with gestures etc.). **punctuated equilibrium** *n.* (*Biol.*) the theory that evolution takes place not as a gradual and steady process, but in short bursts punctuating long periods of relative stability. **punctuation** (-ā´shən) *n.* **punctuation mark** *n.* any of the marks used to punctuate written matter, such as the comma, colon etc. **punctuative** *a.* [med. L *punctuātus*, p.p. of *punctuāre*, as PUNCTUAL]

punctum (pŭngk´təm) *n.* (*pl.* **puncta** (-tə)) (*Biol.*) a point, a speck, a dot, a minute spot of colour etc. [L, POINT]

puncture (pŭngk´chə) *n.* 1 a small hole made with something pointed, a prick. 2 the act of pricking or perforating. 3 the perforation of a pneumatic tyre by e.g. a sharp stone on the road, and the consequent loss of pressure. *~v.t.* 1 to make a puncture in. 2 to pierce or prick with something pointed. 3 (*coll.*) to deflate (a person's self-esteem or pomposity). *~v.i.* (of a tyre, balloon etc.) to sustain a puncture. **puncturable** *a.* **puncturer** *n.* [L *punctūra*, from *pungere punctus*, to prick]

pundit (pŭn´dit) *n.* 1 (*also* **pandit**) a Hindu learned in the Sanskrit language and the science, laws and religion of India. 2 a learned person. 3 a pretender to learning. **punditry** *n.* [Hind. *pandit*, from Sansk. *pandita*, learned]

punga (pŭng´ə) *n.* a New Zealand tree fern, the pith of which is edible. [Maori]

pungent (pŭn´jənt) *a.* 1 sharply affecting the senses, esp. those of smell or taste. 2 pricking or stinging to the sense of touch. 3 acrid, keen, caustic, biting. 4 piquant, stimulating. 5 (*Biol.*) sharp-pointed, adapted for pricking or piercing. **pungency** *n.* **pungently** *adv.* [L *pungens -ntem*, pres.p. of *pungere*, to prick]

Punic (pū´nik) *a.* 1 of or relating to ancient Carthage, the Carthaginians, or the Carthaginian language. 2 (*fig.*) treacherous, faithless. *~n.* the language of the Carthaginians, related to Phoenician. **Punic faith** *n.* bad faith, faithlessness, treachery. [L *Pūnicus*, Poenicus, from *Poenus*, Gr. *Phoinix*, Phoenician]

punily, puniness PUNY.

punish (pŭn´ish) *v.t.* 1 to inflict a penalty on (a person) for an offence. 2 to visit judicially with pain, loss, confinement or other penalty, to chastise. 3 to inflict a penalty for (an offence). 4 to inflict pain or injury on, to handle severely, to maul. 5 to give great trouble to (opponents in a game, race etc.). 6 (*coll.*) to consume large quantities of (food etc.). **punishable** *a.* **punishability** (-bil´-), **punishableness** *n.* **punishably** *adv.* **punisher** *n.* **punishing** *a.* severe, wearing. **punishingly** *adv.* **punishment** *n.* 1 the act, or an instance, of punishing. 2 the state of being punished. 3 the penalty or suffering inflicted. 4 (*coll.*) severe or rough treatment. **punitive** (pū´-), **punitory** (pū´-) *a.* 1 awarding or inflicting punishment. 2 retributive. 3 (of taxes) at a very high rate. **punitive damages** *n.pl.* (*Law*) vindictive damages. **punitively** *adv.* **punitiveness** *n.* [F *puniss-*, pres.p. stem of *punir*, L *pūnīre*, from *poena*, Gr. *poinē*, fine, PENALTY]

Punjabi (pŭnjah´bi) *n.* (*pl.* **Punjabis**) 1 a native or inhabitant of the state of Punjab in India or the province of Punjab in Pakistan, or the larger area comprising both of these, formerly a province of British India. 2 the Indic language of these areas. *~a.* of or relating to these areas, their inhabitants or their language.

punk[1] (pŭngk) *n.* 1 a a worthless person or thing. b worthless articles. 2 nonsense. 3 (a follower of) a youth movement of the late 1970s and 1980s, characterized by a violent rejection of established society, outlandish (often multicoloured) hairstyles, and the use of worthless articles such as safety pins and razor blades as decoration. 4 punk rock. 5 (*N Am.*) a novice. 6 (*N Am.*) a petty criminal. 7 (*N Am.*) a passive male homosexual. 8 †a prostitute. *~a.* 1 associated with the punk movement or punk rock. 2 (*N Am.*) inferior, rotten. **punkish** *a.* **punk rock** *n.* a style of popular music associated with the punk movement and characterized by a driving beat, crude or obscene lyrics and an aggressive performing style. **punk rocker** *n.* **punky** *a.* **punkiness** *n.* [etym. uncertain]

punk[2] (pŭngk) *n.* 1 (*N Am.*) wood decayed through the growth of a fungus, touchwood. 2 a composition for igniting fireworks. [etym. uncertain]

punkah (pŭng´kə) *n.* (*Ind.*) 1 a large portable fan made from a palm leaf. 2 a large screenlike fan suspended from the ceiling and worked by a cord. [Hind. *pankhā*]

punner PUN[2].

punnet (pŭn´it) *n.* a small, shallow basket for fruit, flowers etc. [etym. uncertain]

punster PUN[1].

punt[1] (pŭnt) *n.* a shallow, flat-bottomed, square-ended boat, usu. propelled by pushing against the bottom of the stream with a pole. *~v.t.* 1 to propel (a punt etc.) with a pole. 2 to convey in a punt. *~v.i.* 1 to propel about thus. 2 to go (about) in a punt. **punter**[1] *n.* **punt pole** *n.* [OE, from L *ponto*, prob. from Gallic]

punt[2] (pŭnt) *v.i.* 1 to stake against the bank in some card games. 2 (*coll.*) to bet on a horse etc. 3 (*coll.*) to speculate on the Stock Exchange. *~n.* 1 a bet. 2 a point in the game of faro. 3 the act of playing basset, faro etc. 4 PUNTER. **punter**[2] *n.* 1 a person who bets. 2 a small gambler on the Stock Exchange. 3 a prostitute's client. 4 (*coll.*) any member of the public, esp. when considered as a customer or client. 5 (*sl.*) a victim of a con trick. 6 a point in faro. [F *ponter*, etym. unknown]

punt[3] (pŭnt) *v.t.* in ball games, to kick the ball after dropping it from the hand and before it touches the ground. *~n.* such a kick. **punter**[3] *n.* [etym. uncertain]

punt[4] (punt) *n.* the standard monetary unit of the Republic of Ireland. [Ir., pound]

punter[1] PUNT[1].

punter[2] PUNT[2].
punter[3] PUNT[3].
punto (pŭn´tō) *n.* (*pl.* **puntos**) a thrust or pass in fencing. [It. or Sp., as POINT]
punty (pŭn´ti) *n.* (*pl.* **punties**) a pontil. [PONTIL]
puny (pū´ni) *a.* (*comp.* **punier**, *superl.* **puniest**) **1** small and feeble, tiny, undersized, weak, poorly developed. **2** petty, trivial. **punily** *adv.* **puniness** *n.* [PUISNE]
pup (pŭp) *n.* **1** a puppy. **2** the young of other animals, such as the seal. **3** (*sl.*, *derog.*) a conceited young man. ~*v.t.* (*pres.p.* **pupping**, *past*, *p.p.* **pupped**) to give birth to (pups). ~*v.i.* to give birth to pups, to whelp, to litter. **in pup** pregnant. **to sell a pup to** (*sl.*) to trick into buying something worthless; to swindle. **pup tent** *n.* a very small and basic shelter tent. [PUPPY]
pupa (pū´pə) *n.* (*pl.* **pupae** (-pē), **pupas**) an insect at the immobile, metamorphic stage between larva and imago. **pupal** *a.* **puparium** (-peə´riəm) *n.* (*pl.* **puparia** (-riə)) a hard case containing the pupa of the housefly etc. **puparial** *a.* **pupate** (-pāt´) *v.i.* to become a pupa. **pupation** (-pā´shən) *n.* **pupiparous** *a.* (of insects) giving birth to young which are already at the pupal stage. [L, a girl, a puppet]
pupil[1] (pū´pil, -pəl) *n.* **1** a young person of either sex under the care of a teacher. **2** a person who is being, or has been, taught by a particular person. **3** (*Law*) a boy or girl under the age of puberty and under the care of a guardian, a ward. **4** (*Law*) a trainee barrister. **pupillage** (-ij), **pupilage** *n.* **1** the state or period of being a pupil. **2** (*Law*) the apprenticeship period of a barrister. **pupillarity** (-lar´i-) *n.* (*Sc. Law*) the period before puberty. **pupillary**[1], **pupilary** *a.* **pupilship** *n.* **pupil teacher** *n.* (*Hist.*) a person in apprenticeship as a teacher and receiving general education at the same time. [F *pupille*, L *pūpillum*, nom. *-lus*, dim. of *pūpus*, boy]
pupil[2] (pū´pil, -pəl) *n.* the circular opening of the iris of the eye through which rays of light pass to the retina. **pupillar, pupilar** *a.* **pupillary**[2], **pupilary** *a.* **pupillate** (-lət), **pupilled** *a.* having a central spot like a pupil (of ocelli). [F *pupille*, L *pūpilla*, fem. of *pūpillus*, see PUPIL[1]]
pupillar PUPIL[2].
pupillary[1] PUPIL[1].
pupillary[2] PUPIL[2].
pupiparous PUPA.
puppet (pŭp´it) *n.* **1** an articulated toy figure moved by strings, wires or rods, a marionette. **2** a small figure with a hollow head and cloth body into which the operator's hand is inserted, a glove puppet. **3** a person whose actions are under another's control, a mere tool. **puppet-clack** *n.* a poppet-valve. **puppeteer** (-tiə´) *n.* **1** a person who manipulates puppets. **2** a person who manipulates other people. **puppeteering** *n.* **puppet play, puppet show** *n.* a play with puppets as dramatis personae. **puppetry** *n.* the art of making and manipulating puppets and presenting puppet shows. **puppet state, puppet government** *n.* a country, or government, which appears to be independent but is in fact controlled from another country. **puppet-theatre** *n.* **puppet-valve** *n.* a poppet-valve. [OF *poupette*, dim. from L *puppa*, *pūpa*, see PUPA]
puppy (pŭp´i) *n.* (*pl.* **puppies**) **1** a young dog. **2** a silly young man, a coxcomb, a fop. **puppy-dog** *n.* a puppy. **puppydom** *n.* the state of being a puppy. **puppy fat** *n.* temporary plumpness in children or adolescents. **puppyhood** *n.* **puppyish** *a.* **puppyism** *n.* **puppy love** *n.* temporary infatuation in adolescence. [prob. from F *poupée*, doll, irreg. as PUPPET]
pur- (pœ) *pref.* a form of PRO-[1], as *purchase*. [A-F, from OF *por-*, *pour-*, *pur-*, from L *pro*]
Purana (poorah´nə) *n.* (*pl.* **Puranas**) any of a great class of Sanskrit poems comprising the whole body of Hindu mythology. **Puranic** *a.* [Sansk., from *pura*, formerly]
Purbeck (pœ´bek) *n.* Purbeck stone. **Purbeck marble** *n.* one of the finer varieties of Purbeck stone, used for shafts etc. in architecture. **Purbeck stone** *n.* a hard limestone from Purbeck. [Isle of *Purbeck*, a peninsula in Dorset]
purblind (pœ´blīnd) *a.* **1** partially blind, near-sighted, dim-sighted. **2** obtuse, lacking insight or understanding. **purblindly** *adv.* **purblindness** *n.* [orig. totally blind (perh. PURE, BLIND)]
purchase (pœ´chis) *v.t.* **1** to obtain by payment of an equivalent value, to buy. **2** to acquire at the expense of some sacrifice, exertion, danger etc. **3** (*Naut.*) to haul up, hoist or draw in by means of a pulley, lever, capstan etc. ~*n.* **1** the act, or an instance, of purchasing or buying. **2** a thing which is purchased. **3** annual value, annual return, esp. from land. **4** (*Law*) the acquisition of property by payment of a price or value, any mode of acquiring property other than by inheritance. **5** advantage gained by the application of any mechanical power, leverage. **6** an appliance furnishing this, such as a rope, pulley etc. **7** an effective hold or position for leverage, a grasp, a foothold. **8** (*Hist.*) the system of buying commissions in the army, abolished in 1871. **purchasable** *a.* **purchasability** (-bil´-) *n.* **purchase money** *n.* the price paid or contracted to be paid for anything purchased. **purchaser** *n.* **purchase tax** *n.* (*Hist.*) a differential tax on certain goods sold to the public. **purchasing power** *n.* the ability of a person, or of their money, to buy (an amount of goods or services). [ME *purchasen*, A-F *purchacer*, OF *pur-*, *pourchacier*, to procure (PUR-, CHASE[1])]
purdah (pœ´də) *n.* **1** the custom in some Muslim and Hindu societies of secluding women from the view of strangers. **2** a curtain or screen, esp. one keeping women secluded. **purdahed** (-dəd) *a.* [Urdu and Pers. *pardah*]
pure (pūə) *a.* **1** unmixed, unadulterated. **2** free from anything foul or polluting, clear, clean. **3** free from moral defilement, innocent, guiltless. **4** unsullied, chaste. **5** of unmixed descent, free from admixture with any other breed. **6** mere, sheer, absolute. **7** (of a sound) free from discordance, harshness etc., perfectly correct in tone intervals. **8** (of a vowel) having a single sound or tone, not combined with another. **9** (of sciences) entirely theoretical, not applied. **pure-bred** *a.* of a pure strain through many generations of controlled breeding. ~*n.* such an animal. **pure culture** *n.* a culture consisting of a single species of micro-organism. **purely** *adv.* **1** in a pure way. **2** merely; entirely. **pure mathematics** *n.* the abstract science of magnitudes etc. **pure merino** *n.* (*pl.* **pure merinos**) (*Austral.*, *coll.*) a descendant of an early settler with no convict connection. **pureness** *n.* **pure reason** *n.* reason without the benefit of experience. **pure science** *n.* a science based on self-evident truths, such as logic, mathematics etc., or one studied apart from any practical applications. [OF *pur*, fem. *pure*, L *pūrum*, nom. *-us*]
purée (pū´rā) *n.* (*pl.* **purées**) **1** a smooth thick pulp of fruit, vegetables etc. obtained by liquidizing, sieving etc. **2** a thick soup made by boiling meat or vegetables to a pulp and straining it. ~*v.t.* (*3rd pers. sing. pres.* **purées**, *pres.p.* **puréeing**, *past*, *p.p.* **puréed**) to reduce to a purée. [F, etym. uncertain]
purfle (pœ´fəl) *v.t.* **1** †to decorate with a wrought or ornamental border, to border. **2** to adorn, to beautify. **3** to give a border of fur etc. to. **4** to ornament the edge of (a canopy etc.) with knobs, crockets etc. ~*n.* **1** a border or edging of embroidered work. **2** the ornamental border on the backs and bellies of stringed instruments. **purfling** (-fling) *n.* ornamental bordering. [OF *porfiler*, as PROFILE]
purgation (pœgā´shən) *n.* **1** the act of purging, purification. **2** cleansing of the bowels by the use of

purgatives. 3 (*Hist.*) the act of clearing oneself from an imputed crime by oath or ordeal. 4 in the Roman Catholic Church, the process of spiritual purification of souls in purgatory. **purgative** (pœ´gə-) *a.* having the quality of cleansing, esp. evacuating the intestines, aperient. ~*n.* 1 something that purges. 2 an aperient or cathartic. **purgatively** *adv.* [ME and OF *purgacion*, L *purgātiōnem*, nom. *-tio*, from *purgāre*, to PURGE]

purgatory (pœ´gətri, -təri) *n.* (*pl.* **purgatories**) 1 a place or state of spiritual purging, esp. a place or state succeeding the present life in which, according to the Roman Catholic Church, the souls of the faithful are purified from venial sins by suffering. 2 any place of temporary suffering or tribulation. 3 (*coll.*) an acutely uncomfortable experience. ~*a.* cleansing, purifying. **purgatorial** (-taw´ri-) *a.* **purgatorially** *adv.* [ME and A-F *purgatorie* (OF *purgatoire*), med. L *purgātōrium*]

purge (pœj) *v.t.* 1 to cleanse or purify. 2 to free (of or from impurity, sin etc.). 3 to remove (off or away) by cleansing. 4 to clear (of an accusation, suspicion etc.). 5 to rid (a state or a party) of persons actively in opposition. 6 (*Law*) to clear oneself of, to atone for (an offence). 7 to atone for, expiate or annul (guilt, spiritual defilement etc.). 8 **a** to cleanse (the bowels) by administering a laxative. **b** to empty (the bowels). ~*v.i.* to grow pure by clarification. ~*n.* 1 the act, or an instance, of purging. 2 a purgative medicine. **purger** *n.* **purging** *a.*, *n.* [OF *purger*, L *purgāre*]

puri (poo´ri) *n.* (*pl.* **puris**) an unleavened wholewheat bread, deep-fried and sometimes containing a spicy vegetable etc. mixture. [Hind.]

purify (pū´rifī) *v.t.* (*3rd pers. sing. pres.* **purifies**, *pres.p.* **purifying**, *past, p.p.* **purified**) 1 to make pure, to cleanse. 2 to free from sin, guilt, pollution etc. 3 to make ceremonially clean. 4 to clear of or from foreign elements, corruptions etc. **purification** (-fikā´shən) *n.* 1 the act of physical or spiritual purifying. 2 the act or process of cleansing ceremonially. **purificator** (-fikā´-) *n.* a piece of linen used to wipe the chalice and paten at the Eucharist. **purificatory** *a.* 1 having power to purify. 2 tending to purify. **purifier** *n.* [F *purifier*, late L *pūrificāre*, (*pūrus*, PURE, *-ficāre*, *facere*, to make)]

Purim (puə´rim, purēm´) *n.* a Jewish festival instituted in commemoration of the deliverance of the Jews from the destruction threatened by Haman's plot (Esther ix.20–32). [Heb. *pūrīm*, pl. of *pūr*, prob. lot]

purin (pū´rin), **purine** (-rēn) *n.* (*Chem.*) 1 a crystalline solid derivable from uric acid. 2 any of a group of compounds derived from this, such as guanine and adenine. [G *Purin*, from L *purus*, pure, mod. L *uricus*, uric]

purist (pū´rist) *n.* 1 a person advocating or affecting purity, esp. in art or language. 2 a rigorous critic of literary style. **purism** *n.* **puristic** (-ris´-), **puristical** *a.* [F *puriste*, from *pur*, PURE]

puritan (pū´ritən) *n.* 1 (**Puritan**) any one of a party or school of English Protestants of the 16th and 17th cents., who aimed at purifying religious worship from all ceremonies etc. not authorized by Scripture, and at the strictest purity of conduct. 2 any person practising or advocating extreme strictness in conduct or religion (usu. applied in a deprecatory sense). 3 a purist. ~*a.* 1 (**Puritan**) of or relating to the Puritans. 2 excessively strict in religion or morals. **puritanic** (-tan´-), **puritanical** *a.* **puritanically** *adv.* **puritanism** (pū´-), **Puritanism** *n.* [late L *puritas -tātem*, PURITY]

purity (pū´riti) *n.* 1 the state of being pure, cleanness. 2 freedom from pollution, adulteration or admixture of foreign elements. 3 moral cleanness, innocence, chastity. [F *pureté*, late L *puritas -tātem*]

purl[1] (pœl) *n.* 1 an edging or fringe of twisted gold or silver wire. 2 the thread or cord of which this is made. 3 a small loop on the edges of pillow lace. 4 a series of such loops as an ornamental hem or edging. 5 an inversion of the stitches in knitting. ~*a.* of or relating to an inverted stitch in knitting, made by putting the needle into the front of the stitch, as distinct from *plain*. ~*v.t.* 1 to border or decorate with purl or purls. 2 to knit with a purl stitch. ~*v.i.* to knit with a purl stitch. [perh. from obs. *pirl*, to twist]

purl[2] (pœl) *v.i.* to flow with a soft, bubbling, gurgling or murmuring sound and an eddying motion. ~*n.* a gentle bubbling, gurgling or murmuring sound; an eddying motion. **purling** *n.*, *a.* [cp. Norw. *purla*, Swed. *porla*, to bubble up]

purl[3] (pœl) *v.t.*, *v.i.* to upset, to overturn. ~*n.* a heavy fall, an overturn. **purler**[1] *n.* (*coll.*) a heavy or headlong fall or throw. **to come a purler** to take a heavy fall. [prob. from *pirl*, PURL[1]]

purler[1] PURL[3].

purler[2] (pœ´lə) *n.* (*Austral.*, *coll.*) something which is very good of its kind. [etym. uncertain]

purlieu (pœ´lū) *n.* (*pl.* **purlieus**) 1 (*usu. pl.*) the bounds or limits within which one ranges, one's usual haunts. 2 (*pl.*) outlying parts, outskirts, environs. 3 (*Hist.*) the borders or outskirts of a forest, esp. a tract of land, once included in forest but entirely or partially disafforested. [A-F *puralé*, OF *puralee* (PUR-, *aley*, see ALLEY[1]), assim. to LIEU]

purlin (pœ´lin) *n.* a horizontal timber resting on the principal rafters and supporting the common rafters or boards on which the roof is laid. [etym. uncertain]

purloin (pœloin´) *v.t.* (*formal or facet.*) to steal, to take by theft. ~*v.i.* to practise theft; to pilfer. **purloiner** *n.* [A-F and OF *purloigner* (*loign*, *loin*, L *longe*, FAR)]

purple (pœ´pəl) *a.* 1 of the colour of red and blue blended, the former predominating. 2 (*Hist.*) of the crimson colour obtained from molluscs esp. of the genus *Murex*. 3 dyed with or as if with blood. 4 imperial, regal. 5 (of literary style) florid, highly rhetorical. ~*n.* 1 a purple colour. 2 a purple pigment or dye. 3 a purple dress or robe, esp. of an emperor, king, Roman consul or a bishop. 4 **a** (*fig.*) (**the purple**) imperial or regal power. **b** any position of authority or privilege. 5 the cardinalate. 6 (**the purple**) bishops collectively. ~*v.t.* to make or dye purple. ~*v.i.* to become purple. **born in the purple** of high and wealthy, esp. royal or imperial, family. **purple emperor** *n.* a variety of butterfly, *Apatura iris*, having purple wings. **purple heart** *n.* 1 a mauve, heart-shaped, amphetamine tablet taken as a stimulant. 2 (**Purple Heart**) a US decoration for wounds received on active service. **purple loosestrife** *n.* a waterside plant, *Lythrum salicaria*, with red or purple flowers. **purpleness** *n.* **purple passage** *n.* 1 (*also* **purple patch**) a passage of over-ornate writing. 2 (*coll.*) a period of success or good fortune. **purple prose** *n.* obtrusively elevated or ornate writing. **purplish, purply** *a.* [ME *purpre*, OE *purpure*, L PURPURA]

purport[1] (pəpawt´) *v.t.* 1 to convey as the meaning, to imply, to signify. 2 to profess, to be meant to appear (to). **purportedly** *adv.* [A-F and OF *purporter* (PUR-, *porter*, L *portāre*, to carry)]

purport[2] (pœ´pawt) *n.* 1 meaning, tenor, sense. 2 object, purpose. 3 pretext, disguise. **purportless** *a.* [as PURPORT[1]]

purpose (pœ´pəs) *n.* 1 an end in view, an object, an aim. 2 the reason why something exists. 3 an effect, result, consequence. 4 determination, resolution. ~*v.t.* to intend, to design. **on purpose** 1 intentionally, designedly, not by accident. 2 in order (that). **to no purpose** with no useful result. **to the purpose** 1 with close relation to the matter in hand, relevantly. 2 usefully. **purpose-built** *a.* constructed to serve a specific purpose. **purposeful** *a.* 1 having a definite end in view. 2 determined, resolute. **purposefully** *adv.*

purposefulness *n.* **purposeless** *a.* having no purpose, aimless. **purposelessly** *adv.* **purposelessness** *n.* **purposely** *adv.* on purpose, intentionally, not by accident. **purpose-made** *a.* made for a specific purpose. **purposive** *a.* **1** having or serving a purpose. **2** purposeful. **3** done with a purpose. **purposively** *adv.* **purposiveness** *n.* [ME and OF *pourpos*, L *prōpositum*, p.p. of *prōpōnere*, to propose, see PROPOUND]

purpura (pœ´pūrə) *n.* a skin rash consisting of small purple spots caused by internal bleeding from the small blood vessels. **purpure** *n.* (*Her.*) purple, represented in engraving by diagonal lines from left to right. **purpuric** (-pū´-) *a.* **1** of or relating to the disease purpura. **2** of or relating to a purple colour. **purpurin** (-rin) *n.* a red colouring matter used in dyeing, orig. obtained from madder. [L, from Gr. *porphura*]

purr (pœ) *n.* a soft vibratory murmuring as of a cat when pleased. ~*v.i.* **1** (of a cat) to make this sound. **2** (of a person) to express satisfaction with or as if with this sound. **3** (of machinery, a car engine etc.) to make a similar soft sound. ~*v.t.* to signify, express or utter thus. **purring** *a., n.* **purringly** *adv.* [imit.]

purse (pœs) *n.* **1** a small bag or pouch for money, usu. carried in the pocket. **2** (*N Am.*) a woman's handbag. **3** money, funds, resources, a treasury. **4** a sum of money subscribed or collected or offered as a gift, prize etc. **5** a baglike receptacle, a pouch. ~*v.t.* to wrinkle, to pucker. ~*v.i.* to become wrinkled or puckered. **purseful** *n.* (*pl.* **pursefuls**). **purseless** *a.* **purse net** *n.* a net the mouth of which can be drawn together with cords like an old-fashioned purse. **purse-proud** *a.* proud of one's wealth. **purse seine** *n.* a large purse net for sea-fishing. **purse-seine** *a.* **purse-seiner** *n.* **purse strings** *n.pl.* strings for drawing together the mouth of an old-fashioned purse. **to hold the purse strings** to control the expenditure (of a household etc.). [OE *purs*, late L *bursa*, Gr. *bursa*, hide, leather]

purser (pœ´sə) *n.* an officer on board ship or on an aircraft in charge of the provisions, pay and the general welfare of the passengers. **pursership** *n.*

purslane (pœs´lin) *n.* any of various herbs of the genus *Portulaca*, esp. the succulent herb, *Portulaca oleracea*, used as a salad and pot-herb. [OF *porcelaine*, L *porcilāca*, PORTULACA, assim. to PORCELAIN]

pursue (pəsū´, -soo´) *v.t.* (*pres.p.* **pursuing,** *past, p.p.* **pursued**) **1** to follow with intent to seize, kill etc. **2** to try persistently to gain or obtain, to seek. **3** to continue with, to be engaged in (a course of action, studies). **4** to proceed in accordance with. **5** to apply oneself to, to practise continuously. **6** (of misfortune, consequences etc.) to attend persistently, to haunt. **7** to try persistently to make the acquaintance of, or to gain the attention of (a person). **8** to continue to discuss, to follow up. **9** †to attend, to accompany. ~*v.i.* **1** to follow, to seek (after). **2** to go in pursuit. **3** to go on, to proceed, to continue. **pursuable** *a.* **pursuance** *n.* the carrying out, performance, implementation (of a plan etc.). **pursuant** *a.* **1** in accordance, consonant, conformable (to). **2** pursuing. ~*adv.* in accordance or conformably (to). **pursuantly** *adv.* **pursuer** *n.* **1** a person who pursues. **2** (*Sc. Law*) a plaintiff, a prosecutor. **pursuit** (-sūt, -soot) *n.* **1** the act, or an instance, of pursuing, a following. **2** a prosecution, an endeavour to attain some end. **3** an employment, occupation, business or recreation that one follows persistently. **4** a kind of cycle race in which two competitors at a time set off at opposite sides of the track and try to overtake each other. **in pursuit of** pursuing. **pursuit plane** *n.* a type of military aeroplane used to pursue enemy planes. [A-F *pursuer*, OF *porsievre* (F *poursuivre*), late L *prōsequere* (*sequere, sequī*, to follow)]

pursuivant (pœ´sivənt, -swi-) *n.* **1** (*Her.*) an attendant on a herald, an officer of the College of Arms of lower rank than a herald. **2** (*poet.*) a follower, an attendant. [OF *porsivant* (F *poursuivant*), pres.p., as PURSUE]

pursy[1] (pœ´si) *a.* (*comp.* **pursier,** *superl.* **pursiest**) **1** short-winded, asthmatic. **2** fat, corpulent. **pursiness** *n.* [formerly *pursive*, A-F *prosif*, OF *polsif* (F *poussif*), from *polser* (F *pousser*), to breathe with effort, from L *pulsāre*, to PULSE[1]]

pursy[2] (pœ´si) *a.* (*comp.* **pursier,** *superl.* **pursiest**) **1** like a purse, puckered up like the mouth of a purse. **2** moneyed, purse-proud. [PURSE]

purtenance (pœ´tənəns) *n.* an appurtenance.

purty (pœ´ti) *a.* (*comp.* **purtier,** *superl.* **purtiest**) (*dial., N Am.*) pretty.

purulent (pū´rələnt) *a.* consisting of or discharging pus or matter. **purulence, purulency** *n.* **purulently** *adv.* [F, from L *pūrulentus*, from *pūs pūris*, PUS]

purvey (pəvā´) *v.t.* **1** to provide, to supply, esp. provisions. **2** to procure. ~*v.i.* **1** to make provision. **2** to act as a supplier. **purveyance** *n.* **1** the purveying or providing of provisions. **2** provisions supplied. **3** (*Hist.*) the old royal prerogative of buying up provisions, impressing horses etc. **purveyor** *n.* **1** a person who purveys provisions etc., a caterer, esp. on a large scale. **2** a person who repeats, or sells (information, rumours etc.). [A-F *purveier* (F *pourvoir*), to PROVIDE]

purview (pœ´vū) *n.* **1** extent, range, scope, intention. **2** range of vision, knowledge etc. **3** (*Law*) the body of a statute consisting of the enacting clauses. [A-F *purveu* (F *pourvu*), p.p. of *purveier*, see PURVEY]

pus (pŭs) *n.* the thick yellowish liquid secreted from inflamed tissues, the produce of suppuration. **pussy**[1] (pŭs´i) *a.* (*comp.* **pussier,** *superl.* **pussiest**) full of pus, containing pus. [L]

Puseyism (pū´ziizm) *n.* the High Church tenets of the Oxford Movement, in the Church of England, Tractarianism. **Puseyistical** (-ist´-) *a.* **Puseyite** (-īt) *a., n.* [Edward *Pusey*, 1800–82, English clergyman, a leader of the movement]

push (push) *v.t.* **1** to press against with force, tending to urge forward or away. **2** to move (a body along, up, down etc.) thus. **3** to make (one's way) vigorously. **4** to impel, to drive. **5** to cause to put forth or project. **6** to put pressure on (a person). **7** to pursue (a claim etc.). **8** to develop or carry, as a point, an argument, esp. to extremes. **9** (with a number) to approach. **10** to seek to promote, esp. to promote the sale or use of. **11** (*coll.*) to peddle (drugs). ~*v.i.* **1** to exert pressure (against, upon etc.). **2** to press forward, to make one's way vigorously, to hasten forward energetically. **3** to protrude or project. **4** to thrust or butt (against). **5** to be urgent and persistent. **6** to make a push-stroke in billiards. ~*n.* **1** the act, or an instance, of pushing, a thrust, a shove. **2** a vigorous effort, an attempt, an onset. **3** pressure. **4** an exigency, a crisis, an extremity. **5** persevering energy, self-assertion. **6** the use of influence to help (a person or a cause). **7** (*Mil.*) an offensive. **8** a stroke in billiards in which the ball is pushed, not struck. **9** (*Austral.*) a gang of larrikins, a clique or party. **at a push** if really necessary. **if it comes to the push** if really necessary. **pushing up the daisies** DAISY. **to be pushed for** (*coll.*) to be short of (time or money). **to get/ give the push** (*sl.*) to dismiss, be dismissed, esp. from a job. **to push about/ around 1** (*coll.*) to bully, to treat with contempt. **2** to move around roughly or aimlessly. **to push along** (*coll.*) to go away. **to push for** (*coll.*) to advocate vigorously, to make strenuous efforts to achieve. **to push in** (*coll.*) to force one's way into (esp. a queue) ahead of others. **to push off 1** to push against the bank with an oar so as to move a boat off. **2** (*coll.*) to go away. **to push on 1** to press forward, to hasten. **2** to urge or drive on. **to push one's luck** (*coll.*) to take risks, esp. by overplaying an existing advantage. **to push through** to secure the acceptance of (a plan, proposal etc.)

speedily or by compulsion. **when push comes to shove** (*coll.*) when the time for action comes. **push-bike, push-bicycle** *n.* (*coll.*) a bicycle worked by foot pedals as distinguished from a motor-bicycle. **push-button** *n.* a device for opening or closing an electric circuit by the pressure of the finger on a button. ~*a.* (of machinery etc.) operated by means of a push-button. **pushcart** *n.* (*N Am.*) a barrow. **pushchair** *n.* a light, folding chair on wheels for a child. **pusher** *n.* **1** a person or thing that pushes, esp. a device used in conjunction with a spoon for feeding very young children. **2** (*coll.*) a pushful person. **3** (*coll.*) a drug peddler. **4** (*Austral.*) a pushchair. **pushful** *a.* (*coll.*) self-assertive, energetic, vigorous or persistent in advancing oneself. **pushfully** *adv.* **pushfulness** *n.* **pushing** *a.* **1** enterprising, energetic. **2** self-assertive; encroaching. **3** (*coll.*) having almost reached (a specified age). **pushingly** *adv.* **pushover** *n.* (*coll.*) **1** something easy to do. **2** a person, team etc. easy to defeat. **push-pin** *n.* **1** a pin with a ball-shaped head, used esp. for marking positions on a map. **2** (*Shak.*) a kind of child's game. **push-pull** *a.* of or relating to any piece of apparatus in which electrical or electronic devices, e.g. two transistors in an amplifier, act in opposition to each other. **pushrod** *n.* in an internal-combustion engine, a metal rod that opens and closes the valves. **push-start** *v.t.* to set (a vehicle) in motion by pushing, then engaging a gear to start the engine. ~*n.* the act, or an instance, of starting an engine thus. **push-stroke** *n.* in billiards, a push. **push-up** *n.* (*N Am.*) a press-up. **pushy** *a.* (*comp.* **pushier,** *superl.* **pushiest**) (*coll.*) pushful. **pushily** *adv.* **pushiness** *n.* [OF *pousser*, L *pulsāre*, to PULSATE]

Pushtoo PASHTO.

pusillanimous (pūsilan´iməs) *a.* lacking courage, firmness or strength of mind, faint-hearted. **pusillanimity** (-nim´-) *n.* **pusillanimously** *adv.* **pusillanimousness** *adv.* [eccles. L *pusillanimis* (*pusillus*, small, petty, *animus*, soul)]

puss[1] (pus) *n.* **1** a pet name for a cat, esp. in calling. **2** a hare. **3** (*coll.*) a child, a girl. **puss moth** *n.* a large bombycid moth, *Cerura vinula.* **pussy**[2] *n.* (*pl.* **pussies**) **1** (*coll.*) a cat. **2** (*taboo sl.*) the female pudenda. **3** (*offensive*) women generally considered as sexual objects. **pussy cat** *n.* **1** a cat. **2** anything woolly or fuzzy, such as a willow catkin. **pussyfoot** *v.i.* **1** to move stealthily or warily. **2** to avoid committing oneself. **pussyfooter** *n.* **pussy willow** *n.* **1** a small American willow, *Salix discolor*, with silvery catkins. **2** any of various similar willows. [cp. Dut. *poes*, LG *Puus*, Norw. *puse*, Swed. dial. *pus*; prob. imit.]

puss[2] (pus) *n.* (*sl.*) the face. [Ir. *pus*]

pussy[1] PUS.

pussy[2] PUSS[1].

pustule (pŭs´tūl) *n.* **1** a small vesicle containing pus, a pimple. **2** a small excrescence, a wart, a blister. **pustular** *a.* **pustulate**[1] (-lāt) *v.t., v.i.* to form into pustules. **pustulate**[2] (-lət) *a.* covered with pustules or excrescences. **pustulation** (-lā´shən) *n.* **pustulous** *a.* [F, from L *pustula*, prob. conn. with Gr. *phusalis, phuskē*, a bladder, *phusaein*, to blow]

put[1] (put) *v.t.* (*pres. p.* **putting,** *past, p.p.* **put**) **1** to move so as to place in some position. **2** to set, lay, place or deposit. **3** to bring into some particular state or condition. **4** to append, to affix. **5** to connect, to add. **6** to assign. **7** to express, to state. **8** to render, to translate (into). **9** to substitute (one thing for another). **10** to apply, to set, to impose. **11** to stake (money on). **12** to invest (e.g. money in). **13** to inflict (something on somebody). **14** to subject (a person) to. **15** to subject, to commit (to or upon). **16** to advance, to propose (for consideration etc.), to submit (to a vote). **17** to imagine (oneself) in a position etc. **18** to constrain, to incite, to force, to make (a person do etc.). **19** to make (one) appear in the right, wrong etc. **20** to repose, as trust, confidence etc. **21** to estimate (at a specified amount). **22** to hurl, to cast, to throw (a weight etc.) as a sport. **23** to thrust. **24** to couple (a female animal) with a male. ~*v.i.* **1** (*Naut.*) to go, to proceed, to steer one's course (in a specified direction). **2** (*N Am.*) (of a river) to flow in a specified direction. ~*n.* **1** the act, or an instance, of putting. **2** a cast, a throw (of a weight etc.). **3** an agreement to sell or deliver (stock, goods etc.) at a stipulated price within a specified time. **4** a thrust. **not to know where to put oneself** (*coll.*) to be very embarrassed. **not to put it past somebody** to consider a person capable of (the activity under discussion). **put up or shut up!** either defend yourself or remain silent. **to put a bold/ brave face on** FACE. **to put about** **1** to inconvenience. **2** (*Naut.*) to go about, to change the course of to the opposite tack. **3** (*coll.*) to make public, to spread abroad. **to put across** **1** to communicate effectively. **2** to make acceptable. **to put an end to** END. **to put away** **1** to return to its proper place. **2** to lay by. **3** to shut up (in a prison, mental institution etc.). **4** (*coll.*) to consume (food or drink). **5** to put (an animal) to death because of old age etc. **6** to remove. **to put back** **1** to retard, to check the forward motion of. **2** to postpone. **3** to move the hands of (a clock) back. **4** to replace. **5** (*Naut.*) to return (to land etc.). **to put by** to put, set or lay aside for future use. **to put down** **1** to suppress, to crush. **2** to take down, to snub, to degrade. **3** to confute, to silence. **4** to reduce, to diminish. **5** to write down, to enter, to subscribe. **6** to reckon, to consider, to attribute. **7** to put (a baby) to bed. **8** to kill, esp. an old or ill animal. **9** to pay (as a deposit). **10** (of an aircraft) to land. **11** (of a bus etc.) to stop to let (passengers) off. **12** to preserve, to store, to pickle. **to put forth** **1 a** to present to notice. **b** to publish, to put into circulation. **2** to extend. **3** to shoot out. **4** to exert. **5** (of a plant) to produce (buds, shoots). **to put forward** **1** to set forth, to advance, to propose. **2** to thrust (oneself) into prominence. **3** to move the hands of (a clock) onwards. **to put in** **1** to introduce, to interject, to interpose. **2** to insert, to enter. **3** to install in office etc. **4 a** to present, to submit, as an application, request etc. **b** to submit a claim (for something). **5** to be a candidate (for). **6** to enter a harbour. **7** (*coll.*) to spend, to pass (time), to devote (effort). **to put in mind** MIND. **to put it across someone** (*coll.*) to defeat someone by ingenuity. **to put it on** **1** to pretend (to be ill etc.). **2** to exaggerate. **to put it to someone** **1** to suggest to a person (that). **2** to challenge a person to deny (that). **to put off** **1** to lay aside, to discard, to take off. **2 a** to postpone (an appointment). **b** to postpone an appointment with (a person). **3** to disappoint, to evade (a person). **4** to hinder, to distract the attention of. **5** to dissuade (from). **6** to cause aversion to. **7** to foist, to palm off (with). **to put on** **1** to take on. **2** to clothe oneself with. **3 a** to assume (a disguise etc.). **b** to pretend to feel (an emotion). **4** to add, to affix, to apply. **5** to add on (weight etc.). **6** to bring into play, to exert. **7** to cause to operate (a light etc.). **8** to cause to be available. **9** to stage, to produce (a play etc.). **10** to appoint. **11** to move the hands of (a clock) forward. **12** to send (a bowler) on to the field in cricket. **to put one across** (*coll.*) to deceive into believing or accepting. **to put one over on** (*coll.*) to deceive into believing or accepting. **to put on to** to make (a person) aware of; to put (a person) in touch with. **to put out** **1** to eject. **2** to extinguish (a light). **3** to disconcert; to annoy, to irritate. **4** to inconvenience (oneself). **5** to exert (strength). **6** to dislocate (a joint). **7** to publish, to broadcast. **8** to give out (work) to be done at different premises. **9** to render unconscious. **10** to invest, to place (at interest). **11** in cricket, to dismiss (a batsman or a side). **12** to blind (someone's eyes). **to put out of one's mind** MIND. **to put out of sight** SIGHT. **to put over** **1** to communicate effectively. 2 (*N Am.*) to postpone. 3 (*N Am.*) to pass off. **to put someone's mind at rest** MIND. **to put the boot in** BOOT[1]. **to put the clock back** CLOCK[1]. **to put through 1** to connect (someone) by telephone (to someone else). 2 to see to a conclusion, to accomplish. 3 to cause to undergo (esp. suffering). **to put to bed** BED. **to put together** to assemble (things, parts) to form a finished whole. **to put to it** 1 to distress. 2 to press hard. **to put under** to render unconscious by the use of an anaesthetic. **to put up** 1 to raise (a hand etc.). 2 to erect, to build. 3 to offer, to present, as for sale, auction. 4 to increase (a price etc.). 5 to give, to show, as a fight, resistance etc. 6 to lodge and entertain. 7 to take lodgings. 8 to display (a notice etc.). 9 to publish (banns etc.). 10 to provide (money, a prize). 11 to offer (oneself) as a candidate. 12 to present as a candidate. 13 to pack up. 14 to place in a safe place. 15 to lay aside. 16 to sheathe (a sword). 17 to cause (game birds) to come out of cover. **to put upon** 1 to impose upon; to take undue advantage of. 2 to victimize. **to put up to** 1 to incite to. 2 to make conversant with. **to put up with** to tolerate, to submit to. **to stay put** STAY[1]. **put-down** *n.* a snub, an action or remark intended to humiliate. **put-in** *n.* in rugby football, the action of putting the ball into the scrum. **put-off** *n.* an evasion, an excuse. **put-on** *n.* an attempt to deceive or mislead. **putter**[1] *n.* 1 a person who puts. 2 a shot-putter. **putting (the shot)** *n.* the act or sport of throwing a heavy weight from the shoulder by an outward thrust of the arm. **put-up job** *n.* something secretly pre-arranged for purposes of deception. **put-you-up** *n.* a makeshift temporary bed for a visitor. [late OE *putian* (in *putung*), *potian*, to put, *pȳtan*, to put or thrust out]

put[2] PUTT.

putamen (pūtā´mən) *n.* (*pl.* **putamina** (-minə)) 1 the hard bony stone or endocarp of a fruit such as a peach or cherry. 2 the membrane of skin inside the shell of an egg. 3 (*Anat.*) the outer zone of the lenticular nucleus of the brain. [L, from *putāre*, to prune]

putative (pū´tətiv) *a.* 1 reputed, supposed. 2 commonly regarded as. **putatively** *adv.* [F *putatif*, fem. *-tive*, late L *putātīvus*, from *putāre*, to think]

putlog (pŭt´log), **putlock** (-lok) *n.* a short horizontal piece of timber for the floor of a scaffold to rest on. [etym. uncertain]

put-put (pŭt´pŭt) *v.i.* (*pres.p.* **put-putting,** *past, p.p.* **put-putted**) 1 (of a petrol engine) to make a rapid popping sound. 2 (of a vehicle) to travel along while making this sound. *~n.* this sound. [imit.]

putrefy (pū´trifī) *v.t.* (*3rd pers. sing. pres.* **putrefies,** *pres.p.* **putrefying,** *past, p.p.* **putrefied**) 1 to make putrid, to cause to rot or decay. 2 to make carious or gangrenous. 3 to corrupt. *~v.i.* 1 to become putrid, to rot, to decay. 2 to fester, to suppurate. 3 to become corrupt. **putrefaction** (-fak´-) *n.* **putrefacient** (-fā´shənt) *a.* **putrefactive** *a.* **putrescence** (-tres´əns) *n.* the process of rotting. **putrescent** *a.* **putrescible** *a.* liable to rot. *~n.* a putrescible substance. **putrescibility** (-bil´-) *n.* **putrescine** (-in) *n.* (*Chem.*) a poisonous alkaloid contained in decaying animal matter. [F *putréfier*, L *putrefacere* (*putre-*, as in *putrēre*, to be rotten, *facere*, to make)]

putrid (pū´trid) *a.* 1 in a state of putrefaction, decomposition, or decay. 2 tainted, foul, noxious. 3 (*fig.*) corrupt. 4 (*sl.*) of very poor quality. **putrid fever** *n.* typhus or jail-fever. **putridity** (-trid´-), **putridness** *n.* **putridly** *adv.* [L *putridus*, rotten, see PUTREFY]

putsch (puch) *n.* a sudden rising, revolt; a coup d'état. [Swiss G]

putt (pŭt), **put** *v.i.* (*3rd pers. sing. pres.* **putts, puts,** *pres.p.* **putting,** *past, p.p.* **putted**) to strike a golf ball with a putter. *~v.t.* to strike (the ball) gently with a putter so as to get it into a hole on a putting green. *~n.* this stroke. **to putt out** to putt the ball into the hole and so complete a hole in a round of golf. **putter**[2] *n.* 1 a short, stiff golf club, used for striking the ball on a putting green. 2 a person who putts. **putting green** *n.* 1 the piece of ground around each hole on a golf course, usu. kept rolled, closely mown and clear of obstacles. 2 an area of smooth grass with several holes for putting games. [var. of PUT[1]]

puttee (pŭt´i, -ē) *n.* 1 a long strip of cloth wound spirally round the leg, usu. from ankle to knee, as a form of gaiter. 2 (*N Am.*) a leather legging. [Hind. *patti*, bandage]

putter[1] PUT[1].

putter[2] PUTT.

putter[3] (pŭt´ə) *v.i.* to put-put. *~n.* a put-putting sound.

putter[4] POTTER[2].

putti PUTTO.

puttier PUTTY.

putto (put´ō) *n.* (*pl.* **putti** (-ē)) a figure of a small boy, cherub or cupid in Renaissance and baroque art. [It., from L *putus*, a boy]

putty (pŭt´i) *n.* (*pl.* **putties**) 1 whiting and linseed oil beaten up into a tenacious cement, used in glazing etc. 2 fine lime mortar used by plasterers for filling cracks etc. 3 calcined tin or lead used by jewellers as polishing powder for glass, metal etc. *~v.t.* (*3rd pers. sing. pres.* **putties,** *pres.p.* **puttying,** *past, p.p.* **puttied**) to fix, cement, fill up or cover with putty. **to be putty in someone's hands** to be easily manipulated by someone. **up to putty** (*Austral., sl.*) no good, valueless, of bad quality. **puttier** *n.* a worker with putty, a glazier. **putty-coloured** *a.* pale yellowish-grey. **putty-faced** *a.* having a smooth, colourless face like putty. **putty knife** *n.* a short, blunt, flexible knife for applying putty. **putty powder** *n.* jewellers' putty in the form of powder, used for polishing. **putty-root** *n.* an American orchid, *Aplectrum hyemale*, the root of which contains glutinous matter sometimes used as cement. [F *potée*, orig. potful, see POT[1]]

puy (pwē) *n.* a conical hill of volcanic origin, esp. in the Auvergne, France. **puy lentils** *n.pl.* small green lentils of a type grown in Le Puy, France. [F, ult. from L *podium*, elevation, height]

puzzle (pŭz´əl) *n.* 1 a perplexing problem, question or enigma. 2 a toy, riddle or other contrivance for exercising ingenuity or patience. 3 a state of bewilderment or perplexity. *~v.t.* to perplex, to embarrass, to mystify. *~v.i.* to be bewildered or perplexed. **to puzzle out** to discover, or work out by mental labour. **puzzledom** (-dəm), **puzzlement** *n.* **puzzler** *n.* a person who or a thing which puzzles. **puzzling** *a.* **puzzlingly** *adv.* [etym. uncertain]

puzzolana POZZOLANA.

PVA *abbr.* polyvinyl acetate.

PVC *abbr.* polyvinyl chloride.

PVFS *abbr.* post-viral fatigue syndrome.

PVS *abbr.* 1 persistent vegetative state. 2 post-viral syndrome.

Pvt. *abbr.* (*Mil.*) Private.

PW *abbr.* policewoman.

p.w. *abbr.* per week.

PWA (pēdŭbəlūā´) *n.* (*pl.* **PWAs**) a person with Aids.

PWD *abbr.* Public Works Department.

PWR *abbr.* pressurized-water reactor.

PX *abbr.* (*Mil., US*) post exchange.

PY *abbr.* Paraguay (IVR).

py- PYO-.

pyaemia (piē´miə), (*N Am.*) **pyemia** *n.* (*Med.*) blood poisoning, due to the spread of pus-forming bacteria in the system causing multiple abscesses. **pyaemic** *a.* [Gr. *puon*, pus, *haima*, blood]

pycn- PYCNO-.

pycnic PYKNIC.

pycnidium (piknid´iəm) *n.* (*pl.* **pycnidia** (-diə)) (*Bot.*) a flask-shaped structure in certain fungi which contains spores. [Gr. *puknos*, thick, *-idion*, dim. suf.]

pycnite (pik´nīt) *n.* a columnar variety of topaz.

pycno- (pik´nō), **pycn-** *comb. form* thick, dense. [Gr. *puknos*, thick, dense]

pycnometer (piknom´itə) *n.* a bottle or flask of known volume used in measuring the specific gravity of fluids. **pycnometric** (-met´-) *a.*

pye-dog (pī´dog), **pie-dog, pi-dog** *n.* a stray mongrel dog, esp. in India. [Hind.]

pyel- PYELO-.

pyelitis (pīəlī´tis) *n.* (*Med.*) inflammation of the pelvis of the kidney. **pyelitic** (-lit´-) *a.*

pyelo- (pīə´lō), **pyel-** *comb. form* of or relating to the kidneys. [mod. L (Gr. *puelos*, trough)]

pyelography (pīəlog´rəfi) *n.* the branch of radiology dealing with the kidneys and the surrounding structures. **pyelogram** (pī´ə-) *n.* an X-ray picture of the kidneys etc. **pyelographer** (-log´-) *n.*

pyelonephritis (pīəlōnifrī´tis) *n.* inflammation of the kidney and of the renal pelvis. **pyelonephritic** (-frit´-) *a.*

pyemia PYAEMIA.

pyg- PYGO-.

pygidium (pījid´iəm, -gid´-) *n.* (*pl.* **pygidia** (-iə)) the tail, or other end structure, of certain worms, insects or other invertebrates. [mod. L, from Gr. *pugidion*, dim. of *pugē*, rump]

pygmy (pig´mi), **pigmy** *n.* (*pl.* **pygmies, pigmies**) **1** a member of any of various dwarf peoples living in Malaysia or Central Africa. **2** a dwarf, a small person, anything very diminutive. **3** a person having a certain faculty or quality in relatively a very small degree; an insignificant person. **4** a member of a dwarfish people mentioned by Herodotus and other ancient historians as living in Africa and India. ~*a.* **1** of or relating to pygmies; diminutive, dwarf. **2** small and insignificant. **pygmaean** (-mē´ən), **pygmean** *a.* **pygmy chimpanzee** *n.* an anthropoid ape of central and W Africa, *Pan paniscus*. **pygmy hippopotamus** *n.* (*pl.* **pygmy hippopotamuses, pygmy hippopotami**) a quadruped, *Choeropsis liberiensis*, related to but smaller than *Hippopotamus amphibius*. [L *pygmaeus*, Gr. *pugmaios*, dwarfish, from *pugmē*, fist, the length from elbow to knuckles]

pygo- (pī´gō), **pyg-** *comb. form* **1** diminutive, dwarf. **2** small and insignificant. [Gr. *pugo-*, *pugē*, rump]

pygostyle (pī´gəstīl) *n.* the vomer or ploughshare bone forming the end of the vertebral column in most birds. **pygostyled** *a.*

pyjamas (pəjah´məz), (*N Am.*) **pajamas** *n.pl.* **1** a sleeping suit consisting of a loose jacket and trousers. **2** loose trousers of silk, cotton etc. worn by both sexes among Muslims in India and Pakistan. **pyjama** *a.* of or relating to either the jacket or the trousers of pyjamas. **pyjama cricket** *n.* (*Austral., coll.*) cricket played in the evening under floodlights, the players wearing coloured clothing. **pyjama'd, pyjamaed** *a.* wearing pyjamas. [Pers. and Hind. *pāejāmah* (*pāe*, leg, *jāmah*, clothing, garment)]

pyknic (pik´nik), **pycnic** *a.* (of a body type) characterized by short stature, relatively short arms and legs, a large abdomen and a short neck. ~*n.* a person of this body type. [Gr. *puknos*, thick]

pylon (pī´lən) *n.* **1** a structure, usu. of steel, supporting an electric cable. **2** a rigid, streamlined support (for an engine etc.) on the outside of an aircraft. **3** a stake marking out the path for aircraft at an airfield. **4** a gateway of imposing form or dimensions, esp. the monumental gateway of an Egyptian temple. [Gr. *pulōn*, from *pulē*, gate]

pylorus (pīlaw´rəs) *n.* (*pl.* **pylori** (-rī)) the contracted end of the stomach leading into the small intestine. **pyloric** (-lor´ik) *a.* [late L, from Gr. *pulōros*, gatekeeper (*pulē*, gate, *ouros*, keeper, watcher)]

pyo- (pī´ō), **py-** *comb. form* pus. [Gr. *puon*, pus]

pyoderma (pīōdœ´mə) *n.* (*Med.*) any skin rash characterized by the formation of pus-filled spots. [Gr. *derma dermatos*, skin]

pyogenesis (pīōjen´əsis) *n.* the formation of pus, suppuration. **pyogenetic** (-net´-), **pyogenic** *a.*

pyoid (pī´oid) *a.* of the nature of pus, purulent.

pyorrhoea (pīərē´ə), (*N Am.*) **pyorrhea** *n.* **1** inflammation of the gums leading to the discharge of pus and loosening of the teeth; periodontal disease. **2** any discharge of pus. **pyorrhoeal, pyorrhoeic** *a.*

pyosis (pīō´sis) *n.* suppuration.

pyr- PYRO-.

pyracantha (pī´rəkanthə), **pyracanth** (-kanth) *n.* (*pl.* **pyracanthas, pyracanths**) any evergreen thorny shrub of the genus *Pyracantha*, with white flowers and coral-red berries, also called the firethorn, commonly trained against walls as an ornamental climber. [L *pyracantha*, Gr. *purakantha* (see ACANTHUS)]

pyral PYRE.

pyralid (pīral´id, -rā´lid) *n.* any of various moths of the family *Pyralidae*, small and slender with long legs. ~*a.* of or relating to this family. [mod. L, from Gr. *puralis*, a mythical insect said to live in fire (*pur*, fire)]

pyramid (pir´əmid) *n.* **1** a monumental structure of masonry, with a square base and triangular sloping sides meeting at the apex. **2** a similar solid body, with a triangular or polygonal, but usu. square, base. **3** a pile or heap of this shape. **4** a game of pool played with fifteen coloured balls and a cue ball. **5** a crystal form in which three planes intersect all three axes. ~*v.i.* (*N Am.*) to speculate during a boom by using paper profits to make further purchases. **the Pyramids** the great pyramids of ancient Egypt. **pyramidal** (-ram´-), **pyramidic** (-mid´-), **pyramidical** *a.* **pyramidally, pyramidically** *adv.* **pyramidist** *n.* a student or investigator of the origin, structure etc. of ancient pyramids, esp. those of Egypt. **pyramidism** *n.* **pyramidon** (-ram´idon) *n.* an organ stop having stopped pipes like inverted pyramids, producing very deep tones. **pyramid selling** *n.* a system of selling whereby batches of goods are sold to agents who sell smaller batches at increased prices to subagents and so on. **pyramidwise** *adv.* [L *pyramis -idis*, Gr. *puramis -idos*, prob. of Egypt. orig.]

pyrargyrite (pirah´jirīt) *n.* (*Mineral.*) a dark red mineral consisting of sulphide of silver and antimony. [Gr. *arguros*, silver]

pyre (pīə) *n.* **1** a funeral pile for burning a dead body. **2** any pile of combustibles. **pyral** *a.* [L *pyra*, Gr. *pura*, cogn. with *pur*, fire]

pyrene[1] (pī´rēn) *n.* an aromatic hydrocarbon obtained in the dry distillation of coal. [Gr. *pur*, fire]

pyrene[2] (pī´rēn) *n.* the stone of a fruit such as a peach. [Gr. *purēn*]

pyrethrum (pīrēth´rəm) *n.* (*pl.* **pyrethrums**) **1** any of several plants of the genus *Tanacetum* of the Compositae, esp. *T. coccineum*. **2** an insecticide made from the dried heads of these. **pyrethrin** (-rin) *n.* either of two oily, insecticidal compounds found in pyrethrum flowers. **pyrethroid** *n.* (*Chem.*) any one of a group of synthetic compounds with similar insecticidal properties. [L, from Gr. *purethron*, as PYRE]

pyretic (pīret´ik) *a.* of, relating to or producing fever. [Gr. *puretos*, fever]

Pyrex® (pī´reks) *n.* a heat-resistant glass containing oxide of boron. ~*a.* (of a cooking or laboratory container) made of Pyrex.

pyrexia (pīrek´siə) *n.* (*Med.*) fever, feverish condition. **pyrexial, pyrexic, pyrexical** *a.*

pyrheliometer (pəhēliom´itə) *n.* an instrument for

measuring the intensity of solar radiation. **pyrheliometric** (-met´-) *a.*

pyridine (pir´idēn, pī´-) *n.* (*Chem.*) a liquid alkaloid obtained from bone oil, coal tar etc., used as a solvent etc. **pyridoxine** (-dok´sēn) *n.* a derivative of pyridine found in yeast, vitamin B_6.

pyriform (pir´ifawm) *a.* pear-shaped. [med. L *pyrum*, L *pirum*, PEAR]

pyrimidine (pirim´idēn) *n.* **1** (*Chem.*) a cyclic organic nitrogenous base, with the formula $C_4H_4N_2$. **2** any of several compounds derived from this including constituents of nucleic acids.

pyrites (pīrī´tēz) *n.* a native sulphide of iron, one of two common sulphides, chalcopyrite, yellow or copper pyrites, or marcasite, usu. called iron pyrites. **pyrite** (-´rīt) *n.* iron pyrites. **pyritic** (-rit´-), **pyritous** (pī´ri-) *a.* **pyritiferous** (-tif´-) *a.* **pyritize** (pī´ri-), **pyritise** *v.t.* **1** to convert into pyrites. **2** to replace with pyrites. [L, from Gr. *puritēs*, orig. pertaining to fire, from *pur*, fire]

pyro (pī´rō) *n.* pyrogallic acid. [short for PYROGALLIC]

pyro- (pī´rō), **pyr-** *comb. form* **1** fire, heat. **2** (*Chem.*) obtained (as if) by heating or by the elimination of water. **3** (*Mineral.*) changing under the action of heat. **4** having a red or yellow colour like fire. [Gr. *pur puros*, fire]

pyroacetic (pīrōəsē´tik) *a.* of or derived from acetic acid by heat.

pyrochemical (pīrōkem´ikəl) *a.* of, relating to or involving chemical reactions at very high temperatures.

pyroclastic (pīrōklas´tik) *a.* formed from or consisting of the fragments broken up or ejected by volcanic action. **pyroclast** *n.* **pyroclastic flow** *n.* (*Geol.*) a mixture of hot ash, lava and gases flowing at high speed from a volcanic crater. [Gr. *klastos*, broken]

pyroelectric (pīrōilek´trik) *a.* (of some minerals) becoming electrically charged on heating. **pyroelectricity** (-eliktris´-) *n.*

pyrogallic (pīrōgal´ik) *a.* produced from gallic acid by heat. **pyrogallol** (-ol) *n.* pyrogallic acid, a weak acid used as a developing agent in photography.

pyrogen (pī´rəjen) *n.* a substance, such as ptomaine, that produces fever on being introduced into the body. **pyrogenetic** (-net´-), **pyrogenic** (-jen´-) *a.* **1** producing heat. **2** producing feverishness. **3** pyrogenous. **pyrogenous** (-roj´-) *a.* produced by fire or by volcanic processes, igneous.

pyrognostic (pīrəgnos´tik) *a.* of or relating to pyrognostics. **pyrognostics** *n.pl.* those properties of a mineral, e.g. fusibility, that are determinable by heat.

pyrography (pīrog´rəfi) *n.* (*pl.* **pyrographies**) **1** the art of making designs in wood by means of fire, pokerwork. **2** a design or picture made thus. **pyrographer** *n.* **pyrographic** (-graf´-) *a.* **pyrogravure** (-rōgrəvūə´) *n.* **1** pyrography. **2** a picture produced by this means.

pyroligneous (pīrōlig´niəs) *a.* derived from wood by heat. **pyroligneous acid** *n.* an acidic liquid obtained by the destructive distillation of wood. **pyrolignite** (-nīt) *n.* a salt of pyroligneous acid.

pyrolusite (pīrəloo´sīt) *n.* (*Mineral.*) native manganese dioxide, one of the most important of the ores of manganese. [G *Pyrolusit* (Gr. *lousis*, washing)]

pyrolysis (pīrol´isis) *n.* the chemical decomposition of a substance by heat. **pyrolyse,** (*N Am.*) **pyrolyze** *v.t.* to subject to this process. **pyrolytic** (-lit´-) *a.*

pyromagnetic (pīrōmagnet´ik) *a.* thermomagnetic.

pyromancy (pī´rəmansi) *n.* divination by fire. **pyromancer** *n.* **pyromantic** (-man´-) *a.* [OF *pyromancie*, late L *pyromantīa*, Gr. *puromanteia*]

pyromania (pīrəmā´niə) *n.* an irresistible desire to set things on fire. **pyromaniac** (-ak) *n.* **pyromaniacal** (-mənī´ə-) *a.*

pyrometer (pīrom´itə) *n.* an instrument for measuring high temperatures. **pyrometric** (-met´-), **pyrometrical** *a.* **pyrometrically** *adv.* **pyrometry** (-om´-) *n.*

pyromorphite (pīrōmaw´fīt) *n.* (*Mineral.*) an ore of lead consisting of phosphate and chloride of lead.

†**pyronomics** (pīrənom´iks) *n.* the science of heat. [Gr. *nomos*, a law]

pyrope (pī´rōp) *n.* a deep-red garnet. [OF *pirope*, L *pyrōpus*, Gr. *purōpos* (*pur*, fire, *ōps*, face, eye)]

pyrophoric (pīrəfor´ik) *a.* **1** (of a chemical) igniting spontaneously on contact with air. **2** (of an alloy) emitting sparks when struck. [mod. L *pyrophorus*, from Gr. *purophoros*, fire-bearing]

pyrophosphoric (pīrōfosfor´ik) *a.* derived by heat from phosphoric acid. **pyrophosphate** (-fos´fāt) *n.* a salt or ester of pyrophosphoric acid.

pyrophyllite (pīrōfil´īt) *n.* a mineral occurring in metamorphic rocks, a form of hydrated aluminium silicate.

pyrosis (pīrō´sis) *n.* (*Med.*) heartburn. [Gr. *purōsis*, from *puroein*, to set on fire]

pyrostat (pī´rōstat) *n.* a type of thermostat for use at high temperatures.

pyrosulphate (pīrōsŭl´fāt), (*N Am.*) **pyrosulfate** *n.* a salt of pyrosulphuric acid. **pyrosulphuric acid** *n.* an unstable acid obtained by adding sulphur trioxide to sulphuric acid.

pyrotechnic (pīrōtek´nik) *a.* **1** of or relating to fireworks or their manufacture. **2** of the nature of fireworks. **3** (*fig.*) resembling a firework show, brilliant, dazzling. **pyrotechnical** *a.* **pyrotechnically** *adv.* **pyrotechnics** *n.* **1** the art of making fireworks. **2** (*sing. or pl.*) a display of fireworks. **3** (*sing. or pl.*) a dazzling or virtuoso display. **pyrotechnist** *n.* **pyrotechny** (pī´rətekni) *n.* [Gr. *technē*, art]

pyroxene (pī´roksēn, -rok´-) *n.* any of a group of silicates of lime, magnesium, iron or manganese, of various forms and origin. **pyroxenic** (-sen´-) *a.* **pyroxenite** (-sinīt) *n.* a coarse-grained rock consisting of pyroxene minerals. [Gr. *xenos*, stranger]

pyroxylin (pīrok´silin), **pyroxyle** (-sil) *n.* a nitrocellulose, gun cotton, used in the manufacture of plastics and lacquers. **pyroxylic** (-sil´-) *a.* of or relating to the crude spirit obtained by the distillation of wood in closed vessels. [F *pyroxyline* (Gr. *xulon*, wood)]

Pyrrhic (pir´ik) *a.* of or relating to Pyrrhus. **pyrrhic victory, Pyrrhic victory** *n.* a victory that is as costly as a defeat. [*Pyrrhus*, king of Epirus, who won a victory over the Romans at Asculum (279 BC) but suffered heavy losses]

pyrrhic (pir´ik) *n.* **1** a metrical foot of two short syllables. **2** a warlike dance among the ancient Greeks. ~*a.* **1** of or relating to such a dance. **2** consisting of two short syllables. [L *pyrrhica*, Gr. *purrhichē*, from *Purrhichos*, the inventor]

Pyrrhonism (pir´ənizm) *n.* **1** the sceptical philosophy taught by Pyrrho of Elis, a Greek sceptical philosopher of the 4th cent. BC. **2** universal doubt, philosophic nescience. **Pyrrhonian** (-rō´-), **Pyrrhonic** (-ron´-) *a.* **Pyrrhonist** *n.* [Gr. *Purrhōn*, Pyrrho]

pyrrole (pir´ōl) *n.* (*Chem.*) a colourless toxic liquid found in e.g. porphyrins and chlorophyll. **pyrrolic** (-rol´ik) *a.* **pyrrolidine** (-rol´idēn) *n.* a colourless alkaline liquid found in tobacco leaves or produced from pyrrole. [Gr. *purrhos*, red]

pyruvate (pīroo´vāt) *n.* (*Chem.*) any salt or ester of pyruvic acid. **pyruvic acid** *n.* an organic acid occurring as an intermediate in the metabolism of proteins and carbohydrates. [L *uva*, grape]

Pythagorean (pīthagərē´ən) *n.* a follower of Pythagoras. ~*a.* of or relating to Pythagoras or his philosophy. **Pythagoras's theorem** (pīthag´ərəsiz) *n.* the theorem, attributed to Pythagoras, that the square on the hypotenuse of a right-angled triangle is equal to the sum of the squares on the other two sides. **Pythagoreanism**

(-thag´-), **Pythagorism** *n.* [*Pythagoras* of Samos, 6th cent. BC, philosopher and mathematician]

Pythian (pith´iən) *a.* of or relating to Delphi, Apollo, or his priestess who delivered oracles at Delphi. ~*n.* **1** an inhabitant of Delphi. **2** the priestess of Apollo at Delphi. **Pythian games, Pythic games** *n.pl.* one of the four great Panhellenic festivals, celebrated once every four years near Delphi. **Pythic** *a.* [L *Pythius*, Gr. *Puthios*, from *Puthō*, former name of Delphi]

python[1] (pī´thən) *n.* **1** a large non-venomous serpent of the family Pythonidae, that crushes its prey. **2** in Greek mythology, a gigantic serpent slain by Apollo near Delphi. **pythonic**[1] (-thon´-) *a.* [L, from Gr. *Puthōn*, prob. from *Puthō*, see PYTHIAN]

python[2] PYTHONESS.

Pythonesque (pīthənesk´) *a.* (of humour) surreal, extravagant, absurd. [*Monty Python's Flying Circus*, BBC television series, 1969–74]

pythoness (pī´thənis) *n.* **1** the priestess of the temple of Apollo at Delphi who delivered the oracles. **2** a woman believed to be possessed by a familiar spirit or having the gift of prophecy, a witch. **python**[2] *n.* **1** a familiar spirit or demon. **2** a person supposedly possessed by this, a soothsayer, a diviner. **pythonic**[2] (-thon´-) *a.* inspired, oracular, prophetic. **pythonism** *n.* [late L *pytho -ōnem*, or late Gr. *puthōn*, prob. rel. to PYTHON[1] but history obscure]

pythonic[1] PYTHON[1].

pythonic[2] PYTHONESS.

pyuria (pīū´riə) *n.* (*Med.*) the presence of pus in the urine. [Gr. *puon*, pus, *ouron*, urine]

pyx (piks), **pix** *n.* **1** the covered vessel, usu. of precious metal, in which the Eucharistic host is kept. **2** a box at the Royal Mint in which sample coins are placed for testing at the annual trial by a jury of the Goldsmiths' Company. **pyxidium** (-sid´iəm) *n.* (*pl.* **pyxidia** (-diə)) (*Bot.*) a capsule or seed vessel dehiscing by a transverse suture, as in the pimpernel. **pyxis** (-sis) *n.* (*pl.* **pyxides** (-sidēz)) **1** a box, a casket. **2** (*Bot.*) a pyxidium. [L *pyxis*, Gr. *puxis*, a box, from *puxos*, box tree]

pzazz PIZAZZ.

Q

Q[1] (kū), **q** (*pl.* **Qs, Q's**) the 17th letter of the English and other versions of the Roman alphabet. It is pronounced as a voiceless velar plosive like *k* and is normally followed by *u*, the combination of *qu* usually having the sound of *kw*. ~*symbol* **1** the alleged source of the material found in the gospels of both Matthew and Luke but not in Mark. **2** (*Physics*) heat. **to mind one's P's and Q's** P[1].

Q[2] *abbr.* **1** quality, as in *Q factor.* **2** Quebec. **3** Queen. **4** Queen's. **5** query, as in *Q fever, Q ship.*

q *abbr.* **1** quart. **2** quarter. **3** quarterly. **4** query. **5** question. **6** quintal. **7** quire.

Qaddish KADDISH.

qadi CADI.

Qantas (kwon´təs), **QANTAS** *abbr.* Queensland and Northern Territory Aerial Services, an airline.

QARANC *abbr.* Queen Alexandra's Royal Army Nursing Corps.

QB *abbr.* Queen's Bench.

Q-boat Q-SHIP.

QC *abbr.* Queen's Counsel.

QCD *abbr.* quantum chromodynamic.

QED *abbr. quod erat demonstrandum*, which was to be proved. [L]

Q factor (kū) *n.* **1** the difference between stored energy and the rate at which energy is being expended. **2** the heat released in a nuclear explosion. [*Q*uality *factor*]

Q fever (kū) *n.* an acute disease caused by rickettsiae, whose symptoms include fever and pneumonia. [*Q*uery *fever*, the cause being orig. unknown]

qibla KIBLAH.

qindar (kindah´), **qintar** (-tah´) *n.* a unit of Albanian currency equal to one hundredth of a lek. [Albanian]

Qld. *abbr.* Queensland.

QM *abbr.* quartermaster.

QMG *abbr.* Quartermaster General.

QMS *abbr.* Quartermaster Sergeant.

QPM *abbr.* Queen's Police Medal.

qr. *abbr.* quarter(s).

Q-ship (kū), **Q-boat** *n.* (*Hist.*) an armed navy vessel disguised as a merchant ship, employed as a decoy to lure and surprise enemy submarines. [*Q*uery-ship]

QSO *abbr.* quasi-stellar object, a quasar.

qt. *abbr.* **1** quantity. **2** quart, quarts. **3** (*also* **q.t.**) quiet. **on the qt.** (*coll.*) secretly, on the sly.

qto *abbr.* quart.

qty *abbr.* quantity.

qu *abbr.* **1** query. **2** question.

qua (kwā, kwah) *conj.* in the character of, by virtue of being, as. [L, abl. fem. sing. of *qui*, rel. pron., who]

quack[1] (kwak) *v.i.* **1** to make the harsh cry of a duck or a similar sound. **2** (*coll.*) to chatter loudly or boastfully. ~*n.* the cry of a duck. **quack-quack** *n.* a duck (used by or to children). [imit., cp. Dut. *kwakken*, G *quacken*, Icel. *kvaka*, also L *coaxāre*, Gr. *koax*, a croak]

quack[2] (kwak) *n.* **1** an unqualified practitioner of medicine, esp. one offering ineffectual remedies. **2** (*sl.*) a doctor. **3** a mere pretender to knowledge or skill. ~*a.* of or relating to quacks or quackery (*quack remedies*). **quackery, quackism** *n.* **quackish** *a.* [short for QUACKSALVER]

†**quacksalver** (kwak´salvə) *n.* **1** a person who brags of their medicines or salves. **2** a quack. [Dut. *kwakzalver*, earlier *quacksalver*]

quad[1] (kwod) *n.* a quadrangle or court, as of a college etc. [short for QUADRANGLE]

quad[2] (kwod) *n.* (*coll.*) each child of quadruplets. [short for QUADRUPLET (under QUADRUPLE)]

quad[3] (kwod) *n.* (*Print.*) a block of type metal lower than the type, used for spacing out lines etc. ~*v.t.* (*pres.p.* **quadding,** *past, p.p.* **quadded**) to insert quadrats in (a line of type). [short for earlier QUADRAT]

quad[4] (kwod) *a.* quadraphonic. ~*n.* quadraphonics.

quad[5] QUOD.

quad bike (kwod) *n.* a four-wheeled motorcycle designed for off-road sporting, agricultural etc. use. [QUADRUPLE]

quadr- QUADRI-.

quadragenarian (kwodrəjəneə´riən) *n.* a person who is forty or between 40 and 50 years old. ~*a.* aged forty or between 40 and 50. [L *quadrāgēnārius*, from *quadrāgēnī*, distrib. of *quadrāginta*, 40 (*quadrus*, cogn. with *quatuor*, four, *-ginta*, prob. for *dekinta*, tenth, from *decem*, ten)]

Quadragesima (kwodrəjes´imə) *n.* **1** (*also* **Quadragesima Sunday**) the first Sunday in Lent. **2** †Lent (so called because it consists of 40 days). **quadragesimal** *a.* **1** (of a fast) lasting 40 days. **2** of, relating to or used in Lent; Lenten. [med. L, fem. of *quadrāgēsimus*, 40th, as QUADRAGENARIAN]

quadrangle (kwod´rang·gəl) *n.* **1** a plane figure having four angles and four sides, esp. a square or rectangle. **2** an open square or four-sided court surrounded by buildings. **3** such a court together with the surrounding buildings. **quadrangular** (-rang´gū-) *a.* **quadrangularly** *adv.* [F, from L *quadrangulum*]

quadrant (kwod´rənt) *n.* **1** the fourth part of the circumference of a circle, an arc of 90°. **2** a plane figure contained by two radii of a circle at right angles to each other and the arc between them. **3** a quarter of a sphere. **4** any of the four sections into which something, esp. a plane, is divided by two lines that intersect at right angles. **5** an object or part shaped like a quadrant of a circle. **6** an instrument shaped like a quarter-circle graduated for taking angular measurements, esp. one formerly used by sailors and astronomers for taking the altitude of the sun or stars. **quadrantal** (-ran´-) *a.* [L *quadrans -antis*, as QUADRI-]

quadraphonic (kwodrəfon´ik), **quadrophonic** *a.* of, relating to or being a system of recording and reproducing sound using four independent sound signals or speakers. **quadraphonically** *a.* **quadraphonics** *n.pl.* (*also constr. as sing.*) (the use of) quadraphonic recording or reproduction. **quadraphony** (-raf´əni) *n.*

quadrat (kwod´rət) *n.* **1** a square of vegetation marked out for ecological study. **2** (*Print.*) a quad (of type). [var. of QUADRATE[1]]

quadrate[1] (kwod´rət) *a.* square; rectangular. ~*n.* **1** the quadrate bone. **2** a quadrate muscle. **3** a square, cubical or rectangular object. **quadrate bone** *n.* in birds and reptiles, a bone by means of which the jaws are articulated with the skull. **quadrate muscle** *n.* a square-shaped muscle in the hip, forearm etc. **quadratic** (-rat´-) *a.* **1** involving the second and no higher power of the variable or unknown quantity. **2** square. ~*n.* **1** a quadratic equation. **2** (*pl.*) the part of algebra dealing with quadratic equations. **quadratrix** (-rā´triks) *n.* (*pl.* **quadratrices** (-trisēz)) a curved figure by means of which straight lines can be found equal to the circumferences of circles or other curves. **quadrature** (-rəchə) *n.* **1** the act of constructing or finding a square equal in area to a given curved figure. **2** the position of a heavenly body with respect to another 90° distant. **3** in electronics, a phase difference of one quarter of a cycle between two waves. [L *quadrātus*, p.p. of *quadrāre*, to square, from *quadrus*, square]

quadrate[2] (kwodrāt´, kwod´-) *v.t.* **1** to square. **2** to make conformable. ~*v.i.* to agree, to match, to correspond.

quadratic, quadrature etc. QUADRATE[1].

quadrella (kwodrel´ə) *n.* (*Austral.*) a form of betting where the person making the bet must pick the winners of four races. [dim. of QUADRI-, four]

quadrennial (kwodren´iəl) *a.* **1** lasting four years. **2** recurring every four years. **quadrennially** *adv.* **quadrennium** (-iəm) *n.* (*pl.* **quadrenniums, quadrennia** (-iə)) a period of four years. [L *quadriennium* (QUADRI-, *annus*, year)]

quadri- (kwod´ri), **quadr-** *comb. form* four. [L, rel. to *quattuor*, four]

quadric (kwod´rik) *a.* (*Math.*) of the second degree; quadratic. ~*n.* a curve, surface etc. of the second degree.

quadricentennial (kwodrisenten´iəl) *n.* the 400th anniversary of an event. ~*a.* of or relating to a period of 400 years.

quadriceps (kwod´riseps) *n.* a four-headed muscle at the front of the thigh, acting as extensor to the leg. **quadricipital** (-sip´itəl) *a.* [L (as BICEPS)]

quadricone (kwod´rikōn) *n.* a quadric cone.

quadrifarious (kwodrifeə´riəs) *a.* arranged in four parts or rows.

quadrifid (kwod´rifid) *a.* (*Bot.*) cleft into four parts, segments or lobes.

quadrifoliate (kwodrifō´liət) *a.* having four leaves or leaflets.

quadriga (kwodrē´gə) *n.* (*pl.* **quadrigae** (-jē)) (*pl.*) an ancient Roman two-wheeled chariot drawn by four horses abreast. [L, orig. in pl. form. *quadrīgae* for *quadrijugae* (*jugum*, yoke)]

quadrigeminal (kwodrijem´inəl), **quadrigeminous** (-nəs) *a.* of or relating to four medullary tubercles situated at the base of the brain. **quadrigeminate** (-nət) *a.* **1** fourfold. **2** occurring in fours. [GEMINOUS (under GEMINI)]

quadrigenarious (kwodrijineə´riəs) *a.* consisting of 400.

quadrijugate (kwodrijoo´gət), **quadrijugous** (-gəs) *a.* (*Bot.*) pinnate with four pairs of leaflets.

quadrilateral (kwodrilat´ərəl) *n.* a plane figure or area with four straight sides. ~*a.* having four sides and four angles. **quadrilaterality** (-ral´-), **quadrilateralness** *n.* [L *quadrilaterus*]

quadrilingual (kwodriling´gwəl) *a.* **1** speaking four languages. **2** written in four languages.

quadriliteral (kwodrilit´ərəl) *a.* consisting of four letters. ~*n.* a quadriliteral word, esp. a Semitic root containing four consonants.

quadrille[1] (kwədril´) *n.* **1** a dance consisting of five figures executed by four sets of couples. **2** a piece of music for such a dance. ~*v.i.* **1** to dance a quadrille. **2** to play music for a quadrille. [F, from Sp. *cuadrillo*, a squadron, a band, dim. of *cuadra*, square, as QUADRI-]

quadrille[2] (kwədril´) *n.* a game of cards played by four persons with 40 cards, fashionable in the 18th cent. [F, from Sp. *cuartillo*, from *cuarto*, fourth, assim. to QUADRILLE[1]]

quadrillion (kwədril´yən) *n.* (*pl.* **quadrillion, quadrillions**) **1** the fifth power of a thousand, one followed by 15 zeros. **2** (in Britain, esp. formerly) the number produced by raising a million to its fourth power, represented by one followed by 24 zeros. **quadrillionth** *n., a.* [F (MILLION, cp. BILLION)]

quadrilobate (kwodrilō´bāt) *a.* having four lobes.

quadrilocular (kwodrilok´ūlə) *a.* having four cells or chambers.

†**quadrimanous** QUADRUMANOUS.

quadrinomial (kwodrinō´miəl) *a.* consisting of four terms. ~*n.* a mathematical expression consisting of four algebraic terms.

quadripartite (kwodripah´tīt) *a.* **1** divided into or consisting of four parts. **2** affecting or shared by four parties. **quadripartitely** *adv.* **quadripartition** (-tish´ən) *n.* division by four or into four parts.

quadriplegia (kwodriplē´jə, -jiə) *n.* paralysis of all four limbs. **quadriplegic** *a., n.*

quadrireme (kwod´rirēm) *n.* an ancient Roman galley having four banks of oars. [L *quadrirēmis* (*rēmus*, oar)]

quadrisection (kwodrisek´shən) *n.* division into four usu. equal parts. **quadrisect** (kwod´-) *v.t.*

quadrisyllabic (kwodrisilab´ik) *a.* consisting of four syllables. **quadrisyllable** (-sil´-) *n.* a word consisting of four syllables.

quadrivalent (kwodrivā´lənt) *a.* having a valency or combining power of four, tetravalent. **quadrivalency, quadrivalence** *n.*

quadrivium (kwodriv´iəm) *n.* in the Middle Ages, an educational course consisting of arithmetic, music, geometry, and astronomy. **quadrivial** *a.* **1** having four ways meeting in a point. **2** of or relating to the quadrivium. [L (*via*, way)]

quadroon (kwədroon´) *n.* **1** the offspring of a mulatto and a white person; a person of one quarter black and three-quarters white blood. **2** any similarly proportioned hybrid in human, animal and vegetable stocks. [Sp. *cuarteron*, from *cuarto*, fourth, as QUARTO, assim. to QUADRI-]

quadrophonic QUADRAPHONIC.

quadrumanous (kwodroo´mənəs), †**quadrimanous** *a.* of, relating to or belonging to a group of mammals in which the hind as well as the fore feet have an opposable digit and are used as hands, containing the monkeys, apes, baboons and lemurs. **quadrumana** *n.pl.* **quadrumane** (kwod´rəmān) *n.* [L *quadru-*, QUADRI-, *manus*, hand]

quadruped (kwod´ruped) *n.* a four-footed animal, esp. a mammal. ~*a.* having four legs and feet. **quadrupedal** (-pē´dəl, -ped´əl, -roo´pidəl) *a.* [L *quadrupes -pedis* (*quadru-*, QUADRI-, *pes pedis*, foot)]

quadruple (kwod´rupəl, -roo´-) *a.* **1** consisting of four parts. **2** involving four members, units etc. **3** equal to four times the number or quantity of, fourfold. **4** (of musical time) having four beats in a bar. ~*n.* a number or quantity four times as great as another. ~*v.i.* to increase fourfold, to become four times as much. ~*v.t.* to multiply fourfold, to make four times as much. **quadruplet** (-plit) *n.* **1** any one of four children born of the same mother at one birth. **2** a compound or combination of four things working together. **3** four notes to be played in a time value of three. **4** a bicycle for four. **quadruplex** (-rupleks) *a.* **1** fourfold. **2** (of a telegraphic wire) used four times over. **3** of or relating to a videotape recording system using four rotating recording heads. ~*n.* **1** an electrical apparatus by means of which four messages may be sent simultaneously over one telegraphic wire. **2** a quadruplex recording and reproduction system. ~*v.t.* to arrange (a wire etc.) for quadruplex working. **quadruplicate**[1] (-roo´plikāt) *v.t.* to make fourfold, to quadruple. **quadruplicate**[2] (-roo´plikət) *a.* **1** four times as many or as much, fourfold. **2** four times copied. ~*n.* **1** any one of four copies or similar things. **2** quadruplicity. **in quadruplicate** written out or copied four times. **quadruplication** (-ā´shən) *n.* **quadruplicity** (-plis´-) *n.* the state of being quadruple. **quadruply** *adv.* [F, from L *quadruplus*, acc. *-plum* (*quadru-*, QUADRI-, *-plus*, fold)]

quadrupole (kwod´rupōl) *n.* (*Physics*) a system of two associated dipoles. **quadrupolar** (-pō´-) *a.*

quaere (kwiə´rē) *int.* ask, inquire, it is a question. ~*n.* a question, a query. **quaesitum** (kwēsī´təm) *n.* (*pl.* **quaesita** (-tə)) a query. [L, imp. of *quaerere*, to ask, to INQUIRE]

quaestor (kwēs´tə), **questor** *n.* an ancient Roman magistrate having charge of public funds, a public treasurer, paymaster etc. **quaestorial** (-taw´riəl) *a.* **quaestorship** *n.* †**quaestuary** (-tūəri) *a.* seeking profit or gain. ~*n.* (*pl.* **quaestuaries**) **1** a person employed to collect profits. **2** a pardoner. [L, for *quaesitor*, from *quaerere*, see QUAERE, p.p. *quaesitus*]

quaff (kwof) *v.t.* **1** to drink in large draughts. **2** to drink from in large draughts. ~*v.i.* to drink copiously. ~*n.* a copious draught. **quaffable** *a.* **quaffer** *n.* [etym. uncertain]

quag (kwag, kwog) *n.* a piece of marshy or boggy ground. **quaggy** *a.* (*comp.* **quaggier**, *superl.* **quaggiest**). **quagginess** *n.* [onomat.]

quagga (kwag´ə) *n.* (*pl. in general* **quagga**, *in particular* **quaggas**) a S African quadruped, *Equus quagga*, intermediate between the ass and the zebra, now extinct. [prob. orig. Bantu, imit. of its cry]

quaggy QUAG.

quagmire (kwag´mīə, kwog´-) *n.* **1** an area of soft marshy ground that moves or sinks under the feet. **2** an awkward or difficult predicament.

quahog (kwaw´hog, kwah´-), **quahaug** (-hawg) *n.* a common edible clam, *Venus mercenaria*, of the Atlantic coast of N America. [Narragansett *poquauhock*]

quaich (kwākh), **quaigh** *n.* (*Sc.*) a shallow drinking vessel, usu. of wood. [Gael. *cuach*, prob. from L *caucus*, Gr. *kauka*]

quail[1] (kwāl) *v.i.* **1** to shrink back with fear, to be cowed, to lose heart. **2** to give way (before or to). [etym. uncertain]

quail[2] (kwāl) *n.* (*pl. in general* **quail**, *in particular* **quails**) **1** a small migratory bird of the genus *Coturnix*, allied to the partridge, esp. a European game bird *C. coturnix*. **2** any of various allied American game birds. **quail-pipe** *n.* a whistle imitating the cry of the quail for enticing them to the net. [OF *quaille* (F *caille*), prob. from Gmc. (cp. Dut. *kwakkel*, OHG *quatala*), prob. of imit. orig.]

quaint (kwānt) *a.* **1** old-fashioned and odd, pleasing by virtue of strangeness, oddity or fancifulness. **2** odd, whimsical, singular. **quaintish** *a.* **quaintly** *adv.* **quaintness** *n.* [ME and OF *cointe*, L *cognitus*, acc. *-tum*, p.p. of *cognoscere*, to know, to learn]

quake (kwāk) *v.i.* **1** to shake, to tremble, to quiver. **2** to rock, to vibrate. ~*n.* a tremulous motion, a shudder. **quaking** *a.* **1** trembling. **2** unstable. **quaking ash** *n.* the aspen. **quaking-grass** *n.* a grass of the genus *Briza*, the spikelets of which have a tremulous motion. **quaky** *a.* (*comp.* **quakier**, *superl.* **quakiest**). **quakiness** *n.* [OE *cwacian*, prob. of imit. orig., cp. QUAG]

Quaker (kwā´kə) *n.* a member of the Society of Friends. ~*a.* of or relating to Quakers or their religious belief. **Quakerdom** *n.* **Quakeress** *n.* **Quaker gun** *n.* a model gun mounted to deceive the enemy. **Quakerish** *a.* **Quakerism** *n.* **Quakerly** *a.* like a Quaker. [QUAKE, -ER[1], orig. applied in derision, 1650, perh. from the founder's direction to tremble at the word of the Lord, or from the alleged fits caused by religious emotion]

quaking, quaky QUAKE.

qualify (kwol´ifī) *v.t.* (*3rd pers. sing. pres.* **qualifies**, *pres.p.* **qualifying**, *past*, *p.p.* **qualified**) **1** to invest or furnish with the requisite qualities. **2** to make competent, fit, or legally capable (to be or do, or for any action, place, office or occupation). **3** to modify, to limit, to narrow the scope, force etc. of (a statement, opinion or word). **4** to moderate, to mitigate, to temper. **5** to reduce the strength or flavour of (spirit etc.) with water, to dilute. **6** to attribute a quality to, to describe or characterize as. ~*v.i.* **1** to become qualified or fit. **2** to make oneself competent, suitable or eligible (for). **qualifiable** *a.* **qualification** (-fikā´shən) *n.* **1** the act of qualifying or the state of being qualified. **2** modification, restriction or limitation of meaning; exception or partial negation restricting completeness or absoluteness. **3** any natural or acquired quality fitting a person or thing (for an office, employment etc.). **4** a condition that must be fulfilled for the exercise of a privilege etc. **qualificative, qualificatory** *a.* **qualified** *a.* **qualifier** *n.* **qualifying** *n.*, *a.* **qualifying round** *n.* a preliminary round in a competition. [F *qualifier*, med. L *quālificāre* (L *quālis*, such, *-ficāre*, *facere*, to make)]

quality (kwol´iti) *n.* (*pl.* **qualities**) **1** a distinctive property or attribute, that which gives individuality. **2** relative nature or kind, distinguishing character. **3** a mental or moral trait or characteristic. **4** particular capacity, value, or function. **5** degree of excellence, relative goodness. **6** a high standard of excellence. **7** the affirmative or negative nature of a proposition. **8** that which distinguishes sounds of the same pitch and intensity, timbre. ~*a.* **1** having or displaying excellence. **2** (of a newspaper) aimed at an educated readership. †**the quality** persons of high rank, the upper classes. **qualitative** (-tətiv) *a.* of, relating to or concerned with quality (as opposed to *quantitative*). **qualitative analysis** *n.* (*Chem.*) the detection of the constituents of a compound body. **qualitatively** *adv.* **qualitied** *a.* **quality control** *n.* the testing of manufactured products to ensure they are up to standard. **quality controller** *n.* **quality time** *n.* time spent constructively in improving family relationships, lifestyle etc. [F *qualité*, L *quālitas* acc. *-tātem*, from *quālis*, as QUALIFY]

qualm (kwahm) *n.* **1** a sensation of fear or uneasiness. **2** a misgiving, a scruple, compunction. **3** a sensation of nausea, a feeling of sickness. **qualmish** *a.* **qualmishly** *adv.* **qualmishness** *n.* **qualmy** *a.* (*comp.* **qualmier**, *superl.* **qualmiest**). [perh. from OE *cwealm*, pestilence; or rel. to G *Qualm*, vapour, dial. swoon, Dut. *kwalm*, Dan. *kvalm*, Swed. *qvalm*, vapour, closeness]

qualy (kwol´i) *n.* (*pl.* **qualies**) a method of measuring the quality and length of the life given to a patient by medical treatment, used to assess the cost-effectiveness of treatment, and to compare different, expensive, treatments. [acronym for *qu*ality-*a*djusted *l*ife *y*ear]

quamash CAMASS.

quandang QUANDONG.

quandary (kwon´dəri) *n.* (*pl.* **quandaries**) **1** a state of difficulty or perplexity. **2** an awkward predicament, a dilemma. [etym. uncertain]

quandong (kwan´dong), **quandang** (-dang), **quantong** (-tong) *n.* a small Australian tree, *Fusanus acuminatus*, with edible drupaceous fruit. [Austral. Abor.]

quango (kwang´gō) *n.* (*pl.* **quangos**) a board set up by central government to supervise activity in a specific field, e.g. the Race Relations Board. [acronym for *qu*asi-*a*utonomous *n*on-*g*overnmental *o*rganization]

quant (kwont) *n.* a punting-pole with a flange at the end to prevent its sinking in the mud. ~*v.t.* to propel with a quant. ~*v.i.* to propel a boat with a quant. [perh. from L *contus*, Gr. *kontos*]

quanta, quantal QUANTUM.

quantic (kwon´tik) *n.* (*Math.*) a rational, integrally homogeneous function of two or more variables. **quantical** *a.* [L *quantus*, how much]

quantify (kwon´tifī) *v.t.* (*3rd pers. sing. pres.* **quantifies**, *pres.p.* **quantifying**, *past*, *p.p.* **quantified**) **1** to determine the quantity of, to measure as to quantity. **2** to express the quantity of. **3** (*Logic*) to define the application of as regards quantity. **quantifiable** *a.* **quantification** (-fikā´shən) *n.* **quantifier** *n.* that which indicates quantity. [med. L *quantificāre* (*quantus*, as QUANTIC, *-ficāre*, *facere*, to make)]

quantity (kwon´titi) *n.* (*pl.* **quantities**) **1** that property by virtue of which anything may be measured. **2** extent, measure, size, greatness, volume, amount or number. **3** a sum, a number. **4** a certain or a large number, amount or portion. **5** (*pl.*) large quantities, abundance. **6** (*Math.*) **a** a thing having such relations, of number or extension, as can be expressed by symbols. **b** a symbol representing this. **7** the duration of a syllable or vowel sound. **8** (*Logic*) the extent to which a predicate is asserted of the subject of a proposition. **quantitative** (-tātiv, -tətiv), **quantitive** *a.* **1** of, relating to or concerned with quantity (as opposed to *qualitative*). **2** relating to or based on the quantity of vowels (as accent, verse etc.). **quantitative analysis** *n.* (*Chem.*) the determination of the amounts and proportions of the constituents of a compound body. **quantitatively** *adv.* **quantity mark** *n.* a mark placed over a vowel to indicate quantity. **quantity surveyor** *n.* a person employed to estimate the quantities of materials needed to erect a building. **quantity theory** *n.* the economic theory that prices vary directly with the amount of money in circulation and the speed at which it circulates. [OF *quantité*, L *quantitas*, from *quantus*, as QUANTIC]

quantivalence (kwontiv´ələns) *n.* valency. **quantivalent** *a.* [L *quanti-*, *quantus*, how much, *-valence*, as in EQUIVALENCE (under EQUIVALENT)]

quantize (kwon´tīz), **quantise** *v.t.* **1** to restrict or limit to a set of fixed discrete values or quanta. **2** to express in terms of quantum theory. **quantization** (-zā´shən) *n.* [etym. uncertain, perh. from *quantus*]

quantong QUANDONG.

quantum (kwon´təm) *n.* (*pl.* **quanta** (-tə)) **1** (*Physics*) the smallest possible amount into which a physical property such as energy or momentum can be subdivided and by which the value of that property can change. **2** a quantity, an amount. **3** a portion, a proportion, a share. **4** an amount required, allowed or sufficient. **quantal** *a.* **1** of or relating to a quantum; composed of discrete values. **2** existing in only one of two possible states. **quantum chromodynamics** *n.* (*Physics*) a theory describing the strong interaction between elementary particles in terms of quarks and gluons. **quantum electrodynamics** *n.* a branch of physics which applies quantum mechanics to the interactions between particles and electromagnetic radiation. **quantum jump, quantum leap** *n.* **1** (*coll.*) a sudden transition. **2** an unexpected and spectacular advance. **3** the sudden transition of an atom, electron etc. from one energy level to another. **quantum mechanics** *n.* a branch of physics based on quantum theory, applied to elementary particles and atoms which do not behave according to Newtonian mechanics. **quantum mechanical** *a.* **quantum mechanically** *adv.* **quantum number** *n.* any of a set of integers or half-integers which specifies the value of a quantized property and which together serve to describe the state of a particle or system of particles. **quantum sufficit** (sŭf´isit) *n.* (esp. in prescriptions) a sufficient amount. **quantum theory** *n.* the theory that energy, esp. radiant energy, occurs in quanta and that energy transferences take place in discrete increments. [L, neut. of *quantus*, how much, so much]

quaquaversal (kwahkwəvœ´səl) *a.* **1** pointing in every direction. **2** (*Geol.*) inclined outwards and downwards in all directions. **quaquaversally** *adv.* [late L *quāquāversus* (*quāquā*, whithersoever, *versus*, towards)]

quarantine (kwor´əntēn) *n.* **1** the enforced isolation, esp. of people and animals coming from places infected with contagious disease. **2** the prescribed period of isolation imposed. **3** a place where quarantine is enforced. ~*v.t.* to isolate or put in quarantine. **quarantine flag** *n.* a yellow flag flown from ships in quarantine. [from OF *quarantine* (F *quarantaine*), or from It. *quarantina*, from *quaranta*, L. *quadrāginta*, 40, see QUADRAGENARIAN]

quarant' ore (kwarənt aw´rā, kwor-) *n.* in the Roman Catholic Church, 40 hours' exposition of the Blessed Sacrament. [It., 40 hours]

quarenden (kwor´əndən), **quarender** (-də) *n.* a large red variety of apple, grown in Devon and Somerset. [etym. uncertain]

quark[1] (kwahk) *n.* any of several hypothetical particles thought to be the fundamental units of other subatomic particles. [from a word coined by James Joyce in *Finnegans Wake*, 1939]

quark[2] (kwahk) *n.* a low-fat soft cheese made from skimmed milk. [G]

quarrel[1] (kwor´əl) *n.* **1** a noisy or violent contention or dispute, an altercation, a brawl, a petty fight. **2** a falling-out or breach of friendship. **3** a ground or cause of complaint or dispute, a reason for strife or contention. ~*v.i.* (*pres.p.* **quarrelling,** (*N Am.*) **quarreling,** *past, p.p.* **quarrelled,** (*N Am.*) **quarreled**) **1** to dispute violently, to wrangle, to squabble. **2** to fall out, to break off friendly relations (with). **3** to cavil, to take exception, to find fault (with). **4** (of colours or other qualities etc.) to be at variance, to be discordant or incongruous. **quarreller,** (*N Am.*) **quarreler** *n.* **quarrelling,** (*N Am.*) **quarreling** *n., a.* **quarrelsome** (-səm) *a.* **1** inclined or apt to quarrel, contentious. **2** irascible, choleric, easily provoked. **quarrelsomely** *adv.* **quarrelsomeness** *n.* [ME and OF *querele*, L *querēla*, complaint, from *querī*, to complain]

quarrel[2] (kwor´əl) *n.* **1** a short, heavy bolt or arrow with a square head, formerly used for shooting from crossbows or arbalests. **2** a square or diamond-shaped pane of glass used in lattice windows. [ME and OF *quarel* (F *carreau*), It. *quadrello*, dim. of *quadro*, med. L *quadrus*, square]

quarrian (kwor´iən), **quarrion** *n.* a cockatiel found in inland Australia. [Austral. Abor.]

quarry[1] (kwor´i) *n.* (*pl.* **quarries**) **1** a place from which building-stone, slates etc. are dug, cut, blasted etc. **2** a source from which information is extracted. ~*v.t.* (*3rd pers. sing. pres.* **quarries,** *pres.p.* **quarrying,** *past, p.p.* **quarried**) to dig or take from or as from a quarry. **quarriable** *a.* **quarrier** *n.* **quarryman** *n.* (*pl.* **quarrymen**) a person employed in a quarry. **quarrymaster** *n.* the owner of a quarry. [med. L *quareia*, *quareria*, *quadrāria*, from L *quadrāre*, to square, as QUADRATE[1]]

quarry[2] (kwor´i) *n.* (*pl.* **quarries**) **1** any animal pursued by hounds, hunters, a bird of prey etc. **2** game, prey. **3** any object of pursuit. **4** †a part of the entrails etc. of a deer placed on a skin and given to the hounds. [ME *quirre*, OF *cuirée*, from *cuir*, L *corium*, skin]

quarry[3] (kwor´i) *n.* (*pl.* **quarries**) **1** a square or diamond-shaped pane of glass, a quarrel. **2** a square stone or tile. **quarry tile** *n.* an unglazed floor tile. [later form of QUARREL[2]]

quart[1] (kwawt) *n.* **1** a measure of capacity, the fourth part of a gallon, two pints (1.136 l). **2** a measure, bottle or other vessel containing such a quantity. **to fit a quart into a pint pot 1** (*usu. neg.*) **a** to cram a large amount into a small space, esp. too small a space. **b** to attempt something impossible or barely possible. [F *quarte*, fem. of *quart*, L *quarta*, fem. of *quartus*, fourth]

quart[2] (kaht) *n.* **1** a sequence of four cards of the same suit in piquet etc. **2** QUARTE.

quartan (kwaw´tən) *a.* (esp. of a fever) occurring or recurring every third or (inclusively) fourth day. ~*n.* a quartan fever, esp. malaria. [F *quartaine*, L *quartāna* (*febris*), fem. of *quartānus*, fourth, from *quartus*, see QUART[1]]

quartation (kwawtā´shən) *n.* the addition of silver, usu. in the proportion of 3:1, in the process of separating gold from its impurities by means of nitric acid. [L *quartus*, fourth]

quarte (kaht), **quart**, **carte** *n.* the fourth of eight parrying or attacking movements in fencing. [F, as QUART[1]]

quarter (kwaw´tə) *n.* **1** a fourth part, any of four equal parts. **2** the fourth part of the year, three calendar months. **3** a point of time 15 minutes before or after the hour. **4** the fourth part of a dollar, 25 cents; a coin of this value. **5** any one of four equal periods into which a game or match is divided. **6** (*coll.*) **a** the fourth part of a pound weight (4 oz.). **b** the fourth part of a hundredweight (28 lb., 12.7 kg). **c** a grain measure of 8 bushels (2.91 hl). **d** the fourth part of a fathom. **7 a** the fourth part of a period of the moon. **b** any one of the four phases of increase or decrease of the moon's face during a lunation. **8** one of the four chief points of the compass. **9** a main division of the globe corresponding to this. **10** a particular direction, region, or locality. **11** place of origin or supply, source. **12** a division of a town, esp. one assigned to or occupied by a particular class or group. **13** (*pl.*) a place of lodging or abode, that is occupied by troops etc. **14** (*usu. in pl.*) allotted position, proper place or station, esp. for troops. **15** one of four parts, each comprising a limb, into which the carcass of an animal or bird may be divided. **16** (*pl.*) the similar parts into which the body of a criminal or traitor was formerly divided after execution. **17** a haunch. **18** mercy, clemency. **19** exception from death allowed in war to a surrendered enemy. **20** one of the divisions of a shield when this is divided by horizontal and perpendicular lines meeting in the fesse point. **21** either side of a ship between the main chains and the stern. *~v.t.* **1** to divide into four equal parts. **2** (*Hist.*) to cut the body of (a traitor etc.) into quarters. **3 a** to put into quarters, to assign quarters to. **b** to provide (esp. soldiers) with lodgings and food. **4** (of a hound etc.) to range over (a field) in all directions. **5 a** to bear or arrange (charges or coats of arms) quarterly on a shield etc. **b** to add (other arms) to those of one's family. **c** to divide (a shield) into quarters by vertical and horizontal lines. *~v.i.* **1** to be stationed or lodged. **2** to range in search of game. **3** (of the wind) to blow on a ship's quarter. **quarterage** (-rij) *n.* a quarterly payment, wages, allowance etc. **quarterback** *n.* a player in American football who directs the attacking play of the team. **quarter-bell** *n.* a bell sounding the quarter-hours. **quarter-binding** *n.* a type of bookbinding in which the back is of leather, cloth etc. and the sides and corners of another usu. inferior material. **quarter-bound** *a.* **quarter-boy** *n.* a mechanism used for striking the quarter-hours. **quarter-bred** *a.* (of horses or cattle) having one-fourth pure blood. **quarter-butt** *n.* a long billiard or snooker cue, shorter than a half-butt. **quarter day** *n.* the day beginning each quarter of the year (Lady Day, 25 Mar., Midsummer Day, 24 June, Michaelmas Day, 29 Sept. and Christmas Day, 25 Dec.) on which tenancies etc. begin and end, payments are due etc. **quarterdeck** *n.* the upper deck extending from the stern to the mainmast, usu. assigned for the use of officers and cabin passengers. **quartered** *a.* **quarter-final** *n.* the round before the semi-final, in a knockout competition. **quarter-finalist** *n.* **quarter-horse** *n.* a small stocky horse, orig. bred in the US, that is capable of running short distances at great speed. **quarter-hour** *n.* **1** a quarter of an hour. **2** a point of time 15 minutes before or after the hour or sometimes 30 minutes after the hour. **quarter-hourly** *adv.* **quartering** *n.* **1** a dividing into quarters or fourth parts. **2** the assignment of quarters or lodgings. **3** a length of square-section timber with side 2–6 in. (5–15 cm). **4** the grouping of several coats of arms on a shield. **5** any one of the coats so quartered. **quarter-jack** *n.* a quarter-boy. **quarter-light** *n.* the small window in the front door of a car, often for ventilation. **quarter-line** *n.* a line 22 m from the goal-line in rugby, or the space enclosed by it. **quarterly** *a.* **1** containing a quarter. **2** occurring or done every quarter of a year. **3** (of a shield) divided into quarters. *~adv.* **1** once in each quarter of the year. **2** in quarters, arranged in the four quarters of the shield. *~n.* (*pl.* **quarterlies**) a periodical published every quarter. **quartermaster** *n.* **1** a regimental officer appointed to provide and assign quarters, lay out camps, and issue rations, clothing, ammunition etc. **2** a petty officer, having charge of the steering, signals, stowage etc. **quartermaster sergeant** *n.* a sergeant assisting the quartermaster. **Quartermaster-General** *n.* a staff officer in charge of the department dealing with quartering, encamping, moving, or embarking troops. **quarter-miler** *n.* an athlete who specializes in the quarter-mile race. **quarter note** *n.* (*esp. N Am.*) a crotchet. **quarter of an hour** *n.* a period of 15 minutes. **bad quarter of an hour** BAD. **quarteroon** *n.* QUADROON. **quarter-plate** *n.* **1** a photographic plate measuring 4¼ × 3¼ in. (10.8 × 8.3 cm). **2** a picture produced from this. **quarter-pound** *n.* a quarter of a pound weight, 4 oz. (113 g). **quarter-pounder** *n.* a hamburger weighing a quarter of a pound. **quarter-round** *n.* a convex moulding having the contour of a quarter-circle; an ovolo; an echinus. **quarter sessions** *n.pl.* (*Hist.*) a general court of limited criminal and civil jurisdiction held by the Justices of the Peace in every county (and in boroughs where there was a Recorder). **quarterstaff** *n.* an iron-shod pole about 6½ ft. (2 m) long, formerly used as a weapon of offence or defence, usu. grasped by one hand in the middle and by the other between the middle and one end. **quarter-tone** *n.* an interval of half a semitone. [OF, from L *quartārius*, a fourth part, from *quartus*, fourth]

quartern (kwaw´tən) *n.* a quarter or fourth part of various measures, esp. a pint, peck or pound. **quartern-loaf** *n.* a loaf of the weight of 4 lb. (1.8 kg). [OF *quarteron*, from *quarte*, fourth]

quartet (kwawtet´), **quartette** *n.* **1** a musical composition for four voices or instruments. **2** the performers of such a composition, a group of four musicians playing together. **3** a group or set of four people or four similar things. [F *quartette*, It. *quartetto*, from *quarto*, L *quartus*, fourth]

quartic (kwaw´tik) *a.* (*Math.*) of or relating to the fourth degree. *~n.* a curve, equation etc. of the fourth degree. [L *quartus*, fourth]

quartile (kwaw´tīl) *a.* denoting the aspect of two heavenly bodies when distant from each other a quarter of a circle. *~n.* **1** a quartile aspect. **2** any of three values of a variable that divide a statistical survey into four equal parts, each containing a quarter of the individuals surveyed. **3** a quarter of the individuals studied in a statistical survey, whose characteristics lie within stated limits. [med. L *quartīlis*, from L *quartus*, fourth]

quarto (kwaw´tō) *n.* (*pl.* **quartos**) **1** a size obtained by folding a sheet of paper twice, making four leaves or eight pages (usu. written *4to*). **2** a book, pamphlet etc. having pages of this size. *~a.* having the sheet folded into four leaves (*quarto paper*). [L *in quarto* (abl. of *quartus*, fourth), in a fourth part]

quartz (kwawts) *n.* a mineral consisting of pure silica or silicon dioxide, either massive or crystallizing hexagonally. **quartz clock** *n.* an electric clock of high accuracy in which the alternating current frequency is determined by the mechanical vibrations of a quartz crystal. **quartz crystal** *n.* a piece of piezoelectric quartz cut and ground so that it vibrates at a particular frequency. **quartz glass** *n.* glass made of almost pure silica, transparent to ultraviolet radiation and resistant to high temperatures. **quartziferous** (-if´-) *a.* bearing quartz (*quartziferous rock*). **quartz (iodine) lamp** *n.* a light source, based on iodine vapour, used for high-intensity lighting in car headlamps, cine projectors etc. **quartzite** (-īt) *n.* a massive or schistose metamorphic rock consisting of sandstone with a deposition of quartz about each grain. **quartzitic** (-it´-) *a.* **quartzose** (-ōs) *a.* containing or rich in quartz. **quartz watch** *n.* a watch operated by the vibrations of a piezoelectric quartz crystal as in a quartz clock. **quartzy** *a.* [G *Quarz*, etym. unknown]

quasar (kwā´zah) *n.* any of a group of unusually bright, starlike objects outside our galaxy, that exhibit large red-shifts and are a powerful source of radio waves and other energy emissions. [from *quasi-stellar* radio source]

quash (kwosh) *v.t.* 1 to annul or make void. 2 to put an end to, esp. by legal procedure. 3 to suppress, to extinguish, to crush. [OF *quasser*, L *quassāre*]

Usage note The verbs *quash* and *squash* should not be confused: *quash* means to annul, and *squash* to crush.

Quashie (kwosh´i) *n.* (*W Ind.*, *offensive*) a black person, esp. a simple-minded one. [Ashanti *Kwasi*, boy born on Sunday]

quasi (kwā´zī, -sī, kwah´zi) *adv.* as if; as it were. [L, as if]

quasi- (kwā´zī, -sī, kwah´zi) *comb. form* 1 apparently, seeming, not real, as *quasi-scientific.* 2 partly, not quite, to some degree, as *quasi-judicial.* **quasi-stellar object** *n.* any of various classes of very distant celestial bodies, including quasars. [L, QUASI]

Quasimodo (kwazimō´dō) *n.* the first Sunday after Easter, Low Sunday. [from first words of the introit for that day; L *quasi modo geniti infantes*, as new-born babes]

quassia (kwosh´ə, -iə) *n.* 1 a tree of a S American genus *Quassia*, esp. *Q. amara*, the bitter wood, bark and oil of which yield a tonic and insecticide. 2 the wood or bark of this or a related W Indian tree. [named by Linnaeus after Graham *Quassi*, 18th-cent. black slave who discovered its curative properties]

quatercentenary (kwatəsəntē´nəri, -ten´-) *n.* (*pl.* **quatercentenaries**) 1 a 400th anniversary. 2 its celebration. **quatercentennial** (-ten´-) *a.* [L *quater*, four times, CENTENARY (under CENTENARIAN)]

Usage note Pronunciation and spelling as *quarter-* are best avoided.

quaternary (kwətœ´nəri) *a.* 1 consisting of four, having four parts, esp. being or composed of an atom bound to four other atoms or radicals. 2 fourth in order. 3 (**Quaternary**) of, relating to or being the most recent geological period or rock strata. ~*n.* (*pl.* **quaternaries**) 1 a set of four. 2 the number four. 3 (**Quaternary**) the Quaternary period or system of rock. **quaternate, quaternal** *a.* fourfold, arranged in or composed of four or fours. **quaternity** *n.* (*pl.* **quaternities**) a set of four. [L *quaternārius*, from *quarternī*, four at a time, distrib. of *quater*, four times]

quaternion (kwətœ´niən) *n.* 1 a set, group or system of four. 2 an operator that changes one vector into another and depends on four irreducible geometrical elements. 3 (*pl.*) the form of the calculus of vectors employing this.

quaternity QUATERNARY.

quatorzain (kat´əzān) *n.* a poem or stanza of 14 lines, esp. a sonnet of an irregular form. **quatorze** (kətawz´) *n.* a set of four aces, kings, queens, knaves or tens, scoring 14 in a hand of piquet. [F *quatorzaine*, from *quatorze*, L *quātuordecim* (*quotar*, four, *decem*, ten), 14]

quatrain (kwot´rān) *n.* a stanza of four lines, usu. rhyming alternately. [F, from *quatre*, L *quāttuor*, four]

quatrefoil (kat´rəfoil, kat´ə-), **quaterfoil, quarterfoil** *n.* 1 an opening, panel or other figure in ornamental tracery, divided by cusps into four foils. 2 a leaf or flower composed of four divisions or lobes. [OF *quatre*, L *quāttuor*, four, FOIL[1]]

Quattrocento (kwatrōchen´tō, kwah-) *n.* the 15th cent., regarded as a distinctive period in Italian art and literature. **quattrocentism** *n.* **quattrocentist** *n.* [It., lit. 400 (L *quātuor*, four, *centum*, hundred), usu. 1400]

quaver (kwā´və) *v.i.* 1 to quiver, to tremble, to vibrate. 2 to sing or play with tremulous modulations or trills. ~*v.t.* to sing or utter with a tremulous sound. ~*n.* 1 a shake or rapid vibration of the voice, a trill. 2 a quiver or shakiness in speaking. 3 a note equal in duration to half a crotchet or one-eighth of a semibreve. **quaverer** *n.* **quavering** *a.* **quaveringly** *adv.* **quavery** *a.* [freq. of obs. *quave*, ME *quaven*, rel. to QUAKE]

quay (kē) *n.* a landing place or wharf, usu. of masonry and stretching along the side of or projecting into a harbour, for loading or unloading ships. **quayage** (-ij) *n.* 1 a system of quays. 2 a charge imposed for the use of a quay. **quayside** *n.* the edge of a quay. [ME *key*, A-F *kaie*, OF *kay* (F *quai*), prob. Celt. (cp. Welsh *cae*, Bret. *kaé*, hedge, enclosure)]

quean (kwēn) *n.* 1 †an impudent or disreputable woman, a slut, a hussy. 2 (*Sc.*) a young or unmarried woman, a lass. [OE *cwene*, woman (cp. Dut. *kween*, barren cow, OHG *quena*, Gr. *gunē*, woman, Eng. QUEEN)]

queasy (kwē´zi) *a.* (*comp.* **queasier**, *superl.* **queasiest**) 1 sick at the stomach, affected with nausea. 2 causing or tending to cause nausea. 3 easily nauseated. 4 fastidious, squeamish, uneasy (*a queasy conscience*). **queasily** *adv.* **queasiness** *n.* [formerly *queisy*, *coisy*, perh. from OF *coisié*, p.p. of *coisir*, to hurt]

Quebecker (kwibek´ə), **Quebecer** *n.* a native or inhabitant of Quebec. **Québecois** (kābekwah´) *n.* (*pl.* **Québecois**) a French-speaking inhabitant of Quebec.

quebracho (kibrah´chō) *n.* (*pl.* **quebrachos**) any of several S American trees with hard dense wood. [Sp., contr. of *quebrahacha* (*quebrar*, to break, *hacha*, axe)]

Quechua (kech´wə), **Quichua** (kich´-) *n.* (*pl.* **Quechuas, Quechua, Quichuas, Quichua**) 1 a member of any of various groups of S American Indian peoples, including the Incas. 2 their language. **Quechuan** *a.* [Sp., from Quechua]

queen (kwēn) *n.* 1 a female sovereign, esp. a hereditary sovereign of an independent state. 2 the wife of a king. 3 a queen dowager. 4 a court card bearing a representation of a queen. 5 the most powerful piece in chess. 6 the fertile female in a colony of bees, ants, etc. 7 a woman who or thing which is pre-eminent in any sphere or is regarded as the supreme example of its class. 8 a woman of majestic presence. 9 a woman or girl masquerading as a sovereign or presiding at some festivity. 10 (*sl.*, *derog.*) an effeminate male homosexual, often an ageing one. 11 a female cat. ~*v.t.* 1 to make (a woman) queen. 2 in chess, to make (a pawn) into a queen. ~*v.i.* 1 to act as a queen. 2 to reign as queen. 3 to become a queen in chess. **queen high** in a card game, having the queen as the top-ranking card. **the queen** the national anthem during the reign of a queen. **to queen it** to act in a superior or arrogant way (over). **Queen Anne** *a.* 1 of, relating to or denoting the architectural style prevalent in the reign of Queen Anne (*c.* 1700–20), characterized by plain and unpretentious design with classic details. 2 of or relating to a style of decorative art typified by Chippendale furniture. ~*n.* this style of architecture or furniture. **Queen Anne is dead** stale news. **Queen Anne's Bounty** *n.* (*Hist.*) a provision made in the reign of Queen Anne for augmenting poor church livings. **Queen Anne's lace** *n.* the wild carrot, *Daucus carota.* **queen bee** *n.* 1 a fully-developed female bee. 2 a woman in a dominating position, socially or in business. **queen cake** *n.* a small, soft, usu. heart-shaped currant cake. **queen consort** *n.* the wife of a king. **queencraft** *n.* **queendom** *n.* **queen dowager** *n.* the widow of a king. **queenhood** *n.* **queening** (kwē´ning) *n.* a variety of apple. **queenless** *a.* **queenlike** *a.* **queenly** *a.* (*comp.* **queenlier,** *superl.* **queenliest**) **1** appropriate to a queen. **2** like a queen, majestic. **queenliness** *n.* **queen mother** *n.* a queen dowager who is also the mother of the reigning sovereign. **queen of puddings** *n.* a pudding made with a breadcrumb and custard mixture topped with meringue. **Queen of the May** *n.* MAY QUEEN (under MAY). **queen of the meadows** *n.* meadowsweet. **queen post** *n.* either of two suspending or supporting posts between the tie-beam and rafters in a roof. **Queen regent** *n.* a queen who reigns as regent. **Queen regnant** *n.* a reigning queen. **Queen's Bench** *n.* a division of the High Court of Justice during the reign of a queen (formerly a court presided over by the sovereign). **queen's bishop** *n.* the bishop on the queen's side of a chessboard at the beginning of a game. **Queen's Bounty** *n.* (*Hist.*) a grant made to the mother of three or more children at a birth. **Queen's Champion** *n.* CHAMPION OF ENGLAND (under CHAMPION). **Queen's colour** *n.* a flag carried by a regiment during the reign of a queen. **Queen's Counsel** *n.* counsel to the Crown, an honorary title which gives precedence over ordinary barristers. **Queen's English** *n.* correct English as spoken by educated people. **Queen's evidence** *n.* evidence given against one's accomplice in return for a free pardon or reduction in sentence, during the reign of a queen. **Queen's flight** *n.* a unit of the RAF reserved for the use of the royal family. **Queen's Guide** *n.* a Guide who has reached the highest level of proficiency, during the reign of a queen. **Queen's highway** *n.* a public road, a right-of-way. **queenship** *n.* **queen-size, queen-sized** *a.* (of a bed etc.) larger than is usual or regular but smaller than king-size. **queen's knight** *n.* the knight on the queen's side of a chessboard at the beginning of a game. **Queen's Messenger** *n.* a courier in the diplomatic service, during the reign of the queen. **queen's-metal** *n.* an alloy of tin, antimony, lead and bismuth. **queen's pawn** *n.* the pawn in front of the queen at the beginning of a game of chess. **Queen's peace** *n.* the state of tranquillity, order and absence of hostilities throughout the country, for which the queen is responsible. **Queen's Proctor** *n.* an officer of the Crown during the reign of a queen who intervenes in probate, divorce or nullity cases when collusion or other irregularity is alleged. **Queen's Remembrancer** *n.* an officer of the Exchequer whose business is to collect debts due to the queen. **queen's rook** *n.* the rook on the queen's side of a chessboard at the beginning of a game. **Queen's Scout** *n.* a Scout or Guide who has passed the highest tests of proficiency and ability. **Queen's Speech** *n.* during the reign of a queen, an address by the sovereign to Parliament at the beginning of every session, outlining the government's proposed legislation. **queen substance** *n.* a secretion of the queen bee fed to worker bees to stop the development of their ovaries. **queen's-ware** *n.* glazed Wedgwood earthenware of a creamy colour. **queen truss** *n.* a truss in a roof, framed with queen posts. [OE *cwēn*, cogn. with QUEAN]

Queensberry Rules (kwēnz´bəri) *n.pl.* standard rules of boxing drawn up by the 8th Marquess of Queensberry in 1867.

Queensland nut (kwēnz´lənd) *n.* a macadamia tree or nut.

queer (kwiə) *a.* **1** strange, odd; singular, droll. **2** questionable, suspicious. **3** out of sorts, slightly unwell, faint. **4** (*sl., derog.*) homosexual. **5** (*coll.*) mentally unbalanced. **6** (*coll.*) bad, worthless, counterfeit. ~*n.* (*sl., derog.*) a homosexual, esp. a male homosexual. ~*v.t.* (*coll.*) to spoil, to put out of order. **to queer someone's pitch** to spoil one's chances. **queer fish** *n.* (*coll.*) a strange person. **queerish** *a.* **queerly** *adv.* **queerness** *n.* **Queer Street** *n.* (*coll.*) trouble, esp. financial difficulty. [prob. from LG, cp. G *quer*, crosswise]

Usage note Some homosexuals now use *queer* of themselves, but its use by non-homosexuals remains offensive.

quell (kwel) *v.t.* **1** to suppress, to put down, to subdue. **2** to crush. **3** to cause to subside; to calm, to allay, to quiet. **queller** *n.* [OE *cwellan*, to kill (cp. Dut. *kwellen*, G *kwälen*)]

quench (kwench) *v.t.* **1** to extinguish, to put out, esp. with water. **2 a** to cool (heat or a heated thing), esp. with water. **b** to cool (hot metal) rapidly by immersing in oil, water etc. **3** to satisfy (thirst) by drinking. **4** to allay, to slake. **5** to suppress, to subdue. **6** to reduce or inhibit (luminescence, oscillation etc.). **quenchable** *a.* **quencher** *n.* **1** a person or thing which quenches. **2** (*coll.*) a drink that satisfies thirst. **quenching** *a.* **quenchless** *a.* **1** that cannot be quenched. **2** inextinguishable. **quenchlessly** *adv.* **quenchlessness** *n.* [OE *cwencan*, found in *acwencan*, causal of *cwincan*, to go out (cp. Fris. *kwinka*)]

quenelle (kənel´) *n.* a ball of savoury paste made of meat or fish, usu. served as an entrée. [F, etym. uncertain]

quercetum (kwœsē´təm) *n.* a collection of living oaks, an arboretum of oak trees. [L *quercus*, oak]

quercitron (kwœ´sitrən) *n.* **1** a N American oak, *Quercus velutina*. **2** the bark of this, or a yellow dye made from it. **quercetin** (-tin), **quercitin** *n.* a yellow crystalline substance obtained from the bark of quercitron etc., used esp. formerly to strengthen capillaries. [L *querci-*, *quercus*, oak, CITRON]

querimonious (kwerimō´niəs) *a.* (*formal*) complaining, querulous, discontented. **querimoniously** *adv.* **querimoniousness** *n.* [late L *queri-mōniōsus*, from L *querimōnia*, from *querī*, to complain]

querist (kwiə´rist) *n.* (*formal*) a person who asks questions, an enquirer. [L *quaerere*, see QUAERE]

quern (kwœn) *n.* **1** a simple hand-mill for grinding corn, usu. consisting of two stones resting one on the other. **2** a small hand-mill for grinding spices. **quernstone** *n.* [OE *cweorn* (cp. Dut. *kweern*, Icel. *kvern*)]

querulous (kwer´ələs, -ū-) *a.* **1** complaining. **2** discontented, peevish, fretful. **querulously** *adv.* **querulousness** *n.* [late L *querulōsus*, L *querulus*, from *querī*, to complain]

query (kwiə´ri) *n.* (*pl.* **queries**) **1** a question (often used absolutely as preface to a question). **2** a point or objection to be answered, a doubt. **3** a mark of interrogation (?). ~*v.i.* (*3rd pers. sing. pres.* **queries,** *pres.p.* **querying,** *past, p.p.* **queried**) to put a question. ~*v.t.* **1** to express as a question. **2** to question, to call in question. **3** to express doubt concerning. **4** to mark with a query. **querying** *n., a.* **queryingly** *adv.* **query language** *n.* a set of instructions and commands used for retrieving information from a computer database. [var. of QUAERE]

quesadilla (kāsədē´yə) *n.* a tortilla filled, fried and topped with cheese. [Sp.]

quest (kwest) *n.* **1** the act of seeking, a search. **2** an expedition or venture in search or pursuit of some object, esp. embarked on by a medieval knight. **3** the object of such a venture. **4** an official inquiry. **5** a jury of an inquest. **6** a collection of alms. ~*v.i.* **1** to go on a quest (after), to search (for). **2** (of a dog) to search about for game. ~*v.t.* (*poet.*) to seek out or for. **in quest of** searching for. **quester** *n.* **questing** *a.* **questingly** *adv.* [OF *queste* (F *quête*). p.p. L *questa*, L *quaesita*, p.p. of *quaerere*, to seek]

question (kwes´chən) *n.* **1** a sentence requiring an answer, an interrogative sentence. **2** the act of asking or enquiring. **3** doubt, uncertainty, objection. **4** a point at issue, a matter to be resolved, a problem requiring solution. **5** a subject to be discussed. **6** a proposition or subject to be debated and voted on, esp. in a deliberative assembly. *~v.t.* **1** to ask a question or questions of, to interrogate, to examine by asking questions. **2** to study (phenomena etc.) with a view to acquiring information. **3** to call in question, to treat as doubtful or unreliable, to raise objections to. *~v.i.* **1** to ask a question or questions. **2** to doubt, to be uncertain. **beyond (all) question** undoubtedly, unquestionably. **in question** referred to, under discussion. **out of the question** not worth discussing, impossible. **past question** undoubtedly. **to call in/ into question** to dispute. **to pop the question** POP[1]. **to put the question** to put to the vote, to divide the meeting or House upon. **questionable** *a.* **1** open to doubt or suspicion, esp. with regard to honesty, morality etc. **2** disputable. **questionability** (-bilˊ-), **questionableness** *n.* **questionably** *adv.* **questionary** *n.* (*pl.* **questionaries**) a series of questions for the compilation of statistics, etc. *~a.* questioning, enquiring. **questioner** *n.* **questioning** *n.*, *a.* **questioningly** *adv.* **questionless** *a.* beyond all question or doubt. **question mark** *n.* **1** a mark of interrogation (?). **2** a cause for doubt or suspicion. **question master** *n.* a person who puts questions, esp. the person who asks the questions in a quiz or game. **questionnaire** (-neəˊ) *n.* **1** a series of questions designed to collect information, esp. for statistical purposes. **2** a form containing these. **question time** *n.* time set aside each day in Parliament where ordinary members may question ministers. [OF, from L *quaestio* acc. *-ōnem*, as QUEST]

questor[1] (kwesˊtə) *n.* a pardoner. [med. L, as QUAESTOR]

questor[2] QUAESTOR.

quetzal (kwetˊsəl) *n.* (*pl.* **quetzals, quetzales** (-sahˊlēz)) **1** a Central American bird, *Pheromacrus mocinno*, of the trogon family, with brilliantly coloured plumage. **2** the basic unit of currency of Guatemala. [Sp., from Nahuatl *quetzalli*]

queue (kū) *n.* **1** a line of people, vehicles etc. waiting their turn. **2** a sequence of items to be dealt with or processed in the order in which they were received. **3** WAITING LIST (under WAIT). **4** a plaited tail hanging at the back of the head, either of the natural hair or a wig, a pigtail. *~v.t.* (*pres.p.* **queuing, queueing,** *past, p.p.* **queued**) to arrange or place in a queue. *~v.i.* to form into a waiting queue, to take one's place in a queue. **queue-jumping** *n.* going to the beginning of a queue instead of to the end. **queue-jump** *v.i.* **queue-jumper** *n.* [F, from L *cauda*, tail]

quey (kwā) *n.* (*Sc., North.*) a young cow that has not yet had a calf, a heifer. [from Icel. *kvīga* (prob. cogn, with COW[1])]

quibble (kwibˊəl) *n.* **1** a trivial or petty objection, argument or distinction, esp. one exploiting a verbal ambiguity. **2** an evasion of the point, an equivocation. **3** a play upon words; a pun. *~v.i.* **1** to raise trivial objections, to argue over unimportant, esp. verbal, details. **2** to evade the point in question. **3** to pun. **quibbler** *n.* **quibbling** *a.* **quibblingly** *adv.* [prob. freq. of obs. *quip*, L *quibus*, dat. of *quī*, who, which]

quiche (kēsh) *n.* a pastry shell filled with a savoury egg custard to which cheese, onion or other vegetables, bacon etc. have been added. [F, from G *Kuchen*, cake]

Quichua QUECHUA.

quick (kwik) *a.* **1** rapid in movement, acting swiftly, swift, nimble. **2** done or happening in a short time, taking only a short time. **3** speedy, expeditious, prompt. **4** lively, vigorous, alert, acutely sensitive or responsive, intelligent. **5** (of a temper) irritable, easily aroused. **6** rash, precipitate, hasty. **7** eager, ready (to act or respond). **8** †alive, living. **9** quickset. *~adv.* in a short space of time, at a rapid rate; quickly. *~int.* come, move, act etc. quickly. *~n.* **1** sensitive living flesh, esp. the sensitive flesh under the nails. **2** the feelings, the seat of the feelings. **3** †living people. **in quick succession** SUCCESSION. **quick on the draw 1** fast to draw and shoot a gun. **2** fast to act or respond. **quick on the trigger** fast to react. **quick on the uptake** UPTAKE (under UP- (+ T– WORDS)). †**quick with child** pregnant, esp. when movement of the foetus is perceptible. **the quick and the dead** the living and the dead. **quick assets** *n.pl.* assets easily converted into cash. **quickbeam** *n.* the rowan or mountain ash. **quick buck** *n.* a lot of money, easily earned. **quick-change** *a.* (of actors etc.) making rapid changes of costume or appearance. **quick-change artist** *n.* **1** a performer who executes quick changes. **2** a person who frequently changes their opinions. **quick-eyed** *a.* having sharp sight. **quick-fire** *a.* **1** rapid, following in rapid succession. **2** (of a quiz etc.) consisting of quick-fire questions. **3** designed to fire shots in rapid succession. **quick-firer** *n.* a quick-fire gun. **quick-firing** *a.* **quick fix** *n.* a rapidly accomplished, usu. temporary, solution. **quick-fix** *a.* **quick-freeze** *v.t.* (*past* **quick-froze,** *p.p.* **quick-frozen**) to freeze (food) rapidly in order to retain the natural qualities. **quickie** *n.* (*coll.*) **1** something that is done rapidly. **2** a swift act of sexual intercourse. **3** a swiftly consumed (alcoholic) drink. **quicklime** *n.* burned lime not yet slaked; calcium oxide. **quickly** *adv.* **quick march** *n.* **1** a march in quick time. **2** the music for such a march. *~int.* the command to start a quick march. **quick-match** *n.* a quick-burning match for firing cannon etc., usu. made of cotton wick soaked in a mixture of alcohol, saltpetre etc. **quickness** *n.* **quick one** *n.* (*coll.*) a quickie. **quicksand** *n.* **1** loose wet sand easily yielding to pressure and engulfing people, animals etc. **2** a bed of such sand. **3** something treacherous and engulfing. **quickset** *a.* (of a hedge) composed of living plants, esp. hawthorn bushes. *~n.* **1** slips of plants, esp. hawthorn, put in the ground to form a quickset hedge. **2** a quickset hedge. **quick-sighted** *a.* **1** having acute sight. **2** quick to see or understand. **quick-sightedness** *n.* **quicksilver** *n.* **1** mercury. **2** an unpredictable temperament. *~v.t.* to coat (the glass of a mirror) with an amalgam of quicksilver and tinfoil. **quicksilvered** *a.* **quicksilvering** *n.* **quicksilverish** *a.* **quicksilvery** *a.* **quickstep** *n.* **1** a fast foxtrot. **2** (**quick step**) the step used in marching at quick time. **3** a march tune or lively piece of music to accompany either of these. *~v.i.* (*pres.p.* **quickstepping,** *past, p.p.* **quickstepped**) to dance a quickstep. **quick-tempered** *a.* easily irritated, irascible. **quickthorn** *n.* the hawthorn, esp. when planted as a hedge. **quick time** *n.* the ordinary rate of marching in the British Army, usu. reckoned at about 120 paces to the minute or 4 miles (6.44 km) an hour. **quick trick** *n.* **1** a trick won during the opening rounds of play in a game of bridge. **2** a card that should win this. **quick-witted** *a.* **1** having a keen and alert mind. **2** having a ready wit. **quick-wittedly** *adv.* **quick-wittedness** *n.* [OE *cwic*, *cwicu* (cp. Dut. *kwik*, G *keck*, Icel. *kvikr*, Swed. *quick*, also L *vīvus*, lively, Gr. *bios*, life)]

quicken (kwikˊən) *v.t.* **1** to make faster, to accelerate. **2** to give or restore life or animation to. **3** to stimulate, to rouse, to inspire, to kindle. **4** to cheer, to refresh. *~v.i.* **1** to move with increased rapidity. **2** to receive life, animation or vigour. **3** to come to life. **4** to be in that state of pregnancy in which the child gives signs of life. **5** (of a foetus) to give signs of life in the womb. *~n.* (*chiefly dial.*) the rowan or mountain ash. **quickener** *n.*

quid[1] (kwid) *n.* (*pl.* **quid**) (*sl.*) a pound (sterling). **not the full quid** (*Austral., sl.*) simple-minded. **quids in** (*sl.*) in a profitable position. [etym. uncertain]

quid[2] (kwid) *n.* a piece of tobacco for chewing. [var. of CUD]

quiddity (kwidˊiti) *n.* (*pl.* **quiddities**) 1 the essence of a thing. 2 a quibble, a trifling or captious subtlety. **quiddative, quidditative** (-itātiv) *a.* [med. L *quidditas*, from L *quid*, what, anything]

quidnunc (kwidˊnŭngk) *n.* a person who is curious to know or pretends to know everything that goes on, a newsmonger, a gossip. [L, what now?]

quid pro quo (kwid prō kwōˊ) *n.* (*pl.* **quid pro quos**) something in return or exchange (for something), an equivalent. [L, something for something]

quiescent (kwiesˊənt) *a.* 1 at rest, still, not moving, inert, inactive, dormant. 2 (*formal*) tranquil, calm, free from anxiety, agitation or emotion. 3 (of a letter) not pronounced or sounded. **quiesce** *v.i.* to become silent. **quiescence, quiescency** *n.* **quiescently** *adv.* [L *quiescens -entem*, pres.p. of *quiescere*, from *quies*, QUIET]

quiet (kwīˊət) *a.* 1 making little or no noise, silent, hushed. 2 in a state of rest, motionless. 3 calm, unruffled, placid, tranquil, peaceful, undisturbed. 4 gentle, mild, peaceable. 5 unobtrusive, not glaring or showy. 6 not overt, private. 7 retired, secluded. ~*n.* 1 silence, stillness, peace, calmness. 2 a state of rest or repose. 3 freedom from disturbance, tranquillity. 4 peace of mind, calm, patience, placidness. ~*v.t.*, *v.i.* to quieten. **on the quiet** (*coll.*) secretly. **to keep quiet (about)** to refrain from talking or disclosing information (about). †**quietage** (-ij) *n.* **quieten** *v.t.* 1 to make quiet. 2 to soothe, to calm, to appease. 3 to bring to a state of rest. ~*v.i.* to become quiet or calm. **quieter** *n.* **quietism** *n.* 1 a state of calmness and placidity. 2 (**Quietism**) a form of religious mysticism based on the doctrine that the essence of religion consists in the withdrawal of the soul from external objects and in fixing it upon the contemplation of God. **quietist** *a.*, *n.* **quietistic** (-tisˊ-) *a.* **quietly** *adv.* **quietness, quietude** *n.* [L *quiētus*, p.p. of *quiescere*, to rest, from *quies -ētis*, rest]

quietus (kwīēˊtəs) *n.* (*pl.* **quietuses**) 1 a final discharge or settlement. 2 release from life, death. 3 something that represses or quietens. [med. L *quiētus est*, he is QUIT]

quiff (kwif) *n.* 1 a tuft of hair brushed up and back from the forehead. 2 a curl lying flat on the forehead. [F *coiffure*, hairdressing]

quill (kwil) *n.* 1 the hollow stem or barrel of a feather. 2 any of the large strong feathers of a bird's wing or tail. 3 a pen, esp. one made from such a feather. 4 a spine of a porcupine. 5 a plectrum, toothpick, angler's float etc. made from a bird's quill. 6 a tube or hollow stem on which weavers wind their thread; a bobbin, a spool. 7 a musical pipe made from a hollow cane, reed etc. 8 a strip of cinnamon or cinchona bark rolled into a tube. 9 a fluted fold. ~*v.t.* 1 to form into rounded folds, flutes etc., to goffer. 2 to wind on a quill or quills. **quill-driver** *n.* (*derog.*) a writer, an author, a clerk. **quilled** *a.* (*usu. in comb.*, as *long-quilled*). **quill-feather** *n.* a large wing or tail feather. **quilling** *n.* 1 lace, tulle or ribbon gathered into small rolls resembling quills. 2 the process of making ornamental designs from this. **quill pen** *n.* a pen made from a bird's quill. [etym. uncertain, cp. G *Kiel*]

quillet (kwilˊit) *n.* a quibble, a quirk. [perh. from obs. *quillity*, var. of QUIDDITY]

quillon (kēyōˊ) *n.* either of the arms forming the cross-guard of a sword. [F, from *quille*, ninepin]

quilt (kwilt) *n.* 1 a bed-cover or bedspread made by stitching one cloth over another with some soft warm material as padding between them. 2 a duvet. ~*v.t.* 1 to fill, cover or line with padded material. 2 **a** to stitch together (two pieces of cloth) with soft material in between, esp. using crossing lines of stitching. **b** to make (a cover, jacket etc.) in this way. 3 to stitch in crossing lines or ornamental figures, like the stitching in a quilt. 4 to sew up between two layers of material. 5 to put together (literary extracts etc.). 6 (*Austral.*, *sl.*) to beat, to thrash. **quilted** *a.* **quilter** *n.* **quilting** *n.* 1 the process of making quilted work. 2 material for making quilts. 3 quilted work. [OF *cuilte*, L *culcita*, cushion]

quim (kwim) *n.* (*taboo*) the female genitals. [etym. uncertain]

quin (kwin) *n.* (*coll.*) each child of quintuplets. [short for QUINTUPLET (under QUINTUPLE)]

quina (kēˊnə) *n.* quinine. [Sp., as QUININE]

quinacrine (kwinˊəkrēn) *n.* an anti-malarial drug based on acridine. [*quin*ine, *acridine*]

quinary (kwīˊnəri) *a.* 1 consisting of or arranged in fives. 2 based on the number five. **quinate** (-nət) *a.* (of a leaf) composed of five leaflets. [L *quīnārius*, from *quīnī*, five each, distrib. of *quinque*, five]

quince (kwins) *n.* 1 a hard, acid, yellowish fruit used in cookery for flavouring and for preserves etc. 2 a small tree or shrub, *Cydonia oblonga*, that bears quinces. 3 Japanese quince, japonica. [orig. pl. of obs. *quine*, ME *coine*, OF *cooing*, L *cotōneum*, var. of *cydōnium*, from *Cydōnia* (now Canea), in Crete]

quincentenary (kwinsəntēˊnəri, -tenˊ-) *n.* (*pl.* **quincentenaries**) 1 a 500th anniversary. 2 its celebration. **quincentennial** (-tenˊ-) *a.* [L, irreg. from *quinque*, five, CENTENARY (under CENTENARIAN)]

quincunx (kwinˊkŭngks) *n.* (*pl.* **quincunxes**) an arrangement of five things in a square or rectangle, one at each corner and one in the middle, esp. such an arrangement of trees in a plantation. **quincuncial** (-kŭnˊshəl) *a.* **quincuncially** *adv.* [L *quinque*, five, *uncia*, OUNCE[1]]

quindecagon (kwindekˊəgon) *n.* a plane figure having 15 sides and 15 angles. [from L *quindecim* (*quinque*, five, *decem*, ten), 15, after DODECAGON]

quinella (kwinelˊə) *n.* (*Austral.*) a form of betting where the person placing the bet must pick the first- and second-placed winners. [Am. Sp. *quiniela*]

quingentenary (kwinjəntēˊnəri, -tenˊ-) *n.* (*pl.* **quingentenaries**) a quincentenary. [L *quingentī*, 500]

quinine (kwinˊēn, -ēnˊ) *n.* a bitter alkaloid obtained from cinchona bark formerly widely used, esp. in the form of its salts, to relieve fever, in the treatment of malaria and as a tonic. **quinic** (kwinˊ-) *a.* **quinidine** (kwinˊidēn) *n.* an alkaloid, isomeric with quinine, contained in some cinchona barks. **quinism** (kwinˊ-) *n.* [Sp. *quina*, from Quechua *kina*, bark]

quinnat (kwinˊət) *n.* the chinook salmon of the Pacific coast of N America. [N Am. Ind.]

quinoa (kēˊnōə) *n.* an annual plant, *Chenopodium quinoa*, the ground farinaceous seeds of which are made into cakes in Chile and Peru. [Sp., from Quechua, *kinua*]

quinol (kwinˊol) *n.* hydroquinone. **quinoline** (kwinˊəlēn) *n.* a colourless, pungent, liquid compound, obtained by the dry distillation of bones, coal and various alkaloids, forming the basis of many dyes and medicinal compounds. [QUININE]

quinone (kwinˊōn, -nōnˊ) *n.* 1 a yellow crystalline compound, usu. produced by the oxidation of aniline, used in the manufacture of dyes. 2 any of a series of similar compounds derived from the benzene hydrocarbons by the substitution of two oxygen atoms for two of hydrogen. [as QUININE, -ONE]

quinquagenarian (kwinkwəjəneəˊriən) *n.* a person who is 50 or between 50 and 60 years old. ~*a.* aged 50 or between 50 and 60. **quinquagenary** (-jēˊ-) *a.*, *n.* (*pl.* **quinquagenaries**). [L *quinquāgēnārius*, from *quinquāgēnī*, 50 each, distrib. of *quinquāginta*, 50 (*quinque*, five, *-ginta*, see QUADRAGENARIAN)]

Quinquagesima (kwinkwəjesˊimə) *n.* 1 (*also* **Quinquagesima Sunday**) the Sunday before Lent (about 50 days before Easter). 2 †the period from the Sunday before Lent to Easter Sunday, or the first week of this. **quinquagesimal** *a.* 1 of or relating to the number 50. 2 of or relating to 50 days. [L, 50th, as QUINQUAGENARIAN]

quinquangular (kwinkwang´gūlə) *a.* having five angles.

quinque- (kwin´kwi), **quinqui-** *comb. form* five. [L *quinque*, five]

quinquecostate (kwinkwikos´tāt) *a.* having five ribs.

quinquefarious (kwinkwifeə´riəs) *a.* arranged in five parts or rows.

quinquefoliate (kwinkwifō´liət) *a.* having five leaves or leaflets.

quinqueliteral (kwinkwilit´ərəl) *a.* consisting of five letters. ~*n.* a quinqueliteral word, esp. a Hebrew root-word.

quinquennial (kwinkwen´iəl) *a.* 1 lasting five years. 2 recurring every five years. **quinquenniad** *n.* a quinquennium. **quinquennially** *adv.* **quinquennium** (-iəm) *n.* (*pl.* **quinqenniums, quinquennia**) a period of five years. [L *quinquennis*, (QUINQUE-, *annus*, year)]

quinquepartite (kwinkwipah´tīt) *a.* 1 divided into or consisting of five parts. 2 affecting or shared by five parties.

quinquereme (kwin´kwirēm) *n.* an ancient Roman galley having five banks of rowers. [cp. QUADRIREME]

quinquevalent (kwinkwivā´lənt), **quinquivalent** *a.* having a valency or combining power of five, pentavalent. **quinquevalence, quinquevalency** *n.*

quinqui- QUINQUE-.

quinquivalent QUINQUEVALENT.

quinsy (kwin´zi) *n.* inflammatory sore throat, esp. with suppuration of one tonsil or of both. **quinsied** *a.* [OF *quinancie*, med. L *quinancia*, Gr. *kunanche* (*kun-*, *kuōn*, dog, *anchein*, to throttle)]

quint[1] (kwint) *n.* 1 a sequence of five cards of the same suit in piquet etc. 2 (*Mus.*) a fifth. 3 an organ stop giving tones a fifth above the normal. **quint major** *n.* the cards from ten to ace. **quint minor** *n.* the cards from seven to knave. [F *quinte*, L *quinta*, fem. of *quintus*, fifth, from *quinque*, five]

quint[2] (kwint) *n.* (*N Am.*) QUIN. [from *quintuplet*]

quinta (kin´tə) *n.* a country house or villa in Portugal, Madeira and Spain. [Sp. and Port. (from orig. rent at a fifth of the farm's produce)]

quintain (kwin´tən) *n.* 1 a post, or a figure or other object set up on a post, in the Middle Ages, to be tilted at, often fitted with a sandbag, sword or other weapon that swung round and struck a tilter who was too slow. 2 the exercise of tilting at this. [OF *quintaine*, perh. from L *quintāna*, as QUINTAN, the fifth street of a camp]

quintal (kwin´təl) *n.* 1 a weight of 100 or 112 lb. (45.36 or 50.8 kg). 2 100 kg or 220½ lb. [OF, Sp., and Port., from Arab. *qintār*, L *centum*, 100]

quintan (kwin´tən) *a.* (esp. of a fever) occurring or recurring every fourth (or inclusively, fifth) day. ~*n.* a quintan fever. [L *quintāna* (*febris*), fifth-day fever (*quintāna*, fem. of *quintānus*, from *quintus*, fifth, from *quinque*, five)]

quinte (kāt) *n.* the fifth of eight parrying or attacking movements in fencing. [F, as QUINT[1]]

quintessence (kwintes´əns) *n.* 1 the essential principle or pure embodiment (of a quality, class of things etc.). 2 the pure and concentrated essence of any substance, a refined extract. 3 in ancient philosophy, the fifth, last or highest essence, apart from the four elements of earth, air, fire and water, forming the substance of the heavenly bodies and latent in all things. **quintessential** (-tisen´shəl) *a.* **quintessentially** *adv.* [F, from L *quinta essentia*, fifth ESSENCE]

quintet (kwintet´), **quintette** *n.* 1 a musical composition for five voices or instruments. 2 the performers of such a composition, a group of five musicians playing together. 3 a group or set of five people or five similar things. [F *quintette*, It. *quintetto*, from *quinto*, L *quintus*, fifth]

quintic (kwin´tik) *a.* (*Math.*) of or relating to the fifth degree. ~*n.* a curve, equation etc. of the fifth degree. [L *quintus*, fifth, -IC]

quintile (kwin´tīl) *n.* (*Astrol.*) the aspect of two heavenly bodies when distant from each other one-fifth of a circle or 72°.

quintillion (kwintil´yən) *n.* (*pl.* **quintillion, quintillions**) 1 the sixth power of a thousand, one followed by 18 zeros. 2 in Britain, esp. formerly, the number produced by raising a million to its fifth power, represented by one followed by 30 zeros. **quintillionth** *n., a.* [from L *quintus*, after BILLION]

quintroon (kwintroon´) *n.* the offspring of a white person and an octoroon; a person one-fifth (inclusively) in descent from a black person. [Sp. *quinteron*, from *quinto*, L *quintus*, fifth]

quintuple (kwin´tūpəl, -tū´-) *a.* 1 consisting of five parts. 2 involving five members etc. 3 equal to five times the number of a quantity of, fivefold. 4 (of musical time) having five beats in a bar. ~*n.* a number or amount five times as great as another. ~*v.i.* to increase fivefold, to become five times as much. ~*v.t.* to multiply fivefold, to make five times as much. **quintuplet** (-plit) *n.* 1 a set of five things. 2 any one of five children born of the same mother at one birth. 3 five notes played in the time of four. **quintuplicate**[1] (-tū´plikāt) *v.t.* to make fivefold, to multiply by five. **quintuplicate**[2] (-tū´plikət) *a.* 1 five times as much or as many, fivefold. 2 five times copied. ~*n.* 1 any one of five copies or similar things. 2 fivefoldness. **in quintuplicate** written out or copied five times. **quintuplication** (-ā´shən) *n.* [F, from L *quintus*, fifth, after QUADRUPLE]

quinze (kwinz, kāz) *n.* a card game of chance analogous to vingt-et-un, the object being to score nearest to 15 points without exceeding it. [F, from L *quindecim* (*quinque*, five, *decem*, ten), 15]

quip (kwip) *n.* 1 a sarcastic jest or sally. 2 a witty retort, a smart saying. 3 a quibble. ~*v.i.* (*pres.p.* **quipping,** *past, p.p.* **quipped**) to make quips, to scoff. **quippish** *a.* **quipster** (-stə) *n.* a person known for making witty remarks. [var. of obs. *quippy*, L *quippe*, forsooth]

quipu (kē´poo, kwip´oo) *n.* a contrivance of coloured threads and knots used by the ancient Peruvians in place of writing. [Quechua, knot]

quire[1] (kwīə) *n.* 1 24, or now usu. 25, sheets of paper. 2 a set of four sheets of paper or parchment folded into eight leaves, as in medieval manuscripts. 3 a small book, pamphlet etc. [ME and OF *quaer* (F *cahier*), L *quaternī*, four each, a set of four, from *quāttuor*, four]

†**quire**[2] CHOIR.

Quirites (kwirī´tiz) *n.pl.* the ancient Roman citizens in their civil capacity. [L, pl. of *Quiris -rītis*, inhabitant of the Sabine town *Cures*]

quirk (kwœk) *n.* 1 a mannerism. 2 an artful trick, evasion or subterfuge, a shift. 3 a twist or flourish in drawing or writing. 4 a fantastic turn or flourish in music. 5 (*Archit.*) an acute recess between a moulding proper and a fillet or soffit. **quirkish** *a.* **quirksome** (-səm) *a.* **quirky** *a.* (*comp.* **quirkier**, *superl.* **quirkiest**). **quirkily** *adv.* **quirkiness** *n.* [etym. uncertain]

quirt (kwœt) *n.* a riding whip with a short handle and a long, braided leather lash. ~*v.t.* to strike with a quirt. [Sp. *cuerda*, CORD]

quisling (kwiz´ling) *n.* 1 a person who openly allies themselves with their nation's enemies. 2 a traitor. [Vidkun *Quisling*, 1887–1945, Norwegian collaborator]

quit (kwit) *v.t.* (*pres.p.* **quitting,** *past, p.p.* **quitted, quit**) 1 to give up, to renounce, to abandon, to rid oneself of.

2 to leave, to depart from. 3 (*esp. N Am.*) to cease, to desist from. 4 †to acquit, to behave, to conduct (oneself). 5 †to free, to liberate. 6 †(to pay off) a debt. ~*v.i.* 1 to leave, to depart. 2 to stop doing something, esp. to give up one's job. ~*a.* free, clear, absolved, rid (of). **double or quits** DOUBLE². **to be quits** to be even or left on even terms, so that neither has the advantage. **to call it/ cry quits** to declare things to be even, to agree not to go on with a contest, quarrel etc., to make it a draw. **to quit scores** to balance or make even. **to quit the scene** SCENE. **quitclaim** *n.* 1 a renunciation of right or claim. 2 a deed of release. ~*v.t.* 1 to renounce claim or title to. 2 to release, to discharge. **quit-rent** *n.* a usu. small rent paid by a freeholder or copyholder in discharge of other services. †**quittal** *n.* requital, quittance. **quittance** *n.* 1 (*formal or poet.*) a discharge or release from a debt or obligation. 2 (*formal*) a receipt, an acquittance. 3 †repayment, requital. ~†*v.t.* to repay, to requite. **quitter**¹ *n.* 1 a person who quits. 2 a shirker, a coward. [OF *quiter* (F *quitter*), as QUIET]

qui tam (kwē tam´) *n.* an action brought by an informer under a penal statute. [L, who as well (first words of the clause in the statute)]

quitch (kwich), **quitch-grass** *n.* couch grass. [OE *cwic*, QUICK]

quite (kwīt) *adv.* 1 completely, entirely, altogether, to the fullest extent, absolutely, perfectly. 2 to some extent, somewhat, fairly. 3 certainly, yes (used to indicate agreement). **not quite** NOT. **quite something** a remarkable person or thing. **quite the go** GO². **quite the thing** quite proper or fashionable. **quite so** *int.* certainly, decidedly (a form of affirmation). [from obs. *quite*, a. QUIT]

quittal, quittance QUIT.

quitter¹ QUIT.

quitter² (kwit´ə) *n.* an ulcer or suppurating sore on the quarter of a horse's hoof. [etym. uncertain]

quiver¹ (kwiv´ə) *v.i.* 1 to tremble or be agitated with a rapid tremulous motion. 2 to shake, to shiver. ~*v.t.* to cause (wings etc.) to quiver. ~*n.* a quivering motion. ~†*a.* nimble, active. **quiverer** *n.* **quivering** *a.* **quiveringly** *adv.* **quiverish** *a.* **quivery** *a.* [prob. imit., perh. rel. to QUAVER]

quiver² (kwiv´ə) *n.* a portable case for arrows. **quivered** *a.* **quiverful** *n.* (*pl.* **quiverfuls**). [OF *cuivre*, prob. from Gmc. (cp. OE *cocor*, G *Köcher*)]

qui vive (kē vēv´) *int.* who lives, who goes there? **on the qui vive** on the lookout, alert, expectant. [F, a sentry's challenge]

quixotic (kwiksot´ik) *a.* 1 extravagantly romantic and chivalrous. 2 aiming at lofty but impracticable ideals, visionary. **quixotically** *adv.* **quixotism** *n.* **quixotry** (kwik´sətri) *n.* [after the hero of Cervantes' *Don Quixote*]

quiz (kwiz) *n.* (*pl.* **quizzes**) 1 a set of questions designed to test knowledge. 2 an entertainment, such as a radio or television game based on this. 3 an investigation by questioning, an interrogation. 4 †something designed to puzzle or ridicule, a hoax. 5 †a quizzer. 6 †an odd-looking or eccentric person. ~*v.t.* (*3rd pers. sing. pres.* **quizzes**, *pres.p.* **quizzing**, *past, p.p.* **quizzed**) 1 to examine by questioning. 2 †to make fun of. 3 †to look at in a mocking or offensively curious way. ~†*v.i.* to behave in a bantering or mocking way. **quizmaster** *n.* a person who puts the questions to contestants in a quiz. **quiz show** *n.* a radio or television quiz. **quizzable** *a.* **quizzer** *n.* a person given to quizzing. **quizzery** *n.* **quizzical** *a.* 1 questioning, mocking. 2 slightly eccentric, amusingly odd. **quizzicality** (-kal´-), **quizzicalness** *n.* **quizzically** *adv.* **quizzing** *n.*, *a.* **quizzing-glass** *n.* a small eyeglass, a monocle. **quizzingly** *adv.* [etym. uncertain]

quod (kwod), **quad** *n.* (*sl.*) prison, jail. [etym. uncertain]

quod erat demonstrandum (kwod erat´ demənstran´dum) which was to be proved (used at the conclusion of a proof or demonstration). [L]

quodlibet (kwod´libet) *n.* 1 a fantasia, a medley of popular tunes. 2 (*dated or formal*) a scholastic discussion or argument. **quodlibetarian** (-teə´ri-) *n.* (*dated or formal*) someone fond of quodlibets or subtle arguments. **quodlibetic** (-bet´-), **quodlibetical** *a.* (*dated or formal*) [L, what you please]

quoin (koin) *n.* 1 the external angle of a building. 2 a large stone, brick etc. at the external angle of a wall, a cornerstone. 3 a wedge-shaped block of wood used for various purposes, such as locking up type in a forme, raising the level of a gun etc. ~*v.t.* to raise or secure with a quoin or wedge. **quoining** *n.* [var. of COIN]

quoit (koit, kwoit) *n.* 1 a flattish circular ring of iron, rope etc. for throwing at a peg or similar mark. 2 (*pl., usu. sing. in constr.*) a game of throwing such rings. 3 a dolmen or the horizontal stone cover of this. ~†*v.t.* to throw or pitch as a quoit. **quoiter** *n.* [etym. uncertain]

quokka (kwok´ə) *n.* a small-tailed wallaby, *Setonix brachyurus*. [Austral. Abor.]

quondam (kwon´dam) *a.* having formerly been, sometime, former (*his quondam friend*). [L, formerly]

Quonset hut® (kwon´sit) *n.* (*N Am.*) a hut similar to a Nissen hut.

Quorn® (kwawn) *n.* a textured vegetable protein used as a meat substitute.

quorum (kwaw´rəm) *n.* (*pl.* **quorums**) the minimum number of officers or members of a society, committee etc. that must be present to transact business. **quorate** (-rət, -rāt) *a.* being or consisting of a quorum, having a quorum present. [L, of whom, gen. pl. of *qui*, who]

quota (kwō´tə) *n.* (*pl.* **quotas**) 1 a proportional share, part or contribution. 2 a prescribed number or quantity, e.g. of students to be admitted to a given college at the beginning of each year. [L *quota* (*pars*), how great (a part), fem. of *quotus*, from *quot*, how many]

quote (kwōt) *v.t.* 1 to adduce or cite from (an author, book etc.), esp. in illustration or support of a point, statement etc. 2 to repeat or copy out the words of (another person, a passage in a book etc.). 3 to enclose in quotation marks. 4 to state (the current price) of a commodity, job of work etc. ~*v.i.* 1 to cite or adduce a passage (from). 2 to state a price (for), to supply an estimate of costs (for). ~*n.* (*usu. in pl., coll.*) a quotation mark. **quote...unquote** an expression used to show the beginning and end of a quotation. **quotable** *a.* worth quoting. **quotability** (-bil´-), **quotableness** *n.* **quotably** *adv.* **quotation** (-tā´shən) *n.* 1 the act of quoting. 2 a passage or phrase quoted. 3 a price listed or stated as current on the Stock Exchange. 4 an estimate supplied by a contractor for a job of work. 5 a short passage taken from one piece and used in another. 6 (*Print.*) a quadrat for filling up blanks etc. **quotation mark** *n.* either of a pair of punctuation marks (in English usu. double (" ") or single (' ')) used to indicate the beginning and end of a passage quoted, and sometimes to enclose words considered slang, jargon etc. **quoted** *a.* **quoted company** *n.* a company whose shares are quoted on the Stock Exchange. **quoter** *n.* **quoteworthy** *a.* [orig. to mark the number of (chapters etc.), from med. L *quotāre*, from QUOTA]

†**quoth** (kwōth) *v.t.* (*1st and 3rd pers.*) said, spoke. †**quotha** (-thə) *int.* forsooth, indeed. [past of obs. *quethe*, OE *cwœth*, from *cwethan*, to speak (cp. Icel. *kvetha*, OHG *quedan*)]

quotidian (kwətid´iən) *a.* 1 daily. 2 (esp. of a fever) recurring every day. 3 commonplace, everyday. ~*n.* a fever, esp. malaria, in which the paroxysms return every day. [L *quotīdiānus*, from *quotīdiē*, daily (QUOTA, *dies*, day)]

quotient (kwō´shənt) *n.* 1 the result obtained by dividing one quantity by another. 2 the ratio, usu.

multiplied by 100, of a test score to a measurement on which the score is held to depend. [F, irreg. from L *quotiens*, how many times, as QUOTA]

quo warranto (kwō woran´tō) *n.* (*Law*) a writ requiring a person or body to show by what authority some office or franchise is claimed or exercised. [med. L, by what warrant?]

Quran, Qur'an KORAN.

q.v. *abbr.* L *quod vide*, which see (*imper.*), an instruction to look up a cross-reference. [L]

qwerty (kwœ´ti), **QWERTY** *n.* the standard English typewriter or keyboard layout. [from the first six letters of the top line of keys]

qy. *abbr.* query.

R[1] (ah), **r** (*pl.* **Rs, R's**) the 18th letter of the English and other versions of the Roman alphabet, corresponding to the Greek rho (P, ρ). It has two sounds: (1) when it precedes a vowel, as in *ran, morose*, it is usually an alveolar continuant; (2) at the end of syllables and when it is followed by a consonant, as in *her, martyr, heard*, it is no longer pronounced in standard English. **three R's** THREE. **R months** *n.pl.* those months with an 'r' in the spelling (September to April), when oysters are in season.

R[2] *abbr.* **1** (*Chem.*) radical. **2** radius. **3** rand. **4** Réaumur. **5** Regina. **6** (*also* ®) registered (trademark). **7** (*Physics*) resistance. **8** reverse (gear). **9** Rex. **10** right. **11** River. **12** rook.

r *abbr.* **1** radius. **2** recto. **3** right. **4** run, runs.

RA *abbr.* **1** (*Astron.*) right ascension. **2** Royal Academy; Royal Academician. **3** Royal Artillery.

Ra *chem. symbol* radium.

RAAF *abbr.* Royal Australian Air Force.

rabato (rəbah´tō), **rebato** *n.* (*pl.* **rabatos, rebatos**) **1** a stiff collar worn by either sex in the early 17th cent. **2** a similar collar supporting a ruff. [F *rabat*, turned-down collar]

rabbet (rab´it), **rebate** (rē´bāt, rab´it) *v.t.* (*pres.p.* **rabbeting, rebating,** *past, p.p.* **rabbeted, rebated**) **1** to cut a groove or slot along the edge of (a board) so that it may receive the edge of another piece cut to fit it. **2** to unite or fix in this way. ~*n.* **1** a groove or slot made in the edge of a board so that it may join with another. **2** a joint so made. **rabbet plane** *n.* a plane for cutting rabbets. [OF *rabat*, from *rabattre*, REBATE[1]]

rabbi (rab´ī) *n.* (*pl.* **rabbis**) **1** a Jewish doctor or teacher of the law, esp. one ordained and having certain legal and ritual functions. **2** the leader of a Jewish congregation. **rabbin** (-in) *n.* a rabbi, esp. one of the great scholars and authorities on Jewish law and doctrine flourishing in the Middle Ages. **rabbinate** (-nət) *n.* **1** the office of rabbi. **2** rabbis collectively. **Rabbinic** (rəbin´-) *n.* the language or dialect of the rabbins, late Hebrew. **rabbinical, rabbinic** *a.* of or relating to rabbis, their opinions, learning or language. **rabbinically** *adv.* **rabbinism** (rab´in-) *n.* rabbinic teachings and traditions. **rabbinist** *n.* **rabbinistic** (-nis´-) *a.* **rabbinite** (-nīt) *n.* a person who follows the traditions of the rabbis and the Talmud. [L, from Gr. *rhabbi*, Heb. *rabbī*, my master (*rabh*, master, *ī*, my)]

rabbit (rab´it) *n.* **1** a burrowing mammal, *Oryctolagus cuniculus*, allied to the hare, killed for its flesh and fur and kept as a pet. **2** the fur of a rabbit. **3** (*coll.*) a bungling player at an outdoor game. **4** (*coll.*) a timid person. **5** (*N Am.*) a hare. ~*v.i.* (*pres.p.* **rabbiting,** *past, p.p.* **rabbited**) **1** to hunt rabbits. **2** (*coll.*) (*often with* **on**) to talk at length, often aimlessly. **rabbiter** *n.* **rabbit fever** *n.* tularaemia. **rabbit hutch** *n.* a cage for rearing tame rabbits in. **rabbit punch** *n.* a sharp blow to the back of the neck that can cause unconsciousness or death. **rabbitry** *n.* (*pl.* **rabbitries**) a place where domestic rabbits live and breed. **rabbit warren** *n.* a piece of ground where rabbits live and breed in burrows. **rabbity** *a.* [perh. from Walloon *robett* from Flem. *robbe*]

rabble[1] (rab´əl) *n.* **1** a noisy crowd of people, a mob. **2** the common people, the mob, the lower orders. **rabblement** *n.* **rabble-rouser** *n.* a person who stirs up the common people to mass anger or violence; a demagogue. **rabble-rousing** *a., n.* [ME *rabel*, prob. rel. to Dut. *rabbelen*, to speak in a confused, indistinct way (cp. LG *rabbeln*)]

rabble[2] (rab´əl) *n.* an iron tool consisting of a bar with the end sharply bent, used for stirring molten metal. [F *râble*, ult. from L *rutābulum*, fire-shovel, from *ruere*, to cast, to rake up]

Rabelaisian (rabəlā´ziən) *a.* **1** of, relating to or characteristic of the French satirical humorist François Rabelais, 1483–1553. **2** extravagant, grotesque, coarsely and boisterously satirical. ~*n.* a student or admirer of Rabelais. **Rabelaisianism** *n.*

rabi (rŭb´i) *n.* the grain crop reaped in the spring, the chief of the three crops in India, Pakistan etc. [Hind., from Arab. *rabī'*, spring]

rabic RABIES.

rabid (rab´id) *a.* **1** mad, raging, furious, violent. **2** fanatical, headstrong, excessively zealous or enthusiastic, unreasoning. **3** relating to or affected with rabies. **rabidity** (-bid´-), **rabidness** *n.* **rabidly** *adv.* [L *rabidus*, from *rabĕre*, to rage]

rabies (rā´biz) *n.* an often fatal viral disease of the nervous system transmitted through the saliva of a rabid animal and characterized by hydrophobia and convulsions. **rabic** (rab´-), **rabietic** (-et´-), **rabific** (-bif´-) *a.* [L, as RABID]

RAC *abbr.* **1** Royal Armoured Corps. **2** Royal Automobile Club.

raccoon (rəkoon´), **racoon** *n.* (*pl. in general* **raccoon, racoon,** *in particular* **raccoons, racoons**) **1** a greyish-black furry ring-tailed N American carnivore of the genus *Procyon*, esp. *P. lotor.* **2** the fur of a raccoon. [Algonquian]

race[1] (rās) *n.* **1** a contest of speed between horses, runners, boats, motor-vehicles etc. **2** (*pl.*) a series of racing contests for horses, dogs etc. **3** (*fig.*) any competitive contest or rivalry, esp. one depending chiefly on speed. **4** a rapid current of water, esp. in the sea or a tidal river. **5** a channel of a stream, esp. an artificial one. **6** a channel or groove along which a piece of mechanism, such as a shuttle, glides to and fro. **7** a grooved ring containing the balls in a ball-bearing. **8** (*Austral.*) a fenced passage in a sheepfold. **9** †a course, esp. the course of life. ~*v.i.* **1** to take part in a race. **2** to contend in speed (with). **3** to run or move swiftly. **4** to go at full speed. **5** to go at a violent pace owing to diminished resistance (as a propeller when lifted out of the water). **6** to attend races. ~*v.t.* **1** to contend against in speed or in a race. **2** to cause (e.g. a horse) to participate in a race. **3** to cause to go or move at full speed. **racecard** *n.* a programme of a race meeting with particulars of the horses, prizes etc. **racecourse** *n.* a piece of ground on which horse races are run. **racegoer** *n.* a person who frequently goes to race meetings. **racegoing** *n.* **racehorse** *n.* a horse bred for racing. **race meeting** *n.* a meeting for horse racing. **racer** *n.* **1** a person, animal or machine that races or contends in a race. **2** a yacht, cycle, car etc. built for racing. **3** a rail or turntable for traversing a heavy gun. **racetrack** *n.* **1** a racecourse. **2** a circuit for motor racing. **raceway** *n.* **1** a channel or passage for water, such as a mill-race. **2** a groove for the passage of a shuttle etc. **3** a conduit for electrical wires or a cable. **4** (*esp. N Am.*) a racecourse or racetrack. **racing** *n.* **racing car** *n.* a car specially built to go at high speeds in competition. **racing driver** *n.* a person who drives racing cars. **racy**[1] *a.* (*comp.* **racier**, *superl.* **raciest**) designed or fitted for racing. [Icel. *rās* or OE *ræs*]

race[2] (rās) *n.* **1** a major division of human beings descended from a common stock and distinguished by physical characteristics. **2 a** a particular ethnic stock. **b** a subdivision of this, a tribe, nation or group of peoples, distinguished by less important differences. **3** division of humankind into races. **4** a group or division of living creatures (*the human race*). **5** a genus, species, stock, strain or variety, of plants or animals, persisting through several generations. **6** (*fig.*) lineage, pedigree, descent. **7** a class of people or animals differentiated from others by some common characteristic. **8** a clan, a family, a house. **race-hatred** *n.* hatred of other people on grounds of race. **race memory** *n.* a subconscious memory of past events held to be inherited by successive generations. **race relations** *n.pl.* **1** the relations between people of different races within a single community. **2** (*as sing.*) the study of such relations. **race riot** *n.* a riot caused by a feeling of being discriminated against on grounds of race. **racial** (-shəl) *a.* **1** of or relating to race or lineage. **2** on grounds of or resulting from difference in race. **racially** *adv.* **racism, racialism** *n.* **1** a belief in the superiority of one race over another. **2** discrimination or prejudice based on this belief. **3 a** antagonism between different races or towards races other than one's own. **b** a tendency towards this. **4** the theory that race determines human development. **racist, racialist** *n., a.* [F *race, rasse*, It. *razza*, etym. unknown]

race[3] (rās) *n.* a root of ginger. [OF *raïs*, L *rādīcem*, nom. *-dix*, root]

raceme (ras´ēm, rəsēm´) *n.* (*Bot.*) a centripetal inflorescence in which the flowers are attached separately by nearly equal stalks along a common axis. **racemate** (ras´əmāt) *n.* (*Chem.*) a racemic compound. **racemed** *a.* **racemic** (-sē´-) *a.* **1** (*Chem.*) consisting of equal parts of dextrorotatory and laevorotatory forms of the same compound. **2** of, relating to or obtained from grape juice. **racemiferous** (rasəmif´-) *a.* **racemism** (ras´ə-) *n.* the quality of being racemic. **racemize** (ras´ə-), **racemise** *v.t., v.i.* (*Chem.*) to change into a racemic compound or mixture. **racemization** (-ā´shən) *n.* **racemose** (ras´əmōs), **racemous** (-əs) *a.* having the form of a raceme. **racemose gland** *n.* a gland consisting of branching ducts. [F *racème*, L *racēmus*, bunch of grapes]

racer RACE[1].

rachis (rāk´is), **rhachis** *n.* (*pl.* **rachides** (rak´idēz, rā´-), **rhachides, rachises** (rak´isēz, rā´-), **rhachises**) **1** (*Bot.*) **a** the axis of an inflorescence. **b** the axis of a pinnate leaf or frond. **2** (*Anat.*) the spinal column. **3** the shaft of a feather, esp. the part bearing the barbs. **rachial** (rā´-), **rachidial** (rəkid´-), **rachidian** *a.* vertebral, spinal. [Gr. *rachis*, spine]

rachitis (rəkī´tis) *n.* rickets. **rachitic** (-kit´-) *a.* [Gr. *rhachitis*, see RACHIS]

Rachmanism (rak´mənizm) *n.* the conduct of an unscrupulous landlord who exploits tenants and charges extortionate rents for slum property. [P. *Rachman*, 1920–62, Polish-born landlord, London]

racial, racialism etc. RACE[2].

racily, raciness RACY[2].

racing RACE[1].

racism, racist RACE[2].

rack[1] (rak) *n.* **1** an open framework or set of rails, bars, woven wire etc. for placing articles on. **2** a grating or framework of metal or wooden rails or bars for holding cattle fodder etc. **3** a bar or rail with teeth or cogs for engaging with a gearwheel, pinion or worm. **4** (*Hist.*) an apparatus for torture consisting of a framework on which the victim was laid, the wrists and ankles being tied to rollers which were turned so as to stretch the joints, sometimes to the extent of dislocation. ~*v.t.* **1** to cause intense pain or anguish to. **2** to strain, tear or shake violently. **3** to injure in this manner. **4** (*fig.*) to strain, to stretch. **5** to place on or in a rack. **6** (*Hist.*) to torture on the rack. **7** to extort or exact (rent) in excess or to the utmost possible extent. **8** to harass (tenants) by such exaction of rent. **9** to wrest, to exaggerate, to distort (a meaning etc.). **on the rack 1** under torture. **2** under great stress. **to rack one's brains** to use great mental effort. **to rack up** (*chiefly N Am.*) to accumulate (points or a score). **rack and pinion** *n.* **1** a device for converting rotary motion into linear motion and vice versa, with a gearwheel which engages in a rack. **2** a type of steering gear found in some motor vehicles. **racker**[1] *n.* **racking** *a., n.* **rack railway** *n.* a railway, usu. on a steep incline, with a cogged rail between the bearing rails. **rack-rent** *n.* an exorbitant rent, approaching the value of the property or land. ~*v.t.* to extort such a rent from (a tenant) or for (land etc.). **rack-renter** *n.* **1** a landlord extorting rack-rent. **2** a tenant paying it. **rack-wheel** *n.* a cogwheel. [prob. from MDut. or MLG *recken* (Dut. *rekken*, G *recken*), cp. Icel. *rekja*, OE *reccan*]

rack[2] (rak) *n.* destruction. **to go to rack and ruin** to fall into a state of complete ruin or neglect. [perh. var. of WRACK]

rack[3] (rak) *v.t.* to draw off (wine etc.) from the lees. [OProv. *arracar*, from *raca*, the stems, husks, dregs]

rack[4] (rak) *n.* **1** a joint of lamb comprising the front rib section. **2** the neck and spine of a forequarter of veal or mutton. [etym. unknown]

rack[5] (rak) *n.* light vapoury clouds, cloud-drift. ~*v.i.* to fly, as cloud or vapour before the wind. [perh. from Scand., cp. Norw., Swed. dial. *rak*, wreckage, Icel. *rek*, drift, *reka*, to drive, rel. to WREAK]

rack[6] (rak) *n.* a horse's gait in which both hoofs of one side are lifted from the ground almost or quite simultaneously, all four legs being off the ground entirely at times. ~*v.i.* (of a horse) to go in this manner. **racker**[2] *n.* a horse that goes at a racking pace. [etym. uncertain]

racker[1] RACK[1].

racker[2] RACK[6].

racket[1] (rak´it), **racquet** *n.* **1** a bat with a network of catgut etc. instead of a blade, with which players at tennis, squash, badminton or rackets strike the ball. **2** a snow-shoe resembling this. ~*v.t.* to strike with or as with a racket. **racket court, racket ground** *n.* a four-walled court where the game of rackets is played. **racket-press** *n.* a press for keeping the strings of a wood-framed racket taut. **rackets** *n.* a ball game resembling tennis, played against a wall in a four-walled court. **racket-tail** *n.* a hummingbird, *Loddigesia mirabilis*, with two long, racket-shaped tail feathers. **racket-tailed** *a.* [F *raquette*, perh. dim. from low L *racha*, Arab. *rāha*, palm of the hand]

racket[2] (rak´it) *n.* **1** a clamour, a confused noise, a din. **2** a commotion, a disturbance, a fuss. **3** a frolic, a spree, uproarious gaiety, excitement or dissipation. **4** (*sl.*) a scheme, a dodge, an underhand plan. **5** an organized illegal or unethical activity. **6** (*sl.*) a line of business. **7** a medieval instrument of the woodwind family, with a deep bass pitch, like a bassoon. ~*v.i.* (*pres.p.* **racketing**, *past, p.p.* **racketed**) **1** to make a noise or din. **2** to lead an exciting or dissipated life, to frolic, to revel. **racketeer** (-tiə´) *n.* a member of a gang engaged in systematic blackmail, extortion or other illegal activities for profit. ~*v.t.* to operate an illegal business or enterprise for profit. **racketeering** *n.* **racketer** *n.* **racketing** *n.* confused, tumultuous mirth. **rackety** *a.* [prob. imit.]

racloir (raklwah´) *n.* in archaeology, a flint implement used for scraping sideways. [F *racler*, to scrape]

racon (rā´kon) *n.* a radar beacon. [*ra*dar, bea*con*]

raconteur (rakontœ´) *n.* a (good, skilful etc.) storyteller. **raconteuring** *n.* **raconteuse** (-tœz´) *n.* a female raconteur. [F, from *raconter*, to RECOUNT]

racoon RACCOON.

racquet RACKET[1].

racy[1] RACE[1].

racy[2] (rā´si) *a.* (*comp.* **racier,** *superl.* **raciest)** **1** lively, spirited, stimulating. **2** suggestive, bordering on the indecent, risqué. **3** strongly flavoured, piquant, pungent. **4** having the characteristic qualities in high degree. **racily** *adv.* **raciness** *n.* [RACE[2]]

rad[1] (rad) *n.* (*coll.*) a political radical. [by shortening]

rad[2] (rad) *n.* a unit measuring the dosage of ionized radiation absorbed, equivalent to 0.01 joule of energy per kilogram of mass of irradiated material. [*rad*iation]

rad[3] (rad) *n.* (*coll.*) a radiator. [by shortening]

rad[4] (rad) *a.* (*comp.* **radder,** *superl.* **raddest)** (*sl.*) excellent, very good. [*rad*ical]

rad[5] *abbr.* **1** radian. **2** radius.

RADA (rah´də) *abbr.* Royal Academy of Dramatic Art.

radar (rā´dah) *n.* **1** a system which employs reflected or retransmitted radio waves to locate the presence of objects and to determine their angular position and range. **2** the equipment used for this. **radar beacon** *n.* a fixed radio transmitter which sends out signals which allow an aircraft or ship to determine its own position. **radar gun** *n.* a device which when aimed at a moving car uses radar to record the car's speed, used by the police. **radarscope** *n.* a cathode-ray oscilloscope capable of showing radar signals. **radar trap** *n.* a device which uses radar to allow the police to identify vehicles exceeding the speed limit. [acronym for *ra*dio *d*etection *a*nd *r*anging]

RADC *abbr.* Royal Army Dental Corps.

raddle[1] (rad´əl) *n.* ruddle. ~*v.t.* **1** to paint or colour with ruddle. **2** to apply rouge to (the face) excessively or badly. **raddled** *a.* **1** dilapidated. **2** unkempt. **3** haggard-looking because of age or debauchery. [var. of RUDDLE]

raddle[2] (rad´əl) *n.* **1** a lath, stick or branch interwoven with others to form a fence, usu. plastered over with clay etc. **2** a hurdle or hedge of twisted branches. ~*v.t.* to interweave, to twist (sticks etc.) together. [A-F *reidele*, OF *reddalle* (F *ridelle*), a pole, the back rail of a cart]

radial (rā´diəl) *a.* **1** of, relating to or resembling a ray, rays or radii. **2** extending or directed from a centre as rays or radii; divergent. **3** having radiating parts, lines etc. **4** positional as or acting along a radius. **5** (*Anat.*) of or relating to the radius of the forearm. ~*n.* **1** a radiating part, line, bone, nerve, artery etc. **2** a radial-ply tyre. **radial artery** *n.* (*pl.* **radial arteries)** (*Anat.*) an artery of the forearm, felt at the wrist when taking the pulse. **radial engine** *n.* an internal-combustion engine which has its cylinders arranged radially. **radiality** (-al´-) *n.* (*pl.* **radialities)** radial symmetry. **radialize, radialise** *v.t.* to cause to radiate from or as from a centre. **radialization** *n.* **radial keratotomy** *n.* keratotomy to correct short-sightedness. **radially** *adv.* **radially symmetrical** *a.* showing radial symmetry. **radial-ply** *a.* (of a motor vehicle tyre) having the fabric in the casing placed radially at right angles to the circumference for increased flexibility. **radial symmetry** *n.* the state of having several planes arranged symmetrically around a common axis, as in a starfish. **radial velocity** *n.* (*pl.* **radial velocities)** the component of velocity of an object along the line of sight between the observer and the object. [RADIUS, -AL[1]]

radian (rā´diən) *n.* (*Geom.*) **1** an arc equal in length to the radius of its circle. **2** the angle subtending such an arc, 57.296°. [RADIUS, -AN]

radiant (rā´diənt) *a.* **1** emitting rays of light or heat. **2** issuing in rays. **3** (*fig.*) shining, beaming (with joy, love etc.). **4** splendid, brilliant. **5** extending, arranged or acting radially, radiating. **6** emitting radiant heat. ~*n.* **1** the point from which light or heat radiates. **2** the part of a gas or electric fire that becomes incandescent. **3** the point from which a meteor shower seems to proceed. **4** (*Geom.*) a straight line proceeding from a fixed pole about which it is conceived as revolving. **radiance,** †**radiancy** *n.* (*pl.* **radiances,** †**radiancies**). **radiant energy** *n.* energy given out in the form of electromagnetic waves. **radiant flux** *n.* the rate at which radiant energy is emitted or transmitted. **radiant heat** *n.* heat transmitted by radiation. **radiant heater** *n.* **radiantly** *adv.* **radiant point** *n.* (*Geom., Astron.*) a radiant. [L *radians -ntem*, pres.p. of *radiāre*, from RADIUS]

radiata pine (rādiah´tə) *n.* a pine tree, *Pinus radiata*, grown in Australia and New Zealand for timber. [L, fem. of *radiātus*, see RADIATE]

radiate (rā´diāt) *v.i.* **1** to emit rays of light, heat or other electromagnetic radiation. **2** to issue or be emitted in rays from or as from a centre. **3** to proceed or spread from a central point. ~*v.t.* **1** to emit or send out as rays or from a central point. **2** to exhibit, to demonstrate (vitality, happiness etc.). **3** to send forth in all directions, to disseminate. **radiation** (-ā´shən) *n.* **1** the act of radiating or emitting rays, esp. the emission of heat, light etc. in the form of electromagnetic waves or particles. **2** the transmission of radiant energy from one body to another without raising the temperature of the intervening medium. **3** energy transmitted as waves or particles. **4** a group of rays of the same wavelength. **5** the rays emitted in radioactive decay. **6** a travelling outwards, as radii, to the periphery. **radiational** *a.* **radiation chemistry** *n.* chemistry dealing with the effects of radiation on living matter. **radiation sickness** *n.* illness caused by too great absorption of radiation in the body, whose symptoms include fatigue, nausea, vomiting, internal bleeding, loss of hair and teeth, and in extreme cases, leukaemia. **radiative** (-ətiv), **radiatory** (-ətri) *a.* **radiator** *n.* **1** something that radiates. **2** a vessel, chamber or coil of pipes charged with hot air, water, steam etc. for radiating heat in a building. **3** a device for dissipating the heat absorbed by the cooling water of an engine jacket. **4** the part of an aerial which radiates electromagnetic waves. **radiator grille** *n.* a grille on the front of a motor vehicle that protects the radiator and allows cooling air to circulate round it. [L *radiātus*, p.p. of *radiāre*, from RADIUS]

radical (rad´ikəl) *a.* **1** of or relating to the root, source or origin. **2** inherent, fundamental. **3** going to the root, thorough-going, extreme. **4 a** being, relating to or according to radical politics, favouring extreme action or changes. **b** of or belonging to a political party advocating extreme measures. **5** original, basic, primary. **6** (*Med.*) relating to or being surgery intended to remove all traces of diseased tissue. **7** (*Math.*) of or relating to the root of a number or quantity. **8** (*Bot.*) arising from or close to the root. **9** of or relating to the root of a word, primary, underived. **10** (*sl.*) excellent, very good, outstanding. ~*n.* **1** a person promoting extreme measures or holding advanced views on either side of the political spectrum. **2** (*Math.*) **a** a quantity that is, or is expressed as, the root of another. **b** a radical sign. **3** (*Chem.*) **a** an element, atom or group of atoms forming part of a compound and not decomposed by the reactions that normally alter the compound. **b** a free radical. **4** the root of a word. **5** a fundamental principle. **6** any of the set of basic characters in the Chinese writing system.

radical chic *n.* superficial, dilettantish left-wing radicalism. **radicalism** *n.* the principles of radical politics. **radicalistic** (-lis´-) *a.* **radicalistically** *adv.* **radicality** (-kal´-), **radicalness** *n.* **radicalize, radicalise** *v.t., v.i.* **radicalization** (-zā´shən) *n.* **radically** *adv.* thoroughly, fundamentally, essentially. **radical mastectomy** *n.* surgical removal of the breast including some of the pectoral muscles and the lymph nodes of the armpit. **radical sign** *n.* the symbol √ placed before a number to show that the square root, or some higher root as shown by a superscript number (e.g. $\sqrt[3]{}$), is to be calculated. [F, from late L *rādīcālis*, from *rādix -īcis*, root]

radicand (rad´ikand) *n.* a number from which a root is to be extracted, usu. preceded by a radical sign, e.g. three is the radicand of √3. [L *rādīcandum*, that which is to be rooted]

radicate (rad´ikət) *a.* **1** having a root, rooted. **2** having rootlike organs of attachment, as some molluscs. **radicant** *a.* producing roots from the stem. **radication** (-ā´shən) *n.* **radicel** (-sel) *n.* a rootlet. **radiciform** (rədis´ifawm) *a.* **radicivorous** (-siv´ərəs) *a.* feeding on roots. [L *rādīcātus*, p.p. of *rādīcāre*, as RADICAND]

radicchio (rədē´kiō) *n.* (*pl.* **radicchios**) a type of chicory from Italy with purple and white leaves eaten raw in salads. [It.]

radices RADIX.

radicle (rad´ikəl) *n.* **1** the part of a plant embryo that develops into the main root. **2** a small root, a rootlet. **3** a rootlike part of a nerve, vein etc. **4** (*Chem.*) a radical. **radicular** (-dik´ū-) *a.* [L *rādīcula*, dim. of *rādix*]

radii RADIUS.

radio (rā´diō) *n.* (*pl.* **radios**) **1** electromagnetic waves used in two-way broadcasting. **2** the process or system of transmitting and receiving sound signals, messages, music etc. by means of electromagnetic waves of radio frequency. **3** any device which can send signals through space using electromagnetic waves. **4** an apparatus capable of demodulating and transmitting a signal sent using electromagnetic waves. **5** a radio receiving set. **6** sound broadcasting. **7** the programmes broadcast on the radio. **8** a sound broadcasting station, channel or organization. ~*v.t.* (*3rd pers. sing. pres.* **radioes,** *pres.p.* **radioing,** *past, p.p.* **radioed**) **1** to send or communicate by radio. **2** to send a radio message to. ~*v.i.* to use a radio or the system of radio to communicate. **radio astronomy** *n.* the study of radio waves received back from celestial objects. **radio beacon** *n.* a transmitting station which sends out signals to aid navigators. **radio cab, radio car** *n.* (*dated*) a taxi equipped with a two-way radio. **radio compass** *n.* a device for navigation which can determine the direction of incoming radio waves from a beacon. **radio control** *n.* remote control using radio signals. **radio-controlled** *a.* **radio fix** *n.* the position of a ship, aeroplane etc. as determined by radio signals. **radio frequency** *n.* (*pl.* **radio frequencies**) **1** radio spectrum. **2** a frequency or band of frequencies used for radio transmission. **radio galaxy** *n.* (*pl.* **radio galaxies**) a galaxy which is a strong source of radio waves. **radio ham** *n.* a licensed amateur operator of a radio transmitting and receiving system. **radio source** *n.* a celestial object, e.g. a quasar, which emits radio waves. **radio spectrum** *n.* the range of electromagnetic frequencies, between 10 kHz and 300,000 MHz, used in radio transmissions. **radio star** *n.* a radio source. **radio station** *n.* **1** a radio or television broadcasting organization. **2** an installation of radio transmitters and receivers. **radio telescope** *n.* an apparatus for collecting radio waves from outer space. **radio wave** *n.* an electromagnetic wave of radio frequency. [L *rādius*, a ray, a spoke]

radio-[1] (rā´diō) *comb. form* **1** of or relating to radio, radio frequency or broadcasting. **2** of, relating to or connected with radiation or radioactivity. **3** radioactive, radioactive isotope of (an element). [RADIATION (under RADIATE), RADIO]

radio-[2] (rā´diō) *comb. form* **1** radiate. **2** (*Anat.*) of or relating to the outer bone of the forearm. [RADIUS]

radioactive (rādiōak´tiv) *a.* of or exhibiting radioactivity. **radioactive decay** *n.* the disintegration of an atomic nucleus with accompanying emission of radiation. **radioactively** *adv.* **radioactive series** *n.* a series of nuclides which each undergo radioactive decay, finally creating a stable element, usu. lead. **radioactivity** (-tiv´-) *n.* **1** the spontaneous emission of usu. penetrating radiation, as alpha and beta particles, that accompanies the disintegration of atomic nuclei of unstable elements or isotopes. **2** radioactive substances. **3** radiation emitted by radioactive substances.

radio-assay (rādiōas´ā) *n.* a chemical assay based on the amounts and types of radiation from a sample.

radiobiology (rādiōbīol´əji) *n.* the study of the effects of radiation on the body using radioactive tracers. **radiobiological** (-loj´-) *a.* **radiobiologically** *adv.* **radiobiologist** *n.*

radiocarbon (rādiōkah´bən) *n.* carbon-14, a radioactive carbon isotope. **radiocarbon dating** *n.* CARBON DATING (under CARBON).

radiochemistry (rādiōkem´istri) *n.* the chemistry of radioactive substances. **radiochemical** *a.* **radiochemically** *adv.* **radiochemist** *n.*

radio-element (rādiōel´imənt) *n.* a radioactive chemical element.

radiogenic (rādiōjēn´ik) *a.* **1** produced by radioactivity. **2** suitable for radio broadcasting. **radiogenically** *adv.*

radio-goniometer (rādiōgoniom´itə) *n.* an apparatus used as a radio direction-finding system.

radiogram (rā´diōgram) *n.* (*dated*) **1** a combined radio and record player. **2** a photograph produced by X-rays, gamma rays etc. **3** a radio-telegraphic message.

radiograph (rā´diōgrahf) *n.* **1** a negative produced by X-rays, gamma rays etc. **2** a print from this. ~*v.t.* to obtain a photographic image of by means of such rays. **radiographer** (-og´-) *n.* a person who takes X-ray pictures of parts of the body. **radiographic** (-graf´-) *a.* **radiographically** *adv.* **radiography** (-og´-) *n.*

radioimmunoassay (rādiōimūnōas´ā) *n.* an immunological assay which uses radioactive labelling of various levels, such as hormone levels.

radioimmunology (rādiōimūnol´əji) *n.* immunology that employs the techniques of radiology. **radioimmunological** (-loj´-) *a.*

radioisotope (rādiōī´sətōp) *n.* a radioactive isotope of a chemical element. **radioisotopic** (-top´-) *a.* **radioisotopically** *adv.*

radiolarian (rādiōleə´riən) *n.* a marine rhizopod protozoan of the superclass Actinopoda, having radiating filamentous pseudopodia and abounding in warm seas. ~*a.* of or relating to radiolarians. [L *Radiolaria* (former order name), from *radiolus*, dim. of RADIUS]

radiolocation (rādiōləkā´shən) *n.* the location by radar of the position of an object in space.

radiology (rādiol´əji) *n.* the branch of medical science concerned with radioactivity, X-rays and other diagnostic or therapeutic radiations. **radiologic** (-loj´-), **radiological** *a.* **radiologically** *adv.* **radiologist** *n.* a medical practitioner trained in radiology, e.g. a person who interprets X-ray pictures of parts of the body.

radioluminescence (rādiōloomines´əns) *n.* luminous radiation emitted by radioactive material. **radioluminescent** *a.*

radiometer (rādiom´itə) *n.* an instrument for measuring the intensity of radiant energy. **radiometric** (-met´-) *a.* **radiometrically** *adv.* **radiometric dating** *n.* a method of dating geological material by measuring the relative amounts of the isotopes of a particular radioactive element. **radiometry** *n.*

radiomicrometer (rādiōmīkrom´itə) *n.* an instrument for measuring minute variations of heat etc.

radiomimetic (rādiōmimet´ik) *a.* of or relating to a chemical or substance which affects living tissue in a similar way to ionizing radiation.

radionics (rādion´iks) *n.* a form of complementary medicine that bases diagnoses on the analysis of energy supposedly emitted from items, e.g. hair, belonging to the patient. [RADIO-[1], *-onics*, as electr*onics*]

radionuclide (rādiōnū´klīd) *n.* a radioactive nuclide.

radio-opaque RADIOPAQUE.

radiopaging (rā´diōpājing) *n.* a system for alerting a person, using a small device which emits a sound in response to a signal at a distance.

radiopaque (rādiōpāk´), **radio-opaque** (rādiōōpāk´) *a.* not allowing X-rays or other radiation to pass through. **radiopacity** (-pas´-) *n.*

radiophonic (rādiōfon´ik) *a.* of, relating to or being music or other sounds produced electronically. **radiophone** (rā´-) *n.* **1** a radiotelephone. **2** an instrument for the production of sound by means of radiant energy. **radiophonically** *adv.* **radiophonics, radiophony** (-of´əni) *n.* the art of producing sounds, esp. music, electronically.

radioscopy (rādios´kəpi) *n.* examination of bodies by means of X-rays. **radioscopic** (-əskop´-) *a.* **radioscopically** *adv.*

radiosensitive (rādiōsen´sitiv) *a.* liable to injury from radiation.

radiosonde (rā´diōsond) *n.* a miniature radio transmitter sent up in a balloon and dropped by parachute, for sending information of pressures, temperatures etc.

radio-telegram (rādiōtel´igram) *n.* a message sent by radio-telegraphy, esp. from a ship to land. **radio-telegraph** *n.* **radio-telegraphic** (-graf´-) *a.* **radio-telegraphy** (-təleg´-) *n.* telegraphy which transmits messages using radio waves.

radio-telephone (rādiōtel´ifōn) *n.* an apparatus for sending telephone messages using radio waves. ~*v.t.* to telephone using a radio-telephone. **radio-telephonic** (-fon´-) *a.* **radio-telephony** (-təlef´-) *n.* telephony which transmits messages using radio waves.

radio-teletype (rādiōtel´itīp) *n.* **1** a teleprinter which can transmit or receive messages using radio waves. **2** a network of teleprinters used to communicate news and messages.

radiotelex (rādiotel´eks) *n.* a telex sent using radio-teletype apparatus.

radiotherapy (rādiother´əpi) *n.* the treatment of disease by means of X-rays or other radiation, esp. from radioactive sources. **radiotherapeutic** (-pū´tik) *a.* **radiotherapist** *n.*

radio-ulna (rādiōŭl´nə) *n.* (*Zool.*) a bone in the forelimb of amphibians, equivalent to the radius and ulna of more advanced vertebrates.

radish (rad´ish) *n.* **1** a cruciferous plant, *Raphanus sativus*, cultivated for its pungent root, which is eaten as a salad vegetable. **2** this root. [F *radis*, from L *rādix, -īcem*, see RADIX]

radium (rā´diəm) *n.* (*Chem.*) a highly radioactive metallic element, at. no. 88, chem. symbol Ra, occurring in pitchblende, used in making luminous materials and in radiotherapy. **radium therapy** *n.* the treatment of disease, esp. cancer, using radiation from radium. [as RADIUS, -IUM]

radius (rā´diəs) *n.* (*pl.* **radii** (-diī)) **1** a straight line from the centre of a circle or sphere to any point on the circumference. **2** the length of this, half the diameter. **3 a** a circular area measured by its usu. specified radius. **b** any circumscribed area. **4** the shorter of the two long bones of the forearm. **5** the corresponding bone in animals and birds. **6** a radiating line, part, object etc., such as a spoke. **7** (*Geom.*) the distance from a focus to a point on a curve. **8** (*Bot.*) **a** the outer zone of a composite flower. **b** a floret in this. **c** a branch of an umbel. **9** an arm of a starfish. ~*v.t.* (*3rd pers. sing. pres.* **radiuses,** *pres.p.* **radiusing,** *past, p.p.* **radiused**) to give a rounded edge to. **radius vector** *n.* (*pl.* **radii vectores** (-taw´rēz)) **1** the distance from a fixed point to a curve. **2** a line drawn from the centre of a heavenly body to that of another revolving round it. [L, rod, spoke, ray]

radix (rā´diks) *n.* (*pl.* **radices** (-disēz)) **1** a quantity or symbol taken as the base of a system of numbering, logarithms etc. **2** a source or origin. **3** a root. **radix point** *n.* any point which separates the integral part from the fractional part of a number, such as a decimal point. [L, root]

radome (rā´dōm) *n.* a protective covering for radar antennae, through which radio waves can pass. [*ra*dar, *dome*]

radon (rā´don) *n.* (*Chem.*) a gaseous radioactive element, at. no. 86, chem. symbol Rn, formed by the disintegration of radium.

radula (rad´ūlə) *n.* (*pl.* **radulae** (-lē)) (*Zool.*) a ribbonlike band covered with minute teeth occurring in some molluscs, used for scraping up food and drawing it into the mouth. **radular** *a.* [L, scraper, from *rādere*, to scrape, see RAZE]

RAF (raf) *abbr.* Royal Air Force.

raff (raf) *n.* **1** (*dial.*) sweepings, refuse. **2** †the rabble, the ruck, the lowest class. **3** †a person of this class, a rowdy. [prob. from RIFF-RAFF]

Raffaelesque RAPHAELESQUE.

Rafferty's rules (raf´ətiz) *n.pl.* (*Austral., New Zeal.*) no rules whatsoever. [perh. corr. of REFRACTORY]

raffia (raf´iə), **raphia** *n.* **1** a Madagascan palm, *Raphia ruffia*, with a short stem and gigantic pinnate leaves. **2** fibre prepared from the leaves, used for tying, ornamental work etc. [Malagasy]

raffinate (raf´ināt) *n.* (*Chem.*) the liquid remaining after extraction of a solute with a solvent. [F *raffiner*, to refine, -ATE[1]]

raffish (raf´ish) *a.* **1** disreputable, disorderly, dissipated-looking, rakish. **2** vulgar, tawdry. **raffishly** *adv.* **raffishness** *n.* [RAFF]

raffle[1] (raf´əl) *n.* a lottery in which one or more articles are put up to be disposed of by drawing lots among a number of people buying tickets for the draw. ~*v.t.* to dispose of by means of a raffle. ~*v.i.* to engage in a raffle (for). **raffler** *n.* [ME and F *rafle*, a game with dice]

raffle[2] (raf´əl) *n.* **1** rubbish, lumber, debris. **2** a tangle of cordage, rigging or other nautical material. [OF *rafle* (in *rifle ou rafle*), prob. rel. to RAFF]

rafflesia (rəflē´ziə) *n.* any of a genus, *Rafflesia*, of very large stemless parasitic plants from Java and Sumatra. [Sir Stamford *Raffles*, British colonial governor, 1781–1826]

raft[1] (rahft) *n.* **1** a flat floating framework of planks or other material used for supporting or carrying people, goods etc. on water. **2** a slab of concrete etc. used as a foundation for a building. **3** a small, often inflatable boat for use in an emergency. **4** a floating accumulation of driftwood, ice etc. in a river. **5** a number of logs or pieces of timber fastened together for transport by floating down a river etc. ~*v.t.* **1** to transport on or as on a raft. **2** to cross (a river etc.) on a raft. **3** to make into a raft. **4** to transport in the form of a raft. ~*v.i.* **1** to travel on a raft. **2** to work on a raft. **rafter**[1] *n.* a person who manages or works on a raft. **raftsman** *n.* (*pl.* **raftsmen**). [Icel. *raptr* (cp. Swed. *raft*, Dan. *rafte*)]

raft[2] (rahft) *n.* (*coll.*) a large number, a crowd, a lot. [var. of RAFF]

rafter[1] RAFT[1].

rafter[2] (rahf´tə) *n.* any of the sloping pieces of timber supporting a roof or forming the framework on which the tiles etc. of the roof are laid. *~v.t.* to furnish with rafters. **raftered** *a.* **raftering** *n.* [OE *ræfter*, cp. RAFT[1]]

rag[1] (rag) *n.* **1** a torn or worn piece of cloth, esp. an irregular piece detached from a fabric by wear and tear. **2** (*pl.*) tattered or shabby clothes. **3** (*collect.*) torn fragments of cloth, linen etc., used as material for paper, stuffing etc. **4** (*sl.*) a handkerchief. **5** (*derog.*) a newspaper. **6** (*derog.*) a flag, sail, drop-curtain etc. **7** a remnant, a scrap, the smallest piece (of anything). **rag-and-bone man** *n.* (*pl.* **rag-and-bone men**) an itinerant dealer in old or unwanted clothes, household items etc. **ragbag** *n.* **1** a miscellaneous collection. **2** a bag for scraps of cloth. **3** (*coll.*) a carelessly dressed or dishevelled woman. **rag bolt** *n.* a bolt with jags on the shank to prevent its being easily withdrawn. *~v.t.* to fasten with these. **rag book** *n.* a book for a young child made out of cloth instead of paper. **rag doll** *n.* a doll made from cloth. **rag-fair** *n.* a market for the sale of old clothes. **rag paper** *n.* paper made from rags. **ragpicker** *n.* (*esp. Hist.*) a person who collects, sorts and sells rags. **rag rolling** *n.* a decorating technique in which paint of a contrasting colour is applied over a previously painted surface using a roughly folded cloth to create a textured or marbled effect. **rags-to-riches** *a.* denoting someone who starts off poor and becomes rich, or a story describing this progress. **ragtag, ragtag and bobtail** *n.* the riff-raff, the rabble. **ragtail** *a.* (*esp. N Am.*) confused, badly organized, straggly. **rag trade** *n.* (*coll.*) the clothing industry. **ragweed** *n.* ragwort. **rag-wheel** *n.* a wheel with a notched margin, a sprocket-wheel. **ragworm** *n.* any of several burrowing marine worms used as bait in fishing. **ragwort** *n.* a yellow-flowered plant with deeply cut leaves of the genus *Senecio*, esp. *S. jacobaea*, a common weed. [cp. Icel. *rögg*, Norw., Swed. *ragg*, rough hair]

rag[2] (rag) *v.t.* (*pres.p.* **ragging**, *past, p.p.* **ragged**) **1** to tease, irritate or play rough practical jokes on. **2** to reprove, to talk to severely. *~v.i.* to engage in rough or noisy horseplay. *~n.* **1** a programme of entertainments, stunts, processions etc. organized by students to raise money for charity. **2** a prank. **3** the act of ragging. **4** a piece of boisterous and disorderly conduct. **to lose one's rag** (*sl.*) to lose one's temper. **rag-day, rag-week** *n.* in British universities, a day or week devoted to staging fundraising events for charity. **ragging** *n.* **raggy**[1] *a.* (*comp.* **raggier**, *superl.* **raggiest**) (*sl.*) irritated, angry. [cp. BALLYRAG]

rag[3] (rag) *n.* **1** a piece of ragtime music. **2** ragtime. *~v.t.* (*pres.p.* **ragging**, *past, p.p.* **ragged**) to play in ragtime. [by shortening]

rag[4] (rag) *n.* **1** (*also* **ragstone**) a hard, coarse, rough stone, usu. breaking up into thick slabs. **2** a large roofing slate with a rough surface on one side. **rag work** *n.* thick slabs of masonry. [etym. uncertain]

rag[5] RAGA.

raga (rah´gə), **rag** (rahg) *n.* **1** in traditional Indian music, a form or a mode which forms the basis for improvisation. **2** a composition following such a pattern. [Sansk. *rāga*, tone, colour]

ragamuffin (rag´əmŭfin) *n.* **1** a ragged unkempt person, esp. a child. **2** ragga. **3** (*also* **raggamuffin**) a follower of ragga music. [prob. from RAG[1] (cp. *Ragamoffyn*, a demon in the poem *Piers Plowman* (1393))]

rage (rāj) *n.* **1** violent anger, fury. **2** a fit of passionate anger. **3** (*fig.*) extreme violence, vehemence or intensity (of). **4** a violent desire or enthusiasm (for). **5** (*coll.*) an object of temporary pursuit, enthusiasm or devotion. **6** intense emotion, passion or ardour. **7** (*Austral., New Zeal., coll.*) a party. *~v.i.* (*pres.p.* **raging**) **1** to storm, to rave, to be furious with anger, to be violently incensed or agitated. **2** to express anger or passion violently. **3** to be violent, to be at the highest state of vehemence, intensity or activity. **4** (*Austral., New Zeal., coll.*) to have a good time. *~v.t.* †to enrage. **all the rage** an object of general desire, quite the fashion. **rageful** *a.* **ragefully** *adv.* **rager** *n.* someone who or something which rages. **raging** *a.* **1** violent, extreme. **2** causing extreme pain (*a raging headache*). **3** (*coll.*) immense, considerable (*a raging success*). *~n.* **1** violence. **2** fury. **ragingly** *adv.* [F, late L *rabia*, RABIES]

ragee RAGI.

ragga (rag´ə) *n.* a form of popular dance music incorporating elements of reggae and hip hop. [by shortening from RAGAMUFFIN]

raggamuffin RAGAMUFFIN.

ragged (rag´id) *a.* **1** worn into rags, tattered. **2** rough, shaggy. **3** broken, jagged, or uneven in outline or surface. **4** disjointed, irregular, imperfect. **5** lacking in uniformity, finish etc. **6** harsh, dissonant. **7** wearing tattered clothes. **8** shabby, poor, miserable in appearance. **to run someone ragged** RUN. **raggedly** *adv.* **raggedness** *n.* **ragged robin** *n.* a pink-flowered plant, *Lychnis floscuculi*, the petals of which have a tattered appearance. **ragged school** *n.* (*Hist.*) a free school for the education of poor children. **ragged staff** *n.* a stick with branch stubs. **raggedy** *a.* tattered.

raggee RAGI.

raggle-taggle (ragəltag´əl), **wraggle-taggle** *a.* unkempt, untidy. [RAG[1], TAG]

raggy[1] RAG[2].

raggy[2] RAGI.

ragi (rah´gi, rag´i), **ragee, raggee, raggy** *n.* an Indian food-grain, *Eleusine coracana*. [Hind.]

raging RAGE.

raglan (rag´lən) *n.* a loose overcoat with no seams on the shoulders, the sleeves going up to the neck. *~a.* cut in this way. **raglan sleeve** *n.* a sleeve which continues to the collar, with no seams on the shoulders. [1st Baron *Raglan*, 1788–1855, British commander]

ragout (ragoo´) *n.* a highly seasoned dish of small pieces of stewed meat and vegetables. *~v.t.* to make into a ragout. [F *ragoût*, from *ragoûter*, to bring, to awaken or stimulate the appetite, (RE-, *goût*, taste)]

ragtime (rag´tīm) *n.* a style of jazz music popular esp. in the early 20th cent., characterized by a syncopated melody and played esp. on the piano. *~a.* disreputable, unruly. [prob. from *ragged time*]

raguly (rag´ūli), †**raguled** (-ūld) *a.* (*Her.*) having projections like lopped branches at the sides. [etym. uncertain, prob. rel. to RAG[1]]

rah (rah) *int.* (*esp. N Am., coll.*) hurrah. **rah-rah** *a.* (*N Am., coll.*) marked by or demonstrating extreme, esp. noisy enthusiasm. **rah-rah skirt** *n.* a short flared skirt as worn by a cheerleader. [by shortening]

rai (rī) *n.* a form of popular music originating in Algeria that incorporates elements of traditional Bedouin music and Western rock. [Arab.]

raid (rād) *n.* **1** a sudden hostile or predatory incursion as of armed troops, criminals etc. **2** a sudden surprise invasion or descent of police or customs officers etc. **3** an air raid. **4** an attempt by speculators to lower stock market prices by concerted selling. **5** (*chiefly facet.*) an excursion or foray to obtain something (*a raid on the larder*). *~v.t.* to make a raid upon. *~v.i.* to make a raid. **to raid the market** to upset stock market prices artificially for future gain. **raider** *n.* [Sc., from OE *rād*, ROAD[1]]

rail[1] (rāl) *n.* **1** a bar of wood or metal or series of such bars resting on posts or other supports, forming part of a fence, banisters etc. **2** a continuous line of iron or steel bars, resting on sleepers etc. laid on the ground, usu. forming one of a pair of such lines constituting the track of a railway or tramway. **3** any of the iron or steel bars forming such a line. **4** either of a similar pair of lines serving as track for part of a machine. **5** the railway as a means of travel or transportation. **6** a bar fixed on a wall on which to hang things. **7** a horizontal structural support in a door. **8** (*pl.*) a barrier at the side of a racecourse. ~*v.t.* **1** to enclose with rails. **2** to furnish or fill with rails. **3** to lay down rails upon. **4** to send by rail. ~†*v.i.* to travel by rail. **to go off the rails 1** to go mad. **2** to go awry. **railage** *n.* **railcar** *n.* a self-powered single railway carriage. **rail card** *n.* an identity card issued to certain people (e.g. pensioners and students) allowing the holder cheaper rail fares. **railer**[1] *n.* a person who makes or fits rails. **rail fence** *n.* a fence made of rails. **rail gun** *n.* an electromagnetic anti-missile projectile launcher. **railhead** *n.* **1** a terminus. **2** the farthest point to which rails have been laid. **railing**[1] *n.* **1** (*often pl.*) a fence made of wooden or other rails. **2** materials for railings. **railless** *a.* **railman** *n.* (*pl.* **railmen**) a railway worker. **railroad** *n.* (*esp. N Am.*) a railway. ~*v.t.* **1** to force hurriedly to a conclusion. **2** to send to prison on a false charge. **railroader** *n.* a person employed on a railway. **railway** (rāl´wā) *n.* **1** a permanent track formed of rails of iron or steel along which trains and vehicles are driven, usu. by locomotives. **2** a system of tracks, stations, rolling stock and other apparatus worked by one company or organization. **3** an organization that runs such a system. **4** a track laid with rails for the passage of cranes, trucks etc. **railway carriage** *n.* a railway vehicle for passengers. **railway company** *n.* a joint-stock company owning and managing a railway. **railway-crossing** *n.* a crossing of two railway lines, or a road and a railway. **railwayman, railwaywoman** *n.* (*pl.* **railwaymen, railwaywomen**) a railway worker. **railway station** *n.* a place where railway trains stop to set down or take up passengers or goods, usu. with a platform and administrative buildings and public facilities. **railway yard** *n.* a place where rolling stock is kept. **railwoman** *n.* (*pl.* **railwomen**) a female railway worker. [OF *reille*, L *rēgula*, RULE]

rail[2] (rāl) *v.i.* **1** to use abusive or derisive language. **2** to scoff (at or against). ~†*v.t.* to effect by raillery. **railer**[2] *n.* a person who rails or scoffs. **railing**[2] *n.*, *a.* **railingly** *adv.* **raillery** *n.* (*pl.* **railleries**) **1** good-humoured ridicule or pleasantry, banter. **2** a bantering comment. [F *railler*, etym. uncertain]

rail[3] (rāl) *n.* a wading bird of the family Rallidae, esp. the water rail and the corncrake or landrail. [F *râle*, etym. uncertain]

railer[1] RAIL[1].

railer[2] RAIL[2].

railing[1] RAIL[1].

railing[2] RAIL[2].

raillery RAIL[2].

raiment (rā´mənt) *n.* (*dated or poet.*) dress, apparel, clothes. [short for obs. *arrayment* (ARRAY, -MENT)]

rain (rān) *n.* **1** the condensed moisture of the atmosphere falling in drops. **2** a fall of such drops. **3** a similar fall or shower of liquid, particles or objects. **4** (*fig.*) a large quantity of anything falling quickly. **5** rainy weather. **6** (*pl.*) the rainy season in a tropical country. ~*v.i.* **1** (*usu. impers.*) to fall in drops of water from the clouds. **2** to fall in showers like rain. **3** to send down rain. ~*v.t.* **1** to pour down (rain). **2** to send down in showers like rain. **come rain or come shine** whatever the weather, whatever the circumstances. **rain or shine** come rain or come shine. **to be rained off** to be cancelled or postponed because of rain or bad weather. **to be rained out** (*N Am.*) to be rained off. **to rain cats and dogs** CAT[1]. **rainbird** *n.* any of various birds supposed to foretell rain, esp. the green woodpecker. **rainbow** (-bō) *n.* **1** a luminous arc showing the prismatic colours, appearing opposite the sun during rain, caused by the reflection, double refraction and dispersion of the sun's rays passing through the drops. **2** any similar effect or display of colours. **3** a wide assortment (*a rainbow of opinions*). ~*a.* **1** coloured like the rainbow. **2** many-coloured. **3** consisting of or bringing together groups from different races or of different political views. **to chase rainbows** to pursue an illusory aim. **rainbow coalition** *n.* a political alliance of minority groups. **rainbow-coloured,** (*N Am.*) **rainbow-colored** *a.* **rainbow-tinted** *a.* **rainbow trout** *n.* a brightly-coloured trout, *Onchorhyncus mykiss*, of N American origin. **rainbowy** *a.* **rain check** *n.* (*esp. N Am.*) **1** a ticket for a sports event which allows readmission on another day if rain stops play. **2** an extension of an offer to a later, more convenient time. **3** the postponing of a decision. **to take a rain check** to postpone accepting an invitation till a later date. **rain cloud** *n.* a cloud producing rain, a nimbus. **raincoat** *n.* a waterproof coat or cloak for wearing in wet weather, a mackintosh. **rain-doctor** *n.* a person who professes to cause rain by incantations or magic. **raindrop** *n.* a particle of rain. **rainfall** *n.* **1** a shower of rain. **2** the amount of rain which falls in a particular district in a given period. **rainforest** *n.* a dense tropical forest of mostly evergreen trees with a very heavy rainfall. **rain gauge** *n.* an instrument for measuring the amount of rain falling on a given surface. **rain-glass** *n.* (*coll.*) a barometer. **rainless** *a.* **rainmaker** *n.* **1** a person who professes to cause rain by incantations or magic. **2** (*N Am.*, *sl.*) a successful business person who generates a high level of income for an employer. **rainmaking** *n.* the artificial production of rain, e.g. by seeding clouds. **rainout** *n.* (*N Am.*) the cancellation or interruption of an event because of rain. **rainproof** *a.* impervious or resistant to rain. ~*v.t.* to make impervious to rain. **rain shadow** *n.* the leeward side of hills, which has a relatively light rainfall compared to the windward side. **rainstorm** *n.* a storm with very heavy rain. **rainswept** *a.* exposed to the rain. **raintight** *a.* rainproof. **rain-wash** *n.* **1** the movement of soil and stones effected by rain. **2** matter transported by rain. **rainwater** *n.* water that has fallen in the form of rain. **rainwear** *n.* rainproof clothing. **rain-worm** *n.* an earthworm. **rainy** *a.* (*comp.* **rainier**, *superl.* **rainiest**) **1** characterized by much rain. **2** showery, wet. **3** bearing rain. **rainily** *adv.* **raininess** *n.* **rainy day** *n.* a time of misfortune or distress, esp. pecuniary need. [OE *regn*, *rēn* (cp. Dut. and G *Regen*, Icel., Swed. and Dan. *regn*), whence *regnian*, to rain, *rēnig*, rainy]

raise (rāz) *v.t.* **1** to move or put into a higher position. **2** to cause to rise, to elevate. **3** to cause to stand up, to set upright. **4** to increase the amount or value of. **5** to increase the strength or intensity of (*to raise one's voice*). **6** to erect, to build, to construct. **7** to restore to life or from sleep. **8** to rouse, to excite, to stir up. **9** to produce, to create, to cause. **10** to set up, to cause to be heard or known, to suggest (a point etc.). **11** to occasion. **12** to bring up, to rear. **13** to grow or breed. **14** to collect, to procure, to levy (money etc.). **15** to advance, to promote, to heighten, to make higher or nobler, to cause to ascend. **16** to remove, to bring to an end (a ban, blockade, siege etc.). **17** to multiply (a number) by itself a specified number of times. **18** to cause to increase in volume by the addition of a raising agent. **19** to cause (a blister, lump etc.) to form or swell. **20** to bid more money than (a previous player) at cards. **21 a** in bridge, to make a higher bid in (the suit of one's partner). **b** to increase (a bid) in this way. **22** to establish radio links with. **23** to come in sight of (land etc.). **24** to put a nap on (cloth). ~*n.* (*N Am.*) a rise in salary. **to raise a dust** DUST. **to raise an eyebrow** EYEBROW (under EYE[1]). **to raise a/ one's hand to** to hit. **to raise a stink** STINK. **to raise hell** (*coll.*) to make a lot of trouble. **to raise hob** HOB[2]. **to raise its (ugly) head** HEAD[1]. **to raise one's eyebrows** EYEBROW (under EYE[1]).

to raise one's eyes EYE[1]. to raise one's glass (to) to drink a toast (to). to raise one's guard GUARD. to raise the devil (*coll.*) to make a disturbance or commotion. to raise the roof ROOF. to raise the wind 1 (*sl.*) to make a disturbance or commotion. 2 (*sl.*) to get hold of cash. **raised** *a.* **raised beach** *n.* an ancient beach or shore, of a lake or sea, left high and dry by elevation of the land or recession of the water. **raised pie** *n.* a pie that stands upright without a supporting dish. **raiser** *n.* **raising** *n.* **raising agent** *n.* a natural or chemical substance which causes dough or cakes to rise. [Icel. *reisa* (cp. Dan. *reise*, Swed. *resa*)]

raisin (rā´zin) *n.* a dried grape, the partially dried fruit of various species of vine. **raisiny** *a.* [OF *raizin* (F *raisin*), pop. L *racīmum*, L *racēmum*, RACEME]

raison d'être (rāzõn det´rə) *n.* (*pl.* **raisons d'être** (rāzõn det´rə)) the reason for a thing's existence. [F, reason of being]

raisonné (rā´zənā) *a.* (of a catalogue) arranged systematically. [F, p.p. of *raisonner*, to REASON]

raita (rahē´tə, rāē´tə, rīē´tə, rī´ta) *n.* an Indian side dish of chopped cucumber or other salad vegetables in yogurt. [Hind.]

raj (rahj) *n.* (in the Indian subcontinent) rule, government. **the Raj** the British rule of India before 1947. [Hind.]

raja (rah´jə), **rajah** *n.* 1 an Indian king, prince or tribal chief, a dignitary or noble. 2 a Malayan or Javanese chief. **rajaship** *n.* **raja yoga** *n.* a form of yoga concerned with achieving control over the mind through meditation etc. [Hind., from Sansk. *rāj*, to reign, rel. to L *rex*, king]

Rajput (rahj´put), **Rajpoot** *n.* 1 a member of a Hindu warrior caste who claim descent from the Kshatriyas. 2 a member of a Hindu aristocratic class. [Hind. *rajpūt* (Sansk. *rāja*, see RAJA, *putra*, son)]

rake[1] (rāk) *n.* 1 an implement having a long handle with a cross-bar set with teeth, used for drawing loose material together, smoothing soil etc. 2 (*Hist.*) a two-wheeled implement drawn by a horse for gathering hay together etc. 3 a similar implement for collecting light articles. ~*v.t.* 1 to collect or gather (up or together) with a rake. 2 to scrape, scratch, smooth, clean etc. (soil) with a rake. 3 to search with or as with a rake, to scour, to ransack. 4 to fire along the length of, to enfilade. 5 to sweep (a ship, deck, line of soldiers etc.) from end to end. 6 (of shot) to pass from end to end of. 7 (*fig.*) to command from end to end with the eye. ~*v.i.* 1 to use or work with a rake. 2 to search (about etc.) with or as with a rake. **to rake in** (*coll.*) to accumulate (usu. money). **to rake off** (*coll.*) to receive a share of the profits from an illegal job. **to rake over** (*coll.*) to dwell on the memory of (a quarrel, the past etc.). **to rake up** (*coll.*) to revive the memory of (a quarrel, the past etc.). **rake-off** *n.* (*coll.*) 1 commission on a job. 2 more or less illicit profits from a job. **raker**[1] *n.* **raking** *n.* 1 the act of using or working with a rake. 2 the amount of ground or quantity of material raked. 3 (*usu. pl.*) that which is raked together. [OE *raca* (cp. Dut. *raak*, G *Rechen*, Icel. *reka*)]

rake[2] (rāk) *n.* a dissolute or immoral man, a debauchee, a libertine. †**rakehell** *n.* an utterly abandoned scoundrel, a rake. †**rakehelly** *a.* **rakery** (-əri) *n.* dissoluteness. **rakish**[1] *a.* of, resembling or characteristic of a rake. **rakishly**[1] *adv.* **rakishness** *n.* [short for RAKEHELL (under RAKE[1])]

rake[3] (rāk) *n.* 1 inclination, slope, esp. backward slope. 2 (*Naut.*) projection of the stem or stern of a vessel beyond the extremities of the keel. 3 (*Naut.*) the slope of a mast or funnel towards the stern. 4 the slope of the stage or an auditorium. 5 the angle between the face of a cutting tool and a plane perpendicular to the working surface. 6 the angle of sweepback of an aircraft's wing. ~*v.i.* to slope, esp. backwards, from the perpendicular. ~*v.t.* to give such an inclination to. **raker**[2] *n.* a sloping shore or support. [etym. uncertain]

rakehell RAKE[1].

raker[1] RAKE[1].

raker[2] RAKE[3].

raki (rahkē´, rak´i), **rakee** *n.* (*pl.* **rakis, rakees**) an aromatic liquor made from spirit or grape juice, usu. flavoured with mastic, used in the E Mediterranean region. [Turk. *rāqī*, brandy, spirit]

rakish[1] RAKE[2].

rakish[2] (rā´kish) *a.* 1 (*Naut.*) with masts sharply inclined. 2 apparently built for speed. 3 smart-looking with a suggestion of the pirate or smuggler. 4 dashing, jaunty. **rakishly**[2] *adv.* [RAKE[3] (prob. with alln. to RAKE[2])]

rakishly[1] RAKE[2].

rakishly[2] RAKISH[2].

raku (rah´koo) *n.* Japanese lead-glazed pottery used esp. for tea bowls. [Jap., enjoyment]

rale (rahl), **râle** *n.* (*Med.*) a rattling sound in addition to that of respiration, heard with the stethoscope in lungs affected by disease. [F, from *râler*, etym. uncertain]

rall. (ral) *abbr.* rallentando.

rallentando (raləntan´dō) *adv.*, *a.* (*Mus.*) gradually slower. ~*n.* (*pl.* **rallentandos, rallentandi** (-dē)) 1 a gradual slowing in the speed at which music is played. 2 a passage to be played in this way. [It., gerund of *rallentare*, as RELENT]

ralli car (ral´i), **ralli cart** *n.* (*Hist.*) a two-wheeled horse-drawn carriage seating four. [name of the first buyer]

rallier[1] RALLY[1].

rallier[2] RALLY[2].

ralline (ral´īn) *a.* of or relating to the Rallidae, a family of birds including rails. [mod. L *rallus*, RAIL[3]]

rally[1] (ral´i) *v.t.* (*3rd pers. sing. pres.* **rallies,** *pres.p.* **rallying,** *past, p.p.* **rallied**) 1 to reunite, to bring (disordered troops) etc. together again. 2 to gather or bring together for a common purpose. 3 to restore, to reanimate, to revive, to pull together. ~*v.i.* 1 to reassemble, to come together again after a reverse or rout. 2 to come together for a cause or purpose. 3 to regain strength, to recover tone or spirit, to return to a state of health, vigour or courage. 4 (of share prices) to increase after a period of decline. ~*n.* (*pl.* **rallies**) 1 the act of rallying or recovering order, strength, health, energy etc. 2 an assembly, a reunion. 3 a large gathering of supporters of a cause, or of people with a common interest. 4 in tennis etc., a rapid or lengthy exchange of strokes. 5 a sharp increase in trade on the Stock Exchange after a period of decline. 6 a motoring contest designed to test driving and navigational skills in which cars are raced over a usu. unknown route on public roads and rough terrain. **to rally round** to come to someone's aid morally or financially. **rallier**[1] *n.* **rallycross** *n.* a form of motor racing in which specially adapted saloon cars race over a circuit containing both paved and rough, uneven surfaces (e.g. grass). **rally-driving** *n.* the sport of participating in car rallies. **rally-driver** *n.* **rallying** *n.* rally-driving. **rallying-cry** *n.* a slogan to attract attention to or support for a cause. **rallying-point** *n.* a point or place for a rally, esp. a place for a mass meeting. [F *rallier* (RE-, *allier*, to ALLY[1])]

rally[2] (ral´i) *v.t.* (*3rd pers. sing. pres.* **rallies,** *pres.p.* **rallying,** *past, p.p.* **rallied**) to ridicule or tease in a good-humoured way. **rallier**[2] *n.* **rallyingly** *adv.* [F *railler*, to RAIL[2]]

RAM[1] (ram) *n.* a temporary storage space in a computer from which data can be accessed directly in any order and altered. [acronym for *r*andom-*a*ccess *m*emory]

RAM[2] *abbr.* Royal Academy of Music.

ram (ram) *n.* 1 an uncastrated male sheep, a tup. 2 (*Hist.*) a battering-ram. 3 (*Hist.*) **a** a battleship armed with a beak of steel at the bow for cutting into a hostile vessel. b such a beak. 4 the drop-weight of a piledriver or steam hammer. 5 a hydraulic engine for raising water, lifting etc. 6 a rammer. 7 the compressing piston of a hydrostatic press. 8 the plunger of a force-pump. ~*v.t.* (*pres.p.* **ramming,** *past, p.p.* **rammed)** 1 to beat, drive, press or force (down, in, into etc.) by heavy blows. 2 to stuff, to compress, to force (into) with pressure. 3 to make firm by ramming. 4 to crash against with force. 5 to strike (a ship) with a ram. 6 to drive or impel (a thing against, into etc.) forcefully or with violence. ~*v.i.* to crash or collide violently. **the Ram** the constellation or zodiacal sign Aries. **to ram home** to force recognition or acceptance of. **to ram something down someone's throat** to force someone to accept or listen to an idea, argument etc., esp. by aggressive repetition. **ramjet** *n.* 1 (*also* **ramjet engine**) a form of aero-engine where the compressed air produced by the forward movement of the aircraft is used to burn the fuel. 2 an aircraft powered by such an engine. **rammer** *n.* 1 someone who or something which rams. 2 an instrument for pounding, driving etc. 3 a ramrod. **ram-raid** *n.* a robbery from a shop etc., using a vehicle to break into the premises. **ram-raider** *n.* **ram-raiding** *n.* **ramrod** *n.* 1 a rod for forcing down the charge of a muzzle-loading gun. 2 a stiff or rigid person or thing. ~*a.* stiff as a ramrod, uncompromising, formal. **ram's-horn** *n.* 1 a horn of a male sheep. 2 a scroll-ornament like a ram's skull and horns. **ram's horn snail** *n.* a freshwater snail of the genus *Planorbis* often used in aquaria as scavengers. [OE (cp. Dut. and OHG *ram*, G *Ramme*, prob. rel. to Icel. *ramr*, strong)]

Ramadan (ram´ədan, -dahn´), **Ramadhan** *n.* the ninth and holiest month of the Islamic year, the time of the great annual fast. [Arab. (cp. Pers. and Turk. *Ramazān*), from *ramada*, to be hot]

ramal RAMUS.

Raman effect (rah´mən) *n.* the change in wavelength which light undergoes when it passes through a transparent medium and is scattered by molecules of the medium. **Raman spectroscopy** *n.* the study of the properties of molecules using the Raman effect. [Sir Chandrasekhara *Raman*, 1888–1970, Indian physicist]

ramble (ram´bəl) *v.i.* 1 to walk or move about freely, as for recreation, or aimlessly. 2 to wander or be incoherent in speech, writing etc. 3 (of a plant) to grow in a straggling random manner. ~*n.* 1 a walk for pleasure or without a definite object, a stroll. 2 a roaming about. **rambler** *n.* 1 a person who rambles about, esp. a person who takes long walks in the countryside. 2 a vigorous climbing rose with lax stems. **rambling** *a.* 1 wandering about. 2 desultory, disconnected, incoherent. 3 irregular, straggling. 4 (of a plant) climbing with trailing stems. **ramblingly** *adv.* [ME *ramblen*, poss. from MDut. *rammelen*, to ROAM]

Ramboesque (rambōesk´) *a.* characterized by, using or advocating extreme force, violence or aggression. **Ramboism** (ram´-) *n.* 1 the use of Ramboesque tactics. 2 aggressive or violent behaviour. [John *Rambo*, fictional hero popularized in the film *First Blood* (1982) and *Rambo, First Blood II* (1985)]

rambunctious (rambŭngk´shəs) *a.* (*esp. N Am., coll.*) unruly, boisterous, exuberant. **rambunctiously** *adv.* **rambunctiousness** *n.* [perh. from Icel. *ram, bunctious* from BUMPTIOUS]

rambutan (ramboo´tən) *n.* 1 the red, hairy, pulpy fruit of a Malaysian tree, *Nephelium lappaceum*. 2 this tree. [Malay, from *rambut*, hair]

RAMC *abbr.* Royal Army Medical Corps.

rameal RAMAL (under RAMUS).

ramee RAMIE.

ramekin (ram´ikin), **ramequin** *n.* 1 a dish of cheese, eggs, breadcrumbs etc., baked in a small dish or mould. 2 (*also* **ramekin dish**) the mould itself. [F *ramequin*, etym. uncertain]

ramentum (rəmen´təm) *n.* (*pl.* **ramenta** (-tə)) any of the thin membranous scales formed on leaves and stems esp. of a fern. **ramentaceous** (-tā´shəs) *a.* [L, from *rādere*, to RAZE]

rameous RAMUS.

ramequin RAMEKIN.

rami RAMUS.

ramie (ram´i), **ramee** *n.* 1 a bushy Chinese and E Asian plant, *Boehmeria nivea*, of the nettle family. 2 the fine fibre of this woven as a substitute for cotton. [Malay *rāmī*]

ramification (ramifikā´shən) *n.* 1 the act of ramifying, the state of being ramified. 2 a subdivision in a complex system, structure etc. 3 a consequence, esp. one that causes complications. 4 the production of figures like branches. 5 the arrangement of branches. **ramify** (ram´ifī) *v.i.* (*3rd pers. sing. pres.* **ramifies,** *pres.p.* **ramifying,** *past, p.p.* **ramified)** 1 to divide into branches or subdivisions, to branch out, to send out offshoots. 2 to develop a usu. complicated consequence. ~*v.t.* to cause to divide into branches etc. [F, from *ramifier*, med. L *rāmificāre* (L *rāmus*, branch, *-ficāre, facere*, to make)]

ramiform RAMUS.

rammer RAM.

rammish (ram´ish) *a.* strong-smelling, rank. **rammishness** *n.* [RAM]

rammy (ram´i) *n.* (*pl.* **rammies)** a brawl, a fight, a free-for-all. [perh. from Sc. *rammle*, uproar]

ramose, ramous RAMUS.

ramp[1] (ramp) *v.i.* 1 to dash about, to rage, to storm. 2 to act in a violent or aggressive manner. 3 (of a wall) to ascend or descend to another level. 4 (of a heraldic lion) to rear or stand up on the hind legs, with the forelegs raised. ~*v.t.* to build or provide with ramps. ~*n.* 1 a slope or inclined plane or way, esp. leading from one level to another. 2 a movable stairway for boarding or leaving a plane. 3 a hump in the road, often designed to slow traffic down. 4 a sloping part in the top of a handrail, wall, coping etc. 5 a difference in level between the abutments of a rampart arch. 6 the act of ramping. **to ramp and rage** to act in a violent manner. [OF *ramper*, to creep, crawl, climb, etym. uncertain]

ramp[2] (ramp) *v.t.* (*sl.*) 1 to force to pay large amounts of money, esp. by swindling. 2 to increase (a price) exorbitantly and fraudulently. ~*v.i.* to engage in a ramp. ~*n.* a swindle, esp. one involving artificially inflated prices. **ramper** *n.* a swindler. [etym. uncertain]

rampage[1] (rampāj´) *v.i.* to dash about, to storm, to rage, to behave violently or boisterously. **rampager** *n.* [etym. uncertain]

rampage[2] (ram´pāj, -pāj´) *n.* boisterous, excited, violent behaviour. **on the rampage** 1 violently excited. 2 on a drunken spree. **rampageous** (-pā´-) *a.* **rampageously** *adv.* **rampageousness** *n.* [as RAMPAGE[1]]

rampant (ram´pənt) *a.* 1 unrestrained, aggressive, wild, violent. 2 (of weeds etc.) rank, luxuriant. 3 (of a heraldic animal) standing upright on the hind legs, ramping. 4 (of an arch) springing from different levels. **rampancy** *n.* (*pl.* **rampancies)**. **rampantly** *adv.* [F, pres.p. of *ramper*, to RAMP[1]]

rampart (ram´paht) *n.* 1 an embankment, usu. surmounted by a parapet, round a fortified place, or such an embankment together with the parapet. 2 (*fig.*) a defence. ~*v.t.* to fortify or defend with or as with a rampart. [F *rempart*, from *remparer*, to fortify (RE-, EM-, *parer*, L *parāre*, see PARRY)]

rampion (ram´piən) *n.* 1 a bellflower, *Campanula rapunculus*, with red, purple or blue blossoms. 2 any of several related plants of the genus *Phyteuma* with clusters of bluish flowers. [prob. rel. to F *raiponce* or It. *raperonzolo*, etym. uncertain]

ramrod RAM.

ramshackle (ram´shakəl) *a.* (of a building, vehicle etc.) tumbledown, rickety, shaky. [var. of obs. *ramshackled*, prob. from *ransackle*, freq. of RANSACK]

ramsons (ram´zəns -səns) *n.* (*pl.* **ramsons**) the broad-leaved garlic, *Allium ursinum*, or its bulbous root, eaten as a relish. [OE *hramsan*, pl. of *hramsa* (cp. G, Dan., Swed. *rams*, also Gr. *kromuon*)]

ramus (rā´məs) *n.* (*pl.* **rami** (-mī)) **1** (*Bot.*) a branched or forked part or structure. **2** (*Zool.*) the barb of a feather. **ramal** (-əl), **rameal** (-iəl) *a.* of, relating to or growing on or from a branch. **rameous** (-iəs) *a.* of or belonging to branches. **ramiform** (ram´-) *a.* having a branched or branchlike shape. **ramose** (rā´mōs, rəmōs´), †**ramous** (rā´məs) *a.* **1** branched or branching. **2** full of branches. **ramosely, ramously** *adv.* **ramosity** (-mos´-) *n.* **ramulus** (ram´ūləs) *n.* (*pl.* **ramuli**) a small branch or ramus. **ramuliferous** (-lif´-) *a.* **ramulose** (-ōs), **ramulous** (-əs) *a.* having many ramuli. **ramuscule** (ramŭs´kūl) *n.* a small ramus. [L *rāmus*, a branch]

RAN *abbr.* Royal Australian Navy.

ran RUN.

rance (rahns) *n.* a variegated kind of marble. [etym. uncertain]

ranch (rahnch) *n.* **1** a farm for rearing cattle and horses, esp. in western N America. **2** any large farm devoted to rearing a particular animal or crop. **3** a ranch house. ~*v.t.* to manage or work on a ranch. **rancher** *n.* a person who owns, manages or works on a ranch. **rancheria** (-ərē´ə) *n.* **1** a house or hut of a ranchero. **2** a cluster of south-western N American or Mexican Indian huts. **rancherie** (-ri) *n.* a settlement of N American Indians in British Columbia, Canada. **ranchero** (-chea´rō) *n.* a rancher, esp. in Mexico. **ranch house** *n.* **1** a house belonging to a ranch. **2** (*N Am.*) an open-plan single-storey house. **ranchman** *n.* (*pl.* **ranchmen**) a rancher. **rancho** (-ō) *n.* (*pl.* **ranchos**) a ranch. [Sp. *rancho*, mess, a party eating together, prob. rel. to RANK[1]]

rancid (ran´sid) *a.* **1** having the taste or smell of stale oil or fat. **2** rank, stale. **rancidity** (-sid´-), **rancidness** *n.* **rancidly** *adv.* [L *rancidus*]

rancour (rang´kə), (*N Am.*) **rancor** *n.* inveterate spite, resentment or enmity, malignancy, deep-seated malice. **rancorous** *a.* **rancorously** *adv.* [OF, from L *rancōrem*, nom. *-cor*, cogn. with RANCID]

rand[1] (rand, rant) *n.* **1** the standard monetary unit of S Africa. **2** (*S Afr.*) the high land bordering a river valley. [Afrikaans, rel. to RAND[2], sense 1 from *the Rand*, abbr. of Witwatersrand, the gold and diamond district surrounding Johannesburg]

rand[2] (rand) *n.* **1** a strip of leather between the sole and heel-piece of a boot or shoe. **2** (*dial.*) orig. a border, edge or margin. [OE *rand*, border, also Dut. and G, Swed. and Dan., cp. Icel. *rönd*]

randan[1] (ran´dan, -dan´) *n.* **1** a boat worked by three rowers, the one amidships using two oars. **2** this method of rowing a boat. [etym. uncertain]

randan[2] (randan´) *n.* a spree. [perh. rel. to RANDOM]

R & B, R. & B. *abbr.* (*Mus.*) rhythm and blues.

R & D, R. & D. *abbr.* research and development.

randem (ran´dəm) *a.* having three horses harnessed together. ~*adv.* in this fashion. ~*n.* a team or carriage driven thus. [from RANDOM after TANDEM]

random (ran´dəm) *a.* **1** done, made etc. without calculation or method; left to or occurring by chance. **2** having a value or outcome which cannot be determined, only defined in terms of probability (*a random variable*). **3** relating to, being or consisting of items or individuals having equal probabilities of occurring or being chosen (*a random sample*; *random numbers*). **4** (of masonry) consisting of stones etc. of irregular size and shape. ~†*n.* great speed or impetuosity. **at random** without direction or definite purpose, haphazardly. **random access** *n.* direct access to specific data in a larger store of computer data, without reading the entire store sequentially. **random-access memory** *n.* RAM. **randomize, randomise** *v.t.* **randomization** (-zā´shən) *n.* **randomizer** *n.* **randomly** *adv.* **randomness** *n.* **randomwise** *adv.* [F *randon*, from *randir*, to press forward, to gallop]

R and R, R. and R. *abbr.* **1** rescue and resuscitation. **2** rest and recreation. **3** rock and roll.

randy (ran´di) *a.* (*comp.* **randier**, *superl.* **randiest**) **1** lustful, on heat, sexually eager or excited. **2** (*chiefly Sc.*) loud-tongued, boisterous. **randily** *adv.* **randiness** *n.* [*rand* (RANT), -Y[1]]

ranee (rah´ni), **rani** *n.* (*pl.* **ranees, ranis**) **1** a Hindu queen. **2** the consort of a raja. [Hind. *rānī*, Sansk. *rājnī*, fem. of *rājā*, RAJA]

rang RING[2].

rangatira (rŭng·gətiə´rə) *n.* a Maori chief of either sex. [Maori]

range (rānj) *n.* **1** the extent of variation in something. **2** the limits between which such variation occurs. **3** the area, extent, scope, compass or sphere of power, activity, variation, voice-pitch etc. **4** the entire collection of products of a designer, manufacturer, stockist etc. **5 a** the extreme horizontal distance attainable by a gun or missile. **b** the distance between a gun or missile and its target. **6 a** a piece of ground with targets etc. for firing practice. **b** an area used for testing military equipment. **7** a row, rank, line, chain or series (e.g. of mountains). **8** a cooking-stove or fireplace, usu. containing a boiler, oven or ovens, hotplate etc. **9** a stretch, a tract, esp. of grazing or hunting ground. **10** the distance between a camera and the photographic subject. **11** the geographical area over which a plant or animal is naturally distributed. **12** the set of values of a dependent variable in statistics. ~*v.t.* (*pres.p.* **ranging**) **1** to set in a row or rows. **2** to arrange in definite order, place, company etc., to classify, to array. **3** to roam or pass over, along or through. **4** to make straight, level or flush, to align. ~*v.i.* **1** to lie, extend or reach. **2** to vary (between specified limits or from one specified point to another). **3** to roam, to wander, to rove, to sail (along etc.). **4** to be level, straight or flush. **5** to rank, to be in place (among, with etc.). **6 a** to carry (a specified distance) in a particular direction. **b** (of a gun etc.) to have a specified range. **to range oneself** to take sides (with). **rangefinder** *n.* an instrument for measuring the distance of an object from the observer, used in shooting a gun or focusing a camera. **ranger** *n.* **1** the superintendent of a forest, nature reserve etc. **2** (*N Am.*) a commando in the US army. **3** a member of a body of mounted troops. **4** (**Ranger**) a Guide of 16 and upwards. **5** a person who ranges, a rover, a wanderer. **6** a dog used to scour over ground. **rangership** *n.* **ranging-pole, ranging-rod** *n.* a usu. red and white striped rod used in surveying. **rangy** *a.* (*comp.* **rangier**, *superl.* **rangiest**) **1** tall, wiry, strong. **2** (*Austral.*) mountainous. **rangily** *adv.* **ranginess** *n.* [OF *ranger*, *renger*, from *rang*, RANK[1]]

rangé (rā´zhā), (*fem.*) **rangée** (rā´zhā) *a.* **1** orderly. **2** (of a number of heraldic charges) set in order.

rangiora (rang·giaw´rə) *n.* a broad-leaved shrub or small tree, *Brachyglottis repanda*, found in New Zealand. [Maori]

rani RANEE.

ranine (rā´nīn) *a.* of or relating to the underside of the tip of the tongue, where ranulas occur. **raniform** (ran´ifawm) *a.* frog-shaped. **ranivorous** (rəniv´ərəs) *a.* frog-eating. [L *rāna*, frog]

rank[1] (rangk) *n.* **1** relative degree of excellence etc. **2** high station, dignity, eminence. **3** relative position, degree, standing, station, class. **4** a row, a line. **5** a row of soldiers ranged side by side, as opposed to file. **6** a row of taxis for hire. **7** order, array. **8** a line of squares stretching across a chessboard from side to side. ~*v.t.* **1** to classify, to estimate, to give a (specified) rank to. **2** to draw up or arrange in rank or ranks. **3** (*N Am.*) to take precedence over, to have a higher rank than. ~*v.i.* **1** to hold a (specified) rank. **2** to have a place or position (among, with etc.). **3** to have a place on the list of claims on a bankrupt's estate. **4** (*N Am.*) to take precedence (over). **the ranks** ordinary soldiers, as distinct from officers. **to break rank/ ranks 1** (of soldiers) to fall out of line. **2** to lose solidarity. **to close ranks** to maintain solidarity. **to keep rank** (of soldiers) to remain in line. **to pull rank** to take precedence by virtue of higher rank, sometimes unfairly. **to rise from the ranks 1** (of a soldier) to be promoted from the ranks, to receive a commission. **2** to achieve success by one's own efforts. **to take rank with** to be placed on a level or be ranked with. **rank and file** *n.* (*often constr. as pl.*) **1** common soldiers. **2** (*fig.*) ordinary people. **rank and filer** *n.* **ranker** *n.* **1** a soldier in the ranks. **2** a commissioned officer promoted from the ranks. **3** a person who disposes or arranges in ranks. **ranking** *a.* **1** (*N Am.*) highly placed, prominent. **2** (*W Ind., sl.*) stylish, exciting. ~*n.* a position on a scale of excellence. [F *ranc* (now *rang*), prob. from OHG *hring, hrinc,* RING[1]]

rank[2] (rangk) *a.* **1** excessively luxuriant in growth, over-fertile, over-abundant. **2** rancid, offensive, strong, evil-smelling. **3** indecent, obscene. **4** strongly marked, thorough, flagrant, arrant, utter. **5** coarse, gross. **6** complete, total (*a rank outsider*). ~*adv.* rankly. **rankly** *adv.* **rankness** *n.* [OE *ranc,* cp. Dut. *rank,* Icel. *rakka,* straight, slender]

rankle (rang´kəl) *v.i.* **1** to continue to cause irritation, anger or bitterness. **2** (of a wound etc.) to be inflamed, to fester. [OF *rancler,* from *rancle, drancle,* an eruption or sore, med. L *dracunculus,* dim. of *draco,* DRAGON]

ransack (ran´sak) *v.t.* **1** to pillage, to plunder. **2** to search thoroughly. **ransacker** *n.* [Icel. *rannsaka* (*rann,* house, *sœkja,* to seek, cogn. with OE *sēcan,* SEEK)]

ransom (ran´səm) *n.* **1** a sum of money demanded or paid for the release of a person from captivity or for goods captured by an enemy. **2** release from captivity in return for such a payment. ~*v.t.* **1** to redeem from captivity or obtain the restoration of (property) by paying a sum of money. **2** to demand or exact a ransom for, to hold to ransom. **3** to release in return for a ransom. **4** to redeem from sin, to atone for. **to hold to ransom** to keep in confinement until a ransom is paid. **ransomable** *a.* **ransomer** *n.* **ransomless** *a.* [OF *ranson* (F *rançon*), L *redemptiōnem,* nom. *-tio,* REDEMPTION]

rant (rant) *v.i.* **1** to use loud, bombastic or violent language. **2** to declaim or preach in a theatrical or noisy fashion. ~*v.t.* to declaim or utter loudly or theatrically. ~*n.* **1** bombastic or violent declamation. **2** a tirade, a noisy declamation. **3** inflated talk. **to rant and rave** to express anger in a loud uncontrolled manner. **ranter** *n.* **1** a person who rants. **2** a declamatory preacher. **3** (*derog.*) a Primitive Methodist (in allusion to the declamatory nature of their preaching). **ranterism** *n.* **ranting** *a.* **rantingly** *adv.* [MDut. *randten, ranten,* cp. G *ranzen,* to spring or dance about]

ranula (ran´ūlə) *n.* (*pl.* **ranulas**) (*Med.*) a cystic tumour under the tongue. **ranular** *a.* [L *rānula,* dim. of *rāna,* frog]

ranunculus (rənŭngk´ūləs) *n.* (*pl.* **ranunculuses, ranunculi** (-lī)) a plant of the genus *Ranunculus,* typified by the buttercup. **ranunculaceous** (-ā´shəs) *a.* relating or belonging to the Ranunculaceae, a family of plants including the buttercup. [L, dim. of *rāna,* frog]

RAOC *abbr.* Royal Army Ordnance Corps.

rap[1] (rap) *v.t.* (*pres.p.* **rapping,** *past, p.p.* **rapped**) **1** to strike with a slight, sharp blow. **2** to strike smartly. **3** to rebuke. **4** (*usu. with out*) to utter in a quick, abrupt way. ~*v.i.* **1** to strike a sharp, quick blow, esp. at a door. **2** to make a sharp, quick sound like a light blow. **3** (*sl.*) to talk. **4** to perform a rap or rap music. ~*n.* **1** a slight, sharp blow. **2** a sound like the blow from a knocker, the knuckles etc. on a door. **3** a similar sound made by some agency as a means of communicating messages at a spiritualistic séance. **4** a sharp rebuke. **5** (*coll.*) blame, punishment. **6** (*sl.*) an informal talk, chat. **7 a** a rhythmic, often impromptu monologue, over music. **b** (*also* **rap music**) a style of popular music characterized by a heavy, rhythmic beat over which a rap is recited. **8** (*esp. N Am., sl.*) a legal or criminal charge. **to beat the rap** (*N Am., sl.*) to be acquitted of a crime, to escape punishment. **to rap on the knuckles** to reprove, reprimand. **to rap over the knuckles** to reprove, reprimand. **to take the rap** (*coll.*) to take the blame for another. **rapper** *n.* **1** a person who raps. **2** a spirit-rapper. **3** a door-knocker. **4** a performer of a rap or rap music. **rapping** *n.* the art of performing rhythmic monologues, esp. to music. [prob. imit., cp. Swed. *rappa,* to beat, G *rappeln,* to rattle]

rap[2] (rap) *n.* (*with a neg.*) the least amount. **not worth a rap** worthless. [orig. a counterfeit Irish coin passing for a halfpenny (prob. from Ir. *ropaire,* robber)]

rapacious (rəpā´shəs) *a.* **1** grasping, extortionate. **2** given to plundering or seizing by force, predatory. **3** (of animals) living on food seized by force. **rapaciously** *adv.* **rapaciousness** *n.* **rapacity** (-pas´-) *n.* [L *rapax -pācis,* from *rapere,* to seize, see RAPE[1]]

rape[1] (rāp) *v.t.* **1** to force to have sexual intercourse, to commit rape on. **2** (*fig.*) to despoil, to violate. **3** †to seize, to carry off. ~*n.* **1** penetrative sexual intercourse with someone, usu. a woman, against the person's will. **2** (*fig.*) violation, despoiling (e.g. of the countryside). **3** †seizing or carrying off by force. **raper** *n.* **rapist** *n.* a person who commits rape. [prob. from L *rapere,* to seize]

rape[2] (rāp) *n.* a plant, *Brassica napus,* allied to the turnip, grown as food for animals and for its seed which yields oil. **rape-cake** *n.* the compressed seeds and husks of rape after the oil has been expressed, used for feeding cattle and as manure. **rape-oil, rapeseed oil** *n.* oil obtained from rapeseed, used in cooking and as a lubricant. **rapeseed** *n.* the seed of the rape plant. [L *rāpum, rāpa,* turnip]

rape[3] (rāp) *n.* **1** the refuse stems and skins of grapes after the wine has been expressed, used to make vinegar. **2** a large vessel used in making vinegar. [F *râpe,* med. L *raspa*]

rape[4] (rāp) *n.* (*Hist.*) any of six divisions of the county of Sussex. [prob. from OE, etym. uncertain]

Raphaelesque (rafāelesk´), **Raffaelesque** *a.* after the style of the Italian painter Raphael, 1483–1520. **Raphaelism** *n.* the idealistic principles of Raphael in painting. **Raphaelite** (-līt) *n.* [cp. PRE-RAPHAELITE (under PRE- (+ R– WORDS))]

raphania (rəfā´niə) *n.* (*dated*) a form of the poisoning ergotism, supposed to be due to the use of grain containing seeds of wild radish. [L, from Gr. *raphanos,* radish]

raphe (rā´fē) *n.* (*Biol.*) **1** a seam-like suture or line of union. **2** a median line or rib. **3** a fibrovascular cord connecting the hilum of an ovule with the base of the nucleus. [mod. L and Gr.]

raphia RAFFIA.

raphide (rā´fīd), **raphis** (-fis) *n.* (*pl.* **raphides** (-fidēz)) (*Bot.*) any of numerous needle-shaped transparent crystals, usu. of calcium oxalate, found in the cells of plants. [Gr. *raphis -idos,* needle]

rapid (rap´id) *a.* **1** very swift, quick, speedy. **2** done, acting, moving or completed in a very short time. **3**

descending steeply. *~n.* (*usu. pl.*) a sudden descent in a stream, with a swift current. **rapid eye movement** *n.* the rapid movement of the eyes under closed eyelids which usu. occurs during the dreaming phase of sleep. **rapid-fire** *a.* 1 (of guns) quick-firing. 2 done, occurring etc. in rapid succession. **rapid-firer** *n.* **rapidity** (-pid´-), **rapidness** *n.* **rapidly** *adv.* **rapid transit** *n.* (*N Am.*) fast passenger transport, usu. by underground, in urban areas. [L *rapidus*, from *rapere*, to seize, see RAPE[1]]

rapier (rā´piə) *n.* a light, narrow sword, used only in thrusting. *~a.* sharp, penetrating (*rapier wit*). **rapierlike** *a.* [F *rapière*, etym. uncertain]

rapine (rap´īn) *n.* (*formal or poet.*) 1 the act of plundering or carrying off by force. 2 plunder, spoliation, robbery. [F *rapine*, L *rapīna*, from *rapere*, to seize]

rapist RAPE[1].

rapparee (rapərē´) *n.* (*Hist.*) an Irish irregular soldier, freebooter or robber, esp. during the late 17th and the 18th cents. [Ir. *rapaire*, a small pike, a robber]

rappee (rəpē´) *n.* a coarse kind of snuff. [F *râpé*, from *râper*, to RASP]

rappel (rəpel´) *n.* 1 abseiling. 2 (*Hist.*) the beat of a drum calling soldiers to arms. *~v.i.* (*pres.p.* **rappelling,** *past, p.p.* **rappelled**) to abseil. [F, from *rappeler*, to recall, as REPEAL]

rapper, rapping RAP[1].

rapport (rəpaw´) *n.* 1 correspondence, sympathetic relationship, agreement, harmony. 2 communication via a spiritualist. **rapporteur** (rapawtœ´) *n.* a person responsible for carrying out an investigation and presenting a report on it to a higher committee. [F, from *rapporter* (RE-, AP-[1], *porter*, L *portāre*, to carry)]

rapprochement (raprosh´mã) *n.* reconciliation, re-establishment of friendly relations, esp. between nations. [F, from *rapprocher*]

rapscallion (rapskal´iən) *n.* (*dated or facet.*) a rascal, a scamp, a good-for-nothing. [earlier RASCALLION (under RASCAL)]

rapt (rapt) *a.* 1 transported, carried away by one's thoughts or emotions, enraptured. 2 absorbed, engrossed. **raptly** *adv.* **raptness** *n.* [L *raptus*, p.p. of *rapere*, to seize, see RAPE[1]]

raptor (rap´tə) *n.* a bird of prey. **raptorial** (-taw´ri-) *a.* 1 catching and feeding on prey, predatory. 2 of or relating to a bird of prey. 3 (of a bird's talons) adapted for seizing prey. *~n.* a predatory animal or esp. bird. **raptorious** *a.* [L, plunderer, from *rapere*, as RAPT]

rapture (rap´chə) *n.* 1 ecstasy, transport, ecstatic joy. 2 (*pl.*) a fit or transport of delight. 3 †the act of being transported from one place or level of existence to another, esp. from an earthly existence to heaven or a state of divine knowledge. **raptured** *a.* **rapturist** *n.* an enthusiast. **rapturous** *a.* **rapturously** *adv.* **rapturousness** *n.* [RAPT, -URE]

rara avis (rahrə ah´vis, reərə ā´vis) *n.* (*pl.* **rarae aves** (-rē, -vēz)) a rarity, something very rarely met with. [L, rare bird]

rare[1] (reə) *a.* 1 exceptional, seldom existing or occurring, not often met with, unusual, scarce, uncommon. 2 especially excellent, singularly good, choice, first-rate. 3 (esp. of the atmosphere) of sparse, tenuous, thin or porous substance, not dense. **rare bird** *n.* RARA AVIS. **rare earth** *n.* 1 an oxide of a lanthanide. 2 (*also* **rare-earth element, rare-earth metal**) a lanthanide. **rare gas** *n.* an inert gas. **rarely** *adv.* 1 seldom. 2 exceptionally. 3 remarkably well. **rareness** *n.* **rarity** (reə´riti) *n.* (*pl.* **rarities**) 1 the quality or state of being rare, rareness. 2 a rare thing or person, esp. a thing of exceptional value through being rare. [L *rārus*]

rare[2] (reə) *a.* 1 (of meat) half-cooked, underdone. 2 (of eggs) soft. [var. of *rear*, OE *hrēr*]

rarebit (reə´bit) *n.* WELSH RABBIT (under WELSH). [corr. of RABBIT, after RARE[1]]

raree-show (reə´rēshō) *n.* 1 a show, a spectacle, a carnival. 2 a show carried about in a box, a peep-show. [corr. of RARE[1], SHOW]

rarefy (reə´rifī), **rarify** *v.t.* (*3rd pers. sing. pres.* **rarefies, rarifies,** *pres.p.* **rarefying, rarifying,** *past, p.p.* **rarefied, rarified**) 1 to make rare, thin, porous or less dense and solid. 2 to expand without adding to the substance of. 3 (*fig.*) to purify, to refine, to make less gross. *~v.i.* to become less dense. **rarefaction** (-fak´shən), **rarefication** (-fikā´shən) *n.* **rarefactive** (-fak´-) *a.* **rarefiable** *a.* **rarefied** *a.* 1 thin. 2 exalted. [obs. F *raréfier*, L *rārēfacere* (*rārus*, RARE[1], *facere*, to make)]

rareripe (reə´rīp) *a.* (*N Am.*) ripening early. *~n.* (*N Am.*) an early fruit or vegetable, esp. a variety of peach or an onion that ripens early. [var. of RATHE-RIPE (under RATHE)]

rarify RAREFY.

raring (reə´ring) *a.* ready, eager. **raring to go** eager to get started. [REAR[2]]

RAS *abbr.* 1 Royal Agricultural Society. 2 Royal Astronomical Society.

ras (ras) *n.* an Ethiopian governor or administrator. [Arab.]

☒ **rasberry** common misspelling of RASPBERRY.

rasbora (razbaw´rə) *n.* (*pl.* **rasboras**) any of a genus, *Rasbora*, of small, brightly coloured cyprinid fishes from tropical Asia and E Africa, popular for aquariums. [etym. uncertain]

rascal (ras´kəl, rahs´-) *n.* 1 a mischievous or slightly naughty person or animal, esp. a child (*used playfully or affectionately*). 2 a mean rogue, a tricky, dishonest or contemptible fellow, a knave, a scamp. *~†a.* worthless, low, mean. **rascaldom** *n.* (*dated*) **rascality** (-kal´-) *n.* (*pl.* **rascalities**). **rascallion** (-kal´yən) *n.* (*dated*) a rascal. **rascally** *a.* dishonest, contemptible. *~adv.* in a dishonest manner. [OF *rascaille*, *rescaille* (F *racaille*), rabble, dregs, outcasts]

raschel (rah´shəl, rahshel´) *n.* a type of knitted fabric, often with open patterns. [G *Raschelmaschine*, from Elisa Félix *Rachel*, 1821–58, French actress]

rase RAZE.

rash[1] (rash) *a.* 1 hasty, precipitate, impetuous, venturesome. 2 reckless, thoughtless, acting or done without reflection. **rashly** *adv.* **rashness** *n.* [cp. Dan. and Swed. *rask*, Dut. and G *rasch*, quick, vigorous]

rash[2] (rash) *n.* 1 an eruption of spots or patches on the skin. 2 a series of unwelcome, unexpected events. [perh. from MF *rasche* (F *rache*)]

rasher (rash´ə) *n.* a thin slice of bacon or ham for frying. [perh. from obs. *rash*, to cut, var. of RAZE, or rel. to RASH[1], with the sense rashly or hastily cooked]

raskolnik (raskol´nik) *n.* a dissenter from the Orthodox or Greek Church in Russia. [Rus., a schismatic]

rasorial (rəsaw´riəl) *a.* of, relating to or being a bird (e.g. the common fowl) having toes ending in strong claws for scratching up seeds etc. from the ground. [L *rāsor*, from *rādere*, to scrape, see RAZE]

rasp (rahsp) *v.t.* 1 to rub down, scrape or grate with a coarse, rough implement. 2 to file with a rasp. 3 to utter in harsh or grating tones. 4 to irritate, to grate upon (feelings etc.). *~v.i.* 1 to rub, to grate. 2 to make a grating sound. *~n.* 1 an instrument like a coarse file with projections or raised teeth for scraping away surface material. 2 a harsh, grating noise. **raspatory** *n.* (*pl.* **raspatories**) a rasp for scraping the outer membrane from bones etc. **rasper** *n.* 1 a rasp, scraper, a rasping-machine. 2 (*coll.*) a difficult fence in hunting. **rasping, raspy** *a.* **raspingly** *adv.* **raspings** *n.pl.* crisp dried or browned breadcrumbs. [OF *rasper* (F *râper*), from Gmc. (cp. OHG *raspōn*, G *raspeln*)]

raspberry (rahz´bəri) *n.* (*pl.* **raspberries**) 1 the fruit of various species of *Rubus*, esp. *R. idaeus*, consisting of red or sometimes white or yellow drupes set on a conical receptacle. 2 a shrub that bears raspberries. 3 (*coll.*) a rude derisive sound made with the lips. 4 a pinkish to purplish-red colour. **raspberry cane** *n.* a long woody shoot of a raspberry plant. **raspberry-vinegar** *n.* a sweetened vinegar prepared from raspberry juice. [obs. *rasp, raspis*, perh. rel. to RAPE³]

rasse (ras´i, ras) *n.* a feline carnivore allied to the civet, inhabiting S and SE Asia. [Javanese *rase*]

Rastafarian (rastəfeə´riən) *n.* a member of the religious and political, largely Jamaican, sect which believes Haile Selassie, the former Emperor of Ethiopia, to be God. ~*a.* of or relating to Rastafarians or Rastafarianism. **Rasta** (ras´-) *n., a.* Rastafarian. **Rastaman** (ras´-) *n.* (*pl.* **Rastamen**) a Rastafarian. **Rastafarianism** *n.* [*Ras Tafari*, title of Haile Selassie]

raster (ras´tə) *n.* the pattern of scanning lines which appears as a patch of light on a television screen and which reproduces the image. **rasterize, rasterise** *v.t.* to convert (a digitized image) into a pattern of signals which can be displayed on a screen. **rasterization** (-zā´shən) *n.* **rasterizer** *n.* [L *rastrum*, rake]

rat (rat) *n.* 1 any of several rodents of the genus *Rattus* that are similar to but larger than mice, esp. the black rat, *R. rattus*, and *R. norvegicus*, the grey, brown or Norway rat. 2 any of various similar or related rodents. 3 a person who is considered to have deserted their party or friends, a turncoat. 4 (*coll.*) a contemptible person. 5 (*coll.*) a worker who works for less than the trade-union rate of wages or who stands aloof from or works during a strike, a blackleg. ~*v.i.* (*pres.p.* **ratting,** *past, p.p.* **ratted**) 1 to hunt or kill rats (esp. of dogs). 2 (*coll.*) to play the rat in politics, in a strike etc. **to rat on** to betray, to divulge secret information, to inform against. **to smell a rat** to be suspicious. **rat-arsed** *a.* (*sl.*) drunk. **ratbag** *n.* (*sl.*) a disagreeable or despicable person. **rat-catcher** *n.* a person who earns a living by ridding buildings etc. of rats. **ratfink** *n.* (*chiefly N Am., sl.*) a contemptible or dislikable person. **rat kangaroo** *n.* any kangaroo-like marsupial of the family Potoroidea, about the size of a rabbit. **rat race** *n.* the continual competitive scramble of everyday life. **rat-run** *n.* a minor road or route of minor roads used by drivers to avoid traffic congestion during a rush hour. **rats!** *int.* (*sl.*) an exclamation of incredulity or derision. **ratsbane** *n.* poison for rats. **rat-snake** *n.* any of various snakes of the family Colubridae which prey on rats. **rat's-tail** *n.* a thing, esp. a file, like the tail of a rat. **rat-tail** *n.* 1 the grenadier fish. 2 a horse's tail with little or no hair. 3 a horse with such a tail. 4 a disease in horses in which the hair of the tail is lost. 5 an excrescence growing from the pastern to the middle of the shank of a horse. **rat-tailed** *a.* **rat-tail spoon, rat-tailed spoon** *n.* a spoon with a tapering, ridged moulding along the underside of the bowl. **ratted** *a.* (*sl.*) drunk. **ratter** *n.* 1 a person or animal, esp. a dog or cat, that catches rats. 2 a person who is considered to have deserted their party or friends. **rat-trap** *n.* 1 a trap for catching rats. 2 a rat-trap pedal. ~*a.* (of a bicycle pedal) consisting of two parallel notched or toothed steel plates. **ratty** *a.* (*comp.* **rattier,** *superl.* **rattiest**) 1 infested with or characteristic of rats. 2 (*sl.*) annoyed, ill-tempered. 3 (*coll.*) unkempt, untidy, shabby. **rattily** *adv.* **rattiness** *n.* [OE *ræt* (cp. Dut. *rat*, G *Ratz*, F *rat*)]

rata (rah´tə) *n.* either of two large New Zealand forest trees, *Metrosideros robusta* and *M. lucida*, belonging to the myrtle family, having beautiful crimson flowers and yielding hard red timber. [Maori]

ratable RATEABLE (under RATE¹).

ratafia (ratəfē´ə) *n.* 1 a liqueur or cordial flavoured with the kernels of cherry, peach, almond or other kinds of fruit. 2 a sweet almond-flavoured biscuit eaten with this. [F, etym. uncertain]

ratal RATE¹.

ratan RATTAN¹.

ratany RHATANY.

rataplan (rat´əplan) *n.* a noise like the rapid beating of a drum. ~*v.t.* (*pres.p.* **rataplanning,** *past, p.p.* **rataplanned**) 1 to beat (a drum). 2 to beat out (a tune) on or as if on a drum. ~*v.i.* to make a rataplan on a drum. [F, imit.]

ratatat, rat-a-tat RAT-TAT.

ratatouille (ratətwē´) *n.* a vegetable casserole from Provence, France, made with aubergines, tomatoes, peppers etc., stewed slowly in olive oil. [F *touiller*, to stir]

ratch (rach) *n.* a ratchet or ratchet-wheel. **ratchet** (-it) *n.* 1 a wheel or bar with inclined angular teeth, between which a pawl drops, permitting motion in one direction only. 2 the pawl or detent that drops between the teeth of a ratchet-wheel. ~*v.t.* (*pres.p.* **ratcheting,** *past, p.p.* **ratcheted**) 1 to furnish with a ratchet. 2 to move as if by a ratchet. ~*v.i.* to operate by or as by a ratchet. **ratchet-bar** *n.* a bar with teeth into which a pawl drops to prevent motion in more than one direction. **ratchet screwdriver** *n.* a screwdriver operated by pushing the handle in and out and having a ratchet mechanism that causes the bit to turn in one direction only. **ratchet-wheel** *n.* a wheel with a toothed edge. [etym. uncertain, cp. G *Ratsche*, also F *rochet*, whence prob. the form *ratchet*]

rate¹ (rāt) *n.* 1 the proportional measure of something in relation to some other thing, ratio, comparative amount, degree etc. 2 a standard by which any quantity or value is fixed. 3 a price, cost, charge, value etc. 4 relative speed of movement, change, progress etc. 5 (*usu. pl.*) a sum levied upon commercial property and (formerly) dwellings for local purposes. 6 rank or class. ~*v.t.* 1 to estimate the value or relative worth of. 2 to assign a value, rank, position on a scale etc. to. 3 to consider, to regard as. 4 to merit, to deserve. 5 (*coll.*) to think highly of. 6 a to assess for local rates. b to subject to payment of local rates. 7 to fix the rank of (a seaman etc.). ~*v.i.* to be rated or ranked (as). **at any rate** 1 in any case. 2 even so. **at a rate of knots** KNOT¹. **at that rate** if that is so, typical or true. **at this rate** if this is so, typical or true. **ratal** *n.* (*Hist.*) the amount on which local rates were assessed. **rateable, ratable** *a.* 1 liable to be rated, subject to assessment for local rates. 2 capable of being rated or valued. 3 proportional, estimated proportionally. **rateability** (-bil´-) *n.* **rateable value** *n.* the estimated value of a commercial property and formerly a dwelling, used annually to assess the rates chargeable on the property. **rateably** *adv.* **rate-cap** *v.t.* (*pres.p.* **rate-capping,** *past, p.p.* **rate-capped**) (*Hist.*) to restrict the amount of money that may be levied in rates by (a local authority). **rate-capping** *n.* **rate of exchange** *n.* the rate at which bills drawn upon drawees in a foreign country may be sold where they were drawn. **ratepayer** *n.* a person who was formerly liable to pay rates; a householder. **rater** *n.* 1 a person who rates or assesses. 2 (*in comb.* as *first-rater*) a ship or boat, esp. a yacht, of a specified rate. **rate support grant** *n.* (*Hist.*) the money given to local authorities by central government to supplement the amount raised in rates. [OF from med. L *rata*, fem. of L *ratus*, p.p. of *rērī*, to think, to judge]

rate² (rāt) *v.t.* to chide angrily, to scold. ~*v.i.* to chide, to storm (at). [etym. uncertain]

rate³ RET.

ratel (rā´təl) *n.* a nocturnal carnivore of the genus *Mellivora*, allied to the badger, esp. *M. capensis*, the honey badger of W and S Africa which feeds on small animals and honey, and *M. indicus* from India. [Afrikaans, etym. uncertain]

ratfink RAT.

rath[1] (rahth) *n.* a prehistoric Irish hill fort or earthwork. [Ir.]

rath[2] RATHE.

rathe (rādh), †**rath** (rahth) *adv.* (*poet.*) early, soon, quickly. ~*a.* **1** coming, appearing, ripening etc. early or before the usual time. **2** quick, speedy. **3** of or relating to early morning. **rathe-ripe** *a.* **1** ripening early. **2** precocious. ~*n.* an early kind of apple, pea etc. [OE *hrathe*, adv. from *hræd*, a., quick]

rather (rah´dhə) *adv.* **1** more readily or willingly, preferably, for choice, sooner. **2** with more reason, more properly, rightly, truly or accurately. **3** in a greater degree, to a greater extent. **4** to a certain extent. **5** slightly, somewhat. **6** on the contrary. **7** (*coll.*) very much, assuredly, yes, certainly. **had/ would rather** would prefer to. **the rather** by so much the more. **ratherish, ratherly** *adv.* (*dial.*) somewhat. [comp. of RATHE]

Usage note See note under PREFER.

ratify (rat´ifī) *v.t.* (*3rd pers. sing. pres.* **ratifies,** *pres.p.* **ratifying,** *past, p.p.* **ratified**) to confirm, to establish or make valid (by formal consent or approval). **ratifiable** *a.* **ratification** (-fikā´shən) *n.* **ratifier** *n.* [F *ratifier*, med. L *ratificāre* (*ratus*, RATE[1], *-ficāre, facere*, to make)]

ratine RATTEEN.

rating[1] (rā´ting) *n.* **1** the act of assessing, judging, ranking etc. **2** a classification according to grade, a rank; relative standing or position. **3** an estimate of the financial standing or creditworthiness of a person or business. **4** (*pl.*) an evaluation of the popularity of radio or television programmes based on estimated audience size. **5 a** an ordinary seaman. **b** the class or grade of a seaman as stated in the ship's books. **6** (*Hist.*) the amount fixed as a local rate. **7** the operating limit of an electrical apparatus expressed in watts etc. **8** the tonnage class of a racing yacht.

rating[2] (rā´ting) *n.* a scolding, a harsh reprimand.

ratio (rā´shiō) *n.* (*pl.* **ratios**) the relation of one quantity or magnitude to another of a similar kind, measured by the number of times one is contained by the other, either integrally or fractionally. [L, as RATE[1]]

ratiocinate (rashios´ināt) *v.i.* (*formal*) **1** to reason or argue. **2** to deduce consequences from premises or by means of syllogisms. **ratiocination** (-nā´shən) *n.* **ratiocinative** (-ətiv), **ratiocinatory** (-ətawri, -ətri) *a.* **ratiocinator** *n.* [L *ratiōcinātus*, p.p. of *ratiōcinārī*, as RATIO]

ration (rash´ən) *n.* **1** a fixed statutory allowance of food or other provisions in a time of shortage (e.g. war). **2** (*usu. pl.*) a fixed daily allowance of food, a portion allotted or allowed to an individual. **3** (*pl.*) provisions, esp. food. ~*v.t.* **1** to supply with rations, to put on fixed rations. **2** to limit to a fixed allowance or amount. **3** to distribute in fixed, esp. small, quantities. **ration book, ration card** *n.* a book or card containing coupons etc. authorizing the holder to draw a ration. [F, from L RATIO]

rational (rash´ənəl) *a.* **1** having the faculty of reasoning, endowed with mental faculties. **2** agreeable to reasoning, reasonable, sensible, not foolish, not extravagant. **3** based on or conforming to what can be tested by reason. **4** (of a number, quantity etc.) expressible as the ratio of two integers. ~*n.* a rational number. **rational dress** *n.* (*Hist.*) a style of dress (e.g. knickerbockers) worn by some women in the late 19th cent. and regarded as more sensible than the conventional one. **rationale** (rashənahl´) *n.* **1** a statement or exposition of reasons or principles. **2** the logical basis or fundamental reason (of anything). **rational horizon** *n.* CELESTIAL HORIZON (under CELESTIAL). **rationalism** (rash´-) *n.* **1** reliance on reason rather than intuition, religious authority etc. **2** the determination of all questions of belief, esp. in religious matters, by the reason, rejecting supernatural revelation. **3** the doctrine that reason supplies certain principles for the interpretation of phenomena that cannot be derived from experience alone. **rationalist** *n.* **rationalistic** (-lis´-) *a.* **rationalistically** *adv.* **rationality** (-nal´-) *n.* (*pl.* **rationalities**) **1** the quality of being rational. **2** the power or use of reasoning. **3** reasonableness. **4** a rational opinion, practice etc. **rationalize, rationalise** *v.t.* **1 a** to offer a rational explanation for, esp. to justify, explain or excuse (behaviour, actions etc.) by offering plausible reasons. **b** (*Psych.*) to supply a conscious and apparently rational reason for (one's behaviour etc.) whilst suppressing an unconscious and less rational motive. **2** to render rational or reasonable. **3** to reorganize (e.g. a business) so as to make more efficient and economic. **4** to clear (an equation etc.) of radical signs. **5** to interpret as a rationalist. ~*v.i.* **1** to provide plausible explanations for behaviour, actions etc. **2** to think or act as a rationalist. **rationalization** (-zā´shən) *n.* **rationalizer** *n.* **rationally** *adv.* **rationalness** *n.* [L *ratiōnālis*, as RATION]

ratite (rat´īt) *a.* (*Zool.*) of or belonging to the group of flightless birds with a keelless sternum and abortive wings, such as the ostrich, emu, cassowary, kiwi, moa etc. ~*n.* a bird of this group, a flightless bird. [L *ratis*, raft, -ITE[1]]

ratline (rat´lin), **ratlin, ratling** (-ling) *n.* any of the small ropes extended across the shrouds on each side of a mast, forming steps or rungs. [etym. uncertain, perh. rel. to OF *raalingue*, small cords strengthening a sail etc.]

ratoon (rətoon´), **rattoon** *n.* a sprout from the root of a sugar cane that has been cut down. ~*v.i.* to send up ratoons. ~*v.t.* to cut down so as to encourage growth. [Sp. *retoño*, shoot, sprout]

ratsbane RAT.

rattan[1] (rətan´, rat´-), **ratan** *n.* **1** any of various species of Malaysian climbing palms of the genus *Calamus* with long, thin pliable stems. **2** the stem or part of a stem of such a plant. **3** a switch or walking stick of this material. **4** (*collect.*) such stems used for wickerwork etc. [Malay *rōtan*, from *rāut*, to pare]

rattan[2] (rətan´) *n.* the beat of a drum, a rataplan.

rat-tat (rat·tat´), **ratatat** (ratətat´), **rat-a-tat, ratatat-tat** (ratətat·tat´), **rat-a-tat-tat** *n.* a rapid knocking sound as of a knocker on a door. [imit.]

ratted RAT.

ratteen (rətēn´), **ratine** *n.* a thick quilted or twilled woollen material. [F *ratine*, etym. uncertain]

ratten (rat´ən) *v.t.* to annoy or molest by destroying, injuring or taking away the tools or machinery of (a worker or employer) in a trade-union dispute etc. ~*v.i.* to practise this method. **rattener** *n.* [etym. uncertain, perh. var. of obs. *ratton*, OF *raton*, RAT]

ratter RAT.

rattle (rat´əl) *v.i.* **1** to make a rapid succession of sharp noises, as of things clattered together or shaken in a hollow vessel. **2** to talk rapidly, noisily or foolishly. **3** to move, go or act with a rattling noise. **4** to run, ride or drive rapidly. ~*v.t.* **1** to cause to make a rattling noise, to make (a window, door etc.) rattle. **2** to utter, recite, play etc. (off, away etc.) rapidly. **3** to stir up, to disconcert, to alarm, to frighten. **4** to cause to move quickly with noise, esp. to drive fast. ~*n.* **1** a rapid succession of sharp noises. **2** an instrument, esp. a child's toy, with which such sounds are made. **3** a rattling noise in the throat. **4** rapid, noisy or empty talk, chatter. **5** noise, bustle, racket, boisterous gaiety. **6** the horny articulated rings in the tail of the rattlesnake, which make a rattling noise. **7** a plant having seeds that rattle in their cases. **8** †an incessant chatterer. **to rattle one's dags** DAG. **rattlebag, rattlebox** *n.* a bag or box with loose things inside for rattling. **rattle-brain,**

rattle-head, rattle-pate *n.* (*coll.*) an empty-headed person, full of chatter. **rattle-brained, rattle-headed, rattle-pated** *a.* (*coll.*) giddy, wild, empty-headed. **rattler** *n.* **1** someone who or something which rattles. **2** (*coll.*) a rattlesnake. **3** (*sl.*) a first-rate specimen. **rattlesnake** *n.* any of various snakes of the American genera *Crotalus* or *Sistrurus*, having a tail furnished with a rattle. **rattletrap** *n.* (*coll.*) **1** a rickety object, esp. a vehicle. **2** (*pl.*) valueless articles, rubbishy curios. ~*a.* rickety, rubbishy. **rattling** *a.* **1** making a rapid succession of sharp noises. **2** (*coll.*) brisk, vigorous. **3** (*coll.*) first-rate, excellent. ~*adv.* (*coll.*) extremely, very (*a rattling good time*). **rattly** *a.* **rattliness** *n.* [ME *ratelen* (cp. Dut. *ratelen*, G *rasseln*)]

rattoon RATOON.

ratty RAT.

raucous (raw´kəs) *a.* hoarse, rough or harsh in sound. **raucity** (-si-) *n.* **raucously** *adv.* **raucousness** *n.* [L *raucus*]

raunchy (rawn´chi) *a.* (*comp.* **raunchier**, *superl.* **raunchiest**) (*coll.*) **1** earthy, sexual. **2** smutty. **3** (*esp. N Am.*) slovenly. **raunchily** *a.* **raunchiness** *n.* [etym. unknown]

raupo (row´pō) *n.* (*pl.* **raupos**) (*New Zeal.*) the giant bulrush, *Typha angustifolia*. [Maori]

rauwolfia (row·wool´fiə) *n.* (*pl.* **rauwolfias**) **1** any of several tropical flowering shrubs and trees of the SE Asian genus *Rauwolfia*. **2** the root of *R. serpentina*, which yields the drug reserpine. [Leonhard *Rauwolf*, d. 1596, German botanist]

ravage (rav´ij) *n.* **1** devastation, ruin, havoc, waste. **2** (*usu. pl.*) devastating effects. ~*v.t.* to devastate, to spoil, to pillage. ~*v.i.* to wreak havoc. **ravager** *n.* [F, from *ravir*, to RAVISH]

Usage note The verbs *ravage* and *ravish* should not be confused: *ravage* means to devastate, and *ravish* to rape.

rave[1] (rāv) *v.i.* **1** to wander in mind, to be delirious, to talk wildly, incoherently or irrationally. **2** to speak in a furious way (against, at etc.). **3** to be excited, to go into raptures (about etc.). **4** to act, move or dash furiously, to rage. **5** (*coll.*) to enjoy oneself wildly. ~*v.t.* to utter in a wild, incoherent or furious manner. ~*n.* **1** the act of raving. **2** extravagant enthusiasm (*a rave review*). **3** (*coll.*) (*also* **rave-up**) a very lively party. **4** an often large-scale party for dancing to fast, non-stop electronic music, typically held in the early hours of the morning in a marquee, disused building or outside. **5** (*sl.*) a fad, a fashion. **6** a raving sound as of the wind or sea. **7** (*sl.*) an infatuation. **raver** *n.* **1** (*coll.*) a person who leads a wild social life. **2** (*coll.*) a person who attends raves. **3** a frenzied or delirious person. **raving** *a.* **1** frenzied. **2** (*coll.*) marked (*a raving beauty*). ~*n.* **1** (*pl.*) extravagant, irrational utterances. **2** (*coll.*) fast, athletic dancing associated with the type of music (e.g. techno) played at raves. **ravingly** *adv.* [prob. from OF *raver*, var. of *rêver*, to dream (cp. REVERIE)]

rave[2] (rāv), †**rathe** (rādh) *n.* **1** (*pl.*) a cart-rail. **2** a framework added to the sides of a cart to enable a larger load to be carried. **3** a vertical sidepiece in a wagon, sleigh etc. [etym. uncertain]

ravel (rav´əl) *v.t.* (*pres.p.* **ravelling,** (*N Am.*) **raveling,** *past, p.p.* **ravelled,** (*N Am.*) **raveled**) **1** to entangle, to confuse, to complicate. **2** to untwist, to disentangle, to separate the component threads of. **3** to fray. ~*v.i.* **1** to become tangled. **2** to become untwisted, unravelled or unwoven. **3** to fray (out). **raveller,** (*N Am.*) **raveler** *n.* **ravelling,** (*N Am.*) **raveling** *n.* **1** the act of entangling, confusing etc. **2** the act of unravelling. **3** anything, such as a thread, separated in the process of unravelling. †**ravelly** *a.* **ravelment** *n.* [prob. from MDut. *ravelen*]

ravelin (rav´əlin) *n.* a detached outwork of a fortification with a parapet and ditch forming a salient angle in front of the plain wall of a larger work. [F, from It. *rivellino*, earlier *ravellino*]

raven[1] (rā´vən) *n.* a large, black, omnivorous bird, *Corvus corax*, of the crow family. ~*a.* resembling a raven in colour, glossy black. [OE *hræfn* (cp. Dut. *raaf*, G *Rabe*, Icel. *hragn*, Dan. *ravn*)]

raven[2] (rav´ən) *v.t.* (*chiefly poet.*) **1** to devour with voracity. **2** to ravage, to plunder. ~*v.i.* **1** to plunder. **2** to go about ravaging. **3** to prowl after prey. **4** to be ravenous. **5** to feed with voracity. **ravener** *n.* **ravening** *n.*, *a.* **raveningly** *adv.* [OF *raviner*, from L *rapīna*, RAPINE]

ravenous (rav´ənəs) *a.* **1** voracious, hungry, famished. **2** furiously rapacious, eager for gratification. **ravenously** *adv.* **ravenousness** *n.* [OF *ravineux*, as RAVEN[1]]

ravin (rav´in) *n.* (*poet.*) **1** plundering, rapine, spoliation, ravaging. **2** prey. [OF *ravine*, L *rapīna*, RAPINE]

ravine (rəvēn´) *n.* a long, deep hollow caused esp. by a torrent, a gorge, a narrow gully or cleft. **ravined** *a.* [F, orig. a torrent, as RAVIN]

raving RAVE[1].

ravioli (raviō´li) *n.* small pasta cases with a savoury filling. [It. dial. *raviolo*, little turnip]

ravish (rav´ish) *v.t.* **1** to violate, to rape. **2** to carry away, to enrapture, to transport (with pleasure etc.). **3** †to snatch away or carry off by force. **ravisher** *n.* **ravishing** *a.* enchanting, charming, entrancing, transporting, filling one with rapture. **ravishingly** *adv.* **ravishment** *n.* [F *raviss-*, pres.p. stem of *ravir*, L *rapere*, to seize, to snatch]

Usage note See note under RAVAGE.

raw (raw) *a.* **1** uncooked. **2** in the natural state. **3** not manufactured, processed or refined; requiring further industrial treatment. **4** not modified or adjusted (*raw data*). **5** (of spirits) not blended or diluted. **6** crude, untempered. **7** untrained, unskilled, inexperienced, undisciplined, immature, fresh. **8** having the skin off, having the flesh exposed, galled, inflamed, chafed. **9** sore or sensitive as if from chafing (*a raw throat*; *touched a raw nerve*). **10** (of weather) cold and damp, bleak. **11** (of a fabric edge) unhemmed. ~*n.* a raw place on the body, a sore, a gall. **in the raw 1** in its natural state. **2** naked. **to come the raw prawn** (*Austral., sl.*) to try to deceive. **to touch on the raw** to wound in a sensitive spot. **raw-boned** *a.* having bones scarcely covered with flesh, gaunt. **raw deal** *n.* (*coll.*) unfair treatment. **raw-head** *n.* (*dated*) a spectre or goblin. **raw-head and bloody-bones** *a.* (*dated*) denoting blood-and-thunder fiction etc. **rawhide** *n.* **1** untanned leather. **2** a whip made of this. **rawish** *a.* **rawly** *adv.* **raw material** *n.* the material of any manufacturing process. **rawness** *n.* **raw sienna** *n.* the yellowish-brown colour of untreated sienna. **raw silk** *n.* **1** natural and untreated silk fibre. **2** material made from untreated silk fibres. **raw umber** *n.* umber in the natural state; the colour of this. [OE *hrēaw* (cp. Dut. *raauw*, G *roh*, Icel. *hrār*, also L *crūdus*, *cruor*, blood, Gr. *kreas*, raw flesh)]

rawinsonde (rā´winsond) *n.* a hydrogen balloon which carries meteorological instruments to measure wind velocity. [*ra*dar, *win*d, radio*sonde*]

Rawlplug® (rawl´plŭg) *n.* a thin ridged or toothed tube, usu. of plastic, inserted in masonry to provide a fixing for a screw.

ray[1] (rā) *n.* **1** a line or beam of light proceeding from a radiant point. **2** (*often pl.*) a narrow beam of radiant energy or a stream of particles (*alpha rays*; *cosmic rays*). **3** a straight line along which radiant energy, esp. light or heat, is propagated. **4** (*fig.*) a gleam, a vestige or slight manifestation (of hope, enlightenment etc.). **5** any of a series of radiating lines or parts. **6** (*Math.*) a straight line extending from a point. 7 (*Bot.*) **a** the outer whorl of florets in a composite flower. **b** a wedge-shaped area of tissue running radially through the vascular tissue of a plant. 8 (*Zool.*) **a** any of the bony rods supporting the fin of a fish. **b** any of the radial parts of a starfish or similar animal. ~*v.t.* **1** to shoot out (rays), to radiate. **2** to adorn with rays. ~*v.i.* to issue or shine forth in rays. **rayed** *a.* **ray flower, ray floret** *n.* any of the small strap-shaped flowers in the flower head of some composite plants, such as the daisy. **ray fungus** *n.* an actinomycete bacterium which forms radiating filaments. **ray gun** *n.* in science fiction, a gun which sends out rays to kill or stun. **rayless** *a.* **raylet** *n.* a small ray. [OF *rai, ray,* nom. *rais,* L RADIUS]

ray[2] (rā) *n.* any of several large cartilaginous fish allied to the sharks, with a broad flat body, the eyes on the upper surface and a long, slender tail. [ME and OF *raye* (F *raie*), L *raia*]

ray[3] (rā), **re** (rā) *n.* **1** the second note of a major scale in the tonic sol-fa system of notation. **2** the note *D* in the fixed-doh system. [ME *re,* see GAMUT]

Rayah (rī´ə) *n.* (*Hist.*) a non-Muslim subject in Turkey. [Arab. *ra'ūjah,* flock, from *ra'ā,* to feed]

Raynaud's disease (rā´nōz) *n.* (*Med.*) a disorder of the circulatory system in which spasms in the blood vessels, often intensified by cold or stress, restrict the supply of blood to the fingers and toes resulting in discoloration, numbness and sometimes pain. [Maurice *Raynaud,* 1834–81, French physician]

rayon (rā´on) *n.* an artificial textile fibre or fabric made from cellulose. [F, from *rai,* RAY[1]]

raze (rāz), **rase** *v.t.* **1** to demolish, to level to the ground, to destroy. **2** to erase, to obliterate. **3** to scratch (out). **4** †to graze or shave. **razed** *a.* **razer** *n.* [F *raser,* pop. L *rāsāre,* freq. of L *rādere* (p.p. *rāsus*), to scrape]

razee (rəzē´) *n.* (*Hist.*) a vessel cut down to a fewer number of decks. ~*v.t.* (*pres.p.* **razeeing,** *past, p.p.* **razeed**) (*Hist.*) to reduce (a ship) in height thus. [F *rasée,* p.p. of *raser,* see RAZE]

razoo (rəzoo´) *n.* (*Austral., New Zeal., coll.*) an insignificant sum of money, a farthing. **not a brass razoo** not a farthing. [etym. unknown]

razor (rā´zə) *n.* a sharp-edged cutting instrument for shaving off the hair of the beard, head etc. ~*v.t.* **1** to shave with a razor. **2** to shave, to cut (down) close. **razorback** *n.* **1** an animal with a sharp back like a razor. **2** a rorqual. **3** a semi-wild pig of the south-eastern USA with a sharply ridged back. ~*a.* having a sharp back or ridge like a razor. **razorbacked** *a.* **razorbill** *n.* a bird with a bill like a razor, esp. the razor-billed auk, *Alca torda.* **razor-billed** *a.* **razor blade** *n.* a blade used in a razor, for cutting or shaving. **razor clam** *n.* (*N Am.*) a razor-shell. **razor cut** *n.* a haircut trimmed or shaped with a razor, esp. one tapering at the neck. ~*v.t.* (*pres.p.* **razor cutting,** *past, p.p.* **razor cut**) to cut or trim (hair) with a razor. **razor edge, razor's edge** *n.* **1** the edge of a razor. **2** a keen edge. **3** a sharp crest or ridge, as of a mountain. **4** a critical situation, a crisis. **5** a sharp line of demarcation, esp. between parties or opinions. **razor-edged** *a.* **razor-fish** *n.* (*pl. in general* **razor-fish,** *in particular* **razor-fishes**) a razor-shell. **razor-shell** *n.* a bivalve mollusc with a narrow, curved shell like the handle of a cut-throat razor. **razor-strop** *n.* a leather pad on which a razor is sharpened. **razor wire** *n.* strong wire set across with pieces of sharp metal, used for fences or on top of walls etc. [OF *rasor* (F *rasoir*), late L *rāsōrium,* from *rādere,* to RAZE]

razz (raz) *n.* (*chiefly N Am., sl.*) a sound of contempt, a raspberry. ~*v.t.* to jeer at, to heckle. [*razzberry,* corr. of RASPBERRY]

razzamatazz RAZZMATAZZ.

razzia (raz´iə) *n.* (*pl.* **razzias**) (*Hist.*) a foray or incursion for the purpose of capturing slaves etc., as practised by African Muslims. [F, from Algerian *ghāzīah,* var. of Arab. *ghazwah,* from *ghazw,* making war]

razzle-dazzle (raz´əldazəl) *n.* (*coll.*) **1** bewilderment, excitement, stir, bustle. **2** a spree. **3** noisy or showy fuss. **on the razzle** on a spree or binge, esp. involving excessive drinking. [DAZZLE]

razzmatazz (razmətaz´), **razzamatazz** (razə-) *n.* (*coll.*) **1** colourful, noisy, lively atmosphere or activities, razzle-dazzle. **2** insincere deceptive talk. [prob. from RAZZLE-DAZZLE]

Rb *chem. symbol* rubidium.

RC *abbr.* **1** Red Cross. **2** reinforced concrete. **3** Republic of China (IVR). **4** Reserve Corps. **5** Roman Catholic.

RCA *abbr.* **1** Central African Republic (IVR). **2** Radio Corporation of America. **3** Royal Canadian Academy. **4** Royal College of Art.

RCAF *abbr.* Royal Canadian Airforce.

RCB *abbr.* Republic of the Congo (IVR).

RCD *abbr.* residual current device.

RCH *abbr.* Republic of Chile (IVR).

RCM *abbr.* Royal College of Music.

RCMP *abbr.* Royal Canadian Mounted Police.

RCN *abbr.* **1** Royal Canadian Navy. **2** Royal College of Nursing.

RCO *abbr.* Royal College of Organists.

RCP *abbr.* Royal College of Physicians.

RCS *abbr.* **1** Royal College of Science. **2** Royal College of Surgeons. **3** Royal Corps of Signals.

RCT *abbr.* Royal Corps of Transport.

RCVS *abbr.* Royal College of Veterinary Surgeons.

RD *abbr.* **1** refer to drawer. **2** (Royal Naval) Reserve Decoration.

Rd *abbr.* Road.

rd *abbr.* **1** road. **2** rod. **3** rutherford.

RDA *abbr.* recommended daily allowance.

RDC *abbr.* (*Hist.*) Rural District Council.

RDF *abbr.* radio direction-finder.

RDX *abbr.* Research Department Explosive.

RE *abbr.* **1** religious education. **2** Royal Engineers.

Re *chem. symbol* rhenium.

re[1] (rā) *prep.* **1** in the matter of. **2** (*coll.*) as regards, about. [L, abl. of *rēs,* thing, matter, affair]

Usage note The use of *re* in the middle of a sentence for 'about' is sometimes disapproved of.

re[2] RAY[3].

re- (rē) *pref.* **1** again, again and again, afresh, anew, repeatedly. **2** back, backward, back again. **3** in return, mutually. **4** against, in opposition. **5** after, behind. **6** off, away, down. **7** UN-[1]. [L, back, again]

Usage note In its main productive use, *re-* usually forms hyphenated words where the second element begins with *e* (as *re-echo*), or where a solid form could be confused with another word (as *re-form* and *reform*).

're *contr.* are (*we're; they're; you're*).

re- (+ ab–ac words) reabsorb *v.t.* to absorb anew or again. **reabsorption** *n.* **reaccede** *v.i.* to accede anew or again. **reaccession** *n.* **reaccept** *v.t.* to accept again. **reacceptance** *n.* **reacclaim** *v.t.* to acclaim anew or again. **reacclamation** *n.* **reacclimatize, reacclimatise** *v.t.* to acclimatize anew or again. **reacclimatization** *n.* **reaccommodate** *v.t.* to accommodate or adjust afresh or again. **reaccommodation** *n.* **reaccuse** *v.t.* to accuse again. **reaccusation** *n.* **reaccustom** *v.t.* to accustom again. **reacidify** *v.t.* (*3rd pers. sing. pres.* **reacidifies,** *pres.p.* **reacidifying,** *past, p.p.* **reacidified**) to acidify afresh. **reacidification** *n.* **reacquaint** *v.t.* to make acquainted again. **reacquaintance** *n.* **reacquire** *v.t.* to acquire anew. **reacquisition** *n.* **re-act** (rēakt´) *v.t.* to act or perform again. **reactivate** *v.t.* to restore to a state of activity, to make functional or operational again. **reactivation** *n.*

reach[1] (rēch) *v.t.* 1 to stretch out, to extend. 2 to extend towards so as to touch, to extend as far as, to attain, to arrive at. 3 to make contact with, to communicate with. 4 to affect, to influence. 5 to hand, to deliver, to pass. ~*v.i.* 1 to reach out, to extend. 2 to reach or stretch out the hand. 3 to make a reaching effort, to put forth one's powers, to be extended so as to touch. 4 to have extent in time, space etc. 5 to attain (to). 6 (*Naut.*) to sail on a tack with the wind from the side. ~*n.* 1 the act or power of reaching. 2 extent, range, compass, power, attainment. 3 an unbroken stretch of water, as between two bends on a river. 4 (*Naut.*) the direction or distance travelled by a vessel on a tack. 5 the estimated number of people exposed to a marketing campaign or who select a particular radio or television programme or channel. **out of reach** unable to be reached or gained. **reachable** *a.* **reacher** *n.* **reaching** *a.* **reach-me-down** *a.* (of clothes) cheap ready-made or second-hand. ~*n.pl.* ready-made or second-hand clothes. [OE *rǣcan* (cp. Dut. *reiken*, G *reichen*]

†**reach**[2] (rēch) *v.i.* (*chiefly dial.*) to retch.

react (riakt´) *v.i.* 1 to act in response (to a stimulus etc.). 2 to act or tend in an opposite manner, direction etc. 3 to have a reciprocal effect, to act upon the agent. 4 to exert chemical action upon another substance, to undergo a chemical reaction. 5 to exert an equal and opposite force to that exerted by another body. ~*v.t.* (*Chem.*) to cause to react (with another substance). **reactance** *n.* the part of the opposition to the flow of an electric current that is due to capacitance or inductance in a circuit; the component of impedance that is not due to resistance. **reactant** *n.* a substance that takes part in a chemical reaction, esp. one that undergoes change. **reactive** *a.* 1 reacting or exhibiting reaction. 2 tending to react, liable to react readily. 3 occurring as a reaction, esp. produced in response to stress etc. (*reactive depression*). 4 of or relating to reactance. **reactively** *adv.* **reactivity** (-tiv´-), **reactiveness** *n.* **reactor** *n.* 1 a substance which undergoes a reaction. 2 NUCLEAR REACTOR (under NUCLEAR). 3 a vessel in which chemical reaction takes place. 4 a person sensitive to a given drug or medication. 5 a component that introduces reactance into an electrical circuit.

reaction (riak´shən) *n.* 1 the response of an organ etc. to stimulation. 2 a mental or emotional response. 3 reciprocal action. 4 contrary action or condition following the first effects of an action. 5 action in an opposite direction, esp. in politics after a reform movement, revolution etc. 6 an effect, esp. an adverse effect, produced in response to a drug, medical treatment etc. 7 the chemical action of one substance upon another, resulting in the formation of one or more new substances. 8 a process involving change within atomic nuclei. 9 the equal and opposite force exerted upon the agent by a body acted upon. 10 a phenomenon obtained from a three-electrode valve whereby a small voltage on the grid is strengthened by the amplified currents flowing in the anode circuit. **reactionary** *a.* involving or tending towards reaction, esp. political reaction, retrograde, conservative. ~*n.* (*pl.* **reactionaries**) a reactionary person. **reaction engine, reaction motor** *n.* an engine or motor which develops thrust by expelling gas at high speed. **reactionism** *n.* **reactionist** *n.* **reaction time** *n.* the length of time between stimulation and response. **reaction turbine** *n.* a turbine where the working fluid is accelerated through expansion in the static nozzles and the rotor blades.

read (rēd) *v.t.* (*past, p.p.* **read** (red)) 1 to perceive and understand the meaning of (printed, written or other characters, signs, symbols, significant features etc.); to peruse. 2 to reproduce mentally, vocally or instrumentally (words, notes etc. conveyed by symbols etc.). 3 to discover the meaning of by observation; to interpret, to explain. 4 to assume as implied in a statement etc. 5 to accurately deduce or comprehend. 6 to learn or ascertain by reading. 7 to study by reading. 8 to bring into a specified condition by reading. 9 to study for an examination. 10 a (of a meteorological instrument etc.) to indicate or register. b to take a reading from (such an instrument). 11 to hear and understand a message transmitted by radio from (a person). 12 (*Comput.*) to retrieve copy or transfer (data) from a storage device, such as magnetic tape. 13 to substitute as a (correct or preferred) reading (*read mouse for moose*). ~*v.i.* 1 to follow or interpret the meaning of a book etc. 2 to pronounce written or printed matter aloud. 3 to render written music vocally or instrumentally (well, easily etc.). 4 to acquire information (about). 5 to study by reading. 6 to mean or be capable of interpretation (in a certain way etc.). 7 to sound or affect (well, ill etc.) when perused or uttered. ~*n.* 1 an act of reading, a perusal. 2 something to be read (*an interesting read*). **to read between the lines** LINE[1]. **to read in** to transfer (data) into a computer memory etc. **to read into** to extract or assume (a meaning not explicit). **to read off** to take (a reading or information) from a recording instrument, e.g. a thermometer. **to read oneself in** to enter upon an incumbency by the public reading of the Thirty-nine Articles. **to read out** 1 to read aloud. 2 to retrieve (data) from storage in a computer memory etc. 3 (*N Am.*) to expel from a political party or other organization. **to read someone a lecture/ lesson** to scold, to reprimand someone. **to read someone like a book** to have full understanding of a person's motives etc. **to read someone's mind** to make an accurate guess as to what someone is thinking. **to read the riot act** RIOT ACT (under RIOT). **to read up** to get information about by reading. **to take as read** to assume, to accept without discussion. **readable** *a.* worth reading, interesting, legible. **readability** (-bil´-), **readableness** *n.* **readably** *adv.* **reader** *n.* 1 a person who reads or reads much. 2 a textbook, a book of selections for translation, a reading-book for schools. 3 a person employed by a publisher to read and report upon manuscripts etc. offered for publication. 4 a proof-reader. 5 a person appointed to read aloud, esp. parts of the church service. 6 (*also* **Reader**) a lecturer in some universities ranking below a professor. 7 a device for projecting a large-scale image of microfilm etc. **readership** *n.* 1 a body of readers, esp. of a particular newspaper, magazine etc. or author. 2 (*also* **Readership**) the post of university reader. **read-only memory** *n.* ROM. **read-out** *n.* 1 a record or display of the data retrieved from a computer or of a measurement made by a scientific recording instrument. 2 the act of retrieving data from computer storage facilities for display on screen or as a printout. **read-write head** *n.* the electromagnetic head in a computer disk-drive which reads or writes data on magnetic tape or disk. [OE *rǣdan* (cp. Dut. *raden*, G *rathen*, Icel. *ratha*, Goth. *rēdan*, rel. to Sansk. *rāth*, to succeed)]

re-(+ad–words) readapt *v.t., v.i.* 1 to adapt again or to suit a new purpose. 2 to adjust to new circumstances. **readaptation** *n.* **readd** *n.* to add again. **readdition** *n.* **readdress** *v.t.* 1 to put a new, esp. a corrected address upon. 2 to deal with (a problem etc.) again or in a different way. 3 to write or speak to anew. **readjourn** *v.t.* to adjourn again. **readjust** *v.t.* to arrange or adjust afresh. **readjustable** *a.* **readjustment** *n.* **readmit** *v.t.* (*pres.p.* **readmitting,** *past, p.p.* **readmitted**) to admit again. **readmission, readmittance** *n.* **readopt** *v.t.* to adopt again. **readoption** *n.* **readorn** *v.t.* to adorn afresh. **readornment** *n.* **re-advertise** *v.t., v.i.* to advertise again. **re-advertisement** *n.*

readily, readiness READY.

reading (rē´ding) *n.* 1 the act, practice or art of reading.

2 matter for reading. 3 the study or knowledge of books, literary research, scholarship. 4 a public recital or entertainment at which selections etc. are read to the audience. 5 an observation made by examining a recording instrument, a measurement. 6 the way in which a passage reads. 7 an interpretation of a piece of music. 8 the form of a passage given by a text, editor etc. 9 the recital of the whole or part of a Bill as a formal introduction or measure of approval in a legislative assembly. ~*a.* addicted to reading, studious. **first reading** FIRST. **second reading** SECOND[1]. **third reading** THIRD. **reading age** *n.* a person's reading ability calculated with reference to the average ability of a whole population at a particular age (*a reading age of nine*). **reading-book** *n.* a book of selections to be used as exercises in reading. **reading-desk** *n.* a stand for books etc. for the use of a reader, esp. in church, a lectern. **reading-glass** *n.* a hand magnifying-glass. **reading-lamp** *n.* a lamp for reading by. **reading-room** *n.* a room in a library, club etc. furnished with books, papers etc. for the use of readers.

ready (red´i) *a.* (*comp.* **readier,** *superl.* **readiest**) 1 in a state of preparedness, fit for use or action. 2 willing, apt, disposed. 3 on the point of, about (to). 4 quick, prompt. 5 able, expert, facile. 6 at hand, within reach, handy, quickly available. ~*adv.* (*usu. in comb. with p.p.*) in a state of preparedness, beforehand. ~*n.* 1 (*coll.*) ready money. 2 the position in which a firearm is held before presenting and aiming. ~*v.t.* (*3rd pers. sing. pres.* **readies,** *pres.p.* **readying,** *past, p.p.* **readied**) †to make ready, to prepare. **at/ to the ready** 1 prepared for action. 2 (of a firearm) held in the position preparatory to aiming and firing. **ready, steady, go!** the usual words used to start a race. **ready to drop** DROP. **ready to hand** nearby. **to make ready** to prepare. **readies** *n.pl.* (*coll.*) ready money, esp. banknotes. **readily** *adv.* 1 willingly, without reluctance. 2 without trouble or difficulty, easily. **readiness** *n.* 1 the state of being ready, preparedness. 2 willingness, prompt compliance. 3 facility, ease, aptitude. **ready-made** *a.* 1 (esp. of clothing in standard sizes) made beforehand, not made to order. 2 convenient, suitable. 3 lacking originality. 4 (of a shop etc.) selling ready-made articles. **ready-mix** *n.* 1 a food or concrete mix which only needs liquid to be added to make it ready for use. 2 concrete which is delivered in liquid state ready for use. **ready-mixed** *a.* **ready money** *n.* actual cash, ready to be paid down. **ready-money** *a.* **ready reckoner** *n.* a book with tables of interest etc. for facilitating business calculations. **ready-to-wear** *a.* off-the-peg. ~*n.* an item of off-the-peg clothing. **ready-witted** *a.* quick to understand or perceive. [ME *redi, rædi,* prob. from OE *gerǣde* (cp. OHG *bireiti,* G *bereit,* Dut. *bereid*) -Y[1] from conf. with OE *-ig*]

re- (+ af–al words) reaffirm *v.t.* to affirm again. **reaffirmation** *n.* **reafforest** *v.t.* to convert back into forest. **reafforestation** *n.* **realign** *v.t.* 1 to align again. 2 to group together on a new basis. **realignment** *n.* **reallege** *v.t.* to allege again. **reallocate** *v.t.* to allocate again or differently. **reallocation** *n.* **reallot** *v.t.* (*pres.p.* **reallotting,** *past, p.p.* **reallotted**) to allot again or differently. **reallotment** *n.* **realter** *v.t.* to alter again. **realteration** *n.*

reagent (riā´jənt) *n.* 1 a substance in a chemical reaction, esp. used to detect the presence of other substances or in chemical synthesis. 2 a force etc. that reacts. **reagency** *n.* reciprocal action.

real[1] (riəl) *a.* 1 actually existing; not fictitious, affected, imaginary, apparent, theoretical or nominal. 2 true, genuine, not counterfeit, not spurious. 3 having substantial existence, objective. 4 measured by purchasing power (*real income*). 5 consisting of fixed or permanent things, such as lands or houses, as distinct from *personal.* 6 (*coll.*) complete, utter (*a real beauty*). 7 (*Philos.*) having an absolute and independent existence. 8 (*Math.*) concerned with or containing real numbers. 9 (*Physics*) of or being an image through which light rays pass. ~*adv.* (*N Am., coll.*) very. **for real** 1 (*coll.*) in reality, genuine. 2 in earnest. **the real** that which is actual, esp. as opposed to the ideal; reality. **the real McCoy** 1 the genuine article. 2 the best. **the real thing** the genuine article and not a substitute. **real ale** *n.* beer which is allowed to ferment and mature in the cask and is not pumped up from the keg with carbon dioxide. **real estate** *n.* real property. **real life** *n.* actual human life, as distinct from fictional representation of human life. **real live** *a.* (*coll.*) actual, real. **really** *adv.* 1 in fact, in reality. 2 positively, truly. 3 I assure you. 4 is that so? **realness** *n.* **real number** *n.* any rational or irrational number. **real presence** *n.* the actual presence of the body and blood of Christ in the Eucharist. **real property** *n.* immovable property such as freehold land. **real tennis** *n.* the earliest form of tennis, played in a walled indoor court. **real time** *n.* the actual time during which an event occurs. **real-time** *a.* 1 of or relating to the processing of data by a computer as it is generated. 2 responding instantly to events as they occur. [late L *reālis,* from *rēs,* thing]

real[2] (rā´al) *n.* (*pl.* **reals, reales** (-lēz)) 1 the standard monetary unit of Brazil. 2 (*Hist.*) a Spanish silver coin or money of account. [Sp., from L *rēgālis,* REGAL[1]]

realgar (rial´gah) *n.* an orange-red mineral consisting of a sulphide of arsenic, used as a pigment and in the manufacture of fireworks. [med. L or F *réalgar,* Arab. *rehj alghār,* powder of the mine or cave]

realism (riə´lizm) *n.* 1 the practice of regarding, accepting and dealing with people, circumstances etc. as they are; concern with what is factual and practicable. 2 the practice of representing objects, people, scenes etc. as they are or as they appear to the painter, novelist etc., rather than an idealized or romantic interpretation. 3 the scholastic doctrine that every universal or general idea has objective existence, as distinct from *nominalism* and *conceptualism.* 4 the doctrine that the objects of perception have real existence, as distinct from *idealism.* 5 the doctrine that in perception there is an immediate cognition of the external object. **realist** *n.* 1 a practical person. 2 a believer in or adherent of realism. **realistic** (-lis´-) *a.* 1 of or relating to realism. 2 matter-of-fact, commonsense. **realistically** *adv.* [REAL[1], -ISM]

reality (rial´iti) *n.* (*pl.* **realities**) 1 the quality of being real, actuality, actual existence, being, that which underlies appearances. 2 truth, fact. 3 that which is real and not counterfeit, imaginary, supposed etc. 4 the real nature (of). 5 (*Law*) the permanent quality of real estate. **in reality** in fact. [F *réalité,* med. L *realitātem,* nom. *-tas*]

realize (riə´līz), **realise** *v.t.* 1 to perceive as a reality. 2 to apprehend clearly and vividly, to become aware of. 3 to bring into actual existence, to give reality to, to achieve. 4 to present as real, to impress on the mind as real, to make realistic. 5 to convert into money. 6 to bring in, as a price. 7 (*Mus.*) to reconstruct as complete (a part or composition) from a figured bass etc. **realizable** *a.* **realization** (-ā´shən) *n.* **realizer** *n.*

realm (relm) *n.* 1 a kingdom. 2 domain, region, sphere, field of interest. [OF *realme, reaume* (F *royaume*), prob. through pop. L *rēgālimen,* from L *rēgālis,* REGAL[1]]

realpolitik (rāahl´politēk) *n.* politics based on practical reality rather than moral or intellectual ideals. [G]

realty *n.* (*Law*) real property. **Realtor®** *n.* (*N Am.*) a member of the National Association of Real Estate Boards. **realtor** (-tə, -taw) *n.* (*N Am.*) an estate agent.

ream[1] (rēm) *n.* 1 500 sheets of paper, formerly 480 sheets or 20 quires. 2 (*usu. pl., coll.*) a large amount, esp. of written material. [ME *rēm*, *rīm*, through OF *rayme*, or Dut. *riem*, from Arab. *rizmah*, bundle]

ream[2] (rēm) *v.t.* **1** to enlarge the bore of (a hole in metal etc.). **2** (*Naut.*) to open (a seam) for caulking. **3** (*N Am.*) to squeeze the juice from (citrus fruit). **reamer** *n.* **1** an instrument or tool used in reaming. **2** (*N Am.*) a lemon-squeezer. [OE *ryman*, cogn. with *rūm*, ROOM]

re- (+ an–ap words) reanalyse, (*N Am.*) **reanalyze** *v.t.* to analyse again. **reanalysis** *n.* (*pl.* **reanalyses**). **reanimate** *v.t.* **1** to restore to life. **2** to revive, to encourage, to give new spirit to. **reanimation** *n.* **reannex** *v.t.* **1** to annex anew. **2** to reunite. **reannexation** *n.* **reapparel** *v.t.* (*pres.p.* **reapparelling,** (*N Am.*) **reappareling,** *past, p.p.* **reapparelled,** (*N Am.*) **reappareled**) to clothe again. **reappear** *v.i.* to appear again. **reappearance** *n.* **reapply** *v.t.* (*3rd pers. sing. pres.* **reapplies,** *pres.p.* **reapplying,** *past, p.p.* **reapplied**) to apply again, esp. to submit a second application (e.g. for a job). **reapplication** *n.* **reapplier** *n.* **reappoint** *v.t.* to appoint again. **reappointment** *n.* **reapportion** *v.t.* to share out again. **reapportionment** *n.* **reappraise** *v.t.* to revalue, to reassess. **reappraisal** *n.* **reapproach** *v.t.* to approach again.

reap (rēp) *v.t.* **1** to cut (a crop) with a scythe, sickle or reaping-machine. **2** to gather in (a harvest etc.). **3** to cut the harvest off (ground etc.). **4** to obtain as return for labour, deeds etc. *~v.i.* to perform the act of reaping. **to reap the whirlwind** WHIRLWIND (under WHIRL). **reaper** *n.* **1** a person who reaps. **2** a reaping-machine. **the (Grim) Reaper** death. **reaping-hook** *n.* a sickle. **reaping-machine** *n.* a machine for cutting grain. [OE *rīpan*]

rear[1] (riə) *n.* **1** the back or hindmost part. **2** the hindmost division of a military or naval force. **3** a place or position at the back. **4** (*euphem.*) the buttocks. **5** (*coll.*) a water closet, a latrine. *~a.* of or at the rear. **in the rear** at the back. **to bring up the rear** to come last. **to drop to the rear** DROP. **to take in the rear** to attack from behind. **rear admiral** *n.* a naval officer next below the rank of vice admiral. **rear-arch** (riər´ahch) *n.* an inner arch of a doorway or window opening, differing in size or form from the outer arch. **rear commodore** *n.* an officer of a yacht club below vice commodore. **rear-end** *n.* **1** the back part of anything. **2** (*coll.*) the buttocks. *~v.t.* to crash into the rear of (a vehicle). **rearguard** *n.* **1** a body of troops protecting the rear of an army. **2** an element in a political party, organization etc. holding entrenched or conservative views. *~a.* **1** of or characteristic of the rearguard. **2** defensive in the face of defeat (*rearguard action*). **rear lamp, rear light** *n.* a red light at the back of a bicycle or motor vehicle. **rearmost** *a.* coming or situated last of all. **rear-rank, rear-line** *n.* the rank or line of a body of troops in the rear. **rear sight** *n.* the sight of a firearm nearest the breach. **rear-view mirror** *n.* a small mirror in a motor vehicle which allows the driver to observe the traffic behind. **rearward** (-wəd) *a.* situated in or towards the rear. *~adv.* (*also* **rearwards**) towards the rear. *~n.* **1** the rear. **2** †the rearguard of an army. **3** (*fig.*) those coming last. **rear-wheel drive** *n.* a system in which power is transmitted to and by the rear wheels of a motor vehicle. [shortened from ARREARS]

rear[2] (riə) *v.t.* **1** to bring up, to breed, to educate. **2** to raise, to set up, to elevate to an upright position. **3** to raise, to cultivate, to grow. **4** to build, to erect, to uplift, to place or hold on high. **5** to raise from a prostrate position. *~v.i.* **1** (of a horse) to stand on the hind legs. **2** (*fig.*) to rise to a great height, to tower. **3** to become suddenly roused with anger etc. **to rear its (ugly) head** HEAD[1]. **rearer** *n.* [OE *rǣran*, cogn. with RAISE, which has largely superseded it]

re- (+ ar–at words) reargue *v.t.* (*3rd pers. sing. pres.* **reargues,** *pres.p.* **rearguing,** *past, p.p.* **reargued**) to argue or debate afresh. **reargument** *n.* **rearm** *v.t.* to arm afresh, esp. with more modern weapons. **rearmament** *n.* **rearouse** *v.t.* to arouse again. **rearousal** *n.* **rearrange** *v.t.* **1** to arrange in a new way or order. **2** to alter the arrangements for (a meeting etc.). **rearrangement** *n.* **rearrest** *v.t.* to arrest again. *~n.* a second arrest. **reascend** *v.t., v.i.* to ascend again. **reascension, reascent** *n.* **reassemble** *v.t., v.i.* to assemble or collect together again. **reassembly** *n.* (*pl.* **reassemblies**). **reassert** *v.t.* to assert anew. **reassertion** *n.* **reassess** *v.t.* to make a new assessment of. **reassessment** *n.* **reassign** *v.t.* **1** to assign again. **2** to transfer back or to another what has been already assigned. **reassignment** *n.* **reassimilate** *v.t.* to assimilate again. **reassimilation** *n.* **reassume** *v.t.* **1** to take up again. **2** to take upon oneself again. **reassumption** *n.* **reassure** *v.t.* **1** to assure or confirm again. **2** to give fresh courage to, to restore to confidence. **3** to reinsure. **reassurance** *n.* **reassurer** *n.* **reassuring** *a.* **reassuringly** *adv.* **reattach** *v.t.* to attach afresh. **reattachment** *n.* **reattain** *v.t.* to attain again. **reattainment** *n.* **reattempt** *v.t.* to attempt afresh. *~n.* a new attempt.

reason (rē´zən) *n.* **1** that which is adduced to support or justify, or serves as a ground or motive for an act, opinion etc. **2** that which accounts for anything, a final cause. **3** the intellectual faculties, esp. the group of faculties distinguishing man from animals. **4** the exercise of the rational powers. **5** good sense, judgement, sanity. **6** sensible conduct, moderation. **7** the intuitive faculty which furnishes a priori principles, categories etc. **8** the premise of an argument, esp. the minor premise when stated after the conclusion. **9** the power of consecutive thinking, the logical faculty.*~v.i.* **1** to use the faculty of reason. **2** to argue, esp. to employ argument (with) as a means of persuasion. **3** to reach conclusions by way of inferences from premises. *~v.t.* **1** to debate, discuss or examine by means of the reason or reasons and inferences. **2** to assume, conclude or prove by way of argument. **3** to persuade or dissuade by argument. **4** to set forth in orderly argumentative form. **by reason of** because, on account of, in consequence of. **in/ within reason 1** in moderation. **2** according to good sense. **it stands to reason** it follows logically. **to listen to reason** to be persuaded to act in a sensible manner. **to see reason** to recognize and accept the logical force of an argument. **with reason** with justifiable cause, for a good reason. **reasonable** *a.* **1** rational, reasoning, governed by reason. **2** conformable to reason, sensible, proper. **3** not extravagant, moderate, esp. in price; fair, not extortionate. **4** willing to listen to reason. **5** average, quite good (*reasonable weather*). **6** endowed with the faculty of reason. **reasonableness** *n.* **reasonably** *adv.* **reasoned** *a.* well-thought-out, well-argued. **reasoner** *n.* **reasoning** *n.* **1** the act of drawing conclusions from premises or using the reason. **2** a statement of the reasons justifying a course, opinion, conclusion etc. **3** argumentation. **reasonless** *a.* **reasons of state** *n.pl.* politics or state security used to justify immoral acts. [OF *raisun* (F *raison*), L *ratiōnem*, nom. *-tio*, see RATIO]

Usage note *The reason (why)...is that...* is preferred to *the reason (why)...is because.*

reata (riah´tə) *n.* (*pl.* **reatas**) a lariat. [Sp., from *reatar*, to tie again (RE-, L *aptāre*, to apply, see APT)]

Réaumur (rā´əmuə, rā´ō-) *a.* relating to, conforming to or denoting measurement on the Réaumur scale. **Réaumur scale** *n.* a temperature scale on which 0° corresponds to the freezing point of water and 80° to the boiling point. [René Antoine Ferchault de *Réaumur*, 1683–1757, French physicist]

re- (+ aw– words) reawake *v.t., v.i.* (*past* **reawoke,**

p.p. **reawoken**) to awake again. **reawaken** *v.t., v.i.* 1 to reawake. 2 to arouse afresh. **reawakening** *n.*

†**reave** (rēv) *v.t.* (*past, p.p.* **reaved,** (*poet.*) **reft** (reft)) 1 to take (away or from) by force. 2 to deprive (of) by force, to bereave. ~*v.i.* to pillage, to ravage. **reaver** *n.* [OE *rēafian* (cp. Dut. *rooven*, G *rauben*, Icel. *raufa*, also L *rup-*, *rumpere*, to break)]

re- (+ b– words) rebadge *v.t.* to give a new badge or logo to. **rebarbarize, rebarbarise** *v.t.* to reduce to barbarism again. **rebarbarization** *n.* **rebase** *v.t.* to give a new base or basis to. **rebellow** *v.i.* 1 (*poet.*) to bellow in return. 2 to echo back loudly. ~*v.t.* to re-echo loudly. **rebid**[1] (rēbid´, rē´-) *v.i.* (*pres.p.* **rebidding,** *past, p.p.* **rebid**) to bid again, esp. to bid on the same suit as the previous bid in a game of bridge. ~*v.t.* to bid (the same suit as a previous bid) at a higher level. **rebid**[2] (rē´bid) *n.* 1 an act of rebidding. 2 a bid made in this way. **rebiddable** *a.* **rebind** *v.t.* (*past, p.p.* **rebound**) 1 to bind again. 2 to give a new binding to. **rebirth** *n.* 1 a second birth, esp. an entrance into a new sphere of existence, as in reincarnation. 2 a revival. 3 a spiritual renewal. **rebirther** *n.* **rebirthing** *n.* a type of psychotherapy that involves reliving the experience of being born, used as a treatment for anxieties, neuroses etc. **rebloom** *v.i.* to bloom again **reboil** *v.t., v.i.* to boil again. **reboot** *v.t.* (*Comput.*) to boot again. **rebore**[1] *v.t.* to bore again, esp. to widen the bore of (a cylinder in an internal-combustion engine). **rebore**[2] (rē´baw) *n.* the process of reboring the cylinders of a worn vehicle engine. **reborn** *a.* 1 born again. 2 having undergone spiritual renewal or enlightenment. **rebrace** *v.t.* to brace again. **rebreathe** *v.t.* to breathe again. **rebroadcast** *v.t.* (*past* **rebroadcast, rebroadcasted,** *p.p.* **rebroadcast**) to broadcast again. ~*a.* broadcast again. ~*n.* a second broadcast. **rebuild** *v.t.* to build again, to reconstruct. **rebuilder** *n.* **rebury** *v.t.* (*3rd pers. sing. pres.* **reburies,** *pres.p.* **reburying,** *past, p.p.* **reburied**) to bury again. **reburial** *n.*

REB *abbr.* Revised English Bible.

rebarbative (ribah´bətiv) *a.* (*formal or poet.*) repellent, grim, forbidding. [F *barbe*, a beard]

rebate[1] (rē´bāt, -bāt´) *n.* 1 a refund of part of an amount paid. 2 a deduction from an account payable. ~*v.t.* 1 to give a rebate of. 2 to refund or deduct a portion of (a charge). 3 to give a rebate to. 4 to reduce, to diminish. 5 †to make blunt, to dull. **rebatable, rebateable** *a.* **rebatement** *n.* **rebater** *n.* [OF *rabattre* (RE-, *abattre*, to ABATE)]

rebate[2] (ribāt´) *n.* (*dial.*) a kind of hard freestone. [etym. uncertain]

rebate[3] RABBET.

rebato RABATO.

rebec (rē´bek), **rebeck** *n.* a medieval three-stringed musical instrument played with a bow. [OF *rebec*, var. of *rebebe*, Arab. *rebāb*]

rebel[1] (reb´əl) *n.* 1 a person who forcibly resists the established government or renounces allegiance to it. 2 a person who resists authority or control. 3 a person who refuses to conform to the accepted social norms or conventions. ~*a.* 1 rebellious. 2 of or relating to rebellion or to rebels. **rebeldom** *n.* **rebel-like** *a.*

rebel[2] (ribel´) *v.i.* (*pres.p.* **rebelling,** *past, p.p.* **rebelled**) 1 to act in rebellion (against). 2 to refuse to conform, to revolt (against any authority, control etc.). 3 to feel or show repugnance. **rebellion** (-bel´yən) *n.* 1 organized, esp. armed, resistance to the established government. 2 opposition to any authority. 3 refusal to conform to accepted social norms or conventions. 4 an instance of rebelling. **rebellious** (-bel´yəs) *a.* 1 disposed to rebel, insubordinate, difficult to manage or control. 2 engaged in rebellion. 3 defying or opposing lawful authority. 4 resisting treatment, refractory, unyielding. **rebelliously** *adv.* **rebelliousness** *n.* [F *rebelle*, L *rebellem*, nom. *-llis*, rebellious (RE-, *bellum*, war)]

reboant (reb´ōənt) *a.* (*poet.*) loudly resounding or re-echoing. [L *reboans -ntem*, pres.p. of *reboāre* (*boāre*, to bellow)]

rebound[1] (ribownd´) *v.i.* 1 to bound back, to recoil (from a blow etc.). 2 to react, esp. adversely (on or upon the perpetrator). 3 to re-echo. **rebounder** *n.* a small trampoline used for performing jumping exercises on. **rebounding** *n.* 1 the act of rebounding. 2 a form of exercise involving jumping up and down on a rebounder. [OF *rebondir*]

rebound[2] (rē´bownd) *n.* 1 the act of rebounding, a recoil. 2 a reaction (of feeling etc.). **on the rebound** 1 in the act of bouncing back. 2 as a reaction to a disappointment, esp. in love.

rebound[3] REBIND (under RE- (+ B– WORDS)).

rebuff (ribŭf´) *n.* 1 a rejection, a check (to an offer or a person who makes advances etc.). 2 a curt denial, a snub. 3 a defeat, a sudden or unexpected repulse. ~*v.t.* to give a rebuff to, to repel. [obs. F *rebuffe*, It. *re-*, *ribuffo* (*buffo*, puff, imit. in orig.)]

rebuke (ribūk´) *v.t.* to reprove, to reprimand, to chide. ~*n.* 1 the act of rebuking. 2 a reproof. **rebukable** *a.* **rebukeful** *a.* **rebukefully** *adv.* **rebukefulness** *n.* **rebuker** *n.* **rebukingly** *adv.* [A-F and ONF *rebuker*, OF *rebuchier* (RE-, *bucher*, to beat, perh. orig. to lop, from *busche*, F *bûche*, a log)]

rebus (rē´bəs) *n.* (*pl.* **rebuses**) 1 a picture or figure enigmatically representing a word, name or phrase, usu. by objects suggesting words or syllables. 2 (*Her.*) a device representing a proper name or motto in this way. [L, abl. pl. of *rēs*, thing, etym. uncertain]

rebut (ribŭt´) *v.t.* (*pres.p.* **rebutting,** *past, p.p.* **rebutted**) 1 to contradict or refute by plea, argument or countervailing proof. 2 to thrust back, to check, to repel. **rebutment, rebuttal** *n.* **rebuttable** *a.* **rebutter** *n.* 1 a person who, or argument etc. that rebuts. 2 the answer of a defendant to a plaintiff's surrejoinder. [A-F *reboter*, OF *rebouter*, *-boter* (RE-, *boter*, to BUTT[1])]

rec (rek) *n.* (*coll.*) a recreation ground.

rec. *abbr.* 1 receipt. 2 recipe. 3 record, recorded, recorder.

re- (+ ca– words) recalculate *v.t.* to calculate again. **recalculation** *n.* **recapitalize, recapitalise** *v.t.* 1 to reorganize the capital of (a business organization etc.). 2 to convert into capital again. 3 to supply again with capital. **recapitalization** *n.* **recapture** *v.t.* 1 to capture again, to recover (as a prize from the captor). 2 to re-experience or renew (a past feeling etc.). ~*n.* 1 the act of recapturing. 2 that which is recaptured. **recarburize, recarburise** *v.t.* to carburize (steel) after decarbonization. **recarburization** *n.* **recarburizer** *n.* **recarry** *v.t.* (*3rd pers. sing. pres.* **recarries,** *pres.p.* **recarrying,** *past, p.p.* **recarried**) to carry back or again. **recarriage** *n.* **recarrier** *n.* **recast** *v.t.* (*past, p.p.* **recast**) 1 to put into a new form, to fashion again, to remodel. 2 to cast, found or mould again. 3 a to change the cast of (a play etc.). b to assign a different part to (an actor). 4 to compute or add up again. ~*n.* 1 that which has been recast. 2 the process or result of recasting. **recaster** *n.* **recategorize, recategorise** *v.t.* to categorize again or differently. **recategorization** *n.* **recaution** *v.t.* to caution again.

recalcitrant (rikal´sitrənt) *a.* refractory, obstinately resisting authority or control. ~*n.* a recalcitrant person. **recalcitrance** *n.* **recalcitrantly** *adv.* **recalcitrate** *v.i.* (*formal*) 1 to refuse compliance, to show resistance, to be refractory. 2 to kick (against or at a proposal etc.). **recalcitration** *n.* (*formal*) [F *récalcitrant* or L *recalcitrans -ntem*, pres.p. of *recalcitrāre* (RE-, *calcitrāre*, to strike with the heel, from *calx calcis*, heel)]

recalescence (rēkəles´əns) *n.* a sudden temporary increase in the temperature of iron, steel etc. which occurs at certain temperatures during the cooling process as a result of changes in crystal structure. **recalesce** *v.i.* to undergo recalescence. **recalescent** *a.* [L *recalescere* (RE-, *calescere* to grow hot, incept. of *calēre*, to be warm)]

recall[1] (rikawl´) *v.t.* **1** to call back, to summon to return. **2** to bring back to mind, to recollect. **3** to remind one of. **4** to revoke, to annul, to take back. **5** (*chiefly poet.*) to renew, to revive, to resuscitate. **6** to take back. **recallable** *a.* **recallment** *n.*

recall[2] (rē´kawl) *n.* **1** a calling back, a summons to return. **2** the act or power of remembering. **3** the possibility of revoking, annulling or cancelling. **4** a signal calling back soldiers, a ship etc.

recant (rikant´) *v.t.* to retract, to renounce, to abjure. ~*v.i.* to disavow or abjure opinions or beliefs formerly avowed, esp. with a formal acknowledgement of error. **recantation** (rēkantā´shən) *n.* **recanter** *n.* [L *recantāre* (RE-, *cantāre* freq. of *canere*, to sing)]

recap (rē´kap, -kap´) *v.t.*, *v.i.* (*pres.p.* **recapping,** *past, p.p.* **recapped**) to recapitulate. ~*n.* recapitulation.

recapitulate (rēkəpit´ūlāt) *v.t.* to repeat in brief (as the principal points or headings of a discourse), to sum up, to summarize. ~*v.i.* to sum up an argument, speech etc. **recapitulation** (-lā´shən) *n.* **1** the act of recapitulating, e.g. at the end of a speech. **2** the apparent repetition of the evolutionary stages of a species in the embryonic development of a member of that species. **3** the repeating of earlier themes in a piece of music. **recapitulative** (-lətiv), **recapitulatory** (-lətri) *a.*

recaption (rikap´shən) *n.* (*Law*) recovery of goods, wife, child etc. by peaceful means from someone unlawfully withholding them. [CAPTION (in old sense of seizure, taking)]

recce (rek´i) *n.* (*pl.* **recces**) (*coll.*) a reconnaissance. ~*v.t.*, *v.i.* (*3rd pers. sing. pres.* **recces,** *pres.p.* **recceing,** *past, p.p.* **recced**) to reconnoitre. [by shortening]

☒ **reccommend** common misspelling of RECOMMEND.

recd. *abbr.* received.

re- (+ ce–cl words) re-cede *v.t.* to cede again, to restore to a former possessor. **rechallenge** *v.t.* to challenge again. **rechannel** *v.t.* (*pres.p.* **rechannelling,** (*N Am.*) **rechanneling,** *past, p.p.* **rechannelled,** (*N Am.*) **rechanneled**) to direct into a different channel. **recharge**[1] *v.t.* **1** to charge again. **2** to put a new charge into. **3** to make a new charge against. **4** to charge or attack again or in return. **5** to restore the vitality of (a battery etc.). **recharge**[2] (rē´-) *n.* a new charge or a charge in return. **rechargeable** *a.* **recharger** *n.* **rechart** *v.t.* to chart again. **recharter** *v.t.* **1** to charter again. **2** to give a new charter to. **recheck**[1] *v.t.*, *v.i.* to check again. **recheck**[2] (rē´-) *n.* the act of checking something again. **rechristen** *v.t.* **1** to christen again. **2** to give a new name to. **recirculate** *v.t.*, *v.i.* to pass or go round again. **recirculation** *n.* **recivilize, recivilise** *v.t.* to civilize again. **recivilization** *n.* **reclass** *v.t.* to reclassify. **reclassify** *v.t.* (*3rd pers. sing. pres.* **reclassifies,** *pres.p.* **reclassifying,** *past, p.p.* **reclassified**) to classify again or elsewhere. **reclassification** *n.* **reclimb** *v.t.* to climb again. **reclose** *v.t.*, *v.i.* to shut again. **reclothe** *v.t.* to clothe again.

recede (risēd´) *v.i.* **1** to go back or away (from). **2** to be gradually lost to view by distance. **3** to incline, slope or tend backwards or away. **4** to retreat, to withdraw (from). **5** to decline, to retrograde. **6** (of hair) to cease to grow at the temples. **7** to draw back, e.g. from a promise. [L *recēdere* (RE-, *cēdere*, to go, see CEDE)]

re-cede RE- (+ CE–CL WORDS).

receipt (risēt´) *n.* **1** a written acknowledgement of money or goods received. **2** the act or fact of receiving or being received. **3** (*usu. pl.*) that which is received, esp. money. **4** †a recipe. ~*v.t.* **1** to give a receipt for. **2** (*chiefly N Am.*) to write an acknowledgement of receipt on (a bill etc.). **in receipt of** having received. [ME *receit*, A-F *receite*, OF *recete*, *reçoite*, L *recepta*, fem. p.p. of *recipere* to RECEIVE]

receive (risēv´) *v.t.* **1** to obtain, get or take as a thing due, offered, sent, paid or given. **2** to be given, to be furnished or supplied with, to acquire. **3** to encounter, to experience. **4** to take or stand the onset of. **5** to understand, to perceive, to regard (in a particular light). **6** to support the face or weight of, to bear. **7** to be a receptacle for. **8** to admit to one's presence, to welcome, to entertain as a guest. **9** to accept for consideration. **10** to accept with approval or consent, to admit, as proper or true. **11** to accept (stolen goods) from a thief. **12** to convert (incoming electrical signals) into sounds, pictures etc. by means of a receiver. **13** to return the service in tennis or squash. ~*v.i.* **1** to hold a reception of visitors or callers. **2** to buy and sell stolen goods. **3** to receive incoming electrical signals. **to be at/ on the receiving end** to be the recipient of something unpleasant. **receivable** *a.* **receivability** (-bil´-), **receivableness** *n.* **received** *a.* generally accepted or believed. **received pronunciation, Received Pronunciation** *n.* the non-localized pronunciation of British English, taken as the standard. **Received (Standard) English** *n.* English spoken by educated British people, taken as the standard of the language. **receiver** (risē´və) *n.* **1** a person who receives. **2** a part of a telephonic or telegraphic apparatus for receiving messages or current, esp. the part of a telephone containing the earpiece and mouthpiece. **3** an officer appointed by a court to administer property under litigation, esp. that of bankrupts. **4** an apparatus that converts incoming radio, television or telephone signals into an audible or visual form. **5** a person who receives stolen goods. **6** a vessel for receiving the products of distillation or for collecting gas. **7** the glass vessel of an air pump etc. **8** a player in American football eligible to catch a pass. **9** the catcher in baseball. **official receiver** OFFICIAL (under OFFICE). **receiver-general** *n.* (*pl.* **receivers general**) an officer appointed to receive public revenues. **receivership** *n.* **1** the office of a receiver, esp. an official receiver. **2** the state of being administered by a receiver. **receiving order** *n.* an order from a bankruptcy court staying separate action against a debtor and placing affairs in the hands of an official receiver. [A-F *receivre* (OF *reçoivre*), L *recipere* (RE-, *capere*, to take)]

recency RECENT.

recension (risen´shən) *n.* **1** a critical revision of a text. **2** a revised edition of a text. [L *recensio*, from *recensēre* (RE-, *censēre*, to review)]

recent (rē´sənt) *a.* **1** of, relating to or being the present or time not long past. **2** that happened, existed or came into existence lately. **3** modern, fresh, newly begun or established. **4** (**Recent**) of, relating to or being the existing epoch of geological time; Holocene. ~*n.* (**Recent**) Holocene. **recency** (-si), **recentness** *n.* **recently** *adv.* [F *récent*, L *recentem*, nom. *-cens*, etym. unknown]

receptacle (risep´təkəl) *n.* **1** something which receives, holds or contains. **2** a vessel, space or place of deposit. **3** (*Bot.*) a part forming a support, such as the axis of a flower cluster, the spore-bearing structure of a fern or alga etc. **receptacular** (resiptak´ūlə) *a.* [F, from L *receptāculum*, from *recept-*, p.p. stem of *recipere*, to RECEIVE]

reception (risep´shən) *n.* **1** the act of receiving. **2** the state of being received or the manner in which something is received. **3** receipt, acceptance, admission. **4** the receiving, admitting or accommodating of people, esp. guests, new members of a society etc. **5** an occasion of formal or ceremonious receiving of visitors. **6** a formal welcome. **7** an area of a hotel, office etc. where people report or are received on arrival. **8**

the quality of received radio or television signals. **reception centre** *n.* a place where people can receive immediate assistance for problems, such as drugs or homelessness. **receptionist** *n.* a person at a hotel or elsewhere, whose duty it is to receive and look after visitors or clients. **reception order** *n.* the official order required for detention in a psychiatric hospital. **reception room** *n.* **1** a room for receptions. **2** a room in a house to which visitors are admitted, as distinct from bedrooms, kitchen etc. **receptive** (risep´tiv) *a.* **1** quick to receive impressions, ideas etc. **2** having the ability or capacity to receive. **receptively** *adv.* **receptivity** (rēseptiv´-), **receptiveness** *n.* **receptor** *n.* **1** any of various devices which receive signals or information. **2** an organ adapted for receiving stimuli. **3** a sensory nerve ending which changes stimuli into nerve impulses. **4** a site on or in a cell to which a hormone, neurotransmitter, antigen etc. binds. [F, from L *receptiōnem*, from *recipere*, to RECEIVE, p.p. *receptus*]

recess (rises´, rē´ses) *n.* **1** a part that recedes, a depression, indentation, hollow, niche or alcove. **2 a** a cessation or suspension of public or other business, a vacation. **b** (*N Am.*) a short break (e.g. between school classes). **3** (*often pl.*) a secluded or secret place, a nook. **4** a depression, cavity, indentation or fold. *~v.t.* **1** to put into a recess. **2** to build a recess in (a wall etc.). **3** (*N Am.*) to interrupt temporarily, to adjourn. *~v.i.* (*N Am.*) to adjourn. **recessed** *a.* **recessed arch** *n.* an arch set within another. [L *recessus*, p.p. of *recēdere*, to RECEDE]

recession[1] (risesh´ən) *n.* **1** a slump, esp. in trade or economic activity. **2** the act of receding, withdrawal, retirement. **3** a receding part or object. **4** the withdrawal of the clergy and choir after a church service. **recessional** *a.* of or relating to the recession of the clergy and choir from the chancel. *~n.* a hymn sung during this ceremony. **recessionary** *a.* **recessive** *a.* **1** tending to recede. **2** relating to or controlled by a recessive gene. **3** (of a stress accent) tending to move towards the beginning of a word. **recessive gene** *n.* a gene that must be inherited from both mother and father in order to show its effect in the individual. **recessively** *adv.* **recessiveness** *n.*

recession[2] (risesh´ən) *n.* the act of giving back to a former owner. [RE-CEDE (under RE- (+ CE–CL WORDS))]

Rechabite (rek´əbīt) *n.* a total abstainer from alcohol, esp. a member of a society of the Independent Order of Rechabites, a society of abstainers. **Rechabitism** *n.* [orig. one of the descendants of Jonadab, son of Rechab, who bound themselves to abstain from wine]

réchauffé (rāshōfā´) *n.* **1** a dish warmed up again. **2** a rehash. [F, p.p. of *réchauffer*, to warm up again (RE-, *chauffer*, to CHAFE]

recherché (rəshœ´shā) *a.* **1** out of the common, rare, choice, exotic. **2** affected, precious, far-fetched. [F, p.p. of *rechercher* (RE-, *chercher*, to SEARCH)]

recidivist (risid´ivist) *n.* a relapsed or inveterate criminal, usu. one serving or who has served a second term of imprisonment. **recidivism** *n.* a habitual relapse into crime. **recidivistic** (-vis´-) *a.* [F *récidiviste*, L *recidīvus*, from *recidere* (RE-, *cadere*, to fall)]

☒ **recieve** common misspelling of RECEIVE.

recipe (res´ipi) *n.* **1** a list of ingredients and directions for preparing a dish. **2** a remedy, expedient, device or means for effecting some result. **3** a formula or prescription for compounding medical or other mixtures, a receipt. [L, imper. of *recipere*, to RECEIVE]

recipient (risip´iənt) *n.* a person who receives something. *~a.* **1** receiving. **2** receptive. **recipience, recipiency** *n.* [L *recipiens -entem*, pres.p. of *recipere*, to RECEIVE]

reciprocal (risip´rəkəl) *a.* **1** acting, done or given in return, mutual. **2** mutually interchangeable. **3** inversely correspondent, complementary. **4** (*Gram.*) expressing mutual action or relation. *~n.* (*Math.*) the quotient resulting from dividing unity by a given quantity. **reciprocality** (-kal´-) *n.* reciprocity. **reciprocally** *adv.* **reciprocal pronoun** *n.* a pronoun which expresses a mutual action or relationship. **reciprocant** *n.* (*Math.*) a differential invariant. [L *reciprocus* (prob. RE-, back, *pro*, forward)]

reciprocate (risip´rəkāt) *v.i.* **1** to return an equivalent, to make a return in kind. **2** to alternate, to move backwards and forwards. *~v.t.* **1** to give in return. **2** to give and take mutually, to interchange. **3** to give alternating or backward-and-forward motion to. **reciprocating** *a.* **reciprocating engine** *n.* an engine in which the reciprocating motion of a piston is transformed into rotary motion of a crankshaft. **reciprocating motion** *n.* backward-and-forward or up-and-down motion, as of a piston. **reciprocation** (-kā´shən) *n.* **1** the act of reciprocating. **2** giving and returning. **3** reciprocating motion. **reciprocative** *a.* **reciprocator** *n.* **reciprocatory** *a.* moving backwards and forwards, reciprocating. **reciprocity** (resipros´iti) *n.* (*pl.* **reciprocities**) **1** the state of being reciprocal, reciprocation of rights or obligations. **2** mutual action or the principle of give-and-take, esp. interchange of commercial privileges between two nations. [as RECIPROCAL]

recision (risizh´ən) *n.* the act of rescinding, annulment. [L *recīsio*, from *recīdere* (RE-, *caedere*, to cut)]

recitative[1] (resitətēv´) *n.* **1** a style of rendering vocal passages intermediate between singing and ordinary speaking, as in oratorio and opera. **2** a piece or part to be sung in recitative.

recitative[2] (risī´tativ) *a.* **1** relating to, suitable for or characteristic of recitative. **2** of or relating to a recital. **recitatively** *adv.*

recite (risīt´) *v.t.* **1** to repeat aloud or declaim from memory, esp. before an audience. **2** to give details of, to relate in full. **3** to enumerate. *~v.i.* to give a recitation. **recitable** *a.* **recital** *n.* **1** the act of reciting. **2** a musical performance, esp. by one person or of the works of one person. **3** an enumeration or narrative of facts or particulars, a story. **4** the part of a document formally stating facts, reasons, grounds etc. **5** a public entertainment consisting of recitations. **recitalist** *n.* **recitation** (-ā´shən) *n.* **1** the recital of prose or poetry, esp. the delivery of a composition committed to memory. **2** a composition intended for recital. **reciter** *n.* **1** a person who recites. **2** a book of selections etc. for reciting. **reciting note** *n.* in Gregorian chant, that note on which most of a verse is sung. [F *réciter*, L *recitāre* (RE-, *citāre*, to CITE)]

reck (rek) *v.t.* (*poet.*) to care about, to heed. *~v.i.* **1** to have a care or thought (of). **2** to trouble oneself, to be concerned, to be heedful. [OE *reccan* (cp. OHG *ruohhen*, MHG *ruochen*, Icel. *rækja*)]

reckless (rek´lis) *a.* **1** heedless of the consequences or danger, rash, foolhardy. **2** careless, heedless, regardless, neglectful. **recklessly** *adv.* **recklessness** *n.* [OE *recceleas* (as RECK)]

reckon (rek´ən) *v.t.* **1** to count, to add (up), calculate or compute. **2** to count or include (in or among). **3** to regard (as), to account, to esteem, to consider (to be). **4** to be of the opinion, to calculate, to guess (that). **5** (*sl.*) to think highly of, to regard favourably. *~v.i.* **1** to compute, to calculate. **2** to settle accounts (with). **3** to rely, to count, to place dependence (upon). **4** to suppose, to believe, to guess, to calculate. **to be reckoned with** meriting consideration because formidable, influential etc. **to reckon on 1** to rely upon. **2** to expect. **to reckon with** to take into account. **to reckon without** to fail to take into account. **reckoner** *n.* any of several devices or tables for quick calculations, esp. a ready reckoner. **reckoning** *n.* **1** the act of calculating or counting. **2** an appraisal, an estimation, an opinion. **3**

a statement of accounts or charges, a bill. **4** a settling of accounts. **5** an estimate or calculation of a ship's position. [OE *gerecenian* (cp. MDut. *rekenen*, G *rechnen*, Icel. *reikna*), cogn. with RECK]

reclaim (riklām´) *v.t.* **1** to claim or demand back, to claim the restoration of. **2** to bring (e.g. marshland) under cultivation. **3** to recover (usable substances) from waste products. **4** to bring back from error, vice, wildness etc., to reform, to tame, to civilize. **5** to bring back (a hawk) to the wrist. ~*n.* the act of reclaiming or being reclaimed, reclamation. **reclaimable** *a.* **reclaimably** *adv.* **reclaimer, reclaimant** *n.* **reclamation** (rekləmā´shən) *n.* **1** the act of reclaiming. **2** the state of being reclaimed. **3** the conversion of waste land, marshland etc. into land suitable for human use. **4** the recovery of usable substances from waste products. [OF *reclamer*, L *reclāmāre*, to cry out against (RE-, *clāmāre*, to shout)]

réclame (rāklahm´) *n.* **1** public attention, publicity or notoriety. **2** self-advertisement, puffing. [F, from *réclamer*, see RECLAIM]

recline (riklīn´) *v.i.* **1** to assume or be in a leaning or recumbent posture, to lie down or lean back upon cushions or other supports. **2** to incline backwards. ~*v.t.* **1** to lay or lean (one's body, head, limbs etc.) back, esp. in a horizontal or nearly horizontal position. **2** to cause (e.g. the back of a car seat) to lean backwards from the vertical. **reclinable** *a.* **reclinate** (rek´linăt) *a.* (*Bot.*) (of plant parts) inclined from an erect position, bending downwards. **reclination** (-ā´shən) *n.* **recliner** *n.* **1** a type of armchair having a back which can be adjusted to recline backwards. **2** a person who or thing which reclines. [L *reclīnāre* (RE-, *clīnāre*, to lean), see DECLINE]

recluse (rikloos´) *n.* a person who lives retired from the world, esp. a religious devotee who lives in a solitary cell and practises austerity and self-discipline, a hermit, an anchorite or anchoress. ~*a.* **1** retired from the world. **2** solitary, secluded, retired, sequestered. **reclusely** *adv.* **reclusion** (-kloo´zhən) *n.* **reclusive** *a.* [OF *reclus -cluse*, p.p. of *reclure*, L *reclūdere* (RE-, *claudere*, to shut)]

re- (+ co- words) recoat *v.t.* to coat again (with paint etc.). **recode** *v.t.* to code again or differently. **recodify** *v.t.* (*3rd pers. sing. pres.* **recodifies,** *pres.p.* **recodifying,** *past, p.p.* **recodified**) to codify again or differently. **recodification** *n.* **recoin** *v.t.* to coin over again. **recoinage** *n.* **recoiner** *n.* **re-collect** *v.t.* **1** to collect or gather together again. **2** to collect or compose (one's ideas, thoughts or feelings) again. **3** to summon up, to rally, to recover (one's strength, spirit etc.). ~*v.i.* to come together again. **recolonize, recolonise** *v.t.* to colonize afresh. **recolonization** *n.* **recolour,** (*N Am.*) **recolor** *v.t.* to colour again. **recombine** *v.t., v.i.* to combine or join together again or differently. **recommence** *v.i., v.t.* to begin again. **recommencement** *n.* **recommission** *v.t.* to commission anew. **recommit** *v.t.* (*pres.p.* **recommitting,** *past, p.p.* **recommitted**) **1** to commit again. **2** to refer back (to a committee etc.). **recommitment, recommittal** *n.* **recommunicate** *v.t.* to communicate anew. **recompact** *v.t.* to join together again. **recompare** *v.t.* to compare again. **recomparison** *n.* **recompile** *v.t.* to compile again. **recompilation** *n.* **recompose** *v.t.* **1** to compose or put together again. **2** to rearrange. **3** to restore the composure of, to make tranquil again. **recomposition** *n.* **recompound** *v.t.* to compound afresh. **recompress** *v.t.* to compress again. **recompression** *n.* **recompute** *v.t.* to compute again. **recomputation** *n.* **reconcentrate** *v.t.* to concentrate again, to make more concentrated. **recondense** *v.t.* to condense again. **recondensation** *n.* **recondition** *v.t.* to repair, to make as good as new. **reconditioned** *a.* **reconduct** *v.t.* to conduct back again. **reconfigure** *v.t.* to configure again or differently. **reconfiguration** *n.* **reconfirm** *v.t.* to confirm or ratify again. **reconfirmation** *n.* **reconjoin** *v.t.* to join together again. **reconnect** *v.t., v.i.* to connect again. **reconnection** *n.* **reconquer** *v.t.* **1** to conquer again. **2** to regain. **reconquest** *n.* **reconsecrate** *v.t.* to consecrate afresh. **reconsecration** *n.* **reconsider** *v.t.* to consider (a decision) again (esp. with a view to rescinding). **reconsideration** *n.* **reconsign** *v.t.* to consign again. **reconsignment** *n.* **reconsolidate** *v.t., v.i.* to consolidate again. **reconsolidation** *n.* **reconstitute** *v.t.* **1** to constitute again. **2** to build up again, to reconstruct, to re-form. **3** to restore (esp. dried food) to a former condition by adding liquid. **4** to give a new constitution to, to reorganize. **reconstituent** *n., a.* **reconstitution** *n.* **reconstruct** *v.t.* **1** to construct again. **2** to rebuild. **3 a** to build up a picture of (a past event) from the available evidence. **b** to act out (a crime) as part of a police investigation. **reconstructable, reconstructible** *a.* **reconstruction** *n.* **1** the act or process of reconstructing. **2** (**Reconstruction**) the process by which the Southern States of the USA which had seceded from the Union were restored to Federal rights and privileges after the Civil War of 1861–5. **reconstructive, reconstructional, reconstructionary** *a.* **reconstructively** *adv.* **reconstructor** *n.* **recontaminate** *v.t.* to contaminate again. **recontamination** *n.* **recontest** *v.t.* to contest again. **reconvene** *v.t., v.i.* to convene or assemble again. **reconvention** *n.* a counteraction brought by the defendant in a suit against the plaintiff. **reconvert** *v.t.* to convert again, back to its previous state, religion etc. **reconversion** *n.* **reconvey** *v.t.* **1** to convey back. **2** to restore to a former owner. **reconveyance** *n.* **reconvict** *v.t.* to convict again. **reconviction** *n.* **recopy** *v.t.* (*3rd pers. sing. pres.* **recopies,** *pres.p.* **recopying,** *past, p.p.* **recopied**) to copy again. **re-count** *v.t.* to count over again. **re-count** (rē´-) *n.* a new or second count, esp. of votes in an election. **re-cover** *v.t.* to cover again, to put a new covering on.

recognisance RECOGNIZANCE.

recognise RECOGNIZE.

recognition (rekəgnish´ən) *n.* **1** the act of recognizing. **2** the state of being recognized. **3** acknowledgement, notice taken. **4** a perceiving as being known. **recognitive** (rekog´-), **recognitory** (-kog´-) *a.* [L *recognitio*, from *recognit-*, p.p. stem of *recognoscere*, to RECOGNIZE]

recognizance (rekog´nizəns), **recognisance** *n.* (*Law*) **1** a bond or obligation entered into in a court or before a magistrate to perform a specified act, fulfil a condition etc. (such as to keep the peace or appear when called upon). **2** a sum deposited as pledge for the fulfilment of this. [A-F *reconisaunce*, OF *recoignisance*, as RECOGNIZE]

recognize (rek´əgnīz), **recognise** *v.t.* **1** to know again, to recall the identity of. **2** to be aware, to realize or perceive the nature of. **3** to acknowledge, to admit the truth, validity, existence etc. of. **4** to reward, to thank. **5** to show appreciation of. **6** to give a sign of knowing (a person). **7** (*esp. N Am.*) to allow to speak in a meeting, debate etc. ~*v.i.* (*N Am.*) to enter into recognizances. **recognizable** *a.* **recognizability** (-bil´-) *n.* **recognizably** *adv.* **recognizant** (rikog´nizənt) *a.* (*formal*) **1** conscious (of). **2** showing recognition or acknowledgement (of). **recognizer** *n.* [OF *reconoistre* (F *reconnaître*), L *recognoscere* (RE-, *cognoscere*, to cognosce, to know)]

Usage note Pronunciation with just (-n-), rather than (-gn-) is best avoided.

---

recoil[1] (rikoil´) *v.i.* **1** to shrink back, as in fear or disgust. **2** to start or spring back. **3** to rebound. **4** to go wrong and harm the perpetrator. **5** (of a firearm) to be driven back when fired. **6** to retreat. **7** (*Physics*) to change momentum on emission of a particle. **recoiler** *n.* **recoilingly** *adv.* **recoilment** *n.* [OF *reculer* (RE-, *cul*, L *culum*, nom. *-lus*, the posterior)]

recoil[2] (rikoil′, rē′-) *n.* **1** the act of recoiling. **2** the act or feeling of shrinking back, as in fear or disgust. **3** a rebound. **4** the backward kick of a gun when fired. **5** the change in motion of an atom, elementary particle etc. caused by emission of a particle. **recoil escapement** *n.* a clock escapement in which after each beat the escape wheel recoils slightly. **recoilless** (ri-) *a.*

recollect (rekəlekt′) *v.t.* to recall to memory, to remember, to succeed in recalling the memory of. *~v.i.* to succeed in remembering. **recollection** (-lek′shən) *n.* **1** the act or power of recollecting. **2** a memory, a reminiscence. **3** a person's memory. **4** the period of past time over which a person's memory extends. **recollective** *a.* **recollectively** *adv.* [L *recollectus*, p.p. of *recolligere*, after F *récolliger*]

re-collect RE- (+ CO- WORDS).

recombinant (rikom′binənt) *a.* found by or exhibiting genetic recombination. *~n.* a recombinant organism, cell or cell nucleus. **recombinant DNA** *n.* DNA prepared in the laboratory by combining DNA molecules from different individuals or species. **recombination** *n.* the process whereby genetic material from different sources is combined, esp. the interchange of sections of parental chromosomes resulting in new combinations of genes in the offspring.

recommend (rekəmend′) *v.t.* **1** to commend to another's notice, use or favour, esp. to represent as suitable for an office or employment. **2** to advise (a certain course of action etc.), to counsel. **3** (of qualities etc.) to make acceptable, desirable or serviceable. **4** †to give (one's soul, a person etc.) in charge (to God etc.), to entrust. **recommendable** *a.* **recommendably** *adv.* **recommendation** (-dā′shən) *n.* **1** the act of recommending. **2** something recommended. **3** a letter recommending a person for an appointment etc. **4** a quality or feature that tends to procure a favourable reception, a ground of approbation. **recommendatory** *a.* **recommender** *n.* [from F *recommender*, var. of *recommander*, or med. L *recommendāre* (RE-, *commendāre*, to COMMEND)]

recompense (rek′əmpens) *v.t.* **1** to make a return or give an equivalent for, to requite, to repay (a person, a service, an injury etc.). **2** to indemnify, to compensate (for), to make up (for). *~n.* that which is given as a reward, compensation, requital or satisfaction (for a service, injury etc.). **recompensable** *a.* **recompenser** *n.* **recompensive** *a.* [OF *recompenser*, late L *recompensāre* (RE-, *compensāre*, to COMPENSATE)]

☒ **reconaisance** common misspelling of RECONNAISSANCE.

reconcile (rek′ənsīl) *v.t.* **1** to restore to friendship after an estrangement. **2** to make content, acquiescent or submissive (to). **3** to harmonize, to make consistent or compatible (with). **4** to adjust, to settle (differences etc.). **5** in the Roman Catholic Church, to purify or restore (a desecrated church etc.) to sacred uses, to reconsecrate. **reconcilable** *a.* **reconcilability** (-bil′-), †**reconcilableness** *n.* **reconcilably** *adv.* **reconcilement** *n.* **reconciler** *n.* **reconciliation** (-siliā′shən) *n.* **reconciliatory** (-sil′iətri) *a.* [F *réconcilier*, L *reconciliāre* (RE-, *conciliāre*, to conciliate)]

recondite (rek′əndīt, rikon′-) *a.* **1** out of the way, abstruse, little known, obscure. **2** of or relating to abstruse or special knowledge, profound. **reconditely** *adv.* **reconditeness** *n.* [L *reconditus*, p.p. of *recondere* (RE-, *condere*, to hide, see CONDIMENT)]

☒ **reconize** common misspelling of RECOGNIZE.

reconnaissance (rikon′əsəns) *n.* **1** a preliminary examination or survey. **2** an exploratory survey of a tract of country or a coastline in wartime to ascertain the position of the enemy, the strategic features etc. **reconnaissance in force** *n.* a reconnaissance by a large body of troops or vessels of war. [F, from *reconnaître*, late form of RECONNOITRE]

reconnoitre (rekənoi′tə) *v.t.* to make a reconnaissance of. *~v.i.* to make a reconnaissance. *~n.* a reconnaissance. **reconnoitrer** *n.* [F, now *reconnaître*, L *recognoscere*, to RECOGNIZE]

record[1] (rikawd′) *v.t.* **1** to register, to write an account of, to set down permanent evidence of. **2 a** to transfer (sound, a programme etc.) by electronic means on to a storage medium for later reproduction or broadcast. **b** to make a recording of (the voice etc.). **3** to bear witness to, to be evidence of. **4** to indicate, to register. *~v.i.* to make a recording. **recordable** *a.* **recorded** *a.* **recorded delivery** *n.* a postal service in which an official record of posting and delivery is kept. **recording** *a.* registering waveforms arising from sound sources, or the readings of meteorological and other instruments to make a record automatically. *~n.* **1** the process of making a record of sound or image on record, tape or film. **2** the record, tape or film so produced. **3** a radio or television programme which has been recorded. **recording angel** *n.* an angel supposed to keep a record of every person's good and bad deeds. **recordist** *n.* a person who records a sound. [OF *recorder*, L *recordāre -dārī* (RE-, *cor cordis*, heart)]

record[2] (rek′awd, -əd) *n.* **1** a written or other permanent account or statement of a fact, event etc. **2** a register, a report, a minute or minutes of proceedings. **3** a trace or series of marks made by a recording instrument. **4** a thin plastic disc on to which sound is recorded. **5** an official report of proceedings, judgement etc. to be kept as authentic legal evidence, or an official memorial of particulars, pleadings etc. to be submitted as a case for decision by a court. **6** the past history of a person's career, achievements etc. esp. as an index of character and abilities. **7** a list or history of criminal convictions. **8** the best performance, as in sport, or the most striking event of its kind recorded. **9** the state of being recorded. **10** something that bears witness, testimony, attestation. **11** a portrait, monument or other memento of a person, event etc. **12** (*Comput.*) a group of items handled as a unit. **for the record** for the sake of accuracy. **off the record** in confidence, not said officially. **on record 1** recorded, esp. with legal or official authentication. **2** publicly known. **to beat/ break the record** to surpass all former achievements or events of the kind. **to go on record** to state one's beliefs publicly. **to have a record** to be a known, previously convicted criminal. **to put/ set the record straight** to correct an error or false impression. **record breaker** *n.* a person who breaks a world, national etc. record, esp. in sport. **record-breaking** *n., a.* **record holder** *n.* a person who holds a record, esp. in sport. **Record Office** *n.* an official repository for state papers or public records. **record player** *n.* a machine for playing and reproducing sounds on a gramophone record.

recorder (rikaw′də) *n.* **1** a person or thing which records. **2** a machine for recording sound on to tape, a tape recorder. **3** a form of flute blown through a mouthpiece at the end. **4 a** a barrister or solicitor with a minimum of ten years' standing, appointed as a part-time judge in the Crown court. **b** (*Hist.*) a magistrate having a limited criminal and civil jurisdiction in a city or borough and presiding over quarter sessions. **5** a person who keeps records. **recordership** *n.*

recount (rikownt′) *v.t.* to relate in detail, to narrate. **recountal, recountment** *n.* [OF *reconter* (RE-, COUNT[1])]

re-count RE- (+ CO- WORDS).

recoup (rikoop′) *v.t.* **1** to reimburse, to indemnify for a loss or expenditure. **2** to recover, to make up for (a loss, expenditure etc.). **3** (*Law*) to keep back (a part of something due). *~v.i.* **1** to make up for a loss. **2** (*Law*) to keep back part of something due. **recoupable** *a.* **recouper** *n.* **recoupment** *n.* [F *recouper* (RE-, *couper*, to cut, see COUP[1])]

Usage note The verbs *recoup* and *recuperate* should not be confused: *recoup* refers to recovering loss or expenditure, and *recuperate* to recovering health or strength.

recourse (rikaws´) *n.* **1** resorting or applying (to) as for help. **2** a source of help, that which is resorted to. **3** the right to demand payment, esp. from the drawer or endorser of a bill of exchange or other negotiable instrument. **to have recourse to** to turn or apply to for help. **without recourse** an endorsement of a bill of exchange etc. protecting the endorser from liability for non-payment. **recourseful** *a.* [F *recours*, L *recursum*, nom. *-sus* (RE-, *cursus*, COURSE)]

recover (rikŭv´ə) *v.t.* **1** to regain, to repossess oneself of, to win back. **2** to obtain by legal process. **3** to save (the reusable by-products of an industrial process). **4** to extract (valuable matter) from an ore. **5** to make up for, to retrieve. **6** to bring (a weapon) back after a thrust etc. *~v.i.* **1** to regain a former state, esp. after sickness, misfortune etc. **2** to come back to consciousness, life, health etc. **3** to be successful in a lawsuit. **4** in fencing, to come back to a posture of defence after making an attack. *~n.* **1** the position of a weapon or the body after a thrust etc. **2** the act of coming back to this. **recoverable** *a.* **recoverability** (-bil´-), **recoverableness** *n.* **recoveree** (-rē´) *n.* the person against whom a judgement is obtained in recovery. **recoverer** *n.* someone who or something which recovers. **recoveror** *n.* the person who obtains a judgement in their favour in recovery. **recovery** *n.* (*pl.* **recoveries**) **1** the act of recovering or the state of having recovered. **2** restoration to health after sickness etc. **3** the obtaining of the right to something by the judgement of a court. **4** a golf stroke played on to the fairway or green from a bunker or the rough. **5** the retrieval of by-products from an industrial process. [OF *recovrer* (F *recouvrer*), L *recuperāre*, to RECUPERATE]

re-cover RE- (+ CO– WORDS).

re- (+ cr– words) recreate[1] *v.t.* to create anew. **recreation** *n.* **re-creator** *n.* **recross** *v.t.*, *v.i.* to cross or pass over again. **recrown** *v.t.* to crown again. **recrystallize, recrystallise** *v.t.*, *v.i.* to crystallize again. **recrystallization** *n.*

recreant (rek´riənt) *a.* (*formal or poet.*) **1** craven, cowardly. **2** disloyal. *~n.* a coward, an apostate, a deserter. **recreance, recreancy** *n.* **recreantly** *adv.* [OF, pres.p. of *recroire*, to yield in trial by combat (RE-, *croire*, L *crēdere*, to believe, to entrust)]

recreate[1] RE- (+ CR– WORDS).

recreate[2] RECREATION.

recreation (rekriā´shən) *n.* **1** the act or process of refreshing oneself or renewing one's strength after toil. **2** a pleasurable or entertaining exercise or activity. **recreate**[2] (rek´riāt) *v.t.* (*formal*) **1** to divert, to entertain, to amuse. **2** to refresh after toil. *~v.i.* to take recreation. **recreational** *a.* **1** of, relating to or providing recreation. **2** (of a drug) taken for pleasure rather than for medical reasons. **recreationally** *adv.* **recreation ground** *n.* a communal open space in an urban area. **recreative** *a.* **recreatively** *adv.* **recreativeness** *n.* [L *recreātus*, p.p. of *recreāre*]

re-creation RE- (+ CR– WORDS).

recrement (rek´rimənt) *n.* **1** (*Med.*) fluid separated from the blood and absorbed into it again, such as gastric juice, saliva etc. **2** (*formal*) useless matter separated from that which is useful, refuse. **recremental** (-men´-), **recrementitial** (-tish´-), **recrementitious** *a.* [F *récrément*, L *recrēmentum*, from *recernere* (RE-, *cernere*, to sift)]

recriminate (rikrim´ināt) *v.i.* to return an accusation, to bring countercharges. *~v.t.* to accuse in return. **recrimination** (-ā´shən) *n.* **1** the act of bringing a countercharge or of accusing in return. **2** a countercharge. **recriminative, recriminatory** *a.* **recriminator** *n.* [med. L *recrīminātus*, p.p. of *recrīminārī* (RE-, *crīminārī*, to CRIMINATE)]

recrudesce (rēkrudes´) *v.i.* (*formal*) to break out or become active again. **recrudescence** *n.* a relapse, a breaking-out again, a renewal, a reappearance. **recrudescent** *a.* [L *recrūdescere* (RE-, *crūdescere*, to become raw, from *crūdus*, raw)]

recruit (rikroot´) *v.t.* **1** to enlist (esp. soldiers, sailors or airmen). **2** to raise or increase the strength of (an army, regiment, crew etc.) by enlisting recruits. **3** to enrol (members). **4** to replenish with fresh supplies, to fill gaps in. **5** to restore to health, to refresh, to reinvigorate. *~v.i.* **1** to enlist recruits for military service. **2** to gain new members, supplies etc. *~n.* **1** a serviceman or servicewoman newly enlisted. **2** a person who has newly joined a society etc. **recruitable** *a.* **recruiter** *n.* **recruiting** *n.*, *a.* **recruiting ground** *n.* any source of, or place from which recruits may be gained. **recruiting-officer** *n.* a person, esp. a military officer, engaged in enlisting recruits. **recruitment** *n.* [F *recruter*, from obs. *recrute*, a recruit, prov. form of *recrue*, fem. p.p. of *recroître* (RE-, *croître*, OF *creistre*, L *crescere*, to grow, to INCREASE[1])]

rect-[1] RECTI-.

rect-[2] RECTO-.

recta, rectal etc. RECTUM.

rectangle (rek´tang·gəl) *n.* a plane quadrilateral figure with four right angles. **rectangled** *a.* having an angle or angles of 90°. **rectangular** (-tang´gūlə) *a.* **1** shaped like a rectangle. **2** having an angle or angles of 90°. **3** placed or having parts placed at right angles. **4** having a base, surface or section shaped like a rectangle. **rectangular coordinates** *n.pl.* in a cartesian system, coordinates which have axes perpendicular to each other. **rectangular hyperbola** *n.* a hyperbola with asymptotes at right angles. **rectangularity** (-lar´-) *n.* **rectangularly** *adv.* [F, from late L *rectangulus* (*rectus*, straight, *angulus*, ANGLE[1])]

recti RECTUS.

recti- (rek´ti), **rect-** *comb. form* **1** straight. **2** right. [L *rectus*]

rectify (rek´tifī) *v.t.* (*3rd pers. sing. pres.* **rectifies,** *pres.p.* **rectifying,** *past, p.p.* **rectified**) **1** to set right, to correct, to amend, to adjust, to reform, to supersede by what is right or just. **2** to refine or purify (spirit etc.) by repeated distillations and other processes. **3** to transform (alternating current) into direct current. **4** to determine the length of (an arc etc.). **rectifiable** *a.* **rectification** (-fikā´shən) *n.* **rectified spirit** *n.* a mixture of 95.6% ethanol and water. **rectifier** *n.* **1** someone who or something which rectifies. **2** any of various electrical devices used in power supply circuits to change alternating current into direct current. [F *rectifier*, late L *rectificāre* (RECTI-, *-ficāre*, *facere*, to make)]

rectilinear (rektilin´iə), **rectilineal** (-iəl) *a.* **1** consisting of, lying or proceeding in a straight line. **2** straight. **3** bounded by straight lines. **rectilinearity** (-niar´iti) *n.* **rectilinearly, rectilineally** *adv.* [late L *rectilīneus* (*līnea*, LINE[1])]

rectiserial (rektisiə´riəl) *a.* (*Bot.*) (of leaves) arranged in a straight line, esp. in vertical ranks. [L *recti-*, *rectus*, straight, SERIAL]

rectitis, rectitic RECTUM.

rectitude (rek´titūd) *n.* **1** uprightness, rightness of moral principle, conformity to truth and justice. **2** righteousness. **3** freedom from error, correctness in judgement etc. **rectitudinous** (-tū´-) *a.* [F, from late L *rectitūdo*, from L *rectus*, right]

recto (rek´tō) *n.* (*pl.* **rectos**) 1 the right-hand page of an open book (usu. bearing an odd number) as distinct from *verso.* 2 the front of a printed sheet of paper. [L *recto* (*folio*), on the right (leaf)]

recto- (rek´tō), **rect-** *comb. form* of or relating to the rectum. [L *rectus*, straight]

rectocele (rek´təsēl) *n.* (*Med.*) protrusion of the rectum into the vagina.

rector (rek´tə) *n.* 1 the incumbent of a Church of England parish in which tithes were formerly paid to the incumbent. 2 a Roman Catholic priest in charge of a religious institution or church. 3 a clergyman in charge of a parish in the Episcopalian Church. 4 the head of certain universities, colleges and schools. 5 LORD RECTOR (under LORD). **rectorate** (-rət) *n.* 1 the office or position of rector. 2 a rector's term of office. **rectorial** (-taw´ri-) *a.* 1 of or relating to a rector. 2 of or relating to the election of a Lord Rector. *~n.* the election of a Lord Rector. **rectorship** *n.* **rectory** *n.* (*pl.* **rectories**) 1 the house of a rector. 2 the benefice or living of a Church of England rector with all its rights, property etc. [L, ruler, from *regere* (p.p. *rectus*), to rule]

rectrix (rek´triks) *n.* (*pl.* **rectrices** (-sēz)) the quill-feathers in a bird's tail which guide its flight. **rectricial** (-trish´əl) *a.* [L, fem. of RECTOR]

rectum (rek´təm) *n.* (*pl.* **rectums, recta** (-tə)) (*Anat.*) the lowest portion of the large intestine extending to the anus. **rectal** *a.* **rectally** *adv.* **rectitic** (-tit´-) *a.* **rectitis** (rektī´tis) *n.* (*Med.*) inflammation of the rectum. [L *rectum intestinum*, straight intestine]

rectus (rek´təs) *n.* (*pl.* **recti** (-tī)) (*Anat.*) a straight muscle, esp. of the abdomen, thigh, neck or eyes. [L, straight]

re- (+ cu–cy words) recultivate *v.t.* to cultivate afresh. **recultivation** *n.* **recut** *v.t.* (*pres.p.* **recutting,** *past, p.p.* **recut**) to cut again. **recycle** *v.t.* to pass again through a system of treatment or series of changes, esp. to process (a waste product, such as paper or glass) so as to be reusable. *~v.i.* (esp. of an electrical device) to return to an original position so the operation can begin again. *~n.* the repetition of a sequence of events. **recyclable** *a.* **recyclability** *n.* **recycler** *n.*

recumbent (rikŭm´bənt) *a.* 1 lying down, reclining. 2 (of an organ or structure) resting against a part or surface to which it is attached. 3 (*Geol.*) of or relating to a fold in rock in which the strata are nearly horizontal. *~n.* a bicycle or tricycle having a low, chairlike seat with a backrest against which the rider leans to push forwards against the pedals. **recumbence, recumbency** *n.* **recumbently** *adv.* [L *recumbens -ntem*, pres.p. of *recumbere* (RE-, *cumbere*, to lie)]

recuperate (rikoo´pərāt, -kū´-) *v.i.* to recover from sickness, exhaustion, loss of power, a loss etc. *~v.t.* to recover, to regain (health, strength etc.). **recuperable** *a.* **recuperation** (-ā´shən) *n.* **recuperative** *a.* **recuperator** *n.* †**recuperatory** *a.* [L *recuperātus*, p.p. of *recuperāre*, var. of *reciperāre*, form of *recipere*, to RECEIVE]

Usage note The use of *recuperate* as a transitive verb is sometimes disapproved of. See also note under RECOUP.

recur (rikœ´) *v.i.* (*pres.p.* **recurring,** *past, p.p.* **recurred**) 1 to happen again, to happen repeatedly. 2 to come back to one's mind. 3 (*Math.*) to be repeated indefinitely. 4 to return, to go back (to) in thought etc. **recurrence** (-kŭr´əns) *n.* †**recurrency** *n.* **recurrent** (rikŭr´ənt) *a.* 1 returning, recurring, esp. at regular intervals. 2 (*Anat.*) (of veins, nerves etc.) turning in the opposite direction, running in an opposite course to those from which they branch. *~n.* (*Anat.*) a recurrent nerve or artery, esp. one of the laryngeal nerves. **recurrently** *adv.* **recurring** *a.* happening again or being repeated. **recurring decimal** *n.* (*Math.*) a decimal fraction in which one digit or a sequence of digits recurs over and over again indefinitely. **recursion** (-shən) *n.* 1 the act of returning. 2 (*Math.*) the repeated application of a mathematical procedure to a preceding result to generate a sequence of values. **recursion formula** *n.* (*Math.*) a mathematical formula or expression which enables the computation of successive values of a sequence from a preceding value. **recursive** *a.* 1 recurring, repeating. 2 relating to or involving mathematical recursion. 3 relating to or being a computer program or subroutine which calls itself into operation. **recursively** *adv.* [L *recurrere* (RE-, *currere*, to run)]

recurve (rikœv´) *v.t., v.i.* to bend backwards. **recurvate** (-vət, -vāt) *a.* recurved, reflexed. **recurvature** (-vəchə) *n.* [L *recurvāre*]

recusant (rek´ūzənt) *a.* 1 obstinately refusing to conform. 2 (*Hist.*) refusing to attend the services of the Church of England. *~n.* 1 a person who refuses to submit or comply. 2 (*Hist.*) a person, esp. a Roman Catholic, who refused to attend the services of the Church of England. **recusance, recusancy** *n.* [L *recusans -antem*, pres.p. of *recusāre*, to refuse, to object (RE-, *causa*, CAUSE)]

red[1] (red) *a.* (*comp.* **redder,** *superl.* **reddest**) 1 of a bright warm colour, such as blood, usu. including crimson, scarlet, vermilion etc.; of the colour at the least refracted end of the spectrum or that farthest from the violet. 2 tinged with red. 3 (of hair) reddish-brown, auburn, tawny, ginger, russet. 4 flushed, suffused with blood, esp. as a sign of anger or shame. 5 involving bloodshed or violence, bloody. 6 revolutionary, anarchistic. 7 (*coll. or derog.*) (*also* **Red**) left-wing, communist, socialist. 8 (*Hist.*) (*also* **Red**) Soviet. 9 denoting danger. *~n.* 1 a red colour or a shade of this. 2 a red pigment. 3 red clothes. 4 the red ball in billiards, snooker etc. 5 the red colour in roulette etc. 6 a red light. 7 (*coll. or derog.*) a revolutionary, an extreme radical, an anarchist. 8 a member of a Communist or Socialist party, state or country, esp. the former Soviet Union. **in the red** overdrawn at the bank. **to paint the town red** to have a riotous time. **to see red** to become enraged. **red admiral** *n.* a butterfly, *Vanessa atalanta*, with reddish-banded wings. **red alert** *n.* a state of readiness for a crisis or disaster. **red algae** *n.pl.* seaweed of the family Rhodophycae, having red pigment as well as chlorophyll. **red-and-black** *n.* rouge-et-noir. **red arsenic** *n.* realgar. **red-back, red-back spider** *n.* a venomous Australian spider, *Latrodectus hasselti*, with red spots on its back. **red-backed** *a.* **red-backed shrike** *n.* a shrike, *Lanius collurio*, the male of which has a chestnut-coloured back. **red bark** *n.* a variety of cinchona. **red-bearded** *a.* **red-bellied** *a.* **red-berried** *a.* bearing red berries. **red biddy** *n.* red wine mixed with methylated spirits. **red-billed** *a.* (of a bird) having a red bill. **red blood cell, red blood corpuscle** *n.* a blood cell containing haemoglobin, an erythrocyte. **red-blooded** *a.* vigorous, virile. **red-bloodedness** *n.* **red book** *n.* a book, orig. bound in red, containing a list of the peerage, civil servants etc. **redbreast** *n.* (*coll.*) the robin, *Erythacus rubecula*. **redbrick** *a.* relating to, being or characteristic of any of the pre-1939 provincial universities in Britain. **redbud** *n.* an American leguminous tree of the genus *Cerci*, esp. *C. canadensis*, closely related to the Mediterranean Judas tree. **red cabbage** *n.* a reddish-purple cabbage, used esp. for pickling. **red campion** *n.* a Eurasian plant of the pink family, with red flowers. **redcap** *n.* 1 (*coll.*) a member of the military police. 2 (*N Am.*) a porter at a railway station. 3 any small bird with a reddish head, esp. the goldfinch. **red card** *n.* a piece of red cardboard shown by a soccer referee to a player to indicate that they are being sent off the field. **red carpet** *n.* 1 a strip of red carpet put out for a celebrity or important person to walk on. 2 deferential treatment shown to such a person. **to put out the red carpet** to give an impressive welcome. **red cedar** *n.* 1 any of various species of cedar, esp. a N American juniper, *Juniperus virginiana*, with fragrant, red wood. 2 the timber from such a tree. **red cell** *n.* an erythrocyte. **red cent** *n.* (*N Am., coll.*) a trifling amount of money. **red-cheeked** *a.* having red or rosy cheeks. **redcoat** *n.* 1 (*Hist.*) a British soldier (so called from the scarlet tunics worn by line regiments). 2 an entertainments officer at a Butlin's holiday camp. **red coral** *n.* any of several pinkish-red corals of the genus *Corallium* used to make ornaments and jewellery. **red corpuscle** *n.* an erythrocyte. **Red Crescent** *n.* the equivalent of the Red Cross in Muslim countries. **Red Cross** *n.* 1 an international organization established in accordance with the Geneva Convention of 1864 for the provision of ambulance and hospital services for the wounded in time of war, and later extended to assist in severe epidemics and national disasters in peace time. 2 the emblem of this organization consisting of a red cross on a white background. **red cross** *n.* 1 St George's Cross, the English national emblem. 2 the side of the Christians during the Crusades. **redcurrant** *n.* 1 the small, red, edible berry from a shrub of the gooseberry family. 2 a shrub, *Ribes rubrum*, that bears redcurrants. **red deer** *n.* a large species of deer, *Cervus elaphus*, with reddish coat and branching antlers, occurring wild in the Scottish Highlands, on Exmoor etc. **redden** *v.t.* to make red. ~*v.i.* to become red, esp. to blush. **reddish, reddy** *a.* **reddishness** *n.* **red duster** *n.* (*sl.*) the red ensign. **red dwarf** *n.* a star with a relatively small mass and low luminosity. **red earth** *n.* soil coloured red by iron compounds, found in tropical savanna. **red ensign** *n.* a red flag with the Union Jack in one corner, used as the ensign of the British Merchant Navy. **red-eye** *n.* 1 (*N Am., coll.*) low quality whisky. 2 the effect on a photograph of a person's eyes appearing red, caused by light from a flashgun etc. being reflected from the retina. 3 the rudd. 4 (*N Am., coll.*) (*also* **red-eye flight**) a long-distance overnight aeroplane flight. **red eyes** *n.pl.* bloodshot eyes, with lids red and inflamed with weeping. **red-eyed** *a.* having red eyes from weeping. **red-faced** *a.* 1 flushed with embarrassment. 2 with a red, florid complexion. **redfin** *n.* any of several small aquarium fishes with red fins. **redfish** *n.* 1 a male salmon in the spawning season. 2 any of various fishes with a reddish colour, esp. of the genus *Sebastes*. **red flag** *n.* 1 the symbol of revolution or of communism. 2 a danger signal. **red fox** *n.* the common European fox, *Vulpes vulpes*. **red giant** *n.* a giant star with high luminosity that emits red light. **red grouse** GROUSE[1]. **Red Guard** *n.* (*Hist.*) a member of the militant Maoist youth movement in China, formed to preserve popular support for the regime and active during the cultural revolution in the 1960s. **red gum** *n.* 1 an eruption of red pimples in infants, caused by teething. 2 any of various species of Australian eucalyptus yielding reddish resin. 3 such a resin. **red-haired** *a.* having red hair. **red-handed** *a., adv.* in the very act of committing a crime or doing something wrong. **red hat** *n.* 1 a cardinal's hat. 2 the rank or office of a cardinal. 3 a staff officer. **redhead** *n.* a person with red hair. **red-headed** *a.* 1 (of a person) having red hair. 2 (of a bird etc.) having a red head. **red heat** *n.* 1 the temperature at which a thing is red-hot. 2 the state of being red-hot. **red herring** *n.* 1 herring, dried and smoked. 2 anything which diverts attention from the real issue or line of enquiry. **red-hot** *a.* 1 heated to redness. 2 **a** excited, keen, wildly enthusiastic. **b** full of energy or activity. 3 intense, ardent, passionate. 4 furious, violent. 5 very recent, topical, new. **red-hot poker** *n.* a plant of the S African genus *Kniphofia*, esp. *K. uvaria* cultivated for its tall stout stems bearing terminal spikes of orange and yellow flowers. **Red Indian** *n.* (*offensive*) a N American Indian. **red lead** *n.* red oxide of lead used as a pigment. **redleg** *n.* (*W Ind., derog.*) a poor white. **red-legged** *a.* (of a bird) having red legs. **red Leicester** *n.* orange-coloured Leicester cheese. **red-letter day** *n.* an auspicious or memorable day (because these were marked in red on the calendar). **red light** *n.* 1 a red light used as a signal to stop, esp. a red traffic light. 2 a danger signal. 3 any signal or indication to stop. **red-light area, red-light district** *n.* an area or district in a town where there is a collection of brothels etc. **redly** *adv.* **red man** REDSKIN (under RED[1]). **red meat** *n.* dark-coloured meat, esp. beef or lamb. **red mullet** *n.* an edible mullet of the family Mullidae, found in European waters. **redneck** *n.* (*N Am., derog.*) 1 a poor white farm labourer in the South. 2 a reactionary person or institution. ~*a.* reactionary. **redness** *n.* **red ochre,** (*N Am.*) **red ocher** *n.* any of several red earths, used as pigments. **red orpiment** *n.* REALGAR. **red panda** *n.* a small raccoon-like animal, *Aelurus fulgens*, from the SE Himalayas and Tibet. **red pepper** *n.* 1 the red fruit of the sweet pepper. 2 any of various pepper plants cultivated for their hot red fruits. 3 the fruit of such a plant. 4 cayenne pepper. **Red Planet** *n.* Mars. **Red Poll** *n.* a red-haired breed of hornless cattle. **redpoll** (red´pol, -pōl) *n.* any of several small finches of the genus *Acanthis*, the males of which have a red or rosy crown, esp. *A. flammea* and *A. hornemanni*. **red precipitate** *n.* red oxide of mercury. **red rag** *n.* anything that excites rage (as a red object is supposed to enrage a bull). **red rattle** *n.* a pink-flowered European plant, *Pedicularis palustris*, of marshland. **red ribbon** *n.* 1 the ribbon worn by members of the Order of the Bath. 2 membership of this. **red rose** *n.* the emblem of the House of Lancaster during the Wars of the Roses, 1455–85. **red salmon** *n.* any salmon with red flesh, esp. the sockeye salmon. **red sandalwood** *n.* 1 a SE Asian tree, *Pterocarpus santalinus*, with hard, fragrant dark red wood. 2 the wood of this tree used for cabinetwork and to make dyes. **red sanders** *n.* red sandalwood. **red seaweed** *n.* red algae. **redshank** *n.* 1 either of two red-legged sandpipers, *Tringa totanus* or *T. erythropus*. 2 (*pl., derog.*) †inhabitants of the Scottish Highlands or of Ireland (bare-legged). **red shift** *n.* the shift of lines in the spectrum towards the red, caused by a receding light source. **red-shirt** *n.* 1 (*Hist.*) a follower of Garibaldi, 1807–82. 2 a revolutionary. **red-short** *a.* of iron, brittle when hot, hot-short. **redskin** *n.* (*offensive*) a N American Indian. **red snapper** *n.* any of several edible fish of the snapper family. **red snow** *n.* snow reddened by the growth of a minute alga containing red pigment, such as *Chlamydomonas nivalis*, frequent in Arctic and Alpine regions. **red spider, red spider mite** *n.* a mite of the family Tetranychidae, infesting house and garden plants. **Red Spot** *n.* a reddish spot, oval in shape and about 48,000 km (29,760 miles) long which drifts around the southern hemisphere of Jupiter. **red squirrel** *n.* 1 a reddish squirrel, *Sciurus vulgaris*, found in Europe and some parts of Asia. 2 a small, widely distributed N American squirrel, *Tamiasciurus hudsonicus*. **Red Star** *n.* the emblem of some Communist countries. **red-streak** *n.* a type of cider apple. **red tape** *n.* extreme adherence to official routine and formality (from the red tape once used in tying up official documents). **red-tape** *a.* characterized by red tape. **red-tapery, red-tapism** *n.* **red-tapist** *n.* **red tide** *n.* sea water, when discoloured and made toxic by red protozoans. **red-top** *n.* (*N Am.*) a grass of the genus *Agrostis*, a kind of bent grass. **red underwing** *n.* a large moth with red and black hind wings. **red valerian** *n.* a Mediterranean plant, *Centranthus ruber*, with red spurred flowers. **red vitriol** *n.*

cobalt sulphate. **redwater, redwater fever** *n.* (*Zool.*) 1 haematuria in cattle and sheep, the most marked symptom of which is red urine. 2 a disease of cattle caused by the tick-borne protozoan *Babesia boris*, resulting in haematuria. **red wine** *n.* wine made from black grapes and coloured by grape skins. **redwing** *n.* 1 a European thrush, *Turdus iliacus*, with red patches under the wings. 2 a N American blackbird, *Agelaius phoeniceus*, with red wing patches. **redwood** *n.* any of various trees with reddish timber, esp. the gigantic Californian sequoia, *Sequoia sempervirens*. [OE *read* (cp. Dut. *rood*, G *roth*, Icel. *rauthr*, also L *rufus*, *ruber*, Gr. *eruthros*, Sansk. *rudhira*-)]

red[2] REDD[1].

-red (rid) *suf.* condition, as *hatred*, *kindred*. [OE *rǣdan*]

redaction (ridak´shən) *n.* 1 reduction to order, esp. revising, rearranging and editing a literary work. 2 a revised or rearranged edition. **redact** *v.t.* to reduce to a certain form, esp. a literary form, to edit, to prepare for publication. **redactor** *n.* a person who redacts, an editor. **redactorial** (redaktaw´ri-) *a.* [F *rédaction*, late L *redactiōnem*, nom. *-tio*, from *redigere* (*red-*, RE-, *agere*, to bring), p.p. *redactus*]

redan (ridan´) *n.* a fortification having two faces forming a salient angle towards the enemy. [F, for *redent* (RE-, DENT[1], tooth)]

redd[1] (red), **red** *v.t.* (*pres.p.* **redding**, *past*, *p.p.* **redd, red, redded**) (*chiefly Sc.*) 1 to clear (up), to put in order, to tidy, to make ready or clear. 2 to interfere between, to separate (combatants etc.), to settle (a quarrel). **redder**[2] *n.* [etym. uncertain, cp. Dut. *redden*]

redd[2] (red) *n.* a hollow made in a river bed by a salmon, trout etc. for spawning. [etym. unknown]

redden RED[1].

redder[1] etc. RED[1].

redder[2] REDD[1].

reddish RED[1].

reddle RUDDLE.

reddy RED[1].

re- (+ de–dy words) redecorate *v.t.* to decorate afresh. **redecoration** *n.* **rededicate** *v.t.* to dedicate anew. **rededication** *n.* **rededicatory** *a.* **redefine** *v.t.* to define again or afresh. **redefinition** *n.* **redelegate** *v.t.* to delegate anew. **redelegation** *n.* **redeliver** *v.t.* 1 to deliver back, to restore, to free again. 2 to repeat, to report. **redeliverance, redelivery** *n.* **redemand** *v.t.* to demand again or back. **redemonstrate** *v.t.* to demonstrate again. **redemonstration** *n.* **redeploy** *v.t.* 1 to transfer (troops, labour force) from one area to another. 2 to assign a new task to. **redeployment** *n.* **redescend** *v.t.*, *v.i.* to descend again. **redescribe** *v.t.*, *v.i.* to describe again. **redescription** *n.* **redesign**[1] (rēdizīn´) *v.t.* to make a new design of, incorporating improvements. **redesign**[2] (rē´-) *n.* a new or changed design. **redetermine** *v.t.* to determine again. **redetermination** *n.* **redevelop** *v.t.* 1 to develop again. 2 to renovate and build in (a depressed urban area). **redeveloper** *n.* **redevelopment** *n.* **redevelopment area** *n.* an urban area where existing buildings are either demolished and rebuilt or renovated. **redial** *v.t.*, *v.i.* (*pres.p.* **redialling**, (*N Am.*) **redialing**, *past*, *p.p.* **redialled**, (*N Am.*) **redialed**) to dial again. **redid** REDO (under RE- (+ DE–DY WORDS)). **redigest** *v.t.* to digest again. **redigestion** *n.* **redirect** *v.t.* 1 to direct again. 2 to readdress (a letter, parcel etc.). **redirection** *n.* **rediscount** *v.t.* to discount again. ~*n.* 1 the act of rediscounting. 2 something rediscounted. **rediscountable** *a.* **rediscover** *v.t.* to discover afresh. **rediscovery** *n.* (*pl.* **rediscoveries**). **redispose** *v.t.* to dispose again. **redisposition** *n.* **redissolve** *v.t.*, *v.i.* to dissolve again. **redissoluble** *a.* **redissolution** *n.* **redissolvable** *a.* **redistil**, (*N Am.*) **redistill** *v.t.* (*pres.p.* **redistilling**, *past*, *p.p.* **redistilled**) to distil again or repeatedly. **redistillation** *n.* **redistribute** *v.t.* to distribute again. **redistribution** *n.* the act of distributing again. **redistributive** *a.* **redivide** *v.t.* to divide again. **redivision** *n.* **redo** *v.t.* (*3rd pers. sing. pres.* **redoes**, *pres.p.* **redoing**, *past* **redid**, *p.p.* **redone**) 1 to do again. 2 to redecorate. **redouble** *v.t.* to increase by repeated additions, to intensify, to multiply. ~*v.i.* 1 to become increased by repeated additions, to grow more intense, numerous etc. 2 to be repeated, to re-echo. 3 to double an opponent's double in bridge. ~*n.* the act of redoubling. **redoublement** *n.* **redraft**[1] *v.t.* to draft or draw up a second time. **redraft**[2] (rē´-) *n.* 1 a second or revised draft. 2 a fresh bill of exchange drawn on the drawer or endorser to cover a protested bill plus costs and charges. **redraw** *v.t.* (*past* **redrew**, *p.p.* **redrawn**) to draw again. ~*v.i.* to draw a fresh bill of exchange to cover a protested one. **redrawer** *n.* **re-dress** *v.t.*, *v.i.* 1 to dress again. 2 to dress in different clothes. **redrill** *v.t.* to drill again. **redry** *v.t.* (*3rd pers. sing. pres.* **redries**, *pres.p.* **redrying**, *past*, *p.p.* **redried**) to dry again. **re-dye** *v.t.* (*3rd pers. sing. pres.* **re-dyes**, *pres.p.* **re-dyeing**, *past*, *p.p.* **re-dyed**) to dye again.

†**rede** (rēd) *n.* counsel, advice. ~*v.t.* 1 to counsel, to advise. 2 to read or interpret (a riddle etc.). [OE *rǣd*, from *rǣdan*, see READ]

redeem (ridēm´) *v.t.* 1 to buy back, to recover by paying a price. 2 to recover (mortgaged property), to discharge (a mortgage), to buy off (an obligation etc.). 3 to exchange (coupons, tokens etc.) for goods or cash. 4 to deliver, to save, to rescue, to reclaim. 5 to atone for, to make amends for. 6 to make good. 7 to recover from captivity by purchase, to ransom. 8 (of Christ) to deliver from sin and its penalty. 9 to perform (a promise). **redeemable** *a.* **redeemability** (-bil´-), **redeemableness** *n.* **redeemer** *n.* 1 a person who redeems. 2 (**Redeemer**) Christ, as Saviour of the world. **redeeming** *a.* compensating for faults. [F *redimer*, L *redimere* (*red-*, RE-, *emere*, to buy), p.p. *redemptus*]

redemption (ridemp´shən) *n.* 1 the act of redeeming or the state of being redeemed. 2 salvation from sin and damnation by the atonement of Christ. 3 release by purchase, ransom etc. 4 reclamation (of land etc.). 5 that which redeems. **redemptible** *a.* redeemable. **redemptioner** *n.* (*Hist.*) an emigrant to the US who obtained passage by becoming an indentured servant for a certain time. **redemptive, redemptory** *a.* **Redemptorist** *n.* a member of a Roman Catholic congregation of missionary priests founded at Naples in 1732 by St Alfonso Liguori. [F, from L *redemptiōnem*, nom. *-tio*, from *redimere*, to REDEEM]

rediffusion (rēdifū´zhən) *n.* a system of relaying radio or television programmes via cables.

redingote (red´ing·gōt) *n.* 1 a woman's long double-breasted coat. 2 a similar coat worn by men in the 18th cent. [F, corr. of *riding-coat*]

redintegrate (redin´tigrāt) *v.t.* 1 to restore to completeness, to make united or perfect again. 2 to renew, to re-establish. **redintegration** (-grā´shən) *n.* **redintegrative** (-grətiv) *a.* [L *redintegrātus*, p.p. of *redintegrāre*]

†**redivivus** (redivī´vəs) *a.* (*formal*) come to life again, revived (*usu. following its noun*). [L *redivīvus* (*redi-*, *red-*, RE-, *vīvus*, living)]

redolent (red´ələnt) *a.* 1 suggestive, reminding one (of). 2 fragrant. 3 giving out a strong smell. **redolence, redolency** *n.* **redolently** *adv.* [OF, L *redolentem*, nom. *-lens*, pres.p. of *redolēre* (*red-*, RE-, *olēre*, to smell)]

redoubt (ridowt´) *n.* a detached outwork or fieldwork enclosed by a parapet without flanking defences. [F *redoute*, It. *redotto*, L *reductus*, retired (later, a secret place, a refuge), p.p. of *redūcere*, to REDUCE]

redoubtable (ridow´təbəl) *a.* 1 formidable. 2 valiant. **redoubtableness** *n.* **redoubtably** *a.* [OF *redoutable*, from *redouter*, to fear]

redound (ridownd´) *v.i.* 1 to have effect, to contribute (to one's credit etc.). 2 to result, to act in return or recoil (on or upon). [F *rédonder*, L *redundāre*, to overflow (*red-*, RE-, *undāre*, from *unda*, wave)]

redowa (red´əvə) *n.* a Bohemian round dance of two forms, one resembling a waltz, the other a polka. [F and G, from Czech *reydovák*, from *reydovati*, to whirl round]

redox (rē´doks) *a.* (*Chem.*) of, relating to or being a chemical reaction where one agent is reduced and another oxidized. ~*n.* oxidation and reduction. [*reduction oxidation*]

redress (ridres´) *v.t.* 1 to remedy, to amend, to make reparation for. 2 to set straight or right again, to re-adjust, to rectify. ~*n.* 1 redressing of wrongs or oppression. 2 reparation. 3 rectification. **to redress the balance** to make equal again. **redressable** *a.* capable of being redressed. **redressal, redressment** *n.* redress. **redresser, redressor** *n.*

re-dress RE- (+ DE–DY WORDS).

redstart (red´staht) *n.* 1 a red-tailed migratory songbird, *Phoenicurus phoenicurus*. 2 a N American warbler of the genus *Setophaga*. [RED[1], OE *steort*, tail]

reduce (ridūs´) *v.t.* 1 to make smaller or less in size, number, degree, extent etc. 2 to bring or force into a specified condition, state, action etc. 3 to convert from one form into another, esp. simpler, form. 4 to set out in systematic form, to modify or simplify so as to conform (to a rule, formula, fundamental classification etc.). 5 to bring down, to lower, to degrade, to diminish, to weaken. 6 to lower the price of. 7 to impoverish. 8 to subdue, to conquer. 9 (*Math.*) to change from one denomination to another. 10 (*Chem.*) **a** to cause to lose oxygen atoms from. **b** to cause to combine or react with hydrogen. **c** to cause to gain electrons. 11 to convert (e.g. iron ore) to a metal. 12 to lessen the density of (a photographic print or negative). 13 to correct (a bone fracture, dislocation etc.) by restoring to the proper position. 14 to concentrate (a stock, sauce etc.) by boiling. 15 †to bring to an original condition. 16 †to bring back (to). 17 (*Sc.*) to set aside or annul by judicial action. ~*v.i.* 1 to become smaller or less. 2 to lose weight. 3 (*Chem.*) to become reduced, to undergo reduction. **to reduce to the ranks** (*Mil.*) to demote to the rank of private soldier. **reduced** *a.* **in reduced circumstances** poor, hard-up. **reducer** *n.* 1 someone who or something which reduces. 2 a piece of pipe for connecting two other pieces of different diameter. **reducible** *a.* **reducibility** (-bil´-), **reducibleness** *n.* **reducibly** *adv.* **reducing** *a.* **reducing agent** *n.* a substance which reduces another in a chemical process. **reducing glass** *n.* a lens or mirror which reflects an image smaller than the actual object observed. [L *redūcere* (RE-, *dūcere*, to bring), p.p. *reductus*]

reductio ad absurdum (ridŭktiō ad absœ´dəm) *n.* 1 proof of the falsity of a proposition by showing the absurdity of its logical consequence. 2 proof of the truth of a proposition by showing that its contrary has absurd consequences. 3 (*coll.*) an absurd conclusion. [L, reduction to absurdity]

reduction (ridŭk´shən) *n.* 1 the act or process of reducing. 2 the state of being reduced. 3 the amount by which something is reduced, a decrease, a diminution. 4 a reduced copy of anything. 5 (*Mus.*) a piano score arranged from an orchestral score. 6 (*Math.*) the process of finding an equivalent expression in terms of a different denomination. 7 a process whereby one or more electrons are added to an atom, molecule etc. **reduction division** *n.* (*Biol.*) meiosis. **reductionism** *n.* 1 the explaining of complex data or phenomena in simpler terms. 2 oversimplification. **reductionist** *n.*, *a.* **reductionistic** (-nis´-) *a.* **reductive** *a.*

redundant (ridŭn´dənt) *a.* 1 superfluous, excessive, superabundant, unnecessary. 2 deprived of one's job as no longer necessary. 3 using more words than are necessary, pleonastic, tautological. 4 included as a back-up in case of failure (*redundant components*). **redundancy, redundance** *n.* (*pl.* **redundancies, redundances**). **redundantly** *adv.* [L *redundans -antem*, pres.p. of *redundāre*, to REDOUND]

reduplicate (ridū´plikāt) *v.t.* 1 to double, to repeat. 2 to repeat (a letter or syllable) to form a tense. ~*a.* 1 doubled, repeated. 2 (of petals or sepals) with edges turned out. **reduplication** (-ā´shən) *n.* 1 the act of doubling or repeating. 2 the repetition of a syllable or other part of a word. 3 the part so repeated. 4 the doubling or folding back of a part or organ. **reduplicative** *a.* [med. L *reduplicātus*, p.p. of *reduplicāre* (RE-, *duplicāre*, to DUPLICATE[1])]

reduviid (ridū´viid) *a.* belonging to the Reduviidae, a family of blood-sucking insects. ~*n.* an insect of this family. **reduvioid** (-oid) *n.*, *a.* [mod. L *Reduvius*, -ID]

re- (+ e– words) re-echo *v.t.* (*3rd pers. sing. pres.* **re-echoes,** *pres.p.* **re-echoing,** *past, p.p.* **re-echoed)** 1 to echo or repeat again. 2 to return (an echo). ~*v.i.* 1 to echo again. 2 to reverberate. **re-edify** *v.t.* (*3rd pers. sing. pres.* **re-edifies,** *pres.p.* **re-edifying,** *past, p.p.* **re-edified**) 1 to rebuild. 2 (*fig.*) to reconstruct, to re-establish. **re-edification** *n.* **re-edit** *v.t.* to edit afresh. **re-educate** *v.t.* 1 to cause to develop new or different attitudes, habits, beliefs etc. 2 to teach new skills to. **re-education** *n.* **re-elect** *v.t.* to elect again, esp. for another term in office. **re-election** *n.* **re-elevate** *v.t.* to elevate again. **re-elevation** *n.* **re-eligible** *a.* eligible to be re-elected to the same position. **re-eligibility** *n.* **re-embark** *v.t.*, *v.i.* to embark again. **re-embarkation** *n.* **re-embody** *v.t.* (*3rd pers. sing. pres.* **re-embodies,** *pres.p.* **re-embodying,** *past, p.p.* **re-embodied**) to embody again. **re-embodiment** *n.* **re-embrace** *v.t.* to embrace again. ~*n.* a second embrace. **re-emerge** *v.i.* to emerge again. **re-emergence** *n.* **re-emergent** *a.* **re-emphasize, re-emphasise** *v.t.* to emphasize again or more strongly. **re-employ** *v.t.* to employ again. **re-employment** *n.* **re-enable** *v.t.* to make able again. **re-enact** *v.t.* to enact again, to act out (a past event). **re-enactment** *n.* **re-endorse** *v.t.* to endorse again. **re-endorsement** *n.* **re-endow** *v.t.* to endow again. **re-enforce** *v.t.* 1 to enforce again. 2 to give fresh or additional force or strength to. 3 to reinforce. **re-enforcement** *n.* **re-enforcer** *n.* **re-engage** *v.t.*, *v.i.* to engage again. **re-engagement** *n.* **re-enlarge** *v.t.*, *v.i.* to enlarge again or further. **re-enlargement** *n.* **re-enlighten** *v.t.* **re-enlightenment** *n.* **re-enlist** *v.t.*, *v.i.* to enlist again. **re-enlistment** *n.* **re-enter** *v.t.*, *v.i.* to enter again. **re-entrant** *a.* 1 re-entering. 2 pointing inwards. ~*n.* a re-entrant angle, esp. in fortification, as distinct from *salient*. **re-entrance** *n.* **re-entry** *n.* (*pl.* **re-entries)** 1 the act of re-entering. 2 a new entry in a book etc. 3 (*Law*) an act of retaking possession, esp. of leased premises by the leasor. 4 the re-entry of a spacecraft into the earth's atmosphere. **re-equip** *v.t.* (*pres.p.* **re-equipping,** *past, p.p.* **re-equipped**) to equip again. **re-erect** *v.t.* to erect again. **re-erection** *n.* **re-establish** *v.t.* to establish anew, to restore. **re-establisher** *n.* **re-establishment** *n.* **re-evaluate** *v.t.* to evaluate again or differently. **re-evaluation** *n.* **re-examine** *v.t.* to examine again or further. **re-examinable** *a.* **re-examination** *n.* **re-exchange** *v.t.* to exchange again. ~*n.* 1 a renewed exchange. 2 the difference in the value of a bill of exchange occasioned by its being dishonoured in a foreign country where it was payable. **re-exhibit** *v.t.* to exhibit again. **re-existence** *n.* **re-existent** *a.* **re-experience** *v.t.* to experience again. **re-explore** *v.t.* to explore again. **re-exploration** *n.* **re-export** *v.t.* 1 to export again. 2 to export after having been imported. 3 to export (imported goods) after processing. ~*n.* 1 the act of re-exporting. **2** a commodity re-exported. **re-exportation** *n.* **re-exporter** *n.*

ree (rē) *n.* the female ruff. [var. of REEVE[3]]

reebok RHEBOK.

reed (rēd) *n.* **1** any of various water or marsh plants with long straight stems, esp. of the genera *Phragmites* or *Arundo.* **2 a** the stem of a reed. **b** (*collect.*) reeds as material for thatching etc. **3 a** a thin strip of metal or wood inserted in an opening in a musical instrument and set in vibration by a current of air to produce the sound. **b** (*usu. pl.*) a musical instrument or organ pipe constructed with this. **c** (*usu. pl.*) the section of an orchestra that plays reed instruments. **4** a musical pipe made from a reed, a shepherd's pipe. **5** an implement, a pastoral loom for separating the threads of the warp. **6** a semicylindrical moulding, a reeding. ~*v.t.* **1** to thatch with reed. **2** to fit (an organ pipe etc.) with a reed. **3** to decorate with reeds or reeding. **broken reed** BROKEN. **reed-band** *n.* a group of reed instruments. **reed-bird** *n.* the bobolink. **reedbuck** *n.* a buff-coloured antelope of the genus *Redunca*, found south of the Sahara in Africa. **reed bunting** *n.* a common European bunting with a black head, *Emberiza schoeniclus.* **reeded** *a.* (of a musical instrument) having a reed. **reed-grass** *n.* any of various reeds or reedlike grasses, e.g. of the genera *Arundo* or *Glyceria.* **reeding** *n.* **1** a semicylindrical architectural moulding or series of these set parallel to one another. **2** milling on the edge of a coin. **reed instrument** *n.* a woodwind instrument with a reed, such as an oboe. **reedless** *a.* **reedling** *n.* the bearded titmouse. **reed mace** *n.* a reedlike marsh or water plant of the genus *Typha*, esp. *T. latifolia* which bears tiny spikes of furry brown flowers. **reed-organ** *n.* a musical instrument with a keyboard, the sounds of which are produced by reeds of the organ type. **reed-pheasant** *n.* the bearded tit. **reed pipe** *n.* **1** a reed instrument. **2** a reeded organ pipe. **3** a musical pipe made of a reed. **reed-stop** *n.* an organ stop controlling a set of reed pipes. **reed warbler** *n.* any of various common Eurasian warblers of the genus *Acrocephalus*, esp. *A. scirpaceus*, that frequent marshy areas. **reedy** *a.* (*comp.* **reedier,** *superl.* **reediest**) **1** abounding in reeds. **2** like a reed. **3** sounding like a reed instrument, thin or sharp in tone. **4** thin, frail in form. **reedily** *adv.* **reediness** *n.* [OE *hrēod* (cp. Dut. and G *reet*)]

reef[1] (rēf) *n.* **1** a ridge of rock, coral, sand etc. in the sea at or near the surface of the water. **2** a lode or vein of ore, esp. gold-bearing quartz. **3** the bedrock left after the removal of diamantiferous or other valuable ore. **reefy** *a.* abounding in reefs. [prob. from Dut. *rif*, Icel. *rif*, perh. cogn. with RIB[1]]

reef[2] (rēf) *n.* (*Naut.*) any of the horizontal portions across the top of a square sail or the bottom of a fore-and-aft sail, which can be rolled up or wrapped and secured in order to shorten sail. ~*v.t.* **1** to reduce the extent of (a sail) by taking in a reef or reefs. **2** to take in a part of (a bowsprit, topmast etc.) in order to shorten it. **to take in a reef 1** to reef a sail. **2** to proceed with caution or in moderation. **reefer**[1] *n.* **1** a person who reefs. **2** a reefing-jacket. **3** (*Naut., sl.*) a midshipman. **4** a reef knot. **reefing-jacket** *n.* a stout, close-fitting double-breasted jacket. **reef knot** *n.* a square or symmetrical double knot. **reef-point** *n.* a short length of rope stitched to a sail, for securing a reef. [Icel. *rif*, see REEF[1]]

reefer[1] REEF[2].

reefer[2] (rē´fə) *n.* a marijuana cigarette. [prob. from its resemblance to a rolled sail (see REEF[2])]

reek (rēk) *v.i.* **1** to give off a strong disagreeable odour. **2** to give a strong impression (of something offensive or undesirable). **3** to emit smoke, fumes, vapour or steam. ~*n.* **1** a foul, stale or disagreeable odour, a foul atmosphere. **2** (*chiefly Sc.*) **a** smoke. **b** vapour, steam, fume. **reeking** *a.* **reekingly** *adv.* **reeky** *a.* (*comp.* **reekier,** *superl.* **reekiest**) **1** smoky. **2** filthy, dirty. [OE *rēc* (cp. Dut. *rook*, G *Rauch*, Icel. *reykr*), whence *rēocan*, Dut. *rieken*, G *rauchen*, to smoke]

reel[1] (rēl) *n.* **1** a rotatory frame, cylinder or other device on which thread, cord, wire, paper etc. can be wound, either in the process of manufacture or for winding and unwinding as required. **2** a quantity of material wound on a reel. **3** a bobbin. **4** the spool on which a film is wound. **5** a portion of film to be projected, usu. 1000 ft. (about 300 m). **6** (*coll.*) the film itself. ~*v.t.* **1** to wind on a reel. **2** to unwind or take (off) a reel. **to reel in 1** to draw (a fish etc.) towards one by using a reel. **2** to wind (thread, a line etc.) on a reel. **to reel off 1** to unwind or pay out from a reel. **2** to tell (a story) fluently and without a hitch. **to reel up 1** to wind up entirely on a reel. **2** to reel in. **reelable** *a.* **reeler** *n.* **reel-fed** *a.* of or relating to printing on a web of paper. **reelman** *n.* (*Austral., New Zeal.*) in a beach life-saving team, the person who controls the reel with the rescue line on. **reel-to-reel** *a.* **1** of magnetic tape, wound from one reel to another. **2** using large reels of such tape as distinct from cassettes. [OE *hrēol*]

reel[2] (rēl) *v.i.* **1** to stagger, to sway. **2** to go (along) unsteadily. **3** to have a whirling sensation, to be dizzy. **4** to whirl, to rock. ~*n.* a staggering or swaying motion or sensation. **reeling** *a.* **reelingly** *adv.* [perh. rel. to REEL[1]]

reel[3] (rēl) *n.* **1** a lively esp. Scottish dance in which the couples face each other and describe figures of eight. **2** a piece of music for this. ~*v.i.* to dance a reel. [perh. from REEL[2]]

reest[1] (rēst) *v.t.* (*Sc., North.*) to dry or smoke (bacon, fish etc.), to cure. ~*v.i.* to become smoke-dried. [etym. uncertain]

reest[2] (rēst) *v.i.* (*Sc., North.*) (esp. of a horse) to stop, to refuse to go on, to balk. **reesty** *a.* [prob. var. of REST[1], or a form of Sc. *arreest*, ARREST]

reeve[1] (rēv) *n.* **1** (*Hist.*) a chief officer or magistrate of a town or district, holding office usu. under the monarch but sometimes by election. **2** †a bailiff, a steward. **3** (*Can.*) the presiding officer of a township or village council. [OE *gerēfa*, etym. uncertain]

reeve[2] (rēv) *v.t.* (*past, p.p.* **reeved, rove** (rōv)) (*Naut.*) **1** to pass (the end of a rope, a rod etc.) through a ring, a hole in a block etc. **2** to fasten (a rope etc.) round some object by this means. [prob. from Dut. *reven*, to REEF[2]]

reeve[3] (rēv) *n.* the female of the ruff. [etym. obscure, cp. RUFF[1]]

ref[1] (ref) *n.* a referee. ~*v.t.* (*pres.p.* **reffing,** *past, p.p.* **reffed**) (*coll.*) to referee.

ref[2] *abbr.* **1** reference. **2** refer to. **3** reformed.

re- (+ fa–fl words) reface *v.t.* to put a new face or surface on (a wall, building etc.). **refacing** *n.* **refashion** *v.t.* to fashion anew. **refashionment** *n.* **refasten** *v.t.* to fasten again. **refill**[1] (rēfil´) *v.t.* to fill again. **refill**[2] (rē´-) *n.* **1** something which is used to refill. **2** a fresh or replacement fill (as of lead for a propelling pencil, tobacco for a pipe etc.). **refillable** *a.* **refilm** *v.t.* **1** to film again. **2** to make a new film version of. **refinance** *v.t.* **1** to finance again, to provide further capital for. **2** to pay off (a debt) by borrowing additional capital. **refinancing** *n.* **refind** *v.t.* (*past, p.p.* **refound**) to find again. **refinish** *v.t.* to give a new finish or surface to. **refinisher** *n.* **refit**[1] *v.t.* (*pres.p.* **refitting,** *past, p.p.* **refitted**) to make fit for use again, to repair, to re-equip, to fit out anew (esp. a ship). ~*v.i.* (of ships) to undergo repair of damages. **refit**[2] (rē´-) *n.* the repairing or renewing of what is damaged or worn out, esp. the repairing of a ship. **refitment** *n.* **refitter** *n.* **reflag** *v.t.* (*pres.p.* **reflagging,** *past, p.p.* **reflagged**) to change the country of registration of (a ship). **refloat** *v.t., v.i.* to float again. **reflood** *v.t.* to flood anew. **reflourish** *v.i.* to flourish anew. **reflow** *v.i.* 1 to flow back. 2 to ebb. ~*n.* 1 a reflowing, a reflux. 2 the ebb (of the tide). **reflower** *v.i.* to flower again. **reflowering** *n.*

refectory (rifek´təri) *n.* (*pl.* **refectories**) a room or hall where meals are taken in colleges, religious houses etc. **refection** (rifek´shən) *n.* (*formal*) 1 refreshment by food. 2 a light meal, a repast. **refectory table** *n.* a long narrow dining table, esp. on two trestles. [late L *refectōrium*, from L *reficere*, to refresh]

refer (rifœ´) *v.t.* (*pres.p.* **referring**, *past, p.p.* **referred**) 1 to trace back, to assign (to a certain cause, source, class, place etc.). 2 to hand over (for consideration and decision). 3 to send or direct (a person) for information, aid, treatment etc. 4 to fail (an examinee). ~*v.i.* 1 to apply for information. 2 to appeal, to have recourse. 3 to cite, to allude, to direct attention (to). 4 to be concerned with, to have relation (to). **refer to drawer** the words used by a bank to notify the payee of a cheque that payment of the cheque has been suspended. **referable** (refœ´rəbəl, ref´ə-), **referrable, referrible** (-fœ´-) *a.* †**referment** *n.* **referral** *n.* the act of referring or being referred, esp. to another person or organization for treatment, consideration etc. **referred** *a.* **referred pain** *n.* pain localized at a different point from the part actually causing it. **referrer** *n.* [OF *referer*, L *referre* (RE-, *ferre*, to bear)]

referee (refərē´) *n.* 1 an umpire in football, boxing etc. 2 a person to whom a point or question is referred. 3 a person to whom a matter in dispute is referred for settlement or decision, an arbitrator, an umpire. 4 a person who is prepared to testify to the abilities and character of someone, and who furnishes a reference, testimonial etc. ~*v.i.* (*3rd pers. sing. pres.* **referees**, *pres.p.* **refereeing**, *past, p.p.* **refereed**) to act as a referee (in football etc.).

reference (ref´ərəns) *n.* 1 the act of referring. 2 relation, respect, correspondence (to). 3 allusion, directing of attention (to). 4 a a note or mark referring from a book to another work or from the text to a commentary, diagram etc. b that which is referred to. 5 a testimonial, esp. one not seen by the person described within it. 6 a person referred to for information, evidence of character etc., a referee. ~*v.t.* (*usu. p.p.*) to furnish (a work) with cross-references, references to authorities etc. **in/ with reference to** with regard to, as regards, concerning. **without reference to** irrespective of, regardless of. **reference book** *n.* an encyclopedia, dictionary or the like, consulted when occasion requires, not for continuous reading. **reference library** *n.* a library where books may be consulted but not borrowed. **reference work** *n.* a reference book. **referent** (ref´ə-) *n.* the thing to which a word or phrase refers. **referential** (referen´-) *a.* **referentially** *adv.*

referendum (referen´dəm) *n.* (*pl.* **referendums, referenda** (-də)) 1 the submission of a political question to the whole electorate for a direct decision by general vote. 2 a vote taken in this manner.

Usage note The plural *referendums* is preferred to *referenda*.

referrable, referral etc. REFER.

reffo (ref´ō) *n.* (*pl.* **reffos**) (*Austral., derog.*) a political refugee from Europe. [REFUGEE (under REFUGE)]

refine (rifīn´) *v.t.* 1 to clear from impurities, defects etc., to purify, to clarify. 2 to free from coarseness, to educate, to polish, to cultivate the taste, manners etc. of. 3 to make (a statement, idea etc.) more subtle, complex or abstract. 4 to transform or modify into a subtler or more abstract form. ~*v.i.* 1 to become pure or clear. 2 to become polished or more highly cultivated in talk, manners etc. 3 to affect subtlety of thought or language. 4 to draw subtle distinctions (upon). **refinable** *a.* **refined** *a.* 1 freed from impurities. 2 highly cultivated, polished, elegant. **refinedly** (-nid-) *adv.* **refinedness** *n.* **refinement** *n.* 1 the act or process of refining. 2 the state of being refined. 3 elegance of taste, manners, language etc. 4 high culture, polish. 5 an additional feature or development, an improvement, an elaboration. 6 a subtle distinction or piece of reasoning. 7 subtlety of thought or reasoning. **refiner** (rifī´nə) *n.* 1 someone who or something which refines. 2 a person or company whose business is to refine metals, oil etc. **refinery** *n.* (*pl.* **refineries**) a place for refining raw materials, such as sugar and oil. [RE-, FINE[1]]

refl. *abbr.* 1 reflection, reflective, reflectively. 2 reflex, reflexive, reflexively.

reflate (rēflāt´) *v.t.* to inflate again. **reflation** (-ā´shən) *n.* an increase in economic activity, esp. through an increase in the supply of money and credit. **reflationary** *a.* [RE-, INFLATE]

reflect (riflekt´) *v.t.* 1 to turn or throw back (light, heat, sound etc.) esp. in accordance with certain physical laws. 2 to mirror, to throw back an image of. 3 to reproduce exactly, to correspond to in features or effects. 4 to show, to give an idea of. 5 to cause to accrue or to cast (honour, disgrace etc.) upon. ~*v.i.* 1 to throw back light, heat, sound etc. 2 to turn the thoughts back, to think, to ponder, to meditate. 3 to remind oneself (that). 4 to bring shame or discredit (on or upon). **to reflect on/ upon** to cast censure or blame upon. **reflectance** *n.* a measure of the ability of a surface to reflect light or other radiation; the ratio of the amount of light reflected by a surface to that falling on the surface. **reflecting** *a.* **reflecting factor** *n.* reflectance. **reflectingly** *adv.* 1 thoughtfully, meditatively. 2 reproachfully. **reflecting microscope** *n.* a microscope with a series of mirrors instead of lenses. **reflecting telescope** *n.* a telescope in which the object glass is replaced by a polished reflector, from which the image is magnified by an eyepiece. **reflection** (-flek´shən), **reflexion** *n.* 1 the act of reflecting. 2 the state of being reflected. 3 that which is reflected. 4 rays of light, heat etc. or an image thrown back from a reflecting surface. 5 reconsideration. 6 a continued consideration, thought, meditation. b the act or process by which the mind takes cognizance of its own operations. 7 a thought, idea, comment or opinion resulting from deliberation. 8 discredit, censure, reproach (brought or cast on or upon a person etc.). 9 that which entails censure or reproach (upon). 10 the bending or folding back of an anatomical etc. structure. **reflectional** *a.* **reflection factor** *n.* reflectance. **reflectionless** *a.* **reflective** *a.* 1 throwing back an image, rays of light, heat etc. 2 of, relating to or concerned with thought or reflection. 3 meditative, thoughtful. 4 reflected. **reflectively** *adv.* **reflectiveness** *n.* **reflectivity** (rēflektiv´-) *n.* 1 the ability to reflect light or other radiation. 2 reflectance when measured independently of the thickness of the material of which a reflecting surface is composed. **reflector** *n.* 1 someone who or something which reflects. 2 a reflecting surface that throws back rays of light, heat etc., usu. a polished, concave surface, as in a lamp, lighthouse, telescope, surgical instrument etc. 3 a small piece of red, orange or clear plastic glass used (e.g. on a bicycle) to reflect the light from vehicle headlights. 4 a reflecting telescope. [L *reflectere* (RE-, *flectere*, to bend), p.p. *reflexus*]

reflet (rəflā´) *n.* a metallic lustre or glow, esp. on pottery. [F, from It. *riflesso*, reflection]

reflex (rē´fleks) *a.* 1 involuntary, produced independently of the will under stimulus from impressions on the sensory nerves. 2 done or produced as a reaction or response to a situation without apparent intervention of conscious thought; automatic, mechanical. 3 turned or bent backward. 4 (of an angle) greater than 180°. 5

introspective. 6 reactive, turned back upon itself or the source, agent etc. 7 reflected, lighted by reflected light. ~*n.* 1 a reflex action. 2 a mechanical or automatic response. 3 (*pl.*) the power or capacity to respond rapidly. 4 a reflected image, reproduction or secondary manifestation. 5 a reflection. 6 reflected light, colour etc. 7 a part of a picture represented as lit by the reflected light or colour of other parts. 8 a word formed by development from a form in an earlier stage of a language. **reflex** (rifleks´) *v.t.* 1 to bend or fold back. 2 †to reflect. **reflex action** *n.* the involuntary contraction of a muscle in response to stimulus from without the body. **reflex anal dilatation** *n.* (*Med.*) involuntary widening of the anus on physical examination, used as a diagnostic procedure to detect repeated anal penetration, esp. in cases involving suspected sexual abuse in children. **reflex arc** *n.* the nervous pathway which nerve impulses travel along to produce a reflex action. **reflex camera** *n.* a camera in which the viewfinder is integrated with the main lens. **reflexed** *a.* bent backwards or downwards. **reflexible** *a.* **reflexibility** (-bil´-) *n.* **reflexive** *a.* 1 denoting action upon the agent. 2 (*Gram.*) implying action by the subject upon itself or themselves or referring back to the grammatical subject. **reflexively** *adv.* **reflexiveness, reflexivity** *n.* **reflexive verb** *n.* (*Gram.*) a verb that has for its direct object a pronoun which stands for the agent or subject. **reflexly** *adv.* **reflexology** (rēfleksol´-) *n.* 1 a form of complementary medical therapy where the soles of the feet are massaged to stimulate the circulation and nerves, and so release tension. 2 the interpretation of behaviour in terms of reflex actions and responses. **reflexologist** *n.* [L *reflexus*, p.p. of *reflectere*, to reflect (whence late L *reflexus -ūs*, a reflex)]

reflexion REFLECTION (under REFLECT).

refluent (ref´luənt) *a.* (*formal*) 1 flowing back. 2 ebbing. **refluence** *n.* [L *refluens -entem*, pres.p. of *refluere* (RE-, *fluere*, to flow)]

reflux (rē´flŭks) *n.* 1 (*Chem.*) the boiling of liquid in a flask fitted with a condenser, so that the vapour condenses and flows back into the flask. 2 a flowing back. 3 a return, an ebb. ~*v.t.*, *v.i.* to boil under reflux conditions. [as REFLUENT]

re- (+ fo–fu words) refocus *v.t.* (*3rd pers. sing. pres.* **refocuses, refocusses,** *pres.p.* **refocusing, refocussing,** *past, p.p.* **refocused, refocussed**) 1 to focus again. 2 to change or adjust the focus of. **refold** *v.t.* to fold again. **refoot** *v.t.* to put a new foot to (a stocking, etc.). **reforest** *v.t.* to reafforest. **reforestation** *n.* **reforge** *v.t.* 1 to forge over again. 2 to refashion. **re-form** *v.t.*, *v.i.* to form again or anew. **re-formation** *n.* **re-former** *n.* **reformat** *v.t.* (*pres.p.* **reformatting,** *past, p.p.* **reformatted**) 1 to put into a new format. 2 (*Comput.*) to format again. **reformulate** *v.t.* to formulate again. **reformulation** *n.* **refortify** *v.t.* (*3rd pers. sing. pres.* **refortifies,** *pres.p.* **refortifying,** *past, p.p.* **refortified**) to fortify anew. **refortification** *n.* **refound**[1] *v.t.* to found anew, to recast. **refound**[2] REFIND (under RE- (+ FA–FL WORDS)). **refracture** *v.t.* to fracture again. **reframe** *v.t.* to frame again, to fashion anew. **refreeze** *v.t.* (*past* **refroze,** *p.p.* **refrozen**) to freeze again. **refuel** *v.t.* (*pres.p.* **refuelling,** (*N Am.*) **refueling,** *past, p.p.* **refuelled,** (*N Am.*) **refueled**) to provide with fresh fuel. ~*v.i.* to take on fresh fuel. **re-fund** *v.t.* to pay off (an old debt) by borrowing more money. **refurnish** *v.t.* 1 to furnish anew. 2 to supply with new furniture. **re-fuse** *v.t.* to fuse or melt again. **re-fusion** *n.*

reform (rifawm´) *v.t.* 1 to change from worse to better by removing faults, imperfections, abuses etc. 2 to improve, to amend, to redress, to cure, to remedy. 3 to change the structure of (a hydrocarbon) so as to make suitable for use as petrol. ~*v.i.* 1 to amend one's habits, morals, conduct etc. 2 to abandon evil habits etc. ~*n.* 1 the act of reforming, esp. the correction of political, social or legal abuses. 2 an alteration for the better, an amendment, an improvement. **reformable** *a.* **reformability** (-bil´-) *n.* **Reform Acts** *n.pl.* Acts passed in 1832, 1867 and 1884 for enlarging the electorate and reforming the constitution of the House of Commons. **reformation** (refəmā´shən) *n.* 1 the act of reforming. 2 the state of being reformed. 3 redress of grievances or abuses, esp. a thorough change or reconstruction in politics, society or religion. **the Reformation** the great religious revolution in the 16th cent. which resulted in the establishment of the Protestant Churches. **reformationist** *n.* **reformative** *a.* tending to produce reform. **reformatory** *a.* reformative. ~*n.* (*pl.* **reformatories**) (*N Am. or Hist.*) a reform school. **reformed** *a.* corrected, amended, purged of errors and abuses. **Reformed Church** *n.* a Protestant Church that adopted Calvinistic doctrines and principles, as distinct from Lutheran Churches. **reformer** (rifaw´mə) *n.* 1 a person who effects a reformation. 2 a person who favours political reform. 3 (**Reformer**) a leader of the Reformation of the 16th cent. **reformism** *n.* any policy advocating religious or political reform. **reformist** *n.*, *a.* **Reform Judaism** *n.* a form of Judaism which adapts Jewish Law to contemporary life. **reform school** *n.* an institution for the detention and reformation of juvenile offenders. [F *reformer*, L *reformāre*]

re-form RE- (+ FO–FU WORDS).

refract (rifrakt´) *v.t.* 1 (*Physics*) (of water, glass etc.) to cause (a ray of light etc.) to undergo refraction. 2 to measure the refractive capacity of (the eye, a lens etc.). **refractable** *a.* **refracted** *a.* 1 deflected from a direct course, as a ray of light or heat. 2 bent back at an acute angle. **refracting** *a.* **refracting telescope** *n.* the earliest form of telescope, in which the image of an object is received direct through a converging lens and magnified by an eyepiece. **refraction** *n.* 1 (*Physics*) **a** the deflection that takes place when a ray of light, heat etc. passes at any angle other than a right angle from the surface of one medium into another medium of different density. **b** the amount of deflection which takes place. 2 an apparent change in the position of a heavenly body resulting from the deflection of luminous rays proceeding from it as they enter the earth's atmosphere. **refractive** *a.* 1 of or relating to refraction. 2 having the capacity to cause refraction. **refractive index** *n.* 1 the amount by which a medium refracts light. 2 the ratio of the speed of light or other radiation in free space to its speed in any other medium. **refractively** *adv.* **refractiveness, refractivity** (rēfraktiv´-) *n.* **refractometer** (rēfraktom´itə) *n.* any instrument which measures the refractive index of a medium. **refractometric** (-təmet´-) *a.* **refractometry** *n.* **refractor** *n.* 1 a refracting medium or lens. 2 a refracting telescope. [L *refractus*, p.p. of *refringere* (RE-, *frangere*, to break)]

refractory (rifrak´təri) *a.* 1 perverse, insubordinate, obstinate in opposition or disobedience, unmanageable. 2 (*Med.*) **a** not amenable to ordinary treatment. **b** immune or resistant to infection. 3 **a** not easily fused or reduced, not easily worked. **b** (of a material) capable of resisting high temperatures without change. 4 (of nerves etc.) tardily responsive to stimulus. ~*n.* (*pl.* **refractories**) a piece of refractory ware used in a kiln with a flux for glazing pottery. **refractorily** *adv.* **refractoriness** *n.* [L *refractārius*, as REFRACT]

refrain[1] (rifrān´) *v.i.* to abstain (from an act or doing), to forbear. ~†*v.t.* to hold back, to restrain, to curb (oneself, one's tears etc.). **refrainer** *n.* **refrainment** *n.* [OF *refrener*, L *refrēnāre* (RE-, *frēnum*, bit, curb)]

refrain[2] (rifrān´) *n.* 1 a recurring phrase or line, esp. repeated at the end of every stanza, a chorus. 2 the music to accompany this. [OF, from *refraindre*, pop. L *refrangere*, L *refringere*, to REFRACT]

refrangible (rifran´jibəl) *a.* capable of being refracted. **refrangibility** (-bil´-), **refrangibleness** *n.* [pop. L *refrangibilis*, from *refrangere*, see REFRAIN[2]]

refresh (rifresh´) *v.t.* **1** to make fresh again, to reanimate, to reinvigorate. **2** to revive or restore after depression, fatigue etc. **3** to freshen up, to stimulate (one's memory). **4** to restore, to repair, to renovate. **5** to replenish. **6** (*coll.*) to give (esp. liquid) refreshments to. **7** to pour cold water over blanched food. **8** †to give a sensation of coolness to. **refresher** *n.* **1** someone who or something which refreshes. **2** (*coll.*) a drink. **3** an extra fee paid to counsel when a case is adjourned or continued from one term or sitting to another. **refresher course** *n.* a course to bring up to date knowledge of a particular subject. **refreshing** *a.* **1** reinvigorating, reanimating. **2** welcome or pleasing because different or new. **refreshingly** *adv.* **refreshingness** *n.* **refreshment** *n.* **1** the act of refreshing. **2** the state of being refreshed. **3 a** that which refreshes. **b** (*usu. pl.*) food or drink. **refreshment room** *n.* a room at a railway station etc. for the supply of refreshments. [OF *refreschir*]

refrigerate (rifrij´ərāt) *v.t.* **1** to make cool or cold. **2** to freeze or keep at a very low temperature in a refrigerator so as to preserve in a fresh condition. ~*v.i.* to become cold or chilled. **refrigerant** *n.* **1** that which cools or refreshes. **2** the working fluid in a refrigerator or freezer that removes heat and transfers it to the surroundings. **3** a medicine for allaying fever or inflammation. ~*a.* cooling, allaying heat. **refrigeration** (-ā´shən) *n.* **refrigerative** *a.*, *n.* **refrigerator** (rifrij´ərātə) *n.* an apparatus for keeping meat and other provisions at a low temperature, in order to preserve their freshness. **refrigeratory** *a.* cooling. ~*n.* (*pl.* **refrigeratories**) (*Hist.*) a vessel attached to a still for condensing vapour. [L *refrīgerātus*, p.p. of *refrīgerāre* (RE-, *frīgus -goris*, cold)]

refringent (rifrin´jənt) *a.* refractive. **refringence, refringency** *n.* [L *refringens -entem*, pres.p. of *refringere*, to REFRACT]

reft REAVE.

refuge (ref´ūj) *n.* **1** shelter or protection from danger or distress. **2** a place, thing, person or course of action that shelters or protects from danger, distress or calamity. **3** a stronghold, a retreat, a sanctuary, a house of refuge. **4** an expedient, a subterfuge. **5** a traffic island. **refugee** (-jē´) *n.* a person who flees to a place of refuge, esp. one who takes refuge in a foreign country in time of war or persecution or political commotion. **refugeeism** *n.* **refugium** (rifū´jiəm) *n.* (*pl.* **refugia** (-jiə)) a geographical region which has not been changed by climatic or environmental conditions and so becomes a haven for relict varieties of flora and fauna. [F, from L *refugium* (RE-, *fugium*, from *fugere*, to flee)]

refulgent (riful´jənt) *a.* (*poet.*) shining brightly, brilliant, radiant, splendid. **refulgence, †refulgency** *n.* **refulgently** *adv.* [L *refulgens -ntem*, pres.p. of *refulgēre* (RE-, *fulgēre*, to shine)]

refund[1] (rifŭnd´) *v.t.* **1** to pay back, to repay, to restore. **2** to reimburse. ~*v.i.* to make repayment. **refundable** *a.* **refunder** *n.* **refundment** *n.* [L *refundere*, to pour back (RE-, *fundere*, see FOUND[3])]

refund[2] (rē´fŭnd) *n.* **1** an act of refunding money. **2** an amount refunded.

re-fund RE- (+ FO–FU WORDS).

refurbish (rēfœ´bish) *v.t.* to freshen up by renovating, redecorating etc. **refurbishment** *n.* [RE-, FURBISH]

refuse[1] (rifūz´) *v.t.* **1** to decline (to do, yield, grant etc.). **2** to decline to accept or consent to. **3** to deny the request of. **4** (of a horse) to decline to jump over (a ditch etc.). ~*v.i.* **1** to decline to comply. **2** (of a horse) to fail to jump. **3** to be unable to follow suit in a game of cards. **refusable** *a.* **refusal** (rifū´zəl) *n.* **1** the act of refusing. **2** denial of anything solicited, demanded or offered. **3** (*also* **first refusal**) the choice or option of taking or refusing something before it is offered to others. **refusenik** (-nik), **refusnik** *n.* **1** (*Hist.*) a Soviet Jew who was refused permission to emigrate. **2** (*coll.*) a person who refuses to cooperate in some way. **refuser** *n.* [OF *refuser*, prob. through a pop. L *refūsāre*, from L *refundere*, see REFUND[1], p.p. *refūsus*]

refuse[2] (ref´ūs) *a.* rejected as valueless. ~*n.* something which is refused or rejected as worthless, waste or useless matter. **refuse tip** *n.* a place where refuse is heaped or disposed of. [prob. OF *refus*, *refuse*, p.p. of *refuser*, see REFUSE[1]]

re-fuse RE- (+ FO–FU WORDS).

refusenik REFUSE[1].

refute (rifūt´) *v.t.* **1** to prove (a statement, argument etc.) false or erroneous, to disprove. **2** to prove wrong, to rebut in argument, to confute. **3** to declare to be false, to deny. **refutable** *a.* **refutably** *adv.* **refutal, refutation** (refūtā´shən) *n.* **refuter** *n.* [F *refuter*, L *refūtāre*, see CONFUTE]

Usage note The use of *refute* where there is no argument or proof is often disapproved of: *deny* or *repudiate* can be used instead.

---

reg (rej) *n.* (*coll.*) registration mark.

reg. *abbr.* **1** regiment. **2** register, registered. **3** registrar, registry. **4** regular, regularly. **5** regulation.

re- (+ ga–gi words) regalvanize, regalvanise *v.t.* to galvanize again. **regather** *v.t.*, *v.i.* to gather or collect together again. **regelate** *v.i.* **1** to freeze together again. **2** (of fragments of ice, snow etc.) to unite into a mass by freezing together again following a temporary thawing of the surfaces in contact under pressure. **regelation** *n.* **regenesis** *n.* the state of being born again or reproduced. **regerminate** *v.i.* to germinate anew. **regermination** *n.* **regild** *v.t.* (*p.p.* **regilded, regilt**) to gild again.

regain (rigān´) *v.t.* **1** to recover possession of. **2** to reach again. **3** to gain anew, to recover. **regainable** *a.* **regainer** *n.* **regainment** *n.* [F *regagner*]

regal[1] (rē´gəl) *a.* of, relating to or fit for a king or queen, royal. **regalism** *n.* the doctrine of royal supremacy in ecclesiastical affairs. **regality** (rigal´-) *n.* (*pl.* **regalities**) **1** the state of being royal, royalty. **2** sovereign jurisdiction. **3** an attribute of royalty. **4** (*Sc.*) a territorial distinction formerly conferred on a noble by the sovereign. **5** a country or territory under royal jurisdiction, a monarchical state, a kingdom. **regally** *adv.* [L *rēgālis*, from *rex rēgis*, king]

regal[2] (rē´gəl) *n.* (*Hist.*) a small portable reed-organ held in the hands, in use in the 16th and 17th cents.; also called *pair of regals*. [F *régale*, perh. from REGAL[1]]

regale (rigāl´) *v.t.* **1** to entertain sumptuously with food and drink. **2** to amuse, to divert, to give entertainment to. **3** to delight, to gratify (with something rich or choice). **regalement** *n.* [F *régaler*, It. *regalare*, etym. uncertain]

regalia[1] (rigā´liə) *n.pl.* **1** the insignia of royalty, esp. the emblems worn or displayed in coronation ceremonies etc. **2** the emblems or insignia of an office or order. **3** finery in general. [L, neut. pl. of *rēgālis*, REGAL[1]]

Usage note *Regalia* should not be used as a singular.

---

regalia[2] (rigā´liə) *n.* a Cuban cigar of superior quality. [Sp., royal privilege, as REGALIA[1]]

regally, regality etc. REGAL[1].

regard (rigahd´) *v.t.* **1** to look upon or view in a specified way or with fear, reverence etc., to consider (as). **2** to look at, to observe, to notice. **3** to value, to pay honour to, to esteem. **4** to affect, to relate to, to concern. **5** to give heed to, to pay attention to, to take into account. ~*v.i.* **1** to look. **2** to pay attention. ~*n.* **1**

observant attention, heed, care, consideration. 2 esteem, kindly or respectful feeling. 3 a look, a gaze. 4 reference. 5 relation. 6 (*pl.*) compliments, good wishes. **as regards** regarding. **in this regard** on this point. **in/with regard to** 1 regarding. 2 in connection with. **with kind regards** with good wishes. **regardable** *a.* **regardant** *a.* 1 (*Her.*) looking backwards. 2 observant, watchful. **regarder** *n.* **regardful** *a.* 1 heedful, mindful (of). 2 showing regard, respect or consideration. **regardfully** *adv.* **regardfulness** *n.* **regarding** *prep.* respecting, concerning. **regardless** *a.* heedless, careless, negligent (of). *~adv.* despite everything, without concern for the consequences, drawbacks etc. **regardless of** in spite of. **regardlessly** *adv.* **regardlessness** *n.* [F *regarder*]

regatta (rigat´ə) *n.* a sporting event comprising a series of yacht or boat races. [It., orig. contention]

regd. *abbr.* registered.

regency REGENT.

regenerate[1] (rijen´ərāt) *v.t.* 1 to generate anew, to give new existence to. 2 to impart fresh vigour or higher life to. 3 to change fundamentally and reform the moral and spiritual nature of. 4 to replace (a lost or damaged body part or tissue) by new growth. 5 (*Theol.*) to cause to be born again, to renew the heart of by the infusion of divine grace. 6 to form or produce again from a modified form or derivative by chemical treatment. *~v.i.* to become regenerated. **regenerable** *a.* **regeneracy, regenerateness** *n.* **regeneration** (-ā´shən) *n.* **regenerative** (-rət-), **regeneratory** *a.* **regeneratively** *adv.* **regenerator** *n.* 1 someone who or something which regenerates. 2 a device in furnaces, hot-air engines and gas-burners, by which the waste heat is applied to the incoming current of air or combustible gas. [L *regenerātus*, p.p. of *regenerāre* (RE-, *generāre*, to GENERATE)]

regenerate[2] (rijen´ərət) *a.* 1 regenerated, renewed. 2 reformed, converted.

regent (rē´jənt) *n.* 1 a person appointed to govern a country during the minority, absence or disability of a monarch. 2 (*N Am.*) a member of the governing body of a State university. 3 a ruler, a governor. *~a.* exercising the authority of regent (*usu. following its noun*). **regency** *n.* (*pl.* **regencies**) 1 the office, commission or government of a regent. 2 a body entrusted with the office or duties of a regent. 3 the period of office of a regent or a body so acting. 4 rule, government, control. *~a.* (**Regency**) of the style of architecture, art etc. prevailing during the early 19th cent. in Britain. **the Regency** the period (1810–20) when George, Prince of Wales, was regent for George III. **regent-bird, regent oriole** *n.* an Australian bower bird, *Sericulus chrysocephalus*, having beautiful plumage. **regentship** *n.* [F, from L *regentem*, nom. *-gens*, pres.p. of *regere*, to rule]

reggae (reg´ā) *n.* a form of rhythmical W Indian rock music in 4/4 time. [W Ind.]

regicide (rej´isīd) *n.* 1 the killing of a king. 2 a person who takes part in killing a king. **regicidal** (-sī´-) *a.* [F *régicide* (L *rex rēgis*, king, -CIDE)]

Régie (rāzhē´) *n.* the revenue department in some European countries having sole control of the importation of tobacco and sometimes of salt. [F, from *régir*, L *regere*, see REGENT]

regime (rāzhēm´), **régime** *n.* 1 a mode or prevailing system of government or management. 2 the prevailing social system or general state of things. 3 a prevailing set of conditions. 4 a regimen. [F *régime*, L REGIMEN]

regimen (rej´imən) *n.* 1 a systematic plan or course of diet, exercise etc. for the preservation or restoration of health. 2 †rule, government. 3 a government, a regime, a prevailing system of government. 4 (*Gram.*) the syntactical dependence of one word on another. **regiminal** (rijim´inəl) *a.* [L, from *regere*, to rule]

regiment[1] (rej´imənt) *n.* 1 a body of soldiers forming the largest permanent unit of the army, usu. divided into two battalions comprising several companies or troops, and commanded by a colonel. 2 a large number or a group. 3 †rule, government. **regimental** (-men´-) *a.* of or relating to a regiment. *~n.pl.* military uniform. **regimentally** *adv.* **regimental sergeant major** *n.* the chief sergeant of a regiment, a squadron of cavalry or a battery of artillery. [F, from L *regimentum*, as REGIMEN]

regiment[2] (rejiment´) *v.t.* 1 to force order or discipline on, esp. harshly. 2 to organize into a system of bodies or groups. 3 to form into a regiment or regiments. **regimentation** (-tā´shən) *n.* 1 enforcement of strict order or discipline. 2 organization into a regiment or a system of groups etc.

Regina (rijī´nə) *n.* a reigning queen. **reginal** *a.* [L, fem. of *rex rēgis*, king]

region (rē´jən) *n.* 1 a tract of land, sea, space etc. of large but indefinite extent, often having certain prevailing characteristics, as of fauna or flora. 2 a part of the world or the physical or spiritual universe. 3 a district, a sphere, a realm. 4 a part of the body surrounding an organ etc. 5 a civil division of a town, district or country. 6 one of the strata into which the atmosphere or the sea may be divided. **in the region of** 1 near. 2 approximately. **regional** *a.* **regionalism** *n.* 1 division into sections or administrative areas on a regional basis. 2 loyalty to one's region. 3 a word, accent etc. characteristic of a particular geographical area. **regionalist** *n.*, *a.* **regionalistic** (-lis´-) *a.* **regionalize, regionalise** *v.t.* to organize into administrative regions. **regionalization** (-zā´shən) *n.* **regionally** *adv.* **regionary** *a.* regional. [A-F *regiun*, L *regiōnem*, nom. *-gio*, from *regere*, to rule, to direct]

régisseur (rāzhēsœ´) *n.* an official in a dance company whose responsibilities include directing. **régisseuse** (-œz´) *n.* a female régisseur. [F *régir*, to manage]

register (rej´istə) *n.* 1 an official or authoritative list of names, facts etc., as of births, marriages, deaths, people entitled to vote at elections, shipping etc. 2 an official written record. 3 a book, roll or other document in which such a record is kept. 4 an entry in such a record or list. 5 a mechanical device for recording data automatically. 6 a cash register. 7 a computer device which can store small amounts of data. 8 (*Mus.*) **a** the range or compass of a voice or instrument. **b** a particular portion of this. 9 a form of language used in a particular situation. 10 a contrivance for regulating the admission of air or heat to a room, ventilator, fireplace etc. 11 a sliding device in an organ for controlling a set of pipes. 12 (*Print.*) **a** precise correspondence of lines etc. on one side of the paper to those on the other. **b** exact overlaying of the different colours used in colour printing. **c** correspondence of the surface of a sensitized film to that of the focusing-screen. 13 an act of registering, registration. *~v.t.* 1 to enter or cause to be entered in a register. 2 to record or note as if in a register. 3 to note mentally. 4 to express (an emotion) facially or by one's bearing. 5 (of an instrument) to record, to indicate. 6 to send (a letter etc.) by registered post. 7 to cause (printed material etc.) to correspond precisely. *~v.i.* 1 to enter one's name in or as in a register. 2 to make an impression. 3 (of an emotion) to be expressed in the face, bearing etc. 4 to be shown by a recording instrument. 5 to be in register. 6 to discharge experimental rounds of gunfire in order to ascertain the exact range. **in register** (of printed matter, photographic and colour plates etc.) exactly corresponding. **registered** *a.* **Registered General Nurse** *n.* a fully-trained nurse registered as competent in any type of nursing by the United Kingdom Central Council for Nursing, Midwifery and Health Visiting. **registered nurse** *n.* a nurse registered with the United Kingdom

Central Council for Nursing, Midwifery and Health Visiting. **registered post** *n.* 1 a Post Office service where a registration fee is paid for mail and compensation paid in case of loss. 2 mail sent by this service. **registered trademark** *n.* a trademark which is legally registered and protected. **register office** *n.* a registrar's office where civil marriages are performed and births, marriages and deaths are recorded. **register ton** *n.* a unit used to measure the internal capacity of a ship, equal to 100 cu. ft. (about 3 m^3). **registrable** *a.* **registrant** *n.* a person registering something, esp. a trademark etc. **registrar** (-strah´, rej´-) *n.* 1 an official keeper of a register or record. 2 an official charged with keeping registers of births, deaths and marriages. 3 an administrative officer in a college or university responsible for enrolment, student records etc. 4 a hospital doctor between the grades of houseman and consultant. 5 a court official with administrative and judicial functions. **Registrar General** *n.* a public officer who superintends the registration of births, deaths and marriages. **registrarship** *n.* **registrary** (rej´-) *n.* (*pl.* **registraries**) the registrar of Cambridge University. **registration** *n.* 1 the act of registering. 2 the state of being registered. 3 an entry in a register. 4 a group of people all registered at a single time. **registration document** *n.* a document which shows the official details of a motor vehicle. **registration mark, registration number** *n.* a combination of letters and numbers corresponding to a place and (time of) year of registration, displayed by and identifying every motor vehicle. **registry** *n.* (*pl.* **registries**) 1 an office or other place where a register is kept. 2 registration. 3 the place where a ship is registered. 4 a register. **registry office** *n.* 1 a register office. 2 an employment agency for domestic servants. [F *registre*, or med. L *registrum*, var. of *regestrum*, late L *regesta*, pl. *regest*]

regius (rē´jiəs) *a.* 1 royal. 2 appointed by the sovereign. **Regius Professor** *n.* a professor whose chair was founded by the Crown, esp. any of several professors at Oxford and Cambridge Universities whose chairs were founded by Henry VIII. [L, royal from *rex rēgis*, king]

re- (+ gl–gr words) reglaze *v.t.* to glaze again. **reglazing** *n.* **regorge** *v.t.* 1 to disgorge, to vomit up. 2 to swallow back again. ~*v.i.* to gush or flow back (from a river etc.). **regrade** *v.t.* to grade again or differently. **regraft** *v.t.* to graft again. **regrant**[1] *v.t.* to grant anew. **regrant**[2] (rē´-) *n.* a renewed or fresh grant. **regroup** *v.t.*, *v.i.* to group again. **regroupment** *n.* **regrow** *v.t.*, *v.i.* (*past* **regrew**, *p.p.* **regrown**) to grow again. **regrowth** *n.*

reglet (reg´lit) *n.* 1 (*Print.*) a strip of wood, less than type high, used for separating pages, filling blank spaces etc. 2 a flat, narrow band separating mouldings etc. [F *réglet*, dim. of *règle*, L *rēgula*, RULE]

regma (reg´mə) *n.* (*pl.* **regmata** (-tə)) a dry fruit made up of several cells that burst open when ripe. [Gr. *rhēgma*, fracture]

regnal (reg´nəl) *a.* of or relating to a reign. **regnal day** *n.* the anniversary of a sovereign's accession. **regnal year** *n.* the year of a reign dating from the sovereign's accession (used in dating some documents). **regnant** *a.* 1 reigning, ruling, exercising regal authority (*often following its noun* as *queen regnant*). 2 predominant, prevalent. **regnancy** *n.* [med. L *regnālis*, from *regnum*, see REIGN]

rego (rej´ō) *n.* (*Austral.*, *sl.*) motor vehicle registration.

regolith (reg´əlith) *n.* unconsolidated rock, soil etc. at the earth's surface. [Gr. *rhēgos*, blanket, *lithos*, stone]

regrate (rigrāt´) *v.t.* to buy up (corn, provisions etc.) and sell again in the same or a neighbouring market so as to raise the prices. **regrater** *n.* [OF *regrater* (F *regratter*), prob. RE-, *gratter*, to GRATE[1]]

regrede (rigrēd´) *v.i.* to go back. [L *regredī* (RE-, *gradī*, to go)]

regression (rigresh´ən) *n.* 1 a backward movement, a return. 2 reversion to type. 3 (*Psych.*) return to an earlier stage of development or a form of behaviour characteristic of this. 4 the turning back of a curve upon itself. 5 the statistical analysis between dependent and independent variables. **regress**[1] (rigres´) *v.i.* to move back, to return, esp. to a former state, condition or mode of behaviour. ~*v.t.* to cause psychological regression in. **regress**[2] (rē´gres) *n.* 1 passage back, return, regression. 2 the act of reasoning backwards from effect to cause. **regressive** (ri-) *a.* 1 regressing or characterized by regression. 2 (of a tax) decreasing in rate as the amount to be taxed increases. **regressively** *adv.* **regressiveness, regressivity** (rēgresiv´iti) *n.* **regressor** *n.* [L *regressus*, p.p. of *regredī*, to REGREDE]

regret (rigret´) *n.* 1 distress or sorrow for a disappointment, loss or want. 2 grief, repentance or remorse for a wrongdoing, fault or omission. 3 (*pl.*) an expression of sorrow or disappointment, esp. in declining an invitation. ~*v.t.* (*pres.p.* **regretting**, *past*, *p.p.* **regretted**) 1 to be distressed or sorry for (a disappointment, loss etc.). 2 to regard (a fact, action etc.) with sorrow or remorse. **regretful** *a.* feeling regret, esp. sorry for past action. **regretfully** *adv.* **regretfulness** *n.* **regrettable** *a.* to be regretted, unwelcome, undesirable. **regrettably** *adv.* [F, from *regretter*, OF *regrater*, etym. uncertain]

Usage note *Regretfully* should not be used to express general regret (as a sentence adverb) instead of *regrettably*.

Regt *abbr.* 1 Regent. 2 Regiment.

regulable REGULATE.

regular (reg´ūlə) *a.* 1 conforming to or governed by rule, law, type or principle. 2 systematic, methodical, consistent. 3 acting, done or happening in an orderly, uniform, constant or habitual manner; not casual, fortuitous or capricious. 4 governed throughout by the same law, following consistently the same process. 5 symmetrical, unvarying, harmonious, normal. 6 conforming to custom, etiquette etc.; not infringing conventions. 7 duly authorized, properly qualified. 8 (of a geometrical figure) having the sides and angles equal. 9 (*Gram.*) conforming to the normal type of inflection. 10 belonging to the permanent standing army. 11 (*coll.*) belonging to a religious or monastic order. 12 complete, thorough, out-and-out, unmistakable. 13 (*N Am.*, *Can.*) popular, likeable. 14 defecating or menstruating at uniform or normal intervals. ~*n.* 1 a soldier belonging to a permanent army. 2 (*coll.*) a person permanently employed or constantly attending (as a customer etc.). 3 a member of the regular clergy. **to keep regular hours** HOUR. **regularity** (-lar´-) *n.* **regularize, regularise** *v.t.* **regularization** (-zā´shən) *n.* **regularly** *adv.* **regular octahedron** *n.* an octahedron contained by eight equal equilateral triangles. [OF *reguler* (F *régulier*), L *rēgulāris*, from *rēgula*, rule]

Usage note Pronunciation of *regularly* as (reg´ūli) is best avoided.

regulate (reg´ūlāt) *v.t.* 1 to adjust, control or order by rule. 2 to subject to restrictions. 3 to adjust to requirements, to put or keep in good order. 4 to reduce to order. **regulable** (-ləbəl) *a.* **regulation** (-lā´shən) *n.* 1 the act of regulating. 2 the state of being regulated. 3 a prescribed rule, order or direction. ~*a.* 1 prescribed by regulation. 2 formal, normal, accepted. 3 (*coll.*) ordinary, usual. **regulative** (-lət-), **regulatory** *a.* **regulator** (reg´ūlātə) *n.* 1 someone who or something which regulates. 2 a clock keeping accurate time, used for regulating other timepieces. 3 the lever of a watch or other contrivance for regulating or equalizing motion. **regulator gene** *n.* a gene whose product controls the product of other genes. **regulator valve** *n.* a valve in a locomotive which controls the supply of steam to the cylinders. [late L *regulātus*, p.p. of *regulāre*, as REGULAR]

reguli REGULUS.

regulo (reg´ūlō) *n.* the temperature of a gas oven, expressed as a particular number. [from Regulo®, trademark for a type of thermostat on gas ovens]

regulus (reg´ūləs) *n.* (*pl.* **reguluses, reguli** (-lī)) the purer mass of a metal that sinks to the bottom when ore is being smelted, an intermediate product retaining to a greater or lesser extent the impurities of the ore. **reguline** (-līn) *a.* [L, dim. of *rex rēgis*, king, prob. applied to antimony on account of its readiness to combine with gold]

regurgitate (rigœ´jitāt) *v.t.* **1** to bring back (partially digested food) into the mouth after swallowing. **2** to throw or pour back again. ~*v.i.* to gush or be poured back. **regurgitant** *a.* **regurgitation** (-ā´shən) *n.* [med. L *regurgitātus*, p.p. of *regurgitāre* (RE-, L *gurges -gitis*, eddy, whirlpool)]

re- (+ h- words) rehandle *v.t.* to handle or deal with again. **rehang** *v.t.* (*past, p.p.* **rehung**) to hang again (e.g. curtains). **reharness** *v.t.* to harness again. **rehash**[1] *v.t.* **1** to work over again. **2** to remodel, esp. in a perfunctory or ineffective manner. **rehash**[2] (rē´-) *n.* something presented under a new form. **rehear** *v.t.* (*past, p.p.* **reheard**) **1** to hear a second time. **2** to try over again in a law court. **rehearing** *n.* **1** a second hearing. **2** a retrial. **reheat**[1] *v.t.* **1** to heat again. **2** to inject fuel into (a jet aircraft's exhaust gases) to produce more thrust. **reheat**[2] (rē´-) *n.* the process by which thrust is produced in an aircraft by the ignition fuel added to exhaust gases. **reheater** *n.* an apparatus for reheating, esp. in an industrial process. **reheel** *v.t.* to heel (a shoe etc.) again. **rehire** *v.t.* to hire again (usu. after dismissal). **rehome** *v.t.* to find a new home for. **rehouse** *v.t.* to house anew. **rehumanize, rehumanise** *v.t.* to humanize again. **rehumanization** *n.* **rehung** REHANG (under RE- (+ H- WORDS)). **rehydrate** *v.t.* **1** to add water to (esp. dehydrated food). **2** to restore fluid lost by dehydration to (a person). ~*v.i.* to take up water or other fluid after dehydration. **rehydratable** *a.* **rehydration** *n.* **rehypothecate** *v.t.* **1** to hypothecate again. **2** to pledge again. **rehypothecation** *n.*

rehab (rē´hab) *n.* (*coll.*) rehabilitation. [abbr.]

rehabilitate (rēhəbil´itāt) *v.t.* **1** to make fit after disablement, illness, imprisonment etc. for making a living or playing a part in the life of society. **2** to restore to a former rank, position, office or privilege, to reinstate. **3** to re-establish the character or reputation of. **4** to restore (as a building) to good condition. **rehabilitation** (-ā´shən) *n.* **1** the act or process of rehabilitating. **2** the branch of occupational therapy which deals with the restoration of the injured, disabled etc. in society. **3** re-establishment of character or reputation. **rehabilitative** (-ətive) *a.* [med. L *rehabilitāre* (as RE-, HABILITATE)]

rehearse (rihœs´) *v.t.* **1** to recite or practise (a play, musical performance, part etc.) before public performance. **2** to train for a public performance by rehearsal. **3** to repeat, to recite. **4** to relate, to recount, to enumerate. ~*v.i.* to take part in a rehearsal. **rehearsal** *n.* **1** the act of rehearsing. **2** a preparatory performance of a play etc. **rehearser** *n.* **rehearsing** *n.* [OF *rehercer*, to harrow over again (RE-, HEARSE)]

rehoboam (rēəbō´əm) *n.* a wine bottle, especially a champagne bottle, which holds six times the amount of a standard bottle, approximately 156 fl. oz. (about 4.6 l). [*Rehoboam*, son of King Solomon, and King of Israel]

re- (+ i- words) reignite *v.t.* to ignite again. **reilluminate** *v.t.* to light up again, to illuminate again. **reillume, reillumine** *v.t.* (*poet.*) to reilluminate. **reillumination** *n.* **reimplant** *v.t.* to implant again. **reimplantation** *n.* **reimport**[1] (rēimpawt´) *v.t.* **1** to import again after exportation. **2** to import (goods made from exported raw materials). **reimport**[2] (rēim´pawt) *n.* **1** the act of reimporting. **2** something reimported. **reimportation** *n.* **reimpose** *v.t.* to impose again. **reimposition** *n.* **reimpress** *v.t.* to impress anew. **reimpression** *n.* **reimprint** *v.t.* **1** to imprint again. **2** to reprint. **reimprison** *v.t.* to imprison again. **reimprisonment** *n.* **reinaugurate** *v.t.* to inaugurate anew. **reincarnate** *v.t.* **1** to incarnate anew. **2** to cause to be born again. ~*a.* born again in a new body. **reincarnation** *n.* **1** the rebirth of the soul in a new body after death. **2** the embodiment of a concept, idea etc. in a new form. **reincarnationism** *n.* the belief in the reincarnation of the soul. **reincarnationist** *n.* **reincense** *v.t.* to incense anew. **reincite** *v.t.* to incite anew. **reincorporate** *v.t.* to incorporate again. **reincorporation** *n.* **reincur** *v.t.* (*pres.p.* **reincurring,** *past, p.p.* **reincurred**) to incur again. **reinduce** *v.t.* to induce again. **reinduction** *n.* **reindustrialize, reindustrialise** *v.t.* to redevelop the industry of. **reindustrialization** *n.* **reinfect** *v.t.* to infect again. **reinfection** *n.* **reinfest** *v.t.* to infest again. **reinfestation** *n.* **reinflame** *v.t.* to inflame again. **reinform** *v.t.* to inform again. **reinfuse** *v.t.* to infuse again. **reinfusion** *n.* **reingratiate** *v.t.* to ingratiate (oneself) again. **reinhabit** *v.t.* to inhabit again. **reink** *v.t.* to ink again. **reinoculate** *v.t.* to inoculate again. **reinoculation** *n.* **reinscribe** *v.t.* to inscribe again. **reinsert** *v.t.* to insert again. **reinsertion** *n.* **reinspect** *v.t.* to inspect again. **reinspection** *n.* **reinspire** *v.t.* to inspire again. **reinstall, reinstal** *v.t.* (*3rd pers. sing. pres.* **reinstalls, reinstals,** *pres.p.* **reinstalling,** *past, p.p.* **reinstalled**) to install again. **reinstallation** *n.* **reinstalment,** (*N Am.*) **reinstallment** *n.* **reinstate** *v.t.* **1** to restore, to replace (in a former position, state etc.). **2** to restore to a former rank, status etc. **3** to replace, to repair (property damaged by fire etc.). **reinstatement, reinstation** *n.* **reinstruct** *v.t.* to instruct again or in turn. **reinstruction** *n.* **reinsure** *v.t.* to insure against insurance risks. **reinsurance** *n.* **reinsurer** *n.* **reintegrate** *v.t.* **1** to integrate again (as into society). **2** to redintegrate. **reintegration** *n.* **reinter** *v.t.* to inter or bury again. **reinterment** *n.* **reinterpret** *v.t.* to interpret again or differently. **reinterpretation** *n.* **reinterrogate** *v.t.* to interrogate again. **reinterrogation** *n.* **reintroduce** *v.t.* to introduce or bring back into. **reintroduction** *n.* **reinvade** *v.t.* to invade again. **reinvasion** *n.* **reinvent** *v.t.* **1** to invent again. **2** to produce or create again or in a new or different form. **to reinvent the wheel 1** to devise something that already exists. **2** to spend time unnecessarily on things which have already been done, covered etc. **reinvention** *n.* **reinvest** *v.t.* to invest again. **reinvestment** *n.* **reinvestigate** *v.t.* to investigate again. **reinvestigation** *n.* **reinvigorate** *v.t.* **1** to reanimate. **2** to give fresh vigour to. **reinvigoration** *n.* **reinvite** *v.t.* to invite again. **reinvoke** *v.t.* to invoke again. **reinvolve** *v.t.* to involve again. **reinvolvement** *n.* **reissue** *v.t., v.i.* (*pres.p.* **reissuing,** *past, p.p.* **reissued**) to issue again. ~*n.* a second issue. **reissuable** *a.*

Reich (rīkh) *n.* the German realm considered as an empire made up of subsidiary states. **First Reich** FIRST. **Second Reich** SECOND[1]. **Third Reich** THIRD. **Reichsmark** (rīkhs´mahk) *n.* (*pl.* **Reichsmarks, Reichsmark**) the standard monetary unit of Germany between 1924 and 1948. **Reichsrat** (rīkhs´raht) *n.* the old Austrian parliament. **Reichstag** (-stahg) *n.* the parliament of the German Reich (1867–1933). [G, kingdom]

reify (rē´ifī) *v.t.* (*3rd pers. sing. pres.* **reifies,** *pres.p.* **reifying,** *past, p.p.* **reified**) to make (an abstract idea) concrete, to treat as real. **reification** (-fikā´shən) *n.* **reificatory** *a.* **reifier** *n.* [L *rēs rēi*, thing, -FY]

reign (rān) *n.* **1** the period during which a sovereign reigns. 2 a period during which a person or thing is predominant or prevalent. 3 supreme power, sovereignty, dominion. 4 rule, sway, control, influence. ~*v.i.* 1 to exercise sovereign authority, to be a king or queen. 2 to predominate, to prevail. **reigning** *a.* currently holding the title as most recent winner of a contest etc. **Reign of Terror** *n.* the bloodiest period of the French Revolution (April 1793–July 1794). [ME and OF *regne*, L *regnum*, from *regere*, to rule]

reimburse (rēimbœs´) *v.t.* 1 to repay (a person who has spent money). 2 to refund (expenses etc.). **reimbursable** *a.* **reimbursement** *n.* **reimburser** *n.* [RE-, late L *imbursāre*, to put in a purse (IM-[1], *bursa*, purse)]

rein (rān) *n.* (*often pl.*) 1 a long narrow strip, usu. of leather, attached at each end to a bit for guiding and controlling a horse or other animal in riding or driving. 2 a similar device for controlling a young child. 3 a means of restraint or control. ~*v.t.* 1 to check, to control, to manage with reins. 2 to pull (in, up or back) with reins. 3 to govern, to curb, to restrain. **to draw rein** 1 to stop one's horse, to pull up. 2 to abandon an effort, enterprise etc. **to give (free) rein to** to leave unrestrained, to allow to proceed without check. **to give the reins to** 1 to leave unrestrained. 2 to allow (a horse) to go its own way. **to keep on a tight rein** to control carefully. **to rein in** to cause (a horse) to stop by pulling on the reins. **to take the reins** to assume guidance, direction, office etc. **reinless** *a.* **reinsman** *n.* (*pl.* **reinsmen**) (*N Am.*) a horse driver. [OF *rene*, *reine*, *resne* (F *rêne*), prob. through late L *retina*, from L *retinēre* (RE-, *tenēre*, to hold)]

reindeer (rān´diə) *n.* a deer, *Rangifer tarandus*, now inhabiting the subarctic parts of the northern hemisphere, domesticated for the sake of its milk and as a draught animal. **reindeer lichen, reindeer moss** *n.* a lichen, *Cladonia rangiferina*, which forms the winter food of the reindeer. [Icel. *hreinn* (in *hreindýri*), DEER]

reinforce (rēinfaws´) *v.t.* 1 to add new strength, support or emphasis to. 2 to strengthen or support with additional troops, ships etc. 3 to strengthen by adding to the size, thickness etc.; to add a strengthening part to. 4 (*Psych.*) to encourage (a response or a subject making a particular response) by rewarding. 5 to enforce again. ~*n.* 1 the thicker part of a gun, that next to the breech. 2 a reinforcing or strengthening part, band etc. **reinforceable** *a.* **reinforced concrete** *n.* concrete given great tensile strength by the incorporation of rods, wires etc. of iron or steel; ferroconcrete. **reinforcement** *n.* 1 the act of reinforcing. 2 the state of being reinforced. 3 anything that reinforces. 4 (*usu. in pl.*) additional troops, ships etc. **reinforcer** *n.*

†**reins** (rānz) *n.pl.* 1 the kidneys. 2 the loins (formerly supposed to be the seat of the affections and passions). [OF, from L *rēnēs*]

reinsman REIN.

reiterate (rēit´ərāt) *v.t.* to repeat again and again. **reiterant** *a.* **reiteratedly** *adv.* **reiteration** (-ā´shən) *n.* **reiterative** (-ətiv) *a.* expressing or characterized by reiteration. ~*n.* a word or part of a word repeated so as to form a reduplicated word. **reiteratively** *adv.* [L *reiterāre*]

reive (rēv) *v.i.* (*Sc.*, *North.*) to go on a raid, to plunder. **reiver** *n.* [REAVE]

re- (+ j–k words) rejig[1] (rējig´) *v.t.* (*pres.p.* **rejigging**, *past*, *p.p.* **rejigged**) 1 to re-equip (e.g. a factory). 2 to rearrange or adjust, sometimes in an unethical way. **rejig**[2] (rē´-) *n.* the act of rejigging. **rejigger** *n.* **rejoin**[1] *v.t.* 1 to join again. 2 to join together again, to reunite after separation. ~*v.i.* to come together again. **rejoint** *v.t.* 1 to reunite the joints of. 2 to fill up the joints of (stonework, brickwork etc.) with new mortar, to point. **rejudge** *v.t.* 1 to judge again. 2 to re-examine. **rekey** *v.t.* to retype, esp. to re-enter (data) using a computer keyboard. **rekindle** *v.t.* 1 to kindle again. 2 to inflame or rouse anew. ~*v.i.* to ignite again.

reject[1] (rijekt´) *v.t.* 1 to put aside, to discard, to cast off. 2 to refuse to accept, receive, grant etc., to deny (a request etc.). 3 to fail to accept (an implanted organ, tissue graft etc.) because of immunological incompatibilities. 4 to rebuff (a person). 5 to repel, to cast up again, to vomit. **rejectable** *a.* **rejectamenta** (-təmen´tə) *n.pl.* matter rejected, refuse, excrement. **rejecter, rejector** *n.* **rejection** (-jek´shən) *n.* **rejectionist** *a.* rejecting or showing a tendency to reject a policy, proposal etc., esp. one offering peace. ~*n.* a person who refuses to accept a peace treaty, policy etc. **rejective** *a.* [from F *rejecter* (now *rejeter*) or L *rējectus*, p.p. of *rēicere* (RE-, *jacere*, to throw)]

reject[2] (rē´jekt) *n.* 1 someone who or something which has been rejected. 2 something which is substandard and offered for sale at discount.

rejoice (rijois´) *v.i.* 1 to feel joy or gladness in a high degree. 2 to be glad (that or to). 3 to delight or exult (in). 4 to express joy or gladness, to celebrate, to make merry. ~*v.t.* to make joyful, to gladden. **to rejoice in** 1 to be glad because of. 2 to be fortunate to have (*He rejoices in the name of Rufus T. Firefly*). **rejoiceful** *a.* **rejoicer** *n.* **rejoicing** *n.* 1 joyfulness. 2 (*often pl.*) the expression of joyfulness, making merry, celebrating a joyful event. **rejoicingly** *adv.* [OF *rejoiss-*, pres.p. stem of *rejoir* (F *rejouir*)]

rejoin[1] RE- (+ J–K WORDS).

rejoin[2] (rijoin´) *v.t.* to answer to a reply, to retort. ~*v.i.* to answer to a charge or pleading, esp. as the defendant to the plaintiff's replication. **rejoinder** (-də) *n.* 1 an answer to a reply, a retort. 2 a reply or answer in general. 3 the answer of a defendant to the plaintiff's replication. [F *rejoin-*, stem of *rejoindre*]

rejuvenate (rijoo´vənāt) *v.t.* 1 to make young again. 2 to restore to vitality or a previous condition. ~*v.i.* to become young again. **rejuvenation** (-ā´shən) *n.* **rejuvenator** *n.* **rejuvenesce** (-nes´) *v.i.* 1 to grow young again. 2 (*Biol.*) (of cells) to acquire fresh vitality. ~*v.t.* to give fresh vitality to. **rejuvenescence** *n.* **rejuvenescent** *a.* **rejuvenize, rejuvenise** *v.t.*, *v.i.* [L *juvenis*, young, -ATE[3]]

rel. *abbr.* 1 relating. 2 relative, relatively. 3 religion, religious.

re- (+ la–le words) relabel *v.t.* (*pres.p.* **relabelling,** (*N Am.*) **relabeling**, *past*, *p.p.* **relabelled,** (*N Am.*) **relabeled**) to label again. **relaid** RELAY[1] (under RE- (+ LA–LE WORDS)). **reland** *v.t.*, *v.i.* to land again. **relaunch**[1] *v.t.* 1 to launch again. 2 to reintroduce (a product) on to the market, usu. with some modifications. **relaunch**[2] (rē´-) *n.* 1 the act of relaunching. 2 something relaunched. **relay**[1] (rēlā´) *v.t.* (*past*, *p.p.* **relaid**) to lay again. **relearn** *v.t.* (*past*, *p.p.* **relearned, relearnt**) to learn again. **release**[1] (rēlēs´) *v.t.* to give a new lease to. **relet** *v.t.* (*pres.p.* **reletting,** *past*, *p.p.* **relet**) to let again.

relapse (rilaps´) *v.i.* 1 to fall or slip back (into a former bad state, condition or practice). 2 to become ill again after partial recovery. ~*n.* a falling or sliding back into a former bad state, esp. in a patient's state of health after partial recovery. **relapser** *n.* **relapsing fever** *n.* an epidemic infectious disease characterized by frequent attacks of fever, caused by spirochaetes of the genus *Borrelia*. [L *relapsus*, p.p. of *relābi* (*lābi*, to slip)]

relate (rilāt´) *v.t.* 1 to tell, to narrate, to recount. 2 to bring into relation or connection (with). 3 to ascribe to as source or cause, to show a relation (with). ~*v.i.* 1 to have relation or regard (to). 2 to refer (to). 3 to get on well with. **relatable** *a.* **related** *a.* 1 connected. 2 connected or allied by blood or marriage. 3 narrated. **relatedness** *n.* **relater** *n.* [F *relater*, med. L *relātāre*, from *relātus*, p.p. of *referre*, see REFER]

relation (rilā´shən) *n.* 1 the condition of being related or connected. 2 the way in which a thing or person stands or is conceived in regard to another, as dependence, independence, similarity, difference, correspondence, contrast etc. 3 connection by blood or marriage, kinship. 4 a person so connected, a relative, a kinsman or kinswoman. 5 respect, reference. 6 (*pl.*) dealings, affairs with. 7 (*pl., euphem.*) sexual intercourse. 8 the act of relating. 9 that which is related. 10 a narrative, an account, a story. 11 (*Law*) the laying of an information before the Attorney-General by a person bringing an action. **relational** *a.* 1 of, characterized by or indicating relation. 2 having kinship. **relational database** *n.* (*Comput.*) a database structured so that related items of data are recognized as such and can be accessed together. **relationally** *adv.* **relationless** (-lis) *a.* **relationship** *n.* 1 the state of being related. 2 connection by blood etc., kinship. 3 mutual connection between people or things. 4 an emotional or sexual affair.

relative (rel´ətiv) *a.* 1 not absolute but depending on relation to something else. 2 considered or being in relation to something else, correlative. 3 resulting from relation, proportionate to something else, comparative. 4 a having reference, relating (to). b relevant, pertinent, closely related (to). 5 having mutual relation, corresponding, related. 6 (*Gram.*) referring or relating to another word, sentence or clause (the antecedent). 7 (*Mus.*) having the same key signature. ~*n.* 1 a person connected by blood or marriage, a kinsman or kinswoman, a relation. 2 an animal or plant related to another by common origin. 3 a relative word, esp. a pronoun. 4 something relating to or considered in relation to another thing, a relative term. **relatival** (-tī´vəl) *a.* **relative aperture** *n.* the ratio of the focal length of a camera lens to the diameter of the aperture. **relative atomic mass** *n.* the ratio of the average mass of one atom of an element to one-twelfth of the mass of an atom of carbon-12. **relative density** *n.* the ratio of density of a substance to the density of a standard substance under the same, or specified, conditions. **relative frequency** *n.* in statistics, the actual number of favourable events as compared with the number of total possible events. **relative humidity** *n.* the amount of water vapour present in the air expressed as a percentage of the amount that would be present in the same volume of saturated air at the same temperature. **relatively** *adv.* 1 in relation to something else. 2 comparatively. **relative majority** *n.* the majority held by the winner of an election where no candidate has won more than 50% of the vote. **relative molecular mass** *n.* the ratio of the average mass of one molecule of an element or compound to one-twelfth of the mass of an atom of carbon-12. **relativeness** *n.* **relative permeability** *n.* the ratio of permeability of any medium to that of free space. **relativism** *n.* 1 the doctrine that ethical truths, moral principles etc. are not absolute but may vary between individuals and cultures. 2 the doctrine that knowledge is not absolute but relative to the thinking mind; relativity of knowledge. **relativist** *n.* **relativistic** (-vis´-) *a.* 1 of, concerned with or described by the theory of relativity. 2 of or relating to relativism. **relativity** (-tiv´-) *n.* 1 the fact or condition of being relative, relativeness. 2 (also **relativity theory**) either of two theories enunciated by Albert Einstein founded on the postulates that motion is relative and that the velocity of light is constant, and developing the Newtonian concept of space, time, motion and gravitation. **general theory of relativity** GENERAL. **special theory of relativity** SPECIAL. **relativize, relativise** *v.t.* 1 to make relative. 2 to apply theories of relativity to. ~*v.i.* to become relative. **relativization** (-zā´shən) *n.* [F *relatif -tive*, L *relatīvus*, as RELATE]

relator (rilā´tə) *n.* 1 an informer, a complainant, esp. one who institutes proceedings by way of a relation or information to the Attorney-General. 2 a relater, a narrator.

relax (rilaks´) *v.i.* 1 to become less tense, rigid, stern or severe. 2 to take relaxation. 3 to become less energetic, to diminish. 4 to become less formal or inhibited. ~*v.t.* 1 to allow to become less tense or rigid. 2 to slacken, to loosen. 3 to lessen the force or intensity of. 4 to make less strict or severe. 5 to relieve from strain, effort or nervous tension. **relaxable** *a.* **relaxant** *a.* relaxing. ~*n.* a medicine etc. that relaxes. **relaxation** (rēlaksā´shən) *n.* 1 the act of relaxing. 2 the state of being relaxed. 3 cessation from work, indulgence in recreation, amusement. 4 a diminution of tension, severity, application or attention. 5 remission of a penalty etc. 6 (*Physics*) a return to equilibrium. **relaxative** *a.* **relaxed** *a.* informal. **relaxedly** (-sid-) *adv.* **relaxedness** *n.* **relaxer** *n.* **relaxin** (-in) *n.* 1 a hormone found in pregnant mammals which relaxes the pelvic ligaments and so makes childbirth easier. 2 a preparation of this hormone used in childbirth. **relaxing** *a.* producing or conducive to relaxation. [L *relaxāre* (*laxus*, LAX)]

relay[1] RE- (+ LA–LE WORDS).

relay[2] (rē´lā) *n.* 1 a supply of fresh horses, workers, hounds etc. to relieve others when tired. 2 a supply of materials, people etc. to be ready when required. 3 a relay race. 4 a contrivance for receiving, reinforcing and retransmitting radio, television etc. signals. 5 an electrical control device that responds to variations in the current, voltage etc. of a circuit by activating switches and other devices in the same or a different circuit. 6 a message etc. that is relayed. 7 the passing along of something by stages. **relay race** *n.* a race between teams, each member of which covers a certain distance. [OF *relais*, from *relayer*, to relay]

relay[3] (rē´lā, rilā´) *v.t.* 1 to spread (information etc.) by relays. 2 a to receive and transmit by a relay. b to broadcast (a signal or programme) from a particular place. 3 to operate or control by a relay. 4 to arrange in or provide with relays.

release[1] RE- (+ LA–LE WORDS).

release[2] (rilēs´) *v.t.* 1 to set free from restraint or confinement, to liberate. 2 to free from obligation or penalty. 3 to deliver from pain, care, trouble, grief or other evil. 4 to move from a fixed position. 5 to allow to pass from a place of origin or storage, to emit. 6 to issue (a recording, film etc.) for general sale, exhibition etc. 7 to make (information, news etc.) public. 8 (*Law*) to surrender, to quit, to remit (a right, debt, claim etc.). ~*n.* 1 liberation from restraint, confinement, pain, care, obligation or penalty. 2 a discharge from liability, responsibility etc. 3 the act of releasing or issuing a recording, film etc. 4 anything newly issued for sale or to the public. 5 a news item available for publication or broadcasting. 6 a handle, catch or other device by which a piece of mechanism is released. 7 (*Law*) a surrender or conveyance of property or right to another. b the instrument by which this is carried out. **releasable** *a.* **releasee** (-sē´) *n.* a person to whom property is released. **releaser** *n.* **releasor** *n.* (*Law*) a person releasing property or a claim to another. [OF *relesser*, *relaisser*, var. of *relâcher*, L *relaxāre*, to RELAX]

relegate (rel´igāt) *v.t.* 1 to consign or dismiss (to some inferior position etc.). 2 to demote (e.g. a football team) to a lower division. 3 (*formal*) to refer, commit, or hand over (to). 4 (*formal*) to assign to a category or class. 5 to send away, to banish. **relegable** *a.* **relegation** (-gā´shən) *n.* [L *relegātus*, p.p. of *relegāre* (*legāre*, to send)]

☒ **releive** common misspelling of RELIEVE.

relent (rilent´) *v.i.* 1 to give way to compassion, to yield. 2 to become less harsh, severe or obdurate. 3 to let up, to slacken. **relenting** *n., a.* **relentingly** *adv.* **relentless** (-lis) *a.* **1** inflexible, unyielding, inexorable. **2** merciless, pitiless. **3** sustained, incessant, unremitting. **relentlessly** *adv.* **relentlessness** *n.* [etym. uncertain, perh. through F *ralentir*, to slacken; ult. from RE-, L *lentus*, soft]

relevant (rel´əvənt) *a.* pertinent, applicable, bearing on the matter in hand, apposite. **relevance, relevancy** *n.* **relevantly** *adv.* [med. L *relevans -ntem*, orig. pres.p. of L *relevāre* (*levāre*, to raise)]

re-(+li–lo words) relicense, (*N Am.*) **relicence** *v.t.* **1** to license again. **2** to renew the license of. **relight** *v.t.* (*past, p.p.* **relighted, relit**) to light, kindle or illumine afresh. ~*v.i.* to ignite again. **reline** *v.t.* to line again, to give a new lining to. **relist** *v.t.* to list again. **relisten** *v.i.* to listen again. **relive** *v.t.* to live over again, esp. in the imagination. ~*v.i.* to live again, to revive. **relivable** *a.* **reload** *v.t.* to load again. ~*v.i.* to load a firearm again. **relocate** *v.t.* to move (e.g. a factory, workers, business) to a new location. ~*v.i.* to move to a new place or area, esp. for employment or business reasons. **relocation** *n.* **1** the act of relocating. **2** (*Sc. Law*) renewal of a lease without a fresh agreement.

reliable, reliance etc. RELY.

relic (rel´ik), †**relique** (rəlēk´, rel´ik) *n.* **1** any ancient object of historical interest. **2** something remaining or kept in remembrance of a person, esp. a part of the body or other object religiously cherished from its having belonged to some saint. **3** a custom etc. that has survived from the past. **4** a keepsake, a souvenir, a memento. **5** (*usu. pl.*) some part or thing remaining after the loss or decay of the rest, a remnant, a fragment, a scrap, a survival, a trace. **6** (*pl.*) a dead body, a corpse, remains. **relic-monger** *n.* a person who trades in relics. [OF *relique*, L *reliquiae*, pl., remains, as RELICT]

relict (rel´ikt) *n.* **1** †a plant or animal existing as a remnant of a formerly widely distributed group in a previous geological era. **2** a geological or geographical feature, such as a mountain, which is a remnant of an earlier formation. **3** †a widow. ~*a.* surviving as a relict. [OF *relicte* or L *relicta*, p.p. of *relinquere* (*linquere*, to leave)]

relief[1] (rilēf´) *n.* **1** alleviation of pain, grief, discomfort etc. **2** the feeling of comfort or cheerfulness that follows the removal of pain, distress etc. **3** anything that breaks monotony or relaxes tension. **4** something which alleviates. **5** assistance given to people in poverty, need or distress. **6** release from a post or duty by a person or persons acting as substitute. **7** such a substitute. **8** a supplementary vehicle for transporting passengers at peak times. **9** assistance in time of stress or danger, the raising of the siege of a besieged town. **10** an army or detachment carrying this out. **11** redress of a grievance etc., esp. by legal remedy or compensation. **indoor relief** INDOOR. **on relief** (*esp. N Am.*) in receipt of government financial assistance. **outdoor relief** OUT-. **relief road** *n.* a road taking traffic round a congested urban area. [OF *relef*, from *relever*, to RELIEVE]

relief[2] (rilēf´) *n.* **1** the projecting of carved or moulded figures or designs from a surface in approximate proportion to the objects represented. **2** a piece of sculpture, moulding etc. with the figures etc. projecting. **3** apparent projection of forms and figures due to drawing, colouring and shading. **4** distinctness of contour, clearness, vividness. **relief map** *n.* **1** a map in which hills and valleys are indicated by shading, hachures, contour lines etc. **2** a three-dimensional map in which hills and valleys are shown by prominences and depressions, usu. in exaggerated proportion, instead of contour lines. **relief printing** *n.* printing by letterpress of blocks, as distinct from lithography. [It. *rilievo*, from *rilevare*, L *relevāre*, to RELIEVE, assim. to RELIEF[1]]

relieve (rilēv´) *v.t.* **1** to alleviate, to mitigate, to relax, to lighten. **2** to free wholly or partially from pain, grief, discomfort etc. **3** to provide aid or assistance to. **4** to release from a post, duty, responsibility etc., esp. to take turn on guard or at a post. **5** to remove a burden or responsibility from. **6** to break or mitigate the monotony, dullness etc. of. **7** to raise the siege of. **8** (*coll.*) to take or steal from, to deprive (one of). **9** to give relief or prominence to, to bring out or make conspicuous by contrast. **to relieve oneself** (*euphem.*) to defecate or urinate. **to relieve one's feelings** (*euphem.*) to use strong language when angry. **relievable** *a.* **relieved** *a.* experiencing relief, esp. from worry or emotion. **relievedly** (-vid-) *adv.* **reliever** *n.* **relieving** *n., a.* **relieving arch** *n.* (*Archit.*) an arch constructed in a wall to take the weight off a part underneath. **relieving-officer** *n.* (*Hist.*) an officer appointed by the guardians to superintend the relief of the poor in a parish or union. [OF *relever*, L *relevāre* (*levāre*, to raise, from *levis*, light)]

relievo (relē´vō), **rilievo** *n.* (*pl.* **relievi** (-vē, rilievi) raised or embossed work, relief. [RELIEF[2]]

religieuse (rilēzhœz´) *n.* a nun. **religieux** (-zhœ´) *n.* (*pl.* **religieux** (-zhœ´)) a monk. [F, RELIGIOUS (under RELIGION)]

religio- (rilij´iō) *comb. form* **1** religion. **2** religious.

religion (rilij´ən) *n.* **1** belief in a superhuman being or beings, esp. a personal god, controlling the universe and entitled to worship and obedience. **2** the feelings, effects on conduct and the practices resulting from such belief. **3** a system of faith, doctrine and worship. **4** the monastic state, the state of being bound by religious vows. **5** anything of great personal importance. **6** (*coll.*) spiritual awakening, conversion. **7** (*fig.*) devotion, sense of obligation. **to get religion** (*coll.*) to be converted. **religionary** *a.* **religioner** *n.* a member of an order. **religionism** *n.* **1** excessive or exaggerated religious zeal. **2** a profession or affectation of religion, the outward practice of religion. **religionist** *n., a.* **religionize, religionise** *v.t.* to make religious, to imbue with religion. ~*v.i.* to profess or display religion. **religionless** *a.* **religiose** (-iōs) *a.* **1** morbidly affected with religious emotion. **2** pious, sanctimonious. **religiosely** *adv.* **religiosity** (-ios´-) *n.* religious sentimentality or emotionalism. **religious** *a.* **1** of, relating to or concerned with religion. **2** imbued with religion, pious, devout. **3** bound by vows to a monastic life, belonging to a monastic order. **4** conscientious, rigid, strict. ~*n.* (*pl.* **religious**) a person bound by monastic vows. **religious house** *n.* a house for monks or nuns, a monastery, a convent. **religiously** *adv.* **1** in a religious manner. **2** (*coll.*) scrupulously. **religiousness** *n.* [A-F *religiun* (F *religion*), L *religiōnem*, nom. *-gio*, perh. rel. to *religāre*, to bind (perh. from *religens*, fearing the gods, opp. to *negligens*, NEGLIGENT (under NEGLIGENCE))]

relinquish (riling´kwish) *v.t.* **1** to give up a claim to, to surrender. **2** to forsake, to abandon, to resign. **3** to quit, to desist from. **4** to let go of. **relinquisher** *n.* **relinquishment** *n.* [OF *relinquiss-*, pres.p. stem of *relinquir*, L *relinquere* (*linquere*, to leave)]

reliquary (rel´ikwəri), **reliquaire** (relikweə´) *n.* (*pl.* **reliquaries, reliquaires**) a depository for relics, a casket for keeping a relic or relics in. [F *reliquaire*, from *relique*]

†**relique** RELIC.

reliquiae (rilik´wiē) *n.pl.* **1** remains. **2** fossil remains of organisms. [L]

relish (rel´ish) *n.* **1** great enjoyment, gusto, appetite, zest, fondness, liking. **2** pleasing anticipation. **3** something taken with food to give a flavour, a condiment. **4** the effect of anything on the palate, taste, distinctive flavour, esp. a pleasing taste or flavour. **5** a pleasing quality. **6** a slight admixture or flavouring, a smack, a trace (of). *~v.t.* **1** to be gratified by, to enjoy. **2** to look forward to with pleasure. **3** to partake of with pleasure, to like. **4** to give agreeable flavour to, to make piquant etc. *~v.i.* (*dated*) **1** to have a pleasing taste. **2** to have a flavour, to taste or smack (of). **3** to affect the taste (well etc.). **relishable** *a.* [ME and OF *reles*, var. of *relais*, that left behind, from *relesser*, see RELEASE[2]]

reluctant (rilŭk´tənt) *a.* **1** unwilling, averse, disinclined (to). **2** doing, done or granted unwillingly. **reluctance, †reluctancy** *n.* **1** unwillingness, disinclination. **2** the ratio of the opposition between a magnetic substance and the magnetic flux. **reluctantly** *adv.* **reluctivity** (reləktiv´-) *n.* the reluctance of a magnetic substance. [L *reluctans -antem*, pres.p. of *reluctārī* (*luctārī*, to struggle)]

rely (rilī´) *v.i.* (*3rd pers. sing. pres.* **relies,** *pres.p.* **relying,** *past, p.p.* **relied**) **1** to trust or depend (on or upon) with confidence. **2** to be dependent (on). **reliable** *a.* **1** that may be relied on. **2** trustworthy. **reliability** (-bil´-), **reliableness** *n.* **reliably** *adv.* **reliance** *n.* **1** confident dependence (on or upon), trust. **2** a ground of confidence, that on which one relies. **reliant** *a.* **reliantly** *adv.* [OF *relier*, L *religāre* (*ligāre*, to bind)]

REM (rem) *abbr.* rapid eye-movement. **REM sleep** *n.* paradoxical sleep. [acronym]

rem (rem) *n.* (*pl.* **rems**) a unit of radiation dosage which has the same biological effect as one roentgen of X-ray or gamma radiation. [roentgen equivalent man]

re- (+ ma–mi words) remake[1] (rēmāk´) *v.t.* (*past, p.p.* **remade**) to make again or anew. **remake**[2] (rē´māk) *n.* **1** anything made again from the original materials. **2** a new version of an old film, record etc. **reman** *v.t.* (*pres.p.* **remanning,** *past, p.p.* **remanned**) **1** to man (a ship, gun etc.) again. **2** to equip with a new complement of men. **3** (*poet.*) to imbue with courage again. **remanufacture** *v.t.* to manufacture again. **remargin** *v.t.* to give a fresh margin to (a page etc.). **re-mark** *v.t.* to mark again. **remarry** *v.t., v.i.* (*3rd pers. sing. pres.* **remarries,** *pres.p.* **remarrying,** *past, p.p.* **remarried**) to marry again. **remarriage** *n.* **remaster** *v.t.* to make a new master recording from (an older or original recording to improve the sound quality). **rematch**[1] *v.t.* to match (esp. two contestants or teams) again. **rematch**[2] (rē´-) *n.* a second or return match or game. **remeasure** *v.t.* to measure again. **remeasurement** *n.* **remelt** *v.t.* to melt again. **remend** *v.t.* to mend again. **remerge** *v.t.* to merge again. **remigrate** (rem´igrāt, rēmīgrāt´, rēmī´grāt) *v.i.* to migrate back again, to return to a former place or state. **remigration** (-grā´shən) *n.* **remilitarize, remilitarise** *v.t.* to equip with military forces again. **remilitarization** *n.* **remint** *v.t.* to mint over again. **remix**[1] *v.t.* **1** to mix again. **2** to change the balance of (a sound recording). **remix**[2] (rē´-) *n.* a remixed version of a sound recording. **remixer** *n.*

remain (rimān´) *v.i.* **1** to stay behind or be left after use, separation, destruction etc. **2** to survive. **3** to continue in a place or state. **4** to last, to abide, to continue, to endure. **5** to continue to be. **6** to be still to be done or dealt with. **remainder** (-də) *n.* **1** anything left over after a part has been taken away, used etc.; the rest, the residue. **2** the quantity left over after subtraction, the excess remaining after division. **3** the copies of a book left unsold after the initial demand for it has ceased, offered at a reduced price. **4** (*Law*) an interest in an estate limited to take effect and be enjoyed after a prior estate is determined. *~v.t.* to offer (unsold copies of a book) at a reduced price. **remainder-man** *n.* (*pl.* **remainder-men**) a person to whom an estate in remainder is bequeathed. **remaining** *a.* **remains** *n.pl.* **1** that which remains behind. **2** ruins, relics. **3** a dead body, a corpse. **4** literary productions published after one's death. [OF *remaindre*, L *remanēre* (*manēre*, to stay)]

remand (rimahnd´) *v.t.* **1** to recommit to custody after a partial hearing. **2** to send back (to). *~n.* **1** the act of remanding. **2** the state of being remanded. **to be on remand** to be in custody awaiting trial. **remand centre** *n.* a place of detention for people awaiting trial. **remand home** *n.* (*Hist.*) a place where children aged 8–14 years were remanded or detained as punishment for criminal offences. **remandment** *n.* [OF *remander*, late L *remandāre* (*mandāre*, to commit)]

remanent (rem´ənənt) *a.* remaining, left behind, surviving. **remanence** *n.* the ability of any magnetized substance to remain magnetic when the magnetizing force becomes zero. **remanet** (-nit) *n.* **1** a remainder. **2** a case postponed to another term. **3** a bill deferred to another session. [from L *remanens -ntem*, pres.p. of *remanēre*, to REMAIN]

remark (rimahk´) *v.t.* **1** to utter by way of comment, to comment (that). **2** to take notice of, to observe with particular attention, to perceive. *~v.i.* to make a comment or observation (on). *~n.* **1** an observation, a comment. **2** the act of noticing, observation. **3** (*usu. pl., coll.*) anything said, conversation. **4** (*also* **remarque**) **a** a distinguishing mark indicating the particular state of an engraved plate, usu. as a marginal sketch. **b** a plate so marked or a print or proof from such a plate. **remarked** *a.* **1** conspicuous. **2** (*also* **remarqued**) with a remark etched on. **remarker** *n.* [F *remarquer* (*marquer*, to MARK[1])]

remark- RE- (+ MA–MI WORDS).

remarkable (rimahk´əbəl) *a.* **1** worthy of special observation or notice, notable. **2** unusual, extraordinary, striking. **remarkableness** *n.* **remarkably** *adv.* [as REMARK]

remarque REMARK.

remblai (rã´blā) *n.* the material used to form a rampart or embankment. [F, from *remblayer*, to embank]

Rembrandtesque (rembrantesk´) *a.* in the style of or resembling the effects of the Dutch painter Rembrandt van Rijn, 1609–69, esp. in chiaroscuro. **Rembrandtish** (rem´-) *a.*

REME (rē´mē) *abbr.* Royal Electrical and Mechanical Engineers.

remedy (rem´ədi) *n.* (*pl.* **remedies**) **1** something which cures a disease. **2** medicine, healing treatment. **3** something which serves to remove, counteract or repair any evil. **4** redress, reparation. **5** the tolerated variation in the standard weight of coins. *~v.t.* (*3rd pers. sing. pres.* **remedies,** *pres.p.* **remedying,** *past, p.p.* **remedied**) **1** to cure, to heal. **2** to repair, to rectify, to redress. **remediable** (rimē´-) *a.* **remediableness** *n.* **remediably** *adv.* **remedial** (rimē´-) *a.* **1** affording or intended as a remedy. **2** of or relating to the teaching of slow learners and people with special needs. **remedially** *adv.* **remediless** *a.* **remedilessly** *adv.* **remedilessness** *n.* [A-F *remedie* (F *remède*), L *remedium* (*mederī*, to heal)]

remember (rimem´bə) *v.t.* **1** to bear or keep in mind, not to forget. **2** to recall to mind, to recollect. **3** to hold in the memory, to know by heart. **4** to keep in mind with gratitude, reverence, respect etc. **5** to commemorate (e.g. the dead). **6** (*coll.*) to convey a greeting from (*remember me to your father*). **7** to be good to, to make a present to, to tip. **8** to recall to the memory of someone else. **9** †to remind. *~v.i.* **1** to have the power of memory, to exercise the memory. **2** to have a remembrance or recollection. **to remember oneself** to recover or retain one's good manners. **rememberable** *a.* **rememberability** (-bil´-) *n.* **rememberably** *adv.* **rememberer** *n.* **remembrance** (-brəns) *n.* **1 a** the act of remembering. **b** memory. **2** the state of being remembered. **3** a recollection, a memory. **4** that which serves to recall to or preserve in memory. **5** a keepsake, a memento, a memorial. **6** the time over which memory extends. **7** (*pl.*) regards, greetings. **Remembrance Day, Remembrance Sunday** *n.* the Sunday nearest to 11 Nov., when those who were killed in the two World Wars are remembered. **remembrancer** *n.* **1** someone who or something which puts in mind. **2** a reminder, a memento. [OF *remembrer*, late L *rememorārī* (*memor*, mindful)]

remex (rē´meks) *n.* (*pl.* **remiges** (rem´ijēz)) any of the quill feathers of a bird's wings. **remigate** *v.i.* to row. **remigation** (-ā´shən) *n.* **remigial** (rimij´iəl) *a.* [L, rower, from *rēmus*, oar]

remind (rimīnd´) *v.t.* **1** to put in mind (of). **2** to cause to remember (to do etc.). **reminder** *n.* **1** someone who or something which reminds. **2** a memento. **remindful** *a.* **1** serving to remind. **2** mindful.

reminiscence (reminis´əns) *n.* **1** the act or power of remembering or recalling past knowledge. **2** a past event, experience etc. which is remembered. **3** an account of or the narration of this. **4** (*pl.*) a collection of personal recollections of past events etc. **5** something reminding or suggestive (of something else). **6** the philosophical doctrine that the human mind has seen everything before in an earlier, disembodied, existence. **reminisce** *v.i.* to talk, think or write about past experiences. **reminiscent** *a.* **1** reminding or suggestive (of). **2** of the nature of or relating to reminiscence. **3** recalling or given to recalling past events. **reminiscential** (-sen´shəl) *a.* **reminiscently** *adv.* **reminiscer** *n.* **reminiscitory** *a.* [late L *reminiscentia*, from *reminiscī* (*men-*, stem of *meminī*, I remember, cogn. with MIND)]

remise (rimīz´, rimēz´) *v.t.* (*Law*) to surrender, to release or grant back (a right, claim, property etc.). ~*v.i.* in fencing, to make a remise. ~*n.* **1** a release of property. **2** a surrender of a claim. **3** in fencing, a thrust following up one that misses before the opponent has time to recover. [F, from *remettre*, to REMIT[1]]

remiss (rimis´) *a.* **1** careless or lax in the performance of duty or business, heedless, negligent. **2** slow, slack, languid. **remissly** *adv.* **remissness** *n.* [L *remissus*, p.p. of *remittere*, to REMIT[1]]

remission (rimish´ən) *n.* **1** the act of remitting. **2** the reduction of a prison sentence. **3** abatement (e.g. in the symptoms of a disease), diminution of force or intensity, reduction. **4** the remitting or discharge of a debt, penalty etc. **5** forgiveness, pardon. **6** remittance (of money etc.). **remissible** (rimis´əbəl) *a.* that may be remitted. **remissibility** (-bil´-) *n.* **remissive** (rimis´-), **remissory** *a.* **remissively** *adv.* [OF, from L *remissiōnem*, nom. *-sio*, as REMISS]

remit[1] (rimit´) *v.t.* (*pres.p.* **remitting,** *past, p.p.* **remitted**) **1** to transmit (cash, payment etc.), esp. by post. **2** to refrain from exacting etc., to forgo, to discharge from (a fine, penalty etc.). **3** to relax, to slacken, to mitigate, to desist from partially or entirely. **4** to refer or submit, to send back for consideration. **5** to refer (a case) to a lower court. **6** to defer, to put off. **7** to send or put back. **8** to pardon, to forgive. ~*v.i.* to become less intense, to abate. **remitment** *n.* **1** the act of remitting. **2** remittance. **remittable** *a.* **remittal** *n.* **1** the act of remitting, esp. the referral of a case from one court to another lower one. **2** remission. **remittance** *n.* **1** the act of remitting money or the like, in payment for goods etc. or as an allowance. **2** the sum so remitted. **remittance man** *n.* (*pl.* **remittance men**) (*Hist.*) an emigrant depending on remittances from home for his living. **remittee** (-ē´) *n.* a person receiving a remittance. **remittent** *a.* (of an illness or symptom) having alternate increase and decrease of intensity. **remittence** *n.* **remittently** *adv.* **remitter** (rimit´ə) *n.* **1** a person who remits or sends a remittance. **2** (*Law*) reversion to the more valid of two titles to an estate in favour of the holder entering in possession by the inferior title. **3** remission to another court. [L *remittere* (*mittere*, to send), p.p. *remissus*]

remit[2] (rē´mit, rimit´) *n.* **1** the extent of responsibility, authority or concern of a person, committee etc. **2** the act of remitting. **3** something remitted, esp. a matter remitted for consideration.

remittable, remittal etc. REMIT[1].

remnant (rem´nənt) *n.* **1** that which is left after a larger part has been separated, used, lost or destroyed. **2** the last part of a piece of cloth etc., esp. a portion offered at a reduced price. **3** a scrap, a fragment, a surviving trace. **4** the remainder. ~*a.* remaining. [ME and OF *remenant*, pres.p. of *remenoir*, *manoir*, to REMAIN]

re- (+ mo– words) remodel *v.t.* (*pres.p.* **remodelling,** (*N Am.*) **remodeling,** *past, p.p.* **remodelled,** (*N Am.*) **remodeled**) **1** to model again. **2** to refashion. **remodify** *v.t.* (*3rd pers. sing. pres.* **remodifies,** *pres.p.* **remodifying,** *past, p.p.* **remodified**) to modify again. **remodification** *n.* **remold** REMOULD[1] (under RE- (+ MO– WORDS)). **remonetize, remonetise** *v.t.* to reinstate (a metal etc.) as legal currency. **remonetization** *n.* **remortgage** *v.t.* **1** to mortgage again. **2** to take out a second or further mortgage on (a property). ~*n.* a second or further mortgage. **remould**[1], (*N Am.*) **remold** *v.t.* **1** to mould, fashion or shape anew. **2** to bond a new tread on to (a tyre). **remould**[2] (rē´-) *n.* a used tyre which has a new tread bonded into the casing and the walls coated with rubber. **remount**[1] *v.t.* **1** to mount again. **2** to reascend. **3** to mount or set up (a gun, jewellery, a picture etc.) again. **4** to supply (a person, regiment etc.) with a fresh horse or horses. ~*v.i.* **1** to mount a horse again. **2** to make a fresh ascent. **remount**[2] (rē´-) *n.* a fresh horse for riding on.

remonstrance (rimon´strəns) *n.* **1** the act of remonstrating. **2** an expostulation, a protest. **3** a formal representation or protest against public grievances etc. **remonstrant** *a.* **1** containing or of the nature of remonstrance, remonstrating, expostulatory. **2** (*Hist.*) †(**Remonstrant**) of or relating to the Arminian party in the Dutch Church. ~*n.* **1** a person who remonstrates. **2** (*Hist.*) †(**Remonstrant**) any of the Dutch Arminians who in 1610 presented to the States of Holland a remonstrance formulating their points of departure from Calvinism. **remonstrantly** *adv.*

remonstrate (rem´ənstrāt) *v.i.* to make a protest, to argue or object forcibly. ~*v.t.* to say or state in protest or opposition. **remonstratingly** *adv.* **remonstration** (-strā´shən) *n.* **remonstrative** (rimon´strətiv), **remonstratory** (rem´-) *a.* **remonstrator** *n.* [med. L *remonstrāre* (L *monstrāre*, to show)]

remontant (rimon´tənt) *a.* (esp. of a rose) blooming more than once in the season. ~*n.* a remontant rose. [F, pres.p. of *remonter*, to remount]

remora (rem´ərə) *n.* (*pl.* **remoras**) any of various spiny-finned fishes of the family Echeneidae having a suctorial disc for attaching larger fish and believed by the ancients to have the power of stopping ships in this way. [L, orig. hindrance, impediment (*mora*, delay)]

remorse (rimaws´) *n.* **1** the pain caused by a sense of guilt, bitter regret or repentance. **2** compunction, reluctance to commit a wrong or to act cruelly. **remorseful** *a.* **1** feeling remorse. **2** penitent. **remorsefully** *adv.* **remorsefulness** *n.* **remorseless** *a.* **1** without compassion or compunction, cruel. **2** unrelenting. **3** without remorse. **remorselessly** *adv.* **remorselessness** *n.* [OF *remors*, late L *remorsus*, from *remordere* (*mordere*, to bite, p.p. *morsus*)]

remote (rimōt´) *a.* **1** far off, distant in time or space. **2** out of the way, far away from a centre of population, isolated. **3** not closely connected or related. **4** removed in likeness or relation, separated, different. **5** operated or operating from a distance. **6** (*usu. superl.*) slight, inconsiderable, least. **7** (of a person) aloof, cold. **remote**

control *n.* 1 electronic or radio control of apparatus etc. from a distance. 2 a device allowing remote control (e.g. of a television set). **remote-controlled** *a.* **remotely** *adv.* **remoteness** *n.* **remote sensing** *n.* the scanning of the earth or another planet from space, esp. by satellites equipped with cameras, radar etc., in order to obtain data. **remote sensor** *n.* [L *remōtus*, p.p. of *removēre*, REMOVE]

rémoulade (rāmulahd´) *n.* a sauce, often made with mayonnaise, flavoured with herbs, mustard and capers and served with fish, cold meat, salads etc. [F dial. *ramolas*, horseradish, from L *armoracea*]

remove (rimoov´) *v.t.* 1 to move or take from a place or position. 2 to move to another place. 3 to take away, to get rid of. 4 to transfer to another post or office. 5 to dismiss. 6 (*euphem.*) to kill, to murder. 7 (*formal*) to act as the removers of or for. ~*v.i.* to go away (from), esp. to change one's place or abode. ~*n.* 1 a distance, a degree of separation. 2 a degree of difference or gradation. 3 a class or form (in some public schools). 4 removal, a change of place or position. 5 (*dated*) a dish removed to give place to another, or the dish brought on in its place. **removable** *a.* 1 able to be moved. 2 liable to removal. **removability** (-bil´-) *n.* **removal** *n.* 1 the act of removing or displacing. 2 change of place, site or abode. 3 the transfer of furniture etc. from one house etc. to another. 4 dismissal. 5 (*euphem.*) murder. **removalist** *n.* (*Austral.*) a person or company responsible for moving furniture etc. to a new home. **removed** *a.* 1 distant in space or time. 2 distant in condition, character, association or relationship. 3 separated by a specified number of intervals of descent. **once removed** separated by one generation younger or older. **twice removed** separated by two generations younger or older. **removedness** (-vid-) *n.* **remover** *n.* 1 someone who or something which removes. 2 (*often pl.*) a company whose business is to remove furniture from one house etc. to another. [OF *remouvoir*, *-movoir*, L *removēre* (*movēre*, to MOVE)]

remunerate (rimū´nərāt) *v.t.* 1 to reward, to recompense, to pay for a service etc. 2 to serve as recompense or equivalent for or to. **remunerable** *a.* **remunerability** (-bil´-) *n.* **remuneration** (-ā´shən) *n.* **remunerative** (-ətiv) *a.* 1 producing a due return for outlay. 2 paying, profitable. **remuneratively** *adv.* **remunerativeness** *n.* **remuneratory** *a.* [L *remūnerātus*, p.p. of *remūnerāre*, *-erārī* (*mūnus*, gift)]

re- (+ n– words) rename *v.t.* to name anew, to give a new name to. **renationalize, renationalise** *v.t.* to bring (a privatized industry) back under state control. **renationalization** *n.* **renegotiate** *v.t.* to negotiate again, esp. on different terms. **renegotiable** *a.* **renegotiation** *n.* **renerve** *v.t.* to put fresh nerve or vigour into. **renominate** *v.t.* to nominate again. **renomination** *n.* **renotify** *v.t.* (*3rd pers. sing. pres.* **renotifies**, *pres.p.* **renotifying**, *past, p.p.* **renotified**) to notify again. **renotification** *n.* **renumber** *v.t.* to number again.

Renaissance (rinā´səns) *n.* 1 the revival of art and letters in the 14th–16th cents. 2 the period of this. 3 the style of architecture, painting, literature and science that was developed under it. 4 (**renaissance**) any revival of a similar nature, a rebirth. **Renaissance man** *n.* (*pl.* **Renaissance men**) a person who has wide expertise and learning. [F, from *renaître* (*naître*, to be born), cp. RENASCENCE (under RENASCENT)]

renal (rē´nəl) *a.* of or relating to the kidneys. **renal cortex** *n.* the outer part of the kidney. **renal pelvis** *n.* the cavity joining the kidney and the ureter. [late L *rēnālis*, from *rēn*, kidney]

renascent (rinas´ənt, -nā´-) *a.* coming into being again, reborn, renewed. **renascence** *n.* 1 rebirth, renewal, a springing into fresh life. 2 the Renaissance. [L *renascens -ntem*, pres.p. of *renascī* (*nascī*, to be born)]

rencounter (rənkown´tə), †**rencontre** (rākõn´trə) *n.* 1 an unexpected meeting or encounter. 2 a hostile meeting or collision, an encounter, a combat, a duel, a skirmish. ~†*v.t.* to fall in with unexpectedly. [F *rencontre*, from *rencontrer* (ENCOUNTER)]

rend (rend) *v.t.* (*past, p.p.* **rent** (rent)) (*dated or poet.*) 1 to tear, pull or wrench (off, away, apart, asunder etc.). 2 to tear or pull (one's clothes or hair) as an expression of extreme grief or rage. 3 to split or separate with violence. 4 to lacerate, to cause anguish to. 5 to pierce or disturb (the air, silence etc.), with sound. ~*v.i.* to be or become torn or pulled apart. [OE *rendan*, cp. OFris. *renda*]

render (ren´də) *v.t.* 1 to make, to cause to be. 2 to bestow, to give, to pay, to furnish. 3 to give in return. 4 to pay or give back. 5 to present, to submit, to hand in. 6 to reproduce, to express, to represent, to interpret, to translate, to perform, to execute. 7 to boil down, to melt and clarify (fat). 8 to give the first coat of plaster to. 9 to give up, to surrender. ~*n.* 1 the first coat of plaster on a wall etc. 2 a return, a payment in return, esp. from a feudal tenant to a lord. **renderable** *a.* **renderer** *n.* **rendering** *n.* 1 a performance, an execution, an interpretation (of a piece of music, a dramatic part etc.). 2 a translation, a version. 3 the first coat of plaster on brickwork etc. 4 a return. **rendition** *n.* 1 surrender, giving up. 2 translation, interpretation. 3 execution, performance, rendering (of music etc.). [OF *rendre*, pop. L *rendere*, var. of L *reddere* (*dare*, to give)]

rendezvous (ron´dāvoo, rā´-) *n.* (*pl.* **rendezvous** (-vooz)) 1 a place agreed upon for meeting. 2 a meeting at an arranged place and time. 3 a place appointed for assembling, esp. of troops or warships. 4 an arranged meeting of two spacecraft in preparation for docking. 5 a place of common resort. ~*v.i.* (*3rd pers. sing. pres.* **rendezvouses** (-vooz), *pres.p.* **rendezvousing** (-vooing), *past, p.p.* **rendezvoused** (-vood)) to meet or assemble at a rendezvous. [F *rendez-vous*, render or betake yourselves]

rendition RENDER.

rendzina (rendzē´nə) *n.* a dark rich soil containing lime, found in grassy regions overlying chalk. [Pol.]

renegade (ren´igād) *n.* 1 a deserter. 2 a turncoat. 3 a rebel, an outlaw. 4 an apostate, esp. from Christianity. ~*a.* 1 having deserted or turned against a cause, faith etc., traitorous. 2 rebellious. ~*v.i.* to turn renegade. †**renegado** (renəgā´dō) *n.* (*pl.* **renegadoes**) a renegade. [Sp. *renegado*, med. L *renegātus*, p.p. of *renegāre* (*negāre*, to deny)]

renege (rināg´, -nēg´), **renegue** *v.i.* 1 to go back (on one's promise, commitments etc.). 2 to break one's word. 3 to fail to follow suit in cards, to revoke. ~*v.t.* to deny, to renounce. **reneger** *n.* [L *renegāre*, as RENEGADE]

Usage note Pronunciation of *renege* with (-j-) instead of (-g-) is best avoided.

renew (rinū´) *v.t.* 1 to make new again or as good as new, to renovate. 2 to restore to the original or a sound condition. 3 to make fresh or vigorous again, to reanimate, to revivify, to regenerate. 4 to replace (something old or worn out) with new. 5 to replenish. 6 to get, make, do, say etc. over again, to recommence, to repeat. 7 to grant or be granted a further period of validity or effectiveness of (a lease, patent, mortgage, licence etc.). 8 to grant or be granted a further loan of (esp. a library book). ~*v.i.* 1 to become young or new again. 2 to begin again. 3 to renew a lease, licence etc. **renewable** *a.* 1 able to be renewed. 2 derived from or being natural resources (such as wind and waves) considered to be unlimited in supply. **renewability** (-bil´-) *n.* **renewal** *n.* 1 the act of renewing. 2 the state of being renewed. 3 revival, regeneration. 4 a fee paid for continuance of anything. **renewed** *a.* **renewer** *n.* **renewing** *n.*

reni- (ren´i, rē´ni) *comb. form* of or relating to the kidneys. [L *rēnēs*]

reniform (rē´nifawm) *a.* kidney-shaped.

renin (rē´nin) *n.* a proteolytic enzyme secreted by the kidneys, which helps to maintain blood pressure.

renitence (rinī´təns, ren´i-), **renitency** *n.* **1** resistance, esp. of a body to pressure. **2** moral resistance, reluctance, disinclination. **renitent** *a.* [obs. F *rénitence*, from *rénitent*, L *renitentem*, nom. *-tens*, pres.p. of *renītī* (*nītī*, to struggle)]

rennet[1] (ren´it) *n.* **1** curdled milk containing rennin, obtained from the stomach of an unweaned calf etc. or an aqueous infusion of the stomach membrane of the calf, used to coagulate milk. **2** a similar preparation from seeds or other vegetable sources. **rennin** (-in) *n.* an enzyme occurring in the digestive juice of young calves or related mammals that causes coagulation of milk protein and is used in making cheese, junket etc. [ME, from *renne*, to RUN]

rennet[2] (ren´it) *n.* any of several varieties of apple, esp. the pippin. [F *reinette*, prob. dim. of *reine*, queen (perh. from F *rainette*, dim. of *raine*, frog, with alln. to the speckled skin)]

rennin RENNET[1].

renounce (rinowns´) *v.t.* **1** to surrender or give up (a claim, right etc.) esp. by formal declaration. **2** to declare against, to reject or cast off formally, to repudiate, to disclaim, to disown. **3** to forsake, to abandon, to give up, to withdraw from. *~v.i.* **1** (*Law*) to decline or resign a right or trust. **2** in cards, to fail to follow suit through having none left of that suit. *~n.* a failure to follow suit in a card game. **renouncement** *n.* **renouncer** *n.* [F *renoncer*, L *renuntiāre* (*nuntiāre*, from *nuntius*, messenger, see NUNCIO)]

renovate (ren´əvāt) *v.t.* **1** to restore to a state of soundness or good condition, to repair. **2** to make new again. **3** to restore to vigour. **renovation** (-ā´shən) *n.* **renovator** *n.* [L *renovātus*, p.p. of *renovāre* (*novus*, new)]

renown (rinown´) *n.* exalted reputation, fame, celebrity. *~v.t.* (*poet.*) to make renowned or famous. **renowned** *a.* famous, celebrated. [ME and A-F *renoun*, OF *renon* (F *renommée*), from *renoumer*, *renomer*, L *renomināre*, renominate]

rent[1] (rent) *n.* **1** a sum of money payable periodically for the use of land, buildings etc. **2** payment for the use of any kind of property. **3** the return from cultivated land after production costs have been subtracted. *~v.t.* **1** to occupy, hold in tenancy or use in return for rent. **2** to let for rent. **3** to impose rent upon. **4** (*esp. N Am.*) to hire. *~v.i.* **1** to be let (at a certain rent). **2** to allow or obtain the use of property in return for rent. **for rent** available for use or tenancy on payment of a rent. **rent-a-** *comb. form* rented or hired, e.g. *rent-a-crowd*, *rent-a-mob*. **rentable** *a.* **rentability** (-bil´-) *n.* **rental** *n.* **1** an amount paid or received as rent. **2** the act of renting. **3** income from rents. **4** property available for rent. **5** a rent roll. **rental library** *n.* (*pl.* **rental libraries**) (*N Am.*) a library that hires out books for a fee. **rent boy** *n.* a young male prostitute. **rent-charge** *n.* a periodical charge on land etc. granted by deed to some person other than the owner. **rent collector** *n.* a person who collects rents. **rent control** *n.* government regulation of the amount that can be charged as rent for housing. **rent-controlled** *a.* **rent-day** *n.* the day on which rent is due. **renter**[1] *n.* **1** a tenant. **2** a person who lets property for rent. **3** a distributor of cinema films. **4** (*sl.*) a male prostitute. **rent-free** *a.* exempted from the payment of rent. *~adv.* without payment of rent. **rentless** *a.* **rent restriction** *n.* restrictions on a landlord's powers to charge or raise rents. **rent roll** *n.* **1** a schedule of a person's property and rents. **2** a person's total income from this source. **rent strike** *n.* the refusal by tenants to pay their rent. [OF *rente*, prob. through pop. L *rendita*, var. of *reddita*, fem. p.p. of *reddere*, to RENDER]

rent[2] (rent) *n.* **1** a tear, slit or breach, an opening made by or as if by rending or tearing asunder. **2** a cleft, a fissure, a chasm. **3** a schism, a separation brought about by violent means. [from obs. v. *rent*, var. of REND]

rent[3] REND.

rente (rāt) *n.* (*pl.* **rentes** (rāt)) **1** annual income or revenue from capital investment. **2** (*pl.*) **a** interest or annuities from French and other European government stocks. **b** the stocks themselves. **rentier** (-tiā) *n.* a person drawing income from rentes or investments. [F]

renter[1] RENT[1].

renter[2] (ren´tə) *v.t.* to sew together the edges of two pieces of cloth without doubling them, so that the seam is scarcely visible; to fine-draw. **renterer** *n.* [F *rentrer*, var. of *rentraire*]

rentier RENTE.

renunciation (rinŭnsiā´shən) *n.* **1** the act of renouncing. **2** a declaration or document expressing this. **3** self-denial, self-sacrifice, self-resignation. **renunciant** *n.*, *a.* **renunciative, renunciatory** (-nŭn´-) *a.* [L *renuntiātio*, from *renuntiāre*, to RENOUNCE]

renvoi (ren´voi) *n.* (*Law*) referral of a legal question or dispute to another jurisdiction. [F, from *renvoyer*, to send]

re- (+ o– words) reobtain *v.t.* to obtain again. **reobtainable** *a.* **reoccupy** *v.t.* (*3rd pers. sing. pres.* **reoccupies**, *pres.p.* **reoccupying**, *past, p.p.* **reoccupied**) to occupy again. **reoccupation** *n.* **reoccur** *v.i.* (*pres.p.* **reoccurring**, *past, p.p.* **reoccurred**) to occur again. **reoccurrence** *n.* **reoffend** *v.i.* to offend again, to commit a second offence. **reoffender** *n.* **reoffer** *v.t.* to offer (an issue of shares etc.) for public sale. **reopen** *v.t.*, *v.i.* to open again. **reopening clause** *n.* in collective bargaining, a clause in a contract which allows an issue to be reconsidered before the expiry date of the contract. **reordain** *v.t.* **1** to ordain again. **2** to appoint or enact again. **reordination** *n.* **reorder** *v.t.* **1** to put in order again, to rearrange. **2** to order or command again. *~n.* a repeat order for goods. **reorganize, reorganise** *v.t.* to order anew. **reorganization** *n.* **reorganizer** *n.* **reorient** *v.t.* **1** to orient again. **2** to change the outlook or attitude of or restore the normal outlook of. *~a.* (*poet.*) rising again. **reorientate** *v.t.* to reorient. **reorientation** *n.*

Rep *abbr.* **1** (*N Am.*) Representative. **2** Republic. **3** (*N Am.*) Republican.

rep[1] (rep) *n.* (*coll.*) **1** repertory. **2** a repertory company or theatre.

rep[2] (rep) *n.* a representative, esp. a sales representative. *~v.i.* (*pres.p.* **repping**, *past, p.p.* **repped**) to act or be employed as a sales representative.

rep[3] (rep), **repp** *n.* a textile fabric of wool, cotton or silk, with a finely-corded surface. **repped** *a.* having a surface like rep. [F *reps*, etym. unknown]

rep[4] *n.* (*N Am.*, *sl.*) reputation.

rep. *abbr.* **1** report. **2** reported. **3** reporter.

re- (+ pa–pl words) repacify *v.t.* (*3rd pers. sing. pres.* **repacifies**, *pres.p.* **repacifying**, *past, p.p.* **repacified**) to pacify again. **repack** *v.t.* to pack again. **repacker** *n.* **repackage** *v.t.* to package again. **repackaging** *n.* **repaginate** *v.t.* to renumber the pages of. **repagination** *n.* **repaid** REPAY. **repaint**[1] *v.t.*, *v.i.* to paint again. **repaint**[2] (rē´-) *n.* **1** an act of repainting. **2** something repainted, esp. a golf ball. **repaper** *v.t.* to paper (walls etc.) again. **repartition** *v.t.* to partition, to allot again. *~n.* **1** distribution, allotment. **2** a fresh distribution or allotment. **repass** *v.t.* **1** to pass again. **2** to go past again. **3** to recross. *~v.i.* **1** to pass in the opposite direction. **2** to pass again (into, through etc.). **repassage** *n.* **repeople** *v.t.* to repopulate. **reperuse** *v.t.* to peruse again. **reperusal** *n.* **rephotograph** *v.t.* to photograph again. **rephrase** *v.t.* to express in a different way, esp. so as to make clearer.

repiece *v.t.* to piece together again. **replan** *v.t.* (*pres.p.* **replanning,** *past, p.p.* **replanned**) to plan again or anew. **replant** *v.t.* **1** to plant (a tree etc.) again or in a new site. **2** to plant (ground) again. **3** to reattach (a severed part) by surgery. **4** to re-establish, to resettle. **replantation** *n.* **replay**[1] *v.t.* to play again (a record, game etc.). **replay**[2] (rē´-) *n.* **1** a second game between two contestants. **2** the playing again of a recording or part of a broadcast match or game.

repair[1] (ripeə´) *v.t.* **1** to restore to a good or sound state after dilapidation or wear. **2** to make good the damaged or dilapidated parts of, to renovate, to mend. **3** to remedy, to set right, to make amends for. ~*n.* **1** restoration to a sound state. **2** a part that has been mended or repaired. **3** good or comparative condition. **in bad repair** in a dilapidated condition, needing repair. **in good repair** in sound working condition, in good order. **in repair** in good repair. **out of repair** needing repair. **repairable** *a.* **repairer** *n.* **repairman** *n.* (*pl.* **repairmen**) a person who repairs machinery, appliances etc. [OF *reparer*, L *reparāre* (RE-, *parāre*, to make ready)]

Usage note See note under REPARATION.

repair[2] (ripeə´) *v.i.* to go, to betake oneself, to resort (to). ~*n.* **1** resort. **2** a place to which one goes often or which is frequented by many people. [OF *repairer*, late L *repatriāre* (RE-, *patria*, one's native land)]

repand (ripand´) *a.* (*Bot.*) having an uneven, wavy or sinuous margin. **repandly** *adv.* [L *repandus* (*pandus*, bent)]

reparation (repərā´shən) *n.* **1** the act of making amends. **2** satisfaction for wrong or damage, amends, compensation. **3** (*usu. pl.*) compensation for war damage payable by a defeated nation. **4** the act of repairing or restoring. **5** the state of being repaired. **reparable** (rep´ərəbəl) *a.* capable of being made good, repaired or remedied. **reparative, reparatory** *a.* [REPAIR[1]]

Usage note The uses of the adjectives *reparable* and *repairable* overlap, but *reparable* is usual of abstract effects, and *repairable* of physical damage or wear.

repartee (repahtē´) *n.* **1** sharp, witty remarks or retorts or conversation consisting of these. **2** a smart or witty rejoinder. **3** skill in repartee, adroitness and wit in reply. [F *repartie*, fem. p.p. of *repartir*, to start again (*partir*, to PART)]

repast (ripahst´) *n.* (*formal*) **1** a meal. **2** food, victuals. [OF, from *repaistre* (F *repaître*) (RE-, L *pascere*, to feed, see PASTURE)]

repat (rē´pat, -pat´) *n.* (*coll.*) **1** a repatriate. **2** repatriation.

repatriate (rēpat´riat, -pā´-) *v.t.* to restore (someone) to their country. ~*v.i.* to return to one's country. ~*n.* a person who has been repatriated. **repatriation** (-ā´shən) *n.* [late L *repatriātus*, p.p. of *repatriāre* (*patria*, one's country)]

repay (ripā´) *v.t.* (*past, p.p.* **repaid** (-pād´)) **1** to pay back, to refund. **2** to return, to deal (a blow etc.) in retaliation or recompense. **3** to pay (a creditor etc.). **4** to make recompense for, to requite. ~*v.i.* to make a repayment or requital. **repayable** *a.* **repayment** *n.* [OF *repayer*]

repeal (ripēl´) *v.t.* to revoke, to rescind, to annul (a law etc.). ~*n.* abrogation, revocation, annulment. **repealable** *a.* **repealist** *n.* [A-F *repeler*, OF *rapeler* (*apeler*, to APPEAL)]

repeat (ripēt´) *v.t.* **1** to do, make or say over again. **2** to reiterate. **3** to recite from memory, to rehearse. **4** to reproduce, to imitate. ~*v.i.* **1** to do something over again. **2** to recur, to happen again. **3** (of a watch etc.) to strike over again the last hour or quarter-hour struck. **4** (of food) to rise to the mouth, to be tasted again. **5** (of a firearm) to fire several shots without reloading. **6** (*N Am.*) to vote more than once in an election. ~*n.* **1** the act of repeating, repetition. **2** something repeated. **3** a radio or television programme broadcast for the second time or more. **4 a** a supply of goods corresponding to the previous one. **b** the order for this. **5 a** a passage to be repeated. **b** a sign indicating this. **to repeat itself** to recur in the same form or order. **to repeat oneself** to say or do the same thing over again. **repeatable** *a.* **repeatability** (-bil´-) *n.* **repeated** *a.* **1** done or said again. **2** done or said over and over again. **repeatedly** *adv.* **repeater** *n.* **1** someone who or something which repeats. **2** a repeating firearm. **3** a watch or clock striking the hours and parts of hours when required. **4** a repeating signal etc. **5** a device for transmitting or amplifying electrical signals. **repeating decimal** *n.* a recurring decimal. **repeating firearm** *n.* a rifle etc. constructed usu. with a magazine, to fire several shots without reloading. [F *répéter*, L *repetere* (*petere*, to seek)]

repechage (rep´əshahzh) *n.* a heat, esp. in rowing or fencing, where contestants beaten in earlier rounds get another chance to qualify for the final. [F *repêchage*, fishing out again]

repel (ripel´) *v.t.* (*pres.p.* **repelling,** *past, p.p.* **repelled**) **1** to drive or force back. **2** to repulse, to ward off, to keep at a distance. **3** to produce aversion or disgust in, to be repulsive or distasteful to. **4** to resist mixing with, absorbing or adherence of. **5** to tend to force away or apart. **repellence, repellency** *n.* **repellent** *a.* **1** repelling or tending to repel. **2** repulsive. ~*n.* that which repels. **repellently** *adv.* **repeller** *n.* [L *repeller* (*peller*, to drive, p.p. *pulsus*)]

Usage note See note on *repellent* under REPULSE.

repent[1] (ripent´) *v.i.* **1** to feel sorrow, regret or pain for something done or left undone, esp. to feel such sorrow for sin as leads to amendment, to be penitent or contrite. **2** to be sorry. ~*v.t.* **1** to feel contrition or remorse for, to regret. **2** to affect (oneself) with penitence. **repentance** *n.* **repentant** *a.* **repentantly, repentingly** *adv.* **repenter** *n.* [F *repentir* (RE-, L *paenitēre*, to make contrite, see PENITENT)]

repent[2] (rē´pənt) *a.* (of a plant) creeping, esp. along the ground, and rooting. [L *rēpens -ntem*, pres.p. of *rēpere*, to creep]

☒ **repentence** common misspelling of REPENTANCE (under REPENT[1]).

repercussion (rēpəkŭsh´ən) *n.* **1** an effect or consequence of an act, action or event, esp. one that is indirect and wide-ranging. **2** a recoil after impact. **3** an echo, a reverberation. **4** (*Mus.*) frequent repetition of the same subject, note, chord etc. **repercuss** *v.t.* **repercussive** *a.* [F *répercussion* or L *repercussiōnem*, nom. *-sio*, from *repercutere* (*percutere*, to PERCUSS)]

repertoire (rep´ətwah) *n.* **1** a stock of plays, musical pieces, songs etc., that a person, company etc. is ready to perform. **2** a stock or range of items, techniques, skills etc. available or regularly used. [F *répertoire*, as REPERTORY]

repertory (rep´ətəri) *n.* (*pl.* **repertories**) **1** a repertoire. **2** the staging of several different plays in a season by one company. **3** this as an occupation. **4** a repertory company. **5** a repertory theatre. **6** a store, a collection, esp. of information, statistics etc. **7** a place in which things are so disposed that they can be readily found, a repository. **repertory company** *n.* a theatrical company that presents a number of different plays, esp. at one theatre. **repertory theatre** *n.* a theatre with a permanent repertory company. [L *repertōrium*, from *reperīre* (p.p. *repertus*), to find (OL *parīre*, L *parere*, to produce)]

repetend (rep´ətend, -tend´) *n.* **1** something repeated, a recurring word or phrase. **2** a refrain. **3** that part of a repeating decimal which keeps recurring. [L *repetendum*, ger. of *repetere*, to REPEAT]

répétiteur (repetitœ´, rāpātētœ´) *n.* a person who coaches opera singers. [F, see REPEAT]

repetition (repitish´ən) *n.* **1** the act of repeating, reiteration. **2** recital from memory. **3** that which is repeated, a piece set to be learnt by heart. **4** a copy, a reproduction, a replica. **5** (*Mus.*) the ability of a musical instrument to repeat a note in rapid succession. **repetitional, repetitionary** *a.* of or relating to repetition. **repetitious** (repitish´-) *a.* characterized by repetition, esp. when tedious or superfluous. **repetitiously, repetitively** *adv.* **repetitiousness, repetitiveness** *n.* **repetitive** (ripet´-) *a.* of, relating to or characterized by repetition. **repetitive strain injury** *n.* (*Med.*) a condition in which the joints and tendons of usu. the hands become inflamed, typically as the result of repeated use of (usu. industrial) apparatus, machinery, computers etc. [OF *repeticion* (F *répétition*), L *repetitiōnem*, nom. *-tio*, as REPEAT]

Usage note The meanings of the adjectives *repetitious* and *repetitive* overlap, but *repetitious* suggests undesirable and tedious repetition, whereas *repetitive* can be neutral.

repine (ripīn´) *v.i.* (*formal*) **1** to fret, to be discontented (at). **2** to complain, to grumble. **repiner** *n.* **repiningly** *adv.*

repique (ripēk´) *n.* in piquet, the scoring of 30 points on cards alone before playing. ~*v.t.* (*3rd pers. sing. pres.* **repiques,** *pres.p.* **repiquing,** *past, p.p.* **repiqued**) to make a repique against. ~*v.i.* to make a repique. [F *repic*]

☒ **repitition** common misspelling of REPETITION.

repla REPLUM.

replace (riplās´) *v.t.* **1** to put back again in place. **2** to take the place of, to succeed. **3** to be a substitute for. **4** to supersede, to displace. **5** to put a substitute in place of, to fill the place of (with or by). **6** to put in a fresh place. **replaceable** *a.* **replacement** *n.* **1** the act of replacing. **2** a person who or thing which replaces another. **replacer** *n.*

replenish (riplen´ish) *v.t.* **1** to fill up again. **2** to renew, to replace with new supplies. **3** to fill completely. **replenisher** *n.* **replenishment** *n.* [OF *repleniss-*, pres.p. stem of *replenir* (RE-, L *plēnus*, full)]

replete (riplēt´) *a.* **1** abundantly supplied or stocked (with). **2** filled to excess, sated, gorged (with). **3** completely filled. **repletion** (-ē´shən), **repleteness** *n.* **1** the state of being replete. **2** eating and drinking to satiety. **3** surfeit. [F *replet*, *-plète*, L *replētus*, p.p. of *replēre* (RE-, *plēre*, to fill)]

replevy (riplev´i) *v.t.* (*3rd pers. sing. pres.* **replevies,** *pres.p.* **replevying,** *past, p.p.* **replevied**) (*Law*) to recover possession of (distrained goods) upon giving security to submit the matter to a court and to surrender the goods if required. ~*n.* (*pl.* **replevies**) a replevin. **repleviable, replevisable** (-vis-) *a.* **replevin** (-in) *n.* **1** an action for replevying. **2** the writ by which goods are replevied. [A-F and OF *replevir* (*plevir*, etym. uncertain, cp. PLEDGE)]

replica (rep´likə) *n.* (*pl.* **replicas**) **1** a duplicate of a picture, sculpture etc. by the artist who executed the original. **2** an exact copy, a facsimile. **3** a copy on a smaller scale. [It., from *replicare*, to REPLY]

replicate[1] (rep´likāt) *v.t.* **1** to repeat (e.g. an experiment) exactly. **2** to reproduce, to make a replica of. **3** to fold back on itself. ~*v.i.* to produce a replica of itself, to undergo biological replication. **replicable** (-kəbəl) *a.* **replicability** (-bil´-) *n.* **replication** (-kā´shən) *n.* **1** the act of replicating, repeating or reproducing. **2** a reproduction, a copy. **3** the production of an exact copy or a duplicate of itself by a virus, cell structure or complex molecule, esp. DNA or RNA. **4** an echo. **5** a reply, a rejoinder. **6** (*Law*) the reply of a plaintiff to the defendant's plea. **7** (*Mus.*) a replicate. **replicative** *a.* [L *replicātus*, p.p. of *replicāre* (*plicāre*, to fold)]

replicate[2] (rep´likət) *a.* folded back on itself. ~*n.* (*Mus.*) a tone one or more octaves above or below a given tone.

replication, replicative REPLICATE[1].

replier REPLY.

replum (rep´ləm) *n.* (*pl.* **repla** (-lə)) (*Bot.*) the central process or placenta remaining after the valves of a dehiscent fruit have fallen away. [L, a bolt]

reply (riplī´) *v.i.* (*3rd pers. sing. pres.* **replies,** *pres.p.* **replying,** *past, p.p.* **replied**) **1** to answer, to respond, to make answer orally, in writing, or by action. **2** (*Law*) to plead in answer to a defendant's plea. ~*v.t.* **1** to return as in answer. **2** to answer (that etc.). ~*n.* **1** the act of replying. **2** that which is said, written or done in answer, a response. **replier** *n.* **reply coupon** *n.* a coupon exchangeable in any country for stamps to be used on a letter or reply. **reply-paid** *a.* (of an envelope etc.) provided by and having the postage paid by the person requesting a reply. [OF *replier*, L *replicāre* (*plicāre*, to fold, cp. REPLICATE[1])]

re- (+ po–pu words) repoint *v.t.* to repair the joints of (brickwork etc.) with new cement or mortar. **repolish** *v.t.* to polish again. **repopulate** *v.t.* **1** to populate again. **2** to increase the population of. **repopulation** *n.* **reposition**[1] *v.t.* to place in a new or different position. ~*v.i.* to alter one's position. **repossess** *v.t.* **1** to possess again, to regain possession of. **2** to take back possession of (property and goods) for failure to make loan repayments. **repossession** *n.* **repot** *v.t.* (*pres.p.* **repotting,** *past, p.p.* **repotted**) to put (a plant) into a fresh pot. **re-present** *v.t.* to present again. **re-presentation** *n.* **re-press** *v.t.* to press again. **reprice** *v.t.* to price again or anew. **reprovision** *v.t.* to provision (a ship etc.) again. **reprint**[1] *v.t.* to print (a book etc.) again. **reprint**[2] (rē´-) *n.* a new edition or impression of a printed work without much alteration of the contents. **reprize** *v.t.* to prize anew. **reprocess** *v.t.* **1** to process again. **2** to treat (a substance or material) in order to make it reusable in a new form. **reprocessing** *n., a.* **reprogram, reprogramme** *v.t.* (*pres.p.* **reprogramming,** *past, p.p.* **reprogrammed**) to program again or in a different way. **reprogrammable** *a.* **reproof**[1] *v.t.* **1** to make waterproof again. **2** to make a fresh proof of. **republish** *v.t., v.i.* **1** to publish again. **2** to print a new edition (of). **republication** *n.* **republisher** *n.* **repurchase** *v.t., v.i.* to purchase back or again. ~*n.* **1** the act of buying again. **2** something which is bought again. **repurify** *v.t.* (*3rd pers. sing. pres.* **repurifies,** *pres. p.* **repurifying,** *past, p.p.* **repurified**) to purify again. **repurification** *n.*

report (ripawt´) *v.t.* **1** to give an account of, to describe or to narrate, esp. as an eyewitness. **2** to bring back as an answer. **3** to state as a fact or as news. **4** to prepare a record of, esp. for official use or for publication. **5** to take down in full or to summarize (a speech, sermon etc.). **6** to announce, to make a formal or official statement about, to certify. **7** to give information against. **8** (of a parliamentary committee etc.) to return (a Bill) with conclusions and amendments. ~*v.i.* **1** to make or tender a report. **2** to act as a reporter. **3** to present oneself (at a certain place etc.). **4** to be responsible (to an employer or supervisor). **5** to give an account of one's condition or opinion as specified (*to report sick*). ~*n.* **1** that which is reported, esp. the formal statement of the result of an investigation, trial etc. **2** a detailed account of a speech, meeting etc., esp. for publication in a newspaper. **3** common talk, popular rumour. **4** an account or statement of the merits of a person or thing. **5** an end-of-term statement of a pupil's work and behaviour at school. **6** a loud noise, esp. of an explosive kind. **7** fame, repute, accepted character. **to report back 1** to submit a report to the person, company etc.

for whom one is acting. 2 to present oneself as having returned. **reportable** *a.* **reportage** (ripawt´ij, repawtahj´) *n.* 1 the art of reporting news. 2 writing in a factual or journalistic style. **reported** *a.* **reportedly** *adv.* according to common talk or rumour. **reported speech** *n.* indirect speech. **reporter** *n.* 1 a person who gathers news etc. for a newspaper or broadcasting company. 2 a person who reports. 3 a person authorized to draw up official statements of law proceedings and decisions of legislative debates. **reportorial** (repawtaw´riəl) *a.* (*esp. N Am.*) of or relating to newspaper reporters. **reportorially** *adv.* **report stage** *n.* the stage of progress with a Bill in the House of Commons or House of Lords when a committee has reported. [OF *reporter*, L *reportāre* (*portāre*, to bring)]

reposal[1] REPOSE[1].

reposal[2] REPOSE[2].

repose[1] (ripōz´) *n.* 1 rest, cessation of activity, excitement, toil etc. 2 sleep. 3 quiet, tranquillity, calmness. 4 composure, ease of manner etc. 5 in art, restful effect. 6 in art, moderation and harmony of colour and treatment. ~*v.i.* 1 to lie at rest. 2 to be laid or be in a recumbent position, esp. in sleep or death. 3 to rest or be supported (on). 4 to rest. ~*v.t.* 1 to lay (oneself etc.) to rest, to rest. 2 to refresh with rest. **reposal**[1], **reposedness** *n.* **reposeful** *a.* **reposefully** *adv.* **reposefulness** *n.* [F *reposer*, late L *repausāre* (*pausāre*, to PAUSE, conf. with L *pōnere*, see REPOSE[2])]

repose[2] (ripōz´) *v.t.* to place, to put (confidence etc. in). **reposal**[2] *n.* [L *repos-*, p.p. stem of *repōnere* (*pōnere*, to place, p.p. *positum*)]

reposit (ripoz´it) *v.t.* 1 to store, to deposit, as in a place of safety. 2 to replace, to put back in place. **reposition**[2] *n.* **repositor** *n.* (*Med.*) an instrument for surgically replacing a displaced organ. [L *repositus*, p.p. of *repōnere*, to put back, lay aside, see REPOSE[2]]

reposition[1] RE- (+ PO–PU WORDS).

reposition[2] REPOSIT.

repository *n.* (*pl.* **repositories**) 1 a place or receptacle in which things are deposited for safety or preservation. 2 a depository, a museum, a store, a warehouse, a vault, a sepulchre. 3 a person, book etc. regarded as a store of information or knowledge. 4 a person to whom a secret etc. is confided. [L *repositōrium*, as REPOSIT]

repoussé (ripoo´sā) *a.* (of ornamental metalwork) formed in relief by hammering from behind. ~*n.* metalwork ornamented in this way. **repoussage** (-sahzh´) *n.* [F, p.p. of *repousser* (RE-, *pousser*, to PUSH)]

repp, repped REP[3].

repr. *abbr.* 1 represent, represented. 2 reprint, reprinted.

reprehend (reprihend´) *v.t.* 1 to find fault with. 2 to censure, to blame. **reprehender** *n.* **reprehensible** (-hen´sibəl) *a.* open to censure or blame. **reprehensibility** (-bil´-), **reprehensibleness** *n.* **reprehensibly** *adv.* **reprehension** *n.* **reprehensive, †reprehensory** *a.* [L *reprehendere* (RE-, *prehendere*, to seize, cp. COMPREHEND), p.p. *reprehensus*]

represent (reprizent´) *v.t.* 1 to stand for, to correspond to. 2 to be an example or specimen of. 3 to serve as symbol for. 4 (of a picture etc.) to serve as a likeness of, to depict. 5 to present to or bring before the mind by describing, portraying, imitating etc. 6 to take the place of as deputy, substitute etc. 7 to act as agent or spokesman for (e.g. in a representative chamber). 8 to describe (as), to make out (to be). 9 to set forth. 10 to state (that). 11 to enact (a play etc.) on the stage, to personate, to play the part of. **representable** *a.* **representability** (-bil´-) *n.* **representation** (-tā´shən) *n.* 1 the act of representing. 2 something that represents, a likeness, a picture, an image. 3 a dramatic performance. 4 (*often pl.*) a statement of facts, arguments etc. 5 the system of representing bodies of people in a legislative assembly. 6 representatives collectively. **representational** *a.* 1 of or relating to representation. 2 (of art) depicting objects etc. in a realistic manner. **representationalism** *n.* 1 representational art. 2 representationism. **representationalist** *n.* **representationism** *n.* the doctrine that the immediate object in perception is only an idea, image or other representation of the external thing. **representationist** *n.* **representative** *a.* 1 serving to represent or symbolize, able or fitted to represent, typical. 2 presenting the general characteristics of. 3 similar or corresponding to others of its kind. 4 acting as agent, delegate, deputy etc. 5 consisting of delegates etc. 6 based on representation by delegates. 7 presenting images or ideas to the mind. 8 (of art) representational. ~*n.* 1 someone who or something which represents. 2 an example, a specimen, a typical instance or embodiment. 3 an agent, deputy or substitute, esp. a person chosen by a body of electors. 4 a travelling salesperson, a sales representative. **representatively** *adv.* **representativeness** *n.* **representer** *n.* [OF *representer*, L *repraesentāre*]

re-present RE- (+ PO–PU WORDS).

repress (ripres´) *v.t.* 1 to restrain, to keep under restraint. 2 to put down, to suppress, to quell. 3 to prevent from breaking out etc. 4 to banish (unpleasant thoughts etc.) to the unconscious. **repressed** *a.* (of a person) repressing or tending to repress unacceptable thoughts, feelings etc. **represser** *n.* **repressible** *a.* **repression** (-shən) *n.* 1 the act of repressing. 2 (*Psych.*) unconscious exclusion from the conscious mind of thoughts and memories which are in conflict with conventional standards of behaviour. **repressive** *a.* **repressively** *adv.* **repressor** *n.* a substance, esp. a protein, produced by a regulator gene that indirectly represses the expression of a gene responsible for protein synthesis. [L *repressus*, p.p. of *reprimere* (RE-, *premere*, to PRESS[1])]

re-press RE- (+ PO–PU WORDS).

reprieve (riprēv´) *v.t.* 1 to suspend the execution of (someone) for a time. 2 to grant a respite to. 3 to rescue, to save (from). ~*n.* 1 the temporary suspension of a sentence on a prisoner. 2 the warrant authorizing this. 3 a respite. **reprieval** *n.* [from obs. *repry*, to remand, A-F and OF *repris*, p.p. of *reprendre* (RE-, L *prehendere*, to seize, see COMPREHEND)]

reprimand[1] (rep´rimahnd) *n.* a severe reproof, a rebuke, esp. a public or official one. [F *réprimande, reprimende*, from *reprimer*, to REPRESS]

reprimand[2] (-mahnd´) *v.t.* to reprove severely, to rebuke, esp. publicly or officially.

reprisal (riprī´zəl) *n.* 1 an act of retaliation. 2 (*Hist.*) the act of seizing from an enemy by way of indemnification or retaliation. [OF *reprisaille* (cp. F *représaille*, It. *ripresaglia*), from REPRISE]

reprise (riprēz´) *n.* (*Mus.*) a repeated phrase, theme etc., a refrain. ~*v.t.* 1 to repeat (an earlier phrase, theme etc.). 2 to repeat or restage the performance of. [F, fem. of *repris*, p.p. of *reprendre*, see REPRIEVE]

repro (rē´prō) *n.* (*pl.* **repros**) 1 a reproduction, a copy. 2 a reproduction proof.

reproach (riprōch´) *v.t.* 1 to censure, to upbraid. 2 to find fault with (something done). 3 †to rebuke (an offence). 4 †to disgrace. ~*n.* 1 censure mixed with disappointment. 2 a rebuke, a censure. 3 shame, infamy, disgrace. 4 an object or cause of scorn or derision. 5 (*pl.*) in the Roman Catholic Church, a set of antiphons chanted on Good Friday, representing Christ's reproaches to the Jewish people. **above reproach** perfect, blameless. **beyond reproach** above reproach. **reproachable** *a.* **reproachably** *adv.* **reproacher** *n.* **reproachful** *a.* 1 containing or expressing reproach, upbraiding, opprobrious, abusive. 2 †shameful, infamous, base. **reproachfully** *adv.* **reproachfulness** *n.* **reproachingly** *adv.* **reproachless** *a.* **reproachlessness**

n. [F *reprocher*, etym. uncertain (perh. from a pop. L *repropriāre*, from L *prope*, near, cp. as APPROACH, or from L as APPROVE)]

reprobate (rep´rəbāt) *n.* **1** a wicked, depraved wretch. **2** a person who is condemned by God. **3** (*facet.*) a rogue, a rascal. ~*a.* **1** depraved. **2** abandoned to sin, condemned by God. ~*v.t.* **1** to express disapproval and detestation of, to condemn severely. **2** (of God) to abandon to wickedness and eternal punishment. **reprobater** *n.* **reprobation** (-ā´shən) *n.* **reprobative, reprobatory** *a.* [L *reprobātus*, p.p. of *reprobāre*, see REPROVE (under REPROOF[2])]

reproduce (rēprədūs´) *v.t.* **1** to copy. **2** to produce again. **3** to produce (new life) through sexual or asexual processes. ~*v.i.* **1** to produce offspring. **2** to come out (well, badly etc.) as a copy. **reproducer** *n.* **reproducible** *a.* **reproducibility** (-bil´-) *n.* **reproducibly** *adv.* **reproduction** (-dŭk´-) *n.* **1** the act of reproducing. **2** any of the sexual or asexual processes by which animals or plants produce offspring. **3** a copy, an imitation. **4** the quality of the sound of a recording. ~*a.* made in imitation of a particular style or period. **reproduction proof** *n.* (*Print.*) a high-quality proof reproduced photographically to make a printing plate. **reproductive** *a.* **reproductively** *adv.* **reproductiveness, reproductivity** (-tiv´-) *n.*

reprography (riprog´rəfi) *n.* the art or process of reproducing printed matter e.g. by photocopying. **reprographic** (rēprəgraf´-) *a.* **reprographically** *adv.* **reprographics** *n.* reprography.

reproof[1] RE- (+ PO–PU WORDS).

reproof[2] (riproof´) *n.* **1** censure, blame, reprehension. **2** an expression of blame. **reprove** (-proov´) *v.t.* to rebuke, to censure, esp. to one's face, to chide. **reprovable** *a.* **reproval** *n.* **reprover** *n.* **reprovingly** *adv.* [OF *reprove*, from *reprover*, L *reprobāre*, to disapprove (RE-, *probāre*, to PROVE)]

reptant (rep´tənt) *a.* (*Biol.*) creeping. **reptation** (-tā´shən) *n.* **reptatory** *a.* [L *reptans -ntem*, pres.p. of *reptāre*, freq. of *rēpere*, to creep]

reptile (rep´tīl) *n.* **1** a crawling animal; a member of the Reptilia, a class of animals comprising the snakes, lizards, turtles, crocodiles etc. **2** a grovelling, mean, despicable person. ~*a.* **1** creeping, crawling, moving on the belly or on small, short legs. **2** grovelling, servile, mean, despicable. **reptilian** (-til´-) *a., n.* **reptiliferous** (-tilif´-) *a.* containing fossil reptiles. **reptilious** (-til´-), **reptiloid** (-loid) *a.* [F, from late L *reptilis*, from *rēpere*, to creep, p.p. *reptus*]

republic (ripŭb´lik) *n.* **1** a state or a form of political constitution in which the supreme power is vested in the people or their elected representatives; a commonwealth. **2** a society in which all the members are equal. **republican** *a.* **1** of, relating to or consisting of a republic. **2** characteristic of the principles of a republic. **3** believing in or advocating the principles of a republic. ~*n.* (*also* **Republican**) **1** a person who favours or advocates a republican form of government. **2** a member of the Republican Party in the US. **3** a supporter of republicanism in N Ireland. **republicanism** *n.* **republicanize, republicanise** *v.t.* **Republican Party** *n.* the more conservative of the two political parties in the US, the other being the *Democratic Party*. **Republic Day** *n.* a day commemorating the foundation of a republic, e.g. 26 January in India. **republic of letters** *n.* the world of literature. [F *république*, L *rēspublica* (*rēs*, thing, concern, PUBLIC)]

repudiate (ripū´diāt) *v.t.* **1** to refuse to acknowledge, to disown, to disclaim (a debt etc.). **2** to disavow, to reject, to refuse to admit, accept, recognize etc. **3** (*Hist.*) to divorce (one's wife). **repudiable** *a.* **repudiation** (-ā´shən) *n.* **repudiator** *n.* [L *repudiātus*, p.p. of *repudiāre*, from *repudium*, divorce (RE-, *pud-*, stem of *pudēre*, to feel shame)]

†**repugn** (ripūn´) *v.i.* to oppose, to resist, to strive (against). ~*v.t.* to combat, to oppose, to strive against. [F *répugner*, L *repugnāre* (RE-, *pugnāre*, to fight)]

repugnance (ripŭg´nəns), **repugnancy** *n.* **1** antipathy, dislike, distaste, aversion. **2** inconsistency, incompatibility or opposition, of mind, disposition, statements, ideas etc. **repugnant** *a.* **repugnantly** *adv.* [ME, from F *répugnance* or L *repugnantia*, from *repugnare* (see REPUGN)]

repulse (ripŭls´) *v.t.* **1** to beat or drive back, by force of arms. **2** to reject, esp. in a rude manner, to rebuff, to snub. **3** to disgust, to be repulsive to. **4** to defeat in argument. ~*n.* **1** the act of repulsing. **2** the state of being repulsed. **3** a rebuff, a refusal, a failure, a disappointment. **repulser** *n.* **repulsion** (-shən) *n.* **1** disgust, repugnance, aversion. **2** (*Physics*) the tendency of certain bodies to repel each other, as distinct from *attraction*. **3** the act of repulsing. **4** the state of being repulsed. **repulsive** *a.* **1** repellent, loathsome, disgusting. **2** (*Physics*) acting by repulsion. **3** †acting so as to repel, unsympathetic, forbidding. **repulsively** *adv.* **repulsiveness** *n.* [L *repulsus*, p.p. of *repellere* (RE-, *pellere*, to drive)]

Usage note The meanings of the adjectives *repulsive* and *repellent* overlap, but *repulsive* expresses much stronger aversion than *repellent*.

reputable (rep´ūtəbəl) *a.* being of good repute, respectable, creditable. **reputably** *adv.*

reputation (repūtā´shən) *n.* **1** the estimation in which one is generally held, repute. **2** good estimation, credit, esteem, respectability. **3** the repute, honour or credit derived from favourable public opinion or esteem. **reputative** (rep´-) *a.* reputed, putative. [L *reputātio*, from *reputāre*, to REPUTE]

repute (ripūt´) *n.* character attributed by public report; reputation, fame. ~*v.t.* **1** (*chiefly in p.p.*) to consider, to report, to regard (as). **2** to think, to account, to reckon. **reputed** *a.* generally regarded (usu. with implication of doubt) (*She is reputed to be the richest woman in the country*). **reputedly** *adv.* [F *réputer*, L *reputāre* (RE-, *putāre*, to think)]

re- (+ q–r words) requicken *v.t.* to quicken again, to reanimate. **rerail** *v.t.* to put (rolling stock) on the rails again. **reran** RERUN[1] (under RE- (+ Q–R WORDS)). **reread[1]** (rērēd´) *v.t.* (*past, p.p.* **reread** (rēred´)) to read again. **reread[2]** (rē´rēd) *n.* the act of reading again. **re-readable** *a.* **re-record** *v.t.* to record again. **re-recording** *n.* **re-release** *v.t.* to release (a record etc.) again. ~*n.* a record etc. which has been re-released. **re-roof** *v.t.* to provide with a new roof. **re-route** *v.t.* (*pres.p.* **re-routeing, re-routing,** *past, p.p.* **re-routed**) to transport or redirect by a different route. **rerun[1]** *v.t.* (*pres.p.* **rerunning,** *past* **reran,** *p.p.* **rerun**) **1** to run (a race) again. **2** to show (a film or television programme) again. **rerun[2]** (rē´rŭn) *n.* **1** a repeated film, television programme etc. **2** a race run a second time.

request (rikwest´) *n.* **1** an expression of desire or the act of asking for something to be granted or done; a petition. **2** something which is asked for. **3** the state of being demanded or sought after. **4 a** a request for a particular song to be played by a disc jockey or performer. **b** the song requested. **5** †an inquiry. ~*v.t.* **1** to ask for. **2** to address a request to. **3** to ask (that). **by request** on request. **on request** if or when asked for. **requester** *n.* **request programme** *n.* a radio programme consisting of requests from listeners. **request stop** *n.* a stop on a route where a bus will stop only if signalled to do so. [OF *requeste* (RE-, QUEST)]

requiem (rek´wiəm) *n.* **1** (**Requiem**) in the Roman Catholic Church, a mass for the repose of the soul of a dead person. **2** the musical setting of this, a dirge. **3** a memorial (for). ~*a.* (**Requiem**) of or relating to a Requiem. [L, rest (the first word of the introit *Requiem aeternam dona eis, Domine*)]

requiem shark *n.* any shark of the family Carcharinidae, including tiger sharks and whaler sharks. [from obs. F *requiem*, var. of *requin*, a shark, influ. by REQUIEM]

requiescat (rekwies´kat) *n.* a wish or prayer for the repose of the dead. [L *requiescat in pace*, let him (or her) rest in peace]

require (rikwīə´) *v.t.* **1** to have need of, to depend upon for completion etc. **2** to ask or claim as a right or by authority, to order. **3** to command, to instruct. **4** to demand (something of a person), to insist (on having, that etc.). **5** to want to have. **requirable** *a.* **requirement** *n.* **requirer** *n.* [OF *requerre* (F *requérir*), assim. to L *requīrere* (RE-, *quaerere*, to seek)]

requisite (rek´wizit) *a.* required by the nature of things, necessary for completion etc., indispensable. ~*n.* something which is required, a necessary part or quality. **requisitely** *adv.* **requisiteness** *n.* [L *requīsītus*, p.p. of *requīrere*, as REQUIRE]

requisition (rekwizish´ən) *n.* **1** an authoritative order for the supply of provisions etc. **2** a formal and usu. written demand or request for the performance of a duty. **3** the state of being called upon or put in use. **4** the act of requiring or demanding; application. ~*v.t.* to demand by requisitions. **in requisition** under requisition. **under requisition** in use, being applied. **requisitioner** *n.* **requisitionist** *n.* [F *réquisition*, L *requīsītiōnem*, nom. *-tio*, as REQUISITE]

requite (rikwīt´) *v.t.* **1** to make return for. **2** to reward or avenge. **3** to repay, to make return to, to recompense. **4** to give or deal in return. **requital** *n.* **requiter** *n.* [RE-, *quite*, var. of QUIT]

reredos (riə´dos) *n.* (*pl.* **reredoses**) **1** the ornamental screen at the back of an altar. **2** the back of an open hearth, a fireback. [ME *rere*, REAR[1], F *dos*, L *dorsum*, the back]

res (rās) *n.* (*pl.* **res**) a thing, property. [L]

res. *abbr.* **1** research. **2** reserve. **3** residence. **4** resides. **5** resigned. **6** resolution.

re- (+ sa–so words) resale *n.* **1** a second, i.e. retail, sale. **2** a sale at second hand. **resaleable, resalable** *a.* **resale price maintenance** *n.* the practice by which a manufacturer sets a minimum resaleable price for goods. **resat** RESIT[1] (under RE- (+ SA–SO WORDS)). **reschedule** *v.t.* to change the schedule of. **reseal** *v.t.* to seal again. **resealable** *a.* **re-search** *v.t., v.i.* to search again. **reseat** *v.t.* **1** to seat again. **2** to furnish (a church etc.) with new seats. **3** to provide (a chair, pair of trousers etc.) with a new seat. **4** to realign (a nail etc.) into its correct position. **reseed** *v.t.* to sow (land) with seed again. **reseek** *v.t.* (*past, p.p.* **resought**) to seek again. **reselect** *v.t.* to select again or in a different way. **reselection** *n.* **resell** *v.t.* (*past, p.p.* **resold**) to sell again. **reseller** *n.* **resend** *v.t.* (*past, p.p.* **resent**) to send back or again. **re-serve** *v.t., v.i.* to serve again. **reset**[1] *v.t.* (*pres.p.* **resetting,** *past, p.p.* **reset**) to set (type, a jewel etc.) again. **reset**[2] (rē´-) *n.* (*Print.*) matter set up again. **resettable** *a.* **resettability** *n.* **resettle** *v.t., v.i.* to settle again. **resettlement** *n.* **reshape** *v.t.* to shape again. **resharpen** *v.t., v.i.* to sharpen again. **reship** *v.t., v.i.* (*pres.p.* **reshipping,** *past, p.p.* **reshipped**) to ship again. **reshoe** *v.t.* (*pres.p.* **reshoeing,** *past, p.p.* **reshod**) to shoe again. **reshuffle**[1] *v.t.* **1** to shuffle again. **2** to rearrange or reorganize (esp. the Cabinet or a government department). **reshuffle**[2] (rē´-) *n.* the act of reshuffling. **re-sign** *v.t., v.i.* to sign again. **resignal** *v.t.* (*pres.p.* **resignalling,** (*N Am.*) **resignaling,** *past, p.p.* **resignalled,** (*N Am.*) **resignaled**) to supply with signals again. **resit**[1] *v.t., v.i.* (*pres.p.* **resitting,** *past, p.p.* **resat**) to sit (an examination) again after failing. **resit**[2] (rē´-) *n.* an examination which one must sit again, having failed initially. **resite** *v.t.* to move to another site. **resize** *v.t.* to change the size of. **reskill** *v.t.* to provide with new skills. **resold** RESELL (under RE- (+ SA–SO WORDS)). **resole** *v.t.* to provide (a shoe etc.) with a new sole. **re-soluble** *a.* able to be dissolved again. **re-sort** *v.t.* to sort again.

rescind (risind´) *v.t.* to annul, to cancel, to withdraw. **rescindable** *a.* **rescission** (-sizh´ən) *n.* **rescissory** (-sis´-) *a.* [F *rescinder*, L *rescindere* (RE-, *scindere*, to cut, p.p. *scissus*)]

rescript (rē´skript) *n.* **1** (*Hist.*) the answer or decision of a Roman emperor to a question or appeal, esp. on a point of jurisprudence. **2** a Pope's written reply to a question of canon law, morality etc. **3** an edict, a decree, an order, an official announcement. **4** something rewritten, the act of rewriting. [L *rescriptum*, neut. p.p. of RESCIND]

rescue (res´kū) *v.t.* (*3rd pers. sing. pres.* **rescues,** *pres.p.* **rescuing,** *past, p.p.* **rescued**) **1** to save from confinement, danger, evil or injury. **2** (*Law*) to liberate by unlawful means from custody. **3** (*Law*) to recover (property etc.). ~*n.* **1** the act of saving from confinement, danger, evil or injury. **2** forcible seizure (of a person, property etc.) from the custody of the law. **rescuable** *a.* **rescue bid** *n.* **1** an attempt to rescue someone, esp. in dramatic circumstances. **2** in bridge, a bid made in order to rescue one's partner from a difficult situation. **rescuer** *n.* **1** a person who rescues. **2** (*coll.*) an anti-abortion activist. [OF *rescoure*, ult. L *exutere* (EX-, *cutere*, *quatere*, to shake)]

research (risœch´) *n.* **1** systematic study of phenomena etc., a course of critical investigation. **2** diligent and careful inquiry or investigation. ~*a.* of or relating to research (*a research grant*). ~*v.t.* to make careful and systematic investigation into. ~*v.i.* to make researches. **researchable** *a.* **research and development** *n.* in industry, work concerned with the application of scientific research in the development of new products etc. **researcher** *n.* [F *recerche* (now *recherche*)]

Usage note Pronunciation as (rē´-), with stress on the first syllable, is best avoided.

re-search RE- (+ SA–SO WORDS).

resect (risekt´) *v.t.* **1** (*Med.*) to excise a section of (an organ or part). **2** to cut or pare down (bone etc.). **resection** (-sek´shən) *n.* **resectional** *a.* **resectionist** *n.* [L *resectus*, p.p. of *resecāre* (RE-, *secāre*, to cut)]

reseda (res´idə) *n.* **1** any plant of the genus *Reseda*, containing the mignonette and dyer's weed. **2** a pale or greyish green. ~*a.* pale green. [L, prob. imper. of *resedāre*, to assuage (first word of a charm for allaying tumours)]

resemble (rizem´bəl) *v.t.* to be like, to be similar to; to have features, nature etc., like those of. **resemblance** *n.* similarity, likeness. **resemblant** *a.* **resembler** *n.* [OF *resembler* (F *ressembler*) (RE-, *sembler*, L *similāre*, *simulāre*, from *similis*, SIMILAR)]

resent[1] (rizent´) *v.t.* to regard as an injury or insult, to feel or show displeasure or indignation at, to cherish bitter feelings about. **resenter** *n.* **resentful** *a.* **resentfully** *adv.* **resentfulness** *n.* **resentingly** *adv.* **resentment** *n.* [F *ressentir* (RE-, *sentir*, L *sentire*, to feel)]

resent[2] RESEND (under RE- (+ SA–SO WORDS)).

reserpine (risœ´pin) *n.* an alkaloid extracted from plants of the *Rauwolfia* genus, used to treat high blood pressure and as a sedative. [G *Reserpin*, prob. from the L name of the plant, *Rauwolfia serpentina*]

reservable RESERVE.

reservation (rezəvā´shən) *n.* **1** the act of reserving. **2** something which is reserved. **3** the booking of accommodation in a hotel, train, ship etc. **4** an expressed or tacit limitation, exception, or qualification. **5** a strip of land separating a dual carriageway. **6** a tract of land reserved for indigenous peoples or for public use. 7 (*Law*) the right or interest retained in a property being conveyed. 8 in the Roman Catholic Church, the reserving of the right of nomination to benefices, of the power of absolution or of a portion of the consecrated elements of the Eucharist.

reserve (rizœv´) *v.t.* 1 to keep back for future use, enjoyment, treatment etc.; to postpone, to keep in store. 2 to retain for oneself or another, esp. as an exception from something granted. 3 to book, keep or set apart. 4 (*in p.p.*) to set apart for a certain fate, to destine. ~*n.* 1 something which is reserved. 2 a sum of money or a fund reserved, esp. by bankers, to meet any demand. 3 a reservation of land for a special use. 4 troops kept for any emergency, such as to act as reinforcements or cover a retreat. 5 a part of the military or naval forces not embodied in the regular army and navy, but liable to be called up in case of emergency. 6 a member of these forces, a reservist. 7 the state of being reserved or kept back for a special purpose. 8 in sport, a substitute. 9 (*pl.*) in sport, the second-choice team. 10 mental reservation, exception or qualification. 11 a limitation attached to a price etc. 12 reticence, self-restraint, caution in speaking or action. 13 lack of exaggeration in artistic or literary expression. 14 a company's profit added to capital. 15 the deliberate suppression of the truth. 16 in ceramics or textiles, an area in the original background colour. **in reserve** reserved and ready for use in an emergency. **to reserve judgement** to delay making a judgement about someone or something until more information is available. **with all (proper) reserve** without reserving. **without reserve** 1 fully, without reservation. 2 (offered for sale) to the highest bidder without the condition of a reserve price. **reservable** *a.* **reserve currency** *n.* a foreign currency acceptable as a medium of international banking transactions and held in reserve by many countries. **reserved** *a.* 1 reticent, backward in communicating one's thoughts or feelings, undemonstrative, distant. 2 retained for a particular use, person etc. **reserved list** *n.* a list of naval officers not on active service but liable to be called up in an emergency. **reservedly** (-vid-) *adv.* **reservedness** (-vid-) *n.* **reserved occupation** *n.* vital employment which exempts a person from military service in the event of war. **reserve grade** *n.* (*Austral.*) the second-choice team in a club. **reserve price** *n.* in an auction, a price below which no offer will be accepted. **reserver** *n.* **reservist** *n.* a member of the military or naval reserve. [OF *reserver*, L *reservāre* (*servāre*, to keep)]

re-serve RE- (+ SA–SO WORDS).

reservoir (rez´əvwah) *n.* 1 a receptacle of earthwork or masonry for the storage of water in large quantity. 2 a lake used as a water supply. 3 a receptacle in which a quantity of anything, esp. fluid, may be kept in store. 4 a part of an implement, machine, animal or vegetable organ etc., acting as a receptacle for fluid. 5 a reserve supply or store of anything. ~*v.t.* to collect or store in a reservoir. [F *réservoir*, late L *reservātorium*, as RESERVE]

res gestae (rās jes´tē) *n.pl.* 1 achievements. 2 exploits. 3 (*Law*) relevant facts or circumstances admissible in evidence.

reside (rizīd´) *v.i.* 1 to dwell permanently or for a considerable length of time, to have one's home (at). 2 to be in official residence. 3 (of qualities, rights etc.) to inhere, to be vested (in). 4 to be precipitated, to sink. **residence** (rez´i-) *n.* 1 the act or state of residing in a place. 2 the act of living or remaining where one's duties lie. 3 the place where one dwells, one's abode. 4 a house of some size or pretensions. **in residence** 1 actually resident. 2 (of an artist, writer etc.) acting in a regular capacity for a limited period at a gallery, university etc. **to take up residence** to make one's home or begin to live (in a particular place). **residency** *n.* (*pl.* **residencies**) 1 a residence. 2 (*N Am.*) a period of specialized training undertaken by a doctor following internship. 3 (*Hist.*) the official residence of a resident or governor of a British protectorate in India. 4 a musician's or band's regular engagement at a venue. 5 a group of intelligence agents in a foreign country. **resident** (rez´i-) *n.* 1 a person who dwells permanently in a place, as distinct from a visitor. 2 a non-migratory bird or animal. 3 a hotel guest. 4 (*N Am.*) a boarder at a boarding school. 5 a representative of the British government in a British protectorate. 6 (*N Am.*) a junior doctor who lives and works in a hospital to gain specialized experience. 7 an intelligence agent in a foreign country. ~*a.* 1 residing. 2 having a residence, esp. official quarters in connection with one's duties. 3 working regularly in a particular place. 4 non-migratory. 5 inherent. **residential** (reziden´shəl) *a.* 1 suitable for residence or for residences. 2 of or relating to residence. **residentially** *adv.* **residentiary** (reziden´-) *a.* maintaining or bound to an official residence. ~*n.* (*pl.* **residentiaries**) an ecclesiastic bound to an official residence. **residentship** *n.* [F *résider*, L *residēre* (RE-, *sedēre*, to sit)]

residue (rez´idū) *n.* 1 what is left or remains over, the rest, the remainder. 2 what remains of an estate after payment of all charges, debts and particular bequests. 3 a residuum. **residual** (-zid´-) *a.* 1 of the nature of a residue or residuum, remaining after a part has been taken away. 2 (*Math.*) left by a process of subtraction. 3 remaining unexplained or uneliminated. ~*n.* 1 a residual quantity, a remainder. 2 the difference between the computed and the observed value of a quantity at any given moment, a residual error. 3 a payment to an artist for reuse of a film, recording etc. **residually** *adv.* **residuary** (-zid´-) *a.* 1 of or relating to the residue of an estate. 2 of, relating to or forming a residue, residual, remaining. **residuum** (-zid´ūəm) *n.* (*pl.* **residua** (-ə)) 1 (*Chem.*) a substance which is left after any process of separation or purification, esp. after combustion, evaporation etc. 2 the remainder left by subtraction or division, a residual error. 3 the lowest classes, the dregs of society. [A-F (F *résidu*), L *residuum*, nom. *-duus*, remaining, as RESIDE]

resign (rizīn´) *v.i.* 1 to give up office, to retire (from). 2 in chess, to admit defeat. ~*v.t.* 1 to give up, to surrender, to relinquish. 2 to hand over (to). 3 to give up, to abandon. 4 to yield, to submit, to reconcile (oneself, one's mind etc. to). **resignation** (rezignā´shən) *n.* 1 the act of resigning, esp. an office. 2 a document announcing this. 3 the state of being resigned, patience, acquiescence, submission. **resigned** *a.* submissive, patiently acquiescent or enduring. **resignedly** (-nid-) *adv.* **resignedness** (-nid-) *n.* [OF *resigner*, L *resignare*, to unseal (RE-, *signāre*, to seal, see SIGN)]

re-sign RE- (+ SA–SO WORDS).

resignation RESIGN.

resile (rizīl´) *v.i.* 1 to spring back, to rebound, to recoil, to resume the original shape after compression, stretching etc., to show elasticity. 2 to be able to recover quickly from illness or misfortune. 3 to withdraw (from). [obs. F *resiler*, L *resilīre* (RE-, *salīre*, to leap)]

resilience (rizil´yəns), **resiliency** *n.* 1 elasticity. 2 (of a person) an ability to recover quickly from illness or misfortune. **resilient** *a.* **resiliently** *adv.* [as RESILE]

resin (rez´in) *n.* 1 an amorphous inflammable vegetable substance secreted by plants and usu. obtained by exudation, esp. from the fir and pine. 2 a similar substance obtained by the chemical synthesis of various organic materials, used esp. in making plastics. ~*v.t.* (*pres.p.* **resining,** *past, p.p.* **resined**) to treat with resin. **resinate**[1] (rez´inət) *n.* a salt of any acid occurring in natural resins. **resinate**[2] (rez´ināt) *v.t.* to impregnate with resin. **resiniferous** (-nif´-) *a.* yielding resin. **resinify** (-ifī) *v.t., v.i.* (*3rd pers. sing. pres.* **resinifies,** *pres.p.* **resinifying,** *past, p.p.* **resinified**). **resinification** *n.* **resinoid** (-noid) *a., n.* **resinous** *a.* **resinously** *adv.* **resinousness** *n.* [F *résine,* L *rēsīna,* rel. to Gr. *rhētinē*]

resist (rizist´) *v.t.* **1** to stand or strive against, to act in opposition to, to try to frustrate. **2** to oppose successfully, to withstand, to stop, to repel, to frustrate, to be proof against. **3** not to yield to (temptation or pleasure). ~*v.i.* to offer resistance. ~*n.* a substance applied to a surface etc. to prevent the action of a chemical agent, such as the mordant used in dyeing calico. **unable to resist** strongly inclined to, strongly attracted to. **resistance** *n.* **1** the act or power of resisting. **2** opposition, refusal to comply. **3** something which hinders or retards, esp. the opposition exerted by a fluid to the passage of a body. **4** (*Physics*) the opposition exerted by a substance to the passage of electric current, heat etc. through it, or a measure of this. **5** (*Biol.*) the ability to withstand adverse conditions. **6** the body's natural power to withstand disease. **7** a resistor. **8** a resistance movement. **resistance coil** *n.* a coil of insulated wire used to offer resistance to a current. **resistance movement** *n.* an underground organization of civilians and others in an enemy-occupied country whose aim is to sabotage the invaders' plans and render their position as difficult as possible. **resistance thermometer** *n.* a type of thermometer which accurately measures high temperatures from the change in resistance of a wire coil or semiconductor as the temperature varies. **resistant** *a.* **resister** *n.* **resistible** *a.* **resistibility** *n.* **resistibly, resistingly** *adv.* **resistive** *a.* **resistivity** (rēzistiv´-) *n.* the power of a material to resist the passage of electrical current through it. **resistless** *a.* **1** irresistible. **2** unresisting. †**resistlessly** *adv.* †**resistlessness** *n.* **resistor** *n.* an electronic component with a specified resistance. [OF *resister,* L *resistere* (*sistere,* redupl. of *stare,* to stand)]

Usage note It is conventional to use *resistEr* for a person, *resistOr* for an electrical device.

res judicata (rās joodikah´tə) *n.* (*Law*) an issue that has already been settled in court and cannot be raised again. [L]

resoluble (rizol´ūbəl) *a.* able to be dissolved, resolved or analysed. [F *résoluble* or L *resolubilis*]

re-soluble RE- (+ SA–SO WORDS).

resolute (rez´əloot) *a.* having a fixed purpose, determined, constant in pursuing an object. **resolutely** *adv.* **resoluteness** *n.* **resolution** (-loo´shən) *n.* **1** resoluteness, determination, firmness and boldness in adhering to one's purpose. **2** a resolve, a settled purpose. **3** a formal proposition, statement of opinion, or decision by a legislative or corporate body or public meeting. **4** a proposition put forward for discussion and approval. **5** mental analysis, solution of a problem etc. **6** the act or process of resolving or separating anything into the component parts, decomposition, analysis. **7** analysis of a force into two or more jointly equivalent forces. **8** analysis or conversion into a different format. **9** (*Med.*) the disappearance of inflammation without production of pus. **10** (*Mus.*) the conversion of a discord into a concord. **11** (*Physics*) the smallest interval which can be measured by a scientific instrument. **12** the definition of a television or film image. **13** the substitution of two short syllables for a long one. **resolutionist** *n.* **resolutive** *a.* (*Med.*) having the power or tending to resolve, dissolve or relax. **resolutive condition** *n.* (*Law*) a condition whose fulfilment terminates a contract. [L *resolūtus,* p.p. of *resolvere,* see RESOLVE]

resolve (rizolv´) *v.t.* **1** to cause (someone) to decide or determine. **2** to pass by vote or resolution (that). **3** to separate into the component parts; to dissolve, to analyse, to disintegrate, to dissipate; to reduce to the constituent parts or elements. **4** to distinguish between (adjacent objects). **5** to analyse mentally. **6** to solve, to explain, to clear up, to answer. **7** to convert into by analysis. **8** (*Med.*) to cause to disperse without suppuration. **9** (*Mus.*) to convert (a discord) into a concord. **10** in prosody, to replace (a long syllable) by two short ones. **11** to replace (a force) by two or more jointly equivalent forces. **12** to decide, to determine on. ~*v.i.* **1** to make one's mind up, to decide or determine (upon). **2** to separate into the component parts, to dissolve, to break up, to be analysed. **3** to be converted. **4** to reduce by mental analysis (into). **5** (*Mus.*) to be converted from discord into concord. **6** (*Med.*) to pass away without suppuration. **7** to pass a resolution. ~*n.* **1** a resolution, a firm decision or determination. **2** (*N Am.*) a resolution by a deliberative assembly. **3** resoluteness, firmness of purpose. **resolvable** *a.* **resolvability** (-bil´-) *n.* **resolved** *a.* determined, resolute. **resolvedly** (-vid-) *adv.* **resolvent** *a.* having the power of resolving, dissolving or disintegrating. ~*n.* something which has the power of resolving, esp. a chemical substance, drug or medical application. **resolver** *n.* **resolving power** *n.* **1** the ability of a microscope or telescope to distinguish or produce separable images of small adjacent objects. **2** the ability of a photographic emulsion to produce fine detailed images. [L *resolvere* (RE-, *solvere,* to loosen, see SOLVE)]

resonant (rez´ənənt) *a.* **1** (of a sound) prolonged or reinforced by vibration or reverberation. **2** having the property of prolonging or reinforcing sound, esp. by vibration. **3** capable of returning sound, re-echoing, resounding. **resonance** *n.* **1** the quality or state of being resonant. **2** sympathetic vibration. **3** the specially large vibration of a body or system when subjected to a small periodic force of the same frequency as the natural frequency of the system. **4** the amplification of human speech by sympathetic vibration in the bone structure of the head and chest resounding in the vocal tract. **5** (*Chem.*) the description of the electronic structure of a molecule in certain compounds in terms of different arrangements of two or more bonds. **resonantly** *adv.* **resonate** *v.i.* to resound, to reverberate. **resonator** *n.* (*Mus.*) **1** a body or system that detects and responds to certain frequencies. **2** a device for enriching or amplifying sound. [L *resonans -ntem,* pres.p. of *resonāre* (RE-, *sonāre,* to SOUND[1])]

resorb (risawb´) *v.t.* to absorb again. **resorbence** *n.* **resorbent** *a.* **resorption** (-zawp´-) *n.* **resorptive** *a.* [L *resorbēre* (*sorbēre,* to drink in, p.p. *sorptus*)]

resorcin (rizaw´sin), **resorcinol** (-nol) *n.* (*Chem.*) a crystalline phenol used as a dyestuff in resins, adhesives and in medicine. [RESIN, ORCIN]

resorption, resorptive RESORB.

resort (rizawt´) *n.* **1** a place frequented by holidaymakers. **2** something to which one has recourse, an expedient. **3** recourse (to). **4** the act of frequenting a place. **5** the state of being frequented. ~*v.i.* **1** to go, to repair, to betake oneself. **2** to have recourse, to apply, to turn to (for aid etc.). **resorter** *n.* [OF *resortir* (F *ressortir*), to come out, etym. uncertain]

resound (rizownd´) *v.i.* **1** to ring, to re-echo, to reverberate (with). **2** (of a place) to be filled with sound. **3** (of sounds, instruments etc.) to be re-echoed, to be repeated, reinforced, or prolonged. **4** (of news, events etc.) to be talked about, to make a sensation. ~*v.t.* **1** to spread the fame of. **2** to sound again, to return the sound of. **resounding** *a.* **1** ringing, resonant. **2** clear, decisive (*a resounding success*). **resoundingly** *adv.* [SOUND[1], after F *resonner,* cp. RESONANT]

resource (risaws´, -zaws´) *n.* **1** an expedient, a device. **2** a means of aid, support or safety. **3** (*usu. pl.*) stocks or supply available. **4** (*usu. pl., N Am.*) assets available.

5 (*pl.*) means of support and defence, esp. of a country. 6 a leisure pursuit. 7 capacity for finding or devising means. 8 skill in devising expedients, practical ingenuity. 9 †the possibility of being aided. ~*v.t.* to provide with resources. **one's own resources** one's own abilities. **resourceful** *a.* ingenious, clever. **resourcefully** *adv.* **resourcefulness** *n.* **resourceless** (-lis) *a.* **resourcelessness** *n.* [F *ressource*, from OF *ressourdre*, from L *resurgere* (RE-, *surgere*, to rise)]

re- (+ sp–su words) respell *v.t.* (*past*, *p.p.* **respelt, respelled**) to spell again. **respray**[1] *v.t.* to spray again. **respray**[2] (rē´-) *n.* the act of respraying. **restack** *v.t.* to stack again. **restaff** *v.t.* to appoint or assign replacement staff. **restage** *v.t.* to stage again or in a different way. **restart**[1] *v.t.*, *v.i.* to start afresh. **restart**[2] (rē´-) *n.* 1 a new beginning. 2 a new start to a race, match etc. after a false start, stoppage etc. **restate** *v.t.* to state again or express differently. **restatement** *n.* **restock** *v.t.*, *v.i.* to stock again. **restraighten** *v.t.*, *v.i.* to straighten again. **re-strain** *v.t.* to strain again. **restring** *v.t.* (*past*, *p.p.* **restrung**) 1 to provide (a musical instrument or tennis racket) with new strings. 2 to put (beads etc.) on to a new string. **restructure** *v.t.* to change the structure or organization (of). **restrung** RESTRING (under RE- (+ SP–SU WORDS)). **restudy** *v.t.* (*3rd pers. sing. pres.* **restudies,** *pres.p.* **restudying,** *past, p.p.* **restudied**) to study again. **restyle**[1] *v.t.* 1 to give a new style to. 2 to give a new name or title to. **restyle**[2] (rē´-) *n.* a new or different style. **resubmit** *v.t.* to submit (an application, a proposal etc.) again. **resubscribe** *v.t.*, *v.i.* to subscribe again. **resummon** *v.t.* 1 to summon again. 2 to convene again. **resupply** *v.t.* (*3rd pers. sing. pres.* **resupplies,** *pres.p.* **resupplying,** *past, p.p.* **resupplied**) to provide with fresh supplies. ~*v.i.* to obtain fresh supplies. ~*n.* 1 the act of resupplying. 2 something which is resupplied. **resurface** *v.t.* to put a new surface on (a road etc.). ~*v.i.* to appear again. **resurvey**[1] (rēsəvā´) *v.t.* to survey again, to read and examine again. **resurvey**[2] (rēsœ´vā) *n.* a renewed survey.

respect (rispekt´) *n.* 1 esteem, deferential regard. 2 attention (to), heed (to), regard (to or of). 3 a particular, an aspect. 4 relation, regard, reference. 5 (*pl.*) expressions of esteem sent as a complimentary message. ~*v.t.* 1 to esteem, to regard with deference. 2 to treat with consideration, to spare from insult, injury, interference etc. **in respect of** with regard to, concerning. **in respect that** because. **to pay one's last respects** to show respect for someone who has just died, by attending their funeral. **to pay one's respects** to send a message of esteem or compliment. **with (all due) respect** a polite phrase used to precede an expression of disagreement. **with respect to** with regard to, concerning. **respectable** *a.* 1 worthy of respect, of good repute. 2 of fair social standing. 3 honest, decent, not disreputable. 4 not mean, not inconsiderable, above the average in number, quantity, merit etc. 5 fairly good, tolerable, passable. 6 appropriate for a respectable person. 7 prim and conventional. **respectability** (-bil´-), **respectableness** *n.* 1 the quality or character of being respectable. 2 people who are respectable. **respectably** *adv.* **respecter** *n.* **no respecter of persons** a person who pays no consideration to and is not biased by wealth and social standing. **respectful** *a.* showing respect. **respectfully** *adv.* **respectfulness** *n.* **respecting** *prep.* in regard to, concerning. **respective** *a.* relating severally to each of those in question; several, comparative, relative. **respectively** *adv.* [F, from L *respectus*, p.p. of *respicere* (*specere*, to look)]

respire (rispīə´) *v.i.* 1 to breathe. 2 to inhale or take air into and exhale it from the lungs. 3 (of a plant) to carry out respiration. 4 to recover breath. 5 to recover hope, spirit etc. ~*v.t.* to inhale and exhale, to breathe out, to emit (perfume etc.). **respirable** (res´pir-) *a.* 1 capable of being respired. 2 fit to be breathed. **respirability** (-bil´-) *n.* **respirate** (-rāt) *v.t.* to give artificial respiration to. **respiration** (respirā´shən) *n.* 1 the act or process of breathing. 2 a single act of inhaling and exhaling. 3 (*Biol.*) the absorption of oxygen and emission of carbon dioxide by living organisms. **respirator** (res´pir-) *n.* 1 an appliance worn over the mouth or mouth and nose to exclude poisonous gases, fumes etc., or to protect the lungs from the sudden inspiration of cold air; a gas mask. 2 (*Med.*) an apparatus for providing artificial respiration. **respiratory** (-spir´-) *a.* **respiratory quotient** *n.* (*Biol.*) the ratio of carbon dioxide expired to the volume of oxygen consumed by an organism or tissue in a given period. **respirometer** (respirom´itə) *n.* an instrument for measuring respiration. [F *respirer*, L *respīrāre* (RE-, *spīrāre*, to breathe)]

respite (res´pīt) *n.* 1 an interval of rest or relief, a reprieve. 2 a temporary intermission of labour, effort, suffering etc., esp. a delay in the execution of a sentence. ~*v.t.* 1 to grant a respite to, to reprieve. 2 to suspend the execution of (a sentence). 3 to relieve by a temporary cessation of labour, suffering etc. 4 to postpone, to defer, to delay. **respiteless** *a.* [OF *respit*, from L, as RESPECT]

resplendent (risplen´dənt) *a.* shining with brilliant lustre, vividly or gloriously bright. **resplendence, resplendency** *n.* **resplendently** *adv.* [L *resplendens -ntem*, pres.p. of *resplendēre* (RE-, *splendēre*, to shine, to glitter)]

respond (rispond´) *v.i.* 1 to answer, to reply. 2 (of a congregation) to return set answers to a priest. 3 to perform an act or show an effect in answer or correspondence to something. 4 to react (to an external irritation or stimulus). 5 to be responsive, to show sympathy or sensitiveness (to). 6 in bridge, to bid in response to a partner's bid. ~*v.t.* to answer, to say in response. ~*n.* 1 (*Archit.*) a half-column or half-pier in a wall supporting the impost of an arch. 2 an anthem or versicle sung in response, a responsory. **respondence, †respondency** *n.* **respondent** *n.* 1 (*Law*) a person who answers in a suit at law, a defendant, esp. in a divorce case. 2 a person who answers. 3 a person who maintains a thesis in reply. ~*a.* 1 giving response, answering. 2 responsive (to). 3 in the position of defendant. **respondentia** (responden´shə) *n.* a loan upon a cargo repayable provided that the goods arrive safely. **responder** *n.* [OF *respondre* (F *répondre*), L *respondēre* (RE-, *spondēre*, to pledge, p.p. *sponsus*)]

response (rispons´) *n.* 1 the act of answering. 2 an answer, a reply, a reaction. 3 (*often pl.*) a versicle or other portion of a liturgy said or sung in answer to the priest, a responsory. 4 in bridge, a bid made in responding. 5 the ratio of the output to the input level on an electrical transmission system at any particular frequency. 6 the reaction of an organism to stimulation. **responsion** (-shən) *n.* (*pl.*, *Hist.*) the first of three examinations for the degree of BA at Oxford University **responsive** *a.* 1 answering or inclined to answer. 2 of the nature of an answer. 3 reacting to stimulus. 4 responding readily, sympathetic, impressionable. **responsively** *adv.* **responsiveness** *n.* **responsorial** (-saw´-) *a.* of or relating to liturgical responses. **responsory** *n.* (*pl.* **responsories**) an anthem said or sung alternately by the soloist and a choir after one of the lessons. ~*a.* of, relating to or of the nature of a response. [OF, from L *responsum*, neut. p.p. of *respondēre*, to RESPOND]

responsible (rispon´sibəl) *a.* 1 answerable, liable, accountable (to or for). 2 morally accountable for one's actions, able to discriminate between right and wrong. 3 respectable, trustworthy. 4 being the cause. 5 not autocratic. 6 involving responsibility. **responsibility** (-bil´-) *n.* 1 the state of being responsible. 2 the ability to act according to the laws of right and wrong. 3 something for which one is responsible. **on one's own responsibility** without authorization. **responsibly** *adv.*

responsion, responsive etc. RESPONSE.

rest[1] (rest) *v.i.* 1 to cease from exertion, motion or activity. 2 to be relieved from work or exertion, to repose. 3 to lie in sleep or death, to lie buried. 4 to be still, to be without motion. 5 to be free from care, disturbance or molestation, to be tranquil, to be at peace. 6 (of land) to be allowed to lie fallow. 7 to lie. 8 to be spread out. 9 to be supported or fixed, to be based, to lean, to recline, to stand (on). 10 to depend, to rely (on). 11 to trust or put one's confidence (in). 12 (of eyes) to be fixed, to be directed steadily (upon). 13 to remain without further discussion. 14 (*US*) (of an attorney) to call no more evidence. ~*v.t.* 1 to cause to cease from exertion. 2 to give repose to, to lay at rest. 3 (*in p.p.*) to refresh by resting. 4 to give (oneself) rest. 5 to place for support, to base, to establish, to lean, to lay, to support. ~*n.* 1 cessation from bodily or mental exertion or activity, repose, sleep. 2 freedom from care, disturbance or molestation, peace, tranquillity. 3 a period of such cessation or freedom, esp. a brief pause or interval. 4 a stopping place, a place for lodging. 5 a shelter for taxi drivers, sailors etc. 6 something on which anything stands or is supported, a prop, a support, a device for steadying a rifle on in taking aim, for supporting the cutting tool in a lathe etc. 7 a long cue with a crosspiece at one end used as a support for a snooker cue in playing. 8 (*Mus.*) **a** an interval of silence. **b** the sign indicating this. 9 a pause in a verse, a caesura. 10 death. **at rest** 1 reposing, not in motion, still. 2 not disturbed, agitated or troubled. 3 (*euphem.*) dead, in the grave. **(God) rest his/ her soul** may God grant his/her soul peace. **to rest one's case** to conclude one's arguments. **to rest on one's laurels** LAUREL. **to rest on one's oars** OAR. **to rest up** (*N Am.*) to have a rest. **to set at rest** to ease (someone's mind). **rest-cure** *n.* seclusion and rest (usu. in bed) as a method of treatment for nervous disorders. **rest day** *n.* 1 a day of rest. 2 Sunday. **rested** *a.* invigorated after a rest. **restful** *a.* 1 inducing rest, soothing, free from disturbance. 2 at rest, quiet. **restfully** *adv.* **restfulness** *n.* **rest home** *n.* an institution where old people live and are looked after. **rest house** *n.* in Asia and Africa, a place where travellers can rest. **resting place** *n.* 1 a place for rest. 2 the grave. **restless** *a.* 1 not resting, never still, agitated, uneasy, fidgety, unsettled, turbulent. 2 not affording sleep, sleepless. **restlessly** *adv.* **restlessness** *n.* **rest mass** *n.* (*Physics*) the mass of an object at rest. **restroom** *n.* (*N Am.*) a room with toilet facilities etc. in a public building. [OE *rest, ræst* (cp. Dut. *rust*, G *Raste*, Icel. *röst*), whence *ræstan*, to rest (cp. Dut. *rusten*, G *rasten*)]

rest[2] (rest) *n.* 1 the remaining part or parts, the residue, the remainder; the others. 2 a reserve fund, a balance or surplus fund for contingencies. 3 (*Hist.*) in tennis, a continuous series of quick returns of the ball. ~*v.i.* to remain, to stay, to continue (in a specified state). **and all the rest** and all the others. **as for the rest** for the rest. **for the rest** as regards the remaining persons, matters or things, as regards anything else. **to rest assured** ASSURE. **to rest with** to be left in the hands of. [F *reste*, from *rester*, L *restāre* (RE-, *stāre*, to stand)]

restaurant (res´tərənt, -trənt, -trã) *n.* a place for refreshment, a public eating house. **restaurant car** *n.* a dining car on a train. **restaurateur** (-tərətœ´) *n.* the keeper of a restaurant. [F, from *restaurer*, to RESTORE]

Usage note The form *restauranteur* (after *restaurant*) for *restaurateur* is best avoided.

rest-harrow (rest´harō) *n.* any plant of the genus *Ononis* with a tough woody root. [form of ARREST]

restiform (res´tifawm) *a.* (*Anat.*) (of two bundles of fibrous matter connecting the medulla oblongata with the cerebellum) ropelike or cordlike. [L *restis*, a cord, -FORM]

restitution (restitū´shən) *n.* 1 the act of restoring something taken away or lost. 2 making good, reparation, indemnification. 3 (*esp. Theol.*) restoration to a former state or position. 4 the resumption of its former shape by an elastic body. **restitutive** (res´-), **restitutory** (-tū´-) *a.* [OF, from L *restitutiōnem*, nom. *-tio*, from *restituere* (RE-, *statuere*, to set up)]

restive (res´tiv) *a.* 1 restless, fidgety. 2 (of a horse) unwilling to go forward, standing still, refractory. 3 impatient of control, unmanageable. **restively** *adv.* **restiveness** *n.* [formerly *restiff*, OF *restif*, from *rester*, to REST[1]]

Usage note The meanings of the adjectives *restive* and *restless* overlap, but *restive* should imply some impending (usually rebellious) action, whereas *restless* is more simply descriptive of a state.

restore (ristaw´) *v.t.* 1 to bring back to a former state, to repair, to reconstruct. 2 to put back, to replace, to return. 3 to bring back to health, to cure. 4 to bring back to a former position, to reinstate. 5 to bring into existence or use again, to re-establish, to renew. 6 to reproduce (a text or part of a text) by emendation, conjecture etc. 7 to represent (an extinct animal, mutilated picture, ruin etc.) as it is supposed to have been originally. 8 to give back, to make restitution of. **restorable** *a.* **restoration** (restərā´shən) *n.* 1 the act of restoring. 2 a building etc., restored to its supposed original state. 3 a skeleton of an extinct animal built up of its remains. 4 a drawing, model, or other representation of a building, extinct animal etc., in its supposed original form. 5 the re-establishment of a monarchy, or the period of this. ~*a.* (**Restoration**) of or relating to the literary period following the Restoration of Charles II (*Restoration comedy*). **the Restoration** 1 (*Hist.*) the return of Charles II of England in 1660 and the re-establishment of the monarchy after the Commonwealth. 2 (*Hist.*) the return of the Bourbons to France in 1814. **restorationism, Restorationism** *n.* (*Theol.*) the doctrine of the final restoration of all people to happiness and sinlessness in the future life. **restorationist** *n.*, *a.* **restorative** (-stor´-) *a.* tending to restore health or strength. ~*n.* food, drink, a medicine etc., for restoring strength, vigour etc.; a stimulant, a tonic. **restoratively** *adv.* **restorer** *n.* [OF *restorer*, L *restaurāre* (RE-, *sta-*, root of *stāre*, to stand, cp. Gr. *stauros*, stake)]

restrain (ristrān´) *v.t.* 1 to hold back, to check, to curb. 2 to keep under control, to repress, to hold in check, to restrict. 3 to confine, to imprison. **restrainable** *a.* **restrainedly** (-nid-) *adv.* **restrainer** *n.* **restraint** *n.* 1 the act of restraining. 2 the state of being restrained. 3 check, repression, control, self-repression, avoidance of excess. 4 constraint, reserve. 5 restriction, limitation. 6 deprivation of liberty, confinement. 7 something used to retain a person or animal physically. **in restraint of** in order to restrain. **restraint of trade** *n.* interference with free competition in business. [OF *restraign-*, pres.p. stem of *restraindre* (F *restreindre*), L *restringere* (RE-, *stringere*, to draw tight, p.p. *strictus*)]

re-strain RE- (+ SP–SU WORDS).

restrict (ristrikt´) *v.t.* 1 to limit, to confine, to keep within certain bounds. 2 to subject to limitation. 3 to withhold from disclosure. **restricted** *a.* 1 limited, confined. 2 out of bounds to the general public. 3 denoting a zone where a speed limit or waiting restrictions apply for vehicles. **restricted area** *n.* 1 an area where a speed limit applies for vehicles. 2 (*N Am.*) an area which is out of bounds to the general public or to military personnel. **restrictedly** *adv.* **restrictedness** *n.* **restriction** *n.* 1 something that restricts. 2 a restrictive law or regulation. **3** restricting or being restricted. **restriction enzyme** *n.* any of several enzymes which divide DNA at a specific sequence of bases, for genetic manipulation. **restrictionist** *a., n.* **restrictive** *a.* **1** restricting or tending to restrict. **2** (*Gram.*) denoting a relative clause or phrase which restricts the application of the antecedent noun etc. **restrictively** *adv.* **restrictiveness** *n.* **restrictive practice** *n.* **1** a trading agreement contrary to the public interest. **2** a practice by a trade union, e.g. the closed shop, regarded as limiting managerial flexibility. [L *restrictus*, see RESTRAIN]

result (rizŭlt´) *v.i.* **1** to have an issue, to terminate or end (in). **2** to be the actual, or follow as, the logical consequence; to ensue (from). ~*n.* **1** consequence, issue, outcome, effect. **2** a favourable outcome. **3** a quantity, value, or formula obtained from a calculation. **4** a final score in a game or contest. **without result** in vain. **resultant** *a.* **1** resulting, following as a result. **2** resulting from the combination of two factors, agents etc. ~*n.* (*Math.*) the force resulting from the combination of two or more forces acting in different directions at the same point, ascertained by a parallelogram of forces. **resultful** *a.* **resulting** *a.* **resultless** *a.* [F *résulter*, L *resultāre* (RE-, *saltāre*, freq. of *salīre*, to leap)]

resume (rizūm´) *v.t.* **1** to begin again, to recommence, to go on with after interruption. **2** to take back, to take again, to reoccupy, to recover. **3** †to sum up, to recapitulate, to make a résumé of. ~*v.i.* to continue after interruption, to recommence. **resumable** *a.* [OF *resumer*, L *resūmere* (RE-, *sūmere*, to take, p.p. *sumptus*)]

résumé (rez´ūmā), **resumé** *n.* **1** a summary, a recapitulation, a condensed statement. **2** (*esp. N Am.*) a curriculum vitae. [F, p.p. of *résumer*, to RESUME]

resumption (rizŭmp´shən) *n.* the act of resuming. **resumptive** *a.* [L *resumptio*, from *resūmere*, to RESUME]

resupinate (risoo´pināt) *a.* (*Bot.*) inverted, apparently upside-down. **resupination** (-ā´shən) *n.* [L *resupīnātus*, p.p. of *resupīnāre* (RE-, *supināre*, to make SUPINE)]

resurgent (risœ´jənt) *a.* rising again, esp. in popularity. **resurge** *v.i.* to rise again. **resurgence** *n.* [L *resurgere* (RE-, *surgere*, to rise)]

resurrect (rezərekt´) *v.t.* **1** (*coll.*) to bring again into vogue or currency, to revive. **2** to exhume. **3** to bring back to life. ~*v.i.* to come back to life. **resurrection** *n.* **1** (**Resurrection**) a rising again from the dead, esp. the rising of Christ from the dead, and the rising of all the dead at the Last Day. **2** the state of being risen again. **3** a springing again into life, vigour, vogue or prosperity. **4** exhumation, resurrecting, body snatching. **resurrectional** *a.* **resurrectionism** *n.* belief in the Christian doctrine of Resurrection. **resurrection plant** *n.* any of various desert plants which curl into a tight ball in drought and unfold when moistened. [OF, from late L *resurrectiōnem*, nom. *-tio*, from *resurgere*, to RESURGE (under RESURGENT)]

resuscitate (risŭs´itāt) *v.t.* **1** to revive, to restore from apparent death. **2** to restore to vigour, animation, usage etc. ~*v.i.* to revive, to come to life or prominence again. **resuscitable** *a.* **resuscitant** *n., a.* **resuscitation** (-ā´shən) *n.* **resuscitative** *a.* **resuscitator** *n.* [L *resuscitātus*, p.p. of *resuscitāre* (RE-, SUS-, *citāre*, to CITE)]

ret (ret), **rate** (rāt) *v.t.* (*pres.p.* **retting, rating,** *past, p.p.* **retted, rated**) to subject (flax etc.) to the action of retting. ~*v.i.* (of hay) to be spoilt by wet. **retted** *a.* **rettery** *n.* (*pl.* **retteries**). **retting** *n.* the act or process of steeping flax or hemp to loosen the fibre from the woody portions. [etym. obscure, cp. Dut. *reten*, Swed. *röta*, Norw. *röyta*, rel. to ROT]

ret. *abbr.* **1** retain. **2** retired. **3** return(ed).

re- (+ ta–to words) retake[1] *v.t.* (*pres.p.* **retaking,** *past* **retook,** *p.p.* **retaken**) **1** to take again. **2** to recapture. **3** to shoot (a film scene) again. **4** to record (a performance) again. **retake**[2] (rē´-) *n.* **1** the act of retaking. **2** something retaken. **3** a second photographing (of a scene). **4** a rerecording. **reteach** *v.t.* (*past, p.p.* **retaught**) to teach again or in a different way. **retell** *v.t.* (*past, p.p.* **retold**) to tell again or in a different way. **retest** *v.t., v.i.* to test again. **retestify** *v.i., v.t.* (*3rd pers. sing. pres.* **retestifies,** *pres.p.* **retestifying,** *past, p.p.* **retestified**) to testify again. **retexture** *v.t.* to treat (clothing) so as to restore the original texture. **rethink**[1] *v.t.* (*past, p.p.* **rethought**) to think again, to reconsider (a plan, decision etc.) and take an alternative view. **rethink**[2] (rē´-) *n.* the act of rethinking. **rethread** *v.t., v.i.* to thread again. **retie** *v.t.* (*pres.p.* **retying,** *past, p.p.* **retied**) to tie again. **re-time** *v.t.* to set a new time or timetable for. **retitle** *v.t.* to give a new title to. **retold** RETELL (under RE- (+ TA–TO WORDS)). **retook** RETAKE[1] (under RE- (+ TA–TO WORDS)). **retool** *v.t., v.i.* to replace or re-equip (a factory etc.) with new tools. **retouch** *v.t.* **1** to improve (a photograph, picture etc.) by new touches. **2** to touch again. ~*n.* **1** the act of retouching. **2** a photograph, painting etc. that has been retouched. **retoucher** *n.*

retable (ritā´bəl) *n.* **1** a shelf, ledge or panelled frame above the back of an altar for supporting ornaments. **2** a shelf. [F *rétable*, after med. L *retrotabulum*]

retail[1] (rē´tāl) *n.* the sale of commodities in small quantities, as distinct from *wholesale*. ~*a.* of or relating to selling by retail. ~*adv.* at a retail price. **retail price index** *n.* an index of the cost of living, based on average retail prices of selected goods, usu. updated monthly. [OF *retail*, *retaille*, from *retailler*, to cut off a piece (RE-, *tailler*, see TAILOR)]

retail[2] (rē´tāl, ritāl´) *v.t.* **1** to sell in small quantities. **2** to tell (a story etc.) in detail, to retell, to spread about. ~*v.i.* to be sold by retail (at or for a specified price). **retailer** *n.*

retain (ritān´) *v.t.* **1** to hold or keep possession of, to keep. **2** to continue to have, to maintain, to preserve. **3** to remember. **4** to hold back, to keep in place. **5** to hire, to engage the services of (someone) by paying a preliminary fee. **retainable** *a.* **retainability** (-bil´-) *n.* **retainer** *n.* **1** someone who or something which retains. **2** (*Law*) an agreement by which an attorney acts in a case. **3** a preliminary fee paid (esp. to a counsel) to secure someone's services. **4** an attendant, a follower, esp. of a feudal chieftain. **5** (*facet.*) a long-serving, faithful servant. **6** a reduced rent paid on accommodation during a period of non-occupancy. **7** in dentistry, a structure attaching a bridge to a tooth. **retaining** *n., a.* **retaining fee** *n.* a retainer. **retaining wall** *n.* a massive wall built to support and hold back the earth of an embankment, a mass of water etc. **retainment** *n.* [OF *retenir*, L *retinēre* (RE-, *tenēre*, to hold)]

retaliate (rital´iāt) *v.i.* to repay an injury or result, to make reprisals. ~*v.t.* to repay (an injury or insult). **retaliation** (-ā´shən) *n.* **retaliative** (-tal´yətiv) *a.* **retaliator** *n.* **retaliatory** (-tal´jətəri) *a.* [L *retāliātus*, p.p. of *retāliāre* (RE-, *tāliāre*, from *tālis*, such, cp. *tālio*, retaliation)]

retard[1] (ritahd´) *v.t.* **1** to cause to move more slowly. **2** to hinder, to impede, to delay the growth, advance, arrival or occurrence of. ~*n.* delay, retardation. **in retard** delayed. **retardant** *n.* a substance that slows a process down (*fire retardant*). ~*a.* serving to delay or slow down. **retardate** *a.* (*N Am.*) mentally retarded. ~*n.* a mentally retarded person. **retardation** (rētahdā´shən) *n.* **retardative, retardatory** *a.* **retarded** *a.* underdeveloped intellectually or emotionally. **retarder** *n.* **retardment** *n.* [F *retarder*, L *retardāre* (RE-, *tardus*, slow)]

retard[2] (rē´tahd) *n.* (*N Am., sl., offensive*) a mentally retarded person.

retch (rech) *v.i.* **1** to make an effort to vomit. **2** to strain, as in vomiting. ~*n.* the act or sound of retching. [OE *hræcan*, from *hrāca*, spittle (cp. Icel. *hrækja*, from *hrāki*, spittle)]

retd. *abbr.* 1 retired. 2 retained. 3 returned.
rete (rē´ti) *n.* (*pl.* **retia** (-tiə, -shiə)) (*Anat.*) a network of nerves or blood vessels. **retial** (-shi-) *a.* [L *rēte*, a net]
retention (riten´shən) *n.* 1 the act of retaining. 2 the state of being retained. 3 the power of retaining, esp. ideas in the mind. 4 (*Med.*) failure to evacuate urine etc. **retentive** *a.* **retentively** *adv.* **retentiveness** *n.* [OF from L *retentiōnem*, nom. *-tio*, from *retinēre*, to RETAIN]
retia, retial RETE.
retiarius (retiah´riəs) *n.* (*pl.* **retiarii** (-riī)) (*Hist.*) a Roman gladiator armed with a net and trident. [L *rētiārius*, from *rēte*, a net]
reticent (ret´isənt) *a.* 1 reserved in speech. 2 not disposed to communicate one's thoughts or feelings. 3 keeping something back. 4 inclined to keep one's own counsel. **reticence** *n.* **reticently** *adv.* [L *reticens -ntem*, pres.p. of *reticēre* (RE-, *tacēre*, to be silent)]
reticle (ret´ikəl) *n.* a network of fine lines etc., drawn across the focal plane of an optical instrument.
reticula RETICULUM.
reticular (ritik´ūlə) *a.* 1 having the form of a net or network. 2 formed with interstices.
reticulate[1] (ritik´ūlāt) *v.t.* to make, divide into or arrange in a network, to mark with fine, intersecting lines. ~*v.i.* to be divided into or arranged in a network. **reticulation** (-lā´shən) *n.*
reticulate[2] (ritik´ūlət) *a.* formed into or resembling a network. **reticulately** *adv.*
reticule (ret´ikūl) *n.* 1 a lady's handbag. 2 reticle. 3 a kind of bag, orig. of network.
reticulum (ritik´ūləm) *n.* (*pl.* **reticula** (-lə)) 1 a netlike or reticulated structure, membrane etc. 2 (*Zool.*) the second stomach of a ruminant. **reticulose** (-lōs) *a.* [L *rēticulum*, dim. of *rēte*, net]
retiform (rē´tifawm, ret´-) *a.* netlike, reticulated. [L *rēte*, net]
retina (ret´inə) *n.* (*pl.* **retinas, retinae** (-nē)) (*Anat.*) a netlike layer of sensitive nerve-fibres and cells behind the eyeball in which the optic nerve terminates. **retinal** *a.* [med. L, prob. from L *rēte*, net]
retinaculum (retinak´ūləm) *n.* (*pl.* **retinacula** (-lə)) (*Zool.*) 1 an apparatus by which the wings of insects are interlocked in flight. 2 a connecting band or cord. 3 an apparatus in some insects controlling the sting. [L, from *retinēre*, to RETAIN]
retinalite (ret´inəlīt) *n.* (*Mineral.*) a variety of serpentine with a resinous lustre. **retinite** (-nīt) *n.* pitchstone. **retinol** (-nol) *n.* a liquid hydrocarbon obtained from resin, used in pharmacy etc. [Gr. *rhētinē*, RESIN, -LITE]
retinitis (retinī´tis) *n.* (*Med.*) inflammation of the retina.
retinol RETINALITE.
retinoscopy (retinos´kəpi) *n.* examination of the eye using an instrument that throws a shadow on to the retina. **retinoscopic** (-skop´-) *a.* **retinoscopically** *adv.*
retinue (ret´inū) *n.* the group of attendants accompanying a distinguished person. [ME and OF *retenue*, p.p. of *retenir*, to RETAIN]
retire (ritīə´) *v.i.* 1 to withdraw, to go away, to fall back, to retreat, to recede. 2 to withdraw from business to a private life. 3 to resign one's office or appointment, to cease from or withdraw from active service. 4 to go to or as to bed. 5 to go into privacy or seclusion. 6 in cricket, to end one's innings without being out. 7 in baseball, to put out (a batter). ~*v.t.* 1 to cause to retire or resign. 2 to order (troops) to retire. 3 (of a cricket captain) to cause (a batsman) to end his innings. 4 to withdraw (a bill or note) from circulation or operation. ~*n.* a signal (to troops) to retire. **to retire from the world** to become reclusive. **to retire into oneself** to become withdrawn or uncommunicative. **retiral** *n.* (*esp. Sc.*) retirement from work. **retired** *a.* 1 having retired from work. 2 of or relating to retired people. 3 private, withdrawn from society, given to privacy or seclusion. 4 secluded, sequestered. †**retiredly** *adv.* †**retiredness** *n.* **retirement** *n.* **retirement age** *n.* the age at which people usually retire from work. **retirement home** *n.* 1 a house or flat to which an old person moves after retirement. 2 an institution where old people live and are looked after. **retirement pension** *n.* a state pension paid to people who have reached retirement age. **retirement pregnancy** *n.* (*coll.*) a pregnancy artificially induced in a woman beyond child-bearing age. **retirer** *n.* **retiring** *a.* shy, not forward, unsociable. **retiring age** *n.* retirement age. **retiringly** *adv.* **retiringness** *n.* [OF *retirer* (RE-, *tirer*, to draw, from Gmc.)]
retort[1] (ritawt´) *n.* 1 the turning of a charge, taunt, attack etc. against the originator or aggressor. 2 an angry reply. 3 a retaliation. ~*v.t.* 1 to say, make or do as a retort. 2 to turn (an argument, accusation, etc.) on or against the originator or aggressor. 3 to pay back (an attack, injury etc.) in kind. 4 to turn or throw back. ~*v.i.* to turn an argument or charge against the originator or aggressor. **retorted** *a.* recurved, bent or twisted back. **retorter** *n.* **retortion** (-taw´shən), **retorsion** *n.* 1 bending, turning, or twisting back. 2 the act of retorting. 3 retaliation by a state on the subjects of another without actual war. [L *retortus*, p.p. of *retorquēre* (*torquēre*, to twist)]
retort[2] (ritawt´) *n.* 1 a container with a bulblike receptacle and a long neck bent downwards used for distillation of liquids etc. 2 a large receptacle of fireclay, iron etc., of similar shape, used for the production of coal gas. ~*v.t.* to purify (mercury etc.) by treatment in a retort. [F *retorte*, as RETORT[1]]
re- (+ tr–tu words) retrace *v.t.* 1 to go over (one's course or track) again. 2 to trace back to the beginning, source etc. 3 to go over again in memory, to try to recollect. 4 to trace (an outline) again. **retraceable** *a.* **retrain** *v.t.* to teach new skills to. ~*v.i.* to learn new skills. **retransfer**[1] (rētransfœ´) *v.t.* (*pres.p.* **retransferring**, *past, p.p.* **retransferred**) to transfer again. **retransfer**[2] (rētrans´fœ) *n.* an act of retransferring. **retransform** *v.t.* to transform again. **retransformation** *n.* **retranslate** *v.t.* 1 to translate again. 2 to translate back into the original language. **retranslation** *n.* **retransmit** *v.t.* (*pres.p.* **retransmitting**, *past, p.p.* **retransmitted**) to transmit again or to a greater distance. **retransmission** *n.* **retread**[1] *v.t.* (*past* **retrod**, *p.p.* **retrodden**) 1 to tread again. 2 to remould (a tyre). **retread**[2] (rē´-) *n.* 1 (*Austral.*) a re-enlisting soldier. 2 a retired person who re-enters their employment. 3 something unoriginal, using ideas which have been used before. **retrial** (rē´trīəl) *n.* (*Law*) a second trial. **retrim** *v.t.* (*pres.p.* **retrimming**, *past, p.p.* **retrimmed**) to trim again. **retrod, retrodden** RETREAD[1] (under RE- (+ TR–TU WORDS)). **retry** *v.t.* (*3rd pers. sing. pres.* **retries**, *pres.p.* **retrying**, *past, p.p.* **retried**) to try again. **retune** *v.t.* to tune again or in a different way. **returf** *v.t.* to turf again. **retwist** *v.t., v.i.* to twist again. **retying** RETIE (under RE- (+ TA–TO WORDS)). **retype** *v.t.* to type again, correcting errors.
retract (ritrakt´) *v.t.* 1 to take back, to revoke, to acknowledge to be false or wrong. 2 to draw back or in. ~*v.i.* 1 to withdraw a statement, declaration, promise etc. 2 to withdraw, to shrink back. **retractable** *a.* retractile. **retractability** (-bil´-) *n.* **retractation** (rētraktā´shən) *n.* **retractile** (-tīl) *a.* capable of being retracted. **retractility** (-til´-) *n.* **retraction** (-trak´shən) *n.* **retractive** *a.* **retractor** *n.* 1 a muscle used for drawing back. 2 (*Med.*) an instrument or bandage used by a surgeon for holding back parts. [L *retractus*, p.p. of *retrahere* (*trahere*, to draw), later senses from *retractāre*, to revoke, freq. of *retrahere*]
retreat (ritrēt´) *v.i.* 1 to move back, to retire, esp. before an enemy or from an advanced position. 2 to recede. 3 to withdraw to a place of privacy, seclusion or security. ~*v.t.* 1 to cause to retreat. 2 in chess, to move (a piece)

back. ~*n.* 1 the act of withdrawing or retiring, esp. the retiring of an army before an enemy. 2 (*Mil.*) **a** a signal to retreat. **b** a bugle call at sunset. **c** a flag-lowering ceremony including a retreat. 3 retirement for meditation, prayer etc. 4 a state of retirement or seclusion. 5 a period of retirement. 6 a place of retirement, security, privacy or seclusion. 7 an institution for the care of old or mentally ill people. [OF *retret, -trete* (F *retraite*), p.p. of *retraire*, L *retrahere*, to RETRACT]

retrench (ritrench´) *v.t.* 1 to cut down, to reduce, to curtail, to diminish. 2 to shorten, to abridge, to cut out or pare down. 3 (*esp. Austral.*) to make redundant. 4 (*Mil.*) to furnish with a retrenchment. ~*v.t.* to curtail expenses, to make economies. **retrenchment** *n.* 1 the act of retrenching. 2 a work constructed with or behind another to prolong a defence. [F *retrencher*, obs. var. of *retrancher*, to TRENCH]

retribution (retribū´shən) *n.* recompense, a suitable return, esp. for evil, requital, vengeance. **retributive** (ritrib´-) *a.* **retributor** (ritrib´-) *n.* **retributory** (-trib´-) *a.* [OF *retribucion, -tion*, L *retributio*, acc. *-ōnem*, from *retribuere* (*tribuere*, to assign)]

retrieve (ritrēv´) *v.t.* 1 (of a dog) to find and bring in (game, a stick, a ball etc.). 2 to recover by searching or recollecting, recall to mind. 3 to regain (something which has been lost, impaired etc.). 4 to rescue (from). 5 to restore, to re-establish (one's fortunes etc.). 6 to remedy, to make good, to repair. 7 in tennis etc., to return (a difficult ball) successfully. 8 to recover (data stored in a computer system). ~*v.i.* (of a dog) to fetch. ~*n.* the possibility of being recovered. **retrievable** *a.* **retrievability** (-bil´-) *n.* **retrievably** *adv.* **retrieval** *n.* **retriever** *n.* 1 a dog of a breed used to fetch in game that has been shot. 2 a person who retrieves. [OF *retroev-*, a stem of *retrover* (*trouver*, to find, see TROVER and CONTRIVE)]

retro (ret´rō) *n.* (*pl.* **retros**) 1 an object made in the style of a past era. 2 a style or fashion mimicking one from a past era. ~*a.* mimicking the style of a past era. [F, *rétro*, abbr. of *rétrograde*]

retro- (ret´rō) *comb. form* 1 back, in return. 2 (*Anat., Med.*) located behind. [L, *retro*, backwards]

retroact (retrōakt´) *v.i.* 1 to act backwards or in return. 2 to act retrospectively. 3 to react. **retroaction** (-ak´shən) *n.* **retroactive** *a.* 1 (of a law etc.) applying to the past. 2 operating backwards. **retroactively** *adv.* **retroactivity** (-tiv´-) *n.* [L *retroactus*, p.p. of *retroagere*, to ACT]

retrocede (retrōsēd´) *v.i.* 1 to move backwards. 2 to recede. ~*v.t.* to cede back again, to restore (territory etc.). **retrocedence** *n.* **retrocedent** *a.* **retrocession** (-sesh´ən) *n.* **retrocessive** (-ses´-) *a.* [L *retrōcēdere* (*cēdere*, to yield, to go back, see CEDE)]

retrochoir (ret´rōkwīə) *n.* a part of a cathedral or other large church beyond the high altar.

retrofit (ret´rōfit) *v.t.* (*pres.p.* **retrofitting,** *past, p.p.* **retrofitted**) to equip or modify (an aircraft, car etc.) with new parts or safety equipment after manufacture.

retroflected (retrəflek´tid), **retroflex** (ret´rəfleks), **retroflexed** (ret´rōflekst) *a.* 1 (*Anat., Med., Bot.*) turned or curved backward. 2 (of a vowel or consonant) articulated with the tip of the tongue bent upwards and backwards. **retroflection** (-flek´shən), **retroflexion** *n.* [med. L *retroflexus*, p.p. of *retroflectere* (*flectere*, to bend)]

retrofract (ret´rōfrakt), **retrofracted** *a.* (*Bot.*) bent back so as to look as if broken. [cp. REFRACT]

retrograde (ret´rəgrād) *a.* 1 going, moving, bending or directed backwards. 2 inverted, reversed. 3 declining, degenerating, deteriorating. 4 (*Astron.*) denoting the apparent motion of a planet east to west relative to the stars beyond. ~*n.* 1 a degenerate person. 2 a backward movement or tendency, deterioration, decline. ~*v.i.* 1 to move backwards, to recede. 2 to decline, to deteriorate, to revert. 3 (*Astron.*) to move or appear to move from east to west relatively to the fixed stars. **retrogradation** (-grədā´shən) *n.* 1 (*Astron.*) the backward or apparently backward (east to west) motion of a planet relative to the stars beyond. 2 retrogression. **retrogradely** *adv.* [L *retrōgradus*, from *retrōgradī*, to go backward (*gradī*, to go)]

retrogress (retrōgres´) *v.i.* 1 to go backward, to retrograde. 2 to degenerate. **retrogression** (-gresh´ən) *n.* 1 moving backwards. 2 a move back to an earlier stage of development, deterioration. 3 (*Astron.*) retrogradation. **retrogressive** *a.* **retrogressively** *adv.* [L *retrōgressus*, p.p. of *retrōgradī*, as RETROGRADE]

retroject (retrōjekt´) *v.t.* to throw backwards, as distinct from *project*.

retromingent (retrōmin´jənt) *a.* (*Zool.*) discharging the urine backwards. ~*n.* an animal that discharges the urine backwards. [L *mingens -ntem*, pres.p. of *mingere*, to make water]

retropulsion (retrōpŭl´shən) *n.* (*Med.*) a symptom of locomotory disease in which the patient has a tendency to walk backwards. **retropulsive** (-pŭl´siv) *a.*

retro-rocket (ret´rōrokit) *n.* a small rocket on a spacecraft, satellite etc. which produces thrust in the opposite direction to flight for deceleration or manoeuvring.

retrorse (ritraws´) *a.* (*Biol.*) turned or bent backwards, reverted. **retrorsely** *adv.* [L *retrorsus* (*versus*, p.p. of *vertere*, to turn)]

retrospect (ret´rəspekt) *n.* 1 a looking back on things past. 2 view of, regard to, or consideration of previous conditions etc. 3 a review of past events. **in retrospect** looking back on something that has happened. **retrospection** (-spek´-) *n.* 1 the act of looking back on things past. 2 a tendency to indulge in retrospection. **retrospective** (-spek´-) *a.* 1 in retrospection, viewing the past. 2 of or relating to an exhibition of an artist's life work. 3 applicable to what has happened. 4 towards the rear. 5 licensing, condoning or condemning a past action. ~*n.* an exhibition of an artist's life work. **retrospectively** *adv.* [L *retrospectus*, p.p. of *retrospicere* (RETRO-, *specere*, to look)]

retrosternal (retrōstœ´nəl) *a.* (*Anat., Med.*) behind the breastbone.

retroussé (ritroo´sā) *a.* (of the nose) turned up at the end. [F, p.p. of *retrousser*]

retrovert (rētrəvœt´) *v.t.* to turn back (esp. of the womb). **retroversion** (-vœ´shən) *n.* [late L *retrovertere* (RETRO-, *vertere*, to turn, p.p. *versus*)]

retrovirus (ret´rōvīərəs) *n.* (*pl.* **retroviruses**) (*Biol.*) any of a group of viruses which use RNA to synthesize DNA, reversing the normal process of cellular transcription of DNA into RNA; many cause cancer in animals and one is the cause of Aids in humans.

retsina (retsē´nə) *n.* a resin-flavoured white wine from Greece. [mod. Gr. from It. *resina*, resin]

rettery, retting RET.

return (ritœn´) *v.i.* 1 to come or go back, esp. to the same place or state. 2 to revert, to happen again, to recur. ~*v.t.* 1 to bring, carry or convey back. 2 to give, render or send back. 3 to repay, to put or send back or in return, to requite. 4 to yield (a profit). 5 to say in reply, to retort. 6 in cricket etc., to hit (the ball) back. 7 to report officially. 8 to elect. 9 to lead a card of the same suit as another player has led. 10 to lead (a suit or card) after taking a trick. 11 (*Archit.*) to continue (a wall). ~*n.* 1 the act of coming or going back. 2 the act of giving, paying, putting or sending back. 3 something which is returned. 4 a return ticket. 5 an official account or report. 6 a sheriff's report on a writ or a returning officer's announcement of a candidate's election. 7 the act of electing or returning. 8 the state of being elected. 9 (*often pl.*) the proceeds or profits on labour, investments etc. 10 an electrical conductor bringing a current back to its source. 11 (*Archit.*) a receding part of a façade etc., a part of a moulding etc. bending in another direction. 12 on a typewriter keyboard, a carriage return key or carriage key. 13 in sport, a stroke, thrust etc. in return. 14 a return match or game. 15 (*Law*) the rendering back or delivery of a writ, precept or execution to the proper officer or court. 16 (*pl.*) a mild kind of tobacco. **by return (of post)** by the next post back to the sender. **in return** in reply or response, in requital. **many happy returns (of the day)** a birthday greeting. **to return thanks** 1 to offer thanks. 2 to answer a toast. **to return the compliment** COMPLIMENT[1]. **returnable** *a.* **return crease** *n.* in cricket, either of two lines at right angles to the bowling crease and extending beyond it. **returnee** (-nē´) *n.* 1 a person who returns home after being abroad for a long time. 2 a person who returns to work after a period looking after their children. **returner** *n.* **return game** *n.* a return match. **returning officer** *n.* the presiding officer at an election. **return key** *n.* a key on a computer keyboard pressed to return to the beginning of the next line. **returnless** *a.* **return match** *n.* a second meeting of the same clubs or teams. **return ticket** *n.* a ticket for a journey to a place and back again. [OF *returner* (F *retourner*)]

retuse (ritūs´) *a.* (*esp. Bot.*) having a round end with a depression in the centre. [L *retūsus*, p.p. of *retundere* (RE-, *tundere*, to beat)]

re- (+ u- words) reunify *v.t.* (*3rd pers. sing. pres.* **reunifies,** *pres.p.* **reunifying,** *past, p.p.* **reunified**) to join together (territories which have been divided). **reunification** *n.* **reunite** *v.t.* 1 to join again after separation. 2 to reconcile after variance. ~*v.i.* to become united again. **reupholster** *v.t.* to upholster again. **reupholstery** *n.* **reuse**[1] (rēūz´) *v.t.* to use again. **reusable** *a.* **reusability, reusableness** *n.* **reusably** *adv.* **reuse**[2] (rēūs´) *n.* the act of using again. **reutilize, reutilise** *v.t.* to utilize again or in a different way. **reutilization** *n.*

reunion (rēū´nyən) *n.* 1 the act of reuniting. 2 the state of being reunited. 3 a meeting or social gathering, esp. of friends, associates or partisans. [F *réunion* (UNION)]

re- (+ v- words) revaccinate *v.t.* to vaccinate again. **revaccination** *n.* **revalorization, revalorisation** *n.* restoration of the value of currency. **revalue** *v.t.* (*pres.p.* **revaluing,** *past, p.p.* **revalued**) 1 to adjust the exchange rate of (a currency) usu. upwards, as distinct from *devalue*. 2 to reappraise. **revaluation** *n.* **revamp** *v.t.* to renovate, to restore the appearance of. ~*n.* 1 something renovated or revamped. 2 the act or process of revamping. **revarnish** *v.t.* to varnish again. **revegetate** *v.t.* to produce new vegetation on. **revegetation** *n.* **reverify** *v.t.* (*3rd pers. sing. pres.* **reverifies,** *pres.p.* **reverifying,** *past, p.p.* **reverified**) to verify again. **reverification** *n.* **revictual** *v.t.* (*pres.p.* **revictualling,** (*N Am.*) **revictualing,** *past, p.p.* **revictualled,** (*N Am.*) **revictualed**) to victual again. **reviolate** *v.t.* to violate again. **reviolation** *n.* **revisit** *v.t.* (*pres.p.* **revisiting,** *past, p.p.* **revisited**) to visit again. **revitalize, revitalise** *v.t.* to vitalize again. **revitalization** *n.* **revivify** *v.t.* (*3rd pers. sing. pres.* **revivifies,** *pres.p.* **revivifying,** *past, p.p.* **revivified**) to restore to life, to reanimate, to reinvigorate, to put new life into, to revive. **revivification** *n.*

Rev. *abbr.* 1 (*Bible*) Revelation (of St John the Divine). 2 Reverend.

rev (rev) *n.* a revolution in an engine. ~*v.t., v.i.* (*pres.p.* **revving,** *past, p.p.* **revved**) to run (an engine) quickly by increasing the speed of revolution. **rev counter** *n.* a revolution counter. [abbr. of REVOLUTION]

rev. *abbr.* 1 revenue. 2 reverse(d). 3 review. 4 revise(d). 5 revision. 6 revolution. 7 revolving.

revalenta (revəlen´tə) *n.* lentil meal. [altered from *ervalenta*, from L *ervum lens*, a LENTIL]

revanche (rivahnch´) *n.* a policy directed towards restoring lost territory or possessions. **revanchism** *n.* **revanchist** *n., a.* [F]

Revd *abbr.* Reverend.

reveal[1] (rivēl´) *v.t.* 1 to allow to appear. 2 to disclose, to divulge (something secret, private or unknown), to betray. 3 to make known by supernatural or divine means. ~*n.* †revelation. **to be revealed** to come to attention. **to reveal oneself** to be revealed. **revealable** *a.* **revealed religion** *n.* a religion based on revelation, as distinct from *natural religion*. **revealer** *n.* **revealing** *a.* 1 significant. 2 (of a dress etc.) exposing more of the body than is usual. **revealingly** *adv.* **revealment** *n.* [OF *reveler*, L *revēlāre* (*vēlāre*, from *vēlum*, a VEIL)]

reveal[2] (rivēl´) *n.* the depth of a wall as revealed in the side of an aperture, doorway or window. [earlier *revale*, from OF *revaler* (RE-, *valer, avaler*, to VAIL[1])]

reveille (rival´i) *n.* a morning signal by drum or bugle to awaken soldiers or sailors. [F *réveillez*, awake, pl. imper. of *réveiller* (RE-, *veiller*, L *vigilāre*, to watch, see VIGIL)]

revel (rev´əl) *v.i.* (*pres.p.* **revelling,** (*N Am.*) **reveling,** *past, p.p.* **revelled,** (*N Am.*) **reveled**) 1 to make merry, to carouse, to be boisterously festive. 2 to take great enjoyment (in). ~*v.t.* to spend or waste in revelry. ~*n.* (*often pl.*) an act of revelling, a carousal, a merry-making. **reveller,** (*N Am.*) **reveler** *n.* **revel-rout** *n.* 1 tumultuous festivity. 2 a band of revellers. **revelry** (-ri) *n.* (*pl.* **revelries**). [OF *reveler*, L *revellāre*]

revelation (revəlā´shən) *n.* 1 the act of revealing, a disclosing of knowledge or information. 2 knowledge or information which is revealed, esp. by God to humans. 3 (**Revelation**) the Revelation of St John the Divine, the last book of the New Testament, the Apocalypse. 4 an astonishing disclosure. **revelational** *a.* **revelationist** *n.* 1 a person who believes in divine revelation. 2 the author of the Apocalypse. **Revelations** *n.* (*coll.*) the Revelation of St John the Divine. **revelative** (rev´ələ-), **revelatory** (rev´ələ-) *a.* [ME and OF *revelacion*, L *revēlātiōnem*, nom. *-tio*, from *revēlāre*, to REVEAL[1]]

reveller, revelry etc. REVEL.

revenant (rev´ənənt) *n.* a person who returns from the grave or from exile, esp. a ghost. [F, from *revenir*, L *revenīre* (*venīre*, to come)]

revendication (rivendikā´shən) *n.* (*Law*) a formal claim for the surrender of rights, esp. to territory. **revendicate** (-ven´-) *v.t.* [F]

revenge (rivenj´) *n.* 1 retaliation, retribution or spiteful return for an injury. 2 a means, mode or act of revenging. 3 the desire to inflict revenge, vindictiveness. 4 in a game, the chance to win following an earlier defeat. ~*v.t.* 1 to take satisfaction or retribution for, to retaliate. 2 to avenge or satisfy (oneself) with such retribution or retaliation. 3 to inflict injury on, in a malicious spirit. ~*v.i.* to take vengeance. **revengeful** *a.* **revengefully** *adv.* **revengefulness** *n.* **revengeless** *a.* **revengement** *n.* **revenger** *n.* **revengingly** *adv.* [OF *revenger*]

Usage note The usual constructions of *revenge* are *revenge oneself* (*on* or *upon*) and *be revenged* (*on* or *upon*). See also notes under AVENGE, VENGEANCE.

revenue (rev´ənū) *n.* 1 (*often pl.*) income, esp. of a considerable amount from many forms of property. 2 the annual income of a state, derived from taxation, customs, excise etc. 3 the department of the civil service collecting this. **Inland Revenue** INLAND. **revenue cutter** *n.* a boat employed to prevent smuggling. **revenue tax** *n.* a tax for raising revenue, as distinct from *protective tax*, designed to affect trade. [F, fem. p.p. of *revenir*, to return (L *revenīre*)]

reverb (rē´vœb, rivœb´) *n.* (*coll.*) 1 an electronic device which creates an artificial echo in recorded music. 2 artificial echo effects in recorded music. [REVERBERATION (under REVERBERATE)]

reverberate (rivœ'bərāt) *v.i.* **1** (of sound, light or heat) to be driven back or to be reflected, to resound, to re-echo. **2** (of an event or idea) to have a powerful, long-lasting effect. **3** to rebound, to recoil. *~v.t.* to send back, to re-echo, to reflect (sound, light or heat). **reverberant** *a.* **reverberantly** *adv.* **reverberating furnace** *n.* a reverberatory furnace. **reverberation** (-ā'shən) *n.* **reverberative** (-bərə-) *a.* **reverberator** *n.* **reverberatory** *a.* producing or acting by reverberation. **reverberatory furnace** *n.* a furnace or kiln in which metal or other material is exposed to the action of flame and heat which is thrown back from a vaulted roof. [L *reverberātus*, p.p. of *reverberāre* (*verberāre*, to beat, from *verber*, a scourge)]

revere (riviə') *v.t.* to regard with awe mingled with affection, to venerate. **reverence** (rev'ər-) *n.* **1** the act of revering, veneration. **2** a feeling of or the capacity for feeling reverence. **3** †an act or gesture of respect, an obeisance, a bow, a curtsy. **4** (**Reverence**) a title given to the clergy. *~v.t.* to regard or treat with reverence, to venerate. **saving your reverence** with all respect to you. **reverencer** *n.* **reverend** (rev'ə-) *a.* worthy or entitled to reverence or respect, esp. as a title of respect given to members of the clergy. *~n.* (*coll.*) a member of the clergy. **reverent** (rev'ər-) *a.* **1** feeling or expressing reverence. **2** submissive, humble. **reverential** (revəren'-) *a.* **reverentially** *adv.* **reverently** *adv.* [F *révérer*, L *reverērī* (*verērī*, to fear)]

Usage note (1) In referring to persons with the title 'Reverend', *the Reverend Dr Smith, the Reverend Bill Smith* and *the Reverend W. Smith* are the recommended styles: always include *the* and a name, initial or other title along with the surname. (2) The adjectives *reverend* and *reverent* should not be confused: *reverend* means worthy of reverence, and *reverent* feeling reverence. The uses of *reverent* also overlap with those of *reverential*, but *reverent* is stronger and requires sincere feeling.

reverie (rev'əri) *n.* **1** listless musing, a daydream, a loose or irregular train of thought. **2** †a wild or fantastic conceit, a vision, a delusion. **3** a dreamy musical composition. [F *rêverie*, from *rêver*, to dream, etym. uncertain, cp. RAVE[1]]

revers (riviə') *n.* (*pl.* **revers** (-viəz')) a part of a coat, esp. a lapel, turned back so as to show the lining. [F, as REVERSE]

reverse (rivœs') *v.t.* **1** to turn in the contrary direction, to turn the other way round, upside down, or inside out. **2** to invert, to transpose. **3** to cause to go backwards. **4** to cause to have a contrary motion or effect. **5** to revoke, to annul, to nullify. **6** †to recall, to bring back (to). *~v.i.* **1** to change to a contrary condition, direction etc. **2** to put a car into reverse gear. **3** in dancing, to begin to turn in the opposite direction. *~a.* **1** having an opposite direction, contrary. **2** turned backwards, inverted, reversed, upside down. *~n.* **1** the contrary, the opposite. **2** the opposite of the usual manner. **3** the back surface (of a coin etc.), as distinct from *obverse*. **4** a complete change of affairs for the worse, a check, a defeat. **5** reverse gear. **6** the verso of a page. **to reverse arms** to hold a rifle with the butt upwards. **to reverse the charges** to make a telephone call for which the recipient pays. **reversal** *n.* **reverse-charge** *a.* denoting a telephone call for which the recipient pays. **reversed** *a.* **reversedly** (-sid-) *adv.* **reverse engineering** *n.* the taking apart of a competitor's product in order to study it and reproduce it or improve on it. **reverse fault** *n.* (*Geol.*) an oblique fault with the upper rock strata displaced upwards in relation to the lower strata. **reverse gear** *n.* the gear which makes a vehicle go backwards. **reversely** *adv.* **reverse Polish notation** *n.* (*Comput.*) a notation which does not use brackets or punctuation and places operators after their arguments, also called *postfix notation*. **reverser** *n.* **reverse take-over** *n.* the take-over of a larger company by a smaller one. **reverse video** *n.* (*Comput.*) a technique for highlighting information on a VDU in which the normal colours for text and background are reversed. **reversible** *a.* **reversibility** (-bil'-) *n.* **reversibly** *adv.* **reversing** *n.*, *a.* **reversing light** *n.* a light on the rear of a motor vehicle which is lit when reverse gear is engaged. **reversion** (-shən) *n.* **1** return to a former condition, habit etc. **2** (*Biol.*) the tendency of an animal or a plant to revert to ancestral type or character. **3** the returning of an estate to the grantor or their heirs after a particular period is ended. **4** the right of succeeding to an estate after the death of the grantee etc. **5** a sum payable upon a person's death, esp. an annuity or life assurance. **6** the right or expectation of succeeding to an office etc., on relinquishment by the present holder. **reversional** *a.* **reversionally** *adv.* **reversionary** *a.* **reversioner** *n.* a person who holds the reversion to an estate etc. [OF *revers*, L *reversus*, p.p. of *revertere* (*vertere*, to turn)]

reversi (rovœ'si) *n.* **1** a game played by two people on a draughtboard with pieces differently coloured above and below, which may be reversed. **2** †a card game in which the player who takes fewest tricks wins. [F (see REVERSE)]

reverso (rivœ'sō) *n.* (*pl.* **reversos**) the left-hand page of an open book, usu. even-numbered; the verso.

revert (rivœt') *v.i.* **1** to go back, to fall back, to return (to a previous condition, habits, type etc., esp. to a wild state). **2** (*Law*) to come back by reversion to the possession of the former proprietor. **3** to recur, to turn the attention again (to). *~v.t.* to turn (esp. the eyes) back. **reverter** *a.* **revertible** *a.* [OF *revertir*, L *revertere*, REVERSE]

revet (rivet') *v.t.* (*pres.p.* **revetting**, *past, p.p.* **revetted**) to face (a wall, scarp, parapet etc.) with masonry. **revetment** *n.* **1** a facing of stones, concrete etc. to protect a wall or embankment. **2** a retaining wall. [F *revêtir*]

review (rivū') *n.* **1** a final examination, esp. by people in authority. **2** a repeated examination, a reconsideration, a second view. **3** a retrospective survey. **4** a critical account of a book etc. **5** a periodical publication containing essays and criticisms. **6** a display or a formal or official inspection of military or naval forces. *~v.t.* **1** to view again. **2** to look back on, to go over in memory, to revise. **3** to survey, to look over carefully and critically. **4** to write a critical review of. **5** to hold a review of, to inspect. *~v.i.* to write reviews. **reviewable** *a.* **review copy** *n.* a copy of a new book sent to a periodical for review. **reviewer** *n.*

Usage note The spellings of the nouns *review* (a second view, a critical account, etc.) and *revue* (an entertainment) should not be confused.

revile (rivīl') *v.t.* to abuse, to vilify. *~v.i.* to be abusive. **revilement** *n.* **reviler** *n.* **reviling** *a.* **revilingly** *adv.* [OF *reviler*]

revise (rivīz') *v.t.* **1** to look over, to re-examine for correction or emendation. **2** to correct, alter or amend. **3** to reread (course notes etc.) for an examination. *~v.i.* to reread course notes etc. for an examination. *~n.* **1** (*Print.*) a proof-sheet in which corrections made in rough proof have been embodied. **2** a revision. **3** a revised form or version. **revisable** *a.* **revisal** *n.* **revised** *a.* **Revised Standard Version** *n.* a version of the American Standard Version of the Bible, published in 1946–57. **Revised Version** *n.* a revision of the Authorized Version of the Bible, published in 1870–84. **reviser** *n.* **revising barrister** *n.* a barrister formerly appointed to hold an annual court for the revision of the register of Parliamentary voters. **revision** (-vizh'ən) *n.* **1** the act or process of revising. **2** the process of rereading course notes etc. before an exam. **3** a revised version. **revisional, revisionary** *a.* **revisionist** *n.* **1** a person in favour of revision. **2** a person who believes in the broadening and evolution of the theories of Marxism. **3** (*derog.*) a person who departs from the principles of orthodox Communism. **4** a reviser of the Bible. **revisionism** *n.* **revisory** *a.* [F *reviser* (*viser*, L *vidēre*, to see, p.p. *vīsus*)]

revive (rivīv´) *v.i.* **1** to return to life, consciousness, vigour, popularity, activity, vogue, the stage etc. **2** to gain new life or vigour. **3** to recover from a state of obscurity, neglect, or depression. **4** to come back to the mind again, to reawaken. *~v.t.* **1** to bring back to life, consciousness, vigour, etc. **2** to reanimate. **3** to resuscitate, to renew, to renovate, to reawaken, to re-establish. **4** (*Chem.*) to restore or reduce to its natural or metallic state. **revivable** *a.* **revivably** *adv.* **revival** *n.* **1** the act of reviving. **2** the state of being revived. **3** the return or recovery of life, consciousness, vigour, activity or popularity; a renaissance. **4** a new production of a dramatic work previously neglected or forgotten. **5** a religious awakening, esp. a movement for the renewal of religious fervour by means of special services etc. **revivalism** *n.* **revivalist** *n.* **revivalistic** (-lis´-) *a.* **reviver** *n.* **1** someone who or something which revives. **2** a preparation for renovating leather, cloth etc. **3** (*sl.*) a drink, a stimulant. **revivingly** *adv.* [F *revivre*, L *revīvere* (*vīvere*, to live)]

reviviscent (revivis´ənt) *a.* recovering life and strength, reviving. **reviviscence, reviviscency** *n.* [L *revīviscens -ntem*, pres.p. of *revīviscere*]

revoke (rivōk´) *v.t.* to annul, to cancel (a law etc.). *~v.i.* in cards, to fail to follow suit when this would have been possible. *~n.* the act of revoking at cards. **revocable** (rev´əkəbəl) *a.* **revocableness** *n.* **revocably** *adv.* **revocation** (revəkā´shən) *n.* **revocatory** (rev´əkətəri) *a.* **revokable** *a.* **revokability, revokableness** *n.* **revokably** *adv.* **revoker** *n.* [OF *revoquer*, L *revocāre* (RE-, *vocāre*, to call)]

revolt (rivōlt´) *v.i.* **1** to renounce allegiance, to rise in rebellion or insurrection. **2** to be repelled (by), to feel disgust (at), to feel repugnance (at). *~v.t.* to repel, to nauseate, to disgust. *~n.* **1** a renunciation of allegiance and subjection. **2** a rebellion, an uprising, an insurrection. **3** revulsion. **4** a mood of defiance. **5** a change of sides. **revolted** *a.* having revolted. **revolter** *n.* **revolting** *a.* horrible, digusting, repulsive. **revoltingly** *adv.* [F *révolte*, from *révolter*, MIt. *revoltare* (It. *rivoltare*) (RE-, L *volutāre*, freq. of *volvere*, to roll, p.p. *volūtus*)]

revolute[1] (rev´əloot) *a.* (of a leaf) rolled backwards from the edge. [L *revolūtus*, p.p. of *revolvere* (RE-, *volvere*, to roll)]

revolute[2] REVOLUTION.

revolution (revəloo´shən) *n.* **1** a fundamental change in government, esp. by the forcible overthrow of the existing system and substitution of a new ruler or political system. **2** a radical change or reversal of circumstances, conditions, relations or things. **3** the act or state of revolving. **4** the circular motion of a body on its axis, rotation. **5** the motion of a body round a centre. **6** a complete rotation or movement round a centre. **7** the period of this. **8** a round or cycle or regular recurrence or succession. **revolute**[2] (rev´əloot) *v.i.* **revolutionary** *a.* **1** bringing about great changes. **2** of, relating to or tending to produce a revolution in government. **3** of or relating to a particular revolution. *~n.* **1** an advocate of revolution. **2** a person who takes an active part in a revolution. **revolution counter** *n.* an instrument which shows the speed of the engine in a vehicle. **revolutionism** *n.* **revolutionist** *n.* **revolutionize, revolutionise** *v.t.* **1** to cause radical change in. **2** to bring about a revolution in. [ME and OF *revolucion* (F *révolution*), L *revolūtiōnem*, nom. *-tio*, from *revolvere*, to REVOLVE]

revolve (rivolv´) *v.i.* **1** to turn round. **2** to move round a centre, to rotate. **3** to move in a circle, orbit or cycle. *~v.t.* **1** to cause to revolve or rotate. **2** to turn over and over in the mind, to meditate on, to ponder over. **to revolve around** to have (something) as an important central feature or focus (*His life revolves around his family*). **revolvency** *n.* **revolver** *n.* **1** a pistol having a revolving breech cylinder by which it can be fired several times without reloading. **2** something which revolves. **revolving** *a.* **revolving credit** *n.* credit which allows repeated borrowing of a fixed sum as long as that sum is never exceeded. **revolving door** *n.* a door, usu. with four leaves at right angles, which rotates about a vertical axis. [L *revolvere* (*volvere*, to roll)]

revue (rivū´) *n.* a light entertainment with songs, dances etc., representing topical characters, events, fashions etc. [F]

Usage note See note under REVIEW.

---

revulsion (rivŭl´shən) *n.* **1** a strong feeling of disgust. **2** a sudden or violent change or reaction, esp. of feeling. **3** (*Med.*) reduction of a disease in one part of the body by treatment of another part, e.g. by counterirritation. **revulsive** *a.* (*Med.*) causing or tending to cause revulsion. *~n.* an application causing revulsion, a counter-irritant. **revulsively** *adv.* [F *révulsion*, L *revulsiōnem*, nom. *-sio*, from *revellere* (*vellere*, to pull, p.p. *vulsus*)]

re- (+ w–z words) rewake *v.t., v.i.* (*pres.p.* **rewaking,** *past, p.p.* **rewaked, rewoke**) to wake again. **rewaken** *v.t.* **rewarm** *v.t.* to warm again. **rewash** *v.t.* **reweigh** *v.t.* **reweld** *v.t.* **rewiden** *v.t., v.i.* **rewind**[1] *v.t.* (*past, p.p.* **rewound**) to wind (a film or tape) back to the beginning. **rewind**[2] (rē´-) *n.* **1** a mechanism for rewinding a film or tape. **2** the act of rewinding. **3** something rewound. **rewinder** *n.* **rewire** *v.t.* to install new electrical wiring in (a house etc.). **rewoke** REWAKE (under RE- (+ W–Z WORDS)). **reword** *v.t.* **1** to put into different words. **2** to repeat, to re-echo. **3** to put into words again. **rework** *v.t.* **1** to treat or use again. **2** to revise. **3** to reprocess for renewed use. **reworking** *n.* **rewound** REWIND[1] (under RE- (+ W–Z WORDS)). **rewrap** *v.t.* (*pres.p.* **rewrapping,** *past, p.p.* **rewrapped**) to wrap again or in a different way. **rewrite**[1] *v.t.* (*pres.p.* **rewriting,** *past* **rewrote,** *p.p.* **rewritten**) **1** to write over again. **2** to revise. **rewrite**[2] (rē´-) *n.* **1** the act of rewriting. **2** something rewritten. **rewritten, rewrote** REWRITE[1] (under RE- (+ W–Z WORDS)). **rezone** *v.t.* **1** to distribute in different zones. **2** to assign to a different zone.

reward (riwawd´) *n.* **1** something which is given in return usu. for good done or received. **2** a recompense, a requital, retribution. **3** a sum of money offered for the detection of a criminal or for the restoration of anything lost. *~v.t.* to repay, to requite, to recompense (a service or offence, a doer or offender). **rewardable** *a.* **rewardableness** *n.* **reward claim** *n.* (*Hist., Austral.*) land awarded to a miner who discovers gold in a new area. **rewarder** *n.* **rewarding** *a.* **1** personally satisfying. **2** profitable. **rewardingly** *adv.* **rewardless** *a.* [A-F and ONF *rewarder*, OF *reguarder*, to REGARD]

rewarewa (rā´wərāwə) *n.* a tall tree, *Knightia excelsa*, of New Zealand, having red flowers. [Maori]

Rex (reks) *n.* a reigning king (the official title used by a king, esp. on documents, coins etc.). [L]

Rexine® *n.* a kind of artificial leather used for bookbinding etc. [etym. unknown]

Reynard (ren´əd, -ahd, rā´-) *n.* a proper name for a fox (esp. in stories). [OF *Renart*, name of the fox in the medieval *Roman de Renart*, from Gmc. (cp. OHG *Reginhart*)]

Reynolds number (ren´əldz) *n.* (*Physics*) a number which indicates the degree of turbulence of flow of a fluid in a system. [Osborne *Reynolds*, Eng. physicist, 1842–1912]

RF, r.f. *abbr.* radio frequency.
Rf *chem. symbol* rutherfordium.
RFA *abbr.* Royal Fleet Auxiliary.
RFC *abbr.* **1** (*Hist.*) Royal Flying Corps. **2** Rugby Football Club.
RFU *abbr.* Rugby Football Union.
RGN *abbr.* Registered General Nurse.
RGS *abbr.* Royal Geographical Society.
RH *abbr.* **1** (Republic of) Haiti (IVR). **2** right hand.
Rh[1] *chem. symbol* rhodium.
Rh[2] *abbr.* (*Med.*) rhesus factor.
r.h. *abbr.* right hand.
RHA *abbr.* Royal Horse Artillery.
rhabdomancy (rab´dəmansi) *n.* divination by a rod, esp. the discovery of minerals, underground streams etc. with a divining rod. **rhabdomancer** *n.* [Gr. *rhabdos*, a rod, *manteia*, divination]
rhachis RACHIS.
Rhadamanthine (radəman´thīn) *a.* rigorously just and severe. [L *Rhadamanthus*, judge in Hades]
Rhaetian (rē´shən), **Rhetian** *n.* Rhaeto-Romance. *~a.* of or relating to the Rhaeto-Romance dialects. **Rhaetic, Rhetic** *a.* (*Geol.*) of or relating to the Rhaetian Alps (applied to the group of strata between the Lias and Trias developed there and also in England). *~n.* the Rhaetic formation or strata. **Rhaeto-Romance** (-rōmans´), **Rhaeto-Romanic** (rētōrōman´ik) *a.* of or relating to the Romance peoples of SE Switzerland and the Tyrol or their dialects, esp. Romans and Ladin. *~n.* any of the Rhaeto-Romance dialects.
rhamphoid (ram´foid) *a.* beak-shaped. **rhamphotheca** (-thē´kə) *n.* (*pl.* **rhamphothecas**) the horny sheath of a bird's beak. [Gr. *rhamphos*, a curved beak, *thēkē*, a box, case]
rhapontic (rapon´tik) *n.* a species of rhubarb, *Rheum rhaponticum*. [mod. L *rhaponticum* (*Rha*, see RHUBARB, PONTIC)]
rhapsody (rap´sədi) *n.* (*pl.* **rhapsodies**) **1** a high-flown, enthusiastic composition or utterance. **2** (*Mus.*) an irregular and emotional composition, esp. of the nature of an improvisation. **3** in ancient Greece, an epic poem or a portion of one, for recitation at one time by a rhapsode. **rhapsode** (-sōd) *n.* an ancient Greek reciter of epic poems, esp. one of a professional school who recited the Homeric poems. **rhapsodic** (-sod´-), **rhapsodical** *a.* **1** of or relating to rhapsody. **2** enthusiastic, high-flown, extravagant. **rhapsodically** *adv.* **rhapsodist** *n.* **1** any professional reciter or improviser of verses. **2** a person who writes or speaks rhapsodically. **3** a rhapsode. **rhapsodize, rhapsodise** *v.i.* to recite or write rhapsodies. *~v.t.* to say or write with emotion or enthusiasm. [Gr. *rhapsōdos* (*rhaptein*, to sew, ODE)]
rhatany (rat´əni), **ratany** *n.* (*pl.* **rhatanies, ratanies**) a Peruvian shrub, *Krameria triandra*, or its root, from which an extract is obtained for use in medicine and for adulterating port wine. [Port. *ratanhia* or Sp. *ratania*, Quechua *rataña*]
rhea[1] (rē´ə) *n.* any flightless bird of the family Rheidae of S America, smaller than ostriches and with three toes. [Gr., daughter of Uranas and Gaea, and wife of Kronos]
rhea[2] (rē´ə) *n.* the ramie plant. [Assamese]
rhebok (rē´bok), **reebok** *n.* a small antelope of southern Africa, *Pelea capreolus*, having a long neck and short, straight horns.
rhematic (rēmat´ik) *a.* of or relating to the formation of words, esp. verbs. **rhematics** *n.* the science of propositions. [Gr. *rhēmatikos*, from *rhēma -atos*, a word]
Rhemish (rē´mish) *a.* of or relating to Rheims, NE France (applied esp. to an English translation of the New Testament by Roman Catholic students in 1582).
Rhenish (ren´ish) *a.* of or relating to the Rhine or the Rhineland. *~n.* Rhine wine, hock.
rhenium (rē´niəm) *n.* a metallic element, at. no. 75, chem. symbol Re, occurring in certain platinum and molybdenum ores. [L *Rhenus*, the Rhine]
rheo- (rē´ō) *comb. form* of or relating to a current or flow. [Gr. *rheos*, a stream, a current, rel. to *rheein*, to flow]
rheology (rēol´əji) *n.* the science dealing with the flow and deformation of matter. **rheologic** (-loj´-), **rheological** *a.* **rheologist** *n.*
rheostat (rē´əstat) *n.* a variable resistance for adjusting and regulating an electric current. **rheostatic** (-stat´-) *a.*
rheotropism (riot´rəpizm) *n.* the tendency in growing plant organs exposed to running water to dispose their longer axes either in the direction of or against the current.
rhesus (rē´səs), **rhesus monkey** *n.* a macaque, *Macaca mulatta*, held sacred in some parts of India. **rhesus baby** *n.* (*pl.* **rhesus babies**) a baby born with a blood disorder because its own rhesus-positive blood is incompatible with its mother's rhesus-negative blood. **rhesus factor** *n.* an antigen substance occurring in the red blood corpuscles of most human beings and many mammals (e.g. the rhesus monkey). **rhesus negative** *a.* not having the rhesus factor. **rhesus positive** *a.* having the rhesus factor. [L, from Gr. *Rhēsos*, a king of Thrace]
rhetor (rē´tə) *n.* **1** in ancient Greece, a teacher or professor of rhetoric. **2** a professional orator, a mere orator. [ME, via late L *rethor* and L *rhetor*, from Gr. *rhētōr*]
rhetoric (ret´ərik) *n.* **1** the art of effective speaking or writing, the rules of eloquence. **2** the power of persuading by looks or acts. **3** the use of language for effect or display, esp. affected or exaggerated oratory or declamation. **4** a treatise on rhetoric. **rhetorical** (ritor´-) *a.* **1** designed for effect or display, florid, showy, affected, declamatory. **2** of, relating to or of the nature of rhetoric. **rhetorically** *adv.* **rhetorical question** *n.* a question asked merely for the sake of emphasis and requiring no answer. **rhetorician** (retərish´ən) *n.* **1** a skilled orator. **2** a teacher of rhetoric. **3** a flamboyant or affected speaker. [OF *rethorique* (F *rhétorique*), L *rhētorica*, Gr. *rhētorikē technē*, rhetorical art, *rhētōr*, a public speaker, rel. to *eirein*, to speak. perf. *eirēka*]
rheum (room) *n.* **1** the thin serous fluid secreted by the mucous glands as tears, saliva, or mucus. **2** mucous discharge, catarrh. **3** (*poet.*) tears. **4** (*pl.*) rheumatic pains. **rheumy** *a.* [OF *reume*, L *rheuma*, Gr. *rheuma -atos*, stream, from *rheu-*, root of *rheein*, to flow; L *rheumaticus*, Gr. *rheumatikos*]
rheumatic (roomat´ik) *a.* of, relating to, suffering from or subject to rheumatism. *~n.* a person who suffers from rheumatism. **rheumatically** *adv.* **rheumatic fever** *n.* (*Med.*) a disease characterized by fever, acute pain in the joints and potential inflammation of the heart and pericardium. **rheumaticky** *a.* **rheumatics** *n.* (*coll.*) rheumatism. **rheumatism** (roo´mətizm) *n.* an inflammatory disease which affects the muscles and joints of the human body, causing swelling and pain. **rheumatismal** (roomətiz´-) *a.* rheumatic. **rheumatoid** (roo´mə-) *a.* resembling rheumatism. **rheumatoid arthritis** *n.* (*Med.*) a chronic disease which causes inflammation and pain in the joints. [ME, via OF *reumatique* or L *rheumaticus*, from Gr. *rheumatikos* (as RHEUM)]
rheumatology (roomətol´əji) *n.* the study of rheumatism. **rheumatological** (-loj´-) *a.* **rheumatologist** *n.*
RHG *abbr.* Royal Horse Guards.
rhin- RHINO-.
rhinal (rī´nəl) *a.* (*Anat.*) of or relating to the nose or nostrils. [RHINO-]
rhinencephalon (rīnensef´əlon, -kef´-) *n.* (*pl.* **rhinencephalons, rhinencephala** (-lə)) (*Anat.*) the olfactory lobe of the brain. **rhinencephalic** (-sifal´-, -kefal´-) *a.* **rhinencephalous** *a.*
rhinestone (rīn´stōn) *n.* **1** a colourless artificial gem cut

to look like a diamond. **2** a kind of rock crystal. [River *Rhine*]

Rhine wine (rīn) *n.* a wine made from grapes grown in the neighbourhood of the River Rhine.

rhinitis (rīnī´tis) *n.* (*Med.*) inflammation of the mucous membrane of the nose. [RHINO-]

rhino¹ (rī´nō) *n.* (*pl.* **rhinos, rhino**) a rhinoceros.

rhino² (rī´nō) *n.* (*sl.*) money. [etym. uncertain]

rhino- (rī´nō), **rhin-** *comb. form* (*Anat.*) of or relating to the nose or nostrils. [Gr. *rhis rhinos*, the nose]

rhinobatid (rīnob´ətid) *n.* any bottom-dwelling fish of the family Rhinobatidae. [Gr. *batos*, a ray]

rhinoceros (rīnos´ərəs) *n.* (*pl.* **rhinoceros, rhinoceroses**) a large grey-coloured quadruped of the family Rhinocerotidae, now found only in Africa and S Asia, with one or two horns on the nose. **rhinocerical** (rīnōser´i-) *a.* **rhinoceros beetle** *n.* a large horned beetle of the subfamily Dynastinae. **rhinoceros bird** *n.* the ox-pecker. **rhinoceros horn** *n.* the keratinized fibres, forming rhinoceros's horns, supposed to have aphrodisiac or reinvigorating qualities. **rhinocerotic** (-rot´-) *a.* [late L, from Gr. *rhīnokerōs* (RHINO-, *kerōs, keras*, horn)]

rhinolith (rī´nəlith) *n.* a nasal calculus. [RHINO-, -LITH]

rhinology (rīnol´əji) *n.* the branch of medical science dealing with the nose and nasal diseases. **rhinological** (-loj´-) *a.* **rhinologist** *n.*

rhinopharyngeal (rīnōfərin´jiəl) *a.* of or relating to the nose and pharynx. **rhinopharyngitis** (-farinjī´tis) *n.* (*Med.*) inflammation of the nose and pharynx.

rhinoplasty (rī´nōplasti) *n.* (*Med.*) plastic surgery of the nose. **rhinoplastic** (-plas´-) *a.*

rhinorrhoea (rīnərē´ə), (*N Am.*) **rhinorrhea** *n.* (*Med.*) discharge of blood from the nose.

rhinoscleroma (rīnōsklərō´mə) *n.* (*Med.*) a disease affecting the nose, lips etc. with a tuberculous growth.

rhinoscope (rī´nəskōp) *n.* (*Med.*) an instrument for examining the nasal passages. **rhinoscopic** (-skop´-) *a.* **rhinoscopy** (-nos´kəpi) *n.*

rhiz- RHIZO-.

rhizanthous (rīzan´thəs) *a.* (*Bot.*) flowering or seeming to flower from the roots. [RHIZO-, Gr. *anthos*, flower]

rhizic (rī´zik) *a.* of or relating to the root of an equation.

rhizo- (rī´zō), **rhiz-** *comb. form* having roots or rootlike processes. [Gr. *rhiza*, a root]

rhizobium (rīzō´biəm) *n.* a soil bacterium of the genus *Rhizobium*, occurring in the root nodules of leguminous plants. [mod. L, from RHIZO-, Gr. *bios*, life, -IUM]

rhizocarp (rī´zōkahp) *n.* (*Bot.*) a plant having a perennial root but a flower which withers annually. **rhizocarpean** (-kah´-) *a.* **rhizocarpic, rhizocarpous** *a.* [Gr. *karpos*, fruit]

rhizocephalan (rīzōsef´ələn) *n.* any member of the Rhizocephala, a suborder of parasitic crustaceans related to the barnacles. **rhizocephalous** *a.* [Gr. *kephalē*, the head]

rhizogenic (rīzōjen´ik) *a.* root-producing.

rhizoid (rī´zoid) *a.* (*Bot.*) rootlike. ~*n.* a filament or hairlike organ in mosses etc.

rhizoma (rīzō´mə) *n.* a rhizome.

rhizome (rī´zōm) *n.* (*Bot.*) a prostrate, thickened, rootlike stem, sending roots downwards and producing aerial shoots etc. annually. **rhizomatous** (-zom´-) *a.* [Gr. *rhizōma*, from *rhizoun*, to cause to take root, from *rhiza*, a root]

rhizomorph (rī´zōmawf) *n.* (*Bot.*) a rootlike mycelial growth by which some fungi attach themselves to higher plants. **rhizomorphous** (-maw´-) *a.*

rhizophagous (rīzof´əgəs) *a.* (*Zool.*) feeding on roots. **rhizophagan** (-gən) *n., a.* [Gr. *phagein*, to eat]

rhizophore (rī´zəfaw) *n.* (*Bot.*) a rootlike structure bearing the roots in species of *Selaginella*. **rhizophorous** (-zof´ər-) *a.* root-bearing. [-PHORE]

rhizopod (rī´zōpod) *n.* an animalcule of the class Rhizopoda, comprising those with pseudopodia for locomotion and the ingestion of food. ~*a.* of or relating to the rhizopods. [Gr. *pous podos*, a foot]

rho (rō) *n.* (*pl.* **rhos**) the 17th letter of the Greek alphabet (Ρ, ρ).

rhod- RHODO-.

rhodamine (rō´dəmēn) *n.* any of a group of fluorescent, usu. red dyestuffs.

rhodanic (rōdan´ik) *a.* producing a rose-red colour with ferric salts. [Gr. *rhodon*, rose, -IC]

Rhode Island Red (rōd) *n.* an American breed of domestic fowl with reddish-brown plumage.

Rhodes Scholarship (rōdz) *n.* a scholarship at Oxford founded under the will of Cecil Rhodes for students from the British Commonwealth and the US. **Rhodes Scholar** *n.* [Cecil *Rhodes*, 1853–1902]

Rhodian (rō´diən) *a.* of or relating to Rhodes, an island in the Aegean Sea. ~*n.* a native or inhabitant of Rhodes.

rhodium¹ (rō´diəm) *n.* a greyish-white metallic element, at. no. 45, chem. symbol Rh, belonging to the platinum group. **rhodic, rhodous** *a.* [Gr. *rhodon*, rose, -IUM]

rhodium² (rō´diəm) *n.* **1** a W Indian rosewood, *Amyris balsamifera*. **2** the hard, white, scented wood of either of two shrubby convolvuluses growing in the Canary Islands. **rhodian** *a.* [mod. L, neut. of *rhodius*, roselike, from Gr. *rhodon*, a rose]

rhodo- (rō´dō), **rhod-** *comb. form* **1** rose. **2** roselike. [Gr. *rhodon*, a rose]

rhodochrosite (rōdōkrō´sīt) *n.* (*Mineral.*) a mineral form of manganese carbonate formed of rose-red crystals.

rhododendron (rōdəden´drən) *n.* (*pl.* **rhododendrons**) any evergreen shrub of the genus *Rhododendron* akin to the azaleas, with brilliant flowers. [late L and Gr. (RHODO-, *dendron*, tree)]

rhodolite (rod´əlīt) *n.* a pale pink or purple garnet used as a gemstone.

rhodonite (rod´ənīt) *n.* a rose-pink silicate of manganese. [G *Rhodonit* (Gr. *rhodon*, a rose)]

rhodopsin (rōdop´sin) *n.* a purplish pigment found in the retina, visual purple. [Gr. *opsis*, sight]

rhodora (rōdaw´rə) *n.* a N American flowering shrub, *Rhodora canadensis*, belonging to the family Ericaceae, growing in boggy ground. [Gr. *rhodon*, a rose]

rhoeadine (rē´ədēn) *n.* an alkaloid obtained from the red poppy, *Papaver rhoeas*. [Gr. *rhoias -ados*, a kind of poppy]

rhomb (rom, romb) *n.* **1** a rhombus. **2** in crystallography, a rhombohedron. **rhombencephalon** (rombensef´əlon, -kef´-) *n.* (*Anat.*) the hindbrain. **rhombic** (rom´bik) *a.* [F *rhombe*, L *rhombus*, Gr. *rhombos*]

rhombi RHOMBUS.

rhombohedron (rombōhē´drən) *n.* (*pl.* **rhombohedra** (-drə), **rhombohedrons**) **1** a solid figure bounded by six equal rhombuses. **2** in crystallography, a crystal in the form of a rhombohedron. **rhombohedral** *a.*

rhomboid (rom´boid) *a.* having the shape or nearly the shape of a rhomboid. ~*n.* **1** a parallelogram, the adjoining sides of which are not equal and which contains no right angle. **2** a rhomboid muscle, a rhomboideus. **rhomboidal** (-boi´-) *a.*

rhomboideus (romboi´diəs) *n.* (*pl.* **rhomboidei** (-diī)) (*Anat.*) a muscle which connects the shoulder blade to the vertebrae. [mod. L, a rhomboid]

rhombus (rom´bəs) *n.* (*pl.* **rhombuses, rhombi** (-bī)) (*Geol.*) an oblique parallelogram with equal sides.

rhotacism (rō´təsizm) *n.* **1** exaggerated or erroneous pronunciation of the letter *r*, burring. **2** the change of *s* into *r*, as in Indo-European languages. **rhotacize, rhotacise** *v.t., v.i.* [Gr. *rhōtakizein*, to rhotacize, from *rhō*, the letter *r*, -ISM]

rhotic (rō´tik) *a.* of or relating to a dialect of English in which the letter *r* is pronounced before a consonant and at the end of a word.

RHS *abbr.* 1 Royal Historical Society. 2 Royal Horticultural Society. 3 Royal Humane Society.

rhubarb (roo´bahb) *n.* 1 any herbaceous plant of the genus *Rheum*, esp. *R. rhaponticum*, the fleshy and juicy leaf-stalks of which are cooked and eaten. 2 the root of several central Asian species of *Rheum*, from which purgative medicines are prepared. 3 the sound supposedly made by actors to simulate background conversation. 4 nonsense. 5 (*N Am., sl.*) a loud argument, an angry quarrel. **rhubarby** *a.* [OF *reubarbe* (F *rhubarbe*), med. L *rheubarbum, rheubarbarum*, altered from *rhabarbarum* (*rha barbarum*, foreign *Rha*, the Volga)]

rhumb (rŭm) *n.* 1 any one of the 32 principal points of the compass. 2 the angular distance between any successive pair of these. 3 (*Naut.*) a line cutting all the meridians at the same angle, such as a ship would follow sailing continuously on one course. **rhumbline** *n.* [from F *rumb* or Sp. *rhumbo*]

rhumba RUMBA.

rhyme (rīm), †**rime** *n.* 1 a correspondence of sound in the final accented syllable or group of syllables of a line of verse with that of another line, consisting of identity of the vowel sounds and of all the consonantal sounds but the first. 2 (*sing. or pl.*) verse characterized by rhyme. 3 poetry, verse. 4 a word rhyming with another. ~*v.i.* 1 to make a rhyme with another word or verse. 2 to be in accord, to harmonize (with). 3 to make rhymes, to versify. ~*v.t.* 1 to put into rhyme. 2 to treat (a word) as rhyming with another. 3 to pass or waste (time etc.) in rhyming. **without rhyme or reason** unreasonable, purposeless. **rhymeless** *a.* **rhymer** *n.* **rhyme royal** *n.* a seven-lined decasyllabic stanza rhyming *a b a b b c c* (perh. because employed by James I of Scotland in the *Kingis Quair*). **rhyme-scheme** *n.* the pattern of rhymes in a stanza, poem etc. **rhymester** (-stə), **rhymist** *n.* a poet, esp. of inferior talent; a poetaster. **rhyming slang** *n.* a form of slang originating among Cockneys in London in which a word is replaced by a rhyming phrase of which often only the first element is used, so that the rhyme itself disappears (e.g. *Barnet fair* becomes *Barnet* meaning *hair*). [OF *rime*, L *rhythmum*, nom. *-mus*, Gr. *rhuthmos*, RHYTHM, first form assim. to RHYTHM]

rhyncho- (ring´kō), **rhynch-** *comb. form* (*Zool.*) having a snout or snoutlike process. [Gr. *rhunchos*, a snout]

rhynchocephalian (ringkōsifā´liən) *a.* of or relating to the Rhyncocephalia, an almost extinct order of reptiles. ~*n.* a reptile of this order. [Gr. *kephalē*, the head]

rhynchophore (ring´kəfaw) *n.* a member of the Rhynchophora (now Curculionoidea), a division of tetramerous beetles containing the weevils. **rhynchophorous** (-kof´-) *a.*

rhyolite (rī´əlīt) *n.* (*Geol.*) an igneous rock with a structure showing the effect of lava-flow, composed of quartz and feldspar with other minerals. **rhyolitic** (-lit´-) *a.* [G *Rhyolit* (Gr. *rhuax*, a stream)]

rhyparographer (ripərog´rəfə) *n.* a painter of squalid subjects. **rhyparographic** (-graf´-) *a.* **rhyparography** *n.* [late L *rhyparographus*, Gr. *rhuparographos* (*rhuparos*, filthy)]

rhythm (ridh´m) *n.* 1 movement characterized by action and reaction or regular alternation of strong and weak impulse, stress, accent, motion, sound etc. 2 metrical movement determined by the regular recurrence or harmonious succession of groups of long and short or stressed and unstressed syllables called feet. 3 the flow of words in verse or prose characterized by such movement. 4 the regulated succession of musical notes according to duration. 5 a structural system based on this. 6 in art, correlation of parts in a harmonious whole. 7 any alternation of strong and weak states or movements. 8 a sense of rhythm. **rhythm and blues** *n.* a style of popular music integrating elements of folk, rock and roll, and blues. **rhythmic, rhythmical** *a.* **rhythmically** *adv.* **rhythmic gymnastics** *n.pl.* (*sometimes sing.*) a kind of gymnastics incorporating elements of dance and often using ribbons or hoops. **rhythmicist** (-sist) *n.* **rhythmist** *n.* **rhythmless** *a.* **rhythm method** *n.* a method of contraception requiring sexual abstinence during the period when ovulation is most likely to occur. **rhythm section** *n.* the section of instruments (usu. piano, double bass and drums) in a band whose main task is to provide the rhythm. [F *rithme* (now *rhythme*), L *rhythmus*, Gr. *rhuthmos*, from *rhu-*, root of *rheein*, to flow]

RI[1] *abbr.* 1 King and Emperor (L *rex et imperator*). 2 Queen and Emperor (L *regina et imperatrix*). 3 religious instruction. 4 (Republic of) Indonesia (IVR). 5 Rhode Island. 6 Royal Institution.

RI[2] *abbr.* 1 radio-telegraphy. 2 radio-telephony.

RIA *abbr.* Royal Irish Academy.

ria (rē´ə) *n.* (*pl.* **rias**) a long, narrow inlet into the sea coast. [Sp., river mouth]

rial (rē´ahl), **riyal** *n.* the standard unit of currency in Iran, Oman, Saudi Arabia, Qatar and Yemen. [Arab. *riyal*, from Sp. *real*, REAL[2]]

riant (rī´ənt) *a.* smiling, cheerful. **riancy** (-ənsi) *n.* **riante** *a.* (of a woman or girl) smiling, cheerful. [F, pres.p. of *rire*, L *ridēre*, to laugh]

rib[1] (rib) *n.* 1 (*Anat.*) any one of the bones extending outwards and forwards from the spine, and in human beings forming the walls of the thorax. 2 a ridge, strip, line etc., analogous in form or function to this. 3 a cut of meat including one or more ribs. 4 a curved timber extending from the keel for supporting the side of a ship etc. 5 a raised moulding or groin on a ceiling or vaulted roof. 6 a timber or iron beam helping to support a bridge. 7 a hinged rod forming part of an umbrella-frame. 8 a main vein in a leaf. 9 a spur of a mountain. 10 a raised row in a knitted or woven fabric. 11 a structural member in an aerofoil. 12 (*facet.*) a wife, in allusion to Eve. ~*v.t.* (*pres.p.* **ribbing**, *past, p.p.* **ribbed**) 1 to provide with ribs. 2 to mark with ribs or ridges. 3 to enclose with ribs. 4 to plough leaving spaces between furrows. ~*v.i.* to knit alternate plain and purl stitches to a raised form. **ribbed** *a.* **ribbing**[1] *n.* a system or arrangement of ribs, as in a vaulted roof etc. **ribcage** *n.* the structure of ribs and tissue which forms the enclosing wall of the chest. **ribgrass** *n.* ribwort. **ribless** *a.* **rib-tickler** *n.* something funny, a joke. **rib-vaulting** *n.* **ribwort** *n.* the narrow-leaved plantain, *Plantago lanceolata*. [OE *ribb* (cp. Dut. *rib*, G *Rippe*, Icel. *rif*, Norw. *riv*)]

rib[2] (rib) *v.t.* (*pres.p.* **ribbing**, *past, p.p.* **ribbed**) (*coll.*) to tease, make fun of. **ribbing**[2] *n.* [prob. from tickling of the ribs to cause laughter]

RIBA *abbr.* Royal Institute of British Architects.

ribald (rib´əld) *a.* (of language) coarse, licentious, lewd. ~*n.* a low or indecent person, esp. one using coarse language. **ribaldry** (-ri) *n.* [OF *ribaud* (F *ribaut*), a low ruffian, etym. uncertain]

riband RIBBON.

ribband (rib´ənd) *n.* a piece of timber used in launching a ship, as a stop, guide etc., or in the construction of pontoons, gun-platforms etc. [var. of RIBAND or from RIB[1], BAND[1]]

ribbing[1] RIB[1].

ribbing[2] RIB[2].

ribble-rabble (ribəlrab´əl) *n.* 1 a rabble, a mob. 2 meaningless talk, rigmarole.

ribbon (rib´ən), **riband** (rib´ənd) *n.* 1 a narrow woven strip or band of silk, satin etc., used for ornamenting dress etc. 2 such a strip or band worn as a distinctive mark of an order, college, club etc. 3 a narrow strip of anything. 4 an ink-impregnated cloth strip used in typewriters etc. 5 (*pl.*) driving-reins. 6 (*pl.*) torn shreds, ragged strips. **ribbon development** *n.* urban extension in the form of a single depth of houses along roads radiating from a town. **ribboned** *a.* **ribbonfish** *n.* (*pl.* **ribbonfish**) a long, narrow, flattish fish, esp. of the families Trachipteridae and Regalecidae. **ribbon-grass** *n.* an American grass, *Phalaris arundinacea* var. *picta*, grown for ornamental purposes in gardens. **ribbon-wood** *n.* a small evergreen tree, *Hoheria populnea*, of New Zealand. **ribbon worm** *n.* a nemertean. [F *riban* (now *ruban*), etym. uncertain]

riboflavin (rībōflā´vin), **riboflavine** (-vēn) *n.* a yellow vitamin of the B complex, found esp. in milk and liver, which promotes growth in children; vitamin B_2.

ribonuclease (rībōnū´klēās) *n.* any of several enzymes that catalyse the hydrolysis of ribonucleic acid.

ribonucleic acid (rībōnūklē´ik) *n.* any of a group of nucleic acids present in all living cells and playing an essential role in the synthesis of proteins.

ribose (rī´bōz) *n.* a pentose sugar occurring in ribonucleic acid and riboflavin. [from *arabinose*, (gum) arabic]

ribosome (rī´bəsōm) *n.* any of numerous minute granules containing ribonucleic acid and protein in a cell, which are the site for protein synthesis. **ribosomal** *a.*

Ribston pippin (rib´stən) *n.* a variety of apple first cultivated in England at Ribston Park, Yorkshire.

Ricardian (rikah´diən) *a.* 1 of or relating to the reign of Richard I, II, or III of England. 2 holding the opinion that Richard III has been misrepresented by historians. 3 of or relating to the economist David Ricardo, 1772–1823. ~*n.* 1 a supporter of Richard III. 2 a follower of David Ricardo.

rice (rīs) *n.* the white grain or seeds of *Oryza sativa*, an Asian aquatic grass extensively cultivated in warm climates for food. **ricebird** *n.* 1 the bobolink. 2 the Java sparrow. **rice-biscuit** *n.* a sweet biscuit made of flour mixed with rice. **rice bowl** *n.* an area where rice is produced in large quantities. **rice milk** *n.* milk boiled and thickened with rice. **rice-paper** *n.* 1 a thin edible paper made from rice straw, used in baking. 2 a paper made from the pith of the Taiwanese *Tetrapanax papyriferum* and used by Chinese artists for painting on. **ricer** *n.* a device with small holes through which potatoes etc. are pressed to make a coarse mash. [OF *riz*, It. *riso*, L *oryza*, Gr. *oruza*, prob. from OPers.]

ricercar (rēchəkah´), **ricercare** (-kah´rā) *n.* (*Mus.*) an elaborate, contrapuntal, instrumental composition in a slow tempo. [It., to seek out]

rich (rich) *a.* 1 wealthy, having a lot of valuable possessions, abounding (in resources, productions etc.). 2 abundantly supplied (in or with). 3 producing ample supplies. 4 fertile, abundant, well-filled. 5 valuable, precious, costly. 6 elaborate, splendid. 7 abounding in qualities pleasing to the senses, sweet, luscious, high-flavoured, containing a lot of fat, oil, sugar, spices etc. 8 containing a large proportion of fuel. 9 vivid, bright. 10 (of a sound) mellow, deep, full, musical. 11 comical, funny, full of humorous suggestion. **richen** *v.i.*, *v.t.* **riches** *n.pl.* valuable possessions and large amounts of money. **richly** *adv.* 1 in a rich manner. 2 abundantly, thoroughly. **richness** *n.* [OE *rīce* (cp. Dut. *rijk*, G *Reich*, Icel. *rīkr*), rel. to L *rex*, king, perh. ult. derived from it]

†**richesse** (rishes´) *n.* (*usu. in pl.*) abundant possessions, wealth, opulence, affluence. [F]

Richter scale (rik´tə) *n.* a logarithmic scale for registering the magnitude of earthquakes. [Charles *Richter*, 1900–85, US seismologist]

ricin (rī´sin) *n.* a toxic substance obtained from castor oil beans. [mod. L, *Ricinus communis*, the castor oil plant]

ricinoleic (risinōlē´ik) *a.* derived from castor oil. [L *ricinus*, the castor oil plant]

rick[1] (rik), **wrick** *n.* a stack of corn, hay etc., built in a regular shape and thatched. ~*v.t.* to make or pile into a rick. **rick-barton** (-bahtən) *n.* space on a farm reserved for ricks. **rickstand** *n.* a platform of short pillars and joists for keeping a rick above the ground. **rickyard** *n.* a rick-barton. [OE *hrēac* (cp. Dut. *rook*, Icel. *hraukr*)]

rick[2] (rik), **wrick** *v.t.* to wrench or sprain. ~*n.* a wrench or sprain. [ME, *wricke*, from MG, *wricken*, to move about, to sprain]

rickets (rik´its) *n.* (*Med.*) a disease of children resulting in the softening of the bones, esp. the spine; bow-legs, emaciation etc. owing to lack of mineral matter in the bones. **rickety** *a.* 1 shaky, tumbledown, fragile, unsafe. 2 feeble in the joints. 3 affected with or of the nature of rickets. **ricketiness** *n.* [etym. uncertain]

rickettsia (riket´siə) *n.* (*pl.* **rickettsiae** (-siē)) any of a group of microorganisms of the genus *Rickettsia* found in lice, ticks etc. which when transmitted to human beings cause serious diseases, e.g. typhus. **rickettsial** *a.* [after Howard T. *Ricketts*, 1871–1910, US pathologist]

rickey (rik´i) *n.* (*pl.* **rickeys**) a cocktail made from gin, lime juice and soda water. [prob. from surname *Rickey*]

rickrack RICRAC.

rickshaw (rik´shaw), **ricksha** (-shah) *n.* a light two-wheeled hooded carriage drawn by one or two people, or attached to a bicycle etc. [Jap. *jin-riki-sha* (*jin*, a man, *riki*, strength, *sha*, a vehicle)]

ricochet (rik´əshā) *n.* 1 a rebounding or skipping of a stone, projectile or bullet off a hard or flat surface. 2 the act of aiming so as to produce this, or a hit so made. ~*v.i.* (*pres.p.* **richocheting** (-shāing), **richochetting** (-sheting), *past, p.p.* **ricocheted** (-shād), **richochetted** (-shetid)) to skip or bound in this way. [F, etym. uncertain]

ricotta (rikot´ə) *n.* a soft white Italian cheese made from sheep's milk. [It., from L *recocta*, fem. p.p. of *recoquĕre*, to cook again]

ricrac (rik´rak), **rickrack** *n.* a zigzag braid for trimming garments. [reduplication of RACK[1]]

RICS *abbr.* Royal Institution of Chartered Surveyors.

rictus (rik´təs) *n.* (*pl.* **rictuses, rictus**) 1 (*Zool., Anat.*) the expanse of a person's or animal's open mouth, gape. 2 a grimace. 3 the opening of a two-lipped corolla. **rictal** *a.* [L, p.p. of *ringī*, to open the mouth wide]

rid[1] (rid) *v.t.* (*pres.p.* **ridding,** *past* **rid,** *p.p.* **ridded**) to free, to clear, to disencumber (of). **to be rid of** to get rid of. **to get rid of** to free oneself of or become free of. **riddance** *n.* clearance, deliverance, relief. **good riddance** GOOD. [Icel. *rythja*, conf. with REDD[1]]

†**rid**[2], **ridden** etc. RIDE.

-ridden (rid´ən) *comb. form* oppressed, dominated by or excessively concerned with, as *debt-ridden*.

riddle[1] (rid´əl) *n.* 1 a question or proposition put in ambiguous language to exercise ingenuity; a puzzle, conundrum or enigma. 2 any person, thing or fact of an ambiguous, mysterious or puzzling nature. ~*v.i.* to speak in riddles. ~*v.t.* 1 to solve, to explain (a riddle, problem etc.). 2 to be a riddle to. **riddler** *n.* **riddling** *a.* puzzling. **riddlingly** *adv.* [OE *rædels*, from *rædan*, to READ (cp. Dut. *raadsel*, G *Rätsel*)]

riddle[2] (rid´əl) *v.t.* 1 to pass through a riddle, to sift. 2 to perforate with holes, esp. with gunshot. 3 to assail with arguments, questions, facts etc. ~*n.* a coarse sieve for sifting gravel, cinders etc. or washing ore. **riddled with** full of. **riddlings** *n.pl.* screenings, siftings. [OE *hriddel*, *hridder*, from *hrīd-*, to shake (cp. G *Reiter*, also L *crībrum*)]

riddler, riddling etc. RIDDLE[1].

ride (rīd) *v.i.* (*pres.p.* **riding,** †**rid** (rid), *past* **rode** (rōd), *p.p.* **ridden** (rid´ən), †**rid**) 1 to sit and be carried along, as on a horse, cycle, public conveyance etc., esp. to go on horseback. 2 to practise horsemanship. 3 to float, to seem to float. 4 to lie at anchor. 5 to be supported by, to be on something, esp. in motion. 6 to project, to overlap. 7 to work up. 8 (of an animal) to serve for riding. ~*v.t.* 1 to sit on and be carried along by (a horse etc.). 2 (*N Am.*) to travel in (a vehicle). 3 to traverse on a horse, cycle etc. 4 to compete in (a race). 5 to cause to ride, to give a ride to. 6 to be carried by, to float over. 7 to yield to (a blow). 8 to oppress, to tyrannize, to domineer (over). 9 (*taboo sl.*) to copulate with. 10 (*N Am.*) to annoy, to pester. ~*n.* 1 the act of riding. 2 a journey on horseback or in a public conveyance. 3 a path for riding on, esp. through a wood. 4 a journey or an experience of a specified nature (*a rough ride*). 5 a fairground device or structure, such as a roller-coaster, which people ride for fun. 6 a district under an excise officer. 7 (*taboo sl.*) an act of copulation. 8 (*taboo sl.*) a sexual partner. **riding high** HIGH. **to let something ride** to let something continue without interference. **to ride again** to return to a former activity. **to ride and tie** (of two people having only one horse) to ride and walk alternately. **to ride bodkin** BODKIN. **to ride down** 1 to overtake by riding. 2 to trample on in riding. **to ride for a fall** to act recklessly. **to ride herd on** HERD. **to ride high** to be popular or successful. **to ride out** 1 to come safely through (a storm etc.). 2 to endure successfully. **to ride roughshod over** ROUGH. **to ride shotgun** 1 (*esp. N Am.*) to travel as a guard, sitting beside the driver of a vehicle. 2 (*esp. N Am.*) to travel in the passenger seat of a vehicle. 3 (*esp. N Am.*) to act as a protector. **to ride to hounds** to hunt. **to ride up** (of a skirt etc.) to work up out of the normal position. **to take for a ride** 1 (*coll.*) to play a trick on. 2 (*coll.*) to kidnap and murder. **rideable, ridable** *a.* **ride-off** *n.* in a riding competition, a qualifying round. **ride-on** *a.* (of a lawnmower) designed to be ridden on while operated. **rider** *n.* 1 a person who rides, esp. on a horse. 2 an additional clause to a document, act etc., an opinion, recommendation etc. added to a verdict. 3 a subsidiary problem, a corollary, an obvious supplement. 4 a part in a machine which surmounts or bridges other parts. 5 (*pl.*) an additional timber or plate for strengthening the framework of a ship. **riderless** *a.* **riding**[1] *n.* 1 the act or state of a person who rides. 2 a path for riding on, esp. through a wood. **riding crop** *n.* a whip with a short lash used by riders on horseback. **riding habit** *n.* a woman's costume for riding on horseback. **riding-hood** *n.* (*Hist.*) a hood worn by women when travelling. **riding lamp** *n.* a riding light. **riding light** *n.* a light shown by a ship at anchor. **riding-master** *n.* a man who teaches riding. **riding school** *n.* a place where riding is taught. [OE *rīdan* (cp. Dut. *rijdan*, G *reiten*, Icel. *rīthā*, Dan. *ride*)]

ridge (rij) *n.* 1 the long horizontal angle formed by the junction of two slopes. 2 an elevation of the earth's surface which is long in comparison with its breadth. 3 a long and narrow hilltop or mountain crest. 4 a continuous range of hills or mountains. 5 a strip of ground thrown up by a plough or other implement. 6 the spine of an animal. 7 an elongated area of high pressure on a weather map. 8 a raised hotbed for melons. ~*v.t.* 1 to mark or cover with ridges. 2 to break (a field etc.) into ridges. 3 to plant in ridges. 4 to gather into ridges. ~*v.i.* to gather into ridges. **ridge piece** *n.* a horizontal timber along the ridge of a roof. **ridge-plate** *n.* a ridge piece. **ridge-pole** *n.* 1 the horizontal pole of a long tent. 2 a ridge piece. **ridge tile** *n.* a tile used to make a roof ridge. **ridge tree** *n.* a ridge piece. **ridgeway** *n.* a road or way along a ridge. **ridgy** *a.* [OE *hrycg* (cp. Dut. *rug*, G *Rücken*, Icel. *hryggr*, Dan. *ryg*)]

ridicule (rid´ikūl) *n.* 1 derision, mockery. 2 words or actions intended to express contempt and excite laughter. ~*v.t.* to treat with ridicule, to laugh at, to make fun of, to expose to derision. **ridiculer** *n.* **ridiculous** (-dik´-) *a.* 1 meriting or exciting ridicule. 2 absurd, foolish. **ridiculously** *adv.* **ridiculousness** *n.* [L *ridiculus*, laughable, from *rīdēre*, to laugh]

riding[1] RIDE.

riding[2] (rī´ding) *n.* 1 each of the three former administrative divisions of Yorkshire (*East Riding, North Riding, West Riding*). 2 an electoral division of Canada. [orig. *thriding* THIRD, -ING[1]]

ridotto (ridot´ō) *n.* (*pl.* **ridottos**) (*Hist.*) an entertainment consisting of singing and dancing, esp. a masked ball. [It., from med. L *reductus*, orig. p.p. of *redūcere*, to REDUCE]

riel (rē´əl) *n.* the standard monetary unit of Cambodia.

riem (rēm) *n.* (*S Afr.*) a rawhide strap or thong. **riempie** (rim´pi) *n.* a long narrow riem used for lacing the backs of chairs etc. [Afrikaans, from Dut.]

Riesling (rēz´ling) *n.* a dry white wine, or the grape that produces it. [G]

rieve REAVE.

rifacimento (rēfahchimen´tō) *n.* (*pl.* **rifacimenti** (-tē)) a recast of a literary work etc. [It., from *rifare* (RE-, L *facere*, to make)]

rife (rīf) *a.* 1 occurring in great quantity, number etc., current, prevalent. 2 abundant. **rifely** *adv.* **rifeness** *n.* [late OE *rȳfe* (cp. Icel. *rīfa*, Dut. *rijf*)]

riff (rif) *n.* (*Mus.*) a phrase or figure played repeatedly in jazz or rock music, usu. as background to an instrument solo. ~*v.i.* to play riffs. [perh. altered from *refrain*]

riffle[1] (rif´əl) *v.t.* 1 to ruffle, to flick through rapidly (the pages of a book etc.). 2 to shuffle (playing cards) by halving the deck and flicking the corners together using both thumbs. ~*v.i.* to flick cursorily (through). ~*n.* the act of riffling.

riffle[2] (rif´əl) *n.* 1 in gold mining, a groove, channel, slab, block or cleat set in an inclined trough, sluice or cradle for arresting the particles of auriferous sand etc. 2 (*N Am.*) a timber or plank forming part of a fish ladder. 3 (*N Am.*) an obstruction in a stream. 4 (*N Am.*) a ripple on water. [etym. uncertain]

riffler (rif´lə) *n.* a file with curved ends for working in shallow depressions etc. [F *rifloir*, from *rifler*, to RIFLE]

riff-raff (rif´raf) *n.* worthless people, rabble. [formerly *riff and raff*, F *rif et raf*, prob. from Gmc. (cp. MDut. *rijf ende raf*)]

rifle (rī´fəl) *n.* 1 a firearm having the barrel spirally grooved so as to give a rotary motion to the projectile. 2 (*pl.*) troops armed with rifles. ~*v.t.* 1 to furnish (a firearm or the bore or barrel of a firearm) with spiral grooves in order to give a rotary motion to the projectile. 2 to plunder, to pillage, to strip. 3 to search and rob. 4 to snatch and carry off. ~*v.i.* 1 to search (through). 2 to shoot with a rifle. **rifle bird** *n.* any Australian bird of the genus *Ptilorrhis*, with velvety black plumage. **rifle-corps** *n.* **rifleman** *n.* (*pl.* **riflemen**). **rifler** *n.* a robber, a plunderer. **rifle range** *n.* an area for target practice using rifles. **rifleshot** *n.* 1 the distance a projectile from a rifle will carry. 2 a marksman with a rifle. **rifling** *n.* the spiral grooves in the bore of a firearm which cause the rotation of the projectile fired. [OF *rifler*, to scrape, to scratch, to strip, to plunder (cp. LG *rifeln*, G *riefeln*, Dan. *rifle*, Swed. *reffla*)]

rift (rift) *n.* 1 a cleft, a fissure. 2 a wide crack, rent or opening, made by splitting. 3 a break in cloud. 4 a serious quarrel causing a split between people. ~*v.t.* to cleave, to split. ~*v.i.* to break open. **riftless** *a.* **rift valley** *n.* a narrow valley formed by the subsidence of the earth's crust between two faults. **rifty** *a.* [from Scand. (cp. Dan. and Norw. *rift*, Icel. *ript*, from *rifa*, to RIVE)]

rig[1] (rig) *v.t.* (*pres.p.* **rigging**, *past, p.p.* **rigged**) 1 to furnish or fit (a ship) with spars, gear or tackle. 2 to dress, clothe or fit up or out. 3 to put together or fit up in a hasty or makeshift way. 4 to assemble the parts of (an aircraft). ~*n.* 1 the way in which the masts and sails of a ship are arranged. 2 equipment for a particular purpose. 3 an oil rig. 4 (*coll.*) the style or look of a person's clothes etc., an outfit, a turn-out. 5 (*esp. NAm., Austral.*) an articulated lorry. **in full rig** (*coll.*) smartly or formally dressed. **rigged** *a.* **rigger**[1] *n.* 1 a person who rigs ships etc. 2 a person who erects scaffolding. 3 an outrigger. 4 a person who works on an oil rig. **-rigger** *comb. form* a ship rigged in the specified manner. **rigging** *n.* 1 the system of tackle, ropes etc. supporting the masts and controlling the sails etc. of a ship. 2 the adjustment or alignment of the components of an aeroplane. **rigging loft** *n.* 1 a large room or gallery where rigging is fitted. 2 a space over the stage in a theatre from which the scenery is worked. **rig-out** *n.* (*coll.*) 1 dress, outfit. 2 appearance or look as regards clothing. [etym. uncertain, Norw. and Swed. *rigga*, may be from Eng.]

rig[2] (rig) *v.t.* (*pres.p.* **rigging**, *past*, *p.p.* **rigged**) 1 to manipulate fraudulently. 2 to hoax, to trick. ~*n.* 1 a swindling scheme, a dodge, a trick. 2 a prank, a frolic, a practical joke. **to rig the market** to manipulate the market so as to raise or lower prices for underhand purposes. **rigger**[2] *n.* [etym. uncertain]

rig[3] (rig) *n.* (*Sc., North.*) a ridge.

rigadoon (rigədoon´) *n.* 1 a lively dance performed by one couple. 2 the music in duple time for this dance. [F *rigaudon*, *rigodon*, etym. uncertain, perh. from *Rigaud*, name of a dancing master]

rigger[1] RIG[1].

rigger[2] RIG[2].

rigging RIG[1].

right (rīt) *a.* 1 required by or acting, being or done in accordance with truth and justice. 2 correct, true. 3 fit, suitable, most suitable, the preferable, the more convenient. 4 sound, sane, well. 5 properly done, placed etc., not mistaken, satisfactory. 6 real, genuine, veritable. 7 on or towards the side of the body which is to the south when the face is to the sunrise. 8 straight, direct. 9 formed by lines meeting perpendicularly. 10 (of a cone, pyramid or cylinder) not oblique, involving or based on a right angle or angles. 11 (*also* **Right**) politically conservative, right-wing. ~*adv.* 1 in accordance with truth and justice, justly, equitably, rightly. 2 exactly, correctly, properly. 3 satisfactorily, well. 4 to or towards the right hand. 5 straight. 6 (*coll.*) immediately. 7 all the way (to). 8 completely. 9 †very, quite, to the full. ~*n.* 1 what is right or just. 2 fair or equitable treatment. 3 the cause or party having justice on its side. 4 just claim or title, esp. a claim enforceable at law, justification. 5 something which one is entitled to. 6 (*coll.*) the right hand. 7 the right-hand side, part or surface of anything. 8 a thing, part etc. pertaining or corresponding to this. 9 (*often* **Right**) **a** the party sitting on the right of the president in a foreign legislature, usu. the more conservative party. **b** conservatives collectively. 10 in marching etc., the right foot. 11 the right wing of an army. ~*v.t.* 1 to set in or restore to an upright, straight, correct or proper position; to correct, make right, to rectify. 2 to do justice to, to vindicate, to rehabilitate. 3 to relieve from wrong or injustice. ~*v.i.* to resume a vertical position. ~*int.* (*coll.*) used to express approval, compliance or enthusiasm. **a right one** (*coll.*) a foolish person. **as of right** of right. **by right** properly, with justice. **by rights** by right. **in one's own right** because of one's own efforts. **in one's right mind** sane, lucid. **in the right** correct, in accordance with reason or justice. **in the right ballpark** BALLPARK (under BALL[1]). **of right** legally or morally entitled. **on the right tack** TACK[1]. **on the right track** TRACK. **right and left** 1 in all directions. 2 on every side. **right as a trivet** 1 (*coll.*) firm, stable. 2 (*coll.*) in first-rate health, circumstances, position etc. **right as nails** (*coll.*) perfectly right. **right as rain** (*coll.*) perfectly all right. **right away** at once, immediately. **right face** FACE. **right ho!** righto! **right, left and centre** in or from all directions. **right off** right away. **right oh!** righto! **right on!** (*sl.*) used to express support or approval. **right you are!** (*coll.*) used to express agreement or compliance. **she'll be right** (*Austral., coll.*) that is all right. **too right** (*coll.*) used to express agreement. **to put right** to correct, to rectify. **to put to rights** to put in order. **to see someone right** SEE[1]. **to set right** to put right. **to set to rights** to put to rights. **within one's rights** legally or morally entitled. **rightable** *a.* **right about** *n.* 1 the opposite direction, a reverse to face in the opposite direction. 2 a reversal of policy. 3 a retreat. **right about-face** *n.* a right about. **right about-turn** *n.* a right about. **right angle** *n.* an angle formed by two lines meeting perpendicularly. **at right angles** placing at or forming a right angle. **right-angled** *a.* **right arm** *n.* one's best or most efficient assistant, aid or support. **right ascension** *n.* (*Astron.*) the distance from the first point of Aries, measured along the celestial equator. **right-back** *n.* in football, hockey etc., a defensive player playing mainly on the right side of the pitch. **right bank** *n.* the bank of a river which is on the right facing downstream. **right bower** *n.* the knave of trumps. **righten** *v.t.* **righter** *n.* **right field** *n.* in baseball, the part of the outfield to the right of the batter when facing the pitcher. **right-footed** *a.* 1 using the right foot more readily and effectively than the left, in football etc. 2 done by the right foot. **rightful** *a.* 1 entitled, holding or held by legitimate claim. 2 just, equitable, fair. **rightfully** *adv.* **rightfulness** *n.* **right hand** *n.* 1 one's best assistant etc. 2 the hand on the right side, esp. as the better hand. 3 a position on or direction to this side. **right-hand** *a.* 1 situated on or towards the right hand. 2 done with the right hand. 3 (of a screw) right-handed. 4 denoting a person whose help is most useful or necessary. **right-handed** *a.* 1 (of a screw) turning to the right. 2 (of a tool) used by or fitted for use by the right hand. 3 done with the right hand. 4 using the right hand more readily and effectively than the left. **right-handedly** *adv.* **right-handedness** *n.* **right-hander** *n.* 1 a right-handed person. 2 a blow with the right hand. **right-hand man** *n.* (*pl.* **right-hand men**) one's best or most efficient assistant, aid or support. **Right Honourable** *n.* a title given to peers, peeresses, Privy Counsellors etc. **rightish** *a.* **rightist** *n.* a conservative, an adherent of the right in politics. ~*a.* conservative, right-wing. **rightism** *n.* **rightless** *a.* **rightlessness** *n.* **rightly** *adv.* 1 justly, fairly, equitably. 2 honestly, uprightly. 3 correctly, accurately, properly. **right-minded** *a.* having fair, honourable or sensible views. **right-mindedness** *n.* **rightmost** *a.* furthest right. **rightness** *n.* **righto** (-ō) *int.* used to express agreement or compliance. **right of abode** *n.* a person's right to be resident in a country. **right of common** *n.* the right to pasture cattle, dig turf, cut wood, fish etc. on the property of another. **right of primogeniture** *n.* the right, system or rule under which, in cases of intestacy, the eldest son succeeds to the real estate of his father. **right of search** *n.* the right claimed by a belligerent nation to board neutral vessels and examine their papers and cargo for contraband. **right of user** *n.* (*Law*) 1 a right to use something. 2 a presumptive right arising from the user. **right of visit, right of visitation** *n.* the right to hold a visitation of a ship. **right of way** *n.* 1 the right established by usage or dedication to the public to use a track, path, road etc. across a person's land. 2 a track, path or road subject to such a right. 3 the right of a vehicle or ship to take precedence in passing according to law or custom. **right-on** *a.* (*sl.*) 1 up to date, modern, fashionable. 2 having modern, liberal views. **Right Reverend** *n.* the title of a bishop. **Right Reverend Father in God** *n.* the formal title of a bishop or archbishop. **right side** *n.* the outer side of a fabric or garment. **on the right side of** 1 pleasing, in the favour of. **2** below (a specified age). **right side out** with the correct side facing outwards. **rights issue** *n.* an issue of new shares by a company to its existing shareholders on more favourable terms. **right sphere** *n.* the sphere of the heavens where there is a right angle between the equator and the horizon. **right-thinking** *a.* right-minded. **right-to-life** *a.* pro-life. **right turn** *n.* a turn to the right. **rightward** *a., adv.* **right whale** *n.* any whale of the family Balaenidae, yielding the best whalebone etc. **right wing** *n.* **1** the conservative section of a political party or grouping. **2** the right side of an army, football team etc. **right-wing** *a.* **1** having or relating to conservative political views. **2** of or on the right wing. **right-winger** *n.* **righty-ho** (rītihō´) *int.* righto! [OE *riht* (cp. Dut. *regt*, G *recht*, Icel. *rettr*), cogn. with L *rectus*, rel. to *reg-*, root of *regere*, to rule]

righteous (rī´chəs) *a.* **1** just, upright, morally good. **2** equitable, deserved, justifiable, fitting. **righteously** *adv.* **righteousness** *n.* [OE *rihtwīs* (RIGHT, WISE[1] or -WISE)]

rigid (rij´id) *a.* **1** stiff, not easily bent, not pliant, unyielding. **2** rigorous, strict, inflexible, harsh, stern. **rigid airship** *n.* an airship in which the envelope is attached to a framework of hoops and girders. **rigidify** (-jid´ifī) *v.i.* (*3rd pers. sing. pres.* **rigidifies,** *pres.p.* **rigidifying,** *past, p.p.* **rigidified**) to make or become rigid. **rigidity** (-jid´-), **rigidness** *n.* **rigidly** *adv.* [L *rigidus*]

rigmarole (rig´mərōl) *n.* **1** a long, complicated procedure. **2** a long unintelligible story. **3** loose disjointed talk. *~a.* incoherent. [prob. corr. of *Ragman rolls*, a complex oath to Edward I]

rigor[1] (rī´gaw, rig´ə) *n.* **1** (*Med.*) a feeling of chill, a shivering accompanied by stiffening, premonitory of fever etc. **2** a state of rigidity assumed by certain animals and commonly known as 'shamming dead'. **rigor mortis** (maw´tis) *n.* the stiffening of the body following death. [L, RIGOUR]

rigor[2] RIGOUR.

rigour (rig´ə), (*N Am.*) **rigor** *n.* **1** strictness, exactness in enforcing rules. **2** stiffness or inflexibility of opinion, doctrine, observance etc., austerity of life. **3** sternness, harshness. **4** inclemency of the weather etc., hardship, distress. **5** (*pl.*) harsh conditions. **rigorism** *n.* **rigorist** *a., n.* **rigorous** *a.* **1** strict, precise, severe, stern, inflexible. **2** logically accurate, precise, stringent. **3** inclement, harsh. **rigorously** *adv.* **rigorousness** *n.* [OF, from L *rigōrem*, nom. *-or*, from *rigēre*, to be stiff]

Rigsdag (rigz´dag) *n.* (*Hist.*) the Danish parliament. [Dan. *rige*, a kingdom, *dag*, a DAY]

Rig-Veda (rigvā´də) *n.* the oldest and most original of the Hindu Vedas. [Sansk. *ric*, praise, *veda*, knowledge]

Riksdag (riks´dag) *n.* the Swedish parliament. [Swed., cp. RIGSDAG]

rile (rīl) *v.t.* **1** (*coll.*) to make angry, to vex, to irritate. **2** (*N Am.*) to make turbulent or muddy. [var. of ROIL]

rilievo RELIEVO.

rill (ril) *n.* **1** a small stream, a rivulet. **2** a trench or furrow. **3** a rille. *~v.i.* to issue or flow in a small stream. **rillet** *n.* a little rill. [cp. LG and G *Rille*, Dut. *ril*]

rille (rill) *n.* (*Astron.*) a furrow, trench or narrow valley on Mars or the moon. [G (as RILL)]

RIM *abbr.* (Islamic Republic of) Mauritania (IVR).

rim (rim) *n.* **1** an outer edge, border or margin, esp. of a vessel or other circular object. **2** a ring or frame. **3** the peripheral part of the framework of a wheel, between the spokes or hub and the tyre. *~v.t.* (*pres.p.* **rimming,** *past, p.p.* **rimmed**) **1** to furnish with a rim. **2** to serve as rim to. **3** to edge, to border. **rim-brake** *n.* a brake acting on the rim, not the hub, of a wheel. **rim-fire** *a.* (of a cartridge) having the detonating fulminate in the rim and not the centre. **rimless** *a.* **rimmed** *a.* having a rim (*usu. in comb.*, as *horn-rimmed*). [OE *rima* (cp. Icel. *rime*, *rimi*, strip, ridge)]

rime[1] (rīm) *n.* **1** a deposit of ice caused by freezing fog or low temperatures. **2** (*poet.*) hoar frost. *~v.t.* to cover with rime. **rimy** *a.* (*comp.* **rimier,** *superl.* **rimiest**). [OE *hrīm* (cp. Dut. *rijm*, Icel. *hrīm*, OF *rime*)]

†**rime**[2] RHYME.

rimose (rī´mōs), **rimous** (-məs) *a.* (of the bark of trees) full of chinks or cracks. [L *rīmōsus*, from *rīma*, a chink]

rimu (rē´moo) *n.* **1** the red pine of New Zealand, *Dacrydium cupressinum*. **2** the light brown wood of the rimu. [Maori]

rimy RIME[1].

rind (rīnd) *n.* the outer coating of trees, fruits etc.; bark, peel, husk, skin. *~v.t.* to strip the bark from. **rinded** *a.* (*usu. in comb.*, as *coarse-rinded*). **rindless** *a.* **rindy** *a.* [OE, cp. G *Rinde*]

rinderpest (rin´dəpest) *n.* a malignant contagious disease attacking ruminants, esp. cattle. [G *Rinder*, pl. of *Rind*, an OX, a PEST]

ring[1] (ring) *n.* **1** a circlet. **2** a circlet of gold etc., worn usu. on a finger or in the ear as an ornament, token etc. **3** anything in the form of a circle. **4** a line, mark, moulding, space or band round, or the rim of, a circular or cylindrical object or sphere. **5** an annual ring. **6** a group or concourse of people, things etc. arranged in a circle. **7** a circular space, enclosure or arena for circus performances etc. **8** an enclosed space with seats round it, for boxing or wrestling. **9** a combination of people acting together, often illegally for commercial or political ends. **10** a circular course. **11** a gas ring. **12** (*Astron.*) **a** a thin band of particles round a planet. **b** a halo round the moon. **13** in archaeology, a circular prehistoric earthwork. **14** (*Chem.*) a closed chain of atoms. **15** (*Math.*) a closed set. *~v.t.* (*past, p.p.* **ringed**) **1** to put a ring round. **2** to encircle, to enclose, to hem in. **3** to fit with a ring. **4** to cut a ring of bark from (a tree). **5** to cut into rings. **6** to put a ring on or in. *~v.i.* to form a ring. **the ring 1** boxing. **2** bookmakers collectively. **to make/ run rings round** (*coll.*) to be much more successful or skilful than. **to throw one's hat into the ring** HAT. **ringbark** *v.t.* to cut a ring of bark from (a tree) in order to check growth, kill it or induce it to fruit. **ring-binder** *n.* a binder consisting of metal rings which hold loose-leaf pages by means of perforations in the paper. **ringbolt** *n.* a bolt with a ring or eye at one end. **ringbone** *n.* a deposit of bony matter on the pastern bones of a horse. **ring circuit** *n.* an electrical circuit in which power points are connected to the supply in a continuous closed circuit. **ring-dove** *n.* **1** the wood pigeon. **2** the collared dove. **ringed** *a. often in comb.*, as *three-ringed*. **ringed plover** *n.* either of two small plovers, *Charadrius hiaticula* and *C. dubius*. **ringer**[1] *n.* **1** (*Austral.*) the fastest shearer in a shearing shed. **2** a person who rings. **3** a quoit falling round the pin. **4** a quoit so thrown or a throw resulting in this. **ringette** (-et´) *n.* (*Can.*) a game similar to ice hockey, played mostly by women, with a straight stick and rubber ring. **ring-fence** *n.* **1** a fence encircling a whole estate or piece of land. **2** a complete barrier. *~v.t.* **1** to encircle with a ring-fence. **2** to protect completely. **ring finger** *n.* the third finger, esp. of the left hand, on which the wedding ring is worn. **ringleader** *n.* the leader of a riot, mutiny, piece of mischief etc. **ringless** *a.* **ringlet** *n.* **1** a curl, a curly lock of hair. **2** a butterfly, *Aphantopus hyperantus*, having spots on its wings. **3** a small ring or circle. **ringletted, ringleted** *a.* **ringlety** *a.* **ringlike** *a.* **ring main** *n.* **1** an electrical supply in which outlet sockets are connected to the mains supply through a ring circuit. **2** a ring circuit. **ringmaster** *n.* the manager and master of ceremonies of a circus performance. **ring-neck** *n.* any of various ring-necked birds. **ring-necked** *a.* (*Zool.*) having a band or bands of colour round the neck. **ring ouzel** *n.* a thrush, *Turdus* *torquatus*, having a white band on the breast. **ring-pull** *n.* a metal ring attached to a can of soft drink, beer etc. which opens it when pulled. **ring road** *n.* a road circumnavigating an urban centre. **ringside** *n.* **1** the area or seats immediately beside a boxing or wrestling ring or any sporting arena. **2** any position affording a close and unobstructed view. ~*a.* of or relating to a ringside (*a ringside seat*; *a ringside view*). **ringsider** *n.* **ring-snake** *n.* **1** the grass snake. **2** an American snake of the genus *Diadophis*. **ringster** *n.* a person who participates in a ring for commercial or political ends. †**ring-streaked** *a.* streaked with bands of colour. **ringtail** *n.* **1** a ring-tailed opossum, lemur or phalanger. **2** a young golden eagle. **3** a female hen harrier. **ring-tailed** *a.* **1** having a tail marked with rings or bands of colour. **2** having a tail curled at the end. **ring-wall** *n.* a wall round an estate etc. **ringworm** *n.* a contagious skin disease caused by a white fungus. [OE *hring* (cp. Dut. and G *Ring*, Icel. *hringr*)]

ring[2] (ring) *v.i.* (*past* **rang** (rang), *p.p.* **rung** (rŭng)) **1** to give a clear vibrating sound, like a sonorous metallic body when struck. **2** to re-echo, to resound, to reverberate, to continue to sound. **3** (of the ears) to have a sensation as of vibrating metal, to tingle. **4** to give a summons or signal by ringing. **5** to telephone someone. ~*v.t.* **1** to cause to ring. **2** to telephone. **3** to sound (a knell, peal etc.) on a bell or bells. **4** to summon, signal, announce, proclaim, celebrate etc. by ringing. **5** to usher (in or out) with bell-ringing. ~*n.* **1** the sound of a bell or other resonant body. **2** the act of ringing a bell. **3** a set of bells tuned harmonically. **4** a ringing sound, a continued or reverberated sound. **5** (*coll.*) a telephone call. **6** the quality of resonance. **7** the characteristic sound of a voice, statement etc. **to ring a bell** BELL[1]. **to ring back** to make a return telephone call to. **to ring down the curtain** to lower the curtain in a theatre. **to ring false** to appear insincere. **to ring in** **1** to report in by telephone. **2** (*Austral.*, *New Zeal.*, *sl.*) to substitute fraudulently. **to ring in one's ears/ heart** to stay in one's memory. **to ring off** to end a telephone call; to hang up the receiver. **to ring round** to telephone several people. **to ring the changes** CHANGE. **to ring true** to seem genuine. **to ring up** to call on the telephone. **to ring up the curtain** to raise the curtain in a theatre. **ringer**[2] *n.* **1** a person or thing almost identical to another. **2** a horse, athlete etc. racing under the name of another. **3** a person who rings, e.g. church bells. **4** a device for ringing, a bell pull. **dead ringer** DEAD. **to be a ringer for** to look exactly like. **ringing** *a.*, *n.* **ringingly** *adv.* **ringing tone** *n.* the tone heard on a telephone after an unengaged number is dialled. [OE *hringan* (cp. Dut. and G *ringen*, Icel. *hyringja*), prob. imit.]

Usage note In standard English, the past tense of the verb *ring* is *rang*, not *rung*.

ringent (rin´jənt) *a.* (*Bot.*) (of a flower or corolla) irregular and gaping. [L *ringens -ntem*, pres.p. of *ringere*, to gape]

ringer[1] RING[1].

ringer[2] RING[2].

ringgit (ring´git) *n.* the standard unit of currency of Malaysia, the Malaysian dollar. [Malay]

ringhals RINKHALS.

ringster RING[1].

rink (ringk) *n.* **1** a prepared floor for roller skating or an area of artificially formed ice for ice-skating. **2** the building or structure housing a skating rink. **3** a strip of ice or of a green marked off for curling. **4** a division of a side playing bowls or curling. [prob. rel. to RANK[1] or RING[1]]

rinkhals (ringk´hals), **ringhals** (ring´-) *n.* (*pl.* **rinkhals, rinkhalses, ringhals, ringhalses**) a venom-spitting snake of southern Africa, *Hemachatus hemachatus*. [Afrikaans *ring*, a RING[1], *hals*, the neck]

☒ **rinoceros** common misspelling of RHINOCEROS.

rinse (rins) *v.t.* **1** to wash, to cleanse with clean water. **2** to apply liquid to. **3** to remove (soap) by rinsing. **4** to clear by rinsing. ~*n.* **1** the act of rinsing. **2** an antiseptic mouthwash. **3** a hair tint. **rinser** *n.* [F *rincer*, etym. uncertain]

Rioja (riokh´ə) *n.* a Spanish table wine from Rioja. [a region in N Spain]

riot (rī´ət) *n.* **1** a disturbance, an outbreak of lawlessness, a tumult, an uproar. **2** wanton or unrestrained conduct, loose living, revelry. **3** unrestrained indulgence in something. **4** luxuriant growth, lavish display. **5** (*Law*) a tumultuous disturbance of the peace by three or more persons. **6** (*coll.*) a person or thing which is hilariously funny. ~*a.* of or relating to the suppression of riots (*a riot shield*). ~*v.i.* **1** to take part in a riot. **2** to revel, to behave or live licentiously. **to run riot** **1** to act without control or restraint. **2** to grow luxuriantly. **Riot Act** *n.* (*Hist.*) an Act of 1715 enjoining riotous people to disperse within an hour of the Act being read by a magistrate. **to read the riot act** to give a severe warning that something must stop; to reprimand severely. **rioter** *n.* **riot gear** *n.* protective clothing for police or prison officers in the event of a riot. **riotous** *a.* **riotously** *adv.* **riotousness** *n.* **riot police** *n.* police specially trained and equipped to deal with rioters. **riot shield** *n.* a large transparent shield used as protection by riot police. [OF *riote*, whence *rioter*, to riot (cp. It. *riotta*), etym. uncertain]

RIP *abbr.* may he, she or they rest in peace. [L, *requiescat, requiescant in pace*]

rip[1] (rip) *v.t.* (*pres.p.* **ripping,** *past, p.p.* **ripped**) **1** to tear or cut forcibly (out, off, up etc.). **2** to rend, to split. **3** to saw (wood) with the grain. **4** to make a long tear or rent in. **5** to make (a passage, opening etc.) by ripping. **6** to utter (an oath etc.) with violence. ~*v.i.* **1** to come or be torn forcibly apart, to tear. **2** to go (along) at a great pace. ~*n.* **1** a rent made by ripping, a tear. **2** the act of ripping. **to let it rip** (*coll.*) to allow something to proceed without restraint. **to let rip** **1** (*coll.*) to speak, act or proceed without restraint. **2** (*coll.*) not to check the speed of. **to rip into** to attack or criticize verbally. **to rip off** **1** (*coll.*) to cheat. **2** (*coll.*) to steal (from). **ripcord** *n.* a cord which, when pulled, releases a parachute from its pack or opens the gasbag of a balloon allowing it to descend. **rip-off** *n.* **1** (*coll.*) a cheat. **2** (*coll.*) an exploitative imitation. **3** (*coll.*) a theft. **ripper** *n.* **1** a person who rips or tears. **2** a murderer who mutilates victims' bodies. **3** (*esp. Austral.*, *New Zeal.*, *sl.*) an excellent person or thing. **ripping** *a.* (*dated, coll.*) excellent, fine, splendid. **rippingly** *adv.* **rip-roaring** *a.* (*coll.*) **1** noisy, unrestrained, exuberant. **2** excellent, fine, splendid. **ripsaw** *n.* a saw for sawing along the grain. **ripsnorter** *n.* (*coll.*) a forceful or excellent person or thing. **ripsnorting** *a.* **ripsnortingly** *adv.* **ripstop** *a.* woven in such a way as to prevent tears. ~*n.* a ripstop fabric. [prob. from Scand. (cp. Norw. and Swed. dial. *ripa*, Dan. *rippe*)]

rip[2] (rip) *n.* an eddy, a stretch of broken water, a rip tide. **rip current** *n.* a rip caused by tidal currents flowing away from the land. **rip tide** *n.* **1** a rip current. **2** an eddy, a stretch of broken water. **3** a conflict of psychological forces. [etym. uncertain, perh. from RIP[1]]

rip[3] (rip) *n.* (*coll.*) **1** a disreputable person. **2** a worthless horse. [etym. uncertain, perh. var. of *rep*, short for REPROBATE]

riparian (rīpeə´riən) *a.* of, relating to or dwelling on the banks of a river. ~*n.* an owner of property on the banks of a river. **riparial** *a.* [L *rīpārius*, from *rīpa*, a bank]

ripe (rīp) *a.* **1** ready for reaping or gathering. **2** mature, come to perfection in growth, fully developed, mellow, fit for use, ready or in a fit state (for). 3 resembling ripe fruit, rosy, rounded, luscious. ~*v.t., v.i.* to ripen. **ripely** *adv.* **ripen** *v.t.* to make ripe. ~*v.i.* to become ripe. **ripeness** *n.* [OE *rīpe* (cp. Dut. *rijp*, G *reif*), whence *rīpian*, to ripen]

ripeck RYEPECK.

ripieno (ripiā´nō) *a.* additional, supplementary. ~*n.* (*pl.* **ripienos, ripieni** (-nē)) (*Mus.*) 1 in baroque concerto music, a number of additional accompanying instruments. 2 a ripieno player or instrument. **ripienist** *n.* [It. (*ri*-, RE-, *pieno*, L *plēnus*, full)]

riposte (ripost´) *n.* 1 a quick reply, a retort. 2 in fencing, a quick lunge or return thrust. ~*v.i.* to make a riposte. [F *riposte*, It. *risposta*, repartee]

ripper RIP[1].

ripping RIP[1].

ripple[1] (rip´əl) *v.i.* 1 to run in small waves or undulations. 2 to sound like water running over a rough surface. ~*v.t.* to cause to run in small waves or undulations. ~*n.* 1 the ruffling of the surface of water, a wavelet. 2 a sound as of rippling water. 3 an undulation (of water, hair etc.). 4 a slight variation in the strength etc. of an electric current. 5 a kind of ice cream with streaks of syrup etc. through it. **ripple-mark** *n.* a mark left by ripples or wavelets on sand, mud, rock etc. **ripple-marked** *a.* **ripplet** *n.* **rippling** *n., a.* **ripplingly** *adv.* **ripply** *a.* [etym. uncertain]

ripple[2] (rip´əl) *n.* a large comb for removing the seeds from flax. ~*v.t.* to clean or remove seeds from (flax) with a ripple. [cp. Dut. *repel* (v. *repelen*), G *Riffel* (v. *riffeln*)]

riprap (rip´rap) *n.* (*N Am.*) a foundation of loose stones, e.g. in deep water or on a soft bottom. ~*v.t.* (*pres.p.* **riprapping**, *past, p.p.* **riprapped**) to give a riprap foundation to. [redupl. of RAP[1]]

Ripuarian (ripūeə´riən) *a.* 1 of or relating to the ancient Franks living near the Rhine. 2 of or relating to the Ripuarians' code of laws. ~*n.* a Ripuarian Frank. [med. L *Ripuārius*, perh. from L *rīpa*, a bank]

riroriro (rē´rōrērō) *n.* (*pl.* **riroriros**) a small grey New Zealand bird, *Gerygone igata*. [Maori]

risaldar (risahldah´) *n.* the captain of a troop of Indian cavalry. [Hind.]

RISC (risk) *n.* 1 a computer which performs a limited number of operations at high speed. 2 computing with a RISC computer. [reduced *i*nstruction *s*et *c*omputer]

rise (rīz) *v.i.* (*pres.p.* **rising**, *past* **rose** (rōz), *p.p.* **risen** (riz´ən)) 1 to move upwards, to ascend, to leave the ground, to mount, to soar. 2 to get up from a lying, kneeling or sitting position, or out of bed, to become erect, to stand up. 3 to adjourn, to end a session. 4 to come to life again. 5 to swell or project upwards. 6 to increase, to become high or tall. 7 (of the sun or moon) to appear above the horizon. 8 to be promoted, to thrive. 9 to increase in confidence, cheerfulness, energy, force, intensity, value, price etc. 10 to slope up. 11 to arise, to come into existence, to originate. 12 to come to the surface, to come into sight. 13 to become audible. 14 to become higher in pitch. 15 to respond, esp. with annoyance. 16 to be built. 17 to swell by the action of yeast. 18 to become equal (to). 19 to break into insurrection, to revolt, to rebel (against). 20 (of the wind) to start to blow. 21 (of a barometer) to indicate a higher atmospheric pressure. ~*n.* 1 the act of rising. 2 ascent, elevation. 3 a an upward slope. b the degree of this. 4 a hill, a knoll. 5 source, origin, start. 6 an increase in volume, price, value, power, rank, age, prosperity, height, amount, salary etc. 7 promotion, upward progress in social position, advancement. 8 the rising of a feeding fish to the surface. 9 the vertical part of an arch, step etc. 10 appearance above the horizon, rising (of the sun or moon). **on the rise** increasing. **rise and shine** (*coll.*) get up out of bed. **to get a rise out of** (*coll.*) to tease, to provoke. **to give rise to** to cause. **to rise above** 1 to be superior to. 2 to remain unaffected by (problems or adverse conditions). **to rise in the world** to advance to a higher social position. **to rise to the occasion** OCCASION. **to rise with the lark** LARK[1]. **to rise with the sun** to get up early. **to take a rise out of** to get a rise out of. **riser** *n.* 1 someone who or something which rises (*an early riser*). 2 the vertical part of a step etc. 3 a vertical pipe for liquid or gas. 4 a low platform on a stage etc. **rising** *n.* 1 a revolt, an insurrection. 2 the agent causing dough to rise. 3 a mounting up or ascending. 4 a protuberance, a tumour, a knoll. ~*a.* 1 increasing. 2 growing. 3 advancing. 4 sloping upwards. ~*adv.* (*coll.*) approaching, nearing. **rising damp** *n.* the absorption of ground moisture into the fabric of a building. [OE *rīsan*, cp. Dut. *rijzen*, G *reisen*, Icel. *rīsa*, OHG *rīsan*]

rishi (rish´i) *n.* (*pl.* **rishis**) a seer, a saint, an inspired poet, esp. each of the seven sages said to have communicated the Hindu Vedas to humankind. [Sansk.]

risible (riz´ibəl) *a.* 1 exciting laughter. 2 inclined to laugh. 3 of or relating to laughter. **risibility** (-bil´-) *n.* **risibly** *adv.* [F, from late L *rīsibilis*, from *rīdēre*, to laugh]

rising RISE.

risk (risk) *n.* 1 hazard, a chance of harm, injury, loss etc. 2 a person or thing liable to cause a hazard or loss. ~*v.t.* 1 to expose to risk or hazard. 2 to venture on, to take the chance of. **at one's (own) risk** accepting responsibility. **at risk** in danger, vulnerable. **at the risk of** with the possibility of (unpleasant consequences). **to put at risk** to expose to danger. **to risk one's neck** to do something very dangerous. **to run a risk** to risk danger. **to run the risk** to take the chance (of danger). **to take a risk** to run a risk. **risk capital** *n.* money invested in a speculative enterprise. **risker** *n.* **riskful** *a.* **risky** *a.* (*comp.* **riskier**, *superl.* **riskiest**) 1 dangerous, hazardous, venturesome, daring. 2 risqué. **riskily** *adv.* **riskiness** *n.* [F *risque*, It. *risco*]

Risorgimento (risawjimen´tō) *n.* the rising of the Italian peoples against Austrian and papal rule, culminating in the unification of Italy in 1870. **risorgimento** *n.* (*pl.* **risorgimentos**) a rebirth, a renewal, a revival. [It., RESURRECTION (under RESURRECT)]

risotto (rizot´ō) *n.* (*pl.* **risottos**) an Italian dish of rice cooked in butter and stock or broth, with onions, cheese, chicken, ham etc. [It.]

risqué (rēs´kā) *a.* suggestive of indecency, indelicate. [F, p.p. of *risquer*, to RISK]

rissole (ris´ōl) *n.* a ball or flat cake of minced meat, fish etc., coated with breadcrumbs and fried. [F, from OF *roussole*, perh. from L *russeolus*, reddish, from *russus*, red]

rit. *abbr.* (*Mus.*) 1 ritardando. 2 ritenuto.

ritardando (ritahdan´dō) *adv., a., n.* (*pl.* **ritardandos, ritardandi** (-dē)) (*Mus.*) (a) slowing down. [It., from *ritardare*, to RETARD[1]]

rite (rīt) *n.* 1 a religious or solemn prescribed act, ceremony or observance. 2 (*pl.*) the prescribed acts, ceremonies or forms of worship of any religion. **riteless** *a.* **rite of passage, rite de passage** (rēt də pasahzh´) *n.* a ceremony marking an individual's change of status, esp. into adulthood or matrimony. [L *rītus*]

ritenuto (ritənoo´tō) *a., adv.* (*Mus.*) restrained, held back. ~*n.* (*pl.* **ritenutos**) a passage played in this way. [It., from L *retinēre*, to hold back]

ritornello (ritawnel´ō) *n.* (*pl.* **ritornellos, ritornelli** (-lē)) (*Mus.*) a brief prelude, interlude or refrain. [It., dim. of *ritorno*, a RETURN]

ritual (rich´uəl) *n.* 1 a prescribed manner of performing divine service. 2 performance of rites and ceremonies, esp. in an elaborate or excessive way. 3 a book setting out the rites and ceremonies of a particular Church. 4 any formal or customary act or series of acts consistently followed. 5 (*pl.*) ritual observances. ~*a.* of, relating to, consisting of or involving rites. **ritualism** *n.* punctilious or exaggerated observance of ritual. **ritualist** *n.* **ritualistic** (-lis´-) *a.* **ritualistically** *adv.* **ritualize, ritualise** *v.t., v.i.* **ritualization** (-zā´shən) *n.* **ritually** *adv.* [F, from L *rītuālis*, from *rītus*, RITE]

ritzy (rit´si) *a.* (*comp.* **ritzier**, *superl.* **ritziest**) (*coll.*) elegant, showy, luxurious, rich. **ritzily** *adv.* **ritziness** *n.* [after the *Ritz* hotels established by César Ritz, 1850–1918, Swiss hotelier]

rival (rī´vəl) *n.* 1 one's competitor for something. 2 a person or thing considered as equal to another. 3 a person who strives to surpass another in a quality, pursuit etc. ~*a.* being a rival, having the same claims or pretensions, in competition. ~*v.t.* (*pres.p.* **rivalling,** (*N Am.*) **rivaling,** *past, p.p.* **rivalled,** (*N Am.*) **rivaled**) 1 to vie with, to emulate, to strive to equal or surpass. 2 to be, or almost be, the equal of. **rivalry** (-ri) *n.* (*pl.* **rivalries**). **rivalship** *n.* [F, from L *rīvālis*, orig. on the same stream, from *rīvus*, a stream]

†**rive** (rīv) *v.t.* (*past* **rived,** *p.p.* **riven** (riv´ən)) 1 to tear, split, cleave or rend asunder. 2 to wrench or rend (away, from, off etc.). ~*v.i.* to split, to be split. [Icel. *rīfa*, cp. Dan. *rive*, Swed. *rifva*]

river (riv´ə) *n.* 1 a large stream of water flowing in a channel over a portion of the earth's surface and discharging itself into the sea, a lake, a marsh or another river. 2 a large and abundant stream, a copious flow. ~*a.* of or living in or beside a river or rivers. **to sell down the river** (*coll.*) to let down, to betray. **riverain** (-rān) *a.* of or relating to a river. ~*n.* a person who lives on or near a river. **river bed** *n.* the channel in which a river flows. **river blindness** *n.* a tropical skin disease caused by the parasitic threadworm *Onchocerca volvulus*, whose larvae can cause blindness if they enter the eyes. **riverboat** *n.* a boat for use on rivers. **river capture** *n.* the diversion of a mountain stream into a stronger one. **rivercraft** *n.pl.* small craft plying only on rivers. **river dolphin** *n.* any of several freshwater mammals of the family Platanistidae, found in rivers in S America and S Asia. **rivered** *a.* (*usu. in comb.*, as *many-rivered*). **river god** *n.* a deity presiding over or personifying a river. **river hog** *n.* an African wild pig of the genus *Potamochoerus*, inhabiting river banks etc. **river horse** *n.* (*coll.*) the hippopotamus. **riverine** (-rīn) *a.* of, relating to, resembling or produced by a river; riparian. **riverless** *a.* **river novel** *n.* a roman-fleuve. **riverside** *n.* the ground along the bank of a river. ~*a.* built on the bank of a river. **rivery** *a.* 1 like a river. 2 having many rivers. [A-F *rivere*, OF *riviere*, pop. L *rīpāria*, from *rīpa*, a bank (cp. RIPARIAN)]

rivet (riv´it) *n.* a short bolt, pin or nail, usu. with a flat head at one end, the other end being flattened out and clinched by hammering, used for fastening metal plates together. ~*v.t.* (*pres.p.* **riveting,** *past, p.p.* **riveted**) 1 to join or fasten together with a rivet or rivets. 2 to clinch. 3 to fasten firmly. 4 to fix (attention, eyes etc. upon). 5 to engross the attention of. **riveter** *n.* **riveting** *a.* extremely interesting, engrossing. [F, from *river*, to clinch, etym. uncertain]

riviera (rivieə´rə) *n.* a coastal strip with a subtropical climate. [It., the shore]

rivière (rivieə´) *n.* a necklace of gems, usu. of several strings. [F, a RIVER]

rivulet (riv´ūlit) *n.* a small stream. [perh. through L *rīvulus*, dim. from *rīvus*, a stream]

riyal RIAL.

rizzer (riz´ə) *v.t.* (*Sc.*) to dry (haddocks etc.) in the sun. ~*n.* a rizzered haddock. [Sc., from obs. F *ressoré*, rizzered (*sorer*, to dry, to make red)]

RL *abbr.* 1 (Republic of) Lebanon (IVR). 2 Rugby League.

rly. *abbr.* railway.

RM *abbr.* 1 Malagasy Republic (IVR). 2 Resident Magistrate. 3 Royal Mail. 4 Royal Marines.

rm. *abbr.* 1 ream. 2 room.

RMA *abbr.* Royal Military Academy.

RMM *abbr.* (Republic of) Mali (IVR).

r.m.s. *abbr.* (*Math.*) root-mean-square.

RMT *abbr.* National Union of Rail, Maritime and Transport Workers.

RN *abbr.* 1 Registered Nurse. 2 Royal Navy.

Rn *chem. symbol* radon.

RNA *abbr.* ribonucleic acid.

RNAS *abbr.* 1 Royal National Air Service. 2 Royal Naval Air Station.

RNIB *abbr.* Royal National Institute for the Blind.

RNLI *abbr.* Royal National Lifeboat Institution.

RNZAF *abbr.* Royal New Zealand Air Force.

RNZN *abbr.* Royal New Zealand Navy.

roach[1] (rōch) *n.* (*pl.* **roach**) a freshwater fish, *Rutilus rutilus*, allied to the carp. [OF *roche*, *roce*, perh. from Gmc. (cp. G *Roche*, OE *reohhe*)]

roach[2] (rōch) *n.* 1 (*N Am., coll.*) a cockroach. 2 (*sl.*) the butt or filter of a cannabis cigarette.

roach[3] (rōch) *n.* (*Naut.*) 1 a curved part of a fore-and-aft sail projecting beyond an imaginary straight line between its corners. 2 the extent of such projections. 3 the upward curve in the foot of a square sail. [etym. uncertain]

road[1] (rōd) *n.* 1 a track or way for travelling on, esp. a broad strip of ground suitable for motor vehicles, forming a public line of communication between places, a highway. 2 a way of going anywhere, route, course. 3 an underground passage in a mine. 4 (*N Am.*) a railway. 5 (*usu. pl.*) a place in the open water beyond a harbour where ships can ride at anchor, a roadstead. **by road** using transport on the roads. **in someone's road** (*coll.*) in the road. **in the road** (*coll.*) obstructing someone. **no through road** NO[1]. **one for the road** ONE. **on the road** passing through, travelling, touring (often as a way of life). **rule of the road** a regulation governing the methods of passing each other for vehicles on the road, vessels on the water etc. **to get out of someone's road** (*coll.*) to get out of someone's way. **to get out of the road** (*coll.*) to get out of the way. **to hit the road** (*sl.*) to leave, to begin travelling. **to take to the road** to set out, to begin travelling. **roadbed** *n.* 1 the foundation upon which a railway track or highway is laid. 2 (*N Am.*) the part of a road on which vehicles travel. **roadblock** *n.* a road obstructed by the army or police checking for escaped criminals, terrorists etc. **road book** *n.* a guidebook describing roads, distances etc. **road fund** *n.* (*Hist.*) a fund for the maintenance of roads and bridges. **road fund licence** *n.* a paper disc displayed on a vehicle to prove that the owner has paid road tax. **road hog** *n.* (*coll.*) a selfish motorist or cyclist paying no regard to the convenience of other people using the road. **road-holding** *n.* the capacity of a motor vehicle to remain stable at high speeds, on wet roads etc. **roadhouse** *n.* a public house, restaurant etc. on a highway, which caters for motorists. **road hump** *n.* a sleeping policeman. **roadie** *n.* a person employed to transport, set up and dismantle the instruments and equipment of a touring band. **road kill** *n.* (*esp. N Am.*) 1 the act of killing an animal with a road vehicle. 2 an animal killed by a road vehicle. **roadless** *a.* **roadman** (-mən) *n.* (*pl.* **roadmen**) a person who keeps roads in repair. **road manager** *n.* a person who organizes and supervises a band's tour. **road metal** *n.* broken stones for road-making. **road movie** *n.* a film or genre of film which has a central plot involving a journey by road. **road-pricing** *n.* a method of reducing traffic on busy roads by making drivers pay to use them. **road rage** *n.* violent aggression towards other motorists. **roadroller** *n.* a vehicle with a large metal roller for compacting the surface of a newly-laid road. **roadrunner** *n.* a bird of Mexican and US deserts, *Geococcyx californianus*, which can run very fast. **road sense** *n.* the instinct of a road-user which enables them to cope with a traffic emergency, avoid an accident etc. **roadshow** *n.* **1** a touring group of performers. **2** a musical or theatrical performance by such a group. **3** a live or prerecorded outside broadcast by a touring radio or television unit. **4** a touring political or advertising campaign. **roadside** *n.* the border of a road. ~*a.* situated or growing by the roadside. **road sign** *n.* a sign giving instructions to road users. **roadstead** *n.* an anchorage for ships some distance from the shore. **roadster** (-stə) *n.* **1** a horse, cycle or car suitable for the road. **2** a two-seater car. **road sweeper** *n.* a person whose job is to sweep roads. **road test** *n.* a test of the performance of a vehicle on a road. **road-test** *v.t.* to give a road test to. **road train** *n.* (*esp. Austral.*) a large lorry pulling one or more trailers. **roadway** *n.* **1** a road. **2** the central part of a highway, used by vehicles etc. **roadwork** *n.* **1** (*pl.*) repairs to or under a section of road. **2** physical training comprising running or jogging along roads. **roadworthy** *a.* fit for use or travel on a road. **roadworthiness** *n.* [OE *rād*, from *rīdan*, RIDE]

road² (rōd) *v.t.* (of a dog) to follow (a game bird) by its scent. [etym. unknown]

roading RODING (under RODE²).

roam (rōm) *v.i.* to wander about without any definite purpose, to rove, to ramble. ~*v.t.* to range, to wander, to rove over. ~*n.* the act of roaming. **roamer** *n.* [etym. uncertain]

roan¹ (rōn) *a.* **1** (of an animal, esp. a horse) of a bay, sorrel or dark colour, with spots of grey or white thickly interspersed. **2** of a mixed colour, having a decided shade of red. ~*n.* **1** a roan animal, esp. a horse. **2** a roan colour. [OF (cp. It. and Sp. *roano*, Port. *ruão*), etym. unknown]

roan² (rōn) *n.* a soft flexible leather made of sheepskin tanned with sumac. ~*a.* made of roan. [perh. from *Rouen*, France]

roar (raw) *n.* **1** a loud, deep, hoarse, continued sound, as of a lion etc. **2** a confused din resembling this. **3** a burst of mirth or laughter. **4** a loud engine noise. ~*v.i.* **1** (of a lion etc.) to make a loud, deep, hoarse, continued sound. **2** (of a person in rage or distress; loud laughter, the sea, thunder, guns, a fire) to make a confused din like this. **3** (of a diseased horse) to make a noise in breathing. **4** (of a place) to resound, to re-echo, to be full of din. **5** (of a vehicle) to travel at high speed, making a loud noise. ~*v.t.* to shout, say, sing or utter with a roaring voice. **roarer** *n.* **roaring** *a.* **1** shouting, noisy, boisterous, stormy. **2** brisk, active. ~*n.* **1** a loud, continued or confused noise. **2** a peculiar sound emitted during breathing by some horses, due to disease in the air passages. ~*adv.* extremely, boisterously. **roaring business** *n.* a roaring trade. **roaring drunk** *a.* extremely and noisily drunk. **roaring forties** *n.pl.* the stormy part of the Atlantic Ocean between 39° and 50° S latitude. **roaringly** *adv.* **roaring success** *n.* (*coll.*) a great success. **roaring trade** *n.* (*coll.*) thriving and profitable business. **roaring twenties** *n.pl.* (*coll.*) the 1920s. [OE *rārian* (cp. G *raren*, MDut. *reeren*, G *rehren*), prob. imit.]

roast (rōst) *v.t.* **1** to cook by exposure to the direct action of radiant heat, esp. at an open fire or in an oven. **2** to dry (coffee beans etc.) by exposure to heat. **3** to heat excessively or violently. **4** to heat (ore etc.) highly without fusing, to drive out impurities. **5** (*coll.*) to criticize strongly. ~*v.i.* **1** to be roasted. **2** to heat oneself excessively. ~*a.* roasted. ~*n.* **1** something which is roasted, roast meat or a dish of this, a roast joint. **2** the act or operation of roasting. **3** (*N Am.*) a party where roasted food is served. **to rule the roast** RULE. **roaster** *n.* **1** someone who or something which roasts. **2** a kind of oven for roasting. **3** a contrivance for roasting coffee. **4** a furnace for roasting ore. **5** a fowl, animal, vegetable etc. suitable for roasting. **roasting** *a.* very hot. ~*n.* **1** the act of roasting. **2** a severe criticism. [OF *rostir* (F *rôtir*), from Gmc. (cp. OHG *rōsten*, from *Rōst*, a grate, a gridiron)]

rob (rob) *v.t.* (*pres.p.* **robbing**, *past*, *p.p.* **robbed**) **1** to take something by unlawful violence or secret theft from. **2** to plunder, to pillage, to deprive, to strip (of). **3** (*dial.*) to steal. ~*v.i.* to commit robbery. **to rob Peter to pay Paul 1** to take away from one person in order to give to another. **2** to pay off one debt by incurring a new one. **robber** *n.* **robber-baron** *n.* **1** (*Hist.*) a medieval baron exacting tribute by oppressive means. **2** a wealthy and influential but unscrupulous person. **robber-crab** *n.* a land crab, *Birgus latro*, of the Indian Ocean, which climbs coconut palms to feed on the nuts. **robbery** *n.* (*pl.* **robberies**) **1** the act or practice of robbing. **2** an instance of robbing. **3** extortion, overpricing. [OF *robber*, *rober*, rel. to REAVE]

robe (rōb) *n.* **1** a long, loose outer garment. **2** (*often pl.*) a dress, gown or vestment of state, rank or office. **3** a dressing gown, a bathrobe. **4** a long, white dress worn by a baby at its christening. **5** (*N Am.*) a fur blanket or wrap. ~*v.t.* **1** to clothe, to dress. **2** to invest with a robe or robes. ~*v.i.* to put on a robe or dress. **robe de chambre** (rob də shā´brə) *n.* (*pl.* **robes de chambre** (rob)) a dressing gown or morning dress. [OF, cogn. with ROB, cp. OE *rēaf*, spoil, clothing, Icel. *rauf*, booty]

robin (rob´in) *n.* **1** a small brown European bird, *Erithacus rubecula*, the male adult having a red throat and breast. **2** a N American red-breasted thrush, *Turdus migratorius*. **3** any red-breasted bird. **Robin Goodfellow** *n.* a merry domestic fairy, noted for mischievous pranks. **Robin Hood** *n.* a person who victimizes the rich in favour of the poor (from a legendary outlaw of Sherwood Forest who stole from the rich to give to the poor). **Robin-run-in-the-hedge** *n.* ground-ivy, bindweed or any of various other trailers or climbers. [OF, fam. form of the name, *Robert*]

robinia (rəbin´iə) *n.* any member of the genus *Robinia* of leguminous shrubs and trees including the false acacia. [Jean *Robin*, 1550–1629, French botanist]

roble (rō´bəl) *n.* **1** the Californian white oak, *Quercus lobata*. **2** any of various similar or related trees. [Sp. and Port., from L *rōbur*, an oak]

roborant (rō´bərənt) *a.* (*Med.*) (of a medicine, tonic etc.) strengthening. ~*n.* a strengthening medicine. [L *rōborans -ntem*, pres.p. of *rōborāre*, to strengthen, from *rōbur -boris*, strength]

robot (rō´bot) *n.* **1** a machine capable of acting and speaking in a human manner; a humanoid, an automaton. **2** a brutal, mechanically efficient person who has no sensitivity. **3** (*S Afr.*) a traffic light. **robotic** (-bot´-) *a.* **robotically** *adv.* **robotic dancing** *n.* a style of dancing, popular in the 1980s, with robot-like mechanical movements. **robotics** *n.* the branch of technology concerned with the design, construction, application etc. of robots. **robotize, robotise** *v.t.* to cause (work etc.) to be done by a robot. **robotization** (-zā´shən) *n.* **robot-like** *a.* [from Karel Capek's play *R.U.R.*, 1923]

robust (rōbŭst´) *a.* **1** strong, hardy, vigorous, capable of endurance, having excellent health and physique. **2** (of wine) full-bodied. **3** (of exercise, sport, discipline etc.) requiring muscular strength, invigorating. **4** sinewy, muscular. **5** mentally vigorous, firm, self-reliant. †**robustious** *a.* boisterous, rough, noisy. †**robustiously** *adv.* **robustly** *adv.* **robustness** *n.* [F *robuste*, L *rōbustus*, strong]

robusta (rōbus´tə) *n.* **1** coffee beans from an American plant, *Coffea canephora*. **2** the plant itself. [mod. L, from L *robustus*, robust]

ROC *abbr.* Royal Observer Corps.

roc (rok) *n.* a legendary bird of immense size and strength. [F *rock,* Arab. *rokh, rukh*]

rocaille (rōkī´) *n.* decorative work of rock, shell or a similar material. [F]

rocambole (rok´əmbōl) *n.* a plant related to the leek, *Allium scorodoprasum,* Spanish garlic. [F, etym. uncertain]

Rochelle powder (roshel´) *n.* Seidlitz powder. **Rochelle salt** *n.* a tartrate of soda and potash, used in Seidlitz powder.

roche moutonnée (rosh mooton´ā) *n.* (*pl.* **roches moutonnées** (rosh mooton´ā)) rock ground down by glacial action so as to present a rounded appearance on the side from which the flow came. [F, rock rounded like the back of a sheep]

rochet (roch´it) *n.* an open-sided vestment with tight sleeves, resembling a surplice, worn by bishops and abbots. [OF *rochet, roket,* from Gmc. (cp. Dut. *rok,* G *Rock,* OE *rocc*)]

rock[1] (rok) *n.* **1** the solid matter constituting the earth's crust, or any portion of this. **2** a similar material from any other planet. **3** (*Geol.*) any solid, hard or stony part of this, a mass of it, esp. forming a hill, promontory, islet, cliff etc. **4** a detached block of stone, a boulder. **5** (*N Am.*) a stone, a pebble. **6** (*pl., N Am., sl.*) money. **7** (*sl.*) a diamond or other precious or large gem. **8** a hard sweet, often in the form of a stick, esp. as a souvenir. **9** anything dangerous. **10** a person or thing providing refuge, stability, supportiveness etc. **11** (*sl.*) a solid form of cocaine. **12** (*pl., taboo sl.*) the testicles. **between a rock and a hard place** (*N Am.*) having to decide between two equally unpleasant courses of action. **on the rocks 1** (*coll.*) poor, hard up. **2** (*coll.*) (of a marriage) at an end, destroyed. **3** (of a drink) served with ice. **the Rock** Gibraltar. **to get one's rocks off** (*sl.*) to achieve esp. sexual gratification. **rock-basin** *n.* a hollow occupied by a lake etc., in rock, usually attributed to glacial action. **rock-bed** *n.* a base of rocks. **rock-bottom** *n.* **1** the lowest stratum reached in excavating, mining etc. **2** the lowest point (e.g. of despair). *~a.* (of prices) lowest possible. **rock-bound** *a.* hemmed in by rocks. **rockburst** *n.* a sudden collapse of rock in a mine. **rock cake** *n.* a bun with a hard, rough surface. **rock-candy** *n.* (*N Am.*) a hard sweet often found in the form of a stick. **rock-climber** *n.* a person who climbs rock faces for enjoyment. **rock-climbing** *n.* **rock-cod** *n.* **1** a gadoid fish allied to the cod. **2** a cod caught on a rocky bottom. **rock-cork** *n.* a corklike variety of asbestos. **rock cress** *n.* arabis. **rock-crystal** *n.* the finest and most transparent kind of quartz, usu. found in hexagonal prisms. **rock dove** *n.* the European wild dove, *Columba livia,* supposed to be the ancestor of the domesticated varieties. **Rock English** *n.* the mixed patois of Gibraltar. **rockery** *n.* (*pl.* **rockeries**) a mound or slope of rocks, stones and earth, for growing alpine and other plants. **rock face** *n.* the surface of a vertical or nearly vertical cliff or mountainside. **rockfall** *n.* **1** a fall of loose rocks. **2** a mass of fallen rocks. **rockfish** *n.* (*pl.* **rockfish**) **1** a black goby. **2** any of several wrasses etc. which frequent rocks. **rock garden** *n.* **1** a rockery. **2** a garden containing a rockery or rockeries. **rockhopper** *n.* a crested penguin, *Eudyptes crestatus,* of the Antarctic and New Zealand. **rockless** *a.* **rocklet** *n.* **rocklike** *a.* **rockling** *n.* a small gadoid fish, esp. of the genus *Cilata* or *Rhinomenus,* found in pools among rocks. **rock oil** *n.* petroleum. **rock-pigeon** *n.* the rock dove. **rock pipit** *n.* a kind of pipit, *Anthis spinoletta,* which frequents rocky shores. **rock plant** *n.* any of various plants growing among rocks, esp. alpines. **rock pool** *n.* a small pool between rocks. **rock python** *n.* any large snake of the family Boidae, esp. *Python sebae,* the African python. **rock rabbit** *n.* a hyrax, esp. *Procavia capensis.* **rock rose** *n.* the helianthemum. **rock salmon** *n.* **1** dogfish or other coarse fish disguised for the market. **2** (*N Am.*) an amberjack. **rock salt** *n.* salt found in stratified beds. **rock snake** *n.* any large python of the genus *Python.* **rock tar** *n.* petroleum. **rock tripe** *n.* (*Can.*) any of various types of edible lichen. **rock-wool** *n.* mineral wool. **rockwork** *n.* **1** (*Archit.*) masonry made to resemble rock. **2** a rockery. **3** rock-climbing. **rocky**[1] *a.* (*comp.* **rockier,** *superl.* **rockiest**) **1** full of or abounding with rocks. **2** consisting of or resembling rock. **3** solid. **4** rugged, hard, stony, obdurate, difficult. **the Rockies** the Rocky Mountains in N America. **rockiness**[1] *n.* **Rocky Mountain goat** *n.* an animal of NW America, *Oreamnos americanus,* resembling a goat. **Rocky Mountain spotted fever** *n.* a tick-borne rickettsial disease with high fever and a skin rash. [OF *roke, roque, roche,* etym. uncertain]

rock[2] (rok) *v.t.* **1** to move backwards and forwards. **2** to cause a cradle to move to and fro. **3** to soothe, to lull to sleep. **4** to shake, to cause to sway or reel. **5** to shock, to distress. **6** to shake or sift in a cradle. *~v.i.* **1** to move backwards and forwards. **2** to sway, to reel. **3** to dance to or play rock music. *~n.* **1** an act or spell of rocking. **2** a rocking motion. **3** rock music. **4** rock and roll. *~a.* of or relating to rock music. **rockabilly** (-əbili) *n.* a quick-paced type of Southern US rock and country music originating in the 1950s. **rock and roll, rock 'n' roll** *n.* **1** a type of music, popular from the mid-1950s, which combines blues and country-and-western music. **2** the type of dancing done to this music. *~a.* of or relating to this type of music or style of dancing. *~v.i.* to dance in the rock-and-roll style, to jive. **rock and roller** *n.* **rocker** *n.* **1** someone who or something which rocks. **2** a rocking chair. **3** a curved piece of wood on which a cradle, rocking chair etc., rocks. **4** a rock-music fan. **5** a rock musician. **6** a member of a teenage band of leather-clad motorcyclists of the 1960s, as opposed to the *Mods.* **7** a gold-miner's cradle. **8** a low skate with a curved blade. **9** the curve of this blade. **10** (of machinery) any one of various devices and fittings having a rocking motion. **off one's rocker** (*coll.*) crazy. **rocking** *n., a.* **rocking chair** *n.* a chair mounted on rockers. **rocking horse** *n.* a large toy horse mounted on rockers. **rocking stone** *n.* a stone so balanced on a natural pedestal that it can be rocked. **rocking-tool** *n.* an instrument used in mezzotinting to give the plate a burr. **rock-shaft** *n.* a shaft rocking, instead of revolving, on its bearings, usu. for conveying horizontal motion. **rockumentary** (-ūmen´təri) *n.* (*pl.* **rockumentaries**) a documentary on the subject of rock music. **rocky**[2] *a.* (*comp.* **rockier,** *superl.* **rockiest**) (*coll.*) unsteady, tottering, fragile. **rockily** *adv.* unsteadily. **rockiness**[2] *n.* [OE *roccian,* cp. G *rücken*]

rockery ROCK[1].

rocket[1] (rok´it) *n.* **1** a firework consisting of a cylindrical case of paper or metal filled with a mixture of explosives and combustibles, used for display, signalling, conveying a line to stranded vessels and in warfare. **2** a device with a warhead containing high explosive and propelled by the mechanical thrust developed by gases generated through the use of chemical fuels. **3** (*coll.*) a severe scolding, a telling-off. *~v.t.* (*pres.p.* **rocketing,** *past, p.p.* **rocketed**) **1** to bombard with rockets. **2** to propel by means of a rocket. *~v.i.* **1** to fly straight up or to fly fast and high. **2** (of prices) to rise rapidly. **3** (of a promoted person) to advance to a high position speedily. **rocketeer** (-tiə´) *n.* **1** a person who flies rocket-propelled missiles. **2** a person who works with or is interested in space rockets. **rocketer** *n.* a pheasant etc. that flies straight up in the air when flushed. **rocket range** *n.* a place for testing rocket projectiles. **rocketry** (-ri) *n.* the scientific study of rockets. [F *roquet,* It. *rocchetta,* dim. of *rocca,* ROCK[1]]

rocket[2] (rok´it) *n.* **1** any of various plants of the genus

Hesperis or *Sisymbrium*. 2 (*also* **roquette**) a variety of the cruciferous plant *Eruca vesicaria*, used for salads. [F *roquette*, It. *ruchetta*, dim. of *ruca*, L *ērūca*]
rockiness[1] ROCK[1].
rockiness[2] ROCK[2].
rocky[1] ROCK[1].
rocky[2] ROCK[2].
rococo (rəkō´kō) *n*. 1 a florid style of ornamentation (in architecture, furniture etc.) flourishing in the 18th cent. 2 design or ornament of an eccentric and over-elaborate kind. *~a.* in this style. [F, prob. coined from ROCAILLE]
rod (rod) *n.* 1 a straight, slender piece of wood, a stick, a wand. 2 this or a bundle of twigs etc. as an instrument of punishment. 3 punishment. 4 a baton, a sceptre. 5 a fishing rod. 6 an angler using a fishing rod. 7 a slender, straight stick which grows as a shoot on a tree. 8 a magician's wand. 9 a slender bar of metal, esp. forming part of machinery etc. 10 (*Hist.*) a unit of linear measure, equal to 5½ yards (about 5 m). 11 (*N Am., sl.*) a hot rod. 12 (*N Am., sl.*) a revolver. 13 a rodlike body or structure in the retina of the eye. **to have a rod in pickle** PICKLE. **to make a rod for one's own back** to do something that will cause one trouble later. **rodless** *a.* **rodlet** *n.* **rodlike** *a.* [OE *rodd*, cp. Icel. *rudda*, rel. to ROOD]
rode[1] RIDE.
rode[2] (rōd) *v.i.* (of a woodcock or wildfowl) to fly in the evening. **roding, roading** *n.* [etym. unknown]
rodent (rō´dənt) *n.* any animal of the order Rodentia, having two (or sometimes four) strong incisors and no canine teeth, including the squirrel, beaver, rat etc. *~a.* 1 (*Med.*) gnawing. 2 of or relating to the Rodentia. **rodent officer** *n.* an official employed to destroy rodents and other vermin. [L *rōdens -ntem*, pres.p. of *rōdere*, to gnaw]
rodeo (rō´diō, rədā´ō) *n.* (*pl.* **rodeos**) 1 a driving together or rounding-up of cattle. 2 a place they are rounded up in. 3 an outdoor entertainment or contest exhibiting the skills involved in this. 4 an exhibition of motorcycling skills etc. [Sp., from *rodear*, to go round]
rodham (rod´əm) *n.* in the Fens, a raised bank on the course of a dry river. [etym. unknown]
rodomontade (rodōmontād´, -tahd´) *n.* 1 brag, bluster. 2 an instance of bragging. *~a.* bragging, boastful. *~v.i.* to boast, to bluster. **rodomontader** *n.* [F, from *Rodomont*, *Rodomonte*, leader of the Saracens in Ariosto's *Orlando Furioso*]
roe[1] (rō) *n.* 1 the mass of eggs forming the spawn of fishes, amphibians etc. 2 the sperm or milt. **hard roe** HARD. **soft roe** SOFT. **roed** *a.* **roe-stone** *n.* oolite. [cp. MDut. and MLG *Roge*, OHG *Rogo*]
roe[2] (rō) *n.* (*pl.* **roe, roes**) a small species of deer, *Capreolus capreolus*. **roebuck** *n.* the male roe. **roe-deer** *n.* the roe. [OE *rāha*, cp. Icel. *rā*, Dut. *ree*, G *Reh*]
roentgen (rŭnt´yən, rœnt´-), **röntgen** *n.* the international unit of quantity of X- or gamma-rays. **roentgenography** (-nog´-) *n.* photography using X-rays. **roentgenology** (-nol´-) *n.* radiology. **roentgen rays** *n.pl.* (*Hist.*) X-rays. [W.K. von *Röntgen*, 1845–1923, German physicist]
rogation (rōgā´shən) *n.* (*usu. pl.*) a solemn supplication, esp. one chanted in procession on the Rogation Days. **rogational** *a.* **Rogation Days** *n.pl.* the Monday, Tuesday and Wednesday preceding Ascension Day, marked by prayers, processions and supplications. **Rogation Sunday** *n.* the Sunday preceding Ascension Day. **Rogationtide** *n.* the period of the Rogation Days. **Rogation Week** *n.* the week which includes the Rogation Days. **rogatory** (rog´ə-) *a.* (*Law*) seeking information. [L *rogātio*, from *rogāre*, to ask]
roger (roj´ə) *int.* 1 in radio communication, your message is received and understood. 2 (*sl.*) I agree. *~v.t.* (*taboo sl.*) (of a man) to have sexual intercourse with. *~v.i.* (*taboo sl.*) to have sexual intercourse. **Jolly Roger** JOLLY[1]. [OF, a personal name, prob. from Gmc.]
rogue (rōg) *n.* 1 a dishonest person, a criminal. 2 a mischievous person, esp. a child. 3 a vicious wild animal cast out or separate from the herd, esp. an elephant. 4 a shirking or vicious racehorse or hunter. 5 an inferior or intrusive plant among seedlings. 6 a variation from the standard type or variety. *~a.* 1 irresponsible, destructive. 2 roguish. *~v.t.* to weed out inferior plants from among (seedlings, a crop etc.). **rogue buffalo** *n.* a solitary, savage buffalo. **rogue elephant** *n.* a solitary, savage elephant. **roguery** *n.* (*pl.* **rogueries**). **rogues' gallery** *n.* a collection of photographic portraits kept in police records for identification of criminals. **roguish** *a.* mischievous, high-spirited. **roguishly** *adv.* **roguishness** *n.* [16th-cent. jargon]
roil (roil) *v.t.* 1 to make turbid, as by stirring or shaking up. 2 (*N Am.*) to make angry, to irritate, to rile. [perh. from obs. F *ruiler*, to mix up mortar, cp. RILE]
roister (rois´tə), **royster** *v.i.* 1 to behave uproariously, to revel boisterously. 2 to swagger. **roisterer** *n.* **roistering** *a., n.* **roisterous** *a.* [F *rustre*, a ruffian, var. of *ruste*, L *rusticus*, RUSTIC]
ROK *abbr.* (Republic of) Korea (IVR).
Roland (rō´lənd) *n.* used only as below. **a Roland for an Oliver** 1 an effective retort. 2 a blow for a blow, a story capping another. [a legendary paladin, nephew of Charlemagne and comrade of Oliver]
role (rōl), **rôle** *n.* 1 a part or character taken by an actor. 2 any part or function one is called upon to perform. **role model** *n.* a person who is admired and emulated by many people. **role-play** *n.* role-playing. **role-playing** *n.* an enactment of a possible situation or playing of an imaginary role, as therapy, training etc. **role reversal** *n.* the reversing of roles which have been traditionally or formerly taken. [F, a ROLL]
roll (rōl) *n.* 1 anything rolled up, a cylinder of any flexible material formed by or as by rolling or folding over on itself. 2 a small individual loaf of bread. 3 a pastry or cake rolled round a filling (*a sausage roll*). 4 a document, an official record, a register, a list, esp. of names of solicitors, soldiers, schoolchildren etc. 5 a cylindrical or semicylindrical mass of anything. 6 a fold, a turned-back edge, a convex moulding, a volute. 7 a roller. 8 a rolling motion or gait. 9 the act of rolling. 10 a gymnastic exercise in which the body is curled up and rolled over either forwards or backwards. 11 a resounding peal of thunder etc. 12 a continuous beating of a drum with rapid strokes. 13 a complete lateral revolution of an aircraft. 14 (*N Am.*) a wad of money. *~v.t.* 1 to send, push or cause to move along by turning over and over on its axis. 2 to cause to rotate. 3 to cause to revolve between two surfaces. 4 to knead, press, flatten or level with or as with a roller or rollers. 5 to enwrap (in), to wrap (up in). 6 to form into a cylindrical shape by wrapping round and round or turning over and over. 7 to carry or impel forward with a sweeping motion. 8 to carry (along) with a swinging gait. 9 to convey in a wheeled vehicle. 10 to cause to operate. 11 to display (the credits for a film or television programme) by rolling them up the screen. 12 to utter with a prolonged, deep, vibrating sound. 13 to overturn (a car). 14 to throw (a dice). 15 (*sl.*) to robe. *~v.i.* 1 to move along by turning over and over and round and round. 2 to revolve. 3 to operate or cause to operate. 4 to move along on wheels. 5 to be conveyed (along) in a wheeled vehicle. 6 (*coll.*) to progress. 7 (of eyes etc.) to move or slip about with a rotary motion. 8 to wallow about. 9 to sway, to reel, to go from side to side; to move along with such a motion. 10 (of film or television credits) to be displayed by rolling up the screen. 11 to make a prolonged, deep, vibrating sound.

12 (*sl.*) (of a car) to overturn. 13 (of a ship) to turn back and forth on the longitudinal axis. 14 (of an aircraft) to make a full corkscrew revolution about the longitudinal axis. 15 to undulate or sweep along. 16 to be formed into a cylindrical shape by turning over upon itself. 17 to grow into a cylindrical or spherical shape by turning over and over. 18 to spread (out) under a roller. **a roll in the hay** 1 (*coll.*) sexual intercourse. 2 (*coll.*) a period of sexual play. **heads will roll** people will be severely punished. **on a roll** (*sl.*) having a period of great success. **roll on!** (of a day, date or event) hurry along, come quickly (*Roll on the holidays!*). **to roll along** 1 to walk in a casual manner or with an undulating gait. 2 to have a casual or unambitious approach to life. **to roll back** (*N Am.*) to cause to decrease. **to roll in** 1 to come in quantities or numbers. 2 (*coll.*) to arrive in a casual manner. **to roll on** 1 to knock over. 2 to repay (maturing stock) by an issue of new stock. **to roll up** 1 (*coll.*) to assemble, to come up. 2 to make (a cigarette) by hand. 3 to wind into a cylinder. 4 (*Mil.*) to drive back (an enemy line) so that it is shortened or surrounded. **to roll up one's sleeves** SLEEVE. **to strike off the rolls** to remove from the official list of qualified solicitors, to debar, to expel. **rollable** *a.* **rollaway** *a.* (*N Am.*) (of a bed etc.) able to be wheeled away. **roll-back** *n.* a reduction in prices, taxes or wages. **roll bar** *n.* a metal strengthening bar which reinforces the frame of a (racing) vehicle which may overturn. **roll-call** *n.* the act of calling a list of names to check attendance. **rolled** *a.* **rolled into one** combined together. **rolled gold** *n.* metal covered by a thin coating of gold. **rolled oats** *n.pl.* oats which have been husked and crushed. **roller** *n.* 1 a cylindrical body turning on its axis, employed alone or forming part of a machine, used for inking, printing, smoothing, spreading out, crushing etc. 2 a small cylinder for curling the hair, a curler. 3 a long, heavy, swelling wave. 4 (*also* **roller bandage**) a long, broad bandage, rolled up for convenience. 5 a tumbler pigeon. 6 any bird of the family Coraciidae, remarkable for their habit of turning somersaults in the air. 7 a breed of canary having a trilling song. 8 someone who or something which rolls. **rollerball** *n.* a type of pen with a nib consisting of a rolling ball which controls the flow of ink. **roller bearing** *n.* a bearing comprised of strong steel rollers for giving a point of contact. **Rollerblade®** *n.* a type of roller skate with a single row of small wheels fitted to the side of the boot. **rollerblade** *v.i.* to skate wearing Rollerblades. **rollerblader** *n.* **roller blind** *n.* a window blind fitted on a roller. **roller coaster** *n.* a switchback railway at an amusement park, carnival, fair etc. **roller-coaster** *a.* having many sudden dramatic changes. ~*v.i.* to have many sudden and dramatic changes. **roller-coast** *v.i.* to roller-coaster. **roller derby** *n.* a (boisterous) roller-skating race. **roller skate** *n.* a skate mounted on wheels or rollers for skating on a hard surface etc. ~*v.i.* to skate wearing roller skates. **roller skater** *n.* **roller skating** *n.* **roller towel** *n.* a continuous towel hung on a roller. **rolling** *a., n., adv.* **to be rolling in** to have a lot of. **to be rolling (in it)** (*coll.*) to be extremely wealthy. **rolling barrage** *n.* a creeping barrage. **rolling drunk** *a.* staggering through drunkenness. **rolling mill** *n.* a factory in which metal is rolled out by machinery into plates, sheets, bars etc. **rolling pin** *n.* a hard wooden etc. roller for rolling out dough, pastry etc. **rolling stock** *n.* 1 the carriages, vans, locomotives etc. of a railway. 2 (*N Am.*) the road vehicles of a business firm. **rolling stone** *n.* a person who cannot settle down in one place. **rolling strike** *n.* industrial action consisting of a series of strikes by consecutive groups. **rollmop** *n.* a rolled-up fillet of herring pickled in vinegar. **roll-neck** *n.* 1 a jumper with a high neck folded over. 2 such a neck on a garment. ~*a.* having a roll-neck. **roll of honour** *n.* a list of people who are being honoured. **roll-on** *a.* (of a deodorant) applied by a plastic rolling ball in the neck of its container. ~*n.* 1 a step-in elastic corset which fits by stretching. 2 a roll-on deodorant. **roll-on roll-off** *a.* (of a ship) carrying motor vehicles which drive on and off when embarking and disembarking. **roll-out** *n.* 1 the official presentation of a new aircraft or spacecraft. 2 the official launch of a new product. 3 the part of a landing when an aircraft travels along the runway gradually losing speed. **roll-over** *n.* 1 the extension of a debt for a longer period. 2 (*coll.*) the act of overturning a vehicle. ~*n., a.* (relating to) the extension of the period of validity of a prize, competition etc. **roll-top** *n.* a roll-top desk. **roll-top desk** *n.* a desk with a flexible cover sliding in grooves. **roll-up** *n.* 1 (*coll.*) a hand-made cigarette made with tobacco and a cigarette paper. 2 (*Austral.*) attendance, turnout. **roll-your-own** *n.* (*coll.*) a roll-up. [OF *roler, roller*, It. *rololare*, from L *rotula*, dim. of *rota*, a wheel]

rollick (rol´ik) *v.i.* to behave in a careless, merry fashion; to frolic, to revel, to be merry or enjoy life in a boisterous fashion. ~*n.* 1 exuberance, high spirits. 2 a frolic, a spree, an escapade. **rollicking** *a.* boisterous, carefree. ~*n.* (*coll.*) a severe reprimand (euphem. for *bollocking*). [etym. uncertain]

rollock ROWLOCK (under ROW[2]).

roly-poly (rōlipō´li) *n.* (*pl.* **roly-polies**) 1 (*also* **roly-poly pudding**) a pudding made of a sheet of suet pastry, spread with jam, rolled up and baked or boiled. 2 a plump or dumpy person. 3 (*N Am.*) a tumbler toy. 4 (*Austral.*) a bushy plant, *Salsola kali*, which often breaks off and is rolled by the wind. ~*a.* plump, dumpy. [prob. a redupl. of ROLL]

ROM (rom) *n.* (*Comput.*) a data-storage device in computers which retains information in an unalterable state. [*r*ead *o*nly *m*emory]

Rom (rom) *n.* (*pl.* **Romas, Roma** (-ə)) a male gypsy, a Romany. [Romany, a man]

Rom. *abbr.* 1 Roman. 2 Romance (language). 3 Romania(n). 4 (*Bible*) Romans.

rom. *abbr.* roman (type).

Romaic (rōmā´ik) *n.* the vernacular language of modern Greece. ~*a.* of, relating to or expressed in modern Greek. [Gr. *Rōmaikos*, from *Rōmē*, L *Rōma*, Rome]

romaine (rōmān´) *n.* (*N Am.*) a cos lettuce. [F, fem. of *romain* (as ROMAN)]

romaji (rō´məji) *n.* a system of romanized spelling for the transliteration of Japanese. [Jap.]

romal (rōmahl´), **rumal** (roo-) *n.* 1 a handkerchief worn as a headdress. 2 in the Indian subcontinent, a silk or cotton fabric. [Hind. and Pers. *rūmāl*]

Roman (rō´mən) *a.* 1 of or relating to the modern or ancient city of Rome or its territory or people. 2 †of or relating to the language of ancient Rome. 3 of or relating to the Roman Catholic Church, papal. 4 dating from a period of rule by the ancient Romans. 5 belonging to the Roman alphabet. 6 (**roman**) denoting ordinary upright characters used in print as distinct from italic or Gothic. ~*n.* 1 an inhabitant or citizen of Rome. 2 a soldier of the ancient Roman Empire. 3 a Roman Catholic. 4 (*pl.*) the Christians of ancient Rome. 5 a letter of the Roman alphabet. 6 roman type. **Holy Roman Empire** HOLY. **Roman candle** *n.* a firework consisting of a tube from which coloured fireballs are discharged. **Roman Catholic** *a.* of or relating to the Church of Rome, a Christian denomination with the Pope as its head. ~*n.* a member of this Church. **Roman Catholicism** *n.* **Roman holiday** *n.* an entertainment or enjoyment which depends on others suffering. **Romanic** (-man´-) *a.* 1 derived from Latin, Romance. 2 derived or descended from the Romans. ~*n.* Romance. **Romanish** *a.* (*usu. derog.*) of, relating to or characteristic of the Church of Rome. **Romanism** *n.* Roman Catholicism.

Romanist *n.* 1 a student of Roman history etc. or of the Romance languages. 2 a Roman Catholic. 3 a 16th-cent. Dutch or Flemish painter influenced by Italian Renaissance art. **Romanistic** (-nis´-) *a.* **romanize, romanise** *v.t.* 1 to make Roman in character. 2 to convert to the Roman Catholic religion. 3 to put into the Roman alphabet or roman type. 4 to subject to the authority of ancient Rome. ~*v.i.* to conform to Roman Catholic opinions. **romanization** (-zā´shən) *n.* **romanizer** *n.* **Roman law** *n.* the system of law evolved by the ancient Romans which forms the basis of many modern legal codes. **Roman nose** *n.* a nose with a high bridge, an aquiline nose. **Roman numeral** *n.* a roman letter representing a (cardinal) number as in the ancient Roman system of numbering, occasionally still in use. **Romano-** *comb. form* Roman. **Romans** *n.* an epistolary book in the New Testament written by St Paul to the Christians of Rome. [L *Rōmānus*]

roman-à-clef (rōmahnaklā´) *n.* (*pl.* **romans-à-clef** (rōmahnaklā´)) a novel in which a knowing reader is expected to identify real people under fictitious names, or actual events disguised as fictitious. [F, a novel with a key]

Romance (rōmans´) *n.* any one of a group of languages derived from Latin, e.g. French, Spanish or Romanian. ~*a.* of or relating to this group of languages.

romance (romans´) *n.* 1 the spirit or atmosphere of imaginary adventure, chivalrous or idealized love, strangeness and mystery. 2 an episode, love affair or series of facts having this character. 3 a modern literary genre of sentimental love stories, romantic fiction. 4 a work of this genre. 5 a medieval tale, usu. in verse, describing the adventures of a hero of chivalry. 6 a story, usu. in prose, rarely in verse, with characters, scenery and incidents more or less remote from ordinary life. 7 fiction of this kind. 8 a fabrication, a fiction, a falsehood. 9 a short musical composition of a simple character, usu. suggestive of a love-song. ~*v.i.* 1 to make false, exaggerated or imaginary statements. 2 to imagine or tell romantic or extravagant stories. ~*v.t.* to have a love affair with. **romancer** *n.* 1 a writer or composer of romances. 2 a person who romances or exaggerates. **romancing** *n.*, *a.* [ME, OF *romanz, -ce*, as ROMAN]

Usage note The pronunciation (rō´-), with stress on the first syllable, should only be used facetiously or mockingly.

Romanes (rom´ənis) *n.* the Romany language.

Romanesque (rōmənesk´) *a.* of the styles of architecture that succeeded the Roman and lasted till the introduction of Gothic. ~*n.* Romanesque art, architecture etc. [F]

roman-fleuve (rōmahnflœv´) *n.* (*pl.* **romans-fleuves** (rōmahnflœv´)) a novel sequence or saga chronicling a family history, and thereby a social period. [F, a river novel]

Romanian (rumā´niən), **Rumanian, Roumanian** *a.* of or relating to the country of Romania, its people or language. ~*n.* 1 a native or inhabitant of Romania, or a person of Romanian descent. 2 the language of Romania. [from L *Rōmānus*, Roman]

Romano (rōmah´nō) *n.* a strong-tasting, hard Italian cheese. [It., Roman]

Romansh (rōmansh´), **Rumansh** (ru-) *n.* the Rhaeto-Romance dialects of part of E Switzerland. ~*a.* of or relating to these dialects. [Romansh, *Ruman(t)sch, Roman(t)sch*, from med. L *romanice* (as ROMANCE)]

romantic (rōman´tik) *a.* 1 of, relating to, of the nature of or given to romance. 2 imaginative, visionary, poetic, extravagant, fanciful. 3 (of conduct etc.) fantastic, unpractical, sentimental. 4 (of scenery etc.) wild, picturesque, suggestive of romance. 5 (*also* **Romantic**) of or relating to the movement in literature and art tending away from the moderation and harmonious proportion of classicism towards the less restrained expression of ideal beauty and grandeur. ~*n.* 1 a romantic person, a person given to sentimental thoughts or acts of love. 2 a romantic poet, novelist etc., a romanticist. **romantically** *adv.* **romanticism** (-sizm) *n.* 1 the reaction from classical to medieval forms and to the less restrained expressions of romantic ideals which originated in Germany about the middle of the 18th cent., and reached its culmination in England and France in the first half of the 19th cent. 2 the quality or state of being romantic. **romanticist** *n.* **romanticize** (-sīz), **romanticise** *v.t.*, *v.i.* **romanticization** (-zā´shən) *n.* [F *romantique*, from OF *romant*, var. of *romanz*, ROMANCE]

Romany (rom´əni, rō´-) *n.* (*pl.* **Romanies**) 1 a gypsy. 2 the gypsy language. ~*a.* gypsy. [Romany *Romani*, fem. and pl. of *Romano*, from ROM]

Rome (rōm) *n.* the Roman Catholic Church. **Romish** *a.* (*usu. derog.*) belonging to or tending towards Roman Catholicism. [L *Rōma*, Rome, the capital city of Italy]

Romeo (rō´miō) *n.* a man who is an ardent lover. [the lovelorn hero of Shakespeare's *Romeo and Juliet*]

romer (rō´mə) *n.* a small piece of card or plastic marked with graduations for measuring map references. [C. *Romer*, d. 1951, British inventor]

romneya (rom´niə) *n.* any plant of the genus *Romneya*, having large, poppy-like flowers. [Thomas *Romney* Robinson, 1792–1882, Irish astronomer]

romp (romp) *v.i.* 1 to play or frolic roughly or boisterously. 2 (*coll.*) to go rapidly (along, past etc.) with ease. ~*n.* 1 rough or boisterous play. 2 an easy win. 3 †a child, esp. a girl, fond of romping. 4 a swift run. **to romp home/ in** (*coll.*) to win easily. **romper** *n.* 1 a person who romps. 2 (*also* **romper suit**) a one-piece playsuit for infants. **rompy** *a.* (*comp.* **rompier**, *superl.* **rompiest**). [var. of RAMP[1]]

rondavel (rondah´vəl) *n.* a round hut or building in S Africa. [Afrikaans *rondawel*]

ronde (rond) *n.* 1 a dance in which the dancers move round in a circle. 2 a course of talk etc. 3 an upright angular form of type imitating handwriting. [F, fem. of *rond*, ROUND]

rondeau (ron´dō) *n.* (*pl.* **rondeaux** (ron´dōz, ron´dō)) 1 a poem in iambic verse of eight or ten syllables and ten or thirteen lines, with only two rhymes, the opening words coming twice as a refrain. 2 (*Mus.*) a rondo. **rondel** (-dəl) *n.* a particular form of rondeau, usu. of thirteen or fourteen lines with only two rhymes throughout. **rondelet** (-lit) *n.* a poem of seven lines with a refrain, usu. repeating words from the opening. **rondo** (-dō) *n.* (*pl.* **rondos**) a musical composition having a principal theme which is repeated after each subordinate theme, often forming part of a symphony etc. [F from *rond*, ROUND]

rone (rōn), **ronepipe** (-pīp) *n.* (*Sc.*) a gutter, a pipe for channelling rainwater from a roof.

Roneo® (rō´niō) *n.* (*pl.* **Roneos**) a duplicating machine using stencils. ~*v.t.* (*3rd pers. sing. pres.* **Roneos**, *pres.p.* **Roneoing**, *past, p.p.* **Roneoed**) to make duplicate copies of (a document) with this machine.

ronin (rō´nin) *n.* (*pl.* **ronin, ronins**) 1 (*Hist.*) in Japan, a lordless samurai. 2 a Japanese student retaking an examination. [Jap.]

röntgen ROENTGEN.

roo (roo), **'roo** *n.* (*pl.* **roos, 'roos**) (*Austral., coll.*) a kangaroo.

rood (rood) *n.* 1 the cross of Christ, a crucifix, esp. one set on a beam or screen in a church. 2 a quarter of an acre (about 0.1 ha). **rood-beam** *n.* a beam across the arch opening into a choir, supporting the rood. **rood-loft** *n.* a gallery over the rood-screen. **rood-screen** *n.* a stone or wood screen between the nave and choir of a church, usu. elaborately designed and decorated with carving etc., orig. supporting the rood. [OE *rōd*]

roof (roof) *n.* (*pl.* **roofs, rooves** (roovz)) **1** the upper covering of a house or other building. **2** the covering or top of a vehicle etc. **3** any analogous part, e.g. of a furnace, oven etc. **4** (*Anat.*) the palate. **5** the top of a mountain or plateau. **6** (*poet.*) a covering, a canopy. **7** a house, shelter etc. **8** an upper limit, a ceiling. *~v.t.* **1** to cover with or as if with a roof. **2** to be the roof of. **3** to shelter. **a roof over one's head** a place to live. **to go through the roof 1** (*coll.*) (of prices etc.) to increase suddenly and quickly. **2** to hit the roof. **to hit/ raise the roof** (*coll.*) to lose one's temper. **under one roof** in the same building. **under one's roof** in one's home. **roofage** *n.* the expanse of a roof. **roofed** *a.* (sometimes in comb. as in *red-roofed*). **roofer** *n.* a person who builds and repairs roofs. **roof garden** *n.* a garden of plants and shrubs growing in soil-filled receptacles on a flat roof. **roofing** *n.* **1** material used for roofs. **2** the act of roofing buildings. **roofless** *a.* **roof light** *n.* **1** a window in a roof. **2** a flashing light on the top of a police car, ambulance etc. **3** a light on the ceiling of a vehicle. **rooflike** *a.* **roof of the mouth** *n.* the palate. **roof-rack** *n.* a detachable rack on the roof of a motor vehicle for holding luggage etc. **rooftop** *n.* the outside surface of a roof. **to shout from the rooftops** to announce publicly. **roof-tree** *n.* the ridge-pole of a roof. **roofy** *a.* [OE *hrōf*, cp. Dut. *roef*, Icel. *hrōf*]

Usage note The plural *roofs* is preferred to *rooves.*

rooibos (roi´bos) *n.* (*S Afr.*) **1** an evergreen shrub of the genus *Aspalathus*, whose leaves are used to make tea. **2** a small tree, *Combretum apiculatum*, having spikes of yellow flowers. [Afrikaans, a red bush]

rooinek (roi´inek) *n.* (*S Afr., sl., offensive*) an English-speaking South African. [Afrikaans, red neck]

rook[1] (ruk) *n.* **1** a gregarious bird, *Corvus frugilegus*, of the crow family with glossy black plumage. **2** (*sl.*) a cheat, a swindler, a sharper, esp. at cards, dice etc. *~v.t.* **1** to charge extortionately. **2** to cheat, to swindle. **rookery** *n.* (*pl.* **rookeries**) **1** a colony of rooks. **2** a wood or clump of trees where rooks nest. **3** a place frequented by seabirds or seals for breeding. **4** a colony of seals etc. **rookish** *a.* [OE *hrōc* (cp. Dut. *roek*, G *Ruch*, Icel. *hrōkr*), prob. imit., cp. Gr. *krōzein*, to caw]

rook[2] (ruk) *n.* the castle in chess. [OF *roc*, *rock*, ult. from Pers. *rukh*]

rookie (ruk´i), **rooky** *n.* (*pl.* **rookies**) (*sl.*) a raw recruit or beginner. [from RECRUIT]

rooky ROOKIE.

room (room) *n.* **1** space regarded as occupied or available for occupation, accommodation, capacity, vacant space or standing ground. **2** opportunity, scope. **3** a portion of space in a building enclosed by walls, floor and ceiling. **4** the people present in a room. **5** (*pl.*) apartments, lodgings, accommodation for a person or family. *~v.i.* to occupy rooms, to lodge. **no room to swing a cat** CAT[1]. **to give/ leave/ make room** to withdraw so as to leave space for other people. **-roomed** *a.* (*usu. in comb.*, as *two-roomed*). **roomer** *n.* (*N Am.*) a lodger. **roomette** (-et´) *n.* (*N Am.*) **1** a sleeping compartment in a train. **2** a small bedroom for rent. **roomful** *n.* (*pl.* **roomfuls**). **roomie** *n.* (*N Am., coll.*) a room-mate. **rooming** *a.*, *n.* **rooming house** *n.* a lodging-house. **room-mate**, (*N Am.*) **roommate** *n.* a person with whom someone shares a room or lodgings. **room service** *n.* in a hotel, the serving of food and drink to guests in their rooms. **roomy** *a.* (*comp.* **roomier**, *superl.* **roomiest**) having ample room, spacious, extensive. **roomily** *adv.* **roominess** *n.* [OE *rūm* (cp. G *Raum*, Dan. and Swed. *rum*, also Dut. *ruim* and Icel. *rūmr*, spacious)]

roop (roop) *n.* (*Sc.*) a respiratory disease of poultry caused by a virus. [var. of ROUP[2]]

roost[1] (roost) *n.* **1** a pole or perch for birds to rest on. **2** a place for fowls to sleep on at night. **3** a resting place, a room, esp. a bedroom. *~v.i.* **1** to perch on or occupy a roost, to sleep on a roost. **2** to stay the night. *~v.t.* to provide with a roost or a resting-place. **to come home to roost** COME. **to rule the roost** RULE. **rooster** *n.* (*esp. N Am., Austral.*) the domestic cock. [OE *hrōst*, cp. Dut. *roest*]

roost[2] (roost) *n.* a powerful tidal current, esp. off the Orkney and Shetland Islands. [Icel. *rost*]

root[1] (root) *n.* **1** the descending part of a plant which fixes itself in the earth and draws nourishment from it. **2** (*pl.*) the ramifying parts, rootlets or fibres into which this divides, or the analogous part of an epiphyte etc. **3** a young plant for transplanting. **4** a vegetable with an edible root, such as a carrot or turnip. **5** an edible root. **6** the part of an organ or structure that is embedded. **7** the cause or source. **8** the basis, the bottom, the fundamental part or that which supplies origin, sustenance, means of development etc. **9** (*pl.*) one's ancestry, origins, place of origin or belonging. **10** the elementary, unanalysable part of a word as distinct from its inflectional forms and derivatives. **11** (*Mus.*) the fundamental note of a chord. **12** (*Math.*) **a** the quantity or number that, multiplied by itself a specified number of times, yields a given quantity. **b** a square root. **c** a value of an unknown quantity which satisfies a given equation. **13** (*Bible*) an offshoot. **14** (*Austral., New Zeal., sl.*) **a** an act of sexual intercourse. **b** a sexual partner. *~a.* (of an idea etc.) from which the rest originated. *~v.i.* to take root. *~v.t.* **1** to cause to take root. **2** to fix or implant firmly (to the spot). **3** to pull or dig (up) by the roots. **4** (*Austral., New Zeal., taboo sl.*) **a** to have sexual intercourse with. **b** to exhaust. **root and branch** utterly, radically. **to pull up by the roots 1** to uproot. **2** to destroy. **to put down roots 1** to draw nourishment from the soil. **2** to become established. **to root out 1** to uproot. **2** to extirpate. **to strike at the root/ roots of** to destroy deliberately. **to strike root** to take root. **to take root 1** to become planted and send out living roots or rootlets. **2** to become immovable or established. **rootage** (-ij) *n.* **root beer** *n.* (*N Am.*) a fizzy soft drink made from herbs and the roots of plants. **root canal** *n.* the pulp cavity in the root of a tooth. **root canal treatment** *n.* a procedure to replace infected pulp in the root canal with inert material. **root cap** *a.* a protective covering of cells on the tip of a root. **root crop** *n.* a crop of plants with edible roots. **rooted** *a.* firmly established. **rootedly** *adv.* **rootedness** *n.* **rooter**[1] *n.* **rootless** *a.* **rootlet** *n.* **rootlike** *a.* **root-mean-square** *n.* (*Math.*) the square root of the average of the squares of a set of values. **root sign** *n.* (*Math.*) a radical sign. **rootstock** *n.* **1** a rhizome. **2** a plant into which a graft is inserted. **3** the original source or primary form of anything. **rootsy** *a.* (*coll.*) (of music) authentic, uncommercialized, incorporating elements of traditional folk music. **root vegetable** *n.* a vegetable that is or has an edible root. **rooty** *a.* **rootiness** *n.* [late OE and Icel. *rōt*, rel. to L *rādix* and WORT]

root[2] (root) *v.t.* to dig, turn or grub (up) with the snout, beak etc. *~v.i.* **1** to turn up the ground in this manner in search of food. **2** to hunt (up or out), to rummage (about, in etc.). **rooter**[2] *n.* **rootle** (-təl) *v.t.*, *v.i.* to root. [OE *wrōtan*, from *rōt*, ROOT[1]]

root[3] (root) *v.i.* (*coll.*) to cheer, to shout encouragement, to give support (*I'm rooting for you*). **rooter**[3] *n.* a person who roots, cheers or supports. [perh. var. of ROUT[1]]

rooter[1] ROOT[1].

rooter[2] ROOT[2].

rooter[3] ROOT[3].

rootle ROOT[2].

rooves ROOF.

rope (rōp) *n.* **1** a stout cord of twisted fibres of hemp, flax, sisal, cotton, nylon etc., or wire. **2** a lasso. **3** cordage, over one inch (2.5 cm) in circumference. **4** a series of things strung together in a line, e.g. of garlic, onions, pearls. **5** (*pl.*) the ropes enclosing a boxing or wrestling ring. **6** a slimy or gelatinous formation in beer etc. *~v.t.* **1** to tie, fasten or secure with a rope. **2** to enclose or close (in) with rope. **3** to fasten (people) together or to tie (a person on) with a rope when climbing. **4** to pull (a horse) so as to avoid winning a race. *~v.i.* **1** to put a rope on for climbing. **2** to climb (down or up) using a rope. **3** to form threads or filaments (of glutinous matter in liquid) into a rope. **money for old rope** MONEY. **on the rope** in mountaineering, roped together. **on the ropes 1** in boxing, forced against the ropes by one's opponent. **2** nearly defeated. **the rope 1** a hangman's noose. **2** death by hanging. **to give someone enough/ plenty of rope to hang themselves** to allow someone enough freedom of speech or action to commit a blunder or cause their downfall. **to know the ropes** KNOW. **to rope in** to enlist or persuade (someone) to join a group or enter into an activity. **to rope into** to persuade (someone) to enter into (an activity). **ropeable, ropable** *a.* **1** capable of being roped. **2** (*Austral., New Zeal., sl.*) wild, intractable, bad-tempered. **roped** *a.* **rope-dancer** *n.* a tightrope artist. **rope ladder** *n.* a ladder made of two ropes connected by rungs usu. of wood. **ropemanship** *n.* skill in tightrope walking or climbing with ropes. **rope-moulding** *n.* a moulding cut in imitation of rope-strands. **rope of sand** *n.* a feeble or delusive bond. **roper** *n.* **rope's-end** *n.* (*Hist.*) a short piece of rope used for flogging, esp. on shipboard. **rope-walk** *n.* (*Hist.*) a long piece of usu. covered ground where ropes are made. **rope-walker** *n.* a tightrope artist. **rope-walking** *n.* **ropeway** *n.* a cable railway. **rope-yard** *n.* an establishment where rope is made. **rope-yarn** *n.* **1** the fibres used to make rope. **2** a piece of rope-yarn. **3** a mere trifle. **roping** *n.* **ropy, ropey** *a.* (*comp.* **ropier**, *superl.* **ropiest**) **1** (*coll.*) inferior, shoddy. **2** (*coll.*) unwell. **3** glutinous, sticky. **4** resembling a rope. **ropily** *adv.* **ropiness** *n.* [OE *rāp* (cp. Dut. *reep*, G *Reif*, Icel. and Norw. *reip*, Swed. *rep*)]

Roquefort (rok´faw) *n.* **1** a French blue cheese made from ewes' milk. **2** a salad dressing made from Roquefort. [*Roquefort*, France]

roquelaure (rok´əlaw) *n.* a short cloak for men worn in the 18th cent. [Duc de *Roquelaure*, 1656–1738, French marshal]

roquet (rō´kā) *v.t.* (*pres.p.* **roqueting**, *past, p.p.* **roqueted**) **1** in croquet, to make one's ball strike (another ball). **2** (of a croquet ball) to strike (another ball). *~v.i.* to make this stroke. *~n.* this stroke or a hit with it. [from CROQUET]

roquette ROCKET[2].

†**roral** (raw´rəl), †**roric** (raw´rik) *a.* pertaining to or like dew, dewy. †**roriferous** (-rif´-) *a.* producing dew or moisture. [L *rōs rōris*, dew, -AL[1], -IC]

ro-ro (rō´rō) *a.* roll-on roll-off.

rorqual (raw´kwəl) *n.* a baleen whale with dorsal fins, of the family Balaenopteridae, the finback. [F, from Norw. *röyrkval* (*reythr*, red, *kval*, a whale)]

Rorschach test (raw´shahk) *n.* (*Psych.*) a test for personality traits and disorders based on the interpretation of random ink blots. [Hermann *Rorschach*, 1884–1922, Swiss psychiatrist]

rort (rawt) *n.* (*Austral., sl.*) **1** a deception. **2** a party or boisterous celebration. **3** a noise. **rorter** *n.* **rorty** *a.* (*comp.* **rortier**, *superl.* **rortiest**) (*sl.*) **1** rowdy, noisy. **2** coarse, vulgar. [etym. uncertain, perh. from *rorty*, fine, excellent]

rosace (rō´zās) *n.* **1** a rose window. **2** a rose-shaped centrepiece or other ornament, a rosette. **rosacea** (-zā´shiə) *n.* (*Med.*) a chronic skin disease characterized by redness of the skin. **rosaceous** (-zā´shəs) *a.* **1** of or relating to the Rosaceae family of plants to which the rose belongs. **2** roselike, rose-coloured. **rosarian** (-zeə´ri-) *n.* a cultivator of roses. **rosarium** (-əm) *n.* (*pl.* **rosariums**) a rose garden. [F, from ROSE[1]]

rosaline (rō´zəlēn) *n.* fine needlepoint or pillow lace. [prob. F]

rosaniline (rōzan´ilēn, -līn, -lin) *n.* **1** a compound having powerful basic properties, derived from aniline. **2** a salt of this used as a dyestuff under the names aniline red, magenta etc. [ROSE[1], ANILINE]

rosarian, rosarium ROSACE.

rosary (rō´zəri) *n.* (*pl.* **rosaries**) **1** a form of prayer in the Roman Catholic Church in which three sets of five decades of aves, each decade preceded by a paternoster and followed by a gloria, are repeated. **2** this series of prayers. **3** a string of beads by means of which account is kept of the prayers uttered. **4** a similar string of beads used in other religions. **5** a rose garden, a rose plot.

Roscian (ros´kiən) *a.* of or in the manner of Quintus Roscius Gallus, a Roman actor.

roscoe (ros´kō) *n.* (*N Am., sl.*) a gun. [the name *Roscoe*]

rose[1] (rōz) *n.* **1** any plant or flower of the genus *Rosa*, consisting of prickly bushes or climbing and trailing shrubs bearing single or double flowers, usu. scented, of all shades of colour from white and yellow to dark crimson. **2** any of various other flowers or plants having some resemblance to the rose (*a Christmas rose*). **3** a light crimson or pink colour. **4** (*pl.*) a complexion of this colour. **5** a device, rosette, knot, ornament or other object shaped like a rose. **6** a perforated nozzle for a hose or watering can. **7** a rose window. **8** a rose-shaped ornament on a ceiling. **9** a rose diamond. **10** a circular card, disc or diagram with radiating lines, used in a mariner's compass etc. **11** a beautiful woman. **12** (*Med.*) erysipelas, St Anthony's fire. *~a.* coloured like a rose, pink or pale red. *~v.t.* (*chiefly in p.p., poet.*) to make rosy. **all roses** completely pleasant, unproblematic or easy. **everything is coming up roses** everything is turning out successfully. **roses all the way** all roses. **under the rose** in secret, privately, confidentially, sub rosa. **Wars of the Roses** WAR. **rose acacia** *n.* the locust tree, *Robinia hispida*. **roseal** (-ziəl) *a.* **rose-apple** *n.* **1** a tropical tree of the genus *Syzygium*, cultivated for its foliage, flowers and fruit. **2** the fruit of the rose-apple. **roseate** (-ziət) *a.* **1** rose-coloured, rosy. **2** having a partly pink plumage. **3** smiling, promising, optimistic. **rosebay** *n.* **1** (*also* **rosebay willowherb**) the willowherb *Chamerion angustifolium*. **2** the azalea. **3** the oleander. **4** the rhododendron. **rose-beetle** *n.* the rose-chafer. **rosebowl** *n.* a bowl-shaped ornamental vase for roses. **rosebud** *n.* **1** a flower bud of a rose. **2** an attractive young woman. **rose-bug** *n.* an American beetle destructive to roses. **rose bush** *n.* a rose plant. **rose campion** *n.* a garden plant with crimson flowers, *Lychnis coronaria*. **rose-chafer** *n.* a European beetle, *Cetonia aurata*, infesting roses. **rose colour**, (*N Am.*) **rose color** *n.* a deep pink. **to see through rose-coloured spectacles** to take an overoptimistic or unrealistic view (of). **rose-coloured** *a.* **1** of rose colour. **2** sanguine, optimistic. **rose comb** *n.* the fleshy comb of a fowl. **rose-cut** *a.* (of a diamond etc.) cut with a flat surface below and a hemispherical or pyramidal part above covered with facets. **rosed** *a.* **rose diamond** *n.* a rose-cut diamond. **rose-engine** *n.* a lathe attachment for engraving curved patterns. **rose-fish** *n.* (*pl.* **rose-fish**) a red-coloured food fish, *Sebastes marinus*, of the N Atlantic. **rose geranium** *n.* a sweet-scented pelargonium, *Pelargonium graveolus*. **rose-hip** *n.* a red berry, the fruit of the rose plant. †**rose-hued** *a.* rose-coloured. **rose leaf** *n.* a petal (or leaf) of a rose. **roseless** *a.* **roselike** *a.* **rose madder** *n.* a pale pink pigment. **rose-mallow** *n.* a hibiscus. **rose nail** *n.* a nail with a head in the shape of a rose diamond. **rose of Jericho** (jer´ikō) *n.* a resurrection plant, *Anastatica hierochuntica*, a small annual cruciferous plant of N Africa and the

Levant, having fronds that expand with moisture. **rose of Sharon** (sheə´rən, shar´ən) *n.* 1 a species of hypericum, *Hypericum calycinum*, having golden-yellow flowers. 2 (*Bible*) an Eastern plant not clearly identified. 3 a species of garden hibiscus, *Hibiscus syriacus*. **rose pink** *n.* 1 rose colour. 2 a pigment composed of whiting dyed with Brazil wood. **rose-pink** *a.* rose-coloured. **rose-point** *n.* a point lace with a rose design. **rose quartz** *n.* a rose-pink variety of quartz. **rose-rash** *n.* ROSEOLA. **rose red** *n.* the colour of a red rose. **rose-red** *a.* of the colour of a red rose. **rose-root** *n.* a yellow-flowering plant, *Rhodiola rosea*, having a fragrant root. **rosery** (-zəri) *n.* (*pl.* **roseries**) a place where roses grow, a rose garden. **rose-tinted** *a.* rose-coloured. **to see through rose-tinted spectacles** to take an overoptimistic or unrealistic view (of). **rose tree** *n.* a rose plant. **rose vitriol** *n.* cobalt sulphate. **rose water** *n.* scented water distilled from rose leaves. **rose-water** *a.* affectedly delicate, fine or sentimental. **rose window** *n.* a circular window filled with tracery branching from the centre, usu. with mullions arranged like the spokes of a wheel. **rosewood** *n.* 1 a hard close-grained fragrant wood of a dark-red colour obtained chiefly from various species of *Dalbergia*. 2 any tree yielding rosewood. **rosewood oil** *n.* oil obtained from a species of rosewood. **rosy** *a.* (*comp.* **rosier**, *superl.* **rosiest**) 1 of the colour of a pink or red rose. 2 healthy, blooming. 3 favourable, auspicious. **rosily** *adv.* **rosiness** *n.* **rosy-cheeked** *a.* [OE *rose*, L *rosa*, prob. ult. from Gr. *rhodea*, *rhodon*]

rose[2] RISE.

rosé (rō´zā) *n.* a pink-coloured wine, having had only brief contact with red grape skins. [F, pink]

rosella (rōzel´ə) *n.* (*pl.* **rosellas**) (*Austral.*) a variety of brightly-coloured parakeet, *Platycerus eximius*. [*Rose Hill*, a district near Sydney where it was first observed]

roselle (rōzel´) *n.* a hibiscus, *Hibiscus sabdariffa*, with a red calyx.

rosemaling (rō´səmahling) *n.* the art of painting furniture with flower motifs. [Norw., rose painting]

rosemary (rōz´məri) *n.* (*pl.* **rosemaries**) 1 an evergreen fragrant shrub, *Rosmarinus officinalis*, of the mint family, with leaves which yield a perfume and oil and which are used in cooking etc. 2 a funeral emblem signifying remembrance. [orig. *rosmarine*, OF *rosmarin* (F *romarin*), late L *rōsmarīnum* (*rōs*, dew, *marīnus*, MARINE)]

roseola (rōzē´ələ) *n.* 1 a rash occurring in measles etc. 2 (*Med.*) †rubella. **roseolar** *a.* **roseolous** *a.* [dim. of ROSE[1]]

rosery ROSE[1].

roset (roz´it) *n.* a rosin. ~*v.t.* (*pres.p.* **roseting**, *past, p.p.* **roseted**) to rosin.

Rosetta Stone (rōzet´ə) *n.* a key to understanding something previously unattainable. [a basalt stele with an inscription in hieroglyphics, demotic characters and Greek, discovered at Rosetta in Egypt (1799), from which Egyptian hieroglyphics were deciphered]

rosette (rōzet´) *n.* 1 a rose-shaped ornament, knot or badge. 2 a bunch of ribbons, worsted, strips of leather etc. arranged concentrically more or less as the petals of a rose (usu. worn as a badge or given as a prize). 3 (*Archit.*) a carved or painted ornament in the conventional form of a rose. 4 (*Archit.*) a rose window. 5 (*Bot.*) a a circular group of leaves usu. round the base of a stem. b markings resembling a rose. 6 a rose diamond. **rosetted** *a.* [F]

Rosh Hashana (rosh həshah´nə), **Rosh Hashanah** *n.* the Jewish New Year. [Heb., head of the year]

Roshi (rō´shi) *n.* (*pl.* **Roshis**) the spiritual leader of a community of Zen Buddhist monks. [Jap.]

Rosicrucian (rōzikroo´shən) *n.* 1 (*Hist.*) a member of a secret religious society devoted to the study of occult science, which became known to the public early in the 17th cent., and was alleged to have been founded by a German noble, Christian Rosenkreuz, in 1484. 2 a member of a later society derived from this society. ~*a.* of or relating to the Rosicrucians. **Rosicrucianism** *n.* [from L *rŏsa*, a rose, *crux*, a cross]

rosily ROSY (under ROSE[1]).

rosin (roz´in) *n.* resin, esp. the solid residue left after the oil has been distilled from crude turpentine. ~*v.t.* (*pres.p.* **rosining**, *past, p.p.* **rosined**) to rub, smear etc. (esp. the bow of a stringed instrument) with rosin. **rosined** *a.* **rosiny** *a.* [var. of RESIN]

Rosinante (rozinan´ti) *n.* a worn-out horse, a nag. [horse in Cervantes' *Don Quixote*]

rosiness ROSY (under ROSE[1]).

rosolio (rōzō´liō), **rosoglio** *n.* (*pl.* **rosolios, rosoglios**) a cordial made from raisins, spirits etc. in Italy and S Europe. [It. (L *rōs*, dew, *sōlis*, gen. of *sōl*, the sun)]

RoSPA (ros´pə) *abbr.* Royal Society for the Prevention of Accidents.

rostellum (rostel´əm) *n.* (*pl.* **rostella** (-lə)) (*Biol.*) 1 an elevated portion of the stigma in orchids. 2 any small beaklike part or process, such as the protruding forepart of the head in tapeworms, the mouthpart of lice etc. **rostellar** *a.* **rostellate** (-ət) *a.* [L, dim. of ROSTRUM]

roster (ros´tə) *n.* 1 a list showing the order of rotation in which employees, officers, members etc. are to perform their turns of duty. 2 a list of names, e.g. of sports players, available for selection to a team. ~*v.t.* to put on a roster. [Dut. *rooster*, list, orig. gridiron, from *roosten*, to ROAST]

rostrum (ros´trəm) *n.* (*pl.* **rostra** (-trə), **rostrums**) 1 a platform, a pulpit. 2 (*Zool., Bot.*) a beak, bill or beaklike snout, part or process. 3 (*Hist.*) the beak or prow of a Roman war galley. 4 (*Hist.*) a platform (decorated with beaks of captured galleys) in the Roman forum from which public orations etc. were delivered. **rostral** *a.* 1 of, relating to, situated on or resembling a rostrum or beak. 2 (*Anat.*) nearer the hypophysial area, or the nose-and-mouth area. 3 (of a column etc.) decorated with the beaks of war galleys or representations of these. **rostrally** *adv.* **rostrate** (-trət), **rostrated** (-trātid) *a.* 1 (*Zool., Bot.*) having or ending in a part resembling a bird's beak. 2 (of a column etc.) rostral. **rostriferous** (-strif´-) *a.* **rostriform** (-fawm) *a.* [L, beak, cogn. with *rōdere*, to gnaw, cp. RODENT]

rosula (roz´ūlə) *n.* (*pl.* **rosulas**) a rosette of leaves. **rosulate** (-lət) *a.* with leaves making a small rosette. [ROSE[1]]

rosy ROSE[1].

rot (rot) *v.i.* (*pres.p.* **rotting**, *past, p.p.* **rotted**) 1 to decay, to decompose through natural change, to putrefy. 2 to crumble (away) through decomposition. 3 to be affected with rot or some other decaying disease. 4 to pine away. 5 to die out gradually. 6 to become morally corrupt. 7 (*sl.*) to joke. ~*v.t.* 1 to cause to rot, to decompose, to make putrid. 2 (*sl.*) to tease, to abuse. ~*n.* 1 putrefaction, rottenness. 2 dry rot, wet rot. 3 a malignant liver disease in sheep etc. 4 (*coll.*) nonsense, rubbish. 5 a rapid deterioration. ~*int.* used to express disbelief or disagreement. **rotgut** *n.* (*coll.*) any alcoholic drink of inferior quality. [OE *rotian* (cp. Dut. *rotten*, Icel. *rotna*)]

rota (rō´tə) *n.* (*pl.* **rotas**) 1 a list of names, duties etc., a roster. 2 (**Rota**) in the Roman Catholic Church, the supreme court deciding on ecclesiastical and secular causes. **rotal** *a.* **rotaplane** *n.* a gyroplane. [L, wheel]

rotary (rō´təri) *a.* 1 acting or characterized by rotation. 2 rotating on its axis. ~*n.* (*pl.* **rotaries**) 1 a rotary machine. 2 (*N Am.*) a traffic roundabout. **Rotary, Rotary International** *n.* an international business club for mutual benefit and service. **Rotarian** (-teə´ri-) *n.* a member of Rotary. ~*a.* of or relating to Rotary. **Rotarianism** *n.* **Rotary club** *n.* a local branch of Rotary. **rotary cultivator** *n.* a horticultural machine with revolving blades or claws for tilling. **rotary pump** *n.* a pump in which the liquid is delivered at low pressure by means of shaped rotating members. **rotary-wing** *a.* (of an aircraft) deriving lift from rotary aerofoils. **Rotavator®** (-vātə), (*N Am.*) **Rotovator** *n.* a rotary cultivator. **rotavate,** (*N Am.*) **rotovate** *v.t.* to till with a rotary cultivator. **rotatill** *v.t.* (*N Am.*) to rotovate. [med. L *rotarius* (as ROTA)]

rotate[1] (rōtāt´) *v.i.* **1** to revolve round an axis or centre. **2** to act in rotation. ~*v.t.* **1** to cause (a wheel etc.) to revolve. **2** to arrange (crops etc.) in rotation. **rotatable** *a.* **rotation** (-shən) *n.* **1** the act of rotating, rotary motion. **2** alternation, recurrence, regular succession. **3** a system of growing different kinds of crop in a regular order. **rotational** *a.* **rotationally** *adv.* **rotative** (rō´-) *a.* **rotator** *n.* **1** something which moves in or gives a circular motion. **2** (*Anat.*) a muscle imparting rotatory motion. **rotatory** (rō´tə-) *a.*

rotate[2] (rō´tāt) *a.* (*Bot.*) (of a calyx, corolla etc.) wheel-shaped.

rote (rōt) *n.* mere repetition of words, phrases etc. without understanding; mechanical, routine memory or knowledge. ~*v.t.* **1** to repeat from memory. **2** †to learn by rote. **rote learning** *n.* learning by rote. [etym. uncertain, said to be rel. to ROUTE]

rotenone (rō´tənōn) *n.* a crystalline substance obtained from the roots of derris, used as an insecticide. [Jap. *rotenon*, from *roten*, a derris]

roti (rō´ti) *n.* unleavened bread, food. [Hind.]

rotifer (rō´tifə) *n.* any member of the Rotifera, a phylum of minute aquatic animals with swimming organs appearing to have a rotary movement. **rotiferal** (-tif´-), **rotiferous** *a.* [ROTA, L *-fer*, as -FEROUS]

rotisserie (rōtis´əri) *n.* **1** a device with a spit on which food, esp. meat, is roasted or barbecued. **2** a restaurant specializing in meat cooked in this way. [F, cookshop]

rotogravure (rōtəgrəvūə´) *n.* **1** a process of photogravure printing on a rotary machine. **2** a print produced by this process. [L *rota*, a wheel, F *gravure*, engraving]

rotor (rō´tə) *n.* **1** the rotating part of an electric machine. **2** any system of revolving blades that produces lift in aircraft. [short for ROTATOR (under ROTATE[1])]

rototill, rotovate etc. ROTATE[1].

rotten (rot´ən) *a.* **1** decomposed, decayed, decaying, tainted, putrid, fetid. **2** unsound, liable to break, tear etc. **3** morally corrupt, unhealthy, untrustworthy. **4** (*coll.*) poor or contemptible in quality. **5** (*coll.*) disagreeable, annoying, unpleasant. **6** (*coll.*) unwell. **rotten apple** *n.* (*coll.*) a member of a group who is immoral or corrupt. **rotten borough** *n.* (*Hist.*) a borough (before 1832) having only a nominal constituency. **rottenly** *adv.* **rottenness** *n.* **rotten-stone** *n.* a friable siliceous limestone used for polishing. **rotter** *n.* (*coll.*) a good-for-nothing or detestable person. [prob. from Icel. *rotinn* (cp. Swed. *rutten*), cogn. with ROT and RET]

Rottweiler (rot´vīlə, -wī´-) *n.* a large German breed of dog with a smooth black-and-tan coat. [*Rottweil*, a place in SW Germany]

rotula (rot´ūlə) *n.* (*pl.* **rotulas**) **1** (*Anat.*) the kneecap or patella. **2** (*Zool.*) any one of the radial parts of the oral skeleton of a sea urchin. [L, dim. of ROTA]

rotund (rōtŭnd´) *a.* **1** rounded, circular or spherical. **2** (of speech or language) sonorous, magniloquent. **3** plump, well-rounded. **rotunda** (-də) *n.* (*pl.* **rotundas**) a circular building, hall etc., esp. with a dome. **rotundate** (-dāt) *a.* rounded off. **rotundity** *n.* **rotundly** *adv.* [L *rotundus*, ROUND]

Usage note See note under OROTUND.

roturier (rotoor´yā) *n.* a plebeian. [F, from *roture*, prob. from L *ruptūra*, RUPTURE]

rouble (roo´bəl), **ruble** *n.* the standard monetary unit of Russia, Belarus and Tajikistan. [Rus. *rubl'*]

roué (roo´ā) *n.* a rake, a debauchee. [F, p.p. of *rouer*, to break on the wheel, L *rotāre*, to ROTATE[1]]

rouge (roozh) *n.* **1** a cosmetic used to colour the cheeks red. **2** red oxide of iron used for polishing metal, glass etc. ~*v.t.* to colour with rouge. ~*v.i.* **1** to colour one's cheeks etc. with rouge. **2** to blush. **Rouge Croix** (krwah´) *n.* a pursuivant in the English College of Arms. **Rouge Dragon** *n.* a pursuivant in the English College of Arms. **rouge-et-noir** (ānwah´) *n.* a gambling card game played by a 'banker' and a number of people on a table marked with four diamonds, two red and two black. [F, from L *rubeus* (cp. *ruber*, *rufus*, also RED[1])]

rough (rŭf) *a.* **1** having an uneven, broken or irregular surface, having prominences or inequalities, not smooth, level or polished. **2** shaggy, hairy. **3** of coarse texture. **4** rugged, hilly. **5** harsh to the senses, astringent, discordant, severe. **6** violent, boisterous, tempestuous. **7** (of language) coarse, crude. **8** turbulent. **9** disorderly. **10** (of wine) sharp-tasting. **11** harsh or rugged in temper or manners. **12** cruel, unfeeling. **13** rude, unpolished. **14** lacking finish or completeness, not completely wrought, crude. **15** approximate, not precise or exact, general. **16** difficult, hard (to bear). **17** unwell or low in spirits (*feeling rough*). ~*adv.* roughly, in a rough manner. ~*n.* **1** a rough or unfinished state. **2** rough ground. **3** the rough ground to right and left of a golf fairway. **4** a rough person, a rowdy. **5** a spike put in a horseshoe to prevent slipping. **6** a draft, a rough drawing. **7** rough or harsh experiences, hardships. ~*v.t.* **1** to make rough, to roughen. **2** to provide (a horse or horseshoe) with roughs or spikes. **3** to plan or shape (out) roughly or broadly. **bit of rough** BIT[1]. **in the rough** in general. **roughly speaking** approximately. **the rough edge/ side of one's tongue** (*coll.*) a scolding, a rebuke. **to cut up rough** CUT[1]. **to rough in** to outline, to draw roughly. **to rough it** to put up with hardships, to live without the ordinary conveniences. **to rough up** **1** to ruffle (fur, hair or feathers) by rubbing in the wrong direction. **2** (*sl.*) to beat up, to injure during a beating. **to sleep rough** SLEEP. **to take the rough with the smooth** to be subject to unpleasantness or difficulty as well as ease, happiness etc. **roughage** (-ij) *n.* **1** food materials containing a considerable quantity of cellulose, which resist digestion and promote peristalsis. **2** coarse fodder. **rough-and-ready** *a.* hastily prepared, without finish or elaboration; provisional, makeshift. **rough-and-tumble** *a.* disorderly, irregular, haphazard. ~*n.* an irregular fight, contest, scuffle etc. ~*adv.* in a disorderly, irregular or haphazard manner. **rough breathing** *n.* (*Gram.*) in Greek, a sign (ʽ) over an initial vowel indicating that it is aspirated, as distinct from a *smooth breathing*. **roughcast** *n.* **1** a rough model or outline. **2** a coarse plastering, usu. containing gravel, for outside walls etc. ~*a.* **1** formed roughly, without revision or polish. **2** coated with roughcast. ~*v.t.* (*past, p.p.* **roughcast**) **1** to form or compose roughly. **2** to coat (a wall) with roughcast. **rough coat** *n.* a preliminary coat of plaster applied to a surface. **rough cut** *n.* the first assembly of a film by an editor from the selected takes which are joined in scripted order. **rough deal** *n.* harsh or unfair treatment. **rough diamond** *n.* a person with rough exterior or manners but a genuine or warm character. **rough draft** *n.* a rough sketch. **rough-draw** *v.t.* (*past* **rough-drew,** *p.p.* **rough-drawn**) to rough-draft. **rough-dry** *v.t.* (*3rd pers. sing. pres.* **rough-dries,** *pres.p.* **rough-drying,** *past, p.p.* **rough-dried**) to dry without smoothing or ironing. ~*a.* suitable for rough-drying. **roughen** *v.t., v.i.* **rougher** *n.* a person who works in the rough or in the rougher stages of a process etc. **rough-handle** *v.t.* to handle roughly. **rough-hew** *v.t.* (*past* **rough-hewed,** *p.p.* **rough-hewn**) to hew out roughly, to give the first crude form to. **rough-hewn** *a.* 1 cut out roughly. 2 rugged, rough, unpolished. **rough hound** *n.* a dogfish, *Scyliorhinus canicula.* **rough house** *n.* (*sl.*) horseplay, brawling. **rough-house** *v.t.* to handle roughly. ~*v.i.* to create a disturbance. **roughie** *n.* (*sl.*) 1 (*dial. and Austral.*) a rough person, a hooligan. 2 (*Austral.*) **a** an outsider in a race. **b** an unfair act. **c** a roughy. **roughish** *a.* **rough justice** *n.* 1 justice appropriate to a crime but not strictly legal. 2 a sentence or verdict hastily reached and executed. **roughly** *adv.* 1 in a rough manner. 2 approximately. **roughneck** *n.* 1 a rowdy, a hooligan. 2 an oilworker employed to handle drilling equipment on a rig. **roughness** *n.* **rough passage** *n.* 1 a voyage over rough sea. 2 a difficult period. **rough ride** *n.* a difficult experience. **rough-rider** *n.* 1 a horsebreaker, a bold, skilful horseman able to ride unbroken horses. 2 an irregular horse soldier. **rough-shod** *a.* (of a horse) shod with roughened shoes. **to ride roughshod over** to treat in a domineering and inconsiderate way. **rough shooting** *n.* game shooting without the use of beaters, on rough ground or moorland. **rough-spoken** *a.* having a coarse manner of speech. **rough stuff** *n.* (*sl.*) violence, violent behaviour. **rough tongue** *n.* a rough manner of speech. **rough trade** *n.* (*sl.*) a usu. casual homosexual partner who is uncultivated or aggressive. **rough work** *n.* 1 preliminary work. 2 (*coll.*) violence. 3 a piece of work which requires the use of force. **rough-wrought** *a.* worked only as regards the initial stages. **roughy** *n.* (*pl.* **roughies**) (*esp. Austral.*) either of two fishes having rough scales, the tommy ruff, *Arripis georgianus*, or a reef fish, *Trachichthys australis.* [OE *rūh* (cp. Dut. *ruig*, G *rauh*, Dan. *ru*)]

roulade (rulahd´) *n.* 1 a rolled piece of veal or pork. 2 a thin slice of meat spread with a stuffing and rolled into a sausage shape. 3 (*Mus.*) a run of notes on one syllable, a flourish. [F, from *rouler*, to ROLL]

rouleau (roo´lō) *n.* (*pl.* **rouleaux** (-lōz), **rouleaus**) 1 a small roll, esp. a pile of coins done up in paper. 2 a trimming of decorative piping. [F, from ROLE]

roulette (rulet´) *n.* 1 a gambling game played with a ball on a table with a revolving disc. 2 a wheel with points for making dotted lines, used in engraving, for perforating etc. 3 (*Math.*) a curve that is the locus of a point rolling on a curve. **rouletted** *a.* [F, dim. of *rouelle*, dim. of *roue*, L *rota*, a wheel]

Roumanian ROMANIAN.

rounce (rowns) *n.* in printing on a hand press, the handle by which the bed of the printing press is run in and out under the platen. [Dut. *ronse*, *ronds*]

round (rownd) *a.* 1 spherical, circular, cylindrical or approximately so. 2 convexly curved in contour or surface; full, plump, not hollow, corpulent. 3 going from and returning to the same point, with circular or roughly circular course or motion. 4 continuous, unbroken. 5 plain, open, frank, candid, fair. 6 (of pace etc.) quick, smart, brisk. 7 full-toned, resonant. 8 (of a sound) articulated with lips formed into a circle. 9 liberal, ample, large, considerable. 10 composed of tens, hundreds etc., esp. evenly divisible by ten, approximate, without fractions. ~*n.* 1 a round object, piece, slice etc. 2 a ladder rung, a circle, coil, sphere or globe. 3 a sandwich made with two slices of bread. 4 a thick cut from a joint of beef. 5 something which surrounds, circumference, extent. 6 a circular course, a circuit, a recurrent series. 7 a heat, a cycle. 8 a bout, a session, a spell. 9 an allowance. 10 a series of actions. 11 in archery, a number of arrows fired from a fixed distance. 12 an order of drinks for several people, each of whom is buying drinks for the group in turn. 13 a burst of applause. 14 a single shot or volley fired from a firearm or gun. 15 ammunition for this. 16 the state of being completely carved out in the solid, as distinct from RELIEF[2]. 17 (*Mil.*) a circuit of inspection, the route taken. 18 (*Mus.*) a piece of music sung by several voices each taking it up in succession. 19 the extent (of). ~*adv.* 1 on all sides so as to encircle. 2 so as to come back to the same point. 3 to or at all points on the circumference or all members of a party etc. 4 by a circuitous route. 5 with rotating motion. 6 to an opposite opinion or view. 7 to one's house. 8 into a more convenient position. 9 in girth. ~*prep.* 1 on all sides of. 2 so as to encircle. 3 to or at all parts of the circumference of. 4 in relation to as a body is to its axis or centre, in all directions from. 5 revolving round. 6 visiting each of. 7 to the other side of. ~*v.t.* 1 to make round or curved. 2 to pass, go or travel round. 3 to change (an amount or figure) to the nearest large number or round number. 4 to collect together, to gather (up). 5 to fill out, to complete. 6 to pronounce fully and smoothly. ~*v.i.* 1 to grow or become round. 2 (of a guard etc.) to go the rounds. 3 (*chiefly Naut.*) to turn round. **in round numbers** 1 to the nearest large number. 2 approximately. **in the round** 1 all things considered. 2 able to be viewed from every side. **round about** 1 in or as if in a circle (round), all round. 2 approximately. 3 in an opposite direction. 4 circuitously, indirectly. **round and round** several times round. **round peg in a square hole** PEG. **round the bend** BEND. **round the clock** CLOCK[1]. **round the twist** TWIST. **to be round the bend** BEND. **to get round** 1 to coax by flattery or deception. 2 to evade (a law or rule). **to get round to** GET[1]. **to go one's rounds** to make one's rounds. **to go round in circles** CIRCLE. **to go the round(s)** (of news, a joke etc.) to be passed from person to person. **to make one's rounds** to make a series of visits to different people or places. **to make the round of** to go round. **to round down** to lower (a number) to avoid fractions or reach a convenient figure. **to round off** 1 to finish off, to complete, to perfect. 2 to shape (angles etc.) to a round or less sharp form. **to round on** to turn upon, to attack. **to round out** 1 to finish off, to complete, to perfect. 2 to provide more information about. 3 to fill out, to become more plump. **to round to** to turn the prow of a ship towards the wind, in order to heave to. **to round up** 1 to gather (horse, cattle etc.) together. 2 to raise (a number) to avoid fractions or reach a convenient figure. **roundabout** *n.* 1 a device at a crossroads whereby traffic circulates in one direction only. 2 a merry-go-round. 3 a circuitous or indirect journey, way, course etc. 4 a circular revolving device for riding on in a children's playground. ~*a.* 1 circuitous, indirect, loose. 2 plump, stout. **round-aboutness** *n.* **round-arm** *a.* in cricket, (of bowling) performed with a swing in which the arm turns at shoulder level. **round-backed** *a.* having a round or curved back. **round brackets** *n.pl.* parentheses. **round dance** *n.* a dance in which the performers are ranged or move in a circle, esp. a waltz. **rounded** *a.* **roundedness** *n.* **rounder** *n.* 1 (*pl.*) a game with a short bat and a ball, between two sides, with four bases around which a player hitting the ball has to run without the ball being returned to the base ahead. 2 a complete run through all the bases in rounders. 3 someone who or something which rounds, esp. a tool used in bookbinding, a wheelwright's plane etc. **round-eyed** *a.* **round-faced** *a.* **round game** *n.* any card game in which there are a number of players but no sides or partners. **round-hand** *n.* writing in which the letters are round and full. **Roundhead** *n.* a Parliamentarian in the English Civil War. **roundhouse** *n.* 1 (*Hist.*) a circular building containing a turntable for servicing railway locomotives. 2 (*sl.*) a blow with a wide sweep of the arm. 3 (*Hist.*) a lock-up. 4 (*Naut.*) a cabin on the after part of the quarterdeck, esp. on sailing ships. **round-house kick** *n.* in karate, a kick with a wide sweep of the leg. **rounding** *a.* becoming round, nearly round. **roundish** *a.* **roundly** *adv.* 1 bluntly, straightforwardly, plainly, emphatically. 2 energetically, thoroughly. 3 in a round or roundish form. **roundness** *n.* **round robin** *n.* 1 a petition with the signatures placed in a circle so that no name heads the list. 2 a tournament in which each contestant plays every other contestant. **round-shouldered** *a.* having the shoulders bent forward so that the back is rounded. **roundsman** (-mən) *n.* (*pl.* **roundsmen**) 1 a man who makes calls to collect orders, deliver goods etc. 2 (*N Am.*) a police officer making a round of inspection. 3 (*Austral.*) a journalist covering a particular topic. **Round Table** *n.* an international association of professional and business men who meet to further business activities and undertake community service. **round table** *n.* a conference or meeting at which all parties are on an equal footing. **round-the-clock** *a.* continuous, lasting 24 hours a day. **round top** *n.* a platform at the top of a mast. **round tower** *n.* a high narrow tower, tapering from the base upwards, usu. with a conical top, frequent in Ireland, esp. near an ancient church or monastery. **round trip** *n.* a journey to a place and back. ~*a.* (*N Am.*) return. **round-up** *n.* 1 a gathering together of cattle etc. 2 a similar gathering of people, objects, news, facts etc.; a news round-up. **roundworm** *n.* a parasitic elongated worm, a nematode. [OF *rund, rond, round* (F *rond*), L *rotundus*, from *rota*, wheel]

roundel (rown´dəl) *n.* 1 a round disc, panel, heraldic circular charge etc. 2 a rondel or rondeau. [ME, from OF *rondel(le)* (as ROUND)]

roundelay (rown´dəlā) *n.* 1 a simple song, usu. with a refrain. 2 a round dance. [F *rondelet*, as RONDEL (under RONDEAU), with assim. to LAY[1] or *virelay*, a medieval song]

roup[1] (rowp) *v.t.* (*Sc., North.*) to sell by auction. ~*n.* a sale by auction. [cp. Icel. *raupa*]

roup[2] (roop) *n.* a respiratory viral disease of poultry. **roupy** *a.* [as ROUP[1]]

rouse (rowz) *v.t.* 1 to wake. 2 to excite to thought or action. 3 to provoke, to stir (up), to agitate. 4 (*Naut.*) to haul (in) with vigour. 5 to startle (game) from a covert. 6 to stir. ~*v.i.* 1 to wake or be wakened. 2 to start up, to be excited or stirred (up) to activity etc. **to rouse on** (*Austral.*) to scold, to tell off. **to rouse oneself** to abandon inactivity. **rousable** *a.* **rouseabout** *n.* (*Austral., New Zeal.*) an odd-job man in a shearing shed or on a station. **rouser** *n.* **rousing** *a.* 1 having power to awaken, excite or rouse. 2 blazing strongly. **rousingly** *adv.* [etym. uncertain, perh. rel. to RUSH[1]]

roust (rowst) *v.t.* 1 to rouse, to rout (out). 2 (*N Am., sl.*) to jostle or harass. **to roust around** to rummage. **roustabout** *n.* 1 an unskilled worker on an oil rig. 2 a casual labourer. 3 a labourer on wharves. 4 (*N Am.*) a labourer in a circus. 5 (*Austral.*) a rouseabout. [perh. alt. of ROUSE]

rout[1] (rowt) *n.* 1 an utter defeat and overthrow. 2 a disorderly and confused retreat of a defeated army etc. 3 a crowd, a miscellaneous or disorderly gathering. 4 (*Law*) an assembly and attempt of three or more people to do an unlawful act upon a common quarrel. 5 a riot, a brawl, an uproar, a disturbance. 6 †a large evening party. ~*v.t.* to defeat utterly and put to flight. **to put to rout** to defeat utterly. [OF *route*, a troop, company etc.]

rout[2] (rowt) *v.t.* 1 to root (up or out). 2 to turn (a bed). 3 to fetch, evict from a house etc. 4 to gouge, to scoop, to tear (out etc.). ~*v.i.* to root up or out. **to rout out** to hunt out. **router** *n.* 1 a plane, a saw or any of various other tools for hollowing out or cutting grooves. 2 someone who or something which routs. [var. of ROOT[2]]

rout[3] (rowt) *v.i.* (*Sc., North.*) (of cattle etc.) to bellow, to roar. [from Scand. (cp. Icel. *rauta*, Norw. *ruta*), rel. to ROUT[1]]

route (root) *n.* 1 the course, way or road(s) travelled or to be travelled. 2 (*N Am.*) a course travelled in delivering or selling. ~*v.t.* (*pres.p.* **routeing, routing**) 1 to send by a certain route. 2 to arrange or plan the route of. **routeman** *n.* (*pl.* **routemen**) (*N Am.*) a roundsman. **route march** *n.* 1 an arduous military-training march. 2 (*coll.*) a long, tiring walk. **route-step** *n.* an irregular step allowed in long marching. [F, from L *rupta*, broken (way), fem. p.p. of *rumpere*, to break]

routine (rootēn´) *n.* 1 a course of procedure, business or official duties etc., regularly pursued. 2 any regular or mechanical habit or practice. 3 a sequence of jokes, movements, steps etc. regularly performed by a comedian, dancer, skater, stripper etc. 4 a computer program or part of one which performs a particular task. 5 (*coll.*) insincere speech or behaviour. ~*a.* 1 tiresome, repetitive, commonplace. 2 of or relating to a set procedure. **routinely** *a.* **routinism** *n.* adherence to routine. **routinist** *n., a.* **routinize, routinise** *v.t.* **routinization** (-zā´shən) *n.* [F]

roux (roo) *n.* (*pl.* **roux**) a sauce base, the thickening element in a sauce made from fat and flour cooked together. [F, brown]

rove[1] (rōv) *v.i.* 1 to wander, to ramble, to roam. 2 (of eyes) to look round, to wander. 3 to troll with live bait. ~*v.t.* to wander over, through etc. ~*n.* the act of roving, a ramble. **rove-beetle** *n.* a beetle of the family Staphylinidae, having an elongated body. **rover**[1] *n.* 1 a wanderer. 2 **a** in croquet, a ball that has gone through all the hoops but not pegged out. **b** a person playing this shot. 3 in archery, a mark chosen at random for long-distance shooting. 4 in American football, a defensive linebacker moving around in anticipation of the opposition's play. 5 a fickle person. 6 a pirate, a buccaneer. 7 (**Rover**) a member of the Rover Scouts. **Rovers, Rover Scouts** *n.pl.* (*Hist.*) a branch of the Scouts for boys over 16 years old. **rover ticket** *n.* a ticket which can be used for unlimited travel on public transport within a defined area for a certain period. **roving**[1] *n., a.* **roving commission** *n.* a commission without a rigidly defined area of authority. **roving eye** *n.* a promiscuous sexual interest. **rovingly** *adv.* [etym. uncertain, perh. rel. to Icel. *rāfa* or to Dut. *rooven*, to rob]

rove[2] (rōv) *n.* a small metal plate through which a rivet is passed and clenched over. [etym. unknown]

rove[3] (rōv) *v.t.* to draw out and slightly twist (slivers of wool, cotton etc.) before spinning into thread. ~*n.* a slightly twisted sliver of wool, cotton etc. **rover**[2] *n.* **roving**[2] *n.* [etym. uncertain]

rove[4] REEVE[2].

rover[1] ROVE[1].

rover[2] ROVE[3].

roving[1] ROVE[1].

roving[2] ROVE[3].

row[1] (rō) *n.* 1 a series of persons or things in a straight or nearly straight line. 2 a line, a rank (of seats, vegetables etc.). 3 a street usu. of identical houses. **hard row to hoe** a difficult task. **in a row** 1 (placed) one after the other. 2 (ordered) in succession. **row house** *n.* (*N Am.*) a terrace house. [OE *rāw*, cp. Dut. *rij*, G *Reihe*]

row[2] (rō) *v.t.* 1 to propel by oars. 2 to convey by rowing. 3 to make (a stroke) in rowing. 4 to take part in (a rowing race). 5 to compete against (in a rowing race). ~*v.i.* 1 to row a boat. 2 to labour with an oar. 3 to be impelled by oars. ~*n.* 1 a spell at rowing. 2 an excursion in a rowing boat. **to row down** to overtake by rowing, esp. in a bumping race. **to row over** to win a rowing race very easily. **rowable** *a.* **row-boat** *n.* (*N Am.*) a rowing boat. **rower** *n.* **rowing** *n., a.* **rowing boat** *n.* a boat propelled by rowing. **rowing machine** *n.* an exercise machine fitted with oars and a sliding seat. **rowlock** (rol´ək), **rollock** *n.* a crotch, notch or other device on the gunwale of a boat serving as a fulcrum for an oar. **row-port** *n.* (*Naut.*) a small porthole, cut near the water's edge for the use of oars in a small vessel. [OE *rōwan* (cp. Dut. *roeijen*, Icel. *rōa*, MHG *rüejen*, also L *rēmus*, Gr. *eretmon*, an oar)]

row[3] (row) *n.* (*coll.*) 1 a noisy disturbance, a noise, a din, a commotion, a tumult. 2 a quarrel. 3 a scolding. *~v.t.* to scold, to reprimand. *~v.i.* to make a row, to quarrel. **to kick up a row** to make a row. **to make a row** to make a loud, unpleasant noise. [etym. uncertain, prob. orig. slang]

rowan (row´ən, rō´-) *n.* 1 the mountain ash, *Sorbus aucuparia*. 2 (*N Am.*) a similar tree, *Sorbus americana*, of America. **rowan berry** *n.* the small red fruit of the rowan. **rowan tree** *n.* [Sc. and ONF, from Scand. (cp. Swed. *röun*, Dan. *rön*, Icel. *reynir*)]

rowdy (row´di) *a.* (*comp.* **rowdier**, *superl.* **rowdiest**) rough, riotous. *~n.* (*pl.* **rowdies**) a noisy, rough or disorderly person. **rowdily** *adv.* **rowdiness** *n.* **rowdyish** *a.* **rowdyism** *n.*

rowel (row´əl) *n.* 1 a spiked disc or wheel on a spur. 2 (*Hist.*) a roll or disc of various materials with a hole in the centre for placing under a horse's skin to discharge purulent matter. *~v.t.* (*pres.p.* **rowelling,** (*N Am.*) **roweling,** *past, p.p.* **rowelled,** (*N Am.*) **roweled**) 1 to prick or goad with a rowel. 2 to insert a rowel in (a horse etc.). **rowel-spur** *n.* a spur with a rowel. [OF *rouel*, dim. of *roue*, L *rota*, wheel]

rowen (row´ən) *n.* (*sometimes pl.*, *N Am.*) a second growth of grass, an aftermath. [ME, from OF *regain* (as RE-, GAIN)]

rowlock ROW[2].

Rowton house (row´tən) *n.* (*Hist.*) a cheap lodging house for poor, single men. [Lord *Rowton*, d. 1903, English social reformer]

Roxburghe (roks´bərə) *n.* a style of bookbinding comprising a plain leather back, usu. gilt-lettered, cloth or paper sides, gilt top and the other edges untrimmed. [Duke of *Roxburghe*, 1740–1804, book collector]

royal (roi´əl) *a.* 1 of, relating to, suitable to or befitting a king or queen. 2 under the patronage or in the service of a king or queen. 3 regal, kingly, princely. 4 noble, magnificent, majestic. 5 extremely fine, on a great scale, splendid, first-rate. *~n.* 1 (*coll.*) a member of a royal family. 2 a royal stag. 3 a royal mast or sail next above the topgallant. **rhyme royal** RHYME. **the Royals** 1 the royal family. 2 the Royal Marines. 3 (*Hist.*) the first regiment of foot in the British service, the Royal Scots. **Royal Academy** *n.* an academy of fine arts in London. **Royal Air Force** *n.* the air force of Great Britain. **royal assent** *n.* the sovereign's assent to a bill passed by Parliament. **royal blue** *n.* a deep blue. **royal-blue** *a.* of a deep blue. **Royal British Legion** *n.* an association of ex-servicemen and ex-servicewomen. **royal burgh** *n.* a burgh holding its municipal authority by royal charter. **Royal Commission** *n.* a commission of inquiry ordered by Parliament. **royal duke** *n.* a duke who is also a prince. **Royal Engineers** *n.pl.* the engineering branch of the British army. **royal family** *n.* the sovereign and the sovereign's family. **royal fern** *n.* a flowering fern, *Osmunda regalis*. **royal flush** *n.* a flush with cards in a sequence headed by the ace. **royal icing** *n.* a hard icing on wedding cakes, fruit cakes etc. **Royal Institution** *n.* a British society for the diffusion of scientific knowledge. **royalism** *n.* **royalist** *n.* 1 an adherent or supporter of royalism or of monarchical government, esp. a supporter of the royal cause in the English Civil War. 2 (*N Am.*) a reactionary or conservative person. *~a.* of or relating to royalists. **royal jelly** *n.* the food secreted and fed by worker bees to developing queen bees. **royally** *adv.* **Royal Marines** *n.pl.* a British corps specializing in commando and amphibious operations. **royal mast** *n.* the topmost part of a mast above the topgallant. **Royal Navy** *n.* the British navy. **royal oak** *n.* a sprig of oak worn on 29 May to commemorate King Charles II. **royal palm** *n.* any tall palm of the genus *Roystonea*, of tropical America. **royal plural** *n.* the royal 'we'. **royal prerogative** *n.* the constitutional authority and privilege invested in a sovereign. **royal purple** *n.* a deep violet tending to blue. **royal road** *n.* an easy way or direct route (to a goal etc.). **royal sail** *n.* a sail above a topgallant sail. **Royal Society, Royal Society of London** *n.* a society for the promotion of scientific discussion and research. **royal stag** *n.* a stag with antlers having 12 or more points. **royal standard** *n.* a flag with the royal arms. **royal tennis** *n.* real tennis. **royalty** *n.* (*pl.* **royalties**) 1 the office or dignity of a king or queen, sovereignty. 2 a royal person or persons. 3 a member of a royal family. 4 a right or prerogative of a sovereign. 5 royal rank, birth or lineage. 6 kingliness, queenliness. 7 (*usu. pl.*) a share of profits paid to a landowner for the right to work a mine, to a patentee for the use of an invention, to an author on copies of books sold etc. **Royal Victorian Chain** *n.* an order founded by King Edward VII and conferred by the sovereign on special occasions. **Royal Victorian Order** *n.* an order founded by Queen Victoria and conferred for special services to the sovereign. **royal warrant** *n.* a warrant authorizing the supply of goods to a royal household. **royal 'we'** *n.* the customary use of the first person plural by a sovereign referring to themselves. [OF *roial*, L *rēgālis*, REGAL[1]]

royster ROISTER.

rozzer (roz´ə) *n.* (*sl.*) a police officer. [etym. unknown]

RP *abbr.* 1 received pronunciation. 2 Reformed Presbyterian. 3 Regius Professor.

RPG *abbr.* 1 (*Comput.*) report program generator (a commercial programming language). 2 rocket-propelled grenade. 3 role-playing game.

RPI *abbr.* retail price index.

r.p.m. *abbr.* 1 revolutions per minute. 2 resale price maintenance.

RPO *abbr.* Royal Philharmonic Orchestra.

rpt *abbr.* repeat.

RR *abbr.* 1 (*N Am.*) railroad. 2 Right Reverend. 3 (*N Am.*) rural route.

-rrhagia (rā´jiə) *comb. form* abnormal discharge, excessive flow, as in *menorrhagia*. [L from Gr., a bursting forth, from *rhēgnunai*, to break, to burst]

-rrhoea (rē´ə), (*N Am.*) **-rrhea** *comb. form* a discharge, a flow, as *diarrhoea*. [L from Gr. *-rrhoia*, from *rheein*, to flow]

RS *abbr.* 1 Received Standard. 2 Royal Scots. 3 Royal Society.

Rs. *abbr.* rupee(s).

RSA *abbr.* 1 Republic of South Africa. 2 Royal Scottish Academy or Academician. 3 Royal Society of Arts.

RSC *abbr.* 1 Royal Shakespeare Company. 2 Royal Society of Chemistry.

RSFSR *abbr.* (*Hist.*) Russian Soviet Federative Socialist Republic.

RSI *abbr.* repetitive strain injury.

RSJ *abbr.* rolled steel joist.

RSM *abbr.* 1 Regimental Sergeant Major. 2 (Republic of) San Marino (IVR). 3 Royal Society of Medicine.

RSNO *abbr.* Royal Scottish National Orchestra.

RSPB *abbr.* Royal Society for the Protection of Birds.

RSPCA *abbr.* Royal Society for the Prevention of Cruelty to Animals.

RSV *abbr.* Revised Standard Version (of the Bible).

RSVP *abbr.* please reply. [F, *répondez s'il vous plaît*]

RTE *abbr.* Radio Telefis Éireann (Irish radio and television).

Rt. Hon. *abbr.* Right Honourable.

Rt. Revd., Rt. Rev. *abbr.* Right Reverend.

RU *abbr.* 1 Burundi (IVR). 2 Rugby Union.

Ru *chem. symbol* ruthenium.

rub[1] (rŭb) *v.t.* (*pres.p.* **rubbing,** *past, p.p.* **rubbed**) 1 to apply friction to, to move one's hand or other object over the surface of. 2 to polish, to clean, to scrape, to graze. 3 to slide or pass (a hand or other object) along, over or against something. 4 to make sore by rubbing. 5 to take an impression of (a design) with chalk and graphite on paper laid over it. 6 to reduce to a powder by rubbing. 7 to remove by rubbing. 8 to irritate. 9 to spread on or mix into something by rubbing. ~*v.i.* 1 to move or slide along a surface, to grate, to graze, to chafe (against, on etc.). 2 to cause pain or fraying by rubbing. 3 in bowling, to meet with a hindrance. 4 to get (along, on, through etc.) with difficulty. ~*n.* 1 the act or a spell of rubbing. 2 a hindrance, an obstruction, a difficulty. 3 in bowling, an unevenness of the ground which impedes the bowl. **to rub along** 1 (*coll.*) to manage, to just succeed, to cope despite difficulties. 2 (*coll.*) to keep on friendly terms. **to rub down** 1 to clean or dry by rubbing. 2 to make smooth. **to rub elbows with** (*N Am.*) to rub shoulders with. **to rub in** to force in by friction. **to rub it in** to keep reminding someone of something embarrassing. **to rub noses** to rub one's nose against someone else's as an Eskimo (Inuit) greeting. **to rub off** to remove by rubbing. **to rub off on someone** to pass on to someone by example or close association. **to rub on** (*coll.*) to rub along. **to rub one's hands** to express expectation, glee, satisfaction etc. by rubbing one's hands together. **to rub out** 1 to remove or erase by friction. 2 (*N Am., sl.*) to kill. **to rub shoulders with** to associate or mix with. **to rub someone's nose in it** to refer to or remind someone of an error, indiscretion or misfortune. **to rub up** 1 to polish, to burnish. 2 to freshen (one's recollection of something). 3 to mix into a paste etc. by rubbing. **to rub (up) the wrong way** to irritate. **rubbing** *n.* 1 the act of rubbing. 2 an impression made on paper laid over an image and rubbed with chalk, wax etc. **rub-down** *n.* the act of rubbing down. **rub of the green, rub on the green** *n.* 1 in golf, an accidental interference with the ball. 2 (*coll.*) good fortune. **rubstone** *n.* a stone used for sharpening by rubbing. **rub-up** *n.* the act of rubbing up. [ME *rubben* (cp. LG *rubben*), etym. uncertain]

rub[2] (rŭb) *n.* a rubber of bridge.

rub-a-dub (rŭbədŭb´), **rub-a-dub-dub** *n.* the sound of a rapid drumbeat. [imit.]

rubaiyat (roo´bīyat) *n.* in Persian poetry, a verse form consisting of quatrains. [Arab. *ruba´īyah*, from *ruba´īy*, consisting of four elements]

rubato (rubah´tō) *n.* (*pl.* **rubatos, rubati** (-tē)) (*Mus.*) 1 flexibility of rhythm, fluctuation of tempo within a musical piece. 2 an instance of this. ~*a.* to be performed in this manner. [It., stolen, *tempo rubato*, stolen time, from *rubare*, to rob]

rubber[1] (rŭb´ə) *n.* 1 a soft, elastic substance obtained from the coagulated juice of several tropical plants. 2 a piece of rubber for erasing pencil marks etc. 3 (*coll.*) a condom. 4 (*pl., N Am.*) galoshes, rubber overshoes. 5 someone who or something which rubs. 6 a masseur or masseuse. 7 an instrument used for rubbing, a rubstone. 8 a part of a machine that rubs, grinds, polishes etc. ~*a.* made of, yielding or relating to rubber. **rubber band** *n.* a continuous band of rubber for securing packages, the hair etc. **rubber bullet** *n.* a baton round made of rubber. **rubber cement** *n.* an adhesive containing rubber. **rubberize, rubberise** *v.t.* to treat with rubber. **rubberneck, rubbernecker** *n.* (*coll.*) 1 a sightseer. 2 a person who gapes out of curiosity. ~*v.i.* 1 to sightsee. 2 to gape foolishly. **rubber plant** *n.* 1 a plant, *Ficus elastica*, common to Asia and related to the fig, with large shiny leaves, grown as a popular house plant. 2 (*also* **rubber tree**) any one of various tropical, latex-yielding trees, esp. *Hevea brasiliensis*. **rubber solution** *n.* a liquid adhesive which dries to a rubber-like material. **rubber stamp** *n.* 1 a device with a rubber pad for marking or imprinting. 2 a person who makes routine authorizations, a cipher. 3 a routine seal of approval, an automatic endorsement. ~*v.t.* 1 to approve or endorse as a matter of routine. 2 to imprint with a rubber stamp. **rubber tree** *n.* a rubber plant. **rubbery** *a.* **rubberiness** *n.* [RUB[1], -ER[1]]

rubber[2] (rŭb´ə) *n.* 1 a series of three games at whist, bridge, backgammon etc. 2 two games out of three or the game that decides the contest. [etym. uncertain]

rubbish (rŭb´ish) *n.* 1 waste, broken or rejected matter, refuse, junk, litter, trash. 2 nonsense. ~*a.* (*coll.*) bad, useless, distasteful etc. ~*v.t.* 1 to criticize. 2 to reject as rubbish. **rubbish heap** *n.* 1 a pile of or place for waste. 2 a state of uselessness. **on the rubbish heap** rejected, useless. **rubbishing, rubbishy** *a.* [ME *robows*, A-F *robeux*, prob. pl. of RUBBLE]

rubble (rŭb´əl) *n.* 1 rough, broken fragments of stone, brick etc. 2 rubblework. 3 (*Geol.*) disintegrated rock. 4 water-worn stones. **rubble-stone** *n.* the upper fragmentary and decomposed portion of a mass of rock. **rubblework** *n.* masonry composed of irregular fragments of stone, or in which these are used for filling in. **rubbly** *a.* [prob. from Scand. (cp. Icel. *rubb rubbr*, Norw. *rubl*)]

rube (roob) *n.* (*N Am., coll.*) an unsophisticated country dweller, a country bumpkin. [the name *Reuben*]

rubefy (roo´bifī), **rubify** *v.t.* (*3rd pers. sing. pres.* **rubefies, rubifies,** *pres.p.* **rubefying, rubifying,** *past, p.p.* **rubefied, rubified**) to make red. **rubefacient** (-fā´shənt) *a.* making red. ~*n.* an external application causing redness of the skin. **rubefaction** (-fak´shən) *n.* [F *rubéfier*, L *rubefacere* (*rubēre*, to be red, *facere*, to make)]

rubella (rubel´ə) *n.* (*Med.*) a mild, infectious disorder resembling measles which, if contracted by a pregnant woman, may cause birth deformities in her unborn child; German measles. **rubellite** (roo´bəlīt, rubel´-) *n.* a pinkish-red tourmaline. **rubeola** (-bē´ələ) *n.* measles. [dim. of L *rubeus*, red]

Rubicon (roo´bikən) *n.* 1 an irrevocable step, a point of no return. 2 (**rubicon**) in piquet, the winning of the game before one's opponent has scored 100 points. ~*v.t.* (*pres.p.* **rubiconing,** *past, p.p.* **rubiconed**) to defeat (one's opponent) thus. **to cross the Rubicon** to take an irrevocable step. [a small stream in Italy, bounding the province of Caesar, who crossed it before the war with Pompey, exclaiming, 'The die is cast!']

rubicund (roo´bikənd) *a.* ruddy, rosy, red-faced. **rubicundity** (-kŭn´-) *n.* [F *rubicond*, L *rubicundus*, from *rubēre*, to be red]

rubidium (rubid´iəm) *n.* a silvery-white metallic element, at. no. 37, chem. symbol Rb, belonging to the potassium group. **rubidic** *a.* [L *rubidus*, red, as RUBICUND, -IUM]

rubied RUBY.

rubify RUBEFY.

rubiginous (rubij´inəs) *a.* (*formal*) rusty or brownish-red in colour. [L *rūbīgo -gīnis*, rust]

Rubik's cube® (roo´biks) *n.* a puzzle consisting of a cube, each face of which is divided into nine coloured segments which can be revolved to obtain the same colour on each face. [Erno *Rubik*, b. 1944, Hungarian inventor]

ruble ROUBLE.

rubric (roob´rik) *n.* 1 a title, chapter heading, entry, set of rules, commentary or direction, orig. printed in red or distinctive lettering, esp. a liturgical direction in the Prayer Book etc. 2 explanatory notes, instructions, rules. 3 an established custom. ~*a.* red, marked with red. **rubrical** *a.* **rubrically** *adv.* **rubricate** *v.t.* 1 to mark, distinguish, print or illuminate with red. 2 to furnish with a rubric or rubrics. **rubrication** (-ā´shən) *n.* **rubricator** *n.* **rubrician** (-brish´ən) *n.* a person versed in or adhering strictly to liturgical rubric. [F *rubrique*, L *rubrīca*, from *ruber*, red]

ruby (roo´bi) *n.* (*pl.* **rubies**) **1** a precious stone of a red colour, a variety of corundum. **2** the colour of ruby, a purplish red. **3** (*Hist.*) a size of type between nonpareil and pearl. ~*a.* **1** of the colour of a ruby. **2** marking a 40th anniversary. **rubied** *a.* red as a ruby. **ruby-coloured,** (*N Am.*) **ruby-colored** *a.* of the deep red colour of a ruby. **ruby glass** *n.* glass coloured with oxides of copper, iron, lead etc. **ruby-red** *a.* ruby-coloured. **ruby-tail** *n.* a wasp, *Chrysis ignita*, with a bluish-green back and red abdomen. **ruby wedding** *n.* a 40th wedding anniversary. [OF *rubi, rubis*, ult. from L *rub-*, stem of *rubeus*, red]

RUC *abbr.* Royal Ulster Constabulary.

ruche (roosh) *n.* a pleated strip of gauze, lace, silk or the like used as a frill or trimming. ~*v.t.* to trim with a ruche. **ruched** *a.* **ruching** *n.* [F, from med. L *rusca*, tree bark, of Celtic orig.]

ruck[1] (rŭk) *n.* **1** a multitude, a crowd, esp. the mass of horses left behind by the leaders in a race. **2** the common run of people or things. **3** in rugby, a gathering of players round the ball when it is on the ground. **4** in Australian Rules football, three players who follow the play without fixed positions. **5** a heap, a pile. ~*v.i.* to form a ruck in rugby. [prob. cogn. with RICK[1]]

ruck[2] (rŭk) *v.i., v.t.* to wrinkle, to crease. ~*n.* a crease, a wrinkle, a fold, a pleat. **ruckle**[1] (-əl) *v.t., v.i.* to ruck. ~*n.* a ruck. [Icel. *hrukka*, cp. Norw. *rukka*]

ruckle[1] RUCK[2].

ruckle[2] (rŭk´əl) *v.i.* to make a rattling or gurgling noise. ~*n.* a rattling or gurgling noise, esp. in the throat, a death rattle. [prob. from Scand. (cp. Norw. *rukla*)]

rucksack (rŭk´sak) *n.* a bag carried on the back by means of straps by campers, hikers, climbers etc. [G (*Rücken*, back, SACK[1])]

ruckus (rŭk´əs) *n.* (*chiefly N Am.*) a row, a disturbance, an uproar. [prob. combination of RUCTION and RUMPUS]

ruction (rŭk´shən) *n.* (*coll.*) **1** a commotion, a disturbance, a row. **2** (*pl.*) trouble, arguments.

rudaceous (rudā´shəs) *a.* (of rock) composed of fairly large fragments. [L *rudus*, rubble]

rudbeckia (rŭdbek´iə) *n.* a plant of the genus *Rudbeckia* of N American plants of the aster family. [Olaus *Rudbeck*, 1630–1702, Swedish botanist]

rudd (rŭd) *n.* a fish, *Scardinius erythrophthalmus*, resembling a roach. [prob. from obs. *rud*, OE *rudu*, cogn. with RED[1]]

rudder (rŭd´ə) *n.* **1** a flat wooden or metal framework or solid piece hinged to the sternpost of a boat or ship and serving as a means of steering. **2** a vertical moving surface in the tail of an aircraft for providing directional control and stability. **3** any steering device. **4** a principle etc. which guides, governs or directs the course of anything. **rudderhead** *n.* **rudderless** *a.* **rudderpost** *n.* [OE *rōther* (cp. Dut. *roer*, G *Ruder*, Swed. *roder*), cogn. with ROW[2]]

ruddily, ruddiness RUDDY.

ruddle (rŭd´əl), **reddle** (red´əl) *n.* a variety of red ochre used for marking sheep, raddle. ~*v.t.* to colour or mark with ruddle. [as RUDD]

ruddock (rŭd´ək) *n.* (*dial.*) a robin (the bird). [OE *rudduc*, rel. to RUDD]

ruddy (rŭd´i) *a.* (*comp.* **ruddier**, *superl.* **ruddiest**) **1** of a red or reddish colour. **2** (of a healthy complexion) fresh-coloured. **3** bloody. ~*v.t.* (*3rd pers. sing. pres.* **ruddies,** *pres.p.* **ruddying,** *past, p.p.* **ruddied**) to make ruddy. ~*v.i.* to grow red. **ruddily** *adv.* **ruddiness** *n.* **ruddy duck** *n.* an American duck, *Oxyura jamaicensis*, which has reddish-brown plumage in the male. [OE *rudig* (cp. Icel. *rothi*), from *rudu*, cogn. with *rēad*, RED[1]]

rude (rood) *a.* **1** impolite, uncivil, insolent, offensive, insulting. **2** unformed, unfinished. **3** simple, primitive, crude, uncultivated, uncivilized, unsophisticated, unrefined, rough, rugged. **4** †uneducated. **5** violent, boisterous, abrupt, tempestuous. **6** coarse, uncouth, indecent, vulgar. **7** hearty, robust, strong. **to be rude to** to speak impolitely to. **rudely** *adv.* **rudeness** *n.* **rudery** *n.* **rudish** *a.* [F, from L *rudem*, nom. *-dis*]

ruderal (roo´dərəl) *a.* (of a plant) growing on rubbish. ~*n.* a ruderal plant. [L *rūdera*, pl. of *rūdus*, broken stones]

rudery RUDE.

rudiment (roo´dimənt) *n.* **1** (*usu. pl.*) an elementary or first principle of knowledge etc. **2** (*pl.*) the undeveloped or imperfect form of something, a beginning, a germ. **3** (*Biol.*) a partially developed, aborted or stunted organ, structure etc., a vestige. **rudimental** *a.* **rudimentary** (-men´-) *a.* **rudimentarily** *adv.* **rudimentariness** *n.* [F, from L *rudīmentum*, from *rudis*, RUDE]

rudish RUDE.

rue[1] (roo) *v.t.* (*pres. p.* **rueing, ruing,** *past, p.p.* **rued**) to grieve or be sorry for, to regret, to repent of. ~†*n.* **1** sorrow, regret, repentance. **2** compassion. **rueful** *a.* regretful, sorrowful. **ruefully** *adv.* **ruefulness** *n.* [OE *hrēowan* (cp. Dut. *rouwen*, G *reuen*), rel. to Icel. *hryggr*, grieved]

rue[2] (roo) *n.* a plant of the genus *Ruta*, esp. *R. graveolens*, a shrubby evergreen plant, having a strong smell and acrid taste, formerly used as a stimulant etc. in medicine. [F, from L *rūta*, Gr. *rhutē*]

rufescent (rufes´ənt) *a.* (*Zool., Bot.*) reddish, tinged with red. [L *rūfescens -ntem*, pres.p. of *rūfescere*, from *rūfus*, reddish]

ruff[1] (rŭf) *n.* **1** a broad pleated or fluted collar or frill of linen or muslin worn by both sexes, esp. in the 16th cent. **2** a growth like a ruff, such as the ring of feathers round the necks of some birds. **3** a bird, *Philomachus pugnax*, of the sandpiper family (perh. from the conspicuous ruff in the male in the breeding season). **4** a breed of pigeons related to the jacobin. **ruffed** *a.* having a ruff. **rufflike** *a.* [prob. shortened from RUFFLE]

ruff[2] (rŭf) *n.* **1** (*also* **ruffe**) a small freshwater fish, *Gymnocephalus cernua*, related to and resembling the perch. **2** (*esp. Austral.*) a marine food fish, *Arripis georgianus*, related to the Australian salmon.

ruff[3] (rŭf) *n.* the act of trumping when one cannot follow suit. ~*v.t., v.i.* to trump. [OF *roffle, roufle*, perh. corr. of *triomphe*, cp. TRUMP[1]]

ruffe RUFF[2].

ruffian (rŭf´iən) *n.* a low, lawless, brutal person, a bully, a violent hoodlum. ~*a.* ruffianly, brutal. **ruffianish** *a.* **ruffianism** *n.* **ruffian-like, ruffianly** *a.* [OF, cp. It. *ruffiano*, etym. uncertain]

ruffle (rŭf´əl) *v.t.* **1** to disorder, to disturb the smoothness or order of, to rumple, to disarrange. **2** to annoy, to disturb, to upset, to discompose. **3** to gather into a ruffle. **4** (of a bird) to make (the feathers) stand out, when cleaning or in anger etc. ~*v.i.* to grow rough or turbulent, to move or toss about loosely, to flutter. ~*n.* **1** a strip or frill of fine, pleated or goffered lace etc., attached to some part of a garment, esp. at the neck or wrist. **2** a bird's ruff. **3** a ripple on water. **4** a low, vibrating beat of the drum. **5** †a disturbance, a commotion, a dispute. **ruffled** *a.* **ruffler** *n.* an attachment for a sewing machine for making ruffles. **ruffling** *n., a.* [ME *ruffelen*, etym. uncertain, cp. Dut. *roffelen*, LG *ruffelen*]

rufiyaa (roofē´yah) *n.* the standard unit of currency of the Maldives.

rufous (roo´fəs) *a.* of a brownish red. [L *rūfus*]

rug (rŭg) *n.* **1** a thick, heavy wrap, coverlet etc., usu. woollen with a thick nap, or of skin with the hair or wool left on. **2** a carpet or floor mat of similar material. **3** (*coll.*) a hairpiece, a wig. **to pull the rug from under** to put (someone) in a defenceless or discomposed state, to undermine (someone). **rugging** *n.* material for making rugs. [prob. from Scand. (cp. Norw. dial. *rugga*, Swed. *rugg*, tangled hair, Icel. *rögg*, cp. RAG[1])]

ruga (roo´gə) *n.* (*pl.* **rugae** (-jē)) (*Anat.*) a wrinkle, crease, fold or ridge. **rugose** (-gōs) *a.* **rugosely** *adv.* **rugosity** (-gos´-) *n.* [L]

rugby (rŭg´bi), **Rugby, rugby football** *n.* a game of football in which players are allowed to use their hands in carrying and passing the ball and tackling their opponents. **Rugby fives** *n.* the game of fives in which the court has five walls. **Rugby League** *n.* a form of rugby played by teams consisting of 13 players of amateur or professional status. **Rugby Union** *n.* a form of rugby played by teams of 15 players of largely amateur status. **rugger** *n.* (*coll.*) rugby. [*Rugby*, Warwickshire town with public school]

rugged (rŭg´id) *a.* **1** having an extremely uneven surface full of inequalities; broken and irregular. **2** rocky, craggy, of abrupt contour. **3** (of a man) having strong, virile features. **4** (of a sound) harsh, grating. **5** rough in temper, stern, unbending, severe. **6** rude, unpolished. **7** (*N Am.*) (of weather, waves etc.) tempestuous, turbulent. **8** strenuous, hard. **9** hardy, sturdy. **ruggedized** *a.* (*esp. N Am.*) designed to be hard-wearing. **ruggedization** (-zā´shən) *n.* **ruggedly** *adv.* **ruggedness** *n.* [prob. from Scand., cp. RUG and ROUGH]

rugger RUGBY.

rugging RUG.

rugosa (roogō´zə) *n.* a Japanese rose, *Rosa rugosa*, having deep pink flowers. [L, fem. of *rugosus*, as RUGA]

rugose, rugosity RUGA.

ruin (roo´in) *n.* **1** a disastrous change or state of wreck or disaster, an overthrow, a downfall. **2** bankruptcy. **3** a cause of destruction, downfall or disaster. **4** the state of being ruined or destroyed. **5** (*often in pl.*) the remains of a structure, building, city etc. that has been demolished or has decayed. **6** a person who has suffered a downfall, e.g. a bankrupt. *~v.t.* (*pres.p.* **ruining,** *past, p.p.* **ruined**) **1** to bring to ruin. **2** to reduce to ruins, to dilapidate. **3** to destroy, to overthrow, to subvert. **4** to harm, to spoil, to disfigure. **5** to bankrupt. **in ruins 1** in a state of ruin or decay. **2** completely spoiled. **ruinable** *a.* **ruination** (-ā´shən) *n.* **ruined** *a.* **ruiner** *n.* **ruining** *n., a.* **ruinous** *a.* **1** causing ruin, destructive, pernicious. **2** fallen into ruin, dilapidated. **ruinously** *adv.* **ruinousness** *n.* [F *ruine*, L *ruīna*, from *ruere*, to fall]

rule (rool) *n.* **1** something which is established as a principle, standard or guide of action or procedure. **2** a line of conduct, a regular practice, an established custom, canon or maxim. **3** the act of ruling or the state or period of being ruled, government, authority, sway, direction, control; method, regularity. **4** a strip of wood, plastic, metal etc. usu. graduated in centimetres or inches and millimetres or fractions of an inch, used for linear measurement or guidance. **5** (*Print.*) **a** a thin metal strip for separating columns, headings etc. **b** a thin printed line. **6** an authoritative form, direction or regulation, a body of laws or regulations, to be observed by an association, religious order etc. and its individual members. **7** a prescribed formula, method etc. for solving a mathematical problem of a given kind. **8** an order, direction or decision by a judge or court, usu. with reference to a particular case only. **9** the general way of things. **10** (**Rules**) Australian Rules football. *~v.t.* **1** to govern, to manage, to control, to curb, to restrain. **2** to be the ruler, governor or sovereign of. **3** to lay down as a rule or as an authoritative decision. **4** to mark (paper etc.) with straight lines. **5** to draw (a straight line) using a rule. *~v.i.* **1** to exercise supreme power (usu. over). **2** to decide, to make a decision. **3** (of prices) to stand at or maintain a certain level. **4** to dominate, to be prevalent. **as a rule** usually, generally. **by rule** mechanically, automatically. **to be ruled by** to be guided by. **to rule out** to exclude, to eliminate (as a possibility). **to rule the roast** to rule the roost. **to rule the roost** to be the leader, to be dominant. **to run the rule over** to check quickly for accuracy. **rulable** *a.* **Rule 43** *n.* a prison rule allowing prisoners to be isolated for their own protection. **ruleless** *a.* **rule of the road** ROAD[1]. **rule of three** *n.* (*Math.*) simple proportion. **rule of thumb** *n.* practical experience, as distinct from theory, as a guide in doing anything. **ruler** *n.* **1** a person who rules or governs. **2** an instrument with straight edges or sides, used as a guide in drawing straight lines, a rule. **rulership** *n.* **ruling** *n.* **1** an authoritative decision, esp. with regard to a special legal case. **2** a ruled line or lines. *~a.* **1** predominant, pre-eminent. **2** having or exercising authority or control. **ruling passion** *n.* a strong feeling which influences someone's actions. [A-F *reule*, OF *riule* (F *règle*), L *rēgula*, whence *rēgulāre*, to rule, to REGULATE]

rum[1] (rŭm) *n.* **1** a spirit distilled from fermented molasses or cane juice. **2** (*N Am.*) any alcoholic drink. **rum baba** *n.* a small cake soaked in rum. **rum butter** *n.* butter mixed with sugar and flavoured with rum. **rummy**[1] *a.* (*comp.* **rummier,** *superl.* **rummiest**). **rumminess** *n.* **rum-punch** *n.* punch made with rum. **rum-runner** *n.* (*Hist.*) a smuggler of rum, esp. during the Prohibition era in the US. **rum-running** *n.* [formerly *rumbo, rumbullion* (now, in Devon dial., a great tumult)]

rum[2] (rŭm) *a.* (*comp.* **rummer,** *superl.* **rummest**) (*sl.*) strange, singular, odd, queer. **rum go** *n.* a strange or surprising occurrence. **rumly** *adv.* **rummy**[2] *a.* (*comp.* **rummier,** *superl.* **rummiest**). **rumness** *n.* **rum start** *n.* a rum go. [perh. ident. with 16th-cent. cant *rum*, a fine treat]

rumal ROMAL.

Rumanian ROMANIAN.

Rumansh ROMANSH.

rumba (rŭm´bə), **rhumba** *n.* **1** a complex and rhythmic Cuban dance. **2** a ballroom dance developed from this dance. **3** a piece of music for this dance. *~v.i.* (*3rd pers. sing. pres.* **rumbas, rhumbas,** *pres.p.* **rumbaing, rhumbaing,** *past, p.p.* **rumbaed, rumba'd, rhumbaed, rhumba'd**) to dance the rumba. [Sp.]

rumble (rŭm´bəl) *v.i.* **1** to make a low, heavy, continuous sound, as of thunder, heavy vehicles etc. **2** to move (along) with such a sound. *~v.t.* **1** to cause to move with a rumbling noise. **2** to utter with such a sound. **3** (*sl.*) to discover the truth about, to see through. *~n.* **1** a rumbling sound. **2** (*N Am., sl.*) a gang fight. **3** a seat or place for luggage behind the body of a carriage; a rumble seat. **rumbler** *n.* **rumble seat** *n.* (*N Am.*) an outside folding seat on some early motor vehicles. **rumble strip** *n.* a series of raised strips set into a road to make vehicles vibrate as a warning to drivers. **rumble-tumble** *n.* **1** a rumbling vehicle. **2** a commotion. **rumbling** *a.* **rumblingly** *adv.* **rumblings** *n.pl.* signs that an unpleasant situation is about to develop. **rumbly** *a.* [ME *romblen* (cp. Dut. *rommelen*, G *rummeln*, Dan. *rumle*), prob. of imit. orig.]

rumbustious (rŭmbŭs´chəs) *a.* (*coll.*) boisterous, turbulent, cheerful and noisy. **rumbustiously** *adv.* **rumbustiousness** *n.* [prob. corr. of ROBUSTIOUS (under ROBUST)]

rumen (roo´men) *n.* (*pl.* **rumens, rumina** (-minə)) (*Zool.*) the first cavity of the complex stomach of a ruminant. [from L, the gullet]

ruminant (roo´minənt) *n.* **1** any member of the division of cud-chewing animals with a complex stomach, including cattle, sheep, deer etc. **2** any other cud-chewing animal (e.g. the camel). *~a.* **1** of or relating to the ruminants. **2** meditative, contemplative. **ruminantly** *adv.* **ruminate** (-nāt) *v.i.* **1** to muse, to meditate (over). **2** to chew the cud. *~v.t.* **1** to ponder over. **2** to chew again (what has been regurgitated). **rumination** (-ā´shən) *n.* **ruminative** (-nətiv) *a.* **ruminatively** *adv.* **ruminator** *n.* [L *rūminans -ntem*, pres.p. of *rūminārī*, to ruminate, from RUMEN]

rummage (rŭm´ij) *v.t.* **1** to make a search in or through, to ransack, esp. by throwing the contents about. **2** to find or uncover by such searching. **3** to disarrange or throw into disorder by searching. ~*v.i.* to make a search (through, among, in). ~*n.* **1** the act of rummaging, a search. **2** miscellaneous articles, odds and ends (found by rummaging). **rummager** *n.* **rummage sale** *n.* (*esp. N Am.*) a jumble sale. [F *arrumage* (now *arrimage*), from *arrumer* (*arrimer*), etym. uncertain]

rummer (rŭm´ə) *n.* a large drinking glass. [WFlem. *rummer, rommer*, cp. Dut. *romer*, G *Römer*]

rummy[1] RUM[1].

rummy[2] RUM[2].

rummy[3] (rŭm´i) *n.* any of several card games in which the object is to collect combinations and sequences of cards. [etym. uncertain]

rumour (roo´mə), (*N Am.*) **rumor** *n.* **1** popular report, hearsay, common talk. **2** a current story without any known authority. ~*v.t.* to report or circulate as a rumour. **rumorous** *a.* **rumourer** *n.* **rumour-monger** *n.* a person who spreads rumours. **rumour-mongering** *n.* [A-F, from L *rūmōrem*, nom. *-mor*]

rump (rŭmp) *n.* **1** the end of the backbone of a mammal with the adjacent parts, the posterior, the buttocks. **2** in birds, the terminal part of the body. **3** the tail-end of anything. **the Rump** (*Hist.*) the remnant of the English Long Parliament, after the expulsion of those favourable to Charles I by Pride's Purge in 1648, or after its restoration in 1659. **rump-bone** *n.* the coccyx. **rumpless** *a.* **rump steak** *n.* a beefsteak cut from the rump. [prob. from Scand. (cp. Icel. *rumpr*, Swed. and Norw. *rumpa*, Dan. *rumpe*)]

rumple (rŭm´pəl) *v.t.* to wrinkle, to make uneven, to crease, to disorder. ~*v.i.* to become wrinkled or creased. ~*n.* a fold, a crease, a wrinkle. **rumply** *a.* [Dut. *rompelen*; rel. to OE *gerumpen*, wrinkled]

rumpus (rŭm´pəs) *n.* (*pl.* **rumpuses**) (*coll.*) a disturbance, an uproar, a row. **rumpus room** *n.* (*N Am., Austral., New Zeal.*) a playroom or games room, esp. for children. [etym. uncertain]

run (rŭn) *v.i.* (*pres.p.* **running,** *past* **ran** (ran), *p.p.* **run**) **1** to move or pass over the ground by using the legs more quickly than in walking, esp. with a springing motion, so that both feet are never on the ground at once. **2** to hasten. **3** (of a horse etc.) to amble, trot, or canter. **4** to flee, to try to escape. **5** to make a run at cricket. **6** to compete in a race. **7** to complete a race in a specified position. **8** to seek election etc. **9** to move or travel rapidly. **10** to make a quick or casual trip or visit. **11** to be carried along violently. **12** to move along on or as if on wheels. **13** to revolve. **14** to be in continuous motion, to be in action or operation. **15** to go smoothly. **16** to glide, to elapse. **17** to flow. **18** to fuse, to melt, to dissolve and spread. **19** to flow (with), to be wet, to drip, to emit liquid, mucus etc. **20** to go, to ply. **21** to spread or circulate rapidly or in profusion. **22** (of a shoal of fish) to migrate, esp. upstream for spawning. **23** to range. **24** to extend, to take a certain course, to proceed, to go on, to continue (for a certain distance or duration). **25** to be played, featured or published etc. **26** to tend, to incline. **27** to be current, valid, in force or effect. **28** to occur inherently, persistently or repeatedly. **29** to pass freely or casually. **30** to occur in sequence. **31** to perform quickly or in sequence. **32** to be allowed to wander unrestrainedly or grow (wild). **33** to elapse. **34** (of a loan, debt etc.) to accumulate. **35** (of stockings, tights etc.) to ladder, to unravel. **36** to sail before the wind. ~*v.t.* **1** to cause to run or go. **2** to cause or allow to pass, penetrate etc., to thrust with. **3** to drive, to propel. **4** to track, to pursue, to chase, to hunt. **5** to press (hard) in a race, competition etc. **6** to accomplish (as if) by running. **7** to perform or execute (a race, an errand etc.). **8** to follow or pursue (a course etc.). **9** to cause to ply. **10** to bring to a specific state as if by running. **11** to keep going, to manage, to conduct, to carry on, to work, to operate. **12** to enter or enrol (as a contender). **13** to introduce or promote the election of (a candidate). **14** to get past or through (e.g. a blockade). **15** to cross, to traverse. **16** to cause to extend or continue. **17** to discharge, to flow with. **18** to cause to pour or flow. **19** to fill (a bath) from a flowing tap. **20** to convey in a motor vehicle, to give a lift to. **21** to be affected by or subjected to. **22** to sail with the wind. **23** to graze (animals) in open pasture. **24** in billiards, cricket etc., to hit or score (a successful sequence of shots, runs etc.). **25** to sew quickly. **26** to have or keep current. **27** to publish. **28** to cast, to found, to mould. **29** to deal in, to smuggle. **30** to incur, to expose oneself to, to hazard. **31** to allow (a bill etc.) to accumulate before paying. ~*n.* **1** an act or spell of running. **2** the distance or duration of a run or journey. **3** a trip, a short excursion. **4** the running of two batsmen from one wicket to the other in cricket without either's being put out. **5** a unit of score in cricket. **6** the distance a golf ball rolls along the ground. **7** a complete circuit of the bases by a player in baseball etc. **8** a continuous course, a sustained period of operation or performance. **9** a sequence, series, stretch or succession (e.g. of cards, luck etc.). **10** a succession of demands (on a bank etc.). **11** the quantity of a product produced by a factory at any one time. **12** a pipe or course for flowing liquid. **13** (*N Am.*) a small stream. **14** the ordinary succession, trend or general direction, the way things tend to move. **15** a rapid motion. **16** a ladder or rip in a stocking, jumper, pair of tights etc. **17** a line of goods. **18** general nature, character, class or type. **19** a batch, flock, drove or shoal of animals, fish etc. born together or migrating together. **20** a periodical passage or migration. **21** an inclined course esp. for winter sports. **22** a habitual course or circuit. **23** a regular track (of certain animals), a burrow. **24** a grazing ground. **25** an enclosure for fowls. **26** free use or access, unrestricted enjoyment. **27** a mission involving travel (*a smuggling run*; *a bombing run*). **28** (*Mus.*) a rapid scale passage. **a (good) run for one's money 1** a strong challenge. **2** pleasure derived from an activity. **3** return for one's money or effort. **at a/ the run** running, in haste. **in the long run** LONG[1]. **in the short run** SHORT. **on the run 1** in flight, fugitive. **2** rushing about. **run off one's feet** extremely busy. **the runs** (*coll.*) diarrhoea. **to run a blockade** BLOCKADE. **to run about 1** to rush from place to place. **2** (of children) to play freely, without restraint. **to run across 1** to encounter by chance, to discover by accident. **2** to make a quick visit (to). **3** to cross at a run. **to run afoul of** AFOUL. **to run after 1** to try to form a sexual or romantic relationship with. **2** to cultivate, to devote oneself to. **3** to chase. **to run against 1** to compete against (someone) for election. **2** to happen on. **to run along** (*coll.*) to leave, to go away. **to run a risk** RISK. **to run around 1** to transport from place to place by car. **2** to deceive repeatedly. **3** (*coll.*) to have casual sexual relations (with). **to run at** to rush at, to attack. **to run a temperature** to have an abnormally high body temperature. **to run away 1** to flee, to abscond. **2** to elope. **3** (of a horse) to bolt. **to run away with 1** to carry off. **2** to win (an easy victory). **3** to accept (an idea) rashly. **4** to cost (a lot of money). **5** (of a horse) to bolt with. **6** to elope with. **7** (of enthusiasm, emotions etc.) to deprive of self-control and common sense. **to run down 1** to stop through not being wound up, recharged etc. **2** to make enfeebled by overwork etc. **3** to pursue and overtake. **4** to search for and discover. **5** to disparage, to abuse. **6** to run against or over and sink or collide with. **7** to reduce in size or amount. **to run dry 1** to stop flowing. **2** (of a supply) to end. **to run for it** to make an escape attempt, to run away. **to run foul of** FOUL. **to run high** HIGH. **to run in 1** (*coll.*) to arrest, to take into custody. **2** to break in (a motor vehicle, machine etc.) by running or operating. **3** to insert (printed matter etc.). **4** to approach. **5** to incur (a debt). **6** to drive (cattle etc.) in. **7** to call, to drop in. **to run in the family/ blood** to be hereditary. **to run into 1** to incur, to fall into. **2** to collide with. **3** to reach (a specified number, amount etc.). **4** to meet by chance. **5** to be continuous with. **to run into the ground** (*coll.*) to exhaust or wear out with overwork. **to run it fine** FINE[1]. **to run its course** to develop naturally and come to a natural end. **to run low (on)** to have a depleted supply (of). **to run off 1** to print. **2** to decide (a race or contest) after a series of heats. **3** to cause to pour or flow out. **4** to write fluently. **5** to digress. **to run off with 1** to elope with. **2** to steal, remove. **to run on 1** to continue without a break. **2** to talk volubly or incessantly. **3** to elapse. **4** (of the mind) to be absorbed by. **to run one's head against a brick wall** BRICK. **to run on the spot** SPOT. **to run out 1** to come to an end. **2** to leak. **3** in cricket, to dismiss a batsman by breaking the wicket when they are not in their ground. **4** (of a rope) to pass out. **5** to jut out. **6** to end a contest in a specified position. **7** to finish (a race). **8** to point (a gun). **9** to exhaust oneself by running. **to run out of** to have no more supplies of. **to run out on** (*coll.*) to abandon. **to run over 1** to review or examine cursorily. **2** to recapitulate. **3** to overflow. **4** to pass, ride or drive over. **5** to touch (piano keys) lightly in quick succession. **6** to go for a quick visit (to). **to run rings round** RING[1]. **to run riot** RIOT. **to run round in circles** CIRCLE. **to run scared** SCARE. **to run short** SHORT. **to run someone close/ hard** to be a serious challenge to. **to run someone ragged** to exhaust someone. **to run the gamut of** GAMUT. **to run the gauntlet** GAUNTLET[2]. **to run the risk** RISK. **to run the show** (*coll.*) to manage, to have control of something in one's own hands. **to run through 1** to go through or examine rapidly. **2** to take, deal with, spend etc. one after another, to squander. **3** to pass through by running. **4** to pervade. **5** to transfix, to pierce with a weapon. **6** to strike out by drawing a line through. **to run to 1** to afford. **2** to extend to. **3** to have a tendency to. **4** to amount to. **5** to have the resources for. **6** to fall into (ruin). **to run to earth** to track down, to find after hard or prolonged searching. **to run to ground** to run to earth. **to run to meet** to anticipate (one' s problems or troubles). **to run to seed** SEED. **to run to waste** WASTE. **to run up 1** to grow rapidly. **2** (of prices) to increase quickly. **3** to accumulate (a debt etc.). **4** to force up (prices etc.). **5** to amount (to). **6** to add up (a column of figures). **7** to make a quick visit (to). **8** to build, make or sew in a hasty manner. **9** to raise or hoist. **to run up against** to encounter (problems). **to run upon** to dwell on, to be absorbed by. **to run wild** WILD. **to run with the hare and hunt with the hounds** HARE. **runabout** *n.* a light motor car or aeroplane. **run-around** *n.* evasive and deceitful treatment (*He gave me the run-around*). **runaway** *n.* **1** a person who flees from danger, restraint or service; a deserter, a fugitive. **2** an animal or vehicle which is out of control. **3** an escape, a flight. *~a.* **1** breaking from restraint. **2** out of control. **3** (of a success etc.) prodigious, decisive, easily won. **4** accomplished by flight. **5** fleeing as a runaway. **rundown** *n.* **1** a reduction in number, speed, power etc. **2** a brief or rapid résumé. **run-down** *a.* **1** dilapidated. **2** exhausted, worn out. **run-in** *n.* **1** (*coll.*) an argument, a row. **2** an approach. **3** (*Print.*) an insertion of printed matter within a paragraph. **runnable** *a.* **runner** *n.* **1** a person who runs, a racer. **2** a messenger, a scout, a spy. **3** a person who solicits custom etc., an agent, a collector, a tout. **4** (*sl.*) a smuggler. **5** a blockade-runner. **6** (*Hist.*) a police officer, a detective. **7** something on which anything runs, revolves, slides etc. **8** the blade of a skate. **9** a piece of wood or metal on which a sleigh runs. **10** a groove, rod, roller etc. on which a part slides or runs, esp. in machinery. **11** a sliding ring, loop etc. on a strap, rod etc. **12** (*Naut.*) a rope run through a single block with one end attached to a tackle block and the other having a hook. **13** a revolving millstone. **14** a creeping stem thrown out by a plant, such as a strawberry, tending to take root. **15** a twining or climbing plant, esp. a kidney bean. **16** a running bird, esp. the water rail. **17** in cricket, a player who runs for an injured batsman during their innings. **18** a long strip of carpet for a passage etc., or cloth for a table etc. **19** (*coll.*) a person who receives goods, services etc. but tries to avoid paying for them. **to do a runner** (*sl.*) to leave, esp. in order to avoid paying for something. **runner bean** *n.* a trailing bean plant, *Phaseolus coccineus*, having long, green seed pods. **runner-up** *n.* (*pl.* **runners-up, runner-ups**) the competitor in a race etc. who takes second place. **running** *n.* **1** the action of RUN *v.* **2** the sport of running competitively. **3** management, control, operation. **4** maintenance, working order. **5** competition, the chance of winning a race etc. *~a.* **1** moving at a run. **2** (of handwriting) cursive. **3** flowing. **4** continuous, uninterrupted. **5** discharging matter. **6** following in succession, repeated. **7** (of plants) trailing. **8** current, done at, or accomplished with, a run. **in the running** having a chance of winning. **take a running jump!** (*coll.*) **1** under no circumstances! **2** go away! **to make the running** to set the pace. **to take up the running** to make the running. **running account** *n.* a current account. **running back** *n.* in American football, a back whose main task is to advance the ball from the scrimmage by running with it. †**running banquet** *n.* a meal taken between main meals, a snack. **running battle** *n.* **1** a battle between pursuers and pursued. **2** a continuous or long-running argument. **running-board** *n.* the footboard of an (early) motor-car. **running commentary** *n.* (*pl.* **running commentaries**) an oral description, usu. by broadcasting, of an event in progress, e.g. a race. **running fight** *n.* **1** a fight in which one party flees and the other pursues, the contest being continued during the chase. **2** a protracted battle, esp. one which is continually broken off or renewed. **running fire** *n.* a discharge of firearms in rapid succession by a line of troops. **running gear** *n.* **1** the wheels, axles or other working parts of a vehicle etc. **2** the rope and tackle used in handling a boat. **running hand** *n.* writing in which the pen is not lifted after each letter. **running head, running headline** *n.* the title of a book or similar heading used as a headline throughout a sequence of pages. **running knot** *n.* a knot which slips along the rope, line etc. **running light** *n.* a light visible on a moving vehicle, ship or aircraft at night. **runningly** *adv.* **running mate** *n.* **1** a subordinate candidate, one standing for the less important of two linked offices in a US election, esp. the vice-presidency. **2** (*esp. US*) a horse teamed or paired with another in a race. **running repairs** *n.pl.* repairs carried out while a machine etc. is in operation, minor repairs. **running rope** *n.* a rope which can move freely through a pulley etc. **running sore** *n.* a suppurating sore. **running stitch** *n.* **1** a simple continuous stitch used for gathering or tacking. **2** a line of running stitches. **running title** *n.* a running head. **running water** *n.* water flowing from a tap. **runny** *a.* (*comp.* **runnier**, *superl.* **runniest**) **1** (of a nose or eyes) having liquid flowing from it or them. **2** excessively liquid. **run-off** *n.* **1** an additional tie-breaking contest, race etc. **2** overflow or liquid drained off. **3** (*New Zeal.*) an area of land where young animals are kept. **run-of-the-mill** *a.* undistinguished, ordinary, mediocre. **run-on** *n.* (*Print.*) continuous printed matter. **run-out** *n.* in cricket, the dismissal of a batsman by running them out. **run through** *n.* a quick examination, perusal or rehearsal. **run-up** *n.* **1** an approach. **2** a period preceding an event etc., e.g. a general election. **runway** *n.* **1** a landing strip for aircraft. **2** a trail to a watering place. **3** a ramp, passageway or chute. **4** a raised gangway in a theatre. [ME *rinnen*, *rennen*, OE *rinnan* (also *iernan*), perh. affected by Icel. *rinna* (cp. Dut. and G *rennen*)]

runcible (rŭn´sibəl), **runcible spoon**. ~*n.* a three-pronged fork hollowed out like a spoon and with one of the prongs having a cutting edge. [nonsense word invented by Edward Lear, 1812–88, British humorist]

runcinate (rŭn´sinət) *a.* (*Bot.*) (of a leaf) saw-toothed. [mod. L *runcinatus*, from L *runcina*, a PLANE² (formerly taken to mean 'a saw')]

rune (roon) *n.* **1** a letter or character of the earliest Germanic alphabet, formed from the Greek alphabet by modifying the shape to suit carving, used chiefly by the Scandinavians and Anglo-Saxons. **2** any mysterious mark or symbol. **3** a canto or division in Finnish poetry. **rune-staff** *n.* **1** a magic wand with runic inscriptions. **2** a runic calendar. **runic** *a.* of, relating to, consisting of, written in or cut in runes. [Icel. *rūn*, cogn. with OE *rūn*, secret, mystery, also *round*]

rung¹ (rŭng) *n.* **1** a stick or bar forming a step in a ladder. **2** a rail or spoke in a chair etc. **runged** *a.* **rungless** *a.* [OE *hrung*, cp. Dut. *hronge*, LG *runge*]

rung² RING².

runic RUNE.

runlet (rŭn´lit) *n.* a small stream, a runnel.

runnable RUN.

runnel (rŭn´əl) *n.* **1** a rivulet, a little brook. **2** a gutter. [OE *rynel*, dim. of RUN]

runner, running etc. RUN.

runt (rŭnt) *n.* **1** the smallest or feeblest animal in a litter esp. a piglet. **2** an ox or bullock of a small breed, esp. Welsh or Highland. **3** a large variety of domestic pigeon. **4** any animal or person who is stunted in growth, deficient or inferior. **runtish** *a.* **runty** *a.* **runtiness** *n.* [etym. uncertain]

rupee (rupē´) *n.* the standard monetary unit of various Asian countries including India, Pakistan, Sri Lanka, Nepal, Bhutan, the Maldives, Mauritius and the Seychelles. [Hind. *rūpiyah*, from Sansk. *rūpya*, wrought silver]

rupestrian (roopes´triən) *a.* (of art) done on cave walls. [mod. L *rupestris*, found on rocks, from L *rupes*, rock]

rupiah (roopē´ə) *n.* the standard monetary unit of Indonesia. [Hind., a RUPEE]

rupture (rŭp´chə) *n.* **1** the act of breaking or the state of being broken or violently parted, a break, a breach. **2** a breach or interruption of friendly relations. **3** (*Med.*) hernia. ~*v.t.* **1** to burst, to break, to separate by violence. **2** to sever (a friendship etc.). **3** to affect with a hernia. ~*v.i.* **1** to suffer a breach or rupture. **2** to suffer a hernia. **rupturable** *a.* [F, from L *ruptūra*, from *rumpere*, to break, p.p. *ruptus*]

rural (roo´rəl) *a.* **1** of or relating to the country, as distinct from *urban*. **2** pastoral, agricultural. **3** suiting or resembling the country, rustic. **rural dean** *n.* a member of the clergy, ranking below an archdeacon, charged with the inspection of a district. **rural district** *n.* (*Hist.*) a group of country parishes governed by an elected council. **ruralism** *n.* **ruralist** *n.* **rurality** (-ral´-), **ruralness** *n.* **ruralize, ruralise** *v.i., v.t.* **ruralization** (-zā´shən) *n.* **rurally** *adv.* **ruridecanal** (-dikā´nəl) *a.* of or relating to a rural dean. [F, from L *rūrālis*, from *rus rūris*, the country]

Ruritania (rooritā´niə) *n.* an imaginary mysterious or romantic country. **Ruritanian** *n., a.* [fictitious state in SE Europe, scene of adventures invented by Anthony Hope in *The Prisoner of Zenda*]

rusa (roo´sə) *n.* a large Indonesian deer, *Cervus timorensis*. [Malay]

ruscus (rŭs´kəs) *n.* any plant of the genus *Ruscus* of shrubby evergreen plants, containing the butcher's broom. [L *ruscum*, butcher's broom]

ruse (rooz) *n.* a stratagem, trick or wile. **ruse de guerre** (də geə´) *n.* a war stratagem. **rusée** *a.* (of a woman) wily, sly, cunning. [F, from *ruser*, perh. rel. to RUSH¹]

rush¹ (rŭsh) *v.t.* **1** to drive, urge, force, move or push with violence and haste, to hurry. **2** to perform or complete quickly. **3** to force (someone) to act quickly. **4** to take by sudden assault. **5** to surmount, to pass, to seize and occupy, with dash or suddenness. **6** (*coll.*) to cheat, to swindle by overcharging. **7** in American football, to hinder by charging. **8** (*N Am.*) to try to recruit for a fraternity or sorority. ~*v.i.* **1** to move or run impetuously or precipitately. **2** to enter or go (into) with undue eagerness or lack of consideration. **3** to run, flow or roll with violence and impetuosity. ~*n.* **1** the act of rushing. **2** a violent or impetuous movement, advance, dash or onslaught. **3** a sudden onset of activity, movement or thronging of people (to a gold field etc.). **4** (*pl., coll.*) the first print from a film. **5** a violent demand (for) or run (on) a commodity etc. **6** (*sl.*) a surge of euphoria induced by or as if by a drug. **7** in football, rugby etc., a dash with the ball. **8** in American football, a charge at the quarterback. ~*a.* characterized by or requiring much activity, speed or urgency. **to rush one's fences** to act too hastily or precipitously. **rusher** *n.* **rush hour** *n.* a period when traffic is very congested owing to people going to or leaving work. **rushingly** *adv.* [A-F *russher*, OF *reusser*, *ruser*, perh. from a pop. L *refūsāre*, see REFUSE¹]

rush² (rŭsh) *n.* **1** a plant with long thin stems or leaves, of the family Juncaceae, growing mostly on wet ground, used for making baskets, mats, seats for chairs etc., and formerly for strewing floors. **2** a stem of this plant. **3** any of various other similar plants, e.g. the bulrush. **4** rushes collectively. **5** a rush candle. **6** †something of little or no worth. ~*a.* (made) of rush or rushes. **rush-bearing** *n.* a Northern English festival when rushes and garlands are carried to strew the floor of a church. **rush-bottomed** *a.* having a seat made of rushes. **rush candle** *n.* **1** a small candle made of the pith of a rush dipped in tallow. **2** any weak, flickering light. **rush light** *n.* a rush candle. **rushlike** *a.* **rushy** *a.* **rushiness** *n.* [OE *risc*, *rysc*, cp. G *Rusch*]

rusk (rŭsk) *n.* a piece of bread or cake crisped and browned in the oven, given to babies. [Sp. or Port. *rosca*, twist or roll of bread]

Russ. *abbr.* **1** Russia. **2** Russian.

russel (rŭs´əl), **russel-cord** *n.* a twilled woollen or cotton fabric or rep. [etym. uncertain]

russet (rŭs´it) *a.* **1** of a reddish-brown colour. **2** †coarse, rustic, homely, simple. ~*n.* **1** a reddish-brown colour. **2** a rough-skinned reddish-brown variety of apple. **3** (*Hist.*) a coarse homespun cloth worn by peasants. **russety** *a.* [OF *rousset*, dim. of *rous* (F *roux*), L *russus*, red]

Russian (rŭsh´ən) *a.* of or relating to Russia. ~*n.* **1** a native or inhabitant of Russia, or a descendant of one. **2** the Russian language. **Russia leather** (rŭsh´ə) *n.* a soft leather made from hides prepared with birch-bark oil, used in bookbinding etc. **Russian boot** *n.* a wide-topped, calf-length boot. **Russianism** *n.* **Russianist** *n.* **Russianize, Russianise** *v.t.* **Russianization** (-zā´shən) *n.* **Russianness** *n.* **Russian olive** *n.* an oleaster. **Russian roulette** *n.* **1** a test of courage or act of bravado involving firing a revolver loaded with a single bullet at one's own head after spinning the chamber. **2** any very dangerous undertaking. **Russian salad** *n.* a salad of pickles and diced vegetables in a mayonnaise dressing. **Russian tea** *n.* tea drunk with lemon instead of milk. **Russify** (rŭs´ifī) *v.t.* (*3rd pers. sing. pres.* **Russifies**, *pres.p.* **Russifying**, *past, p.p.* **Russified**) to make

Russian in character. **Russification** (-fikā´shən) *n.* **Russki** (rŭs´ki), **Russky** *n.* (*pl.* **Russkis, Russkies**) (*sl., offensive*) 1 a Russian. 2 (*Hist., loosely*) a Soviet citizen. [med. L *Russiānus*]

Russophile (rŭs´ōfīl) *n.* a friend or admirer of Russia or the Russians. *~a.* friendly to Russia. **Russophilism** (-of´i-) *n.*

Russophobe (rŭs´ōfōb) *n.* a person who fears or is an opponent of Russia or the Russians. *~a.* hating or fearing Russia or the Russians. **Russophobia** (-fō´biə) *n.*

rust (rŭst) *n.* 1 the red incrustation on iron or steel caused by its oxidation when exposed to air and moisture. 2 a similar incrustation on other metals. 3 a plant disease caused by parasitic fungi of the order Urediniomycetes; blight. 4 any of these fungi. 5 a dull or impaired condition due to idleness etc. 6 the colour of rust, an orangey-red shade of brown. 7 any corrosive or injurious accretion or influence. *~a.* rust-coloured. *~v.i.* 1 to contract rust, to be oxidated. 2 to become rust-coloured. 3 to be attacked by blight. 4 to degenerate through idleness or disuse. *~v.t.* 1 to affect with rust, to corrode. 2 to impair by idleness, disuse etc. **rust belt** *n.* (*coll.*) a region of formerly profitable manufacturing industry, now in decline. **rust-coloured,** (*N Am.*) **rust-colored** *a.* **rusted** *a.* **rusting** *n., a.* **rustless** *a.* **rustproof** *a.* impervious to corrosion. *~v.t.* to make rustproof. **rusty** *a.* (*comp.* **rustier,** *superl.* **rustiest**) 1 covered or affected with or as if with rust. 2 faded, discoloured by age. 3 impaired by disuse, inaction, neglect etc. 4 rust-coloured. 5 antiquated in appearance. 6 (of a voice) harsh, husky. **rustily** *adv.* **rustiness** *n.* [OE *rūst* (cp. Dut. *roest*, G and Swed. *rost*, Dan. *rust*) rel. to RED[1]]

rustic (rŭs´tik) *a.* 1 of or relating to the country, rural. 2 like or characteristic of country life or people, unsophisticated, simple, artless. 3 rude, unpolished. 4 awkward, uncouth. 5 of rough workmanship, coarse, plain. 6 made of rough timber. 7 loosely formed. 8 (*Archit.*) having a rough surface. 9 †rusticated. *~n.* 1 a country person or dweller. 2 an artless, unsophisticated or uncouth person. 3 rusticwork. **rustically** *adv.* **rusticate** *v.t.* 1 to suspend for a time from residence at a university; to exile to the country, as a punishment. 2 to make rustic in style, finish etc. 3 to give a rough surface and chamfered joints to (masonry). *~v.i.* 1 to retire or to live in the country. 2 to become rustic. **rusticated** *a.* countrified. **rustication** (-ā´shən) *n.* **rusticator** *n.* **rusticity** (-tis´-) *n.* **rusticize** (-sīz), **rusticise** *v.t., v.i.* **rusticwork** *n.* 1 woodwork made of roughly trimmed trunks, branches etc. 2 masonry with a rough surface and chamfered joints. [L *rusticus*, from *rus*, the country]

rustle (rŭs´əl) *v.i.* 1 to make a quick succession of small sounds like the rubbing of silk or dry leaves. 2 to move or go along with a rustling sound. 3 to steal cattle, horses or sheep. 4 (*N Am., coll.*) to bustle, to move quickly and energetically. *~v.t.* 1 to cause to make a rustling sound. 2 to steal (cattle, horses or sheep). *~n.* a rustling. **to rustle up** 1 (*coll.*) to prepare or make quickly, or without preparation or prior notice. 2 to gather up, to put together. **rustler** *n.* **rustling** *a., n.* **rustlingly** *adv.* [imit., cp. Dut. dial. and LG *russeln*]

rustre (rŭs´tə) *n.* (*Her.*) a lozenge with a round hole. [F]

rut[1] (rŭt) *n.* 1 a sunken track made by wheels or vehicles, a hollow, a groove. 2 a settled habit or course. *~v.t.* (*pres.p.* **rutting,** *past, p.p.* **rutted**) to make ruts in. **in a rut** stuck in tedious routine. **rutty** *a.* **ruttily** *adv.* **ruttiness** *n.* [etym. uncertain]

rut[2] (rŭt) *n.* the sexual excitement or heat of deer and some other animals. *~v.i.* (*pres.p.* **rutting,** *past, p.p.* **rutted**) to be in a period of rut. **ruttish** *a.* **ruttishness** *n.* [OF *rut, ruit*, ult. from L *rugītus*, from *rugīre*, to roar]

rutabaga (rootəbā´gə) *n.* (*N Am.*) a swede. [F, prob. from Swed.]

ruthenium (ruthē´niəm) *n.* a white, spongy metallic element of the platinum group, at. no. 44, chem. symbol Ru. **ruthenic** (-then´-), **ruthenious** *a.* [*Ruthenia*, Russia]

rutherfordium (rŭdhəfaw´diəm) *n.* a proposed name for the artificial radioactive elements of at. nos. 104 and 106. [Ernest *Rutherford*, 1871–1937, British physicist born in New Zealand]

ruthless (rooth´lis) *a.* pitiless, merciless, cruel. †**truth** (rooth) *n.* 1 mercy, pity, compassion, tenderness. 2 remorse. 3 sorrow. †**truthful** *a.* †**truthfully** *adv.* **ruthlessly** *adv.* **ruthlessness** *n.* [RUE[1], -TH[1]]

rutile (roo´til, -tīl) *n.* red titanium dioxide. [F, from L *rutilus*, red]

ruttish RUT[2].

rutty RUT[1].

RV *abbr.* 1 (*N Am.*) recreational vehicle. 2 Revised Version (of the Bible).

RWA *abbr.* Rwanda (IVR).

Rwanda (ruan´də) *n.* the official language of Rwanda, central Africa. **Rwandan** *a.* of or relating to Rwanda. *~n.* a native or inhabitant of Rwanda, or a descendant of one.

-ry (ri), **-ery** (əri) *suf.* a business, a place of business, cultivation etc., conduct, things connected with or of the nature etc., as *foundry, poultry, yeomanry.*

rye (rī) *n.* 1 the seeds or grain of *Secale cereale*, a cereal allied to wheat, used to make (black) bread, whisky etc. 2 the plant bearing this. 3 rye whisky. 4 (*N Am.*) rye bread. *~a.* of rye. **rye bread** *n.* bread (white or dark) made from ryeflour. **ryeflour** *n.* flour made from rye. **ryegrass** *n.* any one of various grasses of the genus *Lolium*, cultivated for fodder grass. **rye whisky** *n.* whisky distilled from rye. [OE *ryge* (cp. Icel. *rūgr*, Dan. *rug*, also Dut. *rogge*, G *Roggen*)]

ryepeck (rī´pek), **rypeck, ripeck** *n.* (*dial.*) an ironshod pole used for driving into the bed of a stream to moor a punt etc. [etym. uncertain]

ryokan (riō´kan) *n.* a traditional Japanese inn. [Jap.]

ryot (rī´ət) *n.* in the Indian subcontinent, a peasant. [Hind. *rāiyat*, also *rayah*]

☒ **rythm** common misspelling of RHYTHM.

S

S[1] (es), **s** (*pl.* **Ss, S's**) the 19th letter of the English and other versions of the Roman alphabet, corresponding to the Greek sigma (Σ, σ). It has four sounds: (1) a voiceless labiodental fricative or sibilant, with a hard sound as in *sin*, *so*; (2) its voiced equivalent, the sound of *z*, as in *music*, *muse* etc.; (3) a voiceless palatal affricate, with the sound of *sh* in *sugar*, *mission*; (4) its voiced equivalent, marked in this dictionary zh, as in *measure*, *vision*. *n.* an S-shaped object or curve. **S-bend** *n.* an S-shaped bend.

S[2] *chem. symbol* sulphur.

S[3], **S.** *abbr.* 1 Sabbath. 2 Saint. 3 Saxon. 4 siemens. 5 Signor. 6 small. 7 society. 8 South. 9 Southern. 10 Special (in *S level*). 11 sun. 12 Sweden (IVR). **S level** *n.* in England, Wales and N Ireland, an examination taken in conjunction with an A level in the same subject, but with a more advanced syllabus.

s *abbr.* 1 second(s). 2 shilling(s). 3 singular. 4 snow. 5 solid. 6 son. 7 succeeded.

†**'s-** (s, z) *pref.* (esp. in oaths) God's. [abbr.]

-s[1] (s, z) *suf.* forming plurals of most nouns. [OE *-as*, nom. and acc. pl. endings of various masculine nouns]

-s[2] (s, z) *suf.* 1 forming adverbs. 2 forming possessive pronouns.

-s[3] (s, z) *suf.* forming nicknames or pet names.

-s[4] (s, z) *suf.* forming the 3rd pers. sing. pres. tense of most verbs. [OE *-es*, *-as*, second pers. sing. ending]

-s' (s, z) *suf.* forming the genitive (possessive) case of plural nouns and sometimes sing. nouns ending in *s*.

-'s[1] (s, z, iz) *suf.* forming the genitive (possessive) case of sing. nouns and pl. nouns not ending in *s*. [OE *-es*]

-'s[2] (s, z, iz) *suf.* var. of -S[1], forming plurals of letters or symbols.

-'s[3] (s, z) *suf.* 1 short for IS, HAS. 2 short for US. 3 short for *does*, 3rd pers. sing. pres. of DO[1].

SA *abbr.* 1 Salvation Army. 2 sex appeal. 3 F *société anonyme*, limited liability company. 4 Society of Antiquaries. 5 Society of Arts. 6 Society of Authors. 7 Soil Association. 8 South Africa. 9 South America. 10 South Australia. 11 (*Hist.*) *Sturmabteilung* (Nazi paramilitary force).

s.a. *abbr. sine anno*, without date.

SAA *abbr.* (*Comput.*) systems application architecture.

sab (sab) *n.* (*sl.*) a hunt saboteur. ~*v.t.* (*pres.p.* **sabbing,** *past*, *p.p.* **sabbed**) to disrupt (a hunt). [abbr.]

sabadilla (sabədil´ə) *n.* 1 a Mexican and Central American liliaceous plant, *Schoenocaulon officinale*, yielding acrid seeds from which veratrine is obtained. 2 a preparation of the barley-like seeds of this. [Sp. *cebadilla*, dim. of *cebada*, barley]

Sabaean (səbē´ən), **Sabean** *n.* a member of the ancient people of Yemen. ~*a.* of or relating to this people. [L *Sabaeus*, Gr. *Sabaios*, from Arab. *Saba'*, Sheba]

Sabaism (sā´bəizm) *n.* the worship of the stars or the host of heaven. **Sabaistic** (-is´-) *a.* [Heb. *çābā*, host, -ISM]

Sabaoth (sab´āoth, -bā´-) *n.pl.* (*Bible*) hosts, armies (in the title 'Lord God of Sabaoth'). [Heb. *çabāōth*, pl. of *çābā*, host]

sabbat (sab´ət) *n.* a witches' sabbath. [var. of SABBATH]

Sabbatarian (sabəteə´riən) *n.* 1 a Jew who strictly observes Saturday as a day of rest and divine worship. 2 a Christian who observes Sunday as a sabbath, or who is specially strict in its observance. 3 a Christian who observes Saturday as the sabbath. ~*a.* observing or inculcating the observance of the sabbath or Sunday. **Sabbatarianism** *n.* [L *Sabbatārius*, see SABBATH]

sabbath (sab´əth) *n.* 1 (*also* **sabbath day**) the seventh day of the week, Saturday, set apart, esp. by the Jews, for rest and divine worship. 2 the Christian Sunday observed as a day of rest and worship. 3 a time of rest. 4 a witches' sabbath. **sabbath-breaker** *n.* a person who profanes the sabbath. **sabbath-breaking** *n.* **sabbathless** *a.* **sabbatic** (-bat´-) *a.* **sabbatical** *a.* 1 of, relating to or befitting the sabbath. 2 of or relating to an extended period of leave from one's work. ~*n.* an extended period of leave from one's work. **sabbatically** *adv.* **sabbatical year** *n.* 1 a year's leave of absence orig. granted every seven years esp. to university teachers. 2 (*Bible*) every seventh year, during which the Hebrews were not to sow their fields or prune their vineyards, and were to liberate slaves and debtors. **sabbatism** *n.* **sabbatismal** (-tiz´-) *a.* **sabbatize, sabbatise** *v.t.* to keep as or turn into a sabbath. ~*v.i.* to keep the sabbath. [L *Sabbatum*, from Gr. *Sabbaton*, Heb. *shabbāth*, from *shābath*, to rest]

SABC *abbr.* South African Broadcasting Corporation.

Sabean SABAEAN.

Sabellian (səbel´iən) *a.* of or relating to Sabellianism. ~*n.* a follower of Sabellius, an African priest of the 3rd cent., who taught that the persons of the Trinity are only different manifestations of one divine person. **Sabellianism** *n.* the doctrines of Sabellius. [late L *Sabelliānus* (*Sabellius*, -AN)]

sabelline (səbel´īn) *a.* 1 of or relating to the sable. 2 coloured like its fur. [med. L *sabellīnus*, from *sabellum*, SABLE]

saber SABRE.

Sabian (sā´biən), **Zabian** (zā´-) *n.* 1 a member of an ancient sect who are classed in the Koran with Muslims, Jews and Christians as worshippers of the true God. 2 a star-worshipper. ~*a.* of or relating to Sabianism. **Sabianism** *n.* 1 the religion of the Sabians. 2 Sabaism. [Arab. *çabi'*, prob. to baptize]

sabicu (sabikoo´) *n.* 1 a W Indian tree, *Lysiloma latisiliqua*. 2 its mahogany-like wood. [Cuban Sp. *sabicú*]

sabin (sab´in, sā´-) *n.* a unit of acoustic absorption. [Wallace C. *Sabine*, 1868–1919, US physicist]

Sabine (sab´īn) *n.* a member of an ancient Italian people inhabiting the central Apennines. ~*a.* of or relating to this people. [L *Sabīnus*]

Sabin vaccine (sā´bin) *n.* a vaccine taken orally to immunize against poliomyelitis. [Albert Bruce *Sabin*, 1906–93, US microbiologist]

sable (sā´bəl) *n.* 1 a small arctic and subarctic carnivorous quadruped, *Martes zibellina*, allied to the marten, the brown fur of which is very highly valued. 2 its skin or fur. 3 a painter's brush made of its hair. 4 (*Her.*) black. 5 (*poet.*) black, esp. as the colour of mourning. 6 (*pl.*) mourning garments. ~*a.* 1 (*Her.*, *poet.*) black. 2 (*poet.*) dark, gloomy. ~*v.t.* to make dark or dismal. **sable antelope** *n.* a large black E African antelope, *Hippotragus niger*, with long, backward-curving horns. **sable-coloured** *a.* black. **sabled** *a.* **sable-stoled, sable-vested** *a.* clothed in sables. **sably** *adv.* [OF, from Slav., cp. Rus., Pol. and Czech *sobol*]

sabot (sab´ō) *n.* **1** a simple wooden shoe, usu. made in one piece. **2** a wooden-soled shoe. **3** a wooden disc fastened to a spherical projectile, or a metal cap on a conical one, to make these fit a gun bore. **4** a cap or shoe for protecting the end of a beam or pile etc. **5** (*Austral.*) a small sailing boat. **saboted** *a.* [F, etym. uncertain]

sabotage (sab´ətahzh) *n.* **1** malicious damage to a railway, industrial plant, machinery etc., as a protest by discontented workers, or as a non-military act of warfare. **2** the operation of cutting shoes or sockets for railway lines. **3** any action designed to hinder or undermine. ~*v.t.* **1** to commit sabotage on. **2** to hinder or undermine. **saboteur** (-tœ´) *n.* a person who commits sabotage. [F from *saboter*, to spoil through clumsiness, lit. to clatter in sabots]

sabra (sab´rə) *n.* an Israeli born in Israel. [Heb.]

sabre (sā´bə), (*NAm.*) **saber** *n.* **1** a cavalry sword having a curved blade. **2** (*pl.*) cavalry. **3** a light fencing-sword with a tapering blade. ~*v.t.* to cut or strike down or kill with the sabre. **sabre-cut** *n.* **1** a blow with a sabre. **2** a wound or scar from such a blow. **sabre-rattling** *n.* a display of military power or aggression. **sabre saw** *n.* a portable electric jigsaw. **sabre-toothed tiger, sabre-toothed cat** *n.* a large extinct feline mammal with long upper canines, esp. of the genus *Smilodon*. **sabreur** (sabrœ´) *n.* a person who fights with the sabre. **sabre-wing** *n.* a S American hummingbird of the genus *Campylopterus*. [F, earlier *sable*, G *Säbel*, cp. Hung. *szablya*, Pol. *szabla*]

sabretache (sab´ətash) *n.* a cavalry officer's leather pocket suspended on the left side from the sword-belt. [F, from G *Säbeltasche* (*Säbel*, sabre, *Tasche*, pocket)]

sabreur SABRE.

sabulous (sab´ūləs), **sabulose** (-lōs) *a.* sandy, gritty. [L *sabulōsus*, from *sabulum*, sand]

SAC *abbr.* **1** Senior Aircraftman. **2** Strategic Air Command.

sac[1] (sak) *n.* **1** a pouch, a cavity or receptacle in an animal or vegetable. **2** a pouch forming the envelope of a tumour, cyst etc. **saccate** (-āt) *a.* **1** having the form of a pouch. **2** contained in a sac. **sacciform** (sak´sifawm) *a.* sac-shaped. [F, from L *saccus*, SACK[1]]

sac[2] (sak) *n.* (*Hist.*) a right or privilege, such as that of holding a court, granted to a lord of a manor by the Crown. [OE *sacu*, dispute, lawsuit]

saccade (sakahd´) *n.* **1** a jump of the eye between fixation points. **2** a sudden check of a horse with the reins. **3** a strong pressure of a violin bow against the strings. **saccadic** (-kad´-) *a.* [F, a jerk, sudden pull, from *saquer*, to pull]

saccate SAC[1].

sacchar- (sak´ə), **saccharo-** (-rō) *comb. form* sugar. **saccharic** (-kar´-) *a.* of, relating to or obtained from sugar. **saccharide** (-īd) *n.* a carbohydrate, esp. a sugar. **sacchariferous** (-if´-) *a.* producing or containing sugar. **saccharify** (-kar´ifī) *v.t.* (*3rd pers. sing. pres.* **saccharifies,** *pres.p.* **saccharifying,** *past, p.p.* **saccharified**) to break down into simple sugars. **saccharimeter** (-im´itə) *n.* an instrument for determining the quantity of sugar in solutions, esp. by means of a polarized light. **saccharimetry** (-tri) *n.* **saccharin** (-ərin) *n.* an intensely sweet compound obtained from toluene, a product of coal-tar, used as a sugar substitute in food. **saccharine** (-īn, -ēn, -in) *a.* **1** of or relating to sugar. **2** having the qualities of sugar. **3** sickly sweet, sugary. **4** ingratiatingly pleasant or polite. **saccharite** (-īt) *n.* a white or whitish granular variety of feldspar. **sacchar-ize, saccharise** *v.t.* to convert into sugar. **saccharoid** (-oid) *a.* (*Geol.*) having a granular structure. ~*n.* a sugar-like substance. **saccharoidal** (-oi´-) *a.* **sacchar-ometer** (-om´itə) *n.* a saccharimeter, esp. a hydrometer for measuring sugar concentration. **saccharose** (-ōs) *n.* sucrose. **saccharous** *a.* [L *saccharum*, from Gr. *sakcharon*, sugar]

sacciform SAC[1].

saccule (sak´ūl), **sacculus** (-ləs) *n.* (*pl.* **saccules, sacculi** (-lī)) a small sac, esp. the smaller of two cavities in the labyrinth of the inner ear. **saccular, sacculate, sacculated** *a.* **sacculation** (-ā´shən) *n.* [L, *sacculus*, dim. of *saccus*, SAC[1]]

sacellum (səsel´əm) *n.* (*pl.* **sacella** (-lə)) **1** a small, usu. roofless sanctuary containing an altar in an ancient Roman building. **2** a chapel, a shrine. [L, dim. of *sacrum*, shrine, neut. of *sacer*, holy]

sacerdotal (sasədō´təl, sak-) *a.* **1** of or relating to priests or the priesthood. **2** priestly. **3** (of a doctrine etc.) attributing sacrificial power and supernatural or sacred character to priests. **4** claiming or suggesting excessive emphasis on the authority of the priesthood. **sacerdocy** (sas´ədōsi, sak´-) *n.* **1** sacerdotalism. **2** the priestly office. **sacerdotalism** *n.* **sacerdotalist** *n.* **sacerdot-alize, sacerdotalise** *v.t.* **sacerdotally** *adv.* [L *sacer-dōtālis*, from *sacerdōs -dōtis*, priest (*sacer*, holy, *dōs dōtis*, cogn. with *dare*, to give)]

sachem (sā´chəm) *n.* **1** a chief of certain tribes of N American Indians. **2** (*NAm., coll.*) a magnate, a prominent person. **3** (*US*) any of the governing officers of the Tammany Society in New York City. **sachemship** *n.* [N Am. Ind.]

sachet (sash´ā) *n.* **1** a small ornamental bag or other receptacle containing perfumed powder for scenting clothes etc. **2** a small packet of shampoo etc. [F, dim. of SAC[1]]

sack[1] (sak) *n.* **1** a large, usu. oblong bag of strong coarse material, for holding corn, raw cotton, wool etc. **2** the quantity a sack contains, as a unit of capacity and weight. **3** a sack together with its contents. **4** a loose coat. **5** a loose-fitting waistless dress. **6** (*coll.*) dismissal from employment. **7** (*Hist.*) a loose garment, gown or appendage to a dress, of various kinds, a sacque. **8** (*esp. NAm., sl.*) bed. ~*v.t.* **1** to put into a sack. **2** (*coll.*) to give the sack to. **to get the sack** to be dismissed from employment. **to give the sack** to dismiss from employment. **to hit the sack** (*coll.*) to go to bed. **sackable** *a.* **sackcloth** *n.* **1** sacking. **2** this worn formerly in token of mourning or penitence. **sackful** *n.* (*pl.* **sackfuls**). **sacking** *n.* coarse stuff of which sacks, bags etc. are made. **sacklike** *a.* **sack race** *n.* a race in which the competitors are tied up to the waist or neck in sacks. [OE *sacc*, L *saccus*, Gr. *sakkos*, Heb. *saq*]

sack[2] (sak) *v.t.* **1** to plunder or pillage (a place taken by storm). **2** to rifle, to ransack, to loot. ~*n.* **1** the pillaging of a captured place. **2** (*poet.*) plunder, booty. **sacker** *n.* [prob. from SACK[1], cp. F *saccager*, It. *saccheggiare*]

sack[3] (sak) *n.* (*Hist.*) a white wine, esp. one from Spain and the Canaries. **sack-posset, sack-whey** *n.* beverages made of sack, milk etc. [orig. *wyne seck*, F *vin sec*, dry wine]

sackbut (sak´būt) *n.* **1** a medieval bass trumpet with a slide like the modern trombone. **2** (*Bible*) an Aramaic musical stringed instrument. [F *saquebote*, prob. conf. with ONF *saqueboute*, a lance with a hook]

sacque (sak) *n.* **1** a loose-fitting woman's gown. **2** a loose-fitting coat hanging from the shoulders. [prob. var. of SACK[1]]

sacra, sacral SACRUM.

sacrament (sak´rəmənt) *n.* **1** a religious rite instituted as an outward and visible sign of an inward and spiritual grace (applied by the Eastern and Roman Catholic Churches to baptism, the Eucharist, confirmation, matrimony, penance, holy orders and anointing of the sick, and by most Protestants to the first two of these). **2** the Lord's Supper, the Eucharist. **3** the consecrated elements of the Eucharist. **4** a sacred token, symbol, influence etc. **5** in Roman times, a military oath. **6** a solemn oath or engagement. *~v.t.* (*usu. in p.p.*) to bind by an oath. **sacramental** (-men´-) *a.* **1** of, relating to or constituting a sacrament. **2** bound by oath, consecrated. *~n.* a rite or observance ancillary or analogous to the sacraments. **sacramentalism** *n.* the doctrine of the spiritual efficacy of the sacraments. **sacramentalist** *n.* **sacramentality** (-tal´-) *n.* sacramental nature. **sacramentally** *adv.* **sacramentarian** (-teə´ri-) *a.* relating to the sacraments or the sacramentarians. *~n.* a person holding extreme or 'high' doctrines regarding the spiritual efficacy of the sacraments. **sacramentarianism** *n.* **sacramentary** (-men´-) *a.* of or relating to a sacrament or to the sacramentarians. *~n.* (*pl.* **sacramentaries**) **1** an ancient book of ritual in the Western Church, containing the rites for Mass and for the administration of the sacraments generally etc. **2** a sacramentarian. [F *sacrement*, L *sacrāmentum*, orig. military oath, from *sacrāre*, to make sacred, from *sacer sacris*, SACRED]

sacrarium (səkreə´riəm) *n.* (*pl.* **sacraria** (-riə)) **1** the sanctuary of a church. **2** in the Roman Catholic Church, a piscina. **3** (*Hist.*) a sacred place where sacred things were kept in ancient Rome, esp. the room in the house where the penates were kept, or the adytum of a temple. [L, from *sacer -cris*, SACRED]

sacred (sā´krid) *a.* **1** dedicated to religious use, consecrated. **2** dedicated or dear to a divinity. **3** set apart, reserved or specially appropriated (to). **4** of, relating to or hallowed by religion or religious service, holy. **5** sanctified by religion, reverence etc., not to be profaned, inviolable. **sacred beetle** *n.* a scarab. **Sacred College** *n.* COLLEGE OF CARDINALS (under COLLEGE). **sacred cow** *n.* (*coll.*) an institution, custom etc. regarded with reverence and as beyond criticism. **Sacred Heart** *n.* **1** the physical heart of Christ. **2** a representation of this. **sacred ibis** *n.* (*pl.* **sacred ibises**) an ibis, *Threskiornis aethiopicus*, venerated by the ancient Egyptians. **sacredly** *adv.* **sacred mushroom** *n.* **1** any of various hallucinogenic mushrooms, esp. species of *Psilocybe* and *Amanita*. **2** a mescal button, chewed for its hallucinogenic effects. **sacredness** *n.* **sacred number** *n.* a number associated with religious symbolism, such as the number seven. [p.p. of ME *sacren*, OF *sacrer*, L *sacrāre*, to consecrate, from *sacer -cris*, holy]

sacrifice (sak´rifīs) *n.* **1** the giving up of anything for the sake of another person, object or interest. **2** that which is offered or given up, a victim, an offering. **3** the act of offering an animal, person etc., esp. by ritual slaughter, or the surrender of a valued possession to a deity, as an act of propitiation, atonement or thanksgiving. **4** the Crucifixion as Christ's offering of himself. **5** the Eucharist as a renewal of this or as a thanksgiving. **6** the sale of goods at a loss. **7** a great loss or destruction (of life etc.). *~v.t.* **1** to surrender for the sake of another person, object etc., to devote. **2** to offer to a deity as a sacrifice. **3** (*coll.*) to sell at a much reduced price. **sacrificatory** *a.* **sacrificeable** *a.* **sacrifice hit** *n.* in baseball, a hit to enable another player to score or reach a base. **sacrificer** *n.* **sacrificial** (-fish´əl) *a.* **sacrificial anode** *n.* a metal anode that protects another more important part by corroding when it is attacked by electrolytic action. **sacrificially** *adv.* [F, from L *sacrificium* (*sacer -cris*, holy, SACRED, *facere*, to make)]

sacrilege (sak´rilij) *n.* **1** the violation or profanation of sacred things, esp. larceny from a consecrated building. **2** irreverence towards something or someone (considered) sacred. **sacrilegious** (-lij´əs) *a.* **sacrilegiously** *adv.* **sacrilegiousness** *n.* **sacrilegist** (-lē´-) *n.* [OF, from L *sacrilegium*, from *sacrilegus*, a sacrilegious person (*sacer -cris*, SACRED, *legere*, to gather, to steal)]

†**sacring** (sā´kring) *n.* consecration, esp. of the Eucharistic elements in the Mass, and of bishops, kings etc. **sacring bell** *n.* the sanctus bell. [ME *sacren*, see SACRED, -ING[1]]

sacrist (sā´krist) *n.* an officer in charge of the sacristy of a church or religious house with its contents. **sacristan** (sak´ristən) *n.* **1** a sacrist. **2** †a sexton. **sacristy** (sak´risti) *n.* (*pl.* **sacristies**) an apartment in a church in which the vestments, sacred vessels, books etc. are kept. [OF *sacriste*, L *sacrista*, from *sacer -cris*, SACRED]

sacro- (sak´rō, sāk´-) *comb. form* sacrum, sacral. **sacrocostal** (-kos´təl) *a.* of or relating to the sacrum and of the nature of a rib. *~n.* a sacrocostal part. **sacroiliac** (-il´iak) *a.* of or relating to the sacrum and the ilium. **sacropubic** (-pū´bik) *a.* of or relating to the sacrum and the pubis.

sacrosanct (sak´rəsangkt) *a.* **1** inviolable by reason of sanctity. **2** regarded with extreme respect, revered. **sacrosanctity** (-sangk´titi) *n.* [L *sacrosanctus* (*sacro-sacer*, SACRED, *sanctus*, see SAINT)]

sacrum (sāk´rəm, sak´-) *n.* (*pl.* **sacra** (-rə), **sacrums**) a composite bone formed by the union of vertebrae at the base of the spinal column, constituting the dorsal part of the pelvis. **sacral** *a.* [L, neut. of *sacer*, holy]

SACW *abbr.* Senior Aircraftwoman.

SAD *abbr.* seasonal affective disorder.

sad (sad) *a.* (*comp.* **sadder**, *superl.* **saddest**) **1** sorrowful, mournful. **2** expressing sorrow. **3** causing sorrow, unfortunate. **4** lamentable, bad, shocking. **5** (of bread, cake etc.) heavy, not well raised. **6** dull, dark-coloured. **7** (*sl.*) pathetic, contemptible. **sadden** *v.t.* **1** to make sad. **2** to tone down (a colour etc.) by certain chemicals, as in dyeing. *~v.i.* to become sad. **saddish** *a.* **sad-eyed, sad-faced, sad-hearted** *a.* (*poet.*) sorrowful or looking sorrowful. **sad-iron** *n.* a solid smoothing iron. **sadly** *adv.* **sadness** *n.* **sad sack** *n.* (*N Am., coll.*) an inept person. [OE *sæd*, sated, cp. Dut. *zat*, G *satt*, also L *satis*]

saddhu SADHU.

saddle (sad´əl) *n.* **1** a seat placed on an animal's back, to support a rider. **2** a similar part of the harness of a draught animal. **3** a seat on a bicycle, agricultural machine etc. **4** an object resembling a saddle. **5** a saddle-shaped marking on an animal's back. **6** the rear part of a male fowl's back. **7** a joint of mutton, venison etc., including the loins. **8** a supporting piece in various machines, suspension bridges, gun-mountings, tackle etc. **9** a depressed part of a ridge between two summits, a col. **10** a raised and symmetrical anticlinal fold. **11** a bar for supporting ceramic ware in a kiln. *~v.t.* **1** to put a saddle on. **2** to load or burden with a duty etc. **3** (of a trainer) to enter (a horse) for a race. **in the saddle** **1** mounted. **2** in control. **saddleback** *n.* **1** a roof or coping sloping up at both ends or with a gable at each end. **2** a saddlebacked hill. **3** an animal with a marking suggestive of a saddle. **4** a black pig with a white band across the back. **5** any of various birds with a saddle-like marking, esp. a New Zealand bird *Creadion carunculatus*. **6** the hooded crow. *~a.* saddlebacked. **saddlebacked** *a.* **1** (of a horse) having a low back with an elevated neck and head. **2** curving up at each end. **saddlebag** *n.* **1** each of a pair of bags connected by straps slung across a horse etc. from the saddle. **2** a bag attached to the back of the saddle of a bicycle etc. **3** a kind of carpeting woven in imitation of Persian saddlebags for camels. **saddle-blanket** *n.* a saddle-cloth. **saddle bow** *n.* the pommel. **saddle-cloth** *n.* a cloth laid on a horse under the saddle. **saddle-corporal, saddle-sergeant** *n.* a regimental saddler. **saddle-horse** *n.* a horse for riding. **saddleless** *a.* **saddle-pillar** *n.* the saddle support of a cycle. **saddler** *n.* **1** a maker or dealer in saddles and harness. **2** (*Mil.*) a non-commissioned officer in charge of the harness in a cavalry regiment. **saddlery** *n.* (*pl.* **saddleries**) **1** the trade or shop of a saddler. **2** saddles and harnesses collectively. **saddle soap** *n.* an oily soap for cleaning and preserving leather. **saddle-sore** *a.* chafed with riding. **saddle-spring** *n.* the spring of a cycle saddle. **saddle stitch** *n.* a stitch or staple passed through the centre of a booklet etc. **saddle-stitch** *v.t.* **saddle tree** *n.* **1** the frame of a saddle. **2** the tulip tree. [OE *sadol* (cp. Dut. *zadel*, G *Sattel*, Icel. *söthull*), whence *sadelian* (cp. Dut. *zadelen*, G *satteln*), prob. rel. to SIT]

Sadducee (sad´ūsē) *n.* a member of a sect among the Jews, arising in the 2nd cent. BC, who adhered to the written law to the exclusion of tradition, and denied the resurrection from the dead, existence of spirits etc. **Sadducean** (-sē´ən) *a.* **Sadduceeism** *n.* [L *Sadducaei*, pl., from Gr. *Saddoukaioi*, prob. from *Zadok*, name of High Priest]

sadhu (sah´doo), **saddhu** *n.* a Hindu usu. mendicant holy man. [Sansk.]

sadism (sā´dizm) *n.* **1** sexual perversion characterized by a passion for cruelty. **2** (*coll.*) pleasure derived from inflicting pain. **sadist** *n.* **sadistic** (sədis´-) *a.* **sadistically** *adv.* **sadomasochism** (-dōmas´əkizm) *n.* sadism and masochism combined in one person. **sadomasochist** *n.* **sadomasochistic** (-kis´-) *a.* [F *sadisme*, from the Marquis de *Sade*, 1740–1814, French writer]

sae *abbr.* **1** self-addressed envelope. **2** stamped addressed envelope.

safari (səfah´ri) *n.* (*pl.* **safaris**) **1** a hunting or scientific expedition, esp. in E Africa. **2** a sightseeing trip to see African animals in their natural habitat. **safari jacket** *n.* a light, usu. cotton jacket with breast pockets and a belt. **safari park** *n.* a park containing uncaged wild animals, such as lions and monkeys. **safari suit** *n.* a suit having a safari jacket. [Arab. *safar*, a journey]

safe (sāf) *a.* **1** free or secure from danger, damage or evil. **2** uninjured, unharmed, sound. **3** affording security. **4** not dangerous, hazardous or risky. **5** cautious, prudent, trusty. **6** unfailing, certain, sure. **7** no longer dangerous, secure from escape or from doing harm. ~*n.* **1** a receptacle for keeping things safe, a steel fireproof and burglarproof receptacle for valuables, a strongbox. **2** a cupboard or other receptacle for keeping meat and other provisions. **on the safe side** as a precaution. **safe and sound** secure and unharmed. **safe as houses** completely safe. **to play safe** PLAY. **safe bet** *n.* a bet that is certain to succeed. **safe-blower, safe-breaker,** (*N Am.*) **safe-cracker** *n.* a person who opens safes to steal. **safe-blowing, safe-breaking,** (*N Am.*) **safe-cracking** *n.* **safe conduct** *n.* **1** an official document or passport ensuring a safe passage, esp. in a foreign country or in time of hostilities. **2** the protection given by such a document. **safe deposit** *n.* a specially-constructed building or basement with safes for renting. **safeguard** *n.* **1** a person who or thing which protects. **2** a proviso, precaution, circumstance etc. that tends to save loss, trouble, danger etc. **3** a safe conduct, a passport. ~*v.t.* to make safe or secure by precaution, stipulation etc. **safeguarding** *n.* protecting specified home industries against foreign competition by customs duties. **safe house** *n.* a place that can be used as a refuge. **safe keeping** *n.* **1** the act of keeping or preserving in safety. **2** secure guardianship. **3** custody. **safe light** *n.* a filtered light used in a darkroom. **safely** *adv.* **safeness** *n.* **safe period** *n.* the part of the menstrual cycle when conception is least likely to occur. **safe seat** *n.* a Parliamentary seat that is certain to be held by the same party as previously. **safe sex** *n.* sexual activity avoiding penetration or using physical protection such as condoms, to prevent the transmission of disease, esp. Aids. [ME and OF *sauf*, L *salvus*, whole, uninjured]

safety (sāf´ti) *n.* (*pl.* **safeties**) **1** the state of being safe, freedom from injury, danger or risk. **2** safe keeping or custody. **3** a safety catch. **4** (*coll.*) a safety bicycle. **5** in American football, the defensive back furthest back in the field. **safety first** used to advise caution. **safety belt** *n.* **1** a seat belt. **2** a belt fastening a person to a fixed object to prevent falling. **safety bicycle** *n.* a low bicycle with wheels of equal size. **safety catch, safety lock** *n.* **1** a lock that cannot be picked easily. **2** a device in a firearm to prevent accidental discharge. **safety curtain** *n.* a fireproof curtain in a theatre that cuts off the stage from the audience. **safety deposit** *n.* a safe deposit. **safety factor** *n.* FACTOR OF SAFETY (under FACTOR). **safety film** *n.* a photographic film with a non-flammable or slow-burning base. **safety fuse** *n.* **1** a fuse that allows an explosive to be fired without danger to the person igniting it. **2** an electrical fuse that protects a circuit from overloading. **safety glass** *n.* **1** glass layered with a sheet of plastic to resist shattering. **2** glass treated to prevent splintering when broken. **safety harness** *n.* a system of belts used to prevent a person falling or being injured. **safety lamp** *n.* a miner's lamp protected by wire or gauze so as not to ignite combustible gas. **safety match** *n.* a match that ignites only on a surface treated with a special ingredient. **safety net** *n.* **1** a net to catch tightrope and trapeze performers if they should fall. **2** a safeguard, precaution. **safety pin** *n.* a pin with a part for keeping it secure and guarding the point. **safety razor** *n.* a razor mounted on a handle with a guard to prevent cutting the skin. **safety valve** *n.* **1** a valve on a boiler automatically opening to let steam escape to relieve pressure and prevent explosion. **2** any harmless means of relieving anger, excitement etc. **safety zone** *n.* (*N Am.*) a marked-off area on a road, where pedestrians etc. can wait safely.

saffian (saf´iən) *n.* leather prepared from goatskin or sheepskin tanned with sumac and dyed yellow or red. [Rus. *safiyanu*]

safflower (saf´lowə) *n.* **1** a thistle-like plant, *Carthamus tinctorius*, with orange flowers yielding a red dye, and seeds rich in oil. **2** the petals of this, or the dye made from them. [Dut. *saffloer*, OF *saffleur*, obs. It. *saffiore*]

saffron (saf´rən) *n.* **1** the dried deep orange stigmas of a crocus, *Crocus sativus*, used for colouring and flavouring food. **2** this plant. **3** the colour deep orange. **4** the meadow saffron, *Colchicum autumnale*. **5** the false saffron or safflower. ~*a.* saffron-coloured, deep yellow. ~*v.t.* **1** to make yellow. **2** to tinge with saffron. **saffrony** *a.* **safranin** (-nin, -nēn), **safranine** *n.* any of a series of basic compounds used in dyeing. [OF *safran*, Arab. *za'frān*]

S Afr. *abbr.* South Africa.

safrole (saf´rōl) *n.* a usually colourless liquid obtained from sassafras and used in soaps and perfumes. [*sassafras*, -OLE]

sag (sag) *v.i.* (*pres.p.* **sagging,** *past, p.p.* **sagged**) **1** to droop, to sink, to yield or give way esp. in the middle, under weight or pressure. **2** to bend, to hang sideways. **3** to lose vigour, to weaken. **4** (of prices, esp. of stocks) to decline. **5** (*Naut.*) to drift to leeward. ~*v.t.* to cause to give way, bend, or curve sideways. ~*n.* **1** the act or state of sagging or giving way. **2** the amount of this. **3** (*Naut.*) a sideways drift or tendency to leeward. **sag bag** *n.* a large bean bag used for sitting on. **saggy** *a.* (*comp.* **saggier,** *superl.* **saggiest**). [prob. of Scand. orig. (cp. Dan. and Norw. *sakke*, Dut. *zakken*)]

saga[1] (sah´gə) *n.* **1** a medieval prose narrative recounting family or public events in Iceland or Scandinavia, usu. by contemporary or nearly contemporary native writers. **2** a story of heroic adventure. **3** a series of books relating the history of a family. **4** a long involved story or account. [Icel., cogn. with SAW[2]]

saga[2] SAGUM.

sagacious (səgā´shəs) *a.* **1** intellectually keen or quick to understand or discern, intelligent, perspicacious, shrewd, wise. **2** (of policy etc.) characterized by wisdom and discernment. **3** (of an animal) sensible, quick-scented. **sagaciously** *adv.* **sagaciousness** *n.*

sagacity (-gas´-) *n.* [L *sagax -ācis* (rel. to *sagīre*, to perceive)]

sagamore (sag´əmaw) *n.* a N American Indian chief, a sachem. [Algonquian *sagamo*]

sagan (sā´gən) *n.* the deputy of the Jewish high priest. [Heb.]

sagapenum (sagəpē´nəm) *n.* a gum resin obtained from *Ferula persica*, formerly used to relieve spasms. [late L, from Gr. *sagapēnon*]

sage[1] (sāj) *n.* a grey-leaved aromatic plant of the genus *Salvia*, esp. *S. officinalis*, formerly much used in medicine, now employed in cookery. **sage and onion** *n.* a kind of stuffing used with meat or poultry. **sagebrush** *n.* **1** a shrubby plant of the various species of *Artemisia*, esp. *A. tridentata*, abounding in the plains of the W US. **2** an area covered in this. **sage cheese** *n.* cheese flavoured and coloured with layers of or an infusion of sage. **sage cock, sage grouse** *n.* the largest of the American grouse, *Centrocercus urophasianus*, frequenting the sagebrush regions. **sage Derby (cheese)** *n.* a cheese flavoured with sage. **sage green** *n.* a greyish green. **sage-green** *a.* **sage tea** *n.* a medicinal infusion of sage leaves. **sagy** *a.* [ME and A-F *sauge*, L *salvia*]

sage[2] (sāj) *a.* **1** wise, discreet, prudent. **2** judicious, well-considered. **3** grave, serious- or solemn-looking. *~n.* a person of great wisdom, esp. one of past times with a traditional reputation for wisdom. **sagely** *adv.* **sageness** *n.* **sageship** *n.* [F, ult. from pop. L *sapius*, from *sapere*, to be wise]

sagene[1] (səjēn´) *n.* a fishing net. [L *sagēna*, Gr. *sagēnē*, cp. SEINE]

sagene[2] (sah´zhen) *n.* a Russian measure of length, about 7 ft. (2 m). [Rus.]

saggar (sag´ə), **sagger** *n.* a vessel of fireproof pottery in which delicate porcelain is enclosed while in a kiln. **saggar-house** *n.* [perh. corr. of SAFEGUARD (under SAFE)]

saggy SAG.

sagittal (səjit´əl) *a.* **1** of, relating to or resembling an arrow. **2** of or relating to the join between the two parietal bones forming the sides and top of the skull. **3** in or parallel to the mid-plane of the body. **Sagittarius** (sajiteə´riəs) *n.* **1** the Archer, a zodiacal constellation and the ninth sign of the zodiac, which the sun enters on 22 Nov. **2** a person born under this sign. **Sagittarian** *n., a.* **sagittary** (saj´-) *n.* (*pl.* **sagittaries**) a centaur. **sagittate** (saj´itāt) *a.* (esp. of a leaf) shaped like an arrowhead. **sagittiferous** (-tif´-) *a.* **sagittiform** (-jit´-) *a.* **sagittilingual** (sajitiling´gwəl) *a.* having an arrow-like tongue. [L *sagitta*, arrow]

sago (sā´gō) *n.* (*pl.* **sagos**) **1** a starchy substance obtained from the soft inner portion of the trunk of several palms or cycads and used as food. **2** a sago palm. **sago palm** *n.* any of several tropical palms and cycads, esp. *Cycas circinalis* and *Metroxylon sagu*. [Malay *sāgu*]

saguaro (səgwah´rō), **sahuaro** (səwah´rō) *n.* (*pl.* **saguaros, sahuaros**) a large Central American cactus, *Carnegiea gigantea*, with edible fruit. [Mex. Sp.]

sagum (sā´gəm) *n.* (*pl.* **saga** (-gə)) the military cloak worn by ancient Roman soldiers. [L]

sagy SAGE[1].

sahib (sah´ib) *n.* (in India) a polite form of address for a man; a gentleman. [Hind. from Arab. *sāhib*, friend, companion]

sahlite (sah´līt) *n.* a green variety of pyroxene. [from *Sahla*, in Sweden]

sahuaro SAGUARO.

sai (sī) *n.* (*pl.* **sais**) a S American capuchin monkey, *Cebus olivaceus*. [Tupi-Guarani *çahy*]

saic (sā´ik) *n.* a sailing vessel of the eastern Mediterranean. [F *saïque*, Turk. *shāïqā*]

said SAY.

SAIDS *abbr.* simian acquired immune deficiency syndrome.

saiga (sī´gə, sā-) *n.* an antelope, *Saiga tartarica*, of the steppes of E Europe and W Asia. [Rus.]

sail (sāl) *n.* **1** a piece of canvas or other fabric spread on rigging to catch the wind, and cause a ship or boat to move in the water. **2** some or all of a ship's sails. **3** a ship or vessel with sails. **4** a specified number of ships in a squadron etc. **5** an excursion by sail or (*loosely*) by water. **6** anything like a sail in form or function. **7** the arm of a windmill. **8 a** the dorsal fin of some fish. **b** the tentacle of a nautilus. **c** the float of a Portuguese man-of-war. **9** a wing. **10** (*pl., sl.*) a maker or repairer of sails. **11** (*pl., Hist.*) a chief petty officer in charge of rigging. *~v.i.* **1** to move or be driven forward by the action of the wind upon sails. **2** to be conveyed in a vessel by water. **3** to set sail. **4** to handle or make journeys in a vessel equipped with sails as a sport or hobby. **5** to pass gently (along), to float (as a bird), to glide. **6** to go along in a stately manner. **7** (*usu. with through, coll.*) to succeed easily. *~v.t.* **1** to pass over in a ship, to navigate. **2** to perform by sailing. **3** to manage the navigation of (a ship). **4** to cause to sail, to set afloat. **to make sail 1** to set sail. **2** to extend an additional quantity of sail. **to sail close to/ near the wind** WIND[1]. **to sail into** (*coll.*) to attack vigorously. **to set sail** to begin a voyage. **to shorten sail** to reduce the amount of sail spread. **to strike sail 1** to lower sails suddenly. **2** to give way, to submit. **to take in sail 1** to furl the sails of a vessel. **2** to moderate one's ambitions. **under sail** with sails spread. **sailable** *a.* **sail-arm** *n.* an arm of a windmill. **sailboard** *n.* a moulded board with a single mast and sail, used in windsurfing. **sailboarder** *n.* **sailboarding** *n.* **sailcloth** *n.* **1** canvas etc. for making sails. **2** a kind of dress material. **sailed** *a.* (*also in comb.*) **sailer** *n.* a ship (with reference to her power or manner of sailing). **sailfish** *n.* (*pl. in general* **sailfish,** *in particular* **sailfishes**) **1** any large fish of the genus *Istiophorus*, with a tall dorsal fin. **2** a basking shark. **sail-fluke** *n.* a deep-water flatfish, the megrim. **sailing** *n.* **sailing boat,** (*N Am.*) **sailboat** *n.* a boat with sails. **sailing master** *n.* an officer whose duty it is to navigate a yacht etc. **sailing orders** *n.pl.* instructions to the captain of a ship. **sailing ship** *n.* a ship with sails. **sailless** *a.* **sail-loft** *n.* a large apartment where sails are cut out and made. **sailmaker** *n.* a person who makes, repairs or alters sails. **sailmaking** *n.* **sailplane** *n.* a glider that rises in an upward air current. **sailroom** *n.* an apartment on board ship where spare sails are stowed. **sailyard** *n.* a horizontal spar on which sails are extended. [OE *segel, segl* (cp. Dut. *zeil*, G *Segel*, Icel. *segl*)]

sailor (sā´lə) *n.* a member of the crew of a boat or ship, as distinguished from an officer. **sailor hat** *n.* a flat-crowned narrow-brimmed straw hat worn by women, or one with a turned-up brim for children. **sailoring** *n.* **sailorless** *a.* **sailorlike, sailorly** *a.* **sailor man** *n.* (*pl.* **sailor men**) (*coll.*) a seaman. **sailor's knot** *n.* a kind of reef knot used in tying a necktie. **sailor suit** *n.* a child's navy and white suit like a sailor's.

sainfoin (sān´foin, san´-) *n.* a leguminous herb, *Onobrychis viciifolia*, resembling clover, grown for fodder. [F *sainfoin*, L *sānum*, SANE, *foenum*, hay]

saint (sānt, sənt) *n.* **1** a person eminent for piety and virtue, a holy person. **2** any of the blessed in heaven. **3** a person canonized or recognized by the Church as pre-eminently holy and deserving of veneration. **4** a member of the Mormons and some other sects (used in speaking of themselves). *~v.t.* **1** to canonize. **2** to regard or address as a saint. *~v.i.* to act as a saint. **saintdom, sainthood** *n.* **sainted** *a.* **1** canonized. **2** gone to heaven. **3** holy, pious. **my sainted aunt** AUNT. **sainting** *n.* **saintlike** *a.* **saintling** *n.* **saintly** *a.*

(*comp.* **saintlier,** *superl.* **saintliest**). **saintliness** *n.* **saintpaulia** (səntpaw´liə) *n.* AFRICAN VIOLET (under AFRICAN). **saint's bell** *n.* the sanctus bell. **saint's day** *n.* a day dedicated to the commemoration of a particular saint, esp. the patron saint of a church, school etc. **saintship** *n.* **St Andrew's cross** *n.* an X-shaped cross. **St Anthony cross, St Anthony's cross** *n.* a T-shaped cross. **St Anthony's fire** *n.* erysipelas (from the tradition that those stricken by the pestilence of erysipelas, or sacred fire, in 1809, were cured through the intercession of St Anthony). **St Bernard (dog)** *n.* a large and powerful breed of dog orig. kept by the monks of the Hospice in the Great St Bernard Pass to rescue travellers. **St Elmo's fire** (el´mōz) *n.* the corposant (from its being regarded as a sign of protection from St Elmo, patron saint of sailors). **St George's cross** *n.* a Greek cross used on the British flag. **St John's wort** *n.* any plant of the genus *Hypericum*, esp. *H. androsaemum*. **St Leger** (lej´ə) *n.* a horse race at Doncaster for three-year-olds. **St Luke's summer** *n.* a spell of mild weather in the autumn (usually around 18 Oct., the feast day of Saint Luke). **St Martin's summer** *n.* a spell of mild weather in late autumn (usually around 11 Nov., the feast day of Saint Martin of Tours). **St Monday** *n.* Monday turned into a holiday by workers. **St Stephen's** *n.* the British parliament (so named from the chapel within the precincts of the Houses of Parliament). **St Valentine's day** *n.* 14 Feb., commemorating the day when St Valentine was beheaded by the Romans and when birds were supposed to begin to mate. **St Vitus's dance** (vī´təsiz) *n.* SYDENHAM'S CHOREA. [OF, from L *sanctus*, p.p. of *sancīre*, to make holy, rel. to *sacer*, SACRED]

Saint-Simonian (sāntsimō´niən) *n.* an adherent of the comte de St-Simon (1760–1825), who advocated the establishment of State ownership and distribution of earnings according to capacity and labour. *~a.* of or relating to his doctrines. **Saint-Simonianism, Saint-Simonism** (-sī´mən-) *n.* **Saint-Simonist** *n.* **Saint-Simonite** (-īt) *n.*

sair (seə) *a.* (*Sc.*) sore.

saithe (sāth) *n.* the coalfish, *Pollachius virens*. [Sc., from Icel. *seithr*, cp. Gael. *saigh*]

sajou (sazhoo´) *n.* (*pl.* **sajous**) a capuchin monkey. [F, also *sajouassu*, Tupi-Guarani *sauiassu*]

sake[1] (sāk) *n.* **1** end, purpose. **2** desire of obtaining. **3** account, reason, cause. **for Christ's sake** used as a solemn adjuration or an expression of exasperation etc. **for conscience' sake 1** for the sake of one's conscientious scruples. **2** for the sake of one's religion. **for God's sake** used as a solemn adjuration or an expression of exasperation etc. **for goodness' sake** a solemn adjuration. **for heaven's sake** a solemn adjuration. **for mercy's sake** used as a solemn adjuration or appeal. **for old sake's sake** for old time's sake. **for old time's sake** in memory of days gone by. **for Pete's sake** used as expression of annoyance. **for pity's sake** a solemn adjuration. **for someone's sake** because of someone, out of consideration for someone. **for something's sake** because of, out of consideration for something. **for the sake of** because of, out of consideration for. [OE *sacu*, SAC[2]]

sake[2] (sak´ā, sah´ki), **saké, saki** *n.* a fermented liquor made from rice. [Jap.]

saker (sā´kə) *n.* **1** a large falcon, *Falco cherrug*, used in hawking, esp. the female. **2** (*Hist.*) a small piece of artillery. **sakeret** *n.* the male of the saker, which is smaller than the female. [F *sacre*, Sp. and Port. *sacro*, Arab. *çaqr*]

saki[1] (sah´ki) *n.* (*pl.* **sakis**) any monkey of the S American genera *Pithecia* or *Chiropotes*. [F, prob. from Tupi-Guarani *çahy*, SAI]

saki[2] SAKE[2].

sakieh (sak´iə) *n.* an apparatus used in Egypt for raising water, consisting of a vertical wheel or wheel and chain carrying pots or buckets. [Arab. *sāqiyah*, fem. pres.p. of *saqā*, to irrigate]

Sakti (shak´ti), **sakti** *n.* in Hinduism, the female principle esp. as personified as the wife of a god. **Sakta** (shahk´tə) *n.* a member of a Hindu sect worshipping the Sakti. [Sansk. *śakti*, divine energy]

sal[1] (sal) *n.* (*Chem.*) salt (used only with qualifying word). **sal alembroth** (əlem´broth) *n.* a compound of corrosive sublimate of mercury and sal ammoniac. **sal ammoniac** (əmō´niak) *n.* ammonium chloride. **sal prunella** (prunel´ə) *n.* nitrate of potash fused and cast into cakes or balls. **sal volatile** (vəlat´ili) *n.* an aromatic solution of ammonium carbonate. [L]

sal[2] (sahl) *n.* a large Indian timber tree, *Shorea robusta*. [Hind.]

salaam (səlahm´) *n.* a ceremonious salutation or obeisance in Eastern countries. *~v.i.* to make a salaam. *~v.t.* to make a salaam to (a person). [Arab. *salam*]

salable SALE.

salacious (səlā´shəs) *a.* **1** lustful, lecherous. **2** arousing lust, erotic, lewd. **salaciously** *adv.* **salaciousness** *n.* **salacity** (-las´-) *n.* [L *salax -ācis*, cogn. with *salīre*, to leap]

salad (sal´əd) *n.* **1** a dish of (mixed) raw vegetables. **2** a cold dish of precooked vegetables, or of fruit, often mixed with a dressing. **3** any herb or other vegetable suitable for eating raw. **salad cream** *n.* a kind of mayonnaise. **salad days** *n.pl.* the time of youth and inexperience. **salad dressing** *n.* a mixture of oil, vinegar, mustard etc., for dressing salads. **salading** *n.* herbs etc. for salads. **salad oil** *n.* a vegetable oil suitable for use in salad dressings. [OF *salade*, OIt. *salata*, pop. L *salāta*, p.p. of *salāre*, to salt, from SAL[1]]

salade SALLET.

salal (sal´əl) *n.* an evergreen shrub, *Gaultheria shallon*, of California etc., bearing grapelike edible berries. [Chinook]

salamander (sal´əmandə) *n.* **1** an amphibian of the family *Urodela*, esp. the genus *Salamandra*. **2** a lizard-like animal anciently believed to be able to live in fire. **3** a spirit or genie fabled to live in fire. **4** anyone who can stand great heat, a soldier who is unperturbed under fire. **5** any of various implements and utensils used in a heated state. **6** (*N Am., dial.*) a gopher. **salamandrian** (-man´dri-), **salamandrine** (-man´drin) *a.* **salamandroid** (-man´droid) *n., a.* [F *salamandre*, L and Gr. *salamandra*]

salami (səlah´mi), **salame** *n.* (*pl.* **salamis, salames**) a highly-seasoned Italian sausage. [It.]

salangane (sal´əng·gān) *n.* a Chinese swift of the genus *Collocalia*, that builds edible nests. [F, from Luzon name *salamga*]

salary (sal´əri) *n.* (*pl.* **salaries**) a fixed payment given periodically, usu. monthly, esp. for work not of a manual or mechanical kind. *~v.t.* (*3rd pers. sing. pres.* **salaries**, *pres.p.* **salarying**, *past, p.p.* **salaried**) to pay a salary to. **salariat** (səleə´riət) *n.* the salaried class. **salaried** *a.* **salaryman** *n.* (*pl.* **salarymen**) in Japan, a white-collar worker. [A-F *salarie* (F *salaire*), L *salārium*, orig. salt-money given to soldiers, from SAL[1]]

salbutamol (salbū´təmol) *n.* a drug used as a bronchodilator to treat asthma.

salchow (sal´kō) *n.* an ice-skating jump with turns in the air. [Ulrich *Salchow*, 1877–1949, Swedish skater]

sale (sāl) *n.* **1** the act of selling. **2** the exchange of a commodity for money or other equivalent. **3** an event at which goods are sold. **4** an auction. **5** a disposal of a shop's remaining goods at reduced prices. **6** demand, market. **7** (*pl.*) quantity of goods sold. **8** (*pl.*) the activities involved in selling goods collectively. **on/for/up for sale** offered for purchase. **saleable, salable**

a. **saleability** (-bil´-) *n.* **saleableness** *n.* **sale of work** *n.* a sale of home-made goods for charitable purposes. **sale or return** *n.* an arrangement by which a retailer may return unsold goods to the wholesaler. **sale ring** *n.* a circle of buyers at an auction. **saleroom,** (*N Am.*) **salesroom** *n.* a room in which goods are sold, an auction room. **sales clerk** *n.* (*N Am.*) a shop assistant. **sales department** *n.* the part of a firm that deals with selling. **sales engineer** *n.* a salesperson who has technical knowledge of their goods and market. **salesgirl** *n.* a saleswoman. **saleslady** *n.* (*pl.* **salesladies**) a saleswoman. **salesman, saleswoman** *n.* (*pl.* **salesmen, saleswomen**) **1** a person employed to sell goods, esp. in a shop. **2** a sales representative. **salesmanship** *n.* the art of selling, skill in persuading prospective purchasers. **salesperson** *n.* (*pl.* **salespersons, salespeople**) a salesman or saleswoman. **sales representative** *n.* a person employed to secure orders for a company's products, usu. in an assigned geographical area. **sales resistance** *n.* opposition of a prospective customer to purchasing a product. **sales talk** *n.* persuasive or attractive arguments to influence a possible purchaser. **sales tax** *n.* a tax on the sale of goods and services. **salework** *n.* **1** work made for sale. **2** work done in a perfunctory way. [OE *sala*, prob. from Icel. *sala*, cogn. with SELL]

salep (sal´əp) *n.* a farinaceous meal made from the dried roots of *Orchis mascula* and other orchidaceous plants. [F and Turk., from Arab. *tha'leb*]

saleratus (salərā´təs) *n.* (*N Am.*) an impure bicarbonate of potash or soda, much used as baking powder. [mod. L *sal aerātus*, aerated salt]

Salesian (səlē´zhən, -ziən) *n.* a member of a religious order founded by St Francis of Sales. *~a.* of or relating to this order. [St Francis of *Sales*, 1567–1622, French ecclesiastic and theologian]

Salian[1] (sā´liən) *a.* of or relating to the Salii or priests of Mars of ancient Rome. [L *Salii*, from *salīre*, to leap, -AN]

Salian[2] (sā´liən) *a.* of or relating to a Frankish tribe on the lower Rhine to which the ancestors of the Merovingians belonged. *~n.* a member of this tribe. **Salic** (sal´-), **Salique** (səlēk´) *a.* Salian. **Salic law** *n.* **1** (*also* **Salic code**) a Frankish law-book written in Latin extant during the Merovingian and Carolingian periods. **2** (*Hist.*) a law derived from this excluding females from succession to the throne, esp. as the fundamental law of the French monarchy. [late L *Salii*, the tribe, -AN]

salic (sal´ik, sā-) *a.* (of minerals) rich in silicon and aluminium.

salicet (sal´iset), **salicional** (-lish´ə-) *n.* organ stops with notes like those of a willow-pipe. **salicetum** (-sē´təm) *n.* (*pl.* **salicetums, saliceta** (-tə)) a garden or arboretum of willows. [L *salix*, *salicis*, a willow]

salicin (sal´isin), **salicine** (-sēn) *n.* a bitter crystalline compound obtained from the bark of willows and poplars, used medicinally. **salicyl** (-sil) *n.* the hypothetical radical of salicylic acid. **salicylate** (-lis´ilāt) *n.* a salt of salicylic acid. *~v.t.* to salicylize. **salicylic** (-sil´-) *a.* **1** derived from the willow. **2** belonging to a series of benzene derivatives of salicin. **3** derived from salicylic acid. **salicylic acid** *n.* an acid whose derivatives, including aspirin, are used to relieve pain and to treat rheumatism. **salicylize** (-lis´-), **salicylise** *v.t.* to impregnate with salicylic acid. **salicylous** (-lis´-) *a.* [F *salicine* (L *salix -icis*, willow)]

salient (sā´liənt) *a.* **1** conspicuous, prominent, noticeable. **2** pointing or projecting outwards. **3** (*Her.*) represented in a leaping posture. **4** †leaping, jumping, springing. **5** †shooting out (of water). *~n.* **1** a salient angle. **2** a portion of defensive works or of a line of defence projecting towards the enemy. **salience, saliency** *n.* **saliently** *adv.* **salient point** *n.* **1** a significant point. **2** †the initial stage, origin, or first beginning. [L *saliens -ntem*, pres.p. of *salīre*, to leap]

salientian (sālien´shiən) *n.*, *a.* ANURAN. [mod. L *Salientia*, as SALIENT]

saliferous (səlif´ərəs) *a.* (of rock strata) bearing or producing salt. **saliferous system** *n.* the Triassic rocks, from the deposits of salt. **salify** (sal´ifī) *v.t.*, *v.i.* (*3rd pers. sing. pres.* **salifies,** *pres.p.* **salifying,** *past, p.p.* **salified**) to form (into) a salt. **salifiable** *a.* **salification** (-fikā´shən) *n.* [L *sal salis*, SAL[1], -FEROUS]

saline (sā´līn) *a.* **1** consisting of or having the characteristics of salt. **2** containing or impregnated with salt or salts. **3** containing a salt or salts of alkaline metals or magnesium. *~n.* **1** a salina. **2** a saline substance, esp. a purgative. **3** a saline solution, esp. with the same concentration as body fluids. **salina** (səlī´nə) *n.* **1** a salt marsh, lake, spring etc. **2** salt works. **salineness** *n.* **saliniferous** (salinif´-) *a.* SALIFEROUS. **salinity** (səlin´-) *n.* **salinization** (salinīzā´shən), **salinisation** *n.* **salinometer** (salinom´itə) *n.* an instrument for ascertaining the density of brine in the boilers of marine steam-engines. **salinoterrene** (-terēn´) *a.* consisting of a salt and earth. [SAL[1], -INE]

Salique SALIAN[2].

saliva (səlī´və) *n.* an odourless, colourless, somewhat viscid liquid secreted by glands into the mouth where it lubricates ingested food, spittle. †**salival** *a.* **salivant** (sal´i-) *n.*, *a.* (a medicine) exciting salivation. **salivary** (sal´i-, səlī´-) *a.* of or producing saliva. **salivate** (sal´iv-) *v.t.* to excite an unusual secretion and discharge of saliva in, as by the use of mercury. *~v.i.* to secrete or discharge saliva in excess. **salivation** (-ā´shən) *n.* **saliva test** *n.* a scientific test based on a sample of saliva. [L]

salix (sal´iks) *n.* a plant of the *Salix* genus, such as the willow. [L]

Salk vaccine (sawlk) *n.* a vaccine against poliomyelitis. [Jonas *Salk*, b. 1914, American virologist]

sallee (sal´i), **sally** *n.* (*pl.* **sallees, sallies**) (*Austral.*) any of several eucalypts and acacias resembling the willow. [Austral. Abor., or SALLOW[1]]

sallee-man (sal´iman), **sallee rover** *n.* (*pl.* **sallee-men**) (*Hist.*) a Moorish pirate or pirate ship. [*Sallee*, port in Morocco]

sallenders (sal´əndəz) *n.* a dry scabby inflammation in the hock-joint of a horse's hind leg. [F *solandre*, etym. uncertain]

sallet (sal´it), **salade** (səlahd´) *n.* (*Hist.*) a light, hemispherical, crestless helmet with the back curving away, worn by 15th-cent. foot soldiers. [earlier *salade*, F *salade*, It. *celata*, prob. from L *caelāta*, fem. p.p. of *caelāre*, to engrave (a helmet)]

sallow[1] (sal´ō) *n.* **1** a willow tree, esp. one of the low shrubby varieties. **2** a willow-shoot, an osier. **3** any of various moths feeding on willows. **sallowy** *a.* [OE *sealh* (cp. Icel. *selja*, OHG *salaha*, also L *salix*, Gr. *helikē*)]

sallow[2] (sal´ō) *a.* of a sickly yellowish or pale brown colour. *~v.t.* to make sallow. *~v.i.* to become sallow. **sallowish** *a.* **sallowness** *n.* [OE *salu* (cp. MDut. *salu*, Icel. *sölr*, OHG *salo*)]

Sally (sal´i) *n.* (*pl.* **Sallies**) (*coll.*) **1** the Salvation Army. **2** a member of this. **Sally Army** *n.* [abbr.]

sally[1] (sal´i) *n.* (*pl.* **sallies**) **1** a sudden rushing out or sortie of troops from a besieged place against besiegers. **2** an issuing forth, an excursion. **3** a sudden or brief outbreak of spirits etc., an outburst. **4** a flight of fancy or wit, a bantering remark etc. **5** †an act of levity, an escapade. *~v.i.* (*3rd pers. sing. pres.* **sallies,** *pres.p.* **sallying,** *past, p.p.* **sallied**) **1** (of troops) to rush out suddenly. **2** to go (out or forth) on a journey, excursion etc. **3** †to leap or come out suddenly. **sally-port** *n.* a postern or passage for making sallies from. [F *saillie*, from *saillir*, to rush out, L *salīre*, to leap]

sally[2] (sal´i) *n.* (*pl.* **sallies**) **1** the part of a bell-ringer's rope covered with wool for holding. **2** the first movement of a bell when set for ringing. **sally-hole** *n.* the hole through which the bell rope is passed. [perh. from SALLY[1]]

sally[3] SALLEE.

Sally Lunn (sali lŭn´) *n.* a sweet teacake eaten hot and buttered. [*Sally Lunn*, who sold them at Bath, *c.* 1800]

salmagundi (salməgŭn´di) *n.* (*pl.* **salmagundis**) **1** a dish of chopped meat, anchovies, eggs, oil, vinegar etc. **2** a multifarious mixture, a medley, a miscellany. [F *salmagondis*, etym. uncertain]

salmanazar (salmənā´zə) *n.* a large wine bottle, holding about 12 times as much as a standard bottle. [*Shalmaneser*, King of Assyria (II Kings xvii.3)]

salmi (sal´mē), **salmis** *n.* (*pl.* **salmis**) a ragout, esp. of game birds stewed with wine. [F, prob. from SALMAGUNDI]

salmiac (sal´miak) *n.* native sal ammoniac.

salmis SALMI.

salmon (sam´ən) *n.* (*pl. in general* **salmon,** *in particular* **salmons**) **1** a larger silvery, pink-fleshed fish of the family Salmonidae, esp. of the genus *Salmo*, fished both for food and sport. **2** any of various fish resembling the salmon such as the Australian salmon and an American sea trout of the genus *Cynoscion*. **3** salmon pink. *~a.* salmon-coloured. **salmonberry** *n.* (*pl.* **salmonberries**) **1** a raspberry bush, *Rubus spectabilis*, which has salmon-coloured berries. **2** the fruit of this. **salmon colour** *n.* the colour of salmon flesh, orangey-pink. **salmon-coloured** *a.* **salmonid** (sal´mənid, -mon´-) *a.* of or relating to the family Salmonidae. *~n.* a fish of this family. **salmon-ladder, salmon-leap, salmon-pass, salmon-stair, salmon-weir** *n.* a series of steps, zigzags, or other contrivances to enable salmon to get past a dam or waterfall. **salmonoid** (sal´mənoid) *n., a.* **salmon-parr** *n.* a parr. **salmon-peal** *n.* a salmon weighing less than 2 lb. (0.9 kg). **salmon pink** *n.* the colour of salmon flesh. **salmon-pink** *a.* **salmon trout** *n.* **1** an anadromous fish, *Salmo trutta*, resembling the salmon but smaller. **2** any of various similar fishes. **salmony** *a.* [ME and A-F *saumoun* (OF and F *saumon*), L *salmōnem*, nom. *-mo*]

salmonella (salmənel´ə) *n.* (*pl.* **salmonellae** (-lē)) **1** any bacterium of the genus *Salmonella*, many of which cause food poisoning. **2** food poisoning caused by infection with salmonellae. **salmonellosis** (-ō´sis) *n.* infection with bacteria of the genus *Salmonella*.

salon (sal´on) *n.* **1** a reception room, esp. in a great house in France. **2** the business premises of a hairdresser, beautician etc. **3** (*Hist.*) a periodical reunion of eminent people in the house of someone socially fashionable, esp. a lady. **4** (*N Am.*) a meeting of esp. intellectuals in the house of a celebrity or socialite. **5** (*pl.*) fashionable circles. **6** a hall for exhibiting paintings etc. **7** (**Salon**) an annual exhibition of paintings etc. held in Paris. **salon music** *n.* light music, usu. classical. [F, from It. *salone*]

saloon (səloon´) *n.* **1** a large room or hall, esp. one suitable for social receptions, public entertainments etc., or used for a specified purpose. **2** a large room for passengers on board ship. **3** (*also* **saloon car**) a closed motor car with no internal partitions. **4** a saloon in a train. **5** (*esp. N Am., coll.*) a drinking bar, a public house. **6** a saloon bar. **7** (*also* **saloon car, saloon carriage**) a large railway carriage without compartments, often arranged as a drawing room. **saloon bar** *n.* the more reserved bar in a public house. **saloon deck** *n.* a deck reserved for first-class or saloon passengers. **saloon-keeper** *n.* (*N Am.*) a publican or bartender. **saloon pistol, saloon rifle** *n.* firearms suitable for short-range practice in a shooting saloon. [from SALON]

saloop (səloop´) *n.* **1** an infusion of sassafras etc., formerly used with milk and sugar as a beverage instead of tea or coffee. **2** salep. [var. of SALEP]

Salop. *abbr.* Shropshire. [see SALOPIAN]

salopettes (saləpets´) *n.pl.* thick usu. quilted trousers with shoulder straps, used for skiing. [F]

Salopian (səlō´piən) *n.* a native or inhabitant of Shropshire. *~a.* of or relating to Shropshire. [*Salop*, Shropshire, from A-F *Sloppesberie*, corr. of OE *Scrobbesbyrig*, Shrewsbury]

salpicon (sal´pikon) *n.* a stuffing or thick sauce made with chopped meat and vegetables. [F and Sp., from *salpicar*, to pickle]

salpiglossis (salpiglos´is) *n.* any plant of the genus *Salpiglossis*, with trumpet-shaped flowers. [Gr. *salpinx -ngos*, trumpet, *glōssa*, tongue]

salping- (sal´ping) *comb. form* denoting the Fallopian tubes. [Gr. *salpinx salpingos*, trumpet]

salpinx (sal´pingks) *n.* (*pl.* **salpinges** (-pin´jēz)) **1** the Eustachian tube. **2** the Fallopian tube. **salpingectomy** (salpinjek´təmi) *n.* (*pl.* **salpingectomies**) the surgical removal of a Fallopian tube. **salpingian** (-pin´jiən) *a.* **salpingitis** (-jī´tis) *n.* inflammation of a Fallopian tube. **salpingitic** (-jit´-) *a.* [Gr. *salpinx -ngos*, trumpet]

salsa (sal´sə) *n.* **1** a Puerto Rican dance or the music for this. **2** a spicy sauce, esp. served with Mexican food. [Sp., sauce]

salse (sals) *n.* a mud volcano. [F, from It. *salsa*, orig. a volcano at Salsuolo, near Modena]

salsify (sal´sifi) *n.* (*pl.* **salsifies**) **1** a composite plant, *Tragopogon porrifolius*, the long whitish root of which is eaten. **2** this root. [F *salsifis*, etym. uncertain]

salsilla (salsil´ə) *n.* the tubers of *Bomarea edulis* and *B. salsilla*, eaten in the W Indies. [Sp., dim. of *salsa*, SAUCE]

SALT (sawlt) *abbr.* **1** Strategic Arms Limitation Talks. **2** Strategic Arms Limitation Treaty.

salt (sawlt) *n.* **1** chloride of sodium, used for seasoning and preserving food, obtained from sea water or brine by evaporation or in crystalline form in beds of various geological age. **2** a compound formed by the union of basic and acid radicals, an acid the hydrogen of which is wholly or partially replaced by a metal. **3** relish, piquancy, pungency, wit, repartee, brilliance in talk etc. **4** that which gives flavour. **5** a salt cellar. **6** (*pl.*) any of various mineral salts used as a medicine, esp. as a purgative. **7** (*pl.*) smelling salts. **8** a salt marsh or salting. **9** a sailor. **10** (*pl.*) an influx of sea water. *~a.* **1** impregnated or flavoured with or tasting of salt, saline. **2** cured with salt (*salt beef*). **3** living or growing in salt water. **4** (of wit etc.) pungent. **5** (of grief) bitter. **6** indecent, salacious. *~v.t.* **1** to sprinkle or cover with salt. **2** to season with salt. **3** to cure or preserve with salt. **4** to make salt. **5** in photography, to treat (paper etc.) with a solution of a salt. **6** to add liveliness to (a story etc.). **7** to misrepresent as valuable by the addition of material, esp. to add pieces of ore etc. to (a mine) so as to represent it as profitable to work. *~v.i.* to deposit salt from a saline substance. **above the salt** at the higher part of a table, above the salt cellar. **below the salt** among the less distinguished company. **in salt** sprinkled with salt or steeped in brine for curing. **not made of salt** not put off by wet weather. **not worth one's salt** not worth keeping, not useful. **to eat someone's salt** to accept someone's hospitality. **to put salt on someone's tail** to find or catch someone. **to salt an account** (*sl.*) to put down excessively high prices. **to salt away/ down** (*sl.*) to save or hoard (money etc.). **to salt the books** (*sl.*) to show receipts as larger than they really are. **with a grain of salt** with doubt or reserve. **with a pinch of salt** with doubt or reserve. **worth one's salt** worth keeping, useful. **salt-and-pepper** *a.* (esp. of hair) with light and dark colours mixed together. **salt bath** *n.* a bath of molten salts used in the hardening or tempering of steel. **saltbox** *n.* **1** a wooden box for holding salt. **2** (*sl.*) a prison cell. **saltbush** *n.* ORACHE. **salt cake** *n.* crude sulphate of soda, prepared for the use of glass- and soap-makers. **salt-cat** *n.* a mixture of salt, gravel, cumin seed and stale urine given to pigeons. **salt cellar** *n.* **1** a vessel for holding salt at table. **2** (*coll.*) either of the two deep hollows formed above the collarbones. **salt dome, salt plug** *n.* a domelike structure formed when rock salt is forced up through upper rock strata. **salted** *a.* **1** seasoned, preserved or treated with salt. **2** experienced or hardened. **salter** *n.* **1** a person who salts (fish etc.). **2** a person who makes or sells salt. **3** a worker at a salt works. **4** a dry-salter. **saltern** (-tən) *n.* **1** a salt manufactory. **2** a series of pools for evaporating sea water. **salt fish** *n.* (*W Ind.*) preserved cod. **salt flat** *n.* a salt-covered flat area formed by the total evaporation of a body of water. **salt-glaze** *n.* a glaze produced on pottery by putting salt into the kiln after firing. ~*v.t.* to apply salt-glaze to. **salt grass** *n.* (*N Am.*) grass growing in salt meadows or alkaline regions. **salt horse** *n.* **1** dry salt beef for use at sea. **2** a naval officer with general duties. **salting** *n.* **1** the application of salt for preservation etc. **2** (*pl.*) saltlands, a salt marsh. **saltish** *a.* **saltishly** *adv.* **saltishness** *n.* **salt-junk** *n.* (*sl.*) salt beef. **salt lake** *n.* an inland body of salt water. **saltless** *a.* **salt lick** *n.* **1** a place to which cattle go to lick ground impregnated with salt. **2** a block of this salt. **salt marsh** *n.* land liable to be overflowed by the sea, esp. used for pasturage or for collecting salt. **salt meadow** *n.* a meadow liable to be overflowed with salt water. **salt mine** *n.* a mine for rock salt. **saltness** *n.* **salt of hartshorn** *n.* impure carbonate of ammonia. **salt of lemon** *n.* acid oxalate of potassium. **salt of the earth** *n.* a person of the utmost worth. **salt pan** *n.* **1** a shallow depression in the land in which salt water evaporates to leave salt. **2** a vessel in which brine is evaporated at a salt works. **salt pit** *n.* a pit where salt is obtained. **salt plug** SALT DOME (under SALT). **salt-rheum** *n.* (*N Am.*) eczema. **salt shaker** *n.* (*N Am.*) a container of salt; a salt cellar. **salt spoon** *n.* a small spoon for use at the table. **salt water** *n.* **1** sea water. **2** (*sl.*) tears. **salt-water** *a.* living in, of or relating to salt water, esp. the sea. **salt well** *n.* a bored well yielding brine. **salt works** *n.* a factory for making salt. **saltwort** *n.* any of various plants of the genus *Salsola* or *Salicornia*, growing in salt marshes and on seashores. **salty** *a.* (*comp.* **saltier,** *superl.* **saltiest**) **1** of or containing salt. **2** tasting (strongly) of salt. **3** of the sea or life at sea. **4** witty. **5** earthy, coarse. **6** (*sl.*) tough, aggressive. **saltily** *adv.* **saltiness** *n.* [OE *sealt* (cp. Dut. *zout*, G *Salz*, Icel., Dan. and Swed. *salt*, also L *sal*, Gr. *hals*)]

saltant (sal´tənt) *a.* **1** (*Her.*) salient (used of figures of small animals). **2** †leaping. [L *saltans -ntem*, pres.p. of *saltāre*, freq. of *salīre*, to leap]

saltarello (saltərel´ō) *n.* (*pl.* **saltarellos, saltarelli** (-li)) **1** an Italian or Spanish dance characterized by sudden skips. **2** the music for such a dance. [It., from L *saltāre*, see SALTANT]

saltation (saltā´shən, sawl-, sol-) *n.* **1** a leaping or bounding. **2** an abrupt transition or variation in the form of an organism. **saltatorial** (-tətaw´ri-), **saltatorian, saltatorious, saltatory** (sal´tətəri) *a.* [L *saltātio*, from *saltāre*, see SALTANT]

saltigrade (sal´tigrād, sawl´-, sol´-) *a.* formed for leaping. ~*n.* a saltigrade arthropod, such as a spider with legs adapted for leaping on its prey. [L *saltus*, leap, from *saltāre*, see SALTANT, *-gradus*, walking]

saltire (sal´tīə, sawl´-) *n.* (*Her.*) an ordinary in the form of a St Andrew's cross or the letter X. **in saltire** arranged in this way. **saltirewise** *adv.* [ME *sawtire*, OF *sauteoir*, *-toir*, a stile, L *saltātōrium*, SALTATION]

saltpetre (sawltpē´tə), (*N Am.*) **saltpeter** *n.* potassium nitrate. **saltpetrous** *a.* [ME and OF *salpetre*, med. L *salpetra* (L *sal petrae*, salt of the rock), assim. to SALT]

saltus (sal´təs) *n.* (*pl.* **saltus**) a sudden starting aside, breach of continuity or jumping to a conclusion. [L, leap, cp. SALTIGRADE]

salubrious (səloo´briəs) *a.* **1** (of climate etc.) promoting health, wholesome. **2** spiritually wholesome, respectable. **3** (of surroundings etc.) agreeable. **salubriously** *adv.* **salubriousness, salubrity** *n.* [L *salūbris*, -OUS]

saluki (səloo´ki) *n.* (*pl.* **salukis**) a Persian greyhound. [Arab.]

salutary (sal´ūtəri) *a.* **1** promoting good effects, beneficial, corrective, profitable. **2** salubrious, wholesome. **salutarily** *adv.* **salutariness** *n.* [L *salūtāris*, from *salus -ūtis*, health]

Usage note The adjectives *salutary* and *salutatory* should not be confused: *salutary* means beneficial, and *salutatory* relating to salutation.

salute (səloot´, -lūt´) *v.t.* **1** to show respect to (a military superior) by a salute. **2** to greet with a gesture or words of welcome, respect or recognition. **3** to accost or welcome (as with a bow, kiss, oath, volley etc.). **4** to praise, acknowledge. **5** to honour by the discharge of ordnance etc. **6** to meet (the eye etc.). **7** †to hail (as king etc.). ~*v.i.* to perform a salute. ~*n.* **1** gesture of welcome, homage, recognition etc., a salutation. **2** a prescribed method of doing honour or paying a compliment or respect, as discharge of ordnance, dipping colours, presenting arms etc. **3** the attitude taken by a soldier, sailor etc. in giving a salute. **4** in fencing, a conventional series of movements performed before engaging. **to take the salute 1** (of an officer) to acknowledge a salute. **2** to receive ceremonial salutes. **salutation** (salūtā´shən) *n.* **1** the act of saluting. **2** that which is said or done in the act of greeting. **3** (*pl.*) words of greeting or communicating good wishes or courteous inquiries. **4** a salute. **salutational** *a.* **salutatorian** (salūtətaw´ri-) *n.* a student at a N American college who pronounces the salutatory. **salutatory** (səlū´tətəri) *a.* **1** of, relating to or of the nature of a salutation. **2** of or relating to a salutatory. ~*n.* (*pl.* **salutatories**) (*N Am.*) an oration delivered by a graduating student at the degree-giving ceremony in colleges. **salutatorily** *adv.* **saluter** *n.* [L *salūtāre*, from *salus -utis*, health]

Usage note See note on *salutatory* under SALUTARY.

salvable (sal´vəbəl) *a.* capable of being saved. **salvability** (-bil´-) *n.* **salvableness** *n.* **salvably** *adv.* [L *salvāre*, to SAVE, -ABLE]

Salvadorean (salvədaw´riən) *a.* of or relating to El Salvador. ~*n.* a native or inhabitant of El Salvador.

salvage (sal´vij) *n.* **1** the act of saving a ship, goods etc. from shipwreck, capture, fire etc. **2** compensation allowed for such saving. **3** property so saved. **4** the saving and recycling of waste or scrap material. **5** material saved for re-use. ~*v.t.* **1** to save or recover from wreck, capture, fire etc. **2** to save from ruin or destruction. **salvageable** *a.* **salvage money** *n.* **salvager** *n.* [OF, from *salver* (F *sauver*), to SAVE]

salvation (salvā´shən) *n.* **1** the act of saving from destruction. **2** deliverance, preservation from danger, evil etc. **3** deliverance of the soul, or of believers from sin and its consequences. **4** a person who or thing which delivers, preserves etc. **Salvation Army** *n.* a religious organization on a military pattern working among the poor. **salvationism** *n.* **1** belief in, or the doctrine of, the salvation of the soul. **2** the principles and practices of the Salvation Army. **salvationist** *n.* **1** a person who advocates salvationism. **2** a member of the Salvation Army. **salvatory** (sal´və-) *a.* saving or tending to save or preserve. ~*n.* (*pl.* **salvatories**) a repository, a safe. [ME and OF *sauvacion* (F *salvation*), L *salvātionem*, nom. *-tio*, from *salvāre*, to SAVE]

salve[1] (salv) *n.* **1** a healing ointment. **2** anything that soothes or palliates. *~v.t.* **1** to soothe, to ease, to palliate, to make good. **2** †to dress or anoint with a salve. [OE *sealf* (cp. Dut. *zalf*, G *Salbe*)]

salve[2] (sal´vā, -vi), **Salve Regina** (rigī´nə) *n.* **1** a Roman Catholic antiphon beginning with the words *Salve Regina*, 'Hail, holy Queen', addressed to the Virgin. **2** music for this. [L, hail, imper. of *salvēre*, to be well]

salve[3] (salv) *v.t.* **1** to save from destruction. **2** to salvage. **3** to preserve unhurt. [back formation from SALVAGE]

salver (sal´və) *n.* a tray, usu. of silver, brass, electroplate etc., on which refreshments, visiting cards etc. are presented. **salver-shaped** *a.* [F *salve*, a tray on which things were presented to a king, from Sp. *salva*, tasting of food before serving, from *salvar*, L *salvāre*, to SAVE]

Salve Regina SALVE[2].

salvia (sal´viə) *n.* any plant of the genus *Salvia*, labiate plants comprising the common sage and many cultivated species with brilliant flowers. [L, SAGE[1]]

Salvo (sal´vō) *n.* (*pl.* **Salvos**) (*Austral., sl.*) a member of the Salvation Army. [abbr.]

salvo[1] (sal´vō) *n.* (*pl.* **salvoes, salvos**) **1** a discharge of guns etc. as a salute. **2** a concentrated fire of artillery, release of missiles etc. **3** a volley of cheers etc. [It. *salva*, salutation, prob. as SALVE[2]]

salvo[2] (sal´vō) *n.* (*pl.* **salvos**) **1** a saving clause, a proviso. **2** a mental reservation, an evasion, an excuse. **3** an expedient to save one's reputation etc. [L, abl. of *salvus*, SAFE]

sal volatile SAL[1].

salvor (sal´və, -vaw) *n.* a person or ship effecting salvage.

SAM *abbr.* surface-to-air missile.

Sam. *abbr.* Samuel.

S Am. *abbr.* South America.

sam (sam), **sammy** (-i) *v.t.* (*3rd pers. sing. pres.* **sams, sammies,** *pres.p.* **samming, sammying,** *past, p.p.* **sammed, sammied**) to dampen (skins) in the process of manufacture, so as to temper them. [etym. uncertain]

samadhi (səmah´di) *n.* **1** in Buddhism and Hinduism, a state of concentration induced by meditation. **2** in Buddhism and Hinduism, a state into which a perfected holy man is believed to pass when he dies. [Sansk. *samādhi*, contemplation]

samara (səmah´rə) *n.* a one-seeded indehiscent dry fruit with winglike extensions, produced by the sycamore, ash etc. [L]

Samaritan (səma´ritən) *n.* **1** a kind, charitable person, in allusion to the 'good Samaritan' of the parable (Luke x.30–37); also *good Samaritan.* **2** a member of a voluntary organization formed to give help to people in despair. **3** a native or inhabitant of Samaria. **4** the language of Samaria. **5** a person adhering to the Samaritan religious system. *~a.* of or relating to Samaria or the Samaritans. **Samaritanism** *n.* **Samaritan Pentateuch** *n.* a form of the Hebrew Pentateuch having archaic characters, used by the Samaritans.

samarium (səmeə´riəm) *n.* a silvery-grey metallic chemical element, at. no. 62, chem. symbol Sm, one of the rare earth metals. **samarskite** (səmah´skīt) *n.* a mineral containing uranium. [Colonel von *Samarski*, 19th-cent. Russian mine inspector]

Sama-Veda (sah´məvādə) *n.* the third of the four Vedas, mainly made up of extracts from hymns in the Rig-Veda. [Sansk.]

samba (sam´bə) *n.* **1** a Brazilian dance. **2** a ballroom dance in imitation of this. **3** music for this. *~v.i.* (*pres.p.* **sambaing,** *past, p.p.* **sambaed, samba'd**) to dance the samba.

sambal (sam´bal) *n.* a side dish eaten with Malayan and Indonesian curries. [Malay]

sambar SAMBUR.

Sambo (sam´bō) *n.* (*pl.* **Sambos, Samboes**) **1** (*sl., offensive*) a black person. **2** (*Hist.*) (**sambo**) a person of three-quarters black African descent. [Sp. *zambo*]

Sam Browne (sam brown´), **Sam Browne belt** *n.* **1** a military officer's belt with a light strap over the right shoulder. **2** a belt of similar design made from a fluorescent material and worn by motor-cyclists, cyclists etc. [Sir *Samuel Browne*, 1824–1901, British military commander]

sambuke (sam´būk), **sambuca** (-bū´kə) *n.* an ancient musical stringed instrument of high-pitched tone. [L *sambuca*, Gr. *sambukē*, cogn. with Aram. *sabbekā*]

sambur (sam´bə), **sambar** *n.* a large deer or elk, *Cervus unicolor*, from S Asia. [Hind. *sābar, sāmbar*]

same (sām) *a.* **1** identical. **2** not other, not different. **3** identical or similar in kind, quality, degree etc. **4** exactly alike. **5** just mentioned, aforesaid. **6** unchanged, unchanging, uniform, monotonous. *~pron.* **1** the same person or thing. **2** the aforesaid. *~adv.* similarly; in the same way. **all the same 1** nevertheless. **2** notwithstanding what is said, done, altered etc. **by the same token** TOKEN. **in the same boat** BOAT. **in the same breath** BREATH. **in the same canoe** CANOE. **just the same** nevertheless, yet. **same here** (*coll.*) me too. **the same old story** STORY[1]. **the same to you!** likewise. **to be all the same to someone** used to express indifference. **to speak the same language** LANGUAGE. **very same** emphatically the same. **sameness** *n.* **samey** *a.* (*comp.* **samier,** *superl.* **samiest**) (*coll.*) monotonous, repetitive. **sameyness** *n.* [Icel. *same*, a., or OE *same*, adv. (cp. OHG and Goth. *sama*, also Gr. *homos*, L *similis*), cogn. with Sansk. *sawa*]

Usage note The adverbial or conjunctive use of *(the) same as* (as in *I use dictionaries, (the) same as you (do)*) is informal and sometimes disapproved of: *in the same way as* can often be used instead. See also note under AS[1].

---

samfu (sam´foo), **samfoo** *n.* an outfit worn esp. by Chinese women, consisting of a blouse or jacket and trousers. [Cantonese]

Samhain (sown, sow´in, saw´in) *n.* 1 Nov., celebrated as a festival marking the beginning of winter by the ancient Celts. [Ir.]

Samian (sā´miən) *a.* of or relating to Samos. *~n.* a native or inhabitant of Samos. **Samian earth** *n.* a kind of bole or marl from Samos. **Samian ware** *n.* red or black pottery made from this or similar earth. [L *Samius*, Gr. *Samios*, from *Samos*, isle in the Aegean]

samiel (sā´miəl) *n.* the simoom. [Turk. *samyel*, from *sam*, Arab. *samm*, cp. SIMOOM]

samisen (sam´isen) *n.* a Japanese three-stringed guitar-like instrument played with a plectrum. [Jap., from Chin. *sanhsien* (*san*, three, *hsien*, string)]

samite (sam´īt) *n.* (*Hist.*) a rich medieval silk fabric with a warp, each thread of which was six strands. [OF *samit*, med. L *samitum, examitum*, Gr. *hexamiton* (*hex*, six, *mitos*, a thread)]

samizdat (sam´izdat, -miz´-) *n.* **1** the clandestine publishing of banned literature in the former Communist countries of eastern Europe. **2** this literature. [Rus.]

samlet (sam´lit) *n.* a young salmon.

sammy SAM.

Samnite (sam´nīt) *n.* **1** a member of an ancient Italian people eventually subjugated by the Romans. **2** the language of these people. *~a.* of or relating to the Samnites or their language. [L *Samnītes*]

Samoan (səmō´ən) *n.* **1** a native or inhabitant of Samoa. **2** the language of Samoa. *~a.* of or relating to Samoa or its language.

samosa (səmō´sə) *n.* (*pl.* **samosas, samosa**) an Indian savoury of spiced meat or vegetables in a triangular pastry case. [Hind.]

samovar (sam´əvah) *n.* a Russian tea urn heated by burning charcoal in an inner tube. [Rus. *samovaru*, self-boiler, prob. from Tatar]

Samoyed (sam´əyed) *n.* (*pl.* **Samoyed, Samoyeds**) **1** a member of a Mongolian people inhabiting middle Siberia. **2** their language. **3** (*also* **samoyed**) a breed of white sledge-dog. **Samoyedic** (-yed´-) *a.* of or relating to this people. ~*n.* their language. [Rus. *Samoyedu*]

samp (samp) *n.* (*N Am.*) maize coarsely ground or made into porridge. [Algonquian *nasamp*]

sampan (sam´pan) *n.* a Chinese flat-bottomed river boat, frequently used as a houseboat. [Chin. (*san*, three, *pan*, board)]

samphire (sam´fīə) *n.* **1** a herb, *Crithmum maritimum*, growing on sea-cliffs, the aromatic leaves of which are pickled as a condiment. **2** a glasswort of the genus *Salicornia*. [formerly *sampire*, F *herbe de St Pierre*, St Peter's herb]

sample (sam´pəl, sahm´-) *n.* **1** a part taken, offered or used as illustrating the whole, a specimen, an example, a pattern, a model. **2** in electronics, a sound created by sampling. ~*v.t.* **1** to take samples of, to test, to try. **2** to have an experience of. **3** to present samples of. **sample bag** *n.* (*Austral.*) a bag of advertisers' samples. **sampler** *n.* **1** a person who or thing which takes samples. **2** a piece of embroidered work done as a specimen of skill. **3** an electronic device used for sampling. **4** (*N Am.*) a collection of representative items etc. **sample room** *n.* **1** a room where samples are shown. **2** (*N Am., sl.*) a grog-shop. **samplery** *n.* **sampling** *n.* **1** the act of sampling. **2** the taking of sounds, such as extracts from existing popular songs, and putting them together to form a new piece. **sampling error** *n.* error in a statistical analysis when the sample is unrepresentative. **sampling frame** *n.* an enumeration of a population for the purposes of sampling. **sampling statistic** *n.* any function of observed data, such as the sample mean. [orig. *essample*, var. of EXAMPLE]

samsara (səmsah´rə) *n.* **1** in Hinduism, the cycle of birth, death and rebirth. **2** in Buddhism, the transmigration or rebirth of a person. **samsaric** *a.* [Sansk. *samsāra*, a passing through]

samshu (sam´shoo), **samshoo** *n.* a Chinese alcoholic drink made from fermented rice. [pidgin, etym. uncertain]

samskara (samskah´rə) *n.* **1** in Hinduism, a purificatory ceremony or rite. **2** in Hinduism, a mental impression, instinct or memory. [Sansk. *samskāra*, a preparation]

samsoe (sam´zō) *n.* a firm-textured Danish cheese with a mild flavour. [the island of Samsø]

Samson (sam´sən) *n.* a man of extraordinary strength (Judges xiv.6 *passim*). **Samson post, Samson's post** *n.* (*Naut.*) **1** a pillar resting on the kelson and passing through the hold or between decks. **2** an upright in whalers for fastening the harpoon rope to. [L and Gr. *Sampsōn*, Heb. *Shimshōn*]

samurai (sam´urī) *n.* (*pl.* **samurai**) **1** a Japanese army officer. **2** (*Hist.*) a member of the military caste under the Japanese feudal regime, or a military retainer. [Jap.]

san (san) *n.* (*sl.*) a sanatorium in a school etc. [abbr.]

sanative (san´ətiv) *a.* healing, tending to cure, curative. [med. L *sānātīvus*, from *sānāre*, to heal, from *sānus*, SANE]

sanatorium (sanətaw´riəm), (*esp. N Am.*) **sanitarium** (-teə´-) *n.* (*pl.* **sanatoriums, sanatoria** (-riə), (*esp. N Am.*) **sanitariums, sanitaria**) **1** an institution for the treatment of chronic diseases, esp. pulmonary tuberculosis. **2** a place to which people resort for the sake of their health. **3** an institution for invalids, esp. convalescents. **4** a sickroom, esp. in a boarding school. **sanatory** (san´-) *a.*

sanbenito (sanbənē´tō) *n.* (*pl.* **sanbenitos**) (*Hist.*) a penitential garment painted with a red St Andrew's cross worn by heretics who recanted, or painted over with flames and figures of devils, worn at an auto-da-fé by persons condemned by the Inquisition. [Sp. (*San Benito*, St Benedict)]

sancho (sang´kō) *n.* (*pl.* **sanchos**) a W African musical instrument like a guitar. [Ashanti *osanku*]

sancta SANCTUM.

sanctify (sangk´tifī) *v.t.* (*3rd pers. sing. pres.* **sanctifies**, *pres.p.* **sanctifying**, *past, p.p.* **sanctified**) **1** to make holy, to consecrate. **2** to set apart or observe as holy. **3** to purify from sin. **4** to give a sacred character to, to sanction, to make inviolable. **5** to render productive of holiness. **sanctification** (-fikā´shən) *n.* **sanctifier** *n.* [ME *seintefie*, OF *saintifier* (F *sanctifier*), late L *sanctificāre* (*sanctus*, holy, *-ficāre*, *facere*, to make)]

sanctimonious (sangktimō´niəs) *a.* making a show of piety or saintliness. **sanctimoniously** *adv.* **sanctimoniousness** *n.* **sanctimony** (sangk´timəni) *n.* affectation of piety, sanctimoniousness. [L *sanctimōnia*, from *sanctus*, holy]

sanction (sangk´shən) *n.* **1** the act of ratifying, ratification, confirmation by superior authority. **2** a provision for enforcing obedience, a penalty or reward. **3** anything that gives binding force to a law, oath etc. **4** countenance, support, encouragement conferred by usage etc. **5** that which makes any rule of conduct binding. **6** (*usu. in pl.*) a coercive measure taken by one state against another to force compliance with international law or a change in policy etc. **7** (*Hist.*) a law or decree. ~*v.t.* **1** to give sanction to, to authorize, to ratify. **2** to countenance, to approve. **3** to enforce by penalty etc. **sanctionable** *a.* **sanctionless** *a.* [F, from L *sanctiōnem*, nom. *-tio*, from *sancīre*, to render sacred, see SAINT]

sanctity (sangk´titi) *n.* (*pl.* **sanctities**) **1** the state of being holy, holiness. **2** spiritual purity, saintliness. **3** sacredness, inviolability. **4** (*pl.*) sacred things, feelings etc. †**sanctitude** *n.* **1** holiness, saintliness. **2** sacredness. [OF *saincteté* (F *sainteté*), L *sanctitātem*, nom. *-tas*, from *sanctus*, SAINT]

sanctuary (sangk´chuəri) *n.* (*pl.* **sanctuaries**) **1** a holy place. **2** a church, temple or other building or enclosure devoted to sacred uses, esp. an inner shrine or most sacred part of a church etc., as the part of a church where the altar is placed. **3** a place where deer, birds etc. are left undisturbed. **4** a place of immunity, an asylum, a refuge. **5** immunity, protection. **6** (*Hist.*) a church or other consecrated place in which debtors and malefactors were free from arrest. **to take sanctuary** to hide in a place of refuge. [A-F *saintuarie*, OF *sainctuarie* (F *sanctuaire*), L *sanctuārium*, from *sanctus*, SAINT]

sanctum (sangk´təm) *n.* (*pl.* **sanctums, sancta** (-tə)) **1** a sacred or private place. **2** (*coll.*) a private room, den or retreat. **sanctum sanctorum** (sangktaw´rəm) *n.* (*pl.* **sancta sanctorum, sanctum sanctorums**) **1** the holy of holies in the Jewish temple. **2** (*coll.*) one's sanctum. [L, neut. of SANCTUS]

sanctus (sangk´təs), **Sanctus** *n.* **1** the liturgical phrase 'Holy, holy, holy', in Latin or English. **2** the music for this. **sanctus bell** *n.* a bell, usu. in a turret or bell-cote over the junction of nave and chancel, rung at the sanctus before the Canon of the Mass. [L, holy]

sand (sand) *n.* **1** comminuted fragments of rock, esp. of chert, flint and other quartz rocks, reduced almost to powder. **2** a particle of this. **3** (*pl.*) tracts of sand, stretches of beach or shoals or submarine banks of sand. **4** (*pl.*) particles of sand in an hourglass. **5** (*pl.*) the time one has to live. **6** (*N Am. coll.*) grit, endurance, pluck.

7 a yellowish-brown colour. ~*v.t.* 1 to smooth or rub with sandpaper or a similar abrasive. 2 to sprinkle or treat with sand. 3 to cover or overlay with or bury under sand. 4 to mix sand with, to adulterate. 5 to drive (a ship) on a sandbank. **sands are running out** the end is approaching. **to bury one's head in the sand** BURY. **sandbag** *n.* a bag or sack filled with sand, used in fortification for making defensive walls, as ballast, for stopping crevices, draughts etc., as a cushion for supporting an engraver's plate, as a weapon for stunning a person etc. ~*v.t.* (*pres.p.* **sandbagging,** *past, p.p.* **sandbagged**) 1 to fortify or stop up with sandbags. 2 to strike or fell with a sandbag. 3 (*N Am.*) to coerce by harsh means. ~*v.i.* to deliberately underperform in e.g. a race, to gain an unfair advantage. **sandbagger** *n.* **sandbank** *n.* a bank or shoal of sand, esp. in the sea, a river etc. **sandbar** *n.* a ridge of sand built up by currents in a sea or river. **sand-bath** *n.* a vessel containing hot sand used for heating, tempering etc. **sand-bed** *n.* a layer of sand. **sandblast** *n.* a jet of sand used for engraving and cutting glass, cleaning stone surfaces etc. ~*v.t.* to cut, clean etc. with a sandblast. **sandblaster** *n.* **sand blight, sandy blight** *n.* (*Austral.*) an eye inflammation caused by sand. **sandbox** *n.* 1 a box containing sand carried by a locomotive etc., for sprinkling the rails when slippery. 2 in golf, a box for sand used in teeing. 3 a large open box containing sand for children to play in, a sandpit. 4 (*Hist.*) a box with a perforated top formerly used for sprinkling paper with sand to dry up ink. **†sandboy** *n.* a boy carting or hawking sand. **happy as a sandboy** happily engrossed. **sandcastle** *n.* a model of a castle in sand. **sand cloud** *n.* driving sand in a simoom. **sand-crack** *n.* 1 a fissure in the hoof of a horse, liable to cause lameness. 2 a crack in the human foot, caused by walking on hot sand. 3 a crack or flaw in a brick due to defective mixing. **sand dab** *n.* any of various small flatfishes of the genus *Citharichthys*, often eaten as food. **sand dollar** *n.* any flat sea urchin of the order Clypeasteroida. **sand dune** *n.* a ridge of loose sand formed by the wind. **sanded** *a.* 1 sprinkled with sand. 2 filled, covered or dusted with sand. 3 sand-blind. **sand eel** *n.* any eel-like fish of the family Ammodytidae or Hypotychidae. **sander** *n.* a person who or thing which sands, esp. a power tool for smoothing etc. by means of an abrasive belt or disc. **sand flea** *n.* 1 a chigger. 2 a sand-hopper. **sand flood** *n.* a mass of sand borne along in a desert. **sandfly** *n.* (*pl.* **sandflies**) 1 any biting blackfly of the genus *Simulium*. 2 any tropical biting fly of the genus *Phlebotomus*. **sand-glass** *n.* an hourglass. **sand-groper** *n.* (*Austral.*) 1 a gold rush pioneer. 2 (*derog.*) a Western Australian. **sandgrouse** *n.* a seed-eating bird of the family Pteroclididae, found in dry regions of the Old World. **sand-heat** *n.* heat imparted by warmed sand in chemical operations. **sandhill** *n.* a sand dune. **sandhog** *n.* (*N Am.*) a person who works underwater or underground on construction projects etc. **sand-hopper** *n.* any of various small jumping crustaceans of the order Amphipoda. **sand-iron** *n.* a golf club used for lifting the ball from sand. **sandlike** *a.* **sand lizard** *n.* a small greyish-brown European lizard, *Lacerta agilis*. **sandlot** *n.* (*N Am.*) a sandy area where children can play. **sandman** *n.* (*pl.* **sandmen**) a being in fairy lore who makes children sleepy by casting sand in their eyes. **sand martin** *n.* a small swallow, *Riparia riparia*, which makes its nest in sandbanks etc. **sand painting** *n.* the making of designs using coloured sand, esp. as done by American Indians. **sandpaper** *n.* a paper or thin cloth coated with sand, used for smoothing wood etc. ~*v.t.* to rub or smooth with this. **sand-pipe** *n.* (*Geol.*) a deep cylindrical hollow, filled with sand and gravel, penetrating chalk. **sandpiper** *n.* any of various wading birds of the family Scolopacidae. **sandpit** *n.* a container of sand for children to play in. **sand-pump** *n.* a pump used for extracting wet sand from a drill-hole, caisson etc. **sand-shoe** *n.* a light shoe, usu. of canvas with a rubber sole, for walking on sand. **sand-skipper** *n.* a sand-hopper. **sandsoap** *n.* a gritty general-purpose soap. **sand spurrey** *n.* a pink-flowered plant, *Spergularia rubra*, which grows on sandy soil. **sandstock** *n.* a brick made with sand dusted on the surface. **sandstone** *n.* stone composed of an agglutination of grains of sand. **sandstorm** *n.* a storm of wind carrying along volumes of sand in a desert. **sand table** *n.* a surface used to demonstrate military tactics by moulding sand. **sand-trap** *n.* (*chiefly N Am.*) on a golf course, a bunker. **sand wasp** *n.* a solitary burrowing wasp of the subfamily Sphecinae. **sand wedge** *n.* a golf club used to hit the ball out of bunkers. **sandworm** *n.* the lugworm. **sandwort** *n.* any plant of the genus *Arenaria*, low herbs growing in sandy soil. **sandy** *a.* (*comp.* **sandier,** *superl.* **sandiest**) 1 consisting of or abounding in sand. 2 of the colour of sand. 3 (of hair) yellowish red. 4 having hair of this colour. 5 (*N Am., coll.*) plucky, brave, having plenty of grit or sand. 6 shifting, unstable. **sandiness** *n.* **sandy blight** SAND BLIGHT (under SAND). **sandyish** *a.* **sand yacht** *n.* a yachtlike vehicle with wheels and sails for use on sand. [OE, cp. Dut. *zand*, G *Sand*, Icel. *sandr*, Swed. and Dan. *sand*]

sandal[1] (san´dəl) *n.* 1 a kind of shoe consisting of a sole secured by straps passing over the foot and often round the ankle. 2 a strap for fastening a low shoe. ~*v.t.* (*pres.p.* **sandalling,** (*N Am.*) **sandaling,** *past, p.p.* **sandalled,** (*N Am.*) **sandaled**) 1 to put sandals on. 2 to fasten with a sandal. **sandalled,** (*N Am.*) **sandaled** *a.* 1 wearing sandals. 2 fitted or fastened with a sandal. [F *sandale*, L *sandalium*, Gr. *sandalion*]

sandal[2] (san´dəl) *n.* sandalwood. **sandal tree** *n.* any tree yielding sandalwood. **sandalwood** *n.* 1 the fragrant wood of various trees of the genus *Santalum*, esp. *S. album*, much used for cabinetwork; also called *white sandalwood*. 2 a tree that yields sandalwood. 3 a similar wood or a tree that yields it. 4 a perfume derived from sandalwood. **sandalwood oil** *n.* an aromatic oil made from the white sandalwood. [med. L *sandalum*, Gr. *sandalon*, Arab. *sandal*, prob. from Sansk. *chandana*]

sandarac (san´dərak), **sandarach** *n.* 1 a whitish-yellow gum-resin obtained from a NW African tree, *Tetraclinis articulata*. 2 this tree. 3 realgar. [L *sandaraca*, Gr. *sandarakē*, etym. uncertain]

sand-blind (sand´blīnd) *a.* half-blind, dim-sighted. [prob. corr. of *sam-blind* (OE *sam-*, cogn. with SEMI-, BLIND)]

Sandemanian (sandimā´niən) *n.* a follower of Robert Sandeman, 1718–81, principal exponent of the views of John Glass and leader of the movement founded by him, a Glassite.

sanderling (san´dəling) *n.* a small wading bird, *Calidris alba*. [etym. uncertain]

sanders (san´dəz, sahn´-), **sanders-wood, saunders** (sawn´-) *n.* the red sandalwood, *Pterocarpus santalinus*. [OF *sandre*, var. of *sandle*, SANDAL[2]]

sandhi (san´di) *n.* (*pl.* **sandhis**) the modification of the sound of a word or affix as a result of its position in an utterance. [Sansk. *samdhi*, placing together]

sandiver (san´divə) *n.* a saline scum rising to the surface of fused glass in the pot. [prob. corr. of OF *sain de verre* (*suin, suint*, exudation, from *suer*, to sweat, *de verre*, of glass)]

sandwich (san´wich, -wij) *n.* 1 two slices of bread, usu. spread with butter or a similar substance, with meat etc. between them. 2 anything resembling a sandwich in layered arrangement. ~*v.t.* to put, lay or insert between two things of a dissimilar kind.

sandwich-board *n.* either of two advertisement boards worn by a sandwich-man. **sandwich course** *n.* an educational course containing one or more periods of practical work. **sandwich-man** *n.* (*pl.* **sandwich-men**) a person carrying two advertisement boards hung from their shoulders, one in front and one behind. [the 4th Earl of *Sandwich*, 1718–92]

Sandwich tern (san´wich) *n.* a crested tern, *Sterna sandvicensis.* [*Sandwich*, Kent]

Sandy (san´di) *n.* (*pl.* **Sandies**) (*coll.*) a Scotsman. [Sc., fam. for *Alexander*]

sandy SAND.

sane (sān) *a.* **1** sound in mind, not deranged. **2** (of views etc.) sensible, reasonable. **sanely** *adv.* **saneness** *n.* [L *sānus*]

Sanforized® (san´fərīzd), **Sanforised** *a.* (of fabric) pre-shrunk by a patented process.

sang[1] SING.

sang[2] (sang) *n.* (*Sc.*) SONG.

sanga (sŭng´gə), **sangar** *n.* a breastwork or wall of loose stones built for defensive purposes in the Himalayas. [Pushtu *sangar*]

sangaree (sang·gərē´) *n.* wine and water sweetened, spiced and usu. iced. [Sp. SANGRIA]

sang-de-boeuf (sādəbœf´) *n.* a dark-red colour such as that of some old Chinese porcelain. ~*a.* of this colour. [F, blood of a bullock]

sang-froid (sāfrwah´) *n.* coolness, calmness, composure in danger etc. [F, cold blood]

sangraal (sang·grāl´, sang´-), **sangrail, sangreal** *n.* GRAIL.

sangria (sang·grē´ə) *n.* a Spanish drink of diluted (red) wine and fruit juices. [Sp., ult. from L *sanguis*, blood]

sanguify (sang´gwifī) *v.i.* (*3rd pers. sing. pres.* **sanguifies,** *pres.p.* **sanguifying,** *past, p.p.* **sanguified**) to produce blood. **sanguiferous** (-gwif´-) *a.* conveying blood. **sanguification** (-fikā´shən) *n.* the formation of blood. **sanguifier** *n.* **sanguifluous** (-gwif´luəs) *a.* running with blood. [L *sanguis*, blood]

sanguinary (sang´gwinəri) *a.* **1** accompanied by bloodshed or carnage. **2** delighting in bloodshed, bloodthirsty, murderous. **3** (of laws) inflicting death freely. **sanguinarily** *adv.* **sanguinariness** *n.* [L *sanguinārius*, from *sanguis -uinis*, blood]

sanguine (sang´gwin) *a.* **1** hopeful, cheerful, confident, optimistic, ardent, enthusiastic. **2** (of the complexion) ruddy, florid. **3** (*Hist.*) (of a temperament) supposed to be due to the predominance of blood over the other humours. **4** having the colour of blood. **5** full of blood, plethoric. **6** †composed of blood. **7** †sanguinary. ~*n.* **1** blood colour, deep red. **2** a crayon of this colour prepared from iron oxide. **3** a drawing with this. ~*v.t.* **1** to stain with blood. **2** to colour red. **sanguinely** *adv.* **sanguineness** *n.* **sanguineous** (-gwin´-) *a.* **1** of, relating to, forming or containing blood. **2** sanguinary. **3** of a blood colour. **4** full-blooded, plethoric. **sanguinity** (-gwin´-) *n.* **1** sanguineness. **2** consanguinity. **sanguinivorous** (-niv´-), **sanguivorous** (-gwiv´-) *a.* feeding on blood. **sanguinolent** (-gwin´ələnt) *a.* **1** of blood. **2** bleeding, suffering from haemorrhage. **sanguisorb** (-sawb) *n.* a plant of the rosaceous genus *Sanguisorba*, containing the burnet, formerly used as a styptic. [F *sanguin*, L *sanguineum*, nom. *-us*, from *sanguis -uinis*, blood]

Sanhedrin (san´idrin, -hē´-, -hed´-), **Sanhedrim** (-rim) *n.* (*Hist.*) the supreme court of justice and council of the Jewish nation, down to AD 425, consisting of 71 priests, elders and scribes. [late Heb., from Gr. *sunedrion* (SYN-, *hedra*, seat)]

sanicle (san´ikəl) *n.* any small woodland plant of the umbelliferous genus *Sanicula*, allied to the parsley. [OF, from med. L *sānicula*, from *sānus*, SANE]

sanies (sā´niēz) *n.* a thin fetid discharge, usu. stained with blood, from sores or wounds. **sanious** *a.* [L]

sanify (san´ifī) *v.t.* (*3rd pers. sing. pres.* **sanifies,** *pres.p.* **sanifying,** *past, p.p.* **sanified**) to make healthy or more sanitary. [L *sānus*, SANE]

sanious SANIES.

sanitary (san´itəri) *a.* **1** relating to or concerned with the preservation of health, of or relating to hygiene. **2** free from dirt, disease-causing organisms etc., hygienic. **sanitarian** (-teə´ri-) *n., a.* **sanitarily** *adv.* **sanitariness** *n.* **sanitarist** *n.* **sanitarium** SANATORIUM. **sanitary cordon** *n.* CORDON SANITAIRE. **sanitary engineer** *n.* a civil engineer dealing with disposal of waste, provision of clean water etc. **sanitary engineering** *n.* **sanitary napkin** *n.* (*esp. N Am.*) a sanitary towel. **sanitary towel** *n.* an absorbent pad used for menstruation. **sanitary wallpaper** *n.* varnished wallpaper that can be sponged. **sanitary ware** *n.* porcelain for lavatories, baths etc. **sanitate** *v.t.* to improve the sanitary condition of. ~*v.i.* to carry out sanitary measures. **sanitation** (-ā´shən) *n.* **1** sanitary conditions. **2** measures for the maintenance of health and the prevention of disease. **sanitationist** *n.* **sanitize, sanitise** *v.t.* **1** to make sanitary. **2** to remove offensive language etc. from, make respectable. **sanitization** (-zā´shən) *n.* **sanitizer** *n.* [cp. F *sanitaire*, from L *sānitas*, from *sānus*, SANE]

sanity (san´iti) *n.* **1** saneness, mental soundness. **2** reasonableness, moderation. [L *sānitas*, from *sānus*, SANE]

sanjak (san´jak) *n.* (*Hist.*) an administrative subdivision of a Turkish vilayet or province. [Turk.]

sank SINK.

sannyasi (sŭnyah´si), **sanyasi** *n.* (*pl.* **sannyasi, sanyasi**) a Hindu religious man who lives by begging. [Sansk. *saṃnyāsin*, casting aside]

sans (sanz, sã) *prep.* (*Shak.*) without. **sans-culotte** (sãkulot´, sanzkū-) *n.* **1** (*Hist.*) a republican in the French Revolution. **2** a radical extremist, a revolutionary. **3** a person without breeches. ~*a.* republican, revolutionary. **sans-culottic** *a.* **sans-culottism** *n.* **sans serif** (san ser´if), **sanserif** *n.* a printing type without serifs. ~*a.* without serifs. [F, from L *sine*, without]

Sansk. *abbr.* Sanskrit.

Sanskrit (sans´krit) *n.* the ancient language of the Hindu sacred writings. **Sanskritic** (-krit´-) *a.* **Sanskritist** *n.* [Sansk. *samskrta* (*sam*, together, cp. SAME, *krta*, made)]

Santa Claus (san´tə klawz, klawz´), **Santa** *n.* a mythical white-bearded old man bringing presents at Christmas and putting them in children's stockings, made popular in Britain in the late 19th cent. [N Am., from Dut. *Sint Klaas*, St Nicholas]

santal (san´təl) *n.* sandalwood. **santalin** (-lin) *n.* the colouring matter of red sandalwood. [F, from med. L *santalum*, Gr. *santalon*, as SANDAL[2]]

santir (santiə´) *n.* an Eastern form of dulcimer played with two sticks. [Arab., corr. of Gr. *psaltērion*, PSALTERY]

santolina (santəlē´nə) *n.* any fragrant shrubby composite plant of the genus *Santolina.* [prob. var. of SANTONICA]

santon (san´ton) *n.* a Muslim hermit, a dervish. [F or Sp., from *santo*, SAINT]

santonica (santon´ikə) *n.* **1** a shrubby plant, *Artemisia cina.* **2** the unexpanded flower heads of this, containing santonin. **santonin** (san´tənin) *n.* the bitter principle of santonica, used as an anthelmintic. **santoninic** (-nin´-) *a.* [L, fem. a., of or relating to the *Santones*, a people of Aquitania]

☒ **sanwich** common misspelling of SANDWICH.

sanyasi SANNYASI.

sap[1] (sap) *n.* **1** the watery juice or circulating fluid of living plants. **2** the sapwood of a tree. **3** vital fluid, strength, vigour. **4** (*sl.*) a gullible person, a saphead. **5** (*N Am., sl.*) any object used as a bludgeon. ~*v.t.* (*pres.p.* **sapping,** *past, p.p.* **sapped**) **1** to draw off sap. **2** to exhaust the strength or vitality of. **3** (*N Am., sl.*) to hit with a sap. **sap colour** *n.* an expressed vegetable colour inspissated by evaporation for use by painters. **sapful** *a.* **sap green** *n.* **1** a green pigment obtained from the juice of blackthorn berries. **2** the colour of this. **sap-green** *a.* of this colour. **saphead** *n.* (*sl.*) a softhead, a ninny. **sap-lath** *n.* a lath of sapwood. **sapless** *a.* **sapling** (-ling) *n.* **1** a young tree. **2** a youth. **3** a young greyhound. **sappy** *a.* (*comp.* **sappier,** *superl.* **sappiest**). **sappily** *adv.* **sappiness** *n.* **sap rot** *n.* dry rot. **sapsucker** *n.* a small woodpecker of the genus *Sphyrapicus*, which feeds on sap from trees. **sap tube** *n.* a plant vessel conducting sap. **sapwood** *n.* the soft new wood next to the bark, alburnum. [OE *sæp* (cp. Dut. *sap*, G *Saft*), prob. cogn. with L *sapa*, must, new wine]

sap[2] (sap) *v.t.* (*pres.p.* **sapping,** *past, p.p.* **sapped**) **1** to undermine. **2** to approach by mines, trenches etc. **3** to render unstable by wearing away the foundation. **4** to subvert or destroy insidiously. ~*v.i.* to make an attack or approach by digging trenches or undermining. ~*n.* **1** the act of sapping. **2** a deep ditch, trench or mine for approach to or attack on a fortification. **3** insidious undermining or subversion of faith etc. **sapper** *n.* **1** a person who digs trenches. **2** (*coll.*) an officer or private of the Royal Engineers. **3** (*N Am.*) a military engineer who lays or detects mines. [F *sapper*, from OF *sappe* (F *sape*) or It. *zappa*, late L *sappa*, spade]

sap[3] (sap) *v.i.* (*pres.p.* **sapping,** *past, p.p.* **sapped**) (*sl.*) to be studious, to grind. ~*n.* **1** a hard-working student, a plodder. **2** a tiring piece of work, a grind. [prob. from SAP[2]]

sapajou (sap´əjoo) *n.* a small S American prehensile-tailed monkey of the genus *Cebus*; a capuchin. [F, perh. from Tupi]

sapanwood (sap´ənwud), **sappanwood** *n.* a brownish-red dyewood obtained from trees of the genus *Caesalpinia*, esp. *C. sappan*, from S Asia and Malaysia. [Dut. *sapan*, Malay *sapang*, wood]

sapele (səpē´li) *n.* **1** any of several W African trees of the genus *Entandrophragma*. **2** the reddish-brown wood, resembling mahogany, obtained from these trees. [W Afr.]

saphena (səfē´nə) *n.* (*pl.* **saphenae** (-nē)) either of two prominent veins of the leg. **saphenal, saphenous** *a.* [med. L, from Arab. *çāfin*]

☒ **saphire** common misspelling of SAPPHIRE.

sapid (sap´id) *a.* **1** possessing flavour that can be relished, savoury. **2** not insipid, vapid or uninteresting. **sapidity** (-pid´-), **sapidness** *n.* [L *sapidus*, from *sapere*, to taste]

sapient (sā´piənt) *a.* wise, sagacious, discerning, sage (often ironical). **sapience** *n.* **sapiential** (-en´shəl) *a.* of or conveying wisdom. **sapiential books** *n.pl.* (*Bible*) Proverbs, Ecclesiastes, Ecclesiasticus, The Book of Wisdom, The Canticles. **sapiently** *adv.* [L *sapiens -entem*, pres.p. of *sapere*, to be wise, as SAPID]

sapindaceous (sapindā´shəs) *a.* of, relating to or belonging to the *Sapindaceae*, a family of trees, shrubs and lianas which includes the soapberry. [L *sāpō*, soap, *Indus*, Indian]

sapi-utan (sapioo´tan), **sapi-outan** *n.* the wild ox of Celebes. [Malay, wild ox]

sapling SAP[1].

sapodilla (sapədil´ə), **zapotilla** (zapətil´ə) *n.* **1** a large evergreen tree, *Manilkara zapota*, growing in the W Indies and Central America. **2** the edible fruit of this. **3** its durable wood. **sapodilla plum** *n.* the fruit of the sapodilla. [Sp. *zapotilla*, dim. of *zapote*, from Nahuatl *zapotl*]

saponaceous (sapənā´shəs) *a.* **1** soapy. **2** resembling, containing or having the qualities of soap. [L *sāpo -pōnis*, soap]

saponaria (sapəneə´riə) *n.* a plant of the genus *Saponaria*, the soapwort.

saponify (səpon´ifī) *v.t.* (*3rd pers. sing. pres.* **saponifies,** *pres.p.* **saponifying,** *past, p.p.* **saponified**) **1** to convert into soap by combination with an alkali. **2** to convert to an acid and an alcohol as a result of treatment with an alkali. ~*v.i.* (of an oil, fat etc.) to become converted into soap. **saponifiable** *a.* **saponification** (-fikā´shən) *n.*

saponin (sap´ənin) *n.* any of various glucosides obtained from the soapwort, horse chestnut etc. that produce a soapy foam and are used in detergents.

saponule (sap´ənūl) *n.* a soaplike compound formed by the action of an alkali on an essential oil.

sapor (sā´pə, -paw) *n.* **1** taste. **2** distinctive flavour. **saporific** (-rif´-) *a.* producing taste or savour. **saporosity** (-ros´-) *n.* **saporous** *a.* [L, from *sapere*, to taste]

sappanwood SAPANWOOD.

sapper SAP[2].

Sapphic (saf´ik) *a.* **1** of or relating to Sappho, a poetess (*c.* 600 BC) from the Greek island of Lesbos. **2** lesbian. **Sapphics, sapphics** (*n.pl.*) sapphic verses or stanzas, esp. stanzas of three pentameters followed by a dipody. **Sapphism, sapphism** *n.* lesbianism. **sapphist** *n.* [L *Sapphicus*, Gr. *Sapphikos*, from *Sapphō*]

sapphire (saf´īə) *n.* **1** any transparent blue variety of corundum. **2** an intense and lustrous blue, azure. **3** a S American hummingbird with a blue throat. ~*a.* sapphire-blue. **sapphire blue** *n.* a bright blue colour. **sapphire-blue** *a.* **sapphire wedding** *n.* a 45th wedding anniversary. **sapphirine** (-rīn) *a.* having the qualities, esp. the colour, of sapphire. ~*n.* a mineral of a pale blue colour, esp. a silicate of alumina and magnesia or a blue spinel. [F *saphir*, L *saphīrus*, Gr. *sappheiros*, prob. from Semitic (cp. Heb. *sappīr*)]

sappy SAP[1].

sapr- SAPRO-.

sapraemia (səprē´miə), (*esp. N Am.*) **sapremia** *n.* septic poisoning. **sapraemic** *a.* [Gr. *haima*, blood]

sapro- (sap´rō), **sapr-** *comb. form* indicating rotting or dead matter. [Gr. *sapros*, rotten]

saprogenic (saprəjen´ik) *a.* producing or produced by putrefaction.

saprolegnia (saprəleg´niə) *n.* any fungus of the genus *Saprolegnia*. **saprolegnious** *a.* [Gr. *legnon*, border]

sapropel (sap´rəpel) *n.* slimy sediment that accumulates at the bottom of lakes, oceans etc., largely organic in origin. **sapropelic** (-pel´-) *a.*

saprophagous (səprof´əgəs) *a.* feeding on decomposing matter. **saprophagan** (səprof´əgən) *n.* a lamellicorn beetle living on decomposed vegetable matter.

saprophile (sap´rəfīl) *n.* a bacterium feeding on decomposed matter. **saprophilic** (-fil´-), **saprophilous** (-prof´-) *a.*

saprophyte (sap´rəfīt) *n.* a plant, bacterium or fungus that grows on decaying organic matter. **saprophytic** (-fit´-) *a.* **saprophytically** *adv.* **saprophytism** *n.*

saprostomus (səpros´təməs) *n.* halitosis, foulness of breath. **saprostomous** *a.* [Gr. *stoma*, mouth]

saprozoic (saprəzō´ik) *a.* saprophagous.

sapsago (sap´səgō) *n.* (*pl.* **sapsagos**) a greenish hard cheese flavoured with melilot, made in Switzerland. [corr. of G *Schabzieger* (*schaben*, to grate, *Zieger*, cheese)]

sapucaia (sapukah´yə), **sapucaya** *n.* a S American tree, *Lecythis zabucajo*, bearing an edible nut. **sapucaia nut** *n.* [Tupi]

SAR *abbr.* search and rescue.

sar (sah), **sargo** (-gō) *n.* (*pl.* **sars, sargos**) any fish of the genus *Sargus*, comprising the sea breams. [F, var. of *sargo*, L *sargus*]

saraband (sar´əband), **sarabande** *n.* **1** a slow and stately Spanish dance. **2** a piece of music for this in strongly accented triple time. [F *sarabande*, Sp. *zarabanda*, prob. from Arab.]

Saracen (sar´əsən) *n.* (*Hist.*) **1** a nomad Arab of the Syrian-Arabian desert in the times of the later Greeks and Romans. **2** a Muslim or Arab at the time of the Crusades. *~a.* of or relating to the Saracens. †**Saracen corn** *n.* buckwheat. **Saracenic** (-sen´-) *a.* **Saracen's head** *n.* the head of a Saracen as a heraldic charge or pub-sign. [late L *Saracēnus*, late Gr. *Sarakēnos*, prob. from Arab.]

SARAH *abbr.* search and rescue and homing.

sarangi (sərang´gi, -rŭng´-) *n.* (*pl.* **sarangis**) an Indian stringed instrument similar to a violin. [Hind.]

sarape SERAPE.

Saratoga (sarətō´gə), **Saratoga trunk** *n.* a large travelling trunk. [*Saratoga* Springs, New York State]

sarc- SARCO-.

sarcasm (sah´kazm) *n.* **1** a bitter, taunting, ironical or wounding remark. **2** bitter or contemptuous irony or invective. **sarcast** *n.* a sarcastic speaker etc. **sarcastic** (-kas´-) *a.* **1** containing or characterized by sarcasm. **2** given to using sarcasm. **sarcastical** *a.* **sarcastically** *adv.* [late L *sarcasmus*, late Gr. *sarkazmos*, from *sarkazein*, to tear flesh, as SARCO-]

sarcenchyme (sahseng´kīm) *n.* the gelatinous tissue of some higher sponges. **sarcenchymatous** (-kim´ə-) *a.* [SARC-, after PARENCHYMA]

sarcenet (sah´snit), **sarsenet** *n.* a thin, fine soft-textured silk used chiefly for linings, ribbons etc. [A-F *sarzinett*, OF *sarcenet*, prob. dim. of *sarzin*, SARACEN]

sarcine (sah´sīn) *n.* a nitrogenous compound existing in the juice of flesh. [G *Sarkin* (*sarc-*, SARCO-, -INE)]

sarco- (sah´kō), **sarc-** *comb. form* flesh. [Gr. *sarx sarkos*, flesh]

sarcobasis (sah´kōbāsis) *n.* (*Bot.*) a fleshy gynobase.

sarcoblast (sah´kōblahst) *n.* a germinating particle of protoplasm. **sarcoblastic** (-blas´-) *a.*

sarcocarp (sah´kōkahp) *n.* the fleshy part of a drupaceous fruit.

sarcocele (sah´kōsēl) *n.* fleshy enlargement of the testicle.

sarcocol (sah´kəkol) *n.* a gum resin from Arabia and Iran. **sarcocolla** (-kol´ə) *n.* sarcocol. [Gr. *kolla*, glue]

sarcode (sah´kōd) *n.* animal protoplasm. **sarcodal, sarcodic** (-kod´-) *a.*

sarcoderm (sah´kōdœm) *n.* an intermediate fleshy layer in certain seeds.

sarcody (sah´kədi) *n.* (*Bot.*) conversion into fleshiness.

sarcoid (sah´koid) *a.* resembling flesh. *~n.* **1** a particle of sponge tissue. **2** a swelling, nodule.

sarcolemma (sahkōlem´ə) *n.* (*pl.* **sarcolemmas, sarcolemmata** (-tə)) the tubular membrane sheathing muscular tissue. **sarcolemmic** *a.*

sarcology (sahkol´əji) *n.* the branch of anatomy concerned with the soft parts of the body. **sarcological** (-loj´-) *a.* **sarcologist** *n.*

sarcoma (sahkō´mə) *n.* (*pl.* **sarcomas, sarcomata** (-tə)) a tumour of connective tissue. **sarcomatosis** (-tō´sis) *n.* the formation and spread of sarcomas. **sarcomatous** *a.* [Gr. *sarkōma*, from *sarkoun*, to become fleshy]

sarcophagous (sahkof´əgəs), **sarcophagic** (-faj´-) *a.* feeding on flesh. **sarcophagon** (-gon) *n.* an insect of the order Sarcophaga, a flesh-fly. **sarcophagy** (-ji) *n.* the practice of eating flesh.

sarcophagus (sahkof´əgəs) *n.* (*pl.* **sarcophagi** (-jī, -gī), **sarcophaguses**) **1** a stone coffin, esp. one of architectural or decorated design. **2** a kind of stone used by the ancient Greeks for coffins, as it was believed to consume the flesh of those buried in it in a few weeks. [L, from Gr. *sarkophagus* (SARCO-, Gr. *phagein*, to eat)]

sarcoplasm (sah´kōplazm) *n.* the substance between the columns of muscle fibre. **sarcoplasmic** (-plaz´-) *a.*

sarcoptes (sahkop´tēz) *n.* an itch mite of the genus *Sarcoptes*. **sarcoptic** *a.* [Gr. *koptein*, to cut]

sarcosis (sahkō´sis) *n.* (*pl.* **sarcoses** (-sēz)) a fleshy tumour, a sarcoma. [Gr. *sarkōsis*, from *sarkoun*, as SARCOMA]

sarcotome (sah´kətōm) *n.* an instrument for cutting through the tissues of the body.

sarcous (sah´kəs) *a.* composed of flesh or muscle tissue.

Sard (sahd) *a., n.* Sardinian. [L *Sardus*]

sard (sahd) *n.* a precious stone, a variety of cornelian. **sardachate** (-dəkāt) *n.* a variety of agate containing layers of cornelian. **sardine**[1] (-dīn) *n.* (*Bible*) the sardius. [F *sarde*, L *sarda*, SARDIUS]

sardar SIRDAR.

sardelle (sahdel´), **sardel** *n.* a small Mediterranean clupeoid fish like, and prepared as, the sardine. [It. *sardella*, dim. of *sarda*, SARDINE[2]]

sardine[1] SARD.

sardine[2] (sahdēn´) *n.* **1** a fish, *Clupea pilchardus*, caught off Brittany and Sardinia, and cured and preserved in oil. **2** any of various other small fish preserved in the same way. **like sardines** (packed) closely together. [F, from It. *sardina*, L *sardīna*, late Gr. *sardēnē*, Gr. *sarda*]

Sardinian (sahdin´iən) *a.* of or relating to the island or the former kingdom of Sardinia, or its language. *~n.* **1** a native or inhabitant of Sardinia. **2** the Romance language of Sardinia.

sardius (sah´diəs) *n.* a precious stone mentioned in Scripture, perhaps the sard or the sardonyx. [L, from Gr. *sardios*, from *Sardeis*, Sardis, an ancient city of W Asia Minor]

sardonic (sahdon´ik) *a.* **1** unnatural, forced, affected, insincere. **2** (of laughter etc.) sneering, malignant, bitterly ironical. **sardonian** (-dō´-) *n., a.* **sardonically** *adv.* **sardonicism** (-sizm) *n.* [F *sardonique*, L *Sardonicus*, *Sardonius*, Gr. *Sardonios*, Sardinian (as if in alln. to the effects of a Sardinian plant in contorting the face), for *Sardonios*, etym. uncertain]

sardonyx (sah´dəniks) *n.* a variety of onyx composed of white chalcedony alternating with layers of sard. [L, from Gr. *sardonux*]

saree SARI.

☒ **sargant** common misspelling of SERGEANT.

sargasso (sahgas´ō), **sargassum** (-gas´əm) *n.* (*pl.* **sargassos, sargassa**) any seaweed of the genus *Sargassum*, found floating esp. in the Sargasso Sea in the N Atlantic. [Port. *sargaço*]

sarge (sahj) *n.* (*sl.*) short for SERGEANT.

sargo SAR.

sari (sah´ri), **saree** *n.* (*pl.* **saris, sarees**) a Hindu woman's traditional dress, formed from a length of material draped around the body. [Hind.]

sarin (sah´rin) *n.* a compound of phosphorus used as a nerve gas. [G]

sark (sahk) *n.* (*Sc., North.*) a shirt or chemise. *~v.t.* **1** to clothe with a sark. **2** to cover (a roof) with sarking. **sarking** *n.* (*Sc., North.*) thin boards for lining, esp. a roof under slates. [OE *serc* or Icel. *serkr*, cp. Swed. *sārk*, Dan. *saerk*]

sarkinite (sah´kinīt) *n.* a mineral composed of red arsenate of manganese. [Gr. *sarkinos*, fleshy, see SARCINE, -ITE[1]]

sarky (sah´ki) *a.* (*comp.* **sarkier**, *superl.* **sarkiest**) **1** (*coll.*) sarcastic. **2** (*sl.*) bad-tempered. **sarkily** *adv.* **sarkiness** *n.* [abbr.]

Sarmatian (sahmā´shən) *a.* **1** of or relating to ancient Sarmatia, now Poland and part of Russia, or its people. **2** (*poet.*) Polish. *~n.* **1** a native or inhabitant of Sarmatia. **2** (*poet.*) a Pole.

sarmentose (sahmen´tōs), **sarmentous** (-təs) *a.* (*Bot.*) having or producing runners. **sarmentum** (-təm) *n.* (*pl.*

sarmenta (-tə)) a prostrate shoot rooting at the nodes, a runner. [L *sarmentōsus*, from *sarmentum*, twigs, brushwood]
sarnie (sah´ni) *n.* (*coll.*) a sandwich. [abbr.]
sarod (sar´od) *n.* an Indian instrument like a cello, that may be played with a bow or plucked. [Hind.]
sarong (sərong´) *n.* a loose, skirtlike garment traditionally worn by men and women in the Malay Archipelago. [Malay *sārung*, from Sansk. *sāranga*, variegated]
saros (seə´ros) *n.* a cycle of 6585⅓ days in which solar and lunar eclipses repeat themselves (a misunderstanding from the original cycle of 3600 years). [Gr. *saros*, from Babylonian *shāru*, 3600]
sarpanch (sœ´pŭnch) *n.* an elected head of an Indian village council. [Hind.]
sarracenia (sarəsē´niə) *n.* any plant of the genus *Sarracenia*, insectivorous plants with pitcher-shaped leaves. [Dr D. *Sarrazen* of Quebec, *c.* 1700]
sarrusophone (sərooz´əfōn) *n.* a brass musical instrument resembling an oboe with a metal tube. [M *Sarrus*, French bandmaster and inventor, *c.* 1860, -PHONE]
sarsaparilla (sahspəril´ə) *n.* **1** the dried roots of various species of smilax, used as a flavouring and formerly in medicine as an alterative and tonic. **2** a plant yielding this. **3** a carbonated drink flavoured with sassafras. [Sp. *zarzaparrilla* (*zarza*, bramble, *-parrilla*, perh. dim. of *parra*, vine)]
SARSAT *abbr.* search and rescue satellite-aided tracking.
sarsen (sah´sən) *n.* a sandstone boulder such as those scattered over the chalk downs of Wiltshire. **sarsen-boulder, sarsen-stone** *n.* [prob. var. of SARACEN]
sarsenet SARCENET.
sartage (sah´tij) *n.* the clearing of woodland for agricultural purposes. [OF, from *sarter*, to clear ground, from *sart*, med. L *sartum*, neut. p.p. of L *sartīre*, to hoe]
sartorial (sahtaw´riəl) *a.* **1** of or relating to a tailor or tailored clothing. **2** of or relating to the elegance etc. of clothes. **3** of or relating to the sartorius. [L *sartōrius*, from *sartor*, mender, tailor, from *sarcīre*, to patch]
sartorius (sahtaw´riəs) *n.* (*pl.* **sartorii** (-riī)) a muscle of the thigh that helps to flex the knee.
Sarum use (seə´rəm) *n.* the rites used at Salisbury cathedral before the Reformation. [L *Sarum*, Salisbury]
SAS *abbr.* Special Air Service.
SASE, s.a.s.e. *abbr.* (*N Am.*) self-addressed, stamped envelope.
sash[1] (sash) *n.* an ornamental band or scarf worn round the waist or over the shoulder, frequently as a badge or part of a uniform. **sashed**[1] *a.* [formerly *shash*, a strip worn as a turban, from Arab. *shāsh*, muslin]
sash[2] (sash) *n.* **1** a frame of wood or metal holding the glass of a window. **2** a sliding light in a greenhouse etc. *~v.t.* to furnish with sashes. **sash cord, sash line** *n.* a stout cord attached to a sash and the sash weights. **sashed**[2] *a.* **sash frame** *n.* the frame in which a sash slides up and down. **sashless** *a.* **sash pocket** *n.* the space in which the sash weights are hung. **sash tool** *n.* a glazier's or painter's brush. **sash weight** *n.* a weight used to balance a sash and hold it in an open position. **sash window** *n.* a window having a movable sash or sashes. [corr. of CHASSIS]
sashay (sashā´) *v.i.* (*chiefly N Am.*) **1** to walk or move in a nonchalant or sauntering manner. **2** to strut, swagger. [alteration of CHASSÉ]
sashed[1] SASH[1].
sashed[2] SASH[2].
sashimi (sashim´i) *n.* a Japanese dish of thin slices of raw fish. [Jap.]
sasin (sas´in) *n.* the common Indian antelope, *Antilope cervicapra*, also called *blackbuck*. [Nepalese]
sasine (sā´sin) *n.* (*Sc. Law*) **1** the act of giving legal possession of feudal property. **2** the instrument by which this is effected. [var. of SEISIN (under SEISE)]
Sask. *abbr.* Saskatchewan.
Sasquatch (sas´kwach) *n.* a hairy humanoid creature reputedly living in W Canada. [Am. Ind.]
sass (sas) *n.* (*N Am., coll.*) impudence, cheek, sauce. *~v.t.* to talk impudently to. **sassy** *a.* (*comp.* **sassier,** *superl.* **sassiest**) cheeky, saucy. **sassily** *adv.* **sassiness** *n.* [var. of SAUCE]
sassaby TSESSEBI.
sassafras (sas´əfras) *n.* **1** a N American tree, *Sassafras albidum*, of the laurel family. **2** the dried bark of its root used as an aromatic stimulant and flavouring. [Sp. *sasafras*, etym. uncertain, perh. from SAXIFRAGE]
Sassanian (səsā´niən) *a.* of or relating to the Sassanids. *~n.* a Sassanian king. **Sassanid** (sas´ənid) *n.* a descendant of Sasan, ancestor of the last pre-Islamic dynasty of Persia (AD 226–642). *~a.* Sassanian. [Pers. *Sāsān*]
Sassenach (sas´ənakh) *n.* (*Sc. and Ir., chiefly derog.*) a Saxon, an English person. *~a.* English. [Gael. and Ir. *Sassunach*, *Sasanach*, SAXON]
sassoline (sas´əlēn) *n.* a mineral composed of a native triclinic form of boric acid. [G *Sassolin* (*Sasso*, Tuscany, -INE)]
sassy SASS.
Sastra SHASTRA.
sastrugi (sastroo´gi), **zastrugi** (zas-) *n.pl.* wavelike ridges on snow-covered plains caused by winds. [Rus. *zastrugi*, small ridges]
SAT *abbr.* **1** (*N Am.*) scholarship aptitude test. **2** standard assessment task.
Sat. *abbr.* Saturday.
sat SIT.
satai SATAY.
Satan (sā´tən), **Satanas** (sat´ənas) *n.* the arch-fiend, the Devil. **satanic** (sətan´-), **satanical** *a.* **1** of, relating to, emanating from or having the qualities of Satan. **2** devilish, infernal. **satanically** *adv.* **Satanism** *n.* **1** a diabolical disposition, doctrine or conduct. **2** the deliberate pursuit of wickedness. **3** Satan-worship. **Satanist** *n.* **Satanize, Satanise** *v.t.* [L and Gr. *Satān*, *Satanās*, Heb. *Sātān*, enemy, adversary]
Satano- (sā´tənō) *comb. form* of or relating to Satan. **Satanology** (-ol´əji) *n.* (*pl.* **Satanologies**) the study of or a treatise on doctrines relating to Satan.
satara (sat´ərə, sətah´-) *n.* a heavy, horizontally-ribbed woollen or broadcloth. [town in India]
satay (sat´ā), **satai, saté** *n.* a Malaysian and Indonesian dish of cubed meat served with a spicy peanut sauce. [Malay]
SATB *abbr.* soprano, alto, tenor, bass.
satchel (sach´əl) *n.* a small rectangular bag, often suspended by a strap passing over one shoulder, esp. for schoolchildren to carry books etc. in. **satchelled,** (*N Am.*) **satcheled** *a.* [ME and OF *sachel*, L *saccellum*, nom. *-lus*, dim. of *saccus*, SACK[1]]
sate[1] (sāt) *v.t.* **1** to satisfy (an appetite or desire). **2** to satiate, to surfeit, to glut, to cloy. **sateless** *a.* (*poet.*) [OF *satier*, to SATIATE, or from OE *sadian*, to make SAD, assim. to this]
†**sate**[2] SIT.
saté SATAY.
sateen (sətēn´) *n.* a glossy woollen or cotton fabric made in imitation of satin. [from SATIN]
satellite (sat´əlīt) *n.* **1** a secondary planet revolving round a primary one. **2** a man-made device projected into space to orbit the earth, moon etc., used for communications, broadcasting, weather forecasting, surveillance etc. **3** something dependent on or subordinate to another. **4** an obsequious follower, dependant or henchman. *~a.* **1** transmitted by satellite. **2** on the periphery. **satellite dish** *n.* a dish-shaped

aerial for receiving broadcasting signals from a satellite. **satellite state** *n.* a country subservient to a greater power. **satellite town** *n.* a small town dependent upon a larger town in the vicinity. **satellitic** (-lit´ik) *a.* **satellitism** *n.* [F, from L *satellitem*, nom. *-telles*, guard, attendant]

sati SUTTEE.

satiate (sā´shiāt) *v.t.* 1 to satisfy (as a desire or appetite) fully. 2 to sate, to glut, to surfeit. ~†*a.* sated, glutted, cloyed. †**satiable** *a.* **satiation** (-ā´shən) *n.* **satiety** (sətī´əti) *n.* 1 the state of being sated or glutted. 2 excess of gratification producing disgust. **to satiety** to an extent beyond what is desired. [L *satiātus*, p.p. of *satiāre*, from *sat*, *satis*, see SATISFY]

satin (sat´in) *n.* a silken fabric with an overshot weft and a highly-finished glossy surface on one side only. ~*a.* made of or resembling this, esp. in smoothness. ~*v.t.* (*pres.p.* **satining**, *past, p.p.* **satined**) to give (paper etc.) a glossy surface like satin. **satinbird** *n.* an Australian bowerbird, *Ptilonorhyncus violoceus.* **satiné** (sətē´nā) *n.* a variety of satinwood from Guiana. **satinet** (-net´), **satinette** *n.* 1 a thin satin. 2 a glossy fabric made to imitate satin. **satin finish** *n.* 1 a lustrous polish given to silverware with a metallic brush. 2 any effect resembling satin produced on materials. **satinflower** *n.* 1 the greater stitchwort, *Stellaria holostea.* 2 any other plant whose flowers have a satiny sheen. **satin gypsum** *n.* a fibrous gypsum used by lapidaries. **satining machine** *n.* a machine for giving paper etc. a satiny surface. **satinize, satinise** *v.t.* to satin. **satinized** *a.* **satin paper** *n.* a fine, glossy writing paper. **satin spar** *n.* a finely fibrous variety of aragonite, calcite, or gypsum. **satin stitch** *n.* a stitch in parallel lines giving the appearance of satin. **satin-stone** *n.* SATIN GYPSUM (under SATIN). **satinwood** *n.* 1 a tree, *Chloroxylon swietenia*; also called *Ceylon satinwood* or *Sri Lanka satinwood.* 2 a tree, *Fagara flava*; also called *West Indian satinwood* or *Jamaican satinwood.* 3 the yellow ornamental wood of these. **satiny** *a.* [F, prob. through late L *sētīnus*, silken, from L *sēta*, silk, orig. bristle]

satire (sat´īə) *n.* 1 ridicule, sarcasm or the use of ridicule, irony and invective ostensibly for the chastisement of vice or folly. 2 a composition, orig. a medley in verse, now either in verse or prose, in which wickedness or folly or individual persons are held up to ridicule. 3 satirical writing as a genre. **satiric** (-tir´-), **satirical** *a.* **satirically** *adv.* **satiricalness** *n.* **satirist** (sat´irist) *n.* a person who writes or employs satire. **satirize** (-i-), **satirise** *v.t.* to ridicule by means of satire. ~*v.i.* to use or write satire. **satirization** (-ā´shən) *n.* [F, from L *satira*, *satura* (*lanx satura*, full dish, medley), rel. to *satur*, *satis*, see SATISFY]

Usage note See note under SATYR.

satisfy (sat´isfī) *v.t.* (*3rd pers. sing. pres.* **satisfies**, *pres.p.* **satisfying**, *past, p.p.* **satisfied**) 1 to supply or gratify to the full. 2 to content, to gratify, to please. 3 to pay (a debt etc.). 4 to fulfil, to comply with. 5 to be sufficient for, to meet the desires, expectations or requirements of. 6 (*Math., Logic*) to fulfil the conditions of. 7 to free from doubt. 8 to convince. 9 to meet (a doubt, objection etc.) adequately. ~*v.i.* 1 to give satisfaction. 2 to make payment, compensation or reparation, to atone. **to satisfy oneself** to be certain in one's own mind. **to satisfy the examiners** to reach the standard required in an examination. **satisfaction** (-fak´-) *n.* 1 the act of satisfying. 2 the state of being satisfied. 3 gratification, contentment. 4 payment of a debt, fulfilment of an obligation. 5 a source of satisfaction. 6 reparation, compensation, amends. 7 atonement, esp. the atonement for sin achieved by Christ's death. 8 the performance of penance. **to one's satisfaction** so that one is satisfied. **satisfactory** (-fak´-) *a.* 1 giving satisfaction, sufficient, adequate, meeting all needs, desires or expectations. 2 relieving the mind from doubt. 3 atoning, making amends. **satisfactorily** *adv.* **satisfactoriness** *n.* **satisfiable** *a.* **satisfiability** (-bil´-) *n.* **satisfiedly** *adv.* **satisfier** *n.* **satisfying** *a.* **satisfyingly** *adv.* [OF *satisfier*, L *satisfacere* (*satis*, enough, *facere*, to make, p.p. *factus*)]

satnav (sat´nav) *abbr.* satellite navigation.

satori (sətaw´ri) *n.* in Zen Buddhism, an intuitive enlightenment. [Jap., awakening]

satrap (sat´rəp) *n.* 1 a governor of a province under the ancient Persian empire, a viceroy. 2 a governor, a ruler of a dependency etc., esp. one who affects despotic ways. **satrapal** (-trā´-), **satrapial** *a.* **satrapess** (-is) *n.* a female satrap. **satrapic** (-trap´-), **satrapical** *a.* **satrapy** *n.* (*pl.* **satrapies**) the territory, office or period of office of a satrap. [L *satrapa*, *satrapes*, Gr. *satrapēs*, OPers. *khsatrapāvā* (*khsatra*, province, *pa-*, to protect)]

satsuma (satsoo´mə, sat´sumə, -sū-) *n.* 1 a seedless type of mandarin orange. 2 a tree that bears such fruit. **Satsuma ware** *n.* a cream-coloured variety of Japanese pottery. [former Japanese province]

saturate[1] (sach´ərāt) *v.t.* 1 to soak, impregnate, or imbue thoroughly. 2 to fill or charge (a body, substance, gas, fluid etc.) with another substance, fluid, electricity etc. to the point where no more can be held. 3 to cause (a chemical compound) to combine until no further addition is possible. 4 to overwhelm (a target) with bombs or projectiles. 5 to supply (a market) with more than is necessary. **saturable** *a.* **saturant** *a.* saturating. ~*n.* a substance neutralizing acidity or alkalinity. **saturated** *a.* 1 (of a solution) containing as much dissolved material as possible at a given temperature. 2 full of water, soaked. 3 (of an organic compound) containing only single bonds between carbon atoms and not reacting to add further groups to the molecule. 4 (of a colour) deep, free from white. **saturated fat** *n.* a fat containing mostly saturated fatty acids. **saturater** *n.* **saturation** (-ā´shən) *n.* 1 the state of being saturated. 2 the presence in the atmosphere of the maximum amount of water vapour at any particular temperature. 3 the point at which increasing magnetizing force fails to increase any further the flux-density of the magnet. 4 the purity of a colour, freedom from mixture with white. **saturation bombing** *n.* bombing that completely covers a target area. **saturation current** *n.* the maximum value of electric current that can be carried. **saturation point** *n.* the point at which no more can be taken in, held etc. [L *saturātus*, p.p. of *saturāre*, from *satur*, cogn. with *satis*, enough]

saturate[2] (sach´ərət) *a.* 1 (of a colour) intense, deep. 2 (*poet.*) saturated.

Saturday (sat´ədi, -dā) *n.* the seventh day of the week, following Friday. ~*adv.* (*coll.*) on Saturday. **Saturdays** *adv.* (*coll.*) on Saturdays, each Saturday. [OE *Sæter-dæg* (*Sæternes*, L *Saturni*, of SATURN, *dies*, DAY)]

Saturn (sat´ən) *n.* 1 the sixth of the major planets in distance from the sun. 2 †in alchemy, lead. **saturnalia** (-nā´liə) *n.* (*pl.* **saturnalia, saturnalias**) 1 (*Hist.*) (*usu.* **Saturnalia**) an ancient Roman annual festival held in December in honour of Saturn, regarded as a time of unrestrained licence and merriment. 2 (*sing. or pl.*) a season or occasion of unrestrained revelry. **saturnalian** *a.* **Saturnian** (-tœ´ni-) *a.* 1 of or relating to the planet Saturn. 2 of a saturnine temperament. 3 of or relating to the god Saturn or the golden age. 4 happy, virtuous, distinguished for purity. 5 denoting the accentual metre of early Latin poetry. ~*n.* 1 an inhabitant of Saturn. 2 (*pl.*) Saturnian verses. †**saturnic** (-tœ´-) *a.* affected with lead poisoning. **saturniid** (sətœ´niid) *n.* any large moth of the family Saturniidae. **saturnine** (-nīn) *a.* 1 dull, phlegmatic, gloomy, morose. 2 †of or relating to lead or lead poisoning. 3 born under the influence of the planet Saturn. **saturninely** *adv.* †**saturnism** *n.* lead poisoning. **saturnite** (-nīt) *n.* a mineral substance containing lead. [L *Saturnus*, the ancient Roman god of agriculture, usu. identified with Gr. *Kronos*, father of Zeus, prob. from *sa-* or *se-* (*serere*, to sow)]

satyagraha (sŭt´yəgrah·hə, -tyah´-) *n.* non-violent resistance to authority as practised orig. by Mahatma Gandhi. [Sansk. *satya*, faithful, *agraha*, obstinacy]

satyr (sat´ə) *n.* **1** any of a class of ancient sylvan Greek gods represented with the legs of a goat, budding horns, and goatlike ears, identified by the Romans with the fauns. **2** a lascivious man. **3** SATYRID (under SATYR). **4** the orang-utan. **satyral** *n.* (*Her.*) a monster with a human head and parts of various animals. **satyriasis** (-rī´əsis) *n.* unrestrained sexual appetite in men. **satyric** (sətir´-) *a.* †**satyrical** *a.* **satyric drama** *n.* a burlesque play with a chorus of satyrs, usu. following a trilogy. **satyrid** (sat´irid) *n.* any butterfly of the family Satyridae. [L *satyrus*, Gr. *saturos*]

Usage note The nouns *satyr* and *satire* should not be confused: a *satyr* is a mythological creature, and a *satire* a work ridiculing vice or folly. The corresponding adjectives *satyric* and *satiric* (pronounced the same) should also be distinguished.

sauce (saws) *n.* **1** a preparation, usu. liquid, taken with foods as an accompaniment or to enhance the taste. **2** anything that gives piquancy or makes palatable. **3** (*coll.*) sauciness, impertinence, impudence, cheek. **4** (*N Am.*) stewed fruit, esp. apples. *~v.t.* **1** (*coll.*) to be saucy or impudent towards. **2** †to treat with sauce, to season. **3** (*fig.*) †to flavour, to make piquant or pungent. **what is sauce for the goose is sauce for the gander** what is appropriate for one person is also appropriate for another. **sauce-boat** *n.* a low broad jug for holding sauce. **saucebox** *n.* (*coll.*) an impudent person, esp. a child. **sauceless** *a.* **saucepan** *n.* a metal pan or pot, usu. cylindrical with a long handle, for boiling or stewing, orig. a pan for cooking sauces. **saucepanful** *n.* (*pl.* **saucepanfuls**). **sauce tartare** *n.* TARTARE SAUCE (under TARTARE). **saucy** *a.* (*comp.* **saucier**, *superl.* **sauciest**) **1** pert, impudent, insolent to superiors, cheeky. **2** (*coll.*) smart, sprightly. **3** (*dial.*) fastidious, dainty. **4** (*coll.*) smutty, suggestive. **saucily** *adv.* **sauciness** *n.* [F, from pop. L *salsa*, fem. of *salsus*, salt, from SAL[1]]

saucer (saw´sə) *n.* **1** a shallow dish for placing a cup on and catching drips. **2** any small flattish vessel, dish or receptacle of similar use. **saucer-eyes** *n.pl.* large, round, staring eyes. **saucer-eyed** *a.* **saucerful** *n.* (*pl.* **saucerfuls**). **saucerless** *a.* [OF *saussiere*, from late L *salsārium*, L *salsa*, SAUCE]

saucisse (sōsēs´), **saucisson** (-sō´) *n.* **1** a long tube of gunpowder, etc., for firing a charge. **2** a long fascine. [F, SAUSAGE]

Saudi (sow´di, saw´-), **Saudi Arabian** *n.* (*pl.* **Saudis, Saudi Arabians**) **1** a native or inhabitant of Saudi Arabia. **2** a member of the dynasty founded by King Saud. *~a.* of or relating to Saudi Arabia or the dynasty founded by King Saud.

sauerkraut (sow´əkrowt) *n.* finely chopped cabbage compressed with salt until it ferments. [G]

sauger (saw´gə) *n.* (*N Am.*) the smaller N American pikeperch, *Stizostedion canadense*. [etym. uncertain]

sault (soo) *n.* (*N Am.*) a rapid in a river. [OF, from L *saltus*, from *salīre*, to leap]

sauna (saw´nə) *n.* **1** a Finnish-style steam bath. **2** a building or room used for saunas. **3** a period spent in a sauna. [Finnish]

saunders SANDERS.

saunter (sawn´tə) *v.i.* **1** to wander about idly and leisurely. **2** to walk leisurely (along). *~n.* **1** a leisurely ramble or stroll. **2** a sauntering gait. **saunterer** *n.* **saunteringly** *adv.* [perh. through A-F *sauntrer*, from med. L *exadventūrāre* (EX-, ADVENTURE)]

saur- SAURO-.

saurian (saw´riən) *a.* of, relating to or resembling the Sauria, an order of reptiles formerly including the crocodiles and lizards, but now the lizards alone. *~n.* a lizard or lizard-like creature, esp. one of the extinct forms such as the ichthyosaurus and plesiosaurus. **sauroid** (-roid) *n.*, *a.* [SAURO-, -IAN]

saurischian (sawris´kiən, -rish´iən) *a.* of or relating to the Saurischia, an order of dinosaurs. *~n.* a dinosaur of this order. [L *Saurischia*, from Gr. *sauros*, lizard, *ischion*, hip joint]

sauro- (saw´rō), **saur-** *comb. form* lizard. [Gr. *saura*, *sauros*, lizard]

saurodont (saw´rədont) *n.* any of the Saurodontidae, an extinct family of fishes of the Cretaceous age. *~a.* of or relating to this family.

saurognathous (sawrog´nəthəs) *a.* (of birds) having a palate similar to that of the lizards. **saurognathism** *n.* [Gr. *gnathos*, jaw]

saurophagous (sawrof´əgəs) *a.* feeding on lizards and other reptiles. [-PHAGOUS]

sauropod (saw´rəpod) *n.* any of the Sauropoda, an extinct order of gigantic herbivores. **sauropodous** (-rop´-) *a.*

saury (saw´ri) *n.* (*pl.* **sauries**) a sea fish, *Scomberesox saurus*, with elongated body ending in a beak. [L *saurus*, lizard]

S Aus. *abbr.* South Australia.

sausage (sos´ij) *n.* **1** an article of food consisting of pork or other meat minced, seasoned and stuffed into a length of animal's gut or a similar receptacle. **2** anything of similar cylindrical shape. **not a sausage** (*coll.*) nothing at all. **sausage balloon** *n.* an observation balloon shaped like an inflated sausage. **sausage-cutter, sausage-filler, sausage-grinder** *n.* appliances used in manufacturing sausages. **sausage dog** *n.* (*coll.*) a dachshund. **sausage machine** *n.* **1** a machine used in manufacturing sausages. **2** a relentlessly uniform process. **sausage meat** *n.* meat used for stuffing sausages, esp. cooked separately as stuffing etc. **sausage roll** *n.* sausage meat enclosed in pastry and baked. [F *saucisse*, late L *salsicia*, from *salsus*, SAUCE]

saussurite (saw´sūrīt) *n.* an impure white, grey or green silicate mineral formed by alteration from feldspar. **saussuritic** (-rit´-) *a.* [H. B. de *Saussure*, 1740–99, Swiss geologist, the discoverer]

sauté (sō´tā) *a.* lightly fried. *~v.t.* (*pres.p.* **sautéing**, *past*, *p.p.* **sautéd, sautéed**) to fry lightly. *~n.* a dish of sautéd food. [F, p.p. of *sauter*, to leap]

Sauternes (sōtœn´) *n.* a sweet white Bordeaux wine. [district on the Garonne, France]

sauve qui peut (sōv kē pœ´) *n.* a state of panic or chaos. [F, save (himself) who can]

savable SAVE.

savage (sav´ij) *a.* **1** fierce, brutal, cruel, violent, ferocious. **2** uncivilized, in a primitive condition. **3** uncultivated, untamed, wild. **4** (*coll.*) extremely angry, enraged. **5** (*Her.*) nude, unclad. *~n.* **1** a person of extreme brutality or ferocity, a brute, a barbarian. **2** †a human being in a primitive state, esp. a member of a nomadic tribe living by hunting and fishing. *~v.t.* **1** (esp. of an animal) to attack violently, to bite, tear or trample. **2** to attack or criticize. **savagedom, savagism** *n.* **savagely** *adv.* **savageness** *n.* **savagery** *n.* (*pl.* **savageries**). [OF *salvage*, L *silvāticus*, from *silva*, wood]

savannah (səvan´ə), **savanna** *n.* an extensive treeless plain covered with low vegetation, esp. in tropical America. **savannah flower** *n.* an evergreen shrub of various species of *Echites*. [Sp. *sabana*, prob. from Carib]

savant (sav´ənt) *n.* a person of learning, esp. an eminent scientist. **savante** (sav´ənt) *n.* a female savant. [F, orig. p.p. of *savoir*, to know]

savarin (sav´ərin) *n.* a ring-shaped cake containing nuts and fruit, often flavoured with rum. [Antheline Brillat-*Savarin*, d. 1826, French politician and gourmet]

savate (savaht´) *n.* a style of boxing in which the feet are used as well as the hands. [F, from It. dial. *ciabatta*, a slipper]

save (sāv) *v.t.* **1** to preserve, rescue or deliver as from danger, destruction or harm of any kind. **2** to deliver from sin, to preserve from damnation. **3** to keep undamaged or untouched. **4** to keep from being spent or lost. **5** to reserve and lay by, to husband, to refrain from spending or using. **6** to spare, to exempt (*with double object*). **7** to obviate, to prevent. **8** to prevent or obviate the need for. **9** to be in time for, to catch. **10** to preserve an opponent from scoring (a goal etc.). *~v.i.* **1** to be economical, to avoid waste or undue expenditure. **2** to set aside money for future use. *~prep.* **1** except, saving. **2** leaving out, not including. *~conj.* unless. *~n.* **1** the act of preventing an opponent from scoring a goal. **2** something saved, an economy. **3** in bridge, a sacrifice-bid. **save the mark** MARK[1]. **saving your reverence** REVERENCE (under REVERE). **to save a person's face** FACE. **to save appearances** to present an appearance of respectability, wealth, harmony etc. **to save face** FACE. **to save one's bacon** BACON. **to save one's breath** BREATH. **to save oneself the bother** to save oneself the trouble. **to save oneself the trouble** to avoid wasted effort. **to save one's life** LIFE. **to save one's neck** NECK. **to save one's skin** SKIN. **to save someone's life** LIFE. **to save the day** to save the situation. **to save the situation** to find a solution that avoids difficulty or disaster. **to save the tide** to get in and out of port etc. while the tide lasts. **savable, saveable** *a.* **save-all** *n.* **1** anything that prevents things from being wasted. **2** (*Hist.*) a contrivance to hold a candle-end in a candlestick. **3** a strip of canvas laced to a sail to catch a light wind. **save-as-you-earn** *n.* a government savings scheme in which regular contributions are deducted from earnings. **saver** *n.* **1** a person who or thing which saves (*usu. in comb.*, as *life-saver*). **2** a cheap fare. **3** (*sl.*) in racing, a hedging bet. **saving** *a.* **1** preserving from danger, loss, waste etc. **2** (*often in comb.*) economical, frugal. **3** reserving or expressing a reservation, stipulation etc. *~n.* **1** the act of economizing. **2** (*usu. pl.*) that which is saved, an economy. **3** (*pl.*) money saved, esp. regularly or over a period of time. **4** an exception, a reservation. *~prep.* **1** save, except. **2** with due respect to. **saving clause** *n.* (*Law*) a clause containing a stipulation of exemption etc. **saving grace** *n.* a virtue or quality in a person or thing that compensates for other less admirable characteristics. **savingly** *adv.* **savings account** *n.* a deposit account. **savings and loan** *n.* (*N Am.*) a cooperative association similar to a building society. **savings bank** *n.* a bank receiving small deposits and usu. devoting any profits to the payment of interest. **savings certificate** *n.* an interest-bearing document issued by the Government for savers. [F *sauver*, L *salvāre*, from *salvus*, SAFE]

saveloy (sav´əloi) *n.* a highly-seasoned dried sausage of salted pork (orig. of brains). [corr. of F *cervelas*, It. *cervelatta*, from *cervello*, L CEREBELLUM]

savin (sav´in), **savine** *n.* **1** an evergreen bush or low tree, *Juniperus sabina*, with bluish-green fruit, yielding an oil formerly used medicinally. **2** (*N Am.*) RED CEDAR (under RED[1]). [OE *safine*, OF *savine*, L *sabīna*, SABINE]

saviour (sāv´yə), (*N Am.*) **savior** *n.* a person who preserves, rescues, or redeems. **our/ the Saviour** Christ, as the redeemer of humankind. [OF *saveor*, *salveor*, L *salvātōrem*, nom. *-tor*, from *salvāre*, to SAVE]

savoir faire (savwah feə´) *n.* quickness to do the right thing, esp. in social situations, tact, presence of mind. [F, to know what to do]

savonette (sav´ənet) *n.* a toilet preparation of various kinds. [F (now *savonnette*), dim. of *savon*, L *sāpo*, soap]

savor SAVOUR.

savory (sā´vəri) *n.* (*pl.* **savories**) a plant of the aromatic genus *Satureja*, esp. *S. hortensis* and *S. montana*, used in cookery. [OF *savereie*, L *saturēia*]

savour (sā´və), (*N Am.*) **savor** *n.* **1** (characteristic) flavour, taste, relish. **2** a particular taste or smell. **3** characteristic quality. **4** suggestive quality, smack or admixture (of). **5** †smell, perfume. *~v.t.* **1** to relish, to enjoy the savour of. **2** to give a flavour to. **3** to perceive, to discern. *~v.i.* to have a particular smell or flavour, to smack (of). **savourless** *a.* **savoury** *a.* **1** having a pleasant savour. **2** palatable, appetizing. **3** free from offensive smells. **4** salty, spicy etc. (as opposed to sweet). **5** respectable, wholesome. *~n.* (*pl.* **savouries**) a savoury dish, esp. as served as an appetizer or digestive. **savourily** *adv.* **savouriness** *n.* [OF, from L *sapōrem*, nom. *sapor*, from *sapere*, to taste]

savoy (səvoi´) *n.* a hardy variety of cabbage with wrinkled leaves. [district in SE France]

Savoyard (səvoi´ahd) *n.* **1** a native or inhabitant of Savoy in SE France. **2** (*Hist.*) a person connected with or a habitué of the Savoy Theatre in the days of the Gilbert and Sullivan operas (1875–96). *~a.* of Savoy.

savvy (sav´i) *v.t.*, *v.i.* (*3rd pers. sing. pres.* **savvies**, *pres.p.* **savvying**, *past*, *p.p.* **savvied**) (*sl.*) to know, to understand. *~n.* understanding, knowingness, cleverness. *~a.* (*comp.* **savvier**, *superl.* **savviest**) (*esp. N Am.*) knowing, wise. [corr. of Sp. *sabe*, know, ult. from L *sapere*, to be wise]

saw[1] (saw) *n.* **1** a cutting-instrument, usu. of steel, with a toothed edge, worked by hand, or power-driven, as in circular or ribbon form. **2** a tool or implement used as a saw. **3** a serrated body part or organ. *~v.t.* (*past* **sawed**, *p.p.* **sawn** (sawn), **sawed**) **1** to cut with a saw. **2** to form or make with a saw. **3** to make motions as if sawing. **4** to make cuts in (the back of a book) to receive the threads in sewing. *~v.i.* **1** to use a saw. **2** to undergo cutting with a saw. **3** to make motions of one sawing. **sawbench** *n.* a circular saw with a bench. **sawbill** *n.* **1** a tropical or subtropical American bird, the motmot, with serrated mandibles. **2** a duck with a serrated beak, esp. the merganser. **sawbones** *n.* (*sl.*) a surgeon or doctor. **sawbuck** *n.* (*N Am.*) **1** a sawhorse. **2** (*sl.*) a $10 note. **saw-doctor** *n.* a machine for cutting teeth in a saw. **sawdust** *n.* small fragments of wood produced in sawing, used for packing etc. **saw-edged** *a.* serrated. **sawfish** *n.* (*pl. in general* **sawfish**, *in particular* **sawfishes**) a fish of the family Pristidae, with an elongated, sawlike snout. **sawfly** *n.* (*pl.* **sawflies**) any of various hymenopterous insects of the superfamily Tenthredinoidea, furnished with a sawlike ovipositor. **saw frame, saw-gate** *n.* a frame in which a saw blade is held taut. **saw-gin** *n.* a cotton gin with serrated edges. **sawgrass** *n.* (*esp. N Am.*) a sedge of the genus *Cladium*. **sawhorse** *n.* a rack on which wood is laid for sawing. **sawlike** *a.* **sawmill** *n.* a mill with machinery for sawing timber. **sawn-off,** (*N Am.*) **sawed-off** *a.* **1** (of a shotgun) having the end of the barrel cut off with or as with a saw. **2** (*coll.*) (of a person) short. **saw-pit** *n.* a pit over which timber is sawed, one person standing above and the other below the log. **saw-set, saw-wrest** *n.* a tool for slanting the teeth of a saw alternately outward. **sawtooth** *a.* **1** (*also* **sawtoothed**) shaped like the teeth of a saw. **2** (of a waveform) showing a slow linear rise and rapid linear fall. **saw-whet** *n.* a small N American owl of the genus *Aegolius*, with a harsh cry. **saw-wort** *n.* a plant of the daisy family, *Serratula tinctoria*, having serrated leaves yielding a yellow dye. **sawyer** (-yə) *n.* **1** a person employed in sawing timber into planks, or wood for fuel. 2 a wood-boring larva. 3 (*N Am.*) a tree fallen into a river and swept along, sawing up and down in the water. 4 (*New Zeal.*) a kind of grasshopper. [OE *saga* (cp. Dut. *zaag*, G *Säge*, Icel. *sög*), cogn. with L *secāre*, to cut]

saw[2] (saw) *n.* a saying, a proverb, a familiar maxim. [OE *sagu*, cogn. with SAY]

saw[3] SEE[1].

sawder (saw´də) *n.* (*coll.*) blarney, flattery. [corr. of SOLDER]

sawn SAW[1].

Sawney (saw´ni) *n.* (*coll.*) a Scotsman. [prob. SANDY]

sawney (saw´ni) *n.* (*coll.*) a simpleton. [prob. from ZANY]

sawyer SAW[1].

sax[1] (saks) *n.* (*coll.*) 1 a saxophone. 2 a saxophone-player. **saxist** *n.* [abbr.]

sax[2] (saks), **zax** (zaks) *n.* a slate-cutter's chopping and trimming tool with a point for making holes. [OE *seax*, knife, cp. Icel. and OHG *sax*]

saxatile (sak´sətīl, -til) *a.* of, relating to or living among rocks. [F, from L *saxātilis*, from *saxum*, rock]

saxboard (saks´bawd) *n.* the uppermost strake of an open boat. [prob. SAX[2], BOARD]

saxe (saks) *n.* 1 an albumenized photographic paper made in Saxony. 2 saxe blue. **saxe blue** *n.* a light greyish blue. **saxe-blue** *a.* [F *Saxe*, Saxony]

saxhorn (saks´hawn) *n.* a brass musical wind instrument with a long winding tube, a wide opening and several valves. [Adolphe *Sax*, 1814–94, inventor (*c.* 1845), HORN]

saxicavous (saksik´əvəs) *a.* 1 hollowing out stone. 2 belonging to the *Saxicava*, a genus of rock-boring molluscs. [L *saxi-*, *saxum*, rock, *cavāre*, to hollow]

saxicolous (saksik´ələs), **saxicoline** (-līn) *a.* inhabiting or growing among rocks, saxatile. [L *saxi-*, *saxum*, rock, *colere*, to inhabit]

saxifrage (sak´sifrāj) *n.* any plant of the genus *Saxifraga*, consisting largely of Alpine or rock plants with tufted, mossy or encrusted foliage and small flowers. **saxifragaceous** (-frəgā´shəs) *a.* [F, from L *saxifraga*, spleenwort (*saxi-*, *saxum*, rock, *frag-*, root of *frangere*, to break)]

Saxon (sak´sən) *n.* 1 (*Hist.*) a member of a Germanic people from N Germany who conquered England in the 5th and 6th cents. 2 an Anglo-Saxon. 3 the Old Saxon or the Anglo-Saxon language. 4 a native or inhabitant of modern Saxony. 5 the Germanic elements of English. ~*a.* 1 (*Hist.*) of or relating to the Saxons, their country or language. 2 Anglo-Saxon. 3 of or relating to Saxony or its inhabitants. **Saxon architecture** *n.* a style of architecture used in England before the Norman Conquest. **Saxon blue** *n.* 1 indigo dissolved in sulphuric acid, used by dyers. 2 saxe blue. **Saxondom** *n.* **Saxonism** *n.* **Saxonist** *n.* **Saxonize, Saxonise** *v.t.*, *v.i.* [F, from late L *Saxonēs*, pl., from OE *Seaxan*, from *seax*, see SAX[2], rel. to L *saxum*, rock]

saxony (sak´səni) *n.* a fine wool or woollen material produced in Saxony. [*Saxony*, in Germany]

saxophone (sak´səfōn) *n.* 1 a brass musical wind instrument with a single reed used as a powerful substitute for the clarinet. 2 a saxophone-player. **saxophonic** (-fon´-) *a.* **saxophonist** (-sof´ə-, -əfōn-) *n.* [A. *Sax*, see SAXHORN, -PHONE]

saxtuba (saks´tūbə) *n.* a bass saxhorn. [A. *Sax*, see SAXHORN, TUBA]

say (sā) *v.t.* (*3rd pers. sing. pres.* **says** (sez), **†saith** (seth), *pres.p.* **saying,** *past, p.p.* **said** (sed)) 1 to utter in or as words, to speak, to pronounce. 2 to recite, to rehearse, to repeat. 3 to tell, to affirm, to assert, to state. 4 to allege, to report. 5 to promise. 6 to suppose, to assume. 7 to give as an opinion or answer, to decide. 8 to convey (meaning or intention). ~*v.i.* to speak, to talk, to answer. ~*n.* 1 what one says or has to say, an affirmation, a statement. 2 (*coll.*) one's turn to speak. 3 authority, influence. ~*adv.* 1 approximately, about. 2 for example. ~*int.* (*N Am.*) used to express surprise, to attract attention etc. **how say you?** (*Law*) how do you find? **I'll say** (*coll.*) used to express agreement. **I say!** an exclamation of mild surprise, protest etc. or calling for attention. **it is said** it is generally reported or rumoured. **needless to say** NEEDLESS (under NEED). **not to say** indeed one might say, perhaps even. **said he/ I etc.** (*coll.*, *poet.*) he/I etc. said. **say cheese!** CHEESE[1]. **says I/ he etc.** (*coll.*) I/he etc. said. **says/ sez you!** (*sl.*) used to express incredulity. **say when** (*coll.*) tell me when to stop. **that is to say** 1 in other words. 2 or at least. **they say** it is said. **to say for oneself** to say by way of conversation etc. **to say much for** to show the high quality of. **to say no** to refuse or disagree. **to say nothing of** not to mention. **to say out** to express fully. **to say something** to make a short speech. **to say something for** to say much for. **to say the least** LEAST. **to say the word** 1 to say that you agree. 2 to give the order etc. **to say yes** to agree. **what do/ would you say to?** how about? **when all is said and done** in the long run. **you can say that again!** (*coll.*) used to express agreement. **you don't say so** (*coll.*) used to express amazement, disbelief etc. **you said it!** (*coll.*) used to express agreement. **said** *a.* before-mentioned. **saying** *n.* a maxim, an adage, a saw. **as the saying goes** used to introduce a proverb, cliché etc. **there is no saying** it is impossible to know. **to go without saying** to be extremely obvious. **say-so** *n.* (*pl.* **say-sos**) 1 a dictum. 2 an unfounded assertion. 3 right of decision, authority. [OE *secgan*, cp. Icel. *segja*, Dan. *sige*, G *sagen*]

SAYE *abbr.* save-as-you-earn.

sayyid (sī´id) *n.* 1 a Muslim title of respect. 2 a descendant of certain members of Muhammad's family. [Arab.]

Sb *chem. symbol* antimony. [L *stibium*]

sbirro (zbē´rō) *n.* (*pl.* **sbirri** (-rē)) 1 an Italian police officer. 2 a police spy. [It.]

SBN *abbr.* Standard Book Number.

S by E *abbr.* South by East.

S by W *abbr.* South by West.

SC *abbr.* 1 (*Austral., New Zeal.*) School Certificate. 2 Security Council. 3 Signal Corps. 4 South Carolina. 5 special constable. 6 Supreme Court.

Sc *chem. symbol* scandium.

Sc. *abbr.* Scottish.

sc *abbr.* 1 scene. 2 *scilicet* (namely). 3 scruple. 4 *sculpsit* (he/she sculptured it). 5 (*also* **s.c.**) small capitals.

s/c *abbr.* self-contained.

SCA *abbr.* sickle-cell anaemia.

scab (skab) *n.* 1 an incrustation formed over a sore etc., in healing. 2 (*coll.*) a worker who refuses to join in a strike or who takes the place of a striker, a blackleg. 3 a highly contagious skin disease resembling mange, attacking horses, cattle and esp. sheep. 4 any one of various fungoid plant diseases. 5 a despicable scoundrel. ~*v.i.* (*pres.p.* **scabbing,** *past, p.p.* **scabbed**) 1 to form a scab. 2 to work as a scab or blackleg. **scabbed** *a.* **scabby** *a.* (*comp.* **scabbier,** *superl.* **scabbiest**). **scabbily** *adv.* **scabbiness** *n.* **scablike** *a.* **scab mite** *n.* the itch mite. [Dan. and Swed. *skabb* (cp. OE *sceab*, *scæb*)]

scabbard (skab´əd) *n.* 1 the sheath of a sword or similar weapon. 2 (*N Am.*) the sheath of a revolver etc. ~*v.t.* to put into a scabbard, to sheathe. **scabbard-fish** *n.* (*pl.* **scabbard-fish**) 1 a small silver sea fish, *Lepidopus caudatus*, with a bladelike body. 2 any of various related fishes. [ME *scauberc*, A-F *escaubers*, pl., prob. from Gmc.]

scabble SCAPPLE.

scabby SCAB.

scaberulous SCABROUS.

scabies (skāˈbiz, -biēz) *n.* a contagious skin disease, caused by the itch mite. [L, from *scabere*, to scratch]

scabious (skāˈbiəs) *a.* **1** consisting of or covered with scabs. **2** affected with itch. ~*n.* a plant of the herbaceous genus *Scabiosa*, *Knautia* etc., having involucrate heads of blue, pink and white flowers. [L *scabiōsus*, from *scabere*, to scratch]

scabrous (skāˈbrəs, skabˊ-) *a.* **1** rough, rugged or uneven. **2** scaly, scurfy. **3** difficult, thorny, awkward to handle. **4** approaching the indecent, indelicate. **scaberulous** (skəberˊūləs) *a.* (*Bot.*) somewhat scabrous. **scabridity** (skəbridˊ-), **scabrousness** *n.* **scabrously** *adv.* [L *scabrōsus*, from *scaber*, rough]

Usage note *Scabrous* should not be used as though it meant scurrilous or scathing.

scad (skad) *n.* (*pl. in general* **scad**, *in particular* **scads**) any fish of the family Carangidae, usu. having large spiky scales, esp. the horse mackerel *Trachurus trachurus*. [etym. unknown]

scads (skadz) *n.pl.* (*N Am., coll.*) large amounts. [etym. unknown]

scaffold (skafˊəld, -ōld) *n.* **1** a temporary structure of poles and ties supporting a platform for the use of workers building or repairing a house or other building. **2** (*Hist.*) a temporary raised platform for the execution of criminals. **3** a platform, or stage for shows or spectators. **4** the bony framework of a structure, esp. one to be covered by developed parts. **5** (*fig.*) capital punishment. ~*v.t.* **1** to furnish with a scaffold. **2** to uphold, to support. **scaffolder** *n.* **scaffolding** *n.* **1** a scaffold or system of scaffolds for builders, shows, pageants etc. **2** a framework. **3** materials for scaffolds. [ONF *escafaut*, OF *escadafault* (F *échafaud*) (perh. EX-, It. *catafalco*, CATAFALQUE)]

scag SKAG.

scaglia (skalˊyə) *n.* a red, white or grey Italian limestone corresponding to chalk. **scagliola** (-yōˈlə) *n.* a hard, polished plaster, coloured in imitation of marble. [It., SCALE[2]]

scalable SCALE[3].

scalar (skāˈlə) *a.* **1** scalariform. **2** of the nature of a scalar. ~*n.* **1** a pure number, esp. the term in a quaternion that is not a vector. **2** a quantity having magnitude but no direction (e.g. time). **scalariform** (skəlarˊifawm) *a.* (of the structure of cells, vessels, veins etc.) ladder-shaped. [L *scālāris*, from *scāla*, SCALE[3]]

scalawag SCALLYWAG.

scald[1] (skawld) *v.t.* **1** to burn with or as with a hot liquid or vapour. **2** to clean (out) with boiling water. **3** to cook briefly in hot water or steam. **4** to raise (milk) nearly to boiling point. **5** to treat (poultry) with boiling water to remove feathers etc. ~*n.* **1** an injury to the skin from hot liquid or vapour. **2** a fruit disease characterized by discoloration, caused by exposure to sunlight, gases etc. **like a scalded cat** moving very fast. **scalder** *n.* **scalding** *n.* **scalding hot** *a.* hot enough to scald. [ONF *escalder*, OF *eschalder*, L *excaldāre* (EX-, *calidus*, hot)]

scald[2] SKALD.

scaldino (skaldēˊnō) *n.* (*pl.* **scaldini** (-nē)) a small earthenware brazier used for warming the hands etc. [It., from *scaldare*, to warm, from L, as SCALD[1]]

scale[1] (skāl) *n.* **1** each of the thin horny plates forming a protective covering on the skin of fishes, reptiles etc. **2** a modified leaf, bract, hair, feather, disc, husk or other structure resembling this. **3** a thin flake of dry skin. **4** a scab. **5** a carious coating. **6** an incrustation. **7** a coating deposited on the insides of pipes, kettles etc. by hard water. **8** a small plate or flake of metal etc. **9** plaque formed on teeth. ~*v.t.* **1** to strip the scales off. **2** to remove in scales or layers. **3** to deposit scale on. **4** to remove (plaque) by scraping. ~*v.i.* **1** to form scales. **2** to come off in scales. **3** to become coated with scale. **4** (*Sc.*) to disperse, to scatter. **5** (*Austral.*) to ride on a tram or bus without paying the fare. **to remove the scales from someone's eyes** to reveal the truth to someone who has been deceived. **scale armour** *n.* (*Hist.*) armour made of small plates overlapping each other like the scales of a fish. **scale-board** *n.* a thin board for the back of a picture etc. **scale-bug** *n.* a scale insect. **scaled** *a.* having scales (*usu. in comb.*, as *thick-scaled*). **scale-fern** *n.* any of various spleenworts, esp. *Asplenium ceterach*. **scale insect** *n.* an insect, esp. of the family Coccidae, whose female secretes a protective waxy shell and lives attached to a host plant. **scale-leaf** *n.* a modified leaf that resembles a scale. **scaleless** *a.* **scale-moss** *n.* a type of liverwort with scalelike leaves. **scaler**[1] *n.* **scale-winged** *a.* having the wings covered with scales, lepidopterous. **scale work** *n.* an arrangement of overlapping scales, imbricated work. **scaly** *a.* (*comp.* **scalier**, *superl.* **scaliest**). **scaliness** *n.* **scaly anteater** *n.* the pangolin. [OF *escale*, OHG *scala* (OE *scealu*, cogn. with SCALE[2], G *Schale*)]

scale[2] (skāl) *n.* **1** the dish of a balance. **2** (*usu. pl.*) a simple balance; also called *pair of scales*. **3** (*usu. pl.*) a machine for weighing. **4** (**Scales**) Libra. ~*v.t.* to amount to in weight. **to throw into the scale** to add as a factor in a contest, debate etc. **to tip the scales 1** to cause one pan of a scales to become lower than the other because of greater weight, to weigh in (at). **2** to make the significant difference. **to turn the scales** to tip the scales. [OF *escale*, cup, Icel. *skāl*, bowl (cp. Dut. *schaal*), cogn. with SCALE[1]]

scale[3] (skāl) *n.* **1** anything graduated or marked with lines or degrees at regular intervals, such as a scheme for classification, gradation etc. **2** a basis for a numerical system in which the value of a figure depends on its place in the order. **3** a system of correspondence between different magnitudes, relative dimensions etc. **4** a set of marks or a rule or other instrument marked with these showing exact distances, proportions, values etc., used for measuring, calculating etc. **5** (*Mus.*) all the tones of a key arranged in ascending or descending order according to pitch. ~*v.t.* **1** to climb by or as by a ladder. **2** to clamber up. **3** to draw or otherwise represent to scale or proper proportions. **4** to alter the scale of. **5** to arrange, estimate or fix according to a scale. **6** to adjust according to a standard. ~*v.i.* to have a common scale, to be commensurable. **in scale** in proportion to the surroundings etc. **to play scales** to play the notes of a scale as a musical exercise. **to scale** in proportion to actual dimensions. **to scale down** to make smaller proportionately. **to scale up** to make larger proportionately. **to sing scales** to sing a scale as an exercise for the voice. **scalable** *a.* **scalability** (-bilˊ-) *n.* **scale of notation** *n.* the ratio between units in a numerical system. **scaler**[2] *n.* **scaling-ladder** *n.* (*Hist.*) a ladder used in storming fortified places. [L *scāla*, ladder, cogn. with *scandere*, to climb]

scalene (skāˈlēn) *a.* **1** (of a triangle) having no two sides equal. **2** (of a cone or cylinder) having the axis inclined to the base. **3** of or relating to the scalenus muscles. ~*n.* **1** a scalene triangle. **2** (*also* **scalene muscle**) a scalenus muscle. **scalene cone** *n.* a cone with the axis not perpendicular to the base. **scalene cylinder** *n.* a cylinder with the axis not perpendicular to the base. **scalenohedron** (skəlēnōhēˊdrən) *n.* a hemihedral form of the hexagonal or the tetragonal crystallographic system with eight similar and equal scalene triangles as faces. **scalenohedral** *a.* **scalenum** (skəlēˊnəm) *n.* a scalene triangle. **scalenus** (skəlēˊnəs) *n.* (*pl.* **scaleni** (-nī)) any one of a series of irregularly triangular muscles at the neck. [late L *scalēnus*, Gr. *skalēnos*, prob. rel. to *skolios*, crooked]

scaler[1] SCALE[1].

scaler[2] SCALE[3].
scaliness SCALE[1].
scallawag SCALLYWAG.
scallion (skal´yən) *n.* a variety of onion or shallot. [ONF *escalogne*, SHALLOT]
scallop (skol´əp, skal´-), **scollop** (skol´-) *n.* **1** any of various bivalve molluscs of the genus *Pecten* or a related genus, with ridges and flutings radiating from the middle of the hinge and an undulating margin. **2** the large adductor muscle of a scallop eaten as food. **3** (*Hist.*) a single shell of a scallop worn as a pilgrim's badge. **4** (*also* **scallop shell**) such a shell or a small shallow dish or pan used for cooking and serving oysters etc. in. **5** (*pl.*) an ornamental undulating edging cut like that of a scallop shell. **6** ESCALOPE. *~v.t.* (*pres.p.* **scalloping,** *past, p.p.* **scalloped**) **1** to cut or indent the edge of, like a scallop shell. **2** to cook in a scallop. **scalloper** *n.* **scalloping** *n.* **scalloping tool** *n.* [OF *escalope*, from Gmc. (cp. MDut. *schelpe*), cogn. with SHELL]
scallywag (skal´iwag), **scalawag** (-əwag), **scallawag** *n.* **1** a scamp, a rascal. **2** a poor, ill-conditioned or undersized animal (used orig. of Shetland ponies). [poss. corr. of *Scalloway*, Shetland]
scalp (skalp) *n.* **1** the top of the head. **2** (*Hist.*) the skin of this with the hair belonging to it, torn off by N American Indians as a trophy of victory. **3** a trophy or token signifying conquest. **4** (*Sc., poet.*) a bare hilltop or rock. **5** a whale's head without the lower jaw. *~v.t.* **1** (*Hist.*) to tear or take the scalp from. **2** to criticize or abuse savagely. **3** (*N Am.*) to defeat or humiliate. **4** (*esp. N Am., coll.*) to buy (cheaply) and resell so as to make a large profit. **5** (*N Am.*) to buy and sell so as to take small quick profits on (stocks etc.). **6** to cut the top part, layer etc. off (anything). **7** to flay, to lay bare. *~v.i.* (*N Am.*) to take small profits to minimize risk. **scalper** *n.* **1** a person who or thing which scalps. **2** (*esp. N Am.*) a ticket tout. **3** a wood engraver's tool. **scalping** *n., a.* **scalping iron** *n.* a raspatory. **scalping knife** *n.* **scalpless** *a.* **scalp lock** *n.* a solitary tuft of hair left on the shaven crown of the head as a challenge by the warriors of some N American Indian tribes. [prob. Scand. (cp. MSwed. *skalp*, Icel. *skālpr*, sheath), cogn. with SCALLOP]
scalpel (skal´pəl) *n.* a small knife used in surgical operations and anatomical dissections. [L *scalpellum*, dim. of *scalprum*, knife, from *scalpere*, to scrape]
scalpriform (skal´prifawm) *a.* chisel-shaped (as the teeth of rodents). [L *scalpri-*, *scalprum*, see SCALPEL, -FORM]
scaly SCALE[1].
scam (skam) *n.* (*N Am., sl.*) **1** a trick or swindle. **2** a story or rumour. *~v.i.* (*pres.p.* **scamming,** *past, p.p.* **scammed**) to commit fraud. *~v.t.* to swindle. **scammer** *n.* [etym. unknown]
scammony (skam´əni) *n.* (*pl.* **scammonies**) **1** an Asian plant, *Convolvulus scammonia.* **2** a purgative gum resin from the root of this. [OF *scammonie*, L *scammōnia*, Gr. *skammōnia*]
scamp[1] (skamp) *n.* (*coll.*) **1** a worthless person, a knave, a rogue. **2** a mischievous child. **scampish** *a.* [prob. as SCAMPER]
scamp[2] (skamp) *v.t.* to do or execute (work etc.) in a careless manner or with bad material. [prob. var. of SCANT]
scamper (skam´pə) *v.i.* to run rapidly, playfully, hastily, or impulsively. *~n.* **1** a hasty or playful run. **2** a hurried excursion, a hurried tour. [orig. to run away, OF *escamper* (EX-, L *campus*, field)]
scampi (skam´pi) *n.* **1** (*pl.*) large prawns such as the Norway lobster or Dublin (Bay) prawn, esp. when fried in breadcrumbs or batter. **2** (*sing.*) (*pl.* **scampi, scampis**) a dish of these. [It.]
scan (skan) *v.t.* (*pres.p.* **scanning,** *past, p.p.* **scanned**) **1** to examine closely or intently, to scrutinize. **2** to examine and produce an image of (a body part) using ultrasound, X-rays etc. **3** to observe with a radar beam. **4** to continuously traverse (an area or object) with a beam of laser light, electrons etc. in order to examine or to produce or transmit an image. **5** to count, mark or test the metrical feet or the syllables of (a line of verse). **6** to examine sequentially or systematically. **7** to glance at or read through hastily. *~v.i.* to be metrically correct, to agree with the rules of scansion. *~n.* **1** an act of scanning. **2** an image or display produced by scanning. **scannable** *a.* **scanner** *n.* **1** a person who or thing which scans. **2** the aerial of a radar device. **3** an instrument used in scanning the human body, esp. one that takes radiographic photographs from various angles and combines them into a three-dimensional image. **scanning** *n., a.* **scanning beam** *n.* the beam of light or electrons with which an image is scanned for television. **scanning disc** *n.* a disc with a spiral of holes with or without lenses, used for dividing a transmitted picture into a series of narrow strips. **scanning electron microscope** *n.* an electron microscope in which a beam of electrons scans an object to produce a three-dimensional image. [L *scandere*, to climb (*d* prob. conf. with -ED)]
Scand. *abbr.* Scandinavian.
scandal (skan´dəl) *n.* **1** a disgraceful action, person etc., an affront. **2** indignation, offence or censure at some act or conduct, esp. as expressed in common talk. **3** damage to reputation, reproach, shame, disgrace. **4** malicious gossip, aspersion of character. **5** (*Law*) a defamatory statement, esp. of an irrelevant nature. *~†v.t.* (*pres.p.* **scandalling,** *past, p.p.* **scandalled**) to speak scandal of, to defame, to traduce. **scandalize, scandalise** *v.t.* **1** to offend by improper or outrageous conduct, to shock. **2** (*coll.*) to talk scandal about. **scandalmonger** *n.* a person who disseminates scandal. **scandalous** *a.* **scandalously** *adv.* **scandalousness** *n.* **scandal sheet** *n.* a newspaper which publishes scandal or gossip. [ME *scandle*, ONF *escandle* (F *scandale*), L *scandalum*, Gr. *skandalon*, snare, stumbling block]
scandent (skan´dənt) *a.* climbing, as ivy. [L *scandens -ntem*, pres.p. of *scandere*, to climb]
Scandinavian (skandinā´viən) *a.* of or relating to Scandinavia (Norway, Sweden, Denmark and Iceland), its language or literature. *~n.* **1** a native or inhabitant of Scandinavia. **2** the languages of Scandinavia collectively. [L]
scandium (skan´diəm) *n.* a rare metallic element, at. no. 21, chem. symbol Sc, discovered in certain Swedish yttrium ores. [obs. *Scandia*, Scandinavia]
scannable, scanner etc. SCAN.
scansion (skan´shən) *n.* **1** the act of scanning verse. **2** a system of scanning. [L *scansio*, from *scandere*, to SCAN]
scansorial (skansaw´riəl) *a.* climbing, adapted for climbing. [mod. L, from *scandere*, to climb]
scant (skant) *a.* **1** not full, large or plentiful. **2** scarcely sufficient, not enough, deficient. **3** short (of). **4** (*chiefly dial. N Am.*) sparing, stingy. *~†v.t.* **1** to limit, to skimp, to stint. **2** to dole out grudgingly. *~v.i.* (*Naut.*) (of the wind) to fail, to decrease in force, to become unfavourable. **scantly** *adv.* **scantness** *n.* **scanty** *a.* (*comp.* **scantier,** *superl.* **scantiest**) **1** scant, deficient, insufficient. **2** limited or scarcely adequate in extent, size or quantity. **scantily** *adv.* **scantiness** *n.* [Icel. *skamt*, short]
scantle (skan´təl) *v.t.* to divide into small pieces, to partition. *~n.* **1** a gauge by which slates are cut. **2** a small kind of slate. [perh. from SCANTLING]
scantling (skant´ling) *n.* **1** a beam less than 5 in. (12.7 cm) in breadth and thickness. **2** the sectional

measurement of timber. **3** the measurement of stone in all three dimensions. **4** a set of fixed dimensions, esp. in shipbuilding. **5** †a specimen, a sample, a pattern. **6** †a small quantity or portion. **7** a rough draft or sketch. **8** a trestle for a cask. [ME *scantilone*, OF *escantillon* (F *échantillon*), etym. uncertain (perh. EX-, CANTLE)]

scanty SCANT.

SCAO *abbr.* Senior Civil Affairs Officer.

SCAP *abbr.* Supreme Command (Commander) Allied Powers.

scape (skāp) *n.* **1** a leafless radical stem bearing the flower. **2** the basal part of an insect's antenna. **3** the spring or shaft of a column. **4** the shaft of a feather. **scapeless** *a.* **scapiferous** (skəpif´-) *a.* bearing a scape. **scapiform** (-fawm) *a.* [L *scapus*, cogn. with SCEPTRE]

-scape (skāp) *comb. form* scene, view, as in *seascape*, *townscape*. [LANDSCAPE]

scapegoat (skāp´gōt) *n.* **1** a person made to bear blame due to another. **2** (*Bible*) a goat on whose head the high priest laid the sins of the people and then sent it away into the wilderness. ~*v.t.* to make a scapegoat of. **scapegoater** *n.* **scapegoating** *n.* [ESCAPE, GOAT]

scapegrace (skāp´grās) *n.* a graceless, good-for-nothing person, esp. a child. [ESCAPE, GRACE]

scapement (skāp´mənt) *n.* ESCAPEMENT (under ESCAPE).

scaph- SCAPHO-.

scaphite (skaf´īt) *n.* a cephalopod of the fossil genus *Scaphites*.

scapho- (skaf´ō), **scaph-** *comb. form* boat-shaped. [Gr. *skaphē*, boat]

scaphocephalic (skafōsifal´ik, -kef-) *a.* having a boat-shaped skull, owing to premature union of the parietal bones at the sagittal suture. **scaphocephalous** (-sef´-, -kef´-) *a.* **scaphocephalus** (-sef´-, -kef´-), **scaphocephaly** (-sef´-, -kef´-) *n.* [Gr. *kephalē*, head, -IC]

scaphoid (skaf´oid) *a.* boat-shaped, navicular. ~*n.* a scaphoid bone. **scaphoid bone** *n.* a bone of the carpus or tarsus.

scapi SCAPUS.

scapiferous, scapiform SCAPE.

scapolite (skap´əlīt) *n.* any of a group of tetragonal silicate minerals of calcium, aluminium and sodium. [G *Skapolith* (Gr. *skapos*, cp. SCAPE, -LITE)]

scapple (skap´əl), **scabble** (skab´əl) *v.t.* to reduce (stone) to a level surface without smoothing. [OF *escapeler*, to dress timber]

scapula (skap´ūlə) *n.* (*pl.* **scapulae** (-lē), **scapulas**) the shoulder blade. **scapular** *a.* of or relating to the scapula or shoulder. ~*n.* **1** in the Roman Catholic Church, a vestment usu. consisting of two strips of cloth worn by certain monastic orders across the shoulders and hanging down the breast and back. **2** an adaptation of this worn as a badge of affiliation to a religious order. **3** a bandage for the shoulder blade. **4** any of a series of feathers springing from the base of the humerus in birds, and lying along the side of the back. **scapular feather** *n.* a feather covering the shoulder. **scapulary** *n.* (*pl.* **scapularies**) **1** in the Roman Catholic Church, a scapular. **2** a scapular feather. **scapulated** (-lātid) *a.* having the scapular feathers conspicuous, esp. by their white colour. **scapulimancy** (-limansi) *n.* divination by a shoulder blade. **scapulo-** (skap´ūlō) *comb. form* **scapulo-humeral** (-hū´-) *a.* of or relating to the scapula and the humerus. **scapulo-ulnar** (-ŭl´-) *a.* of or relating to the scapula and the ulnus. [late L, sing. of L *scapulae*]

scapus (skā´pəs) *n.* (*pl.* **scapi** (-pī)) SCAPE. [L]

scar[1] (skah) *n.* **1** a mark left by a wound, burn, ulcer etc., a cicatrice. **2** the mark left by the fall of a leaf, stem, seed, deciduous part etc. **3** the after-effects of emotional distress, a psychological trauma etc. ~*v.t.* (*pres.p.* **scarring**, *past, p.p.* **scarred**) **1** to mark with a scar or scars. **2** to leave with lasting adverse effects. ~*v.i.* to form a scar, to cicatrize. **scarless** *a.* **scarry** *a.* [OF *escare*, L and Gr. *eschara*, hearth, scar of a burn]

scar[2] (skah), **scaur** (skaw) *n.* a crag, a cliff, a precipitous escarpment. [Icel. *sker*, SKERRY, cogn. with SHEAR]

scar[3] (skah) *n.* a parrotfish. [L *scarus*, Gr. *skaros*]

scarab (skar´əb) *n.* **1** an ancient Egyptian sacred beetle, *Scarabaeus sacer*. **2** a seal or gem cut in the shape of a beetle, worn as an amulet by the Egyptians. **3** a scarabaeid. **scarabaeid** (-bē´id) *a.* of or relating to the Scarabaeidae, a family of beetles containing the dung-beetles. ~*n.* a beetle of this family. **scarabaeist** *n.* **scarabaeoid** (-oid) *a.*, *n.* **scarabaeus** (-bē´əs) *n.* (*pl.* **scarabaeuses, scarabaei** (-bēī)) a scarab. **scarabee** (-bē) *n.* a scarab. [F *scarabée*, L *scarabaeus*]

†**scaramouch** (skar´əmowch, -mooch) *n.* a coward and braggart. [It. *Scaramuccia*, a character in old Italian comedy, characterized by great boastfulness and poltroonery]

scarbroite (skah´brəīt) *n.* a clayey hydrous silicate mineral of alumina found near Scarborough, Yorks. [*Scarbro'*, *Scarborough*]

scarce (skeəs) *a.* **1** infrequent, seldom met with, rare, uncommon. **2** insufficient, not plentiful, scantily supplied. **3** †parsimonious. ~*adv.* hardly, scarcely. **to make oneself scarce 1** (*coll.*) to keep out of the way. **2** (*coll.*) to be off, to decamp. **scarcely** *adv.* **1** hardly, barely, only just. **2** only with difficulty. **3** not quite (used as a polite negative). **scarceness** *n.* **1** deficiency. **2** rareness. **3** a dearth (of). **4** a famine. **5** parsimoniousness, stinginess. **scarcity** *n.* (*pl.* **scarcities**) a deficiency or dearth (of); lack of food or some commodity etc. [ONF *escars* (cp. It. *scarso*), perh. from late L *scarpsus*, *excarpsus*, L *excarptus* (EX-, *carptus*, p.p. of *carpere*, to pluck)]

Usage note When *scarcely* refers to time ('only just'), a following *when* is preferable to *than* (so *She had scarcely got in when the phone rang*).

scarcement (skeəs´mənt) *n.* (*Sc.*, *North.*) a set-off in a wall, or a plain flat ledge resulting from this. [etym. uncertain]

scarcity SCARCE.

scare (skeə) *v.t.* **1** to frighten, to alarm, to strike with sudden fear. **2** to drive (away) through fear. ~*v.i.* to become frightened. ~*n.* **1** a sudden fright, a panic. **2** a widespread terror of e.g. invasion, epidemic etc. **3** a financial panic. **to run scared** to panic. **to scare out** to scare up. **to scare the hell out of** HELL. **to scare the (living) daylights out of** DAYLIGHT. **to scare the pants off someone** PANTS. **to scare up 1** (*esp. N Am.*) to beat up (game). **2** (*coll.*) to find or produce quickly. **scarecrow** *n.* **1** a figure set up to frighten birds away from crops etc. **2** (*coll.*) a shabby or absurd-looking person, a guy. **3** †a bugbear. **scared** *a.* **scaredy-cat** (skeə´di-) *n.* (*coll.*) a person who is easily frightened. **scaremonger** *n.* a person who causes scares, esp. by circulating unfounded reports etc. **scaremongering** *n.* **scarer** *n.* **scary** *a.* (*comp.* **scarier**, *superl.* **scariest**). **scarily** *adv.* **scariness** *n.* [prob. from ME *skerren*, Icel. *skjarr*, shy, timid]

scarf[1] (skahf) *n.* (*pl.* **scarfs, scarves** (-vz)) **1** a long strip or square of some material worn round the neck and shoulders or over the head for warmth or decoration. **2** a neckcloth or necktie. **3** a stole. **4** a (military or official) sash. ~*v.t.* **1** to clothe or cover with or as with a scarf. **2** to wrap (around or about) as a scarf. **scarfed** *a.* **scarf pin, scarf ring** *n.* a pin or ring, usu. of gold, used to fasten a scarf. **scarf-skin** *n.* the outer layer of skin, the cuticle. **scarf-wise** *adv.* used or worn as a scarf. [perh. from Dut. *scherf*, a shred, or ONF *escarpe*, OF *escharpe*, cp. SCRIP[2] and SCRAP[1]]

Usage note The plural *scarfs* is preferred to *scarves*.

scarf[2] (skahf) *v.t.* **1** to join the ends of (timber) by means of a scarf joint. **2** to cut a scarf in or on. **3** to strip the blubber or skin from (a whale). ~*n.* (*pl.* **scarfs**) **1** (*also* **scarf joint**) a joint made by bevelling or notching so that the thickness is not increased, and then bolting or strapping together. **2** a bevelled or notched end that forms such a joint. **3** an incision or groove cut along the body of a whale before stripping off the blubber. **scarfing** *n.* **scarfing machine** *n.* **scarf weld** *n.* a welded joint between two pieces of metal. [perh. from Swed. *skarfva*, from *scarf*, a seam, cogn. with SCARF[1]]

scarf[3] (skahf) *n.* (*Sc.*) a cormorant. [Icel. *skarfr*, cp. Norw. and Swed. *skarf*]

scarf[4] (skahf) *v.t.* (*N Am., coll.*) to eat or drink greedily (usu. with *down*). [var. of SCOFF[2]]

scarify[1] (skeə´rifī, skar´-) *v.t.* (*3rd pers. sing. pres.* **scarifies,** *pres.p.* **scarifying,** *past, p.p.* **scarified**) **1** to scratch or make slight incisions in. **2** to loosen the surface of (soil). **3** to pain, to torture, to criticize mercilessly. **scarification** (-fikā´shən) *n.* **scarificator** (-fikātə) *n.* a surgical instrument with lancet points used in scarifying. **scarifier** *n.* **1** a person who scarifies. **2** a scarificator. **3** an implement or machine for breaking up soil etc. [F *scarifier*, L *scarīficāre*, Gr. *skariphasthai*, from *skariphos*, pencil, style, cogn. with L *scrībere*, to write]

scarify[2] (skeə´rifī) *v.t.* (*3rd pers. sing. pres.* **scarifies,** *pres.p.* **scarifying,** *past, p.p.* **scarified**) (*coll.*) to scare, frighten. ~*v.i.* to be scared or frightened. **scarifyingly** *adv.* [SCARE, -FY]

scarily, scariness SCARY (under SCARE).

scarious (skeə´riəs), **scariose** (-ōs) *a.* (of bracts etc.) membraneous and dry. [F *scarieux* (prob. from L *scaria*, thorny shrub)]

scarlatina (skahlətē´nə) *n.* (a mild form of) scarlet fever. [It. *scarlattina*]

scarlet (skah´lit) *n.* **1** a bright red colour tending towards orange. **2** cloth or dress of this colour, esp. official robes or uniform. ~*a.* **1** of a scarlet colour. **2** dressed in scarlet. **scarlet admiral** *n.* a butterfly, the red admiral, *Vanessa atalanta.* **scarlet bean** *n.* a scarlet runner. **scarlet fever** *n.* an infectious fever characterized by the eruption of red patches on the skin. **scarlet hat** *n.* **1** a cardinal's hat. **2** the rank of cardinal. **scarlet pimpernel** *n.* a small annual wild plant, *Anagallis arvensis*, which has flowers that close in bad weather; also called *poor man's weather-glass.* **scarlet rash** *n.* roseola. **scarlet runner** *n.* a trailing bean, *Phaseolus coccineus*, with scarlet flowers. **scarlet woman** *n.* (*pl.* **scarlet women**) **1** a prostitute. **2** worldliness or sensuality. **3** pagan or papal Rome (see Rev. xvii.4–5). [OF *escarlate* (F *écarlate*), Pers. *saqalāt*, scarlet cloth]

scaroid SCARUS.

scarp[1] (skahp) *n.* **1** a steep or nearly perpendicular slope. **2** the interior slope of the ditch at the foot of the parapet of a fortification. ~*v.t.* to cut down so as to be steep or nearly perpendicular. **scarped** *a.* precipitous, abrupt. [OF *escarpe*, It. *scarpa*, perh. from OHG *scarpōn*, cp. SHARP]

scarp[2] (skahp) *n.* (*Her.*) a diminutive of the bend sinister, half its width. [OF *escarpe*, SCARF[1]]

scarper (skah´pə) *v.i.* (*sl.*) **1** to leave in a hurry. **2** to go away without notice or warning. [prob. from It. *scappare*, to escape]

scarpines (skah´pinz) *n.pl.* an instrument of torture similar to the boot. [It. *scarpino*, dim. of *scarpa*, shoe]

scarry SCAR[1].

Scart (skaht), **SCART** *n.* a 24-pin socket used to connect video equipment. [*S*yndicat des *C*onstructeurs des *A*ppareils *R*adiorécepteurs et *T*éléviseurs]

scarus (skeə´rəs) *n.* any fish of the genus *Scarus*, which have brightly coloured scales; also called *parrotfish.* **scaroid** (-roid) *a., n.* [L, from Gr. *skaros*]

scarves SCARF[1].

scary SCARE.

scat[1] (skat) *int.* go away!, be off! ~*v.i.* (*pres.p.* **scatting,** *past, p.p.* **scatted**) (*coll.*) **1** to depart hastily. **2** (*chiefly N Am.*) to move quickly. [etym. uncertain]

scat[2] (skat) *n.* jazz singing in meaningless syllables. ~*v.i.* (*pres.p.* **scatting,** *past, p.p.* **scatted**) to sing in this way. [perh. imit.]

scat[3] (skat) *n.* **1** excrement. **2** animal droppings. [Gr. *skōr skatos*, dung]

scat[4] (skat) *n.* (*dial.*) **1** a blow. **2** the noise of a blow or hit. **3** a brisk shower or squall. **scatty**[1] *a.* showery. [perh. imit.]

scat[5] (skat), **scatt** *n.* (*Hist.*) **1** tax, tribute. **2** a land tax in Orkney and Shetland from a udaller to the Crown. **scat field, scat hold, scat land** *n.* land subject to this. [Icel. *skattr*, cp. OE *sceatt*]

scathe (skādh) *v.t.* **1** (*poet.*) to hurt, to harm, to injure, esp. by scorching. **2** to attack severely with sarcasm, criticism etc. ~*n.* †hurt, harm, injury. **scatheless** *a.* **scathing** *a.* **1** hurtful, harmful. **2** (of sarcasm etc.) very bitter or severe, withering. **scathingly** *adv.* [Icel. *skatha*, cp. Swed. *skada*, Dan. *skade*, OE *scathan*, G and Dut. *schaden*, also Gr. *askēthēs*, unharmed]

scatology (skətol´əji) *n.* **1** interest in or literature characterized by obscenity. **2** the study of fossil excrement or coprolites. **3** the biological study of excrement, esp. to determine diet. **scatological** (skatəloj´-) *a.* **scatomancy** (skat´əmansi) *n.* divination by means of faeces. **scatophagous** (-tof´əgəs) *a.* feeding on dung. **scatoscopy** (-tos´kəpi) *n.* diagnosis by means of faeces. [Gr. *skatos*, gen. of *skōr*, dung, -LOGY]

scatt SCAT[5].

scatter (skat´ə) *v.t.* **1** to throw loosely about, to fling in all directions. **2** to strew, to bestrew. **3** to cause to separate in various directions, to disperse. **4** to dissipate. **5** to diffuse (radiation etc.) or cause to spread out. **6** to fire (a charge) diffusely. ~*v.i.* **1** to disperse. **2** to be dissipated or diffused. **3** to fire a charge of shot diffusely. ~*n.* **1** the act of scattering. **2** a small number scattered about. **3** the extent of scattering. **scatterbrain** *n.* a person who is incapable of thinking seriously or unable to concentrate. **scatterbrained** *a.* **scatter cushion, scatter rug** *n.* a small cushion or rug which can be moved to any position in a room. **scatter diagram, scatter plot** *n.* a graph that plots the values of two variables along two axes at right angles to each other. **scattered** *a.* **1** irregularly situated, not together. **2** widely apart. **scatterer** *n.* **scatter-gun** *n.* (*esp. N Am.*) a shotgun. ~*a.* scattershot. **scattering** *n.* **1** the act of dispersing or strewing something. **2** a small amount or number irregularly strewn. **3** the deflecting or spreading out of a beam of radiation in passing through matter. **scatteringly** *adv.* **scattershot** *a.* (*esp. N Am.*) random, haphazard. **scattery** *a.* [ME *scateren*, freq. of SCAT[1], cogn. with Gr. *skedannunai*, to scatter, Sansk. *skhad*, to cut]

†**scattermouch** (skat´əmowch, -mooch) *n.* SCARAMOUCH.

scatty[1] SCAT[4].

scatty[2] (skat´i) *a.* (*comp.* **scattier,** *superl.* **scattiest**) (*coll.*) incapable of prolonged concentration, empty-headed, giddy. **scattily** *adv.* **scattiness** *n.* [prob. from *scatterbrain*]

scaturient (skətū´riənt) *a.* gushing out, as from a fountain. [L *scatūriens -ntem*, pres.p. of *scatūrīre*, from *scatere*, to flow]

scaup (skawp), **scaup duck** *n.* a diving duck of the genus *Aythya*, esp. *A. marila*, found in the northern regions. [var. of SCALP]

scauper (skaw´pə) *n.* a wood engraver's gougelike tool. [prob. var. of SCALPER (under SCALP)]

scaur SCAR[2].

scavenger (skav´ənjə) *n.* **1** a person who collects waste or discarded objects. **2** an organism feeding on refuse, carrion etc. **3** †a person employed to clean the streets by sweeping, scraping, and carrying away refuse. **4** a chemical added to remove or neutralize unwanted material. **5** (*Hist.*) a child employed in a spinning mill to collect loose cotton. **6** anyone willing to do 'dirty work' or delighting in filthy subjects. **scavenge** *v.t.* **1** to search for or salvage (something usable) from among waste or discarded material. **2** to remove impurities from (molten metal) by causing their chemical combination. **3** to remove (impurities etc.). **4** to clean (streets etc.). ~*v.i.* **1** to act as a scavenger. **2** to search for usable material. ~*n.* the action or process of scavenging. **scavenger beetle, scavenger crab** *n.* a beetle or crab feeding on carrion. **scavenger hunt** *n.* a game in which players are given a list of miscellaneous items to collect. **scavengery** *n.* [orig. *scavager*, collector of scavage]

scavenger's daughter (skav´ənjəz) *n.* an instrument of torture for compressing the body, invented by Leonard Skevington or Skeffington, Lieutenant of the Tower, under Henry VIII. [alt. of *Skevington*]

scazon (skā´zən, skaz´-) *n.* a satiric metre of an irregular or faltering character, esp. an iambic trimeter ending with a spondee or trochee, a choliamb. **scazontic** (skəzon´-) *a.* [L, from Gr. *skazōn*, orig. pres.p. of *skazein*, to limp]

SCB *abbr.* Solicitors Complaints Bureau.

SCBU *abbr.* special care baby unit.

SCC *abbr.* Sea Cadet Corps.

SCCL *abbr.* Scottish Council for Civil Liberties.

Sc.D *abbr.* Doctor of Science.

SCE *abbr.* Scottish Certificate of Education.

scena (shā´nə) *n.* (*pl.* **scene** (-nā)) a long elaborate solo piece or scene in opera. [It., from L *scēna*, SCENE]

scenario (sinah´riō) *n.* (*pl.* **scenarios**) **1** a sketch or outline of the scenes and main points of a play etc. **2** the script of a film with dialogue and directions for the producer during the actual shooting. **3** an account or outline of projected, expected or imagined future events. **scenarist** *n.* [It.]

Usage note *Scenario* should not be used as though it meant simply a scene or situation.

scene (sēn) *n.* **1** the place where anything occurs or is exhibited as on a stage. **2** the place in which the action of a play or story is supposed to take place. **3** a single event, situation or incident in a play or film. **4** a description of an incident, situation etc. from life. **5** a striking incident, esp. an exhibition of feeling or passion. **6** a division of a play comprising so much as passes without change of locality or break of time, or, in French drama, without intermediate entrances or exits. **7** a film or television sequence. **8** a landscape, a view, regarded as a piece of scenery. **9** (*coll.*) one's usual or preferred social environment, area of interest etc. **10** (*coll.*) an area of activity or business. **11** †the stage in a Greek or Roman theatre. **12** the stage, the theatre. **13** any of the painted frames, hangings or other devices used to give an appearance of reality to the action of a play. **behind the scenes 1** at the back of the stage. **2** in possession of facts etc., not generally known. **to come on the scene** to arrive, appear. **to hit the scene** to arrive, to appear. **to make the scene** (*N Am.*) to arrive, to appear. **to quit the scene** to die or to leave. **to set the scene 1** to describe the location of events. **2** to give background information. **scene-dock** *n.* a place near the stage in a theatre for storing scenery. **scene-painter** *n.* a person who paints scenery for theatres. **scene painting** *n.* **scenery** (-əri) *n.* (*pl.* **sceneries**) **1** the various parts or accessories used on the stage to represent the actual scene of the action. **2** the views presented by natural features, esp. when picturesque. **scene-shifter** *n.* a person employed in a theatre to move scenery. **scene shifting** *n.* **scenic** *a.* **1** characterized by beautiful natural scenery, picturesque. **2** of or relating to natural scenery. **3** (of a painting etc.) depicting a scene or incident. **4** of or relating to the stage. **5** arranged for effect, dramatic, theatrical. **scenically** *adv.* **scenic railway** *n.* **1** a miniature railway that runs through artificial representations of picturesque scenery. **2** a switchback railway at a funfair. [L *scēna*, Gr. *skēnē*, tent, stage]

scenography (sēnog´rəfi) *n.* **1** the painting or design of scenes in a theatre. **2** the representation of an object in perspective. **scenograph** (sē´nəgrahf) *n.* **scenographer** *n.* **scenographic** (-graf´-) *a.* **scenographically** *adv.* [Gr. *skēnographia* (*skēnē* as SCENE, -GRAPHY)]

scent (sent) *v.t.* **1** to perceive by smell. **2** to recognize the odour of. **3** to begin to suspect. **4** to trace or hunt (out) by or as by smelling. **5** to perfume. ~*v.i.* **1** to exercise the sense of smell. **2** to give forth a smell. ~*n.* **1** odour, esp. of a pleasant kind. **2** the odour left by an animal forming a trail by which it can be followed (as by hounds). **3** pieces of paper left as a trail in a paperchase. **4** a trail to be pursued. **5** a clue. **6** a liquid essence containing fragrant extracts from flowers etc., a perfume. **7** the sense of smell, esp. the power of recognizing or tracing things by smelling. **on the scent** having a useful clue, lead etc. **to put someone off the scent** to throw someone off the scent. **to scent out** to discover by smelling or searching. **to throw someone off the scent** to mislead someone. **scent-bag** *n.* **1** an external pouchlike scent gland, as in the musk deer. **2** a bag containing aniseed etc., used to leave a track of scent for hounds to follow. **scent-bottle** *n.* a bottle for holding perfume. **scented** *a.* having a scent (*usu. in comb.*, as *keen-scented*). **scent gland** *n.* a gland secreting an odorous substance, as in the musk deer, civet etc. **scentless** *a.* **scentless mayweed** *n.* the plant *Tripleurospermum inodorum*. **scent organ** *n.* a scent gland. [orig. *sent*, F *sentir*, L *sentīre*, to perceive]

scepter SCEPTRE.

sceptic (skep´tik), (*esp. N Am.*) **skeptic** *n.* **1** a person of a questioning, doubting or incredulous habit of mind. **2** a person who casts doubt on any statement, theory etc., esp. in a cynical manner. **3** a person who doubts the truth of a revealed religion. **4** an agnostic. **5** an atheist. **6** a person who questions or denies the possibility of attaining knowledge of truth. **7** (*Hist.*) an adherent of philosophical scepticism, a Pyrrhonist. ~*a.* sceptical. **scepsis** (-sis) *n.* **1** scepticism, sceptical philosophy. **2** the attitude of philosophic doubt. **sceptical** *a.* **1** given to doubting or questioning, incredulous. **2** doubting or denying the truth of revelation, or the possibility of knowledge. **3** of, relating to or characteristic of a sceptic. **sceptically** *adv.* **scepticism** (-sizm) *n.* **scepticize** (-sīz), **scepticise** *v.i.* to act as a sceptic. [F *sceptique*, L *scepticus*, Gr. *skeptikos*, from *skeptesthai*, to examine]

sceptre (sep´tə), (*esp. N Am.*) **scepter** *n.* **1** a staff or baton borne by a sovereign as a symbol of authority. **2** royal authority. **sceptred** *a.* invested with a sceptre or with royal authority. **sceptreless** *a.* [ME and OF *ceptre*, *sceptre*, L *scēptrum*, Gr. *skēptron*, from *skēptein*, to prop]

SCF *abbr.* **1** Save the Children Fund. **2** Senior Chaplain to the Forces.

scfh *abbr.* standard cubic feet per hour.

scfm *abbr.* standard cubic feet per minute.

sch. *abbr.* **1** scholar. **2** (*also* **Sch.**) school. **3** schooner.

schadenfreude (shah´dənfroidə) *n.* pleasure in others' misfortunes. [G *Schaden*, damage, *Freude*, joy]
schappe (shap, shap´ə) *n.* a fabric or yarn made from waste silk. [G]
schechita, schechitah SHECHITA.
schedule (shed´ūl, sked´-) *n.* **1** a timetable. **2** a planned programme of events, tasks etc. **3** a written or printed table, list, catalogue or inventory (appended to a document). *~v.t.* **1** to enter in a schedule. **2** to make a schedule or list of. **3** to arrange for a particular time. **4** to include (a building) in a list for preservation or protection. **according to schedule** as planned. **behind schedule** late; not keeping up to an arranged timetable. **on schedule** on time. **schedular** *a.* **scheduled castes** *n.pl.* in India, the former untouchables. **scheduled flight, scheduled service** *n.* a flight or service that is part of a regular service. **scheduled territories** *n.pl.* STERLING AREA (under STERLING). **scheduler** *n.* **schedulize, schedulise** *v.t.* [ME and OF *cedule*, from late L *scedula, schedula*, dim. of L *scheda*, strip of papyrus, Gr. *schidē*, splint, from *schizein*, to cleave]
scheelite (shē´līt) *n.* a vitreous variously-coloured mineral, a tungstate of calcium. [K. W. *Scheele*, 1742–86, Swedish chemist, -ITE[1]]
schema (skē´mə) *n.* (*pl.* **schemata** (-tə), **schemas**) **1** a scheme, summary, outline or conspectus. **2** a chart or diagram. **3** the abstract figure of a syllogism. **4** a figure of speech. **5** in Kant's philosophy, the form, type or rule under which the mind applies the categories to the material of knowledge furnished by sense perception. **schematic** (-mat´-) *a.* having, or in the nature of, a plan or schema. *~n.* a schematic diagram, esp. of an electrical circuit. **schematically** *adv.* **schematism** *n.* **schematist** *n.* a person given to forming schemes. **schematize, schematise** *v.t.* **1** to formulate or express by means of a scheme. **2** to apply the Kantian categories to. **schematization** (-ā´shən) *n.* [L, from Gr. *schēma -atos*, from *schē-*, base of *schēsō*, fut. of *echein*, to have]
scheme (skēm) *n.* **1** a plan, a project, a proposed method of doing something. **2** a contrivance, an underhand design. **3** a table or schedule of proposed acts, events etc., a syllabus. **4** a systematic statement, representation, diagram or arrangement of facts, objects, principles etc. **5** a table of classification. *~v.t.* to plan, to design, to contrive, to plot. *~v.i.* **1** to form plans. **2** to plot. **schemer** *n.* **scheming** *a., n.* (given to) forming schemes. **schemingly** *adv.* [L SCHEMA]
schemozzle SHEMOZZLE.
scherzo (skœt´sō) *n.* (*pl.* **scherzi** (-sē), **scherzos**) a light playful movement in music, usu. following a slow one, in a symphony or sonata. **scherzando** (-san´dō) *adv.* (*Mus.*) playfully. *~n.* (*pl.* **scherzandi** (-dē), **scherzandos**) a passage or movement played in this way. [It., from Gmc. (cp. G *Scherz*, jest)]
schiavone (skyavō´nā) *n.* a 17th-cent. basket-hilted broadsword, so called because the Schiavoni or Slav bodyguards of the Doge were armed with it. [It.]
schicksa SHIKSA.
Schick test (shik), **Schick's test** *n.* a test to determine susceptibility to diphtheria by injecting diluted diphtheria toxin into the skin. [Bela *Schick*, 1877–1967, US paediatrician]
schiedam (skēdam´) *n.* a type of Dutch gin. [town where made]
schiller (shil´ə) *n.* the peculiar bronzelike sheen or iridescence characteristic of certain minerals. **schillerization** (-ā´shən), **schillerisation** *n.* a process by which minute crystals are deposited in other minerals so as to produce this peculiar sheen. **schillerize** *v.t.* **schiller-spar, schillerite** *n.* a rock allied to diallage which has undergone schillerization. [G]
schilling (shil´ing) *n.* **1** the standard monetary unit of Austria. **2** a coin of this value. [G]
schindylesis (skindilē´sis) *n.* (*pl.* **schindyleses** (-sēz)) an articulation in which a thin part of one bone fits into a groove in another. **schindyletic** (-let´-) *a.* [Gr. *schindulēsis*, cleaving]
schipperke (skip´əki, ship´-, -kə) *n.* a small black variety of lapdog. [Dut., little boatman]
schisiophone (shiz´iəfōn) *n.* an instrument comprising a hammer and induction-balance for detecting flaws in iron rails. [Gr. *schisis, schiseōs*, from *schizein*, to cleave, -PHONE]
schism (siz´m, skiz´m) *n.* **1** a split or division in a community. **2** division in a Church, esp. secession of a part or separation into two Churches. **3** the sin of causing such division. **schismatic** (-mat´-) *n., a.* **schismatical** *a.* **schismatically** *adv.* **schismaticalness** *n.* **schismatist** *n.* **schismatize, schismatise** *v.t., v.i.* **schismless** *a.* [F *schisme*, late L and Gr. *schisma*, from *schizein*, to split]
schist (shist) *n.* a rock of a more or less foliated or laminar structure, tending to split easily. **schistaceous** (-tā´shəs) *a.* slate-grey. **schistoid** (-toid), **schistose** (-tōs), **schistous** *a.* of the nature or structure of schist. [F *schiste*, L and Gr. *schistos*, easily split, as SCHISM]
schistosome (shis´təsōm) *n.* a tropical flatworm of the genus *Schistosoma*. **schistosomiasis** (-səmī´əsis) *n.* a disease caused by infestation with worms of the genus *Schistosoma*; bilharzia.
schiz- SCHIZO-.
schizanthus (skitsan´thəs) *n.* any plant of the genus *Schizanthus*, with much-divided leaves and showy flowers. [Gr. *anthos*, flower]
schizo (skit´sō) *n.* (*pl.* **schizos**) (*coll., offensive*) a schizophrenic. *~a.* schizophrenic.
schizo- (skit´sō, skī´zō), **schiz-** *comb. form* **1** marked by a cleft or clefts. **2** tending to split. [Gr. *schizein*, to cleave]
schizocarp (skit´səkahp) *n.* a fruit splitting into several one-seeded portions without dehiscing. **schizocarpic** (-kah´-), **schizocarpous** *a.*
schizocoele (skī´zəsēl) *n.* a perivisceral cavity produced by a splitting of the mesoblast of the embryo. **schizocoelous** (-sē´-) *a.* [Gr. *koilos*, hollow]
schizogenesis (skitsəjen´əsis) *n.* reproduction by fission. **schizogenetic** (-net´-) *a.* **schizogenetically** *adv.* **schizogenic** *a.* **schizogenically** *adv.* **schizogony** (-sog´əni) *n.* schizogenesis.
schizognathous (skitsog´nəthəs) *a.* having the bones of the palate cleft from the vomer and each other, as in the gulls, plovers etc. **schizognathism** *n.* [Gr. *gnathos*, jaw]
schizoid (skit´soid, skid´zoid) *a.* **1** showing qualities of a schizophrenic personality. **2** (*coll.*) characterized by inconsistency, contradiction etc. *~n.* a schizoid person. **schizoidal** (-soi´-) *a.*
schizomycete (skitsəmī´sēt) *n.* (*Bot.*) any organism of the class Schizomycetes, a class of microscopic organisms comprising bacteria. **schizomycetic** (-set´-) *a.* **schizomycetous** (-sē´-) *a.* [Gr. *mukēs*, pl. *mukētes*, a fungus]
schizophrenia (skitsəfrē´niə) *n.* **1** a severe psychological disorder characterized by loss of contact with reality, personality disintegration, hallucinations, delusions etc. **2** (*coll.*) behaviour characterized by inconsistency, contradictions etc. **schizophrenic** (-fren´-) *a., n.*
schizophyte (skit´sōfīt) *n.* any of various plants that reproduce by fission, such as bacteria and certain fungi. **schizophytic** (-fit´-) *a.* [Gr. *phuton*, plant]
schizopod (skit´səpod) *n.* any of the Schizopoda, a suborder of podophthalmate crustaceans with the feet apparently cleft. **schizopodous** (-sop´ədəs) *a.* [Gr. *pous podos*, foot]
schizothecal (skitsəthē´kəl) *a.* (of birds) having the

tarsus divided by scutellation or reticulation. [Gr. *thēkē*, case]

schizothymia (skitsəthī´miə) *n.* introversion exhibiting elements of schizophrenia but within normal limits. **schizothymic** *a.* [Gr. *thumos*, mind, spirit]

schläger (shlā´gə) *n.* a German student's duelling sword, pointless, but with sharpened edges towards the end. [G, from *schlagen*, to beat]

schlemiel (shləmēl´), **schlemihl, shlemiel** *n.* (*chiefly N Am., coll.*) a bungling clumsy person who is easily victimized. [Yiddish]

schlepp (shlep), **shlep** *v.t.* (*pres.p.* **schlepping,** *past, p.p.* **schlepped**) (*chiefly N Am., coll.*) to drag, pull. ~*n.* **1** a tedious journey. **2** an unlucky or incompetent person. [Yiddish]

schlieren (shlē´rən) *n.* **1** small streaks of different composition in igneous rock. **2** streaks in a transparent fluid caused by regions of differing density and refractive index. [G]

schlimazel (shlimaz´əl), **shlimazel** *n.* (*N Am., sl.*) an unlucky person; a born loser. [Yiddish]

schlock (shlok) *n.* (*N Am., coll.*) shoddy, cheap goods; trash. ~*a.* shoddy, cheap, trashy. [Yiddish]

schloss (shlos) *n.* a castle (in Germany). [G]

schlump (shlump) *n.* (*esp. N Am., sl.*) a slovenly person, a slob. [Yiddish]

schmaltz (shmawlts), **schmalz** *n.* (*esp. N Am., coll.*) over-sentimentality, esp. in music. **schmaltzy** *a.* (*comp.* **schmaltzier,** *superl.* **schmaltziest**). [Yiddish *schmalts*, fat, dripping]

schmelze (shmelt´sə) *n.* any one of various kinds of coloured glass, esp. that coloured red and used to flash white glass. [G *Schmelz*, enamel, cp. SMELT[1]]

schmo (shmō), **schmoe, shmo** *n.* (*pl.* **schmoes, shmoes**) (*N Am., sl.*) a stupid or boring person. [Yiddish]

schmooze (shmooz), **schmoose, shmooze** *v.i.* (*esp. N Am., sl.*) to gossip, chat. ~*n.* chitchat. [Yiddish]

schmuck (shmŭk) *n.* (*esp. N Am., sl.*) a fool. [Yiddish, penis, from G *Schmuck*, jewel]

schnapps (shnaps) *n.* any of various spirits resembling genever gin. [G, from Dut. *snaps*, mouthful, from *snappen*, to SNAP]

schnauzer (shnow´zə, -tsə) *n.* a breed of wire-haired German terrier. [G *Schnauze*, snout]

Schneiderian (shnīdiə´riən) *a.* of or relating to the German anatomist Konrad Victor Schneider, 1610–80. **Schneiderian membrane** *n.* the mucous membrane of the nose, first investigated by Schneider.

schnitzel (shnit´səl) *n.* an escalope of meat, esp. veal. [G]

schnorkel SNORKEL.

schnorrer (shnor´ə, shnaw´-) *n.* (*esp. N Am., sl.*) a beggar. [Yiddish]

schnozzle (shnoz´əl) *n.* (*chiefly N Am., coll.*) a nose. [Yiddish *shnoitsl*, G *Schnauze*]

scholar (skol´ə) *n.* **1** a learned person, esp. one with a profound knowledge of literature. **2** an undergraduate on the foundation of a college and receiving assistance from its funds, usu. after a competitive examination. **3** a person acquiring knowledge, a (good or apt) learner. **4** a disciple. **5** †a pupil, a student, a person attending school. **6** (*coll.*) †a person who can read and write. **scholarlike** *a.* **scholarly** *a.* **1** befitting a scholar. **2** learned. **scholarliness** *n.* **scholarship** *n.* **1** high attainments in literature or science. **2** education, instruction. **3** education, usu. with maintenance, free or at reduced fees, granted to a successful candidate after a competitive examination. **4** the emoluments so granted to a scholar. **5** the qualities of a scholar. **scholar's mate** *n.* in chess, a series of four moves by a player resulting in checkmate. [A-F *escoler* (F *écolier*), cp. OE *scolere* (SCHOOL[1], -ER[1]), assim. to late L *scholāris*]

scholastic (skəlas´tik) *a.* **1** of or relating to school, schools, universities etc. **2** educational, academic. **3** pedagogic, pedantic. **4** (*Hist.*) of, relating to or characteristic of the schoolmen of the Middle Ages. **5** given to precise definitions and logical subtleties. ~*n.* **1** (*Hist.*) a schoolman of the Middle Ages. **2** a person characterized by the method and subtlety of the schoolman. **3** a mere scholar, an academic person. **4** a Jesuit of the third grade. **scholastically** *adv.* **scholasticism** (-sizm) *n.* [L *scholasticus*, Gr. *scholastikos*, from *scholazein*, to be at leisure, see SCHOOL[1]]

scholiast (skō´liast) *n.* (*Hist.*) a commentator, esp. an ancient grammarian who annotated the classics. **scholiastic** (-as´-) *a.* **scholium** (-əm) *n.* (*pl.* **scholia** (-liə)) a marginal note, esp. an explanatory comment on the Greek and Latin authors by an early grammarian. [Gr. *scholiastēs*, from *scholiazein*, to write scholia]

school[1] (skool) *n.* **1** an institution for education or instruction, esp. one for instruction of a more elementary kind than that given at universities. **2** a faculty of a university. **3** an establishment offering specialized teaching. **4** the building or buildings of a school. **5** the body of pupils of a school. **6** a session or time during which teaching is carried on. **7** a lecture room. **8** (*Hist.*) a seminary in the Middle Ages for teaching logic, metaphysics and theology. **9** (*pl., Hist.*) the medieval universities, professors, teaching etc. **10** scholasticism. **11** any of the branches of study with separate examinations taken by candidates for honours. **12** the hall where such examinations are held. **13** (*pl.*) the final BA examination at Oxford University. **14** the body of disciples or followers of a philosopher, artist etc., or of adherents of a cause, principle, system of thought etc. **15** (*Mus.*) a book of instruction, a manual. **16** any sphere or circumstances serving to discipline or instruct. **17** a group of people assembled for a common purpose, such as playing poker. ~*v.t.* **1** to instruct, to educate. **2** to train, to drill. **3** to discipline, to bring under control. **4** to send to school. ~*a.* of school, schools or the school. **at school** attending lessons etc. **in school** (*N Am.*) attending lessons, at school. **of the old school** OLD. **to go to school** **1** to begin one's schooling. **2** to attend lessons. **to leave school** to finish one's education. **schoolable** *a.* **school age** *n.* the age at which children attend school. **school-age** *a.* **schoolbag** *n.* a bag for carrying schoolbooks etc. **school board** *n.* **1** (*Hist.*) a public body (1870–1902) elected to provide for the elementary instruction of children in their district. **2** (*N Am.*) a local education board. **schoolbook** *n.* a book for use in schools. **schoolboy** *n.* a boy attending a school. ~*a.* of or relating to schoolboys. **schoolboyish** *a.* **schoolchild** *n.* (*pl.* **schoolchildren**) a child attending a school. **school dame** *n.* **1** (*N Am.*) a schoolmistress. **2** (*Hist.*) the keeper of a dame school. **schoolday** *n.* **1** a day on which schools are open. **2** (*pl.*) the time of being a school pupil. **school-divine** *n.* a person who adopts scholastic theology. **school-divinity** *n.* **schoolfellow** *n.* a person who attends the same school. **schoolfriend** *n.* a friend from school. **schoolgirl** *n.* a girl attending a school. ~*a.* of or relating to schoolgirls. **schoolgirlish** *a.* **schoolhouse** *n.* **1** a building used as a school. **2** a dwelling house provided for a schoolmaster or schoolmistress. **3** the head teacher's house or the chief boarding house at a public school. **schoolie** *n.* (*Austral., sl.*) a schoolteacher. **schooling** *n.* **1** instruction or education at school. **2** training, tuition, coaching, guidance. **3** school fees. **4** discipline. **5** the training of a horse for riding, or in dressage, jumping etc. **school inspector** *n.* an official appointed to examine schools. **school leaver** *n.* a pupil who is about to leave or has recently left school. **school-leaving age** *n.* the minimum age at which a child may leave school. **school-ma'am, school-marm** *n.* (*N Am., coll.*) a schoolmistress. **school-marmish** *a.* (*esp. N Am., coll.*) prim and fussy.

schoolman *n.* (*pl.* **schoolmen**) **1** (*Hist.*) a teacher or professor in a medieval university. **2** (*Hist.*) a person versed in the theology, logic or metaphysics of the medieval schools or the niceties of academic disputation. **3** (*N Am.*) a male teacher. **school-marm, school-marmish** SCHOOL-MA'AM (under SCHOOL[1]). **schoolmaster** *n.* **1** a male head or assistant teacher in a school. **2** a pedagogue. **3** a person who or something which trains or disciplines. **schoolmastering** *n.* **schoolmasterly** *a.* **schoolmate** *n.* a person attending the same school. **school-miss** *n.* **1** a schoolgirl. **2** an inexperienced or bashful girl. **schoolmistress** *n.* a female head or assistant teacher in a school. **schoolmistressy** *a.* **school nurse** *n.* a nurse who works in a school or schools. **school of hard knocks** *n.* experience gained from a difficult life. **school phobia** *n.* a fear of attending school. **schoolroom** *n.* a room where teaching is given, in a school, house etc. **school-ship** *n.* a training ship. **schoolteacher** *n.* a person who teaches in a school. **schoolteaching** *n.* **school time** *n.* **1** lesson time. **2** schooldays. **schoolward** *a., adv.* **schoolwards** *adv.* **schoolwork** *n.* work done at or for school. **school year** *n.* an academic year, usu. from September to the end of July. [A-F *escole*, L *schola*, Gr. *scholē*, rest, leisure, philosophy, lecture-place]

school[2] (skool) *n.* a shoal of fish, porpoises etc. ~*v.i.* to form a school, swim in a school. **schoolfish** *n.* a fish that usually appears in shoals, esp. the menhaden. **schoolwhale** *n.* [Dut., cp. SHOAL[1]]

schooner (skoo'nə) *n.* **1** a vessel with two or more masts with fore-and-aft rigging. **2** (*Hist., N Am.*) a large emigrant-wagon or van. **3** (*N Am., Austral.*) a tall glass for beer or ale. **4** a tall glass for sherry. [etym. uncertain]

schorl (shawl) *n.* black tourmaline. [F, from G *Schörl*]

schottische (shotēsh', shot'ish) *n.* **1** a dance resembling a polka. **2** the music for it. [G, Scottish]

Schottky effect (shot'ki) *n.* (*Physics*) a reduction in the energy required to remove an electron from a solid surface when an electric field is present. [Walter *Schottky*, 1886–1976, German physicist]

schout (skowt) *n.* a municipal officer in the Netherlands and Dutch colonies. [Dut., cogn. with OE *sculthēta*, *scyldhæta*]

Schrödinger equation (shrœ'dingə, shrō'-) *n.* (*Physics*) an equation used in quantum mechanics for the wave function of a particle. [Erwin *Schrödinger*, 1887–1961, Austrian physicist]

schtick, schtik SHTICK.

schtook, schtuck SHTOOK.

schtoom SHTOOM.

schul SHUL.

schuss (shus) *n.* **1** a straight fast ski slope. **2** a run made on this. ~*v.i.* to make such a run. [G, shot]

schwa (shwah, shvah) *n.* **1** a neutral unstressed vowel sound. **2** the symbol ə used to represent this. [G, from Heb. *schĕwā*]

Sci. *abbr.* Science.

sci. *abbr.* science, scientific.

sciagraphy (sīag'rəfi), **skiagraphy** (skī-) *n.* (*pl.* **sciagraphies, skiagraphies**) **1** the art of drawing objects with correct shading. **2** a sciagraph. **3** (*Astron.*) the art of finding the hour by the shadow of the sun, moon, or stars. **4** dialling. **sciagram** (sī'ə-) *n.* **1** the outline of a figure filled in with black, a silhouette. **2** a sciagraph. **sciagraph** (sī'əgrahf) *n.* **1** a photograph by roentgen rays. **2** a vertical section of a building showing the interior. **sciagraphic** (-graf'-), **sciagraphical** *a.* **sciagraphically** *adv.* [F *sciagraphie*, L and Gr. *skiagraphia* (*skia*, shadow, -GRAPHY)]

sciamachy (sīam'əki), **skiamachy** (skī-) *n.* (*pl.* **sciamachies, skiamachies**) **1** (*formal*) a fight with a shadow. **2** a sham fight, a visionary fight. [Gr. *skia*, shadow, *mache*, a fight]

sciascopy (sīas'kəpi), **skiascopy** (skī-) *n.* a method of measuring the refractive power of the eye by projecting light into it from a small mirror, the shadow test. [Gr. *skia*, shadow, -SCOPY]

sciatheric (sīəther'ik), **sciotheric** *a.* of or relating to a sundial. **sciatherically** *adv.* [late Gr. *skiathērikos*, from Gr. *skiathēros*, sundial (*skia*, shadow, *thēran*, to catch)]

sciatic (sīat'ik) *a.* **1** of or relating to the hip. **2** of or affecting the sciatic nerve. **3** of the nature of or affected by sciatica. **sciatica** (-kə) *n.* **1** neuralgia of the hip and thigh. **2** pain in the great sciatic nerve. **sciatically** *adv.* **sciatic nerve** *n.* the nerve that extends from the pelvis down the back of the thigh. [F *sciatique*, late L *sciaticus*, L *ischiadicus*, Gr. *ischiadikos*, from *ischias -ados*, pain in the loins, from *ischion*, socket of the thigh bone]

SCID *abbr.* severe combined immune deficiency.

science (sī'əns) *n.* **1** systematized knowledge about the physical world, developed by observation and experiment. **2** a department of systematized knowledge, a system of facts and principles concerning any subject. **3** a natural science. **4** the pursuit of such knowledge or the principles governing its acquirement. **5** exceptional skill due to knowledge and training, as distinguished from natural ability, esp. in boxing. **6** †knowledge. **to blind someone with science** to overawe someone with esp. spurious knowledge. **science fiction** *n.* fiction dealing with space travel, life on one of the planets etc. **science of self-defence** *n.* boxing or fencing. **science park** *n.* a place where academic scientific research is applied to commercial developments. **sciential** (-en'shəl) *a.* **1** of or producing science. **2** having knowledge. **scientially** *adv.* **scientific** (-tif'-) *a.* **1** of, relating to, used or engaged in science. **2** treating of or devoted to science. **3** made or done according to the principles of science, systematic, exact. **4** (of boxing etc.) skilful, expert. **scientifically** *adv.* **scientism** *n.* **1** scientific methods or attitudes. **2** (belief in) the application of scientific methods to investigate and explain social and psychological phenomena. **scientistic** *a.* **scientist** *n.* a person who studies or is expert in a (physical or natural) science. **Scientology**® (-tol'əji) *n.* a religious movement advocating self-improvement of one's physical and mental condition through psychological and scientific means. **Scientologist** *n.* [F, from L *scientia*, from *scīre*, to know]

scienter (sīen'tə) *adv.* (*Law*) with knowledge, wittingly, deliberately. [L]

sci-fi (sī'fī) *n.* (*coll.*) science fiction.

scil. *abbr.* scilicet.

scilicet (sī'liset, skē'liket) *adv.* to wit, videlicet, namely. [L (*scīre licet*, it is permitted to know)]

scilla (sil'ə) *n.* (*pl.* **scillas**) any plant of the genus *Scilla*, liliaceous plants with bell-shaped flowers. **scillitin** (-itin) *n.* the chemically active principle of *Scilla maritima*. [L, from Gr. *skilla*]

Scillonian (silō'niən) *n.* a native or inhabitant of the Scilly Isles. ~*a.* of or relating to the Scilly Isles.

scimitar (sim'itə) *n.* a short Oriental sword, single-edged, curved and broadest towards the point. [orig. OF *cimiterre*, It. *scimitarra*, prob. from Pers. *shimshīr*]

scincoid (sing'koid) *a.* of, relating to or resembling the Scincidae or skinks. ~*n.* a skinklike lizard. **scincoidian** (-koi'-) *n., a.* [L *scincus*, SKINK, -OID]

scintigraphy (sintig'rəfi) *n.* a diagnostic technique that uses the radiation emitted following administration of a radioactive isotope to produce a picture of an internal body organ. **scintigram** (sin'tigram) *n.* a picture produced by scintigraphy. [*scintil*lation, -GRAPHY]

scintilla (sintil'ə) *n.* (*pl.* **scintillas**) **1** a spark. **2** a trace, hint. **scintillant** *a.* **scintillate** (sin'-) *v.i.* **1** to be brilliantly witty or interesting. **2** to sparkle, to twinkle. **3** to emit sparks. **4** to emit flashes of light when bombarded by electrons, photons etc. **scintillating** *a.* **scintillatingly** *adv.* **scintillation** (-āʹshən) *n.* **scintillation counter** *n.* an instrument for measuring radiation from a source by electronically counting the flashes of light produced by the absorption of radioactive particles by a phosphor. **scintillometer** (-omʹitə) *n.* **1** an instrument attached to a telescope for measuring the amount of scintillation of a star. **2** a scintillation counter. **scintiscan** (sinʹtiskan) *n.* an image or other record showing radioactive traces in the body. [L]

sciography (sīogʹrəfi) *n.* (*pl.* **sciographies**) sciagraphy.

sciolist (sīʹəlist) *n.* a person who knows many things superficially, a pretender to knowledge. **sciolism** *n.* **sciolistic** (-lisʹ-) *a.* [L *sciolus*, smatterer, dim. of *scius*, knowing, from *scīre*, to know]

sciolto (sholʹtō) *adv.* (*Mus.*) **1** freely, to one's taste. **2** staccato. [It.]

sciomachy (sīomʹəki) *n.* (*pl.* **sciomachies**) sciamachy.

sciomancy (sīʹəmansi) *n.* divination through the shades of the dead. **sciomantic** (-manʹ-) *a.* [Gr. *skia*, shadow, -MANCY]

scion (sīʹən) *n.* **1** (*N Am. also* **cion**) a shoot, esp. for grafting or planting. **2** a descendant, a child. [F, perh. from *scier*, to saw, L *secāre*, to cut]

sciotheric SCIATHERIC.

scire facias (sīəri fāʹshias) *n.* (*Law*) a writ to enforce the execution of or annul judgements etc. [L, make (him) to know]

scirocco SIROCCO.

scirrhus (sirʹəs, skirʹ-) *n.* (*pl.* **scirrhi** (-ī)) a hard (cancerous) tumour. **scirrhoid** (-oid), **scirrhous** *a.* **scirrhosity** (-osʹ-) *n.* [late L, from Gr. *skirros*, *skīros*, hardened swelling, from *skiros*, hard]

scissel (sisʹəl) *n.* **1** metal clippings. **2** the remainder of plates after discs have been punched out in coining. [F *cisaille*, from *ciseler*, to CHISEL]

scissile (sisʹīl) *a.* that may be cut. **scission** (sishʹən) *n.* **1** the act of cutting or dividing. **2** a division, separation or split. [L *scissilis*, from *scindere*, to cut, p.p. *scissus*]

scissors (sizʹəz) *n.pl.* **1** a cutting instrument consisting of two blades pivoted together that cut objects placed between them; also called *pair of scissors*. **2** a gymnastic movement in which the legs open and close with a scissor-like action. **3** a scissors hold. **scissor** *v.t.* **1** to cut with scissors. **2** to clip or cut (out) with scissors. **scissor-beak, scissor-bill** *n.* a skimmer, a bird of the genus *Rhynchops*. **scissor-bird, scissor-tail** *n.* a N American fork-tailed flycatcher, *Tyrannus forficatus*. **scissoring** *n.* **scissors-and-paste** *a.* of compilation, as distinguished from original literary work. **scissors and paste** *n.* **scissors-grinder** *n.* (*Austral.*) a kind of flycatcher. **scissors hold** *n.* a wrestling hold in which the legs lock round the opponent's head or body. **scissors kick** *n.* a swimming kick in which the legs move in a scissor-like action. **scissor-tooth** *n.* a tooth working against another like a scissor-blade, in certain carnivores. **scissorwise** *adv.* [ME *sisoures*, OF *cisoires*, L *cīsorium*, from *cīs-*, *caes-*, p.p. stem of *caedere*, to cut]

scissure SCISSILE.

sciurine (sīʹūrin, -rīn) *a.* **1** of, relating to or resembling the family Sciuridae, the squirrel family. **2** squirrel-like. ~*n.* a squirrel. **sciuroid** (-roid) *a.* [L *sciūrus*, Gr. *skiouros* (*skia*, shadow, *oura*, tail)]

scler- SCLERO-.

sclera (skliəʹrə) *n.* the white of the eye; the sclerotic. **scleral** *a.* **scleritis** (sklərīʹtis) *n.* sclerotitis.

sclerenchyma (sklərengʹkimə) *n.* **1** the strong tissue forming the hard or fibrous parts of plants, such as the walls of nuts and fruit-stones, leaf midribs etc. **2** the calcareous tissue in coral. **sclerenchymatous** (-kimʹətəs) *a.* [Gr. *enchuma*, infusion, see PARENCHYMA]

scleriasis (sklərīʹəsis) *n.* hardening or induration of tissue.

sclerite (skliəʹrīt) *n.* any one of the definite component parts of the hard integument of various invertebrates. **scleritic** (-ritʹ-) *a.*

scleritis SCLERA.

sclero- (sklerʹō), **scler-** *comb. form* **1** hard, dry. **2** sclerotic. [Gr. *sklēros*]

scleroderm (sklerʹədœm) *n.* **1** a hardened integument or exoskeleton, esp. of corals. **2** a fish of the family Sclerodermi, having hard scales. **scleroderma** (-dœʹ-), **sclerodermia** (-miə) *n.* a chronic induration of the skin. **sclerodermatous** (-dœʹ-), **sclerodermic** *a.* **sclerodermite** (-dœʹmīt) *n.* any of the hard segments of the body in crustaceans. **sclerodermitic** (-mitʹ-) *a.*

sclerogen (skliəʹrəjən) *n.* the hard matter deposited in the cells of certain plants, as the ivory-nut. **sclerogenous** (skləroj´-) *a.*

scleroid (skliəʹroid) *a.* (*Bot., Zool.*) hard in texture.

scleroma (sklərōʹmə) *n.* (*pl.* **scleromata** (-tə)) hardening of cellular tissue, scleriasis.

sclerometer (skliəromʹitə, sklər-) *n.* an instrument for determining the hardness of a mineral or a metal.

sclerophyll (skliəʹrəfil) *n.* any woody plant with leathery leaves. **sclerophyllous** (-rofʹ-) *a.*

scleroprotein (skliərōprōʹtēn) *n.* an insoluble protein, such as keratin, forming the skeletal tissues of the body.

sclerosis (sklərōʹsis) *n.* (*pl.* **scleroses** (-ōʹsēz)) **1** hardening of a plant cell wall by the deposit of sclerogen. **2** thickening or hardening of a body tissue. **3** MULTIPLE SCLEROSIS (under MULTIPLE). **sclerosed** (skliəʹrōzd) *a.*

scleroskeleton (skliərōskelʹitən) *n.* the skeletal parts resulting from ossification of tendons, ligaments etc. **scleroskeletal** *a.*

sclerotia SCLEROTIUM.

sclerotic (sklərotʹik) *a.* **1** (of the outer coat or tunic of the eye) hard, indurated. **2** of or affected with sclerosis. ~*n.* **1** the firm white membrane forming the outer coat of the eye, the white of the eye. **2** a medicine hardening the parts to which it is applied. **sclerotal** (-ōʹtəl) *n.* **1** any of the bony plates of the sclerotic coat in some birds and reptiles. **2** the sclerotic. ~*a.* **1** of or relating to the sclerotal of a bird or reptile. **2** sclerotic. **sclerotitis** (skliərətīʹtis) *n.* inflammation of the sclerotic. **sclerotized** (skliərʹətīzd), **sclerotised** *a.* (esp. of the insect exoskeleton) hardened, indurated. **sclerotization** (-āʹshən) *n.* **sclerotome** (skliəʹrətōm) *n.* a knife used in cutting the sclerotic coat of the eye. **sclerotomy** (sklərotʹəmi) *n.* (*pl.* **sclerotomies**) surgical incision into the sclera.

sclerotium (sklərōʹshiəm) *n.* (*pl.* **sclerotia** (-shiə)) **1** a compact tuberous mass formed on the mycelium of certain higher fungi, such as ergot. **2** a cystlike part of a plasmodium in the Mycetozoa. **sclerotial** *a.* **sclerotioid** (-oid) *a.* resembling a sclerotium.

sclerotized, sclerotome etc. SCLEROTIC.

sclerous (skliəʹrəs) *a.* hard, indurated, ossified.

SCM *abbr.* **1** State Certified Midwife. **2** Student Christian Movement.

scoff[1] (skof) *v.i.* to speak in derision or mockery, to mock or jeer (at). ~*n.* **1** an expression of contempt, derision or mockery. **2** a gibe, a taunt. **3** an object of derision, a laughing stock. **scoffer** *n.* **scoffingly** *adv.* [prob. from Scand. (cp. MDan. *skof*, Icel. *skaup*, also OFris. *schof*, MDut. *schobben*), perh. rel. to SHOVE]

scoff[2] (skof) *v.t.* (*coll.*) to eat ravenously. ~*n.* food. [Afrikaans]

scold (skōld) *v.i.* **1** to find fault noisily or angrily. **2** to rail (at). ~*v.t.* **1** to chide or find fault with noisily or angrily. **2** to chide, to rate, to rail at. ~*n.* **1** †a noisy, railing, nagging woman. **2** a scolding. **scolder** *n.* **scolding** *a.*, *n.* **scoldingly** *adv.* [ME *scolden*, cp. Dut. *schelden*, G *schelten*, OFris. *skelda*]

scolex (skōʹleks) *n.* (*pl.* **scoleces** (-lēʹsēz), **scolices** (-lisēz)) **1** the larva or embryo in metagenesis. **2** the head of the larval or adult tapeworm. **scoleciform**

(-sifawm), **scolecoid** (-koid) *a.* **scolecite** (-sīt) *n.* 1 the vermiform body formed in the fructification of some fungi. 2 a hydrous silicate mineral of aluminium and calcium. [Gr. *skōlēx*, worm]

scoliosis (skoliō´sis) *n.* lateral curvature of the spine. **scoliotic** (-ot´-) *a.* [Gr. *skoliōsis*, from *skolios*, bent]

scollop SCALLOP.

scolopendrid (skolәpen´drid) *n.* any centipede of the family Scolopendridae. **scolopendra** (-pen´drә) *n.* a fabulous marine animal. **scolopendrine** (-drīn, -drin) *a.* [L and Gr. *skolopendra*, legendary sea fish]

scolopendrium (skolәpen´driәm) *n.* any of a genus of ferns containing the hart's tongue, *Phyllitis scolopendrium*. [L, from Gr. *skolopendrion*, from a supposed resemblance to a centipede]

scombroid (skom´broid) *n.* any marine fish of the family Scombridae or the superfamily Scombroidea including the mackerels, tunas and swordfishes. *~a.* of or belonging to the Scombridae or Scombroidea. **scombrid** (-brid) *n.* [L, from Gr. *skombros*]

sconce[1] (skons) *n.* 1 a flat candlestick with a handle. 2 a candleholder fixed to a wall. 3 the socket of a candlestick into which the candle is inserted. [OF *esconse*, hiding place, concealed light, dark-lantern, L *absconsa*, fem. of *-sus*, var. of *absconditus*, p.p. of *abscondere*, to hide]

sconce[2] (skons) *n.* 1 a blockhouse, a bulwark, a small detached fort. 2 †a shelter, a covering, a shed. *~v.t.* to fortify with a sconce. [Dut. *schans*]

†**sconce**[3] (skons) *n.* a fine at Oxford or Cambridge University for a light offence. *~v.t.* to exact such a fine from. [etym. unknown]

scone (skon, skōn) *n.* 1 a soft plain cake, usu. in small round or triangular pieces, cooked on a griddle or in an oven. 2 (*Austral., sl.*) the head. **off one's scone** 1 (*Austral., sl.*) angry. 2 (*Austral., sl.*) insane. [cp. MDan. *skon-roggen*, muffin of bolted rye flour (LG *schön*, fine, *Roggen*, rye)]

scoop (skoop) *n.* 1 a short-handled shovel-like implement for drawing together, lifting and moving loose material such as coal, grain, sugar, potatoes etc. 2 a large ladle or dipping-vessel. 3 a gougelike implement used by grocers, surgeons etc. or for spooning out shaped pieces of ice cream or other soft food. 4 the bucket of a dredging machine. 5 a coal scuttle. 6 the act or movement of scooping. 7 the amount scooped at once. 8 a large profit made in a speculation or competitive transaction. 9 the publication or broadcasting of a piece of sensational news in advance of rival newspapers etc. 10 a news item so published. 11 (*Mus.*) a singer's exaggerated portamento. 12 a scooped-out hollow etc. *~v.t.* 1 to ladle or dip (out) or to hollow (out) with a scoop. 2 to lift (up) with a scoop. 3 to scrape, gouge or hollow (out). 4 to gain (a large profit) by a deal etc. 5 to forestall (rival newspapers etc.) with a piece of sensational news. **to scoop the pool** POOL[2]. **scooper** *n.* 1 a person who or thing which scoops. 2 a tool used by engravers. **scoopful** *n.* (*pl.* **scoopfuls**). **scoop neck** *n.* a rounded low neckline on a garment. **scoop-net** *n.* a net so formed as to sweep the bottom of a river etc. **scoop-wheel** *n.* a wheel with buckets round it used to raise water or for dredging. [perh. through OF *escope*, from Swed. *skopa*, or MDut. *schōpe*, bailing-vessel, or MDut. *schoppe* (Dut. *schop*), shovel, cp. G *schöpfen*, to draw water]

scoot (skoot) *v.i.* (*coll.*) to dart off, bolt, to scurry away. *~n.* the act or an instance of scooting. **scooter** *n.* 1 a two-wheeled toy vehicle on which a child can ride with one foot, propelling with the other. 2 a larger, motorized two-wheeled vehicle with a seat. 3 (*N Am.*) a sailboat that can travel on water or ice. *~v.i.* to travel or ride on a scooter. **scooterist** *n.* a rider on a scooter. [var. of SHOOT]

scopa (skō´pә) *n.* (*pl.* **scopae** (-pē)) a brushlike tuft of bristly hairs as on the legs of bees. **scopate** (-pāt) *a.* 1 brush-shaped. 2 covered with brushlike hairs. **scopiform** (-fawm) *a.* brush-shaped. **scopiped** (-ped) *a.* (of certain bees) having a brushlike contrivance on the hind legs for collecting pollen. **scopula** (skop´ūlә) *n.* (*pl.* **scopulas, scopulae** (-lē)) a small brushlike tuft on the legs of bees and spiders, a scopa. **scopulate** (skop´ūlәt) *a.* **scopuliform** (-pū´lifawm) *a.* [L, in pl., twigs]

scope[1] (skōp) *n.* 1 range of action or observation, outlook, reach, sphere. 2 extent of or room for activity, development etc. 3 outlet, opportunity, vent. 4 (*Naut.*) the length of cable at which a vessel rides. 5 †end, aim, purpose or intention. **scopeless** *a.* [prob. through It. *scopo*, from Gr. *skopos*, a watcher, a mark, rel. to *skeptesthai*, to look out]

scope[2] (skōp) *n.* (*coll.*) a periscope, telescope, oscilloscope etc.

-scope (skōp) *comb. form* denoting an instrument of observation etc., as in *microscope, spectroscope*. **-scopic** (skop´ik) *comb. form* of or relating to this or to observation etc., as in *microscopic, spectroscopic*. **-scopy** (skәpi) *comb. form* observation by the instrument etc., specified, as in *microscopy, spectroscopy*. [Gr. *skopos*, see SCOPE[1]]

scopelid (skop´әlid) *n.* a fish of the deep-water, teleostean group Scopelidae. **scopeloid** (-loid) *a., n.* [Gr. *skopelos*, a rock, -ID]

-scopic -SCOPE.

scopiform, scopiped SCOPA.

scopolamine (skәpol´әmēn) *n.* hyoscine hydrobromide, a hypnotic drug used, among other purposes, with morphine for producing twilight sleep. [*Scopolia*, genus of plants yielding this, from G. A. *Scopoli*, 1723–88, Italian naturalist, AMINE]

scops owl (skops) *n.* an owl of the genus *Scops*, having erect tufts of feathers on the side of the head. **scops-eared** *a.* [Gr. *skōps*]

scopula, scopulate etc. SCOPA.

-scopy -SCOPE.

scorbutic (skawbū´tik) *a.* of, relating to, like or affected with scurvy. *~n.* a person affected with scurvy. **scorbutically** *adv.* [obs. *scorbute* (F *scorbut*), low L *scorbūtus*, scurvy, prob. from LG, cp. SCURF]

scorch (skawch) *v.t.* 1 to burn the outside of so as to injure or discolour without consuming, to singe, to parch, to dry or shrivel (up). 2 to affect harmfully with or as with heat. 3 to criticize or censure severely. *~v.i.* 1 to be parched, singed or dried up with or as with heat. 2 (*coll.*) to go at an excessive rate of speed. *~n.* 1 a burn or mark caused by scorching. 2 (*coll.*) an act or spell of scorching. **scorched** *a.* **scorched earth** *n.* the destruction of everything in a country that might be of service to an invading army. **scorched earth policy** *n.* **scorcher** *n.* 1 a person who or thing which scorches. 2 an extremely hot day. 3 (*coll.*) a striking or staggering example, a stunner. **scorching** *a.* **scorchingly** *adv.* [OF *escorcher*, late L *excorticāre* (EX-, L *cortex -ticis*, bark)]

scordato (skawdah´tō) *a.* (*Mus.*) put out of tune. **scordatura** (-too´rә) *n.* (*pl.* **scordature** (-rā)) an intentional departure from normal tuning to secure special effects. [It., from *scordare*, to be out of tune, for *discordare*, see DISCORD[1]]

score (skaw) *n.* 1 the points made by a player or side at any moment in, or in total in certain games and contests. 2 the record of this. 3 the act of gaining a point in a game or contest. 4 (*pl.* **score, scores**) twenty, a set of twenty. 5 (*pl.*) large numbers. 6 account, category, reason. 7 a copy of a musical work in which all the component parts are shown, either fully or in a compressed form, so called from the line orig. drawn through all the staves. 8 the music for a film, play etc.

9 the notation for a choreographed work. 10 (*sl.*) a remark etc. in which one scores off another person. 11 (*coll.*) the situation, the facts. 12 a scratch, incision. 13 an account, a bill, a debt. 14 a reckoning orig. kept on a tally, esp. a running account for liquor marked up against a customer's name at a tavern. 15 (*Naut.*) a groove in a block etc., for receiving a strap. 16 a notch or mark on a tally. 17 anything laid up or recorded against one, a grudge. 18 a mark from which a race starts, competitors fire in a shooting match etc. 19 a weight of 20 or 21 lb. (about 9 or 9.5 kg) used in weighing pigs and cattle. 20 a line drawn or scratched through writing etc. ~*v.t.* 1 to gain (a point, a win etc.) in a game or contest. 2 to count for a score of (points etc.). 3 to mark (up) or enter in a score. 4 to mark with notches, cuts, scratches, lines etc. 5 to orchestrate. 6 to arrange for an instrument. 7 to prepare the sound script for (a film). 8 to arrange in score. 9 to gash, to groove, to furrow. 10 to make or mark (lines etc.). 11 to mark (out) with lines. 12 to mentally record (an offence etc.). 13 (*N Am.*) to criticize severely. ~*v.i.* 1 to win points, advantages etc. 2 to keep a score. 3 (*sl.*) to obtain illegal drugs. 4 (*sl.*) to successfully seduce someone into having sexual intercourse. **on that score** so far as that is concerned. **on the score of** for the reason that; because of. **to keep (the) score** to record the score during a game etc. **to know the score** KNOW. **to pay off old scores** to pay someone out or have revenge for an offence of old standing. **to quit scores** QUIT. **to run up a score** to run up a debt. **to score a hit (with)** HIT. **to score an own goal** OWN[1]. **to score off** 1 (*coll.*) to get the better of. 2 (*coll.*) to triumph over in argument, repartee etc. **to score out** to cross out, cancel. **to score points** to outdo someone else; make a better impression. **to score points off** to get the better of in an argument. **to score under** to underline. **to settle old scores** to pay off old scores. **scoreboard** *n.* a board on which the score at any point in a game or contest is displayed. **scorebook** *n.* a book for recording the score in a game. **scorecard** *n.* **score draw** *n.* a draw in football in which goals are scored. **scoreless** *a.* **scoreline** *n.* a score in a match etc. **scorer** *n.* **scoresheet** *n.* **scoring** *n.* [OE *scor*, twenty, Icel. *skor*, twenty, notch, cogn. with SHEAR]

scoria (skaw´riə) *n.* (*pl.* **scoriae** (-riē)) 1 cellular lava or ashes. 2 the refuse of fused metals, dross. **scoriaceous** (-ā´shəs), **scoriform** (-fawm) *a.* **scorify** (-rifī) *v.t.* (*3rd pers. sing. pres.* **scorifies,** *pres.p.* **scorifying,** *past, p.p.* **scorified**) 1 to reduce to dross. 2 to assay (metal) by fusing its ore in a scorifier with lead and borax. **scorification** (-fikā´shən) *n.* **scorifier** *n.* [L, from Gr. *skōria*, refuse, from *skōr*, dung]

scorn (skawn) *n.* 1 contempt, disdain. 2 mockery, derision. 3 a subject or object of extreme contempt. ~*v.t.* 1 to hold in extreme contempt or disdain. 2 to regard as unworthy, paltry or mean. **to laugh to scorn** LAUGH. **to pour scorn on** to express contempt or disdain for. †**to think scorn of** to despise or disdain. **scorner** *n.* **scornful** *a.* **scornfully** *adv.* **scornfulness** *n.* [from ME *scorn*, OF *escorne*, perh. from *escorner*, to deprive of horns (EX-, L *cornu*, horn), or ME *scarn*, OF *escarn*, OHG *Skern*, mockery, sport]

scorodite (skor´ədīt) *n.* a mineral consisting of a native arsenate of iron. [G *Skorodit*, from Gr. *skorodon*, garlic]

scorpaenid (skawpē´nid) *n.* any spiny-finned fish of the family Scorpaenidae, including the scorpion fishes. **scorpaenoid** (-noid) *a., n.* [mod. L, from Gr. *skorpaina*, prob. from *skorpios*, SCORPION]

scorper (skaw´pə) *n.* a gouging-tool for working in concave surfaces in wood, metal or jewellery. [var. of SCAUPER]

Scorpio (skaw´piō) *n.* (*pl.* **Scorpios**) 1 (*usu.* **Scorpius**) a zodiacal constellation. 2 the eighth sign of the zodiac. 3 a person born under this sign. **Scorpian** *a., n.*

scorpioid (-oid) *a.* 1 (*Bot.*) curled up like the end of a scorpion's tail and uncurling as the flowers develop. 2 of, relating to or resembling a scorpion. ~*n.* a scorpioid inflorescence. [as SCORPION]

scorpion (skaw´piən) *n.* 1 an arachnid of the order Scorpiones, with claws like a lobster and a sting in the jointed tail. 2 a smaller, similar arachnid of the order Pseudoscorpiones, a false scorpion. 3 the constellation Scorpio. 4 the zodiacal sign Scorpio. 5 (*Bible*) a whip armed with points of iron. 6 a form of ballista. **scorpion fish** *n.* any of various marine fish of the family Scorpaenidae. **scorpion fly** *n.* any insect of the order Mecoptera, esp. of the genus *Panorpa*, named from the forceps-like point of the abdomen. **scorpion grass, scorpion wort** *n.* the myosotis or forget-me-not. **scorpion plant** *n.* 1 a Javan orchid with large spider-like flowers. 2 scorpion broom. [L *scorpiōnem*, nom. *-pio*, Gr. *skorpios*]

Scorpius SCORPIO.

scorzonera (skawzəniə´rə) *n.* 1 a plant of the family *Scorzonera hispanica* with long tapering roots. 2 this root eaten as a vegetable. [It., perh. from *scorzone*, a snake]

Scot (skot) *n.* 1 a native of Scotland. 2 a person of Scottish descent. 3 (*Hist.*) a member of a Gaelic people migrating to Scotland from Ireland in the 5th or 6th cent. [OE *Scottas*, pl.]

Scot. *abbr.* Scotland, Scottish.

scot (skot) *n.* (*Hist.*) a payment, an assessment, a tax. **scot and lot** *n.* a town or parish tax levied according to ability to pay. **to pay scot and lot** to settle outstanding accounts, obligations etc. **scot-free** *a.* 1 unhurt, safe. 2 unpunished. 3 free from payment, untaxed. [OF *escot*, Icel. *skot*, cp. OE *sceot*, Dut. *schot*, G *Schoss*, SHOT[1]]

Scotch (skoch) *a.* Scottish. ~*n.* 1 (Scotch) whisky. 2 a drink of this. 3 the Scots. **Scotch barley** *n.* pot or husked barley. **Scotch bonnet** *n.* a round, flat woollen cap, like a beret, with a tassel in the middle; also called *Lowland bonnet*. **Scotch broth** *n.* a clear broth containing barley and chopped vegetables. **Scotch cap** *n.* a brimless woollen cap, either a balmoral or a glengarry. **Scotch catch, Scotch snap** *n.* a short note followed by a long note in two played to the same beat. **Scotch egg** *n.* a hard-boiled egg encased in sausage meat and breadcrumbs. **Scotch fir** *n.* the Scots pine. **Scotchman** *n.* (*pl.* **Scotchmen**) a Scotsman. **Scotchman grass** *n.* (*New Zeal.*) a variety of grass with sharp points. **Scotch mist** *n.* 1 a wet dense mist. 2 fine drizzle. 3 a retort made to someone who hasn't understood something. **Scotchness** *n.* **Scotch pancake** *n.* a drop scone. **Scotch pebble** *n.* agate, jasper, cairngorm etc. found in Scotland. **Scotch snap** SCOTCH CATCH (under SCOTCH). **Scotch tape®** *n.* adhesive transparent tape. **Scotch terrier** *n.* a Scottish terrier. **Scotch thistle** *n.* any of various thistles regarded as the Scottish national emblem, esp. *Carduus lanceolatus* or *C. nutans.* **Scotch whisky** *n.* whisky distilled in Scotland. **Scotchwoman** *n.* (*pl.* **Scotchwomen**) a Scotswoman. **Scotch woodcock** *n.* hot toast with anchovy paste and scrambled eggs on top.

Usage note The use of *Scotch* other than of whisky or in the established compounds above can offend Scots: *Scottish* and *Scots* are acceptable alternatives.

scotch[1] (skoch) *v.t.* 1 to put an end to, frustrate. 2 †to wound slightly, to cripple, to disable. 3 †to cut with narrow incisions. ~*n.* 1 †a slight cut or incision. 2 a mark for hopping from, as in the game of hopscotch. [ME *scocche*, prob. from SCORE]

scotch[2] (skoch) *n.* a block for a wheel or other round object. ~*v.t.* 1 to block, wedge or prop (a wheel, barrel etc.) to prevent rolling. 2 to frustrate (a plan etc.). [etym. uncertain]

scoter (skō´tə) *n.* (*pl.* **scoter, scoters**) a large sea duck of the genus *Melanitta.* [etym. uncertain]

scotia (skō´shə) *n.* a hollow moulding in the base of a column. [Gr. *skotia*, darkness, cp. SCOTO-]

Scotice (skot´isi) *adv.* in a or the Scottish manner.

Scoticism SCOTTICISM (under SCOTTISH).

Scoticize SCOTTICIZE (under SCOTTISH).

Scotism (skō´tizm) *n.* the scholastic philosophy of Johannes Duns Scotus, *c.* 1265–1308. **Scotist** *a., n.*

Scotland Yard (skot´lənd) *n.* **1** the headquarters of the London Metropolitan Police. **2** the Criminal Investigation Department of the police. **3** police detectives. [locality in London]

scoto- (skot´ō) *comb. form* dark, dullness. [Gr. *skotos*]

scotodinia (skotōdin´iə) *n.* dizziness, vertigo, with dimness of vision.

scotograph (skot´əgrahf) *n.* an instrument for writing in the dark or by the blind.

scotoma (skotō´mə) *n.* (*pl.* **scotomas, scotomata** (-tə)) **1** a blind spot in the field of vision. **2** dizziness or swimming of the head with dimness of sight. **scotomatous** (-tom´-, -tō´-) *a.*

scotoscope (skot´əskōp) *n.* a telescope enabling one to see objects at night.

Scots (skots) *a.* Scottish (applied to the people, language and law). *~n.* **1** the form of the English language used in Scotland. **2** the people of Scotland. **Scots fir** *n.* a Scots pine. **Scotsman, Scotswoman** *n.* (*pl.* **Scotsmen, Scotswomen**). **Scots pine** *n.* a European pine, *Pinus sylvestris*, prob. indigenous in N Britain. [ME *Scottis*, Scottish]

Scottish (skot´ish) *a.* of or relating to Scotland or its people. *~n.* **1** the Scots language. **2** (*as pl.*) the people of Scotland. **Scotticism** (-sizm), **Scoticism** *n.* a Scottish idiom. **Scotticize, Scoticize, Scotticise** *v.t.* to make Scottish. *~v.i.* to imitate the Scottish. **Scottie, Scotty** *n.* (*pl.* **Scotties**) (*coll.*) **1** a nickname for a Scotsman. **2** (*also* **Scottie dog**) a Scottish terrier. **Scottify** (-fī) *v.t.* (*3rd pers. sing. pres.* **Scottifies,** *pres.p.* **Scottifying,** *past, p.p.* **Scottified**) to make Scottish. **Scottishness** *n.* **Scottish terrier** *n.* a breed of small terrier with short legs and a rough coat. [ME *Scottes*]

scoundrel (skown´drəl) *n.* an unprincipled person, a rogue, a rascal, a villain. *~a.* base, villainous, unprincipled. **scoundreldom, scoundrelism** *n.* **scoundrelly** *a.* [etym. unknown]

scour[1] (skow´ə) *v.t.* **1** to clean, polish or brighten by friction. **2** to remove or clean (away, off etc.) by rubbing. **3** to flush or clear out. **4** (of water etc.) to pass swiftly through or over. **5** (*Hist.*) to purge violently. *~v.i.* **1** to clean. **2** to be scoured or cleaned (well, easily etc.). **3** to be purged to excess. **4** (of cattle etc.) to have diarrhoea. *~n.* **1** scouring. **2** a swift, deep current. **3** a rapid. **4** the clearing action of this. **5** dysentery in cattle etc. **6** a cleanser for various fabrics. **scourer** *n.* **scouring** *n.* **scouring pad** *n.* an abrasive pad used for cleaning pans etc. **scouring powder** *n.* an abrasive powder used esp. in the kitchen. **scouring-rush** *n.* any of various horsetails, esp. *Equisetum hyemale*, formerly used for scouring and polishing. [prob. through MDut. *schūren*, OF *escurer*, pop. L *excūrāre* (EX-, *cūrāre*, to CURE)]

scour[2] (skow´ə) *v.i.* **1** to rove, to range. **2** to skim, to scurry. **3** to search about. *~v.t.* **1** to move rapidly over, esp. in search. **2** to search thoroughly. [OF *escourre*, L *excurrere* (EX-; *currere*, to run)]

scourge (skœj) *n.* **1** a whip with thongs used as an instrument of punishment. **2** any means of inflicting punishment, vengeance or suffering. **3** a pestilence or plague. *~v.t.* **1** to whip with or as with a scourge. **2** to afflict, to harass, to chastise. **scourger** *n.* [A-F *escorge* (F *écourgée*), ult. from L *excoriāre*, to strip the skin off (EX-, *corium*, hide)]

Scouse (skows) *n.* **1** the dialect of Liverpool. **2** (*also* **Scouser**) a native or inhabitant of Liverpool. **3** (**scouse**) LOBSCOUSE. *~a.* of or relating to Liverpool. [short for LOBSCOUSE]

scout[1] (skowt) *n.* **1** a person sent out to bring in information, esp. one employed to watch the movements etc. of an enemy. **2** a person employed to search for people with talent in a particular field, new sales markets etc. **3** the act of watching or bringing in such information. **4** a scouting expedition. **5** (**Scout**) a member of an organization, established in Great Britain by Lord Baden-Powell in 1908 and now worldwide, intended to train and develop qualities of leadership, responsibility etc., orig. in boys. **6** a domestic worker at an Oxford college. **7** †a person, a fellow. **8** a ship or aircraft used for reconnaissance. *~v.t.* (*coll.*) to explore to get information about. *~v.i.* **1** to act as a scout. **2** to make a search. **Boy Scout** BOY. **scout car** *n.* an armoured car used for reconnaissance. **Scouter** *n.* an adult leader of Scouts. **scouter** *n.* **Scouting** *n.* **scouting** *n.* **Scoutmaster** *n.* **1** the leader of a group of Scouts. **2** (*Hist.*) a person in charge of a troop of scouts. [OF *éscoute*, eavesdropper, from *escouter* (F *écouter*), to listen, L *auscultāre*, see AUSCULTATION]

scout[2] (skowt) *v.t.* to treat with contempt and disdain, to reject contemptuously. [perh. from Scand. (cp. Icel. *skuti*, a taunt, rel. to *skjōta*, to SHOOT)]

scow (skow) *n.* a large flat-bottomed, square-ended boat. *~v.t.* to transport in a scow. [Dut. *schouw*]

scowl (skowl) *v.i.* **1** to frown, to look sullen or ill-tempered. **2** to have a threatening aspect. *~n.* **1** an angry frown. **2** a look of sullenness, ill-temper or discontent. **scowler** *n.* **scowlingly** *adv.* [ME *scoulen*, Dan. *skule*, cp. Icel. *skolla*, to skulk]

SCP *abbr.* single-cell protein.

SCPS *abbr.* Society of Civil and Public Servants.

SCR *abbr.* **1** senior common (combination) room. **2** silicon-controlled rectifier.

scr. *abbr.* scruple(s) (of weight).

scrabble (skrab´əl) *v.i.* **1** to scrape, scratch or grope (about) as if to obtain something. **2** to scramble. **3** to scrawl, to scribble. **4** to make irregular or unmeaning marks. *~v.t.* to scribble on or over. *~n.* **1** a scramble, struggle. **2** a scribble, scrawl. **3** a scratching or scraping. **Scrabble®** *n.* a word-building board game. **Scrabbler** *n.* (*coll.*) a person who plays Scrabble. [var. of *scrapple*, freq. of SCRAPE]

scrag (skrag) *n.* **1** a lean or bony piece of meat, esp. the lean end of neck of mutton. **2** a lean or bony person or animal. **3** anything thin, lean or shrivelled. **4** (*coll.*) a person's neck. *~v.t.* (*pres.p.* **scragging,** *past, p.p.* **scragged**) (*sl.*) **1** to wring the neck of, to throttle. **2** to kill by hanging. **3** in football, to tackle by the neck. **4** to handle roughly; beat up. **scrag-end** *n.* the scrag of a neck, esp. of mutton. **scragged** *a.* **scraggedness** (-gid-) *n.* **scraggy** *a.* (*comp.* **scraggier,** *superl.* **scraggiest**). **scraggily** *adv.* **scragginess** *n.* **scrag-necked** *a.* having a long, thin neck. [cp. Norw. *skragg*, a poor creature, Dan. *skrog*, carcass, a poor creature, NFris. *skrog*, a lean man]

scraggly (skrag´li) *a.* (*comp.* **scragglier,** *superl.* **scraggliest**) sparse and irregular.

scram (skram) *int.* (*coll.*) get out of it! go away! [SCRAMBLE]

scramble (skram´bəl) *v.i.* **1** to climb or move along by clambering, crawling, wriggling etc., esp. with the hands and knees. **2** to move with urgent or disorderly haste. **3** to seek or struggle (for, after etc.) in a rough-and-tumble or eager manner. **4** to climb or spread irregularly. **5** (of an aircraft or its crew) to take off immediately. *~v.t.* **1** to put or collect together hurriedly or haphazardly. **2** to mix or jumble up. **3** to prepare (eggs) by breaking into a pan and stirring up during cooking. **4** to order (an aircraft or crew) to scramble.

5 to make (a radiotelephonic conversation) unintelligible without a decoding receiver by altering the frequencies. 6 (*coll.*) to execute (an action etc.) inefficiently. ~*n.* 1 the act of scrambling. 2 a climb or walk over rocks etc., or in a rough-and-tumble manner. 3 a rough or unceremonious struggle for something. 4 an emergency take-off of fighter aircraft. 5 a motorcycle race over rough ground. **scrambled egg** *n.* 1 a dish of eggs cooked by scrambling. 2 (*coll.*) gold embroidery on a military officer's cap. **scrambler** *n.* 1 a person who scrambles. 2 an electronic device for scrambling speech transmitted by radio or telephone. 3 a motorcycle for racing over rough ground. 4 a plant with long weak shoots which it uses to climb over other plants. [prob. var. of SCRABBLE]

scran (skran) *n.* (*dial. or sl.*) 1 (leftover) food. 2 scraps, refuse. ~*v.t.* (*pres.p.* **scranning,** *past, p.p.* **scranned**) to collect or gather up scran. **bad scran to you!** (*Ir.*) bad luck to you! [etym. uncertain]

scrap[1] (skrap) *n.* 1 a small detached piece, a bit, a fragment. 2 a picture, paragraph etc., cut from a newspaper etc., for preservation. 3 refuse, waste, esp. old pieces of discarded metal collected for melting down etc. 4 (*pl.*) bits, odds-and-ends, leavings. 5 (*pl.*) leftover fragments of food. 6 (*usu. pl.*) refuse of fat from which the oil has been expressed. ~*v.t.* (*pres.p.* **scrapping,** *past, p.p.* **scrapped**) 1 to make scrap of, to consign to the scrap heap. 2 to condemn and discard as worn out, obsolete etc. **scrapbook** *n.* a blank book into which pictures, cuttings from newspapers etc. are pasted for preservation. **scrap-cake** *n.* fish scrap compressed into cakes. **scrap heap** *n.* 1 a heap of scrap metal. 2 a rubbish heap. **on the scrap heap** no longer useful. **scrap iron, scrap metal** *n.* discarded metal for reprocessing. **scrap merchant** *n.* a dealer in scrap. **scrappy** *a.* (*comp.* **scrappier,** *superl.* **scrappiest**) 1 consisting or made up of scraps. 2 disconnected. **scrappily** *adv.* **scrappiness** *n.* **scrapyard** *n.* a place where scrap, esp. scrap metal, is collected or stored. [Icel. *skrap,* SCRAPE]

scrap[2] (skrap) *n.* (*coll.*) a fight, a scuffle, a dispute. ~*v.i.* (*pres.p.* **scrapping,** *past, p.p.* **scrapped**) to engage in a fight. **scrapper** *n.* **scrapping-match** *n.* [etym. uncertain]

scrape (skrāp) *v.t.* 1 to rub the surface of with something rough or sharp. 2 to abrade, smooth or shave (a surface) thus. 3 to remove, to clean (off, out etc.) thus. 4 to erase. 5 to rub or scratch (out). 6 to excavate or hollow (out) by scraping. 7 to rub against with a rasping or grating noise. 8 to draw or rub along something with a scraping noise. 9 to damage or graze by rubbing on a rough surface. 10 to collect or get together by scraping. 11 to save or amass with difficulty or by small amounts. 12 to clear (a ship's bottom) of barnacles etc. 13 to draw (the hair) tightly back off the forehead. ~*v.i.* 1 to rub the surface of something with a rough or sharp instrument. 2 to abrade, to smooth, to clean something thus. 3 to rub (against something) with a scraping or rasping noise. 4 to make such a noise. 5 to get through with difficulty or by a close shave. 6 to be saving or parsimonious. 7 to play awkwardly on a violin etc. 8 to make an awkward bow with a drawing back of the foot. 9 to barely manage. 10 to pass an examination etc. with difficulty. ~*n.* 1 the act, sound or effect of scraping. 2 a scraped place (on the skin etc.). 3 a thin layer of butter etc. 4 an awkward bow with a drawing back of the foot. 5 (*coll.*) an awkward predicament, esp. one due to one's own conduct. **to bow and scrape** BOW[2]. **to scrape acquaintance with** to contrive to make the acquaintance of. **to scrape along** (*coll.*) to keep going somehow. **to scrape away** to abrade, to reduce by scraping. **to scrape by** (*coll.*) to keep going somehow. **to scrape down** 1 to scrape away. 2 to scrape from head to foot or top to bottom. 3 to silence or put down by scraping the feet. **to scrape the barrel** BARREL. **scraper** *n.* 1 a person who scrapes. 2 an instrument for scraping, esp. for cleaning the dirt off one's boots before entering a house. 3 an awkward fiddler. 4 a miser. 5 a prehistoric flint implement used for scraping skins etc. **scraperboard** *n.* 1 a board with a surface that can be scraped off to form a design. 2 this method of producing designs. **scraping** *n.* [ME *scrapien,* Icel. *skrapa* (cp. Dan. *skrabe,* Dut. *schrapen*), cogn. with OE *screpan,* to scratch]

scrapie (skrā´pi) *n.* an encephalopathy affecting sheep, thought to be caused by a prion. [because affected animals support themselves by scraping against trees etc.]

scrapper SCRAP[2].

scrappy SCRAP[1].

Scratch (skrach) *n.* the Devil; also *Old Scratch.* [cp. Icel. *skratte,* OHG *Scrato,* goblin]

scratch (skrach) *v.t.* 1 to tear or mark the surface of lightly with something sharp. 2 to wound slightly. 3 to rub or scrape with the nails. 4 to hollow out with the nails or claws. 5 to chafe the surface of. 6 to write hurriedly; to scribble. 7 to erase, to obliterate, to score (out, through etc.). 8 to expunge (esp. the name of a horse in a list of entries for a race). 9 to withdraw from a contest. 10 to cancel (a match, game etc.). 11 to form by scratching. 12 to scrape (up or together). ~*v.i.* 1 to use the nails or claws in tearing, scraping, marking, hollowing out etc. 2 to rub or scrape one's skin with the nails. 3 to chafe, rub. 4 to scrape the ground as in searching. 5 to make a grating noise. 6 to withdraw one's entry from a contest. 7 to get by or manage with difficulty. ~*n.* 1 a mark made by scratching. 2 a slight wound. 3 a sound of scratching. 4 an act or spell of scratching. 5 a mark from which competitors start in a race, or a line across a prize ring at which boxers begin. 6 in golf, a handicap of zero. 7 (*pl.*) a horse-disease characterized by scabs or chaps between the heel and pastern-joint. 8 (*sl.*) money. 9 in music, the technique of scratching. 10 a scratch-wig. ~*a.* 1 improvised. 2 put together hastily or haphazardly, multifarious, nondescript. 3 in sport, without handicap. **to scratch along** to scrape along. **to scratch one's head** to be puzzled. **to scratch the surface** 1 to gain a superficial understanding. 2 to investigate further. **to start from scratch** to start from the very beginning, with no advantage. **to toe the scratch** 1 to be ready when wanted. 2 to stand the test. **up to scratch** satisfactory, fulfilling the desired standard or requirements. **you scratch my back and I'll scratch yours** if you do me a favour, I'll do you one in return. **scratch card** *n.* a lottery card etc. whose surface has an opaque coating which is scratched off to reveal the figures, letters etc. underneath. **scratcher** *n.* 1 a person who or thing which scratches. 2 a bird that scratches for food, one of the Rasores. **scratch file** *n.* a temporary file for use during the execution of a computer program. **scratchies** *n.pl.* (*Austral., coll.*) instant lottery tickets. **scratching** *n.* 1 a scratchy sound effect produced by manually rotating a (pop) record backwards and forwards, used in some styles of pop music. 2 (*pl.*) PORK SCRATCHINGS (under PORK). **scratch pad** *n.* 1 (*chiefly N Am.*) a notebook, a scribbling block. 2 a small fast memory for storing computer data. **scratch test** *n.* a test for allergy to a certain substance by placing it on a scratched area of skin. **scratch video** *n.* 1 a collage on video of previously existing pieces of television and cinema film. 2 the technique or genre of making scratch videos. **scratch-wig** *n.* a wig covering a bald part of the head. **scratchy** *a.* (*comp.* **scratchier,** *superl.* **scratchiest**) 1 consisting of or characterized by scratches. 2 tending to scratch or rub, rough. 3 making a noise like scratching. 4 uneven, irregular, heterogeneous. **scratchily** *adv.*

scratchiness *n.* [prob. from *scrat* (perh. from Swed. *kratta*, to scrape) and ME *cracchen*, MDut. *kratsen*]

scrawl (skrawl) *v.t.* to draw, write or mark clumsily, hurriedly or illegibly, to scribble. ~*v.i.* to scribble, to mark with illegible writing etc. ~*n.* a piece of hasty, clumsy or illegible writing. **scrawler** *n.* **scrawly** *a.* (*comp.* **scrawlier,** *superl.* **scrawliest**). [perh. var. of SCRABBLE]

scrawny (skraw´ni) *a.* (*comp.* **scrawnier,** *superl.* **scrawniest**) **1** excessively lean, thin, bony. **2** meagre. **scrawnily** *adv.* **scrawniness** *n.* [var. of dial. *scranny*]

scream (skrēm) *v.i.* **1** to make a shrill, piercing, prolonged cry as if in extreme pain or terror. **2** to give out a shrill sound, to whistle, hoot or laugh loudly. **3** to speak or write excitedly or violently. **4** to be over-conspicuous or vivid. **5** (*coll.*) to turn informer. ~*v.t.* to utter or say in a screaming tone. ~*n.* **1** a loud, shrill, prolonged cry, as of one in extreme pain or terror. **2** a similar, loud sound. **3** (*coll.*) something or someone excruciatingly funny. **to scream blue/ bloody murder** MURDER. **screamer** *n.* **1** a person who or something which screams, esp. the swift. **2** any bird of the S American semiaquatic family Anhimidae, from their harsh cry. **3** (*N Am.*, *coll.*) a sensational headline. **4** (*coll.*) a person who or thing which makes one laugh. **5** (*sl.*) an exclamation mark. **6** (*Austral.*, *sl.*) a person who or thing which is excellent. **screamingly** *adv.* extremely. **screamy** *a.* **screamily** *adv.* **screaminess** *n.* [cp. Icel. *skraema*, to scare, to terrify]

scree (skrē) *n.* **1** loose fragments or debris of rock on a steep slope. **2** a slope covered with this. [Icel. *skritha*, landslip, from *skrītha*, to glide, cp. OE *scrithan*]

screech (skrēch) *v.i.* **1** to scream out with a sharp, harsh, shrill voice. **2** to make a shrill, strident noise. ~*v.t.* to utter or say with such a voice. ~*n.* a shrill, harsh cry as of terror or pain. **screecher** *n.* **screech hawk** *n.* (*dial.*) the nightjar. **screech martin** *n.* the swift. **screech owl** *n.* an owl that screeches instead of hooting, esp. the barn owl or a small American owl, *Otus asio.* **screechy** *a.* (*comp.* **screechier,** *superl.* **screechiest**). **screechily** *adv.* **screechiness** *n.* [ME *scriken*, *schriken*, from Icel., as *screak*, to shriek (prob. imit.)]

screed (skrēd) *n.* **1** a long harangue or tirade. **2** a strip of mortar, wood etc. put on a wall etc. that is to be plastered, as a guide to evenness of surface etc. **3** a screeding. **4** a piece, a fragment, a strip. **5** a long and tedious piece of writing. **screeding** *n.* the final rendering of concrete to get a smooth surface. [North. var. of SHRED]

screen (skrēn) *n.* **1** a partition separating a portion of a room or of a church from the remainder, esp. one between the choir and the nave or ambulatory. **2** a movable piece of furniture, usu. consisting of a light framework covered with paper, cloth etc., used to shelter from excess of heat, draught etc. **3** anything serving to shelter, protect or conceal. **4** a surface on which images can be projected. **5** the film industry, moving pictures collectively. **6** the part of a television set, VDU etc. on which the image appears. **7** in cricket, a sight-screen. **8** a windscreen. **9** a frame containing a mesh placed over a window, door etc. to keep out flies. **10** a body affording a shield against electric or magnetic induction. **11** in photography, a device for modifying the effect of light passing through a lens. **12** a coarse sieve or riddle, esp. for sorting coal. **13** a board or structure on which notices etc. can be posted. **14** a system for selecting, checking etc. **15** (*Print.*) a plate or film for half-tone reproduction. **16** a body of troops etc. used as a cover. ~*v.t.* **1** to shelter or protect from inconvenience, injury, hurt or pain, to shield. **2** to hide, to conceal wholly or partly. **3** to prevent from causing, or protect from, electrical interference. **4** to separate with a screen. **5** to test for the presence of disease, weapons etc. **6** to examine or check thoroughly in order to assess suitability, sort into categories etc. **7** to project (a film) on a screen. **8** to portray in film. **9** to sift, to riddle. **screenable** *a.* **screener** *n.* **screening** *n.* **screening-machine** *n.* a machine for sifting and assorting coal etc. **screenings** *n.pl.* small stuff or refuse separated by screening. **screenplay** *n.* a film script including stage directions and details of characters and sets. **screen printing, screen process** *n.* SILK-SCREEN PRINTING (under SILK). **screen print** *n.* **screen-print** *v.t.* **screen-printed** *a.* **screen saver** *n.* a computer program which uses moving images to prevent a monitor becoming damaged. **screen test** *n.* a filmed test of an actor to judge their suitability for a film. **screenwriter** *n.* a writer of screenplays. **screenwriting** *n.* [ME *scren*, OF *escren* (F *écran*), prob. from OHG *skrank*, barrier (cp. G *Schranke*)]

screeve (skrēv) *v.t.* (*sl.*) to write. ~*v.i.* **1** to write or draw with coloured chalk etc. on pavements. **2** to write begging letters. [perh. through It. *scrivere*, from L *scrībere*, to write]

screw (skroo) *n.* **1** a cylinder with a spiral ridge or groove round its outer surface (called a male or exterior screw) or round its inner surface (called a female or internal screw). **2** a male screw used for fastening boards etc. together. **3** a male or female screw forming part of a tool, mechanical appliance or machine and conveying motion to another part or bringing pressure to bear. **4** (*also* **screw-bolt**) a metal male screw with a blunt end, used to bolt things together. **5** something resembling a screw in spiral form. **6** (*sing. or pl.*) an instrument of torture. **7** a screw propeller. **8** a turn of a screw. **9** a screw steamer. **10** a sideways motion or tendency like that of a screw, a twist. **11** backspin given to a ball in snooker, billiards etc. **12** a twisted-up paper (of tobacco etc.). **13** (*sl.*) a stingy person. **14** (*sl.*) salary. **15** (*sl.*) a prison warder. **16** (*sl.*) an act of sexual intercourse. **17** (*sl.*) a partner in sexual intercourse. **18** (*sl.*) a broken-down or vicious horse. ~*v.t.* **1** to fasten, secure, tighten, join etc. with a screw or screws. **2** to turn (a screw). **3** to turn round or twist as a screw. **4** to give a spiral thread or groove to. **5** to press hard, to oppress, esp. by exactions, to grind. **6** to extort, to squeeze (money etc.) out of. **7** to cheat. **8** to twist, to contort, to distort (as the face). **9** (*sl.*) to have sexual intercourse with. **10** to cause (esp. a billiard ball) to swerve. **11** (*sl.*) to bungle. ~*v.i.* **1** to turn as a screw. **2** to twist, to move obliquely or spirally, to swerve. **3** (*sl.*) to have sexual intercourse. **to have a screw at** (*Austral.*, *coll.*) to take a look at. **to have a screw loose** (*coll.*) to be slightly crazy. **to have one's head screwed on the right way** HEAD[1]. **to put the screws on** (*coll.*) to put pressure on. **to screw around** (*sl.*) to have sexual intercourse with many partners. **to screw up 1** to tighten up with or as with a screw. **2** to fasten with a screw or screws. **3** to shut (a person) in thus. **4** to twist. **5** (*sl.*) to bungle, mess up. **6** (*sl.*) to make confused or neurotic, to disturb. **to screw up courage** to summon up resolution. **screwable** *a.* **screwball** *a.* (*chiefly N Am.*, *coll.*) eccentric, crazy, zany. ~*n.* **1** an eccentric person. **2** in baseball, a ball that spins against the natural curve. **screw cap** *n.* SCREW TOP (under SCREW). **screw-coupling** *n.* a collar with threads for joining pipes etc. together. **screw-cutter** *n.* a tool for cutting screws. **screwdriver** *n.* **1** a tool like a blunt chisel for turning screws. **2** a cocktail of vodka and orange juice. **screwed** *a.* **1** twisted. **2** (*sl.*) ruined. **3** (*sl.*) drunk, tipsy. **screwer** *n.* **screw eye** *n.* a screw with a loop instead of a slotted head, for attaching cords to picture frames etc. **screw gear** *n.* an endless screw or worm for working a cogwheel etc. **screw hook** *n.* a hook which has a screw point for fastening it. **screw-jack** *n.* **1** a lifting-jack with a screw rotating in a nut. **2** a dentist's implement for pressing teeth apart etc. **screw-pile** *n.* a pile armed with a screw point, sunk by turning instead of hammering. **screw pine** *n.* any tree of the tropical genus *Pandanus*, with leaves clustered spirally. **screw-plate** *n.* a steel plate used for making male screws. **screw-press** *n.* a press worked by means of a screw. **screw propeller** *n.* a form of propeller with twisted blades which act like a screw. **screw steamer** *n.* a steamer driven by a screw propeller. **screw-tap** *n.* a tool for making female screws. **screw top** *n.* a top for a bottle, jar etc., that opens and closes with a screwing motion. **screw-top, screw-topped** *a.* **screw-up** *n.* (*sl.*) a mess, bungle. **screw valve** *n.* a stopcock opened and shut by a screw. **screw wrench** *n.* **1** a tool for gripping the head of a large screw or nut. **2** a wrench with jaws worked by a screw. **screwy** *a.* (*comp.* **screwier,** *superl.* **screwiest**) **1** (*coll.*) mad, crazy. **2** (*coll.*) eccentric, absurd, zany. **3** (of a horse) worn-out, broken down. **screwiness** *n.* [formerly *scrue*, OF *escroue* (F *écrou*), etym. uncertain]

scribal, scribaceous SCRIBE.

scribble[1] (skrib´əl) *v.i.* **1** to write hastily, illegibly or without regard to correctness of handwriting or composition. **2** to make random or meaningless marks with a pen, crayon etc. **3** (*derog.*) to be a journalist or author. ~*v.t.* to write hastily, carelessly or without regard to correctness. ~*n.* **1** hasty or careless writing. **2** a scrawl. **3** something written hastily or carelessly. **scribblement** *n.* **scribbler**[1] *n.* a minor author. **scribbling** *a.*, *n.* **scribblingly** *adv.* **scribbling paper** *n.* paper for making hasty notes on. **scribbly** *a.* [SCRIBE]

scribble[2] (skrib´əl) *v.t.* **1** to card roughly. **2** to pass through a scribbler. **scribbler**[2], **scribbling machine** *n.* a carding machine used for the first rough process in preparing wool, cotton etc. [Swed. *skrubbla*, freq. of *skrubba*, to SCRUB[1]]

scribbler[1] SCRIBBLE[1].

scribbler[2] SCRIBBLE[2].

scribe (skrīb) *n.* **1** a writer, a penman. **2** a secretary, a copyist. **3** (*Hist.*) an ancient Jewish writer or keeper of official records, one of a class of commentators, interpreters and teachers of the sacred law. **4** (*also* **scribe-awl**) a pointed instrument for marking lines on wood, bricks etc., a scriber. ~*v.t.* **1** to mark with a scriber. **2** to mark and fit one piece to the edge of another. **scribal** *a.* **scribedom** *n.* **scriber, scribing-awl, scribing-iron, scribing-tool** *n.* a tool used for scoring or marking lines etc. **scribing-compasses** *n.pl.* compasses used for scoring circles etc. **scribism** *n.* [L *scrība*, from *scrībere*, to write]

scrim (skrim) *n.* strong cotton or linen cloth used for lining in upholstery and for cleaning. [etym. uncertain]

scrimmage (skrim´ij) *n.* **1** a tussle, a confused or rough-and-tumble struggle, a skirmish. **2** in rugby football, a scrummage. **3** in American football, the period or activity between the ball coming into play and the time it is dead. ~*v.i.* to engage in a scrimmage. ~*v.t.* in American football, to put (the ball) into a scrimmage. **scrimmager** *n.* [var. of SKIRMISH]

scrimp (skrimp) *v.t.* **1** to make small, scant or short. **2** to limit or straiten, to skimp. ~*v.i.* to skimp, to be niggardly. ~*a.* scanty, narrow. ~*n.* (*N Am.*) a niggard, a pinching miser. **scrimply** *adv.* **scrimpness** *n.* **scrimpy** *a.* **scrimpily** *adv.* **scrimpiness** *n.* [cp. Swed. and Dan. *skrumpen*, shrivelled, G *schrumpfen*, cogn. with OE *scrimman*]

scrimshander (skrim´shandə) *v.t.* to scrimshaw. ~*n.* a person who scrimshaws.

scrimshank (skrim´shangk) *v.i.* (*sl.*) to avoid work, to get out of doing one's duty. **scrimshanker** *n.* [etym. unknown]

scrimshaw (skrim´shaw) *v.t.* to decorate (ivory, shells etc.) with carvings and coloured designs. ~*v.i.* to produce decorated work of this kind. ~*n.* a piece of such work. [prob. a surname]

scrip[1] (skrip) *n.* **1** a provisional certificate given to a subscriber for stock of a bank or company. **2** such certificates collectively. **3** an extra share or shares instead of a dividend. **4** a piece of writing, a list, as of names, a schedule. **scrip-holder** *n.* **scrip issue** *n.* a bonus issue. [SCRIPT]

scrip[2] (skrip) *n.* a small bag, a wallet or satchel. [OE *scripp*, cp. Icel. *skreppa*, rel. to SCRAP[1]]

Script. *abbr.* Scripture.

script (skript) *n.* **1** a piece of writing. **2** handwriting as distinct from print. **3** printed cursive characters, type in imitation of writing. **4** an alphabet or system of writing. **5** handwriting in imitation of type. **6** the written text or draft of a film, play or radio or television broadcast as used by the actors or performers. **7** (*Law*) a writing, an original document. **8** an answer paper in an examination. ~*v.t.* to write the script for. **scription** (-shən) *n.* **scriptorium** (-taw´ri-) *n.* (*pl.* **scriptoriums, scriptoria** (-riə)) a writing room, esp. in a monastery. **scriptorial** *a.* **scriptwriter** *n.* a person who writes scripts, esp. for broadcasting or for the cinema. **script-writing** *n.* [OF *escript* (F *écrit*), L *scriptum*, something written, neut. p.p. of *scrībere*, see SCRIBE]

scripture (skrip´chə) *n.* **1** a sacred writing or book. **2** (**Scripture**) the Bible, esp. the books of the Old and New Testament without the Apocrypha. **3** a passage from the Scriptures. **the Scriptures** the Bible. **scriptural** *a.* of, relating to, derived from, based upon, or contained in a scripture, esp. the Bible. **scripturalism** *n.* **scripturalist, scripturist** *n.* **scripturally** *adv.* **scripturalness** *n.* **scripture-reader** *n.* (*Hist.*) a person employed to read the Scriptures publicly. [ME from OF *escripture*, L *scriptūra*, as SCRIPT]

†**scritch** (skrich) *n.* a screech. ~*v.t.*, *v.i.* to screech. **scritch owl** *n.* SCREECH OWL (under SCREECH). [imit., cp. SCREECH]

scrivener (skriv´ənə) *n.* (*Hist.*) **1** a person whose business was to draw up contracts or other documents, a notary. **2** a financial agent, a broker, a moneylender. [ME *scriveyn*, OF *escrivain* (F *écrivain*), It. *scrivano*, late L *scrībānus*, SCRIBE, -ER[1]]

scrobe (skrōb) *n.* a groove, as that receiving the base of the antenna in a weevil. **scrobicular** (skrəbik´-), **scrobiculate** (-lət), **scrobiculated** (-lātid), **scrobiculous** *a.* **scrobicule** (-ikūl) *n.* (*Biol.*) a small pit or depression. **scrobiculus** (-bik´ūləs) *n.* (*pl.* **scrobiculi** (-lī)) a scrobicule. [L *scrobis*, trench]

scrod (skrod) *n.* (*N Am.*) a young cod or haddock, esp. when prepared for cooking. [perh. from obs. Dut. *schrood*, a shred]

†**scrofula** (skrof´ūlə) *n.* a form of tuberculosis affecting esp. the lymph glands of the neck. **scrofulous** *a.* **scrofulously** *adv.* **scrofulousness** *n.* [L, orig. dim. of *scrōfa*, breeding sow]

scrog (skrog) *n.* (*chiefly Sc.*) **1** a stunted bush. **2** brushwood, undergrowth, thicket. **3** (*Her.*) a branch of a tree. **scrogged, scroggy** *a.* [etym. uncertain]

scroll (skrōl) *n.* **1** a roll of paper or parchment. **2** an ancient book or volume in this form. **3** a convolved or spiral ornament more or less resembling a scroll of parchment, such as a volute, the curved head of a violin etc., a band or ribbon bearing an inscription, a flourish, or tracery consisting of spiral lines. **4** (*Her.*) the ribbon upon which a motto is inscribed. ~*v.t.* **1** to roll up like a scroll. **2** to decorate with scrolls. **3** to enter in a scroll. **4** (*Comput.*) to move (text) up, down or across a screen. ~*v.i.* **1** to curl up like a scroll. **2** (*Comput.*) to move text up, down or across a screen so as to display the next line or section. **scroll bar** *n.* the part at the edge of a computer display which can be clicked on to scroll text etc. **scrolled** *a.* **scroller** *n.*

scroll-head *n.* a volute-shaped timber at a ship's bow. **scroll saw** *n.* a fretsaw for cutting scrolls. **scrollwork** *n.* ornamental work in spiral lines, esp. cut out with a scroll saw. [formerly *scrowl*, dim. of ME *scrowe*, *scroue*, OF *escroue*, from Gmc. (cp. MDut. *schroode*, OHG *scrōt*, strip) SHRED]

Scrooge (skrooj) *n.* a miserly person. [Ebenezer *Scrooge*, a character in Dickens's *A Christmas Carol*]

scrophularia (skrofūleə´riə) *n.* any plant of the genus *Scrophularia*, typical of the family Scrophulariaceae, containing the figwort. **scrophulariaceous** (-ā´shəs) *a.* [mod. L from med. L *scrophula*, SCROFULA]

scrotum (skrō´təm) *n.* (*pl.* **scrota** (-tə), **scrotums**) the pouch enclosing the testes in the higher mammals. **scrotal** *a.* **scrotiform** (-tifawm) *a.* **scrotitis** (-tī´tis) *n.* inflammation of the scrotum. **scrotocele** (-təsēl) *n.* a scrotal hernia. [L]

scrounge (skrownj) *v.t.* (*coll.*) **1** to pilfer. **2** to cadge. *~v.i.* **1** to forage or hunt around. **2** to cadge things. *~n.* an act of scrounging. **on the scrounge** engaged in scrounging. **scrounger** *n.* [etym. uncertain]

scrub[1] (skrŭb) *v.t.* (*pres.p.* **scrubbing**, *past, p.p.* **scrubbed**) **1** to rub hard with something coarse and rough, esp. with soap and water used with a scrubbing-brush for the purpose of cleaning or scouring. **2** to purify (a gas) with a scrubber. **3** (*coll.*) to get rid of, cancel, delete, erase. **4** to slow down by allowing one's tyres to scrape the road. *~v.i.* **1** to clean, scour or brighten things by rubbing hard. **2** to work hard and penuriously, to drudge. **3** to scrub the hands and arms before carrying out surgery. **4** (of tyres) to scrape, esp. when cornering. *~n.* **1** the act of scrubbing. **2** a worn-out brush or broom. **3** a lotion containing abrasive granules for cleansing the skin. **to scrub round** (*coll.*) to avoid or ignore. **scrubber**[1] *n.* **1** a person who or thing which scrubs. **2** a scrubbing-brush. **3** a gas-purifier for removing tar and ammonia by spraying with water. **4** (*sl.*) a prostitute or promiscuous woman. **scrubbing** *n., a.* **scrubbing-board** *n.* a ribbed board used in washing for rubbing clothes on. **scrubbing-brush**, (*N Am.*) **scrub-brush** *n.* a stiff brush for scrubbing floors etc. **scrub-woman** *n.* (*pl.* **scrubwomen**) (*N Am.*) a charwoman. [ME *scrobben*, MDan. *skrubbe* (cp. Swed. *skrubba*, Dut. *schrobben*)]

scrub[2] (skrŭb) *n.* **1** (a tract of) brushwood, undergrowth or stunted trees. **2** a stunted tree, bush etc. **3** a paltry, stingy person. **4** (*esp. N Am.*) an inferior animal. **5** something mean or despicable. **6** (*N Am.*) a player not of the first team. *~a.* mean, paltry, petty, niggardly, contemptible. †**scrubbed** *a.* **scrubber**[2] *n.* (*Austral.*) a bullock that has run wild. **scrub bird** *n.* either of two Australian passerine birds, *Atrichornis clamosus* or *A. rufescens*. **scrubby** *a.* (*comp.* **scrubbier**, *superl.* **scrubbiest**) **1** mean, stunted, insignificant. **2** covered with brushwood. **3** rough, unshaven. **scrubbiness** *n.* **scrub cattle** *n.* (*Austral.*) cattle that have run wild and deteriorated. **scrub fowl** *n.* a megapode. **scrubland** *n.* **scrub oak** *n.* any one of several N American dwarf oaks. **scrub rider** *n.* (*Austral.*) a person who goes out in search of scrub cattle. **scrub turkey** *n.* a megapode. **scrub typhus** *n.* a febrile disease transmitted by mites. [SHRUB[1]]

scrubber[1] SCRUB[1].

scrubber[2], **scrubby** SCRUB[2].

scruff[1] (skrŭf) *n.* the nape or back of the neck, esp. as grasped by a person dragging another. [formerly *scuft*, Icel. *skopt* (*skoft*), hair of head]

scruff[2] (skrŭf) *n.* **1** (*coll.*) an unkempt or scruffy person. **2** (*dial.*) dandruff, scurf. **scruffy** *a.* (*comp.* **scruffier**, *superl.* **scruffiest**) **1** untidy, dirty, shabby, down-at-heel. **2** scurvy. **scruffily** *adv.* **scruffiness** *n.* [SCURF]

scrum (skrŭm) *n.* **1** a set struggle in rugby between the forwards of both sides grappling in a compact mass with the ball on the ground in the middle. **2** a scuffle. **3** (*coll.*) a disorderly crowd. *~v.i.* (*pres.p.* **scrumming**, *past, p.p.* **scrummed**) **1** to form a scrum. **2** (*coll.*) to jostle or crowd. **to scrum down** to scrum. **scrum-half** *n.* the half-back who puts the ball into the scrum. [short for SCRUMMAGE]

scrummage (skrum´ij) *n.* a rugby scrum. *~v.i.* to scrum in rugby. **scrummager** *n.* [var. of SCRIMMAGE]

scrump (skrŭmp) *v.t., v.i.* (*coll.*) to steal (apples) from an orchard. **scrumpy** *n.* (*pl.* **scrumpies**) (*coll.*) (a) rough cider. [*scrump*, orig. mean. something withered or shrivelled, a shrivelled apple, from SCRIMP]

scrumple (skrŭm´pəl) *v.t.* to crumple, wrinkle. [var. of CRUMPLE]

scrumptious (skrŭmp´shəs) *a.* (*coll.*) **1** (of food) delicious. **2** first-class, stylish. **scrumptiously** *adv.* **scrumptiousness** *n.* [perh. orig. mean, stingy, from SCRIMP, perh. var. of SUMPTUOUS]

scrumpy SCRUMP.

scrunch (skrŭnch) *v.t.* **1** to crunch. **2** to crush, to crumple. **3** to hunch up. **4** to style (hair) by crushing it. *~v.i.* to make or move with a crunching sound. *~n.* a crunch. **scrunch-dry** *v.t.* (*3rd pers. sing. pres.* **scrunch-dries**, *pres.p.* **scrunch-drying**, *past, p.p.* **scrunch-dried**) to dry (the hair) with a hairdryer whilst crushing in the hand, to give body. **scrunchy**, **scrunchie** *n.* (*pl.* **scrunchies**) an elastic loop covered in pleated fabric, for holding the hair in a ponytail. [var. of CRUNCH]

scruple (skroo´pəl) *n.* **1** a doubt, objection or hesitation from conscientious or moral motives. **2** (*Hist.*) a weight of 20 grains (1.296 g), the third part of a dram (apothecaries' weight). **3** †a small quantity, a tiny fraction, a particle. *~v.i.* to have scruples, to doubt, to hesitate, to be reluctant (to do etc.). **scrupler** *n.* **scrupulous** (-pū-) *a.* **1** influenced by scruples. **2** careful, cautious, extremely conscientious, punctilious, precise, exact. **scrupulosity** (-los´-) *n.* **scrupulously** *adv.* **scrupulousness** *n.* [F *scrupule*, L *scrūpulum*, nom. *-lus*, dim. of *scrūpus*, sharp stone]

scrutator (skrootā´tə) *n.* a person who scrutinizes, a close inquirer. **scrutable** (skroo´-) *a.* [L, as SCRUTINY]

scrutiny (skroo´tini) *n.* (*pl.* **scrutinies**) **1** close observation or investigation. **2** minute inquiry. **3** critical examination. **4** an official examination of votes given at an election to verify the correctness of a declared result. **5** a searching look. **scrutineer** (-niə´) *n.* a person who examines something, esp. who acts as examiner in a scrutiny of votes. **scrutinize**, **scrutinise** *v.t.* to examine narrowly or minutely. **scrutinization** (-zā´shən) *n.* **scrutinizer** *n.* **scrutinizingly** *adv.* [late L *scrūtinium*, from *scrūtārī*, to search carefully, from *scrūta*, broken pieces, cogn. with SHRED]

scruto (skroo´tō) *n.* (*pl.* **scrutos**) a trapdoor with springs, made flush with a theatre stage, for rapid disappearances etc. [etym. uncertain]

scry (skrī) *v.t.* (*3rd pers. sing. pres.* **scries**, *pres.p.* **scrying**, *past, p.p.* **scried**) **1** to practise crystal-gazing. **2** to descry. **scryer** *n.* [DESCRY]

SCSI *abbr.* small computer systems interface.

scuba (skoo´bə, skū´-) *n.* (*pl.* **scubas**) an aqualung. **scuba-diving** *n.* underwater swimming with an aqualung. **scuba-dive** *v.i.* **scuba-diver** *n.* [acronym for *s*elf-*c*ontained *u*nderwater *b*reathing *a*pparatus]

scud (skŭd) *v.i.* (*pres.p.* **scudding**, *past, p.p.* **scudded**) **1** to run or fly swiftly. **2** (*Naut.*) to run fast before a gale with little or no sail spread. *~v.t.* to move swiftly over. *~n.* **1** the act or a spell of scudding. **2** a scudding motion. **3** loose, vapoury clouds driven swiftly by the wind. **4** a light passing shower. **5** wind-blown spray. **6** (*usu.* **Scud**) a surface-to-surface missile which can carry nuclear warheads. **scudder** *n.* [Norw. *skudda*, allied to SHOOT]

scudo (skoo´dō) *n.* (*pl.* **scudi** (-dē)) an old Italian silver coin and money of account. [It., from L *scūtum*, shield]

scuff[1] (skŭf) *v.i.* **1** to drag or scrape with the feet in walking, to shuffle. **2** to become abraded or roughened, esp. by use. ~*v.t.* **1** to scrape or shuffle (the feet). **2** to touch lightly, to graze. **3** to abrade, scratch or roughen the surface of. ~*n.* **1** the act or noise of scuffing. **2** a mark or roughened place caused by scuffing. **scuffed** *a.* worn, shabby. **scuffy** *a.* (*Sc.*) [etym. uncertain, cp. Swed. *skuffa*, Icel. *skūfa*, to SHOVE, perh. conf. with SCRUFF[1] or SCURF in some senses]

scuff[2] (skŭf) *n.* SCRUFF[1].

scuffle (skŭf´əl) *v.i.* **1** to fight or struggle in a rough-and-tumble way. **2** to shuffle, to scrape with the feet. **3** to scamper, to scurry. ~*n.* **1** a confused and disorderly fight or struggle. **2** a soft, shuffling sound. **scuffler** *n.* [freq. of SCUFF[1]]

sculduggery SKULDUGGERY.

scull (skŭl) *n.* **1** either of a pair of short oars used by one person for propelling a boat. **2** an oar used with twisting strokes over the stern. **3** a person who sculls a boat. **4** a boat propelled by sculling. **5** (*pl.*) a race between boats rowed by one person. ~*v.t.* to propel (a boat) by a scull or sculls. ~*v.i.* to propel a boat thus. **sculler** *n.* **1** a person who sculls. **2** a boat rowed thus. [etym. uncertain]

Usage note The spellings of the nouns *scull* (an oar) and *skull* (the cranium) should not be confused.

scullery (skŭl´əri) *n.* (*pl.* **sculleries**) a place where dishes and utensils are washed up, vegetables prepared etc. [OF *escuelier*, L *scutellārius*, dish-keeper, from *scutella*, see SCUTTLE[1], -ERY]

†**scullion** (skŭl´yən) *n.* a servant who cleans pots, dishes etc., a kitchen drudge. [OF *escouillon*, *escouvillon*, Sp. *escobillon*, sponge for a cannon, from *escobilla*, sponge, dim. of *escoba*, L *scōpa*, pl. *scōpae*, a besom]

sculp (skŭlp) *v.t.* (*coll.*) to carve, to sculpture. [short for SCULPTURE]

sculp., Sculp. *abbr.* sculptor, sculpture.

sculpin (skŭl´pin) *n.* any of various N American sea fishes with large spiny heads. [perh. corr. of obs. *scorpene*, *scorpaena*]

sculpture (skŭlp´chə) *n.* **1** the art of cutting, carving, modelling or casting wood, stone, clay, metal etc. into representations of natural objects or designs in round or in relief. **2** carved or sculptured work collectively. **3** a piece of this. **4** raised or sunk markings on a shell etc. ~*v.t.* **1** to represent in or by sculpture. **2** to ornament with sculpture. **3** to shape by or as by carving, moulding etc. ~*v.i.* to practise sculpture. **sculpt** *v.t.*, *v.i.* to sculpture. **sculptor** *n.* a person who sculptures. **sculptress** *n.* a female sculptor. **sculptural** *a.* **sculpturally** *adv.* **sculpturesque** (-resk´) *a.* [F, from L *sculptūra*, from *sculpere*, to carve]

scum (skŭm) *n.* **1** impurities that rise to the surface of liquid, esp. in fermentation or boiling. **2** the scoria of molten metal. **3** froth, foam or any film of floating matter. **4** (*fig.*) refuse, dregs, the vile and worthless part. **5** (*coll.*) a worthless person or group. ~*v.t.* (*pres.p.* **scumming**, *past, p.p.* **scummed**) **1** to clear of scum, to skim. **2** to be or form a scum on. ~*v.i.* **1** to rise as scum, to form a scum. **2** to become covered with scum. **scumbag** *n.* (*sl.*) a despicable or disgusting person. **scummer** *n.* **scummings** *n.pl.* skimmings. **scummy** *a.* (*comp.* **scummier**, *superl.* **scummiest**). [Dan. *skum* (cp. Icel. *skūm*, G *Schaum*), rel. to SKIM]

scumble (skŭm´bəl) *v.t.* **1** to cover (an oil painting) lightly with opaque or semi-opaque colours so as to soften the outlines or colours. **2** to produce a similar effect on (a drawing) by lightly rubbing. **3** to soften (a colour) thus. **4** to prepare (a painted wall) for repainting. ~*n.* **1** a material for scumbling. **2** the effect produced. [freq. of SCUM]

scummer, scummings etc. SCUM.

scuncheon (skŭn´chən) *n.* **1** a bevelling, splay or elbow in a window opening etc. **2** arching etc. across the angles of a square tower supporting a spire. [OF *escoinson*]

scunge (skŭnj) *n.* (*Austral.*, *New Zeal.*, *coll.*) **1** dirt, scum. **2** a dirty or worthless person. **scungy** *a.* (*comp.* **scungier**, *superl.* **scungiest**). [etym. uncertain]

scunner (skŭn´ə) *v.t.* (*Sc.*) to disgust, to nauseate. ~*v.i.* to feel loathing, to be sickened. ~*n.* **1** loathing, disgust. **2** an object of loathing. [etym. uncertain]

scupper[1] (skŭp´ə) *n.* a hole or tube through a ship's side to carry off water from the deck. [prob. from OF *escope*, SCOOP]

scupper[2] (skŭp´ə) *v.t.* **1** (*sl.*) to sink (a ship). **2** (*sl.*) to ruin, to do for. **3** (*sl.*) to kill. [etym. uncertain]

scuppernong (skŭp´ənong) *n.* (*N Am.*) **1** a sweet American wine made from a variety of muscadine grape. **2** the purple grape, muscadine, esp. the variety from which this wine is made. [river in N Carolina]

scurf (skœf) *n.* **1** flakes or scales thrown off by the skin, esp. of the head. **2** any loose scaly matter adhering to a surface. **scurfy** *a.* **scurfiness** *n.* [OE (cp. Swed. *skorf*, Icel. *skurfur*), rel. to *sceorfan*, to scarify]

scurrilous (skŭr´iləs) *a.* using or expressed in low, vulgar, grossly abusive or indecent language. **scurrility** (-ril´-) *n.* (*pl.* **scurrilities**). **scurrilously** *adv.* **scurrilousness** *n.* [L *scurrīlis*, from *scurra*, buffoon]

scurry (skŭr´i) *v.i.* (*3rd pers. sing. pres.* **scurries**, *pres.p.* **scurrying**, *past, p.p.* **scurried**) to go with great haste, to hurry, to scamper. ~*n.* (*pl.* **scurries**) **1** an act or the noise of scurrying. **2** bustle, haste. **3** a flurry of rain or snow. [perh. from obs. *scurrier*, a scout, as SCOUR[2], perh. from *hurry-scurry*, reduplication of HURRY]

scurvy (skœ´vi) *n.* a disease caused by lack of vitamin C and characterized by swollen gums, extravasation of blood and general debility, arising orig. esp. among those on shipboard from a deficiency of vegetables. ~*a.* (*comp.* **scurvier**, *superl.* **scurviest**) mean, paltry, base, shabby, contemptible. **scurvied** *a.* **scurvily** *adv.* **scurviness** *n.* **scurvy grass** *n.* any plant of the genus *Cochlearia*, formerly used as a remedy for scurvy. [SCURFY (under SCURF)]

scut (skŭt) *n.* a short tail, esp. of a hare, rabbit or deer. [cp. Icel. *skott*]

scuta SCUTUM.

scutage (skū´tij) *n.* (*Hist.*) money paid by a feudal tenant in lieu of personal attendance on his lord in war. [med. L *scūtāgium*, from *scūtum*, shield (cp. OF *escuage*)]

scutal, scutate SCUTUM.

scutch (skŭch) *v.t.* to dress (cotton, flax etc.) by beating. ~*n.* **1** a scutcher. **2** coarse tow separated from flax by scutching. **scutcher** *n.* an implement used in scutching flux. [OF *escoucher*, *escousser*, perh. from Scand. (cp. Norw. *skoka*, scutcher)]

scutcheon (skŭch´ən) *n.* **1** an escutcheon. **2** a cover or frame for a keyhole. **3** a nameplate. **scutcheoned** *a.* [ESCUTCHEON]

scute SCUTUM.

scutellum (skūtel´əm) *n.* (*pl.* **scutella** (-lə)) a small shield, plate, scale or horny segment in or on a plant or animal. **scutellar, scutellate** (skū´tələt), **scutellated** (-lātid) *a.* **scutellation** (-ā´shən) *n.* **scutelliform** (-tel´ifawm) *a.* shield-shaped. [dim. of SCUTUM]

scutter (skŭt´ə) *v.i.* to scurry, scuttle. ~*n.* the act or an instance of scuttering. [SCUTTLE[3]]

scuttle[1] (skŭt´əl) *n.* **1** a metal or other receptacle for carrying or holding coals, esp. for a fireplace, usu. called a coal scuttle. **2** the part of a motor-car body immediately behind the bonnet. **scuttleful** *n.* (*pl.*

scuttlefuls). [OE *scutel*, dish, L *scutella*, salver, dim. of *scutra*, tray, platter]

scuttle[2] (skŭt´əl) *n.* **1** a hole with a movable lid or hatch in a wall or roof or the deck or side of a ship. **2** the lid or hatch covering this. ~*v.t.* **1** to cut holes through the bottom or sides of (a ship). **2** to sink by cutting such holes. **scuttlebutt** *n.* **1** a cask of drinking water, usu. with a hole for dipping through, kept on the deck of a ship. **2** (*coll.*) rumour, gossip. **scuttlecask** *n.* a scuttlebutt on a ship. **scuttler**[1] *n.* [OF *escoutilles*, pl., hatches (cp. F *écoutille*), Sp. *escotilla*, from *escotar*, to cut out round the neck, from *escote*, tucker, from Gmc. (cp. Dut. *schoot*, G *Schoss*, bosom)]

scuttle[3] (skŭt´əl) *v.i.* **1** to hurry along, to scurry. **2** to make off, to bolt. ~*n.* **1** a hurried run or gait. **2** a hasty flight, a bolt. **scuttler**[2] *n.* [orig. *scuddle*, freq. of SCUD]

scuttler[1] SCUTTLE[2].

scuttler[2] SCUTTLE[3].

scutum (skū´təm) *n.* (*pl.* **scuta** (-tə)) **1** a scute. **2** the kneecap. **3** (*Hist.*) the shield of the heavy-armed Roman legionaries. **scutal** *a.* **scutate** (-tət) *a.* **1** covered with scutes or bony plates. **2** shield-shaped. **scute** *n.* a shieldlike plate, scale or bony or horny segment as of the armour of a crocodile, turtle etc. **scutiform** (-tifawm) *a.* **scutulum** (-tūləm) *n.* (*pl.* **scutula** (-lə)) a shield-shaped scale or scab, esp. in ringworm of the scalp. **scutulate** (-lət) *a.* [L, from *sku-*, to cover, cogn. with SKY]

scuzzy (skŭz´i) *a.* (*comp.* **scuzzier**, *superl.* **scuzziest**) (*sl.*) squalid or disgusting. **scuzz** *n.* [prob. abbr. of DISGUSTING (under DISGUST)]

scye (sī) *n.* the opening of a coat etc. where the sleeve is inserted. [Sc. dial.]

Scylla (sil´ə) *n.* either of a pair of alternative risks. **between Scylla and Charybdis** caught between alternative risks, escape from one of which entails danger from the other. [L, from Gr. *Skulla*, a rock on the Italian shore of the Straits of Messina, facing Charybdis, described by Homer as a monster devouring sailors]

scyphozoan (sīfəzō´ən, skī-, skif-) *n.* any marine jellyfish of the class Scyphozoa. ~*a.* of or relating to this class. [Gr. *skuphos*, bowl, *zōion*, animal]

scyphus (sī´fəs) *n.* (*pl.* **scyphi** (-fī)) **1** a bowl-shaped footless Greek cup with two handles. **2** a cup-shaped plant part or organ. **scyphiform** (-fifawm), **scyphose** (-fōs) *a.* [L, from Gr. *skuphos*]

scythe (sīdh) *n.* **1** a long curved blade with a crooked handle used for mowing or reaping. **2** a curved blade projecting from the axle of an ancient war chariot. ~*v.t.* to cut with a scythe. **scythed** *a.* **scytheman** *n.* (*pl.* **scythemen**) a person who uses a scythe, a mower. **scythe stone** *n.* a whetstone for sharpening scythes. [OE *sīthe* (cp. Dut. *zeis*, Icel. *sigthr*, LG *Saged*), cogn. with L *secāre*, to cut]

Scythian (sidh´iən) *a.* of or relating to ancient Scythia, the region north of the Black Sea, the Caspian and the Sea of Aral, or the ancient people inhabiting it. ~*n.* **1** a member of this people. **2** the Scythian language. **Scythic** *a.* **Scythism** *n.* **Scytho-** *comb. form.*

SD *abbr.* **1** senile dementia. **2** Social Democrat. **3** South Dakota. **4** standard deviation. **5** Swaziland (IVR).

sd *abbr.* indefinitely. [L *sine die*]

s.d. *abbr.* **1** semi-detached. **2** standard deviation.

SDA *abbr.* **1** Scottish Development Agency. **2** Seventh Day Adventists.

S.Dak. *abbr.* South Dakota.

SDAT *abbr.* senile dementia of the Alzheimer type.

S-DAT *abbr.* stationary digital audio tape.

SDD *abbr.* **1** Scottish Development Department. **2** subscriber direct dialling.

SDI *abbr.* Strategic Defence Initiative.

SDLP *abbr.* Social Democratic and Labour Party.

SDP *abbr.* (*Hist.*) Social Democratic Party.

SDR *abbr.* **1** special discretion required. **2** special drawing right(s).

SDS *abbr.* sodium dodecyl sulphate.

SE *abbr.* **1** Society of Engineers. **2** south-east. **3** south-eastern.

Se *chem. symbol* selenium.

s.e. *abbr.* standard error.

se- (sə, si) *pref.* away from, apart, without, as in *secede*, *secure*. [L]

sea (sē) *n.* **1** the body of salt water covering the greater part of the earth's surface, the ocean. **2** a definite part of this, or a very large enclosed body of (usu. salt) water. **3** the swell or motion of the sea. **4** a great wave, a billow. **5** the set or direction of the waves. **6** a vast quantity or expanse, an ocean, a flood (of people, troubles etc.). ~*a.* of, relating to, living, growing or used in, on or near the sea, marine, maritime. **all at sea** perplexed, uncertain, wide of the mark. **at full sea** **1** at high tide. **2** at the acme or culmination. **at sea** **1** on the open sea. **2** out of sight of land. **3** perplexed, uncertain, wide of the mark. **beyond seas** overseas. **by sea** in a ship. **on the sea** **1** in a ship at sea. **2** situated on the coast. **to follow the sea** to go to sea. **to go to sea** to become or to be a sailor. **to put (out) to sea** to leave port or land. **sea acorn** *n.* a barnacle. **sea anchor** *n.* a sail stretched by spars and thrown overboard to lessen the leeway of a drifting ship. **sea anemone** *n.* any of various coelenterates of the order Actinaria, having a polypoid body with oral rings of tentacles. **sea-angel** *n.* the angelfish. **sea ape** *n.* **1** the sea fox. **2** the sea otter. **sea aster** *n.* a perennial plant, *Aster tripolium*, growing on salt marshes. **sea bass** *n.* a serranoid food-fish, esp. *Centropristis striatus*, common on the Atlantic shores of the US. **sea bat** *n.* **1** a flying fish. **2** a fish of the genus *Platax* (from the length of its dorsal and ventral fins). **sea bear** *n.* **1** a polar bear. **2** the N Pacific fur seal. **sea-beaten** *a.* beaten by the waves. **seabed** *n.* the floor of the sea. **sea beet** *n.* the wild form of *Beta vulgaris*. **sea-belt** *n.* a species of fucus with beltlike fronds. **seabird** *n.* **seablite** *n.* an annual of the goosefoot family, *Suaeda maritima*, which grows on salt marshes. **seaboard** *n.* **1** land bordering on the sea. **2** the seacoast. **3** the seashore. ~*a.* bordering on the sea. **sea-boat** *n.* a ship (with regard to her seagoing qualities). **seaborne** *a.* conveyed by sea. **sea-bow** *n.* a bow like a rainbow produced in sea spray. **sea bream** *n.* a marine fish of the family Sparidae, esp. of the genus *Pagellus* or *Spondyliosoma*. **sea breeze** *n.* a breeze blowing from the sea, usu. by day, in alternation with a land breeze at night. **sea buckthorn** *n.* a shrub, *Hippophae rhamnoides*, which grows on seacoasts. **sea butterfly** *n.* a pteropod. **sea calf** *n.* the common seal. **sea campion** *n.* a plant of the pink family, *Silene maritima*. **sea-cap** *n.* **1** the cap of a wave. **2** (*N Am.*) a large basket-shaped sponge. **sea captain** *n.* **1** the captain of a vessel, as distinct from a military officer. **2** a great commander or admiral. **sea card** *n.* **1** the card of the mariner's compass. **2** a map or chart. **sea change** *n.* a transformation or transmutation. **sea-chest** *n.* a sailor's storage chest. †**sea coal** *n.* coal (orig. brought from Newcastle by sea) as distinct from charcoal. **seacoast** *n.* a coast. **seacock** *n.* a valve through which the sea can be admitted into the hull of a ship. **sea-colander** *n.* an olive-coloured seaweed with perforated fronds. **sea cow** *n.* **1** a sirenian. **2** a walrus. **sea cucumber, sea gherkin** *n.* a holothurian such as the trepang. **sea deity** SEA GOD (under SEA). **sea devil** *n.* **1** the angler fish. **2** any holothurian, esp. the bêche-de-mer. **sea dog** *n.* **1** an old sailor, esp. of the Elizabethan era. **2** the common seal. **3** the dogfish. **sea dragon** *n.* any of various fishes having some resemblance to a dragon. **sea eagle** *n.* **1** any of various fishing eagles, esp. of the genus *Haliaeetus*, and other large seabirds. **2** the osprey. **sea-ear** *n.* an ormer or mollusc of the genus *Haliotis*. **sea egg** *n.* a sea urchin. **sea elephant** *n.* the elephant seal. **sea fan** *n.* a coral of the genus *Gorgonia* or a related genus, having fanlike branches. **seafarer** *n.* **1** a sailor. **2** a traveller by sea. **seafaring** *a.* **1** travelling by sea. **2** following the occupation of a sailor. ~*n.* **1** travel by sea. **2** the occupation of a sailor. **sea fennel** *n.* samphire. **sea fight** *n.* a naval engagement. **sea fir** *n.* a hydroid colony. **sea flower** *n.* the sea anemone. **sea foam** *n.* froth on the sea's surface. **seafood** *n.* edible salt-water fish and crustaceans, esp. shellfish. **sea fowl** *n.* **sea fox** *n.* the long-tailed shark, *Alopias vulpes*. **sea fret** *n.* a fog or mist coming off the sea. **seafront** *n.* the part of a town that faces the sea. **sea gauge** *n.* **1** a self-registering apparatus for taking deep-sea soundings. **2** the draught of a ship. **sea gherkin** SEA CUCUMBER (under SEA). **sea gilliflower** *n.* the sea pink. **sea-girt** *a.* (*poet.*) surrounded by the sea. **sea god, sea deity** *n.* a deity supposed to preside over the sea. **sea goddess** *n.* **seagoing** *a.* **1** making foreign voyages, as opposed to *coasting*. **2** seafaring. **sea gooseberry** *n.* any ctenophore with a rounded body and numerous cilia. **sea green** *n.* a faint bluish green. **sea-green** *a.* **seagull** *n.* a gull (family Laridae). **sea hare** *n.* any mollusc of the genus *Aplysia* with earlike tentacles. **sea heath** *n.* a small wiry perennial plant, *Frankenia laevis*. **sea hedgehog** *n.* a sea urchin. **sea hog** *n.* the common porpoise. **sea holly** *n.* an umbelliferous plant, *Eryngium maritimum*, with spiny leaves. **sea horse** *n.* **1** any of various upright fish of the family Syngnathidae, esp. *Hippocampus hippocampus*. **2** a fabulous animal, half horse and half fish. **sea-island cotton** *n.* a fine variety of cotton originally grown on the islands off the coasts of Georgia, S Carolina and Florida. **seajack** *v.t.* to hijack at sea. ~*n.* an act of sea-jacking. **seajacker** *n.* **seakale** *n.* a cruciferous plant, *Crambe maritima*, grown as a culinary vegetable for its young shoots. **seakale beet** *n.* CHARD. **sea king** *n.* (*poet.*) a viking or piratical Scandinavian chieftain. **sea lane** *n.* a route for ships at sea. **sea lavender** *n.* any maritime plant of the genus *Limonium*, which have spikes of white, pink or mauve flowers. **sea lawyer** *n.* **1** a sailor given to arguing and criticizing. **2** a shark. **sea legs** *n.pl.* ability to walk on the deck of a vessel at sea on a stormy day. **sea lemon** *n.* a yellow oval gastropod of the genus *Doris*. **sea leopard** *n.* a spotted seal from the S Pacific and Antarctic. **sea letter, sea pass** *n.* a document from the custom house carried by a neutral ship in time of war, specifying the nature of the cargo etc. **sea lettuce** *n.* any of various green seaweeds of the genus *Ulva*, with edible fronds. **sea level** *n.* a level continuous with that of the surface of the sea at mean tide, taken as a basis for surveying etc. (in Britain at Newlyn, Cornwall). **sea lily** *n.* (*pl.* **sea lilies**) any echinoderm of the class Crinoidea, esp. of the genus *Ptilocrinus*. **sealine** *n.* the horizon at sea. **sea lion** *n.* **1** a large-eared seal, esp. of the genus *Zalophus* or *Otaria*. **2** (*Her.*) a fabulous animal, half lion and half fish. **sea loch** *n.* (*Sc.*) a lakelike arm of the sea. **Sea Lord** *n.* either of two senior naval officers (First Sea Lord and Second Sea Lord) on the admiralty board of the Ministry of Defence. **sea magpie** SEA-PIE[1] (under SEA). **sea maid** *n.* **1** (*Shak.*) a mermaid. **2** a sea-nymph. **seaman** *n.* (*pl.* **seamen**) **1** a mariner, a sailor, esp. one below the rank of officer. **2** a person able to navigate a ship, a navigator. **seamanlike, seamanly** *a.* **seamanship** *n.* **seamark** *n.* an elevated object, such as a lighthouse or beacon, serving as a guide to vessels at sea. **sea mat** *n.* a polyzoan forming a flat matted coral. **sea melon** *n.* a holothurian, sea cucumber. **seamew** *n.* a seagull. **sea mile** *n.* a nautical mile. **sea milkwort** *n.* a trailing, primulaceous plant, *Glaux maritima*, with small pink flowers. **sea monster** *n.* a huge sea creature, natural or mythical. **sea moss** *n.* **1** a mosslike coralline or seaweed. **2** corrageen. **seamount** *n.* a mountain under the sea that rises more than 1000 metres above the ocean floor. **sea mouse** *n.* an iridescent sea worm, *Aphrodite aculeata*. **sea nettle** *n.* a jellyfish. **sea onion** *n.* the squill. **sea otter** *n.* a marine otter, *Enhydra lutris*, of the shores of the N Pacific. **sea pass** SEA LETTER (under SEA). **sea pen** *n.* any of various coelenterates of the genus *Pennatula*, which form feather-like colonies. **sea perch** *n.* **1** any of various serranid fishes, such as the bass and stone bass. **2** the surfperch, a viviparous percoid fish of the family Embiotocidae. **sea-pie[1], sea magpie, sea pilot** *n.* the oystercatcher, *Haematopus ostralegus*. **sea-pie[2]** *n.* a sailors' dish of crust and meat in alternate layers, baked together. **sea-piece** *n.* a seascape. **sea pig** *n.* **1** a porpoise. **2** a dugong. **sea pike** *n.* **1** the garfish. **2** the hake. **sea pilot** SEA-PIE[1] (under SEA). **sea pink** *n.* thrift, *Armeria maritima*. **seaplane** *n.* an aeroplane fitted with floats to enable it to take off from and alight on the water. **seaport** *n.* a town with a harbour on the coast. **sea power** *n.* **1** a nation that has great naval strength. **2** naval strength. **sea pumpkin** *n.* a holothurian, a sea cucumber. **sea purse** *n.* the leathery envelope in which sharks and rays deposit their eggs. **sea purslane** *n.* a small shrub, *Halimione portulacoides*, that grows on salt marshes. **seaquake** *n.* an earthquake at sea. **sea ranger** *n.* a ranger in the Girl Guide Association who trains in seamanship. **searat** *n.* a pirate. **sea-raven** *n.* **1** a large fish, *Hemitripterus americanus* of the N American Atlantic. **2** a cormorant. **sea-risk** *n.* hazard of injury or loss at sea. **searobber** *n.* a pirate. **sea robin** *n.* any of various gurnards of the genus *Prionotus* and related genera. **sea roll** *n.* a holothurian. **sea room** *n.* room to handle a ship without danger of running ashore or of collision. **sea rosemary** *n.* the sea lavender. **sea-rover** *n.* **1** a pirate. **2** a piratical vessel. **sea salt** *n.* salt obtained from sea water by evaporation. **seascape** *n.* a picture representing a scene at sea. **sea scorpion** *n.* **1** any fish of the genus *Scorpaena*. **2** the sculpin, *Cottus scorpius*. **Sea Scout** *n.* a member of a branch of the Scouts specializing in sailing etc. **sea serpent** *n.* **1** a sea snake. **2** a creature of immense size and serpentine form, believed by mariners to inhabit the depths of the ocean. **sea shanty** *n.* SHANTY[2]. **seashell** *n.* the shell of a marine mollusc. **seashore** *n.* **1** the shore, coast or margin of the sea. **2** (*Law*) the space between high and low water marks. **3** land adjacent to the sea. **seasick** *a.* suffering from seasickness. **seasickness** *n.* a peculiar functional disturbance characterized by nausea and vomiting, brought on by the motion of a ship. **seaside** *n.* a place or district close to the sea, esp. a holiday resort. ~*a.* bordering on the sea. **sea-sleeve** *n.* a cuttlefish. **sea slug** *n.* **1** any of various shell-less marine gastropod molluscs, esp. of the order *Nudibranchia*. **2** a trepang. **sea snail** *n.* **1** any snail-like marine gastropod such as a whelk. **2** a slimy fish of the family Liparididae, esp. *Liparis liparis*, the unctuous sucker. **sea snake** *n.* a venomous marine snake of the family Hydrophidae inhabiting the Indian Ocean and other tropical seas. **sea snipe** *n.* **1** the snipe fish. **2** the dunlin, *Calidris alpina*. **sea spider** *n.* a small marine arachnid, resembling a spider. **sea squirt** *n.* an ascidian. **sea sunflower** *n.* a sea anemone. **sea swallow** *n.* the tern. **sea tang, sea tangle** *n.* a seaweed of the genus *Laminaria*. **sea-term** *n.* a word or phrase peculiar to seamen. **sea toad** *n.* **1** the toadfish. **2** the angler fish. **3** the sculpin. **sea trout** *n.* the salmon trout, bulltrout and some other fishes. **sea unicorn** *n.* the narwhal. **sea urchin** *n.* an echinus. **sea wall** *n.* a wall or embankment for protecting land against encroachment by the sea. **seaward** *a.* directed or situated towards the sea. ~*adv.* towards the sea. ~*n.* a seaward side or aspect. **seawards** *adv.* **seaware** *n.* any large coarse seaweed, esp. when used as a fertilizer. **sea wasp** *n.* a jellyfish of the order Cubomedusae, of Australian tropical waters. **sea water** *n.* water of or from the sea. **seaway** *n.* **1** an inland waterway on which ocean-going ships can travel. **2** a ship's progress. **3** a clear way for a ship at sea. **seaweed** *n.* **1** any alga or other plant growing in the sea. **2** such algae collectively. **seaweeded, seaweedy** *a.* **sea whip** *n.* a whip-shaped coral. **sea whipcord** *n.* a variety of seaweed. **sea-wife** *n.* a variety of wrasse. **sea wolf** *n.* **1** a viking. **2** a pirate. **3** a large voracious fish, esp. the wolf-fish, *Anarhicas lupus.* **4** the sea elephant. **seaworthy** *a.* (of a ship) in a fit state to go to sea. **seaworthiness** *n.* **sea wrack** *n.* coarse seaweed, esp. thrown up by the waves. [OE *sǣ*, cp. Dut. *zee*, G *See*, Icel. *saer*]

seaborgium (sēbaw´giəm) *n.* (a name proposed for) the artificial radioactive element, at. no. 106, chem. symbol Sg. [Glenn Theodore *Seaborg*, b. 1912, US chemist and physicist]

SEAC *abbr.* (*Hist.*) School Examination and Assessment Council.

SEAL *abbr.* sea, air, land (team).

seal[1] (sēl) *n.* **1** a carnivorous amphibious marine mammal of various species of the family Phocidae, having flipper-like limbs adapted for swimming and thick fur. **2** any allied mammal belonging to the family Otariidae, distinguished by having visible external ears, comprising the sea lions and fur seals. **3** sealskin. *~v.i.* to hunt seals. **sealer[1]** *n.* a ship or person engaged in hunting seals. **seal-fishery** *n.* (*pl.* **seal-fisheries**). **seal-rookery** *n.* (*pl.* **seal-rookeries**) a breeding-place of seals. **sealskin** *n.* **1** the underfur of the fur seal, esp. prepared for use as material for jackets etc. **2** a sealskin garment. [OE *seolh*, cp. Icel. *selr*, Dan. *sæl*, Swed. *själ*]

seal[2] (sēl) *n.* **1** a die or stamp having a device, usu. in intaglio, for making an impression on wax or other plastic substance. **2** a piece of wax, lead or other material stamped with this and attached to a document as a mark of authenticity etc., or to an envelope, package, box etc. to prevent its being opened without detection etc. **3** the impression made thus on wax, lead etc. **4** a stamped wafer- or other mark affixed to a document in lieu of this. **5** any device that must be broken to give access. **6** any act, gift or event regarded as authenticating, ratifying or guaranteeing. **7** a symbolic, significant or characteristic mark or impress. **8** a decorative adhesive stamp. **9** a vow of secrecy. **10** anything used to close a gap, prevent the escape of gas etc. **11** water in the trap of a drainpipe preventing the ascent of foul air. *~v.t.* **1** to affix a seal to. **2** to stamp with a seal or stamp, esp. as a mark of correctness or authenticity. **3** to fasten with a seal. **4** to close hermetically, to shut up. **5** to close (the lips etc.) tightly. **6** to confine securely. **7** to secure against leaks, draughts etc. **8** to make (e.g. wood) impermeable to rain, etc. by applying a coating. **9** to fix or fill with plaster etc. **10** to confirm. **11** to ratify, to certify. **12** to set a mark on, to designate or destine irrevocably. **one's lips are sealed** one must keep a secret. **to set one's seal on** to authorize. **to set one's seal to** to authorize. **under seal** in a document authenticated by a seal. **sealable** *a.* **sealant** *n.* a substance for sealing wood, stopping up gaps etc. **sealed** *a.* **sealed-beam** *a.* of or relating to electric lights, such as car headlights, in which the reflector and bulb are in one sealed unit. **sealed book** *n.* something beyond one's knowledge or understanding. **sealed orders** *n.pl.* orders that must not be read until a specified time. **sealer[2]** *n.* **1** a device or substance that seals. **2** (*Can.*) (*also* **sealer jar**) a jar used for preserving fruit etc. **3** (*Hist. or N Am.*) an official who examines weights and measures for accuracy. **sealing** *n.* **sealing wax** *n.* a composition of shellac and turpentine with a pigment used for sealing letters etc. **seal-pipe** *n.* a dip-pipe. **seal-ring** *n.* a finger ring with a seal. **seals of office** *n.pl.* seals held by the Lord Chancellor, Secretary of State etc. as a symbol of office. **sealwort** *n.* Solomon's seal. [OF *seel* (F *sceau*), L *sigillum*, cogn. with *signum*, SIGN]

sealer[1] SEAL[1].

sealer[2] SEAL[2].

Sealyham (sē´lihəm, -liəm), **Sealyham terrier** *n.* a breed of Welsh terrier. [village in SW Wales]

seam (sēm) *n.* **1** a ridge or other visible line of junction between two parts or things, esp. two pieces of cloth etc. sewn together, planks fitted edge to edge, or sheet metal lapped over at the edges. **2** (*Anat.*) a suture. **3** a mark of separation, a crack, a fissure. **4** a line on the surface of anything, esp. the face, a wrinkle, a cicatrix, a scar. **5** a thin layer separating two strata of rock. **6** a thin stratum of coal. **7** (*N Am.*) a piece of sewing. *~v.t.* **1** to join together with or as with a seam. **2** to mark with a seam, furrow, scar etc. **bursting at the seams** BURST. **seam bowler** *n.* in cricket, a bowler who makes the ball bounce on its seam so that it changes direction. **seam bowling** *n.* **seamed** *a.* **seamer, seaming machine** *n.* a sewing machine for making seams. **seaming plough** *n.* a seam presser. **seam-lace, seaming-lace** *n.* galloon, braid etc., used to cover the seams in upholstery. **seamless** *a.* **seamlessly** *adv.* **seam presser** *n.* **1** a heavy iron used by tailors for pressing seams. **2** an implement used to flatten down the ridges after ploughing. **seam-rent** *n.* a rent along a seam. *~a.* ragged. **seamstress** (-stris), **sempstress** (semp´-) *n.* a woman whose occupation is sewing. **seamy** *a.* (*comp.* **seamier,** *superl.* **seamiest**) **1** showing the seams. **2** disreputable, sordid, unpleasant. **seaminess** *n.* [OE (cp. Dut. *zoom*, G *Saum*, Icel. *saumr*), rel. to SEW]

Seanad (shan´ədh), **Seanad Eireann** (eə´rən) *n.* the upper house, or senate, of the parliament of the Republic of Ireland. [Ir.]

seance (sā´ons, -ās), **séance** *n.* **1** a meeting for exhibiting, receiving or investigating spiritualistic manifestations. **2** a session, as of a society, deliberative body etc. [F, a sitting, from OF *seoir*, L *sedēre*, to sit]

SEAQ *abbr.* Stock Exchange Automated Quotations (a computerized system for recording trade and price changes in shares, used by the London Stock Exchange).

sear (siə), **sere** *v.t.* **1** to burn or scorch the surface of to dryness and hardness. **2** to cauterize. **3** (*fig.*) to brand. **4** to cause pain or anguish to. **5** to brown (meat) at a high temperature so that the juices are retained. **6** to make callous or insensible. **7** †to wither up, to blast. *~a.* (*poet.*) (of leaves etc.) dried up, withered. **seared** *a.* hardened, insensible, callous. **searedness** *n.* **searing** *a.* **searingly** *adv.* [OE *sear*, a. from Gmc. (cp. Gr. *auos*, for *sausos*, dry, and AUSTERE), whence *sēarian*, to sear]

search (sœch) *v.t.* **1** to go over and examine for what may be found or to find something. **2** to examine (esp. a person) for concealed weapons etc. **3** to explore, to probe. **4** to look for, to seek (out). *~v.i.* to make a search, inquiry or investigation. *~n.* **1** the act of seeking, looking or inquiring. **2** investigation, exploration, inquiry, quest, examination. **in search of** trying to find. **search me!** (*coll.*) how should I know?, I have no idea. **searchable** *a.* **search engine** *n.* (*Comput.*) a program that searches for data, files etc. **searcher** *n.* **searching** *a.* **1** making search or inquiry. **2** penetrating, thorough, minute, close. **searchingly** *adv.* **searchingness** *n.* **searchless** *a.* **searchlight** *n.* an electric arc light or other powerful illuminant concentrated into a beam that can be turned in any direction for lighting channels, discovering an enemy etc. **search party** *n.* a party going out to search for a lost, concealed or abducted person or thing. **search warrant** *n.* a warrant granted by a Justice of the Peace, authorizing entry into a house etc. to search for stolen property etc. [ME *serchen*, OF *cercher* (F *chercher*), L *circāre*, to go round, from CIRCUS]

season (sē´zən) *n.* **1** any one of the four divisions of the year, spring, summer, autumn, winter. **2** a period of time of a specified or indefinite length. **3** the period of the greatest activity of something, or when it is in vogue, plentiful, at its best etc. **4** a favourable, opportune, fit, suitable or convenient time. **5** a period when a mammal is on heat. **6** (*coll.*) a season ticket. **7** †seasoning. ~*v.t.* **1** to render palatable or give a higher relish to by the addition of condiments etc. **2** to make more piquant or pleasant, to add zest to. **3** to make sound or fit for use by preparation, esp. by tempering, maturing, acclimatizing, inuring, habituating or hardening. **4** to make mature or experienced. **5** to mitigate, to moderate, to qualify (justice with mercy etc.). ~*v.i.* **1** to become inured, habituated, accustomed etc. **2** (of timber) to become hard and dry. **in season 1** in vogue. **2** in condition for shooting, hatching, use, mating, eating etc. **3** (of a mammal) on heat. **4** at a fit or opportune time. **in season and out of season** at all times, continuously or indiscriminately. **seasonable** *a.* **1** occurring or done at the proper time, opportune. **2** suitable to the season. **seasonableness** *n.* **seasonably** *adv.* **seasonal** *a.* **1** of or occurring at a particular season. **2** required, done etc. according to the season. **seasonal affective disorder** *n.* a state of fatigue and depression occurring in the winter months, thought to be caused by lack of sunlight. **seasonality** (-nal´-) *n.* **seasonally** *adv.* **seasoner** *n.* **seasoning** *n.* **1** anything added to food to make it more palatable. **2** anything that increases enjoyment. **seasonless** *a.* **season ticket** *n.* a railway or other ticket, usu. issued at a reduced rate, valid for any number of journeys etc., for the period specified. [OF *seson* (F *saison*), L *satiōnem*, nom. *-tio*, from *serere*, to sow]

Usage note The adjectives *seasonable* and *seasonal* should not be confused: *seasonable* means suitable to the season, and *seasonal* relating to or done at a particular season.

seat (sēt) *n.* **1** something on which a person sits or may sit, a chair, bench, stool etc. **2** the part of a chair etc. on which a person's weight rests in sitting. **3** the part of a machine or other structure on which another part or thing is supported. **4** the buttocks or the part of trousers etc. covering them. **5** a place for sitting or where one may sit. **6** the place where anything is, location, site, situation. **7** a place in which authority is vested. **8** a country residence, a mansion. **9** the right of sitting, esp. in a legislative body. **10** manner or posture of sitting. ~*v.t.* **1** to cause to sit down, to place or set on a seat. **2** to assign seats to. **3** to provide (a church etc.) with seats. **4** to provide (a chair, trousers etc.) with a seat. **5** to settle, to locate, to install, to establish, to fix in place. ~*v.i.* **1** (of a garment) to become baggy from sitting. **2** to settle. **be seated** sit down. **by the seat of one's pants** (*coll.*) by intuition or instinct. **to take a seat** to sit down. **to take one's seat** to sit down. **seatage** (-ij) *n.* **seat back** *n.* a loose ornamental covering for the back of a chair etc. **seat belt** *n.* a strap to hold a person in a seat in a car, aeroplane etc. **seated** *a.* sitting. **seater** *n.* (*usu in comb.*, as *two-seater*). **seating** *n.* **1** the provision of seats. **2** the seats provided or their arrangement. **3** material for seats. **4** a support on which something rests. **seatless** *a.* [ME *sete*, Icel. *saeti*, cogn. with SIT]

SEATO (sē´tō) *abbr.* South-East Asia Treaty Organization.

sebaceous (sibā´shəs) *a.* **1** fatty. **2** made of fatty or oily matter. **3** (of glands, ducts, follicles etc.) containing, conveying, or secreting fatty or oily matter to the skin or hair. **sebacic** (-bas´-) *a.* **sebacic acid** *n.* an acid derived from various oils. **sebate** (sē´bāt) *n.* a salt of this. **sebiferous** (-bif´-), **sebific** (-bif´-) *a.* **seborrhoea** (sebərē´ə), (*N Am.*) **seborrhea** *n.* excessive secretion of sebum. **seborrhoeic** *a.* **sebum** (sē´bəm) *n.* the fatty matter secreted by the sebaceous glands, which lubricates the hair and skin. [L *sēbāceus*, from *sēbum*, tallow]

Sebat SHEBAT.

sebate, sebiferous etc. SEBACEOUS.

SEC *abbr.* Securities and Exchange Commission.

Sec. *abbr.* secretary.

sec[1] (sek) *n.* (*coll.*) a second (of time).

sec[2] (sek) *a.* (of wine) dry. [F, from L *siccus*]

sec[3] (sek) *abbr.* secant.

sec. *abbr.* **1** second(s). **2** secondary. **3** secretary. **4** section.

secability (sekəbil´iti) *n.* capability of being cut or divided into parts. [late L *secābilitas*, from *secāre*, to cut]

SECAM *abbr.* *sequentiel couleur à mémoire* (a French colour television broadcasting system).

secant (sē´kənt) *a.* **1** cutting. **2** dividing into two parts. ~*n.* **1** a straight line intersecting a curve, esp. a radius of a circle drawn through the second extremity of an arc of this and terminating in a tangent to the first extremity. **2** the ratio of this to the radius. **3** the ratio of the hypotenuse to the base of a right-angled triangle formed by drawing a perpendicular to either side of the angle. [L *secans -antem*, pres.p. of *secāre*, to cut]

secateurs (sekətœz´) *n.pl.* pruning scissors. [F]

secco (sek´ō) *n.* (*pl.* **seccos**) tempera-painting on dry plaster. ~*a.* (*Mus.*) plain, unadorned. [It., dry]

secede (sisēd´) *v.i.* to withdraw from membership, association or communion, as with a Church. **seceder** *n.* **1** a person who secedes. **2** (*pl.*, *Hist.*) those who seceded from the Scottish Church in 1733. [L *sēcēdere* (SE-, *cedere*, to go, p.p. *cessus*)]

secern (sisœn´) *v.t.* **1** to separate, to distinguish. **2** to secrete or excrete. **secernent** *a.* secretory. ~*n.* **1** a secretory organ. **2** a drug etc. promoting secretion. **secernment** *n.* [L *sēcernere* (SE-, *cernere*, to separate)]

secesh (sisesh´) *n.* (*N Am.*, *coll.*) a secessionist. ~*a.* of or relating to the Secession or secessionists. **secesher** *n.*

secession (sisesh´ən) *n.* **1** the act of seceding. **2** (*Hist.*) (**Secession**) the withdrawal of 11 southern states from the US Union in 1860. **secessional** *a.* **secessionism** *n.* **secessionist** *n.* a seceder or advocate of secessionism, esp. one who took part with the southern states in the American Civil War of 1861–5. [L *sēcessio*, see SECEDE]

Sec. Gen. *abbr.* Secretary-General.

sech (sesh) *abbr.* hyperbolic secant.

seckel (sek´əl) *n.* a small, pulpy variety of pear. [*Seckel*, of Pennsylvania, who introduced it]

seclude (siklood´) *v.t.* **1** to shut up or keep (a person, place etc.) apart or away from society. **2** to cause to be solitary or retired. **secluded** *a.* **1** hidden from view, private. **2** away from others, solitary. **secludedly** *adv.* **secludedness** *n.* **seclusion** (-zhən) *n.* **seclusionist** *n.* **seclusive** *a.* [L *sēclūdere* (SE-, *claudere*, to shut)]

second[1] (sek´ənd) *a.* **1** immediately following the first in time, place or position. **2** next in value, authority, rank or position. **3** secondary, inferior. **4** other, alternate. **5** additional, supplementary. **6** subordinate, derivative. **7** (*Mus.*) lower in pitch. **8** (*Mus.*) performing a subordinate part. ~*n.* **1** the next after the first in rank, importance etc. **2** a second class in an examination etc. **3** a person taking this. **4** another or an additional person or thing. **5** a person who supports another, esp. one who attends on the principal in a duel, boxing match etc. **6** the 60th part of a minute of time or angular measurement. **7** (*coll.*) a very short time. **8** (*pl.*) goods that have a slight flaw or are of second quality. **9** (*pl.*) coarse, inferior flour, or bread made from this. **10** (*Mus.*) the interval of one tone between two notes, either a whole tone or a semitone. **11** (*Mus.*) the next tone above or below. 12 (*Mus.*) two tones so separated combined together. 13 (*Mus.*) a lower part added to a melody when arranged for two voices or instruments. 14 (*coll.*) an alto. 15 second gear. 16 (*pl., coll.*) a second helping or course of a meal. ~*v.t.* 1 to forward, to promote, to support. 2 to support (a resolution) formally to show that the proposer is not isolated. **in the second place** as a second consideration etc. **second to none** unsurpassed. **to play second fiddle** FIDDLE. **second advent** *n.* the return of Christ to establish His personal reign on earth. **second adventist** *n.* a premillenarian. **second ballot** *n.* a procedure in an election to choose a clear winner after some candidates have been eliminated in a first ballot. **second-best** *a.* next after best, of second quality. ~*n.* an alternative. **second cause** *n.* (*Logic*) a cause that is itself caused. **second chamber** *n.* the upper house in a legislative body having two chambers. **second childhood** *n.* a person's dotage. **second class** *n.* 1 the category next to the first or highest. 2 the second level of an honours degree. 3 the class of mail not given priority. 4 (*N Am.*) a class of mail for newspapers etc. **second-class** *a.* 1 of second or inferior quality, rank etc., second-rate. 2 treated as inferior or second-rate. 3 of the second class. ~*adv.* by second class. **second coming** *n.* the second advent. **second cousin** *n.* the child of a parent's cousin. **second-degree** *a.* (of burns) that cause blistering but not permanent scars. **Second Empire** *n.* the empire of Napoleon III (1852–70). **seconder** *n.* **second floor** *n.* 1 the second from the ground floor. 2 (*US*) the first storey. **second gear** *n.* the forward gear next above first gear in a car etc. **second generation** *n.* children of parents who were the first of their families to be born in a given country. **second-generation** *a.* 1 of an improved stage of development. 2 denoting the children of a first generation. **second-guess** *v.t.* 1 (*coll.*) to forestall (a person) by guessing their actions, reactions etc. in advance. 2 to re-evaluate (a situation etc.) with hindsight. **second hand** *n.* the hand on a watch or clock that indicates seconds. **second-hand** *a.* 1 not primary or original. 2 not new, sold or for sale after having been used or worn. 3 dealing in second-hand goods. ~*adv.* at second hand. **at second hand** as one deriving or learning through another purchaser, owner, hearer etc. **second honeymoon** *n.* a holiday taken by a married couple after some years of marriage. **second in command** *n.* the next under the commanding officer, person in charge etc. **second intention** *n.* 1 (*Med.*) the healing of a wound by granulation after suppuration. 2 (*pl., Logic*) secondary conceptions formed by the action of the mind upon first intentions and their interrelations. **second lieutenant** *n.* the lowest commissioned rank in the British army. **secondly** *adv.* 1 in the second place. 2 as the second item. **second name** *n.* a surname. **second nature** *n.* something that has become effortless or instinctual through constant practice. **second officer** *n.* an assistant mate on a merchant ship. **second-pair back** *n.* a room in the back of the house on the floor two flights of stairs above the ground floor. **second-pair front** *n.* a room in the front of the house on the floor two flights of stairs above the ground floor. **second person** *n.* (*Gram.*) the form of a pronoun, verb etc. indicating the person or persons addressed. **second-rate** *a.* of inferior quality, size, value etc. **second rater** *n.* **second reading** *n.* a general approval of the principles of a bill. **Second Reich** *n.* Germany under the Hohenzollern emperors, 1871–1918. **second self** *n.* a close friend or associate. **second sight** *n.* the power of seeing things at a distance in space or time as if they were present, clairvoyance. **second-sighted** *a.* **second-sightedness** *n.* **second string** *n.* 1 an alternative course of action. 2 (*N Am.*) a reserve for a sports team etc. **second teeth** *n.pl.* a mammal's permanent teeth. **second thoughts** *n.pl.* reconsideration of a previous opinion or decision. **second wind** *n.* a renewed burst of energy, stamina etc. after a concentrated effort. [F, from L *secundus*, orig. following, from *sequī*, to follow]

second² (sikond´) *v.t.* 1 to retire (a military officer) temporarily without pay in order that they may take a civil or other appointment. 2 to transfer temporarily or release for temporary transfer to another position, branch of an organization etc. **secondee** (-dē´) *n.* **secondment** *n.* [F *en second*]

secondary (sek´əndəri) *a.* 1 coming next in order of place or time to the first. 2 not primary, not original, derivative, supplementary, subordinate. 3 of the second or of inferior rank, importance etc. 4 revolving round a primary planet. 5 between the tertiary geological formation above and the primary below, Mesozoic. 6 of or being a feather on the second joint of a bird's wing. 7 of, relating to or carrying an induced current. ~*n.* (*pl.* **secondaries**) 1 a delegate or deputy. 2 a cathedral dignitary of secondary rank. 3 a secondary planet, a satellite. 4 the secondary geological epoch or formation. 5 a secondary feather. 6 a hind wing in an insect. 7 a secondary coil, circuit etc. **secondarily** *adv.* **secondariness** *n.* **secondary cell** *n.* a rechargeable cell or battery using reversible chemical reactions to convert chemical into electrical energy. **secondary coil** *n.* a coil in which the current in the primary winding induces the electric current. **secondary colour,** (*N Am.*) **secondary color** *n.* any of the colours produced by combinations of two primary colours. **secondary education** *n.* education provided for children who have received primary education. **secondary electrons** *n.pl.* the electrons emitted by secondary emission. **secondary emission** *n.* the emission of electrons from a surface or particle bombarded by primary electrons at high velocity. **secondary growth** SECONDARY TUMOUR (under SECONDARY). **secondary picketing** *n.* picketing of an organization by workers with whom there is no direct dispute. **secondary rainbow** *n.* a reversed rainbow sometimes seen inside or outside a rainbow. **secondary school** *n.* a school for pupils in secondary education. **secondary sex characteristics, secondary sexual characteristics** *n.pl.* attributes related to the sex of an individual that develop from puberty. **secondary smoking** *n.* passive smoking. **secondary tumour, secondary growth** *n.* a tumour occurring somewhere other than at the site of the original cancer. **secondary winding** *n.* a secondary coil.

seconde (sikond´, səgõd´) *n.* in fencing, a position in parrying or lungeing. [F]

secondo (sikon´dō) *n.* (*pl.* **secondi** (-di)) (*Mus.*) the second part or the second performer in a duet. [It.]

☒ **secratary** common misspelling of SECRETARY.

secrecy (sē´krəsi) *n.* (*pl.* **secrecies**) 1 the state of being secret, concealment. 2 the quality of being secretive, secretiveness. 3 solitude, retirement, seclusion. **sworn to secrecy** having promised to keep something a secret.

secret (sē´krit) *a.* 1 concealed from notice, kept or meant to be kept private, hidden, not to be revealed or exposed. 2 unseen, occult, mysterious. 3 given to secrecy, secretive, close, reserved, reticent. 4 secluded, private. ~*n.* 1 something to be kept back or concealed. 2 a thing kept back from general knowledge. 3 a mystery, something that cannot be explained. 4 the explanation or key to a mystery. 5 secrecy. 6 in the Roman Catholic Church, a prayer in a low tone recited by the celebrant at Mass. **in (on) the secret** among the people who know a secret. **in secret** secretly, privately. **to keep a secret** not to reveal a secret. **secretage** (-tij) *n.* a process of preparing furs. **secret agent** *n.* an agent of the secret service. **secret ballot** *n.* a ballot in which votes are cast in secret. **secretly** *adv.* **secretness** *n.* **secret police** *n.* a police force operating in secret, usu. dealing with political rather than criminal matters. **secret service** *n.* **1** a government service for obtaining information, or other work of which no account is given to the public. **2** (**Secret Service**) in the US, a branch of the Treasury Department responsible for protecting the President etc. **secret society** *n.* a society that is kept secret from non-members. [OF, from L *sēcrētus*, p.p. of *sēcernere*, to SECERN]

secretaire (sekrəteə´) *n.* an escritoire, a bureau. [F *secrétaire*, as SECRETARY]

secretary (sek´rətəri) *n.* (*pl.* **secretaries**) **1** a person employed to assist in clerical work, correspondence, arranging meetings etc., either by an individual or in an office. **2** an officer appointed by a company, firm, society etc. to conduct its correspondence, keep its records and represent it in business transactions etc. **3** a Secretary of State. **4** the principal assistant or deputy of an ambassador. **5** an escritoire. **6** a secretary bird. **secretarial** (-teə´ri-) *a.* **secretariat** (-teə´riət) *n.* **1** the post of a secretary. **2** an administrative office headed by a secretary. **3** the administrative workers of an organization. **secretary bird** *n.* a S African bird, *Sagittarius serpentarius*, preying on snakes etc. (named from its penlike tufts in the ear). **Secretary-General** *n.* (*pl.* **Secretary-Generals**) the person in charge of the administration of an organization. **secretary hand** *n.* (*Hist.*) a style of handwriting used for legal documents until the 17th cent. **Secretary of State** *n.* **1** a minister in charge of a government department. **2** the Foreign Secretary of the US. **secretaryship** *n.* [F *secrétaire*, late L *sēcrētārius*, orig. a confidential officer, as SECRET]

Usage note Pronunciation as (sek´ət-), without the first *r*, is best avoided.

secrete (sikrēt´) *v.t.* **1** to conceal, to hide. **2** to keep secret. **3** to separate from the blood, sap etc. by the process of secretion. **secretin** *n.* a peptic hormone that stimulates the pancreas. **secretion** (-shən) *n.* **1** the process of separating materials from the blood, sap etc. for the service of the body or for rejection as excreta. **2** any matter thus secreted, such as mucus, gastric juice, urine etc. **3** the act of secreting or concealing. **secretional, secretionary** *a.* **secretive**[1] *a.* promoting or causing secretion. **secretor** *n.* **secretory** *a.* [L *sēcrētus*, SECRET]

secretive[1] SECRETE.

secretive[2] (sē´krətiv) *a.* given to secrecy, reserved, uncommunicative. **secretively** *adv.* **secretiveness** *n.*

secretor, secretory SECRETE.

sect (sekt) *n.* **1** a body of persons who have separated from a larger body, esp. an established Church, on account of philosophical or religious differences. **2** a religious denomination, a nonconformist church (as regarded by opponents). **3** the body of adherents of a particular philosopher, school of thought etc. **4** a party, a faction. **sectarial** (-teə´ri-) *a.* **sectarian** *n., a.* **sectarianism** *n.* **sectarianize, sectarianise** *v.t.* **sectary** *n.* (*pl.* **sectaries**) **1** a member of a sect. **2** (*Hist.*) a Dissenter, esp. an Independent or Presbyterian at the time of the Civil War. [OF *secte*, L *secta*, a following, faction (med. L, suite, suit, costume), from *sequī*, to follow]

sect. *abbr.* section.

sectant (sek´tənt) *n.* (*Geom.*) a portion of space separated by three intersecting planes but extending to infinity. [L *sectum*, neut. p.p. of *secāre*, to cut]

sectarian, sectary etc. SECT.

sectile (sek´tīl) *a.* capable of being cut. [F, from L *sectilis*, as SECTION]

section (sek´shən) *n.* **1** separation by cutting. **2** that which is cut off or separated, a part, a portion. **3** each of a series of parts into which anything naturally separates or is constructed so as to separate for convenience in handling etc. **4** a division or subdivision of a book, chapter, statute etc. **5** a section-mark. **6** a distinct part of a country, people, community, class etc. **7** (*Biol.*) a group, a subgenus. **8** (*Mil.*) a subdivision of an army platoon. **9** (*N Am.*) any one of the portions of a square of 640 acres (259 hectares) into which public lands are divided. **10** a thin slice of any substance prepared for microscopic examination. **11** a cutting of a solid figure by a plane, or the figure so produced. **12** a vertical plan of a building etc. as it would appear upon an upright plane cutting through it. **13** a part of an orchestra consisting of all the instruments of one class. **14** (*N Am.*) a particular district of a town. *~v.t.* **1** to divide or arrange in sections. **2** to represent in sections. **3** to cause (a person) to be committed to a psychiatric hospital under the mental health legislation. **4** (*Biol.*) to cut into thin slices for microscopic examination. **sectional** *a.* **sectionalism** *n.* **sectionalist** *n.* **sectionalize, sectionalise** *v.t.* **sectionally** *adv.* **section-mark** *n.* the sign § marking a reference or the beginning of a section of a book, chapter etc. [F, from L *sectio*, acc. *-ōnem*, from *secāre*, to cut, p.p. *sectus*]

sector (sek´tə) *n.* **1** a distinct part, a section. **2** a section of a battle front. **3** a portion of a circle or other curved figure included between two radii and an arc. **4** a mathematical rule consisting of two hinged arms marked with sines, tangents etc. **sectoral** *a.* **sectorial** (-taw´ri-) *a.* **1** denoting a tooth on each side of either jaw, adapted for cutting like scissors with the corresponding one, as in many Carnivora. **2** sectoral. *~n.* a sectorial tooth. **sector of a sphere** *n.* a solid figure generated by the revolution of a plane sector round one of the radii. [L, orig. cutter, as SECTION (late L, sector)]

secular (sek´ūlə) *a.* **1** of or relating to the present world or to things not spiritual or sacred, not ecclesiastical or monastic. **2** (of education etc.) not concerned with religion. **3** worldly, temporal, profane. **4** lasting, extending over, occurring in or accomplished during a century, an age or a very long period of time. **5** of or relating to secularism. *~n.* **1** a lay person. **2** a Roman Catholic priest bound only by the vow of chastity and belonging to no regular order. **3** a church official who is not ordained. **secularism** *n.* **1** the state of being secular. **2** the belief that religion should not be part of education etc. **3** a doctrine opposed to religious education or ecclesiasticism, founded by George Jacob Holyoake. **secularist** *n., a.* **secularity** (-lar´-) *n.* **secularize, secularise** *v.t.* **secularization** (-zā´shən) *n.* **secularly** *adv.* [OF *seculier*, L *saeculāris*, from *saeculum*, generation, age, perh. cogn. with *serere*, to sow]

secund (sikŭnd´, sek´-, sē´-) *a.* (of flowers etc.) arranged all on one side of the rachis. **secundly** *adv.* [L, SECOND[1]]

secundine (sek´əndin, -dīn, -kŭn´-) *n.* **1** (*often pl.*) the placenta and other parts connected with the foetus, ejected after parturition, the afterbirth. **2** (*Bot.*) the membrane immediately surrounding the nucleus. [late L *secundīnae*, pl., as SECUND]

secundogeniture (sikŭndōjen´ichə) *n.* the right of inheritance belonging to a second son. [L *secundō*, abl. of *secundus*, SECOND[1], *geniture*, procreation (see GENITOR)]

secundum (sikŭn´dəm) *prep.* according to. **secundum artem** (ah´tem) *adv.* according to art. **secundum legem** (leg´em) *adv.* according to law. **secundum naturam** (nətoo´ram) *adv.* according to nature. **secundum regulam** (reg´ūlam) *adv.* according to rule. [L]

secure (sikūə´) *a.* **1** free from danger, risk or apprehension. **2** safe from attack, impregnable. **3** reliable, confident, certain, sure (of). **4** in safe keeping, safe not to escape. **5** firmly fixed or held. **6** trustworthy. *~v.t.* **1** to make safe or secure. **2** to put into a state of safety from danger. 3 to fasten, to close securely, to enclose or confine securely. 4 to make safe against loss, to guarantee payment of. 5 to get, to obtain, to gain possession of. 6 to compress (a vein etc.) to prevent bleeding. **to secure arms** to hold rifles muzzle downwards with the lock under the armpit as a protection from rain. **securable** *a.* **securely** *adv.* **securement** *n.* **secureness** *n.* security. **securer** *n.* [L *sēcūrus* (SE-, *cūra*, care)]

securi- (sikū´ri) *comb. form* of or relating to an axe. [L *secūris*, axe]

securiform (sikū´rifawm) *a.* axe-shaped.

securite (sek´ūrīt) *n.* a high explosive composed of nitrated hydrocarbons, used chiefly for blasting. [SECURE, -ITE[1]]

security (sikū´riti) *n.* (*pl.* **securities**) 1 the state of being or feeling secure. 2 freedom from danger or risk, safety. 3 certainty, assurance, over-confidence. 4 that which guards or secures. 5 (an organization which sees to) the protection of premises etc. against burglary, espionage etc. 6 a pledge, a guarantee. 7 something given or deposited as a pledge for payment of a loan, fulfilment of obligation etc., to be forfeited in case of non-performance. 8 a person who becomes surety for another. 9 a document constituting evidence of debt or of property, a certificate of stock, a bond etc. **on security of** using as a guarantee. **securitization** (-zā´shən), **securitisation** *n.* the putting together of a number of stocks, mortgages etc. into a single bond which is traded like a security. **securitize** *v.t.* **security blanket** *n.* 1 an official sanction or set of measures used in the interest of security. 2 a blanket or piece of material used to comfort a young child. **Security Council** *n.* a body of the United Nations charged with the maintenance of international security and peace. **security guard** *n.* a person employed to guard buildings, money in transit etc. **security risk** *n.* a person or thing considered to be a threat to (national) security. [F *sécurité*, L *securitās -tātem*, from *sēcūrus*, SECURE]

SED *abbr.* Scottish Education Department.

sedan (sidan´) *n.* 1 (*also* **sedan chair**) a covered chair for one person, carried by two people by means of a pole on each side. 2 (*N Am.*) a closed car with a single compartment for driver and passengers, a saloon car. [town in France]

sedate (sidāt´) *a.* composed, calm, tranquil, staid, not impulsive. ~*v.t.* to administer a sedative to. **sedately** *adv.* **sedateness** *n.* **sedation** (-ā´shən) *n.* 1 a state of calmness or relaxation, esp. produced by a sedative drug. 2 the administration of a sedative. **sedative** (sed´ə-) *a.* allaying nervous irritability, soothing, assuaging pain. ~*n.* a sedative medicine, influence etc. [L *sēdātus*, p.p. of *sēdāre*, causal of *sedēre*, to sit]

sedentary (sed´əntəri) *a.* 1 sitting. 2 accustomed or inclined, or obliged by occupation, to sit a great deal. 3 involving or requiring much sitting. 4 caused by sitting much. 5 not migratory, attached to one place, not free-moving. **sedentarily** *adv.* **sedentariness** *n.* **sedentism** *n.* the abandonment of a nomadic way of life in favour of living in permanent settlements. [F *sédentaire*, L *sedentārius*, from *sedēre*, to sit]

Seder (sā´də) *n.* a ceremonial meal eaten on the first night (or the first two nights) of Passover. [Heb. *sēdher*, order]

sederunt (sideə´rənt) *n.* (*Sc.*) 1 a sitting of a court etc. 2 a list of persons present. ~*v.i.* (*Sc. Law*) were present at the sitting of a court etc. [L, they sat, see SEDENTARY]

sedge (sej) *n.* 1 any coarse grasslike plant of the genus *Carex*, usu. growing in marshes or beside water. 2 any coarse grass growing in such spots. 3 a sedge fly. **sedge bird, sedge warbler, sedge wren** *n.* a reed warbler, *Acrocephalus schoenoboenus*, haunting sedgy places. **sedged** *a.* **sedge fly** *n.* (*pl.* **sedge flies**) 1 a caddis-fly or mayfly. 2 an imitation of this, used by anglers. **sedgy** *a.* (*comp.* **sedgier**, *superl.* **sedgiest**). [OE *secg*, cp. LG *Segge*, rel. to SAW[1], L *secāre*, to cut]

sedile (sidī´li) *n.* (*pl.* **sedilia** (-dil´iə)) (*usu. pl.*) each of usu. three stone seats, usu. canopied and decorated, on the south side of the chancel in churches, for the priest, deacon and subdeacon. [L, seat, cogn. with *sedēre*, to sit]

sediment (sed´imənt) *n.* 1 the matter which subsides to the bottom of a liquid. 2 lees, dregs, settlings. 3 (*Geol.*) deposited material. **sedimentary** (-men´-) *a.* **sedimentary rocks** *n.pl.* rocks or strata laid down as sediment from water. **sedimentation** (-ā´shən) *n.* **sedimented** *a.* [OF, from L *sedimentum*, as SEDILE]

sedition (sidish´ən) *n.* 1 agitation, disorder or commotion in a state, not amounting to insurrection. 2 conduct tending to promote treason or rebellion. **seditionary** *n.*, *a.* **seditious** *a.* **seditiously** *adv.* **seditiousness** *n.* [OF, from L *sedītio -ōnem* (L *sed-*, SE-, *īre*, to go, supine *-itum*)]

seduce (sidūs´) *v.t.* 1 to lead astray, to entice from rectitude or duty, esp. to induce (someone) to sexual intercourse. 2 to entice or lure, esp. by offering rewards. **seduced** *a.* beguiled. **seducement** *n.* **seducer** *n.* **seducible** *a.* **seducing** *a.* **seducingly** *adv.* **seduction** (-dŭk´shən) *n.* 1 the act of seducing, esp. of persuading someone to sexual intercourse. 2 the state of being seduced. 3 that which seduces, an enticement, an attraction, a tempting or attractive quality, a charm. **seductive** *a.* **seductively** *adv.* **seductiveness** *n.* **seductress** (-tris) *n.* a female seducer. [L *sēdūcere* (SE-, *dūcere*, to lead, p.p. *ductus*)]

sedulous (sed´ūləs) *a.* assiduous, constant, steady and persevering in business or endeavour; industrious, diligent. **sedulity** (-dū´-), **sedulousness** *n.* **sedulously** *adv.* [L *sēdulus*, from *sēdulō*, honestly, diligently (SE-, *dolō*, abl. of *dolus*, guile)]

sedum (sē´dəm) *n.* any fleshy-leaved plant of the genus *Sedum*, including the stonecrop, orpine etc. [L, houseleek]

see[1] (sē) *v.t.* (*past* **saw** (saw), *p.p.* **seen** (sēn)) 1 to perceive by the eye. 2 to discern, to descry, to observe, to look at. 3 to perceive mentally, to understand, to apprehend, to have an idea of. 4 to witness, to experience, to go through, to have knowledge of. 5 to watch; be a spectator of. 6 to imagine, to picture to oneself. 7 to ascertain or establish. 8 to call on, to pay a visit to, to grant an interview to, to receive. 9 to escort, to attend, to conduct (a person home etc.). 10 in poker etc., to accept (a challenge, bet etc., or person offering this). 11 to consider; deduce. 12 to meet socially, esp. regularly as a boyfriend or girlfriend. 13 to consult. 14 to find attractive (*What does he see in her?*). 15 to supervise (an action etc.). ~*v.i.* 1 to have or exercise the power of sight. 2 to discern, to comprehend. 3 to inquire, to make an investigation (into). 4 to reflect, to consider carefully. 5 to ascertain by reading. 6 to take heed. 7 to give attention. 8 to make provision for. 9 to look out. 10 to take care (that). 11 (*imper.*) to refer to. **as far as I can see** to the best of my understanding, judgement etc. **as I see it** in my opinion. **do you see?** do you understand? **I'll be seeing you** (*coll.*) goodbye. **I see** I understand. **let me see** used to ask for time to consider or reflect. **not to see (someone) for dust** DUST. **not to see the wood for the trees** WOOD. **see here!** used to get attention etc. **see you (later)** (*coll.*) goodbye for the present. **to be ill seen in** not to be versed in. **to be well seen in** to be versed in. **to have seen better days** to be on the decline. **to see about** 1 to give attention to. 2 to make preparations etc. **to see after** 1 to take care of. 2 to see about. **to see daylight** (*coll.*) to begin to comprehend. **to see eye to eye** EYE[1]. **to see fit** to think advisable. **to see good** to see fit. **to see into** to investigate. **to see life** to gain experience of the world, esp. by dissipation. **to**

see no further than one's nose NOSE. **to see off 1** to escort on departure. **2** (*coll.*) to get rid of. **to see one's way clear to** to feel able to. **to see out 1** to escort out of a house etc. **2** to outlive, outlast. **3** to last to the end of. **4** to finish. **to see over** to inspect. **to see reason** REASON. **to see red** RED¹. **to see service** SERVICE¹. **to see someone damned first** (*coll.*) to refuse categorically to do what someone wants. **to see someone right** (*coll.*) to make sure that someone is taken care of, rewarded etc. **to see stars** STAR. **to see the back of** BACK¹. **to see the light 1** to be born. **2** to realize the truth. **3** to be converted to a religion or to any other belief. **to see the light of day** to come into existence. **to see the world** WORLD. **to see things** to see things that are not there. **to see through 1** to penetrate, not to be deceived by. **2** to persist (in a task etc.) until it is finished. **3** to help through a difficulty, danger etc. **to see through a brick wall** BRICK. **to see to** to look after. **to see to it that** to take care that. **we shall see 1** we will see what happens. **2** used to ask for time to consider something. **we will see about it** used to ask for time to consider something. **you see 1** you understand. **2** you will understand when I have explained. **seeable** *a.* **seeing** *n.* **1** sight. **2** (*Astron.*) atmospheric conditions for observation. *~conj.* inasmuch as, since, considering (that). **seeing eye** *n.* a guide dog for the blind. **seer**¹ *n.* **1** a person who sees. **2** a person who foresees, a prophet. **seership** *n.* **see-through** *a.* (esp. of clothing) (semi-) transparent. [OE *sēon*, cp. Dut. *zien*, G *sehen*, Icel. *sjā*, Dan. and Swed. *se*]

see² (sē) *n.* the diocese or jurisdiction of a bishop or archbishop. **See of Rome** *n.* the papacy. [OF *se*, *sed*, L *sēdes*, from *sedēre*, to sit]

seed (sēd) *n.* **1** the mature fertilized ovule of a flowering plant, consisting of the embryo germ or reproductive body and its covering. **2** (*collect.*) seeds, esp. in quantity for sowing. **3** the male fertilizing fluid, semen. **4** the germ from which anything springs, first principle, beginning or source. **5** (*Bible*) †progeny, offspring, descendants. **6** †birth, descent. **7** a seeded player. **8** a crystal added to induce crystallization. **9** a small container for the application of radium etc. *~v.t.* **1** to sow or sprinkle with seed. **2** to put a small crystal into (a solution) to start crystallization. **3** to scatter solid particles in (a cloud) to bring on rain. **4** to remove the seeds from (fruit etc.). **5** in sport, to arrange the draw in (a tournament) so that the best players do not meet in the early rounds. **6** to classify (a good player) in this way. *~v.i.* **1** to sow seed. **2** to run to seed. **3** to produce or drop seed. **to go to seed** to run to seed. **†to raise up seed** to have children. **to run to seed 1** to cease flowering as seeds are produced. **2** to become shabby. **3** to lose self-respect. **seedbed** *n.* **1** a piece of ground where seedlings are grown. **2** a place where anything develops. **seed-bud** *n.* an ovule. **seed cake** *n.* a sweet cake containing aromatic seeds, esp. caraway. **seed-coat** *n.* the integument of a seed. **seed coral** *n.* coral in small seedlike pieces. **seedcorn** *n.* **1** corn set aside for sowing. **2** assets reused for future profit. **seed crystal** *n.* a crystal used to cause crystallization. **seed-eater** *n.* a granivorous bird. **seeded** *a.* **seeder** *n.* **1** a seed-drill or other device for planting seeds. **2** a device for removing the seeds from raisins etc. **3** a seed-fish. **4** a person who seeds. **seed-fish** *n.* (*pl. in general* **seed-fish,** *in particular* **seed-fishes**) a fish that is ready to spawn. **seed grain** *n.* corn set aside for sowing. **seed-head** *n.* a flower head in seed. **seed-lac** *n.* lac dried. **seed-leaf** *n.* a cotyledon. **seedless** *a.* **seedling** (-ling) *a.* raised from seed. *~n.* **1** a plant reared from seed. **2** a very young plant. **seed-lip** *n.* a basket in which a sower carries seed. **seed-loaf, seed-lobe** *n.* a cotyledon or primary leaf. **seed money** *n.* the money with which a project is set up. **seed oyster** *n.* a young oyster. **seedpearl** *n.* a small seedlike pearl. **seed plant** *n.* **1** a spermatophyte. **2** a plant grown from seed, or for seed. **seed-plot** *n.* **1** a piece of ground on which seeds are sown. **2** a nursery or hotbed (of seditions etc.). **seed potato** *n.* (*pl.* **seed potatoes**) a potato tuber used for planting. **seedsman** *n.* (*pl.* **seedsmen**) a person who deals in seeds. **seed-time** *n.* the season for sowing. **seed vessel** *n.* the pericarp. **seed-wool** *n.* raw cotton from which the seeds have not yet been removed. **seedy** *a.* (*comp.* **seedier,** *superl.* **seediest**) **1** abounding in seeds. **2** run to seed. **3** (of some French brandies) having a peculiar flavour, derived from weeds among the vines. **4** (*coll.*) shabby, down-at-heel. **5** (*coll.*) off colour, as after a debauch. **6** (*coll.*) out of sorts. **seedily** *adv.* **seediness** *n.* **1** shabbiness, near poverty. **2** a state of poor health. [OE *saed* (cp. Dut. *zaad*, G *Saat*, Icel. *saethi*, Dan. *saed*, Swed. *säd*), cogn. with SOW¹]

seek (sēk) *v.t.* (*past, p.p.* **sought** (sawt)) **1** to go in search of. **2** to try to find, to look for. **3** to ask, to solicit (a thing of a person). **4** to search (a place etc. through). **5** to resort to. **6** †to aim at, to try to gain, to pursue as an object. *~v.i.* **1** to make search or inquiry (after or for). **2** to endeavour, to try (to do). **far/ much to seek 1** seriously lacking or insufficient. **2** a long way off being found yet. **seek dead** used to tell a retriever to find game that has been killed. **to seek 1** lacking, insufficient. **2** not found yet. **to seek out 1** to search for. **2** to cultivate the friendship of. **seeker** *n.* **1** a person who seeks, an inquirer. **2** (*Hist.*) a member of an English sect of the time of Cromwell, somewhat akin to the Quakers. **Seekerism** *n.* **sought-after** *a.* desired as a possession etc., much in demand. [OE *sēcan* (cp. Dut. *zoekan*, G *suchen*, Icel. *saekja*, also L *sāgīre*, to perceive, Gr. *hēgeisthai*, to lead)]

†seel (sēl) *v.t.* to close the eyes of (a hawk), or close (its eyes) by threads drawn through the lids. [OF *siller*, *ciller*, from *cil*, eyelid, see CILIUM]

seem (sēm) *v.i.* **1** to give the impression of being, to be apparently though not in reality. **2** to appear (to do, to have done, to be true or the fact that). **3** to be evident or apparent. **do not seem to** (*coll.*) somehow do not. **I can't seem to** (*coll.*) I am unable to. **it seems** it appears, it is reported (that). **it would seem** it appears, it seems to one. **seeming** (sē´ming) *a.* **1** appearing, apparent, but not real. **2** apparent and perhaps real. *~n.* appearance, semblance, esp. when false. **seemingly** *adv.* **seemingness** *n.* [OE *sēman*, to conciliate, cogn. with SAME]

seemly (sēm´li) *a.* (*comp.* **seemlier,** *superl.* **seemliest**) **1** becoming, decent. **2** suited to the occasion, purpose etc. **seemliness** *n.* [ME *semlish*, Icel. *saemiligr* (*saemr*, becoming, from *samr*, SAME, -LY¹)]

seen SEE¹.

seep (sēp) *v.i.* to soak, to percolate, to ooze. *~n.* (*N Am.*) a spring or place where oil, water etc. oozes out of the ground. **seepage** (-ij) *n.* [OE *sipian*, rel. to SIP]

seer¹ SEE¹.

seer² (siə) *n.* an Indian weight of about one kilogram or liquid measure of about one litre. [Hind.]

seersucker (siə´sŭkə) *n.* a thin striped linen or cotton fabric with a puckered appearance. [corr. of Pers. *shīr o shakkar*, milk and sugar]

see-saw (sē´saw) *n.* **1** a game in which two persons sit one on each end of a board balanced on a support in the middle and move alternately up and down. **2** the board so used. **3** alternate or reciprocating motion. **4** a contest in which the advantage changes sides repeatedly. *~a.* **1** moving up and down or to and fro. **2** vacillating. *~adv.* with a see-saw movement. *~v.t.* to cause to move in a see-saw fashion. *~v.i.* **1** to play on a see-saw. **2** to move up and down or backwards and forwards. **3** to act in a vacillating manner. **to go see-saw** to vacillate. [redupl. of SAW¹]

seethe (sēdh) *v.t.* (*past* **seethed, †sod** (sod), *p.p.* **seethed, †sodden** (sod´ən)) **1** to boil. **2** †to prepare by boiling or steeping in hot liquid. ~*v.i.* **1** to be in a state of ebullition. **2** to be agitated, to bubble over. **seether** *n.* **seethingly** *adv.* [OE *sēothan*, cp. Dut. *zieden*, G *sieden*, Icel. *sjotha*]

segment (seg´mənt) *n.* **1** a portion cut or marked off as separable, a section, a division, esp. one of a natural series (as of a limb between the joints, the body of an articulate animal, a fruit or plant organ divided by clefts). **2** (*Geom.*) a part cut off from any figure by a line or plane. **3** in linguistics, the smallest distinct part of a spoken utterance. ~*v.i.* **1** to divide or be divided into segments. **2** (of a cell) to undergo cleavage. ~*v.t.* to divide into segments. **segmental** (-men´-), **segmentary, segmentate** (-tət) *a.* **segmentalize** (-men´-), **segmentalise** *v.t.* **segmentalization** (-ā´shən) *n.* **segmentally** *adv.* **segmentation** (-ā´shən) *n.* **segmented** *a.* **1** composed of segments. **2** divided into segments. [L *segmentum*, from *secāre*, to cut]

segno (sā´nyō) *n.* (*pl.* **segni** (-nyē), **segnos**) (*Mus.*) a sign marking the beginning or end of a section to be repeated. [It., from L *signum*, a mark]

sego (sē´gō), **sego lily** *n.* (*pl.* **segos, sego lilies**) a N American liliaceous plant, *Calochortus nuttallii*. [Paiute]

segregate[1] (seg´rigāt) *v.t.* **1** to separate from others, to set apart, to isolate. **2** to place in a separate class. **3** to split (a community) into separate parts on the basis of race. ~*v.i.* **1** (of a pair of alleles) to become separated during meiosis. **2** (of crystals) to separate from a mass and collect about nuclei and lines of fracture. **segregable** *a.* **segregation** (-ā´shən) *n.* **1** the act of segregating. **2** separation of a community on racial grounds. **segregational** *a.* **segregationist** *n.* a believer in racial segregation. **segregative** *a.* [L *sēgregātus*, p.p. of *sēgregāre* (SE-, *grex gregis*, flock)]

segregate[2] (seg´rigət) *a.* **1** (*Zool.*) simple, solitary, not compound. **2** †separate, set apart, select.

segregation, segregative etc. SEGREGATE[1].

segue (seg´wā) *v.i.* (*3rd pers. sing. pres.* **segues,** *pres.p.* **seguing,** *past, p.p.* **segued**) (*Mus.*) to follow on immediately. ~*n.* an act or result of seguing. [It., follows]

seguidilla (segidēl´yə) *n.* **1** a lively Spanish dance in triple time. **2** the music for this. [Sp., dim. of *seguida*, a continuation, from *seguir*, L *sequī*, to follow]

Sehnsucht (zān´zookht) *n.* yearning. [G]

sei (sā), **sei whale** *n.* a rorqual, *Balaenoptera borealis*. [Norw. *sejhval*]

seicento (sāchen´tō) *n.* the 17th cent. in Italian art, architecture or literature. **seicentist** *n.* **seicentoist** *n.* [It., short for *mille seicento*, one thousand six hundred]

seiche (sāsh) *n.* an undulation, somewhat resembling a tidal wave, in the water of Lake Geneva and other Swiss lakes, usu. due to disturbance of atmospheric pressure or to subterranean movements. **seichometer** (-shom´itə) *n.* an instrument for measuring seiches. [Swiss F, prob. G *Seiche*, sinking]

Seidlitz powder (sed´lits), (*N Am.*) **Seidlitz powders** *n.* a mild aperient, composed of a mixture of Rochelle salt, bicarbonate of soda and finely powdered tartaric acid, mixed separately in water to form an effervescing drink. **Seidlitz water** *n.* a sparkling mineral water of the same composition as that of the Seidlitz spring. [*Seidlitz* (mod. *Sedlčancy*), a village in Bohemia, with a mineral spring]

seif (sēf, sāf), **seif dune** *n.* a long sand dune in the form of a ridge. [Arab. *saif*, sword]

☒ **seige** common misspelling of SIEGE.

seigneur (senyœ´), **†seignior** (sān´yə) *n.* **1** (*Hist.*) a feudal lord. **2** (*Can.*) the holder of a seigneury. **seigneurial** *a.* **seigneury** (sā´-) *n.* (*pl.* **seigneuries**) **1** (*Hist.*) the territory or lordship of a seigneur. **2** (*Can.*) an estate formerly held on a feudal tenure. **3** the mansion of a seigneur. **seigniorage** (sān´yərij), **seignorage** *n.* **1** (*Hist.*) something claimed by the sovereign or by a feudal superior as a prerogative, esp. an ancient right of the Crown to a percentage on bullion brought to the mint to be coined. **2** (*Hist.*) the profit derived from issuing coins at a rate above their intrinsic value. **3** a royalty. **seigniorial** (-yaw´ri-) *a.* seigneurial. **seigniorship** *n.* **seigniory** *n.* (*pl.* **seigniories**) **1** feudal lordship. **2** power as sovereign lord. **3** the territory or domain of a feudal lord. **4** SIGNORY (under SIGNOR). [F, as SENIOR]

seine (sān) *n.* a large fishing net with floats at the top and weights at the bottom for encircling. ~*v.t.* to catch with this. ~*v.i.* to fish with it. **seine-fishing** *n.* **seine-net** *n.* **seiner** *n.* [F, from L *sagēna*, Gr. *sagēnē*]

seise (sēz) *v.t.* (*usu. in p.p.*, *Law*) to put in possession of. **seised of** in legal possession of. **seisable** *a.* **seisin** (-zin) *n.* **1** possession of land under a freehold. **2** the act of taking such possession. **3** the thing so possessed. **seisor** *n.* [SEIZE]

seismic (sīz´mik), **seismal** (-məl) *a.* **1** of, relating to or produced by an earthquake. **2** of, relating to or involving artificially induced vibrations of the earth. **3** of enormous proportions or effect. **seismical** *a.* **seismically** *adv.* **seismicity** (-mis´iti) *n.* seismic activity, esp. liability to or frequency of earthquakes. **seismic survey** *n.* a survey which uses seismic methods to find oil and gas. [Gr. *seismos*, earthquake, from *seiein*, to shake]

seismo- (sīz´mō) *comb. form* of or relating to an earthquake.

seismogram (sīz´məgram) *n.* a record given by a seismograph. **seismograph** (sīz´məgrahf) *n.* an instrument for recording the period, extent and direction of the vibrations of an earthquake. **seismographer** (-mog´-) *n.* **seismographic** (-graf´-), **seismographical** *a.* **seismography** (-mog´-) *n.*

seismology (sīzmol´əji) *n.* the study or science of earthquakes. **seismological** (-məloj´-) *a.* **seismologically** *adv.* **seismologist** *n.*

seismometer (sīzmom´itə) *n.* **1** a seismograph. **2** a seismoscope. **seismometric** (-məmet´-), **seismometrical** *a.* **seismometry** *n.*

seismoscope (sīz´məskōp) *n.* a simple form of seismograph. **seismoscopic** (-məskop´-) *a.*

seismotic (sīzmot´ik) *a.* seismic.

seisor SEISE.

seize (sēz) *v.t.* **1** to grasp or lay hold of suddenly, to snatch, to take possession of by force. **2** to grasp mentally, to comprehend. **3** to come upon, to affect suddenly and forcibly. **4** (*Naut.*) to fasten, to lash with cord etc. **5** (*Law*) to seise. **6** to take possession of. **7** to impound, to confiscate. ~*v.i.* **1** to lay hold (upon). **2** to jam, to become stuck. **3** (of a body part) to become stiff. **seized of 1** in legal possession of. **2** aware or informed of. **seizable** *a.* **seizer** *n.* **seizin** (-zin) *n.* SEISIN (under SEISE). **seizing** *n.* (*Naut.*) a cord or cords used for seizing. **seizing-up** *n.* the locking or partial welding together of sliding surfaces from lack of lubrication. **seizure** (-zhə) *n.* **1** the act of seizing. **2** a sudden attack, as of a disease. [OF *seisir*, *saisir*, to put in possession of, late L *sacīre*, to take possession of, perh. from Gmc. and cogn. with SET[1]]

sejant (sē´jənt), **sejeant** *a.* (*Her.*) sitting with the forelegs erect. [A-F *seiant*, pres.p. of *seier*, OF *seoir*, L *sedēre*, to sit]

Sekt (zekt, sekt) *n.* a German sparkling white wine. [G]

selachian (silā´kiən) *n.* a fish of the subclass Selachii comprising the sharks, dogfish etc. ~*a.* of or relating to this subclass. **selachoid** (sel´əkoid) *n., a.* [Gr. *selachos*, shark]

seladang (səlah´dang) *n.* a Malayan gaur. [Malay]

selaginella (seləjinel´ə) *n.* any moss of the genus

Selaginella, many of which are cultivated for ornamental purposes. [L dim. of *selāgo -ginis*, club moss]

selah (sē´lə) *n.* a word occurring in the Psalms and in Habakkuk, always at the end of a verse, variously interpreted as indicating a pause, a repetition, the end of a strophe etc. [Heb.]

seldom (sel´dəm) *adv.* rarely, not often. ~*a.* rare. [OE *seldan, -don, -dom* (*seld, -om*, dat. pl.), cp. Dut. *zelden*, G *selten*, Icel. *sjaldan*]

select (silekt´) *a.* **1** chosen, picked out, choice. **2** taken as superior to or more suitable than the rest. **3** strict in selecting new members etc., exclusive, more valuable. ~*v.t.* to choose, to pick out (the best etc.). **select committee** *n.* members of parliament specially chosen to examine a particular question and to report on it. **selectee** (-tē´) *n.* (*N Am.*) a conscript. **selection** *n.* **1** the act of selecting. **2** the right or opportunity of selecting, choice. **3** that which is selected. **4** a natural or artificial process of sorting out organisms suitable for survival. **5** a range of goods (as in a shop) from which to choose. **6** (*Austral.*) FREE SELECTION (under FREE[1]). **selectional** *a.* **selectionally** *adv.* **selective** *a.* **1** of or relating to selection. **2** capable of selecting. **3** given to selecting only what suits. **selectively** *adv.* **selectiveness** *n.* **selective service** *n.* (*Hist.*, *N Am.*) service in the armed forces under conscription. **selectivity** (sēlektiv´-, sil-, sel-) *n.* **1** the quality of being selective. **2** the efficiency of a wireless receiver in separating the different broadcasting stations. **selectman** *n.* (*pl.* **selectmen**) any one of a board of officers chosen annually by the freemen of towns in New England to manage local affairs. **selectness** *n.* **selector** *n.* **1** a person who or thing which selects. **2** (*Austral.*) a settler who takes up a piece of select land. [L *sēlectus*, p.p. of *sēligere* (SE-, *legere*, to choose)]

selen- SELENO-.

selenate SELENIUM.

seleni- SELENO-.

selenium (silē´niəm) *n.* a non-metallic element, at. no. 34, chem. symbol Se, obtained as a by-product in the manufacture of sulphuric acid, similar in chemical properties to sulphur and tellurium, utilized for its varying electrical resistance in light and darkness. **selenate** (sel´ināt) *n.* a salt of selenic acid. **selenic** (silen´ik, -lē´-) *a.* **1** containing or derived from (high valency) selenium. **2** of or derived from the moon. **selenide** (sel´inīd) *n.* a compound of selenium with an element or radical. **selenious** *a.* containing or derived from (low valency) selenium. **selenite** (sel´inīt) *n.* **1** a transparent variety of gypsum or sulphate of lime. **2** a salt of selenious acid. **3** an inhabitant of the moon. **selenitic** (selinit´-) *a.* **selenitiferous** (-nitif´-) *a.* **selenium cell** *n.* a type of photoelectric cell using a strip of selenium. [Gr. *Selēnē*, the moon]

seleno- (silē´nō), **selen-**, **seleni-** (-ni) *comb. form* **1** of or relating to the moon. **2** of, relating to or containing selenium. [G *Selen* or SELENIUM, or Gr. *Selēnē*, the moon]

selenocentric (silēnōsen´trik) *a.* referred to, seen from or measured from the moon as centre.

selenodont (silē´nədont) *a.* **1** (of molar teeth) having crescent-shaped ridges. **2** having such teeth. ~*n.* a selenodont mammal. [Gr. *odous odontos*, tooth]

selenography (selinog´rəfi) *n.* **1** a description of the moon and its phenomena. **2** the art of delineating the face of the moon. **selenograph** (silē´nəgrahf) *n.* **selenographer** (-nog´-) *n.* **selenographic** (-əgraf´-), **selenographical** *a.*

selenology (selinol´əji) *n.* the branch of astronomical science treating of the moon. **selenological** (-lēnəloj´-) *a.* **selenologically** *adv.* **selenologist** *n.*

selenotropic (silēnətrop´ik) *a.* (of plant organs) curving towards the moon. **selenotropism** (selənot´rə-), **selenotropy** (-pi) *n.* [F *sélénotropique* (Gr. *tropos*, from *trepein*, to turn)]

self (self) *n.* (*pl.* **selves** (selvz)) **1** the individuality of a person or thing, as the object of reflexive consciousness or action. **2** one's individual person. **3** one's private interests etc. **4** furtherance of these. **5** (*pl.* **selfs**) a flower of a uniform or of the original wild colour. ~*a.* **1** self-coloured. **2** uniform, pure, unmixed. **3** of one piece or the same material throughout. ~*pron.* (*coll.*, *facet.*) myself, yourself etc. ~*v.t.* to self-fertilize. **one's better self** one's nobler impulses. **one's former self** oneself as one was before. **one's old self** one's former self. **selfhood, selfness** *n.* **selfish** *a.* **1** attentive only to one's own interests. **2** not regarding the interests or feelings of others. **3** actuated by or proceeding from self-interest. **selfishly** *adv.* **selfishness** *n.* **selfless** *a.* having no regard for self, unselfish. **selflessly** *adv.* **selflessness** *n.* [OE, cp. Dut. *zelf*, G *Selbe*, Icel. *sjālfr*, Dan. *selv*, Swed. *sjelf*]

self- (self) *comb. form* **1** expressing direct or indirect reflexive action, as in *self-command*. **2** expressing action performed independently, or without external agency, as in *self-acting*, *self-fertilization*. **3** expressing relation to the self, as in *self-conscious*, *self-suspicious*. **4** expressing uniformity, naturalness etc., as in *self-coloured*, *self-glazed*.

self-(+a–i words) self-abandon *n.* the abandonment of oneself. **self-abandoned** *a.* **self-abandonment** *n.* **self-abasement** *n.* the abasement or humiliation of oneself. **self-abhorrence** *n.* self-hatred. **self-abnegating** *a.* **self-abnegation** *n.* self-denial. **self-absorbed** *a.* absorbed in oneself. **self-absorption** *n.* **1** absorption in oneself. **2** (*Physics*) the absorption of radiation in a material by the material itself. **self-abuse** *n.* **1** masturbation. **2** the revilement of oneself. **self-abuser** *n.* **self-accusation** *n.* the accusation of oneself. **self-accusatory** *a.* **self-accused** *n.*, *a.* **self-accuser** *n.* **self-accusing** *a.* **self-acknowledged** *a.* acknowledged by oneself. **self-acting** *a.* automatic. **self-action** *n.* **self-activity** *n.* **self-actualization, self-actualisation** *n.* (*Psych.*) the realization of one's personality and development of this. **self-addressed** *a.* (of an envelope) addressed to oneself (for the sending of a reply). **self-adhesive** *a.* (of a label etc.) adhesive; able to stick without extra glue etc. **self-adjusting** *a.* (of machinery etc.) adjusting itself. **self-adjustment** *n.* **self-administered** *a.* administered by oneself. **self-admiration** *n.* the admiration of oneself. **self-advancement** *n.* the advancement of oneself or one's interests. **self-advertisement** *n.* the promotion of oneself. **self-advertiser** *n.* **self-affirmation** *n.* (*Psych.*) the recognition of the existence of the self. **self-aggrandizement, self-aggrandisement** *n.* the act or process of trying to make oneself more important. **self-aggrandizing** *a.* **self-amendment** *n.* **self-analysis** *n.* (*Psych.*) the analysis of oneself. **self-analysing,** (*N Am.*) **self-analyzing** *a.* **self-annealing** *a.* (of metals) recrystallizing at air temperature, so that they can be cold-worked without strain-hardening. **self-annihilation** *n.* the surrender of one's sense of self in mystical contemplation; a sense of union with God. **self-appointed** *a.* appointed by oneself. **self-appointment** *n.* **self-appreciation** *n.* appreciation of oneself. **self-approbation** *n.* approval of oneself. **self-approval** *n.* self-appreciation. **self-approving** *a.* **self-assembly** *n.* the construction of furniture etc. using parts that come in a kit. **self-assertion** *n.* the assertion of one's views etc. **self-asserting, self-assertive** *a.* **self-assertiveness** *n.* **self-assumed** *a.* assumed by one's own act. **self-assumption** *n.* self-conceit. **self-assured** *a.* confident in one's own abilities etc. **self-assurance** *n.* **self-assuredly** *adv.* **self-aware** *a.* conscious of one's own feelings, motives etc. **self-awareness** *n.* **self-basting** *a.* (of poultry etc.) not requiring basting during cooking. **self-begot, self-begotten, self-born** *a.* begotten by or born of oneself or one's own powers. **self-betrayal** *n.* 1 the betrayal of oneself. 2 the revelation of one's real thoughts etc. **self-binder** *n.* 1 a reaping machine with an automatic binding device. 2 this device. **self-blinded** *a.* blinded by oneself. **self-born** *a.* born of itself. **self-build** *n.* the building of a house by the person who is going to live in it. ~*a.* of or relating to such building. **self-builder** *n.* **self-catering** *a.* (of holiday accommodation) not providing meals, cleaning etc. **self-censorship** *n.* censorship of oneself. **self-centred,** (*N Am.*) **self-centered** *a.* interested solely in oneself and one's own affairs, egotistic. **self-centredly** *adv.* **self-centredness** *n.* **self-certify** *v.t.* (*3rd pers. sing. pres.* **self-certifies,** *pres.p.* **self-certifying,** *past, p.p.* **self-certified**) to attest to in writing (one's financial standing etc.). **self-certification** *n.* **self-certified** *a.* **self-cleaning** *a.* (esp. of an oven) cleaning itself. **self-closing** *a.* (of a door etc.) closing automatically. **self-cocking** *a.* (of a gun or gun hammer) cocking automatically. **self-collected** *a.* self-possessed, composed. **self-colour,** (*N Am.*) **self-color** *n.* 1 a colour uniform throughout. 2 a pure or unmixed colour. 3 a colour not changed by cultivation. **self-coloured** *a.* **self-command** *n.* self-control. **self-communion** *n.* meditation, mental converse with oneself. **self-complacent** *a.* pleased with oneself. **self-complacency** *n.* **self-conceit** *n.* self-satisfaction. **self-conceited** *a.* **self-conceitedness** *n.* **self-concentration** *n.* concentration of one's thoughts on oneself. **self-concept** *n.* one's concept of oneself. **self-condemned** *a.* condemned by oneself (openly or inadvertently). **self-condemnation** *n.* **self-confessed** *a.* openly admitting oneself to be. **self-confident** *a.* self-assured. **self-confidence** *n.* **self-confidently** *adv.* **self-congratulation** *n.* congratulation of oneself. **self-congratulatory** *a.* **self-conquest** *n.* the overcoming of one's weak points etc. **self-conscious** *a.* 1 conscious of one's actions, behaviour, situation etc., esp. as observed by others. 2 (*Philos.*) conscious of one's own activities, states etc. 3 able to reflect on these. **self-consciously** *adv.* **self-consciousness** *n.* **self-consistent** *a.* consistent with other parts (of a whole). **self-consistency** *n.* **self-constituted** *a.* self-appointed. **self-consumed, self-consuming** *a.* consuming itself or oneself. **self-contained** *a.* 1 reserved, not communicative. 2 complete in itself. **self-containment** *n.* **self-contempt** *n.* contempt for oneself. **self-contemptuous** *a.* **self-content** *n.* satisfaction with oneself. **self-contented** *a.* **self-contradiction** *n.* internal inconsistency. **self-contradictory** *a.* **self-control** *n.* power of controlling one's feelings, impulses etc. **self-controlled** *a.* **self-convicted** *a.* convicted by one's own acts etc. **self-correcting** *a.* correcting itself. **self-created** *a.* brought into existence by one's or its own power or vitality. **self-creation** *n.* **self-critical** *a.* critical of oneself. **self-criticism** *n.* **self-culture** *n.* the education of oneself. **self-deceiver** *n.* a person who deceives themselves. **self-deceit, self-deception** *n.* **self-deceiving** *a.* **self-deceptive** *a.* **self-defeating** *a.* doomed to failure because of flaws within it. **self-defence,** (*N Am.*) **self-defense** *n.* the act or art of defending one's own person, property or reputation. **self-defensive** *a.* **self-degradation** *n.* degradation of oneself. **self-delight** *n.* delight in oneself. **self-delusion** *n.* the delusion of oneself. **self-denial** *n.* 1 refusal to gratify one's own appetites or desires. 2 self-abnegation. **self-denying** *a.* **self-denying ordinance** *n.* (*Hist.*) a resolution in 1645 which deprived Members of Parliament of civil and military office. **self-dependent** *a.* dependent on oneself. **self-dependence** *n.* **self-deprecation** *n.* the disparagement of oneself. **self-deprecating** *a.* **self-deprecatingly** *adv.* **self-deprecatory** *a.* **self-depreciation** *n.* self-deprecation. **self-depreciative** *a.* **self-depreciatory** *a.* **self-despair** *n.* despair with oneself. **self-destroying** *a.* destroying oneself or itself. **self-destruct** *v.i.* (of a bomb etc.) to explode automatically at a pre-set time. ~*a.* able to self-destruct. **self-destruction** *n.* 1 the destruction of something by itself. 2 suicide. **self-destructive** *a.* **self-destructively** *adv.* **self-determination** *n.* 1 determination of one's own will, as opposed to *fatalism*. 2 the right of a group (local or racial) to decide to what state it will adhere. 3 the liberty of a state to determine its own form of government. **self-determined, self-determining** *a.* **self-development** *n.* the development of oneself. **self-devotion** *n.* the devotion of oneself to a cause; self-sacrifice. **self-discipline** *n.* discipline of oneself; self-control. **self-disciplined** *a.* **self-discovery** *n.* the process of gaining insight into one's character etc. **self-disgust** *n.* disgust with oneself. **self-distrust** *n.* distrust of oneself. **self-doubt** *n.* lack of confidence in one's abilities. **self-drive** *a.* (of a hired vehicle) driven by the hirer. **self-educated** *a.* educated by oneself. **self-education** *n.* **self-effacement** *n.* modesty; timidity. **self-effacing** *a.* **self-effacingly** *adv.* **self-elect, self-elected** *a.* elected by oneself or (as a committee) by its own members, co-opted. **self-election** *n.* **self-elective** *a.* **self-employed** *a.* running one's own business, or working freelance. **self-employment** *n.* **self-esteem** *n.* a good opinion of oneself. **self-estimation** *n.* **self-evident** *a.* obvious of itself, not requiring proof or demonstration. **self-evidence** *n.* **self-evidently** *adv.* **self-examination** *n.* 1 the examination of one's own behaviour etc. 2 the examination of one's body. **self-excited** *a.* (of electrical machines) supplying their own exciting current. **self-exciting** *a.* **self-executing** *a.* (of a law) providing for its own enforcement independently of other legislation. **self-existent** *a.* existing independently, underived, unconditioned. **self-existence** *n.* **self-explanatory, self-explaining** *a.* not needing explanation. **self-expression** *n.* the expression of one's own personality (through art etc.). **self-expressive** *a.* **self-faced** *a.* (of stone) having its natural face, unhewn. **self-feeder** *n.* 1 a machine, furnace etc. that feeds itself. 2 a machine for feeding animals automatically. **self-feeding** *a.* **self-fertile** *a.* (of plants) fertilized by their own pollen. **self-fertility** *n.* **self-fertilization, self-fertilisation** *n.* **self-fertilized, self-fertilizing** *a.* **self-financing** *a.* (of a project etc.) that finances itself. **self-financed** *a.* **self-flattery** *n.* self-appreciation. **self-flattering** *a.* **self-forgetful** *a.* oblivious of self, unselfish. **self-forgetfulness** *n.* **self-fulfilling** *a.* (of a prophecy etc.) bound to come true as a result of its being made. **self-fulfilment,** (*N Am.*) **self-fulfillment** *n.* the fulfilment of one's desires etc. **self-generating** *a.* generated by itself or oneself. **self-glazed** *a.* covered with glaze of uniform colour. **self-glorification** *n.* the glorification of oneself. **self-governing** *a.* 1 controlling oneself. 2 autonomous. **self-governed** *a.* **self-government** *n.* **self-hate** *n.* self-hatred. **self-hatred** *n.* hatred of oneself. **self-heal** *n.* a plant having healing virtues, esp. *Prunella vulgaris*. **self-help** *n.* the act or practice of attaining one's ends without help from others. ~*a.* of or relating to self-help. **self-helpful** *a.* **self-humiliation** *n.* humiliation of oneself. **self-hypnotism** *n.* hypnotism of oneself. **self-hypnosis** *n.* **self-hypnotic** *a.* **self-identity** *n.* the conscious realization of the self as having a unique identity. **self-image** *n.* one's own idea of what one is. **self-immolation** *n.* the offering of oneself as a sacrifice. **self-important** *a.* important in one's own conceit, pompous. **self-importance** *n.* **self-importantly** *adv.* **self-imposed** *a.* imposed on and by oneself. **self-improvement** *n.* improvement of one's social or economic position by one's own efforts. **self-inductance** *n.* the property of an electric circuit that causes an electromotive force to be generated in it by a change in the current flowing through it. **self-induced** *a.* 1 induced by oneself or itself. 2 produced by self-induction. **self-induction** *n.* production of an induced electric current in the circuit by the variation of the current in the circuit. **self-inductive** *a.* **self-indulgent** *a.* gratifying one's inclinations etc. **self-indulgence** *n.* **self-indulgently** *adv.* **self-inflicted** *a.* inflicted by and on oneself. **self-insurance** *n.* insuring oneself or one's possessions by putting money aside, rather than by taking out an insurance policy. **self-interest** *n.* 1 one's personal advantage. 2 absorption in selfish aims. **self-interested** *a.* **self-invited** *a.* invited only by oneself. **self-involved** *a.* wrapped up in oneself. **self-involvement** *n.*

selfish SELF.

self- (+ j–l words) self-justification *n.* justifying or providing excuses for oneself. **self-justifying** *a.* **self-knowledge** *n.* the understanding of oneself. **self-knowing** *a.* **self-loading** *a.* (of a firearm) reloading automatically. **self-loader** *n.* **self-locking** *a.* locking itself. **self-love** *n.* 1 undue regard for oneself or one's own interests. 2 selfishness. 3 conceit.

selfless SELF.

self- (+ m–w words) self-made *a.* 1 successful, wealthy etc. through one's own exertions. 2 made by oneself. **self-mastery** *n.* self-control. **selfmate** *n.* in chess, checkmate in which a player is forced to achieve checkmate. **self-mocking** *a.* mocking oneself or itself. **self-mockery** *n.* **self-motivated** *a.* motivated by one's own interest, enthusiasm etc. **self-motivation** *n.* **self-moved, self-moving** *a.* moving spontaneously. **self-motion** *n.* **self-murder** *n.* suicide. **self-murderer** *n.* **self-mutilation** *n.* mutilation of oneself. **self-neglect** *n.* neglect of oneself. **self-observation** *n.* (*Psych.*) the observation of one's own behaviour, personality etc. **self-operating** *a.* operating itself. **self-opinion** *n.* high opinion of oneself or one's opinion. **self-opinioned, self-opinionated** *a.* conceitedly or obstinately adhering to one's own views. **self-parody** *n.* (*pl.* **self-parodies**) (a) parody of oneself or one's work. **self-parodying** *a.* **self-partial** *a.* favouring oneself, biased towards one's own interest. **self-partiality** *n.* **self-perpetuating** *a.* perpetuating itself or oneself. **self-perpetuation** *n.* **self-pity** *n.* pity for oneself. **self-pitying** *a.* **self-pityingly** *adv.* **self-planted** *a.* planted without outside help. **self-pleasing** *a.* pleasing oneself. **self-poised** *a.* balanced without help from outside. **self-pollination** *n.* pollination by pollen from the same plant. **self-pollinated** *a.* **self-pollinating** *a.* **self-pollinator** *n.* **self-pollution** *n.* masturbation. **self-portrait** *n.* a portrait of oneself. **self-portraiture** *n.* **self-possessed** *a.* calm, imperturbable, having presence of mind. **self-possessedly** *adv.* **self-possession** *n.* **self-praise** *n.* praise of oneself; boasting. **self-preservation** *n.* 1 preservation of oneself from injury. 2 the instinct impelling one to this. **self-proclaimed** *a.* proclaimed by oneself or itself. **self-profit** *n.* self-interest. **self-promotion** *n.* promotion of oneself. **self-propagating** *a.* able to propagate itself. **self-propelled** *a.* moving using its own means of propulsion. **self-propelling** *a.* **self-protection** *n.* self-defence; protecting oneself. **self-protecting** *a.* **self-protective** *a.* **self-publicist** *n.* a person who tries to get publicity for themselves. **self-publicity** *n.* **self-punishment** *n.* punishment of oneself. **self-questioning** *a.* questioning oneself. **self-raising,** (*N Am.*) **self-rising** *a.* (of flour) having the raising agent already added. **self-raker** *n.* a reaping machine automatically gathering corn into sheaves for binding. **self-realization** *n.* 1 full development of one's faculties. 2 this as an ethical principle. **self-recording** *a.* self-registering. **self-referential** *a.* making reference to itself or oneself. **self-referentiality** *n.* **self-regard** *n.* 1 consideration or respect for oneself. 2 selfishness. 3 conceit. **self-regarding** *a.* **self-registering** *a.* (of a scientific instrument etc.) recording its movements etc. automatically. **self-regulating** *a.* regulating oneself or itself. **self-regulation** *n.* **self-regulatory** *a.* **self-regulatory organization** *n.* an organization set up to regulate the London investment markets. **self-reliant** *a.* independent; confident in one's abilities. **self-reliance** *n.* **self-reliantly** *adv.* **self-renewal** *n.* renewing oneself or itself. **self-renunciation** *n.* 1 self-sacrifice. 2 unselfishness. **self-renunciatory** *a.* **self-repression** *n.* repression of one's expression etc. **self-reproach** *n.* blame directed at oneself. **self-reproachful** *a.* **self-reproof** *n.* reproof of oneself. **self-reproving** *a.* **self-repugnant** *a.* self-contradictory, inconsistent. **self-respect** *n.* 1 due regard for one's character and position. 2 observing a worthy standard of conduct. **self-respectful, self-respecting** *a.* **self-restrained** *a.* restrained by oneself. **self-restraint** *n.* **self-revealing** *a.* revealing one's character, motives etc. **self-revelation** *n.* **self-reverence** *n.* self-respect, esp. in a spiritual sense. **self-righteous** *a.* pharisaical. **self-righteously** *adv.* **self-righteousness** *n.* **self-righting** *a.* righting itself (as when capsized). **self-rising** SELF-RAISING (under SELF- (+ M–W WORDS)). **self-rule** *n.* self-government. **self-sacrifice** *n.* surrender or subordination of one's own interests and desires to those of others. **self-sacrificing** *a.* **selfsame** *a.* exactly the same, absolutely identical. **self-satisfaction** *n.* conceit; complacence. **self-satisfied** *a.* **self-satisfying** *a.* **self-schooled** *a.* taught by oneself. **self-sealing** *a.* able to seal itself. **self-seed** *v.i.* (of a plant) to propagate itself by seed. **self-seeder** *n.* **self-seeding** *a.* **self-seeker** *n.* a person selfishly pursuing their own interests. **self-seeking** *n.*, *a.* **self-selection** *n.* the act of selecting oneself or itself. **self-selecting** *a.* **self-service** *n.*, *a.* (a restaurant, shop etc.) where customers help themselves and pay a cashier on leaving. **self-serving** *a.* giving priority to one's own interests. **self-shielding** *n.* (*Physics*) the absorption of radiation by another part of a radioactive source. **self-slaughter** *n.* suicide. **self-sown** *a.* growing from seed sown naturally by the parent plant. **self-starter** *n.* 1 an automatic device for starting a motor car. 2 a person who is ambitious and strongly motivated. **self-sterile** *a.* incapable of self-fertilization. **self-sterility** *n.* **self-styled** *a.* assuming a name or title oneself without authorization, would-be, pretended. **self-substantial** *a.* consisting of one's own substance. **self-sufficient, self-sufficing** *a.* 1 capable of fulfilling one's own requirements, needs etc. without aid. 2 conceited, overbearing. **self-sufficiency** *n.* **self-sufficiently** *adv.* **self-suggestion** *n.* suggestion arising reflexively within the self, esp. in hypnotic states. **self-supporting** *a.* 1 financially independent. 2 able to support itself without help. **self-support** *n.* **self-surrender** *n.* surrender of oneself or one's will. **self-sustained, self-sustaining** *a.* sustaining oneself or itself. **self-tapping** *a.* (of a screw) able to cut its own thread. **self-taught** *a.* taught by oneself. **self-torment** *n.* the inflicting of (esp. emotional) pain on oneself. **self-tormenting** *a.* **self-tormentor** *n.* **self-torture** *n.* the inflicting of pain on oneself. **self-trust** *n.* reliance on oneself. **self-understanding** *n.* 1 comprehension of one's actions etc. 2 awareness of oneself. **self-violence** *n.* violence to oneself, esp. suicide. **self-will** *n.* obstinacy. **self-willed** *a.* **self-winding** *a.* (of a clock etc.) winding itself automatically. **self-worship** *n.* worship of oneself. **self-worth** *n.* self-esteem.

Seljuk (sel´jook) *n.* a member of any of various Muslim dynasties in Central and W Asia during 11th–13th cents., descended from the Turkish chieftain Seljuk. ~*a.* of or relating to the Seljuks. **Seljukian** (-joo´-) *n.*, *a.* [Turk. *seljūg*]

sell (sel) *v.t.* (*past, p.p.* **sold** (sōld)) **1** to transfer or dispose of (property) to another for an equivalent in money. **2** to yield or give up (one's life etc.) exacting some return. **3** to be a regular dealer in. **4** to surrender, betray or prostitute for a price, reward or bribe. **5** (*sl.*) to disappoint, to cheat, to play a trick upon. **6** to inspire others with a desire to possess. **7** (of a publication or recording) to attain sales of (a specified number of copies). **8** to cause to be sold. ~*v.i.* **1** to be a shopkeeper or dealer. **2** to be purchased, to find purchasers. **3** to have a specified price (*to sell for £10*). ~*n.* **1** (*sl.*) a disappointment, a fraud. **2** a manner of selling. **sold on** enthusiastic about. **to sell a dummy** DUMMY. **to sell a pup to** (*sl.*) PUP. **to sell down the river** RIVER. **to sell off 1** to sell the remainder of (goods). **2** to clear out (stock), esp. at reduced prices. **to sell oneself 1** to try to persuade someone of one's abilities. **2** to offer one's services for money etc. **to sell one's life dear** to injure one's enemy before they kill you. **to sell one's life dearly** to sell one's life dear. **to sell out 1** to sell off (one's stock etc.). **2** to sell completely. **3** to dispose of (one's shares in a company etc.). **4** to betray. **to sell short** SHORT. **to sell the pass** PASS. **to sell up 1** to sell the goods of (a debtor) to pay their debt. **2** to sell one's business, one's house and possessions etc. **sellable** *a.* **sell-by date** *n.* **1** a date marked on the packaging of a perishable product, by which day the product should be withdrawn from sale. **2** (*coll.*) a date after which decay or decline begins. **seller** *n.* **1** a person who sells. **2** something that sells well or badly. **seller's market, sellers' market** *n.* a market in which demand exceeds supply and sellers make the price. **selling** *n.* **selling point** *n.* a good feature. **selling race** *n.* a horse race, the winner of which is sold by auction. **sell-off** *n.* **1** the privatization of a company by selling shares. **2** (*esp. N Am.*) a sale of bonds, shares etc. leading to a fall in price. **3** a sale. **sell-out** *n.* **1** a betrayal. **2** a performance etc. for which all the tickets have been sold. **sell-through** *n.* the retail of articles also commonly rented out, such as videos. [OE *sellan* (cp. ON *selja*, OHG *saljan*), cogn. with SALE]

Sellotape® (sel´ətāp) *n.* a cellulose or plastic adhesive tape for mending, binding etc. **sellotape** *v.t.* to fix or fasten with Sellotape.

seltzer (selt´sə), **seltzer water** *n.* **1** an effervescing mineral water. **2** an artificial substitute for this. **seltzogene** (-əjēn) *n.* a gazogene. [G *Selterserwasser*, water from (Nieder-)Selters, near Wiesbaden, Germany]

selva (sel´və) *n.* tropical rain forest in the Amazon basin. [Sp., Port., from L *silva*, wood]

selvage (sel´vij) *n.* **1** a rope or ring made of spun yarns etc., laid parallel and secured by lashings. **2** SELVEDGE. **selvaged** *a.* **selvagee** (-jē´) *n.* [SELVEDGE]

selvedge (sel´vij) *n.* **1** the edge of cloth woven so as not to unravel. **2** a narrow strip of different material woven along the edge of cloth etc. and removed or hidden in seaming. **3** the edge-plate of a lock with an opening for the bolt. **4** (*Geol.*) an alteration zone at the edge of a rock mass. [MDut. *selfegge* (SELF, EDGE)]

selves SELF.

SEM *abbr.* **1** scanning electron microscope. **2** standard error of the mean.

Sem. *abbr.* **1** seminary. **2** Semitic.

semanteme (siman´tēm) *n.* a unit of meaning conveying an image or idea.

semantic (siman´tik) *a.* of or relating to semantics; concerned with the meaning of words and symbols. **semantically** *adv.* **semantician** (-tish´ən) *n.* **semanticist** (-sist) *n.* **semantics** *n.* the area of linguistics concerned with meaning. [Gr. *semantikos*, significant]

semaphore (sem´əfaw) *n.* **1** a system of signalling using the arms or two flags to represent letters of the alphabet. **2** an apparatus for signalling by means of oscillating arms or flags or the arrangement of lanterns etc. **semaphoric** (-for´-), **semaphorical** *a.* **semaphorically** *adv.* **semasphere** (-sfiə) *n.* an electric aerostatic signalling apparatus. [F *sémaphore* (Gr. *sēma*, sign, *pherein*, to bear)]

semasiology (simāziol´əji) *n.* semantics. **semasiological** (-əloj´-) *a.* **semasiologically** *adv.* **semasiologist** *n.* [Gr. *sēmasia*, signification, as SEMAPHORE]

semasphere SEMAPHORE.

sematic (simat´ik) *a.* of the nature of a sign, significant, esp. of or relating to markings on animals serving to attract, to warn off enemies etc. **sematography** (semətog´-) *n.* the use of signs or symbols instead of letters in writing. **sematology** (semətol´-) *n.* **1** the science of signs as expressions of thought etc. **2** semantics. [Gr. *sēma -matos*, sign, -IC]

semblance (sem´bləns) *n.* **1** external appearance, seeming. **2** a mere show. **3** a likeness, an image. **semblable** (sem´bləbəl) *n.* (one's) like or fellow. ~†*a.* like, similar, seeming. [OF, from *sembler*, L *simulāre*, see SIMULATE]

semé (sem´ā), **semée** *a.* (*Her.*) (of a field or charge) strewn over with figures, such as stars, crosses etc. [F, p.p. of *semer*, L *sēmināre*, to sow, from SEMEN]

semeiology SEMIOLOGY.

semeiotics SEMIOTICS.

sememe (sem´ēm, sē´-) *n.* in linguistics, the meaning of a morpheme. [Gr. *sēma*, a sign]

semen (sē´mən) *n.* the fertilizing fluid containing spermatozoa, produced by the generative organs of a male animal. [L, seed, cogn. with *serere*, to sow]

semester (simes´tə) *n.* a college half-year in German, some American and other universities. [F *semestre*, L *semestris* (*se-* sex, six, *mensis*, month)]

semi (sem´i) *n.* (*pl.* **semis**) (*coll.*) **1** a semi-detached house. **2** a semi-final.

semi- (semi) *pref.* **1** half. **2** partially, imperfectly. **3** once every half. [L, cp. Gr. *hēmi-*, OE *sam-*, Sansk. *sāmi-*, prob. cogn. with SAME]

semi- (+ a–m words) semiacid *a.* subacid. **semi-annual** *a.* occurring every six months, half-yearly. **semi-annually** *adv.* **semiaquatic** *a.* living or growing close to or partly in water. **semi-attached** *a.* **1** partially attached. **2** semi-detached. **semi-automatic** *a.* **1** partly automatic. **2** (of a firearm) self-loading. ~*n.* such a firearm. **semi-autonomous** *a.* **1** partly self-governing. **2** having some freedom to act independently. **semi-bajan** *n.* (*Hist.*) a second-year student at a Scottish university. **semi-barbarous** *a.* half-barbarous. **semi-barbarian** *n., a.* **semi-barbarism** *n.* **semi-basement** *n.* a storey in a building which is partly below ground level. **semi-bold** *a.* printed in a darker type than normal but not bold. **semibreve** (sem´-) *n.* a note equal to half a breve, or two minims. **semibull** *n.* a bull issued by a Pope between his election and coronation. **semicentennial** *a.* happening, celebrated etc. at the end of every 50 years. **semicircle** (sem´-) *n.* **1** a half circle. **2** half the circumference of a circle. **3** a series of objects etc. arranged like this. **semicircled** *a.* **semicircular** *a.* **semicircular canal** *n.* each of three fluid-filled tubes in the inner ear, concerned with the maintenance of balance. **semi-civilized, semi-civilised** *a.* partially civilized. **semicolon** *n.* a mark (;) used in punctuation, now usu. intermediate in value between the period and the comma. **semiconductor** *n.* **1** a substance (such as silicon) whose electrical conductivity lies between those of metals and insulators and increases as its temperature rises. **2** a device using such a substance. **semiconducting** *a.* **semi-conscious** *a.* partially conscious. **semicylinder** *n.* half of a cylinder divided along the plane of its axis. **semicylindric, semicylindrical** *a.* **semi-darkness** *n.* partial darkness. **semidemisemiquaver** *n.* HEMIDEMISEMIQUAVER. **semi-deponent** *a.* (of a Latin verb) passive in form in the perfect tenses only.

semi-derelict *a.* partially derelict. **semi-detached** *a.* partially detached, esp. being one of two houses built as a pair. *~n.* a semi-detached house. **semidiameter** *n.* half a diameter. **semi-diurnal** *a.* consisting of, relating to or lasting half a day or in half the time between the rising and setting of a heavenly body. **semi-documentary** *n.* (*pl.* **semi-documentaries**) a film using a mixture of fact and fiction. **semi-dome** *n.* **1** a half-dome, usu. a structure like a dome divided vertically. **2** a structure resembling a dome. **semi-double** *a.* (of a flower) intermediate between single and double. **semi-elliptical** *a.* shaped like half an ellipse divided by either axis. **semi-ellipse** *n.* **semi-final** *n.* the match or round before the final. **semi-finalist** *n.* **semi-finished** *a.* (of metal etc.) prepared for the final stage in the manufacturing process. **semi-fitted** *a.* (of a garment) shaped but not closely fitted. **semi-fluid** *a.* imperfectly fluid. *~n.* a semi-fluid substance. **semi-fused** *a.* in a half-molten condition. **semi-independent** *a.* partially independent. **semi-infinite** *a.* limited in one direction and extending to infinity in the other. **semi-instinctive** *a.* partly instinctive. **semi-instinctively** *adv.* **semi-invalid** *n.* a person who is partially disabled. **semi-liquid** *n., a.* semi-fluid. **semi-literate** *a.* **1** hardly able to read and write. **2** (of a text) showing a lack of literacy. **semi-literacy** *n.* **semi-lunar** *a.* resembling or shaped like a half-moon or crescent. *~n.* a semi-lunar bone. **semi-lunar bone** *n.* a bone of this shape in the carpus. **semi-lunar cartilage** *n.* a cartilage of this shape in the knee. **semi-lunar valve** *n.* either one of two half-moon-shaped valves in the heart. **semi-lunary, semi-lunate** *a.* **semi-metal** *n.* an element having metallic properties but non-malleable. **semi-metallic** *a.* **semi-monthly** *a.* **1** occurring twice a month. **2** issued at half-monthly intervals. *~adv.* twice a month. *~n.* (*pl.* **semi-monthlies**) a half-monthly periodical. **semi-mute** *a.* without the power of speech or having it poorly developed. *~n.* a semi-mute person.

seminal (sem´inəl) *a.* **1** of or relating to semen or reproduction. **2** germinal, propagative. **3** important to the future development of anything. **4** containing new ideas, original. **seminal fluid** *n.* semen. **seminally** *adv.* [OF from L *sēminālis*, from SEMEN]

seminar (sem´inah) *n.* **1** a group of students undertaking an advanced course of study or research together, usu. under the guidance of a professor. **2** such a course. **3** a discussion group, or a meeting of it. [G, as SEMINARY]

seminary (sem´inəri) *n.* (*pl.* **seminaries**) a place of education, a school, academy or college, esp. a (foreign) Roman Catholic school for training priests. **seminarian** (-neə´ri-) *n., a.* **seminarist** *n.* [L *sēminārium*, seed-plot, as SEMINATION]

semination (seminā´shən) *n.* the natural dispersal of seeds by plants. **seminiferous** (-nif´-) *a.* **1** bearing or producing seed. **2** conveying semen. [L *sēminātio*, from *sēmināre*, to sow, from SEMEN]

semi- (+ o– words) semi-official *a.* partly or virtually official. **semi-officially** *adv.* **semi-opal** *n.* a non-opalescent variety of opal. **semi-opaque** *a.* partly opaque. **semi-opacity** *n.* **semi-osseous** *a.* partially ossified. **semi-oval** *a.* semi-elliptical. **semioviparous** *a.* imperfectly viviparous, producing young only partially developed beyond the egg, as the marsupials.

semiochemical (semiōkem´ikəl) *n.* a chemical substance such as a pheromone, used for communication between animals. [Gr. *sēmeion*, sign]

semiology (semiol´əji), **semeiology** *n.* **1** the study of signs and symbols. **2** the study of the symptoms of disease. **semiological** (-loj´-) *a.* **semiologist** *n.* [Gr. *sēmeion*, sign]

semiotics (semiot´iks), **semeiotics** *n.* **1** the study of signs and symbols and their relationships in language. **2** symptomatology. **semiotic** *a.* **semiotical** *a.* **semiotically** *adv.* **semiotician** (-tish´-) *n.* [Gr. *sēmeiōtikos*, a., from *sēmeion*, sign]

semi- (+ p–t words) semipalmate, semipalmated *a.* half-webbed, as the toes of many shorebirds. **semi-parabola** *n.* a curve of such a nature that the powers of its ordinates are to each other as the next lower powers of its abscissae. **semiparabolic** *a.* **semiparasitic** *a.* partially parasitic. **semiparasite** *n.* **semiparasitism** *n.* **semiped** (sem´-) *n.* in verse, a half-foot. **semi-permanent** *a.* long-lasting, but not permanent. **semi-permeable** *a.* permeable by small molecules but not by large ones. **semipiscine** *a.* partly resembling a fish. **semi-plume** (sem´-) *n.* a feather with a stiff stem but a downy web. **semi-plumaceous** *a.* **semiporcelain** *n.* a coarse ware that resembles porcelain. **semi-precious** *a.* valuable, but not regarded as a precious stone. **semi-pro** *n.* (*pl.* **semi-pros**) (*NAm., coll.*) a semi-professional. *~a.* semi-professional. **semi-professional** *n.* a person who is paid for an activity but does not do it for a living. *~a.* of or relating to semi-professionals. **semi-professionally** *adv.* **semiquaver** (sem´-) *n.* (*Mus.*) a note of half the duration of a quaver. **semi-retired** *a.* partially retired. **semi-retirement** *n.* **semi-rigid** *a.* (of an airship) having a flexible gas container and a rigid keel. **semi-rotary** *a.* capable of turning half round. **semisex** *n.* (*Biol.*) a group in a bisexual species capable of breeding with other groups. **semisexual** *a.* **semi-sextile** *n.* the aspect of two planets when distant from each other 30° or one-twelfth of a circle. **semi-skilled** *a.* (of a worker) having some basic skills but not highly trained. **semi-skimmed** *a.* (of milk) containing less fat than full-cream milk. **semi-smile** *n.* a half or forced smile. **semi-soft** *a.* (of cheese) fairly soft. **semi-solid** *a.* so viscous as to be almost solid. *~n.* a substance in this state. **semi-sweet** *a.* slightly sweetened. **semi-synthetic** *a.* (of a substance) prepared synthetically but deriving from a material that occurs naturally. **semi-tone** (sem´-) *n.* (*Mus.*) an interval equal to half a major tone on the scale. **semitonal, semitonic** *a.* **semitonically** *adv.* **semi-trailer** *n.* a trailer which has back wheels but is supported in front by the towing vehicle. **semi-transparent** *a.* almost transparent. **semitransparency** *n.* **semi-tropical** *a.* partly within or bordering on the tropics. **semi-tropics** *n.pl.* **semi-tubular** *a.* having the shape of a tube divided lengthwise.

Semit. *abbr.* Semitic.

Semite (sem´īt, sē´-) *n.* a descendant of Shem, or a member of one of the peoples (including Jews, Phoenicians, Assyrians, Arabs and Ethiopians) reputed to be descended from Shem. *~a.* Semitic. **Semitic** (simit´-) *a.* of or relating to the Semites or their languages. *~n.* any one of the Semitic group of languages, including Arabic and Hebrew. **Semiticize** (-mit´isīz), **Semiticise** *v.t.* **Semitism** (semi´-) *n.* **Semitist** *n.* **Semitize** (semi´-), **Semitise** *v.t.* **Semitization** (-ā´shən) *n.* [late L and Gr. *Sēm*]

semi- (+ u–w words) semi-uncial *a.* (of letters) half-uncial, between uncial and cursive. **semi-vitreous** *a.* partially vitreous. **semivitrify** *v.t.* (*3rd pers. sing. pres.* **semivitrifies**, *pres.p.* **semivitrifying**, *past, p.p.* **semi-vitrified**). **semivitrification** *n.* **semivocal, semivocalic** *a.* of or relating to a semivowel. **semivowel** (sem´-) *n.* **1** a sound having the character of both vowel and consonant, as *w* and *y*. **2** a consonant such as *l*, *m*, *r* and *z*, that is not plosive. **3** a character representing such a sound. **semi-weekly** *a.* occurring, issued etc. twice a week. *~adv.* twice a week.

semmit (sem´it) *n.* (*Sc.*) a vest or undershirt. [etym. unknown]

semnopithecus (semnōpithē´kəs) *n.* any monkey of the genus *Semnopithecus*, having long limbs and tails. **semnopithecine** (-sīn) *a.* **semnopithecoid** (-koid) *a., n.* [Gr. *semnos*, sacred, *pithekos*, ape]

semolina (semәlē´nә) *n.* the hard grains of wheat left after bolting, used for puddings etc. [It. *semolino*, dim. of *semola*, bran, L *simila*, fine wheat flour]
semper (sem´pә) *adv.* always. **semper fidelis** (fidā´lis) *a.* always faithful. **semper idem** (id´em) *a., pron.* (*pl.* **semper eadem** (āah´dem)) always the same. **semper paratus** (pәrah´tәs) *a.* always ready. [L]
sempervirent (sempәvī´rәnt) *a.* evergreen. [L *semper*, always, *virens -entem*, pres.p. of *virēre*, to be green, from *vis*, pl. *vires*, strength]
sempervivum (sempәvē´vәm) *n.* a fleshy plant of the genus *Sempervivum*, containing the houseleeks. [L, neut. of *sempervīvus* (as SEMPERVIRENT, *vīvus*, living)]
sempiternal (sempitœ´nәl) *a.* everlasting, eternal, endless. **sempiternally** *adv.* **sempiternity** *n.* **sempiternous** *a.* [OF *sempiternel*, L *sempiternus* (*sempi-semper*, always), *-ternus*, cp. *nocturnus*]
semplice (sem´plichi) *adv.* (*Mus.*) simply, plainly, without embellishment. [It.]
sempre (sem´pri) *adv.* (*Mus.*) in the same manner throughout. [It., from L *semper*, always]
sempstress SEAMSTRESS (under SEAM).
Semtex® (sem´teks) *n.* a malleable plastic explosive.
semuncia (simŭn´shә) *n.* (*Hist.*) a Roman coin equal to half an uncia. **semuncial** *a.* [L (SEMI-, *uncia*, a twelfth)]
SEN *abbr.* **1** special educational needs. **2** State Enrolled Nurse.
Sen. *abbr.* **1** (*N Am.*) Senate. **2** (*N Am.*) Senator. **3** Senior.
sen (sen) *n.* (*pl.* **sen**) a Japanese monetary unit, one-hundredth of a yen. [Jap.]
senarius (sineә´riәs) *n.* (*pl.* **senarii** (-iī)) in Latin prosody, a verse of six feet, esp. the iambic trimeter. **senary** (sē´nәri) *a.* **1** containing six units. **2** by sixes. [L (*sēnī*, six each)]
senate (sen´әt) *n.* **1** (*also* **Senate**) an assembly or council performing legislative or administrative functions. **2** (*Hist.*) (*also* **Senate**) the state council of the ancient Roman republic and empire of ancient Athens, Sparta etc., of the free cities of the Middle Ages etc. **3** (*also* **Senate**) the upper legislative house in various bicameral parliaments, as of the US and France. **4** the governing body of various universities. **5** any venerable deliberative or legislative body. **senate house** *n.* a building in which a senate meets. **senator** *n.* **1** a member of a senate. **2** in Scotland, a Lord of Session. **senatorial** (-taw´ri-) *a.* **senatorially** *adv.* **senatorship** *n.* **senatus** (sәnah´tәs) *n.* (*pl.* **senatus, senatuses**) **1** (*Hist.*) the ancient Roman senate. **2** the governing body of some universities. **senatus consultum** (kәnsŭl´tәm) *n.* (*pl.* **senatus consulta** (kәnsŭl´tә)) (*Hist.*) **1** a decree of the Roman Senate. **2** a decree of Napoleon I. **senatus populusque Romanus** (populuskwi rәmah´nus) *n.pl.* the Roman senate and people. [OF *senat*, L *senātus*, from *sen-*, base of *senex*, old]
send (send) *v.t.* (*past, p.p.* **sent** (sent), (*Naut.*) **sended**) **1** to cause or bid to go or pass or to be conveyed or transmitted to some destination. **2** to cause to go (in, up, off, away etc.). **3** to propel, to hurl, to cast. **4** to cause to come or befall. **5** to grant, to bestow, to inflict. **6** to cause to be, to bring about. **7** (*sl.*) to affect emotionally; to move to rapture. ~*v.i.* **1** to dispatch a messenger or letter. **2** (*Naut. also* **scend**) to pitch or plunge deeply into the trough of the sea. ~*n.* **1** (*Naut. also* **scend**) **a** the impetus or drive of the sea. **b** the act of sending or pitching into the trough of the sea. **to send away for** to order (goods) by post. **to send down 1** to suspend from university. **2** to send to prison. **3** in cricket, to bowl (a ball or an over). **to send for 1** to require the attendance of a person or the bringing of a thing. **2** to summon. **3** to order. **to send forth 1** to put forth. **2** to emit. **to send in 1** to cause to go in. **2** to submit (something, such as a competition entry). **to send in one's papers** PAPER. **to send off 1** to dispatch. **2** to give a send-off to (a person who is departing). **3** in sport, to order (a player) off the field because of an infringement of the rules. **to send off for** to send away for. **to send on 1** to forward (mail). **2** to send (luggage) in advance. **to send out** to send forth. **to send packing** PACK. **to send round the hat** HAT. **to send someone about their business** BUSINESS. **to send to Coventry** COVENTRY. **to send up 1** to parody. **2** to ridicule. **3** to cause to go up. **4** (*N Am.*) to send to prison. **5** to pass to a higher authority. **to send word** to send information. **sendable** *a.* **sender** *n.* **send-off** *n.* **1** a start, as in a race. **2** a leave-taking, a friendly demonstration to a person departing on a journey. **send-up** *n.* (*coll.*) a parody or imitation. [OE *sendan*, cp. Dut. *zenden*, G *senden*, Icel. *sende*]
sendal (sen´dәl) *n.* (*Hist.*) a light, thin silken fabric used in the Middle Ages for costly attire, banners etc. [OF *sendal, cendal*, low L *cendalum*, Sansk. *sindhu-*, of or relating to the Indus or Scinde]
Senecan (sen´ikәn) *a.* of, relating to or in the style of Seneca. [L, Annaeus *Seneca*, d. AD 65, Roman Stoic, dramatist etc.]
senecio (sinē´shiō) *n.* (*pl.* **senecios**) any plant of the genus *Senecio*, including the groundsel and the ragwort. **senecioid** (-oid) *a.* [mod. L, from *senex*, old man]
senescent (sines´әnt) *a.* growing old. **senesce** *v.i.* to grow old. **senescence** *n.* [L *senescens -ntem*, pres.p. of *senescere*, from *senex*, old]
seneschal (sen´ishәl) *n.* **1** (*Hist.*) an officer in the houses of princes and high dignitaries in the Middle Ages having the superintendence of feasts and domestic ceremonies, sometimes dispensing justice; a steward or major-domo. **2** a judge in Sark. **seneschalship** *n.* [OF, from Gmc. (cp. Goth. *sins*, cogn. with L *senex*, old, *skalks*, servant)]
senhor (senyaw´) *n.* **1** a man, in a Portuguese-speaking country. **2** the Portuguese or Brazilian title corresponding to the English Mr or sir. **senhora** (-rә) *n.* **1** a lady (in Portugal, Brazil etc.). **2** Mrs, madam. **senhorita** (-rē´tә) *n.* **1** a young unmarried girl (in Portugal, Brazil etc.). **2** Miss. [Port.]
senile (sē´nīl) *a.* **1** of, relating to or proceeding from the infirmities etc. of old age. **2** suffering from the (mental) infirmities associated with old age. ~*n.* a senile person. **senile dementia** *n.* dementia starting in old age, characterized by the loss of memory and inability to control one's bodily functions. **senility** (sinil´-) *n.* **1** old age. **2** the (mental) infirmity associated with old age. [L *senīlis*, see SENIOR]
senior (sēn´yә) *a.* **1** older, elder (appended to names to denote the elder of two persons with identical names, esp. father and son). **2** older or higher in rank or service. **3** (of a school) having pupils in an older age range. **4** (*N Am.*) of the final year at university or high school. ~*n.* **1** a person older than another. **2** a person older or higher in rank, service etc. **3** (*N Am.*) a student in their third or fourth year. **4** an aged person. **senior aircraftman** *n.* (*pl.* **senior aircraftmen**) the rank above aircraftman in the RAF. **senior aircraftwoman** *n.* (*pl.* **senior aircraftwomen**). **senior citizen** *n.* an elderly person, usu. an old-age pensioner. **senior college** *n.* (*N Am.*) a college in which students complete the last two years of a bachelor's degree. **senior combination room** *n.* a senior common room. **senior common room** *n.* a common room for the use of staff at a college. **senior high school** *n.* (*N Am.*) a secondary school comprising usu. the three highest grades. **seniority** (-nior´-) *n.* (*pl.* **seniorities**). **senior management** *n.* the highest level of management below the board of directors. **senior nursing officer** *n.* a person in a hospital who is in charge of the nursing services. **senior officer** *n.* an

officer to whom a junior officer is responsible. **senior partner** *n.* the head of a firm. **senior registrar** *n.* a hospital doctor one grade below a consultant. **senior service** *n.* the Royal Navy. **senior tutor** *n.* a college tutor in charge of teaching arrangements. [L, older, comp. of *senex senis*, old]

Usage note An implicit double comparative *more senior* is occasionally encountered, but is best avoided: *senior* already includes the notion of 'more'. However *senior* does not function as a true comparative in English, and should not be followed by *than* (the correct form is *senior to*).

senna (sen´ə) *n.* **1** the dried, purgative leaflets or pods of several species of cassia. **2** a cassia tree. [It. *sena*, Arab. *sanā*]

sennet (sen´it) *n.* (*Hist.*) a trumpet-signal for stage entrances and exits in the Elizabethan theatre. [OF *segnet*, dim. of *seing*, L *signum*, SIGN]

†**sennight** (sen´īt) *n.* seven nights, a week. [contr. of SEVEN-NIGHT (under SEVEN)]

sennit SINNET.

señor (senyaw´) *n.* (*pl.* **señores** (-riz)) **1** a man, in a Spanish-speaking country. **2** the Spanish form of address equivalent to Mr or sir. **señora** (-rə) *n.* **1** a lady (in Spain etc.). **2** Mrs, madam. **señorita** (-yərē´tə) *n.* **1** a young unmarried girl (in Spain etc.). **2** Miss. [Sp.]

Senr. *abbr.* Senior.

sensa SENSUM.

sensation (sensā´shən) *n.* **1** the mental state or affection resulting from the excitation of an organ of sense, the primary element in perception or cognition of an external object. **2** the content of such a mental state or affection, a state of excited feeling or interest, esp. affecting a number of people. **3** the thing or event exciting this. **to create a sensation** to cause surprise and excitement. **sensate**[1] (sensāt´) *v.t.* to perceive by the senses. **sensate**[2] (sen´sət) *a.* **1** perceived by the senses. **2** having bodily senses. **sensational** *a.* **1** causing, of or relating to sensation. **2** (*coll.*) very good. **sensationalism** *n.* **1** the employment of sensational methods in literary composition, political agitation etc. **2** (*Philos.*) the theory that all knowledge is derived from sensation. **sensationalist** *n.* **sensationalistic** (-lis´-) *a.* **sensationalize, sensationalise** *v.t.* **sensationally** *adv.* [med. L *sensātio*, from late L *sensātus*, sensate, from L *sensus*, SENSE]

sense (sens) *n.* **1** any one of the five faculties by which sensation is received through special bodily organs (sight, hearing, touch, taste, smell). **2** the muscular sense giving a sensation of physical effort. **3** the faculty of sensation, perception or ability to perceive through the senses, sensitiveness. **4** bodily feeling, sensuousness. **5** intuitive perception, comprehension, appreciation. **6** consciousness, conviction (of). **7** sound judgement, sagacity, common sense, good mental capacity. **8** meaning, signification. **9** general feeling or judgement, consensus of opinion. **10** (*pl.*) normal command or possession of the senses, sanity. **11** (*Math.*) a direction of movement. ~*v.t.* **1** to be aware of, to perceive by the senses. **2** (of a computer) to detect (a signal, a hole in a punched tape etc.). **3** (*N Am.*) to understand. **in a sense** in a way. **in one sense** in a sense. **in one's senses** sane. **out of one's senses** insane. **to bring someone to their senses 1** to make someone understand that they are doing something wrong, silly etc. **2** to make someone conscious after they have been unconscious. **to come to one's senses** COME. **to make sense** to be intelligible. **to make sense of** to understand. **to take leave of one's senses** LEAVE[2]. **under a sense of wrong** feeling wronged. **sense datum** *n.* an item of experience received directly through a sense organ. **senseful** *a.* significant. **sense impression** *n.* an impression on the mind through the medium of sensation. **senseless** *a.* **1** incapable of sensation, insensible. **2** contrary to reason, foolish, nonsensical. **senselessly** *adv.* **senselessness** *n.* **sense of direction** *n.* the ability to know in which direction one should be travelling. **sense of humour** *n.* the capacity of perceiving the ludicrous elements in life or art. **sense organ** *n.* a bodily organ concerned in the production of sensation. **sense-perception** *n.* perception by the senses. [F *sens*, L *sensus*, feeling, from *sentīre*, to feel, p.p. *sensus*]

sensible (sen´sibəl) *a.* **1** acting with or characterized by good sense or judgement, judicious, reasonable. **2** perceptible by the senses. **3** appreciable. **4** (of clothing etc.) practical. **5** having perception (of). ~*n.* that which is sensible or perceptible. **sensibility** (-bil´-) *n.* (*pl.* **sensibilities**) **1** capacity to see or feel. **2** susceptibility of impression. **3** sensitivity to sensory stimuli. **4** (*often pl.*) †acute or delicate susceptibility, oversensitiveness. **sensible horizon** *n.* the circular line where the sky and the earth seem to meet. **sensibleness** *n.* **sensible note** *n.* LEADING NOTE (under LEADING[2]). **sensibly** *adv.* **sensile** (-sīl) *a.* **1** sentient. **2** capable of affecting the senses. **sensism** *n.* SENSATIONALISM (under SENSATION). **sensist** *n.* SENSATIONALIST (under SENSATION). [F, from late L *sensibilis*, as SENSE]

Usage note The nouns *sensibility* and *sensibleness* should not be confused: *sensibility* is the capacity to feel, and *sensibleness* reasonableness or common sense.

sensillum (sensil´əm) *n.* (*pl.* **sensilla** (-ə)) a sense organ in insects. [L, dim. of *sensus*, sense]

sensitive (sen´sitiv) *a.* **1** readily or acutely affected by external influences. **2** impressible, delicately susceptible, excitable or responsive. **3** of or depending on the senses, sensory. **4** (of photographic materials) susceptible to the action of light. **5** (of information) secret, classified. **6** (of a market) liable to quick price changes. ~*n.* a person who is sensitive or abnormally sensitive. **sensitively** *adv.* **sensitiveness, sensitivism** *n.* **sensitive plant** *n.* **1** a plant, *Mimosa pudica* or *M. sensitiva*, the leaves of which shrink from the touch. **2** a sensitive person. **sensitivity** (-tiv´-) *n.* (*pl.* **sensitivities**). **sensitize, sensitise** *v.t.* **1** to make sensitive. **2** to render (paper etc.) sensitive to light. **3** to render (a person) sensitive (to an allergen, drug etc.). **sensitization** (-zā´shən) *n.* **sensitizer** *n.* **sensitometer** (-tom´itə) *n.* an apparatus for determining the sensitiveness of photographic plates, films etc. [OF *sensitif -tive*, med. L *sensitīvus*, see SENSE]

sensor (sen´sə) *n.* an instrument which responds to, and signals, a change in a physical stimulus, for information or control purposes. [see SENSE]

sensorium (sensaw´riəm) *n.* (*pl.* **sensoria** (-riə), **sensoriums**) **1** the seat or organ of sensation, the brain. **2** the nervous system, comprising the brain, spinal cord etc. **3** the grey matter of these. **sensorial** *a.* **sensorially** *adv.* **sensory** (sen´səri) *a.* **1** sensorial. **2** of the senses or of sensation. ~*n.* (*pl.* **sensories**) the sensorium. **sensorily** *adv.* [late L, see SENSE]

sensual (sen´shuəl, -sū-) *a.* **1** of, relating to or affecting the senses, carnal as distinct from spiritual or intellectual. **2** of, relating to or devoted to the indulgence of the appetites or passions, esp. those of sex, voluptuous. **3** (*Philos.*) of, relating to or according to sensationalism. **4** of or relating to sense or sensation, sensory. **sensualism** *n.* **sensualist** *n.* **sensualistic** (-lis´-) *a.* **sensuality** (-al´-) *n.* indulgence of the appetites or passions, voluptuousness. **sensualize, sensualise** *v.t.* **sensualization** (-zā´shən) *n.* **sensually** *adv.* [late L *sensuālis*, see SENSE]

Usage note The adjectives *sensual* and *sensuous* should not be confused: *sensual* is more associated with bodily appetites, and *sensuous* with aesthetic pleasures.

sensum (sen´səm) *n.* (*pl.* **sensa** (-sə)) (*Philos.*) a sense datum. [mod. L, neut. p.p. of *sentīre*, to feel]

sensuous (sen´shuəs, -sū-) *a.* **1** of, relating to or derived from the senses. **2** abounding in or suggesting sensible images. **3** readily affected through the senses. **sensuously** *adv.* **sensuousness** *n.* [L *sensus*, SENSE]

Usage note See note under SENSUAL.

sensu stricto (sensoo strik´tō) *adv.* strictly speaking, in the narrow sense. [L, in the restricted sense]

sent SEND.

sentence (sen´təns) *n.* **1** a series of words, containing a subject, predicate etc., expressing a complete thought. **2** a penalty or declaration of penalty upon a condemned person. **3** a judicial decision, verdict. **4** (*Logic*) an expression that is well-formed, without variables. **5** †a decision, judgement or opinion. **6** a pithy saying, a maxim, a proverb. **7** two or more musical phrases forming a unit. ~*v.t.* **1** to pronounce judgement on. **2** to condemn to punishment. **under sentence of** condemned to. **sentential** (-ten´shəl) *a.* of a sentence. [OF, from L *sententia*, from *sentīre*, to feel]

sententious (senten´shəs) *a.* **1** characterized by many pithy sentences, axioms or maxims. **2** terse, brief and energetic. **3** pompous in tone. **sententiously** *adv.* **sententiousness** *n.* [L *sententiosus*]

sentient (sen´shiənt, -tiənt) *a.* **1** having the power of sense-perception. **2** having sense of feeling. ~*n.* a sentient person or thing. **sentience** *n.* **sentiency** *n.* **sentiently** *adv.* [L *sentiens -entem*, pres.p. of *sentīre*, to feel]

sentiment (sen´timənt) *n.* **1** (*often pl.*) an opinion or attitude. **2** a thought, view or mental tendency derived from or characterized by emotion. **3** mental feeling excited by aesthetic, moral or spiritual ideas. **4** susceptibility to emotion. **5** †a thought or wish as formulated for a toast. [ME and OF *sentement*, med. L *sentīmentum*, as SENTIENT]

sentimental (sentimen´təl) *a.* **1** characterized by sentiment. **2** swayed by emotion. **3** mawkish. **4** displaying unbalanced tenderness. **sentimentalism** *n.* **1** unreasonable or uncontrolled emotion. **2** mawkishness. **sentimentalist** *n.* **sentimentality** (-tal´-) *n.* **sentimentalize, sentimentalise** *v.i.* to affect sentimentality. ~*v.t.* to make sentimental. **sentimentalization** (-zā´shən) *n.* **sentimentally** *adv.* **sentimental value** *n.* the value of an object in terms not of money but of associations, memories etc.

sentinel (sen´tinəl) *n.* **1** a person who keeps watch to prevent surprise, esp. a soldier on guard. **2** a sentinel crab. ~*v.t.* (*pres.p.* **sentinelling,** (*N Am.*) **sentineling,** *past, p.p.* **sentinelled,** (*N Am.*) **sentineled**) **1** to watch over, to guard. **2** to set sentinels at or over. **sentinel crab** *n.* a crab with long eye-stalks found in the Indian and Pacific Oceans. [OF *sentinelle*, from It. *sentinella* or dim. of *sentine*, dim. of *sente*, L *sēmita*, path]

sentry (sen´tri) *n.* (*pl.* **sentries**) **1** a sentinel, a soldier on guard. **2** the duty of a sentinel. **sentry box** *n.* a shelter for a sentry. **sentry-go** *n.* a sentry's duty of pacing to and fro. [perh. corr. of SENTINEL, or from OF *senteret*, from *sentier*, med. L *sēmitārius*, from *sēmita*, path]

senza (sent´sə) *prep.* (*Mus.*) without. **senza sordino** *adv.* to be played without mute. **senza tempo** *adv.* without strict time. [It.]

Sep. *abbr.* **1** September. **2** Septuagint.

sepal (sep´əl) *n.* any one of the segments, divisions or leaves of a calyx. **sepaline** (-īn), **sepaloid** (-oid), **sepalous** *a.* **sepalody** (-ōdi) *n.* reversion of petals etc. into sepals by metamorphosis. [F *sépale* (L *sēpar-*, SEPARATE[1], assim. to PETAL)]

separata SEPARATUM.

separate[1] (sep´ərāt) *v.t.* **1** to disunite, to set or keep apart. **2** to break up into distinct parts, to disperse. **3** to come or be between, to be the boundary of. **4** to sort or divide. **5** (*N Am.*) to discharge, dismiss. ~*v.i.* **1** to part, to be disconnected, to withdraw (from). **2** to disperse. **3** (of a married couple) to agree to live apart. **to separate the men from the boys** MAN. **to separate the sheep from the goats** SHEEP. **separable** *a.* **separability** (-bil´-) *n.* **separableness** *n.* **separably** *adv.* **separation** (-ā´shən) *n.* **1** the act of separating or the state of being separated, esp. partial divorce, consisting of cessation of cohabitation between married persons. **2** any of three or more monochrome reproductions which can combine to make a full colour picture. **separation order** *n.* a court order for judicial separation. **separatism** *n.* **separatist** *n.* a person who advocates secession, from a Church, political party, federation etc. **separative** *a.* **separator** *n.* **1** a person who separates. **2** a machine that separates the cream from milk. **separatory** (-rətəri) *a.* [L *sēparātus*, p.p. of *sēparāre* (SE-, *parāre*, to arrange)]

separate[2] (sep´ərət) *a.* **1** disconnected, considered apart. **2** distinct, individual. ~*n.* **1** (*pl.*) women's clothes that cover part of the body and are worn together, e.g. skirts and jackets. **2** an offprint. **under separate cover** COVER. **separately** *adv.* **separateness** *n.* [as SEPARATE[1]]

separatrix (sep´ərātriks) *n.* (*pl.* **separatrices** (-trisēz)) a separating mark, such as a decimal point, or line marking off corrections in the margin of proof, the line of demarcation between light and shade in a picture etc. [L, fem. of *sēparātor*, SEPARATOR (under SEPARATE[1])]

separatum (sepərā´təm) *n.* (*pl.* **separata** (-tə)) a reprint of one of a series of papers etc. [L *sēparātum*, neut. of *sēparātus*, see SEPARATE[1]]

☒ **seperate** common misspelling of SEPARATE[1].

Sephardi (sifah´di) *n.* (*pl.* **Sephardim** (-dim)) a Jew of Spanish, Portuguese or N African descent. **Sephardic** *a.* [mod. Heb.]

sepia (sē´piə) *n.* **1** a dark reddish-brown colour. **2** a dark brown pigment. **3** this pigment prepared from the black secretion of the cuttlefish. **4** the fluid secreted by cuttlefish. **5** a watercolour drawing in sepia. **6** any cuttlefish of the genus *Sepia*. ~*a.* **1** made in sepia. **2** of the colour sepia. [L and Gr.]

sepoy (sē´poi) *n.* (*Hist.*) an Indian soldier under European discipline, esp. one in the former British Indian army. [perh. through Port. *sipae*, from Hind., Pers. *sipāhī*, from *sipāh*, army]

seppuku (sepoo´koo) *n.* hara-kiri. [Jap.]

sepsis (sep´sis) *n.* (*pl.* **sepses** (-sēz)) **1** septic condition, putrefaction. **2** infection by disease-causing bacteria, e.g. from a wound, blood poisoning. [Gr. *sēpsis*, from *sēpein*, to make rotten]

Sept. *abbr.* **1** September. **2** Septuagint.

sept (sept) *n.* a clan or branch of a clan, esp. in Scotland or Ireland. **septal**[1] *a.* [OF *septe*, var. of *secte*, SECT]

sept-[1] SEPTI-[1].

sept-[2] SEPTI-[2].

septa SEPTUM.

septal[1] SEPT.

septal[2] SEPTUM.

septarium (septeə´riəm) *n.* (*pl.* **septaria** (-riə)) a nodule of limestone, ironstone etc., with radiating fissures in the middle filled with some extraneous deposit. **septarian** *a.*

septate (sep´tāt) *a.* provided with or divided by a septum or septa, partitioned. **septation** (-tā´shən) *n.* [late L *sēptatus*, see SEPTUM]

septavalent SEPTIVALENT.

septcentenary (septsentē´nəri, -ten´-, -sen´tin-) *n.* (*pl.*

septcentenaries) 1 a seven-hundredth anniversary. 2 a festival celebrating this. ~*a.* of or relating to a septcentenary.

September (septem´bə) *n.* the ninth month of the year (the seventh after March, first month of the ancient Roman year). **Septembrist** *n.* a member of the Paris mob that massacred political prisoners in Sept. 1792. [ME and OF *Septembre*, L *September* (*septem*, seven, cp. DECEMBER)]

septemvir (septem´viə) *n.* (*pl.* **septemviri** (-virī)) each of seven people forming a government, committee etc. **septemvirate** (-virət) *n.* [L *vir*, man]

septenarius (septineə´riəs) *n.* (*pl.* **septenarii** (-riī)) a verse of seven feet, esp. a trochaic trimeter catalectic. [L, from *septēnī*, seven apiece, from *septem*, seven]

septenary (sep´tinəri) *a.* 1 consisting of or relating to seven. 2 by sevens. 3 lasting seven years. ~*n.* (*pl.* **septenaries**) 1 a set of seven years, things etc. 2 a septenarius. **septenate** (-nət) *a.* (*Bot.*) growing in sevens. [as SEPTENARIUS]

septennium (septen´iəm) *n.* (*pl.* **septenniums, septennia** (-niə)) a period of seven years. **septennial** *a.* 1 lasting seven years. 2 happening every seven years. **septennially** *adv.* [L *annus*, year]

septet (septet´), **septette** *n.* 1 a group of seven, esp. singers, voices, instruments etc. 2 a musical composition for seven performers. [G, from L]

septfoil (set´foil) *n.* 1 a figure of seven equal segments of a circle, used as a symbol of the seven sacraments etc. 2 †the tormentil, *Potentilla erecta*. [FOIL[1]]

septi-[1] (sep´ti), **sept-** *comb.form* seven. [L *septem*, seven]

septi-[2] (sep´ti), **sept-**, **septo-** (sep´tō) *comb.form* septum.

septic (sep´tik) *a.* (*Med.*) causing or tending to promote putrefaction, not aseptic. ~*n.* a septic substance. **septicaemia** (-sē´miə), (*N Am.*) **septicemia** *n.* an abnormal state of the blood caused by the absorption of poisonous or putrid matter, blood poisoning. **septicaemic** *a.* **septically** *adv.* **septicity** (-tis´-) *n.* **septic tank** *n.* a tank in which sewage is partially purified by the action of bacteria. [Gr. *sēptikos*, from *sēptos*, rotten, from *sēpein*, to cause to rot]

septicidal (septisī´dəl) *a.* (of the dehiscence of a fruit) taking place through the partitions. **septicidally** *adv.* [SEPTI-[2], L *caedere*, to cut]

septiferous (septif´ərəs) *a.* bearing septa. [see SEPTI-[2]]

septiform[1] (sep´tifawm) *a.* sevenfold. [SEPTI-[1]]

septiform[2] (sep´tifawm) *a.* shaped like a septum. [SEPTI-[2]]

septifragal (septif´rəgəl) *a.* (*Bot.*) breaking away from the partitions (of or relating to a mode of dehiscence in which the septa break away from the valves). [SEPTI-[2], L *frangere*, to break]

septilateral (septilat´ərəl) *a.* seven-sided.

septillion (septil´yən) *n.* (*pl.* **septillion**) 1 the seventh power of a million. 2 (*N Am.*) the eighth power of a thousand. **septillionth** *n., a.*

septimal (sep´timəl) *a.* of, relating to or based on the number seven. **septime** (sep´tēm) *n.* the seventh parry in fencing.

septivalent (septivā´lənt), **septavalent** *a.* (*Chem.*) having a valency of seven; heptavalent.

septo- SEPTI-[2].

septuagenarian (septūəjineə´riən) *n.* a person of 70 years of age, or between 70 and 80. ~*a.* of such an age. **septuagenary** (-aj´-, -jen´ə-) *a.* containing or consisting of 70. [L *septuāgēnārius*, from *septuāgēnī*, seventy each, from *septuāginta*, seventy]

Septuagesima (septūəjes´imə), **Septuagesima Sunday** *n.* the third Sunday before Lent, so called because about 70 days before Easter.

Septuagint (sep´tūəjint) *n.* a Greek version of the Old Testament including the Apocrypha (*c.* 3rd cent. BC) (so called because, according to tradition, about 70 persons were employed on the translation). [L *septuāginta*, seventy]

septum (sep´təm) *n.* (*pl.* **septa** (-tə)) a partition, as in a chambered cell, the cell of an ovary, between the nostrils etc. **septal**[2] *a.* of or relating to a septum or septa. **septulate** (-ūlət) *a.* **septulum** (-tūləm) *n.* (*pl.* **septula** (-lə)) a small septum. [L, from *sē-*, *saepīre*, to enclose, from *sēpes*, *saepes*, hedge]

septuple (sep´tūpəl) *a.* sevenfold. ~*n.* 1 a set of seven things. 2 a sevenfold number or amount. ~*v.t., v.i.* to multiply by seven. **septuplet** (-tū´plit) *n.* each of seven children born at a birth. [late L *septuplus*, from *septem*, seven]

sepulchre (sep´əlkə), (*N Am.*) **sepulcher** *n.* 1 a tomb, esp. one hewn in the rock or built in a solid and permanent manner. 2 a burial vault. ~*v.t.* 1 to place in a sepulchre, to entomb. 2 to serve as a sepulchre for. **sepulchral** (-pŭl´krəl) *a.* 1 of or relating to burial, the grave or to monuments raised over the dead. 2 suggestive of a sepulchre, grave, dismal, funereal. **sepulchrally** *adv.* [OF *sepulcre*, L *sepulcrum* (*sepelīre*, to bury, p.p. *sepultus*, *-crum*, suf.)]

sepulture (sep´əlchə) *n.* (*formal*) interment, burial. [OF, from L *sepultūra*, as SEPULCHRE]

seq. *abbr.* 1 the following (L *sequens*). 2 and in what follows (L *sequente*). 3 it follows (L *sequitur*).

seqq. *abbr.* 1 (*pl.*) the following (L *sequentes*, *sequentia*). 2 in the following places (L *sequentibus*).

sequacious (sikwā´shəs) *a.* 1 logically consistent and coherent. 2 †following, inclined to follow. 3 †servile, ductile, pliant. **sequaciously** *adv.* **sequacity** (-kwas´-) *n.* [L *sequax -ācis*, from *sequī*, to follow, -OUS]

sequel (sē´kwəl) *n.* 1 that which follows. 2 a succeeding part, a continuation (of a story etc.). 3 the upshot, consequence or result (of an event etc.). **in the sequel** as things developed afterwards. [OF *sequele*, L SEQUELA]

sequela (sikwē´lə) *n.* (*pl.* **sequelae** (-lē)) 1 an abnormal condition occurring as the consequence of some disease. 2 an inference, a consequence. [L, from *sequī*, to follow]

sequence (sē´kwəns) *n.* 1 succession, the process of coming after in space, time etc. 2 a series of things following one another consecutively or according to a definite principle. 3 a set of consecutive cards. 4 (*Mus.*) a succession of similar harmonious formations or melodic phrases at different pitches. 5 a scene in a film. 6 a set of poems on a theme. 7 a hymn in rhythmical prose sung before the Gospel. 8 succession without implication of causality. ~*v.t.* 1 to arrange in definite order. 2 to discover the sequence of. **sequence of tenses** *n.* the relation of tense in a subordinate clause to the tense of the principal verb. **sequencer** *n.* 1 an electronic device which can be programmed with musical notes, chords etc., connected to a synthesizer. 2 a device for performing operations in a sequence, esp. in data processing. 3 an apparatus for determining the sequence of monomers in a biological polymer. **sequent** *a.* **sequential** (sikwen´shəl) *a.* **sequentiality** (-shial´-) *n.* **sequentially** *adv.* **sequently** *adv.* [OF, from L *sequentia*, from *sequens -ntis*, pres.p. of *sequī*, to follow]

sequester (sikwes´tə) *v.t.* 1 (*esp. in p.p.*) to set apart, to isolate, to seclude. 2 (*Law*) to separate (property etc.) from the owner temporarily. 3 to take possession of (property in dispute) until some case is decided or claim is paid. 4 to confiscate, to appropriate. 5 (*Chem.*) to remove (a metal ion) by adding a reagent that forms a complex with it. ~*v.i.* (*Law*) (of a widow) to renounce or decline any concern with the estate of a late husband. **sequestrable** *a.* **sequestrate** (sē´kwistrāt) *v.t.* (*Law*) to sequester. **sequestration** (-ā´shən) *n.* **sequestrator** *n.* [OF *sequestrer*, late L *sequestrāre*, to surrender, to commit, from *sequester*, agent, trustee, from *sequī*, to follow]

sequestra SEQUESTRUM.

sequestrable SEQUESTER.

sequestral SEQUESTRUM.

sequestrate, sequestration etc. SEQUESTER.

sequestrum (sikwes´trəm) *n.* (*pl.* **sequestra** (-trə)) a piece of dead and separated bone remaining in place. **sequestral** *a.* **sequestrotomy** (sēkwistrot´əmi) *n.* (*pl.* **sequestrotomies**) the removal of this. [med. L, as SEQUESTER]

sequin (sē´kwin) *n.* **1** a small disc of shiny metal, jet etc., used as trimming for dresses etc. **2** (*Hist.*) a Venetian gold coin. **sequinned, sequined** *a.* [F, from It. *zecchino*, from *zecca*, mint, Arab. *sikka*, die]

sequoia (sikwoi´ə) *n.* either of two gigantic conifers of California, *Sequoia sempervirens* and *Sequoiadendron giganteum*. [name of a Cherokee]

sera SERUM.

serac (serak´, ser´-) *n.* any of the large angular or tower-shaped masses into which a glacier breaks up at an icefall. [Swiss F, orig. a cheese in the form of a cube]

seraglio (siral´yō) *n.* (*pl.* **seraglios**) **1** a harem. **2** (*Hist.*) a walled palace, esp. the old palace of the Turkish Sultan, with its mosques, government offices etc. at Istanbul. [It. *serraglio*, enclosure, ult. from Pers. *sarāy*, palace]

serai (sərī´) *n.* a caravanserai. [Pers., as SERAGLIO]

seral SERE[1].

serang (sərang´) *n.* a boatman; the leader of a Lascar crew. [Hind.]

serape (sərah´pā), **sarape** (sar-), **zarape** (zar-) *n.* a Mexican blanket or shawl. [Mex. Sp.]

seraph (ser´əf) *n.* (*pl.* **seraphs, seraphim** (-fim)) an angel of the highest order. **seraphic** (-raf´-) *a.* **1** of or like a seraph. **2** ecstatic, rapturous. **3** (*coll.*) very good, well-behaved. **seraphically** *adv.* [orig. *seraphin*, Heb. *serāphīm*, pl., from Arab. *sharaf*, high]

seraphina (serəfē´nə), **seraphine** (ser´əfēn) *n.* a form of harmonium (invented 1883) with reeds, a keyboard etc. [as SERAPH, -INE]

seraskier (serəskiə´) *n.* (*Hist.*) a Turkish commander, esp. the commander-in-chief or minister of war. **seraskierate** (-rət) *n.* [F *sérasquieur*, Turk. *ser'asker* (Pers. *ser*, head, Arab. *'asker*, army)]

Serb (sœb) *n.* **1** a native or inhabitant of Serbia in SE Europe. **2** a person of Serbian descent; a person belonging to a Slav ethnic group of Serbia. **3** Serbian. *~a.* of or relating to the Serbs, Serbian. **Serbian** *a.* of or relating to Serbia, its people or their language. *~n.* **1** a native or inhabitant of Serbia, a Serb. **2** the language of Serbia, one of the two main dialects of Serbo-Croat. **Serbo-** (sœ´bō) *comb. form* Serbian (and). **Serbo-Croat** (-krō´at), **Serbo-Croatian** (-krōā´shən) *n.* the Slavonic language which has Serbian and Croat as its main dialects. *~a.* of or relating to this language. [Serb. *Srb*]

Serb. *abbr.* Serbian.

SERC *abbr.* (*Hist.*) Science and Engineering Research Council.

sere[1] (siə) *n.* a series of ecological communities following one another in one area. **seral** *a.* [SERIES]

sere[2] SEAR.

serein (sərān´) *n.* a fine rain falling from a clear sky after sunset, esp. in tropical regions. [F, as SERENE]

serenade (serənād´) *n.* **1** a song or piece of music played or sung in the open air at night, esp. by a lover beneath his lady's window. **2** a nocturne, a serenata. *~v.t.* to sing or play a serenade to or in honour of. *~v.i.* to perform a serenade. **serenader** *n.* **serenata** (-nah´tə) *n.* a cantata or simple form of symphony, usu. with a pastoral subject, for the open air. [F *sérénade*, It. *serenata*, orig. fem. p.p. of *serenare*, to make serene, see SERENE]

serendipity (serəndip´iti) *n.* the happy knack of making unexpected and delightful discoveries by accident. **serendipitous** *a.* **serendipitously** *adv.* [coined by Horace Walpole, after the fairy tale *The Three Princes of Serendip* (an old name for Sri Lanka)]

serene (sərēn´) *a.* **1** placid, tranquil, undisturbed. **2** (of the sky, atmosphere etc.) calm, fair and clear. **3** honoured; applied as a title to certain continental princes. **all serene** (*sl.*) all right. **Serene Highness** *n.* title accorded to certain European princelings. **serenely** *adv.* calmly, quietly, deliberately. **serenity** (-ren´-), **sereneness** *n.* [L *serēnus*]

serf (sœf) *n.* **1** (*Hist.*) a feudal labourer attached to an estate, a villein. **2** a slave, a drudge. **serfage** (-ij), **serfdom, serfhood** (-hud), **serfism** *n.* [F, from L *servus*, slave]

Serg. *abbr.* Sergeant.

serge (sœj) *n.* a strong and durable twilled cloth, of worsted, cotton, rayon etc. [F, from L *sērica*, fem. of *sēricus*, silken, orig. Chinese, from L and Gr. *Sēres*, the Chinese]

sergeant (sah´jənt) *n.* **1** a non-commissioned Army or Air Force officer ranking next above corporal, teaching drill, commanding small detachments etc. **2** a police officer ranking next below an inspector. **3** (*N Am.*) a police officer ranking next below a lieutenant. **sergeancy** (-si) *n.* (*pl.* **sergeancies**). **Sergeant Baker** *n.* (*Austral.*) a large brightly coloured fish, *Aulopus purpurissatus*, found in temperate waters. **sergeant-fish** *n.* (*pl. in general* **sergeant-fish,** *in particular* **sergeant-fishes**) a fish with lateral stripes resembling a chevron, *Rachycentron canadum*. **sergeant major** *n.* the chief sergeant of a regiment, a squadron of cavalry or a battery of artillery. **sergeantship** *n.* **serjeant-at-arms, sergeant-at-arms** *n.* (*pl.* **serjeants-at-arms, sergeants-at-arms**) **1** an officer of the Houses of Parliament attending the Lord Chancellor or the Speaker, and carrying out arrests etc. **2** an officer with corresponding duties attached to other legislative bodies. **3** any one of several court and city officers with ceremonial duties. **serjeant-at-law** *n.* (*pl.* **serjeants-at-law**) (*Hist.*) a member of the highest order of barristers, abolished in 1877. **serjeantship** *n.* [OF *sergant*, *serjant* (F *sergent*), late L *serviens -entem*, orig. pres.p. of *servīre*, to SERVE]

Sergt. *abbr.* Sergeant.

serial (siə´riəl) *a.* **1** of, relating to, consisting of or having the nature of a series. **2** (of a novel, story etc.) published, broadcast or shown at a cinema in instalments. **3** occurring as part of a series of a set of repeated occurrences (*serial murder*). **4** of or relating to the computer processing of tasks one after another. **5** (of music) based on a fixed, arbitrary series of notes, not on a traditional scale. *~n.* **1** a serial story, play, film etc. **2** a serial publication, a periodical. **serialism** *n.* **serialist** *n.* **seriality** (-al´-) *n.* **serialize, serialise** *v.t.* **1** to publish (a novel) in instalments. **2** to arrange in a series. **3** to compose (music) using a serial technique. **serial killer** *n.* a killer who commits a series of apparently unconnected murders. **serially** *adv.* **serial number** *n.* a number stamped on an item which identifies it in a large series of identical items. **serial rights** *n.pl.* the right to publish as a serial. **seriate**[1] (-āt) *v.t.* to arrange in a series or regular sequence. **seriate**[2] (-ət), **seriated** (-ātid) *a.* arranged in a series or regular sequence. **seriately** *adv.* **seriatim** (-ā´tim) *adv.* **1** in regular order. **2** one point etc. after the other. **seriation** (-ā´shən) *n.*

Seric (ser´ik) *a.* (*poet.*) Chinese. [L *sēricus*]

sericeous (sirish´iəs), **sericate** (ser´ikət), **sericated** (-kātid) *a.* **1** of, relating to or consisting of silk. **2** silky, downy, soft and lustrous. [late L *sericeus*, silken, L *sericum*, silk, as SERIC]

sericin (ser´isin) *n.* a gelatinous substance contained in silk.

sericulture (ser´ikūlchə) *n.* the breeding of silkworms

and the production of raw silk. **sericultural** (-kŭl´-) *a.* **sericulturist** (-kŭl´-) *n.*
seriema (seriē´mə), **cariama** (kariah´mə) *n.* any long-legged S American bird of the family Cariamidae. [Tupi-Guarani]
series (siə´riz) *n.* (*pl.* **series**) **1** a number, set or continued succession of things similar to each other or each bearing a definite relation to that preceding it; a sequence, a row, a set. **2** a set of radio or television programmes or of lectures complete in themselves but featuring the same characters, subject matter etc. **3** a set of volumes, parts, articles, periodicals etc., consecutively numbered or dated or issued in the same format under one general title. **4** a sequence of games between the same teams. **5** (*Math.*) a number of terms, the successive pairs of which are related to each other according to a common law or mode of derivation, a progression. **6** the connection of two or more electric circuits so that the same current traverses all the circuits. **7** (*Geol.*) a group of allied strata forming a subdivision of a geological system. **8** (*Mus.*) an arrangement of 12 notes used as a basis for composition. **9** (*Chem.*) a set of related elements or compounds. **in series 1** in ordered succession. **2** (of circuits etc.) arranged in a series. [L, from *serere*, to join together, cp. Gr. *eirein*, to bind]
serif (ser´if), **ceriph** *n.* any of the fine cross-lines at the top and bottom of printed letters of the alphabet. **seriffed** *a.* [etym. uncertain; perh. from Dut. and Flem. *schreef*, a line]
serigraph (ser´igrahf) *n.* a silk-screen print. **serigrapher** (-ig´rəphə) *n.* **serigraphic** (-graf´-) *a.* **serigraphy** (-ig´-) *n.* [L *sericum*, silk, -GRAPH]
serin (ser´in) *n.* a small yellow or green finch, *Serinus serinus*, the wild canary. [F, etym. uncertain]
serine (siə´rēn, ser´-) *n.* a hydrophilic amino acid involved in the synthesis of cysteine. [L *sericum*, silk, -INE]
seringa (səring´gə) *n.* **1** a Brazilian rubber tree, *Hevea brasiliensis*. **2** syringa. [F, Port., from L SYRINGA]
serious (siə´riəs) *a.* **1** grave, sober, sedate, thoughtful. **2** in earnest, not ironical or pretended, sincere. **3** not merely entertaining, not frivolous. **4** of great importance, momentous. **5** having serious consequences, dangerous. **6** sincerely concerned about religious matters, esp. one's own salvation. **7** (*coll.*) significantly costly or substantial in value. **serio-comic, serio-comical** *a.* mingling the serious and the comic; serious in meaning with the appearance of comedy, or comic with a grave appearance. **serio-comically** *adv.* **serioso** (seriō´sō) *adv.* (*Mus.*) with gravity, solemnly. **seriously** *adv.* **1** in a serious manner. **2** to a serious extent. **3** (*coll.*) very. **seriousness** *n.* [OF *serieux*, late L *sēriōsus*, L *serius*, etym. uncertain]
serjeant SERGEANT.
sermon (sœ´mən) *n.* **1** a discourse founded on a text of Scripture delivered in church in exposition of doctrine or instruction in religion or morality. **2** a similar discourse delivered elsewhere. **3** a moral reflection. **4** a serious exhortation or reproof. *~v.t.* **1** to deliver a sermon to. **2** to lecture. **sermonet** (-nit), **sermonette** (-net´) *n.* a short sermon. **sermonize, sermonise** *v.i.*, *v.t.* **sermonizer** *n.* **Sermon on the Mount** *n.* Christ's sermon which included the Lord's Prayer (Matthew v–vii). [OF, from L *sermo -ōnem*, speech, discourse]
sero- (siə´rō) *comb. form* serum.
serology (siərol´əji) *n.* the study of blood serum, its composition and properties. **serological** (-əloj´-) *a.* **serologist** *n.*
seronegative (siərōneg´ətiv) *a.* (of a person whose blood has been tested) not showing the presence of a virus etc.
seropositive (siərōpoz´itiv) *a.* (of a person whose blood has been tested) showing the presence of a virus etc.
seropurulent (siərōpū´rulənt) *a.* composed of serum and pus.
serosa (sirō´sə) *n.* serous membrane. [L, fem. of *serosus*, from SERUM]
serosity SEROUS.
serotherapy (siərōther´əpi) *n.* serum therapy.
serotine (ser´ətīn), **serotine bat** *n.* a small reddish bat, *Eptesicus serotinus*, flying in the evening. [F *sérotine*, L *sērōtinus*, from *sērō* (adv.), *sērus*, late]
serotinous (sirot´inəs) *a.* (*Bot.*) appearing late in the season. [from L, as SEROTINE]
serotonin (serətō´nin, sirot´ənin) *n.* a compound found in many body tissues which acts as a vasoconstrictor.
serous (siə´rəs) *a.* **1** of, relating to or resembling serum. **2** thin, watery. **3** like whey. **serosity** (-os´-) *n.* **serous gland, serous membrane** *n.* a thin, transparent membrane lining certain large body cavities, and secreting a thin fluid which allows movement of the organs in the cavities.
serow (ser´ō) *n.* a goat-antelope with a thick, dark coat and conical horns, *Capricornus sumatrensis* of S and E Asia, or *C. crispus* of Taiwan and Japan. [Lepcha *sā-rō*]
serpent (sœ´pənt) *n.* **1** a reptile with an elongated scaly body and no limbs, a snake. **2** a treacherous, insinuating person. **3** an old-fashioned wind instrument of serpentine form. **4** (*Bible*) (**Serpent**) the Devil. **serpent charmer** *n.* a snake charmer. **serpent-charming** *n.* **serpent-eater** *n.* the secretary bird. **serpent-grass** *n.* the bistort. **serpentiform** (-pen´tifawm), **serpent-like** *a.* serpentine. **serpentine** (-tīn) *a.* **1** of, relating to, resembling or having the qualities of a serpent. **2** coiling, winding, twisting, sinuous. **3** subtle, wily, treacherous. *~n.* **1** a massive or fibrous rock consisting of hydrated silicate of magnesia richly coloured and variegated and susceptible of a high polish, used for making various ornamental articles. **2** a skating figure consisting of three circles in a line. *~v.i.* **1** to wind in and out like a serpent. **2** to meander. **serpentinely** *adv.* **serpentine verse** *n.* a verse beginning and ending with the same word. **serpent-lizard** *n.* the seps. †**serpentry** *n.* serpents collectively. **serpent's tongue** *n.* the adder's tongue. [F, from L *serpens -entem*, orig. pres.p. of *serpere*, to creep, cogn. with Gr. *herpein*, to creep, and Sansk. *sarpa-*, snake]
serpigo (səpī´gō) *n.* (*pl.* **serpigines** (-pij´inēz), **serpigoes**) a skin disease, esp. a form of herpes or spreading ringworm. **serpiginous** (-pij´i-) *a.* **1** like a serpent; winding. **2** (of a skin lesion) having a wavy margin. [med. L *serpīgo -piginis*, from *serpere*, to creep, cp. HERPES]
SERPS (sœps), **Serps** *abbr.* State earnings-related pension scheme.
serpula (sœ´pūlə) *n.* (*pl.* **serpulae** (-lē)) a serpulid, esp. of the genus *Serpula*. **serpulid** (-lid) *n.* a brilliantly coloured marine worm of the family Serpulidae, living in a contorted or spiral shell. *~a.* of or relating to this family. **serpulite** (-līt) *n.* a fossil serpula or similar formation. **serpuloid** (-loid) *a.* [late L, small serpent]
serra (ser´ə) *n.* (*pl.* **serrae** (-ē)) **1** a sawlike organ, part or structure. **2** a sawfish. [L, saw]
serradilla (serədil´ə) *n.* (*pl.* **serradillas**) a species of clover, *Ornithopus sativus*, grown for fodder. [Port., dim. of *serredo*, SERRATE[1]]
serrae SERRA.
serranid (səran´id, ser´ə-) *n.* any marine fish of the family Serranidae, comprising the sea basses, sea perches and groupers. *~a.* of or relating to this family. **serranoid** *n.*, *a.* [mod. L *Serranus*, from L *serra*, saw]
serrate[1] (ser´āt) *a.* notched on the edge, like a saw, serrated. [L *serrātus*, from SERRA]
serrate[2] (sərāt´) *v.t.* (*usu. p.p.*) to cut into notches and teeth, to give a sawlike edge to. **serration** (-ā´shən), **serrature** (ser´əchə) *n.* [as SERRATE[1]]

serried (ser'id) *a.* (esp. of soldiers) close-packed, in compact order. **serry** *v.t.* (*3rd pers. sing. pres.* **serries,** *pres.p.* **serrying,** *past, p.p.* **serried**). [F *serré*, p.p. of *serrer*, to close, from late L *serāre*, see SERAGLIO]

serrulate (ser'ūlāt), **serrulated** (-lātid) *a.* finely serrated, having minute notches. **serrulation** (-ā'shən) *n.*

serry SERRIED.

serum (siə'rəm) *n.* (*pl.* **serums, sera** (-rə)) **1** the thin transparent part that separates from the blood in coagulation. **2** animal serum used as an antitoxin etc. **3** a constituent of milk and other animal fluids, lymph. **4** whey. **serum hepatitis** *n.* an acute viral infection of the liver, marked by inflammation and jaundice, spread by contact with infected blood. **serum sickness** *n.* an allergic reaction to a serum injection, such as fever, rashes etc. **serum therapy** *n.* the treatment or prevention of disease by injecting blood containing the appropriate antibodies. [L, whey, cp. Gr. *oros*, Sansk. *saras*, flowing]

serval (sœ'vəl) *n.* an African wild cat with long legs and a black-spotted tawny coat, *Felis serval*. [F, from Port., from late L *cervālis*, from L *cervus*, a stag]

servant (sœ'vənt) *n.* **1** a person employed by another person or body of persons to work under direction for wages, esp. in the house of the employer and undertaking domestic tasks or acting as a personal attendant, and often receiving board and lodging as part of the wages. **2** a devoted follower, a person willing to perform the will of another. **servant-girl, servant maid** *n.* a female domestic servant. **servants' hall** *n.* the room in a large domestic establishment where servants have their meals etc. together. [OF, orig. pres.p. of *servir*, to SERVE]

serve (sœv) *v.t.* **1** to act as servant to, to be in the employment of. **2** to be useful to, to render service to. **3** to attend to as a shop assistant. **4** to be subservient or subsidiary to. **5** to satisfy, to avail, to suffice. **6** to supply, to perform (a purpose, function etc.). **7** to carry out the duties of, to do the work of (an office etc.). **8** to undergo the punishment prescribed by (a sentence) or for (a specified time). **9** to behave towards, to treat (well, badly etc.). **10** to dish (up) for eating, to bring to and set on the table. **11** to distribute to those at table. **12** to furnish, to supply (a person with). **13** to deliver (a summons, writ etc.) in the manner prescribed by law. **14** to throw or send (a ball etc.) to begin or resume play in tennis, badminton etc. **15** (of a male animal) to mate with, to cover, esp. for hire. **16** (*Mil.*) to keep (a gun etc.) firing. **17** (*Naut.*) to lash or whip (a rope) with thin cord to prevent fraying. **18** †to worship. **19** †to play (a trick) on. ~*v.i.* **1** to be employed, to perform the duties of or to hold an office etc. **2** to perform a function, to take the place of. **3** to be used (as), to be a satisfactory substitute (for), to suffice, to avail. **4** to be satisfactory, favourable or suitable. **5** to be in subjection. **6** to deliver the ball to begin or resume play in tennis, badminton etc. **7** to attend a celebrant at the altar. **8** to be a member of an armed force. **9** to act as a waiter. ~*n.* **1** the act of or turn for serving at tennis, badminton etc. **2** (*Austral., sl.*) a reprimand. **it will serve** it will be adequate. **to serve at table** to act as waiter or waitress. **to serve one's need/needs** to be adequate. **to serve one's time 1** to serve one's sentence. **2** to go through an apprenticeship. **3** to hold an office etc. for the full period. **to serve one's turn** TURN. **to serve out 1** to distribute (portions of food) to those at table. **2** †to have one's revenge on. **to serve out one's time** (*esp. N Am.*) to serve one's time. **to serve someone right** to be what someone deserved (as a punishment or misfortune). **to serve the purpose of** to be used as. **to serve the turn** to be adequate. **to serve up** to serve out (food). **server** *n.* **1** a person who serves at table. **2** a utensil (such as a tray or spoon) used to serve food. **3** in tennis, badminton etc., the person who serves. **4** a person who assists the celebrant at mass. **5** a computer program to manage shared access to a network service. **6** a device on which this is run. **servery** (-vəri) *n.* (*pl.* **serveries**) a counter or room from which food is served. **serving** *n.* a portion of food, a helping. [OF *servir*, L *servīre*, from *servus*, slave]

service[1] (sœ'vis) *n.* **1** the act of serving. **2** work done for an employer or for the benefit of another. **3** a benefit or advantage conferred on someone. **4** the state of being a servant, esp. the place or position of a domestic servant. **5** a department of state or public work or duty, the organization performing this or the persons employed in it. **6** willingness to work or act. **7** use, assistance. **8** a liturgical form for worship, an office. **9** a performance of this. **10** a musical setting of a liturgical office or part of it. **11** formal legal delivery, posting up or publication (of a writ, summons etc.). **12** a set of dishes, plates etc. required for serving a meal. **13** that which is served at table. **14** the act of serving the ball at tennis, badminton etc. **15** maintenance work undertaken by the vendor after a sale. **16** (*pl.*) the armed forces. **17** (*pl.*) the service area of a motorway. **18** (*pl.*) provision of water, electricity etc. to a property. ~*v.t.* **1** to repair or maintain (a car etc.) after sale. **2** to meet interest on (a debt). **3** (of a male animal) to serve. **4** to provide service or services for. ~*a.* **1** of the armed forces. **2** for the use of servants. **3** providing services. **at someone's service** ready to help someone. **in/ on active service** on service. **in service 1** working as a servant. **2** available for use. **on service** engaged in actual duty in the army, navy etc. **out of service** not available for use. **to be of service** to be available to help. **to see service 1** to have experience, esp. as a soldier or sailor. **2** to be put to long or hard use. **to take service with** to become a servant to. **serviceable** *a.* **1** able or willing to render service. **2** useful, beneficial, advantageous. **3** durable, fit for service. **serviceability** (-bil'-), **serviceableness** *n.* **serviceably** *adv.* **service area** *n.* **1** an area served by a broadcasting station within which efficient transmission can be guaranteed. **2** a place beside a motorway where petrol, food etc. are available. **service book** *n.* a book containing the church offices, esp. the Book of Common Prayer. **service bus, service car** *n.* (*New Zeal.*) a long-distance bus. **service charge** *n.* a percentage of a bill, charged in addition to the total, to pay for service. **service dress** *n.* in the armed forces, uniform other than full dress. **service engineer** *n.* a person who services and repairs (electrical) equipment. **service flat** *n.* a flat for which an inclusive sum is charged for rent and full hotel service. **service game** *n.* in tennis etc., a game in which a particular player serves. **service industry** *n.* (*pl.* **service industries**) an industry concerned with providing a service to its customers, rather than with manufacturing. **service line** *n.* in tennis etc., either of two lines marking the limit within which the serve must fall. **serviceman** *n.* (*pl.* **servicemen**) **1** a member of the armed forces. **2** a man whose job is to provide service or maintenance. **service pipe** *n.* a pipe from the water or gas main to a building. **service road** *n.* a minor road running alongside a main road and carrying local traffic only. **service station** *n.* a roadside establishment providing petrol etc. to motorists. **servicewoman** *n.* (*pl.* **servicewomen**) a woman member of the armed forces. [OF, from L *servitium*, as SERVE]

service[2] (sœ'vis) *n.* the service tree. **service-berry** *n.* (*pl.* **service-berries**) **1** the fruit of the service tree. **2** any shrub of the genus *Amelanchier*. **3** the fruit of this. **service tree** *n.* **1** a European tree, *Sorbus domestica*, with small pearlike fruit. **2** the wild service tree, *Sorbus torminalis*. [ME *serves*, pl., from OE *syrpe*, ult. from L *sorbus*]

serviette (sœviet´) *n.* a table napkin. [F, related to *servir*, to SERVE]

servile (sœ´vīl) *a.* 1 slavish, abject, mean, cringing, fawning, menial, dependent. 2 of, relating to or befitting a slave or slaves. **servilely** *adv.* **servility** (-vil´-) *n.* [OF, from L *servīlis*, from *servus*, slave]

serving SERVE.

servitor (sœ´vitə) *n.* 1 †a male servant or attendant. 2 (*poet.*) a follower, an adherent, a henchman. 3 (*Hist.*) an undergraduate at Oxford University partly supported out of the college funds, who waited at table on the fellows and gentlemen-commoners. **servitorship** *n.* [OF, from late L *servītor -tōrem*, from *servīre*, to serve]

servitude (sœ´vitūd) *n.* 1 the condition of a slave, slavery, bondage. 2 subjection to or as to a master. 3 (*Law*) the subjection of property to an easement for the benefit of a person other than the owner or of another estate. [F, from L *servitūdo*, as SERVITOR]

servo (sœ´vō) *n.* (*pl.* **servos**) a servo-mechanism or servo-motor. **servo-** (sœ´vō) *comb. form* involving a servo-mechanism. **servo-mechanism** *n.* an automatic device using a small amount of power which controls the performance of a much more powerful system. **servo-motor** *n.* a motor which powers a servo-mechanism. [L *servus*, servant, slave]

sesame (ses´əmi) *n.* 1 an African plant, *Sesamum orientale*, with oily seeds used as food. 2 these seeds. **open sesame** OPEN. **sesame oil** *n.* an edible oil from sesame seeds. **sesamoid** (-moid) *a.* shaped like a sesame seed, nodular. ~*n.* a sesamoid bone, any of several small bones developed in tendons as in the kneecap, the sole of the foot etc. [F *sésame*, ult. from Gr. *sesamon -mē*, prob. of Oriental orig.]

sesqui- (ses´kwi) *comb. form* 1 denoting a proportion of 1½ to 1 or 3 to 2. 2 denoting combinations of three atoms of one element with two of another. [L (*semis*, half, *-que*, and), more by one half]

sesquialtera (seskwial´tərə) *n.* (*Mus.*) 1 an interval with the ratio of 3 to 2, a perfect fifth. 2 a rhythm in which three minims equal two minims preceding. 3 a compound organ stop.

sesquicentenary (seskwisəntē´nəri, -ten´-, -sen´tin-) *n.* (*pl.* **sesquicentenaries**) a 150th anniversary. **sesquicentennial** (-ten´-) *n.*, *a.*

sesquipedal (seskwip´idəl) *a.* 1 measuring a foot and a half. 2 sesquipedalian. ~*n.* a sesquipedalian person or thing. **sesquipedalian** (-dā´-) *a.* 1 (of words) many-syllabled. 2 given to using long words. 3 characterized by long words. ~*n.* a sesquipedalian word. **sesquipedalianism** *n.* **sesquipedality** (-dal´-) *n.*

sess (ses) *n.* CESS[1]. [ASSESS]

sessile (ses´īl) *a.* 1 (*Zool.*, *Bot.*) attached by the base, destitute of a stalk or peduncle. 2 sedentary; immobile. **sessile oak** *n.* the durmast. **sessility** (-sil´-) *n.* [L *sessilis*, from *sess-*, see SESSION]

session (sesh´ən) *n.* 1 a sitting or meeting of a court, council, legislature, academic body etc. for the transaction of business. 2 the time of such meeting. 3 the period during which such meetings are held at short intervals. 4 a period devoted to an activity. 5 (*coll.*) a period of heavy drinking. 6 the period from the meeting of Parliament till its prorogation or dissolution. 7 the lowest court of the Presbyterian Church. 8 the act of sitting or being assembled. **in session** assembled for business. **sessional** *a.* **session-clerk** *n.* the clerk of the Kirk-session. [F, from L *sessio -ōnem*, from *sedēre*, to sit, p.p. *sessus*]

sesterce (ses´təs), **sestertius** (sistœ´shəs) *n.* (*pl.* **sesterces, sestertii** (-shiī)) an ancient Roman silver (afterwards bronze) coin and money of account worth 2½ asses or ¼ denarius. **sestertium** (-shiəm) *n.* (*pl.* **sestertia** (-shiə)) an ancient Roman money of account equivalent to 1000 sesterces. [F *sesterce*, L *sestertius*, orig. a. (*semis*, SEMI-, *tertius*, third)]

sestet (sestet´) *n.* 1 the last six lines of a sonnet. 2 a composition for six instruments or voices, a sextet. **sestetto** (-ō) *n.* (*pl.* **sestettos**). [It. *sestetto*, dim. of *sesto*, L *sextus*, sixth]

sestina (sestē´nə) *n.* a form of verse consisting of six six-lined stanzas with a final triplet, each stanza having the same terminal words to the lines but in different order. [It., as SESTET]

set[1] (set) *v.t.* (*pres.p.* **setting,** *past, p.p.* **set**) 1 to place, to put, to stand. 2 to fix. 3 to plant (usu. *out*). 4 to bring, put, place or station in a specified or right position, posture, direction or state. 5 to arrange or dispose for use, action, display etc. 6 to apply (a thing to something else). 7 to attach, to fasten, to join. 8 to determine, to appoint, to settle, to establish. 9 to cause to sit. 10 to apply (oneself, one's energies etc., to). 11 to cause (to work etc.). 12 to present, to offer (an example, task etc.). 13 to stud, to make insertions in (a surface etc.). 14 to arrange, to compose (type). 15 to fix (the hair) in waves etc. 16 to adapt or fit (words etc.) to music usu. composed for the purpose. 17 (*Naut.*) to hoist, to spread (sail). ~*v.i.* 1 to become solid, hard or firm from a fluid condition, to congeal, to solidify. 2 to take shape, to become fixed. 3 to move, tend or incline in a definite or specified direction. 4 (of flowers or fruit) to mature, to develop. 5 (of a dog) to point. 6 to face one's partner (in dancing). 7 to pass below the horizon. 8 to decline, to pass away. 9 (*dial.*, *sl.*) to sit. ~*a.* 1 fixed, unyielding, immovable. 2 determined, intent (on or upon). 3 rigid, motionless. 4 stationary. 5 established, prescribed. 6 regular, in due form. **dead set against** utterly opposed to. **dead set on** determined on. **in set terms** TERM. **of set purpose** intentionally, deliberately. **set to music** MUSIC. **to get set** GET[1]. **to set about** 1 to begin. 2 to prepare or take steps (to do etc.). 3 (*coll.*) to attack. **to set against** 1 to oppose. 2 to balance (one thing) against another. 3 to make (a person) unfriendly to or prejudiced against. **to set apart** to separate, to reserve (for some special purpose). **to set a person's teeth on edge** EDGE. **to set aside** 1 to reserve. 2 to reject. 3 to annul, to quash. **to set at defiance** to defy. **to set at ease** 1 to relieve of anxiety, fear, bashfulness etc. 2 to make comfortable. **to set at naught** NAUGHT. **to set back** 1 to turn backwards, to reverse the movement of. 2 to hinder the progress of, to impede. 3 (*coll.*) to cost. **to set by** 1 (*esp. NAm.*) to reserve. 2 (*esp. NAm.*) to lay by, to save. **to set by the compass** to observe the compass bearings of. **to set by the ears** EAR[1]. **to set down** 1 to put on the ground. 2 to let (a passenger) alight from a vehicle. 3 to put in writing, to note. 4 to attribute. 5 to explain (as). 6 to snub, to rebuke. **to set eyes on** EYE[1]. **to set fire to** FIRE. **to set foot** FOOT. **to set foot on/ in** FOOT. **to set forth** 1 to start (on a journey etc.). 2 to show, to demonstrate, to expound, to make known. **to set forward** 1 to promote, to help. 2 to begin going forward. **to set free** to release. **to set in** 1 to begin in a steady manner. 2 to come into fashion. 3 (of the tide) to move steadily shoreward. 4 (of the weather) to become settled. 5 to insert (esp. a sleeve). **to set in order** 1 to arrange, to adjust. 2 to reform. **to set little by** to value little. **to set much by** to value highly. **to set off** 1 to make more attractive or brilliant by contrast. 2 to act as a foil to. 3 to beautify, to adorn. 4 to place over, against, as an equivalent. 5 to start (laughing etc.). 6 to set out. 7 to detonate. **to set on** 1 to incite, to instigate, to urge (to attack). 2 to employ (on a task). 3 to make an attack on. **to set oneself** 1 to apply oneself, to undertake. 2 to resolve. **to set oneself up as** to pretend to be. **to set one's face against** FACE. **to set one's hand to** 1 to begin (a task). 2 to sign (a document). **to set one's heart on** HEART. **to set one's mind on** MIND. **to set one's seal**

to to seal (a document). **to set one's sights on** SIGHT. **to set one's teeth 1** to clench the teeth. **2** to be obstinate or determined. **to set on fire** FIRE. **to set on foot** FOOT. **to set out 1** to start (upon a journey etc.). **2** to intend. **3** to display, to expound, to state at length, to publish. **4** to mark off. **5** to assign, to allot. **6** to equip. **7** to adorn, to embellish. **8** to plant out. **9** to lay (a stone etc.) so as to project. **to set over** to put in authority over or in control of. **to set right** to correct. **to set sail** SAIL. **to set someone's heart at rest** HEART. **to set someone's mind at rest** MIND. **to set store by** STORE. **to set the pace** PACE[1]. **to set the scene** SCENE. **to set the stage** to prepare for (an event etc.). **to set the watch** WATCH. **to set to 1** to apply oneself vigorously. **2** to begin to fight. **to set to work 1** to begin on a task. **2** to cause to begin working. **to set up 1** to erect, to fix up, to post up or display. **2** to raise, to exalt. **3** to establish. **4** to start a business (as). **5** to cause to develop, to occasion. **6** to begin to utter. **7** (*coll.*) to arrange for (someone else) to be blamed, to frame. **8** to compose (type). **9** to put (copy etc.) in type. **10** to supply the needs of. **11** to prepare. **12** to restore the health of. **13** to put forward (a theory). **to set upon** to set on. **set-aside** *n.* **1** the act of setting aside. **2** the policy of taking farmland out of production to reduce surpluses or maintain prices of a crop. *~a.* that is set aside; of or relating to set-aside. **setback** *n.* **1** a check, an arrest. **2** an overflow, a counter-current. **3** a relapse. **setdown** *n.* a rebuke, a snub, a rebuff. **set fair** *a.* (of the weather) fine and settled. **set-in** *a.* (of a part of a garment) made up separately and then sewn in. **set-line** *n.* a long fishing line with shorter lines attached to it. **set menu** *n.* a limited menu which has a set number of courses. **set-off** *n.* **1** a thing set off against another. **2** an offset, a counterpoise, a counter-claim. **3** a decorative contrast, an embellishment. **4** a ledge or sloping projection between the thicker part of a wall and a receding portion above. **5** (*Print.*) an accidental transference of ink from one printed sheet to another. **set-out** *n.* **1** beginning, start, outset. **2** preparations or equipment. **3** a display. **set phrase** *n.* an invariable combination of words. **set piece** *n.* **1** a carefully prepared and usually elaborate performance. **2** an elaborate, formalized piece of writing, painting etc. **3** a carefully arranged display of fireworks or a large firework built up with scaffolding. **4** a set scene. **5** in sport, a formal movement to put the ball back into play. **set scene** *n.* a theatre scene of more or less solid and permanent construction. **set screw** *n.* a screw which secures parts of machinery together and prevents relative movement. **set scrum** *n.* a scrum in rugby ordered by the referee. **set square** *n.* a right-angled triangular piece of wood etc. used in mechanical drawing. **setter** *n.* **1** a person who or thing which sets (type, gems, music to words etc.). **2** a large dog trained to point at game by standing rigid. **setter-on** *n.* an instigator. **setter-up** *n.* a person who sets up, establishes etc. **setting** *n.* **1** the action of a person who or thing which sets. **2** the result of this. **3** solidification, hardening, concretion. **4** the framing etc. in which something (such as a jewel) is set. **5** the framing, surroundings or environment of a thing, event etc. **6** the scenery and other stage accessories of a play. **7** a set of eggs. **8** the music to which words, a song etc. are fitted. **9** one person's cutlery etc. at a table. **10** a level at which a machine or device is set to operate. **setting lotion** *n.* lotion used for setting hair. **set-to** *n.* (*pl.* **set-tos**) (*coll.*) **1** a fight, esp. with the fists. **2** a heated argument. **set-up** *n.* **1** an arrangement. **2** a situation. **3** (*N Am., sl.*) a situation which has a predetermined outcome. **4** (*coll.*) a situation in which someone is tricked or framed. [OE *settan*, causal of *sittan*, to SIT (cp. Dut. *zetten*, G *setzen*, Icel. *setja*)]

set² (set) *n.* **1** a number of similar, related or complementary things or persons, a collection, a group, a company, a clique. **2** a number of things intended to be used together or required to form a whole. **3** a collection of mathematical objects, numbers etc. **4** a clutch or sitting of eggs. **5** a group of games played together, counting as a unit, esp. in tennis. **6** the direction of a current, opinion etc., drift, tendency, trend. **7** a predisposition to respond in a certain way to a psychological stimulus. **8** confirmation, posture, pose, carriage. **9** the way a dress etc. sits. **10** permanent inclination, bend, displacement, bias. **11** the spread or deflection of the teeth of a saw alternately to right or left. **12** the amount of this. **13** the act of pointing at game etc. (by a setter). **14** a young plant for setting out, a shoot, a slip for planting. **15** the last coat of plaster on a wall. **16** a mine or group of mines leased together. **17** a distance set off for excavation. **18** a timber framing for supporting the roof. **19** the amount of margin in type determining the distance between letters. **20** a set theatre scene. **21** a built-up cinema scene. **22** an apparatus for radio or television receiving. **23** a class of pupils of the same or similar ability. **24** the adjustment or setting of a machine. **25** (*Austral., coll.*) a grudge. **26** a sequence of songs or pieces of music to be performed. **27** a set hairstyle. **28** a badger's sett. **29** a sett used for paving. **30** a number of people performing a square dance. **to have a set on** (*Austral.*) to intend mischief to. **to make a dead set at 1** to attack with determination. **2** to try to win the affections of. **set point** *n.* in tennis etc., a point which, if won by one of the players, will win the set. **set theory** *n.* a branch of mathematics which studies the properties and relationships of sets. [OF *sette*, var. of *secte*, SECT, in some senses blended with SET[1]]

seta (sē´tə) *n.* (*pl.* **setae** (-tē)) a bristle or bristle-like plant or animal part. **setaceous** (sitā´shəs) *a.* **1** bristly. **2** set with, consisting of or resembling bristles. **setaceously** *adv.* **setiferous** (-tif´-), **setiform** (sē´tifawm), **setigerous** (-tij´-), **setose** (sē´tōs) *a.* [L *sēta*, bristle, -ACEOUS]

SETI *abbr.* search for extraterrestrial intelligence.

setiferous, setiform etc. SETA.

seton (sē´tən) *n.* a twist of silk, cotton or similar material inserted in a wound to maintain drainage and as a counterirritant, esp. in veterinary surgery. [F *séton*, ult. from L *sēta*, see SETA]

setose SETA.

Setswana (setswah´nə) *n.* the Bantu language Tswana. *~a.* of or relating to Setswana.

sett (set) *n.* **1** a small rectangular block of stone used for road paving. **2** a badger's burrow. [var. of SET[2]]

settee (sitē´) *n.* a long seat with a back for several persons; a sofa. [prob. var. of SETTLE[2]]

setter SET[1].

setterwort (set´əwœt) *n.* the bear's foot or stinking hellebore, *Helleborus fetidus*. [*setter*, etym. uncertain, WORT]

setting SET[1].

settle¹ (set´əl) *v.t.* **1** to place firmly, to put in a permanent or fixed position, to establish. **2** to put in order. **3** to cause to sit down or to become fixed. **4** to determine, to decide. **5** to plant with inhabitants, to colonize. **6** to settle in as colonists. **7** to cause to sink or subside, to precipitate. **8** to clear of dregs. **9** to deal with, to dispose of, to finish with, to do for. **10** to adjust and liquidate (a disputed account). **11** to pay (an account). **12** to secure (property, an income etc., on). **13** to arrange, to adjust, to accommodate (a quarrel, dispute etc.). *~v.i.* **1** to sit down, to alight. **2** to cease from movement, agitation etc. **3** to become motionless, fixed or permanent. **4** to take up a permanent abode, mode of life etc. **5** to become established, to become a colonist (in). **6** to subside, to sink to the bottom. **7** to become clarified. **8** to determine, to resolve (upon). **9** to adjust differences, claims or accounts. **to settle down 1** to become regular in one's mode of life, to become established. 2 to begin to apply oneself (to a task etc.). **to settle for** to accept, to be content with. **to settle in** to make or become comfortably established. **to settle old scores** SCORE. **to settle one's affairs** to make sure one's finances etc. are in order before one dies. **to settle someone's hash** HASH[1]. **to settle up 1** to pay what is owing. 2 to finally arrange (a matter). **to settle with 1** to pay money due to (a creditor). 2 to deal with. 3 to get one's revenge for. **settleable** *a.* **settlement** *n.* 1 the act of settling. 2 the state of being settled. 3 a subsidence. 4 a place or region newly settled, a colony. 5 a community or group of persons living together, esp. in order to carry out social work among the poor. 6 (*Law*) the conveyance of property or creation of an estate to make provision for the support of a person or persons or for some other object. 7 the property so settled. **Act of Settlement** ACT. **settler** *n.* 1 a person who settles, esp. a colonist. 2 (*sl.*) a knock-down blow, a decisive argument etc. **settler's clock** *n.* (*Austral.*) the kookaburra. **settler's matches** *n.pl.* (*Austral.*) pieces of dry bark used as tinder. **settling** *n., a.* **settling day** *n.* a day for the settling-up of accounts, esp. on the Stock Exchange. **settlings** *n.pl.* sediment, lees, dregs. **settlor** *n.* (*Law*) a person who makes a settlement. [OE *setlan*, as SETTLE[2], combined with *sahtlian*, to reconcile, from *saht*, Icel. *saetl*, peace]

settle[2] (set´əl) *n.* a long, high-backed seat or bench for several persons. [OE *setl* (cp. Dut. *zettel*, G *Sessel*), cogn. with SIT]

seven (sev´ən) *n.* 1 the number or figure 7 or vii. 2 the age of seven. 3 the seventh hour after midnight or midday. 4 (*pl.*) a rugby game or tournament played with teams of seven players. 5 a set of seven persons or things, esp. a card with seven pips. 6 a size etc. denoted by the number seven. 7 a team or set of seven people. ~*a.* 1 seven in number. 2 aged seven. **seven deadly sins** *n.pl.* pride, covetousness, lust, gluttony, anger, envy, sloth. **seven dolours** *n.pl.* seven sorrowful experiences in the life of the Virgin Mary. **sevenfold** *a., adv.* **seven-knit** *n.* SINNET. **seven-league boots** *n.pl.* magical boots enabling the wearer to travel seven leagues at a stride. **seven-night** *n.* a week. **seven seas** *n.pl.* the N and S Atlantic, N and S Pacific, Arctic, Antarctic and Indian oceans. **Seven Sisters** *n.pl.* PLEIADES (under PLEIAD). **seven-up** *n.* (*N Am.*) a card game, all fours. **seven wonders of the world** *n.pl.* the pyramids, the Hanging Gardens of Babylon, the Temple of Diana at Ephesus, the tomb of Mausolus of Caria, the Colossus of Rhodes, the statue of Zeus by Phidias and the Pharos of Alexandria. **seven year itch** *n.* the supposed onset of boredom, leading to infidelity, after seven years of marriage. [OE *seofon* (cp. Dut. *zeven*, G *sieben*, Dan. *syv*, L *septem*, Gr. *hepta*, Sansk. *saptan*)]

seventeen (sevəntēn´, sev´-) *n.* 1 the number or figure 17 or xvii. 2 the age of 17. 3 a size etc. denoted by the number seventeen. ~*a.* 1 17 in number. 2 aged 17. **seventeenth** *n.* 1 any one of 17 equal parts. 2 the last of 17 (people, things etc.). 3 the next after the 16th. ~*a.* that is the seventeenth.

seventh (sev´ənth) *n.* 1 any one of seven equal parts. 2 (*Mus.*) the interval between a given tone and the seventh above it (inclusively) on the diatonic scale. 3 a combination of these two tones. 4 the last of seven (people, things etc.). 5 the next after the sixth. ~*a.* 1 the last of seven (people, things etc.). 2 the next after the sixth. **Seventh-Day Adventist** *n.* a member of a sect that believes in the imminent second advent of Christ and observes Saturday as the sabbath. **seventh heaven** *n.* 1 the highest of the seven heavens believed by cabbalists and Muslims to be the dwelling place of God. 2 a state of supreme happiness (*in seventh heaven*). **seventhly** *adv.*

seventy (sev´ənti) *n.* (*pl.* **seventies**) 1 the number or figure 70 or lxx. 2 the age of 70. ~*a.* 1 70 in number. 2 aged 70. **the Seventy 1** the translators of the Septuagint. 2 the 70 evangelists mentioned in Luke x.1–24. 3 the Jewish Sanhedrin. **seventies** *n.pl.* 1 the period of time between one's 70th and 80th birthdays. 2 the range of temperature between 70° and 80°. 3 the period of time between the 70th and 80th years of a century. **seventieth** (-əth) *n.* 1 any one of 70 equal parts. 2 the last of 70 (people, things etc.). 3 the next after the 69th. ~*a.* that is the seventieth. **seventy-eight** *n.* (*Hist.*) a gramophone record playing at 78 revolutions per minute. **seventy-first, seventy-second** etc. *a., n.* the ordinal numbers corresponding to seventy-one, seventy-two etc. **seventy-four** *n.* (*Hist.*) a warship with 74 guns. **seventy-one, seventy-two** etc. *n.* the cardinal numbers between seventy and eighty. [OE *seofontig* (SEVEN, -TY[1])]

sever (sev´ə) *v.t.* 1 to part, to separate, to disjoin. 2 to divide, to cleave, to sunder. 3 to cut or break off (apart from the whole). 4 to keep distinct or apart. 5 to conduct or carry on independently. 6 to end the contract of. ~*v.i.* to separate, to part. **severable** *a.* **severance** *n.* **severance pay** *n.* a sum of money paid to a worker as compensation for loss of employment. [OF *sevrer*, L *sēparāre*, to SEPARATE[1]]

several (sev´ərəl) *a.* 1 consisting of a number, more than two but not many. 2 separate, distinct, individual, single, particular. 3 not common, not shared with others, of or relating to individuals. ~*n.* 1 a few, an indefinite number, more than two but not many. 2 an enclosed piece of ground, pasture or field. **severally** *adv.* **severalty** (-ti) *n.* (*pl.* **severalties**) (*Law*) exclusive tenure or ownership. [OF, from late L *sēparāre*, to SEPARATE[1]]

severance SEVER.

severe (siviə´) *a.* 1 rigorous, strict, austere, harsh, merciless. 2 trying, hard to endure or sustain. 3 distressing, bitter, painful. 4 grave, serious, sedate. 5 rigidly conforming to rule, unadorned, restrained. **severely** *adv.* **severity** (-ver´i-) *n.* (*pl.* **severities**). [OF, from L *sevērus*]

severy (sev´əri) *n.* (*pl.* **severies**) a compartment in a vaulted ceiling. [ME, from OF *civoire*, as CIBORIUM]

Seville orange (səvil´, sev´-) *n.* a bitter orange used to make marmalade. [city in Spain]

Sèvres (sev´rə) *n.* porcelain made at Sèvres. [town in Seine-et-Oise, France]

sew (sō) *v.t.* (*p.p.* **sewn** (sōn), **sewed**) 1 to fasten together by thread worked through and through with a needle. 2 to make, mend, close up, attach, fasten on or in etc. by sewing. ~*v.i.* to work with a needle and thread. **to sew up 1** to mend, join etc. by sewing. 2 (*sl.*) to exhaust, to nonplus. 3 (*sl.*) to complete satisfactorily. **sewer**[1] *n.* **sewing** *n.* **sewing machine** *n.* a machine for stitching etc. driven electrically or by a treadle or a crank turned by hand. [OE *siwian* (cp. Icel. *sȳja*, OHG *siwan*), cogn. with L *suere*, Gr. *kassuein*, Sansk. *sīv*]

Usage note The spellings of the verbs *sew* (of needlework) and *sow* (of seed) should not be confused.

sewage SEWER[2].

sewen SEWIN.

sewer[1] SEW.

sewer[2] (soo´ə, sū´ə) *n.* a channel, underground conduit or tunnel for carrying off the drainage and liquid refuse of a town etc. **sewage** (-ij) *n.* the waste matter, esp. excrement, carried off through the sewers. ~*v.t.* to manure with sewage. **sewage farm** *n.* a place where sewage is treated for use as manure. **sewage works** *n.* a place where sewage is treated before being discharged (into the sea etc.). **sewerage** (-rij) *n.* 1 the system of draining by means of sewers. 2 sewers, drains etc. collectively. 3 (*N Am.*) sewage. **sewer gas** *n.* foul air from a sewer. **sewer rat** *n.* the common brown rat. [OF *seuwiere seweria*, sluice (EX-, L *aqua*, water), cp. med. L *exaquātōrium*]

sewin (sū´in), **sewen** *n.* a variety of sea or salmon trout. [etym. uncertain]

sewn SEW.

sex (seks) *n.* **1** the sum total of the physiological, anatomical and functional characteristics which distinguish male and female. **2** either of the divisions according to this. **3** the quality of being male or female. **4** (*collect.*) males or females, men or women. **5** (*coll.*) sexual intercourse. **6** sexual instincts, desires etc. ~*v.t.* to determine the sex of. ~*a.* **1** of or relating to sex. **2** arising from or based on sexual differences. **the sex** (*dated, coll.*) women. **sex act** *n.* an act of sexual intercourse. **sex appeal** *n.* what makes a person attractive to the opposite sex. **sex change** *n.* the use of surgery, hormone treatment etc. to enable a person to change sex. **sex chromosome** *n.* the chromosome responsible for the initial determination of sex. **sex determination** *n.* the factors which decide whether a particular organism will evolve into a male or a female. **sexed** *a.* **sexer** *n.* **sex hormone** *n.* a hormone involved in sexual development. **sexism** *n.* discrimination (esp. against women) on the grounds of sex. **sexist** *n.* **sex kitten** *n.* (*coll.*) a young woman who plays up her sex appeal. **sexless** *a.* **sexlessly** *adv.* **sexlessness** *n.* **sex life** *n.* a person's sexual activity. **sex-limited** *a.* restricted to one sex. **sex-linked** *a.* **1** (of a gene) located on a sex chromosome. **2** (of a character) determined by a sex-linked gene. **sex maniac** *n.* (*coll.*) a person who needs or wants sexual gratification to an excessive degree. **sex object** *n.* a person perceived solely as an object of sexual desires and fantasies. **sex offender** *n.* a person who commits a crime of a sexual nature. **sexology** (-ol´-) *n.* the science dealing with the sexes and their relationships. **sexological** (-əloj´-) *a.* **sexologist** (-ol´-) *n.* **sexpot** *n.* (*coll.*) a sexy person. **sex shop** *n.* a shop selling sexual aids, pornography etc. **sex-starved** *a.* suffering from a lack of sexual activity. **sex symbol** *n.* a person who is acknowledged to have sex appeal. **sexy** *a.* (*comp.* **sexier**, *superl.* **sexiest**) **1** sexually stimulating. **2** sexually aroused. **3** of or relating to sex. **4** (*coll.*) interesting, in fashion, appealing. **sexily** *adv.* **sexiness** *n.* [F *sexe*, L *sexus -ūs*, perh. cogn. with *secāre*, to cut]

sex- (seks), **sexa-** (sek´sə), **sexi-** (sek´si) *comb. form* **1** containing six. **2** sixfold. [L *sex*, six]

sexagenarian (seksəjineə´riən) *a.* 60 years of age or between 60 and 70. ~*n.* a sexagenarian person. **sexagenary** (-saj´inəri) *a.* **1** of or relating to 60. **2** sexagesimal. **3** sexagenarian. ~*n.* (*pl.* **sexagenaries**) **1** a sexagenarian. **2** a thing composed of 60 parts. [L *sexāgēnārius*, from *sexāgēnī*, sixty each, from *sexāginta*, sixty]

Sexagesima (seksəjes´imə), **Sexagesima Sunday** *n.* the second Sunday before Lent, so called as being about the 60th day before Easter. **sexagesimal** *a.* **1** 60th. **2** of or relating to 60. **3** proceeding by or based on 60s. **sexagesimal fraction** *n.* a fraction in which the denominator is some power of 60. **sexagesimally** *adv.* [L, fem. of *sexāgēsimus*, sixtieth, from *sexāginta*, sixty]

sexcentenary (seksəntē´nəri, -ten´-, -sen´tin-) *a.* of, relating to or consisting of 600 years. ~*n.* (*pl.* **sexcentenaries**) **1** a 600th anniversary. **2** a celebration of this.

sexennial (seksen´iəl) *a.* **1** occurring once every six years. **2** lasting six years. **sexennially** *adv.*

sexfoil (seks´foil) *n.* **1** a six-leaved flower, a six-lobed leaf. **2** an architectural or other ornament of six-lobed foliation.

sexi- SEX-.

sexivalent (seksivā´lənt), **sexvalent** (seksvā´-) *a.* having a valency or combining power of six; hexavalent.

sexology SEX.

sexpartite (sekspah´tīt) *a.* divided into six.

sexploitation (seksploitā´shən) *n.* the portrayal or manipulation of sex for financial profit in films, magazines etc. [*sex*, ex*ploitation*]

sext (sekst) *n.* in the Roman Catholic Church, the office for the sixth hour or noon. [F *sexte*, med. L *sexta*, orig. fem. of L *sextus*, sixth]

sextant (sek´stənt) *n.* **1** the sixth part of a circle. **2** an instrument used in navigation and surveying for measuring angular distances or altitudes. **sextantal** (-tan´-) *a.* [L *sextans -ntem*, from *sextus*, sixth]

sextet (sekstet´), **sextette** *n.* **1** a composition for six instruments or voices. **2** a group of six musicians or singers performing such a composition. **3** any group of six. [as SESTET]

sextillion (sekstil´yən) *n.* (*pl.* **sextillion, sextillions**) **1** the seventh power of a thousand, 1 followed by 21 ciphers. **2** †the sixth power of a million, represented by 1 followed by 36 ciphers. **sextillionth** *n.*, *a.* [L *sex*, SIX, after MILLION]

sexto (sek´stō) *n.* (*pl.* **sextos**) a book formed by folding sheets into six leaves each. **sextodecimo** (-des´imō) *n.* (*pl.* **sextodecimos**) **1** a book formed by folding sheets into 16 leaves each. **2** a sheet of paper folded thus.

sexton (sek´stən) *n.* an officer having the care of a church, its vessels, vestments etc., and frequently acting as parish clerk and a gravedigger. **sexton beetle** *n.* a beetle of the genus *Nicrophorus* that buries carrion to serve as a nidus for its eggs. **sextonship** *n.* [ME *sekesteyn*, corr. of SACRISTAN (under SACRIST)]

sextuple (sek´stūpəl) *a.* **1** six times as many. **2** having six parts. ~*n.* a sextuple amount. ~*v.t.*, *v.i.* to multiply by six. **sextuplet** (-tū´plit) *n.* **1** each of six born at one birth. **2** (*Mus.*) a group of six notes played in the time of four. **sextuply** *adv.* [from L *sextus*, after QUADRUPLE etc.]

sexual (sek´sūəl, -shəl) *a.* **1** of, relating to or based on sex or the sexes or on the distinction of sexes. **2** of or relating to generation or copulation, venereal. **sexual harassment** *n.* unwanted attention of a sexual nature, esp. in the workplace. **sexual intercourse** *n.* a sexual act in which the male's erect penis is inserted into the female's vagina. **sexualist** *n.* **sexuality** (-al´-) *n.* **sexualize, sexualise** *v.t.* **sexualization** (-ā´shən) *n.* **sexually** *adv.* **sexually transmitted disease** *n.* a venereal disease. **sexual reproduction** *n.* reproduction which involves the union of a male and female gamete or gametic nuclei. **sexual selection** *n.* a method of selection based on the struggle for mating which, according to one school of thought, accounts for the origin of secondary sexual characteristics. [late L *sexuālis*, from *sexus*, SEX]

sexvalent SEXIVALENT.

sexy SEX.

sez you! SAY.

SF *abbr.* **1** Finland (IVR). **2** San Francisco. **3** science fiction. **4** Sinn Féin. **5** Society of Friends.

sf. *abbr.* (*Mus.*) **1** sforzando. **2** sforzato.

SFA *abbr.* **1** Scottish Football Association. **2** (*sl.*) Sweet Fanny Adams.

SFC *abbr.* specific fuel consumption.

sfm *abbr.* surface feet per minute.

SFO *abbr.* Serious Fraud Office.

sforzando (sfawtsan´dō), **sforzato** (-tsah´tō) *adv.* (*Mus.*) emphatically, with sudden vigour. ~*a.* emphatic, vigorous. ~*n.* (*pl.* **sforzandos, sforzandi** (-dē), **sforzatos, sforzati** (-tē)) **1** a note or group of notes emphasized in this way. **2** an increase in emphasis. [It., from *sforzare*, to FORCE[1]]

sfumato (sfumah´tō) *a.* (of art) with misty outlines. ~*n.* (*pl.* **sfumatos**) **1** the technique of blending areas of different colours. **2** this effect. [It., p.p. of *sfumare*, to shade off]

sfz *abbr.* (*Mus.*) sforzando.
SG *abbr.* 1 Secretary-General. 2 (*N Am.*) senior grade. 3 Solicitor-General. 4 specific gravity. 5 Surgeon General.
sg *abbr.* specific gravity.
sgd. *abbr.* signed.
S. Glam. *abbr.* South Glamorgan.
SGML *abbr.* (*Comput.*) Standard Generalized Mark-up Language.
SGP *abbr.* Singapore (IVR).
sgraffito (sgrafē´tō) *n.* (*pl.* **sgraffiti** (-tē)) 1 decoration by means of scratches through plaster or slip, revealing a differently coloured ground. 2 an example of this. [It., p.p. of *sgraffire*, to scratch]
sgt, Sgt *abbr.* sergeant.
sh (sh) *int.* used to call for silence.
s.h. *abbr.* second-hand.
sh. *abbr.* (*Hist.*) shilling(s).
shabby (shab´i) *a.* (*comp.* **shabbier**, *superl.* **shabbiest**) 1 ragged, threadbare. 2 in ragged or threadbare clothes. 3 mean, paltry, despicable. 4 of poor quality. **shabbily** *adv.* **shabbiness** *n.* **shabby-genteel** *a.* aspiring to gentility, although shabby. **shabbyish** *a.* [OE *scæb sceab*, SCAB, -Y]
shabrack (shab´rak) *n.* (*Hist.*) the housing or saddle-cloth of a cavalry saddle. [G *Schabracke*, Turk. *chāprāq*]
Shabuoth SHAVUOTH.
shack (shak) *n.* a rude cabin or shanty, esp. one built of logs. **to shack up (with)** (*sl.*) to live (with), usu. having a sexual relationship. [perh. from Mex. Sp. *jacal*, Aztec *xacatli*, wooden hut]
shackle (shak´əl) *n.* 1 a fetter, gyve or handcuff. 2 the bow of a padlock. 3 a coupling link. 4 an insulating spool or support for a telegraph wire. 5 (*pl.*) fetters, restraints, impediments. ~*v.t.* 1 to chain, to fetter. 2 to restrain, to impede, to hamper. 3 (*N Am.*) to couple (railway carriages). **shackle-bolt** *n.* 1 a bolt passing through holes in a shackle to fasten it. 2 a bolt with a shackle at the end. [OE *sceacul* (cp. Icel. *skökull*, Swed. *skakel*, carriage-pole), rel. to SHAKE]
shad (shad) *n.* (*pl. in general* **shad**, *in particular* **shads**) any of several anadromous deep-bodied food-fish of the genus *Alosa*, esp. the American or white shad. **shadbush** *n.* the June-berry, *Amelanchier canadensis*. [OE *sceadda* (cp. G and Gael. *sgaden*), etym. uncertain]
shaddock (shad´ək) *n.* 1 the large orange-like fruit of a Malaysian and Polynesian tree, *Citrus grandis*. 2 the tree bearing this. [Capt. *Shaddock*, who took it to the W Indies in the 17th cent.]
shade (shād) *n.* 1 obscurity or partial darkness caused by the interception of the rays of light. 2 gloom, darkness. 3 a place sheltered from the sun, a secluded retreat. 4 the dark or darker part of a picture. 5 a screen for protecting from or moderating light, esp. a covering for a lamp, or a shield worn over the eyes. 6 (*N Am.*) a window blind. 7 a glass cover for protecting an object. 8 a colour. 9 gradation of colour, esp. with regard to its depth or its luminosity. 10 a scarcely perceptible degree, a small amount. 11 something unsubstantial, unreal or delusive. 12 the soul after its separation from the body, a spectre. 13 (*pl.*) the abode of spirits, Hades. 14 (*pl.*) wine and spirit or beer vaults. 15 (*pl., coll.*) sunglasses. 16 (*pl.*) undertones (of). ~*v.t.* 1 to shelter or screen from light or heat. 2 to cover, to obscure, to darken (an object in a picture) so as to show gradations of colour or effects of light and shade. 3 to graduate as to light and shade or colour. 4 to cause to pass or blend with another colour. ~*v.i.* to pass off by degrees or blend (with another colour). **to put in the shade** to be superior to; to outdo. **shadeless** *a.* **shading** *n.* **shady** (shā´di) *a.* (*comp.* **shadier**, *superl.* **shadiest**) 1 sheltered from the light and heat of the sun. 2 casting shade. 3 shunning the light. 4 disreputable, of equivocal honesty. **shadily** *adv.* **shadiness** *n.* [OE *scæd*, *sceadu* (cp. Dut. *schaduw*, G *Schatten*, Ir. and Gael. *sgath*, also Gr. *skotos*), cogn. with SKY]
shadoof (shədoof´) *n.* a water-raising contrivance consisting of a long pole with bucket and counterpoise, used on the Nile etc. [Arab. *shādūf*]
shadow (shad´ō) *n.* 1 shade. 2 a patch of shade. 3 the dark figure of a body projected on the ground etc. by the interception of light. 4 an inseparable companion. 5 a person who follows another closely and unobtrusively. 6 darkness, obscurity, privacy. 7 protection, shelter. 8 the dark part of a picture, room etc. 9 a reflected image. 10 an imperfect or faint representation, an adumbration, a type. 11 a dim foreshadowing, a premonition. 12 a faint trace, the slightest degree. 13 something unsubstantial or unreal. 14 a phantom, a ghost. 15 eyeshadow. 16 gloom or sadness. ~*v.t.* 1 to darken, to cloud. 2 to set (forth) dimly or in outline, to adumbrate, to typify. 3 to watch secretly, to spy upon, to dog. 4 to accompany so as to learn what a job involves. **shadow-boxing** *n.* boxing against an imaginary opponent when training. **shadow cabinet** *n.* a group of leading members of a party out of office, who would probably constitute the cabinet if in power. **shadower** *n.* **shadowgraph** *n.* 1 an image or photograph produced by X-rays. 2 an image produced by a shadow on a screen. 3 an image formed by light refracted by a fluid. **shadowless** *a.* **shadow mark** *n.* the trace of an ancient archaeological site as observed from the air. **shadow theatre**, (*N Am.*) **shadow theater** *n.* a puppet show using shadows on a screen. **shadowy** *a.* **shadowiness** *n.* [OE *sceadu*, see SHADE]
shady SHADE.
shaft (shahft) *n.* 1 the slender stem or stock of a spear, arrow etc. 2 an arrow. 3 anything more or less resembling this, such as a ray (of light), a bolt or dart (of lightning, ridicule etc.). 4 a column between the base and the capital. 5 a small column in a cluster or in a window joint. 6 a stem, a stalk, a trunk. 7 the scape of a feather. 8 any long, straight and more or less slender part. 9 (*sl.*) a penis. 10 the handle of a tool. 11 either one of the bars between a pair of which a horse is harnessed. 12 a large axle, arbor or long cylindrical bar, esp. rotating and transferring motion. 13 a well-like excavation, usu. vertical, giving access to a mine. 14 the tunnel of a blast furnace. 15 an upward vent to a mine, tunnel etc. 16 (*N Am., coll.*) unfair treatment. ~*v.t.* 1 (*N Am., coll.*) to cheat, to treat unfairly. 2 (*sl.*) to have sexual intercourse with. 3 to fit with a shaft. **shafted** *a.* **shaft-horse** *n.* a horse harnessed between the shafts. **shafting** *n.* 1 a system of shafts for the transmission of power. 2 material from which shafts are cut. **shaftless** *a.* [OE *sceaft*, spear-shaft, orig. shaved, from *scafan*, to SHAVE (cp. Dut. *schacht*, G *Schaft*, Icel. *skapt*)]
shag (shag) *n.* 1 a rough coat of hair, a bushy mass. 2 cloth having a long coarse nap. 3 strong tobacco cut into fine shreds. 4 the crested cormorant, *Phalacrocorax aristotelis*. 5 (*taboo sl.*) an act of sexual intercourse. ~*a.* shaggy. ~*v.t., v.i.* (*pres.p.* **shagging**, *past, p.p.* **shagged**) (*taboo sl.*) to have sexual intercourse (with). †**shagged** (shagd, shag´id) *a.* shaggy. **shagged out** *a.* tired out. **shagger** *n.* **shaggy** *a.* (*comp.* **shaggier**, *superl.* **shaggiest**) 1 rough-haired, hairy, hirsute. 2 coarse, tangled, unkempt. 3 overgrown with trees or coarse vegetation, scrubby, rugged. **shaggily** *adv.* **shagginess** *n.* **shaggy-dog story** *n.* a long, inconsequential story, funny but lacking a punchline. [OE *sceacga* (cp. Icel. *skegg*, beard, *skaga*, to jut)]
shagreen (shəgrēn´) *n.* 1 a kind of leather with a granular surface which is prepared without tanning from the skins of horses, asses, camels, sharks and seals, usu. dyed green. 2 the skins of various sharks,

rays etc., covered with hard papillae, used for polishing etc. [var. of CHAGRIN]

shah (shah) *n.* (*Hist.*) a sovereign of Iran. **shahdom** *n.* [Pers.]

shaikh SHEIK.

Shak. *abbr.* Shakespeare.

shake (shāk) *v.t.* (*past* **shook** (shuk), *p.p.* **shaken** (shā´kən)) 1 to move forcibly or rapidly to and fro or up and down. 2 to cause to tremble or quiver. 3 to shock, to convulse, to agitate, to disturb. 4 to brandish, to weaken the stability of, to impair, to shatter. 5 to trill. 6 (*coll.*) to upset the composure of another. 7 to cause (another) to doubt. 8 (*Austral., sl.*) to steal. 9 (*esp. N Am., coll.*) to shake off. ~*v.i.* 1 to move quickly to and fro or up and down, to tremble, to totter, to shiver. 2 to quiver, to rock. 3 to change the pitch or power of the voice, to make trills. 4 (*coll.*) to shake hands. ~*n.* 1 the act or an act of shaking. 2 a jerk, a jolt, a shock, a concussion. 3 the state of being shaken, agitation, vibration, trembling. 4 a trill. 5 a milk shake. 6 a crack in growing timber. 7 (*N Am., Austral.*) an earthquake. **in two shakes (of a lamb's/ dog's tail)** very quickly. **no great shakes** (*coll.*) of no great account. **the shakes** (*coll.*) a fit of trembling, caused by fever, withdrawal from alcohol etc. **to shake a leg** LEG. **to shake down** 1 to bring down (fruit etc.) by shaking. 2 to cause (grain etc.) to settle into a compact mass. 3 to become compact. 4 to settle down into a comfortable or harmonious state. 5 (*N Am., sl.*) to extort money from. **to shake hands** HAND. **to shake in one's shoes** to be very frightened. **to shake off** 1 to get rid of by shaking, to cast off. 2 to get rid of (someone who is following one). **to shake one's head** to move the head from side to side in token of refusal, dissent, disapproval etc. **to shake out** 1 to open out or empty by shaking. 2 (*coll.*) to reduce (staff) as part of a drastic reorganization. **to shake someone by the hand** to shake hands. **to shake the dust off one's feet** DUST. **to shake up** 1 to mix, disturb etc. by shaking. 2 (*coll.*) to reorganize drastically. 3 to reshape by shaking. 4 to rouse or shock. **shakeable, shakable** *a.* **shakedown** *n.* 1 a makeshift bed. 2 a period or process of adjustment. 3 (*esp. N Am., sl.*) a swindle. ~*a.* of or relating to a familiarization or test voyage. **shake-out** *n.* **Shaker** *n.* a member of an American millenarian sect believing in a life of simplicity and celibacy (from their religious dances). **Shakeress** (-ris) *n.* a female Shaker. **Shakerism** *n.* **shaker** *n.* 1 a container for mixing or sprinkling by shaking. 2 a person who or thing which shakes. **shake-up** *n.* **shaky** *a.* (*comp.* **shakier**, *superl.* **shakiest**) 1 liable to shake, unsteady, rickety, unstable, tottering. 2 of doubtful integrity, solvency, ability etc. **shakily** *adv.* **shakiness** *n.* **shook**[1] *a.* (*coll.*) **shook on** (*Austral., coll.*) keen on. **shook up** (*coll.*) disturbed emotionally or physically; upset. [OE *sceacan*, cp. Icel. and Swed. *skaka*, Dan. *skage*]

Shakespearean (shākspiə´riən), **Shakespearian** *a.* of, relating to or resembling Shakespeare or his style. ~*n.* a student of Shakespeare's works. **Shakespeareana** (-ah´nə) *n.pl.* items connected with Shakespeare. **Shakespeareanism** *n.* [William *Shakespeare*, 1564–1616, dramatist and poet]

shako (shak´ō) *n.* (*pl.* **shakos**) a military cylindrical hat, usu. flat-topped, with a peak in front, usu. tilting forward, and decorated with a pompom, plume or tuft. [F, from Hung. *csako*]

shakuhachi (shakuhach´i) *n.* (*pl.* **shakuhachis**) a Japanese bamboo flute. [Jap.]

shaky SHAKE.

shale (shāl) *n.* a laminated argillaceous rock resembling soft slate, often containing much bitumen. **shale oil** *n.* oil obtained from bitumen shale. **shaly** *a.* [G *Schale*, cogn. with obs. Eng. *shale*, shell, var. of SCALE[1]]

shall (shal) *v.aux.* (*2nd pers. sing. pres.* **†shalt** (shalt), *3rd pers. sing. pres.* **shall**, *past, subj.* **should** (shud, shəd), *2nd pers.* **†shouldst, †shouldest**) 1 (in the 1st pers.) used to express simple futurity or a conditional statement or (stressed) strong intention. 2 (in the 2nd and 3rd pers.) used to express a command, intention, promise, permission etc. 3 used to express future or conditional obligation, duty etc. 4 used to form a conditional protasis etc. **shall I?** do you want me to? [OE *sceal*, past of *sculan*, to owe (cp. Dut. *zal*, G *soll*, Icel. *skal*), cogn. with *scyld*, G *Schuld*, and prob. L *scelus*, guilt]

Usage note In British English, *shall* is now used less frequently than *will* (or, in spoken and informal written English, *'ll*, which blurs the distinction between the two). The traditional rules for using *shall* (or *should*) and *will* (or *would*) are basically as follows: in expressing the future and in conditional sentences (with *if, lest*) *shall* is used in the first person and *will* in the second and third persons (*I shall go*; *If you go we will be sad*; *They will go*; *If she goes you will be sad* etc.); in other contexts the distribution is reversed, with *will* for the first person and *shall* for others (*I will go, you can't stop me*; *He shall go, I'll force him* etc.). Nowadays, however, uses such as *I will go* (future) and *We shall go, definitely* are also generally acceptable.

shallot (shəlot´) *n.* a plant, *Allium ascalonicum*, allied to garlic with similar but milder bulbs. [OF *eschalote* (F *échalote*), corr. of *escalogne*, L *escalōnia*, fem. a. from *Ascalon* in ancient Palestine]

shallow (shal´ō) *a.* 1 not having much depth. 2 superficial, trivial, silly. ~*n.* a shallow place, a shoal. ~*v.i.* to become shallow or shallower. ~*v.t.* to make shallow. **shallowly** *adv.* **shallowness** *n.* [ME *schalowe*, perh. rel. to OE *sceald* (cp. Icel. *skālgr*, wry, also SHOAL[2], SHELVE[2])]

shalom (shəlom´) *n., int.* peace (a greeting used esp. by Jewish people). [Heb.]

†shalt SHALL.

shaly SHALE.

sham (sham) *v.t.* (*pres.p.* **shamming**, *past, p.p.* **shammed**) to feign, to make a pretence of. ~*v.i.* to feign, to pretend. ~*n.* 1 an imposture, a false pretence. 2 a fraud, a person who or thing which pretends to be someone or something else. ~*a.* feigned, pretended, counterfeit. **shammer** *n.* [var. of SHAME]

shamanism (shah´mənizm, shā´-) *n.* a form of religion based on the belief in good and evil spirits which can be influenced by shamans, prevailing among some Siberian and N American peoples. **shaman** *n.* a priest, exorcist or medicine man among shamanists. **shamanist** *n., a.* **shamanistic** (-nis´-) *a.* [Rus., from Tungus (Siberian language)]

shamateur (sham´ətə) *n.* a person classed as an amateur in sport, but who accepts payment. **shamateurism** *n.* [*sham*, *amateur*]

shamble (sham´bəl) *v.i.* to walk in an awkward, shuffling or unsteady manner. ~*n.* a shambling walk or gait. **shambling** *a.* [etym. uncertain, cp. SCAMPER]

shambles (sham´bəlz) *n.* 1 (*coll.*) utter confusion, a disorganized mess. 2 a butcher's slaughterhouse. 3 a place of carnage or execution. 4 (*dial.*) butcher's stalls, a meat market. [pl. of obs. *shamble*, OE *scamel*, L *scamellum*, stool, dim. of *scamnum*, bench, step, cogn. with Gr. *skēptein*, to prop]

shambolic (shambol´ik) *a.* (*coll.*) chaotic, utterly confused. [SHAMBLES]

shame (shām) *n.* 1 a painful feeling due to consciousness of guilt, degradation, humiliation etc. 2 the instinct to avoid this, the restraining sense of pride, modesty, decency, decorum. 3 a state of disgrace, discredit or ignominy. 4 anything that brings reproach, a disgrace. **5** (*coll.*) an unfairness. ~*v.t.* **1** to make ashamed. **2** to bring shame on, to cause to blush or feel disgraced. **3** to disgrace. **4** to force (into or out of) by shame. ~*v.i.* to be ashamed. **for shame!** used to reprove someone who should be ashamed. **shame on you!** you should be ashamed. **to put to shame** to humiliate by exhibiting better qualities. **what a shame!** how unfortunate! **shame!** *int.* that is unfair! disgraceful! **shamefaced** *a.* bashful, shy, easily confused or abashed, modest, retiring. **shamefacedly** (-fāst´li, -fā´sid-) *adv.* **shamefacedness** *n.* **shameful** *a.* **shamefully** *adv.* **shamefulness** *n.* **shameless** *a.* immodest. **shamelessly** *adv.* **shamelessness** *n.* **shamer** *n.* [OE *sceamu, scamu* (cp. G *Scham*, Dan. *skam*, Icel. *skömm*), whence *sceamian, scamian*, to shame]

shammer SHAM.

shammy (sham´i), †**shamoy** (-oi) *n.* (*pl.* **shammies,** †**shamoys**) (*coll.*) CHAMOIS LEATHER (under CHAMOIS).

shampoo (shampoo´) *v.t.* (*3rd pers. sing. pres.* **shampoos,** *pres.p.* **shampooing,** *past, p.p.* **shampooed**) **1** to wash with shampoo. **2** to wash the hair of with shampoo. ~*n.* (*pl.* **shampoos**) **1** a liquid soap or detergent used for washing the hair. **2** a similar cleaner for a car, carpet, upholstery etc. **3** an act of shampooing. [Hind. *chāmpnā*, to press, to shampoo]

shamrock (sham´rok) *n.* a species of trefoil, esp. *Trifolium minus, T. repens* or *Medicago lupulina*, forming the national emblem of Ireland. [Ir. *seamrōg*]

shamus (shā´məs) *n.* (*pl.* **shamuses**) (*N Am., sl.*) a detective. [etym. uncertain]

Shan (shan) *n.* (*pl.* **Shan, Shans**) **1** a member of a people living on the borders of N Thailand, E Burma (Myanmar) and Yunnan province (China). **2** the language of this people. ~*a.* of or relating to the Shan or their language. [Burmese]

shandy (shan´di) *n.* (*pl.* **shandies**) a mixture of beer and ginger beer or lemonade. [etym. uncertain]

shanghai (shanghī´) *v.t.* (*3rd pers. sing. pres.* **shanghais,** *pres.p.* **shanghaiing,** *past, p.p.* **shanghaied**) **1** to drug and ship as a sailor while stupefied. **2** to kidnap. **3** (*coll.*) to trick into performing an unpleasant task. **4** (*Austral.*) to shoot with a catapult. ~*n.* (*pl.* **shanghais**) (*Austral.*) a catapult. [town in China]

Shangri-La (shang-grilah´) *n.* a paradise on earth. [name of a hidden Tibetan valley in *Lost Horizon* (1933) by James Hilton]

shank (shangk) *n.* **1** the leg, esp. the part from the knee to the ankle. **2** the shin bone. **3** a bird's tarsus. **4** the shaft of a column. **5** the straight part of an instrument, tool etc. connecting the acting part with the handle. **6** the narrow part of the sole of a shoe. **7** the lower foreleg of an animal, esp. as a cut of meat. ~*v.i.* to be affected or fall (off) with decay in the footstalks. **shanked** *a.* having a shank (*esp. in comb.*, as *short-shanked*). **shanks's pony, shanks's mare** *n.* one's legs for walking as opposed to riding etc. [OE *sceanca, scanca* (cp. Dut. *schonk*, Dan. and Swed. *skank*), perh. rel. to SHAKE]

shanny (shan´i) *n.* (*pl.* **shannies**) the smooth blenny, *Blennius pholis*. [etym. unknown]

shan't (shahnt) *contr.* shall not.

shantung (shantŭng´) *n.* a plain fabric woven in coarse silk yarns. [province in China]

shanty[1] (shan´ti) *n.* (*pl.* **shanties**) **1** a rude hut or cabin. **2** a hastily built or rickety building. **3** (*Austral.*) a low public house, a grogshop. **shanty town** *n.* a poor part of a town consisting mainly of shanties. [Can. F *chantier*, lumber camp, hut]

shanty[2] (shan´ti), **chanty** *n.* (*pl.* **shanties, chanties**) a song sung by sailors, esp. one with a strong rhythm sung while working. [F *chanter*, to sing, see CHANT]

shapable SHAPEABLE (under SHAPE).

SHAPE (shāp) *abbr.* Supreme Headquarters Allied Powers Europe.

shape (shāp) *v.t.* (*p.p.* **shaped,** †**shapen** (-pən)) **1** to form, to create, to construct. **2** to make into a particular form, mould, to fashion. **3** to adapt, to fit, to adjust, to make conform (to). **4** to regulate, to direct. **5** to conceive, to conjure up. ~*v.i.* **1** to take shape, to come into shape, to develop (well, ill etc.). **2** to become fit or adapted (to). ~*n.* **1** the outward form, figure, configuration or contour. **2** outward aspect, form, guise, appearance. **3** concrete form, embodiment, realization. **4** definite, fit or orderly form or condition. **5** kind, sort. **6** an image, an appearance, an apparition. **7** a pattern, a mould, a confection shaped in a mould. **to knock into shape** KNOCK. **to lick into shape** LICK. **to shape up 1** to develop a shape. **2** to develop satisfactorily. **to take shape** to become recognizable as or develop into something definite. **shapeable, shapable** *a.* **shaped** *a.* having a shape (*usu. in comb.*, as *square-shaped*). **shapeless** *a.* **1** having no regular form. **2** lacking in symmetry. **shapelessly** *adv.* **shapelessness** *n.* **shapely** *a.* (*comp.* **shapelier,** *superl.* **shapeliest**) **1** well-formed, well-proportioned. **2** having beauty or regularity. **shapeliness** *n.* **shaper** *n.* [OE *scieppan* (p.p. *gescapen*), cp. G *schaffen*, to create, also -SHIP]

sharable SHAREABLE (under SHARE[1]).

shard (shahd), **sherd** (shœd) *n.* **1** a potsherd. **2** a fragment of volcanic rock. **3** the wing-case of a beetle. ~*v.t., v.i.* †to break or flake off. [OE *sceard*, cogn. with SHEAR, SHARE[1]]

share[1] (sheə) *n.* **1** a part or portion detached from a common amount or stock. **2** a part to which one has a right or which one is obliged to contribute, a fair or just portion. **3** a lot, an allotted part, esp. any one of the equal parts into which the capital of a company is divided. ~*v.t.* **1** to divide into portions, to distribute among a number, to apportion. **2** to give away a portion of. **3** to partake of, to have or endure with others, to participate in. ~*v.i.* **1** to have a share or shares (in). **2** to be a sharer or sharers (with). **3** to participate. **share and share alike** in equal shares. **to go shares** to divide equally with others. **to share out** to divide into equal shares and distribute. **shareable, sharable** *a.* **sharebroker** *n.* a dealer in shares. **share certificate** *n.* a document showing entitlement to a share or shares in a company. **sharecropper** *n.* (*esp. N Am.*) a tenant farmer who pays over part of the crop as rent. **sharecrop** *v.i., v.t.* (*pres.p.* **sharecropping,** *past, p.p.* **sharecropped**). **shared care** *n.* a system of caring for a person with a disability or illness, whereby the care is shared between the person's family and a welfare agency. **share-farmer** *n.* (*Austral.*) a tenant farmer who shares in the profits. **shareholder** *n.* a person who holds a share or shares in a joint-stock company etc. **shareholding** *n.* **share index** *n.* the index which shows the movement of share prices. **share list** *n.* a list of the current prices of shares. **share-out** *n.* **sharer** *n.* **shareware** *n.* computer software which is free to users for a certain time. [OE *scearu*, from *sceran*, to SHEAR]

share[2] (sheə) *n.* **1** a ploughshare. **2** a blade of a cultivator, seeder etc. [OE *scear*, from *sceran*, to SHEAR]

sharia (shərē´ə), **shariah** *n.* the body of Islamic religious law. [Arab.]

sharif SHERIF.

shark (shahk) *n.* **1** a selachoid sea fish of various species with lateral gill openings and an inferior mouth, mostly large and voracious and armed with formidable teeth. **2** (*coll.*) a grasping, rapacious person. **3** (*coll.*) a rogue, a swindler. ~*v.i.* to play the part of a shark or swindler. ~*v.t.* **1** to gain or pick (up) by underhand, fraudulent or disreputable means. **2** to swallow greedily. **shark-bait** *n.* (*Austral., coll.*) a bather or surfer who goes too far out to sea. **sharkskin** *n.* **1** the skin of a shark. **2** a smooth woven fabric of rayon etc. [etym. uncertain, perh. from

L *carcharus*, Gr. *karcharias*, from *karcharos*, jagged (in alln. to its teeth)]

sharon fruit (shar´ən) *n.* a kind of persimmon. [grown in the *Sharon* Valley, Israel]

sharp (shahp) *a.* **1** having a keen edge or fine point. **2** terminating in a point or edge. **3** peaked, pointed, edged. **4** angular, abrupt. **5** clean-cut, clearly outlined or defined. **6** pungent, acid, sour. **7** (of sand) gritty. **8** shrill, biting, piercing. **9** harsh, sarcastic, acrimonious, severe, painful, intense. **10** acute, keen-witted. **11** vigilant, attentive, alert, penetrating. **12** alive to one's interests, unscrupulous, dishonest, underhand. **13** quick, speedy, energetic, brisk, vigorous, impetuous. **14** in phonetics, voiceless. **15** (*Mus.*) above the true pitch, esp. a semitone higher. **16** (*coll.*) stylish. **17** (*coll.*) too flashy or too smart. *~adv.* **1** punctually, exactly. **2** at a sharp angle. **3** above the true pitch. **4** suddenly, abruptly. *~n.* **1** a note a semitone above the true pitch. **2** the sign # indicating this. **3** a long and slender sewing-needle. **4** (*coll.*) a cheat. *~v.t.* **1** to raise the pitch of (a note). **2** to mark with a #. **3** (*N Am.*) to make sharp. *~v.i.* †to swindle, to cheat. **to look sharp** LOOK. **sharp-cut** *a.* clearly outlined, well-defined. **sharpen** *v.t.*, *v.i.* to make sharp. **sharpener** *n.* **sharp end** *n.* **1** the bow of a ship. **2** (*coll.*) the place where things are happening. **at the sharp end** taking the most important or difficult part in any enterprise. **sharper** *n.* **1** a person who or thing which sharpens. **2** (*coll.*) a swindler, a rogue. **3** a person who lives by their wits. **sharp-featured** *a.* having well-defined facial features. **sharpish** *a.* (*coll.*) rather sharp. *~adv.* **1** rather quickly. **2** rather sharply. **sharply** *adv.* **sharpness** *n.* **sharp practice** *n.* (*coll.*) underhand or questionable dealings. **sharp-set** *a.* **1** set with a sharp edge. **2** ravenous. **sharpshooter** *n.* a skilled marksman. **sharpshooting** *n.* **sharp-sighted** *a.* **1** having keen sight. **2** sharp-witted. **sharp-tongued** *a.* having critical or sarcastic speech. **sharp-witted** *a.* having a keen wit, judgement or discernment. **sharp-wittedly** *adv.* **sharp-wittedness** *n.* [OE *scearp* (cp. Dut. *scherp*, G *scharf*, Icel. *skarpr*), perh. rel. to SCRAPE]

shashlik (shash´lik) *n.* a lamb kebab. [Rus. *shashlyk*]

Shasta daisy (shas´tə) *n.* a Pyrenean plant, *Leucanthemum maximum*, which has white daisy-like flowers. [Mount *Shasta* in California]

Shastra (shas´trə), **Shaster** (-tə), **Sastra** (sah´strə) *n.* any of the Vedas and other sacred scriptures of Hinduism. [Hind. *shāstr*, Sansk. *shastra*]

shat SHIT.

shatter (shat´ə) *v.t.* **1** to break up at once into many pieces. **2** to smash, to shiver. **3** to destroy, to dissipate, to overthrow, to ruin. **4** to upset, distress. **5** (*sl.*) to tire out. *~v.i.* to break into fragments. **shattered** *a.* **shatterer** *n.* **shattering** *a.* **shatteringly** *adv.* **shatter-proof** *a.* made so as to be proof against shattering. **shatters** *n.pl.* fragments into which anything is smashed. [var. of SCATTER]

shave (shāv) *v.t.* (*p.p.* **shaved, †shaven** (-vən)) **1** to remove hair from (the face, a person etc.) with a razor. **2** to remove (usu. off) from a surface with a razor. **3** to pare or cut thin slices off the surface of (leather, wood etc.). **4** to pass by closely with or without touching, to brush past, to graze. *~v.i.* to shave oneself. *~n.* **1** the act of shaving or the process of being shaved. **2** a knife for shaving, paring or scraping, esp. a blade with a handle at each end for shaving hoops etc. **3** a thin slice. **4** a narrow escape or miss. **5** (*sl.*) a swindle. **6** a doubtful report. **shavegrass** *n.* the scouring-rush, *Equisetum hyemale*. **†shaveling** (-ling) *n.* a man shaved (used contemptuously for a monk or friar). **shaver** *n.* **1** a barber. **2** an electric razor. **3** (*coll.*) a young boy. **4** a humorous fellow, a wag. **shaving** *n.* **1** the act of a person who shaves. **2** a thin slice pared off. **shaving-basin, shaving-bowl, shaving-brush, shaving-cup** *n.* utensils employed for lathering the face before shaving. [OE *sceafan*, *scafan* (cp. Dut. *schaven*, G *schaben*, Icel. *skafa*), cogn. with L *scabere*, to scratch, Gr. *skaptein*, to dig]

Shavian (shā´viən) *a.* of, relating to or characteristic of the writings of George Bernard Shaw, 1856–1950. *~n.* a follower of Shaw. [*Shavius*, mod. L form of *Shaw*]

shaving SHAVE.

Shavuoth (shəvoo´əs, shahvuot´), **Shavuot** *n.* the Jewish Pentecost. [Heb.]

shaw (shaw) *n.* the stalk and leaves of a root-crop plant, e.g. a potato. [form of SHOW]

shawl (shawl) *n.* a square or oblong garment worn chiefly by women as a loose wrap for the upper part of the person. *~v.t.* to wrap with a shawl. **shawl collar** *n.* (on a coat etc.) a collar of a rolled shape that tapers down the front of the garment. **shawl-dance** *n.* an Oriental dance in which the performer waves a shawl. **shawled** *a.* **shawlless** *a.* **shawl-pattern** *n.* a variegated pattern with a design characteristic of Oriental shawls. [Pers. *shāl*, cp. F *châle*]

shawm (shawm) *n.* an ancient wind instrument similar to the oboe. [OF *chalemie* (cp. *chalemelle*, *chalumeau*, also *chaume*, straw), L *calamus*, Gr. *kalamos*, reed]

shchi (shchē) *n.* cabbage soup. [Rus.]

she (shē) *pron.* **1** the female person, animal or personified thing mentioned or referred to. **2** (*Austral.*, *coll.*) it. *~n.* **1** a female. **2** †a woman. *~a.* female (*esp. in comb.*, as *she-cat*, *she-devil*, *she-goat* etc.). **she'll be right** RIGHT. **she's apples** APPLE. **she-devil** *n.* a spiteful woman. **she-oak** *n.* an Australian tree of the genus *Casuarina* (*she* here orig. meaning 'inferior'). [etym. uncertain, perh. phonetic devel. of OE *hīo*, *hēo*, fem. of HE, or from OE *sēo*, fem. definite article]

Usage note *She* is sometimes used as an objective pronoun (after a verb or preposition), especially when joined by *and* to a personal name or pronoun, *she and X*, but this is best avoided. See also note under THEY.

---

s/he *pron.* a written representation of 'he or she'.

shea (shē, shē´ə) *n.* a tropical African tree, *Vitellaria paradoxa*, yielding a kind of butter. **shea-butter** *n.* [Afr. name]

sheading (shē´ding) *n.* any one of the six divisions of the Isle of Man. [var. of SHED[1], -ING[1]]

sheaf (shēf) *n.* (*pl.* **sheaves** (-vz)) a quantity of things bound or held together lengthwise, esp. a bundle of wheat, oats, barley etc. *~v.t.* to collect and bind into sheaves, to sheave. **sheafy** *a.* [OE *scēaf* (cp. Dut. *schoof*, G *Schaub*, Icel. *skauf*), cogn. with SHOVE]

shealing SHIELING.

shear (shiə) *v.t.* (*past* **sheared, †shore** (shaw), *p.p.* **shorn** (shawn), **sheared**) **1** to cut or clip with shears. **2** to reduce or remove nap from (cloth etc.) by clipping. **3** to remove (wool etc.) thus. **4** to fleece, to plunder, to strip. **5** to reap. **6** to subject to a shear. *~v.i.* **1** to use shears. **2** to cut, to penetrate. **3** to undergo a shear. *~n.* **1** (*pl.*) a cutting instrument with two large blades crossing each other like scissors and joined together by a spring; also called *pair of shears*. **2** a strain caused by pressure upon a solid body in which the layers of its substance move in parallel planes. **3** (*Geol.*) alteration of structure by transverse pressure. **4** (*pl.*) SHEERLEGS. **to shear off** to break off vertically. **shearer** *n.* a person who shears sheep. **shearlegs** SHEERLEGS. **shearling** (-ling) *n.* **1** a sheep that has been shorn once. **2** wool from a shearling. **shear steel** *n.* blister steel, heated, rolled etc. to improve the quality. **shearwater** *n.* **1** any seabird of the family Procellariidae, allied to the petrels. **2** any seabird of the genus *Rhynchops*; the skimmer. [OE *sceran* (cp. Dut. and G *scheren*, Icel. *skera*, also Gr. *keirein*), cogn. with SCAR[1], SHARD, SHORT etc.]

sheatfish (shēt´fish) *n.* (*pl. in general* **sheatfish,** *in particular* **sheatfishes**) a large catfish, *Silurus glanis*, the largest European freshwater fish. [OE *scēota*, trout, rel. to SHOOT, FISH[1]]

sheath (shēth) *n.* (*pl.* **sheaths** (shēths, shēdhz)) **1** a case for a blade, weapon or tool, a scabbard. **2** (*Biol., Zool.*) an envelope, a case, a cell-covering, investing tissue, membrane etc. **3** a structure of loose stones for confining a river within its banks. **4** a condom. **5** the protective covering of an electric cable. **sheathe** (shēdh) *v.t.* **1** to put into a sheath. **2** to protect by a casing or covering. **3** to hide, to conceal. **to sheathe the sword** to make peace. **sheathing** (-dh-) *n.* anything which sheathes, esp. a metal covering for a ship's bottom. **sheath knife** *n.* (*pl.* **sheath knives**) a large case knife. **sheathless** *a.* [OE *scæth*, cp. Dut. *scheede*, G *Scheide*, Icel. *skeithir*, Dan. *skede*]

sheave[1] (shēv) *n.* the grooved wheel in a block or pulley over which the rope runs. **sheave-hole** *n.* (*Naut.*) a groove or channel in which to fix a sheave. [ME *schīve* (cp. Dut. *schijf*, G *Scheibe*, Icel. *skīfa*)]

sheave[2] (shēv) *v.t.* to gather into sheaves, to sheaf. **sheaved** *a.* put up in sheaves. [from SHEAF]

sheaves SHEAF.

shebang (shibang´) *n.* (*N Am., sl.*) **1** a business, concern, affair. **2** a shed or hut. **3** a store, a saloon, gaming house etc. **4** a brothel. [etym. unknown]

Shebat (shebat´), **Sebat** (seb-) *n.* the 11th ecclesiastical month, or fifth civil month, of the Jewish year (corresponding to parts of January and February). [Heb.]

shebeen (shibēn´) *n.* **1** (*Ir.*) a low public house. **2** an unlicensed house where excisable liquors are sold. [Ir. *síbín*]

Shechinah SHEKINAH.

shechita (shehē´ta), **schechita, shehita, schechitah, shehitah** *n.* the Jewish method of killing animals for food. [Heb.]

shed[1] (shed) *v.t.* (*pres.p.* **shedding,** *past, p.p.* **shed**) **1** to pour out, to let fall, to drop, to spill, to effuse. **2** to throw off, to emit, to diffuse, to spread around. **3** to take off (clothes). **4** to reduce (an electrical power load). **5** to reduce one's number of (employees). *~v.i.* **1** to cast off seed, a covering, clothing etc. **2** (of an animal) to moult. *~n.* **1** a division, a parting. **2** the ridge of a hill. **3** a divide, a watershed. **4** in weaving, the opening between the warp threads in a loom through which the shuttle carries the weft. **to shed light on** LIGHT[1]. **shedder** *n.* **1** a person who or thing which sheds. **2** a female salmon after spawning. [OE *scēadan*, *scādan*, to separate, to scatter (cp. G *scheiden*, also L *scindere*, Gr. *schizein*, to cleave, to split)]

shed[2] (shed) *n.* **1** a slight simple building, usu. a roofed structure with the ends or ends and sides open. **2** a hovel, a hut. *~v.t.* (*pres.p.* **shedding,** *past, p.p.* **shedded**) to park in a shed. **shedding** *n.* **shedhand** *n.* (*Austral.*) a worker in a sheep-shearing shed. [var. of SHADE]

she'd (shid, shēd) *contr.* **1** she had. **2** she would.

shedder SHED[1].

shedding SHED[2].

sheeling SHIELING.

sheen (shēn) *n.* **1** brightness, splendour. **2** lustre, glitter. **sheeny** *a.* [OE *scēne* (cp. Dut. *schoon*, G *schön*), not rel. to SHINE]

sheep (shēp) *n.* (*pl.* **sheep**) **1** a gregarious ruminant animal of the genus *Ovis*, esp. the domesticated *O. aries*, or any of its numerous breeds, reared for the sake of their flesh and wool. **2** a timid, subservient, unoriginal person who follows the crowd. **3** a bashful or embarrassed person. **4** (*pl.*) the members of a minister's flock. **5** (*pl.*) God's people, as the flock of the Good Shepherd. **6** sheepskin used as a leather. **black sheep** BLACK. **to separate the sheep from the goats** to sort a group into inferior and superior members. **sheep-bot** *n.* a botfly infesting sheep. **sheepcote** *n.* a sheepfold. **sheep-dip** *n.* **1** a preparation for killing vermin or preserving the wool on sheep. **2** a place for dipping sheep in this. **sheepdog** *n.* **1** a collie. **2** a breed of heavy, rough-coated, short-tailed dogs employed by shepherds. **sheep-faced** *a.* sheepish, bashful. **sheepfold** *n.* a pen or enclosure for sheep. **sheep-hook** *n.* a shepherd's crook. **sheepish** *a.* **1** like a sheep. **2** bashful, diffident, timid. **3** ashamed. **sheepishly** *adv.* **sheepishness** *n.* **sheeplike** *a.* **sheep louse** *n.* an insect parasitic on sheep. **sheep market** *n.* a place where sheep are sold. **sheepmaster** *n.* an owner of sheep. **sheepmeat** *n.* mutton or lamb. **sheep-pen** *n.* a sheepfold. **sheep-pox** *n.* an eruptive contagious disease resembling smallpox, affecting sheep. **sheep-run** *n.* a large tract of land for pasturing sheep. **sheep's-bit** *n.* a plant with blue flowers like the scabious, *Jasione montana.* **sheep's eye** *n.* (*usu. pl.*) **1** a bashful or diffident look. **2** a wishful or amorous glance. **sheepshank** *n.* a knot used to shorten a rope temporarily. **sheep's head** *n.* **1** the head of a sheep. **2** an important food-fish, *Archosargus rhomboidalis*, abundant on the Atlantic coasts of the US. **sheepshearer** *n.* a person who shears sheep. **sheep-shearing** *n.* **sheepskin** *n.* **1** the skin of a sheep, esp. used as a coat or rug. **2** leather prepared therefrom, used for bookbinding etc. **3** parchment made therefrom or a document or diploma of this. **sheep tick** *n.* a sheep louse. **sheeptrack** *n.* a path trodden by the feet of sheep. **sheepwalk** *n.* land for pasturing sheep, usu. of less extent than a sheep-run. **sheep-wash** *n.* sheep-dip. [OE *scēap*, cp. Dut. *schaap*, G *Schaf*, OHG *scaf*]

sheer[1] (shiə) *a.* **1** pure, unmixed, simple, mere, absolute, bitter, downright. **2** perpendicular, unbroken by a ledge or slope. **3** (of a fabric) very thin, diaphanous. *~adv.* **1** vertically, plumb. **2** entirely, outright. **sheerly** *adv.* **sheerness** *n.* [Icel. *skoerr*, cogn. with *skīna*, to SHINE, and OE *skir*]

sheer[2] (shiə) *v.i.* **1** (*esp. Naut.*) to deviate from a course. **2** (of a horse) to start aside, to shy. **3** to go (away or off), esp. from someone or something one does not like. *~n.* **1** the upward curvature of a vessel towards the bow and stern. **2** the position of a ship riding at single anchor. **3** a swerving or curving course. **to sheer off** to move off, to go away. [Dut. *scheren*, to SHEAR]

sheerlegs (shiə´legz), **shearlegs** *n.* an apparatus consisting of two masts, or legs, secured at the top, for hoisting heavy weights, esp. in dockyards. **sheerhulk** *n.* a dismantled hull of a vessel fitted with sheers for hoisting out and putting in the masts of other ships etc.

sheers (shiəz) *n.* [var. of SHEAR]

sheet[1] (shēt) *n.* **1** a thin, flat, broad piece of anything, esp. a rectangular piece of linen, cotton or nylon used in a bed to keep the blankets etc. from a sleeper's body. **2** a piece of metal etc., rolled out, hammered, fused etc. into a thin sheet. **3** a piece of paper of a regular size, esp. complete as it was made, reckoned as the 24th part of a quire. **4** a newspaper. **5** a broad expanse or surface. **6** a set of unseparated postage stamps. *~v.t.* **1** to cover, wrap or shroud in a sheet or sheets. **2** to form into sheets. *~v.i.* (of rain) to come down in sheets, very heavily. **in sheets 1** (of a book) not bound. **2** (of rain) very heavy. **sheet copper, sheet iron, sheet lead, sheet metal** *n.* metal rolled out, hammered or fused into thin sheets. **sheet glass** *n.* **sheeting** *n.* fabric used for making sheets. **sheet lightning** *n.* lightning in wide extended flashes. **sheet music** *n.* music printed on unbound sheets of paper. [OE *scēte*, *scyte*, rel. to and blended with *scēat*, a corner, a fold, from *scēotan*, to shoot]

sheet[2] (shēt) *n.* **1** a rope attached to the clew of a sail for moving, extending it etc. **2** (*pl.*) the space at the bow or stern of a boat. **three sheets in the wind** (*Naut., sl.*)

drunk. **to sheet home** to secure a sail with the sheet. **sheet anchor** *n.* **1** a large anchor, usu. one of two carried outside the waist of a ship for use in emergencies. **2** a chief support, a last refuge. **sheet bend** *n.* a kind of knot used for joining ropes of different thicknesses. [OE *scēata*, Icel. *skaut*, rel. to SHEET[1]]

sheik (shāk, shēk), **sheikh, shaikh** *n.* **1** the head of a Bedouin family, clan or tribe. **2** a Muslim leader. **sheikdom** *n.* **Sheikh ul Islam** (ul) *n.* the grand mufti or head of the Muslim hierarchy in Turkey. [Arab.]

sheila (shē´lə) *n.* (*Austral., sl.*) a girl, a young woman. [Eng. dial. *shaler*, assim. to girl's name *Sheila*]

shekel (shek´əl) *n.* **1** the main unit of currency of Israel. **2** (*pl., coll.*) money, riches. **3** a Hebrew weight of 1/60 of a mina. **4** (*Hist.*) a silver coin of this weight. [Heb. *sheqel*, from *shāqal*, to weigh]

Shekinah (shikī´nə), **Shechinah** *n.* the visible presence of Jehovah above the mercy-seat in the Tabernacle and Solomon's Temple. [Heb. from *shākan*, to dwell]

sheldrake (shel´drāk) *n.* (*pl.* **sheldrake, sheldrakes**) a large wild duck with vivid plumage, of the genus *Tadorna* or *Cascarca*, esp. *T. tadorna*, breeding on sandy coasts. **shelduck** *n.* (*pl.* **shelduck, shelducks**) a female sheldrake. [OE *scild*, SHIELD (cp. G *schildern*, to paint, with alln. to plumage), DRAKE[1]]

shelf[1] (shelf) *n.* (*pl.* **shelves** (-vz)) **1** a horizontal board or slab set in a wall or forming one of a series in a bookcase, cupboard etc., for standing vessels, books etc. on. **2** a projecting layer of rock, a ledge. **3** a reef, a shoal, a sandbank. **on the shelf 1** put aside, discarded. **2** (of a woman) considered too old to marry. **shelfful** *n.* (*pl.* **shelffuls**). **shelf-life** *n.* (*pl.* **shelf-lives**) the length of time a foodstuff or manufactured item can be stored before deteriorating. **shelflike** *a.* **shelf mark** *n.* a mark on a library book indicating its place on the shelves. **shelf room** *n.* room available on a shelf. [OE *scylfe*, cogn. with SCALE[1] and SHELL]

shelf[2] (shelf) *n.* (*pl.* **shelfs**) (*Austral., sl.*) an informer. *~v.t.* to inform upon. [from SHELF[1]]

shell (shel) *n.* **1** a hard outside covering etc. **2** the hard but fragile outside covering of an egg. **3** the hard outside case of a mollusc. **4** the wing-case or pupa-case of an insect. **5** the carapace of a tortoise, turtle etc. **6** the exoskeleton of an arthropod. **7** the hard outside covering of a nut-kernel, seed etc., a husk, a pod. **8** the framework or walls of a house, ship etc., with the interior removed or not yet built. **9** the outline of a plan etc. **10** a light, long and narrow racing boat. **11** an inner coffin. **12** a hollow pastry case. **13** the handguard of a sword. **14** a hollow projectile containing a bursting-charge, missiles etc., exploded by a time or percussion fuse. **15** a case of paper or other material containing the explosive in fireworks, cartridges etc. **16** (*N Am.*) a cartridge. **17** mere outer form or semblance. **18** a spherical area outside the nucleus of an atom occupied by electrons of almost equal energy. **19** a shell program. **20** an intermediate form in some schools. **21** (*poet.*) a lyre, orig. a stringed tortoise shell. *~v.t.* **1** to strip or break off the shell from. **2** to take out of the shell. **3** to cover with a shell or with shells. **4** to throw shells at, to bombard. *~v.i.* **1** to come away or fall (off) in scales. **2** to cast the husk or shell. **to come out of one's shell** to stop being shy or reserved. **to shell out** (*coll.*) to pay up, to pay the required sum. **shellback** *n.* an old sailor. **shell-bark** *n.* either of two kinds of hickory. **shell-bit** *n.* a gouge-shaped boring bit. **shell company** *n.* a company with a Stock Exchange listing used to form a new company. **shelled** *a.* (*usu. in comb.*, as *hard-shelled*). **shell egg** *n.* an egg in its shell. **shellfire** *n.* the firing of artillery shells. **shellfish** *n.* (*pl. in general* **shellfish**, *in particular* **shellfishes**) any aquatic mollusc or crustacean having a shell. **shell game** *n.* (*N Am.*) thimblerig. **to play a shell game** (*coll.*) to trick or deceive someone. **shell-heap** *n.* (*Hist.*) a kitchen midden. **shell-jacket** *n.* (*Mil.*) an undress or fatigue jacket. **shell-less** *a.* **shell-like** *a.* **shell-lime** *n.* lime obtained by burning seashells. **shell-money** *n.* wampum. **shell-mound** *n.* (*Hist.*) a shell-heap. **shell-out** *n.* **1** the act of shelling out. **2** a variety of pool etc. played on the billiard table. **shell pink** *n.* a pale yellow-tinged pink colour. **shell-pink** *a.* **shell program** *n.* a basic computer program used as a framework to develop one's own requirements. **shellproof** *a.* impenetrable to shells, bombproof. **shell-shock** *n.* COMBAT FATIGUE (under COMBAT). **shell-shocked** *a.* **shell suit** *n.* a nylon tracksuit worn as leisure wear. **shell-work** *n.* work composed of or ornamented with shells. **shelly** *a.* [OE *scell* (cp. Dut. *schel*, Icel. *skel*), cogn. with SCALE[1]]

she'll (shēl) *contr.* she will, she shall.

shellac (shəlak´) *n.* a thermoplastic resin obtained by purifying the resinous excreta of certain jungle insects, used in the manufacture of varnishes. *~v.t.* (*pres.p.* **shellacking**, *past, p.p.* **shellacked**) **1** to varnish with this. **2** (*N Am.*) to defeat or thrash. [SHELL, LAC[1]]

Shelta (shel´tə) *n.* a secret jargon made up largely of Gaelic or Irish words, used by tinkers, beggars etc. [etym. uncertain]

shelter (shel´tə) *n.* **1** anything that covers or shields from injury, danger, heat, wind etc. **2** being sheltered, security. **3** a place of safety. **4** a light building affording protection from the weather to persons, instruments etc. **5** an air-raid shelter. *~v.t.* **1** to shield from injury, danger etc. **2** to protect, to cover. **3** to conceal, to screen. *~v.i.* to take shelter (under). **shelter belt** *n.* a row of trees planted to provide shelter for crops. **sheltered** *a.* **1** protected from weather or from outside influence. **2** (of housing) providing a safe, supervised environment for the disabled or elderly. **sheltered accommodation, sheltered housing** *n.* accommodation consisting of individual homes which have some shared facilities and are looked after by a warden, used esp. by elderly people. **shelterer** *n.* **shelterless** *a.* [ME *sheld-trume*, OE *scild-trume* (SHIELD, *truma*, hand, rel. to *trum*, firm)]

shelty (shel´ti), **sheltie** *n.* (*pl.* **shelties**) **1** a Shetland pony or sheepdog. **2** any pony. **3** a Shetlander. [prob. from Icel. *Hjalti*, Shetlander]

shelve[1] (shelv) *v.t.* **1** to place on a shelf or shelves. **2** to put aside, to defer indefinitely. **3** to fit with shelves. **shelver** *n.* **shelving[1]** *n.* **1** shelves collectively. **2** material for making shelves. **shelvy** *a.* projecting, overhanging. [see SHELF[1]]

shelve[2] (shelv) *v.i.* to slope gradually. **shelving[2]** *a.* [cp. Icel. *skelgjask*, to be askew, also SHOAL[2]]

shelver, shelves SHELF[1].

shelving[1] SHELVE[1].

shelving[2] SHELVE[2].

shelvy SHELVE[1].

shemozzle (shimoz´əl), **schemozzle** *n.* (*sl.*) **1** an uproar, a violent row. **2** a confused situation. [Yiddish]

shenanigan (shinan´igən) *n.* (*often pl., coll.*) **1** trickery, deception. **2** noisy, boisterous behaviour. [etym. unknown]

Sheol (shē´ōl, -əl) *n.* the Hebrew place of the dead, often translated 'hell' in the Authorized Version. [Heb., from *shā'al*, to dig]

shepherd (shep´əd) *n.* **1** a person employed to tend sheep at pasture. **2** a pastor, a Christian minister. **3** (*Austral.*) a person who holds legal rights on a mining claim. *~v.t.* **1** to tend, as a shepherd. **2** to drive or gather together. **3** (*Austral.*) to preserve legal rights on (a mining claim). **Good Shepherd** GOOD. **shepherd dog** *n.* a sheepdog. **shepherdess** *n.* a female shepherd. **shepherd's clock** *n.* (*Austral.*) the kookaburra. **shepherd's crook** *n.* a long staff armed with an iron crook, used to catch or hold sheep. **shepherdship** *n.* **shepherd's knot** *n.* the tormentil. **shepherd's needle**

n. **1** a plant, *Scandix pecten-veneris*; also called *Venus's comb.* **2** the cranesbill. **shepherd's pie** *n.* cooked minced meat, covered with mashed potatoes and baked in an oven. **shepherd's plaid** *n.* **1** black and white checked cloth. **2** this pattern. **shepherd's purse** *n.* a common cruciferous weed, *Capsella bursa-pastoris*. **shepherd's rod** *n.* the teasel. **shepherd's staff** *n.* the common mullein. [OE *scēaphyrde*, SHEEP, HERD]

sherardize (sher´ədīz), **sherardise** *v.t.* to coat (iron or steel) with zinc by heating it in a container with zinc dust. [*Sherard* Cowper-Coles, d. 1936, English inventor]

Sheraton (sher´ətən) *a.* (of furniture) of a severe style designed and introduced into England by Sheraton towards the end of the 18th cent. ~*n.* this style. [Thomas *Sheraton*, 1751–1806, English furniture-maker]

sherbet (shœ´bit) *n.* **1** an effervescent powder used in sweets or to make fizzy drinks. **2** (*esp. N Am.*) a water ice. **3** an oriental cooling drink, made of diluted fruit juices. **4** (*Austral.*) beer. [Pers., from Arab. *shariba*, to drink, cp. SYRUP]

sherd SHARD.

sherif (shərēf´), **shereef, sharif** *n.* **1** a descendant of Muhammad through his daughter Fatima and Hassan Ibn Ali. **2** the chief magistrate of Mecca. [Arab. *sherif*, lofty]

sheriff (sher´if) *n.* **1** HIGH SHERIFF (under HIGH). **2** (*N Am.*) an elected county official responsible for keeping the peace etc. **3** an honorary elected official in some towns. **sheriffalty** *n.* (*pl.* **sheriffalties**) SHRIEVALTY (under SHRIEVAL). **sheriff court** *n.* (*Sc.*) a sheriff's court, hearing civil and criminal cases. **sheriffdom, sheriffhood, sheriffship** *n.* SHRIEVALTY (under SHRIEVAL). [OE *scīr-gerēfa* (SHIRE, REEVE[1])]

Sherpa (shœ´pə) *n.* (*pl.* **Sherpa, Sherpas**) a member of a mountaineering people living on the southern slopes of the Himalayas. [Tibetan *shar*, east, *pa*, inhabitant]

sherry (sher´i) *n.* (*pl.* **sherries**) **1** a fortified Spanish white wine orig. from Xeres. **2** a glass of this. **sherry cobbler** *n.* a cobbler (iced drink) made with sherry. **sherry glass** *n.* a small glass for sherry. [*Xeres*, now Jerez de la Frontera, in S Spain]

she's (shiz, shēz) *contr.* **1** she is. **2** she has.

Shetland (shet´lənd) *n.* a Shetland pony. **Shetlander** *n.* a native of the Shetland Islands. **Shetland lace** *n.* an ornamental openwork trimming made of woollen yarn. **Shetland pony** *n.* a very small variety of horse with flowing mane and tail, orig. from Shetland. **Shetland sheepdog** *n.* a small collie-like dog. **Shetland wool** *n.* the fine wool from Shetland sheep. [group of islands to the NE of Scotland]

sheva (shəvah´) *n.* **1** the Hebrew sign (:) put under a consonant to denote the absence of a following vowel sound. **2** SCHWA. [Rabbinic Heb. *shewā*]

†**shew** SHOW.

shewbread SHOW.

Shia (shē´ə), **Shiah, Shi'a** *n.* (*pl.* **Shia, Shias, Shiah, Shiahs, Shi'a, Shi'as**) **1** one of the two main branches of Islam (see also SUNNA), which regards Ali (Muhammad's cousin and son-in-law) as the first rightful imam or caliph and rejects the three Sunni caliphs. **2** a Shi'ite. ~*a.* belonging to, or characteristic of, the Shia sect. **Shi'ism, Shiism** *n.* adherence to Shia. **Shi'ite** (-īt), **Shiite** *n.* a member of the Shia branch of Islam. ~*a.* of or relating to Shia. **Shiitic** (-it´-) *a.* [Arab. *shi'a*, sect]

shiatsu (shiat´soo) *n.* a massage in which pressure is applied to the acupuncture points of the body. [Jap.]

shibboleth (shib´əlǝth) *n.* **1** a criterion, test or watchword of a party etc. **2** an old-fashioned or discredited doctrine etc. [Heb., a word used as a test to distinguish the Ephraimites from the Gileadites, the former calling it *sibboleth* (Judges xii)]

shicer (shī´sə) *n.* (*Austral.*) **1** (*sl.*) a crook, a welsher. **2** a useless mine. **3** (*sl.*) a useless thing. [G *Scheisser*, contemptible person]

shicker (shik´ə) *a.* (*Austral., New Zeal., sl.*) drunk. ~*n.* drink, excessive drinking. **shickered** *a.* drunk. [Yiddish]

shield (shēld) *n.* **1** a broad piece of defensive armour made of wood, leather or metal, usu. carried on the left arm to protect the body, usu. straight across the top and tapering to a point at the bottom. **2** a shield-shaped trophy in, e.g., a sporting competition. **3** a wooden screen or framework or a metal plate used in tunnelling, machinery etc., as a protection when working a gun etc. **4** a shieldlike part in an animal or a plant. **5** (*Her.*) an escutcheon or field bearing a coat of arms. **6** defence, a protection, a defender. **7** (*N Am.*) a sheriff's or detective's badge. **8** a structure of lead, concrete etc., round something highly radioactive to protect against radiation. **9** a mass of very ancient rock at the centre of a continent. ~*v.t.* to screen or protect with or as with a shield. **shield bug** *n.* a shield-shaped insect of the family Pentatomidae. **shield fern** *n.* **1** a fern of the genus *Polystichum* having shield-shaped covers protecting the fruit-dots. **2** a fern of the genus *Dryopteris*; also called *buckler*. **shieldless** *a.* **shield volcano** *n.* a broad domed volcano. [OE *scild*, cp. Dut. and G *Schild*, Icel. *skjöldr*, perh. rel. to SHELL and SCALE[1]]

shieling (shē´ling), **shealing** *n.* (*Sc.*) **1** a hut used by shepherds, sportsmen etc. **2** a small house or cottage. **3** a piece of summer pasturage. [North. ME *shāle*, *schele*, perh. from Icel. *skjōl*, shelter, rel. to SKY]

shift (shift) *v.t.* **1** to move from one position to another. **2** to change the position of. **3** to remove, esp. with an effort. **4** to change (one thing) for another. **5** (*N Am.*) to change (gear). **6** (*sl.*) to dispose of, sell. **7** (*sl.*) to consume hastily or in large quantities. ~*v.i.* **1** to move or be moved about. **2** to change place or position. **3** to change into a different place, form, state etc. **4** to resort to expedients, to do the best one can, to manage, to contrive. **5** to prevaricate, to practise evasion. **6** (*sl.*) to move quickly. **7** (*N Am.*) to change gear. ~*n.* **1** a shifting, a change of place, form or character. **2** a substitution of one thing for another, a vicissitude. **3** a change of clothing. **4** a relay of workers. **5** the period of time for which a shift works. **6** a chemise. **7** a woman's loose, unshaped dress. **8** a device, a contrivance, an expedient. **9** a dodge, a trick, an artifice, an evasion. **10** a displacement of spectral lines. **11** SOUND SHIFT (under SOUND[1]). **12** a key on a keyboard which switches between upper and lower case. **13** in bridge, a change of suit in bidding or playing. **14** the overlapping of bricks so that the ends of rows do not coincide. **15** (*N Am.*) a gear lever or its mechanism. **to make shift** to manage, to contrive (to do, to get on etc.). **to shift about 1** to turn right round. **2** to prevaricate. **3** to be shifted from side to side. **to shift for oneself** to depend on one's own efforts. **to shift off** to get rid of, to defer. **to shift one's ground** GROUND[1]. **shiftable** *a.* **shifter** *n.* **shiftingly** *adv.* **shiftless** *a.* **1** lazy. **2** incompetent, incapable, without forethought. **shiftlessly** *adv.* **shiftlessness** *n.* **shift work** *n.* work in shifts. **shifty** *a.* (*comp.* **shiftier**, *superl.* **shiftiest**) (*coll.*) furtive, sly, unreliable. **shiftily** *adv.* **shiftiness** *n.* [OE *sciftan*, to divide (cp. Dut. *schiften*, Icel. *skipta*, Swed. *skifta*)]

shigella (shigel´ə) *n.* any bacterium of the genus *Shigella*, some of which cause dysentery in human beings. [K. *Shiga*, 1870–1957, Japanese bacteriologist]

shih-tzu (shētsoo´) *n.* a small dog with long silky hair, of a Tibetan and Chinese breed. [Chin. *shizi*, lion]

Shi'ism, Shi'ite etc. SHIA.

shiitake (shitah´kā), **shiitake mushroom** *n.* a mushroom, *Lentinus edodes*, used in Oriental cookery. [Jap. *shii*, an oak, *take*, mushroom]

shikar (shikah´) *n.* (*Ang.-Ind.*) hunting, sport, game. **shikari** (-ri), **shikaree** (-rē) *n.* a hunter. [Hind.]

shiksa (shik´sə), **schicksa, shikse** *n.* (*offensive*) a non-Jewish woman. [Yiddish]

shill (shil) *n.* (*N Am.*) a decoy or person employed to entice others into buying etc. [prob. from *shillaber*, etym. uncertain]

shillelagh (shilā´li, -lə) *n.* (*Ir.*) an oak or blackthorn sapling used as a cudgel. [place in Co. Wicklow, Ireland]

shilling (shil´ing) *n.* **1** (*Hist.*) a former British silver (or, later, cupronickel), coin and money of account, equal in value to 12 old pence (5 new pence). **2** the standard monetary unit of several E African countries. **to take the King's shilling** (*Hist.*) to enlist during the reign of a king (with alln. to the former practice of giving recruits a shilling as token of a contract). **to take the Queen's shilling** to enlist during the reign of a queen. **shilling-mark** *n.* (*Hist.*) a solidus sign. [OE *scilling* (cp. Dut. *schelling*, G *Schilling*, Icel. *skillingr*) perh. from Gmc. *skel-*, to divide, cp. SKILL]

shilly-shally (shil´ishali) *v.i.* (*3rd pers. sing. pres.* **shilly-shallies,** *pres.p.* **shilly-shallying,** *past, p.p.* **shilly-shallied**) **1** to act in an irresolute manner, to hesitate. **2** to be undecided. *~n.* **1** irresolution, hesitation. **2** foolish trifling. *~a.* vacillating. **shilly-shallyer, shilly-shallier** *n.* [redupl. of *shall I*]

shim (shim) *n.* a wedge, piece of metal etc., used to tighten up joints, fill in spaces etc. *~v.t.* (*pres.p.* **shimming,** *past, p.p.* **shimmed**) to fill in, wedge or fit with this. [etym. uncertain]

shimmer (shim´ə) *v.i.* **1** to emit a faint or tremulous light. **2** to glimmer, beam or glisten faintly. *~n.* a faint or tremulous light. **shimmeringly** *adv.* **shimmery** *a.* [OE *scymrian*, freq. of *scīmian*, to shine (cp. Dut. *schemeren*, G *schimmern*)]

shimmy (shim´i) *n.* (*pl.* **shimmies**) **1** (*coll.*) †a chemise. **2** (*Hist.*) an orig. N American dance in which the body is shaken rapidly. **3** abnormal vibration in an aircraft or motor car. *~v.i.* (*3rd pers. sing. pres.* **shimmies,** *pres.p.* **shimmying,** *past, p.p.* **shimmied**) **1** (*Hist.*) to dance a shimmy. **2** (of a car or aircraft) to vibrate. [CHEMISE]

shin (shin) *n.* **1** the forepart of the human leg between the ankle and the knee. **2** a cut of beef, the lower foreleg. *~v.i.* (*pres.p.* **shinning,** *past, p.p.* **shinned**) **1** to climb up a tree etc. by means of the hands and legs alone. **2** to trudge, to trot. **3** (*N Am., sl.*) to borrow money in a hurry. *~v.t.* **1** to kick on the shins. **2** to climb. **shin bone** *n.* the tibia. **shin-guard** *n.* a padded guard for the shin worn at football etc. **shin-pad** *n.* a shin-guard. [OE *scinu* (cp. Dut. *scheen*, G *Schiene*), prob. cogn. with SKIN]

shindig (shin´dig) *n.* (*coll.*) a noisy or rowdy ball or dance. [SHINDY]

shindy (shin´di) *n.* (*pl.* **shindies**) **1** a row, a disturbance, a rumpus, a brawl. **2** a rowdy party or dance. [perh. corr. of SHINNY or SHINTY]

shine (shīn) *v.i.* (*past, p.p.* **shone** (shon), **shined**) **1** to emit or reflect rays of light. **2** to be bright, to beam, to glow. **3** to be brilliant, eminent or conspicuous. **4** to be lively or animated. *~v.t.* **1** to cause to shine, to make bright, to polish. **2** (*N Am.*) to clean (shoes etc.). *~n.* **1** (*coll.*) fair weather, sunshine, brightness, lustre. **2** (*sl.*) a row, a shindy. **3** an act of shining esp. shoes. **to take a shine to** to like at first sight. **to take the shine out of** **1** to surpass, eclipse. **2** to spoil the brilliance etc. of. **shiner** *n.* **1** a person who or thing which shines. **2** (*sl.*) †a coin, esp. a sovereign; money. **3** any of several silvery fishes, esp. of the genus *Notropis*. **4** (*coll.*) a black eye. **shiningly** *adv.* **shiny** *a.* (*comp.* **shinier,** *superl.* **shiniest**). **shinily** *adv.* **shininess** *n.* [OE *scīnan*, cp. Dut. *schijnen*, G *scheinen*, Icel. *skīna*]

shingle[1] (shing´gəl) *n.* **1** a thin piece of wood laid in overlapping rows as a roof-covering. **2** †a woman's haircut in which the hair is layered like shingles, showing the shape of the head. **3** (*N Am.*) a small signboard or plate, such as that of a doctor. *~v.t.* **1** to roof with shingles. **2** †to cut (hair) in a shingle. **shingler** *n.* **shingling** *n.* **shingly**[1] *a.* [corr. of *shindle*, L *scindula*, from *scindere*, to split (cp. G *Schindel*)]

shingle[2] (shing´gəl) *n.* coarse rounded gravel on the seashore. **shingly**[2] *a.* [cp. Norw. *singl*]

shingles (shing´gəlz) *n.pl.* (*usu. treated as sing.*) a viral infection, *Herpes zoster*, marked by pain and inflammation of the skin along the path of an affected nerve (usu. on the chest or abdomen). [OF *cengle*, L *cingulum*, girth, from *cingere*, to gird]

shingling SHINGLE[1].

shingly[1] SHINGLE[1].

shingly[2] SHINGLE[2].

shinny (shin´i) *v.i.* (*3rd pers. sing. pres.* **shinnies,** *pres.p.* **shinnying,** *past, p.p.* **shinnied**) (*N Am., coll.*) to shin (up, down). [SHIN]

Shinto (shin´tō) *n.* the indigenous religion of the people of Japan existing along with Buddhism, a species of nature- and ancestor-worship. **Shintoism** *n.* **Shintoist** *n.* [Jap., from Chin. *shen dao*, way of the gods]

shinty (shin´ti) *n.* (*pl.* **shinties**) **1** a game somewhat resembling hockey, played by teams of 12 people. **2** a stick or ball used in shinty. [perh. from the cry *shin (to) ye*, used in the game]

shiny SHINE.

ship (ship) *n.* **1** a large seagoing vessel. **2** a large sailing vessel with three or more square-rigged masts. **3** (*coll.*) an aircraft, a spacecraft. **4** a boat, esp. a racing boat. *~v.t.* (*pres.p.* **shipping,** *past, p.p.* **shipped**) **1** to put on board a ship. **2** to send, take or carry in a ship. **3** to engage for service on board a ship. **4** to fix (a mast, rudder etc.) in the proper place on a ship. **5** to send (goods) by any recognized means of conveyance. **6** (*Naut.*) to take in (water) over the side. **7** to bring (oars) inside a vessel. *~v.i.* **1** to embark on a ship. **2** to engage for service as a sailor. **to ship a sea** to have a wave come over the side of a vessel. **to ship off** **1** to send by ship. **2** (*coll.*) to send (a person) away. **to take ship** to embark. **when one's ship comes home** when one's ship comes in. **when one's ship comes in** when one becomes rich. **ship biscuit, ship's biscuit** *n.* (*Hist.*) a hard coarse kind of bread or biscuit used on board ship, hard tack. **shipboard** *n.* the deck or side of a ship. *~a.* happening etc. on board ship. **on shipboard** on board ship. **ship-breaker** *n.* a contractor who breaks up old ships. **shipbroker** *n.* **1** a person who transacts all necessary business for a ship when in port. **2** a marine insurance agent. **shipbuilder** *n.* **1** a shipwright. **2** a naval architect. **shipbuilding** *n.* **ship burial** *n.* burial in a wooden ship under a mound. **ship canal** *n.* a canal along which ocean-going vessels can pass. **ship chandler, ship's chandler** *n.* a person who deals in cordage, canvas and other commodities for fitting out ships. **ship chandlery** *n.* **ship-fever** *n.* typhus. **shiplap** *n.* cladding consisting of overlapping boards. *~v.t.* (*pres.p.* **shiplapping,** *past, p.p.* **shiplapped**) to fit (boards) in this way. **shipless** *a.* **shipload** *n.* the quantity of cargo, passengers etc. that a ship carries. **shipman** *n.* (*pl.* **shipmen**) **1** a sailor. **2** the captain or master of a ship. **shipmaster** *n.* the master, captain or commander of a vessel. **shipmate** *n.* a person who serves or sails in the same ship, esp. a fellow-sailor. **shipment** *n.* **1** the act of shipping. **2** goods or commodities shipped, a consignment. **ship money** *n.* (*Hist.*) a tax formerly charged on the ports, towns, cities, boroughs and counties of England for providing certain ships for the navy. **ship of the desert** *n.* a camel. **ship of the line** *n.* (*Hist.*) a warship suitable for taking its place in a line of battle. **shipowner** *n.* a person who owns a ship or ships or shares therein. **shippable** *a.* **shipped** *a.* put on board a ship. **shipper** *n.* a person who ships or sends goods by a common carrier. **shipping** *a.* of or relating to ships. ~*n.* 1 the act of putting on board ship, sending goods etc. 2 ships collectively, esp. the ships of a country or port. 3 tonnage. 4 sailing. **to take shipping** to embark on board ship. **shipping agent** *n.* a person or company managing the administrative business of a ship. **shipping-articles, ship's articles** *n.pl.* articles of agreement between the captain of a vessel and the crew as to wages etc. **shipping-bill** *n.* an invoice of goods shipped. **shipping-master** *n.* an official superintending the signing of shipping-articles, paying off of workers etc. **shipping-office** *n.* the office of a shipping agent or shipping master. **ship-rigged** *a.* having three or more square-rigged masts. **ship's articles** *n.pl.* shipping-articles. **ship's biscuit** SHIP BISCUIT (under SHIP). **ship's boat** *n.* a small boat carried on a ship. **ship's chandler** *n.* a ship chandler. **ship's company** *n.* the crew of a ship. **ship's corporal** *n.* a sailor who attends to police matters under the master-at-arms. **shipshape** *adv.* in a seaman-like manner, in good order. ~*a.* well arranged, neat, trim. **ship's husband** *n.* a person who attends to the repairs, provisioning and other necessaries of a ship, a shipbroker. **ship's papers** *n.pl.* documents carried by a ship containing details of ownership, nationality, destination and cargo. **ship-to-shore** *a.* from a ship to land. ~*n.* a radio-telephone used from a ship to the land. **shipway** *n.* a timber structure forming an inclined way for building or launching ships. **shipworm** *n.* a bivalve that bores into ships' timbers, piles etc.; a teredo. **shipwreck** *n.* 1 the destruction or loss of a ship, by foundering, striking a rock or other cause. 2 destruction, ruin. ~*v.t.* 1 to cause to suffer shipwreck. 2 to ruin. ~*v.i.* 1 to suffer shipwreck. 2 to be ruined. **shipwright** *n.* 1 a shipbuilder. 2 a ship's carpenter. **shipyard** *n.* a yard etc. where ships are built and repaired. [OE *scip* (cp. Dut. *schip*, G *Schiff*, Icel. *skip*), cogn. with SKIFF[1], Gr. *skaphos*]

-ship (ship) *suf.* 1 denoting state, condition, the quality of being so-and-so, as in *fellowship*, *friendship*. 2 status, office, as in *judgeship*, *ladyship*. 3 tenure of office, as in *chairmanship*. 4 skill in the capacity specified, as in *marksmanship*, *scholarship*. 5 the whole group of people of a specified type, as in *membership*. [OE *-scipe*, cogn. with SHAPE]

shiralee (shir´əlē) *n.* (*Austral.*) a swag, a tramp's bundle. [etym. unknown]

shire (shīə) *n.* 1 an administrative division of England, a county, esp. one whose name ends in '-shire'. 2 (*pl.*) (**Shires**) the predominantly rural midland counties of England, esp. Leicestershire and Northamptonshire, noted for foxhunting. 3 (*Austral.*) a rural district with an elected council. **-shire** (shə, shiə) *suf.* forming the names of counties. **shire county** *n.* a non-metropolitan county. **shire-horse** *n.* a large breed of draught horse, orig. raised in the midland shires. [OE *scīr*, etym. uncertain; not rel. to SHEAR or SHARE[1]]

shirk (shœk) *v.t.* to avoid or get out of unfairly. ~*v.i.* to avoid the performance of work or duty. ~*n.* a person who shirks. **shirker** *n.* [prob. var. of SHARK]

shirr (shœ) *n.* 1 an elastic cord or thread inserted in cloth etc. to make it elastic. 2 a gathering or fulling. ~*v.t.* 1 to draw (a sleeve, dress etc.) into gathers by means of elastic threads. 2 (*N Am.*) to bake (eggs) in a buttered dish. **shirring** *n.* [etym. uncertain]

shirt (shœt) *n.* 1 a loose garment of linen, cotton, wool, silk or other material, extending from the neck to the thighs, and usu. showing at the collar and wristbands, worn by men and boys under the outer clothes. 2 (*also* **shirt blouse**) a woman's blouse with collar and cuffs. 3 a lining or inner casing. 4 a nightshirt. **the shirt off one's back** (*coll.*) one's last remaining possessions. **to keep one's shirt on** (*coll.*) to keep calm. **to lose one's shirt** (*coll.*) to lose all one has. **to put one's shirt on** (*coll.*) to bet all one has. **shirt-dress** *n.* a shirtwaister. **shirted** *a.* **shirt-front** *n.* 1 the part of a shirt covering the breast, esp. if stiffened and starched. 2 a dicky. **shirting** *n.* **shirtless** *a.* **shirtsleeve** *n.* (*usu. in pl.*) the sleeve of a shirt. **in one's shirtsleeves** with one's coat off. **shirt-tail** *n.* the curved part at the back of a shirt below the waist. **shirtwaist** *n.* (*esp. N Am.*) a woman's blouse similar to a shirt. **shirtwaister** *n.* a woman's dress with a bodice similar to a shirt. **shirty** *a.* (*comp.* **shirtier**, *superl.* **shirtiest**) (*sl.*) cross, ill-tempered. **shirtily** *adv.* **shirtiness** *n.* [from OE *scyrte*, from *scort*, SHORT, or the cogn. Icel. *skyrta*, SKIRT]

shishkebab (shish kibab´) *n.* a skewer of marinated and cooked meat and vegetables. [Turk.]

shit (shit) *v.i.* (*pres.p.* **shitting**, *past*, *p.p.* **shit, shitted, shat** (shat)) (*taboo sl.*) to empty the bowels. ~*n.* 1 ordure, excrement. 2 an act of defecating. 3 a worthless or despicable person or thing. 4 nonsense. 5 a drug such as cannabis. ~*int.* used to express anger, disappointment etc. **in the shit** in trouble. **no shit!** (*esp. N Am.*) no fooling. **not to give a shit** not to care at all. **the shits** diarrhoea. **up shit creek** in an awkward situation. **shitbag, shithead** *n.* a worthless person. **shite** (shīt) *n.*, *int.* **shithouse** *n.* 1 a lavatory. 2 a dirty or inferior place. **shitless** *a.* **to be scared shitless** to be very scared. **shit-scared** *a.* terrified. **shitty** *a.* (*comp.* **shittier**, *superl.* **shittiest**) 1 soiled with excrement. 2 very bad or inferior. 3 despicable. **shittily** *adv.* **shittiness** *n.* [ON *skita*, cp. Dut. *schijten*]

shittim (shit´im) *n.* (*Bible*) 1 the wood of the shittah tree used in constructing the Ark of the Covenant and the tabernacle. 2 the shittah tree. **shittah** (-tə), **shittah tree** *n.* a kind of acacia. [Heb.]

Shiva SIVA.

shivaree CHARIVARI.

shiver[1] (shiv´ə) *v.i.* to tremble or shake, as with fear, cold or excitement. ~*n.* the act of shivering, a shivering movement. **the shivers** 1 a feeling or movement of horror. 2 a chill, ague. **shiverer** *n.* **shiveringly** *adv.* **shivery[1]** *a.* [ME *chiveren*, perh. rel. to QUIVER[2], cp. Norw. and Swed. dial. *kippa*]

shiver[2] (shiv´ə) *n.* 1 a tiny fragment, a sliver, a shive. 2 a species of blue slate. 3 (*Naut.*) a sheave, a pulley. ~*v.t.*, *v.i.* to break into shivers. **shiver my timbers** an oath supposedly used by pirates. **shivery[2]** *a.* [ME *schīve*, (cp. Dut. *schift*, G *Scheibe*, Icel. *skīfa*)]

shivery[1] SHIVER[1].

shivery[2] SHIVER[2].

shivoo (shivoo´) *n.* (*Austral.*, *coll.*) 1 a (noisy) party. 2 an entertainment. [etym. uncertain]

shlemiel SCHLEMIEL.

shlep SCHLEPP.

shlimazel SCHLIMAZEL.

shmo SCHMO.

shmooze SCHMOOZE.

shoal[1] (shōl) *n.* a large number, a multitude, a crowd, esp. of fish moving together. ~*v.i.* (of fish) to form a shoal or shoals. [OE *scolu*, cp. SCHOOL[2]]

shoal[2] (shōl) *a.* (*esp. dial.*) (of water) shallow, of little depth. ~*n.* 1 a shallow, a submerged sandbank. 2 (*esp. pl.*) hidden danger or difficulty. ~*v.i.* to become shallower. **shoaly** *a.* **shoaliness** *n.* [var. of SHALLOW]

shoat (shōt) *n.* (*N Am.*) a young hog. [Flem. *schote*]

shochet (shokh´ət) *n.* (*pl.* **shochetim** (-tim)) a slaughterer who is qualified to prepare meat and poultry according to Jewish ritual. [Heb.]

shock[1] (shok) *n.* 1 a violent collision of bodies, a concussion, an impact, a blow, a violent onset. 2 a sudden and violent sensation, such as that produced on the nerves by a discharge of electricity. 3 prostration brought about by a violent and sudden disturbance of the system. 4 (*coll.*) a stroke caused by thrombosis etc. 5 a sudden mental agitation, a violent disturbance (of belief, trust etc.). 6 (*esp. N Am.*) a shock absorber. ~*v.t.* 1 to give a violent sensation of disgust, horror or indignation to. 2 to shake or jar by a sudden collision. 3 to affect with a shock. ~*v.i.* 1 to behave or appear in an improper or scandalous fashion. 2 (*poet.*) to collide. **shockable** *a.* **shockability** (-bil´-) *n.* **shock absorber** *n.* an apparatus to neutralize the shock of axle-springs on recoil. **shock-brigade** *n.* in the former USSR, a body of workers engaged in a particularly arduous task. **shock cord** *n.* 1 heavy elasticated cord designed to absorb shock. 2 a piece of this. **shocker** *n.* (*coll.*) 1 something that shocks, esp. a sensational story. 2 a staggering specimen or example of anything. 3 a shock absorber. **shocking** *a.* 1 causing a shock. 2 disgraceful. 3 dreadful. ~*adv.* (*coll.*) shockingly; extremely. **shockingly** *adv.* **shockingness** *n.* **shocking pink** *n.* a garish, intense shade of pink. **shocking-pink** *a.* **shockproof** *a.* resistant to damage from shock. **shock stall** *n.* loss of lift and air resistance experienced by aircraft approaching the speed of sound. **shock tactics** *n.pl.* 1 any sudden and violent action. 2 a cavalry charge relying on weight of numbers for success. **shock therapy, shock treatment** *n.* the treatment of certain mental and other disorders by administering an electric shock. **shock troops** *n.pl.* selected soldiers employed on tasks requiring exceptional endurance and courage. **shock wave** *n.* a very strong sound wave, accompanied by a rise in pressure and temperature, caused by an explosion or by something travelling supersonically. **shock-workers** *n.pl.* a shock-brigade. [prob. through F *choc*, from OHG *scoc* (cp. Dut. *schok*, Icel. *skykkr*), cogn. with SHAKE]

shock[2] (shok) *n.* a collection of sheaves of grain, usu. 12 but varying in number. ~*v.i.* to collect sheaves into shocks. [cp. MDut. *schocke*, Swed. *skock*, prob. rel. to SHOCK[1]]

shock[3] (shok) *n.* 1 a thick, bushy mass or head of hair. 2 a dog with shaggy hair, esp. a poodle. ~*a.* shaggy. [prob. var. of SHAG, or rel. to SHOCK[2]]

shod SHOE.

shoddy (shod´i) *a.* (*comp.* **shoddier,** *superl.* **shoddiest**) 1 inferior. 2 not genuine, sham. 3 made of shoddy. ~*n.* (*pl.* **shoddies**) 1 fibre obtained from old cloth torn to pieces and shredded. 2 inferior cloth made from a mixture of this with new wool etc. 3 anything of an inferior, sham or adulterated kind. **shoddily** *adv.* **shoddiness** *n.* [prob. from OE *scēadan*, to SHED[1]]

shoe (shoo) *n.* (*pl.* **shoes, †shoon** (shoon)) 1 an outer covering for the foot, esp. one distinguished from a boot by not coming up to the ankles. 2 (*N Am.*) a boot. 3 a metallic rim or plate nailed to the hoof of a horse, ox or ass, to preserve it from wear and damage. 4 anything resembling a shoe in form or function, such as a socket, ferrule, wheel-drag or parts fitted to implements, machinery etc. to take friction, thrust etc. 5 the apparatus by which a tractor collects current from a live rail. ~*v.t.* (*pres.p.* **shoeing,** *past, p.p.* **shod** (shod)) 1 to furnish (esp. a horse) with shoes. 2 to cover at the bottom or tip. **another pair of shoes** a different matter or state of things altogether. **if the shoe fits** (*N Am.*) if the cap fits. **to be in another's shoes** to be in another's place or plight. **to die in one's shoes** to meet with a violent death, esp. by hanging. **to shake in one's shoes** SHAKE. **where the shoe pinches** where one's problem is. **shod** *a.* having shoes (*esp. in comb.*, as *dry-shod*). **shoebill, shoe-billed stork** *n.* a whale-headed stork. **shoeblack** *n.* a person earning a living by cleaning the shoes of passers-by. **shoebox** *n.* 1 a box for shoes. 2 (*coll.*) a very small space, house etc. **shoe-buckle** *n.* a buckle for fastening a shoe over the instep. **shoehorn** *n.* a device to assist one in putting on a shoe. ~*v.t.* to force into a space that is too small. **shoelace** *n.* a string of cotton etc. for fastening on a shoe. **shoe leather** *n.* 1 leather for making shoes. 2 shoes. **shoeless** *a.* **shoemaker** *n.* **shoemaking** *n.* **shoer** *n.* 1 a person who makes or puts on shoes. 2 a farrier. **shoeshine** *n.* (*esp. N Am.*) a polish on shoes. **shoe shop** *n.* **shoestring** *n.* 1 a shoelace. 2 (*coll.*) an inadequate or barely adequate sum of money. ~*a.* 1 barely adequate. 2 produced, run etc. on a minimum of capital. **shoe-tie** *n.* a shoelace. **shoe-tree** *n.* a shaped block inserted in a shoe when it is not being worn. [OE *scēo, scōh, scō* (cp. Dut. *schoen*, G *Schuh*, Icel. *skōr*, Swed. and Dan. *sko*)]

shofar (shō´fah) *n.* (*pl.* **shofars, shofroth** (-frō´)) a trumpet made from a ram's horn used in Jewish religious ceremonies and as a battle-signal in ancient times. [Heb.]

shogun (shō´gun) *n.* (*Hist.*) the hereditary commander-in-chief of the army and virtual ruler of Japan under the feudal regime, abolished in 1868. **shogunate** (-ət) *n.* [Jap., general]

shoji (shō´jē) *n.* (*pl.* **shoji, shojis**) a paper screen forming a wall or partition in a Japanese home. [Jap.]

shone SHINE.

shonky (shong´ki) *a.* (*comp.* **shonkier,** *superl.* **shonkiest**) (*Austral., sl.*) unreliable; unsound. ~*n.* (*pl.* **shonkies**) a disreputable person. **shonk** *n.* a disreputable person. [perh. Eng. dial. *shonk*, smart]

shoo (shoo) *int.* begone, be off. ~*v.t.* (*pres.p.* **shooing,** *past, p.p.* **shooed**) to drive (birds etc. away) by crying 'shoo'. ~*v.i.* to cry 'shoo'. **shoo-in** *n.* (*N Am.*) a sure thing; a certain winner. [instinctive sound]

shook[1] SHAKE.

shook[2] (shuk) *n.* 1 (*N Am.*) a set of staves and headings for a cask ready for setting up. 2 a set of boards for a box etc. ~*v.t.* to pack in shooks. [prob. var. of SHOCK[2]]

†shoon SHOE.

shoot (shoot) *v.i.* (*past, p.p.* **shot** (shot)) 1 to dart, rush or come (out, along, up etc.) swiftly. 2 to sprout, to put out buds etc. to extend in growth. 3 to protrude, to project, to jut out. 4 to discharge a missile, esp. from a firearm. 5 to hunt game etc. thus. 6 (of a ball in cricket) to dart along the ground after pitching. ~*v.t.* 1 to propel, let fly, discharge, eject or send with sudden force. 2 to cause (a bow, firearm etc.) to discharge a missile. 3 to hit, wound or kill with a missile from a bow, firearm etc. 4 to hunt thus over (ground, an estate etc.). 5 to pass swiftly through, over or down. 6 to protrude, to push out. 7 to put forth. 8 in various games, to hit or kick at a goal. 9 to take (photographs) or record (on film). 10 (*N Am., coll.*) to play a game of (pool etc.). 11 (*N Am., coll.*) to throw (a die or dice). 12 (*coll.*) in golf, to make (a specified score). 13 (*coll.*) to go through (a red traffic light). 14 to plane (a board) to produce a straight edge. ~*n.* 1 a young branch, sprout or sucker. 2 an inclined plane or trough down which water, goods etc. can slide, a chute, a rapid. 3 a place where rubbish can be shot. 4 a shooting party, match or expedition, a hunt. 5 an act or an instance of shooting. ~*int.* 1 (*esp. N Am.*) speak out! say it! 2 (*N Am., sl.*) used to express disappointment, disgust etc. **the whole shoot** (*coll.*) the whole amount, everything. **to shoot ahead** to get swiftly to the front in running, swimming etc. **to shoot a line** (*sl.*) to boast, to exaggerate. **to shoot down** 1 to destroy, kill, by shooting. 2 to defeat the argument of. **to shoot down in flames** 1 to criticize severely. 2 to defeat soundly. **to shoot from the hip** (*coll.*) to speak plainly or carelessly. **to shoot home** to hit the target or mark. **to shoot it out** (*sl.*) to fight using guns in order to settle a dispute. **to shoot one's bolt** to do all in one's power. **to shoot one's mouth off** (*sl.*) to speak boastfully or ill-advisedly. **to shoot the sun** SUN. **to shoot through** (*Austral., sl.*) to depart; to escape. **to shoot up** 1 to grow rapidly. 2 (*sl.*) to inject a drug into a vein. **3** to terrorize (an area) by shooting. **shootable** *a.* **shooter** *n.* **1** a person who or thing which shoots, *usu. in comb.*, as *six-shooter.* **2** in cricket, a ball that darts along the ground without bouncing. **3** a person who throws a die or dice. **shooting** *n.* **1** the act of discharging firearms or arrows. **2** a piece of land rented for shooting game. **3** the right to shoot over an estate etc. *~a.* moving or growing quickly. **whole shooting match** (*coll.*) everything. **shooting box** *n.* a small house or lodge for use during the shooting season. **shooting brake, shooting break** *n.* an estate car. **shooting coat** *n.* a coat worn when shooting game. **shooting gallery** *n.* a piece of ground or an enclosed space with targets and measured ranges for practice with firearms. **shooting iron** *n.* (*esp. N Am., coll.*) a firearm, esp. a revolver. **shooting jacket** *n.* a shooting coat. **shooting range** *n.* a shooting gallery. **shooting star** *n.* an incandescent meteor shooting across the sky. **shooting stick** *n.* a walking stick that may be adapted to form a seat. **shooting war** *n.* a war in which there is shooting. **shoot-out** *n.* (*coll.*) **1** a fight, esp. to the death, using guns. **2** a direct confrontation. **3** in football, a tie-breaker decided by shots at goal. [OE *scotian*, to shoot, dart, rush (intr.), *scēotan*, to shoot or throw (tr.) (cp. Dut. *schieten*, G *schiessen*, Icel. *skjōta*)]

shop (shop) *n.* **1** a building in which goods are sold by retail. **2** a building in which a manufacture, craft or repairing is carried on. **3** (*coll.*) one's business, profession etc. or talk about this. **4** (*sl.*) a berth, a job. **5** (*coll.*) an act of shopping. **6** (*coll.*) an institution, place of business etc. *~v.i.* (*pres.p.* **shopping,** *past, p.p.* **shopped**) to visit shops for the purpose of purchasing goods. *~v.t.* **1** (*sl.*) to inform against to the police. **2** (*coll.*) to discharge from employment. **all over the shop 1** (*coll.*) scattered around. **2** (*coll.*) in every place. **3** (*coll.*) wildly. **to set up shop** to start a business. **to shop around** to try several shops to find the best value. **to shut up shop** to give up doing something. **to talk shop** TALK. **shopaholic** *n.* (*coll.*) a compulsive shopper. **shop assistant** *n.* a person who serves in a retail shop. **shop bell** *n.* an automatic bell giving notice of the entry of a customer. **shop board** *n.* a bench on which work is done, esp. by tailors. **shop-bought** *a.* bought rather than made at home. **shop boy** *n.* a boy employed in a shop. **shopfitter** *n.* a person who fits shelves etc. in shops. **shopfitting** *n.* **shop floor** *n.* **1** the part of a workshop where the machinery is situated. **2** the workforce as opposed to the management. **shopfront** *n.* a shop's façade. **shop girl** *n.* a girl employed in a shop. **shopkeeper** *n.* the owner of a shop, a trader who sells goods by retail. **shopkeeping** *n.* **shopless** *a.* **shoplifter** *n.* a person who steals from a shop under pretence of purchasing. **shoplift** *v.t., v.i.* **shoplifting** *n.* **shopman** *n.* (*pl.* **shopmen**) **1** a shopkeeper or a man employed to assist in a shop. **2** a workman in a repair shop. **shopper** *n.* **1** a person who shops. **2** a bag or trolley for carrying shopping. **3** a small-wheeled bicycle. **4** (*sl.*) an informer. **shopping** *n.* **1** the act or an instance of buying goods from shops. **2** goods purchased from shops. **shopping cart** *n.* a supermarket trolley. **shopping centre,** (*N Am.*) **shopping center** *n.* an area where there are many shops. **shopping mall** *n.* a shopping centre with covered walkways. **shopping precinct** *n.* a pedestrian area containing shops. **shoppy** *a.* **1** having many shops. **2** given to talking shop. **shop-soiled** *a.* **1** dirty or faded from being displayed in a shop. **2** tarnished. **3** hackneyed. **shop steward** *n.* a trade union member elected from the workforce to represent them. **shop talk** *n.* talk about one's job. **shop-till-you-drop** *a.* of or relating to the activity of shopping pursued obsessively for its own sake. **shopwalker** *n.* a person employed in a large shop to direct customers etc. **shop window** *n.* **1** a shop's display window. **2** a place or opportunity for one to display one's talents. **shop woman** *n.* a female shopkeeper or a woman employed to assist in a shop. **shop worker** *n.* a worker in a shop. **shopworn** *a.* shop-soiled. [OE *sceoppa*, stall, booth (cp. LG *schup*, med. OHG *scopf*, whence F *échoppe*)]

shoran (shaw´ran, shor´-) *n.* a system of aircraft navigation using two radar signals. [*sho*rt *ra*nge *n*avigation]

shore[1] (shaw) *n.* **1** the land on the borders of a large body of water, the sea, a lake etc. **2** (*usu. pl.*) a country or sea coast. **3** (*Law*) the land between high- and low-water marks. **in shore** on the water near to the shore. **on shore** ashore. **shore-based** *a.* operating from a base on shore. **shorebird** *n.* a bird such as a wader which frequents the shore, esp. those of the families Charadriiformes or Scolopacidae. **shore leave** *n.* (*Naut.*) **1** permission to go on shore. **2** the period of this. **shoreless** *a.* **shoreline** *n.* the line along which water meets the shore. **shoreward** *a., adv.* **shorewards** *adv.* **shoreweed** *n.* a perennial plant, *Littorella uniflora*, which grows in shallow water. [OE *score*, from *sceran*, to SHEAR]

shore[2] (shaw) *n.* **1** a prop, a stay. **2** a support for a building or a vessel on the stocks. *~v.t.* to support or hold (up) with shores. **shoring** *n.* [ME *schore* (cp. MDut. *schōre*, Dut. *schoor*, Icel. *skortha*), etym. uncertain]

†**shore**[3], **shorn** SHEAR.

short (shawt) *a.* **1** measuring little in linear extension, not long. **2** not extended in time or duration, brief. **3** below the average in stature, not tall. **4** not coming up to a certain standard. **5** deficient, scanty, defective, in want (of). **6** breaking off abruptly. **7** brief, concise, abrupt, curt. **8** brittle, friable, crumbling or breaking easily. **9** (*coll.*) neat, undiluted. **10** (of vowels and syllables) not prolonged, unaccented. **11** not having goods, stocks etc. in hand at the time of selling. **12** (of stocks etc.) not in hand, sold. *~adv.* **1** abruptly, at once. **2** so as to be short or deficient. *~n.* **1** a short syllable or vowel, or a mark (˘) indicating that a vowel is short. **2** a short circuit. **3** a single-reel film. **4** the bran and coarse part of meal mixed together. **5** (*pl.*) knee- or thigh-length trousers; also called *pair of shorts.* **6** (*pl., chiefly N Am.*) underpants; also called *pair of shorts.* **7** a drink of, or containing, spirits. **8** (*pl.*) short-dated bonds. **9** a person who sells short on the Stock Exchange. *~v.t.* **1** to shorten. **2** to make of no effect. **3** to short-circuit. *~v.i.* to short-circuit. **at short notice** NOTICE. **for short** as an abbreviation. **in short** briefly, in few words. **in short order** (*N Am.*) straightaway. **in short supply** scarce. **in the short run** over a short period of time. **in the short term** in the short run. **long and the short of it** LONG[1]. **short and sweet** (*esp. facet.*) brief and pleasant. **short for** a shortened form of. **short of 1** deficient in; lacking. **2** less than. **3** distant from. **4** except. **short of breath** short-winded. **short on** (*coll.*) deficient in; lacking. **to be caught short** to be taken short. **to be taken short 1** (*coll.*) to feel a sudden need to urinate or defecate. **2** to be put at a disadvantage. **to bring up short** to check or pause abruptly. **to come short** to be deficient, to fail. **to cut up short** to bring up short. **to draw the short straw** STRAW. **to fall short** FALL. **to get by the short and curlies** (*coll.*) to get (someone) in one's power. **to go short** not to have enough. **to have by the short and curlies** (*coll.*) to get someone in one's power. **to make short work of** to deal with quickly and expeditiously. **to pull up short** to bring up short. **to run short** to exhaust the stock in hand (of a commodity). **to sell short 1** to sell (stocks) for future delivery. **2** to cheat. **3** to disparage. **to stop short 1** to come to a sudden stop. **2** to fail to reach the point aimed at. **shortage** (-tij) *n.* **1** a deficiency. **2** the amount of this. **short-arm** *a.* (of a blow) delivered with the arm not fully stretched. **short back and sides** *n.* a short haircut. **shortbread** *n.* a brittle, dry cake like a biscuit made with much butter and sugar. **shortcake** *n.* **1** shortbread. **2** a cake made with short pastry and containing fruit and cream in layers. **short-change** *v.t.* **1** to give too little money as change to. **2** (*sl.*) to cheat. **short change** *n.* **short circuit** *n.* an accidental crossing of two conductors carrying a current by another conductor of negligible resistance, which shortens the route of the current. **short-circuit** *v.t.* **1** to form or introduce a short circuit. **2** to dispense with intermediaries. **3** to take a short cut. **shortcoming** *n.* **1** a failure of performance of duty etc. **2** a falling short of supply, produce etc. **short commons** *n.pl.* a scanty allowance of food. **shortcrust (pastry)** *n.* a crumbly type of pastry. **short cut** *n.* **1** a shorter route than the usual. **2** a quicker way of doing something. **short date** *n.* an early date for the maturing of a bill etc. **short-dated** *a.* (of a security etc.) having only a little time to run. **short-day** *a.* (of a plant) able to flower only when exposed to short periods of daylight and long periods of darkness. **short division** *n.* the division of numbers that can be worked out in one's head rather than on paper. **short drink** *n.* a small measure of a strong alcoholic drink. **short-eared owl** *n.* a migratory owl, *Asio flammeus.* **shorten** *v.t.* **1** to make short in time, extent etc. **2** to curtail. **3** to reduce the amount of (sail spread). ~*v.i.* to become short, to contract. **shortener** *n.* **shortening** *n.* **1** making or becoming shorter. **2** fat used for making pastry. **shortfall** *n.* the amount by which something falls short, deficit. **short fuse** *n.* (*coll.*) a quick temper. **short game** *n.* in golf, play on and around the green. **shorthair** *n.* a cat of a short-haired breed. **shorthand** *n.* a system of contracted writing used for reporting etc., stenography. **shorthand typist** *n.* a typist qualified to use shorthand. **short-handed** *a.* short of workers, helpers etc. **short haul** *n.* **1** transport etc. over a short distance. **2** a short-term effort. **short head** *n.* in racing, a distance less than the length of a horse's head. **short-head** *v.t.* to beat by this length. **shorthold** *a.* (of a tenancy or lease) lasting a short fixed term. **shorthorn** *n.* an animal of a breed of cattle with short horns. **short hundredweight** *n.* (*N Am.*) a measure of weight equal to 100 lb. (about 45.4 kg). **shortie** (-ti), **shorty** *n.* (*pl.* **shorties**) (*coll.*) a shorter than average person, garment etc. **shortish** *a.* **shortlist,** (*esp. Sc.*) **short leet** *n.* a selected list of candidates from whom a final choice will be made. ~*v.t.* to put on such a list. **short-lived** (-livd′) *a.* not living or lasting long, brief. **shortly** *adv.* **short mark** *n.* a breve indicating an unstressed or short vowel. **short measure** *n.* less than the correct or promised amount. **short metre,** (*N Am.*) **short meter** *n.* a metre for hymns, four lines of 6, 6, 8, 6 syllables. **shortness** *n.* **short notice** *n.* a small length of warning time. **short odds** *n.pl.* in betting, a nearly equal chance. **short order** *n.* (*N Am.*) an order in a restaurant for food that can be prepared quickly. **short-order** *a.* **short-pitched** *a.* (of a cricket ball) pitching relatively near the bowler. **short-range** *a.* having a small range, in time or distance. **short rib** *n.* a false rib. **short score** *n.* a musical score using a small number of staves. **short sea** *n.* short broken waves. **short shrift** *n.* summary treatment. **short sight** *n.* **1** inability to see clearly at a distance, myopia. **2** lack of foresight. **short-sighted** *a.* **short-sightedly** *adv.* **short-sightedness** *n.* **short-sleeved** *a.* having sleeves reaching not below the elbow. **short-spoken** *a.* curt and abrupt in speech. **short-staffed** *a.* short-handed. **shortstop** *n.* in baseball, a fielder between second and third base. **short story** *n.* a story that is not as long as a novel. **short suit** *n.* in cards, a suit of which one has fewer than four cards. **short supply** *n.* general shortage of a commodity. **short temper** *n.* **short-tempered** *a.* having little self-control, irascible. **short-term** *a.* of or covering a short period of time. **short-termism** *n.* concentrating on short-term gain. **short time** *n.* the condition of working fewer than the normal number of hours per week. **short title** *n.* an abbreviated title. **short ton** *n.* (*N Am.*) a measure of weight equal to 2000 lb. (907.18 kg). **short view** *n.* a view only of the present. **short waist** *n.* **1** a high waist of a dress. **2** a short upper body. **short-waisted** *a.* (of a dress) having the waist high up. **short wave** *n.* a radio wave of between 10 and 100 metres wavelength. **short weight** *n.* weight less than it should be. **short whist** *n.* a short form of whist. **short wind** *n.* breath that is quickly exhausted. **short-winded** (-win′-) *a.* **1** easily put out of breath. **2** incapable of sustained effort. **3** (of writing) terse. **short-windedness** *n.* **shorty** SHORTIE (under SHORT). [OE *sceort*, cogn. with SHEAR (cp. L *curtus*, CURT, Gr. *keirein*, to cut)]

shot[1] (shot) *n.* **1** a missile for a firearm, esp. a solid or non-explosive projectile. **2** the act of shooting. **3** the discharge of a missile from a firearm or other weapon. **4** an attempt to hit an object with such a missile. **5** a photographic exposure. **6** the film taken between the starting and stopping of a cine-camera. **7** (*coll.*) an injection by hypodermic needle. **8** a stroke at various games. **9** an attempt to guess etc. **10** the distance reached by a missile, the range of a firearm, bow etc. **11** a marksman. **12** (*pl.* **shot, shots**) a small lead pellet, a quantity of which is used in a charge or cartridge for shooting game. **13** a remark aimed at someone. **14** (*coll.*) a drink of esp. spirits. ~*v.t.* (*pres.p.* **shotting,** *past, p.p.* **shotted**) to load or weight with shot. **big shot** BIG. **like a shot** immediately, eagerly. **not a shot in one's locker** LOCKER. **not by a long shot** LONG[1]. **to get shot of** (*coll.*) to get rid of. **to give it one's best shot** (*coll.*) to try one's very best. **to have shot one's bolt** to be unable to take further action. **to make a bad shot** to guess incorrectly. **shot across the bows** *n.* a warning. **shotbelt** *n.* a belt with pouches etc. for carrying shot. **shot-blasting** *n.* cleaning using a stream of shot. **shot-blast** *v.t.* **shot-firer** *n.* a person who fires a blasting-charge. **shotgun** *n.* a light gun for firing small shot. ~*a.* enforced. **shotgun marriage, shotgun wedding** *n.* (*coll.*) a hurried wedding esp. because the bride is pregnant. **shot-hole** *n.* a hole made by a shot. **shot in the arm** *n.* (*coll.*) **1** a hypodermic injection. **2** something which encourages or invigorates. **shot in the dark** *n.* a random guess. **shotproof** *a.* impenetrable to shot. **shot-put** *n.* an athletic contest in which a shot is thrown. **shot-putter** *n.* **shot-putting** *n.* **shot-tower** *n.* (*Hist.*) a tower in which shot is made by pouring molten lead through a rotating sieve at the top and letting it fall into water at the bottom. **shot-window** *n.* a window projecting from a wall. [OE *gesceot*, from *scēotan*, to SHOOT]

shot[2] (shot) *a.* **1** that has been shot. **2** (of fabric) having a changeable colour. **shot silk** *n.* silk with warp and weft of different colours, chatoyant silk. [p.p. of SHOOT]

shot[3] (shot) *n.* a reckoning, a bill. [var. of SCOT]

shot[4] SHOOT.

shotten (shot′ən) *a.* (of a herring etc.) having ejected the spawn. **shotten herring** *n.* **1** a herring that has spawned. **2** †a weakened or dispirited person. [old p.p. of SHOOT]

should SHALL.

shoulder (shōl′də) *n.* **1** the part of the body at which the arm, foreleg or wing is attached to the trunk. **2** one's power to sustain burdens, responsibility etc. **3** (*pl.*) the upper part of the back. **4** the forequarter of an animal cut up as meat. **5** anything resembling a shoulder. **6** a projecting part of a mountain, tool etc. **7** the obtuse angle formed by the face and flank of a bastion. **8** the verge of a road. ~*v.t.* **1** to push with the shoulder. **2** to jostle, to make (one's way) thus. **3** to take on one's shoulders. **4** to accept (a responsibility). **5** to carry vertically (a rifle etc.) at the side of the body. ~*v.i.* to make one's way by jostling. **shoulder to shoulder** 1 (standing in rank) with shoulders nearly touching. 2 with hearty cooperation, with mutual effort. **straight from the shoulder** STRAIGHT. **to give someone the cold shoulder** (*coll.*) to shun or snub someone. **to put one's shoulder to the wheel** to set to work enthusiastically or in earnest. **to rub shoulders with** RUB[1]. **to set one's shoulder to the wheel** to put one's shoulder to the wheel. **to shoulder arms** to hold a rifle with the barrel against one's shoulder. **shoulder bag** *n.* a bag worn over the shoulder. **shoulder-belt** *n.* a baldric, bandolier etc. passing across the shoulder. **shoulder blade, shoulder bone** *n.* the scapula. **shouldered** *a.* having shoulders, *usu. in comb.*, as *broad-shouldered.* **shoulder-high** *a.*, *adv.* up to the shoulders. **shoulder holster** *n.* a gun holster worn in the armpit. **shoulder joint** *n.* the place where the upper arm joins the collarbone and blade-bone. **shoulder-knot** *n.* an ornamental knot of ribbons etc. worn on the shoulder by livery servants. **shoulder-length** *a.* (of hair) down to one's shoulders. **shoulder loop** *n.* (*N Am.*) a shoulder strap worn on a uniform to show rank. **shoulder mark** *n.* (*N Am.*) a badge of rank worn on the shoulder by a naval officer. **shoulder note** *n.* (*Print.*) a note at the upper outside corner of a page. **shoulder-of-mutton sail** *n.* a triangular fore-and-aft sail with a boom at the bottom. **shoulder pad** *n.* a pad sewn into the shoulder of a garment. **shoulder strap** *n.* 1 a strap worn over the shoulder, esp. by soldiers, bearing the initials or number of the regiment etc. 2 either one of two strips of cloth that suspend a garment from the shoulders. 3 a strap of a bag. [OE *sculdor* (cp. Dut. *schouder*, G *Schulter*, Swed. *skuldra*), etym. uncertain]

†**shouldest,** †**shouldst** SHALL.

shouldn't (shud´ənt) *contr.* should not.

shout (showt) *n.* 1 a loud, vehement and sudden call or outcry of joy, triumph or the like. 2 (*coll.*) a round of drinks; one's turn to buy this. ~*v.i.* 1 to utter a loud cry or call. 2 to speak at the top of one's voice. 3 (*Austral.*, *coll.*) to buy a round of drinks. ~*v.t.* 1 to utter with a shout. 2 to say at the top of one's voice. 3 (*Austral.*, *coll.*) to buy or stand someone (a drink). **all over bar the shouting** (*coll.*) virtually decided. **to shout down** to silence or render inaudible by shouting. **to shout for** to call for by shouting. **to shout from the rooftops** ROOFTOP (under ROOF). **to shout the odds** ODD. **shouter** *n.* **shout-up** *n.* (*coll.*) a noisy argument. [etym. uncertain]

shove (shŭv) *v.t.* 1 to push, to move forcibly along. 2 to push against, to jostle. 3 (*coll.*) to put. ~*v.i.* 1 to push. 2 to make one's way (along etc.) by pushing. 3 to jostle. ~*n.* 1 a strong or hard push. 2 an act of prompting into action. **to shove off** 1 to push off from the shore etc. 2 (*sl.*) to go away. **shove-halfpenny** *n.* a game in which coins are slid over a flat board which is marked off into sections. [OE *scūfan*, cp. Dut. *schuiven*, G *schieven*, Icel. *skūfa*]

shovel (shŭv´əl) *n.* 1 an implement consisting of a wide blade or scoop with a handle, used for shifting loose material. 2 a machine with a similar function. ~*v.t.* (*pres.p.* **shovelling,** (*N Am.*) **shoveling,** *past*, *p.p.* **shovelled,** (*N Am.*) **shoveled**) 1 to shift, gather together or take up and throw with a shovel. 2 (*coll.*) to move (esp. food) roughly. **shovelful** *n.* (*pl.* **shovelfuls**). **shovel hat** *n.* a hat with a broad brim turned up at the sides, worn by Anglican clergy. **shovelhead** *n.* the shark *Sphyrna tibura*; also called *bonnethead.* **shoveller,** (*N Am.*) **shoveler** *n.* 1 a person who shovels. 2 (*also* **shoveler**) the spoonbill duck, *Anas clypeata.* **shovelnose** *n.* the freshwater sturgeon, *Scaphirhynchus platorhyncus*, which has a snout like a shovel. [OE *scofl* (*scof-*, base of SHOVE)]

shovelboard (shŭv´əlbawd) *n.* a game played (now usu. on a ship's deck) by shoving wooden discs with the hand or a mace towards marked compartments. [orig. *shoveboard*]

show (shō), †**shew** *v.t.* (*past* **showed,** †**shewed,** *p.p.* **shown** (shōn), †**shewn,** †**showed,** †**shewed**) 1 to cause or allow to be seen, to disclose, to offer to view, to exhibit, to expose, to reveal. 2 to give, to bestow, to offer. 3 to make clear, to point out, to explain, to demonstrate, to prove. 4 to cause (a person) to see or understand. 5 to conduct (round or over a house etc.). ~*v.i.* 1 to become visible or noticeable, to appear. 2 to have a specific appearance. 3 (*N Am.*) to finish third or in the first three in a race. ~*n.* 1 the act of showing. 2 outward appearance, semblance, pretence. 3 display, ostentation, parade, pomp. 4 a spectacle, a pageant, a display, an entertainment, an exhibition, esp. one of a petty kind shown for money. 5 (*coll.*) an opportunity, a chance, a concern, a business. 6 (*Med.*) a discharge from the vagina marking the start of childbirth. **bad show!** BAD. **good show!** GOOD. **nothing to show for** no visible result of (one's efforts etc.). **on show** being displayed. **to give someone a fair show** to let someone have a chance. **to give the (whole) show away** 1 to let out the real nature of something pretentious. 2 to blab. **to run the show** RUN. **to show a clean pair of heels** HEEL[1]. **to show a leg** LEG. **to show around** (*N Am.*) to show round. **to show cause** (*Law*) to allege with justification. **to show fight** not to give in without resistance. †**to show forth** to display, to make manifest. **to show in** to lead in. **to show off** 1 to set off, to show to advantage. 2 (*coll.*) to make a display of oneself, one's talents etc. **to show one's cards** to show one's hand. **to show one's colours** COLOUR. **to show oneself** 1 to appear in public. 2 to exhibit oneself (to be). **to show one's face** FACE. **to show one's hand** HAND. **to show one's teeth** TOOTH. **to show out** to lead out. **to show round** to guide round. **to show the door** DOOR. **to show the flag** FLAG[1]. **to show the way** to show what has to be done, which way to go etc. by leading. **to show the white feather** FEATHER. **to show through** 1 to be visible through. 2 to be revealed inadvertently. **to show up** 1 to expose. 2 to be clearly visible. 3 to be present. 4 (*coll.*) to embarrass or humiliate. **to show willing** WILLING. **showband** *n.* 1 a jazz band. 2 a band playing cover versions of popular songs. **showbiz** *n.* (*coll.*) show business. **showboat** *n.* (*N Am.*) a steamboat fitted as a theatre. **showbread, shewbread** *n.* 12 loaves (one for each tribe) displayed by the Jewish priests in the Temple, and renewed every Sabbath. **show business** *n.* (*coll.*) the entertainment industry, theatre, television, cinema. **showcard** *n.* an advertising card. **showcase** *n.* 1 a glass case for exhibiting specimens, articles on sale etc. 2 a place where something is presented. ~*v.t.* to display in or as in a showcase. **showdown** *n.* 1 an open or final confrontation. 2 in poker, putting one's cards face up on the table. **shower**[1] *n.* **showgirl** *n.* an actress working in variety theatre. **showground** *n.* a piece of land where a show is staged. **show house, show home** *n.* one of a group of new houses, open to the public as an example of the type. **showing** *n.* **showjumping** *n.* competitive riding over a set course containing obstacles. **showjump** *v.i.* **showjumper** *n.* **showman** *n.* (*pl.* **showmen**) 1 the manager or proprietor of a menagerie, circus etc. 2 a person skilled in publicizing esp. themselves. **showmanship** *n.* 1 the showman's art. 2 the ability to display goods etc. most attractively. **show-off** *n.* (*coll.*) a person who shows off, an exhibitionist. **show of force** *n.* a demonstration of willingness to use force. **show of hands** *n.* the raising of hands in voting. **showpiece** *n.* a particularly fine specimen, used for display. **showplace** *n.* a place tourists etc. go to see. **showroom** *n.* a room where goods are set out for inspection. **show-stopper** *n.* (*coll.*)

a performance where the audience applaud for such a long time that the show is interrupted. **show-stopping** *a.* **show trial** *n.* a judicial trial to demonstrate a state's power. **show-window** *n.* **showy** *a.* (*comp.* **showier,** *superl.* **showiest**) ostentatious, gaudy. **showily** *adv.* **showiness** *n.* [OE *scēawian*, to see, to point out (cp. Dut. *schouwen*, G *schauen*, Dan. *skue*), cogn. with L *cavēre*, to take heed, Gr. *koein*, to observe]

shower[1] SHOW.

shower[2] (show´ə) *n.* **1** a fall of rain, hail or snow of short duration. **2** a brief fall of arrows, bullets etc. **3** a copious supply (of). **4** a shower-bath. **5** (*chiefly N Am.*) a party (e.g. for a bride-to-be or expectant mother) at which gifts are given. **6** (*sl., derog.*) a collection of (inferior etc.) people. **7** a group of particles caused by a cosmic-ray particle colliding with a particle in the earth's atmosphere. ~*v.t.* **1** to sprinkle or wet with a shower. **2** to discharge or deliver in a shower. ~*v.i.* **1** to fall in a shower. **2** to have a shower. **shower-bath** *n.* a bath in which a stream of water is sprayed over the body. **showerless** *a.* **showerproof** *a.* **showery** *a.* **showeriness** *n.* [OE *scūr*, cp. Dut. *schoer*, G *Schauer*, Icel. *skūr*]

shown SHOW.

s.h.p. *abbr.* shaft horsepower.

shrank SHRINK.

shrapnel (shrap´nəl) *n.* **1** bullets enclosed in a shell with a small charge for bursting in front of the enemy and spreading in a shower. **2** shell-splinters from a high-explosive shell. [Gen. Henry *Shrapnel*, 1761–1842, English inventor]

shred (shred) *n.* **1** a piece torn off. **2** a strip, a rag, a fragment, a bit, a tiny particle. ~*v.t.* (*pres.p.* **shredding,** *past, p.p.* **shredded, shred**) to tear or cut into shreds. **to tear to shreds** to completely refute or demolish (an argument). **shredder** *n.* **shredding** *n.* **shreddy** *a.* **shredless** *a.* [OE *screade* (cp. MDut. *schroode*, G *Schrot*), doublet of SCREED]

shrew (shroo) *n.* **1** a small mouselike mammal of the family Soricidae. **2** a bad-tempered, scolding woman, a virago. **shrewish** *a.* **shrewishly** *adv.* **shrewishness** *n.* **shrew mole** *n.* a N American mole such as *Neurotrichus gibbsi*. **shrewmouse** *n.* (*pl.* **shrewmice**) a shrew, esp. the common shrew. [OE *scrēawa*, shrew-mouse]

shrewd (shrood) *a.* **1** astute, sagacious, discerning. **2** †wicked, vixenish, shrewish, troublesome, spiteful. **3** †sharp to the senses, biting. **shrewdly** *adv.* **shrewdness** *n.* [ME *schrewed*, p.p. of *schrewen*, to curse, as SHREW]

shriek (shrēk) *v.i.* **1** to utter a sharp, shrill, inarticulate cry, to scream, to screech, as in a sudden fright. **2** to laugh wildly. ~*v.t.* **1** to utter with a shriek. **2** to reveal blatantly. ~*n.* a sharp, shrill, inarticulate cry. **to shriek of** to give a clear indication of, to reveal blatantly. **to shriek out** to utter in a shriek. **to shriek with laughter** to laugh uncontrollably. **shrieker** *n.* [var. of SCREECH]

shrieval (shrē´vəl) *a.* of or relating to a sheriff. **shrievalty** (-ti) *n.* (*pl.* **shrievalties**) **1** the office or jurisdiction of a sheriff. **2** the tenure of this. [obs. *shrieve*, SHERIFF, *-alty*, as in COMMONALTY]

shrift (shrift) *n.* **1** †confession to a priest. **2** †absolution, esp. of one about or appointed to die. **short shrift** SHORT. [OE *scrift*, from *scrīfan*, to SHRIVE]

shrike (shrīk) *n.* a bird of the family Laniidae, especially the butcher-bird, feeding on insects and small birds and having the habit of impaling them on thorns for future use. [OE *scrīc*, cp. SCREECH, from its cry]

shrill (shril) *a.* **1** high-pitched and piercing in tone, sharp, acute. **2** noisy, importunate. ~*n.* a shrill sound. ~*v.i.* **1** to utter a piercing sound. **2** to sound shrilly. ~*v.t.* to cause to utter in a shrill tone. **shrillness** *n.* **shrilly** *adv.* [cp. SKIRL, LG *schrell*, G dial. *schrill*]

shrimp (shrimp) *n.* (*pl. in general* **shrimp,** *in particular* **shrimps**) **1** a slender long-tailed edible crustacean, allied to the prawn. **2** (*coll.*) a very small person. ~*v.i.* to fish for shrimps. **shrimper** *n.* **shrimp plant** *n.* an evergreen shrub, *Justicia brandegeana*, with small white flowers. [cogn. with SCRIMP and SHRINK]

shrine (shrīn) *n.* **1** a chest or casket in which sacred relics were deposited. **2** a tomb, altar, chapel etc. of special sanctity. **3** a place hallowed by its associations. **4** a Shinto place of worship. ~*v.t.* (*poet.*) to place in a shrine. [OE *scrīn*, L *scrīnium*, writing-chest, cogn. with *scrībere*, to write]

shrink (shringk) *v.i.* (*past* **shrank** (shrangk), *p.p.* **shrunk** (shrŭngk), **shrunken** (-kən)) **1** to grow smaller, to contract, to shrivel. **2** to give way, to recoil. **3** to flinch. ~*v.t.* to cause to shrink, to make smaller. ~*n.* **1** shrinkage, shrinking. **2** (*sl.*) a psychiatrist. **to shrink into oneself** to become withdrawn. **to shrink on** to put (a tyre etc.) on in a heated condition so that it may become firmly fixed in contracting. **shrinkable** *a.* **shrinkage** (-ij) *n.* **1** the process of shrinking, a shrunken condition. **2** the amount of this. **3** a deduction from one's takings to allow for loss. **shrinker** *n.* **shrinking** *a.* **shrinkingly** *adv.* **shrinking violet** *n.* (*coll.*) a shy, hesitant person. **shrink-proof** *a.* **shrink-resistant** *a.* resistant to shrinkage. **shrink-wrap** *v.t.* (*pres.p.* **shrink-wrapping,** *past, p.p.* **shrink-wrapped**) to wrap in plastic film, which is then shrunk, e.g. by heating, to make a tight-fitting, sealed package. ~*n.* such plastic film. **shrunken** (-ən) *a.* [OE *scrincan*, cp. MDut. *schrinken*, Swed. *skrynka*]

Usage note In standard English, the past tense of *shrink* is *shrank*, not *shrunk*.

†**shrive** (shrīv) *v.t.* (*past* **shrove** (shrōv), *p.p.* **shriven** (shriv´ən)) **1** to receive the confession of. **2** to confess, impose penance on and absolve. **3** to confess (oneself) and receive absolution. ~*v.i.* to confess, impose penance and administer absolution. **shriver** *n.* a confessor. [OE *scrīfan*, from L *scrībere*, to write]

shrivel (shriv´əl) *v.i.* (*pres.p.* **shrivelling,** (*N Am.*) **shriveling,** *past, p.p.* **shrivelled,** (*N Am.*) **shriveled**) to contract, to wither, to become wrinkled. ~*v.t.* to cause to contract or become wrinkled. [cogn. with Swed. dial. *skryvla*]

shriven SHRIVE.

shroud (shrowd) *n.* **1** a winding sheet. **2** anything that covers or conceals. **3** (*pl.*) ropes extending from the lower mast-heads to the sides of the ship, serving to steady the masts. **4** the ropes from a parachute to its burden. ~*v.t.* **1** to dress for the grave. **2** to cover, disguise or conceal. **shroud-laid** *a.* (of a rope) having four strands laid right-handed on a core. **shroudless** *a.* [OE *scrūd* (cp. Icel. *skrūth*, Dan., Norw. and Swed. *skrud*), cogn. with SHRED]

shrove SHRIVE.

Shrovetide (shrōv´tīd) *n.* the period before Lent, when people formerly went to confession and afterwards made merry. **Shrove Tuesday** *n.* the day before Ash Wednesday. [cp. OE *scrīfan*, to shrive]

shrub[1] (shrŭb) *n.* a woody plant smaller than a tree, with branches proceeding directly from the ground without any supporting trunk. **shrubbery** *n.* (*pl.* **shrubberies**) a plantation of shrubs. **shrubby** *a.* (*comp.* **shrubbier,** *superl.* **shrubbiest**). **shrubbiness** *n.* **shrubless** *a.* [OE *scrybb*, cp. Norw. *skrubba*, SCRUB[2]]

shrub[2] (shrŭb) *n.* a drink composed of the sweetened juice of lemons or other fruit with spirit. [Arab. *sharāb* or *shurb*, drink; see SHERBET]

shrug (shrŭg) *v.t.* (*pres.p.* **shrugging,** *past, p.p.* **shrugged**) to draw up (the shoulders) to express dislike, doubt etc. ~*v.i.* to draw up the shoulders. ~*n.* this gesture. **to shrug off 1** to disregard, to ignore. **2** to throw off, to get rid of. [cp. Dan. *skrugge*, Swed. *skrukka*, cogn. with SHRINK]

shrunk, shrunken SHRINK.

shtick (shtik), **schtick, schtik** *n.* (*sl.*) a comedian's or performer's routine, patter etc. [Yiddish]

shtook (shtuk), **schtook, schtuck, shtuck** *n.* (*sl.*) trouble, bother. **in shtook** in trouble. [etym. unknown]

shtoom (shtum), **schtoom, shtum, shtumm** *a.* (*sl.*) quiet, silent. **to keep shtoom** to keep quiet. [Yiddish]

shtuck SHTOOK.

shubunkin (shubŭng´kin) *n.* a type of large-finned goldfish. [Jap.]

shuck (shŭk) *n.* (*chiefly N Am.*) **1** a shell, husk or pod. **2** (*pl.*) something utterly valueless. *~v.t.* to remove the shell etc. from. **to shuck off** to strip off. **shucker** *n.* **shucks** *int.* (*coll.*) used to express contempt, annoyance, embarrassment etc. [etym. uncertain]

shudder (shŭd´ə) *v.i.* **1** to shiver suddenly as with fear. **2** to tremble, to quake, to shrink. **3** to vibrate. *~n.* a sudden shiver or trembling. **the shudders** (*coll.*) a state of shuddering. **shudderingly** *adv.* **shuddery** *a.* [ME *schuderen*, cp. MDut. *schudden*, EFris. *schüdden*, G *schüttern*]

shuffle (shŭf´əl) *v.t.* **1** to shift or shove to and fro or from one to another. **2** to move (cards) over each other so as to mix them up. **3** to mix (up), to throw into disorder. **4** to put aside, to throw (off). **5** to put or throw (on) hastily. *~v.i.* **1** to change the relative positions of cards in a pack. **2** to shift ground. **3** to prevaricate. **4** to move (along) with a dragging gait. *~n.* **1** the act of shuffling. **2** a shuffling movement of the feet etc. **3** the shuffling of cards. **4** a mix-up, a general change of position. **5** an evasive or prevaricating piece of conduct. **to shuffle the cards** to change policy etc. **shuffle-board** *n.* (*N Am.*) SHOVELBOARD. **shuffler** *n.* **shufflingly** *adv.* [var. of SCUFFLE; cp. LG *schuffeln*]

shufti (shŭf´ti, shuf´-), **shufty** *n.* (*pl.* **shuftis, shufties**) (*sl.*) a (quick) look (at something). [Arab.]

shul (shool) *n.* a synagogue. [Yiddish]

shun (shŭn) *v.t.* (*pres.p.* **shunning,** *past, p.p.* **shunned**) to avoid, to eschew, to keep clear of. [OE *scunian*, etym. uncertain]

'shun (shŭn) *int.* (*Mil.*) short for ATTENTION.

shunt (shŭnt) *v.t.* **1** to turn (a train etc.) on to a side track. **2** to get rid of, suppress or defer discussion or consideration of. **3** to get (a person) out of the way, or keep (a person) inactive. *~v.i.* (of a train etc.) to turn off on to a side track. *~n.* **1** the act of shunting. **2** a conductor joining two points of a circuit through which part of an electric current may be diverted. **3** a passage connecting two blood vessels, diverting blood from one to the other. **4** (*sl.*) a car crash. **shunter** *n.* [ME *shunten*, OE *scyndan*, to hasten]

shush (shush, shŭsh) *int.* used to call for silence. *~v.i.* to be quiet. *~v.t.* to make quiet. *~n.* an utterance of 'shush' to call for silence. [redupl. of SH]

shut (shŭt) *v.t.* (*pres.p.* **shutting,** *past, p.p.* **shut**) **1** to close by means of a door, lid, cover etc. **2** to cause (a door, lid, cover etc.) to close an aperture. **3** to keep (in or out) by closing a door. **4** to bar (out), to exclude, to keep from entering or participating in. **5** to bring (teeth etc.) together. *~v.i.* **1** to become closed. **2** (of teeth, scissor-blades etc.) to come together. **to be shut of** (*sl.*) to be rid of. **to get shut of** (*sl.*) to get rid of. **to shut down 1** to pull or push down (a window-sash etc.). **2** (of a factory) to stop working. **3** to stop (a factory etc.) from operating. **to shut in 1** to confine. **2** to encircle. **3** to prevent egress or prospect from. **to shut off 1** to stop the inflow or escape of (gas etc.) by closing a tap etc. **2** to separate. **to shut one's eyes to** EYE[1]. **to shut one's heart to** to refuse to or pretend not to feel sympathy for. **to shut one's mind to** MIND. **to shut out 1** to exclude, to bar. **2** to prevent the possibility of. **3** to block from the memory. **4** (*N Am.*) to prevent from scoring. **to shut the door on** to prevent the possibility of. **to shut to 1** to close (a door). **2** (of a door) to shut. **to shut up 1** to close all the doors, windows etc. of (a house). **2** to close and fasten up (a box etc.). **3** to put away in a box etc. **4** to confine. **5** (*coll.*) to stop, to make an end. **6** to confute, to silence. **to shut up shop** SHOP. **shutdown** *n.* **shut-eye** *n.* (*coll.*) sleep. **shut-off** *n.* **1** something used for stopping an operation. **2** cessation. **shutout** *n.* (*N Am.*) the act of preventing an opponent from scoring. **shut-out bid** *n.* in bridge, a pre-emptive bid. **shut up!** *int.* be quiet!, stop talking! **shut your face!, shut your head!, shut your mouth!, shut your trap!** *int.* (*sl.*) shut up! [OE *scyttan*, cogn. with SHOOT, from shooting the bolt]

shutter (shŭt´ə) *n.* **1** a person who or thing which shuts. **2** a cover of wooden battens or panels or metal slats for sliding, folding, rolling or otherwise fastening over a window to exclude light, burglars etc. **3** a device for admitting and cutting off light to a photographic lens. **4** a device in a camera which allows exposure of the film for a predetermined period. **5** a contrivance for closing the swell-box of an organ. *~v.t.* **1** to put up the shutters of. **2** to provide or fit with a shutter or shutters. **to put up the shutters** to cease business. **shuttering** *n.* **1** temporary support for concrete work. **2** material used for shutters. **shutterless** *a.* [as SHUT]

shuttle (shŭt´əl) *n.* **1** a boat-shaped contrivance enclosing a bobbin, used by weavers for passing the thread of the weft between the threads of the warp. **2** the sliding holder carrying the lower thread for making lock-stitches in a sewing machine. **3** a shuttle service. **4** a vehicle used on a shuttle service or one that goes between two points. **5** a space shuttle. *~v.i.* to move or travel regularly between two points or places. *~v.t.* to cause to move in this way. **shuttle armature** *n.* an H-shaped armature used in direct-current motors. **shuttle diplomacy** *n.* negotiations by a mediator travelling between two heads of state etc. **shuttle service** *n.* transport service running to and fro between two points. **shuttlewise** *adv.* [OE *scyttel*, bolt, cogn. with SHUT and SHOOT]

shuttlecock (shŭt´əlkok) *n.* **1** a light cone-shaped object with feathered flights, used in the games of battledore and badminton. **2** anything repeatedly passed to and fro.

shy[1] (shī) *a.* (*comp.* **shyer, shier,** *superl.* **shyest, shiest**) **1** easily frightened, fearful, timid. **2** bashful, coy, shrinking from approach or familiarity. **3** wary, cautious, suspicious. **4** circumspect, careful, watchful (of). **5** difficult to secure, understand etc., elusive. *~adv.* (*coll.*) short of, lacking. *~v.i.* (*3rd pers. sing. pres.* **shies,** *pres.p.* **shying,** *past, p.p.* **shied**) **1** (of a horse) to start or turn aside suddenly. **2** to shrink from. *~n.* (*pl.* **shies**) the act of shying. **-shy** *comb. form* showing reluctance or aversion, as in *work-shy*. **shyer**[1] *n.* **shyly** *adv.* **shyness** *n.* [OE *scēoh*, cp. Dan. *shy*, Dut. *schuw*, G *scheu*]

shy[2] (shī) *v.t., v.i.* (*3rd pers. sing. pres.* **shies,** *pres.p.* **shying,** *past, p.p.* **shied**) (*coll.*) to fling, to throw. *~n.* (*pl.* **shies**) **1** the act of shying. **2** a try, an attempt. **to have a shy at 1** (*coll.*) to try to hit with an object. **2** (*coll.*) to try. **3** (*coll.*) to jeer at. **shyer**[2] *n.* [etym. uncertain]

shyer[1] SHY[1].

shyer[2] SHY[2].

Shylock (shī´lok) *n.* a miser; a ruthless creditor or money-lender. [character in Shakespeare's *The Merchant of Venice*]

shyster (shī´stə) *n.* (*esp. N Am.*) **1** a tricky or disreputable lawyer. **2** (*coll.*) a tricky person. [etym. uncertain]

SI *abbr.* **1** (Order of the) Star of India. **2** *Système International* (*d'Unités*), the now universally used system of scientific units, the basic units of which are the metre, second, kilogram, ampere, kelvin, candela and mole.

Si *chem. symbol* silicon.

si (sē) *n.* (*Mus.*) te. [perh. from initials of *Sanctus Johannes*, see GAMUT]

sial (sī´əl) *n.* the outer layer of the earth's crust, rock rich in silicon and aluminium. **sialic**[1] (sīal´ik) *a.* [*si*licon, *al*uminium]

sial- SIALO-.

sialagogue SIALOGOGUE.

sialic[1] SIAL.

sialic[2] (sīal´ik) *a.* of or relating to saliva. [as SIALO-]

sialo- (sī´əlō), **sial-** *comb. form* saliva. [Gr. *sialon*, saliva]

sialogogue (sī´ələgog), **sialagogue** *n.* (*Med.*) a drug or other substance that stimulates the flow of saliva. **sialogogic** (-goj´ik) *a.*

sialoid (sī´əloid) *a.* resembling saliva.

sialorrhoea (sīələrē´ə), (*N Am.*) **sialorrhea** *n.* excessive flow of saliva.

siamang (sī´əmang) *n.* a large gibbon of the Malay peninsula and Sumatra. [Malay]

Siamese (sīəmēz´) *a.* of or relating to Siam, now Thailand, a country of SE Asia, or to its inhabitants or their language. ~*n.* **1** (*pl.* **Siamese**) a native or inhabitant of Siam, now a Thai. **2** the language of Siam, now Thai. **3** (*pl.* **Siameses**) a Siamese cat. **Siamese cat** *n.* a breed of cat with blue eyes and dark-coloured ears, face, tail and paws. **Siamese fighting fish** *n.* a colourful freshwater fish, *Betta splendens*, of SE Asia, the male of which has sail-like fins and is highly aggressive. **Siamese twins** *n.pl.* identical twins born joined together at some part of the body.

SIB *abbr.* Securities and Investments Board.

sib (sib) *n.* **1** a brother or sister. **2** any blood relative. **3** those regarded as blood relatives, kindred. ~*a.* (*esp. Sc.*) related, akin (to). **sibling** (-ling) *n.* each of two or more children that have one or both parents in common. **sibship** *n.* **1** the circumstance of being children of the same two parents. **2** a group of children that have the same two parents. [OE, from *sib*, *sibb*, relationship, peace (cp. Icel. *sif*, G *Sippe*, affinity)]

sibilant (sib´ilənt) *a.* **1** hissing. **2** (of a letter of the alphabet etc.) having a hissing sound. ~*n.* a letter which is pronounced with a hissing sound, as *s* or *z*. **sibilance, sibilancy** *n.* **sibilantly** *adv.* **sibilate** *v.t.*, *v.i.* **sibilation** (-ā´shən) *n.* [L *sībilans -ntem*, pres.p. of *sībilāre*, from *sībilus*, a hissing, prob. imit. in orig.]

sibling SIB.

sibyl (sib´il) *n.* **1** (*also* **Sibyl**) one of a number of women who prophesied in ancient times under the supposed inspiration of a deity. **2** a prophetess, a sorceress. **3** a fortune-teller, a gypsy, an old hag. **sibylline** (-īn) *a.* **1** of or relating to, or composed or uttered by, a sibyl. **2** prophetic, oracular, cryptic, mysterious. **Sibylline Books, Sibylline Oracles** *n.pl.* a collection of oracles of mysterious origin preserved by the ancient Romans and consulted by the senate in times of disaster or emergency. **sibyllism** *n.* **sibyllist** *n.* **sibyllistic** (-lis´-) *a.* [L *Sibylla*, Gr. *Sibulla*]

sic[1] (sik) *a.*, *adv.*, *pron.* (*Sc.*) such.

sic[2] (sēk, sik) *adv.* thus, so (usu. printed after a doubtful word or phrase to indicate that it is quoted exactly as in the original). [L]

sic[3] SICK[2].

Sicanian (sikā´niən) *n.* a native or inhabitant of Sicily, esp. any of the aboriginal inhabitants of Sicily at the time of Greek colonization. ~*a.* of or relating to the Sicanians. [L *Sīcanius*, from *Sicāni*, pl., Gr. *Sikanoi*]

siccative (sik´ətiv) *a.* drying, causing to dry. ~*n.* a siccative substance, esp. one used with oil paint. [late L *siccātivus*, from L *siccāre*, to dry, from *siccus*, dry]

sice[1] (sīs) *n.* the number six on dice. [OF *sis*, SIX]

sice[2] SYCE.

Sicilian (sisil´yən) *a.* of or relating to Sicily, an island off S Italy, or its inhabitants. ~*n.* a native or inhabitant of Sicily. **siciliana** (-siliah´nə), **siciliano** (-ah´nō) *n.* (*pl.* **sicilianas, sicilianos**) **1** a graceful dance of the Sicilian peasantry. **2** the music (in 6/8 time) for this. **Sicilian Vespers** *n.pl.* a great massacre of the French in Sicily, which began at the first stroke of the vesper bell on Easter Monday in 1282. **sicilienne** (-ien´) *n.* **1** a fine ribbed silk or poplin. **2** (*Mus.*) a siciliana.

sick[1] (sik) *a.* **1** ill, affected by some disease, in bad health. **2** affected with nausea, inclined to vomit. **3** disgusted, feeling disturbed, upset. **4** pining or longing (for). **5** mentally ill, or having a warped personality. **6** tired (of). **7** (of a ship) needing repair. **8** (of a room, quarters etc.) set apart for sick people. **9** (of humour) macabre, cruel, referring to subjects not usu. considered suitable for jokes. **10** tending to cause sickness. ~*n.* (*coll.*) vomit. ~*v.t.* (*coll.*) to vomit (up) (food etc.). **sick and tired of** bored and exhausted by, fed up with. **sick to/ at one's stomach 1** (*chiefly N Am.*) affected with nausea, vomiting. **2** (*chiefly N Am.*) disgusted, revolted. **the sick** those who are ill. **to be sick** to vomit. **to feel sick** to feel like being sick. **to go sick** to be absent from one's work or duties through illness (real or claimed). **to look sick** (*coll.*) to be outranked or outshone, to be deficient in comparison. **to make one sick** to disgust or nauseate one. **to report sick** to inform someone in authority that one is ill and unable to attend to one's work or duties. **to sick out** (*N Am.*, *W Ind.*) (of a workforce) to report sick universally and simultaneously. **to take sick** (*esp. N Am.*) to take ill. **sickbay** *n.* **1** a part of a ship used for the sick and injured. **2** any area set aside for the sick. **sickbed** *n.* a bed occupied by someone who is ill. **sick benefit** *n.* SICKNESS BENEFIT (under SICK[1]). **sick building syndrome** *n.* (*Med.*) a combination or pattern of ailments, such as headaches and dizziness, thought to be caused by working in a fully air-conditioned building. **sick call** *n.* **1** a doctor's visit to the home of a sick person. **2** (*Mil.*) a call for the sick to attend a muster etc. **sicken** *v.i.* **1** to grow ill. **2** to develop the symptoms (for a particular illness). **3** to feel disgust (at). ~*v.t.* **1** to make sick. **2** to affect with nausea. **3** to disgust. **sickener** *n.* **1** (*coll.*) a circumstance that causes disgust or acute disappointment. **2** a toadstool of the genus *Russula*, esp. a poisonous one. **sickening** *a.* **1** disgusting, offensive. **2** horrifying. **3** (*coll.*) very annoying, or acutely disappointing. **sickeningly** *adv.* **sick flag** *n.* a yellow flag flown on ship or at a quarantine station to show the presence of infectious illness. **sick headache** *n.* a migraine. **sickie** *n.* (*coll.*) **1** (*Austral.*, *New Zeal.*) a day's sick leave, sometimes taken when one is not ill. **2** (*N Am.*) someone physically or mentally ill. **sickish** *a.* **sickishly** *adv.* **sickishness** *n.* **sick leave** *n.* leave of absence on account of illness. **sick list** *n.* a list of people, e.g. staff, students, or members of a military unit, laid up by illness. **on the sick list** laid up by illness. **sick-listed** *a.* **sickly** *a.* (*comp.* **sicklier**, *superl.* **sickliest**) **1** habitually indisposed or ailing, weak in health, affected by illness. **2** languid, faint, ill-looking. **3** nauseating. **4** sentimental, mawkish. **sickliness** *n.* **sick-making** *a.* (*coll.*) sickening. **sickness** *n.* **1** the condition of being ill. **2** nausea, vomiting. **3** an illness, a disease. **sickness benefit** *n.* a benefit paid to someone who is off work through illness. **sick note** *n.* (*coll.*) a note given to an employer, signed either by the employee or their doctor, certifying that absence from work was due to illness. **sick nurse** *n.* a person trained to care for the sick. **sicko** (sik´ō) *n.* (*pl.* **sickos**) (*N Am.*, *coll.*) someone mentally ill, or with a warped personality. **sick-out** *n.* (*N Am.*, *W Ind.*) a form of industrial action whereby the whole workforce reports sick simultaneously. **sick pay** *n.* the salary or wages paid to a worker on sick leave.

sickroom *n.* 1 a room in which a sick person is laid up. 2 a room adapted to accommodate the sick. [OE *sēoc*, cp. Dut. *ziek*, G *siech*, Icel. *sjūkr*, Dan. *syg*]

sick[2] (sik), **sic** *v.t.* (*pres.p.* **sicking**, *past, p.p.* **sicked**) to chase or attack, to set upon. [SEEK]

sickle (sik´əl) *n.* 1 an implement consisting of a long curved blade with a short handle, used for reaping, lopping etc. 2 a reaping-hook. **sickle-bill** *n.* a bird of various species with a sickle-shaped beak. **sickle-cell anaemia**, (*N Am.*) **sickle-cell anemia** *n.* a severe form of anaemia, hereditary and typically affecting black peoples, in which the red blood cells become narrow and curved like a sickle, as a result of the production of abnormal haemoglobin. **sickled** *a.* bearing a sickle. **sickle-feather** *n.* any of the long curved feathers of a cock's tail. **sickleman** *n.* (*pl.* **sicklemen**) a reaper. [OE *sicol*, L *secula*, cogn. with *secāre*, to cut]

sickly, sicko etc. SICK[1].

sidalcea (sidal´siə) *n.* any plant of the genus *Sidalcea*, resembling a mallow.

siddur (sid´uə) *n.* (*pl.* **siddurim** (siduə´rim)) the Jewish prayer book used for daily worship.

side (sīd) *n.* 1 any of the bounding surfaces (or lines) of a material object, esp. a more or less vertical inner or outer surface (as of a building, a room, a natural object etc.). 2 such a surface as distinct from the top and bottom, back and front, or the two ends. 3 a part of an object, region etc. to left or right of its main axis or aspect facing oneself. 4 **a** either surface of a plate, sheet, layer etc. (*Write on one side only*). **b** the writing etc. on one side of a sheet of paper etc. 5 the right or left half of a person or animal, esp. of the part between the hip and shoulder. 6 a direction or position, esp. to right or left, in relation to a person or thing. 7 (*esp. in combination*) a position close to something or someone (*on the lakeside*; *never left my side*). 8 an aspect or partial view of a thing (*see the funny side*; *his nice side*). 9 either of two opposing bodies, parties, teams or sects. 10 either of the opposing views or causes represented. 11 the line of descent through one's father or mother (*There's red hair on my mother's side*). 12 twist or spin given to a billiard or snooker ball. 13 a television channel (*Try the other side*). 14 (*sl.*) swagger, bumptiousness, pretentiousness. ~*v.i.* to align oneself (with one of two opposing parties). ~*a.* 1 situated at or on the side, lateral. 2 being from or towards the side, oblique, indirect. **bit on the side** BIT[1]. **by the side of** 1 alongside, close to. 2 in comparison with. **from side to side** 1 all the way across. 2 one way then the other from a central line or path. **on one side** 1 away in one direction from a central or principal position. 2 aside. **on the short/ long/ narrow/ raw etc. side** slightly too short, long, narrow, raw etc. **on the side** 1 in addition to the usual, principal or known. 2 in addition to, or apart from, the main aim, or one's main occupation or income, applied esp. to an underhand or illicit arrangement. **on this side of the grave** during one's life. **side by side** close together (for strength or support etc.). **the other side of the coin** COIN. **this side of** not going as far as, short of (*Keep this side of plagiarism*). **to change sides** to alter one's allegiance, to change one's party. **to choose sides** (of team leaders) to select team members from the group available. **to let the side down** (*coll.*) to disgrace one's colleagues, relations etc. by failing to live up to their standards. **to take sides** to support one side in an argument etc. **side arms** *n.pl.* weapons, such as swords or pistols, carried at the side. **side band** *n.* the band of radio frequencies on either side of the carrier frequency, caused by modulation. **side-bet** *n.* a bet in addition to the ordinary stakes. **sideboard** *n.* 1 a flat-topped table or cabinet placed at the side of a room to support decanters, dining utensils etc. 2 (*pl.*) side-whiskers. **sidebone** *n.* 1 either of the small bones under the wings of a fowl, easily separated in carving. 2 ossification of the cartilage in the pasterns of a horse. **sideburns** *n.pl.* side-whiskers. **sidecar** *n.* 1 a car with seats, attached to the side of a motorcycle. 2 a kind of cocktail with citrus fruit and brandy. 3 a small jaunting car. **side chain** *n.* (*Chem.*) a group of atoms attached to a particular atom that is part of the main ring or chain of a molecule. **side chapel** *n.* a chapel at the side of a church, in or with an entrance from an aisle. **sided** *a.* having sides or a specified number or type of sides (*usu. in comb.*, as *many-sided*). **sidedly** *adv.* **sidedness** *n.* **side dish** *n.* a supplementary dish accompanying a course at dinner etc. **side door** *n.* 1 a door at the side of a building, or beside the main entrance. 2 an indirect or unexpected means of attaining something. **side-dress** *v.t.* to add fertilizer to the soil near the roots of (a plant). **side drum** *n.* a small double-headed drum with snares, orig. carried at the drummer's side. **side effect** *n.* a secondary effect (e.g. of a drug), often adverse. **side glance** *n.* a sideways glance, a surreptitious look. **sidehill** *n.* (*N Am.*) a hillside. **side issue** *n.* a subsidiary matter. **sidekick** *n.* (*coll.*) a close associate or assistant, often in a shady enterprise. **sidelamp** *n.* a lamp at the side of something, esp. at the side of a vehicle for warning of its presence. **sideless** *a.* **sidelight** *n.* 1 light admitted into a building etc. from the side. 2 an incidental illustration or piece of information. 3 either of two small lights at the side of a vehicle, for warning of its presence. 4 either of the two navigational lights carried by a ship at night. **sideline** *n.* 1 an incidental branch of business. 2 a line marking the side of a sports pitch, tennis court etc. ~*v.t.* to remove from participation in a game or other activity. **from the sidelines** 1 watching a game etc. from the side of the pitch etc. 2 without participating directly in an activity. **on the sidelines** 1 watching a game etc. from the side of the pitch etc. 2 not participating directly in an activity. **sidelong** *adv.* from the side, obliquely rather than directly. ~*a.* (of a look or glance) oblique, rather than direct. **sideman** *n.* (*pl.* **sidemen**) a member of a band or jazz group who performs occasional solo passages. **side note** *n.* a marginal note as distinct from a footnote. **side-on** *adv., a.* 1 with a side facing in the forward or leading direction. 2 in profile, showing the profile. **side plate** *n.* the smallest size of plate in a dinner service, laid to the side of a place setting, and used for bread etc. **side road, side street** *n.* a minor road or street leading off the main road or street. **sidesaddle** *n.* a saddle designed for sitting on a horse with both legs on one side. ~*adv.* in this position on horseback. **side salad** *n.* a portion of salad served as a side dish. **side seat** *n.* a seat in a vehicle etc. in which the occupant faces the side rather than the front (or rear). **sideshow** *n.* a subordinate show, business affair etc. **side-slip** *n.* 1 a skid. 2 a movement of an aeroplane downwards and outwards from its true course. 3 a groove at the wings for moving scenery on and off the stage. 4 a slip or shoot from a plant. ~*v.i.* (*pres.p.* **sideslipping,** *past, p.p.* **sideslipped**) 1 (esp. of a bicycle or motor vehicle) to skid, to slip sideways. 2 (of an aeroplane) to move downwards and outwards from its true course. **sidesman** *n.* (*pl.* **sidesmen**) a church officer assisting the churchwarden. **sidespin** *n.* a horizontal spinning motion imparted to a ball in various ball games. **side-splitting** *a.* (of laughter, a joke etc.) causing one to double up. **sidestep** *n.* a step or movement to one side. ~*v.t.* (*pres.p.* **sidestepping,** *past, p.p.* **sidestepped**) 1 to dodge (a tackle in football etc.) by stepping sideways. 2 to avoid confronting and dealing with (a question or issue), to evade. **sidestepper** *n.* **sidestroke** *n.* 1 a stroke delivered sideways or on the side of a thing. 2 a swimming stroke performed lying on one's side. 3 an incidental action. **sideswipe** *n.* 1 a glancing blow. 2 an incidental criticism. ~*v.t.* to hit with a sideswipe. **side table** *n.* a table for use at the side of a room or alongside a main table. **sidetrack** *n.* **1** a diversion or digression. **2** a railway siding. ~*v.t.* **1** to divert or distract from the main purpose or intended course. **2** to defer indefinitely. **3** (*N Am.*) to turn into a railway siding. **side trip** *n.* a detour, a trip in addition to or in the course of a main trip. **side valve** *n.* a valve operated from the side of the cylinder of an internal-combustion engine. **side view** *n.* a view from the side, a profile. **sidewalk** *n.* (*N Am.*) a pavement. **sidewall** *n.* the part of a pneumatic tyre between the tread and the rim. **sideward** (-wəd) *adv., a.* sideways. **sidewards** (-wədz) *adv.* sideways. **sideways, sidewise** *adv.* **1** towards or from the side. **2** with one side facing forward (*sitting sideways on the chair*). ~*a.* **1** directed or moving towards or from the side (*a sideways movement, glance*). **2** unconventional, from an unusual point of view. **side-wheeler** *n.* (*US*) a paddle steamer. **side-whiskers** *n.pl.* hair grown by a man on either side of the face in front of the ears. **side wind** *n.* **1** a wind from the side. **2** an indirect influence, agency etc. **sidewinder**[1] (-wīndə) *n.* a N American rattlesnake that moves by a kind of sideways looping movement. **sidewinder**[2] (-wində) *n.* (*N Am.*) a heavy punch from the side. **siding** *n.* **1** a short track connected to and positioned alongside a railway line, for shunting trains or facilitating overtaking. **2** weatherproof cladding for the outside of a building. [OE *sīde* (cp. Dut. *zijde*, G *Seite*, Icel. *sītha*), prob. rel. to *sīd*, spacious]

sidereal (sīdiə´riəl) *a.* **1** of or relating to the fixed stars or the constellations. **2** (of time) measured or determined by the movement of the earth in relation to the fixed stars. **sidereal day** *n.* the time between two successive upper culminations of a fixed star or of the vernal equinox, about four minutes shorter than the solar day. **sidereal month** *n.* the mean period required by the moon to make a circuit among the stars, amounting to 27.32166 days. **sidereal time** *n.* time as measured by the movement of the earth in relation to the fixed stars. **sidereal year** *n.* the time occupied by a complete revolution of the earth round the sun, longer than the solar year. [L *sīderius*, as SIDERO-[2]]

siderite (sid´ərīt) *n.* **1** native ferrous carbonate. **2** an iron meteorite. **sideritic** (-rit´-) *a.* [F, from L and Gr. *sidērītē*, as SIDERO-[1]]

sidero-[1] (sid´ərō) *comb. form* iron. [Gr. *sidēros*, iron]

sidero-[2] (sī´dərō, sid-) *comb. form* the stars. [L *sīdus*, *-deris*, star]

siderolite (sid´ərəlīt) *n.* a meteorite consisting partly of stone and partly of iron.

siderosis (sidərō´sis) *n.* a lung disease caused by breathing iron or other metal dust.

siderostat (sid´ərōstat) *n.* an astronomical instrument by which a star under observation is kept within the field of the telescope. **siderostatic** (-stat´-) *a.*

siding SIDE.

sidle (sī´dəl) *v.i.* to move or edge sideways (e.g. up to someone), esp. in a stealthy or ingratiating manner. [back-formation, from old adv. *sideling*, sideways]

SIDS *abbr.* sudden infant death syndrome.

siege (sēj) *n.* **1** the military operation of surrounding a town or fortified place with troops, cutting its supply lines, and subjecting it to constant bombardment, in order to force its surrender. **2** a police operation conducted on comparable lines, usu. to force an armed and dangerous person out of a building. **state of siege** STATE. **to lay siege to** LAY[1]. **under siege 1** being besieged. **2** subjected to constant attack or criticism. **siege basket** *n.* a gabion. **siege economy** *n.* the economic practice of limiting imports in order to protect home products and industry. **siege gun** *n.* a heavy cannon adapted for breaching fortifications etc. **siege mentality** *n.* a mental or emotional condition characterized by the feeling that one is under attack from all sides. **siege piece** *n.* **1** a siege gun. **2** a coin issued at a place in a state of siege. **siege train** *n.* the artillery and other equipment carried by an army for conducting a siege. [ME and A-F *sege*, OF *siege*, ult. from L *sedes*, seat]

siemens (sē´mənz) *n.* the SI unit of electrical conductance, equal to one reciprocal ohm. [E. W. *Siemens*, 1816–92, German engineer]

Sienese (sēənēz´) *a.* of or relating to Siena, a city of Italy, esp. in reference to its 13th- and 14th-cent. school of painting. ~*n.* (*pl.* **Sienese**) **1** a native or inhabitant of Siena. **2** a member of the Sienese school of painters. **3** (*as pl.*) the people of Siena.

sienna (sien´ə) *n.* **1** a pigment composed of a native clay coloured with iron and manganese. **2** the colour of this pigment, raw or burnt sienna. **burnt sienna** BURN[1]. **raw sienna** RAW. [It. *terra di Siena*, earth of Siena]

sierra (sieə´rə) *n.* (*pl.* **sierras**) in Spanish-speaking countries and the US, a long mountain chain, jagged in outline. [Sp. from L *serra*, saw]

siesta (sies´tə) *n.* (*pl.* **siestas**) a short midday sleep, esp. in hot countries. [Sp., from L *sexta (hora)*, sixth (hour)]

sieve (siv) *n.* an instrument for separating the finer particles of substances from the coarser, or liquids from solids, having meshes or perforations through which liquid or fine particles pass, while solids or coarse particles are retained. ~*v.t.* **1** to pour or pass through a sieve, to sift. **2** to examine minutely to identify or separate out elements of (*They sieved the evidence for clues*). **to have a head like a sieve** (*coll.*) to be very forgetful. **sievelike** *a.* **sieve tube** *n.* (*Bot.*) a nutrient-conducting chain of thin-walled cells in the phloem tissue of flowering plants. [OE *sife*, cp. Dut. *zeef*, G *Sieb*]

sievert (sē´vət) *n.* the SI unit of ionizing radiation, equal to 100 rems. [R. M. *Sievert*, 1896–1966, Swedish physicist]

☒ **sieze** common misspelling of SEIZE.

sifaka (sifah´kə) *n.* the long-tailed black-and-white lemur of the genus *Propithecus*, native to Madagascar.

siffleur (sēflœ´) *n.* a whistling artiste. **siffleuse** (-flœz´) *n.* a female siffleur. [F, from *siffler*, late L *siffilāre*, form of L *sibilāre*, see SIBILANT]

sift (sift) *v.t.* **1** to separate into finer and coarser particles by means of a sieve. **2** to separate (from, out etc.). **3** to sprinkle (sugar, flour etc.) as with a sieve. **4** to examine minutely, to scrutinize, to analyse critically (evidence etc.). ~*v.i.* **1** (of snow etc.) to fall or be sprinkled sparsely or lightly. **2** to search (through a quantity of things). **sifter** *n.* (*usu. in comb.*, as *sugar-sifter*). [OE *siftan*, from SIEVE]

Sig. *abbr.* **1** signor. **2** signore.

sig. *abbr.* signature.

sigh (sī) *v.i.* **1** to inhale and exhale deeply and audibly, as an involuntary expression of grief, fatigue, relief etc. **2** to yearn (for). **3** to make a sound like sighing. ~*v.t.* to utter with sighs (*'It's too late,' she sighed*). ~*n.* an act or sound of sighing. **sigher** *n.* **sighingly** *adv.* [OE *sīcan* (cp. Swed. *sucka*, Dan. *sukke*), prob. imit.]

sight (sīt) *n.* **1** the faculty of seeing. **2** the act of seeing. **3** vision, view, range of vision, visibility (*The island was already within sight*). **4** one's point of view, judgement or estimation (*In his sight she was perfect*). **5** that which is seen, a scene, esp. a delightful or shocking one. **6** something interesting, or worth going, to see (*the sights of London*). **7** a device on a firearm, optical instrument etc. for enabling one to direct it accurately to any point. ~*v.t.* **1** to see, catch sight of (*The vehicle was sighted again at 10.45 heading for the coast*). **2** to adjust the sights of (a firearm or optical instrument). **3** to aim (a firearm) by means of sights. **a sight** (*coll.*) a great deal

(*She's got a sight more common sense than you have*). **at first sight** immediately on seeing someone or something, as a first impression. **at sight** on sight. **by a long sight** by a long way (*not finished by a long sight*). **in sight 1** visible. **2** having a view (of). **3** not far off. **on sight 1** as soon as seen, immediately. **2** (of a bill, to be paid) on presentation. **out of sight 1** not in a position to be seen, or to have a view, or be in view (of). **2** having disappeared, e.g. into the distance. **3** forgotten, ignored. **4** (*coll.*) excellent. **to catch sight of** to begin to see, to glimpse or notice. **to get a sight of** to glimpse, to manage to see. **to have lost sight of** to have fallen out of touch with, no longer to know the whereabouts of. **to look a sight** to look untidy or disreputable. **to lose sight of 1** to cease to see. **2** to overlook, to forget, to cease to take cognizance of. **to lower one's sights** to settle for less, to become less ambitious. **to put out of sight** to put away, to ignore. **to set one's sights on** to have as one's goal, or the object of one's desires or ambition. **within sight** in sight. **sighted** *a.* **1** having the faculty of sight. **2** (*in comb.*) having vision of a specified kind, as *short-sighted*. **3** (of a gun) fitted with a sight. **sighter** *n.* **sight for sore eyes, sight for the gods** *n.* (*coll.*) a person or thing one is pleased to see, a welcome visitor. **sight-glass** *n.* a transparent tube, window etc. for checking the inside of an apparatus. **sighting** *n.* an instance of seeing or catching sight of someone or something. **sighting shot** *n.* a shot to help gunners to adjust their sights. **sightless** *a.* **1** not having the faculty of sight, blind. **2** (*poet.*) invisible. **sightlessly** *adv.* **sightlessness** *n.* **sightline** *n.* **1** the line from one's eye to the object one is seeing. **2** (*pl.*) the view one has e.g. of the stage in a theatre, or of a cinema screen, from where one is sitting. **sightly** *a.* **1** pleasing to the eye, attractive. **2** (*N Am.*) affording a pleasant view. **sightliness** *n.* **sight-read** *v.t.* (*past, p.p.* **sight-read**) to play or sing (music) at sight, without having previously seen it. **sight-reader** *n.* **sight-reading** *n.* **sight screen** *n.* a white screen set on the boundary of a cricket field to help the batsman see the ball. **sightseeing** *n.* the activity of going to see the sights or notable features of a place. **sightsee** *v.i., v.t.* **sightseer** (-sēə) *n.* **sight-sing** *v.t., v.i.* (*past* **sight-sang,** *p.p.* **sight-sung**) to sing (music) at sight. **sight unseen** *adv.* without previous inspection (of the object to be bought etc.). **sightworthy** *a.* worth seeing. [OE *gesihth* (cp. Dut. *gezigt*, G *Sicht*), from *sēon*, to SEE[1]]

sigil (sij´il) *n.* a seal, a signet. **sigillate** (-lət) *a.* **1** having seal-like marks or markings. **2** (of pottery) decorated with impressed marks. **sigillography** (-log´rəfi) *n.* the study or science of seals used on documents, esp. as a means of identifying and dating them. **sigillographer** *n.* **sigillographical** (-graf´-) *a.* [late L *sigillum*, dim. of L *signum*, SIGN]

siglum (sig´ləm) *n.* (*pl.* **sigla** (-lə)) a symbol, sign or abbreviation used in a manuscript or document.

sigma (sig´mə) *n.* the eighteenth letter of the Greek alphabet, Σ, σ, or when final, ς, or, in uncial form, C or c. **sigmate** (-māt) *a.* sigma- or S-shaped. ~*v.t.* to add *S* or a sigma to. **sigmatic** (-mat´-) *a.* (*Gram.*) (of certain tenses etc.) formed with a sigma. **sigmoid** (-moid) *a.* **1** curved like the uncial sigma C, crescent-shaped. **2** curved like an S, having a double or reflexed curve. ~*n.* **1** the sigmoid flexure. **2** a double or reflexed curve. **sigmoidal** (-moi´-) *a.* sigmoid. **sigmoid colon** *n.* (*Anat.*) the sigmoid flexure in the descending colon. **sigmoid flexure** *n.* (*Anat.*) a C-shaped or S-shaped curve or bend, esp. the final section of the descending colon, leading to the rectum. **sigmoidoscope** (-moi´-) *n.* (*Med.*) an instrument that is inserted through the anus for examining the inside of the rectum and the sigmoid colon. **sigmoidoscopy** (-os´kəpi) *n.* [Gr.]

sign (sīn) *n.* **1** a mark expressing a particular meaning. **2** a conventional mark used for a word or phrase to represent a mathematical process (as + or -). **3** a symbol, a token, a symptom or proof (of), esp. a miracle as evidence of a supernatural power. **4** (*Med.*) any external indication of illness, as distinct from symptoms felt by the patient. **5** a password, a secret formula, motion or gesture by which confederates etc. recognize each other. **6** a motion, action or gesture used instead of words to convey information, commands etc., e.g. one used in a sign language. **7** a board or panel giving information or indicating directions etc. **8** a device, usu. painted on a board, displayed as a token or advertisement of a trade, esp. by innkeepers. **9** any of 12 ancient divisions of the zodiac named after the constellations formerly in them but now not corresponding through the precession of the equinoxes. ~*v.t.* **1** to mark with a sign, esp. with one's signature, initials or an accepted mark as an acknowledgement, guarantee, ratification etc. **2** to write (one's name) by way of official acknowledgement, ratification etc. **3** to order, request or make known by a gesture. ~*v.i.* **1** to write one's name by way of official acknowledgement, ratification etc. **2** to communicate by gesture or movement. **3** to communicate in a sign language. **to sign away** to transfer or convey by signing a deed. **to sign for** to acknowledge receipt of by signing. **to sign in** to record arrival by signing. **to sign off 1** to stop work for the time. **2** to end a letter by signing. **3** to stop broadcasting, with a verbal announcement etc. **4** to discharge from employment. **5** formally to cease collecting unemployment benefit. **6** in bridge, to make a conventional bid indicating that one wishes to end the bidding. **to sign on 1** to commit (oneself or another) to an undertaking or employment. **2** to register as unemployed. **3** to begin broadcasting, with a verbal announcement etc. **to sign out** to record departure by signing. **to sign up 1** to commit (oneself or another) to an undertaking or employment. **2** to enlist, enrol. **signable** *a.* **signage** *n.* **1** signs collectively, advertising boards, or their design. **2** the use of a sign language, signing. **signboard** *n.* a board on which a tradesman's sign or advertisement is painted. **signer** *n.* **signing** *n.* **1** the use of, or the art of using, a sign language. **2** a recently signed-up member of a professional sports team. **sign language** *n.* a system of communication that uses visual signals rather than the spoken word, esp. any system of hand and finger movements used by the deaf. **sign manual** *n.* one's signature written by one's own hand. **sign-off** *n.* in bridge, an act of signing off. **sign of the cross** *n.* in Christianity, a gesture made tracing the shape of a cross, either in front of one in the air, or from the forehead to chest and to each shoulder, as a way of invoking God's grace. **sign of the times** *n.* anything that serves as an indication of sociological change or development. **sign of the zodiac** *n.* each of the 12 equal parts into which the zodiac has anciently been divided, orig. corresponding to the constellations bearing the same names, but now, through the precession of the equinoxes, coinciding with the constellations bearing the names next in order. **sign-painter** *n.* a person whose job is painting signboards etc. **signpost** *n.* **1** a post supporting a sign, e.g. at a crossroads, indicating the direction of, and often distance to, particular places. **2** (*fig.*) something that indicates the right direction or course, a pointer. ~*v.t.* **1** to provide with signposts. **2** to point to or indicate (a direction or course to be followed). **signwriter** *n.* a person who paints the lettering on signboards. **signwriting** *n.* [ME and OF *signe*, L *signum*]

signal (sig´nəl) *n.* **1** a sign in the form of an action, light or sound, agreed upon or understood as conveying information, or providing the prompt for a certain move, esp. to someone at a distance. **2** an event that is the occasion or cue for some action. **3** the apparatus used for conveying information, e.g., on the railway, a pole with a movable arm or coloured light, indicating whether the line is clear. 4 a set of transmitted electrical impulses received as a sound or image on radio or television. ~*v.t.* (*pres.p.* **signalling,** (*N Am.*) **signaling,** *past, p.p.* **signalled,** (*N Am.*) **signaled**) 1 to make signals to (*to signal someone to move on*). 2 to convey, announce, order etc. by signals (*to signal one's assent*). 3 (of an event) to signify, indicate or herald (a certain change or development). ~*v.i.* to make signals. ~*a.* conspicuous, notable, extraordinary (*a signal victory*). **signal book** *n.* (*esp. Mil.*) a list of prescribed signals. **signal box** *n.* an elevated cabin beside a railway track, from which signals and points are worked. **signalize, signalise** *v.t.* 1 to make signal or remarkable, to give distinction to. 2 to point out or indicate particularly. **signaller,** (*N Am.*) **signaler** *n.* **signally** *adv.* **signalman** *n.* (*pl.* **signalmen**) 1 a person who works railway signals. 2 (*Mil.*) a person who receives or transmits signals. **signal of distress** *n.* (*Naut.*) a signal, esp. the firing of a gun, urgently requesting help. **signal-to-noise ratio** *n.* the ratio of the strength of a desired electrical signal to that of the noise or interference from an unwanted signal, usu. expressed in decibels. **signal tower** *n.* (*N Am.*) a signal box. [F, from late L *signāle* (SIGN, -AL[2])]

signature (sig´nəchə) *n.* 1 one's name, initials or mark written or impressed with one's own hand in signing a document etc. 2 the act of signing one's name on a document etc. 3 in older books, a distinguishing letter or number at the bottom of the first page, and often several subsequent pages, of each of the sheets that are folded to compose the book, as a guide to folding and binding. 4 such a sheet after folding, the resulting gathering of pages. 5 (*Mus.*) a symbol indicating key (*key signature*) or time (*time signature*) at the beginning of a stave to the right of the clef, or wherever there is a change. 6 a distinguishing mark, feature, characteristic or pattern. 7 (*N Am.*) on a medical prescription, a set of directions for use. 8 a signature tune. **signatory** (-təri) *n.* (*pl.* **signatories**) any one of those who have signed an agreement, treaty etc., e.g. on behalf of a state; the state thus represented. ~*a.* having signed a document or agreement, bound by one's signature. **signature dish** *n.* a particular dish invented by, and regarded as the speciality of, a certain chef. **signature tune** *n.* a distinctive piece of music used to introduce a particular programme, performer etc., and therefore associated with them. [F, from med. L *signātūra*, from *signāre*, to SIGN]

signet (sig´nit) *n.* 1 a small seal, esp. for use in lieu of or with a signature as a mark of authentication. 2 (*Hist.*) such a seal used by the English or Scottish sovereigns either privately or for certain official purposes. 3 in Scotland, the royal seal used as the seal of the Court of Session. **signet ring** *n.* a finger ring set with a seal. [F, dim. of *signe*, SIGN]

signify (sig´nifī) *v.t.* (*3rd pers. sing. pres.* **signifies,** *pres.p.* **signifying,** *past, p.p.* **signified**) 1 to make known by signs, gestures or words (*to signify one's agreement with a nod*). 2 to communicate, to announce. 3 to be a sign of, to indicate (*Raised eyebrows usually signify surprise*). 4 to mean or denote, to have as its meaning (*A thumbs-up sign signifies OK*). ~*v.i.* (*dated*) to be of consequence, to matter. **significance** (-nif´ikəns) *n.* 1 importance, moment, consequence (*an event of little significance*). 2 meaning, real import (*The significance of this passage has evidently escaped most of you*). 3 the quality of being significant. 4 in statistics, the measurable probability that data not conforming to a hypothesis are substantial enough to refute the hypothesis. 5 particular emphasis or expressiveness used to convey a hint. **significance test** *n.* in statistics, a test to establish whether data not conforming to a hypothesis are significant. **significant** *a.* 1 meaning something. 2 meaning something important, and relevant. 3 expressing or suggesting something more than appears on the surface (*with a significant nod*). 4 in statistics, having significance. **significant figures, significant digits** *n.pl.* (*Math.*) digits that contribute to a number, as distinct from zeros filling vacant spaces at the beginning or end. **significantly** *adv.* **significant other** *n.* (*N Am., coll.*) one's spouse, partner or lover. **signification** (-fikā´shən) *n.* 1 the act of signifying. 2 that which is signified, the precise meaning, sense or implication (of a term etc.). **significative** (-nif´ikətiv) *a.* 1 conveying a meaning or signification. 2 serving as a sign or evidence (of), significant. **significatory** (-kətəri) *a., n.* [F *signifier*, L *significāre* (SIGN, -FY)]

signor (sēn´yaw) *n.* (*pl.* **signori** (sēnyaw´rē)) 1 an Italian man. 2 the Italian form of address corresponding to *sir* or *Mr.* **signora** (-yaw´rə) *n.* (*pl.* **signore** (-yaw´rā)) 1 a married Italian woman. 2 the Italian form of address to a married woman, corresponding to *Madam* or *Mrs.* **signorina** (-yərē´nə) *n.* (*pl.* **signorine** (-nā)) 1 an Italian unmarried girl. 2 the Italian form of address to an unmarried girl or woman, corresponding to *Miss* or to French *mademoiselle.* **signory** (sē´nyəri) *n.* (*pl.* **signories**) (*Hist.*) 1 a seigniory. 2 the municipal council of an Italian republic. [It., from L *senior*, older, cp. SENIOR, SEIGNEUR, SEÑOR]

sika (sē´kə) *n.* a small deer, *Cervus nippon*, native to Japan but introduced into other countries, including Britain. [Jap. *shika*]

Sikh (sēk) *n.* a member of a monotheistic religion that takes the Granth as its scripture, founded in the 16th cent. in the Punjab. ~*a.* of or relating to Sikhs or Sikhism. **Sikhism** *n.* [Hind., from Sansk. *sishya*, disciple]

silage (sī´lij) *n.* 1 any green crop, esp. grass or clover, stored by ensilage, that is, compressed into pits, for use as fodder. 2 the making of silage. ~*v.t.* to store in a silo.

sild (sild) *n.* a young herring, esp. one canned in Norway. [Norw.]

sile (sīl), **seil** *v.t.* to strain (esp. milk). ~*v.i.* (*North.*) to rain heavily, to pour. [prob. from Icel., cp. Norw. and Swed. *sil*]

silence (sī´ləns) *n.* 1 the absence of noise, stillness. 2 avoidance of comment, or withholding of information, secrecy. 3 uncommunicativeness, taciturnity. 4 absence of mention, oblivion. 5 a period during which conversation or communication lapses. ~*v.t.* 1 to reduce to silence with an unanswerable argument. 2 to fit (e.g. a firearm) with a silencer. **in silence** without a word or sound. **to put to silence** to reduce to silence. **to reduce to silence** to defeat with an unanswerable argument, to have the last word. **silencer** *n.* 1 a person who or something that silences. 2 a device for reducing or muffling noise, fitted to firearms, or to the exhaust of a motor on a vehicle etc. [F, from L *silentium*, from *silēre*, to be silent]

sileni SILENUS.

silent (sī´lənt) *a.* 1 not speaking, not making any sound, noiseless, still. 2 (of a letter) written but not pronounced, as the unpronounced *k* in *knee.* 3 uncommunicative, taciturn. 4 saying nothing (about or on a topic), making no mention. 5 (of a film) not having a synchronized soundtrack. **silentiary** (-len´shiəri) *n.* (*pl.* **silentiaries**) 1 a person appointed to maintain silence in a court etc. 2 (*Hist.*) someone sworn to secrecy in affairs of state, esp. a confidential officer of the Byzantine court. **silently** *adv.* **silent majority** *n.* the large majority of a population who have moderate views but who do not bother to express them. **silentness** *n.* **silent partner** *n.* a partner in a business who has no voice in its management.

silenus (sīlē´nəs) *n.* (*pl.* **sileni** (-nī)) a woodland satyr in the shape of a riotous and drunken old man. [L, from

Gr. *Seilēnos*, attendant and tutor of Bacchus and oldest of the satyrs]

silesia (sīlē´zhə) *n.* a type of twilled cotton or linen cloth used for blinds, dress-linings etc. [orig. made in *Silesia* (now part of Poland)]

silex (sī´leks) *n.* **1** silica, esp. in the form of quartz or flint. **2** a heat- and shock-resistant glass made of fused quartz. [L, flint]

silhouette (siluet´) *n.* **1** a portrait in profile or outline, usu. black on a white ground or cut out in paper etc. **2** the outline of a figure as seen against the light or cast as a shadow. *~v.t.* (*usu. in pass.*) to represent or cause to be visible in silhouette. **in silhouette** as a dark shape or outline. [Étienne de *Silhouette*, 1709–67, French minister of finance, whose name became a synonym for anything cheap]

silica (sil´ikə) *n.* a hard, crystalline silicon dioxide, occurring in various mineral forms, esp. as sand, flint, quartz etc. **silica gel** *n.* a granular form of hydrated silica, used to absorb water and other vapours. **silicate** (-kət) *n.* any of many salts of silicic acid, common in the rocks forming the earth's crust. **silicated** (-kātid) *a.* **1** combined or impregnated with silica. **2** coated with silica. **siliceous** (-lish´əs), **silicious** *a.* of or containing silica. **silicic** (-lis´-) *a.* of or containing silica or silicon. **siliciferous** (-sif´ərəs) *a.* containing silica. **silicify** (-lis´ifī) *v.t.* (*3rd pers. sing. pres.* **silicifies,** *pres.p.* **silicifying,** *past, p.p.* **silicified**) to convert into or impregnate with silica. *~v.i.* to become or be impregnated with silica. **silicification** (-fikā´shən) *n.* **silicium** (-lis´iəm) *n.* silicon. **silicon** (-kən) *n.* a non-metallic semi-conducting element, at. no. 14, chem. symbol Si, usu. occurring in combination with oxygen as quartz or silica, and next to oxygen the most abundant of the elements. **silicon carbide** *n.* CARBORUNDUM. **silicon chip** *n.* a microchip composed of silicon, on to which an integrated microcircuit can be printed. **silicone** (-kōn) *n.* any of numerous water-repellent oils of low melting-point, the viscosity of which changes little with temperature, used as lubricants, constituents of polish etc. *~v.t.* to treat with silicone. **silicone rubber** *n.* a synthetic rubber stable up to comparatively high temperatures. **Silicon Valley** *n.* an area that has a high concentration of industries concerned with information technology and electronics. **silicosis** (-kō´sis) *n.* an occupational disease of the lungs occasioned by the inhalation of silica dust. **silicotic** (-kot´-) *a.* [from L *silex -licis*, see SILEX]

silici- (sil´isi), **silico-** (sil´ikō) *comb. form* silicon, silica.

silicle (sil´ikəl), **silicula** (-lik´ūlə) *n.* a short siliqua or seed pod. **siliculose** (-lik´ūlōs) *a.* [F *silicule* or L *silicula*, dim. of *siliqua*]

silico- SILICI-.

silicon, silicone etc. SILICA.

silicula, siliculose SILICLE.

siliqua (sil´ikwə) *n.* (*pl.* **siliquae** (-kwē)) **1** a dry, elongated pericarp or pod containing seeds, as in plants of the mustard family. **2** (*Anat.*) a podlike envelope. **silique** (silēk´) *n.* (*Bot.*) a siliqua. **siliquiform** (-lik´wifawm) *a.* **siliquose** (sil´ikwōs), **siliquous** *a.* [L]

silk (silk) *n.* **1** a fine soft glossy fibre spun by the larvae of certain moths, esp. the common silkworm, *Bombyx mori*. **2** similar thread spun by the silk spider and other arachnids. **3** cloth made of silk. **4** (*pl.*) varieties of this or garments made of it, esp. as worn by jockeys. **5** (a skein of) fine thread for embroidery. **6** the silky lustre seen in some gems, e.g. rubies. **7** the styles of the female maize flower. **8** a King's or Queen's Counsel, or their rank (from their right to wear a silk gown). *~a.* made of silk, silken, silky. **to take silk** to exchange a gown of ordinary fabric for one of silk, esp. to become a KC or QC. **silk cotton** *n.* the silky covering of the seed pods of the bombax and other trees. **silken** *a.* **1** made of silk. **2** soft and glossy like silk. **3** silk-clad. **4** (of someone's manner) suave, plausible, ingratiating. **silk-fowl** *n.* a breed of fowl that has silky plumage. **silk-gland** *n.* a gland in the silkworm, certain spiders etc., secreting silk. **silk hat** *n.* a top hat. **silklike** *a.* **silkman** *n.* (*pl.* **silkmen**) a maker of or dealer in silk. **silk moth** *n.* any of various moths whose caterpillars make a silken cocoon, esp. the moth which metamorphoses from the silkworm. **silk-screen** *a.* denoting a stencil method of printing in which paint or ink is forced through a screen of silk or other fine-meshed fabric. *~v.t.* to print or decorate using the silk-screen method. **silk-screen printing** *n.* **silk spider** *n.* a spider spinning a silky substance, esp. *Nephela plumipes*. **silk-thrower, silk-throwster** *n.* a person who winds, twists or throws silk to prepare it for weaving. **silk-weaver** *n.* **silkworm** *n.* the larva of *Bombyx mori* or allied moths which enclose their chrysalis in a cocoon of silk. **silkworm gut** *n.* a fine gut used for angling, drawn from the glands of the silkworm. **silky** *a.* (*comp.* **silkier,** *superl.* **silkiest**) **1** like silk, glossy, soft. **2** silken. **silkily** *adv.* **silkiness** *n.* **silky oak** *n.* an Australian tree yielding wood suitable for furniture, fittings etc. [OE *seolc*, L *sēricum*, see SERICEOUS]

sill (sil), **cill** *n.* **1** a block or timber forming a basis or foundation in a structure, esp. a slab of timber or stone at the foot of a door or window. **2** a piece of timber forming the horizontal base of a lock or dock gate. **3** the top level of a weir. **4** a sheet of intrusive igneous rock between other strata. [OE *syll*, cp. Icel. *syll, svill*, Swed. *syll*, Dan. *syld*]

sillabub SYLLABUB.

siller (sil´ə) *n.* (*Sc.*) silver, money.

sillimanite (sil´imənīt) *n.* the mineral aluminium silicate, found as orthorhombic crystals or fibrous masses. [Benjamin *Silliman*, 1779–1864, American scientist]

silly (sil´i) *a.* (*comp.* **sillier,** *superl.* **silliest**) **1** foolish, fatuous, weak-minded. **2** showing poor judgement, unwise, imprudent. **3** mentally weak, imbecile. **4** senseless as a result of a blow (*The blow knocked him silly*). **5** in cricket, close to the batsman's wicket. **6** †innocent, simple-minded, guileless. *~n.* (*pl.* **sillies**) a silly person. **sillily** *adv.* **silliness** *n.* **silly billy** *n.* (*pl.* **silly billies**) (*coll.*) a foolish person. **silly season** *n.* the late summer, when newspapers are traditionally full of trivial stories, for lack of anything serious to print. [OE *sǣlig*, happy, fortunate (cp. Dut. *zalig*, G *selig*, Icel. *sæll*, blessed)]

silo (sī´lō) *n.* (*pl.* **silos**) **1** a store-pit or airtight chamber for pressing and preserving green fodder. **2** a tall construction in which grain etc. can be stored. **3** an underground store and launch pad for a guided missile. *~v.t.* (*3rd pers. sing. pres.* **siloes,** *pres.p.* **siloing,** *past, p.p.* **siloed**) **1** to put in a silo. **2** to convert into silage. [Sp., from L *sīrus*, Gr. *siros*]

☒ **silouette** common misspelling of SILHOUETTE.

silphium (sil´fiəm) *n.* (*pl.* **silphia** (-fiə), **silphiums**) a plant of the Mediterranean region, the juice of which was used by the ancients as a condiment and as a medicine. [L, from Gr. *silphion*]

silt (silt) *n.* fine sediment deposited by water. *~v.t.* to choke or fill (up) with silt. *~v.i.* to be choked (up) with silt. **siltation** (-tā´shən) *n.* **siltstone** *n.* a type of rock composed of solidified silt. **silty** *a.* (*comp.* **siltier,** *superl.* **siltiest**). [MG *Silte*, cp. MSwed. *sylta*, mud, Dan. *sylt*, Norw. *sylta*, salt-marsh, G *Sülze*, brine]

Silurian (silūə´riən, sī-) *a.* **1** (*Geol.*) of or relating to the period called Silurian or its rock system. **2** of or relating to the Silures, an ancient British people living in SE Wales. *~n.* **1** the lowest subdivision of the Palaeozoic strata, next above the Cambrian (well developed in S Wales, where these strata were first examined). **2** the geological period during which these strata formed. [L]

silurid (silūə´rid, -oo´-) *n.* any fish belonging to a

freshwater family that includes the European catfish or sheatfish, *Silurus glanis*. ~*a.* of or relating to these fishes. [L, from Gr. *Silouros*]

silva SYLVA.

silver (sil´və) *n.* **1** a precious ductile and malleable metallic element of a white colour, at. no. 47, chem. symbol Ag. **2** domestic utensils, esp. cutlery, implements, ornaments etc. made of silver, usu. combined with a harder metal. **3** silver or cupronickel coins. **4** (*esp. Sc.*) money. **5** salts of silver employed in photography. **6** the colour or lustre of or as of silver. **7** a silver medal. ~*a.* **1** made of silver. **2** resembling silver, white or lustrous like silver. **3** denoting second-best quality or rank, esp. coming after gold or golden, but before bronze. **4** denoting a 25th anniversary. **5** (of sounds) clear and ringing. ~*v.t.* **1** to coat or plate with silver or a silver substitute. **2** to back (mirror glass) with an amalgam of tin and mercury. **3** to give a silvery colour or lustre to. **4** to tinge (hair) with white or grey. ~*v.i.* to acquire a silvery appearance, e.g. (of hair) to turn grey or white. **born with a silver spoon in one's mouth** SPOON. **silver age** *n.* **1** in Greek and Roman mythology, the age of Zeus, following the golden age, the happy innocent reign of Cronos. **2** the period of Latin literature following the classical period, the age of writers such as Tacitus, Juvenal and Martial. **silver band** *n.* a band whose instruments are silver-plated. **silver bath** *n.* a solution of nitrate of silver for sensitizing photographic plates. **silver-beater** *n.* a person who beats silver into thin sheets. **silver birch** *n.* a common variety of birch, *Betula alba*, with a silvery-white trunk. **silver bromide** *n.* a pale yellow salt used in the production of photographic emulsions. **silver chloride** *n.* a white salt that darkens when exposed to light, used in the production of photographic paper and emulsions, and antiseptics. **silverer** *n.* **silver fern** *n.* **1** a tree fern of New Zealand, *Cyaltea dealbata*, with leathery leaves. **2** a silver fern leaf on a black background, as the symbol of New Zealand. **silver fir** *n.* any of various fir trees of the genus *Abies* with needles that are silvery-white on the underside. **silverfish** *n.* **1** any of various small wingless insects of the *Lepisma* genus, esp. *Lepisma saccharina*, which infest buildings and can be destructive to books, cloth etc. **2** a silvery fish of various species, esp. a white variety of goldfish. **silver foil** *n.* **1** silver leaf. **2** tin foil. **silver fox** *n.* **1** a variety of common American red fox in a phase during which its coat becomes black mixed with silver. **2** the pelt of this animal. **silver gilt** *n.* **1** gilded silver or silverware. **2** an imitation gilding consisting of silver foil varnished with yellow lacquer. **silver grey** *n.*, *a.* pale luminous grey. **silver-haired** *a.* **silvering** *n.* **silver iodide** *n.* a yellow salt used in medicine, photography, and in seeding clouds to make artificial rain. **silverize, silverise** *v.t.* to treat or coat with silver. **silver jubilee** *n.* (a celebration of) a 25th anniversary, esp. of a monarch's reign. **silver Latin** *n.* the Latin of writers such as Tacitus, Juvenal and Martial, of the early imperial period. **silver leaf** *n.* **1** silver beaten out into thin leaves or plates. **2** (**silver-leaf**) a disease of plum trees. **silverless** *a.* **silverlike** *a.* **silver lining** *n.* the bright or compensating side of any misfortune, trouble etc. (from the proverb 'Every cloud has a silver lining'). **silver medal** *n.* in athletics competitions etc., the silver-coloured medal awarded as a second prize. **silvern** (-vən) *a.* (*poet.*) **1** made of silver. **2** silvery. **silver nitrate** *n.* a poisonous crystalline salt that turns grey or black on exposure to light, used in photography, and as an antiseptic. **silver paper** *n.* **1** silver-coloured wrapping material, e.g. for confectionery, usu. consisting of aluminium foil or sometimes tin foil, often with a backing of greaseproof paper. **2** fine tissue paper, (orig. for wrapping silverware). **silver plate** *n.* **1** silverware. **2** (metal articles coated with) a thin layer of silver, electroplate. **silver-plate** *v.t.* to coat with a thin layer of silver, to electroplate. **silver-plated** *a.* **silver-plating** *n.* the process of coating metal articles with a layer of silver, esp. by electroplating. **silverpoint** *n.* **1** the process of drawing with a pencil with a tip of silver wire. **2** a sketch so made. **3** a pencil used in silverpoint. **silver salmon** *n.* COHO. **silver sand** *n.* fine white sand used in gardening. **silver screen** *n.* **1** the cinema screen. **2** motion pictures generally, cinematography. **silver service** *n.* **1** a set of silver cutlery. **2** a manner of serving food in restaurants using a fork and spoon in one hand. **silverside** *n.* **1** the upper and choicer part of a round of beef. **2** (*also* **silversides**) any of several small sea fishes with a silver side-marking, e.g. *Atherina presbyter*. **silversmith** *n.* a maker of or worker in silver articles. **silversmithing** *n.* **silver solder** *n.* solder that contains silver. **silver standard** *n.* a monetary system in which a currency is defined in terms of the fineness and weight of its silver content, and may be exchanged for silver. **silver-stick** *n.* a court official (a field officer of the Life Guards) who attends the sovereign on state occasions, carrying a silver staff. **silver thaw** *n.* a thin glassy layer of ice formed by freezing rain or re-freezing slush, also its forming process. **silver tongue** *n.* eloquence. **silver-tongued** *a.* **silverware** *n.* articles of silver or silver plate, esp. cutlery and often tableware. **silver wedding** *n.* a 25th wedding anniversary. **silverweed** *n.* any of various silvery-leaved plants, esp. *Potentilla anserina*. **silvery** *a.* **1** having the appearance of silver. **2** (of hair) white, with a bright sheen. **3** having a soft clear sound. **silveriness** *n.* [OE *seolfor* (cp. Dut. *zilver*, G *Silber*, Icel. *silfr*), etym. uncertain]

silviculture (sil´vikŭlchə), **sylviculture** *n.* the cultivation of trees, forestry. **silvicultural** (-kŭl´-) *a.* **silviculturist** (-kŭl´-) *n.* [F, from L *silva*, a wood]

sima (sī´mə) *n.* **1** the inner part of the earth's crust, lying deep to the ocean bed as well as to the continental masses. **2** the silica- and magnesia-rich material of which this layer consists. [*si*lica, *ma*gnesia]

simar CYMAR.

simaruba (simərooʹbə) *n.* **1** a tropical American tree of the genus *Simaruba*, esp. *Simaruba amara*. **2** the bark of this tree, containing quassia and used medicinally. [prob. Guianan name]

Simeonite (sim´iənīt) *n.* **1** a person of low-church sympathies, an evangelical. **2** (*Hist.*) a follower of Charles Simeon. [Charles *Simeon*, 1759–1836, of Cambridge, distinguished for his evangelism]

simian (sim´iən) *a.* **1** of or relating to the anthropoid apes. **2** apelike or monkey-like in appearance or movement. ~*n.* an ape or monkey. **simious** *a.* [L, ape]

similar (sim´ilə) *a.* **1** having a resemblance (to) (*Her nose was similar to her mother's*; *They've got a van similar to ours*). **2** resembling each other, alike (*Our views are similar, though not exactly the same*; *We have similar interests*). **3** (*Geom.*) made up of the same number of parts arranged in the same manner, corresponding. **similarity** (-lar´-) *n.* (*pl.* **similarities**). **similarly** *adv.* [F *similaire*, L *similis*, like]

Usage note *Similar* should be followed by *to* (and not *as*).

simile (sim´ili) *n.* a figure of speech that highlights a particular quality that something has by comparing it, esp. using *like* or *as*, to something else proverbial for that quality, as of *eyes like stars*; *a heart as pure as the driven snow*. **similitude** (-mil´itūd) *n.* **1** likeness, resemblance. **2** semblance, guise. **3** †a comparison, simile or metaphor. **4** †a facsimile, duplicate, counterpart or equal.

similor (sim´ilaw) *n.* a gold-coloured alloy of copper

and zinc used for cheap jewellery. [F (L *similis*, SIMILAR, F *or*, gold)]
simious SIMIAN.
simmer (sim´ə) *v.i.* 1 to boil gently. 2 to be just below boiling point. 3 to be in a state of suppressed emotion, esp. rage. ~*v.t.* 1 to boil gently. 2 to keep just below boiling point. ~*n.* a state of simmering. **to simmer down** to become less agitated or excited, to calm down. [cp. Dan. *summe*, G *summen*, to hum, -ER]
simnel (sim´nəl), **simnel cake** *n.* a rich fruit cake decorated with marzipan, traditionally eaten on Mothering Sunday, Easter Day and Christmas Day. [OF *simenel*, late L *siminellus*, fine bread, from L *simila*, the finest wheat flour, rel. to Gr. *semidalis*]
simoniac, simonist etc. SIMONY.
Simon Pure (sī´mən) *n.* the genuine article, the real person. **simon-pure** *a.* genuine, authentic, real. [character in Mrs Centlivre's *A Bold Stroke for a Wife*, 1717]
simony (sim´əni, sī´-) *n.* the buying or selling of ecclesiastical preferments or privileges. **simoniac** (-mō´niak), **simoniacal** (-nī´əkəl) *a.* 1 guilty of simony. 2 of the nature of or obtained by simony. **simoniacally** *adv.* **simonist** (sī´-, sim´-) *n.* [F *simonie*, late L *simōnia*, from *Simon* Magus, who wished to buy the gift of the Holy Ghost with money (Acts viii.18)]
simoom (simoom´), **simoon** (-moon´) *n.* a hot dry wind blowing over the desert, esp. of Arabia, raising great quantities of sand and causing intense thirst. [Arab. *samūm*, from *samma*, to poison]
simorg SIMURG.
simp (simp) *n.* (*N Am., coll.*) a simpleton. [shortened form]
simpatico (simpat´ikō) *a.* congenial, agreeable, likeable. [It., Sp.]
simper (sim´pə) *v.i.* to smile in an affected manner, to smirk. ~*v.t.* to utter with a simper. ~*n.* an affected smile or smirk. **simperer** *n.* **simpering** *a.* **simperingly** *adv.* [cp. Norw. *semper*, smart, Dan. dial. *semper*, Swed. *sipp*, prim, prudish]
simple (sim´pəl) *a.* (*comp.* **simpler**, *superl.* **simplest**) 1 clear, intelligible, easy to understand. 2 not difficult, easy to do. 3 not complicated, not complex, straightforward. 4 not elaborate, not adorned, not sumptuous or luxurious. 5 uncompounded, unmingled, all of one kind or consisting of only one thing, not analysable, not subdivided, elementary. 6 absolute, mere, nothing but, sheer (*It's simple jealousy*). 7 weak in intellect, silly, inexperienced, ignorant. 8 credulous. 9 unaffected, unsophisticated, natural, artless, sincere. 10 plain, homely, humble, of low degree. 11 insignificant, trifling. 12 (*Bot.*) **a** composed of one part only. **b** (of fruit) formed from a single pistil. ~†*n.* 1 a medicinal herb or a medicine made from it. 2 a simpleton. 3 something not mixed or compounded. **simple eye** *n.* in insects etc., an eye that has only one lens. **simple fraction** *n.* a fraction expressed as a ratio, as distinct from a decimal, having whole numbers for the denominator and numerator, a common or vulgar fraction. **simple fracture** *n.* a fracture in which the surrounding skin is not injured. **simple harmonic motion** *n.* HARMONIC MOTION (under HARMONIC). **simple-hearted** *a.* 1 genuine, sincere. 2 uncomplicated, guileless. **simple interest** *n.* in money loans, interest payable upon the principal, i.e. the capital sum, only. **simple interval** *n.* (*Mus.*) an interval of an octave or less. **simple machine** *n.* any of various simple mechanisms, including the pulley, wedge, lever, wheel and axle, screw, and inclined plane, which overcome resistance at one point by applying force usu. at another point. **simple-minded** *a.* 1 foolish, stupid. 2 mentally deficient, feeble-minded. **simple-mindedly** *adv.* **simple-mindedness** *n.* **simpleness** *n.* simplicity. †**simpler** *n.* a person who gathers simples, a herbalist. **simple sentence** *n.* a sentence consisting of a single main clause. **Simple Simon** *n.* a simpleton (from the nursery-rhyme character). **simple time** *n.* (*Mus.*) a tempo that has two, three or four beats to the bar. **simpleton** (-tən) *n.* a silly, gullible or feeble-minded person. **simplex** (-pleks) *a.* 1 simple, not compound. 2 in computing and telecommunications, allowing the transmission of a signal in only one direction at a time. ~*n.* (*pl.* **simplexes, simplices** (-plisēz)) 1 the most rudimentary geometric figure of a given dimension (e.g. a line in one-dimensional space, a triangle in two-dimensional space). 2 in linguistics, a simple word, as distinct from a compound. **simplicity** (-plis´-) *n.* **simplify** (-plifī) *v.t.* (*3rd pers. sing. pres.* **simplifies**, *pres.p.* **simplifying**, *past, p.p.* **simplified**) 1 to make simple. 2 to make simpler or easier to understand, to reduce to essentials. **simplification** (-fikā´shən) *n.* **simplifier** *n.* **simplism** *n.* 1 the affectation of simplicity. 2 the fault of being simplistic, oversimplification. †**simplist** *n.* a simpler, an expert in medicinal herbs. **simpliste** (-plēst´, sã´-) *a.* simplistic, naive. **simplistic** (-plis´-) *a.* 1 oversimplified, naive, superficial, unrealistically limited, shallow etc. 2 oversimplifying. **simplistically** *adv.* **simply** *adv.* 1 in a simple manner. 2 absolutely, without qualification (*simply delicious*). 3 merely, only, just (*I'm simply wanting to help*). [F, from L *simplicem*, nom. *-plex*, onefold (*sim-*, cp. *semel*, once, *simul*, at once, *singulī*, one by one, *-plic-*, as in *plicāre*, to fold)]
simulacrum (simūlā´krəm) *n.* (*pl.* **simulacra** (-krə)) 1 an image or likeness. 2 a deceptive or superficial likeness, a spurious substitute. 3 a mere semblance or pretence. [L, from *simulāre*, to imitate, from *similis*, SIMILAR]
simulate (sim´ūlāt) *v.t.* 1 to assume the likeness or mere appearance of. 2 to counterfeit, to feign, to imitate, to put on, to mimic. 3 to reproduce the structure, movement or conditions of (a situation or environment) e.g. in an experiment, by computer etc. 4 (of a word or expression) to alter in form by mistaken association with an unrelated word. **simulated** *a.* 1 pretended, false, feigned, counterfeited. 2 (of leather, fur etc.) imitation. 3 (of the flight of an aircraft, spaceship etc.) reproduced or represented by a model. **simulation** (-lā´shən) *n.* **simulative** (-lətiv) *a.* **simulatively** *adv.* **simulator** (-lātə) *n.* 1 a person or thing that simulates something. 2 a device that simulates a certain environment, set of conditions, or process, used for testing or training purposes. [L *simulātus*, p.p. of *simulāre*, from *similis*, SIMILAR]
simulcast (sim´əlkahst) *n.* (the transmission of) a simultaneous broadcast on radio and television. ~*v.t.* to broadcast (a programme) simultaneously on radio and television. [*simul*taneous, broad*cast*]
simultaneous (siməltā´niəs) *a.* 1 happening, done or acting at the same time. 2 coincident or concurrent (with). **simultaneity** (-tənā´-) *n.* **simultaneous equations** *n.pl.* a set of two or more equations in both or all of which the variables have the same values. **simultaneously** *adv.* **simultaneousness** *n.* [late L *simultāneus* (*simultim*, adv., from L *simul*, together, -ANEOUS)]
simurg (simœg´), **simorg** (-mawg´), **simurgh** *n.* an enormous fabulous bird of Persian mythology with the ability to think and speak. [Pers. *sīmurgh*]
sin[1] (sin) *n.* 1 transgression of duty, morality, or the law of God. 2 wickedness, moral depravity. 3 a transgression, an offence. 4 a breach of etiquette, social standards etc. 5 (*dated, coll.*) a shame, a pity. ~*v.i.* (*pres.p.* **sinning**, *past, p.p.* **sinned**) 1 to commit a sin. 2 to offend (against). ~†*v.t.* to commit (a crime, sin etc.). **as sin** (*coll.*) to a degree, extremely, very (*ugly as sin*). **for one's sins** (*facet.*) literally, as a judgement upon one, meaning little more than 'as it happens'. **like sin** (*coll.*)

intensely (*She hates him like sin*). **mortal sin** MORTAL. **original sin** ORIGINAL (under ORIGIN). **seven deadly sins** SEVEN. **to live in sin** (of a couple) to cohabit without being married. **sin bin** *n.* 1 (*sl.*) in ice hockey etc., an area to the side of the pitch where players who have committed fouls are temporarily sent. 2 (*coll.*) an independent unit where disruptive school pupils can be sent for temporary attendance. 3 (*euphem.*) a brothel. **sin-eater** *n.* (*Hist.*) a person who took on the sins of a deceased person by eating beside the corpse. **sinful** *a.* 1 (of a person) frequently or habitually sinning. 2 (of an act) culpable, reprehensible, or entailing sin. **sinfully** *adv.* **sinfulness** *n.* **sinless** *a.* **sinlessly** *adv.* **sinlessness** *n.* **sinner** *n.* someone who habitually sins, a sinful person. **sin-offering** *n.* a sacrifice to atone for sin. **sins of the flesh** *n.pl.* unchastity. [OE *synn*, cp. Dut. *zonde*, G *Sünde*, Icel., Dan. and Swed. *synd*]

sin[2] (sin) *abbr.* SINE[1].

Sinaitic (sīnāit´ik) *a.* of or relating to, or given at, Mount Sinai or the peninsula of Sinai.

Sinanthropus (sinan´thrəpəs) *n.* any of the primitive apelike hominids represented by Peking man, now regarded as a subspecies of *Homo erectus*. [late L *Sīnae*, the Chinese, Gr. *anthrōpos*, a man]

sinapism (sin´əpizm) *n.* a mustard plaster. [late L, from Gr. *sinēpi*, mustard]

since (sins) *adv.* 1 after or from a time specified or implied till now (*I've been scared ever since*). 2 at some time after such a time and before now (*It's happened twice since*). 3 before this, before now, ago (*I gave up hoping long since*). ~*prep.* 1 from the time of. 2 throughout or during the time after. 3 after (a certain event, time or date) and before now. ~*conj.* 1 from the time when, during the time after. 2 inasmuch as. 3 because. [ME *sithens*, thence, OE *siththan* (*sith*, after, *thon*, that)]

sincere (sinsiə´) *a.* (*comp.* **sincerer**, *superl.* **sincerest**) 1 being in reality as in appearance or profession. 2 not feigned or put on, genuine, honest, undissembling, frank. **sincerely** *adv.* in a sincere manner. **yours sincerely** a conventional way of ending a formal or business letter. **sincereness** *n.* **sincerity** (-ser´i-) *n.* [OF, from L *sincērus*, pure, sincere]

Usage note In closing letters, *Yours sincerely* is a formal style, and goes with an opening in which an individual is addressed by name (*Dear John*, *Dear Miss X* etc.).

---

sinciput (sin´sipŭt) *n.* the upper part of the head, especially from the forehead to the crown. **sincipital** (-sip´-) *a.* [L SEMI-, *caput*, head]

sine[1] (sīn) *n.* 1 a trigonometric function that is the ratio of the length of the line opposite the angle to the length of the hypotenuse in a right-angled triangle. 2 a function of the straight line drawn from one extremity of an arc perpendicular to the diameter passing through the other extremity. **sine curve** *n.* a curve representing the relationship between the size of an angle and its sine, a sinusoid. **sine wave** *n.* any oscillation whose representation is a sine curve. **sinical** (sin´ikəl) *a.* of or relating to a sine or sines. [L *sinus*, curve]

sine[2] (sin´i, sī´-) *prep.* without, lacking. **sine cura** (kū´rə) *adv.*, *a.* without duties or office. **sine die** (dī´ē, dē´ā) *adv.*, *a.* without any day (being fixed). **sine qua non** (sī´ni kwā non, sin´i kwah nōn) *n.* (*pl.* **sine qua nons**) an essential condition or indispensable requirement. [L]

sinecure (sin´ikūə, sī´-) *n.* 1 an ecclesiastical benefice without cure of souls. 2 any paid office with few or no duties attached. **sinecurism** *n.* **sinecurist** *n.* [L *sine cura*, without care]

sinew (sin´ū) *n.* 1 a tendon, a fibrous cord connecting muscle and bone. 2 (*pl.*) muscles. 3 (*often in pl.*) that which gives strength or power, e.g. to a state, organization or policy, muscle, clout. ~*v.t.* (*poet.*) 1 to knit strongly together. 2 to strengthen or furnish with sinews. **sinewed** *a.* **sinewless** *a.* **sinews of war** *n.pl.* the availability of money. **sinewy** *a.* **sinewiness** *n.* [OE *sinu*, *seono* (cp. Dut. *zenuw*, G *Sehne*, Icel. *sin*)]

sinfonia (sinfō´niə) *n.* 1 a symphony. 2 an orchestral piece introducing a baroque opera, suite etc. 3 a symphony orchestra. **sinfonietta** (-fōniet´ə) *n.* 1 a short or light symphony. 2 a small symphony orchestra. [It.]

sing (sing) *v.i.* (*past* **sang** (sang), *p.p.* **sung** (sŭng)) 1 to utter words in a tuneful manner, to render a song vocally, to make vocal melody. 2 (of birds, or certain insects) to emit sweet or melodious sounds. 3 (of a kettle, the wind etc.) to make a murmuring or whistling sound. 4 (of the ears) to ring, to buzz. 5 (*sl.*) to confess, to inform, to grass. 6 to tell (of) in song or poetry. 7 (*poet.*) to compose poetry. ~*v.t.* 1 to utter (words, a song, tune etc.) in a tuneful or melodious manner. 2 to relate, proclaim or celebrate in verse or poetry. 3 to celebrate. 4 to accompany with singing; to greet, acclaim, lull (to sleep), usher (in or out) etc., with singing. 5 to chant. **to sing out** to call out loudly, to shout. **to sing the praises of** to commend warmly, to proclaim the virtues of. **to sing up** to sing more loudly and enthusiastically. **singable** *a.* **singalong** *n.* 1 (*often attrib.*) a tune or song that an audience can join in with, or sing in accompaniment to. 2 an occasion or event at which the audience can join in with the performer in singing popular or familiar songs. **to sing along** (of an audience) to accompany a performer in singing popular songs. **singer** (sing´ər) *n.* **singer-songwriter** *n.* someone who writes songs and performs them, esp. professionally. **singing** *a.*, *n.* **singing bird** *n.* **singing hinny** *n.* (*pl.* **singing hinnies**) (*North.*) a currant cake that hisses as it cooks on the griddle. **singingly** *adv.* **singing master** *n.* (*dated*) a teacher of singing. **singing saw** *n.* MUSICAL SAW (under MUSIC). **singing telegram** *n.* a (usu. congratulatory) telegram with a message which is delivered in song (often by someone in costume). **singing voice** *n.* the voice as used in singing. **sing-song** *a.* 1 (of a voice, accent etc.) having a rising and falling inflection. 2 having a monotonous rhythm. ~*n.* 1 a monotonous rising and falling (of a voice etc.). 2 an informal session of singing usu. well-known songs. ~*v.i.*, *v.t.* (*past*, *p.p.* **sing-songed**) to utter, to recite, sing etc. in a sing-song manner. [OE *singan*, cp. Dut. *zingen*, G. *singen*, Icel. *syngja*]

Usage note In standard English, the past tense of *sing* is *sang*, not *sung*.

---

sing. *abbr.* singular.

singe (sinj) *v.t.* (*pres.p.* **singeing**, *past*, *p.p.* **singed**) 1 to burn slightly, to scorch, to burn the surface of. 2 to burn bristles or nap off (an animal carcass or fabric). 3 in hairdressing, to burn the tips off (the hair). ~*n.* a slight or superficial burn. **to singe one's wings** to take a risk and come off badly. **singed** *a.* [OE *sengan*, cp. Dut. *zengen*, G *sengen*, cogn. with Icel. *sangr*, burnt, singed]

Singhalese SINHALESE.

single (sing´gəl) *a.* 1 consisting of one only, sole. 2 simple, not compound, double or complex, not combined with others. 3 particular, individual, separate, solitary, alone, unaided, unaccompanied. 4 (*with neg.*) even one (*not a single offer*). 5 (*used for emphasis*) individual (*every single person*). 6 unmarried, or without a current partner. 7 involving or performed by one or by one on each side. 8 designed for use by or with one person, thing etc. 9 (of a travel ticket) valid for the outward journey only. 10 (*poet.*) sincere, ingenuous, consistent. 11 (of petals or blooms) not double, not clustered. ~*n.* 1 a single thing, item, quantity or measure. 2 a rail, bus etc. ticket for a journey in one direction. **3** a gramophone record with only one track recorded on each side. **4** a single round or game, a hit for one run in cricket or a one-base hit in baseball. **5** (*pl.*) a game, esp. of tennis, consisting of a single player on either side. **6** (*usu. in pl.*) an unmarried person. **7** (*N Am., coll.*) a one-dollar bill. ~*v.t.* to pick (out) from among others. **single acrostic** *n.* an acrostic that uses only the first letter of each line. **single-acting** *a.* (of an engine or pump) working by means of pressure on one side of the piston or pistons only. **single-action** *a.* (of a gun) that must be cocked before firing. **single bed** *n.* a bed intended to be used by one person. **single blessedness** *n.* the state of being unmarried. **single-breasted** *a.* (of a jacket, coat etc.) having only one thickness of cloth over the breast when closed, with one central set of buttons, holes etc.; not overlapping. **single combat** *n.* a duel. **single cream** *n.* pouring cream of a less fatty consistency than double cream. **single-cut** *a.* (of a metal file) having grooves incised in one direction only, not criss-crossing. **single-decker** *n.* a bus with a single floor or deck of seats. **single-end** *n.* (*Sc.*) a one-room dwelling, typically in a tenement. **single entry** *n.* in bookkeeping, the system of entering transactions in one account only. **single figures** *n.pl.* a number etc. under ten. **single file** *n.* a line of people, vehicles etc. standing or moving one behind the other. ~*adv.* one behind the other. **single-handed** *a.* **1** done without assistance. **2** unassisted, alone. **3** (of e.g. a player in certain games etc.) using only one hand. ~*adv.* without assistance, alone. **single-handedly** *adv.* **single-handedness** *n.* **single-hearted** *a.* **1** free from duplicity, sincere. **2** devoted. **single-issue** *a.* (of a political party) founded for the achievement of one particular aim only. **single-lens reflex** *a.* (of a camera) with a reflex system that has a single lens serving both viewfinder and film. **single-line** *a.* (of a thoroughfare) only allowing traffic in one direction at a time. **single market** *n.* an association of countries trading freely with one another, esp. the single internal market of the European Union. **single-minded** *a.* **1** intent on one purpose only. **2** dedicated. **single-mindedly** *adv.* **single-mindedness** *n.* **singleness** *n.* **single parent** *n.* one parent raising a child or children alone. **single-parent family** *n.* a one-parent family. **single phase** *n.* an alternating-current supply using an outward wire and a return wire. **single-phase** *a.* denoting such a system. **single pneumonia** *n.* pneumonia affecting one lung only. **singles bar, singles club** *n.* a bar or club where unmarried people meet. **single-seater** *n., a.* of a vehicle, vessel etc., having seating for only one person. **single-sex** *a.* (of a school or other institution) admitting members of one sex only. **single stick** *n.* **1** a wooden stick or sword formerly used in a kind of fencing. **2** fencing with this, cudgel-play. **singlet** (-glit) *n.* **1** an undershirt, a vest. **2** (*Physics*) a single line in a spectrum. **singleton** (-tən) *n.* **1** a card that is the only one of its suit in a player's hand at whist, bridge etc. **2** a single object, person etc. as opposed to a group or pair. **3** an only child. **4** the only child of a birth, as opposed to twins etc. **5** (*Math.*) a mathematical set of one. **single-track** *a.* **1** (of a railway) having a single line, so that only one train can use it at a time. **2** (of a road) too narrow to accommodate two vehicles abreast. **singletree** *n.* (*N Am., Austral.*) a swingletree. **singly** *adv.* [late L *singulus*, from L *singulī*, one by one]

singspiel (sing´shpēl, zing´-) *n.* a dramatic entertainment in which the action is expressed alternately in dialogue and song. [G (*singen*, to SING, *Spiel*, play)]

singular (sing´gūlə) *a.* **1** standing alone, out of the usual course, strange, remarkable, extraordinary, unique, distinguished. **2** peculiar, odd, eccentric. **3** (of a word or inflected form of a word) denoting or referring to one person or thing; not plural. **4** (*Math.*) having unique properties. **5** (of a logical proposition) referring to a specific thing or person, not general. **6** single, individual, particular. ~*n.* **1** (*Gram.*) the singular number. **2** a word denoting this. **singularity** (-lar´-) *n.* (*pl.* **singularities**) **1** the state of being singular. **2** an odd mannerism or trait. **3** (*Physics, Math.*) a point in space-time at which matter is compressed to an infinite density, as in a black hole. **singularize, singularise** *v.t.* **1** to distinguish, or make striking or eye-catching. **2** to alter (a word) that sounds like a plural to a singular form (as the form *pease* was supplanted by *pea*). **singularization** (-zā´shən) *n.* **singularly** *adv.* [ME *singuler*, F *singulier*, L *singulāris*, as SINGLE]

singultus (sing·gŭl´təs) *n.* (*Med.*) hiccups, hiccuping. [L]

sinh (shīn, sinch, sīnăch´) *abbr.* (*Math.*) a hyperbolic sine. [*sine*, *hyperbolic*]

Sinhalese (sinhəlēz´), **Singhalese, †Cingalese** (sing·gə-) *a.* of or relating to Sri Lanka (formerly Ceylon), or to its majority people or their language; Sri Lankan. ~*n.* (*pl.* **Sinhalese, Singhalese, †Cingalese**) **1** a native or inhabitant of Sri Lanka. **2** a member of the Sinhalese people constituting the majority of the inhabitants of Sri Lanka. **3** the official language of Sri Lanka and the Sinhalese people. **Sinhala** (sin´hələ) *a., n.* [Sansk. *Siinhala*, Sri Lanka]

Sinic (sin´ik) *a.* Chinese. **Sinicism** (-sizm) *n.* a Chinese idiom, custom etc. **Sinicize** (-sīz), **Sinicise** *v.t.* to make Chinese or impart Chinese characteristics to. **Sinicization** (-zā´shən) *n.* **Sinify** (-fī) *v.t.* (*3rd pers. sing. pres.* **Sinifies**, *pres.p.* **Sinifying**, *past, p.p.* **Sinified**) to Sinicize. **Sinification** (-fikā´shən) *n.* [med. L *sinicus*, from late L *Sīnae*, the Chinese]

sinical SINE[1].

sinister (sin´istə) *a.* **1** ill-looking, malignant, malevolent, villainous. **2** nefarious or criminal. **3** ill-omened, inauspicious. **4** (*Her.*) on the left side (of a shield etc.), the side to the right of the observer. **5** †in left-hand. **sinisterly** *adv.* **sinisterness** *n.* **sinistral** *a.* **1** left-handed. **2** of, on, or towards the left. **3** (of a flatfish) having the left side uppermost. **4** (of a spiral shell) with a whorl turning (unusually) to the left. **sinistrality** (-tral´-) *n.* **sinistrally** *adv.* **sinistro-** *comb. form* on or towards the left; laevo-. **sinistrorse** (-traws) *a.* (*Bot.*) rising and twining to the left, from the observer's point of view. **sinistrorsal** (-traw´-) *a.* **sinistrorsally** *adv.* **sinistrous** *a.* **1** ill-omened, unlucky, sinister. **2** being on, of or relating to, directed towards, or inclined to the left. **sinistrously** *adv.* [F *sinistre*, L *sinistrum*, nom. *-ter*, left]

sink (singk) *v.i.* (*past* **sank** (sangk), **sunk** (sŭngk), *p.p.* **sunk**, *part. a.* **sunken** (-kən)) **1** to go downwards, to descend, to fall gradually. **2** to disappear below the horizon. **3** to drop below the surface of a liquid. **4** (of a ship) to go down to the sea bed etc. **5** to fall or descend by force of gravity. **6** to decline to a lower level of health, morals etc. **7** to deteriorate. **8** to droop, to despond. **9** to subside or decline. **10** to expire or come to an end by degrees. **11** to become lower in intensity, pitch, value, price etc. **12** to become shrunken or hollow, to slope downwards, to recede. **13** to go deep or deeper (into), to be impressed (into) to be absorbed. **14** (of darkness) to fall (on a place). ~*v.t.* **1** to cause to sink. **2** to submerge (as) in a fluid, to send below the surface. **3** to excavate, to make by excavating, to bore (a shaft) or dig (a well). **4** to inset or inlay into a surface. **5** to cause to disappear. **6** to pocket (the ball) in snooker etc. **7** in golf, to hole (the ball or a putt). **8** to put out of sight, to conceal, to suppress, to lose sight of. **9** to allow to fall or droop. **10** to lower, to degrade, to ruin. **11** to reduce, to diminish, to lessen the value of. **12 a** to invest (money in an enterprise). **b** to invest unprofitably, to lose, to waste, to squander. **13** (*coll.*) to drink, to quaff. **14** (*usu. in pass.*) to absorb or preoccupy (*to be sunk* *in thought*). ~*n.* **1** a plastic, porcelain or metal basin, usu. fitted to a water supply and drainage system in a kitchen. **2** a cesspool or sewer. **3** a place of iniquity. **4** (*Geol.*) a depression esp. in limestone where a stream disappears underground, a sink-hole, a swallow-hole. **5** (*Physics*) a device, body or process which absorbs or dissipates energy, as *heat sink*. **to sink in 1** to become absorbed, to penetrate. **2** to become understood. **to sink or swim** to either succeed or fail (in a venture etc.). **sinkable** *a.* **sinkage** (-kij) *n.* **1** the act, operation or process of sinking. **2** the amount of sinking. **3** a depression, a shaft, a sinking or hollow area. **sinker** *n.* **1** a person who or something that sinks. **2** a weight used to sink a fishing line, net etc. **3** (*N Am.*) a doughnut. **4** (*N Am.*) in baseball, a ball that drops after being pitched or hit. **sink-hole** *n.* **1** (*Geol.*) a hole or series of holes in limestone strata through which water sinks below the surface or a stream disappears underground, a swallow-hole. **2** a hole for the discharge of foul waste. **sinking** *a.*, *n.* **sinking feeling** *n.* the uncomfortable feeling in the abdomen brought on by e.g. nervousness or hunger. **sinking fund** *n.* a fund set aside for the reduction of a debt. **sink-tidy** *n.* (*pl.* **sink-tidies**) **1** a receptacle with a perforated bottom for holding washing-up utensils. **2** a small sieve placed over a plughole for catching refuse. **sink unit** *n.* a sink and draining board set in a structure with a drawer and cupboards. **sinky** *a.* (*comp.* **sinkier**, *superl.* **sinkiest**) (of the ground) soft or yielding to the foot. **sunken garden** *n.* a garden at a lower level than the surrounding land. **sunk fence** *n.* **1** a fence set along the bottom of a ditch. **2** a ditch forming an enclosing barrier. [OE *sincan* (cp. Dut. *zinken*, G *sinken*, Dan. *synke*, also Sansk., *sich*, to sprinkle)]

Usage note In standard English, the past tense of *sink* is *sank*, not *sunk*.

sinkie (sing´ki) *n.* (*sl.*) a single person with a good income and no children. [from *s*ingle *i*ncome *n*o *k*ids, after TWINKIE]

sinner SIN[1].

sinnet (sin´it), **sennit** (sen´it) *n.* (*Naut.*) braided cordage made with three to nine cords.

Sinn Fein (shin fān´) *n.* the Irish republican party which was formed in 1905 by the coalescence of all the Irish separatist organizations, and is the political wing of the Irish Republican Army. **Sinn Feiner** *n.* a member of Sinn Fein. [Ir., ourselves]

Sino- (sī´nō) *comb. form* Chinese, or Chinese and, as in *Sino-Tibetan*.

sinology (sīnol´əji) *n.* the study of Chinese languages, culture, literature etc. **sinological** (-nəloj´-) *a.* **sinologist** *n.* **sinologue** (sī´nəlog, sin´-) *n.* an expert or specialist in sinology, a sinologist. [Gr. *Sinae*, late L *Sinae*, see SINIC]

Sino-Tibetan (sīnōtibet´ən) *n.* a family of languages comprising most Chinese languages, Tibetan, Burmese and usu. Thai. ~*a.* of or relating to this family of languages.

sinsemilla (sinsəmē´lyə) *n.* **1** a specially potent type of marijuana. **2** the seedless variety of cannabis plant from which it is obtained. [Am. Sp., without seed]

sinter (sin´tə) *n.* a calcareous or siliceous rock precipitated from (hot) mineral waters. ~*v.t.* to form (metal powder, ceramics, glass etc.) into a solid mass by pressure or heating at a temperature below melting point. ~*v.i.* to be formed into such a mass. [G, CINDER]

sinuate (sin´ūət), **sinuated** (-ātid) *a.* (esp. of the edges of leaves etc.) bending, curving or winding in and out. **sinuately** *adv.* [L *sinuātus*, p.p. of *sinuāre* to bend, from SINUS]

sinuous (sin´ūəs) *a.* **1** bending in and out. **2** winding, serpentine, tortuous. **sinuosity** (-os´-) *n.* (*pl.* **sinuosities**) **1** the quality of being sinuous. **2** a bend or series of bends and curves. **sinuously** *adv.* **sinuousness** *n.* [F *sinueux*, L *sinuosus*, from SINUS]

sinupallial (sinūpal´iəl), **sinupalliate** (-iət) *a.* (of a division of bivalve molluscs) having a deeply incurved pallial line for the passage to and fro of the pallial siphons.

sinus (sī´nəs) *n.* (*pl.* **sinuses**) **1** a cavity or pouchlike hollow, esp. in bone or tissue. **2** the cavity in the skull which connects with the nose. **3** (*Med.*) a fistula. **4** (*Bot.*) a rounded recess or curve, as in the margin of a leaf. **sinusitis** (-sī´tis) *n.* (painful) inflammation of a nasal sinus. **sinusoid** *n.* **1** (*Math.*) a sine curve. **2** any of the small blood vessels that replace the capillaries in a bodily organ, esp. the liver. **sinusoidal** (-soi´-) *a.* **sinusoidally** *adv.* [L, a curve, a recess]

Sion ZION.

-sion (shən, zhən) *suf.* forming nouns from Latin past participles with a stem in *-s-*, as *revulsion*, *immersion*, *fusion*.

Sioux (soo) *n.* (*pl.* **Sioux**) **1** a member of a N American Indian people of the upper Mississippi and Missouri rivers, a Dakota. **2** any of the various Siouan languages spoken by this group. ~*a.* of or relating to the Sioux. **Siouan** *n.* **1** a family of central and eastern N American languages. **2** a Sioux. ~*a.* of or relating to the Sioux or their languages. [F, from N Am. Ind.]

sip (sip) *v.t.*, *v.i.* (*pres.p.* **sipping**, *past*, *p.p.* **sipped**) to drink or imbibe in small quantities using the lips. ~*n.* **1** a very small draught of liquid. **2** an act of sipping. **sipper** *n.* **sippet** (-it) *n.* **1** a small piece of toast or fried bread garnishing a dish of mince etc. **2** a small piece of bread or other food soaked in broth etc. **3** any small piece or fragment. [OE *sypian*, cogn. with *sūpan*, to SUP (cp. MDut. *sippen*, Swed. dial. *syppa*)]

sipe[1] (sīp) *v.i.* to soak through, to ooze or seep. [OE *sīpian*, var. of SEEP]

sipe[2] (sīp) *n.* a groove in the tread of a tyre, for improving its grip and helping the dispersal of water. [from SIPE[1]]

siphon, siphonal etc. SYPHON.

siphonophore (sī´fənəfaw, -fon´-) *n.* any member of an order of marine life (the Siphonophora) variously regarded as a colony of medusoid zooids or as a single individual composed of a cluster of tubular organs. **siphonophoran** (-nof´ərən) *a.*, *n.*

siphuncle (sī´fŭngkəl) *n.* **1** the tube connecting the chambers of the shell in many cephalopods. **2** the suctorial or other tubes in insects etc.

sipper, sippet SIP.

sir (sœ) *n.* **1** a form of courteous address to a man. **2** (**Sir**) a title prefixed to the names of baronets and knights and formerly clergymen. [SIRE]

sirdar (sœ´dah), **sardar** (sœ´dah) *n.* **1** a military leader or commander in the Indian subcontinent or in other Eastern countries. **2** (**Sirdar**) the former commander-in-chief of the Egyptian army. **3** a title used before the names of Sikh men. **4** a leader, chief, foreman etc. [Pers. *sar*, head, *-dār*, holding]

sire (sīə) *n.* **1** the male parent of an animal, esp. a stallion. **2** †a title used in addressing a king or a sovereign prince. **3** (*poet.*) †a father, a progenitor. ~*v.t.* (esp. of stallions or male domestic animals) to beget. [OF, earlier *senre*, L SENIOR]

siren (sī´rən) *n.* **1** an apparatus for producing a loud warning sound by means of a rotating perforated disc through which steam or compressed air is emitted. **2** an electrical warning device emitting a similarly piercing sound. **3** in Greek mythology, any of several sea nymphs, half woman and half bird, dwelling on rocky isles and luring sailors to shipwreck by their singing. **4 a** a charming or seductive woman, esp. a dangerous temptress. **b** (*sometimes attrib.*) an alluring distraction. **5** a sweet singer. **6** any of the Sirenidae, a family of American eel-like amphibians, with two anterior feet and permanent branchiae. **sirenian** (-rē´-) *n.* any of the Sirenia, an order of marine herbivorous mammals, allied to the whales, but having the fore limbs developed into paddles, comprising the manatees and dugongs. ~*a.* of or relating to the Sirenia. **siren suit** *n.* a suit in one piece, closed with a zip fastening (designed for wearing in air-raid shelters). [L *sīrēn*, Gr. *seirēn*]

sirih (siə´ri) *n.* betel. [Malay]

sirloin (sœ´loin) *n.* the loin or upper part of the loin of beef. [orig. *surloine*, OF *surlonge* (*sur*, over, *longe*, LOIN)]

sirocco (sirok´ō), **scirocco** (shi-) *n.* (*pl.* **siroccos, sciroccos**) **1** a hot oppressive wind blowing from N Africa across to Italy etc., often carrying dust or rain. **2** a sultry southerly wind in Italy. [It. *sirocco*, Arab. *sharq*, east]

†**sirrah** (sir´ə) *n.* fellow, sir (a term of address used in anger or contempt). [Prov. *sira*, F *sire*, SIRE]

sirree (sirē´) *n.* (*N Am., coll.*) sir (used for emphasis often with *yes* or *no*). [SIR]

sirup SYRUP.

sirvente (sœvãt´) *n.* a form of ballad or lay, usu. satirical, used by the medieval trouvères and troubadours. [F, *servir*, L *servīre*, to SERVE]

☒ **sirynge** common misspelling of SYRINGE.

sis (sis), **siss** *n.* (*coll.*) short for SISTER. **sissy** (sis´i), **cissy** *n.* (*pl.* **sissies, cissies**) an effeminate, feeble or cowardly boy or man. ~*a.* (*comp.* **sissier**, *superl.* **sissiest**) effeminate, feeble, cowardly. [SISTER]

sisal (sī´səl), **sisal-grass, sisal-hemp** *n.* the fibre of the Mexican agave used for cordage etc. [*Sisal*, a port in Yucatan from where it was first exported]

siskin (sis´kin) *n.* a small migratory songbird, *Carduelus spinus*, related to the goldfinch. [MDut. *cijsken*, LG *zieske*, Pol. *czyzik*]

☒ **sisors** common misspelling of SCISSORS.

siss, sissy SIS.

sist (sist) *v.t.* (*Sc. Law*) **1** to stop, to stay. **2** to summon. ~*n.* a stay of proceedings. [L *sistere*, to cause to stand, from *stāre*, to stand]

sister (sis´tə) *n.* **1 a** a female born of the same parents as oneself. **b** a half-sister, a foster sister or, formerly, a sister-in-law. **2** (*esp. N Am., coll.*) used as a form of address to a female companion or friend. **3** a female fellow member of the same group, society, trade union etc., esp. now a fellow feminist. **4** a senior nurse, usu. one in charge of a hospital ward. **5** a member of a female religious order. **6** any thing, quality etc. closely resembling the one in question. ~*a.* closely related, similar, of the same design, type, origins, as *sister ships*. ~*v.t.* **1** to be sister to. **2** to call sister. ~*v.i.* to be closely allied or to have a sisterly resemblance (to). **sister city** *n.* (*pl.* **sister cities**) a city that is twinned with one's own. **sister german** *n.* (*pl.* **sisters german**) a sister having the same parents as oneself. **sisterhood** *n.* **1** the state of being a sister, the relationship of sisters. **2** a religious community of women bound together by monastic vows. **3** a community or body of women, such as the Women's Movement, bound together by common interests. **sister hook** *n.* either of a pair of hooks opening to receive a rope etc., and overlapping. **sister-in-law** *n.* (*pl.* **sisters-in-law**) **1** one's husband's or wife's sister. **2** one's brother's wife. **sisterless** *a.* **sisterlike** *a.* **sisterly** *a.* **sisterliness** *n.* **Sister of Mercy** *n.* (*pl.* **Sisters of Mercy**) a member of a teaching or charitable order, esp. that founded in 1827 in Dublin. **sister uterine** *n.* (*pl.* **sisters uterine**) a sister having the same mother, but not the same father, as another. [OE *sweoster*, *swuster* (cp. Dut. *zuster*, G *Schwester*, Icel. *systir*, also L *soror*, Sansk. *svasā*)]

Sistine (sis´tēn, -tīn) *a.* of or relating to any of the Popes named Sixtus, esp. Sixtus IV (*the Sistine Chapel*). [It. *Sistino*, from *Sisto*, Sixtus]

sistrum (sis´trəm) *n.* (*pl.* **sistrums, sistra** (-trə)) a jingling instrument used by the ancient Egyptians in the worship of Isis. [L, from Gr. *seistron*, from *seiein*, to shake]

Sisyphean (sisifē´ən) *a.* (of a task) unceasingly or fruitlessly laborious. [from *Sisuphos*, one of the Titans, condemned to push up a hill a stone that everlastingly rolled back again]

sit (sit) *v.i.* (*pres.p.* **sitting**, *past*, *p.p.* **sat** (sat)) **1** to set oneself or be in a resting posture with the body nearly vertical supported on the buttocks. **2** (of birds and various animals) to be in a resting posture. **3** to perch, to roost. **4** (of a bird) to cover eggs in order to hatch, to brood. **5** to be in a specified position, quarter etc. **6** to be situated. **7** (of clothes etc.) to suit, to fit. **8** to rest, press or weigh (on). **9** to meet, to hold a session. **10** to hold or occupy a seat (on a deliberative body or in a specified capacity e.g. as a magistrate). **11** to babysit (for someone). **12** to take up a position, to encamp (before) so as to besiege. **13** †to remain, to abide. ~*v.t.* **1** to cause to sit, to set. **2** to place (oneself) in a seat. **3** to hold or keep a sitting position on (a horse etc.). **4** to be a candidate for (an examination). **5** (*in comb.* as *babysit*) to stay in with so as to look after. ~*n.* **1** an act or time of sitting. **2** a sit-down, a rest. **sitting pretty** in an advantageous position. **to make someone sit up** to surprise someone, or rivet their attention. **to sit at the feet of** to be taught by (a certain teacher, esp. a famous one). **to sit back** to withdraw from active participation. **to sit bodkin** BODKIN. **to sit by** to observe without taking an active part. **to sit down 1** to place oneself on a seat, or in a sitting position, after standing. **2** to place in a sitting position, to cause to sit. **3** to begin a siege. **to sit down under** to submit meekly to (an insult or insulting treatment). **to sit for 1** to take (an examination). **2** to represent (a constituency in parliament). **3** to pose for (a portrait). **to sit heavy on the stomach** to be difficult to digest. **to sit in** to take part in a sit-in. **to sit in judgement** to pass judgement on the actions of others, to be critical. **to sit in on** to observe, be present at, or participate in (a discussion, meeting, lecture etc.) as a visitor. **to sit loosely on** (of the duties of office) to be taken rather lightly by. **to sit on 1** to hold a meeting, discussion or investigation over. **2** (*coll.*) to repress severely, to snub. **3** (*coll.*) to suppress or prevent from circulating. **to sit on one's hands 1** not to act or intervene. **2** not to applaud. **to sit on the fence** FENCE. **to sit out 1** to sit out of doors. **2** to sit apart from (a dance, meeting etc.). **3** to stay till the end of (a concert etc., or an uncomfortable episode). **4** to stay longer than (other visitors). **to sit tight** to hold firm and do nothing. **to sit under** to attend the ministrations of (a member of the clergy). **to sit up 1** to rise from a recumbent position. **2** to sit with the body erect. **3** suddenly to pay attention, take notice, become alert, esp. in *to sit up and take notice*. **4** not to go to bed. **sit-down** *n.* **1** (*coll.*) a spell of sitting, a rest, a break. **2** a protest in which participants sit down in a public place, or occupy their workplace, as a form of passive resistance. **3** a sit-down strike. ~*a.* (of a meal) eaten while seated at a table. **sit-down strike** *n.* a strike in which employees occupy their place of work. **sit-in** *n.* the occupation of premises (e.g. at a university) as a form of protest. **sitter** *n.* **1** a person who sits, esp. for a portrait. **2** (*coll.*) something easy to achieve or accomplish, esp. an easy catch or shot. **3** a babysitter. **4** a hen that sits on a clutch of eggs to incubate them. **sitting** *n.* **1** a period of continuous sitting (e.g. for a portrait). **2** a session of one particular activity. **3** a meeting of a body, esp. the time when business is officially in progress. **4** a meal-serving session (*first sitting for lunch*). **5** (*Law*) a term. **6** a clutch of eggs for hatching or the process of brooding on them. ~*a.* **1** seated. **2** (of a bird or animal) remaining still, not flying or running. 3 (of a hen) sitting on eggs to hatch them, brooding. 4 holding office or (of a Member of Parliament) current. 5 in session. **sitting duck** *n.* an easy target, someone in a defenceless position. **sitting room** *n.* 1 a room for sitting in, a living room or lounge. 2 room or space for people to sit down. **sitting target** *n.* a sitting duck. **sitting tenant** *n.* the person currently occupying or in possession of a flat, house etc. **sit-up** *n.* a physical exercise in which the upper torso is raised from a reclining into a sitting position using the abdominal muscles without the help of the hands. **sit-upon** *n.* (*coll.*) the bottom, buttocks. [OE *sittan* (cp. Dut. *zitten*, G *sitzen*, Icel. *sitja*, also L *sedēre*, Gr. *hezesthai*, Sansk. *sad*)]

sitar (sitah´, sit´-) *n.* an Indian stringed musical instrument with a long neck. **sitarist** (-tah´-) *n.* [Hind., three-stringed]

sitatunga (sitətŭng´gə) *n.* a grey or brown antelope, *Tragelaphus spekii*, of central and E Africa, the male having spiral horns. [Swahili]

sitcom (sit´kom) *n.* (*coll.*) a situation comedy. [*sit*uation *com*edy]

site (sīt) *n.* 1 the ground on which anything, esp. a building, stands, has stood, or will stand. 2 (*esp. in comb.*) a place or centre of a particular activity or procedure (*a camping site*; *building site*). ~*v.t.* to position, locate. **on site** (available) at the workplace or place of activity. [F, from L *situs*]

sitiology (sitiol´əji), **sitology** (sītol´-) *n.* dietetics. **sitiophobia** (-fō´biə) *n.* morbid repugnance to food. [Gr. *sitos*, food, *sition*, bread, -LOGY]

Sitka (sit´kə), **Sitka spruce** *n.* a quick-growing spruce fir, *Picea sitchensis*, cultivated for its timber, native to N America. [*Sitka*, a town of Alaska]

sitrep (sit´rep) *n.* (*coll.*) a (military) report on the current situation. [*sit*uation *rep*ort]

sits vac (sits vak´) *n.pl.* (*coll.*) situations vacant, jobs offered.

sitter, sitting SIT.

situate[1] (sit´ūāt) *v.t.* (*usu. in pass.*) 1 to place. 2 to locate. 3 to place in certain circumstances. **situation** (-ā´shən) *n.* 1 the place in which something is situated, position, locality. 2 a state of affairs or set of circumstances. 3 a critical juncture, e.g. in a story or play. 4 (*dated*) a paid office, post or place, esp. of a domestic servant. **situations vacant** a heading used to introduce lists of jobs offered. **situations wanted** a heading used to introduce lists of jobs sought. **situational** *a.* **situation comedy** *n.* a serialized comedy on radio or esp. television involving the same set of characters in a different comic situation in each episode. **situationism** *n.* the argument that people's behaviour is influenced or dictated more by their circumstances or environment than by their qualities or personality. **situationist** *n.* [late L *situātus*, p.p. of *situāre*, to locate, from *situs*, SITE]

situate[2] (sit´ūət) *a.* (*usu. Law*) situated.

situation SITUATE[1].

sitz-bath (sits´bahth) *n.* 1 a bath in which a person sits, a hip bath. 2 a therapeutic bath taken thus. [G *Sitzbad* (*sitzen*, to sit, BATH[1])]

Siva (sē´və), **Shiva** (shē´-) *n.* the god who is associated with Brahma and Vishnu in the Hindu triad, known as the destroyer and reproducer of life. **Sivaism** *n.* **Sivaistic** (-is´-) *a.* **Sivaite** (-īt) *n.* [Hind., from Sansk. *çiva*, auspicious]

Sivan (sivahn´) *n.* the third month of the Jewish ecclesiastical year and ninth of the civil year, comprising parts of May and June. [Heb.]

six (siks) *n.* 1 the number or figure 6 or vi. 2 the age of six. 3 the time of six o'clock, the sixth hour after midday or midnight. 4 the sixth in a series. 5 a size represented by 6. 6 a card etc. bearing six symbols. 7 that which represents, amounts to or is worth six, e.g. a hit to the boundary, worth six runs in cricket. 8 a set or team of six, e.g. any of the divisions in a Cub-Scout or Brownie pack. ~*a.* 1 six in number. 2 aged six. **at sixes and sevens** in disorder or confusion. **six and half a dozen** six of one and half a dozen of the other. **six of one and half a dozen of the other** a dilemma presenting alternatives of equal acceptability, merit etc. **to knock for six** 1 to overcome completely, to defeat. 2 to astonish. 3 to stagger. **sixain** (sik´sān), **sixaine** *n.* in poetry, a six-line stanza. **Six Counties** *n.pl.* the counties that make up Northern Ireland. **sixer** *n.* 1 the leader of a Cub-Scout or Brownie six. 2 anything representing, worth or equal to six, e.g. a boundary hit in cricket. **sixfold** *a., adv.* 1 six times as much or as many. 2 in six parts or divisions. **six-footer** *n.* (*coll.*) a person six ft. tall. **six-gun** *n.* a six-shooter. **sixmo** (-mō) *n.* in bookbinding, sexto. **six of the best** *n.* a severe beating, esp. with a cane. **six-pack** *n.* a pack of six cans or bottles, esp. of beer. **six-pack ribs** *n.pl.* prominent torso muscles, due to body-building etc. **sixpence** *n.* (*Hist.*) a cupronickel coin equivalent to six old pennies, the equivalent of 2½p. **on a sixpence** 1 within a small area. 2 easily, quickly. **sixpenny** *a.* worth or costing sixpence, esp. before decimalization. **six-shooter** *n.* a six-chambered revolver. **sixth** *n.* 1 any one of six equal parts. 2 a sixth form. 3 (*Mus.*) **a** a musical interval of six consecutive notes on the diatonic scale. **b** a note separated from another by this interval. **c** a tone and the sixth note above or below it sounded together. ~*n., a.* 1 (the) last of six (people, things etc.). 2 the next after the fifth. **sixth form** *n.* the highest form in a secondary school. **sixth-form college** *n.* a college for pupils over 16, where subjects are taught at sixth-form level. **sixth-former** *n.* a sixth-form pupil. **sixthly** *adv.* **sixth sense** *n.* the power of intuition, or extrasensory perception. [OE (cp. Dut. *zes*, G *sechs*, Icel., Dan. and Swed. *sex*, also L *sex*, Gr. *hex*, Sansk. *shash*)]

sixte (sikst) *n.* a parry in fencing (the sixth of eight parrying positions) in which the hand is opposite the right breast and the point of the sword raised and a little to the right. [F, from L *sextus*, sixth]

sixteen (sikstēn´) *n.* 1 the number/figure 16 or xvi. 2 the age of 16. 3 a size etc. represented by 16. ~*a.* 1 16 in number. 2 aged 16. **sixteenmo** (-mō) *n.* in bookbinding, sextodecimo. **sixteenth** *n.* any one of 16 equal parts. ~*n., a.* 1 (the) last of 16 (people, things etc.). 2 the next after the 15th. **sixteenth note** *n.* (*Mus., N Am.*) a semiquaver.

Sixtine (siks´tēn, -tīn) *a.* SISTINE.

sixty (siks´ti) *n.* (*pl.* **sixties**) 1 the number/figure 60 or lx. 2 the age of 60. 3 60°F. ~*a.* 1 60 in number. 2 aged 60. **sixties** *n.pl.* 1 the period of time between one's 60th and 70th birthdays. 2 the range of temperature (Fahrenheit) between 60 and 70 degrees. 3 the period of time between the 60th and 70th years of a century. **sixtieth** *n.* any one of 60 equal parts. ~*n., a.* 1 (the) last of 60 (people, things etc.). 2 the next after the 59th. **sixty-first, sixty-second** etc. *n., a.* the ordinal numbers corresponding to sixty-one etc. **sixty-fourmo** *n.* in bookbinding, a book size in which the printing sheet has been folded into 64 leaves (by analogy with DUODECIMO (under DUODECIMAL) etc.). **sixty-fourth note** *n.* (*Mus., N Am.*) a hemidemisemiquaver. **sixty-four thousand dollar question** *n.* the crucial question (from the top prize-winning question in a television quiz show). **sixty-one, sixty-two** etc. *n.* the cardinal numbers between 60 and 70.

sizar (sī´zə) *n.* any of a number of students at Cambridge University or Trinity College, Dublin, who receive a college allowance towards expenses, and formerly acted as servitors. [from an old sense of SIZE[1], allowance, portion of food]

size[1] (sīz) *n.* 1 measurement, extent, dimensions,

magnitude. 2 any one of a series of standard grades or classes with which garments and other things are divided according to their relative dimensions. ~*v.t.* 1 to sort, grade or arrange according to size. 2 to cut or shape to a required size. **of a size** all having the same size. **of some size** fairly big. **the size of** as large as. **the size of it** the situation as it really is. **to size up** 1 to form a rough estimate of the size of. 2 to judge the capacity of (a person). **what size?** how big? **sizeable, sizable** *a.* of considerable size. **sizeableness** *n.* **sizeably** *adv.* **sized** *a.* 1 having a particular size (*usu. in comb.*, as *small-sized*). 2 sorted or graded according to size. **sizeism, sizism** *n.* discrimination on the grounds of size. **sizeist** *n., a.* **sizer**[1] *n.* **size-stick** *n.* a shoemaker's rule for measuring people's feet. **sizing**[1] *n.* the process or result of sorting or arranging according to size. [orig. short for ASSIZE]

size[2] (sīz) *n.* a gluey, gelatinous solution used to glaze surfaces (e.g. of paper), stiffen fabrics, prepare walls for papering etc. ~*v.t.* to coat, glaze or prepare with size. **sizer**[2] *n.* **sizing**[2] *n.* materials for making size. **sizy** *a.* (*comp.* **sizier**, *superl.* **siziest**). **siziness** *n.* [It. *sisa*, short for *assisa*, painter's size, as ASSIZE]

sizer[1] SIZE[1].

sizer[2] SIZE[2].

sizing[1] SIZE[1].

sizing[2] SIZE[2].

sizism SIZEISM (under SIZE[1]).

sizy SIZE[2].

sizzle (siz´əl) *v.i.* 1 to make a hissing noise as of frying. 2 (*coll.*) to be extremely hot. 3 (*coll.*) to be in a rage or in a state of extreme excitement. ~*n.* 1 a hissing noise. 2 a state of heat or excitement. **sizzler** *n.* (*coll.*) 1 a hot day. 2 anything which is striking or racy (e.g. a dress, a novel). **sizzling** *a.* 1 very hot. 2 scurrilous or risqué. ~*adv.* (*coll.*) very, as in *sizzling hot.* [imit.]

SJ *abbr.* Society of Jesus.

SJAA *abbr.* St John Ambulance Association.

SJAB *abbr.* St John Ambulance Brigade.

sjambok (sham´bok), **jambok** (jam´-) *n.* (*S Afr.*) a short heavy whip, usu. of rhinoceros hide. ~*v.t.* (*pres.p.* **sjambokking, sjamboking, jambokking, jamboking,** *past, p.p.* **sjambokked, sjamboked, jambokked, jamboked**) to flog with this kind of whip. [Afrikaans, from Malay (*chambuk*, from Urdu *chābuk*, a horse-whip)]

SJC *abbr.* in the US, Supreme Judicial Court.

ska (skah) *n.* an early form of reggae music originating in Jamaica. [etym. uncertain]

skag (skag) *n.* (*esp. N Am., sl.*) 1 a cigarette or the stub of one. 2 heroin. [etym. uncertain]

skald (skawld, skald), **scald** *n.* in ancient Scandinavia, a bard, a writer and reciter of epic poetry. **skaldic** *a.* [Icel. *skald*]

skat (skat) *n.* a three-handed card game resembling piquet. [G, from It. *scarto*]

skate[1] (skāt) *n.* 1 (each of a pair of boots fitted with) a steel blade or runner for gliding on ice, an ice-skate. 2 a four-wheeled device for fitting to the sole of a shoe, for gliding on a smooth surface, a roller skate. 3 a board or plate, often with wheels, for putting under a heavy or cumbersome object to enable it to be moved around. 4 a period of skating. ~*v.i.* to move over ice or a smooth surface on skates. ~*v.t.* to perform or describe (a particular figure) on skates. **to get one's skates on** (*coll.*) to hurry up. **to skate around** to avoid talking about or confronting (an issue, subject etc.) directly. **to skate on thin ice** to take up a risky stance when not altogether certain of one's ground. **to skate over** to gloss over or hurry over (a topic that calls for direct confrontation). **skateboard** *n.* a board mounted on roller-skate wheels on which both feet can be placed when momentum is achieved, propulsion being effected by pushing one foot against the ground. ~*v.i.* to ride on a skateboard. **skateboarder** *n.* **skateboarding** *n.* **skatepark** *n.* a place designed for skateboarding, with ramps etc. **skater** *n.* **skating** *a., n.* **skating rink** *n.* a place with an artificial floor or sheet of ice for skating. [formerly *schates, scates*, Dut. *schaats*, pl. *schaatsen*, OF *eschace* (F *échasse*), stilt, LG *schake*, SHANK]

skate[2] (skāt) *n.* (*pl. in general* **skate**, *in particular* **skates**) a fish of the genus *Raja*, distinguished by having a long pointed snout. [Icel. *skata*, cp. Norw. *skata*, Dan. *skade*]

skate[3] (skāt) *n.* (*sl.*) a mean or dishonest person. [etym. uncertain]

skean (skē´ən) *n.* (*Hist.*) a long knife or dagger used in Scotland and Ireland. **skean-dhu** (-doo´) *n.* (*pl.* **skean-dhus**) a knife or dagger worn (in the stocking) with Scottish Highland dress. [Gael. *sgian*, knife, cp. OIr. *scīan*; Gael. *dhu*, black]

sked (sked) *n.* (*N Am., coll.*) a schedule. ~*v.t.* (*pres.p.* **skedding,** *past, p.p.* **skedded**) to schedule. [abbr.]

skedaddle (skidad´əl) *v.i.* (*coll.*) to run away, as in haste or panic. ~*n.* a hasty flight, retreat or dispersal.

skeet (skēt) *n.* a type of clay-pigeon shooting in which targets are hurled in different directions, angles etc. from two traps, to simulate a bird in flight. [from Icel. *skjōta*, to shoot]

skeeter[1] (skē´tə) *n.* (*N Am., Austral., coll.*) a mosquito. [shortening]

skeeter[2] SKITTER.

skeg (skeg) *n.* 1 a stabilizing fin on the underside of a surfboard or sailboard. 2 any of various finlike projections under the stern of a ship, e.g. one for protecting the rudder. [Icel. *skeg*, beard, cp. Dut. *scheg*, cutwater]

skegger (skeg´ə) *n.* a little salmon. [etym. uncertain]

skein (skān) *n.* 1 a quantity of yarn, silk, wool, cotton etc., wound in a coil which is folded over and knotted. 2 something resembling this. 3 a flock of wild geese, swans etc. in flight. 4 a tangle, a web. [OF *escaigne*, prob. from Celt. (cp. Ir. *sgainne*, Gael. *sgeinnidh*)]

skeleton (skel´itən) *n.* 1 the hard supporting or protective framework of an animal or vegetable body, comprising bones, cartilage, shell and other rigid parts. 2 the bones of a person or animal dried, preserved and fastened together in the posture of the living creature. 3 a very lean person or emaciated animal. 4 the supporting framework of any structure. 5 the essential portions, the nucleus (of an organization). 6 an outline or rough draft. 7 all that is left of something when bereft of life or purpose, a hulk. ~*a.* reduced to the essential parts or a minimum. **skeletal** (skel´itəl, skəlē´təl) *a.* 1 of or relating to the skeleton. 2 thin, emaciated. **skeletal muscle** *n.* striated muscle, associated with voluntary movements. **skeleton in the cupboard, skeleton in the closet** *n.* an unpleasant or shameful secret from the past. **skeletonize, skeletonise** *v.t.* to reduce to or as to a skeleton framework or outline. **skeleton key** *n.* a key with most of the inner bits removed or filed down, used as a master key or pass-key, or for picking locks. **skeleton staff** *n.* a staff reduced to the minimum number able to run a factory, office etc. [Gr., a mummy, orig. neut. of *skeletos*, dried up, from *skellein*, to dry, to parch]

skelf (skelf) *n.* (*Sc.*) 1 a splinter. 2 (*coll.*) a rogue. [as SHELF[1]]

skelly (skel´i) *a.* (*Sc.*) squint. ~*n.* (*pl.* **skellies**) a squint. ~*v.i.* (*3rd pers. sing. pres.* **skellies,** *pres.p.* **skellying,** *past, p.p.* **skellied**) to squint. **skelly-eye** *n.* **skelly-eyed** *a.* [prob. from Icel., cp. Norw. *skjegla*, OE *sceolh*, squint]

skelp (skelp) *n.* (*Sc., dial.*) a blow, a smack. ~*v.t.* to strike, to slap. **skelping** *n.* a spanking. ~*a.* large, smacking. [Sc., from Gael. *sgealp*, a slap]

skep (skep) *n.* 1 a basket or similar receptacle of wicker, wood etc., or the amount it can carry. 2 a beehive of straw or wicker. [Icel. *skeppa*, cp. Dut. *schepel*, G *Scheffel*, basket]

skeptic SCEPTIC.
skerrick (sker´ik) *n.* (*chiefly Austral., New Zeal.*) a tiny amount.
skerry (sker´i) *n.* (*pl.* **skerries**) (*Sc.*) **1** a rocky islet in the sea. **2** a reef. [Orkney, from Icel. *sker*, cp. SCAR[2]]
sketch (skech) *n.* **1** a rough, hasty, unfinished or tentative drawing or painting, often one done in preparation for a larger work. **2** a preliminary study, a rough draft, an outline, a short account without details. **3** a comedy act, or humorous one-scene play, esp. as part of a programme or revue. **4** a one-movement musical composition. **5** a descriptive essay of a brief, unelaborated or slight character. **6** (*dated, coll.*) an amusing person or thing. *~v.t.* **1** to make a sketch of. **2** to present in rough draft or outline without details. *~v.i.* to make a sketch or sketches. **to sketch in/ out** to indicate roughly or in outline only. **sketchable** *a.* **sketch-block** *n.* a sketch pad. **sketchbook** *n.* **1** a book for sketching in. **2** a collection of descriptive essays etc. **sketcher** *n.* **sketch map** *n.* a map drawn quickly and roughly, e.g. to show the position of something. **sketch pad** *n.* a pad of drawing paper for sketching on. **sketchy** *a.* (*comp.* **sketchier**, *superl.* **sketchiest**) **1** like a sketch in being rough or vague, with few details. **2** hasty and inadequate. **sketchily** *adv.* **sketchiness** *n.* [Dut. *schets*, It. *schizzo*, L *schedius*, Gr. *schedios*, hasty, off-hand, cogn. with *schein*, to hold]
skeuomorph (skū´ōmawf) *n.* **1** a decorative feature in architecture etc. derived from the material used, or the means of working it. **2** in archaeology, a retained but non-functional feature in an artefact. **skeuomorphic** (-maw´-) *a.* [Gr. *skeuos*, implement, vessel]
skew (skū) *a.* **1** oblique, slanting, crooked, twisted, turned askew. **2** distorted, unsymmetrical. *~n.* **1** a slant or oblique position, an oblique course or movement. **2** in statistics, skewness. **3** a sloping coping, or a stone supporting the coping of a gable. *~v.i.* to move sideways, to turn aside, to swerve or twist. *~v.t.* **1** to make skew. **2** to distort. **on the skew** skewed, slanting, crooked. **skew arch** *n.* an arch (e.g. that of a bridge) set obliquely to its span or abutments. **skewback** *n.* a stone, plate or course of masonry at the top of an abutment taking the spring of an arch. **skewbacked** *a.* **skew bridge** *n.* a bridge having its arch or arches set obliquely to its span or abutments. **skew chisel** *n.* a chisel that has an oblique edge. **skewed** *a.* **skew gear** *n.* a gear consisting of two cogwheels whose axes are not parallel and do not intersect. **skewness** *n.* **1** the quality of being skew. **2** in statistics, a measure, or the degree, of asymmetry in a frequency distribution. **skew-whiff** *a., adv.* (*coll.*) askew, to one side. [ONF *eskiuer*, rel. to MDut. *schuwen*, to avoid (cp. G *scheuen*, also ESCHEW, SHY[1])]
skewbald (skū´bawld) *a.* (of an animal, esp. a horse) with spots of white and a colour other than black, as distinct from piebald. *~n.* an animal of this colour. [SKEW, PIEBALD]
skewer (skū´ə) *n.* **1** a long pin of wood or metal for holding meat together during cooking. **2** a similar implement used for various other purposes. *~v.t.* **1** to fasten with a skewer. **2** to pierce with or as with a skewer, to transfix. **3** (*esp. N Am.*) to criticize harshly. [rel. to SHIVER[1]]
ski (skē) *n.* (*pl.* **skis, ski**) **1** either of a pair of long narrow runners of waxed wood, metal, plastic etc., usu. pointed and curved upwards at the front, fastened one to each foot and used for sliding over snow. **2** a similar piece of apparatus fitted to the underside of a vehicle or aircraft. **3** WATER-SKI (under WATER). *~a.* for use or wear while skiing. *~v.i.* (*3rd pers. sing. pres.* **skis,** *pres.p.* **skiing, ski-ing,** *past, p.p.* **skied** (skēd), **ski'd**) to move on skis. *~v.t.* to ski at (a certain venue) or on (a certain route, slope etc.). **skiable** *a.* **ski-bob** (-bob) *n.* a bicycle-like snow vehicle with a low seat and steering device, supported on two skis. **ski-bobber** *n.* **ski-bobbing** *n.* **skier**[1] *n.* **ski-joring** (skē´jawring, shē´yœring) *n.* a winter sport in which a skier is towed by a horse or vehicle. **ski-jorer** *n.* **ski jump** *n.* a ski slope or run surmounted by a ramp from which skiers jump. **ski-jump** *v.i.* to execute a jump from this. **ski jumper** *n.* **ski jumping** *n.* **ski lift** *n.* any of various forms of lifting apparatus for transporting skiers up a slope (e.g. a chair lift). **ski-pants** *n.pl.* stretch trousers with stirrups which fit under the feet. **ski-plane** *n.* an aeroplane with skis fitted to its undercarriage for landing on snow or ice. **ski pole** *n.* a ski stick. **ski run** *n.* a slope for skiing on. **ski slope** *n.* a ski run. **ski stick** *n.* each of a pair of pointed sticks used in skiing to balance or propel. [Norw., from Icel. *skīth*, billet of wood, snowshoe]
skiagraphy SCIAGRAPHY.
skiamachy SCIAMACHY.
skiascopy SCIASCOPY.
skid (skid) *v.i.* (*pres.p.* **skidding,** *past, p.p.* **skidded**) **1** (of wheels or vehicles) to slip sideways or diagonally on a slippery surface. **2** to slide or slip. **3** (of wheels) to slide along without revolving. **4** (*coll.*) to decline or fail, or to err or slip up. *~v.t.* **1** to move, support, check or brake with a skid. **2** to cause to skid. *~n.* **1** an instance of skidding, a slip on muddy ground, an icy road etc. **2** a support or prop, usu. of wood. **3** a ship's fender. **4** a plank, log, or other device used for sliding heavy things on. **5** a shoe or other device acting as a brake. **6** the runner on the underside of an aircraft. **on the skids 1** (*coll.*) due to be abandoned or defeated. **2** (*coll.*) due to be launched. **to hit the skids** (*coll.*) to deteriorate fast. **to put the skids under 1** (*coll.*) to speed the collapse or departure of. **2** (*coll.*) to hurry (someone) up. **skid-lid** *n.* (*sl.*) a crash helmet. **skid-pad** *n.* a slippery area of ground for training drivers to control a skidding vehicle. **skid-pan** *n.* **1** a skid-pad. **2** a shoe or drag usu. put under a wheel as a brake on a slope etc. **skid road** *n.* (*N Am.*) **1** a road along which logs can be hauled. **2** (*coll.*) a quarter frequented by loggers and homeless people. **skid row** *n.* (*N Am., coll.*) a quarter inhabited by alcoholics and vagrants. [cp. Icel. *skīth*, SKI, also ME *shide*, OE *scid*, a thin piece of wood, rel. to SHEATH]
skidoo (skidoo´), **skiddoo** *v.i.* (*3rd pers. sing. pres.* **skidoos, skiddoos,** *pres.p.* **skidooing, skiddooing,** *past, p.p.* **skidooed, skiddooed**) (*N Am., sl.*) to make off, decamp. [perh. from SKEDADDLE]
skier[1] SKI.
skier[2] SKYER (under SKY).
skiey SKYEY (under SKY).
skiff[1] (skif) *n.* a small light boat. *~v.i.* to row or scull in a skiff. [F *esquif*, It. *schifo*, prob. from OHG *skif* (cp. G *Schiff*), SHIP]
skiff[2] (skif) *v.i., v.t.* to skim (as a stone on water). *~n.* a skimming action, a grazing blow. [prob. imit.]
skiffle (skif´əl) *n.* a type of music popular in the 1950s played on unconventional percussion instruments and guitars. **skiffle band, skiffle group** *n.* a band that performs this music. [perh. imit.]
skill (skil) *n.* **1** familiar knowledge of any art or science combined with dexterity. **2** expertness, ability, practical mastery of a craft, trade, sport etc., often attained by training. **3** tact, diplomacy. **skilful,** (*N Am.*) **skillful** *a.* **1** having or showing skill (at or in something). **2** expert, adept, clever, adroit, dexterous. **3** requiring or involving skill. **skilfully** *adv.* **skilfulness** *n.* **skilled** *a.* **1** having skill, skilful (in or at something). **2** (of a worker) experienced, highly trained. **3** (of a job) involving or requiring skill or specialized training. **skill-less, †skilless** *a.* [Icel. *skil*, discernment, from *skilja*, to separate, distinguish, cogn. with SHELL and SCALE[1]]
skillet (skil´it) *n.* **1** a long-handled cooking pot. **2** (*N*

Am.) a frying pan. [OF *escuellette*, dim. of *escuelle*, L *scutella*, dim. of *scutra*, dish (cp. SCUTTLE[1])]

skilling (skil´ing), **skillion** (skil´yən) *n.* (*esp. Austral.*) an out-house, a lean-to, a shed, esp. with a sloping roof. [etym. uncertain]

skilly (skil´i) *n.* (*pl.* **skillies**) **1** thin broth, soup or gruel. **2** a weak beverage. [shortened from *skilligalee*, prob. a fanciful formation]

skim (skim) *v.t.* (*pres.p.* **skimming**, *past, p.p.* **skimmed**) **1** to clear the scum etc. from the surface of. **2** to take (cream etc.) from the surface of a liquid. **3** to touch lightly or nearly touch the surface of, to graze. **4** to throw so as to cause to graze or pass lightly over a surface. **5** to glance over or read superficially. **6** to deal with cursorily. **7** (*N Am., sl.*) to redirect or conceal (income) to avoid tax. *~v.i.* **1** to pass lightly and rapidly (over or along a surface). **2** to glance (over or through) rapidly and superficially. **3** to pass (over a subject) briefly. *~n.* **1** the act or process of skimming. **2** the thick matter which forms on or is removed from, the surface of a liquid, scum. **to skim the cream off** to remove the best part from. **skimmer** *n.* **1** someone who or something that skims. **2** a perforated ladle for skimming. **3** a flat, usu. broad-brimmed, straw hat. **4** a bird of the N American genus *Rhynchops*, which takes small fishes from the water by flying along with its lower mandible under the surface. **5** a craft that skims over the water, such as a hovercraft, hydroplane or hydrofoil. **6** (*N Am.*) a close-fitting sheath dress. **skim milk, skimmed milk** *n.* milk from which the cream has been skimmed. **skimming** *n.* **skimmingly** *adv.* [from SCUM, cp. DINT and DENT[1], FILL and FULL[1]]

skimmia (skim´iə) *n.* any evergreen shrub of the Asian genus *Skimmia*, with red berries.

skimp (skimp) *v.t.* **1** to supply in a niggardly manner, to stint (a person, provisions etc.). **2** to perform with insufficient attention or inadequate effort. *~v.i.* to be stingy or parsimonious. **skimpingly** *adv.* **skimpy** *a.* (*comp.* **skimpier**, *superl.* **skimpiest**) **1** meagre, inadequate. **2** (of clothing) covering the body minimally, scanty, short or tight. **skimpily** *adv.* **skimpiness** *n.* [perh. from Icel. *skemma*, to shorten, from *skamr*, short]

skin (skin) *n.* **1** the natural membraneous outer covering of an animal body. **2** the hide or integument of an animal removed from the body, with or without the hair. **3** one's colouring or complexion (*people with fair skins*). **4** a vessel made of the skin of an animal for holding liquids (e.g. wine). **5** the outer layer or covering of a plant, fruit etc. **6** a film, e.g. the skinlike film that forms on certain liquids. **7** a membrane. **8** the outer layer or covering of an object, structure etc. **9** the outer cladding of a vessel, rocket etc. **10** (*sl.*) a skinhead. **11** (*N Am.*) a card game in which each player is dealt a single card and bets that it will not be the first to be paired with one dealt from the pack. **12** GOLD-BEATER'S SKIN (under GOLD). **13** a duplicating stencil. *~a.* made of, intended for, or used on the skin. *~v.t.* (*pres.p.* **skinning**, *past, p.p.* **skinned**) **1** to strip the skin from, to flay, to peel. **2** to graze (e.g. one's knee). **3** to cover (over) with or as with skin. **4** (*sl.*) to cheat, to swindle, to rip off. *~v.i.* to become covered (over) with skin, to cicatrize. **by/ with the skin of one's teeth** very narrowly, by a close shave. **no skin off someone's nose** making no difference to someone, possibly even encouraging rather than perturbing to someone. **to be skin and bone** to be extremely thin or emaciated. **to change one's skin** to suffer an unlikely change of character. **to get under one's skin** to interest or annoy one intensely. **to have a thick skin** to be impervious to insults or criticism. **to have a thin skin** to be sensitive to slights or criticism. **to save one's skin** to escape injury, to get off unscathed. **to the skin** right through one's clothing, as in *soaked to the skin*. **with a whole skin** unharmed or unwounded. **skincare** *n.* the care and protection of the skin and complexion through the use of beauty products and cosmetics. **skin-deep** *a.* superficial, not deep. *~adv.* superficially. **skin diver** *n.* someone who dives in deep water usu. with flippers and an aqualung, but no diving suit, as, orig., a pearl-diver. **skin-diving** *n.* **skin effect** *n.* the tendency of an alternating electric current to be diffused over the surface of a conductor instead of being equally distributed over the whole area. **skin-flick** *n.* (*sl.*) an overtly pornographic film that features nudity and sex scenes. **skinflint** *n.* a niggardly person, a miser. **skin-food** *n.* a cosmetic that nourishes the skin. **skin friction** *n.* the friction between the surface of a solid body and the fluid it is moving through. **skinful** *n.* (*pl.* **skinfuls**) (*sl.*) enough alcohol to intoxicate one. **skin game** *n.* (*N Am., sl.*) **1** in gambling, a rigged game. **2** a swindle. **skin graft** *n.* the transfer of skin from a sound to a disfigured or injured part. **skin-grafting** *n.* **skinhead** *n.* **1** a young person with close-cropped hair, esp. as a member of a gang of aggressive and often racist youths wearing heavy-duty boots and braces. **2** (*N Am.*) a recruit in the Marines. **skinless** *a.* **skinlike** *a.* **skinned** *a.* having skin, esp. of a certain type (*usu. in comb.*, as in *thin-skinned, dark-skinned*). **skinner** *n.* **1** a person who skins animals or prepares hides or skins. **2** a person who deals in skins, a furrier. **skinny** *a.* (*comp.* **skinnier**, *superl.* **skinniest**) **1** very lean or thin. **2** (of garments, esp. knitted ones) tight-fitting. **3** resembling skin. **skinniness** *n.* **skinny-dip** *v.i.* (*pres.p.* **skinny-dipping**, *past, p.p.* **skinny-dipped**) (*coll.*) to swim in the nude. **skinny-dipping** *n.* **skin test** *n.* a test performed on the skin to determine its resistance to disease or to detect substances liable to cause an allergic reaction. **skintight** *a.* (of garments) tight, clinging. [Icel. *skinn*, cogn. with G *schinden*, to skin, to flay]

skink (skingk) *n.* a small lizard of the family Scincidae, of Africa and SW Asia. [F *scinc* (now *scinque*), L *scincus*, Gr. *skinkos*]

skinner, skinny SKIN.

skint (skint) *a.* (*sl.*) hard up for money, penniless. [var. of *skinned*, p.p. SKIN]

skip[1] (skip) *v.i.* (*pres.p.* **skipping**, *past, p.p.* **skipped**) **1** to progress by hopping on each foot in turn. **2** to move about with light bounds or capers. **3** to frisk, to gambol. **4** to jump repeatedly over a skipping rope. **5** to pass rapidly (from one thing to another). **6** to make omissions. **7** (*sl.*) to make off hurriedly, to bolt (off), to abscond. *~v.t.* **1** to cause (a stone) to skim over water, bouncing off its surface at intervals. **2** to omit, to miss deliberately, to absent oneself from (a meal, a class, a church service etc.). **3** (*chiefly N Am.*) to leave (town) quickly and quietly, to abscond from. *~n.* **1** a step and a hop on one foot, or a type of forward movement hopping on each foot in turn. **2** a light leap or spring. **3** an act of omitting, leaving out or passing over. **4** a belt of inaudibility in radio transmissions. **5** a college servant. **skip it!** (*coll.*) forget it! never mind! **skip distance** *n.* the minimum distance around a radio transmitter at which it is possible to receive an ionospheric wave. **skipjack** *n.* **1** any of various kinds of fish that jump out of the water. **2** (*also* **skipjack tuna**) a striped tropical tuna, *Katsuwonus pelamis*, important as a food fish. **3** a click beetle. **skipper**[1] *n.* **1** someone who or something that skips. **2** a saury. **3** a member of the butterfly family Hesperidae (from their short, jerky flight). **skipping** *n.* the act, recreation or exercise of jumping over a rope repeatedly. **skippingly** *adv.* in a skipping manner, by skipping. **skipping rope,** (*N Am.*) **skip-rope** *n.* a rope or cord used for skipping over as a game or form of physical exercise. **skip zone** *n.* an area around a broadcasting station where it is impossible to receive a transmission. [ME *skippen* (cp. Norw. and Swed. dial. *skopa*, also Icel. *skoppa*, to spin)]

skip[2] (skip) *n.* **1** a container for collecting and moving refuse, building materials etc. **2** a box cage or bucket lift in a mine for hoisting people or materials. [var. of SKEP]

skip[3] (skip) *n.* **1** (*coll.*) short for SKIPPER. **2** in bowls or curling, the captain of a side. *~v.t.* (*pres.p.* **skipping,** *past, p.p.* **skipped**) to be the skip of (a side).

skipper[1] SKIP[1].

skipper[2] (skip´ə) *n.* **1** a sea captain, the master of a vessel. **2** the captain of a team or side. **3** an aircraft captain. *~v.t.* to act as skipper of. [Dut. *schipper* (*schip*, SHIP, -ER)]

skippet (skip´it) *n.* a flat round box for holding the seal attached to a document. [dim. of SKIP[2]]

skipping SKIP[1].

skirl (skœl) *n.* (*Sc.*) **1** the shrill sound of the bagpipes. **2** a shrill cry or noise. *~v.i.* **1** (of bagpipes) to produce their characteristic shrill sound. **2** to give a shrill cry or make a shrill sound. [var. of SHRILL]

skirmish (skœ´mish) *n.* **1** a slight or irregular fight, esp. between small parties or scattered troops. **2** a contest, clash, struggle, esp. of a preliminary, brief or minor nature. **3** an altercation or clash of wit. *~v.i.* to engage in a skirmish. **skirmisher** *n.* [OF *eskermiss-*, stem of *eskermir*, to fence; from OHG *scirman*, from *scirm* (cp. G *Schirm*, shelter, cover)]

skirr (skœ) *v.t.* to pass over rapidly, to range, to scour. *~v.i.* to move rapidly, to scud or scurry. [prob. rel. to SCOUR[2]]

skirret (skir´it) *n.* a water parsnip, *Sium sisarum*, with an edible tuberous root. [ME *skyrwyt*, prob. from OF *eschervis*, Sp. *chirivia*, Arab. *karawiyā*, CARAWAY]

skirt (skœt) *n.* **1** a woman's garment hanging from the waist. **2** the part of a dress or coat hanging below the waist. **3** the outer flap surrounding the base of a hovercraft. **4** a part of an aircraft or vehicle that hides and protects the wheels or underside. **5** the flap of a saddle. **6** (*often pl.*) the edge, border, margin or outer extremities of something. **7** a cut of beef from the flank. **8** the diaphragm and other membranes as a meat dish. **9** (*sl.*, *offensive*) a woman or girl as a sexual object. *~v.t.* **1** to lie or go along or by the edge of. **2** to pass round (the edge of), to avoid. **3** to border. *~v.i.* to lie or move (along, round the side or edge of something). **bit of skirt** BIT[1]. **skirted** *a.* **skirter** *n.* **1** a horse or huntsman that goes round obstacles instead of over them. **2** a hound that runs wide of the pack. **3** (*Austral.*) someone that trims fleeces. **skirting** *n.* **1** a skirting board. **2** material suitable for skirts. **3** (*pl.*, *Austral.*, *New Zeal.*) the inferior parts of wool trimmed from a fleece. **skirting board** *n.* a narrow board running round the bottom of the wall of a room. **skirtless** *a.* [ME *skyrt*, Icel. *skyrta*, shirt]

skit[1] (skit) *n.* a satirical piece, lampoon or humorous theatrical sketch (on a certain situation or topic). [perh. Icel. *skjōta*, to shoot]

skit[2] *n.* (*coll.*) **1** a large number or crowd. **2** (*pl.*) masses, lots. [etym. uncertain]

skite[1] (skīt) *v.i.* to dart aside, to slip, to slide. *~v.t.* to hit with a darting blow. *~n.* **1** an act or instance of darting aside or slipping. **2** a sharp blow, esp. in a slanting direction. **3** (*Sc.*) a drinking spree. **on the skite** on a drinking spree. [prob. from Icel. *skȳt*, stem of *skjōta*, to SHOOT]

skite[2] (skīt) *v.i.* (*Austral.*, *New Zeal.*, *coll.*) to boast or brag. *~n.* **1** a braggart or boaster. **2** boastful talk, swagger. [cp. BLETHERSKATE (under BLETHER)]

skitter (skit´ə), **skeeter** (skē´tə) *v.i.* **1** to glide, skim or skip rapidly (esp. along a surface). **2** to dart or scurry (about, off). **3** to fish by drawing a bait etc. along the surface. *~v.t.* to cause to skitter. *~n.* an act or instance of skittering. **skittery** *a.* nervous, restless, fidgety. [prob. freq. of SKITE[1]]

skittish (skit´ish) *a.* **1** (of horses) excitable, nervous, easily frightened. **2** capricious, uncertain, coquettish, wanton, too lively. **skittishly** *adv.* **skittishness** *n.* [etym. uncertain]

skittle (skit´əl) *n.* **1** any one of the pins set up to be bowled at in skittles or ninepins. **2** (*pl.*) ninepin bowling, a game in which nine wooden pins are set up at the far end of an alley, and the player has to knock as many as possible down by bowling a wooden ball or disc at them. **3** TABLE SKITTLES (under TABLE). *~v.i.* to play at ninepins. **to skittle out** in cricket, to dismiss (batsmen) in quick succession. **skittle-alley, skittle-ball, skittle-ground** *n.* [Dan. *skyttel*, an earthen ball used in child's game, as SHUTTLE]

skive[1] (skīv) *v.t.* **1** to split (leather) into thin layers. **2** to shave or pare (hides). **skiver**[1] *n.* **1** a paring tool for leather. **2** thin leather split from a sheepskin, used for bookbinding. [Icel. *skīfa*, cogn. with *shive*, a thin slice (from ME *schīve*), see also SHEAVE[1]]

skive[2] (skīv) *v.i.* (*coll.*) **1** to avoid performing a duty, task etc. **2** to take time (off work or school) illicitly. *~n.* **1** a period of shirking or an evasion of duty etc. **2** a task or piece of work etc. which is far from onerous. **skiver**[2] *n.* [etym. uncertain]

skiver[1] SKIVE[1].

skiver[2] SKIVE[2].

skivvy (skiv´i) *n.* (*pl.* **skivvies**) (*sl.*) **1** a maid or general servant. **2** a person who does menial work. *~v.i.* (*3rd pers. sing. pres.* **skivvies,** *pres.p.* **skivvying,** *past, p.p.* **skivvied**) to work as a skivvy, do menial work (for someone). [etym. uncertain]

skol (skōl), **skoal** *int.* cheers! good health! (usu. as a toast). [Icel. *skāl*, Dan. *skaal*, a bowl, a cup]

Skt, Skr. *abbr.* Sanskrit.

skua (skū´ə) *n.* (*pl.* **skuas**) a dark-coloured predatory seabird of the family Stercorariidae, allied to the gulls. [Icel. *skūfr*, *skŭmr* (cp. *skūmi*, shade, Norw. and Swed. *skum*, dull, dusky)]

skulduggery (skŭldŭg´əri), **sculduggery, skullduggery** *n.* (*coll.*) underhand behaviour, trickery, cheating or malpractice. [from earlier form *skulduddery*, orig. Sc., meaning 'unchastity']

skulk (skŭlk) *v.i.* **1** to lurk, to withdraw and conceal oneself. **2** to move about furtively. **3** to sneak away, esp. from duty, work, danger etc. *~n.* **1** a person who skulks, a skulker. **2** a company of foxes. **skulker** *n.* **skulking** *n., a.* **skulkingly** *adv.* [Dan. *skulk* (cp. Swed. *skolka*, Dut. *schuilen*)]

skull (skŭl) *n.* **1** the bony case enclosing the brain, the cranium. **2** the whole head, esp. as part of the skeleton, without skin or soft tissue. **3** an image or representation of this. **out of one's skull 1** (*sl.*) out of one's mind, crazy. **2** (*sl.*) helplessly drunk. **skull and crossbones** *n.* (*usu. sing.*) a representation of a human skull surmounting two crossed thigh bones, used as an emblem of death or danger. **skullcap** *n.* **1** a light, brimless cap fitting closely to the head. **2** the sinciput. **3** a plant of the genus *Scutellaria*, with blue, helmet-shaped flowers. **4** (*usu. derog.*) the brain, the intelligence. **skulled** *a.* having a skull, esp. of a certain kind (*usu. in comb.*, as in *thick-skulled*). **skull session** *n.* (*N Am.*, *sl.*) a debate, discussion or conference. [ME *skulle*, *scolle* (cp. Swed. dial. *skulle*, Norw. *skult*), cogn. with SCALE[2]]

Usage note See note under SCULL.

skunk (skŭngk) *n.* **1** a N American carnivorous quadruped, *Mephitis mephitica*, with a bushy tail and white stripes down the back, which when on the defence ejects a fetid secretion from the anal glands. **2** the pelt of this animal. **3** (*coll.*, *offensive*) a base or obnoxious person. *~v.t.* **1** (*N Am.*, *sl.*) to defeat, esp. without allowing to score. **2** to fail to pay (a debt or bill). **skunk-bear** *n.* (*N Am.*) the wolverine or glutton. **skunkbird, skunk-blackbird** *n.* the bobolink (from its colouring). **skunk-cabbage** *n.* (*N Am.*) either of two plants of the arum family, *Symplocarpus foetidus* or *Lysichitum americanum*, which give off a fetid odour. [Algonquian *segongw*]

sky (skī) *n.* (*pl.* **skies**) (*used in sing. or pl.*) **1** the apparent vault of heaven, the firmament. **2** the upper region of the atmosphere, the region of clouds. **3** the climate, the weather. **4** the celestial regions, the heavens. ~*v.t.* (*3rd pers. sing. pres.* **skies,** *pres.p.* **skying,** *past, p.p.* **skied**) **1** to hit (a ball) high into the air. **2** to hang (a picture) in the top tier at an exhibition. **the sky is the limit** there's virtually no limit (e.g. to a potential sum, or to the possibilities for achievement). **to the skies** lavishly, extravagantly (*praise someone to the skies*). **under the open sky** outside, out of doors. **sky-blue** *n., a.* (of) a pale blue. **sky-blue pink** *n., a.* (*facet.*) (of) some unlikely or fantastic colour. **sky-clad** *a.* naked, as in pagan rituals. **sky cloth** *n.* in the theatre, a backcloth painted to look like sky. **skydive** *v.i.* to jump from an aircraft and delay opening the parachute, esp. in order to execute acrobatic manoeuvres. ~*n.* an instance of this. **skydiver** *n.* **skydiving** *n.* **skyer, skier** *n.* a cricket ball hit high into the air. **skyey, skiey** *a.* **sky-high** *adv., a.* high as the sky, very high. **to blow sky-high** to blow up, to destroy completely. **skyjack** (-jak) *v.t.* to hijack (an aircraft). ~*n.* an act of skyjacking. **skyjacker** *n.* **skyjacking** *n.* **skylark** *n.* a lark, *Alauda arvensis*, that flies singing high into the air. ~*v.i.* (*coll.*) to lark, to frolic, to play practical jokes etc. **skyless** *a.* **skylight** *n.* a window set in a roof or ceiling. **skyline** *n.* **1** the outline against the sky of the configuration of the land or buildings. **2** the horizon. **sky pilot** *n.* (*sl.*) a clergyman, a priest, a preacher. **skyrocket** *n.* a rocket. ~*v.i.* (*pres.p.* **skyrocketing,** *past, p.p.* **skyrocketed**) to rise rapidly to a high level. **skysail** (skī´səl, -sāl) *n.* a light sail set above the royal in a square-rigged ship. **skyscape** *n.* a picture or view chiefly of the sky or clouds. **skyscraper** *n.* **1** a very high multi-storeyed building. **2** a triangular skysail. **sky-shouting** *n.* communication by loudspeaker between an aircraft and the ground. **sky-sign** *n.* an advertisement on a roof. **skywalk** *n.* a high-level covered walkway bridging two buildings. **skyward** *a., adv.* **skywards** *adv.* **skyway** *n.* **1** a route or lane used by aircraft. **2** the sky as a means of transport. **3** SKYWALK (under SKY). **sky-writing** *n.* (the formation of) writing, esp. for advertising purposes, traced in the sky by smoke discharged from an aeroplane. **sky-writer** *n.* [Icel. *skȳ* (cp. OE *scēo*, cloud, *scuwa*, shadow), cogn. with SHOWER[2], L *obscūrus*, OBSCURE]

Skye (skī), **Skye terrier** *n.* a small rough-haired variety of Scotch terrier with a long body and short legs. [Isle of *Skye*]

skyey SKY.

skyr (skiə) *n.* a dish of curds. [Icel.]

slab[1] (slab) *n.* **1** a thin, flat, regularly shaped piece of anything, esp. of stone, concrete etc. **2** a large slice of bread, cake etc. **3** the outside piece sawn from a log in squaring the side. **4** (*Austral., New Zeal.*) a plank. **5** the table on which a corpse is laid out in a mortuary. ~*a.* (*Austral., New Zeal.*) (of a hut etc.) made of rough planks. ~*v.t.* (*pres.p.* **slabbing,** *past, p.p.* **slabbed**) **1** to saw slabs from (a log etc.). **2** to square (a tree) in order to saw it into planks. **3** to cut or form into a slab or slabs. **4** to cover or line with slabs. **slabbed** *a.* **slabbing** *a., n.* **slabstone** *n.* a flagstone. [etym. uncertain, cp. OF *esclape*, splinter (*es-*, EX-, LG *klappen*, to cleave noisily, cp. G *klaffen*, to split)]

slab[2] (slab) *a.* thick, slimy, viscous, sticky. ~*n.* ooze, mud, slime. **slabby** *a.* (*comp.* **slabbier,** *superl.* **slabbiest**). **slabbiness** *n.* [dial. *slab*, puddle, Icel. *slabb*, mire (cp. Swed. dial. and Norw. *slabb*, MDan. *slab*)]

slabber (slab´ə) *v.i., v.t., n.* (*dial.*) SLOBBER.

slack[1] (slak) *a.* **1** not drawn tight, loose. **2** limp, relaxed. **3** lax, careless, negligent, not zealous, eager or active. **4** (of trade or the market) tardy, sluggish, dull, slow. **5** (of the tide) neither ebbing nor flowing. **6** in phonetics, pronounced with relaxed vocal muscles. ~*adv.* **1** in a slack manner. **2** insufficiently or slowly. ~*n.* **1** the part of a rope etc. that hangs loose. **2** a slack period in trade etc. **3** a lazy fit, a spell of inactivity. **4** a cessation of flow, slack water. **5** (*pl.*) loosely cut casual trousers. ~*v.i.* **1** to abate. **2** to become loose or looser. **3** to become slower, to fail. **4** to neglect, or take a break from, one's work, to become remiss or lazy. ~*v.t.* **1** to slow. **2** to lessen. **3** to cause to abate. **4** to loosen, to relax. **5** to slake (lime). **to slack off 1** to loosen, to reduce the tension on (a rope etc.). **2** to shirk work. **3** to lose speed or momentum. **to slack up 1** to slow down (a train) before stopping. **2** to ease off. **to take up the slack 1** to gather up the loose portion of a rope. **2** to use surplus resources or time to good effect. **slacken** *v.i., v.t.* to become or make slack or slacker. **to slacken off** to slack off. **slacker** *n.* a shirker, a lazy or remiss person. **slack lime** *n.* slaked lime. **slackly** *adv.* **slackness** *n.* **slack suit** *n.* (*N Am.*) a casual outfit of slacks and coordinating jacket or shirt. **slack water** *n.* an interval of still water at the turn of the tide, esp. at low water, between the ebb and flow. [OE *sleac* (cp. Icel. *slakr*, Swed. and Dan. *slak*, OHG *slah*), cogn. with LAG[1] and LAX]

slack[2] (slak) *n.* (*Sc.*) **1** a hollow, a dip, a dell. **2** a bog, a morass. [Icel. *slakki*, cp. Norw. *slakke*]

slack[3] (slak) *n.* small pieces of coal, or coal dust. [ME, cp. G *Schlacke*]

slacken SLACK[1].

slag (slag) *n.* **1** the fused refuse or dross separated in the reduction of ores, clinker. **2** volcanic scoria. **3** a mixture of mineral dross and dust produced in coal mining. **4** (*sl.*) a slovenly or immoral woman. ~*v.i.* (*pres.p.* **slagging,** *past, p.p.* **slagged**) to form slag, to combine in a slaggy mass. ~*v.t.* **1** to convert into slag. **2** (*sl.*) to criticize, to disparage. **to slag off** (*sl.*) to make disparaging remarks about. **slaggy** *a.* (*comp.* **slaggier,** *superl.* **slaggiest**). **slagheap** *n.* a hill or heap of waste material produced in coal mining. **slag-wool** *n.* mineral wool. [Swed. *slagg*, cp. Norw. *slagga*, to flow over, G *Schlacke*, slag]

slain SLAY[1].

slake (slāk) *v.t.* **1** to quench, to assuage, to satisfy, to appease (one's thirst, desire etc.). **2** to mix (lime) with water so as to form a chemical combination. ~*v.i.* (of lime) to become slaked. **slakeable, slakable** *a.* **slaked lime** *n.* calcium hydroxide, produced by adding water to quicklime. **slakeless** *a.* that cannot be quenched. [OE *slacian*, from *slæc*, *sleac*, SLACK[1]]

slalom (slah´ləm) *n.* **1** a downhill ski race on a zigzagged course marked with artificial obstacles. **2** a similarly zigzagged obstacle race in canoes or vehicles, or on water-skis or skateboards. [Norw.]

slam[1] (slam) *v.t.* (*pres.p.* **slamming,** *past, p.p.* **slammed**) **1** to shut (a door, lid etc.) suddenly with a loud noise. **2** to put (a thing down on a surface) thus. **3** (*coll.*) to hit, to thrash, to defeat completely. **4** (*coll.*) to criticize severely. **5** to put into action suddenly or violently (*He slammed the brakes on*). ~*v.i.* **1** (of a door) to shut violently or noisily. **2** (*coll.*) to move, esp. to enter or leave, angrily or violently (*She slammed out of the room*). ~*n.* **1** a noise as of the violent shutting of a door. **2** an act of slamming. **3** (*N Am., sl.*) prison. **slambang** (slambang´) *adv.* **1** with a slamming sound. **2** (*esp. N Am.*) SLAP BANG (under SLAP). ~*a.* (*coll.*) vigorous, all-out. **slam dunk, slamdunk** *n.* in basketball, the action of jumping high and ramming the ball down through the basket. **slammer** *n.* (*sl.*) prison. [cp. Norw. *slemba*, Icel. *slambra*, prob. imit. in orig.]

slam[2] (slam) *n.* in whist etc., the winning of every trick (a *grand slam*), or all but one trick (a *little slam* or *small slam*). *~v.t.* (*pres.p.* **slamming**, *past, p.p.* **slammed**) to beat (one's opponents) by achieving a slam. [from the name of an old card game, perh. from old word *slampant*, trickery]

slammer SLAM[1].

slander (slahn´də) *n.* **1** a false statement maliciously uttered to injure a person. **2** the making of malicious and untrue statements, defamation, calumny. **3** (*Law*) false defamatory language or statements. *~v.t.* to injure by the malicious utterance of a false report, to defame falsely. **slanderer** *n.* **slanderous** *a.* **slanderously** *adv.* **slanderousness** *n.* [OF *esclander*, L *scandalum*, SCANDAL]

slang (slang) *n.* very informal vocabulary or phraseology that would be out of place in a formal context, and is often confined to a specific context, culture or profession. *~a.* of the nature of slang (*slang expressions*). *~v.i.* to use slang. *~v.t.* to abuse with slang. **slanging** *n.*, *a.* **slanging match** *n.* a quarrel in which strong insults are exchanged. **slangy** *a.* (*comp.* **slangier**, *superl.* **slangiest**) **1** (of an expression) classifiable as slang. **2** (of written or spoken language) interspersed with slang expressions. **slangily** *adv.* **slanginess** *n.* [prob. from Norw. *sleng*, slinging, from *slengja*, to SLING[1]]

slant (slahnt) *v.i.* **1** to slope. **2** to incline from or be oblique to a vertical or horizontal line. **3** to be biased (towards). *~v.t.* **1** to cause to slant. **2** to present (a report etc.) in a biased or unfair way. *~a.* **1** sloping, oblique. **2** inclined from a horizontal or perpendicular line. *~n.* **1** a slope. **2** inclination from the vertical or horizontal. **3** an oblique line, a solidus. **4** an angle of approach, a point of view. **5** a bias or unfair emphasis. **on a/ the slant** sloping, aslant. **slanted** *a.* **1** sloping, inclined, oblique. **2** (of language or reporting style) biased, unfair. **slant-eyed** *a.* having slanting eyes. **slant height** *n.* the height of a cone from its vertex to the edge of its base. **slanting** *a.* **slantingly** *adv.* **slantly, slantways, slantwise** *adv.* [prob. through ME *slenten*, *sclenten*, from Norw. *slenta*]

slap (slap) *v.t.* (*pres.p.* **slapping**, *past, p.p.* **slapped**) **1** to strike with the open hand, to smack. **2** to lay or throw forcefully or quickly (*He slapped a note on the counter*). **3** to put (on) or apply hastily (*She slapped on some make-up*). *~n.* a blow, esp. with the open hand. *~adv.* with the suddenness and impact of a slap, headlong, slap bang. **to slap down** to rebuff or rebuke curtly and unequivocally. **to slap on the back** to congratulate. **slap and tickle** *n.* flirtatious romping, kissing and cuddling. **slap bang** *adv.* **1** suddenly, violently, headlong. **2** exactly, precisely. **3** conspicuously, in an obvious position. **slapdash** *a.* hasty, impetuous, careless, happy-go-lucky. *~adv.* in a careless, rash, impetuous manner. *~n.* **1** rough and haphazard work. **2** roughcast. *~v.t.* **1** to roughcast. **2** to do hastily or carelessly. **slap-happy** *a.* **1** careless, irresponsible. **2** happy-go-lucky, carefree. **3** punch-drunk. **slaphead** *n.* (*derog.*) someone with very little hair or very short hair. **slap in the face** *n.* a rebuff. **slapjack** *n.* (*N Am.*) a flapjack, pancake. **slap on the back** *n.* an offer of congratulations. **slap on the wrist** *n.* a reprimand. **slapstick** *n.* **1** broad comedy or knockabout farce. **2** a clown's implement that makes a noise like a resounding slap when used to strike someone. *~a.* of, relating to or in the style of slapstick. **slap-up** *a.* (*coll.*) **1** first-rate. **2** lavish. [cp. LG *slapp*, imit. of sound]

slash (slash) *v.t.* **1** to cut by striking violently at random. **2** to make long incisions or narrow gashes in, to slit. **3** to reduce (prices etc.) drastically. **4** to criticize severely. **5 a** to lash (with a whip etc.). **b** to crack (a whip). *~v.i.* **1** to strike (at etc.) violently and at random with a knife, sword etc. **2** (of a tail etc.) to lash. *~n.* **1** a long cut, slit or incision. **2** a slashing cut or stroke. **3** a slit in a garment designed to reveal the lining as a decorative feature. **4** a solidus. **5** (*sl.*) an act of urinating. **slash-and-burn** *a.* denoting a cultivation technique whereby vegetation is cut down and left to dry, and then burnt off before seed-planting begins. **slashed** *a.* (of sleeves etc.) having decorative slits revealing the lining, or with a contrasting material projecting through. **slasher** *n.* **1** a person or thing that slashes. **2** a slasher film or movie. **slasher film, slasher movie** *n.* a film showing violent knife attacks. **slashing** *a.* trenchant and incisive. **slashingly** *adv.* [OF *esclachier* (*es-*, EX-, MHG *klecken*, to break noisily, from *klac*, noise), perh. conf. with *esclicier*, to SLICE]

slat[1] (slat) *n.* a thin narrow strip, usu. of wood or metal, used in Venetian blinds, crates etc. *~v.i.* (*pres.p.* **slatting**, *past, p.p.* **slatted**) to make or equip with slats. **slatted** *a.* having slats, fitted with slats. [ME, from OF *esclat*, splinter]

slat[2] (slat) *v.t.* (*pres.p.* **slatting**, *past, p.p.* **slatted**) **1** to fling, to dash, to slap, to jerk. **2** to beat, to bang. *~v.i.* **1** to beat, to bang. **2** (of sails) to flap violently. *~n.* a sharp blow, a violent flap. [perh. rel. to Icel. *sletta*, to slap]

slate[1] (slāt) *n.* **1** a fine-grained laminated rock easily splitting into thin, smooth, even slabs. **2** a slab or trimmed piece of this, esp. for use as a roofing-tile. **3** a tablet of slate, usu. with a wooden frame, for writing on. **4** (*chiefly N Am.*) a preliminary list of candidates liable to revision. **5** the colour of slate, a dull blue-grey. *~v.t.* **1** to cover or roof with slates. **2** (*chiefly N Am.*) to place (a candidate) on a list. *~a.* **1** made or consisting of slate. **2** slate-coloured. **on the slate** on credit, on the tab, recorded as a debt. **to have a slate loose** (*coll.*) to be slightly mentally unbalanced. **to wipe the slate clean** to start afresh, to erase past crimes, errors etc. **slate-black, slate-grey** *a.* of the dark, blue or grey colour characteristic of slate. **slate colour,** (*N Am.*) **slate color** *n.* a dark greenish or bluish shade of grey. **slate-coloured** *a.* **slate-pencil** *n.* a stick of soft slate for writing on slates with. **slater** *n.* **1** a person who manufactures slates. **2** a person who slates roofs. **3** a woodlouse. **slating** *n.* **slaty** *a.* (*comp.* **slatier**, *superl.* **slatiest**). **slatiness** *n.* [ME *slat*, *sclat*, OF *esclat* (F *éclat*), from *esclater*, to break to pieces, late L *exclapitāre* (EX-, LG *klappen*, to CLAP[1])]

slate[2] (slāt) *v.t.* to criticize savagely, to abuse, to berate. [etym. unknown; perh. conn. with SLATE[1], or with OE *slætan*, to bait]

slattern (slat´ən) *n.* an untidy or sluttish woman. **slatternly** *a.* **slatternliness** *n.* [from obs. *slatter*, to be wasteful or untidy, freq. of obs. *slat*, to splash, cp. Icel. *sletta*]

slaty SLATE[1].

slaughter (slaw´tə) *n.* **1** the killing of animals for market. **2** wholesale or indiscriminate killing, butchery, carnage. *~v.t.* **1** to kill wantonly or ruthlessly, to massacre. **2** to kill (animals) for market. **3** (*coll.*) to defeat decisively. **slaughterer** *n.* **slaughterhouse** *n.* a place where beasts are slaughtered, a shambles. **slaughterman** *n.* (*pl.* **slaughtermen**) a person who kills livestock for market. **slaughterous** *a.* **slaughterously** *adv.* [Icel. *slātr*, slaughtering, meat, cogn. with SLAY[1]]

Slav (slahv) *n.* a member of any of various peoples inhabiting eastern Europe who speak a Slavonic language, including the Russians, Poles, Serbs, Croats, Bulgarians and Slovenes. *~a.* **1** of or relating to the Slavs. **2** Slavonic. **Slavic** *a.*, *n.* Slavonic. **Slavism** *n.* **Slavonian** (sləvō´ni-) *n.*, *a.* (an inhabitant) of Slavonia, a part of Croatia between the Drava and Sava rivers. **Slavonic** (sləvon´-) *a.* **1** of or relating to a group of languages belonging to the Indo-European family including Russian, Bulgarian, Polish, Serbo-Croat and Czech etc. 2 of or relating to the peoples who speak these languages. ~*n.* the Slavonic group of languages. **Slavophil** (-əfil), **Slavophile** (-əfīl) *n., a.* (a person who is) favourable or friendly towards the Slavs. [F *slave* or G *Sklave*, med. L *slavus, sclavus*, or late Gr. *sklabos, sklabēnos*]

slave (slāv) *n.* **1** a person who is the property of and bound in obedience to another. **2** a person who is entirely under the domination (of another person), the influence (of e.g. fashion) or a helpless victim (to a habit, drugs, alcohol etc.). **3** a person who works like a slave esp. for low wages, a drudge. **4** a machine or device which is entirely controlled by another, or imitates the action of a similar device. ~*v.i.* to toil like a slave, to drudge. **slave-bangle, slave bracelet** *n.* a bangle of gold, silver, glass etc. worn usu. above the elbow. **slave-born** *a.* born in slavery or of slave parents. **slave-driver** *n.* **1** an overseer of slaves. **2** an exacting or over-demanding taskmaster. **slave-drive** *v.t.* **slave-holder** *n.* a person who owns slaves. **slave-holding** *n.* **slave labour,** (*N Am.*) **slave labor** *n.* (the work of) people employed as or like slaves. **slavelike** *a.* **slaver**[1] *n.* **1** a person who deals in slaves. **2** a slave ship. **slavery**[1] (-vəri) *n.* **1** the condition of being a slave. **2** the practice of owning slaves. **slave ship** *n.* a vessel engaged in the slave trade. **Slave State** *n.* any of the southern states of N America in which slavery flourished prior to the Civil War. **slave trade** *n.* the trade of procuring, buying and transporting slaves, esp. from Africa to America in the 16th–18th cents. **slave trader** *n.* **slavey** *n.* (*pl.* **slaveys**) (*coll.*) a maidservant, a household drudge. **slavish** *a.* **1** of or relating to or characteristic of a slave. **2** subservient, servile, base, abject, ignoble. **3** entirely imitative, devoid of originality. **4** consisting in drudgery. **slavishly** *adv.* **slavishness** *n.* **slavocracy** (-vok´rəsi) *n.* (*pl.* **slavocracies**) slave-owners collectively, esp. as a dominating political or social power. [F *esclave*, med. L *sclavus*, a SLAV captive]

slaver[1] SLAVE.

slaver[2] (slav´ə) *v.i.* **1** to let saliva flow from the mouth, to slabber, to dribble. **2** to fawn, to flatter, to drool. ~*v.t.* to let saliva dribble upon or over. ~*n.* **1** saliva dribbling from the mouth. **2** (*coll.*) nonsense, drivel. **slaverer** *n.* **slavering** *a.* **slavery**[2] *a.* [Icel. *slafra* (cp. LG *slabbern*)]

slavery[1] SLAVE.

slavery[2] SLAVER[2].

slavey SLAVE.

Slavic SLAV.

slavish, slavocracy SLAVE.

Slavonian, Slavonic SLAV.

slaw (slaw) *n.* (*N Am.*) sliced cabbage served as a salad, coleslaw. [Dut. *sla*, SALAD]

slay[1] (slā) *v.t.* (*past* **slew** (sloo), *p.p.* **slain** (slān)) **1** to put to death, to kill. **2** (*coll.*) (*past, p.p. also* **slayed**) **a** to impress powerfully. **b** to amuse to an overwhelming degree. **slayer** *n.* [OE *slēan* (cp. Dut. *slaan*, G *schlagen*, Icel. *slā*)]

slay[2] SLEY.

sleaze (slēz) *n.* (*coll.*) **1** that which is squalid, distasteful, disreputable, esp. with reference to corrupt behaviour by politicians. **2** sleazy conditions, sleaziness. **3** a person of doubtful morality. ~*v.i.* to move sleazily. **sleazeball, sleazebag** *n.* (*sl.*) a morally disreputable person. **sleaze factor** *n.* the invasion of political life by corruption or dishonest dealing. **sleazy** *a.* (*comp.* **sleazier,** *superl.* **sleaziest**) **1** squalid, sordid or seedy (*sleazy nightclubs*). **2** slatternly. **3** (of fabric) thin, wanting in substance, flimsy. **sleazily** *adv.* **sleaziness** *n.* [etym. uncertain]

sled (sled) *n.* (*N Am.*) a sledge. ~*v.i.* (*pres.p.* **sledding,** *past, p.p.* **sledded**) to travel by sled. ~*v.t.* to convey by sled. [MLG *sledde*, rel. to SLIDE]

sledge[1] (slej) *n.* **1** a vehicle on runners instead of wheels, used for carrying passengers or hauling loads etc., esp. over snow or ice, drawn variously by dogs, horses, reindeer or people; a sleigh. **2** a toboggan. ~*v.i.* to travel by sledge. ~*v.t.* to carry or convey on a sledge. **sledger** *n.* **sledging**[1] *n.* **1** travelling by sledge. **2** tobogganing. [MDut. *sleedse*, rel. to SLED]

sledge[2] (slej) *n.* a sledgehammer. **sledgehammer** *n.* a heavy hammer wielded by both hands. ~*a.* (of a blow etc.) imitating the action of a sledgehammer, clumsy, hardhitting. **sledging**[2] *n.* (*esp. Austral., sl.*) in cricket, the practice of baiting batsmen so as to distract them. [OE *slecge* (cp. Dut. *slegge*, Icel. *sleggja*), cogn. with SLAY[1]]

sledging[1] SLEDGE[1].

sledging[2] SLEDGE[2].

sleek (slēk) *a.* **1** (of fur, skin etc.) smooth, glossy. **2** well-groomed and well-fed, prosperous-looking. **3** oily, unctuous, smooth-spoken. **4** (of a surface) polished, smooth. ~*v.t.* **1** to make (hair etc.) sleek. **2** to make pleasant or less disagreeable, to smooth (over). **sleeken** *v.t.* **sleekly** *adv.* **sleekness** *n.* **sleeky** *a.* (*comp.* **sleekier,** *superl.* **sleekiest**). [var. of SLICK]

sleep (slēp) *n.* **1** a state of rest in which consciousness is almost entirely suspended, the body is relaxed, the eyes are closed, and the vital functions are inactive. **2** a period or spell of this (*have a short sleep*). **3** a state with the characteristics of sleep, such as torpor, rest, quiet, death or the hibernating state of certain animals. **4** (*coll.*) mucous matter which collects at the corner of the eye, esp. during sleep. ~*v.i.* (*past, p.p.* **slept** (slept)) **1** to take rest in sleep, to be asleep. **2** to be or lie dormant, inactive or in abeyance. **3** to be dead. **4** to fall asleep. **5** (of a top) to spin rapidly and smoothly so as to seem motionless. ~*v.t.* **1** to spend (time) in sleep (*slept the night on the floor, sleep the whole morning away*). **2** to provide with accommodation for sleeping, to lodge (a certain number). **3** to rest in (sleep, as cognate object). **in one's sleep** while asleep (*talks in her sleep*). **to get to sleep** to manage to go to sleep. **to go to sleep** to fall asleep. **to let sleeping dogs lie** DOG. **to put to sleep 1** to anaesthetize. 2 to kill (an animal) painlessly, usu. by injection. **to sleep around** (*coll.*) to be sexually promiscuous. **to sleep in 1** to sleep on the premises. 2 to oversleep. **to sleep like a log** LOG[1]. **to sleep like a top** TOP[2]. **to sleep off** to rid or recover from (e.g. the effects of alcohol) by sleeping. **to sleep on it** to postpone making a decision until the next day. **to sleep out** 1 to sleep out of doors. 2 to have one's sleeping accommodation away from one's place of work. **to sleep over** to spend the night where one is visiting. **to sleep rough** to sleep out of doors, esp. on the street. **to sleep the sleep of the just** (*usu. facet.*) to enjoy sound untroubled sleep. **to sleep together/ with** to have sexual intercourse (with), esp. in bed. **sleeper** *n.* **1** a person who sleeps, or is asleep. **2** a wooden beam or other support for the rails on a railway track. **3** a sleeping berth, compartment or carriage on a train. **4** a train with these. **5** a small stud or hoop earring worn to keep the hole in a pierced ear open. **6** a sleeping suit. **7** (*coll.*) a person (e.g. a secret agent) who lies dormant before coming into action. **8** (*coll.*) something (e.g. a film, a book) which becomes valuable or popular after a period of being neither. **sleeping** *a., n.* **sleeping bag** *n.* a padded bag of warm material for sleeping in, esp. when camping. **sleeping car, sleeping carriage** *n.* a railway carriage fitted with berths for sleeping in. **sleeping draught** *n.* a drink containing a drug to make one go to sleep. **sleeping partner** *n.* a partner having no share in the management of a business, a silent partner. **sleeping pill** *n.* a sedative in tablet form for inducing sleep.

sleeping policeman *n.* (*pl.* **sleeping policemen**) (*coll.*) a hump on the surface of a road for slowing traffic. **sleeping sickness** *n.* a disease characterized by fever and mental and physical lethargy, almost always fatal, endemic in tropical Africa, and caused by a parasite *Trypanosoma gambiense*. **sleeping suit** *n.* a baby's one-piece suit for sleeping in. **sleep-learning** *n.* learning by hearing and assimilating during sleep. **sleepless** *a.* **1** unable to sleep. **2** (of a night) during which one cannot get to sleep. **3** constantly watchful and active, never resting. **sleeplessly** *adv.* **sleeplessness** *n.* **sleep-out** *n.* (*Austral., New Zeal.*) a porch, veranda or outbuilding for use as sleeping accommodation. **sleepover** *n.* a night that one spends where one is visiting. *~a.* of or relating to a night spent away from home. **sleepwalk** *v.i.* to walk about or perform actions while asleep. **sleepwalker** *n.* a person who sleepwalks, esp. habitually, a somnambulist. **sleepwalking** *n.* **sleepy** *a.* (*comp.* **sleepier**, *superl.* **sleepiest**) **1** inclined to sleep, drowsy, somnolent. **2** dull, lazy, indolent, habitually inactive. **3** tending to induce sleep. **sleepily** *adv.* **sleepiness** *n.* **sleepyhead** *n.* a lazy or sleepy person. **sleepy sickness** *n.* encephalitis lethargica, acute inflammation of certain portions of the brain, causing drowsiness and eventual mental disease. [OE *slæpan, slēpan* (cp. Dut. *slapen*, G *schlafen*), from *slæp*, rel. to G *schlaff*, loose]

sleet (slēt) *n.* hail or snow mingled with rain. *~v.i.* to snow or hail with a mixture of rain. **sleety** *a.* (*comp.* **sleetier**, *superl.* **sleetiest**). **sleetiness** *n.* [cp. EFris. *slaite*, Norw. *slūtr*, hail, G *Schlosse*, hailstone]

sleeve (slēv) *n.* **1** the part of a garment that covers the arm. **2** the cardboard cover for a gramophone record. **3** a tube, pipe or cylindrical sheath enclosing a revolving shaft, connecting lengths of pipe etc. **4** a windsock. **5** a windsock used by an aircraft as a brake, a drogue. *~v.t.* to provide or fit with a sleeve or sleeves. **to have up one's sleeve** to hold secretly in reserve or in readiness. **to roll up one's sleeves** to get ready for hard work, a fight etc. **sleeve board** *n.* a small narrow ironing board for pressing sleeves. **sleeve-coupling** *n.* a tube-shaped connection for joining pipes or shafts. **sleeved** *a.* having sleeves (of a stated type) (*usu. in comb.* as in *long-sleeved*). **sleeveless** *a.* (of a dress, blouse etc.) without sleeves. **sleeve link** *n.* a cuff link. **sleeve note** *n.* a note providing information on a record sleeve about the recorded work. **sleeve-nut** *n.* a long nut with a right-hand and a left-hand screw-thread at the ends for drawing together and connecting conversely threaded pipes, shafts etc. **sleeve valve** *n.* a cylinder-shaped valve with a sliding operation. **sleeving** *n.* the outer insulating cover on an electric cable. [OE *slyf*, rel. to SLIP[1]]

sleigh (slā) *n.* a vehicle mounted on runners for driving over snow or ice, a sledge, esp. for carrying passengers rather than goods. *~v.i.* to travel by sleigh. **sleigh bell** *n.* any of a set of small bells hung on a sleigh or its harness. **sleighing** *n.* [form of SLED]

sleight (slīt) *n.* **1** dexterity, skill in manipulating things. **2** a trick or stratagem so dexterously performed as to escape detection. **3** trickery, cunning. *~a.* deceitful, artful. **sleight of hand** *n.* deceptive movement of the hands, esp. in conjuring, legerdemain. [Icel. *slaegth*, from *slaegr*, SLY]

slender (slen´də) *a.* (*comp.* **slenderer**, *superl.* **slenderest**) **1** small in circumference or width as compared with length. **2** attractively or gracefully thin, slim. **3** slight, scanty, meagre, inadequate, small, poor. **4** (of hopes etc.) feeble, not strong or well-founded. **slenderize, slenderise** *v.t.* to make slender or slim. *~v.i.* to slim. **slender loris** *n.* one of two types of loris, *Loris tardigradus*. **slenderly** *adv.* **slenderness** *n.* [etym. uncertain]

slept SLEEP.

sleuth (slooth) *n.* (*coll.*) a detective. *~v.i.* to act as a detective. *~v.t.* to track or investigate. **sleuth-hound** *n.* **1** a bloodhound. **2** (*coll.*) a detective. [var. of SLOT[2]]

slew[1] SLAY[1]

slew[2] (sloo), **slue** *v.t., v.i.* to turn, twist or swing (round, about etc.) as on a pivot. *~n.* such a turn or twist. **slewed, slued** *a.* (*sl.*) tipsy, drunk. [etym. uncertain]

slew[3] (sloo), **slue** *n.* (*N Am., coll.*) a great quantity or large number. [Ir. *slaugh*]

sley (slā), **slay** *n.* a weaver's reed for separating threads. [OE *slege*, conn. with SLAY[1]]

slice (slīs) *n.* **1** a broad thin piece cut off, esp. from bread etc., or a wedge cut from a circular pie, tart, cake etc. **2** a part, share etc., separated or allotted from a larger quantity. **3** a spatula or other similarly shaped blade for lifting fish etc. from a frying pan or for serving it. **4** a slicing stroke in tennis or golf. *~v.t.* **1** to cut (*usu.* up) into broad, thin pieces. **2** to cut (off) slices from. **3** to cut, to divide. **4** to strike (a ball) with a drawing motion so that it curves to the right (or to the left for a left-handed player). *~v.i.* to cut (through a medium) with a slicing action. **sliceable** *a.* **slicer** *n.* **1** someone who or something that slices. **2** a broad flat-bladed knife or other slicing implement. **slice of life** *n.* an experience that brings home the grim realities of life. **slice of the cake** *n.* one's fair share of the benefits. **slicing** *a., n.* [ME *slice*, OF *esclice*, from *esclicier*, to slit, from Gmc., cogn. with SLIT]

slick (slik) *a.* **1** (*coll.*) dexterous, adroit. **2** neatly or deftly performed. **3** clever, smart, specious. **4** oily, smooth of speech, glib etc. **5** smooth, sleek. **6** polished, glossy. *~adv.* **1** smoothly, deftly, smartly. **2** quickly, immediately. *~n.* **1** a smooth or slippery surface patch, esp. of oil spilt on water. **2** a smooth racing-car tyre. **3** (*N Am.*) a glossy magazine. **4** (*N Am.*) a slick person. *~v.t.* to make smooth or sleek, esp. to flatten or smooth (the hair back or down). **slicker** *n.* (*N Am.*) **1** a waterproof, an oilskin. **2** (*coll.*) a plausible, cunning person, a swindler. **3** CITY SLICKER (under CITY). **slickly** *adv.* **slickness** *n.* [Icel. *slīkr*, cp. Dut. *slijk*, G *Schlick*, grease]

slickenside (slik´ənsīd), **slickensides** (-sīdz) *n.* (*Geol.*) a polished and grooved rock surface produced by friction, as in faults, the sides of a vein etc. [dial. *slicken*, SLICK, SIDE]

slide (slīd) *v.i.* (*past* **slid** (slid), *p.p.* **slid**, †**slidden** (-dən)) **1** to move smoothly along a surface with continuous contact, to glide, to slip, esp. to glide over ice, snow or other slippery surface, without skates. **2** to pass (away, into etc.) smoothly, gradually or imperceptibly, to drift, to take its own course. **3** to move secretly or unobtrusively, to slip. **4** to glide or gloss (over a subject best avoided). *~v.t.* **1** to cause to move smoothly along with a slippery motion (*slid the glass across the bar*). **2** to cause to move or slip unobtrusively (*She slid her hand into his*). *~n.* **1** **a** an act of sliding. **b** a downward turn (e.g. in value), a rapid deterioration. **2** a piece or part that slides (e.g. on a machine). **3** a thin glass plate carrying an object to be viewed in a microscope. **4** a photographic transparency mounted in card or plastic, for projection on to a screen. **5** the moving part on a trombone. **6** a surface, series of grooves, guide-bars etc., on which a part slides, a slideway. **7** an inclined channel, chute etc., esp. which children slide down for fun. **8** a polished track on ice for people to slide on. **9** a prepared slope on snow for tobogganing. **10** a landslip. **11** a clasp for the hair, a hairslide. **12** a series of musical tones passing smoothly one into another. **13** in guitar-playing, a device fitted on the finger and pressed against the frets to produce this effect. **14** a style of guitar-playing characterized by the use of this device. **to let things slide** to leave things undone, or take no positive action over them, to allow things to deteriorate. **slidable** *a.* **slidably** *adv.* **slide fastener** *n.* (*NAm.*) a zip fastener. **slider** *n.* **slide rule** *n.* a device, consisting of one rule sliding within another, whereby several mathematical processes can be performed mechanically. **slide-valve** *n.* a valve that slides across an opening to expose or cover it. **slideway** *n.* in machinery etc., the projection, channel or grooves along which a sliding part moves. **sliding** *a.*, *n.* **sliding door** *n.* a door that slides along a groove etc. to open or shut, as distinct from turning on hinges. **sliding gear** *n.* a gear sliding along an axle or shaft, and thereby being capable of being instantly disconnected. **sliding keel** *n.* a centreboard. **sliding roof** *n.* a moving section, e.g. in a motor vehicle, covering an opening in the roof, that can be slid back to provide fresh air etc. **sliding scale** *n.* a scale of duties, prices, wages etc., varying directly or inversely according to fluctuations of value or other conditions. **sliding seat** *n.* a seat moving on a track, esp. one in a racing boat (enabling a rower to lengthen the stroke). [OE *slīdan*, cp. LG *sliddern*, G *schlittern*, freq. from *slid-*]

slight (slīt) *a.* (*comp.* **slighter**, *superl.* **slightest**) **1** inconsiderable, insignificant. **2** small in amount, intensity etc., hardly perceptible. **3** inadequate, paltry, superficial, negligible. **4** frail, flimsy, weak. **5** (of a person's figure) small and slender. **6** (*in superl.*) (*usu. with neg. or interrog.*) the least (*hadn't the slightest inkling this would happen*). ~*n.* an act of disregard, disrespect or neglect, a snub. ~*v.t.* **1** to treat, or speak about, as of little importance, to disregard. **2** to treat disrespectfully, to snub. **3** (*Hist. Mil.*) to raze (a fortification), or render it useless by partial demolition. **not in the slightest** NOT. **to put a slight upon** to belittle or disparage. **slighter** *n.* **slightingly** *adv.* **slightish** *a.* **slightly** *adv.* **slightness** *n.* [MDut. *slicht*, cp. OLG *sligt*, G *schlicht*, Icel. *slēttr*]

slily SLYLY (under SLY).

slim (slim) *a.* (*comp.* **slimmer**, *superl.* **slimmest**) **1** tall and narrow in shape. **2** slender, gracefully thin, of slight shape or build. **3** poor, slight, inadequate. **4** slick, crafty, clever. **5** economically streamlined. ~*v.i.* (*pres.p.* **slimming**, *past*, *p.p.* **slimmed**) to diet and exercise in order to become slimmer. ~*v.t.* to make slim or slimmer. ~*n.* (*also* **slim disease**) Aids (used esp. by Africans). **slimline** *a.* **1** slim in shape. **2** (of a drink etc.) aiding slimness. **slimly** *adv.* **slimmer** *n.* a person who loses or attempts to lose weight through dieting or exercise. **slimmers' disease** *n.* anorexia nervosa. **slimming** *n.* **slimmish** *a.* **slimness** *n.* [cp. MDut. *slim*, sly, G *schlimm*, bad, cunning]

slime (slīm) *n.* any soft, glutinous or viscous substance, esp. mucus or soft, moist and sticky earth. ~*v.t.* to smear or cover with slime. **slime mould**, (*NAm.*) **slime mold** *n.* a myxomycete or other micro-organism that secretes slime. **slimy** *a.* (*comp.* **slimier**, *superl.* **slimiest**) **1** consisting of, or of the nature of, slime. **2** covered with or abounding in slime. **3** slippery, difficult to grasp. **4** repulsively mean, dishonest, cringing or obsequious. **slimily** *adv.* **sliminess** *n.* [OE *slīm*, cp. Dut. *slijm*, G *Schleim*, Icel. *slīm*, also L *līmus*, mud]

slimmer, slimming etc. SLIM.

slimy SLIME.

sling[1] (sling) *n.* **1** a band, loop, or other arrangement of rope, chains, straps etc., for suspending, hoisting or transferring anything. **2** a band of cloth for supporting an injured arm, suspended from the neck. **3** a short leather strap having a string at each end for hurling a small missile by hand. **4** an act of slinging. **5** a throw. ~*v.t.* (*past*, *p.p.* **slung** (slŭng)) **1** to hurl from a sling. **2** (*coll.*) to throw, to hurl. **3** (*coll.*) to cast (out). **4** to suspend in or as in a swing, to hang loosely so as to swing. **5** to hoist by means of a sling. **6** (*coll.*) to pass, hand, give (someone something). ~*v.i.* **1** to hurl missiles with or as with a sling. **2** to move swiftly or violently. **to sling off at** (*Austral.*, *New Zeal.*, *sl.*) to jeer at or disparage. **to sling one's hook** HOOK. **sling-back** *n.* **1** a backless shoe with a narrow strap round the back of the ankle. **2** (*in full* **sling-back chair**) a chair with a loose seat of e.g. fabric, slung from a rigid frame. **sling-bag** *n.* a bag with a long strap, for carrying over the shoulder. **slinger** *n.* **slingshot** *n.* **1** SLUNG SHOT (under SLING[1]). **2** (*chiefly NAm.*) a catapult. **slung shot** *n.* a heavy metal ball attached by a thong or strap to the wrist for use as a weapon. [Icel. *slyngva*, cp. G *schlingen*, to wind, twist, sling]

sling[2] (sling) *n.* a sweetened drink of water mixed with spirits, esp. gin. [prob. from G *schlingen*, to swallow]

slink (slingk) *v.i.* (*past*, *p.p.* **slunk** (slŭngk)) **1** to steal or sneak (away etc.) in a furtive, ashamed or cowardly manner. **2** to move sinuously and provocatively. ~*v.t.* (of an animal) to give birth to prematurely. ~*n.* **1** an animal, esp. a calf, born prematurely. **2** its flesh. **slinky** *a.* (*comp.* **slinkier**, *superl.* **slinkiest**) **1** sinuous, slender. **2** (of clothes) clinging, figure-hugging. **slinkily** *adv.* **slinkiness** *n.* [OE *slincan*, cp. G *schleichen*]

slip[1] (slip) *v.i.* (*pres.p.* **slipping**, *past*, *p.p.* **slipped**) **1** to slide unintentionally and miss one's footing or lose one's balance. **2** to slide, to glide. **3** to move, go or pass unnoticed, furtively or quickly. **4** to go (along) swiftly. **5 a** to get (out, through etc.), become free, or escape thus. **b** to drop (out of someone's grasp, fingers etc.). **6** to commit a small mistake or oversight. **7** to decline (*Standards are slipping*). **8** (*coll.*) to lose one's customary skill or grip, to lose control of a situation. **9** (of time) to elapse. **10** (of a clutch) to fail to engage. ~*v.t.* **1** to cause to move in a sliding manner. **2** to put (on or off) or to insert (into) with a sliding, stealthy, hasty or careless motion. **3** to let loose, to unleash, to undo. **4** to put (a garment on) or take (a garment off) speedily or easily. **5** to escape or free oneself from (*The dog slipped its collar*). **6** to escape (one's memory). **7** (of animals) to give birth to prematurely. **8** to dislocate (a bone). **9** to keep (a clutch) partially engaged. **10** to transfer (an unworked stitch) from one knitting needle to the other. **11** to detach (a carriage) from a train in motion. **12** to detach (an anchor) from a ship. ~*n.* **1** an instance of slipping. **2** an unintentional error, a small offence, a lapse, an indiscretion. **3** a garment etc., easily slipped on or off, such as a loose petticoat, pillowcase. **4** a leash for slipping a dog or hounds. **5** (*sing. or pl.*) **a** an inclined ramp, dock or movable structure on which vessels are built, repaired or laid up temporarily. **b** an artificially constructed slope of stone for launching or landing vessels. **6** a landslide. **7** (*pl.*) in cricket, any of three off-side positions or the fielders playing in these positions. **8** (*pl.*) in a theatre, the sides of the stage, from which the scenes are slipped on, where actors stand before coming on the stage. **9 a** backward movement of a belt on a pulley, due to slipping. **b** the difference between the pitch of a propeller and the distance travelled through the surrounding medium in a single revolution. **to give the slip** to escape from, to evade. **to let slip through one's fingers 1** to lose hold of. **2** to miss the chance of getting. **to slip away/ off** to leave quickly or unobtrusively. **to slip up** to make a mistake. **slip-carriage, slip-coach** *n.* a railway carriage detached at a station from an express train in motion. **slip case** *n.* an open-ended cover for one or more books which reveals the spines. **slip cover** *n.* **1** a loose cover for fitting over a chair or sofa. **2** a dust jacket or slip case for a book. **slip form** *n.* a mould for casting a structure with a uniform cross-section. **slip hook** *n.* a hook with a quick-release mechanism. **slip-knot** *n.* **1** a knot that can be undone with a pull. **2** a knot that slips up and down the string etc. on which it is made, a running knot. **slip of the pen** *n.* a mistake in writing.

slip of the tongue *n.* a mistake in speaking. **slip-on** *a.*, *n.* (a garment or item of footwear) which can be put on or removed easily and quickly, usu. without fasteners. **slipover** *a.* (of a garment) easily put on over the head. ~*n.* a pullover. **slippage** (-ij) *n.* an act, instance, amount or degree of slipping or failure to meet a target. **slipped disc** *n.* a displacement of one of the discs between the vertebrae, causing painful pressure on spinal nerves. **slipper** *n.* **1** a loose comfortable shoe, for wearing indoors, esp. with nightclothes. **2** a light slip-on dancing shoe. **3** (*Hist.*) a skid or shoe for braking a wheel. **4** a person who or something that slips. ~*v.t.* (*coll.*) to beat with a slipper. **slipper bath** *n.* a bath with a covered end, roughly resembling a slipper. **slippered** *a.* wearing slippers. **slipper sock** *n.* a thick sock with a leather sole, used as a slipper. **slipperwort** *n.* a calceolaria. **slippery** *a.* **1** so smooth, wet or slimy as to be difficult to hold. **2** so smooth, wet, muddy etc. as to cause slipping, not allowing a firm footing or hold. **3** elusive. **4** unreliable, shifty, dishonest. **5** unstable. **slipperiness** *n.* **slippery elm** *n.* **1** a N American elm, *Ulmus fulvus.* **2** its medicinal inner bark. **slippery slope** *n.* a disastrous course. **slippy** *a.* (*comp.* **slippier,** *superl.* **slippiest**) (*coll.*) slippery. **to look slippy** (*coll.*) to hurry, to look sharp. **slippiness** *n.* **slip ring** *n.* in a dynamo or electric motor, a conducting ring that makes sliding contact with the brushes. **slip road** *n.* an access or exit road on to or off a motorway. **slip-rope** *n.* (*Naut.*) a rope both ends of which are on board, so that the ship is released from its moorings when either end is cast off. **slipshod** *a.* **1** careless, slovenly. **2** down-at-heel. **slip stitch** *n.* **1** a hidden stitch used in hemming. **2** in knitting, a stitch passed unworked from one needle to the other. **slip-stitch** *v.t.* **1** to sew with a slip stitch. **2** to slip (an unworked stitch) from one knitting needle to the other. **slipstream** *n.* **1** the stream of air behind an aircraft propeller. **2** a similar stream behind any moving body, object, vehicle etc. **slip-up** *n.* an error, a blunder. **slipway** *n.* a slip for the repair, laying up or launch of vessels. [ME *slippen* (cp. Dut. *slippen*, G *schleifen*), cogn. with OE *slūpan*, also with L *lūbricus*, slippery]

slip² (slip) *n.* a creamy mixture of clay and water used to coat or decorate pottery. **slip casting** *n.* a process of making pottery in which slip is allowed to solidify in a mould. **slipware** *n.* pottery which has been decorated with slip. [OE *slypa*, slime]

slip³ (slip) *n.* **1** a small piece of paper for writing messages etc. on. **2** a small form for filling in. **3** a long narrow strip of paper, wood or other material. **4** (*Print.*) a galley proof. **5** a cutting for grafting or planting. **6** a scion, a descendant. **7** a slight young person, a stripling. ~*v.t.* (*pres.p.* **slipping,** *past, p.p.* **slipped**) to take a cutting from (a plant). **a slip of a** merely a slight young (girl etc.). [prob. from MLG *slippe*, to strip, to cut]

slipper, slippery etc. SLIP¹.

slit (slit) *n.* a long cut or narrow opening. ~*v.t.* (*pres.p.* **slitting,** *past, p.p.* **slit**) **1** to make a long cut in. **2** to cut into long pieces or strips. **3** to cut or tear lengthways. **slit-eyed** *a.* having narrow eyes. **slit pocket** *n.* a pocket with a vertical opening. **slitter** *n.* **slit trench** *n.* a narrow trench for one or two soldiers, or their weapons. **slitty** *a.* (*comp.* **slittier,** *superl.* **slittiest**) (of eyes) narrow. [OE *slītan*, cp. Icel. *slīta*, Dut. *slijten*, G *schleissen, schlitzen*]

slither (slidh´ə) *v.i.* **1** to slip, to slide unsteadily (along etc.). **2** to move with a slipping or sliding motion like a snake. ~*n.* a sliding motion. **slithery** *a.* [OE *slēfan*, to slip on]

slitter, slitty SLIT.

sliver (sliv´ə) *n.* **1** a thin piece cut from something. **2** a piece of wood or similar material torn off. **3** a splinter from an exploded shell. **4** a fleecy strand or twist pulled out from wool or other textile fibre. ~*v.t.* **1** to form or divide into long, thin pieces. **2** to cut or break into slivers. ~*v.i.* **1** to break off in the form of a sliver. **2** to split, to splinter, to break into slivers. [dim. of obs. *slive*, a slip, from OE *slīfan*, to cast off (in *tō-slāf*)]

slivovitz (sliv´əvits) *n.* a dry plum brandy. [Serbo-Croat *sljivovica*, from *sl(j)iva*, plum]

Sloane (slōn), **Sloane Ranger** *n.* (*dated*) an upper-class young person, typically female and cultivating the casually elegant look, living in any of the fashionable parts of London. [*Sloane* Square, London, with a pun on the *Lone Ranger*, a television cowboy hero]

slob (slob) *n.* **1** (*coll.*) a messy, slovenly or boorish person. **2** (*Ir.*) a mire. **slobbish** *a.* **slobby** *a.* (*comp.* **slobbier,** *superl.* **slobbiest**) slovenly, messy. [Ir. *slab*]

slobber (slob´ə) *v.i.* **1** to let saliva run from the mouth, to dribble, to slaver. **2** to talk or behave sentimentally (over). ~*v.t.* to wet with saliva, to dribble over. ~*n.* **1** saliva or spittle running from the mouth. **2** over-sentimental talk or behaviour. **slobberer** *n.* **slobbery** *a.* **slobberiness** *n.* [var. of SLUBBER]

slobbish SLOB.

sloe (slō) *n.* the fruit of the blackthorn, *Prunus spinosa*, or the shrub bearing it. **sloe-eyed** *a.* having dark, slanted or almond-shaped eyes. **sloe gin** *n.* gin flavoured with sloes. [OE *slā*, cp. Dut. *slee*, G *Schlehe*, Dan. *slaaen*]

slog (slog) *v.t.* (*pres.p.* **slogging,** *past, p.p.* **slogged**) to hit vigorously and at random, esp. in batting or with the fists. ~*v.i.* **1** to work (away) hard. **2** to move slowly or cumbersomely. ~*n.* **1** a spell of hard work. **2** a heavy blow. **3** an exhausting walk. **slogger** *n.* [etym. uncertain, cp. SLUG²]

slogan (slō´gən) *n.* **1** a catchy advertising phrase or word. **2** a political catchword. **3** (*Hist.*) the war cry of the old Highland clans. [Gael. *sluagh-ghairm* (*sluagh*, host, *gairm*, outcry)]

slogger SLOG.

sloop (sloop) *n.* **1** a fore-and-aft rigged vessel with one mast. **2** (*Hist.*) a small warship with guns on one deck only. [Dut. *sloep*, LG *Sluup*, from *slupen*, to glide along]

sloot (sloot), **sluit** *n.* (*S Afr.*) **1** an irrigation ditch, a drainage channel. **2** a channel or gully formed by heavy rain. [Afrikaans, from Dut. *sluit*, *sluis*, SLUICE]

slop¹ (slop) *v.t.* (*pres.p.* **slopping,** *past, p.p.* **slopped**) **1** to spill or allow to overflow. **2** to soil by spilling liquid upon. **3** to feed liquid food refuse to. **4** to serve (food) in a messy or clumsy way. ~*v.i.* **1** to spill (over), to overflow the side of a vessel. **2** to tramp through slush or mud. ~*n.* **1** water or other liquid carelessly thrown about. **2** sentimental or maudlin speech or writing. **3** (*pl.*) dirty water, liquid refuse. **4** (*pl.*) liquid food, weak or non-alcoholic liquors. **5** (*pl.*) liquid food refuse fed to animals, esp. pigs. **6** (*Naut.*) a rough sea. **to slop about** to shamble or slouch. **to slop out** (of prisoners) to clean out slops from a chamber pot. **to slop over** (*chiefly N Am.*) to be too effusive, to gush. **slop basin, slop bowl** *n.* a basin for emptying the dregs of cups etc. into at table. **slop bucket** *n.* a bucket for taking away slops from the bedroom or kitchen. **sloppy** *a.* (*comp.* **sloppier,** *superl.* **sloppiest**) **1** wet, splashed, covered with spilt water or puddles. **2** (of food) watery and insipid. **3** (of work) slovenly, done carelessly. **4** (of clothes) untidy, badly fitting. **5** weakly sentimental, maudlin or effusive. **6** (*Naut.*) (of the sea) rough, choppy. **sloppily** *adv.* **sloppiness** *n.* [OE, *sloppe*, *slyppe*, in *cū slyppe*, see COWSLIP, rel. to SLIP¹]

slop² (slop) *n.* **1** a workman's loose overall. **2** (*pl.*) ready-made cheap clothing. **3** (*pl.*) clothing, bedding etc., sold to sailors. **4** (*pl., Hist.*) wide loose breeches, esp. the kind worn by sailors. **slop shop** *n.* a shop selling ready-made clothes. [Icel. *sloppr*, cogn. with SLIP¹]

slope (slōp) *n.* **1** an inclined surface, line or direction. **2** an incline, a declivity or acclivity, a piece of ground whose surface makes an angle with the horizon. **3** the degree of such inclination, the difference in level between two ends or sides of something, or the rate at which this becomes greater with distance. **4** a downhill skiing course on a hillside. **5** the position of a rifle when carried on the shoulder. *~v.i.* to be inclined at an angle to the horizon, to lie obliquely, to slant. *~v.t.* to place or form with a slope, to hold or direct obliquely. **to slope arms** to position a rifle on the shoulder with the barrel pointing up and back. **to slope off** (*coll.*) to leave, esp. furtively, to sneak away. **sloping** *a.* **slopingly** *adv.* **slopy** *a.* (*comp.* **slopier,** *superl.* **slopiest**). [ME, *cogn.* with SLIP[1]]

sloppy SLOP[1].

slosh (slosh) *v.t.* **1** (*coll.*) to strike hard. **2** (*coll.*) to splash, spread or pour (liquid) carelessly. **3** to move (something) about in liquid. **4** to wet by splashing. *~v.i.* **1** to move or splash through slush, mud, water etc. **2** (*coll.*) to hit. *~n.* **1** (*coll.*) a heavy blow. **2** a liquid or semi-liquid medium, such as slush, mud etc. **3** the slapping or splashing sound of liquid. **sloshed** *a.* (*coll.*) drunk. [prob. from SLOP[1] and SLUSH]

slot[1] (slot) *n.* **1** the aperture into which coins are put in a slot machine. **2** a groove, channel, depression or opening, esp. in a machine for some part to fit into. **3** a place or niche (e.g. in an organization). **4** a (usu. regular) position in a sequence or schedule (e.g. of a television programme). *~v.t.* (*pres.p.* **slotting,** *past, p.p.* **slotted**) **1** to fit or place (as) into a slot. **2** to make a slot in. *~v.i.* to fit (together or into) by means of a slot or slots. **slot machine** *n.* **1** a machine for dispensing sweets, drinks etc., operated by means of coins or tokens pushed or dropped through a narrow aperture, a vending machine. **2** a similarly operated machine allowing a spell of play at pinball. **3** (*N Am.*) a fruit machine. **slotted** *a.* having a slot or slots. **slotter** *n.* [perh. from OF *esclot*, pit of the breast or stomach]

slot[2] (slot) *n.* **1** the track of a deer. **2** a deer's foot. [A-F and OF *esclot*, horse's hoofprint, Icel. *sloth*, trail, cp. SLEUTH]

slot[3] (slot) *n.* **1** a bar or bolt fastening a door. **2** a metal rod, bar etc. [ME, cp. MDut. *slot*, lock]

sloth (slōth) *n.* **1** laziness, indolence, sluggishness, reluctance to exert oneself. **2** a S American arboreal edentate mammal of the family Bradypodidae characterized by its slow and awkward movements on the ground. **sloth bear** *n.* a long-snouted bear, *Melursus ursinus*, of India and Sri Lanka which feeds on termites. **slothful** *a.* **slothfully** *adv.* **slothfulness** *n.* [ME *slouthe*, OE *slæwth*, from *slāw*, SLOW]

slotted, slotter SLOT[1].

slouch (slowch) *n.* **1** an ungainly or negligent drooping or stooping attitude, gait, or movement. **2** a downward bend of the hat-brim. **3** (*sl.*) an awkward, slovenly or incapable person. **4** a slouch hat. *~v.i.* **1** to stand or move in a loose, drooping, negligent or ungainly attitude. **2** to droop or hang down. *~v.t.* to bend the brim of (a hat) so that it hangs down on one side. **to be no slouch** (*coll.*) to be quick and efficient (at doing something). **sloucher** *n.* **slouch hat** *n.* any soft hat with a brim that can be pulled down, esp. one worn with the brim down at one side. **slouching** *a.* **slouchy** *a.* (*comp.* **slouchier,** *superl.* **slouchiest**). **slouchiness** *n.* [Icel. *slōkr*, cp. Norw. *slōk*, slouching fellow, cogn. with SLACK[1]]

slough[1] (slow) *n.* **1** a place full of mud, a bog, a quagmire. **2** a marsh, a swamp. **3** a state of abject depression or degradation. **Slough of Despond** *n.* extreme despondency (from the name of a place in John Bunyan's *Pilgrim's Progress*). **sloughy[1]** *a.* (*comp.* **sloughier,** *superl.* **sloughiest**). [OE *slōh*, cogn. with G *schlingen*, to devour]

slough[2] (slŭf) *n.* **1** the cast skin of a snake. **2** a covering or other part or thing cast off. **3** dead tissue separating from a living part. **4** a habit that one has abandoned. *~v.t.* to cast off (a skin, dead tissue etc.). *~v.i.* **1** to peel and come (off, away etc.). **2** to cast off slough. **sloughy[2]** *a.* (*comp.* **sloughier,** *superl.* **sloughiest**). [ME *sloh*, etym. uncertain, cp. LG *slu, sluwe*, husk, covering, perh. rel. to SLEEVE]

sloughy[1] SLOUGH[1].

sloughy[2] SLOUGH[2].

Slovak (slō´vak) *n.* **1** any member of a Slavonic people inhabiting Slovakia, formerly the eastern part of Czechoslovakia, but now an independent republic. **2** the Slavonic language of this people, closely related to Czech. *~a.* of or relating to this people, their language or the region they inhabit. **Slovakian** (-vak´-) *n., a.* [Slovak *Slovák*, rel. to SLOVENE]

sloven (slŭv´ən) *n.* a person who is careless about dress or negligent about cleanliness; an untidy, careless, lazy person. **slovenly** *a., adv.* **slovenliness** *n.* [ME *sloveyn* (perh. MDut. *slof*, Flem. *sloef*, -EN)]

Slovene (slōvēn´, slō´-) *n.* **1** a member of a S Slavonic people inhabiting Slovenia, a republic of S central Europe, formerly part of Yugoslavia. **2** the language of this people. *~a.* of or relating to the Slovenes, their language or the region they inhabit. **Slovenian** (-vē´-) *n., a.* [Gr. *Sklabēnos*, see SLAV]

slovenly SLOVEN.

slow (slō) *a.* **1** not quick, of low velocity, moving at a low speed. **2** taking a long time in acting or doing something. **3** deliberate (of speech etc.). **4** gradual, e.g. in growth or development. **5** not prompt or willing (to do something). **6** not hasty, not precipitate. **7** tardy, backward (*slow learners*). **8** stupid, dull. **9** (of a party or similar event) tedious, lifeless. **10** (of business, trade etc.) slack. **11** (of a clock or watch) behind the right time. **12** not allowing fast movement (*in the slow lane*). **13** (of a fire or oven) producing little heat. **14** (of a cricket pitch or tennis court) causing the ball to roll or bounce sluggishly. **15** (of a photographic film) needing a long exposure. **16** (of a lens) having a small aperture. *~adv.* slowly. *~v.i.* to slacken or moderate speed (up or down), to go slower. *~v.t.* to reduce the speed of. **slow and sure** steady and methodical. **slow but sure** finally achieving results. **slowcoach** *n.* a person who is slow in moving, acting, deciding etc. **slow cooker** *n.* an electrically powered cooking pot used for slow stewing etc. **slowdown** *n.* **1** the act or process of slowing down. **2** a go-slow protest. **slow fuse, slow match** *n.* a fuse or match burning slowly for igniting explosives. **slow handclap** *n.* a slow regular clapping by an audience, expressing discontent. **slowish** *a.* **slow loris** *n.* (*pl.* **slow loris**) one of two types of loris, *Nycticebus coucang*. **slowly** *adv.* **slow march** *n.* a marching tempo used by the military at funerals etc. **slow motion** *n.* **1** in film and video, a slow-projection or fast-exposure technique which allows action to appear slower than normal. **2** artificially slow movement or action imitating this. **slow-motion** *a.* **1** of or relating to the technique of slowing down action on film or video. **2** operating or moving at a slower speed than is normal. **slowness** *n.* **slow neutron** *n.* a neutron with kinetic energy not greater than 10 electrovolts. **slowpoke** *n.* (*N Am., coll.*) a slowcoach. **slow puncture** *n.* a small puncture that causes the tyre to deflate only gradually. **slow reactor** *n.* (*Physics*) a nuclear reactor that uses chiefly slow neutrons. **slow track** *n.* a course characterized by slow progress, as distinct from *fast track*. **slow virus** *n.* a virus that breeds slowly in its host and has a long incubation period. **slow-witted** *a.* dull, slow to react. [OE *slāw*, cp. Dut. *sleeuw*, Icel. *sloer*]

slow-worm (slō´wœm) *n.* a small limbless viviparous snakelike lizard, *Anguis fragilis*, the blindworm. [OE *slā-wyrm* (prob. *slā*, *slah*, from *slēan*, to SLAY[1], WORM, from its being formerly supposed to be venomous)]

SLR *abbr.* **1** self-loading rifle. **2** single-lens reflex.

slub[1] (slŭb) *n.* **1** a knob or lump in yarn. **2** fabric woven with this kind of yarn. ~*a.* (of a fabric) having a lumpy appearance. [etym. uncertain]

slub[2] (slŭb) *n.* wool slightly twisted before spinning. ~*v.t.* (*pres.p.* **slubbing**, *past*, *p.p.* **slubbed**) to form into slubs, in preparation for spinning. [etym. uncertain]

slubber (slŭb´ə) *v.t.* (*dial.*) **1** to do lazily, carelessly, or bunglingly. **2** to stain, to daub, to soil. **slubberingly** *adv.* [cp. Dan. *slubbre*, to slaver, also LG *slubbern*, to lap up, to scamp]

sludge (slŭj) *n.* **1** thick mud. **2** an oozy or slimy sediment, as of ore and water. **3** a hard precipitate produced in the treatment of sewage. **4** a residue of dirty oil in the sump of an internal-combustion engine. **5** sea ice beginning to form in small accumulations. **6** (*also* **sludge green**) a muddy green colour. **sludgy** *a.* (*comp.* **sludgier**, *superl.* **sludgiest**). [ME *sluche*, etym. uncertain]

slue[1] SLEW[2].

slue[2] SLEW[3].

slug[1] (slŭg) *n.* **1** a shell-less air-breathing gastropod, very destructive to plants. **2** a sea slug. **3 a** a bullet, esp. an irregularly shaped one. **b** a pellet for an airgun. **4** a small, roughly rounded lump of metal. **5** a strip of metal for spacing between lines of type. **6** a line of type from a Linotype machine. **7** (*coll.*) a quantity of liquor which can be gulped at one go. **8** in the foot-per-second system, a unit of mass equal to 32.174 lb. (14.6 kg). **9** (*N Am.*) a token for a slot machine. ~*v.t.* (*pres.p.* **slugging**, *past*, *p.p.* **slugged**) to gulp (liquor) down, to swig. †**slugabed** *n.* a person who stays in bed late in the morning out of laziness. **sluggard** (-əd) *n.* a habitually lazy person. ~†*a.* sluggish, lazy. **sluggardly** *a.* **sluggish** *a.* **1** habitually lazy, dull, inactive. **2** slow in movement or response, inert, torpid. **sluggishly** *adv.* **sluggishness** *n.* [orig. *sluggard*, from obs. *slug*, ME *sluggen* (cp. Dan. *slug*, Swed. *sloka*, Norw. *sloka*, to SLOUCH)]

slug[2] (slŭg) *v.t.* (*pres.p.* **slugging**, *past*, *p.p.* **slugged**) to hit hard. ~*n.* a hard blow. **to slug it out 1** to fight it out. **2** to stick it out, to keep going to the end. **slugger** *n.* [etym. uncertain, cp. SLOG]

†**slugabed, sluggard** etc. SLUG[1].

slugger SLUG[2].

sluice (sloos) *n.* **1** a waterway with a sliding gate or hatch by which the level of a body of water is controlled, a sluice-gate or floodgate. **2** the stream above, below, or passing through a floodgate. **3** an inclined trough or channel for washing ore, floating logs down etc., a sluice-way. **4** a place for, or an act of, rinsing. ~*v.t.* **1** to flood or drench by means of a sluice or sluices. **2** to provide with a sluice. **3** to drench, to wash thoroughly, to rinse. **4** to let out or drain by a sluice. ~*v.i.* to pour out (as) through a sluice. **sluice-gate** *n.* a floodgate. **sluice-valve** *n.* a valve controlling the level of a sluice. **sluice-way** *n.* a channel into which water passes from a sluice. **sluicy** *a.* (*comp.* **sluicier**, *superl.* **sluiciest**) **1** flowing as though from a sluice. **2** soaking. [ME *scluse*, OF *escluse*, late L *exclūsa*, floodgate, orig. fem. p.p. of *exclūdere*, to EXCLUDE]

sluit SLOOT.

slum[1] (slŭm) *n.* **1** a squalid, usu. overcrowded, neighbourhood in a town or city, inhabited by the very poor. **2** a house, flat etc. which is overcrowded, in a deteriorated condition etc. ~*v.i.* (*pres.p.* **slumming**, *past*, *p.p.* **slummed**) **1** to live in squalid or poverty-stricken conditions. **2** to visit a place or affect a lifestyle inferior to what one is accustomed to, out of curiosity or for amusement. **to slum it** (*coll.*) to make do with less comfortable or luxurious conditions than one is used to. **slummer** *n.* **slummy** *a.* (*comp.* **slummier**, *superl.* **slummiest**). **slumminess** *n.* [orig. sl., etym. uncertain]

slum[2] (slŭm) *n.* **1** the non-lubricating part of crude oil. **2** the sticky residue of lubricating oil. [perh. G *Schlamm*, mud, dirt]

slumber (slŭm´bə) *v.i.* **1** to sleep, esp. lightly. **2** to be inactive or dormant. ~*v.t.* to waste (time away) in sleep. ~*n.* **1** light sleep, or a spell of this. **2** a state of dormancy, inactivity. **slumberer** *n.* **slumberingly** *adv.* **slumberous** *a.* **slumberously** *adv.* **slumberousness** *n.* **slumberwear** *n.* nightclothes. [ME *slumeren*, freq. of *slumer* (from n. *slume*, OE *slūma*, slumber), cp. Dut. *sluimeren*, G *schlummern*, Swed. *slumra*]

slumgullion (slŭmgŭl´yən) *n.* (*N Am.*, *sl.*) watery stew, or other sloppy matter. [perh. SLUM[2], slime, and N Am. *cullion*, testicles, or fanciful formation]

slummer, slummy SLUM[1].

slump (slŭmp) *v.i.* **1** to fall or sink (down) heavily. **2** (of prices, prosperity etc.) to fall, to collapse. **3** to decline quickly or drastically. ~*n.* **1** an act of slumping. **2** a heavy fall or decline, a collapse (of prices etc.). [cp. Dan. *slumpe*, Norw. and Swed. *slumpa*, to fall; prob. imit.]

slung SLING[1].

slunk SLINK.

slur (slœ) *v.t.* (*pres.p.* **slurring**, *past*, *p.p.* **slurred**) **1** to pronounce indistinctly. **2** to blur or smudge (writing). **3** (*Mus.*) **a** to sing or play legato. **b** to mark (notes) to be slurred. **4** to calumniate, to speak slightingly of. **5** to pass lightly over. ~*v.i.* **1** to speak or articulate indistinctly. **2** to pass lightly or slightingly (over). ~*n.* **1** a stain, a stigma, a reproach or disparagement. **2** a blurred impression in printing. **3** a slurring in pronunciation or singing. **4** a curved line (∪ ∩) placed over or under notes, denoting that they are to be played or sung legato. **5** the performance of such notes. **slurred** *a.* [MDut. *sleuren*, to trail]

slurp (slœp) *n.* a sucking sound produced when eating or drinking noisily. ~*v.i.*, *v.t.* to eat or drink noisily. [Dut. *slurpen*, *slorpen*, to gulp, to sip]

slurry (slŭr´i) *n.* (*pl.* **slurries**) **1** a thin, fluid paste made by mixing certain materials (esp. cement) with water. **2** liquid manure. **3** a mixture of coal dust and water remaining at the washing plant of a mine. [obs. *slur*, fluid mud, cogn. with SLUR, -Y[1]]

slush (slŭsh) *n.* **1** half-melted snow. **2** liquid mud, sludge. **3** (*sl.*) mawkishly sentimental talk or writing, gush. ~*v.i.* to move (as) through slush. **slush fund** *n.* a fund of money used to finance corrupt business or political practices. **slushy** *a.* (*comp.* **slushier**, *superl.* **slushiest**). **slushiness** *n.* [perh. from Norw. *slush* or var. of SLUDGE]

slut (slŭt) *n.* a dirty, slovenly or sexually promiscuous woman. **sluttery** *n.* sluttishness. **sluttish** *a.* **sluttishly** *adv.* **sluttishness** *n.* [cp. Swed. dial. *slata*, Norw. *slott*, Dan. *slatte*]

sly (slī) *a.* (*comp.* **slyer, slier**, *superl.* **slyest, sliest**) **1** crafty, cunning, stealthily artful. **2** underhand, furtive, not open or frank. **3** playfully roguish, knowing, arch. **on the sly** slyly, in secret, on the quiet. **slyboots** *n.* (*coll.*) a sly person, esp. in keeping something dark. **sly dog** *n.* a cunning or secretive person. **slyly, slily** *adv.* **slyness** *n.* [ME *sleigh*, Icel. *slægr*, cogn. with SLAY[1]]

slype (slīp) *n.* a covered passage between the transept of a cathedral and the chapter house, deanery etc. [var. of SLIP[1]]

SM *abbr.* **1** sadomasochism. **2** sergeant major.

Sm *chem. symbol* samarium.

smack[1] (smak) *n.* **1** a blow with the flat of the hand, a slap. **2** in cricket, a hard hit. **3** a loud kiss. **4** a quick, smart report as of a blow with something flat, a crack of a whip etc. ~*v.t.* **1** to strike with the flat of the hand, to slap. **2** to separate (the lips) with a sharp noise, as an indication that one is enjoying, or is about to enjoy, something, esp. food. **3** to hit, put down, crack (a whip), kiss etc. with a sharp noise. *~v.i.* to produce a sharp noise. *~adv.* headlong, plump, directly (*ran smack into her*). **to have a smack at** (*coll.*) to tackle, have a go at. **to smack one's lips** to gloat (over something) or anticipate something with relish. **smack-dab** *adv.* (*N Am.*) headlong, directly. **smacker** *n.* **1** a noisy kiss. **2** a resounding blow. **3** (*sl.*) a pound or dollar note. **smack in the eye, smack in the face** *n.* (*coll.*) a snub or rebuff. [prob. onomat., cp. Swed. *smacka,* Dan. *smække,* to bang, to slam]

smack[2] (smak) *n.* **1** a slight taste or flavour (of). **2** a suggestion, trace, tincture or dash (of). **3** a very tiny amount, a smattering (of). *~v.i.* to have a taste, flavour or suggestion (of). [OE *smæc,* cp. MDut. *smac,* LG *smakk,* Swed. *smak,* G *Geschmack*]

smack[3] (smak) *n.* a one-masted vessel, like a sloop or cutter, used in fishing etc. [MDut. *smacke,* cp. LG *smakk,* perh. rel. to SNAKE, cp. OE *snacc*]

smack[4] (smak) *n.* (*sl.*) heroin or some other illegally sold drug. [perh. alteration of Yiddish *schmeck,* sniff]

small (smawl) *a.* **1** deficient or relatively little in size, age, stature, degree, power, amount, number, weight etc. **2** of less dimensions than the standard kind, belonging to the lesser kind. **3** composed of little pieces (*small shot*). **4** of minor importance, slight, trifling, petty. **5** concerned or dealing with business etc., of a restricted or minor kind (*small shopkeepers*). **6** of low degree, poor, humble, plebeian. **7** unpretentious. **8** paltry, mean, ignoble, narrow-minded. *~adv.* **1** into small pieces (*cut the vegetables up small*). **2** quietly, gently, softly, in a low voice. *~n.* **1** the slender part of anything (*a pain in the small of the back*). **2** (*pl., coll.*) small items of washing, esp. undergarments. **in a small way** on a small or unambitious scale. **no small** considerable, substantial, significant, rather a lot of (*no small feat; with no small dismay*). **small profits and quick returns** the policy of selling cheap but on a large scale. **small wonder 1** it is hardly surprising (that etc.). **2** naturally, of course. **to feel small** to feel humiliated or insignificant. **to look small** to be publicly humiliated, to appear insignificant. **to make someone look small** to humiliate publicly, to cause to appear insignificant. **small ads** *n.pl.* classified advertisements. **small arms** *n.pl.* portable firearms, such as rifles, pistols etc. **small beer** *n.* beer of a mild, light or weak quality. **to be small beer 1** to be unimportant, trivial or insignificant. **2** to lack power and influence. **small-bore** *a.* (of a low-calibre gun) having a chamber with a narrow bore. **small bower** *n.* the port bower. **small calorie** *n.* a unit of heat, equalling 4.1868 joules; the quantity of heat required to raise the temperature of 1 gram of water by 1°C. **small capital** *n.* a capital letter lower in height than the regular capital of the same font. **small change** *n.* coins as distinct from notes, esp. of low denominations. **small circle** *n.* a circle dividing a sphere into two unequal parts. **small claims court** *n.* a local court that can decide speedily and economically cases involving claims for small amounts of money. **small craft** *n.pl.* fishing vessels and other small boats. **small deer** *n.pl.* small insignificant animals. **small fortune** *n.* a large sum of money. **small fry** *n.pl.* **1** small or young fishes. **2** (*coll.*) children. **to be small fry** to be insignificant or unimportant. **smallgoods** *n.pl.* (*Austral.*) cold or cured meats from a delicatessen. **smallholder** *n.* the farmer or tenant of a smallholding. **smallholding** *n.* (the working of) a portion of agricultural land of limited area smaller than a farm. **small hours** *n.pl.* the time from midnight till 3 or 4 a.m., the early hours of the morning. **small intestine** *n.* the long narrow part of the intestine comprising the duodenum, jejunum and the ileum. **smallish** *a.* **small letter** *n.* a lower-case letter. **small mercies** *n.pl.* minor benefits or lucky breaks that one is reminded to be grateful for. **small-minded** *a.* restricted in outlook, petty. **small-mindedly** *adv.* **small-mindedness** *n.* **smallness** *n.* **small potatoes** *n.* (*sl.*) an insignificant person or unimportant matter. **smallpox** *n.* variola, an acute contagious disease with fever and an outbreak of pustules on the skin that leave permanent pockmarks, now eradicated through vaccination and surviving only in a few laboratories. **small print** *n.* **1** matter printed in a small typeface. **2** the unobtrusively printed reservations or restrictions in a policy or contract document. **small-scale** *a.* of limited scope or extent. **small screen** *n.* television. **small slam** *n.* in bridge, the winning of 12 tricks, that is all but one, as distinct from a *grand slam.* **small-sword** *n.* (*Hist.*) a short light duelling sword used for thrusts. **small talk** *n.* light social conversation on superficial topics. **small-time** *a.* (*coll.*) **1** insignificant, unimportant. **2** amateurish. **small-timer** *n.* **small-town** *a.* (*derog.*) characteristic of a small town in all its lack of sophistication, provinciality and pettiness. [OE *smæl,* cp. Dut., Dan. and Swed. *smal,* G *schmal*]

†**smallage** (smawˈlij) *n.* wild celery. [small, F *ache,* L *apium,* parsley]

smalt (smawlt) *n.* a blue glass coloured with cobalt, used in a pulverized state as a pigment. [F, from It. *smalto,* from Gmc., cp. G *Schmalz,* cogn. with SMELT[1]]

smarm (smahm) *v.t.* (*coll.*) to plaster, to flatten (hair down) with hair oil etc. *~v.i.* to fawn, to ingratiate oneself, to make (up to someone). *~n.* gush, fawning behaviour. **smarmy** *a.* (*comp.* **smarmier,** *superl.* **smarmiest**) **1** sleek and smooth. **2** having a wheedling manner. **smarmily** *adv.* **smarminess** *n.* [onomat.]

smart (smaht) *a.* **1** astute, clever, intelligent, ingenious. **2** shrewd, wide-awake, sharp, quick to spot a chance and take advantage of it. **3** quick at repartee, witty, esp. impertinently so. **4** (of dealings) verging on the unethical (*a bit of smart practice*). **5** spruce, well-groomed. **6** (of equipment etc.) clean, bright and in good repair. **7** (of a resort, rendezvous etc.) stylish, fashionable. **8** (of people in society) sophisticated, admired. **9** vigorous, lively, brisk. **10** stinging, pungent, keen, severe, poignant. **11** computer-controlled, electronically operated or technologically advanced. *~v.i.* **1** to feel or give or cause sharp pain or mental distress (*The chlorine made his eyes smart*). **2** (of a rebuff or injustice) to rankle. **3** to feel wounded (*was smarting from the rebuff*). **4** to suffer punishment (*You'll smart for this!*). *~adv.* smartly. *~n.* **1** a sharp, lively pain, a stinging sensation. **2** a feeling of resentment. **3** distress, anguish. **4** smart money. **to look smart** to hurry up, be quick. **smart alec** (alik), **smart aleck, smart alick** *n.* (*coll.*) a know-all. **smart-alecky** *a.* **smart-arse,** (*N Am.*) **smart-ass** *n.* (*sl.*) a smart alec. **smart bomb** *n.* a bomb containing a device enabling it to be guided to its target. **smart card** *n.* a plastic card containing a microprocessor for effecting point-of-sale debits etc. **smarten** *v.t., v.i.* **smartish** *adv.* **smartly** *adv.* **smart money** *n.* **1** money paid to buy oneself off from an unpleasant engagement etc., or paid as a penalty or in compensation. **2** money bet or invested by experienced gamblers or business people. **3** (*Law*) excessive damages. **smartness** *n.* **smart set** *n.* those in society who are admired for their sophistication, glamour and know-how. **smartweed** *n.* the water-pepper, *Polygonum hydropiper.* **smarty** *n.* (*pl.* **smarties**) (*coll.*) **1** a smart alec. **2** a smartly dressed person, a member of the smart set. **smarty pants, smarty boots** *n.* (*pl.* **smarty pants, smarty boots**) (*coll.*) a know-all, a smart alec. [OE *smeortan* (cp. Dut. *smarten,* G *schmerzen,* Swed. *smarta,* also L *modēre,* to bite, Gr. *smerdaleos,* terrible)]

smash (smash) *v.t.* **1** to break to pieces by violence, to shatter, to dash, to wreck, to crash. **2** to hit with a crushing blow. **3** to overthrow completely, to rout, to crush. **4** to hit (a shuttlecock, tennis ball etc.) with a forceful overhead stroke. *~v.i.* **1** to break to pieces. **2** to go bankrupt. **3** to collide or crash (into). **4** to perform a smash (in badminton, tennis etc.). **5** to come to pieces under force. *~n.* **1** an act or instance of smashing; a breaking to pieces or the sound this makes. **2** a smash-up, a crash between vehicles. **3** (*coll.*) a smash hit. **4** in badminton, tennis etc., a forceful overhead stroke. **5** a violent blow with the fist. **6** a break-up, a collapse; a disaster; the bankruptcy or ruin of a person or concern. *~adv.* with a smash. **to go to smash** (*coll.*) to suffer financial ruin. **smashable** *a.* **smash-and-grab** *a.* (*coll.*) (of a theft) in which a shop window is broken and goods inside hurriedly removed. **smashed** *a.* **1** broken. **2** (*sl.*) very drunk. **smasher** *n.* **1** (*sl.*) an outstandingly attractive or amiable person. **2** (*sl.*) something of staggering size, quality, effectiveness etc. **3** someone who or something that smashes. **smash hit** *n.* (*coll.*) a song, show, performer etc. that is a great success. **smashing** *a.* (*coll.*) very fine, wonderful. **smashingly** *adv.* **smash-up** *n.* a violent collision between vehicles, a car crash. [prob. onomat.]

smatter (smat´ə) *n.* a smattering. **smatterer** *n.* a dabbler. **smattering** *n.* **1** a slight superficial knowledge. **2** a small quantity. [ME *smateren*, to chatter, to prattle]

smear (smiə) *v.t.* **1** to rub or daub with anything greasy or sticky. **2** to rub (a screen, a lens etc.) so as to blur. **3** to apply thickly. **4** to soil, stain or dirty. **5** to malign (someone) or blacken (their name) publicly. *~v.i.* **1** to make a smear. **2** to become blurred, smudged etc. *~n.* **1** a stain or mark made by smearing. **2** an attack on a person's reputation. **3** a substance (e.g. vaginal secretion) smeared on a glass slide for examination under a microscope. **smear campaign** *n.* a series of orchestrated attacks on the reputation of a politician, institution etc. **smearer** *n.* **smear test** *n.* a microscopic examination of a smear, e.g. for cervical cancer. **smeary** *a.* (*comp.* **smearier**, *superl.* **smeariest**). **smearily** *adv.* **smeariness** *n.* [OE *smerien* (cp. Dut. *smeren*, G *schmieren*, Icel. *smyrja*), from *smeru*, fat, cogn. with Gr. *muron*, ointment]

smectic (smek´tik) *a.* (*Chem.*) denoting, of or relating to the state, e.g. of liquid crystal, between solid and liquid, with atoms and molecules oriented in parallel planes. *~n.* a smectic substance. [L *smecticus*, Gr. *smēktikos*, cleansing, from the soapy consistency]

smeddum (smed´əm) *n.* (*Sc.*) **1** fine powder. **2** spirit, mettle, go. [OE *smedma*, etym. uncertain]

smegma (smeg´mə) *n.* a sebaceous soapy secretion found in the folds of the skin, esp. under the foreskin. [Gr. *smēgma*, soap, from *smēchein*, to wipe]

smell (smel) *n.* **1** the sense by which odours are perceived. **2** the sensation or the act of smelling. **3** that which affects the organs of smell, scent, odour. **4** a bad odour, a stench. **5** a characteristic quality, a trace, an aura, a suggestion. *~v.t.* (*past*, *p.p.* **smelt** (smelt), **smelled** (smeld, smelt)) **1** to notice or perceive through the sense of smell (*I smell burning*). **2** to scent or detect (*She could smell a bargain a mile off*). *~v.i.* **1** to give out an odour (of etc.) (*His breath smelt of garlic*). **2** to have a specified smell (*You smell lovely*). **3** to suggest, to indicate, to smack (of) (*It smells of corruption*). **4** to have or exercise the sense of smell (*Here, smell*). **5** to stink. **to smell out 1** to detect by instinct or prying. **2** to pollute (e.g. a room with smoke). **smeller** *n.* **1** a person who smells. **2** (*sl.*) the nose. **3** (*sl.*) a hit on the nose. **smelling** *n.* **smelling bottle** *n.* a small bottle or phial for holding smelling salts. **smelling salts** *n.pl.* an aromatic preparation of ammonium carbonate used in cases of faintness etc. **smell-less** *a.* **smelly** *a.* (*comp.* **smellier,** *superl.* **smelliest**) malodorous. **smelliness** *n.* [ME *smel*, v. *smelen*, (cp. Dut. *smeulen*, LG *smelen*, to SMOULDER)]

smelt[1] (smelt) *v.t.* **1** to fuse (an ore) so as to extract the metal. **2** to extract (metal) from ore thus. **smelter** *n.* **smeltery** *n.* (*pl.* **smelteries**) a place where smelting is done. **smelting** *n.* **smelting furnace** *n.* [cp. MDut. *smelten*, G *schmelzen*, Dan. *smelta*, OHG *smelzen*]

smelt[2] (smelt) *n.* (*pl.* **smelt, smelts**) a small food fish, *Osmerus eperlanus*, allied to the salmon. [OE cp. *smeolt*, smooth]

smelt[3] SMELL.

smew (smū) *n.* a small merganser or diving duck, *Mergus albellus*. [var. of obs. *smee*, *smeath*, SMOOTH]

smidgen (smij´in), **smidgeon, smidgin** *n.* (*coll.*) a tiny amount.

smilax (smī´laks) *n.* (*pl.* **smilaxes**) **1** any climbing shrub of the genus *Smilax*, the roots of many species of which yield sarsaparilla. **2** a S African twining plant of the asparagus family with bright green foliage, often used by florists. [Gr.]

smile (smīl) *v.i.* **1** to express kindness, love, pleasure, amusement or contempt by an instinctive lateral movement of the lips with an upward turn at the corners. **2** (of the weather, fortune etc.) to look bright and cheerful, or favourably (on or upon someone). *~v.t.* **1** to express by or as by a smile. **2** to bring or drive (into, out of, away etc.) thus. *~n.* **1** an act of smiling. **2** a gay, cheerful or favourable expression, aspect or disposition. **to come up smiling** to end up in a favourable state, esp. after misfortune. **smileless** *a.* **smiler** *n.* **smiley** *a.* **smilingly** *adv.* [ME *smīlen* (cp. OHG *smîlen*, MHG *smielen*), cogn. with L *mīrārī*, to wonder, and Gr. *meidân*, to smile]

smir, smirr SMUR.

smirch (smœch) *v.t.* to soil, to smear, to stain, to defile, to defame (someone's name or reputation). *~n.* **1** a stain, a smear. **2** a stain or blot on one's reputation. **3** an act of smirching. [extension of ME *smeren*, to SMEAR]

smirk (smœk) *v.i.* to smile affectedly or smugly, to simper. *~n.* an affected or smug smile, a simper. **smirker** *n.* **smirkingly** *adv.* **smirky** *a.* (*comp.* **smirkier,** *superl.* **smirkiest**). **smirkily** *adv.* [OE *smercian*, cp. MHG *smieren*, *smielen*, to SMILE]

smite (smīt) *v.t.* (*past* **smote** (smōt), †**smit** (smit), *p.p.* **smitten** (smit´ən)) (*poet.* or *facet.*) **1** to strike, to deal a severe blow to. **2** to inflict injury, death, defeat, damage or disaster upon. **3** (*usu. p.p.*) to strike or affect (by or with a feeling, disease etc.) (*smitten with paralysis*; *smitten by her charms*). *~v.i.* to strike, to knock, to come (on, against etc.) with force. *~n.* a blow. **to smite hip and thigh** HIP[1]. **smiter** *n.* **smitten** *a.* (*coll.*) enamoured. [OE *smitan*, cp. Dut. *smijten*, G *schmeissen*, MSwed. *smīta*]

smith (smith) *n.* **1** a person who works in metals, esp. someone who forges iron with the hammer, a blacksmith. **2** (*usu. in comb.*) a person who makes or crafts something (*a locksmith*; *a wordsmith*; *a songsmith*). **smithery** (smith´əri) *n.* (*pl.* **smitheries**) **1** the craft, trade or occupation of a smith. **2** a smithy. **smithy** (smidh´i) *n.* (*pl.* **smithies**) a blacksmith's workshop. [OE, cp. Dut. *smid*, G *Schmied*, Icel. *smithr*, Dan. and Swed. *smed*]

smithereens (smidhərēnz´), **smithers** (smidh´əz) *n.pl.* little bits, tiny fragments (*blew the place to smithereens*). [Ir. *smidirín*, *smiodar*]

smithery, smithy SMITH.

smithsonite (smith´sənīt) *n.* carbonate of zinc, calamine. [J. L. M. *Smithson*, *c.*1765–1829, British chemist]

smitten SMITE.

smock (smok) *n.* **1** a loose dress or shirt with a yoke, or smocking forming one, or an artist's overall of similar shape. **2** (*Hist.*) (*also* **smock-frock**) a farm labourer's yoked or smocked shirtlike overall. **3** (*Hist.*) a woman's undergarment, a chemise. ~*v.t.* **1** to decorate with smocking. **2** to clothe in a smock. **smock-faced** *a.* (*dated*) having an effeminate appearance or complexion. **smocking** *n.* decorative gathering on a shirt or dress, across the yoke or round the wrists or waist. [OE *smoc*, cogn. with *smūgan*, to creep into, cp. SMUGGLE]

smog (smog) *n.* fog thickened by smoke and by fumes from industrial plants or motor vehicles. **smoggy** *a.* (*comp.* **smoggier**, *superl.* **smoggiest**). [comb. of SMOKE and FOG[1]]

smokable SMOKE.

smoke (smōk) *n.* **1** volatile products of combustion, esp. carbonaceous and other matter in the form of visible vapour or fine particles escaping from a burning substance. **2** a suspension of particles in gas. **3** an act of smoking a cigarette, pipe, cigar etc. (*was outside having a quick smoke*). **4** (*sl.*) a cigarette. **5** insubstantiality, nothingness. ~*v.i.* **1** to draw into the mouth or inhale and exhale the smoke of tobacco etc. **2** to emit smoke. **3** to emit vapour, fumes etc., to reek. **4** (of a chimney etc.) to send smoke into a room, to fail to draw. ~*v.t.* **1** to draw with the mouth or inhale and exhale the smoke of (a cigarette, pipe etc.). **2** to apply smoke to. **3** to blacken, colour, cure, flavour etc., with smoke. **4 a** to cleanse (a place) of infestation, e.g. by insects, with smoke. **b** to stupefy or suffocate (insects, e.g. bees) with smoke. **big smoke** BIG. **no smoke without fire** rumours are usually not without foundation. **the Smoke** (*coll.*) a big city, esp. London. **to end up in smoke** to go up in smoke. **to go up in smoke 1** (of a scheme, a desire) to come to nothing. **2** to be destroyed by fire. **to smoke out 1** to exterminate or drive out with smoke. **2** to discover, to force into the open. **smokable, smokeable** *a.* **smoke-ball** *n.* **1** a puffball. **2** a projectile containing a composition that emits a dense smoke, used as a screen for military operations. **smoke-black** *n.* lampblack. **smoke bomb** *n.* a bomb that produces dense smoke on exploding. **smoke box** *n.* in a steam locomotive, the chamber through which smoke and gases pass from the boiler tubes to the funnel. **smoke bush** *n.* SMOKE PLANT (under SMOKE). **smoked** *a.* **smoked glass** *n.* glass darkened by being exposed to smoke. **smoked herring** *n.* a kipper. **smoke-dried** *a.* cured by smoking. **smoke-dry** *v.t.* **smoke-ho** SMOKE-OH (under SMOKE). **smokehouse** *n.* a building where meat, fish etc. is cured by smoking. **smoke-jack** *n.* (*Hist.*) an apparatus for turning a roasting-spit by using the current of hot air in a chimney. **smokeless** *a.* (of e.g. fuel) emitting little or no smoke. **smokeless zone** *n.* an area in which it is forbidden to emit smoke from chimneys, and where smokeless fuel only may be burnt. **smoke-oh** (-ō), **smoko, smoke-ho** *n.* (*Austral.*, *New Zeal.*, *coll.*) **1** a break from work for a smoke or rest. **2** a tea break. **smoke plant** *n.* an ornamental shrub or tree with long, feathery fruit stalks. **smoker** *n.* **1** a person who smokes tobacco. **2** a person who dries, cures, fumigates etc., with smoke. **3** a smoking compartment. **4** (*N Am.*) an all-male get-together. **5** an apparatus for smoking bees. **smoke ring** *n.* cigarette smoke exhaled in the shape of a ring. **smoke-room** *n.* a smoking room. **smokescreen** *n.* **1** a dense volume of smoke produced by chemicals used to conceal the movements of ships, troops etc., from the enemy. **2** a ploy used to obscure or deceive. **smoke signal** *n.* **1** a message conveyed by a series of puffs of smoke. **2** (*coll.*) a private signal from one person to another. **smokestack** *n.* a funnel, esp. on a steamer. **smoke-stone** *n.* a cairngorm. **smoke tree** *n.* SMOKE PLANT (under SMOKE). **smoke-tunnel** *n.* a wind tunnel using wisps of smoke to show wind direction. **smoking** *n.*, *a.* **smoking cap** *n.* a decorated cap, formerly worn by men when smoking. **smoking carriage, smoking compartment, smoking room** *n.* a railway carriage or compartment, or a room in a club etc., reserved for smokers. **smoking gun, smoking pistol** *n.* a piece of incontestably incriminating evidence. **smoking jacket** *n.* a velvet jacket, orig. used by men when smoking. **smoky** *a.* (*comp.* **smokier,** *superl.* **smokiest**) **1** resembling smoke in colour, smell, flavour etc. **2** filled with smoke. **3** emitting smoke. **4** dirtied by smoke. ~*n.* (*pl.* **smokies**) (*Sc.*) a smoked haddock. **smokily** *adv.* **smokiness** *n.* [OE *smoca* (cp. Dut. *smook*, G *Schmauch*), rel. to *smēocan*, cogn. with Gr. *smuchein*, to smoulder]

smolder SMOULDER.

smolt (smōlt) *n.* a salmon in its second year when it acquires its silvery scales. [perh. from OE *smolt*, serene, shining]

smooth (smoodh) *a.* (*comp.* **smoother,** *superl.* **smoothest**) **1** having a continuously even surface, free from roughness, projections or indentations. **2** not hairy. **3** (of water) unruffled. **4** (of liquids or semi-liquids) without lumps, of an even texture. **5** free from obstructions or impediments. **6** offering no resistance. **7** (of sound, taste etc.) not harsh. **8** (of e.g. breathing or movement) flowing rhythmically or evenly. **9** equable, calm, pleasant, bland, suave, polite, flattering. **10** (of wine) not harsh-tasting or astringent. ~*v.t.* (*also* **smoothe**) **1** to make smooth, to even (out). **2** to flatten (lumps or projections out) or ease (difficulties or problems away). **3** to free from harshness, discomforts, obstructions, irregularities etc. **4** to extenuate, to soften, to alleviate, to dispel. ~*v.i.* **1** to become smooth, to even (out). **2** (of problems or upsets) to abate, to heal (over). ~*n.* **1** an act of smoothing, stroking or patting down. **2** a smooth place or part. **3** (*coll.*) that which is pleasant or easy (*take the rough with the smooth*). **in smooth water** out of difficulty, having passed the worst. **to smooth over** to gloss over (a difficulty). **smoothable** *a.* **smooth-bore, smooth-bored** *a.* (of a gun) not rifled. ~*n.* a smooth-bore gun. **smooth breathing** *n.* (*Gram.*) in Greek, a sign (') over an initial vowel indicating that it is unaspirated, as distinct from a *rough breathing*. **smooth-chinned** *a.* beardless. **smooth-coated** *a.* (of an animal) having a smooth pelt or fur. **smoothen** *v.t.*, *v.i.* to make or become smooth or smoother. **smoother** *n.* **smooth-faced** *a.* **1** beardless. **2** having a suave, specious, flattering appearance or expression, hypocritical. **3** unwrinkled. **4** having a smooth surface. **smooth hound** *n.* a small shark of the genus *Mustelus*, found in shallow water. **smoothie** (-i), **smoothy** *n.* (*pl.* **smoothies**) (*coll.*) an excessively suave or plausible person, esp. a man. **smoothing** *n.*, *a.* **smoothing iron** *n.* (*dated*) a flat iron, an iron for pressing clothes and linen. **smoothing-plane** *n.* a short plane, finely set, used for finishing. **smoothish** *a.* **smoothly** *adv.* **smooth muscle** *n.* muscle (e.g. in the intestine, the wall of a blood vessel) capable of involuntary contractions, as distinct from striated muscle. **smoothness** *n.* **smooth-spoken, smooth-tongued** *a.* polite, plausible, flattering. **smooth talk** *n.* suave, specious or hypocritical talk. **smooth-talk** *v.t.* to attempt to win over by such talk. [OE *smethe* (rare *smōth*)]

smorgasbord (smaw´gəsbawd) *n.* **1** a buffet or hors d'œuvre of open sandwiches. **2** a buffet comprising an assortment of hors d'oeuvres and other dishes. [Swed. *smörgås*, open sandwich, *bord*, table]

smorzando (smawtsan´dō), **smorzato** (-sah´tō) *a.*, *adv.* (*Mus.*) with a gradual fading or dying away. ~*n.* (*pl.* **smorzandos, smorzandi** (-dē), **smorzatos, smorzati** (-tē)) a smorzando or smorzato passage. [It. pres.p. and p.p. of *smorzare*, to extinguish]

smote SMITE.

smother (smŭdh´ə) *v.t.* **1** to suffocate, to stifle. **2** to kill by suffocation etc. **3** to keep (a fire) down by covering it with ashes etc. **4** to hide, to suppress, to keep from being divulged, to conceal (the truth etc.). **5** to overcome, to overwhelm (*smothered the baby with kisses*). **6** to cover thickly, to enclose, to envelop (*likes his food smothered in gravy*). **7** (*N Am.*) to defeat fast and thoroughly. **8** to cook in a covered pot. *~v.i.* to be suffocated, to be prevented from breathing freely. *~n.* **1** a stifling cloud of dust, smoke, vapour etc. **2** a smouldering state. **smothered mate** *n.* in chess, a checkmate by a knight when the king is surrounded and unable to move. **smotheringly** *adv.* **smothery** *a.* **smotheriness** *n.* [ME *smorther*, from OE *smorian*, to choke, stifle, cp. Dut. *smooren*, G *schmoren*, cogn. with SMOKE and SMOULDER]

smoulder (smōl´də), (*esp. N Am.*) **smolder** *v.i.* **1** to burn in a smothered way without flames. **2** to exist in a suppressed or latent condition. **3** to feel or show strong repressed emotions (such as anger, jealousy). *~n.* **1** a smouldering state. **2** a smouldering fire. **smoulderingly** *adv.* [ME *smolderen*, from *smolder*, smoke, cogn. with SMELL and SMOTHER]

smriti (smrit´i) *n.* a body of Hindu religious teachings from the Vedas. [Sansk. *smrti*, what one remembers, from *samarati*, he remembers]

smudge[1] (smŭj), **smutch** (smŭch) *n.* a dirty mark, a smear, a blur. *~v.t.* **1** to smear or blur (writing, drawing etc.). **2** to make a dirty smear, blot or stain on. **3** to soil, to smirch, to defile, to sully (purity, reputation etc.). *~v.i.* to become smeared or blurred. **smudgeless** *a.* **smudgy** *a.* (*comp.* **smudgier**, *superl.* **smudgiest**). **smudginess** *n.* [ME *smogen*, cogn. with SMUT]

smudge[2] (smŭj) *n.* (*N Am.*) a smouldering fire for driving away mosquitoes etc. *~v.t.* to fumigate (a place) with smoke to drive mosquitoes away. [etym. uncertain]

smudgy SMUDGE[1].

smug (smŭg) *a.* (*comp.* **smugger**, *superl.* **smuggest**) self-satisfied, complacent. **smugly** *adv.* **smugness** *n.* [cp. MDan. *smug*, smooth, LG *smuk*, G *schmuck*, neat, spruce]

smuggle (smŭg´əl) *v.t.* **1** to import or export illegally without paying customs duties. **2** to take (out) or bring (in) secretly, to convey clandestinely. **3** to hide (away). **smuggled** *a.* **smuggler** *n.* **smuggling** *n.* [LG *smuggeln* (cp. Dan. *smöge*, Icel. *smuga*, lurking-hole), cogn. with SMOCK]

smur (smœ), **smir, smirr** *n.* (*chiefly Sc.*) fine misty rain, drizzle. *~v.i.* (*pres.p.* **smurring, smirring**, *past, p.p.* **smurred, smirred**) to drizzle. **smurry, smirry** *a.* (*comp.* **smurrier, smirrier**, *superl.* **smurriest, smirriest**). [etym. uncertain]

smut (smŭt) *n.* **1** a particle of soot or other dirt, a mark or smudge made by this. **2** obscene or ribald talk, language, stories etc. **3** a disease of corn caused by parasitic fungi, that turns parts of the ear to black powder. **4** any fungus of the order *Ustilaginales* that causes smut. *~v.t.* (*pres.p.* **smutting**, *past, p.p.* **smutted**) **1** to stain or mark with smut. **2** to infect with smut. *~v.i.* (of corn etc.) to be attacked by smut. **smut-ball** *n.* a grain affected by smut. **smut-mill** *n.* a machine for removing smut from grain. **smutty** *a.* (*comp.* **smuttier**, *superl.* **smuttiest**). **smuttily** *adv.* **smuttiness** *n.* [cp. LG *Schmutt*, G *Schmutz*, Swed. *smuts*]

smutch SMUDGE[1].

smutty SMUT.

Sn *chem. symbol* tin. [late L *stannum*]

snack (snak) *n.* **1** a quick light meal. **2** a dish of something, or a small quantity of food, taken between main meals. *~v.i.* to have a snack. **snack bar** *n.* a café, self-service restaurant or other place offering light meals or refreshments. [var. of SNATCH]

snaffle (snaf´əl) *n.* a bridle-bit usu. with a joint in the middle. *~v.t.* **1** to provide or control with a snaffle. **2** (*coll.*) to steal, to appropriate for oneself. **snaffle-bit** *n.* a snaffle. [cp. Dut. *snavel*, muzzle, G *Schnabel*, bill, snout]

snafu (snafoo´) *n.* (*esp. N Am., sl.*) a state of total confusion or chaos. *~a.* in total chaos or confusion. *~v.t.* (*3rd pers. sing. pres.* **snafues**, *pres.p.* **snafuing**, *past, p.p.* **snafued**) to throw into confusion. [*s*ituation *n*ormal *a*ll *f*ucked *u*p]

snag[1] (snag) *n.* **1** an unexpected or concealed difficulty, an obstacle. **2** a jagged projection, as the stumpy base of a branch left in pruning, a branch broken off, a knot, a stump of a tooth. **3** a tree stump projecting from the bed of a river (constituting a navigational hazard). **4** a tear, a pull, a flaw in fabric. **5** a short tine on an antler. *~v.t.* (*pres.p.* **snagging**, *past, p.p.* **snagged**) **1** to catch or damage on a snag. **2** to clear of snags. **3** (*N Am.*) to catch, seize (an opportunity etc.), to obtain by seizing or taking quick action. **4** (*chiefly N Am.*) to hinder, to halt, to impede. *~v.i.* to become snagged. **snagged** *a.* **snaggy** *a.* (*comp.* **snaggier**, *superl.* **snaggiest**). [prob. from Scand. (cp. Norw. dial. *snag*, Icel. *snagr*), perh. rel. to KNAG]

snag[2] (snag) *n.* (*Austral., sl.*) a sausage. [etym. uncertain]

snail (snāl) *n.* **1** a gastropod mollusc of various species with a spirally coiled shell. **2** the sea snail. **3** a sluggish person or thing. **snailery** *n.* (*pl.* **snaileries**) a place where edible snails are cultivated. **snail-like** *a.* **snail mail** *n.* (*sl.*) (mail sent by) the ordinary postal system, not e-mail. **snail-paced** *a.* slow-moving. **snail's pace** *n.* a slow rate of progress. **snail-wheel** *n.* a rotating part of a clock, usu. spiral or snail-shaped in outline, with notches determining the number of strokes to be given in striking. **snaily** *a.* (*comp.* **snailier**, *superl.* **snailiest**). [OE *snægl*, dim. of *snaca*, SNAKE]

snake (snāk) *n.* **1** a limbless reptile of the suborder Ophidia, of a venomous or non-venomous type and having a forked tongue and the ability to swallow prey whole. **2** a snakelike limbless lizard or amphibian. **3** a sneaking, treacherous person. **4** anything resembling a snake in appearance or movement, esp. a tool for unblocking drains, a plumber's snake. **5** in the EU, a system which allows the currencies of member countries to fluctuate within narrow limits. *~v.t.* to make (one's way) sinuously, to follow (a winding course). *~v.i.* to wind, to move quietly or snakily. **snake bird** *n.* the darter or anhinga. **snake bite** *n.* **1** the venomous bite of a snake. **2** (*coll.*) a drink of lager and cider. **snake-charmer** *n.* an entertainer who appears to mesmerize snakes by playing music. **snake-charming** *n.* **snake in the grass** *n.* a treacherous or underhand person. **snakelike** *a.* **snake oil** *n.* (*coll.*) a panacea or quack remedy. **snake-pit** *n.* **1** a pit full of snakes. **2** any arena where people are viciously fighting each other for power. **snakeroot** *n.* **1** the root of various N American plants supposed to be an antidote for snake bites. **2** any of these plants. **snakes and ladders** *n.pl.* a board game in which counters can advance more speedily up ladders or move backwards down snakes. **snake's-head** *n.* the fritillary. **snakeskin** *n., a.* (made of) the skin of a snake. **snake-stone** *n.* an ammonite. **snake-weed** *n.* the bistort. **snakish** *a.* **snaky** *a.* (*comp.* **snakier**, *superl.* **snakiest**). **snakily** *adv.* **snakiness** *n.* [OE *snaca* (cp. LG *Snake*, Icel. *snākr*, Dan. *snog*), cogn. with SNEAK]

snap (snap) *v.i.* (*pres.p.* **snapping**, *past, p.p.* **snapped**) **1** to break with a sharp report. **2** to make a sharp, quick sound, like a crack or slight explosion. **3** to part, close or fit into place suddenly with a sharp click. **4** (of a dog) to make a biting movement (at). **5** to snatch or grasp (at an opportunity, chance etc.). **6** to speak or shout sharply or irritably (at someone). **7** to collapse (under pressure, strain of work etc.), to break down. **8** to move smartly (e.g. into action). *~v.t.* **1** to break (something) with a sharp report. **2** to cause to click (shut, open etc.). **3** to cause (a whip, one's fingers etc.) to make a sharp crack or report. **4** to say abruptly or irritably. **5** to photograph casually. **6** to seize suddenly, to snatch (up); to take advantage of eagerly. **7** in American football, to put (the ball) into play by sending it backwards from the line of scrimmage. **8** to interrupt or take (up) in the midst of a speech etc. ~*n.* **1** the act or an instance or the sound of snapping. **2** a crisp ginger-flavoured biscuit (*a ginger snap*; *a brandy snap*). **3** a snapshot. **4** a sudden spell of severe weather. **5** a children's card game in which players shout 'Snap!' when two identical cards are turned face up. **6** vigour, briskness, dash, go. **7** (*N Am., coll.*) something that is easy or profitable, a cinch. **8** an abrupt reply or retort. ~*a.* **1** done, taken etc., suddenly, offhand or on the spur of the moment (*snap judgements*). **2** closing or fastening with a snap. **3** (*N Am., coll.*) easy, profitable, cheap. ~*adv.* with (the sound of) a snap. ~*int.* **1** uttered when playing the game of snap. **2** used to indicate similarity, identicalness or synchronicity. **to snap off 1** to break off. **2** to bite off. **to snap one's fingers (at)** to show contempt or defiance (of). **to snap out** to say crossly. **to snap out of it** to change one's mood abruptly (for the better). **to snap someone's head off** to retort abruptly, irritably or rudely. **to snap someone's nose off** to snap someone's head off. **to snap up 1** to take quick advantage of (a bargain etc.), to purchase eagerly. **2** to grab quickly. **3** to interrupt (someone) while they are still speaking. **snap bean** *n.* a bean whose pods are broken in pieces and eaten. **snap-bolt** *n.* an automatically operating bolt on a door or window. **snap-brim** *a.* denoting a kind of hat of which the brim can be turned up and down on opposite sides. **snap decision** *n.* a decision taken without deliberation. **snapdragon** *n.* **1** a plant of the genus *Antirrhinum*, with a flower opening like a dragon's mouth. **2** a game of snatching raisins from a dish of burning spirit. **snap fastener** *n.* a press-stud. **snap-link, snap-ring** *n.* a karabiner. **snap-on** *a.* designed to be attached by a snap fastening or spring clip. **snappable** *a.* **snapper** *n.* **1** any of various toothed fish related to the bass which inhabit warm waters. **2** any of a number of reddish sea fish of the family Lutjanidae. **3** a spotted food fish of Australia and New Zealand. **4** a snapping turtle. **5** a person who or something that snaps. **6** a party cracker. **snapper-up** *n.* **snapping** *n., a.* **snappingly** *adv.* **snapping turtle** *n.* a fierce and voracious N American freshwater turtle, *Chelydra serpentina*, a snapper. **snappish** *a.* given to snapping or biting, given to sharp replies, spiteful, irascible. **snappishly** *adv.* **snappishness** *n.* **snappy** *a.* (*comp.* **snappier,** *superl.* **snappiest**) **1** snappish. **2** irritable, cross. **3** brisk, sharp, lively. **4** smart, up-to-date, stylish. **to make it snappy** to hurry up. **snappily** *adv.* **snapshot** *n.* a photograph taken casually, as distinct from a posed photograph taken in a studio. [prob. from MDut. *snappen*, cp. G *schnappen*, Dan. *snappe*, cogn. with SNAFFLE]

snare (sneə) *n.* **1** a trap, usu. consisting of a noose, for catching birds or other animals. **2** a trick, trap, stratagem or allurement by which one is brought into difficulty, defeat, disgrace, sin etc. **3** a string of gut, wire or hide stretched inside the head of a drum making a rattling sound when the head is struck. **4** a surgical instrument for removing tumours and other tissue matter, consisting of a wire loop. ~*v.t.* **1** to catch in a snare. **2** to ensnare, entrap or inveigle. **snare drum** *n.* a small drum with two heads, the lower of which is fitted with a snare. **snarer** *n.* **snary** *a.* (*comp.* **snarier,** *superl.* **snariest**). [OE *snear*, cp. Dut. *snaar*, G *Schnur*, Icel. *snara*, string]

snark (snahk) *n.* an imaginary creature sought in Lewis Carroll's nonsense poem, *The Hunting of the Snark*. [fanciful name]

snarl[1] (snahl) *v.i.* **1** (of a dog) to growl in a sharp tone with teeth bared. **2** to speak in a harsh, surly or savage manner. ~*v.t.* to express or say with a snarl. ~*n.* **1** a sharp-toned growl. **2** a savage remark or exclamation. **snarler**[1] *n.* **snarling** *a., n.* **snarlingly** *adv.* **snarly** *a.* (*comp.* **snarlier,** *superl.* **snarliest**). [orig. *snar*, MDut. *snarren*, to trawl, cp. G *schnarren*, Swed. *snarra*, to make guttural noises, prob. imit.]

snarl[2] (snahl) *v.t.* **1** to entangle. **2** to cause to become confused or complicated. **3** to flute or emboss (metalware) by hammering the inside with a snarling iron. ~*v.i.* to become entangled, muddled, complicated, jammed etc. ~*n.* **1** a tangle, a knot of hair, thread etc. **2** a knot in wood. **3** (*fig.*) an entanglement, embarrassing difficulty. **to snarl up** to (cause to) become tangled, disordered, inoperable, immobile etc. **snarled** *a.* **snarler**[2] *n.* **snarling iron, snarling tool** *n.* a curved tool used for snarling metalware. **snarl-up** *n.* an instance or state of confusion, obstruction, disorder etc. (e.g. a traffic jam). [SNARE]

snarler[1] SNARL[1].

snarler[2] SNARL[2].

snary SNARE.

snatch (snach) *v.t.* **1** to seize suddenly, eagerly or without permission or ceremony. **2** to steal, grab. **3** to remove or rescue (from, away etc.) suddenly or hurriedly. **4** to win or gain narrowly, to manage to get. **5** to grab (a chance or opportunity). ~*v.i.* to try to seize, to make a sudden motion (at) as if to seize. ~*n.* **1** an act of snatching, a grab (at). **2** that which is snatched; a short spell e.g. of rest, work. **3** a fragment of talk, song etc. **4** in weightlifting, a kind of lift in which the weight is raised overhead in one motion. **5** (*coll.*) a robbery, a kidnapping. **by/ in snatches** desultorily, in fits and starts. **snatchblock** *n.* a single block with an opening in one side to receive a rope. **snatcher** *n.* (*often in comb.*, as *body-snatcher*). **snatchingly** *adv.* **snatch squad** *n.* a group of police officers who enter a rioting crowd etc. to arrest troublemakers. **snatchy** *a.* (*comp.* **snatchier,** *superl.* **snatchiest**). **snatchily** *adv.* [ME *snacchen*, cogn. with SNACK and SNECK (cp. Dut. *snakken*)]

snazzy (snaz´i) *a.* (*comp.* **snazzier,** *superl.* **snazziest**) (*sl.*) up to date, showy, smart, attractive (e.g. of clothes). **snazzily** *adv.* **snazziness** *n.* [perh. from SNAPPY (under SNAP) and JAZZY (under JAZZ)]

sneak (snēk) *v.i.* (*past, p.p.* **sneaked,** (*coll.*) **snuck** (snŭk)) **1** to creep, slink or steal (about, away, off etc.), as if afraid or ashamed to be seen. **2** to behave in a mean, cringing, cowardly or underhand way. **3** to tell tales. ~*v.t.* **1** (*sl.*) to steal. **2** to place or remove stealthily. ~*n.* **1** a person who sneaks. **2** a tale-bearer. **3** in cricket, a ball bowled along the ground. **to sneak away/ off** to leave unobtrusively. **sneaker** *n.* **1** a rubber-soled shoe. **2** a person who sneaks. **sneaking** *a.* **1** unacknowledged but persistent (*have a sneaking admiration for someone*). **2** niggling, half-formed (*a sneaking suspicion*). **sneakingly** *adv.* **sneak thief** *n.* a pilferer, someone who steals from open windows or doors. **sneaky** *a.* (*comp.* **sneakier,** *superl.* **sneakiest**). **sneakily** *adv.* **sneakiness** *n.* [OE *snīcan*, to creep, cogn. with SNAKE (cp. Icel. *snikja*, to hanker after)]

sneck (snek) *n.* (*dial.*) a latch or catch. ~*v.t., v.i.* to latch, to fasten, to lock (up). [cp. SNACK and SNATCH]

sneer (sniə) *n.* a smile, laugh or verbal expression of contempt or derision. ~*v.i.* **1** to show contempt by a smile, grin or laugh. **2** to scoff, to jibe, to express derision or contempt (at). ~*v.t.* **1** to say or express with a sneer. **2** to treat or put (down etc.) with a sneer. **sneerer** *n.* **sneering** *n., a.* **sneeringly** *adv.* **sneery** *a.* (*comp.* **sneerier,** *superl.* **sneeriest**). [ME *sneren*, cp. NFris. *sneere*, MDan. *snarre*, rel. to SNARL[1]]

sneeze (snēz) *v.i.* to eject air etc. through the nostrils audibly and convulsively, owing to irritation of the inner membrane of the nose. ~*n.* an act of sneezing or the noise produced by it. **not to be sneezed at** not to be despised, worth consideration. **sneezer** *n.* **sneezewort** *n.* the wild yarrow or pellitory, *Achillea ptarmica*, whose dried leaves induce sneezing and can be used as a substitute for snuff. **sneezy** *a.* (*comp.* **sneezier,** *superl.* **sneeziest**). [ME *snesen*, OE *fnēosan* (cp. Dut. *fniezen*, Icel. *fnasa*, also Gr. *pneein*, to breathe)]

snell (snel) *a.* (*chiefly Sc.*) active, keen, smart, severe, stinging, pungent. [OE *snel*, cp. LG and OHG *snel*, G *schnell*, Icel. *snjallr*]

Snell's law (snelz) *n.* (*Physics*) the law of refraction, stating that the sine of the angle of incidence divided by the sine of the angle of refraction is a constant. [W. *Snell*, 1591–1626, Dutch mathematician]

snib (snib) *n.* (*esp. Ir., Sc.*) a bolt or catch. ~*v.t.* (*pres.p.* **snibbing,** *past, p.p.* **snibbed**) to fasten with a bolt or catch. [etym. uncertain]

snick (snik) *v.t.* **1** to cut, to nick, to notch, to snip. **2** in cricket, to hit (the ball) lightly with a glancing stroke. ~*n.* **1** a slight cut, nick or notch. **2** a light glancing hit, in cricket. [etym. uncertain]

snicker (snik´ə) *v.i.* **1** to snigger. **2** to neigh, to nicker. ~*v.t.* to say with a snigger. ~*n.* a snigger. **snickerer** *n.* **snickeringly** *adv.* **snickery** *a.* [imit., cp. SNIGGER]

snickersnee (snik´əsnē) *n.* a big knife, esp. a bowie. [prob. corr. of obs. *snick or snee*, a fight with knives]

snide (snīd) *a.* (*comp.* **snider,** *superl.* **snidest**) **1** malicious, sneering, disparaging, sly, mean. **2** sham, bogus, counterfeit. ~*n.* **1** a snide person. **2** a snide remark. **3** (*sl.*) sham jewellery etc. **snidely** *adv.* **snideness** *n.* [etym. uncertain]

sniff (snif) *v.i.* to draw air audibly up the nose in order to smell, clear the nasal passages, inhale a drug, express contempt etc. ~*v.t.* **1** to draw (up) with the breath through the nose. **2** to smell, to perceive or investigate by sniffing. ~*n.* **1** an act or the sound of sniffing. **2** that which is sniffed in (e.g. a scent). **to sniff at 1** to investigate by sniffing. **2** to express contempt or disdain for. **to sniff out** to discover (as if) by sniffing, to find through investigation. **sniffer** *n.* **1** (*often in comb.*) someone who sniffs, esp. a person who sniffs a drug, glue etc. (*glue-sniffers*). **2** (*sl.*) the nose. **3** (*coll.*) any of various devices for detecting gas, drugs, explosives, radiation etc. **sniffer dog** *n.* a dog trained to smell out drugs or explosives. **sniffle** (-əl) *v.i.* to sniff (as with a cold, when weeping etc.), to snuffle. ~*n.* **1** an act or sound of sniffling. **2** a snuffle. **3** (*usu. pl.*) a slight cold, a runny nose. **sniffler** *n.* **sniffly** *a.* **sniffy** *a.* (*comp.* **sniffier,** *superl.* **sniffiest**) (*coll.*) given to sniffing, disdainful. **sniffily** *adv.* **sniffiness** *n.* [ME *sneven*, cp. Dan. *snive*, Icel. *snippa*, MDan. *snifte*, imit. in orig.]

snifter (snif´tə) *n.* **1** (*coll.*) a small drink of spirits. **2** a short-stemmed glass with a wide bowl and narrow top (for brandy, liqueur etc.). **snifter-valve, snifting valve** *n.* a valve in a steam cylinder for the escape of air. [dial. *snift*, sniff]

snig[1] (snig) *v.t.* (*pres.p.* **snigging,** *past, p.p.* **snigged**) (*Austral., New Zeal.*) to drag (a heavy log etc.) by means of a rope or chain. **snigging chain** *n.* a chain for dragging logs. [etym. uncertain]

snig[2] (snig) *n.* a small eel. [etym. uncertain]

snigger (snig´ə) *v.i.* to laugh in a half-suppressed or discourteous manner. ~*n.* a suppressed laugh. **sniggerer** *n.* **sniggeringly** *adv.* [var. of SNICKER]

sniggle (snig´əl) *v.i.* to fish for eels by thrusting the bait into their holes. ~*v.t.* to catch (eels) by this means. [SNIG[2]]

snip (snip) *v.t.* (*pres.p.* **snipping,** *past, p.p.* **snipped**) **1** to cut (cloth etc.) or cut (a hole) in something, quickly and sharply with scissors or shears. **2** to cut or clip (off) sharply or quickly with shears or scissors. ~*v.i.* to make a quick sharp cutting movement with scissors or shears (at). ~*n.* **1** an act, movement or sound of snipping. **2** a cut with scissors or shears. **3** a small piece snipped off. **4** (*coll.*) a certainty, a cinch, a bargain. **5** (*pl.*) shears used to cut sheet metal by hand. **snipper** *n.* **snippet** (-it) *n.* **1** a small bit snipped off. **2** a scrap of information or news. **3** a short extract from a book etc. **snippety** *a.* **snippetiness** *n.* **snipping** *n.* a piece snipped off. **snippy** *a.* (*comp.* **snippier,** *superl.* **snippiest**) **1** bad-tempered, irritable, cross. **2** hypercritical, severe, fault-finding. [cp. Dut. and LG *snippen*, G *schnippen*, cogn. with SNAP]

snipe (snīp) *n.* (*pl. in general* **snipe,** *in particular* **snipes**) **1** a long-billed marsh- and shore-bird of the genus *Gallinago*, esp. the British *G. coelestis*. **2** a gunshot, usu. fired from cover. **3** a verbal attack or criticism, usu. made from a secure position. ~*v.i.* **1** to criticize, to find fault, carp (at), esp. slyly or snidely. **2** to pick off members of the enemy, usu. from cover. **3** to shoot or hunt snipe. ~*v.t.* to shoot at or kill from cover. **snipe eel** *n.* any long-snouted eel of the *Nemichthyidae*. **snipe fish** *n.* any long-snouted fish of the Macrorhamphosidae. **sniper** *n.* **sniping** *n.* [Icel. *snīpa*, cp. Dut. *snip*, G *Schnepfe*, cogn. with SNAP]

snipper, snippet etc. SNIP.

snit (snit) *n.* (*N Am., coll.*) a rage. **in a snit** sulking, in a rage. [etym. uncertain]

snitch (snich) *v.i.* (*sl.*) to inform, to peach (on). ~*v.t.* to steal, to pilfer. ~*n.* **1** the nose. **2** a tell-tale, an informer. **3** a minor robbery. [etym. uncertain]

snivel (sniv´əl) *v.i.* (*pres.p.* **snivelling,** (*N Am.*) **sniveling,** *past, p.p.* **snivelled,** (*N Am.*) **sniveled**) **1** to weep with nose running, to whimper or whine; to be tearful. **2** to run at the nose, sniffing continually. ~*n.* **1** mucus running from the nose. **2** audible or affected weeping. **3** hypocrisy, cant. **sniveller,** (*N Am.*) **sniveler** *n.* **snivellingly** *adv.* **snivelly,** (*N Am.*) **snively** *a.* [ME *snevelen*, cogn. with OE *snofl*, mucus, cp. SNUFF[1], SNUFFLE]

SNO *abbr.* (*Hist.*) Scottish National Orchestra.

snob (snob) *n.* **1** a person who cultivates or behaves obsequiously towards those of higher social position, or regards the claims of wealth and position with an exaggerated and contemptible respect. **2** a person who condescends to, patronizes, or avoids those felt to be of lower standing. **snobbery** *n.* (*pl.* **snobberies**). **snobbish** *a.* **snobbishly** *adv.* **snobbishness** *n.* **snobby** *a.* (*comp.* **snobbier,** *superl.* **snobbiest**). [etym. uncertain, orig. cobbler]

SNOBOL (snō´bol) *n.* a language used in computer programming for handling strings of symbols. [acronym for String Orientated Symbolic Language]

Sno-Cat® (snō´kat) *n.* a type of vehicle designed to travel on snow. [SNOW and CATERPILLAR]

snoek (snook) *n.* (*S Afr.*) **1** a barracouta. **2** SNOOK[2]. [Dut., pike]

snog (snog) *v.i.* (*pres.p.* **snogging,** *past, p.p.* **snogged**) (*coll.*) to kiss and cuddle. ~*n.* an act or an instance of this. **snogger** *n.* [etym. unknown]

snood (snood) *n.* **1** a fillet or ribbon formerly worn round the hair in Scotland by unmarried girls. **2** a crocheted net to contain a woman's back-hair. **3** a knitted tube worn as a hood. **4** a gut- or hair-line by which a fish-hook is fastened to the main line. **snooded** *a.* [OE *snōd*, from *snā-*, to spin, cogn. with SNARE]

snook[1] (snook) *n.* a gesture of derision made with the thumb to the nose and the fingers spread. **to cock a snook 1** to make this gesture (at). **2** to express defiance or laugh (at someone's authority etc.). [etym. uncertain]

snook[2] (snook) *n.* the tropical American fish *Centropomus undecimalis*, and various kinds of sea fish used for food, esp. the S African and Australian pike. [Dut. *snoek*, pike]

snooker (snoo´kə) *n.* **1** a game played on a billiard table, in which a white cue ball is used to pocket the other 21 balls (15 red and 6 coloured). **2** a shot or situation in this game in which the cue ball is blocked by another ball, making a direct stroke impossible. ~*v.t.* **1** to put (one's opponent or oneself) in this position. **2** to put (someone) in a difficult position, to obstruct, to thwart. **3** to defeat. **snookered** *a.* thwarted, foiled, outwitted. [etym. uncertain]

snoop (snoop) *v.i.* to go about in an inquisitive or sneaking manner, to pry. ~*n.* **1** an act or instance of snooping. **2** a snooper, a detective. **snooper** *n.* a prying busybody. **snooperscope** *n.* a device used for seeing in the dark, which makes infra-red radiation visible as an image. **snoopy** *a.* (*comp.* **snoopier,** *superl.* **snoopiest**). [Dut. *snoepen*]

snoot (snoot) *n.* (*coll.*) the nose. **snooty** *a.* (*comp.* **snootier,** *superl.* **snootiest**) supercilious, snobbish. **snootily** *adv.* **snootiness** *n.* [var. of SNOUT]

snooze (snooz) *v.i.* to take a short sleep, esp. in the day. ~*v.t.* to pass or waste (time) in slumber or indolence. ~*n.* a short sleep, a nap. **snoozer** *n.* **snoozy** *a.* (*comp.* **snoozier,** *superl.* **snooziest**). [etym. uncertain, prob. onomat.]

snore (snaw) *v.i.* to breathe through the mouth and nostrils with a snorting noise in sleep. ~*v.t.* to pass (time away) in snoring or sleeping. ~*n.* an act or sound of snoring. **snorer** *n.* **snoring** *n.* [prob. imit.]

Snorkel® (snaw´kəl) *n.* a fire-fighting platform that is elevated electronically.

snorkel (snaw´kəl), **schnorkel** (shnaw´-) *n.* **1** a breathing apparatus used in diving and swimming consisting of a tube which extends from the mouth to above the surface of the water. **2** a device on a submarine for taking in and expelling air when at periscope depth. ~*v.i.* (*pres.p.* **snorkelling,** (*N Am.*) **snorkeling,** *past, p.p.* **snorkelled,** (*N Am.*) **snorkeled**) to swim with a snorkel. **snorkelling,** (*N Am.*) **snorkeling** *n.* [from G *Schnorchel*]

snort (snawt) *v.i.* **1** to force air violently and loudly through the nostrils like a frightened or excited horse (e.g. as an expression of contempt). **2** (of e.g. an engine) to make a noise like this. **3** (*sl.*) to inhale drugs, esp. habitually. ~*v.t.* **1** to utter or throw (out) with a snort. **2** (*sl.*) to inhale (a drug). ~*n.* **1** an act or sound of snorting. **2** (*sl.*) an instance of inhaling a drug, or the amount inhaled in one snort. **3** (*coll.*) a small drink of spirits, a snifter. **snorter** *n.* **1** a person or animal that snorts. **2** (*coll.*) anything of extraordinary size, excellence, violence etc. (such as a strong wind). **snortingly** *adv.* [ME *snorten*, prob. imit. (cp. SNORKEL, also LG *snurten*, Dut. *snorken*, Swed. *snarka*)]

snot (snot) *n.* (*sl.*) **1** mucus from the nose. **2** a low or contemptible person. **snot-rag** *n.* a handkerchief. **snotter** *n.* **1** a turkeycock's wattles. **2** (*Sc.*) snot. ~*v.i.* to snivel, to weep. **snotty** *a.* (*comp.* **snottier,** *superl.* **snottiest**) **1** (*coll.*) soiled with nasal mucus. **2** (*sl.*) contemptible, low. **3** (*sl.*) snobbish, snooty. **snottily** *adv.* **snottiness** *n.* **snotty-nosed** *a.* [OE *gesnot* (cp. LG *Snotte*, Dut. and Dan. *snot*), cogn. with SNOUT]

snout (snowt) *n.* **1** the projecting nose or muzzle of an animal. **2** (*sl.*) the human nose. **3** a nozzle. **4** a projecting front, as of a glacier, a cliff etc. **5** (*sl.*) cigarette tobacco. **6** (*sl.*) an informer, esp. a police one. **snout-beetle** *n.* a weevil. **snouted** *a.* (*usu. in comb.*, as *long-snouted*). **snoutless** *a.* **snoutlike** *a.* **snouty** *a.* (*comp.* **snoutier,** *superl.* **snoutiest**). [ME *snute*, cogn. with OE *snȳtan*, to blow the nose (cp. Dut. *snuit*, G *Schnauze*, Swed. *snut*)]

snow (snō) *n.* **1** watery vapour in the atmosphere frozen into crystals and falling to the ground in flakes. **2** a fall of this or the layer it forms on the ground. **3** anything resembling snow, esp. in whiteness. **4** a gas in the form of frozen vapour, esp. carbon dioxide. **5** (*sl.*) cocaine. **6** a mass of white dots on a television or radar screen caused by interference. **7** a dessert resembling snow in appearance, texture and whiteness. ~*v.i.* **1** (with subject *it*) to fall in or as snow. **2** to come or arrive in large quantities. ~*v.t.* **1** to cover (over) or block (up) with snow. **2** to confine or hem (in) with snow. **3** to send, sprinkle or scatter down as snow. **4** (*chiefly N Am., coll.*) to overwhelm or charm with persuasive, glib or deceiving talk. **to snow under** (*usu. pass.*) to overwhelm (with work etc.). **snowball** *n.* **1** a round mass of snow pressed together in the hands and flung as a missile. **2** a round pudding or confection of various kinds. **3** a drink of advocaat and lemonade. **4** something that accumulates ever faster, like a snowball rolled in snow. ~*v.t.* to pelt with snowballs. ~*v.i.* **1** to throw snowballs. **2** to accumulate with increasing rapidity, to accelerate. **snowball tree** *n.* the sterile-flowered variety of guelder rose. **snowberry** *n.* (*pl.* **snowberries**) **1** the N American shrub, *Symphoricarpos racemosus.* **2** any of various other white-berried ornamental shrubs. **3** the berry of these shrubs. **snowbird** *n.* a small finch, bunting or sparrow, esp. the snow bunting. **snow-blind** *a.* partially or totally blinded, usu. temporarily, through the glare of reflected light from the surface of snow. **snow-blindness** *n.* **snow-blink** *n.* a luminous reflection over the horizon from snowfields. **snowblower** *n.* a machine which clears snow from a road by blowing it to the side. **snowboard** *n.* a wide ski for sliding downhill on. **snow boot** *n.* any of various kinds of boot or overshoe for walking in snow. **snowbound** *a.* imprisoned or kept from travelling by snow. **snow-broth** *n.* melted or melting snow. **snow bunting** *n.* a northern finch, *Plectrophenax nivalis*, visiting Britain in winter. **snowcap** *n.* the cap of snow on top of a mountain. **snow-capped** *a.* (of a mountain) crowned with snow. **snowdrift** *n.* a mass of snow accumulated by the wind. **snowdrop** *n.* a bulbous plant, *Galanthus nivalis*, with a white drooping flower appearing in early spring. **snowfall** *n.* **1** a fall of snow. **2** the amount of snow falling in a given place during a given time. **snowfield** *n.* an expanse of snow, esp. in polar or lofty mountain regions. **snowfinch** *n.* an alpine bird resembling the snow bunting. **snowflake** *n.* **1** a fleecy cluster of ice crystals, or a single six-branched ice crystal, falling as snow. **2** a plant of the genus *Leucojum*, a European flower resembling the snowdrop. **snow goose** *n.* a white Arctic goose with black wing-tips. **snow gum** *n.* any of various types of eucalyptus growing in the mountains of SE Australia. **snow-ice** *n.* opaque white ice formed as snow melts. **snow-in-summer** *n.* a plant of S Europe and Asia, *Cerastium tomentosum*, cultivated as a rockery plant for its white flowers. **snow job** *n.* (*chiefly N Am., coll.*) an instance of, or attempt to overwhelm with, persuasive, flattering or deceiving talk. **snow leopard** *n.* the ounce. **snowless** *a.* **snowlike** *a., adv.* **snowline** *n.* the lowest limit of perpetual snow on mountains etc. **snowman** *n.* (*pl.* **snowmen**) a humanlike figure built with packed snow. **snowmobile** *n.* a motor vehicle with runners or caterpillar tracks enabling it to travel over snow. **snow-on-the-mountains** *n.* the arabis, N American spurge (*Euphorbia marginata*) or certain other plants with white flowers or leaves. **snow owl** *n.* SNOWY OWL (under SNOW). **snow partridge** *n.* a predominantly white partridge, *Lerwa lerwa.* **snow pea** *n.* (*esp. N Am.*) a mangetout. **snowplough,** (*N Am.*) **snowplow** *n.* **1** an implement used to clear a road or railway track of snow. **2** a skiing position in which the tips of the skis meet to form a V shape. ~*v.i.* to ski in this position in order to slow or stop. **snowscape** *n.* a snow-covered landscape. **snowshoe** *n.* a long, light, racket- or ski-shaped frame worn to prevent sinking when walking on snow. **snowshoe hare, snowshoe rabbit** *n.* a N American hare, white-coated in winter, that has long hind feet. **snowshoer** *n.* **snow-slip** *n.* an avalanche.

snowstorm *n.* a heavy fall of snow, esp. accompanied by wind. **snow tyre,** (*N Am.*) **snow tire** *n.* a heavy tyre with deep treads for use on snow. **snow-white** *a.* as white or pure as snow. **snowy** *a.* (*comp.* **snowier,** *superl.* **snowiest**) **1** resembling snow, white like snow. **2** (of weather etc.) bringing a lot of snow. **3** covered with snow. **4** spotless, unblemished. **snowily** *adv.* **snowiness** *n.* **snowy owl** *n.* a white, black-barred northern owl, *Nyctea scandiaca.* [OE *snāw*, Dut. *sneeuw*, G *Schnee*, Dan. *snee*, Icel. *snaeo*, also L *nix nivis*, Gr. *nipha*]

SNP *abbr.* Scottish National Party.

Snr., snr. *abbr.* senior.

snub (snŭb) *v.t.* (*pres.p.* **snubbing,** *past, p.p.* **snubbed**) **1** to rebuke with sarcasm or contempt, to slight in a pointed or offensive manner. **2** to stop (a cable, ship etc.) suddenly, esp. by tying a rope round a post. ~*n.* **1** an act of snubbing, a rebuff, a slight. **2** a snub nose. ~*a.* short, stubby. **snubber** *n.* **snubbing** *n., a.* **snubbingly** *adv.* **snubby** *a.* (*comp.* **snubbier,** *superl.* **snubbiest**). **snub nose** *n.* a short upturned nose. **snub-nosed** *a.* **1** having a snub nose. **2** (of a gun) having a short barrel. [Icel. *snubba*, to chide, cp. Dan. *snubbe*, to nip off]

snuck SNEAK.

snuff[1] (snŭf) *n.* the charred part of the wick in a candle or lamp. ~*v.t.* **1** to trim (a wick, candle etc.) by removing this. **2** to extinguish (a flame) by or as by snuffing. **to snuff it** (*sl.*) to die. **to snuff out 1** to put out, extinguish (a candle etc.). **2** (*sl.*) to kill. **snuffer**[1] *n.* **1** a long-handled instrument with a cone-shaped cap at the end for extinguishing candles. **2** (*pl.*) a scissor-like instrument for trimming away snuff from the wick of a candle. **snuff movie, snuff film, snuff video** *n.* (*sl.*) a pornographic film whose climax is the actual murder of an unsuspecting member of the cast. [etym. uncertain, cp. prov. *snop*, to crop shoots, cogn. with SNUB]

snuff[2] (snŭf) *n.* **1** powdered tobacco or other substance inhaled through the nose. **2** a pinch of this. **3** an act of snuffing. **4** a sniff. **5** a state of resentment, a huff. ~*v.t.* to draw in through the nostrils, to sniff, to scent. ~*v.i.* **1** to sniff. **2** to take snuff. **up to snuff 1** knowing, sharp, not easily imposed upon. **2** in good condition, up to scratch. **snuffbox** *n.* a small container for carrying snuff. **snuff-coloured,** (*N Am.*) **snuff-colored** *a.* of a dark yellowish- or greyish-brown colour. **snuffer**[2] *n.* a person who takes snuff. **snuffing** *n., a.* **snuff-mill** *n.* **1** a factory or a hand-mill for grinding snuff. **2** a snuffbox. **snuffy** *a.* (*comp.* **snuffier,** *superl.* **snuffiest**) **1** annoyed, irritable. **2** disdainful, supercilious. **3** like snuff in colour or texture. **snuffiness** *n.* [prob. from MDut. *snuffen*, to clear the nose, prob. cogn. with MDut. *snuyven* (Dut. *snuiven*)]

snuffer[1] SNUFF[1].

snuffer[2] SNUFF[2].

snuffle (snŭf´əl) *v.i.* **1** to breathe noisily or make a sniffing noise as when the nose is obstructed. **2** to talk through the nose. **3** to snivel, to whine. ~*v.t.* **1** to say through the nose. **2** to sniff. ~*n.* **1** an act or sound of snuffling. **2** (*pl.*) a slight cold, the sniffles. **3** a nasal tone or voice. **snuffler** *n.* **snuffly** *a.*

snug (snŭg) *a.* (*comp.* **snugger,** *superl.* **snuggest**) **1** lying close, sheltered, and comfortable. **2** cosy, comfortable. **3** compact, trim, well secured. **4** not exposed to view. ~*v.i.* (*pres.p.* **snugging,** *past, p.p.* **snugged**) to lie close, to nestle, to snuggle. ~*n.* a snuggery. **snuggery** *n.* (*pl.* **snuggeries**) a snug place or room, esp. in a pub or bar. **snuggle** (-əl) *v.i.* to move or lie close (up to) for warmth. ~*v.t.* to draw close to one, to cuddle. ~*n.* an act of snuggling. **snugly** *adv.* **snugness** *n.* [cp. LG *snügger*, Dan. *snugg*, neat, tidy, smooth, short-haired]

So. *abbr.* south, southern.

so[1] (sō) *adv.* **1** (*usu. with neg.*) in such a manner or to such an extent, degree etc. (with *as* expressed or understood) (*not so confident now; not so easy as it used to be; not so stupid as to believe that; never heard so blatant a lie!*). **2** in the manner or to the extent, degree, intent, result etc. (with *that*) (*was so tired that he fell asleep in the armchair*). **3** also, in addition (*He needs a holiday and so do I*). **4** therefore; with the result that (*I've got a dental appointment, so I'll be a bit late*). **5** on condition, provided (that) (*just so (that) you realize you're not the only one round here*). **6** well (*So, next we tried the window*). **7** extremely, very (*You've been so patient; Things are not so good*). **8** thus, this, that, as follows, as demonstrated (*I think so too; People thought her bad-tempered, but I never found her so; Place your feet so*). **9** in such a case, or state (*He's in a coma and likely to remain so for weeks*). ~*conj.* in order that (*Listen carefully so you miss nothing*). ~*int.* used to express surprise, dawning awareness or dissent etc. (*So! This is where you've been hiding!*). ~*a.* **1** true (*That is so*). **2** put in a set order, right (*likes things just so*). ~*pron.* the same, as much (*If you haven't yet registered, please do so now; You're too shy—you told me so yourself*). **and so forth** and the rest, and so on, and the like. **and so on** and so forth. **or so** or thereabouts, or about that. **so as to** in order to (*I kept pinching myself so as to keep awake*). **so be it** let it be thus (in affirmation, resignation etc.). **so far** FAR. **so far as** FAR. **so help me (God)** HELP. **so long!** (*coll.*) au revoir, goodbye. **so long as** as long as, on condition that (*So long as you play quietly, you can stay up till 9.30*). **so much 1** a great deal, to a great extent (*She's so much better!*). **2** a certain (limited) amount (*I only have so much patience*). **3** (*with neg.*) to a lesser degree (*not so much a fashion as a fad*). **so much as** (*with neg.*) (not) even (*without so much as a wave*). **so much for 1** I don't think much of (*So much for her fabled speed, if she can't be accurate*). **2** there is nothing more to be said about (*So much for that*). **so much so** to such a degree, extent (that). **so that** in order that (*We moved into town so that we could be nearer my mother*). **so what?** what about it? **so-and-so** *n.* (*pl.* **so-and-sos**) **1** an indefinite person or thing. **2** an unpleasant person or disliked thing. **so-called** *a.* usually called thus (with implication of doubt). **so so** *a.* indifferent, middling, mediocre. ~*adv.* indifferently. [OE *swā*, cp. Dut. *zoo*, G *so*, Icel. *svā*, Dan. *saa*]

so[2] SOH.

-so (sō) *comb. form* of any kind, -soever.

soak (sōk) *v.t.* **1** to put (something) in liquid to become permeated, to steep. **2** to wet thoroughly, to drench. **3** to suck (in or up), to absorb (liquid). **4** to extract, remove or wash (out) by steeping in a liquid. **5** (*coll.*) to overcharge, or to tax heavily. ~*v.i.* **1** to lie in liquid so as to become permeated, to steep. **2** to penetrate, to permeate (into, through etc.). **3** (*coll.*) to drink excessively, to tipple, to booze. ~*n.* **1** an act of soaking or an instance of being soaked. **2** the liquid that something is immersed in or the period for which something is immersed. **3** (*sl.*) a heavy drinker. **4** (*coll.*) a drinking bout. **5** (*Austral.*) low-lying land where water is retained. **to soak in** to become fully understood, appreciated, felt etc., to penetrate. **to soak oneself in** to become thoroughly acquainted or steeped in (a subject etc.). **soakage** (-ij) *n.* **soakaway** *n.* a hole or depression dug in the ground to allow drainage to percolate into the soil. **soaker** *n.* **soaking** *a.* wet through. ~*n.* an act of wetting, steeping etc.; the state of being soaked. **soaking wet** *a.* wet through. [OE *socian*, cogn. with SUCK]

so-and-so SO[1].

soap (sōp) *n.* **1** a compound of a fatty acid and a base of sodium or potassium, producing a lather in water, and used for washing and cleansing. **2** a solid piece or bar of this, esp. for cleansing the body with. **3** INSOLUBLE SOAP (under INSOLUBLE). **4** a salt of a fatty acid. **5** (*sl.*)

flattery, glib or persuasive talk, soft soap. **6** (*coll.*) a soap opera. ~*v.t.* **1** to rub or wash with soap. **2** to flatter. **soft soap** SOFT. **soapbark** *n.* **1** any tree bark that contains saponia. **2** any tree with this type of bark, esp. the Chilean *Quillaja saponaria.* **soapberry** *n.* (*pl.* **soapberries**) (*Bot.*) the fruit of *Sapindus saponaria* and related shrubs and trees, which contains saponin. **soapbox** *n.* **1** a box for packing soap. **2** a box or improvised stand used as a platform by a street orator. **soap-bubble** *n.* a thin inflated film of soapy water. **soap flakes** *n.pl.* soap in the form of fine flakes, for washing clothes with. **soapless** *a.* **soap opera** *n.* a serialized, long-running television or radio drama usu. following a regular set of characters through various domestic or sentimental situations (orig. sponsored by soap manufacturers). **soap powder** *n.* powdered soap or detergent for washing clothes etc. **soapstone** *n.* steatite. **soapsuds** *n.pl.* water impregnated with soap to form a foam. **soap-works** *n.sing. or pl.* a factory manufacturing soap. **soapwort** *n.* a trailing herbaceous plant, *Saponaria officinalis,* the juice of which forms a lather with water. **soapy** *a.* (*comp.* **soapier,** *superl.* **soapiest**) **1** of the nature of or resembling soap. **2** smeared or combined with soap. **3** unctuous, flattering, smooth. **soapily** *adv.* **soapiness** *n.* [OE *sāpe*, cp. Dut. *zeep*, G *Seipe*, also L *sēbum*, tallow]

soar (saw) *v.i.* **1** to fly into the air, to rise. **2** (of a bird, aircraft etc.) to sail, float at a great height. **3** to rise or mount intellectually or in spirit, status, position etc. **4** to increase or rise rapidly in amount, degree etc. **5** to tower. ~*n.* a towering flight. **soarer** *n.* **soaringly** *adv.* [F *essorer*, prob. from a pop. L *exaurare* (EX-, *aura*, air)]

sob (sob) *v.i.* (*pres.p.* **sobbing,** *past, p.p.* **sobbed**) **1** to weep violently, catching one's breath in a convulsive manner. **2** to gasp convulsively from physical exhaustion or distress. ~*v.t.* **1** to say with a sob or sobs. **2** to bring (oneself into a certain state) by sobbing (*She sobbed herself to sleep*). ~*n.* a convulsive catching of the breath, as in weeping. **sobbingly** *adv.* **sob sister** *n.* (*coll.*) **1** a female journalist who writes about personal relationships and problems. **2** a female actor who plays sentimental roles. **sob story** *n.* (*pl.* **sob stories**) a hard-luck story intended to elicit pity. **sob-stuff** *n.* sentimental talk, writing, films etc. intended to prompt tears or sympathy. [ME *sobben*, prob. imit., perh. rel. to OE *siofian*]

sober (sō´bə) *a.* (*comp.* **soberer,** *superl.* **soberest**) **1** not drunk. **2** temperate in the use of alcoholic liquors etc. **3** moderate, well-balanced, sane. **4** self-possessed, calm, serious, solemn, sedate. **5** (of a view, facts, the truth etc.) objective, not exaggerated. **6** (of colours etc.) subdued, quiet. ~*v.t., v.i.* **1** to make or become sober. **2** to make or become calm, quiet or grave, to cool (down) or steady (up). **sober as a judge** entirely sober. **sobering** *a.* **soberingly** *adv.* **soberly** *adv.* **soberminded** *a.* **sobermindedness** *n.* **soberness** *n.* **sobersided** *a.* of a sober, serious or sedate disposition. **sobersides** *n.* (*pl.* **sobersides**) a person of this disposition. **sobriety** (-brī´ə-) *n.* [F *sobre*, L *sōbrius* (*sō-*, SE-, *ēbrius*, drunk), see EBRIETY]

soboles (sob´əlēz), **sobole** (sō´bōl) *n.* a creeping or underground stem, a sucker. [L]

sobriety SOBER.

sobriquet (sō´brikā), **soubriquet** (soo´-) *n.* **1** a nickname. **2** an assumed name. [F, perh. from *soubriquet*, a tap under the chin]

Soc., soc. *abbr.* **1** socialist. **2** society.

soc (sok), **soke** (sōk) *n.* (*Hist.*) **1** the right of holding a local court. **2** a district under such jurisdiction. **socage** (-ij), **soccage** *n.* a feudal tenure by any certain and determinate service distinct from military service and villainage. [OE *sōcn*, cogn. with SEEK (cp. Icel. *sōkn*, Norw. *sokn*, Dan. *sogn*, parish, Goth. *sōkns*, enquiry)]

soca (sō´kə) *n.* a type of music popular in the E Caribbean which blends elements of soul and calypso. [*so*ul, *ca*lypso]

soccage SOCAGE (under SOC).

soccer (sok´ə) *n.* Association Football.

sociable (sō´shəbəl) *a.* **1** fit or inclined to associate or be friendly, companionable, affable. **2** (of a party etc.) of a friendly, not stiff or formal, character. ~*n.* **1** an open carriage with side seats facing each other. **2** an S-shaped couch designed so that the two occupants partly face each other. **3** (*chiefly N Am.*) a social gathering. **sociability** (-bil´-), **sociableness** *n.* **sociably** *adv.*

social *a.* **1** of or relating to society, its organization or its divisions, or to the intercourse, behaviour or mutual relations of humans. **2** living in communities, gregarious, not solitary, tending to associate with others, fitted for existence in an organized, cooperative system of society. **3 a** needing the company of others. **b** accommodating the needs of others (*social awareness*). **4** practising the division of labour, cooperative. **5** existing only as a part or member of a multiple organism. **6** (of insects) organized or existing in such a community. **7** (of plants) growing in clumps and monopolizing the ground they grow on. **8** of, relating to, or conducive to shared activities or companionship (*social gatherings*). **9** of or relating to the social services. **10** relating to the classes in society, esp. the upper class or fashionable society (*social background*; *social poise*). **11** sociable, companionable, consisting in friendly converse, convivial. ~*n.* a social gathering, a community party. **the social** (*coll.*) social security. **social anthropology** *n.* a discipline within the social sciences concerned with systems of belief and cultural organization in a society. **social climber** *n.* a person who constantly looks for ways of improving their social status, esp. by ingratiating themselves with people of a higher class. **social climbing** *n.* **social contract, social compact** *n.* a collective agreement between members of a society and a government that secures the rights and liberties of each individual to the extent of not interfering with another's rights and liberties. **social credit** *n.* the doctrine that the general public should be given the profits from industry. **social democracy** *n.* the theories and practices of socialists who believe in transforming a capitalist society into a socialist one by democratic means. **social democrat** *n.* a supporter of social democracy. **social disease** *n.* venereal disease. **social engineering** *n.* the management and adjustment of society carried out on sociological principles. **social engineer** *n.* **social insurance** *n.* insurance against unemployment, sickness or old age provided by the state out of contributions from employers and wage-earners. **socialism** *n.* the doctrine that the political and economic organization of society should be based on the subordination of the individual to the interests of the community, involving the collective ownership of the sources and instruments of production, democratic control of industries, cooperation instead of individual private gain, state distribution of the products instead of payment by wages, free education etc. **socialist** *n., a.* **socialistic** (-is´-) *a.* **socialistically** *adv.* **socialite** (-līt) *n.* a person who is constantly to be found in fashionable society. **sociality** (-shial´-) *n.* **socialize, socialise** *v.i.* to behave in a convivial or sociable manner, to mix socially. ~*v.t.* **1** to prepare, make fit for social life. **2** (*chiefly N Am.*) to constitute or transform according to socialist principles. **socialization** (-zā´shən) *n.* **socialized medicine** *n.* (*N Am., derog.*) the providing of medical services to all through public funds. **socially** *adv.* **social order** *n.* the complex interdependent hierarchy that constitutes society, esp. with reference to one's place in it. **social realism** *n.* the realistic presentation of social conditions in art etc. **social science** *n.*

1 the study of society and the interaction and behaviour of its members. 2 any one of the subjects included in this, e.g. sociology, economics, political science, anthropology and psychology. **social scientist** *n.* **social secretary** *n.* a person whose job is to arrange the social engagements and activities of an organization or individual. **social security** *n.* state provision for the unemployed, aged or sick through a system of pensions or benefits. **social service** *n.* work for the benefit of one's fellow human beings, philanthropic work. **social services** *n.pl.* welfare services provided by the state or a local authority. **social war** *n.* a war between allies. **social work** *n.* any of various types of welfare service (for the aged, disabled etc.) provided by the social services and carried out by trained employees. **social worker** *n.* [L *socius*, companion, rel. to *sequī*, to follow]

society (səsī´əti) *n.* (*pl.* **societies**) 1 a social community. 2 the general body of persons, communities or nations constituting mankind regarded as a community. 3 social organization. 4 the privileged and fashionable classes of a community or some subdivision or quasi-subdivision of them, as *high society, polite society*. 5 a body of persons associated for some common object or collective interest, a club or an association. 6 the company of other people, companionship, fellowship (*She enjoyed his society; She began to shun society*). 7 a group of plants or animals of the same species or sharing the same needs, characteristics etc. ~*a.* of or relating to fashionable society. **societal** *a.* of or relating to (human) society. **societally** *adv.* **Society of Friends** *n.* the religious body of Quakers founded by George Fox in the mid 17th cent., whose members reject the ritual of church services and instead hold religious meetings at which any member may speak. **Society of Jesus** *n.* the Roman Catholic order of Jesuits. [F *société*, L *societātem*, nom. *-tas*, from *socius*, see SOCIABLE]

socio- (sō´siō) *comb. form* 1 social. 2 society. [L *socius*, a companion]

sociobiology (sōsiōbīol´əji) *n.* the study of human or animal behaviour from a genetic or evolutionary basis. **sociobiological** (-əloj´-) *a.* **sociobiologically** *adv.* **sociobiologist** *n.*

sociocultural (sōsiōkŭl´chərəl) *a.* of, relating to or involving social and cultural factors. **socioculturally** *adv.*

socio-economic (sōsiōēkənom´ik, -ek-) *a.* of, relating to or involving social and economic factors. **socio-economically** *adv.*

sociolinguistic (sōsiōling·gwis´tik) *a.* of or relating to the social aspects of language. **sociolinguist** (-ling´gwist) *n.* **sociolinguistically** *adv.* **sociolinguistics** *n.* the study of language as a social tool.

sociology (sōsiol´əji) *n.* 1 the science of the organization and dynamics of human society. 2 the study or investigation of social problems. **sociological** (-əloj´-) *a.* **sociologically** *adv.* **sociologist** *n.* [F *sociologie*]

sociometry (sōsiom´ətri) *n.* the study of social relationships within a group. **sociometric** (-əmet´-) *a.* **sociometrically** *adv.* **sociometrist** *n.*

sociopath (sō´siōpath) *n.* a person affected by a personality disorder, manifesting itself in antisocial or asocial behaviour, e.g. a psychopath. **sociopathic** (-əpath´-) *a.* **sociopathy** (-op´-) *n.*

sociopolitical (sōsiōpəlit´ikəl) *a.* of, relating to or involving social and political factors.

sock[1] (sok) *n.* (*pl.* **socks,** (*commercial*) **sox**) 1 a short stocking. 2 a removable inner sole. 3 the light shoe worn by the comic actors of ancient Greece and Rome. **put a sock in it** (*sl.*) be quiet, shut up. **to blow the socks off** to astonish. **to knock the socks off** 1 (*coll.*) to defeat resoundingly. 2 to astonish. **to pull one's socks up** to make a vigorous effort to do better. [OE *socc*, L *soccus*, a shoe worn by comic actors]

sock[2] (sok) *v.t.* (*sl.*) to hit or punch (esp. a person) hard with a blow. ~*n.* 1 a hard hit, punch or blow. 2 (*N Am.*) the power behind a punch or blow. **to sock it to** to address or attack with great vigour or force. [etym. uncertain]

socket (sok´it) *n.* 1 a natural or artificial hollow place or fitting adapted for receiving and holding another part or thing, e.g. an implement or electric plug, or for holding a revolving part such as a limb, eye, head of an instrument etc. 2 an electric power point. 3 the part of an iron golf club that the shaft is fitted into. ~*v.t.* (*pres.p.* **socketing,** *past, p.p.* **socketed**) 1 to fit into or furnish with a socket. 2 in golf, to hit (the ball) with the socket of a club. **socketed** *a.* **socket joint** *n.* BALL-AND-SOCKET JOINT (under BALL[1]). [etym. uncertain; ME and OF *soket*, perh. dim. of *souche*, tree-stump, from Gmc.]

sockeye (sok´ī) *n.* a Pacific blueback salmon, *Oncorhynchus nerka*, with red flesh highly esteemed as a food. [by folk etym. from N Am. Ind. *suk-kegh*]

socle (sō´kəl) *n.* a plain low rectangular block or plinth, forming a base for a statue, column etc. [G, from *zoccolo*, L *socculus*, dim. of *soccus*, SOCK[1]]

Socratic (səkrat´ik), †**Socratical** *a.* of, relating to or according to Socrates, Greek philosopher, 469–399 BC. ~*n.* an adherent of Socrates or his philosophy. **Socratically** *adv.* **Socratic elenchus** *n.* the refutation of an opponent's argument by the method of short question and answer. **Socratic irony** *n.* simulation of ignorance in order to lead on and eventually confute an opponent. **Socratic method** *n.* the dialectical method of procedure by question and answer introduced by Socrates, designed to trap an opponent into exposing the weakness in their own argument.

sod[1] (sod) *n.* 1 a piece of surface soil cut away, a turf. 2 surface soil filled with the roots of grass etc., turf, sward. ~*v.t.* (*pres.p.* **sodding,** *past, p.p.* **sodded**) to cover with sod. **under the sod** in one's grave. [cp. MDut. *sode*, Dut. *zode*, perh. cogn. with SEETHE, cp. SOD[2]]

sod[2] (sod) *n.* (*sl.*) 1 a despicable person, esp. male. 2 a person, chap (*the lucky sod*). ~*int.* curse (someone or something). **sod all** nothing at all. **sod off** go away, get lost. **sodding** *a.* accursed. ~*adv.* used as an intensive before adjectives and adverbs. **Sod's law** (sodz) *n.* a wry maxim saying that anything which can possibly go wrong will do so. [short for SODOMITE (under SODOM)]

soda (sō´də) *n.* 1 any of various compounds of sodium, e.g. sodium carbonate, sodium hydroxide, sodium bicarbonate. 2 soda water. 3 (*N Am.*) a fizzy soft drink. **soda bread, soda scone** *n.* a type of bread or scone made with baking soda, esp. in Ireland. **soda fountain** *n.* 1 a device for dispensing soda water. 2 (*N Am.*) a counter serving soft drinks, ice creams etc. **sodaic** (-dā´-) *a.* **soda lime** *n.* a mixture of sodium hydroxide and calcium oxide. **soda syphon** *n.* a pressurized bottle for dispensing soda water. **soda water** *n.* an effervescent drink composed of water charged with carbon dioxide. [It., prob. fem. of *sodo, solido*, glasswort, prob. from L, as SOLID]

sodality (sədal´iti) *n.* (*pl.* **sodalities**) a fellowship, a confraternity, esp. a charitable association in the Roman Catholic Church. [F *sodalité*, L *sodālitas*, from *sodālis*, comrade]

sodden (sod´ən) *a.* 1 soaked, saturated. 2 (of bread etc.) not properly baked, heavy, doughy. 3 bloated and stupid, esp. with drink. ~*v.t.* to soak, to saturate, esp. with drink. ~*v.i.* to become sodden. **soddenly** *adv.* **soddenness** *n.* [p.p. of SEETHE]

sodding SOD[2].

sodium (sō´diəm) *n.* a silver-white metallic element, at. no. 11, chem. symbol Na, the base of soda. **sodium bicarbonate** *n.* a white powder used in baking powder, effervescent drinks, antacid preparations and fire extinguishers, baking soda. **sodium carbonate** *n.* a crystalline salt used in the manufacture of cleaning agents, glass etc., washing soda. **sodium chloride** *n.* a colourless crystalline compound occurring in sea water, common salt. **sodium hydroxide** *n.* a deliquescent alkali used in manufacturing paper and soap, caustic soda. **sodium lamp, sodium-vapour lamp** *n.* an electric lamp used esp. in street lighting, consisting of a glass tube containing sodium vapour and neon which emits an orange light when current is passed through it. **sodium nitrate** *n.* a white crystalline salt occurring naturally as Chile saltpetre, used in fertilizers, explosives etc. [SODA, -IUM]

Sodom (sod´əm) *n.* a place of utter wickedness or depravity. **sodomite** (-mīt) *n.* a person who practises sodomy. **sodomitic** (-mit´-), **sodomitical** *a.* **sodomy** (-i) *n.* anal intercourse with a man or woman, or sexual relations with an animal (supposedly the characteristic sexual behaviour of the people of Sodom, Gen.xix.24). [from the name of the corrupt city destroyed by God in the Old Testament, Gen. xix.24]

soever (sōev´ə), **-soever** *adv.* appended, sometimes as a suffix, and sometimes after an interval, to pronouns, adverbs or adjectives to give an indefinite or universal meaning (*wheresoever I find her; in what place soever she dwells*).

sofa (sō´fə) *n.* a long stuffed couch or seat with raised back and ends. **sofa bed** *n.* a sofa that can be extended so as to serve as a bed. [prob. through F, from Arab. *suffah*]

soffit (sof´it) *n.* the undersurface of a cornice, lintel, balcony, arch etc. [F *soffite*, It. *soffitta*, ceiling, fem. of *soffitto*, p.p. (SUB-, L *figere*, to FIX)]

S. of S. *abbr.* The Song of Songs (Old Testament).

soft (soft) *a.* **1** yielding easily to pressure, easily moulded, cut or worked, malleable, pliable, plastic, as opposed to *hard*. **2** smooth to the touch, not rough or coarse. **3** not loud or harsh, low-toned. **4** affecting the senses in a mild, delicate, or gentle manner. **5** (of a day, a breeze etc.) balmy, gentle. **6 a** (of air, climate etc.) not hot or cold, mild, genial. **b** (of the weather) damp or thawing. **7 a** (of light colours, outlines etc.) not brilliant, glaring, or abrupt. **b** (of an image) blurred. **8** easily magnetized and demagnetized. **9** (of radiation rays) low in energy. **10 a** (of water) free from mineral salts that prevent lathering, suitable for washing. **b** in the form of rain. **11** (of a drug) relatively harmless or non-addictive. **12** (of coal) bituminous. **13** (of pornography) titillating but not explicit. **14** (of prices etc.) likely to drop. **15** gentle or mild in disposition, yielding, conciliatory. **16** (of the wing of a political party) willing to compromise, moderate. **17** impressionable, sympathetic, compassionate. **18** low-key, non-insistent. **19** easily imposed on, lenient. **20** weak, timorous, effeminate. **21** silly, simple. **22** amorous, sentimental, tender-hearted. **23** flaccid, out of condition, pampered. **24** (of a job) easy. **25 a** in phonetics, not guttural or explosive, sibilant (as *c* in *cede* or *g* in *gem*). **b** voiced or unaspirated (as *b*, *d* and *g*). ~*n.* **1** a soft part, object or material. **2** a weak or silly person, a softie. ~*adv.* softly, gently, quietly. **soft in the head** feeble-minded, foolish. **to be soft on 1** to be lenient or sympathetic towards. **2** to be amorously inclined towards. **to have a soft spot for** to be fond of (a person). **soft answer** *n.* a complaisant response to abuse or accusations. **softball** *n.* **1** a game resembling baseball played with a larger and softer ball. **2** the ball used in this game. **soft-boiled** *a.* (of an egg) lightly boiled, so as to leave the yolk runny. **soft-centred,** (*N Am.*) **soft-centered** *a.* **1** (of a chocolate) with a soft filling. **2** (of a person) kind or sentimental at heart. **soft-core** *a.* (of pornography) relatively inexplicit. **soft-cover** *n., a.* (a) paperback. **soft currency** *n.* a currency that is unstable owing to the uncertainty of its gold backing. **soft detergent** *n.* a detergent that is biodegradable. **soft drink** *n.* a non-intoxicant beverage. **soften** (sof´ən) *v.t.* **1** to make soft or softer. **2** to palliate, to mitigate, tone down. ~*v.i.* to become soft or softer. **to soften up 1** to make more sympathetic to. **2** to break down the resistance of. **3** to reduce the effectiveness of the defences of (a targeted position etc.) e.g. by preliminary bombing. **softener** *n.* **softening** *n.* **softening of the brain** *n.* **1** a softening of cerebral tissue resulting in mental deterioration. **2** (*coll.*) stupidity, excessive credulity. **soft-focus** *n., a.* (having, designed to produce) a slightly out-of-focus image with blurred edges. **soft fruit** *n.* small stoneless berries such as strawberries, raspberries, blackcurrants, redcurrants and blackberries. **soft furnishings** *n.pl.* textile furnishings such as carpets, curtains, chair covers etc. **soft goods** *n.pl.* textiles. **soft-headed** *a.* silly, stupid. **soft-headedness** *n.* **soft-hearted** *a.* tender-hearted, compassionate. **soft-heartedly** *adv.* **soft-heartedness** *n.* **softie, softy** *n.* (*pl.* **softies**) **1** a silly, weak-minded person. **2** a person who is physically unfit or flaccid. **3** a tender-hearted person. **softish** *a.* **soft-land** *v.i., v.t.* to land or cause (a spacecraft) to land gently on the moon or a planet, without incurring damage. **soft landing** *n.* **softly** *adv.* **softly-softly** *a.* (of tactics) deceptively gentle, but insidious nonetheless. **softness** *n.* **soft option** *n.* an option offering least difficulty. **soft palate** *n.* the posterior part of the palate terminating in the uvula. **soft-paste** *n.* porcelain, made from bone ash, clay etc. **soft pedal** *n.* a foot pedal for subduing the tone of notes played on the piano. **soft-pedal** *v.i., v.t.* (*pres.p.* **soft-pedalling,** (*N Am.*) **soft-pedaling,** *past, p.p.* **soft-pedalled,** (*N Am.*) **soft-pedaled**) to play down, avoid the issue of. **soft porn** *n.* soft-core pornography. **soft roe** *n.* the roe of a male fish. **soft sell** *n.* selling by means of gentle persuasiveness or suggestion. **soft-sell** *v.t.* (*past, p.p.* **soft-sold**). **soft-shoe** *a.* of or relating to a style of tap dancing performed in soft-soled shoes. **soft soap** *n.* **1** semi-liquid soap made with potash. **2** (*coll.*) flattery, blarney. **soft-soap** *v.t.* (*coll.*) to flatter for some ulterior object. **soft-spoken** *a.* **1** speaking softly. **2** mild, affable, conciliatory. **soft sugar** *n.* granulated or powdered sugar. **soft tack** *n.* bread, as distinct from *hard tack* or biscuit. **soft target** *n.* an easily attacked, undefended target. **soft tissues** *n.pl.* the soft bodily parts as distinct from bone or cartilage. **soft-top** *n.* **1** a car with a flexible roof that can be folded back. **2** the roof of a car like this. **soft touch** *n.* (*sl.*) someone easily influenced or imposed upon. **software** *n.* computer programs designed to perform various applications, e.g. word processing. **soft wicket** *n.* in cricket, a wicket with soft-wet turf. **softwood** *n.* **1** the wood of a coniferous tree such as the pine. **2** a conifer yielding this wood. **softy** SOFTIE (under SOFT). [OE *sōfte*, adv. (*sēfte*, a.), cp. G *sanft*, Dut. *zacht*, also Gr. *hēmeros*, mild, Sansk. *sāmen*, mildness]

softa (sof´tə) *n.* a student of Muslim theology and sacred law. [Turk., from Pers. *sūhtah*, lighted]

soften, softie etc. SOFT.

SOGAT (sō´gat) *abbr.* (*Hist.*) Society of Graphical and Allied Trades.

soggy (sog´i) *a.* (*comp.* **soggier,** *superl.* **soggiest**) **1** soaked, sodden, thoroughly wet. **2** heavy with moisture. **3** (*coll.*) dull, heavy, spiritless. **soggily** *adv.* **sogginess** *n.* [dial. *sog*, a swamp]

soh (sō), **so, sol** (sol) *n.* **1** the fifth note of a major scale in the tonic sol-fa system. **2** the note G in the fixed-doh system. [L *sol-ve*, see GAMUT]

soi-disant (swahdēzā´) *a.* self-styled, pretended, so-called. [F, *soi*, L *se*, self, *disant*, pres.p. of *dire*, L *dīcere*, to say]

soigné (swahn´yā), (*fem.*) **soignée** *a.* **1** well-turned-out, well-groomed. **2** elegant, tasteful. [F]

soil[1] (soil) *n.* **1** the ground, esp. the top stratum of the earth's crust, composed of a mixture of crumbled rock and organic matter, whence plants derive their mineral food. **2** land, country, territory, region (*on German soil; back on my native soil*). **3** the earth with reference to agriculture and cultivation (*a man of the soil*). **4** that which nourishes or promotes development. **soil-less** *a.* **soil mechanics** *n.* the study of the aspects and properties of soil that are relevant to civil engineering. **soil science** *n.* the scientific study of soils, pedology. **soily** *a.* (*comp.* **soilier**, *superl.* **soiliest**). [A-F, prob. from L *solium*, seat, or late L *solea*, sole, ground, conf. with *solum*, ground]

soil[2] (soil) *v.t.* **1** to make dirty, to stain or mark with dirt. **2** to sully, to tarnish, to pollute. ~*v.i.* to become sullied or dirty, to tarnish. ~*n.* **1** a dirty spot, stain, taint or defilement. **2** any foul matter, filth, refuse, dung, compost. **soiled** *a.* **soil pipe** *n.* a pipe carrying waste material and water from a toilet. [A-F *soyler*, OF *soillier*, *suillier* (F *souiller*), prob. from *soil*, a boar's soil, L *suillus*, of, relating to swine, from *sus*, pig (cp. SULLY)]

soil[3] (soil) *v.t.* to feed (cattle etc.) with green food, in order to fatten, orig. to purge. [perh. from SOIL[2], or from OF *soeler* (F *soûler*), to satiate, ult. from L *satullus*, dim. of *satur*, full]

soirée (swah´rā) *n.* an evening party or gathering for conversation and social intercourse etc., usu. with music. [F, orig. evening, from L *sērus*, late]

soixante-neuf (swasãtnœf´) *n.* (*sl.*) sixty-nine, a sexual position or activity in which a couple engage in oral stimulation of each other's genitals at the same time. [F]

sojourn (soj´œn, sō´-) *v.i.* to stay or reside (in, among etc.) temporarily. ~*n.* a temporary stay or residence. **sojourner** *n.* [OF *sojourner* (F *séjourner*), (SUB-, L *diurnāre*, to stay, from *diurnus*, DIURNAL)]

soke SOC.

Sol (sol) *n.* (*poet.*) the sun personified. [L, the sun]

Sol. *abbr.* (The Song of) Solomon (Old Testament).

sol[1] (sol) *n.* a colloidal solution. [short for SOLUTION (under SOLUBLE)]

sol[2] SOH.

sol. *abbr.* **1** soluble. **2** solution.

sola[1] (sō´lə) *n.* **1** an E Indian plant with a pithy stem, *Aeschynomene indica*. **2** the pith of this plant, used for making sun helmets. **sola topi, sola topee** *n.* a helmet affording protection from the sun, made from sola. [Hind. *solā*]

sola[2] SOLUS.

solace (sol´əs) *n.* comfort in grief, trouble etc., consolation, compensation. ~*v.t.* **1** to comfort or console in trouble etc. **2** to alleviate, to allay. **to solace oneself with** to find comfort in. **solacement** *n.* **solacer** *n.* [OF *solaz*, L *sōlācium*, cogn. with *sōlārī*, to console]

solan (sō´lən), **solan goose** *n.* the gannet, *Sula bassana*. [Icel. *sūla*, perh. *ond*, goose]

solanaceous, solanine SOLANUM.

solano (sōlah´nō) *n.* a hot oppressive SE wind in Spain. [Sp., from L *Solānus*, from SOL]

solanum (səlā´nəm) *n.* any plant of the genus *Solanum*, containing the potato, eggplant, nightshades and tobacco. **solanaceous** (solənā´shəs) *a.* **solanine** (sol´ənin, -nēn) *n.* a poisonous alkaloid found in several species of *Solanum*, esp. in green potatoes. [late L, nightshade]

solar (sō´lə) *a.* of or relating to, proceeding from, measured by or powered by the sun. ~*n.* **1** a solarium. **2** an upper room, garret or loft in a medieval house. **3** a platform or raised floor between ladders in a mine. **solar battery** *n.* a battery consisting of one or more solar cells. **solar cell** *n.* a cell that converts solar energy into electricity. **solar constant** *n.* the rate at which the sun's energy reaches the earth's surface, estimated to be 1,388 watts per square metre. **solar cycle** *n.* a period of 28 years, after which the days of the month recur on the same days of the week. **solar day** *n.* the interval between successive traverses of the meridian (at any particular place) by the sun. **solar eclipse** *n.* an eclipse of the sun in which it is obscured by the moon. **solar energy** *n.* **1** radiant energy produced by the sun. **2** energy derived from the sun, solar power. **solarium** (-leə´riəm) *n.* (*pl.* **solaria** (-riə), **solariums**) a room or building constructed for the enjoyment of, or therapeutical exposure of the body to, the rays of the sun. **solarize, solarise** *v.t.* **1** to expose (photographic material) to sunlight, esp. for too long. **2** to affect in this way. ~*v.i.* to be spoiled by over-exposure. **solarization** (-zā´shən) *n.* **solar month** *n.* one-twelfth of a solar year. **solar myth** *n.* a myth that allegorizes the course and properties of the sun in terms of the activities and attributes of a god or hero. **solar panel** *n.* a panel of solar cells functioning as a power source. **solar plexus** *n.* the epigastric plexus, a network of nerves behind the stomach. **solar power** *n.* solar energy. **solar system** *n.* the sun and the various heavenly bodies revolving about it. **solar time** *n.* time as reckoned by the apparent motion of the sun. **solar wind** *n.* the streams of protons and electrons emitted by the sun. **solar year** *n.* the time taken by the earth to make a single circuit of the sun, 365 days, 5 hours, 48 minutes and 46 seconds. [L *sōlāris*, from *sol*, sun]

solatium (səlā´shiəm) *n.* (*pl.* **solatia** (-shiə)) something given as compensation for suffering or loss. [L, SOLACE]

sold SELL.

soldanella (soldənel´ə) *n.* any plant of the dwarf Alpine genus *Soldanella*, with bell-shaped flowers that have fringed petals.

solder (sōl´də) *n.* **1** a fusible alloy for uniting the edges etc. of less fusible metals. **2** anything that cements or unites. ~*v.t.* to unite or mend with or as with solder. ~*v.i.* to become united or mended (as) with solder. **solderable** *a.* **solderer** *n.* **soldering** *n., a.* **soldering iron** *n.* a tool used hot for melting and applying solder. [ME *soudur*, *soudre*, OF *soudure*, from *souder*, L *solidāre*, to make firm, as SOLDIER]

soldier (sōl´jə) *n.* **1** a person engaged in military service, esp. a private or non-commissioned officer. **2** a person of military skill or experience, esp. a tried and successful commander. **3** a person who works diligently for a cause. **4** a soldier ant, soldier beetle, or soldier crab. **5** an upright brick set in a wall. **6** an oblong piece of toast for dipping into a soft-boiled egg. ~*v.i.* to serve as a soldier. **to soldier on** to persevere doggedly in the face of difficulty. **soldier ant** *n.* any of the asexual fighting ants or termites of a community, with a large head and jaws. **soldier beetle** *n.* a reddish beetle that preys on the larvae of other insects. **soldier crab** *n.* a species of hermit crab. **soldiering** *n.* service in the army. **soldier-like** *a.* soldierly. **soldierly** *a.* **1** having a soldier's appearance or bearing. **2** like a soldier in being brave, staunch etc. **soldier of Christ** *n.* a Christian who actively tries to make converts to Christianity. **soldier of fortune** *n.* **1** a military adventurer ready to fight in any army for pay, a mercenary. **2** a person who lives on their wits. **soldiership** *n.* **soldiery** *n.* (*pl.* **soldieries**) **1** soldiers collectively. **2** a body of soldiers. **3** the profession of soldiers, soldiership. [OF, from late L *soldārius*, *solidārius*, from L *solidus*, a gold coin, the pay of a soldier]

sole[1] (sōl) *n.* **1** the flat underside or bottom of the foot. **2** the part of a boot or shoe under the foot, esp. the part in front of the heel. **3** the bottom or lower part (of a plane, a plough, the head of a golf club, various engines etc.). **4** the floor of a ship's cabin. ~*v.t.* to provide or fit (a boot etc.) with a sole. **-soled** *a.* (*in comb.*, as in *leather-soled, rubber-soled*). **sole-plate** *n.* the bedplate of a machine, an iron etc. [OE, from L *solea*, from *solum*, the ground]

sole[2] (sōl) *n.* a flatfish of various species of the family Soleidae, highly esteemed as food. [L *solea*, see SOLE[1]]

sole[3] (sōl) *a.* **1** single, only, unique, alone in its kind (*Her sole aim in life is shopping; is the sole prerogative of the Speaker*). **2** (*Law, Hist.*) unmarried. **3** †solitary, alone. **solely** *adv.* **soleness** *n.* [A-F, from OF *sol*, L *sōlum*, nom. *-lus*]

solecism (sol´isizm) *n.* **1** a deviation from correct idiom or grammar. **2** any incongruity, error or absurdity. **3** a breach of good manners, an impropriety. **solecist** *n.* **solecistic** (-sis´-), **solecistical** *a.* **solecistically** *adv.* †**solecize, solecise** *v.i.* [L *solaecismus*, Gr. *soloikismos*, from *soloikos*, speaking incorrectly (*Soloi*, in Cilicia, Asia Minor, where the Attic colonists spoke bad Greek, *-oikos*, dwelling)]

Usage note The nouns *solecism* and *solipsism* should not be confused: a *solecism* is a lapse in language or manners, and *solipsism* a philosophical theory.

solemn (sol´əm) *a.* **1** performed with or accompanied by rites, ceremonies or due formality. **2** awe-inspiring, impressive. **3** grave, serious, momentous. **4** formal, affectedly grave, self-important, pompous. **5** dull, sombre. **solemness, solemnness** *n.* **solemnify** (-lem´nifī) *v.t.* (*3rd pers. sing. pres.* **solemnifies,** *pres.p.* **solemnifying,** *past, p.p.* **solemnified**) to make solemn. **solemnification** (-fikā´shən) *n.* **solemnity** (-lem´ni-) *n.* (*pl.* **solemnities**) **1** solemness, impressiveness. **2** affected gravity or formality. **3** (*often pl.*) a rite or ceremony, esp. one performed with religious reverence. **solemnize** (-nīz), **solemnise** *v.t.* **1** to dignify or to celebrate with solemn formalities or ceremonies. **2** to make solemn. **solemnization** (-zā´shən) *n.* **solemnizer** *n.* **Solemn League and Covenant** *n.* the Presbyterian compact of 1643 between Scotland and England. **solemnly** *adv.* **Solemn Mass** *n.* HIGH MASS (under HIGH). [ME and OF *solempne*, L *sōlemnis, sollennis*, prob. from *sollus*, whole, entire, cp. Gr. *holos*]

solenoid (sol´ənoid, sō´-) *n.* a magnet consisting of a cylindrical coil traversed by an electric current. **solenoidal** (-noi´-) *a.* [F *solenoïde*, from Gr. *sōlēnoeides*, pipe-shaped, from *solēn*, pipe, -OID]

soleus (sō´liəs) *n.* a muscle of the calf of the leg beneath the gastrocnemius concerned with plantar flexion, i.e. helping to extend the foot. [from L *solea*, SOLE[1]]

sol-fa (solfah´) *v.i.* (*3rd pers. sing. pres.* **sol-fas,** *pres.p.* **sol-faing,** *past, p.p.* **sol-faed**) to sing the notes of the musical scale up or down to the syllables *doh* (or *ut*), *re, mi, fa, sol* (or *soh*), *la, si* (or *ti*). *~v.t.* to sing (a musical composition) thus. *~n.* solmization, tonic sol-fa. **solfège** (-fezh), **solfeggio** (-fej´ō) *n.* (*pl.* **solfèges** (-fezh), **solfeggi** (-fej´i), **solfeggios**) **1** a singing exercise in solmization. **2** solmization, sol-fa. [SOL[2], FA]

solfatara (solfətah´rə) *n.* a volcanic vent emitting sulphurous gases. [It., from *solfo*, sulphur]

solfège, solfeggio SOL-FA.

soli SOLO.

solicit (səlis´it) *v.t.* (*pres.p.* **soliciting,** *past, p.p.* **solicited**) **1** to make earnest or importunate requests for. **2** to make earnest or persistent requests or appeals to. **3** to entice or incite (someone) to do something illegal or immoral. **4** (of a prostitute) openly to offer sexual relations in exchange for money. *~v.i.* **1** to make earnest or importunate appeals. **2** (of a prostitute) to proposition someone as a potential client. **solicitant** *n., a.* **solicitation** (-ā´shən) *n.* **solicitor** *n.* **1** a legal practitioner authorized to advise clients and prepare causes for barristers but not to appear as advocate in the higher courts. **2** a person who solicits. **Solicitor General** *n.* (*pl.* **Solicitors General**) a law officer of the British Crown ranking next to the Attorney General, appointed by the government in power to advise and represent it in legal matters. **solicitorship** *n.* **solicitous** *a.* **1** anxious, concerned, apprehensive, disturbed (about, for etc.). **2** eager (to). **solicitously** *adv.* **solicitousness** *n.* **solicitude** (-tūd) *n.* **1** a solicitous state of mind, or solicitous behaviour. **2** anxiety, concern. [OF *soliciter*, L *sollicitāre*, from *sollicitus*, from *sollus*, whole, *citus*, aroused]

solid (sol´id) *a.* (*comp.* **solider,** *superl.* **solidest**) **1** firm, unyielding, stable, rigid, not fluid or liquid. **2** composed of particles closely cohering, dense, compact; not hollow, devoid of cavities, interstices or crevices, not porous (*a solid block of concrete*). **3** uniform, uninterrupted; the same throughout, homogeneous (*solid gold*). **4** sound, substantial, not flimsy (*good solid walls*). **5** (*Geom.*) of or in three dimensions. **6** real, genuine, reliable, well-grounded (*a solid argument*). **7** thinking, feeling or acting unanimously. **8** (*Print.*) having no leads between the lines of type. **9** (of a compound word) printed or written as one word, without a hyphen. *~adv.* **1** in a solid manner. **2** so as to be solid (*set solid*). **3** unanimously. *~n.* **1** a rigid, compact body. **2** (*Geom.*) a body or magnitude possessing length, breadth and depth, having thickness or volume. **solid angle** *n.* the angle at any corner of a solid figure such as a cube, or at the vertex of a cone, from which there is a three-dimensional spread of direction. **solid colour,** (*N Am.*) **solid color** *n.* colour that covers an object etc. uniformly, without a pattern. **solid-drawn** *a.* (of e.g. a tube) drawn from a solid bar of metal. **solid fuel** *n.* **1** fuel composed of solid matter (e.g. coal) rather than gas or liquid. **2** solid propellant. **solid geometry** *n.* the branch of geometry dealing with three-dimensional figures. **solidify** (-lid´ifī) *v.t., v.i.* (*3rd pers. sing. pres.* **solidifies,** *pres.p.* **solidifying,** *past, p.p.* **solidified**) to make or become solid. **solidifiable** *a.* **solidification** (-fikā´shən) *n.* **solidifier** *n.* **solidity** (-lid´-), **solidness** *n.* **solidly** *adv.* **solid propellant** *n.* solid fuel for rockets. **solid solution** *n.* a solid material consisting of a substance in which another substance is uniformly distributed. **solid state** *n.* the state that matter is in when it can maintain its shape or boundaries without support. **solid-state** *a.* **1** of or relating to solid matter or substances. **2** of, composed of, or relating to semiconductor materials. **solid-state physics** *n.* a branch of physics dealing with the properties and nature of solid matter, esp. now electrical conduction in the crystals of semiconductors, photoconductivity, superconductivity and ferromagnetism. [OF *solide*, L *solidum*, nom. *-dus*, cogn. with Gr. *bolos*, Sansk. *sarva(s)*, whole]

solidarity (solidar´iti) *n.* **1** cohesion, mutual dependence. **2** community of interests, feelings, responsibilities etc. **solidary** (sol´-) *a.* united in nature, interests, responsibility etc. [F *solidarité, solidaire*, from L *solidum*, see SOLID]

solidi SOLIDUS.

solidungulate (solidŭng´gūlət) *a.* solid-hoofed, not cloven. [L *solidus*, solid, *ungula*, a hoof]

solidus (sol´idəs) *n.* (*pl.* **solidi** (-dī)) **1** the stroke (/) formerly denoting a shilling (as in 2/6), also used in writing fractions (e.g. 1/4), separating numbers (e.g. in dates) or alternative words (as in *him/her*) etc. **2** (*in full* **solidus curve**) in a graph representing the composition and temperature of a mixture, a curve below which the mixture is completely solid. **3** a Roman gold coin introduced by Constantine. [late L, see SOLID]

solifluction (soliflŭk´shən), **solifluxion** *n.* a slow downwards slip of waterlogged soil which usu. occurs in areas of permanent frost (e.g. tundra regions). [from L *solum*, soil, *fluctio*, an act of flowing]

soliloquy (səlil´əkwi) *n.* (*pl.* **soliloquies**) **1** the activity of talking to oneself. **2** a speech or discourse, esp. in a play, uttered to oneself, a monologue. **soliloquist**

n. **soliloquize, soliloquise** *v.i.* **soliloquizer** *n.* [L *sōliloquium* (from *sōlus*, SOLE[3], *loquī*, to speak)]

soliped (sol´iped) *n.*, *a.* (an animal) having solid, as distinct from cloven, hoofs. [mod. L *solipedem* (nom. *solipēs*), from *sōlus*, alone, *pēs*, foot]

solipsism (sol´ipsizm) *n.* the philosophical theory that the only knowledge possible is that of oneself, absolute egoism. **solipsist** *n.*, *a.* **solipsistic** (-sis´-) *a.* [L *soli-*, *sōlus*, SOLE[3], *ipse*, self, -ISM]

Usage note See note under SOLECISM.

solitaire (sol´iteə) *n.* **1** a gem, esp. a diamond, set singly in a ring or other jewel. **2** a jewel, esp. a ring, set with a single gem. **3** a game for one player, played on a board with hollows and marbles or holes and pegs, in which marbles or pegs are removed from the board as others are jumped over them, till only one remains. **4** (*esp. N Am.*) a card game for one player, patience. **5** an American or W Indian rock-thrush. **6** an extinct flightless bird, *Pezophaps solitarius*, related to the dodo. [F, as SOLITARY]

solitary (sol´itəri) *a.* **1** living or being alone, lonely, not gregarious. **2** (of plants) growing singly. **3** passed or spent alone (*a solitary life*). **4** (of a place) unfrequented, sequestered, secluded. **5** single, individual, sole (*can't think of a solitary reason*). ~*n.* (*pl.* **solitaries**) **1** a person who lives in solitude, a recluse. **2** (*coll.*) solitary confinement. **solitarily** *adv.* **solitariness** *n.* **solitary confinement** *n.* in a prison, incarceration without the company of others, isolation. [A-F *solitaire* (F *solitaire*), L *sōlitārius* (*sōlitas*, loneliness, from *sōlus*, SOLE[3])]

solitude (sol´itūd) *n.* **1** the condition of being solitary, seclusion, loneliness. **2** somewhere isolated and empty of people. **solitudinous** (-tū´dinəs) *a.* [L *sōlitūdo*, from *sōlus*, alone]

solmization (solmizā´shən), **solmisation** *n.* **1** the association of the syllables *doh, ray, me, fah, soh, lah, te* with the notes of the musical scale, *doh* being C in the fixed-doh system, or the keynote in tonic sol-fa. **2** a recital of the notes of the gamut, sol-faing. [F, from *solmiser* (SOL[2], MI (ME[1]), -IZE)]

solo (sō´lō) *n.* (*pl.* **solos, soli** (-lē)) **1** a composition or passage played by a single instrument or sung by a single voice, usu. with an accompaniment. **2 a** solo whist. **b** a bid in this game to win five tricks, or the accomplishment of this. **3** a solo flight. **4** any unaided or unaccompanied effort by one person. ~*a.*, *adv.* unaccompanied, alone. ~*v.i.* (*3rd pers. sing. pres.* **soloes,** *pres.p.* **soloing,** *past, p.p.* **soloed**) **1** to perform a musical solo. **2** to fly an aircraft unaccompanied. **solo climbing** *n.* rock-climbing without ropes or the assistance of a partner. **solo flight** *n.* a flight in an aircraft by a single person. **soloist** *n.* **solo stop** *n.* any of the organ stops adapted for imitating a solo performance on a particular musical instrument. **solo whist** *n.* a card game for four people somewhat resembling whist. [It., as SOLE[3]]

Solomon (sol´əmən) *n.* a very wise man (after King Solomon of Israel, d. *c.* 930 BC). **Solomonic** (-mon´-) *a.* **Solomon's seal** *n.* **1** a plant, *Polygonatum multiflorum*, with drooping white flowers and a root-stalk marked with scars which are said to account for the name. **2** a six-pointed star, the Star of David.

Solon (sō´lon) *n.* a sage, esp. a wise law-maker. [*Solon*, Athenian statesman and sage, *c.* 638–*c.* 558 BC]

solstice (sol´stis) *n.* either of the times (about 21 June and 22 Dec.) and points at which the sun is farthest from the celestial equator (north in summer and south in winter). **solstitial** (-stish´əl) *a.* [F, from L *sōlstitium* (*sol*, sun, *-stitium*, from *statum*, neut. p.p. of *sistere*, to cause to stand)]

soluble (sol´ūbəl) *a.* **1** capable of being dissolved in a fluid. **2** capable of being solved. **solubility** (-bil´-) *n.* **1** the quality or state of being soluble. **2** the number of grams of substance required to saturate 100 grams of solvent. **solubilize, solubilise** *v.t.* to render soluble, or more soluble. **solubilization** (-zā´shən) *n.* **soluble glass** *n.* water-glass. **solute** (-ūt) *n.* a dissolved substance. **solution** (səloo´shən) *n.* **1** the resolution or act or process of solving a problem, difficulty etc. **2** the correct answer to a problem, puzzle etc. or the means of solving it. **3** the liquefaction of a solid or gaseous body by mixture with a liquid. **4** the liquid combination so produced. **5** the condition of being dissolved. **6** RUBBER SOLUTION (under RUBBER[1]). **7** separation, dissolution, disintegration. **solution set** *n.* (*Math.*) a full set of solutions, e.g. of an equation. [F, from L *solvere*, to SOLVE]

solus (sō´ləs), (*fem.*) **sola** (-lə) *a.*, *adv.* in stage directions etc., alone. [L]

solute, solution SOLUBLE.

Solutrean (solū´triən, -loo´-), **Solutrian** *a.* of or relating to the period of Upper Palaeolithic culture between the Aurignacian and Magdalenian periods, including flint and bone instruments and carvings on stone. [*Solutre*, France]

solve (solv) *v.t.* **1** to resolve or find an answer to (a problem etc.). **2** to clear up, to settle, to put an end to. **3** to dissolve. **solvable** *a.* **solvability** (-bil´-) *n.* **solvate**[1] (sol´vāt, solvāt´) *n.* a combination of a solute with a solvent. **solvate**[2] (-vāt) *v.t.* to combine (a solute) with a solvent. ~*v.i.* (of a solute) to combine with a solvent. **solvation** (-vā´shən) *n.* **solvent** (-vənt) *a.* **1** having the power to dissolve. **2** able to pay all just debts or claims. ~*n.* **1** a liquid that can dissolve a substance. **2** something which solves. **solvency** *n.* **solvent abuse** *n.* the using of solvents (such as glue or petrol) as drugs by inhaling their fumes. **solver** *n.* [L *solvere*]

Som. *abbr.* Somerset.

soma[1] (sō´mə) *n.* (*pl.* **somata** (sō´mətə)) **1** the body as distinguished from soul and spirit. **2** the body of an organism excluding its reproductive cells. **somatic** (səmat´ik) *a.* of or relating to the body as distinct from the mind, corporeal, physical. **somatically** *adv.* **somatic cell** *n.* any non-reproductive cell of a living organism. **somato-** (sō´mətō) *comb. form* body. **somatogenic** (-jen´ik) *a.* originating in the somatic cells of an organism. **somatology** (-ol´əji) *n.* the science of organic bodies, esp. human anatomy and physiology. **somatological** (-loj´-) *a.* **somatologist** *n.* **somatotonic** (-ton´ik) *a.* showing the extrovert and assertive behaviour thought typical of mesomorphs. **somatotrophin** (-trō´fin) *n.* a growth-promoting hormone secreted by the pituitary gland. **somatotype** (sō´mətōtīp) *n.* a physical type (e.g. an endomorph, mesomorph or ectomorph). [Gr. *soma*, the body, a dead body]

soma[2] (sō´mə) *n.* **1** an intoxicating liquor used in connection with ancient Vedic worship. **2** the plant whose juice it is made from. [Sansk.]

Somali (səmah´li) *n.* (*pl.* **Somalis, Somali**) **1** a member of a people inhabiting Somalia in NE Africa. **2** the language of this people. ~*a.* of or relating to this people, their language or their country.

somatic, somato- etc. SOMA[1].

sombre (som´bə), (*N Am.*) **somber** *a.* **1** dark, gloomy. **2** solemn, melancholy. **3** grave, worrying (*a sombre outlook*). **sombrely** *adv.* **sombreness** *n.* **sombrous** *a.* [F (perh. EX-, or SUB-, L *umbra*, shade)]

sombrero (sombreə´rō) *n.* (*pl.* **sombreros**) a wide-brimmed hat worn esp. in Mexico. [Sp., from *sombra*, shade, as SOMBRE]

sombrous SOMBRE.

some (sŭm) *a.* **1** an indeterminate quantity, number etc. of. **2** an appreciable if limited amount etc. of. **3** several. **4** (at least) a few, a little (*I do have some common sense*). **5** a considerable quantity, amount etc. of (*It'll take some time to sort out*). **6** a certain, a particular but not definitely known or specified (person or thing) (*Some psychologist said so*). 7 certain (members of a group) or a certain (proportion of a total amount) in contrast to the others or the rest (*Some people are allergic to gluten*). 8 used to present an approximate number (*some 200 people*). 9 (*chiefly N Am.*) striking, outstanding (*That's some kitchen*). ~*adv.* (*coll.*) to some extent (*You've certainly improved some*). ~*pron.* 1 a particular but unspecified amount or quantity. 2 certain unspecified ones. **and then some** (*sl.*) and a lot more. **some few** FEW. **somebody** *pron.* some person. ~*n.* (*pl.* **somebodies**) a person of consequence. **someday, some day** *adv.* at some unspecified time in the future. **somehow** *adv.* 1 in some indeterminate way, for some unknown reason (*Somehow I miss him still*). 2 in some way or other, no matter how (*I must see you somehow*). 3 by some indeterminate means. **someone** *pron.*, *n.* somebody. **someone or other, something or other** *pron.* an unspecified person or thing. **someplace** *adv.* (*esp. N Am.*) somewhere. **something** *pron.*, *n.* 1 some indeterminate, unknown or unspecified thing (*Have something to eat; Something's happened; He's an expert on something, I forget what*). 2 some quantity or portion (*She has something of her mother in her*). 3 a thing of consequence or importance (*You made it - that's quite something*). ~†*adv.* in some degree, somewhat. **or something** used to indicate a further unspecified possibility (*The train must be late or something*). **something like** LIKE[1]. **something of** by way of being (*She's something of an expert on early music*). **something of the kind** KIND. **to have something on someone** HAVE. **to see something of** to meet (someone) occasionally. **something else** *n.* (*chiefly N Am., sl.*) a person or thing inspiring wonder, awe, disbelief etc. **sometime** *adv.* 1 at some unspecified time. 2 †once, formerly, at one time. ~*a.* former, late. **sometimes** *adv.* occasionally, now and then. **someway** *adv.* in some unspecified way. **somewhat** *adv.* to some extent, rather. ~†*n.* 1 a certain amount or degree. 2 something. **more than somewhat** considerably (*I was more than somewhat annoyed*). **somewhen** *adv.* (*coll.*) at some time. **somewhere** *n., adv.* 1 (in, at or to) some unknown or unspecified place. 2 (in) some place or other. **somewhere about** approximately (*aged somewhere about 45*). **to get somewhere** to make headway, to progress. [OE *sum* (cp. Icel. *sumr*, Dan. *somme*, pl., OHG *sum*), cogn. with SAME]

-some[1] (səm) *suf.* 1 forming adjectives from verbs, nouns or adjectives, denoting qualities, as *wearisome, loathsome, toothsome, wholesome.* 2 forming nouns from numbers, denoting groups of a certain number of people, as *threesome, foursome, eightsome* etc. [OE *-sum* (cp. Dut. *-zaam*, G *-sam*, Icel. *-samr*), as SOME]

-some[2] (sōm) *comb.form* a body, as in *chromosome.* [Gr. *soma*, body]

somebody, somehow etc. SOME.

somersault (sŭm´əsawlt), **summersault** *n.* a leap, or a forward roll on the ground, in which one turns head over heels and lands on one's feet. ~*v.i.* to execute a somersault. [OF *sombresaut*, Prov. *sobresaut* (L *suprā*, above, *saltum*, nom. *-tus*, a leap)]

something, sometime etc. SOME.

somite (sō´mīt) *n.* a segment of the body of an invertebrate animal such as an earthworm, or of the embryo of a vertebrate animal, a metamere. **somitic** (-mit´-) *a.* [Gr. *sōma*, body, -ITE[1]]

sommelier (som´əlyā, sŭm´-, səmel´-) *n.* a wine waiter. [F from OF from OProv. *saumalier*, pack-animal driver, from L *sagma*, a packsaddle, from Gr.]

somnambulance (somnam´būləns) *n.* sleepwalking. **somnambulant** *n., a.* **somnambulate** *v.i.* to sleepwalk. **somnambulation** (-lā´shən) *n.* **somnambulator** *n.* **somnambulism** *n.* the activity or phenomenon of walking or performing other actions in sleep or a condition resembling sleep. **somnambulist** *n.* **somnambulistic** (-lis´-) *a.* [L *somnus*, sleep, *ambulāre*, to walk]

somniferous (somnif´ərəs) *a.* causing or inducing sleep. **somniferously** *adv.* **somnific** *a.* [L *somnifer* (*somni-*, *somnus*, sleep, -FEROUS)]

somniloquism (somnil´əkwizm), †**somniloquence,** †**somniloquy** (-kwi) *n.* the activity or habit of talking in one's sleep. **somniloquist** *n.* [L *loquī*, to talk]

somnolent (som´nələnt) *a.* 1 sleepy, drowsy. 2 inducing sleep or drowsiness. 3 (*Med.*) in an unnaturally drowsy state. **somnolence, somnolency** *n.* **somnolently** *adv.* [earlier and OF *sompnolent*, L *somnolentus* (*somno-*, *somnus*, sleep, suf. *-lentus*)]

son (sŭn) *n.* 1 a male child in relation to a parent or parents. 2 a male descendant. 3 a form of address used by an old person to a youth, or by a priest or teacher to a disciple etc. 4 a native (of a country). 5 an inheritor, exponent or product (of a quality, art, occupation etc.) (*the sons of toil*). **the Son** Christ as the second person of the Trinity. **son-in-law** *n.* (*pl.* **sons-in-law**) a daughter's husband. **sonless** *a.* **sonny** *n.* a familiar, often patronizing or belittling term of address to a boy or man. **son of a bitch, sonofabitch** *n.* (*pl.* **sons of bitches**) (*derog.*) a man. **son of a gun** *n.* a rascal. **Son of Man** *n.* the second person in the Trinity, Christ, the Messiah. **son of the manse** *n.* the son of a minister. **sonship** *n.* the state of being a son. [OE *sunu*, cp. Dut. *zoon*, G *Sohn*, Icel. *sunr*, *sonr*, OHG *sunu*]

sonant (sō´nənt) *a.* voiced and syllabic. ~*n.* 1 a vowel or other voiced sound or letter. 2 a syllabic consonant, e.g. syllabic *l*, *m* or *n*. 3 any of the frictionless continuants or nasals, e.g. *l, m, n, ng, r.* **sonance** *n.* [L *sonans -ntem*, pres.p. of *sonāre*, to SOUND[1]]

sonar (sō´nah) *n.* a device which detects the presence and position of underwater objects by means of echo-soundings or emitted sound. [*so*und *na*vigation *r*anging]

sonata (sənah´tə) *n.* a musical composition for one instrument, or for one instrument accompanied on the piano, usu. of three or four movements in different rhythms. **sonata form** *n.* a musical form used esp. in the first movement of a sonata, typically consisting of an exposition, a development and a recapitulation. **sonatina** (sonətē´nə) *n.* a short or simple sonata. [It., from L *sonāta*, fem. p.p. of *sonāre*, to SOUND[1]]

sondage (sondahzh´, sō-) *n.* (*pl.* **sondages** (-dahzh´)) in archaeology, a trial excavation or inspection trench. [F, a sounding]

sonde (sond) *n.* a scientific device for gathering information about atmospheric conditions at high altitudes, a radiosonde. [F, sounding line]

son et lumière (son ā loomieə´) *n.* an outdoor entertainment at a historic location which recreates past events associated with it using sound effects, a spoken narration, music, and special lighting. [F, sound and light]

song (song) *n.* 1 a short poem intended or suitable for singing, esp. one set to music. 2 a musical composition accompanied by words for singing. 3 an instrumental piece of a similar character. 4 musical or modulated utterance with the voice, singing (*She would break into song occasionally*). 5 a melodious utterance, as the musical cry of a bird. 6 poetry, verse. **for a song** for a trifle, very cheaply (*bought it for a song; going for a song*). **to be on song** to be in top form, to be performing at one's best. **to make a song and dance** to make a fuss (about). **songbird** *n.* 1 any bird with a musical cry or call. 2 any perching bird of the suborder Oscines, having a syrinx or song-organ. **songbook** *n.* a book of songs with music. **song cycle** *n.* a sequence of songs concerned with the same subject or theme. **songless** *a.* **Song of Songs, Song of Solomon** *n.* an Old Testament book attributed to Solomon, containing love songs. **songsmith** *n.* a composer or writer of songs, a songwriter. **song sparrow** *n.* an American songbird, *Melospiza melodia.* **songster** (-stə) *n.* **1** a person skilled in singing. **2** a songbird. **songstress** (-stris) *n.* a female singer. **song thrush** *n.* a European thrush, *Turdus philomelos,* whose song is partly imitated from that of other birds. **songwriter** *n.* a writer or composer of esp. popular songs. **songwriting** *n.* [OE *sang, song,* cp. Dut. *zang,* G and Dan. *sang,* Icel. *söngr,* rel. to SING]

sonic (son´ik) *a.* **1** of, relating to or producing sound waves. **2** travelling at about the speed of sound. **sonically** *adv.* **sonic barrier** *n.* the sound barrier. **sonic boom, sonic bang** *n.* the loud noise caused by a shock wave produced by an aircraft or projectile travelling at supersonic speed. **sonics** *n.* the branch of physics concerned with sound waves.

sonnet (son´it) *n.* a poem of 14 iambic pentameter (ten-syllable) lines, usu. consisting of an octave rhyming *a b b a a b b a,* and a sestet with three rhymes variously arranged. ~*v.i.* (*pres.p.* **sonneting,** *past, p.p.* **sonneted**) to compose sonnets. ~*v.t.* to address sonnets to. **sonneteer** (-tiə´) *n.* (*usu. derog.*) a writer of sonnets. [F, from It. *sonetto,* dim. of *sono,* L *sonus,* SOUND[1]]

sonny SON.

sonobuoy (sō´nəboi) *n.* a buoy fitted with instruments for detecting underwater sounds and communicating them by radio to surface vessels etc. [L *sonus,* sound; BUOY]

sonofabitch SON.

sonogram (sō´nəgram) *n.* **1** a visual representation of a sound produced by means of a sonograph. **2** a sonogram produced from an ultrasound examination. **sonograph** (-grahf) *n.* an instrument for scanning and recording sound, showing the distribution of energy at various frequencies. [L *sōnus,* sound, -GRAM]

sonometer (sənom´itə) *n.* **1** (*Mus.*) a device for determining the vibration frequency of a string etc. **2** an audiometer. [L *sōnus,* sound, -METER]

sonorous (son´ərəs) *a.* **1** giving out sound, resonant. **2** loud-sounding, sounding rich or full. **3** high-sounding, impressive. **sonorant** *n.* **1** a frictionless continuant or nasal (*l, r, m, n, ng*) which has a consonantal or vocalic function depending on its position within a syllable. **2** either of the consonants represented by *w* or *y* which have consonantal or vocalic articulations, a semivowel. **sonority** (sənor´-), **sonorousness** *n.* **sonorously** *adv.* [L *sonōrus,* from *sonor,* sound, from *sonāre,* to SOUND[1]]

sonsy (son´si), **sonsie** *a.* (*comp.* **sonsier,** *superl.* **sonsiest**) (*chiefly Sc., Ir.*) **1** happy or jolly-looking, buxom, well-favoured, plump. **2** good-natured, tractable. **3** lucky. [Sc. *sonse,* Gael. *sonas,* good fortune, -Y[1]]

sook[1] (sook) *n.* **1** (*dial.*) a baby. **2** (*derog.*) a timid person, a coward. **3** (*New Zeal., coll.*) a calf. [dial. *suck,* a hand-reared calf, used to call a calf]

sook[2] (sook) *n.* (*Sc.*) a person who tries to ingratiate themselves, a toady or sycophant. [var. of SUCK]

sool (sool) *v.t.* (*Austral., New Zeal., coll.*) **1** to incite (esp. a dog) to attack. **2** (of a dog) to attack or worry (an animal). **sooler** *n.* [SOWL]

soon (soon) *adv.* (*comp.* **sooner,** *superl.* **soonest**) **1** in a short time from now (*You'll be eighteen soon*). **2** in a short time after a specified or established time (*I soon regretted it*). **3** early (*How soon can you come?*). **4** quickly, readily, willingly (*We'd as soon pay now*). **as soon as 1** at the moment that (*I'll ring as soon as I hear; Ring as soon as possible*). **2** immediately after (*As soon as she'd said it, she realized her gaffe*). **3** not later than (*He went to bed as soon as the clock struck eleven*). **so soon as** as soon as. **sooner** *adv.* **1** in a shorter time. **2** earlier. **3** rather, more willingly. **no sooner...than** immediately (*No sooner did she make the promise than she withdrew it*). **sooner or later 1** sometime or other. **2** inevitably, eventually. **soonest** *adv.* (*coll.*) **1** in the shortest time. **2** earliest. **3** as soon as possible. **soonish** *adv.* [OE *sōna,* cp. OS and OHG *sān,* Goth. *suns*]

Usage note *No sooner...than* is preferred to *no sooner...when.*

soot (sut) *n.* a black substance composed of carbonaceous particles rising from fuel in a state of combustion and deposited in a chimney etc. ~*v.t.* to cover, manure or soil with soot. **sootless** (-lis) *a.* **sooty** *a.* (*comp.* **sootier,** *superl.* **sootiest**). **sootily** *adv.* **sootiness** *n.* [OE *sōt,* cp. Icel. *sōt,* Dan. *sod,* Swed. *sot*]

sooth (sooth) †*n.* **1** truth, reality. **2** (*Shak.*) cajolery, blandishment. **in good sooth** in truth. **soothsay** *v.i.* (*past, p.p.* **soothsaid**) to prognosticate, to divine. **soothsayer** *n.* a prognosticator, a diviner. [OE *sōth,* for *santh* (cp. Icel. *sannr,* Swed. *sann*), from root *es-,* to be]

soothe (soodh) *v.t.* **1** to calm, to tranquillize. **2** to soften, to mitigate, to assuage. **3** †to humour, to flatter, to gratify. **soother** *n.* **soothing** *a.* **soothingly** *adv.* [OE *gesōthian,* to confirm, to assent to, from *sōth,* truth]

sop (sop) *n.* **1** a piece of bread etc. steeped or dipped and softened in milk, broth, gravy etc. **2** something done or given to bribe or pacify. ~*v.t.* (*pres.p.* **sopping,** *past., p.p.* **sopped**) **1** to dip or steep in broth etc. **2** to take (up) by absorption. ~*v.i.* (*usu. pres.p.*) to be thoroughly wet or soaked. **sopping** *a.* wet through, soaking. **sopping wet** *a.* wet through. **soppy** *a.* (*comp.* **soppier,** *superl.* **soppiest**) (*coll.*) **1** maudlin, sentimental, weak-minded. **2** foolishly doting (on). **3** wet through. **soppily** *adv.* **soppiness** *n.* **sop to Cerberus** *n.* a propitiatory bribe. [OE *sopp* (cp. Icel. *soppa*), cogn. with SUP]

Sophi SOPHY.

sophism (sof´izm) *n.* a plausible but specious or fallacious argument. **sophist** *n.* **1** any one of a class of men in ancient Athens who taught philosophy, dialectic, rhetoric etc., for pay. **2** a plausible but fallacious reasoner, a quibbler or casuist. **sophistic** (səfis´-), **sophistical** *a.* **sophistically** *adv.* **sophisticate**[1] (-fis´tikāt) *v.t.* **1** to make (a person) more cultivated or refined. **2** to make (machinery or methods) more complex or refined. **3 a** to envelop or obscure (a subject) with sophistry. **b** to mislead or delude (someone) thus. **4** to deprive (a person or thing) of simplicity, to make perverted, affected or artificial. **5** to alter or garble (a text etc.) in order to support one's arguments etc. **6** to make (wine etc.) spurious by admixture, to adulterate. ~*v.i.* to be sophistical. **sophisticate**[2] (-kət) *n.* a sophisticated person. **sophisticated** *a.* **1** worldly-wise; self-assured. **2** refined; cultured. **3** complex, highly developed. **4** subtle. **5** adulterated. **sophisticatedly** *adv.* **sophistication** (-kā´shən) *n.* **sophisticator** *n.* **sophistry** *n.* (*pl.* **sophistries**) **1** the use, or art of using, plausible but specious arguments to persuade hearers, casuistry, sophism. **2** a plausible but fallacious argument. [OF *sophisme,* L and Gr. *sophisma,* from *sophizein,* to instruct, from *sophos,* wise]

Sophoclean (sofəklē´ən) *a.* of, relating to or characteristic of Sophocles, the Greek tragic poet (*c.* 496–*c.* 406 BC). [L *Sophoclēus,* Gr. *Sophokleios* (*Sophocles,* -AN)]

sophomore (sof´əmaw) *n.* (*chiefly N Am.*) a second-year student. **sophomoric** (-mor´-), **sophomorical** *a.* **sophomorically** *adv.* [earlier *sophumer,* perh. *sophum,* old form of SOPHISM, -ER[1]; or Gr. *sophos,* wise, *mōros,* foolish]

Sophy (sō´fi), **Sophi** *n.* (*pl.* **Sophies**) (*Hist.*) the title of a Persian sovereign, the shah. [from the Persian *Ṣafi* dynasty (1502–1736), descended from *Ṣafi-ud-dīn*]

-sophy (səfi) *comb. form* denoting (a branch of) knowledge.

soporific (sopərif´ik) *a.* **1** causing or tending to cause sleep. **2** drowsy, sleepy. ~*n.* a soporific medicine or agent. **soporiferous** *a.* **soporifically** *adv.* [L *sopor, sopōris*, sleep, -FIC]

sopping, soppy SOP.

soprano (səprah´nō) *n.* (*pl.* **sopranos, soprani** (-nē)) **1** the highest singing voice, treble. **2** a boy or female singer with this voice. **3** a musical part for this voice. **4** an instrument that has the highest range within a family of instruments. **5** the player of such an instrument. ~*a.* of, or having, a treble part, voice or pitch. **sopranino** (soprənē´nō) *n.* (*pl.* **sopraninos, sopranini** (-nē)) an instrument, esp. a recorder or saxophone, with a pitch higher than soprano. **sopranist** *n.* **soprano clef** *n.* (*Hist.*) a clef that placed middle C on the lowest line of the stave. **soprano recorder** *n.* (*N Am.*) a descant recorder. [It., from *sopra*, above, from L *suprā*]

sora (saw´rə), **sora rail** *n.* a bird, *Porzana carolina*, inhabiting the Carolina marshes and caught for food. [prob. from N Am. Ind.]

Sorb (sawb) *n.* **1** a member of a Slavonic people primarily of E Germany, a Wend. **2** the language of this people, Wendish. **Sorbian** *a., n.* [G *Sorbe*, var. of *Serbe*, SERB]

sorb (sawb) *n.* **1** (*also* **sorb-apple**) the service tree. **2** its fruit. **sorbate** (-bāt) *n.* a salt of sorbic acid. **sorbic** *a.* **sorbic acid** *n.* an acid obtained from rowan berries, used in preserving food. **sorbitol** (-itol) *n.* a white crystalline substance obtained from sugar and often used as a sugar substitute or in the manufacture of synthetic resins. [F *sorbe*, L *sorbus*]

sorbefacient (sawbifā´shənt) *a.* promoting absorption. ~*n.* a substance or preparation promoting absorption. [L *sorbēre*, to ABSORB, -FACIENT]

sorbet (saw´bā) *n.* **1** an ice flavoured with fruit juice, spirit etc., a water ice. **2** sherbet. [F, as SHERBET]

sorbic, sorbitol SORB.

Sorbo® (saw´bō), **Sorbo rubber** *n.* a spongy kind of rubber. [ABSORB, -O]

sorcerer (saw´sərə) *n.* a person who uses magic, witchcraft, spells or enchantments, a wizard or magician. **sorceress** (-ris) *n.* a female magician or enchanter, a witch. **sorcerous** *a.* **sorcery** *n.* (*pl.* **sorceries**). [ME (*sorser*, OF *sorcier*, late L *sortiārius*, from *sortiāre*, to cast lots, from L *sors sortis*, lot]

sordavalite (saw´dəvəlīt) *n.* a vitreous silicate of alumina and magnesia found in diabase. [Swed. *sordawalit*, *Sordavala*, Finland]

sordid (saw´did) *a.* **1** foul, squalid, dirty. **2** mean, base, ignoble, vile. **3** avaricious, niggardly. **4** of a dull, muddy colour. **sordes** (-dēz) *n.* foul matter, filth, esp. foul discharges, excretions, encrustations etc. **sordidly** *adv.* **sordidness** *n.* [F *sordide*, L *sordidus*, from *sordes*, dirt, filth]

sordino (sawdē´nō) *n.* (*pl.* **sordini** (-nē)) a contrivance for deadening the sound of a bowed instrument or wind instrument, a mute, a damper. [It. *sordino*, L *surdus*, deaf, see SURD]

sore (saw) *a.* **1 a** (of a part of the body) tender and painful to the touch, esp. through disease, injury or irritation. **b** (of a person) suffering pain. **2** mentally distressed, aggrieved, vexed (at). **3** (*coll.*) annoyed. **4** causing annoyance or distress, irritating, exasperating. **5** †grievous, grave. **6** easily annoyed; touchy. ~†*adv.* sorely, grievously, severely, intensely. ~*n.* **1** a sore place on the body where the surface is bruised, broken or inflamed by a boil, ulcer etc. **2** that which excites resentment, remorse, grief etc. **a sight for sore eyes** SIGHT. **to stand out like a sore thumb** to be highly conspicuous. **sorehead** *n.* (*N Am., coll.*) an irritable person. **sorely** *adv.* **1** extremely, strongly (*was sorely tempted to be rude back*). **2** severely, gravely (*sorely insulted*). **soreness** *n.* **sore point** *n.* a subject etc. which arouses irritation, annoyance, retrospective hurt feelings etc. **sore throat** *n.* an inflamed condition of the membranous lining of the gullet etc., usu. due to a cold. [OE *sār* (cp. Dut. *zeer*, Icel. *sārr*), G *sehr*, sorely, very]

sorel (sor´əl), **sorell** *n.* a male fallow deer in its third year. [var. of SORREL[2]]

sorghum (saw´gəm) *n.* any member of the genus *Sorghum*, which includes the Indian millet, durra etc., much cultivated in the US for fodder etc. [mod. L, from F *sorgho*, etym. uncertain]

sori SORUS.

sorites (sərī´tēz) *n.* **1** a series of syllogisms so connected that the predicate of one forms the subject of that which follows, the subject of the first being ultimately united with the predicate of the last. **2** a sophistical argument in this form. **soritic** (-rit´-), **soritical** *a.* [L, from Gr. *sōritēs*, from *sōros*, heap]

soroptimist (sərop´timist) *n.* a member of an international organization of women's clubs, Soroptimist International. [L *soror*, sister, and OPTIMIST (under OPTIMISM)]

sororal (səraw´əl), **sororial** (-riəl) *a.* of, relating to or characteristic of a sister or sisters. **sororicide** (-ror´isīd) *n.* **1** the murder of a sister. **2** the murderer of a sister. **sorority** (-ror´i-) *n.* (*pl.* **sororities**) **1** (*N Am.*) a society of women students. **2** a body or association of women, a sisterhood. [F (L *soror*, sister, -AL[1])]

sorosis (sərō´sis) *n.* (*pl.* **soroses** (-sēz)) a fleshy fruit formed by the cohesion of numerous flowers etc., e.g. the pineapple. [mod. L (Gr. *sōros*, heap, -OSIS)]

sorption (sawp´shən) *n.* the separate processes, or simultaneous process, of absorption and adsorption. [back-formation from ABSORPTION (under ABSORB), ADSORPTION (under ADSORB)]

sorrel[1] (sor´əl) *n.* **1** a herb with acid leaves, *Rumex acetosa*, allied to the dock. **2** any of various plants with similar leaves, as wood sorrel. [OF *sorel* (F *surelle*), from MHG *sūr*, SOUR]

sorrel[2] (sor´əl) *a.* of a reddish- or yellowish-brown. ~*n.* **1** this colour. **2** a horse or other animal of this colour. **3** a sorel. [OF *sorel*, dim. of *sor*, sorrel horse]

sorrily, sorriness SORRY.

sorrow (sor´ō) *n.* **1** mental pain or distress from loss, disappointment etc., grief, sadness. **2** an event, thing or person causing this, an affliction, a misfortune. **3** mourning, lamentation. ~*v.i.* **1** to grieve. **2** to lament. **to drown one's sorrows** DROWN. **sorrower** *n.* **sorrowful** *a.* **sorrowfully** *adv.* **sorrowfulness** *n.* **sorrowing** *a., n.* [ME *sorwe*, OE *sorg* (cp. Dut. *zorg*, G *Sorge*, Icel., Dan. and Swed. *sorg*)]

sorry (sor´i) *a.* **1** penitent, apologetic (*I'm sorry for causing all this trouble*; *Sorry about the mess*). **2** feeling or showing grief, regretful (that) (*I'm sorry (that) you've been ill*). **3** feeling pity (for) (*was very sorry for the victims*). **4** poor, paltry, pitiful, despicable (*a sorry sight*; *a sorry effort*). ~*int.* used to express apology. **sorrily** *adv.* **sorriness** *n.* [OE *sārig* (*sār*, SORE, -Y)]

sort (sawt) *n.* **1** a group of instances of a certain thing identifiable, by having the same set of characteristics, as a subgroup or subdivision, a class, kind, type or species (*What sort of dog?*; *several sorts of humour*). **2** a more or less adequate example or instance of a kind (*A cassowary is a sort of bird*; *thinks she's some sort of expert*). **3** (*coll.*) a person, a type (of person) (*She's a good sort*; *He's not the complaining sort*). **4** a letter or other piece of printing type considered as part of a font. ~*v.t.* **1** to separate into sorts, classes etc. **2** to arrange. **3** (*esp. Sc.*) to resolve, deal with, fix or punish, to sort out. ~†*v.i.* to agree or accord (with). **after a sort** in a (usu. inadequate) way or fashion. **in some sort** after a sort, to a certain extent. **of a sort** of sorts. **of sorts** of an inferior or inadequate kind (*a dancer of sorts*). **out of sorts** **1** irritable, moody. **2** slightly unwell. **sort of** rather, to a degree, as it were (*sort of unsettled*). **to sort out** **1** to solve or resolve. **2** to clear out; to tidy up. **3** to separate.

4 to arrange. 5 (*coll.*) to beat, to punish. **to sort out the men from the boys** MAN. **sortable** *a.* **sorter** *n.* a person who or something that sorts (e.g. mail). **sorting** *n.* **sorting office** *n.* an office where mail is sorted. **sort-out** *n.* an act of sorting out. [OF *sorte*, L *sortem*, nom. *sors*, lot, chance, condition]

Usage note *Sort of* should not be used as a plural (as in *those sort of men*) or followed by the indefinite article *a, an* (as in *this sort of a woman*).

sortie (saw´ti) *n.* 1 a sally, esp. of troops from a besieged place in order to attack or raid. 2 a mission or attack by a single aircraft. ~*v.i.* (*3rd pers. sing. pres.* **sorties,** *pres.p.* **sortieing,** *past, p.p.* **sortied**) 1 to sally. 2 to make a sortie. [F, fem. p.p. of *sortir*, to go out]

sortilege (saw´tilij) *n.* divination by drawing lots. [OF (F *sortilège*), med. L *sortilegium*, from L *sortilegus*, diviner (*sors sortis*, lot, *legere*, to choose)]

sorus (saw´rəs) *n.* (*pl.* **sori** (-rī)) (*Bot.*) a cluster of spore-producing bodies (sporangia) esp. on the underside of a fern leaf. [mod. L, from Gr. *sōros*, heap]

SOS (esōes´) *n.* (*pl.* **SOSs**) 1 an internationally recognized distress call in Morse code. 2 any distress call or plea for help (e.g. an emergency broadcast on television or radio). ~*v.i.* (*3rd pers. sing. pres.* **SOS-es,** *pres.p.* **SOS-ing,** *past, p.p.* **SOS-ed**) to call for help or rescue. [Morse letters, chosen for easy transmission]

sostenuto (sostinū´tō) *a., adv.* (*Mus.*) (played) in a steadily sustained manner. ~*n.* (*pl.* **sostenutos**) a passage to be played thus. [It., p.p. of *sostenere*, to SUSTAIN]

sot (sot) *n.* a habitual drunkard, a person habitually muddled (as if) with excessive drinking. ~*v.i.* (*pres.p.* **sotting,** *past, p.p.* **sotted**) to tipple, to get drunk habitually. **sottish** *a.* [ME, prob. from OF (F *sot sotte*), cp. MDut. *zot*, MHG *sot*]

soterial (sətiə´riəl) *a.* of or relating to salvation. **soteriology** (-ol´əji) *n.* the doctrine of salvation. **soteriological** (-loj´-) *a.* [Gr. *sōtēria*, salvation, from *sōtēr*, saviour, cogn. with *sōzein*, to save]

Sothic (sō´thik, soth´-) *a.* of or relating to the star Sirius, esp. with reference to the 1460-year cycle in Egyptian reckoning, which began with a year whose start coincided with the heliacal rising of Sirius. [*Sōthis*, Egyptian name of Sirius]

sotto voce (sotō vō´chi) *adv.* under one's voice, in an undertone. [It.]

sou (soo) *n.* (*pl.* **sous**) 1 (*Hist.*) a French copper coin worth 1/12 of a livre. 2 (*Hist.*) the 5-centime piece. 3 (*with neg.*) a very small amount of money (*haven't a sou*). [F, from OF *sol*, L *solidum*, cp. SOLD]

soubise (soobēz´), **soubise sauce** *n.* a white sauce made from onions, butter, béchamel sauce and consommé. [Prince de *Soubise*, 1715–87, a French marshal]

soubrette (soobret´) *n.* 1 a lady's maid. 2 a mischievous coquettish scheming female character in a comedy, esp. the role of a lady's maid, or an actress or singer practised in such roles. 3 a person who displays similar characteristics, a flirt, a coquette. [F, from Prov. *soubreto*, fem. of *soubret*, affected, from *soubra*, to exceed, from L *superāre*, to be above]

soubriquet SOBRIQUET.

souchong (soo´shong) *n.* a black China tea made from the youngest leaves. [F, from Chin. *hsiao-chung* (*hsiao*, small, *chung*, sort)]

souffle (soo´fəl) *n.* (*Med.*) a low whispering or murmur heard in the auscultation of an organ etc. [F, from *souffler*, L *sufflare* (SUF-, *flāre*, to blow)]

soufflé (soo´flā) *n.* any of various savoury or sweet, cooked or uncooked dishes made of beaten whites of eggs etc. ~*a.* made light and frothy by beating etc. **souffléed** *a.* [F, p.p. of *souffler*, see SOUFFLE]

sough[1] (sow, sŭf, sookh) *v.i.* to make a murmuring, sighing sound, like the wind. ~*n.* such a sound. [OE *swōgan*, prob. imit. in orig., cp. Goth. *ufswōgjan*]

sough[2] (sŭf) *n.* a drain, a sewer, a water-channel, esp. in a mine. [etym. uncertain]

sought SEEK.

souk (sook) *n.* an outside, often covered market in a Muslim country (esp. in N Africa and the Middle East). [Arab. *sūq*, market]

soul (sōl) *n.* 1 the spiritual part of a person. 2 a spiritual being. 3 the moral and emotional part of a person. 4 the rational part of a person, consciousness. 5 the vital principle and mental powers possessed by humans in common with lower animals. 6 the essential or animating or inspiring force or principle, the life, the energy in anything. 7 a person regarded as providing this, a leader, a moving spirit. 8 the heart. 9 spirit, courage, nobility. 10 a disembodied spirit (*lost souls*). 11 a human being, a person (*haven't seen a soul all day*). 12 an epitome, embodiment or exemplification (*I'll be the soul of tact*). 13 soul music. ~*a.* 1 of or relating to soul music. 2 of, relating to or characteristic of black Americans or their culture, food etc. **to be the life and soul of** to be the liveliest or most entertaining person at (a party etc.). **to be the soul of honour** to be incapable of acting dishonourably. **upon my soul!** good gracious! goodness me! **soul brother, soul sister** *n.* a fellow black person. **soul-destroying** *a.* unrewarding, frustrating, boring. **souled** *a.* (*usu. in comb.*, as *high-souled*). **soul food** *n.* (*coll.*) the traditional foods of American blacks in the south (e.g. yams, chitterlings). **soulful** *a.* 1 rich in, satisfying or expressing the spiritual, emotional or higher intellectual qualities. 2 sad, longing, yearning, mournful. **soulfully** *adv.* **soulfulness** *n.* **soulless** *a.* 1 impersonal, dull, uninteresting. 2 lacking sensitivity or finer feeling. 3 having no soul. **soullessly** *adv.* **soullessness** *n.* **soul mate** *n.* a person with whom one feels a close affinity. **soul music** *n.* a type of music made popular by American blacks, combining elements of blues, gospel, jazz and pop. **soul-searching** *n.* a critical and close examination of one's motives, actions etc. ~*a.* manifesting a tendency towards such self-examination. [OE *sāwel*, *sāwl*, cp. Dut. *ziel*, G *Seele*, Dan. *sjæl*, Swed. *själ*]

sound[1] (sownd) *n.* 1 the sensation produced through the organs of hearing. 2 that which causes this sensation, the vibrations affecting the ear. 3 (*also* **musical sound**) vibrations of a regular and continuous nature as opposed to noise. 4 other similar vibrations, whether audible or inaudible. 5 that which can be heard. 6 a specific tone or note. 7 an articulate utterance corresponding to a particular vowel or consonant. 8 an impression given by words (*don't like the sound of his illness*). 9 mere talk. 10 dialogue, music etc. accompanying visual images. 11 (*pl., sl.*) music, esp. popular music. 12 hearing distance, earshot. ~*a.* of or relating to, or broadcast on, radio as opposed to television. ~*v.i.* 1 to make or give out sound. 2 to convey a particular impression by sound or word (*She sounded upset; Their kitchen sounds great*). 3 to give out a sound by way of summons, call or signal (*when the alarm sounded*). 4 to resonate. ~*v.t.* 1 to cause to sound. 2 to utter (a letter etc.) audibly. 3 to give a signal for by sound (*sound the alarm*). 4 to cause to resound, to make known, to proclaim (*sounding her praises*). 5 to test (e.g. the lungs) by the sound produced. **to sound off** 1 to boast. 2 to speak loudly, volubly, angrily etc. **soundalike** *n.* a thing or person closely similar in sound to the one in question. **sound barrier** *n.* the build-up of air resistance to an aircraft etc. as it attains the speed of sound. **sound bite** *n.* a brief pithy, telling or representative extract from a recorded interview. **soundboard** *n.* 1 a board for enhancing the sounds made by various musical instruments. 2 a sounding board. **sound bow** *n.* the thick curved edge against which the tongue strikes in a bell. **soundbox** *n.* the hollow belly of a stringed instrument, responsible for its resonance. **sound card** *n.* a device that can be inserted into a computer to allow the use of audio applications. **soundcheck** *n.* a check made on sound equipment prior to recording. **sound effect** *n.* (*often pl.*) an imitation or reproduction of a sound used in the performance of a play or on the soundtrack of a film or broadcast. **sound engineer** *n.* an engineer responsible for the acoustics of a musical performance, broadcast etc. **sounder**[1] *n.* a person or thing that causes something to sound, or something that emits a sound. **sound film** *n.* a combination of the projection of a film and the synchronized sounds proper to it. **soundhole** *n.* an opening in the belly of some stringed musical instrument, such as the guitar. **sounding**[1] *a.* **1** making or giving out sound. **2** sonorous, resonant, noisy. **3** plausible, pompous, high-flown. **sounding board** *n.* **1** a canopy-like structure of wood or metal placed over a pulpit etc. to reflect sound towards the audience. **2** a sound board. **3** a person, institution, group etc., used to test reaction to a new idea or plan. **soundless** *a.* without a sound, silent. **soundlessly** *adv.* **soundlessness** *n.* **sound post** *n.* an upright supporting the belly of a violin etc., and transmitting sound-vibrations to the back. **soundproof** *a.* impenetrable to sound. *~v.t.* to make impenetrable to sound, to insulate against sound. **sound shift** *n.* in linguistics, a general or systematic change in pronunciation in any language. **sound spectrograph** *n.* an instrument for making a graphic representation of the frequency, intensity etc. of sound. **sound system** *n.* a set of apparatus for sound reproduction. **soundtrack** *n.* **1** the synchronized sound recording accompanying a film etc. **2** the portion along the side of a film which bears the continuous recording of the accompanying sound. **soundwave** *n.* a sound-propagating wave of disturbance in a medium such as air. [ME *soun*, F *son*, L *sonus*, whence *sonāre*, F *sonner*, to sound]

sound[2] (sownd) *a.* **1** whole, unimpaired, free from injury, defect or decay. **2** not diseased or impaired, healthy. **3** well-grounded, wise, well-established. **4** orthodox. **5** based on truth or reason, valid, correct. **6** thorough, complete. **7** solid, stable, firm. **8** trustworthy, honest. **9** solvent. **10 a** (of sleep) deep, unbroken. **b** (of a sleeper) tending to sleep deeply. *~adv.* soundly, fast (asleep). **sound as a bell** perfectly sound, free from any flaw. **soundly** *adv.* **soundness** *n.* [OE *sund*, cp. Dut. *gezond*, G *gesund*, Dan. and Swed. *sund*]

sound[3] (sownd) *v.t.* **1** to measure the depth of (a sea, channel etc.) or test the quality of (its bed) with a sounding line or sounding rod. **2** to find the depth of water in (the hold of a ship). **3** to gather information about pressure, temperature and humidity from (the upper atmosphere). **4** to test or examine (e.g. someone's bladder etc.) by means of a probe etc. *~v.i.* **1** to take soundings, to ascertain the depth of water. **2** (of a whale etc.) to dive deeply. *~n.* an instrument for exploring cavities of the body, a probe. **to sound out 1** to test, to examine, to endeavour to discover (intentions, feelings etc.). **2** to test the reaction of (someone) to a proposed move etc. **sounder**[2] *n.* a device for taking soundings. **sounding**[2] *n.* **1** the act of measuring the depth of water, esp. by means of an echo. **2** (*usu. pl.*) a measurement of depth taken thus. **3** (*pl.*) a part of the sea where the bottom can be reached by sounding. **4** the act of collecting a sample of opinions etc., esp. unofficially. **5** a test, an examination, a probe. **sounding-balloon** *n.* a balloon for gathering information above the upper atmosphere. **sounding lead** *n.* the weight on the end of a sounding line. **sounding line** *n.* a weighted wire or line for measuring the depth of water. **sounding rod** *n.* a graduated iron rod, used to ascertain the depth of water in a ship's hold. [F *sonder*, prob. from Scand. *sund*]

sound[4] (sownd) *n.* **1** a narrow passage of water, such as a strait connecting two seas. **2** the swim-bladder of a fish. [OE *sund*, cp. G, Icel., Dan. and Swed. *sund*, related to SWIM]

sounder[1] SOUND[1].

sounder[2] SOUND[3].

sounding[1] SOUND[1].

sounding[2] SOUND[3].

soup (soop) *n.* **1** a liquid food made from meat, fish or vegetables and stock. **2** anything resembling soup in consistency etc. **3** (*coll.*) a thick fog. **4** (*coll.*) a photographic developer. **5** (*sl.*) nitroglycerin or gelignite for safe-breaking. **in the soup** (*sl.*) in difficulties, in trouble. **to soup up** to modify (the engine of a car or motorcycle) in order to increase its power. **soup and fish** *n.* (*coll.*) men's evening dress. **souped-up** *a.* (of a vehicle engine) modified to increase its power. **soup kitchen** *n.* **1** a public establishment for supplying soup to the poor. **2** a mobile army kitchen. **soup-maigre** *n.* thin soup, made with fish or vegetables rather than meat, orig. for use on fast days. **soup plate** *n.* a deep plate for holding soup. **soup spoon** *n.* a large, or round-bowled, spoon, for drinking soup with. **soupy** *a.* (*comp.* **soupier**, *superl.* **soupiest**). **soupily** *adv.* **soupiness** *n.* [F *soupe*, from *souper*, to SUP]

soupçon (soop´sõ) *n.* a mere trace, taste or flavour (of). [F, as SUSPICION]

sour (sowə) *a.* **1** sharp or acid to the taste, like a lemon, tart. **2 a** tasting thus through fermentation, rancid. **b** tasting thus through unripeness. **3** bad-tempered, crabbed, morose, peevish. **4** disagreeable, jarring, inharmonious. **5** (of soil) excessively acidic or infertile. **6** (of petroleum gas etc.) containing sulphur compounds. *~v.t.* to make sour. *~v.i.* to become sour. *~n.* **1** (*chiefly N Am.*) a cocktail usu. made with a spirit and lemon juice, sugar and ice. **2** a solution of acid used for bleaching, curing hides etc. **3** something sour to the taste etc. **to go/ turn sour 1** to become sour. **2** to lose attraction or become distasteful. **sour cream** *n.* fresh cream soured by the introduction of bacteria, used in salads, cooking etc. **sourdough** *n.* **1** fermenting dough, orig. from a previous baking, used as leaven. **2** (*N Am.*) an old-time prospector in Alaska etc. *~a.* (of bread) made with fermenting yeast. **sour grapes** *n.pl.* peevish disdain for a desired object that is out of one's reach. **souring** *n.* **1** the process of becoming or turning sour. **2** a process of bleaching with acid etc. **3** (*dial.*) a crab apple. **sourish** *a.* **sourly** *adv.* **sour mash** *n.* (*N Am.*) a mash for brewing or distilling, acidified to speed up fermentation. **sourness** *n.* **sourpuss** *n.* (*coll.*) a habitually morose person. **soursop** *n.* the W Indian evergreen tree *Annona muricata*, or its large juicy fruit. [OE *sūr*, cp. Dut. *zuur*, G *sauer*, Icel. *sūrr*, Swed. *sur*, Dan. *suur*]

source (saws) *n.* **1** the spring or fountainhead from which a stream of water proceeds, a first cause, a generating force etc. **2** an origin, a beginning. **3** a person who or something that gives out, initiates or creates something. **4** a person or thing that provides inspiration or information. **5** a body that emits radiation. **6** part of a transistor from which carriers flow into the interelectrode conductivity channel. **7** (*Physics*) a point from which a current or fluid flows. *~v.t.* **1** to obtain (components, materials etc.) from a particular source. **2** to establish the source of. **at source** at the point of issue. **sourcebook** *n.* a book containing original documents for study. **source-criticism** *n.* the assessment of available, esp. successive, historical or literary sources. **source program** *n.* an original computer program which has been converted into machine language. [OF *sorse*, p.p. of *sordre* (F *sourdre*), L *surgere*, to rise, see SURGE]

sourdine (suədēn´) *n.* **1** a soft stop on an organ etc. **2** SORDINO. [F, as SORDINO]

sous- (soo) *pref.* (used before French-derived nouns) under-, subordinate, assistant etc. (*a sous-chef*).

sousaphone (soo´zəfōn) *n.* a brass wind instrument like a long curved tuba, carried so as to encircle the player's waist. **sousaphonist** *n.* [J. P. *Sousa*, 1854–1932, US composer and bandmaster]

souse (sows) *v.t.* **1** to pickle. **2** to plunge into or drench thoroughly with water etc. **3** (*usu. p.p.*, *sl.*) to inebriate. ~*v.i.* **1** to plunge into water or another liquid. **2** to become drenched. ~*n.* **1** pickle made with salt. **2** anything steeped or preserved in pickle, esp. mackerel and herring. **3** a dip or plunging into liquid. **4** (*sl.*) a drunkard. **5** (*sl.*) a drinking bout. **soused** *a.* **1** (*sl.*) drunk. **2** pickled. **3** drenched. [OF *sorse*, SAUCE, combined in some senses with obs. *sorse*, to swoop, as SOURCE]

souslik (soos´lik), **suslik** (sŭs´-) *n.* any ground squirrel of the genus *Spermophilus*, of Europe and Asia. [Rus.]

soutache (sootash´) *n.* a narrow, ornamental braid. [F, from Hung. *szuszak*, a curl, a lock]

soutane (sootan´) *n.* a cassock. [F, from It. *sottana*, L *subtus*, under]

souteneur (sootənœ´) *n.* a pimp. [F, a protector]

souter (soo´tə) *n.* (*chiefly Sc.*) a shoemaker, a cobbler. [OE *sūtere*, L *sūtor*, from *suere*, see SEW]

souterrain (soo´tərān) *n.* an esp. Iron-Age underground chamber. [F, *sous*, under, *terre*, earth]

south (sowth) *n.* **1** that one of the four cardinal points of the compass directly opposite to the north, or the direction in which this lies. **2** (*usu.* **the South**) **a** the southern part of a region, e.g. the part of England south of the Wash, or the American states south of the Mason–Dixon line. **b** the less developed countries of the world. **3** a wind from the south. **4** at cards, the player or position facing north. ~*a.* **1** situated in the south. **2** facing in the southern direction. **3** (of the wind) coming from the south. ~*adv.* **1** towards the south. **2** (of the wind) from the south. **south by east** between south and south-south-east. **south by west** between south and south-south-west. **south of** further south than. **to the south** in a southerly direction. **South African** *a.* of or relating to the Republic of South Africa, its inhabitants or any of their languages. ~*n.* a native, citizen or inhabitant of South Africa. **South American** *a.* of or relating to South America, its inhabitants or any of their languages. ~*n.* a native, citizen or inhabitant of any of the South American countries. **southbound** *a.* going or leading south. **Southdown** *a.* of or relating to the South Downs, Sussex. ~*n.* a breed of hornless sheep originating there. **south-east** *n.* **1** the point of the compass equally distant from the south and the east, or the direction in which this lies. **2** (*usu.* **the South-East**) the part of a town or a region lying towards the south-east, esp. the south-eastern area of Britain, including London. ~*a.* of or relating to, approaching or coming from the south-east. ~*adv.* at, towards or near the south-east. **southeaster** *n.* a south-east wind. **south-easterly** *a.*, *adv.* south-east. ~*n.* (*pl.* **south-easterlies**) a south-east wind. **south-eastern** *a.* **south-easternmost** *a.* **south-eastward** *a.*, *adv.* (moving) towards the south-east. ~*n.* a south-easterly direction or south-eastern area. **south-eastwardly** *a.*, *adv.* **south-eastwards** *adv.* **souther** *n.* a south wind. **southerly** (sŭdh´əli) *a.*, *adv.* **1** (positioned) in, or (tending) towards the south. **2** (of a wind) blowing from the south. ~*n.* (*pl.* **southerlies**) a south wind. **southerliness** *n.* **southern** (sŭdh´ən) *a.* **1** of or relating to or situated in or towards the south. **2** coming from or inhabiting the south. ~*n.* a southerner. **Southern Cone** *n.* the part of South America comprising Brazil, Paraguay, Uruguay and Argentina. **Southern Cross** *n.* a cross-shaped constellation visible in the southern hemisphere. **Southerner, southerner** *n.* an inhabitant or native of the south, esp. of southern England or the southern states of the US. **southern hemisphere** *n.* the half of the earth south of the equator. **southern lights** *n.pl.* the aurora australis. **southernmost** *a.* **southernwood** *n.* a shrubby species of wormwood, *Artemisia abrotanum*. **southing** *n.* **1** movement south. **2** the passing of the meridian, e.g. the transit of the moon or a star across it. **3** deviation, or distance travelled, towards the south. **4** the declination, or angular distance, of a star south of the celestial equator. **southmost** *a.* **southpaw** *n.*, *a.* (of or relating to) a left-handed person, esp. a left-handed boxer. **South Pole** *n.* **1** the most southerly point on the earth's axis or the celestial sphere. **2** (**south pole**) the south-seeking pole on a magnet. **South Sea** *n.* the southern Pacific Ocean. **south seas** *n.pl.* the seas south of the equator. **south-south-east** *n.* the compass point, or the direction, midway between south and south-east. **south-south-west** *n.* the compass point, or the direction, midway between south and south-west. **southward** (sowth´wəd, sŭdh´əd) *a.*, *adv.* (moving) towards the south. **southwardly** *a.*, *adv.* **southwards** *adv.* towards the south. **south-west** *n.* **1** the point of the compass equally distant from the south and the west, or the direction in which this lies. **2** (*usu.* **the South-West**) the part of a town or region lying towards the south-west, esp. the south-western part of Britain. ~*a.* of or relating to, approaching or coming from the south-west. ~*adv.* at, towards or near the south-west. **southwester** *n.* a wind from the south-west. **southwesterly** *a.*, *adv.* south-west. ~*n.* (*pl.* **south-westerlies**) a south-west wind. **south-western** *a.* **south-westernmost** *a.* **south-westward** *a.*, *adv.* (moving) towards the south-west. ~*n.* a south-westerly direction or south-western area. **south-westwards** *adv.* **sou'wester** (sow·wes´tə) *n.* **1** a southwester. **2** a waterproof hat with a wide brim hanging down behind, worn by sailors etc. **south wind** *n.* a wind blowing from the south. [OE *sūth* (cp. Dut. *zuid*, G *sud*, Icel. *suther*, *sunnr*, OHG *sund*), perh. rel. to SUN]

souvenir (soovəniə´) *n.* a keepsake, a memento. ~*v.t.* (*Austral.*, *New Zeal.*, *sl.*) to pilfer, to steal. [F, orig. to remember, L *subvenīre*, (SUB-, *venīre*, to come)]

souvlaki (soovlah´ki) *n.* (*pl.* **souvlakis, souvlakia** (-kiə)) a Greek dish consisting of small pieces of meat grilled on a skewer. [mod. Gr.]

sou'wester SOUTH-WEST (under SOUTH).

sov (sov) *abbr.* (*Hist.*, *coll.*) a sovereign (the gold coin).

sovereign (sov´rən) *a.* **1** supreme. **2** possessing supreme power, dominion or jurisdiction. **3** royal. **4** (of a remedy) efficacious, effectual. **5** utter, absolute (*sovereign disdain*). ~*n.* **1** a supreme ruler, a king or queen, an emperor or empress, a monarch. **2** a former English gold coin, worth one pound. **sovereign good** *n.* the greatest (esp. universal or common) good. **sovereignly** *adv.* **sovereign pontiff** *n.* the Pope. **sovereignty** (-ti) *n.* (*pl.* **sovereignties**) **1** lordship, supremacy. **2** an independent, self-governing state. **3** self-government, independence. [ME *soverein*, OF *soverain*, late L *superānus*, (*super*, suf. *-ānus*), assim. to REIGN]

Usage note The form *sovereignity* for *sovereignty* is best avoided.

soviet (sō´viət, sov´-) *n.* **1** a local council elected by workers and inhabitants of a district in the former Soviet Union. **2** a regional council selected by a number of these. **3** the national congress consisting of delegates from regional councils. **4** (*pl.*) (*usu.* **Soviet**) the government or people of the former Soviet Union. ~*a.* **1** (*usu.* **Soviet**) of or relating to the former Soviet Union, its government or its people. **2** of or relating to a soviet. **sovietic** (-viet´-) *a.* **sovietism** *n.* **sovietize, sovietise** *v.t.* to transform (a country etc.) to the Soviet model of economic, social and political activity. **sovietization** (-zā´shən) *n.* **sovietologist** (-ol´əjist) *n.* a person who studies the former Soviet Union. [Rus. *sovet*, council]

†**sovran** (sov´rən) *n., a.* (a) sovereign.

sow[1] (sō) *v.t.* (*past* **sowed,** *p.p.* **sown** (sōn), **sowed**) **1** to scatter (seed) for growth. **2** to scatter seed over (ground etc.). **3** to scatter over, to cover thickly with. **4** to disseminate, to spread. **5** to implant, to initiate. *~v.i.* to scatter seed for growth. **to sow one's oats/ wild oats** OAT. **to sow the seeds/ seed of** to introduce, initiate or implant (a doubt, a suspicion etc.). **sower** *n.* **sowing** *n.* [OE *sāwan* (cp. Dut. *zaaĭjen*, G *säen*, Icel. *sā*, also L *serere*)]

Usage note See note under SEW.

sow[2] (sow) *n.* **1** a female pig. **2** the female of other animals, e.g. the guinea pig. **3** the main channel through which molten iron flows to solidify as pigs in side channels. **4** a block of iron solidified in this. **5** (*esp. N Am.*) (*also* **sow bug**) a woodlouse. **sowback** *n.* a long ridged hill, a hogsback. **sowbread** *n.* a type of cyclamen, *Cyclamen hederifolium*, whose tubers are eaten by pigs. **sowthistle** *n.* a plant of the genus *Sonchus*, with toothed leaves and milky juice. [OE *sugu*, *sū* (cp. Dut. *zog*, G *Sau*, Icel. *sȳr*, Dan. and Swed. *so*, also L *sūs*, Gr. *hus*, *sus*), from root *su-*, to produce, cogn. with SWINE]

sowens (sow´ənz, soo´ənz) *n.* (*Sc.*) a kind of pudding made from the husks of oats. [Gael. *súghan*, *súbhan*, from *súgh*, *súbh*, sap]

Sowetan (səwā´tən, -et´-) *n.* a native or inhabitant of Soweto in S Africa. *~a.* of or relating to Soweto.

sowl (sowl) *v.t.* (*dial.*) to drag about, to tug, to pull by the ears. [etym. uncertain]

sox SOCK[1].

soy (soi) *n.* **1** (*also* **soy sauce**) a thin brown salty sauce made from fermented soya beans, used extensively in Japanese and Chinese cookery. **2** the soya plant. [Jap. *shō-yu*, from Chin. *shi-you*, from *shi*, salted beans, *you*, oil]

soya (soi´ə) *n.* **1** a leguminous herb, *Glycine soja*, native to SE Asia, grown for its seeds. **2** (*also* **soya bean**) the seed of this plant, used as a source of oil and flour, as a substitute for animal protein and to make soy sauce and tofu. **3** (*also* **soya sauce**) soy. [Jap. *si-yan*; Chin. *shi-yu*]

sozzled (soz´əld) *a.* (*coll.*) drunk. [onomat.]

SP *abbr.* starting price.

Sp. *abbr.* **1** Spain. **2** Spaniard. **3** Spanish.

sp *abbr. sine prole*, without issue. [L]

sp. *abbr.* **1** special. **2** (*pl.* **spp.**) species. **3** specific. **4** spelling.

spa (spah) *n.* (*pl.* **spas**) **1** a mineral spring. **2** a resort or place where there is such a spring. [town in Belgium]

space (spās) *n.* **1** continuous extension in three dimensions or any quantity or portion of this. **2** the universe beyond the earth's atmosphere, outer space; the vacuum or near-vacuum between heavenly bodies. **3** an interval between points etc. **4** emptiness. **5** room. **6 a** an unoccupied seat, an empty place. **b** welcome isolation. **7** an interval of time. **8** advertising slots in newspapers etc., or on radio or television. **9** COMMERCIAL SPACE (under COMMERCIAL). **10** an interval between signals or characters in Morse code. **11** a thin piece of type metal used to separate words or lines. **12** an interval between written or printed words or lines. **13** any one of the blanks between the lines of the music staff. *~v.t.* **1** to set so that there will be spaces between. **2** to put the proper spaces between (words, lines etc.). **to space out** to place at wider intervals. **space age** *n.* the era in which space travel and exploration have become possible. **space-age** *a.* **1** of or relating to the space age. **2** modern. **space bar** *n.* a bar on a typewriter or computer keyboard for making spaces (between words etc.). **space blanket** *n.* a heat-retaining aluminium-coated wrapping for the body, carried e.g. by mountaineers for emergencies. **space capsule** *n.* a small information-gathering spacecraft. **spacecraft** *n.* a manned or unmanned craft for travelling through outer space. **spaced-out** *a.* (*pred.* **spaced out**) (*dated sl.*) unnaturally euphoric, high on drugs. **space flight** *n.* **1** a voyage in space. **2** space travel. **Space Invaders®** *n.* a video game in which the object is to shoot down images of alien invaders from outer space. **spaceman, spacewoman** *n.* (*pl.* **spacemen, spacewomen**) a space traveller. **space platform, space station** *n.* a large artificial satellite serving as a landing stage in space travel and as a base for scientific investigations. **space probe** *n.* an unmanned spacecraft carrying equipment for collecting scientific measurements of conditions in space. **spacer** *n.* **space rocket** *n.* a rocket for launching spacecraft or for travelling in space. **space-saving** *a.* economic on space, occupying very little space. **spaceship** *n.* a manned spacecraft. **space shuttle** *n.* **1** a spacecraft designed to carry people and materials to and from a space station. **2** a reusable rocket-launched manned spacecraft that returns to earth. **space station** SPACE PLATFORM (under SPACE). **spacesuit** *n.* an all-in-one garment specially adapted for space travel. **spacetime, space-time continuum** *n.* the four-dimensional manifold for continuum which in accordance with Einstein's theory of relativity, is the result of fusing time with three-dimensional space. **space travel** *n.* travel in outer space. **space traveller,** (*N Am.*) **space traveler** *n.* **space vehicle** *n.* a spacecraft. **space walk** *n.* a trip by an astronaut outside a spacecraft when it is in space. **spacewalk** *v.i.* to float or move in space while attached by a line to a spacecraft. **spacey, spacy** *a.* (*comp.* **spacier,** *superl.* **spaciest**) **1** large, roomy, commodious. **2** (*N Am., sl.*) dreamy, behaving as if spaced out. **spacial** SPATIAL. **spacing** *n.* **spacious** (-shəs) *a.* **1** having ample room. **2** commodious, roomy, wide, extensive. **spaciously** *adv.* **spaciousness** *n.* [OF *espace*, L *spatium*]

spade[1] (spād) *n.* **1** an implement for digging, having a broad blade fitted on to a long handle, and worked with both hands and one foot. **2** a tool of similar form employed for various purposes. **3** anything resembling a spade in shape etc. *~v.t.* **1** to dig with a spade. **2** to cut out with a spade. **to call a spade a spade** to be outspoken, not to mince matters. **spade beard** *n.* a stiff square outward-curving beard. **spade foot** *n.* (*pl.* **spade feet**) a spade-shaped foot on a piece of furniture. **spadeful** *n.* (*pl.* **spadefuls**). **spade guinea** *n.* a guinea (minted 1787–99) having a shield like a pointed spade on the reverse. **spadework** *n.* tedious but necessary preliminary work. [OE *spædu*, *spadu*]

spade[2] (spād) *n.* **1** a playing card with a black figure or figures shaped like a heart with a small triangular handle. **2** (*pl.*) this suit of cards. **3** (*offensive, sl.*) a black person. **in spades** (*coll.*) to an extreme degree. [Sp. *espada*, sword, from L *spatha*; Gr. *spathē*, a broad blade]

spadille (spədil´) *n.* **1** in the card games ombre and quadrille, the ace of spades. **2** the highest trump, esp. the ace of spades, in various card games. [F, from Sp. *espadilla*, dim. of *espada*, sword]

spadix (spā´diks) *n.* (*pl.* **spadices** (-sēz)) (*Bot.*) a spike of flowers on a fleshy stem, usu. enclosed in a spathe. **spadiceous** (spədish´əs) *a.* [L and Gr., from *spaein*, to draw out, to rend]

spae (spā) *v.t., v.i.* (*3rd pers. sing. pres.* **spaes,** *pres.p.* **spaeing,** *past, p.p.* **spaed**) (*Sc.*) to prophesy or foretell. **spaewife** *n.* (*pl.* **spaewives**) a female fortune-teller. [ME, from ON *spā*]

spaghetti (spəget´i) *n.* a variety of pasta made in long thin cylindrical strings. **spaghetti Bolognese** (bolənāz´) *n.* spaghetti with a minced-beef sauce. **spaghetti junction** *n.* a multi-intersection road junction, esp. at a motorway, with criss-crossing flyovers. **spaghetti western** *n.* a film about the American West made cheaply in Italy or Spain, often with a violent or melodramatic content. [It., pl. dim. of *spago*, cord]

spahi (spah´hē), **spahee** *n.* (*pl.* **spahis, spahees**) **1** a Turkish irregular cavalryman. **2** (*Hist.*) an Algerian cavalryman in the French army. [Turk. *sipāhī*, SEPOY]

†**spake** SPEAK.

spall (spawl) *n.* a chip, splinter or flake. ~*v.t.* to break up (ore etc.) for sorting. ~*v.i.* to splinter, to chip. **spallation** (spəlā´shən) *n.* (*Physics*) the disintegration of a nucleus on bombardment by high-energy particles. [etym. uncertain, cp. ME *speld*, Sc. *spale*, splinter, Dut. *spald*, pin, MDut. *spalden*, G *spalten*, to split]

spalpeen (spalpēn´) *n.* (*chiefly Ir.*) a scamp, a young rascal. [Ir. *spailpin*]

Spam® (spam) *n.* a tinned luncheon meat of chopped and spiced ham. [*sp*iced h*am*]

Span. *abbr.* Spanish.

span[1] (span) *n.* **1** the space from end to end of a bridge etc. **2** the horizontal distance between the supports of an arch. **3** an entire stretch of distance or time (e.g. a lifespan, attention span). **4** a brief space of distance or time. **5** the wingspan of a bird or aeroplane. **6** the space from the tip of the thumb to the tip of the little finger when extended, esp. as a former measure, 9 in. (23 cm). ~*v.t.* (*pres.p.* **spanning**, *past*, *p.p.* **spanned**) **1** (of a bridge etc.) to extend from side to side of (a river etc.). **2** (of an engineer etc.) to build a bridge across (a river etc.). **3** to measure or cover the extent of (e.g. an octave) with one's hand expanded. **4** to encompass, to cover, to extend across (a range, a period of time). ~*v.i.* (*N Am.*) to progress in distinct stretches, like a span-worm. **spanless** *a.* measureless. **span-long** *a.* of the length of a span. **spanner**[1] *n.* **span roof** *n.* an ordinary roof with two sloping sides. **span-worm** *n.* (*N Am.*) the larva of the geometer moth. [OE *spannan* (Dut. and G *spannen*, Icel. *spenna*, also Gr. *spaein*, to draw)]

span[2] (span) *n.* **1** (*Naut.*) a rope or chain fastened at both ends to take a purchase. **2** a pair of horses, usu. matched in colour etc., harnessed side by side. **3** a yoke or team of oxen etc. [Dut. and G *span*, from *spannen*, to unite]

span[3] (span) *a.* absolutely new, brand new. [ON *spān*, chip]

span[4] SPIN.

spanaemia (spənē´miə), (*N Am.*) **spanemia** *n.* a blood condition in which there is a deficiency of red corpuscles. **spanaemic** *a.* [Gr. *spanos*, *spanios*, scanty, *haima*, blood]

Spandex® (span´deks) *n.* a stretchy fabric made from polymethane fibre.

spandrel (span´drəl), **spandril** *n.* the space between the shoulder of an arch and the rectangular moulding etc enclosing it, or between the shoulders of adjoining arches and the moulding etc. [etym. uncertain]

spanemia SPANAEMIA.

spangle (spang´gəl) *n.* **1** a small disc of glittering metal or metallic material, used for ornamenting dresses etc., a sequin. **2** any small sparkling object. **3** (*in full* **spangle gall**) a spongy growth on the surface of oak leaves. ~*v.t.* to set or adorn with spangles. ~*v.i.* to glitter (as though) with spangles. **spangled** *a.* **spangler** *n.* **spangly** *a.* [ME *spangel*, dim. of obs. *spang*, OE *spang*, a metal clasp, cp. MDut. and G *Spange*, rel. to Gr. *sphingein*, to bind lightly]

Spaniard (span´yəd) *n.* **1** a native or inhabitant of Spain. **2** (*usu.* **spaniard**) any of various sharp-leaved plants of the New Zealand genus *Aciphylla*; also called *wild spaniard*. [alt. of ME *Spaynyell*, as SPANIEL]

spaniel (span´yəl) *n.* **1** any of various breeds of dog, distinguished by large drooping ears, long silky or curly coat and a gentle disposition. **2** a servile, cringing person, esp. someone's minion. [ME, from OF *espagneul*, Sp. *español*, Spanish, from *España*, L *Hispania*, Spain]

Spanish (span´ish) *a.* of or relating to Spain, its people or their language. ~*n.* **1** the language of Spain and South America. **2** (*as pl.*) the Spaniards. **Spanish America** *n.* the predominantly Spanish-speaking parts of Central and South America, and the West Indies, orig. settled by the Spanish. **Spanish-American** *a.*, *n.* **Spanish bayonet** *n.* a species of yucca, *Yucca aloifolia*, with lanceolate leaves. **Spanish broom** *n.* a Mediterranean shrub, *Spartium junceum*, with rushlike branches and fragrant yellow flowers. **Spanish chestnut** *n.* the true chestnut tree, *Castanea sativa*. **Spanish fly** *n.* (*pl.* **Spanish flies**) **1** a bright green beetle that raises blisters, *Lytta vesicatoria*. **2** a (supposedly aphrodisiac) preparation made from this, cantharides. **Spanish fowl** *n.* a breed of domestic fowl of a glossy black colour. **Spanish grass** *n.* esparto grass. **Spanish guitar** *n.* **1** a traditional six-stringed acoustic guitar. **2** classical guitar music. **Spanish ibex, Spanish goat** *n.* a Pyrenean ibex, *Capra pyrenaica*. **Spanish mackerel** *n.* any of several large Atlantic fishes related to the mackerel, esp. *Scomberomorphus maculatus*. **Spanish Main** *n.* the northern coast of South America and the adjacent part of the Caribbean Sea. **Spanish moss** *n.* any of various parasitic trailing ferns, esp. *Tillandsia usneoides*. **Spanishness** *n.* **Spanish omelette** *n.* an omelette with a filling of tomato, peppers (traditionally pimento) or other chopped vegetables. **Spanish onion** *n.* a large variety of onion with a mild flavour. **Spanish windlass** *n.* a rope-tightening device in which a stick is used as a lever. [ME, from *Spain*, with vowel-shortening]

spank (spangk) *v.t.* to strike with the open hand, to slap, esp. on the buttocks. ~*v.i.* (of a horse) to trot fast, almost approaching a gallop. ~*n.* a resounding blow with the open hand, a slap, esp. on the buttocks. **spanker** *n.* **1** a person who spanks another. **2** a fore-and-aft sail set by two spars on the after side of the mizzen-mast. **3** a fast horse. **4** (*coll.*) an exceptionally fine specimen, a stunner. **spanking** *n.* a series of slaps on the buttocks, as a punishment. ~*a.* (*coll.*) **1** dashing, brisk, stunning. **2** (of a breeze) strong. ~*adv.* exceptionally. [prob. onomat.]

spanner[1] SPAN[1].

spanner[2] (span´ə) *n.* **1** an instrument for tightening up or loosening the nuts on screws, a wrench. **2** the cross-brace of a bridge or similar structure. **spanner in the works** *n.* an impediment, a cause of confusion or difficulty.

Spansule® (span´sūl) *n.* a capsule for swallowing that releases one or more drugs into the system over a predetermined period. [SPAN[1], CAPSULE]

spar[1] (spah) *n.* **1** a round timber, a pole, esp. used as a mast, yard, boom, shears etc. **2** the longitudinal supporting beam of an aircraft wing. **spar buoy** *n.* a buoy consisting of a spar with one end moored, so that the other end floats upright. **spar-deck** *n.* the upper deck of a vessel stretching from stem to stern. [ME *sparre* (cp. Dut. *spar*, G *sparren*, Icel. *sparri*, Dan. and Swed. *sparre*), perh. cogn. with SPEAR]

spar[2] (spah) *v.i.* (*pres.p.* **sparring**, *past*, *p.p.* **sparred**) **1** to move the arms about in defence or offence as in boxing. **2** (of gamecocks etc.) to strike out, esp. with protected spurs. **3** to engage in a contest of words etc. ~*n.* **1** a sparring movement. **2** a boxing match. **3** a cockfight. **4** a verbal contest, an argument. **sparrer** *n.* **sparring** *n.* **sparring partner** *n.* **1** a boxer with whom one in training practises. **2** a person with whom another engages in lively repartee. [perh. OF *esparer*, to strike out with the heels, perh. from Gmc. and rel. to SPUR, SPURN]

spar[3] (spah) *n.* any of various lustrous minerals occurring in crystalline or vitreous form, e.g. *feldspar, fluorspar.* **sparry** *a.* (*comp.* **sparrier,** *superl.* **sparriest**). [OE *spær*]

sparable (spar´əbəl) *n.* a headless nail for boot soles. [corr. of SPARROW and BILL[2]]

spare (speə) *a.* 1 not needed for routine purposes, extra, able to be spared. 2 that can be spared, kept in reserve, available for use in emergency etc. 3 unoccupied, not in use (*a spare seat; a spare keyboard*). 4 (of someone's figure) thin, lean, wiry. 5 (of style) concise, not wasting words (*her spare prose*). 6 (of diet etc.) meagre, scanty, frugal, sparse. *~v.t.* 1 to be able to afford (*can't spare the money; Can you spare a moment?*). 2 to dispense with or do without (*can't spare her just now*). 3 to relieve, to release (*was trying to spare her feelings*). 4 to refrain from punishing, injuring, destroying etc. (*spared the prisoners*). 5 to refrain from inflicting (*Spare us the sob story*). 6 to use frugally, to be chary of using (*no expense spared; Don't spare the horses*). 7 to refrain from using (*Spare the rod and spoil the child*). 8 †to forbear (to do something). *~v.i.* to live sparingly or frugally. *~n.* that which is surplus to immediate requirements and available for use, such as a copy or duplicate of something (*I'd lend you a key but I haven't got a spare*). **not to spare oneself** to do one's utmost, to give utterly dedicated service. **to go spare** (*coll.*) to become excessively angry, agitated or distraught. **to spare** extra, surplus, more than required (*plenty to spare*). **to spare someone's blushes** BLUSH. **sparely** *adv.* **spareness** *n.* **spare part** *n.* a replacement for a machine part which may break, wear out etc. **spare-part surgery** *n.* surgery involving the transplanting of organs or parts, or the implanting of artificial ones. **sparer** *n.* **spare rib** *n.* a piece of pork consisting of a rib with only a little meat. **spare room** *n.* a guest bedroom in a private household. **spare time** *n.* time when one is at leisure, or not engaged in one's regular work or activities. **spare-time** *a.* relating to one's spare time (*spare-time occupations*). **spare tyre** *n.* 1 a tyre carried in a vehicle as a replacement in case of a puncture. 2 (*coll.*) a bulge of fat around the midriff. **sparing** *a.* **sparingly** *adv.* **sparingness** *n.* [OE *spær*, whence *sparian*, to spare (cp. Icel. *sparr*, G *spärlich*, also Dut. and G *sparen*, Icel. and Swed. *spara*), prob. cogn. with L *parcere*, to spare]

sparge (spahj) *v.t.* to sprinkle; to moisten by sprinkling, e.g. in brewing. **sparger** *n.* a sprinkling apparatus used in brewing. [obs. *sparge*, L *spargere*, to sprinkle, -ER]

sparing SPARE.

spark (spahk) *n.* 1 an incandescent particle thrown off from a burning substance, or produced from a match, flint etc. 2 the luminous effect of a disruptive electrical discharge. 3 such an electrical discharge as the igniting device in an internal-combustion engine. 4 a flash of wit, a particle of life or energy. 5 a trace, a hint (of kindled interest etc.). 6 a gallant, a beau. 7 a vivacious and witty person. 8 a brilliant point, facet, gleam etc. *~v.i.* 1 to give out sparks. 2 to produce sparks at the point of broken continuity in an electrical circuit. **to make sparks fly** to start a violent quarrel, to cause a row. **to spark off** 1 to kindle (a process, someone's interest etc.). 2 to galvanize into activity. **spark chamber** *n.* a radiation-detecting apparatus that shows the sparks caused by ionizing particles. **spark coil** *n.* an instrument for producing a high electromotive force from a supply of low electromotive force, an induction coil. **spark-gap** *n.* the space between electrodes where electric sparks occur. **sparkish** *a.* **sparkless** *a.* **sparklet** *n.* a small spark. **spark plug, sparking plug** *n.* a device for igniting the explosive mixture in the cylinder of an internal-combustion engine. **sparks** *n.* (*coll.*) 1 the radio operator esp. on board ship. 2 an electrician. **sparky** *a.* (*comp.* **sparkier,** *superl.* **sparkiest**). [OE *spearca*, cp. MDut. *sparcke*, LG *sparke*, Icel. *spraka*, to crackle, prob. imit.]

sparkle (spah´kəl) *n.* 1 a gleam, a glittering, glitter, brilliance. 2 vivacity, wit. 3 effervescence. *~v.i.* 1 to emit sparks. 2 to glisten, to glitter, to twinkle. 3 (of some wines, mineral waters etc.) to emit carbon dioxide in little bubbles. 4 to be vivacious, witty, or scintillating. *~v.t.* to cause to glitter, twinkle, shine etc. **sparkler** *n.* 1 something that sparkles. 2 (*sl.*) a diamond. 3 a hand-held firework that emits fizzling sparks. **sparkling** *a.* 1 effervescent. 2 twinkling, scintillating. **sparklingly** *adv.* [dim. of SPARK]

sparrer, sparring SPAR[2].

sparrow (spar´ō) *n.* 1 a small brownish-grey bird of the genus *Passer*, esp. *P. domesticus*, the house sparrow. 2 any of various other small birds resembling this, e.g. the hedge sparrow, *Prunella modularis.* **sparrow-grass** *n.* (*coll., dial.*) corr. of ASPARAGUS. **sparrowhawk** *n.* a small hawk, *Accipiter nisus*, preying on small birds etc. [OE *spearwa* (cp. Icel. *spörr*, Dan. *spurv*, Swed. *sparf*) cogn. with SPAR[2]]

sparry SPAR[3].

sparse (spahs) *a.* thinly scattered, set or occurring at considerable intervals, not dense. **sparsely** *adv.* **sparseness, sparsity** *n.* [L *sparsus*, p.p. of *spargere*, to scatter]

Spartan (spah´tən) *n.* 1 a native or inhabitant of Sparta. 2 a person bearing pain, enforcing discipline etc., like a Spartan. *~a.* 1 of or relating to Sparta or the Spartans. 2 like a Spartan, hardy, strict etc. 3 austere, rigorous, frugal. [ME, from L *Spartānus*, from Gr. *Spartē*]

spartina (spahtī´nə, -tē´nə) *n.* any grass of the genus *Spartina*, having rhizomatous roots, growing in marshy ground. [Gr. *spartinē*, rope]

spasm (spaz´m) *n.* 1 a convulsive and involuntary muscular contraction. 2 a sudden or convulsive act, movement etc. 3 a burst of emotion or effort. **spasmodic** (-mod´-) *a.* 1 caused or affected by a spasm or spasms. 2 happening at irregular intervals. **spasmodical** *a.* **spasmodically** *adv.* **spastic** (spas´tik) *a.* 1 of, affected by, resembling or characterized by spasms. 2 (*sl., offensive*) ineffectual, incapable. *~n.* 1 a sufferer from cerebral palsy. 2 (*sl., offensive*) an ineffectual, clumsy person. **spastically** *adv.* **spasticity** (-tis´-) *n.* **spastic paralysis** *n.* a condition characterized by spasms in the affected muscles. [F *spasme*, L *spasmus*, Gr. *spasmos*, from *spaein*, to draw out]

Usage note The term *spastic* gives offence: it is better to express in terms of *cerebral palsy* instead.

spat[1] (spat) *n.* 1 (*usu. pl., Hist.*) a short gaiter fastening over and under the shoe. 2 a cover for the top part of an aircraft wheel. [short for SPATTERDASH (under SPATTER)]

spat[2] (spat) *n.* 1 (*chiefly N Am.*) a petty quarrel. 2 (*chiefly N Am.*) a splash, a drop, a smattering (e.g. of rain). 3 a slap, a smack. *~v.t.* (*pres.p.* **spatting,** *past, p.p.* **spatted**) to slap. *~v.i.* (*N Am., New Zeal.*) to engage in a petty argument. [prob. imit.]

spat[3] (spat) *n.* the spawn of shellfish, esp. oysters. *~v.i.* (*pres.p.* **spatting,** *past, p.p.* **spatted**) (of an oyster) to spawn. *~v.t.* to deposit (spawn). [A-F, etym. uncertain]

spat[4] SPIT[1].

spatangoid (spətang´goid) *a., n.* (an urchin) of the Spatangoidea, an order of heart-shaped sea urchins. [mod. L, from Gr. *spatangēs*, a sea urchin]

spatchcock (spach´kok) *n.* 1 a fowl opened out along the backbone and fried or grilled flat. 2 a fowl killed and immediately cooked. *~v.t.* 1 to cook (poultry) in this way. 2 to insert or interpolate (a phrase etc.)

hurriedly. [said to be short for *dispatch-cock* (perh. conf. with SPITCHCOCK)]

spate (spāt) *n.* **1** a heavy flood, esp. in a mountain stream or river. **2** a sudden onrush, influx or outburst. **3** a sudden downpour. [etym. uncertain]

spathe (spādh) *n.* a large bract or pair of bracts enveloping the spadix of a plant. **spathaceous** (spədhā´shəs) *a.* [L *spatha*, Gr. *spathē*, a broad blade, sword etc.]

spathic (spath´ik), **spathose** (-ōs) *a.* resembling spar, esp. in cleavage. **spathic iron ore** *n.* siderite. [G *Spath*, SPAR[3], -IC]

spatial (spā´shəl), **spacial** *a.* of, relating to, existing or occurring in space. **spatiality** (-al´-) *n.* **spatialize, spatialise** *v.t.* to make spatial, to apply spatial qualities to. **spatially** *adv.* **spatio-temporal** (spāshiōtem´pərəl) *a.* **1** of space-time. **2** of, concerned with or existing in both space and time. **spatio-temporally** *adv.* [L *spatium*, space]

Spätlese (shpet´lāzə) *n.* (*pl.* **Spätleses, Spätlesen** (-zən)) a (German etc.) white wine made from late-harvested grapes. [G *spät*, late, *Lese*, a picking]

spatter (spat´ə) *v.t.* **1** to scatter or splash (water etc.) about. **2** to sprinkle or splash (someone etc.) with water, mud etc. **3** to slander, to smear, to defame. ~*v.i.* **1** to sprinkle drops about. **2** to be scattered about in drops. ~*n.* **1** a shower, a sprinkling, a pattering. **2** something spattered or soiled. **spatterdash** *n.* **1** (*usu. pl.*) a legging or gaiter for protecting against mud etc. **2** (*N Am.*) roughcast, pebbledash. [freq. of *spat*, cogn. with dial. *spat*, to spit]

spatula (spat´ūlə) *n.* a broad knife or trowel-shaped tool used for spreading plasters, working pigments, mixing foods etc. **spatular** *a.* **spatulate** (-lət) *a.* **spatule** *n.* a spatula. [L, dim. of *spatha*, SPATHE]

spavin (spav´in) *n.* a disease in horses affecting the hock joint with swelling or a hard excrescence. **spavined** *a.* [OF *esparvin*, prob. through a late L *sparvānus*, from OHG *sparwe*, SPARROW, with alln. to birdlike motion of a spavined horse]

spawn (spawn) *v.t.* **1** (of fish, amphibians etc.) to deposit or produce (eggs, young etc.). **2** (*derog.*) (of human beings) to give birth to, to beget (children). **3** (*coll.*) to produce, to generate, to give rise to. ~*v.i.* **1** (of fish etc.) to deposit eggs. **2** (*derog.*) to issue, to be brought forth, esp. in abundance. ~*n.* **1** the eggs of fish, frogs and molluscs. **2** white fibrous matter from which fungi are produced, mycelium. **3** (*derog.*) offspring. **spawner** *n.* [OF *espandre*, L *expandere*, to EXPAND]

spay (spā) *v.t.* to destroy or remove the ovaries of (female animals) so as to make them infertile, to sterilize. [prob. through OF, from late L *spadāre*]

SPCK *abbr.* Society for Promoting Christian Knowledge.

speak (spēk) *v.i.* (*past* **spoke** (spōk), †**spake** (spāk), *p.p.* **spoken** (spō´kən)) **1** to utter articulate sounds or words in the ordinary tone as distinct from singing. **2** to talk, to converse. **3** to deliver a speech or address. **4** to communicate by other means. **5** (of a picture etc.) to be highly expressive or lifelike. **6** to be on speaking terms. **7** (of a musical instrument etc.) to produce a (characteristic) sound. **8** (of a dog) to bark. **9** to communicate (with a ship) by hailing etc. ~*v.t.* **1** to utter articulately. **2** to make known, to tell, to declare (one's thoughts, opinions etc.). **3** to talk or converse in (a language). †**4 a** (of behaviour) to reveal (someone) as (*a gesture that speaks him honourable*). **b** to be proof or evidence of (*the hard mouth that spoke the ruthless will*). **none to speak of** nothing to speak of. **nothing to speak of** nothing important or significant, none worth mentioning. **speak of the devil** DEVIL. **spoken for** allocated, reserved, claimed. **to speak by the card** CARD[1]. **to speak for 1** to be spokesperson for. **2** to act as an advocate for, to represent, to witness to. **to speak for itself** (of a circumstance) to be of self-evident significance. **to speak for oneself** to be one's own advocate. **to speak ill** ILL. **to speak of** to mention. **to speak one's mind** to speak freely and frankly. **to speak out 1** to speak loudly and articulately. **2** to express one's opinion frankly. **to speak the same language** LANGUAGE. **to speak to 1** to address. **2** to speak in support or confirmation of (*spoke to the general view*). **3** (*coll.*) to reprimand, to reprove (*shall have to speak to him*). **to speak to someone's heart** HEART. **to speak up 1** to speak loudly. **2** to speak without constraint, to express one's opinion freely. **to speak volumes 1** (of a circumstance) to be of great or peculiar significance. **2** to constitute abundant evidence (for). **to speak well 1** to make favourable mention (of). **2** to be abundant evidence (for). **speakable** *a.* **speakeasy** *n.* (*pl.* **speakeasies**) (*Hist., N Am.*) a premises where illicit liquor was sold during the time of Prohibition. **speaker** *n.* **1** a person who speaks, esp. someone who delivers a speech. **2** (*in comb.*) a person who speaks a specified language (*English-speakers*). **3** (**Speaker**) an officer presiding over a deliberative assembly, esp. the House of Commons. **4** a loudspeaker. **speakerphone** *n.* (*N Am.*) a telephone that does not have to be held in the hand. **speakership** *n.* **speaking** *n.* the activity or an instance of uttering words etc. ~*a.* **1** (of a likeness etc.) animated, vivid, expressive. **2** able to speak. **3** (*in comb.*) able to speak a specific language, or having a specific language as one's native tongue (*the German-speaking Czechs*). **4** transmitting speech. **5** giving an estimate or opinion from a specified angle (*technically speaking; roughly speaking*). **on speaking terms 1** amicable towards one another. **2** slightly acquainted. **speaking acquaintance** *n.* **1** a person whom one knows slightly. **2** slight familiarity with someone. **speaking clock** *n.* a recorded-speech telephone service giving the correct time. **speaking in tongues** *n.* GIFT OF TONGUES (under GIFT). **speaking-trumpet** *n.* (*Hist.*) an instrument for amplifying the voice. **speaking-tube** *n.* a tube through which one can communicate with another room, building etc. [OE *sprecan*, later *specan* (cp. Dut. *spreken*, G *sprechen*, also Icel. *spraka*, SPARK)]

spear (spiə) *n.* **1** a weapon with a pointed head on a long shaft. **2** a sharp-pointed instrument with barbs, for stabbing fish etc. **3** a pointed shoot, esp. a stem of broccoli or asparagus. **4** a blade or stalk of grass. **5** †a spearman. ~*v.t.* to pierce, kill or capture with a spear. **spear-grass** *n.* grass of various species having long, sharp leaves. **speargun** *n.* a gun for firing spears under water. **spearhead** *n.* **1** the pointed end of a spear. **2** the person or group leading a campaign, thrust or attack. ~*v.t.* to lead (a campaign, an assault etc.). †**spearman** *n.* (*pl.* **spearmen**) a soldier etc. armed with a spear. **spearmint** *n.* the garden mint, *Mentha spicata*, used as a flavouring. **spear side** *n.* the male members of a family, as distinct from the *distaff side*. **spear-thistle** *n.* a common thistle, *Carduus lanceolatus*. **spearwort** *n.* any of several species of ranunculus, esp. the aquatic *Ranunculus lingua*. [OE *spere* (cp. Dut. and G *speer*, Icel. *spjör*), perh. cogn. with SPAR[1]]

spec[1] (spek) *n.* (*coll.*) short for SPECIFICATION (under SPECIFY) (*a job spec*).

spec[2] (spek) *n.* (*coll.*) short for SPECULATION (under SPECULATE). ~*a.* (*Austral., New Zeal.*) short for SPECULATIVE (under SPECULATE). **on spec** (*coll.*) on the off chance, in the hope of success, as a gamble.

spec. *abbr.* special.

speccy SPECS.

special (spesh´əl) *a.* **1** exceptionally good or important (*a special day*). **2** particular, peculiar, not ordinary or general (*has a special meaning in this context*). **3** for a particular purpose, environment or occasion (*requires no special qualifications*). **4** close, intimate (*a special friend*). **5** additional, extra (*special buses*). **6** individual

(*They have their own special chairs*). 7 denoting the educational needs of children who are handicapped etc. ~*n.* 1 a person or thing dedicated to a special purpose etc. 2 a special train, constable, edition of a newspaper, item on a menu etc. **special area** *n.* a district for which exceptional arrangements are made in economic legislation. **Special Branch** *n.* a branch of the British police force dealing with political security. **special case** *n.* 1 a written statement of fact given to a court by litigants. 2 an exceptional case. **special constable** *n.* a citizen sworn in to aid the police force in times of war, civil commotion etc. **special correspondent** *n.* a journalist or reporter who writes on special topics for a newspaper. **special delivery** *n.* express delivery. **special drawing rights** *n.pl.* the right to buy extra foreign currency from the International Monetary Fund. **special edition** *n.* an extra edition of a newspaper with updated news. **special effect** *n.* an extraordinary visual or sound effect, esp. one created on a film, video tape, or television or radio broadcast. **special intention** *n.* in the Roman Catholic church, a special cause or purpose for which a Mass is held or prayers said. **specialism** *n.* a special area of expertise etc., a speciality. **specialist** *n.* 1 a person who is trained in a particular branch of a profession etc. (*a specialist in obstetrics*). 2 a person whose studies particularly or exclusively concern a certain subject or branch of one. **specialistic** (-lis´-) *a.* **speciality** (-shial´-) *n.* (*pl.* **specialities**) 1 a particular area of expertise, a pursuit, occupation, service, commodity, product etc., which is the special concern of a certain person or business. 2 a person's special characteristic or feature, peculiarity or skill. **specialize, specialise** *v.t.* to differentiate, limit, adapt or apply to a specific use, function, environment, purpose or meaning. ~*v.i.* 1 to become differentiated, adapted or applied thus. 2 to employ oneself as or train oneself to be a specialist. **specialization** (-zā´shən) *n.* **special jury** *n.* (*pl.* **special juries**) (*Hist.*) a jury selected from people of a certain social standing, or of a certain profession. **special licence** *n.* a licence authorizing marriage without banns. **specially** *adv.* **specialness** *n.* **special offer** *n.* the offering of a certain product, service etc. at a lower price than normal, for a limited period. **special pleading** *n.* 1 the allegation of special or new matter in a legal case. 2 specious or unfair argument. **special providence** *n.* a particular example of the working of God's providence. **special school** *n.* a school established to meet the educational needs of handicapped children. **special theory of relativity** *n.* the theory that in systems moving close to or beyond the speed of light, normal laws of physics do not hold and that time, dimension and mass will change as velocity increases. **specialty** *n.* (*pl.* **specialties**) 1 a legal agreement expressed in a sealed deed. 2 (*chiefly N Am.*) a speciality. **special verdict** *n.* a verdict stating the facts but leaving the decision to be determined by the court. [shortened from ESPECIAL, or directly from L *speciālis*, as SPECIES]

species (spē´shiz) *n.* (*pl.* **species**) 1 a class of things with certain characteristics in common. 2 a group of organisms (taxonomically subordinate to a genus) generally resembling each other and capable of reproduction. 3 (*Logic*) a group of individuals having certain common attributes and designated by a common name (subordinate to a genus). 4 a kind, a sort, a variety. 5 (*Law*) the form or shape given to any material. 6 an element in the Eucharist in its visible form. **speciation** (-ā´shən) *n.* the development of new biological species in the course of evolution. **specie** (-shē) *n.* coin as distinct from paper money. **in specie** 1 in coin. 2 in kind. **speciesism** (spē´shizizm) *n.* the assumption that human beings are superior to all other animal species, and are therefore justified in exploiting them. **speciesist** *a.*, *n.* [L, appearance, sort, from *specere*, to look]

specify (spes´ifī) *v.t.* (*3rd pers. sing. pres.* **specifies,** *pres.p.* **specifying,** *past, p.p.* **specified**) 1 to mention expressly, to name distinctively. 2 to stipulate, to state as a condition (that). 3 to include in a specification. **specifiable** *a.* **specific** (spəsif´-) *a.* 1 clearly specified or particularized, explicit, definite, precise (*Can you be more specific?*; *specific instructions*). 2 constituting, of or relating to, characterizing or particularizing a species (*specific difference*; *the creature's specific name*). 3 distinctive, special, peculiar (to) (*no specific treatment for Aids-related illnesses*; *symptoms specific to mercurial poisoning*; *gender-specific diseases*). 4 (of a tax or duty) assessed according to the quantity or weight of goods rather than their value. ~*n.* 1 †a medicine, remedy, agent etc. for a particular part of the body. 2 that which is particular or specific, a factor or detail. **specifically** *adv.* **specificate** *v.t.* to specify. **specification** (spesifikā´shən) *n.* 1 the act of specifying. 2 an article or particular specified. 3 a detailed statement of particulars, esp. of materials, work, workmanship to be undertaken or supplied by an architect, builder, manufacturer etc. 4 a detailed description of an invention by an applicant for a patent. 5 (*Law*) the converting of materials into a product that is not held to be the property of the owner of the materials. **specific cause** *n.* the cause of a particular form of an illness. **specific difference** *n.* a characteristic that differentiates a species. **specific gravity** *n.* the relative weight or density of a solid or fluid expressed by the ratio of its weight to that of an equal volume of a substance taken as a standard, water in the case of liquids and solids, air for gases. **specific heat, specific heat capacity** *n.* the heat required to raise the temperature of one unit of a given substance by one degree. **specificity** (spesifis´-) *n.* **specific medicine** *n.* a medicine that is successful in treating a particular illness. **specificness** *n.* **specific performance** *n.* (*Law*) the performance of a contractual duty where compensatory damages would be inadequate. **specific resistance** *n.* resistivity. **specified** *a.* **specifier** *n.* [F *specifique*, L *specificus*, from *specere*, to look, -IC]

specimen (spes´imən) *n.* 1 a part or an individual intended to illustrate or typify the nature of a whole or a class, an example, an illustration, an instance. 2 a sample of blood, urine etc. taken for medical analysis. 3 (*coll.*) a person or animal (*a splendid specimen*). [L, from *specere*, to look]

specious (spē´shəs) *a.* 1 apparently, but not actually, right or fair, plausible (*specious arguments*). 2 deceptively pleasing to the eye, showy. **speciosity** (-shios´-), **speciousness** *n.* **speciously** *adv.* [F *spécieux*, L *speciōsus*, from *specere*, to see]

speck (spek) *n.* 1 a small spot, fleck, stain or blemish. 2 a minute particle (*not a speck of dust anywhere*). 3 a rotten patch in a piece of fruit. ~*v.t.* to mark with a speck or specks. **specked** *a.* **speckle** *n.* a small spot, stain or patch of colour, light etc. ~*v.t.* to mark (as) with speckles. **speckled** *a.* **speckless** *a.* **specky** *a.* (*comp.* **speckier,** *superl.* **speckiest**). [OE *specca*, cp. LG *spaken*, to be spotted, MDut. *spickelen*, to speckle]

specky SPECK.

specs (speks) *n.pl.* (*coll.*) spectacles, glasses. **speccy** *a.* bespectacled.

spectacle (spek´təkəl) *n.* 1 something exhibited to the view, a show, pageant, sight etc. 2 (*coll.*) a sight attracting ridicule, laughter etc. **to make a spectacle of oneself** to do something that makes people stare or laugh at one. **spectacled** *a.* 1 wearing spectacles. 2 (of an animal etc.) having eye markings like spectacles. **spectacled bear** *n.* the S American bear *Tremarctos ornatus*, which has white markings round the eyes.

spectacled cobra *n.* the Asian cobra *Naja naja*, which has markings like spectacles on its hood. **spectacles** *n.pl.* an optical instrument, consisting of a lens for each eye mounted in a light frame for resting on the nose and ears, used to assist the sight; also called *pair of spectacles*. **spectacular** (-tak´ū-) *a.* **1** of the nature of a public spectacle. **2** marked by great display, lavish. **3** dramatic; thrilling; stunning, striking. ~*n.* an elaborate show, esp. a musical, in a theatre, on television etc. **spectacularly** *adv.* [F, from L *spectāculum*, from *specere*, to look]

spectator (spektā´tə) *n.* a person who looks on, esp. at a show or spectacle. **spectate** *v.i.* to look on, to be an observer or onlooker. **spectatorial** (-tətaw´ri-) *a.* **spectatorship** *n.* **spectator sport** *n.* a sport that attracts a large number of spectators or viewers. **spectatress** (-tā´tris), **spectatrix** (-tā´triks) *n.* (*rare*) a female spectator. [L, from *spectāre*, to behold, from *specere*, to look]

specter SPECTRE.

spectra SPECTRUM.

spectral[1] SPECTRE.

spectral[2] SPECTRUM.

spectre (spek´tə), (*N Am.*) **specter** *n.* **1** an apparition, a ghost. **2** an unpleasant thought or image that haunts one (*the spectre of poverty*). **spectral**[1] *a.* **1** of or relating to ghosts. **2** ghostlike, phantom-like. **3** (*in comb.*) denoting an animal with a very thin or diaphanous body, as in *spectre-bat*, *spectre-crab*, *spectre-insect*, *spectre-lemur*, *spectre shrimp*. **spectrality** (-tral´-) *n.* **spectrally** *adv.* [OF, from L SPECTRUM, image, apparition]

spectro- (spek´trō) *comb. form* spectrum.

spectrochemistry (spektrōkem´istri) *n.* a branch of chemistry that studies the spectra of substances.

spectrograph (spek´trəgrahf) *n.* an apparatus for photographing or otherwise reproducing spectra. **spectrogram** (-gram) *n.* a record produced by a spectrograph. **spectrographic** (-graf´-) *a.* **spectrographically** *adv.* **spectrography** (-trog´rəfi) *n.*

spectroheliograph (spektrōhē´liəgrahf) *n.* an instrument for photographing the sun using a particular wavelength of light. **spectroheliogram** *n.* a photograph taken by a spectroheliograph. **spectroheliographic** (-graf´ik) *a.* **spectroheliography** (-og´rəfi) *n.* **spectrohelioscope** *n.* a device for viewing the sun.

spectrology (spektrol´əji) *n.* the science of spectrum analysis. **spectrological** (-trəloj´-) *a.* **spectrologically** *adv.*

spectrometer (spektrom´itə) *n.* an instrument for measuring the refractive index of substances. **spectrometric** (-met´-) *a.* **spectrometry** *n.*

spectrophotometer (spektrōfōtom´itə) *n.* an instrument for measuring the intensity of light in different areas of the spectrum, esp. as transmitted by substances or solutions at various wavelengths. **spectrophotometric** (-fōtəmet´-), **spectrophotometrical** *a.* **spectrophotometrically** *adv.* **spectrophotometry** *n.*

spectroscope (spek´trəskōp) *n.* an instrument for forming and analysing the spectra of rays emitted by bodies. **spectroscopic** (-skop´-), **spectroscopical** *a.* **spectroscopically** *adv.* **spectroscopist** (-tros´-) *n.* **spectroscopy** (-tros´-) *n.*

spectrum (spek´trəm) *n.* (*pl.* **spectra** (-trə)) **1** the rainbow-like range of colours into which white light is dispersed, according to the degrees of refrangibility of its components, when passing through a prism, from violet (with the shortest wavelength) to red (with the longest wavelength). **2** the complete range of wavelengths of electromagnetic radiation. **3** any particular distribution of electromagnetic radiation, esp. as characteristic of a particular substance when emitting or absorbing radiation. **4** any similar range, e.g. of sound frequencies, or of particles distributed according to energy. **5** a complete range, of e.g. opinion, interests, activities, abilities etc. **6** OCULAR SPECTRUM (under OCULAR). **spectral**[2] *a.* of or relating to, or like a spectrum. **spectral type, spectral class** *n.* any of the various groups into which stars can be classified according to the bands or lines of their spectra. **spectrum analyser,** (*N Am.*) **spectrum analyzer** *n.* a device for breaking down oscillation into its individual components. **spectrum analysis, spectral analysis** *n.* chemical analysis with a spectroscope. [L, a vision, an image, from *specere*, to look]

specula, specular SPECULUM.

speculate (spek´ūlāt) *v.i.* **1** to pursue an inquiry or form conjectures or views (on or upon). **2** to guess or conjecture (e.g. how, or that, something is the case). **3** to make purchases, investments etc. on the chance of profit. **4** to gamble wildly or recklessly. **speculation** (-lā´shən) *n.* **1** the act or practice of speculating. **2** a mental inquiry, train of thought or series of conjectures about a subject. **3** a speculative business transaction, investment or undertaking. **4** a game in which the players speculate on the value of their cards. **speculative** (-lətiv) *a.* **speculatively** *adv.* **speculativeness** *n.* **speculator** *n.* [L *speculātus*, p.p. of *speculāri*, to behold, from *specula*, a watchtower]

speculum (spek´ūləm) *n.* (*pl.* **specula** (-lə)) **1** a surgical instrument for dilating the passages or cavities of the body, to facilitate inspection. **2** a mirror, esp. one of polished metal, used as a reflector in a telescope. **3 a** a lustrous spot or coloured area on the wing of certain birds. **b** an ocellus. **specular** *a.* **1** of or relating to a speculum. **2** of or relating to a mirror, mirror-like, reflecting. **specular iron, specular iron ore** *n.* a bright crystalline variety of haematite. **speculum-metal** *n.* an alloy of copper and tin used for mirrors or reflectors. [L, mirror, from *specere*, to look]

sped SPEED.

speech (spēch) *n.* **1** the faculty or act of uttering articulate sounds or words. **2** a public address, an oration. **3** an individual's characteristic manner of speech. **4** that which is spoken, an utterance, a remark. **5** the language or dialect of a nation, region etc. **6** in linguistics, parole. **7** the sounding-quality of a musical instrument, esp. of an organ pipe, inexpressible in words. **speech community** *n.* a community sharing a common dialect or language. **speech day** *n.* the annual prize-giving day in some schools, with ceremonial speeches etc. **speechful** *a.* **speechify** *v.i.* (*3rd pers. sing. pres.* **speechifies**, *pres.p.* **speechifying**, *past, p.p.* **speechified**) (*often derog.*) to make a speech or speeches, esp. pompous or lengthy, to harangue. **speechification** (-fikā´shən) *n.* **speechifier** *n.* **speechless** *a.* **1** unable to speak, silent, esp. through emotion. **2** dumb, dumbfounded. **speechlessly** *adv.* **speechlessness** *n.* **speech-reading** *n.* lip-reading. **speech therapy** *n.* treatment for improving speech, enunciation etc. **speech therapist** *n.* **speech-writer** *n.* a person who writes the speeches delivered by a politician etc. [OE *spæc*, *spræc*, see SPEAK]

speed (spēd) *n.* **1** rapidity, swiftness, celerity. **2** rate of motion, the ratio of the distance covered to the time taken by a moving body. **3** the numerical expression of the sensitivity of a photographic plate, film or paper to light. **4** a measure of the power of a lens to take in light. **5 a** any of the gear ratios on a bicycle. **b** (*esp. N Am.*) †a gear in a motor vehicle. **6** (*sl.*) amphetamine. **7** †success or good fortune (*Wish us good speed*). ~*v.i.* (*past, p.p.* **sped** (sped)) **1** to move rapidly, to hasten. **2** (*past, p.p.* **speeded**) to drive, to travel at an excessively high, dangerous or illegal speed. **3** †to fare, to be successful. ~*v.t.* **1** (*past, p.p.* **speeded**) to regulate the speed of, to set (an engine etc.) at a fixed rate of speed. **2** to cause to go fast, to urge, to send at great speed. **3** †to promote, to make prosperous, to cause to succeed. **at speed** while moving quickly. **to speed up** 1 to progress faster. 2 to cause to progress faster, to expedite. **speedball** *n.* 1 (*sl.*) a mixture of cocaine with morphine or heroin. 2 a game resembling soccer with some permitted handling of the ball. **speedboat** *n.* a light motor boat designed for high speed. **speed bump, speed hump** *n.* a widthways ridge on a road for slowing traffic down. **speeder** *n.* **speeding** *n.* (the offence of) driving at an excessive, dangerous or illegal speed. ~*a.* travelling at such a speed. **speed limit** *n.* the legal limit of speed for a road vehicle, vessel etc. in a particular area or in particular conditions. **speed merchant** *n.* (*coll.*) a motorist who habitually drives fast. **speedo** (-ō) *n.* (*pl.* **speedos**) (*coll.*) a speedometer. **speedometer** (-dom´itə) *n.* a device fitted in a vehicle to measure and indicate its speed. **speedster** (-stə) *n.* 1 a fast car, a sports car. 2 a speedboat. 3 a person who speeds. **speed trap** *n.* a stretch of road monitored by police using radar devices to catch speeding drivers. **speed-up** *n.* an increase in speed, an acceleration. **speedway** *n.* 1 the sport of motorcycle racing on a track. 2 a racecourse, stadium or track for motorcycle racing. 3 (*N Am.*) a road or track for motor-car racing. 4 (*N Am.*) a highway for fast traffic. **speedwell** *n.* a flowering herb, any of various species of *Veronica*. **speedy** *a.* (*comp.* **speedier,** *superl.* **speediest**). **speedily** *adv.* **speediness** *n.* [OE *spēd* (whence *spēdan*, v.), from *spōwan*, to succeed (cp. Dut. *spoed*, OHG *spuot*, *spōt*, success, *spuon*, to prosper, also L *spatium*, space, *spēs*, hope)]

speer (spēr), **speir** *v.i.*, *v.t.* (*Sc.*) to question, to inquire, to ask. [OE *spyrian*, to follow a track, cogn. with SPOOR]

speiss (spīs) *n.* a compound of arsenic, nickel, copper etc., produced in the smelting of various ores such as lead. [G *Speise*, orig. food, It. *spesa*, from L, as EXPENSE]

spekboom (spek´bōm) *n.* (*S Afr.*) a large shrub with succulent leaves, *Portulacaria afra*. [Afrikaans *spek*, fat meat, *boom*, tree]

spelean (spilē´ən), **spelaean** *a.* 1 of or relating to a cave or caves. 2 cave-dwelling. **speleology** (spēliol´əji) *n.* the scientific study or exploration of caves. **speleological** *a.* **speleologist** *n.* [L *spēlaeum*, Gr. *spēlaion*, cave, -AN]

spelk (spelk) *n.* (*Sc.*, *North.*) a splinter. [OE *spelc*, cp. Dut. *spalk*]

spell[1] (spel) *v.t.* (*past*, *p.p.* **spelt** (spelt), **spelled** (speld, spelt)) 1 to say or write the letters forming (a word). 2 (of letters) to form (a word). 3 to mean, to import, to portend, entail or involve (*a formula that spells disaster*). 4 †to read or decipher with difficulty. ~*v.i.* to put letters together in such a way as to (correctly) form a word (*He never could spell*). **to spell it out** to explain things fully and simply, as distinct from hinting or alluding. **to spell out** 1 to utter or write letter by letter. 2 to make clear, easy to understand. 3 to puzzle out. **spellable** *a.* **spell-check** *n.* a check made by a spelling checker of the spelling in a computer file. ~*v.t.* to check the spelling in (a file) with a spelling checker. **spell-checker** *n.* a spelling checker. **speller** *n.* 1 a person who spells well, badly etc. (*a good speller*). 2 a spelling-book. **spelling** *n.* 1 the activity or process of writing or saying the letters of a word. 2 the particular formation of letters making up a word, orthography. 3 one's ability to spell (*My spelling's awful*). **spelling-bee** *n.* a competition in spelling. **spelling-book** *n.* a book for teaching spelling. **spelling checker** *n.* a computer program that checks the spelling of words keyed, usu. against a stored list of vocabulary. [OF *espeler*, cp. Dut. *spelen*, OE *spellian*, from SPELL[3]]

spell[2] (spel) *n.* 1 a series of words used as a charm, an incantation. 2 the power of an occult force; a state of enchantment. 3 a powerful attraction or fascination. **under a spell** dominated by, or as if by, a spell. **spellbind** *v.t.* (*past*, *p.p.* **spellbound**) 1 to put a spell on. 2 to entrance. **spellbinder** *n.* a person or thing that entrances, esp. an eloquent speaker, film, book etc. **spellbinding** *a.* **spellbindingly** *adv.* **spellbound** *a.* 1 under the influence of a spell. 2 enchanted, fascinated. [OE *spel*, *spell*, cp. Icel. *spjall*, OHG *spel*, narrative, story, cogn. with SPELL[1]]

spell[3] (spel) *n.* 1 a shift or turn of work. 2 a (usu. short) period of time. 3 a period of weather of a certain kind (*a cold spell*). 4 a period characterized by some experience (*a spell of ill health*; *having a bad spell*). 5 (*Austral.*) a rest from work. ~*v.t.* to take the turn of at work, to relieve or allow to rest. ~*v.i.* (*Austral.*) to rest briefly. [OE *spelian*, perh. cogn. with *spilian*, to play, cp. G *spielen* and *Spiel*]

spell[4] (spel) *n.* a splinter of wood etc. [perh. from obs. *speld*, chip]

spellican SPILLIKIN.

spelt[1] SPELL[1].

spelt[2] (spelt) *n.* a variety of wheat, *Triticum spelta*, formerly much cultivated in S Europe etc. [OE, from late L *spelta*]

spelter (spel´tə) *n.* commercial or impure smelted zinc. [from Gmc. (cp. Dut. and G *Spialter*), rel. to PEWTER]

spelunker (spilŭng´kə) *n.* (*N Am.*) a person who explores or studies caves as a sport or hobby. **spelunking** *n.* [from L *spēlunca*, a cave]

†**spence** (spens) *n.* a larder or pantry. [ME, from OF *despense*, from L *dispensa*, fem. p.p. of *dispendere*, as DISPENSE]

spencer[1] (spen´sə) *n.* 1 a short overcoat or jacket, for men or women. 2 a woman's undergarment, a vest. [Earl *Spencer*, 1758–1834]

spencer[2] (spen´sə) *n.* (*Naut.*) a fore-and-aft trysail abaft the foremast or mainmast on a barque or ship. [etym. uncertain, perh. the name *Spencer*]

spend (spend) *v.t.* (*past*, *p.p.* **spent** (spent)) 1 to pay out (money etc. on something or someone) (*spent £40 on a new pair of shoes*; *seemed reluctant to spend money on his children*). 2 to consume, to use up, to expend (time, energy, effort etc.). 3 to pass (time) (*spending a week in Venice*). 4 to wear out, to exhaust (*The storm had spent itself*). ~*v.i.* to expend money. ~*n.* 1 the activity of spending money. 2 a sum spent, expenditure. **to spend a penny** (*coll.*) to urinate. **spendable** *a.* **spender** *n.* **spending** *n.* **spending money** *n.* pocket money, money for spending. **spendthrift** *n.* a prodigal or wasteful person. ~*a.* prodigal, wasteful. **spent** *a.* exhausted, burnt out, used up (*feeling spent*; *spent inspiration*). **spent force** *n.* a person who or thing that is used up, exhausted, useless etc. **spent tan** *n.* tan with the tannic acid extracted, used as a road surface etc. [OE *spendan*, late L *dispendere*, to weigh out, see DISPENSE]

Spenserian (spensiə´riən) *a.* of or relating to or in the style of the poet Edmund Spenser, 1552–99, or his verse. ~*n.* 1 a student of Spenser. 2 a poet writing in a style resembling that of Spencer. 3 a Spenserian stanza. **Spenserian stanza** *n.* a stanza with eight iambic pentameters and an alexandrine, rhyming *a b a b b c b c c*, as used in his *Faerie Queene* or in Byron's *Childe Harold*.

spent SPEND.

sperm (spœm) *n.* (*pl.* **sperm, sperms**) 1 a spermatozoon, a male gamete. 2 the seminal or reproductive fluid of male animals. 3 a sperm whale or cachalot. 4 spermaceti. 5 sperm oil. **sperm bank** *n.* a supply of semen stored ready for using in artificial insemination. **sperm count** *n.* the number of spermatozoa found in a single ejaculation, or in any measured quantity of semen. **spermic** *a.* SPERMATIC. **spermicide** (-misīd) *n.* a substance that kills spermatozoa. **spermicidal** (-sī´-) *a.* **sperm oil** *n.* oil from the head of a sperm whale, used as a lubricant. **spermous** *a.* SPERMATIC. **sperm whale** *n.* a large whale, *Physeter macrocephalus*, yielding sperm oil, spermaceti and ambergris. [F *sperme*, from L and Gr. *sperma*, seed, from *speirein*, to sow]

sperm- SPERMATO-.
-sperm (spœm) *comb. form* a seed. [Gr. *sperma*]
spermaceti (spœməsē´ti, -set´i) *n.* a white waxy, buoyancy-promoting substance, existing in solution in the oily matter in the head of the sperm whale, used for candles, ointments etc. **spermacetic** *a.* [Gr. *sperma*, seed, L, *cētī*, gen. of *cētus*, Gr. *kētos*, whale]
spermary (spœ´məri), **spermarium** (-meə´riəm) *n.* (*pl.* **spermaries, spermaria** (-riə)) the male spermatic gland, testicle or other organ. [from mod. L]
spermat- SPERMATO-.
spermatheca (spœməthē´kə) *n.* a receptacle in female insects and other invertebrates for spermatozoa. [Gr. *thēkē*, repository]
spermatic (spœmat´ik) *a.* **1** consisting of, of or relating to or conveying sperm or semen. **2** of or relating to the spermary. **spermatical** *a.* **spermatically** *adv.* **spermatic cord** *n.* a cord running to and from each testicle, consisting of blood vessels, nerves etc. **spermatic fluid** *n.* semen. [F *spermatique*, L *spermaticus*, from Gr. *sperma -matos*, sperm]
spermatid (spœ´mətid) *n.* a male sex cell that may develop directly into a spermatozoon. **spermatidal** (-tī´dəl) *a.*
spermato- (spœ´mətō), **spermat-, sperm-, spermo-** *comb. form* a seed or sperm. [Gr. *sperma, spermatos*, seed]
spermatoblast (spœ´mətōblast) *n.* a cell from which a spermatozoon develops.
spermatocyte (spœ´mətōsīt, -mat´-) *n.* a cell produced from a spermatogonium that may divide into spermatids.
spermatogenesis (spœmətōjen´isis) *n.* the development or production of mature spermatozoa. **spermatogenetic** (-jinet´-) *a.*
spermatogonium (spœmətōgō´niəm) *n.* (*pl.* **spermatogonia** (-niə)) a primitive male germ cell which divides to form spermatocytes. [mod. L *gonium*, from Gr. *gonos*, seed, offspring]
spermatophore (spœ´mətōfaw, -mat´ə-) *n.* a capsule holding spermatozoa, in molluscs and other invertebrates. **spermatophoric** (-for´-) *a.*
spermatophyte (spœ´mətōfīt, -mat´ə-) *n.* a seed-bearing plant. **spermatophytic** (-fit´-) *a.*
spermatorrhoea (spœmətərē´ə), (*esp. N Am.*) **spermatorrhea** *n.* involuntary discharge of seminal fluid. [Gr. *rheein*, to flow]
spermatozoon (spœmətōzō´on, -mat´ə-) *n.* (*pl.* **spermatozoa** (-zō´ə)) any of the millions of mature male sex cells contained in the semen. **spermatozoal** (-zō´əl), **spermatozoan** (-zō´ən), **spermatozoic** (-zō´ik) *a.* **spermatozoid** (-zō´id) *n.* the mature male sex cell of some plants, an antherozoid.
spermic, spermicide SPERM.
spermo- SPERMATO-.
spew (spū), **spue** *v.t.* **1** to vomit (up). **2** to spit out. **3** to emit or eject violently or in great quantity. ~*v.i.* **1** to vomit. **2** to stream, gush or flood out. ~*n.* vomit, matter ejected with great force or in great quantity. **spewer** *n.* **spewy** *a.* (*comp.* **spewier,** *superl.* **spewiest**). [OE *speowan, spīwan* (cp. MDut. *spouwen*, G *spein*, Icel. *spȳja*, also L *spuere*, Gr. *ptuein*), imit. in orig.]
SPF *abbr.* sun protection factor (an indication of the protective strength of sun creams or lotions).
sp. gr. *abbr.* specific gravity.
sphagnum (sfag´nəm) *n.* (*pl.* **sphagna** (-nə)) any moss of the genus *Sphagnum*, found in peat or bogs, and used as a fertilizer and as packing material. **sphagnous** *a.* **sphagnum moss** *n.* [Gr. *sphagnos*]
sphalerite (sfal´ərīt) *n.* blende. [Gr. *sphaleros*, deceptive]
sphen- SPHENO-.
sphene (sfēn) *n.* titanite, occurring as wedge-shaped crystals. **sphenic** *a.* wedge-shaped. [F *sphène*, Gr. *sphēn, sphēnos*, a wedge]
spheno- (sfē´nō), **sphen-** *comb. form* **1** (*Anat.*) the sphenoid bone. **2** of or relating to a wedge. [Gr. *sphēn, sphēnos*, a wedge]
sphenodon (sfē´nədon) *n.* any member of the genus *Sphenodon* of nocturnal lizard-like reptiles, now confined to New Zealand. [Gr. *odous odontos*, tooth]
sphenogram (sfē´nəgram) *n.* a cuneiform or wedge-shaped written character. **sphenography** (-nogrəfi) *n.* writing in such characters. **sphenographic** (-graf´-) *a.*
sphenoid (sfē´noid) *a.* **1** wedge-shaped. **2** (*Anat.*) of or relating to the sphenoid bone. ~*n.* **1** the sphenoid bone. **2** a wedge-shaped crystal enclosed by four equal isosceles triangles. **sphenoidal** (-noi´-) *a.* **sphenoid bone** *n.* a compound butterfly-shaped bone at the base of the cranium behind the eyes.
sphere (sfiə) *n.* **1** a solid bounded by a surface every part of which is equally distant from a point within called the centre. **2** a figure approximately spherical, a ball, a globe, esp. one of the heavenly bodies. **3 a** a globe representing the earth or the apparent heavens. **b** any of the spherical shells revolving round the earth as centre in which, according to ancient astronomy, the heavenly bodies were set. **c** the sky, the heavens. **4** an area of knowledge or a discipline. **5** field of action, influence etc., scope, range, province, place, position; social class. ~†*v.t.* **1** to enclose in or as in a sphere. **2** to make spherical. **harmony of the spheres** HARMONY. **music of the spheres** MUSIC. **spheral** *a.* **1** spherical. **2** of or relating to the celestial spheres or the music of the spheres. **spheric** (sfer´ik) *a.* spherical. **spherical** (sfer´ikəl) *a.* **1** sphere-shaped, globular. **2** relating to spheres or their properties. **spherical aberration** *n.* the deterioration of an image from a lens or mirror with a spherical surface as a result of the different focal points of rays striking its edge and centre. **spherical angle** *n.* the angle between two intersecting great circles of a sphere. **spherical coordinates** *n.pl.* coordinates used to locate a point in space comprising a radius vector and two angles measured from a vertical and a horizontal line. **spherically** *adv.* **spherical triangle** *n.* a figure on the surface of a sphere bounded by the arcs of three great circles. **spherical trigonometry** *n.* the trigonometry concerned with spherical triangles. **sphericity** (-ris´-) *n.* **spherics** (sfer´iks) *n.* spherical geometry and trigonometry. **spheroid** (sfiə´roid) *n.* **1** a body nearly spherical. **2** a solid generated by the revolution of an ellipse about its minor axis (called an *oblate spheroid*) or its major axis (called a *prolate spheroid*). **spheroidal** (-roi´-) *a.* **spheroidally** *adv.* **spheroidic, spheroidical** *a.* **spheroidically** *adv.* **spheroidicity** (-dis´-) *n.* [ME *spere*, OF *espere*, L *sphæra*, Gr. *sphaira*, ball]
spherometer (sfiərom´itə) *n.* an instrument for measuring the radii and curvature of spherical surfaces.
spherule (sfer´ūl) *n.* a small sphere. **spherular** *a.* **spherulite** (-līt) *n.* a radiating globular mass of crystalline fibres occurring in certain rocks, e.g. obsidian. **spherulitic** (-lit´-) *a.* [late L *sphaerula*, dim. of *sphaera*, ball, sphere]
sphincter (sfingk´tə) *n.* a ring muscle that contracts or shuts any orifice or tube. **sphincteral, sphincterial** (-tiə´riəl), **sphincteric** (-ter´ik) *a.* [L and Gr., from Gr. *sphingein*, to bind tight]
sphingid (sfin´jid) *n.* a hawkmoth of the family Sphingidae. [SPHINX, -ID]
sphinx (sfingks) *n.* **1** (**Sphinx**) in Greek mythology, a winged monster, half woman and half lion, said to have devoured the inhabitants of Thebes till a riddle she had proposed should be solved, and on its solution by Oedipus to have flung herself down and perished. **2** any of several ancient Egyptian figures with the body of a lion and a human or animal head. **3** (**the Sphinx**) the

huge figure near the Pyramids at Giza. **4** a taciturn or enigmatic person. **5** a hawkmoth. **6** a variety of baboon, *Mandrillus sphinx*. [L and Gr., prob. of foreign etym., pop. from Gr. *sphingein*, to squeeze, strangle]

sphragistics (sfrəjis´tiks) *n.* the study of engraved seals and signets. **sphragistic** *a.* [Gr. *sphrāgistikos*, from *sphrāgis*, seal]

sphygmic SPHYGMUS.

sphygmo- (sfig´mō) *comb. form* of or relating to a pulse. [Gr. *sphugmos*, pulse, from *sphuzein*, to beat, to throb]

sphygmograph (sfig´məgrahf) *n.* an instrument for recording the movements of the pulse. **sphygmogram** (-gram) *n.* a record produced by a sphygmograph. **sphygmographic** (-graf´-) *a.* **sphygmographically** *adv.* **sphygmography** (-mog´rəfi) *n.*

sphygmology (sfigmol´əji) *n.* the branch of physiology concerned with the pulse. **sphygmological** (-məloj´ikəl) *a.*

sphygmomanometer (sfigmōmənom´itə) *n.* an instrument for measuring the tension of blood in an artery. **sphygmomanometric** (-manōmet´-) *a.*

sphygmophone (sfig´məfōn) *n.* an instrument for enabling one to hear the action of the pulse.

sphygmoscope (sfig´məskōp) *n.* an instrument for rendering the movements of the pulse visible.

sphygmus (sfig´məs) *n.* a pulse, a pulsation. **sphygmic** *a.*

spic (spik), **spick, spik** *n.* (*N Am., offensive*) **1** a Spanish-speaking American, esp. a Mexican. **2** the Spanish spoken by such a person. [shortening of *spiggoty*, perh. an alt. of *speak the*, as in 'no speak the English']

spica (spī´kə) *n.* (*pl.* **spicas, spicae** (-kē)) **1** (*Bot.*) a spike. **2** a spiral surgical bandage with the turns reversed. **spicate** (-kāt, -kət), **spicated** (-kā´tid) *a.* (*Bot.*) pointed, having spikes. [L, ear of corn, spike]

spic and span SPICK AND SPAN.

spiccato (spikah´tō) *n.* a staccato style on a stringed instrument in which the player makes the bow rebound lightly from the strings. ~*a., adv.* (played) in this style. [It., detached]

spice (spīs) *n.* **1** any aromatic and pungent vegetable substance used for seasoning food. **2** such substances collectively (*sugar and spice*). **3** a flavour, a touch, a trace. **4** zest or interest (*adds a bit of spice*). ~*v.t.* **1** to season with spice. **2** to add interest to. **spicebush,** (*N Am.*) **spicewood** *n.* the wild allspice, *Lindera benzoin*, an American shrub. **spicery** (-əri) *n.* (*pl.* **spiceries**) **1** spices generally. **2** the piquancy associated with spices. **spicy, spicey** *a.* (*comp.* **spicier,** *superl.* **spiciest**) **1** flavoured with spice. **2** abounding in spices. **3** pungent, piquant. **4** suggestive of scandal. **5** showy, smart. **spicily** *adv.* **spiciness** *n.* [OF *espice*, L *speciēs*, kind, late L, spice]

spick and span (spik ən span´), **spic and span** *a.* new and fresh, clean and smart. [orig. *spick and span new*, extension of *span new*, see SPAN[3]]

spicknel SPIGNEL.

spicule (spik´ūl) *n.* **1** a small sharp needle-shaped body, such as the calcareous or siliceous spikes in sponges etc. **2** (*Bot.*) a small or subsidiary spike. **3** a spiked flare of hot gas ejected from the surface of the sun. **spicular** (-lə), **spiculate** (-lət), **spiculiform** (-fawm) *a.* **spiculiferous** (-lif´-), **spiculigerous** (-lij´-) *a.* **spiculum** (-ləm) *n.* (*pl.* **spicula** (-lə)) a spicule. [L *spīculum*, dim. of SPICA]

spicy SPICE.

spider (spī´də) *n.* **1** an eight-legged arachnid of the order Araneae, usu. equipped with a spinning apparatus utilized by most species for making webs to catch their prey. **2** an arachnid resembling this. **3** a spider-like thing, esp. a three-legged frying-pan, gridiron, frame etc. **4** an arrangement of elastic ropes with hooks attached, used for fastening loads to car roofs, motorcycles etc. **5** a long-legged rest for a cue in snooker. ~*v.i., v.t.* to (cause to) move in a spider-like way. **spider crab** *n.* a crab with long thin legs. **spidering** *a.* spider-like in shape, movement or manner. **spiderish** *a.* **spider-like** *a., adv.* **spider-line** *n.* a filament of spider's web used in the reticle of astronomical instruments etc. **spiderman** *n.* (*pl.* **spidermen**) (*coll.*) a construction worker who works at great heights. **spider mite** *n.* RED SPIDER (under RED[1]). **spider monkey** *n.* any monkey belonging to the American genus *Ateles* or *Brachyteles* with long limbs, a slender body, and a prehensile tail. **spider plant** *n.* a southern African house plant of the lily family, *Chlorophytum comosum*, having streamers of long narrow leaves with central white or yellow stripes. **spider's web, spider-web, spiderweb** *n.* **spider wasp, spider-hunting wasp** *n.* a wasp of the family Pompiloidea, that preys on spiders and other insects and stores them in its nest as food for its larvae. **spiderwort** *n.* any plant of the genus *Tradescantia*, esp. *Tradescantia virginiana*, whose flowers have long hairy stamens. **spidery** *a.* (esp. of handwriting) attenuated, spindly. [OE *spīthra*, from *spinnan*, to spin, see SPIN]

spiegeleisen (spē´gilīzən) *n.* a white variety of cast iron containing manganese, used in making Bessemer steel. [G *Spiegel*, mirror, SPECULUM, *Eisen*, iron]

spiel (shpēl, spēl) *n.* the sales patter of a practised dealer, or anyone's well-rehearsed or familiar tale. ~*v.i.* to talk with glib or practised ease. ~*v.t.* to reel off (patter). **spieler** *n.* (*sl.*) **1** (*esp. N Am.*) a person who spiels or holds forth. **2** (*Austral., New Zeal.*) a gambler, card-sharper or trickster. [G, a game]

spiffing (spif´ing) *a.* (*dated coll.*) **1** excellent. **2** smart, spruce, well-dressed. **spiffy** *a.* (*comp.* **spiffier,** *superl.* **spiffiest**) (*esp. N Am.*) spiffing. [etym. uncertain]

spiflicate (spif´likāt), **spifflicate** *v.t.* (*esp. facet.*) to smash, to crush, to destroy. **spiflication** (-kā´shən) *n.* [fanciful 18th-cent. coinage]

spignel (spig´nəl), **spicknel** (spik´nəl) *n.* an umbelliferous plant, *Meum athamanticum*, with an aromatic root used in medicine, and finely cut, ornamental leaves, also called *baldmoney*. [perh. ME *spigurnel*, a plant name, from med. L *spigurnellus*]

spigot (spig´ət) *n.* **1** a peg or plug for stopping the vent-hole in a cask. **2** (*N Am.*) a faucet, a tap. **3** (*N Am.*) the turning-plug in a tap. [prob. from OProv. *espigot*, dim. of *espiga*, L SPICA]

spik SPIC.

spike[1] (spīk) *n.* **1** any pointed object, a sharp point. **2** a pointed piece of metal, e.g. one of a number fixed on the top of a railing, fence, or wall. **3** **a** any of a number of metal points fitted to the sole of a boot or running shoe, to prevent slipping. **b** (*pl.*) a pair of running shoes with spikes. **4** a pointed metal rod set vertically into a base, on which to impale bills or, in journalism, rejected news stories. **5** a large nail or pin, used in structures built of large timbers, on railways etc. **6** (*sl.*) a hypodermic needle. **7** (*sl.*) a doss-house. **8** an electrical pulse characterized by a rapid increase and equally rapid decrease in voltage. ~*v.t.* **1** to fasten with spikes. **2** to provide or fit with spikes. **3** **a** to pierce with or impale on a spike. **b** (of a news editor) to file (a story) as rejected (by impaling it on a spike). **4** to plug the touch-hole of (a cannon) with a spike. **5** to lace (a drink) with spirits. **6** to render useless. **7** in volleyball, to punch (the ball) sharply down into the opposing court. **to spike someone's guns** to foil someone's plans. **spike heel** *n.* a high heel tapering to a point. **spike-nail** *n.* a large nail with a small head. **spiky** *a.* (*comp.* **spikier,** *superl.* **spikiest**). **spikily** *adv.* **spikiness** *n.* [perh. from Scand. (cp. Icel. *spīk*, Swed. *spik*), cogn. with SPOKE[1]]

spike[2] (spīk) *n.* **1** (*Bot.*) an inflorescence closely attached to a common stem. **2** spike lavender. **spike lavender** *n.* a species of lavender, *Lavandula latifolia*, that yields an oil used in paints. **spikelet** (-lit) *n.* a small spike, esp. as part of the inflorescence of most grasses, with two bracts at the base. [ME, ear of corn, from L *spīca*]

spikenard (spīk´nahd) *n.* **1 a** a Himalayan herb, *Nardostachys jatamansi*, related to the valerian. **b** an ancient and costly aromatic ointment prepared chiefly from the root of this. **2** a European and African plant, *Inula conyza*, with yellow flowers and aromatic roots. **3** any of various vegetable oils. [OF *spiquenare* (L SPICA, *nardī*, gen. of *nardus*, NARD)]

spiky SPIKE[1].

spile (spīl) *n.* **1** a small wooden plug, a spigot. **2** a large timber driven into the ground to protect a bank etc., a pile. **3** (*N Am.*) a small spout used for tapping sap from a sugar maple. ~*v.t.* to pierce (a cask) with a hole and furnish with a spile. [cp. Dut. *spijl*, LG *spile*, bar, spile, G *Speiler*, skewer]

spill[1] (spil) *v.t.* (*past, p.p.* **spilt** (spilt), **spilled** (spild, spilt)) **1** to cause (liquid, powder etc.) to fall or run out of a vessel, esp. accidentally. **2** to shed. **3** (*coll.*) to throw out of a vehicle or from a saddle. **4** (*Naut.*) **a** to empty (a sail) of wind. **b** to lose (wind) from a sail. **5** (*sl.*) to give away, disclose (information). ~*v.i.* **1** (of liquid) to run or fall out of a vessel. **2** (of a crowd) to pour (out of a place). ~*n.* **1** an instance of spilling, or the amount spilt. **2** a tumble, a fall, esp. from a vehicle or saddle. **3** (*Austral.*) the vacating of a number of political posts to make way for reorganization. **to spill over 1** to overflow. **2** (of excess population) to be forced to move or spread. **to spill someone's blood** to be responsible for someone's death. **to spill the beans** to divulge a secret. **spillage** (-lij) *n.* **spilling line** *n.* a rope for spilling the wind out of a square sail to enable it to be reefed. **spillover** *n.* **1** an instance, or the process, of spilling over. **2** that which spills over. **3** a repercussion or knock-on effect. **spillway** *n.* a passage for the overflow of water from a reservoir etc. **spilth** (-th) *n.* **1** that which is spilt. **2** an instance of spilling. **3** excess of supply. [OE *spillan*, to destroy, Icel. *spilla*, cp. Swed. *spilla*]

spill[2] (spil) *n.* a slip of paper or wood used to light a candle, pipe etc. [ME, rel. to SPILE]

spillikin (spil´ikin), **spellican** (spel´ikən) *n.* a small strip or pin of bone, wood etc., used in spillikins. **spillikins** *n.* a game in which players attempt to remove spillikins from a pile one at a time without disturbing the others. [prob. dim. of SPILL[2]]

spilosite (spī´ləsīt) *n.* a greenish schistose rock spotted with chlorite concretions or scales. [Gr. *spilos*, spot, -ITE[1]]

spilt, spilth SPILL[1].

spin (spin) *v.t.* (*pres.p.* **spinning**, *past* **spun** (spŭn), **span** (span), *p.p.* **spun**) **1** to make (something or someone) rotate or whirl round rapidly. **2 a** to draw out and twist (wool, cotton etc.) into threads. **b** to make (yarn etc.) thus. **3** (of spiders etc.) to produce (a web, cocoon etc.) by drawing out a thread of viscous substance. **4** to tell, compose etc. (a tale), at great length. **5** to hit (a ball) so that it twists in flight. **6** to shape in a lathe etc. **7** to fish with a revolving bait. **8** to toss (a coin). **9** to spin-dry. **10** (*sl.*) to reject after examination. ~*v.i.* **1** to whirl round. **2** to turn round quickly. **3** (of a ball) to twist in flight. **4** (of one's head) to be dizzy with amazement or excitement. **5** to draw out and twist cotton etc., into threads. **6** to make yarn etc., thus. **7** to fish with a spinning bait. **8** (of a vehicle etc.) to go (along) with great swiftness. ~*n.* **1** the act or motion of spinning, a whirl. **2** a rapid diving descent by an aircraft accompanied by a continued gyration. **3** a twisting motion imparted to a ball, or to a rifle bullet. **4** (*coll.*) a brief run in a car, aircraft etc. **5** (*Physics*) the angular momentum of a subatomic particle in default of orbital motion. **6** (*Austral.*) a piece of luck. **7** (*N Am.*) a cosmetic twist given to information in presentation. **in a flat spin** in a state of agitation. **to spin a yarn** to tell a story. **to spin off** to throw off, or be thrown off, by centrifugal force while spinning. **to spin out 1** to compose or tell (a yarn etc.) at great length. **2** to prolong, to protract, to make to last. **3** to spend (time) in tedious discussion etc. **4** (*N Am.*) (of e.g. a vehicle) to go out of control in a skid etc. **5** (of a bowler in cricket) to dismiss (a batsman) by spin bowling. **spin bowling** *n.* in cricket, a style of bowling in which the ball is delivered slowly with an imparted spin to make it bounce unpredictably. **spin bowler** *n.* **spin doctor** *n.* (*coll.*) in politics, a spokesperson employed to give a favourable twist to events for the benefit of the media. **spin-dryer, spin-drier** *n.* a machine with a rotating perforated drum in which the water is extracted from washing by centrifugal force. **spin-dry** *v.t.* (*3rd pers. sing. pres.* **spin-dries,** *pres.p.* **spin-drying,** *past, p.p.* **spin-dried**). **spinner** *n.* **1** a person or thing that spins. **2** a machine for spinning thread. **3 a** in cricket, a ball bowled with a spin. **b** a spin bowler. **4 a** a spider's spinneret. **b** †a spider. **5** in fishing, a lure designed to revolve in the water. **6** a mayfly or other fly used in fishing. **7** a spin-dryer. **spinneret** (spin´əret) *n.* **1** the spinning organ of a spider through which the silk issues. **2** the orifice through which liquid cellulose is projected to form the threads of rayon or artificial silk. **spinnery** *n.* (*pl.* **spinneries**) a spinning mill. **spinning** *n.* **spinning jenny** *n.* (*pl.* **spinning jennies**) a spinning frame with several spindles invented by Hargreaves in 1764 for spinning more than one thread at once. **spinning machine** *n.* a machine for spinning fibres continuously. **spinning mill** *n.* a factory where spinning is carried on. **spinning mule** *n.* an early form of spinning machine. **spinning top** TOP[2]. **spinning wheel** *n.* a machine for home spinning, with a spindle driven by a wheel operated by the foot or hand, formerly used for spinning wool, cotton, or flax. **spin-off** *n.* a by-product or incidental benefit, something derived from an existing idea or product. [OE *spinnan* (cp. Dut. and G *spinnen*, Icel. and Swed. *spinna*), cogn. with SPAN[1]]

spina bifida SPINE.

spinach (spin´ich, -ij) *n.* **1** an annual herb of the genus *Spinacia*, esp. *S. oleracea*, with succulent leaves cooked as food. **2** the leaves of this plant. **spinaceous** (-nā´shəs) *a.* **spinach beet** *n.* a variety of beet of which the leaves are eaten as spinach. **spinachy** *a.* [OF *espinache*, *espinage*, Sp. *espinaca*, Arab. *'isfānākh*, prob. from Pers.]

spinal SPINE.

spindle (spin´dəl) *n.* **1** a pin or rod in a spinning wheel for twisting and winding the thread. **2** a rod used for the same purpose in hand-spinning. **3** a pin bearing the bobbin in a spinning machine. **4** a rod, axis, or arbor which revolves, or on which anything revolves. **5** a spindle-shaped structure formed in a cell during cell division. **6** a measure of length for yarn. **7** a slender object or person. ~*v.i.* to grow into a long slender stalk, shape etc. **spindle-berry** *n.* (*pl.* **spindle-berries**) the fruit of the spindle tree. **spindle-legged, spindle-shanked** *a.* having long, thin legs. **spindle-legs, spindle-shanks** *n.* **1** (*as pl.*) long thin legs. **2** (*as sing.*) a person with long thin legs. **spindle-shaped** *a.* tapering from the middle towards both ends, fusiform. **spindle side** *n.* the female members of a family, the distaff side. **spindle tree** *n.* a shrub or small tree, *Euonymus europaeus*, the hard wood of which is used for spindles, pins, skewers etc. **spindly** *a.* (*comp.* **spindlier,** *superl.* **spindliest**) **1** tall and thin. **2** elongated. [OE *spinl*, from *spinnan*, to SPIN]

spindrift (spin´drift) *n.* fine spray blown up from the surface of water. [var. of *spoondrift* (*spoon*, to scud before the wind, DRIFT)]

spine (spīn) *n.* **1** the spinal column, the backbone. **2** a sharp, stiff woody process, a thorn. **3** (*esp. Zool.*) a sharp ridge, projection, out-growth etc. **4** the narrow back part of a book or its cover, that usu. faces outwards on a shelf and bears the title and the author's name. **spina bifida** (spīnə bif´idə) *n.* a congenital condition in which one or more vertebrae fail to unite during the embryo stage, so that the spinal cord and meninges protrude, resulting in paralysis of the lower body in some cases. **spinal** *a.* of or relating to the spine. **spinal canal** *n.* a passage through the vertebrae that contains the spinal cord. **spinal column** *n.* the backbone, an interconnected series of vertebrae in the skeleton which runs the length of the trunk and encloses the spinal cord, giving support to the thorax and abdomen. **spinal cord** *n.* a cylindrical structure of nerve fibres and cells within the vertebral canal, forming part of the central nervous system. **spinally** *adv.* **spine-chiller** *n.* a book, film, event etc. that causes terror. **spine-chilling** *a.* **spined** *a.* **spineless** *a.* **1** without a spine; invertebrate. **2** (of a plant or animal) without spines. **3** of weak character, lacking decision. **spinescent** (-nes´ənt) *a.* **1** (*Bot.*) tending to be spinous. **2** spinous, thorny. **spinescence** *n.* **spiniferous** (-nif´-), **spinigerous** (-nij´-) *a.* having spines or thorns. **spinose** (-nōs), **spinous** *a.* having spines, spiny. **spinosity** (-nos´-) *n.* **spiny** *a.* (*comp.* **spinier**, *superl.* **spiniest**). **spininess** *n.* **spiny anteater** *n.* ECHIDNA. **spiny lobster** *n.* any of several large spiny crustaceans, lacking large anterior claws, esp. *Palinuris vulgaris.* [OF *espine* (F *épine*), L *spīna*, thorn, backbone]

spinel (spinel´) *n.* **1** a vitreous aluminate of magnesium, of various colours, crystallizing isometrically. **2** any of various other minerals of similar structure. **spinel ruby** *n.* a dark red variety of spinel, used in jewellery etc. [F *spinelle*, from It. *spinella*, dim. of *spina*, thorn, from L]

spinescence SPINE.

spinet (spinet´) *n.* **1** an obsolete musical instrument, similar in construction to but smaller than the harpsichord. **2** (*N Am.*) a kind of small upright piano. [MF *espinette*, It. *spinetta*, dim. of *spina*, thorn, or perh. from *Spinetti*, possibly name of inventor]

spini- (spī´ni) *comb. form* of or relating to the spine. [L *spīna*, spine]

spiniferous SPINE.

spinifex (spī´nifeks) *n.* any coarse, spiny Australian grass of the genus *Spinifex*, growing in sandhills etc. in the arid regions of Australia, and often covering enormous areas of ground. [L *spīna*, SPINE, *-fex*, maker, from *facere*, to make]

spinigerous SPINE.

spinnaker (spin´əkə) *n.* a large jib-shaped sail carried opposite the mainsail on the mainmast of a racing yacht. [perh. from *Sphinx*, name of a yacht]

spinner, spinneret etc. SPIN.

spinney (spin´i) *n.* (*pl.* **spinneys**) a small wood with undergrowth, a copse. [OF *espinei*, *espinoye* (F *épinaie*), L *spīnētum*, from *spīna*, thorn, SPINE]

spinning SPIN.

spinode (spī´nōd) *n.* a stationary point on a curve, a cusp.

spinose, spinous SPINE.

Spinozism (spinō´zizm) *n.* the monistic system of Baruch de Spinoza, 1632–77, who resolved all being into extension and thought, which he considered as attributes of God. **Spinozist** *n.* **Spinozistic** (-zis´-) *a.*

spinster (spin´stə) *n.* **1** an unmarried woman. **2** a woman unlikely to get married, esp. an elderly one. **spinsterhood** *n.* **spinsterish** *a.* **spinsterishness** *n.* [SPIN, -STER]

spinthariscope (spinthar´iskōp) *n.* an instrument for showing the rays emitted by radium by the scintillations caused by their impact against a fluorescent screen. **spinthariscopic** (-skop´-) *a.* [Gr. *spintharis*, spark, -SCOPE]

spinule (spin´ūl) *n.* a minute spine. **spinuliferous** (-lif´-) *a.* bearing spinules. **spinulose** (-lōs), **spinulous** *a.* [L *spīnula*, dim. of *spīna*, SPINE]

spiny SPINE.

spiracle (spī´rəkəl), **spiraculum** (-rak´ūləm) *n.* (*pl.* **spiracles, spiracula** (-lə)) **1** an external breathing hole in insects, certain fish, and whales. **2** (*Geol.*) a vent-hole for lava. **spiracular** (-rak´ū-), **spiraculate** (-lət), **spiraculiform** (-kū´lifawm) *a.* [F, from L *spīrāculum*, from *spīrāre*, to breathe]

spiraea (spīrē´ə), (*N Am.*) **spirea** *n.* any flowering plant belonging to the *Spiraea* genus of Rosaceae, including the meadowsweet. [L, from Gr. *speiraia*, meadowsweet, from *speira*, SPIRE[2]]

spiral (spī´rəl) *a.* **1** forming a spire, spiral, or coil. **2** continually winding about, and receding from, or advancing on, a centre, in a flat plane, or rising or descending in a cone. **3** continually winding, as the thread of a screw. *~n.* **1** a plane or three-dimensional spiral curve, formed by a point revolving round a central point while continuously advancing on or receding from it. **2** formations or objects with this shape, such as a spring, a shell formation, or a spiral galaxy. **3** a helix. **4** a continuous upward or downward movement, e.g. of prices and wages, a decrease or increase in the one causing a corresponding movement in the other. **5** flight in a spiral motion. *~v.i.* (*pres.p.* **spiralling,** (*N Am.*) **spiraling,** *past, p.p.* **spiralled,** (*N Am.*) **spiraled**) **1** to move upwards, downwards, or in a plane, in a spiral. **2** (esp. of prices and wages) to rise or fall rapidly. *~v.t.* to make spiral. **spiral balance** *n.* a weighing device operating by means of the torsion of a spiral spring. **spiral galaxy** *n.* (*pl.* **spiral galaxies**) a galaxy comprising an ellipsoidal nucleus around which two arms revolve and spiral outwards. **spirality** (-ral´-) *n.* **spiralled,** (*N Am.*) **spiraled** *a.* **spirally** *adv.* **spiral staircase** *n.* a staircase rising in a spiral round a central column. [F, from L *spīrālis*, from *spīra*, SPIRE[2]]

spirant (spī´rənt) *n.* a consonant produced with a continuous expulsion of breath, esp. a fricative. *~a.* denoting this kind of consonant. [L *spirans -ntem*, pres.p. of *spīrāre*, to breathe]

spire[1] (spīə) *n.* **1** a tapering, conical, or pyramidal structure, esp. the tapering portion of a steeple. **2** a stalk of grass, the tapering part of a tree above the point where branching begins. **3** the spike of a flower, or any similarly tapering object. *~v.i.* to shoot up like a spire. *~v.t.* to furnish with a spire or spires. **spiry** *a.* (*comp.* **spirier**, *superl.* **spiriest**). [OE *spīr*, cp. Dut. and G *Spier*, Dan. *spire*, Swed. *spira*]

spire[2] (spīə) *n.* **1** a spiral, a coil. **2** a single turn in this, a whorl, a twist. [F, from L *spīra*, Gr. *speira*, coil]

spirea SPIRAEA.

spirillum (spīril´əm) *n.* (*pl.* **spirilla** (-lə)) any bacterium of a genus, *Spirillum*, of bacteria having a spiral structure. **spirillar** *a.* **spirilliform** (-ifawm) *a.* [dim. of L *spīra*, SPIRE[2]]

spirit (spir´it) *n.* **1 a** the vital principle animating a person or animal. **b** the non-physical, immaterial part of a person, the soul. **c** †an immaterial principle thought to control vital phenomena. **2 a** a rational being unconnected with a physical body. **b** (**Spirit**) the Holy Spirit. **3** a disembodied soul; an incorporeal or supernatural being, such as a ghost, fairy, sprite, elf. **4** a person considered with regard to their individual qualities of mind or temperament. **5** a person of strong mental or moral force. **6** vigour of mind or intellect. **7** vivacity, energy, ardour, enthusiasm (*lacks spirit*).

8 (*often pl.*) mood, humour (*in high spirits*). 9 mental attitude (*take it in the right spirit*). 10 real meaning or intent (*the spirit of the law*). 11 actuating principle, pervading influence, characteristic quality or tendency (*the spirit of the age*). 12 (*usu. pl.*) distilled alcoholic liquors, such as brandy, whisky, gin etc. 13 (*often pl., N Am.*) a liquid distilled essence. 14 distilled alcohol. 15 a solution of a volatile principle in alcohol. ~*v.t.* (*pres.p.* **spiriting,** *past, p.p.* **spirited**) 1 to convey (away, off etc.) secretly and rapidly. 2 to animate, to inspirit. **if the spirit moves one** if one feels inclined. **in spirit** 1 inwardly, in one's heart. 2 as a supportive presence, though not in person (*They are with us today in spirit*). **to spirit up** to cheer or encourage. **spirit duck** *n.* the bufflehead and other ducks that dive with striking rapidity. **spirit duplicator** *n.* a duplicator that reproduces copies from a master sheet with the use of an alcoholic solution. **spirited** *a.* 1 full of spirit, fire, or life, animated, lively, courageous. 2 (*in comb.*) having a particular mental attitude, as in *high-spirited.* **spiritedly** *adv.* **spiritedness** *n.* **spirit gum** *n.* a fast-drying gum solution used for sticking on false hair etc. **spiritism** *n.* SPIRITUALISM (under SPIRIT). **spiritist** *n.* **spiritistic** (-tis´-) *a.* **spirit lamp** *n.* a lamp burning methylated or other spirit. **spiritless** *a.* lacking strength of character or purpose. **spiritlessly** *adv.* **spiritlessness** *n.* **spirit level** *n.* an instrument used for determining the horizontal through the position of an air bubble in a glass tube containing alcohol. **spirit of hartshorn** *n.* a solution of ammonia in water, smelling salts. **spirit of wine, spirits of wine** *n.* pure alcohol. **spiritoso** (-tō´sō) *adv.* (*Mus.*) in a spirited manner. **spiritous** *a.* spirituous. **spirit-rapper** *n.* a person professing to communicate with spirits by means of raps on a table etc. **spirit-rapping** *n.* †**spirits of salt** *n.* hydrochloric acid. **spiritual** (-chuəl, -tūəl) *a.* 1 of or relating to the spirit as distinct from matter. 2 immaterial, incorporeal. 3 of or relating to the soul or the inner nature. 4 derived from or of or relating to God, pure, holy, sacred, divine, inspired. 5 of or relating to sacred things, not lay or temporal. ~*n.* a type of hymn sung by black people of the southern US, a negro spiritual. **spiritualism** *n.* 1 a system of professed communication with the spirits of the dead, chiefly through people called mediums; belief in this. 2 (*Philos.*) the doctrine that the spirit exists as distinct from matter or as the only reality. **spiritualist** *n.* **spiritualistic** (-lis´-) *a.* **spirituality** (-al´-) *n.* 1 immateriality, incorporeity. 2 the quality of being spiritual or unworldly. 3 (*esp. Hist.*) that which belongs to the Church, or to an ecclesiastic on account of a spiritual office. **spiritualize, spiritualise** *v.t.* 1 to elevate (thoughts etc.), to render spiritual. 2 to give a spiritual rather than literal meaning to. **spiritualization** (-zā´shən) *n.* **spiritualizer** *n.* **spiritually** *adv.* **spiritualness** *n.* **spirituel** (-tūel´), (*fem.*) **spirituelle** *a.* characterized by refinement, grace or delicacy of mind. **spirituous** (-tūəs) *a.* containing spirit, alcoholic; distilled as distinct from fermented. **spirituousness** *n.* **spiritus** (spī´ritus, spir´-) *n.* (*Gram.*) a breathing in Greek. **spiritus asper** (as´pə) *n.* a rough breathing or aspirate, in Greek marked (῾). **spiritus lenis** (lē´nis) *n.* a smooth breathing, in Greek (᾿), denoting the absence of an aspirate. [OF *espirit* (F *esprit*), L *spīritum*, nom. *-tus*, from *spīrāre*, to breathe]

spiro-[1] (spī´rō) *comb. form* of or relating to a coil. [Gr. *speira*, a coil]

spiro-[2] (spī´rō) *comb. form* of or relating to breathing. [L *spīro*, I breathe]

spirochaete (spī´rōkēt), (*N Am.*) **spirochete** *n.* any spiral-shaped bacterium of the genus *Spirochaeta*, which includes the causative agents of syphilis, relapsing fever, and epidemic jaundice.

spirograph (spī´rəgrahf) *n.* an instrument for recording the movement in breathing. **spirographic** (-graf´-) *a.* **spirographically** *adv.*

spirogyra (spīrəjī´rə) *n.* (*pl.* **spirogyras**) any alga of the genus *Spirogyra*, whose cells contain spiral bands of chlorophyll.

spirometer (spīrom´itə) *n.* an instrument for measuring the capacity of the lungs. **spirometric** (-rəmet´-) *a.* **spirometry** (-rom´itri) *n.*

spirophore (spī´rəfaw) *n.* an instrument for inducing respiration when animation is suspended.

spiroscope (spī´rōskōp) *n.* a spirometer.

spirt SPURT.

spirtle SPURTLE.

spirula (spī´rūlə) *n.* a tropical cephalopod mollusc, *Spirula peronii* of the order Decapoda, having a flat spiral shell. [dim. of L *spīra*, SPIRE[2]]

spiry SPIRE[1].

†**spissitude** (spis´itūd) *n.* density, inspissation. [L *spissitūdo*, from *spissus*, thick, compact]

spit[1] (spit) *v.t.* (*pres.p.* **spitting,** *past, p.p.* **spat** (spat), †**spit**) 1 to eject (saliva etc.), throw (out) from the mouth. 2 to utter or throw (out) in a violent or spiteful way (*'Bitch!' he spat; He spat out a curse*). ~*v.i.* 1 to eject saliva from the mouth. 2 (of an angry cat) to make a spitting noise. 3 (of a frying pan, fire, pen etc.) to throw out hot fat, sparks, spurts of ink etc. 4 (*impers.*) to drizzle with rain. ~*n.* 1 spittle, saliva. 2 an act of spitting. 3 the foamy liquid that certain insects secrete to protect their young. 4 the exact likeness or double (of). **to spit chips** (*Austral., sl.*) to be furious. **to spit it out** (*coll.*) to say what is concerning one, to come clean. **to spit up** (*N Am.*) (usu. of a baby) to vomit. **spit and polish** *n.* 1 the activities of cleaning and polishing, esp. as a soldier's duties. 2 (*coll.*) (obsessive) cleanliness, attention to details, as in the army. **spitball** *n.* (*N Am.*) 1 a ball of chewed paper thrown as a missile. 2 a baseball that the pitcher has illegally moistened to influence its flight. ~*v.i.* to toss out ideas for discussion. **spitballer** *n.* **spitfire** *n.* an irascible person. **spitter** *n.* **spitting** *n.* **spitting cobra** *n.* a black-necked cobra native to Africa that spits out its venom, as distinct from striking. **spitting distance** *n.* a very small distance. **spitting image** *n.* (*coll.*) an exact likeness; a person or thing that exactly resembles another. **spittle** (spit´əl) *n.* saliva, esp. ejected from the mouth. **spittly** *a.* **spittoon** (-toon´) *n.* a receptacle for spittle. [OE *spittan*, cogn. with *spætan*, and prob. with Icel. *spyta*, Dan. *spytte*, Swed. *spotta*, rel. to SPOUT]

spit[2] (spit) *n.* 1 a long pointed rod on which meat for roasting is skewered and rotated over a fire. 2 a skewer. 3 a point of land or a narrow shoal extending into the sea. 4 a long narrow underwater ridge. ~*v.t.* (*pres.p.* **spitting,** *past, p.p.* **spitted**) 1 to fix (meat) upon a spit. 2 to pierce, to transfix. **spitty** *a.* (*comp.* **spittier,** *superl.* **spittiest**). [OE *spitu*, cp. Dut. *spit*, G *Spiess*, Dan. *spīd*, Swed. *spětt*]

spit[3] (spit) *n.* (*pl.* **spit, spits**) a spade's depth of earth. [MDut., MLG, cp. OE *spittan*, to dig with a spade]

spitchcock (spich´kok) *v.t.* to split and broil (an eel etc.). ~*n.* an eel split and broiled. [perh. from MHG *spiz*, SPIT[2], G *kochen*, to cook]

spite (spīt) *n.* 1 ill will, malice, malevolence. 2 a grudge. ~*v.t.* 1 to thwart maliciously. 2 to vex or annoy. **in spite of** notwithstanding, despite. **in spite of oneself** though behaving contrary to one's inclinations. **spiteful** *a.* **spitefully** *adv.* **spitefulness** *n.* [short for DESPITE]

spitter, spittle etc. SPIT[1].

spitz (spits) *n.* a sharp-muzzled breed of dog, also called *Pomeranian.* [G]

spiv (spiv) *n.* a man who dresses flashily and lives by dubious dealing and trading, e.g. in black-market goods. **spivvish** *a.* **spivvy** *a.* (*comp.* **spivvier,** *superl.* **spivviest**). [etym. unknown]

splake (splāk) *n.* a hybrid trout found in the lakes of N America. [*sp*eckled trout, *lake* trout]

splanchnic (splangk´nik) *a.* of or relating to the bowels, intestinal. [Gr. *splanchnikos*, from *splanchna*, entrails]

splanchnology (splangknol´əji) *n.* the branch of medical science dealing with the viscera.

splanchnotomy (splangknot´əmi) *n.* (*pl.* **splanchnotomies**) dissection of the viscera.

splash (splash) *v.t.* **1** to bespatter with water, mud etc. **2** to dash (liquid etc., about, over, etc.). **3** to make (one's way) e.g. through water, scattering it about. **4** to spend recklessly, throw (one's money about). **5** to display prominently in a newspaper (*Her name was splashed across the front page*). **6** to decorate with bright scattered patches of colour. ~*v.i.* **1** to dash water or other liquid about. **2** to dabble, to plunge. **3** to move or to make one's way (along etc.) thus. ~*n.* **1** the act of splashing. **2** water or mud splashed about. **3** a noise as of splashing. **4** a spot or patch of liquid, colour etc. **5** a vivid display. **6** a conspicuously presented news item. **7** a dash; a small amount of soda water etc. mixed with an alcoholic drink. **to make a splash** (*sl.*) to make a sensation, display, etc. **to splash down** (of a spacecraft) to land on water when returning to earth. **splashback** *n.* a washable surface or panel behind a sink to protect the wall from splashes. **splashboard** *n.* a mudguard on a vehicle. **splashdown** *n.* the landing of a spacecraft on the ocean. **splasher** *n.* **1** a person or thing that splashes. **2** a guard over the wheels of locomotives; a splashboard. **3** a screen hung behind a washstand to keep splashes off the wall. **splashy** *a.* (*comp.* **splashier**, *superl.* **splashiest**). [*s*-, F *es*-, EX-, PLASH[1]]

splat[1] (splat) *n.* a flat strip of wood forming the central part of a chair back. [rel. to ME *splātan*, to split]

splat[2] (splat) *n.* **1** the slapping sound made by a soft or wet object striking a surface. **2** a cracking, splitting or squashing sound. ~*adv.* with such a sound (*was spread-eagled splat against the wall*). ~*v.t.*, *v.i.* (*pres.p.* **splatting**, *past*, *p.p.* **splatted**) to hit or fall with a splat. [onomat., or shortening of SPLATTER]

splatter (splat´ə) *v.t.* **1** to bespatter, to splash with dirt, mud, water etc. **2** to display or present (news, pictures etc.) conspicuously. **3** to splutter. ~*v.i.* **1** to spatter. **2** to make a continuous splash or splashing noise. ~*n.* **1** a noisy splash. **2** an untidy spread of colour. **splatter movie** *n.* (*sl.*) a very violent film dwelling on bloody deaths and mutilations. [onomat.]

splay (splā) *v.t.* **1** to form (a window opening, doorway etc.) with diverging sides. **2** to spread out (one's arms, legs etc.). ~*v.i.* (of e.g. an embrasure or other opening, or its sides) to widen, to diverge. ~*n.* an oblique surface, side, or widening of a window etc. ~*a.* **1** wide and flat. **2** turned outwards. **splay-foot** *n.* (*pl.* **splay-feet**) a broad flat foot turned outwards. **splay-footed** *a.* [ME, from DISPLAY]

spleen (splēn) *n.* **1** a soft vascular organ situated to the left of the stomach in most vertebrates which produces lymphocytes and antibodies, and filters the blood. **2** spitefulness, ill temper. **3** low spirits, melancholy. **spleenful** *a.* **spleenfully** *adv.* **spleenish** *a.* **spleenishly** *adv.* **spleenless** *a.* **spleenwort** *n.* any fern of the genus *Asplenium*, formerly supposed to be a specific for spleen. **spleeny** *a.* (*comp.* **spleenier**, *superl.* **spleeniest**). [L and Gr. *splēn*]

splen- (splin) *comb.form* of or relating to the spleen. [Gr. *splēn*, SPLEEN]

splendid (splen´did) *a.* **1** magnificent, gorgeous, sumptuous. **2** glorious, illustrious. **3** brilliant, lustrous, dazzling. **4** fine, excellent, first-rate. **splendent** *a.* (*formal*) **1** shining, lustrous, brilliant; splendid. **2** very conspicuous. **3** illustrious. **splendidly** *adv.* **splendidness** *n.* **splendiferous** (-dif´-) *a.* (*facet.*) splendid. **splendiferously** *adv.* **splendiferousness** *n.* **splendour**, (*N Am.*) **splendor** *n.* **splendorous** *a.* [L *splendidus*, from *splendēre*, to shine]

splenectomy (splinek´təmi) *n.* (*pl.* **splenectomies**) the surgical removal of the spleen.

splenetic (splinet´ik) *a.* **1** affected with spleen; peevish, ill-tempered. **2** of or relating to the spleen. ~*n.* a person affected with spleen, a peevish, irritable person. **splenetically** *adv.* [late L *splēnēticus*, from L *splēn*, SPLEEN]

splenial SPLENIUS.

splenic (splen´ik, splē´nik) *a.* of or relating to or affecting the spleen. **splenic fever** *n.* anthrax. **splenitis** (-nī´tis) *n.* inflammation of the spleen. **splenoid** (splē´noid) *a.* [L *splēnicus*, Gr. *splēnikos*, from *splēn*, SPLEEN]

splenius (splē´niəs) *n.* (*pl.* **splenii** (-niī)) a muscle extending in two parts on either side of the neck and upper back, serving to bend the head backwards. **splenial** *a.* **1** of or relating to this muscle. **2** splintlike. [Gr. *splēnion*, bandage]

splenization (splēnīzā´shən), **splenisation** *n.* conversion of a portion of the lung into spongy tissue resembling the spleen. [F *splénisation*]

splenology (splinol´əji) *n.* scientific study of the spleen. **splenological** (splēnəloj´-) *a.*

splenomegaly (splēnōmeg´əli) *n.* morbid enlargement of the spleen. [Gr. *megas*, *megal*-, large]

splenotomy (splinot´əmi) *n.* (*pl.* **splenotomies**) the dissection of or an incision into the spleen.

spleuchan (sploo´khən) *n.* (*Sc.*, *Ir.*) a small bag, pouch or purse, esp. a tobacco pouch. [Gael. *spliùchan*]

splice (splīs) *v.t.* **1** to unite (two ropes etc.) by interweaving the strands of the ends. **2** to unite (timbers etc.) by bevelling, overlapping, and fitting the ends together. **3** (*coll.*) to unite in marriage (*get spliced*). ~*n.* **1** a union of ropes, timbers etc., by splicing. **2** the point of juncture between two pieces of film. **3** the joint on the handle of a cricket bat which fits into the blade. **to splice the main brace** MAIN[1]. **splicer** *n.* [Dut. *splitsen*, to splice, from *splijten*, to SPLIT (cp. Dan. *splidse*, Swed. *splissa*, G *splissen*, to splice)]

spliff (splif) *n.* (*sl.*) a cannabis cigarette. [etym. uncertain]

spline (splīn) *n.* **1** a key fitting into a groove in a shaft and wheel to make these revolve together. **2** a flexible strip of wood or rubber used in laying down large curves in mechanical drawing. **3** a slat. ~*v.t.* to apply a spline to, to fit with a spline. [etym. uncertain, orig. E Anglian dial.]

splint (splint) *n.* **1** a thin piece of wood or other material used to keep the parts of a broken bone together. **2** a thin strip of wood used in basketmaking etc., or one used to light a fire, pipe etc. **3** a splint-bone. **4** a callous tumour on the splint-bone of a horse. ~*v.t.* to secure or support with splints. **splint-bone** *n.* **1** either of two small bones in a horse's leg extending from the knee to the fetlock. **2** a human fibula. **splint-coal** *n.* a slaty variety of cannel coal. [MDut. *splinte*, cp. Dut., G, Dan., Swed., and Norw. *splint*]

splinter (splin´tə) *n.* **1** a thin piece of wood, glass, stone, metal etc. broken, split, or shivered off. **2** a needle-like piece of wood, esp. when embedded in the flesh. ~*v.t.* to split, shiver or rend into splinters or fragments. ~*v.i.* to split or shiver into splinters. **splinter-bar** *n.* a crossbar in front of a horse-drawn vehicle to which the traces are attached or which supports the springs, a swingletree. **splinter group, splinter party** *n.* a small group that has broken away from its parent political etc. organization. **splinter-proof** *a.* proof against the splinters of bursting shells or bombs. **splintery** *a.* [MDut., rel. to SPLINT]

split (split) *v.t.* (*pres.p.* **splitting**, *past*, *p.p.* **split**) **1** to break, cleave, tear or divide, esp. longitudinally or with the grain. **2** to divide into two or more thicknesses, sections etc. **3** to break or separate (off or away). **4** to divide (up) into parts or groups. **5** to divide into opposed parties (*The issue has split the government; are split over finance; split on education*). **6** (of a candidate or a minority party) to attract (the votes of the electorate from another candidate or party), with the possibility that both will be defeated by a third. **7** (*coll.*) (esp. of accomplices) to divide (a haul of money etc.) between members of the group; to divide (proceeds) in this way. **8** to cause (one's head) to ache or throb. **9** to bring about the fission of (an atom). ~*v.i.* **1** to be broken or divided, esp. longitudinally or with the grain. **2** to break (up), to come to pieces. **3** to divide into opposed parties. **4** (of a couple etc.) to break (up), to separate or stop associating (with one another). **5** (*sl.*) to betray the secrets of, to inform (on). **6** (*coll.*) (of one's head) to ache acutely. **7** (*coll.*) to burst with laughter. **8** (*sl.*) to depart. **9** (of a ship) to be wrecked. ~*n.* **1** an instance, or the resultant state, of splitting. **2** a crack, rent, tear or fissure. **3** a separation, a rupture, a schism, a division into opposing parties. **4** (*pl.*) an acrobat's feat of leaping, or sitting down, with the legs fully stretched out forwards and backwards, or right and left. **5** a dessert of sliced fruit, esp. banana, and ice cream etc. **6** something split, a split osier for basketwork, a single thickness of split hide etc. **7** any one of the strips or splints forming the reed of a loom. **8** (*sl.*) a half bottle of soda water. **9** a half glass of liquor. **10** in faro, the turning up of two cards of equal value, dividing the stakes. **11** (*coll.*) a division of proceeds, a haul of money etc. ~*a.* **1** having been split. **2** fractured. **3** having splits. **to split hairs** HAIR. **to split one's sides** to laugh uproariously. **to split one's vote** (*N Am.*) to vote for candidates of more than one party. **to split the difference** to compromise by taking the average of two amounts. **to split the ticket** (*N Am.*) to split one's vote. **split end** *n.* **1** (*usu. pl.*) the tip of a hair that has split from dryness etc. **2** in American football, an offensive player who lines up some distance from the formation. **split gear, split pulley** *n.* a gear or pulley made in halves to ease removal from a shaft. **split infinitive** *n.* an infinitive phrase where an adverb has been inserted between *to* and the verb, as in *to completely destroy*, considered by some a stylistic solecism, but in many cases allowable. **split-level** *a.* (esp. of a one-storey house) built on more than one level. **split pea** *n.* a dried pea split in half and used in soups etc. **split personality** *n.* (*pl.* **split personalities**) a personality comprising two or more dissociated groups of attitudes and behaviour, as a manifestation of mental illness. **split pin** *n.* a pin with a divided end which is splayed apart to keep the pin in place. **split ring** *n.* a metal ring constructed in two spiral turns, so that keys etc. can be put on it or taken off. **split-screen** *n.* a cinematic or computing technique in which different images are displayed simultaneously on separate sections of the screen. ~*a.* (of cinematic or computing technique) displaying two or more images in this way. **split second** *n.* an instant, a fraction of a second. **split-second** *a.* **1** very rapid. **2** precise to a fraction of a second (*split-second timing*). **split shift** *n.* a work period divided into two parts separated by a long interval. **split shot, split stroke** *n.* in croquet, a stroke that hits two touching balls in different directions. **splitter** *n.* a person who splits. **splitting** *a.* (of a headache) acute, severe. [MDut. *splitten*, rel. to Dut. *splijten*, G *spleissen*]

splodge (sploj) *n.* a daub, a blotch, an irregular stain. ~*v.t.* to make a daub or blotch on. **splodgy** *a.* (*comp.* **splodgier**, *superl.* **splodgiest**). [perh. onomat.]

splore (splaw) *n.* (*Sc.*) a noisy frolic, a carousal, a spree. [etym. uncertain]

splosh (splosh) *v.i.*, *v.t.* (*coll.*) to splash; to move with a splashing sound. ~*n.* **1** a splash or a splashing sound. **2** (*sl.*) money. [onomat.]

splotch (sploch) *n.* a splodge. ~*v.t.* to make a splodge on, to cover with splodges. **splotchy** *a.* (*comp.* **splotchier**, *superl.* **splotchiest**). [perh. OE *splott*, spot, or a combination of *spot* and *blotch*]

splurge (splœj) *n.* **1** an exuberant or extravagant display. **2** a bout of extravagance. ~*v.i.* **1** to make an exuberant or extravagant display. **2** to spend a lot of money (on). [N Am., onomat.]

splutter (splŭt´ə) *v.i.* **1** to speak in an agitated, incoherent manner. **2** to emit drops of saliva etc. from the mouth. **3** (of a fire, frying food etc.) to emit sparks, hot fat etc. with a spitting noise. ~*v.t.* to utter in a spluttering way. ~*n.* a spluttering sound or utterance. **splutterer** *n.* **spluttering** *a.* **splutteringly** *adv.* **spluttery** *a.* [imit., prob. a combination of *sputter* and *splash*]

Spode® (spōd) *n.* porcelain made by the factory of Josiah Spode, 1754–1827.

†**spodium** (spō´diəm) *n.* fine powder obtained from calcined bone and other substances. [L, from Gr. *spodion*, dim. of *spodos*, ashes, dust]

spodumene (spod´ūmēn) *n.* a monoclinic silicate of aluminium and lithium. [F *spodumène*, G *Spodumen*, Gr. *spodoumenos*, p.p. of *spodousthai*, to be turned to ashes, from *spodos*, ash]

spoffish (spof´ish) *a.* (*dated sl.*) fussy, officious. **spoffy** *a.* (*comp.* **spoffier**, *superl.* **spoffiest**). [etym. uncertain]

spoil (spoil) *v.t.* (*past*, *p.p.* **spoilt** (spoilt), **spoiled** (spoild, spoilt)) **1** to mar, to damage, to vitiate; to impair the goodness, usefulness, value etc., of. **2** to detract from one's enjoyment of, to mar (*The rain completely spoilt our holiday*). **3** to impair the character of by over-indulgence (*mustn't spoil the children*). **4** to invalidate (a ballot paper) by marking it incorrectly. **5** †to plunder, to deprive (of) by violence. ~*v.i.* **1** (of perishable food) to decay, to deteriorate through keeping. **2** (*with neg.*) (of long-sustained jokes or secrets) to get stale. **3** to be eager or only too ready (for a fight). ~*n.* **1** (*usu. pl.*) plunder, booty. **2** offices, honours, or emoluments acquired as the result of a party victory, esp. in the US. **3** waste material obtaining in mining, quarrying, excavating etc. **4** pillage, spoliation, rapine. **spoilt for choice** faced with so many attractive possibilities that one cannot choose between them. **spoilage** (-ij) *n.* **1** an amount wasted or spoiled, e.g. of paper in the printing process. **2** the act of spoiling or process of being spoiled. **spoiler** *n.* **1** a person or thing that spoils something. **2** an aerodynamic device fitted to an aircraft wing to increase drag and reduce lift. **3** a similar device fitted to the front or rear of a motor vehicle to maintain stability at high speeds. **4** an electronic device incorporated into sound-recording equipment, or sound recordings, which produces a disruptive signal and so discourages unauthorized recording or copying. **spoilfive** *n.* a card game in which unless a player makes three out of five possible tricks the hand is 'spoilt'. **spoilsman** *n.* (*pl.* **spoilsmen**) **1** a supporter of the spoils system. **2** (*N Am.*) a politician working for a share of the spoils. **spoilsport** *n.* a person who interferes with other people's enjoyment. **spoils system** *n.* in US politics, the practice by a successful political party of giving office to its loyal backers. [OF *espoiller*, L *spoliāre*, from *spolium*, a skin stripped off, (in pl.) booty]

spoke[1] (spōk) *n.* **1** any one of the rods connecting the hub with the rim of a wheel. **2** a rung of a ladder. **3** any of the projecting radial handles of a ship's steering wheel. ~*v.t.* **1** to fit or provide with spokes. **2** to check (a wheel) with a spoke. **to put a spoke in someone's wheel** to thwart someone. **spokeshave** *n.* a plane with a handle at each end for dressing spokes, curved work etc. [OE *spāca* (cp. Dut. *speek*, G *Speiche*), rel. to SPIKE[1]]

spoke[2], **spoken** SPEAK.

spokesman (spōks´mən), **spokesperson, spokeswoman** *n.* (*pl.* **spokesmen, spokespersons, spokespeople, spokeswomen**) **1** a person who speaks on behalf of another or others. **2** a person delegated to give the views etc. of a group or body. [formed irreg. from SPOKE[2]]

spoliation (spōliā´shən) *n.* **1** robbery, pillage, the act or practice of plundering, esp. of neutral commerce, in time of war. **2** extortion. **3** (*Law*) destruction, mutilation, or alteration of a document to prevent its use as evidence. **4** taking the emoluments of an ecclesiastical benefice under an illegal title. **spoliator** (spō´-) *n.* **spoliatory** (spō´liətəri) *a.* [ME, from L *spoliātio*]

spondee (spon´dē) *n.* a metrical foot consisting of two long syllables. **spondaic** (-dā´ik) *a.* **1** of or relating to spondees. **2** (of a hexameter) having a spondee as the fifth foot. [L *spondēus*, Gr. *spondeios*, from *spondai*, a solemn treaty, pl. of *spondē*, libation, in ref. to the typical rhythm of libation-accompanying music]

spondulicks (spondū´liks) *n.pl.* (*sl.*) money, cash. [etym. unknown]

spondyl (spon´dil), †**spondyle** *n.* a vertebra. [F *spondyle*, L *spondylus*, Gr. *spondulos*]

spondylitis (spondilī´tis) *n.* inflammation of the vertebrae.

sponge (spŭnj) *n.* **1** any marine animal of the phylum Porifera, with pores in the body wall. **2** the skeleton or part of the skeleton of a sponge or colony of sponges, esp. of a soft, elastic kind used as an absorbent pad in bathing, cleansing etc. **3** a synthetic imitation of this. **4** any spongelike substance or implement, e.g. a piece of absorbent material impregnated with spermicide, used in the vagina as a contraceptive. **5** an act of cleansing or wiping with a sponge. **6** dough for baking before it is kneaded. **7** sponge cake. **8** a swab for cleansing a cannon bore after a discharge. **9** a parasite, a sponger. **10** (*coll.*) a heavy drinker. *~v.t.* (*pres.p.* **sponging, spongeing**) **1** to wipe, wet or cleanse with a sponge; to sluice (down or over). **2** to obliterate, to wipe (out or away) with or as with a sponge. **3** to absorb, to take (up) with a sponge. **4** to put paint on (walls etc.) with a sponge. **5** to extort or obtain by scrounging. *~v.i.* **1** to suck in like a sponge. **2** to live parasitically (on) or scrounge (off). **3** to gather sponges. **to throw in the sponge 1** to acknowledge oneself beaten. **2** to give up the contest (orig. of a boxer, on the tossing of the sponge into the air by their second as token of defeat). **to throw up the sponge** to throw in the sponge. **spongeable** *a.* **sponge bag** *n.* a small waterproof bag for carrying toiletries. **sponge bath** *n.* a cleansing of the body e.g. of a bedridden patient, with a wet sponge or cloth. **sponge cake** *n.* **1** a light porous cake, made with eggs, sugar and flour but without fat. **2** a basic cake made with eggs, fat, sugar and flour. **sponge cloth** *n.* **1** loosely-woven fabric with a wrinkled surface. **2** (a piece of) thin spongy material used for cleaning. **spongelike** *a.* **sponge pudding** *n.* a baked or steamed pudding usu. made of a Victoria sponge mixture. **sponger** *n.* **1** a scrounger or parasite. **2** a person or thing that sponges. **sponge tree** *n.* a thorny tropical acacia, *Acacia farnesiana*, with rounded heads of yellow flowers that yield a perfume; the opopanax. **spongiform** (-jifawm) *a.* **1** like a sponge in porosity or texture. **2** denoting diseases in which diseased tissues have a spongelike appearance or texture. **sponging house** *n.* (*Hist.*) a house where people arrested for debt were lodged temporarily before being put in prison. **spongy** *a.* (*comp.* **spongier**, *superl.* **spongiest**). **spongily** *adv.* **sponginess** *n.* [OE, from L *spongia*, Gr. *spongia*, *-gos*, cogn. with FUNGUS]

spongio- (spŭn´jiō), **spongi-, spongo-** (spong´gō) *comb. form* of or relating to sponge(s). [see SPONGE]

spongiole (spŭn´jiōl, spon´-) *n.* (*Bot.*) the spongy extremity of a radicle.

spongo- SPONGIO-.

spongology (spong·gol´əji) *n.* the scientific study of sponges. **spongologist** *n.*

spongy SPONGE.

sponsal (spon´səl) *a.* of or relating to marriage. [L *sponsālis*, from *sponsus*, SPOUSE]

sponsion (spon´shən) *n.* **1** the act of becoming surety for another. **2** (*Law*) an act or engagement on behalf of a state by an agent not specially authorized. [L *sponsio*, from *spondēre*, to promise, p.p. *sponsus*]

sponson (spon´sən) *n.* **1** a projection from the sides of a vessel, as supporting the wheel on a paddle steamer, for a gun on a warship, or to support a bearing etc. **2** a device attached to the wings of a seaplane to give it steadiness when resting on the water. [etym. uncertain]

sponsor (spon´sə) *n.* **1** a person or organization that provides esp. financial support for another person or group or for some activity. **2** a person who promises to pay a sum of money usu. to charity, the amount of which is determined by the performance of an entrant in a fund-raising event. **3** a person or firm that pays the costs of mounting a radio or TV programme in exchange for advertising time. **4** a member who introduces a bill into a legislative assembly. **5** a godfather or godmother. **6** a surety, a person who undertakes to be responsible for another. *~v.t.* to act as a sponsor for. **sponsorial** (-saw´ri-) *a.* **sponsorship** *n.* [L (*spons-*, see SPONSION, -OR[1])]

spontaneous (spontā´niəs) *a.* **1** arising, occurring, done, or acting without external cause. **2** not due to external constraint or suggestion, voluntary. **3** not due to conscious volition or motive. **4** instinctive, automatic, involuntary. **5** self-originated, self-generated. **spontaneity** (-tənē´-, -nā´-) *n.* **spontaneous combustion** *n.* the ignition of a body by the development of heat within itself. **spontaneous generation** *n.* the supposed emergence of living matter from non-living matter, abiogenesis. **spontaneously** *adv.* **spontaneousness** *n.* **spontaneous suggestion** *n.* a suggestion generated by an association of ideas, not consciously thought up. [L *spontāneus*, from *sponte*, of one's own accord]

spontoon (spontoon´) *n.* (*Hist.*) a kind of short pike or halberd carried by British infantry officers in the 18th cent. [F *sponton*, It. *spontone*, from *punto*, point]

spoof (spoof) *n.* **1** a deception, a hoax. **2** a parody, humorous take-off (of a play, poem etc.). *~v.t.* **1** to hoax, to fool. **2** to parody. **spoofer** *n.* **spoofery** *n.* (*pl.* **spooferies**). [after a hoaxing game invented by Arthur Roberts, 1852–1933, British comedian]

spook (spook) *n.* (*coll.*) **1** a ghost. **2** (*chiefly N Am.*) a spy. *~v.t.* (*chiefly N Am.*) to startle or frighten. *~v.i.* (*chiefly N Am.*) to become frightened. **spookish** *a.* **spooky** *a.* (*comp.* **spookier**, *superl.* **spookiest**) **1** ghostly. **2** (*coll.*) eerie, weird. **3** frightening. **4** (*N Am., sl.*) of or relating to spies. **spookily** *adv.* **spookiness** *n.* [Dut., cp. G *Spuk*]

spool (spool) *n.* **1** a small cylinder for winding thread, photographic film etc., on. **2** the central bar of an angler's reel. **3** a reel (of cotton etc.). *~v.t.* to wind on a spool. [MDut. *spoele* (perh. through ONF *espole*), cp. Dut. *spoel*, G *Spule*]

spoon (spoon) *n.* **1** a domestic utensil consisting of a shallow bowl on a stem or handle, used for conveying liquids or liquid food to the mouth etc. **2** an implement or other thing shaped like a spoon, such as an oar with the blade curved lengthwise, a golf club with a lofted face, a spoon-bait etc. **3** a spoonful. **4** (*pl.*) a pair of spoons played as a musical instrument. **5** (*coll.*) a mawkish or foolishly demonstrative lover. **6** (*dated, coll.*) a silly fellow. *~v.t.* **1** to take (up etc.) with a spoon. **2** in cricket etc., to hit a ball (usu. up) with little force. ~*v.i.* **1** to fish with a spoon-bait. **2** (*dated*) to indulge in demonstrative lovemaking. **born with a silver spoon in one's mouth** fortunate in being born into a family with wealth and social class. **spoon-bait** *n.* a spoon-shaped piece of bright metal with hooks attached used as a revolving lure in fishing. **spoon-beak, spoonbill** *n.* a bird with a broad, flat bill, esp. of the genus *Platalea*. **spoon-bread** *n.* (*N Am.*) soft bread made from maize. **spooner** *n.* (*coll.*) a person who behaves in a foolishly or mawkishly amorous way. **spoon-feed** *v.t.* (*past, p.p.* **spoon-fed**) **1** to feed (a baby) with a spoon. **2** to teach by presenting (information) to (students etc.) in such a manner that no individual effort or research is required on the part of those being taught. **spoon-fed** *a.* **spoonful** *n.* (*pl.* **spoonfuls**). **spoony, spooney** *a.* (*comp.* **spoonier,** *superl.* **spooniest**) (*dated coll.*) foolishly or mawkishly amorous. **spoonily** *adv.* **spooniness** *n.* [OE *spōn*, chip, splinter (cp. Dut. *spaan*, G *Span*, Icel. *spānn*, *spōnn*, also Gr. *sphēn*, wedge)]

spoonerism (spooʹnərizm) *n.* an accidental or facetious transposition of the initial letters or syllables of words, e.g. 'I have in my breast a half-warmed fish'. [Rev. W. A. *Spooner*, 1844–1930, Warden of New College, Oxford]

spoor (spuə) *n.* the track of a wild animal. ~*v.i.* to follow a spoor. **spoorer** *n.* [Dut., cogn. with SPEER]

spor- SPORO-.

sporadic (spəradʹik), †**sporadical** *a.* separate, scattered, occurring here and there or irregularly. **sporadically** *adv.* **sporadicalness** *n.* [Gr. *sporadikos*, from *sporas -ados*, scattered, from *speirein*, to sow]

sporangium (spəranʹjiəm) *n.* (*pl.* **sporangia** (-jiə)) (*Bot.*) a sac in which spores are formed. **sporangial** *a.* [mod. L, from Gr. *spora*, spore, *angeion*, vessel]

spore (spaw) *n.* **1** the reproductive body in a cryptogam, usu. composed of a single cell not containing an embryo. **2** a minute organic body that develops into a new individual, as in protozoa etc. **3** a germ. [Gr. *spora*, sowing, as SPORADIC]

sporo- (sporʹō, spawʹrō) *comb. form* of or relating to spores. [Gr. *spora*, spore]

sporocarp (sporʹəkahp, spawʹrə-) *n.* a fructification containing spores or sporangia. [Gr. *karpos*, fruit]

sporocyst (sporʹəsist, spawʹrə-) *n.* a cyst containing spores or an encysted organism giving rise to spores. **sporocystic** (-sisʹ-) *a.*

sporogenesis (sporōjenʹəsis) *n.* spore formation. **sporogenous** (-rojʹinəs) *a.*

sporogony (spərogʹəni) *n.* the process of spore formation. [Gr. *-goneia*, from *gonos*, seed, reproduction]

sporophore (sporʹəfaw, spawʹrə-) *n.* a spore-bearing branch, process etc.

sporophyte (sporʹəfīt, spawʹrə-) *n.* the nonsexual phase in certain plants exhibiting alternation of generations. **sporophytic** (-fitʹ-) *a.* **sporophytically** *adv.*

sporozoan (sporəzōʹən, spawrə-) *n.* any of a group of spore-producing parasitic protozoans, that includes the malaria parasite. **sporozoite** (-zōʹīt) *n.* an infective form of some sporozoans, produced by sporogony. [Gr. *zoion*, animal]

sporran (sporʹən) *n.* a pouch, usu. covered with fur, hair etc., worn by Scottish Highlanders in front of the kilt. [Gael. *sporan*, from med. L *bursa*, purse]

sport (spawt) *n.* **1** a game, a competitive pastime, esp. an athletic or outdoor pastime, such as hunting, fishing, football, racing, running etc. **2** such games or pastimes collectively. **3** (*pl.*) a meeting for outdoor games etc. **4** diversion, amusement, fun, jest, pleasantry. **5** (*coll.*) a sportsman, a fair or obliging person. **6** a person who behaves in a specified way on losing (*a good sport*). **7** (*Austral.*) used as a form of address, esp. between males. **8** (*N Am., coll.*) a playboy. **9** an animal or plant deviating remarkably from the normal type. **10** a plaything. ~*v.i.* **1** to play, to divert oneself. **2** to trifle, to jest, to make merry (with a person's feelings etc.). **3** to vary remarkably from the normal type. ~*v.t.* to wear or display in an ostentatious manner. **in sport** in fun, as a joke. **to have good sport** to have a successful time hunting, shooting etc. **to make sport of** to jeer at, to ridicule. **sporter** *n.* **sportful** *a.* **sportfully** *adv.* **sportfulness** *n.* **sporting** *a.* **1** relating to, used in, or fond of sports. **2** calling for sportsmanship. **3** involving a risk, as in sports competition. **sporting chance** *n.* some chance of succeeding. **sportingly** *adv.* **sportive** *a.* frolicsome, playful. **sportively** *adv.* **sportiveness** *n.* **sportless** *a.* **sport of kings** *n.* **1** horse racing. **2** hunting. **3** fighting wars. **4** surfing. **sports** *a.* (of clothing etc.) suitable for sports. **sports car** *n.* a low usu. two-seater car built for high-speed performance. **sportscast** *n.* (*N Am.*) a broadcast of sports news. **sportscaster** *n.* **sports coat, sports jacket** *n.* a casual jacket for men, usu. made of tweed. **sports ground** *n.* an area of ground equipped for competitive outdoor sports. **sportsman** *n.* (*pl.* **sportsmen**) **1** a person who participates in sport, esp. professionally. **2** a person who goes hunting or shooting. **3** a person who acts fairly towards opponents or who faces good or bad luck with equanimity. **sportsmanlike** *a.* **sportsmanly** *a.* **sportsmanship** *n.* **sports medicine** *n.* the medical supervision of athletes in training and in competition and the treatment of their injuries. **sportsperson** *n.* (*pl.* **sportspeople, sportspersons**). **sportswear** *n.* clothes worn for sport, or for casual wear. **sportswoman** *n.* (*pl.* **sportswomen**). **sports writer** *n.* a newspaper columnist who writes on sport. **sporty** *a.* (*comp.* **sportier,** *superl.* **sportiest**) **1** taking pleasure in sports. **2** (of clothes etc.) suitable as sportswear. **3** (of a car etc.) resembling a sports car. **4** vulgar, showy. **sportily** *adv.* **sportiness** *n.* [short for DISPORT]

sporule (sporʹūl, -ool) *n.* a spore, esp. a small or secondary spore. **sporular** *a.* **sporulation** (-lāʹshən) *n.* [F, dim. of SPORE]

spot (spot) *n.* **1** a small part of a surface of distinctive colour or texture, esp. round or roundish in shape. **2** a small mark or stain, a speck, a blot. **3** a pimple or blemish on the skin. **4** a mark, e.g. a circle, or one of a set of such marks, distinguishing the face of a playing card, dice, domino etc. **5** a stain on one's character or reputation. **6** a small extent of space (*find a sheltered spot*). **7** **a** a particular place, a definite locality (*landed on this spot*). **b** the place where one is, or is standing or sitting (*remain on the spot*; *move off the spot*). **8** (*often in comb.*) a place used for a certain activity; a place of entertainment. **9** PENALTY SPOT (under PENALTY). **10** a place on one's body (*a tender spot*). **11** an aspect of one's character (*a weak spot*). **12** an aspect of a situation (*a bright spot*). **13** (*coll.*) a small amount (of anything) (*a spot of dinner*; *a spot of luck*; *a spot of bother*; *a spot of rain*). **14** (*coll.*) a drink. **15** a place on a television or radio programme for an entertainer. **16** an opportunity in the interval between programmes for advertisers. **17** a spotlight. **18** **a** a mark near the top of a billiard or snooker table on which the red ball or cue ball is placed at certain times. **b** SPOT-STROKE (under SPOT). **c** SPOT-BALL (under SPOT). **19** a sea fish, esp. the redfish, marked with a spot. **20** a breed of domestic pigeon, white, with a spot on its forehead. ~*v.t.* (*pres.p.* **spotting,** *past, p.p.* **spotted**) **1** to pick out beforehand (e.g. the winner of a race). **2** to recognize, to detect. **3** to watch out for and note (*train-spotting*). **4** to catch sight of (*spotted her in the crowd*). **5** (*Mil.*) to pinpoint (the enemy's position), esp. from the air. **6** to mark, stain, or discolour with a spot or spots. **7** to sully, to blemish (someone's reputation). **8** to place (a ball) on the spot at billiards. **9** (*impers.*) to rain slightly. ~*v.i.* to become or be liable to be marked with spots. **in a spot** in an awkward situation. **in a tight spot** in a dangerous or complicated situation. **on the spot** 1 at the scene of action. 2 in the position of having to act or respond quickly. 3 at once, without change of place, there and then. 4 alert, wide awake. **to change one's spots** to reform one's ways. **to hit the spot** (*coll.*) to be just what is needed. **to knock spots off** to outdo easily. **to put someone on the spot** to put someone in an awkward position, to force someone to think fast. **to run on the spot** to make running movements with the legs without moving forwards, for exercise. **spot-ball** *n.* in billiards, a white ball marked with two black spots. **spot-barred** *a.* in billiards, denoting a game in which the spot-stroke is not allowed more than twice in succession. **spot cash** *n.* (*coll.*) money down. **spot check** *n.* a random examination or check without prior warning. **spot-check** *v.t.* to make a random check on. **spot height** *n.* (a number on a map indicating) the altitude above sea level of a certain point. **spotlamp** *n.* a spotlight. **spotless** *a.* **spotlessly** *adv.* **spotlessness** *n.* **spotlight** *n.* 1 a lamp for throwing a concentrated beam of light, esp. on a performer on the stage. 2 the patch of light thus thrown. 3 the glare of publicity. ~*v.t.* (*past, p.p.* **spotlighted, spotlit**) 1 to direct a spotlight on to. 2 to direct attention towards. **spot-on,** (*pred.*) **spot on** *a.* (*coll.*) absolutely accurate. **spot-stroke** *n.* in billiards, a winning hazard off the red ball when on the spot. **spotted** *a.* **spotted dick** *n.* a steamed suet pudding with currants. **spotted dog** *n.* 1 a Dalmatian. 2 spotted dick. **spotted fever** *n.* 1 cerebrospinal meningitis, characterized by spots on the skin. 2 typhus. 3 ROCKY MOUNTAIN SPOTTED FEVER (under ROCK[1]). **spotted gum** *n.* (*Austral.*) a eucalyptus tree, *Eucalyptus maculata*, marked on the bark with spots. **spottedness** *n.* **spotter** *n.* 1 (*Mil.*) an observer trained to detect the approach of enemy aircraft. 2 (*in comb.*) a person whose hobby or job is spotting or noting things (*a talent-spotter, a plane-spotter*). **spotting** *n.* (*often in comb.*, as *talent-spotting, train-spotting*). **spotty** *a.* (*comp.* **spottier,** *superl.* **spottiest**) 1 covered or marked with spots. 2 having pimples or blemishes on the skin. 3 patchy, uneven, irregular. **spottily** *adv.* **spottiness** *n.* **spot-weld** *v.t.* to join (two pieces of metal) with a circular weld. **spot weld** *n.* a weld of this type. **spot-welder** *n.* **spot-welding** *n.* [ME (cp. EFris. *spot*, MDut. *spotten*, Icel. *spotte*, Norw. *spott*), cogn. with SPOUT]

spouse (spows) *n.* a husband or wife. **spousal** (-zəl) *a.* 1 of or relating to marriage. 2 nuptial, matrimonial. **spouseless** *a.* [ME *spuse*, OF *spus, spuse*, var. of *éspus* (F *époux*), L *sponsus*, p.p. of *spondēre*, to promise]

spout (spowt) *n.* 1 a short pipe, tube, or channelled projection for carrying off water from a gutter, conducting liquid from a vessel etc. 2 a chute or trough down which things may be shot into a receptacle. 3 (*Hist.*) a chute or lift in a pawnbroker's shop. 4 a continuous stream, jet, or column of water etc. 5 a waterspout. 6 (*also* **spout-hole**) a whale's spiracle or blowhole. ~*v.t.* 1 to pour out or discharge with force or in large volume. 2 to utter or recite in a declamatory manner. ~*v.i.* 1 to pour out or issue forcibly or copiously. 2 to declaim, to hold forth. **up the spout** 1 (*sl.*) ruined, failed. 2 (*sl.*) at the pawnbroker's, in pawn. 3 (*sl.*) pregnant. **spouter** *n.* **spoutless** *a.* [ME *spouten* (cp. Dut. *spuiten*, Swed. *sputa, spruta*), prob. by-form of SPROUT]

spp. SP.

SPQR *abbr.* 1 (*Hist.*) the Senate and the people of Rome (L *Senatus Populusque Romanus*). 2 small profits and quick returns.

Spr. *abbr.* sapper.

spraddle (sprad´əl) *v.i., v.t.* (*dial., N Am.*) to straddle, spread, sprawl or splay. [prob. rel. to SPREAD]

sprag (sprag) *n.* 1 a chock of wood for locking the wheel of a vehicle. 2 a billet of wood, esp. a prop for the roof of a mine. ~*v.t.* (*pres.p.* **spragging,** *past, p.p.* **spragged**) to support or lock with sprags. [etym. uncertain]

sprain (sprān) *v.t.* to twist or wrench the muscles or ligaments of (a joint) so as to injure without dislocation. ~*n.* such a twist or wrench or the bruising and swelling caused by it. [etym. uncertain]

spraint (sprānt) *n.* (*usu. pl.*) the dung of an otter. [OF *espreintes*, from *espreindre*, to squeeze out, rel. to EXPRESS[1]]

sprang SPRING.

sprat (sprat) *n.* 1 a small food fish, *Clupea sprattus*, related to the herring. 2 the young of the herring and other small fish. ~*v.i.* (*pres.p.* **spratting,** *past, p.p.* **spratted**) to fish for sprats. **spratter** *n.* [OE *sprott*, cp. Dut. *sprot*, also OE *sprot, sprota*, SPROUT]

sprauncy (sprawn´si) *a.* (*comp.* **sprauncier,** *superl.* **spraunciest**) (*sl.*) smart, dapper, swish. [perh. dial. *sprouncey*, cheerful]

sprawl (sprawl) *v.i.* 1 to lie or stretch out the body and limbs in a careless or awkward posture. 2 (of a town, plant etc.) to straggle, to be spread out in an irregular or ungraceful form. ~*v.t.* to spread out (one's body or limbs) in an ungainly fashion. **sprawler** *n.* **sprawling** *a.* **sprawlingly** *adv.* **sprawly** *a.* [OE *sprewlian*, cp. Norw. *sprala*, Dan. *spraelle*]

spray[1] (sprā) *n.* 1 water or other liquid flying in small, fine drops. 2 a perfume or other liquid applied in fine particles with an atomizer. 3 (*often in comb.*) an appliance for spraying (*a hairspray*). ~*v.t.* 1 to throw or apply (liquid) in the form of spray. 2 to treat with a spray, e.g. to sprinkle (a plant) with an insecticide. ~*v.i.* (of a male cat or other male animal) to sprinkle its territory with urine, so that the smell will attract females. **sprayable** *a.* **spray-dry** *v.t.* (*3rd pers. sing. pres.* **spray-dries,** *pres.p.* **spray-drying,** *past, p.p.* **spray-dried**) to dry (a liquid, e.g. milk) by spraying it into hot air etc. **sprayer** *n.* **spray gun** *n.* a gunlike appliance which sprays paint etc. **spray-paint** *v.t.* to paint (a surface) using a spray. [cp. LG *sprei*, drizzle, MDut. *sprayen*, G *sprühen*, to drizzle]

spray[2] (sprā) *n.* 1 a small branch or sprig, esp. with branchlets, leaves, flowers etc. 2 a decorative bouquet of this shape. 3 a corsage of flowers and foliage. 4 a brooch or other ornament resembling a sprig of leaves, flowers etc. **sprayey** (-i) *a.* [ME, from OE *(e)sprei*]

spread (spred) *v.t.* (*past, p.p.* **spread**) 1 to extend in length and breadth by opening (out), unrolling, unfolding, flattening out etc. 2 to scatter, to diffuse, to smooth into a thin wide layer (*spread jam on bread*). 3 to disseminate, to publish (*spread the word*). 4 to cover the surface of (*spread bread with jam*). 5 to display, lay (out) before the eye or mind (*the landscape that was spread out before us*). 6 to lay (a table). ~*v.i.* 1 to be extended in length and breadth. 2 to be scattered, diffused, smoothed out thinly or disseminated. 3 to extend, stretch (out) widely. ~*n.* 1 an act of spreading. 2 breadth, extent, compass, expansion. 3 an aircraft's wingspan. 4 diffusion, dissemination. 5 expanding girth (*middle-age spread*). 6 the gap between two prices, e.g. the bid and offer price of shares. 7 (*coll.*) a meal set out, a feast. 8 a sweet or savoury paste for spreading over bread etc. 9 a coverlet, a bedspread. 10 two facing pages in a book, magazine etc. 11 (*N Am.*) an extensive ranch. **to spread like wildfire** WILDFIRE (under WILD). **to spread one's wings** WING. **spreadable** *a.* **spread eagle** *n.* 1 (*Her.*) an eagle with wings and legs extended. 2 (*Hist.*) a seaman lashed with outstretched limbs to the rigging for punishment. **spreadeagle** *v.t.* 1 to fix (a person) with outstretched limbs for punishment. 2 to cause to stand or lie with arms and legs stretched out. ~*v.i.* to stand or lie with arms and legs stretched out. **spreadeagled** *a.* **spread-eagle** *a.* 1 bombastic. 2 aggressively patriotic.

3 lying or standing with the arms and legs stretched out. **spreader** *n.* **spreadsheet** *n.* a computer program which can perform rapid calculations on figures displayed on a VDU in rows and columns, used for business accounting and financial planning. [OE *sprǣdan*, cp. Dut. *spreiden*, G *spreiten*]

Sprechgesang (shprekh´gəzang) *n.* (*Mus.*) a style of vocalization between singing and speaking. [G, speaking song]

Sprechstimme (shprekh´shtimə) *n.* (*Mus.*) **1** the type of voice used in Sprechgesang. **2** Sprechgesang. [G, speaking voice]

spree (sprē) *n.* **1** a lively frolic, esp. with drinking. **2** a bout of extravagance or excess, esp. involving an outing (*a spending spree; a shopping spree*). ~*v.i.* (*3rd pers. sing. pres.* **sprees**, *pres.p.* **spreeing**, *past, p.p.* **spreed**) to have a spree. **on the spree** having a spree. [etym. uncertain]

sprig[1] (sprig) *n.* **1** a small branch, twig, or shoot. **2** an ornament resembling this, esp. as a pattern on fabric. **3** (*derog.*) a scion, a young fellow. ~*v.t.* (*pres.p.* **sprigging**, *past, p.p.* **sprigged**) **1** to print or embroider (fabric) with sprigs. **2** to ornament (pottery) with applied decoration. **sprigged** *a.* **sprigging** *n.* **spriggy** *a.* (*comp.* **spriggier**, *superl.* **spriggiest**). [ME, rel. to LG *sprick*]

sprig[2] (sprig) *n.* a small headless nail or brad. ~*v.t.* (*pres.p.* **sprigging**, *past, p.p.* **sprigged**) to drive small brads into. [ME, etym. uncertain]

sprightly (sprīt´li), **spritely** *a.* (*comp.* **sprightlier**, *superl.* **sprightliest**) lively, spirited, gay, vivacious, brisk or agile. †**sprightful** *a.* **sprightliness** *n.* [*spright*, var. of SPRITE, -LY[1]]

spring (spring) *v.i.* (*past* **sprang** (sprang), *p.p.* **sprung** (sprŭng)) **1** to leap, to bound, to jump (*sprang to her feet; sprang across the room; sprang to my help*). **2** to move suddenly by or as by the action of a spring (*The lid sprang open; The branches sprang back*). **3** to rise, to come (up) from or as from a source, to arise, to originate, to appear, esp. unexpectedly (*A storm sprang up; Where could that idea have sprung from?*). **4** (of wood etc.) to warp, to split. **5** (*N Am., Austral., sl.*) to pay (for a treat etc.). ~*v.t.* **1** to cause to move, fly, act etc., suddenly by or as by releasing a spring (*sprang the trap*). **2** to produce unexpectedly (*always springing surprises*). **3** (*sl.*) to bring about the escape from prison of. **4** to rouse or start (game) from earth or covert. **5** to provide (a vehicle etc.) with springs (*fully sprung seats*). **6** (*coll.*) to spend (cash). **7** to cause (a mine) to explode. **8** to cause (timber, a wooden implement etc.) to warp, crack, or become loose. **9** (of a vessel) to develop (a leak) thus. ~*n.* **1** a leap, jump. **2** a backward movement as from release from tension, a recoil, a rebound. **3** the starting of a plank, seam, leak etc. **4** elasticity, resilience (*a dance floor with plenty of spring; My feet are losing their spring*). **5** an elastic body or structure, usu. of bent or coiled metal used to prevent jar, to convey motive power in a watch etc. **6** the first of the four seasons of the year, preceding summer, roughly March, April and May in the N hemisphere. **7** (*Astron.*) the period lasting from the vernal equinox to the summer solstice. **8** the early part (of life, a relationship etc.), youth. **9** the spring tide. **10** a natural issue of water, oil etc. from the earth, or the site of this. **11** a source, an origin. **12** a source of energy, a cause of action, a motive. **13** (*sl.*) an escape by prisoners. **14** the upward curve of a beam from the horizontal. **15** the giving way or splitting of a plank etc. **to spring a leak** LEAK. **to spring to mind** MIND. **spring balance** *n.* a balance weighing objects by the tension of a spring. **spring bed** *n.* a bed with a spring mattress. **springboard** *n.* **1** a springy board giving impetus in leaping, diving etc. **2** anything that provides a starting point or initial impetus. **3** (*N Am., Austral.*) a platform inserted into the trunk of a tree for a lumberjack to stand on so as to operate at some distance from the ground. **spring-carriage, spring-cart** *n.* a carriage or cart mounted on springs. **spring chicken** *n.* **1** (*N Am.*) a tender young chicken, usu. from 2 to 10 months old. **2** (*usu. with neg., coll.*) a young, active, inexperienced person (*and he's no spring chicken*). **spring-clean** *v.t.* to clean (a house) thoroughly in preparation for summer. ~*n.* a thorough cleaning of this kind. **spring equinox** *n.* **1** the equinox that occurs about 20 March in the N hemisphere and 22 September in the S hemisphere. **2** (*Astron.*) the March equinox. **springer** *n.* **1** a person or thing that springs. **2** a breed of spaniels used to rouse game; a spaniel of this breed. **3** (*Archit.*) **a** the part or stone where the curve of an arch begins. **b** the rib of a groined roof. **c** the lowest stone of a gable-coping. **4** the springbok. **spring fever** *n.* **1** a restless feeling associated with spring. **2** (*facet.*) lethargy, lassitude. **spring greens** *n.pl.* the young leaves of a type of cabbage that does not develop a heart. **springless** *a.* **springlet** *n.* **springlike** *a.* **spring-loaded** *a.* having a spring, secured by means of a stretched or compressed spring. **spring lock** *n.* a lock with a spring-loaded bolt. **spring mattress** *n.* **spring onion** *n.* an onion with a tiny thin-skinned bulb and long leaves, eaten in salads. **spring roll** *n.* a Chinese dish comprising a thin deep-fried pancake filled with a savoury mixture. **springtail** *n.* any insect of the wingless order Collembola, having bristles on its under side enabling it to leap. **spring tide** *n.* **1** a high tide occurring a day or two after the new or the full moon. **2** (*poet.*) (*usu.* **springtide**) springtime. **springtime** *n.* the season of spring. **spring washer** *n.* a washer consisting of one or two coils of spiral-spring form, used to prevent nuts from becoming slack with vibration. **spring water** *n.* water from a spring, as distinct from rainwater or river water. **springy** *a.* (*comp.* **springier**, *superl.* **springiest**) **1** elastic or resilient, like a spring. **2** (of movement) lively, bouncy. **springily** *adv.* **springiness** *n.* [OE *springan, sprincan*, cp. Dut. and G *springen*, Icel. *springa*, to burst]

Usage note In standard English, the past tense of *spring* is *sprang*, not *sprung*.

springbok (spring´bok) *n.* **1** a southern African gazelle, *Antidorcas marsupialis*, that runs with a high leaping movement. **2** (**Springbok**) a sportsman or sportswoman representing South Africa in international competitions. [Afrikaans, from Dut. *springen*, to spring, *bok*, buck, antelope]

springe (sprinj) *n.* a noose, a snare, usu. for small game. ~*v.t.* to catch in a springe. [ME, var. of SPRING]

springhalt STRINGHALT.

sprinkle (spring´kəl) *v.t., v.i.* to scatter in small drops or particles. ~*v.t.* to shower (a surface with) small drops or particles. ~*n.* a sprinkling, a light shower. **sprinkler** *n.* that which sprinkles, e.g. a rotating device that waters a lawn. **sprinkler system** *n.* a system for extinguishing fires, in which a sudden rise in temperature triggers the release of water from overhead nozzles. **sprinkling** *n.* a small quantity or number (of). [formerly *sprenkle*, prob. freq. from OE *sprengan*, causal of *springan*, to SPRING]

sprint (sprint) *v.i., v.t.* to run (a short distance) at top speed. ~*n.* **1** a short burst of running, cycling etc. at top speed. **2** a running race of 400 metres or less. **sprinter** *n.* [from Icel., etym. uncertain, cp. Swed. *spritta*]

sprit (sprit) *n.* a small spar set diagonally from the mast to the top outer corner of a sail. **spritsail** (-səl, -sāl) *n.* **1** a sail extended by a sprit. **2** (*Hist.*) a sail extended by a yard fitted under the bowsprit. [OE *sprēot*, pole, cogn. with SPROUT]

sprite (sprīt) *n.* **1** a fairy, an elf. **2** a computer-generated display shape that can be manipulated by a programmer to create fast and complex animation sequences. [ME, as SPIRIT]

spritely SPRIGHTLY.

spritz (sprits) *v.t.* (*N Am.*) to squirt or spray. ~*n.* an act of spritzing. [G *spritzen*, to squirt]

spritzer (sprit´sə) *n.* a drink made from white wine and soda water. [G *Spritzer*, a splash]

sprocket (sprok´it) *n.* **1** each of a set of teeth on a wheel etc., engaging with the links of a chain. **2** a sprocket-wheel. **3** a wheel with teeth for advancing film in a camera or projector, or paper, tape etc. in a printer. **sprocket-wheel** *n.* a wheel set with sprockets. [etym. uncertain]

sprog (sprog) *n.* (*coll.*) a baby, an infant, a child. [orig. air force sl., a recruit; etym. uncertain]

sprout (sprowt) *v.i.* **1** to shoot forth, to develop shoots, to germinate. **2** to grow, like the shoots of plants. ~*v.t.* **1** to put forth or produce (shoots etc.). **2** to grow (e.g. a beard or moustache) or put forth (e.g. a television aerial). **3** to cause to put forth sprouts or to grow. ~*n.* **1** a new shoot on a plant. **2** a Brussels sprout. [OE *sprūtan*, cp. Dut. *spruiten*, G *spriessen*, cogn. with SPOUT and SPURT]

spruce[1] (sproos) *a.* neat, trim, smart. ~*v.t.* to smarten (up). **sprucely** *adv.* **spruceness** *n.* [prob. from OF *Pruce*, G *Preussen*, Prussia (orig. applied to Prussian leather)]

spruce[2] (sproos) *n.* any conifer of the genus *Picea*, of a distinctive cone shape, with dense foliage and four-angled needles. **spruce beer** *n.* a fermented liquor made from the needles and twigs of the spruce fir. **spruce fir** *n.* [alt. of obs. *Pruce*, Prussia]

spruce[3] (sproos) *v.t.* (*sl.*) to deceive. ~*v.i.* **1** to engage in deception. **2** to malinger or dodge a duty. **sprucer** *n.* [etym. uncertain]

sprue[1] (sproo) *n.* **1** a hole or channel through which molten metal or plastic is poured into a mould. **2** the corresponding projection in a casting. [etym. uncertain]

sprue[2] (sproo) *n.* a tropical disease characterized by diarrhoea, anaemia, and wasting, with ulceration of the mucous membrane of the mouth. [Dut. *spruw*, thrush]

spruik (sprook) *v.i.* (*Austral.*, *New Zeal.*, *coll.*) to speak in public, to harangue people. **spruiker** *n.* a barker at a fair booth. [etym. uncertain]

spruit (sprāt) *n.* (*S Afr.*) a small tributary stream, esp. one that is dry in summer. [Afrikaans]

sprung[1] SPRING.

sprung[2] (sprŭng) *a.* provided with, or as if with, springs (*fully sprung seats*; *a sprung dance floor*). **sprung rhythm** *n.* a metre used in poetry (e.g. by Gerard Manley Hopkins) imitating natural speech, with one stressed syllable in each foot, followed by a varying number of unstressed syllables. [p.p. of SPRING]

spry (sprī) *a.* (*comp.* **spryer**, **sprier**, *superl.* **spryest**, **spriest**) active, lively, nimble, agile. **spryly** *adv.* **spryness** *n.* [cp. Swed. dial. *sprygg*]

spud (spŭd) *n.* **1** (*coll.*) a potato. **2** a short spadelike tool for cutting up weeds by the roots etc. **3** a short, thick person or thing. ~*v.t.* (*pres.p.* **spudding**, *past*, *p.p.* **spudded**) to dig (up) or clear (out) with a spud. **to spud in 1** to begin drilling an oil well. **2** (*coll.*) to start work. **spud-bashing** *n.* (*coll.*) peeling potatoes. **spuddy** *a.* (*comp.* **spuddier**, *superl.* **spuddiest**) plump, podgy. [ME *spudde*, a short knife, cp. Dan. *spydd*, MDan. *spjud*, Swed. *spujt*, Icel. *spjōt*]

spue SPEW.

spumante (spooman´ti) *n.* (*pl.* **spumantes** (-tiz)) a sparkling Italian wine. [It., sparkling]

spume (spūm) *n.* froth, foam. ~*v.i.* to froth, to foam. **spumescent** (-mes´ənt) *a.* foaming, frothing. **spumy** *a.* (*comp.* **spumier**, *superl.* **spumiest**). **spuminess** *n.* [L *spūma*]

spun[1] SPIN.

spun[2] (spŭn) *a.* produced by a spinning process. **spun glass** *n.* glass that is spun, when heated, into filaments that retain their pliancy when cold. **spun gold, spun silver** *n.* gold or silver thread spun for weaving. **spun silk** *n.* yarn made from silk waste and spun like woollen yarn. **spun sugar** *n.* sugar spun into soft fibres, for candyfloss etc. **spun yarn** *n.* a line made of twisted rope-yarns. [p.p. of SPIN]

spunk (spŭngk) *n.* **1** mettle, spirit, pluck. **2** touchwood, tinder. **3** (*taboo, sl.*) semen. **4** (*Austral.*, *sl.*) a sexually attractive person. **5** (*Sc.*) a match (for ignition). **spunky** *a.* (*comp.* **spunkier**, *superl.* **spunkiest**) **1** plucky, spirited. **2** (*Austral.*, *sl.*) sexually attractive. [Ir. *sponc*, tinder, L and Gr. *spongia*, SPONGE]

spur (spœ) *n.* **1** an instrument worn on a horseman's heel having a sharp or blunt point or a rowel. **2** instigation, incentive, stimulus, impulse. **3** a spur-shaped projection, attachment, or part, such as the pointed projection on a cock's leg, or a steel point or sheath fastened on this in cockfighting. **4** the largest root of a tree. **5** a ridge or buttress projecting from a mountain range. **6** a tubular projection on the columbine and other flowers. **7** a short fruit-bearing shoot. **8** a climbing-iron. **9** a branch road, or a railway siding or branch line. ~*v.t.* (*pres.p.* **spurring**, *past*, *p.p.* **spurred**) **1** to prick with spurs. **2** to urge (on), to incite. **3** to stimulate (interest, enthusiasm etc.). **4** to provide or fit with spurs. ~*v.i.* to ride hard, to press (on or forward). **on the spur of the moment** on impulse, impromptu. **to set/ put spurs to 1** to spur (a horse). **2** to whet, to put an edge on (one's resolution). **to win one's spurs 1** to achieve distinction, to make oneself famous. **2** (*Hist.*) to gain knighthood. **spur-gear** *n.* a spur-wheel. **spurless** *a.* **spurred** *a.* **spurrer** *n.* **spurrier** (spŭr´-) *n.* a person who makes spurs. **spur royal** *n.* a gold coin of James I having on the reverse a sun with rays, somewhat resembling a spur. **spur-wheel** *n.* a gearwheel with radial teeth projecting from the rim. [OE *spura*, *spora*, cp. Dut. *spoor*, G *Sporn*, Icel. *spori*, Dan. *spore*]

spurge (spœj) *n.* a plant of the genus *Euphorbia* with milky, usu. acrid juice. **spurge laurel** *n.* a bushy evergreen shrub, *Daphne laureola*, with glossy leaves, greenish flowers, and poisonous berries. [A-F, from OF *espurge*, from *espurger*, L *expurgāre*, to EXPURGATE]

spurious (spū´riəs) *a.* **1** not genuine, not proceeding from the true or pretended source, false, counterfeit (*a spurious interest*). **2** like a specified part or organ in form or function but physiologically or morphologically different. **3** (of children) illegitimate. **spuriously** *adv.* **spuriousness** *n.* [L *spurius*]

spurn (spœn) *v.t.* **1** to reject with disdain; to treat with scorn. **2** to thrust or kick away with the foot. ~*v.i.* to kick (at or against). ~*n.* the act of spurning, scornful rejection. **spurner** *n.* [OE *spornan spurnan* (cp. Icel. *sperna*, also L *spernere*), cogn. with SPUR]

spurrer SPUR.

spurrey (spŭr´i), **spurry** *n.* (*pl.* **spurreys, spurries**) a low annual weed of the genus *Spergula* of the family Silenaceae. [OF *spurrie*, late L *spergula*, perh. from G]

spurrier SPUR.

spurry SPURREY.

spurt (spœt) *v.i.* **1** (*also* **spirt**) to gush out in a jet or sudden stream. **2** to make a sudden intense effort. ~*v.t.* to send or force out in a jet or stream. ~*n.* **1** (*also* **spirt**) a forcible gush or jet of liquid. **2** a short burst of intense effort or speed. [etym. uncertain]

spurtle (spœ´təl), **spirtle** *n.* (*Sc.*) a stirring stick for porridge. [etym. uncertain]

sputa SPUTUM.

sputnik (spŭt´nik, sput´-) *n.* any of a series of Russian artificial earth satellites, the first of which was launched in 1957. [Rus., a travelling-companion]

sputter (spŭt´ə) *v.i.* **1** (of frying food etc.) to emit spitting sounds. **2** to emit saliva in scattered drops, to splutter. **3** to speak in a jerky, incoherent, or excited way. *~v.t.* **1** to emit with a spluttering noise. **2** to utter rapidly and indistinctly. **3** (*Physics*) to remove atoms from (a surface) by bombardment with high-energy ions. **4** to coat a surface with (a metallic film) by such a process. *~n.* **1** an act, or a sound, of sputtering. **2** (an instance of) confused, incoherent speech. **sputterer** *n.* **sputteringly** *adv.* [Dut. *sputteren*, imit.]

sputum (spū´təm) *n.* (*pl.* **sputa** (-tə)) **1** spittle, saliva. **2** (*Med.*) a morbid mixture of saliva and mucus expectorated from the respiratory tract. [L, neut. p.p. of *spuere*, to spit]

spy (spī) *n.* (*pl.* **spies**) **1** a person employed by a government or business to obtain information about, and report on, the movements and operations of an enemy, business rival etc. **2** a person who keeps a constant secret or surreptitious watch on the actions, movements etc., of others. *~v.t.* (*3rd pers. sing. pres.* **spies**, *pres.p.* **spying**, *past, p.p.* **spied**) **1** to see, to detect, to discover, esp. by close observation. **2** to explore or search (out) secretly. **3** to discover thus. *~v.i.* **1** to act as a spy, to keep a surreptitious watch (on). **2** to search narrowly, to pry (into). **spyglass** *n.* a small telescope. **spyhole** *n.* a peephole. **spymaster** *n.* the person at the head of a spy organization. [OF *espier*, to ESPY]

Sq *abbr.* Square (in addresses).

sq., sq *abbr.* **1** (*pl.* **sqq.**) *sequens*, following. **2** square.

SQL *abbr.* (*Comput.*) structured query language.

Sqn *abbr.* squadron. **Sqn Lr** *abbr.* Squadron Leader.

sqq. SQ.

squab (skwob) *n.* **1** a short fat person. **2** a young bird, esp. an unfledged pigeon. **3** a stuffed cushion; a sofa padded throughout; an ottoman; the padded side or back of a car seat. *~a.* fat, short, squat. *~adv.* **1** with a heavy fall. **2** plonk, plump. *~v.i.* to fall plonk or plump. **squabby** *a.* (*comp.* **squabbier**, *superl.* **squabbiest**) short and fat, squat. **squab pie** *n.* **1** a pigeon pie. **2** a pie made of mutton, pork, apples, and onions. [cp. Swed. dial. *squabb*, loose, fat flesh, *squabba*, fat woman]

squabble (skwob´əl) *n.* a petty or noisy quarrel, a wrangle. *~v.i.* to engage in a petty or noisy quarrel, to wrangle. **squabbler** *n.* [cp. Swed. dial. *skvabbel*, dispute, *skvappa*, to chide, from *skvapp*, splash, imit.]

squacco (skwak´ō) *n.* (*pl.* **squaccos**) a small crested heron, *Ardeola ralloides*, of S Europe, Asia and Africa. **squacco heron** *n.* [imit. of cry]

squad (skwod) *n.* **1** a small party of people, e.g. engaged in a task together. **2** a small number of soldiers assembled for drill or inspection. **3** a sports team. **4** a specialized body within the police force (*usu. in comb.*, as *the drug squad*). **5** FLYING SQUAD (under FLYING). **6** a party of people of specified type. **squad car** *n.* a police car linked to headquarters by radio. **squaddie, squaddy** *n.* (*pl.* **squaddies**) (*coll.*) a private soldier. [MF *esquadre* (F *escadre*), It. *squadra*, SQUARE]

squadron (skwod´rən) *n.* **1** an organized group of people. **2** a main division of a cavalry regiment, usu. consisting of two troops containing 120 to 200 men. **3** a detachment of several warships employed on some particular service. **4** a division of a naval fleet under a flag-officer. **5** a Royal Air Force unit with 10 to 18 aircraft. *~v.t.* to arrange in squadrons. **squadron leader** *n.* a commissioned officer in the Royal Air Force immediately junior to a wing commander, the equivalent in rank to a major in the army. [MF *esquadron*, It. *squadrone*, as SQUAD]

squail (skwāl) *n.* **1** (*pl.*) a game played on a small table or board with discs which are snapped from the edge towards a mark in the centre. **2** a disc used in the game of squails. *~v.t.* to pelt with a stick etc. *~v.i.* to throw a stick etc. (at). **squail-board** *n.* **squailer** *n.* a stick with a leaded knob for squailing birds etc. [etym. uncertain]

squalid (skwol´id) *a.* **1** repulsively dirty, filthy. **2** mean, poverty-ridden. **3** sordid. **squalidity** (-lid´-) *n.* **squalidly** *adv.* **squalidness** *n.* **squalor** (skwol´ə) *n.* [L *squālidus*, from *squālēre*, to be stiff, dirty etc.]

squall (skwawl) *n.* **1** a sudden, violent gust or succession of gusts of wind, esp. accompanied by rain, hail, snow etc. **2** a harsh, discordant scream, esp. of a child. **3** (*often pl.*) an upset, quarrel or commotion (*domestic squalls*). *~v.i., v.t.* **1** to cry out. **2** to scream discordantly. **squaller** *n.* **squally** *a.* (*comp.* **squallier**, *superl.* **squalliest**). [prob. imit., or from SQUEAL influ. by BAWL]

squaloid (skwā´loid) *a.* **1** resembling a shark. **2** belonging to the Squalidae, a family of sharks. [L *squalus*, a sea fish, prob. a shark]

squalor SQUALID.

squama (skwā´mə) *n.* (*pl.* **squamae** (skwā´mē)) **1** a scale on a plant or animal. **2** (*Anat.*) a thin plate of bone. **squamate** (-mət, -māt), **squamose** (-mōs), **squamous** *a.* scaly. **squamule** (-mūl) *n.* a small scale. [L]

squander (skwon´də) *v.t.* **1** to spend (money, time etc.) wastefully. **2** to dissipate by foolish prodigality. **3** to waste (one's talents etc.) by misapplication. **squanderer** *n.* **squanderingly** *adv.* [etym. uncertain]

square (skweə) *n.* **1** a rectangle with equal sides. **2** any surface, area, object, part etc., of this shape. **3** a rectangular division of a chessboard or draughtboard, window pane etc. **4** an academic cap with a stiff flat square top. **5** a square scarf. **6** an open quadrilateral area surrounded by buildings, usu. laid out with trees, flower beds, lawns etc. **7** an open area at a street junction. **8** (*N Am.*) a block of buildings bounded by four streets. **9** in cricket, a close-trimmed area at the centre of the ground, from which the playing strip can be selected. **10** a body of infantry formed into a rectangular figure. **11** a drilling area inside barracks. **12** the product of a quantity multiplied by itself (*The square of 9 is 81*). **13** an L- or T-shaped instrument for laying out and testing right angles. **14** (*sl.*) a conventional, old-fashioned person, someone out of touch with modern ways of thought. **15** an arrangement of words, figures etc., with as many rows as columns (usu. reading alike perpendicularly or across). **16** a unit of measure for flooring, 100 square feet. **17** (*N Am., coll.*) a square meal. **18** order, regularity, proper proportion. **19** equity, fairness, honesty. *~a.* **1** having four equal sides and four right angles. **2** (of corners or angles) of right-angled shape, measuring 90°, rectangular. **3** at right angles (to). **4** angular as distinct from rounded (*a square jaw*). **5** broad with straight sides or outlines (*He was square rather than fat*). **6** denoting a unit of measure representing the area of a square whose side is the unit specified (*a square metre*). **7** level or parallel (with). **8** even (with), quits (with). **9** in football, in a straight line across the pitch. **10** in cricket, at right angles to the wicket, on a line through the stumps. **11** just, fair, honest. **12** in proper order. **13** not in debt, owing no money. **14** evenly balanced, even, settled, complete, thorough, absolute. **15** in golf etc., having the same score as one's opponent. **16** (of scores) equal. **17** direct, uncompromising (*a square denial*). **18** (*coll.*) (of a person or their tastes) dull, conventional, old-fashioned. **19** (*Mus.*) (of rhythms) simple, uncomplicated, straightforward. *~adv.* **1** evenly (*not lying square*). **2** honestly; fairly (*not playing square with me*). **3** at right angles (*a workbench placed square to the window*). *~v.t.* **1** to make square or rectangular. **2** to give a rectangular cross-section to (timber). **3** to multiply (a number or quantity) by itself. **4** to adjust, to bring into conformity (with or to), to reconcile (*square the account with the facts*). **5** to mark (paper etc.) out in squares. **6** to settle, to pay (a bill). **7** to hold (one's shoulders) back, and at an even height, presenting a square front. **8** (*coll.*) to bribe, to win over with gifts, money etc. **9** to even the scores in (a match etc.). **10** (*Naut.*) **a** to lay (a vessel's yards etc.) at right angles to the plane of the keel. **b** to make (deadlines or ratlines) horizontal. ~*v.i.* **1** to conform precisely, to agree, to harmonize (with) (*Your story doesn't square with the facts*). **2** to put oneself in an attitude for boxing. **3** to be at right angles (with). **all square** with no party in debt to any other, even, quits. **back to square one** back to where one started without having made any progress. **on the square 1** at right angles. **2** fair, honest; fairly, honestly. **3** belonging to the Freemasons. **out of square** not square, not at right angles. **square peg in a round hole** PEG. **to get square with** to pay or make terms with (a creditor). **to square accounts with** ACCOUNT. **to square away** (*N Am.*, *coll.*) to put in order, tidy up. **to square off 1** to assume a posture of defence or attack. **2** (*Austral.*) to placate. **3** to mark off in squares. **to square the circle 1** to construct geometrically a square equal in area to a given circle. **2** to attempt impossibilities. **to square up** to settle an account. **to square up to 1** to face (someone) in a fighting attitude. **2** to face up to, to tackle positively (one's problems etc.). **square-bashing** *n.* (*sl.*) military drill. **square brackets** *n.pl.* a pair of angular brackets [] as distinct from parentheses. **square-built** *a.* broadly built. **square dance** *n.* a dance for four couples forming a square set. **square-dancer** *n.* **square-dancing** *n.* **square deal** *n.* **1** a fair bargain. **2** a fair deal, fair treatment. **square dinkum** *a.*, *adv.* (*Austral.*, *coll.*) absolutely honest(ly). **squared paper** *n.* paper marked out in squares, for graphs etc. **square-eyed** *a.* (*facet.*) watching, or affected by watching, too much television. **square knot** *n.* a reef knot. **square leg** *n.* in cricket, a fielder standing about 20 metres directly behind the batsman on strike. **squarely** *adv.* **square meal** *n.* a meal which is full and satisfying. **square measure** *n.* a system of measures expressed in square feet, square metres etc. **Square Mile** *n.* the City, the financial heart of London. **squareness** *n.* **square number** *n.* the product of a number multiplied by itself. **square perch** *n.* a square measure, 30¼ square yards. **square piano** *n.* an early piano, of rectangular design. **squarer** *n.* a person or thing that squares. **square-rigged** *a.* (*Naut.*) having the principal sails extended by horizontal yards suspended by the middle from the mast. **square root** *n.* the quantity that, multiplied by itself, will produce the given quantity (*The square root of 49 is 7*). **square sail** (səl, sāl) *n.* a four-cornered sail set on a yard, esp. on a fore-and-aft rigged vessel. **square-shouldered** *a.* having the shoulders held well up and back, as opposed to round sloping shoulders. **square-toed** *a.* **1** (of shoes or boots) square at the front end, not pointed. **2** wearing shoes or boots like this. **3** precise, prim. **square wave** *n.* (*Physics*) an oscillation that gives a rectangular waveform. **squarish** *a.* [OF *esquarre*, from p.p. of nonextant late L *exquadrāre*, (EX-, L *quadrāre*, to make square, from *quadrus*, four-cornered, cogn. with *quattuor*, four)]

squarrose (skwor´ōs, skwar´-, -rōs´), **squarrous** *a.* rough with scalelike projections. [said to be from late L *squarrōsus*, perh. *squāmōsus*]

squash[1] (skwosh) *v.t.* **1** to crush, to press flat or into a pulp. **2** to pack (people or things) tight, to crowd. **3** to put down, to snub (someone) with a crushing remark. **4** to dismiss (a suggestion, proposal etc.). **5** to put down, to quash (a rebellion). ~*v.i.* **1** to be crushed or beaten to pulp by a fall. **2** to squeeze (into). ~*n.* **1** a throng, a crowd packed tight. **2** the fall of a soft body. **3** the sound of this. **4** a drink made from usu. concentrated fruit juice from crushed fruit, diluted with water. **5** (*also* **squash rackets**) a game with rackets and a small soft ball, played against the walls of a closed court. **6** a thing or mass crushed or squeezed to pulp. **squasher** *n.* **squashy** *a.* (*comp.* **squashier**, *superl.* **squashiest**). **squashily** *adv.* **squashiness** *n.* [alt. of QUASH]

Usage note See note under QUASH.

squash[2] (skwosh) *n.* **1** the fleshy edible gourdlike fruit of any of several trailing plants of the genus *Cucurbita*, cooked and eaten as a vegetable. **2** the plant producing this fruit. **3** (*N Am.*) a vegetable marrow. [Narragansett *asquutasquash*]

squat (skwot) *v.i.* (*pres.p.* **squatting**, *past*, *p.p.* **squatted**) **1** to sit down or crouch on the haunches. **2** (chiefly of animals) to crouch close to the ground, to cower. **3** (*coll.*) to sit. **4** to settle on land or occupy a building without any title. ~*v.t.* to put (oneself) in a crouching posture. ~*a.* (*comp.* **squatter**, *superl.* **squattest**) **1** short, thick, dumpy. **2** in a squatting position. ~*n.* **1** a squatting posture. **2** a building occupied by squatters, or the illegal occupation of a building by squatters. **squatly** *adv.* **squatness** *n.* **squatter** *n.* **1** a person who occupies property or land without legal title to it. **2** (*Austral.*) **a** a person who leases land for pasturage from the Government, a stock-owner. **b** a sheep farmer. **3** a person who sits on the haunches. **squat thrust** *n.* an exercise in which, from a squatting position with hands on the floor in front, the legs are thrust out backwards to full length, and then drawn in again. **squattocracy** (-ok´rəsi) *n.* (*Austral.*) squatters as a corporate body. [OF *esquatir*, to flatten, crush (EX-, *quatir*, as SQUASH[1])]

squaw (skwaw) *n.* (*now offensive*) a N American Indian woman or wife. **squaw-man** *n.* a white or black man married to a N American Indian. **squaw winter** *n.* in N America, a short spell of chilly weather before an Indian summer. [Algonquian *squa*, Narragansett *squaws*]

squawk (skwawk) *n.* **1** a raucous squeal, esp. as the cry of a fowl. **2** (*coll.*) a complaint or protest. ~*v.i.* **1** to utter a squawk. **2** (*coll.*) to protest loudly. ~*v.t.* to utter with a squawk. **squawk-box** *n.* an intercom or loud speaker. **squawker** *n.* [imit.]

squeak (skwēk) *n.* **1** a sharp, shrill cry, like that of a mouse. **2** a high-pitched whine produced e.g. by an unoiled door hinge. **3** (*coll.*) a narrow escape or margin, a close shave. ~*v.i.* **1** to utter or make a squeak. **2** (*coll.*) to get (by, through, past etc.) narrowly. **3** (*sl.*) to break silence or secrecy, esp. to turn informer. ~*v.t.* to utter with a squeak. **squeaker** *n.* **1** a person or thing that squeaks. **2** a young bird, esp. a pigeon. **3** (*esp. N Am.*) something won narrowly, e.g. an election or game. **4** (*sl.*) an informer, a traitor. **squeaky** *a.* (*comp.* **squeakier**, *superl.* **squeakiest**). **squeakily** *adv.* **squeakiness** *n.* **squeaky-clean** *a.* **1** utterly clean (orig. from the squeaking noise made by newly washed hair when rubbed). **2** above reproach. [ME, imit., cp. MSwed. *sqwæka*, cp. Norw. *skvaka*, Icel. *skvakka*]

squeal (skwēl) *n.* a more or less prolonged shrill cry, like that made by a pig or a baby. ~*v.i.* **1** to utter a more or less prolonged shrill cry as in pain, etc. **2** (*sl.*) to turn informer. **3** (*coll.*) to complain loudly. ~*v.t.* to utter with a squeal. **squealer** *n.* [ME, imit., cp. SQUEAK]

squeamish (skwē´mish) *a.* **1** easily nauseated, disgusted or offended. **2** fastidious, finicky, hypercritical, excessively nice, prudish, unduly scrupulous. **squeamishly** *adv.* **squeamishness** *n.* [ME *squeamous*, A-F *escoymous*, etym. uncertain]

squeegee (skwē´jē) *n.* **1** a rubber-bladed implement fixed to a handle, for cleaning surfaces such as windows or wiping them dry. **2** a similar implement, usu. with a rubber roller, used by photographers for squeezing and flattening. ~*v.t.* (*3rd pers. sing. pres.* **squeegees**, *pres.p.* **squeegeeing**, *past*, *p.p.* **squeegeed**) to wipe, smooth etc., with a squeegee. [formerly *squilgee*, etym. uncertain, perh. reinforcement of SQUEEZE]

squeeze (skwēz) *v.t.* **1** to press closely, esp. between two bodies or with the hand, so as to force moisture etc., out. **2** to crush (out), to extract (moisture etc.) thus. **3** to reduce the size of, or alter the shape of, by pressing closely. **4** to force (oneself etc., or one's way, into, out of etc. a narrow space etc.). **5** to extort money etc., from, to harass by exactions. **6** to exact (money etc.) by extortion etc. **7** to put pressure on, to oppress, to constrain by arbitrary or illegitimate means. **8** in bridge, to subject (an opponent) to a squeeze. **9** to press (someone's hand) to express affection, sympathy etc. **10** to force (a tear etc. out). *~v.i.* to press, to push, to force one's way (into, through etc.). *~n.* **1** an act of squeezing or the condition of being squeezed. **2** pressure. **3** a close embrace. **4** a throng, a crush. **5** a small amount of juice etc. produced by squeezing (*a squeeze of lemon*). **6** an illicitly exacted commission, or other such extortion. **7** an economic situation, e.g. during a financial crisis, in which there are restrictions on investment and borrowing. **8** an impression taken of an inscription, coin etc., by pressing wax, damp paper etc. against it. **9** (*also* **squeeze play**) in bridge, the practice of leading winning cards till an opponent is forced to discard a valuable card. **10** in baseball, the practice of hitting the ball short, into the infield, so that a runner on third base can set off for home as soon as the ball is pitched. **to put the squeeze on** (*coll.*) to put pressure on (someone), to coerce. **squeezable** *a.* **squeezability** (-bil´-) *n.* **squeeze bottle, squeezy bottle** *n.* a flexible plastic bottle that is squeezed to extract the contents. **squeeze-box** *n.* (*coll.*) an accordion or concertina. **squeezer** *n.* **1** a person or thing that squeezes. **2** (*pl.*) playing cards marked at the top right-hand corner with the value to save spreading out in the hand. **squeezy** *a.* (*comp.* **squeezier,** *superl.* **squeeziest**) **1** (of a container) flexible, able to be squeezed to extract the contents. **2** cramped, confined, suggestive of squeezing. [OE *cwīesan*, cp. LG *quōsen*]

squelch (skwelch) *v.i.* **1** to make a noise as of treading in wet snow. **2** to move with this sound (*squelched across the field*). *~v.t.* **1** to crush. **2** to silence, to extinguish, to discomfit. *~n.* **1** an act of squelching; a squelching noise. **2** a heavy blow. **3** a crushing retort. **4** (*also* **squelch circuit**) a circuit that cuts off the audio-frequency amplifier of a radio in response to a low input signal, to suppress background noise. **squelcher** *n.* **squelchy** *a.* (*comp.* **squelchier,** *superl.* **squelchiest**). [imit., or perh. rel. to QUELL]

squib (skwib) *n.* **1** a firework emitting sparks and hisses, and exploding with a bang. **2** a short satire or lampoon. **3** (*Austral., New Zeal., coll.*) a coward, a sneak. *~v.i.* (*pres.p.* **squibbing,** *past, p.p.* **squibbed**) to write squibs. *~v.t.* **1** in American football, to kick (the ball) only a short distance, or execute (a kick) like this. **2** to satirize in a squib. **damp squib** DAMP. [etym. uncertain, prob. imit.]

squid (skwid) *n.* (*pl.* **squid, squids**) **1** any cephalopod mollusc of the order Teuthoidea, similar to a cuttlefish but with eight arms and two long tentacles, esp. an edible variety of the genus *Loligo*. **2** an artificial bait roughly imitating a squid in shape. *~v.i.* (*pres.p.* **squidding,** *past, p.p.* **squidded**) to fish with this. [etym. uncertain, cp. Swed. dial. *skvitta*, Icel. *skvetta*, to squirt]

squidgy (skwij´i) *a.* (*comp.* **squidgier,** *superl.* **squidgiest**) (*coll.*) soft and squashy. [imit.]

squiffy (skwif´i) *a.* (*comp.* **squiffier,** *superl.* **squiffiest**) (*coll.*) slightly drunk. **squiffed** *a.* squiffy. [imit.]

squiggle (skwig´əl) *n.* a wriggly line. *~v.i.* **1** to squirm, to wriggle, to twist. **2** to make wriggly lines. **3** (*dial.*) to shake a fluid about in the mouth. *~v.t.* to scrawl or scribble (a word, signature etc.). **squiggler** *n.* **squiggly** *a.* (*comp.* **squigglier,** *superl.* **squiggliest**). [prob. imit.]

squill (skwil) *n.* **1** any of several liliaceous plants of the genus *Scilla*, e.g. the striped squill, *Puschkinia scilloides*, typically with small blue flowers. **2** a white-flowered Mediterranean plant *Drimia* or *Urginea maritima*; also called *sea onion*. **3** the sliced bulb of this used as an expectorant, diuretic etc. **4** a shrimp of the genus *Squilla*, with front legs like those of a mantis. [MF *squille*, L *squilla*, Gr. *skilla*]

squinch[1] (skwinch) *n.* an arch across the internal angle of a square tower to support a superstructure such as an octagonal spire, dome etc. [var. of SCUNCHEON]

squinch[2] (skwinch) *v.t.* **1** to screw (one's face or one's eyes up). **2** to squeeze or compress, to squash (up, down). *~v.i.* (of eyes) to squint or narrow. [perh. comb. of SQUEEZE, PINCH]

squint (skwint) *v.i.* **1** to look with the eyes differently directed. **2** to be affected with strabismus, to have a squint. **3** to look obliquely or with half-closed eyes (at). *~v.t.* **1** to shut or contract (the eyes) quickly. **2** to keep (the eyes) half shut. **3** to cause to squint. *~a.* **1** squinting. **2** looking obliquely; looking askance. **3** (*coll.*) askew, crooked. *~n.* **1** an affection of the eyes causing the axes to be differently directed, strabismus. **2** a stealthy look, a sidelong glance. **3** (*coll.*) a look (*had a squint at the document*). **4** an obliquely set opening through the wall of a church, giving a view of the altar. **5** a leaning (towards). **squinter** *n.* **squint-eye, squint-eyes** *n.* a person who squints. **squint-eyed** *a.* **1** squinting. **2** ill-willed, malevolent. **squinting** *a.* **squintingly** *adv.* **squinty** *a.* (*comp.* **squintier,** *superl.* **squintiest**). [aphetic from ASQUINT]

squire (skwīə) *n.* **1** a country gentleman, esp. the chief landowner in a place. **2** (*Hist.*) an attendant on a knight. **3** a man who attends a lady, a beau, a gallant. **4** (*facet.*) used as a form of address to a man. **5** (*N Am.*) a rural judge or magistrate. **6** (*Austral.*) an immature snapper fish. *~v.t.* to attend as a squire, to escort (a woman). **squirearchy** (-ahki), **squirarchy** *n.* (*pl.* **squirearchies, squirarchies**) **1** landed proprietors collectively. **2** the political influence of, or government by these. **squirearch** *n.* a member of the squirearchy. **squirearchical** (-ah´-), **squirarchal** *a.* **squiredom** *n.* **squireen** (-rēn´) *n.* a petty squire, esp. in Ireland. **squirehood** *n.* **squirelet, squireling** *n.* **squirely** *a.* **squireship** *n.* [ESQUIRE]

squirm (skwœm) *v.i.* **1** to wriggle, to writhe about; to move (up, through etc.) by wriggling. **2** to display discomfort, embarrassment etc. *~n.* a wriggling movement. **squirmer** *n.* **squirmy** *a.* (*comp.* **squirmier,** *superl.* **squirmiest**). [perh. from ME *quirr*, var. of WHIR]

squirrel (skwir´əl) *n.* **1** any bushy-tailed rodent of the family Sciuridae, with reddish fur (*red squirrel*) or grey fur (*grey squirrel*) living chiefly in trees. **2** the fur of a squirrel. **3** (*coll.*) a person who hoards things. *~v.t.* (*pres.p.* **squirrelling,** (*N Am.*) **squirreling,** *past, p.p.* **squirrelled,** (*N Am.*) **squirreled**) to hoard or hide (things away). *~v.i.* to bustle or scurry (about). **squirrel cage** *n.* **1** a small cylindrical cage for a squirrel, with a treadmill. **2** the rotor of an induction motor with cylindrically arranged copper bars. **3** a life of frustratingly humdrum routine. **squirrel-fish** *n.* any brightly coloured tropical marine teleost fish of the family Holocentridae. **squirrel grass, squirrel-tail, squirrel-tail grass** *n.* a type of grass, *Hordeum jubatum*, related to barley, with long hairlike awns. **squirrelly** *a.* **squirrel-monkey** *n.* a small S American monkey, *Saimiri sciureus*, with soft golden fur. [OF *escuirel, escurel*, late L *scūrellus*, dim. of *sciūrus*, Gr. *skiouros*, perh. shadow-tail (*skia*, shadow, *oura*, tail)]

squirt (skwœt) *v.t.* **1** to eject (liquid etc.) in a jet or stream from a narrow orifice. **2** to splash with such a jet or stream (*squirted her with water from the hosepipe*). *~v.i.* (of liquid) to be so ejected. *~n.* **1** a jet (of liquid etc.), or a small quantity produced by squirting (*a squirt* *of soda water*). 2 a syringe. 3 (*coll.*) a pert, conceited or insignificant person. **squirter** *n.* [ME, imit.]

squish (skwish) *n.* a moist squashing or squelching sound. ~*v.t.* to crush so as to make a squelching or sucking noise. ~*v.i.* to make a squelching or sucking sound. **squishy** *a.* (*comp.* **squishier,** *superl.* **squishiest**). [imit.]

squit (skwit) *n.* 1 (*sl.*) an insignificant person. 2 (*dial.*) nonsense. 3 (*pl., coll., dial.*) (*usu.* **the squits**) diarrhoea. **squitters** *n.pl.* (*coll., dial.*) diarrhoea. [var. of SQUIRT]

squitch (skwitch), **squitch-grass** *n.* quitch, couch grass. [alt. of QUITCH]

squiz (skwiz) *n.* (*Austral., New Zeal., sl.*) a glance. [perh. from QUIZ]

SR *abbr.* (*Hist.*) Southern Railway.

Sr *chem. symbol* strontium.

Sr. *abbr.* 1 Senior. 2 Señor. 3 Signior. 4 Sir. 5 Sister.

sr *abbr.* steradian, steradians.

Sra. *abbr.* Señora.

SRC *abbr.* 1 Science Research Council. 2 Student Representative Council.

Sri Lankan (shrēlang´kən, srē-) *n.* 1 a native or inhabitant of Sri Lanka (formerly Ceylon). 2 a person of Sri Lankan parentage or descent. ~*a.* of or relating to Sri Lanka or its people.

SRN *abbr.* State Registered Nurse.

SRO *abbr.* 1 self-regulatory organization. 2 standing room only. 3 Statutory Rules and Orders.

SS *abbr.* 1 Saints. 2 (*Hist.*) Hitler's bodyguard, used as security police, concentration-camp guards etc. (G *SchutzStaffel*, elite guard). 3 steamship.

SSAFA *abbr.* Soldiers', Sailors' and Airmen's Families Association.

SSC *abbr.* 1 in Scotland, Solicitor in the Supreme Court. 2 superconducting super collider.

SSE *abbr.* south-south-east.

SSP *abbr.* statutory sick pay.

SSR *abbr.* Soviet Socialist Republic.

SSRC *abbr.* Social Science Research Council.

SSSI *abbr.* Site of Special Scientific Interest.

SST *abbr.* supersonic transport.

SSW *abbr.* south-south-west.

St, St. *abbr.* 1 Saint. 2 statute. 3 stokes. 4 Strait. 5 Street.

Usage note Names spelt St are conventionally alphabetized as if *Saint*: see SAINT for entries.

st. *abbr.* 1 stanza. 2 stone. 3 in cricket, stumped by.

-st -EST².

Sta. *abbr.* station.

stab (stab) *v.t.* (*pres.p.* **stabbing,** *past, p.p.* **stabbed**) 1 to pierce or wound with a pointed, usu. short, weapon. 2 to plunge (a weapon, into). 3 to inflict pain upon or to injure by slander etc. 4 to roughen (a wall) with a pick to make it hold plaster. ~*v.i.* 1 to aim a blow with or as with a pointed weapon (at). 2 (of a pain etc.) to produce a feeling like being stabbed. ~*n.* 1 a blow or thrust with a pointed weapon. 2 a wound inflicted thus. 3 a secret malicious injury. **to have/ make a stab at** (*coll.*) to attempt, to have a go at (doing something). **to stab in the back** 1 (*fig.*) to betray. 2 (*fig.*) to injure the reputation of (esp. a colleague, friend etc.). **stabber** *n.* **stabbing** *a., n.* **stabbingly** *adv.* **stab in the back** *n.* a treacherous act. [ME *stabbe*, cp. Swed. dial. *stabbe*, Icel. *stabbi*, stump]

Stabat Mater (stahbat mah´tə, stā´bat mā´tə) *n.* 1 a Latin hymn reciting the seven dolours of the Virgin at the Cross, beginning with these words. 2 a musical setting of this. [L, the Mother was standing]

stable¹ (stā´bəl) *a.* (*comp.* **stabler,** *superl.* **stablest**) 1 firmly fixed, established. 2 not to be moved, shaken or destroyed easily. 3 firm, resolute, constant, not changeable, unwavering. 4 mentally and emotionally steady. 5 (*Chem.*) durable, not readily decomposed. 6 (*Physics*) not radioactive, not subject to radioactive decay. **stabilator** (-bilātə) *n.* a device combining the functions of stabilizer and elevator at the tail of an aircraft. **stabile** (-bīl) *a.* 1 fixed. 2 stable. ~*n.* an abstract art form similar to a mobile but stationary. **stability** (stəbil´-) *n.* 1 the quality of being stable. 2 the property of mechanical, electrical or aerodynamic systems that makes them return to a state of equilibrium after disturbance. **stabilize, stabilise** *v.t.* to make stable. **stabilization** (-zā´shən) *n.* **stabilizer** *n.* 1 anything that stabilizes. 2 a device working on gyroscopic principles that prevents a ship from rolling. 3 (*N Am.*) the horizontal member of the tailplane of an aircraft. 4 (*pl.*) a pair of small wheels fitted on either side of the rear wheel of a child's bicycle. 5 a food additive which retards chemical action. **stable equilibrium** *n.* the tendency of any body to recover equilibrium when moved. **stableness** *n.* **stably** *adv.* [ME, from A-F *stable*, OF *estable*, from L *stabilis*, from *stāre*, to stand]

stable² (stā´bəl) *n.* 1 a building or part of a building for horses or (sometimes) cattle. 2 an establishment for housing and training racehorses. 3 the racehorses belonging to a particular stable. 4 a group of people with particular skills, e.g. athletes under one manager. 5 any collection or group, e.g. of products, from a common source. 6 a source from which such a group or collection proceeds. ~*v.t.* to put or keep (a horse) in a stable. ~*v.i.* (of horses etc.) to lodge in a stable. **stable boy** *n.* a boy employed in a stable. **stable companion** *n.* a person with whom one shares rooms etc. **stable door** *n.* 1 a horizontally divided door for a stable, of which the upper half can be left open while the lower half remains closed. 2 a similarly designed door as the door, esp. the front door, of a house. **stableful** *n.* (*pl.* **stablefuls**). **stable girl** *n.* a girl or woman employed at a stable. **stable lad** *n.* a groom in a racing stable. **stableman** *n.* (*pl.* **stablemen**) a person employed at a stable. **stable mate** *n.* a stable companion. **stabling** *n.* accommodation for horses. [OF *estable*, L *stabilem*, as STABLE¹]

stably STABLE¹.

staccato (stəkah´tō) *a., adv.* (*Mus.*) (played) with each note sharply distinct and detached, as opposed to *legato*. ~*n.* (*pl.* **staccatos**) 1 a passage of music played in this way. 2 a staccato style of playing. **staccato mark** *n.* a dot or stroke printed above or below a note to indicate that it should be played staccato. [It., p.p. of *staccare*, to detach, from *distaccare*, to separate]

stachys (stā´kis) *n.* any labiate plant of the genus *Stachys*, with white or reddish spikes of flowers, also called *woundworts*. [L, from Gr. *stachus*, ear of corn]

stack (stak) *n.* 1 a pile, a heap, esp. of an orderly kind. 2 a round or rectangular pile of corn in the sheaf, or of hay, straw etc., usu. with a thatched top, a rick. 3 (*often pl., coll.*) a great quantity (*stacks of homework*). 4 a funnel, a smokestack. 5 a tall factory chimney. 6 the part of a chimney projecting above the roof of a building, supporting one or more chimney pots. 7 an accumulation of aircraft circling an airport at different altitudes waiting for instructions to land. 8 (*usu. pl.*) compact bookshelves in a library, usu. with restricted public access. 9 a temporary storage area in a computer memory, from which the most recently accessed or saved item can be retrieved first. 10 a vertically arranged set of hi-fi or public-address-system components. 11 a towering isolated mass of rock, esp. off the coast of N Britain. 12 a pyramidal pile of rifles standing on their butts with the muzzles together. 13 a measure of wood in piles, 108 cu. ft. (3.05 m³). ~*v.t.* 1 to pile in a stack or stacks. 2 to assign (waiting aircraft) to a particular altitude in preparation for landing at an airport. **to stack arms** to pile arms. **to stack the cards** CARD¹.

to stack up (*N Am., coll.*) to measure up, to compare satisfactorily. **stackable** *a.* **stacked** *a.* **1** piled or elevated in a stack, or (of aircraft) allotted a place in a stack. **2** (of shelves etc.) piled with goods. **3** (of odds) weighted (against one). **4** (*sl.*) (of a woman) having large breasts. **stacker** *n.* **stack-room** *n.* in a library, the area containing the stacks. **stack-stand** *n.* a platform for supporting a stack of hay etc. **stack-yard** *n.* a yard or enclosure for stacks of hay, straw etc. [Icel. *stakkr*, Swed. *stack*, Dan. *stak*]

stacte (stak´tē) *n.* one of the spices used by the ancient Jews in the preparation of incense. [L from Gr. *staktē*, from *stazein*, to drip]

staddle (stad´əl) *n.* a stack-stand. **staddle-stone** *n.* a mushroom-shaped stone used for supporting a rick or staddle. [OE *stathol*, foundation, base, cp. G *Stadel*]

stadia[1] (stā´diə) *n.* an instrument, usu. composed of a graduated rod and a telescope, for measuring distances. **stadiometer** (-om´itə) *n.* any of various instruments for measuring length or distance. [late L, from STADIUM]

stadia[2] STADIUM.

stadium (stā´diəm) *n.* (*pl.* **stadiums, stadia** (-diə)) **1** a sports arena with tiers of benches for spectators. **2** (*Hist.*) a racecourse for foot races or chariot races. **3** an ancient measure of length, about 185 metres. **4** a stage of development, e.g. in geology, or in the course of a disease. [L, from Gr. *stadion*]

Usage note The plural *stadiums* is preferred to *stadia* when referring to modern structures.

stadtholder (stat´hōldə, stad´-), **stadholder** (stad´-) *n.* (*Hist.*) **1** the chief magistrate of the United Provinces. **2** a viceroy, governor or deputy governor of a province or town in the Netherlands. **stadtholderate** (-rət), **stadtholdership** *n.* [Dut. *stadhouder*, deputy, from *stad*, stead, *houder*, holder]

staff[1] (stahf) *n.* **1** a stick carried for help in walking, climbing etc., or as a weapon. **2** a rod carried as a symbol of authority. **3** a shaft or pole serving as a support, e.g. a flagstaff. **4** a thing or person that affords support or sustenance (*Bread is the staff of life*; *the staff of my old age*). **5** a rod used in surveying etc. **6** a token passed to an engine-driver on a single-track railway as authorization to proceed along a certain section of the track. **7** a spindle in a watch. **8** a body of employees, e.g. in a firm under a manager, or on a newspaper under an editor. **9** the body of those in authority in an organization, esp. the teachers of a school collectively. **10** (*Mil.*) a body of officers assisting an officer in high command, whose duties are concerned with a regiment, or with an army, fleet or air force as a whole. **11** (**Staff**) a staff sergeant. **12** (*Mus.*) (*pl.* **staffs, staves**) the set of five parallel lines on which and between which notes are written, their position indicating their pitch. ~*v.t.* to supply (a firm, hospital, school etc.) with staff (*inadequately staffed wards*). **staff college** *n.* **1** a college at which military officers receive training for staff duties. **2** a college for the staff of a particular organization. **staffed** *a.* **staffer** *n.* (*N Am.*) a member of a staff, esp. that of a newspaper. **staff notation** *n.* (*Mus.*) notation by the staff as distinct from tonic sol-fa. **staff nurse** *n.* a qualified nurse immediately below a sister in rank. **staff officer** *n.* an officer serving on a staff. **staffroom** *n.* **1** a common room for staff, esp. in a school or college. **2** the staff using such a room (*staffroom politics*). **staff sergeant** *n.* **1** the senior sergeant of a non-infantry company. **2** (*N Am.*) a non-commissioned officer immediately above a sergeant in rank. [OE *stæf*, cp. Dut. *staf*, G *Stab*, Icel. *stafr*]

staff[2] (stahf) *n.* a composition of plaster of Paris, cement etc., used as building material etc., esp. in temporary structures. [perh. var. of STUFF]

staffage (stəfahzh´) *n.* additional or accessory objects in a painting, such as sheep or cattle in a landscape painting. [sham F, from G *staffieren*, to garnish]

Staffordshire bull terrier (staf´ədshə) *n.* a smooth-coated breed of terrier of stocky build. [from the county *Staffordshire*]

stag (stag) *n.* **1** the male of the red deer, esp. from its fifth year. **2** the male of other large deer. **3** a bull castrated when nearly full-grown. **4** (*sl.*) an informer. **5** a male unaccompanied by a woman at a social function. **6** in Stock Exchange dealings, a person who stags. ~*v.t.* (*pres.p.* **stagging,** *past, p.p.* **stagged**) (*sl.*) to watch closely, to spy on. ~*v.i.* in Stock Exchange dealings, to apply for or to purchase stock or shares in a new issue solely with the object of selling at a profit immediately on allotment. **stag beetle** *n.* any beetle of the family Lucanidae, with large mandibles, in the male branching like a stag's horns. **stag-horn, stag's horn** *n.* **1** antler as a craft material, used to make knife handles etc. **2** any of several ferns, esp. of the genus *Platycerium*, with antler-like fronds. **staghound** *n.* a large hound used for hunting stags. **stag-night, stag-party** *n.* (*coll.*) a party for men only, esp. one given for a man about to be married. [OE *stagga*, ON *steggr*, he-bird, male animal]

stage (stāj) *n.* **1** a point in a progressive movement, a definite period or phase in development (*is at a difficult stage*; *in the early stages*; *at the planning stage*; *at the embryonic stage*). **2 a** a raised platform on which theatrical or other performances take place before an audience. **b** any elevated platform, such as a scaffold for workers erecting or repairing a building, or a shelf on which objects may be exhibited or examined etc. **3** the theatre, drama, the profession of an actor, actors collectively. **4** the scene of action. **5** a dock, often floating, for the embarkation or disembarkation of passengers or goods. **6** any one of a series of regular stopping places on a route. **7** the distance between two such places. **8** a definite portion of a journey (*a fare stage*). **9** (*Hist.*) a stagecoach. **10** a detachable propulsion unit of a rocket. **11** (*Geol.*) a band of strata constituting a subdivision of a series or formation. **12** part of a complex electronic circuit, esp. any one of a series of transistors with associated equipment. **13** the small platform on a microscope where the slide is mounted for examination. ~*v.t.* **1** to put (a play etc.) on the stage. **2** to plan and execute (an event). **to go on the stage** to become a professional actor or actress. **to hold the stage** to dominate proceedings, to take the leading role, e.g. in a discussion. **to set the stage** to arrange things in preparation (for an event etc.). **to tread the stage** TREAD. **stageable** *a.* **stageability** (-bil´-) *n.* **stagecoach** *n.* (*Hist.*) a horse-drawn coach that ran regularly by stages for conveyance of parcels, passengers etc. **stagecoachman** *n.* (*pl.* **stagecoachmen**) the driver of a stagecoach. **stagecraft** *n.* the art of writing or staging plays. **stage direction** *n.* an instruction respecting the movements etc. of actors in a play. **stage door** *n.* a door to a theatre for the use of actors, workers etc. **stage effect** *n.* **1** in the theatre, an effect contrived by lighting etc. **2** generally, something done to add theatricality to an occasion. **stage fever** *n.* intense desire to become an actor. **stage fright** *n.* a fit of nervousness in facing an audience. **stagehand** *n.* a worker who moves scenery etc. in a theatrical production. **stage left** *n., adv.* (the area of the stage) to the left of an actor facing the audience. **stage-manage** *v.t.* to direct or supervise (a play, performance, show etc.) from behind the scenes. **stage management** *n.* **stage manager** *n.* a person who superintends the scenic effects etc. of a play. **stage name** *n.* a professional name used by an actor etc. **stage play** *n.* a play performed on stage, as distinct from radio or television. **stager** *n.* a person of long experience in anything (esp. in *old-stager*). **stage right** *n., adv.* (the area of the stage) to the right of an actor facing the audience. **stage rights**

n.pl. exclusive legal rights to perform a certain play. **stage-struck** *a.* smitten with the theatre, esp. with an overwhelming desire to act. **stage whisper** *n.* **1** an audible aside. **2** something meant for the ears of people other than the person ostensibly addressed. **stagey** STAGY (under STAGE). **staging** *n.* **1** the business or process of putting a play on the stage. **2** a platform or scaffolding, usu. temporary. **3** shelving for greenhouse plants. **4** (*Hist.*) the driving or running of stagecoaches. **staging area** *n.* an assembly point for troops in transit. **staging post** *n.* a regular stopover point on an air route. **stagy, stagey** *a.* (*comp.* **stagier,** *superl.* **stagiest**) theatrical, melodramatic, histrionic, artificial. **stagily** *adv.* **staginess** *n.* [OF *estage*, (F *étage*), prob. through a L *staticum*, from *stāre*, to stand]

stagflation (stagflā´shən) *n.* a state of the economy in which there is a combination of high inflation and falling industrial output and employment. [STAGNATION (under STAGNANT), INFLATION (under INFLATE)]

staggard (stag´əd) *n.* a male red deer in its fourth year. [STAG, -ARD]

stagger (stag´ə) *v.i.* **1** to move unsteadily in walking, to totter, to reel. **2** to begin to give way, to waver, to hesitate. ~*v.t.* **1** to cause to reel. **2** to cause to hesitate. **3** to amaze or shock. **4** to overlap, to place zigzag. **5** to arrange (working hours, holidays etc.) so as not to coincide. **6** to design (a crossroads) so that the side roads do not meet opposite one another. **7** to set (the spokes of a wheel) alternately leaning in and out. ~*n.* **1** a staggering movement. **2** an overlapping, overhanging, zigzag or slantwise arrrangement of things in a series or structure. **staggerer** *n.* **1** a person who staggers. **2** a staggering blow, argument etc. **staggering** *a.* **staggeringly** *adv.* **staggers** *n.* **1** a disease affecting the brain and spinal cord of horses and cattle, causing staggering and a loss of balance. **2** giddiness, vertigo. [ME *stakeren*, Icel. *stakra*, freq. of *staka*, to push]

stagnant (stag´nənt) *a.* **1** (of water) still, without current, motionless. **2** (of people or their lives, of business etc.) dull, sluggish. **stagnancy** *n.* **stagnantly** *adv.* **stagnate** (-nāt´, stag´-) *v.i.* to become stagnant. **stagnation** (-nā´shən) *n.* [L *stagnāre*, from *stagnum*, pool]

stagy STAGE.

staid (stād) *a.* sober, steady, sedate. **staidly** *adv.* **staidness** *n.* [*stayed*, p.p. of STAY[1]]

stain (stān) *v.t.* **1** to discolour, to soil, to sully. **2** to tarnish, to blemish (a reputation etc.). **3** to colour by means of dye or another agent acting chemically or by absorption. **4** to impregnate (an object for microscopic examination) with a colouring matter affecting certain parts more powerfully than others. **5** to dim, to obscure. ~*v.i.* **1** to cause discoloration. **2** to take stains. ~*n.* **1** a discoloration. **2** a spot of a distinct colour. **3** a blot, a blemish. **stainable** *a.* **stained glass** *n.* glass coloured for use in windows. **stainer** *n.* **stainless** *a.* **1** without a stain, immaculate. **2** resistant to rust or tarnish. **stainlessly** *adv.* **stainlessness** *n.* **stainless steel** *n.* a rustless alloy steel used for cutlery etc. [ME *steinen*]

stair (steə) *n.* **1** each one of a series of steps, esp. for ascending from one storey of a house to another. **2** (*usu. pl.*) a flight of stairs. **below stairs 1** in the basement. **2** in the servants' quarters or relating to their affairs. **stair carpet** *n.* a narrow carpet used to cover stairs. **staircase** *n.* a flight of stairs with banisters, supporting structure etc. **moving staircase** MOVE. **stairhead** *n.* the landing at the top of a flight of stairs. **stairlift** *n.* a mechanism fitted to a staircase, with a chair in which an elderly or disabled person can be carried up and down stairs. **stair-rod** *n.* a rod for fastening a stair carpet into the angle between two stairs. **stairway** *n.* a staircase. **stairwell** *n.* the vertical shaft which contains a staircase. [OE *stǣger* (cp. Dut. *steiger*, G *Steg*, Icel. *stigi*), from Gmc. *steigan*, to climb, cogn. with Gr. *steichein*, to ascend, to go]

staithe (stādh, stāth), **staith** *n.* (*dial.*) a landing stage, a wharf, esp. a staging laid with rails from which coal-wagons etc. may discharge their loads into vessels. [OE *stæth*, bank, shore, Icel. *stoth*]

stake[1] (stāk) *n.* **1** a stick or post pointed at one end and set in the ground, as a support, part of a railing etc. **2** (*Hist.*) a post to which persons condemned to death by burning were bound. **3** death by this method; martyrdom. **4** a prop or upright part or fitting for supporting a machine etc. **5** a tinsmith's small anvil that may be set in a bench. **6** in basket-weaving, any of the uprights acting as supports for the woven strands. ~*v.t.* **1** to fasten, support, or protect with a stake or stakes. **2** to mark (out or off) with stakes. **to pull up stakes** to move home, to move on. **to stake one's claim** to assert one's right to possess something, to register or establish one's claim (to something). **to stake out** to place under surveillance. **stake-boat** *n.* an anchored boat marking a point on a boat-race course. **stake-body** *n.* (*pl.* **stake-bodies**) (*NAm.*) a kind of body for a lorry, consisting of an open platform with posts along its sides. **stake-net** *n.* a fishing net stretched on stakes. **stake-out** *n.* **1** a place, person etc. under surveillance. **2** a (police) surveillance operation covering a particular building or area. [OE *staca*, (cp. MDut. and Swed. *stake*, Icel. *stjaki*, Dan. *stage*), cogn. with STACK]

stake[2] (stāk) *n.* **1** anything, esp. a sum of money, wagered on a competition or contingent event, esp. deposited with a stakeholder. **2** (*pl.*) money competed for in a race etc. **3** (*pl.*) the race itself. **4** an interest or involvement (in some concern). ~*v.t.* **1** to wager, to venture (something, esp. a sum of money, on an event etc.). **2** to risk. **3** (*NAm., coll.*) to support financially or otherwise. **at stake 1** likely to be lost or damaged, at risk, endangered (*Many lives are at stake*). **2** at issue. **stakebuilding** *n.* in the Stock Exchange, the accumulation of a shareholding. **stakeholder** *n.* **1** an independent person with whom each party making a wager deposits their stake. **2** a person with an interest or involvement in something, such as a business concern or the society in which they live. **staker** *n.* [perh. from STAKE[1]]

Stakhanovism (stəkhan´əvizm) *n.* in the former Soviet Union, a system for increasing production by utilizing each worker's initiative. **Stakhanovist** *n.* **Stakhanovite** (-īt) *n.* an outstandingly keen and productive worker. [A. G. *Stakhanov*, 1906–77, Soviet miner]

stalactite (stal´əktīt) *n.* a deposit of carbonate of lime, hanging from the roof of a cave etc., in the form of a thin tube or a large icicle, produced by the evaporation of percolating water. **stalactic** (-lak´-), **stalactiform** (-lak´tifawm) *a.* **stalactitic** *a.* **stalactitically** *adv.* [Anglicization of mod. L *stalactītes*, from Gr. *stalaktos*, dripping, from *stalassein*, to drip]

Usage note See note under STALAGMITE.

Stalag (stah´lag) *n.* a German prisoner-of-war camp, esp. for men from the ranks and non-commissioned officers. [short for *Stammlager*, *Stamm*, base, *Lager*, camp]

stalagmite (stal´əgmīt) *n.* a deposit of the same material as in a stalactite, in the form of a pointed column or a mound, rising from the floor of a cave. **stalagmitic** (-mit´-) *a.* **stalagmitically** *adv.* [mod. L *stalagmītes*, from Gr. *stalagma*, a drop, from *stalassein*, to drip]

Usage note A *stalagmite* (with *g* for *ground*) rises from the floor, and a *stalactite* (with *c* for *ceiling*) hangs from the roof.

stale[1] (stāl) *a.* (*comp.* **staler,** *superl.* **stalest**) **1** not fresh; dry, musty. **2** insipid or tasteless from being kept too long. **3** (of jokes etc.) trite; (of news) old. **4** (of e.g. an athlete or person studying) in a debilitated condition from overtraining or overexertion. ~*v.t.* to make stale. ~*v.i.* to become stale. **stalely** *adv.* **staleness** *n.* [OF *estaler*, to come to a stand, rel. to STALL[1]]

stale[2] (stāl) *n.* the urine of horses or cattle. ~*v.i.* (of horses or cattle) to urinate. [perh. from OF *estaler*, to stand in a certain position]

stalemate (stāl´māt) *n.* **1** in chess, the position when the king, not actually in check, is unable to move without placing itself in check, and there is no other piece that can be moved. **2** a situation of deadlock. ~*v.t.* **1** in chess, to reduce (one's opponent) to a stalemate. **2** to bring to a standstill. [A-F *estale*, a fixed position, from *estaler*, to be placed (cp. STALE[1])]

Stalinism (stah´linizm) *n.* the rigid authoritarianism, totalitarianism and centralization associated with the regime of the dictator of the former Soviet Union Joseph Stalin, 1879–1953, developed from the communist ideology of Marxism–Leninism. **Stalinist** *n.*

stalk[1] (stawk) *n.* **1** the stem or axis of a plant. **2** in a plant, a slender attachment such as the peduncle of a flower or petiole of a leaf. **3** the supporting peduncle of a crinoid, barnacle etc.; any slender attachment for an organ in an animal. **4** any long slender linking or supporting shaft, such as the stem of a wineglass. **5** a high factory chimney. **stalked** *a.* (*often in comb.*, as *thick-stalked*). **stalk-eyed** *a.* (of certain crustaceans) having the eyes set on peduncles. **stalkless** *a.* **stalklet** *n.* **stalklike** *a.* **stalky** *a.* (*comp.* **stalkier**, *superl.* **stalkiest**). [ME *stalke*, dim. of *stale*, OE *stalu*, cp. Dut. *steel*]

stalk[2] (stawk) *v.t.* **1** to pursue (game or other prey, or an enemy) stealthily by the use of cover. **2** to follow (a person, esp. a public figure) persistently and with a sinister or unwelcome purpose. ~*v.i.* **1** to go stealthily, to steal (up to game or prey) under cover. **2** to walk with a stately stride. ~*n.* **1** the act of stalking game or prey. **2** stately gait. **stalker** *n.* **stalking-horse** *n.* **1** a horse or figure like a horse behind which a hunter hides when stalking game. **2** a mask or pretence concealing one's true purpose. [OE *bestealcian*, to walk stealthily, rel. to STEAL]

stall[1] (stawl) *n.* **1** a booth or shed in a market, street etc., or a bench, table etc. in a building for the sale of goods. **2** a cowshed or stable. **3** a division or compartment for a horse, ox etc. in a stable or byre. **4** a seat in the choir of a large church, enclosed at the back and sides and usu. canopied, for a clergyman, chorister etc. **5** the office of a canon, dean etc. **6** (*usu. pl.*) each one of a set of seats in a theatre, usu. in the front part of the pit. **7** in public washing or toilet facilities, a compartment for one person, containing a shower or lavatory. **8** STARTING STALL (under START). **9** an instance of an aircraft or motor stalling, or the resulting condition. **10** a sheath or holder for something (*a finger-stall*). ~*v.i.* **1** (of a vehicle or its engine) to cease working suddenly, e.g. when the fuel supply is inadequate. **2** (of an aircraft or pilot) to lose forward impetus and thus sustaining power if there is not enough airspace underneath for recovering lift. **3** (*esp. N Am.*) to stick fast (in mire etc.). ~*v.t.* **1** to cause (a vehicle, aircraft or engine) to stall. **2** to put or keep (esp. cattle) in a stall for fattening. **3** to furnish (a stable etc.) with stalls. **stallage** *n.* **1** accommodation for or by stalls in a market etc. **2** the rent for such accommodation. **3** the right of erecting a stall in a market etc. **stall-feed** *v.t.* (*past, p.p.* **stall-fed**) to fatten (cattle) in a stall. [OE *steal, steall* (cp. Dut. *stal*, G *Stall*, Icel. *stallr*, OHG *stal*), rel. to STABLE[2], STEAD]

stall[2] (stawl) *v.i.* to play for time; to be evasive. ~*v.t.* to obstruct or delay. ~*n.* **1** an act of stalling. **2** the confederate of a thief or pickpocket who diverts attention while the theft is committed and helps the thief to escape. **to stall off** to evade, to stave off. [A-F *estale*, a decoy]

stallion (stal´yən) *n.* an uncastrated male horse, esp. one kept for breeding purposes. [OF *estalon* (F *étalon*), rel. to STALL[1]]

stalwart (stawl´wət, stal´-) *a.* **1** strong in build, sturdy. **2** stout-hearted, determined, resolute. ~*n.* a strong, resolute, dependable person, esp. a valiant supporter or partisan. **stalwartly** *adv.* **stalwartness** *n.* [OE *stǣlwyrthe* (*stathol*, foundation, WORTH[1])]

stamen (stā´mən) *n.* (*pl.* **stamens, stamina** (stam´inə)) the pollen-bearing male organ of a flower. **stamened** *a.* **staminal** *a.* of or relating to stamens. **staminate** (-nāt) *a.* having stamens (but no pistils). **stamineous** (-min´-) *a.* of or relating to stamens. **staminiferous** (-nif´-) *a.* having stamens. [L *stāmen stāminis*, orig. warp in an upright loom, from *stāre*, to stand]

stamina[1] (stam´inə) *n.* **1** strength, vigour. **2** power of endurance, ability to tolerate long periods of mental or physical stress. [L, pl. of STAMEN]

stamina[2], **staminal** etc. STAMEN.

stammel (stam´əl) *n.* (*Hist.*) **1** a woollen cloth for making underclothes, usu. dyed red. **2** the red colour of this cloth. [prob. from obs. *stamin*, OF *estamine* (F *étamine*), L STAMEN]

stammer (stam´ə) *v.i.* to speak with halting articulation, nervous hesitation, or repetitions of the same sound; to stutter. ~*n.* **1** this kind of speech disorder; a tendency to stammer or stutter. **2** a stammering utterance. **stammerer** *n.* **stammeringly** *adv.* [ME *stameren* (cp. OE *stamm, stamor*, stammering, Dut. *stameren*, G *stammern*)]

stamp (stamp) *v.t.* **1** to bring (one's foot) down heavily. **2** to crush or flatten with one's foot thus. **3** to extinguish (e.g. the remains of a fire) thus, to put (out). **4** to impress (a mark, pattern, initials etc.) on a surface with a die or similar rubber, metal or wooden implement. **5** to make a mark or impression upon (a surface) thus. **6** to impress (a scene, an experience, a fact, on or in the mind or memory). **7** to affix a postage stamp or other stamp to (an envelope etc.). **8** to characterize distinctively (*the pusillanimous attitude that stamps a coward; They were put in the top class and stamped as bright*). **9** to crush, to pulverize (ore etc.). ~*v.i.* **1** to bring one's foot down heavily or forcibly on the ground. **2** to walk heavily. ~*n.* **1** an instrument for stamping marks, designs etc. **2** the mark made, or the blow imparted, by this. **3** an official mark set on things chargeable with some duty or tax, to show that it is paid. **4** a small piece of adhesive paper for affixing to letters, receipts etc., to show that the required charge has been paid. **5** a label, imprint, or other mark certifying ownership, quality, genuineness etc., affixed to or impressed on goods etc. **6** a distinguishing mark or impress. **7** a kind, sort or type (*people of this stamp*). **8** a downward blow with the foot, or an act of bringing it down heavily. **9** the sound of this. **10** the block for crushing ore in a stamp-mill. **to stamp on** to suppress, to crush out of existence. **to stamp out 1** to extinguish (a fire) by stamping. **2** to suppress, extirpate. **Stamp Act** *n.* an Act dealing with stamp duties, esp. that of 1765 imposing duty on the American colonies, one of the causes of the Revolution. **stamp album** *n.* a book to hold a postage stamp collection. **stamp-collector** *n.* **1** a person who collects specimens of postage stamps. **2** (*Hist.*) a collector of stamp-duties. **stamp collecting** *n.* **stamp duty** *n.* a duty imposed on certain legal documents. **stamper** *n.* **stamp hinge** *n.* a transparent paper holder with adhesive backing for sticking postage stamps into a stamp album. **stamping ground** *n.* a habitual meeting place, a favourite resort. **stamp-mill** *n.* a mill for crushing ore, fruit etc. **stamp office** *n.* an office issuing official stamps and receiving stamp duty. **stamp paper** *n.* **1** paper bearing the government revenue stamp. **2** the gummed paper forming the margin of a sheet of postage stamps. [ME, from OE unrecorded vb. (cp. Dut. *stampen*, G *stampfen*, ON *stappa*), influ. by OF *estamper*]

stampede (stampēd´) *n.* **1** a sudden headlong rush of startled animals, esp. cattle. **2** a sudden rush of people, esp. in panic. **3** any impulsive or unreasoning movement on the part of a large number of people. ~*v.i.* to take part in a stampede. ~*v.t.* **1** to cause to do this. **2** to rush (people into acting without due thought). [Sp. and Port. *estampido*, from *estampar*, to STAMP]

stance (stans, stahns) *n.* **1** the position taken for a stroke in golf, cricket etc. **2** a personal attitude, political position etc. **3** the position adopted by a person when standing. **4** (*Sc.*) a site, station, taxi rank etc. [OF *estance*, late L *stantia*, see STANZA]

stanch[1] STAUNCH[1].

stanch[2] STAUNCH[2].

stanchion (stan´shən) *n.* **1** a prop, post, pillar etc., forming a support or part of a structure. **2** a vertical bar or pair of bars for confining cattle in a stall. ~*v.t.* **1** to fit with a stanchion. **2** to fasten (cattle) to a stanchion. [ONF *estanchon*, (F *etançon*), dim. of *estance*, STANCE]

stand (stand) *v.i.* (*past*, *p.p.* **stood** (stud)) **1** to be in, take or keep an upright position, esp. on the feet, or on a base. **2** to be located or situated (*On this spot stood the gallows*). **3** to have a specified height or stature (*stood barely five foot*). **4** to be in a specified state, attitude, position, situation, rank etc. (*The score stands at three-nil*; *He stood in awe of the prefects*; *stand accused of murder*). **5** to move into a specified position and remain in it (*stood to one side*). **6** to take a certain attitude (*stand aloof*). **7** to remain firm or constant, to abide, to endure, to persist. **8** to be or remain in a stationary position, to cease from motion, to stop, to be or remain immovable, not to give way. **9** (of rules, laws, conditions etc.) to hold good, to remain valid or unimpaired. **10** (of water) to be motionless, to lie stagnant. **11** (*Naut.*) to hold a specified course, to steer. **12** (of a setter) to point. **13** (*also* **stand at stud**) (of a stallion) to be available to breed from. **14** to become a candidate (for). **15** to act or serve in a specified role or capacity (*stand surety*; *stand proxy*). **16** in cricket, to be umpire. ~*v.t.* **1** to set in an erect or a specified position (*stood the vase on the piano*). **2** to endure, to sustain, without giving way or complaining (*can't stand the pain*). **3** to treat (someone) to (a drink etc.) (*I'll stand you dinner*). **4** to undergo (a trial etc.). ~*n.* **1** a cessation of motion or progress, a stop, a halt, a state of inactivity, a standstill, a stoppage. **2** the act of standing, esp. with firmness, in a fixed or stationary position, place or station (*took her stand at the entrance*). **3** a show of resistance, opposition, defensive effort etc. (*make a stand against racism*). **4** in cricket, a lengthy partnership between two batsmen at the wicket. **5** someone's attitude, position or standpoint in regard to an issue. **6** a small frame or piece of furniture for supporting anything, a base, rack or holder (*an inkstand*; *a hatstand*). **7** a trading stall in a street or market, or a commercial company's information booth at a conference etc. **8** a place in a town where cabs etc. stand for hire. **9** an erection with banks of seats or steps for spectators to stand or sit on. **10** (*N Am.*) the witness box in a court of law. **11** a halt somewhere for a performance by a performer on tour. **12** a clump of plants or trees (*a stand of willows*). **as it stands 1** in its present state, without alteration. **2** in the present circumstances, as things are. **as things stand** in the present circumstances, as things are. **it stands to reason** REASON. **stand and deliver!** (*Hist.*) the traditional utterance of a highwayman at a hold-up, ordering the victims to hand over their money and valuables. **stand easy!** EASY. **stand on me** (*sl.*) depend on me. **to be at a stand 1** to be perplexed. **2** to be in doubt as to further progress. **to stand a chance** CHANCE. **to stand a good chance** CHANCE. **to stand alone** to be unique or unrivalled. **to stand aloof** ALOOF. **to stand at bay** BAY[3]. **to stand at ease** EASE. **to stand back 1** to retire to a position further from the front. **2** to withdraw mentally from close involvement, usu. in order to get an objective view. **to stand bail** BAIL[1]. **to stand by 1** to be present as a bystander; to look on passively. **2** to uphold, to support firmly. **3** to abide by (one's decision etc.). **4** to stand near in readiness to act promptly as directed. **5** (*Naut.*) to post oneself ready to operate (the anchor etc.). **to stand comparison** COMPARISON. **to stand corrected** CORRECT. **to stand down 1** to withdraw or resign from a body, competition etc. **2** to leave the witness box in a law court. **3** (*Mil.*) to come off duty. **4** (of a committee) to be dissolved. **to stand fast** to stay firm, to be unmoved. **to stand for 1** to represent, to imply. **2** (*usu. with neg.*) to allow, to tolerate, to endure. **3** to support the cause of. **to stand good** to remain valid. **to stand guard** GUARD. **to stand high** to have a high reputation. **to stand in for 1** to deputize for, to act in place of. **2** to take the place of (an actor etc. whose special skills are temporarily not required). **to stand in good stead** STEAD. **to stand in the breach** BREACH. **to stand in the gap** GAP. **to stand in with** to have an understanding or community of interest with, to league oneself with. **to stand off 1** to move away; to keep at a distance. **2** to suspend (an employee). **to stand off and on** (*Naut.*) to tack in and out along shore. **to stand on 1** to insist on (ceremony etc.). **2** (*Naut.*) to keep on the same course. **to stand one's ground** to remain resolute, to stay fixed in position. **to stand on one's dignity** DIGNITY. **to stand on one's own (two) feet** to manage without the help of others. **to stand out 1** to be conspicuous, prominent or outstanding. **2** to persist in opposition or support, to hold out (for or against). **3** to endure without giving way. **to stand over 1** to supervise closely in an irksome or threatening way. **2** to be deferred, to be postponed. **to stand pat** PAT. **to stand someone in good stead** STEAD. **to stand the pace** PACE[1]. **to stand to 1** (*Mil.*) to stand ready for an attack, e.g. after dark or before dawn. **2** to abide by. **3** not to desert. **4** to be liable to (lose, gain etc. something). **5** to fall to, to set to work. **to stand treat** TREAT. **to stand up 1** to rise to one's feet. **2** to be or remain erect; to set erect. **3** (of an argument etc.) to be valid, to hold water. **4** (*coll.*) to fail to keep an appointment with. **to stand up for** to maintain, to support, to take the side of. **to stand upon** to stand on. **to stand up to** to oppose with determination. **to stand well with** to be on good terms with, to be in the favour of. **to take one's stand on** to have as the basis of one's argument. **stand-alone** *a.* (of a computer) working independently, not part of an interdependent network etc. **standby** *n.* (*pl.* **standbys**) **1** a substitute or replacement kept esp. for use in an emergency. **2** a thing or person to be confidently relied upon. ~*a.* (of a ticket) not booked in advance, subject to availability. **on standby 1** held in readiness for use or service in an emergency etc. **2** (of an airline passenger) awaiting an empty seat, not having booked in advance. **stand camera** *n.* a camera designed to be mounted on a tripod, not hand-held. **standee** *n.* (*coll.*) a person who is having to stand because all the seats are occupied. **stander** *n.* **stander-by** *n.* (*pl.* **standers-by**). **stand-in** *n.* **1** a substitute or deputy. **2** a minor actor who takes the place of a star at points when the latter's acting skills are not essential. **standing** *a.* **1** erect. **2** not cut down. **3** remaining on the spot, not moving or progressing. **4** fixed, established, permanent, not temporary or for a special occasion. **5** stagnant. ~*n.* **1** repute, estimation, esp. good estimation. **2** relative place or position. **3** the position or activity of a person that stands. **4** duration, existence (*a partnership of long standing*). **to be in good standing with** to be on good or friendly terms with. **to**

be left standing to prove much the weaker competitor, to be left at the starting post. **standing army** *n.* (*pl.* **standing armies**) a peacetime army of professional soldiers. **standing joke** *n.* a subject of constant ridicule. **standing order** *n.* **1** an instruction to a bank by a customer to pay fixed sums at regular intervals in payment of bills etc. **2** (*pl.*) orders made by a deliberative assembly as to the manner in which its business should be conducted. **standing ovation** *n.* a prolonged spell of applause during which the audience rise to their feet in their enthusiasm. **standing rigging** *n.* the fixed ropes and chains by which the masts etc. on a ship, are secured. **standing room** *n.* room for standing, esp. after all seats are filled. **standing stone** *n.* a large erect stone set in the ground in prehistoric times. **standing wave** *n.* (*Physics*) the pattern of maximum and minimum amplitude that occurs when two waves vibrating at the same frequency are travelling in opposed directions. **stand of arms** *n.* (*Mil.*) a complete outfit of arms and ammunition for one person. **stand of colours** *n.* (*Mil.*) the flags of a regiment. **stand-off, stand-off half** *n.* a rugby half-back acting as a link between the scrum-half and the three-quarters. **stand-offish** *a.* cold, distant, reserved in manner. **stand-offishly** *adv.* **stand-offishness** *n.* **standout** *n.*, *a.* (*N Am.*, *coll.*) (a person who is) outstanding or extraordinary. **standpipe** *n.* an upright pipe serving as a hydrant, to provide a head of water for pressure etc. **standpoint** *n.* a point of view or viewpoint, whether topographical or mental. **standstill** *n.* a stoppage, a cessation of progress. **stand-to** *n.* (*Mil.*) a state of readiness for action, the activity of standing ready. **stand-up** *a.* **1** (of a meal) taken standing. **2** **a** (of a fight) fully physical and violent. **b** in boxing, unflinching. **3** (of a collar) upright. **4** (of a comedian) telling jokes etc. directly to the audience in a solo performance. **stand-up fight** *n.* an open encounter. [OE *standan, stondan*, cp. Dut. *staan*, G *stehen*, Icel. *standa*, Swed. *stā*, also L *stāre*, Gr. *histanai*]

standard (stan´dəd) *n.* **1** a measure of extent, quantity, value etc. established by law or custom as an example or criterion for others. **2** any type, fact, thing etc. serving as a criterion. **3** the degree of excellence required for a particular purpose (*not up to standard*; *below standard*). **4** any particular level of quality or competence (*a low standard of workmanship*). **5** the ordinary quality of product etc., as distinct from one including extra features. **6** a flag as the distinctive emblem of an army, government etc. **7** an upright pillar, post or other support. **8** an upright water pipe or standpipe. **9** a tree or shrub growing on a single upright stem, or supported on its own stem. **10** a shrub grafted on to an upright stem. **11** a document dictating the required specifications, nationally or internationally, of manufactured goods. **12** something taken as a model to imitate. **13** a well-established and popular tune or song. **14** **a** in coinage, the system of defining the value of a currency in terms of gold or silver. **b** the proportion of gold or silver and alloy in coins fixed by authority. **15** (*Hist.*) a measure for timber, equivalent to 165 cubic feet (4.67 cubic metres). **16** (*Hist.*) a grade of classification in elementary schools. *~a.* **1** serving as a standard; used as a standard. **2** being of the normal or regulation quality, size etc. **3** recognized as having lasting value; accepted as authoritative. **4** (of language) conforming to the usage of educated native speakers. **to raise the standard** to rally supporters to the cause in preparation for war or some other campaign. **standard assessment task** *n.* a standard test taken by schoolchildren in any of the core subjects in the national curriculum, which indicates their progress in it. **standard-bearer** *n.* **1** a soldier carrying a standard. **2** a leader of a movement or cause. **Standardbred** *n.* (a horse of) a breed developed in the US for trotting or pacing in harness to a standard minimum speed. **standard candle** *n.* a candela. **standard deviation** *n.* a measure of the scatter of the value of a variable about a mean in a frequency distribution. **standard gauge** *n.* the standard distance between the two rails of a railway track, 1.43 m (4 ft. 8½in.). **Standard Grade** *n.* in Scotland, a national examination equivalent to GCSE, testing application of knowledge rather than mere knowledge. **standardize, standardise** *v.t.* **1** to bring into line with a standard. **2** to compare with a standard. *~v.i.* to model oneself (on). **standardizable** *a.* **standardization** (-zā´shən) *n.* **standardizer** *n.* **standard lamp** *n.* a movable lamp on a tall pedestal. **standard of living** *n.* the level of subsistence or material welfare of an individual, group or community. **standard time** *n.* the method of reckoning time from a conventionally adopted meridian (for most purposes this is the meridian of Greenwich). **standard wire gauge** *n.* a standard system of sizes designating the diameter of wire. [OF *estandard*, from OHG *standan*, to STAND, combined with OF *estendard*, from L, as EXTEND]

stanhope (stan´əp) *n.* a light open two- or four-wheeled carriage (first built for Fitzroy Stanhope, 1787–1864).

staniel (stan´yəl) *n.* a kestrel. [OE *stāngiella* (*stān*, STONE, *giellan*, to YELL)]

stank STINK.

Stanley knife® (stan´li) *n.* a sharp trimming knife with a replaceable blade. [F. T. *Stanley*, founder of US hand-tool manufacturing company]

stannary (stan´əri) *n.* (*pl.* **stannaries**) **1** a tin-mining district. **2** a tin mine, tinworks. *~a.* of or relating to tin mines etc. **stannary court** *n.* (*Hist.*) any of the legal courts administering justice among the tin-miners and tinsmiths of Devon and Cornwall, abolished in 1896. [late L *stannāria*, from *stannum*, tin]

stannic (stan´ik) *a.* (*Chem.*) of or containing (tetravalent) tin. **stannate** (-āt) *n.* a salt of stannic acid. **stanniferous** (-if´-) *a.* **stannous** *a.* of or containing (divalent) tin.

stanza (stan´zə) *n.* **1** a recurring group of lines of poetry adjusted to each other in a definite scheme, often with rhyme. **2** in classical prosody, a group of four lines in some metres. **stanza'd, stanzaed** (-zəd), **stanzaic** (-zā´-) *a.* [It., from late L *stantia*, abode, from *stāre*, to stand]

stapelia (stəpē´liə) *n.* any southern African plant of the genus *Stapelia*, whose flowers have an unpleasant smell of carrion. [mod. L, from J. B. von *Stapel*, d. 1636, Dutch botanist]

stapes (stā´pēz) *n.* (*pl.* **stapes**) the innermost of the three small bones of the middle ear, shaped like a stirrup and transmitting vibrations to the middle ear from the incus. **stapedial** (stəpē´di-) *a.* [med. L, stirrup, prob. from Gmc.]

staphyl- STAPHYLO-.

staphyline (staf´ilīn) *a.* shaped like a bunch of grapes.

staphylitis (stafilī´tis) *n.* inflammation of the uvula.

staphylo- (staf´ilō), **staphyl-** *comb. form* **1** shaped like a bunch of grapes. **2** of or relating to the uvula. [Gr. *staphulē*, a bunch of grapes, the uvula, swollen at the tip]

staphylococcus (stafiləkok´əs) *n.* (*pl.* **staphylococci** (-kok´sī)) any micro-organism of the genus *Staphylococcus*, forming the bacteria most frequently found in suppurative infections of the skin or mucous membrane. **staphylococcal** *a.*

staphyloma (stafilō´mə) *n.* an abnormal protrusion of the sclera or the cornea. **staphylomatous** *a.*

staple¹ (stā´pəl) *n.* **1** a U-shaped piece of metal driven into a post, wall etc., to receive part of a fastening or to hold wire etc. **2** a similarly shaped piece of thin wire for driving through sheets of paper and clamping them together. **3** the boxlike part receiving the bolt of a lock. **4** a bent wire used in wire-stitching. *~v.t.* to fasten, attach or support with staples. **staple gun** *n.* a hand tool for propelling staples into a surface. **stapler** *n.* a device for inserting or driving in staples. [OE *stapol*, cp. Dut. *stapel*, G *Staffel*, step, rung, G and Swed. *stapel*, heap, emporium, Dan. *stabel*, hinge, pile]

staple[2] (stā´pəl) *n.* 1 the principal commodity sold or produced in any place, country etc. 2 the main element of diet etc. 3 the chief material or substance of anything. 4 raw material. 5 the length, strength etc. of the fibre of wool, cotton etc., as a criterion of quality. ~*a.* 1 (of a commodity or product) predominating in the home consumption or exports of a nation or region. 2 chief, principal, main. ~*v.t.* to sort or classify (wool etc.) according to staple. [OF *estaple*, LG *stapel*, rel. to STAPLE[1]]

star (stah) *n.* 1 any celestial body appearing as a luminous point, esp. one of the fixed stars or those so distant that their relative position in the heavens appears constant, as distinct from planets or comets. 2 any heavenly body that is really a gaseous mass giving out heat and light. 3 a heavenly body regarded as having influence over a person's life. 4 an object, figure or device resembling a star. 5 such a figure with radiating points used as an emblem, e.g. as a military decoration, part of the insignia of an order or as indicating a grade of excellence (*a three-star hotel*). 6 an asterisk (*). 7 a white spot on the forehead of a horse etc. 8 a brilliant or prominent person, esp. an actor or singer. 9 a star connection. 10 (*sl.*) a star prisoner. ~*a.* 1 outstanding, brilliant (*a star student*). 2 of or relating to stars of the stage or screen (*star quality*). ~*v.t.* (*pres.p.* **starring,** *past, p.p.* **starred**) 1 to set, spangle, or decorate with stars. 2 to put an asterisk against (a name etc.). ~*v.i.* (of an actor, singer etc.) to appear as a star. **my stars!** (*coll.*) used as an expression of astonishment. **to see stars** (*coll.*) to have flashes or dots before one's eyes, as when dazed or stunned. **star-apple** *n.* the edible purple fruit of a tropical evergreen tree, *Chrysophyllum cainito*, with a star-shaped cross-section. **starburst** *n.* 1 a pattern of diverging lines around a source of light. 2 the explosion of a star. 3 a photographic lens attachment that makes a light source appear with divergent rays. 4 a period of star-formation in a galaxy. **Star Chamber** *n.* 1 a court of civil and criminal jurisdiction at Westminster (abolished 1641), famous under Charles I for its arbitrary proceedings. 2 any similarly arbitrary tribunal. **star connection** *n.* a three-way Y-shaped electrical connection, e.g. in a motor. †**star-crossed** *a.* unfortunate, ill-fated. **stardom** *n.* the state or status of being a star in films etc. **star-drift** *n.* the common proper motion of stars in the same region of the heavens. **stardust** *n.* 1 a large concentration of distant stars appearing as dust. 2 dust that supposedly fills the eyes with romantic illusions. **starfish** *n.* (*pl. in general* **starfish**, *in particular* **starfishes**) an echinoderm, *Asterias rubens*, with five or more rays or arms. **star fruit** *n.* the yellow edible fruit, star-shaped in section, of a SE Asian tree, *Averrhoa carambola*. **stargazer** *n.* 1 an astronomer or astrologer. 2 (*Austral.*, *sl.*) a horse that is inclined to turn its head while galloping. **stargaze** *v.i.* 1 to gaze at the stars. 2 to daydream. **stargazing** *n.* **starless** *a.* **starlet** *n.* 1 a young actress who is being trained and promoted as a future star performer. 2 a little star. **starlight** *n.* the light of the stars. ~*a.* starlit. **starlike** *a.* **starlit** *a.* 1 lit by the stars. 2 with the stars visible in the heavens. **star of Bethlehem** *n.* a bulbous plant, *Ornithogalum umbellatum*, of the lily family, with star-shaped white flowers striped outside with green. **Star of David** *n.* the emblem of Judaism and the State of Israel, consisting of a six-pointed star made from two superimposed equilateral triangles. **star prisoner** *n.* (*sl.*) a convict serving a first sentence. **star route** *n.* (*N Am.*) a privately contracted-out postal delivery route. **star ruby, star sapphire** *n.* a ruby or sapphire exhibiting asterism. **starry** *a.* (*comp.* **starrier**, *superl.* **starriest**) 1 filled or adorned with stars. 2 shining like, or illuminated by, stars. 3 resembling a star. 4 featuring many star actors or singers etc. **starrily** *adv.* **starriness** *n.* **starry-eyed** *a.* acting or thinking in a dreamy, over-optimistic manner. **Stars and Bars** *n.pl.* the flag of the Confederate States of the US. **Stars and Stripes** *n.pl.* the national flag of the US. **star shell** *n.* a shell bursting in the air and emitting luminous stars, used to light up an enemy's position. **starship** *n.* in science fiction, a manned spacecraft for interstellar travel. **star-spangled** *a.* covered with stars. **Star-Spangled Banner** *n.* 1 the Stars and Stripes. 2 the national anthem of the US. **star stone** *n.* a star ruby or star sapphire, or other gem exhibiting asterism. **star stream** *n.* a systematic movement or drift of stars. **star-struck** *a.* obsessed with the glamour of stardom or of film stars etc. **star-studded** *a.* 1 covered with stars. 2 (of a film, play etc.) having a large proportion of famous performers. **star turn** *n.* the principal performance in an entertainment. **Star Wars** *n.pl.* (*coll.*) the strategic defence initiative. **starwort** *n.* a plant of the genera *Stellaria* (esp. *Stellaria holostea*, the stitchwort) or *Aster*. [OE *steorra*, cp. Dut. *ster*, G *Stern*, Icel. *stjarna*, Swed. *stjerna*, also L *stella*, Gr. *astēr*]

starboard (stah´bawd, -bəd) *n.* the right-hand side of a vessel looking forward. ~*v.t.* 1 to put (the helm) to starboard. 2 to make (a vessel) turn to starboard. **starboard tack** *n.* a ship's direction as determined by the wind direction and the position of the sails. **starboard watch** *n.* the watch taken by crew members with bunks on the starboard side. [OE *stēorbord* (*stēor*, rudder, as STEER[1], *bord*, side)]

starch (stahch) *n.* 1 a white, tasteless, odourless, amorphous compound, found in all plants except fungi, but esp. in cereals, potatoes, beans etc., an important constituent of vegetable foods, and used as a soluble powder to stiffen linen etc. 2 food, e.g. potatoes, which contains a lot of starch. 3 stiffness, preciseness, formality. ~*a.* stiff, precise, prim. ~*v.t.* to stiffen with starch. **starched** *a.* **starchedly** (stah´chidli) *adv.* primly. **starchedness** (stah´chid-) *n.* **starcher** *n.* **starchly** *adv.* **starchness** *n.* **starch-reduced** *a.* having the starch content reduced, as in bread etc. made specially for slimmers. **starchy** *a.* (*comp.* **starchier**, *superl.* **starchiest**) 1 of or relating to starch. 2 stiff, unyielding. **starchily** *adv.* **starchiness** *n.* [ME *sterch*, strong, cp. OE *stercan*, to stiffen, cogn. with STARK]

stare (steə) *v.i.* 1 to look with eyes fixed and wide open, as in admiration, surprise, horror etc. 2 (of the eyes) to be wide open and gazing fixedly. 3 to stand out, to be prominent. ~*v.t.* to reduce to a specified state by staring (*stared her into submission*). ~*n.* a staring gaze. **to be staring one in the face** 1 to be only too obvious. 2 to be imminent, to be inexorably awaiting one. **to stare down** to outstare. **to stare out** to outstare. **starer** *n.* **staring** *a.* [OE *starian* (cp. Dut. *staren*, Icel. *stara*, also G *starr*, stiff), prob. rel. to Gr. *stereos*, firm]

stark (stahk) *a.* 1 (of a landscape etc.) bare, desolate. 2 plain, simple, esp. harshly so (*a stark contrast*; *the stark realities*). 3 stubborn, inflexible. 4 complete, downright, sheer (*stark madness*). 5 completely naked. 6 †strong, stiff, rigid. ~*adv.* wholly, absolutely (*stark mad*). **stark staring mad** completely crazy. **starkers** (-kəz) *a.* (*coll.*) stark naked. **starkly** *adv.* **stark naked** *a.* completely naked. **starkness** *n.* [OE *stearc* (cp. Dut. *sterk*, G *stark*, Icel. *sterkr*); in *stark naked* corr. of OE *steort*, tail (cp. Dut. *stert*, G *Sterz*, Icel. *stertr*)]

Stark effect (stahk) *n.* (*Physics*) the splitting of the spectrum into components by applying an electric field. [J. *Stark*, 1874–1957, German physicist]

starkers STARK.

starling[1] (stah´ling) *n.* a small black and brown speckled bird of the genus *Sturnus*, esp. *S. vulgaris.* [OE *stær* (cp. G *Star*, Icel. *stari, starri*)]

starling[2] (stah´ling) *n.* an enclosure of piles round or (esp.) upstream of a bridge pier, to protect it from floating rubbish. [cp. Dan. and Swed. *stor*, stake]

starry STAR.

START *abbr.* Strategic Arms Limitation Treaty (or Talks).

start (staht) *v.i.* **1** to commence, to come into existence (*The programme starts at 8.30*). **2 a** to make a beginning (on a task, journey etc.). **b** to begin a meal etc. (with a certain item) (*usually start with soup*). **3** to begin moving, to make as if to move (*She started after him, then changed her mind*). **4** to set out, to leave, to begin a journey (*If we start at six, we'll be there by eleven*). **5** (of a machine, engine etc.) to begin operating (*The car won't start*). **6** (*coll.*) to begin complaining (*Now don't you start*). **7** to make a sudden involuntary movement, as from fear, surprise etc. **8** to shrink, to wince. **9** to move abruptly, to spring (aside etc.). **10** (of timber, rivets etc.) to give way, to become loose etc. **11** to appear or well up suddenly (*The pain made tears start in his eyes*). **12** (of eyes) to open wide, to stare, to appear prominent. ~*v.t.* **1** to begin (*started work; start singing; started to laugh*). **2** to set going, to set in motion (*start the proceedings; started a fire*). **3** to set (someone) up (in business etc.). **4** to originate, to set going (*start a business*). **5** to set (people) working. **6** to cause (someone) to begin (reacting in some way) (*started us all laughing; started me coughing*). **7** to cause (a machine, engine etc.) to begin operating. **8** to give the signal to (competitors) to start in a race. **9** to cause to start, to rouse (game etc.). **10** to conceive (a baby). **11** to cause (timbers etc.) to start. **12** (*Naut.*) to draw (liquor) from, or draw liquor from (a cask). ~*n.* **1** the beginning of a journey, enterprise etc., a setting-out. **2** a starting-place. **3** the amount of lead given to a competitor at the beginning of a race etc. (*a ten-second start*). **4** an advantageous initial position in life, in business etc. **5** a sudden involuntary movement, as of fear, surprise etc. **6** (*usu. pl.*) a spasmodic effort, as in *fits and starts.* **7** (*coll.*) an odd or queer occurrence (*a rum start*). **by fits and starts** FIT[2]. **for a start** in the first place, as the first consideration of several. **to get the start of** to obtain an advantage over. **to start a hare** HARE. **to start in 1** to begin. **2** (*N Am.*) to make a beginning (on). **to start off 1** to begin (*start off with introductions*). **2** to set out on a journey. **to start on** (*coll.*) to pick a fight with, to nag, to bully. **to start out 1** to begin a journey. **2** to begin in a certain way (*He started out as an airman but eventually became an archaeologist*). **3** to take the first steps in a particular activity (*We started out making the usual mistakes of first-time buyers*). **to start over** OVER. **to start something** (*coll.*) to cause trouble or complications, esp. inadvertently. **to start up 1** to come into notice or occur to the mind suddenly; to arise, to occur. **2** (of an engine, machine etc.) to start. **3** to rise suddenly. **4** to establish (a business etc.). **to start with 1** in the first place, as the first consideration (*should never have bought it to start with*). **2** in the beginning (*There were eight of us to start with*). **starter** *n.* **1** a person who or thing that starts. **2** a device for starting an internal-combustion engine. **3** a person who gives the signal for starting a race etc. **4** a horse or other competitor starting in a race (*There are ten starters*). **5** (*sometimes pl.*) the first course of a meal. **6** anything that initiates a process. **for starters** (*coll.*) in the first place, to begin with, as the first consideration. **under starter's orders** (of racehorses etc.) ready to race, awaiting the signal to go. **starting** *n., a.* **starting block** *n.* (*usu. pl.*) a device consisting of angled wooden blocks or metal pads used by sprinters to brace their feet in crouch starts. **starting gate** *n.* in horse racing, a set of starting stalls. **starting grid** *n.* in motor racing, a system of markings on the track to indicate starting positions. **starting-handle** *n.* a crank for starting the engine of a car etc. **starting pistol** *n.* a pistol used to give the starting signal for a race. **starting point** *n.* a point of departure for a journey, argument, procedure etc. **starting post** *n.* a post from which competitors start in a race. **starting price** *n.* the odds on a horse at the beginning of a race. **starting stall** *n.* a compartment for one horse in the line-up for a race, with a movable barrier that is lifted at the starting signal. **start-up** *n.* an act, or the process, of starting, esp. in reference to setting a machine in motion or establishing a business. [ME *sterten*, cp. Dut. *storten*, G *sturzen*, Dan. *styrte*, Swed. *störta*, to cast down, etc.]

startle (stah´təl) *v.t.* to alarm, to shock; to cause to start in surprise etc. **startler** *n.* **startling** *a.* surprising, alarming. **startlingly** *adv.* [ME *stertlen*, freq. of START]

starve (stahv) *v.i.* **1** to die of hunger. **2** to suffer severely from hunger or malnourishment. **3** to be in need or penury. **4** (*used in continuous tenses, coll.*) to be very hungry (*I'm starving*). **5** to suffer from the lack of mental or spiritual nourishment. **6** to long (for e.g. affection, stimulation). **7** (*dial.*) to die or suffer severely from cold. ~*v.t.* **1** to cause to die, or suffer extremely, from lack of food. **2** to deprive (of affection etc.). **3** to deprive of mental or spiritual nourishment. **4** to force (into surrender, out of a stronghold etc.) by starving. **5** (*dial.*) to cause to die, or suffer severely, from cold. **starvation** (-vā´shən) *n.* **starved** *a.* †**starveling** (-ling) *n.* a starving or malnourished person or animal. ~*a.* **1** starving. **2** lean, meagre. **starving** *a.* [OE *steorfan*, to die, cp. *sterfan*, to kill, Dut. *sterven*, G *sterben*]

stases STASIS.

stash (stash) *v.t.* (*coll.*) to store, (money etc.) in a secret place (usu. with *away*). ~*n.* **1** a secret store. **2** a hiding place, hideaway or hideout. [etym. uncertain]

Stasi (shtah´zi) *n.* in the German Democratic Republic before 1989, the internal security force. [G *Sta*ats*si*cherheitsdienst]

stasimon (stas´imən) *n.* (*pl.* **stasima** (-mə)) in ancient Greek drama, an ode sung by the entire chorus, having taken their places after the opening ode, or one sung without interruption by dialogue. [Gr., short for *stasimon melos*, stationary song]

stasis (stā´sis, stas´-) *n.* (*pl.* **stases** (-sēz)) **1** a state of equilibrium or inaction. **2** stagnation of the blood, esp. in the small vessels or capillaries, or any stoppage in the flow of a bodily fluid. **-stasis** (stā´sis, stəsis) *comb. form* (*pl.* **-stases** (-sēz)) denoting a stoppage or slowing down. [mod. L, from Gr., from *sta-*, root of *histanai*, to stand]

stat[1] (stat) *n.* (*coll.*) a thermostat.

stat[2] (stat) *n.* **1** (*esp. pl.*) a statistic. **2** statistics.

-stat (stat) *comb. form* designating a device that causes something to remain stationary or constant, as in *thermostat.* [Gr. *-statēs*, from *histanai*, to cause to stand]

state (stāt) *n.* **1** the condition, mode of existence, situation, or relation to circumstances, of a person or thing (*in a poor state of health; in a reasonable state*). **2** (*coll.*) a nervous or excited condition (*Don't get in such a state*). **3** (*coll.*) an untidy or confused condition. **4** (*often* **State**) a political community organized under a government, a commonwealth, a nation, the body politic. **5 a** such a community forming part of a federal republic, esp. *the United States.* **b** (**the States**) the US. **6** civil government (*Ministers of State; Church and State*). **7** dignity, rank, pomp, splendour. **8** (**the States**) the legislative body in Jersey, Guernsey or Alderney. **9** each of two or several different forms of the same edition of a book. 10 an engraved or etched plate at a certain stage of its development, or an impression taken from this. ~*a*. 1 (*often* **State**) **a** of or relating to the state or body politic (*state secrets*; *state papers*). **b** used or reserved for ceremonial occasions (*the State apartments*). **c** involving ceremony (*a state visit*; *the state opening of Parliament*). ~*v.t.* 1 to set forth in speech or writing, esp. with explicitness and formality (*stated her intentions*). 2 to declare (*has stated his innocence*). 3 to fix, to determine, to specify (*only at stated times*). 4 (*Law*) to present the facts of (a case) for review. 5 (*Mus.*) to play (a theme) so as to acquaint the listener with it. **in state** with proper ceremony (*was received in state*). **of state** relating to government (*affairs of state*). **to lie in state** (of an important dead person) to lie in a coffin in some place where the public may come to visit as a token of respect. **statable** *a*. **state capitalism** *n*. the control and deployment of capital by the state. **statecraft** *n*. statesmanship. **State Department** *n*. that part of the US government responsible for foreign affairs. **statedly** *adv*. **statehood** *n*. **state house** *n*. 1 the building which houses a US state legislature. 2 in New Zealand, a private residence built with government funds. **stateless** *a*. 1 (of a person) without nationality or citizenship. 2 having no state or political community. **statelessness** *n*. **stately** *a*. (*comp*. **statelier**, *superl*. **stateliest**) grand, lofty, dignified, elevated, imposing. **stateliness** *n*. **stately home** *n*. a large country mansion, usu. of historic interest and open to public view. **statement** *n*. 1 the act of stating; the expression of something in words. 2 that which is stated; a declaration. 3 a formal account, recital, or narration (*make a statement to the police*). 4 an itemized record of additions to and withdrawals from a bank account. 5 a formal presentation of money owed for goods, services etc. 6 in the UK, a local education authority's assessment of a child's special educational requirements. ~*v.t.* to assess as having special educational requirements. **statemented** *a*. assessed as having such needs. **state of affairs, state of things, state of play** *n*. 1 a certain situation. 2 the present circumstances. **state of emergency** *n*. the situation of a country at a time of peril or disaster, esp. justifying the suspension of the normal running of the constitution. **state of grace** *n*. the spiritual condition of forgiveness or release from one's sins. **state of life** *n*. one's rank or occupation. **state of siege** *n*. a situation in which civil law is abandoned, esp. in favour of military law. **state-of-the-art** *a*. using the most advanced technology available at the time. **state of war** *n*. the situation following a declaration of war, or when war is in progress. **state paper** *n*. a document relating to state affairs. **state pension** *n*. a pension paid by the state to a person of pensionable age. **state prisoner** *n*. a person imprisoned for an offence against the state. **State Registered Nurse** *n*. a fully qualified nurse. **stateroom** *n*. 1 a room reserved for ceremonial occasions, a state apartment. 2 a private sleeping apartment on a liner etc. or, in N America, a train. **state school** *n*. a government-financed school for the provision of free education. **state's evidence** *n*. King's or Queen's evidence. **States General** *n*. the legislative assembly in the Netherlands and in France before the 1789 Revolution. **stateside** *a*., *adv*. (*coll.*) of, in or towards the US. **statesman, stateswoman** *n*. (*pl*. **statesmen, stateswomen**) 1 a person skilled in the art of government. 2 a person taking a leading part in the administration of the state. **statesmanlike, statesmanly** *a*. **statesmanship** *n*. **state socialism** *n*. government ownership of the leading industries, services, financial institutions etc., in the public interest. **statesperson** *n*. (*pl*. **statespersons, statespeople**) a statesman or stateswoman. **state's rights** *n.pl*. rights reserved by the individual states of the US. **stateswoman** STATESMAN (under STATE). **state trial** *n*. a trial for offences against the state. **state university** *n*. (*N Am.*) a university run by the public authorities of a state. **statewide** *a*., *adv*. (*N Am.*) (happening, applying etc.) throughout the whole state. **statism** *n*. (belief in) the centralized control of economic and social affairs by the state. **statist** *n*. 1 a statistician. 2 a believer in statism. [OF *estat*, L STATUS]

stater (stā´tə) *n*. a coin of ancient Greece, esp. the standard gold coin of 20 drachmas. [Gr., orig. a pound weight, from *histanai*, to establish, to weigh]

static (stat´ik) *a*. 1 stationary; not moving, acting or altering; stable, passive. 2 of or relating to bodies at rest or in equilibrium. 3 acting as weight without producing motion. 4 of or relating to or causing stationary electric charges. 5 of or relating to interference of radio or television signals. 6 of or relating to statics. ~*n*. 1 static electricity. 2 atmospherics; electrical interference of radio or television signals causing crackling, hissing and a speckled picture. **statical** *a*. static. **statically** *adv*. **static electricity** *n*. electrical effects caused by stationary charges, as opposed to charged particles flowing in a current. **static energy** *n*. potential energy. **static line** *n*. a cord attaching the pack of a parachute to an aircraft, so that the parachute opens without the use of a ripcord. **statics** *n*. the branch of dynamics concerned with the relations between forces in equilibrium. [Gr. *statikos*, from *histanai*, to stand]

statice (stat´isē) *n*. any plant of a genus *Limonium* that includes the sea lavender. [Gr. *statikē*, fem. of *statikos*, staunching (blood etc.)]

station (stā´shən) *n*. 1 a place where railway trains stop to set down or take up passengers or goods, usu. with a platform and administrative buildings and public facilities. 2 such buildings and facilities. 3 a similarly equipped terminus or assembly point for coaches or buses. 4 the place where a person or thing stands, esp. an appointed or established place. 5 a place where a particular service or operation is based (*a police station*; *a coastguard station*; *a polling station*; *a petrol station*). 6 (*N Am.*) a subsidiary post office. 7 a particular broadcasting establishment, or the radio or television channel it serves. 8 a military or naval base, esp., formerly, in India, or its personnel or inhabitants. 9 position, occupation, standing, rank, esp. high rank (*one's station in life*; *ideas above one's station*). 10 (*Austral.*) the ranch house or homestead of a sheep farmer. 11 (*Bot.*) the area inhabited by a particular species, a habitat. 12 in the Roman Catholic Church, a church to which a procession resorts for devotion. 13 a station of the cross. ~*v.t.* to assign to or place in a particular station, to post. **stational** *a*. **stationary** *a*. 1 remaining in one place, not moving. 2 intended to remain in one place; fixed, not portable. 3 not changing in character, condition, magnitude etc. 4 (of planets) having no apparent movement in longitude. ~*n*. (*pl*. **stationaries**) 1 a person who is stationary. 2 (*pl.*) stationary troops. **stationariness** *n*. **stationary air** *n*. the air that remains in the lungs during normal respiration. **stationary bicycle** *n*. an exercise machine with a similar operation to that of a bicycle. **stationary point** *n*. (*Math.*) a point of zero gradient on a curve. **stationary wave** *n*. STANDING WAVE (under STAND). **station-bill** *n*. (*Naut.*) a list giving each crew member's station in an emergency, or for drilling purposes. **station break** *n*. (*N Am.*) a break between broadcast programmes, during which the broadcasting station is identified. **station hand** *n*. (*Austral.*) a worker on a sheep farm or cattle farm. **station house** *n*. a police station. **station-keeping** *n*. (*Naut.*) the maintaining of one's position in a flotilla etc., relative to other vessels. **stationmaster** *n*. the official in charge of a railway station. **station of the cross** *n*. in the Roman Catholic Church, any of a series of 14 images or pictures in a church etc. depicting successive scenes in Christ's passion. **station pointer** *n.* (*Naut.*) a navigational instrument for fixing the vessel's place on a chart from landmarks or objects at sea. **station sergeant** *n.* the sergeant in charge of a police station. **station wagon** *n.* (*chiefly N Am.*) an estate car. [F, from L *statiōnem*, nom. *-tio*, from *stāre*, to stand]

Usage note The spellings of the adjective *stationary* (not moving) and the noun *stationery* (writing materials) should not be confused.

stationer (stā´shənə) *n.* a person who sells papers, pens, ink and writing materials. **Stationers' Hall** *n.* the hall of the Stationers' Company in London at which, formerly, every new book had to be registered to establish copyright. **stationery** *n.* writing materials and related goods sold by a stationer. **Stationery Office** *n.* the government department for the preparation and issue of official books and documents. [orig. a bookseller, having a STATION, stall or stand]

Usage note See note on *stationery* under STATION.

statism, statist STATE.

statistics (stətis´tiks) *n.* **1** (*as sing.*) the science of collecting, organizing, and analysing numerical data, esp. on a large scale, with the purpose of extrapolating trends in a whole from the representative sample studied. **2** (*as pl.*) numerical facts, arranged and classified, esp. respecting social conditions. **statistic** *n.* a statistical fact, a figure or total. ~*a.* statistical. **statistical** *a.* of or relating to statistics. **statistically** *adv.* **statistical physics** *n.* the application of statistics to the behaviour of large numbers of physical particles. **statistical significance** *n.* a measure of the amount of significance assignable to a deviant result. **statistician** (statistish´ən) *n.* [G *Statistik*, *statistisch*, from *Statist*, a statist]

stative (stā´tiv) *a.* **1** (of verbs) expressing a state of mind as distinct from an action, e.g. *know, like, believe.* **2** (of some Hebrew verbs) expressing past action etc. as still continuing. **3** (*Hist.*) denoting an ancient Roman fixed camp or military post. [L *statīvus*, from *stāre*, to stand, p.p. *status*]

statoblast (stat´ōblahst) *n.* an internal bud developed in freshwater sponges and polyzoa. [Gr. *statos*, fixed, from *histanai*, to stand, -BLAST]

stator (stā´tə) *n.* the fixed part of an electrical generator. [from STATIONARY (under STATION), on the analogy of ROTOR from ROTARY]

statoscope (stat´əskōp) *n.* a sensitive aneroid barometer for showing minute fluctuations of pressure.

stats (stats) *n.* (*coll.*) statistics.

statue (stat´ū) *n.* a representation of a person or animal sculptured or cast, e.g. in marble or bronze, esp. about life-size. **statuary** *a.* of or for statues. ~*n.* (*pl.* **statuaries**) **1** statues collectively. **2** the art of making statues. **3** a sculptor. **statued** *a.* **statuesque** (-esk´) *a.* like a statue; having the dignity or beauty of a statue. **statuesquely** *adv.* **statuesqueness** *n.* **statuette** (-et´) *n.* a small statue, less than life-size. [OF, from L *statua*, from *statuere*, to cause to stand, as STATURE]

stature (stach´ə) *n.* **1** the natural height of a body, esp. of a person. **2** eminence or social standing. **3** mental or moral standing. **statured** *a.* [F, from L *statūra*, upright posture, from *stāre*, to stand, p.p. *status*]

status (stā´təs) *n.* **1** relative standing, rank, or position in society. **2** (*Law*) a person's legal identity, e.g. whether alien or citizen. **3** the current situation or state of affairs. **status symbol** *n.* a possession regarded as indicative of a person's elevated social rank or wealth. [L, standing, from *stāre*, to stand]

status quo (stātəs kwō´) *n.* the existing state of affairs. **status quo ante** (an´ti) *n.* the situation immediately preceding the current state of affairs or the one in question. [L, state in which, *ante*, before]

statute (stat´ūt) *n.* **1** a written law enacted by a legislative body. **2** an ordinance of a corporation or its founder intended as a permanent law. **statutable** *a.* **statutably** *adv.* **statute-barred** *a.* (of a case etc.) no longer legally enforceable because of the lapse of time. **statute book** *n.* a book in which statutes are published. **statute law** *n.* law enacted by a legislative body. **statute mile** *n.* a unit of distance equivalent to 1,760 yards (1.609 kilometres). **statute of limitations** *n.* a statute prescribing a period of time within which proceedings must be taken to enforce a right or bring an action at law. **statute roll** *n.* **1** any one of the rolls housed in the Public Record Office containing the statutes of the Parliament of England. **2** the roll on which statutes are engrossed; a statute book. **statutes at large** *n.pl.* the statutes as first enacted, without regard to later alterations. **statutory** *a.* enacted, regulated, enforced or recognized by statute. **statutorily** *adv.* **statutory rape** *n.* (*Law, N Am.*) the act of having sexual intercourse with a minor. [L, as STATUS]

staunch[1] (stawnch), **stanch** (stawnch) *a.* **1** loyal, constant, trustworthy. **2** (of a ship) seaworthy, watertight. **3** (of a joint etc.) firm, stout. **staunchly** *adv.* **staunchness** *n.* [OF *estanche*, fem. of *estanc*]

staunch[2] (stawnch), **stanch** (stahnch, stawnch) *v.t.* to stop (blood) flowing, or stop blood flowing from (a wound). ~†*v.i.* (of blood) to stop flowing. [OF *estanchier*, from late L *stancare*, from *stagnāre*, to stagnate]

staurolite (staw´rəlīt) *n.* (*Mineral.*) an orthorhombic ferrous silicate of aluminium occurring in crosslike twin crystals. **staurolitic** (-lit´ik) *a.* **stauroscope** (-skōp) *n.* an instrument for observing the effects of parallel polarized light in crystals. [Gr. *stauros*, cross, -LITE]

stave (stāv) *n.* **1** each of the curved strips forming the side of a cask etc. **2** a strip of wood or other material used for a similar purpose. **3** a stanza, a verse. **4** (*Mus.*) a staff. ~*v.t.* (*past, p.p.* **staved, stove** (stōv)) **1** to crush the staves of (a cask, boat etc.). **2** to make (a hole) thus. **3** to furnish or fit with staves. **4** (*past, p.p.* **staved**) to stop, avert or ward (off). **to stave in** to crush. **stave rhyme** *n.* alliteration, esp. in older German poetry. [var. of STAFF[1], from ME dat. sing.]

staves STAFF[1].

stavesacre (stāv´zākə) *n.* a species of larkspur, *Delphinium staphisagria*, the seeds of which were formerly used as a poison for lice etc. [OF *stavesaigre*, *staphisaigre*, L *staphisagria* (Gr. *staphis*, raisins, *agria*, wild)]

stay[1] (stā) *v.i.* **1** to continue in a specified place or state, not to move or change. **2** to remain (e.g. calm, cheerful). **3** to reside temporarily (at, with etc.). **4** (*Sc., S Afr.*) to live, to dwell permanently (somewhere). **5** to remain somewhere long enough to be included in something (*stay to dinner; stay for evensong*). **6** to keep going or last out in a race etc., or till some other conclusion. **7** †to pause, to stand still. **8** †to tarry, to wait. ~*v.t.* **1** to spend (a period of time) somewhere (*stayed a week with her parents*). **2** to hinder, to stop the progress etc. of (e.g. a disease). **3** temporarily to satisfy (someone's hunger). **4** to postpone, to suspend (judgement, a decision etc.). ~*n.* **1** the circumstance, or a period, of staying or dwelling. **2** continuance in a place etc. **3** a suspension of judicial proceedings (*a stay of execution*). **4** †a check, a restraint or deterrent. **to be here to stay** to be a fixture, to have come for good. **to have come to stay** to be here to stay. **to stay in** to remain at home, to remain indoors. **to stay one's hand** HAND. **to stay over** (*coll.*) to remain overnight. **to stay put** to remain where put or placed; to remain on the spot. **to stay the course** COURSE. **to stay the night** to remain somewhere, esp. to sleep, until the next day. **to stay the pace** PACE[1]. **to stay up** not to go to bed till after one's normal bedtime.

stay-at-home *a., n.* (a person who is) unenterprising or unadventurous. **stayer**[1] *n.* a person with stamina and the will-power to go on; a horse or person that can stay the course. **staying power** *n.* stamina. **stay-in strike** *n.* a sit-down strike. **stay-up** *a.* (of stockings) having elasticated tops to keep them up without suspenders. *~n.* such a stocking. [OF *ester*, L *stāre*, STAND]

stay[2] (stā) *n.* **1** a support, a prop. **2** (*pl.*) a corset. *~v.t.* to prop (usu. up), to support. **stay-bar, stay-rod** *n.* a bar or rod used as a stay or support in a building etc. **stayer**[2] *n.* **stay lace** *n.* a string used to lace a corset. **stayless** *a.* **stay-maker** *n.* a corset-maker. [OF *estayer*, to prop, *estaye*, prop, MDut. *stade*, *staeye*, OHG *stata*, fit place or time, cogn. with STEAD]

stay[3] (stā) *n.* **1** a rope supporting a mast. **2** a guy rope or other rope supporting a flagstaff. **3** a supporting brace in an aircraft. *~v.t.* **1** to support by stays. **2** to put (a sailing ship) on the other tack. **staysail** (-səl) *n.* a sail extended by a stay. [perh. from OE *stæg*, etym. uncertain, or STAY[2]]

stayer[1] STAY[1].

stayer[2] STAY[2].

STD *abbr.* **1** *Sanctae Theologiae Doctor*, Doctor of Sacred Theology. **2** sexually transmitted disease. **3** subscriber trunk dialling.

stead (sted) *n.* place or room which another had or might have had. **in someone's stead** instead of someone. **in something's stead** instead of something. **to stand someone in good stead** to be of service to someone. [OE *stede* (cp. Dut. *stede*), cogn. with *stæth*, bank, Dut. *stad*, G *Stadt*, town, L *statis*, Gr. *statis*, and STAND]

steadfast (sted´fəst, -fahst) *a.* firm, resolute, unwavering. **steadfastly** *adv.* **steadfastness** *n.* [OE *stedefæst*]

steading (sted´ing) *n.* (*Sc., North.*) a farmstead. [OE *stede*, place]

steady (sted´i) *a.* (*comp.* **steadier**, *superl.* **steadiest**) **1** firmly fixed, not wavering. **2** moving or acting in a regular way, uniform, constant. **3** free from intemperance or irregularity, constant in mind or conduct. **4** persistent, tenacious. **5** serious, reliable and conscientious. **6** well controlled (*a steady hand; steady nerves*). **7** (of a ship) upright and on course. *~v.t.* (*3rd pers. sing. pres.* **steadies**, *pres.p.* **steadying**, *past*, *p.p.* **steadied**) to make steady. *~v.i.* to become steady. *~n.* (*pl.* **steadies**) **1** (*coll.*) a regular boyfriend or girlfriend. **2** a rest or support for keeping the hand etc. steady. *~adv.* steadily (*held them steady*). *~int.* careful! take care! **steady on!** calm down! take it easy! **to go steady** GO[1]. **to steady down** to become steady. **steadier** *n.* **steadily** *adv.* **steadiness** *n.* **steady-going** *a.* sober, dependable. **steady state** *n.* (*Physics*) a state of dynamic equilibrium. **steady-state theory** *n.* in cosmology, the theory that the universe has always existed in a steady state, matter being created continuously as it expands. [STEAD, -Y[1]]

steak (stāk) *n.* **1** a thick slice of beef, other meat, or fish cut for grilling, frying etc. **2** any of several cuts of beef such as *stewing steak, braising steak*. **steakhouse** *n.* a restaurant that specializes in serving steaks. **steak knife** *n.* (*pl.* **steak knives**) a knife with a serrated blade, for eating steak with. **steak tartare** *n.* uncooked minced beef steak served with onions, raw egg and seasoning. [ME *steike*, Icel. *steik*, from *steikja*, to roast on a spit, cogn. with STICK[2]]

steal (stēl) *v.t.* (*past* **stole** (stōl), *p.p.* **stolen** (stō´lən)) **1** to take (someone else's property) away without right or permission or intention of returning it, to take feloniously. **2** to secure covertly or by surprise (*steal a kiss*). **3** to secure (e.g. someone's affections) insidiously. **4** in various sports, to get (a run, the ball etc.) stealthily or fortuitously. **5** in baseball, to run to (a base) while the pitcher is delivering. *~v.i.* **1** to take anything feloniously. **2** to go or come furtively, silently or unnoticed (*She stole out of the house; The minutes stole past; A thought stole into his head*). *~n.* (*coll.*) **1** an act of stealing. **2** something stolen. **3** a bargain. **to steal a march on** MARCH[1]. **to steal someone's thunder 1** to spoil the effect someone had hoped to achieve with a particular idea by using the idea oneself first. **2** to attract publicity away from someone towards oneself. **stealer** *n.* **stealingly** *adv.* [OE *stelan*, cp. Dut. *stelen*, G *stehlen*, Icel. *stela*]

stealth (stelth) *n.* **1** furtiveness, secrecy. **2** secret procedure. **by stealth** furtively, surreptitiously. **stealthy** (-thi) *a.* (*comp.* **stealthier**, *superl.* **stealthiest**). **stealthily** *adv.* **stealthiness** *n.* [STEAL, -TH[1]]

steam (stēm) *n.* **1** water in the form of vapour or the gaseous form to which it is changed by boiling. **2** the visible mass of particles of water into which this condenses. **3** any vaporous exhalation. **4** power or energy generated by steam under pressure. **5** (*coll.*) energy, force, go. *~a.* powered by steam, as in *steam engine*, or relating to energy from steam under pressure. *~v.i.* **1** to give off steam. **2** to rise in steam or vapour. **3** to move by the agency of steam (*steamed across the bay*). **4** (*sl.*) (of a gang) to push through a crowd robbing people in the process. *~v.t.* **1** to cook (food) in steam. **2** to treat (e.g. timber) with steam for the purpose of softening. **3** to ease (an envelope) open or (a stamp) off by applying steam to the gum. **to get up steam 1** to build up steam pressure, esp. sufficient to run a steam engine. **2** to collect one's forces or energy. **3** to work oneself up into an excited state. **to let off steam** to give vent to one's feelings. **to run out of steam** to lose momentum or energy. **to steam in** (*sl.*) to initiate or join a fight, to weigh in. **to steam up** to (cause to) become covered with condensed steam. **under one's own steam** by one's own efforts, without help. **steam age** *n.* the era of steam power, when trains were pulled by steam-powered locomotives. **steam bath** *n.* a steam-filled room in which to cleanse oneself. **steamboat** *n.* a vessel propelled by a steam engine. **steam boiler** *n.* a boiler in a steam engine. **steam-chest** *n.* in a steam boiler, the box-shaped part through which steam is conveyed from the boiler to the cylinder. **steamed up** *a.* **1** (of windows etc.) clouded by steam. **2** (*coll.*) angry, indignant. **steam engine** *n.* an engine worked by the pressure of steam on a piston moving in a cylinder etc. **steamer** *n.* **1** a person or thing that steams. **2** a vessel propelled by steam. **3** a steam fire engine. **4** a receptacle for steaming articles, esp. for cooking food. **steamer rug** *n.* (*N Am.*) a travelling rug. **steam gauge** *n.* an instrument attached to a boiler to indicate the pressure of steam. **steam hammer** *n.* a steam-powered forging hammer. **steam-heat** *n.* heat produced by steam, as in a steam-using central heating system. *~v.t.* to heat by means of steam. **steam iron** *n.* an electric iron with a compartment in which water is heated and then emitted as steam through holes in its base to aid pressing and ironing. **steam-jacket** *n.* a hollow casing round a cylinder etc., for receiving steam to heat the latter. **steam navvy** *n.* (*pl.* **steam navvies**) a steam shovel. **steam organ** *n.* a pipe organ used e.g. at fairgrounds, played by keyboard or by a punched-card system. **steam power** *n.* force applied by the agency of steam to machinery etc. **steamroll** *v.t.* (*N Am.*) to steamroller. **steamroller** *n.* **1** a heavy roller propelled by steam, used in road-making and road-repairing. **2** any crushing force. *~v.t.* **1** to crush (opposition etc.) by overwhelming pressure. **2** to force (legislation through) in a legislative assembly by such means. **steamship** *n.* a ship propelled by a steam engine. **steam shovel** *n.* a mechanical excavator consisting of a large bucket working from a long beam. **steam-tight** *a.* impermeable by steam. **steam train** *n.* a train powered or drawn by a steam engine. **steam tug**

n. a small steam vessel used for towing ships. **steam turbine** *n.* a machine in which steam acts on moving blades attached to a drum. **steamy** *a.* (*comp.* **steamier,** *superl.* **steamiest**) **1** of, like, full of, emitting or covered with steam. **2** (*sl.*) erotic. **steamily** *adv.* **steaminess** *n.* [OE *stēam*, cp. Dut. *stoom*]

stearin (stiə´rin), **stearine** *n.* **1** a usu. white crystalline glyceryl ester of stearic acid. **2** stearic acid as used for candles. **3** a fatty compound contained in the more solid animal and vegetable fats. **stearate** (-rāt) *n.* a salt of stearic acid. **stearic** (stiar´-) *a.* of or relating to stearin or stearic acid. **stearic acid** *n.* a fatty acid obtained from solid animal or vegetable fats and used in making candles and soap. [F *stéarine* (Gr. *stear*, fat)]

steat- STEATO-.

steatite (stē´ətīt) *n.* soapstone or some other impure form of talc. **steatitic** (-tit´-) *a.* [F *stéatite*]

steato- (stē´ətō) *comb. form* fat. [Gr. *stear, steatos*, fat]

steatocele (stē´ətəsēl) *n.* a fatty tumour of the scrotum.

steatoma (stēətō´mə) *n.* (*pl.* **steatomas, steatomata** (-mətə)) a fatty encysted tumour. **steatomatous** *a.*

steatopygous (stēətop´igəs) *a.* having fat buttocks. **steatopygia** (-pij´iə), **steatopygy** (-top´iji) *n.* [Gr. *pugē*, rump]

steatorrhoea (stiətərē´ə), (*N Am.*) **steatorrhea** *n.* **1** a condition in which there is excessive fat in the faeces. **2** seborrhoea.

steed (stēd) *n.* (*poet.*) a horse, esp. a warhorse. [OE *stēda*, cogn. with STUD[2]]

steel (stēl) *n.* **1** iron combined with carbon in various proportions, remaining malleable at high temperatures and capable of being hardened by cooling. **2** a quality of hardness, toughness etc. in a person. **3** a steel rod with a roughened surface for sharpening knives. **4** a steel strip for stiffening clothing or corsets. **5** (*poet.*) weaponry consisting of a sword or swords. ~*a.* **1** made of steel. **2** like steel in being e.g. hard and cold. ~*v.t.* **1** to harden (one's heart etc. against), to brace (oneself for). **2** to cover, point or face with steel. **steel band** *n.* a type of band (orig. from the Caribbean islands) which plays percussion instruments made from oil drums. **steel-clad** *a.* clad in armour. **steel engraving** *n.* **1** the art of engraving upon steel-coated copper plates. **2** an engraving on a steel plate. **3** an impression taken from this. **steel grey, steel blue** *a., n.* bluish-grey like steel. **steelhead** *n.* a large rainbow trout. **steel-plated** *a.* plated with steel. **steel wool** *n.* fine steel shavings bunched together for cleaning and polishing. **steelwork** *n.* articles or parts of a structure made of steel. **steelworker** *n.* **steelworks** *n.sing. or pl.* a plant where steel is made. **steely** *a.* (*comp.* **steelier,** *superl.* **steeliest**) **1** of steel; like steel in being cold, bright, hard or grey. **2** strong, cold and ruthless or inflexible (*steely determination*). **steeliness** *n.* [OE *style*, cp. Dut. *staal*, G *Stahl*, Icel. *stal*, Dan. *staal*]

steelyard (stēl´yahd) *n.* a balance with unequal arms, the article weighed being hung from the shorter arm and a weight moved along the other till they balance. [STEEL, YARD[1], a rod]

steenbok (stēn´bok, stān´-) *n.* a small S African antelope, *Raphicerus campestris.* [Dut., stone buck, cp. G *Steinbock*]

steep[1] (stēp) *a.* **1** sharply inclined, sloping at a high angle. **2** (of a rise or fall) swift, sudden. **3** (*coll.*) (of a price, demand etc.) excessive, exorbitant, unreasonable. **4** (of a story) difficult to credit, incredible. ~*n.* **1** a steep slope. **2** a precipice. **steepen** *v.t., v.i.* to make or become steep or steeper. **steepish** *a.* **steeply** *adv.* **steepness** *n.* **steepy** *a.* (*comp.* **steepier,** *superl.* **steepiest**) (*poet.*) steep. [OE *stēap*, cp. Icel. *steypthr*, rel. to *steypa*, to overthrow, causal of *stūpa*, to stoop]

steep[2] (stēp) *v.t.* **1** to soak (in liquid); to wet thoroughly. **2** to imbue, to immerse (in a subject, tradition etc.). ~*n.* **1** an act of steeping; the process of being steeped. **2** a liquid for steeping. **steeped in** imbued with, having a thorough knowledge of or familiarity with. **steeper** *n.* [ME *stepen*, Icel. *steypa*, to pour out or cast metals, see STEEP[1]]

steeple (stē´pəl) *n.* a lofty structure rising above the roof of a building, esp. a church tower with a spire. **steeplechase** *n.* **1** a horse race across country (orig. with a visible steeple as the finishing point) in which hedges etc. have to be jumped. **2** a track race over obstacles including hurdles and water jumps. **steeplechaser** *n.* **steeplechasing** *a., n.* **steeple-crowned** *a.* (of a hat) having a tall, tapering crown. **steepled** *a.* **steeplejack** *n.* a person who climbs steeples etc., to do repairs etc. [OE *stypel*, rel. to STEEP[1]]

steer[1] (stiə) *v.t.* **1** to guide (a ship, aeroplane, vehicle etc.) by a rudder, wheel, handle etc. **2** to direct (one's course) in this way. **3** to guide the movement or direction of by suggestion, instruction etc. ~*v.i.* **1** to guide a ship, vehicle etc., or direct one's course by or as by this means. **2** (of a vehicle etc.) to allow itself to be steered (easily etc.). ~*n.* (*N Am.*) steering; guidance. **to steer clear of** to avoid. **steerable** *a.* **steerage** (-rij) *n.* **1** the activity or process of steering. **2** the effect of the helm on a ship. **3** (*esp. Hist.*) the part of a ship, usu. forward and on or below the main deck, allotted to passengers travelling at the lowest rate. **4** the part of the berth-deck on a warship just forward of the ward-room, allotted as quarters to midshipmen etc. **steerage-way** *n.* sufficient motion of a vessel to enable it to answer the helm. **steerer** *n.* **steering** *n.* **steering column** *n.* a shaft in a motor vehicle carrying the steering wheel at the top. **steering committee** *n.* a committee which determines the order of business for a legislative assembly or other body. **steering gear** *n.* the mechanism transmitting motion from the steering wheel of a vehicle, enabling it to be steered. **steering wheel** *n.* the wheel which controls the rudder of a ship, or the stub axles of the front wheels of a vehicle. **steersman** *n.* (*pl.* **steersmen**) a person who steers a vessel, a helmsman. [OE *stēoran*, rel. to *stēor*, rudder (cp. Dut. *sturen, stuur*, G *steuern, Steuer*)]

steer[2] (stiə) *n.* a young male of the ox kind, esp. a castrated bullock. **steerling** *n.* [OE *stēor*, cp. Dut. and G *Stier*, Icel. *stjörr*, also L *taurus*, Gr. *tauros*]

steeve[1] (stēv) *n.* (*Naut.*) the angle of elevation of a bowsprit. ~*v.i.* (of a bowsprit) to have a certain angle of elevation. ~*v.t.* to give (a bowsprit) this angle. [OE *stīfian*, from *stīf*, STIFF]

steeve[2] (stēv) *n.* (*Naut.*) a spar or derrick for stowing cargo. ~*v.t.* to stow with a steeve. [OF *estiver*, L *stīpāre*, to press, rel. to STEEVE[1]]

stegano- (steg´ənō) *comb. form* **1** covered. **2** hidden. **3** watertight. [Gr. *steganos*, covered, from *stegein*, to cover]

steganography (stegənog´rəfi) *n.* the art of secret writing or writing in cipher. **steganographer, steganographist** *n.*

stegosaur (steg´əsaw), **stegosaurus** (-saw´rəs) *n.* a quadrupedal herbivorous dinosaur of the Jurassic period, with a double ridge of bony plates along its back. [Gr. *stego-*, covering, *sauros*, lizard]

stein (stīn) *n.* a large, usu. earthenware beer mug, often with a hinged lid. [G, stone]

steinbock (stīn´bok) *n.* **1** an Alpine ibex. **2** a steenbok. [G *Stein*, stone, *Bock*, buck]

stela (stē´lə) *n.* (*pl.* **stelae** (-lē)) an upright stone slab or column, usu. with sculptured figures and an inscription. [L, from Gr. *stēlē*, a standing block]

stele (stēl, stē´li) *n.* **1** (*Bot.*) the central cylinder in stems and roots of the higher plants, consisting of vascular bundles with pith and pericycle. **2** a stela. **stelar** *a.* [Gr. *stēlē*, a standing block]

stellar (stel´ə) *a.* of or relating to stars. **stellaria** (-leə´riə) *n.* any tufted herb of the genus *Stellaria*, containing the chickweeds or starworts. **stellate** (-āt, -ət), **stellated** (-ātid) *a.* star-shaped, radiating. **stellately** *adv.* **stelliferous** (-lif´-) *a.* **stelliform** (-ifawm) *a.* **stellular** (-ū-), **stellulate** (-lət) *a.* set with or shaped like small stars. [late L *stellāris*, from L *stella*, star]

stellion (stel´yən) *n.* a lizard belonging to the family Agamidae. [L *stellio -opis*, from *stella*, star]

stellular, stellulate STELLAR.

stem[1] (stem) *n.* **1** the stock, stalk, or ascending axis of a tree, shrub, or other plant. **2** the slender stalk or peduncle of a flower, leaf etc. **3** the slender part between the body and foot of a wineglass etc. **4** the tube of a tobacco-pipe. **5** a vertical stroke e.g. in a letter or musical note. **6** the winding-shaft of a watch. **7** the main part of a noun, verb etc., to which inflectional endings etc. are affixed, or that remains unchanged when suffixes etc. are added to form derivatives. **8** the upright piece of timber or iron at the fore end of a ship to which the sides are joined. **9** the stock of a family, a branch of a family. **10** DRILL STEM (under DRILL[1]). *~v.t.* (*pres.p.* **stemming,** *past, p.p.* **stemmed**) **1** to remove the stem or stems of. **2** (of a ship) to make headway or hold its position against (the tide etc.). **from stem to stern** from one end of the ship to the other. **to stem from** to originate in, to spring from. **stem cell** *n.* (*Biol.*) an undifferentiated parent cell from which specialized cells arise. **stemless** *a.* **stemlet** *n.* **stemlike** *a.* **stemmed** *a.* **stemmer** *n.* **stem stitch** *n.* an embroidery stitch used for the stems of flowers etc. **stemware** *n.* (*N Am.*) glasses with stems, wineglasses. **stem-winder** *n.* (*N Am.*) a watch which may be wound by the stem without a key. [OE *stæfn*, *stefn*, *stemn*, cp. Dut. *stam*, trunk, *steven*, prow, Icel. *stafn*, *stamn*, stem of ship, G *Stamm*, trunk, *Steven*, stem of ship]

stem[2] (stem) *v.t.* (*pres.p.* **stemming,** *past, p.p.* **stemmed**) **1** to draw up, to check, to hold back. **2** to dam up (a stream etc.). **3** in skiing, to slow down by pushing the heel of one or both skis outward from the direction of travel. *~n.* in skiing, the process of stemming, used to turn or slow down. **stem turn** *n.* in skiing, a turn executed by stemming with one ski. [Icel. *stemma*, cp. G *stemmen*]

stemma (stem´ə) *n.* (*pl.* **stemmata** (-tə)) **1** pedigree, a family tree. **2** a diagrammatical representation of the lines of descent of the surviving manuscripts of a text. **3** a simple eye, an ocellus. **4** any one of the facets of a compound eye. [Gr., a wreath]

stemmer STEM[1].

stemple (stem´pəl) *n.* a crossbar serving as a step or support in the shaft of a mine. [etym. uncertain, cp. MHG *stempfel*]

stemson (stem´sən) *n.* a curved timber behind a ship's apron, supporting the scarfs. [etym. uncertain]

stench (stench) *n.* a foul or offensive smell. **stench trap** *n.* a trap in a sewer to prevent the escape of noxious gas. [OE *stenc*, from *stincan*, to STINK]

stencil (sten´sil) *n.* **1** (*also* **stencil-plate**) a thin plate of metal or other material out of which patterns have been cut for painting through the spaces on to a surface. **2** the decoration, lettering etc. produced thus. **3** a waxed sheet used for preparing a stencil with a typewriter. *~v.t.* (*pres.p.* **stencilling,** (*N Am.*) **stenciling,** *past, p.p.* **stencilled,** (*N Am.*) **stenciled**) **1** to paint (letters, designs etc.) by means of a stencil. **2** to decorate (a wall etc.) thus. **stenciller,** (*N Am.*) **stenciler** *n.* [prob. from OF *estenceler*, to sparkle, to cover with stars, from *estencele*, spark, as TINSEL]

Sten gun (sten) *n.* a light sub-machine gun. [*S*hepherd and *T*urpin, the designers, and *En*field, as in BREN]

steno (sten´ō) *n.* (*pl.* **stenos**) (*N Am., coll.*) a stenographer.

steno- (sten´ō) *comb. form* contracted. [Gr. *stenos*, narrow]

stenochrome (sten´əkrōm) *n.* a print taken at one impression from several differently-coloured blocks. **stenochromy** (-nok´rəmi) *n.* [Gr. *chrōma*, colour]

stenograph (sten´əgrahf) *n.* **1** a character used in shorthand. **2** a form of typewriter using stenographic characters. **stenographer** (-nog´-), **stenographist** (-nog´-) *n.* a shorthand writer. **stenography** (-nog´-) *n.* the art of writing in shorthand by hand or by machine.

stenosis (stənō´sis) *n.* (*Med.*) **1** constriction of a bodily passage or orifice. **2** constipation. **stenotic** (-not´-) *a.* [Gr. *stenōsis*, a narrowing, from *stenoun*, to make narrow, from *stenos*, narrow]

stenotype (sten´ətīp) *n.* **1** a typewriter-like machine for recording speech as symbols representing phonemes or syllables. **2** a symbol, or the set of symbols, used in such a machine. **stenotypic** (-tip´-) *a.* **stenotypist** *n.* **stenotypy** (-tīpi) *n.*

Stentor (sten´taw), **stentor** *n.* a person with a loud, strong voice. **stentorian** (-taw´ri-) *a.* (of someone's voice) carrying, powerful, loud. [L and Gr. *Stentōr*, herald in Trojan war]

step (step) *v.i.* (*pres.p.* **stepping,** *past, p.p.* **stepped**) **1** to lift and set down a foot or the feet alternately, to walk a short distance in a specified direction. **2** to walk or dance slowly or with dignity. *~v.t.* **1** to go through, perform, or measure by stepping. **2** to insert the foot of (a mast etc.) in a step. *~n.* **1** a single complete movement of one leg in the act of walking, dancing etc. (*Take one step back*). **2** the distance traversed in this. **3** a sequence constituting a unit of movement in dancing. **4** an action or measure taken in a series directed to some end (*take steps to halt the spread of the disease*; *What's the next step?*). **5** the level-topped, block-shaped structure on which the foot is placed in ascending or descending, a single stair or a tread in a flight of stairs. **6** a rung of a ladder, a support for the foot in stepping in or out of a vehicle, a doorstep etc. **7** in climbing, a foothold cut in ice or snow. **8** a footprint. **9** the noise made by a foot in walking etc. **10** the distinctive sound or look of someone's manner of walking. **11** a short distance. **12** (*pl.*) a self-supporting stepladder with fixed or hinged prop; also called *pair of steps.* **13** a degree or grade in progress, rank or precedence. **14** one of a sequence of fixed levels on a payscale etc. **15** (*Mus., N Am.*) the interval of a tone or semitone. **16** (*Naut.*) a socket supporting a frame, etc. for the end of a mast, shaft, etc. **in someone's steps** following the example of someone. **in step 1** in marching, dancing etc., in conformity or time with others. **2** (*coll.*) in agreement (with). **out of step 1** not in step. **2** (*coll.*) not in agreement or harmony (with others). **step by step** gradually, with deliberation, taking one step at a time. **step this way** please come this way, please follow me. **to break step** to cease marching in unison. **to change step** in marching, to adjust one's step so as to make one's other leg mark the main beat. **to keep step** to stay in step. **to mind one's step** to watch one's step. **to step down 1** to resign, retire, relinquish one's position etc. **2** to decrease the voltage of. **to step in 1** to enter a house or room, esp. briefly. **2** to intervene. **3** to stand in as a substitute for someone. **to step into the breach** BREACH. **to step it** (*poet.*) to dance. **to step on it** to hurry, to increase speed. **to step on the gas** GAS. **to step on the juice** JUICE. **to step out 1** to leave a room, house etc. briefly. **2** to be socially active. **3** (*N Am., coll.*) to date, to go out (with). **4** to take longer, faster strides. **to step out of line** to depart from normal or acceptable behaviour. **to step up 1** to advance by one or more stages. **2** to increase the voltage of. **3** to come forward. **to turn one's steps towards** to head for, to walk in the direction of. **to watch one's step** to take care, to guard one's behaviour. **step aerobics** *n.* a form of aerobics in which participants step on to and down from a portable plastic block. **step-by-step** *a.* (of progress etc.) gradual, a little at a time. **step-cut** *a.* (of a gem) cut in straight facets around the centre. **step-down** *a.* (of a transformer) reducing voltage. **step-in** *a.* (of clothes) that can be stepped into without undoing etc. ~*n.* a garment like this. **stepladder** *n.* a ladder with flat treads or rungs. **steplike** *a.* **stepped** *a.* **stepper** *n.* **stepping** *n., a.* **stepping stone** *n.* 1 a raised stone in a stream or swampy place on which one steps in crossing. 2 a means to an end. **step-up** *a.* (of a transformer) increasing the voltage. **stepwise** *adv.* proceeding, or arranged, in steps. [OE *steppan*, cogn. with STAMP, *stæpe*, cp. Dut. *stap*, G *Stapfe*]

step- (step) *comb. form* denoting a family relationship resulting from a remarriage. [OE *steop-*, orphan-]

stepbrother (step´brŭdhə) *n.* a son of a step-parent by a marriage other than with one's mother or father.

stepchild (step´chīld) *n.* (*pl.* **stepchildren** (-childrən)) a child of one's husband or wife by a previous marriage.

stepdad (step´dad) *n.* (*coll.*) a stepfather.

stepdaughter (step´dawtə) *n.* a female stepchild.

stepfamily (step´famili) *n.* (*pl.* **stepfamilies**) a family that contains a stepchild or stepchildren.

stepfather (step´fahdhə) *n.* a male step-parent.

stephanite (stef´ənīt) *n.* a metallic black sulphantimonite of silver. [Archduke *Stephan*, of Austria, d. 1867]

stephanotis (stefənō´tis) *n.* any tropical climbing plant of the genus *Stephanotis*, with fragrant waxy flowers. [Gr. *stephanos*, wreath, *ous*, *ōtos*, ear]

stepmother (step´mŭdhə) *n.* a female step-parent.

stepmum (step´mŭm) *n.* (*coll.*) a stepmother.

step-parent (step´peərənt) *n.* the later husband or wife of a mother or father.

steppe (step) *n.* a vast plain devoid of forest, esp. in Russia and Siberia. [Rus. *stepe*]

stepped, stepping etc. STEP.

stepsister (step´sistə) *n.* a daughter of a step-parent by a marriage other than with one's mother or father.

stepson (step´sŭn) *n.* a male stepchild.

-ster (stə) *suf.* denoting a person belonging to a certain category, or involved in a certain activity, as in *youngster, songster, gamester, gangster.* [OE *-estre*, from Gmc.]

steradian (stərā´diən) *n.* the SI unit of solid angle, that is the angle subtended at the centre of a sphere by an area on its surface numerically equal to the square of the radius. [Gr. *stereos*, solid, RADIAN]

stercoraceous (stœkərā´shəs) *a.* 1 of or relating to, composed of, or like dung. 2 (of an insect) living on dung. **stercoral** (stœ´-) *a.* **stercorary** (stœ´-) *a.* stercoraceous. [L *stercus -coris*, dung, -ACEOUS]

stere (stiə) *n.* a cubic metre (35.147589 cu. ft.) used to measure timber. [F *stère*, as STEREO-]

stereo (ster´iō, stiə´riō) *n.* (*pl.* **stereos**) 1 stereophonic reproduction, stereophony. 2 a piece of stereophonic equipment such as a record player, tape deck etc. 3 stereoscopic photography. 4 a stereoscope. 5 a stereoscopic photograph. 6 (*Print.*) (a) stereotype. ~*a.* 1 stereophonic. 2 stereoscopic.

stereo- (ster´iō, stiə´riō) *comb. form* solid, three-dimensional. [Gr. *stereos*, stiff, solid]

stereobate (ster´iōbāt, stiə´riō-) *n.* a solid substructure or base for a building. [Gr. *batēs*, base, from *bainein*, to go]

stereochemistry (steriōkem´istri, stiəriō-) *n.* chemistry concerned with the three-dimensional disposition of atoms in molecules.

stereochromy (ster´iōkrōmi, stiə´riō-) *n.* wall-painting with pigments mixed or fixed with water-glass.

stereogram (ster´iōgram, stiə´riō-) *n.* 1 a three-dimensional picture or image, a stereograph. 2 a stereo radiogram. **stereograph** (-grahf) *n.* a pair of almost identical images which when viewed together through a stereoscope give a three-dimensional effect. **stereographic** (-graf´-) *a.* **stereographically** *adv.* **stereography** (-og´-) *n.* the art of delineating solid forms on a plane.

stereoisomer (steriōī´sōmə, stiə´riō-) *n.* an isomer of a molecule in which the atoms are linked in the same order but have a different spatial arrangement. **stereoisomerism** *n.*

stereome (ster´iōm, stiə´ri-) *n.* a strengthening tissue in vascular plants composed of thick-walled, elongated prosenchymatous cells.

stereometer (steriom´itə, stiə´ri-) *n.* 1 an instrument for measuring the volume of solid bodies. 2 an instrument for determining the specific gravity of liquids, powders etc. **stereometric** (-met´-), **stereometrical** *a.* **stereometry** (-tri) *n.*

stereophonic (steriōfon´ik, stiəriō-) *a.* denoting a sound-recording or reproduction system involving the use of two or more separate microphones and loudspeakers to split the sound into separate channels to create a spatial effect. **stereophonically** *adv.* **stereophony** (-of´əni) *n.*

stereopsis (steriop´sis, stiəri-) *n.* the perception of depth imparted by the combining of images from both eyes, binocular vision. **stereoptic** *a.* **stereoptics** *n.* the study of stereopsis. **stereopticon** (-op´tikon) *n.* a double magic-lantern for producing dissolving views or for giving a stereoscopic effect. [Gr. *opsis*, vision, image]

stereoscope (ster´iōskōp, stiə´riō-) *n.* a binocular instrument for blending into one two pictures taken from slightly different positions, thus giving an effect of three dimensions. **stereoscopic** (-skop´-), **stereoscopical** *a.* giving the effect of solidity. **stereoscopically** *adv.* **stereoscopy** (-os´-) *n.*

stereospecific (steriōspəsif´ik, stiəriō-) *a.* (*Chem.*) of or relating to a certain stereoisomer of a substance. **stereospecifically** *adv.* **stereospecificity** (-fis´-) *n.*

stereotaxis (steriōtak´sis, stiəriō-), **stereotaxy** (-si) *n.* surgery involving precision-placing of probes in the brain. **stereotaxic, stereotactic** *a.*

stereotropic (steriōtrop´ik, stiəriō-) *a.* (*Bot.*) denoting a tendency to turn in response to contact with a solid object. [Gr. *tropē*, turning, from *trepein*, to turn]

stereotype (ster´iōtīp, stiə´riō-) *n.* 1 a person or thing that conforms to a standardized image. 2 a hackneyed convention, idea etc. 3 a printing-plate cast from a mould taken from movable type. ~*v.t.* 1 to fix or establish in a standard form. 2 to print from a stereotype. 3 to make a stereotype of. **stereotyped** *a.* hackneyed, unoriginal; formulaic, conventional. **stereotyper** *n.* **stereotypic** (-tip´-), **stereotypical** *a.* **stereotypically** *adv.* **stereotypist** *n.* **stereotypy** (-tīpi) *n.* 1 the process of making stereotype plates. 2 meaningless, repetitive action or thought.

steric (ster´ik), **sterical** (-kəl) *a.* (*Chem.*) of or relating to the spatial arrangement of atoms in a molecule. **steric hindrance** *n.* the hindrance of a chemical reaction due to obstruction by reacting atoms.

sterigma (stərig´mə) *n.* (*pl.* **sterigmata** (-mətə)) (*Bot.*) a stalk or support. [Gr. *stērigma stērigmatos*, a support]

sterile (ster´īl) *a.* 1 barren, unfruitful; not producing crops, fruit, young etc. 2 (of arguments etc.) barren of results; unproductive, pointless. 3 containing no living bacteria, microbes etc., sterilized. 4 destitute of ideas or sentiment; mentally unproductive. **sterilely** *adv.* **sterility** (stəril´-) *n.* **sterilize** (-ri-), **sterilise** *v.t.* 1 to rid of living bacteria; to make sterile. 2 to render incapable of procreation. **sterilizable** *a.* **sterilization** (-zā´shən) *n.* **sterilizer** *n.* [OF, from L *sterilis*, rel. to Gr. *stereos*, stiff, G *starr*, rigid]

sterlet (stœ´lit) *n.* a small sturgeon of the Caspian Sea, *Acipenser ruthenus.* [F, from Rus. *sterlyad'*]

sterling (stœ´ling) *a.* 1 of, relating to, or in, British money (*in pounds sterling*). 2 (of coins and precious metals) of standard value, genuine, pure. 3 (of work, efforts etc.) sound, of intrinsic worth, not showy. ~*n.* 1 British (as distinct from foreign) money. 2 genuine British money. **sterling area** *n.* a group of countries that keep their reserves in sterling rather than in gold or dollars. **sterlingness** *n.* **sterling silver** *n.* silver that is 92¼ per cent pure. [perh. from unrecorded OE *steorling*, little star, from *steorra*, star (early Norman pennies having borne a small star)]

stern[1] (stœn) *a.* 1 severe, grim, forbidding, austere. 2 harsh, rigid, strict. 3 ruthless, unyielding, resolute. **sterner sex** *n.* the male sex, men. **sternly** *adv.* **sternness** *n.* [OE *styrne*, perh. rel. to Gr. *stereos*, hard, stiff]

stern[2] (stœn) *n.* 1 the hind part of a ship or boat. 2 any rear part, e.g. the rump or tail of an animal. **stern foremost** (moving) backwards. **stern on** with the stern to the fore. **stern-chase** *n.* a chase in which one vessel follows the other straight behind. **stern-chaser** *n.* a cannon mounted in the stern of a vessel. **sterned** *a.* (*usu. in comb.*, as *flat-sterned*). **stern-fast** *n.* a rope or chain mooring the stern to a wharf etc. **sternmost** *a.* **sternpost** *n.* a timber or iron post forming the central upright of the stern and usu. carrying the rudder. **sternsheets** *n.pl.* the space in a boat between the stern and the aftermost thwart. **sternward** *a.*, *adv.* **sternwards** *adv.* **sternway** *n.* the movement of a ship backwards. **sternwheeler** *n.* a river steamer or lake steamer with a paddle wheel at its stern. [ME *stēorne*, Icel. *stjōrn*, steering, cogn. with STEER[1]]

sternum (stœ´nəm) *n.* (*pl.* **sternums, sterna** (-nə)) the breastbone. **sternal** *a.* of or relating to the sternum. **sternal rib** *n.* a true rib, attached to the breastbone, not floating. **sternalgia** (-nal´jə) *n.* pain in the chest, esp. angina pectoris. **sternebra** (-nəbrə) *n.* (*pl.* **sternebrae** (-brē)) each of the serial segments of the sternum of a vertebrate. [L, from Gr. *sternon*]

sternutation (stœnūtā´shən) *n.* (*Med.*, *or facet.*) the act of sneezing, a sneeze. **sternutative** (-nū´tətiv) *a.* causing one to sneeze. ~*n.* a sternutative substance, such as snuff. **sternutatory** (-nū´tətəri) *a.*, *n.* (*pl.* **sternutatories**) (a) sternutative. [L *sternūtātio*, from *sternūtāre*, freq. of *sternuere*, to sneeze, cp. Gr. *ptarnusthai*]

steroid (stiə´roid, ster´-) *n.* any of a group of compounds of similar chemical structure, including sterols, bile acids and various hormones. **steroidal** *a.* [STEROL, -OID]

sterol (ster´ol, stiə´rol) *n.* any of various solid alcohols, such as cholesterol, ergosterol. [shortened from CHOLESTEROL, ERGOSTEROL etc.]

stertorous (stœ´tərəs) *a.* (of breathing) characterized by deep snoring or snorelike sounds. **stertorously** *adv.* **stertorousness** *n.* [L *stertere*, to snore, -OR, -OUS]

stet (stet) *v.i.* (*pres.p.* **stetting**, *past, p.p.* **stetted**) in proof-reading etc., to let the original stand (cancelling a previous correction), usu. as an instruction 'let it stand'. ~*v.t.* to write 'stet' against. [L, 3rd pers. sing. pres. subj. of *stāre*, to stand]

stethoscope (steth´əskōp) *n.* an instrument used in listening to the movement of the heart and lungs, consisting of a disc for placing against the chest, attached to a tube dividing into two branches with earpieces. **stethoscopic** (-skop´-) *a.* **stethoscopically** *adv.* **stethoscopist** (-thos´-) *n.* **stethoscopy** (-thos´kəpi) *n.* [Gr. *stēthos*, breast, -SCOPE[1]]

stetson (stet´sən) *n.* a broad-brimmed slouch hat. [John *Stetson*, 1830–1906, American hatmaker]

stevedore (stē´vədaw) *n.* a person whose occupation is to load and unload ships. [Sp. *estivador*, from *estivar*, L *stīpāre*, see STEEVE[2]]

stevengraph (stē´vəngrahf) *n.* a brightly coloured woven-silk picture. [T. *Stevens*, 1828–88, whose weaving company made such pictures]

stew[1] (stū) *v.t.*, *v.i.* to cook by boiling slowly or simmering in a closed dish or pan. ~*v.i.* 1 to be stifled or oppressed by a close atmosphere. 2 (*coll.*) to be anxious or agitated; to fret or agonize (over). 3 (of tea) to become bitter from overlong brewing. 4 (*coll.*) to study hard, to sweat or pore (over). ~*n.* 1 a meat dish etc. cooked by stewing. 2 (*coll.*) a state of mental agitation or worry (*get in a stew*). †3 a a hot bath. b (*pl.*) a brothel. **to stew in one's own juice** to suffer alone the consequences of one's folly. **stewed** *a.* 1 (of meat etc.) cooked by stewing. 2 (*coll.*) drunk. **stewpan, stewpot** *n.* a cooking pot for stewing. [ME *stuwen* from *stuwe*, *stue*, OF *estuve*, bath, perh. from EX-, Gr. *tuphos*, steam, perh. rel. to STOVE[1]]

stew[2] (stū) *n.* 1 an artificial oyster bed. 2 a fish pond or tank for keeping fish alive for the table. [ME *stewe* (cp. LG *stau*, dam, *stauen*, to dam), rel. to STOW]

steward (stū´əd) *n.* 1 a passengers' attendant on a ship, aircraft or train, in charge of provisions, accommodation etc. 2 any one of the officials superintending a ball, show, public meeting etc. 3 a shop steward. 4 a person employed to manage the property or affairs of another person, esp. the paid manager of a large estate or household. 5 a person in charge of provisions etc., in a college, club etc. 6 the title of certain officers of state, or of the royal household. **stewardess** (-dis) *n.* a female steward, esp. on an aircraft. **stewardship** *n.* the office of a steward. [OE *stigweard* (STY[1], WARD)]

stg. *abbr.* sterling.

Sth. *abbr.* South.

sthenic (sthen´ik) *a.* 1 (*Med.*) having a strong athletic physique. 2 (*Psych.*) exhibiting an extreme degree of energy, vigour and aggressiveness. [Gr. *sthenos*, strength, -IC]

stibium (stib´iəm) *n.* (*dated*) antimony. **stibial** *a.* **stibialism** *n.* antimonial poisoning. **stibnite** (-nīt) *n.* a grey mineral consisting of antimony sulphide. [L, from Gr. *stibi*]

stich (stik) *n.* 1 a metrical line, a verse. 2 a unit of prose of comparable length, e.g. a line of the Bible, esp. one of the rhythmic lines exhibiting the parallelism of the poetic books. **stichic** *a.* [Gr. *stichos*]

stichomancy (stik´əmansi) *n.* divination by passages taken at random in a book.

stichomythia (stikəmith´iə), **stichomythy** (-kom´ithi) *n.* in ancient Greek drama, dialogue in which the interlocutors speak alternate lines. [Gr. *stichomuthia*, from *stichos*, line, *muthos*, speech]

stick[1] (stik) *n.* 1 a shoot or branch of a tree or shrub broken or cut off. 2 a slender piece of wood or other material used, esp. specially trimmed and shaped, as a rod, staff, walking cane etc. 3 (*often in comb.*) any of various long slender implements with a specialized use, e.g. a *candlestick, drumstick, cocktail stick, fiddlestick, broomstick, matchstick*, or for hitting the ball with in games, e.g. a *hockey stick, polo stick, lacrosse stick*. 4 (*pl.*) in hockey, the offence of raising the stick above the shoulder. 5 a slender piece of something, e.g. *a stick of celery, rhubarb, rock*. 6 a conductor's baton. 7 the gear lever of a motor vehicle or the control rod of an aircraft. 8 a number of bombs or paratroops dropped in succession. 9 (*Naut.*) a mast, a spar. 10 (*coll.*) blame, hostile criticism (*got a lot of stick for his opinions*). 11 (*coll.*) a piece of wood representing an item of furniture etc. (*one or two sticks of furniture*). 12 a person, esp. someone elderly and old-fashioned. 13 (*coll.*) (**the sticks**) areas remote from the city, esp. as rustic and unsophisticated, or inaccessible. 14 (*pl.*, *Austral.*, *coll.*) goalposts. ~*v.t.* (*past, p.p.* **sticked**) to provide (a plant) with sticks for support. **to up sticks** UP. **wrong end of**

the stick WRONG. **stick insect** *n.* an insect belonging to the Phasmidae, which resembles dry twigs. **stickless** *a.* **sticklike** *a.* [OE *sticca*, peg, rel. to *stician*]

stick[2] (stik) *v.t.* (*past, p.p.* **stuck** (stŭk)) **1** to thrust the point of (in, into, through etc.). **2** to pierce, to stab. **3** to fix or insert (in, into) (*stuck posts into the ground*). **4** to fix or impale on or as on, by or as by, a point. **5** to thrust (out, up, through etc.). **6** to set with pointed objects (*an orange stuck with cloves*). **7** to cause to adhere (*sticking stamps on envelopes; stuck a poster on the wall*). **8** (*coll.*) to put (something somewhere) (*Stick those boxes in the spare room*). **9** (*coll.*) to tolerate, endure. **10** (*sl.*) to try to put the blame for (something on someone) (*You can't stick that one on me*). *~v.i.* **1** to be inserted or thrust, to poke (into). **2** to protrude, project, or stand (up, out etc.). **3** to become fixed, to adhere (*These stamps don't stick very well*). **4** to remain attached (to) (*The burrs stuck to her clothing*). **5** to be inseparable, to be constant (to), to stay (with) (*Stick with me; She stuck to him loyally*). **6** to endure or persist (*The image stuck in her mind*). **7** to stay, remain (*I'll stick here for a while*). **8** to persist, to persevere (at) (*I stuck at that job for four years*). **9** to be stopped, hindered, or checked (*We got so far, then stuck*). **10** to have scruples or misgivings, to hesitate (at). **stick 'em up!** (*coll.*) hands up! **to be stuck** **1** to be unable to progress further. **2** to be confined (somewhere) (*I don't want to be stuck in the house all day*). **to be stuck for** to lack, to need (*I'm a bit stuck for cash*). **to be stuck on** (*coll.*) to be very keen on, or infatuated with. **to be stuck with** (*coll.*) to have no choice but to have, to be landed with (*I'm stuck with a husband who won't dance*). **to get stuck in(to)** GET[1]. **to stick around** (*coll.*) to remain in the vicinity. **to stick at it** to persevere. **to stick at nothing** not to be deterred or feel scruples. **to stick by** **1** to stay close to. **2** to remain faithful to, to support. **to stick fast** **1** to adhere strongly. **2** to be fixed or trapped immovably. **to stick in one's gizzard** GIZZARD. **to stick in one's throat** to be repugnant to one, to be against one's principles. **to stick it on** **1** (*coll.*) to overcharge. **2** (*coll.*) to exaggerate. **to stick it out** to put up with something as long as is demanded of one. **to stick one's bib in** BIB. **to stick one's chin out** to be resolute, to show determination. **to stick one's neck out** **1** (*coll.*) to invite trouble. **2** (*coll.*) to take a risk. **to stick out** **1** to (cause to) protrude. **2** to be conspicuous or obvious. **to stick out a mile** to be only too obvious. **to stick out for** to demand, to insist upon. **to stick out like a sore thumb** SORE. **to stick pigs** to go in for the sport of pigsticking. **to stick the boot in** BOOT[1]. **to stick together** to remain loyal to one another. **to stick to it** to persevere. **to stick to one's guns** GUN. **to stick to one's last** LAST[1]. **to stick to someone's fingers** (*coll.*) (of money) to be embezzled by someone. **to stick up** **1** to put up, to erect. **2** to stand up, to be prominent. **3** to paste or post up. **4** (*coll.*) to hold up; to rob at gunpoint. **to stick up for** to take the part of, to defend. **to stick up to** to stand up against, to resist. **stickability** (-bil´-) *n.* (*coll.*) perseverance, staying power. **sticker** *n.* **1** an adhesive label or poster. **2** a person or thing that sticks. **3** a conscientious, persevering person. **4** an importunate person. **5** a knife used for piercing; a butcher's knife. **6** in an organ, a rod connecting two reciprocating levers. **sticking** *n.*, *a.* **sticking place, sticking point** *n.* **1** the place where a screw etc., becomes fixed or jammed. **2** the point at which difficulties arise, and prevent progress. **sticking plaster** *n.* an adhesive plaster for wounds etc. **stick-in-the-mud** *a.* dull, slow, unprogressive. *~n.* an unenterprising person. **stickpin** *n.* (*N Am.*) a tiepin. **stick-up** *n.* (*sl.*) an armed robbery. **stickweed** *n.* **sticky** *a.* (*comp.* **stickier,** *superl.* **stickiest**) **1** tending to stick, adhesive. **2** viscous, glutinous. **3** (*coll.*) difficult, painful. **on a sticky wicket** WICKET. **stickily** *adv.* **stickiness** *n.* **stickybeak** *n.* (*Austral., New Zeal., sl.*) an inquisitive person, a nosy parker. *~v.i.* to be inquisitive, to pry. **sticky end** *n.* (*coll.*) a disagreeable end or death. **sticky-fingered** *a.* (*coll.*) given to stealing. **sticky wicket** *n.* **1** a damp cricket pitch which is difficult to bat on. **2** (*coll.*) a difficult situation. **stuck-up** *a.* puffed up, conceited, giving oneself airs. [ME *steken*, to pierce (cp. LG *steken*, G *stechen*, also Gr. *stizein*, L *instīgāre*, to INSTIGATE), coalescing with ME *stikien*, OE *stician*, to stick, to be fixed, to prick etc.]

stickle (stik´əl) *v.i.* **1** to contend pertinaciously (for some trifle). **2** †to interfere, to take part with one side or the other. **stickler** *n.* a person who argues contentiously (for something, esp. a nice point of style, punctuation or etiquette). [prob. from ME *stightlen*, to be umpire, freq. from OE *stihtan*, to arrange, to regulate]

stickleback (stik´əlbak) *n.* a small spiny-backed, freshwater fish, esp. *Gasterosteus aculeatus.* [OE *sticel*, prickle, from *stician*, to STICK[1]]

stickler STICKLE.

sticky STICK[2].

stiff (stif) *a.* **1** rigid, not easily bent or moved. **2** not pliant, not flexible, not yielding, not working freely. **3** hard to deal with or accomplish; difficult. **4** (of a person or their manner) constrained, not easy, not graceful, awkward, formal, precise, affected. **5** obstinate, stubborn, firm, persistent (*stiff resistance*). **6** severe, harsh, strong (*a stiff fine; encountered a stiff breeze*). **7** (of muscles or limbs) painful to use because of immediately previous, esp. unwonted, exercise. **8** (*used predic., coll.*) to an intense degree (*worried stiff; bored stiff; frozen stiff*). **9** (of liquor) strong. **10** (of prices) high. **11** (of a mixture etc.) not fluid, thick and tenacious, viscous. *~n.* (*sl.*) **1** a corpse. **2** a racehorse that is sure to lose. **3** a bill of exchange, a negotiable paper. **4** a forged paper. **stiff with** (*coll.*) packed with, full of (*stiff with holidaymakers*). **stiffen** *v.t., v.i.* to make or become stiff or stiffer. **stiffener** *n.* **1** something which stiffens. **2** (*coll.*) a strong alcoholic drink. **stiffening** *n.* **stiffish** *a.* **stiffly** *adv.* **stiff neck** *n.* rheumatism affecting the muscles of the neck. **stiff-necked** *a.* stubborn, self-willed. **stiff-neckedness** *n.* **stiffness** *n.* **stiff upper lip** *n.* fortitude in adversity (*keep a stiff upper lip*). [OE *stīf*, cp. Dut. *stijf*, Dan. *stiv*, Swed. *styf*, cp. STEEVE[2]]

stifle[1] (stī´fəl) *v.t., v.i.* to smother, to suffocate; to kill or die by suffocation (*nearly stifled by the heat; We'll stifle if we stay indoors*). *~v.t.* **1** to suppress (*I had to stifle a yawn*). **2** to stamp out, quash, extinguish. **stifler** *n.* **stifling** *a.* (of heat, the atmosphere etc.) choking, suffocating. **stiflingly** *adv.* [Icel. *stīfla*, freq. of *stiva*, to stiffen, rel. to STIFF]

stifle[2] (stī´fəl) *n.* **1** the stifle-joint. **2** a disease affecting this or the stifle-bone. **stifle-bone** *n.* a horse's knee-pan or patella. **stifle-joint** *n.* the joint of a horse's hind leg between the femur and tibia. [perh. from STIFF]

stigma (stig´mə) *n.* (*pl.* **stigmas, stigmata** (-mətə, -mah´tə)) **1** a mark of discredit or infamy. **2** a distinguishing mark (of), a typical characteristic (of). **3** (*Bot.*) the part of a pistil of a flower that receives the pollen. **4** (*pl.*) in Christian dogma, the marks left on Christ's body from the process of crucifixion, believed also to have been divinely imprinted on the body of St Francis of Assisi and other saintly people. **5** a natural mark on the skin; a pore. **6** a mark or spot on a butterfly's wing. **7** a visible sign of a disease. **8** an insect's spiracle. **9** a mark branded on to the skin (e.g. of a slave or criminal). **stigmatic** (-mat´-) *a.* **1** of or relating to stigmas. **2** ANASTIGMATIC (under ANASTIGMAT). *~n.* a person marked with stigmata like those of Christ. **stigmatically** *adv.* **stigmatiferous** (-tif´-) *a.* (*Bot.*) having stigmas. **stigmatism** *n.* **1** the condition of a stigmatic. **2** anastigmatism. **stigmatist** *n.* a stigmatic. **stigmatize** (stig´mətīz), **stigmatise** *v.t.* **1** to represent (as something disgraceful or unworthy). **2** to produce stigmata on. **stigmatization** (-zāˊshən) *n.* **stigmatose** (-tōs) *a.* (*Bot.*) stigma-bearing. [L, from Gr. *stigma stigmatos*, a branded mark]

stilb (stilb) *n.* (*Physics*) a unit of luminance equivalent to one candela per square centimetre. **stilbene** (stilˊbēn) *n.* (*Chem.*) a hydrocarbon used in dye manufacture, that forms phosphorescent crystals. **stilboestrol** (stilbēˊstrəl), (*N Am.*) **stilbestrol** *n.* a synthetic oestrogen produced from stilbene. [Gr. *stilbein*, to shine]

stilbite (stilˊbīt) *n.* a vitreous silicate of the zeolite group. [Gr. *stilbein*, to shine]

stile[1] (stīl) *n.* a series of steps or other contrivance by which one may get over a wall etc. [OE *stigel*, from *stīgan*, to climb]

Usage note See note under STYLE.

stile[2] (stīl) *n.* a vertical piece in the frame of a panelled door or wainscot, or in a window frame. [prob. from Dut. *stijl*, doorpost, pillar]

Usage note See note under STYLE.

stiletto (stiletˊō) *n.* (*pl.* **stilettos**) **1** a small dagger. **2** a pointed instrument for making eyelet-holes etc. **3** a stiletto heel. **4** a shoe with a stiletto heel. *~v.t.* (*3rd pers. sing. pres.* **stilettoes,** *pres.p.* **stilettoing,** *past, p.p.* **stilettoed**) to stab with a stiletto. **stiletto heel** *n.* a high, very tapered heel for a woman's shoe. [It., dim. of *stilo*, L *stīlus*, STYLE]

still[1] (stil) *a., adv.* **1** at rest, motionless. **2** (of sea, weather, air etc.) quiet, calm. **3** (of e.g. an audience) silent, noiseless, hushed. **4** (of drinks) not effervescent or sparkling. *~n.* **1** stillness, calm, quiet (*in the still of the evening*). **2** an ordinary photograph, or one from a single frame of a cinema film for record or publicity purposes. *~adv.* **1** without moving. **2** as previously, without stopping or altering (*still jogs several miles a day; They're still in love*). **3** even to this or that time, yet (*It's still dark; happened when I was still a child*). **4** nevertheless, all the same, in spite of that (*I'm still unconvinced; Still, there are advantages*). *~v.t.* **1** to quiet, to calm. **2** to silence. **3** to appease. *~†v.i.* to grow calm. **still and all** (*coll.*) nevertheless, in spite of that. **stillbirth** *n.* **1** the birth of a dead child. **2** a child born dead. **stillborn** *a.* **still life** *n.* (*pl.* **still lifes**) the representation of fruit, flowers and other inanimate objects in painting; a painting of this kind. **stillness** *n.* **still waters** *n.pl.* the calm or inscrutable exterior that is supposed to conceal an active mind (in reference to the proverb 'still waters run deep'). **stilly**[1] (stilˊli) *adv.* **†stilly**[2] (stilˊi) *a.* (*poet.*) calm, still. [OE *stille*, (cp. Dut. *stil*, G *still*, Dan. *stille*), rel. to *stillan*, to rest, cogn. with *stellan*, to place]

still[2] (stil) *n.* a vessel or apparatus employed in distillation, esp. of spirits, consisting of a boiler, a tubular condenser or worm enclosed in a refrigerator, and a receiver. *~v.t.* to distil. **stilliform** (-fawm) *a.* drop-shaped. **still room** *n.* **1** a room for distilling. **2** a store-room for liquors, preserves etc. [L *stillāre*, to drip; sometimes short for DISTIL]

stillage (stilˊij) *n.* a frame, stool, bench etc., for placing things on for draining, waiting to be packed up etc. [cp. STILLING]

stilliform STILL[2].

stilling (stilˊing) *n.* a stand for a cask. [cp. LG *stelling*, G *Stellung*, from *stellen*, to place, cp. STILL[1]]

Stillson (stilˊsən), **Stillson wrench** *n.* a powerful wrench whose jaws tighten with increased pressure. [D. C. *Stillson*, 1830–99, inventor]

stilt (stilt) *n.* **1** a pole having a rest for the foot, used in pairs, to raise a person above the ground in walking. **2** any of a number of tall supports or columns for raising a building above the ground. **3** a long-legged three-toed wading bird related to the plover. **4** a three-legged support for pottery in a kiln. **on stilts 1** mounted on stilts. **2** stilted, bombastic, stiltedly, bombastically. **stilt-bird, stilt-plover** *n.* the common stilt, *Himantopus candidus*. **stilted** *a.* **1** raised on or as if on stilts. **2** (of literary style etc.) bombastic, inflated. **3** (of an arch) springing from vertical masonry set on the imposts. **stiltedly** *adv.* **stiltedness** *n.* [ME *stilte*, Swed. *stylta* (cp. Dut. *stelt*, G *Stelze*), prob. cogn. with OHG *stellan*, to place]

Stilton® (stilˊtən) *n.* a rich white or blue veined cheese orig. sold at Stilton, in Cambridgeshire.

stimulus (stimˊūləs) *n.* (*pl.* **stimuli** (-lī)) **1** something that stimulates one to activity, or energizes one; an incitement, a spur. **2** something that excites reaction in a living organism. **3** (*Med.*) a stimulant. **stimulant** *a.* **1** serving to stimulate. **2** producing a quickly diffused and transient increase in physiological activity. *~n.* something that stimulates, such as a drug or alcoholic drink. **stimulate** *v.t.* **1** to rouse to action or greater exertion. **2** to spur on, to incite. **3** to excite (organic action). *~v.i.* to act as a stimulus. **stimulating** *a.* **stimulatingly** *adv.* **stimulation** (-lāˊshən) *n.* **stimulative** (-lətiv) *a.* **stimulator** *n.* **stimulatory** (-lətəri) *a.* [L *stimulus*, a goad or incentive]

Usage note The meanings of the nouns *stimulus* and *stimulant* overlap, but *stimulant* is usual for something that stimulates physiological activity (as alcohol or drugs), and *stimulus* for an incitement or incentive.

stimy STYMIE.

sting (sting) *n.* **1** a sharp-pointed defensive or offensive organ, often conveying poison, with which certain insects, scorpions and plants are armed. **2** the act of stinging. **3** the wound or pain so caused. **4** any acute pain, ache, smart, stimulus etc. **5** pungent or forceful quality. **6** (*sl.*) a swindle. *~v.t.* (*past, p.p.* **stung** (stŭng)) **1** to pierce or wound with a sting. **2** to cause acute physical or mental pain to (*was stung by his criticism*). **3** to goad (into). **4** (*coll.*) to cheat, to overcharge. *~v.i.* **1** to have or use a sting (*Do those insects sting?*). **2** to have an acute and smarting pain. **stingaree** (-ərē, -ərēˊ) *n.* a stingray. **sting-bull, sting-fish** *n.* the greater weaver, *Trachinus draco*. **stinger** *n.* **1** something that stings, such as a nettle, insect, snake etc. **2** a smarting blow. **stinging** *a.* **stingingly** *adv.* **stinging nettle** *n.* a nettle, *Urtica dioica*, covered with stinging hairs. **sting in the tail** *n.* an unexpected or ironic twist to finish with. **stingless** *a.* **stingray** *n.* a tropical ray with a venomous spine on its tail. [OE *stingan* (cp. Icel. and Swed. *stinga*, Dan. *stinge*), perh. rel. to STICK[1]]

stingily, stinginess STINGY.

stingo (stingˊgō) *n.* (*sl.*) strong ale. [from STING]

stingy (stinˊji) *a.* (*comp.* **stingier,** *superl.* **stingiest**) tight-fisted, mean, parsimonious, niggardly. **stingily** *adv.* **stinginess** *n.* [STING, -Y]

stink (stingk) *v.i.* (*past* **stank** (stangk), **stunk** (stŭngk), *p.p.* **stunk**) **1** to emit a strong, offensive smell. **2** (*coll.*) to have an evil reputation. **3** (*coll.*) to smack of disreputable dealings; to be scandalous. *~v.t.* to drive (someone out of a place) by a stink. *~n.* **1** a strong, offensive smell, a stench. **2** (*sl.*) a disagreeable exposure, a scandal, a row. **like stink** (*sl.*) intensely, very hard. **to raise a stink 1** (*sl.*) to complain. **2** (*sl.*) to stir up trouble, esp. adverse publicity. **to stink out 1** to drive out by creating an offensive smell. **2** to cause (a room etc.) to stink. **stink bomb** *n.* a small glass sphere which releases a foul-smelling liquid when broken. **stinker** *n.* **1** a stinking person, animal etc. **2** (*sl.*) an unpleasant person or thing. **3** (*sl.*) a difficult task or problem. **4** (*sl.*) a strongly-worded letter of disapproval or objection. **stinkhorn** *n.* an evil-smelling fungus, esp. *Phallus impudicus*. **stinking** *a.* **1** emitting an offensive smell. **2** (*coll.*) offensive, repulsive, objectionable. **3** (*coll.*)

extremely drunk. ~*adv.* (*coll.*) extremely, very (*They're stinking rich*). **stinking badger** *n.* the teledu. **stinking iris** *n.* GLADDON. **stinkingly** *adv.* **stinking mayweed** *n.* the odorous plant *Anthemis cotula.* **stinko** (sing´kō) *a.* (*sl.*) drunk. **stinkpot** *n.* (*sl.*) **1** a term of abuse for a person. **2** a vessel or vehicle emitting foul fumes. **stinkstone** *n.* a limestone or other rock emitting a fetid odour when struck. **stink-trap** *n.* a stench trap. **stinkweed** *n.* wall rocket. **stinkwood** *n.* a tree, *Ocotea bulleta,* native to Africa, with foul-smelling timber. **stinky** *a.* (*comp.* **stinkier,** *superl.* **stinkiest**). [OE *stincan,* cp. Dut., G *stinken,* Dan. *stinke,* Swed. *stinka*]

Usage note In standard English, the preferred past tense of *stink* is *stank,* not *stunk.*

stint (stint) *v.t.* **1** to give or allow (someone) money, food etc. scantily or grudgingly. **2** to supply (food etc.) scantily or grudgingly. ~*v.i.* **1** to be too sparing or parsimonious (of a certain commodity). **2** †to cease, to leave off. ~*n.* **1** limit, bound, restriction (*gave her services without stint*). **2** an allotted amount, quantity, turn of work etc. (*when you've done your stint*). **3** a small sandpiper, esp. the dunlin. **stintingly** *adv.* **stintless** *a.* **1** unstinted. **2** abundant. [OE *styntan,* from *stunt,* dull, witless, cp. Icel. *stytta,* to shorten, from *stuttr,* short]

stipe (stīp) *n.* a stalk, stem or stemlike support. **stipes** (-pēz) *n.* (*pl.* **stipites** (stip´itēz)) a stipe. **stipiform** (-fawm), **stipitate** (-tāt), **stipitiform** (-tifawm) *a.* [F, from L *stīpes -pitis*]

stipel (stī´pəl) *n.* (*Bot.*) a secondary stipule at the base of a compound leaf. **stipellate** *a.* [F *stipelle,* from mod. L *stipellus,* dim. of *stipula,* straw]

stipend (stī´pend) *n.* a periodical payment for services rendered, a salary, esp. of a member of the clergy. **stipendiary** (-pen´-) *a.* performing services for or receiving a stipend. ~*n.* (*pl.* **stipendiaries**) a person receiving a stipend, esp. a paid magistrate. **stipendiary magistrate** *n.* a magistrate who receives a salary. [L *stipendium* (*stīps, stipis,* wages, gift in small coin, *pendere,* to pay)]

stipes, stipiform etc. STIPE.

stipple (stip´əl) *v.t.* **1** to engrave, paint or draw by means of dots or light dabs instead of lines etc. **2** to roughen the surface of (wall paint, cement etc.). ~*v.i.* to use dots or light dabs in engraving, painting or drawing. ~*n.* **1** the technique or work of stippling. **2** the effect produced by stippling. **stippler** *n.* **stippling** *n.* [Dut. *stippelen,* from *stippel,* dim. of *stip,* point, cp. G *Stift,* pin]

stipular STIPULE.

stipulate[1] (stip´ūlāt) *v.t.* to lay down or specify as an essential condition to an agreement, contract or bargain. ~*v.i.* **1** to make a specific demand (for). **2** to settle terms. **stipulated** *a.* laid down as a condition. **stipulation** (-lā´shən) *n.* **stipulator** *n.* [L *stipulātus,* p.p. of *stipulārī,* from OL *stipulus,* firm, fast, cogn. with *stīpes,* post]

stipulate[2] STIPULE.

stipule (stip´ūl) *n.* a small leaflike appendage, usu. in pairs at the base of a petiole. **stipular** *a.* **stipulate**[2] (-lət) *a.* having stipules. [L *stipula,* dim. of *stipes,* STIPE]

stir[1] (stœ) *v.t.* (*pres.p.* **stirring,** *past, p.p.* **stirred**) **1** to move a spoon etc. round and round in (a liquid or liquid mixture) to blend the ingredients. **2** to cause to move, to agitate, to disturb. **3** to move vigorously, to bestir (oneself etc.). **4** to rouse (up), to excite, to animate, to inflame (*stirred their imaginations; were stirred to fury*). ~*v.i.* **1** to move, to be in motion, not to be still. **2** to wake up, or get up after sleep. **3** (*esp. with neg.*) to go (out of the house etc.). **4** (*coll.*) to cause trouble by gossip or subversive innuendo. ~*n.* **1** an act of stirring (*give it another stir*). **2** agitation, commotion, bustle, excitement (*caused a stir in the community*). **3** (*with neg.*) a movement (*not a stir*). **not to stir a finger** not to lift a finger, to make no effort or attempt. **to stir in** to mix (an ingredient) into a mixture by stirring. **to stir one's stumps** (*coll.*) to become active, to get going. **to stir the blood** to rouse one emotionally, to evoke strong feelings, e.g. of patriotism. **to stir up 1** to mix by stirring vigorously. **2** to incite (trouble, rebellion etc.). **3** to agitate, to excite, to arouse. **to stir up a hornets' nest** HORNET. **stir-fry** *v.t.* (*3rd pers. sing. pres.* **stir-fries,** *pres.p.* **stir-frying,** *past, p.p.* **stir-fried**) to cook by the Chinese method of frying in hot oil while stirring and tossing. ~*n.* (*pl.* **stir-fries**) a stir-fried meal or dish. **stir-frying** *n.* **stirless** *a.* **stirrer** *n.* **1** a person or thing that stirs. **2** (*coll.*) a person who likes fomenting ill feeling, a troublemaker. **stirring** *a.* **1** moving. **2** animating, rousing, exciting, stimulating. ~*n.* (*pl.*) initial signs or indications of something (*the first stirrings of a renaissance; felt the stirrings of an unfamiliar emotion*). **stirringly** *adv.* [OE *styrian,* cp. Dut. *storen,* G *stören,* Icel. *styrr,* a stir]

stir[2] (stœ) *n.* (*sl.*) prison. **stir-crazy** *a.* (*sl.*) mentally unhinged as a result of prolonged imprisonment or confinement. [etym. uncertain]

stirk (stœk) *n.* (*dial.*) a yearling ox or cow. [OE *styric,* dim. of *stēor,* STEER[2]]

stirps (stœps) *n.* (*pl.* **stirpes** (-pēz)) **1** (*Zool.*) a classificatory group. **2** (*Law*) a branch of a family; the progenitor of a branch of a family. **stirpiculture** (-pikŭlchə) *n.* selective breeding, eugenics. [L]

stirrup (stir´əp) *n.* **1** a horse rider's foot support, usu. consisting of an iron loop suspended from the saddle by a strap. **2** the stapes or stirrup bone. **3** (*Naut.*) a rope with an eye for carrying a footrope. **stirrup bone** *n.* the stapes. **stirrup cup** *n.* a parting cup, orig. given to someone about to leave on horseback. **stirrup iron** *n.* the iron loop of a stirrup. **stirrup leather** *n.* the leather strap suspending the stirrup from the saddle. **stirrup pump** *n.* a portable hand pump with a length of hose, to be worked by one or two people, for extinguishing small fires. **stirrup strap** *n.* a stirrup leather. [OE *stīrāp* (*stīgan,* to climb, *rāp,* ROPE)]

stitch (stich) *n.* **1** a single pass of the needle in sewing. **2** a single turn of the wool or thread round a needle in knitting, crocheting etc. **3** the link of thread, wool etc., thus inserted. **4** a sequence of moves in knitting or sewing that produces a distinctive pattern (*Can you teach me cable stitch?*). **5** (*with neg.*) the least item of clothing (*emerged without a stitch on*). **6** a sharp intense pain in the side, brought on by running or other exercise. ~*v.t., v.i.* to sew. **in stitches** helpless with laughter. **to drop a stitch** DROP. **to stitch up 1** to sew together or mend. **2** (*sl.*) to incriminate by informing on or concocting evidence against. **stitcher** *n.* **stitchery** *n.* **stitch in time** *n.* a timely repair or remedy. **stitchless** *a.* **stitch-up** *n.* (*sl.*) **1** an act of incriminating someone for a crime. **2** an act of securing a desirable outcome for oneself, esp. unfairly. **stitchwort** *n.* any plant of the genus *Stellaria,* esp. *Stellaria holostea,* with starry white flowers, common in hedges. [OE *stice,* from *stician,* see STICK[1] (cp. *stich* and *stechen*)]

stiver (stī´və) *n.* **1** (*Hist.*) any very small coin. **2** (*with neg.*) the least possible bit (*couldn't care a stiver*). [Dut. *stuiver,* a former Dutch coin]

stoa (stō´ə) *n.* (*pl.* **stoas, stoae** (-ē)) **1** in ancient Greek architecture, a portico or colonnade. **2** (*usu.* **the Stoa**) the Stoic school of philosophy. [Gr.]

stoat (stōt) *n.* **1** the ermine, *Mustela erminea,* esp. in its brownish summer coat. **2** a weasel, ferret etc. [ME *stot,* male animal, stoat, cp. Icel. *stūtr,* Swed., Norw. *stut,* bull, Dut. *stooten,* G *stossen,* to push]

stob (stob) *n.* **1** in coal mining, a steel wedge used for bringing down coal. **2** (*Sc.*) a small post, a stake, a stump, a splinter. [var. of STUB]

stochastic (stəkas'tik) *a.* 1 resulting from a randomly distributed set of probabilities. 2 (of a process) involving a sequence of independent random variables. 3 determined by the laws of probability. **stochastically** *adv.* [Gr. *stochastikos*, skilful in aiming]

stock (stok) *n.* 1 the aggregate of goods ready for sale or distribution. 2 a supply of anything, available for use (*the stock of data*). 3 equipment or raw material for use in the course of business etc. (*new rolling stock; run down stationery stocks*). 4 the beasts, or livestock, on a farm, or implements of husbandry and produce. 5 livestock where fattened for slaughter, fatstock. 6 the capital of a corporate company divided into shares entitling the holders to a proportion of the profits. 7 (*pl.*) the shares of such capital. 8 money lent to a government represented by certificates entitling the holders to fixed interest; the right to receive this interest. 9 (*N Am.*) a stock company, a repertory company, or its repertoire. 10 one's reputation or standing (*My stock is low enough as it is*). 11 any cruciferous plant of the genus *Matthiola* or *Malcolmia*, esp. the stock-gillyflower. 12 a plant that receives a graft. 13 the trunk or main stem of a tree or other plant. 14 a a family, a breed, a line of descent (*came of Manx stock*). b any analogous system of branches emerging from a main stem, such as a distinct group of languages. 15 liquor from boiled meat, bones etc., used as a basis for soup, sauce, gravy etc. 16 (*pl.*) a frame of timber with holes in which the ankles, and sometimes also the wrists, of petty offenders were formerly confined as a punishment. 17 (*pl.*) a timber framework on which a vessel rests during building. 18 the principal supporting or holding part of anything, the handle, block, base, body etc. 19 a headstock or tailstock. 20 a band of silk, leather etc., worn as a cravat e.g. by horse-riders. 21 solid brick pressed in a mould. ~*a.* 1 kept in stock (*stock sizes*). 2 habitually used, standing, permanent (*the stock reply*). ~*v.t.* 1 to provide (e.g. shops) with goods, (farms) with livestock etc. 2 to keep (goods) in stock. 3 to fit with a handle, butt etc. ~*v.i.* 1 to take in supplies. 2 (of a plant) to put out new shoots, to tiller. **in stock** available to be sold immediately. **on the stocks** in preparation or construction. **out of stock** not available for sale, not in stock. **to stock up** to take in supplies, lay in stock. **to take stock** 1 to make an inventory of goods etc. on hand. 2 to survey one's position, prospects etc. 3 to examine, to form an estimate (of a person, etc.). **to take stock in** to attach importance to. **stock-book** *n.* a book recording quantities of goods received and disposed of. **stockbreeder** *n.* a farmer who raises livestock. **stockbreeding** *n.* **stockbroker** *n.* a person engaged in the purchase and sale of stocks on commission. **stockbrokerage** *n.* **stockbroker belt** *n.* (*coll., usu. derog.*) the prosperous commuter area around London. **stockbroking** *n.* **stock car** *n.* 1 a production (saloon) car modified for racing. 2 (*N Am.*) a railway truck for transporting livestock. **stock company** *n.* (*pl.* **stock companies**) (*N Am.*) a repertory company. **stock dove** *n.* a European wild pigeon, *Columba oenas*, smaller and darker than the ring-dove. **stocker** *n.* **Stock Exchange** *n.* 1 (*also* **stock exchange**) the place where stocks or shares are publicly bought and sold. 2 the dealers who work there. **stock-farmer** *n.* a farmer who raises livestock. **stock-gillyflower** *n.* a fragrant, bright-flowered herbaceous plant, *Matthiola incana*. **stockholder** *n.* 1 a proprietor of stock in the public funds or shares in a stock company. 2 (*Austral.*) a grazier. **stockholding** *n.* **stock-in-trade** *n.* 1 goods, tools and other requisites of a trade etc. 2 resources, capabilities. 3 a person's range of skills or ploys. †**stockish** *a.* stupid, dull. **stockist** *n.* a shopkeeper etc. who keeps certain goods in stock. **stockjobber** *n.* 1 (*Hist.*) a dealer who speculated in stocks so as to profit by fluctuations of price and acted as an intermediary between the buying and selling stockbrokers. 2 (*N Am.*) a broker. **stockjobbing, stockjobbery** *n.* **stockkeeper** *n.* 1 a person in charge of the stock of a warehouse etc. 2 a stockman. **stockkeeping** *n.* **stockless** *a.* **stocklist** *n.* a publication giving current prices etc. of stocks. **stockman** *n.* (*pl.* **stockmen**) a man in charge of livestock. **stock market** *n.* a Stock Exchange or the business transacted there. **stockout** *n.* an occurrence of an item being out of stock when asked for by a customer. **stockpile** *n.* an accumulated reserve of goods, weapons etc. ~*v.t.* to accumulate (commodities, esp. reserves of raw materials). **stockpiler** *n.* **stockpot** *n.* a pot for making or storing stock for soup, sauces etc. **stock-rider** *n.* (*Austral.*) a herdsman in charge of stock. **stock-room** *n.* a room for storing the stock of goods available for sale. **stock-still** *a., adv.* motionless. **stocktaking** *n.* 1 the job of preparing an inventory of the stock in a shop, warehouse etc. 2 the activity of reviewing one's position and assets. **stocktake** *n.* **stocktaker** *n.* **stock-whip** *n.* a short-handled whip with a long lash for herding cattle. **stocky** *a.* (*comp.* **stockier**, *superl.* **stockiest**) thick-set, short and stout, stumpy. **stockily** *adv.* **stockiness** *n.* **stockyard** *n.* an enclosure with pens etc., for cattle at market etc. [OE *stocc*, cp. Dut. *stok*, G *Stock*, Icel. *stokkr*]

stockade (stokād') *n.* 1 a line or enclosure of posts or stakes. 2 (*N Am.*) a prison, esp. a military one. ~*v.t.* to surround or fortify with a stockade. [Sp. *estacada*, from *estaca*, MDut. *stake*, see STAKE[1], assim. to STOCK]

stockfish (stok'fish) *n.* (*pl.* **stockfish**) cod, ling etc. split open and dried in the sun without salting. [prob. from Dut. *stokvisch*]

stocking (stok'ing) *n.* 1 (*usu. in pl.*) a close-fitting covering for the foot and leg. 2 an elastic covering used as a support for the leg in cases of varicose veins etc. 3 (*esp. N Am.*) a sock. 4 a close-fitting garment (*a body-stocking*). 5 a horse's lower leg when of a contrasting colour, esp. white. 6 CHRISTMAS STOCKING (under CHRISTMAS). **in one's stocking feet/ soles** without one's shoes, e.g. when having one's height measured. **stockinet** (-net'), **stockinette** *n.* an elastic knitted material for undergarments etc. **stocking cap** *n.* a knitted conical cap. **stockinged** *a.* **in one's stockinged feet/ soles** in one's stocking feet. **stocking filler,** (*N Am.*) **stocking stuffer** *n.* a gift suitable for inclusion in a Christmas stocking. **stockingless** *a.* **stocking mask** *n.* a nylon stocking pulled over the head to distort and disguise the features, e.g. as worn by burglars. **stocking stitch** *n.* in knitting, alternate rows of plain and purl stitches, giving a smooth surface on one side. [dim. of STOCK, in sense of trunk or docked part, earlier *stocks*, short for *netherstocks*, the *upper-stocks* being the knee-breeches]

stocky STOCK.

stodge (stoj) *n.* (*coll.*) 1 heavy, starchy, filling food, esp. steamed or baked pudding. 2 turgid literary matter. 3 anything boring, a dull person etc. ~*v.t.* to feed, to stuff. **stodgy** *a.* (*comp.* **stodgier**, *superl.* **stodgiest**) 1 (of food) heavy, stiff, indigestible, lumpy. 2 dull, turgid, matter-of-fact. **stodgily** *adv.* **stodginess** *n.* [etym. uncertain]

stoep (stoop) *n.* (*S Afr.*) an open, roofed platform in front of a house, a veranda. [Afrikaans, from Dut.]

stogy (stō'gi), **stogie** *n.* (*pl.* **stogies**) (*N Am.*) 1 a long cheaply made cigar. 2 a heavy boot. [orig. *stoga*, from *Conestoga*, Pennsylvania]

Stoic (stō'ik) *n.* 1 a philosopher or member of the school founded by Zeno, *c.* 308 BC, teaching that virtue is the highest good, and that the passions and appetites should be rigidly subdued. 2 (**stoic**) a stoical, long-suffering person. ~*a.* 1 of or relating to the Stoics. 2 stoical. **stoical** *a.* resigned, impassive. **stoically** *adv.* **stoicism** (-sizm) *n.* 1 (**Stoicism**) the philosophy of the

Stoics. 2 indifference to pleasure or pain. 3 fortitude in pain or adversity. [L *Stoicus*, Gr. *Stoikos*, from STOA, with ref. to the *Stoa Poikilē*, painted porch, at Athens, where Zeno taught]

stoichiology (stoikiol´əji) *n.* (*Biol.*) the study of the elements that compose animal tissue. **stoichiological** (-loj´-) *a.* **stoichiometry** (-om´ətri) *n.* the branch of chemistry dealing with chemical combination in definite proportions, the mathematics of chemistry. **stoichiometric** (-met´-), **stoichiometrical** *a.* [Gr. *stoicheion*, dim. of *stoichos*, post]

stoke (stōk) *v.t.* to tend (a furnace, esp. of a steam engine). ~*v.i.* to act as stoker. **to stoke up** 1 to feed a fire or furnace with fuel. 2 to fill oneself with food. **stokehold** *n.* the compartment on a steamship where the furnaces are tended. **stokehole** *n.* 1 the mouth of a furnace. 2 an aperture in a blast furnace etc. for a stirring tool and adding fuel. 3 a stokehold. **stoker** *n.* a person who stokes a furnace. [back-formation from Dut. *stoker* (*stoken*, to make fire, prob. from MDut. *stock*, stick or poker, -ER[1])]

stokes (stōks) *n.* (*pl.* **stokes**) (*Physics*) the centimetre-gram-second unit of kinematic viscosity. [G. G. *Stokes*, 1819–1903]

STOL (stol) *n.* 1 a system by which aircraft take off and land over a short distance. 2 an aircraft using this system; cp. VTOL. [acronym for *s*hort *t*ake-*o*ff and *l*anding]

stole[1] (stōl) *n.* 1 a broad band of fabric, fur etc. worn round the neck and shoulders by women. 2 a narrow band of silk etc. worn over both shoulders as an ecclesiastical vestment by priests. [L *stola*, the outer garment of a Roman matron, Gr. *stolē*, from *stellein*, to array]

stole[2], **stolen** STEAL.

stolid (stol´id) *a.* dull, impassive, phlegmatic; lacking emotion, or showing none. **stolidity** (-lid´-), **stolidness** *n.* **stolidly** *adv.* [L *stolidus*]

Stollen (shtol´ən) *n.* a spicy German bread containing dried fruit and coated with icing sugar. [G, a prop or strut]

stolon (stō´lən) *n.* 1 (*Bot.*) a trailing or prostrate shoot that takes root and develops a new plant. 2 (*Zool.*) a branched structure connecting parts of a coral etc. 3 (*Bot.*) an underground shoot in mosses developing leaves. **stolonate** (-nət), **stoloniferous** (-nif´-) *a.* [L *stolo -onis*]

stoma (stō´mə) *n.* (*pl.* **stomas, stomata** (-mətə)) 1 a minute orifice, a pore. 2 an aperture for respiration in a leaf. 3 a surgically made opening in the abdominal wall. **stomal** *a.* **stomatic** (-mat´-) *a.* **stomatopod** (-pod) *n.* any member of the Stomatopoda, a suborder of crustaceans with gills attached to natatory feet. [Gr. *stōma*, *stōmatos*, mouth]

stomach (stŭm´ək) *n.* 1 the digestive cavity, formed by a dilatation of the alimentary canal, or (in certain animals) one of several such cavities. 2 the belly, the abdomen; a prominent belly. 3 appetite (for food) or an inclination or liking (for some enterprise). ~*v.t.* 1 to accept as palatable. 2 to put up with, to brook. **on a full stomach** after a large meal. **on an empty stomach** not having eaten recently. **stomach-ache** *n.* an abdominal pain. **stomachal** *a.* **stomacher** *n.* (*Hist.*) 1 an ornamental covering for the breast and upper abdomen, tapering to a point, worn by women in the 15th–17th cents. 2 an ornament worn on the front of the bodice. **stomachful** *n.* (*pl.* **stomachfuls**). **stomachic** (-mak´-) *a.* 1 of or relating to the stomach. 2 stimulating the action of the stomach or aiding digestion. ~*n.* a stomachic medicine. **stomach pump** *n.* a syringe for withdrawing the contents of the stomach, or for forcing liquid etc. into it. **stomach tube** *n.* a tube that is fed into the alimentary canal through the mouth and used to cleanse or empty the stomach. **stomach upset** *n.* a spell of nausea, diarrhoea or abdominal pain caused by a disorder of the digestive system. [ME *stomak*, OF *estomac*, L *stomachus*, Gr. *stomachos*, gullet, dim. of *stoma*, mouth]

stomal, stomata STOMA.

stomatitis (stōmətī´tis) *n.* inflammation of the mouth. **stomatogastric** (-tōgas´trik) *a.* of or relating to the mouth and the stomach. **stomatology** (-tol´əji) *n.* the study of diseases of the mouth. **stomatological** (-loj´-) *a.* **stomatologist** *n.* [STOMA]

stomatopod STOMA.

stomp (stomp) *v.i.* to stamp with the feet. ~*n.* 1 a lively jazz dance involving heavy stamping of the feet. 2 an early jazz composition with a heavily stressed rhythm. **stomper** *n.* [N Am. dial. var. of STAMP]

stone (stōn) *n.* 1 the non-metallic mineral material of which rock is composed. 2 an esp. small piece of this, a pebble, cobble, or chip etc. used e.g. in road-making. 3 rock as material for building, paving etc., often specifically limestone or sandstone. 4 (*in comb.*) a piece of stone shaped and prepared for a specific purpose, e.g. *a millstone, grindstone, tombstone, curling stone* etc. 5 a gem, a precious stone. 6 a thing like stone in its hardness or form (*a hailstone*). 7 the hard case of the kernel in a drupe or stone fruit (*peach stones*). 8 (*Med.*) **a** a concretion in a bodily organ, a calculus (*gallstones*; *a kidney stone*). **b** the condition of a person with such a concretion. 9 a stony meteorite, an aerolite. 10 (*usu pl.*) a testicle. 11 (*pl.* **stone**) a unit of weight equivalent to 14 lb. (6.35 kg). 12 a greyish-brown colour. ~*a.* 1 made of stone or a hard material like stone. 2 of a greyish-brown colour. ~*v.t.* 1 to pelt with stones. 2 to put to death by this means. 3 to remove stones from (fruit). 4 to face, wall or pave with stone. **stone the crows!** CROW[1]. **to cast/ throw stones** to go in for criticizing people. **to cast/ throw the first stone** to be the first to accuse or criticize, though not oneself blameless. **to leave no stone unturned** to use all available means to effect an object. **Stone Age** *n.* the period in which primitive humans used implements of stone, not metal. **stone axe,** (*N Am.*) **stone ax** *n.* a stonecutter's axe with two blunt edges. **stone-blind** *a.* (*dated*) completely blind. **stone-cast** *n.* a stone's cast. **stonechat** *n.* the wheatear, *Saxicola torquata*. **stone circle** *n.* a ring of prehistoric monoliths. **stone-coal** *n.* anthracite. **stone-cold** *a.* completely cold. **stone-cold sober** *a.* utterly sober. **stonecrop** *n.* any species of *Sedum*, esp. *S. acre*. **stone curlew** *n.* a curlew-like bird, *Burhinus oedicnemus*, frequenting stony open ground, or any bird of the family Burhinidae. **stonecutter** *n.* a person whose occupation is to cut stones for building etc. **stonecutting** *n.* **stoned** *a.* (*sl.*) under the influence of drugs or alcohol. **stone-dead** *a.* completely dead. **stone-deaf** *a.* completely deaf. **stone-dresser** *n.* a person who trims and prepares stones for building, a stonemason. **stonefish** *n.* (*pl.* **stonefish**) the devilfish, *Synanceia verrucosa*, a poisonous tropical fish with venom glands under its dorsal spines. **stonefly** *n.* (*pl.* **stoneflies**) an insect of the order Plecoptera with aquatic larvae harbouring under stones, used as bait for trout. **stone fruit** *n.* a fruit with seeds covered by a hard shell, such as peaches, plums etc., a drupe. **stone-ground** *a.* (of flour) ground between millstones. **stone-hatch** *n.* the ringed plover. **stoneless** *a.* **stone marten** *n.* a brown marten, *Martes foina*, with a white throat, native to S Europe and S Asia; the beech marten. **stonemason** *n.* a person who dresses stones or builds with stone. **stonemasonry** *n.* **stone parsley** *n.* a hedge parsley, *Sison amomum*, the meadow saxifrage. **stone pine** *n.* the Mediterranean pine, *Pinus pinea*, with a spreading top. **stone-pit** *n.* a stone quarry. **stone plover** *n.* a stone curlew. **stoner** *n.* **stonerag** *n.* a lichen, *Parmelia saxatilis*. **stone's throw, stone's cast** *n.* a short distance. **stone-still** *a.* perfectly still. **stonewall** *v.t.* to obstruct (e.g. parliamentary business, a discussion etc.) by giving lengthy or evasive answers etc. *~v.i.* **1** to behave obstructively in this way. **2** in cricket, to stay in batting without trying to make runs. **stoneware** *n.* pottery made from clay and flint or a hard siliceous clay. **stone-washed** *a.* (of clothes, denim etc.) given a faded surface by the abrasive action of small pieces of pumice. **stoneweed** *n.* gromwell. **stonework** *n.* masonry. **stonewort** *n.* **1** the stone parsley, or certain other plants. **2** any freshwater alga of the genus *Cara*, having a calcareous deposit on its stem. **stony** *a.* (*comp.* **stonier,** *superl.* **stoniest**) **1** of or relating to, made or consisting of, abounding in or resembling stone. **2** (of a meteorite) composed of silicates and other non-metals. **3** hard, cruel, pitiless; incapable of feeling or emotion. **4** obdurate, perverse. **stonily** *adv.* **stoniness** *n.* **stony-broke** *a.* (*sl.*) destitute or nearly destitute of money. **stony coral** *n.* any reef-forming coral of the order Madreporaria. **stony-hearted** *a.* unfeeling. [OE *stān*, cp. Dut. *steen*, G *Stein*, Icel. *steinn*]

stonkered (stong´kəd) *a.* (*Austral., New Zeal., sl.*) totally exhausted. **stonking** *a.* (*sl.*) great, impressive. *~adv.* extremely. [*stonk*, a marble, game of marbles, bombardment, perh. imit.]

stony STONE.

stood STAND.

stooge (stooj) *n.* **1** a butt, a confederate, a decoy. **2** a subordinate. **3** a meek or complaisant person. *~v.i.* **1** to act as a stooge (for). **2** to move or potter (about, around) aimlessly. [onomat.]

stook (stuk) *n.* a bundle of sheaves set up on end. *~v.t.* to set up in stooks. [etym. uncertain, cp. LG, Dan. and Swed. dial. *stuke*]

stool (stool) *n.* **1** a seat without a back, for one person, usu. with three or four legs. **2** a low bench for kneeling or resting the feet on; a footstool. **3** (*esp. pl.*) the faeces. **4** the stump of a timber tree from which shoots are thrown up. **5** a plant or stock from which young plants are produced by layering etc. **6** (*N Am.*) a decoy bird used in hunting. *~v.i.* (of a plant) to shoot out stems from the root. **to fall between two stools** FALL. **stool-ball** *n.* a game like cricket, played in S England. **stoolie** *n.* (*N Am., sl.*) a stool-pigeon, an informer. **stool of repentance** *n.* (*Hist.*) a stool in a church where sinners were made to sit. **stool-pigeon** *n.* **1** a person used as a decoy. **2** an informer for the police. **3** (*Hist.*) a pigeon fixed to a stool as a decoy. [OE *stōl*, cp. Dut. *stoel*, G *Stuhl*, Icel. *stōll*, rel. to STAND]

stoop[1] (stoop) *v.i.* **1** to bend the body downward and forward. **2** to have a habitual forward inclination of the head and shoulders. **3** to condescend, to lower or bring oneself down (to some demeaning act). **4** (of a hawk etc.) to pounce, to swoop towards a prey. *~v.t.* to incline (one's head, shoulders etc.) downwards and forwards. *~n.* **1** the act of stooping. **2** a habitual inclination of the shoulders etc. **3** the swoop of a bird on its prey. **stoopingly** *adv.* [OE *stūpian* (cp. MDut. *stupyen*, Icel. *stūpa*), rel. to STEEP[1], STEEP[2]]

stoop[2] (stoop) *n.* (*N Am.*) a flight of steps, a porch, or a small veranda in front of a house. [Dut. *stoep*, see STOEP]

stoor STOUR.

stop (stop) *v.t.* (*pres.p.* **stopping,** *past, p.p.* **stopped**) **1** to cause to cease moving, going, working, or acting. **2** to impede; to hinder; to prevent (from doing something). **3** to prevent the doing or performance of. **4** to discontinue (*stopped talking; stopped work*). **5** to cause to cease action; to foil or defeat. **6 a** in boxing, to knock out, or defeat with a knockout. **b** to parry (a blow). **7** (*coll.*) to be the target or recipient of (a blow, bullet etc.). **8** to close by filling or obstructing, to staunch, to plug (up). **9** to fill (a crack or a cavity); to put a filling in (a tooth etc.). **10** to keep back, to cut off, to suspend (wages etc.). **11** to instruct a bank to withhold payment on (a cheque). **12** (*Mus.*) to press (a string), close (an aperture etc.) so as to alter the pitch. **13** to plug the upper end of (an organ pipe) to lower its note by an octave. **14** to make (a sound) inaudible. **15** in bridge, to prevent one's opponents from taking all the tricks in (a suit). **16** to remove leaves or buds from (a plant) to encourage thick growth, to pinch back. **17** to make (something, e.g. a clock) cease working. **18** to punctuate, to insert punctuation into. **19** (*Naut.*) to secure (a rope) with a clamp or other device. *~v.i.* **1** to come to an end; to discontinue, to cease or desist. **2** to halt; to pause; to come to rest. **3** (*coll.*) to stay, to remain temporarily, to sojourn (*Why not stop here for the night?*). *~n.* **1** an act of stopping or state of being stopped, a cessation, a pause, an interruption. **2** a regular halt for a bus or train, a place where passengers get on or off. **3** a punctuation mark indicating a pause, esp. a full point; in telegrams etc., a full point. **4** a block, peg, pin etc. used to stop the movement of something at a particular point. **5** (*Mus.*) the pressing down of a string, closing of an aperture etc., effecting a change of pitch. **6** a key, lever or other device employed in this. **7** a set of pipes in an organ having tones of a distinct quality. **8** a knob bringing these into play. **9** a way of talking assumed for a particular purpose or effect. **10** a perforated diaphragm for regulating the passage of light in a camera. **11** the diameter of a camera lens. **12** a device for reducing the diameter of a lens. **13** a unit of alteration of exposure or aperture such that a reduction of one stop is the equivalent of halving it. **14** a sound produced by closure of the mouth or throat, a plosive or mute consonant. **15** in bridge, a card or cards that stop a suit. **16** (*Naut.*) a clamp or lashing securing a rope. **to pull out all the stops 1** to make the utmost effort. **2** to play at maximum volume. **to put a stop to** to cause to cease, esp. abruptly. **to stop a gap** GAP. **to stop at nothing** to be ruthless, to be ready to do anything to achieve one's ends. **to stop by** to break one's journey (at a particular place) for a visit. **to stop dead** to stop short. **to stop down** in photography, to reduce the aperture of (a lens) by means of a diaphragm. **to stop off/ over** to break one's journey (at a particular place). **to stop one's ears 1** to put one's fingers in one's ears so as not to hear. **2** to refuse to listen. **to stop out 1** to stay out. **2** in printing etc., to cover (part of a surface) to prevent printing, etching etc. **to stop payment 1** to declare oneself insolvent. **2** to instruct a bank to withhold payment on a cheque etc. **to stop short** SHORT. **to stop the mouth of** MOUTH[1]. **stopbank** *n.* (*Austral., New Zeal.*) an embankment to prevent a river from flooding. **stop bath** *n.* an acidic solution used to halt the action of a developer or a photographic negative or print. **stopcock** *n.* a valve operated externally to stop the flow of fluid in a pipe. **stop-drill** *n.* a drill with a shoulder that prevents penetration beyond a certain depth. **stopgap** *n.* a temporary substitute or expedient. **stop-go** *a.* (of a policy etc.) alternately active and inactive or stimulating and restrictive. **stop-knob** *n.* (*Mus.*) a knob that controls an organ stop. **stop lamp** *n.* a rear light on a vehicle showing when the brake is being used. **stopless** *a.* **stop light** *n.* **1** a traffic light at red. **2** a stop lamp. **stopoff, stopover** *n.* a break in a journey. **stoppable** *a.* **stoppage** (-ij) *n.* **1** the state of being hindered or stopped. **2** a deduction from pay. **3** a cessation of work, as in a strike. **stopper** *n.* **1** a plug for closing a bottle etc. **2** a person or thing that stops, or stops something. **3** (*Naut.*) a rope, plug, clamp etc. for checking the motion of a cable etc. *~v.t.* to close or secure with a stopper. **to put a stopper on 1** to prevent the continuance of. **2** to keep (someone) quiet. **stopping** *n.* **1** a filling in a tooth or material for this; the dental operation itself. **2** plastic material for filling holes and cracks in wood etc. before painting. **3** (*Mus.*) the action of altering pitch by pressing a string (as in *double-stopping*) or closing an aperture. **stopple** (stop´əl) *n.* **1** something that stops or closes the mouth of a vessel, a stopper, plug, bung etc. **2** (*N Am.*) an earplug, EARSTOPPLE (under EAR[1]). *~v.t.* to close with a stopple. **stop press** *n.* **1** late news inserted in a paper after the printing has commenced. **2** a newspaper column reserved for such insertions. **stop-press** *a.* designating a news item worthy of late insertion. **stop valve** *n.* a valve that stops the flow of liquid through a pipe. **stop-volley** *n.* in tennis, a volley close to the net and not followed through, dropping the ball just over the net. **stopwatch** *n.* a watch with an additional hand which can be stopped by a special device at any second or fraction of a second, used for timing races etc. [OE *stoppian*, in *forstoppian*, from late L *stuppāre*, from *stūpa*, *stuppa*, tow, oakum (cp. Gr. *stupē*, *stuppē*)]

stope (stōp) *n.* a steplike area of a mine, where ore is being extracted. [rel. to STEP]

storage STORE.

storax (staw´raks) *n.* **1** a vanilla-scented resin obtained from *Styrax officinalis*, formerly used in medicine etc. **2** the tree itself. **3** a balsam obtained from *Liquidambar orientalis*. [L, from Gr. *sturax*]

store (staw) *n.* **1** a stock laid up for drawing upon. **2** (*often pl.*) an abundant supply, plenty, abundance. **3** a place where things are laid up or kept for sale, a storehouse, a warehouse. **4** a large establishment where articles of various kinds are sold, a department store. **5** (*N Am.*) a shop. **6** (*sometimes in pl.*) a shop selling basic commodities. **7** (*pl.*) articles kept on hand for special use, esp. ammunition, arms, military and naval provisions etc.; a supply of such articles. **8** the memory in a computer. *~v.t.* **1** to deposit (furniture etc.) in a warehouse etc. for safe keeping. **2** to accumulate or lay (usu. up or away) for future use. **3** to stock or supply (with). **4** to have a capacity for holding a reserve, e.g. of water (*The leaves store moisture*). **5** to enter (data) into a computer memory or in a storage device. **in store 1** in reserve. **2** ready for use. **3** on hand. **4** awaiting one in the future. **to lay store by/ on** to value highly. **to put store by/ on** to value highly. **to set store by/ on** to value highly. **storable** *a.* **storage** (-rij) *n.* **1** the storing or warehousing of goods etc. **2** the price paid for or the space reserved for this. **3** the storing of data in a computer memory or on disk etc. **storage battery, storage cell** *n.* an accumulator. **storage capacity** *n.* the maximum amount of data that can be held in a computer memory. **storage device** *n.* a piece of computer hardware such as a magnetic tape, optical disk etc. that can store data. **storage heater** *n.* a type of radiator which stores heat during periods of off-peak electricity. **store card** *n.* a credit card issued to customers by a department store etc. **storefront** *n.* **1** (*esp. N Am.*) the side of a shop that faces the street. **2** a room in the front of a shop. **storehouse** *n.* **1** a place where things are stored up, a warehouse, granary, repository etc. **2** a great quantity. **storekeeper** *n.* **1** a person who has the charge of stores. **2** (*N Am.*) a shopkeeper. **storeman** *n.* (*pl.* **storemen**) a person in charge of stored goods or equipment. **storer** *n.* **storeroom** *n.* **storeship** *n.* a supply vessel for a fleet etc. [OF *estor*, late L *staurum*, *instaurum*, from *instaurāre* (IN-[1], *staurāre*, see RESTORE)]

storey (staw´ri), (*N Am. also*) **story** *n.* (*pl.* **storeys, stories**) a horizontal division of a building, esp. a set of rooms on the same floor. **storeyed, storied** *a.* (*often in comb.*) having storeys, esp. of a certain number, as *four-storeyed*. [L *historia*, HISTORY, but the line of sense-development is uncertain]

storiated (staw´riātid) *a.* historiated, decorated with historical or mythical scenes. **storiation** (-ā´shən) *n.*

storied[1] STORY[1].

storied[2] STOREYED (under STOREY).

stork (stawk) *n.* **1** a long-necked, long-legged wading bird of the genus *Ciconia*, allied to the heron, esp. the white or house-stork *C. alba*, nesting on buildings. **2** this bird as the traditional bringer of babies. **stork's-bill** *n.* a plant of the genus *Erodium* allied to the cranesbill. [OE *storc*, prob. rel. to STARK, cp. Dut. *stork*, G *Storch*, Icel. *storkr*, also Gr. *torgos*, vulture]

storm (stawm) *n.* **1** a violent disturbance of the atmosphere accompanied by wind, rain, snow, hail, or thunder and lightning, a tempest. **2** a wind of force 10 or 11, between a gale and a hurricane. **3** a violent disturbance or agitation of society, life, the mind etc., a tumult, commotion etc. **4** a hail or shower (of blows or missiles). **5** a violent outburst (of cheers etc.). **6** a direct assault on, or the capture of, a fortified place. *~v.i.* **1** to bluster, to fume, to rage (at etc.), to behave violently. **2** to move somewhere in violent and angry haste (*stormed out of the house*). **3** (of wind, rain etc.) to rage. *~v.t.* to take (a stronghold etc.) by storm. **to take by storm 1** to capture by means of a violent assault. **2** to captivate, overwhelm (an audience, (the people of) a city etc.). **storm-beat, storm-beaten** *a.* beaten or injured by storms. **storm belt** *n.* a zone where storms are frequent. **storm-bird** *n.* the storm petrel. **storm-bound** *a.* stopped or delayed by storms. **storm centre,** (*N Am.*) **storm center** *n.* **1** the place of lowest pressure in a cyclonic storm. **2** any focus of violent debate, controversy or conflict. **storm cloud** *n.* **1** a heavy dark rain cloud. **2** a threat of imminent trouble. **storm-cock** *n.* the mistle thrush, fieldfare, or green woodpecker. **storm collar** *n.* a jacket collar that can be turned up and fastened. **storm cone** *n.* a storm-warning device consisting of a tarred cone, hoisted upright to warn of a north wind, and inverted, of a south. **storm-door** *n.* an extra outer door for protection in severe weather. **storm-finch** *n.* the storm petrel. **stormful** *a.* **stormfulness** *n.* **storm-glass** *n.* a sealed tube containing an alcoholic solution of camphor etc. which is affected by changes of temperature, and was formerly used as a weather-glass. **storm in a teacup** *n.* a fuss about nothing. **storming** *a.* **1** that storms or rages. **2** characterized by vigour, speed, dynamism etc. **storming-party** *n.* a detachment of soldiers detailed to start an assault. **storm lantern** *n.* HURRICANE LAMP (under HURRICANE). **stormless** *a.* **storm petrel** *n.* **1** a small black and white petrel of the N Atlantic, *Hydrobates pelagicus*. **2** a seditious person, a troublemaker. **storm-proof** *a.* giving protection against, or withstanding storms. **storm-sail** *n.* a sail of smaller size and stouter canvas, for heavy weather. **storm-signal** *n.* a signal of any of various sorts (such as a storm cone or flag) hoisted as warning of an approaching storm. **storm troops** *n.pl.* **1** shock troops. **2** (*Hist.*) the Nazi political militia. **storm trooper** *n.* **storm window** *n.* an outer sash window to provide extra insulation. **stormy** *a.* (*comp.* **stormier**, *superl.* **stormiest**) **1** characterized or affected by storms. **2** (of winds) tempestuous. **3** violent, vehement, passionate. **stormily** *adv.* **storminess** *n.* **stormy petrel** *n.* STORM PETREL (under STORM). [OE (cp. Dut., Swed., and Dan. *storm*, G *Sturm*, Icel. *stormr*), cogn. with STIR[1]]

stornello (stawnel´ō) *n.* (*pl.* **stornelli** (-lē)) an Italian form of short improvised song. [It.]

Storting (staw´ting), **Storthing** *n.* the Norwegian parliament. [Norw. *stor*, great, *thing*, meeting, assembly, parliament]

story[1] (staw´ri) *n.* (*pl.* **stories**) **1** a narrative or recital in prose or verse, of actual or fictitious events, a tale, short novel, romance, anecdote, legend or myth. **2** the plot or incidents of a novel, epic or play; a storyline. **3** a series of facts of special interest connected with a person, place etc. 4 an account of an incident, experience etc. 5 a descriptive article in a newspaper. 6 (*coll.*) a falsehood, a fib. 7 †history. **the story goes** it is commonly said. **to cut/ make a long story short** used to announce that one is omitting many details and coming directly to the point. **storied**[1] *a.* (*poet.*) 1 adorned with scenes from stories or history. 2 celebrated in stories or history. **storyboard** *n.* (a board displaying) a series of shots or sketches indicating the sequence of images to be used in a cinema film, television programme or television advertisement. **story book** *n.* a book containing a story or stories. **story-book** *a.* fairy-tale, romantic. **storyline** *n.* the main plot of a book, film etc. **story-teller** *n.* 1 a person who tells stories. 2 (*coll.*) a person who tells lies. **storytelling** *n.* **story-writer** *n.* [A-F *storie*, OF *estoire*, L *historia*, HISTORY]

story[2] STOREY.

stot (stot) *n.* (*dial.*) a bullock, a steer. [ME, see STOAT]

stoup (stoop) *n.* 1 a basin for holy water. 2 †a flagon, a drinking vessel. [Icel. *staup*, cp. Dut. *stoop*, G *Stauf*, Icel. *steap*]

stour (stow´ə, stuə), **stoor** (stuə) *n.* (*esp. Sc., North.*) 1 a cloud of dust. 2 a turmoil, a stir. 3 a battle, a tumult. [OF *estour*, *estor*, tumult, armed combat, OHG *stōr*]

stoush (stowsh) *v.t.* (*Austral.*, *New Zeal.*, *coll.*) 1 to fight with or hit. 2 to make a verbal assault on. ~*n.* a fight, a brawl. [perh. from Sc. *stoushie*, a row, a fight]

stout (stowt) *a.* 1 corpulent, bulky, fleshy. 2 strong, sound, sturdy, well-built. 3 staunch, lusty, vigorous, brave, resolute, intrepid. ~*n.* a type of strong beer made from roasted malt or barley. **stout heart** *n.* courage, fortitude. **stout-hearted** *a.* **stout-heartedly** *adv.* **stout-heartedness** *n.* **stoutish** *a.* **stoutly** *adv.* **stoutness** *n.* [OF *estout*, MDut. *stolt*, stout (cp. G *stolz*, proud), perh. from L *stultus*, stupid]

stove[1] (stōv) *n.* 1 an apparatus, wholly or partially closed, in which fuel is burned for heating, cooking etc. 2 a hothouse in which a high temperature is maintained. 3 a kiln or other heating apparatus used in manufacture. ~*v.t.* to heat, dry, force etc. in a stove. **stove-enamel** *n.* enamel made heatproof by treating in a stove. **stove-enamelled,** (*N Am.*) **stove-enameled** *a.* **stove-pipe** *n.* a pipe for conducting smoke etc. from a stove to a chimney. **stove-pipe hat** *n.* a high silk hat. [orig. a bath or hothouse, OE *stofa* (cp. MDut. *stove*, G *Stube*, Icel. *stofa*, *stufa*), prob. rel. to STEW[1]]

stove[2] STAVE.

stow (stō) *v.t.* 1 to put or pack (often away) in a suitable or convenient place or position. 2 to pack or fill compactly with things. **stow it** (*sl.*) drop it! stop joking etc. **to stow away** 1 to put (something) where it will be tidily out of the way; to pack or fold away. 2 to be a stowaway on board a ship or aircraft. **stowage** (-ij) *n.* 1 an area or place for stowing goods or the charge for this. 2 the act of stowing or state of being stowed. 3 things for stowing. **stowaway** *n.* a person who conceals themselves on a ship, aircraft etc. in order to get a free passage. **stower** *n.* [OE *stōwigan*, from *stōw*, place, cogn. with STAND]

STP *abbr.* 1 Professor of Sacred Theology. 2 standard temperature and pressure.

str. *abbr.* 1 strait. 2 stroke (of an oar).

strabismus (strəbiz´məs) *n.* squinting, a squint, produced by a muscular defect of the eye. **strabismal, strabismic** *a.* [Gr. *strabismos*, from *strabos*, crooked]

Strad (strad) *n.* a Stradivarius.

straddle (strad´əl) *v.t.* 1 to stand or sit astride of (something) with legs well apart. 2 (of a town etc.) to be situated on both sides of, or across (e.g. a border, road etc.). 3 to part (one's legs) widely. 4 to shoot or drop bombs beyond and short of (a target) to determine the range. ~*v.i.* 1 to stand, walk or sit with the legs wide apart. 2 (of the legs) to be well apart. 3 to trim, to sit on the fence. ~*n.* 1 an act of straddling. 2 on the Stock Exchange, a contract securing the right of either a put or call. 3 a high-jumping technique in which the legs straddle the bar while the body is parallel to it. 4 a non-committed position on some issue. **straddle-legged** *a.* **straddler** *n.* [earlier *striddle*, freq. of STRIDE]

Stradivarius (stradiveə´riəs) *n.* a stringed instrument, esp. a violin, made by Antonio Stradivari of Cremona, 1644–1737.

strafe (strāf, strahf) *v.t.* 1 to bombard heavily. 2 to rake with machine-gun fire from the air. 3 to reprimand or punish severely. 4 to abuse or do a serious and deliberate injury to. ~*n.* 1 an act of strafing. 2 an attack from the air. [G *strafen*, to punish]

straggle (strag´əl) *v.i.* 1 to spread irregularly, to lose tightness or compactness. 2 to become dispersed, sporadic or irregular. 3 to wander away from or trail behind the main body. 4 (of e.g. a beard or a plant) to grow in an uncontrolled, untidy way. ~*n.* a straggling group or growth. **straggler** *n.* **stragglingly** *adv.* **straggly** *a.* (*comp.* **stragglier**, *superl.* **straggliest**). [perh. freq. of ME *straken*, to roam]

straight (strāt) *a.* 1 extending uniformly in one direction, not bent, curved or crooked. 2 (*Geom.*) (of a line) lying along the shortest path between any two of its points. 3 (*esp. N Am.*) successive, in an unbroken run (*got straight As in her grade exams*). 4 unobstructed, uninterrupted; coming direct from its source. 5 level, even (*That picture's not straight*). 6 in proper order or condition; arranged to one's satisfaction. 7 clear (*Let's get this straight*). 8 **a** upright, honest, not deviating from truth or fairness, correct, accurate, right. **b** reliable, trustworthy, authoritative; not evasive or ambiguous. 9 (of drama or some other art) serious, not comic or popular; using conventional techniques and ideas. 10 **a** unmodified, unmitigated. **b** (of a drink) undiluted. 11 (of a person) conventional, not outrageous. 12 (*sl.*) heterosexual. 13 (of an arch) flat rather than curved. 14 (of hair) not curly or wavy. 15 (of legs or back) not bent, bowed or bandy. 16 (of a garment) not full or flared. 17 (of an aim or shot) going direct to its mark. 18 (of a look) direct, uncompromising. ~*n.* 1 a straight part, piece or stretch of anything. 2 a straight condition or state. 3 in poker, five cards in sequence irrespective of suit. 4 (*coll.*) a conventional person. 5 (*sl.*) a heterosexual person. 6 the straight part of a racetrack. ~*adv.* 1 in a straight line, direct. 2 directly. 3 without deviation, ambiguity or circumlocution. 4 with an accurate aim (*can't shoot straight*). 5 clearly (*can't see straight*). 6 †immediately, at once. **straight as a die** DIE[2]. **straight away** at once, without delay. **straight from the shoulder** 1 (of a physical blow) squarely delivered. 2 (of criticism etc.) frank, direct. **straight off/ out** (*coll.*) without needing time for checking or deliberation (*couldn't tell you the date straight off*). **straight up** 1 (*coll.*) honestly, truly. 2 (*N Am.*, *coll.*) without dilution or admixture. **the straight and narrow** the honest and virtuous way of life. **to go straight** to abandon criminal activities and become honest. **straight angle** *n.* an angle of 180°. **straightaway** *adv.* straight away, immediately. ~*a.* (*esp. N Am.*) (of a course) direct, straight. ~*n.* (*esp. N Am.*) a straight course. **straight-bred** *a.* not cross-bred; from a single breed. **straight chain** *n.* (*Chem.*) a chain of atoms, esp. of carbon, without branches or circular formation. **straight-cut** *a.* (of tobacco) cut lengthwise. **straight-edge** *n.* a strip of metal or wood having one edge straight, used as a ruler etc. **straight-eight** *n.* 1 an internal-combustion engine with eight cylinders in line. 2 a motor vehicle with this arrangement. **straighten** *v.t.* to make straight or symmetrical. **to straighten out** to resolve, unscramble. **to straighten up** to stand erect after bending. **straightener** *n.* **straight eye** *n.* a talent for spotting irregularities of line. **straight face** *n.* a controlled expression, usu. concealing an inclination to laugh. **straight-faced** *a.* **straight fight** *n.* a contest between two candidates or sides only. **straight flush** *n.* a flush with cards in a sequence. **straightforward** *a.* **1** upright, honest, frank, open. **2** (of a task) simple, presenting no difficulties. **3** straight. **straightforwardly** *adv.* **straightforwardness** *n.* **straightish** *a.* **straightjacket** STRAITJACKET (under STRAIT). **straight-laced** STRAIT-LACED (under STRAIT). **straightly** *adv.* **straight man** *n.* (*pl.* **straight men**) a person who acts as a stooge to a comedian. **straightness** *n.* **straight-out** *a.* (*N Am., coll.*) outright, complete, blunt, honest. **straight razor** *n.* (*N Am.*) a cut-throat razor. **straight-up** *a.* (*coll.*) **1** trusty, honest, reliable. **2** (*N Am.*) pure, unmixed, unadulterated. †**straightway** *adv.* straight away, forthwith, at once. [OE *streht*, p.p. of *streccan*, to STRETCH]

Usage note The spellings of the current adjective *straight* (not curved) and the noun *strait* (a narrow passage of water) should not be confused. The archaic adjective *strait* (narrow) is represented in the verb *straiten*, which should be distinguished from *straighten*, and in *straitjacket* and *strait-laced*, which now vary with *straightjacket* and *straight-laced*, but remain the preferred spellings.

strain[1] (strān) *v.t.* **1** to stretch tight; to make taut. **2** to exert (e.g. oneself, one's senses, one's eyes, ears etc.) to the utmost. **3** to force beyond due limits. **4** to apply (rules etc.) beyond the proper scope or intent. **5** to weaken, injure or distort by excessive effort or overexertion. **6** to purify from extraneous matter by passing through a colander or other strainer. **7** to remove (solid matter) by filtering (out). **8** to constrain, to make unnatural, artificial, or uneasy. **9** to press closely, to embrace. *~v.i.* **1** to become taut, tense or fully stretched. **2** to exert oneself, to make violent efforts (after etc.). **3** to pull or tug (at). **4** to toil or labour (under a burden etc.). **5** to be filtered, to percolate. *~n.* **1** an act of straining, a violent effort, a pull. **2** the force thus exerted; tension. **3** an injury, distortion, or change of structure, caused by excessive effort, exertion, or tension. **4** mental tension, fatigue from overwork etc. **5** a song, a tune, a melody, a piece of poetry. **6** tone, spirit, manner, style, pitch. **7** (*Physics*) a molecular displacement occurring in a body subjected to stress. **b** a measure of such displacement, being the amount of deformation divided by the original dimension. **at full strain** stretched or exerted to the utmost. **at strain** fully stretched or exerted. **straining at the leash** LEASH. **to strain oneself** **1** to do oneself an injury through effort or straining. **2** (*often with neg., facet.*) to try unduly hard. **strainable** *a.* **strained** *a.* **1** unnatural. **2** forced. **3** tense. **4** stressful. **strainer** *n.* **1** a filter. **2** a sieve, colander. **strain gauge** *n.* an engineer's device for testing the strain being put on a material or structure, at any point where it is attached. [ME *streinen*, OF *estraign-*, stem of *estraindre*, L *stringere*, see STRINGENT]

strain[2] (strān) *n.* **1** race, stock, family, breed. **2** natural tendency or disposition. [OE *strēon*, rel. to L *struere*, to build]

strait (strāt) *n.* **1** (*often pl.*) a narrow passage of water between two seas. **2** (*usu. pl.*) a trying position, distress, difficulty. *~*†*a.* **1** narrow, confined, restricted, tight. **2** strict, rigorous. **straiten** *v.t.* **1** to distress. **2** to place in difficulty. **straitened circumstances** *n.pl.* poverty, financial hardship. **straitjacket, straightjacket** *n.* a garment with very long sleeves that are crossed in front and tied behind, for confining the arms of a violent prisoner or mental patient. *~v.t.* (*pres.p.* **straitjacketing, straightjacketing,** *past, p.p.* **straitjacketed, straightjacketed**) **1** to confine in a straitjacket. **2** to restrict irksomely. **strait-laced, straight-laced** *a.* **1** puritanically strict in morals or manners. **2** laced or braced tightly. †**straitly** *adv.* †**straitness** *n.* [A-F *estreit*, OF *estroict* (F *étroit*), L *strictum*, STRICT]

Usage note See note under STRAIGHT.

strake (strāk) *n.* **1** a continuous line of planking or plates from stem to stern of a vessel. **2** part of the metal rim on a cartwheel. [rel. to STRETCH, overlapping with STREAK]

stramash (strəmash´) *n.* (*Sc.*) a disturbance, a fray, a struggle. *~v.t.* **1** to strike, beat, or bang. **2** to break, to destroy. [etym. uncertain, cp. OF *estramaçon*, It. *stramazzone*, a cut with a sword]

stramineous (strəmin´iəs) *a.* **1** straw-coloured. **2** consisting of straw, light or worthless like straw. [L *strāmineus*, from *strāmen -minis*, straw, from *sternere*, to strew]

stramonium (strəmō´niəm) *n.* a drug prepared from the thorn apple, *Datura stramonium*, used for asthma and nervous complaints. [etym. uncertain]

strand[1] (strand) *v.t.* **1** to run or force aground. **2** (*esp. in p.p.*) to bring to a standstill or into straits, esp. from lack of funds. *~v.i.* to run aground. *~n.* a shore or beach of the sea, lake or large river. **stranded** *a.* **1** left in difficulties. **2** without resources. [OE, cp. Dut., G, Swed., Dan. *strand*, Icel. *strönd*]

strand[2] (strand) *n.* **1** each of the fibres, threads, wires etc. of which a rope etc. is composed. **2** a thin lock of hair. **3** a string (of pearls, beads etc.). **4** any of the threads or elements composing a complex structure. *~v.t.* **1** to break a strand in (a rope). **2** to make (a rope etc.) by twisting strands together. [ONF *estran*, OHG *Streno* (cp. G *Strähne*), cord]

strange (strānj) *a.* **1** unusual, singular, extraordinary, queer, surprising, unaccountable. **2** not well known, unfamiliar, new (to) (*an experience quite strange to us*). **3** alien, foreign (*strange lands*). **4** not one's own (*strange customs*). **5** fresh or unused (to), unacquainted (*was strange to the work*). **6** awkward, shy. *~adv.* (*coll.*) oddly (*began acting strange*). **strange to say** oddly enough; it is strange to report that. **to feel strange** FEEL. **strange attractor** *n.* (*Math.*) (an equation or fractal set representing) a complex pattern of non-repetitive behaviour in a chaotic system. **strangely** *adv.* **strangeness** *n.* **1** the quality of being strange. **2** (*Physics*) the quantum number, conserved in strong but not in weak interactions, introduced to explain the paradoxically long lifetimes of certain elementary particles. **strange particle** *n.* (*Physics*) an elementary particle (e.g. a hyperon) which possesses a quantum strangeness number different from zero. [OF *estrange* (F *étrange*), L *extrāneus*, EXTRANEOUS]

stranger (strān´jə) *n.* **1** a person from another place; someone who does not know, or is not known in, a certain place. **2** a foreigner. **3** a guest, a visitor. **4** a person unknown (to one). **5** a person unaccustomed (to) (*a stranger to violence*). **6** a person who is neither a member nor an official of the House of Commons. **7** (*Law*) a person not privy or party to an act. [OF *estrangier*, from L *extrāneus*, foreign]

strangle (strang´gəl) *v.t.* **1** to kill by compressing the windpipe, to choke, to throttle. **2** to suppress, to stifle. **stranglehold** *n.* **1** a choking grip used in wrestling. **2** a restrictive force or influence that squeezes the life out of something. **3** a monopoly; exclusive control. **strangler** *n.* **strangles** *n.* an infectious disease of the respiratory tract, affecting horses etc. [OF *estrangler*, L *strangulāre*, Gr. *strangalizein*, from *strangalē*, halter, from *strangos*, twisted]

strangulate (strang´gūlāt) *v.t.* **1** to strangle. **2** to compress (a blood vessel, intestine etc.). **strangulated** *a.* **strangulated hernia** *n.* a hernia so constricted by surrounding tissue that its blood supply is cut off. **strangulation** (-lā´shən) *n.* [L *strangulātus*, p.p. of *strangulāre*, to strangle]

strangury (strang´gūri) *n.* **1** a disease characterized by pain in passing the urine, which is excreted in drops. **2** an abnormal condition produced in plants by bandaging. **strangurious** (-gū´-) *a.* [L *strangūria*, Gr. *strangouria* (*stranx strangos*, a drop, trickle, *ouron*, urine)]

strap (strap) *n.* **1** a long narrow strip of leather or similar material, usu. with a buckle, for fastening round things. **2** a strip of fabric holding a garment in position on the body (*a shoulder strap*). **3** in a vehicle, train etc., a loop for grasping to steady oneself. **4** a strip, band or plate for holding parts together or for mounting things on. **5** †a strop. **6** (*Bot.*) a strap-shaped blade or part, a ligula. **7** (*usu.* **the strap**) chastisement, corporal punishment, with a leather strap. ~*v.t.* (*pres.p.* **strapping,** *past, p.p.* **strapped**) **1** to fasten (down, up etc.) with a strap. **2** to beat with a strap. **3** to sharpen, to strop. **straphanger** *n.* **1** (*coll.*) a standing passenger in a bus or train. **2** a commuter using the bus or train to get to and from work. **strap-hang** *v.i.* **strapless** *a.* **strap-oil** *n.* (*sl.*) a thrashing. **strapped** *a.* (*coll.*) short, in difficulties (for something) (*a bit strapped for cash*). **strapper** *n.* **1** a person who uses or applies straps. **2** (*esp. Austral.*) a person who grooms racehorses. **3** a tall sturdy person. **strapping** *a.* tall, lusty, strong, muscular. **strappy** *a.* (*comp.* **strappier,** *superl.* **strappiest**). **strap-work** *n.* ornamentation in the form of crossed or interlacing bands. [OE *stropp* (cp. Dut. *strop*), L *struppus* (cp. Gr. *strophos*, cogn. with *strephein*, to twist)]

strappado (strəpā´dō, -pah´-) *n.* (*pl.* **strappados**) (*Hist.*) **1** a punishment involving drawing up an offender by a rope and letting them fall to the end of this. **2** the rope etc. used in this. ~*v.t.* (*3rd pers. sing. pres.* **strappadoes,** *pres.p.* **strappadoing,** *past, p.p.* **strappadoed**) to torture or punish in this way. [It. *strappata*, from *strappare*, to pull, Swiss G *strapfen*, prob. from Dut. *straffen*, to punish, from *straf*, severe]

strapped, strapper etc. STRAP.

strass (stras) *n.* paste for making false gems. [Joseph *Strasser*, 18th-cent. German jeweller]

strata STRATUM.

stratagem (strat´əjəm) *n.* **1** an artifice, trick or manoeuvre, esp. for deceiving an enemy. **2** trickery, deception. [OF *stratageme*, L and Gr. *stratēgēma*, from *stratēgein*, to act as general (*stratos*, army, *agein*, to lead)]

stratal STRATUM.

strategy (strat´əji) *n.* (*pl.* **strategies**) **1** the art of war, generalship, esp. the art of directing military movements so as to secure the most advantageous positions and combinations of forces. **2** a long-term plan aimed at achieving a specific goal. **3** a political or economic plan of action. **4** a stratagem. **strategic** (-tē´-), **strategical** *a.* **1** of, relating to, used in or of the nature of strategy. **2** (of materials) essential for the conduct of war. **3** (of missiles etc.) for use against an enemy's homeland rather than on the battlefield. **strategically** *adv.* **strategic defence initiative** *n.* a proposed US defence strategy against nuclear attack, using satellites equipped with lasers. **strategics** *n.* **strategist** (strat´ijist) *n.* an expert in strategy. [Gr. *stratēgia*, from *stratēgein*, see STRATAGEM]

strath (strath) *n.* in the Scottish Highlands, a wide valley through which a river runs. **strathspey** (-spā´) *n.* **1** a Scottish dance slower than a reel. **2** music in 4/4 time for this. [Gael. *srath*, rel. to STRATUM]

strati STRATUS.

strati- (strat´i) *comb. form* layer. [as STRATUM]

straticulate (strətik´ūlət) *a.* (*Geol.*) (of rock) composed of narrow layers. [STRATUM, on the analogy of *denticulate*, *vermiculate* etc.]

stratiform (strat´ifawm) *a.* **1** composed of layers. **2** forming or constituting a layer.

stratify (strat´ifī) *v.t.* (*3rd pers. sing. pres.* **stratifies,** *pres.p.* **stratifying,** *past, p.p.* **stratified**) **1** to form, deposit or arrange in strata. **2** to construct or design in layers, or according to a hierarchy. **stratification** (-fikā´shən) *n.* **stratified** *a.* [F *stratifier*, STRATUM, -FY]

stratigraphy (strətig´rəfi) *n.* **1** the branch of geology dealing with the succession, classification, nomenclature etc. of stratified rocks. **2** the analysis of layers in archaeology. **stratigrapher** *n.* **stratigraphic** (-graf´-), **stratigraphical** *a.*

strato- (strat´ō) *comb. form* **1** layer, esp. with reference to cloud formations. **2** stratosphere. [as STRATUM]

stratocirrus (stratōsir´əs) *n.* (*pl.* **stratocirri** (-ī)) a cloud formation more compact than cirrostratus.

stratocracy (strətok´rəsi) *n.* (*pl.* **stratocracies**) **1** a military government. **2** government by a military class. [Gr. *stratos*, army, -CRACY]

stratocumulus (stratōkū´mūləs) *n.* (*pl.* **stratocumuli** (-lī)) a layer of low cloud in dark round masses.

stratopause (strat´əpawz) *n.* the upper boundary of the stratosphere. [L *pausa*, Gr. *pausis*, cessation]

stratosphere (strat´əsfiə) *n.* the layer of atmosphere above the troposphere, extending to about 50 km above the earth's surface, in the lower part of which temperature does not vary very much and in the upper part of which temperature increases with height. **stratospheric** (-fer´-) *a.*

stratum (strah´təm, strā´-) *n.* (*pl.* **strata** (-tə)) **1** a horizontal layer of any material. **2** a bed of sedimentary rock. **3** a layer of tissue or cells. **4** a layer of sea or atmosphere. **5** a social level, a class. **6** in statistics, each of the bands into which a population is divided for the purpose of stratified sampling. **stratal** *a.* [L, something laid flat, orig. neut. p.p. of *sternere*, to strew]

Usage note *Strata* is sometimes used as a singular noun (*a strata*), and a plural *stratas* may also be encountered, but both uses are best avoided.

stratus (strah´təs) *n.* (*pl.* **strati** (-tī)) a continuous horizontal sheet of cloud. [L, nom. masc. p.p. of *sternere*, to strew, lay flat]

stravaig (strəvāg´) *v.i.* (*Sc.*) to roam about idly, to ramble. [OF *estravaguer*, late L *extrāvagārī*, see EXTRAVAGANT]

straw (straw) *n.* **1** the dry, ripened stalks of certain species of grain, esp. wheat, rye, oats etc., used as cattle fodder or material for packing, thatching, hat-making etc. **2** a single stalk of this kind, or a piece of one. **3** a long narrow plastic or paper tube for sucking up a drink. **4** (*usu. with neg.*) anything proverbially worthless (*not worth a straw*). **5** the colour of straw, a pale yellow. **6** a straw hat. ~*a.* **1** made of straw. **2** pale yellow. **to catch at straws/ a straw** to resort to desperate or manifestly inadequate remedies or measures. **to clutch at straws/ a straw** to catch at straws. **to draw the short straw** to be the one selected, orig. by lot, for a difficult or unpleasant task. **to grasp at straws/ a straw** to catch at straws. **strawboard** *n.* a type of building board consisting of pulped straw faced with paper. **straw boss** *n.* (*N Am.*) an assistant foreman. **straw colour,** (*N Am.*) **straw color** *n.* a pale yellow. **straw-coloured** *a.* **straw hat** *n.* a hat made of plaited straw. **straw in the wind** *n.* a hint or indication of future events. **straw poll, straw vote** *n.* an unofficial ballot taken as a test of opinion. **straw-worm** *n.* the caddis-worm. **strawy** *a.* [OE *strēaw* (cp. Dut. *stroo*, G *Stroh*, Icel. *strā*), cogn. with STRATUM]

strawberry (straw´bəri) *n.* (*pl.* **strawberries**) **1** a low, stemless perennial plant of the genus *Fragaria*, with trifoliate leaves and white flowers, bearing a fleshy red fruit. 2 the fruit itself, its surface studded with small achenes. ~*a.* of the colour (pinkish-red) or flavour of strawberries. **strawberry blonde** *a.*, *n.* (a woman) with reddish-blonde hair. **strawberry mark** *n.* a soft reddish birthmark. **strawberry pear** *n.* (the fruit of) a W Indian cactus, *Hylocereus undatus*. **strawberry roan** *a.* (of an animal's coat) chestnut mixed with grey or white. ~*n.* an animal with a coat of this colour. **strawberry tree** *n.* an evergreen arbutus, *Arbutus unedo*, bearing a strawberry-like fruit. [OE *strēa(w)berige*, lit. strawberry, connection with straw unexplained]

stray (strā) *v.i.* 1 to wander from the direct or proper course, to go wrong, to lose one's way. 2 to wander from the path of rectitude, to err or sin, to go astray. ~*n.* 1 any domestic animal that has gone astray. 2 a straggler, a waif. 3 (*esp. in pl.*) electrical interference with radio reception, atmospherics. ~*a.* 1 gone astray. 2 straggling, occasional, sporadic (*a stray visitor*; *heard a few stray shots*). 3 (*Physics*) waste, unwanted (*stray light*; *stray magnetic fields*). **strayed** *a.* having strayed or gone astray. **strayer** *n.* [OF *estraier*, from late L *extrāvagāri*, to wander abroad]

streak (strēk) *n.* 1 an esp. irregular line or long narrow mark of a distinct colour from the background; a strip or band. 2 a vein or element (*had a streak of selfishness*). 3 a run or stretch, esp. of good or bad luck (*on a winning streak*). 4 a line of bacteria etc. on a culture medium. ~*v.t.* to mark with streaks. ~*v.i.* 1 to move in a straight line at speed. 2 (*coll.*) to run naked through a public place as a prank. **streaker** *n.* **streaking** *n.* **streak of lightning** *n.* a jagged flash of lightning. **streaky** *a.* (*comp.* **streakier**, *superl.* **streakiest**) 1 marked with streaks; striped. 2 (of bacon) having alternate layers of meat and fat. **streakily** *adv.* **streakiness** *n.* [ME *streke*, from Scand. (cp. Swed. *streck*) or OE *strica*, STROKE[1] (cp. G *Strich*), cogn. with STRIKE]

stream (strēm) *n.* 1 a body of flowing water; a small river, a brook. 2 a moving body of fluid, e.g. lava, or anything in a state of continuous progressive movement, a moving throng of people etc. 3 a steady flow, a current, a drift (*against the stream*). 4 a band of schoolchildren of the same general academic ability, taught as a group. ~*v.i.* 1 to flow, move or issue in or as a stream. 2 to pour out or emit liquid abundantly (*eyes streaming with tears*). 3 to float, hang or wave in the wind etc. (*hair streaming in the wind*). ~*v.t.* 1 to pour out or flow with (liquid) abundantly (*The wound was streaming blood*). 2 to group (schoolchildren) into streams. **on stream** (of a factory etc.) in operation, in production. **to go with the stream** to do the same as other people, to behave conventionally. **stream-anchor** *n.* an anchor used for warping, between a bower and a kedge in size. **streamer** *n.* 1 a long narrow flag, a pennon. 2 a narrow roll of paper or ribbon that unrolls when thrown. 3 a column of light shooting across the sky, as in the aurora borealis or australis. 4 (*Comput.*) a device which copies data from a hard disk on to magnetic tape as a backup against accidental erasure or loss. **streamless** *a.* **streamlet** *n.* **streamline** *n.* 1 the direction of an air current or of the particles of air impinging on a moving body. 2 the shape given to aircraft, vehicles etc., in order to cause the minimum of resistance. ~*v.t.* 1 to shape an aircraft, vehicle etc. in this manner. 2 to make an organization, process etc. simpler or more efficient. **streamlined** *a.* 1 having a contoured shape to offer minimum resistance to air or liquid. 2 effectively organized, efficient, simplified. 3 graceful. **stream of consciousness** *n.* 1 the flow of thoughts and feelings forming an individual's conscious experience. 2 a literary technique used to express the unspoken thoughts and emotions of a fictional character, without using conventional narrative or dialogue. **streamy** *a.* (*comp.* **streamier**, *superl.* **streamiest**). [OE (cp. Dut. *stroom*, G *Strom*, Icel. *straumr*), from Gmc. *streu-*, cogn. with Sansk. *sru*, Gr. *rheein*, to flow]

street (strēt) *n.* 1 a road in a city or town with houses on one side or on both. 2 the part of the road used by vehicles. 3 the people living in a street. ~*a.* of or relating to life in urban centres. **in the street** outside the houses. **not in the same street as/ with** not to be compared with, quite inferior to. **on the streets** 1 living by prostitution. 2 homeless, destitute. **streets ahead of** far better than. **streets apart** completely different. **up one's street** ideally suited to one's talents, inclinations etc. **street arab** *n.* an outcast or vagrant child, cp. ARAB. **streetcar** *n.* (*N Am.*) a tram. **street credibility**, (*coll.*) **street cred** *n.* knowledge of the customs, language etc. associated with the urban subculture. **street door** *n.* a main house door opening on to the street. **streeted** *a.* (*often in comb.*, as *narrow-streeted*). **street entertainer** *n.* a juggler, musician, mime or other performer who entertains people in the street, usu. for donations of money. **street entertainment** *n.* **street furniture** *n.* objects for public use or convenience in the street such as litter bins, postboxes, lamp-posts etc. **street jewellery, street jewelry** *n.* enamel advertising plates etc. regarded as collectors' items. **street lamp** *n.* a street light. **street light** *n.* a light, esp. on a post, illuminating a street. **street lighting** *n.* **street-sweeper** *n.* a person or machine that sweeps streets. **street trader** *n.* a person who sells goods from a street stall. **street value** *n.* the monetary value of a commodity, esp. drugs, in terms of the price paid by the ultimate user. **streetwalker** *n.* a prostitute. **streetwalking** *n.*, *a.* **streetward** *a.*, *adv.* **streetwise** *a.* familiar with life among the poor, criminals etc. in an urban environment. [OE]

strelitzia (strəlit´siə) *n.* any southern African plant of the genus *Strelitzia*, with showy flowers that have a projecting tongue. [Charlotte of Mecklenburg-*Strelitz*, 1744–1818, wife of George III]

strength (strength) *n.* 1 the quality of being strong. 2 the relative degree to which, or aspect in which, a person or thing is strong. 3 muscular force. 4 firmness, solidity. 5 power, potency. 6 someone or something that supplies support, power or force. 7 intensity. 8 an attribute or quality seen as a character asset (*Detachment is her great strength*). 9 the number of people present or available. 10 the full number or complement (*The staff is below strength*). **from strength** from a strong position, for the purpose of negotiation etc. **from strength to strength** with continually increasing success. **in strength** in considerable numbers. **on the strength of** 1 in reliance on. 2 on the faith of. **the strength of** the essence, gist or main thrust of (*That's about the strength of it*). **strengthen** *v.t.* to make strong or stronger. ~*v.i.* to increase in strength. **to strengthen someone's hand/ hands** to empower someone to take action. **strengthener** *n.* **strengthless** *a.* [OE *strengthu*, from *strang*, STRONG]

Usage note Pronunciation as (strenth) is best avoided.

strenuous (stren´ūəs) *a.* 1 energetic, vigorous, zealous, ardent. 2 requiring effort. 3 eagerly persistent. **strenuously** *adv.* **strenuousness** *n.* [L *strēnuus*, cp. Gr. *strēnēs*, strong, *stereos*, STEREO-]

strep (strep) *n.* (*coll.*) streptococcus. ~*a.* streptococcal (*a strep throat*).

strepitoso (strepitō´sō) *adv.* (*Mus.*) in a noisy, impetuous manner. [It., from L *strepitus*, noise, from *strepere*, to make a noise]

strepto- (strep´tō) *comb. form* 1 twisted chain. 2 flexible. [Gr. *streptos*, twisted]

streptocarpus (streptəkah´pəs) *n.* any southern African plant of the genus *Streptocarpus*, with violet or pink funnel-shaped flowers and spirally twisted fruits. [Gr. *karpos*, a fruit]

streptococcus (streptōkok´əs) *n.* (*pl.* **streptococci** (-kok´sī)) any bacterium of the chain-forming genus *Streptococcus*, some of which cause infectious diseases. **streptococcal** (-kok´əl), **streptococcic** (-kok´sik) *a.* [Gr. *kokkos*, a seed, berry]

streptokinase (streptōkī´nāz) *n.* (*Med.*) an enzyme effective in treating blood clots and inflammation, produced by certain streptococci. [Gr. *kinein*, to move, -ASE]

streptomycin (streptōmī´sin) *n.* an antibiotic obtained from a soil bacterium and used in the treatment of tuberculosis and other bacterial infections. [Gr. *mukēs*, fungus]

stress (stres) *n.* **1** tension, pressure or strain exerted on an object; a measure of this, or its amount. **2** constraining or impelling force. **3** demands made on one physically, mentally or emotionally. **4** physical, mental or emotional strain resulting from this. **5** weight, importance, emphasis. **6** accentuation of, or emphasis on, a word or syllable; the chief accent in a word (*The stress comes on the third syllable*). **7** in mechanics, force exerted upon or between the parts of a body. ~*v.t.* **1** to emphasize. **2** to put the stress or accent on. **3** to subject to physical or mental stress or mechanical force. **to lay stress on** to emphasize, to accord importance to. **stress disease** *n.* an illness caused by unremitting mental stress. **stressed out** *a.* frantic or exhausted as a result of stress. **stressful** *a.* **stressfully** *adv.* **stressfulness** *n.* **stressless** *a.* [OF *estrecier*, pop. L *strictiāre*, see DISTRESS]

stretch (strech) *v.t.* **1** to draw out, to extend in any direction or to full length. **2** to tighten, to draw tight, to make taut; to make longer or wider by tension. **3** to extend lengthwise, to straighten (a limb etc.). **4** to hit so as to prostrate (*The blow stretched him full length*). **5** to distend, to strain. **6** to do violence to; to exaggerate (e.g. the truth). **7** to utilize fully or challenge sufficiently (*I don't feel this job is stretching me*). **8** (*sl.*) to hang by the neck. ~*v.i.* **1** to be extended in length or breadth. **2** to have a specified extension in space or time, to reach or last. **3** to be drawn out or admit of being drawn out (*fabrics that stretch*). **4** to extend or straighten one's body or limbs (*yawned and stretched*). ~*n.* **1** a reach, sweep, or tract (of land, water etc.). **2** an act of stretching or state of being stretched. **3** extent or reach. **4** (*coll.*) a period of a prison sentence. **5** (*coll.*) a period of service. **6** (*N Am.*) a straight section of a racetrack. **7** (*Naut.*) the distance covered in one tack. ~*a.* **1** (of fabric etc.) able to stretch (*stretch jeans*). **2** (of a vehicle, aircraft etc.) modified to accommodate extra seating etc. (*a stretch limousine*). **at a stretch 1** at one go. **2** continuously. **at full stretch** working etc. to full capacity, using all resources. **to stretch a point** to go beyond what might be expected. **to stretch forth one's hand against** HAND. **to stretch one's legs/ a leg** LEG. **to stretch one's wings** WING. **to stretch out 1** to extend (e.g. a hand or foot). **2** to lie or recline at full length. **3** to eke (money etc.) out. **4** to prolong. **stretchable** *a.* **stretchability** (-bil´-) *n.* **stretched** *a.* **stretcher** *n.* **1** a framework consisting of canvas extended on two poles, for carrying a sick, wounded, dead or disabled person in a recumbent position. **2** a brick or stone laid lengthwise in a course in a wall (cp. HEADER). **3** a cross-piece in a boat for a rower to press their feet against. **4** a horizontal rod fitted between chair legs. **5** a wooden frame with canvas stretched across it. **6** (*sl.*) †a lie or exaggeration. ~*v.t.* to carry on a stretcher (*stretchered off the field*). **stretcher-bearer** *n.* a person who helps to carry a stretcher bearing the wounded etc. **stretcher-bond** *n.* in bricklaying, a form of bond in which nothing but stretchers are used, though the joints come against the middles of the bricks in the contiguous course. **stretch marks** *n.pl.* translucent linear markings on the skin resulting from weight gain or pregnancy. **stretchy** *a.* (*comp.* **stretchier**, *superl.* **stretchiest**). **stretchiness** *n.* [OE *streccan*, from *stræc*, strong, violent (cp. Dut. *strekken*, G *strecken*, also L *stringere*, and Gr. *strangos*, twisted) cogn. with STRING, STRONG]

stretto (stret´ō) *adv.* (*Mus.*) at a quicker tempo. [It., narrow]

strew (stroo) *v.t.* (*p.p.* **strewn** (stroon), **strewed**) **1** to scatter, to spread. **2** to cover (with) by scattering over. **3** to be scattered over, to cover sporadically. **strewer** *n.* [OE *strēowian*, from *strēaw*, STRAW]

strewth (strooth), **struth, 'struth** *int.* used to express surprise or alarm etc. [derived from *God's truth*]

stria (strī´ə) *n.* (*pl.* **striae** (strī´ē)) **1** a superficial furrow, a thin line or groove, mark or ridge. **2** (*Archit.*) each of the fillets between the flutes of a column. **striate**[1] (-ət) *a.* marked with striae. **striately** *adv.* **striate**[2] (strīāt´) *v.t.* to mark with striae. **striated** (-ā´tid) *a.* **striated muscle** *n.* skeletal or voluntary muscle, with contractile fibrils lying side by side, having a striped appearance, as distinct from smooth, or visceral, muscle. **striation** (-ā´shən), **striature** (strī´əchə) *n.* [L]

stricken (strik´ən) *a.* (*often in comb.*) affected, esp. severely, by e.g. disease, disaster or sorrow (*the stricken city*; *disaster-stricken areas*; *grief-stricken parents*; *stricken by polio*). †**stricken in years** elderly, feeble with age. [old p.p. of STRIKE]

strickle (strik´əl) *n.* **1** a straight-edge for levelling grain in a measure. **2** a template. **3** a straight-edge for sharpening curved blades. [dim. of *strick*, cogn. with STRIKE]

strict (strikt) *a.* **1** defined or applied exactly, accurate, precise; admitting of no exception (*must be kept in strict isolation*). **2** enforcing or observing rules precisely, not lax. **3** rigorous, severe, stringent. **strict counterpoint** *n.* (*Mus.*) counterpoint written more as an academic exercise than as a composition. **strictly** *adv.* **1** in a strict manner. **2** (*also* **strictly speaking**) confining words to their exact sense (*strictly (speaking), the spider is not an insect*). **3** (*N Am., coll.*) definitely. **strictness** *n.* [L *strictus*, p.p. of *stringere*, see STRINGENT]

stricture (strik´chə) *n.* **1** a censure, a sharp criticism. **2** (*Med.*) a morbid contraction of a duct or channel, as of the urethra. **strictured** *a.* [L *strictūra*, from *stringere*, to tighten]

stride (strīd) *v.i.* (*past* **strode** (strōd), *p.p.* **stridden** (strid´ən)) **1** to walk with long steps. **2** to sit or stand with legs apart, to straddle. ~*v.t.* **1** to pass over in one step. **2** to bestride. ~*n.* **1** a long or measured step or the distance covered by this. **2** (*pl., chiefly Austral., coll.*) men's trousers. **to make great strides** to progress or develop rapidly. **to take in one's stride 1** to jump (an obstacle) without adjusting one's gait. **2** to achieve (something) or override (something) without difficulty or effort. **stride piano** *n.* a style of jazz piano in which the right hand plays the melody, while the left alternates in a swinging rhythm between single bass notes (on strong beats) and chords. **strider** *n.* [OE *strīdan*, cp. LG *strīden*, Dut. *strijden*, to stride, to strive, G *streiten*, to strive]

stridence (strī´dəns), **stridency** (-si) *n.* loudness or harshness of tone. **strident** *a.* sounding harsh, grating. **stridently** *adv.* **stridor** (strī´daw) *n.* **1** a harsh, whistling noise made during respiration, caused by blockage of the air passages. **2** a harsh high-pitched sound. **stridulate** (strid´ūlāt) *v.i.* (of insects, esp. cicadas and grasshoppers) to make a shrill creaking noise by rubbing the legs or wing-cases or other hard parts together. **stridulant**, **stridulous** *a.* **stridulation** (-lā´shən) *n.* **stridulator** *n.* **stridulatory** (-lā´təri) *a.* [L *strīdens -entis*, pres.p. of *stridēre*, to creak]

strife (strīf) *n.* **1** contention, conflict, hostile struggle. **2** (*Austral., coll.*) any kind of trouble. **strifeful** *a.* [OF *estrif*, Icel. *strīth*, cogn. with STRIDE]

striga (strī´gə) *n.* (*pl.* **strigae** (-jē)) **1** a short stiff hair, bristle or hairlike scale. **2** a fluting on a column. **strigose** (-gōs) *a.* [L, a swath, rel. to *stringere*, to bind]

strigil (strij´il) *n.* **1** a skin-scraper used in baths by the ancient Romans and Greeks. **2** a comblike structure on an insect's leg, used to clean antennae etc. [L *strigilis*, rel. to *stringere*, to graze]

strike (strīk) *v.t.* (*past* **struck** (strŭk), *p.p.* **struck, †stricken** (strik´ən)) **1** to hit, to deliver a blow or blows upon; to deliver, to deal, to inflict (a blow etc.) (*struck him a blow on the shoulder*). **2** to come into violent contact with; to bring or cause to come into violent contact (*struck his fist on the table*; *The ship struck a sandbank*). **3** to drive, to send (a ball etc.) with force. **4** to attack (an enemy craft, location etc.). **5 a** to produce, make, form, effect, or bring into a particular state by a stroke, e.g. to ignite (a match), to stamp or mint (a coin), to render (deaf, dumb or blind). **b** to afflict (*was struck by a virus*). **6** to effect forcibly, to impress strongly, to occur suddenly to the mind of (*A thought struck me*; *That strikes me as a waste of time*). **7** to cause (a bell, musical note etc.) to sound. **8** to notify (the time) by sound (*The clock struck twelve*). **9** to cause to penetrate, to thrust (into) (*The noise struck fear into us*). **10** to make (a bargain). **11** to hook (a fish) by jerking the tackle upwards. **12** (of a snake) to attack or wound with its fangs. **13** to cause (a cutting etc.) to take root. **14** to lower (sails, a flag, tent etc.). **15** to level corn etc. in (a measure) by scraping off the surplus. **16** to determine or find (a balance, average etc.). **17** to assume (an attitude). **18** to discover, to come across. **19** to find by drilling, excavating etc. (*strike oil*; *strike gold*). **20** to put together (a jury), usu. by allowing both sides in the case to reject the same number. **21** †to leave off (work), esp. to enforce a demand for higher wages etc. ~*v.i.* **1** to try to hit, to deliver a blow or blows (at, upon); to collide, to dash (against, upon etc.); to be driven on shore, a rock etc. **2** to sound the time; (of time) to be sounded (*Has the clock struck yet?*; *Twelve had already struck*). **3** to leave off work to enforce a demand for higher wages etc. **4** to arrive suddenly, to happen (upon). **5** to enter or turn (in a certain direction) (*We struck south-west*). **6** to lower sails, a flag etc. in token of surrender etc. **7** (of a cutting) to take root. **8** (of an oyster) to attach itself to a bed. **9** (of a snake) to attack with its fangs. **10** (*Geol.*) (of strata) to extend in a particular direction. ~*n.* **1** an act of striking. **2** an act of striking for an increase of wages etc. **3** a refusal to take part in some other activity or perform a task expected of one. **4** an attack upon an enemy location, craft etc.; an attack on a target from the air. **5** a straight-edge for levelling something, e.g. a measure of grain. **6** (*Geol.*) the horizontal direction of an outcrop. **7** a discovery (as of oil). **8** a lucky find, unexpected success. **9** in tenpin bowling, the knocking down of all ten pins with the first bowl, or the score in doing this. **10** in baseball, a good pitched ball missed by the batter and counting against them. **11** in cricket, a position to receive the bowling. **12** a strickle. **on strike** participating in an industrial strike. **strike a light!** used to express astonishment. **struck on** (*coll.*) enamoured of, infatuated with. **to strike a balance** BALANCE. **to strike a blow for** BLOW[2]. **to strike a chord** CHORD[1]. **to strike a light** to strike a match. **to strike at the root/ roots of** ROOT[1]. **to strike back 1** to return a blow, retaliate. **2** (of a gas burner) to burn from an internal point before the gas mixes with air. **to strike down 1** to knock down. **2** to make ill or cause to die, esp. suddenly. **3** to bring low. **to strike dumb** DUMB. **to strike home 1** to hit the intended target. **2** to achieve the desired effect. **to strike in 1** to break into a conversation. **2** (of a disease) to spread into the interior of the body from the skin or surface. **to strike (it) lucky** to have a success. **to strike it rich 1** to find a deposit of oil, minerals etc. **2** to make an unexpected large financial gain. **to strike off 1** to remove, separate, dislodge etc. by a blow. **2** to erase, to delete, to strike out (e.g. someone, or their name, from a register). **3** to print (copies of a document). **to strike oil 1** to find oil by sinking a shaft. **2** to have a success, to strike lucky. **to strike out 1** to hit from the shoulder (e.g. in boxing). **2** to take vigorous action. **3** to delete, to expunge. **4** to set off (*We struck out northwards*). **5** to make vigorous strokes (in skating, swimming etc.). **6** to devise, to contrive (a plan etc.). **7** to produce (coins, medals etc.) by striking. **8** in baseball, to dismiss (a batter) or be dismissed after three strikes. **to strike root** ROOT[1]. **to strike the flag** FLAG[1]. **to strike the right note** NOTE. **to strike through** to delete (a word etc.) by drawing a line through it. **to strike up 1** to enter into, to start (a conversation etc.). **2** to begin to play or sing. **3** to drive up with a blow. **to strike upon 1** to think of or hit upon (an idea, solution etc.). **2** (of light) to shine upon, to illuminate. **to strike while the iron is hot** to take an opportunity while it presents itself. **strikebound** *a.* (of a factory etc.) closed or disrupted because of a strike. **strike-breaker** *n.* **1** a blackleg. **2** a worker brought in to replace one out on strike. **strike-break** *v.i.* (*past* **strike-broke,** *p.p.* **strike-broken**). **strike-breaking** *n.* **strike call** *n.* a directive to union members to go on strike. **strike force** *n.* **1** a police force or military force equipped for immediate action. **2** in football, the forwards of a team. **strike-measure** *n.* measurement carried out by passing a rod across the top of a heaped container, to ensure that it is completely and exactly full. **strike-out** *n.* in baseball, an out called after three strikes by the batter. **strike pay** *n.* an allowance for subsistence from a trade union to workers on strike. **striker** *n.* **1** a person or thing that strikes, esp. a worker on strike. **2** in soccer, an attacking player, a forward. **strike rate** *n.* a success rate e.g. in goal-scoring or run-scoring. **strike-slip fault** *n.* (*Geol.*) a fault characterized by the horizontal displacement of strata. **strike zone** *n.* in baseball, the rectangular zone between the armpits and knees of a batter. **striking** *a.* surprising, forcible, impressive, noticeable. **within striking distance** near enough to strike, reach or achieve. **striking-circle** *n.* in hockey, the semi-circular area in front of the goal from within which the ball must be struck to score. **striking force** *n.* a military force equipped for immediate action or attack. **strikingly** *adv.* **strikingness** *n.* [OE *strīcan*, to go (cp. Dut. *strijken*, G *streichen*, Icel. *strjūka*, to stroke, rub, smooth etc.), cogn. with L *stringere*, to graze]

Strimmer® (strim´ə) *n.* an electrically operated grass-trimmer with a rapidly rotating nylon cutting cord.

Strine (strīn) *n.* Australian English, comically transliterated, e.g. *afferbeck lauder*, for *alphabetical order*. [a rendering of *Australian* in an Australian accent]

string (string) *n.* **1** twine, a fine line, usu. thicker than thread and thinner than cord. **2** a length of this or strip of leather, tape, or other material, used for tying, fastening, binding together, connecting etc. **3** a stringlike fibre, tendon, nerve etc., e.g. the tough piece connecting the two halves of a bean pod. **4** a piece of wire, catgut etc., yielding musical sounds or notes when caused to vibrate in a piano, violin etc.; each of the interwoven pieces of catgut stretched across the head of a tennis racket. **5** (*pl.*) the stringed instruments in an orchestra. **6** a cord or thread upon which anything is strung; a series of things or persons connected together or following in close succession (*a string of pearls*; *a string of visitors*; *came out with a string of expletives*). **7** in billiards, the apparatus for keeping the score, or the score itself. **8** the horses under training at a particular racing stable. **9** (*pl.*) conditions, complications. **10** a sequence of alphabetic or numeric characters in a computer program. **11** a stringboard. **12 a** a hypothetical subatomic particle behaving like a flexible loop. **b** a hypothetical threadlike concentration of energy within space-time. *~v.t.* (*past, p.p.* **strung** (strŭng)) **1** to supply with a string or strings. **2** to fit the strings on (a bow). **3** to tie with string. **4** to thread (beads etc.) on a string. **5** to strip (beans etc.) of strings or fibres. **6** (*esp. N Am., sl.*) to hoax. *~v.i.* **1** to become stringy. **2** in billiards, to send the ball against the top cushion and back to decide which player is to begin. **no strings attached** (*coll.*) with no conditions or restrictions. **on a string 1** totally dependent, e.g. emotionally. **2** held in suspense. **to pull strings** to exert influence unobtrusively. **to string along 1** (*coll.*) to accompany. **2** to agree with, go along with. **3** (*coll.*) to fool, deceive. **to string out** to prolong, esp. unnecessarily. **to string together** to join up in a series (*stringing together sentences with commas*). **to string up** (*coll.*) to hang (by the neck). **two/ many strings to one's bow** BOW[1]. **string band** *n.* a band of stringed instruments. **string bass** *n.* (*Mus.*) a double bass. **string bean** *n.* **1** (*esp. N Am.*) a runner bean, a French bean. **2** (*coll.*) a tall thin person. **stringboard** *n.* a timber receiving the ends of stairs in a staircase. **string-course** *n.* a projecting horizontal band, moulding or raised course of bricks running along a building. **stringed** *a.* **stringed instrument** *n.* a musical instrument in which sounds are generated by the vibration of strings. **stringer** *n.* **1** a long horizontal member in a structural framework. **2** a stringboard. **3** (*coll.*) a journalist who works part-time for a newspaper or news agency in a particular area. **4** a person who strings. **stringless** *a.* **stringlike** *a.* **string-piece** *n.* **1** a supporting timber forming the edge of a framework, esp. of a floor. **2** a stringboard. **string quartet** *n.* **1** a combination of four stringed instruments, usu. two violins, a viola and a cello. **2** a piece of music written for this combination. **string tie** *n.* a narrow necktie. **string vest** *n.* a wide-meshed vest. **stringy** *a.* (*comp.* **stringier**, *superl.* **stringiest**) consisting of strings or small threads, fibrous, ropy, viscous. **stringiness** *n.* **stringy-bark** *n.* any of various Australian gum trees, from their fibrous bark. **strung up** *a.* (*coll.*) **1** in a highly nervous state. **2** hanged. [OE *streng*, cogn. with STRONG]

stringendo (strinjen´dō) *adv.* (*Mus.*) in accelerated time. [It., as STRINGENT]

stringent (strin´jənt) *a.* **1** strict, precise, binding, rigid. **2** (of the money market) hampered, tight, unaccommodating. **stringency** *n.* **stringently** *adv.* **stringentness** *n.* [L *stringens, stringentis*, pres.p. of *stringere*, to draw tight, p.p. *strictus*]

stringhalt (string´hawlt), **springhalt** (spring´-) *n.* a convulsive movement of a horse's hind legs in walking. [STRING, HALT[1]; alt. spelling influenced by appearance of the movement]

strip[1] (strip) *v.t.* (*pres.p.* **stripping**, *past, p.p.* **stripped**) **1** to pull the clothes or covering from, to denude, to skin, to peel, to husk, to clean. **2** to deprive (of e.g. titles or property), to despoil, to plunder. **3** to remove (clothes, bark, rigging, branches etc.) (*stripped off his clothes; stripped the leaves off the stem*). **4** to remove fittings from. **5** to sell off (the assets of a company) for profit. **6** to milk (a cow) to the last drop. **7** to remove old hair from (a dog). **8** to remove the stems from (tobacco). **9** to tear the thread from (a screw), or the teeth from (a gear). **10** to remove (paint) from (a surface). *~v.i.* **1** to take (off) one's clothes, to undress. **2** to come away in strips. **3** (of a screw) to have the thread torn off. **4** (of a projectile) to be discharged without spin. *~n.* **1** an act of stripping. **2** a striptease. **3** the clothes worn by a football team etc. **to strip down** to dismantle. **stripagram, strippergram** *n.* a telegram delivered by a person who does a striptease for the entertainment of the recipient. **strip club** *n.* a club in which striptease artistes perform. **stripmine** *n.* an opencast mine. **stripper** *n.* **strippergram** STRIPAGRAM (under STRIP[1]). **strippings** *n.pl.* the last milk drawn from a cow. **stripsearch** *n.* a body search requiring the removal of all clothing. *~v.t.* to search in this way. **striptease** *n.* a cabaret turn in which a performer partially or wholly undresses. [OE *bestrīepan*, to plunder]

strip[2] (strip) *n.* **1** a long narrow piece. **2** a narrow stretch of land (*an airstrip*). **3** a flat narrow bar of iron or steel. **4** a strip cartoon. **to tear someone off a strip** (*coll.*) to scold someone angrily. **strip cartoon** *n.* a comic strip. **strip light** *n.* a tubular fluorescent light. **strip lighting** *n.* **strip mill** *n.* a mill where steel slabs are rolled out into strips. [rel. to MLG *Strippe*, strap, rel. to STRIPE]

stripe (strīp) *n.* **1** a long, narrow band of a distinctive colour or texture. **2** a chevron on the sleeve of a uniform indicating rank. **3** (*N Am.*) a cast of character or opinion (*people of that stripe*). **4** †a stroke with a whip, scourge etc. *~v.t.* to mark with stripes. **striped** *a.* **striped squill** *n.* a liliaceous plant, *Puschkinia scilloides*. **stripy** *a.* (*comp.* **stripier**, *superl.* **stripiest**). **stripiness** *n.* [prob. from MDut. *strijpe*, cp. Norw. *stripa*, LG *Stripe*, G *Streifen*]

stripling (strip´ling) *n.* a youth, a lad. [dim. of STRIP[1]]

strive (strīv) *v.i.* (*past* **strove** (strōv), **strived,** *p.p.* **striven** (striv´ən), **strived**) **1** to try hard, to make a great effort (for something, to do something etc.). **2** to struggle or contend (against). **striver** *n.* **strivingly** *adv.* [OF *estriver*, rel. to *estrif*, STRIFE]

strobe (strōb) *n.* **1** a stroboscope. **2** a stroboscopic lamp. **3** (*N Am.*) an electronic flash for a camera. *~v.t.* to illuminate intermittently as though by stroboscope. *~v.i.* **1** to flash intermittently. **2** (of a television screen etc.) to show strobing. **strobe lighting** *n.* **1** high-intensity flashing light. **2** the apparatus that produces this. **strobing** *n.* **1** the appearance of jerkily moving lines or stripes in a television picture. **2** in cinematography, undesirable jerkiness in the movement portrayed. **stroboscope** (-bəskōp) *n.* an instrument for observing or timing periodic motion such as rotation by making the moving body visible at intervals through the use of an intermittently flashing light. **stroboscopic** (-skop´-), **stroboscopical** *a.* **stroboscopically** *adv.* [Gr. *strobos*, twisting, from *strephein*, to turn]

strobila (strō´bilə, strəbī´-) *n.* (*pl.* **strobilae** (-lē)) **1** a chain of segments forming the body of a tapeworm. **2** a polyp-like segment of a jellyfish that divides to produce larvae. [mod. L from Gr. *strobilē*, a twisted plug of lint, from *strephein*, to twist]

strobile (strō´bīl), **strobilus** (-biləs) *n.* **1** a pine cone or a multiple fruit such as this. **2** a conelike structure, such as the flower of the hop plant. **strobilaceous** (-lā´shəs), **strobiliform** (-bil´ifawm), **strobiline** (strō´bilīn) *a.* [Gr. *strobilos*, cogn. with *strephein*, to turn]

stroboscope STROBE.

strode STRIDE.

Stroganoff (strog´ənof) *n., a.* (*usu. following the n.*) denoting a dish of meat, usu. beef in strips, cooked with onions and mushrooms in a sour-cream sauce. [Count *Stroganoff*, 19th-cent. Russian diplomat]

stroke[1] (strōk) *n.* **1** an act of striking, a blow; the impact, shock, noise etc., of this. **2** a sudden attack of illness etc., esp. a thrombosis in the brain, sometimes causing unconsciousness or paralysis. **3** a player's action in hitting the ball etc. in various games, such as golf, tennis, cricket; such a hit as the scoring unit in golf. **4** a single movement of something, esp. any one of a series of recurring movements, as of the heart, an oar, wing, piston etc. **5** the length, manner, rate etc. of such a movement. **6** (*with neg.*) the slightest such movement or action (*haven't done a stroke of work*). **7** a mark made by a single movement of a pen, pencil etc.; a touch or detail, e.g. in a description. **8** a move, action or happening (*a stroke of policy; a stroke of fate*). 9 each strike of a clock. 10 the stroke oar of a boat. ~*v.t.* to act as stroke for (a boat or crew). ~*n.* the aftermost rower in a boat who sets the time of the stroke for the rest. **at a stroke** by a single action. **off one's stroke** not at one's best. **on the stroke** punctually. **on the stroke of** exactly at the time when the clock starts striking (a particular time). **stroke oar** *n.* 1 the rower nearest the stern, who sets the rowing speed. 2 the oar of this rower. **stroke of business** *n.* a financially rewarding transaction. **stroke of genius** *n.* a brilliantly inspired idea. **stroke of (good) luck** *n.* a piece of good fortune. **stroke play** *n.* in golf, scoring by counting the number of strokes played as opposed to the number of holes won. [OE *strāc*, from *strican*, to STRIKE]

stroke[2] (strōk) *v.t.* to pass the hand over the surface of (fur, hair, an animal etc.) caressingly. ~*n.* an act of stroking or a spell of this. **to stroke down** to mollify, to appease. **to stroke someone's hair the wrong way** to ruffle, to annoy. **to stroke the wrong way** to ruffle, to annoy. **stroker** *n.* [OE *strācian*, from *strāc*, see STROKE[1]]

stroll (strōl) *v.i.* 1 to walk in a leisurely way, to saunter. 2 to achieve the desired result easily. ~*v.t.* to saunter or ramble along on foot. ~*n.* 1 a leisurely ramble. 2 an easy success. **stroller** *n.* 1 a person who strolls. 2 (*N Am.*) a pushchair. **strolling players** *n.pl.* (a troupe of) actors who move from place to place giving performances. [perh. G *strollen*, *strolchen*, from *Strolch*, a vagabond]

stroma (strō´mə) *n.* (*pl.* **stromata** (-mətə)) 1 the framework of tissue of an organ or cell. 2 a dense mass of hyphae produced by some fungi, in which fructification may develop. 3 the dense framework of a chloroplast etc. **stromatic** (-mat´-) *a.* **stromatolite** *n.* (*Biol.*) a mound composed of blue-green algae and trapped sediment, found as a fossil, or in lagoons in Australasia. [Gr. *strōma*, bed, rel. to *strōnnunai*, to spread]

stromb (stromb) *n.* 1 any gastropod of the genus *Strombus* or the family Strombidae, chiefly found in tropical seas. 2 a shell of this, used for ornament. **strombuliform** (-bū´lifawm) *a.* (*Bot.*) twisted spirally like a screw. [mod. L *strombus*, Gr. *strombos*, pine cone, rel. to *strephein*, to turn]

strong (strong) *a.* (*comp.* **stronger** (strong´gə), *superl.* **strongest** (strong´gist)) 1 able to withstand or resist force; not easily damaged (*strong walls*). 2 able to withstand opposition or bear adverse fortune etc. (*a strong will; a strong personality*). 3 (of a person or their constitution) able to fight off illness, or not prone to suffer from it. 4 fully healthy, esp. after illness (*strong and well*). 5 (of people's nerves) not easily shattered; proof against shocks. 6 (of a market) maintaining high or rising prices. 7 powerful; muscular; full of stamina; capable of sustained effort. 8 effective, forceful (*strong opposition; a strong lobby*). 9 firm, not wavering (*strong beliefs*). 10 (of a position or argument) difficult to attack, invulnerable, convincing. 11 (of the wind or weather) violent. 12 having a powerful impact on the senses or emotions (*strong sunlight; a strong performance*). 13 (of e.g. a military force, team etc.) powerful, numerous, well-trained, of high quality. 14 likely to be successful or to win (*a strong contestant; a strong combination*). 15 (of a beverage or a solution) concentrated; containing a high proportion of the active ingredient (*strong black coffee*). 16 (*Chem.*) (of an acid or base) having a high concentration of hydrogen or hydroxide ions in aqueous solution. 17 used (following the number) to specify numbers present, the size of a gathering etc. (*a band of protesters about 300 strong*). 18 (of someone's voice) loud, carrying, powerful. 19 (of food, its flavour or smell) pungent. 20 (of someone's breath) foul-smelling. 21 (of written style) telling; forceful, succinct or compact. 22 (of moves or measures) forceful, drastic. 23 (*Gram.*) **a** (of Germanic verbs) forming inflections through a vowel change (as *run, ran, sing, sang, sung*), not by the addition of a suffix (as *walk, walked*). **b** (of Germanic nouns and adjectives) belonging to a declension in which the stem terminated otherwise than with *n*. ~*adv.* (*rare*) strongly. **going strong** 1 continuing to flourish. 2 still in action. **to come it strong** COME. **to come on strong** to behave forcefully or aggressively. **strong-arm** *a.* using or involving physical force. ~*v.t.* to show violence towards. **strongbox** *n.* a safe or robust trunk for storing valuables. **strong drink** *n.* alcoholic liquors. **strong force** *n.* (*Physics*) the force mediating the strong interaction between subatomic particles. **strong grade** *n.* in Germanic philology, the stressed ablaut form. **stronghold** *n.* 1 a fortress, a fastness. 2 a refuge. **strong interaction** *n.* (*Physics*) an interaction between elementary particles responsible for the forces that bind nucleons together in an atomic nucleus, but effective only at comparatively short distances. **strongish** *a.* **strong language** *n.* 1 swearing. 2 forceful or emphatic phraseology. **strongly** *adv.* **strongman** *n.* (*pl.* **strongmen**) 1 a person who performs muscular feats of strength. 2 (*coll.*) an autocratic leader. **strong meat** *n.* theories or doctrines demanding courageous thought. **strong-minded** *a.* 1 resolute, determined. 2 having a vigorous mind. **strong-mindedly** *adv.* **strong-mindedness** *n.* **strong point** *n.* 1 something at which one excels; one's forte. 2 a particularly strongly fortified or defended position. **strongroom** *n.* a specially reinforced room for storing valuables. **strong stomach** *n.* a constitution or digestive system not prone to nausea. **strong suit** *n.* 1 in card-playing, a suit in which one can take tricks. 2 one's forte or strong point. [OE *strang* (cp. Dut. and Dan. *streng*, Icel. *strangr*, Swed. *sträng*, G *streng*, strict), cogn. with L *stringere*, see STRICT]

strontium (stron´tiəm, -shəm) *n.* a soft silvery-white metallic element, at. no. 38, chem. symbol Sr, resembling calcium. **strontia** (-tiə, -shə) *n.* strontium oxide. **strontian** (-tiən, -shən) *n.* strontium, strontia or strontianite. ~*a.* of or relating to any of these. **strontianite** (-nīt) *n.* a carbonate of strontia. **strontium-90** *n.* strontium with atomic weight of 90, a radioactive product of nuclear fission which tends to accumulate in bones. **strontium oxide** *n.* a white compound used in manufacturing fireworks. [*Strontian*, in the Highland Region of Scotland, where first found]

strop (strop) *n.* 1 a strip of leather etc., for sharpening razors etc. on. 2 (*Naut.*) a leather, rope or iron collar used in handling cargo. ~*v.t.* (*pres.p.* **stropping,** *past, p.p.* **stropped**) to sharpen with or on a strop. [var. of STRAP]

strophanthus (strəfan´thəs) *n.* any plant of the genus *Strophanthus* of Asia and Africa, belonging to the periwinkle family. **strophanthin** (-thin) *n.* a poisonous drug made from strophanthus seeds, used as arrow poison, its medicinal uses being similar to those of digitalis. [Gr. *strophos*, a twisted band; *anthos*, a flower]

strophe (strō´fi) *n.* 1 the turning of the chorus from right to left in an ancient Greek drama. 2 a part of the ode (consisting of strophe, antistrophe, and epode) sung whilst so turning, esp. the first part, the strophe proper. 3 a number of lines constituting a section of a lyric poem. **strophic** *a.* [Gr. *strophē*, orig. a turning, from *strephein*, to turn]

strophiole (strof´iōl) *n.* (*Bot.*) an appendage like an aril attached to the hilum of some seeds. **strophiolate** (-lāt) *a.* [L *strophiolum*, dim. of *strophium*, Gr. *strophion*, dim. of *strophos*, a band, from *strophē*, a turn]

stroppy (strop´i) *a.* (*comp.* **stroppier,** *superl.* **stroppiest**) (*coll.*) 1 rowdy, angry. 2 awkward, quarrelsome.

stroppily *adv.* **stroppiness** *n.* [perh. alteration of OBSTREPEROUS]

strove STRIVE.

struck STRIKE.

structure (strŭk´chə) *n.* **1** a combination of parts, as a building, machine, organism etc., esp. the supporting or essential framework. **2** the manner in which a complex whole is constructed, put together, or organically formed. **3** the arrangement of parts, organs, atoms etc., in a complex whole (*sentence structure*). ~*v.t.* to create a structure. **structural** *a.* **1** of or relating to structure. **2** having a structure. **3** forming part of a structure, integral to the structure. **structural engineering** *n.* (the branch of engineering concerned with) the construction of large modern buildings etc. **structural formula** *n.* (*pl.* **structural formulas, structural formulae**) a chemical formula showing the arrangement of atoms and bonds in a molecule. **structural geology** *n.* the study of the relations between the rock masses forming the earth's crust and of their physical causes. **structuralism** *n.* an approach to the human sciences, literature, linguistics etc. as coded systems comprising self-sufficient and self-determining structures of interrelationships and rules of combination through which meaning or function is generated and communicated. **structuralist** *n., a.* **structural linguistics** *n.* the study of language as a complex structure of interconnected elements. **structurally** *adv.* **structural psychology** *n.* the study of the nature and arrangement of mental states and processes. **structural steel** *n.* strong mild steel in prepared shapes suitable for construction work. **structured** *a.* (*sometimes in comb., as loose-structured*). **structureless** *a.* [F, from L *structūra*, from *struere*, to build, p.p. *structus*]

strudel (stroo´dəl) *n.* a thin pastry rolled up with a filling (e.g. apple) and baked. [G, lit. whirlpool]

struggle (strŭg´əl) *v.i.* **1** to make violent movements in trying to break free from restraint etc. **2** to make great efforts, esp. against difficulties or opposition. **3** to strive (for something, or to do something). **4** to contend (with or against). **5** to make one's way (along etc.) against difficulties, opposition etc. **6** (of a writer, artist etc.) to have difficulty making a name for oneself. ~*n.* **1** an act or spell of struggling. **2** a strenuous effort. **3** a fight or contest, esp. of a confused character. **struggle for existence, struggle for life** *n.* the struggle for survival or domination that goes on between natural organisms or between people trying to gain a living. **struggler** *n.* **struggling** *a.* **strugglingly** *adv.* [ME *strogelen*, cp. Swed. dial. *strug*, contention, Norw. *stru*, refractory]

strum (strŭm) *v.t., v.i.* (*pres.p.* **strumming,** *past, p.p.* **strummed**) to play noisily or carelessly, to thrum on a stringed instrument. ~*n.* **1** the sound of strumming. **2** an act of strumming. **strummer** *n.* [imit.]

struma (stroo´mə) *n.* (*pl.* **strumae** (-mē)) **1** (*Med., dated*) scrofula. **2** (*Med.*) goitre. **3** (*Bot.*) a cushion-like swelling on a petiole etc. **strumose** (-mōs), **strumous** *a.* [L, from *struere*, to build]

†**strumpet** (strŭm´pit) *n.* a prostitute, a harlot. ~*v.t.* (*pres.p.* **strumpeting,** *past, p.p.* **strumpeted**) to debauch. [etym. uncertain, perh. from OF *strupe, strupre*, concubinage, L *stuprum*, defilement]

strung STRING.

strut[1] (strŭt) *v.i.* (*pres.p.* **strutting,** *past, p.p.* **strutted**) to walk with a pompous, conceited gait. ~*n.* such a gait. **strutter** *n.* **struttingly** *adv.* [ME *strouten*, prob. from Dan. *strutte* (cp. Swed. dial. *strutta*), cogn. with LG *strutt*, rigid]

strut[2] (strŭt) *n.* a timber or iron beam inserted in a framework so as to keep other members apart, a brace. ~*v.t.* (*pres.p.* **strutting,** *past, p.p.* **strutted**) to brace with a strut or struts. [rel. to STRUT[1]]

struth, 'struth STREWTH.

struthious (stroo´thiəs) *a.* of or relating to the ostrich; ostrich-like. [Gr. *strouthiōn*, ostrich, from *strouthos*, sparrow]

strutter, struttingly STRUT[1].

strychnine (strik´nēn) *n.* a highly poisonous alkaloid obtained from certain plant species of the genus *Strychnos*, esp. *S. nux-vomica*, used in medicine as a stimulant etc. †**strychnia** (-niə) *n.* strychnine. **strychnic** *a.* **strychninism, strychnism** *n.* strychnine poisoning. [L *strychnos*, Gr. *struchnos*, nightshade, -INE]

Sts *abbr.* Saints.

stub (stŭb) *n.* **1** a stump, end or remnant of anything, e.g. of a cigarette or a pencil. **2** the stump of a tree, tooth etc. **3** a counterfoil, esp. of a cheque or receipt. ~*v.t.* (*pres.p.* **stubbing,** *past, p.p.* **stubbed**) **1** to strike (one's toe) against something. **2** to extinguish (a cigarette etc.), to put (out) with a squashing action. **3** to grub (up) by the roots. **4** to clear (land) of stubs. **stub-axle** *n.* an axle that supports only one wheel of a pair. **stubbed** *a.* stubby. **stubby** *a.* (*comp.* **stubbier,** *superl.* **stubbiest**) short and thickset. ~*n.* (*pl.* **stubbies**) (*Austral., coll.*) a small squat beer bottle. **stubbily** *adv.* **stubbiness** *n.* [OE *stybb*, cp. Dut. *stobbe*, Icel. *stubbi*, Dan. *stub*, also Gr. *stupos*]

stubble (stŭb´əl) *n.* **1** the stumps of wheat, barley etc. covering the ground after harvest. **2** short, bristly hair, whiskers etc. **3** an unshaven growth of facial hair. **stubbled** *a.* **stubble-fed** *a.* fed on the grass growing amongst stubble, split grain etc. **stubbly** *a.* (*comp.* **stubblier,** *superl.* **stubbliest**). [ME *stobil*, OF *estoubie*, late L *stupula*, L *stipula*, see STIPULE]

stubborn (stŭb´ən) *a.* **1** unreasonably obstinate, not to be persuaded. **2** obdurate, inflexible, intractable, refractory. **3** unyielding, immovable. **stubbornly** *adv.* **stubbornness** *n.* [ME *stoburn, stiborn*, prob. from OE *stybb*, STUB]

stubby STUB.

stucco (stŭk´ō) *n.* (*pl.* **stuccoes, stuccos**) **1** fine plaster for coating walls or moulding into decorations in relief. **2** any plaster used for coating the outside of buildings. ~*v.t.* (*3rd pers. sing. pres.* **stuccoes,** *pres.p.* **stuccoing,** *past, p.p.* **stuccoed**) to coat with stucco. **stuccoer** *n.* [It., from OHG *stucchi*, crust (cp. G *Stück*, OE *stycce*, piece), cogn. with STOCK]

stuck STICK[2].

stud[1] (stŭd) *n.* **1** a large-headed nail, knob, head of a bolt etc., esp. fixed as an ornament. **2** a small jewel for wearing in pierced ears or a pierced nose. **3** an ornamental button for wearing in a shirt-front etc. **4** a crosspiece in each link of chain cable. **5** a marker let into a road surface so as to project slightly. **6** a stud-bolt. **7** a small spindle, pin, or dowel, in a lathe, watch etc. **8** a post or scantling to which laths are nailed in a partition. **9** (*N Am.*) the height of a room as represented by the length of such a post. ~*v.t.* (*pres.p.* **studding,** *past, p.p.* **studded**) **1** to set with studs or ornamental knobs. **2** to set thickly, to bestrew. **stud-bolt** *n.* a bolt with a thread for screwing into a fixed part at one end and having a nut screwed on it at the other. **studded** *a.* set or scattered (with e.g. gems, stars). **studding** *n.* the wooden framework of a lath-and-plaster wall. [OE *studu*, a post, cp. Dan. and Swed. *stöd*, Icel. *stoth*, G *Stütze*, prop]

stud[2] (stŭd) *n.* **1** a number of horses kept for riding, racing, breeding etc. **2** an animal-breeding establishment. **3** a stallion or other male animal used for breeding. **4** (*sl.*) a sexually potent esp. young man. **5** stud poker. ~*a.* (of a stallion or other male animal) kept for breeding. **at stud** (of a stallion) available for breeding, for a fee. **out to stud** at stud. **stud book** *n.* a register of pedigrees of horses or cattle. **stud farm** *n.* a farm where horses are bred. **stud-horse** *n.* a stallion. **stud poker** *n.* a variety of poker in which cards are dealt face up. [OE *stōd* (cp. Icel. *stōth*, Dan. *stod*, G *Gestüt*), cogn. with STAND]

studded, studding STUD[1].

studding-sail (stŭd´ingsāl, stŭn´səl), **stunsail** (stŭn´səl), **stuns'l** *n.* (*Naut.*) an additional sail set beyond the sides of a square sail in light winds. [etym. uncertain]

student (stū´dənt) *n.* **1** a person engaged in study, esp. someone receiving instruction at a university, college or other institution for higher education or technical training. **2** (*esp. N Am.*) a schoolboy or schoolgirl. **3** a studious person. **4** a person receiving an annual grant for study or research from a foundation etc. **5** a person at the trainee or apprentice stage (*student nurses*). **studentship** *n.* a grant for study at a university. [L *studens -dentis*, pres.p. of *studēre*, see STUDY]

studied STUDY.

studio (stū´diō) *n.* (*pl.* **studios**) **1** the working room of a sculptor, painter, photographer etc. **2** the room in which records, radio and television programmes are recorded, or films made. **3** the place from which television and radio programmes are broadcast. **4** (*pl.*) the buildings used for making films by a television or film company. **studio couch** *n.* a couch that converts into a bed. **studio flat** *n.* a flat with one main room, or with a room suitable as an artist's studio. [It., from L *studium*, STUDY]

studious (stū´diəs) *a.* **1** devoted to study. **2** studied, deliberate, intended. **3** eager, diligent, anxious (to do something, in something). **4** desirous, careful, observant (of). **studiously** *adv.* **studiousness** *n.* [F *studieux*, L *studiōsus*, as STUDY]

study (stŭd´i) *n.* (*pl.* **studies**) **1** mental application to books, art, science etc., the pursuit of knowledge. **2** (*usu. pl.*) a subject that is studied or worth studying; the pursuit of such subjects (*She returned to England to complete her studies*). **3** a room devoted to study, literary work etc. **4** a sketch or other piece of work done for practice or as a preliminary design for a picture etc. **5** (*Mus.*) a composition designed to test or develop technical skill. **6** a person who learns a part in a play etc.; the activity of memorizing a part. **7** a reverie, a fit of musing; a brown study. **8** †(a thing to be attained by) earnest endeavour, watchful attention. ~*v.t.* (*3rd pers. sing. pres.* **studies**, *pres.p.* **studying**, *past, p.p.* **studied**) **1** to apply the mind to for the purpose of learning. **2** to inquire into, to investigate. **3** to contemplate, to consider attentively. **4** to commit (the words of one's role etc.) to memory. **5** to read (a book etc.) carefully and analytically. **6** to apply thought and pains to, to be zealous for. ~*v.i.* **1** to apply oneself to study, esp. to reading. **2** †to meditate, to cogitate, to muse, to rack one's brains. **3** †to be assiduous, diligent, or anxious (to do). **brown study** BROWN. **to make a study of** to examine or investigate thoroughly. **studied** *a.* deliberate; contrived (*with studied indifference*). **studiedly** *adv.* **studiedness** *n.* **study-bedroom** *n.* a room, esp. for a student, in which to sleep and to study. **study group** *n.* a number of people involved in investigating a particular topic, meeting regularly for discussion etc. [A-F and OF *estudie*, L *studium*, eagerness, zeal, whence, med. L *studiāre*, OF *estudier*, F *étudier*, to study]

stuff (stŭf) *n.* **1** the material of which anything is made or may be made. **2** the fundamental substance, essence, or elements of anything. **3** household goods, furniture, utensils etc. **4** clothes, belongings etc. (*helped me shift my stuff*). **5** things said, done, written etc. (*all that stuff about Aids prevention*). **6** a textile fabric, esp. woollen, as opposed to silk or linen. **7** worthless matter, nonsense, trash. ~*v.t.* **1** to cram, to pack, to fill or stop (up). **2** to cram, press, ram, or crowd into a receptacle, confined space etc.; to push roughly (*stuffed my books into my rucksack*). **3** to fill the skin of (a dead animal) so as to restore its natural form. **4** to fill (a fowl etc.) with stuffing or seasoning for cooking. **5** to fill with food (*stuffing themselves as usual*). **6** to fill with ideas, notions, nonsense etc. **7** (*coll.*) to impose on, to hoax. **8** (*sl., offensive*) used to express contemptuous dismissal or rejection (*Tell them to stuff their offer*). **9** (*N Am.*) to put bogus votes into (a ballot box). **10** (*sl.*) to have sexual intercourse with (a woman). ~*v.i.* to cram oneself with food. **bit of stuff** BIT[1]. **stuff and nonsense!** an expression of contemptuous disbelief. **that's the stuff!** that is just what is needed. **to do one's stuff** (*coll.*) to act as one is expected. **to know one's stuff** KNOW. **stuffed** *a.* **1** (of poultry etc.) filled with stuffing. **2** having blocked nasal passages, bunged (up). **get stuffed!** (*offensive*) used to express anger, contempt etc. against another person. **stuffed shirt** *n.* (*coll.*) a pompous person. **stuffer** *n.* **stuff gown** *n.* the gown of woollen or other ordinary cloth worn by a barrister who has not taken silk. **stuffing** *n.* **1** material used to stuff something. **2** a mixture of ingredients used to stuff poultry etc. before it is cooked. **to knock the stuffing out of** to beat (an opponent) thoroughly. **stuffing box** *n.* a chamber packed with stuffing so as to be airtight or watertight, in which a piston rod etc. can work freely. **stuffy** *a.* (*comp.* **stuffier**, *superl.* **stuffiest**) **1** ill-ventilated, close, fusty. **2** boring, uninspiring. **3** strait-laced, conventional, dull. **4** (of one's nose etc.) stuffed up. **stuffily** *adv.* **stuffiness** *n.* [OF *estoffe* (F *étoffe*), L *stuppa*, *stūpa*, see STOP]

stultify (stŭl´tifī) *v.t.* (*3rd pers. sing. pres.* **stultifies**, *pres.p.* **stultifying**, *past, p.p.* **stultified**) **1** to dull the mind of. **2** to render absurd, to cause to appear self-contradictory, inconsistent, or ridiculous. **3** (*Law*) to allege or prove to be insane or of unsound mind. **stultification** (-fikā´shən) *n.* **stultifier** *n.* [L *stultus*, foolish, -FY]

stum (stŭm) *n.* unfermented grape juice, must. ~*v.t.* (*pres.p.* **stumming**, *past, p.p.* **stummed**) **1** to prevent (wine) from fermenting further by using sulphur etc. **2** to renew the fermentation of (wine) by the addition of stum. [Dut. *stom*, orig. a., quiet, cp. G *stumm*, dumb]

stumble (stŭm´bəl) *v.i.* **1** to trip in walking or to strike the foot against something without falling, to have a partial fall. **2** to move (along) unsteadily. **3** to read or speak blunderingly. **4** to come (upon) by chance. ~*n.* an act of stumbling. **stumblebum** *n.* (*N Am., coll.*) a clumsy person. **stumbler** *n.* **stumbling** *n., a.* **stumbling-block** *n.* an obstacle, an impediment, a cause of difficulty or hesitation etc. **stumblingly** *adv.* [ME *stumblen*, freq. of *stum-*, cogn. with STUM and STAMMER]

stumer (stū´mə) *n.* (*sl.*) **1** a cheque that has no money to back it; a returned cheque. **2** a counterfeit note or coin. **3** a dud; a sham; a failure. **4** a disappointing racehorse. [etym. unknown]

stump (stŭmp) *n.* **1** the part left in the earth after a tree has fallen or been cut down. **2** any part left when the rest of a branch, limb, tooth etc., has been cut away, amputated, destroyed, or worn out; a stub, a butt. **3** in cricket, each of the three posts of a wicket. **4** (*pl., facet.*) the legs. **5** the stump of a tree used by a speaker as a platform from which to address a gathering. **6** a pointed roll of leather or paper used to rub down the strong lines of a crayon or pencil drawing etc. ~*v.i.* **1** to walk stiffly, awkwardly, or noisily, as on wooden legs. **2** to make stump speeches, to go about doing this. ~*v.t.* **1** (of a question or problem) to baffle; to be too difficult for. **2** to put out (the batsman) at cricket by touching the wicket while they are out of the crease. **3** to go about (a district) making stump speeches. **4** to work upon (a drawing etc.) with a stump. **on the stump** going about making political speeches. **to stump up** **1** to pay up. **2** to produce the money required. **up a stump** (*N Am.*) in difficulties. **stumped** *a.* baffled, nonplussed, beaten by a question, problem etc. **stumper** *n.* **1** a baffling question. **2** a wicketkeeper. **stump orator** *n.* a person who makes stump speeches. **stump oratory** *n.* **stump speech** *n.* **1** a speech from some improvised platform, orig. a tree stump. **2** an electioneering speech. **stumpy** *a.* (*comp.* **stumpier**, *superl.* **stumpiest**) **1** short, thickset, stocky. **2** full of stumps, stubby. **stumpily** *adv.* **stumpiness** *n.* [Icel. *stumpr* (cp. Dan. and Swed. *stump*, Dut. *stomp*, G *Stumpf*), cogn. with STAMP and STUB]

stun (stŭn) *v.t.* (*pres.p.* **stunning**, *past*, *p.p.* **stunned**) **1** to render senseless with a blow. **2** to stupefy, to shock or overwhelm. **3** to daze or deafen with noise. **stun gun** *n.* a gun that stuns, using ultrasound or electric shock, without causing serious injury. **stunner** *n.* **1** (*sl.*) something astonishing or first-rate. **2** a person or thing that stuns. **stunning** *a.* **1** stupefying. **2** (*sl.*) wonderfully good, fine etc. **stunningly** *adv.* [OE *stunian*, to make a din, cp. Icel. *stynja*, G *stöhnen*, to groan, also Gr. *steinein*]

stung STING.

stunk STINK.

stunsail, stuns'l STUDDING-SAIL.

stunt[1] (stŭnt) *v.t.* to check in growth or development, to dwarf, to cramp. ~*n.* **1** a check in growth. **2** a stunted animal or thing. **stunted** *a.* **stuntedness** *n.* [OE, dull, obtuse (cp. Icel. *stuttr*, short), rel. to STINT]

stunt[2] (stŭnt) *n.* **1** a thing done to attract attention. **2** a performance serving as a display of strength, skill, or the like, a feat. **3** a feat of aerobatics. **stuntman** *n.* (*pl.* **stuntmen**) a person who performs dangerous feats (esp. as a stand-in for an actor). **stuntwoman** *n.* (*pl.* **stuntwomen**). [etym. unknown]

stupa (stooʹpə) *n.* a domed Buddhist shrine, a tope. [Sansk., see TOPE[2]]

stupe[1] (stūp) *n.* a compress of flannel or other soft material used in fomentations etc. ~*v.t.* to treat with this, to foment. [L *stūpa*, STUFF]

stupe[2] (stūp) *n.* (*sl.*) a stupid person.

stupefy (stūʹpəfī) *v.t.* (*3rd pers. sing. pres.* **stupefies**, *pres.p.* **stupefying**, *past*, *p.p.* **stupefied**) **1** to make stupid or senseless. **2** to stun, to astonish. **stupefacient** (-fāʹshənt) *a.*, *n.* **stupefaction** (-fakʹshən) *n.* **1** astonishment. **2** the act of stupefying or state of being stupefied. **stupefactive** *a.* **stupefier** *n.* **stupefying** *a.* **stupefyingly** *adv.* [F *stupéfier*, L *stupefacere* (*stupēre*, to be amazed, *facere*, to make)]

stupendous (stūpenʹdəs) *a.* astounding in magnitude, force, degree etc., marvellous, amazing, astonishing. **stupendously** *adv.* **stupendousness** *n.* [L *stupendus*, from *stupēre*, to be amazed]

stupid (stūʹpid) *a.* (*comp.* **stupider**, *superl.* **stupidest**) **1** slow or dull in apprehension, wit or understanding, unintelligent, obtuse. **2** senseless, nonsensical. **3** in a state of stupor, stupefied. **4** used in irritation for general disparagement (*Move your stupid guitar, can't you?*). ~*n.* (*coll.*) a stupid person. **stupidity** (-pidʹ-) *n.* (*pl.* **stupidities**). **stupidly** *adv.* **stupidness** *n.* [F *stupide*, L *stupidus*, from *stupēre*, see STUPEFY]

stupor (stūʹpə) *n.* a dazed condition, torpor, deadened sensibility. **stuporous** *a.* [L]

sturdy[1] (stœʹdi) *a.* (*comp.* **sturdier**, *superl.* **sturdiest**) **1** robust, lusty, vigorous, hardy. **2** of strong or stocky build. **3** determined (*sturdy opposition*). **sturdily** *adv.* **sturdiness** *n.* [OF *estourdi*, p.p. of *estourdir* (F *étourdir*), to astound, to amaze]

sturdy[2] (stœʹdi) *n.* a disease in sheep characterized by giddiness caused by a tapeworm in the brain. **sturdied** (-did) *a.* [OF *estourdie*, giddiness, as STURDY[1]]

sturgeon (stœʹjən) *n.* a large anadromous fish of the genus *Acipenser*, characterized by bony scales, esp. *A. sturio*, which yields caviare and isinglass. [OF *esturgeon*, med. L *sturiō*, *sturiōnis*, OHG *Sturjo*, cp. OE *styria*, G *Stör*]

Sturm und Drang (shtuəm unt drangʹ) *n.* a late 18th-cent. German literary and artistic genre typified by stirring action, and the expression of strong passion or emotional unrest. [G, storm and stress]

sturnoid (stœʹnoid) *a.* **1** like a starling. **2** belonging to the Sturnidae, a family of birds including the starlings. [L *sturnus*, starling, -OID]

stutter (stŭtʹə) *v.i.* to keep hesitating or repeating sounds spasmodically in the articulation of words. ~*v.t.* to utter in this way, to stammer (out). ~*n.* the act or habit of stuttering or stammering. **stutterer** *n.* **stutteringly** *adv.* [freq. of obs. *stut*, ME *stoten*, cp. Dut. *stottern*, G *stottern*, also G *stossen* and L *tundere*, to beat]

sty[1] (stī) *n.* (*pl.* **sties**) **1** a pen or enclosure for pigs. **2** a mean or filthy habitation. **3** a place of debauchery. ~*v.t.* (*3rd pers. sing. pres.* **sties**, *pres.p.* **stying**, *past*, *p.p.* **stied**) to shut up in or as if in a sty. ~*v.i.* to live in or as if in a sty. [OE *stīgo* (cp. Icel. *stīa*, *stī*, Dan. *sti*, Swed. *stia*, OHG *Stiga*, cattle-pen), prob. from *stīgan*, to climb]

sty[2] (stī), **stye** *n.* (*pl.* **sties, styes**) a small inflamed swelling on the edge of the eyelid. [prob. from OE *stīgend*, pres.p. of *stīgan*, to rise]

Stygian (stijʹiən) *a.* **1** of or relating to the river Styx, in Greek mythology. **2** (of darkness) gloomy, impenetrable.

style (stīl) *n.* **1** a sort, kind, make, pattern, esp. with reference to appearance. **2** manner of writing, expressing ideas, speaking, behaving, doing etc., as distinct from the matter expressed or done. **3** the general characteristics of literary diction, artistic expression, or mode of decoration, distinguishing a particular people, person, school, period etc. **4** a manner or form of a superior or fashionable kind, fashion, distinction (*arrived in style*). **5** the proper expression of thought in language. **6** a mode of designation or address, title, description. **7** a method of reckoning dates, as in *Old Style*, the Julian method, used till 1582, and *New Style*, the Gregorian method introduced in 1582. **8** a pointed instrument used by the ancients for writing on wax-covered tablets. **9** a writing instrument or other thing shaped like this, an etching needle, a graver, a blunt-pointed surgical instrument, a pointed or styloid projection, cusp, or process in a bone etc. **10** the gnomon of a sundial. **11** (*Bot.*) the extension of an ovary supporting the stigma. ~*v.t.* **1** to design or shape. **2** to designate, to describe formally by name and title. **stylar** *a.* of or relating to a style or pointer. **-style** (stīl) *suf.* forming adjectives and adverbs with the meaning 'in the specified style or manner' (*a blues-style rendering*; *congratulated me American-style*). **stylebook** *n.* a book containing rules of grammar, typography etc. for printers and editors. **styleless** *a.* **stylelessness** *n.* **styler** *n.* **styliform** (-lifawm) *a.* **stylish** *a.* fashionable in style, smart, showy. **stylishly** *adv.* **stylishness** *n.* **stylist** *n.* **1** a clothes designer. **2** a hairdresser who styles hair. **3** a writer having or cultivating a good style. **4** a person, esp. an athlete or musician, who performs stylishly. **stylistic** (-lisʹ-) *a.* **stylistically** *adv.* **stylistics** *n.* the study of style in literary language. **stylize, stylise** *v.t.* to give (something) a conventional, non-naturalistic form in drawing, painting or other artistic representation. **stylization** (-zāʹshən) *n.* **stylized** *a.* [ME and OF *stile*, L *stilus*, sometimes written *stylus*, assim. to Gr. *stulos*, pillar]

Usage note The spellings of the nouns *style* (a manner etc.) and *stile* (steps, part of a door frame etc.) should not be confused.

stylet (stīʹlit) *n.* **1** a long pointed instrument, a stiletto. **2** (*Med.*) the stiffening wire of a catheter; a surgical probe. **3** (*Zool.*) a small style, e.g. the piercing mouth-part of an insect. [OF, from It. STILETTO]

styli STYLUS.

styliform, stylish etc. STYLE.

stylite (stīʹlīt) *n.* a religious recluse in ancient and

medieval times who lived on the top of a pillar. [late Gr. *stulitēs*, from *stulos*, pillar]
stylo (stī´lō) *n.* (*pl.* **stylos**) (*coll.*) a stylograph.
stylobate (stī´ləbāt) *n.* (*Archit.*) a continuous base for a range of columns. [Gr. *stulobatēs* (*stulos*, pillar, *bainein*, to stand)]
stylograph (stī´ləgrahf) *n.* a pen with a tubular point fed with ink from a reservoir in the shaft. **stylographic** (-graf´-) *a.* **stylographically** *adv.* **stylography** (-log´-) *n.* the art, process etc. of using a style or stylograph. [see STYLE]
styloid (stī´loid) *a.* penlike, stylus-like. ~*n.* (*also* **styloid process**) a spine projecting from the base of the temporal bone. [STYLUS, -OID]
stylus (stī´ləs) *n.* (*pl.* **styli** (-lī, -li), **styluses**) **1** a pointed instrument for writing by means of carbon paper, a style. **2** a device, esp. a diamond or sapphire point, attached to the cartridge in the arm of a record player that follows the groove in a record. [mistaken spelling of L *stilus*, influenced by Gr. *stulos*, a pillar]
stymie (stī´mi), **stimy** *n.* (*pl.* **stymies, stimies**) **1** in golf, the position when an opponent's ball lies between the player's ball and the hole. **2** a difficult position or situation. ~*v.t.* (*3rd pers. sing. pres.* **stymies, stimies,** *pres.p.* **stymieing, stymying, stimying,** *past, p.p.* **stymied, stimied**) **1** to cause difficulties for, to check. **2** in golf, to hinder by a stymie. [etym. uncertain]
styptic (stip´tik) *a.* **1** (of a drug or application) that stops bleeding. **2** †astringent. ~*n.* a drug that arrests bleeding. **stypticity** (-tis´-) *n.* [F *styptique*, L *stypticus*, Gr. *stuptikos*, from *stuphein*, to contract, prob. cogn. with STOP]
styrax (stī´raks) *n.* any tree or shrub of the genus *Styrax*, certain species of which yield benzoin and storax. **styrene** *n.* a colourless volatile liquid derived from benzene used in the manufacture of plastics and synthetic rubber. [L, from Gr. *sturax*]
styrofoam (stī´rəfōm) *n.* (*esp. NAm.*) a type of expanded polystyrene. [POLYSTYRENE, FOAM]
suable (sū´əbəl) *a.* capable of being sued. **suability** (-bil´-) *n.*
suasion (swā´zhən) *n.* (*formal*) persuasion as opposed to compulsion. **suasive** (-siv) *a.* **suasively** *adv.* [F, from L *suāsio -iōnis*, from *suādēre*, to persuade, p.p. *suāsus*, rel. to SUAVE]
suave (swahv) *a.* agreeable, bland, gracious, polite. **suavely** *adv.* **suaveness** *n.* **suavity** *n.* (*pl.* **suavities**). [F, from L *suāvis*, cogn. with SWEET]
sub (sŭb) *n.* (*coll.*) **1** short for SUBMARINE. **2** short for SUBSCRIPTION (under SUBSCRIBE). **3** short for SUBSTITUTE. **4** short for SUB-EDITOR (under SUB-EDIT). **5** short for SUBALTERN. **6** short for SUBORDINATE[1]. **7** a small loan or advance payment of wages etc. ~*v.i.* (*pres.p.* **subbing,** *past, p.p.* **subbed**) **1** to act as a substitute (for) or as a sub-editor. **2** to receive pay in advance on account of wages due later. ~*v.t.* **1** to grant (a small loan or advance) to. **2** to sub-edit.
sub- (sŭb) *pref.* **1** to, at or from a lower position, as in *submerge, substratum, subvert.* **2** inferior in importance, secondary, as in *subcommittee, subplot.* **3** almost, bordering on, as in *subarctic, subtropical.* **4** forming verbs expressing secondary action, as in *subcontract, subdivide.* **5** signifying support, as in *subsistence.* **6** (*Chem.*) (of a salt) basic. [L *sub, sub-*, under, towards, close to]
subabdominal (sŭbəbdom´inəl) *a.* situated below the abdomen.
subacid (sŭbas´id) *a.* slightly acid or sour. **subacidity** (-sid´-) *n.*
subacute (sŭbəkūt´) *a.* (*Med.*) (of illness) intermediate between acute and chronic.
subadult (sŭbad´ŭlt, -ədŭlt´) *a.* (*Zool.*) (of an animal) not quite adult. ~*n.* a subadult animal.
subaerial (sŭbeə´riəl) *a.* (*Geol.*) being, acting or produced in the open air, as opposed to *submarine, subterranean*, etc. **subaerially** *adv.*
subagent (sŭbā´jənt) *n.* a person employed by an agent. **subagency** *n.* (*pl.* **subagencies**) a subordinate agency.
subalpine (sŭbal´pīn) *a.* of or relating to elevated regions not above the timberline.
subaltern (sŭb´əltən) *n.* a junior army officer, one below the rank of captain. ~*a.* **1** subordinate; of inferior rank. **2** (*Logic*) particular, ranking below universal. **subalternant** (-tœ´-) *n.* (*Logic*) a universal in relation to the subaltern particular. **subalternate** (-tœ´nət) *n.* (*Logic*) a particular proposition in relation to the subaltern universal. ~*a.* inferior in status. **subalternation** (-awltənā´shən) *n.* (*Logic*) the relation between a particular and a universal proposition of the same quality. [F *subalterne*, med. L *subalternus* (*alternus*, see ALTERNATE[1])]
subantarctic (sŭbantahk´tik) *a.* of or relating to the region bordering on the Antarctic.
subapostolic (sŭbapəstol´ik) *a.* of or relating to the period succeeding that of the apostles.
sub-aqua (sŭbak´wə) *a.* of or relating to underwater sports. **subaquatic** (-kwat´-) *a.* **1** partially aquatic. **2** subaqueous. **subaqueous** (-kwiəs) *a.* **1** being or formed under water. **2** feeble, wishy-washy.
subarctic (sŭbahk´tik) *a.* of or relating to the region bordering on the Arctic.
subassembly (sŭb´əsembli) *n.* (*pl.* **subassemblies**) an assembled unit forming part of a larger product.
subastral (sŭbas´trəl) *a.* terrestrial.
subatomic (sŭbətom´ik) *a.* **1** of or occurring inside an atom. **2** making up an atom. **3** smaller than an atom.
subaudition (sŭbawdish´ən) *n.* **1** the act of understanding something not expressed or of mentally supplying a missing word etc. **2** something implied but not expressed. [L *subauditio*, from *subaudīre* (*audīre*, to hear)]
subaxillary (sŭbak´siləri) *a.* situated beneath the armpit or the wing cavity, or under the axil formed by a petiole and stem etc.
sub-base (sŭb´bās) *n.* (*Archit.*) the lowest part of a base horizontally divided.
sub-basement (sŭb´bāsmənt) *n.* a storey underneath a basement.
sub-branch (sŭb´brahnch) *n.* a subordinate branch.
sub-breed (sŭb´brēd) *n.* a secondary or less distinguished breed.
subcategory (sŭb´katəgəri) *n.* (*pl.* **subcategories**) a secondary or subordinate category. **subcategorize, subcategorise** *v.t.* **subcategorization** (-zā´shən) *n.*
subcaudal (sŭbkaw´dəl) *a.* situated under the tail, or relating to this part.
subcelestial (sŭbsiles´tiəl) *a.* terrestrial.
subclass (sŭb´klahs) *n.* **1** a secondary or subordinate class. **2** (*Bot.*) a taxonomic subdivision of a class.
sub-clause (sŭb´klawz) *n.* **1** (*Law*) a subsidiary part of a clause. **2** (*Gram.*) a subordinate clause.
subclavian (sŭbklā´viən) *a.* situated or extending under the clavicle.
subclinical (sŭbklin´ikəl) *a.* having symptoms sufficiently slight as to be undetectable clinically.
subcommittee (sŭb´kəmiti) *n.* a small committee appointed from among its members by a larger committee to consider and report on a particular matter.
subconical (sŭbkon´ikəl) *a.* roughly conical.
subconscious (sŭbkon´shəs) *a.* **1** existing in the mind but without one's full awareness. **2** of or relating to the subconscious. **3** slightly or partially conscious. ~*n.* **1** (*usu.* **the subconscious**) that part of the field of consciousness which at any given moment is outside the range of one's attention. **2** (*usu.* **the subconscious**) the accumulation of past conscious experiences which are

forgotten or for the moment are out of one's thoughts. **subconsciously** *adv.* **subconsciousness** *n.*

subcontinent (sŭbkon´tinənt) *n.* **1** a large land mass, not of sufficient size to be a continent. **2** a large geographically independent land mass forming part of a continent. **subcontinental** (-nen´-) *a.*

subcontract[1] (sŭbkəntrakt´) *v.t.* to employ a company etc. to carry out (work) as part of a larger project. *~v.i.* to make a subcontract or carry out a subcontract. **subcontractor** *n.*

subcontract[2] (sŭbkon´trakt) *n.* a secondary or subsidiary contract, e.g. to supply labour, materials or equipment.

subcontrary (sŭbkon´trəri) *a.* (*Logic*) (of a proposition in relation to another differing from it only in quality) contrary in an inferior degree, such that at least one must be true. *~n.* (*pl.* **subcontraries**) a subcontrary proposition. **subcontrariety** (-rī´ə-) *n.*

subcordate (sŭbkaw´dāt) *a.* roughly heart-shaped.

subcortical (sŭbkaw´tikəl) *a.* (*Anat.*) below the cortex.

subcostal (sŭbkos´təl) *a.* (*Anat.*) below the ribs.

subcranial (sŭbkrā´niəl) *a.* (*Anat.*) below the cranium.

subcritical (sŭbkrit´ikəl) *a.* (of or relating to nuclear fuel) of insufficient mass to sustain a chain reaction.

subculture (sŭb´kŭlchə) *n.* a social or ethnic group with a characteristic culture differing from that of the national or predominant culture. **subcultural** (-kŭl´-) *a.*

subcutaneous (sŭbkūtā´niəs) *a.* beneath the skin. **subcutaneously** *adv.*

subdeacon (sŭbdē´kən) *n.* a minister of the church ranking below a deacon.

subdelirium (sŭbdilir´iəm) *n.* a mild or intermittent form of delirium. **subdelirious** *a.*

subdivide (sŭbdivīd´) *v.t.*, *v.i.* to divide again or into smaller parts. **subdivisible** (-viz´-) *a.* **subdivision** (-vizh´ən, sub´-) *n.* **1** the act of subdividing, or an instance of this. **2** a secondary or subsidiary division. **3** (*N Am.*, *Austral.*) a piece of land divided into plots for sale.

subdominant (sŭbdom´inənt) *a.*, *n.* (*Mus.*) (of or relating to) the tone next below the dominant, the fourth of the scale.

subduction (sŭbdŭk´shən) *n.* (*Geol.*) the sideways and downward thrust of the edge of a tectonic plate into the mantle beneath another plate. **subduct** (səbdukt´) *v.t.* to withdraw or draw downwards; to take away, to subtract. [L *subdūcere* (*dūcere*, to lead, p.p. *ductus*)]

subdue (səbdū´) *v.t.* (*3rd pers. sing. pres.* **subdues**, *pres.p.* **subduing**, *past*, *p.p.* **subdued**) **1** to conquer, to reduce to subjection, to vanquish, to overcome. **2** to check, to curb. **3** to tame, to render gentle or mild. **4** to tone down, to soften, to make less glaring. **subduable** *a.* **subdued** *a.* **1** quiet, passive, cowed. **2** (of e.g. light or sound) toned down, not harsh or glaring. **subduedness** (-id-) *n.* **subduement** *n.* **subduer** *n.* [ME *soduen*, from p.p. *sodued*, OF *subduz*, pl., subdued, prob. through a late L *subdutus*, L *subditus*, p.p. of *subdere*, to conquer]

subdural (sŭbdū´rəl) *a.* (*Anat.*, *Med.*) sited or occurring between the dura mater and the arachnoid membrane of the brain and spinal chord.

sub-edit (sŭb´edit) *v.t.* (*pres.p.* **sub-editing**, *past*, *p.p.* **sub-edited**) to prepare (a manuscript) for printing. **sub-editor** *n.* **1** a person who sub-edits manuscripts. **2** an assistant editor. **sub-editorial** (-taw´-) *a.*

subentry (sŭb´entri) *n.* (*pl.* **subentries**) a subsidiary entry.

suberect (sŭbirekt´) *a.* (of an animal or plant) more or less erect.

subereous (sūbiə´riəs), **suberic** (-ber´ik), **suberose** (sū´bərōs) *a.* of the nature or texture of cork; of, relating to or derived from cork. **suberin** (sū´bərin) *n.* a waxy substance found in cork. **suberize** (sū´-), **suberise** *v.t.* to impregnate (plant-cell walls) with suberin to form cork. **suberization** (-zā´shən) *n.* [L *sūber*, cork]

subfamily (sŭb´famili) *n.* (*pl.* **subfamilies**) **1** (*Biol.*) a taxonomic subdivision of a family. **2** any subdivision or subclass of a group.

subfloor (sŭb´flaw) *n.* a foundation for a floor.

subform (sŭb´fawm) *n.* a secondary form.

sub-frame (sŭb´frām) *n.* a supporting frame, e.g. for a door frame or window frame.

subfusc (sŭb´fŭsk) *a.* **1** dusky, sombre. **2** drab, dingy. *~n.* formal academic dress at Oxford University. **subfuscous** (-fŭs´-) *a.* dusky. [L *fuscus*, FUSCOUS]

subgenus (sŭb´jenəs, -jē´-) *n.* (*pl.* **subgenera** (-ərə), **subgenuses**) a taxonomic subdivision of a genus. **subgeneric** (-jiner´ik) *a.*

subglacial (sŭbglā´shəl, -siəl) *a.* at the bottom of, or next to, a glacier.

sub-group (sŭb´groop), (*Math.*) **subgroup** *n.* a subdivision of a group.

sub-head (sŭb´hed), **sub-heading** (-heding) *n.* a heading, often explanatory, underneath the main heading of a book, article etc.

subhuman (sŭbhū´mən) *a.* **1** less than human or that which is normal to humans. **2** of or relating to animals lower than, or closely related to, humans.

subimago (sŭbimā´gō) *n.* (*pl.* **subimagines** (-jinēz), **subimagos**) a stage in the metamorphosis of certain insects preceding the imago.

subintrant (sŭbin´trənt) *a.* (of a fever) characterized by paroxysms that succeed each other so rapidly as to be almost continuous. [late L *subintrans*, *subintrantis*, pres.p. of *subintrāre* (*intrāre*, ENTER)]

sub-irrigation (sŭbirigā´shən) *n.* **1** irrigation by underground pipes. **2** irrigation from beneath the surface.

subito (soo´bitō) *adv.* (*Mus.*) suddenly, immediately. [It.]

subj. *abbr.* **1** subject. **2** subjunctive.

subjacent (sŭbjā´sənt) *a.* underlying; lower in position. [L *subjacens -ntem*, pres.p. of *subjacēre* (*jacēre*, to lie)]

subject[1] (sŭb´jikt) *n.* **1** the topic under consideration. **2** the theme of discussion or description, or artistic expression or representation. **3 a** that which is treated or to be treated in any specified way. **b** the cause or occasion (for) (*a subject for rejoicing*). **4** a branch of learning or study. **5** (*Gram.*) the noun or its equivalent about which something is affirmed, the nominative of a sentence. **6** someone under the dominion or political rule of a person or state; a person owing allegiance to a sovereign; a member of a state as related to the sovereign or government; any person bound in obedience to another. **7** the ego, as distinguished from the object or non-ego, the mind, the conscious self. **8** the substance or substratum to which attributes must be referred. **9** the leading phrase or motif in music. **10** (*also* **subject for dissection**) a dead body for dissection etc. **11** a person regarded as subject to any specific disease, mental tendency, psychic influence etc. (*a neurotic subject*). **12** (*Logic*) that member of a proposition about which something is predicated. *~a.* **1** being under the power, control or authority of another, owing obedience (to). **2** exposed, liable, prone, disposed (to) (*subject to pneumonia*). **3** dependent, conditional (*subject to their approval*). **on the subject of** concerning. **subject to** conditional(ly) upon. **to change the subject** **1** to abandon the topic under discussion and introduce another. **2** the formula one uses when doing this. **subject catalogue,** (*N Am.*) **subject catalog** *n.* a library catalogue arranged by subject. **subject-heading** *n.* a heading in an index, catalogue etc. under which references are given. **subjective** (-jek´-) *a.* **1** due to or proceeding from the individual mind, personal. **2** concerned with or proceeding from the consciousness or the mind, as opposed to objective or external things. **3** lacking reality, fanciful, imaginary. **4** (of works of art) characterized by the prominence given to the individuality of the author or artist. 5 (*Gram.*) denoting the case of the subject of a verb, nominative. ~*n.* the subjective case. **subjectively** *adv.* **subjectiveness** *n.* **subjectivism** *n.* the doctrine that human knowledge is purely subjective, and therefore relative. **subjectivist** *n.* **subjectivity** (-tiv´-) *n.* **subjectless** *a.* **subject matter** *n.* the object of consideration, discussion etc. **subject-object** *n.* the immediate object in thought as distinguished from an external thing. [ME and OF *suget* (F *sujet*), assim. to L *subjectus*, p.p. of *subjicere* (*jacere*, to cast)]

subject[2] (səbjekt´) *v.t.* 1 to expose, to make liable (to). 2 to cause to undergo. 3 to subdue, to reduce to subjection (to). **subjection** *n.* the act of subjecting people, or the state of being subjected, to authority, control etc.

subjoin (sŭbjoin´) *v.t.* to add at the end, to append, to affix. **subjoinder** (-də) *n.* a remark made in response to a previous one, a rejoinder. **subjoint** (sŭb´joint) *n.* a secondary joint e.g. in an insect's leg. [OF *subjoign-*, stem of *subjoindre*, L *subjungere* (*jungere*, to join, p.p. *junctus*)]

sub judice (sŭb joo´disi) *a.* (*Law*) under consideration, esp. by a court or judge. [L]

subjugate (sŭb´jugāt) *v.t.* to subdue, to conquer, to bring into subjection, to enslave. **subjugable** *a.* **subjugation** (-gā´shən) *n.* **subjugator** *n.* [L *subjugātus*, p.p. of *subjugāre*, to bring under the yoke (*jugum*, cogn. with YOKE)]

subjunctive (səbjŭngk´tiv) *a.* (*Gram.*) denoting the mood of a verb expressing condition, wishes, hypothesis or contingency. ~*n.* 1 the subjunctive mood. 2 a word or form in the subjunctive mood. **subjunctively** *adv.* [L *subjunctīvus*, from *subjunct-*, see SUBJOIN]

subkingdom (sŭb´kingdəm) *n.* a primary division of the animal or plant kingdom.

sublapsarian (sŭblapseə´riən) *n.* any member of a group of moderate Calvinists believing that God permitted the Fall of Adam without preordaining it; an infralapsarian. ~*a.* of or relating to sublapsarians or their doctrine. **sublapsarianism** *n.* [L *sub*, to some extent, *lapsus*, fall]

sublate (səblāt´) *v.t.* (*Logic*) to treat as untrue, to deny. **sublation** *n.* [L *sublātus* (*lātus*, p.p. of *tollere*, to take away)]

sub-lease[1] (sŭb´lēs) *n.* a lease of property by a tenant or lessee.

sub-lease[2] (sŭblēs´) *v.t.* to grant or obtain a sublease of (property). **sub-lessee** (-ē´) *n.* **sub-lessor** (-les´ə) *n.*

sub-let[1] (sŭb´let) *n.* 1 a sub-letting, a sub-lease. 2 (*coll.*) a sub-let property.

sub-let[2] (sŭblet´) *v.t.* (*pres.p.* **sub-letting,** *past, p.p.* **sub-let**) to sub-lease, to let (property already rented or held on lease).

sublibrarian (sŭblībreə´riən) *n.* a subordinate librarian.

sub lieutenant (sŭb leften´ənt) *n.* a British naval officer next in rank below a lieutenant.

sublimate[1] (sŭb´limāt) *v.t.* 1 (*Psych.*) to divert by sublimation. 2 (*Chem.*) to convert (a solid substance) by heat directly to vapour without passing through the liquid state (followed by an equivalent return to solidity by cooling). 3 to refine, to purify, to etherealize. **sublimation** (-ā´shən) *n.* 1 (*Psych.*) the diversion by the subject of certain instinctive impulses, esp. sexual, into altruistic or socially acceptable channels. 2 the act of sublimating a solid etc. 3 the result of sublimating. [L *sublimātus*, p.p. of *sublimāre*, as SUBLIME]

sublimate[2] (sŭb´limət) *n.* (*Chem.*) 1 the product of sublimation. 2 CORROSIVE SUBLIMATE (under CORRODE).

sublime (səblīm´) *a.* (*comp.* **sublimer,** *superl.* **sublimest**) 1 of the most lofty or exalted nature. 2 characterized by grandeur, nobility or majesty. 3 inspiring awe. 4 (of e.g. indifference, ignorance, impudence) unparalleled, outstanding. ~*v.t.* 1 (*Chem.*) to sublimate. 2 to elevate, to purify. 3 to make sublime. ~*v.i.* 1 to pass directly from solid to vapour, to be sublimated. 2 to be elevated or purified. **sublimely** *adv.* **sublimeness** *n.* **Sublime Porte** *n.* (*Hist.*) PORTE. **sublimity** (-lim´-) *n.* [F, from L *sublīmis* (SUB-, and perh. *līmen*, threshold, *limus*, oblique]

subliminal (səblim´inəl) *a.* (*Psych.*) 1 not reaching the threshold of consciousness, hardly perceived. 2 of or relating to subconsciousness. **subliminal advertising** *n.* advertising directed to and acting on the unconscious. **subliminally** *adv.* **subliminal self** *n.* that part of one's personality that is outside one's conscious awareness.

sublingual (sŭbling´wəl) *a.* under the tongue.

sublittoral (sŭblit´ərəl) *a.* 1 (of plants, creatures etc.) found close to the low-water mark on the seashore. 2 of or relating to this part of the seashore.

Sub-Lt. *abbr.* Sub Lieutenant.

sublunary (sŭbloo´nəri), **sublunar** *a.* 1 situated beneath the moon. 2 (*Astron.*) **a** within the orbit of the moon. **b** subject to the moon's influence. 3 of or relating to this world, mundane.

subluxation (sŭblŭksā´shən) *n.* (*Med.*) partial dislocation.

sub-machine gun (sŭbməshēn´) *n.* a light automatic or semiautomatic rapid-firing gun fired from the hip or shoulder.

subman (sŭb´man) *n.* (*pl.* **submen** (-men)) a brutal, subhuman or stupid person.

submarginal (sŭbmah´jinəl) *a.* 1 not meeting minimum requirements, esp. in economic terms. 2 (of land) that cannot be farmed to advantage.

submarine (sŭbmərēn´, sŭb´-) *n.* a vessel, esp. a warship, that may be submerged, equipped with a periscope. ~*a.* situated, acting or growing beneath the surface of the sea. **submariner** (-mar´inə) *n.* a sailor in a submarine.

submaster (sŭb´mahstə) *n.* an assistant master in, or the assistant headmaster of, a school.

submaxillary (sŭbmaksil´əri) *a.* of or relating to the lower jaw, esp. to a pair of salivary glands situated beneath it.

submediant (sŭbmē´diənt) *a.*, *n.* (*Mus.*) (of) the sixth note of the diatonic scale.

submental (sŭbmen´təl) *a.* (*Anat.*) situated below the chin.

submerge (səbmœj´) *v.t.* 1 to put under water etc., to flood. 2 to inundate, to overwhelm. ~*v.i.* to sink or dive under water etc. **submerged tenth** *n.* the proportion of the population said to be living in permanent poverty. **submergence** *n.* **submergible** *a.* **submerse** (-mœs´) *v.t.* to submerge. **submersed** *a.* being or growing under water. **submersible** *n.*, *a.* (a vessel) capable of being submersed. **submersion** (-shən) *n.* [F *submerger*, L *submergere* (*mergere*, to dip, p.p. *mersus*)]

submicroscopic (sŭbmīkrəskop´ik) *a.* too small to be viewed under a normal microscope.

subminiature (sŭbmin´ichə) *a.* 1 of very reduced size. 2 (of a camera) very small, using a 16mm film.

submission (səbmish´ən) *n.* 1 the act of submitting, or the process of being submitted. 2 something that is submitted. 3 the state of being submissive; compliance, obedience, resignation, meekness. 4 (*Law*) a theory or argument presented by counsel to a judge or jury. 5 the surrender of a wrestler overcome by the pain of a hold. **submissive** (-mis´-) *a.* **submissively** *adv.* **submissiveness** *n.* [L *submissio*, *submissiōnis*, see SUBMIT]

submit (səbmit´) *v.t.* (*pres.p.* **submitting,** *past, p.p.* **submitted**) 1 to yield or surrender (oneself) to the domination of someone else. 2 to present or refer for consideration, decision etc. (*submit my application*). 3 to put forward (a theory etc.) deferentially. 4 to subject (to a process, treatment etc.). ~*v.i.* 1 to yield, to surrender, to give in (*refuse to submit; submit to defeat and humiliation*). 2 to be submissive. **submitter** *n.* [L *submittere* (*mittere*, to send, p.p. *missus*)]

submontane (sŭbmon´tān) *a.* situated at the foot of a mountain or range of mountains.

submultiple (sŭbmŭl´tipəl) *n.* (*Math.*) a number capable of dividing another without remainder, a factor or aliquot part.

subnivean (sŭbniv´iən), **subniveal** (-iəl) *a.* situated beneath the snow.

subnormal (sŭbnaw´məl) *a.* 1 less than normal, below the normal standard. 2 having lower intelligence than is normal. **subnormality** (-mal´-) *n.*

sub-nuclear (sŭbnū´kliə) *a.* (*Physics*) occurring in, or smaller than, an atomic nucleus.

subocular (sŭbok´ūlə) *a.* situated below the eyes.

suboptimal (sŭbop´timəl) *a.* less than optimal; not of the best kind or quality.

sub-orbital (sŭbaw´bitəl) *a.* 1 beneath the orbit of the eye. 2 (of a spaceship) achieving less than a complete orbit of the earth, moon etc.

suborder (sŭb´awdə) *n.* a subdivision of a taxonomic order. **subordinal** (-aw´-) *a.*

subordinary (sŭbaw´dinəri) *n.* (*pl.* **subordinaries**) (*Her.*) a device or bearing that is common, but not as common as an ordinary.

subordinate[1] (səbaw´dinət) *a.* 1 inferior (to) in order, rank, importance, power etc. 2 subject, subservient, subsidiary (to). ~*n.* a person working under another or inferior in official standing. **subordinate clause** *n.* (*Gram.*) a clause that functions as a noun, adjective or adverb and qualifies the main clause. **subordinately** *adv.* **subordinateness** *n.* [med. L *subordinātus*, p.p. of *subordināre* (*ordo -dinem*, ORDER)]

subordinate[2] (səbaw´dināt) *v.t.* 1 to make subordinate. 2 to treat or consider as of secondary importance (to). 3 to make subject or subservient (to). **subordination** (-ā´shən) *n.* **subordinationism** *n.* (*Theol.*) the doctrine of the priority of the first to the second and third persons of the Trinity as regards order (the orthodox view) or as regards essence (the Arian view). **subordinative** (-ətiv) *a.*

suborn (səbawn´) *v.t.* to induce (e.g. a witness) by underhand means, esp. bribery, to commit perjury or some other criminal act. **subornation** (-nā´shən) *n.* **suborner** *n.* [F *suborner*, L *subornāre* (*ornāre*, to furnish, to incite)]

suboxide (sŭbok´sīd) *n.* (*Chem.*) an oxide of an element that contains less oxygen than its common oxide (*carbon suboxide*).

subpanation (sŭbpənā´shən) *n.* (*Theol.*) the doctrine that the body and blood of Christ are locally and materially present in the Eucharist in the form of the bread and wine. [cp. IMPANATION (under IMPANATE)]

subphylum (sŭbfī´ləm) *n.* (*pl.* **subphyla** (-lə)) (*Biol.*) a taxonomic subdivision of a phylum.

sub-plot (sŭb´plot) *n.* a secondary or subordinate plot in a novel, play etc.

subpoena (səpē´nə) *n.* a writ commanding a person's attendance in a court of justice under a penalty. ~*v.t.* (*pres.p.* **subpoenaing**, *past, p.p.* **subpoenaed** (-nəd), **subpoena'd**) to serve with such a writ. [L, under penalty]

sub-postmaster (sŭbpōst´mahstə), **subpostmistress** (sŭbpōst´mistris) *n.* a person in charge of a sub-post office.

sub-post office (sŭbpōst´ofis) *n.* a small local post office offering a restricted range of services.

subprogram (sŭbprō´gram) *n.* (*Comput.*) a subroutine.

subregion (sŭb´rējən) *n.* a division of a region, esp. in relation to natural life. **subregional** *a.*

subreption (səbrep´shən) *n.* the act of obtaining something by surprise or fraudulent representation. [L *subreptio*, from *subripere* (*rapere*, to seize)]

subrogation (sŭbrəgā´shən) *n.* (*Law*) the substitution of one person in the place of another with succession to their rights to a debt etc. **subrogate** (sŭb´-) *v.t.*

sub rosa (sŭb rō´zə) *adv.* 1 secretly. 2 in confidence. [L, lit., under the rose, from its use as an emblem of secrecy]

subroutine (sŭb´rootēn) *n.* a sequence of computer instructions for a particular, usu. recurring, task that can be used at any point in a program.

sub-Saharan (sŭbsəhah´rən) *a.* of, relating to, or forming part of the regions of Africa south of the Sahara desert.

subscribe (səbskrīb´) *v.t.* 1 to contribute or pledge to contribute (an annual or other specified sum) to or for a fund, object etc. 2 to write (one's name etc.) at the end of a document etc. 3 to sign (a document, promise etc.). 4 to publish by securing subscribers beforehand. ~*v.i.* 1 to engage to pay a contribution, to allow one's name to be entered in a list of contributors. 2 to assent or give support (to an opinion etc.). 3 to write one's name at the end of a document. 4 to undertake to receive and pay for shares or a periodical, service etc. **to subscribe for** to agree to purchase (a copy or copies of a book) before publication. **to subscribe oneself** to sign one's name as. **to subscribe to** to arrange to take (a periodical) regularly. **subscribable** *a.* **subscriber** *n.* **subscriber trunk dialling** *n.* a telephone dialling system allowing subscribers to dial direct to any number in the system. **subscript** (sŭb´skript) *n., a.* (a character) written or printed below and usu. to the right of another or below the base line. **subscription** (-skrip´-) *n.* 1 the act of subscribing. 2 a contribution to a fund etc. 3 a membership fee. 4 an advance payment for several issues of a periodical. 5 a raising of money from subscribers. 6 a signature. 7 an application to purchase shares. **subscription concert** *n.* each concert of a series for which seats are sold in advance. [L *subscrībere* (*scrībere*, to write)]

subsection (sŭb´sekshən) *n.* a subdivision of a section.

subsellium (sŭbsel´iəm) *n.* (*pl.* **subsellia** (-liə)) a misericord. [L (*sella*, seat)]

sub-sequence (sŭb´sēkwəns) *n.* a subdivision of a sequence, a sequence forming part of a larger one.

subsequent (sŭb´sikwənt) *a.* coming immediately after in time or order; following, succeeding, posterior (to). **subsequence**, †**subsequency** *n.* **subsequently** *adv.* [L *subsequens -ntem*, pres.p. of *subsequī* (*sequī*, to follow)]

subserve (səbsœv´) *v.t.* to serve as a means or instrument in promoting (an end etc.). **subservient** *a.* 1 obsequious, servile. 2 useful as an instrument or means. 3 subordinate (to). **subservience**, **subserviency** *n.* **subserviently** *adv.* [L *subservīre* (*servīre*, to SERVE)]

subset (sŭb´set) *n.* (*esp. Math.*) a set contained within a larger set.

subshrub (sŭb´shrŭb) *n.* a low-growing woody plant with nonwoody tips.

subside (səbsīd´) *v.i.* 1 to settle down, to abate, to become tranquil. 2 to sink, to fall in level. 3 to sink in, to collapse. 4 to settle lower into the ground. 5 (*facet.*) (of a person) to drop plumply (into a chair etc.). **subsidence** (-sī´-, sŭb´si-) *n.* [L *subsīdere* (*sīdere*, to settle, cogn. with *sedēre*, to sit)]

subsidiary (səbsid´iəri) *a.* 1 aiding, auxiliary, supplemental. 2 subordinate or secondary in importance. 3 of, relating to or of the nature of a subsidy. 4 (of troops) paid for by subsidy, or hired by another state. ~*n.* (*pl.* **subsidiaries**) 1 a subsidiary person or thing, an auxiliary, an accessory. 2 a company whose shares are mostly owned by another. **subsidiarily** *adv.* **subsidiarity** (-ar´-) *n.* 1 the state of being subsidiary. 2

the principle of keeping central authorities subsidiary and devolving or delegating power to the lowest practicable level. [L *subsidiārius*, as SUBSIDY]

subsidy (sŭb´sidi) *n.* (*pl.* **subsidies**) **1** money granted by the state or a public body to keep down the price of essential commodities. **2** a contribution by the state, a public corporation etc., to a commercial or charitable undertaking of benefit to the public. **3** financial aid. **4** (*Hist.*) pecuniary aid granted by parliament to the sovereign for purposes of state, a tax to defray special expenses. **5** a sum paid by one government to another, usu. to meet the expenses of a war. **subsidize, subsidise** *v.t.* **subsidization** (-zā´shən) *n.* **subsidizer** *n.* [ME and A-F *subsidie*, L *subsidium* (*sedēre*, to sit)]

subsist (səbsist´) *v.i.* **1** to exist, to remain in existence. **2** to live, to have means of living, to find sustenance, to be sustained (on). **3** to inhere (in), to be attributable to. ~†*v.t.* to supply sustenance to. **subsistence** *n.* **1** the state or means of subsisting. **2** the minimum required to support life. **subsistence allowance, subsistence money** *n.* **1** an advance of wages, or a special payment, made to enable an employee to meet immediate needs. **2** a payment for food etc. made in addition to salary or wages. **subsistence farming** *n.* farming in which most of the yield is consumed by the farmer with little over for sale. **subsistence level** *n.* a living standard that provides only the basic necessities for life. **subsistence wage** *n.* a wage sufficient only to provide the basic necessities of life. **subsistent** *a.* [F *subsister*, L *subsistere* (*sistere*, causal of *stāre*, to stand)]

subsoil (sŭb´soil) *n.* the stratum of earth immediately below the surface soil.

subsonic (sŭbson´ik) *a.* of, relating to, using or travelling at speeds less than that of sound.

subspecies (sŭb´spēshiz, -siz) *n.* (*Biol.*) a taxonomic subdivision of a species. **subspecific** (-spəsif´-) *a.*

substage (sŭb´stāj) *n.* an apparatus underneath the stage of a microscope carrying the condenser etc.

substance (sŭb´stəns) *n.* **1** that of which a thing consists. **2** matter, material, as opposed to form. **3** matter of a definite or identifiable chemical composition. **4** the essence, the essential part, pith, gist or main purport. **5** that which is real, solidity, firmness, solid foundation. **6** material possessions, property, wealth, resources. **7** (*Philos.*) the permanent substratum in which qualities and accidents are conceived to inhere, the self-existent ground of attributes and phenomena. **8** a narcotic or intoxicating drug or chemical, esp. an illegal one. [F, from L *substantia* (*stāre*, to stand)]

sub-standard (sŭbstan´dəd) *a.* below an accepted or acceptable standard.

substantial (səbstan´shəl) *a.* **1** of considerable importance, value, extent, amount etc. **2** material, practical, virtual. **3** solid, stout, strongly constructed, durable. **4** possessed of substance, having sufficient means, well-to-do, financially sound. **5** having physical substance; real, actually existing, not illusory. ~*n.* (*usu. pl.*) the essential parts, reality. **substantialism** *n.* the doctrine that there are substantial realities underlying phenomena. **substantialist** *n.* **substantiality** (-shial´-) *n.* **substantialize, substantialise** *v.t., v.i.* to impart to, or acquire, reality, existence or substance. **substantially** *adv.*

substantiate (səbstan´shiāt) *v.t.* **1** to establish, to prove, to make good (a statement etc.). **2** to make real or actual. **substantiation** (-ā´shən) *n.*

substantive (sŭb´stəntiv) *a.* **1** independently existent, not merely implied, inferential or subsidiary. **2** of or relating to the essence or substance of anything. **3** solidly based; important, substantial. **4** (*Law*) concerning rights and duties. **5** (of an enactment, resolution etc.) not amended. **6** (*Gram.*) **a** expressing existence. **b** denoting or functioning as a noun. **7** (of a dye or dyeing process) not requiring a mordant. **8** (*Mil.*) (of rank) permanent. ~*n.* (*Gram.*) a noun or part of a sentence used as a noun. **substantival** (-tī´-) *a.* **substantivally** *adv.* **substantively** *adv.* **substantive verb** *n.* the verb 'to be'. [ME and F *substantif*, L *substantīvus*, as SUBSTANCE]

sub-station (sŭb´stāshən) *n.* a subsidiary station, esp. one in which electric current from a generating station is modified before distribution.

substituent (səbstit´ūənt) *a.* (*Chem.*) (of a group of atoms) replacing another atom or group in a compound. ~*n.* such a group of atoms.

substitute (sŭb´stitūt) *n.* **1** a person or thing put in the place of or serving for another. **2** an artificial replacement for a natural substance (*milk substitute*). **3** (*Sc. Law*) a deputy. ~*v.t.* **1** to put or use in exchange (for) another person or thing. **2** (*coll.*) to replace (a person or thing by or with another). **3** to replace (an atom or group in a molecule) with another. ~*v.i.* to act as a substitute (for). **substitutable** *a.* **substitutability** (-bil´-) *n.* **substitution** (-ū´shən) *n.* **1** the act of substituting. **2** a replacement. **substitutionally** *adv.* **substitutionary** *a.* **substitutive** *a.* [F *substitut*, L *substitūtus*, p.p. of *substituere* (*statuere*, see STATUTE)]

substratum (sŭb´strahtəm) *n.* (*pl.* **substrata** (-tə)) **1** that which underlies anything. **2** a layer or stratum lying underneath. **3** the subsoil. **4** the ground or basis of phenomena etc., foundation. **substrate** (-strāt) *n.* **1** a substratum. **2** a surface for painting or printing on. **3** the substance on which an enzyme acts. **4** a base on which something lives or is formed. [L, neut. p.p. of *substernere* (see STRATUM)]

substructure (sŭb´strŭkchə) *n.* an understructure or foundation. **substructural** (-strŭk´-) *a.*

substyle (sŭb´stīl) *n.* the line on which the style or gnomon of a dial stands. **substylar** *a.*

subsume (səbsūm´) *v.t.* to include under a more general class or category. **subsumable** *a.* **subsumption** (-sŭmp´-) *n.* **subsumptive** *a.* [L *sūmere*, to take (p.p. *sumptus*)]

subsurface (sŭb´sœfis) *n.* the stratum or strata below the surface of the earth. ~*a.* **1** of or relating to the subsurface. **2** below the ground.

subsystem (sŭb´sistəm) *n.* a system within a larger system.

subtangent (sŭbtan´jənt) *n.* (*Geom.*) the portion of the axis of a curve intercepted between an ordinate and a tangent both drawn from the same point.

subtemperate (sŭbtem´pərət) *a.* of or relating to slightly colder than temperate regions.

subtenant (sŭbten´ənt) *n.* a tenant holding property from someone who is also a tenant. **subtenancy** *n.* (*pl.* **subtenancies**).

subtend (sŭbtend´) *v.t.* **1** (of a chord relatively to an arc, or the side of a triangle to an angle) to extend under or be opposite to. **2** (*Bot.*) to be lower than and enclose. **subtense** (-tens´) *n.* something which subtends. [L *subtendere* (*tendere*, to stretch, p.p. *tensus*)]

subterfuge (sŭb´təfūj) *n.* **1** a deception, prevarication etc. used to avoid an inference, censure etc., or to evade or conceal something. **2** the practice of using subterfuges. [F, from late L *subterfugium* (*fugere*, to flee)]

subterminal (sŭbtœ´minəl) *a.* almost at the end.

subterranean (sŭbtərā´niən) *a.* **1** underground. **2** hidden, concealed. **subterraneous** *a.* underground. **subterraneously** *adv.* **subterrestrial** (-res´tri-) *a.* existing underground. [L *subterrāneus* (*terra*, earth, -ANEOUS)]

subtext (sŭb´tekst) *n.* an unstated message or theme in a speech or piece of writing, conveyed in the tone of voice, choice of words etc.

subtilize (sŭt´ilīz), **subtilise** *v.t.* **1** to make subtle. **2** to refine. ~*v.i.* to reason subtly. **subtilization** (-zā´shən) *n.*

subtitle (sŭb´tītəl) *n.* **1** an additional or subsidiary title of a book etc. 2 a half-title, usu. placed before the title page in books. 3 a printed explanatory caption to a silent film or a printed translation of the dialogue in a foreign film. ~*v.t.* to provide a subtitle for.

subtle (sŭt´əl) *a.* 1 rarefied, attenuated, delicate, hard to seize, elusive. 2 difficult to comprehend, not obvious, abstruse. 3 making fine distinctions, acute, discerning. 4 ingenious, skilful, clever. 5 †artful, cunning, crafty, insidious. **subtleness** *n.* **subtlety** (-ti) *n.* (*pl.* **subtleties**) 1 the quality of being subtle. 2 an instance of being subtle. **subtly** (sut´li) *adv.* [ME *sotil*, OF *sutil*, L *subtilis*, acc. *-lem* (prob. finely woven, SUB-, *tela*, a web)]

subtonic (sŭbton´ik) *n.* (*Mus.*) the note next below the tonic.

subtopia (sŭbtō´piə) *n.* (*derog.*) unsightly suburbs, badly planned rural or urban areas. **subtopian** *a.*

subtopic (sŭb´topik) *n.* a secondary topic.

subtotal (sŭb´tōtəl) *n.* the total resulting from adding a group of figures which form part of the overall total.

subtract (səbtrakt´) *v.t.* to take away (a part, quantity etc.) from the rest, to deduct. **subtracter** *n.* **subtraction** *n.* **subtractive** *a.* **subtractor** *n.* an electrical circuit which produces an output depending on the difference of two inputs. **subtrahend** (sŭb´trəhend) *n.* (*Math.*) the number or quantity to be subtracted from another. [L *subtractus*, p.p. of *subtrahere* (*trahere*, to draw)]

subtriangular (sŭbtrīang´gūlə) *a.* approximately triangular.

subtribe (sŭb´trīb) *n.* a subdivision of a tribe.

subtriplicate (sŭbtrip´likət) *a.* expressed by the cube root.

subtropical (sŭbtrop´ikəl) *a.* 1 characterized by features common to both the temperate and tropical zones. 2 of or relating to the regions near the tropics. **subtropics** *n.pl.*

subulate (sū´būlət) *a.* (*Bot.*, *Zool.*) awl-shaped. [L *subula*, an awl]

subungulate (sŭbŭng´gūlət) *a.* hoofed, but having several digits.

subunit (sŭb´ūnit) *n.* a distinct part, esp. one of the polypeptide chains in a large protein.

suburb (sŭb´œb) *n.* 1 an outlying part of a city or town. 2 (*pl.*) the residential outskirts of a city or large town. **suburban** (-œ´-) *a.* 1 of or relating to a suburb or the suburbs. 2 (*derog.*) denoting an outlook on life limited by certain narrow conventions. **suburbanite** (-nīt) *n.* a person who lives in the suburbs. **suburbanize, suburbanise** *v.t.* **suburbanization** (-zā´shən) *n.* **suburbia** (-œ´biə) *n.* (*often derog.*) 1 (the inhabitants of) residential suburbs collectively. 2 the lifestyle, culture etc. held to be characteristic of suburbia. [A-F and OF *suburbe*, L *suburbium* (*urbs urbis*, a city)]

subvariety (sŭb´vərīəti) *n.* (*pl.* **subvarieties**) a subdivision of a variety.

subvene (səbvēn´) *v.i.* to happen so as to aid or effect a result. **subvention** (-ven´-) *n.* a grant in aid, a subsidy. [F *subvenir*, L *subvenīre* (*venīre*, to come)]

subvert (səbvœt´) *v.t.* 1 to overthrow, to destroy, to overturn. 2 to corrupt, to pervert. **subversion** (-shən) *n.* **subversive** *a.* intending to weaken or destroy a government etc. ~*n.* a subversive person. **subversively** *adv.* **subversiveness** *n.* **subverter** *n.* [F *subvertir*, L *subvertere* (*vertere*, to turn, p.p. *versus*)]

subvocal (sŭbvō´kəl) *a.* subtonic.

subway (sŭb´wā) *n.* 1 an underground passage, tunnel, conduit etc. 2 (*Sc.*, *N Am.*) an underground railway.

subwoofer (sŭb´wufə) *n.* a component in a loudspeaker which reproduces very low bass frequencies.

sub-zero (sŭbziə´rō) *a.* below zero (degrees).

suc- (sŭk) *pref.* var. of SUB-, used before *c.*

succade (sŭkād´) *n.* a fruit candied and preserved in syrup. [L *succus*, juice]

succedaneum (sŭksidā´niəm) *n.* (*pl.* **succedanea** (-niə)) something used instead of something else, a substitute. **succedaneous** *a.* [L *succēdāneus*, as SUCCEED]

succeed (səksēd´) *v.i.* 1 to be successful, to attain a desired object, to end well or prosperously. 2 to follow in time or order, to be subsequent. 3 to be the heir or successor (to an office, estate etc.). ~*v.t.* 1 to follow, to come after (in time or order), to be subsequent to. 2 to take the place previously occupied by, to be heir or successor to. **nothing succeeds like success** success engenders further success. **succeeder** *n.* [F *succéder*, L *succēdere* (*cēdere*, see CEDE, p.p. *cessus*)]

succentor (səksen´tə) *n.* 1 a deputy precentor in a cathedral. 2 the leading bass in a choir. **succentorship** *n.* [late L, from L *succinere* (*canere*, to sing), p.p. *succentus*]

succès de scandale (suksā də skondahl´) *n.* success owing to notoriety. [F, lit., success of scandal]

success (səkses´) *n.* 1 the act of succeeding, favourable result, attainment of what is desired or intended. 2 attainment of prosperity or high position. 3 †the issue or result of an undertaking. **nothing succeeds like success** SUCCEED. **successful** *a.* **successfully** *adv.* **successfulness** *n.* **successless** *a.* **successlessly** *adv.* **successlessness** *n.* **success story** *n.* (*pl.* **success stories**) a person who or something which is very successful despite unfavourable circumstances. [OF *succes*, L *successum*, nom. *-sus*, from *succēdere*, to succeed]

succession (səksesh´ən) *n.* 1 a following in order. 2 a series of things following in order. 3 the act or right of succeeding to an office or inheritance. 4 the order in which persons so succeed. 5 the line of persons so succeeding. 6 the order of descent in the development of species. 7 (*Geol.*) **a** a sequence of fossil forms which represents an evolutionary series. **b** a group of strata which represents a chronological sequence. **in quick succession** one soon after another. **in succession** one after another. **in succession to** as the successor to or of. **successional** *a.* **successionally** *adv.* **succession duty** *n.* DEATH DUTIES (under DEATH). **succession state** *n.* a state which results from the partition of a country. **successor** *n.* a person who or something which succeeds another. [F, from L *successio*, acc. *-ōnem*, as SUCCESS]

successive (səkses´iv) *a.* following in order or uninterrupted succession, consecutive. **successively** *adv.* **successiveness** *n.* [F *successif*, fem. *-ive*, med. L *successīvus*, from L *successus*, SUCCESS]

succi SUCCUS.

succinct (səksingkt´) *a.* compressed into few words, brief, concise. **succinctly** *adv.* **succinctness** *n.* [L *succinctus*, p.p. of *succingere* (*cingere*, to gird)]

succinite (sŭk´sinīt) *n.* amber; a yellow variety of garnet. **succinate** (-nāt) *n.* a salt of succinic acid. **succinic** (-sin´-) *a.* derived from or contained in amber. **succinic acid** *n.* a colourless water-soluble dibasic acid which is important as an intermediate in glucose metabolism. [late L *succinum*, from *succus*, juice]

succor SUCCOUR.

succory (sŭk´əri) *n.* chicory. [by corr.]

succose (sŭk´ōs) *a.* juicy. [L *succus*, juice]

succotash (sŭk´ətash) *n.* (*N Am.*) a dish made of green maize and beans cooked together. [Narragansett]

Succoth (sukōt´, sŭk´əth) *n.* the Jewish harvest festival commemorating the Israelites' sheltering in the wilderness. [Heb. *sukkôth*, pl. of *sukkāh*, a thicket, a hut]

succour (sŭk´ə), (*N Am.*) **succor** *n.* 1 aid in time of difficulty or distress. 2 (*pl.*) †reinforcements. ~*v.t.* to come to the aid of; to help or relieve in difficulty or distress. **succourer** *n.* **succourless** *a.* [OF *sucurre*, L *succurrere* (*currere*, to run, p.p. *cursus*)]

succuba (sŭk´ūbə), **succubus** (-bəs) *n.* (*pl.* **succubae** (-bē), **succubi** (-bī)) a demon believed to assume the shape of a woman and have sexual intercourse with men in their sleep. **succubine** (-bīn) *a.* [L, from *succumbere* (*cumbere*, to lie)]

succulent (sŭk´ūlənt) *a.* 1 juicy and delicious. 2 (*coll.*) desirable. 3 (of a plant, stem etc.) thick and fleshy. ~*n.* a succulent plant, such as a cactus. **succulence** *n.* **succulently** *adv.* [F, from L *succulentus*, from SUCCUS]

succumb (səkŭm´) *v.i.* 1 to cease to resist etc., to give way (to); to yield, to submit (to). 2 to die. [L *succumbere* (*cumbere*, to lie)]

succursal (səkœ´səl) *a.* (of an ecclesiastical building, such as a chapel of ease) auxiliary. [F *succursale* (*église*), subsidiary (church), from med. L *succursus*, SUCCOUR]

succus (sŭk´əs) *n.* (*pl.* **succi** (sŭk´sī)) 1 a body juice or fluid secretion. 2 the expressed juice of a plant, used medicinally. [L, also *sūcus*, juice, sap]

succuss (səkŭs´) *v.t.* to shake suddenly, esp. in medical diagnosis. **succussation** (sŭkŭsā´shən) *n.* a shaking, a succussion. **succussion** (-kŭsh´ən) *n.* 1 a shaking. 2 (*Med.*) a shaking of the thorax to detect pleural effusion. **successive** *a.* [L *succussus*, p.p. of *succutere* (*quatere*, to shake)]

☒ **sucess** common misspelling of SUCCESS.

such (sŭch) *a.* 1 of that, or the same, or the like kind or degree (as). 2 of the kind or degree mentioned or implied. 3 being the same in quality, degree etc. 4 so great, intense etc. (as, that). 5 (*Law*) of the aforesaid kind. ~*adv.* so (*such a nice day*). ~*pron.* 1 such a person, persons or things (as). 2 the aforesaid thing or things. 3 suchlike. **as such** loosely as described (*He has no qualifications as such*). **such a one** 1 such a person or thing. 2 †some unspecified person or thing. **such as** 1 for example. 2 of a kind that. 3 those who. **such as it is** despite its inadequacies. **such-and-such** *a.* not known or specified, some. ~*n.* an unknown or unspecified person or thing. **such-and-such a person** *n.* an unknown or unspecified person. **suchlike** *pron.* things of that sort. ~*a.* of such a kind. [OE *swylc*, (*swā*, so, *līc*, LIKE[1], -LY[1]), cp. Dut. *zulk*, G *solch*, Icel. *slīkr*, Swed. *slik*]

suck (sŭk) *v.t.* 1 to draw (milk etc.) into the mouth by the action of the lips. 2 to draw liquid from with or as with the mouth. 3 to dissolve or eat thus. 4 to take and hold in the mouth with a sucking action. 5 to imbibe, to drink in, to absorb, to gain. 6 to engulf, to draw (in). ~*v.i.* 1 to draw liquid etc. in by suction. 2 to draw milk, nourishment etc. in thus. 3 to make the sound of sucking or a sound like sucking. 4 (*N Am., sl.*) to be very bad or contemptible. ~*n.* 1 an act or spell of sucking, suction. 2 force of suction. 3 a small draught or drink. **†to give suck (to)** to suckle. **to suck dry** 1 to empty by sucking. 2 to use up the sympathy, tolerance etc. of. **to suck in** 1 to absorb. 2 to engulf, to draw (in). 3 to involve unwillingly in a bad situation. **to suck up** 1 (*coll.*) to act in an obsequious manner, toady. 2 to absorb. **sucker** *n.* 1 a person who or something which sucks. 2 a sucking pig. 3 a newborn whale. 4 a suckling. 5 (*coll.*) a gullible person. 6 (*coll.*) a person who is very fond of or unable to resist a specified thing (*I'm a sucker for romance*). 7 (*esp. N Am., coll.*) something not named or specified. 8 a sucking-disc. 9 (*Biol.*) an organ acting on the same principle as a sucking-disc. 10 (*Bot.*) a shoot from a root or a subterranean part of a stem. 11 a fish which sucks in food or has a suctorial mouth. 12 the piston of a suction pump. 13 a pipe or tube through which anything is drawn by suction. 14 (*N Am., coll.*) a lollipop. ~*v.t.* 1 (*Bot.*) to strip suckers from. 2 (*esp. N Am., coll.*) to dupe, to trick. ~*v.i.* (*Bot.*) to send out suckers. **suck-in** *n.* (*sl.*) a deception, a fiasco. **sucking** *a.* 1 deriving nourishment from the breast; not yet weaned. 2 (*Zool.*) unfledged. **sucking-bottle** *n.* a baby's feeding bottle. **sucking-disc** *n.* a disc of leather, rubber etc. adhering firmly to a smooth surface when wetted. **sucking-fish** *n.* a remora. **sucking-pig** *n.* a pig not yet weaned. **sucks** *int.* (*coll.*) used to express disappointment or derision. [OE *sūcan*, cp. L *sugere*, p.p. *suctus*]

suckle (sŭk´əl) *v.t.* 1 to give milk from the breast or udder to. 2 to nourish. ~*v.i.* to feed by sucking milk from the mother's breast or udder. **suckler** *n.* **suckling** *n.* a child or animal not yet weaned. [freq. of SUCK]

sucre (soo´krā) *n.* the standard unit of currency of Ecuador.

sucrose (soo´krōz) *n.* (*Chem.*) sugar as obtained from sugar cane or sugar beet. [F *sucre*, SUGAR, -OSE[1]]

suction (sŭk´shən) *n.* 1 the act or process of sucking. 2 the production of a vacuum in a confined space causing fluid to enter, or a body to adhere to something, under atmospheric pressure. 3 the force produced by this process. **suction pump** *n.* a pump in which liquid is forced up by atmospheric pressure. **suctorial** (-taw´ri-) *a.* (*Zool.*) adapted for sucking or for adhering by suction. **suctorian** (-riən) *n.* [F, from L *suctus*, p.p. of *sugere*, to SUCK]

☒ **suculent** common misspelling of SUCCULENT.

☒ **sucumb** common misspelling of SUCCUMB.

sudamina (soodam´inə) *n.pl.* (*Med.*) minute transparent vesicles arising from a disorder of the sweat glands. **sudaminal** *a.* [pl. of late L *sudāmen*, from L *sudāre*, to sweat]

Sudanese (soodənēz´) *a.* of or relating to Sudan, NE Africa. ~*n.* (*pl.* **Sudanese**) a native or inhabitant of Sudan, or a descendant of one.

sudatory (soo´dətəri) *a.* promoting perspiration. ~*n.* (*pl.* **sudatories**) 1 a sudatory drug. 2 a sudatorium. **sudarium** (-deə´riəm) *n.* (*pl.* **sudaria** (-riə)) a cloth for wiping away sweat, esp. that of St Veronica, believed to have been miraculously impressed with the face of Christ at the Crucifixion. **sudation** (-ā´shən) *n.* 1 sweating. 2 sweat. **sudatorium** (-dətaw´riəm) *n.* (*pl.* **sudatoria** (-iə)) in ancient Rome, a hot-air bath, or a room where such baths were taken. [L *sūdātio*, from *sūdāre*, cogn. with SWEAT]

sudd (sŭd) *n.* a floating mass of vegetation, trees etc. obstructing navigation in the White Nile. [Arab.]

sudden (sŭd´ən) *a.* 1 happening unexpectedly, without warning. 2 instantaneous, abrupt, swift, rapid. **all of a sudden** suddenly; unexpectedly. **of a sudden** suddenly; unexpectedly. **†on a sudden** suddenly; unexpectedly. **sudden death** *n.* (*coll.*) an extended period of play to decide a tie in a game or contest, ending when one side scores. **sudden infant death syndrome** *n.* (*Med.*) cot death. **suddenly** *adv.* **suddenness** *n.* [ME and OF *sodain*, L *subitāneus*, from *subitus*, sudden, from *subīre*, to come up (*īre*, to come)]

sudoriferous (soodərif´ərəs) *a.* producing or secreting perspiration. **sudorific** *a.* causing perspiration. ~*n.* a sudorific drug. [L *sūdōrifer* (*sūdor -dōris*, sweat, -FEROUS)]

Sudra (soo´drə) *n.* (*pl.* **Sudras**) a member of the lowest of the four great Hindu castes. [Hind., from Sansk. *çūdra*]

suds (sŭdz) *n.pl.* 1 soapy water forming a frothy mass. 2 (*N Am., coll.*) beer. ~*v.i.* to form suds. ~*v.t.* to wash in soapy water. **sudsy** *a.* [lit., things sodden, see SEETHE]

sue (soo) *v.t.* (*3rd pers. sing. pres.* **sues,** *pres.p.* **suing,** *past, p.p.* **sued**) 1 (*Law*) to prosecute or to pursue a claim (for) by legal process. 2 to entreat, to petition. ~*v.i.* 1 (*Law*) to take legal proceedings (for). 2 to make entreaty or petition (to or for). **to sue out** to petition for and obtain (a writ, pardon etc.). **suer** *n.* [OF *suir* (F *suivre*), late L *sequere*, L *sequī*, to follow]

suede (swād) *n.* 1 undressed kid or similar leather given a nap surface by rubbing. 2 (*also* **suede-cloth**) a fabric resembling suede. ~*a.* made of suede. [F, *Suède*, Sweden]

suet (soo´it) *n.* the hard fat about the kidneys and loins of oxen, sheep etc. **suet pudding** *n.* a boiled or steamed pudding made of suet etc. **suety** *a.* [dim. from OF *seu*, L *sebum*, tallow]

suf., suff. *abbr.* suffix.

suf- (sŭf) *pref.* var. of SUB-, used before *f.*

suffer (sŭf´ə) *v.i.* **1** to undergo or endure pain, grief, injury, loss etc. **2** to be at a disadvantage. **3** †to undergo punishment, esp. to be executed. ~*v.t.* **1** to experience or undergo (something painful, disagreeable or unjust). **2** to endure, to sustain, to support (unflinchingly etc.). **3** to tolerate, to put up with. **4** †to permit, to allow (of). **sufferable** *a.* **sufferableness** *n.* **sufferably** *adv.* **sufferance** *n.* **1** tacit or passive permission, toleration, allowance. **2** suffering. **3** †endurance, patience, submissiveness. **on sufferance** merely tolerated. **sufferer** *n.* **suffering** *n., a.* **sufferingly** *adv.* [OF *suffrir*, L *sufferre* (*ferre*, to bear)]

suffice (səfīs´) *v.i.* to be enough, to be adequate or sufficient (for or to do etc.). ~*v.t.* to be enough for, to content, to satisfy. **suffice it to say** I will say only this. **sufficiency** (-fish´ənsi) *n.* (*pl.* **sufficiencies**) **1** an adequate supply (of). **2** †the quality of being sufficient. **3** †a competence; adequate qualification, competence, efficiency. **sufficient** (-fish´ənt) *a.* enough, adequate, sufficing (for). ~*n.* (*coll.*) enough, a sufficiency. **sufficiently** *adv.* [ME *suffisen*, OF *suffis-*, stem of *suffire*, L *sufficere* (*facere*, to make)]

suffix[1] (sŭf´iks) *n.* **1** a letter or syllable appended to the end of a word to form an inflection or derivative. **2** (*Math.*) a subscript. **suffixal** *a.* [L *suffixus*, p.p. of *suffigere* (*figere*, to FIX, p.p. *fixus*)]

suffix[2] (sŭf´iks, səfiks´) *v.t.* to add as a suffix, to append. **suffixion** (sŭfik´shən), **suffixation** (-sā´shən) *n.*

suffocate (sŭf´əkāt) *v.t.* **1** to choke, to kill by stopping respiration. **2** to smother, to stifle. **3** to cause difficulty of respiration to. ~*v.i.* to be or feel suffocated. **suffocating** *a.* **suffocatingly** *adv.* **suffocation** (-ā´shən) *n.* **suffocative** *a.* [L *suffōcātus*, p.p. or *suffōcāre* (*fōcāre*, from *fauces*, pl., the throat)]

Suffolk (sŭf´ək) *n.* a breed of black-faced sheep. **Suffolk punch** *n.* a short-legged draught horse, orig. bred in Suffolk.

suffragan (sŭf´rəgən) *a.* assisting: denoting a bishop consecrated to assist another bishop or any bishop in relation to the metropolitan (*suffragan bishop; bishop suffragan*). ~*n.* a suffragan or auxiliary bishop. **suffraganship** *n.* [ME, from F *suffragant*, med. L *suffrāgans -ntem*, pres.p., or *suffrāgāneus*, from L *suffrāgārī*, to vote for, as SUFFRAGE]

suffrage (sŭf´rij) *n.* **1** the right to vote, esp. in parliamentary elections. **2** a vote in support of an opinion etc., or of a candidate for office. **3** approval, consent. **4** (*often pl.*) a prayer by the priest in the liturgy. **5** (*often pl.*) a short intercessory prayer by the congregation, esp. one of the responses in the Litany. **suffragette** (-rəjet´) *n.* (*Hist.*) a female agitator for women's right to vote. **suffragist** *n.* (*esp. Hist.*) an advocate of extension of the right to vote, esp. to women. **suffragism** *n.* [F, from L *suffrāgium*, perh. from *suffrāgo -gīnis*, ankle bone (used for voting) or perh. orig. a potsherd, from *suffringere*, to break]

suffruticose (səfroo´tikōz), **suffrutescent** (sŭfrətes´ənt) *a.* having a woody perennial base with nonwoody branches. [SUF-, L *frutex -ticis*, a shrub, prob. cogn. with Gr. *bruein*, to sprout]

suffuse (səfūz´) *v.t.* **1** (of a blush, fluid etc.) to overspread from within. **2** to cover with colour. **suffusion** (-zhən) *n.* [L *suffūsus*, p.p. of *suffundere* (*fundere*, to pour)]

Sufi (soo´fi) *n.* (*pl.* **Sufis**) a Muslim pantheistic philosopher and mystic. **Sufic** *a.* **Sufism** *n.* [Arab. *sūfī*, pure, wise]

sug (sŭg) *v.t.* (*pres.p.* **sugging,** *past, p.p.* **sugged**) (*sl.*) to pretend to be conducting market research while actually trying to sell a product to. [*s*ell *u*nder the *g*uise]

sug- (sŭj) *pref.* var. of SUB- used before *g.*

sugar (shug´ə) *n.* **1** a sweet, crystalline substance obtained from the expressed juice of various plants, esp. the sugar cane and the sugar beet. **2** (*Chem.*) any one of various sweet or sweetish soluble carbohydrates, such as glucose, sucrose, lactose etc. **3** (*esp. N Am., coll.*) a term of affection, dear. **4** flattering or seductive words, esp. used to mitigate or disguise something distasteful. **5** something used to make an unpleasant thing more acceptable. **6** (*sl.*) heroin or LSD taken on a sugar lump. ~*v.t.* **1** to sweeten, cover or sprinkle with sugar. **2** to mitigate, disguise or render palatable. **to sugar the pill** PILL. **sugar bean** *n.* the lima bean. **sugar beet** *n.* a beet, *Beta vulgaris*, from which sugar is extracted. **sugar-candy** *n.* candy. **sugar cane** *n.* a very tall grass, *Saccharum officinarum*, with tall jointed stems, from the juice of which sugar is made. **sugar-coated** *a.* **1** covered with sugar. **2** made superficially attractive, esp. to hide something less pleasant. **3** excessively sentimental. **sugar daddy** *n.* (*pl.* **sugar daddies**) (*sl.*) a well-to-do, elderly man who spends money on a young woman. **sugar-gum** *n.* a large Australian eucalyptus, *Eucalyptus cladocalyx*, with sweet foliage. **sugarhouse** *n.* a factory in which sugar is made. **sugarless** *a.* **sugar loaf** *n.* (*pl.* **sugar loaves**) a conical mass of refined sugar. **sugar maple** *n.* a N American tree, *Acer saccharum*, the sap of which yields sugar. **sugar mill** *n.* a mill for expressing the juice from sugar cane. **sugar mite** *n.* a mite infesting unrefined sugar. **sugar of lead** *n.* (*Chem.*) acetate of lead. **sugar pea** *n.* a mangetout. †**sugarplum** *n.* a sweet, esp. boiled sugar formed into a ball etc. **sugar-refiner** *n.* **sugar-refinery** *n.* (*pl* **sugar-refineries**). **sugar snap, sugar snap pea** *n.* a mangetout. **sugar soap** *n.* an alkaline preparation for cleaning or stripping paint. **sugar tongs** *n.pl.* a pair of small tongs for lifting lumps of sugar at table. **sugary** *a.* **1** containing or resembling sugar. **2** excessively sweet or sentimental. **3** exaggeratedly charming or flattering. **sugariness** *n.* [ME *sugre*, F *sucre*, Sp. *azucar*, Arab. *sakkar*, *sokkar*, Pers. *shakar*, Sansk. *çarkarā*, gravel, candy, whence Gr. *sacharon*, L *saccharum*]

suggest (səjest´) *v.t.* **1** to propose (a plan, idea etc.) for consideration. **2** to cause (an idea etc.) to arise in the mind. **3** to hint at, indicate. **to suggest itself** to arise in the mind. **suggester** *n.* **suggestible** *a.* **1** able to be suggested. **2** readily yielding to suggestion. **suggestibility** (-bil´-) *n.* **suggestion** (-jes´chən) *n.* **1** the act of suggesting. **2** something which is suggested. **3** a hint, an insinuation. **4** (*Psych.*) insinuation of an idea or impulse into the mind. **suggestive** *a.* **1** containing or conveying (a) suggestion. **2** tending to suggest thoughts of a prurient nature. **suggestively** *adv.* **suggestiveness** *n.* [L *suggestus*, p.p. of *suggerere* (*gerere*, to bring)]

suicide (soo´isīd) *n.* **1** the act of intentionally taking one's own life. **2** a person who takes their own life intentionally. **3** any self-inflicted action of a disastrous nature. ~*a.* (*Mil.*) denoting an extremely dangerous operation. ~*v.i.* to commit suicide. **suicidal** (-sī´-) *a.* **suicidally** *adv.* **suicide pact** *n.* an agreement between people to commit suicide at the same time. [L *suī*, of oneself, gen. of *se*, the self]

sui generis (sooī jen´əris, sooē) *a.* unique, of its own kind. [L]

sui juris (sooī juə´ris, sooē) *a.* (*Law*) of age; legally competent. [L, lit., of one's own right]

suilline (sū´ilīn) *a.* piglike. [L *suillus*, from *sus suis*, a swine]

suint (swint) *n.* the natural grease of wool. [F, from Gmc., cogn. with SWEAT]

suit (soot, sūt) *n.* **1** a set of outer clothes (now usu. a jacket and trousers or a skirt), esp. when made of the same cloth. **2** a set of clothes or an article of clothing for a particular purpose (*a diving suit*). **3** any one of the four sets in a pack of playing cards. **4** those cards in a hand belonging to one of these suits. **5** (*also* **suit at law**) a legal prosecution or action for the recovery of a right etc. **6** the act of suing, a petition, a request. **7** courtship. **8** a set (of sails or other articles used together). **9** (*sl.*) a person who wears a business suit, esp. a bureaucrat without character or individuality. ~*v.t.* **1** to agree with, to be appropriate to, to make (one) look attractive. **2** to satisfy, to please, to meet the desires etc. of. **3** to adapt, to accommodate, to make fitting (to). ~*v.i.* to agree, to accord, to correspond; to be convenient. **to follow suit 1** to play a card of the suit led by someone else. **2** (*fig.*) to follow someone's example. **to suit oneself 1** to do what one wants, regardless of other people's feelings. **2** to find something which pleases one. **to suit the action to the word** to carry out a promise or threat. **suitable** *a.* suited, fitting, convenient, proper, becoming. **suitability** (-bil´-) *n.* **suitableness** *n.* **suitably** *adv.* **suitcase** *n.* a travelling case. **to live out of a suitcase** LIVE[1]. **suitcaseful** *n.* (*pl.* **suitcasefuls**). **suiting** *n.* cloth for suits. †**suit of dittos** *n.* a suit of clothes of the same material. [F *suite*, med. L *secūta*, from *secut-*, p.p. stem of *sequī*, to follow]

suite (swēt) *n.* **1** a set (of connecting rooms, matching furniture etc.). **2** (*Mus.*) a series of instrumental compositions, orig. of dance tunes. **3** (*Mus.*) a set of selected musical pieces played as one instrumental work. **4** a company, a retinue. [F, see SUIT]

suitor (soo´tə, sū´-) *n.* **1** a man who wants to marry a particular woman. **2** a party to a lawsuit. **3** a company seeking to buy another company.

suivez (swē´vā) *v.i.* (*imper., Mus.*) follow (a direction to the accompanist to adapt their time to the soloist). [F, imper. of *suivre*]

suk, sukh SOUK.

sukiyaki (sukiyak´i) *n.* a Japanese dish of thin slices of meat and vegetables cooked together with soy sauce, saki etc. [Jap.]

sulcate (sŭl´kāt) *a.* having longitudinal furrows, grooves or channels. †**sulcated** *a.* **sulcus** (-kəs) *n.* (*pl.* **sulci** (-sī)) **1** a groove, a furrow. **2** (*Anat.*) a furrow separating convolutions of the brain. [L *sulcātus*, p.p. of *sulcāre*, from *sulcus*, a furrow]

sulf- SULPH-.

sulfur SULPHUR.

sulk (sŭlk) *v.i.* to be silent and bad-tempered. ~*n.* (*often pl.*) a fit of sulking. **sulker** *n.* **sulky** *a.* (*comp.* **sulkier**, *superl.* **sulkiest**) **1** sullen, morose, bad-tempered, resentful. **2** slow, sluggish. ~*n.* (*pl.* **sulkies**) a light, two-wheeled vehicle for a single person. **sulkily** *adv.* **sulkiness** *n.* [from *sulky*, from *sulkenness*, OE *solcennes* in *āsolcennes* (*solcen*, slothful)]

sullage (sŭl´ij) *n.* filth, refuse; sewage; silt. [F *souiller*, to soil]

sullen (sŭl´ən) *a.* **1** persistently morose, bad-tempered, cross. **2** slow, sluggish. **3** dismal, forbidding. ~†*n.pl.* a fit of sullenness, the sulks. **sullenly** *adv.* **sullenness** *n.* [ME and OF *solain*, SOLE[3]]

sully (sŭl´i) *v.t.* (*3rd pers. sing. pres.* **sullies**, *pres.p.* **sullying**, *past, p.p.* **sullied**) **1** to defile, to disgrace. **2** (*poet.*) to soil, to tarnish. ~*v.i.* to be soiled or tarnished. ~*n.* (*pl.* **sullies**) a spot, a blemish. [OE *sylian*, from *sol*, mud (prob. with mixture of OF *soillier*, to SOIL[2])]

sulph- (sŭlf), (*esp. N Am.*) **sulf-**, **sulpho-** (sŭl´fō), (*esp. N Am.*) **sulfo-** *comb. form* containing sulphur.

sulpha (sŭl´fə), (*esp. N Am.*) **sulfa** *n.* any drug derived from sulphanilamide. **sulpha drug** *n.* a sulphonamide drug with a powerful antibacterial action.

sulphadiazine (sŭlfədī´əzēn), (*esp. N Am.*) **sulfadiazine** *n.* a sulpha drug used to treat pneumonia and meningitis.

sulphadimidine (sŭlfədim´idēn), (*esp. N Am.*) **sulfadimidine** *n.* a sulpha drug used to treat urinary infections in humans and respiratory disease in pigs.

sulphamic acid (sŭlfam´ik), (*esp. N Am.*) **sulfamic acid** *n.* an amide of sulphuric acid, used in weedkiller. **sulphamate** (sŭl´fəmāt) *n.*

sulphanilamide (sŭlfənil´əmīd), (*esp. N Am.*) **sulfanilamide** *n.* a sulphonamide drug administered orally and by injection for combating streptococcal and other bacterial diseases.

sulphate (sŭl´fāt), (*esp. N Am.*) **sulfate** *n.* a salt of sulphuric acid.

sulphide (sŭl´fīd), (*esp. N Am.*) **sulfide** *n.* a compound of sulphur, with an element or radical.

sulphite (sŭl´fīt), (*esp. N Am.*) **sulfite** *n.* a salt of sulphurous acid.

sulphonamide (sŭlfon´əmīd), (*esp. N Am.*) **sulfonamide** *n.* **1** an amide of a sulphonic acid. **2** a sulpha drug.

sulphonate (sŭl´fənāt), (*esp. N Am.*) **sulfonate** *n.* a salt or ester of sulphonic acid. ~*v.t.* to convert into a sulphonate by treating with sulphuric acid.

sulphone (sŭl´fōn), (*esp. N Am.*) **sulfone** *n.* an organic compound containing the divalent group SO_2 linked to two carbon atoms. **sulphonic** (-fon´-) *a.* **sulphonic acid** *n.* any of a class of strong organic acids used in making dyes, drugs and detergents.

sulphur (sŭl´fə), (*esp. N Am.*) **sulfur** *n.* **1** a pale yellow non-metallic element, at. no. 16, chem. symbol S, insoluble in water, occurring in crystalline or amorphous forms, used in the manufacture of chemicals, gunpowder, matches etc. **2** the material of which hellfire was supposed to consist; brimstone. **3** any one of various pale yellow butterflies. ~*a.* of the colour of sulphur, pale yellow. **sulphurate** (-fūrāt) *v.t.* to impregnate with or subject to the action of sulphur, esp. in bleaching. **sulphuration** (-ā´shən) *n.* **sulphurator** *n.* **sulphur-bottom** *n.* the blue whale. **sulphur candle** *n.* a candle which, when burnt, produces sulphur dioxide for fumigation. **sulphur dioxide** *n.* a pungent gas used industrially and as a bleach and food preservative, which is a major source of air pollution. **sulphureous** (-fū´ri-) *a.* **1** consisting of or having the qualities of sulphur. **2** sulphur-coloured. **sulphureously** *adv.* **sulphureousness** *n.* †**sulphuretted** (-ret´-) *a.* saturated, impregnated or combined with sulphur. **sulphuretted hydrogen** *n.* hydrogen sulphide. **sulphuric** (-fū´-) *a.* (*Chem.*) derived from or containing sulphur, esp. in its highest valency. **sulphuric acid** *n.* a corrosive, oily, liquid acid, oil of vitriol. **sulphurize** (-fū-), **sulphurise** *v.t.* to sulphurate. **sulphurization** (-zā´shən) *n.* **sulphurous**[1] (sŭl´fərəs) *a.* sulphureous. **sulphurous**[2] (sŭlfū´rəs) *a.* containing sulphur in its lower valency. **sulphurous acid** *n.* an unstable acid used as a preservative and a bleaching agent. **sulphur spring** *n.* a spring of water impregnated with sulphur or sulphide etc. **sulphury** (-fəri) *a.* [L]

sultan (sŭl´tən) *n.* **1** a Muslim sovereign, esp. a former ruler of Turkey. **2** a white-crested variety of domestic fowl, orig. from Turkey. **sultana** (-tah´nə) *n.* **1** a seedless raisin. **2** a small yellow grape from which a sultana is produced. **3** the wife, mother or daughter of a sultan. **4** the mistress of a king, prince etc. **sultanate** (-nāt) *n.* **sultaness** (-nis) *n.* **sultanic** (-tan´-) *a.* **sultanship** *n.* [F, from Arab. *sultān*]

sultry (sŭl´tri) *a.* (*comp.* **sultrier**, *superl.* **sultriest**) **1** very hot, close and heavy, oppressive. **2** passionate, sensual. **sultrily** *adv.* **sultriness** *n.* [var. of obs. *sweltry*, from SWELTER]

sum (sŭm) *n.* **1** the aggregate of two or more numbers, magnitudes, quantities or particulars, the total. 2 substance, essence, summary. 3 a particular amount of money. 4 an arithmetical problem or the process of working it out. 5 (*pl.*) elementary arithmetic. ~*v.t.* (*pres.p.* **summing**, *past, p.p.* **summed**) to add, collect or combine into one total or whole. **in sum** briefly, in summary. **to sum up 1** to recapitulate. 2 to form a rapid opinion or estimate of. 3 to put in a few words, to condense. **summing-up** *n.* 1 a summary of the evidence and arguments of a case by the judge to the jury at the end of a trial. 2 a recapitulation. **sum total** *n.* the sum of two or more numbers etc., the total. [ME and F *somme*, L *summa*, orig. fem. of *summus*, super. of *superus*, higher, see SUPER-]

sumac (soo´mak, shoo´-), **sumach** *n.* 1 a tree or shrub of the genus *Rhus or Cotinus*, the dried and powdered leaves of which are used in tanning, dyeing etc. 2 a preparation of the dried leaves. [F, from Sp. *zumaque*, Arab. *summāq*]

Sumatran (sumah´trən) *a.* of or relating to Sumatra, in Indonesia. ~*n.* 1 a native or inhabitant of Sumatra, or a descendant of one. 2 the language of Sumatra.

Sumerian (sumiə´riən) *a.* of or relating to Sumer, an ancient region of Babylonia. ~*n.* 1 a native or inhabitant of Sumeria. 2 the language of Sumeria.

summa (sum´ə, sŭm´ə) *n.* (*pl.* **summae** (-mē)) a comprehensive survey of a subject. [ME, from L (see SUM)]

summa cum laude (sŭmə kŭm law´dē, sumə kum low´dā) *adv., a.* (*esp. N Am.*) with the highest distinction. [L, with highest praise]

summary (sŭm´əri) *n.* (*pl.* **summaries**) an abridged or condensed statement. ~*a.* 1 condensed into few words, abridged, concise. 2 done briefly or unceremoniously. **summarily** *adv.* **summariness** *n.* **summarist** *n.* **summarize, summarise** *v.t.* to make or be a summary of. **summarizable** *a.* **summarization** (-zā´shən) *n.* **summarizer** *n.* **summary conviction** *n.* a conviction made by a judge or magistrate with no jury. **summary jurisdiction** *n.* the authority of a court to adjudicate summarily on a matter arising during proceedings. **summary offence** *n.* an offence tried in a magistrate's court. [L *summārium*, from *summa*, a SUM]

summation (səmā´shən) *n.* 1 the act or process of making a sum, addition. 2 a summing-up; a summary. **summational** *a.* **summative** (sŭm´ətiv) *a.*

summer[1] (sŭm´ə) *n.* 1 the season of the year when the sun shines most directly upon a region, the warmest season of the year. 2 (*Astron.*) the period from the summer solstice to the autumnal equinox. 3 the hot weather associated with the summer. 4 the time of greatest happiness or achievement. 5 (*pl., poet.*) years of age. ~*a.* of, relating to or used in summer. ~*v.i.* to pass the summer. ~*v.t.* to feed or keep (cattle etc.) during the summer. **summer house** *n.* a light building in a garden, for shade etc. in summer. **summering** *n.* **summerless** *a.* **summer lightning** *n.* sheet lightning seen too far off for the thunder to be heard. **summerly** *adv.* **summer pudding** *n.* a pudding of soft fruit in a bread casing. **summer school** *n.* a course of study held during the summer vacation. **summer season** *n.* the time, during the summer, when people are employed in holiday entertainment and related occupations. **summer solstice** *n.* one of the times (about 21 June in the northern hemisphere) and points at which the sun is farthest from the celestial equator. **summer time** *n.* the official time of one hour in advance of Greenwich Mean Time which comes into force between stated dates in the summer in Britain. **summertime** *n.* the period of summer. **summer-weight** *a.* (of clothes) lightweight, suitable for wearing in warm weather. **summery** *a.* [OE *sumor* (cp. Dut. *zomer*, G *Sommer*, Icel. *sumar*), cogn. with Sansk. *samē*, a year]

summer[2] (sŭm´ə) *n.* 1 (*also* **summer-tree**) a heavy horizontal beam or glider. 2 a lintel. 3 a large stone laid on a column as the beginning of an arch, vault etc. [F *sommier*, L *sagmarius*, from L and Gr. *sagma*, a packsaddle]

summersault SOMERSAULT.

summing-up SUM.

summit (sŭm´it) *n.* 1 the highest point, the top. 2 the utmost elevation, degree etc. 3 a summit conference. **summit conference** *n.* a conference between heads of states. **summiteer** (-tiə´) *n.* 1 a person taking part in a summit conference. 2 a person who has climbed to the summit of a mountain. **summitless** *a.* **summit-level** *n.* the highest level. **summit meeting** *n.* a summit conference. **summit talks** *n.pl.* a summit conference. [F *sommet*, dim. of OF *som*, L *summum*, neut. of *summus*, see SUM]

summon (sŭm´ən) *v.t.* 1 to call, cite or command to meet or attend. 2 to order by a summons to appear in court. 3 to call upon to do something. 4 to call together. 5 to rouse, to call (up) (courage etc.). **summonable** *a.* **summoner** *n.* [OF *somoner*, L *submonēre* (*monēre*, to warn)]

summons (sŭm´ənz) *n.* (*pl.* **summonses**) 1 the act of summoning. 2 an authoritative call or citation, esp. to appear before a court or judge. ~*v.t.* to serve with a summons, to summon.

summum bonum (sumәm bon´əm) *n.* the highest or supreme good. [L]

summum genus (sumәm jen´əs, jē´nəs) *n.* a genus which cannot be considered as a species of another genus. [L]

sumo (soo´mō) *n.* traditional Japanese wrestling in which a contestant attempts to force his opponent out of the designated area or to touch the ground with a part of the body other than the feet. ~*a.* of or relating to sumo (*a sumo wrestler*). [Jap. *sumō*]

sump (sŭmp) *n.* 1 a well in the floor of a mine, to collect water for pumping. 2 a receptacle for lubricating oil in the crankcase of an internal-combustion engine. 3 a pit to collect metal at its first fusion. 4 a pond at a saltworks. [cp. Swed. and Dan. *sump*, Dut. *somp*, G *Sumpf*]

sumph (sŭmf) *n.* (*Sc.*) a stupid person, a simpleton. [etym. uncertain]

sumpitan (sŭm´pitan), **sumpit** *n.* a Malay blowpipe. [Malay]

†**sumpter** (sŭmp´tə) *n.* an animal employed to carry packs, a packhorse etc. [OF *sommetier*, a packhorse driver, prob. through late L *sagmatārius*, from Gr. *sagma -atos*, a burden, see SUMMER[2]]

sumptuary (sŭmp´tūəri) *a.* of, relating to or regulating expenditure. **sumptuary edict** *n.* an edict restraining private excess in dress, luxury etc. **sumptuary law** *n.* a law restraining private excess in dress, luxury etc. [L *sumptuārius*, as SUMPTUOUS]

sumptuous (sŭmp´tūəs) *a.* 1 costly, expensive. 2 showing lavish expenditure. 3 splendid, magnificent. **sumptuosity** (-os´-) *n.* **sumptuously** *adv.* **sumptuousness** *n.* [F *somptueux*, L *sumptuōsus*, from *sumptus -tūs*, expense, cost]

Sun. *abbr.* Sunday.

sun (sŭn) *n.* 1 the heavenly body round which the earth revolves and which gives light and heat to the earth and other planets of the solar system. 2 the light or warmth of the sun, sunshine, a sunny place. 3 a fixed star that has satellites and is the centre of a system. 4 (*poet.*) a day, a sunrise. 5 (*poet.*) anything splendid or luminous, or a chief source of light, honour etc. ~*v.t.* (*pres.p.* **sunning**, *past, p.p.* **sunned**) to expose to the rays of the sun. ~*v.i.* to sun oneself. **against the sun** anticlockwise. **beneath the sun** under the sun. **in the sun** exposed to the rays of the sun. **one's sun is set** one's prosperous period is over. **on which the sun never sets** worldwide. **to catch the sun 1** to be in a sunny place. 2 to become sunburnt. **to have the sun in one's eyes** to be intoxicated. **to shoot the sun** (*Naut.*, *sl.*) to take the sun. **to take the sun** (*Naut.*) to ascertain the sun's altitude in order to determine the latitude. **under the sun** in the world, on earth. **with the sun** clockwise. **sun and planet** *n.* a system of gearing cog-wheels. **sun-baked** *a.* dried or hardened by the sun's heat. **sun bath** *n.* exposure to the sun or a sunlamp; insolation. **sunbathe** *v.i.* to expose the body to the sun in order to get a suntan. **sunbather** *n.* **sunbeam** *n.* a ray of sunlight. **sun bear** *n.* a small black bear, *Helarctos malayanus*, of SE Asia, having a pale marking on its chest. **sunbed** *n.* 1 an array of ultraviolet-emitting light tubes under which one lies to tan the skin. 2 a portable folding bed used for sunbathing. **sunbelt** *n.* a strip of land which has a warm, sunny climate. **sunbird** *n.* any bird of the family Nectariniidae, having brilliant metallic plumage with a striking resemblance to hummingbirds. **sunblind** *n.* a window shade or awning. **sunblock** *n.* a cream, lotion etc. for the skin which blocks out the sun's ultraviolet rays; a sunscreen. **sunbonnet** *n.* a large bonnet of light material with projections at the front and sides and a pendant at the back. **sunbow** *n.* a rainbow formed by sunlight on spray etc. **sunburn** *n.* reddening and inflammation of the skin due to over-exposure to the sun. ~*v.i.* (*past, p.p.* **sunburnt, sunburned**) to suffer from sunburn. **sunburnt, sunburned** *a.* **sunburst** *n.* 1 an object made in the shape of the sun with its rays. 2 a strong or sudden burst of sunlight. **sun cream** *n.* cream used to protect the skin from the sun's rays. **sun-dance** *n.* an American Indian dance in honour of the sun. **sun deck** *n.* 1 the upper deck of a passenger ship. 2 (*N Am.*) a terrace, attached to a house, used for sunbathing. **sundew** *n.* any low, hairy, insectivorous bog plant of the genus *Drosera*. **sundial** *n.* an instrument for telling the time of day by means of the shadow of a gnomon cast on a dial etc. **sun-disc** *n.* a winged disc, as an emblem of the sun-god. **sun-dog** *n.* a parhelion. **sundown** *n.* sunset. **sundowner** *n.* (*coll.*) 1 (*Austral., New Zeal.*) a tramp who times his arrival at sundown in order to get a night's lodging. 2 an alcoholic drink taken at sunset. **sundress** *n.* a lightweight, lowcut, sleeveless dress for wearing in the sun. **sun-dried** *a.* dried in the sun. **sunfast** *a.* (*N Am.*) not fading in sunlight. **sunfish** *n.* (*pl.* **sunfish**) a large fish of various species with a body like a sphere truncated behind. **sunflower** *n.* any plant of the genus *Helianthus*, esp. *H. annus*, with yellow-rayed flowers. **sunglasses** *n.pl.* darkened glasses for protecting the eyes from glare. **sun-god** *n.* the sun worshipped as a deity. **sunhat** *n.* a light hat with a broad brim etc., to protect the head from the sun. **sun-helmet** *n.* (*Hist.*) a cork or pith helmet worn by white people in the tropics. **sun in splendour** *n.* (*Her.*) the sun with its rays and a human face. **sun-kissed** *a.* lightened or warmed by the sun. **sunlamp** *n.* 1 a lamp which gives out ultraviolet rays for curative purposes or tanning the skin. 2 in film-making, a large lamp with a parabolic reflector. **sunless** *a.* **sunlessness** *n.* **sunlight** *n.* **sunlit** *a.* **sunlike** *a.* **sun lounge** *n.* a room with large windows to admit sunlight. **sunlounger** *n.* a portable folding bed used for sunbathing. **sun myth** *n.* a solar myth. **sunny** *a.* (*comp.* **sunnier**, *superl.* **sunniest**) 1 bright with or warmed by sunlight. 2 bright, cheerful, cheery, genial. 3 proceeding from the sun. **sunnily** *adv.* **sunniness** *n.* **sunny side** *n.* 1 the side of a street or building which gets most sunshine. 2 the more cheerful or positive aspect of any situation. **sunny side up** (*esp. N Am.*) (of an egg) fried on one side only. **Sun of righteousness** *n.* Jesus Christ. **sun parlor** *n.* (*N Am.*) a sun lounge. **sunproof** *a.* **sunray** *n.* 1 (*usu. pl.*) a sunbeam. 2 (*pl.*) ultraviolet rays used in heat treatment. **sunray pleats** *n.pl.* pleats widening out from the waistband of a skirt to the hem. **sunrise** *n.* 1 the first appearance of the sun above the horizon. 2 the colours and light in the sky at sunrise. 3 the time of sunrise. **sunrise industry** *n.* a high-technology industry with good prospects for the future. **sunroof** *n.* (*pl.* **sunroofs, sunrooves**) 1 a car roof with a panel that slides or lifts open. 2 such a panel. **sunroom** *n.* 1 a sun lounge. 2 (*esp. N Am.*) a solarium. **sunscreen** *n.* a substance included in suntan preparations to protect the skin by screening out some of the ultraviolet radiation from the sun. **sunset** *n.* 1 the disappearance of the sun below the horizon. 2 the colours and light in the sky at sunset. 3 the time of sunset. 4 the decline (of life etc.). **sunset provision** *n.* (*N Am.*) a provision for a programme to be terminated after a fixed period unless it is formally renewed. **sunshade** *n.* a parasol, awning, blind etc. used as a protection against the sun. **sunshine** *n.* 1 the light of the sun. 2 the space lit by this. 3 warmth, brightness. 4 cheerfulness, favourable influence. 5 (*coll.*) a form of address. **sunshine law** *n.* (*N Am.*) a law which requires that certain official records of government agencies be made available to the public. **sunshine roof** *n.* (*pl.* **sunshine roofs, sunshine rooves**) a sunroof. **Sunshine State** *n.* any one of the US States of California, Florida, New Mexico and South Dakota. **sunshiny** *a.* **sunspot** *n.* a dark patch sometimes seen on the surface of the sun. **sunstar** *n.* any starfish of the genus *Solaster*, having many arms. **sunstone** *n.* a feldspar with flecks of haematite etc. **sunstroke** *n.* heatstroke due to exposure to the sun in hot weather. **sunsuit** *n.* a children's playsuit suitable for wearing in sunny weather. **suntan** *n.* a browning of the skin caused by the formation of pigment induced by exposure to the sun or a sunlamp. ~*v.i.* (*pres.p.* **suntanning**, *past, p.p.* **suntanned**) to get a suntan. **suntanned** *a.* **suntrap** *n.* a sheltered sunny place, for example in a garden. **sunup** *n.* (*chiefly N Am.*) sunrise. **sun visor** *n.* a movable shield attached to the top of a car's windscreen to shield the eyes from the sun. **sunward** *a., adv.* **sunwards** *adv.* **sun worship** *n.* **sun worshipper,** (*N Am.*) **sun worshiper** *n.* [OE *sunne* (cp. Dut. *zon*, G *Sonne*, Icel. *sunna*), cogn. with Goth. *sauil*, Icel. *sōl*, L *sōl*]

sundae (sŭn´dā, -di) *n.* an ice cream served with fragments of nuts and various fruits. [perh. from SUNDAY]

Sunday (sŭn´dā, -di) *n.* 1 the 1st day of the week, the Christian Sabbath. 2 a newspaper published on a Sunday. ~*adv.* (*coll.*) on Sunday. **month of Sundays** MONTH. **Sunday best** *n.* (*coll.*) one's best clothes. **Sunday driver** *n.* a person who drives mainly at weekends, esp. one who is slow or lacks confidence. **Sunday letter** *n.* a dominical letter. **Sunday painter** *n.* an amateur painter with little or no training. **Sundays** *adv.* (*coll.*) every Sunday. **Sunday school** *n.* a school held on Sundays for the religious instruction of children. [OE *sunnan dæg*, the day of the sun]

†**sunder** (sŭn´də) *v.t.* to part, to separate. ~*v.i.* to be separated. **in sunder** apart, in two. **sunderance** *n.* [OE *sundrian*, from *sundor*, asunder (cp. Icel. *sundra*, Dan. *sōndre*, G *sondern*)]

sundry (sŭn´dri) *a.* several, various, miscellaneous. ~*n.* (*pl.* **sundries**) 1 (*pl.*) matters, items or miscellaneous articles, too trifling or numerous to specify. 2 (*Austral.*) in cricket, a run scored otherwise than off the bat, an extra. **all and sundry** ALL. [OE *syndrig*, as SUNDER]

sung SING.

sunk, sunken SINK.

sunn (sŭn), **sunn hemp** *n.* a hemplike fibre obtained from an S Asian plant. [Hind. *san*, from Sansk., *śāṇá*, hempen]

Sunna (sun´ə, sŭn´ə) *n.* the traditional part of the Muslim law, based on the sayings or acts of

Muhammad, accepted as of equal authority to the Koran by one branch of Islam, the Sunni, but rejected by the Shiites. **Sunni** (-i) *n.* (*pl.* **Sunni, Sunnis**) **1** the branch of Islam which rejects Ali as Muhammad's first successor, as distinct from *Shia.* **2** an adherent of the Sunni. ~*a.* of or relating to Sunni. **Sunnite** (-īt) *n.* an adherent of the Sunni. [Arab.]

sunn hemp SUNN.

sunny SUN.

sup (sŭp) *v.t.* (*pres.p.* **supping,** *past, p.p.* **supped**) **1** to take (soup etc.) in successive sips or spoonfuls. **2** (*esp. North., coll.*) to drink (alcohol). ~*v.i.* **1** to take in liquid or liquid food by sips or spoonfuls. **2** †to take supper. ~*n.* a mouthful (of a drink, soup etc.). [OE *sūpan* (cp. Dut. *zuipen,* LG *supen,* Icel. *sūpa,* OHG *sūfan*), partly from OF *souper,* see SUPPER]

sup. *abbr.* **1** superior. **2** superlative. **3** supine. **4** supplement, supplementary. **5** supra (above).

sup- (sŭp) *pref.* var. of SUB-, used before *p.*

Supadriv® (soo´pədrīv) *n.* a type of screwdriver which holds a screw on its tip until the hole is located.

super[1] (soo´pə) *a.* **1** (*coll.*) excellent, very good, enjoyable. **2** (of a measure) square, not lineal or solid. **Super Bowl®** *n.* in American football, the annual deciding game between the champions of the National Football League and the American Football Conference. **super-duper** (-doo´pə) *a.* (*coll.*) excellent, very good, enjoyable. [SUPER-]

super[2] (soo´pə) *n.* (*coll.*) **1** a supernumerary actor. **2** a superintendent. **3** superphosphate. **4** an extra or superfluous person, a supernumerary. **5** superfine cloth or manufacture. [abbr.]

super- (soo´pə) *comb. form* **1** above, beyond or over. **2** to a great degree or extent. **3** particularly good or large of its kind. **4** of a higher kind. [L, from *super,* above, beyond]

superable (soo´pərəbəl) *a.* able to be overcome, conquerable. **superableness** *n.* **superably** *adv.* [L *superābilis,* from *superāre,* as SUPER-]

superabound (soopərəbownd´) *v.i.* to be more than enough. **superabundance** (-bŭn´-) *n.* **superabundant** *a.* **superabundantly** *adv.*

superaccommodating (soopərəkom´ədāting) *a.* extremely accommodating.

superaccomplished (soopərəkŭm´plisht) *a.* extremely accomplished.

superactive (soopərak´tiv) *a.* extremely active.

superadd (soopərad´) *v.t.* to add over and above (something else). **superaddition** (-ish´ən) *n.*

superaltar (soo´pərawltə) *n.* a consecrated slab for placing on an unconsecrated altar.

superambitious (soopərambish´əs) *a.* extremely ambitious.

superannuate (soopəran´ūāt) *v.t.* **1** to pension off on account of age. **2** to dismiss, discard, disqualify or incapacitate on account of age. **3** to make pensionable. **superannuable** *a.* **superannuated** *a.* too old, no longer for use. **superannuation** (-ā´shən) *n.* **1** a regular payment made by an employee to a pension scheme. **2** the pension paid after retirement. **3** the act of superannuating. **4** the state of being superannuated. [SUPER-, L *annus,* a year, cp. ANNUAL]

superaqueous (soopərā´kwiəs) *a.* above water.

superb (soopœb´) *a.* **1** grand, majestic, imposing, magnificent, splendid, stately. **2** (*coll.*) excellent, first-rate. **superbly** *adv.* **superbness** *n.* [F *superbe,* L *superbus* (*super,* see SUPER-, *fu-,* stem of *fuī,* I was)]

superbold (soopəbōld´) *a.* extremely bold.

supercalendered (soopəkal´indəd) *a.* (of paper) highly finished.

supercargo (soopəkah´gō) *n.* (*pl.* **supercargoes, supercargos**) an officer in a merchant ship who superintends sales etc. and has charge of the cargo.

supercede SUPERSEDE.

supercelestial (soopəsiles´tiəl) *a.* **1** above the heavens. **2** more than heavenly.

supercession SUPERSESSION (under SUPERSEDE).

supercharge (soo´pəchahj) *v.t.* **1** to charge or fill greatly or to excess with emotion, vigour etc. **2** to fit a supercharger to. **3** (*Her.*) to superimpose on another charge. ~*n.* (*Her.*) one charge borne upon another. **supercharger** *n.* a mechanism in an internal-combustion engine which provides for the complete filling of the cylinder with explosive material when going at high speed.

superciliary (soopəsil´iəri) *a.* (*Anat.*) of, relating to or situated above the eyebrows. [as SUPERCILIOUS]

supercilious (soopəsil´iəs) *a.* contemptuous, overbearing, haughtily indifferent, arrogant, disdainful. **superciliously** *adv.* **superciliousness** *n.* [L *superciliōsus,* from *supercilium,* see CILIUM (with alln. to raising the eyebrows)]

superclass (soo´pəklahs) *n.* a taxonomic category between a phylum or division and a class.

supercolossal (soopəkəlos´əl) *a.* extremely huge.

supercolumnar (soopəkəlŭm´nə) *a.* (*Archit.*) having one order of columns placed over another. **supercolumniation** (-niā´shən) *n.*

supercomplex (soopəkom´pleks) *a.* extremely complex.

supercomputer (soo´pəkəmpūtə) *n.* a very powerful computer capable of over 100 million arithmetic operations per second. **supercomputing** *n.*

superconductivity (soopəkondŭktiv´iti) *n.* (*Physics*) the total loss of electrical resistance exhibited by some metals and alloys at very low temperatures. **superconducting** (-kəndŭk´-), **superconductive** *a.* **superconductor** (-kəndŭk´-) *n.*

superconfident (soopəkon´fidənt) *a.* extremely confident.

superconformity (soopəkənfaw´miti) *n.* extreme conformity.

supercongested (soopəkənjes´tid) *a.* extremely congested.

superconscious (soopəkon´shəs) *a.* beyond human consciousness. **superconsciously** *adv.* **superconsciousness** *n.*

superconservative (soopəkənsœ´vətiv) *a.* extremely conservative.

supercontinent (soo´pəkontinənt) *n.* (*Geol.*) any of several large land masses believed to have split to form the present continents.

supercool (soo´pəkool) *v.t.* (*Chem.*) to cool (a liquid) below its freezing point without solidification. ~*v.i.* to be cooled in this way. ~*a.* (*sl.*) extremely cool, wonderful.

supercriminal (soopəkrim´inəl) *n.* an arch-criminal.

supercritical (soopəkrit´ikəl) *a.* (*Physics*) of more than critical mass.

supercurious (soopəkū´riəs) *a.* extremely curious.

supercynical (soopəsin´ikəl) *a.* extremely cynical.

superdeficit (soopədef´isit) *n.* a very large deficit.

superdevotion (soopədivō´shən) *n.* extreme devotion.

superdifficult (soopədif´ikəlt) *a.* extremely difficult.

superdiplomacy (soopədiplō´məsi) *n.* extreme diplomacy.

superdominant (soopədom´inənt) *n.* (*N Am.*) the submediant.

superdose (soopədōs´) *n.* a larger-than-usual dose.

super-duper SUPER[1].

supereffective (soopərifek´tiv) *a.* extremely effective.

superefficient (soopərifish´ənt) *a.* extremely efficient.

superego (soopərē´gō) *n.* (*pl.* **superegos**) (*Psych.*) the unconscious inhibitory morality in the mind which criticizes the ego and condemns the unworthy impulses of the id.

superelevation (soopərelivā´shən) *n.* the difference in height between the opposite sides of a curved section of road, railway track etc.

supereminent (soopərem´inənt) *a.* extremely remarkable. **supereminence** *n.* **supereminently** *adv.*

supererogation (soopərerəgā´shən) *n.* performance of more than duty requires. **supererogate** (-er´ə-) *v.i.* **supererogatory** (-irog´ətəri) *a.* [late L *superērogātio*, from *superērogāre*, to pay out beyond what is expected]

superexcited (soopəriksī´tid) *a.* extremely excited.

superexpressive (soopərikspres´iv) *a.* extremely expressive.

superfamily (soo´pəfamili) *n.* (*pl.* **superfamilies**) **1** a taxonomic category between a suborder and a family. **2** an analogous category of languages.

superfatted (soopəfat´id) *a.* (of soap) containing excess of fatty matter relatively to alkali.

superfecundation (soopəfekəndā´shən) *n.* the conception of two embryos from ova produced at one time, by separate acts of sexual intercourse.

superfetation (soopəfētā´shən), **superfoetation** *n.* **1** (*Med., Zool.*) the conception of a second embryo or litter during the gestation of the first. **2** (*Bot.*) the fertilization of an ovule by different kinds of pollen. **3** the accretion of one thing on another. [F, *superfétation*, or via mod. L, *superfetatio*, from L, *superfetare*, (as SUPER-, *fetus*, a FOETUS)]

superficial (soopəfish´əl) *a.* **1** of or relating to or lying on the surface. **2** not penetrating deep, cursory. **3** apparent, but not in reality. **4** not deep or profound in character, shallow. **5** (of a measure) square, not lineal or solid. **superficiality** (-shial´-) *n.* (*pl.* **superficialities**). **superficially** *adv.* **superficialness** *n.* [as SUPERFICIES]

superficies (soopəfish´iēz) *n.* (*pl.* **superficies**) **1** (*Geom.*) a surface. **2** the area of a surface. **3** external appearance or form. [L]

superfine (soo´pəfīn) *a.* **1** exceedingly fine, of extra quality. **2** extremely fine in size. **3** over-refined. **superfineness** *n.*

superfinite (soopəfī´nīt) *a.* absolutely finite.

superfluidity (soopəflooid´iti) *n.* the property of flowing without friction or viscosity. **superfluid** *n., a.*

superfluous (supœ´fluəs) *a.* more than is necessary or sufficient, excessive, redundant. **superfluity** (soopəfloo´-) *n.* (*pl.* **superfluities**) **1** the state of being superfluous. **2** something unnecessary. **3** an excess, a superabundance. **superfluously** *adv.* **superfluousness** *n.* [L *superfluus* (*fluere*, to flow)]

superfoetation SUPERFETATION.

superfrontal (soopəfrŭn´təl) *n.* the part of an altar cloth covering the top.

supergenerous (soopəjen´ərəs) *a.* extremely generous.

supergiant (soo´pəjīənt) *n.* a very large, very bright star of low density.

superglue (soo´pəgloo) *n.* an adhesive that gives an extremely strong bond on contact. ~*v.t.* (*3rd pers. sing. pres.* **superglues**, *pres.p.* **supergluing, superglueing**, *past, p.p.* **superglued**) to stick with superglue.

supergrass (soo´pəgrahs) *n.* (*coll.*) a police informer whose information implicates many people or concerns major criminals or criminal activities.

superheat (soopəhēt´) *v.t.* (*Physics*) **1** to heat (a liquid) above boiling point without vaporization. **2** to heat to excess, to heat (steam) above the boiling point of water so no condensation occurs. **superheater** (soo´-) *n.*

superhero (soo´pəhiərō) *n.* (*pl.* **superheroes**) a comic-strip character with superhuman powers who fights against evil.

superhet (soo´pəhet) *n.* (*coll.*) superheterodyne.

superheterodyne (soopəhet´ərədīn) *n.* a radio receiver with a high degree of selectivity. ~*a.* of or relating to superheterodynes.

superhighway (soo´pəhīwā) *n.* **1** (*N Am.*) a motorway. **2** INFORMATION SUPERHIGHWAY (under INFORM[1]).

superhive (soo´pəhīv) *n.* a removable upper storey of a beehive.

superhuman (soopəhū´mən) *a.* **1** beyond normal human ability. **2** higher than human. **superhumanly** *adv.*

superhumeral (soopəhū´mərəl) *n.* something worn upon the shoulders, such as an archbishop's pallium, or a Jewish sacerdotal ephod.

superignorant (soopərig´nərənt) *a.* extremely ignorant.

superimportant (soopərimpaw´tənt) *a.* extremely important.

superimpose (soopərimpōz´) *v.t.* to lay on top of something else. **superimposition** (-pəzish´-) *n.*

superincumbent (soopərinkŭm´bənt) *a.* lying or resting on something.

superindifference (soopərindif´rəns) *n.* extreme indifference.

superinduce (soopərindūs´) *v.t.* to bring in as an addition. **superinduction** (-dŭk´-) *n.*

superinsist (soopərinsist´) *v.i., v.t.* to insist strongly.

superintellectual (soopərintilek´chūəl) *a.* extremely intellectual.

superintelligent (soopərintel´ijənt) *a.* extremely intelligent.

superintend (soopərintend´) *v.t.* to have or exercise the management or oversight of, to direct, to control. ~*v.i.* to supervise, to inspect. **superintendence** *n.* **superintendency** *n.* (*pl.* **superintendencies**). **superintendent** *n.* **1** a person who superintends. **2** a director of an institution. **3** a police officer ranking above an inspector. **4** (*N Am.*) any high-ranking official, esp. the chief of a police department. **5** (*N Am.*) the caretaker of a building. ~*a.* superintending. [L *superintendere* (*intendere*, see INTEND)]

superior (supiə´riə) *a.* **1** upper, of higher position, class, grade, rank, excellence, degree etc. **2** better or greater relatively (to). **3** of a quality above the average. **4** situated near the top, in the higher part or above. **5** (*Bot.*) (of the calyx or the ovary) growing above another. **6** above being influenced by or amenable (to). **7** supercilious. **8** of wider application. **9** (*Print.*) set above the line. ~*n.* **1** a person superior to another or others, one's better. **2** the head of a monastery or other religious house. **superioress** *n.* the head of a convent or other religious house. **superiority** (-or´i-) *n.* **superiority complex** *n.* (*Psych.*) an inflated opinion of one's worth. **superiorly** *adv.* **superior numbers** *n.pl.* (*esp. Mil.*) more men or greater force. **superior planet** *n.* any planet further from the sun than the earth is. [OF *superieur*, L *superior -ōrem*, compar. of *superus*, high (from *super*, above, see SUPER-)]

Usage note *Superior* does not function as a true comparative in English, and should not be followed by *than* (the correct form is *superior to*).

superjacent (soopəjā´sənt) *a.* lying on or above something. [SUPER-, *jacent*, recumbent]

superl. *abbr.* superlative.

superlative (supœ´lətiv) *a.* **1** of the highest degree, consummate, supreme. **2** (*Gram.*) expressing the highest or utmost degree. ~*n.* **1** (*Gram.*) **a** the superlative degree. **b** a word or phrase in the superlative degree. **2** something which is supreme or excellent. **3** an exaggeration. **superlatively** *adv.* **superlativeness** *n.* [L *superlatīvus*, from *superlātus*, exaggerated (*lātus*, p.p. of *ferre*, to carry)]

superlogical (soopəloj´ikəl) *a.* extremely logical.

superlucky (soopəlŭk´i) *a.* extremely lucky.

superluminal (soopəloo´minəl) *a.* (*Physics*) of or relating to a speed greater than the speed of light. [L *lumen luminis*, a light]

superlunar (soopəloo´nə), **superlunary** (-nəri) *a.* above the moon, celestial, not mundane.

superluxurious (soopəlŭgzhuə´riəs) *a.* extremely luxurious.
superman (soo´pəman) *n.* (*pl.* **supermen**) **1** (*Philos.*) a hypothetical superior being, esp. one who is advanced in intellect and morals. **2** (*coll.*) a man of outstanding ability or strength.
supermarket (soo´pəmahkit) *n.* a large, self-service shop where food and domestic goods are sold.
supermodel (soo´pəmodəl) *n.* a well-known, highly-paid fashion model.
supermundane (soopəmŭn´dān) *a.* above or superior to worldly things.
supernal (supœ´nəl) *a.* (*poet.*) **1** divine, lofty. **2** of a loftier kind, nature or region. **3** celestial, heavenly. **supernally** *adv.* [MF *supernel* (L *supernus*)]
supernatant (soopənā´tənt) *a.* (*esp. Chem.*) floating on the surface of a solid residue after precipitation etc. ~*n.* a supernatant surface. **supernatation** (-ā´shən) *n.*
supernatural (soopənach´ərəl) *a.* existing by, due to, or exercising powers above the usual forces of nature, outside the sphere of natural law. **the supernatural** supernatural forces. **supernaturalism** *n.* **supernaturalist** *n.* **supernaturalistic** (-lis´-) *a.* **supernaturalize, supernaturalise** *v.t.* **supernaturally** *adv.* **supernaturalness** *n.*
supernegligent (soopəneg´lijənt) *a.* extremely negligent.
supernormal (soopənaw´məl) *a.* beyond what is normal. **supernormality** (-mal´-) *n.* **supernormally** *adv.*
supernova (soopənō´və) *n.* (*pl.* **supernovae** (-vē), **supernovas**) (*Astron.*) a nova up to 100 million times brighter than the sun, produced by the eruption of a star following its implosion.
supernumerary (soopənū´mərəri) *a.* **1** being in excess of a prescribed or customary number. **2** employed for extra work. **3** (of an actor) having a non-speaking role. ~*n.* (*pl.* **supernumeraries**) a supernumerary person or thing, esp. a person appearing on the stage without a speaking role.
superobligation (soopərobligā´shən) *n.* a pressing obligation.
superoctave (soo´pəroktiv) *n.* **1** a coupler in an organ causing a note to sound an octave higher than the key struck. **2** an organ stop one 15th above the principal.
superofficious (soopərəfish´əs) *a.* extremely officious.
superoptimist (soopərop´timist) *n.* a supreme optimist.
superorder (soo´pərawdə) *n.* (*Biol.*) a taxonomic category between an order and a subclass or a class. **superordinal** *a.*
superordinate (soopəraw´dinət) *a.* **1** superior in rank or status. **2** having the relation of superordination. ~*n.* **1** a superordinate person or thing. **2** a word whose meaning includes the meaning of another word. **superordination** (-ā´shən) *n.* (*Logic*) the relation of a universal proposition to a particular proposition that it includes.
superorganic (soopərawgan´ik) *a.* **1** superior or external to the organism, psychical. **2** of or relating to a higher grade of organism, social.
superovulation (soopərovūlā´shən) *n.* the production of large numbers of ova at a single time. **superovulate** (-ov´-) *v.i.*
superphosphate (soopəfos´fāt) *n.* **1** a mixture of phosphates used as a fertilizer. **2** a phosphate containing the greatest amount of phosphoric acid that can combine with the base.
superphysical (soopəfiz´ikəl) *a.* **1** unable to be explained by physical causes. **2** beyond the physical.
superpose (soopəpōz´) *v.t.* (*esp. Geom.*) to lay over or on something. **superposable** *a.* **superposition** (-ish´ən) *n.*
superpower (soo´pəpowə) *n.* a very powerful nation, esp. the US or the former USSR.
superrefine (soopərifīn´) *v.t.* to refine to a high degree.
super-royal (soopəroi´əl) *a.* larger than royal (denoting a size of printing paper).
supersaturated (soopəsach´urātid) *a.* containing more material than a saturated solution or vapour. **supersaturate** *v.t.* **supersaturation** (-ā´shən) *n.*
superscribe (soo´pəskrīb, -skrīb´) *v.t.* **1** to write on the top or outside of something or above. **2** to write a name, inscription, address etc. on the outside or top of. **superscript** (soo´-) *a.* **1** written at the top or outside. **2** set above the line, superior. ~*n.* a superior character. **superscription** (-skrip´shən) *n.* [L *scrībere*, to write]
supersede (soopəsēd´), **supercede** *v.t.* **1** to put a person or thing in the place of. **2** to set aside, to annul. **3** to take the place of, to displace, to supplant. **supersedeas** (-diəs) *n.* a legal writ to stay proceedings etc. **supersedence** *n.* **supersedure** (-jə) *n.* **supersession** (-sesh´ən), **supercession** *n.* [OF *superseder*, to leave off, to desist, L *supersedēre* (*sedēre*, to sit, p.p. *sessus*)]
supersensitive (soopəsen´sitiv) *a.* extremely sensitive.
supersession SUPERSEDE.
☒ **supersilious** common misspelling of SUPERCILIOUS.
supersimplicity (soopəsimplis´iti) *n.* extreme simplicity.
supersonic (soopəson´ik) *a.* **1** of or relating to sound waves with such a high frequency that they are inaudible. **2** above the speed of sound. **3** travelling at or using such speeds. **supersonically** *adv.* **supersonics** *n.* ultrasonics.
supersophisticate (soopəsəfis´tikət) *n.* an extremely sophisticated person. **supersophisticated** (-kātid) *a.*
superspecialize (soopəspesh´əlīz), **superspecialise** *v.i.*, *v.t.* to specialize to a high degree.
superstar (soo´pəstah) *n.* a very popular film, music, sports etc. star. **superstardom** *n.*
superstate (soo´pəstāt) *n.* a powerful political state formed from a union of several nations.
superstition (soopəstish´ən) *n.* **1** credulity regarding the supernatural, the occult or the mysterious. **2** an ignorant or unreasoning dread of the unknown. **3** a religion, particular belief or practice originating in this, esp. a belief in omens, charms etc. **superstitious** *a.* **superstitiously** *adv.* **superstitiousness** *n.* [F, from L *superstitio -ōnem*, standing over, amazement (*stat-*, p.p. stem of *stāre*, to stand)]
superstore (soo´pəstaw) *n.* a very large supermarket; a very large store selling goods other than food.
superstratum (soopəstrah´təm, -strā´-) *n.* (*pl.* **superstrata** (-tə)) a stratum resting on another.
superstring (soo´pəstring) *n.* (*Physics*) a particle in superstring theory. **superstring theory** *n.* a theory of cosmic strings that incorporates supersymmetry.
superstructure (soo´pəstrŭkchə) *n.* **1** the part of a building above the ground. **2** an upper part of a structure. **3** a concept or idea based on another. **superstructural** *a.*
supersymmetry (soopəsim´itri) *n.* (*Physics*) a postulated type of symmetry relating fermions and bosons.
supertanker (soo´pətangkə) *n.* a very large tanker ship.
supertax (soo´pətaks) *n.* a tax in addition to the basic income tax, levied on incomes above a certain level.
superterrestrial (soopətəres´triəl) *a.* **1** of or relating to a region above the earth. **2** celestial.
supertonic (soopəton´ik) *n.* (*Mus.*) the note next above the tonic in the diatonic scale.
supervene (soopəvēn´) *v.i.* to come or happen as something extraneous or additional. **supervenient** *a.* **supervention** (-ven´-) *n.* [L *sūpervenīre* (*venīre*, to come)]
supervise (soo´pəvīz) *v.t.* to have oversight of, to oversee, to superintend. **supervision** (-vizh´ən) *n.* **supervisor** *n.* **supervisory** *a.* [L *supervīsum*, supine of *supervidēre* (*vidēre*, to see)]

superwaif (soo´pəwāf) *n.* a young, very thin, childlike fashion model.

superwoman (soo´pəwumən) *n.* (*pl.* **superwomen** (-wimin)) (*coll.*) an exceptionally strong or capable woman.

supinate (soo´pināt) *v.t.* to turn the palm of (the hand) upwards or forwards, as distinct from *pronate.* **supination** (-ā´shən) *n.* **supinator** *n.* (*Anat.*) either of two muscles which supinate the hand. [L *supīnātus*, p.p. of *supīnāre*, as SUPINE]

supine (soo´pīn) *a.* **1** lying on the back with the face upwards, as distinct from *prone.* **2** having the front or the palm upwards. **3** negligent, indolent, listless, careless. ~*n.* (*Gram.*) a Latin verbal noun formed from the past participial stem and ending in *-um* or *-u.* **supinely** *adv.* **supineness** *n.* [L *supīnus*, from *sup-*, *sub*, under, see SUB-]

☒ **supose** common misspelling of SUPPOSE.

supp. *abbr.* supplement.

suppedaneum (sŭpədā´niəm) *n.* (*pl.* **suppedanea** (-niə)) a footrest on a cross or crucifix. **suppedaneous** *a.* placed or being under the feet. [late L *sup-* (SUB-), L *pes pedis*, the foot)]

supper (sŭp´ə) *n.* **1** the last meal of the day, esp. a light one. **2** an evening social affair including supper. **to sing for one's supper** to perform a task in order to receive a benefit. **supperless** *a.* [OF *soper, super* (F *souper*), from *soper*, LG *supen*, cogn. with SUP]

suppl. *abbr.* supplement.

supplant (səplahnt´) *v.t.* to take the place of or oust, esp. by craft or treachery. **supplantation** (sŭplahntā´shən) *n.* **supplanter** *n.* [OF *supplanter*, L *supplantāre* (*plantāre*, from *planta*, the sole of the foot)]

supple (sŭp´əl) *a.* **1** pliant, flexible, easily bent. **2** lithe, able to move and bend easily. **3** yielding, compliant, soft, submissive, obsequious, servile. ~*v.t.* **1** to make pliant or flexible. **2** to make compliant. ~*v.i.* to become pliant. **supplejack** *n.* a tough climbing shrub, from which walking sticks are made. **supplely** (sŭp´əlli) *adv.* **suppleness** *n.* **supply**[1] (sŭp´li) *adv.* [ME and F *souple*, L *supplex -icem* (*plic-*, base of *plicāre*, to fold)]

supplement[1] (sŭp´limənt) *n.* **1** an addition, esp. one that supplies a deficiency. **2** an addition or update to a book, newspaper or periodical. **3** an additional charge for additional facilities or services. **4** (*Geom.*) the angle that added to another will make the sum two right angles. **supplemental** (-men´-) *a.* **supplementally** *adv.* **supplementary** *a.* serving as a supplement, additional. ~*n.* (*pl.* **supplementaries**) a supplementary thing, esp. a question. **supplementarily** *adv.* **supplementary benefit** *n.* (*Hist.*) money paid regularly by the state to people whose income fell below a certain minimum level. **suppletion** (səplē´shən) *n.* the act of supplementing. **suppletive** *a.* [F *supplément*, L *supplēmentum*, from *supplēre* (*plēre*, to fill)]

supplement[2] (sŭp´limənt, sŭpliment´) *v.t.* to make additions to; to complete by additions. **supplementation** (-tā´shən) *n.* [as SUPPLEMENT[1]]

suppletion, suppletive SUPPLEMENT[1].

suppliant (sŭp´liənt) *a.* **1** entreating, supplicating. **2** expressing entreaty or supplication. ~*n.* a person making a humble request. **suppliance** *n.* **suppliantly** *adv.* [F, pres.p. of *supplier*, as SUPPLICATE]

supplicate (sŭp´likāt) *v.t.* (*formal*) **1** to beg or ask for earnestly and humbly. **2** to beg humbly (to grant etc.). **3** to address in earnest prayer. ~*v.i.* to petition earnestly, to beseech. **supplicant** *a., n.* **supplicatingly** *adv.* **supplication** (-ā´shən) *n.* **supplicatory** (-kətəri) *a.* [L *supplicātus*, p.p. of *supplicāre*, as SUPPLE]

supplier SUPPLY[2].

supply[1] SUPPLE.

supply[2] (səplī´) *v.t.* (*3rd pers. sing. pres.* **supplies,** *pres.p.* **supplying,** *past, p.p.* **supplied**) **1** to furnish with what is wanted, to provide (with). **2** to furnish, to provide. **3** to serve instead of. **4** to fill (the place of), to make up for (a deficiency etc.). **5** to satisfy. ~*n.* (*pl.* **supplies**) **1** the act of supplying things needed. **2** what is supplied; a sufficiency of things available for use. **3** (*often pl.*) necessary stores or provisions. **4** the quantity of goods or services offered for sale at a particular time. **5** (*pl.*) a grant of money by Parliament to meet the expenses of government, an allowance. **6** a person who fills a position temporarily, a substitute. ~*a.* **1** filling a position temporarily (*a supply teacher*). **2** providing supplies. **on supply** (of a teacher etc.) acting as a supply. **to supply a gap** GAP. **supplier** *n.* **supply and demand** *n.* the amount of a product that is available and the amount that is required, as factors in regulating price. **supply-side** *a.* denoting an economic policy of low taxation and other incentives to stimulate production. [OF *suploier* (F *suppléer*), L *supplēre* (*plēre*, to fill)]

support (səpawt´) *v.t.* **1** to bear the weight of, to hold up, to sustain. **2** to keep from yielding or giving way. **3** to give strength or endurance to. **4** to furnish with necessaries, to provide for. **5** to give assistance to. **6** to advocate, to defend, to back up, to second. **7** to promote, to encourage. **8** to bear out, to substantiate, to corroborate. **9** to take a keen interest in (a sports team etc.); to want (a team etc.) to win. **10** to bear; to endure, to put up with. **11** to maintain. **12** to act as, to represent (a character etc.). **13** to subscribe to (a charity or other institution). **14** to play a secondary role to (the main character) in a film or play. **15** to accompany (a band, feature film etc.) in a subordinate role. ~*n.* **1** the act of supporting or the state of being supported. **2** a person who or something which supports. **3** a band etc. supporting another in a concert. **4** subsistence, livelihood. **5** aid, assistance. **in support of** in order to support. **supportable** *a.* **supportability** (-bil´-) *n.* **supportableness** *n.* **supportably** *adv.* **supporter** *n.* **1** a person who or something which supports or maintains. **2** (*Her.*) a figure on each side of a shield etc., appearing to support it. **3** a jockstrap. **supporting** *a.* **1** playing or having a secondary or subordinate role. **2** giving support. **supporting film** *n.* a less important film in a programme. **supportingly** *adv.* **supportive** *a.* providing support, esp. moral or emotional encouragement. **supportively** *adv.* **supportiveness** *n.* **supportless** *a.* **support price** *n.* a minimum price which is guaranteed to farmers for agricultural produce. [F *supporter*, L *supportāre*, (*portāre*, to carry)]

suppose (səpōz´) *v.t.* **1** to take to be the case, to accept as probable, to surmise. **2** to lay down without proof, to assume by way of argument or illustration. **3** to imagine, to believe. **4** to involve or require as a condition, to imply. **5** (*usu. pass.*) to require or expect, to oblige (to). **6** to believe (to). **I suppose so** used to express agreement with a degree of uncertainty. **supposable** *a.* **supposed** *a.* believed to be so. **supposedly** (-zid-) *adv.* allegedly. **supposer** *n.* **supposition** (sŭpəzish´ən) *n.* **suppositional** *a.* **suppositionally** *adv.* [F *supposer* (*poser*, to POSE[1])]

suppositious (sŭpəzish´əs), **supposititious** (səpoziti sh´əs) *a.* substituted for something else, not genuine, spurious. **suppositiously** *adv.* **suppositiousness** *n.* **supposititiously** *adv.* **supposititiousness** *n.* [L *suppositīcius*, from *supposit-*, p.p. stem of *suppōnere*, to substitute (*pōnere*, to put)]

suppositive (səpoz´itiv) *a.* including or implying supposition. ~*n.* (*Gram.*) a conjunction implying supposition. **suppositively** *adv.* [as SUPPOSITIOUS]

suppository (səpoz´itəri) *n.* (*pl.* **suppositories**) a solid block of medicine introduced into the vagina or rectum, and left to dissolve. [late L *suppositorium*, as SUPPOSITIVE]

suppress (səpres´) *v.t.* **1** to put down, to overpower, to subdue, to quell. **2** to keep in or back, to withhold, to stifle, to repress. **3** to keep back from disclosure or circulation, to conceal. **4** to eliminate (electrical interference). **suppressant** *n.* something which suppresses, esp. a drug which suppresses the appetite. **suppressible** *a.* **suppression** (-presh´ən) *n.* **suppressive** *a.* **suppressor** *n.* [L *suppressus*, p.p. of *supprimere* (*premere*, to press)]

suppurate (sŭp´ūrāt) *v.i.* to generate pus, to fester. **suppuration** (-ā´shən) *n.* **suppurative** (-rətiv) *a.* [L *suppūrātus*, p.p. of *suppūrāre* (*pūrāre*, from *pur-*, base of PUS)]

supra (soo´prə) *adv.* above; earlier on. [L, above]

supra- (soo´prə) *pref.* **1** above. **2** beyond. [L *supra-*, from *supra*, above, beyond, before]

supraciliary (sooprəsil´iəri) *a.* (*Anat.*) SUPERCILIARY.

supralapsarian (sooprəlapseə´riən) *n.* a Calvinist holding that God decreed the salvation of the elect before the Fall (as opposed to INFRALAPSARIAN). ~*a.* of or relating to supralapsarians or supralapsarianism. **supralapsarianism** *n.*

supramaxillary (sooprəmaksil´əri) *a.* of or relating to the upper jaw.

supramundane (sooprəmŭn´dān) *a.* above the world.

supranational (sooprənash´ənəl) *a.* overriding national sovereignty. **supranationalism** *n.* **supranationality** (-nal´-) *n.*

supraorbital (sooprəaw´bitəl) *a.* being above the eye socket.

suprarenal (sooprərē´nəl) *a.* situated above the kidneys. **suprarenal gland** *n.* an adrenal gland.

supreme (suprēm´) *a.* **1** highest in authority or power. **2** highest in degree or importance, utmost, extreme, greatest possible. **3** last, final. ~*n.* a rich, creamy sauce or a dish served in this. **supremacy** (-prem´-) *n.* **1** the quality or state of being supreme. **2** the highest authority or power. **supremacist** (-prem´əsist) *n.* a person who believes or promotes the supremacy of a particular group, esp. a racial group. ~*a.* of or relating to supremacism. **supremacism** *n.* **Supreme Being** *n.* the deity, God. **Supreme Court** *n.* the highest judicial court in a state. **Supreme Court of Judicature** *n.* the court in England established by Acts in 1873 and 1875, combining the functions of the former Courts of Chancery, King's Bench, Common Pleas, Exchequer, Admiralty etc. **supremely** *adv.* **supremeness** *n.* **supreme pontiff** *n.* the Pope. **Supreme Soviet** *n.* the governing council of the former USSR or of one of the republics of the USSR. [F, from L *suprēmus*, superl. of *superus*, see SUPRA-]

suprême (sooprem´) *n.* a rich, creamy sauce or a dish served in this. [F]

supremo (suprē´mō) *n.* (*pl.* **supremos**) a supreme leader or head. [Sp., from L *suprēmus*, SUPREME]

Supt. *abbr.* Superintendent.

sur-[1] (sœ) *pref.* super-. [OF]

sur-[2] (sœ) *pref.* var. of SUB-, used before *r.*

sura (suə´rə), **surah** *n.* a chapter of the Koran. [Arab. *sūra*]

surah[1] (sūə´rə) *n.* a soft, twilled, usu. self-coloured silk material. [F pronunciation of *Surat*, India, where orig. made]

surah[2] SURA.

sural (sūə´rəl) *a.* of or relating to the calf of the leg. [L *sūra*, the calf]

surat (sūrat´) *n.* (*Hist.*) **1** coarse, short cotton grown near Surat, India. **2** cloth made from this.

surbase (sœ´bās) *n.* the cornice or moulding at the top of a pedestal or base. **surbased** *a.* [SUR-[1], BASE[1]]

†**surcease** (sœsēs´) *n.* cessation. ~*v.i.*, *v.t.* to cease. [A-F *sursise*, fem. of *sursis*, p.p. of *surseer*, F *surseoir*, L *supersedēre*, to SUPERSEDE]

surcharge[1] (sœ´chahj) *n.* **1** an extra charge or cost. **2** an additional charge imposed as a penalty for false returns of income or other taxable property. **3** another valuation or other matter printed on a postage or revenue stamp. **4** a stamp so treated. **5** an excessive load, burden or charge. **6** an overcharge. **7** an amount surcharged on official accounts. [A-F (SUR-[1], CHARGE)]

surcharge[2] (sœ´chahj, sœchahj´) *v.t.* **1** to put an extra charge on. **2** to overprint (a stamp) with a surcharge. **3** to overload, to overburden, to overfill. **4** to overcharge. **5** to show an omission in (an account) for which credit should be allowed. **6** to impose payment of (a sum) or on (a person) for amounts in official accounts disallowed by an auditor. **surchargement** *n.* **surcharger** *n.*

surcingle (sœ´sing·gəl) *n.* **1** a belt or girth put round the body of a horse etc., for holding a saddle or blanket on its back. **2** the girdle of a cassock. ~*v.t.* **1** to put a surcingle on. **2** to fasten with a surcingle. [ME and OF *surcengle* (*cengle*, a girth, L *cingula*, a belt, from *cingere*, to gird)]

surcoat (sœ´kōt) *n.* **1** (*Hist.*) an outer coat, esp. a loose robe worn over armour. **2** a similar sleeveless garment as part of the insignia of an order of knighthood. **3** an outer jacket worn by women in the 14th–16th cents. [A-F *surcote*]

surculus (sœ´kūləs) *n.* (*pl.* **surculi** (-lī)) (*Bot.*) a shoot rising from a rootstock, a sucker. **surculose** (-lōs) *a.* producing surculi. [L, a twig]

surd (sœd) *a.* **1** (*Math.*) not capable of being expressed in rational numbers. **2** (of a sound) uttered with the breath and not with the voice. ~*n.* **1** (*Math.*) an irrational quantity. **2** a surd consonant, such as *p*, *f* or *s*. [L *surdus*, deaf]

sure (shuə, shaw) *a.* **1** certain, confident, undoubting. **2** free from doubts (of). **3** positive, believing, confidently trusting (that). **4** infallible, certain (to). **5** safe, reliable, trustworthy, unfailing. **6** unquestionably true. **7** certain (of finding, gaining etc.). ~*adv.*, *int.* (*coll.*) surely, certainly; yes. **for sure** (*coll.*) surely, certainly. **sure as death** quite certain(ly). **sure as eggs is eggs** EGG[1]. **sure as fate** without doubt, undoubtedly. **sure enough 1** (*coll.*) in reality, not merely in expectation. **2** (*coll.*) with near certainty. **to be sure 1** not to fail (to). **2** without doubt, certainly, of course. **3** it must be admitted. **to make sure 1** to make certain, to ascertain. **2** to make secure. **to make sure of** to establish the truth of. **sure-fire** *a.* (*coll.*) bound to succeed, assured. **sure-footed** *a.* not liable to stumble or fall. **sure-footedly** *adv.* **sure-footedness** *n.* **surely** *adv.* **1** undoubtedly. **2** certainly (frequently used by way of asseveration or to deprecate doubt). **3** securely, safely. **sureness** *n.* **sure thing** *n.* (*N Am.*, *coll.*) something certain of success. ~*int.* certainly, yes. [OF *sur*, *seur*, L *sēcūrus*, SECURE]

surety (shuə´rəti, shaw´ti) *n.* (*pl.* **sureties**) **1** a person undertaking responsibility for payment of a sum, discharge of an engagement or attendance in court by another, a guarantor. **2** a pledge deposited as security against loss or damage or for payment or discharge of an engagement etc. **3** a guarantee. **4** certainty. †**for a surety** of a surety. †**of a surety** certainly. **to stand surety** to act as a surety. **suretyship** *n.*

surf (sœf) *n.* **1** the swell of the sea breaking on the shore, rocks etc. **2** the foam produced by this. ~*v.i.* **1** to ride on the surf, to engage in surfing. **2** (*sl.*) to travel illicitly on the roof or outside of a train. ~*v.t.* to browse electronically through (esp. the Internet). **surfbird** *n.* a plover-like bird, *Aphriza virgata*, of the Pacific coasts of N America, related to the sandpiper. **surfboard** *n.* a long narrow board used in surfing. **surfboat** *n.* a strong, buoyant boat for use in rough surf. **surfboatman** *n.* (*pl.* **surfboatmen**). **surf-casting** *n.* fishing by casting into the sea from the shore. **surfduck** *n.* the scoter. **surfer** *n.* **surfie** *n.* (*esp. Austral.*) a person whose life centres round surfing. **surfing** *n.* **1** surf-riding. **2** browsing through the Internet. **3** (*sl.*) travelling illicitly on the roof or outside of a train. **surf-riding** *n.* the sport of surfing. **surfy** *a.* [formerly *suffe*, prob. var. of SOUGH[1]]

surface (sœ´fis) *n.* **1** the exterior part of anything, the outside, the superficies. **2** any one of the limits bounding a solid. **3** (*Geom.*) something which has length and breadth but no thickness. **4** something which is apparent at first view or on slight consideration. *~a.* **1** of or relating to the surface. **2** superficial. *~v.t.* **1** to put a surface on. **2** to bring to the surface. *~v.i.* **1** to rise to the surface. **2** to become known. **3** (*coll.*) to wake up or get out of bed. **to come to the surface** to appear after being hidden. **to scratch the surface** SCRATCH. **surface-active** *a.* capable of lessening the surface tension of a liquid. **surfaced** *a.* (*usu. in comb.*, as *smooth-surfaced*). **surface mail** *n.* mail sent by land or sea. **surfaceman** *n.* (*pl.* **surfacemen**) a man employed in keeping the permanent way of a railway in order. **surface noise** *n.* extraneous noise from a record player caused by imperfections in the record or in the pick-up system. **surfacer** *n.* **surface tension** *n.* the tension of a liquid causing it to act as an elastic enveloping membrane tending to contract to the minimum area, as seen in the bubble, the drop etc. **surface-to-air** *a.* of or relating to missiles launched from land to an airborne target. **surface-to-surface** *a.* of or relating to missiles launched from one point on land to another. **surface-water** *n.* water collecting on the surface of the ground. **surficial** (səfish´əl) *a.* (*Geol.*) of or relating to the earth's surface. **surficially** *adv.* [F]

surfactant (səfak´tənt) *n.* a surface-active substance, such as a detergent. [*surf*ace-*act*ive *a*ge*nt*]

surfeit (sœ´fit) *n.* **1** excess, esp. in eating or drinking. **2** oppression resulting from this, satiety, nausea. **3** an excessive supply or amount. *~v.t.* **1** to fill or feed to excess. **2** to overload, to cloy. *~v.i.* **1** to overeat. **2** to feel uncomfortable through excess. **surfeiter** *n.* [A-F *surfet*, OF *sorfait*, p.p. of *sorfaire* (SUR-[1], *faire*, L *facere*, to do)]

surficial SURFACE.

surg. *abbr.* **1** surgeon. **2** surgery. **3** surgical.

surge (sœj) *n.* **1** a sudden onset. **2** a large wave, a billow, a swell. **3** a heaving and rolling motion. **4** a sudden increase or rise. *~v.i.* **1** (of waves) to swell, to heave, to move up and down. **2** to well up, to move with a sudden rushing or swelling motion. **3** to increase or rise suddenly. **4** (*Naut.*) (of a rope or chain) to jerk back. **surge chamber, surge tank** *n.* a chamber which neutralizes sudden changes of pressure in a flow of liquid. [F *surgir*, L *surgere*, *surrigere* (*sur-*, SUB-, *regere*, to direct)]

surgeon (sœ´jən) *n.* **1** a medical practitioner treating injuries, deformities and diseases by manual procedure, often involving operations. **2** a practitioner holding the diploma of the Royal College of Surgeons. **3** a medical officer in the army or navy or in a military hospital. **4** a surgeonfish. **surgeoncy** *n.* (*pl.* **surgeoncies**). **surgeonfish** *n.* any sea fish of the genus *Acanthurus*, with lancelike spines at the tail. **surgeon general** *n.* (*pl.* **surgeons general**) **1** the head of the public health service in the US. **2** the chief medical officer in the US Army or Navy. **surgeonship** *n.* **surgeon's knot** *n.* a reef knot with a double twist. [contr. of *chirurgeon*, from OF *cirurgien*, from *cirurgie*, L *chīrurgia* (CHEIR-, *ergein*, to work)]

surgery (sœ´jəri) *n.* (*pl.* **surgeries**) **1** (the branch of medicine dealing with) the treatment of injuries, deformities or diseases by manual procedure, often operations. **2** the office or consulting room of a doctor, dentist etc., or its hours of opening. **3** a place where an MP is available for consultation, or the time when they are available. **surgical** *a.* **surgically** *adv.* **surgical spirit** *n.* methylated spirit with oil of wintergreen and castor oil used for sterilizing, cleaning the skin etc.

suricate (sū´rikāt) *n.* a small S African meerkat, *Suricata suricata*, allied to the weasel. [S Afr. name]

Surinamese (suərinamēz´) *a.* of or relating to Suriname, S America. *~n.* (*pl.* **Surinamese**) a native or inhabitant of Suriname. **Surinamer** (-nam´-) *n.* a Surinamese. **Suriname toad** (-nam´) *n.* a S American toadlike amphibian, *Pipa pipa*.

surly (sœ´li) *a.* (*comp.* **surlier**, *superl.* **surliest**) rude and bad-tempered. **surlily** *adv.* **surliness** *n.* [SIR, -LY[1]]

surmise (səmīz´) *n.* a supposition on slight evidence, a guess, a conjecture. *~v.t.* **1** to guess, to imagine, with little evidence; to conjecture, to suspect. **2** to suspect the existence of. *~v.i.* to conjecture, to guess, to suppose. **surmisable** *a.* **surmiser** *n.* [OF, fem. of *surmis*, p.p. of *surmettre* (*mettre*, to put, from L *mittere*, to send, p.p. *missus*)]

surmount (səmownt´) *v.t.* **1** to overcome, to vanquish, to rise above. **2** to overtop, to cap. **3** to get or climb to the top of and beyond. **surmountable** *a.* **surmountableness** *n.* **surmounter** *n.* [F *surmonter* (MOUNT[1])]

surmullet (sœmŭl´it) *n.* the red mullet. [OF *surmulet* (*sur*, *sor*, SORREL[2]), MULLET[1]]

surname (sœ´nām) *n.* a name added to the first or Christian name; a family name (orig. an appellation signifying occupation etc., or a nickname ultimately becoming hereditary). *~v.t.* **1** to call by a surname. **2** to give a surname to. **surnamed** *a.* having as a surname. **surnominal** (-nom´-) *a.* [F *surnom* (SUR-[1], *nom*, L *nomen*, assim. to NAME)]

surpass (səpahs´) *v.t.* **1** to excel, to go beyond in amount, degree etc. **2** to go beyond the range or capacity of, to transcend. **surpassable** *a.* **surpassing** *a.* excellent, exceptional. **surpassingly** *adv.* **surpassingness** *n.* [F *surpasser*]

surplice (sœ´plis) *n.* a loose, flowing vestment of white linen, with full sleeves, worn by clergy and choristers at divine service. **surpliced** *a.* [F *surplis*, med. L *superpelliceum* (*pelliceum*, L *pellicius*, PELISSE)]

surplus (sœ´pləs) *n.* **1** an amount which remains over, excess beyond what is used or required. **2** the balance in hand after all liabilities are paid. **3** the residuum of an estate after all debts and legacies are paid. *~a.* being more than is needed. **surplusage** (-ij) *n.* **surplus value** *n.* the difference between the value of work that has been done and the wages paid for it. [F]

surprise (səprīz´) *n.* **1** an unexpected event. **2** emotion excited by something sudden or unexpected, astonishment. **3** the act of taking someone unawares or unprepared. *~a.* unexpected. *~v.t.* **1** to strike with astonishment, to be contrary to or different from expectation. **2** (*usu. p.p.*) to shock, to scandalize. **3** to come or fall upon suddenly and unexpectedly, esp. to attack unawares. **4** to disconcert. **5** to lead or drive unawares (into an act etc.). **to take by surprise** to strike with astonishment, to take unawares. **surprisal** *n.* **surprisedly** (-zid-) *adv.* **surpriser** *n.* **surprising** *a.* **surprisingly** *adv.* **surprisingness** *n.* [OF, fem. of *surpris*, *sorpris*, p.p. of *sur-*, *sorprendre* (*prendre*, L *prehendere*, to take)]

surra (suə´rə) *n.* a serious disease of horses, cattle etc. in Asia and NE Africa, transmitted by horseflies. [Marathi]

surreal (səriəl´) *a.* **1** having the qualities of surrealism. **2** strange, weird, bizarre. **surreality** (-al´-) *n.* **surreally** *adv.*

surrealism (səriə´lizm) *n.* an artistic and literary movement of the 20th cent. which aimed at expressing the subconscious activities of the mind by presenting images with the chaotic incoherency of a dream. **surrealist** *n.*, *a.* **surrealistic** (-lis´-) *a.* **surrealistically** *adv.* [F *surréalisme*]

surrebut (sŭribŭt´) *v.i.* (*pres.p.* **surrebutting,** *past, p.p.* **surrebutted**) (*Law*) to reply to a defendant's rebutter. **surrebutter** *n.* the plaintiff's reply to the defendant's rebutter.

surrejoin (sŭrijoin´) *v.i.* (*Law*) to reply to a defendant's rejoinder. **surrejoinder** (-də) *n.* the plaintiff's reply to the defendant's rejoinder.

surrender (səren´də) *v.t.* **1** to give up possession of, esp. upon compulsion or demand. **2** to yield up to the power or control of another. **3** to yield (oneself) to any influence, habit, emotion etc. **4** to relinquish (a life-insurance policy) in return for a smaller, immediate payment. **5** to give up (a lease) before it expires. **6** to give up (hope). ~*v.i.* **1** to yield something or to give oneself up into the power of another, esp. to an enemy in war. **2** to give in, to yield, to submit. **3** to yield to any influence, habit, emotion etc. **4** to appear in court in discharge of bail etc. ~*n.* the act of surrendering or the state of being surrendered. **to surrender at discretion** DISCRETION. **to surrender to bail** to appear in court in discharge of bail. **surrenderee** (-ē´) *n.* (*Law*) a person to whom an estate is surrendered. **surrenderer** *n.* **surrender value** *n.* a payment made in return for the voluntary relinquishing of a life insurance policy by its holder. [OF *surrendre*]

surreptitious (sŭrəptish´əs) *a.* **1** done by stealth or fraud. **2** secret, clandestine. **surreptitiously** *adv.* **surreptitiousness** *n.* [L *surreptīcius*, from *surripere*, to purloin (*sur-*, SUB-, *rapere*, to snatch), p.p. *surreptus*]

surrey (sŭr´i) *n.* (*pl.* **surreys**) (*N Am.*) a light, four-wheeled horse-drawn carriage. [orig. an adapt. of *Surrey cart*, first made in *Surrey*, England]

surrogate (sŭr´əgət) *n.* **1** a deputy; a substitute. **2** a deputy of a bishop or his chancellor appointed to grant marriage licences and probates. **3** (*N Am.*) a judge with jurisdiction over inheritance, probate etc. **surrogacy** (-si), **surrogateship** *n.* **surrogate mother** *n.* **1** a person taking the role of a mother. **2** a woman who bears a child for a childless couple, often after artificial insemination or embryo implantation. **surrogatum** (-gā´təm) *n.* (*pl.* **surrogata** (-tə)) (*Sc. Law*) a substitute. [L *surrogātus*, p.p. of *surrogāre*, to elect as substitute (*sur-*, SUB-, *rogāre*, to ask)]

surround (sərownd´) *v.t.* **1** to lie or be situated all round, to encompass, to encircle, to enclose. **2** to cause to be surrounded in this way. ~*n.* **1** an edging, a border. **2** the floor covering, or staining of floorboards, between the skirting and the carpet. **3** the structure built round a fire etc. **surrounding** *a.* **surroundings** *n.pl.* things around a person or thing, environment, circumstances. [OF *soronder*, *surunder*, to overflow (SUR-², over, L *undāre*, to flow, cp. ABOUND, conf. with ROUND)]

surtax (sœ´taks) *n.* **1** an additional tax. **2** (*Hist.*) an additional graduated income tax formerly imposed in the UK in place of the supertax on all incomes above a certain amount. ~*v.t.* to impose a surtax on.

surtitle (sœ´tītəl) *n.* a printed translation of part of the text of an opera etc. projected on a screen above the stage. ~*v.t.* to provide with surtitles.

surtout (sœ´too) *n.* (*Hist.*) a man's overcoat, esp. one like a frock coat. [F (SUR-¹, *tout*, all, L *tōtum*, nom. *-tus*, whole)]

surv. *abbr.* surveyor.

surveillance (səvā´ləns, -vā´əns) *n.* observation, close watch, supervision. [F, from *surveiller* (*veiller*, L *vigilāre*, to watch, see VIGIL)]

Usage note The pronunciation with (l) is preferred to that without.

---

survey¹ (səvā´) *v.t.* **1** to look over, to take a general view of. **2** to view with a scrutinizing eye; to examine closely. **3** to examine and ascertain the condition, value etc. of (a building etc.). **4** to determine by accurate observation and measurement the boundaries, extent, position, contours etc. of (a tract of country, coast, estate etc.). ~*v.i.* to carry out a survey. **surveyable** *a.* **surveying** *n.* **surveyor** *n.* **1** a person who surveys, esp. one who measures land. **2** an inspector (of customs, weights and measures etc.). **surveyorship** *n.* [A-F *surveier* (OF *veeir*, L *vidēre*, to see)]

survey² (sœ´vā) *n.* **1** the act or process of surveying. **2** a general view. **3** a careful examination, investigation, inspection or scrutiny. **4** an account based on this. **5** the operation of surveying land etc. **6** a department carrying this out. **7** a map, plan etc. recording the results of this. [as SURVEY¹]

survive (səvīv´) *v.i.* to be still alive or in existence. ~*v.t.* **1** to live longer than, to outlive, to outlast. **2** to be alive after, to live through, to outlive or outlast (an event, period etc.). **survivable** *a.* **survival** *n.* **1** the act or condition of surviving. **2** a person, thing, custom, opinion etc. surviving into a new state of things. **3** the activity of coping with harsh conditions, either as a sport or as a training exercise. **survivalism** *n.* **1** a policy of taking measures to ensure one's own survival. **2** the activity of practising outdoor survival skills as a sport. **survivalist** *n., a.* **survival kit** *n.* emergency rations etc., carried by members of the armed forces etc. **survival of the fittest** *n.* **1** the preservation of forms of life that have proved themselves best adapted to their environment, the process or result of natural selection. **2** the success of the most adaptable or efficient businesses, people etc. **survivor** *n.* **survivorship** *n.* [F *survivre*, L *supervīvere* (*vīvere*, to live)]

Sus. *abbr.* Susanna (Apocrypha).

sus¹ (sŭs) *n.* (*sl.*) suspicion of loitering with criminal intent. [short for SUSPICION]

sus² SUSS.

sus- (sŭs) *pref.* var. of SUB-, used before *p*, *t* and in some L derivatives before *c*.

susceptible (səsep´tibəl) *a.* **1** impressionable, sensitive. **2** capable of being influenced or affected, accessible, liable (to). **3** admitting (of). **susceptibility** (-bil´-) *n.* (*pl.* **susceptibilities**) **1** the condition or quality of being susceptible. **2** (*pl.*) sensitive feelings, sensibilities. **3** (*Physics*) the ratio of magnetization to a magnetizing force. **susceptibleness** *n.* **susceptibly** *adv.* **susceptive** *a.* **1** readily receiving impressions etc., susceptible. **2** receiving emotional impressions. **susceptiveness, susceptivity** (sŭseptiv´-) *n.* [F, from L *suscipere* (*capere*, to take), p.p. *susceptus*]

†**suscitate** (sŭs´itāt) *v.t.* to rouse, to excite. **suscitation** (-ā´shən) *n.* [L *suscitātus*, p.p. of *suscitāre* (*citāre*, to CITE)]

sushi (soo´shi) *n.* a Japanese dish of cold rice cakes with a vinegar dressing and garnishes of raw fish etc. [Jap.]

suslik SOUSLIK.

suspect¹ (səspekt´) *v.t.* **1** to imagine to exist, to have an impression of the existence of without proof, to surmise. **2** to be inclined to think. **3** to be inclined to believe to be guilty but upon slight evidence, to doubt the innocence of. **4** to believe to be uncertain, to doubt, to mistrust. ~*v.i.* to be suspicious. **suspectable** *a.* **suspectedly** *adv.* [F *suspecter*, L *suspectāre*, from *suspectus*, suspected, p.p. of *suspicere* (*specere*, to look)]

suspect² (sŭs´pekt) *n.* a person suspected of crime etc. ~*a.* **1** suspected, under suspicion, suspicious. **2** doubtful, uncertain.

suspend (səspend´) *v.t.* **1** to hang up, to hang from something above. **2** to sustain from falling or sinking. **3** to hold (particles) in a suspension. **4** to render temporarily inoperative or cause to cease for a time, to intermit; to defer. **5** to debar temporarily from a privilege, office etc. **to suspend payment** to be unable to meet one's financial engagements. **suspended** *a.* (of particles) to be held in a suspension. **suspended animation** *n.* temporary ceasing of the body's vital functions. **suspended sentence** *n.* a prison sentence that is not served unless a further crime is committed. **suspender** *n.* **1** an attachment to hold up a stocking or sock. **2** (*pl., N Am.*) braces. **3** a person who or something which suspends. **suspender belt** *n.* a belt with stocking suspenders attached. **suspensible** *a.* **suspensibility** (-bil´-) *n.* [F *suspendre*, L *suspendere* (*pendere*, to hang), p.p. *suspensus*]

suspense (səspens´) *n.* **1** a state of uncertainty, doubt or apprehensive expectation or waiting. **2** (*Law*) a temporary cessation of a right etc. **to keep in suspense** to delay giving (someone) vital information. **suspense account** *n.* an account in which items are entered until they are properly allocated. **suspenseful** *a.* **suspension** (-shən) *n.* **1** the act of suspending. **2** the state of being suspended. **3** a system of springs etc. that supports the body of a vehicle on the axles. **4** a dispersion of solid particles in a fluid. **5** (*Mus.*) the prolongation of a note to form a discord with the following chord. **suspension bridge** *n.* a bridge sustained by flexible supports passing over a tower or elevated pier and secured at each extremity. **suspensive** *a.* **1** having the power to suspend. **2** causing suspense. **suspensively** *adv.* **suspensiveness** *n.* **suspensor** *n.* (*Bot.*) a row of cells to which a plant embryo is fixed. **suspensorium** (-saw´riəm) *n.* (*pl.* **suspensoriums**) a supporting ligament, part etc., esp. the bone or bones by which the lower jaw is suspended from the cranium in vertebrates. **suspensory** *a.* having power to suspend. [F *suspens*, suspended, L *suspensus*, see SUSPEND]

suspensible SUSPEND.

suspicion (səspish´ən) *n.* **1** the act or feeling of a person who suspects. **2** belief in the existence of wrong or guilt on inadequate proof, doubt, mistrust. **3** a very slight amount; a trace. **above suspicion** too honest or good to be suspected. **under suspicion** suspected. **suspicionless** *a.* **suspicious** *a.* **1** inclined to suspect. **2** entertaining suspicion. **3** expressing or showing suspicion. **4** exciting or likely to excite suspicion. **suspiciously** *adv.* **suspiciousness** *n.* [OF *souspeçon* (F *soupçon*), L *suspitio -ōnem*, from *suspicere*, to SUSPECT[1]]

suss (sŭs), **sus** *v.t.* (*pres.p.* **sussing**, *past, p.p.* **sussed**) (*sl.*) **1** to suspect of a crime. **2** to work out or discover the true facts of. ~*n.* **1** a suspect. **2** a suspicion. ~*a.* suspect. **on suss** on suspicion (of having committed a crime). **to suss out** to investigate, to find out about. **sussed** *a.* well informed. [SUSPECT[1], SUSPICION]

Sussex (sŭs´iks) *n.* an English breed of fowl. [*Sussex*, a former county in S England]

sustain (səstān´) *v.t.* **1** to bear the weight of, to hold up, to keep from falling. **2** to bear up against or under. **3** to stand, to undergo without yielding. **4** to experience, to suffer. **5** to nourish, to provide sustenance for. **6** to enable to bear something, to keep from failing, to strengthen, to encourage, to keep up. **7** to prolong. **8** to maintain, to uphold. **9** to establish by evidence. **10** to support, to confirm, to bear out, to substantiate. **sustainable** *a.* **1** (of sources of raw materials) capable of being replaced at the same rate as they are used, minimizing damage to the environment. **2** able to be sustained. **sustainedly** (-idli) *adv.* **sustainer** *n.* **sustainment** *n.* [OF *sustenir* (F *soutenir*), L *sustinēre* (*tenēre*, to hold)]

sustenance (sŭs´tinəns) *n.* **1** something which sustains, the means of support or maintenance. **2** the nourishing element in food. **3** food, subsistence. **4** the act of sustaining.

sustentaculum (sŭstentak´ūləm) *n.* (*pl.* **sustentaculums**) a supporting body part, tissue etc. **sustentacular** *a.*

sustentation (sŭstəntā´shən) *n.* (*formal*) support, maintenance. **sustentation fund** *n.* a fund to assist indigent clergy. **sustentator** (sŭs´-) *n.*

susurrant (sūsŭr´ənt) *a.* (*poet.*) whispering, rustling, murmuring. **susurration** (sūsərā´shən) *n.* (*poet.*) whispering, rustling. [L *susurrans -ntem*, pres.p. of *susurrāre*, from *susurrus*, a whisper]

☒ **sutle** common misspelling of SUBTLE.

sutler (sŭt´lə) *n.* (*Hist.*) a person following an army and selling provisions, liquor etc. **sutlership** *n.* **sutlery** *n.* (*pl.* **sutleries**) a sutler's work or stall. [Dut. *zoetelaar*, from *zoetelen*, cp. G *sudeln*, to sully (cogn. with SUDS and SEETHE)]

Sutra (soo´trə) *n.* **1** in Hindu literature, a rule, a precept, an aphorism. **2** (*pl.*) Brahminical books of rules, doctrine etc. [Sansk.]

suttee (sŭtē´, sŭt´i), **sati** (sŭt´i) *n.* (*pl.* **suttees, satis**) (*Hist.*) **1** a Hindu custom by which the widow was burnt on the funeral pyre with her dead husband. **2** a widow so burnt. **sutteeism** *n.* [Sansk. *satī*, a virtuous wife]

suture (soo´chə) *n.* **1** the junction of two parts by their margins as if by sewing, esp. of the bones of the skull. **2** the uniting of two body surfaces, esp. the edges of a wound, by stitching. **3** catgut, silk etc. used in uniting body surfaces. **4** a stitch or seam made in this way. ~*v.t.* to unite by a suture. **sutural** *a.* **suturally** *adv.* **suturation** (-ā´shən) *n.* **sutured** *a.* [F, from L *sūtūra*, from *suere*, to sew, p.p. *sūtus*]

suzerain (soo´zərān) *n.* **1** (*Hist.*) a feudal lord. **2** a state having sovereignty or control over another. **suzerainty** *n.* [F, from *sus*, L *susum*, *sursum*, above, after *souverain*, the SOVEREIGN]

s.v. *abbr.* **1** side valve. **2** (L) *sub verbo*, *sub voce*, under the word or heading.

svelte (svelt) *a.* (esp. of a woman's figure) slender, lissom. [F, from It. *svelto*]

Svengali (sven·gah´li) *n.* (*pl.* **Svengalis**) a person who control's another's mind, esp. for a sinister purpose. [character in George Du Maurier's *Trilby*]

SW *abbr.* **1** south-west. **2** south-western. **3** short wave.

swab (swob), **swob** *n.* **1** a mop for cleaning floors, decks, the bore of a gun etc. **2** a small piece of cotton wool or gauze used for removing blood, dressing wounds, taking specimens etc. **3** a specimen taken with a swab for examination. **4** (*sl.*) a clumsy person. **5** (*Naut., sl.*) an officer's epaulette. ~*v.t.* (*pres.p.* **swabbing, swobbing**, *past, p.p.* **swabbed, swobbed**) to rub, wipe or clean with a swab or mop. **swabber** *n.* [back-formation from *swabber*, Dut. *zwabber*, drudge, from *zwabberen*, to do dirty work, cp. G *schwabbern*, prob. cogn. with *schwappen*, to spill]

Swabian (swā´biən) *a.* of or relating to Swabia, a duchy of medieval Germany. ~*n.* a native or inhabitant of Swabia.

swaddle (swod´əl) *v.t.* **1** to wind or swathe in or as in a bandage, wrap or wraps. **2** to wrap in swaddling-clothes to restrict movement. **swaddler** *n.* (*Ir., sl.*) a Protestant, a Methodist. **swaddling** *n.* **†swaddling-bands** *n.pl.* swaddling-clothes. **swaddling-clothes** *n.pl.* (*Hist.*) cloth bands used for swaddling an infant. **†swaddling-clouts** *n.pl.* swaddling-clothes. [OE *swethel*, a swaddling-band, from *swathu*, a SWATH]

Swadeshi (swədā´shi) *n.* (*Hist.*) a movement in India for self-government, and agitation until this was obtained. [Hind.]

swag (swag) *n.* **1** (*sl.*) booty obtained by robbery, esp. burglary. **2** an ornamental festoon. **3** a heavy, loosely hanging fold of fabric. **4** (*Austral., New Zeal.*) a pack or bundle of personal effects, baggage. ~*v.t.* (*pres.p.* **swagging**, *past, p.p.* **swagged**) **1** to hang or arrange in swags. **2** to cause to sway or sag. ~*v.i.* to hang loose and heavy; to sag. **swag-bellied** *a.* having a large, prominent belly. **swag-belly** *n.* (*pl.* **swag-bellies**).

swagman *n.* (*pl.* **swagmen**) (*Austral., New Zeal.*) a man who carries his swag about with him in search of work. **swag shop** *n.* (*sl.*) a shop where cheap and trashy goods are sold. [cp. Norw. *svagga*, cogn. with SWAY]

swage (swāj) *n.* **1** a tool for shaping wrought iron etc. by hammering or pressure. **2** a tool for bending metal etc. ~*v.t.* to shape with a swage. **swage-block** *n.* a heavy iron block or anvil with grooves etc., used for shaping metal. [F *suage*, etym. uncertain]

swagger (swag´ə) *v.i.* **1** to walk, strut or go (about etc.) with an air of defiance, self-confidence or superiority. **2** to talk or behave in a blustering, boastful or hectoring manner. ~*v.t.* to bluster or bluff (a person into, out of etc.). ~*n.* **1** a swaggering walk, gait or manner. **2** bluster, dash, conceit. **3** smartness. ~*a.* (*coll.*) smart, fashionable. **swagger cane** *n.* a swagger stick. **swagger coat** *n.* a loose coat made on full lines which sways when the wearer walks. **swaggerer** *n.* **swaggeringly** *adv.* **swagger stick** *n.* a short cane with a metal head, carried by soldiers. [freq. of SWAG]

Swahili (swəhē´li, swah-) *n.* (*pl.* **Swahili**) **1** a member of a Bantu-speaking people of Tanzania. **2** their language, Kiswahili. [Arab. *Waswahili*, coast people]

swain (swān) *n.* **1** †a young rustic; a country gallant. **2** (*poet.*) a male lover. **swainish** *a.* [Icel. *sveinn*, cp. OE *swān*]

swale (swāl) *n.* (*esp. N Am., dial.*) a moist depression between ridges. [etym. unknown]

swallow[1] (swol´ō) *v.t.* **1** to take through the mouth and throat into the stomach. **2** to absorb, to engulf, to overwhelm, to consume (up). **3** to accept with credulity. **4** to accept without resentment, to put up with. **5** to refrain from showing or expressing. **6** to retract, to recant. **7** to say indistinctly. ~*v.i.* to perform the action of swallowing. ~*n.* **1** the act of swallowing. **2** the amount swallowed at once. **3** the gullet, the oesophagus. **4** a swallow-hole. **swallett** (-it) *n.* a sink-hole. **swallowable** *a.* **swallower** *n.* **swallow-hole** *n.* a sink-hole. [ME *swolowen*, OE *swelgan*, cp. Dut. *zwelgen*, G *schwelgen*, Icel. *svelgja*]

swallow[2] (swol´ō) *n.* **1** any small, swift, migratory bird of the family Hirundinidae, with long, pointed wings and a forked tail. **2** a swift or other bird resembling the swallow. **one swallow does not make a summer** used as a warning against jumping to conclusions from a single piece of evidence. **to swallow a camel** CAMEL. **swallow-dive** *n.* a dive with the arms outstretched. **swallowtail** *n.* **1** a deeply forked tail. **2** a butterfly or hummingbird with such a tail. **3** (*often pl.*) a swallow-tailed coat, a dress coat. **swallow-tailed** *a.* with a deeply forked tail. [OE *swalewe* (cp. Dut. *zwaluw*, G *Schwalbe*, Icel. *svala*), cogn. with SWELL]

swam SWIM.

swami (swah´mi) *n.* (*pl.* **swamis**) a Hindu religious teacher. [Sansk. *svamin*, a master]

swamp (swomp) *n.* a tract of wet, spongy land, a bog, a marsh. ~*v.t.* **1** to cause (a boat etc.) to be filled with or to sink in water. **2** to plunge or sink into a bog. **3** to overwhelm, to render helpless with difficulties, numbers etc. ~*v.i.* to fill with water, to sink, to founder. **swampland** *n.* land consisting of swamps. **swamp oak** *n.* the casuarina. **swamp sparrow** *n.* a New Zealand warbler, *Bowdleria punctata*. **swampy** *a.* (*comp.* **swampier,** *superl.* **swampiest**). [cp. SUMP, Dut. *zwamp*; perh. rel. to OE *swamm*, G *Schwamm*, a sponge]

swan (swon) *n.* **1** a large, web-footed aquatic bird of the genus *Cygnus*, with a long neck and usu. white plumage, noted for its grace in the water. **2** (*poet.*) a poet, a singer. ~*v.i.* (*pres.p.* **swanning,** *past, p.p.* **swanned**) to wander aimlessly (about, around etc.). **swan-dive** *n.* (*N Am.*) a swallow-dive. **swanherd** *n.* a person who tends swans, esp. a royal officer superintending swan-marks. **swanlike** *a.* **swan-maiden** *n.* in German folklore, a maiden able to take the shape of a swan. **swan-mark** *n.* a mark on a swan showing ownership, usu. a notch on the upper mandible. **swan-neck** *n.* a pipe, tube, rail etc. curved like a swan's neck, esp. the end of a discharge pipe. **swannery** *n.* (*pl.* **swanneries**) a place where swans are kept or bred. **Swan of Avon** (ā´vən) *n.* (*poet.*) William Shakespeare. **swansdown** *n.* **1** down obtained from a swan. **2** a thick cotton cloth with a downy nap on one side. **swan-shot** *n.* a large size of shot. **swanskin** *n.* **1** a swan's skin with the feathers on. **2** a soft, fine-twilled flannel. **swansong** *n.* **1** the last or dying work, esp. of a poet. **2** any final work, performance etc. **3** the song traditionally believed to be sung by a dying swan. **swan-upping** (-ŭp´ing) *n.* the annual inspection and marking of Thames swans. [OE (cp. Dut. *zwaan*, G *Schwan*, Icel. *svanr*), perh. cogn. with Sansk. *swan*, L *sonāre*, to SOUND[1]]

swank (swangk) *n.* (*coll.*) swagger, bluster. ~*v.i.* to swagger, to show off, to bluster. ~*a.* (*esp. N Am.*) swanky. **swankpot** *n.* (*coll.*) a person who swanks. **swanky** *a.* (*comp.* **swankier,** *superl.* **swankiest**) (*coll.*) **1** stylish, showy. **2** showing off. **swankily** *adv.* **swankiness** *n.* [etym. uncertain, perh. MG *swanken*, to sway]

swap (swop), **swop** *v.t., v.i.* (*pres.p.* **swapping, swopping,** *past, p.p.* **swapped, swopped**) to exchange, to barter. ~*n.* **1** an act of exchanging, a barter. **2** something suitable for swapping. **3** something exchanged in a swap. **swap meet** *n.* (*esp. N Am.*) **1** a meeting of collectors or traders for the purpose of swapping items. **2** a flea market. **swapper** *n.* [prob. from obs. *swap*, ME *swappen*, to strike]

Swapo (swah´pō) *abbr.* South-West Africa People's Organization.

Swaraj (swərahj´) *n.* (*Hist.*) home rule for India. **Swarajist** *n., a.* [Sansk. *svaraj*, self-ruling]

sward (swawd) *n.* (*poet.*) **1** a surface of land covered with thick short grass. **2** turf. **swarded** *a.* **swardy** *a.* [OE *sweard*, skin, cp. Dut. *zwoord*, G *Schwarte*, Icel. *svörthr*, skin, hide]

†sware SWEAR.

swarf (swawf) *n.* **1** grit, metal filings, chips, grindings. **2** (*Hist.*) wax removed when cutting a gramophone record. [Icel. *svarf*, file dust]

swarm[1] (swawm) *n.* **1** a cluster of bees issuing from a hive with a queen bee and seeking a new home. **2** a large number of small animals, insects, people etc., esp. when moving in a confused mass. **3** (*pl.*) great numbers. **4** a group of zoospores. ~*v.i.* **1** (of bees) to collect together in readiness for emigrating, to leave (or go out of) a hive in a swarm. **2** to move (about etc.) in a swarm. **3** to congregate, to throng, to be very numerous. **4** (of places) to be thronged or overcrowded (with). **swarm cell, swarm spore** *n.* a zoospore. [OE *swearm* (cp. Dut. *zwerm*, G *Schwarm*, Icel. *svarmr*), perh. cogn. with Sansk. *svr*, to sound, L *susurrus*, see SUSURRANT]

swarm[2] (swawm) *v.i.* (*with up*) to climb up (a tree, rope, pole etc.) by embracing it with the arms and legs. ~*v.t.* to swarm up. [etym. uncertain]

†swart (swawt) *a.* of a dark colour; swarthy. [OE *sweart* (cp. Dut. *zwart*, G *schwarz*, Icel. *svartr*), cogn. with L *sordidus*, SORDID]

swarthy (swaw´dhi) *a.* (*comp.* **swarthier,** *superl.* **swarthiest**) dark or dusky in complexion. **swarthily** *adv.* **swarthiness** *n.* [obs. *swarth*, var. of SWART]

swash[1] (swosh) *v.i.* **1** to make a noise as of splashing water. **2** (of liquid) to wash or splash about. **3** †to swagger. **4** †to strike noisily or violently. ~†*v.t.* to strike noisily or violently. ~*n.* **1** a washing, dashing or splashing of water. **2** a blustering noise. **swashbuckler** *n.* **1** an adventurer, a daredevil. **2** a bully, a bravo. **3** a film or book about the adventures of a swashbuckler. **swashbuckling** *a.* **swash-plate** *n.* an inclined disc on a revolving axis transmitting an up-and-down motion to a bar. [imit., cp. Swed. dial. *svasska*]

swash[2] (swosh) *a.* **1** sloping. **2** (of a letter) formed with a flourished stroke. [etym. unknown]

swastika (swos´tikə) *n.* a cross with arms bent at a right angle, used as a symbol of anti-Semitism or Nazism. [Sansk., fortunate (*su*, well, *asti*, being)]

swat (swot) *v.t.* (*pres.p.* **swatting,** *past, p.p.* **swatted**) **1** to hit sharply. **2** to crush (a fly) with a sharp blow. ~*n.* a sharp blow. **swatter** *n.* [onomat.]

Usage note The spellings of the verbs *swat* (to crush) and *swot* (to study hard) should not be confused.

swatch (swoch) *n.* **1** a sample of cloth. **2** a collection of samples. [etym. uncertain]

swath (swawth, swoth), **swathe** (swādh) *n.* (*pl.* **swaths** (swawths, swawdhz, swoths), **swathes**) **1** a row or ridge of grass, corn etc. cut and left lying on the ground. **2** the space cut by a scythe, machine etc. in one course. **3** a broad strip or band. **to cut a wide swath** (*N Am.*) to make a bold or stylish impression. [OE *swæth, swathu,* track (cp. Dut. *zwaad,* G *Schwad,* swath, LG *swade,* a scythe, Norw. *swada,* to slice off)]

swathe[1] (swādh) *v.t.* to bind or wrap in or as in a bandage, cloth etc. ~*n.* a bandage, a wrapping. [ME *swathen,* cp. *swethel,* SWADDLE, perh. as SWATH]

swathe[2] SWATH.

swatter SWAT.

sway (swā) *v.i.* **1** to move backwards and forwards, to swing, to oscillate irregularly. **2** to be unsteady, to waver, to vacillate. **3** to lean or incline to one side or in different directions. ~*v.t.* **1** to cause to oscillate, waver, or vacillate. **2** to bias; to influence, to control, to rule. **3** to cause to incline to one side. ~*n.* **1** rule, dominion, control. **2** the act of swaying, a swing. **3** (*Sc., North.*) an iron rod in a fireplace for hanging kettles and pots on. **sway-back** *n.* (esp. of a horse) a hollowed or sagging back. **sway-backed** *a.* [ME *sweyen,* cp. Dan. *svaie,* Norw. *svaga,* Swed. *svaja,* to jerk]

Swazi (swah´zi) *a.* of or relating to Swaziland, southern Africa. ~*n.* (*pl.* **Swazis, Swazi**) **1** a native or inhabitant of Swaziland. **2** the language of the Swazis.

swear (sweə) *v.i.* (*past* **swore** (swaw), †**sware** (sweə), *p.p.* **sworn** (swawn)) **1** to affirm solemnly invoking God or some other sacred person or object as witness or pledge, to take an oath. **2** to appeal (to) as witness of an oath. **3** to use profane or obscene language. **4** to give evidence on oath. **5** to make a promise on oath. ~*v.t.* **1** to utter or affirm with an oath, to take an oath (that). **2** to take (an oath). **3** to administer an oath to, to bind by an oath. **4** (*coll.*) to declare, to vow. **5** to promise or testify on oath. **6** to utter profanely or obscenely. ~*n.* **1** an act or spell of swearing. **2** a profane oath. **to swear at** (*coll.*) (of colours or patterns) to clash with. **to swear blind** (*coll.*) to state solemnly or emphatically. **to swear by** (*coll.*) to have or profess great confidence in. **to swear in** to induct into office with the administration of an oath. **to swear off** (*coll.*) to renounce solemnly. **to swear out** (*N Am.*) to secure the issue of (a warrant for arrest) by making a charge on oath. **to swear to** to testify firmly to the truth of. **swearer** *n.* **swear word** *n.* an obscene or taboo word. [OE *swerian* (cp. Dut. *zweren,* G *schwören,* Icel. *sverja,* Swed. *svara,* to answer), cogn. with SWARM[1]]

sweat (swet) *n.* **1** the moisture exuded from the skin of a person or animal. **2** the act or state of sweating. **3** (*coll.*) a state of anxiety, a flurry. **4** (*coll.*) drudgery, toil, hard labour, exertion. **5** moisture exuded from or deposited in drops on any surface. **6** (*pl., esp. N Am., coll.*) **a** a sweatsuit. **b** sweatpants. **7** (*sl.*) an old soldier. ~*v.i.* (*past, p.p.* **sweated,** (*N Am.*) **sweat**) **1** to exude sweat, to perspire. **2** to emit moisture. **3** (of moisture) to exude. **4** to collect surface moisture. **5** to be in a flurry or state of anxiety, panic etc. **6** to toil, to labour, to drudge. ~*v.t.* **1** to cause to emit moisture in drops on a surface. **2** to emit as or like sweat. **3** to make (an animal or athlete) sweat by exertion. **4** to employ at starvation wages, to exact the largest possible amount of labour from at the lowest pay, by utilizing competition. **5** (*coll.*) to subject to extortion, to bleed. **6** to subject (hides, tobacco etc.) to fermentation. **7** to wear away (coins) by friction etc. **8** to melt (solder etc.) by heating. **9** to unite (metal pieces) in this way. **10** to heat (meat or vegetables) in fat until the juices exude. **by the sweat of one's brow** by working hard. **no sweat** (*sl.*) no difficulty or problem, without trouble. **to sweat blood** (*sl.*) to work or worry to an extreme degree. **to sweat bullets** (*N Am., sl.*) to sweat profusely. **to sweat out 1** to remove or get rid of by sweating. **2** (*coll.*) to endure, to live through. **sweatband** *n.* a band of absorbent material round the forehead or wrist, worn in some sports to keep sweat out of the eyes or from the hands. **sweated** *a.* of, relating to or produced by the sweating system. **sweater** *n.* **1** a pullover. **2** a person who or something which causes sweating. **3** a person who employs people at starvation wages in unhealthy conditions and for long hours. **sweat gland** *n.* a gland below the skin which exudes sweat. **sweating** *a., n.* **sweating-iron** *n.* a scraper for removing sweat from horses. **sweating-room** *n.* **1** a sudatorium, esp. in a Turkish bath. **2** a room for sweating superfluous moisture from cheese. **sweating-sickness** *n.* any of various fevers accompanied by heavy sweating, epidemic in the 15th and 16th cents. **sweating system** *n.* the practice of employing workers at starvation wages in unhealthy conditions and for long hours. **sweatpants** *n.pl.* loose, warm trousers with an elasticated or drawstring waist, worn for leisure or exercise. **sweatshirt** *n.* a loose, long-sleeved sweater made from cotton jersey. **sweatshop** *n.* a factory or other workplace that employs the sweating system. **sweat sock** *n.* (*N Am.*) either one of a pair of thick, absorbent, cotton socks, worn with trainers. **sweatsuit** *n.* a suit consisting of a sweatshirt and sweatpants, worn for leisure or exercise. **sweaty** *a.* (*comp.* **sweatier,** *superl.* **sweatiest**) covered with or causing sweat. **sweatily** *adv.* **sweatiness** *n.* [OE *swat,* cp. Dut. *zweet,* G *Schweiss,* Icel. *sveiti,* also Sansk. *svēda-,* Gr. *hidrōs,* L *sūdor*)]

Swede (swēd) *n.* a native or inhabitant of Sweden, or a descendant of one. **swede, swede turnip** *n.* a large turnip, *Brassica rutabaga,* having yellow flesh.

Swedenborgian (swēdənbaw´jiən) *a.* of or relating to Swedenborg or Swedenborgianism. ~*n.* a member of the Swedenborgian or New Church, or a believer in the doctrines of Emanuel Swedenborg. **Swedenborgianism** *n.* [Emanuel *Swedenborg,* 1688–1772, Swedish philosopher and mystic]

Swedish (swē´dish) *a.* of or relating to Sweden. ~*n.* the language of the Swedes.

Sweeney (swē´ni) *n.* (*sl.*) the members of a flying squad. [rhyming sl., from *Sweeney* Todd, a barber who murdered customers]

sweeny (swē´ni) *n.* atrophy of a muscle, esp. of the shoulder in horses. [etym. uncertain]

sweep (swēp) *v.t.* (*past, p.p.* **swept** (swept)) **1** to clear dirt etc. from or clean with or as with a broom. **2** to collect or gather (up) with or as with a broom. **3** to propel with sweeps. **4** to cause to move with a sweeping motion. **5** to carry (along, away etc.) with powerful or unchecked force. **6** to wipe out, remove, destroy. **7** to move swiftly and powerfully over, across or along, to range, to scour. **8** (esp. of the eyes) to pass over in swift survey. **9** to pass over destructively. **10** to rake, to enfilade. **11** (*N Am.*) to gain an overwhelming victory in. **12** to dredge (the bottom of a river etc.). ~*v.i.*

1 to clear or clean a place with a broom. 2 to glide, move or pass along with a strong, swift continuous motion. 3 to go with a stately motion. 4 (of land, a curve etc.) to extend continuously. 5 (of the eye) to range unchecked. ~*n.* 1 the act of sweeping. 2 a clearance, a riddance. 3 a sweeping motion. 4 a sweeping curve, direction, piece of road etc. 5 a broad expanse. 6 the range, reach or compass of a sweeping motion or of an instrument, weapon, implement etc. having this motion. 7 a long oar used to propel barges or sailing vessels in a calm. 8 a sail of a windmill. 9 a survey of an area made in an arc. 10 a chimney sweep. 11 a sortie by aircraft. 12 (*dated sl.*) a blackguard. 13 (*coll.*) a sweepstake. 14 (*pl., N Am.*) a periodic survey of the viewing ratings of local television stations, used to calculate advertising rates. **to make a clean sweep of** 1 to get rid of entirely. 2 to win all the prizes in (a competition etc.). **to sweep aside** to remove quickly and completely. **to sweep away** to sweep aside. **to sweep off one's feet** FOOT. **to sweep the board** BOARD. **to sweep under the carpet** CARPET. **sweepback** *n.* the angular relation of an aircraft wing to the axis. **sweeper** *n.* 1 a person who sweeps. 2 a carpet sweeper. 3 a defensive player in soccer positioned behind the main defensive line. **sweeping** *a.* 1 covering a wide area. 2 wide-ranging, comprehensive. 3 without discrimination or qualification. 4 that sweeps. **sweepingly** *adv.* **sweepingness** *n.* **sweepings** *n.pl.* things collected by sweeping. **sweep-net** *n.* 1 a sweep-seine. 2 a butterfly net. **sweep second hand** *n.* a watch or clock hand that registers seconds. **sweep-seine** *n.* a long seine used for sweeping a large area. **swept-back** *a.* (of an aircraft wing) slanting backwards, set back at an angle. **swept-up** *a.* (of hair) upswept. **swept-wing** *a.* (of an aircraft) having swept-back wings. [ME *swepen*, from *swǣp-*, stem of OE *swāpan*, to SWOOP]

sweepstake (swēp´stāk), (*esp. N Am.*) **sweepstakes** *n.* 1 a lottery in which a number of people stake sums on an event, esp. on a horse race, the total amount staked being divided among the winning betters. 2 a race with betting of this kind. 3 a prize won in a sweepstake.

sweet (swēt) *a.* 1 having a taste like the taste of honey or sugar. 2 containing sugar or a sweetening ingredient. 3 pleasing to the senses. 4 fragrant. 5 pleasant or melodious in sound. 6 fresh, not salt or salted, not sour, bitter, stale or rancid. 7 free from acids or other corrosive substances. 8 pleasant to the mind, agreeable, delightful. 9 charming, amiable, gracious. 10 (*coll.*) lovable, dear, beloved. 11 (of butter) fresh, unsalted. ~*n.* 1 a sweet thing. 2 a piece of confectionery, such as a toffee or a chocolate. 3 a sweet dish, such as a tart, pudding or ice cream; this served as a course of a meal, after the main course. 4 the sweetness or the sweet part of anything. 5 (*pl.*) pleasures, delights, pleasant experiences. 6 dear one, darling. ~*adv.* (*coll.*) sweetly. **she's sweet** (*Austral., sl.*) everything is all right. **short and sweet** SHORT. **to be sweet on** to be in love with; to be very fond of. **to go one's own sweet way** to follow one's own plan; to be headstrong or independent. **sweet alyssum** *n.* a cruciferous plant, *Lolularia maritima*, with clusters of small flowers. **sweet and sour** *a.* cooked in a sauce made with sugar and vinegar or lemon juice. **sweet basil** *n.* the culinary herb *Ocimum basilicum*. **sweet bay** *n.* the bay tree or bay laurel, *Laurus nobilis*. **sweetbread** *n.* the pancreas or thymus gland of a calf or sheep, used as food. **sweet-brier** *n.* a Eurasian wild rose, *Rosa eglanteria*, having small, fragrant flowers. **sweet chestnut** *n.* the tree *Castanea sativa*. **sweet cicely** *n.* MYRRH². **sweetcorn** *n.* 1 a variety of maize with kernels rich in sugar. 2 the kernels eaten as a vegetable when young. **sweeten** *v.t.* 1 to make sweet or sweeter. 2 to make more agreeable or less unpleasant. 3 to mollify, to pacify. ~*v.i.* to become sweet or sweeter. **to sweeten the pill** PILL. **sweetener** *n.* 1 a sugar-free sweetening agent. 2 (*sl.*) a bribe. **sweetening** *n.* **sweet fennel** FENNEL. **sweet flag** *n.* the sweet rush. **sweet gale** *n.* the bog myrtle, the gale. **sweetheart** *n.* a lover, a boyfriend or girlfriend (used as a term of endearment). ~*v.i.* to court. **sweetheart agreement, sweetheart contract, sweetheart deal** *n.* (*coll.*) an agreement reached between an employer and a trade union with advantages to both parties. **sweetie, sweety** *n.* (*pl.* **sweeties**) 1 a piece of confectionery, a sweet. 2 (*also* **sweetie-pie**) a term of endearment. **sweeting** *n.* 1 a sweet variety of apple. 2 †a term of endearment. **sweetish** *a.* **sweetishness** *n.* **sweetly** *adv.* **sweet marjoram** *n.* the herb *Marjorana hortensis*, used in cooking. **sweetmeal** *n.* 1 sweetened wholemeal. 2 a biscuit made of sweetmeal. †**sweetmeat** *n.* 1 a piece of confectionery, a sweet. 2 a fruit candied with sugar. 3 a small, fancy cake. **sweetness** *n.* **all sweetness and light** an apparently amiable attitude. **sweet nothings** *n.pl.* words of endearment. **sweet oil** *n.* olive oil. **sweet pea** *n.* an annual leguminous climbing plant, *Lathyrus odoratus*, with showy flowers. **sweet pepper** *n.* a mild-flavoured capsicum. **sweet potato** *n.* (*pl.* **sweet potatoes**) a tropical climbing plant, *Ipomoea batatas*, with an edible root. **sweet rocket** *n.* any of various plants of the genus *Hesperis* or *Sisymbrium*. **sweet rush** *n.* a sedge with an aromatic rootstock used in medicine, confectionery etc. **sweet-scented** *a.* **sweet sedge** *n.* a sweet rush. **sweetshop** *n.* a shop where sweets are sold. **sweetsop** *n.* a tropical American shrub, *Anona squamosa*, with sweet, pulpy fruit. **sweet sultan** *n.* a fragrant plant, *Centaurea moschata* or *C. suaveolus*, of the daisy family. **sweet talk** *n.* (*coll.*) flattery, blandishment. **sweet-talk** *v.t.* (*coll.*) to flatter, esp. in order to coax or persuade. **sweet-tempered** *a.* **sweet tooth** *n.* a fondness for sweet-tasting things. **sweet violet** *n.* the violet *Viola odorata*. **sweetwater** *n.* a sweet, watery variety of white grape. **sweet william** (wil´yəm) *n.* a biennial species of pink, *Dianthus barbatus*, with dense clusters of showy, fragrant flowers. **sweet willow** *n.* the sweet gale. **sweetwood** *n.* 1 the bay tree or bay laurel, *Laurus nobilis*. 2 any one of various other trees and shrubs of the family Lauraceae. **sweety** SWEETIE (under SWEET). [OE *swēte*, cp. Dut. *zoet*, G *süss*, Icel. *soetr*, Sansk. *svad*, to please, L *suāvis*, Gr. *hēdus*, sweet]

swell (swel) *v.i.* (*p.p.* **swollen** (swō´lən), **swelled**) 1 to dilate or increase in bulk or extent, to expand. 2 to rise (up) from the surrounding surface. 3 to bulge, to belly (out). 4 to become greater in volume, strength or intensity. 5 to be puffed up, to be elated, to strut. 6 to be inflated with emotion. 7 to rise in altitude. ~*v.t.* 1 to increase the size, bulk, volume or dimensions of. 2 to raise (up) from the surrounding surface. 3 to inflate, to puff up. ~*n.* 1 the act or effect of swelling. 2 a rise, an increase, an augmentation. 3 a succession of long, unbroken waves in one direction, for example after a storm. 4 a bulge, a bulging part. 5 (*Mus.*) an increase followed by a decrease in the volume of sound; a combined crescendo and diminuendo. 6 (*Mus.*) a contrivance for gradually increasing and diminishing sound in an organ etc. 7 a swell-organ. 8 †a person of high standing or importance, a showy, dashing or fashionable person. ~*a.* 1 (*esp. N Am., coll.*) excellent, fine. 2 †smart, foppish, dandified. **swell-box** *n.* a chamber containing the pipes of a swell-organ, which is opened and closed to change the volume. **swelled head** *n.* (*coll.*) a high opinion of oneself. **swelling** *n.* 1 an unnatural enlargement or protuberance of a body part. 2 the act of expanding, or the state of being swollen or augmented. **swellish** *a.* **swell-organ** *n.* an organ or partial organ with the pipes enclosed in a swell-box. **swollen head** *n.* (*coll.*) a swelled head. [OE *swellan* (cp. Dut. *zwellen*, G *schwellen*, Icel. *svella*), perh. cogn. with Gr. *saluein*, to surge]

swelter (swel´tə) *v.i.* **1** (of the weather etc.) to be hot, moist and oppressive, to cause faintness, languor or oppression. **2** to be overcome and faint with heat. **3** to sweat profusely. ~*n.* a sweltering condition. **sweltering** *a.* oppressively hot. **swelteringly** *adv.* **sweltry** (-tri) *a.* oppressively hot. [OE *sweltan* (cp. Icel. *svelta*, Goth. *swiltan*, OHG *schwelzan*, to be consumed), cogn. with SULTRY]

swept SWEEP.

swerve (swœv) *v.i.* to turn to one side, to deviate, to diverge from the direct or regular course. ~*v.t.* to cause to diverge, to deflect. ~*n.* **1** the act of swerving. **2** a sudden divergence or deflection. **swerveless** *a.* **swerver** *n.* [OE *sweorfan*, to rub, to file, to polish (cp. Dut. *zwerven*, to swerve, Icel. *sverfa*, to file)]

SWG *abbr.* standard wire gauge.

swift (swift) *a.* **1** moving or able to move with great rapidity, rapid, quick, speedy. **2** ready, prompt, expeditious. **3** passing rapidly, soon over, brief, unexpected, sudden. ~†*adv.* swiftly. ~*n.* **1** a small, long-winged insectivorous bird of the family Apodidae, closely resembling the swallow. **2** a reel for winding yarn etc. **3** the common newt. **4** the ghost moth. **swifter** *n.* (*Naut.*) a rope used to fasten, hold or tighten something. **swift-footed** *a.* running swiftly. **swiftie** *n.* (*Austral., sl.*) **1** a trick or deception. **2** a person who acts quickly. **swiftlet** *n.* a small swift of the genus *Collocalia*. **swiftly** *adv.* **swiftness** *n.* **swift-winged** *a.* flying swiftly. [OE, from *swifan*, to move quickly (cp. Icel. *svīfa*, OHG *sweibōn*), cogn. with SWEEP]

swig (swig) *v.t., v.i.* (*pres.p.* **swigging**, *past, p.p.* **swigged**) (*coll.*) to drink in large draughts. ~*n.* a large drink of liquor. **swigger** *n.* [perh. from OE *swelgan*, SWALLOW[1]]

swill (swil) *v.t., v.i.* **1** to wash, to rinse. **2** to drink greedily. ~*n.* **1** the act of rinsing. **2** liquid food for animals, esp. pigs. **3** (liquid) rubbish, slops. **4** poor-quality alcoholic liquor. **5** a swig. **swiller** *n.* [OE *swillian*, to wash, cp. Icel. *skyla*]

swim (swim) *v.i.* (*pres.p.* **swimming**, *past* **swam** (swam), *p.p.* **swum** (swŭm)) **1** to move progressively in the water by the motion of the hands and feet, or fins, tail etc. **2** to float or be supported on water or other liquid. **3** to glide along. **4** to be drenched or flooded (with water etc.). **5** to seem to reel or whirl round one. **6** to have a feeling of dizziness. ~*v.t.* **1** to pass, traverse or accomplish by swimming. **2** to compete in (a race) by swimming. **3** to perform (a particular swimming stroke). **4** to cause (a horse, boat etc.) to swim or float. **5** to bear up, to float (a ship etc.). ~*n.* **1** the act or a spell of swimming. **2** a pool or run frequented by fish in a river. **3** the main current of life, business etc. **4** †a swim-bladder. **in the swim** involved in the main current activity. **swim-bladder** *n.* the air-bladder or sound of a fish. **swimmable** *a.* **swimmer** *n.* **swimmeret** (-ret) *n.* any one of the appendages of a crustacean serving as a swimming organ. **swimming** *n., a.* **swimming bath** *n.* an artificial pool for swimming in. **swimming-bell** *n.* a bell-shaped swimming organ, for example of a jellyfish. **swimming costume** *n.* a swimsuit. **swimmingly** *adv.* smoothly, easily, without impediment. **swimming pool** *n.* an artificial pool for swimming in. **swimming trunks** *n.pl.* a man's or boy's shorts worn for swimming. **swimsuit** *n.* a woman's or girl's one-piece garment for swimming. **swimsuited** *a.* **swimwear** *n.* clothes worn for swimming. [OE *swimman*, cp. Dut. *zwemmen*, G *schwimmen*, Icel. *svimma*), blended with OE *swīma*, a swoon (cp. Dut. *zwijm*, Icel. *svimi*, G *Schwindel*)]

Usage note In standard English, the past tense of *swim* is *swam*, not *swum*.

swindle (swin´dəl) *v.t., v.i.* **1** to cheat. **2** to obtain by cheating. ~*n.* **1** the act or process of swindling. **2** a thing that is not what it pretends to be, a deception, a fraud. **3** a gross fraud or imposition, a fraudulent scheme. **swindler** *n.* [earliest as *swindler*, from G *Schwindler*, a thoughtless person, cheat, from *schwindeln*, to be dizzy, from *Schwindel*, cp. SWIM]

swine (swīn) *n.* (*pl.* **swine, swines**) **1** (*formal or N Am.*) a pig, a hog. **2** (*coll.*) a greedy, vicious or debased person. **3** (*coll.*) something difficult or unpleasant. **swine fever** *n.* an infectious lung disease affecting pigs. **swineherd** *n.* a person who tends pigs. **swinepox** *n.* a form of chickenpox affecting pigs. **swine vesicular disease** *n.* an infectious viral disease of pigs causing fever and blisters. **swinish** *a.* **swinishly** *adv.* **swinishness** *n.* [OE *swīn* (cp. Dut. *swijn*, G *Schwein*, Icel. *svīn*), perh. orig. a., cp. L *suīnus*, pertaining to swine, from *sus*, a sow]

swing (swing) *v.i.* (*past, p.p.* **swung** (swŭng)) **1** to move to and fro, like an object suspended by a point or one side, to sway, hang freely like a pendulum, to oscillate, to rock. **2** to turn on or as on a pivot, to move or wheel (round etc.) through an arc. **3** to go with a swaying, undulating or rhythmical gait or motion. **4** to go to and fro by swinging. **5** (*coll.*) to hit out (at) with a swinging arm movement. **6** (*coll.*) to be hanged. **7** to play swing-music. **8** to have the rhythmical quality of swing-music. **9** to fluctuate between emotions, decisions etc. **10** (*coll.*) to be lively or up to date. **11** (*coll.*) to be promiscuous. **12** (*coll.*) (of a party) to be lively and exciting. **13** (of a cricket ball) to be bowled with a swing. ~*v.t.* **1** to cause to move to and fro, to sway, to oscillate. **2** to wave to and fro, to brandish. **3** to cause to turn or move around, as on a pivot or through an arc. **4** to throw (a punch). **5** to play or perform in the style of swing-music. **6** (*coll.*) to manipulate, to influence. **7** (*coll.*) to cause to happen, to bring about. **8** in cricket, to cause (the ball) to swing. ~*n.* **1** the act or state of swinging. **2** a swinging or oscillating motion. **3** a swinging gait or rhythm. **4** the compass or sweep of a moving body. **5** a curving or sweeping movement. **6** a blow delivered with a sweeping arm movement. **7** free course, unrestrained liberty. **8** regular course of activity. **9** a seat suspended by ropes etc., on which a person, esp. a child, may swing to and fro. **10** a spell of swinging on this. **11** swing-music. **12** the rhythmic feeling of swing-music. **13** a shift in opinion, condition etc. **in full swing** in full activity or operation. **no room to swing a cat** CAT[1]. **swings and roundabouts** a situation in which there are as many gains as losses. **to swing it** to play music with swing. **to swing the lead** LEAD[2]. **swing-back** *n.* an arrangement for adjusting the screen and plate-holder at the back of a camera at different angles. **swingbin** *n.* a plastic bin with a lid which can be swung open and shut. **swingboat** *n.* a boat-shaped carriage for swinging in at fairs etc. **swing bowler** *n.* in cricket, a bowler who swings the ball. **swing bowling** *n.* **swing-bridge** *n.* a drawbridge opening by turning horizontally. **swing-door** *n.* a door which can swing open in either direction. **swinger** *n.* **swinging** *a.* **1** that swings. **2** (*coll.*) lively or up to date. **3** (*coll.*) promiscuous. **swingingly** *adv.* **swing-music** *n.* a style of playing jazz in which the basic melody and rhythm persist through individual interpretations of the theme, impromptu variations etc. **swing of the pendulum** *n.* the regular pattern of change in public opinion, political power etc. **swingometer** (-om´itə) *n.* a device showing the extent of swings in opinion, voting preferences etc. (in an election). **swing-plough**, (*N Am.*) **swing-plow** *n.* a plough without wheels. **swing**

shift *n.* (*N Am.*) a working shift from afternoon until late evening. **swing-wheel** *n.* the wheel driving a clock pendulum, corresponding to the balance wheel of a watch. **swing-wing** *n.* an aircraft having movable wings allowing varying degrees of sweepback at different speeds. **swingy** *a.* (*comp.* **swingier,** *superl.* **swingiest**) **1** (of music) having swing. **2** (of a skirt or dress) designed to swing as the wearer moves. **swung dash** *n.* (*Print.*) a wavy dash (~). [OE *swingan*, cp. Swed. *svinga*, Dan. *svinge*, G *schwingen*]

swingeing (swin´jing) *a.* severe, great, huge. **†swinge** *v.t.* (*pres.p.* **swingeing**) to strike hard, to beat, to thrash. **†swinge-buckler** *n.* a bully; a swashbuckler. **swingeingly** *adv.* [OE *swengan*, causal of *swingan*, SWING]

swingle (swing´gəl) *n.* **1** a wooden instrument for beating flax to separate the woody parts from the fibre. **2** the swinging part of a flail. *~v.t.* to clean (flax) by beating with a swingle. **swingle-bar** *n.* a swingletree. **swingletree** *n.* a crossbar pivoted in the middle, to which traces are attached on a cart etc. [ME *swingelen*, freq. from OE *swingan*, to beat, to SWING]

swinish SWINE.

†swink (swingk) *n.* labour, toil, drudgery. **swinker** *n.* [OE *swincan*, perh. cogn. with SWING]

swipe (swīp) *v.t.* (*coll.*) **1** to hit with great force. **2** to pilfer. **3** to pass (a swipe card) through a machine which can electronically read its encoded information. *~v.i.* to hit out with a swipe. *~n.* a hard, swiping blow. **swipe card** *n.* a credit card, debit card etc. having magnetically encoded information which can be read by an electronic device. **swiper** *n.* [OE *swipian*, cogn. with SWEEP]

swipple (swip´əl) *n.* the swingle of a flail. [ME, prob. SWEEP, -LE[1]]

swirl (swœl) *v.i.* to form eddies, to whirl about. *~v.t.* to carry (along, down etc.) with an eddying motion. *~n.* **1** a whirling motion, an eddy. **2** the act of swirling. **3** a winding or curling pattern or figure. **4** the furious rush of a fish through water, or the disturbance so caused. **swirly** *a.* (*comp.* **swirlier,** *superl.* **swirliest**). [cp. Norw. *svirla*, freq. of *sverra*, to hum, to whirl; cogn. with SWARM[1]]

swish (swish) *v.i.* **1** to make a whistling sound in cutting through the air. **2** to move with such a sound. *~v.t.* **1** to make such a whistling movement with. **2** to strike or cut (off) with such a sound. **3** (*sl.*) to flog, to thrash, esp. with a birch. *~n.* **1** a whistling sound, movement or blow. **2** a stroke with a birch etc. *~a.* (*coll.*) smart, elegant. **swishy** *a.* (*comp.* **swishier,** *superl.* **swishiest**) **1** making a swishing sound. **2** (*sl.*) effeminate. [imit.]

Swiss (swis) *a.* of or relating to Switzerland. *~n.* (*pl.* **Swiss**) a native or inhabitant of Switzerland, or a descendant of one. **Swiss chard** *n.* a variety of beet, *Beta vulgaris*, with stalks and leaves eaten as a vegetable. **Swiss cheese plant** *n.* a climbing house plant, *Monstera deliciosa*, with holes in the leaves. **Swiss Guard, Swiss Guards** *n.* mercenaries formerly employed as bodyguards in France, Naples etc., and still at the Vatican. **Swiss roll** *n.* a thin sponge cake, rolled up around a filling, esp. of jam.

switch (swich) *n.* **1** a mechanism for diverting railway trains or vehicles from one line to another, or for completing or interrupting an electric circuit, transferring current from one wire to another etc. **2** a shift, change. **3** an exchange. **4** a small flexible twig or rod. **5** a (false) tress of hair. **6** a computer system which transfers funds between point-of-sale terminals and institutions. *~v.t.* **1** to turn (on or off) with a switch. **2** to move, to whisk or snatch (away etc.) with a jerk. **3** (*esp. N Am.*) to shift (a train etc.) from one line to another. **4** to lash or beat with a switch. **5** to change, to divert. *~v.i.* **1** to turn an electrical device (on or off) with a switch. **2** to make a change, to shift. **3** to move or swing with a careless or jerking movement, to whisk. **4** to cut (off) connection on a telephone etc. **to switch off** (*coll.*) to stop listening or paying attention, to lose interest. **to switch on** (*coll.*) to become alive or responsive (to). **to switch over** to change, to change over. **Switch®** *n.* a British EFTPOS system. **switchable** *a.* **switchback** *n.* **1** a railway on which the vehicles are carried over a series of ascending inclines by the momentum of previous descents, used for amusement at fairs etc. **2** a zigzag railway for ascending or descending steep inclines. **3** a steeply ascending and descending road, track etc. *~a.* of or relating to a switchback. **switchblade** *n.* a flick knife. **switchboard** *n.* a board on which switches are fixed controlling electric or telephonic circuits. **switched-on** *a.* (*sl.*) **1** up to date, clued up. **2** high, under the influence of drugs. **switcher** *n.* **switchgear** *n.* **1** the switching equipment used to open and close electric circuits. **2** the switches in a motor vehicle. **switchman** *n.* (*pl.* **switchmen**) (*N Am.*) a pointsman. **switch-over** *n.* the act of switching over. [MDut. *swick* (cp. LG *swikk*, G *Swecke*, a tack, a peg, *zwecken*, to prick), cogn. with TWITCH[1]]

swither (swidh´ə) *v.i.* (*Sc.*) to hesitate, to vacillate. *~n.* hesitation, vacillation. [etym. uncertain]

Switzer (swit´sə) *n.* a Swiss, esp. a member of the Swiss Guard.

swivel (swiv´əl) *n.* **1** a link or connection comprising a ring and pivot or other mechanism allowing the two parts to revolve independently. **2** a support allowing free horizontal rotation. **3** a swivel gun. *~v.i., v.t.* (*pres.p.* **swivelling,** (*N Am.*) **swiveling,** *past, p.p.* **swivelled,** (*N Am.*) **swiveled**) to turn on a swivel or pivot. **swivel chair** *n.* a chair that revolves on its base. **swivel-eye** *n.* a squinting eye. **swivel gun** *n.* a gun mounted on a pivot. **swivel-hook** *n.* [OE *swīfan*, see SWIFT, -LE[1]]

swivet (swiv´it) *n.* (*esp. N Am.*) a panic, a fluster. **in a swivet** panicking, flustered. [etym. unknown]

swizz (swiz), **swiz** *n.* (*coll.*) **1** something unfair; a disappointment. **2** a swindle. [abbr. of SWIZZLE]

swizzle (swiz´əl) *n.* (*coll.*) **1** a mixed alcoholic drink of various kinds. **2** a cheat, a fraud. *~v.t.* **1** to stir with a swizzle-stick. **2** (*dial.*) to drink immoderately. **swizzle-stick** *n.* a stick used for frothing or mixing drinks. [perh. rel. to SWIG]

swob SWAB.

swollen SWELL.

swoon (swoon) *v.i.* (*poet.*) **1** to fall into a fainting fit, esp. from excitement. **2** (of music etc.) to sink or die away. *~n.* a faint. **swooningly** *adv.* [ME *swownen*, *swoghenen*, from OE *swogan*, see SOUGH[1]]

swoop (swoop) *v.i.* **1** (of a bird of prey) to descend upon prey etc. suddenly. **2** to come (down upon), to attack suddenly. *~v.t.* (*coll.*) to snatch (up). *~n.* **1** a sudden plunge of or as of a bird of prey on its quarry. **2** a sudden descent, attack, seizing or snatching. **3** (*coll.*) a snatching up of all at once. [OE *swāpan*, to rush (cp. Icel. *sveipa*, G *schweifen*, to rove), cogn. with SWEEP]

swoosh (swoosh) *v.i.* to move with or make a rushing sound. *~n.* such a sound.

swop SWAP.

sword (sawd) *n.* **1** a weapon, usu. consisting of a long blade fixed in a hilt with a guard for the hand, used for cutting or thrusting. **2** the power of the sword, military power or sovereignty. **3** a swordlike body part or object. **4** war, destruction or death in war. **to cross swords** CROSS. **to draw one's sword against** DRAW. **to put to the sword** to kill (esp. those captured or defeated in war). **to sheathe the sword** SHEATHE (under SHEATH). **sword-arm** *n.* the right arm, the arm which wields the sword. **sword bayonet** *n.* a sword-shaped bayonet. **sword-bearer** *n.* an officer who carries a sword of state. **sword belt** *n.* a belt from which a sword is slung.

swordbill *n.* a S American hummingbird, *Ensifera ensifera*, with a long, sword-shaped bill. **sword cane** *n.* a swordstick. **sword dance** *n.* 1 a dance in which swords are brandished or clashed together or in which women pass under crossed swords. 2 a Highland dance performed over two swords laid crosswise on the floor. **swordfish** *n.* (*pl.* **swordfish**) a sea fish, *Xiphias gladius*, allied to the mackerel, having the upper jaw prolonged into a swordlike weapon. **sword grass** *n.* a species of sedge, *Scirpus americanus*, with swordlike leaves. **sword-guard** *n.* the part of a sword hilt protecting the hand. **sword-hand** *n.* the right hand, the hand which wields the sword. **sword knot** *n.* a ribbon or tassel tied to the hilt of a sword, orig. used for securing it to the wrist. **swordless** *a.* **swordlike** *a.* **sword lily** *n.* GLADIOLUS. **sword of Damocles** *n.* a situation of impending disaster. **sword of justice** *n.* judicial authority. **sword of state** *n.* a sword carried before the sovereign on ceremonial occasions. **swordplay** *n.* 1 a combat between gladiators, fencing. 2 repartee. **swordplayer** *n.* **swordproof** *a.* **sword-shaped** *a.* **swordsman** (-mən) *n.* (*pl.* **swordsmen**) 1 a man who carries a sword. 2 a man skilled in the use of the sword. **swordsmanship** *n.* **swordstick** *n.* a hollow walking stick enclosing a long, pointed blade. **sword-swallower** *n.* an entertainer who swallows or appears to swallow sword blades. **swordtail** *n.* 1 a tropical fish, *Xiphophorus helleri*, having a long, swordlike tail. 2 a horseshoe crab. [OE *sweord* (cp. Dut. *zwaard*, G *Schwert*, Icel. *sverth*), etym. uncertain]

swore, sworn SWEAR.

swot (swot) *v.i.*, *v.t.* (*pres.p.* **swotting,** *past, p.p.* **swotted**) (*coll.*) to study hard. ~*n.* 1 a person who studies hard. 2 hard study. 3 a piece of hard work. [var. of SWEAT]

Usage note See note under SWAT.

SWT *abbr.* sheer weight of traffic.

swum SWIM.

swung SWING.

swy (swī) *n.* (*Austral.*) the game of two-up. [G *zwei*, two]

SY *abbr.* 1 Seychelles (IVR). 2 steam yacht.

-sy (si) *suf.* forming diminutive adjectives and nouns, as in *folksy*, *mumsy* etc.

sybarite (sib´ərīt) *n.* a sensual and luxurious person. ~*a.* sensual and luxurious. **sybaritic** (-rit´-), **sybaritical** *a.* **sybaritically** *adv.* **sybaritism** *n.* [*Sybarite*, a native or inhabitant of Sybaris, an ancient Greek colony in S Italy, noted for voluptuousness and luxury]

sybil SIBYL.

sycamine (sik´əmin) *n.* (*Bible*) the black mulberry tree, *Morus nigra* (Luke xvii.6). [L *sȳcamīnus*, Gr. *sukaminos*, perh. from Heb. *shiqmāh*, the SYCAMORE]

sycamore (sik´əmaw) *n.* 1 a large Eurasian maple, *Acer pseudoplatanus*, having winged seeds. 2 the wood of the sycamore. 3 the sycamore fig. **sycamore fig** *n.* (*Bible*) a Syrian and Egyptian fig tree, *Ficus sycomorus*. **sycamore maple** *n.* the Eurasian sycamore. [var. of SYCOMORE]

syce (sīs), **sice** *n.* esp. in the Indian subcontinent, a groom. [Hind., from Arab. *sā'is*, *sāyis*]

sycee (sīsē´), **sycee silver** *n.* pure uncoined silver cast into ingots, usu. bearing the seal of a banker or assayer, and formerly used in China by weight as a medium of exchange. [Chin. *si sze*, fine silk]

sycomore (sik´əmaw) *n.* the sycamore fig. [L *sȳcomorus*, Gr. *sukomoros*, perh. as SYCAMINE, assim. to *sukon*, the fig, *moron*, the mulberry]

syconium (sīkō´niəm) *n.* (*pl.* **syconia** (-niə)) (*Bot.*) an enlarged receptacle which develops into a multiple fruit, such as the fig. [mod. L, from Gr. *sukon*, the fig]

sycophant (sik´əfant) *n.* a servile flatterer, a parasite. ~*v.i.*, *v.t.* to act or flatter in the manner of a sycophant. **sycophancy** *n.* **sycophantic** (-fan´-) *a.* **sycophantically** *adv.* **sycophantish** (-fan´-) *a.* **sycophantize, sycophantise** *v.i.* [L *sȳcophanta*, Gr. *sukophantēs*, etym. uncertain, said to mean orig. an informer against persons exporting figs or plundering the sacred fig trees (*sukon*, a fig, *phainein*, to show)]

sycosis (sīkō´sis) *n.* a pustular eruption or inflammation of the scalp or bearded part of the face. [Gr. *sukōsis*, a figlike ulcer (*sukon*, a fig, -OSIS)]

Sydenham's chorea (sid´ənəmz) *n.* a form of chorea in children, associated with rheumatic fever. [T. *Sydenham*, 1624–89, English physician]

Sydneysider (sid´nisīdə) *n.* (*chiefly Austral.*) a resident of Sydney. **Sydney silkie** (sidni sil´ki) *n.* (*Austral.*) a small, long-haired terrier.

syenite (sī´ənīt) *n.* a granular igneous rock consisting of orthoclase and hornblende, with or without quartz. **syenitic** (-nit´-) *a.* [L *Syēnītes lapis*, the stone of *Syene*, Egypt]

syl- (sil) *pref.* var. of SYN-, used before *l*.

syllabary SYLLABLE.

syllabi SYLLABUS.

syllable (sil´əbəl) *n.* 1 a sound forming a word or part of a word, containing one vowel sound, with or without a consonant or consonants, and uttered at a single effort or vocal impulse. 2 the characters representing a syllable. 3 the least expression or particle of speech. ~*v.i.* to pronounce by syllables, to articulate. **in words of one syllable** expressed clearly or plainly. **syllabary** *n.* (*pl.* **syllabaries**) 1 a catalogue of characters representing syllables. 2 such characters collectively, serving the purpose of an alphabet in certain languages. **syllabic** (-ab´-) *a.* 1 of, relating to, consisting of or based on a syllable or syllables. 2 in prosody, based on the number of syllables. 3 having each syllable distinctly articulated. 4 representing the sound of a whole syllable, as distinct from *alphabetic*. **syllabically** *adv.* **syllabicate** (-lab´-) *v.t.* to syllabify. **syllabication** (-ā´shən) *n.* **syllabicity** (-bis´-) *n.* **syllabify** (-lab´ifī) *v.t.* (*3rd pers. sing. pres.* **syllabifies,** *pres.p.* **syllabifying,** *past, p.p.* **syllabified**) to separate into or pronounce by syllables. **syllabification** (-fikā´shən) *n.* **syllabize, syllabise** *v.t.* to syllabify. **syllabled** *a.* (*usu. in comb.*, as *two-syllabled*). [ME and OF *sillabe*, L *syllaba*, Gr. *sullabē* (*lab-*, base of *lambanein*, to take), assim. to PRINCIPLE etc.]

syllabub (sil´əbŭb), **sillabub** *n.* a dessert made by mixing cream with wine etc., adding flavouring and frothing it up. [etym. unknown]

syllabus (sil´əbəs) *n.* (*pl.* **syllabuses, syllabi** (-bī)) 1 a list, outline, summary, abstract etc., giving the principal points or subjects of a course of lectures, teaching or study, examination requirements, hours of attendance etc. 2 a statement of requirements for an examination. 3 a summary of points decided by the Curia, esp. the list of heretical doctrines etc., forming the appendix to the encyclical letter *Quanta cura* of Pius IX in 1864. [late L, from late Gr. *sullabos*, as SYLLABLE]

syllepsis (silep´sis) *n.* (*pl.* **syllepses** (-sēz)) 1 the application of a word in both the literal and metaphorical senses at the same time. 2 the connection of a verb or adjective with two nouns, with only one of which it is in syntactical agreement. **sylleptic** *a.* **sylleptically** *adv.* [L, from Gr., *sullēpsis*, comprehension (*-lepsis*, from *lambanein*, see SYLLABLE)]

syllogism (sil´əjizm) *n.* 1 a form of argument consisting of three propositions, a major premiss or general statement, a minor premiss or instance, and a third deduced from these, called the conclusion. 2 deductive, as distinct from inductive, reasoning. **syllogistic** (-jis´-) *a.* **syllogistically** *adv.* **syllogize, syllogise** *v.i.*, *v.t.* to reason or deduce by syllogisms. **syllogization** (-zā´shən) *n.* **syllogizer** *n.* [ME and OF *silogime*, L *syllogismum*, nom. *-mus*, Gr. *sullogismos*, from *sullogizesthai*, to reason (*logos*, reason)]

sylph (silf) *n.* **1** a supposed elemental being inhabiting the air, intermediate between material and immaterial beings. **2** a graceful and slender woman or girl. **3** any S American hummingbird of the genus *Aglaiocercus*, with a long, brilliantly-coloured tail. **sylphlike** *a.* [F *sylphe*, prob. from Gr. *silphē*, some beetle or grub]

sylva (sil´və), **silva** *n.* (*pl.* **sylvae** (-vē), **sylvas, silvae, silvas**) **1** the trees of a particular time or place. **2** a catalogue or study of such trees. **sylvan** *a.* (*poet.*) **1** wooded. **2** of or relating to a wood or forest. **3** growing in woods. **4** rural, rustic. ~*n.* **1** a deity of the woods, a satyr. **2** a rustic, a forest-dweller. **sylvatic** (-vat´-), **sylvestrian** (-ves´tri-) *a.* [L *silva*, a wood]

sylvanite (sil´vənīt) *n.* a gold or silver telluride mineral. [Tran*sylvania*, where it was found]

sylviculture SILVICULTURE.

sym- (sim) *pref.* var. of SYN-, used before *b, m* or *p.*

symbiont (sim´biont) *n.* an organism living in a state of symbiosis. **symbiontic** (-on´-) *a.* **symbiosis** (-ō´sis) *n.* (*pl.* **symbioses** (-sēz)) **1** the vital union or partnership of certain organisms, such as the fungus and alga in lichens, as distinct from *antibiosis.* **2** a mutually beneficial relationship between people, things or groups. **3** an instance of symbiosis. **symbiotic** (-ot´-) *a.* **symbiotically** *adv.* [Gr. *sumbiōn -biountos*, pres.p. of *sumbiōnai* (*biōnai*, from *bios*, life)]

symbol (sim´bəl) *n.* **1** an object typifying or representing something by resemblance, association etc., a type, an emblem. **2** a mark, character or letter accepted as representing or signifying some thing, idea, relation, process etc., such as the letters of the alphabet, those representing chemical elements or the signs of mathematical relations. ~*v.t.* (*pres.p.* **symbolling,** (*N Am.*) **symboling,** *past, p.p.* **symbolled,** (*N Am.*) **symboled**) to symbolize. **symbolic** (-bol´-), **symbolical** *a.* of, relating to, serving as or using symbols. **symbolically** *adv.* **symbolicalness** *n.* **symbolic logic** *n.* logic that uses symbols to represent and clarify principles etc. **symbolics** *n.* the study of creeds. **symbolism** *n.* **1** representation by symbols or signs. **2** a system of symbols. **3** symbolic significance. **4** the use of symbols, esp. in art and literature. **5** a late-19th-cent. movement among artists and writers using symbolic images to express or suggest the essential nature of things, mystical ideas, emotions etc. **symbolist** *n.* **symbolistic** (-lis´-) *a.* **symbolize, symbolise** *v.t.* **1** to be the symbol of, to typify. **2** to represent by symbols. **3** to treat as symbolic, not literal, to make symbolic or representative of something. ~*v.i.* to use symbols. **symbolization** (-zā´shən) *n.* **symbolizer** *n.* †**symbology** (-bol´-) *n.* **symbological** (-loj´-) *a.* **symbologist** *n.* **symbololatry** (-lol´-) *n.* symbol-worship. [F *symbole*, L *symbolum*, Gr. *sumbolon*, a token, a pledge, from *sumballein* (*ballein*, to throw)]

symmetry (sim´itri) *n.* (*pl.* **symmetries**) **1** due proportion of the several parts of a body or any whole to each other, congruity, parity, regularity, harmony. **2** beauty of form arising from this. **3** arrangement of parts on either side of a dividing line or point so that the opposite parts are exactly similar in shape and size. **4** regularity of structure so that opposite halves exactly correspond. **5** (*Bot.*) regularity of number in sepals, petals, stamens etc., each whorl composed of the same number or multiples of this. **symmetral** *a.* **symmetric** (-met´-), **symmetrical** *a.* **symmetrically** *adv.* **symmetricalness** *n.* **symmetrize, symmetrise** *v.t.* **symmetrization** (-zā´shən) *n.* [F *symmetrie*, L *symmetria*, Gr. *summetria*, from *summetros*, commensurate (*metron*, measure)]

sympathy (sim´pəthi) *n.* (*pl.* **sympathies**) **1** the quality of being affected with the same feelings as another person, or of sharing emotions, affections, inclinations etc. with another person. **2** fellow feeling, agreement, harmony. **3** (*often pl.*) a feeling of accord (with). **4** loyalty or support. **5** compassion (for). **6** unity or correlation of action. **7** response of an organ or part to an affection in another without actual transmission of the cause. **8** the relation between inanimate bodies by which the vibration of one sets up a corresponding vibration in another. ~*a.* showing loyalty or support (*a sympathy strike*). **in sympathy with 1** showing sympathy for. **2** showing loyalty or support for. **sympathectomy** (-ek´-) *n.* (*pl.* **sympathectomies**) surgical removal of a sympathetic ganglion etc. **sympathetic** (-thet´-) *a.* **1** of, relating to, expressive of or due to sympathy. **2** having sympathy or common feeling with another, sympathizing. **3** being or acting in sympathy or agreement, concordant. **4** in accord with one's mood or disposition, congenial. **5** proceeding from or due to pain or injury in another organ or part. **6** of, relating to or mediated by the sympathetic nervous system. **7** (of acoustic, electrical, and other vibrations) produced by impulses from other vibrations. **sympathetically** *adv.* **sympathetic ink** *n.* invisible ink. **sympathetic magic** *n.* a type of magic involving performing an associated action or using an associated thing. **sympathetic nervous system** *n.* the part of the autonomic nervous system in which nerve impulses are transmitted chiefly by adrenalin and related substances. **sympathize, sympathise** *v.i.* **1** to have or express sympathy with another, in pain, pleasure etc. **2** to be of the same disposition, opinion etc. **sympathizer** *n.* **sympathomimetic** (-thōmimet´-) *a.* having or causing physiological effects like those produced by the sympathetic nervous system. [F *sympathie*, L *sympathīa*, Gr. *sumpatheia*, from *sumpathēs*, sympathetic (*pathein*, *paschein*, to suffer)]

sympatric (simpat´rik) *a.* (*Biol.*) occurring in the same geographical area, as distinct from *allopatric.* [Gr., *patra*, fatherland]

sympetalous (simpet´ələs) *a.* having the petals joined.

symphony (sim´fəni) *n.* (*pl.* **symphonies**) **1** a complex and elaborate composition for an orchestra, usu. consisting of four varied movements. **2** an instrumental passage or composition occurring as an interlude in or introduction to a vocal work. **3** a symphony orchestra. **4** a harmonious composition. **symphonic** (-fon´-) *a.* **symphonically** *adv.* **symphonic poem** *n.* a tone poem. **symphonious** (-fō´-) *a.* **symphonist** *n.* a composer or performer of symphonies. **symphony orchestra** *n.* a large orchestra containing wind, string and percussion sections. [OF *symphonie*, L *symphōnia*, Gr. *sumphōnia*, from *sumphōnos*, agreeing in sound (*phōnē*, sound)]

symphyllous (sim´filəs) *a.* (*Bot.*) having the leaves joined. [Gr. *phullon*, a leaf]

symphysis (sim´fisis) *n.* (*pl.* **symphyses** (-sēz)) **1** (*Anat.*) (the joint formed by) the union of two parts of the skeleton by growing together or the intervention of cartilage. **2** (*Bot.*) the growing together or union of two plant parts. **symphyseal** (-fiz´iəl), **symphysial** *a.* [Gr. *sumphusis*, from *sumphuēs*, grown together (*phuein*, to grow)]

sympiesometer (simpiizom´itə) *n.* **1** an instrument for measuring the pressure or velocity of a current of water. **2** a barometer in which atmospheric pressure is measured by the compression of a small quantity of gas behind a column of liquid. [Gr. *sumpiezein* (*piezein*, to squeeze)]

symploce (sim´plōsē) *n.* the repetition of a word or phrase at the beginning and of another at the end of successive clauses. [Gr. *sumplokē* (*plekein*, to twine)]

sympodium (simpō´diəm) *n.* (*pl.* **sympodia** (-diə)) (*Bot.*) a false plant axis or stem composed of superimposed branches. **sympodial** *a.* [Gr. *pous podos*, a foot]

symposia SYMPOSIUM.
symposiarch (simpō´ziahk) *n.* **1** the president or director of a feast. **2** a toastmaster. **3** the leading spirit of a social or convivial meeting.
symposium (simpō´ziəm) *n.* (*pl.* **symposia** (-ziə), **symposiums**) **1** a conference or formal meeting at which several speakers give addresses on a particular topic. **2** a series of brief articles expressing the views of different writers, in a magazine etc. **3** a drinking party. **4** in ancient Greece, a drinking together, a convivial party, usu. following a banquet, with music, dancing etc. **symposiac** (-ak) *a.* **symposial** *a.* [L, from Gr. *sumposion* (*po-*, base of *pinein*, to drink, cp. *posis*, drink)]
symptom (simp´təm) *n.* **1** (*Med.*) a perceptible change in the appearance or functions of the body indicating disease. **2** a sign, a token, an indication. **symptomatic** (-mat´-), **symptomatical** *a.* **symptomatically** *adv.* **symptomatology** (-mətol´-) *n.* **1** a branch of medicine concerned with disease symptoms. **2** the symptoms associated with a disease. **symptomless** *a.* [OF *symptome*, L *symptōma*, Gr. *sumptōma -matos*, a chance, a casualty, from *sumpiptein* (*piptein*, to fall)]
syn. *abbr.* **1** synonym. **2** synonymous.
syn- (sin) *pref.* **1** with. **2** together. **3** alike. [Gr. *sun-* (pref.) *sun* (prep.) with]
synaeresis (siniə´risis), (*N Am.*) **syneresis** *n.* (*pl.* **synaereses** (-sēz), (*N Am.*) **synereses**) **1** the contraction of two vowels or syllables into one. **2** (*Chem.*) the expulsion of liquid from a gel by contraction. [L, from Gr. *sunairesis* (*haireein*, to take)]
synaesthesia (sinisthē´ziə), (*N Am.*) **synesthesia** *n.* **1** (*Psych.*) the subjective sensation of a sense other than the sense being stimulated. **2** sensation experienced at a point distinct from the point of stimulation. **synaesthetic** (-thet´-) *a.* [cp. HYPERAESTHESIA]
synagogue (sin´əgog) *n.* **1** a Jewish congregation for religious instruction and observances. **2** a building or place of meeting for this. **synagogal** (-gog´-), **synagogical** (-goj´-) *a.* [F, from L *synagōga*, Gr. *sunagōgē* (*agein*, to bring)]
synalepha (sinəlē´fə) *n.* a blending of two syllables into one, esp. by the suppression of a final vowel before an initial vowel. [Gr. *sunaloiphē* (*aleiphein*, to smear)]
synallagmatic (sinəlagmat´ik) *a.* (of a contract or treaty) imposing reciprocal obligations. [Gr. *sunallagmatikos* (*allassein*, to exchange)]
synantherous (sinan´thərəs) *a.* (*Bot.*) having the anthers growing together.
synanthous (sinan´thəs) *a.* (*Bot.*) having flowers and leaves appearing at the same time. [Gr. *anthos*, a flower]
synaphea (sinəfē´ə) *n.* continuity between lines or portions of lines in verse, esp. when the last syllable of a line is made long or elided by synalepha with the initial syllable of the next. [Gr. *sunapheia* (*haptein*, to join)]
synapse (sī´naps) *n.* (*Anat.*) the point at which a nerve impulse is transmitted from one neuron to another. **synapsis** (sinap´sis) *n.* (*pl.* **synapses** (-sēz)) **1** (*Anat.*) a synapse. **2** (*Biol.*) the pairing of homologous chromosomes occurring at the start of cell division by meiosis. **synaptic** (sin-) *a.* **synaptically** *adv.* [Gr. *synapsis*, junction, from *sunaptein* (*haptein*, to fasten)]
synarthrosis (sinahthrō´sis) *n.* (*pl.* **synarthroses** (-sēz)) (*Anat.*) a fixed bone joint. [Gr. *arthrōsis*, jointing, from *arthron*, a joint]
sync (singk), **synch** *n.* (*coll.*) synchronization. ~*v.t.*, *v.i.* (*pres.p.* **syncing, synching,** *past, p.p.* **synced, synched**) to synchronize. **in sync** well matched, working well together. **out of sync** badly matched, not working well together.
syncarp (sin´kahp) *n.* an aggregate fruit, such as the blackberry. **syncarpous** (-kah´-) *a.* [Gr. *karpos*, fruit]
syncategorematic (sinkatigawrəmat´ik) *a.* (*Logic*) denoting words that can express only parts of terms, such as adverbs, prepositions etc. [Gr. *sunkatēgorēmatikos*]
synch SYNC.
synchondrosis (singkondrō´sis) *n.* (*pl.* **synchondroses** (-sēz)) (*Anat.*) the almost immovable articulation of bones by means of cartilage, as in the vertebrae. [Gr. *sunchondrōsis* (*chondros*, cartilage)]
synchoresis (sinkōrē´sis) *n.* in rhetoric, a concession made for the purpose of retorting more effectively. [Gr. *sunchoresis* (*choros*, space)]
synchro- (sing´krō) *comb. form* **1** synchronized. **2** synchronous.
synchrocyclotron (singkrōsī´klətron) *n.* (*Physics*) a cyclotron which can achieve higher frequencies by decreasing the frequency of the accelerating field as the energy and mass of the particles increase.
synchromesh (sing´krəmesh) *a.* of or relating to a system of gearing in which the drive and driving members are automatically synchronized before engagement, thus avoiding shock and noise in changing gear. ~*n.* such a system.
synchronology (singkrənol´əji) *n.* comparative chronology.
synchronous (sing´krənəs) *a.* **1** occurring simultaneously. **2** operating or recurring together at the same rate. **synchronal** *a.* **synchronic** (-kron´-) *a.* applied to the study of a subject, e.g. language, at a particular time, as distinct from *diachronic*. **synchronically** *adv.* **synchronicity** (-nis´-) *n.* **1** an apparently significant simultaneous occurrence of events with no obvious connection. **2** synchrony. **synchronism** *n.* **1** synchrony. **2** the process of matching the soundtrack of a film exactly with the picture. **synchronistic** (-nis´-) *a.* **synchronistically** *adv.* **synchronize, synchronise** *v.t.* **1** to cause to occur in unison or at the same time. **2** (*loosely*) to combine, coordinate. **3** to cause to agree in time or indicate the same time. **4** to match the soundtrack of (a film) exactly with the picture. ~*v.i.* **1** to concur in time, to happen at the same time. **2** (of clocks or watches) to be synchronized. **synchronization** (-zā´shən) *n.* **synchronized swimming** *n.* a sport in which a team of swimmers performs a series of coordinated dancelike movements to music. **synchronizer** *n.* **synchronously** *adv.* **synchronous motor** *n.* an electric motor whose speed is proportional to the frequency of the supply current. **synchrony** *n.* **1** the state of being synchronous or synchronic. **2** the treatment of occurrences as being synchronous. [late L, *synchronus*, from Gr. *sugkhronos* (as SYN-, *chronos*, time]

Usage note The use of *synchronize* to mean combine or coordinate is sometimes disapproved of.

synchrotron (sing´krətron) *n.* (*Physics*) a very high-energy particle accelerator. **synchrotron radiation** *n.* (*Physics*) electromagnetic radiation emitted by a charged particle spinning in a magnetic field.
synchysis (sing´kisis) *n.* **1** a confused arrangement of words in a sentence. **2** (*Med.*) a diseased condition of the eye caused by cholesterol floating in the vitreous humour. [Gr. *sunchusis*, confusion (*cheein*, to pour)]
synclastic (sinklas´tik) *a.* (*Geom.*) having uniform curvature, convex or concave in every direction. [Gr. *klastos*, broken]
synclinal (singklī´nəl) *a.* sloping downwards towards a common point or line, as distinct from *anticlinal*. **syncline** (sing´-) *n.* a synclinal flexure or axis. [Gr. *klīnein*, to lean]
syncopate (sing´kəpāt) *v.t.* **1** (*Mus.*) to modify (a musical note, rhythm etc.) by beginning on an unaccented and continuing with an accented beat. **2** to contract (a

word) by omitting one or more letters or syllables from the middle. **syncopation** (-āʹshən) *n.* **syncopator** *n.* [L *syncopātus*, p.p. of *syncopāre*, orig. to swoon, as SYNCOPE]

syncope (singʹkəpi) *n.* **1** (*Gram.*) the elision of a letter or syllable from the middle of a word. **2** (*Med.*) a faint. **syncopal, syncopic** (-kopʹ-) *a.* **syncoptic** (-kopʹ-) *a.* [L *syncopē*, Gr. *sunkopē* (*koptein*, to strike)]

syncretism (singʹkritizm) *n.* **1** the attempted reconciliation of various philosophic or religious schools or systems of thought, for example against a common opponent. **2** the fusion of inflectional varieties in the development of a language. **syncretic** (-kretʹ-) *n.* **syncretist** *n.* **syncretistic** (-tisʹ-) *a.* **syncretize, syncretise** *v.t.* [Gr. *sunkrētismos*, from *sunkrētizein* (*krētizein*, etym. uncertain)]

syncytium (sinsitʹiəm) *n.* (*pl.* **syncytia** (-tiə)) (*Biol.*) a mass of cytoplasm containing several nuclei. **syncytial** *a.*

syndactyl (sindakʹtil) *a.* having the digits united, as in webbed feet. **syndactylism** *n.* **syndactylous** *a.* syndactyl. [Gr. *daktūlos*, a finger]

syndesis (sinʹdisis) *n.* (*pl.* **syndeses** (-sēz)) (*Biol.*) synapsis. [mod. L, from Gr. *sundesmos*, see SYNDESMOSIS]

syndesmosis (sindezmōʹsis) *n.* (*pl.* **syndesmoses** (-sēz)) an articulation of bones by ligaments. **syndesmotic** (-motʹ-) *a.* [Gr. *sundesmos*, binding (*desmos*, a bond, from *deein*, to bind), -OSIS]

syndetic (sindetʹik) *a.* (*Gram.*) serving to connect, copulative. [cp. ASYNDETON]

syndic (sinʹdik) *n.* **1** an officer or magistrate invested with varying powers in different places and times. **2** a member of a special committee of the senate of Cambridge University. **3** a business agent of a university, corporation etc. **syndical** *a.* [F, from L *syndicus*, Gr. *sundikos* (*dikē*, justice)]

syndicalism (sinʹdikəlizm) *n.* (*Hist.*) the economic doctrine that all the workers in any trade or industry should participate in the management and control and in the division of the profits. **syndicalist** *n.* [see SYNDIC]

syndicate[1] (sinʹdikət) *n.* **1** an association of people or firms formed to promote some special interest or undertake a joint project. **2** an agency which supplies material for simultaneous publication in several newspapers or periodicals. **3** a body of syndics, esp. at Cambridge University. [F *syndicat*, from med. L *syndicatus*, from late L *syndicus*, see SYNDIC]

syndicate[2] (sinʹdikāt) *v.t.* **1** to combine in a syndicate. **2** to sell for simultaneous publication in several newspapers or periodicals. **3** to sell (a television programme) for broadcasting by several different stations. **4** to manage by means of a syndicate. **syndication** (-āʹshən) *n.*

syndrome (sinʹdrōm) *n.* **1** the aggregate of symptoms characteristic of any disease or disorder. **2** a pattern or set of feelings, actions etc. characteristic of a condition or problem. **3** concurrence. **syndromic** (-dromʹ-) *a.* [Gr. *sundromē* (*dramein*, to run)]

syne (sīn), **sine** *adv.*, *conj.*, *prep.* (*Sc.*) since. **auld lang syne** AULD. [SINCE]

synecdoche (sinekʹdəki) *n.* a figure of speech by which a part is put for the whole or the whole for a part. **synecdochic** (-dokʹ-), **synecdochical** *a.* [L, from Gr. *sunekdochē* (*ek*, out, *dechesthai*, to receive)]

synechia (sinekīʹə) *n.* (*Med.*) an abnormal adhesion of the iris to the cornea or to the capsule of the crystalline lens. [Gr. *sunecheia* (*echein*, to have, to hold)]

synecious SYNOECIOUS.

synecology (sinikolʹəji) *n.* the ecology of plant and animal communities. **synecologic** (-ēkəlojʹ-), **synecological** *a.* **synecologist** *n.*

synecphonesis (sinekfōnēʹsis) *n.* synaeresis. [Gr. *synekphōnēsis* (*ek-*, out, *phōnein*, to sound)]

syneresis SYNAERESIS.

synergy (sinʹəji) *n.* (*pl.* **synergies**) **1** the working together of two drugs, muscles etc. so that their combined action exceeds the sum of their individual actions. **2** an instance of synergy. **synergism** (-jizm) *n.* **1** synergy. **2** an instance of synergy. **3** (*Theol.*) the doctrine that human energy cooperates with divine grace in the work of salvation. **synergetic** (-jetʹ-) *a.* **synergetically** *adv.* **synergic** *a.* **synergist** *n.* something that acts with, or increases the effect of, another thing. **synergistic** (-jisʹ-) *a.* [Gr. *sunergos* (*ergos*, work)]

synesis (sinʹisis) *n.* a grammatical construction according to the sense rather than syntax. [Gr. *sunesis*, understanding (*hienai*, to send)]

synesthesia SYNAESTHESIA.

syngamy (singʹgəmi) *n.* (*Biol.*) sexual reproduction by union of gametes. **syngamic** (-gamʹ-), **syngamous** (singʹ-) *a.*

syngenesious (sinjinēʹsiəs) *a.* (*Bot.*) having the anthers cohering.

syngenesis (sinjenʹisis) *n.* reproduction by the union of the ovum and the spermatozoon. **syngenetic** (-jinetʹ-) *a.*

synizesis (sinizēʹsis) *n.* (*pl.* **synizeses** (-ēsēz)) synaeresis involving the combination into one syllable in the pronunciation of two vowels that cannot make a diphthong. [Gr. *sunizēsis* (*hizein*, to seal)]

synod (sinʹəd) *n.* **1** an ecclesiastical council. **2** a Presbyterian council intermediate between the presbyteries and the General Assembly. **3** a deliberative assembly, a meeting for discussion. **synodal** *a.* **synodic** (-nodʹ-) *a.* (*Astron.*) of or relating to the conjunction of heavenly bodies. **synodical** *a.* **synodically** *adv.* **synodic period** *n.* the time between the conjunctions of a planet with the sun. [F *synode*, L *synodum*, nom. *-dus*, Gr. *sunodos* (*hodos*, way)]

synoecious (sinēʹshəs), (*NAm.*) **synecious** *a.* (*Bot.*) having male and female organs in the same inflorescence or receptacle. [Gr. *sunoikia* (*oikos*, a house), -OUS]

synonym (sinʹənim) *n.* **1** a word having much the same meaning as another of the same language. **2** a word denoting the same thing but differing in some senses, or in range of application. **synonymatic** (-nonimatʹ-), **synonymatical, synonymic** (-nimʹ-) *a.* **synonymicon** (-nimʹikon) *n.* (*pl.* **synonymicons**) a dictionary of synonyms. **synonymist** (-nonʹ-) *n.* **synonymity** (-nimʹ-) *n.* **synonymize** (-nonʹ-), **synonymise** *v.t.* to express by synonyms or a synonym. **synonymous** (-nonʹ-) *a.* **1** having the same meaning, conveying the same idea. **2** expressing the same thing by a different word or words. **synonymously** *adv.* **synonymousness** *n.* **synonymy** (-nonʹimi) *n.* (*pl.* **synonymies**) **1** the condition or fact of being synonymous, synonymity. **2** the use of synonyms for emphasis. **3** a treatise on synonyms; a dictionary or list of synonyms. [F *synonime*, L *synōnyma*, Gr. *sunōnumos*, of like meaning or name (*onuma -atos*, name)]

synopsis (sinopʹsis) *n.* (*pl.* **synopses** (-sēz)) a general view, a conspectus, a summary. **synopsize, synopsise** *v.t.* **synoptic** *a.* **1** of or relating to a synopsis. **2** affording a general view. **3** of or relating to the Synoptic Gospels. **4** giving a general view of the weather. **synoptical** *a.* **synoptically** *adv.* **Synoptic Gospels** *n.pl.* the Gospels of Matthew, Mark and Luke. **synoptist** *n.* the writer of any of the Synoptic Gospels. [L, from Gr. *synopsis* (*opsis*, seeing, from *op-*, to see)]

synostosis (sinostōʹsis) *n.* (*Anat.*) union of different parts of the skeleton by means of bone. **synosteotomy** (-otʹəmi) *n.* (*pl.* **synosteotomies**). [Gr. *osteon*, bone]

synovia (sīnōʹviə) *n.* an albuminous lubricating fluid secreted by the synovial membranes lining joints and tendon sheaths. **synovial** *a.* of, relating to or secreting synovia. **synovial membrane** *n.* a membrane of connective tissue secreting synovial fluid. **synovitis** (-əvī´tis) *n.* inflammation of the synovial membrane. [L *ovum*, an egg]

syntactic, syntactical etc. SYNTAX.

syntagma (sintag´mə) *n.* (*pl.* **syntagmas, syntagmata** (-mətə)) **1** a word or phrase forming a syntactic unit. **2** a systematic collection of statements. **syntagmatic** (-mat´-) *a.* **syntagmic** *a.* [late L, from Gr. *suntagma* (as SYNTAX)]

syntax (sin´taks) *n.* **1** (the part of grammar that deals with) the due arrangement of words forming units or the construction of sentences etc. **2** a set of rules for constructing sentences etc. **3** a treatise on syntax. **syntactic** (-tak´-) *a.* of, relating to or according to the rules of syntax. **syntactical** *a.* **syntactically** *adv.* **syntactics** *n.* the branch of semiology dealing with the formal relations and properties of signs. [F *syntaxe*, late L *syntaxis*, Gr. *suntaxis* (*tassein*, to arrange)]

synteresis (sintərē´sis) *n.* the habit of mind which enables one to make primary moral judgements, conscience; remorse. [Gr. *sunteresis*, watching closely]

synth (sinth) *n.* (*coll.*) a synthesizer.

synthesis (sin´thəsis) *n.* (*pl.* **syntheses** (-sēz)) **1** the building up of a complex whole by the union of elements, esp. the process of forming concepts, general ideas, theories etc. **2** the putting of two or more things together, combination, composition. **3** (*Chem.*) the production of a substance by chemical reaction. **4** the formation of compound words by means of composition and inflection, as distinct from *analysis*. **5** the uniting of divided parts in surgery. **synthesist** *n.* a user of synthesis. **synthesize, synthesise** *v.t.* **1** to make a synthesis of. **2** to combine into a synthesis. **synthesizer** *n.* **1** a keyboard-operated electronic instrument which can produce and manipulate a wide variety of sounds, imitate conventional musical instruments etc. **2** a person who or something which synthesizes. **synthetic** (-thet´-), **synthetical** *a.* **1** artificially produced, man-made. **2** false, sham. **3** of, relating to or consisting in synthesis. **synthetically** *adv.* **synthetic resin** *n.* a substance similar to vegetable resin obtained by the chemical synthesis of various organic materials. **synthetist** *n.* a synthesist. [L, from Gr. *sunthesis*, (*thesis*, putting, see THESIS)]

sypher (sī´fə) *v.t.* to join (planks etc.) with bevelled and overlapping edges so as to leave a flush surface. [etym. uncertain]

syphilis (sif´ilis) *n.* an infectious venereal disease caused by the spirochaete *Treponema*, introduced into the system by direct contact or due to heredity, affecting first the genitals, then the skin and mucous membranes and finally the muscles, bones and brain. **syphilitic** (-lit´-) *a.* **syphilize, syphilise** *v.t.* **syphilization** (-zā´shən) *n.* **syphiloid** *a.* **syphilology** (-ol´-) *n.* the branch of medicine dealing with the study and treatment of syphilis. [F, from mod. L *Syphilus*, shepherd in a poem by Frascatorio (16th cent.)]

syphon (sī´fən), **siphon** *n.* **1** a tube shaped like an inverted U or V, having one branch longer than the other, used for conveying liquid over the edge of a cask, tank etc., to a lower level, through the force of atmospheric pressure. **2** a bottle for holding aerated water, discharging through a syphon-like tube through the pressure of the gas, a soda syphon. **3** (*Zool.*) (**siphon**) a suctorial or other tubular organ, esp. in cephalopods, gastropods etc. ~*v.t.* to convey or draw (off) by a syphon. ~*v.i.* to flow or be conveyed by a syphon. **siphonal** *a.* **siphonet** (-nit) *n.* any one of the abdominal tubes through which the honeydew is exuded by an aphis. **syphonage** (-nij) *n.* **syphon bottle** *n.* (*chiefly N Am.*) a soda syphon. **syphonic** (-fon´-) *a.* [F, from L *sīphōnem*, nom. *-pho*, Gr. *siphōn*, pipe]

SYR *abbr.* Syria (IVR).

syren SIREN.

Syrian (sir´iən) *a.* of or relating to Syria in the Middle East. ~*n.* a native or inhabitant of Syria, or a descendant of one. **Syriac** (sir´iak) *n.* the language of the ancient Syrians, western Aramaic. ~*a.* of or relating to Syria. [L *Syriacus*, Gr. *Suriakos*, from *Suria*, from *Suros*, Syrian]

syringa (siring´gə) *n.* (*pl.* **syringas**) **1** the mock orange. **2** any plant of the genus *Syringa*, containing the lilacs. [SYRINX (the stems being formerly used for the stems of Turkish pipes)]

syringe (sirinj´) *n.* a cylindrical instrument with a piston used to draw in a quantity of liquid by suction and eject or inject it in a stream, spray or jet. ~*v.t.* (*pres.p.* **syringing**) to water, spray or cleanse with a syringe. [OF *seringue*, L *syrinx -ingem*, from Gr. SYRINX]

syringo- (siring´gō) *comb. form* a syrinx.

syrinx (sir´ingks) *n.* (*pl.* **syrinxes, syringes** (-in´jēz)) **1** a set of pan pipes. **2** a narrow gallery cut in the rock in ancient Egyptian tombs. **3** the organ of song in birds, the inferior larynx, a modification of the trachea where it joins the bronchi. **4** the Eustachian tube. **5** a surgically made passage or fistula. **syringeal** (-rin´jiəl) *a.* **syringitis** (-jī´-) *n.* inflammation of the Eustachian tube. [L, from Gr. *surinx -ingos*, reed, shepherd's pipe]

Syro- (sī´rō) *comb. form* Syrian, Syriac. [Gr. *Suros*, SYRIAN]

Syroarabian (sīrōərā´biən) *a.* of, relating to or comprising Syriac and Arabic.

Syrophoenician (sīrōfənish´ən) *a.* (*Hist.*) of or relating to Syrophoenicia, a Roman province in W Asia.

syrphid (sœ´fid) *a.* of or relating to the dipteran family Syrphidae, including the hoverflies. ~*n.* a fly belonging to the Syrphidae. [mod. L *Syrphidae*, from the genus name *Syrphis*, from Gr. *surphos*, a gnat]

syrup (sir´əp), (*N Am.*) **sirup** *n.* **1** a saturated solution of sugar in water, usu. combined with fruit juice etc. for use in cookery, as a beverage etc., or with a medicinal substance. **2** the uncrystallizable fluid separated from sugar-cane juice in the process of refining molasses, treacle. **3** excessive sweetness or sentimentality. **syrupy** *a.* [OF *syrop* (F *sirop*), Arab. *sharāb*, a beverage, see SHERBET]

sys- (sis) *pref.* var. of SYN-, used before *s*.

SYSOP (sis´op) *n.* (*Comput.*) a system operator.

syssarcosis (sisahkō´sis) *n.* (*pl.* **syssarcoses** (-ō´sēz)) (*Anat.*) a connection of parts of the skeleton by intervening muscle. [Gr. *sussarkōsis* (*sarkoein*, from *sarx sarkos*, flesh)]

systaltic (sistal´tik) *a.* (of the heart) alternately contracting and dilating, pulsatory. [late L *systalticus*, Gr. *sustaltikos* (*stellein*, to place)]

system (sis´təm) *n.* **1** coordinated arrangement, organized combination, organization, method. **2** an established method or procedure. **3** a coordinated body of principles, facts, theories, doctrines etc. **4** a logical grouping, a method or plan of classification. **5** a coordinated arrangement or organized combination or assembly of things or parts, for working together, performing a particular function etc. **6** a group of related or linked natural objects, such as mountains, the rocks of a geological period etc. **7** any complex and coordinated whole. **8** any organic structure taken as a whole, such as the animal body, the universe etc. **9** a method of selecting one's procedure in gambling etc. **10** (*Comput.*) a group of related hardware units or programs. **11** any of seven types of crystal structure. **12** a major group of geological strata. **13** (*Mus.*) the braced staves of a score. **the system** the establishment, bureaucracy or society generally, esp. when regarded as a destroyer of individualism. **to get something out of one's system** (*coll.*) to rid oneself of a worry or a preoccupation. **systematic** (-mat´-), **systematical** *a.* **1** methodical. **2** done, formed or arranged on a regular plan, not haphazard. **3** taxonomic. **systematically** *adv.* **systematics** *n.* the study of classification, taxonomy. **systematic theology** *n.* a kind of theology in which religious truths are arranged into a self-consistent whole. **systematism** *n.* **systematist** *n.* **systematize, systematise** *v.t.* **1** to make systematic. **2** to create a system for. **systematization** (-zā´shən) *n.* **systematizer** *n.* **systematology** (-tol´-) *n.* systematics. **system building** *n.* a method of building using factory-made standardized components. **systemic** (-stem´-, -stē´-) *a.* **1** of, relating to or affecting the bodily system as a whole. **2** (of blood circulation) not pulmonary. **3** (of an insecticide etc.) absorbed by the tissues of a plant etc., thus making it toxic. **systemically** *adv.* **systemize, systemise** *v.t.* to systematize. **systemization** (-zā´shən) *n.* **systemizer** *n.* **systemless** *a.* **system-maker, system-monger** *n.* a person who is keen on forming systems. **system operator** *n.* (*Comput.*) a person who is in charge of the running of an electronic bulletin board. **systems analysis** *n.* the analysis of an industrial, medical, business etc. procedure or task in order to identify its requirements and devise a computer system to fulfil these. **systems analyst** *n.* **systems operator** *n.* (*Comput.*) a person who is in charge of the running of complex electronic systems. [L *systēma*, Gr. *sustēma -matos* (SYN-, *stē-*, to set, from *sta-*, see STASIS)]

systole (sis´təli) *n.* the contraction of the heart forcing the blood outwards, as distinct from *diastole*. **systole and diastole 1** the pulse. **2** (*fig.*) regular reaction. **3** fluctuation. **systolic** (-tol´-) *a.* [Gr. *sustolē*, from *sustellein*, to draw together, see SYSTALTIC]

systyle (sis´tīl) *a.* (*Archit.*) having columns set only two diameters apart. [late L *systylos*, Gr. *sustulos* (SYN-, STYLE)]

syzygy (siz´iji) *n.* (*pl.* **syzygies**) **1** (*Astron.*) the conjunction or opposition of any two of the heavenly bodies, esp. of a planet with the sun. **2** a pair of connected things. **3** conjunction or union. **syzygetic** (-jet´-) *a.* **syzygetically** *adv.* [L *syzygia*, Gr. *suzugia*, from *suzeugnunai*, to yoke together (SYN-, *zugon*, a yoke)]

T

T[1] (tē), **t** (*pl.* **Ts, T's**) the 20th letter of the English and other versions of the Roman alphabet, corresponding to the Greek tau (Τ, τ). It is pronounced as a voiceless dental or alveolar plosive or, if followed by *h*, as a voiced or voiceless dental or alveolar fricative, as in *then, think* etc. ~*n.* a T-shaped thing or part. **to a T** perfectly, to a nicety (*The working hours suit her to a T*). **T-bandage** *n.* a bandage in the shape of a T. **T-bar** *n.* **1** a metal etc. bar in the shape of a 'T'. **2** a T-bar lift. **3** a shoe or sandal fastening with one strap coming up the foot and another crossing over it. **T-bar lift** *n.* a ski lift made up of a series of inverted T-bars. **T-bone** *n.* a bone in the shape of a T, as in a sirloin steak. **T-junction** *n.* a place where a road joins another road at right angles without crossing over it. **T-shirt** *n.* an informal light-weight, short-sleeved garment for the upper body (so called because when it is laid out flat it resembles the shape of the letter T). **T-square** *n.* a T-shaped ruler used for measuring and drawing right angles.

T[2] *chem. symbol* tritium.

T[3] *abbr.* **1** temperature. **2** tera-. **3** tesla. **4** Thailand (IVR). **5** thymus. **T-lymphocyte, T-cell** *n.* a type of lymphocyte produced or processed by the thymus gland.

t, t. *abbr.* **1** TARE[1]. **2** teaspoon, teaspoonful. **3** temperature. **4** tempo. **5** tense. **6** tenor. **7** ton(s). **8** tonne(s). **9** town. **10** transitive.

t' (tə) *a.* (*dial.*) the (*trouble at t'mill*).

't (t) *pron.* (*poet. or coll.*) it (*'Tis true*).

TA *abbr.* Territorial Army.

Ta *chem. symbol* tantalum.

ta (tah) *int.* (*coll.*) thank you. [etym. uncertain]

taal (tahl) *n.* (*S Afr.*) the Afrikaans language. [Dut., language]

TAB *abbr.* **1** (*Austral.*) Totalizator Agency Board. **2** typhoid-paratyphoid A and B (vaccine).

tab[1] (tab) *n.* **1** a small flap, tag, tongue etc., as the flap of a shoe, the tag or tip of lace etc. **2** a small paper flap attached to a file for identification purposes. **3** a strap, a loop. **4** military insignia. **5** (*N Am., coll.*) the bill, the cost (*The company picked up the tab for the meal*). **6** a check, close surveillance. **7 a** any of several loops that hold up a stage curtain. **b** the stage curtain itself. ~*v.t.* (*pres.p.* **tabbing,** *past, p.p.* **tabbed**) to put a tab or tabs on something. **to keep tabs on 1** (*coll.*) to keep a watch on. **2** (*coll.*) to keep a record or account of. [prob. rel. to TAPE]

tab[2] (tab) *n.* (*coll.*) a tabulator on a computer or type-writer keyboard (*Input the data and then press tab*). ~*v.t.* (*pres.p.* **tabbing,** *past, p.p.* **tabbed**) to tabulate.

tab[3] (tab) *n.* (*sl.*) a tablet or small piece of paper impregnated with a drug, esp. an illegal one.

tabard (tab´əd) *n.* **1** a sleeveless jacket, tunic or overall. **2** an outer garment worn over armour. **3** a herald's sleeveless coat blazoned with the arms of the sovereign. [OF, etym. uncertain]

tabaret (tab´əret) *n.* a fabric of alternate satin and watered-silk stripes used for upholstery. [prob. from TABBY]

Tabasco® (təbas´kō) *n.* a hot, capsicum sauce, used for flavouring Mexican dishes, tomato juice etc. [*Tabasco*, Mexican state]

tabbouleh (təboo´lā) *n.* a type of Mediterranean salad made from cracked wheat, tomatoes and cucumber and flavoured with mint, lemon juice and olive oil. [Arab. *tabbulah*]

tabby (tab´i) *n.* (*pl.* **tabbies**) **1** a tabby cat. **2** a cat, esp. a female cat. **3 a** silk or other fabric with a watered appearance. **b** a garment of this. **4** (*coll.*) a gossipy or interfering old woman. ~*v.t.* (*3rd pers. sing. pres.* **tabbies,** *pres.p.* **tabbying,** *past, p.p.* **tabbied**) to give a wavy or watered appearance to. ~*a.* **1** wavy, watered. **2** striped. **tabby cat** *n.* a grey or brownish cat with dark stripes. [F *tabis*, Arab. *'utābī*, from *al-'attabiya*, the quarter in Baghdad where the fabric was first made]

tabernacle (tab´ənakəl) *n.* **1** (*Bible*) a tent, booth or other building of light construction, and usu. movable, used as a habitation, temple etc. **2** (*fig.*) the human body as the temporary abode of the soul. **3** (*Hist.*) a tentlike structure used by the Jews as a sanctuary before settlement in Palestine. **4** a place of nonconformist worship. **5** an ornamental receptacle for the consecrated elements or the pyx. **6** a canopy, canopied stall or niche. **7** a canopy-like structure over a tomb etc. **8** (*Naut.*) a socket or hinged post for unstepping the mast on a river-boat. **9** a socket or other holder or retainer for a hinged mast. **Feast of Tabernacles** FEAST. **tabernacled** *a.* **tabernacle work** *n.* carved canopies and tracery over a pulpit, stall etc. **tabernacular** (-nak´ū-) *a.* [F, from L *tabernāculum*, tent, dim. of *taberna*, hut]

tabes (tā´bēz) *n.* (*pl.* **tabes**) **1** wasting away, emaciation. **2** a wasting disease, esp. locomotor ataxy. **tabescent** (təbes´-) *a.* **1** wasting away. **2** of or relating to tabes. **tabescence** *n.* **tabes dorsalis** (dawsah´lis) *n.* an advanced form of syphilis which attacks the spinal cord. **tabetic** (təbet´-) *a.* [L, cogn. with Gr. *tēkein*, to melt, and THAW]

tabla (tab´lə) *n.* a pair of small Indian drums with variable pitch, played with the hands. [Hind. *tabla*, from Arab. *tabla*, drum]

tablature (tab´lətyə, -chə) *n.* **1** (*Mus.*) a system of notation for instruments such as the lute, violin or guitar, showing string and fret position, and indicating rhythm and fingering. **2** a painting on a wall or ceiling. **3** a picture. **4** (*fig.*) a vivid description, mental image etc. [F, from TABLE]

table (tā´bəl) *n.* **1** an article of furniture consisting of a flat surface resting on one or more supports, used for serving meals, working, writing, playing games etc. **2** this used for meals. **3** the food served on a table, fare, cuisine. **4** the company sitting at a table. **5 a** a table or board adapted for a particular game (*usu. in comb.*, as *billiard-table*). **b** a table or board designed for a particular purpose (*bird table*). **6** each half or quarter of a backgammon table. **7** (*pl.*) the game of backgammon. **8** a part of a machine or machine-tool where the work to be operated on is put. **9** any apparatus consisting of a plane surface. **10** a slab of wood or other material. **11** such a slab with writing or an inscription. **12** the contents of such writing etc. **13** a list of numbers, references, or other items arranged systematically, esp. in columns. **14** a multiplication table. **15** a plateau, a tableland. **16** the flat face of a gem. **17** a gem cut with two flat faces. **18** (*Archit.*) a flat surface, usu. rectangular, a horizontal band of moulding. **19** the sound board of a guitar, cello etc. ~*v.t.* **1** to lay (a bill etc.)

on the table in front of the Speaker in the House of Commons, i.e. to submit for discussion. 2 to put forward (a motion) for debate at a meeting. 3 to fit (timbers) together with alternate feathers and grooves to prevent separation or slipping. 4 to strengthen (a sail) with wide hems. **at table** taking a meal. **to lay on the table** 1 to put forward for debate or discussion. 2 (*esp. N Am.*) to set aside indefinitely. **to lie on the table** 1 to be up for debate or discussion. 2 (*esp. N Am.*) to be set aside indefinitely. **to turn the tables** to reverse the conditions or relations. **under the table** 1 illicit, secret. 2 (*coll.*) drunk. **table book** *n.* an ornamental book for keeping on a table. **tablecloth** *n.* a cloth for covering a table, esp. at mealtimes. **table-cut** *a.* (of gems) cut with a flat face. **tabled** *a.* **table d'hôte** (tahbəl dōt´) *n.* (*pl.* **tables d'hôte** (tahbəl)) a hotel or restaurant meal at a fixed price, limited to certain dishes arranged by the proprietor. **tableful** *n.* **table knife** *n.* a knife for use at meals. **table lamp** *n.* a small lamp for standing on a table etc. **tableland** *n.* a plateau. **table licence** *n.* a licence which permits the holder, usually a restaurateur, to serve alcohol with food. **table-lifting, table-moving, table-rapping, table-turning** *n.* making a table rise, move or turn over without apparent cause, as by spiritualistic agency. **table linen** *n.* (*collect.*) tablecloths, napkins etc. **table manners** *n.pl.* accepted behaviour during meals. **table mat** *n.* a mat placed on a table to protect the surface from hot dishes or moisture. **table money** *n.* 1 an allowance to army officers for official hospitality. 2 a charge to members of clubs for use of the dining room. **table napkin** *n.* a napkin used to wipe the hands at table etc., a serviette. **table of contents** *n.* a list or summary of the chapters etc. in a book or periodical. †**tabler** *n.* **table salt** *n.* fine, free-flowing salt used at table. **table skittles** *n.pl.* a game of skittles set up on a board, and knocked down by a ball suspended above the board. **tablespoon** *n.* 1 a large spoon, usu. four times the size of a teaspoon and holding a fluid ounce (approx. 0.028 l). 2 a tablespoonful. **tablespoonful** *n.* the amount contained in a tablespoon. **table talk** *n.* 1 talk at table or meals. 2 familiar conversation, miscellaneous chat. **table tennis** *n.* a game based on tennis and played with small bats and hollow balls on a table with a net. **table top** *n.* 1 the flat top of a table. 2 any flat top. **table-top** *a.* that can be put on a table top. **table-topped** *a.* **table-top sale** *n.* a sale at which people sell their unwanted belongings laid out on tables. **tableware** *n.* dishes, plates, knives, forks etc., for use at meals. **table wine** *n.* an unfortified wine drunk with meals. **tabling** *n.* [OF, from L *tabula*, a board, a table]

tableau (tab´lō) *n.* (*pl.* **tableaux** (-lōz, -lō)) 1 a presentation resembling a picture. 2 a striking or vivid representation or effect. **tableau vivant** (vē´vã) *n.* (*pl.* **tableaux vivants** (-lō vē´vã)) a motionless group of performers dressed and arranged to represent some scene or event. [F, dim. of TABLE]

tablet (tab´lit) *n.* 1 a small solid measure of medicine or other substance. 2 a thin flat piece of wood, ivory or other material for writing on. 3 (*pl.*) a set of these. 4 a small table or slab, esp. used as a memorial. 5 a shaped slab (of soap). 6 (*N Am.*) a writing pad. 7 (*Sc.*) a sweet made from butter, sugar and condensed milk. **tablette** *n.* a flat, projecting coping stone, on a wall etc. [OF *tablete* (F *tablette*), dim. of TABLE]

tablier (tab´liā) *n.* (*Hist.*) a small apron or apron-like part of a woman's dress. [F, from L *tabulārium*, from *tabula*, TABLE]

tabling TABLE.

tabloid (tab´loid) *n.* 1 (*coll.*) a cheap daily newspaper that usually offers a more sensationalist view of the news than the broadsheet papers give. 2 a newspaper measuring about 12 in. (30 cm) by 16 in. (40 cm), informal in style, often with lots of photographs. 3 a compressed dose of a drug etc. **tabloid journalism** *n.* newspaper writing that tends to highlight the sensational and salacious issues of the day. **tabloid TV, tabloid television** *n.* television concentrating on gossip, sensational news and light entertainment.

taboo (təboo´), **tabu** *n.* (*pl.* **taboos, tabus**) 1 something which is very strongly disapproved of in a particular society etc. (*Most societies label incest as a taboo*; *Smoking is a taboo in this office*). 2 a custom among the Polynesians etc., of prohibiting the use of certain persons, places or things. 3 (*fig.*) ban, prohibition. 4 any ritual restriction, usu. of something considered to be unclean or unholy. *~a.* banned, prohibited, by social, religious or moral convention. *~v.t.* (*3rd pers. sing. pres.* **taboos, tabus,** *pres.p.* **tabooing, tabuing,** *past, p.p.* **tabooed, tabued**) 1 to put under taboo. 2 to forbid the use of (something). [Tongan *tabu*]

tabor (tā´bə), **tabour** *n.* (*Hist.*) a small drum used to accompany the pipe. **taborer** *n.* [OF *tabour* (F *tambour*), Arab. *tambūr*, lute, drum]

tabouret (tab´ərit), (*N Am.*) **taboret** *n.* 1 a small seat, usu. without arms or back. 2 an embroidery frame. [OF, dim. of TABOR]

tabu TABOO.

tabular (tab´ūlə) *a.* 1 set out, arranged in, or computed from tables. 2 made up of thin plates. 3 in the form of a table, having a broad flat surface. 4 (of a crystal) having two flat faces. **tabula** (-lə) *n.* (*pl.* **tabulae** (-lē)) 1 a flat surface. 2 a writing tablet. **tabula rasa** (rah´zə) *n.* (*pl.* **tabulae rasae** (-zē)) 1 the mind in its supposedly original state, before any impressions have been made on it. 2 a fresh start. 3 a tablet with no writing on it. **tabularize, tabularise** *v.t.* **tabularly** *adv.* **tabulate**[1] (-lāt) *v.t.* 1 to reduce to or arrange (figures etc.) in tabular form. 2 to shape with a flat surface. *~v.i.* to operate the tabulator on a computer or typewriter keyboard. **tabulate**[2] (-lət) *a.* 1 table-shaped, broad and flat. 2 arranged in laminae. **tabulation** (-lā´shən) *n.* **tabulator** *n.* 1 a key on a computer or typewriter keyboard (orig. a separate attachment to a typewriter) which moves to a preset position to facilitate tabulation work etc. 2 (*Hist.*) a machine which prints data from punched cards, producing tables etc. 3 someone or something that tabulates. **tabulatory** *a.* [L *tabula*]

tabun (tah´boon) *n.* an organic phosphorus compound, formula $C_2H_5OP(O)(CN)N(CH_3)_2$, used as a lethal nerve gas in chemical warfare. [G]

tacamahac (tak´əməhak) *n.* 1 a resin obtained from various S American trees, esp. of the genus *Calophyllum*. 2 the balsam poplar. 3 the resin of this tree. [Nahuatl *tecomahiyac*]

tac-au-tac (takōtak´) *n.* 1 in fencing, the parry combined immediately with the riposte. 2 a series of attacks and parries in swift succession. [F, imit.]

tacet (tas´it) *v.i.* (*Mus.*) to be silent (used in the imperative as an instruction to a particular voice or instrument). [L]

tach (tak) *n.* (*N Am., coll.*) short for TACHOMETER.

tache TASH.

tacheometer TACHYMETER.

tachism (tash´izm), **tachisme** *n.* a form of action painting with haphazard blobs of colour. **tachist, tachiste** *n., a.* [F *tache*, spot]

tachistoscope (takis´təskōp) *n.* an instrument which flashes images on to a screen for very brief spaces of time, usually a fraction of a second, used in the study of learning and perception. **tachistoscopic** (-skop´-) *a.* [Gr. *tachistos*, swiftest]

tacho (tak´ō) *n.* (*pl.* **tachos**) (*coll.*) 1 short for TACHOMETER. 2 short for TACHOGRAPH.

tacho- (tak´ō) *comb. form* speed. [Gr. *tachos*, speed]

tachogram (tak´əgram) *n.* a visual record produced by a tachograph.

tachograph (tak´əgrahf) *n.* a tachometer in a motor vehicle, esp. a lorry or bus, which records its speed and the distance travelled between stops.

tachometer (takom´itə) *n.* an instrument for measuring the rate of rotation of a revolving shaft in a vehicle's engine and which can therefore also indicate the vehicle's speed. **tachometry** *n.*

tachy- (tak´i) *comb. form* swift. [Gr. *tachus*, swift]

tachycardia (takikah´diə) *n.* (*Med.*) abnormally rapid beating of the heart.

tachygraphy (takig´rəfi) *n.* shorthand, stenography, esp. any of the ancient Greek or Roman systems. **tachygrapher** *n.* **tachygraphic** (-graf´-), **tachygraphical** *a.*

tachylyte (tak´ilīt) *n.* a black, vitreous basalt. **tachylytic** (-lit´-) *a.*

tachymeter (təkim´itə), **tacheometer** (takiom´-) *n.* **1** a surveying instrument for measuring distances rapidly. **2** an instrument for indicating speed. **tachymetrical** (-met´-) *a.* **tachymetry** *n.*

tachyon (tak´ion) *n.* a hypothetical elementary particle which travels faster than the speed of light.

tachyphylaxis (takifilak´sis) *n.* the rapid development of tolerance or immunity to the effects of a specific drug.

tacit (tas´it) *a.* implied but not actually expressed. **tacitly** *adv.* **tacitness** *n.* [L *tacitus*, silent, from *tacēre*, to be silent]

taciturn (tas´itœn) *a.* habitually silent, reserved or uncommunicative. **taciturnity** (-tœ´-) *n.* **taciturnly** *adv.* [F *taciturne*, from L *taciturnus*, as TACIT]

tack[1] (tak) *n.* **1** a small, sharp, flat-headed nail. **2** (*esp. N Am.*) a drawing pin. **3** a stitch, esp. one of a series of long stitches for fastening fabric in dressmaking temporarily. **4** the course of a ship as determined by the position of the sails. **5** the act of tacking or changing direction to take advantage of a side wind etc. **6** a course of action, a policy (*and, if that doesn't work, try a different tack*). **7** a rope by which the forward lower corner of certain sails is fastened. **8** the part of a sail to which such rope is fastened. **9** stickiness, tackiness. **10** a clause appended to a parliamentary bill. *~v.t.* **1** to fasten with tacks. **2** to stitch (fabric) temporarily or together in a hasty manner. **3** to change the course of a ship to the opposite tack. **4** to annex, to append (to or on to). **5** to append (another clause) to a parliamentary bill. *~v.i.* **1** to change the course of a ship by shifting the tacks and position of the sails. **2** to zigzag. **3** to alter one's conduct or policy. **on the right tack** on the right lines. **on the wrong tack** on the wrong lines. **to come down to brass tacks** to face realities, to state facts. **tacker** *n.* **1** a person who tacks. **2** a person who makes additions. **tacket** (-it) *n.* (*Sc.*) a hobnail. **tackety** *a.* **tack hammer** *n.* a small hammer for driving in tacks. **tacky** *a.* (*comp.* **tackier**, *superl.* **tackiest**) **1** sticky. **2** (*coll.*) cheap or shoddy, vulgar and ostentatious, seedy. **tackily** *adv.* **tackiness** *n.* [ONF *taque* (OF *tache*), fastening, nail, peg, EFris. and Dan. *takke*, pointed thing (cp. LG *takk*, G *Zacke*, point, prong, Dut. *tak*, twig)]

tack[2] (tak) *n.* a horse's saddle, bridle, harness etc. **tack room** *n.* a room or area in a riding stable where the horses' tack is kept and cleaned. [TACKLE]

tack[3] (tak) *n.* (*coll.*) **1** something shoddy, cheap or vulgarly ostentatious. **2** shoddiness, cheapness, vulgar ostentation. [TACKY (under TACK[1])]

tack[4] (tak) *n.* food, fare. [etym. unknown]

tack[5] (tak) *n.* **1** (*Sc. Law*) a letting contract, a lease. **2** land or pasturage leased. **tacksman** *n.* (*pl.* **tacksmen**) a person who holds a tack or lease of land from another. [prob. from Icel. *tak*, seizure, hold, rel. to TAKE[1]]

tacket TACK[1].

tackle (tak´əl) *n.* **1** apparatus, esp. of ropes, pulleys etc., for lifting, hoisting etc., or for working spars, sails etc. **2** a windlass or winch with its ropes etc. **3** the implements, gear or outfit for carrying on any particular work or sport (*fishing tackle*). **4** in football, hockey etc., an attempt to get the ball etc. away from the player who currently has possession of it (*got booked for a reckless tackle on the keeper*). **5** in American football, the position outside the guard, next to the end in the forward line, or the player in this position. *~v.t.* **1** to grapple with. **2** in football, hockey etc., to make a tackle on (an opponent). **3** to collar. **4** (*coll.*) to set to work vigorously upon. **5** to secure or make fast with tackle. **tackle-block** *n.* the pulley that a rope runs over. **tackle-fall** *n.* a rope that allows force to be applied to the blocks of a tackle. **tackler** *n.* **tackling** *n.* (*collect.*) tackle. [prob. from MLG or Dut. *takel*, from MLG *taken*, to TAKE[1], to lay hold of]

tacksman TACK[5].

tacky TACK[1].

taco (tah´kō) *n.* (*pl.* **tacos**) a type of thin pancake or tortilla from Mexico, usually with a spicy meat or vegetable filling. [Sp., a bite to eat]

tact (takt) *n.* **1** an intuitive sense of what is fitting or right. **2** adroitness in doing or saying the proper thing. **tactful** *a.* **tactfully** *adv.* **tactfulness** *n.* **tactless** *a.* **tactlessly** *adv.* **tactlessness** *n.* [L *tactus*, *-tūs*, touch, from *tactus*, p.p. of *tangere*, see TANGENT]

tactics (tak´tiks) *n.* **1** (*sing. or pl.*) the art of manoeuvring military or naval forces, esp. in actual contact with the enemy. **2** (*pl.*) procedure or devices to attain some end (*stooped to using devious tactics*). **tactic** (tak´tik) *n.* a way of doing or achieving something (*His usual tactic is just to wait and see what happens*). **tactical** *a.* **1** skilful, diplomatic. **2** (of a military strike or the weapons used in one) immediately supportive, as opposed to *strategic*. **3** carefully planned or executed. **tactically** *adv.* **tactical voting** *n.* the practice of voting for the candidate most likely to defeat the favourite candidate, rather than for one's preferred candidate. **tactician** (-tish´ən) *n.* [Gr. *taktika*, neut. pl. of *taktikos*, from *taktos*, ordered, from *tassein*, to arrange]

tactile (tak´tīl) *a.* **1** of, relating to or perceived by the sense of touch. **2** capable of being touched. **3** pleasant or distinctive to the touch (*Velvet is a very tactile material*). **4** (of a person) not inhibited in touching others (*French people are generally very tactile*). **tactility** (-til´-) *n.* **tactual** *a.* **1** caused by touch. **2** tactile. **tactually** *adv.* [F, from L *tactilis* (TACT, -ILE)]

tad (tad) *n.* (*N Am.*, *coll.*) a small amount. **a tad** slightly, a little (*This wine is a tad too sweet for me*). [TADPOLE]

Tadjik TAJIK.

tadpole (tad´pōl) *n.* the larva of an amphibian, esp. of a frog or toad, before the gills and tail disappear. [ME *tadpolle* (TOAD, POLL[1], head)]

taedium vitae (tēdiəm vē´tī, vī´tē) *n.* weariness of life. [L]

tae kwon do (tī kwon dō´) *n.* a type of Korean martial art, similar to karate, involving kicks and punches. [Korean, *tae*, kick, *kwon*, punch, *do*, method]

tael (tāl) *n.* **1** a Chinese and Far Eastern weight of 1⅓ oz. (38 g) or a weight close to this. **2** (*Hist.*) a monetary unit equal to a tael of silver. [Malay *tahil*]

ta'en TAKE[1].

taenia (tē´niə), (*N Am.*) **tenia** *n.* (*pl.* **taeniae** (-ē), **taenias**, (*N Am.*) **teniae**, **tenias**) **1** (*Archit.*) a band or fillet separating a Doric frieze from an architrave. **2** (*Anat.*) a band or ribbon-like part. **3** an internal parasite of the genus *Taenia*, which includes the tapeworm. **4** in ancient Greece, a headband. **taeniacide** (-sīd) *n.* a chemical or substance which destroys tapeworms. **taeniasis** (-nī´əsis) *n.* infestation with tapeworms. **taeniate** (-āt), **taenioid** (-oid) *a.* [L, from Gr. *tainia*, a ribbon, from *teinein*, to stretch]

taffeta (taf´itə) *n.* **1** a light, thin, glossy silk fabric. **2** (*loosely*) a silk and linen or silk and wool fabric. [F *taffetas*, It. *taffetà*, Pers. *tāftah*, from *tāftan*, to twist]

taffia TAFIA.

taffrail (taf´rāl) *n.* (*Naut.*) the rail round a ship's stern. [corr. of *tafferel*, from Dut. *tafereel*, dim. of *tafel*, from L, as TABLE]

Taffy (taf´i) *n.* (*pl.* **Taffies**) (*coll., often offensive*) a Welshman. [Welsh pron. of *Davy*, short for *David*, a common first name in Wales and the name of the country's patron saint]

taffy (taf´i) *n.* (*pl.* **taffies**) **1** TOFFEE. **2** (*esp. US, coll.*) insincere flattery.

tafia (taf´iə), **taffia** *n.* a variety of rum distilled from molasses. [etym. uncertain; cp. RATAFIA]

tag (tag) *n.* **1** any small appendage, such as a metal point at the end of a lace. **2** a label, esp. one tied on to an item for sale to show its price or on to a suitcase etc. to show its intended destination. **3** an electronic device attached to goods for sale which will set off an alarm if taken out of the shop door. **4** an electronic tracking device, used to monitor prisoners on remand or wildlife. **5** a loop for pulling a boot on. **6** (*N Am.*) a vehicle licence plate. **7** a loose or ragged end or edge. **8** a loose tuft of wool on a sheep. **9** the tail or tip of the tail of an animal. **10** anything tacked on at the end. **11** the refrain of a song, the closing speech in a play addressed to the audience. **12** a well-worn phrase or quotation. **13** a children's game in which the players try to escape being touched by the one chosen to be 'it'. **14** the act of tagging in wrestling. **15** the act of tagging a runner out in baseball. ~*v.t.* (*pres.p.* **tagging,** *past, p.p.* **tagged**) **1** to fit or mark with a tag, to attach a tag to. **2** (*Comput.*) to attach a special code to (a piece of data) so that it can be easily identified or retrieved. **3** to attach (to, on to or together). **4** to touch in the game of tag. **5** in wrestling, to touch a team-mate's hand as a signal that it is their turn in the ring. **6** in baseball, to touch (a runner) with the ball or with a hand with the ball in it, putting the runner out. **7** (*coll.*) to follow closely or persistently (after). **8** to call or name. **9** to remove tags from (a sheep). **10** to find appropriate tags or trite phrases for. **to tag along with** to go along with (someone), to follow. **tag end** *n.* (*esp. N Am.*) the final part of something. **tagged** *a.* **tagged atom** *n.* the radioactive isotope of a tracer element. **tagger** *n.* **1** a person who tags, esp. the pursuer in the game of tag. **2** (*pl.*) thin tin plate or sheet iron. **tag team** *n.* a pair of wrestlers who either fight together as a team or who take alternate turns in the ring. **tag-team** *a.* denoting this type of wrestling. [cp. Swed. *tagg*, prickle, Norw. *tagge*, tooth, also TACK[1]]

tagetes (təjē´tēz) *n.* any plant of the genus *Tagetes* of the aster family. [mod. L, from L *Tages*, Etruscan divinity]

tagliatelle (talyətel´i) *n.* pasta in the form of thin strips. [It. *tagliare*, to cut]

tahini (təhē´ni) *n.* a thick paste made from ground sesame seeds. [Arab. *tahina*]

Tahitian (tah·hē´shən) *n.* **1** a native or inhabitant of Tahiti, an island in the S Pacific. **2** the language spoken there. ~*a.* belonging or relating to Tahiti, its people or its language.

tahr (teə), **thar** (tah) *n.* a beardless Himalayan goatlike mammal, *Hemitragus jemlahicus*. [Nepali *thar*]

tahsil (tahsēl´) *n.* a division for revenue and other administrative purposes in some Indian states. **tahsildar** (-dah´) *n.* a tahsil officer. [Hind. from Arab.]

taiaha (tī´əhah) *n.* a Maori carved long-handled club, now ceremonial. [Maori]

t'ai chi ch'uan (tī chē chwahn´), **t'ai chi** (chē´) *n.* a Chinese form of exercise and self-defence based on slow controlled movements. [Chin., great ultimate boxing]

Taig (tāg) *n.* (*sl., offensive*) in N Ireland, a Roman Catholic. [Ir. *Tadhg*, a nickname for any Irishman]

taiga (tī´gə) *n.* the spruce-dominated coniferous forests found in subarctic N America and Eurasia. [Rus. *taiga*]

tail[1] (tāl) *n.* **1** the part of an animal, bird, fish or insect that extends from the end or the back of the body, esp. when it forms a movable or flexible appendage. **2** anything that resembles this kind of appendage in form, position or function (*a shirt tail; a long tail of traffic*). **3** the rear or last part or parts of something (*joined the tail of the queue; the tail of the storm*). **4** the rear of an aeroplane, including the rudder and the tailplane. **5** the rear part of a motor vehicle. **6** (*Astron.*) the luminous trail of particles that can be seen to follow a comet. **7** (*in pl.*) **a** a tailcoat. **b** (*coll.*) men's evening wear. **8** (*in pl.*) the obverse side of a tossed coin. **9** (*sl.*) the buttocks. **10** (*sl.*) the female genitals. **11** (*sl.*) a woman, esp. one thought of in sexual terms. **12** (*sl.*) sexual intercourse. **13** the route that someone or something travelling or running away takes (*That police car's been on my tail since we left*). **14** (*coll.*) a person who follows and watches another person or people (*put a tail on the suspected drug dealer*). **15** in music notation, the lower part of a note. **16** the part of a written letter such as a *g, j, p, q* or *y* that lies below the line. **17** the exposed end of a slate or roof tile. **18** the unexposed end of a brick or tile in a wall. **19** in cricket, the less talented batsmen who play last in a batting order. **20** the lower part of a stream or pool, esp. a calm section following rough water. **21** a retinue or following. **22** the thin elongated part on the wing of some butterflies that points backwards. ~*v.t.* **1** to follow and keep under surveillance. **2** to dock the tail of (a lamb). **3** (*coll.*) to remove the tails or ends from (fruit) (*top and tail the blackcurrants*). **4** to provide with a tail. **5** to join (on to another thing). **6** to insert one end of (a timber etc.) into a wall etc. ~*v.i.* **1** to follow closely (after). **2** (*Austral.*) to herd sheep or cattle. **3** to fall behind or drop (away or off) in a scattered line. **4** (of a vessel) to swing (up and down stream) with the tide. **bit of tail** BIT[1]. **on someone's tail** very close behind someone. **the tail wags the dog** WAG[1]. **to tail away** to dwindle. **to tail back** to form a tailback. **to tail off** to come to and end, or almost to an end (*Public interest in the issue has tailed off*). **to turn tail 1** to run away. **2** to turn one's back. **with one's tail between one's legs** beaten, in a state of defeat. **with one's tail up** in good spirits. **tailback** *n.* a queue of traffic stretching back from an obstruction or traffic problem. **tailboard** *n.* the hinged or sliding board at the back of a cart, wagon etc. **tailcoat** *n.* a man's morning or evening coat that is elongated and divided in two at the back. **tailcoated** *a.* **tail covert** *n.* any of the covert feathers around a bird's tail. **tailed** *a.* (*usu. in comb.*, as *long-tailed*). **tail-end** *n.* **1** the last or concluding part (*only heard the tail-end of the story*). **2** the lowest or rearmost part. **3** in cricket, the last of the batting order. **tail-end Charlie** *n.* a person bringing up the rear. **tail-ender** *n.* **1** a person who arrives last or almost last (*The tail-enders are just crossing the finishing line now*). **2** in cricket, a batsman in the tail-end. **tail-feather** *n.* **1** a flight feather in a bird's tail. **2** a feather forming a train. **tailgate** *n.* **1** the lower gate of a canal lock. **2** (*esp. N Am.*) a tailboard. **3** (*esp. N Am.*) the upward-lifting door at the back of a hatchback or estate car. ~*v.t.* (*esp. N Am., coll.*) to follow (the vehicle in front) very closely, often too closely to allow for a safe braking distance. ~*v.i.* to drive very closely behind another vehicle. **tailgater** *n.* **tailing** *n.* **1** the part of a stone or brick inserted into a wall. **2** (*pl.*) the refuse part of ore, grain etc. **tailless** *a.* **tail light, tail lamp** *n.* a red warning light at the rear of a motor vehicle etc. **tail-off** *n.* a dwindling, a gradual ending. **tailpiece** *n.* **1** an ornamental design at the end of a chapter or section of a book. **2** a triangular block on a violin etc., to which the strings are attached. 3 the end or last part of something. 4 any rear appendage. **tail-pipe** *n.* 1 the rearmost part of a vehicle's exhaust pipe. 2 the suction pipe in a pump. **tailplane** *n.* the fixed horizontal portion of the tail of an aeroplane. **tail-race** *n.* the part of a mill-race below a waterwheel. **tailskid** *n.* 1 a device to take the weight at the rear end of an aeroplane's fuselage while taxiing. 2 a type of skid involving loss of control of a motor vehicle's rear wheels. **tailspin** *n.* 1 a vertical, nose-foremost dive by an aeroplane, during which it describes a spiral. 2 a state of upheaval or loss of control. *~v.i.* (*pres.p.* **tailspinning,** *past* **tailspun, tailspan,** *p.p.* **tailspun**) to put an aeroplane into a tailspin. **tailstock** *n.* an adjustable casting on a lathe which supports the free end of a workpiece. **tailwheel** *n.* a supporting wheel below the tail of an aeroplane. **tailwind** *n.* a wind blowing in the same direction as one is travelling in. [OE *taegl, taegel,* cp. Icel. *tagl,* Swed. *tagel,* G *Zegel*]

tail[2] (tāl) *n.* (*Law*) 1 limitation of ownership, limited ownership. 2 an estate of inheritance limited to a person and their heirs, esp. just their offspring. *~a.* limited in this way. **in tail** controlled by or under limited ownership (*estate in tail*).

tailor (tā´lə) *n.* a person whose occupation is to cut out and make clothes, esp. outer clothes for men. *~v.i.* to work as a tailor. *~v.t.* 1 to make (clothes) (*tailored the jacket to a perfect fit*). 2 (*coll.*) to adapt for a particular purpose or need (*tailored her working hours to give her time with the children*). **tailor-bird** *n.* any of several Asian warblers of the genus *Orthotomus,* that sew together leaves to form their nests. **tailored** *a.* 1 well-cut, close-fitting. 2 adapted to a specific purpose. 3 dressed by a tailor. **tailoress** *n.* a female tailor. **tailoring** *n.* **tailor-made** *a.* 1 made by a tailor, well cut and close-fitting. 2 perfectly suited or adapted (*The flats are tailor-made for elderly people*). *~n.* a tailored article of clothing. **tailor's chair** *n.* a legless chair (such as those used by tailors). **tailor's chalk** *n.* pipeclay used by tailors and dressmakers to mark material. **tailor's tack** *n.* loose tacking stitches used to transfer marks from the pattern to the material. **tailor's twist** *n.* a strong silk thread. [OF *tailleor, taillour,* from *tailler,* to cut, see TAIL[2]]

Taino (tī´nō) *n.* (*pl.* **Taino, Tainos**) 1 a member of an extinct American Indian people of the W Indies. 2 their language.

taint (tānt) *n.* 1 a stain, a blemish, a disgrace. 2 a corrupting influence, infection. 3 a trace of decay, unsoundness, disease etc. *~v.t.* 1 to imbue or infect with a noxious, poisonous, or corrupting element. 2 to dirty, sully or tarnish. *~v.i.* 1 to be infected or affected with incipient putrefaction. 2 to weaken. **tainted** *a.* **taintless** *a.* [F *teint,* p.p. of *teindre,* L *tingere,* to tinge, perh. conf. with ATTAINT]

taipan[1] (tī´pan) *n.* a large and extremely venomous Australian snake, *Oxyuranus microlepidotus.* [Austral. Abor.]

taipan[2] (tī´pan) *n.* the head of a foreign business in China. [Chin.]

Taiwanese (tīwanēz´) *n.* (*pl.* **Taiwanese**) 1 a native or inhabitant of Taiwan, an island in SE Asia. 2 (*as pl.*) the people of this island.

taj (tahj) *n.* a crown, a head-dress of distinction, esp. a tall cap worn by Muslim dervishes. [Pers.]

Tajik (tah´jēk), **Tadjik** *n.* 1 a native or inhabitant of Tajikistan, a republic in central Asia. 2 the Iranian language of the Tajiks. [Pers.]

takable TAKE[1].

takahe (tah´kəhē) *n.* NOTORNIS. [Maori]

take[1] (tāk) *v.t.* (*past* **took** (tuk), *p.p.* **taken** (tā´kən)) 1 to lay hold of, grasp, seize, capture, steal, catch, arrest, gain possession of, win, captivate, transport, escort etc. (*took the CD from its case; took his rook easily; broke into the off-licence and took hundreds of cigarettes; took her to the dance*). 2 to carry off, remove, carry away, carry with one, convey etc. (*took the cat to the vet; took the wrong jacket by mistake*). 3 to remove without permission (*OK, who's taken my pen?*). 4 to go by means of (*took the bus; let's take the shortcut*). 5 to lead in a certain direction (*the road that takes you into town*). 6 to have, receive, obtain, procure, acquire, appropriate, opt for etc. (*took a look out of the window; take the opportunity to thank everyone; took early retirement*). 7 to eat, consume, drink or swallow (*We usually take lunch at one o'clock; Do you take sugar in your coffee?*). 8 to indulge in (*used to take cocaine*). 9 to use or make use of (*Take 100g of butter and 175g of sugar; a car that takes unleaded petrol*). 10 to choose to go along (a specified road, direction etc.) (*Take the first right; took a wrong turning*). 11 to go for or perform (an action) (*took a walk; took a run in the car*). 12 to put up with, endure, accept etc. (*told the class she wouldn't take any nonsense; I really can't take her rudeness*). 13 to ascertain and record by weighing, measuring etc. (*had her temperature taken*). 14 to understand, detect, apprehend, grasp, suppose, consider, infer, conclude, interpret etc. (*took him to be telling the truth; took what he said to be true*). 15 to be infected or ill with (a disease, virus etc.). 16 to feel or show (a specified response, esp. an emotional one) (*took offence at her criticisms; takes great pride in her work*). 17 to treat or regard in a specified way (*takes his duties as a father very seriously; took the whole thing as a joke*). 18 (*coll.*) to need (a specified person or thing, esp. to ensure the desired outcome or action) (*took four of us to move the piano; It will take a miracle for us to win now*). 19 to have or spend (time etc.) (*took a day's sick leave; took his annual holiday in France*). 20 to use up or last (a specified length of time) (*The flight takes six hours*). 21 to accommodate or have room for (*This box will take up to 30 CDs*). 22 to act upon or learn from (*Take my advice and stay in bed*). 23 to note down or write up (*The police took her name and address; Take the minutes of the meeting*). 24 to put (a specified course of action) in place or into effect (*took preventative measures; took the decision to expand the company*). 25 to choose to pursue (a specified course of action etc.) (*took the initiative; always takes the easy way out*). 26 to accept or choose to accept (*took £200 for the car; took a job in London; took his word for it*). 27 to hold, believe in or support (*took the party line; took a different view*). 28 to follow or teach (a specified subject, course of study etc.) (*is taking a degree in physics; He takes the senior classes*). 29 to sit an examination in (a specified subject or at a particular level) (*took her English finals last month*). 30 to photograph (*took over 50 holiday snaps; I'll take you with the Eiffel Tower in the background*). 31 to buy or subscribe to (a specified newspaper or other publication), esp. on a regular basis (*We take 'The Guardian'*). 32 to occupy, esp. temporarily (*You can take the seat next to me*). 33 to act as the leader, speaker, chairperson etc. of (*He takes a local scout group; took the floor; Will you take this meeting?*). 34 to look at, use or cite as a prime or illustrative example (*Underfunding is widespread—take education or health for a start*). 35 to wear (a specified size of clothes or shoes) (*What shoe size do you take?*). 36 (*Gram.*) (of a part of speech) to have as the usual syntactic construction (*The noun 'deer' can take singular and plural verb forms*). 37 to use (text written by someone else) as a quote etc. (*took a passage from Ulysses to illustrate the point*). 38 (*dated*) to have sexual intercourse with (a woman). *~v.i.* 1 to be successful or have the desired effect (*The skin graft has taken well*). 2 (of plants) to begin to grow by sending out roots (*The* *seedlings have taken and we can put them outside now*). 3 (*coll.*) to become suddenly ill (*took sick at school and was sent home*). **take that!** used when delivering a blow etc. **to be taken with** to be charmed by or very pleased with. **to have what it takes** (*coll.*) to show the necessary talent, qualities or stamina. **to take after** 1 to resemble physically, mentally etc. 2 to follow, esp. in the same career etc. **to take against** to form a dislike for. **to take apart** 1 to separate. 2 (*coll.*) to criticize severely. 3 (*coll.*) esp. in sport, to outplay, outclass or defeat (*Aberdeen took Rangers apart*). **to take aside** to disengage and talk privately to. **to take away** 1 to subtract. 2 to remove. 3 to buy ready to eat, for consumption elsewhere. **to take away from** to detract from. **to take back** 1 to withdraw, to retract. 2 to stimulate the memory of, esp. nostalgically (*These photos take me back to when I was a lad*). 3 (*Print.*) to reset on the previous line. 4 to return or accept the return of (something bought) for a replacement or refund. 5 to accept back into a relationship that had earlier been ended. **to take down** 1 to write down. 2 to lower (a garment) to one's knees or ankles, esp. temporarily (*took down her jeans*). 3 to swallow, to gulp down. 4 to take apart, to pull to pieces. 5 to humiliate, to humble. **to take down a peg (or two)** PEG. **to take for** to mistake for. **to take for a ride** RIDE. **to take for granted** GRANT. **to take from** 1 to deduct from. 2 to diminish, to lessen. 3 to quote from (*This passage is taken from Joyce's 'Ulysses'*). **to take ill** ILL. **to take in** 1 to admit, to receive (*takes in lodgers*). 2 to undertake (washing, typewriting etc.) at home for pay. 3 to include, to comprise. 4 to understand, to receive into the mind, to accept as true. 5 to deceive, to cheat. 6 to contract, to furl (sails). **to take into custody** to arrest. **to take it** 1 to accept misfortune or punishment. 2 to understand by deduction (*So am I to take it that you want to hand in your notice?*). **to take it on/upon oneself** to decide (to do) without prompting or authority. **to take it or leave it** 1 to accept something, including its problems, or not at all. 2 to have a lukewarm reaction to something. **to take it out of** 1 (*coll.*) to get revenge, compensation or satisfaction from. 2 (*coll.*) to exhaust the strength or freshness of. **to take it out on** to vent one's anger or frustration on. **to take kindly to** KINDLY (under KIND). **to take off** 1 to remove, to withdraw. 2 to begin flight. 3 to become popular (*Cyber cafés are taking off in a big way now*). 4 to carry away. 5 to deduct (from). 6 to spend (an amount of time) away from work etc., esp. by choice. 7 to jump (from). 8 to leave suddenly or hastily. 9 (*coll.*) to mimic, to ridicule (*an impersonator who takes off MPs so well*). 10 (*dated*) to drink off, to swallow. **to take on** 1 to engage for work etc. 2 to undertake to do (work etc.). 3 to accept a challenge from, to engage in a contest with. 4 to acquire, to adopt. 5 (*coll.*) to be violently affected, to be upset. **to take oneself off** to go away, to leave. **to take out** 1 to remove, to bring, lead or convey out. 2 to invite and accompany on an outing etc. 3 to obtain for oneself, to procure. 4 (*Law*) to have (a summons, injunction etc.) put in place. 5 (*N Am.*) to buy ready to eat, for consumption elsewhere. 6 (*sl.*) to murder, to put out of action. 7 in bridge, to remove by bidding differently or no trumps. **to take over** 1 to assume the management, ownership etc. of. 2 to assume control of. 3 (*Print.*) to reset on the next line. **to take sick** SICK[1]. **to take someone out of themselves** to distract someone from their problems or shyness. **to take someone up on** 1 to argue or disagree with someone about. 2 to accept someone's challenge or offer of (*I'll take you up on that offer of a lift*). **to take to** 1 to resort to. 2 to form a habit or liking for. 3 to adapt to. **to take to heart** HEART. **to take to one's bed** BED. **to take to one's heels** HEEL[1]. **to take to pieces** PIECE. **to take to task** TASK. **to take to the cleaner's** CLEANER (under CLEAN). **to take to the road** ROAD[1]. **to take up** 1 to lift (up). 2 to begin to engage or take an interest in. 3 to adopt as a protégé. 4 to agree to act on. 5 to resume, to pursue. 6 (of an object) to occupy or fill physically. 7 (of an activity) to occupy, to engage, to engross. 8 to accept as an office. 9 to interrupt, esp. to criticize. 10 to shorten, esp. by sewing in place. 11 to receive into a vehicle. 12 to absorb. **to take up residence** RESIDENCE (under RESIDE). **to take up with** to begin to associate with. **takable** *a.* **takeaway** *a.* denoting food bought from a restaurant for consumption elsewhere. ~*n.* 1 takeaway food. 2 a restaurant or shop where takeaway food is bought. 3 a takeaway meal. **take-down** *a.* made to be disassembled. ~*n.* a humiliation. **take-home pay** *n.* the amount of salary left after deductions (income tax, national insurance etc.). **take-in** *n.* a deception, a fraud, an imposition. **take-off** *n.* 1 the rising of an aircraft into the air. 2 an act of mimicking, a caricature. 3 the spot from which one's feet leave the ground in leaping. 4 a stroke in croquet by which a player sends their own ball forward and touches another ball without shifting it. **take-out** *a.*, *n.* (*esp. N Am.*) TAKEAWAY (under TAKE[1]). **takeover** *n.* 1 an act of seizing control. 2 the buying out by one company of another. **takeover bid** *n.* an offer to purchase enough shares to obtain control of a company. **taker** *n.* a person who takes something, esp. a person who accepts a bet (*I reckon he'll get the sack—any takers?*). **take-up** *n.* the act of claiming something, esp. of services or state benefit. **taking** *a.* 1 pleasing, alluring, attractive. 2 infectious. ~*n.* 1 the act of someone who takes. 2 capture, arrest. 3 (*pl.*) money taken (*The takings are well down on last week's*). **takingly** *adv.* **takingness** *n.* [late OE *tacan*, Icel. *taka*, cogn. with TACK[1]]

take[2] (tāk) *n.* 1 the act of taking. 2 something which is taken. 3 the amount (of fish etc.) taken at one catch or in one season. 4 takings. 5 the amount of copy taken at one time. 6 a scene that has been filmed. **on the take** making money dishonestly.

takin (tah´kin, -kēn) *n.* a hollow-horned ruminant, *Budorcas taxicolor*, of SE Tibet. [local name]

talapoin (tal´əpoin) *n.* 1 a Buddhist priest or monk in Burma (Myanmar), Sri Lanka etc. 2 an African monkey, *Miopithecus talapoin*. [Port. *talapão*, from a local language, *tala pói*, my lord]

talaria (təleə´riə) *n.pl.* in Roman mythology, the winged boots or sandals of Hermes, Iris etc. [L, pl. of *tālāris*, from TALUS[1]]

talbot (tawl´bət) *n.* a large variety of hound, usu. white with large pendulous ears and massive jaws, now extinct but formerly used for tracking and hunting. [prob. from the surname]

talbotype (tawl´bətīp) *n.* a process invented in 1840 of producing a latent image upon sensitized paper, the basis of the photographic process. [William Henry Fox *Talbot*, 1800–77, British scientist who invented it]

talc (talk) *n.* 1 talcum powder. 2 a fibrous, greasy magnesium silicate occurring in prisms and plates, used as a lubricator etc. 3 (*coll.*) mica. ~*v.t.* (*pres.p.* **talcing, talcking**, *past, p.p.* **talced, talcked**) to treat (something) with talc in order to dry it or lubricate it. **talcite** (-īt) *n.* a massive variety of talc. **talcoid** (-oid), **talcose** (-ōs), **talcous, talcy** *a.* **talcum** (-kəm) *n.* 1 cosmetic talcum powder. 2 talc (magnesium silicate). ~*v.t.* (*pres.p.* **talcuming**, *past, p.p.* **talcumed**) to use talcum powder to dry or freshen (the body) (*talcumed the baby's bottom*). **talcum powder** *n.* 1 a usu. perfumed powder made from purified talc, used, esp. after a bath or shower, to absorb excess body moisture. 2 powdered magnesium silicate. [F, from Arab. *talq*]

tale (tāl) *n.* 1 a narrative, an account, a story, true or fictitious, esp. an imaginative or legendary story. 2 an idle or malicious report. 3 †a number, a total, a reckoning. **to tell a tale** to have clear significance. **to tell its own**

tale 1 to be self-evident. 2 to have clear significance. **to tell one's own tale** to speak for oneself. **to tell tales** 1 to report malicious stories to someone in authority. 2 to tell lies. **to tell tales out of school** to give away secrets, to break confidences. **to tell the tale** (*coll.*) to tell a piteous story. **talebearer** *n.* a person who spreads malicious reports or breaks confidences. **talebearing** *n., a.* **taleteller** *n.* 1 a storyteller. 2 a talebearer. [OE *tael*, number, *talu*, story (cp. TAAL, Icel. *tal*, story, *tala*, number), cogn. with TELL[1]]

Taleban TALIBAN.

talent (tal´ənt) *n.* 1 a particular aptitude, gift or faculty. 2 mental capacity of a superior order. 3 a talented person; talented people (*an exhibition of work from the talent of this year's art department*). 4 (*coll.*) attractive members of the opposite sex, collectively. 5 a weight and denomination of money in ancient Greece, Rome, Assyria etc. differing in various countries at different times (the later Attic talent was 56 lb. 14 oz. troy (29.4 kg)). **talented** *a.* endowed with talents or ability. **talentless** *a.* **talent scout** *n.* a person who is employed to discover talented people, e.g. for sports clubs or the entertainment industry. **talent show** *n.* a show which gives amateur entertainers the chance to display their ability. **talent spotter** *n.* a talent scout. **talent-spot** *v.t., v.i.* (*pres.p.* **talent-spotting,** *past, p.p.* **talent-spotted**). [F, from L *talentum*, Gr. *talanton*, balance, a talent, cogn. with *talas -ntos*, enduring, cp. L *tollere*, to lift]

tales (tā´lēz) *n.* (*Law*) 1 a writ for summoning jurors to make up a deficiency. 2 a list of people who can be summoned for this purpose. **talesman** (tā´lēzmən, tālz´-) *n.* (*pl.* **talesmen**) a person summoned by a tales. [L, pl. of *tālis*, such (first word of writ)]

tali TALUS[1].

Taliban (tal´iban), **Taleban** *n.pl.* members of a fundamentalist Islamic militia in Afghanistan. [Arab., students]

taligrade (tal´igrād) *a.* (*Zool.*) walking on the outer side of the foot. [TALUS[1], L *-grādus*, walking]

taliped (tal´iped) *a.* (*Med.*) club-footed. **talipes** (-pēz) *n.* club foot. [TALUS[1], L *pes pedis*, foot]

talipot (tal´ipot) *n.* a S Indian palm, *Corypha umbraculifera*, with very large fan-shaped leaves used in thatching and as sunshades. [Hind. *tālpāt*]

talisman (tal´izmən) *n.* (*pl.* **talismans**) 1 a charm or an amulet that is believed to have magical powers, esp. one thought to protect the wearer from evil and to bring them good luck. 2 (*fig.*) something producing wonderful effects. **talismanic** (-man´-) *a.* **talismanically** *adv.* [F and Sp., from It. *talismano*, Arab. *tilsam*, Gr. *telesma*, payment, late Gr., mystery, from *teleein*, to accomplish, to pay, from *telos*, end]

talk (tawk) *v.i.* 1 to communicate ideas or exchange thoughts in spoken words. 2 to have the power of speech. 3 to reveal secret or confidential information. 4 to be influential (*money talks*). 5 to communicate by radio or electronic signals. 6 to make sounds as in speech. ~*v.t.* 1 to express in speech. 2 to converse about, to discuss. 3 to speak as a language, to use (a specified language) (*They talk Gaelic at home*). 4 to persuade or otherwise affect by talking. ~*n.* 1 conversation, chat. 2 a subject of conversation. 3 gossip, rumour. 4 a short speech or address. 5 a specified form of speaking (*small talk*). 6 boastful claims (*says her dad's a millionaire, but I think it's all talk*). 7 (*in pl.*) discussion to negotiate something (*held talks about the gun control proposals*). **now you're talking** (*coll.*) at last you're saying something I can agree with or relate to. **talking of** while on the subject of, concerning (*Talking of Helen, where is she working now?*). **talk of the devil** DEVIL. **to know what one is talking about** to be an expert on a particular subject. **to talk about** 1 to discuss. 2 to gossip about. 3 used to express ironic or disparaging emphasis (*Talk about ignorant! He thought Cyprus was in Asia!*). **to talk at** 1 to address remarks to, often indirectly or incessantly. 2 to talk, esp. offensively, about (a person) in their presence. **to talk away** 1 to spend or use up (time) in talking. 2 to speak or carry on speaking. **to talk back** 1 to reply. 2 to answer impudently. **to talk big** to boast. **to talk down** 1 to silence by loud or persistent talking. 2 to guide (a pilot or aeroplane) in to land by giving verbal instructions. **to talk down to** to speak to in a patronizing or condescending way. **to talk into** to persuade to do by argument. **to talk nineteen to the dozen** DOZEN. **to talk of** 1 to discuss. 2 to mention. 3 (*coll.*) to suggest, esp. tentatively. **to talk out** to kill (a motion) by discussing it until the time of adjournment. **to talk out of** to dissuade from doing by argument. **to talk over** 1 to discuss at length. 2 to persuade or convince by talking. **to talk round** 1 to discuss without coming to a decision. 2 to persuade. **to talk shop** to talk about work, esp. tediously or at an inappropriate time. **to talk tall** to boast. **to talk the hind legs off a donkey** DONKEY. **to talk through** 1 to explain the stages of (a procedure). 2 to discuss thoroughly and come to a resolution about. **to talk through one's hat** HAT. **to talk to** 1 to speak to. 2 (*coll.*) to remonstrate with, to reprove. **to talk turkey** TURKEY. **to talk up** 1 to speak loudly, boldly. 2 to praise. **you can/can't talk** used to remind the listener that what is being said also applies to them. **talkative** *a.* given to talking a lot. **talkatively** *adv.* **talkativeness** *n.* **talkback** *n.* a two-way radio system. **talker** *n.* a person who speaks, esp. in a specified way (*a bit of a smooth talker*). **talkie** *n.* (*coll.*) an early film with sound. **talking** *a.* 1 that talks. 2 able to talk. **talking book** *n.* an audiotape of someone reading a book, usu. a novel in abridged form. **talking film, talking picture** *n.* a film with a soundtrack. **talking head** *n.* (*coll.*) on television, a person shown from the shoulders up only, unaccompanied by action or illustrative material. **talking point** *n.* a matter to be or being talked about. **talking shop** *n.* (*often derog.*) a meeting or institution where issues will be discussed but no action will follow. **talking-to** *n.* (*coll.*) a telling-off, a reproof. **talk of the town** *n.* the thing that everyone is discussing or is interested in. **talk show** *n.* a chat show. [ME *talken*, freq. of OE *tal-*, see TALE]

tall (tawl) *a.* 1 high in stature, above the average height. 2 having a specified height. 3 (*sl.*) extravagant, boastful, exorbitant, excessive (*a bit of a tall story; a tall order*). ~*adv.* 1 in a way that suggests great height. 2 proudly (*walk tall*). **tallboy** *n.* a high chest of drawers, often on legs. **tall drink** *n.* a drink served in a long narrow glass. **tall hat** *n.* TOP HAT (under TOP[1]). **tallish** *a.* **tallness** *n.* **tall order** *n.* a difficult or demanding task, an exacting or unreasonable demand. **tall ship** *n.* a square-rigged sailing ship. **tall story** *n.* an exaggerated account. **tall talk** *n.* (*coll.*) exaggeration. [representing or rel. to OE *getael*, swift, prompt, cp. OHG *gizal*, quick]

tallage (tal´ij) *n.* (*Hist.*) 1 a tax on towns levied by the king (abolished 1340). 2 a tax on vassals levied by a lord or liege. [OF *taillage*, from *tailler*, to cut, see TAIL[2]]

tallier TALLY.

tallith (tal´ith) *n.* a fringed scarf worn over the head and shoulders by Jewish men during prayer. [Heb.]

tallow (tal´ō) *n.* a substance composed of the harder or less fusible fats, chiefly of animals, esp. beef or mutton fat, used for making candles, soap etc. ~*v.t.* 1 to grease or smear with tallow. 2 to fatten, to cause to have a large quantity of tallow. **tallow candle** *n.* **tallower** *n.* **tallow face** *n.* a person with a pale complexion. **tallow-faced** *a.* **tallowish, tallowy** *a.* **tallow tree** *n.* any of various trees yielding vegetable tallow, esp. *Sapium sebiferum*. [ME *talgh*, cp. MDut. *talgh*, Dut. *talk*, LG, Dan., and Swed. *talg*, Icel. *tōlgr*]

tally (tal´i) *n.* (*pl.* **tallies**) **1** a reckoning, an account. **2** a number reckoned or registered, a score. **3** (*Hist.*) a stick in which notches are cut as a means of keeping accounts. **4** a mark registering number (of things received, delivered etc.). **5** anything made to correspond with something else, a counterpart, a duplicate (of). **6** a label or tag for identification. ~*v.t.* (*3rd pers. sing. pres.* **tallies,** *pres.p.* **tallying,** *past, p.p.* **tallied**) to score as on a tally, to record, to register. ~*v.i.* to agree, to correspond (with). **tallier** *n.* **tally clerk** *n.* an official on a wharf who checks a ship's cargo against its cargo list. **tallyman, tallywoman** *n.* (*pl.* **tallymen, tallywomen**) **1** a person who keeps a tally. **2** a person who keeps a tallyshop. **3** a person who collects hire purchase payments. **tally sheet** *n.* a sheet of paper on which a tally is kept. **tally shop** *n.* a shop where goods are sold on the tally system. **tally system** *n.* the system of giving and receiving goods on credit, to be paid for by regular instalments. [F *taille,* notch, incision, as TAIL[2]]

tally-ho (talihō´) *int.* used to encourage hounds when the quarry is sighted. ~*n.* (*pl.* **tally-hos**) a shout of this. ~*v.i.* (*3rd pers. sing. pres.* **tally-hoes,** *pres.p.* **tally-hoing,** *past, p.p.* **tally-hoed**) to utter this cry. ~*v.t.* to urge on (hounds) with this cry. [prob. F *taïaut*]

Talmud (tal´mud) *n.* the body of Jewish civil and religious law not included in the Pentateuch, including the Mishna and the Gemara. **Talmudic** (-mud´-), **Talamudical** *a.* **Talmudism** *n.* **Talmudist** *n.* a student of or expert in the Talmud. **Talmudistic** (-dis´-) *a.* [late Heb. from *lāmad,* to teach]

talon (tal´ən) *n.* **1** a claw, esp. of a bird of prey. **2** anything hooked or clawlike. **3** the cards left in the pack after dealing. **4** on the Stock Exchange, a detachable part of a certificate which, when surrendered, entitles the holder to a new sheet of coupons, esp. for bearer bonds. **5** the projection on a bolt against which the key of the lock presses. **6** (*Archit.*) an ogee moulding. **taloned** *a.* [F, heel, late L *tālōnem,* nom. *tālo,* L TALUS[1]]

†**talpa** (tal´pə) *n.* an encysted tumour, a wen. [L, mole]

talus[1] (tā´ləs) *n.* (*pl.* **tali** (-lī)) (*Anat.*) the ankle-bone. [L, ankle, heel]

talus[2] (tā´ləs) *n.* (*pl.* **taluses**) **1** a mass or sloping heap of fragments accumulated at the base of a cliff or scree. **2** the slope or inclination of a wall etc., tapering towards the top. [F, perh. from *talūtium,* slope]

tam (tam) *n.* (*coll.*) a tam-o'-shanter.

tamable TAMEABLE (under TAME).

tamale (təmah´li) *n.* a Mexican dish of highly seasoned maize and meat. [Sp. *tamal*]

tamandua (təman´dūə) *n.* (*pl.* **tamanduas**) any small tropical American anteater of the genus *Tamandua.* [Tupi-Guarani]

tamarack (tam´ərak) *n.* **1** an American larch, *Larix laricina.* **2** the wood of this. [N Am. Ind.]

tamari (təmah´ri) *n.* a concentrated wheat-free sauce made from soya beans. [Jap.]

tamarillo (tamərilʹō) *n.* (*pl.* **tamarillos**) the fruit of the tree tomato. [invented name]

tamarin (tam´ərin) *n.* any small monkey of the genera *Saguinus* or *Leontopithecus* of the forests of Central and S America. [F, from Carib]

tamarind (tam´ərind) *n.* **1** a tropical tree, *Tamarindus indica.* **2** its pulpy leguminous fruit, used in making drinks, as a food flavouring and as a laxative. **3** its wood. [MF, from Sp. *tamarindo,* Arab. *tamr,* ripe date, *Hind,* India]

tamarisk (tam´ərisk) *n.* an evergreen shrub of the genus *Tamarix,* with slender feathery branches and white and pink flowers. [L *tamariscus*]

tamasha (təmah´shə) *n.* in the Indian subcontinent, a show, a public function. [Urdu, from Arab., a stroll]

tambour (tam´buə) *n.* **1** a drum, esp. a bass drum. **2** a circular frame on which silk etc., is embroidered. **3** silk or other fabric embroidered thus. **4** a cylindrical stone, such as one of the courses of the shaft of a column. **5** a vestibule with a ceiling and folding doors in a porch etc., for preventing draughts. **6** a palisade defending an entrance. **7** a sliding door, or rolling top, on cabinets and desks etc. **8** a sloping buttress that allows the ball in a game of real tennis or fives to be deflected. ~*v.t., v.i.* to embroider with or on a tambour. **tamboura** (-boo´rə) *n.* an eastern stringed instrument, plucked like a guitar. **tambourin** (-rin) *n.* **1** a Provençal tabor or drum. **2** a dance accompanied by this and the pipe. **3** the music for such a dance. [F, see TABOR]

tambourine (tambərēn´) *n.* a small percussion instrument composed of a hoop with parchment stretched across one head and loose jingling discs in the sides, played by striking with the hand etc. **tambourinist** *n.* [F, dim. of TAMBOUR]

tame (tām) *a.* **1** (of an animal) having lost its native wildness, domesticated, not wild. **2** tractable, docile. **3** subdued, spiritless. **4** dull, insipid (*an incredibly tame production of 'Hamlet'*). **5** (*US, coll.*) (of land) cultivated. **6** (of a plant) produced by cultivation. ~*v.t.* **1** to make tame. **2** to domesticate, to make docile. **3** to subdue, to humble. **tameable, tamable** *a.* capable of being tamed. **tameability** (-bil´-) *n.* **tameableness** *n.* **tamely** *adv.* **tameness** *n.* **tamer** *n.* [OE *tam,* whence *temian,* v. (cp. Dut. *tam,* G *Zahm,* Dan. and Swed. *tam,* also L *domāre,* Gr. *damaein,* to tame)]

Tamil (tam´il) *n.* **1** a member of the Dravidian people who inhabit S India and Sri Lanka. **2** the language of this people. ~*a.* of or relating to the Tamils or their language. **Tamilian** (-il´iən) *a.* [Tamil]

Tammany (tam´əni), **Tammany Hall** *n.* (*US*) **1** a corrupt political organization. **2** political corruption. **Tammanyism** *n.* [*Tammany* Hall, meeting place of a political organization in New York affiliated to the Democratic party, named after Indian chief *Tamanend*]

Tammuz (tam´uz) *n.* the fourth month in the Jewish calendar according to biblical reckoning, the tenth in the civil year, usually falling in June and July. [Heb.]

tammy (tam´i) *n.* (*pl.* **tammies**) (*coll.*) a tam-o'-shanter.

tam-o'-shanter (taməshan´tə) *n.* a cap fitted closely round the brows but wide and full above. [Burns's poem *Tam o' Shanter*]

tamoxifen (tamok´sifen) *n.* (*Med.*) a drug that suppresses the effects of the hormone oestrogen and which is used in the treatment of women's breast cancer and infertility. [from elements of the drug's chemical formula]

tamp (tamp) *v.t.* **1** to fill up (a blast-hole) with rammed clay above the charge. **2** to ram down (railway ballast, road-metal, soil, tobacco etc.). ~*n.* **1** a person who or device that tamps. **2** a reflective casing around the core of a nuclear weapon which increases its efficiency. **tamper**[1] *n.* **tamping** *n.* material used to tamp a hole. **tampion** (-piən), **tompion** (tom-) *n.* **1** a stopper for the mouth of a gun. **2** a stopper for the top of an organ pipe. **tampon** (-pon) *n.* a plug of lint etc. used for stopping haemorrhage and to absorb bodily secretions such as menstrual blood. ~*v.t.* (*pres.p.* **tamponing,** *past, p.p.* **tamponed**) to plug with a tampon. **tamponade** (-nād´) *n.* **1** cardiac tamponade. **2** the surgical use of a tampon. **tamponage** (tam´pənij) *n.* TAMPONADE (under TAMP). [F *tampon,* a plug]

tamper[1] TAMP.

tamper[2] (tam´pə) *v.i.* **1** to meddle (with). **2** to interfere illegitimately (with), esp. to alter documents etc., to adulterate, or to employ blackmail. **tamperer** *n.* **tampering** *n.* **tamper-proof** *a.* made to be very difficult to tamper with. [var. of TEMPER]

tampion, tampon etc. TAMP.

tam-tam (tam´tam) *n.* a large metal gong. [Hind.]

tan[1] (tan) *n.* 1 a deepening of the skin's colour, esp. from pinkish-white to bronze, caused by exposure to the sun's rays or to artificial ultraviolet rays. 2 a yellowish-brown colour. 3 the bark of the oak or other trees, bruised and broken in a mill and used for tanning hides. 4 SPENT TAN (under SPEND). *~a.* yellowish-brown. *~v.t.* (*pres.p.* **tanning**, *past, p.p.* **tanned**) 1 to make brown by exposure to the sun or to artificial ultraviolet rays. 2 to convert (raw hide) into leather by steeping in an infusion of tannin or by the action of some mineral or chemical salt. 3 (*coll.*) to flog, to thrash. *~v.i.* to become brown by exposure to the sun or to artificial ultraviolet rays. **to tan someone's hide** to beat someone very badly, to thrash. **tanbark** *n.* the bark of some trees, such as the oak, a source of tannin. **tan-coloured,** (*N Am.*) **tan-colored** *a.* yellowish-brown. **tannable** *a.* **tannage** (-ij) *n.* 1 tanning. 2 material to be tanned. **tannate** (-ət) *n.* tannic acid salt. **tanned** *a.* 1 bronzed by the sun or artificial ultraviolet rays. 2 treated by a tanning process. **tanner**[1] *n.* a person who tans hides. **tannery** *n.* (*pl.* **tanneries**) a place where tanning is done. **tannic** *a.* of, relating to or derived from tanbark. **tannic acid** *n.* tannin. **tanniferous** (-if´-) *a.* **tannin** (-in) *n.* an astringent substance obtained from oak-bark etc., used in tanning leather, making writing ink etc., and in medicine. **tanning** *n.* **tannish** *a.* tending towards yellowish brown. [F *tan* (whence *tanner*, to tan), G *Tanne*, fir tree, OHG *Tanna*, fir, oak]

tan[2] (tan) *abbr.* tangent.

tanager (tan´əjə) *n.* an American bird of the subfamily Thraupinae, related to the finches, usu. with brilliantly coloured plumage. [Tupi-Guarani *tangara*]

tandem (tan´dəm) *n.* 1 a bicycle or tricycle for two riders one behind the other. 2 a vehicle with two or more horses harnessed one behind the other. 3 an arrangement of two things one behind the other. *~adv.* 1 with horses harnessed one behind the other. 2 (harnessed) one behind the other. *~a.* harnessed or arranged in this way. **in tandem** 1 with one thing behind another. 2 in partnership, together. [L, at length]

tandoor (tanduə´) *n.* a clay oven as used in N India and Pakistan. **tandoori** (-doo´ri) *a.* cooked in such a clay oven (*tandoori chicken*). *~n.* food so cooked. [Hind. *tandur*, oven, from Arab. *tanur*, oven]

Tang (tang) *n.* a dynasty that ruled in China, AD 618–906. *~a.* of or relating to this dynasty. [Chin.]

tang[1] (tang) *n.* 1 a strong taste or flavour. 2 a distinctive quality. 3 a projecting piece, tongue etc., such as the shank of a knife, chisel etc., inserted into the haft. **tangy** *a.* (*comp.* **tangier**, *superl.* **tangiest**). **tanginess** *n.* [Icel. *tange*, point]

tang[2] (tang) *n.* a ringing or clanging sound. *~v.t.* to ring or clang. *~v.i.* to cause to ring or clang. [imit.]

tanga (tang´gə) *n.* pants, briefs or bikini bottoms that consist of two small joined triangular pieces, held in place by a string or thong waistband. [Bantu]

tangelo (tan´jəlō) *n.* (*pl.* **tangelos**) a tangerine and pomelo hybrid. [*tang*erine, pom*elo*]

tangent (tan´jənt) *n.* 1 a straight line meeting a circle or curve without intersecting it. 2 in trigonometry, the ratio of the sine to the cosine. *~a.* meeting at a single point without intersection. **to go/ fly off at a tangent** to diverge suddenly from a course of thought or action. **tangency** *n.* **tangent galvanometer** *n.* a galvanometer that has a horizontal magnetic needle which is deflected when a current is passed through the vertical coil. **tangential** (-jen´shəl) *a.* 1 relating to or characteristic of a tangent. 2 along the line of a tangent. 3 digressive, irrelevant. **tangentiality** (-shial´-) *n.* **tangentially** *adv.* [L *tangens -ntem*, pres.p. of *tangere*, to touch]

tangerine (tanjərēn´) *n.* 1 a small, loose-skinned orange. 2 a bright orange colour. *~a.* bright orange. [*Tangier*, a Moroccan seaport]

tangible (tan´jibəl) *a.* 1 perceptible by touch. 2 definite, capable of realization, not visionary. 3 corporeal. *~n.* (*usu. pl.*) a tangible thing or property as opposed to goodwill. **tangibility** (-bil´-), **tangibleness** *n.* **tangibly** *adv.* [F, from late L *tangibilis*, from *tangere*, to touch]

tangle[1] (tang´gəl) *v.t.* 1 to knot together or intertwine in a confused mass. 2 to entangle, to ensnare, to entrap. 3 to complicate. *~v.i.* 1 to become thus knotted together or intertwined. 2 to come into conflict with. 3 to embrace. *~n.* 1 a confused mass of threads, hairs etc., intertwined. 2 a state of confusion. 3 a complicated situation or problem. **tangled** *a.* **tanglement** *n.* **tangler** *n.* **tanglesome** *a.* tangling. **tanglingly** *adv.* **tangly** *a.* (*comp.* **tanglier**, *superl.* **tangliest**). [ME var. of *tagle*, etym. uncertain]

tangle[2] (tang´gəl) *n.* any of various seaweeds, esp. the edible ones of the genus *Laminaria*. [Icel. *thöngull*]

tango[1] (tang´gō) *n.* (*pl.* **tangos**) 1 a Latin American dance that is characterized by highly stylized, often erotic, body movements punctuated by glides and pauses. 2 a piece of music for this dance. *~v.i.* (*3rd pers. sing. pres.* **tangoes**, *pres.p.* **tangoing**, *past, p.p.* **tangoed**) to dance the tango. [Am. Sp.]

tango[2] (tang´gō) *n.* a bright orange colour. *~a.* bright orange. [abbr. of TANGERINE, infl. by TANGO[1]]

tangram (tang´gram) *n.* a Chinese puzzle consisting of a square cut into seven differently shaped pieces which have to be fitted together. [etym. uncertain]

tanh (than, tansh, tanāch´) *n.* hyperbolic tangent. [*tan*gent, *h*yperbolic]

tank (tangk) *n.* 1 a cistern or vessel of large size for holding liquid, gas etc. 2 a heavily-armoured motor vehicle running on caterpillar tractors and carrying guns of various calibres. 3 a reservoir in a motor vehicle where the fuel goes. 4 a reservoir for water. 5 an excavation in which water collects. 6 the part of a locomotive tender containing the supply of water for the boiler. *~v.t.* 1 to store or treat in a tank. 2 (*sl.*) to defeat. *~v.i.* to move quickly and deliberately (*tanked up the road*). **to tank up** 1 to fill a vehicle with fuel. 2 to drink, or cause to drink, a large quantity of alcohol. **tankage** (-ij) *n.* 1 storage in tanks. 2 a charge for this. 3 the cubic capacity of a tank or tanks. 4 the residue from rendering refuse fats, bones etc., used as a fertilizer. **tanked-up** *a.* (*sl.*) drunk, inebriated with drugs. **tank engine** *n.* a locomotive with a water tank over the boiler, and without a tender. **tanker** *n.* 1 a specially-built ship, aircraft or vehicle fitted with tanks for carrying a cargo of oil or other liquids. 2 an aircraft for refuelling other aircraft in the air. *~v.t.* to transport using a tanker. **tank-farming** *n.* cultivation of crops etc. that involves growing plants in water without any soil. **tank-farmer** *n.* **tankful** *n.* (*pl.* **tankfuls**). **tanking** *n.* (*sl.*) a defeat. **tankless** *a.* **tanklike** *a.* **tank top** *n.* a sleeveless top with low neck, usually worn over a shirt or blouse. [Port. *tanque* (cp. Sp. *estanque*), from late L, as STAUNCH[2]]

tanka (tang´kə) *n.* a Japanese verse form with five lines and thirty-one syllables, the first and third lines having five syllables and the others having seven. [Jap. *tan*, short, *ka*, verse]

tankard (tang´kəd) *n.* 1 a large drinking-vessel, usu. of metal and often with a cover. 2 the amount a tankard holds. [F *tanquard*, MDut. *tanckaert*]

tannable, tannage etc. TAN[1].

tanner[1] TAN[1].

tanner[2] (tan´ə) *n.* (*Hist.*, *sl.*) a sixpence. [etym. uncertain]

tannery, tannic etc. TAN[1].

Tannoy® (tan´oi) *n.* a public announcement and loudspeaker system.

tanrec TENREC.

tansy (tan´zi) *n.* (*pl.* **tansies**) a yellow-flowered perennial herb, *Tanacetum vulgare*, with much-divided, bitter, aromatic leaves, formerly used in cookery and medicine. [OF *tanasie, athanasie*, L and Gr. *athanasia*, immortality (*a-*, not, without, *thanatos*, death)]

tantalate, tantalic TANTALUM.

tantalise TANTALIZE.

tantalite TANTALUM.

tantalize (tan´təlīz), **tantalise** *v.t.* 1 to torment or tease by seeming to offer something badly wanted but continually withholding it. 2 to raise and then disappoint the hopes of. **tantalization** (-zā´shən) *n.* **tantalizer** *n.* **tantalizing** *a.* **tantalizingly** *adv.* [as TANTALUS]

tantalum (tan´tələm) *n.* a rare hard greyish-white metallic element, at. no. 73, chem. symbol Ta, which is highly resistant to heat and acid corrosion. **tantalate** (-lāt) *n.* a salt of tantalic acid. **tantalic** *a.* relating to or derived from tantalum. **tantalic acid** *n.* a white hydrated oxide of pentavalent tantalum. **tantalite** (-līt) *n.* a black mineral found in granite, an ore of tantalum. [as TANTALUS]

tantalus (tan´tələs) *n.* 1 a spirit-stand in which the decanters remain in sight but are secured by a lock. 2 a wading bird, *Mycteria americana*, similar to the ibis. [L *Tantalus*, from Gr. *Tantalos*, who, in Greek mythology, was condemned to stand waist-deep in water which would recede if he tried to drink it and with branches laden with fruit which would draw back if he tried to pick it]

tantamount (tan´təmownt) *a.* equivalent (to) in value or effect. [A-F *tant amunter*, to amount to so much]

tantivy (tantiv´i) *n.* (*pl.* **tantivies**) 1 a hunting cry. 2 a rushing movement, a furious gallop, great speed. ~*a.* swift, speedy. ~*adv.* swiftly, speedily. [prob. imit.]

tant mieux (tõ myœ´) *int.* so much the better. [F]

tanto (tan´tō) *adv.* (*Mus.*) too much. [It.]

tant pis (tõ pē´) *int.* so much the worse. [F]

tantra (tan´trə) *n.* any of a class of later Sanskrit Hindu and Buddhist textbooks dealing chiefly with magical powers. **tantric** *a.* **tantrism** *n.* 1 the teaching of the tantras. 2 a mystical movement based on tantra texts in Hinduism and Buddhism. **tantrist** *n.* [Sansk., orig. thread]

tantrum (tan´trəm) *n.* a burst of ill temper, a fit of passion. [perh. from Welsh *tant*, passion, impulse]

Taoiseach (tē´shəkh, -shək) *n.* the Prime Minister of the Republic of Ireland. [Ir., leader]

Taoism (tow´izm, tah´ōizm) *n.* the Chinese religious system based on the teachings of Laoze (b. 604 BC), primarily concerned with achieving harmony with the universe. **Tao** *n.* in Taoism, the principle of creative harmony in the universe, the relation between human life and eternal truth. **Taoist** (-ist) *n.* **Taoistic** (-is´-) *a.* [Chin. *tao*, way, -ISM]

tap[1] (tap) *v.t.* (*pres.p.* **tapping**, *past, p.p.* **tapped**) 1 to strike lightly or gently. 2 to strike lightly with. 3 to make with a tapping noise (*tapped the beat with her fingers*). ~*v.i.* 1 to strike a gentle blow. 2 to tap-dance. ~*n.* 1 a light or gentle blow, a rap. 2 the sound of this. 3 (*pl.*) a military signal for putting lights out in quarters or given at a military funeral. 4 a small piece of metal on the heel or toe of a tap-dancer's shoe designed to make the tapping noise. 5 tap-dancing (*learning ballet and tap*). **tap-dance** *n.* a step dance where the performers wear shoes with metal studs in the heels and toes to make a rhythmic sound as they dance. ~*v.i.* to perform such a dance. **tap-dancer** *n.* **tap-dancing** *n.* **tap-in** *n.* a strike, esp. on goal in football, that does not require much power or skill. **tapper**[1] *n.* **tapping** *n., a.* **tap-shoe** *n.* a shoe with specially fitted metal studs in the heels and toes, for tap-dancing. [F *taper, tapper*, prob. from Gmc. (cp. LG and G *tappen*, Icel. *tapsa*), prob. imit.]

tap[2] (tap) *n.* 1 a device that allows water or other fluid to be drawn out at a controlled rate; a faucet, a spigot. 2 a device connected secretly to a telephone and allowing someone other than the user to listen in to calls. 3 an act of listening in to a telephone call between other people. 4 (*coll.*) a taproom. 5 a tool for cutting female or internal screw-threads. 6 a plug or bung for closing a hole in a cask etc. ~*v.t.* (*pres.p.* **tapping**, *past, p.p.* **tapped**) 1 to pierce (a cask etc.) so as to let out a liquid. 2 to let out or draw off (a liquid) in this way. 3 to provide with a tap or cock. 4 to draw (fluid) from a person's body. 5 to draw fluid from (a person) in this way. 6 (*fig.*) to draw upon (a source of supply) usually for the first time. 7 (*coll.*) to obtain money etc. from (*tapped his mum for £10*). 8 to divert current from (a wire). 9 to attach a device to (a telephone) in order to listen in to other people's conversations. 10 to make an internal screw in. **on tap** 1 (of a cask etc.) tapped so that liquor can be drawn off. 2 (of liquor) ready to be drawn off by tap. 3 (*coll.*) freely available for use. **taphole** *n.* a hole in a furnace through which molten lead can be run off. **tappable** *a.* (of rubber trees etc.) able or suitable to be tapped. **tapper**[2] *n.* **taproom** *n.* a room where alcoholic drinks, esp. beer on tap, are served. **tap root** *n.* the main root of a plant penetrating straight downwards for some depth. **tapster** (-stə) *n.* a person who serves liquor in a bar. **tap water** *n.* water from a tap, rather than from a bottle. [OE *taeppa*, cp. Dut. *tap*, G *zappen*, Icel. *tappi*, OHG *Zapho*]

tapa (tah´pə) *n.* 1 a kind of tough clothlike paper made from the bark of a tree, used by Polynesians for clothes, nets etc. 2 the bark this material is made from. [Polynesian]

tapadero (tapədeə´rō) *n.* (*pl.* **tapaderos**) a leather guard worn in front of the stirrup in California and other parts of the western US. [Sp., cover, from *tapar*, to stop up, to cover]

tapas (tap´as) *n.pl.* various light savoury snacks or appetizers, as served in Spain. **tapas bar** *n.* a bar serving this kind of food. [Sp.]

tape (tāp) *n.* 1 a continuous strip of paper or magnetized flexible material that sound, pictures or other data can be recorded on by various types of recording machines. 2 a unit containing a roll of tape for recording (*put the tape into the video*). 3 a narrow strip of woven linen, cotton etc., used for tying things together, in dressmaking, bookbinding etc. 4 a narrow strip of adhesive material, used for sticking things down or together, as insulation etc. 5 a strip of material stretched across a racecourse at the winning post. 6 a tape-measure. 7 a strong flexible band rotating on pulleys in printing and other machines. ~*v.t.* 1 to record (sound, pictures or other data) on magnetic tape. 2 to provide, fasten or tie up with tapes. 3 to bind (sections of a book) with narrow bands. 4 to get a measure of. **on tape** recorded on magnetic tape. **to breast the tape** in a race on foot, to touch or break the tape across the course to win. **to have taped** (*coll.*) to have a complete understanding of (a person or thing). **tapeable** *a.* **tape deck** *n.* a machine for recording sound on to magnetic tape and which replays this sound through an independent amplifier. **tape machine** *n.* a telegraphic instrument that receives and records news, stock prices etc. **tape-measure, tape-line** *n.* a tape or strip of metal, marked with centimetres, inches etc. for measuring, usu. coiled in a round flat case. **taper**[1] *n.* **tape-record** *v.t.* to record using a tape recorder. **tape recorder** *n.* an electronic apparatus for recording music etc. on magnetic tape and which can also reproduce recorded sounds from such tapes. **tape recording** *n.* 1 an act or the process of recording sound on magnetic tape. 2 a tape that has music etc. recorded on it. **tapeworm** *n.* a cestoid worm that parasitically infests the alimentary canal of humans and other vertebrates. [OE *taeppe*, L *tapēte*, cp. TAPPET and TAPESTRY]

taper[1] TAPE.

taper[2] (tā´pə) *n.* **1** a small wax candle. **2** anything giving a very feeble light. ~*v.i.* **1** to become gradually smaller or narrower towards one end. **2** to become gradually smaller or less important. ~*v.t.* to make gradually smaller, narrower or less important. **tapered** *a.* tapering in form. **taperer** *n.* a person who carries a taper, esp. in a religious ceremony. **tapering** *a.* **taperingly** *adv.* [OE *tapor*, cp. Ir. *tapar*, Welsh *tampr*]

tapestry (tap´istri) *n.* (*pl.* **tapestries**) **1** a textile fabric in which the wool is supplied by a spindle instead of a shuttle, with designs or pictures applied by stitches across the warp. **2** any ornamental fabric with designs or pictures applied in this manner. **3** anything that is perceived as being intricate or interwoven (*the tapestry of life*). ~*a.* of tapestry. **tapestried** *a.* [F *tapisserie*, from *tapisser*, to furnish with tapestry, from TAPIS]

tapetum (təpē´təm) *n.* (*pl.* **tapeta** (-tə)) **1** a layer of cells lining the cavity of anthers in flowering plants or of the sporangia in ferns. **2** a part of the choroid membrane in the eye of certain vertebrates, such as cats, which reflects light and allows them to see in the dark. [late L, from L *tapēte*, carpet]

taphonomy (tafon´əmi) *n.* the study of fossilization processes. **taphonomic** (-fənom´ik) *a.* **taphonomist** *n.* [Gr. *taphos*, grave]

tapioca (tapiō´kə) *n.* a starchy, granular substance produced by beating cassava, forming a light farinaceous food. [Port., from Tupi-Guarani *tipioka*, cassava juice]

tapir (tā´pə) *n.* an ungulate mammal of the genus *Tapirus* of Central and S America and parts of Asia, related to the rhinoceros and the horse, with a short, flexible snout which it uses for feeding on vegetation. **tapiroid** (-roid) *a.*, *n.* [Tupi-Guarani *tapīra*]

tapis (tap´ē) *n.* (*pl.* **tapis**) a tapestry, a thick table-covering. **on the tapis** under consideration. [F, tapestry, from med. L *tapētium*, Gr. *tapētion*, dim. of *tapēs-pētos*]

tapotement (təpōt´mənt) *n.* the use of light rapid tapping as a form of massage. [F *tapoter*, to tap]

tappable TAP[2].

tapper[1] TAP[1].

tapper[2] TAP[2].

tappet (tap´it) *n.* a projecting arm or lever that gives intermittent motion to some part in machinery. **tappet loom** *n.* a loom in which the heddles are worked by tappets. [perh. dim. of TAP[1]]

tappit (tap´it) *a.* (*Sc.*) topped, crested. **tappit hen** *n.* **1** a hen with a topknot or tuft. **2** a pewter drinking-vessel that has a lid with a fancy decoration on the top. [Sc. var. of *topped* (TOP[1], -ED)]

tapster TAP[2].

tapu (tah´poo) *a.* (*esp. New Zeal.*) sacred, taboo. [Maori]

tar[1] (tah) *n.* **1** a thick, dark, viscid oily liquid produced by the dry distillation of organic bodies and bituminous minerals, used in surfacing roads, preserving wood and the manufacture of antiseptics. **2** a similar by-product of burning tobacco. ~*v.t.* (*pres.p.* **tarring**, *past*, *p.p.* **tarred**) to cover with tar. **tarred with the same brush** having the same bad characteristics. **to tar and feather** to smear with tar and then cover with feathers as a form of punishment. **tarbrush** *n.* a brush used to apply tar. **Tarmac** (-mak), **tarmac** *n.* **1** TARMACADAM (under TAR[1]). **2** a road or other surface made of this (*The plane taxied down the tarmac*). **tarmac** *v.t.* (*pres.p.* **tarmacking**, *past*, *p.p.* **tarmacked**) to put a layer of tarmacadam on (a surface such as a road). **tarmacadam** (-məka´dəm) *n.* a mixture of stones or slag held together by tar and used in surfacing roads, runways etc. **tar-paper** *n.* paper treated with tar, used in the building trade. **tarry**[1] *a.* (*comp.* **tarrier**, *superl.* **tarriest**). **tarriness** *n.* **tar sand** *n.* (*Geol.*) sand or sandstone that has been naturally impregnated with bitumen. **tar-seal** *v.t.* to cover the surface of (a road) with tarmacadam. ~*n.* the bitumen surface of a road. **tar-sealed** *a.* [OE *teoru* (cp. Dut. *teer*, Icel. *tjara*, Dan. *tjaere*, Swed. *tjära*), cogn. with TREE]

tar[2] (tah) *n.* (*coll.*) a sailor. [short for TARPAULIN]

ta-ra (tərah´) *int.* (*coll.*) goodbye. [North. var. of TA-TA]

taradiddle (tar´ədidəl), **tarradiddle** *n.* (*coll.*) **1** a lie, a fib. **2** nonsense. [etym. uncertain]

taraire (tərī´rē) *n.* a New Zealand forest tree, *Beilschmiedia tarairi*, with white wood. [Maori]

tarakihi (tarəkē´hē), **terakihi** (ter-) *n.* an edible fish, *Cheilodactylus macropterus*, found in the waters of New Zealand. [Maori]

taramasalata (tarəməsəlah´tə), **tarama** (tar´əmə) *n.* a pale pink creamy Greek pâté, made from smoked cod roe or, less commonly, the roe of other fish, blended with olive oil and garlic. [Gk. *tarama*, cod roe, *salata*, salad]

tarantass (tarəntas´) *n.* a large four-wheeled Russian carriage without springs. [Rus. *tarantasu*]

tarantella (tarəntel´ə), **tarantelle** (-tel´) *n.* **1** a rapid S Italian dance in triplets for one couple. **2** the music for such a dance. [It., from *Taranto*, L *Tarentum*, S Italian town]

tarantism (tar´əntizm) *n.* (*Hist.*) a form of nervous disorder characterized by uncontrollable dancing movements, prevalent in S Italy during the 15th, 16th and 17th cents. and at that time believed to be caused by venom from the bite of a tarantula. [as TARANTELLA]

tarantula (təran´tūlə) *n.* (*pl.* **tarantulas**) **1** any large hairy spider of the family Theraphosidae, found in tropical regions. **2** a large, hairy, black wolf spider, *Lycosa tarentula*, found in S Europe, whose bite was formerly believed to cause tarantism. [as TARANTELLA]

taraxacum (tərak´səkəm) *n.* **1** any plant of the genus *Taraxacum*, which includes the dandelion. **2** a drug prepared from the roots of one of these plants, formerly used as a tonic or laxative. [mod. L, prob. from Arab. or Pers.]

tarboosh (tahboosh´), **tarboush, tarbush** *n.* a brimless cap or fez, usu. red. [Arab. *tarbūsh*, head covering]

Tardenoisian (tahdinoi´ziən) *a.* belonging or relating to a mesolithic culture known to exist in S and W Europe and characterized by the use of small flint tools. ~*n.* this culture. [*Tardenois*, town in France where remains of the tools were found]

tardigrade (tah´digrād) *n.* any of various slow-moving invertebrates of the phylum Tardigrada, which have eight legs and live in wet soil, ditches etc. ~*a.* slow-moving. [L *tardigradus* (*tardus*, slow, *gradī*, to walk)]

tardy (tah´di) *a.* (*comp.* **tardier**, *superl.* **tardiest**) **1** moving slowly, slow, sluggish. **2** late, delayed, after the expected or proper time. **3** reluctant. **tardily** *adv.* **tardiness** *n.* [F *tardif*, L *tardus*, slow]

tare[1] (teə) *n.* **1** a vetch, esp. *Vicia sativa*, the common vetch. **2** (*Bible*) a weed that grows in fields of grain and which, when it is young, resembles corn. [ME, cp. MDut. *terwe*, Dut. *tarwe*, wheat]

tare[2] (teə) *n.* **1** an allowance for the weight of boxes, wrapping etc. in which goods are packed. **2** the weight of a motor vehicle without fuel, load, passengers or equipment. **3** the weight of the vessel in which a substance is weighted. ~*v.t.* to ascertain the amount of tare of. **tare and tret** *n.* the arithmetic rule for calculating the net weight of goods. [F, from Sp. *tara*, Arab. *tarhah*, rejected, from *taraha*, to fling]

targa (tah´gə) *n.* a sports car that has a removable hard roof which fits over a roll bar or goes into the boot when not in use. ~*a.* relating to this kind of sports car (*a targa top*). [It. *targa*, shield]

†**targe** (tahj) *n.* a light shield. [OF *targe*, from ON *targe*, shield]

target (tah´git) *n.* **1** an object set up as a mark to be fired at in archery, musketry etc., orig. a circular pad of twisted straw etc. painted with concentric bands surrounding a bull's eye. **2** any person or thing made the object of attack, criticism etc., a butt. **3** the aim, sum of money etc., to be reached by a combined effort. **4** the specific objective or aim of any (concerted) effort. **5** the objective of an air-raid. **6** the anticathode used in a discharge tube to set up X-rays. **7** (*Hist.*) a shield, a buckler, esp. a small round one. ~*v.t.* (*pres.p.* **targeting,** *past, p.p.* **targeted**) **1** to make a target of. **2** to aim at. **3** to direct the resources of the social services to. **on target 1** on the right course. **2** on schedule. **targetable** *a.* able or liable to be aimed at. **target area** *n.* **1** an area with a target located in it. **2** an area which is a target. **targeted** *a.* **targeteer** (-tiə´) *n.* (*Hist.*) a soldier armed with a target. **target language** *n.* the language into which a text etc. is to be translated. **target practice** *n.* shooting practice to improve one's aim. [OF *targuete*, dim. of *targue*, var. *targe* (cp. Icel. *targa*, OE *targe*, OHG *Zarga*)]

Targum (tah´gəm) *n.* any of various ancient Aramaic versions or paraphrases of the Old Testament Scriptures. **Targumic** (-goo´-), **Targumistic** (-mis´-) *a.* **Targumist** *n.* [Chaldee, interpretation]

tariff (tar´if) *n.* **1** a table of charges. **2** a list or table of duties or customs payable on the importation or export of goods. **3** a duty on any particular kind of goods. **4** a law imposing such duties. **5** a method of charging for gas and electricity. **6** the charges imposed on these. ~*v.t.* **1** to draw up a list of duties or charges on (goods etc.). **2** to price, to put a valuation on. [OF *tariffe*, arithmetic, Sp. *tarifa*, Arab. *ta'rīf*, information, from *'irf*, knowledge, from *'arafa*, to know]

tarlatan (tah´lətən) *n.* a fine, transparent muslin. [F *tarlatane*, etym. uncertain]

Tarmac, tarmacadam TAR[1].

tarn (tahn) *n.* a small mountain lake. [Icel. *tjörn*, gen. *tjarnar*, Swed. dial. *tjärn*, *tärn*]

tarnish (tah´nish) *v.t.* **1** to diminish or destroy the lustre of. **2** to sully, to stain. ~*v.i.* to lose lustre. ~*n.* **1** loss of lustre, a stain, a blemish. **2** the film of discoloration forming on the exposed face of a mineral or metal. **tarnishable** *a.* **tarnished** *a.* **tarnisher** *n.* [F *terniss-*, stem of *ternir*, MHG *ternen*, cp. OHG *tarnan*, to obscure, to darken, from *tarni*, secret]

taro (tah´rō) *n.* (*pl.* **taros**) a tropical plant of the arum family, esp. *Colocasia esculenta* and *C. macrorhiza*, the roots of which are used as food by Pacific islanders. [Polynesian]

tarot (tar´ō) *n.* **1** a figured playing card, one of a pack of 78, used in an old (orig. Italian) card game. **2** a pack of such cards, consisting of four suits of 14 plus a fifth suit of 22 permanent trump cards, used for fortune-telling. **3** (any of) these 22 cards. **4** any game played with tarot cards. ~*a.* belonging or relating to these cards or to fortune-telling using them (*had a tarot reading done*). [F *tarots*, spotted cards, It. *tarrocchi*, etym. uncertain]

tarp (tahp) *n.* (*coll.*) (a) tarpaulin. [abbr.]

tarpan (tah´pan) *n.* an extinct small wild horse that formerly lived on the steppes of Russia and central Asia. [Tartar]

tarpaulin (tahpaw´lin) *n.* **1** a canvas cloth coated with tar or other waterproof compound. **2** a sheet of this. **3** a sailor's broad-brimmed tarred or oiled hat. **4** (*dated, coll.*) a sailor. [TAR[1], *palling*, covering, from PALL[1]]

tarpon (tah´pon) *n.* **1** a large and powerful game fish, *Tarpon atlanticus*, of the herring family, found in tropical Atlantic waters. **2** a similar fish, *Megalops cyprinoides*, found in the Pacific. [etym. uncertain]

tarradiddle TARADIDDLE.

tarragon (tar´əgən) *n.* a perennial herb, *Artemisia dracunculus*, related to wormwood, used as a flavouring in cookery etc. **tarragon vinegar** *n.* vinegar flavoured with tarragon. [Sp. *taragona*, Arab. *tarkhūn*, Gr. *drakōn*, DRAGON]

tarras TRASS.

☒ **tarrif** common misspelling of TARIFF.

tarry[1] TAR[1].

†**tarry**[2] (tar´i) *v.i.* (*3rd pers. sing. pres.* **tarries,** *pres.p.* **tarrying,** *past, p.p.* **tarried**) **1** to stay, to remain behind, to wait. **2** to linger, to delay, to be late. ~*v.t.* to wait for. [ME *tarien*, to irritate, to delay, OE *tergan*, to vex (infl. by ME *targen*, OF *targer*, late L *tardicāre*, L *tardāre*, to delay, from *tardus*, see TARDY)]

tarsal, tarsi TARSUS.

tarsia (tah´siə) *n.* an Italian mosaic or inlaid woodwork. [It.]

tarsier (tah´siə) *n.* a small nocturnal arboreal primate of the genus *Tarsius* found in the Philippines and Malaysia, with very large eyes and ears, and long tarsal bones. **tarsioid** (-sioid) *a.* resembling or related to the tarsier. [F, as TARSUS]

tarsus (tah´səs) *n.* (*pl.* **tarsi** (-sī)) **1** the set of bones (seven in humans) between the lower leg and the metatarsus, the ankle. **2** the shank of a bird's leg. **3** the terminal segment in the leg of an insect or crustacean. **4** a plate of connective tissue in the eyelid. **tarsal** *a.* of or relating to the tarsus or the ankle. ~*n.* a tarsal bone. **tarso-** (tah´sō), **tarsi-** (-si) *comb. form* tarsus. **tarsometatarsus** (metətah´səs) *n.* (*pl.* **tarsometatarsi** (-sī)) a bone in the lower leg of birds and some reptiles, consisting of metatarsal and tarsal structures fused together. **tarsometatarsal** (-səl) *a.* **1** of or relating to the tarsus and the metatarsus. **2** of or relating to the tarsometatarsus. [Gr. *tarsos*, flat surface]

tart[1] (taht) *n.* **1** a pie containing fruit or some other sweet filling. **2** a pastry case with a covering or filling of jam etc. **tartlet** *n.* a small savoury or sweet tart. [OF *tarte*, prob. var. of *tourte*, *torte*, L *torta*, fem. p.p. of *torquēre*, to twist]

tart[2] (taht) *n.* (*sl.*) **1** a prostitute, a promiscuous woman. **2** a girl or woman, esp. when thought of in sexual terms. **to tart up 1** to make more showy. **2** to dress cheaply, in a vulgar way. **tarted-up** *a.* **tarty** *a.* (*comp.* **tartier,** *superl.* **tartiest**) **1** cheap. **2** promiscuous. **tartiness** *n.* [perh. from SWEETHEART (under SWEET)]

tart[3] (taht) *a.* **1** sharp to the taste, acid. **2** biting, cutting, piercing. **tartish** *a.* **tartly** *adv.* **tartness** *n.* [OE *teart*, prob. cogn. with TEAR[1]]

tartan[1] (tah´tən) *n.* **1** a chequered pattern of crossing stripes of various colours, esp. one of those distinguishing the various Scottish Highland clans. **2** a woollen etc. fabric with this pattern. ~*a.* consisting of, made of or like tartan. [etym. uncertain]

tartan[2] (tah´tən), **tartane** (-tān) *n.* a small Mediterranean one-masted vessel with bowsprit and lateen sail. [F *tartane*, perh. from Arab. *taridah*]

Tartar (tah´tə), **Tatar** *n.* **1** a member of a group of peoples, such as the Mongols and Turks, who live in central Asia. **2** their language. **3** (**tartar**) a person of an intractable, irritable temper or more than one's match. ~*a.* **1** of or relating to the Tartars or their language. **2** of or relating to the area of Central Asia that lies to the east of the Caspian Sea. **Tartarian** (-teə´ri-) *a., n.* [Pers. *Tātār*]

tartar (tah´tə) *n.* **1** a yellowish incrustation of calcium phosphate deposited on the teeth. **2** partially purified argol, the impure tartrate of potassium deposited from wines. **3** CREAM OF TARTAR (under CREAM). **tartar emetic** *n.* a tartrate of potassium and antimony formerly used as an emetic and purgative, and now used in dyeing and veterinary medicine. **tartaric** (-tar´-) *a.* of, relating to or containing tartar or tartaric acid. **tartaric acid** *n.* a crystalline acid from plants, used as a food additive (E334) and in medicines. **tartarize, tartarise** *v.t.* **tartar sauce** *n.* TARTARE SAUCE (under TARTARE). **tartrate** (-trāt) *n.* a salt or ester of tartaric acid. **tartrazine** (-trəzēn) *n.* a yellow dye used in textiles, medicines and food (E102). [F *tartre*, late L *tartarum*, Arab. *durd*, dregs, tartar of wine]

tartare (tahtah´) *a.* (*usu. following the n.*) in cookery, in a Tartar style. **steak tartare** STEAK. **tartare sauce** (tah´tə) *n.* a relish made from mayonnaise, chopped capers, herbs etc. and usually served with fish. [F, tartar]

Tartarean TARTARUS.

tartaric, tartarize TARTAR.

Tartarus (tah´tərəs) *n.* **1** in Greek mythology, a deep abyss below Hades where the Titans were confined. **2** the place in Hades reserved for the wicked. **Tartarean** (-teə´ri-) *a.* [L, from Gr. *Tartaros*]

tartrate, tartrazine TARTAR.

Tartuffe (tahtuf´, -toof´) *n.* a hypocritical pretender. [F, a character in Molière's *Tartuffe*]

tarwhine (tah´wīn) *n.* any of several edible Australian sea fish, esp. a bream, *Rhabdosargus sarga*. [Austral. Abor.]

Tarzan (tah´zən) *n.* a man of great physical strength and agility. [from the stories of Edgar Rice Burroughs, 1875–1950]

Tas. (tas) *abbr.* Tasmania.

tash (tash), **tache** *n.* (*coll.*) short for MOUSTACHE.

Tashi Lama (tashi lah´mə) *n.* PANCHEN LAMA. [*Tashi* Lhunpo, a monastery in Tibet, LAMA]

tasimeter (təsim´itə) *n.* an instrument for measuring changes in atmospheric pressure. [Gk. *tasis*, a stretch, *metron*, measure]

task (tahsk) *n.* **1** a definite amount of work imposed. **2** (*Comput.*) an action or process to be carried out. **3** a piece of work undertaken voluntarily. ~*v.t.* **1** to impose a task upon. **2** to strain, to overtax. **to take to task** to reprove, to reprimand. **tasker** *n.* **task force, task group** *n.* **1** a group formed to carry out a specific task. **2** a military or police group formed to undertake a specific mission. **taskmaster, taskmistress** *n.* a person who gives someone else some work to do, esp. on a regular basis or with a strict deadline. [ONF *tasque*, OF *tasche* (F *tâche*), late L *tasca*, TAX]

Tasmanian (tazmā´niən) *a.* of or relating to Tasmania. ~*n.* a native or inhabitant of Tasmania. **Tasmanian devil** *n.* a small fierce carnivorous nocturnal marsupial, *Sarcophilus harrisii*, now found only in Tasmania. **Tasmanian tiger, Tasmanian wolf** *n.* THYLACINE.

Tass (tas) *n.* (*Hist.*) the official news agency of the Soviet Union. [Rus., acronym of *Telegrafnoe agentstvo Sovetskogo Soyuza*, Telegraphic Agency of the Soviet Union]

tass (tas) *n.* **1** a cup, a goblet. **2** a small draught of brandy etc. **tassie** *n.* (*Sc.*) a small cup. [OF *tasse*, goblet, prob. from Arab. *tass*, basin]

tasse (tas) *n.* (*usu. in pl., Hist.*) any of a series of overlapping plates of armour hanging from a corslet as a sort of kirtle to protect the thighs. [OF]

tassel[1] (tas´əl) *n.* **1** a pendent ornament, usu. composed of a tuft of threads, cords, silk etc. attached to the corners of cushions, curtains etc. **2** the pendent head of a flower, esp. one, such as the maize plant, with visible tassel-like stamens. ~*v.t.* (*pres.p.* **tasselling,** (*N Am.*) **tasseling,** *past, p.p.* **tasselled,** (*N Am.*) **tasseled**) **1** to provide or adorn with tassels. **2** to remove the tassels from (maize) to strengthen the plant. ~*v.i.* to form tassels. **tasselled,** (*N Am.*) **tasseled** *a.* **tasselling,** (*N Am.*) **tasseling** *n.* **tasselly** *a.* (*comp.* **tassellier,** *superl.* **tasselliest**). [OF *tasel*, *tassel*, It. *tassello*, med. L *tassellus*, etym. uncertain]

tassel[2] (tas´əl), **torsel** (taw´səl) *n.* a small piece of wood or stone fixed into a wall for a beam or joist to rest on. [L *taxillus*, small die]

taste (tāst) *n.* **1** the sensation excited by the contact of various soluble substances with certain organs in the mouth, flavour. **2** the sense by which this is perceived. **3** the act of tasting. **4** a small quantity tasted, drunk, eaten or experienced, a bit taken as a sample. **5** the mental faculty or power of apprehending and enjoying the beautiful and the sublime in nature and art, or of appreciating and discerning between degrees of artistic excellence. **6** manner, style, execution, as directed or controlled by this. **7** an inclination, a predilection (for). ~*v.t.* **1** to try the flavour of by taking into the mouth. **2** to perceive the flavour of. **3** to experience. **4** (*coll.*) to eat a little of. **5** †to enjoy, to relish. ~*v.i.* **1** to have a specified taste, to have a smack or flavour (of) (*This tastes awful*; *This tastes of vinegar*). **2** to experience the sensation of taste. **3** to take or eat a small portion of food etc., to partake (of). **4** to have experience (of). **a taste of one's own medicine** MEDICINE. **in bad/ poor taste** unacceptable, tactless, lacking discernment (*a joke in poor taste*). **to leave a bad/ bitter taste (in one's mouth)** (of an unpleasant experience etc.) to make one upset, regretful, etc. **to one's taste** to one's liking. **to taste** in the amount preferred or needed to give a pleasant taste (*Add seasoning to taste*). **to taste blood** BLOOD. **tasteable, tastable** *a.* **taste bud** *n.* any of the tiny organs on the tongue sensitive to taste. **tasteful** *a.* having, characterized by, or done with good taste; having or showing aesthetic taste. **tastefully** *adv.* **tastefulness** *n.* **tasteless** *a.* **1** having no flavour, insipid. **2** vapid, dull. **3** having, characterized by or done with bad taste. **tastelessly** *adv.* **tastelessness** *n.* **taster** *n.* **1** a person who tastes, esp. a person employed to test the quality of teas, liquors etc. by tasting, orig. one employed to taste food and drink before it was served. **2** an implement for cutting a small cylindrical sample from cheese. **3** a small cup used by a wine taster etc. **4** a small sample. **tasting** *n.* a social event where samples, esp. of wine, are tasted and assessed for quality, sometimes as a prelude to buying. **tasty** *a.* (*comp.* **tastier,** *superl.* **tastiest**) **1** noticeably pleasant to the taste. **2** (*coll.*) in good taste. **3** (*coll.*) attractive. **4** (*coll.*) sexually alluring. **tastily** *adv.* **tastiness** *n.* [OF *taster*, to handle, feel, taste (F *tâter*), L *taxāre*, from *tag-*, base of *tangere*, to touch]

-tastic (tas´tik) *suf.* (*sl.*) added to words to indicate approval, enthusiasm etc. (*a soul-tastic club*; *a funtastic holiday*). [modelled on FANTASTIC]

tat[1] (tat), **tatt** *n.* **1** rubbish, rags. **2** something which is pretentious but of little real value. **3** an unkempt or shabby person. [TATTY[1]]

tat[2] (tat) *v.t.* (*pres.p.* **tatting,** *past, p.p.* **tatted**) to make by knotting. ~*v.i.* to make tatting. ~*n.* tatting. **tatting** *n.* **1** knotted work or lace used for edging etc. **2** the process of making this. [orig. Sc., rel. to TATTER]

ta-ta (tatah´) *int.* (*coll.*) goodbye. [etym. uncertain]

tatami (tətah´mi) *n.* (*pl.* **tatamis**) a traditional woven straw or rush mat of standard size, used as a floor covering in Japanese houses. **tatami mat** *n.* [Jap.]

Tatar TARTAR.

tater (tā´tə), **tatie** (-ti) *n.* (*coll.*) a potato. [corr.]

tatt TAT[1].

tatter (tat´ə) *n.* (*usu. in pl.*) **1** a rag. **2** a torn and hanging piece or shred. ~*v.i.* to fall into tatters. **in tatters 1** torn to pieces. **2** in a state of ruin or irretrievable breakdown. **tattered** *a.* in tatters. **tattery** *a.* [cp. Icel. *tötrar*, LG *taltern*, rags, EFris. *talte*, rag]

tattersall (tat´əsawl), **tattersall check** *n.* material with stripes in a checked pattern. [Richard *Tattersall*, 1724–95, English horseman]

tattie (tat´i) *n.* (*coll.*) a potato.

tatting TAT[2].

tattle (tat´əl) *v.i.* **1** to chatter, to gossip. **2** to tell tales or secrets. ~*n.* **1** prattle, gossip, idle talk. **2** a gossip.

tattler *n.* a person who tattles, a gossip. **tattle-tale** *n.* (*N Am.*) a tell-tale. ~*a.* that tells tales. [freq. of obs. *tat*, imit.]

tattoo[1] (tatoo´) *n.* (*pl.* **tattoos**) **1** the beat of drum recalling soldiers to their quarters. **2** a military pageant, esp. by night. **3** (the sound of) a regular or rhythmic tapping or drumming. ~*v.i.* (*3rd pers. sing. pres.* **tattoos,** *pres.p.* **tattooing,** *past, p.p.* **tattooed**) to beat the tattoo. [Dut. *taptoe* (TAP[2], *toe*, put to, closed), signal for closing tavern taps]

tattoo[2] (tatoo´) *v.t.* (*3rd pers. sing. pres.* **tattoos,** *pres.p.* **tattooing,** *past, p.p.* **tattooed**) to mark (the skin) by pricking and inserting pigments. ~*n.* (*pl.* **tattoos**) a mark or pattern so produced. **tattooer** *n.* **tattooist** *n.* [Tahitian *tatan*]

tatty[1] (tat´i) *a.* (*comp.* **tattier,** *superl.* **tattiest**) (*coll.*) **1** untidy, unkempt. **2** shabby, of poor quality. **3** gaudy, tawdry. **tattily** *adv.* **tattiness** *n.* [ult. rel. to TATTER]

tatty[2] (tat´i) *n.* (*pl.* **tatties**) in the Indian subcontinent, a matting of khus-khus for hanging in doorways and other openings, usu. kept wet to cool the air. [Hind. *tatti*]

tau (taw, tow) *n.* **1** the 19th letter of the Greek alphabet (Τ, τ). **2** a tau cross. **tau cross** *n.* a cross shaped like a T, a St Anthony's cross. **tau particle** *n.* (*Physics*) an elementary particle of the lepton family that has a negative electric charge. [Gr.]

taught TEACH.

taunt[1] (tawnt) *v.t.* **1** to reproach or upbraid sarcastically or contemptuously. **2** to tease or tantalize. ~*n.* a bitter or sarcastic reproach. **taunter** *n.* **taunting** *n., a.* **tauntingly** *adv.* [from OF *tanter, tenter*, L *tentāre*, to TEMPT, or from F *tant*, L *tantum*, so much]

taunt[2] (tawnt) *a.* (*Naut.*) (of masts) exceptionally tall. [from obs. *ataunt*, in full rig, F *autant*, as much]

taupe (tōp) *n.* a brownish-grey colour. ~*a.* of this colour. [F *taupe*, mole, L *talpa*]

Taurus (taw´rəs) *n.* **1** (*Astron.*) a constellation close to Orion, said to represent a bull; the Bull. **2** (*Astrol.*) **a** the second sign of the zodiac, which the sun enters around 21 April. **b** a person born under this sign. **Taurean** *n.* a person born under the sign of Taurus. ~*a.* born under Taurus. **tauric** *a.* of or relating to a bull. **tauriform** (-fawm) *a.* having the form of a bull. **taurine** (-rīn) *n.* (*Chem.*) a colourless amino acid derivative that was first discovered in ox bile and which plays an important part in metabolizing fats. ~*a.* **1** bull-like. **2** bovine. **3** of or relating to Taurus. **tauromachy** (-rom´əki) *n.* (*pl.* **tauromachies**) (*formal or facet.*) **1** bullfighting. **2** a bullfight. [L, from Gr. *tauros*]

taut (tawt) *a.* **1** tight, not slack. **2** (of nerves) tense. **3** (of a ship) in good order, trim. **tauten** *v.t., v.i.* to make or become taut. **tautly** *adv.* **tautness** *n.* [ME *togt, toght*, prob. p.p. of *togen*, to TOW[1]]

tauto- (taw´tō) *comb. form* same, identical. [Gr., for *to auto*, the same]

tautog (tawtog´) *n.* a food fish, *Tautoga onitis*, common on the Atlantic coast of the US. [Narragansett, *tautauog*]

tautology (tawtol´əji) *n.* (*pl.* **tautologies**) **1** repetition of the same thing in different words, e.g. in *free, gratis and for nothing.* **2** (*Logic*) a statement that is always true. **tautologic** (-loj´-), **tautological** *a.* **tautologically** *adv.* **tautologist** *n.* **tautologize, tautologise** *v.i.* **tautologous** (-gəs) *a.* [L and Gr. *tautologia*]

tautomerism (tawtom´ərizm) *n.* (*Chem.*) the ability of two isomers to change into one another so that they may co-exist in equilibrium. **tautomer** (taw´-) *n.* a readily changing isomer. **tautomeric** (-mer´-) *a.*

tautonym (taw´tənim) *n.* a two-part taxonomic name in which the specific name repeats or reflects the generic name, e.g. *Rattus rattus* (black rat). **tautonymic** (-nim´-), **tautonymous** (-ton´-) *a.* **tautonymy** (-ton´imi) *n.*

tautophony (tawtof´əni) *n.* the repetition of sounds. **tautophonical** (-fon´-) *a.*

tavern (tav´ən) *n.* (*dated or poet.*) a public house, an inn. **taverna** (-vœ´nə) *n.* **1** a Greek hotel with its own bar. **2** a Greek restaurant. [F *taverne*, L *taberna*, hut, tavern]

TAVR *abbr.* (*Hist.*) Territorial and Army Volunteer Reserve.

taw[1] (taw) *v.t.* to dress or make (skins) into leather with mineral agents, as alum, instead of tannin. **tawer** *n.* [OE *tawian*, cp. Dut. *touwen*, to curry, OHG *zouwan*, to make, to prepare]

taw[2] (taw) *n.* **1** a game of marbles. **2** the line from which players throw their marbles. **3** a large marble. [etym. uncertain]

tawdry (taw´dri) *a.* (*comp.* **tawdrier,** *superl.* **tawdriest**) **1** showy without taste or elegance. **2** gaudy and of little or no value. ~*n.* tasteless or worthless finery. **tawdrily** *adv.* **tawdriness** *n.* [from *St Audrey* (corr. of *Etheldrida*, founder of Ely cathedral), whose fair was held in the Isle of Ely etc. on 17 Oct.]

tawny (taw´ni) *a.* (*comp.* **tawnier,** *superl.* **tawniest**) brownish-yellow, tan-coloured. ~*n.* this colour. **tawniness** *n.* **tawny eagle** *n.* a tawny-coloured eagle, *Aquila rapax*, found in Africa and Asia. **tawny owl** *n.* **1** a European owl, *Strix aluco*, with reddish-brown plumage. **2** (*coll.*) (**Tawny Owl**) an assistant leader of a Brownie Guide pack (officially an *Assistant Brownie Guider*). [ME *tanny*, F *tanné*, p.p. of *tanner*, to TAN[1]]

taws (tawz), **tawse** *n.* (*chiefly Sc.*) a leather strap, usually with the end cut into thin strips, formerly used as an instrument of punishment, esp. in schools. [prob. pl. of obs. *taw*, lash, from TAW[1]]

tax (taks) *n.* (*pl.* **taxes**) **1** a compulsory contribution levied on a person, property or business to meet the expenses of government or other public services. **2** a heavy demand, requirement, strain etc. ~*v.t.* (*3rd pers. sing. pres.* **taxes**) **1** to impose a tax on. **2** to deduct tax from (someone's income, etc.). **3** to lay a heavy burden or strain upon, to make demands upon. **4** to pay a tax on (*taxed the car for a year*). **5** (*formal*) to accuse (of) (*taxed him with taking the money*). **6** (*Law*) to assess (costs of an action etc.). **taxable** *a.* **taxability** (-bil´-) *n.* **taxation** (-sā´shən) *n.* **tax avoidance** *n.* legal minimization of tax. **tax break** *n.* (*coll.*) an opportunity to reduce or minimize tax, allowed by the government. **tax-collector, tax-gatherer** *n.* **tax-deductible** *a.* (of expenses) able or liable to be legally deducted before assessment for tax. **tax disc, tax disk** *n.* a paper disc on a motor vehicle's windscreen showing payment of road tax. **taxer** *n.* **tax evasion** *n.* illegal non-payment or underpayment of tax. **tax exile** *n.* a person who lives abroad to avoid paying (high) taxes. **tax-free** *a.* exempt from taxation. **tax haven** *n.* a country where taxes are low, and which attracts tax exiles. **taxing** *a.* demanding, difficult (*a very taxing job*). **taxman** *n.* (*pl.* **taxmen**) (*coll.*) **1** a person employed by the Inland Revenue (Inland Revenue Service in US) to collect taxes and often adjudicate on matters relating to taxes. **2** the department responsible for tax collection, typically represented as uncaring and money-grasping. **taxpayer** *n.* **tax return** *n.* a (usu. yearly) statement of one's income and tax paid. **tax shelter** *n.* a financial arrangement to lessen tax payable. **tax year** *n.* FINANCIAL YEAR (under FINANCE). [F *taxe*, from *taxer*, L *taxāre*, from *tag-*, base of *tangere*, to touch]

taxa TAXON (under TAXONOMY).

taxation TAX.

taxi (tak´si) *n.* (*pl.* **taxis**) a motor car usu. fitted with a taximeter and licensed to carry fare-paying passengers. ~*v.i.* (*3rd pers. sing. pres.* **taxies,** *pres.p.* **taxiing, taxying,** *past, p.p.* **taxied**) (of an aircraft or pilot) to travel along the ground before take-off or after landing. **taxicab** *n.* a taxi. **taxi rank, taxi stand** *n.* a place where taxis can queue to pick up fares. **taxiway** *n.* a marked path from an airport terminal to a runway. [short for TAXIMETER]

taxidermy (tak´sidœmi) *n.* the art of preparing and mounting the skins of animals so that they resemble the living forms. **taxidermal** (-dœ´-), **taxidermic** *a.* **taxidermist** *n.* [TAXIS, DERM]

taximeter (tak´simētə) *n.* an automatic instrument fitted in a cab for registering the distance travelled on a particular journey and the fare to be paid. [F *taximètre* (*taxe*, TAX, -METER)]

taxis (tak´sis) *n.* **1** the methodical application of manual pressure to restore displaced body parts to their normal positions. **2** (*Biol.*) the movement of a cell or organism in a specified direction because of some external stimulus. **3** order or arrangement of words. [Gr., from *tassein*, to arrange]

taxonomy (takson´əmi) *n.* (*pl.* **taxonomies**) **1** the branch of natural history that deals with the principles, theories and techniques of classification. **2** a scheme of classification. **taxon** (tak´-) *n.* (*pl.* **taxa** (-sə)) any taxonomical category or group. **taxonomic** (-nom´-), **taxonomical** *a.* **taxonomically** *adv.* **taxonomist** *n.* [F *taxonomie* (TAXIS, Gr. *nom-*, from *nemein*, to deal out)]

tayberry (tā´bəri) *n.* (*pl.* **tayberries**) **1** a type of hybrid plant produced by crossing blackberry and raspberry plants. **2** the fruit of this plant. [*Tay*side, in central Scotland, where developed]

Tay–Sachs disease (tāsaks´) *n.* (*Med.*) a rare hereditary genetic disorder affecting the brain and spinal cord, causing death in early childhood. [Warren *Tay*, 1843–1927, British physician, and Bernard *Sachs*, 1858–1944, US neurologist]

tazza (tat´sə) *n.* (*pl.* **tazze** (-sā)) a flattish or saucer-shaped cup, esp. one on a high foot. [It.]

TB *abbr.* **1** torpedo boat. **2** tubercle bacillus. **3** tuberculosis.

Tb *chem. symbol* terbium.

t.b.a. *abbr.* to be announced, to be arranged.

tbs, tbsp *abbr.* tablespoon(s), tablespoonful(s).

tbsps *abbr.* tablespoonfuls.

Tc *chem. symbol* technetium.

TCCB *abbr.* Test and County Cricket Board.

TCD *abbr.* Trinity College Dublin.

TCDD *abbr.* tetrachlorodibenzoparadioxin.

TCP® *abbr.* trichlorophenylmethyliodasalicyl, a disinfectant and germicide.

TD *abbr.* **1** Teachta Dála, member of the Dáil. **2** Territorial Decoration.

Te *chem. symbol* tellurium.

te (tē), (*N Am.*) **ti** *n.* (*pl.* **tes,** (*N Am.*) **tis**) (*Mus.*) **1** the seventh note of a major scale in the sol-fa system of notation. **2** the note B in the fixed-doh system.

tea (tē) *n.* (*pl.* **teas**) **1** a small evergreen shrub or tree, *Camellia sinensis*, grown in India, China, Japan and other parts of SE Asia for its leaves. **2** the leaves of this plant dried and shredded. **3** a drink made from these leaves by infusing them in boiling water. **4** a similar drink made by infusing the leaves of another plant, or by infusing another substance, in boiling water (*blackcurrant tea*; *beef tea*). **5** AFTERNOON TEA (under AFTERNOON). **6** a substantial meal, usu. served in the early evening. **7** the main meal of the day, usu. served in the early evening and often consisting of a cooked dish followed by a pudding or cakes, biscuits etc. **8** (*esp. N Am.*) an afternoon social gathering at which tea is drunk. ~*v.i.* (*3rd pers. sing. pres.* **teas,** *pres.p.* **teaing,** *past, p.p.* **teaed, tea'd**) to take tea. ~*v.t.* to supply with tea. **black tea** BLACK. **green tea** GREEN. **high tea** HIGH. **Russian tea** RUSSIAN. **tea and sympathy** *n.* (*coll.*) support and hospitality given to someone in trouble. **tea bag** *n.* a small perforated bag containing tea. **teaball** *n.* (*esp. N Am.*) a small perforated metal ball in which tea is put for infusion. **tea-bread** *n.* light, spongy fruit bread. **tea caddy** *n.* a small box in which tea is kept. **teacake** *n.* a bun of light sweet bread, often toasted for eating at tea. **tea ceremony** *n.* (*pl.* **tea ceremonies**) in Japan, a ritualized procedure for preparing, serving and drinking green tea. **tea chest** *n.* **1** a light box lined with thin sheet metal, in which tea is imported. **2** †a tea caddy. **tea cloth** *n.* a tea towel. **tea cosy** *n.* (*pl.* **tea cosies**) a cover for a teapot to keep the contents hot. **teacup** *n.* a small cup for drinking tea from. **teacupful** *n.* **tea dance** *n.* an afternoon tea combined with a dance. **tea fight** *n.* (*coll.*) a tea party. **tea garden** *n.* a garden where tea and other refreshments are served to the public. **tea gown** *n.* a woman's loose gown for wearing at afternoon tea. **tea-kettle** *n.* a kettle for boiling water to make tea. **tea lady** *n.* (*pl.* **tea ladies**) a woman employed to make tea for workers in an office etc. **tea leaf** *n.* (*pl.* **tea leaves**) **1** a leaf of tea or the tea plant. **2** (*pl.*) such leaves after infusion. **3** (*sl.*) a thief. **tea meeting** *n.* a religious meeting at which there is an interval for tea and social chat. **tea party** *n.* (*pl.* **tea parties**) a party at which tea is served. **tea plant** *n.* the plant *Camellia sinensis*. **tea planter** *n.* a person who cultivates tea plants. **teapot** *n.* a vessel in which tea is infused, with a handle and spout for pouring. **tearoom** *n.* a restaurant etc. where afternoon teas are provided. **tea rose** *n.* a rose, *Rosa odorata*, with scent supposed to resemble tea. **tea saucer** *n.* a saucer for a teacup. **tea service, teaset** *n.* a collection of crockery used in serving tea, including teacups, tea saucers and teapot. **teaspoon** *n.* **1** a small spoon for stirring tea in a teacup. **2** a teaspoonful. **teaspoonful** *n.* (*pl.* **teaspoonfuls**) **1** the quantity contained in a teaspoon. **2** a unit of capacity equal to 4 ml or ¼ fl. oz., used in recipes, administering medicine etc. **tea-strainer** *n.* a small perforated device for straining tea. **tea-taster** *n.* a person whose business it is to test and sample tea by the taste. **tea things** *n.pl.* (*coll.*) cups, saucers etc. for tea. **teatime** *n.* the time of the day when the meal called tea is eaten. **tea towel** *n.* a small towel used for drying dishes etc. that have been washed. **tea tray** *n.* a tray on or from which tea is served. **tea-tree** *n.* **1** any Australasian myrtaceous plant of the genera *Melaleuca*, *Leptospermum* etc., used as a tea substitute by early settlers. **2** a red-berried shrub, *Lycium barbarum*, of the nightshade family. **3** the tea plant. **tea trolley, tea wagon** *n.* a trolley that can be wheeled around and from which tea is served. **tea urn** *n.* a vessel for supplying hot water for tea, or tea in large quantities. [Chin. (Amoy) *tē* (pron. tā), *ch'a*]

teach (tēch) *v.t.* (*past, p.p.* **taught** (tawt)) **1** to cause (a person etc.) to learn (to do) or acquire knowledge or skill in, to instruct or train in (*taught her brother to drive*; *taught me how to knit*). **2** to impart knowledge or information concerning (a subject etc.), to give lessons in (*teaches English*). **3** to impart instruction to, to educate (*teaches the sixth form*). **4** to explain, to show, to disclose, to make known. **5** to make (someone) understand by example, experience, etc. (*Her lies taught him not to trust her*). ~*v.i.* to teach people as an occupation. **to teach one's grandmother to suck eggs** GRANDMOTHER (under GRAND). **to teach school** (*esp. N Am.*) to be a schoolteacher. **to teach someone a lesson** LESSON. **teachable** *a.* **1** (of a subject etc.) able to be taught. **2** disposed to learn, docile. **teachability** (-bil´-) *n.* **teachableness** *n.* **teacher** *n.* a person who teaches others, esp. a schoolteacher. **teacherly** *a.* **teach-in** *n.* **1** an informal conference on a specific subject involving specialists and students. **2** a group of these, usu. on a connected theme. **teaching** *n.* **1** the work or profession of a teacher. **2** (*often in pl.*) something which is taught, a doctrine (*according to the teachings of Freud*). **teaching aid** *n.* any device which helps in teaching.

teaching hospital *n.* a hospital where medical students are trained. **teaching machine** *n.* any machine which gives information to the user and corrects the user's answers to questions set. [OE *taecan*, cogn. with TOKEN]

teak (tēk) *n.* **1** a large tree, *Tectona grandis*, grown in India and SE Asia for its heavy timber which does not crack, warp, shrink or corrode iron, used largely for shipbuilding, furniture etc. **2** this timber. [Port. *teca*, Malayalam *tekka*]

teal (tēl) *n.* (*pl.* **teal, teals**) **1** a small Eurasian freshwater duck of the genus *Anas*, esp. *A. crecca*, the common teal, related to the mallard. **2** teal blue. ~*a.* of the colour teal blue. **teal blue** *n., a.* (of) a deep greenish-blue colour. [ME *tele*, cp. MDut. *teelingh*]

team (tēm) *n.* **1** a group of people who form a side in a game or sport. **2** a group of people who work together etc. **3** two or more horses, oxen etc., harnessed together. ~*v.t.* **1** to join (with others) in a common bond or for the same purpose (*Workers teamed up with the management against the takeover*). **2** to harness or join together in a team. **3** to match (*teamed a plain black sweater with her orange and black skirt*). **team-mate** *n.* a fellow member of a team, group, playing side etc. **team player** *n.* a person who works or plays well in a team and who puts this before personal achievement. **team spirit** *n.* the willingness to act as a team, or for the good of the team. **teamster** (-stə) *n.* **1** (*N Am.*) a person who drives a lorry or truck. **2** a person who drives a team of oxen, horses etc. **team-teaching** *n.* teaching done by two or more teachers each of whom has specialist knowledge, skills etc. **teamwise** *adv.* **teamwork** *n.* effective co-operation with other members of a team or group. [OE *tēam*, family, team (cp. Dut. *toom*, G *Zaum*, bridle, Icel. *taumr*, rein), cogn. with TOW[1]]

teapoy (tē´poi) *n.* a small three- or four-legged table for holding a tea service etc. [Hind. *tīn*, three, Pers. *pāē*, *pāī*, foot, *sipāī*, assim. to TEA]

tear[1] (teə) *v.t.* (*past* **tore** (taw), *p.p.* **torn** (tawn)) **1** to pull forcibly apart. **2** to make a hole in, to rip, to lacerate. **3** to make (a hole, rent, tear, wound etc.) by tearing (*tore a hole in my tights*). **4** to pull violently (away, out etc.). **5** to drag, remove or sever. **6** (*usu. pass.*) to split into factions, to divide in sympathy or allegiance. ~*v.i.* **1** to pull violently (at). **2** to part or separate on being pulled. **3** (*coll.*) to rush, move or act with speed or violence (*tore up the road to catch the bus*). ~*n.* **1** a hole or rip. **2** a torn part of cloth etc. **that's torn it** (*sl.*) that's spoiled things. **to be torn between** to be unable to choose, or have difficulty choosing, between. **to tear apart 1** to devastate, disrupt or divide. **2** to make a mess of (a place), esp. when trying to find something. **3** to criticize severely. **to tear a strip off** (*coll.*) to reprimand. **to tear into 1** to reprimand or criticize forcefully. **2** to embark on energetically. **to tear limb from limb** LIMB[1]. **to tear oneself away** to leave reluctantly. **to tear one's hair 1** to be overcome with grief. **2** to be very puzzled. **to tear to shreds 1** to ruin or destroy completely. **2** to ridicule or criticize mercilessly. **tearable** *a.* **tearaway** *n.* (*coll.*) a reckless, sometimes violent, young person. ~*a.* reckless, impetuous. **tearer** *n.* **tearing** *a.* (*coll.*) violent, furious, tremendous (*Can't stop, I'm in a tearing hurry*). **tear-off** *a.* (of a strip of paper etc.) able to be easily detached, usu. along a perforation. **tear sheet** *n.* a page in a publication that is designed to be torn out. [OE *teran*, cp. Goth. *gatairan*, G *zehren*, to destroy, Icel. *taera*, to consume, also Gr. *derein*, to flay]

tear[2] (tiə) *n.* **1** a drop of the saline liquid secreted by the lachrymal glands, moistening the eyes or flowing down in strong emotion etc. **2** a drop of liquid. **3** a solid, transparent drop or droplike object. **in tears** crying, weeping. **without tears** that is in a form that can be easily mastered. **teardrop** *n.* **tear duct** *n.* a short tube that runs from the inner corner of the lower eyelid down into the nasal passage, allowing tears to drain away. **tearful** *a.* **1** shedding or about to shed tears. **2** causing or characterized by sadness. **tearfully** *adv.* **tearfulness** *n.* **tear gas** *n.* (*pl.* **tear gases,** (*N Am.*) **tear gasses**) a poison gas that affects the lachrymal glands and causes violent watering of the eyes. **tear-gas** *v.t.* (*3rd pers. sing. pres.* **tear-gases,** (*N Am.*) **tear-gasses,** *pres.p.* **tear-gassing,** *past, p.p.* **tear-gassed**) to attack using tear gas. **tear-jerker** *n.* a book, film or song which is excessively sentimental. **tear-jerking** *n., a.* **tearless** *a.* not tearful or crying. **tearlessly** *adv.* **tearlessness** *n.* **tear-stained** *a.* **1** wet with tears. **2** (*poet.*) sorrowful, sad. [OE *tēar*, *taer* (cp. Icel. *tār*, Dan. *taar*, Goth. *tagr*, also Gr. *dakru*, L *lacrima*, OL *dacrima*)]

tease (tēz) *v.t.* **1** to annoy, torment, irritate or vex with petty requests, importunity, jesting or raillery. **2** to arouse sexual desire in without any intention of satisfying it. **3** to pull apart or separate the fibres of. **4** to comb or card (wool or flax). **5** to importune (to do something). **6** to backcomb (hair). **7** to dress (cloth), esp. using teasels. ~*n.* **1** a person who teases or irritates. **2** an act or instance of teasing. **to tease out** to disentangle. **teaser** *n.* **1** (*coll.*) an awkward question, problem, or situation, a poser. **2** (*esp. N Am.*) a short trailer for a film etc. **3** a stallion or ram, not the intended stud animal, used to make a female sexually receptive before serving by the actual stud. **4** a machine for teasing wool etc. **5** a person who teases. **teasing** *a.* **teasingly** *adv.* [OE *taesan*, to pluck, pull (cp. MDut. *teesen*, Dan. *taese*)]

teasel (tē´zəl), **teazel, teazle** *n.* **1** a plant of the genus *Dipsacus*, with large burs or heads covered with stiff, hooked awns, which are used for raising a nap on cloth. **2** a bur or head of this kind. **3** a machine used as a substitute for this. ~*v.t.* (*pres.p.* **teaselling,** (*N Am.*) **teaseling,** *past, p.p.* **teaselled,** (*N Am.*) **teaseled**) to dress (cloth) with teasels. **teaseller,** (*N Am.*) **teaseler** *n.* [OE *tasl*, *taesel*, from TEASE]

teat (tēt) *n.* **1** the nipple of the mammary gland, esp. of an animal, through which milk is drawn. **2** a projection or appliance resembling this, such as the attachment on a baby's feeding bottle through which milk etc. is sucked. [ME and OF *tete* (F *tette*), LG *titte* (cp. MDut. *titte*, G *Zitze*, OE *tit*, also Gr. *titthē*)]

teazel, teazle TEASEL.

Tebeth (teb´əth) *n.* the fourth month of the civil and tenth month of the Jewish ecclesiastical year, comprising parts of December and January. [Heb.]

Tebilise® (teb´ilīz) *v.t.* to treat (cotton and linen fabrics) by a proprietary method to prevent creasing and shrinking.

tec[1] (tek) *n.* (*coll.*) a detective, esp. a private detective. [abbr.]

tec[2] TECH.

tech (tek) *n.* **1** (*also* **tec**) a technical college. **2** technology (esp. in *high-tech*).

techie (tek´i), **techy** *n.* (*pl.* **techies**) (*coll.*) a person with a great enthusiasm for or a good understanding of the latest technology (esp. computing).

technetium (teknē´shiəm) *n.* a chemical element, at. no. 43, chem. symbol Tc, whose radioisotope is used in radiotherapy. [Gr. *technētos*, man-made]

technic (tek´nik) *n.* **1** (*usu. in pl.*) **a** technology. **b** technical jargon, procedures etc. **2** technique. ~*a.* technical. **technicist** (-sist) *n.* a technician. [Gr. *technikos*, from *technē*, art]

technical (tek´nikəl) *a.* **1** of or relating to the mechanical arts and applied sciences. **2** of or relating to any particular art, science, business etc. **3** using or requiring specialist knowledge, language etc. (*This manual is far too technical*). **4** caused by a problem or breakdown in machinery etc. (*We've got some technical difficulties*). **5** due to or existing because of the strict interpretation of a law, rule etc. (*got off due to a technical loophole in the law*). ~*n.* 1 a type of armoured vehicle, often mounted with machine guns. 2 the person who fires these guns. **technical college** *n.* a further education college specializing in technical, secretarial and industrial skills. **technical drawing** *n.* the study and practice of draughtsmanship. **technical hitch** *n.* 1 a failure or breakdown, usually temporary, caused by a fault in a mechanism etc. 2 a snag or hold-up. **technicality** (-kal´-) *n.* (*pl.* **technicalities**) 1 technicalness. 2 a technical term, expression etc. 3 a petty or formal detail. **technical knockout** *n.* in boxing, the referee's decision to end the fight because one boxer is too badly injured to continue and to award the fight to the other boxer. **technically** *adv.* **technicalness** *n.*

technician (teknish´ən) *n.* 1 a person skilled in the technical side of a subject, a technical expert. 2 a person employed in a laboratory etc. to use and look after technical equipment.

Technicolor® (tek´nikŭlə) *n.* 1 a colour cinematography process. 2 (*coll.*) (*also* **technicolor, technicolour**) vivid colour or detail.

technique (teknēk´) *n.* 1 a mode of artistic performance or execution. 2 mechanical skill in art, craft etc. 3 proficiency in some skill. 4 a particular way of carrying out or performing something.

techno (tek´nō) *n.* a type of dance music with insistent repetitive beats performed on electronic instruments (*techno-beat, techno-music*).

techno- (tek´nō) *comb. form* technology, technological. [Gr. *technē*, art]

technobabble (tek´nōbabəl) *n.* (*coll.*) meaningless technical jargon.

technocracy (teknok´rəsi) *n.* (*pl.* **technocracies**) 1 government or industrial control by technical experts. 2 an example of this. **technocrat** (tek´nōkrat) *n.* **technocratic** (-krat´-) *a.* **technocratically** *adv.*

technology (teknol´əji) *n.* (*pl.* **technologies**) 1 the study of the mechanical arts and applied sciences; the practical application of science to industry and other fields. 2 the total technical means and skills available to a particular human society. **technological** (-loj´-) *a.* **technologist** *n.*

technophile (tek´nōfīl) *n.* a person with an enthusiasm for new technology. ~*a.* 1 of or relating to technophiles. 2 conforming to or compatible with new technology. **technophilia** (-fil´-) *n.* **technophilic** *a.*

technophobe (tek´nōfōb) *n.* a person who distrusts, avoids or cannot master new technology. **technophobia** (-fō´-) *n.* **technophobic** *a.*

techy TECHIE.

tectonic (tekton´ik) *a.* 1 of or relating to building or construction. 2 (*Geol.*) relating to, resulting from or causing structural deformation of the earth's crust. **tectonically** *adv.* **tectonics** *n.* 1 (*Geol.*) the study of the structure of the earth's crust and the forces that cause it to change. 2 the art of designing and constructing buildings etc. that combine practicality and beauty. [L *tectonicus*, Gr. *tektonikos*, from *tektōn*, *-tonos*, carpenter]

tectorial (tektaw´riəl) *a.* (*Anat.*) forming a covering. ~*n.* the tectorial membrane. **tectorial membrane** *n.* a membrane in the inner ear covering the organ of Corti. [L *tectōrius*, from *tect-*, p.p. stem of *tegere*, to cover]

tectrix (tek´triks) *n.* (*pl.* **tectrices** (-trisēz, -trī´-)) the covert of a bird's flight feather. [L *tect-* (as TECTORIAL)]

Ted (ted), **ted** *n.* (*coll.*) a Teddy boy. [abbr.]

ted[1] (ted) *v.t.* (*pres.p.* **tedding,** *past, p.p.* **tedded**) to turn over and spread (hay, grass or straw) so as to expose to the sun and air. **tedder** *n.* an implement for doing this. [prob. from OE *teddan* (cp. Icel. *tethja*, past *tadda*, to spread manure, from *tath*, manure)]

ted[2] TED.

teddy (ted´i) *n.* (*pl.* **teddies**) 1 (*also* **teddy bear**) a stuffed toy bear. 2 a woman's one-piece undergarment. [Theodore (*Teddy*) Roosevelt, 1858–1919, US president, a noted bear-hunter]

Teddy boy (ted´i) *n.* (*coll.*) a young man, esp. of the 1950s, characteristically wearing a long jacket, drainpipe trousers and other styles of dress associated with the Edwardian period. [pet form of *Edward*]

Te Deum (tē dē´əm) *n.* 1 a hymn of praise sung at morning service or as a special thanksgiving. 2 a musical setting for this. 3 a thanksgiving service at which it is sung. [from the first words '*Te Deum* laudamus', We praise Thee, O God]

tedious (tē´diəs) *a.* tiresome, wearisome, monotonous, fatiguing. **tediously** *adv.* **tediousness** *n.* **tedium** (-əm) *n.* monotony, boredom. [late L *taediōsus*, from *taedium*; from *taedet*, it wearies]

tee[1] (tē) *n.* 1 in golf, the area at the start of each hole where players strike the first ball of the hole. 2 a means of raising and steadying a golf ball for the first stroke at each hole, now usu. a small wooden or plastic cup with a pointed stem to dig into the ground. ~*v.t.* (*3rd pers. sing. pres.* **tees,** *pres.p.* **teeing,** *past, p.p.* **teed**) to put (the ball) on a tee. **to tee off** 1 to play from a tee. 2 (*coll.*) to begin. [etym. uncertain]

tee[2] (tē) *n.* (*pl.* **tees**) the 20th letter of the alphabet, T, t. **to a tee** perfectly, to a nicety. **tee shirt** *n.* T-SHIRT (under T[1]).

tee-hee (tēhē´), **te-hee** *int.* used to express restrained amusement. ~*n.* a restrained laugh, a chuckle, a titter. ~*v.i.* (*3rd pers. sing. pres.* **tee-hees, te-hees,** *pres.p.* **tee-heeing, te-heeing,** *past, p.p.* **tee-heed, te-heed**) to give a restrained laugh, to titter. [imit.]

teem[1] (tēm) *v.i.* 1 to be prolific or abundant (*flies teeming in the heat*). 2 to be abundantly stocked (with) (*The place was teeming with flies*). [OE *tȳman*, *tīeman*, from *tēam*, or TEAM]

teem[2] (tēm) *v.i.* to pour (down), as rain etc. (*Rain was teeming down the window*). [Icel. *tœma*, from *tōmr*, empty]

teen (tēn) *a.* teenage (*teen culture*). ~*n.* a teenager. [abbr.]

-teen (tēn) *suf.* denoting the addition of 10 (in numbers 13–19). **-teenth** (-th) *suf.* forming ordinal numbers from the cardinals 13–19. [OE *-tȳne*, *tīen*, TEN]

teens (tēnz) *n.pl.* the time in a person's life from age 13 to 19 years. **teenage, teenaged** *a.* 1 aged between 13 and 19 years. 2 of or relating to teenagers. **teenager** *n.* a person aged between 13 and 19 years. **teeny-bopper** *n.* (*coll.*) a young teenager, usu. a girl, who follows the latest trends in clothes and pop music with great enthusiasm. [from -TEEN]

teensy (tēn´zi, -si) *a.* (*comp.* **teensier,** *superl.* **teensiest**) (*coll.*) tiny. **teensy-weensy** (-wēn´zi, -si) *a.* (*comp.* **teensy-weensier,** *superl.* **teensy-weensiest**) (*coll.*) very tiny.

teeny (tē´ni) *a.* (*comp.* **teenier,** *superl.* **teeniest**) (*coll.*) tiny. **teeny-weeny** (-wē´ni) *a.* (*comp.* **teeny-weenier,** *superl.* **teeny-weeniest**) very tiny.

teeny-bopper TEENS.

teepee TEPEE.

teeter (tē´tə) *v.i.* 1 to move to and fro unsteadily, to sway or wobble. 2 to hesitate or waver. ~*v.t.* to move to and fro, to tip up, to tilt. **to teeter on the brink/ edge** to be close to taking a step or decision that could prove disastrous. [var. of TITTER, ME *titer*, Icel. *titra*, to shake]

teeth TOOTH.

teethe (tēdh) *v.i.* to cut or develop teeth, esp. first or milk teeth. **teething** *n., a.* **teething ring** *n.* a ring for a teething baby to chew on. **teething troubles** *n.pl.* 1 the problems or difficulties that arise at the beginning of a new venture etc. and which can usu. be put right quite easily. 2 the soreness and irritation caused when cutting the first teeth. [from TEETH]

teetotal (tētō´təl) *a.* characterized by, relating to, pledged to or advocating total abstinence from intoxicants, esp. alcoholic drink. **teetotalism** *n.* **teetotaller,** (*N Am.*) **teetotaler** *n.* **teetotally** *adv.* [redupl. of TOTAL]

teetotum (tētō´təm) *n.* **1** a toy, orig. four-sided, turning like a top, used in a game of chance. **2** any top that is spun using the fingers. [for *T-totum*, take all (T, L *tōtum*, the whole), marked on one of the sides]

teff (tef) *n.* an African cereal, *Eragrostis tef*, used as a fodder-plant and sometimes as a source of flour. [Amharic]

TEFL (tef´əl) *abbr.* teaching English as a foreign language.

Teflon® (tef´lon) *n.* polytetrafluoroethylene, used as a non-stick coating for saucepans etc. [*tetra-*, *fl*uor-, *-on*]

teg (teg) *n.* **1** a sheep in its second year. **2** the fleece of such a sheep. [etym. uncertain, cp. Swed. *tacka*, ewe]

tegmen (teg´mən) *n.* (*pl.* **tegmina** (-minə)) **1** a covering of an organ or part in an animal or plant. **2** the leathery forewing in insects such as locusts and cockroaches in the Orthoptera class. **tegmental** (-men´-) *a.* **tegminal** *a.* **tegument** (-ūmənt) *n.* a protective covering, envelope or membrane in animals. **tegumental** (-men´-), **tegumentary** (-men´-) *a.* [L, var. *tegimen, tegumen*, from *tegere*, to cover]

te-hee TEE-HEE.

tektite (tek´tīt) *n.* (*Geol.*) a small, dark, glassy stone, thought to be of meteoric origin. [Gk. *tektos*, molten]

tel. (tel), **Tel.** *abbr.* telephone.

tela (tē´lə) *n.* (*pl.* **telae** (-lē)) (*Anat.*) a web, a weblike membrane, structure etc. **telar, telary** *a.* [L]

telaesthesia (teləsthē´ziə, -zhə), (*esp. N Am.*) **telesthesia** *n.* (*Psych.*) the supposed perception of objects or events beyond the normal range of sense perceptions. **telaesthetic** (-thet´-) *a.* [TELE-, Gr. *aisthesia*, sensation]

telamon (tel´əmən) *n.* (*pl.* **telamones** (-mō´nēz)) (*Archit.*) a male figure functioning as a column or pilaster supporting an entablature. [L, from Gr. *Telamōn*, mythical hero]

telco (tel´kō) *n.* (*pl.* **telcos**) (*N Am.*) a company in the telecommunications industry. [abbr.]

tele- (tel´i) *comb. form* **1** far, distant, as in *teleport*. **2** television, as in *teletext*. **3** relating to instruments that function over long distances, as in *telephone*. **4** relating to or conducted over the telephone, as in *telemarketing*. [Gr. *tele*, far off]

tele-ad (tel´iad) *n.* a classified advertisement sent to a newspaper etc. by telephone.

telebanking (tel´ibangking) *n.* a computerized system of banking that allows transactions to be carried out by telephone.

telecamera (tel´ikamərə) *n.* **1** a camera designed for filming in television studios. **2** a camera fitted with a telephoto lens.

telecast (tel´ikahst) *n.* a programme or item broadcast by television. ~*v.t.* (*past*, *p.p.* **telecast**) to broadcast by television. **telecaster** *n.*

telecine (tel´isini) *n.* **1** the broadcasting of film, esp. cinema film, on television. **2** the equipment used for this.

telecommunication (telikəmūnikā´shən) *n.* **1** communication at a distance, by cable, telephone, radio etc. **2** (*pl.*) the science or technology of telecommunication.

telecommute (telikəmūt´) *v.i.* to work at home, keeping in contact with the office etc. by telephone, e-mail, fax, the Internet etc. **telecommuter** *n.* **telecommuting** *n.*

telecoms (tel´ikomz), **telecomms** *n.* (*coll.*) telecommunications.

teleconference (tel´ikonfərəns) *n.* a meeting, discussion or conference where the participants are linked by video, audio or computer connections. **teleconferencing** *n.*

telecottage (tel´ikotij) *n.* a place with personal computers, fax, e-mail, Internet etc. facilities where people can work away from a central office while still being in close contact with it. **telecottaging** *n.*

teledu (tel´ədoo) *n.* (*pl.* **teledus**) a badger, *Mydaus javanensis*, of Java and Sumatra, which emits an offensive odour if disturbed or attacked. [Javanese]

tele-evangelist TELEVANGELIST.

telefacsimile (telifaksim´ili) *n.* an act or the process of sending a fax.

Telefax® (tel´ifaks), **telefax** *n.* **1** TELEFACSIMILE. **2** a document etc. sent by telefacsimile. [abbr.]

telefilm (tel´ifilm) *n.* **1** TELECINE. **2** a film made specifically to be shown on television.

telega (tilā´gə) *n.* a four-wheeled springless Russian cart. [Rus. *telêjga*]

telegenic (telijen´ik) *a.* (of a person) having the looks or personal qualities desirable for working in or appearing on television.

telegnosis (telinō´sis, -gnō´-) *n.* knowledge of distant events not obtained through normal sense perceptions. [Gr. *tele*, far off, *gnosis*, knowledge]

telegony (tileg´əni) *n.* (*Biol.*) the supposed influence that a female's first mate has on her offspring by subsequent mates. **telegonic** (-gon´-), **telegonous** *a.* [Gr. *tele*, far off, *gonos*, offspring]

telegram (tel´igram) *n.* a communication sent by telegraph, now only used for international messages and superseded in 1981 by the telemessage for internal messages.

telegraph (tel´igrahf) *n.* **1** an apparatus or device for transmitting messages or signals to a distance, esp. by making and breaking electrical connections. **2** (*in full* **telegraph-board**) a board at sports grounds, racecourses etc. displaying scores and other information in a format large enough to be read at a distance. ~*v.t.* **1** to transmit (a message etc.) by telegraph. **2** to signal in any way. **3** to give advance warning (of something). ~*v.i.* **1** to send a message by telegraph. **2** to signal (to etc.). **bush telegraph** BUSH[1]. **telegrapher** (tel´-, tileg´-) *n.* **telegraphese** (-ēz´) *n.* **1** jargon used in telegrams. **2** contracted language. **telegraphic** (-graf´-) *a.* **1** of or relating to the telegraph, sent by telegraph. **2** suitable for the telegraph, esp. in being brief, concisely worded. **telegraphic address** *n.* a registered address, often abbreviated, for receiving and/or sending telegrams. **telegraphically** *adv.* **telegraphist** (tileg´-) *n.* **telegraph key** *n.* a device that makes and breaks the electrical connections in sending telegraphic messages. **telegraph line, telegraph cable** *n.* a wire designed to carry telegraph messages. **telegraph plant** *n.* an Asian plant, *Codariocalyx motorius*, which has leaves that make jerking movements in response to being stimulated by sunshine. **telegraph pole, telegraph post** *n.* a pole that supports telegraph and telephone wires. **telegraph wire** *n.* a cable used for carrying telegraphic messages.

telegraphy (tileg´rəfi) *n.* the art or practice of communicating by telegraph or of constructing or managing telegraphs.

Telegu TELUGU.

telekinesis (telikinē´sis) *n.* the movement of objects at a distance supposedly without their being physically touched or interfered with. **telekinetic** (-net´-) *a.* [Gr. *kinesis*, motion]

telemark (tel´imahk) *n.* a swinging turn in skiing, performed to change direction or to stop. ~*v.i.* to make this kind of turn. [district in Norway]

telemarketing (tel´imahkiting) *n.* a way of trying to boost the sales of a product by making unsolicited telephone calls to potential customers. **telemarketer** *n.*

telemessage (tel´imesij) *n.* a message sent by telex or telephone (superseding the telegraph).

telemeter (tilem´itə) *n.* **1** a device that records readings, esp. meteorological data, and transmits it by way of electric or radio signals to a distant point. **2** an instrument for determining distances, used in surveying, artillery practice etc. *~v.t.* to obtain and transmit (data) from a distance. *~v.i.* to record and send data readings. **telemetric** (telimet´-) *a.* **telemetry** (-tri) *n.* the use of radio waves to transmit data.

telencephalon (telənsef´əlon, -kef´-) *n.* the front part of the brain, made up of the cerebrum, parts of the hypothalamus and the third ventricle. **telencephalic** (-fal´-) *a.* [Gr. *telos*, end, *enkephalos*, brain]

teleology (teliol´əji, tē-) *n.* (*pl.* **teleologies**) **1** (*Philos.*) the doctrine that asserts that everything in the universe has been designed for a purpose. **2** (*Theol.*) the belief that, as things can be shown to have a design and purpose, there must be some form of designer (God) in control. **teleologic** (-loj´-), **teleological** *a.* **teleologically** *adv.* **teleologism** *n.* **teleologist** *n.* [Gr. *telos teleos*, end, -LOGY]

teleosaur (tel´iəsaw) *n.* a Mesozoic fossil saurian of the genus *Teleosaurus*. [Gr. *teleos*, complete (*telos*, end), *saurus*, lizard]

teleost (tel´iost) *n.* any fish of the subclass Teleostei, which includes all fish with bony skeletons, but excludes those such as sharks, rays, skates etc., which have cartilaginous skeletons. *~a.* belonging or relating to this subclass of fish. **teleostean** (-os´-) *a.* [Gr. *teleo-*, whole, *osteon*, bone]

telepathy (tilep´əthi) *n.* the supposed communication between minds at a distance without using any of the five recognized senses, thought-transference, mind-reading. **telepathic** (telipath´-) *a.* **telepathically** *adv.* **telepathist** *n.* **telepathize, telepathise** *v.t., v.i.*

telephone (tel´ifōn) *n.* **1** a means of transmitting sounds to distances by a wire or cord, esp. by converting sound vibrations into electrical signals. **2** an instrument for sending and receiving messages of this kind. **3** a communications network of telephones. *~v.t.* **1** to speak to (a person) by means of a telephone. **2** to transmit by means of a telephone. *~v.i.* to make a telephone call. **on the telephone 1** connected to a telephone system. **2** using the telephone. **over the telephone** by means of or using the telephone. **telephone book** *n.* a telephone directory. **telephone box, telephone booth, telephone kiosk** *n.* a public place where telephone calls can be made. **telephone call** *n.* **1** a conversation by way of a telephone. **2** an act of telephoning. **telephone directory** *n.* (*pl.* **telephone directories**) a book listing names, addresses and telephone numbers in a given area. **telephone exchange** *n.* a centralized place where telephone connections are made, formerly by operators but now usu. by a system of computers. **telephone number** *n.* **1** a particular number that is assigned to a specified telephone and which callers must dial to be connected to that telephone. **2** (*usu. in pl., coll.*) any very high number with lots of digits, esp. one that refers to money (*I don't know how much her new car cost, but we're talking telephone numbers*). **telephone operator** *n.* a person who works in a telephone exchange, making connections and sometimes also helping callers and answering queries. **telephonic** (-fon´-) *a.* **telephonically** *adv.* **telephonist** (tilef´-) *n.* a person who operates a telephone switchboard. **telephony** (-lef´əni) *n.* **1** a system of telephones. **2** communication by way of this.

telephotograph (telifō´təgrahf) *n.* **1** a picture reproduced at a distance. **2** a picture obtained by telephotography. *~v.t.* to take this kind of photograph of. **telephoto** (tel´ifōtō) *a.* telephotographic. *~n.* (*pl.* **telephotos**) a telephoto lens. **telephoto lens** *n.* a lens of long focal length, for obtaining photographs of very distant objects. **telephotographic** (-graf´-) *a.* **telephotography** (-fətog´rəfi) *n.* the act or process of photographing objects beyond the limits of ordinary vision. [TELE-, Gr. *phōs phōtos*, light]

telepoint (tel´ipoint) *n.* **1** a type of socket where a cordless telephone can be connected to a telephone system. **2** a system of such sockets.

teleport (tel´ipawt) *v.t.* (*Psych.*) to move (an object, oneself or another person) by telekinesis. **teleportation** (-tā´shən) *n.*

telepresence (tel´iprezəns) *n.* **1** the use of virtual reality technology esp. for remotely controlling machinery or for allowing someone to seem to take part in events that are happening at some distance. **2** the sensation of taking part in distant events that using this technology creates.

teleprinter (tel´iprintə) *n.* a telegraphic apparatus with a keyboard transmitter and a receiver which prints incoming messages.

teleprompter (tel´iprompte) *n.* an apparatus which enables a speaker on television to see the text without this being visible to the viewers.

telerecording (tel´irikawding) *n.* a recording for broadcasting on television. **telerecord** *v.t.* to make a telerecording of.

telesales (tel´isālz) *n.pl.* the selling of items by telephone.

telescope (tel´iskōp) *n.* **1** an optical instrument that uses lenses, mirrors or both for increasing the apparent size of distant objects. **2** RADIO TELESCOPE (under RADIO). *~v.t.* **1** to drive or force (sections, trains etc.) into each other, like the sliding sections of a telescope. **2** to condense (something) so that it takes up less space or time (*telescoped two lectures into one hour*). *~v.i.* to move or be forced into each other in this way. **telescopic** (-skop´-) *a.* **1** performed by, characteristic of or relating to, a telescope. **2** capable of retraction and protraction. **3** only able to be seen by using a telescope. **telescopically** *adv.* **telescopic sight** *n.* a small telescope mounted on a rifle, used as a sight to increase the accuracy of aim.

teleshopping (tel´ishoping) *n.* the buying of goods (usu. displayed or listed on a television or computer screen) through a telephone or computer link.

telesoftware (telisoft´weə) *n.* (*Comput.*) software that is sent to and downloaded from remote terminals.

telespectroscope (telispek´trəskōp) *n.* an instrument for spectroscopic examination of the heavenly bodies.

telestereoscope (telister´iōskōp) *n.* an optical instrument presenting distant objects in relief.

telesthesia TELAESTHESIA.

telestich (tiles´tik, tel´i-) *n.* a poem in which the final letters of each line make up a word or words. [Gr. *telos*, end, *stichos*, row, verse]

teletext (tel´itekst) *n.* data, such as news, local information etc., transmitted by television companies and viewable as text and graphics on a television that has a special adaptor or decoder. **Teletex®** *n.* a form of teletext system.

telethon (tel´ithon) *n.* a very long television programme, usu. to raise funds for charities. [*tele*vision, mara*thon*]

Teletype® (tel´itīp) *n.* a brand of teleprinter. **teletype** *v.t.* to send (a message etc.) using this kind of teleprinter. *~v.i.* to use this kind of teleprinter. **teletypewriter** (-tīp´-) *n.* a teleprinter.

teleutospore (tilū´tōspaw) *n.* a spore produced at the end of the season of fructification in the rust-fungi. [Gr. *teleutē*, completion, from *telos*, end, SPORE]

televangelist (telivan´jəlist), **tele-evangelist** (teliiv-) *n.* a person who regularly appears on television to hold religious services, preach (often a fundamentalist doctrine) and appeal for funds. **televangelism** *n.*

televiewer (tel´ivūə) *n.* a person who watches television. **televiewing** *a.*

television (tel´ivizhən) *n.* **1** the transmission by radio or other means of visual images, usu. with accompanying sound, so that they are displayed on a cathode-ray tube screen. 2 (*in full* **television set**) a device designed to receive and decode incoming electrical television signals. 3 the business of broadcasting television programmes (*works in television*). **televise** (-vīz) *v.t.* to transmit by television. **televisable** *a.* **televisual** (-vizh´ūəl) *a.* of or relating to television. **televisually** *adv.*

telework (tel´iwœk) *v.i.* TELECOMMUTE. **teleworker** *n.*

telex (tel´eks), **Telex** *n.* 1 an international telegraphy service that uses public telecommunications systems to send and receive printed messages by way of teleprinters. 2 a teleprinter used for this service. 3 the message sent. ~*v.t.* to send a message by telex. [*tele*typewriter *ex*change]

telic (tel´ik) *a.* 1 (*Gram.*) (of a clause or phrase) expressing end or purpose. 2 purposeful. [Gr. *telos*, end, -IC]

tell[1] (tel) *v.t.* (*past*, *p.p.* **told** (tōld)) 1 to relate, to recount. 2 to make known, to express in words, to communicate, to divulge. 3 to inform, to assure. 4 to give an order to, to direct. 5 to distinguish, to ascertain (*I can tell you are lying*). 6 to show or explain in writing, diagrams etc. 7 to predict, to warn. 8 to judge, to decide, to find out. 9 †to count, to enumerate. ~*v.i.* 1 to give information or an account (of). 2 (*coll.*) to inform (*If you do that, I'll tell*). 3 to produce a marked effect. 4 to reveal the truth (*Only time will tell*). 5 to be an implicating factor. **all told** all included. **as far as one can tell** using whatever evidence, information etc. is known or available. **tell me another** (*coll.*) used to express disbelief. **tell that to the marines** MARINE. **that would be telling** (*coll.*) used to express a disinclination to give out any more information, esp. because doing so would disclose a secret. **there's no telling** it would be impossible to know or guess. **to tell apart** to distinguish between. **to tell a tale** TALE. **to tell its own tale** TALE. **to tell off** 1 (*coll.*) to scold. 2 to count off. 3 to select or detach on some special duty. **to tell on** to report (someone). **to tell one's beads** to recite the rosary. **to tell one's own tale** TALE. **to tell tales** TALE. **to tell the tale** TALE. **to tell the time** to read the time from a clock or watch. **to tell the truth** TRUTH. **you're telling me** (*coll.*) I completely agree with what you are saying. **tellable** *a.* **teller** *n.* 1 an officer in a bank etc. appointed to receive or pay out money. 2 a person who numbers or counts, esp. one of four appointed to count votes in the House of Commons. 3 a person who tells. **tellership** *n.* **telling** *a.* 1 producing a striking effect. 2 revelatory, significant (*a telling remark*). **tellingly** *adv.* **telling-off** *n.* (*pl.* **tellings-off**) a rebuke, a mild scolding. **tell-tale** *n.* 1 a person who tells tales, esp. about the private affairs of others. 2 any automatic device for giving information as to condition, position etc. ~*a.* 1 revealing, implicating (*left tell-tale footprints*). 2 given to telling tales about people. [OE *tellan*, from *talu*, TALE]

tell[2] (tel) *n.* in Middle Eastern archaeology, a mound that is composed of the remains of successive settlements. [Arab. *tall*, hillock]

tellurian (telūə´riən) *a.* of, relating to or living on the earth. ~*n.* an inhabitant of the earth. **tellural** (-rəl) *a.* of, relating to or living on the earth. ~*n.* esp. in science fiction, a person who lives on or comes from the earth. **tellurion** (-riən) *n.* an apparatus for illustrating the real and apparent movements of the earth, the phenomena of eclipses, day and night, the seasons etc. **tellurometer** (-ūrom´itə) *n.* in surveying, an electronic instrument which measures distances using radio waves. [L *tellus -lūris*, the earth, -IAN]

telluric (telūə´rik) *a.* 1 of or relating to the earth's status as a planet. 2 of or relating to soil. 3 (*Chem.*) of or relating to tellurium, esp. in its higher valency.

tellurion TELLURIAN.

tellurium (telūə´riəm) *n.* a rare silvery-white non-metallic element, at. no. 52, chem. symbol Te, found in association with gold, silver and bismuth. **tellurate** (tel´ūrāt) *n.* a salt of telluric acid. **telluride** (tel´ūrīd) *n.* **tellurite** (tel´ūrīt) *n.* 1 native oxide of tellurium. 2 a salt of tellurous acid. **tellurous** *a.* of or relating to tellurium, esp. in its lower valency. [as TELLURIAN, -IUM]

tellurometer TELLURIAN.

telly (tel´i) *n.* (*pl.* **tellies**) (*coll.*) 1 television. 2 a television set.

telophase (tē´ləfāz) *n.* (*Biol.*) the final stage in cell division which results in the formation of the nuclei of the daughter cells. [Gr. *telos*, end, PHASE]

telpher (tel´fə) *n.* a form of suspended monorail on which a truck runs, carrying its load hanging below the level of the truck and rail. **telpherage** *n.* transportation of this nature, operated usually by electricity. [for *telephore* (TELE-, -PHORE)]

telson (tel´sən) *n.* the last segment in the abdomen of crustaceans and arachnids. [Gr., limit]

Telugu (tel´əgoo), **Telegu** *n.* (*pl.* **Telugu, Telugus, Telegu, Telegus**) 1 a Dravidian language spoken in parts of SE and central India and parts of Sri Lanka. 2 a person who speaks this language. [Telugu]

temazepam (təmaz´ipam) *n.* a sedative drug used as a premedication or as a treatment for insomnia, and sometimes taken in quantity for a euphoric effect.

temblor (temblaw´) *n.* (*US*) an earthquake or tremor. [Am. Sp., from Sp. *tremblar*, to shake]

temerity (timer´iti) *n.* 1 excessive rashness, recklessness. 2 impertinence, audacity. **temerarious** (temərea´riəs) *a.* (*formal*) 1 rash, reckless, headstrong. 2 careless, done at random. **temerariously** *adv.* [L *temeritas*, from *temere*, rashly]

temp (temp) *n.* a temporary, usu. secretarial or clerical, worker. ~*v.i.* to work as a temp. [TEMPORARY]

temp. *abbr.* 1 temperature. 2 temporary. 3 *tempore*, in the time of (L).

temper (tem´pə) *n.* 1 a disposition of mind, esp. with regard to emotional stability (*a volatile temper, an even temper*). 2 composure, self-command (*always losing his temper*). 3 anger, irritation, passion (*stamped her feet in temper*). 4 a tendency to have angry emotional outbursts (*He's got a real temper*). 5 the state of a metal as regards hardness and elasticity. ~*v.t.* 1 (*fig.*) to qualify, to modify, to moderate, to tone down, to mitigate (*Temper your disgust with some sympathy*). 2 to bring (steel etc.) to a proper degree of hardness by heating and cooling. 3 to bring (clay etc.) to a proper consistency by mixing, kneading etc. 4 to adjust the tones of (an instrument) according to a particular temperament. **out of temper** irritable, in a bad temper. **to keep one's temper** to remain calm and rational. **to lose one's temper** to become angry. **to show temper** to be irritable or moody. **temperable** *a.* **temperative** *a.* **tempered** *a.* 1 (*usu. in comb.*) having a specified kind of temper (*ill-tempered, even-tempered*). 2 adjusted according to equal temperament. **-temperedly** *adv.* **-temperedness** *n.* **temperer** *n.* [OE *temprian*, L *temperāre*, from *tempus -poris*, time, season]

tempera (tem´pərə) *n.* 1 a method of artistic painting that uses an emulsion of powdered pigment mixed with egg yolk and water. 2 the emulsion itself. [It.]

temperament (tem´pərəmənt) *n.* 1 a person's individual character, natural disposition (formerly supposed to be determined by the relative predominance of certain humours, and classified as sanguine or full-blooded, lymphatic or phlegmatic, bilious, and melancholic). 2 manifest sensitivity or emotionality. 3 the adjustment of the tones of an instrument to fit the scale in any key, esp. by a compromise in the case of instruments of fixed intonation, such as an organ or piano. **temperamental** (-men´-) *a.* 1 having an erratic or neurotic temperament. 2 (*coll.*) unreliable, liable to break down (*a temperamental old car*). 3 resulting from or connected with temperament. **temperamentally** *adv.* [L *temperāmentum*, as TEMPER]

temperance (tem´pərəns) *n.* 1 moderation, self-restraint, esp. where indulgence in food, alcohol etc. is concerned. 2 moderation or abstinence in the use of intoxicants. ~*a.* advocating or promoting moderation, esp. in alcoholic drinks. [OF, from L *temperantia*, as TEMPER]

temperate (tem´pərət) *a.* 1 self-restrained. 2 moderate. 3 (of climate) not liable to excess of heat or cold, mild. 4 abstemious. **temperately** *adv.* **temperateness** *n.* **temperate zone** *n.* the part of the earth which lies between the tropics and the polar circles and has a moderate climate. [L *temperātus*, p.p. of *temperāre*, to TEMPER]

temperative TEMPER.

temperature (tem´prəchə) *n.* 1 degree of heat or cold in a body or the atmosphere, esp. as registered by a thermometer. 2 (*Med.*) the degree of the body's internal heat. 3 (*coll.*) body temperature above normal. 4 the extent of excitement, enthusiasm etc. that a subject, discussion etc. generates. **to take someone's temperature** to use a device such as a thermometer to measure a person's (or an animal's) body heat, esp. as a way of checking on their health. **temperature-humidity index** *n.* an index which measures temperature and humidity and the effect of these on human comfort. **temperature inversion** *n.* the reversal of the usual variation of air temperature with height. [F, from L *temperātūra*, as TEMPERATE]

tempest (tem´pəst) *n.* 1 a violent storm of wind, esp. with heavy rain, hail or snow. 2 (*fig.*) violent tumult or agitation. **tempestuous** (-pes´tū-) *a.* 1 (of the weather) very stormy. 2 (of a person, relationship etc.) turbulent, emotional, passionate. **tempestuously** *adv.* **tempestuousness** *n.* [OF *tempeste* (F *tempête*), L *tempestātem*, nom. *-tas*, weather, from *tempus*, time]

tempi TEMPO.

Templar (tem´plə) *n.* a lawyer or a law student having chambers in the Temple, in London. **Knight Templar** KNIGHT. [A-F *templer*, OF *templier*, med. L *templārius*, from *templum*, TEMPLE[1]]

templar TEMPLE[1].

template (tem´plət), **templet** *n.* 1 a pattern, gauge or mould, usu. of thin wood or metal, used as a guide in shaping, turning or drilling. 2 a short timber or stout stone placed in a wall to distribute the pressure of beams etc. 3 (*Chem.*) the coded information that is contained in the structure of a molecule which serves as the pattern for the production of another specific compound. [F, dim. of *temple*, L *templum*, a small timber]

temple[1] (tem´pəl) *n.* 1 an edifice dedicated to the service of some deity or deities, esp. of the ancient Egyptians, Greeks or Romans. 2 either of the two successive buildings that were the seat of Jewish worship at Jerusalem. 3 a place of public Christian worship, esp. a Protestant church in France. 4 (*N Am.*) a synagogue. 5 a place in which the divine presence is believed to reside, esp. a Christian person's body. 6 something that is thought of as housing something valuable, precious etc. (*treats her body as a temple*; *a home that is a temple to the arts*). **templar** *a.* of or relating to a temple. [OE *templ*, L *templum*]

temple[2] (tem´pəl) *n.* the flat part at either side of the head between the forehead and ear. **temple block** *n.* a hollow wooden percussion instrument played by striking it with a stick. [OF *temples*, L *tempora*, pl. of *tempus*, time]

temple[3] (tem´pəl) *n.* an attachment in a loom for keeping the fabric stretched. [F, see TEMPLATE]

templet TEMPLATE.

tempo (tem´pō) *n.* (*pl.* **tempi** (-pē), **tempos**) 1 (*Mus.*) the specified speed at which a piece of music is or should be played. 2 pace or rate (*the tempo of modern life*). [It., from L *tempus*, time]

temporal[1] (tem´pərəl) *a.* 1 of or relating to this life. 2 secular, as opposed to spiritual. 3 of, relating to or expressing time. 4 (*Gram.*) denoting or relating to tense or to the linguistic expression of time (*'Slowly' is a temporal adverb*). **temporality** (-ral´-) *n.* (*pl.* **temporalities**) 1 temporariness. 2 (*pl.*) a secular possession, esp. the revenues of a religious corporation or an ecclesiastic. **temporal lords** *n.pl.* the peers of the realm, as distinguished from the archbishops and bishops. **temporally** *adv.* **temporalness** *n.* **temporal power** *n.* the power of the Pope or the Church in temporal, as distinct from ecclesiastical, affairs. [OF, from L *temporālis*, from *tempus -poris*, time]

temporal[2] (tem´pərəl) *a.* positioned at the temples. **temporal bone** *n.* either of the two compound bones at the sides of the skull. **temporal lobe** *n.* a large lobe on either side of the brain, associated with hearing and speech.

temporary (tem´pərəri) *a.* 1 lasting, designed or intended only for a limited length of time (*temporary staff*). 2 transient or provisional (*a temporary claim to fame*). ~*n.* (*pl.* **temporaries**) a person working on a short-term contract. **temporarily** (tem´-, rar´i-, -reə´ri-) *adv.* **temporariness** *n.* [L *temporārius*, as TEMPORAL[1]]

Usage note The pronunciation of *temporarily* with stress on the third syllable is sometimes disapproved of.

temporize (tem´pərīz), **temporise** *v.i.* 1 to pursue an indecisive, procrastinating or time-serving policy. 2 to comply with or humour or yield to the requirements of time and occasion. **temporization** (-zā´shən) *n.* **temporizer** *n.* **temporizingly** *adv.* [F *temporiser*, as TEMPORAL[1]]

☒ **temprature** common misspelling of TEMPERATURE.

tempt (tempt) *v.t.* 1 to incite or entice (to or to do something wrong or forbidden). 2 to attract, to allure, to invite. 3 to risk provoking (*You're tempting fate*). 4 †to test (someone's faith, resolve etc.). 5 †to attempt. **to be tempted to** to be inclined to (*I'm tempted to tell her*). **temptable** *a.* **temptability** (-bil´-) *n.* **temptation** (-tā´shən) *n.* 1 the act or an instance of tempting, enticement to do something, esp. something wrong. 2 the condition of being tempted. 3 an inviting prospect or thing. 4 †trial, putting someone to the test. **the Temptation** the tempting of Christ by the Devil, as recorded in Matt. iv. **tempter** *n.* 1 a person who tempts. 2 (*often* **the Tempter**) the Devil. **tempting** *a.* 1 enticing, inviting. 2 enticing to evil. **temptingly** *adv.* **temptress** (-tris) *n.* a female tempter. [OF *tenter*, *tempter*, L *tentāre*, *temptāre*, freq. of *tenēre*, to hold]

tempura (tem´purə) *n.* a Japanese dish of vegetables, seafood and fish coated in batter and deep-fried. [Jap.]

ten (ten) *n.* 1 the number or figure 10 or X. 2 the age of 10. 3 the 10th hour after midnight or midday. 4 a group of 10 people or things. 5 a playing card with 10 pips. 6 a size of shoe or article of clothing designated by the number 10. ~*a.* 1 10 in number. 2 aged 10. 3 an arbitrary use of the number used to express a large amount (*earns ten times as much as me*). **ten to one** very likely or probably. **Ten Commandments** *n.pl.* the rules of behaviour reported in Exod. as given by God to Moses on Mt. Sinai. **tenfold** *a.*, *adv.* 1 10 times as much. 2 made up of 10 parts. **ten-gallon hat** *n.* a wide-brimmed hat worn by some Texans and American cowboys. **ten-minute rule** *n.* in Parliament, a procedure where a member may make a short, ten-minute speech, introducing a bill. **tenner** *n.* (*coll.*) a ten-pound or ten-dollar note. **tenpence** *n.* **tenpenny** *a.* priced or sold at tenpence. **tenpenny nail** *n.* a large nail orig. costing 10d.

per 100. **tenpin** *n.* a type of skittle used in tenpin bowling. **tenpin bowling, tenpins** *n.* a game similar to ninepins but played with ten pins in a skittle-alley. **tenth** (-th) *n.* any one of 10 equal parts. ~*n., a.* **1** (the) last of 10 (people, things etc.). **2** the next after the 9th. **tenthly** *adv.* **tenth-rate** *a.* of very poor quality. **ten-week stock** *n.* a particularly fast-growing variety of stock, *Matthiola incana*, that can flower as soon as ten weeks after the seeds are sown. [OE *tiēn, tȳn* (Anglian *tēn*), (cp. Dut. *tien*, G *zehn*, also L *decem*, Gr. *deka*)]

ten. *abbr.* tenuto.

tenable (ten´əbəl) *a.* **1** capable of being held, retained or maintained against attack. **2** (of a position, office etc.) intended to be held (for a specified period or by a particular person). **tenability** (-bil´-) *n.* **tenableness** *n.* [F, from *tenir*, L *tenēre*, to hold]

tenace (ten´ās) *n.* **1** in whist, etc., the best and third best cards of a suit held in the same hand. **2** the holding of these cards. [F, as TENACIOUS]

tenacious (tənā´shəs) *a.* **1** holding fast. **2** inclined to hold fast, obstinate, unyielding. **3** persistent, determined. **4** retentive, adhesive, sticky. **5** highly cohesive, tough. **tenaciously** *adv.* **tenaciousness** *n.* **tenacity** (-nas´-) *n.* [L *tenax -ācis*, from *tenēre*, to hold]

tenaculum (tənak´ūləm) *n.* (*pl.* **tenacula** (-lə)) (*Med.*) a sharp hook used in surgery for picking up blood vessels. [L, a holding instrument]

tenaille (tənāl´), **tenail** *n.* in fortification works, a low outwork in the enceinte ditch in front of the curtain between two bastions. [F *tenaille*, L TENACULUM]

tenant (ten´ənt) *n.* **1** a person who rents land or property from a landlord. **2** (*Law*) a person who holds land or property by any kind of title. **3** (*loosely*) an occupant, a dweller, an inhabitant. ~*v.t.* to hold as tenant, to occupy. **tenancy** (-si) *n.* (*pl.* **tenancies**) **1** the holding of land, property etc. under a lease. **2** the period of this. **3** the status of being a tenant. **tenantable** *a.* fit for occupation by a tenant. **tenant farmer** *n.* a person who cultivates land leased from the owner. **tenant-in-chief** *n.* (*pl.* **tenants-in-chief**) a person who holds land that is granted directly by the sovereign. **tenantless** *a.* **tenant right** *n.* the right allowed by custom to a well-behaved tenant not to be liable to injurious increase of rent or to be deprived of tenancy without compensation. **tenantry** (-ri) *n.* **1** (*collect.*) tenants. **2** the state of being a tenant. **tenantship** *n.* [OF, pres.p. of *tenir*, see TENABLE]

tench (tench) *n.* (*pl.* **tench**) a freshwater fish, *Tinca tinca*, of the carp family. [OF *tenche* (F *tanche*), L *tinca*]

tend[1] (tend) *v.i.* **1** to have a bent, inclination or attitude, to be inclined (to). **2** to move, hold a course or be directed (in a certain direction etc.). **tendency** (-dənsi) *n.* (*pl.* **tendencies**) **1** bent, drift, inclination, disposition. **2** a faction or sub-group within a political party or movement. **tendentious** (-den´shəs) *a.* (*derog.*) with an underlying purpose, intended to further a cause. **tendentiously** *adv.* **tendentiousness** *n.* [A-F *tendre*, L *tendere*, to stretch (p.p. *tensus, tentus*), cogn. with TENABLE]

tend[2] (tend) *v.t.* to attend, to watch, to look after, to take charge of. ~*v.i.* **1** to attend, to wait (upon). **2** to pay attention (to). **tended** *a.* **tender**[1] (ten´də) *n.* **1** a person who tends. **2** a truck attached to a steam locomotive carrying the supply of fuel, water etc. **3** a vessel attending a larger one, to supply provisions, carry dispatches etc. [shortened from ATTEND]

tendency, tendentious TEND[1].

tender[1] TEND[2].

tender[2] (ten´də) *a.* **1** (of food) easily chewed. **2** sensitive, easily pained or hurt, susceptible to pain, grief etc. **3** easily broken, bruised etc., soft, delicate, fragile, weakly, frail. **4** loving, affectionate, fond. **5** careful, solicitous, considerate (of), requiring to be treated delicately or cautiously, ticklish. **6** young, early. **tender-eyed** *a.* **1** having gentle eyes. **2** weak-eyed. **tenderfoot** *n.* (*pl.* **tenderfoots, tenderfeet**) **1** (*N Am., Austral., sl.*) a newcomer in the bush etc., a novice. **2** a newly enrolled Scout or Guide. **tender-hearted** *a.* **1** kind and thoughtful. **2** easily made to feel pity or love. **tender-heartedly** *adv.* **tender-heartedness** *n.* **tenderize, tenderise** *v.t.* to make tender (e.g. meat), e.g. by pounding and so breaking down the fibres. **tenderization** (-zā´shən) *n.* **tenderizer** *n.* **1** an instrument for pounding meat. **2** a substance which makes (meat) tender. **tenderling** (-ling) *n.* **tenderloin** *n.* **1** the tenderest part of the loin in beef or pork. **2** (*N Am.*) the undercut, fillet. **3** (*N Am.*) an area in a city renowned for prostitution, drug dealing, crime etc. **tenderly** *adv.* **tender mercies** *n.pl.* (*iron.*) care or treatment which may ultimately be beneficial but which also involves a degree of discomfort, unpleasantness etc. **tenderness** *n.* **tender spot** *n.* (*fig.*) a subject or issue that someone is inclined to be touchy about. [ME and OF *tendre*, L *tenerum*, nom. *tener*]

tender[3] (ten´də) *v.t.* **1** to offer, to present for acceptance (*tendered her resignation*). **2** to offer in payment. ~*v.i.* to make a tender (to do certain work or supply goods etc.). ~*n.* **1** an offer in writing to do certain work or supply certain articles, at a certain sum or rate. **2** an offer for acceptance. **3** (*Law*) a formal offer of money or other things in satisfaction of a debt or liability. **legal tender** LEGAL. **to put out to tender** to invite or seek tenders (for work, services etc.). **tenderer** *n.* **tendering** *n.* [F *tendre*, to TEND[1]]

tendon (ten´dən) *n.* (*Anat.*) **1** any of the strong bands or cords of connective tissue forming the termination or connection of the fleshy part of a muscle. **2** the hamstring of a quadruped. **tendinitis** (-ī´tis), **tendonitis** *n.* inflammation of a tendon. **tendinous** *a.* [F, from med. L *tendōnem*, nom. *-do*, from L *tendere*, to stretch]

tendril (ten´dril) *n.* a leafless organ by which a plant clings to another body for support. **tendrilled** *a.* [etym. uncertain, prob. from L as TENDON]

Tenebrae (ten´ibrē) *n.pl.* **1** in the Roman Catholic Church, the offices of matins and lauds for the last three days in Holy Week. **2** these offices set to music. **tenebrism** *n.* a 17th cent. Spanish and Neapolitan school of painting, characterized by the use of much shadow and areas of dark colour. **tenebrous** *a.* (*formal*) dark, gloomy. [L, darkness]

tenement (ten´əmənt) *n.* **1** an apartment or set of apartments used by one family or set of residents. **2** a dwelling house. **3** (*Sc., US*) (*also* **tenement house**) a house that is divided into separate flats or apartments. **4** (*Law*) any kind of permanent property that may be held, such as lands, houses etc. **tenemental** (-men´-) *a.* **tenementary** *a.* [OF, from med. L *tenementum*, from *tenēre*, to hold]

tenesmus (tinez´məs) *n.* a continual need accompanied by effort and straining, to evacuate the bowels or bladder. [med. L, from Gr. *teinesmos*, from *teinein*, to stretch, to strain]

tenet (ten´it, tē´-) *n.* an opinion, principle, doctrine or dogma held by a person, school or organization. [L, he holds, see TENEMENT]

tenfold TEN.

tenia TAENIA.

Tenn. *abbr.* Tennessee.

tenné (ten´i), **tenny** *n.* (*Her.*) an orangish-brown colour. ~*a.* having this colour. [F *tanné*, tawny]

tenner TEN.

tennis (ten´is) *n.* a racket game for two (singles) or four (doubles) players where the object is to hit the ball over a net so that it lands within the confines of a grass or hard court. **lawn tennis** LAWN[1]. **real tennis** REAL[1]. **table tennis** TABLE. **tennis ball** *n.* a ball used in playing tennis. **tennis court** *n.* a court laid out for playing tennis. **tennis elbow** *n.* an elbow strained or sprained in playing tennis, or through other exercise. **tennis racket** *n.* a racket used in playing tennis. **tennis shoe** *n.* a light shoe worn for playing tennis or with casual clothing. [ME *tenetz, tenys*, perh. from OF *tenez*, hold, take, as TENON]

tenno (ten´ō) *n.* (*pl.* **tennos**) the Emperor of Japan, esp. in his capacity as divine ruler. [Jap.]

tenny TENNÉ.

Tennysonian (tenisō´niən) *a.* of, relating to or in the style of Alfred, Lord Tennyson, 1809–92, British poet.

tenon (ten´ən) *n.* the projecting end of a piece of timber fitted for insertion into a mortise etc. *~v.t.* **1** to cut a tenon on. **2** to join by a tenon. **tenoner** *n.* **tenon saw** *n.* a thin saw with a strong brass or steel back used for cutting tenons etc. [F, from *tenir*, L *tenēre*, to hold]

tenor (ten´ə) *n.* **1** the highest of male voices between baritone and alto. **2** a musical part for this voice. **3** a person with such a voice. **4** an instrument, esp. a recorder, saxophone or viola, playing a part between bass and alto. **5** a tenor bell. **6** the exact purport or meaning, also an exact transcript or copy. **7** a settled course, tendency or direction. **8** general purport or drift (of thought etc.). **9** (*Law*) the wording of a document. **10** the subject in a simile or metaphor, e.g. 'My love' in Burns's 'My love is like a red, red rose'. *~a.* **1** (of a voice, singer, instrument etc.) that is a tenor. **2** of, relating to or adapted for singing or playing the tenor part. **tenor bell** *n.* the largest bell in a set. **tenor clef** *n.* the C clef placed upon the fourth line of the stave. **tenorist** *n.* a person who sings or plays a tenor part. [ME and OF *tenour*, L *tenor*, *-ōrem*, a holding on, (later) melody or canto fermo, from *tenēre*, to hold]

tenore (tinaw´rā) *n.* (*pl.* **tenori** (-rē)) a tenor voice or singer. **tenorino** (-rē´nō) *n.* (*pl.* **tenorini** (-nē)) a falsetto tenor voice or singer, a high tenor. [It.]

tenosynovitis (tēnōsīnōvī´tis, ten-) *n.* swelling and inflammation in the tendons, usu. in joints, caused by repetitive use of the joint concerned. [Gr. *tenōn*, tendon, *-itis*, inflammation]

tenotomy (tinot´əmi) *n.* (*pl.* **tenotomies**) the cutting of a tendon. [Gr. *tenōn*, tendon, -TOMY]

tenrec (ten´rek), **tanrec** (tan´-) *n.* any of several small insectivorous mammals similar to the hedgehog, esp. the tailless variety, *Tenrec ecaudatus*, found in Madagascar. [F *tanrec*, Malagasy *tandraka*]

TENS *abbr.* transcutaneous electrical nerve stimulation.

tense[1] (tens) *a.* **1** stretched tight, strained to stiffness (*a tense rope; tense nerves*). **2** under or producing emotional stress (*felt tense before the interview*). **3** (of a phonetic sound) produced with relatively great muscular effort. *~v.t.* to make tense. *~v.i.* to become tense. **to tense up** to make or become tense. **tensely** *adv.* **tenseness** *n.* **tensible** *a.* tensile. **tensibility** (-bil´-) *n.* **tensile** (-sīl) *a.* **1** of or relating to tension. **2** capable of extension. **tensile strength** *n.* the greatest stress a given substance can withstand before breaking. **tensility** (-sil´-) *n.* **tensimeter** (-sim´-) *n.* **1** an instrument for comparing vapour pressure. **2** MANOMETER. **tensiometer** (-siom´-) *n.* **1** TENSIMETER (under TENSE[1]). **2** an instrument for measuring the surface tension of liquid. **3** an instrument which measures the moisture content of soil. **tensiometry** (-siom´itri) *n.* **tensity** *n.* **tensor** (-sə, -saw) *n.* **1** (*Anat.*) a muscle that stretches or tightens a body part. **2** (*Math.*) an array of components which are the functions of the coordinates of any point in space and which have a definite relation to any new components resulting from a transformation of coordinates. **tensorial** (-saw´riəl) *a.* [L *tensus*, p.p. of *tendere*, see TEND[1]]

tense[2] (tens) *n.* (*Gram.*) **1** a form taken by a verb to indicate the time, and also the continuance or completedness, of an action. **2** a set of forms of this kind indicating also person and number. **tenseless** *a.* [OF *tens* (F *temps*), L *tempus*, time]

tensible, tensile etc. TENSE[1].

tension (ten´shən) *n.* **1** the act of stretching or the state of being stretched. **2** strain, stress, effort. **3** mental strain, stress or excitement. **4** a state of hostility, strain or anxiety. **5** in mechanics, a state of strain that results from forces acting in opposition to each other. **6** the expansive force of a gas or vapour. **7** electromagnetic force. **8** in knitting, the relative tightness or looseness of a piece of work. **tensional** *a.* **tensionally** *adv.* **tensioner** *n.* **tensionless** *a.* **tension rod** *n.* a rod in a structure preventing the spreading of opposite members. [TENSE[1]]

tensity, tensor TENSE[1].

tent[1] (tent) *n.* **1** a portable shelter consisting of canvas or other flexible material stretched over and supported on poles. **2** (*Med.*) OXYGEN TENT (under OXYGEN). *~v.t.* to cover with or lodge in a tent. *~v.i.* to camp in a tent. **tentage** *n.* tents and camping equipment generally. **tent-bed** *n.* a bed with curtains which hang from a central point, in the style of a tent. **tent coat, tent dress** *n.* a very roomy style of coat or dress. **tented** *a.* consisting of tents (*a tented village*). **tent-fly** *n.* (*pl.* **tent-flies**) **1** a loose piece of canvas etc., fastened over the ridge pole to shelter a tent from sun and rain. **2** a flysheet. **tent peg, tent pin** *n.* a strong peg or pin driven into the ground to hold the tent loops or guy ropes in place. **tent pole** *n.* a pole supporting a tent. **tent stitch** *n.* **1** embroidery consisting of a series of close parallel stitches made diagonally on a canvas etc. **2** a single stitch of this kind. [OF *tente*, L *tenta*, pl. of *tentum*, neut. p.p. of *tendere*, to stretch]

tent[2] (tent) *n.* a Spanish wine of a deep red colour, used for sacramental purposes. [Sp. *vino tinto*, deep-coloured wine (*tinto*, L *tinctus*, see TINGE)]

tent[3] (tent) *n.* (*Med.*) a small roll of lint, sponge etc., inserted in a wound, ulcer etc., to keep it open. *~v.t.* to keep open with a tent. [OF, from *tenter*, to probe, see TEMPT]

tentacle (ten´təkəl) *n.* **1** (*Zool.*) a long slender organ, esp. in invertebrates, such as an arm of an octopus, used for touching, grasping, moving etc. and, if suckers are present, for attaching the animal to a surface. **2** anything, such as a feeler, that resembles this. **3** (*Bot.*) a sensitive hair. **tentacled** *a.* **tentacular** (-tak´ū-), **tentaculate** (-tak´ūlət), **tentaculated** (-lātid), **tentaculoid** (-loid) *a.* [from L *tentāre*, see TEMPT, after SPECTACLE etc.]

tentative (ten´tətiv) *a.* **1** consisting or done as a trial or essay, experimental. **2** hesitant, uncertain. *~n.* an experiment, a trial, a conjecture. **tentatively** *adv.* **tentativeness** *n.* [med. L *tentātīvus*, from *tentāre*, see TEMPT]

tenter[1] (ten´tə) *n.* **1** a frame or machine for stretching cloth to dry to make it set even and square. **2** a tenter-hook. **tenterhook** *n.* any one of a set of hooks used in stretching cloth on the tenter. **on tenterhooks** in a state of suspense and anxiety, usu. because of uncertainty or awaiting an outcome or result. [prob. through A-F and OF *tentour*, from *tendere*, to stretch]

tenter[2] (ten´tə) *n.* **1** a person who is in charge, esp. of factory machinery. **2** an unskilled assistant to a worker. [perh. TENDER]

tenth TEN.

tenuity (tinū´iti) *n.* **1** thinness, slenderness. **2** rarity. **3** meagreness. **tenuis** (ten´ūis) *n.* in ancient Greek, a voiceless plosive *k, p* or *t*. [F *ténuité*, L *tēnuitātem*, nom. *-tas*, from *tenuis*, thin]

tenuous (ten´ūəs) *a.* **1** insignificant, not able to stand up to much scrutiny (*formed a tenuous connection*). **2** thin, slender, small, minute. **3** rare, rarefied, subtle, over-refined. **tenuously** *adv.* **tenuousness** *n.* [see TENUITY]

tenure (ten´yə) *n.* **1** the act, manner or right of holding property, esp. real estate or office. **2** the manner or conditions of holding. **3** the period or term of holding. **4** the holding of a university or college post for an assured period of time, esp. following a probationary period. **tenured** *a.* **1** (of a teaching or lecturing post) guaranteed to be permanent or to last for a specified time. **2** (of a teacher or lecturer) holding this kind of post. **tenurial** (tenūə´riəl) *a.* **tenurially** *adv.* [A-F and OF, from med. L *tenitūra, tenūra*, cp. TENOR]

tenuto (tinoo´tō) *a., adv.* (*Mus.*) sustained, held on for the full time. ~*n.* (*pl.* **tenutos**) a note or chord played in this way. [It., held, from L, as TENURE]

teocalli (tēōkal´i, tā-) *n.* (*pl.* **teocallis**) a pyramidal mound or structure, usu. surmounted by a temple, used for worship by the ancient peoples of Mexico, Central America etc. [Nahuatl *teotl*, god, *calli*, house]

teosinte (tēōsin´ti) *n.* a type of Mexican fodder grass, *Zea mexicana*. [F, from Nahuatl *teocintli*]

tepal (tep´əl) *n.* (*Bot.*) any of the subdivisions of a perianth which is not clearly differentiated into the calyx and corolla. [F *tépale*, influ. by PETAL, SEPAL]

tepee (tē´pē), **teepee, tipi** *n.* (*pl.* **tepees, teepees, tipis**) a N American Indian tent, usu. cone-shaped and made by stretching animal skins over a framework of poles. [Sioux *tipi*, dwelling]

tepefy (tep´ifī) *v.t.* (*3rd pers. sing. pres.* **tepefies**, *pres.p.* **tepefying**, *past, p.p.* **tepefied**) to make tepid. ~*v.i.* to become tepid. **tepefaction** (-fak´-) *n.* [L *tepefacere* (*tepēre*, see TEPID, *facere*, to make)]

tephra (tef´rə) *n.* the solid debris thrown up in a volcanic eruption. **tephrite** (-rīt) *n.* a volcanic rock allied to basalt. **tephritic** (-frit´-) *a.* [Gr., ash]

tepid (tep´id) *a.* **1** moderately warm, lukewarm. **2** unenthusiastic. **tepidarium** (-deə´riəm) *n.* (*pl.* **tepidaria** (-riə)) (*Hist.*) in ancient Rome, the warm room between the hot and cold rooms in a bathhouse. **tepidity** (-pid´-), **tepidness** *n.* **tepidly** *adv.* [L *tepidus*, from *tepēre*, to be warm]

tequila (tikē´lə) *n.* **1** a Mexican spirit distilled from agave which forms the basis of many drinks. **2** the plant from which this spirit is distilled. [Mex. Sp., *Tequila* district in Mexico]

ter. *abbr.* **1** terrace. **2** territory.

ter- (teə) *comb. form* three, thrice, three times, as in *tertiary*. [L]

tera- (ter´ə) *comb. form* 10 to the power of 12. [Gr. *teras*, monster]

teraflop (ter´əflop) *n.* (*Comput.*) a unit of computing speed equal to one million million floating-point operations per second.

terai (ter´ī), **terai hat** *n.* a wide-brimmed felt hat, often with ventilation holes and a double crown, worn in subtropical regions. [*Terai*, a marshy area in India]

teraph (ter´əf) *n.* (*pl.* **teraphim** (-fim)) a small household god or image which ancient Semitic peoples consulted as an oracle. [Heb.]

teratism (ter´ətizm) *n.* a monster, a malformed person or animal, esp. at the foetal stage.

terato- (ter´ətō) *comb. form* of or relating to a monster. [Gr. *teras -atos*, monster]

teratogen (ter´ətəjən, tərat´-) *n.* (*Med.*) something which results in the malformation of an embryo. **teratogenic** (-jen´-) *a.* **teratogeny** (-toj´-) *n.*

teratology (terətol´əji) *n.* **1** (*Med., Biol.*) the study of congenital malformations. **2** mythological stories that involve monsters or grotesque or fanciful creatures. **teratological** (-loj´-) *a.* **teratologist** *n.*

teratoma (terətō´mə) *n.* (*pl.* **teratomata** (-tə), **teratomas**) (*Med.*) a tumour or group of tumours composed of tissue that is foreign to the site of growth, most usually occurring in the testes or ovaries.

terawatt (ter´əwot) *n.* a unit of power equivalent to 10^{12} watts or a million megawatts.

terbium (tœ´biəm) *n.* a rare metallic element, at. no. 65, chem. symbol Tb, found in association with erbium and yttrium. **terbic** *a.* [*Ytterby*, in Sweden, cp. ERBIUM, -IUM]

terce (tœs) *n.* in the Roman Catholic Church, the third canonical hour of divine office when prayers are said around 9 a.m. [see TIERCE]

tercel TIERCEL.

tercentenary (tœsəntē´nəri) *n.* (*pl.* **tercentenaries**) **1** a 300th anniversary. **2** a celebration to mark this. ~*a.* of or relating to a tercentenary. **tercentennial** (-ten´-) *a.* **1** happening every 300 years. **2** lasting for 300 years. ~*n.* a 300th anniversary.

tercet (tœ´sit), **tiercet** (tiə´-) *n.* in prosody, a set of three consecutive lines of verse that either all rhyme or which rhyme with another set of three lines coming before it or after it. [It. *terzetto*, dim. of *terzo*, L *tertius*, third]

terebene (ter´ibēn) *n.* a liquid hydrocarbon obtained by treating oil of turpentine with sulphuric acid, used as an antiseptic, disinfectant, expectorant etc. **terebic** (-reb´-) *a.* [TEREBINTH, -ENE]

terebinth (ter´əbinth) *n.* **1** a small tree, *Pistacia terebinthus*, found around the Mediterranean and once used as a source of a form of turpentine. **2** its resin. **terebinthine** (-bin´thīn) *a.* **1** of or relating to the terebinth. **2** relating to or characteristic of turpentine. [L *terebinthus*, Gr. *terebinthos*]

teredo (tərē´dō) *n.* (*pl.* **teredos**) any of several molluscs, esp. *Teredo navalis*, that bore into submerged timber, the shipworm. **teredine** (ter´ədin) *n.* [L, from Gr. *terēdōn*, from *teirein*, to bore]

Terentian (tiren´shiən) *a.* of, relating to or in the style of the Roman comic dramatist Terence.

terephthalic acid (terəfthal´ik) *n.* (*Chem.*) a white crystalline carboxylic acid which is insoluble in water and is widely used in the manufacture of synthetic fibres, esp. plastics and polyesters. [from TEREBENE, PHTHALIC ACID (under PHTHALIC)]

terete (tərēt´) *a.* (*Biol.*) rounded, cylindrical and smooth. [L *teres -retis*, from *terere*, see TEREBRA]

terga, tergal TERGUM.

tergiversate (tœ´jivəsāt) *v.i.* **1** to change sides. **2** to practise evasions or subterfuges, to equivocate. **3** to turn one's back. **tergiversation** (-ā´shən) *n.* **tergiversator** *n.* [L *tergiversatus*, p.p. of *tergiversārī* (*tergum*, back, *versārī*, freq. of *vertere*, to turn)]

tergum (tœ´gəm) *n.* (*pl.* **terga** (-gə)) the upper or dorsal plate of a somite or segment of an articulate animal. [L, back]

-teria (tiə´riə) *suf.* indicating that an establishment is self-service, as in *washeteria*. [modelled on CAFETERIA]

term (tœm) *n.* **1** a word or expression that has a precise meaning and is used in a particular, often specialized, field (*a computing term*). **2** (*pl.*) any language or expressions used (*gave an answer in ambiguous terms*). **3** (*pl.*) conditions, stipulations, price, charge, rate of payment (*under the terms of the contract*). **4** (*pl.*) relative position, relation, footing (*on friendly terms*). **5 a** a limited period of time, bounded by holidays or vacations, during which students etc. are taught. **b** a similar period during which a law court is in session. **c** a period of imprisonment (*did a two-year term for robbery*). **6 a** a limited period of time during which a specified state pertains or a particular activity is carried out (*her term of office*). **b** a less specific period of time (*in the long term*). **7** an appointed day or date, such as a Scottish quarter day. **8** (*Law*) an estate to be enjoyed for a fixed period. **9** the end of the normal length of a pregnancy (*carried the baby to term this time*). 10 (*Logic*) a word or group of words that may be the subject or predicate of a proposition. 11 (*Math.*) the antecedent or consequent of a ratio. 12 (*Math.*) any one of the parts of an expression connected by the plus or minus signs. 13 (*Math.*) each value in a sequence or series. 14 (*Archit.*) a terminus. 15 †a limit, a boundary, esp. of time. ~*v.t.* to designate, to call, to denominate. **in set terms** expressed in a specific way. **in terms** explicitly. **in terms of** 1 as measured or indicated by. 2 in relation to, with reference to. **on terms** 1 friendly. 2 of equal status or standing. **to bring to terms** to force or induce to accept conditions. **to come to terms** 1 to conclude an agreement (with). 2 to yield, to give way. **to come to terms with** 1 to find a way of coping and living with (some difficulty). 2 to make an agreement with. **to make terms** to conclude an agreement. **term insurance** *n.* insurance of a specific period only. †**termless** *a.* unlimited, boundless. **termly** *a.* occurring every term. ~*adv.* 1 term by term. 2 every term. 3 periodically. **term of years,** (*N Am.*) **term for years** *n.* (*Law*) an estate to be enjoyed for a fixed period. **term paper** *n.* an essay, report, exercise etc. done to show what has been learned in a term. **terms of reference** *n.pl.* 1 the specific points which a committee or other body is charged to decide. 2 the outlined scope for an inquiry, report etc. **terms of trade** *n.pl.* the ratio of export prices to import prices. **term-time** *n.* the period of time when teaching is done. ~*a.* of, relating to or characteristic of this period. [OF *terme*, L *terminus*, cp. Gr. *terma*, limit]

termagant (tœ´məgənt) *n.* 1 a shrewish, abusive, violent woman. 2 (**Termagant**) a mythical deity believed in the Middle Ages to be worshipped by Muslims and introduced into morality plays as a stereotypical scolding character. ~*a.* violent, boisterous, turbulent, shrewish. **termagancy** *n.* **termagantly** *adv.* [ME *Tervagant*, OF *Tervagan*, It. *Trivigante* (per. L *tri-*, TER-, *vagans -ntem*, pres.p. of *vagārī*, to wander)]

terminal (tœ´minəl) *a.* 1 (of a disease) ending in death. 2 (of someone suffering from a disease) about to die. 3 (of a morbid condition) forming the final stage of a fatal disease. 4 (*coll.*) extreme, acute, incurable (*suffers from terminal pessimism*). 5 (*Zool.*) occurring at the end of a series. 6 (*Bot.*) growing or appearing at the end of a stem (*terminal buds*). 7 relating to, done, submitted etc. during or at the end of a term or each term. ~*n.* 1 a building or area at an airport that arriving and departing passengers pass through. 2 a main terminus or station at the end of a railway line or for long-distance buses or coaches. 3 (*Comput.*) a device, usu. consisting of a screen and keyboard, that allows data or information to enter or leave a computer or communications system. 4 something that forms an end, an extremity. 5 a point in an electric circuit or device where a connection can be made or broken. 6 (*Archit.*) (*in full* **terminal figure**) a sculpted terminus. 7 a storage point at a port or at the end of a pipeline where oil is stored until distribution. 8 a patient in the final stages of a fatal disease. **terminally** *adv.* **terminal velocity** *n.* a maximum constant velocity of an object falling through a fluid such as air which is prevented from further acceleration by gravity. [L *terminālis*, as TERMINUS]

terminate (tœ´mināt) *v.t.* 1 to put an end to. 2 (*Med.*) to bring (a pregnancy) to an end artificially and prematurely. 3 to bound, to limit. 4 to form the extreme point or end of. ~*v.i.* to stop, to end (in etc.). **terminable** *a.* 1 capable of being terminated. 2 having a given term or period. **terminableness** *n.* **termination** (-ā´shən) *n.* 1 the act, process or state of terminating or of being terminated. 2 (*Med.*) the act or an instance of artificially and prematurely bringing a pregnancy to an end. 3 a specific kind of ending or outcome. **to bring to a termination** to put a termination to. **to put a termination to** to end with no possibility of resumption. **terminational** *a.* **terminative** *a.* **terminator** *n.* 1 a person who or thing which terminates. 2 the dividing line between the illuminated and the dark part of a heavenly body. **terminatory** *a.* [L *terminātus*, p.p. of *termināre*, from TERMINUS]

termini TERMINUS.

terminism (tœ´minizm) *n.* 1 (*Theol.*) the doctrine that there is a limited period in each person's life for repentance and grace. 2 NOMINALISM (under NOMINAL). **terminist** *n.*

terminology (tœminol´əji) *n.* (*pl.* **terminologies**) 1 the set of terms used in any art, science, discipline etc. 2 the science or study of the (correct) use of terms. **terminological** (-loj´-) *a.* **terminological inexactitude** *n.* (*facet.*) a lie. **terminologically** *adv.* **terminologist** *n.* [as TERMINUS, -LOGY]

terminus (tœ´minəs) *n.* (*pl.* **termini** (-nī), **terminuses**) 1 the point where a railway or bus route ends. 2 the town, building or buildings at this point. 3 a storage place at the end of an oil pipeline etc. 4 a final point, a goal. 5 a starting point. 6 (*Archit.*) a sculpted figure, usu. of an animal or of the armless bust of a human, placed on top of a square pillar so that the figure seems to be springing from the post, orig. as a boundary marker. 7 (*Math.*) the end point of a vector etc. **terminus ad quem** (ad kwem´) *n.* the end or finishing point of an argument, period of time, particular policy etc. **terminus ante quem** (anti kwem´) *n.* the specified time or date before which something must have been achieved or done. **terminus a quo** (ah kwō´) *n.* the beginning or starting point of an argument, period of time, particular policy etc. **terminus post quem** (pōst kwem´) *n.* the specified time or date before which something cannot or should not be started. [L, end, limit, boundary]

termite (tœ´mīt) *n.* any of several kinds of small social insects of the order Isoptera, found chiefly in tropical regions and often causing damage to trees and wood in buildings, also called *white ant.* **termitarium** (-teə´riəm), **termitary** (-təri) *n.* (*pl.* **termitaria** (-riə), **termitaries**) a nest of a termite colony. [L *termes -mitis*, woodworm, cogn. with TEREDO]

tern[1] (tœn) *n.* any small gull-like seabird of the family Sternidae, having slenderly-built bodies, forked tails and narrow, sharp-pointed wings. [prob. from Dan. *terne*, cp. Icel. *therna*, Swed. *tärna*]

tern[2] (tœn) *a.* ternate. ~*n.* 1 a set of three, esp. three lottery numbers winning a large prize if won together. 2 the prize won in this way. **ternary** *a.* 1 consisting of three parts. 2 (*Math.*) based on the number three (*ternary scale*). ~*n.* (*pl.* **ternaries**) a group of three, a triad. **ternary form** *n.* (*Mus.*) a structured form, aba, where the first subject is repeated after a second subject in a related key has been introduced. **ternate** (-nət, -nāt) *a.* 1 arranged in threes. 2 (*Bot.*) **a** composed of three leaflets. **b** in whorls of three. **ternately** *adv.* [L *ternī*, by threes, from TER-]

terne (tœn) *n.* 1 (*in full* **terne metal**) an alloy of lead and 10–20% tin, often also with a small percentage of antimony. 2 (*in full* **terne-plate**) thin sheet iron or steel coated with this alloy. [F, dull, tarnished]

terotechnology (terōteknol´əji) *n.* the application of managerial, financial and engineering skills to the installation and efficient operation of equipment and machinery. [Gr. *tereo*, to watch, TECHNOLOGY]

terpene (tœ´pēn) *n.* (*Chem.*) any one of various isomeric oily hydrocarbons derived chiefly from coniferous plants. [obs. *terp-*, TURPENTINE, -ENE]

Terpsichorean (tœpsikərē´ən, -kaw´ri-) *a.* 1 characteristic of or relating to dancing or Terpsichore, the Muse of dancing. 2 (*formal or facet.*) dancing.

terra (ter´ə) *n.* (*pl.* **terrae** (-rē)) in legal contexts, earth or land. **terra alba** (al´bə) *n.* any of various white, earthy substances, e.g. gypsum, kaolin, pipeclay, magnesia etc. **terra firma** (fœ´mə) *n.* dry land, firm ground. **terraform** (ter´əfawm) *v.t.* esp. in science fiction, to adapt (a planet, its atmosphere etc.) so that it more closely resembles earth conditions. **terra incognita** (inkognē´tə) *n.* unknown country, unexplored territory. **terra sigillata** (sijilā´tə) *n.* **1** (*Hist.*) a type of astringent clay found on the Aegean islands of Lemnos and Samos and used in medicine and for making pottery. **2** earthenware, e.g. Samian ware, made from this clay. [It. and L]

terrace (ter´əs) *n.* **1** a raised level space or platform, artificially constructed or natural and used for growing grapes etc. **2** a paved patio or balcony next to a house. **3** a row of houses, esp. running along the side of a slope. **4** a row of houses all of the same kind. **5** (*pl.*) **a** open tiers around a sports stadium, formerly esp. a football stadium, where spectators stand. **b** (*usu.* **the terraces**) the standing spectators themselves. **6** (*Geol.*) an old shoreline or raised beach. *~v.t.* to form into or provide with terraces. **terraced** *a.* in terraces. **terraced house, terrace house** *n.* a house which is usu. joined to its neighbour on either side and which forms part of a terrace. **terraced roof** *n.* a flat roof, esp. on an Indian or other Asian house. [OF, from It. *terraccia*, *terrazza*, from TERRA]

terracotta (terəkot´ə) *n.* **1** a hard, unglazed earthenware used as a decorative building material and for making pottery, models etc. **2** a statue or figure in this. **3** the brownish-orange colour of terracotta. *~a.* **1** made of this earthenware. **2** having a brownish-orange colour. [It.]

terrain (tərān´) *n.* **1** a region, a tract, an extent of land of a definite geological character or as thought of in terms of military operations. **2** a field or sphere of interest, influence or knowledge. [F, TERRENE]

terramare (terəmah´ri), **terramara** (-rə) *n.* (*pl.* **terramares, terramare** (-rā)) **1** a dark earthy deposit found at the sites of some prehistoric lakeside settlements, esp. in Italy. **2** a dwelling or settlement that once stood at such a site. [F, from It. dial. *terra mara*, from *terra*, earth, *marna*, marl]

Terramycin® (terəmī´sin) *n.* an antibiotic used to treat a wide range of bacterial infections.

terrapin (ter´əpin) *n.* **1** any of several small turtles of the family Emydidae, esp. *Emys orbicularis*, which lives on land and in freshwater ponds and rivers in Europe. **2** a small edible turtle, *Malaclemys terrapin*, which lives in the marshy areas along the S Atlantic and Gulf coasts in the US. **Terrapin®** *n.* a type of prefabricated house with only one storey. [Algonquian]

terrarium (tereə´riəm) *n.* (*pl.* **terrariums, terraria** (-riə)) **1** an enclosed container where small land animals are kept. **2** a large heavy sealed glass bulb where a variety of plants can be grown. [L *terra*, earth, AQUARIUM]

terrazzo (terat´sō) *n.* (*pl.* **terrazzos**) a mosaic floor-covering made by setting marble or other chips into cement, which is then polished. [It.]

terrene (terēn´) *a.* **1** of or relating to the earth, earthly. **2** characteristic of or relating to earth or soil, earthy. **3** terrestrial. *~n.* a region. **terenely** *adv.* [L *terrēnus*, from TERRA]

terreplein (teə´plān) *n.* **1** the upper surface of a rampart where guns are mounted. **2** the level surface around a fieldwork. [F (*terre*, as TERRENE, *plein*, PLAIN[1])]

terrestrial (təres´triəl) *a.* **1** of or relating to or existing on the earth, not celestial. **2** consisting of land, not water. **3** living on the ground, not aquatic, arboreal etc. **4** (*Astron.*) (of a planet) similar in size, density etc. to the earth. **5** of or relating to this world, worldly. **6** (of broadcasting) not done by way of satellites. **7** (of a telephone) connected to a telephone system as opposed to using a cellular radio system. *~n.* an inhabitant of the earth. **terrestrial globe** *n.* a sphere representing the earth and its geography. **terrestrially** *adv.* **terrestrial magnetism** *n.* the magnetic properties possessed by the earth as a whole, which actuate the magnetic compass. **terrestrial telescope** *n.* a type of telescope designed for looking at the earth's surface rather than for astronomical observations. [L *terrestris*]

terret (ter´it), **territ** *n.* **1** each of the rings or loops on harness through which the driving reins pass. **2** the ring on a dog's collar for attaching the lead. [etym. uncertain]

terre-verte (teəveət´) *n.* a soft green mineral used by artists as a pigment. [F, green earth]

terrible (ter´ibəl) *a.* **1** (*coll.*) dreadful, appalling. **2** (*coll.*) very great or bad, extreme (*a terrible gossip*). **3** (*coll.*) completely useless or incompetent. **4** (*coll.*) ill or unwell. **5** (*coll.*) remorseful, regretful, guilty. **6** causing real terror, fear or dread (*a terrible curse*). **terribleness** *n.* **terribly** *adv.* **1** (*coll.*) very, extremely (*That's terribly good of you*). **2** to a great extent, in a terrible way. [OF, from L *terribilis*, from *terrēre*, to terrify]

terricolous (terik´ələs) *a.* living on or in the earth. [L *terricola*, earth-dweller (TERRA, *colere*, to dwell)]

terrier[1] (ter´iə) *n.* **1** a small active dog of various breeds orig. bred to pursue its quarry underground. **2** any of these breeds. **3** a tenacious and hard-working person or animal. **4** (*coll.*) (**Terrier**) a member of the Territorial Army. [F, from med. L *terrārius*, from TERRA]

terrier[2] (ter´iə) *n.* (*Hist.*) **1** a book or roll in which the lands of private persons or corporations are described by site, boundaries, acreage etc. **2** a rent roll. **3** a collection that comprises vassals' or tenants' acknowledgements of a lordship. [F *papier terrier*, as TERRIER[1]]

terrific (tərif´ik) *a.* **1** (*coll.*) excellent, wonderful. **2** (*coll.*) huge (*made a terrific effort*). **3** (*coll.*) dreadful, very unpleasant (*a terrific mess*). **4** (*coll.*) very powerful, forceful etc. **5** causing real fear, terror, awe etc. (*a terrific scream*). **terrifically** *adv.* **1** (*coll.*) exceedingly, surprisingly. **2** frighteningly. **terrify** (ter´ifī) *v.t.* (*3rd pers. sing. pres.* **terrifies,** *pres.p.* **terrifying,** *past, p.p.* **terrified**) to strike with terror, to frighten. **terrifier** *n.* **terrifying** *a.* **terrifyingly** *adv.* [L *terrificus* (*terrēre*, to frighten, -FIC)]

terrigenous (tərij´inəs) *a.* **1** (*Geol.*) formed in the sea from debris from land erosion. **2** produced by or derived from the earth. [L *terrigena*, earth-dweller]

terrine (tərēn´) *n.* **1** a type of coarse pâté, usu. made by incorporating vegetables into a meat or fish base. **2** an earthenware container, esp. one that this type of pâté is cooked in and which is sometimes sold along with the pâté. [F, TUREEN]

territ TERRET.

territory (ter´itəri) *n.* (*pl.* **territories**) **1** the extent of land within the jurisdiction of a particular sovereign, state or other power. **2** (**Territory**) a division of a country not yet granted full state rights. **3** a field of action, interest, thinking etc. **4** an assigned area of a commercial traveller, goods distributor etc. **5** (*Zool.*) the area defended by an animal or bird. **6** in sport, an area that a player or team tries to defend. **7** a large tract of land. **territorial** (-taw´ri-) *a.* **1** of or relating to territory. **2** limited to a given district. **3** (of an animal, bird etc.) characterized by marking out and defending its own territory. **4** (of a person) inclined to be possessive about a particular field of action, interest etc. **5** (**Territorial**) of or relating to a Territory, esp. one of the US or Canada. **6** (**Territorial**) of or relating to the Territorial Army. *~n.* (*coll.*) (**Territorial**) a member of the Territorial Army. **Territorial Army** *n.* a reserve military force of trained volunteers intended to provide a back-up service to the regular armed forces in an emergency. **territoriality** (-al´-) *n.* **territorialize, territorialise** *v.t.*

territorialization (-zāˊshən) *n.* **territorially** *adv.* **territorial waters** *n.pl.* the area of sea, usu. three miles out, adjoining the coast and adjudged to be under the jurisdiction of the country occupying that coast. [L *territōrium*, from TERRA]

terror (terˊə) *n.* **1** extreme fear. **2** a person or thing that causes fear. **3** (*coll.*) an exasperating nuisance, bore, troublesome child etc. **4** government or revolution by terrorism. **Reign of Terror** REIGN. **terrorism** *n.* **1** organized violence and intimidation, usu. for political ends. **2** the act of terrorizing. **terrorist** *n.* a person who uses or advocates intimidation, violence etc., esp. for political reasons. **terroristic** (-risˊ-) *a.* **terroristically** *adv.* **terrorize, terrorise** *v.t.* **1** to terrify. **2** to coerce with threats of violence etc. **terrorization** (-zāˊshən) *n.* **terrorizer** *n.* **terror-stricken, terror-struck** *a.* terrified, paralysed with fear. [ME *terrour*, F *terreur*, L *terror*, from *terrēre*, to frighten]

terry (terˊi) *n.* (*pl.* **terries**) a pile fabric in which the loops are not cut, used esp. for towels, bathrobes etc. ~*a.* made from this material. **terry towelling,** (*N Am.*) **terry toweling** *n.* [etym. uncertain]

terse (tœs) *a.* (*comp.* **terser,** *superl.* **tersest**) **1** (of style, language etc.) neat and compact. **2** concise, abrupt, often to the point of being rude. **tersely** *adv.* **terseness** *n.* [L *tersus*, p.p. of *tergere*, to wipe]

tertial (tœˊshəl) *a.* of or relating to a bird's tertiary feathers. ~*n.* any one of the tertiary feathers. [from L (*tertius*, third)]

tertian (tœˊshən) *a.* (of a fever) occurring or recurring every third day, taking the first and last days into account. ~*n.* a fever in which the symptoms recur every other day. [ME *terciane*, L *tertiānus*, from *tertius*, third]

tertiary (tœˊshəri) *a.* **1** of the third order, rank or formation. **2** (*Geol.*) (**Tertiary**) of or relating to the first period of the Cenozoic period. **3** of or relating to higher education. ~*n.* (*pl.* **tertiaries**) **1** (*Geol.*) (**Tertiary**) the first period of the Cenozoic era, characterized by the appearance of modern flora and mammals. **2** in the Roman Catholic Church, a member of the third order of a monastic body. **3** any one of the feathers attached to the proximal joint of a bird's wing. **tertiary college** *n.* a sixth-form college which teaches vocational courses. **tertiary education** *n.* education that follows primary and secondary education, usu. at a college or university. [L *tertiārius*, as TERTIAN]

tertium quid (tœshəm kwidˊ) *n.* a third (or intermediate) something. [L, from Gr. *triton ti*, some third thing]

tervalent (tœvāˊlənt) *a.* TRIVALENT.

Terylene® (terˊilēn) *n.* a synthetic polyester used as a textile fibre.

terza rima (tœtsə rēˊmə) *n.* in prosody, an arrangement of tercets with a linking rhyme scheme of aba, bcb, cdc etc. [It., third rhyme]

terzetto (tœtsetˊō) *n.* (*pl.* **terzettos, terzetti** (-tē)) (*Mus.*) a group of three performers or singers. [It., see TERCET]

TESL (tesˊəl) *abbr.* teaching of English as a second language.

tesla (tesˊlə) *n.* the SI unit of magnetic flux density equal to a flux of one weber per square metre. **tesla coil** *n.* a transformer which produces high voltages at high frequencies. [Nikola *Tesla*, 1857–1943, US inventor]

TESOL (tesˊol) *abbr.* teaching of English to speakers of other languages.

TESSA (tesˊə), **Tessa** *n.* a tax exempt special savings account. [acronym]

tessellate (tesˊəlāt) *v.t.* **1** to make (a mosaic, pattern etc.) using tesserae or checks. **2** (*Math.*) to cover (a plane surface) by repeatedly using the same shape. **tessellated** *a.* **1** composed of tesserae, inlaid, like a mosaic. **2** (*Bot., Zool.*) coloured or marked in chequered squares. **tessellation** (-āˊshən) *n.* [L *tessellātus*, from *tessela*, dim. of TESSERA]

tessera (tesˊərə) *n.* (*pl.* **tesserae** (-rē)) **1** a small cubical piece of marble, earthenware etc., used in mosaics. **2** in ancient Greece and Rome, a small piece of bone etc. used as a token. [L, from Gr. *tessares*, four]

tessitura (tesituəˊrə) *n.* (*Mus.*) **1** the range that encompasses most of the tones of a voice part. **2** the natural pitch of a voice or piece of vocal music. [It., texture]

test[1] (test) *n.* **1** a critical trial or examination. **2** a means of trial, a standard, a criterion. **3** a minor examination in a school etc. **4** TEST MATCH (under TEST[1]). **5** judgement, discrimination. **6** (*Chem.*) a substance employed to detect one or more of the constituents of a compound. **7** a movable hearth in a reverberatory furnace with a cupel, used in separating gold or silver from lead. ~*v.t.* **1** to put to the test, to try, to prove by experiment. **2** to try severely, to tax (someone's endurance etc.). **3** (*Chem.*) to examine by the application of some reagent. **4** to refine (metal), esp. in a cupel. **to test out** to put to a practical test. **testable** *a.* **testability** (-bilˊ-) *n.* **Test Act** *n.* **1** an act of 1672 (repealed in 1828) requiring persons holding office, receiving pay from the Crown etc., to take the oaths of allegiance and supremacy, and which effectively excluded Roman Catholics from public office. **2** an act of 1871 which relaxed conditions of university degrees. **test ban** *n.* the banning, by agreement, of the testing of nuclear weapons. **test bed** *n.* an area for testing machinery etc., esp. aircraft engines under simulated working conditions. **test card** *n.* a still television image that is broadcast outside the usual hours of programme transmission and designed to be used as a guide for optimum reception. **test case** *n.* a case taken to trial in order that the court may decide some question that affects other cases. **test drive** *n.* a trial drive of a car or other motor vehicle to assess its performance, before purchase. **test-drive** *v.t.* (*past* **test-drove,** *p.p.* **test-driven**) to give a test drive to. **testee** (-tēˊ) *n.* a person tested. **tester**[1] *n.* **1** a person or thing that tests. **2** a sample, esp. of a cosmetic, paint etc., that allows a customer to try a product out before buying it. **test flight** *n.* a trial flight of a new aircraft to assess its performance. **test-fly** *v.t.* (*3rd pers. sing. pres.* **test-flies,** *pres.p.* **test-flying,** *past* **test-flew,** *p.p.* **test-flown**) to make a test flight of. **testing** *n.* an act or the process of putting someone or something through a test. ~*a.* **1** characterized by trouble, difficulties etc. (*living in testing times*). **2** causing or requiring a lot of effort. **testing ground** *n.* **1** a means of trying something out to gauge its merits, value etc. **2** a site set aside for trying out new weapons etc. **test match** *n.* a cricket or rugby match forming one of a series of international matches. **test meal** *n.* (*Med.*) food of a known quantity and composition, given in order to assess a person's gastric secretion. **test paper** *n.* **1** an examination, usu. one that is taken prior to sitting a more important examination. **2** (*Chem.*) bibulous paper saturated with a chemical solution that changes colour when exposed to the action of certain chemicals. **test pilot** *n.* a pilot who test-flies new aircraft. **test tube** *n.* a narrow glass tube closed at one end, used in chemical tests. **test-tube** *a.* **test-tube baby** *n.* **1** a baby born from an ovum fertilized in vitro in a laboratory, then implanted into the mother's womb. **2** (*loosely*) a baby conceived by artificial insemination. [OF (F *tête*), L *testum*, cp. TESTA]

test[2] (test) *n.* (*Biol.*) a shell, a hard covering or exoskeleton. [L TESTA]

testa (tesˊtə) *n.* (*pl.* **testae** (-tē)) (*Bot.*) a hard seed covering. [L]

testaceous (testāˊshəs) *a.* (*Biol.*) **1** characterized by a hard outer covering. **2** reddish-brown in colour. [L *testaceus*, from TESTA]

testacy TESTATE.
testament (tes´təmənt) *n.* **1** a solemn instrument in writing by which a person disposes of their personal estate after death, a will. **2** something which testifies proof, attestation. **3** (*Bible*) a covenant made between God and humankind. **4** either of the two main divisions of the Christian Scriptures. **5** (*coll.*) a copy of the New Testament. **New Testament** NEW. **Old Testament** OLD. **testamentary** (-men´-), †**testamental** (-men´-) *a.* of or relating to a will, by a will. †**testamentation** (-tā´shən) *n.* [OF, from L *testāmentum*, from *testārī*, to testify]
testate (tes´tāt) *a.* having made and left a valid will. *~n.* a person who has left a will in force. **testacy** (-təsi) *n.* (*pl.* **testacies**) the state or an instance of being testate. **testation** (-tā´shən) *n.* **testator** (-tā´-) *n.* a person who dies testate. **testatrix** (-tā´triks) *n.* a female testator. [L *testātus*, p.p. of *testārī*, to testify]
tester[1] TEST[1].
tester[2] (tes´tə) *n.* a canopy, esp. over a four-poster bedstead. [med. L *testerium*, from L *testa*, tile]
†**tester**[3] (tes´tə) *n.* **1** a shilling of Henry VIII. **2** (*coll.*) a sixpence. [corr. of earlier *teston*, OF *teston*, as TESTER[2]]
testes TESTIS.
testicle (tes´tikəl) *n.* (*Anat.*) either of the two reproductive glands which secrete the seminal fluid in males. **testicular** (-tik´ū-) *a.* **testiculate** (-tik´ūlət) *a.* **1** having testicles. **2** shaped like testicles; having a part so shaped. [L *testiculus*, dim. of TESTIS]
testify (tes´tifī) *v.i.* (*3rd pers. sing. pres.* **testifies,** *pres.p.* **testifying,** *past, p.p.* **testified**) **1** to bear witness (to, against, concerning etc.). **2** (*Law*) to give evidence. **3** to make a solemn declaration. *~v.t.* **1** to bear witness to. **2** to affirm or declare. **3** to be evidence of, to serve as proof of. **testification** (-fikā´shən) *n.* **testifier** *n.* [F *testifier*, L *testificāre* (*testis*, witness, *-ficāre, facere*, to make)]
testily TESTY.
testimony (tes´timəni) *n.* (*pl.* **testimonies**) **1** (*Law*) a statement under oath or affirmation. **2** a solemn declaration or statement. **3** evidence, proof, confirmation. **4** †a solemn declaration of approval or protest. **5** (*Bible*) the Ten Commandments, the Scriptures. *~*†*v.t.* to prove by evidence, to attest. **testimonial** (-mō´-) *n.* **1** a certificate of character, services, qualifications etc., of a person. **2** a formal statement of fact. **3** a gift formally (and usu. publicly) presented to a person as a token of esteem and acknowledgement of services etc. **4** in football, a match or series of matches played in honour of a specified player, usu. towards the end of their career, with the gate receipts being donated to the player. [L *testimonium*, from *testis*, witness]
testiness TESTY.
testis (tes´tis) *n.* (*pl.* **testes** (-tēz)) a testicle. [L, a witness]
testosterone (testos´tərōn) *n.* (*Biol.*) a steroid hormone secreted by the testes, controlling the growth and functioning of male sex organs and stimulating the development of male secondary sexual characteristics. [TESTIS, STEROL]
testudo (testū´dō) *n.* (*pl.* **testudos, testudines** (-dinēz)) **1** (*Hist.*) a type of protective barrier formed by attacking Roman soldiers who raised their shields above their heads so that they overlapped and made a screen. **2** (*Hist.*) a movable screen used for protecting besieging Roman troops. **3** any similar screen, esp. one used by miners working in places liable to cave in. **testudinal** *a.* of, relating to or resembling a tortoise. [L *testūdo -dinis*, tortoise, from TESTA]
testy (tes´ti) *a.* (*comp.* **testier,** *superl.* **testiest**) irritable, peevish, pettish, petulant. **testily** *adv.* **testiness** *n.* [ME and A-F *testif*, from OF *teste* (F *tête*), head]
tetanus (tet´ənəs) *n.* **1** a disease caused by the bacterium *Clostridium tetani* and marked by long-continued spasms of voluntary muscles, esp. those of the jaws. **2** the long-continued spasm of a muscle. **tetanic** (titan´-) *a.* of, relating to or characteristic of tetanus. **tetanically** *adv.* **tetanize, tetanise** *v.t.* **tetanization** (-zā´shən) *n.* **tetanoid** (-noid) *a.* **tetany** (-ni) *n.* a disease brought on by a deficiency of calcium in the blood which causes intermittent painful muscular spasms. [L, from Gr. *tetanos*, redupl. from *ten-*, stem of *teinein*, to stretch]
tetchy (tech´i) *a.* (*comp.* **tetchier,** *superl.* **tetchiest**) fretful, irritable, touchy. **tetchily** *adv.* **tetchiness** *n.* [etym. uncertain]
tête-à-tête (tātahtāt´, tetahtet´) *n.* (*pl.* **têtes-à-têtes** (tātahtāts´, tetahtets´), **tête-à-têtes**) **1** a private interview, a close or confidential conversation. **2** a sofa for two persons, esp. with seats facing in opposite directions so that the occupants face one another. *~a.* private, confidential. *~adv.* in private or close intimacy. [F, head to head]
tête-bêche (tātbesh´, tet-) *a.* (of a postage stamp) printed so that it is upside down or facing the other way in comparison to the other stamps on a sheet. [F, head, *béchevet*, double bedhead]
tether (tedh´ə) *n.* **1** a rope or halter by which an animal is prevented from moving too far. **2** prescribed range, scope. *~v.t.* to confine with or as with a tether. **at the end of one's tether** END. [ME *tedir*, cp. Icel. *tjōthr*, Swed. *tjuder*, MDut. *tūder*, Dut. *tuier*]
tetr- TETRA-.
tetra (tet´rə) *n.* (*pl.* **tetras**) any of various small tropical fish of the characin family that are often kept in home aquaria for their attractive brightly-coloured appearance. [from the former genus name, *Tetragonopterus*]
tetra- (tet´rə), **tetr-** *comb. form* **1** four, as in *tetragon*. **2** (*Chem.*) containing four atoms, radicals or groups, as in *tetraethyl*. [Gr., from *tettares*, four]
tetrabasic (tetrəbā´sik) *a.* (of an acid) having four replaceable hydrogen atoms.
tetrabranchiate (tetrəbrang´kiət) *a.* having four branchiae or gills.
tetrachord (tet´rəkawd) *n.* (*Mus.*) **1** a scale series of four notes where the interval between the first and last notes encompasses a perfect fourth, esp. as used in ancient music. **2** a musical instrument that has four strings.
tetracyclic (tetrəsī´klik) *a.* **1** (*Bot.*) having four circles or whorls. **2** (*Chem.*) having four fused hydrocarbon rings. **tetracycline** (tetrəsī´klēn, -klin) *n.* any of several antibiotics with molecules of four rings.
tetrad (tet´rad) *n.* **1** a collection, group or set of four things. **2** the number four. **3** (*Chem.*) an atom or element that can unite with or replace four atoms of hydrogen. **tetradic** (-trad´-) *a.* [Gr. *tetras -ados*, as TETRA-]
tetradactyl (tetrədak´til) *n.* (*Zool.*) an animal having four digits on each limb. *~a.* tetradactylous. **tetradactylous** *a.* having four digits on each limb. [Gr. *tetradaktulos* (*daktūlos*, finger)]
tetraethyl (tetrəē´thīl, -eth´il) *a.* having four ethyl groups. **tetraethyl lead** *n.* an antiknock, insoluble liquid used in petrol.
tetragon (tet´rəgon) *n.* a plane figure having four angles and four sides. **tetragonal** (titrag´ə-) *a.* **1** having the form of a tetragon. **2** of or relating to the crystal system characterized by three axes at right angles, of which only two are equal. **tetragonally** *adv.* [Gr. *tetragōnon*]
tetragram (tet´rəgram) *n.* a word of four letters. **Tetragrammaton** (-gram´ətən) *n.* the group of four letters representing the name Jehovah or some other sacred word.
tetragynous (titraj´inəs) *a.* (*Bot.*) (of a flower) having four pistils. [Gr. *gunē*, female]
tetrahedron (tetrəhē´drən) *n.* (*pl.* **tetrahedra** (-drə), **tetrahedrons**) a solid figure bounded by four planes,

esp. equilateral, triangular faces. **tetrahedral** *a.* [Gr. *hedra*, base]

tetrahydrocannabinol (tetrəhīdrōkan´əbinol) *n.* THC.

tetralogy (titral´əji) *n.* (*pl.* **tetralogies**) a collection of four dramatic works, esp. in ancient Greek a trilogy or three tragedies, followed by a satyric piece.

tetramerous (titram´ərəs), **tetrameral** (-ərəl) *a.* consisting of four parts. [Gr. *tetramerēs* (*meros*, part)]

tetrameter (titram´itə) *n.* in prosody, a verse consisting of four measures. [L *tetrametrus*, Gr. *tetrametros*]

tetrandrous (titran´drəs) *a.* (*Bot.*) (of a flower) having four stamens.

tetraplegia (tetrəplē´jə) *n.* quadriplegia, paralysis of both arms and both legs. **tetraplegic** *n., a.*

tetraploid (tet´rəploid) *a.* (*Biol.*) having four times the haploid number of chromosomes. *~n.* a tetraploid nucleus or cell.

tetrapod (tet´rəpod) *n.* **1** (*Zool.*) a four-footed animal. **2** an object or structure with four supporting legs. **tetrapodous** (titrap´-) *a.* **tetrapody** (titrap´ədi) *n.* in prosody, a group or a verse of four feet. [Gr. *pous podos*, foot]

tetrapterous (titrap´tərəs) *a.* **1** (*Zool.*) having four wings. **2** (*Bot.*) having winglike appendages, as certain fruits. [Gr. *pteron*, wing]

tetrarch (tet´rahk) *n.* **1** a governor of the fourth part of a province under the Roman empire. **2** a tributary prince under the Roman empire. **3** the commander of a subdivision of the ancient Greek phalanx. **4** each of four people who together rule a province etc. **tetrarchate** (-kāt) *n.* **tetrarchical** (-trah´-) *a.* **tetrarchy** *n.* (*pl.* **tetrarchies**). [late L *tetrarcha*, L and Gr. *tetrarchēs* (*archein*, to rule)]

tetraspore (tet´rəspaw) *n.* a group of four spores asexually produced, as in some algae.

tetrastich (tet´rəstik) *n.* a stanza, poem or epigram consisting of four lines of verse. [Gr. *stichos*, row]

tetrastyle (tet´rəstīl) *n.* a building, portico etc. having four pillars. *~a.* having four pillars. [STYLE]

tetrasyllable (tet´rəsiləbəl) *n.* a word of four syllables. **tetrasyllabic** (-lab´-) *a.*

tetratheism (tetrəthē´izm) *n.* (*Theol.*) the doctrine that the Godhead comprises four elements, the three persons of the Trinity and a divine essence from which each of these proceeds.

tetrathlon (tetrath´lon) *n.* a competition that comprises four distinct events, esp. a sporting one featuring running, swimming, shooting and riding events. [modelled on PENTATHLON]

tetratomic (tetrətom´ik) *a.* (*Chem.*) having four atoms to a molecule.

tetravalent (tetrəvā´lənt) *a.* (*Chem.*) having a valency of four, quadrivalent.

tetrode (tet´rōd) *n.* a thermionic valve containing four electrodes.

tetroxide (tetrok´sīd) *n.* any oxide having four oxygen atoms per molecule.

tetryl (tet´ril) *n.* a yellow crystalline explosive solid, used as a detonator.

tetter (tet´ə) *n.* any of several skin conditions such as eczema. [OE *teter*, cp. Sansk. *dadru*]

Teucrian (tū´kriən) *a.* of or relating to ancient Troy. *~n.* an ancient Trojan. [L *Teucri*, from Gr. *Teukros*, king of Troy]

Teuton (tū´tən) *n.* **1** a member of any Teutonic people, esp. a German. **2** a member of the German tribe, first mentioned as dwelling near the Elbe, *c.* 300 BC, which attacked and was defeated by the Roman army in 102 BC. **Teuto-** *comb. form* **Teutonic** (-ton´-) *a.* **1** of or relating to the Germanic peoples, including Scandinavians, Anglo-Saxons etc., as well as the Germans, or to their languages. **2** German. **3** of or relating to the Teutons. *~n.* **1** early Germanic. **2** the language or languages of the Teutons collectively. **Teutonicism** (-ton´-), **Teutonism** *n.* **Teutonize, Teutonise** *v.t.* **Teutonization** (-zā´shən) *n.* [L *Teutoni*, *Teutonēs*, from Gmc., cp. Goth. *thiuda*, people, G *deutsch*, German]

Tex. *abbr.* Texas, Texan.

Texan (tek´sən) *n.* a native or inhabitant of Texas, a southern US state. *~a.* of or relating to Texas.

Tex-Mex (teks´meks) *a., n.* (of, relating to or denoting) the Texan version of something Mexican, such as food, music, language etc.

text (tekst) *n.* **1** the words of something as printed, written or displayed on a video display unit. **2** the original words of an author, esp. as opposed to a translation, commentary or revision etc. **3** the actual words of a book or poem, as opposed to notes, appendices etc. **4** a verse or passage of Scripture, esp. one selected as the theme of a discourse. **5** a subject, a topic. **6** any book or novel which is studied as part of an educational course. **7** a textbook. **8** (*Comput.*) any display of non-graphic information on a VDU screen, including alphabetic, non-alphabetic and numeric characters, punctuation marks and other symbols. **9** TEXT-HAND (under TEXT). **textbook** *n.* **1** a standard book for a particular branch of study. **2** a manual of instruction. *~a.* **1** conforming to textbook descriptions. **2** ideal. **3** typical. **textbookish** *a.* **text editor** *n.* (*Comput.*) a program that will allow the user to enter and edit text while simultaneously displaying the text entered or changes made on a VDU screen. **text-hand** *n.* a large style of handwriting (from the practice of writing the text in a larger hand than the commentary). **textless** *a.* **text processing** *n.* (*Comput.*) the management of textual data, esp. when it involves converting the data into different formats. **textual** (-tū-) *a.* belonging or relating to or contained in the text. **textual criticism** *n.* **1** the study of texts, esp. the Bible, to establish the original text. **2** a close reading and analysis of any literary text. **textualism** *n.* **textualist** *n.* a person who adheres strictly to the text. **textuality** (-al´-) *n.* **textually** *adv.* [ME and F *texte*, L *textus -tūs*, style, later the Scriptures, from *texere*, to weave]

Usage note The adjectives *textual* and *textural* should not be confused: *textual* relates to text, and *textural* to texture.

textile (teks´tīl) *n.* **1** a woven, bonded or felted fabric. **2** raw material suitable to for making into cloth. **3** a fibre or yarn for making into cloth. *~a.* **1** woven. **2** suitable for weaving. **3** of or relating to weaving. [L *textilis*, as TEXT]

textual TEXT.

texture (teks´chə) *n.* **1** the quality of something as perceived by touch. **2** the particular arrangement or disposition of threads, filaments etc., in a textile fabric. **3** the disposition of the constituent parts of any body, structure or material. **4** the structure of tissues, tissue. **5** the representation of the surface of objects in works of art. **6** (*Mus.*) the particular quality of sound produced by the combination of parts. **7** the particular literary quality of a piece of writing. **8** the particular quality produced by the combination of events etc. *~v.t.* to give texture to. **textural** *a.* **texturally** *adv.* **textured** *a.* **textureless** *a.* **texturize, texturise** *v.t.* to give a particular texture to. **texturized vegetable protein** *n.* a meat substitute made from soya beans to resemble meat in texture and taste. [F, from L *textūra*, from *textus*, TEXT]

Usage note See note on *textural* under TEXT.

TGWU *abbr.* Transport and General Workers Union.

Th *chem. symbol* thorium.

Th. *abbr.* **1** Thomas. **2** Thursday.

-th[1] (th), **-eth** (əth) *suf.* forming ordinal and fractional numbers from the cardinal number four and upwards, as in *sixth, sixteenth, sixtieth*. [from OE *-tha*, *-the*, *-otha*, *-othe*]

-th[2] (th) *suf.* **1** forming nouns from verbs of action of process, as in *growth*. **2** forming nouns from adjectives, as in *width*, *strength*. [from OE *-tha*, *-tho*, *-th*]

-th[3] -ETH[2].

Thai (tī) *n.* (*pl.* **Thai, Thais**) **1** a native or inhabitant of Thailand (formerly Siam). **2** a member of the predominant ethnic group in Thailand. **3** the language of Thailand. *~a.* of or relating to Thailand, its people or its language. [Thai, free]

thalamus (thal´əməs) *n.* (*pl.* **thalami** (-mī)) **1** (*Anat.*) either of two oval masses of grey matter at the base of the brain whose function is to relay sensory information to the cerebral cortex. **2** (*Bot.*) the receptacle of a flower. **3** in ancient Greece, an inner room, the women's apartment, a nuptial chamber. **thalamic** (thəlam´-) *a.* [L, from Gr. *thalamos*]

thalassaemia (thaləsē´miə), (*N Am.*) **thalassemia** *n.* (*Med.*) a hereditary disorder of the blood due to defects in the synthesis of haemoglobin, sometimes fatal in children. [Gr. *thalassa*, sea, *-aemia*, because of its prevalence in the eastern Mediterranean]

thalassic (thəlas´ik) *a.* of or relating to the sea or seas, marine. **thalassocracy** (thaləsok´rəsi) *n.* naval supremacy, sea power. **thalassocrat** (-əkrat) *n.* **thalassotherapy** (-ōther´-) *n.* a type of alternative medicine using mud, seaweed, seawater etc. as relaxing agents and for detoxifying the body. [F *thalassique* (Gr. *thalassa*, the sea, -IC)]

thaler (tah´lə) *n.* (*Hist.*) an old German silver coin. [G, see DOLLAR]

thalidomide (thəlid´əmīd) *n.* a drug formerly used as a sedative, withdrawn from use in 1961, as it was shown to be associated with malformation of the foetus when taken by pregnant women. **thalidomide baby, thalidomide child** *n.* a baby or child born showing the effects, such as shortened malformed limbs, of thalidomide. [ph*thali*c acid, *-id-* (from *imide*), IMIDE]

thalli THALLUS.

thallium (thal´iəm) *n.* a rare soft, white, crystalline metallic element, at. no. 81, chem. symbol Tl, the spectrum of which contains a bright-green line from which it was named, used in alloys and glass-making. **thallic, thallous** *a.* [Gr. *thall-os*, see THALLUS, -IUM]

thallophyte (thal´ōfīt) *n.* (*Bot.*) any plant, such as algae, fungi and lichens, that has a thallus. **thallophytic** (-fit´-) *a.* [as THALLUS]

thallus (thal´əs) *n.* (*pl.* **thalluses, thalli** (-ī)) a plant-body without vascular tissue and lacking differentiation into root, stem or leaves. **thalloid** (-oid) *a.* [L, from Gr. *thallos*, green shoot, from *thallein*, to bloom]

thalweg (tahl´veg), **talweg** *n.* **1** the longitudinal line where the opposite slopes of a river, valley or lake meet. **2** (*Law*) a state boundary that follows the course of a valley or river at its centre. [G *Thal* or *Tal*, valley, *Weg*, way]

than (dhan, dhən) *conj., prep.* **1** used to introduce the second element in a comparison (*taller than his brother*; *colder than yesterday*). **2** used after adverbs, such as *rather*, *other*, *otherwise*, *sooner*, to introduce a less preferable or rejected option or to introduce an alternative (*try to keep calm rather than panic*; *had no choice other than to agree*). [OE *thanne*, *thonne*, etc., a development from THEN]

Usage note After *than*, the objective pronoun (*me*, *him*, *us* etc.) is the everyday choice. The subjective (*I*, *he*, *we* etc.), though formerly demanded by strict grammatical rule, is now considered rather pedantic except with a following verb. So *I am better than him*, *He hit harder than her* are generally acceptable; *I am better than he is*, *He hit harder than she did* are more formal equivalents, with *better than he*, *harder than she* very careful and formal alternatives indeed.

thanage THANE.

thanatology (thanətol´əji) *n.* the scientific study of death. [Gr. *thanatos*, death]

thane (thān) *n.* (*Hist.*) **1** in feudal times in England, a freeman holding land by military service and ranking between ordinary freemen and the nobles. **2** in medieval Scotland, a man who held land from a king (not necessarily in return for military service or support), ranking with the son of an earl; a clan chief. **thanage** (-ij) *n.* **1** the rank of a thane. **2** the land held by a thane. **thanedom** *n.* [OE *thegen*, *thegn* (cp. Icel. *thegn*, G *Degen*, OHG *Degan*), cogn. with Gr. *teknon*, child]

thank (thangk) *v.t.* **1** to express gratitude (to or for). **2** to blame or hold responsible (*I have only myself to thank for the mess I'm in*). *~n.* (*pl.*) **1** an expression of gratitude (*Pass on my thanks for the flowers*). **2** a formula of acknowledgement of a favour, kindness, benefit etc. (*gave thanks to God*). **3** used as a formula expressing gratitude, thank you (*Thanks a lot*). **I will thank you** (*iron.*) used to express disapproval, reproach, polite annoyance etc. (*I will thank you not to smoke in here*). **no (small) thanks to** despite having the handicap of. **thank goodness/ God/ heavens/ the Lord etc.** **1** (*coll.*) used to express relief, pleasure etc. **2** used to express pious gratitude. **thanks to** because of, owing to. **thank you** used as a formula expressing thanks, polite refusal etc. **to give thanks** to say grace before a meal. **to thank kindly** KINDLY (under KIND). **thankful** *a.* **1** grateful, glad, appreciative. **2** expressive of thanks. **thankfully** *adv.* **1** in a grateful, appreciative etc. way. **2** (*coll.*) fortunately, we should all be glad that (*Thankfully, the police arrived*). **thankfulness** *n.* **thankless** *a.* **1** insensible to kindness, ungrateful. **2** not deserving thanks. **3** not appreciated or profitable. **thanklessly** *adv.* **thanklessness** *n.* **thank-offering** *n.* an offering made as an expression of gratitude, esp. a Jewish sacrifice of thanksgiving. **thanksgiving** *n.* **1** the act of returning thanks or expressing gratitude, esp. to God. **2** a form of words expressive of this. **3** (**Thanksgiving**) Thanksgiving Day. **4** (*Bible*) a thank-offering. **thanksgiver** *n.* **Thanksgiving Day** *n.* (*N Am.*) a day set apart annually for thanksgiving to God for blessings enjoyed individually and nationally (the fourth Thursday in Nov. in the US, usu. the second Monday in Oct. in Canada). **thank-you** *n.* (*coll.*) **1** an instance of saying 'thank you'. **2** a gift etc. given in appreciation. *~a.* expressing gratitude, appreciation etc. (*a thank-you present*). [OE *thanc*, *thonc*, thought, grace (cp. Dut. and G *Dank*, Icel. *thökk*), whence *thancian*, cp. Dut. and G *danken*]

Usage note The use of *thankfully* to express thankfulness (as a sentence adverb) is sometimes disapproved of, though it is quite common.

thar TAHR.

that (dhat, dhət) *pron.* (*pl.* **those** (dhōz)) **1** used to refer to someone or something already known, indicated, mentioned etc. **2** used to refer to the more distant, less obvious etc. example of two similar things, often contrasting with *this* (*This book is more interesting than that*). **3** (*coll.*) used as an emphatically positive response to what has just been said (*'You must have been relieved.' 'I was that!'*). **4** the one, usu. used with relative or complementary information (*Those who were late must stay behind*; *has a fiery temper just like that of her brother*). **5** (*pl.* **that**) used like *which* or *who* to introduce defining information (*the recipe that Martin gave me*; *the people that enjoyed her first film*). *~a.* (*pl.* **those**) **1** denoting someone or something already known, indicated, mentioned etc. 2 used with *this* in contrasting or differentiating statements. 3 used for emphasis (*With all its mishaps, that holiday is one I'll never forget*). ~*adv.* 1 to the degree or extent specified or understood (*I can't walk that fast*). 2 (*coll.*) very, much, so, too (*The play wasn't that enjoyable*; *I was that annoyed I nearly hit him*). 3 at which, on which, when etc. (*was away on holiday the day that it happened*). ~*conj.* 1 indicating reason, purpose, consequence etc. (*so drunk that he couldn't stand*; *What happened next was that he fell over*). 2 expressing a wish or desire (*Oh, that this night would never end!*). **all that** (*coll.*) very, particularly (*wasn't all that bad*). **and (all) that** (*coll.*) and all the other things associated with what has just been mentioned. **just like that** effortlessly, without hesitation. **like that** 1 of the kind referred to. 2 in that way. 3 (*coll.*) effortlessly, without hesitation. **that is (to say)** used to introduce a rewording, a simpler version or an explanation of what has just been said. **that's** (*coll.*) you are (*You got an A+! That's my clever girl!*). **that's more like it** used to acknowledge an improvement, something preferable etc. **that's right** used to express approval, agreement etc. **that's that** used to indicate that there is nothing more to be said or done about something. **that there** (*coll.*) used to indicate something emphatically (*That there dress is the one I want*). **that will do** used to indicate that no more is wanted or needed. [OE *thaet*, orig. neut. of THE]

Usage note The introductory *that* of a defining or object clause is often omitted: *the dictionary* (*that*) *I bought*, *I said* (*that*) *I bought a dictionary*.

thatch (thach) *n.* (*pl.* **thatches**) 1 a roof covering of straw, rushes, reeds etc. 2 (*coll.*) anything that resembles this, esp. a thick head of hair. ~*v.t.* to cover with this. ~*v.i.* to do thatching. **thatched** *a.* **thatcher** *n.* **thatching** *n.* 1 the act of thatching. 2 the materials used in thatching. [OE *thaec* (cp. Dut. *dak*, G *Dach*, Icel. *thak*, also Gr. *tegos*, roof, L *tegere*, to cover), whence *theccan*, to thatch]

Thatcherism (thach´ərizm) *n.* the political, economic etc. philosophy and policies of Margaret Thatcher, British Prime Minister, 1979–90. **Thatcherite** (-īt) *n.* a supporter of Margaret Thatcher or her policies. ~*a.* of or relating to Margaret Thatcher or her policies.

thaumato- (thaw´mətō), **thaumat-** *comb. form* of or relating to wonder or miracles. [Gr. *thauma*, wonder]

thaumatrope (thaw´mətrōp) *n.* 1 an optical toy consisting of a disc with figures on opposite sides which appear to combine and perform movements when the disc is rotated. 2 ZOETROPE. [Gr. *-tropos*, turning, from *trepein*, to turn]

thaumaturge (thaw´mətœj) *n.* a worker of miracles; a wonder-worker, a magician or conjuror. **thaumaturgic** (-tœ´-), **thaumaturgical** *a.* **thaumaturgist** *n.* **thaumaturgy** *n.* [med. L *thaumaturgus*, Gr. *thaumatourgos* *-ergos*, working)]

thaw (thaw) *v.i.* 1 (of ice, snow etc.) to melt, dissolve or become liquid. 2 (of the weather) to become warm enough to melt frost, ice or snow. 3 to become warm enough to lose numbness etc. 4 to relax one's stiffness, to unbend, to become genial. ~*v.t.* 1 to cause to melt, dissolve etc. 2 to infuse warmth, animation, conviviality etc. into. ~*n.* 1 the act of thawing or the state of being thawed. 2 warm weather that thaws. 3 a relaxation of tension, an increase in friendliness. **to thaw out** 1 to return to normal from a frozen condition. 2 to become more relaxed or more friendly. **thawless** *a.* [OE *thāwian*, cp. Dut. *dooijen*, G *tauen*, Icel. *theyja*]

THC *abbr.* tetrahydrocannabinol, the main active principle in cannabis.

the (dhə, dhi, dhē) *a.* 1 used to refer to a particular person or thing, or to particular people or things, already mentioned, known to be familiar etc. (*took the dog to the vet*; *laid the table*). 2 used to refer to a unique person or thing (*the Pope*; *Aberdeen straddles the Dee and the Don*). 3 used before an adjective to denote which is, who are etc. (*Pitt the Younger*). 4 used before an adjective functioning as a collective or generic noun (*the poor*). 5 used before a gerund or verbal noun (*The singing was beautiful*). 6 used to denote a familiar cultural concept or activity (*goes to the football every week*; *reads the news*; *off to the cinema*). 7 (pronounced with stress) used to denote something or someone considered to be the best, most desirable etc. of its kind (*Planet Hollywood is the place to be seen*). 8 used before a noun that is followed by some defining, qualifying, relative, complementary etc. information (*the least you could do*; *the first of many*; *the love between them*; *the film we watched last night*). 9 used before a singular noun when it functions generically (*The pig is a clean animal*; *teaches a course on the Western*; *is learning the piano*). 10 used before a figurative noun (*end up in the gutter*; *wants to take her band on the road*). 11 used after a preposition to introduce a quantity, time etc. (*does 45 miles to the gallon*; *gets paid by the hour*). 12 (*coll. or dated*) used before a noun denoting an affliction, condition etc. (*in bed with the cold*; *enough to give you the willies*). 13 used in formulaic constructions of time etc. to denote a notion of currency, the present etc. (*man of the match*). 14 (*coll.*) my, our (*Come back to the house for a drink*; *I'd better ask the wife first*). 15 used before the surname of a clan chief in Scotland and Ireland (*the MacPherson of MacPherson*). 16 in Wales, used, after a name and before the defining function or occupation of a person or thing, to form a title (*Jones the Steam*). ~*adv.* 1 used in comparative constructions to indicate correlation or interdependency (*the sooner the better*). 2 used for emphasis or to indicate supremacy etc., usu. before comparatives or superlatives (*felt the better for telling him*; *This one is the most useful*). **all the** to, into, in etc. an even greater extent. [OE *the*, fem. *theo*, neut. *thaet* (earlier *sē*, *sēo*, *thaet*)]

theandric (thian´drik) *a.* (*Theol.*) relating to or existing by the union of divine and human nature in Christ. [Gr. *theandrikos* (*anēr andros*, man)]

theanthropic (thēənthrop´ik), **theanthropical** (-kəl) *a.* 1 being both human and divine. 2 tending to embody deity in human forms. **theanthropism** (-an´thrə-) *n.* [Gr. *anthrōpos*, man]

thearchy (thē´ahki) *n.* (*pl.* **thearchies**) 1 government by God or gods. 2 a body, class or order of gods or deities. [Gr. *-archia*, rule, from *archein*, to rule]

theatre (thē´ətə), (*N Am.*) **theater** *n.* 1 a building or outdoor area designed for the performance of plays, ballets, operas etc. 2 (*esp. N Am., Austral., New Zeal.*) (*in full* **picture theatre**) a cinema. 3 the business of writing, directing, producing etc. plays. 4 the acting profession (*been in the theatre since she was five*). 5 suitable material for putting on the stage. 6 (*in full* **lecture theatre**) a large room with rising tiered seating suitable for delivering lectures etc. 7 OPERATING THEATRE (under OPERATE). 8 a place where action or events take place (*Bombing turned the city into a theatre of destruction*). 9 the audience of a play, ballet, opera etc. (*The whole theatre was in convulsions*). 10 a naturally occurring land formation that resembles an ancient Greek or Roman amphitheatre, being circular or almost so and having sides that gradually rise in tiers. ~*a.* (*attrib.*) (of weapons etc.) between strategic and tactical. **theatregoing** *n.* attendance at the theatre, esp. regularly or frequently. ~*a.* that attends the theatre, of or relating to attendance at the theatre. **theatregoer** *n.* **theatre-in-the-round** *n.* (*pl.* **theatres-in-the-round**) 1 a theatre which has the stage at the middle with sections of rising tiered seats all around it. 2 drama written or adapted to be staged in this kind of setting. **Theatre of Cruelty** *n.* drama that seeks to provoke a sense of evil and an awareness of suffering in the audience. **Theatre of the Absurd** *n.* drama that seeks to show the impossibility of understanding the world or the human condition by emphasizing the arbitrary nature of events and the ultimate futility of life, esp. through the use of comedy and burlesque. **theatre organ** *n.* an organ that can produce a wider range of musical effects than a church organ and which is used in theatres and cinemas. **theatre sister** *n.* the nurse in charge of the nursing staff, equipment etc. in an operating theatre.

theatrical (thiat´rikəl) *a.* **1** of or relating to the theatre. **2** befitting the stage, dramatic. **3** suitable or calculated for display, pompous, showy. **4** befitting or characteristic of actors, stagy, affected. ~*n.* a professional theatre actor or actress. **theatric** *a.* theatrical. **theatrics** *n.pl.* theatrical actions, gestures etc. **theatricality** (-kal´-) *n.* **theatricalize, theatricalise** *v.t.* **theatricalization** (-zā´shən) *n.* **theatrically** *adv.* **theatricals** *n.pl.* **1** dramatic performances, esp. private ones. **2** theatrical actions, gestures etc. **3** professional theatre actors.

thebaine (thē´bāēn) *n.* (*Chem.*) a poisonous crystalline alkaloid obtained from opium. [as THEBAN]

Theban (thē´bən) *a.* of or relating to ancient Thebes (in Greece or in Egypt). ~*n.* a native or inhabitant of Thebes. [L *Thēbānus*, from *Thēbae*, Gr. *Thebai*]

theca (thē´kə) *n.* (*pl.* **thecae** (-sē)) **1** (*Bot.*) a part in a non-flowering plant such as moss that functions in a similar way to a receptacle. **2** (*Zool.*) a sheath or casing covering an organ or organism. **thecal** *a.* **thecate** (-kət, -kāt) *a.* **thecodont** (-dont) *a.* **1** of or relating to an order of extinct reptiles having the teeth in distinct sockets. **2** (of certain mammals) having teeth set in distinct sockets. ~*n.* a thecodont reptile. [L, from Gr. *thēkē*, case]

thé dansant (tā dāsā´) *n.* (*pl.* **thés dansants** (tā dāsā´)) a dance held during afternoon tea, popular in the 1920s and 1930s. [F, lit. dancing tea]

†**thee** (dhē) *pron.* objective (accusative and dative) of THOU[1].

theft (theft) *n.* **1** the act or an instance of stealing. **2** (*Law*) the dishonest taking of another person's property with no intention of ever returning it. **3** something which is stolen. [OE *thīefth, thēofth, thēoft*]

thegn (thān) *n.* (*Hist.*) an English thane. [OE, as THANE]

theine (thē´ īn, -in) *n.* caffeine (found in tea leaves). [mod. L *thea*, TEA, -IC]

their (dheə) *a.* **1** possessive of THEY. **2** (**Their**) used in titles (*Their Royal Highnesses*). **3** (*coll.*) his or her (*Everyone must make up their own mind*). [ME from ON *their(r)a*, of them, gen. pl. of *sá*, as THE and THAT]

Usage note The spellings of the adjective *their*, adverb *there* and contraction *they're* (they are) should not be confused. See also note under THEY.

theirs (dheəz) *pron.* something belonging to or associated with them (*It's good, but theirs is better*). **of theirs** belonging or relating to, known by etc. them (*a cousin of theirs*). [ME, from THEIR]

Usage note The pronoun *theirs* does not have an apostrophe (not *their's*), and should be distinguished from the contraction *there's* (there is).

theism (thē´izm) *n.* **1** belief in the existence of gods or a God, as opposed to atheism. **2** belief in a righteous God supernaturally revealed, as opposed to deism. **theist** *n.* **theistic** (-is´-), **theistical** *a.* **theistically** *adv.* [Gr. *theos*, god, -ISM]

them (dhem, dhəm) *pron.* **1** objective (accusative and dative) of THEY. **2** (*coll.*) they (esp. after *to be*). **3** †themselves. ~*a.* (*esp. dial.*) those.

Usage note See note under THEY.

theme (thēm) *n.* **1** a subject on which a person thinks, writes or speaks. **2** (*esp. N Am.*) a short dissertation or essay by a student, school pupil etc. on a certain subject. **3** (*Gram.*) the part of a noun or verb remaining unchanged by inflections. **4** (*Mus.*) a melodic subject usu. developed with variations. **5** (*Logic*) the subject of thought. **6** an underlying unifying principle. **7** (*Hist.*) any of the 29 provinces of the Byzantine empire. ~*v.t.* to use a particular theme in the design of (a restaurant, leisure complex etc.). **thematic** (thimat´-) *a.* **1** of or relating to topics, by topics (*a thematic thesaurus*). **2** (*Mus.*) of or relating to melodic subjects. **3** (*Gram.*) **a** of or relating to the stem or a noun of verb. **b** (of a form of a verb) having a thematic vowel. **thematically** *adv.* **thematic catalogue,** (*N Am.*) **thematic catalog** *n.* a catalogue giving the opening theme of each piece of music. **thematics** *n.pl.* **1** the themes, topics or subjects to be studied, discussed, debated etc. **2** (*sing.*) a body of such themes etc. **theme park** *n.* a park designed for leisure, where all the activities are based on a single subject. **theme song, theme tune, theme music** *n.* **1** a recurring melody in a film, musical etc. which is associated with the production or a specific character. **2** a signature tune. **3** (*coll.*) a person's characteristic complaint, repeated phrase etc. [L *thema*, Gr. *thema -atos*, from *the-*, root of *tithenai*, to put]

themselves (dhəmselvz´) *pron.* **1** the emphatic and reflexive form of THEM. **2** himself or herself. **3** their usual or normal selves. **to be themselves** to act in their normal unconstrained manner. **themself** *pron.* (*coll.*) **1** himself, herself. **2** himself or herself (*anyone could teach themself*).

Usage note When referring to a singular indefinite form, *themselves* should still be used, not *themself*. See note under THEY.

then (dhen) *adv.* **1** at that time. **2** afterwards, soon after, after that, next. **3** at another time. ~*conj.* in that case, therefore, consequently, this being so, accordingly. ~*a.* (*coll.*) of or existing at that time. ~*n.* that time, the time mentioned or understood. **by then** by that time. **then and there** on the spot, immediately. **then or thenabouts** about that time. [ME *thenne*, OE *thanne, thonne, thaenne* (cogn. with THAT, THE), cp. THAN]

thenar (thē´nah) *n.* (*Anat.*) **1** the part of the palm at the base of the thumb. **2** the palm of the hand. ~*a.* of or relating to the thenar. [Gr.]

thence (dhens) *adv.* (*formal*) **1** from that place. **2** for that reason, from that source. **3** from that time. **from thence** thence. **thenceforth, thenceforward** *adv.* from that time onward. **from thenceforth** thenceforth. [ME *thennes* (*thenne*, -ES[1]), OE *thanon, thonan*, cogn. with THAT, THE]

theo- (thē´ō), **the-** *comb. form* of or relating to God or a god. [Gr. *theos*, god]

theobromine (thēōbrō´mēn, -min) *n.* a bitter alkaloid resembling caffeine contained in cacao seeds. [Gr. *broma*, food]

theocentric (thēōsen´trik) *a.* having God as its centre.

theocracy (thiok´rəsi) *n.* (*pl.* **theocracies**) **1** government by the immediate direction of God or through a class of priests. **2** a state so governed. **the Theocracy** (*Bible*) the commonwealth of Israel from the time of Moses until Saul became king. **theocrat** (thē´əkrat) *n.* **theocratic** (-krat´-), **theocratical** *a.* **theocratically** *adv.* **theocratist** *n.*

theocrasy (thiok´rəsi) *n.* **1** mixed worship of different gods, polytheism. **2** the union of the soul with God in contemplation. [CRASIS]

theodicy (thiod´isi) *n.* (*pl.* **theodicies**) a vindication of divine justice in respect to the existence of evil.

theodicean (-sē´ən) *n.* [F *théodicée* (THEO-, Gr. *dikē*, justice)]
theodolite (thiod´əlīt) *n.* a portable surveying instrument for measuring horizontal and vertical angles. **theodolitic** (-lit´-) *a.* [etym. uncertain]
theogony (thiog´əni) *n.* (*pl.* **theogonies**) **1** the genealogy of the gods. **2** an account of this, esp. in the form of an epic poem. **theogonic** (thēəgon´-) *a.* **theogonist** *n.* [L and Gr. *theogonia* (*gonia*, from *gen-*, to beget)]
theol. *abbr.* **1** theologian. **2** theological. **3** theology.
theology (thiol´əji) *n.* (*pl.* **theologies**) **1** the study of theistic religion, esp. Christianity. **2** a system of theistic religion, esp. Christianity. **3** an analysis of a religion. **4** a rigid ideology. **theologian** (thēəlō´-), **theologist** *n.* **1** a person versed in theology. **2** a professor of theology. **theological** (thēəloj´-) *a.* **theologically** *adv.* **theologize, theologise** *v.i.* to speculate on theology. ~*v.t.* to make theological. **theologizer** *n.* [ME and OF *theologie*, L and Gr. *theologia* (THEO-, -LOGY)]
theomachy (thiom´əki) *n.* (*pl.* **theomachies**) **1** a combat against or among the gods. **2** opposition to divine will. **theomachist** *n.* [L and Gr. *theomachia* (*-machia*, fighting)]
theomancy (thē´əmansi) *n.* divination by oracle or by people inspired by a god. [Gr. *theomanteia*]
theomania (thēəmā´niə) *n.* **1** religious insanity. **2** a delusion that one is God. **theomaniac** (-ak) *n.*
theomorphic (thēəmaw´fik) *a.* having the form or semblance of God. **theomorphism** *n.* [Gr. *morphē*, form]
theopathy (thiop´əthi) *n.* emotion excited by the contemplation of God. **theopathetic** (thēəpəthet´-) *a.*
theophany (thiof´əni) *n.* (*pl.* **theophanies**) a manifestation or appearance of God to humans. **theophanic** (thēəfan´-) *a.* [L *theophania*, Gr. *theophania* (*ephainein*, to show)]
theophoric (thēəfor´ik) *a.* derived from or bearing the name of a god.
theophylline (thēəfil´ēn, -in) *n.* a white alkaloid similar to theobromine found in plants such as tea, used to treat heart disease and headaches. [L *thea*, tea, Gr. *phullon*, leaf]
theopneusty (thēopnū´sti) *n.* divine inspiration. **theopneustic** *a.* [Gr. *theopneustos*, inspired (*pnein*, to blow)]
theorbo (thiaw´bō) *n.* (*pl.* **theorbos**) (*Mus.*) a stringed instrument resembling a two-necked lute used in the 16th–17th cents. **theorbist** *n.* [It. *tiorba*, etym. uncertain (cp. F *théorbe*)]
theorem (thē´ərəm) *n.* **1** (*Math.*) a rule or law, esp. one expressed by symbols etc. **2** a proposition to be proved. **3** a principle to be demonstrated by reasoning. **theorematic** (-mat´-), **theorematical** *a.* **theorematist** (-rem´ətist) *n.* [late L and Gr. *theōrēma*, from *theōrein*, to behold]
theoretical (thēəret´ikəl) *a.* of, relating to or founded on theory not facts or knowledge, not practical, speculative. **theoretic** *n.* theoretics. ~*a.* theoretical. **theoretically** *adv.* **theoretician** (-ritish´ən) *n.* a person interested in the theory rather than the practical application of a given subject. **theoretics** *n.* the speculative parts of a science. [late L *theōrēticus*, Gr. *thēōretikos*, from *theōrētos*, as THEORY]
theory (thē´əri) *n.* (*pl.* **theories**) **1** a supposition explaining something, esp. a generalization explaining phenomena as the results of assumed natural causes. **2** a speculative idea of something. **3** mere hypothesis, speculation, abstract knowledge. **4** an exposition of the general principles of a science etc. **5** a body of theorems illustrating a particular subject. **theorist** *n.* **1** a person who theorizes. **2** a person given to forming theories. **theorize, theorise** *v.i.* **theorization** (-zā´shən) *n.* **theorizer** *n.* **theory of preformation** *n.* the now exploded theory (prevalent in the 18th cent.) that the organism exists in all its parts in the germ and is merely developed. [A-F *theorie*, L and Gr. *theōria*, from *theōrein*, to behold, to contemplate]
theosophy (thios´əfi) *n.* (*pl.* **theosophies**) **1** a form of speculation, mysticism or philosophy aiming at the knowledge of God by means of intuition and contemplative illumination or by direct communion. **2** a system founded in the US, in 1875, which claims to show the unity of all religions in their esoteric teaching, manifested by occult phenomena. **theosopher** *n.* **theosophic** (thēəsof´-), **theosophical** *a.* **theosophically** *adv.* **theosophism** *n.* **theosophist** *n.* **theosophistical** (-fis´-) *a.* **theosophize, theosophise** *v.i.* [med. L and late Gr. *theosophia* (THEO-, *sophos*, wise)]
theotechny (thē´ōtekni) *n.* the employment of supernatural intervention in a literary composition. **theotechnic** (-tek´-) *a.* [THEO-, *technē*, art]
therapeutic (therəpū´tik) *a.* **1** of or relating to healing or curing disease. **2** curative. **3** contributing to well-being. **therapeutical** *a.* **therapeutically** *adv.* **therapeutics** *n.* (*Med.*) the branch of medical science dealing with the treatment of disease and the action of remedial agents in both health and disease. **therapeutist** *n.* **therapy** (ther´əpi) *n.* (*pl.* **therapies**) **1** the treatment of disease or physical and mental disorders from a curative and preventive point of view, therapeutics. **2** psychiatric or psychological therapy. **3** physiotherapy. **therapist** *n.* a practitioner of therapy, esp. a psychologist or psychiatrist. [from Gr. *therapeutikos*, from *therapeuein*, to wait on (also to heal), from *theraps -apos*, servant]
therapsid (therap´sid) *n.* any fossil reptile of the order Therapsida, considered to be the ancestors of mammals. ~*a.* of or relating to this order. [L, *Therapsida*, from Gr. *thēr*, beast, *apsis*, *apsidos*, arch (of the skull)]
Theravada (therəvah´də) *n.* a form of Buddhism practised esp. in SE Asia. [Pali *theravāda*, from *thera*, elder, *vāda*, doctrine]
there (dheə, dhə) *adv.* **1** in or at that place, point or stage. **2** to that place, thither. **3** used before or (in questions) after the verb *to be* to express fact or existence (*Is there a doctor in the house?*; *There was an old woman who lived in a shoe*). **4** in that regard. ~*n.* that place. ~*int.* **1** used to express direction, confirmation, triumph, alarm etc. **2** used (esp. redupl.) to soothe a child. **all there 1** (*coll.*) of normal intelligence. **2** (*coll.*) fully competent, knowing all about it. **here and there** HERE. **not all there 1** (*coll.*) of less than normal intelligence. **2** (*coll.*) not fully competent. **so there!** used to express derision or triumph. **there and then** at that place and immediately. **there it is** that is the situation. **there you are 1** here is what you wanted. **2** used to express confirmation of a situation in a triumphant or resigned way. **there you go** there you are. **to get there** GET[1]. **to have been there before** to have experienced the same thing previously and to know all about it. **thereabouts, thereabout** *adv.* near that place, number, degree etc. **thereafter** (-ah´-) *adv.* (*formal*) **1** after that. **2** according to that. **thereanent** (-ənent´) *adv.* (*formal, Sc.*) as regards that matter. †**thereat** (-at´) *adv.* **1** at that place. **2** thereupon. **3** on that account. **thereby** (-bī´) *adv.* (*formal*) **1** by that means. **2** in consequence of that. **3** †near that place, thereabouts. **thereby hangs a tale** there are things that could be said by way of background, explanation etc. †**therefor** (-faw´) *adv.* for that object. **therefore** *adv.* for that reason, consequently, accordingly. †**therefrom** (-from´) *adv.* from this or that time, place etc. **therein** (-in´) *adv.* (*formal*) in that or this time, place, respect etc. **thereinafter** (-ah´-) *adv.* (*formal*) later in the same (document etc.). **thereinbefore** (-faw´) *adv.* (*formal*) earlier in the same (document etc.). †**thereinto** (-in´-) *adv.* into that place or matter. **thereof** (-ov´) *adv.* (*formal*) of that or it. †**thereon** (-on´) *adv.* on that or it. †**thereout** (-owt´) *adv.* out of

that or this. **there's** *contr.* 1 there is. 2 (*coll.*) and by that you are or will be (*Fill my glass, there's a love*). †**therethrough** (-throo´) *adv.* through that. **thereto** (-too´) *adv.* (*formal*) 1 to that or this. 2 besides, over and above. **theretofore** (-faw´) *adv.* (*formal*) before that time. †**thereunder** (-ŭn´-) *adv.* 1 under that or this. 2 in accordance with that or this. †**thereunto** (-ŭn´-) *adv.* (*formal*) to that or this, thereto. **thereupon** (-pon´) *adv.* 1 immediately after or following that. 2 in consequence of that. 3 †upon that. †**therewith** (-widh´) *adv.* 1 with that. 2 immediately after or following that, thereupon. †**therewithal** (-awl´) *adv.* with all this, besides. [OE *thaēr*, *thēr* (cp. Dut. *daar*, G *da*, Icel. *thar*, Dan and Swed. *der*), cogn. with THAT, THE]

†**theriac** (thiə´riak) *n.* an antidote against the bite of poisonous animals. [late L *thēriaca*, *thēriacē*, Gr. *thēriakē*, orig. fem. a., from *thērion*, dim. of *thēr*, wild beast]

therianthropic (thiərianthrop´ik) *a.* of or relating to deities represented as half man and half beast or to their worship. **therianthropism** (-an´thrə-) *n.* **theriomorphic** (-maw´fik), **theriomorphous** *a.* having the form of a beast. [Gr. *thērion*, see THERIAC]

therm (thœm) *n.* a British unit of heat, equal to 100,000 British thermal units. [Gr. *thermē*, heat]

thermae (thœ´mē) *n.pl.* (*Hist.*) public baths in ancient Greece and Rome.

thermal (thœ´məl) *a.* 1 of or relating to heat. 2 (of clothing) insulating the body against very low temperatures. ~*n.* 1 a rising current of warm air. 2 (*pl.*) thermal (under)clothes. **thermal barrier** *n.* HEAT BARRIER (under HEAT). **thermal capacity** *n.* (*Physics*) the number of heat units required to raise the temperature of a body, system etc. by one degree. **thermal imaging** *n.* the use of the heat given off by a person, object etc. to produce a visual image, for the purposes of medical diagnosis, location of bodies underground etc. **thermalize, thermalise** *v.i.*, *v.t.* **thermalization** (-zā´shən) *n.* **thermally** *adv.* **thermal neutron** *n.* (*Physics*) a very low energy neutron in thermal equilibrium with its surroundings. **thermal printer** *n.* a printer that produces characters by burning them with fine heated pins on to heat-sensitive paper. **thermal reactor** *n.* a nuclear reactor in which fission is induced using mainly thermal neutrons. **thermal springs** *n.pl.* hot springs. **thermal unit** *n.* a unit for measuring heat. **thermic** *a.*

thermion (thœ´mion) *n.* (*Physics*) an ion or electron emitted by an incandescent body. **thermionic** (-on´-) *a.* **thermionic emission** *n.* the emission of electrons from hot bodies. **thermionics** *n.* 1 the branch of electronics dealing with the emission of electrons from hot bodies. 2 the study of the behaviour of these electrons in a vacuum. **thermionic valve,** (*NAm.*) **thermionic tube** *n.* a vacuum tube in which a stream of electrons flows from one electrode to another and is controlled by one or more other electrodes. [Gr. *thermos*, warm, ION]

thermistor (thœmis´tə) *n.* (*Physics*) a semiconducting device whose resistance decreases with rising temperature. [*thermal resistor*]

thermite (thœ´mīt), **thermit** (-mit) *n.* a mixture of finely divided aluminium and a metallic oxide, esp. of iron, producing intense heat on combustion, used in welding, incendiary bombs etc. [G *Thermit* (Gr. *thermē*, heat)]

thermo- (thœ´mō) *comb. form* heat. [Gr. *thermos*, warm, see THERM]

thermochemistry (thœmōkem´istri) *n.* the branch of chemistry dealing with the relations between chemical reactions and the heat liberated or absorbed. **thermochemical** *a.*

thermocline (thœ´mōklīn) *n.* a layer of water in a lake etc., in which the water temperature decreases rapidly between the epilimnion and hypolimnion.

thermocouple (thœ´mōkŭpəl) *n.* a device for measuring temperature consisting of two wires of differing metals joined at both ends, one wire of a fixed temperature, the other at the temperature to be measured, the voltage developed being proportional to the difference in temperature.

thermodynamics (thœmōdīnam´iks) *n.* the branch of physics dealing with the relations between heat and other forms of energy. **thermodynamic, thermodynamical** *a.* **thermodynamically** *adv.* **thermodynamicist** (-sist) *n.*

thermoelectricity (thœmōilektris´iti) *n.* electricity generated by differences of temperature. **thermoelectric** (-lek´-) *a.* **thermoelectrically** *adv.* **thermoelectrometer** (-trom´itə) *n.* an instrument for ascertaining the heating power of an electric current.

thermogenesis (thœmōjen´əsis) *n.* the production of heat, esp. by physiological processes. **thermogenetic** (-net´-), **thermogenic** *a.*

thermography (thœmog´rəfi) *n.* (*Med.*) the use of thermographic imaging to detect abnormalities in the body. **thermogram** (thœ´məgram) *n.* **thermograph** (-grahf) *n.* 1 an instrument for automatically recording variations of temperature. 2 (*Med.*) an instrument for obtaining an image produced by infrared radiation in the body. **thermographic** (-graf´-) *a.*

thermolabile (thœmōlā´bīl) *a.* (*Chem.*) (of a substance) unstable when subjected to heat.

thermoluminescence (thœmōloomines´əns) *n.* phosphorescence produced by heating an irradiated substance. **thermoluminescent** *a.*

thermolysis (thəmol´isis) *n.* 1 loss of body heat. 2 decomposition due to the action of heat. **thermolytic** (-lit´-) *a.*

thermometer (thəmom´itə) *n.* an instrument for measuring temperature, usu. by the expansion or contraction of a column of mercury or alcohol in a graduated tube of small bore with a bulb at one end. **thermometric** (thœmōmet´-), **thermometrical** *a.* **thermometrically** *adv.* **thermometry** (-tri) *n.*

thermomotor (thœmōmō´tə) *n.* an engine producing force from the expansion of hot air or fluid. **thermomotive** *a.* of or relating to motion produced by heat.

thermonuclear (thœmōnū´kliə) *a.* 1 (*Physics*) relating to the fusion of nuclei at very high temperatures. 2 of or relating to weapons in which an explosion is produced by thermonuclear reaction. **thermonuclear reaction** *n.* the fusion of nuclei at very high temperatures, as in the hydrogen bomb.

thermophile (thœ´məfīl), **thermophil** (-fil) *n.* (*Biol.*) a bacterium thriving in a high temperature. ~*a.* thermophilic. **thermophilic** (-fil´-) *a.* thriving in a high temperature.

thermopile (thœ´məpīl) *n.* a series of thermocouples, esp. one employed to measure small quantities of radiant heat.

thermoplastic (thœmōplas´tik) *n.*, *a.* (a substance) which softens under heat without undergoing any chemical change, and can therefore be heated repeatedly.

Thermos® (thœ´mos), **thermos, thermos flask,** (*NAm.*) **thermos bottle** *n.* a vacuum flask.

thermoscope (thœ´məskōp) *n.* an instrument for indicating changes of temperature without measuring them. **thermoscopic** (-skop´-) *a.*

thermosetting (thœ´mōseting) *a.* (of plastics) softening initially under heat but subsequently hardening and becoming infusible and insoluble. **thermoset** *a.*

thermosphere (thœ´məsfiə) *n.* the part of the earth's atmosphere above the mesosphere, from about 50 miles (80 km), in which the temperature rises steadily with height.

thermostable (thœmōstā´bəl) *a.* (*Chem.*) (of a substance) stable when subjected to heat.

thermostat (thœ´məstat) *n.* an automatic device for regulating temperatures. **thermostatic** (-stat´-) *a.* **thermostatically** *adv.*

thermotaxis (thœmōtak´sis) *n.* (*Biol.*) the movement of an organism in reaction to heat stimulus. **thermotactic** (-tak´tik), **thermotaxic** *a.*

thermotropism (thœmōtrō´pizm) *n.* (*Bot.*) the orientation of a plant in response to temperature difference. **thermotropic** (-trop´-) *a.*

theroid (thiə´roid) *a.* relating to or resembling a beast. [Gr. *thēr-ros*, wild beast, -OID]

theropod (thiə´rəpod) *n.* any carnivorous saurischian dinosaur of the genus *Theropoda*, including the tyrannosaurs and megalosaurs. ~*a.* of or relating to the Theropoda. [as THEROID, Gr. *pous podos*, foot]

THES *abbr.* Times Higher Education Supplement.

thesaurus (thisaw´rəs) *n.* (*pl.* **thesauruses, thesauri** (-rī)) **1** a collection of words, phrases etc. arranged as groups of synonyms or by concept. **2** a dictionary or encyclopedia. [L, from Gr. *thēsauros*, TREASURE]

these THIS.

thesis (thē´sis) *n.* (*pl.* **theses** (-sēz)) **1** a proposition advanced or maintained. **2** an essay or dissertation, esp. one submitted by a candidate for a degree etc. **3** a school or college exercise. **4** (*Logic*) an affirmation, as opposed to a hypothesis. **5** in prosody, the unaccented part of a metrical foot, as opposed to *arsis*. [L, from Gr. *thesis*, from *the-*, root of *tithenai*, to set]

Usage note In prosody also pronounced (thes´is).

thespian (thes´piən) *a.* of or relating to tragedy or drama. ~*n.* an actor. [*Thespis*, traditional Greek dramatic poet]

Thess. *abbr.* Thessalonians.

theta (thē´tə) *n.* the eighth letter of the Greek alphabet (Θ, θ), corresponding to *th.* [Gr. *thēta*]

theurgy (thē´œji) *n.* **1** divine or supernatural agency, esp. in human affairs. **2** supernatural as distinct from natural magic. **theurgic** (-oe´-), **theurgical** *a.* **theurgist** *n.* [late L *theurgia*, Gr. *theourgia* (*theos*, god, *ergon*, work)]

thew (thū) *n.* **1** (*usu. in pl.*, *poet.*) muscles, sinews. **2** (*poet.*) strength, vigour. **3** †manners, mental qualities. **thewless** *a.* **thewy** *a.* [OE *thēaw*, habit, cp. OHG *thau*, *dau*, discipline, etym. uncertain]

they (dhā) *pron.* **1** the plural of HE, SHE or IT[1] (subjective). **2** people in general. **3** those in authority. **4** (*coll.*) he or she (referring to an indefinite pron.). **they'd** (dhād) *contr.* **1** they had. **2** they would. **they'll** (dhāl) *contr.* they will. **they're** (theə) *contr.* they are. **they've** (dhāv) *contr.* they have. [OE *thā*, pl. of THE, THAT]

Usage note This dictionary accepts and uses the (plural) pronouns *they, them, their* to refer back to singular indefinites (*someone, a person* etc.). The traditionally prescribed masculine singular (*he, him, his*) has increasingly come to be regarded as sexist. *They* and its forms are already the natural choices in spoken English, and the explicit alternatives *he or she, him or her, his or her* can be cumbersome. In other formal written contexts, however, *he or she* etc. may be preferred, and outside dictionary definitions indefinite sentences can often conveniently be recast in the plural.

THI *abbr.* temperature-humidity index.

thiamine (thī´əmēn), **thiamin** (-min) *n.* a vitamin found in unrefined cereals, beans and liver, important for metabolism and nerve function, the lack of which can cause beriberi; vitamin B_1. [Gr. *theion*, sulphur, AMINE]

thick (thik) *a.* **1** having great or specified extent or depth from one surface to the opposite. **2** arranged, set or planted closely, crowded together, close packed or abounding (with), following in quick succession. **3** dense, muddy, impure, cloudy, foggy. **4** (*coll.*) not very intelligent, stupid. **5** (of articulation etc.) indistinct, muffled. **6** (*coll.*) very friendly, familiar (*as thick as thieves*). ~*adv.* **1** thickly. **2** in close succession (*thick and fast*). **3** indistinctly. ~*n.* the thickest part. **a bit thick** (*coll.*) unreasonable. **in the thick** at the busiest part (of). **through thick and thin** under any conditions, undauntedly, resolutely. **thick ear** *n.* (*coll.*) a swollen ear as a result of a blow. **thicken** *v.t.*, *v.i.* to make or become thick or thicker. **thickener** *n.* **1** something to thicken a liquid. **2** a thickened part or place. **thickening** *n.* **thicket** *n.* a thick growth of small trees, bushes, etc. **thickhead** *n.* **1** (*coll.*) a blockhead. **2** any Australian perching bird of the Pachycephalidae family, related to the flycatchers, a whistler. **thick-headed** *a.* **thick-headedness** *n.* **thickish** *a.* **thick-knee** *n.* the stone curlew. **thickly** *adv.* **thickness** *n.* **1** extent from upper surface to lower, the dimension that is neither length nor breadth. **2** the state of being thick. **3** a sheet or layer of cardboard etc. **4** a thick part. **thicko** *n.* (*pl.* **thickos**) (*coll.*) an unintelligent person. **thick-set** *a.* **1** solidly built, stout, stumpy. **2** planted, set or growing close together. ~*n.* a thicket. **thick-skinned** *a.* insensitive to taunts, criticism etc. **thick-skulled, thick-witted** *a.* dull, slow to learn. **thick type** *n.* (*Print.*) a type composed of thick lines. **thicky** (-i) *n.* (*pl.* **thickies**) (*sl.*) a stupid person. [OE *thicce*, cp. Dut. *dik*, G *dick*, Icel. *thykkr*]

thief (thēf) *n.* (*pl.* **thieves** (thēvz)) a person who steals, esp. furtively and without violence. **thieve** (thēv) *v.i.* to practise theft, to be a thief. ~*v.t.* to take by theft. **thievery** (-vəri) *n.* (*pl.* **thieveries**) the act or practice of stealing. **thieves' Latin** *n.* cant or jargon employed as a secret language by thieves. **thievish** *a.* **thievishly** *adv.* **thievishness** *n.* [OE *thēof*, cp. Dut. *dief*, G *Dieb*, Icel. *thjōfr*]

thigh (thī) *n.* **1** the thick, fleshy portion of the leg between the hip and knee in humans. **2** the corresponding part in other animals. **thigh bone** *n.* (*Anat.*) the principal bone between the hip and the knee, the femur. **thighed** *a.* (*usu. in comb.*, as *slim-thighed*). [OE *thēok*, *thēo*, cp. Dut. *dij*, Icel. *thjō*, *OHG dioh*]

thigmotropism (thigmətrō´pizm) *n.* (*Biol.*) movement when touched. **thigmotropic** (-trop´-) *a.* [Gr. *thigma*, touch, TROPISM]

thill (thil) *n.* the shaft of a cart, carriage or other vehicle. [OE *thille*, plank, flooring, cogn. with DEAL[2]]

thimble (thim´bəl) *n.* **1** a cap of metal, plastic etc., worn to protect the end of the finger in sewing. **2** a sleeve or short metal tube. **3** a ferrule. **4** (*Naut.*) an iron ring having an exterior groove worked into a rope or sail to receive another rope or lanyard. **thimbleful** *n.* (*pl.* **thimblefuls**) **1** as much as a thimble holds. **2** a very small quantity. **thimblerig** (-rig) *n.* a sleight-of-hand trick with three thimbles or cups and a pea, persons being challenged to guess which cover the pea is under. ~*v.t.*, *v.i.* (*pres.p.* **thimblerigging,** *past, p.p.* **thimblerigged**) to cheat by means of thimblerigging. **thimblerigger** *n.* [OE *thȳmel*, thumb stall]

thin (thin) *a.* (*comp.* **thinner,** *superl.* **thinnest**) **1** having the opposite surfaces close together, of little thickness, slender. **2** not close-packed, not dense. **3** sparse, scanty, meagre. **4** lean, not plump. **5** not full, scant, bare. **6** flimsy, easily seen through. **7** of a watery consistency. **8** weak in sound, not full-toned. ~*adv.* thinly. ~*v.t.* (*pres.p.* **thinning,** *past, p.p.* **thinned**) **1** to make thin or thinner. **2** to make less crowded. **3** to thin out. ~*v.i.* **1** to become thin or thinner. **2** to waste away. **on thin ice** in a vulnerable or dangerous situation. **the thin end of the wedge** WEDGE. **thin on the ground** not numerous, sparse. **thin on top** balding. **to thin out** to remove fruit, flowers etc. from (a tree or plant) or some of a crop of (seedlings etc.) to improve the rest. **thin air** *n.* invisibility, a state of apparent non-existence. **thinly** *adv.* **thinner, thinners** *n.* a solvent used to thin, e.g. paint. **thinness** *n.* **thinnings** *n.pl.* branches, trees etc. removed in the course of thinning out an overgrown area. **thinnish** *a.* **thin-skinned** *a.* sensitive, easily offended. **thin time** *n.* a period of hardship, misery etc. **thin type** *n.* (*Print.*) a type composed of thin lines. [OE *thynne*, cp. Dut. *dun*, G *dünn*, Icel. *thunnr*, also L *tenuis*, Gr. *tanaos*]

†**thine** (dhīn) *a.* THY (before a vowel). ~*pron.* something or someone of or belonging to thee (you).

thing[1] (thing) *n.* **1** any object or thought. **2** whatever exists or is conceived to exist as a separate entity, esp. an inanimate object as distinct from a living being. **3** an act, a fact, affair, circumstance, quality etc. **4** (*coll.*) a person or other animate object regarded with commiseration, disparagement etc. **5** a specimen, a style. **6** a remarkable fact. **7** (*pl.*) clothes, belongings, luggage etc. **8** (*pl.*) the current or usual state of affairs. **9** (*pl., Law*) property. **(just) one of those things** a happening that one cannot do anything about. **one's thing** (*coll.*) one's usual sphere of interest or competence. **the thing** **1** the proper thing (to do etc.). **2** the thing to be decided. **3** the important thing. **to do one's own thing** (*coll.*) to do what one likes or what one pleases. **to do things to** to affect (someone) in a strange and remarkable way. **to have a thing about** to have an unaccountable prejudice or fear about. **to make a good thing of** to make a profit out of. **to make a thing** **1** to make an issue (of), to cause a fuss. **2** to exaggerate the importance (of). **to see things** SEE[1]. **thingamabob** (-əməbob), **thingamajig** (-jig), **thingumabob, thingumajig, thingummygig** *n.* (*coll.*) THINGUMMY (under THING[1]). **thingummy** (-əmi), **thingamy, thingy** (-i) *n.* (*pl.* **thingummies, thingamies, thingies**) (*coll.*) **1** a thing whose name one is unable to specify (through ignorance, forgetfulness or reluctance), a what-d'you-call-it. **2** used instead of a person's name (one does not know, has forgotten or wishes not to specify). [OE, cause, sake, office, reason, council (cp. Dut. *ding* and G *Ding*, Icel. *thing*, Dan. and Swed. *ting*)]

thing[2] (thing) *n.* a Scandinavian public assembly, esp. a legislative body. [Icel., as THING[1]]

think (thingk) *v.t.* (*past, p.p.* **thought** (thawt), (*facet.*) **thunk** (thŭngk)) **1** to regard or examine in the mind, to reflect, to ponder (over etc.). **2** to consider, to be of the opinion, to believe (that), to judge (to be). **3** to design, to intend (to do). **4** to effect by thinking. **5** (*coll.*) to remember, to recollect (to do). **6** to imagine, to recognize. ~*v.i.* **1** to exercise the mind actively, to reason. **2** to meditate, to cogitate, to consider (on, about etc.). ~*n.* (*coll.*) **1** an act of thinking. **2** a thought. **think nothing of it** NOTHING. **to have another think coming** (*coll.*) to be wrong about what one assumes will happen. **to think again** **1** to reconsider a previous decision. **2** to change a previous plan or decision. **to think a lot of** to think highly of. **to think aloud** to speak about one's thoughts as they occur. **to think back** to reflect on the past, a past event etc. **to think better of** to change one's mind, to decide not to pursue (a course of action). **to think big** BIG. **to think fit** FIT[1]. **to think for oneself** to be independent-minded. **to think highly of** to hold in high regard. **to think less of** to regard (someone) in lower esteem than previously. **to think little of** to consider (something) to be of little significance or unremarkable. **to think much of** to think highly of. **to think nothing of it** NOTHING. **to think of** **1** to have in mind, to conceive, to imagine. **2** to call to mind, to remember. **3** to have a particular opinion or feeling about, to esteem. **to think on one's feet** FOOT. **to think on/ upon** to consider, to think about. **to think out** **1** to devise. **2** to solve by long thought. **to think over** to consider (a proposition etc.). **to think through** to think fully about a situation, decision etc. and its consequences. **to think twice** **1** to give extra thought to, to hesitate. **2** to change a decision. **to think up** to devise, to invent. **thinkable** *a.* **thinker** *n.* **thinking** *n.* **1** the process of thought. **2** the opinion, received viewpoint etc. at a given time. ~*a.* of or related to thought. **to put on one's thinking cap** to think hard about a problem. **thinkingly** *adv.* **think-tank** *n.* a group of experts in any field who meet to solve problems and produce new ideas in that field. [cp. G *denken*, Icel. *thekkja*, Dan. *tænke*, cogn. with THANK]

thinner, thinnings etc. THIN.

thio- (thīʹō) *comb.form* sulphur. [Gr. *theion*]

thiol (thīʹol) *n.* (*Chem.*) any organic compound analogous to alcohol containing sulphur in place of oxygen.

thiopentone (thīōpenʹtōn) *n.* (*Chem.*) a barbiturate drug used, as a sodium salt, in medicine as a general anaesthetic and hypnotic.

thiosulphuric (thīōsŭlfūʹrik), (*esp. NAm.*) **thiosulfuric** *a.* (*Chem.*) applied to an acid corresponding to sulphuric acid in which one atom of oxygen is replaced by one of sulphur. **thiosulphate** (-sŭlʹfāt) *n.*

thiourea (thīōūrēʹə) *n.* a white crystalline compound used in photographic fixing, rubber vulcanization and the manufacture of synthetic resins.

third (thœd) *n.* **1** any one of three equal parts. **2** the 60th part of a second of time or angular measurement. **3** (*Mus.*) **a** an interval between a tone and the next but one on the diatonic scale. **b** a tone separated by this interval. **c** the consonance of two such tones. **4** (*pl.*) the third part of a deceased husband's estate, sometimes assigned as her share to the widow. **5** a third-class honours degree. **6** the third gear in a motor vehicle. ~*n., a.* **1** (the) last of three (people, things etc.). **2** the next after the second. **third age** *n.* old age, the period of retirement. **third-best** *a.* of third highest quality. ~*n.* a thing or person in this category. **third-class, third-rate** *a.* **1** inferior, worthless. **2** of the class coming next to the second. ~*adv.* by the third class. ~*n.* the third-best category of hotel, train travel etc. **third cousin** *n.* the child of a parent's second cousin. **third degree** *n.* (*sl.*) intimidation or torture, esp. to extract information. **third-degree** *a.* **1** (of burns) most severe, affecting lower layers of tissue. **2** (of an interrogation etc.) very demanding, perh. using torture. **third estate** *n.* the bourgeoisie of France before the Revolution, as distinguished from the nobles and the clergy. **third eye** *n.* **1** in Hinduism and Buddhism, the eye in the forehead of a deity, esp. Siva, associated with the gift of insight. **2** the gift of insight, the ability to foretell events. **3** in certain vertebrates, the pineal gland. **third force** *n.* a moderate political party acting as a check on two parties with more extreme views. **third gear** *n.* in a motor vehicle, cycle etc., the third lowest gear. **thirdly** *adv.* **third man** *n.* (*pl.* **third men**) **1** in cricket, a fielder placed towards the boundary behind the slips. **2** this position. **third party** *n.* (a person) other than the principals (in a contract etc.). **third-party** *a.* (of insurance) covering damage, injury etc. to those other than the insured person(s). **third person** *n.* (*Gram.*) the form of a pronoun, verb etc. indicating persons or things referred to, as distinct from the speaker or addressee(s). **third rail** *n.* an extra rail through which electricity is supplied to an electric train. **third reading** *n.* the final acceptance of a bill together with the amendments passed in committee. **Third Reich** *n.* Germany under the Nazi regime, 1933–45. **Third World** *n.* (*Hist.*) **1** the developing countries, esp. in Africa, Asia and S America. **2** the countries not aligned with either the USA or the Soviet Union. [OE *thridda*, from *thrī*, THREE]

†**thirl** (thœl) *v.t.* to pierce through, to perforate. ~*n.* a

hole, an aperture. [OE *thyrlian*, from *thyrel*, a hole, from *thurh*, THOROUGH]

thirst (thœst) *n.* **1** the uneasiness or suffering caused by the need to drink liquid. **2** a desire to drink liquid. **3** eager longing or desire. ~*v.i.* **1** to feel thirst (for or after). **2** to feel eager longing or desire (for or after). **thirstless** *a.* **thirsty** *a.* (*comp.* **thirstier**, *superl.* **thirstiest**) **1** feeling thirst, dry, parched. **2** (*coll.*) causing thirst (*thirsty work*). **thirstily** *adv.* **thirstiness** *n.* [OE *thurst* (cp. Dut. *dorst*, G *Durst*, Icel. *thorsti*), whence *thyrstan*, cp. Dut. *dorsten*, G *dürsten*, cogn. with L *torrēre*, Gr. *tersesthai*, to dry up]

thirteen (thœtēn´) *n.* **1** the number or figure 13 or xiii. **2** the age of 13. ~*a.* **1** 13 in number. **2** aged 13. **thirteenth** (-th) *n.* any one of 13 equal parts. ~*n., a.* **1** (the) last of 13 (people, things etc.). **2** the next after the 12th. [OE *thrēotēne* (THREE, -TEEN)]

thirty (thœ´ti) *n.* (*pl.* **thirties**) **1** three times ten. **2** the number or figure 30 or xxx. **3** the age of 30. ~*a.* **1** 30 in number. **2** aged 30. **thirties** *n.pl.* **1** the period of time between one's 30th and 40th birthdays. **2** the range of temperature between 30 and 40 degrees. **3** the period of time between the 30th and 40th years of a century. **thirtieth** (-əth) *n.* any one of 30 equal parts. ~*n., a.* **1** (the) last of 30 (people, things etc.). **2** the next after the 20th. **thirty-first, thirty-second etc.** *n., a.* the ordinal numbers corresponding to thirty-one etc. **thirtyfold** *a., adv.* **1** made up of 30 parts. **2** 30 times as much or as many. **Thirty-nine Articles** *n.pl.* the thirty-nine statements subscribed to by the clergy of the Church of England. **thirty-one, thirty-two etc.** *n., a.* the cardinal numbers between thirty and forty. **thirty-second note** *n.* (*Mus., N Am.*) a demisemiquaver. **thirty-something** *n., a.* (of) an unspecified age between 30 and 40. **thirty-two-mo** *n.* (*pl.* **thirty-two-mos**) **1** (of a book) a size in which each leaf is one-thirty-second the size of a printing sheet. **2** a book of this size. **thirty-year rule** *n.* a rule that certain records, e.g. cabinet papers, may be made public only after 30 years. [OE *thrītig*, *thrittig* (THREE, -TY[1])]

this (dhis) *a., pron.* (*pl.* **these** (dhēz)) used to denote the person or thing that is present or near in place or time, or already mentioned, implied or familiar. ~*adv.* to this extent. **this and that** (*coll.*) random and usu. unimportant subjects of conversation. **this here** (*sl.*) this particular (person, object etc.). **this side of** SIDE. **this world** existence, this mortal life. **thisness** *n.* the quality of being this, Haecceity. [OE *thes*, fem. *theos*, neut. *this* (cp. Dut. *deze*, G *dieser*, Icel. *thessi*), cogn. with THAT, THE]

thistle (this´əl) *n.* any plant of the genera *Circium*, *Carlina*, *Carduus* etc. having prickly stems, leaves and involucres. **thistledown** *n.* the light fluffy down surrounding thistle seeds. **thistly** *a.* [OE *thistel*, cp. Dut. *distel*, G *Distel*, Icel. *thistill*]

thither (dhidh´ə) *adv.* (*formal, poet.*) **1** to that place. **2** to that end, point or result. **thitherward** *adv.* [OE *thider*, *thyder*, cogn. with THAT, cp. HITHER]

thixotropic (thiksətrop´ik) *a.* (of certain gels, e.g. non-drip paints) becoming fluid when shaken or stirred. **thixotropy** (-sot´rəpi) *n.* [Gr. *thixis*, act of touching, *tropos*, turn]

tho' THOUGH.

thole[1] (thōl), **thole-pin** *n.* a pin in the gunwale of a boat serving as fulcrum for the oar. [OE *thol*, cp. Dut. *dol*, Icel. *thollr*, tree, peg, thole]

thole[2] (thōl) *v.t.* (*Sc.*) **1** to suffer, to endure, to bear, to undergo. **2** to permit, to put up with. [OE *tholian*, cp. Icel. *thola*, OHG *dolēn*, Goth. *thulan*, also L *tollere*, Gr. *tlènai*]

tholus (thō´ləs) *n.* (*pl.* **tholi** (-lī)) a dome, cupola, or lantern. **tholos** (-los) *n.* (*pl.* **tholoi** (-oi)) (*Hist.*) a dome-shaped tomb of ancient Greece. [Gr. *tholos*, *-balos*, from *bainein*, to go]

Thomism (tō´mizm) *n.* the scholastic philosophy and theology of St Thomas Aquinas, 1227–74. **Thomist** *a., n.* **Thomistic** (-mis´-), **Thomistical** *a.*

-thon (thon) *comb. form* a large-scale event or related series of events lasting a long time or demanding endurance of the participants, as *telethon*. [MARATHON]

thong (thong) *n.* **1** a strip of leather used as a whiplash, for reins, or for fastening anything. **2** (*Austral., N Am.*) a flip-flop (sandal). **3** a skimpy bathing garment that covers the genitals while leaving the buttocks bare. ~*v.t.* **1** to fit or provide with a thong. **2** to fasten or thrash with a thong. [OE *thwang* (cp. Icel. *thvengr*), cogn. with TWINGE]

thorax (thaw´raks) *n.* (*pl.* **thoraces** (-rəsēz), **thoraxes**) **1** (*Anat.*) the part of the trunk between the neck and the abdomen. **2** (*Zool.*) the middle division of the body of insects. **3** (*Hist.*) a breastplate, cuirass or corselet of ancient Greece. **thoracal** (-rəkəl) *a.* **thoracic** (thəras´-) *a.* **thoraco-** (thor´əkō), **thorac-** *comb. form* [L, from Gr. *thōrax -akos*]

thorium (thaw´riəm) *n.* (*Chem.*) a radioactive metallic element, at. no. 90, chem. symbol Th, found chiefly in thorite and monazite. **thoria** (-riə) *n.* oxide of thorium, used in the manufacture of heat-resistant materials. **thorite** (-rīt) *n.* a massive dark hydrous thorium silicate, found in Norway. [*Thor*, the Scandinavian god of thunder etc.]

thorn (thawn) *n.* **1** a spine, a sharp-pointed projection on a plant, a prickle. **2** a thorny shrub, tree or herb (*usu. in comb.* as *blackthorn*, *whitethorn*). **3** an annoyance, a trouble, a care. **4** the Old English and Icelandic letter þ (th). **on thorns** restless, uneasy. **thorn apple** *n.* **1** a plant with prickly seed capsules, *Datura stramonium*. **2** the fruit of this. **thornback** *n.* a ray, *Raja clavata*, the back and tail of which are covered with spines. **thornbill** *n.* **1** any Australian warbler of the genus *Acanthiza*. **2** any of several S American hummingbirds, esp. of the genus *Chalcostigma*, having thornlike bills. **thorn bush, thorn tree** *n.* a thorn-bearing tree. **thorn in one's side, thorn in one's flesh** *n.* a constant source of trouble. **thornless** *a.* **thornproof** *a.* **thorntail** *n.* any S American hummingbird of the genus *Popelairia*. **thorny** *a.* (*comp.* **thornier**, *superl.* **thorniest**) **1** having many thorns. **2** difficult to resolve, problematical. **thornily** *adv.* **thorniness** *n.* [OE, cp. Icel. *thorn*, Dut. *doorn*, G *Dorn*]

thorough (thŭr´ə) *a.* complete, total, unqualified, not superficial. ~*n.* (*Hist.*) (**Thorough**) the uncompromising absolutist policy of Strafford, under Charles I. **thorough bass** (bās) *n.* (*Mus.*) a bass part accompanied by shorthand marks, usu. figures, written below the stave, to indicate the harmony. **thorough brace** *n.* a leather strap passing between two C-springs to support the body of a carriage. **thoroughbred** *a.* **1** of pure breed. **2** high-spirited, mettlesome. **3** of the best quality. ~*n.* **1** a thoroughbred animal, esp. a horse. **2** (**Thoroughbred**) a British breed of racehorses originating from Arab sires and English mares. **thoroughfare** *n.* **1** a road or street for public traffic. **2** a passage through from one street etc., to another, an unobstructed road or street. **thoroughgoing** *a.* **1** thorough, uncompromising. **2** going or ready to go to any lengths. **thoroughly** *adv.* **thoroughness** *n.* **thorough-paced** *a.* **1** trained to all paces (as a horse). **2** thoroughgoing, out-and-out. **thoroughpin** *n.* a swelling in the hollow of a horse's hock. [THROUGH]

†**thorp** (thawp), **thorpe** *n.* a village, a hamlet (esp. in place names). [OE *thorp*, cp. Dut. *dorp*, G *Dorf*, Icel. *thorp*]

Thos. *abbr.* Thomas.

those THAT.

†**thou**[1] (dhow) *pron.* the second personal pronoun singular (subjective), denoting the person spoken to.

[OE *thū*, cp. G, Dan., and Swed. *du*, Icel. *thū*, L *tu*, Gr. *su, tu*]

thou[2] (thow) *n.* (*pl.* **thou, thous**) **1** (*coll.*) short for THOUSAND. **2** a thousandth of an inch (0.0254 mm).

though (dhō), **tho'** *conj.* **1** notwithstanding that, despite the fact that. **2** even if, granting or supposing that. **3** nevertheless. **4** in spite of being. *~adv.* (*coll.*) however, all the same. **as though** AS[1]. [ME *thogh*, Icel. *thō*, cp. Dut. and G *doch*, OE *thēah, thæh, thāh*]

thought[1] (thawt) *n.* **1** the act or process of thinking. **2** reflection, serious consideration, meditation. **3** deep concern or solicitude. **4** the faculty of thinking or reasoning. **5** that which is thought. **6** a conception, an idea, a reflection, a judgement, conclusion etc. **7** (*pl.*) one's views, ideas, opinions etc. **a thought** (*coll.*) a very small degree, etc. a shade, somewhat. **in thought** in the act of thinking, meditating. **to give thought to** to consider. **to take thought** to consider something carefully. **thoughted** *a.* (*usu. in comb.*) having a (usu. specified kind of) thought or thoughts (*evil-thoughted*). **thoughtful** *a.* **1** engaged in thinking. **2** reflecting serious consideration. **3** considerate, careful. **thoughtfully** *adv.* **thoughtfulness** *n.* **thoughtless** *a.* **1** inconsiderate, careless. **2** reflecting absence of serious consideration. **thoughtlessly** *adv.* **thoughtlessness** *n.* **thought-provoking** *a.* mentally stimulating, engendering serious thought. **thought-reader** *n.* a person who appears to perceive by telepathy what is passing through another person's mind. **thought-reading** *n.* **thought-transference** *n.* telepathy. **thought-wave** *n.* a telepathic undulation or vibration. [OE *thōht*, as THINK]

thought[2] THINK.

thousand (thow´zənd) *n.* (*pl.* **thousand, thousands**) **1** ten hundred, 1000. **2** a great many. *~a.* amounting to a thousand. **thousandfold** *a., adv.* **thousandth** (-th) *a., n.* [OE *thūsend* (cp. Dut. *duizend*, G *tausend*, Icel. *thūsund*), etym. uncertain]

thrall (thrawl) *n.* (*poet.*) **1** a state of slavery or enthralment. **2** a slave, a serf. *~v.t.* to enthral, to enslave. **thraldom, thralldom** *n.* [ME *thral*, Icel. *thræll* (cp. Dan. *træl*, Swed. *trāl*), cogn. with OE *thrægan*, to run]

thrang (thrang) *a.* (*Sc.*) thronged, busy. [THRONG]

thrash (thrash) *v.t.* **1** to beat severely, esp. with a stick etc. **2** to defeat, conquer, beat convincingly. *~v.i.* **1** to strike out wildly and repeatedly. **2** (*Naut.*) to strike the waves repeatedly. *~n.* **1** a thrashing. **2** (*sl.*) a party. **to thrash out** to discuss thoroughly in order to find a solution. **thrasher**[1] *n.* **1** a person who thrashes. **2** a thresher. **thrashing** *n.* a severe beating. [THRESH]

thrasher[1] THRASH.

thrasher[2] (thrash´ə) *n.* (*N Am.*) a N American songbird of the family Mimidae, resembling the thrush. [prob. var. of THRUSH[1]]

†**thrasonical** (thrəson´ikəl) *a.* bragging, boastful. **thrasonically** *adv.* [*Thraso*, the braggart in Terence's comedies, -ICAL (under -IC)]

thrave (thrāv) *n.* (*Sc.*) 24 sheaves or two stooks of corn. [from Scand., cp. Icel. *threfi*, Norw. *treve*, Swed. *trafue*]

thrawn (thrawn) *a.* (*Sc.*) **1** twisted, misshapen. **2** perverse, stubborn. [THROW]

thread (thred) *n.* **1** a slender cord consisting of two or more yarns doubled or twisted, for sewing or weaving. **2** a single filament of cotton, silk, wool etc. **3** anything resembling this. **4** the continuing theme or linking element in an argument or story. **5** the spiral on a screw. **6** a fine line of colour etc. **7** a thin seam or vein. **8** a continuous course (of life etc.). *~v.t.* **1** to pass a thread through the eye or aperture of (a needle etc.). **2** to string (beads etc.) on a thread. **3** to pick (one's way) or to go through an intricate or crowded place etc. **4** to streak (the hair) with grey etc. **5** to cut a thread on (a screw). **to hang by a thread** to be in a very precarious state. **threadbare** *a.* **1** so worn that the thread is visible, having the nap worn off. **2** (of an excuse, phrase etc.) worn, trite, hackneyed. **threadbareness** *n.* **threader** *n.* **threadfin** *n.* (*pl. in general* **threadfin**, *in particular* **threadfins**) any small tropical seafish of the family Polynemidae, having long threadlike streamers from its pectoral fins. **threadlike** *a., adv.* **thread mark** *n.* a mark produced by coloured silk fibres in banknotes to prevent counterfeiting. **thread vein** *n.* (*Med.*) a very fine vein on the surface of the skin. **threadworm** *n.* a threadlike nematode worm, esp. a pinworm. **thready** *a.* (*comp.* **threadier**, *superl.* **threadiest**) **1** threadlike. **2** (of the pulse) very weak, only faintly perceptible. [OE *thræd*, from *thrāwan*, to THROW (cp. Dut. *draad*, G *Draht*, Icel. *thrāthr*)]

threap (thrēp) *v.t.* **1** to scold. **2** to contradict. **3** (*Sc., North.*) to assert with pertinacity, to persist in saying. *~v.i.* to quarrel, to wrangle. [OE *thrēapian*, to rebuke]

threat (thret) *n.* **1** a declaration of an intention to inflict punishment, loss, injury etc. **2** a menace. **3** (*Law*) such a menace as may interfere with freedom, business etc., or a menace of injury to life, property or reputation. **4** an indication of an imminent danger. **threaten** *v.t.* **1** to use threats to. **2** to announce a damaging intention (to do). **3** to announce one's intention to inflict (injury etc.). **4** to indicate an imminent danger of. *~v.i.* **1** to use threats. **2** to have a threatening appearance. **threatened** *a.* (of a species of animal, plant etc.) at risk, endangered. **threatener** *n.* **threateningly** *adv.* [OE *thrēat*, crowd, trouble, threat, from *āthrēotan*, to afflict (cp. Icel. *thrjōta*, cogn. with L *trūdere*, to push)]

three (thrē) *n.* **1** the number or figure 3 or iii. **2** the age of three. **3** the third hour after midnight or midday. **4** a group of three. *~a.* **1** three in number. **2** aged three. **the three professions** divinity, law, medicine. **three sheets in the wind** SHEET[2]. **three balls** *n.pl.* a pawnbroker's sign. **three-card monte** *n.* a Mexican game of sleight of hand with three cards. **three-card trick** *n.* a gambling game in which bets are placed on which is the queen among three cards lying face downwards, also known as *find the lady*. **three cheers** *n.pl.* three successive shouts of 'hurrah'. **three-colour process** *n.* the printing of coloured illustrations by the combination of the three primary colours. **three-cornered** *a.* having three corners or angles. **three-day event** *n.* an equestrian competition taking place over three days and including dressage, show-jumping and cross-country riding. **three-decker** *n.* (*Hist.*) **1** a vessel carrying guns on three decks. **2** a pulpit in three storeys. **three dimensions** *n.pl.* **1** length, breadth and thickness. **2** a line, a surface, a volume, constituting the three degrees of measurement. **three-dimensional** *a.* having or seeming to have three dimensions. **threefold** *a., adv.* **1** made up of three parts. **2** three times as much or as many. **three-handed** *a.* **1** (of a card game) for three players. **2** having three hands. **three-headed** *a.* **three-legged race** *n.* a novelty race in which people run in pairs with one leg tied to a leg of their partner. **three-line whip** *n.* a written notice to MPs urging them to attend a parliamentary vote, underlined three times to denote its importance. **three-master** *n.* (*Naut.*) a vessel, esp. a schooner, with three masts. **three parts** *n.pl.* three-quarters. **three-parts** *a.* **threepence** (threp´əns, thrip´-, thrŭp´-) *n.* the sum of three pence, esp. before decimal currency. **threepenny** (threp´ni, thrip´-, thrŭp´-) *a.* **threepenny bit** *n.* (*Hist.*) a small coin of the value of three old pence. **three-phase** *a.* denoting an alternating-current system in which the currents flow in three separate circuits. **three-piece** *a.* consisting of three matching pieces, as a suit of clothes, a suite of furniture etc. **three-ply** *a.* having three strands, thicknesses etc. *~n.* plywood of three layers. **three-point landing** *n.* a perfect landing in which an aeroplane touches all three wheels down simultaneously. **three-point turn** *n.* an about-turn in a narrow space made by a vehicle moving obliquely forwards, backwards and forwards again. **three-pronged** *a.* (of an attack, strategy etc.) having three elements, goals etc. **three-pronged attack** *n.* an attack on three separate points at the same time. **three-quarters** *n.pl.* three parts out of four equal parts of a whole. ~*adv.* 1 to the extent of three-quarters. 2 almost (*three-quarters drowned*). **three-quarter** *a.* 1 of three-fourths the usual size or number. 2 (of portraits) showing three-quarters of the face, or going down to the hips. ~*n.* a three-quarter back. **three-quarter back** *n.* in rugby football, each of three or four players between the full-back and the half-backs. **three-ring circus** *n.* 1 (*N Am.*) a circus with three rings. 2 an extravagant event or display. 3 a scene of confusion and complexity. **three R's** *n.pl.* reading, writing, arithmetic, the basic subjects of education. †**threescore** *a.* sixty. ~*n.* the age of 60. **threesome** (-səm) *n.* 1 a group of three. 2 a game for three. **three-way** *a.* involving three things or people. **three-wheeler** *a.* a vehicle with three wheels. [OE *thrēo*, *thrī*, cp. Dut. *drie*, G *drei*, Icel. *thrīr*, also L *trēs*, Gr. *treis*]

thremmatology (thremətol´əji) *n.* the branch of biology dealing with the breeding of animals and plants. [Gr. *thremma -atos*, nursling, from *trephein*, to nourish, -LOGY]

threnody (thren´ədi), **threnode** (thrē´nōd, thren´-) *n.* (*pl.* **threnodies, threnodes**) 1 a song of lamentation. 2 a poem on the death of a person. **threnodial** (thrinō´-), **threnodic** (-nod´-) *a.* **threnodist** (thren´-) *n.* [Gr. *thrēnōdia* (*thrēnos*, dirge, *ōidē*, see ODE)]

threonine (thrē´ənēn) *n.* an amino acid essential for growth and health found in certain proteins. [20th cent., *threose* (a tetrose sugar), from Gr. *eruthros*, red, -INE]

thresh (thresh) *v.t.* 1 to beat out or separate the grain (from corn etc.). 2 to thrash. ~*v.i.* 1 to thresh corn. 2 to thrash. **to thresh out** to thrash out. **thresher** *n.* 1 a person who threshes. 2 a threshing machine. 3 a shark, *Alopias vulpinus*, having a long whiplike tail with which it directs its prey. **threshing** *n.* **threshing floor** *n.* a floor or area on which grain is threshed. **threshing machine** *n.* a powered machine for threshing corn etc. [OE *therscan*, cp. Dut. *dorschen*, G *dreschen*, Icel. *threskja*]

threshold (thresh´ōld) *n.* 1 the stone or plank at the bottom of a doorway. 2 an entrance, a doorway, a beginning. 3 the minimum strength of a stimulus etc., that will produce a response (*threshold of pain*). 4 (*Physics*) the minimum quantity that will produce a particular effect. 5 the minimum level at which changes in taxation etc. become operative. [OE *therscold* (THRESH, suf. doubtful)]

threw THROW.

thrice (thrīs) *adv.* 1 three times. 2 (*usu. in comb., poet.*) very much. [ME *thries*]

thrift (thrift) *n.* 1 frugality. 2 good husbandry, economical management. 3 any plant of the genus *Armeria*, esp. the sea pink, *A. maritima*. **thriftless** *a.* **thriftlessly** *adv.* **thriftlessness** *n.* **thrift shop, thrift store** *n.* (*N Am.*) a shop selling things for charity, a charity shop. **thrifty** *a.* (*comp.* **thriftier**, *superl.* **thriftiest**) frugal, careful, economical. **thriftily** *adv.* **thriftiness** *n.* [Icel. *thrīfa*, to seize; see THRIVE]

thrill (thril) *v.t.* 1 to affect with emotion so as to give a sense as of vibrating or tingling. 2 (of emotion) to excite greatly. 3 to penetrate. ~*v.i.* 1 (of emotion) to penetrate, vibrate, or quiver (through, along etc.). 2 to have a vibrating, shivering or tingling sense of emotion. ~*n.* 1 an intense vibration, shiver or wave of emotion. 2 (*coll.*) anything exciting. 3 (*Med.*) a vibratory or tremulous resonance observed in auscultation. **thrilled** *a.* **thriller** *n.* a sensational or exciting novel, film etc., esp. one involving crime and detection. **thrilling** *a.* **thrillingly** *adv.* **thrillingness** *n.* [OE *thyrlian*, from *thȳrel*, bore, from *thurh*, THROUGH]

thrips (thrips) *n.* (*pl.* **thrips**) a minute insect of the order Thysanoptera, often injurious to plants, esp. grain, the thunderfly. [Gr., woodworm]

thrive (thrīv) *v.i.* (*past* **throve** (thrōv), **thrived,** *p.p.* **thriven** (thriv´ən), **thrived**) 1 to prosper, to be fortunate, to be successful. 2 to grow vigorously. **thriver** *n.* **thriving** *a.* **thrivingly** *adv.* **thrivingness** *n.* [ME *thriven*, Icel. *thrīfask*, reflex. of *thrīfa*, to seize, cp. Swed. *trifvas*, Dan. *trives* (reflex.), to thrive]

thro' THROUGH.

throat (thrōt) *n.* 1 the front part of the neck, containing the gullet and windpipe. 2 the gullet, the pharynx; the windpipe, the larynx. 3 a throat-shaped inlet, opening, or entrance, a narrow passage, strait etc. 4 (*Naut.*) the crotch of a gaff where it rests against the mast. 5 (*poet.*) a voice; a bird's song. **to be at one another's throats** to be fighting or quarrelling violently. **to cut one another's throats** to engage in a mutually ruinous competition. **to cut one's own throat** to adopt a policy that will harm or ruin one. **to lie in one's throat** to lie outrageously. **throated** *a.* having a throat (*often in comb.*, as *black-throated diver*). **throaty** *a.* (*comp.* **throatier**, *superl.* **throatiest**) 1 guttural. 2 hoarse. 3 having a large or prominent throat. **throatily** *adv.* **throatiness** *n.* [OE *throte* (cp. G *Drossel*, OHG *drozza*), perh. cogn. with Dut. *strot*, throat, Icel. *throti*, swelling, from *thrūtna*, to swell]

throb (throb) *v.i.* (*pres.p.* **throbbing,** *past, p.p.* **throbbed**) 1 to vibrate, to quiver. 2 (of the heart or pulse) to beat rapidly or forcibly. ~*n.* a strong pulsation, a palpitation. **throbbingly** *adv.* [ME *throbben*, prob. imit]

throe (thrō) *n.* 1 (*pl.*) the pains of childbirth or death. 2 a violent pain, a pang of anguish. **in the throes of** struggling with (a task etc.). [ME *throwe*, Icel. *thrā*, cp. OE *thrōwian*, to suffer]

Usage note The spellings of the noun *throe* (a pang), and especially its plural *throes*, and the verb and noun *throw(s)* (cast) should not be confused.

thrombosis (thrombō´sis) *n.* (*pl.* **thromboses** (-sēz)) 1 (*Med.*) local coagulation of the blood in the heart or a blood vessel. 2 (*coll.*) a coronary thrombosis. **thrombin** (-bin) *n.* an enzyme concerned in the clotting of blood. **thrombocyte** (-bəsīt) *n.* a blood platelet. **thrombocytopenia** (-pē´niə) *n.* (*Med.*) a deficiency of platelets in the blood. **thrombose** (throm´bōz) *v.t., v.i.* to affect with or undergo thrombosis. **thrombosed** *a.* **thrombotic** (-bot´-) *a.* **thrombus** (-bəs) *n.* (*pl.* **thrombi** (-bī)) the clot of blood closing a vessel in thrombosis. [Gr., from *thrombousthai*, to become clotted, from *thrombos*, thrombus]

throne (thrōn) *n.* 1 a royal seat, a chair or seat of state for a sovereign, bishop etc. 2 sovereign power. 3 any one of the third order of angels. ~*v.t.* to enthrone. ~*v.i.* to sit on a throne. **throneless** *a.* [ME and OF *trone*, L *thronus -um*, Gr. *thronos*, seat, support]

throng (throng) *n.* a multitude of people or living things pressed close together, a crowd. ~*v.i.* 1 to crowd or press together. 2 to come in multitudes. ~*v.t.* 1 to crowd, to fill to excess. 2 to fill with a crowd. 3 to press or impede by crowding upon. [OE *gethrang*, from *thringan*, to crowd (cp. Dut. *drang*, G *Drang*, Icel. *thröng*)]

throstle (thros´əl) *n.* 1 the song thrush. 2 (*Hist.*) a throstle frame. **throstle frame** *n.* (*Hist.*) a machine for continuously twisting and winding wool, cotton etc. [OE, cp. MHG *trostel*, also THRUSH[1], L *turdus*]

throttle (throt´əl) *n.* 1 a throttle-lever. 2 a throttle-valve. 3 the windpipe, the gullet, the throat. ~*v.t.* 1 to choke, to strangle. 2 to use a throttle-lever to control (an engine). **to throttle back** to reduce the speed of an engine by controlling the throttle. **to throttle down** to throttle back. **throttle-lever** *n.* a pedal, lever etc. operating a throttle-valve. **throttler** *n.* **throttle-valve** *n.* a valve to shut off, reduce or control the flow of steam in a steam engine or of explosive mixture to an internal-combustion engine. [dim. of THROAT]

through (throo), **thro'**, (*N Am.*) **thru** *prep.* 1 from end to end of, from side to side of, between the sides or walls of. 2 over the whole extent of, in the midst of, throughout. 3 by means, agency or fault of, on account of. 4 (*N Am.*) up to and including (*Monday through Friday*). 5 during. 6 past. 7 at or to the end of. ~*adv.* 1 from end to end or side to side, from beginning to end. 2 to a final (successful) issue. 3 completely. ~*a.* 1 going through or to the end, proceeding right to the end or destination, esp. (of travel tickets etc.) involving several legs of a journey. 2 direct. 3 completed. **all through** all the time, throughout. **through and through** 1 completely, in every way. 2 searchingly. 3 through again and again. **to be through** (*coll.*) to have finished. **to get through** GET[1]. †**throughly** *adv.* THOROUGHLY (under THOROUGH). **throughout** *adv.* right through, in every part, from beginning to end. ~*prep.* right through, from beginning to end of. **throughput** *n.* the amount of raw material put through or processed in e.g. a factory, computer. **throughway,** (*N Am.*) **thruway** *n.* 1 a thoroughfare. 2 (*N Am.*) a motorway. [OE *thurh, thuruh* (cp. Dut. *door,* G *durch*), cogn. with Goth. *thairh*]

Usage note The spellings of *through* and *threw*, the past tense of *throw*, should not be confused.

throve THRIVE.

throw (thrō) *v.t.* (*past* **threw** (throo), *p.p.* **thrown** (thrōn)) 1 to fling, to hurl, to cast, esp. to a distance with some force. 2 to cast down, to cause to fall, to prostrate. 3 to drive, to impel, to dash. 4 to make (a cast) with dice; to score with a cast of a dice. 5 to turn or direct quickly or suddenly (the eyes etc.). 6 to put on (clothes etc.) hastily or carelessly. 7 to cast off (the skin, as a snake). 8 (of rabbits etc.) to give birth to (young). 9 to twist, to wind into threads. 10 to shape on a potter's wheel. 11 to move so as to operate (a lever etc.). 12 (*coll.*) to hold (a party). 13 (*coll.*) to puzzle or astonish. 14 (*sl.*) to lose (a contest) deliberately. 15 in cricket, to bowl illegally with a straightening of the arm. ~*v.i.* 1 to hurl or fling a missile (at etc.). 2 to cast dice. ~*n.* 1 the act of throwing. 2 a cast of the dice. 3 the distance to which a missile is thrown. 4 the extent of motion (of a crank etc.). 5 a device for giving rapid rotation to a machine. 6 (*Geol.*) a a faulting, a dislocation. b the extent of dislocation. 7 (*N Am.*) a throw rug. **to be thrown away (on)** to be wasted (on). **to be thrown back on** to be forced to resort to or rely on. **to throw about** 1 to throw carelessly in various directions. 2 to spend (money) recklessly or ostentatiously. **to throw around** to throw about. **to throw away** 1 to cast from one, to discard. 2 to reject carelessly. 3 to spend recklessly, to squander. 4 to lose through carelessness or neglect. 5 to fail to take advantage of. 6 to say in a deliberately unemphatic way. **to throw away the baby with the bathwater** BABY. **to throw back** 1 to reflect, as light etc. 2 to revert (to ancestral traits). **to throw cold water on** COLD. **to throw dirt at** DIRT. **to throw down** 1 to overturn. 2 to lay (oneself) down prostrate. **to throw down the gauntlet** GAUNTLET[1]. **to throw down the glove** GLOVE. **to throw dust in someone's eyes** DUST. **to throw good money after bad** to waste further money in a futile attempt to rectify a bad situation that has already cost money. **to throw in** 1 to interject, to interpolate. 2 to put in without extra charge, to add as a contribution or extra. 3 in soccer, to restart play by throwing the ball two-handed from the place at which it went out. 4 in cricket etc., to throw (the ball) from the outfield. 5 in cards, to give the lead to to that player's detriment. **to throw in one's lot with** LOT. **to throw in the sponge** SPONGE. **to throw in the towel** TOWEL. **to throw into the scale** SCALE[2]. **to throw light on** LIGHT[1]. **to throw off** 1 to cast off, to get rid of, to abandon, to discard. 2 to produce without effort. 3 to evade (pursuit). 4 to begin hunting. **to throw one's cap over the windmill** WINDMILL (under WIND[1]). **to throw oneself at** to make a determined and blatant attempt to make (someone) become a sexual partner or spouse. **to throw oneself into** to take up (an activity) with enthusiasm and energy. **to throw oneself on/ upon** to commit oneself to the protection, favour etc. of. **to throw one's hand in** 1 to stop participating in a particular hand of a gambling card game. 2 to give up a job etc. as hopeless. **to throw one's hat into the ring** HAT. **to throw one's weight about/ around** WEIGHT. **to throw open** 1 to open suddenly and completely. 2 to make freely accessible. 3 to open (a discussion etc.) to the audience. **to throw out** 1 to cast out, to reject, to expel. 2 to emit. 3 to give utterance to, to suggest. 4 to cause (a building etc.) to stand out or project. 5 to confuse. 6 in cricket, baseball etc., to run (someone) out by throwing the ball directly at the stumps, base etc. 7 to discomfit so as to lose the thread of argument etc. **to throw out the baby with the bathwater** BABY. **to throw over** to abandon, to desert. **to throw someone off the scent** SCENT. **to throw stones** to criticize, to cast aspersions. **to throw together** 1 to put together hurriedly or carelessly. 2 to bring into casual contact. **to throw to the wolves** WOLF. **to throw up** 1 to raise, erect or lift quickly. 2 to abandon, to resign from. 3 (*coll.*) to vomit. 4 to draw attention to. **to throw up the cards** CARD[1]. **to throw up the sponge** SPONGE. **throwable** *a.* **throwaway** *a.* 1 disposable. 2 (of something written or said) deliberately casual (*a throwaway line*). ~*n.* a disposable item. **throwback** *n.* a reversion to an earlier type. **thrower** *n.* **throw-in** *n.* in soccer, an act of throwing in the ball back in play from touch to restart play. **throwing** *n.* the operation of shaping clay on a potter's wheel. **throw-off** *n.* the start (of a race etc.). **throw-over** *a.* able to be thrown over a bed, sofa etc. as a decorative cover. **throw rug** *n.* (*N Am.*) a rug or decorative cloth put over a piece of furniture. **throwster** (-stə) *n.* a person who throws silk. [OE *thrāwan*, to twist, to hurl, cp. G *drehen*, Dut. *draaien*, to twist, to twirl]

Usage note See notes under THROE, THROUGH.

thru THROUGH.

thrum[1] (thrŭm) *v.i.* (*pres.p.* **thrumming,** *past, p.p.* **thrummed)** 1 to play carelessly or unskilfully (on a stringed instrument). 2 to tap, to drum monotonously (on a table etc.). ~*v.t.* 1 to play (an instrument) in this way. 2 to tap or drum on. ~*n.* the act or sound of such drumming or playing. [Icel. *thruma*, to rattle, to thunder, cogn. with DRUM[1]]

thrum[2] (thrŭm) *n.* 1 the fringe of warp threads left when the web has been cut off, or one of such threads. 2 a loose thread, fringe etc., a tassel. 3 (*pl.*) coarse or waste yarn. ~*v.t.* (*pres.p.* **thrumming,** *past, p.p.* **thrummed)** to cover or trim with thrums. **thrummer** *n.* **thrummy** *a.* [OE *tungethrum*, cp. Icel. *thrömr*, edge, Dut. *dreum*, G *Trumm*]

thrush[1] (thrŭsh) *n.* a bird of the family Turdidae, esp. the song thrush, *Turdus philomelos* or mistle thrush, *T. viscivorus.* [OE *thrysce*, cp. G *Drossel*, OHG *droscel*, also THROSTLE]

thrush[2] (thrŭsh) *n.* 1 a disease of the mouth and throat, usu. affecting children, caused by the fungus *Candida albicans* and resulting in white patches. 2 a similar infection of the vagina, caused by the same fungus. 3 an inflammatory affection of the frog in the feet of horses. [cp. Dan. *tröske*, Swed. *törsk*, also Norw. *frosk*, prob. ident. with *frosk*, frog]

thrust (thrŭst) *v.t.* (*past, p.p.* **thrust**) 1 to push suddenly or forcibly, to stab. 2 to impose forcibly (on). 3 to force (one's way). ~*v.i.* 1 to make a sudden push or lunge (at), to stab (at). 2 to force or squeeze (in etc.). ~*n.* 1 a sudden or violent push or lunge. 2 an attack as with a pointed weapon, a stab. 3 a pointed remark. 4 force exerted by one body against another, esp. horizontal outward pressure, as of an arch against its abutments. 5 the forceful part, or gist, of an argument etc. 6 (*Geol.*) a thrust fault. **to thrust oneself in** 1 to intrude. 2 to interfere. **to thrust one's nose in** to interfere. **to thrust something down someone's throat** to ram something down someone's throat. **to thrust through** to pierce. **thrust bearing** *n.* a low-friction bearing on a rotating shaft designed to take a load exerted in the direction of the shaft's axis. **thrust block** *n.* a casting or frame holding the bearings which come into contact with the rotating collars of a propeller shaft. **thruster** *n.* 1 a person who or thing which thrusts. 2 a small rocket engine used to correct altitude, course etc. on a spacecraft. **thrust fault** *n.* (*Geol.*) a fault of low angle in which older strata have been pushed horizontally over newer strata. **thrusting** *a.* aggressively ambitious. **thrust stage** *n.* in a theatre, a stage extending beyond the proscenium arch into the auditorium. [ME *thrusten, thrysten*, Icel. *thrysta*, perh. cogn. with L *trūdere*]

thruway THROUGHWAY (under THROUGH).

thud (thŭd) *n.* a dull sound as of a blow on something soft. ~*v.i.* (*pres.p.* **thudding,** *past, p.p.* **thudded**) 1 to make a thud. 2 to fall with a thud. **thuddingly** *adv.* [cp. OE *thyddan*, to strike, to thrust]

thug (thŭg) *n.* 1 a violent or brutal ruffian. 2 (**Thug**) a member of a fraternity of religious assassins in India (suppressed 1828–35). **thuggee** (-ē), **thuggism** *n.* (*Hist.*) the murderous methods and practices of the Thugs. **thuggery** *n.* brutal behaviour. **thuggish** *a.* **thuggishly** *adv.* **thuggishness** *n.* [Hind. *thag, thug*]

thuja (thū´jə), **thuya** (-yə) *n.* any coniferous tree or shrub of the genus *Thuja*, also called *arbor vitae*. [Gr. *thuia*]

thulium (thū´liəm) *n.* a rare silver-grey malleable metallic element, at. no. 69, chem. symbol Tm. **thulite** (-līt) *n.* a rose-red variety of zoisite. [L, from Gr. *Thoulē*, the northernmost land]

thumb (thŭm) *n.* 1 the short thick digit of the human hand. 2 the corresponding digit in animals. 3 the part of a glove which covers the thumb. ~*v.t.* 1 to turn (the pages of a book) with the thumb. 2 to handle, perform or play awkwardly. 3 to soil or mark with the thumb. ~*v.i.* to thrum. **one's fingers all thumbs** fumbling, clumsily. **rule of thumb** RULE. **to be all thumbs** to be clumsy and fumbling with one's hands. **to thumb a lift** to get a lift from a passing car by signalling with a raised thumb. **to thumb one's nose** to cock a snook. **under someone's thumb** completely under someone's power or influence. **thumbed** *a.* **thumb index** *n.* an index in a book in which the letters are printed on the fore-edge, spaces being cut away from preceding pages to expose them to sight. **thumb-index** *v.t.* **thumb-indexed** *a.* **thumb latch** *n.* a latch with a broad-ended lever for pressing down with the thumb. **thumbless** *a.* **thumbmark** *n.* a mark made with a (dirty) thumb. **thumbnail** *n.* the nail of one's thumb. **thumbnail sketch** *n.* a brief, vivid description. **thumb nut** *n.* a nut with wings for screwing up with the thumb, a wing nut. **thumbprint** *n.* the impression left by the markings of a person's thumb. **thumbscrew** *n.* 1 an instrument of torture for compressing the thumb. 2 a screw adapted to be turned with the finger and thumb. **thumbs down** *n.* an indication of failure or disapproval. **thumbstall** *n.* a case, sheath, or covering for an injured or sore thumb. **thumbs up** *n.* an indication of success or approval. **thumbtack** *n.* (*N Am.*) a drawing pin. [OE *thūma* (cp. Dut. *duim*, G *Daumen*, Swed. *tumme*), cogn. with TUMID]

thump (thŭmp) *v.t.* 1 to strike with something giving a dull sound, esp. with the fist. 2 to hammer out (a tune) on a piano etc. ~*v.i.* 1 to beat, to knock, to hammer (on, at etc.). 2 to throb or pulsate violently. ~*n.* 1 a blow giving a dull sound. 2 the sound of this. **thumper** *n.* 1 a person who or thing which thumps. 2 (*coll.*) anything very large, excellent or remarkable. **thumping** *a.* (*coll.*) very large. [imit.]

thunder (thŭn´də) *n.* 1 the sound following a flash of lightning, due to the disturbance of the air by the electric discharge. 2 a thunderbolt. 3 a loud noise resembling atmospheric thunder. 4 a vehement denunciation or threat. ~*v.i.* 1 (*impers.*) to produce thunder. 2 to make the noise of thunder. 3 to make a loud noise. 4 to make loud denunciations etc. ~*v.t.* to emit or utter as with the sound of thunder. **to steal someone's thunder** STEAL. **thunderbird** *n.* a legendary bird that is said to bring rain and storms according to N American Indian folklore. **thunderbolt** *n.* 1 an electric discharge with lightning and thunder. 2 an irresistible force, hero, a daring denunciation etc. 3 a supposed missile or mass of heated matter formerly believed to be discharged in a thunderbolt. **thunderbox** *n.* (*coll.*) a lavatory. **thunderclap, thundercrack, thunderpeal** *n.* 1 the noise of a single instance of thunder. 2 something alarming and unexpected. **thundercloud** *n.* a cloud from which lightning and thunder are produced. **thunderer** *n.* 1 a person who or thing which thunders. 2 (*facet., dated*) *The Times* newspaper. **thunderflash** *n.* a blank shell, cartridge etc. which when fired makes a flash and a loud noise, used in military exercises. **thunderfly** *n.* (*pl.* **thunderflies**) a thrips. **thunderhead** *n.* an anvil-shaped cumulonimbus cloud indicative of thunder. **thundering** *a.* 1 producing thunder or a loud sound like thunder. 2 (*sl.*) extreme, remarkable, tremendous, out-and-out. ~*adv.* unusually, remarkably, tremendously. **thunderingly** *adv.* **thunderless** *a.* **thunderous** *a.* 1 very loud. 2 angry, threatening. **thunderously** *adv.* **thunderousness** *n.* **thundershower, thunderstorm** *n.* a storm with thunder. **thunderstruck** *a.* 1 amazed, astounded. 2 struck by lightning. **thundery** *a.* characterized by or giving a warning of thunder. [OE *thunor* (cp. Dut. *donder*, G *Donner*, Icel. *thōrr*), whence *thunrian*, cogn. with L *tonāre*, to thunder, Gr. *stenein*, to groan]

thunk[1] (thŭngk) *n.* (*coll.*) a thud. ~*v.i.* to thud.

thunk[2] THINK.

Thur. *abbr.* Thursday.

thurible (thū´ribəl) *n.* a censer. **thurifer** (-fə) *n.* an acolyte who carries a censer. **thuriferous** (-rif´-) *a.* producing frankincense. **thurification** (-fikā´shən) *n.* the act of burning incense. [L *thūribulum*, from *thūs, thūris*, frankincense, Gr. *thuos*, from *thuein*, to sacrifice]

Thurs. *abbr.* Thursday.

Thursday (thoez´dā, -di) *n.* the fifth day of the week, following Wednesday. ~*adv.* (*coll.*) on Thursday. **Thursdays** *adv.* (*coll.*) on Thursday, every Thursday. [OE *Thūres* (*Thunres*) *dæg*, Icel. *thōrs-dagr*, Thor's day, after *dies Jovis*, Jupiter's day]

thus (dhŭs) *adv.* 1 in this manner. 2 in the way indicated or about to be indicated. 3 accordingly. 4 to this extent. [OE, cp. OFris. and OS *thus*, Dut. *dus*, prob. cogn. with THAT]

thuya THUJA.

thwack (thwak) *v.t.* to hit with a loud heavy blow, esp. with something flat. ~*n.* this blow or its sound.

thwaite (thwāt) *n.* (*dial.*) a piece of ground reclaimed and converted to cultivation. [Icel. *thveit*, paddock, a piece cut off, cogn. with OE *thwitan*, to WHITTLE]

thwart (thwawt) *v.t.* to cross, to frustrate. ~*n.* a transverse plank in a boat serving as seat for a rower. ~†*prep., adv.* across, athwart. ~†*a.* transverse, oblique. **thwarter** *n.* **thwartingly** *adv.* [ME, from Icel. *thvert*, cp. OE *thwerh, thweorh*, perverse]

†**thy** (dhī) *a.* of or relating to you (*thy goodness and mercy*). †**thyself** *pron.* 1 emphatic form of THOU[1]. 2 reflexive form of THEE. [OE *thin*, gen. of *thū*, THOU[1] (cp. Icel. *thinn*, Dan. and Swed. *din*, G *dein*)]

thylacine (thī´ləsēn, -sīn, -sin) *n.* a carnivorous marsupial of Tasmania, *Thylacinus cynocephalus*, perhaps extinct. [F (Gr. *thulakos*, pouch)]

thyme (tīm) *n.* any plant of the genus *Thymus*, esp. the garden thyme, *T. vulgaris*, a pungent aromatic herb used in cookery. **thymy** (-i) *a.* [OF *tym* (F *thym*), L *thymum*, nom. *-us*, Gr. *thumos*]

Usage note The name of the plant should not be spelt *time*.

thymi THYMUS.

thymine (thī´mēn) *n.* one of the bases in DNA and RNA, containing nitrogen. [THYMUS, -INE]

thymol (thī´mol) *n.* a phenol obtained from oil of thyme, used as an antiseptic.

thymus (thī´məs) *n.* (*pl.* **thymi** (-mī)) a gland situated in the lower region of the neck, usu. degenerating after puberty. **thymus gland** *n.* [Gr. *thumos*]

thyreo- THYRO- (under THYROID).

thyristor (thīris´tə) *n.* (*Physics*) a semiconductor rectifier in which the flow of current between the anode and the cathode is initiated by a signal applied to a third electrode, the gate. [Gr. *thura*, gate, TRANSISTOR]

thyroid (thī´roid) *n.* 1 the thyroid gland. 2 the thyroid cartilage. 3 a thyroid artery. ~*a.* 1 shield-shaped. 2 of or connected with the thyroid gland or cartilages. 3 (*Zool.*) having a shield-shaped marking. 4 (*Bot.*) peltate. **thyro-** (-rō), **thyreo-** (-riō) *comb. form* **thyroid cartilage** *n.* (*Anat.*) a large cartilage in the larynx, the Adam's apple. **thyroid extract** *n.* an extract prepared from the thyroid glands of oxen, sheep and pigs, and used therapeutically. **thyroid gland, thyroid body** *n.* a large ductless gland consisting of two lobes situated on each side of the larynx and the upper part of the windpipe, which regulates metabolism and hence growth and development. **thyroxine** (thīrok´sēn), **thyroxin** *n.* the main hormone produced by the thyroid gland, an amino acid containing iodine. [Gr. *thureoeidēs* (*thureos*, shield, from *thura*, door, -OID)]

thyrsus (thœ´səs) *n.* (*pl.* **thyrsi** (-sī)) 1 (*Hist.*) in ancient Greece and Rome, a spear or shaft wrapped with ivy or vine branches and tipped with a fir cone, an attribute of Bacchus. 2 (*Bot.*) an inflorescence consisting of a panicle with the longest branches in the middle. **thyrse** *n.* **thyrsoid** (-soid) *a.* [L, from Gr. *thursos*]

thysanuran (thisənū´rən) *a.* belonging to the Thysanura, a division of wingless insects comprising the springtails. ~*n.* one of these insects. **thysanurous** *a.* [Gr. *thusanos*, tassel, *oura*, tail]

thyself THY.

Ti *chem. symbol* titanium.

ti[1] (tē) *n.* (*pl.* **tis**) a cabbage tree. [Polynesian]

ti[2] TE.

TIA *abbr.* (*Med.*) transient ischaemic attack.

tiara (tiah´rə) *n.* 1 a jewelled coronet or headband worn as an ornament by women. 2 the headdress of the ancient Persian kings, resembling a lofty turban. 3 the triple crown worn by the Pope as a symbol of his temporal, spiritual, and purgatorial power. 4 the papal dignity. **tiaraed** *a.* [L and Gr., prob. from Pers.]

Tibetan (tibet´ən) *a.* of or relating to the country of Tibet or its language. ~*n.* 1 a native or inhabitant of Tibet. 2 the language of Tibet. [*Tibet*, in Central Asia]

tibia (tib´iə) *n.* (*pl.* **tibiae** (-biē), **tibias**) 1 (*Anat.*) the shin bone, the anterior and inner of the two bones of the leg. 2 (*Zool.*) the fourth joint of the leg in an insect. 3 (*Zool.*) the tibiotarsus of a bird. 4 (*Hist.*) a pipe or flute. **tibial** *a.* **tibio-** *comb. form* **tibiotarsus** (-tah´səs) *n.* (*pl.* **tibiotarsi** (-sī)) (*Zool.*) in a bird, the bone that corresponds to the tibia. [L.]

tic (tik) *n.* a habitual convulsive twitching of muscles, esp. of the face. **tic douloureux** (doolərœ´, dooləroo´) *n.* trigeminal neuralgia characterized by spasmodic twitching. [F, prob. from Gmc.]

tich TITCH.

tick[1] (tik) *v.i.* 1 to make a small regularly recurring sound like that of a watch or clock. 2 to function, to operate. ~*v.t.* to mark (off) with a tick. ~*n.* 1 the sound made by a going watch or clock. 2 (*coll.*) a moment. 3 a small mark used in checking items and indicating correctness. **in two ticks** (*coll.*) in a very short time. **to tick off** 1 to mark off (a series) by ticks. 2 (*coll.*) to reprimand, to tell off. **to tick over** 1 (of an engine) to run slowly with gear disconnected. 2 to operate smoothly, at a low level of activity. **what makes a person tick** (*coll.*) a person's main motivation or interest. **ticker** *n.* (*coll.*) 1 the heart. 2 a watch. 3 (*N Am.*) a tape machine printing up-to-date information on Stock Exchange prices. **ticker tape** *n.* 1 the long strip of material from a ticker machine. 2 similar material thrown from city windows during a procession etc. **tickless** *a.* **tick-tack, tic-tac** *n.* 1 a code of signalling employed by bookmakers at race meetings whereby their agents can keep them informed of the betting odds. 2 a recurring, pulsating sound. **tick-tack-toe** *n.* (*N Am.*) noughts and crosses. **tick-tock** (-tok) *n.* the noise of a clock ticking. [ME *tek*, a light touch, prob. imit., cp. Dut. *tik, tikken*, Norw. *tikka*]

tick[2] (tik) *n.* 1 any of various parasitic arachnids of the order Acarina, infesting some animals and occasionally humans. 2 any of various insects of the family Hippoboscidae, infesting sheep and birds. 3 (*sl., dated*) an unpleasant or despicable person. **tick-bird** *n.* the oxpecker. **tick fever** *n.* a disease transmitted by ticks. [OE *ticia*, cp. MDut. *teke*, G *Zecke*]

tick[3] (tik) *n.* (*coll.*) credit, trust. ~*v.i.* to give credit. **on tick** bought on credit, hire purchase etc. [shortened from TICKET]

tick[4] (tik) *n.* 1 a cover or case for the filling of mattresses and beds. 2 ticking. **ticking** *n.* the material for this, usu. strong striped cotton or linen cloth. [formerly *teke*, L *thēca*]

ticket (tik´it) *n.* 1 a card or paper with written or printed contents entitling the holder to admission to a concert etc., conveyance by train etc., or other privilege. 2 a tag or label giving the price etc. of a thing it is attached to. 3 a receipt for something to be collected later. 4 (*coll.*) a parking ticket. 5 (*coll.*) the correct thing. 6 (*coll.*) a certificate of discharge from the Army. 7 (*Naut.*) a master's certificate. 8 (*coll.*) a pilot's certificate. 9 (*N Am.*) **a** the list of candidates put up by a party. **b** the principles or programme of a party. 10 (*sl.*) a visiting card. ~*v.t.* (*3rd pers. sing. pres.* **tickets**, *pres.p.* **ticketing**, *past, p.p.* **ticketed**) to put a ticket on. **(just) the ticket** (*coll.*) the right, desirable or appropriate thing. **to have tickets on oneself** (*Austral.*) to be conceited. **ticket collector** *n.* a person employed to collect tickets from rail passengers etc. **ticket-day** *n.* the day before settling day on the Stock Exchange when the brokers learn the amount of stocks and shares that are passing between them and are due for settlement, and the names of the actual purchasers. **ticketed** *a.* **ticket-holder** *n.* a person with a valid ticket for a match, concert, journey etc. **ticketless** *a.* **ticket office** *n.* an office where tickets for travel, entertainment etc. are sold. **ticket of leave** *n.* (*Hist.*) a licence to a prisoner to be at large under certain restrictions before the expiration of the sentence. **ticket-of-leave man** *n.* a person holding a ticket of leave. **ticket-punch** *n.* a punch for cancelling or marking tickets. **ticket tout** *n.* a person who offers scarce tickets for unauthorized resale at inflated prices, esp. outside the venue concerned. **ticket-writer** *n.* an expert in lettering cards for window displays. [ME *etiquet*, OF *etiquet*, *estiquette*, ticket, bill, from G *stecken*, to STICK[1]]

tickety-boo (tikətiboo´) *a.* (*coll.*) satisfactory, all right, fine. [etym. unknown]

ticking TICK[4].

tickle (tik´əl) *v.t.* **1** to touch lightly so as to cause a thrilling sensation usually producing laughter. **2** to please, to gratify, to amuse. **3** to rub (a trout etc.) so that it backs into the hand and can be caught. ~*v.i.* **1** to feel the sensation of tickling. **2** to produce the sensation of tickling. ~*n.* the act or sensation of tickling. ~*a.* (*coll.*) ticklish, uncertain. **to tickle someone's fancy** FANCY. **tickled pink, tickled to death** *a.* (*coll.*) very amused, very pleased. **tickler** *n.* **1** a person who or thing which tickles. **2** something difficult to deal with. **ticklish** *a.* **1** sensitive to the feeling of tickling. **2** difficult, critical, precarious, needing tact or caution. **ticklishly** *adv.* **ticklishness** *n.* [ME *tikelen*, freq. of TICK[1]]

tick-tack, tick-tock etc. TICK[1].

tidal TIDE.

tidbit TITBIT.

tiddledywink TIDDLYWINK.

tiddler (tid´lə) *n.* (*coll.*) **1** a stickleback or other very small fish. **2** anything very small. **tiddling** *a.* tiddly. **tiddly**[1] *a.* (*comp.* **tiddlier,** *superl.* **tiddliest**) very small or insignificant. [corr. of *tittlebat*, from STICKLEBACK]

tiddly[1] TIDDLER.

tiddly[2] (tid´li) *a.* (*comp.* **tiddlier,** *superl.* **tiddliest**) (*coll.*) slightly drunk, drunk. ~*n.* (*pl.* **tiddlies**) an intoxicating drink. [etym. unknown]

tiddlywink (tid´liwingk), (*N Am.*) **tiddledywink** (tid´əldi-) *n.* **1** a small counter or disc flicked into a cup or tray with another. **2** (*pl.*) the game involving flicking such counters. [etym. uncertain]

tide (tīd) *n.* **1** the alternative rise and fall of the sea, due to the attraction of the sun and moon. **2** a rush of water, a flood, a torrent, a stream. **3** the course or tendency of events. **4** time, season, hour. **5** a regular period of time (for a day's work etc.). ~*v.i.* (*Naut.*) (of a ship) to work in or out of a river or harbour by the help of the tide. **to save the tide** SAVE. **to tide over** (to help) to surmount difficulties in a small way or temporarily. **to work double tides** to work twice as hard or twice as long as usual. **tidal** *a.* **1** of or relating to the tides. **2** periodically rising and falling or ebbing and flowing, as the tides. **tidal basin, tidal dock, tidal harbour** *n.* one in which the level of the water rises or falls with the tide. **tidal bore** *n.* a large wave caused by water from a spring tide entering a constricted and shallower stretch of a river. **tidal flow** *n.* the regulated movement of traffic along the central lanes of a road in differing directions according to the time of the day. **tidally** *adv.* **tidal river** *n.* a river in which the tides act a long way inland. **tidal wave** *n.* **1** a large wave due to an earthquake etc. **2** a great movement of popular feeling. **3** a wave following the sun and moon from east to west and causing the tides. **tide-gauge** *n.* an instrument registering the rise and fall of the tide. **tideland** *n.* (*N Am.*) land that is submerged at high tide. **tideless** *a.* **tideline** *n.* the farthest extent of the tide's ingress, often defined by a line of driftwood, seaweed etc. on the shore. **tidemark** *n.* **1** a line along a shore showing the highest level of the tide. **2** (*coll.*) a dirty line round a bath indicating the level of the bath water. **3** (*coll.*) a line on the body showing the limit of washing. **tide-rip** *n.* **1** rough water occurring esp. where opposing tides meet. **2** a patch of rough water caused by this. **tide table** *n.* a table of times of high and low tides in a place. **tide-waiter** *n.* (*Hist.*) a customs officer who boarded ships entering port in order to enforce customs regulations. **tidewater** *n.* **1** water affected by the movement of the tide. **2** (*N Am.*) low-lying coastal land. **tidewave** *n.* the global undulation of water that causes high and low tides. **tideway** *n.* **1** the channel in which the tide runs. **2** the ebb or flow of the tide in this. [OE *tīd*, time, hour, cp. Dut. *tijd*, G *Zeit*, Icel. *tīth*, Dan. and Swed. *tid*]

tidings (tī´dingz) *n.pl.* (*poet.*) news, intelligence, a report. [ME *tidinde*, Icel. *tīthindi*, cp. OE *tiding*, as TIDE]

tidy (tī´di) *a.* (*comp.* **tidier,** *superl.* **tidiest**) **1** in good order, neat, trim. **2** (*coll.*) considerable, pretty large (*a tidy sum*). ~*n.* (*pl.* **tidies**) **1** a receptacle for odds and ends. **2** an act of tidying a room etc. **3** (*N Am.*) an ornamental covering for a chair-back etc. ~*v.t.* (*3rd pers. sing. pres.* **tidies,** *pres.p.* **tidying,** *past, p.p.* **tidied**) to make tidy, to put in order, to clear (up). **tidily** *adv.* **tidiness** *n.* [orig. seasonable, TIDE, -Y[1]]

tie (tī) *v.t.* (*3rd pers. sing. pres.* **ties,** *pres.p.* **tying,** *past, p.p.* **tied**) **1** to fasten with a cord etc., to secure, to attach, to bind. **2** to arrange together and draw into a knot, bow etc. **3** to form (a knot, bow etc.) by securing cords etc. together. **4** to bind together, to unite. **5** to confine, to restrict, to bind (down etc.). **6** (*Mus.*) **a** to unite (notes) by a tie. **b** to perform as a single note. ~*v.i.* to be exactly equal (with) in a score. ~*n.* **1** something used to tie things together. **2** a necktie. **3** a bond, an obligation. **4** a beam or rod holding parts of a structure together. **5** (*Mus.*) a curved line placed over two or more notes to be played as one. **6** an equality of votes, score etc., among candidates, competitors etc. **7** a match between any pair of a number of players or teams. **8** (*N Am.*) a railway sleeper. **9** (*N Am.*) a lace-up shoe. **fit to be tied** (*coll.*) very angry. **tied to the apron-strings** APRON. **to tie in 1** to agree or coordinate (with). **2** to be associated or linked (with). **to tie someone's hands** HAND. **to tie up 1** to fasten securely to a post etc. **2** to restrict, to bind by restrictive conditions. **3** to be compatible or coordinated (with). **4** to keep occupied to the exclusion of other activities. **tie-back** *n.* a strip of fabric, cord etc. holding a curtain at the side of a window. **tie-beam** *n.* a horizontal beam connecting rafters. **tie-break, tie breaker** *n.* a contest to decide the winner after a tied game etc. **tie-clip** *n.* a clasp which holds a necktie against a shirt. **tied** *a.* **1** (of a public house) bound to obtain its supplies from one brewer etc. **2** (of a dwelling house) owned by an employer and rented to a current employee. **3** (of a game etc.) ending with an equal score on each side. **tie-dye, tie and dye** *n.* a method of dyeing in which parts of the fabric are knotted or tied tightly to avoid being coloured. ~*v.t.* to dye by this process. **tie-dyed** *a.* **tie-in** *n.* **1** a connection. **2** something linked to something else, esp. a book to a film. **tie line** *n.* a telephone line between parts of a system, esp. a line between private exchanges. **tiepin** *n.* a pin for holding a necktie in place. **tie-up** *n.* **1** a link or connection. **2** (*N Am.*) a deadlock, a standstill, esp. in business or industry, through a strike etc. [ME *tigen*, OE *tīegan*, from *tēag*, *tēah*, bond, rope etc., from *tēon*, to pull (cp. Icel. *tang*, tie)]

tier (tiə) *n.* **1** a row, a rank, esp. one of several rows placed one above another. **2** (*Naut.*) a length of coiled cable; a place for this. ~*v.t.* to pile in tiers. **tiered** *a.* [OF *tire*, prob. from Gmc.]

tierce (tiəs) *n.* **1** in fencing, the third position for guard, parry or thrust. **2** (*Mus.*) a third. **3** the canonical office for the third hour. **4** a sequence of three cards of the same suit. **5** (*Hist.*) a wine cask of 42 gallons (about 191 l), or one-third of a pipe. **tierced** *a.* (*Her.*) (of a field) divided into three parts of different tinctures. [F *tiers*, fem. *tierce*, L *tertius*, third]

tiercel (tiə´səl), **tercel** *n.* a male falcon. [OF, dim of *tiers*, TIERCE]

tiercet TERCET.

tiff (tif) *n.* **1** a slight quarrel. **2** a fit of peevishness. ~*v.t.* †to sip, to drink. ~*v.i.* to be in a tiff. [cp. Norw. *tev*, a sniff, a scent, Icel. *thefa*, to sniff]

tiffany (tif´əni) *n.* (*pl.* **tiffanies**) a kind of thin silklike gauze. [OF *tiffanie*, THEOPHANY (orig. a Twelfth Night dress)]

tiffin (tif´in) *n.* (*Hist.*) a lunch or light repast between breakfast and dinner, formerly taken by the British in India. ~*v.i.* (*pres.p.* **tiffining**, *past, p.p.* **tiffined**) to take this. [etym. uncertain]

tig (tig) *v.t.* (*pres.p.* **tigging**, *past, p.p.* **tigged**) to touch in the game of tag. ~*n.* the children's game of tag. [perh. var. of TICK[4]]

tiger (tī´gə) *n.* **1** a large Asian carnivorous feline mammal, *Panthera tigris*, tawny with black stripes. **2** any of various other large feline animals such as the American tiger or jaguar, the red tiger or cougar etc. **3** a fierce, relentless, very energetic and forceful or cruel person. **4** (*coll.*) a swaggering ruffian, a bully. **5** (*Hist.*) †a liveried groom attending a person in a light vehicle. **tiger beetle** *n.* a predatory beetle of the family Cicindelidae, with striped or spotted wing-cases. **tiger-cat** *n.* **1** a wild cat of various species. **2** (*Austral.*) the dasyure. **tiger-flower** *n.* a plant of the genus *Tigridia* spotted with orange and yellow. **tigerish** *a.* **tigerishly** *adv.* **tiger lily** *n.* a lily, *Lilium tigrinum*, with orange-spotted flowers. **tiger moth** *n.* any moth of the family Arctiidae, with streaked hairy wings. **tiger's-eye, tiger-eye** *n.* a semi-precious variety of quartz with brilliant chatoyant lustre. **tiger shark** *n.* a striped or spotted shark, esp. *Galeocerdo cuvieri* or *Stegosoma tigrinum*. **tiger-wood** *n.* a black-striped wood used for cabinetmaking. **tigress** (-gris) *n.* **1** a female tiger. **2** a fierce or forceful woman. **tigrine** (-grīn) *a.* [ME and OF *tigre*, L and Gr. *tigris*, perh. from OPers. *tighri*, arrow, in alln. to its swiftness]

tight (tīt) *a.* (*comp.* **tighter**, *superl.* **tightest**) **1** drawn, fastened, held, or fitting closely. **2** compactly built or put together, not leaky. **3** impervious, impermeable (*often in comb.* as *water-tight*). **4** tense, stretched to the full, taut. **5** involving great pressure. **6** (*coll.*) mean, parsimonious, tight-fisted. **7** under strict control. **8** demanding effort, stringent. **9** (of money etc.) not easily obtainable. **10** (*coll.*) awkward, difficult. **11** (*sl.*) drunk. **12** neat, trim, compact. ~*adv.* tightly. **tight corner, tight spot, tight place** *n.* a difficult situation with little scope for manoeuvre. **tighten** *v.t., v.i.* to make or become tight or tighter. **to tighten one's belt** BELT. **tightener** *n.* **tight end** *n.* in American football, a player positioned at the outside of the offensive line, close to the tackle. **tight-fisted** *a.* mean, stingy. **tight-fitting** *a.* (of a garment) fitting close or too close to the body. **tight-knit, tightly-knit** *a.* tightly integrated or organized. **tight-lipped** *a.* **1** having the lips pressed tightly together, in anger etc. **2** taciturn. **tightly** *adv.* **tightness** *n.* **tightrope** *n.* a rope stretched between two points upon which an acrobat walks, dances etc. **tights** *n.pl.* a close-fitting garment made of nylon or wool etc. covering the legs and the body below the waist and worn by women, male acrobats, ballet dancers etc., also called *pair of tights*. **tightwad** *n.* (*NAm., sl.*) a mean or tight-fisted person. [ME *tigt*, Icel. *thēttr*, cp. Swed. *tät*, Dan. *tœt*, NFris. *tacht*]

tigon (tī´gən), **tiglon** (tī´glon, tig´-) *n.* the offspring of a tiger and a lioness. [*tiger, lion*]

Tigrayan (tigrā´ən), **Tigrean** *a.* of or relating to Tigray, a province of N Ethiopia. ~*n.* a native or inhabitant of Tigray.

tigress, tigrine TIGER.

tike TYKE.

tiki (tē´ki) *n.* (*pl.* **tikis**) a Maori neck ornament or figurine, a stylized representation of an ancestor etc. [Maori]

tikka (tik´ə, tē´-) *n.* an Indian dish of kebabs (esp. chicken or lamb) marinated in spices and dry-roasted in a clay oven.

tilapia (tilā´piə, -lap´-) *n.* any freshwater mouthbrooding fish of the African genus *Tilapia* or related genera. [L]

tilbury (til´bəri) *n.* (*pl.* **tilburies**) a light, two-wheeled open horse-drawn carriage. [name of a London coachbuilder]

tilde (til´də, tild) *n.* a diacritical sign (~) in Spanish put over *n* to indicate the sound *ny* as in *señor*, in Portuguese and phonetics put over vowels to indicate nasalization. [Sp., var. of *titulo*, TITLE]

tile (tīl) *n.* **1** a thin slab of baked clay, used for covering roofs, paving floors, constructing drains etc. **2** a similar slab of porcelain or other material used for ornamental paving. **3** a rectangular block used in playing games, esp. mah-jong, and Scrabble. **4** (*coll., dated*) a silk hat. ~*v.t.* **1** to cover with tiles. **2 a** in Freemasonry, to secure against intrusion by stationing the tiler at the door. **b** to bind to secrecy. **on the tiles** (*coll.*) enjoying oneself wildly, usu. drunkenly. **to have a tile loose** to be eccentric or half-crazy. **tiler** *n.* **1** a person who makes or lays tiles. **2** in Freemasonry, the doorkeeper of a lodge. **tilery** (-ləri) *n.* (*pl.* **tileries**) a place where tiles are made. **tilestone** *n.* a flat stone used for tiling, stone, esp. one from the uppermost group of the Silurian formation. **tiling** *n.* an area of tiles. [OE *tigele*, L *tēgula*, from *tegere* to cover]

tiliaceous (tiliā´shəs) *a.* of or relating to the family Tiliaceae of flowering plants and trees, related to or resembling the linden or lime tree. [L *tilia*, linden, -ACEOUS]

till[1] (til) *prep.* up to, up to the time of, until. ~*conj.* up to the time when. **till now** up to the present time. **till then** up to that time. [Icel. *til*, cp. Dan. *til*, Swed. *till*, G *Ziel*, purpose]

Usage note See note under UNTIL.

till[2] (til) *n.* **1** a money drawer in or on a counter. **2** a cash register. [earlier and dial. *tiller*, drawer, from ME *tillen*, OE *tyllan* (in *fortyllan*), to draw]

till[3] (til) *v.t.* to cultivate for crops. **tillable** *a.* **tillage** (-ij) *n.* **1** the cultivation of land for crops. **2** tilled land. **tiller[1]** *n.* [OE *tilian*, *teolian*, to labour, to strive for, to till, from *til*, good, goodness]

till[4] (til) *n.* (*Geol.*) an unstratified clay containing boulder, pebbles, sand etc., deposited by glaciers. [etym. uncertain]

tiller[1] TILL[3].

tiller[2] (til´ə) *n.* the lever on the head of a rudder by which this is turned. [ME *tillen*, see TILL[2], -ER[1]]

tiller[3] (til´ə) *n.* **1** the shoot of a plant springing from the base of the original stalk, a sucker. **2** a sapling. ~*v.i.* to grow tillers. [OE *telgor*, *tealgor*, from *telga*, cp. Dut. *telg*]

Tilley lamp® (til´i) *n.* a portable oil or paraffin lamp where the burner is supplied with fuel by air pressure. [name of manufacturer]

tilt (tilt) *v.i.* **1** to heel over, to tip, to be in a slanting position. **2** to charge with a lance, to joust, as in a tournament. **3** to compete (with). ~*v.t.* **1** to raise at one end, to cause to heel over, to tip, to incline. **2** to thrust or aim (a lance). **3** to hammer or forge with a tilt-hammer. ~*n.* **1** an inclination from the vertical, a slanting position. **2** a tilting, a tournament, a charge with the lance. **3** an attack on an opponent, a jibe. **4** a tilt-hammer. **5** a contrivance, usu. of crossed sticks, for showing a bite in angling through ice. **at full tilt** at full speed or force. **to tilt at windmills** WINDMILL (under WIND[1]). **tilter** *n.* **tilt-hammer** *n.* a large hammer on a pivoted lever, usu. worked by steam or water-power. **tilt-yard** *n.* (*Hist.*) a place where the sport of tilting took place. [ME *tilten*, from OE *tealt*, unsteady (cp. Icel. *tölta*, to amble, Norw. *tylta*, to go tiptoe, Swed. *tulta*, to waddle)]

tilth (tilth) *n.* **1** tillage, cultivation. **2** the depth or condition of soil tilled. [OE (TILL[3], -TH[1])]

Tim. *abbr.* (*Bible*) Timothy.

†**timbal** (tim´bəl), **tymbal** *n.* a kettledrum. [F *timbale*, It. *timballo*, Arab. *tabl*, drum]

timbale (tambahl´) *n.* a dish of meat or fish pounded and mixed with white of egg, cream etc., and cooked in a drum-shaped mould. [F]

timber (tim´bə) *n.* **1** wood suitable for building, carpentry etc. **2** trees yielding wood suitable for constructive purposes, trees generally. **3** a piece of wood prepared for building, esp. one of the curved pieces forming the ribs of a ship. *~v.t.* to provide or construct with timber. *~int.* used as a warning shout that a tree is about to fall. **timbered** *a.* **1** (of a building) made of or containing timber. **2** (of countryside) wooded (*usu. in comb.*, as *well-timbered*). **timber-frame** *a.* **1** built using prefabricated timber sections. **2** timber-framed. *~n.* a prefabricated timber section of a building. **timber-framed** *a.* having a timber frame. **timber-getter** *n.* (*Austral.*) a lumberjack. **timberhead** *n.* (*Naut.*) a timber rising above the deck level for use as a bollard etc. **timber hitch** *n.* a knot used for tying around a log, a spar etc. in order to haul it. **timbering** *n.* **1** the using of timber. **2** temporary timber supports for the sides of an excavation. **timberland** *n.* (*N Am.*) a forested area yielding timber. **timberline** *n.* the line or level on a mountain above which no trees grow, the tree line. **timberman** *n.* (*pl.* **timbermen**) **1** a person who works with timber. **2** any of various longhorn beetles with wood-boring larvae, esp. *Acanthocinus aedilis.* **timber wolf** *n.* (*pl.* **timber wolves**) a grey-coloured type of wolf once common in N America. **timberyard** *n.* a yard where timber is stored etc. [OE (cp. Dut. and Swed. *timmer*, G *Zimmer*, room, timber, Icel. *timbr*)]

timbre (tam´bə) *n.* the quality of tone distinguishing particular voices, instruments etc., due to the individual character of the sound waves. [F, from *tymbre*, L *tympanum*]

timbrel (tim´brəl) *n.* (*Mus.*) an ancient instrument like the tambourine. [ME dim. of *timber*, as TIMBRE]

Timbuctoo (timbŭktoo´) *n.* any distant place. [*Timbuktu*, a town in Mali, W Africa]

time (tīm) *n.* **1** the general relation of sequence or continuous or successive existence. **2** duration or continuous existence regarded as divisible into portions or periods, a particular portion of this. **3** (*sometimes in pl.*) a period characterized by certain events, persons, manners etc., an epoch, an era. **4** a portion of time allotted to one or to a specified purpose, the time available or at one's disposal. **5** the end of an allotted portion of time, as of legal drinking hours. **6** the period of an apprenticeship, of gestation, of a round at boxing etc. **7** a portion of time as characterized by circumstances, conditions of existence etc. **8** a point in time, a particular moment, instant or hour. **9** a date, a season, an occasion, an opportunity. **10** time as reckoned by conventional standards, as sidereal time, solar time etc. **11** the relation of a verb as regards past, present or future, or as regards tenses. **12** the relative duration of a note or rest. **13** rate of movement, tempo. **14** style of movement, rhythm. **15** the duration of a vowel, syllable etc., in pronunciation. **16** (*sl.*) a term of imprisonment. *~v.t.* **1** to ascertain or mark the time, duration or rate of. **2** to adapt to the time or occasion. **3** to do, begin or perform at the proper season. **4** to regulate as to time. **5** to measure, as in music. *~v.i.* to keep time (with). **against time** in a great hurry, at utmost speed in order to achieve a goal by a specified time, to a deadline. **ahead of one's time** having progressive or revolutionary ideas that it is thought would be more generally acceptable at a future time. **ahead of time** earlier than anticipated. **all the time 1** continuously. **2** throughout a given period of time. **3** at all times. **apparent time** APPARENT. **at a time** separately at any one time (referring to a specified group or number) (*two at a time*). **at one time 1** once, in the past (referring to an unspecified time). **2** simultaneously. **at times** at intervals, now and then. **before one's time** prematurely. **behind the times** BEHIND. **behind time** BEHIND. **Father Time** FATHER. **for the time being** for the present. **from time to time** FROM. **in good time 1** at the right moment. **2** early. **3** (*often iron.*) fortunately, happily. **in less than no time** very quickly. **in no time** very quickly. **in one's own good time** at a pace and time decided by oneself. **in one's own time** outside working hours. **in one's time 1** in one's prime, in one's heyday. **2** in a previous period of one's life. **in time 1** not too late, early enough. **2** in course of time, some time or other, eventually. **3** in accordance with the time, rhythm etc. **mean time** MEAN[2]. **not before time 1** at the appropriate moment. **2** later than the appropriate moment (*You're here, and not before time!*). **no time** a very short space of time. **on one's own time** (*N Am.*) in one's own time, outside working hours. **on time** punctually. **out of time 1** unseasonable. **2** too late. **3** not keeping rhythm correctly. **solar time** SOLAR. **the time of one's life** LIFE. **time after time** repeatedly. **time and again** repeatedly. **time and a half** payment at one and a half times the normal rate, usu. for working overtime, weekends etc. **time and time again** repeatedly. **time enough** soon enough. **time immemorial** time beyond legal memory, a very long time ago. **time is up** UP. **time of day 1** the hour by the clock. **2** a greeting appropriate to this. **3** (*sl.*) the latest aspect of affairs. **time out of mind 1** a longer time than anyone can remember. **2** many times. **time was** (*coll.*) there was once a time (*Time was when you could buy a loaf for a halfpenny*). **to do time** to serve a prison sentence. **to have a time of it** to have difficulty or trouble in doing something. **to have no time for 1** to dislike. **2** to be unwilling or unable to spend time on (something). **to have the time 1** to be able to spend the required time. **2** to know what the time is. **to keep bad time 1** to be habitually unpunctual. **2** (of a clock etc.) to be unreliable. **to keep good time 1** to be habitually punctual. **2** (of a clock etc.) to be reliable. **to keep time** to move, sing etc. in time with something else, esp. music. **to know the time of day** to know what is going on, to be well informed. **to lose no time** to act immediately. **to lose time 1** to delay or be delayed. **2** (of a watch) to go more slowly than required. **to make time 1** to make oneself available (for) an activity. **2** (*N Am., sl.*) to make sexual advances (to a person). **to mark time** MARK[1]. **to pass the time of day** to greet each other, to exchange casual remarks. **to take one's time** to proceed steadily and without hurry. **to take time by the forelock** FORELOCK[1]. **to waste no time** to act immediately. **time-and-motion** *a.* relating to the investigation of working methods with a view to increasing efficiency. **time-and-motion study** *n.* **time bomb** *n.* a bomb set to explode at some prearranged time. **timebook, timecard** *n.* a book specifying or recording hours of work for workers etc. **time capsule** *n.* a box containing objects typical of the period in which it was prepared, hidden, e.g. within a memorial, for later generations to examine. **time clock** *n.* **1** a clock that records the hours of workers' arrival and departure. **2** a switch activated at pre-set times by a built-in-clock. **time-consuming** *a.* (of an activity) occupying a considerable amount of one's time. **time-expired** *a.* applied to soldiers whose period of service is completed. **time**

exposure *n.* (a photograph taken by) exposure of a film for a relatively long time. **time factor** *n.* time as an element in scheduling a task etc. **time-frame** *n.* a limited period of time, e.g. as allotted for a planned activity. **time-fuse** *n.* a fuse in a bomb etc., graduated to ignite the charge at a certain time. **time-honoured,** (*N Am.*) **time-honored** *a.* of venerable age. **timekeeper** *n.* **1** a person who records time, e.g. of workers, races. **2** a clock, watch or chronometer. **3** a person considered in terms of punctuality (*a good timekeeper*). **timekeeping** *n.* **time lag** *n.* the interval that elapses between cause and result. **time-lapse photography** *n.* a method of filming a slow process by taking still photographs at regular intervals and showing them as a normal-speed film. **timeless** *a.* **1** without end, eternal, ageless. **2** not restricted to a particular period. **3** untimely, premature. **timelessly** *adv.* **timelessness** *n.* **time limit** *n.* the period within which a task must be completed. **time lock** *n.* a security device by which safes, computer programs etc. can only be operated at certain times. **time-locked** *a.* **timely** *a.* (*comp.* **timelier,** *superl.* **timeliest**) opportune, occurring at the right time. **timeliness** *n.* **time off** *n.* time away from work, for rest, recreation etc. **timeous** (tī´məs), **timous** *a.* (*Sc.*) in good time, sufficiently early. **timeously** *adv.* **time-out** *n.* **1** (*N Am.*) a short break in a game such as basketball. **2** time off. **timepiece** *n.* a clock or watch. **timer** *n.* **1** an instrument which measures or records time. **2** an instrument which operates a machine etc., at a pre-set time. **times** *prep.* multiplied by. **timescale** *n.* the time period in which something is expected or scheduled to happen expressed in broad terms. **time-served** *a.* having completed a substantial period of occupational training, such as an apprenticeship. **time-server** *n.* a person who suits their conduct, opinions and manners to those in power. **time-serving** *a., n.* **time-serving man** *n.* a soldier in the regular army. **time-sharing** *n.* **1** the purchase of the use of holiday accommodation for the same period every year. **2** simultaneous access to a computer by several users on different terminals. **timeshare** *n.* **1** a share in property under a time-sharing scheme. **2** this property. **time sheet** *n.* a sheet of paper on which hours of work are recorded. **time-shift** *n.* a rapid movement from one time to another. ~*v.t.* to move (something) in this way. **time signal** *n.* a signal issued by an observatory or broadcasting station to indicate the exact time. **time signature** *n.* an indication of time at the beginning of a piece of music. **time span** *n.* the amount of time taken up by an activity, historical period etc. **time switch** *n.* a switch with a built-in clock that operates at pre-set times. **timetable** *n.* **1** a printed list of the times of departure and arrival of trains etc. **2** a record of times of events, school lessons etc. **3** a table containing the relative value of every note in music. ~*v.t.* **1** to put (an event etc.) on a timetable. **2** to arrange in a timetable. **time travel** *n.* (in stories, films etc.) travel through time. **time trial** *n.* a race (esp. cycling, motor sports) in which competitors are timed individually rather than racing together. **time warp** *n.* **1** (in science fiction) a hypothetical distortion of space and time in which people or objects from one age can be directly transferred to another. **2** a situation where people living in one period retain the dress, mannerisms, lifestyle etc. of a past period. **time-waster** *n.* a person who wastes their own or other people's time. **time-wasting** *n.* **1** the act of wasting time. **2** in sport, the deliberate slowing down of play in order to preserve the current score. **timework** *n.* work paid for by time, as opposed to *piecework.* **timeworn** *a.* antiquated, dilapidated. **time zone** *n.* a geographical region in which the same standard time is used. **timing** *n.* **1** reckoning the time taken. **2** the choosing of the best time (to do something). **3** the precise instant at which ignition occurs in an internal-combustion engine, and at which the valves open and close. **4** the controlling mechanism for this. [OE *tīma* (cp. Icel. *tīmi*, Dan. *time*, Swed. *tīmme*)]

timid (tim´id) *a.* (*comp.* **timider,** *superl.* **timidest**) easily frightened, shy. **timidity** (-id´-), **timidness** *n.* habitual shyness or fear. **timidly** *adv.* [F *timide*, L *timīdus*, from *timēre*, to fear]

timing TIME.

timocracy (tīmok´rəsi) *n.* (*pl.* **timocracies**) a form of government in which a certain amount of property is a necessary qualification for office. **timocratic** (-krat´-) *a.* [Gr. *timokratia* (*timē*, honour, -CRACY)]

Timorese (tēməwrēz´) *n.* (*pl.* **Timorese**) a native or inhabitant of Timor. ~*a.* of or relating to Timor or its people. [*Timor*, an island of Indonesia]

timoroso (timərō´sō) *adv.* (*Mus.*) with hesitation. [It.]

timorous (tim´ərəs) *a.* fearful, timid. **timorously** *adv.* **timorousness** *n.* [med. L *timorōsus*, from L *timor*, fear, from *timēre*, to fear]

timothy (tim´əthi), **timothy grass** *n.* a valuable fodder grass, *Phleum pratense.* [*Timothy* Hanson, an American through whom it first came into use, *c.* 1720]

timous TIMEOUS (under TIME).

timpani (tim´pəni), **tympani** *n.pl.* (*Mus.*) orchestral kettledrums. **timpanist** *n.* [It., from L *tympanum*]

tin (tin) *n.* **1** a lustrous white metallic element, at. no. 50, chem. symbol Sn, easily beaten into thin plates, much used for cooking utensils etc., esp. in the form of thin plates of iron coated with tin. **2** a tin can. **3** a pot or other utensil made of tin. **4** (*sl.*) money. ~*v.t.* (*pres.p.* **tinning,** *past, p.p.* **tinned**) **1** to preserve (meat, fruit etc.) in tins. **2** to coat or overlay with tin. **to put the tin lid on** LID. **tin can** *n.* a tin plate container that can be hermetically sealed to preserve food or drink. **tinfoil** *n.* tin, tin alloy or aluminium beaten into foil for wrapping foodstuffs etc. **tin-glaze** *n.* a glaze for pottery etc. made white and opaque by the addition of tin oxide. **tin god** *n.* **1** a person of local, undeserved importance. **2** a self-important person. **tin hat** *n.* a steel shrapnel helmet. **tinhorn** *n.* (*N Am.*) a cheap, flashy, pretentious person, esp. a small-time gambler. ~*a.* flashy, pretentious. **tin lizzie** (liz´i) *n.* (*dated sl.*) an old or decrepit motor car. **tinner** *n.* a tin-miner or tinsmith. **tinny** *a.* (*comp.* **tinnier,** *superl.* **tinniest**) **1** of or like tin. **2** making a thin, metallic sound. **3** cheap, made of flimsy materials. **tinnily** *adv.* **tinniness** *n.* **tinny, tinnie** *n.* (*pl.* **tinnies**) (*Austral., sl.*) a can of beer. **tin-opener** *n.* an implement for opening airtight tins of preserved meat, fruit etc. **Tin Pan Alley** *n.* **1** the world of popular music. **2** the writers and publishers of such music. **tin plate** *n.* sheet iron or sheet steel coated with tin. **tin-plate** *v.t.* to coat with tin. **tinpot** *a.* worthless, rubbishy. **tin roof** *n.* a roof made of corrugated iron. **tinsmith** *n.* a person who makes articles of tin or tin plate. **tinsnips** *n.pl.* hand-held cutters for cutting sheet tin. **tin soldier** *n.* **1** a toy soldier made of tin or other metal. **2** (*often derog.*) a person who enjoys playing at being a soldier. **tinstone** *n.* cassiterite, the commonest form of tin ore. **tin-tack** *n.* **1** a carpet tack. **2** a tack coated with tin. **tintype** *n.* ferrotype. **tinware** *n.* vessels or utensils of tin or tin plate. **tin whistle** *n.* a penny whistle. [OE, cp. Dut., Icel. and Dan. *tin*, G *Zinn*]

tinamou (tin´əmoo) *n.* any S American quail-like game bird of the family Tinamidae. [F, from Carib]

tincal (ting´kəl) *n.* borax in the crude state. [Malay *tingkal*]

tincture (tingk´chə) *n.* **1** a slight taste or flavour, a spice (of). **2** a tinge or shade (of colour), a tint. **3** an alcoholic or other solution of some principle, usu. vegetable, used in medicine. **4** (*sl.*) a drink of spirits. **5** (*Her.*) any one of the colours, metals or furs used in emblazoning. ~*v.t.* **1** to imbue with a colour or tint, to tinge. **2** to flavour. **3** to give a flavour or tinge (of some quality etc.). †**tinct** *v.t.* to tincture, to tint. ~*n.* a stain, colour or tint. ~*a.* tinctured. **tinctorial** (-taw´ri-) *a.* **1** of or relating to colour or dyes. **2** colouring. [L *tinctūra*, from *tingere*, to TINGE, p.p. *tinctus*]

tinder (tin´də) *n.* any dry, very combustible substance used to kindle fire from a spark. **tinderbox** *n.* (*Hist.*) a box furnished with tinder, flint and steel, for this purpose. **tindery** *a.* [OE *tyndre*, from *tendan*, to kindle]

tine (tīn) *n.* the prong, point or spike of an antler, fork, harrow etc. **tined** *a.* [OE *tind*, cp. Icel. *tindr*, Swed. *tinne*, also L *dens dentis*, tooth]

tinea (tin´iə) *n.* (*Med.*) a fungal disease of the skin, athlete's foot, ringworm. [L, worm, moth]

ting (ting) *n.* a tinkling sound, as of a small bell. ~*v.i.* to make this sound. ~*v.t.* to cause to make this sound. **ting-a-ling** (-əling´) *n.* [imit.]

tinge (tinj) *v.t.* (*pres.p.* **tingeing, tinging**) **1** to colour slightly, to stain (with). **2** to modify the character or qualities of. ~*n.* **1** a slight admixture of colour, a tint. **2** a smack, flavour. [L *tingere*, cogn. with Gr. *tengein*, to wet]

tingle (ting´gəl) *v.i.* **1** to feel a stinging, prickly sensation. **2** to give this sensation. ~*v.t.* to cause to tingle. ~*n.* a tingling sensation. **tingly** *a.* (*comp.* **tinglier,** *superl.* **tingliest**). [ME *tinglen*, freq. from TING]

tinker (ting´kə) *n.* **1** an itinerant mender of pots, kettles, pans etc. **2** (*Sc., Ir.*) a gypsy. **3** (*coll.*) a mischievous or troublesome person or animal. **4** a rough-and-ready worker or repairer. **5** the act of tinkering, patching, botching. ~*v.t.* **1** to mend, alter or patch up in a rough-and-ready way, or in a clumsy, makeshift or ineffective manner. **2** to mend pots, kettles etc. ~*v.i.* **1** to work in this way (at or with). **2** to interfere, to meddle. **3** to experiment (with). **not to give a tinker's cuss/ damn** not to care at all. **tinkerer** *n.* [ME *tinkere*, from *tinken*, see TINKLE]

tinkle (ting´kəl) *v.i.* **1** to make a succession of sharp, metallic sounds as of a bell. **2** (*coll.*) to urinate. ~*v.t.* to cause to tinkle, to ring. ~*n.* **1** a tinkling sound. **2** (*coll.*) a telephone call. **3** (*coll.*) the act of urination. **tinkler** *n.* **1** a person who or thing which tinkles. **2** (*sl.*) a small bell. **tinkly** *a.* [ME *tinklen*, freq. of *tinken*, to ring, of imit. orig.]

tinner TIN.

tinnitus (tinī´təs, tin´itəs) *n.* (*Med.*) ringing in the ears. [L, from *tinnīre*, to ring]

tinny TIN.

tinsel (tin´səl) *n.* **1** brass, tin or other lustrous metallic substances in extremely into thin sheets and used in strips, discs or spangles to give a sparkling effect in decoration. **2** a fabric adorned with this. **3** a cloth composed of silk and silver. **4** superficial brilliance, gaudy display. ~*a.* gaudy, showy, superficially fine. ~*v.t.* (*pres.p.* **tinselling,** (*N Am.*) **tinseling,** *past, p.p.* **tinselled,** (*N Am.*) **tinseled**) to adorn with tinsel. **tinselled, tinselly** *a.* **Tinseltown** *n.* (*coll.*) Hollywood. [OF *estincelle* (F *étincelle*), L *scintilla*, spark]

tint (tint) *n.* **1** a variety of colour, esp. one produced by admixture with another colour, esp. white. **2** a slight tinge (of another colour). **3** a faint or pale colour spread over a surface. **4** in engraving, an effect of shading texture obtained by a closed series of parallel lines. ~*v.t.* **1** to give a tint or tints to. **2** to tinge. **tinter** *n.* **1** a person who or thing which tints. **2** an engraving tool or machine for tinting. **tintometer** (-tom´itə) *n.* a colorimeter. **tint tool** *n.* a tool for engraving parallel lines etc. [see TINCTURE]

tintinnabulation (tintinabūlā´shən) *n.* a ringing, tinkling or jingling of bells, plates etc. **tintinnabular** (-ab´-), **tintinnabulary, tintinnabulous** *a.* **tintinnabulum** (-ab´ūləm) *n.* (*pl.* **tintinnabula** (-lə)) a bell, esp. a small tinkling one for signalling, fitting to harness etc. [L, from *tintinnāre*, redupl. from *tinnīre*]

tintometer TINT.

tiny (tī´ni) *a.* (*comp.* **tinier,** *superl.* **tiniest**) very small. **tinily** *adv.* **tininess** *n.* [formerly *tine, tyne*, something small, etym. uncertain]

-tion (shən) *suf.* denoting action or condition, as in *mention, expectation, vacation.* [L *-tiōnem*, acc. sing. of nouns in *-tio*, cp. -ION]

tip[1] (tip) *n.* **1** the point, end or extremity, esp. of a small or tapering thing. **2** a small piece or part attached to anything to form a point or end, such as a ferrule or the tip of a cue. **3** a brush used in laying on gold leaf. **4** a leaf bud of tea. ~*v.t.* (*pres.p.* **tipping,** *past, p.p.* **tipped**) **1** to put a tip on. **2** to form the tip of. **on the tip of one's tongue** about to be uttered, esp. if difficult to recall. **tipless** *a.* **tip of the iceberg** *n.* the small and most obvious part of a difficulty, problem etc., that is much larger. **tippy** *a.* (of tea) having a high proportion of leaf buds. **tipstaff** *n.* **1** a metal-tipped staff carried by a sheriff's officer. **2** a sheriff's officer. **tiptoe** *v.i.* (*3rd pers. sing. pres.* **tiptoes,** *pres.p.* **tiptoeing,** *past, p.p.* **tiptoed**) to walk or stand on tiptoe. ~*adv.* on the tips of the toes. ~*n.* the tips of the toes. **on tiptoe** on the tip of the toes. **tiptop** *a.* of extremely high quality. ~*adv.* in a first-rate way. ~*n.* the highest point, the very best. **tip-topper** *n.* [ME *typ*, cp. Dut., Dan. and Swed. *tip*]

tip[2] (tip) *v.t.* (*pres.p.* **tipping,** *past, p.p.* **tipped**) **1** to cause to lean, to tilt (up, over etc.). **2** to overturn, to upset. **3** to discharge (the contents of a cart, vessel etc.) thus. **4** to strike lightly, to tap, to touch. **5** to give a small gratuity to. **6** to toss or throw lightly. **7** (*coll.*) to give private information to about a horse, an investment etc. ~*v.i.* **1** to lean over, to tilt. **2** to upset. ~*n.* **1** a small present in money, a gratuity. **2** a piece of private information, esp. for betting or investment purposes. **3** a place where rubbish is dumped. **4** a slight touch, push or hit. **to tip off 1** to give a warning hint. **2** in basketball, to start play by throwing the ball high between players of the two sides. **to tip one's hat/ cap** to touch or raise one's hat etc. in greeting, acknowledgement. **to tip (someone) the wink** (*coll.*) to give a hint, to inform furtively. **to tip the balance** to make a significant difference, perh. by something in itself insignificant. **to tip the scales** SCALE[2]. **tip-and-run** *a.* **1** relating to a variety of cricket in which the batsman must run every time the ball is hit. **2** (of a raid etc.) carried out swiftly and followed by an immediate getaway. **tipcat** *n.* **1** a game with a piece of wood pointed at both ends which is hit with a stick. **2** the tapering piece of wood. **tip-off** *n.* a piece of confidential information, warning etc., esp. given discreetly and in advance of the events concerned. **tipper** *n.* **1** someone who or something which tips. **2** a lorry or truck whose platform can be tilted towards the rear to empty out the load. **tipster** (-stə) *n.* a person who supplies tips about races etc. **tip-up** *a.* (of a (theatre) seat) able to be tilted up on a hinge or pivot. [ME *tippen* (cp. Swed. *tippa*), cogn. with TAP[2]]

tipi TEPEE.

tipper TIP[2].

tippet (tip´it) *n.* **1** (*Hist.*) a fur covering for the neck and shoulders, worn by women. **2** an ecclesiastical vestment. **3** part of the official costume of judges etc. [OE *tæppet*, L *tapēta*, Gr. *tapēs -ētos*, carpet]

Tipp-Ex® (tip´eks), **Tippex** *n.* a usu. white correction fluid. ~*v.t.* to blank out (typing, writing etc.) using correction fluid. [G *tippen*, to type, L *ex*, out]

tipple (tip´əl) *v.i.* to drink alcoholic liquors habitually. ~*v.t.* **1** to drink (alcoholic liquors) habitually. **2** to sip repeatedly. ~*n.* **1** one's favourite (alcoholic) drink. **2** strong drink. **tippler** *n.* [freq. of TIP[1], cp. Norw. *tipla*, from *tippa*, to drip, from *tipp*]

tipster TIP[2].

tipsy (tip´si) *a.* (*comp.* **tipsier,** *superl.* **tipsiest**) **1** fuddled, partially intoxicated. **2** proceeding from or inducing intoxication. **tipsily** *adv.* **tipsiness** *n.* **tipsy-cake** *n.* a sponge cake soaked in wine served with custard. [prob. rel. to TIP[1], cp. Swiss G *tipseln*, to fuddle oneself]

tiptoe, tip-top TIP[1].

tipula (tip´ūlə) *n.* any fly of the family Tipulidae, a group of dipterous insects containing the crane-flies. [L *tippula*, water-spider]

TIR *abbr.* international road transport. [F, *Transports Internationaux Routiers*]

tirade (tīrād´) *n.* **1** a long, vehement speech, declamation, or harangue, esp. of censure or reproof. **2** (*Mus.*) a diatonic run filling an interval between two notes. [F, from It. *tirata*, p.p. of *tirare*, late L *tīrāre*, to draw, to pull]

tirailleur (tērahyœ´, tirəlœ´) *n.* **1** a skirmisher. **2** a sharpshooter. [F, from *tirailler*, to skirmish, from *tirer*, to shoot]

tire[1] (tīə) *v.t.* **1** to exhaust the strength of by toil or labour, to fatigue, to weary. **2** to exhaust the patience or attention of. ~*v.i.* to become weary or exhausted. **tired** *a.* **1** fatigued. **2** bored, impatient, irritated. **3** stale, hackneyed. **tiredly** *adv.* **tiredness** *n.* **tireless** *a.* unwearied, endlessly energetic. **tirelessly** *adv.* **tirelessness** *n.* **tiresome** *a.* **1** fatiguing, tiring. **2** wearisome, tedious, annoying. **tiresomely** *adv.* **tiresomeness** *n.* **tiring** *a.* [ME *tiren*, *teorian*, OE *tyrigan*, etym. uncertain]

Usage note See note under TYRE.

tire[2] (tīə) *n.* **1** a band of iron, steel etc., placed round the rim of a wheel. **2** see TYRE. [etym. uncertain, see TYRE]

tireless, tiresome TIRE[1].

tiro TYRO.

Tirolean, Tirolese TYROLEAN.

†**'tis** (tiz) *contr.* it is.

tisane (tizan´), **ptisan** *n.* **1** a herbal tea. **2** a medicinal infusion of dried leaves or flowers, orig. made with barley. [F, from L *ptisana*, Gr. *ptisanē*, peeled barley, from *ptissein*, to peel]

Tishri (tish´ri) *n.* the first month of the Hebrew civil year and the seventh of the ecclesiastical year, corresponding to parts of September and October. [Heb. *tishrī*]

tissue (tish´oo) *n.* **1** a fabric of cells and their products, forming the elementary substance of plant and animal organs. **2** a paper handkerchief. **3** tissue paper. **4** a fabrication, a connected series (of lies, accidents etc.). **5** any fine, gauzy or transparent woven fabric. **tissue culture** *n.* the growing of pieces of biological tissue in a nutritive medium in a laboratory. **tissued** *a.* **tissue paper** *n.* a thin, gauzy, unsized paper, used for wrapping articles, protecting engravings etc. **tissue-typing** *n.* the ascertaining of types of body tissue, e.g. in order to match organs for transplant. [F *tissu*, p.p. of *tistre*, now *tisser*, L *tesere*, to weave]

Tit. *abbr.* (*Bible*) Titus.

tit[1] (tit) *n.* **1** any small songbird, esp. of the family Paridae and esp. of the genus *Parus*, e.g. the blue tit, great tit, a titmouse. **2** †a small horse. **3** †a child, a girl. **4** †a bit, a morsel. **titlark** *n.* a pipit, esp. *Anthus pratensis*, the meadow pipit. **titling**[1] *n.* **1** a titmouse. **2** a titlark. [Icel. *tittr*, bird, something small, cp. Norw. *tita*]

tit[2] (tit) *n.* **1** (*sl.*) a woman's breast. **2** a teat or nipple. **titty** *n.* (*pl.* **titties**) **1** (*sl.*) a woman's breast. **2** a teat or nipple (used by or to children). [OE, cp. TEAT]

tit[3] (tit) *n.* (*sl.*) an unpleasant or contemptible person. [etym. uncertain, perh. TIT[2]]

tit[4] (tit) *n.* a tap, a slight blow. **tit for tat** blow for blow, retaliation in kind. [perh. corr. of TIP[2]]

titan (tī´tən) *n.* **1** a person of superhuman strength or genius. **2** (**Titan**) in Greek mythology, each of the 12 children of Uranus and Ge of gigantic size and strength. ~*a.* titanic. **titanic**[1] (-tan´-) *a.* **1** huge, colossal. **2** of or relating to the Titans. **titanically** *adv.* [L and Gr., cogn. with Sansk. *tithā*, fire]

titanic[1] TITAN.

titanic[2] TITANIUM.

titanium (titā´niəm, tī-) *n.* a dark-grey metallic element, at. no. 22, chem. symbol Ti, found in small quantities in various minerals. **titanate** (tī´tənāt) *n.* a salt of titanic acid. **titanic**[2] (tītan´ik) *a.* of titanium, esp. in tetravalent form. **titaniferous** (tītənif´-) *a.* of or containing titanium. **titanium dioxide, titanium oxide** *n.* a naturally occurring white pigment. [as TITAN]

titbit (tit´bit), (*NAm.*) **tidbit** (tid´-) *n.* a delicate or dainty morsel of food or gossip. [perh. from dial. *tid*, tender, BIT[1]]

titch (tich), **tich** *n.* (*coll.*) **1** a very small person. **2** a very small amount. **titchy** *a.* (*comp.* **titchier,** *superl.* **titchiest**). [Little *Tich*, d. 1928, music-hall comedian]

titer TITRE (under TITRATE).

titfer (tit´fə) *n.* (*sl.*) a hat. [rhyming sl. *tit for tat*]

tithe (tīdh) *n.* **1** (*Hist.*) a tax of one-tenth, esp. of the yearly proceeds from land and personal industry, payable for the support of the clergy and Church. **2** the tenth part of anything. ~*v.t.* to impose tithes upon. **tithable** *a.* **tithe barn** *n.* a barn in which the corn and other tithes of a parish were formerly stored. **tithe-pig** *n.* (*Hist.*) one pig out of ten set apart for tithe. **tither** *n.* **tithing** *n.* **1** the taking or levying of tithes. **2** (*Hist.*) a civil division consisting of ten householders living near each other and bound as sureties for each other's good behaviour. [OE *tēodha* (TEN, -TH[1]), whence *tēothian*]

titi[1] (tē´tē) *n.* (*pl.* **titis**) any small brightly-coloured S American monkey of the genus *Callicebus*. [Sp., from Tupi]

titi[2] (tī´tī, tē´tē) *n.* any evergreen shrub or small tree of the family Cyrillaceae, found in the south-eastern US. [perh. from Amer. Indian]

Titian (tish´ən) *a.* (of hair) reddish-brown in colour. **Titian-haired** *a.* [Italian artist *Titian*, 1477–1576]

titillate (tit´ilāt) *v.t.* **1** to excite or stimulate pleasurably. **2** to tickle. **titillatingly** *adv.* **titillation** (-ā´shən) *n.* [L *titallātus*, p.p of *titillāre*, to tickle]

Usage note The verbs *titillate* and *titivate* should not be confused: *titillate* means to excite pleasantly, and *titivate* to dress up or smarten.

titivate (tit´ivāt), **tittivate** *v.t.*, *v.i.* to dress up, to adorn, to make smart. **titivation** (-ā´shən) *n.* [prob. arbitrary]

Usage note See note under TITILLATE.

titlark TIT[1].

title (tī´təl) *n.* **1** an inscription serving as a name or designation, esp. of a book, chapter, poem etc. **2** a personal appellation denoting office, nobility, distinction, or other qualification. **3** (*Law*) the right to ownership of property. **4** the legal evidence of this, a title deed. **5** an acknowledged claim, the grounds of this. **6** the entire contents of the title-page of a book. **7** a book or publication. **8** (*often pl.*) a credit or caption in a film, broadcast etc. **9** in a sport, a championship. **10** fineness, esp. of gold, expressed in carats. **11** a source of income and a fixed sphere of duty required as a condition precedent to ordination. **12** in the Roman Catholic Church, a church or parish under a cardinal. **13** the distinguishing formula at the head of a legal document, statute etc. **14** a division of a document, treatise etc., including caption and text, as arranged for reference. ~*v.t.* to give a title to. **titled** *a.* bearing a title of nobility. **title deed** *n.* a legal instrument giving the evidence of a person's right to property. **title-holder** *n.* a person or team holding a title in sport. **titleless** *a.* **title-page** *n.* the page at the beginning of a book giving the subject, author's name etc. **title role** *n.* the character or part from whose name the title of a play is taken. **titling**[2] *n.*

the act of impressing the title on the cover of a book. [OF, from L *titulus*]

titling[1] TIT[1].

titling[2] TITLE.

titmouse (tit´mows) *n.* (*pl.* **titmice** (-mīs)) the small insectivorous songbird, the tit. [TIT[1] and OE *mase*, a name for several small birds]

Titoism (tē´tōizm) *n.* (*Hist.*) the kind of Communism introduced by Marshal Tito in Yugoslavia as opposed to that of the USSR. **Titoist** *n., a.* [from *Tito*, the adopted name of V. Broz (1892–1980)]

titrate (tī´trāt) *v.t.* (*Chem.*) to determine the amount of a particular constituent in (a solution) by adding a known quantity of another chemical capable of reacting with it. **titratable** *a.* **titration** (-rā´shən) *n.* **titre** (-tə), (*N Am.*) **titer** *n.* **1** the concentration of a substance in a solution, as ascertained by titration. **2** (*Med.*) the concentration of an antibody, as ascertained from the highest dilution at which it remains active. [F *titre*, proportion of fine metal in an alloy (cp. TITLE, -ATE[3])]

ti-tree (tē´trē) *n.* **1** a ti, a cabbage tree. **2** a tea tree.

titter (tit´ə) *v.i.* to laugh in a restrained manner, to snigger, to giggle. *~n.* a restrained laugh. **titterer** *n.* **titteringly** *adv.* [ME *titeren*, freq. of *tit-*, imit.]

tittivate TITIVATE.

tittle (tit´əl) *n.* **1** any small diacritic or punctuation mark. **2** a particle, an iota. **not one jot or tittle** JOT. [ME *titel*, from L *titulus*, TITLE; cp. TILDE]

tittle-tattle (tit´əltatəl) *n.* gossip. *~v.i.* to gossip. [redupl. from TATTLE]

tittup (tit´əp) *v.i.* (*pres.p.* **tittuping, tittupping,** *past, p.p.* **tittuped, tittupped**) (*coll.*) to go, act or behave in a lively manner, to prance, to frisk. *~n.* a tittuping action or movement. **tittupy** *a.* [etym. uncertain]

titty TIT[2].

titubation (titūbā´shən) *n.* (*Med.*) fidgeting or stumbling caused by nervous disorder. [L *titubātio*, from *titubāre*, to totter]

titular (tit´ūlə) *a.* **1** existing in name or in title only, or holding a title without the office or duties attached, nominal. **2** of, relating to or held in virtue of a title. **3** conferring a title. *~n.* a person who holds the title of an office or benefice without the authority or duties of or relating to it. **titular bishop** *n.* a bishop without a diocese whose title is taken from a former, now defunct, diocese. **titularly** *adv.* **titular saint** *n.* the patron saint that gives their name to a particular church. **titulary** *a., n.* (*pl.* **titularies**). [F *titulaire*, from L *titulus*]

tizzy (tiz´i), **tizz, tiz** *n.* (*pl.* **tizzies, tizzes**) (*coll.*) a state of extreme agitation. [corr. of TESTER[3]]

TKO *abbr.* technical knockout.

Tl *chem. symbol* thallium.

TLC *abbr.* (*coll.*) tender loving care.

TLS *abbr.* Times Literary Supplement.

TM *abbr.* **1** trademark. **2** Transcendental Meditation.

Tm *chem. symbol* thulium.

tmesis (tmē´sis) *n.* (*pl.* **tmeses** (-sēz)) (*Gram.*) the separation of the parts of a compound word by inserting one or more words between (e.g. *Get it your-blooming-self!*). [L and Gr., from Gr. *temnein*, to cut]

TN *abbr.* **1** Tennessee. **2** trade name. **3** Tunisia (IVR).

tn *abbr.* **1** (*N Am.*) ton(s). **2** town.

TNT *abbr.* trinitrotoluene (an explosive).

to (tu, tə, too) *prep.* **1** in a direction towards (a place, person, thing, state or quality). **2** as far as. **3** no less than, in comparison with, in respect of, in correspondence with. **4** concerning. **5** with the result of becoming. **6** against, adjoining. **7** before. **8** accompanied by (music). **9** preceding the indirect object or the person or thing affected by the action etc. **10** the sign of the infinitive, expressing futurity, purpose, consequence etc., limiting the meaning of adjectives, or forming verbal nouns. **11** (*ellipt.*) denoting the infinitive of a verb mentioned or understood. **12** as the cost of (in accounting). **13** †in the relation of, for, as. *~adv.* **1** towards the condition or end required. **2** into the normal condition, esp. to a standstill or a state of adjustment. **3** †forward, on. **as to** AS[1]. **to and fro** FRO. **to-be** *a.* about to be (always after the noun, as *mother-to-be*). **to-do** (tədoo´) *n.* (*pl.* **to-dos**) (*coll.*) a fuss, a commotion. **toing and froing** *n.* (*pl.* **toings and froings**) bustle, constant movement back and forth, coming and going. [OE *tō*, cp. Dut. *toe*, G *zu*, Rus. *do*]

Usage note See note under TOO.

toad (tōd) *n.* **1** a tailless amphibian of the family Bufonidae, esp. of the genus *Bufo*, being like a frog, usu. with a warty body, terrestrial except during breeding. **2** a repulsive or detestable person. **3** any of various other tailless amphibians. †**toad-eater** *n.* an obsequious person, a sycophant, a toady. **toadfish** *n.* (*pl. in general* **toadfish**, *in particular* **toadfishes**) any fish of the family Batrachoididae of the Atlantic coast of N America. **toadflax** *n.* a perennial herb of the genus *Linaria*, usu. with yellow or bluish personate flowers. **toad-in-the-hole** *n.* sausages etc. baked in batter. **toadlet** *n.* a small or young toad. **toad spit** *n.* cuckoo spit. [OE *tādige*, etym. uncertain]

toadstone (tōd´stōn) *n.* **1** a stone coloured and shaped somewhat like a toad, or supposed to have been found in the body of a toad, formerly worn as a talisman. **2** an igneous rock of Carboniferous age, occurring in veins and sheets in limestone, named from its barrenness in metalliferous ores. [sense 2 perh. from G *totes Gestein*, dead stone]

toadstool (tōd´stool) *n.* an umbrella-shaped fungus, esp. a poisonous mushroom. [from TOAD, STOOL]

toady (tō´di) *n.* (*pl.* **toadies**) an obsequious person, a sycophant. *~v.t.* (*3rd pers. sing. pres.* **toadies,** *pres.p.* **toadying,** *past, p.p.* **toadied**) to fawn upon, to be obsequious to. **toadyish** *a.* **toadyism** *n.*

toast (tōst) *n.* **1** a slice of bread browned by radiant heat. **2** a drinking or a call for drinking to the health of some person, cause, sentiment etc. **3** the person or other object of this. **4** a celebrity (of a place), a person thought to be toasted often (*the toast of the town*). *~v.t.* **1** to brown (bread), cook (bacon etc.) by radiant heat. **2** to warm (the feet etc.) at a fire. **3** to drink to the health or in honour of. *~v.i.* to be toasted. **on toast 1** (of food) served on a piece of toast. **2** (*coll.*) at one's mercy. **toaster** *n.* an electrical apparatus for making toast. **toasting** *n.* **toasting-fork** *n.* a fork to hold bread etc., for toasting by a fire. **toastmaster, toastmistress** *n.* an official who announces the toasts at public dinners etc. **toastrack** *n.* a rack for holding slices of toast. **toasty** *a.* (*comp.* **toastier,** *superl.* **toastiest**) **1** warm and comfortable. **2** (of wine) having an aroma of maturation in oak casks. **3** of or resembling toast. *~n.* (*pl.* **toasties**) (*coll.*) a toasted sandwich. [ME *tost*, from *toster*, to toast, L *torrēre*, to parch, p.p. *tostus*]

tobacco (təbak´ō) *n.* (*pl.* **tobaccos**) **1** a plant of American origin of the genus *Nicotiana*, with narcotic leaves which are used, after drying and preparing, for smoking, chewing, snuff etc. **2** the leaves of this, esp. prepared for smoking. **tobacco mosaic virus** *n.* a virus causing mosaic disease in tobacco. **tobacconist** *n.* a retailer of tobacco products. **tobacco pipe** *n.* a pipe used in smoking tobacco. **tobacco plant** *n.* **tobacco-pouch** *n.* a pouch for carrying a small quantity of tobacco in. **tobacco-stopper** *n.* an instrument for pressing down tobacco in a pipe. [Sp. *tabaco*, prob. from Taino, roll of leaves for smoking]

toboggan (təbog´ən) *n.* a long low sled used for sliding down snow or ice-covered slopes. *~v.i.* to slide on a toboggan. **tobogganer, tobogganist** *n.* **tobogganing** *n.* **toboggan-shoot, toboggan-slide** *n.* a prepared course for tobogganing, on a hillside or a timber structure. [Algonquian]

toby jug (tō´bi) *n.* a mug or jug shaped like an old man wearing a three-cornered hat. [personal name, *Tobias*]

toccata (təkah´tə) *n.* (*Mus.*) a keyboard composition orig. designed to exercise or display the player's touch. [It., p.p. of *toccare*, to TOUCH]

Toc H (tok āch´) *n.* a society formed after the First World War to encourage Christian fellowship and perform social work, esp. among ex-servicemen. [*toc*, obsolete telegraphy code for T, *H*, after *T*albot *H*ouse, Poperinge, Belgium, the society's first building]

Tocharian (təkeə´riən, təkah´riən) *n.* **1** an extinct Indo-European language of central Asia from the first millennium AD. **2** a member of the people speaking this. ~*a.* of or relating to this language. [F *tocharien*, from Gr. *Tokharoi*, the name of a Scythian tribe]

tocher (tokh´ə) *n.* (*Sc.*) a woman's dowry. ~*v.t.* to give a dowry to. **tocherless** *a.* [Gael. *tochar*]

tocology (təkol´əji) *n.* obstetrics. [Gr. *tokos*, birth, from *tiktein*, to bring forth, -LOGY]

tocopherol (təkof´ərol) *n.* any of a group of antioxidants thought to be required for healthy animal and human reproduction and found in wheatgerm, egg yolk etc.; vitamin E. [Gr. *tokos*, birth, *pherein*, to bear, bring, -OL]

tocsin (tok´sin) *n.* **1** an alarm bell, signal etc. **2** the ringing of this. [MF *toquesing* (OF *toquer*, to TOUCH, *sing*, SIGNAL)]

tod[1] (tod) *n.* own: only as below. **on one's tod** (*sl.*) on one's own. [rhyming slang, *on one's Tod Sloan* (name of an American jockey)]

tod[2] (tod) *n.* **1** a bush, esp. of thick ivy. **2** a bunch, a mass. **3** an old weight for wool, usu. 28 lb. (12.7 kg). **4** a fox (from its bushy tail). [Icel. *toddi*, tod or wool, cp. Dut. *todde*, G *Zolle*, rag]

today (tədā´) *adv.* **1** on or during this or the present day. **2** at the present day, nowadays. ~*n.* **1** this day. **2** this present era. **today fortnight** on this day a fortnight hence, two weeks today. **today week** on this day next week, a week today. [OE *todæge*, for or on (this) day]

toddle (tod´əl) *v.i.* **1** to walk with short unsteady steps, as a child. **2** to walk in a careless or leisurely way, to saunter. ~*v.t.* to walk (a certain distance etc.) in this way. ~*n.* **1** a toddling walk. **2** a stroll. **toddler** *n.* (*coll.*) a toddling child. **toddlerhood** *n.* the time of a child's life during which it is a toddler. [var. of TOTTER[2]]

toddy (tod´i) *n.* (*pl.* **toddies**) **1** a beverage of spirit and hot water sweetened. **2** the fermented juice of various palm trees. [Hind. *tādi*, *tāri*, from Hind. and Pers. *tār*, palm]

to-do TO.

tody (tō´di) *n.* (*pl.* **todies**) any small W Indian insectivorous bird of the genus *Todus*, related to the American kingfishers. [L *tōdus*, a small bird]

toe (tō) *n.* **1** any one of the five digits of the foot. **2** the part of a shoe, sock etc., covering the toes. **3** the forepart of the hoof of a horse etc. **4** the calk in the front of a horseshoe. **5** a projection from the foot of a buttress etc., to give it greater stability. **6** the end of the head of a golf club. **7** the lower end or a projecting part in a shaft, spindle, rod, lever, organ pipe etc. ~*v.t.* (*3rd pers. sing. pres.* **toes**, *pres.p.* **toeing**, *past, p.p.* **toed**) **1** to touch (a line, mark etc.) with the toes. **2** to furnish (socks, shoes etc.) with toes. **3** in golf, to strike (a ball) with the toe of a club. **4** (*sl.*) to kick. **on one's toes** alert, ready to act. **to toe in** to turn the toes in, in walking etc. **to toe out** to turn the toes out, in walking etc. **to toe the line** to conform, to bow to discipline. **to toe the mark** MARK[1]. **to toe the scratch** SCRATCH. **to turn up one's toes** (*sl.*) to die. **toecap** *n.* a stiffened part of a boot or shoe covering the toes. **toe clip** *n.* a clip on the pedal of a bicycle to prevent the foot from slipping. **toed** *a.* **toehold** *n.* **1** in climbing, a small foothold. **2** any slight or precarious means of access or progress. **toeless** *a.* **toenail** *n.* **1** the nail at the end of each toe. **2** a nail driven at an angle through the end of a board etc. ~*v.t.* to fasten (a board) with nails driven in this way. **toe-rag** *n.* (*sl.*) **1** a mean or despicable person. **2** a tramp, a toe-ragger. **toe-ragger** *n.* (*Austral., sl.*) a tramp. **toey** *a.* (*Austral., coll.*) restless, nervous, anxious. [OE *tā*, cp. Dut. *teen*, G *Zehe*, Icel. *tā*, Dan. *taa*]

toff (tof) *n.* (*sl.*) a swell, a dandy, a person of consequence. ~*v.t.* to dress (up) like a toff. [perh. from *tuft*, a titled undergraduate]

toffee (tof´i), **toffy** *n.* (*pl.* **toffees, toffies**) **1** boiled sugar or molasses and butter made for sucking or chewing. **2** a sweet made of this. **for toffee** (*coll.*) at all (*he couldn't play for toffee*). **toffee apple** *n.* a toffee-coated apple on a stick. **toffee-nosed** *a.* (*sl.*) conceited, arrogant, snobbish. [F and Malay *tafia*]

toft (toft) *n.* **1** a homestead. **2** (*Law*) a place where a dwelling has stood. **3** (*dial.*) a hillock or knoll. [late OE, from Icel. *topt* (pronounced 'toft')]

tofu (tō´foo) *n.* unfermented soya bean curd. [Jap.]

tog[1] (tog) *v.t.* (*pres.p.* **togging,** *past, p.p.* **togged**) (*coll.*) to dress (up or out), esp. in one's best (*all togged up*). **toggery** *n.* clothes. **togs** *n.pl.* clothes. [perh. from obs. *togemans*, coat, from TOGA]

tog[2] (tog) *n.* a unit of measurement of the heat insulation of clothing, fabrics etc. [TOG[1]]

toga (tō´gə) *n.* a loose flowing robe, the principal outer garment of an ancient Roman citizen. **togaed** (-gəd), **toga'd** *a.* **toga virilis** (virī´lis) *n.* in ancient Rome, the toga worn on reaching the age of 14, a symbol of manhood. [L, cogn. with *tegere*, to cover]

together (təgedh´ə) *adv.* **1** in company or union, conjointly, unitedly. **2** in the same place or at the same time. **3** into union, so as to unite or be joined. **4** without cessation or intermission. ~*a.* (*coll.*) competent, assured, composed, well-organized. **together with** as well as, in addition to. **togetherness** *n.* a friendly feeling of being together as a group. [OE *tōgædere* (TO, *gador*, together, see GATHER)]

toggery TOG[1].

toggle (tog´əl) *n.* **1** a crosspiece for fastening a garment, securing a watch-chain etc. **2** a pin put through a loop or eye at the end of a rope for securing this. **3** (*Comput.*) a switch which is pressed in the same way to turn a feature both on and off. **4** the barb of a toggle iron. **5** a toggle joint. **6** (*pl.*) a kind of rope ladder made with a single rope having crosspieces fastened in the middle. **toggle iron, toggle harpoon** *n.* a harpoon with a movable barb pivoted so as to turn in an animal's flesh. **toggle joint** *n.* a knee joint formed by two plates hinged together so as to change the direction of pressure from vertical to horizontal. **toggle switch** *n.* **1** an electric switch with a projecting lever which is pushed, usu. up or down. **2** (*Comput.*) a toggle. [prob. dim. of *tog*, cogn. with TUG]

Togolese (tōgōlēz´) *a.* of or relating to Togo in W Africa. ~*n.* (*pl.* **Togolese**) a native or inhabitant of Togo.

toheroa (tōərō´ə) *n.* an edible mollusc, *Mesodesma ventricosum*, of New Zealand shores. [Maori]

toil (toil) *v.i.* **1** to labour with pain and fatigue of body or mind. **2** to move or progress painfully or laboriously. ~*n.* hard and unremitting work, labour, drudgery. **toiler** *n.* **toilful** *a.* **toilfully** *adv.* **toilless** *a.* **toilsome** *a.* **toilsomely** *adv.* **toilsomeness** *n.* **toil-worn** *a.* worn with toil. [A-F *toiler*, to strive, prob. from OF *toillier*, to mix, to trouble, L *tudiculāre*, from *tudicula*, machine for bruising olives, dim. of *tudes*, mallet, cogn. with *tundere*, to beat]

toile (twahl) *n.* **1** cloth, esp. for clothes. **2** a model of a garment made up in cheap cloth. [F, from L TELA]

toilet (toi´lit) *n.* **1** a lavatory. **2** the act or process of washing oneself, dressing etc. ~*v.t.* (*pres.p.* **toileting,**

past, p.p. **toileted**) to assist (a child, invalid etc.) to use the lavatory. **toilet bag** *n.* a washbag. **toilet paper** *n.* paper for wiping oneself after urination or defecation. **toilet roll** *n.* a roll of toilet paper. **toiletry** (-ri) *n.* (*pl.* **toiletries**) (*often pl.*) an article or preparation used in washing or beautifying oneself. **toilet set** *n.* a set of utensils for a dressing table. **toilet soap** *n.* a soap for personal washing. **toilet table** *n.* a dressing table with mirror etc. **toilette** (twahlet´) *n.* the process of washing, dressing etc. **toilet tissue** *n.* soft toilet paper. **toilet-training** *n.* training a child to use a lavatory correctly and at the appropriate time. **toilet-train** *v.t.* **toilet water** *n.* a form of perfume lighter than an essence. [F *toilette*, dim. of TOILE]

toils (toilz) *n.pl.* a net or snare. [see TOILE]

tokamak (tō´kəmak) *n.* (*Physics*) a toroidal reactor used in thermonuclear experiments involving magnetic effects on hot plasma. [Rus. acronym, *to*roidalnaya *ka*mera s *ma*gnitym polem, toroidal chamber with magnetic field]

Tokay (tōkā´, tō´-) *n.* **1** a rich aromatic wine made around Tokaj in Hungary and elsewhere. **2** a white grape from which it is made.

tokay (tō´kā), **tokay gecko** *n.* a grey gecko with orange and blue spots, *Gekko gecko*, of SE Asia. [Malay *toke*, from Javanese *tekèk*, imit.]

token (tō´kən) *n.* **1** something representing or recalling another thing, event etc. **2** a sign, a symbol. **3** an evidence, an indication, a symptom. **4** a memorial of love or friendship, a keepsake. **5** a metal or plastic disc used instead of a coin, e.g. in a slot machine. **6** a voucher that can be used as payment for goods to a certain value. **7** (*Hist.*) a piece of metal like a coin, formerly issued by tradesmen, banks etc., representing money of greater intrinsic value. **8** a sign proving authenticity. ~*a.* **1** serving as a token. **2** nominal, perfunctory, done, given, invited etc. for form's sake only (*a token gesture*). ~†*v.t.* to make known, to betoken. **by the same token** similarly, in corroboration. **by this token** by the same token. **tokenism** *n.* the practice of making only a token effort, esp. as a political gesture. **tokenistic** (-is´-) *a.* **tokenless** *a.* **token money** *n.* coins which have a higher face value than their intrinsic value. **token payment** *n.* a small payment made to indicate that the debt or obligation is not repudiated. **token vote** *n.* a parliamentary vote of money in which the sum stipulated is not binding. [OE *tācen*, *tācn* (cp. Dut. *teeken*, G *Zeichen*, Icel. *teikn*), cogn. with TEACH]

tola (tō´lə) *n.* a unit of weight for gold and silver, usu. about 180 grains troy. [Hind.]

tolbooth TOLL-BOOTH (under TOLL[1]).

told TELL[1].

Toledo (təlā´dō, -ē´-) *n.* (*pl.* **Toledos**) a sword or sword blade made at Toledo in Spain.

tolerate (tol´ərāt) *v.t.* **1** to suffer, to endure, to permit by not preventing or forbidding. **2** to abstain from judging harshly or condemning (persons, religions, votes, opinions etc.). **3** to sustain, to endure (pain, toil etc.). **4** to sustain (a drug etc.) with impunity. **tolerable** *a.* **1** endurable, supportable. **2** passable, fairly good. **tolerability** (-bil´-) *n.* **tolerableness** *n.* **tolerably** *adv.* **tolerance** *n.* **1** the act or state of toleration. **2** permissible variation in weight, dimension, fitting etc. **tolerant** *a.* showing toleration. **tolerantly** *adv.* **toleration** (-ā´shən) *n.* **1** the act of tolerating. **2** the spirit of tolerance. **3** recognition of the right of private judgement in religious matters and of freedom to exercise any forms of worship. **tolerationist** *n.* **tolerator** *n.* [L *tolerātus*, p.p. of *tolerāre*, cogn. with *tollere*, to bear, cp. Gr. *tlēnai*, to suffer]

toll[1] (tōl) *n.* **1** a tax or duty charged for some privilege, service etc., esp. for the use of a road, bridge, market etc. **2** damage, deaths etc., suffered in an accident, natural disaster etc. **3** (*N Am.*) the charge for a long-distance telephone call. **4** (*Hist.*) a portion of grain taken by a miller as compensation for grinding. **to take its toll** to have a damaging effect in terms of loss, injury, deterioration etc. **toll-booth, tolbooth** *n.* **1** a booth by a roadside for collecting tolls. **2** (*Hist.*) a temporary structure for the collection of market tolls. **3** (*Hist., Sc.*) a town jail. **toll bridge** *n.* a bridge where a toll is charged for passing over it. **toll call** *n.* (*N Am.*) a long-distance telephone call. **toll gate, toll bar** *n.* a gate or bar placed across a road to stop passengers or vehicles till a toll is paid. **toll-house** *n.* (*Hist.*) the house at a toll gate occupied by a toll collector. **toll-road** *n.* a road on which a toll is charged. [OE *toll*, *toln* (cp. Dut. *tol*, G *Zoll*, Icel. *tollr*), perh. from late L *tollōnium*, *telōnium*, Gr. *telōnion* toll-house, from *telos*, tax]

toll[2] (tōl) *v.t.* **1** to cause (a bell) to sound with strokes slowly and uniformly repeated. **2** (of a bell, clock etc.) to give out (a knell etc.) with a slow, measured sound. **3** to ring on account of. ~*v.i.* (of a bell) to sound or ring with slow, regular strokes. ~*n.* a tolling or a stroke of a bell. **toller** *n.* [ME *tollen*, to attract, to entice, etym. uncertain]

Toltec (tol´tek) *n.* a member of a people who ruled in Mexico during the 7th–11th cents., before the Aztecs. ~*a.* of or relating to this people. **Toltecan** *a.* [Mex. Sp. *tolteca*]

tolu (təloo´) *n.* a balsam derived from the S American trees *Myroxylon balsamum* and *M. toluifera*. **toluate** (tol´ūāt) *n.* a salt of toluic acid. **toluene** (tol´ūēn), **toluol** *n.* (*Chem.*) a liquid compound belonging to the aromatic series, methyl benzene, orig. obtained from tolu. **toluic** (tol´-) *a.* [Santiago de *Tolú*, seaport in Colombia]

tom (tom) *n.* **1** a male animal, esp. a tom-cat. **2** (*sl.*) a prostitute. ~*v.i.* (*pres.p.* **tomming**, *past, p.p.* **tommed**) (*sl.*) **1** to practise prostitution. **2** to behave promiscuously. **long tom** LONG[1]. **Tom and Jerry** *n.* (*N Am.*) a hot drink of rum and water with eggs beaten up etc. **tomboy** *n.* **1** a girl who likes boys' activities. **2** †a boisterous boy. **tomboyish** *a.* **tomboyishness** *n.* **tom-cat** *n.* a male cat. **Tom Collins** (-kol´inz) *n.* a long iced drink made with gin or whisky, lime or lemon juice, soda water and sugar or syrup. **Tom, Dick and Harry** *n.* (*derog.*) average commonplace people, any taken at random. **tomfool** *n.* a ridiculous fool, a trifler. ~*a.* very foolish. **tomfoolery** *n.* (*pl.* **tomfooleries**). **Tom Thumb** *n.* **1** a very short man. **2** (*also* **tom thumb**) **a** a dwarf variety of a plant or vegetable. **b** a small wild flower. **tomtit** *n.* a small bird, a tit, esp. a blue tit. [short for *Thomas*]

tomahawk (tom´əhawk) *n.* **1** a N American Indian battleaxe or hatchet with a stone, horn or steel head. **2** (*Austral.*) a hatchet. ~*v.t.* **1** to strike or kill with a tomahawk. **2** to criticize or review savagely. **3** (*Austral.*) to cut (a sheep) when shearing. [Algonquian]

tomalley (təmal´i) *n.* the soft, fatty, greenish so-called liver of the lobster. [var. of TOURMALINE]

toman (təmahn´) *n.* (*Hist.*) a former Persian gold coin worth about 10,000 dinars. [Pers. *tūmān*]

tomatillo (tomətil´yō, -til´ō) *n.* (*pl.* **tomatillos**) **1** a Mexican ground cherry, *Physalis philadelphica*. **2** the edible berry of this. [Sp., dim. of *tomate*, tomato]

tomato (təmah´tō) *n.* (*pl.* **tomatoes**) **1** the red or yellow pulpy edible fruit (used as a vegetable) of a trailing plant, *Lycopersicon esculentum*, of the nightshade family or Solanaceae, orig. S American. **2** the plant itself. **tomatoey** *a.* [Sp. and Port. *tomate*, Nahuatl *tomatl*]

tomb (toom) *n.* **1** a grave. **2** a vault for the dead. **3** a sepulchral monument. ~*v.t.* to bury, to entomb. **the tomb** the state of death. **tombless** *a.* **tombstone** *n.* a stone placed as a memorial over a grave. [OF *tumbe* (F *tombe*), late L *tumba* from Gr. *tumbos*, prob. cogn. with TUMULUS]

tombac (tom´bak) *n.* any one of various copper and zinc alloys, used for making cheap jewellery. [F *tombac*, Port. *tambaca*, Malay *tambaga*, Sansk. *tāmrakam*, copper]

tombola (tombō´lə) *n.* an instant lottery at a fête etc. [It., from *tombolare*, to TUMBLE]

tombolo (tombō´lō) *n.* (*pl.* **tombolos**) a narrow spit joining an island to the mainland or to another island. [It., sand dune]

tome (tōm) *n.* a volume, esp. a ponderous one. [F, from L *tomus*, Gr. *tomos*, section, from *temnein*, to cut]

-tome (tōm) *comb. form* **1** forming nouns denoting instruments for cutting. **2** forming nouns denoting a section or segment. [Gr. *tomios*, see TOME]

tomentum (təmen´təm) *n.* (*pl.* **tomenta** (-tə)) **1** (*Bot.*) a down on stems and leaves consisting of matted woolly hairs. **2** (*Anat.*) the inner surface of the pia mater, tufted with tiny vessels. **tomentose** (-tōs), **tomentous** *a.* [L, wool-stuffing]

tommy (tom´i) *n.* (*pl.* **tommies**) **1** (**Tommy**) a British private soldier (from *Tommy Atkins*, a name used on sample forms). **2** (*Hist.*, *sl.*) **a** bread, food, provisions, esp. carried by workers or given to them in lieu of wages. **b** this method of payment, the truck system. **3** a form of wrench. **4** a tommy bar. **tommy bar** *n.* a short rod inserted to turn a box spanner. **tommy-gun** *n.* a short-barrelled sub-machine gun (from General J. T. Thompson, US soldier and inventor). **tommyrot** *n.* (*coll.*) nonsense. **tommy ruff** *n.* (*esp. Austral.*) the ruff, *Arripis georgianus*. **tommy-shop** *n.* (*Hist.*) a shop or other place where the truck system was in force. [familiar form of TOM]

tomography (təmog´rəfi) *n.* diagnostic radiography of plane sections of the human body. **tomogram** (tō´-, tom´-) *n.* a record obtained in this way. [Gr. *tomos*, a slice, -GRAPHY]

tomorrow (təmor´ō) *n.* **1** the next day after today. **2** the near future. ~*adv.* on, during or in this. **like there's no tomorrow** (*coll.*) recklessly, extravagantly. **tomorrow afternoon** (on) the afternoon of tomorrow. **tomorrow morning** (on) the morning of tomorrow. **tomorrow week** on the day a week later than tomorrow, a week tomorrow. [TO, MORROW, as TODAY]

tompion TAMPION (under TAMP).

tom-tom (tom´tom) *n.* a long, narrow, hand-beaten drum used in India, Africa etc. ~*v.i.* (*pres.p.* **tom-tomming,** *past, p.p.* **tom-tommed**) to beat this. [Hind. *tam-tam*, imit.]

-tomy (təmi) *comb. form* (*pl.* **-tomies**) forming nouns denoting cutting, esp. of the surgical type, as in *lobotomy*, *phlebotomy*. [as -TOME, -Y[2]]

ton[1] (tŭn) *n.* **1** any of various measures of weight or volume, usu. large, as the long ton, short ton etc. **2** a measure of refrigeration, the power able to freeze 2,000 lb. (907.2 kg) of water at 0°C in 24 hours. **3** a measure of timber, 40 cu. ft. (1.132 cu. m). **4** an unspecified great weight. **5** (*usu. pl., coll.*) a large quantity. **6** (*sl.*) £100. **7** (*sl.*) 100 m.p.h. **displacement ton** DISPLACEMENT (under DISPLACE). **freight ton** FREIGHT. **gross ton** GROSS. **like a ton of bricks** BRICK. **long ton** LONG[1]. **metric ton** METRIC. **net ton** NET[1]. **register ton** REGISTER. **short ton** SHORT. **to weigh a ton** to be heavy to lift, carry etc. **ton-mile** *n.* a unit of traffic equivalent to one ton of goods carried one mile. **-tonner** *comb. form* a ship of a specified tonnage (*3,000-tonner*). **ton-up** *n.* 100 m.p.h. ~*a.* achieving this speed, esp. recklessly and on a regular basis (*ton-up kid*). [var. of TUN]

ton[2] (tō) *n.* the prevailing fashion or mode. **tonish** (tō´nish) *a.* **tonishness** *n.* **tony** (tō´ni) *a.* (*comp.* **tonier,** *superl.* **toniest**) (*N Am.*) stylish, fashionable. [F, TONE]

tonal (tō´nəl) *a.* **1** of or relating to tone or tonality. **2** having tonality. **3** (of a fugue etc.) repeating the subject in the same key but at different pitches. **tonality** (-nal´-) *n.* (*pl.* **tonalities**) **1** (*Mus.*) the character or quality of a tone or tonal system. **2** a system of tones, a key. **3** adherence to a single tonic key. **4** in fine art, the general colour scheme of a picture. **tonally** *adv.*

to-name (too´nām) *n.* (*Sc.*) **1** a distinguishing name added to a surname. **2** a nickname.

tondo (ton´dō) *n.* (*pl.* **tondi** (-di)) **1** a circular easel painting, relief carving etc. **2** a maiolica plate with a wide decorated rim. [It., from L *rotundus*, ROUND]

tone (tōn) *n.* **1** sound, with reference to pitch, quality and volume. **2** modulation or inflection of the voice to express emotion etc. **3** general disposition, temper, mood, prevailing sentiment, spirit. **4** a musical sound. **5** an interval of a major second. **6** an ancient psalm tune, esp. a Gregorian plainsong melody. **7** syllabic stress or accent. **8** an intonation distinguishing sounds otherwise similar. **9** degree of luminosity of a colour. **10** the general effect of a picture, esp. as regards colour and luminosity, the tint or shade of colour. **11** the shade or colour of a photographic print. **12** healthy general condition of the bodily organs, tissues etc. ~*v.t.* **1** to give tone or quality to. **2** to modify the tone of, to tune. **3** to modify the colour of (a photographic picture). ~*v.i.* **1** to attune (to). **2** to harmonize in colour, tint etc. **3** to receive a particular tone or tint. **to tone down 1** to subdue, to soften (the tint, tone, pitch, intensity etc. of). **2** to modify, to reduce, to soften (a statement, demands etc.). **3** to become softer, less emphatic etc. **to tone up 1** (of muscles etc.) to become firmer or more vigorous. **2** to heighten, to intensify. **tone arm** *n.* the pick-up arm of a record player. **toneburst** *n.* an audio signal used to test transient response in audio equipment. **tone control** *n.* a switch to vary the frequencies of sound from a radio, hi-fi unit etc. **toned** *a.* **tone-deaf** *a.* unable to distinguish accurately between musical sounds of different pitch. **tone-deafness** *n.* **tone language** *n.* a language such as Chinese in which variation of tone serves to distinguish between words otherwise pronounced in the same way. **toneless** *a.* **tonelessly** *adv.* **toneme** (-nēm) *n.* in linguistics, a phoneme which can be distinguished from another only by its particular tone. **tonemic** (-nē´-) *a.* **tonepad** *n.* a device that enables data to be put into a computer over a telephone line by emitting electronic sounds. **tone poem** *n.* an orchestral composition in one movement which illustrates a train of thought external to the music. **toner** *n.* **1** a black powder used in photocopiers, computer printers etc. **2** a lotion applied to the face to tighten the pores. **3** a person or thing which tones. **4** a chemical used in photographic processing. **tone-row** *n.* the basic series of notes in serial music. **tonometer** (-om´itə) *n.* **1** (*Mus.*) a tuning fork or other instrument for determining the pitch of a tone. **2** an instrument for measuring strains in liquids. **3** (*Med.*) an instrument for measuring pressure in body fluids, vapour etc., e.g. in the eyeball. [ME and F *ton*, L *tonus*, Gr. *tonos*, from *teinein*, to stretch]

tong[1] (tong) *n.* a Chinese secret society. [Chin. *t'ang*, a meeting place]

tong[2] TONGS.

tonga (tong´gə) *n.* a light two-wheeled horse-drawn cart for four persons used in India. [Hind.]

Tongan (tong´gən) *a.* of or relating to Tonga, its people or language. ~*n.* a native or inhabitant of Tonga.

tongs (tongz) *n.pl.* an implement consisting of two limbs, usu. connected near one end by a pivot, used for grasping coals etc.; also called *pair of tongs*. **tong**[2] *v.t.* (*pres.p.* **tonging,** *past, p.p.* **tonged**) to style (the hair) using curling tongs. [OE *tange*, sing. (cp. Dut. and Dan. *tang*, G *Zange*, Icel. *töng*), cogn. with Gr. *daknein*, to bite]

tongue (tŭng) *n.* 1 a fleshy muscular organ in the mouth, used in tasting, swallowing and (in humans) speech. 2 the tongue of an ox, sheep etc., as food. 3 a tongue-shaped thing or part. 4 the clapper of a bell. 5 the pin in a buckle. 6 a piece of leather closing the gap in the front of a laced shoe. 7 the index of a scale or balance. 8 (*Mus.*) a vibrating slip in the reed of a flageolet and other instruments. 9 a pointed rail as part of railway points. 10 a projecting edge for fitting into a groove in wood. 11 a long low promontory, a long narrow inlet. 12 speech, utterance, the voice. 13 manner of speech. 14 a language. 15 a nation, a group of peoples with a shared language. ~*v.t.* (*pres.p.* **tonguing,** *past, p.p.* **tongued**) 1 to modify (the sounds of a flute etc.) with the tongue. 2 to put a tongue on (board etc.). 3 (*poet.*) to speak. 4 †to reproach, to reprove. ~*v.i.* to use the tongue in playing some wind instruments. **the rough edge/ side of one's tongue** ROUGH. **to find one's tongue** to express oneself after a period of remaining silent. **to give tongue** 1 to speak one's mind. 2 to bark esp. (of a hound) when in contact with the quarry. **to hold one's tongue** to keep quiet. **to keep a civil tongue in one's head** to remain polite. **to lose one's tongue** to become silent. **with one's tongue hanging out** eagerly, with avid expectation. **with one's tongue in one's cheek** ironically. **tongue-and-groove** *n.* planking that fits together for floors, walling etc. with a projecting strip on one side and a corresponding groove on the other. ~*v.t.* to panel with this. **tongue-and-grooved** *a.* **tongue-bit** *n.* a bit with a plate to prevent a horse from getting its tongue over the mouthpiece. **tongue-bone** *n.* the hyoid bone. **tongued** *a.* (*usu. in comb.*, as *loud-tongued*). **tongue-in-cheek** *a.* said with irony, mischievously and drily humorous. ~*adv.* 1 ironically. 2 insincerely. **tongue-lashing** *n.* a severe scolding. **tongueless** *a.* **tonguelet** *n.* **tongue-tie** *n.* shortness of fraenum impeding movement of the tongue. **tongue-tied** *a.* 1 afraid of or prevented from speaking freely. 2 impeded in speech by tongue-tie. **tongue-twister** *n.* a series of words difficult to articulate without stumbling. **tonguing** *n.* (*Mus.*) the technique of playing wind instruments, using the tongue to control the notes produced. [OE *tunge* (cp. Dut. *tong*, G *Zunge*, Icel. and Swed. *tunga*), cogn. with L *lingua*, earlier, *dingua*]

tonic (ton´ik) *n.* 1 a tonic medicine. 2 tonic water. 3 (*Mus.*) the keynote. ~*a.* 1 invigorating, bracing. 2 of or relating to tones. 3 (*Mus.*) of, relating to or founded on the keynote. 4 in phonetics, denoting a voiced sound. 5 stressed. 6 (*Med.*) of or relating to tension, unrelaxing (of spasms). **tonic accent** *n.* in phonetics, an emphasis given to a syllable through a change in pitch. **tonically** *adv.* **tonicity** (-nis´-) *n.* 1 the state of being tonic. 2 tone. 3 elasticity or contractility of the muscles. **tonic sol-fa** *n.* (*Mus.*) a system of notation in which diatonic scales are written always in one way (the keynote being indicated), the tones being represented by syllables or initials, and time and accents by dashes and colons. **tonic sol-faist** *n.* a person versed in or advocating the tonic sol-fa system. **tonic spasm** *n.* (*Med.*) a continuous muscular spasm, as opposed to *clonus.* **tonic water** *n.* a carbonated drink flavoured with quinine, often used as a mixer with alcoholic drinks. [Gr. *tonikos* (TONE, -IC]

tonight (tənīt´) *n.* 1 the present night. 2 the night of today. ~*adv.* on or during this.

tonka bean (tong´kə) *n.* the fragrant seed of a S American tree, *Dipteryx odorata*, used in perfumery. [Tupi *tonka*]

tonnage (tŭn´ij) *n.* 1 the carrying capacity or internal cubic capacity of a vessel expressed in tons. 2 the aggregate freightage of a number of vessels, esp. of a country's merchant navy. 3 a duty on ships, formerly assessed on tonnage, now on dimensions. [TON[1]]

tonne (tŭn) *n.* the metric ton.

tonneau (ton´ō) *n.* the rear part of a car containing the back seats, esp. of an open car. **tonneau cover** *n.* a removable cover for the seats of an open car, boat etc. when the vehicle is not in use. [F, cask]

-tonner TON[1].

tonometer TONE.

tonsil (ton´sil) *n.* (*Anat.*) either of two organs situated to the rear of the mouth on each side of the fauces. **tonsillar** *a.* **tonsillectomy** (-lek´təmi) *n.* (*pl.* **tonsillectomies**) surgical removal of the tonsils. **tonsillitis** (-lī´tis) *n.* inflammation of the tonsils. **tonsillitic** (-lit´-) *a.* [F *tonsille*, L *tonsilla*, a sharp stake, tonsils, prob. dim. of *tonsa*, oar]

tonsorial (tonsaw´riəl) *a.* of or relating to a hairdresser or hairdressing. [L *tonsōrius*, from *tonsor -sōris*, barber, from *tondere*, to shave, p.p. *tonsus*]

tonsure (ton´shə) *n.* 1 the shaving of the crown (as in the Roman Catholic Church before 1972) or of the whole head (as in the Greek Church) on admission to the priesthood or a monastic order. 2 the part of the head shaved in this way. 3 admission into holy orders. ~*v.t.* to shave the head of, to confer the tonsure on. [F, from L *tonsūra*, as TONSORIAL]

tontine (ton´tēn, -tēn´) *n.* a form of annuity in which the shares of subscribers who die are added to the profits shared by the survivors, the last of whom receives the whole amount. [F, from Lorenzo *Tonti*, *c.* 1653, Italian banker, the originator]

tonus (tō´nəs) *n.* 1 the normal elasticity of a muscle at rest, tonicity. 2 (*Med.*) a tonic spasm. [L, TONE]

Tony (tō´ni) *n.* (*pl.* **Tonys, Tonies**) an annual American award for work in the theatre. [Antoinette (*Tony*) Perry, d. 1946, US actress]

too (too) *adv.* 1 in excessive quantity, degree etc. 2 as well, also, in addition, at the same time. 3 moreover. 4 more than enough (*You are too kind!*). 5 (*coll.*) extremely, superlatively. **none too** hardly, not very, rather less than (*The weather was none too promising*). **too bad** (of circumstances etc.) beyond rectification, esp. in a dismissive sense (*It's too bad we didn't win the lottery*). **too clever/ cocky etc. by half** HALF. **too much** MUCH. **too much for** MUCH. **too right!** RIGHT. **too-too** (-too´) *a.* (*dated*) gushing, affected. [TO]

Usage note The spellings of the adverb *too*, the numeral *two*, and the preposition and adverb *to* should not be confused.

tooart TUART.

toodle-oo (toodəloo´) *int.* (*coll.*) goodbye. [etym. uncertain]

took TAKE[1].

tool (tool) *n.* 1 a simple implement, esp. one used in manual work. 2 a machine used in the making of machines. 3 anything used as a means to an end in one's occupation (*a mathematical tool*). 4 (*sl.*) the penis. 5 a person employed as an instrument or agent, a cat's-paw. 6 in bookbinding, a hand-stamp or design used in tooling. ~*v.t.* to impress designs on (a book cover). ~*v.i.* 1 to work with a tool. 2 (*sl.*) to drive, to ride, esp. at a moderate speed (*tooling along*). **tool bag** *n.* a large flexible bag for carrying or keeping tools in. **toolbox** *n.* a rigid container for carrying or keeping tools in. **tooled-up** *a.* (*sl.*) carrying firearms. **tooler** *n.* 1 a person who or thing which tools. 2 a stonemason's broad chisel. **tooling** *n.* 1 the process of dressing stone with a chisel. 2 the process of decorating leather, book covers etc. with tools. **tool kit** *n.* 1 a set of tools. 2 (*Comput.*) a set of software utilities. **toolmaker** *n.* a worker who makes and repairs machine tools in a workshop etc. **toolmaking** *n.* **tool post** *n.* a device for supporting or holding the tool in a lathe. **tool-pusher** *n.* the supervisor of drilling at an oil rig or oil well. **toolroom** *n.* the part of a workshop where tools are made or repaired. **tool shed** *n.* a shed in which tools are kept. [OE *tōl* (cp. Icel. *tōl*, pl.), cogn. with *tawian*, see TAW[1]]

toon (toon) *n.* a large Indian, SE Asian and Australian tree, *Cedrela toona*, with close-grained red wood. [Hind. *tun*]

toot (toot) *v.i.* **1** to make a short sharp noise like that of a horn, whistle etc. **2** (of a horn, whistle etc.) to give out its characteristic sound. **3** (of grouse) to call. *~v.t.* **1** to sound (a horn etc.). **2** to give out (a blast etc.) on a horn. *~n.* **1** a tooting sound or blast. **2** (*N Am., sl.*) cocaine; a snort of this. **tooter** *n.* [cp. MSwed. and Norw. *tuta*, Icel. *thjōta*, LG *tuten*, MDut. *tuyten*, of imit. orig.]

tooth (tooth) *n.* (*pl.* **teeth** (tēth)) **1** any one of the hard dense structures, originating in the epidermis, growing in the mouth or pharynx of vertebrates, and used for mastication. **2** a false or artificial tooth made by a dentist. **3** a toothlike projection on the margin of a leaf etc. **4** a projecting pin, point, cog etc. **5** a discriminating taste, a palate. **6** (*pl.*) powers, esp. to compel compliance. *~v.t.* **1** to furnish with teeth. **2** to indent. *~v.i.* to interlock. **armed to the teeth** armed with every possible weapon. **in the teeth of 1** in spite of. **2** in direct opposition to. **3** in the face of (the wind). **long in the tooth** elderly, old (as in horses). **to fight tooth and nail** to fight with all one's power. **to get one's teeth into** to tackle (a task etc.) in a determined and satisfying manner. **to one's teeth 1** to one's face. **2** in open opposition. **to set one's teeth on edge** EDGE. **to show one's teeth** to adopt a threatening attitude. **toothache** *n.* pain in the teeth. **tooth-billed** *a.* (*Zool.*) having toothlike processes on the bill. **toothbrush** *n.* a small brush for the teeth. **toothcomb** *n.* a fine-tooth comb. **toothed** *a.* **1** (of a wheel etc.) having teeth. **2** (*usu. in comb.*) having teeth of a certain type, as in *gap-toothed.* **toothed whale** *n.* any whale of the suborder Odonticeti, having simple teeth, such as porpoises etc. **tooth fairy** *n.* (in stories for young children) a fairy who leaves a coin in exchange for a child's milk tooth. **tooth-glass** *n.* a glass for holding dentures or for rinsing the mouth out after cleaning the teeth. **toothing** *n.* **1** fitting with teeth. **2** projecting stones or bricks left in the end of a wall for bonding it to a continuation. **toothless** *a.* **toothlike** *a.* **toothpaste, tooth powder** *n.* paste or powder for cleaning the teeth. **toothpick** *n.* a pointed instrument of plastic, wood etc., for removing particles of food etc., from between the teeth. **tooth shell** *n.* the tusk shell. **toothsome** *a.* palatable, pleasing to the taste. **toothsomely** *adv.* **toothsomeness** *n.* **toothwort** *n.* a herb, *Lathraea squamaria*, allied to the broomrape, with toothlike scales on the rootstock. **toothy** *a.* (*comp.* **toothier,** *superl.* **toothiest**) having prominent teeth. [OE *tōth*, cp. Dut. *tand*, G *Zahn*, Icel. *tönn*, also L *dens dentis*, Gr. *odous odontos*]

tootle (too´təl) *v.i.* **1** to toot gently or continuously, as on a flute. **2** (*coll.*) to amble, to trot. [freq. of TOOT]

tootsy (tut´si), **tootsie** *n.* (*pl.* **tootsies**) **1** a foot or toe (used by or to children). **2** (*N Am.*) a woman. **3** (*N Am.*) a female lover. [alt. of FOOT, -SY]

top[1] (top) *n.* **1** the highest part or point of anything, the summit. **2** the upper side or surface. **3** the upper part of a shoe etc. **4** the cover of a carriage etc. **5** (*N Am.*) the hood of a car. **6** the head of a page in a book. **7** the part of a plant above ground. **8** the uppermost part of a jointed fishing rod. **9** the crown of the head. **10** the upper end or head of a table. **11** the highest position, place, rank etc. **12** the highest degree, the apex, the culmination, the height. **13** (*Naut.*) a platform round the head of a lower mast, forming an extended base for securing the topmast shrouds. **14** (*pl.*) metal buttons plated or washed only on the face. *~v.t.* (*pres.p.* **topping,** *past, p.p.* **topped**) **1** to rise to the top of, to surmount. **2** to excel, to surpass, to be higher than. **3** to remove the top or extremity of (a plant etc.). **4** to put a top or cap on. **5** to be (of a specified height). **6** to cover the top of. **7** (*Naut.*) to tip (a yard) so as to bring one end above the other. **8** (*sl.*) to execute by hanging. **9** in golf, to hit (a ball) above its centre, thus reducing the distance it travels. *~a.* **1** being on or at the top or summit. **2** highest in position, degree etc. **at the top (of the tree)** being the most successful, esp. in a particular field of achievement. **big top** BIG. **from top to toe** completely, from head to foot. **in the top flight** FLIGHT[1]. **off the top of one's head** without preparation, impromptu. **on top 1** in the lead. **2** in control. **on top of 1** added to. **2** in control of. **on top of the world 1** very happy indeed, exuberant. **2** at the height of fame, achievement etc. **over the top 1** on the attack. **2** to excess. **the tops** someone or something that is absolutely the best in quality. **to come to the top** to achieve distinction. **to top off 1** to complete by putting the top or uppermost part to. **2** to finish, to complete. **to top oneself** (*sl.*) to commit suicide. **to top one's part** in the theatre, to play one's role to perfection. **to top out** to put the last or highest girder etc. on (a building). **to top the bill** BILL[1]. **to top up** to fill up (with petrol, oil etc.). **top banana** *n.* (*sl.*) **1** the comedian at the top of the bill. **2** (*N Am.*) the leader of an organization. **top-boot** *n.* a boot having high tops, usu. of distinctive material and colour. **top brass** *n.* (*sl.*) the highest-ranking officials or officers. **topcoat** *n.* **1** an overcoat. **2** a final coat of paint. **top copy** *n.* (*pl.* **top copies**) the uppermost or original copy of a series of copied documents, such as invoices, receipts. **top dog** *n.* (*coll.*) the uppermost person, the boss. **top-down** *a.* **1** hierarchical, controlled from the top echelons of management. **2** going from the general to the particular. **top drawer** *n.* **1** the uppermost drawer in a chest of drawers. **2** the highest social background or status. **out of the top drawer** of the highest quality or social status. **top-drawer** *a.* of the highest quality or social status. **top dress** *v.t.* to manure on the surface, as distinct from digging or ploughing in. **top dressing** *n.* **top-flight** *a.* of the highest rank or quality. **topgallant** (təgal´ənt, top-) *n., a.* (*Naut.*) (denoting) the mast, rigging and sail, next above the topmast. **top gear** *n.* the highest gear in a motor vehicle or on a bicycle. **top-hamper** *n.* (*Naut.*) **1** the light upper sails and rigging. **2** unnecessary tackle, anchors, casks etc., encumbering the deck. **top hat** *n.* a tall silk cylindrical hat. **top-heavy** *a.* **1** having the top or upper part too heavy for the lower. **2** (*coll.*) intoxicated. **top-heavily** *adv.* **top-heaviness** *n.* **top-hole** *a.* (*dated sl.*) excellent, first-rate. **topknot** *n.* **1** an ornamental knot or bow worn on the top of the head. **2** a tuft or crest growing on the head. **topless** *a.* **1** without a top. **2** (of women's clothing) leaving the breasts bare. **3** (of an entertainment etc.) featuring women who are topless. **toplessness** *n.* **top-level** *a.* at the highest level, of the greatest importance, prestige etc. **top-line** *a.* of the highest quality or popular status (*top-line entertainers*). **topman** *n.* (*pl.* **topmen**) (*Naut.*) a sailor stationed in one of the tops. **topmast** *n.* (*Naut.*) the mast next above the lower mast. **topmost** *a.* highest, uppermost. **top-notch** *a.* (*coll.*) first-rate, excellent. **top-notcher** *n.* **top of the pops** *n.* **1** (a record, singer etc.) currently (among) the most popular in terms of sales. **2** a person or thing which is currently enjoying great popularity. **topper** *n.* **1** (*coll.*) a top hat. **2** a person who or thing which tops. **topping** *n.* something which forms a top layer, esp. a sauce for food. *~a.* (*dated sl.*) very fine, excellent. **toppingly** *adv.* **topping-up** *n.* the addition of distilled water to a battery to compensate for loss by evaporation. **topsail** (top´səl) *n.* (*Naut.*) **1** a square sail next above the lowest sail on a mast. **2** a fore-and-aft sail above the gaff. **top secret** *a.* requiring the highest level of secrecy. **topside** *n.* **1** a cut of beef from the thigh. **2** (*pl.*) the sides of a vessel above the waterline. **top-slicing** *n.* a method of assessing the tax payable on a lump sum. **topsoil** *n.* the upper layer of soil. ~*v.t.* to remove this from (a piece of ground). **topsoiling** *n.* **topspin** *n.* in tennis etc., a forward spin imparted to the ball by hitting the top of the ball with the racket etc. angled forward and upward. **topstitch** *v.t.* to stitch decoratively on the outer visible side of (a garment etc.). **topstitching** *n.* **top ten, top twenty** etc. *n.* a list of the highest-selling CDs, tapes etc. in a particular week, esp. one for single releases. **top-up** *n.* an additional amount of something that raises or returns it to the desired level. ~*a.* used as a top-up. **top whack** *n.* the maximum price, rate etc. [OE, cp. Dut. and Dan. *top*, Icel. *toppr*, Swed. *topp*, G *Zopf*, tuft, treetop]

top² (top) *n.* a wooden or metal toy, usu. conical or pear-shaped, made to rotate with great velocity on a metal point underneath, by the rapid unwinding of a string or spring or with the hand. **to sleep like a top** to sleep very soundly. **top-shell** *n.* any marine gastropod mollusc of the family Trochidae, having a conical, top-shaped shell. [late OE *topp*, ult. from MHG *Topf*, cogn. with DIP]

toparch (top´ahk) *n.* the ruler of a small place or country, a petty king. **toparchy** *n.* (*pl.* **toparchies**) a small state or country governed by a toparch. [Gr. *toparchos* (*topos*, place, *-archos*, ruler, from *archein*, to rule)]

topaz (tō´paz) *n.* **1** a transparent or translucent aluminium silicate, usu. white or yellow, but sometimes green, blue, red or colourless, valued as a gem. **2** a large and brilliant hummingbird of the genus *Topaza*. **topazolite** (-paz´əlīt) *n.* a yellow or green variety of garnet resembling topaz. [OF *topaze*, L *topazus*, Gr. *topazos*, *topazion*, cp. Sansk. *tapas*, fire, from *tap*, to shine]

tope¹ (tōp) *v.i.* to drink alcoholic liquors excessively or habitually, to tipple. **toper** *n.* a tippler, a heavy drinker. [perh. from F *tôpe* (from *tôper*, to cover a stake in dicing), as an int. 'accepted! agreed!' afterwards a drinking phrase; or from Gmc. as TOP¹, in alln. to putting the tops of the thumbs together and crying *topp*]

tope² (tōp) *n.* a grove, esp. of mango trees. [Tamil *toppu*]

tope³ (tōp) *n.* a Buddhist monument in the form of a dome, tower or mound, usu. containing relics, a stupa. [Hind. *top*, corr. from Sansk. *stūpa*, mound]

tope⁴ (tōp) *n.* a small European shark, *Galeorhinus galeus*. [prob. Cornish]

topee TOPI¹.

tophaceous TOPHUS.

Tophet (tō´fit) *n.* (*Bible*) hell. [Heb. *Tōpheth*, a place in the valley of Hinnom, SE of Jerusalem, once used for idolatrous worship, and afterwards for the deposit of the city refuse, to consume which fires were continually kept burning]

tophus (tō´fəs) *n.* (*pl.* **tophi** (-fī)) (*Med.*) calcareous matter deposited round the teeth and at the surface of the joints in gout. **tophaceous** (-fā´shəs) *a.* [L *tōphus*, TUFA]

topi¹ (tō´pi), **topee** *n.* (*pl.* **topis, topees**) a sunhat, a pith helmet. **sola topi** SOLA¹. [Hind., hat]

topi² (tō´pi) *n.* (*pl.* **topi, topis**) a large African antelope, *Damaliscus lunatus*, with a sloping back and reddish-brown colouring. [W Afr.]

topiary (tō´piəri) *n.* (*pl.* **topiaries**) **1** the art of cutting and clipping trees or shrubs etc. into fanciful shapes. **2** an example of this. ~*a.* shaped by cutting or clipping. **topiarian** (-eə´ri-) *a.* **topiarist** *n.* [L, fancy gardening, from Gr. *topos*, place]

topic (top´ik) *n.* the subject of a discourse, argument, literary composition or conversation. **topical** *a.* **1** of or relating to news and current affairs. **2** of or relating to a particular place, local. **3** (*Med.*) of or relating to a particular external part of the body. **4** of or relating to topics. **topicality** (-kal´-) *n.* **topically** *adv.* [F *topiques*, L *topica*, Gr. *topika*, topics, neut. pl. of *topikos*, local, from *topos*, place]

topography (təpog´rəfi) *n.* **1** the detailed description of particular places. **2** representation of local features on maps etc. **3** the artificial or natural features of a place or district. **4** (*Anat.*) the mapping of the surface or the anatomy of particular regions of the body. **topographer** *n.* **topographic** (topəgraf´ik), **topographical** *a.* **topographically** *adv.* [F *topographie*, late L and Gr. *topographia* (*topos*, place, -GRAPHY)]

topoi TOPOS.

topology (təpol´əji) *n.* (*Math.*) the study of geometrical properties and relationships which are not affected by distortion of a figure. **topological** (topəloj´-) *a.* **topologically** *adv.* **topologist** *n.*

toponym (top´ənim) *n.* **1** a place name. **2** a descriptive place name, usu. derived from a geographical feature. **toponymic** (-nim´-), **toponymical** *a.* **toponymics** *n.* toponymy. **toponymy** (təpon´-) *n.* **1** the science of place names. **2** a register of place names of a district etc. **3** (*Anat.*) †the naming of regions of the body.

topos (top´os) *n.* (*pl.* **topoi** (-oi)) a basic theme or concept in literature, rhetoric etc. [Gr., commonplace]

topper, topping TOP¹.

topple (top´əl) *v.i.* **1** to totter and fall. **2** to project as if about to fall. ~*v.t.* to cause to topple, to overturn. [freq. of TOP¹]

topsy-turvy (topsitœ´vi) *a.* **1** upside down. **2** in an upset or disordered condition. ~*adv.* in a confused manner. ~*n.* a topsy-turvy state. **topsy-turvily** *adv.* **topsy-turviness** *n.* **topsy-turvyism** *n.* [perh. from TOP¹, SO¹, obs. *terve*, allied to OE *tearflian*, to turn, to roll over, cp. LG *tarven*, OHG *zerben*]

toque (tōk) *n.* **1** a small, brimless, close-fitting hat. **2** (*Hist.*) a cap or headdress, usu. small and close-fitting, worn at various periods by men and women. [F, prob. from Breton *tok*, cp. Welsh *toc*]

toquilla (təkē´yə) *n.* **1** a S American palmlike tree, *Carludovica palmata*. **2** a fibre obtained from the leaves of this. [Sp., dim. of *toca*, toque, a small gauze headdress]

tor (taw) *n.* a prominent hill or rocky peak, esp. on Dartmoor and in the Peak District. [OE *torr*, Welsh *tor*, knob, cogn. with L *turris*, whence Welsh *twr*, tower]

Torah (taw´rə) *n.* **1** the Pentateuch. **2** the scroll containing this, used in synagogue services. **3** the will of God, the Mosaic law. [Heb.]

torc (tawk) *n.* (*Hist.*) a twisted necklace of gold or other metal, worn by the ancient Gauls etc. [as TORQUE]

torch (tawch) *n.* **1** an electric torch. **2** a light made of resinous wood, twisted flax, hemp etc., soaked in oil or tallow, for carrying in the hand. **3** an oil, electric or other lamp used for this purpose, esp. when raised aloft on a pole etc. ~*v.t.* (*sl.*) to set fire to (something) deliberately. **to carry a torch** to suffer from unrequited love (for). **to put to the torch** to burn down (as an act of war etc.). **torch-bearer** *n.* **1** a person who leads the way or inspires others. **2** a person who carries a torch in ceremonies etc. **torch-dance** *n.* a dance in which each performer carries a torch. **torchère** (-sheə´) *n.* an ornamental stand for a lamp. **torch-fishing** *n.* fishing at night by torchlight. **torching** *n.* setting something alight deliberately, esp. with malice. **torchlight** *n.* **torchlit** *a.* **torch race** *n.* (*Hist.*) a race among the ancient Greeks, in which the runners carried lighted torches. **torch song** *n.* a sad song about unrequited love. **torch singer** *n.* **torch-thistle** *n.* any cactus of the genus *Cereus*, having flowers which open at night. [ME and F *torche*, late L *tortica*, from *torquēre*, to twist, p.p. *tortus*]

torchon (taw´shən) *n.* **1** torchon lace. **2** a dishcloth. **torchon lace** *n.* a kind of coarse bobbin lace. **torchon paper** *n.* a rough-surfaced paper used for watercolours etc. [F *torcher*, to wipe, as TORCH]

tore[1] TEAR[1].
tore[2] (taw) *n.* a torus.
toreador (toriədaw´, tor´-) *n.* a bullfighter, esp. one who fights on horseback. **toreador pants** *n.pl.* close-fitting calf-length trousers worn by women. [Sp., from *torear*, to fight bulls, from *toro*, L *taurus*]
torero (toreə´rō) *n.* (*pl.* **toreros**) a bullfighter, esp. one who fights on foot. [Sp., from late L *taurārius*, from L *taurus*, a bull]
toreutic (təroo´tik) *a.* of or relating to carved, chased or embossed work, esp. in metal. **toreutics** *n.* the art of carving, chasing or embossing work, esp. in metal. [Gr. *toreutikos*, from *toreuein*, to bore, to chase]
torgoch (taw´gokh) *n.* a red-bellied Welsh variety of char. [Welsh *tor*, belly, *goch*, red]
tori, toric TORUS.
torii (taw´riē) *n.* (*pl.* **torii**) a gateless gateway composed of two uprights with (usu.) three superimposed cross-pieces, at the approach to a Shinto temple. [Jap.]
torment[1] (taw´ment) *n.* **1** extreme pain or anguish of body or mind. **2** a source or cause of this. **3** †torture. **4** †an instrument of torture. [OF, from L *tormentum*, a machine for hurling stones, a rack, torment, from *torquēre*, to twist]
torment[2] (tawment´) *v.t.* **1** to subject to torment, to afflict, to vex, to irritate. **2** †to torture. **tormentedly** *adv.* **tormentingly** *adv.* **tormentor** *n.* **1** a person who or thing which torments. **2** (*Naut., Hist.*) a long fork for lifting meat from the coppers.
tormentil (taw´məntil) *n.* a low-growing herb, *Potentilla erecta*, with four-petalled yellow flowers, the astringent rootstock of which is used for medicine. [F *tormentille*, late L *tormentilla*, perh. from TORMENT[1], with ref. to curing toothache]
tormina (taw´minə) *n.pl.* severe griping pains in the bowels. [L, from *torquēre*, see TORMENT[1]]
torn TEAR[1].
tornado (tawnā´dō) *n.* (*pl.* **tornadoes, tornados**) **1** a storm of extreme violence covering a very small area at once, but progressing rapidly, usu. having a rotary motion with electric discharges. **2** (*loosely*) a very strong wind, a hurricane. **3** a sudden strong outburst, discharge etc. (of). **tornadic** (-nad´-) *a.* [Sp. *tronada*, thunderstorm, from *tronar*, to thunder]
toroid (tor´oid) *n.* a figure shaped like a torus. **toroidal** (-roi´-) *a.* of or like a torus. **toroidally** *adv.*
torose (tawrōs´), **torous** (taw´rəs) *a.* **1** (*Zool.*) muscular, knobby. **2** (*Bot.*) cylindrical with protuberances at intervals. [L *torōsus*, from TORUS]
torpedo (tawpē´dō) *n.* (*pl.* **torpedoes**) **1** a long, cigar-shaped, self-propelled apparatus charged with explosive, used for attacking a hostile ship below the waterline. **2 a** a detonating fog-signal placed on a railway track to be exploded by the wheels of a train. **b** (*Hist.*) a mixture of fulminate and grit exploded on the ground as a toy. **3** a cartridge for exploding in an oil well etc. **4** (*Zool.*) an electric ray, a sea fish having an electrical apparatus for disabling or killing its prey. **5** †a submarine mine for defending harbours etc. ~*v.t.* (*3rd pers. sing. pres.* **torpedoes,** *pres.p.* **torpedoing,** *past, p.p.* **torpedoed**) **1** to attack, blow up or sink with a torpedo. **2** to destroy or wreck suddenly. **aerial torpedo** AERIAL. **torpedo boat** *n.* a small swift vessel fitted for firing torpedoes. **torpedo-like** *a.* **torpedo-net, torpedo-netting** *n.* a wire net hung round a ship to intercept torpedoes. **torpedo tube** *n.* a tube for the discharge of torpedoes. [L, numbness (also the fish), from *torpēre*, to be numb]
torpid (taw´pid) *a.* **1** dull, sluggish, inactive. **2** numb. **3** (of a hibernating animal) dormant. **4** having lost the power of motion or feeling. **torpefy** (-pifī) *v.t.* (*3rd pers. sing. pres.* **torpefies,** *pres.p.* **torpefying,** *past, p.p.* **torpefied**) to make numb or torpid. **torpidity** (-pid´-) *n.* **torpidly** *adv.* **torpidness** *n.* **torpor** *n.* **torporific** (-rif´-) *a.* [L *torpidus*, from *torpēre*, to be numb]
torque (tawk) *n.* **1** the movement of a system of forces causing rotation. **2** TORC. ~*v.t.* to apply a twisting force to, to apply torque to. **torquate** (-kwāt), **torquated** *a.* (*Zool.*) having a ring of distinctive colour about the neck. **torque converter** *n.* a device applying the correct amount of torque from an engine to the driving axle of a motor vehicle. **torqued** *a.* **1** twisted. **2** (*Her.*) wreathed. **torquey** *a.* [L *torquēs*, from *torquēre*, to twist]
torr (taw) *n.* (*pl.* **torr**) a unit of pressure, equal to 133.32 pascals, 1/760 of a standard atmosphere. [after E. *Torricelli* (see TORRICELLIAN)]
torrefy (tor´ifī) *v.t.* (*3rd pers. sing. pres.* **torrefies,** *pres.p.* **torrefying,** *past, p.p.* **torrefied**) **1** to dry or parch. **2** to roast (ores etc.). **torrefaction** (-fak´shən) *n.* [L *torrefacere* (*torrēre*, to parch, *facere*, to make)]
torrent (tor´ənt) *n.* **1** a violent rushing stream (of water, lava etc.). **2** a flood (of abuse, passion etc.). ~*a.* rushing, impetuous. **torrential** (tərən´shəl) *a.* **torrentially** *adv.* [F, from L *torrens -rentem*, pres.p. of *torrēre*, to parch]
Torricellian (torichel´iən) *a.* of or relating to the Italian physicist and mathematician E. Torricelli, 1608–47. **Torricellian tube** *n.* a mercury barometer. **Torricellian vacuum** *n.* a vacuum above mercury, as in a barometer.
torrid (tor´id) *a.* **1** dried up with heat, parched, scorching, very hot. **2** intense, passionate. **torridity** (-rid´-), **torridness** *n.* **torridly** *adv.* **torrid zone** *n.* the broad belt of the earth's surface between the tropics. [F *torride*, L *torridus*, from *torrēre*, to parch]
torsade TORSE[1].
torsal TORSE[2].
torse[1] (taws) *n.* (*Her.*) a wreath. **torsade** (-sād´) *n.* an ornamental twisted cord, ribbon etc. [F, also *torce*, ult. from L *tors-*, p.p. stem of *torquēre*, to twist]
torse[2] (taws) *n.* (*Geom.*) a surface generated by a straight line continuously moving about some point or other in its length. **torsal** *a.* [L *torsus*, p.p. of *torquēre*, see TORSE[1]]
torsel (taw´səl) *n.* a twisted ornament, such as a scroll. [prob. var. of TASSEL[1]]
torsion (taw´shən) *n.* **1** the act of twisting or the state of being twisted. **2** (*Physics*) the force with which a body tends to return to its original state after being twisted. **3** (*Med.*) the twisting of the cut end of an artery for checking haemorrhage after an operation. **torsibility** (-sibil´-) *n.* **torsional** *a.* **torsionally** *adv.* **torsion balance** *n.* an instrument for estimating very minute forces by the action of a twisted wire. **torsion bar** *n.* a metal bar, part of a vehicle's suspension, that twists to absorb the vertical movement of the wheels. **torsionless** *a.* **torsion pendulum** *n.* a pendulum that works by rotation rather than by swinging back and forth. [F, from L *tortiōnem*, nom. *-tio*, from *torquēre*, to twist]
torsk (tawsk) *n.* an edible fish, *Brosme brosme*, allied to the cod. [Dan. and Swed., cp. Icel. *thorskr*]
torso (taw´sō) *n.* (*pl.* **torsos,** (*N Am.*) **torsi** (-sē)) **1** the trunk of a statue or body without the head and limbs. **2** an unfinished or partially destroyed work of art or literature. [It., stump, stalk, from L THYRSUS]
tort (tawt) *n.* (*Law*) a private or civil wrong leading to liability for damages. **tortfeasor** *n.* a person guilty of tort. **tortious** (-shəs) *a.* **tortiously** *adv.* [F, wrong, harm, L *tortus*, p.p. of *torquēre*, to twist]
torte (taw´tə, tawt) *n.* (*pl.* **torten, tortes**) a rich gateau or tart, with fruit, cream etc. [G, from It. *torta*, from L; see TART[1]]
tortelli (tawtel´i) *n.* a dish of small pasta parcels filled with a meat, cheese or vegetables mixture. **tortellini** (-lē´ni) *n.* tortelli rolled and formed into small rings. [It., small cakes, fritters]
tortfeasor TORT.

torticollis (tawtikol´is) *n.* (*Med.*) a rheumatic disease of the neck muscles, causing abnormal bending and stiffness. [L *tortus*, see TORT, *collum*, neck]

tortile (taw´tīl) *a.* twisted, wreathed, coiled, curved. **tortility** (-til´-) *n.* [L *tortilis*, from *tortus*, see TORT]

tortilla (tawtē´yə) *n.* in Mexican cooking, a thin flat maize cake baked on an iron plate. [Sp., dim. of *torta*, TART[1]]

tortious TORT.

tortoise (taw´təs) *n.* **1** a slow-moving herbivorous land reptile of the family Testudinidae, having a dome-shaped leathery shell. **2** (*Mil.*, *Hist.*) in ancient Rome, a testudo. **3** a very slow person. **tortoise-like** *a.*, *adv.* **tortoiseshell** *n.* the mottled horny plates of the carapace of some marine turtles, used for combs, ornaments, inlaying etc. ~*a.* **1** made of this. **2** resembling this in marking and colour. **tortoiseshell butterfly** *n.* (*pl.* **tortoiseshell butterflies**) any butterfly of the genera *Nymphalis* and *Aglais*, with mottled yellow, orange and black wings. **tortoiseshell cat** *n.* a domestic cat with a mottled yellow, brown and black coat. [ME *tortuce*, *tortu*, OF *tortue*, late L *tortūca*, from *tortus*, see TORT]

tortrix (taw´triks) *n.* any moth of the family Tortricidae, esp. *Tortrix viridana*, whose larvae live in rolled-up leaves. [mod. L, fem. of *tortor*, from *tort-*, p.p. stem of *torquēre*, to twist]

tortuous (taw´tūəs) *a.* **1** twisting, winding, crooked. **2** roundabout, devious, not open and straightforward. **tortuously** *adv.* **tortuousness** *n.* [ME and OF *tortuos* (F *tortueux*), L *tortūosus*, from *tortus*, twist, see TORT]

Usage note The adjectives *tortuous* and *torturous* should not be confused: *tortuous* means twisting, and *torturous* relating to torture.

torture (taw´chə) *n.* **1** the infliction of extreme physical pain as a punishment or to extort confession etc. **2** excruciating pain or anguish of mind or body. ~*v.t.* **1** to subject to torture. **2** to wrest from the normal position, to distort. **3** to pervert the meaning of (a statement etc.). **torturable** *a.* **torturer** *n.* **torturingly** *adv.* **torturous** *a.* **torturously** *adv.* [F, from L *tortura*, twisting, as TORT]

Usage note See note on *torturous* under TORTUOUS.

torula (tor´ūlə) *n.* (*pl.* **torulae** (-lē)) **1** a microscopic yeastlike fungus of the genus *Torula*. **2** a chain of these. **3** a yeast, *Candida utilis*. [dim. of TORUS]

torus (taw´rəs) *n.* (*pl.* **tori** (-rī), **toruses**) **1** (*Geom.*) a ring-shaped surface generated by a circle rotated about a line which does not intersect the circle. **2** (*Bot.*) the receptacle or thalamus of a flower, the modified end of a stem supporting the floral organs. **3** (*Archit.*) a semicircular projecting moulding, esp. in the base of a column. **4** (*Anat.*) a rounded ridge of bone or muscle. **toric** *a.* [L, a prominence, a couch]

Tory (taw´ri) *n.* (*pl.* **Tories**) **1** (*coll.*) a member of the Conservative Party. **2** (*pl.*, *coll.*) the Conservative Party. **3** (*Hist.*) a member of the party opposed to the exclusion of the Duke of York (James II) from the throne and to the Revolution of 1688, opposed to *Whig*. **4** (*Hist.*) an American opposed to independence during the American Revolution. ~*a.* of or relating to the Tories. **Toryism** *n.* [orig. an Irish mosstrooper, from Ir. *toiridhe*, from *toir*, pursuit]

tosa (tō´sə) *n.* a smooth-haired large heavy dog bred from the mastiff, orig. kept for dogfighting. [*Tosa*, a former province of Japan]

tosh[1] (tosh) *n.* (*sl.*) rubbish, nonsense. [etym. uncertain, cp. TUSH[1]]

tosh[2] (tosh) *n.* (*sl.*) used as a casual form of address, esp. to an unknown person, pal, chum. [etym. unknown]

toss (tos) *v.t.* **1** to throw up with the hand, esp. palm upward. **2** to throw, to pitch, to fling, with an easy or careless motion. **3** to throw back (the head) with a jerk. **4** to throw about or from side to side, to cause to rise and fall, to agitate. **5** to exchange views on, to debate. **6 a** to throw up (a coin) into the air to decide a bet etc., by seeing which way it falls. **b** to settle a wager or dispute with (a person) in this way. **7** to turn or shake (a salad etc.) with a dressing or coating. **8** to separate the heavy from the lighter parts of (tin ore) by agitating the slime. ~*v.i.* **1** to roll and tumble about, to be agitated. **2** to throw oneself from side to side. **3** to toss a coin (for). ~*n.* **1** the act of tossing. **2** the state of being tossed. **3** a fall from a horse etc. **to take a toss** to be thrown by a horse. **to toss a pancake** to turn a pancake over in the pan by flipping it in the air. **to toss oars** to salute by raising oars to an upright position. **to toss off** **1** to swallow at a draught. **2** to produce or do quickly or perfunctorily. **3** (*sl.*) to masturbate. **to toss one's head** to throw one's head back in anger, disgust, impatience etc. **to toss up** to toss a coin. **to win the toss** to have something decided in one's favour by tossing up a coin. **tosser** *n.* **1** (*sl.*) an unpleasant or contemptible person. **2** a person who or thing which tosses. **tossing the caber** *n.* a Scottish sport which involves heaving a large pole as far as possible having balanced it upright by the end. **tosspot** *n.* (*sl.*) **1** a toper, a drunkard. **2** an unpleasant or contemptible person. **toss-up** *n.* **1** the tossing up of a coin. **2** a doubtful point, an even chance. [Norw. *tossa*, cp. LG *teusen*]

tot[1] (tot) *n.* **1** a small child. **2** (*coll.*) a dram of liquor. **3** anything small or insignificant. **tottie** (-i), **totty** *a.* (*Sc.*) very small. ~*n.* (*pl.* **totties**) (*sl.*) a woman, a girl, a girlfriend. [Icel. *tottr*, cp. Dan. *tot*]

tot[2] (tot) *v.t.* (*pres.p.* **totting**, *past*, *p.p.* **totted**) to add (up). ~*v.i.* to mount (up). **to tot up to** to total, to amount to. **totting-up** *n.* adding together to make a total, esp. driving offences until there are sufficient to cause disqualification. [L, so many, or short for TOTAL]

tot[3] (tot) *v.i.* (*pres.p.* **totting**, *past*, *p.p.* **totted**) to collect items for resale from waste disposal sites etc. esp. as a licensed operator. ~*n.* (*sl.*) something reusable salvaged from a dustbin etc. **totter**[1] *n.* **1** a person who is licensed to engage in totting. **2** a person who scavenges from dustbins etc. **totting** *n.* [etym. uncertain]

total (tō´təl) *a.* **1** complete, comprising everything or constituting the whole. **2** absolute, entire, thorough. ~*n.* **1** the total sum or amount. **2** the aggregate. ~*v.t.* (*pres.p.* **totalling,** (*N Am.*) **totaling,** *past*, *p.p.* **totalled,** (*N Am.*) **totaled**) **1** to ascertain the total of. **2** to amount to as a total. **3** (*N Am.*, *sl.*) to wreck (a vehicle) completely in a crash. ~*v.i.* to amount (to) as a total. **total abstinence** *n.* complete abstinence from alcoholic drink. **total eclipse** *n.* an eclipse in which the entire visible surface of the sun, moon etc. is temporarily obscured. **total internal reflection** *n.* (*Physics*) the complete reflection of a light ray without refraction at the interface between two media when the ray meets a medium with a higher refractive index. **totalitarian** (-taliteə´ri-) *a.* **1** permitting no rival parties or policies. **2** controlling the entire national resources of trade, natural wealth and manpower. ~*n.* a person in favour in such a system. **totalitarianism** *n.* **totality** (-tal´-) *n.* **1** the total sum or amount. **2** the period of total eclipse during an eclipse. **totalize, totalise** *v.t.* to total. ~*v.i.* to use a totalizator. **totalization** (-zā´shən) *n.* **totalizator** *n.* a machine for showing the total amount of bets staked on a race in order to divide the whole among those betting on the winner. **totally** *adv.* **Total Quality Management** *n.* in industry, a systematic commitment to quality of product and customer service while increasing efficiency and reducing costs. **total recall** *n.* the ability to remember the past in great detail. **total war** *n.* warfare in which all available resources, military and civil, are employed. [F, from late L *tōtālis*, from *tōtus* entire]

totara (tōˊtərə) *n.* a New Zealand conifer, *Podocarpus totara*, yielding dark red wood. [Maori]

tote[1] (tōt) *v.t.* **1** to carry, to bear. **2** to lead, to haul. **tote bag** *n.* a large bag for shopping etc. **tote box** *n.* (*N Am.*) a small rigid container for goods. [etym. uncertain]

tote[2] (tōt) *n.* short for TOTALIZATOR (under TOTAL).

totem (tōˊtəm) *n.* **1** a natural object, usu. an animal, taken as a badge or emblem of an individual or clan on account of a supposed relationship. **2** an image of this. **totemic** (-temˊ-), **totemistic** (-misˊ-) *a.* **totemism** *n.* **totemist** *n.* **totem pole** *n.* a post on which totems are carved or hung. [Algonquian]

tother (tŭdhˊə), **t'other** *a.*, *pron.* (*dial. or facet.*) the other. **to tell tother from which** to distinguish between two people or things. [ME *thet* (THAT), OTHER]

totipalmate (tōtipalˊmət, -māt) *a.* (*Zool.*) having all four toes webbed. **totipalmation** (-māˊshən) *n.* [L *tōti-*, *tōtus*, whole, PALMATE (under PALM[2])]

totter[1] TOT[3].

totter[2] (totˊə) *v.i.* **1** to walk or stand unsteadily, to stagger. **2** to be on the point of falling. **totterer** *n.* **totteringly** *adv.* **tottery** *a.* [for *tolter*, freq. cogn. with ME *tulten*, *tilten*, TILT]

tottie, totty TOT[1].

toucan (tooˊkən) *n.* a brilliantly-coloured tropical American bird of the family Ramphastidae, with an enormous beak. [Tupi *tucana* (Port. *tucano*)]

touch (tŭch) *v.t.* **1** to meet the surface of, to have no intervening space between at one or more points, to be in contact with, to come into contact with. **2** to bring or put the hand or other part of the body or a stick etc., into contact with. **3** to cause (two objects) to come into contact. **4** to put the hand to (the hat etc.). **5** to reach, to attain. **6** to meddle, to interfere with. **7** to affect with tender feeling, to soften. **8** to approach, to compare with. **9** (*sl.*) to beg or borrow money from. **10** to concern, to relate to. **11** to mention hastily or lightly. **12** to strike lightly, to tap, to play upon lightly, to mark or delineate lightly, to put (in) fine strokes with a brush etc. **13** to be tangent to. **14** to produce a mental impression on. **15** to injure slightly. **16** to excite the anger of, to rouse, to irritate. **17** to impair. ~*v.i.* **1** (of two or more objects) to come into contact. **2** to deal with or mention in a slight or hasty manner, to touch on. ~*n.* **1** the act of touching. **2** the state of touching or being touched, contact. **3** the junction of two bodies at the surface, so that there is no intervening space. **4** the sense by which contact, pressure etc. are perceived. **5** a slight effort, a light stroke with brush or pencil. **6** a stroke, a twinge (*a touch of gout*). **7** a trace, a minute quantity, a tinge. **8 a** characteristic manner or method of handling, working, executing, playing on the keys or strings of a musical instrument etc. **b** the manner in which the keys of a piano etc. respond to this. **9** characteristic impress (*the master's touch*). **10** intimate correspondence, intercourse or communication, accord, sympathy. **11** magnetization of a steel bar by contact with magnets. **12** a test, a proof, a touchstone. **13** (*Med.*) the exploring of organs etc. by touch. **14** in football, rugby etc., the part of the field outside the touchlines and between the goal lines. **at a touch** with very little manual effort (*The door opened at a touch*). **in touch 1** in communication (with). **2** up to date, au fait with events etc. **3** aware, understanding of, conscious of, empathetic. **out of touch 1** not up to date or well-informed. **2** not in regular communication (with). **to get in/ into touch** to communicate (with). **to keep in touch 1** to maintain regular communication (with). **2** to be up to date, well-informed. **to lose one's touch** to cease to be skilful. **to lose touch 1** to cease regular communication (with). **2** to cease to be well-informed. **to put in/ into touch** to cause or facilitate communication. **to touch a nerve** NERVE. **to touch at** (of a ship) to come to land or call at (a port etc.). **to touch base** BASE[1]. **to touch bottom** BOTTOM. **to touch down 1** in rugby, American football etc., to touch the ground with the ball behind the opponents' goal. **2** (of an aircraft or spacecraft) to make contact with the ground after a flight. **to touch lucky** to have a stroke of luck. **to touch off** to cause to begin, to trigger. **to touch one's forelock** FORELOCK[1]. **to touch on/ upon 1** to allude to. **2** to deal with or mention in a slight or hasty manner. **to touch the right chord** CHORD[2]. **to touch up 1** to correct or improve by slight touches, as paint or make-up, to retouch. **2** to fondle (someone) in a sexual way. **3** to strike (a horse etc.) gently with a whip. **to touch wood** to touch something wooden as a supposed protection against bad luck. **would not touch with a bargepole** BARGEPOLE (under BARGE). **touchable** *a.* **touch-and-go** *a.* highly uncertain, very risky or hazardous. **touchback** *n.* in American football, a touchdown behind one's own goal. **touchdown** *n.* the moment of touching down. **touched** *a.* **1** moved by some emotion, e.g. pity or gratitude. **2** (*coll.*) slightly insane. **toucher** *n.* a person who or thing which touches. **touch-hole** *n.* the priming hole or vent of a gun. **touching** *a.* affecting, moving, arousing pathos. ~*prep.* concerning, with regard to. **touchingly** *adv.* **touchingness** *n.* **touch-in-goal** *n.* in rugby, the areas at the end of the pitch between the goal line and the dead-ball line. **touch judge** *n.* a linesman in rugby. **touchlines** *n.pl.* in certain sports, the two longer or side boundaries of the field. **touch-mark** *n.* the maker's mark on an item made of pewter. **touch-me-not** *n.* any of several plants of the genus *Impatiens* whose ripe seed pods burst open when touched, noli-me-tangere. **touch-needle** *n.* a needle of gold alloy of known composition employed in assaying other alloys by comparison of the marks made on the touchstone. **touch of nature** *n.* **1** a natural characteristic. **2** overt human feelings with which others sympathize. **touch of the sun** *n.* **1** slight sunstroke. **2** a brief period of sunlight. **touch-paper** *n.* paper saturated with nitre for igniting gunpowder, fireworks etc. **touch rugby, touch football** *n.* a form of rugby or American football, used esp. in training, where touching replaces tackling. **touch screen** *n.* a VDU screen that can be touched to activate menu choices. **touchstone** *n.* **1** a dark stone, usu. jasper, schist or basanite used in conjunction with touch-needles for testing the purity of gold and other alloys. **2** a standard, a criterion. **touch-type** *v.i.* to type without looking at the typewriter keyboard. **touch-typing** *n.* **touch-typist** *n.* **touch-up** *n.* a small action or series of actions to improve something in a minor way. **touchwood** *n.* a soft white substance into which wood is converted by the action of fungi, easily ignited and burning like tinder. **touch wood** *int.* used esp. within a sentence as a substitute for the superstitious practice of touching wood to avert bad luck (*The weather, touch wood, will be fine*). [ME *touchen*, OF *tuchier*, *tochier* (F *toucher*), It. *toccare*, prob. of imit. orig.]

touché (tooshāˊ) *int.* used to acknowledge a hit in fencing, or a point scored in argument. [F, p.p. of *toucher*, to TOUCH]

touchy (tŭchˊi) *a.* (*comp.* **touchier,** *superl.* **touchiest**) apt to take offence, irascible, irritable. **touchily** *adv.* **touchiness** *n.* [corr. of TETCHY]

tough (tŭf) *a.* **1** firm, strong, not easily broken, resilient, not brittle. **2** able to endure hardship. **3** stiff, tenacious. **4** stubborn, unyielding. **5** aggressive, violent. **6** laborious (*tough work*). **7** difficult (*a tough question*). **8** (*coll.*) (of luck etc.) unjust, hard, severe. ~*n.* a burly lout, a bully. **to tough it (out)** to withstand difficult circumstances, to persevere with something difficult. **toughen** *v.t.*, *v.i.* **toughener** *n.* **tough guy** *n.* (*coll.*) **1** a hard, resilient person. **2** an aggressive person. **toughie** *n.* (*coll.*) a tough person or problem. **toughish** *a.* **tough**

luck *n., int.* (*sl.*) hard luck (used esp. where no sympathy is being offered). **toughly** *adv.* **tough-minded** *a.* **1** practical and realistic, not sentimental. **2** resilient in the face of opposition or hardship. **tough-mindedness** *n.* **toughness** *n.* **tough nut to crack** *n.* a difficult problem to solve. **tough shit, tough titty** *n.; int.* (*sl.*) tough luck. [OE *tōh*, cp. Dut. *taai*, G *zähe*]

toupee (too´pā), **toupet** (too´pā, -pit) *n.* **1** a small wig to cover a bald spot, a hairpiece. **2** †an artificial lock or curl of hair. [F *toupet*, dim. of OF *toup*, tuft, see TOP[1]]

tour (tuə) *n.* **1** a journeying round from place to place in a district, country etc. **2** an extended excursion or ramble. **3** a circuit. **4** a shift or turn of work or duty, esp. a period of service abroad. **5** a trip made by a theatre company, band, sports team etc., stopping at various places to play. *~v.i.* to make a tour. *~v.t.* to make a tour through. **on tour** (of a sports team, theatre company, band etc.) engaged in touring. **touring car, tourer** *n.* (*dated*) a large, long car with room for a lot of luggage. **tourism** *n.* the business of attracting and providing for holidaymakers. **tourist** *n.* a person making a tour, esp. a holidaymaker or member of a sports team. **tourist class** *n.* the lowest category of passenger accommodation in a ship or aircraft. **touristed** *a.* frequented by tourists. **touristic** *a.* **touristically** *adv.* **tourist trap** *n.* a place showily got up to appeal to the undiscriminating holidaymaker. **touristy** *a.* **1** full of tourists. **2** designed to attract tourists. **tour operator** *n.* a travel agency which organizes package tours. [F, from *tourner*, to TURN]

touraco TURACO.

tourbillion (tuəbil´yən) *n.* **1** a whirlwind. **2** (*Hist.*) a firework revolving in the air so as to represent a fiery scroll or spiral. [F *tourbillon*, whirlwind]

tour de force (tuə də faws´) *n.* (*pl.* **tours de force** (tuə)) an outstanding feat of performance, skill, strength etc. [F]

Tourette's syndrome (turets´) *n.* (*Med.*) a neurological disorder characterized by involuntary outbursts of shouting, swearing etc. and sudden involuntary movements. [G. de la *Tourette*, 1857–1904, French neurologist]

tourism, tourist etc. TOUR.

tourmaline (tuə´məlēn) *n.* a black or coloured transparent or translucent silicate with electrical properties, some varieties of which are used as gems. [F, from Sinhalese *tōramalli*]

tournament (tuə´nəmənt) *n.* **1** any contest of skill in which a number of people take part. **2** (*Hist.*) a contest, exercise or pageant in which mounted knights contested, usu. with blunted lances etc. [ME *tornement*, OF *torneiement*, from *torneier*, to TOURNEY]

tournedos (tuə´nədō) *n.* (*pl.* **tournedos** (-dōz)) a thick round fillet steak. [F *tourner*, to TURN, *dos*, the back]

tourney (tuə´ni) *n.* (*pl.* **tourneys**) a tournament. *~v.i.* (*3rd pers. sing. pres.* **tourneys,** *pres.p.* **tourneying,** *past, p.p.* **tourneyed**) to engage in a tournament. [ME and OF *tornei*, from *torneier*, L *tornāre*, to TURN]

tourniquet (tuə´nikā) *n.* a bandage for compressing an artery and checking haemorrhage. [F, from *tourner*, to TURN]

tousle (tow´zəl) *v.t.* **1** to disarrange, to rumple, to dishevel, to put into disorder. **2** to pull about. *~n.* a tousled mass (of hair etc.). **tousle-haired** *a.* having untidy hair. **tously** *a.* [freq. of *touse*, ME *tūsen*, cp. G *zausen*]

tous-les-mois (toolāmwah´) *n.* a food starch from the roots of species of a canna, esp. *Canna indica*, a perennial Peruvian herb. [F, every month]

tout[1] (towt) *v.i.* **1** to solicit custom in an obtrusive way. **2** to observe secretly, to spy (esp. on horses in training for a race). *~n.* **1** a person employed to tout. **2** a person who watches horses in training and supplies information. **3** TICKET TOUT (under TICKET). **touter** *n.* [ME *tūten*, var. of *toten*, OE *tōtian*, to project, to peep out]

tout[2] (too) *a.* all, whole. *~adv.* entirely. **tout à fait** (toot a fā´) *adv.* entirely. **tout court** (kuə´) *adv.* simply, without further addition (*called Morse tout court*). **tout de suite** (toot swēt´) *adv.* immediately. **tout ensemble** (toot ãsã´blə) *adv.* all together. **tout le monde** (lə mõd´) *pron.* everybody. [F]

tovarish (təvah´rish), **tovarich** *n.* in Russia, the former Soviet Union etc., comrade. [Rus. *tovarishch*]

tow[1] (tō) *v.t.* **1** to pull (a vehicle) behind another. **2** to pull (a boat, ship etc.) through the water by a rope etc. **3** to drag (a net) over the surface of water to obtain specimens. **4** to pull, to drag behind one. *~n.* **1** the act of towing. **2** the state of being towed. **in tow 1** being towed. **2** following. **3** under control or guidance. **on tow** (of a vehicle) being towed. **to have in tow 1** to have on tow (a boat etc.). **2** to be accompanied by, esp. as the person in charge. **to have on tow** to be towing (a vehicle etc.). **towable** *a.* **towage** (-ij) *n.* **tow bar** *n.* a strong bar on the back of a vehicle for attaching a trailer. **towboat** *n.* a tug. **towpath, towing-path** *n.* a track beside a canal or river, formerly for horses towing barges etc. **towplane** *n.* an aircraft that tows gliders prior to release. **towrope, towing-rope, towline** *n.* a hawser or rope used in towing. [OE *togian*, cp. Icel. *toga*, OHG *zogōn*, also L *dūcere*, to lead, and TUG]

tow[2] (tō) *n.* the coarse broken part of hemp or flax after combing out. **tow-coloured,** (*N Am.*) **tow-colored** *a.* (of hair) very light in colour. **tow-headed** *a.* having very pale hair. **tow-head** *n.* **towy** *a.* [OE *tow-*, spinning (in *towlīc*, fit for spinning)]

toward[1] (təwawd´, twawd, tawd) *prep.* TOWARDS.

†**toward**[2] (tō´əd) *a.* **1** docile, obedient. **2** ready to learn or do, apt. **3** forward, advanced. **towardly** *a.* **towardliness** *n.* **towardness** *n.* [as TOWARDS]

towards (təwawdz´, twawdz, tawdz) *prep.* **1** in the direction of. **2** as regards, with respect to. **3** for, for the purpose of. **4** near, about. [OE *tōweard* (TO, -WARDS)]

towel (tow´əl) *n.* **1** an absorbent cloth for wiping and drying after washing, washing up etc. **2** a piece of absorbent paper similarly used. **3** SANITARY TOWEL (under SANITARY). *~v.t.* (*pres.p.* **towelling,** (*N Am.*) **toweling,** *past, p.p.* **towelled,** (*N Am.*) **toweled**) to wipe with a towel. *~v.i.* to wipe oneself with a towel. **to throw in the towel 1** (of a boxer or their second) to throw a towel into the ring as a sign of submission. **2** (*coll.*) to admit defeat. **towel-horse** *n.* a wooden stand on which to hang towels. **towelling,** (*N Am.*) **toweling** *n.* cloth for making towels. **towel rail** *n.* a rail, esp. in a bathroom, on which towels are hung. [ME *towaille*, OF *toaille* (F *touaille*), OHG *twahila, dwahila* (whence G *Zwehle*), from *twahan*, to wash, cp. OE *thwēan*]

tower (tow´ə) *n.* **1** a structure lofty in proportion to the area of its base, and circular, square or polygonal in plan, frequently of several storeys, often forming part of a church, castle or other large building. **2** a similarly-proportioned structure for industrial or other purposes (*cooling tower, control tower, scaffold tower*). **3** an electricity pylon. **4** a place of defence, a protection. *~v.i.* **1** to rise to a great height, to soar. **2** to be relatively high, to reach high (above). **tower block** *n.* a very tall residential or office building. **towered** *a.* **towering** *a.* **1** very high, lofty. **2** (of passion etc.) violent, outrageous. **Tower of Babel** *n.* a visionary or impractical plan (Gen. xi.1–9). **tower of silence** *n.* an open-topped tower on which Parsees place their dead. **tower of strength** *n.* a person who gives strong, stable, reliable support, esp. in another's time of difficulty. **towery** *a.* [ME *tour, tūr* (later OE *torr*), OF *tor* (F *tour*), L and Gr. *turris*]

towhee (tow´hē, tō´hē) *n.* any of several buntings of the genus *Pipilo*, found in N America. [imit. of its call]

town (town) *n.* 1 an urban area larger than a village, esp. one not constituting a city. 2 such an area as contrasted with the country. 3 the centre of a town. 4 the chief town of a district or neighbourhood, esp. London. 5 the people of a town. 6 the people of a university town who are not members of the university. 7 (*N Am.*) a township. 8 †a collection of dwellings enclosed by a wall or other defence. **on the town** (*coll.*) out to enjoy oneself amongst the amusements and entertainments of a city at night. **to go to town** to let oneself go, to drop all reserve. **to paint the town red** RED[1]. **town and gown** GOWN. **town adjutant, town major** *n.* (*Hist.*) a garrison officer appointed to maintain discipline. **town clerk** *n.* (*Hist.*) 1 the clerk to a municipal corporation. 2 the keeper of the records of a town. **town council** *n.* the governing body in a town. **town councillor** *n.* **town crier** *n.* an officer who makes public proclamations e.g. of sales, lost articles etc. **town gas** *n.* (*Hist.*) manufactured coal gas, as opposed to *natural gas.* **town hall** *n.* a large public building for the transaction of municipal business, public meetings, entertainments etc. **town house** *n.* 1 a private residence in town, as opposed to a country house. 2 a modern urban terraced house, often with a garage at the front on the ground floor. 3 a town hall. **townie, townee** (-i) *n.* (*derog.*) a person who habitually or for preference lives in town. **townish** *a.* **townless** *a.* **townlet** *n.* **town mayor** *n.* the chairman of a town council, often as distinct from the mayor of a wider civic authority under which the town is administered. **town meeting** *n.* (*N Am.*) a public meeting of voters to transact a town's business. **town planning** *n.* the regulating of the laying out or growth of a town. **town planner** *n.* **townscape** *n.* 1 the visual design of an urban development. 2 a picture of an urban scene. **townsfolk** *n.pl.* the people of a town or city. **township** *n.* 1 (*Hist.*) in S Africa, an urban area formerly designated for black people. 2 (*N Am.*) a territorial district subordinate to a county invested with certain administrative powers. 3 (*Austral.*) any town or settlement, however small. 4 a new area being developed by settlers, speculators etc. 5 (*Hist.*) the inhabitants of a parish, village etc., regarded as a corporate body. 6 a division of a large parish, comprising a village or town. **townsman, townswoman** *n.* (*pl.* **townsmen, townswomen**) 1 an inhabitant of a town. 2 a fellow citizen. **townspeople** *n.pl.* townsfolk. **townward** *a., adv.* **townwards** *adv.* [OE *tūn* (cp. Dut. *tuin*, Icel. *tūn*, G *Zaun*, hedge), cogn. with DUN[3], GOWN]

towy TOW[2].

toxaemia (toksē´miə), (*esp. N Am.*) **toxemia** *n.* (*Med.*) 1 blood poisoning. 2 a condition during pregnancy in which there is a sudden rise in blood pressure. **toxaemic** *a.* [Gr. *haima*, blood]

toxi- (tok´si), **toxico-** (-kō), **toxo-** (tok´sō) *comb. form* poisonous; poison. [TOXIC]

toxic (tok´sik) *a.* 1 poisonous. 2 of or relating to poison. **toxically** *adv.* **toxicant** *n.* a poison. ~*a.* poisonous. **toxicity** (-sis´-) *n.* **toxic shock syndrome** *n.* (*Med.*) a group of symptoms in women including vomiting, fever and diarrhoea, usu. attributable to bacterial infection from an unremoved tampon or an IUD etc. [med. L *toxicus*, from L *toxicum*, Gr. *toxikon* (*pharmakon*), (poisonous drug) for arrows, from *toxa*, pl., arrows, from *toxon*, bow]

toxico- TOXI-.

toxicology (toksikol´əji) *n.* the branch of medicine treating of poisons and their antibodies. **toxicological** (-loj´-) *a.* **toxicologically** *adv.* **toxicologist** *n.*

toxicosis (toksikō´sis) *n.* any disease or condition due to the action of toxic matter.

toxin (tok´sin) *n.* 1 a poisonous compound causing a particular disease. 2 any poisonous ptomaine.

toxo- TOXI-.

toxocara (toksəkah´rə) *n.* any parasitic worm of the genus *Toxocara*, esp. the common roundworm causing toxocariasis. **toxocariasis** (-kərī´əsis) *n.* a disease in humans caused by the larvae of the toxocara worm found in cats and dogs, causing damage to the liver and eyes. [Gr. *kara*, head]

toxophilite (toksof´ilīt) *n.* a person skilled in or devoted to archery. ~*a.* of or relating to archery. **toxophilitic** (-lit´-) *a.* **toxophily** *n.* archery. [Gr. *toxon*, bow]

toxoplasmosis (toksōplazmō´sis) *n.* (*Med.*) an infectious disease caused by the sporozoan *Toxoplasma gondii*, characterized by jaundice, enlarged liver and spleen and convulsions, transmitted esp. through badly-prepared food and cat faeces. [TOXO-, PLASMA, -OSIS]

toy (toi) *n.* 1 a plaything, esp. for a child. 2 something of an amusing or trifling kind, not serious or for actual use. 3 a very small breed of dog etc. 4 a replica in miniature. ~*v.i.* to trifle, to amuse oneself, to sport, to dally. **to toy with** 1 to trifle with. 2 to touch or move idly. 3 to touch and nibble rather than eating normally. **toy-box** *n.* a large box for keeping toys in. **toyboy** *n.* (*coll.*) a (woman's) much younger lover. **toy dog, toy spaniel, toy terrier** *n.* a very small variety of dog. **toyer** *n.* **toyingly** *adv.* **toylike** *a.* **toymaker** *n.* a manufacturer or maker of toys. **toyshop** *n.* a shop where toys are sold. **toy soldier** *n.* 1 a miniature model of a soldier. 2 (*coll., derog.*) a peacetime soldier, i.e. one who has not experienced battle conditions. **toytown** *a.* like a model town, small, quaint, over-dainty. [etym. uncertain]

Tpr. *abbr.* Trooper.

TQM *abbr.* Total Quality Management.

TR *abbr.* Turkey (IVR).

tra- (tra, trə) *pref.* across, through, as in *tradition*, *travesty*. [TRANS-]

trabeate (trā´biət) *a.* (*Archit.*) built of horizontal beams, as distinct from arches and vaults. **trabeation** (-ā´shən) *n.* [L *trabs -bem*, beam, -ATE[2]]

trabecula (trəbek´ūlə) *n.* (*pl.* **trabeculae** (-lē)) 1 (*Anat.*) a band or bar of connective tissue, esp. one forming the framework of an organ. 2 (*Bot.*) a beamlike projection, crossbar etc. **trabecular, trabeculate** (-lət), **trabeculated** (-lātid) *a.*

tracasserie (trəkas´əri) *n.* 1 a turmoil, an annoyance. 2 a fuss, a minor dispute. [F]

trace[1] (trās) *n.* 1 a token, vestige, or sign of something that has existed or taken place. 2 a minute quantity. 3 (*usu. in pl.*) a mark left by a person or animal walking or thing moving, a track, a trail, a footprint, a rut etc. 4 a line made by a recording instrument. 5 a change in the brain when learning takes place. ~*v.t.* 1 to follow the traces or track of. 2 to note the marks and vestiges of. 3 to ascertain the position or course of. 4 to pursue one's way along. 5 to copy (a drawing etc.) by marking the lines on transparent paper etc. laid on it or on carbon paper. 6 to delineate, to mark out. 7 to sketch out (a plan, scheme etc.). ~*v.i.* to be followed back to the origins, to date back. **traceable** *a.* **traceability** (-bil´-), **traceableness** *n.* **traceably** *adv.* **trace element** *n.* a chemical element present in small quantities, esp. one that is valuable for an organism's physiological processes. **trace fossil** *n.* the fossilized remains of the traces of an organism, i.e. its track, print, burrow etc. **traceless** *a.* **tracer** *n.* 1 a person who or thing which traces. 2 a tracer bullet, shell etc. 3 an artificially produced radioactive isotope introduced into the human body where its course can be followed by the radiation it emits. **tracer bullet, tracer shell** *n.* a bullet or shell whose course is marked by a smoke trail or a phosphorescent glow. **tracery** (-əri) *n.* (*pl.* **traceries**) 1 ornamental stone openwork in Gothic windows etc. 2 any decorative work or natural markings resembling this. **traceried** *a.* **tracing** *n.* 1 a traced copy of a drawing etc. 2 a trace made by a recording instrument.

tracing paper *n.* a thin transparent paper used for copying drawings etc. by tracing. [F, from *tracer*, OF *tracier*, L *tractus*, p.p. of *trahere*, to draw]

trace[2] (trās) *n.* either of the two straps, chains or ropes by which a vehicle is drawn by horses etc. **in the traces** in harness. **to kick over the traces** KICK[1]. **trace-horse** *n.* a horse that draws a vehicle, using traces. [ME and OF *trays*, pl. of TRAIT]

tracery TRACE[1].

trachea (trəkē´ə, trā´kiə) *n.* (*pl.* **tracheae** (trəkē´ē, trā´kiē), **tracheas**) **1** (*Anat.*) the windpipe, the air passage from the larynx to the bronchi and lungs. **2** (*Zool.*) any one of the tubes by which air is conveyed from the exterior in insects and arachnids. **3** (*Bot.*) a duct, a vessel. **tracheal** *a.* **tracheate** (trā´kiət) *a.* **tracheitis** (trakiī´tis), **trachitis** (trəkī´tis) *n.* (*Med.*) inflammation of the trachea. [L, from Gr. *tracheia*, orig. fem. of *trachus*, rough]

tracheo- (trəkē´ō, trak´iō, trā´kiō) *comb. form* of or relating to the trachea.

tracheotomy (trakiot´əmi) *n.* (*pl.* **tracheotomies**) (*Med.*) the operation of making an opening into the windpipe. **tracheotomy tube** *n.* a tube inserted in the windpipe to enable breathing after a tracheotomy. [-TOMY]

trachitis TRACHEITIS (under TRACHEA).

trachoma (trəkō´mə) *n.* (*Med.*) a disease of the eye characterized by papillary or granular growths on the inner surface of the lids. **trachomatous** (-kō´mətəs, -kom´-) *a.* [Gr., roughness, from *trachus*, rough]

trachyte (trā´kīt, trak´-) *n.* a gritty-surfaced volcanic rock containing glassy feldspar crystals. **trachytic** (-kit´-) *a.* [Gr. *trachutēs*, roughness, as TRACHOMA]

tracing TRACE[1].

track (trak) *n.* **1** a series of marks left by the passage of a person, animal or thing, a trail. **2** (*usu. in pl.*) a series of footprints. **3** a path, esp. one not constructed but beaten by use. **4** a racecourse, a route for racing. **5** a course of action. **6** a process of thought. **7** a set of rails, a monorail or a continuous line of railway. **8** the distance between the points where a pair of wheels are in contact with the ground, or rails etc. **9** a soundtrack. **10** the groove in a gramophone record in which the needle travels. **11** any one of several paths on a magnetic recording device on which esp. sound from a single input channel is recorded. **12** a course, the route followed by ships etc. **13** (*N Am.*) an educational stream of schoolchildren taught together. **14** the endless band on which a Caterpillar tractor, tank etc. propels itself. **15** the conveyor which carries the items being assembled in a factory. **16** a single item, e.g. a song, recorded on a CD, tape etc. ~*v.t.* **1** to follow the track or traces of. **2** to trace, to follow out (the course of anything). **3** to follow the flight of (a spacecraft etc.) by receiving signals emitted by or reflected from it. **4** to film (a subject) by moving the camera along a fixed path. **5** (*N Am.*) to stream (a pupil) according to educational attainment. **6** (*N Am.*) to leave a track of (dirt etc.); to leave a track of dirt etc. on. ~*v.i.* **1** (of the stylus of a pick-up arm) to follow the groove on a record. **2** (of a camera) to move along a fixed path while shooting. **3** (of wheels) to take exactly the same track. **across the tracks** on the wrong side of the tracks. **in one's tracks** where one stands. **off the track** away from the subject in hand. **on someone's track 1** in pursuit of a person. **2** having knowledge of someone's plans, conduct etc. **on the right track** following the correct line of thought, inquiry etc. **on the wrong side of the tracks** in a poor, less socially prestigious area of town. **on the wrong track** following the incorrect line of thought, inquiry etc. **to cover one's tracks** COVER. **to keep track of** to remain aware of (events, developments etc.). **to lose track of** to cease to be aware of (events, developments etc.). **to make tracks** to run away, to bolt, to leave. **to make tracks for 1** to head for. **2** to go in pursuit of. **to track down** to discover by tracking. **to track with** (*Austral.*) to associate with, to go out with. **trackage** (-ij) *n.* **1** railway tracks in general. **2** (*Hist.*) the right to use the tracks of another company. **trackball** *n.* on a portable computer, a built-in rolling ball that guides the cursor on screen. **trackbed** *n.* the foundation of stones etc. beneath a railway track. **tracker** *n.* **tracker dog** *n.* a dog that uses its sense of smell to find e.g. drugs, persons or smuggled goods, used by the police etc. **track events** *n.pl.* in athletics, running events on the track, as distinct from field events such as throwing and jumping. **tracking** *n.* **1** the act or process of following someone or something. **2** a leakage of electric current from an insulated unit along a conducting path created by dirt, moisture etc. **tracking station** *n.* an establishment using radio signals, radar etc. to track objects in the sky. **tracklayer** *n.* **1** (*N Am.*) a platelayer, a trackman. **2** a vehicle with continuous tracks, e.g. a tank. **track-laying** *n.*, *a.* **trackless** *a.* **1** pathless, unmarked by feet. **2** untrodden, untravelled, leaving no track. **tracklessly** *adv.* **tracklessness** *n.* **trackless trolley** *n.* (*N Am.*) a trolleybus. **trackman** *n.* (*pl.* **trackmen**) (*N Am.*) a platelayer. **track record** *n.* the past achievements, performance, experience etc. of a person or thing. **track shoe** *n.* a light running shoe with spikes on the sole to improve grip. **tracksuit** *n.* a light, loose-fitting suit for wearing before and after vigorous exercise, or as a leisure garment. **track system** *n.* (*N Am.*) the educational system of streaming in schools. **trackway** *n.* a long-established path or track. [OF *trac*, prob. from Gmc. (cp. Dut. *treck*, TREK, from *trekken*, to pull)]

tracklement (trak´əlmənt) *n.* a condiment, an accompaniment to food, esp. a jam, jelly etc. [etym. uncertain]

tract[1] (trakt) *n.* **1** a region or area of land or water of a considerable but undefined extent. **2** (*Anat.*) the region of an organ or system. **3** †a period (of time). [L *tractus -tūs*, from *trahere*, to draw, p.p. *tractus*]

tract[2] (trakt) *n.* a short treatise or pamphlet, esp. on religion or morals. [short for TRACTATE]

tract[3] (trakt) *n.* in the Roman Catholic Church, an anthem sung in place of the Alleluia. [med. L *tractus* (*cantus*), extended (song)]

tractable (trak´təbəl) *a.* easily led, managed, or controlled, docile, manageable. **tractability** (-bil´-) *n.* **tractableness** *n.* **tractably** *adv.* [L *tractābilis*, from *tractāre*, to TREAT]

Tractarian (trakteə´riən) *n.* **1** any one of the authors of *Tracts for the Times*, 1833–41, a series enunciating the principles of the Oxford Movement. **2** an adherent of this, a High Churchman. ~*a.* of or relating to Tractarianism. **Tractarianism** *n.* the principles of the Oxford Movement.

tractate (trak´tāt) *n.* a treatise. [L *tractātus*, orig. p.p. of *tractāre*, to TREAT]

tractile (trak´tīl) *a.* capable of being drawn out, ductile.

traction (trak´shən) *n.* **1** the act of drawing something along a surface, esp. by motive power. **2** the state of being drawn in this way. **3** (*Med.*) **a** the sustained pulling on muscles, tone structure etc. by a system of weights and pulleys. **b** contraction. **4** grip on a surface, as of a tyre on the road. **tractional** *a.* **traction engine** *n.* a steam locomotive formerly used for drawing heavy loads on ordinary roads. **traction wheel** *n.* the wheel to which the force is applied in a locomotive etc. **tractive** *a.* [F, from L *tractiō -onem*, from *trahere*, to draw, p.p. *tractus*]

tractor (trak´tə) *n.* **1** a motor vehicle capable of drawing other vehicles, farm implements etc. **2** the front section of an articulated lorry, consisting of a chassis, engine and driver's cab, which pulls the trailer. **3** an aircraft with its propeller or propellers mounted in front of the engine. **4** a traction engine.

trad (trad) *n.* traditional jazz. ~*a.* (*coll.*) traditional.

trade (trād) *n.* **1** the exchange of commodities, buying and selling, commerce. **2** a business, handicraft, mechanical or mercantile occupation carried on for subsistence or profit, distinct from agriculture, unskilled labour, the professions etc. **3** a business, handicraft etc., requiring training or an apprenticeship. **4** the amount of business done in a particular year, place etc. **5** the people engaged in a particular trade (*the motor trade*). **6** an exchange of one thing for another. **7** (*coll.*) in business or politics, a deal, a bargain. **8** (*pl.*) the trade winds. **9** (*sl.*) a homosexual sexual partner. **10** a track, a path, a way. ~*v.i.* **1** to buy and sell, to barter, to exchange, to traffic, to deal (in). **2** to carry on commerce or business (with). **3** to carry merchandise (between etc.). **4** to be bought and sold. ~*v.t.* **1** to sell or exchange in commerce, to barter. **2** to swap. **3** to exchange verbally. **the trade 1** (*coll.*) the brewing industry, licensed victuallers. **2** (*sl.*) the submarine service. **to be in trade** (*usu. derog.*) to be in commerce, esp. to run a shop. **to trade in** to give in part payment. **to trade off** to exchange (one thing for another), esp. as a compromise. **to trade on** to take advantage of. **tradable, tradeable** *a.* **Trade Board** *n.* (*Hist.*) a council for settling industrial disputes. **trade book** *n.* a book produced to be sold to the general public in shops, as distinct from educational, occupational, mail-order etc. books. **trade cycle** *n.* the recurrent alternation of prosperity and depression in trade. **trade gap, trade deficit** *n.* the amount by which a country's visible imports exceeds its visible exports. **trade-in** *n.* **1** a transaction in which an item is given in part payment for another. **2** the item given in part payment. **trade journal, trade paper** *n.* a periodical containing information and comment concerning a particular industry, trade, profession etc. **trade-last** *n.* (*N Am.*) a compliment about someone passed on to that person in response to a compliment about the reporter. **tradeless** *a.* **trade mark, trademark** *n.* **1** a registered symbol or name used by a manufacturer or merchant to guarantee the genuineness of goods. **2** a distinguishing feature of a person or thing. **trademark** *v.t.* to provide with a trade mark. **trade name** *n.* **1** the name by which an article is called in the trade. **2** the name of a proprietary article. **trade-off** *n.* the exchange of one thing for another, esp. as a compromise. **trade paper** TRADE JOURNAL (under TRADE). **trade plates** *n.pl.* number plates used by people in the motor trade in moving otherwise unlicensed cars. **trade price** *n.* the price charged to dealers for articles to be sold again. **trader** *n.* **1** a person engaged in trade, a merchant, a tradesman. **2** a vessel employed in trade, a merchant ship. **trade secret** *n.* a process, formula etc. used to make a commercial product, known to only one manufacturer. **tradesman, tradeswoman** *n.* (*pl.* **tradesmen, tradeswomen**) **1** a retail dealer, a shopkeeper. **2** a craftsman. **tradespeople** *n.pl.* people engaged in trades, tradesmen or tradeswomen and their families. **trade union, trades union** *n.* an organized body of workers in any trade, formed for the promotion and protection of their common interests. **Trades Union Congress** *n.* the body representing trade unions collectively. **trade unionism, trades unionism** *n.* **trade unionist, trades unionist** *n.* **trade-weighted** *a.* (of exchange rates) weighted according to the significance of the trade with the various countries listed. **trade wind** *n.* **1** a wind blowing from the north or south towards the equator and deflected in a westerly direction by the easterly rotation of the earth. **2** (*pl.*) these and the anti-trades. **trading** *n.* the act or process of engaging in trade. **trading estate** *n.* an area of buildings intended for commercial or light industrial use, an industrial estate. **trading post** *n.* a store established in a remote, esp. little-populated, region. **trading stamp** *n.* a stamp given free with a purchase, which can be saved and later exchanged for goods. **trading station** *n.* (*Hist.*) an overseas settlement established or place visited for trading purposes. [MLG, track, cogn. with TREAD]

tradescantia (tradiskan´tiə) *n.* any usu. trailing plant of the genus *Tradescantia*, with large colourful flowers and striped variegated leaves. [L, after J. *Tradescant*, 1570–1638, English naturalist]

trading TRADE.

tradition (trədish´ən) *n.* **1** the handing down of opinions, practices, customs etc., from ancestors to posterity, esp. by oral communication. **2** a belief, custom etc. so handed down. **3** (*coll.*) a regular practice, a custom. **4** a doctrine believed to have divine authority but not found in Scripture, such as the oral law said to have been given by God to Moses on Mount Sinai, the oral teaching of Christ not recorded in the New Testament, or the acts and sayings of Muhammad not recorded in the Koran. **5** the principles, maxims etc., derived from the usage and experience of artists, dramatists, actors etc. **6** (*Law*) formal delivery (of property). **traditional** *a.* **1** of or relating to tradition, based on tradition. **2** of or relating to a type of jazz which began in New Orleans in the 1900s. **traditionalism** *n.* **1** adherence to tradition, esp. superstitious regard to tradition in religious matters. **2** a philosophical system attributing human knowledge, esp. of religion and ethics, to revelation and tradition. **traditionalist** *n.* **traditionalistic** (-lis´-) *a.* **traditionally** *adv.* **traditionary** *a.* [ME and OF *tradicion*, L *traditio -onem*, from *trādere*, to hand over]

traditor (trad´itə) *n.* (*pl.* **traditors, traditores** (-aw´rēz)) (*Hist.*) any one of the early Christians who, to save their lives, gave up copies of the Scriptures or the goods of the Church to their persecutors. [L, from *trādere*, see TRADITION]

traduce (trədūs´) *v.t.* to defame, to misrepresent, to speak ill of. **traducement** *n.* **traducer** *n.* **traducible** *a.* **traducingly** *adv.* [L *tradūcere* (TRA-, *dūcere*, to lead)]

traducianist (trədū´shənist) *n.* a person believing in the transmission of souls by parents to children. **traducianism** *n.* [late L *trāduciānus*, from *trādux -ducis*, layer, shoot, as TRADUCE]

traffic (traf´ik) *n.* **1** the people, vehicles etc. passing on a road etc. **2** the passing to and fro of people, vehicles etc. on a road etc. **3** the movement of ships, aircraft etc. **4** the transportation of people, animals or goods by road, rail, sea or air. **5** the amount of goods or number of people conveyed. **6** the trade in a particular commodity etc., esp. the illegal trade. **7** the exchange of goods by barter or by the medium of money, trade, commerce. **8** the messages, signals etc. handled by a communications system. **9** communication or dealing (with). ~*v.i.* (*pres.p.* **trafficking,** *p.p.* **trafficked**) **1** to deal (in), esp. illegally. **2** to trade, to buy and sell goods, to have business (with). ~*v.t.* to barter. **trafficator** (-kātə) *n.* (*Hist.*) a movable arm on a car that indicated the driver's intention to turn to right or left. **traffic calming** *n.* measures taken to slow traffic down in locations where speed would be dangerous. **traffic circle** *n.* (*N Am.*) a roundabout. **traffic cop** *n.* (*sl.*) a traffic policeman. **traffic island** *n.* an area in the middle of a road that acts as a refuge for pedestrians. **traffic jam** *n.* a line or build-up of vehicles that are stationary or slow-moving because of the large volume of traffic, an obstruction in the road etc. **trafficker** *n.* a person who deals in a commodity, esp. illegally (*drug trafficker*). **trafficless** *a.* **traffic light, traffic lights, traffic signal** *n.* coloured lights at street intersections to control the flow and direction of traffic. **traffic sign** *n.* a sign giving warning or instruction to drivers of vehicles. **traffic warden** *n.* a person employed to enforce observance of parking restrictions, esp. by issuing parking tickets. [F *trafique* (*trafiquer*, to traffic), It. *traffico*, from *trafficare*, to traffic, etym. uncertain]

tragacanth (trag´əkanth) *n.* **1** a whitish or reddish demulcent gum obtained from the Asian plant of *Astragalus gummifer*, used in pharmacy, calico-printing etc. **2** this plant. [F *tragacanthe*, L *tragacantha*, Gr. *tragakantha* (*tragos*, goat, ACANTHUS)]

tragedy (traj´idi) *n.* (*pl.* **tragedies**) **1** a fatal or calamitous event, esp. a murder or fatal accident. **2** a serious event, a misfortune. **3** a drama in verse or elevated prose dealing with a lofty theme of a sad, pathetic or terrible kind, usu. with an unhappy ending. **4** the genre of such drama. **5** tragedy personified, the Muse of Tragedy. **tragedian** (trəjē´diən) *n.* **1** a writer of tragedies. **2** an actor in tragedy. **tragedienne** (trəjēdien´) *n.* an actress in tragedy. [ME and OF *tragedie*, L *tragoedia*, Gr. *tragōidia*, prob. *goat-song* (*tragos*, he-goat, *ōdē*, see ODE)]

tragi TRAGUS.

tragic (traj´ik) *a.* **1** lamentable, sad, calamitous. **2** characterized by loss of life. **3** of the nature or in the style of tragedy. **tragical** *a.* lamentable, sad, calamitous. **tragicality** (-kal´-), **tragicalness** *n.* **tragically** *adv.* **tragic irony** *n.* a situation in a play etc. where the irony is clear to the audience but not to the characters. **tragicomedy** (-kom´-) *n.* (*pl.* **tragicomedies**) a drama in which tragic and comic scenes or features are mingled. **tragicomic, tragicomical** *a.* **tragicomicality** (-kal´-) *n.* **tragicomically** *adv.* [F *tragique*, as TRAGEDY]

tragopan (trag´əpan) *n.* any Asian pheasant of the genus *Tragopan*, having brilliant plumage and erect fleshy processes on its head. [L, from Gr. *tragos*, goat, *Pan*, the god]

tragus (trā´gəs) *n.* (*pl.* **tragi** (-jī)) (*Anat.*) a small process on the front of the orifice in the external ear. [L, from Gr. *tragos*, he-goat]

trahison des clercs (trah·izō dā kleə´) *n.* the betrayal of standards by intellectuals influenced by politics. [F, title of a book by J. Benda, 1927]

trail (trāl) *v.t.* **1** to drag along behind, esp. along the ground. **2** to follow by the track or trail. **3** to tread down (grass) to make a path. **4** to lag behind in a contest, race etc. **5** to show an excerpt of as advance publicity. ~*v.i.* **1** to be dragged along behind, to hang down loosely or grow to some length along the ground, over a wall etc. **2** to lag behind. **3** to be losing in a contest etc. **4** to tail (off), to fall (away). ~*n.* **1** a track left by an animal etc. **2** the scent followed in hunting. **3** a beaten track through forest or wild country. **4** anything trailing behind a moving thing, a train, a floating appendage etc. **5** (*Mil., Hist.*) the end of a gun carriage resting on the ground when the gun was unlimbered. **at the trail** (*Mil.*) with arms trailed. **to hit the trail** (*N Am.*) to hit the road. **to trail arms** (*Mil.*) to carry (a rifle etc.) in a horizontal or oblique position in the right hand with the arm extended. **to trail one's coat/ coat-tails** COAT. **to trail oneself** to move wearily or reluctantly. **trail bike** *n.* a light motorcycle for riding on rough tracks etc. **trailblazer** *n.* **1** a pioneer in a field of endeavour. **2** a person who blazes a trail. **trailblazing** *n., a.* **trailer** *n.* **1** any vehicle, sled etc. drawn behind another. **2** a person who or thing which trails. **3** a trailing plant. **4** (*N Am.*) a caravan. **5** a short piece of film, video etc. giving advance publicity to a forthcoming item. **trailer park** *n.* a caravan park or caravan site. **trailing** *a.* **trailing arbutus** *n.* (*N Am.*) the mayflower, *Epigaea repens*. **trailing edge** *n.* in aircraft, the rear edge of a wing or of a control surface. **trailing wheel** *n.* a wheel on a vehicle without motive power of its own. **trail-net** *n.* a dragnet. [ME *trailen*, prob. from OF *trailler*, to tow, prob. ult. from L *trahere*, to draw]

train (trān) *n.* **1** a series of railway carriages or trucks, either self-powered or drawn by an engine. **2** a line or long series or succession of people or things. **3** process, orderly succession, progressive condition. **4** something drawn or dragged along behind. **5** an extended part of a gown, robe etc. trailing behind the wearer. **6** a retinue, a suite. **7** a long trailing tail or tail feathers of a bird. **8** the tail of a comet. **9** the trail of a gun carriage. **10** a set of wheels, pinions etc., transmitting motion. **11** a line of combustible material leading fire to a charge or mine. ~*v.t.* **1** to bring to a state of proficiency by prolonged instruction, practice etc. **2** to instruct, to drill, to accustom (to perform certain acts or feats). **3** to prepare by diet and exercise (for a race etc.). **4** to bring (a plant etc.) by pruning, manipulation etc. into a desired shape, position etc. **5** to bring to bear, to point or aim (a cannon, camera etc. on). ~*v.i.* **1** to prepare oneself or come into a state of efficiency (for a race, match etc.). **2** (*coll.*) to go by train. **in someone's train** following behind a person. **in the train of** as a consequence or sequel of. **in train** in progress, happening according to an organized schedule. **to train down** to lose weight by training. **to train it** (*coll.*) to go by train. **trainable** *a.* **trainability** (-bil´-) *n.* **trainband** *n.* (*Hist.*) a company of citizen soldiers organized at various dates during the 16th–18th cents. **train-bearer** *n.* an attendant employed to hold up the train of a robe etc. **trained** *a.* **trainee** (-nē´) *n.* a person undergoing training. **traineeship** *n.* **trainer** *n.* **1** a person who trains, esp. one who prepares athletes, sportspeople, horses etc. **2** a training shoe; a similar shoe worn for leisure purposes. **3** an aircraft or simulator for training pilots. **train ferry** *n.* a ferry on to which a train is run to be conveyed across water to a track on the farther side. **training** *n.* **1** the preparation of a person or animal for a particular activity, occupation etc. **2** the state of being trained or physically fit. **in training** **1** at present undergoing physical training. **2** physically fit because of this. **out of training** not physically fit. **to go into training** to begin physical training, usu. for a particular event etc. **training college** *n.* (*Hist.*) a college for training teachers. **training ship** *n.* a ship for instructing young people in navigation, seamanship etc. **training shoe** *n.* a shoe made of light leather, canvas, plastic etc. for physical training. **trainload** *n.* the quantity of people or goods on a train. **trainman** *n.* (*pl.* **trainmen**) a railway employee who works on a train. **train-mile** *n.* a mile travelled by a train, the unit of work in railway statistics. **train of artillery** *n.* a siege-train. **train-shed** *n.* the usu. glass and metal roof over the platforms of a railway station, as distinct from other buildings at the station. **trainsick** *a.* affected by nausea during train travel. **train-spotter** *n.* a person whose hobby is to collect train numbers. **train-spotting** *n.* **1** this hobby. **2** (*sl.*) looking for a vein in which to inject (a narcotic drug). **train station** *n.* a railway station. [F *train*, m., retinue, series, and *traîne*, f., that which is trailed, from *trainer*, ult. from L *trahere*, to draw]

train-oil (trā´noil) *n.* oil obtained from the blubber or fat of whales. [formerly *train*, *trane*, MG *trān*, MDut. *traen* (Dut. *traan*), orig. tear, resin]

traipse (trāps), **trapes** *v.i.* (*coll.*) **1** to trudge, to drag along wearily. **2** to go (about) on errands on foot. ~*n.* **1** a trudge, a weary journey on foot. **2** †a slattern. [rel. to obs. *trape*, perh. from MDut. *trappen*, to tramp]

trait (trāt, trā) *n.* **1** a distinguishing or peculiar feature, esp. of a person's character or behaviour. **2** a stroke, a touch (of). [F, orig. p.p. of *traire*, L *trahere*, to draw, p.p. *tractus*]

traitor (trā´tə) *n.* a person guilty of disloyalty, treason or treachery, esp. to their country. **traitorous** *a.* **traitorously** *adv.* **traitorousness** *n.* **traitress** (-tris) *n.* a female traitor. [ME and OF *traitre* (A-F and OF *traitour*, acc.), L *traditor -torem*, from *trādere*, to hand over (TRA-, *-dere*, *dare*, to give)]

trajectory (trəjek´təri) *n.* (*pl.* **trajectories**) **1** the path taken by a body, comet, projectile etc., under the action of given forces. 2 (*Geom.*) a curve or surface cutting the curves or surfaces of a given system at a constant angle. †**traject** *v.t.* 1 to transmit. 2 to transport. **trajection** (-jek´shən) *n.* [L *trājectus*, p.p. of *trājicere* (TRA-, *jacere*, to throw), -ORY[1]]

tra-la (trahlah´) *int.* 1 used to express joy, pleasure etc. 2 used as a nonsense syllable in the humming of tunes.

tram[1] (tram) *n.* 1 (*also* **tramcar**) a public passenger vehicle, usu. powered electrically from an overhead cable, running on lines set in or near ordinary roads. 2 a four-wheeled truck or car used in coal mines. 3 TRAMWAY (under TRAM[1]). **tramline** *n.* 1 a rail of a tramway. 2 each of the lines at the side of a tennis court which mark the boundaries of the singles and doubles court. 3 a course which cannot be deviated from. **tram road** *n.* (*Hist.*) a road laid with tracks of timber, stone or iron. **tramway** *n.* 1 a public transport system using trams. 2 the route of this. 3 (*Hist.*) a tram road. [cp. LG *traam*, balk, beam, G *Trumm*, lump, slump, Norw. *tram*, doorstep, Swed. dial. *tromm*, log]

tram[2] (tram), **tram silk** *n.* silk thread made up of two or more strands twisted together, used for the weft of the finer kinds of silk goods. [MF *trame*, It. *trama*, L *trāma*, weft]

trammel (tram´əl) *n.* 1 (*usu. in pl.*) anything restraining freedom or activity. 2 a trammel net. 3 an instrument for drawing ellipses. 4 a beam-compass. 5 (*N Am.*) a shackle or fetter, esp. one used in teaching a horse to amble. 6 (*Hist.*) a hook in a fireplace for pots, kettles etc. ~*v.t.* (*pres.p.* **trammelling**, (*N Am.*) **trammeling**, *past, p.p.* **trammelled**, (*N Am.*) **trammeled**) to confine, to hamper, to restrict. **trammelled**, (*N Am.*) **trammeled** *a.* 1 confined, hampered. 2 (of a horse) with white marks on the feet of one side. **trammeller**, (*N Am.*) **trammeler** *n.* **trammel net** *n.* a dragnet formed by a combination of three seines, in which fish become entangled. [ME *tramayle*, MF *tramail* (F *trémail*), pop. L *tramaculum*, *-la* (perh. TRI-, *macula*, mesh)]

tramontane (trəmon´tān) *a.* 1 lying, situated or coming from beyond the mountains, esp. the Alps (as seen from Italy), transmontane. 2 foreign, barbarous. ~*n.* 1 a tramontane person. 2 the tramontana. **tramontana** (tramontah´nə) *n.* the cold north wind in the Adriatic Sea. [It. *tramontana* (perh. through F), L *transmontānus* (TRANS-, *mons montis*, MOUNT[2])]

tramp (tramp) *v.i.* 1 to walk, to go on foot, esp. for a considerable distance. 2 to walk or tread heavily. 3 to live as a tramp. ~*v.t.* 1 to go over or traverse, or to perform (a journey etc.) on foot. 2 to tread heavily on, to trample. ~*n.* 1 an itinerant beggar, a vagrant. 2 the sound of the tread of people etc. walking or marching, or of horses' hoofs. 3 a walk, a journey on foot. 4 (*sl.*) a promiscuous girl or woman. 5 (*Hist.*) a merchant ship having no regular route. 6 an iron plate worn to protect the sole of the boot in digging. **tramper** *n.* **trampish** *a.* [ME, LG and G *trampen*, cp. Dan. *trampe*, Swed. and Norw. *trampa*]

trample (tram´pəl) *v.t.* 1 to tread underfoot, esp. carelessly or in scorn, triumph etc. 2 to tread down, to crush in this way. 3 to treat with arrogance or contemptuous indifference. ~*n.* the act or sound of trampling. **to trample on** 1 to tread heavily on. 2 to tread on in contempt. **trampler** *n.* [freq. of TRAMP]

trampoline (tram´pəlēn) *n.* a sheet of canvas suspended by springs from a frame, used for bouncing on or for assisting jumps in gymnastics. ~*v.i.* to use a trampoline. **trampolinist** *n.* [Sp. *trampolin*, from It. *trampolino*, of Gmc. origin: cp. *trampen*, to stamp]

trance (trahns) *n.* 1 a state of mental abstraction, with no response to external surroundings or stimuli. 2 a hypnotic state, esp. of a spiritualistic medium. 3 a cataleptic state. 4 a state of ecstasy, rapture. 5 (*in full* **trance music**) a hypnotic style of electronic dance music. ~*v.t.* (*poet.*) to entrance, to enchant. **trancelike** *a.* [OF *transe*, from *transir*, to depart, to die, to be numbed, L *transīre* (TRANS-, *īre*, to go)]

tranche (trahnsh) *n.* a portion, esp. of a larger sum of money, block of shares etc. [F, slice]

tranny (tran´i) *n.* (*pl.* **trannies**) (*coll.*) 1 a transistor radio. 2 (*N Am.*) a transmission mechanism.

tranquil (trang´kwil) *a.* calm, peaceful, serene, quiet, undisturbed. **tranquillity** (-kwil´-), **tranquility** *n.* **tranquillize, tranquillise**, (*N Am.*) **tranquilize** *v.t.* to make calm, to reduce anxiety in, esp. with a sedative drug. **tranquillization** (-zā´shən) *n.* **tranquillizer** *n.* 1 a sedative drug, a drug to reduce anxiety. 2 anything that promotes tranquillity. **tranquillizingly** *adv.* **tranquilly** *adv.* **tranquilness** *n.* [F *tranquille*, L *tranquillus*]

trans. *abbr.* 1 transitive. 2 translated. 3 translation. 4 translator.

trans- (tranz) *pref.* 1 across, over. 2 beyond, on the other side. 3 through. 4 into another state or place. 5 surpassing. 6 (*Chem.*) higher in atomic number than. 7 (*Chem.*) being an isomer with two atoms or groups on the opposite side of a given plane. [L, across, beyond]

transact (tranzakt´) *v.t.* to do, to perform, to manage, to carry out. ~*v.i.* to do business, to conduct matters (with). **transaction** *n.* 1 the management or carrying out of a piece of business etc. 2 something transacted, a piece of business, an affair, a proceeding. 3 (*pl.*) the reports of the proceedings of a learned society. 4 adjustment of a dispute by mutual concessions etc. **transactional** *a.* **transactionally** *adv.* **transactor** *n.* [L *transactus*, p.p. of *transigere* (TRANS-, *agere*, to act)]

transalpine (tranzal´pīn) *a.* lying or situated beyond the Alps (usu. as seen from Italy). ~*n.* a person living beyond the Alps.

transatlantic (tranzətlan´tik) *a.* 1 lying or being beyond the Atlantic; American as seen from Europe, European as seen from N America. 2 crossing the Atlantic.

transceiver (transē´və) *n.* a device for transmitting and receiving radio signals. [*trans*mitter, re*ceiver*]

transcend (transend´) *v.t.*, *v.i.* 1 to rise above, to surpass, to excel, to exceed. 2 to pass or be beyond the range, sphere or power (of human understanding etc.). **transcendent** *a.* 1 excelling, surpassing, supremely excellent. 2 in scholastic philosophy, applied to concepts higher or of wider signification than the categories of Aristotle. 3 in Kantian philosophy, beyond the sphere of knowledge or experience. 4 above and independent of the material universe. ~*n.* that which is transcendent. **transcendence, transcendency** *n.* **transcendental** (-den´-) *a.* 1 in Kantian philosophy, transcendent, beyond the sphere of experience. 2 belonging to the a priori elements of experience, implied in and necessary to experience. 3 explaining matter and the universe as products of mental conception. 4 transcending ordinary ideas. 5 abstruse, speculative, vague, obscure. 6 (*Math.*) not capable of being produced by the fundamental operations of algebra, addition, multiplication etc. ~*n.* a transcendent concept, a term. **transcendental cognition** *n.* a priori knowledge. **transcendentalism** *n.* 1 the state of being transcendental. 2 a transcendental philosophy, such as that of Schelling. **transcendentalist** *n.* **transcendentalize, transcendentalise** *v.t.* **transcendentally** *adv.* **Transcendental Meditation** *n.* a form of meditation intended to induce spiritual balance and harmony through silent repetition of a mantra. **transcendental object** *n.* an object that is real but beyond the sphere of knowledge or experience. **transcendental unity** *n.* unity through knowledge and perception. **transcendently** *adv.* [OF *transcender*, L *transcendere* (TRAN-, *scandere*, to climb)]

transcode (tranzkōd´) *v.t.*, *v.i.* to convert (information represented in one code) into another code.

transcontinental (tranzkontinen´təl) *a.* extending or travelling across a continent. ~*n.* a transcontinental railway or train. **transcontinentally** *adv.*

transcribe (transkrīb´) *v.t.* **1** to copy in writing, to write out in full (shorthand notes etc.). **2** to translate, to transliterate. **3** to transfer (data) from one recording medium to another. **4** (*Mus.*) to arrange (a vocal composition) for an instrument, to readjust (a composition) for another instrument. **5** to record (spoken sounds) in the form of phonetic symbols. **6** to record for broadcasting. **transcriber** *n.* **transcript** (tran´skript) *n.* **1** a written or recorded copy. **2** any form of copy. **transcription** (-krip´shən) *n.* **1** the act of transcribing, the state of being transcribed. **2** a transcript. **3** the arrangement of a vocal composition for an instrument, or the readjustment of a composition for another instrument. **4** (*Biol.*) the copying of nucleotides from DNA during the synthesis of an RNA molecule. **transcriptional, transcriptive** *a.* [L *transcrībere* (TRAN-, *scrībere*, p.p. *scriptus*)]

transcurrent (tranzkŭr´ənt) *a.* running or passing across or transversely. [L *transcurrens -ntem*, pres.p. of *transcurrere* (TRANS-, *currere*, to run)]

transducer (tranzdū´sə) *n.* a power-transforming device for which the input and output are of different kinds, electrical, acoustic, optical etc., e.g. loudspeaker, microphone, photoelectric cell etc. **transduce** *v.t.* **transduction** (-dŭk´shən) *n.* **1** transformation by a transducer. **2** †a carrying or leading across. [L *trans-, dūcere*, to lead]

transect[1] (transekt´) *v.t.* **1** to cut across. **2** (*Anat.*) to dissect transversely. **transection** *n.* [TRANS-, L *sectum*, neut. p.p. of *secāre*, to cut]

transect[2] (tran´sekt) *n.* a sample strip of land used to study the geography, natural history etc. of a wider area.

transept (tran´sept) *n.* **1** either of the transverse arms extending north and south in a cruciform church. **2** the area including both these arms. **transeptal** *a.* [TRAN-, SEPTUM]

transexual TRANSSEXUAL.

transfer[1] (transfœ´) *v.t.* (*pres.p.* **transferring,** *past, p.p.* **transferred)** **1** to convey, remove or shift from one place or person to another. **2** to make over the possession of. **3** to remove to another club, department etc. **4** to convey (a design etc.) from one surface to another, esp. in lithography. **5** to remove (a picture etc.) from a wall etc. to canvas or other surface. **6** to use in a figurative or extended sense; to change (meaning) in this way. ~*v.i.* **1** to move from one place to another. **2** to change from one bus, train etc. to another. **3** to move to another club, department etc. **transferable** *a.* **transferability** (-bil´-) *n.* **transferable vote** *n.* in a system of proportional representation, a vote that can be transferred to a second candidate if the first loses a preliminary ballot. **transferee** (-rē´) *n.* **transference** (trans´fər-) *n.* **1** the act of transferring. **2** (*Psych.*) the transferring of emotions, attitudes etc. of childhood towards a substitute object, esp. to a psychotherapist. **transferential** (-ren´shəl) *a.* **transferral** *n.* **transferrer, transferror** *n.* [L *transferre* (TRANS-, *ferre*, to bear)]

transfer[2] (trans´fœ) *n.* **1** the removal or conveyance of a thing from one person or place to another. **2** the act of conveying a right, property etc. from one person to another. **3** the deed by which this is effected. **4** something which is transferred. **5** a design conveyed from paper etc. to some other surface. **6** a soldier transferred from one regiment, troop etc. to another. **7** a footballer etc. transferred from one club to another. **8** (*N Am.*) a ticket which allows a passenger on public transport to change routes. **transfer-book** *n.* a register of transfers of stocks, shares etc. **transfer company** *n.* (*N Am.*) a company that conveys passengers, luggage etc. between stations. **transfer fee** *n.* the fee paid to one sports club by another for the transfer of a player. **transfer ink** *n.* lithographic ink for transferable drawing, writing etc. on lithographic stone, transfer-paper etc. **transfer list** *n.* a list of footballers available for transfer to other clubs. **transfer-paper** *n.* prepared paper for receiving impressions and transferring to stone. **transfer RNA** *n.* an RNA that carries a particular amino acid to a ribosome in protein synthesis.

transferase (trans´fərās) *n.* (*Chem.*) an enzyme that acts as a catalyst in the transfer of a chemical group from one molecule to another.

transferral, transferrer TRANSFER[1].

transferrin (transfœ´rin) *n.* a blood protein that transports iron. [TRANS-, L *ferrum*, iron]

transfiguration (transfigūrā´shən) *n.* **1** a change of form or appearance, esp. that of Christ on the Mount (Matt. xvii.1–9). **2** **(Transfiguration)** a festival on 6 Aug. in commemoration of this. **transfigure** (-fig´ə) *v.t.* to change the outward appearance of, esp. so as to elevate and glorify. [F, from L *transfiguratio -tionem*, from *transfigūrāre* (TRANS-, *figūrāre*, to change the figure of, from *figūra*, figure)]

transfinite (transfī´nīt) *a.* **1** beyond or surpassing what is finite. **2** (*Math.*) (of a number) surpassing all finite numbers.

transfix (transfiks´) *v.t.* **1** to pierce through, to impale. **2** to render motionless with shock, fear etc. **transfixion** (-fik´shən) *n.* **1** the act of transfixing. **2** amputation by piercing and cutting outwards. [L *transfixus*, p.p. of *transfigere* (TRANS-, *figere*, to fix)]

transform[1] (transfawm´) *v.t.* **1** to change the form, shape or appearance of, to metamorphose. **2** to change in disposition, character etc. **3** to change the voltage etc. of (an electrical current). **4** (*Math.*) to change (a figure or expression) by transformation. ~*v.i.* to undergo a transformation. **transformable** *a.* **transformation** (-fəmā´shən) *n.* **1** the act of transforming. **2** the state of being transformed. **3** (*Zool.*) a metamorphosis resulting in a complete change of form. **4** a change from solid to liquid or liquid to gaseous form or the reverse. **5** (*Math.*) the change of a figure or expression to another equivalent to it. **6** (*Med.*) a change of tissue from a normal state to a malignant state. **7** (*Biol.*) the change of the genetic structure of a cell through the introduction of extraneous DNA. **8** in linguistics, a rule for the transforming of the underlying structures of a language into actual sentences. **9** in the theatre, a sudden dramatic change of scene. **10** †a woman's wig. **transformational** *a.* **transformational grammar** *n.* a grammar which describes the structure of a language in terms of a set of rules for transforming the underlying structures of the language into an infinite number of actual sentences. **transformationally** *adv.* **transformation scene** *n.* **1** a scene in a pantomime etc. which changes suddenly and dramatically as the audience looks on. **2** (*Hist.*) a scene in a pantomime in which the principal characters are supposed to be transformed into the chief characters of the harlequinade. **transformative** *a.* **transformer** *n.* **1** a device which changes the circuit of an alternating electrical supply, thereby altering the voltage. **2** a person or thing which transforms. **transformism** *n.* the theory of the development of one species from another, i.e. evolution. **transformist** *n.* [F *transformer*, L *transformāre* (TRANS-, *formāre*, to form)]

transform[2] (trans´fawm) *n.* the result of a mathematical or linguistic transformation.

transfuse (transfūz´) *v.t.* **1** to permeate, to cause to pass from one vessel etc. into another. **2** to transfer (blood) from the veins of one person or animal to those of another. **3** to inject (a liquid) into a blood vessel or cavity to replace loss or wastage. **transfusible** *a.*

transfusion (-zhən) *n.* **transfusive** *a.* [L *transfūsus*, p.p. of *transfundere* (TRANS-, *fundere*, to pour)]

transgenic (tranzjen´ik) *a.* (*Biol.*) (of an animal or plant) containing genetic material artificially transferred from another species.

transgress (tranzgres´) *v.t.* **1** to break (a rule or rules), to violate, to infringe. **2** (*Geol.*) (of the sea) to overspread (the land). ~*v.i.* to offend by violating a law or rule, to sin. **transgression** (-shən) *n.* **transgressive** *a.* **transgressively** *adv.* **transgressor** *n.* [L *transgressus*, p.p. of *transgredī* (TRANS-, *gradī*, to walk)]

tranship TRANS-SHIP.

transhumance (tranzhū´məns) *n.* the seasonal migration of livestock from one grazing ground to another. [from F *transhumer*, from L *trans-*, *humus*, ground]

transient (tran´siənt, -ziənt) *a.* **1** not lasting or durable, temporary. **2** transitory, momentary, hasty, brief. **3** (*Mus.*) passing, serving merely to connect or introduce. **4** (*N Am.*) (of a hotel guest) staying one night only. ~*n.* **1** a transient person or thing. **2** a transient fluctuation in the amount of current flowing through an electrical circuit. **transience, transiency** *n.* **transiently** *adv.* [L *transiens*, pres.p. of *transīre* (TRANS-, *īre*, to go)]

transilluminate (tranzilū´mināt, -loo´-) *v.t.* to send a powerful light through (an organ or part) in diagnosis. **transillumination** (-ā´shən) *n.*

transire (tranzī´ri, tranzīə´) *n.* a customs warrant authorizing the passage of dutiable goods. [L, TRANS-, *īre*, to go]

transistor (tranzis´tə) *n.* **1** a device made primarily of a semiconductor (germanium or silicon) capable of giving current and power amplification. **2** (*coll.*) a transistor radio. **transistorize, transistorise** *v.t.* **1** to equip with transistors. **2** to design with or convert to transistors. **transistorization** (-zā´shən) *n.* **transistor radio** *n.* a small portable radio with transistors. [*trans*fer, re*sistor*]

transit (tran´zit, -sit) *n.* **1** the act of passing, conveying or being conveyed, across, over or through. **2** a line of passage, a route. **3** (*Astron.*) **a** the apparent passage of a heavenly body over the meridian of a place. **b** the passage of a heavenly body across the disc of another, esp. of Venus or Mercury across the sun's disc. **4** (*N Am.*) local public transport. **5** a transit-theodolite. ~*v.t.* (*pres.p.* **transiting,** *past, p.p.* **transited**) to pass across (the disc of the sun etc.). ~*v.i.* to make a transit. **in transit** being conveyed. **transit camp** *n.* a camp where people stay temporarily before moving on to another place. **transit-circle, transit-instrument** *n.* (*Astron.*) MERIDIAN CIRCLE (under MERIDIAN). **transit-duty** *n.* duty paid upon goods passing through a country. **transit lounge** *n.* a lounge at an airport for passengers from one flight waiting to join another. **transit-theodolite, transit-compass** *n.* a rotatable theodolite for measuring horizontal angles. **transit visa** *n.* a visa allowing a person only to pass through a country, not to stay there. [L *transitus -tūs*, from *transīre*, see TRANSIRE]

transition (tranzish´ən) *n.* **1** passage or change from one place, state or action to another. **2** a change in architecture, painting, literature etc. **3** a change from one musical key to another or from the major to the relative minor. **4** in rhetoric, a passing from one subject to another. **5** (*Physics*) a change from one quantum stage to another. **transitional, transitionary** *a.* **transitionally** *adv.* **transition element, transition metal** *n.* (*Chem.*) any of a set of metallic elements in the periodic table with an incomplete penultimate electron shell, tending to exhibit more than one valency and to form coloured complexes. **transition point** *n.* (*Chem.*) the temperature at which different forms of the same substance can be in equilibrium.

transitive (tran´sitiv) *a.* **1** (*Gram.*) (of verbs) expressing an action passing over from a subject to an object, having a direct object. **2** (*Logic*) denoting a relation between members of a sequence that necessarily holds between any two members if it holds between every pair of successive members. **transitively** *adv.* **transitiveness** *n.* **transitivity** (-tiv´-) *n.* [late L *transitivus*]

transitory (tran´sitəri) *a.* lasting only a short time, transient, not durable, short-lived. **transitorily** *adv.* **transitoriness** *n.* **transitory action** *n.* (*Law*) an action that can be brought in any country regardless of where the issue concerned originated. [OF *transitoire*, late L *transitōrius*, as TRANSIT]

Transjordanian (tranzjawdā´niən) *n.* **1** (*Hist.*) a native or inhabitant of the former Transjordan. **2** a person living beyond the River Jordan. ~*a.* of or relating to the land beyond the River Jordan.

translate (translāt´) *v.t.* **1** to render or express the sense of (a word, passage or work) into or in another language. **2** to express in clearer terms. **3** to express, paraphrase or convey (an idea etc.) from one art or style into another. **4** to interpret (as). **5** to transform, to change. **6** to remove from one office to another (esp. a bishop to another see). **7** (*Theol.*) to convey to heaven without death. **8** to move (a body) so that all parts follow the same direction, to give motion without rotation. **9** (*Biol.*) to use as a template for a sequence of amino acids. **10** (*Comput.*) to convert into another programming language. **11** to retransmit (a message). **12** †to transport, to enrapture. ~*v.i.* **1** to be engaged in translation. **2** to allow of translation, to be translatable. **3** to be changed (into). **translatable** *a.* **translatability** (-bil´-) *n.* **translation** *n.* **1** the act or process of translating. **2** the product of translating; a rendition of the sense of a passage etc. in another language. **translational** *a.* **translationally** *adv.* **translator** *n.* **1** a person engaged in translation. **2** a computer program that translates from one (natural or programming) language to another. **3** a television transmitter. **translatory** *a.* [OF *translater*, L *translātus*, p.p. of *transferre*, to TRANSFER[1]]

transliterate (tranzlit´ərāt) *v.t.* to represent (words, sounds etc.) in the corresponding or approximately corresponding characters of another language or alphabet. **transliteration** (-ā´shən) *n.* **transliterator** *n.* [TRANS-, L *littera*, LETTER]

translocation (tranzləkā´shən) *n.* **1** movement from one place to another. **2** (*Biol.*) the transfer of soluble substances from one part of an organism to another. **3** (*Biol.*) the movement of a portion of a chromosome to a new position (on the same or another chromosome). **translocate** *v.t.*

translucent (transloo´sənt) *a.* **1** allowing light to pass through but not transparent. **2** (*loosely*) transparent. **translucence, translucency** *n.* **translucently** *adv.* [L *translūcens -ntem*, pres.p. of *translūcēre* (TRANS-, *lūcēre*, to shine, see LUCID)]

translunar (tranzloo´nə), **translunary** (-nəri) *a.* **1** situated beyond the moon, opposed to *sublunary*. **2** ethereal, visionary.

transmarine (tranzmərēn´) *a.* situated beyond the sea.

transmigrate (tranzmīgrāt´) *v.i.* **1** to pass through one place, country or jurisdiction en route to another, to migrate. **2** (*Theol.*) (of the soul) to pass from one body into another, to undergo metempsychosis. **transmigrant** (-mī´-) *n.* **1** an alien passing through one country on the way to another. **2** a person who transmigrates, a migrant. ~*a.* in the process of transmigrating. **transmigration** *n.* **transmigrationism** *n.* the doctrine of metempsychosis. **transmigrator** *n.* **transmigratory** (-mī´grə-) *a.* [L *transmigrātus*, p.p. of *transmigrāre* (TRANS-, MIGRATE)]

transmit (tranzmit´) *v.t.* (*pres.p.* **transmitting,** *past, p.p.* **transmitted**) **1** to send, transfer, convey or communicate from one person or place to another. **2** to suffer to pass through, to act as a medium for, to conduct. **3** to broadcast (a TV or radio programme). **transmissible** (-mis´-) *a.* **transmissibility** (-bil´-) *n.* **transmission** (-shən) *n.* 1 the act of transmitting. 2 signals sent out by a transmitter. 3 a radio or TV broadcast. 4 the gear by which power is conveyed from an engine to the live axle in a motor vehicle. **transmission line** *n.* a cable or other system of conductors transferring electricity from one location to another. **transmissive** (-mis´-) *a.* **transmittable** *a.* **transmittal** *n.* **transmittance** *n.* (*Physics*) the ratio of the light energy falling on a body to that transmitted onward by it. **transmitter** *n.* 1 a person or thing that transmits. 2 any form of machine that transmits electromagnetic waves, esp. for radio and television. 3 the apparatus required for this. 4 a neurotransmitter. [L *transmittere* (TRANS-, *mittere*, to send)]

transmogrify (tranzmog´rifī) *v.t.* (*3rd pers. sing. pres.* **transmogrifies**, *pres.p.* **transmogrifying**, *past, p.p.* **transmogrified**) (*esp. facet.*) to transform, esp. as if by magical means. **transmogrification** (-fikā´shən) *n.* [TRANS-, *mogrify*, appar. an arbitrary coinage]

transmontane (tranzmon´tān) *a.* situated beyond the mountains, tramontane.

transmute (tranzmūt´) *v.t.* to change from one form, nature or substance into another; to transform (into). **transmutable** *a.* **transmutability** (-bil´-) *n.* **transmutably** *adv.* **transmutation** (-tā´shən) *n.* 1 the act of transmuting. 2 the state of being transmuted. 3 the supposed change of base metals into gold or silver sought by alchemists. 4 (*Biol.*) the supposed change of one species into another. 5 (*Geom.*) the reduction of one figure or body into another of the same area or content. 6 (*Physics*) the conversion of one element or nuclide into another either naturally or artificially. **transmutational** *a.* **transmutationist** *n.* (*Biol.*) a person who believes in the transmutation of species. **transmutative** *a.* **transmuter** *n.* [L *transmūtāre* (TRANS-, *mūtāre*, to change)]

transoceanic (tranzōshian´ik) *a.* 1 situated or coming from beyond the ocean. 2 crossing the ocean. [OCEANIC (under OCEAN)]

transom (tran´səm) *n.* 1 a horizontal bar of wood or stone across a window or other opening. 2 a horizontal bar across the top of a doorway separating it from the fanlight. 3 (*N Am.*) a fanlight. 4 each of the beams bolted across the sternpost of a ship, supporting the after-end of the deck. 5 a horizontal piece connecting the cheeks of a gun carriage. 6 a beam across a saw-pit. 7 the vane of a cross-staff. **transomed** *a.* **transom window** *n.* 1 a window divided by a transom. 2 a window over the transom of a door. [ME *traunsum*, prob. corr. of L *transtrum*, from *trans*, see TRANS-]

transonic (transon´ik), **trans-sonic** *a.* relating to or being a speed near the speed of sound. [SONIC]

transpacific (tranzpəsif´ik) *a.* 1 lying or being beyond the Pacific. 2 crossing the Pacific.

transparent (transpar´ənt, -peə´-) *a.* 1 having the property of transmitting rays of light without diffusion, so that objects are distinctly visible. 2 easily seen through. 3 plain, evident, clear. 4 frank, sincere. 5 permitting heat or electromagnetic radiation to pass through. **transparency** *n.* (*pl.* **transparencies**) 1 transparentness. 2 a thing that is transparent, esp. a picture, inscription, photograph etc. painted on glass, muslin or other transparent or semi-transparent material, to be exhibited by means of light shining through it. 3 a positive photograph on a transparent base mounted on a frame for viewing by means of a projector. **transparence** *n.* **transparently** *adv.* **transparentness** *n.* [F, from med. L *transparens -ntem*, pres.p. of *transpārēre* (TRANS-, *pārēre*, to appear)]

transpersonal (tranzpœ´sənəl) *a.* 1 going beyond the personal. 2 of or relating to psychology or psychotherapy based on mystical, psychical or spiritual experience.

transpierce (transpiəs´) *v.t.* to pierce through.

transpire (transpīə´) *v.t.* to emit through the excretory organs (of the skin or lungs), to emit as vapour, to exhale. ~*v.i.* 1 (of perspiration etc.) to be emitted through the the excretory organs, to pass off as vapour. 2 to leak out, become known. 3 to happen. **transpirable** *a.* **transpiration** (-pirā´shən) *n.* **transpiratory** *a.* [TRAN-, L *spīrāre*, to breathe]

Usage note The use of *transpire* to mean to happen is sometimes disapproved of.

transplant[1] (transplahnt´) *v.t.* 1 to remove and plant in another place. 2 to remove from one place and establish in another. 3 to transfer (living tissue) from one part or person to another. **transplantable** *a.* **transplantation** (-tā´shən) *n.* **transplanter** *n.* 1 a person who or thing which transplants. 2 a machine for removing trees with earth and replanting. 3 a tool for taking up plants in this way. [F *transplanter*, L *transplantāre*]

transplant[2] (trans´plahnt) *n.* 1 the surgical procedure for transplanting an organ. 2 an organ surgically transplanted. 3 a thing which is transplanted, such as a plant.

transponder (transpon´də) *n.* a radio or radar device which automatically transmits a signal in response to a signal received. [*trans*mitter, res*ponder*]

transpontine (transpon´tīn) *a.* 1 on the other side of a bridge. 2 on or from the other side of the ocean. 3 †belonging to the Surrey side of London or the part across London Bridge. [TRANS-, L *pons pontis*, bridge]

transport[1] (transpawt´) *v.t.* 1 to carry or convey from one place to another. 2 (*Hist.*) to remove (a criminal) to a penal colony. 3 (*chiefly in p.p.*) to carry away by powerful emotion, to entrance, to ravish. **transportable** *a.* 1 that may be transported. 2 (*Hist.*) (of an offence) involving transportation. **transportability** (-bil´-) *n.* **transportation** (-tā´shən) *n.* 1 the act of transporting or conveying. 2 the state of being transported. 3 (means of) conveyance. 4 carriage of persons or things from one place to another. 5 (*Hist.*) banishment to a penal colony. **transportedly** *adv.* **transporter** *n.* 1 a person who or device that transports. 2 a large vehicle for transporting goods. **transporter bridge** *n.* a device for carrying road traffic across a river on a moving platform. [F *transporter*, L *transportāre* (*portāre*, to carry)]

transport[2] (trans´pawt) *n.* 1 transportation, conveyance from one place to another. 2 a transport ship or aircraft. 3 a vehicle, aircraft etc. used for transporting people or goods. 4 (*Hist.*) a transported convict or a convict sentenced to transportation. 5 ecstasy. **transport café** *n.* a roadside café used predominantly by lorry drivers. **transport ship, transport vessel** *n.* a ship used to carry troops, munitions of war, stores etc. **transport-worker** *n.* a worker on any system of transport.

transpose (transpōz´) *v.t.* 1 to cause to change places. 2 to change the order or position of (words or a word) in a sentence. 3 (*Math.*) to transfer (a term) from one side of an equation to the other, changing the sign. 4 (*Mus.*) to write or play in a different key. **transposable** *a.* **transposal** *n.* **transposer** *n.* **transposing** *n., a.* **transposing instrument** *n.* a musical instrument, esp. a horn or a clarinet, which produces notes that are different in pitch from the music written for it. **transposing piano, transposing organ** *n.* a piano or organ on which music is transposed mechanically. **transposition** (-pəzish´ən) *n.* 1 the act of transposing. 2 the state of being transposed. **transpositional** *a.* **transpositive** (-poz´-) *a.* [ME *transposen*, F *transposer* (POSE[1])]

transputer (transpū´tə) *n.* a powerful microchip which has its own RAM facility and is designed to process in parallel rather than sequentially. [*trans*istor, com*puter*]

transsexual (trans·sek´shuəl), **transexual** (tran-sek´shuəl) *n.* 1 a person who dresses and lives for all or most of the time as a member of the opposite sex. 2 a person who has undergone surgery and medical treatment to adopt the physical characteristics of the opposite sex. ~*a.* that is a transsexual; of or relating to transsexuals. **transsexualism** *n.*

trans-ship (trans·ship´), **tranship** (tranship´) *v.t.* (*pres.p.* **trans-shipping, transhipping,** *past, p.p.* **trans-shipped, transhipped**) to transfer from one ship, vehicle etc., to another. **trans-shipment** *n.*

trans-sonic TRANSONIC.

transubstantiate (transəbstan´shiāt) *v.t.* to change the substance of. **transubstantiation** (-ā´shən) *n.* 1 change from one substance into another, a change of essence. 2 (*Theol.*) conversion of the whole substance of the bread and wine in the Eucharist into the body and blood of Christ. **transubstantiative** *a.* [med. L *transubstantiātus*, p.p. of *transubstantiāre* (*substantia*, SUBSTANCE)]

transude (transūd´) *v.i.* to pass or ooze through the pores or interstices of a membrane etc. **transudation** (-dā´shən) *n.* **transudatory** (-dətəri) *a.* [F *transsuder* (L *sūdāre*, to sweat)]

transuranic (tranzūran´ik) *a.* (of an atomic element) having an atomic number higher than uranium.

Transvaal daisy (tranzvahl´) *n.* a S African gerbera, *Gerbera jamesonii*, which has large daisy-like flowers. [*Transvaal*, South Africa]

transvalue (tranzval´ū) *v.t.* (*3rd pers. sing. pres.* **trans-values,** *pres.p.* **transvaluing,** *past, p.p.* **transvalued**) to evaluate by a different or new principle. **trans-valuation** (-ā´shən) *n.* **transvaluer** *n.*

transverse (tranzvœs´, tranz´-) *a.* lying, being or acting across or in a cross direction. ~*n.* that which is transverse, esp. a transverse muscle. ~*v.t.* 1 to lie or pass across. 2 †to overturn. 3 to thwart, to cross. **transversal** (-vœ´-) *a.* 1 transverse. 2 running or lying across. ~*n.* a straight line cutting a system of lines. **transversally** *adv.* **transverse flute** *n.* FLUTE. **transverse jury** *n.* (*pl.* **transverse juries**) a petty jury. **transversely** *adv.* **transverse magnet** *n.* a magnet with poles at the sides. **transverse wave** *n.* (*Physics*) a wave in which the disturbance of the medium occurs at right angles to the direction of propagation. **transverso-** (-vœ´sō) *comb. form* [L *transversus*, p.p. of *transvertere* (*vertere*, to turn)]

transvestism (tranzves´tizm) *n.* the wearing of clothing belonging to the opposite sex, esp. for sexual stimulation. **transvestist** *n.* **transvestite** (-tīt) *n.* a person who practises transvestism. **transvestitism** (-tit-) *n.* [TRANS-, L *vestire*, to dress]

Transylvanian (transilvā´niən) *a.* of or belonging to Transylvania, in Romania.

trap[1] (trap) *n.* 1 a contrivance for catching game, vermin and other animals, consisting of a pitfall, enclosure or mechanical arrangement, esp. with a door or lid closing with a spring, often baited. 2 a trick or artifice for misleading or betraying a person, an ambush, a stratagem. 3 a device to catch someone, such as a motorist who is speeding. 4 a device for suddenly releasing a bird or propelling an object into the air to be shot at. 5 a compartment from which a racing greyhound is released. 6 a device for hurling clay pigeons into the air. 7 the game of trap-ball. 8 the wooden instrument used in this game. 9 a U-shaped bend or other contrivance in a soil pipe etc., for sealing this with a body of liquid and preventing the return flow of foul gas. 10 a trapdoor. 11 a two-wheeled vehicle on springs. 12 (*sl.*) the mouth. 13 in golf, a bunker. 14 (*esp. pl., sl.*) a percussion instrument in a jazz band. ~*v.t.* (*pres.p.* **trapping,** *past, p.p.* **trapped**) 1 to catch in or as in a trap. 2 to retain, to hold back. 3 to furnish (a drain) with a trap. 4 to stop or hold (gas etc.) in a trap. 5 to make trapdoors in (a stage). 6 to provide (a place) with traps. ~*v.i.* to catch animals in traps. **trap-ball** *n.* a children's game played with a wooden device having a pivoted bar for sending a ball into the air on being hit with a bat. **trap-cellar** *n.* the space under the stage in a theatre. **trapdoor** *n.* a door in a floor or roof opening and shutting like a valve. **trapdoor spider** *n.* any of various spiders of the family Ctenizidae, that construct a hinged cover like a trapdoor in their burrows. **traplike** *a.* **trapper** *n.* 1 a person who traps animals, esp. for furs. 2 a person in charge of airdoors in mines. **trap-shooting** *n.* clay pigeon shooting. **trap-shooter** *n.* [OE *treppe*, cp. MDut. *trappe*, WFlem. *traap*, OF *trape*]

trap[2] (trap), **trap-rock** *n.* a dark igneous rock, esp. a variety of dolerite or basalt, presenting a columnar or stairlike aspect. [Swed. *trapp*, from *trappa*, stair]

trap[3] (trap) *v.t.* (*pres.p.* **trapping,** *past, p.p.* **trapped**) to adorn, to caparison. **trappings** *n.pl.* 1 decorations, adornments, esp. those of or relating to an office etc., finery. 2 ornamental harness or housing. **traps** *n.pl.* (*coll.*) one's personal belongings, luggage, baggage. [F *drap*, cloth, etym. uncertain]

trapes TRAIPSE.

trapeze (trəpēz´) *n.* an apparatus consisting of a suspended bar or set of bars on which acrobats perform swinging, balancing and other feats. **trapezial** *a.* 1 trapezoid. 2 (*Anat.*) of or relating to the trapezium. **trapeziform** (-ifawm) *a.* trapezoidal. **trapezium** (-iəm) *n.* (*pl.* **trapezia** (-ziə), **trapeziums**) 1 a quadrilateral figure only two sides of which are parallel. 2 (*Anat.*) the outermost bone of the distal row in the carpus. 3 (*N Am.*) a trapezoid. **trapezius** *n.* (*pl.* **trapezii** (-ziī), **trapeziuses**) (*Anat.*) either of two flat triangular muscles on the back and shoulders that rotate the shoulder blades. **trapezoid** (trap´izoid, trəpē´-) *n.* 1 a quadrilateral no two of whose sides are parallel. 2 (*N Am.*) a quadrilateral figure only two sides of which are parallel. ~*a.* shaped like a trapezoid, trapezoidal. **trapezoidal** (-zoi´-) *a.* [F *trapèze*, L *trapezium*, Gr. *trapezion*, dim. of *trapeza*, table (*tra-*, *tetra*, four, *peza*, foot, cogn. with *pous podos*)]

trapper TRAP[1].

trappings TRAP[3].

Trappist (trap´ist) *n.* a member of a Cistercian order, following the strict rule of La Trappe, a monastery founded at Soligny-la-Trappe, France, in 1664. ~*a.* of or relating to this order. **Trappistine** (-tin, -tēn) *n.* a member of an order of nuns allied to the Trappists.

traps TRAP[3].

trash (trash) *n.* 1 any waste or worthless matter, refuse, rubbish. 2 (*esp. N Am.*) domestic refuse. 3 (*esp. N Am.*) nonsense. 4 a poor or worthless person or group of people. 5 (*W Ind.*) bruised sugar canes. 6 a rubbishy article or production of any kind. 7 loppings of trees. ~*v.t.* 1 (*esp. N Am., coll.*) to wreck. 2 to strip (sugar canes) of their outer leaves. 3 to lop. 4 (*coll.*) to subject to criticism, to denigrate. **trash can** *n.* (*N Am.*) a dustbin. **trashery** *n.* **trash-ice** *n.* broken ice on a sea or lake mixed with water. **trashy** *a.* (*comp.* **trashier,** *superl.* **trashiest**). **trashily** *adv.* **trashiness** *n.* [etym. uncertain]

trass (tras), **tarras** (təras´) *n.* a light-coloured type of tuff rock, often used to make hydraulic cement. [Dut., from F *terrasse*, pile of earth]

trattoria (tratərē´ə) *n.* (*pl.* **trattorias, trattorie** (-rē´ā)) an Italian restaurant. [It.]

trauma (traw´mə, trow´-) *n.* 1 (*Psych.*) a psychological shock having a lasting effect on the subconscious. 2 a distressing experience. 3 a wound or external injury. 4 physical shock produced by a wound or injury. **traumatic** (-mat´-) *a.* 1 of or causing trauma. 2 (*coll.*) distressing. 3 of, relating to or adapted to the cure of wounds. ~*n.* a medicine for wounds. **traumatism** *n.*

traumatize, traumatise *v.t.* to inflict a trauma on. **traumatization** (-zāˊshən) *n.* **traumato-** (-mətō) *comb. form* [Gr. *trauma -atos*, wound]

travail (travˊāl) *n.* (*poet.*) **1** painful toil, painful exertion or effort. **2** the pangs of childbirth. *~v.i.* **1** to toil painfully. **2** to suffer the pangs of childbirth. [OF, from *travailler*, to toil, prob. from late L *trepālium*, instrument of torture (*trēs*, three, *pālus*, stake, PALE[2])]

travel (travˊəl) *v.i.* (*pres.p.* **travelling,** (*N Am.*) **traveling,** *past, p.p.* **travelled,** (*N Am.*) **traveled**) **1** to make a journey, esp. to distant or foreign lands. **2** (of a machine or part) to move (along, in, up and down etc.). **3** to move, to go, to pass through space. **4** to make journeys as a commercial traveller for securing orders etc. **5** (*coll.*) (of food or drink) to survive transportation in a specified way. **6** (*coll.*) to move quickly. **7** (of deer etc.) to move onwards in feeding. *~v.t.* **1** to journey over. **2** to cause to travel. *~n.* **1** the act of travelling. **2** (*pl.*) an account of travelling, usu. in distant countries. **3** the length of stroke, the range or scope of a piston etc. **travel agent** *n.* a person who sells holidays, air, train or bus tickets etc. **travel agency** *n.* (*pl.* **travel agencies**). **travel bureau** *n.* a travel agency. **travelled,** (*N Am.*) **traveled** *a.* **1** having travelled. **2** experienced in travelling (*often in comb.*, as *much-travelled*). **traveller,** (*N Am.*) **traveler** *n.* **1** a person who travels. **2** a commercial traveller. **3** (*Austral.*) a swagman. **4** a gypsy. **5** (*Naut.*) an iron ring etc. sliding on a spar, rope etc. **6** an itinerant person who lives an alternative or New Age lifestyle. **traveller's cheque,** (*N Am.*) **traveler's check** *n.* a cheque available in various denominations, sold by a financial institution for use abroad by a traveller, who signs it on receipt and countersigns it in order to cash it. **traveller's joy** *n.* the wild clematis, *Clematis vitalba*. **traveller's tale** *n.* an untrue or unlikely story told by a traveller. **travelling** *a., n.* **travelling crane** *n.* a crane that can move on rails. **travelling expenses** *n.pl.* expenses incurred by a commercial traveller etc. and paid by the employers. **travelling rug** *n.* a rug used while travelling. **travelling salesman** *n.* (*pl.* **travelling salesmen**) a person who travels from place to place promoting and selling the products or services of their company. **travelling salesperson** *n.* **travelling wave** *n.* (*Physics*) a wave in which the medium moves in the direction of propagation. **travelogue** (-log), (*N Am.*) **travelog** *n.* a lecture or talk on travel illustrated by pictures or films. **travel-sick** *a.* suffering from nausea caused by being in a moving car, ship etc. **travel-sickness** *n.* [var. of TRAVAIL]

travelator TRAVOLATOR.

traverse[1] (trəvœsˊ, travˊ-) *v.t.* **1** to travel across. **2** to make a traverse along (a cliff etc.). **3** to lie across or through. **4** to examine, consider or discuss thoroughly. **5** to thwart, to frustrate, to bring to naught. **6** to plane (wood) across the grain. **7** (*Law*) to deny (a plea or allegation). **8** to turn and point (a large gun). *~v.i.* **1** to turn, as on a pivot. **2** to make a traverse. **traversable** *a.* **traversal** *n.* **traverser** *n.* a person who or thing which traverses. **traversing** *n.* a method of plane-table surveying by measured connected lines. [OF *traverser*, from as TRAVERSE[2]]

traverse[2] (travˊœs) *a.* lying or being across, transverse. *~n.* **1** the act of traversing or travelling across. **2** the sideways travel of part of a machine. **3** anything, esp. a part of a building or mechanical structure, crossing something else. **4** a gallery or loft communicating between opposite sides of a church or other large building. **5** a survey using measurements between points, and the angles between the resulting straight lines. **6** (*Naut.*) a zigzag line described by a ship owing to contrary winds etc. **7** a sideways movement of climbers or skiers on a mountainside or precipice to avoid obstacles. **8** a mound or earthwork protecting a covered way etc., from enfilading fire. **9** (*Law*) a denial of a formal allegation by the opposite party. **10** the horizontal sweep of a gun. **11** a transversal. [F *travers -rse*, L *transversus*, TRANSVERSE]

travertine (travˊətin) *n.* a light yellow porous rock formed by calcareous deposit from streams, hardening on exposure, used for building. [It. *travertino*, L *tiburtīnus*, from *Tibur*, Tivoli]

travesty (travˊəsti) *n.* (*pl.* **travesties**) **1** a burlesque imitation. **2** a ridiculous misrepresentation. **3** a parody. *~v.t.* (*3rd pers. sing. pres.* **travesties,** *pres.p.* **travestying,** *past, p.p.* **travestied**) to make a travesty of, to burlesque. [F *travesti*, p.p. of *travestir*, It. *travestire*, to disguise (TRA-, L *vestīre*, to clothe)]

travois (trəvoiˊ) *n.* (*pl.* **travois** (-voizˊ)) a N American Indian vehicle consisting of two poles joined by a frame and pulled by a horse etc. [Can. F, from F *travail*]

travolator (travˊəlātə), **travelator** *n.* a moving pavement. [TRAVEL, in imit. of ESCALATOR]

trawl (trawl) *n.* **1** (*also* **trawl net**) a net, shaped like a flattened bag, for dragging along the sea bottom. **2** a trawl line. **3** the act of trawling. *~v.i.* **1** to fish with a trawl net. **2** to gather data etc. from a great number of different sources. **trawl boat** *n.* **trawler** *n.* **1** a person who trawls. **2** a fishing vessel using a trawl net. **trawlerman** *n.* (*pl.* **trawlermen**) a man who works on a trawler. **trawling** *n.* **trawl line** *n.* a line of great length, with short lines carrying baited hooks, buoyed up at intervals, for deep-sea fishing. [etym. uncertain]

tray (trā) *n.* **1** a flat shallow vessel, used for holding or carrying small articles on. **2** a shallow coverless box, esp. one forming a compartment in a trunk etc. **trayful** *n.* (*pl.* **trayfuls**). [OE *trig*, perh. cogn. with TREE]

treacherous (trechˊərəs) *a.* **1** violating allegiance, disloyal, perfidious. **2** deceptive, illusory. **3** unreliable, unsafe. **treacherously** *adv.* **treacherousness** *n.* **treachery** *n.* (*pl.* **treacheries**). [OF *trecheros*, *tricheros*, from *trecheur*, traitor, from *trechier*, *trichier*, to cheat, It. *treccare*, perh. from L *trīcārī*, to make difficulties, from *trīcae*, wiles]

treacle (trēˊkəl) *n.* **1** a syrup drained from sugar in refining. **2** molasses. **3** a saccharine fluid consisting of the inspissated juices or decoctions of certain plants. **4** excessive sentimentality. **treacly** *a.* (*comp.* **treaclier,** *superl.* **treacliest**). **treacliness** *n.* [ME and OF *triacle*, L *thēriaca*, THERIAC]

tread (tred) *v.i.* (*past* **trod** (trod), *p.p.* **trod, trodden** (trodˊən)) **1** to set the foot on the ground. **2** to walk, to step, to go. **3** to deal (cautiously etc.). **4** to follow (in a person's footsteps). **5** (of a male bird) to copulate with a hen. *~v.t.* **1** to step or walk on. **2** to crush with the feet. **3** to trample on. **4** to walk (a distance, journey etc.). **5** to dance (a measure etc.). **6** (of a male bird) to copulate with, to cover. *~n.* **1** the act or manner of walking. **2** the sound of walking, a footstep. **3** (*also* **tread-board**) the flat part of a stair or step. **4** a piece of rubber, metal etc., placed on this to reduce wear or noise. **5** the part of a wheel that bears upon the ground. **6** the outer face of a tyre that is in contact with the road. **7** the part of a rail on which the wheels bear. **8** the part of a sole that rests on the ground. **9** the lateral distance between the pedals of a bicycle etc. **10** the act of copulating in birds. **11** the cicatricle of an egg. **to tread down 1** to press down or crush with the feet. **2** to trample on. **3** to destroy. **to tread in** to press in or into with the feet. **to tread on 1** to trample on. **2** to set the foot on. **3** to follow closely. **to tread on air** AIR. **to tread on someone's corns** CORN[2]. **to tread on someone's toes** to offend someone's susceptibilities. **to tread out 1** to press out (wine etc.) with the feet. **2** to extinguish by stamping on. **to tread the boards** to go on stage, to be an actor. **to tread the stage** to tread the boards. **to tread under foot 1** to destroy. **2** to treat with scorn. **to**

tread water 1 to remain upright and afloat by making walking motions with the legs. 2 to undergo a period of relative inactivity. **treader** *n.* **treadmill** *n.* 1 a mechanism, usu. in the form of a revolving cylinder driven by the weight of a person or people, horses etc., treading on movable steps on the periphery, formerly used as a punishment in prisons. 2 a similar mechanism used for physical exercise. 3 wearisome monotony or routine. **treadwheel** *n.* a treadmill. [OE *tredan*, cp. Dut. *treden*, G *treten*, Icel. *trotha*, Dan. *træde*]

treadle (tred´əl) *n.* a lever worked by the foot giving motion to a lathe, sewing machine, bicycle etc. ~*v.i.* to work a treadle. [OE *tredel* (TREAD, -LE[1])]

Treas. *abbr.* 1 treasurer. 2 treasury.

treason (trē´zən) *n.* 1 a violation of allegiance by a subject against the sovereign or government, esp. an overt attempt to subvert the government, high treason. 2 (*Hist.*) murder of one's master or husband, petty treason. 3 an act of treachery, a breach of faith. **high treason** HIGH. **petty treason** PETTY. **treasonable** *a.* consisting of or involving treason. **treasonableness** *n.* **treasonably** *adv.* **treasonous** *a.* [ME *trayson*, A-F *treysoun*, OF *traïson* (F *trahison*), L *trāditio*, TRADITION]

treasure (trezh´ə) *n.* 1 precious metals in any form, or gems. 2 a quantity of these hidden away or kept for future use, a hoard. 3 accumulated wealth. 4 anything highly valued, a precious or highly-prized thing, esp. if portable. 5 (*coll.*) a person greatly valued, a beloved person. ~*v.t.* 1 to lay (up) as valuable, to hoard, to store (up). 2 to prize, to lay (up) in the memory as valuable. **treasure-house** *n.* a building in which treasures or highly-valued things are kept. **treasure hunt** *n.* a game in which people compete to be the first to find something hidden. **treasure trove** *n.* 1 money, gold, silver, plate or bullion found hidden in the earth or a private place, the owner being unknown, but now becoming the property of the Crown. 2 a collection of valuable etc. items. [OF *tresor*, L THESAURUS]

treasurer (trezh´ərə) *n.* 1 a person who has charge of a treasure or treasury. 2 an officer who receives and disburses the public revenue from taxes, duties etc. 3 a person who has the charge of the funds of a company, society, club etc. **treasurership** *n.*

treasury (trezh´əri) *n.* (*pl.* **treasuries**) 1 a place or building in which treasure is stored. 2 (**Treasury**) a place where the public revenues are kept. 3 (**Treasury**) a government department in charge of the public revenue. 4 (**Treasury**) the offices of this. 5 a repository, a book etc. full of information on any subject. 6 the funds or revenue of a society etc. **Treasury bench** *n.* the front bench on the right hand of the Speaker in the House of Commons, appropriated to the First Lord of the Treasury, the Chancellor of the Exchequer and other members of the ministry. **treasury bill** *n.* an instrument of credit issued by the government as an acknowledgement of money lent by a private person for three, six or twelve months. **treasury note** *n.* (*Hist.* or *N Am.*) a note issued by the Treasury for use as currency. **treasury tag** *n.* a piece of string with a metal pin at each end, used for holding papers together.

treat (trēt) *v.t.* 1 to act or behave to or towards. 2 to deal with or manipulate for a particular result, to apply a particular process to, to subject to the action of a chemical agent etc. 3 to apply medical care to. 4 to handle or present or express (a subject etc.) in a particular way. 5 to supply with food, drink or entertainment at one's expense, esp. to supply (electors) with these in order to secure votes. ~*v.i.* 1 to arrange terms (with), to negotiate. 2 to discuss, to discourse (of). ~*n.* 1 an entertainment, esp. out of doors, given to schoolchildren etc. 2 an unusual pleasure or gratification. **a treat** (*coll.*) excellently, very well. **to stand treat** (*coll.*) to pay for drinks etc. **to treat like dirt** DIRT. **treatable** *a.* **treater** *n.* **treating** *n.* [ME *treten*, F *traiter*, L *tractāre*, to handle, freq. of *trahere*, to draw]

treatise (trē´tiz, -is) *n.* a literary composition expounding, discussing and illustrating some particular subject in a thorough way. [ME, from A-F *tretis*, from OF *traitier*, to treat]

treatment (trēt´mənt) *n.* 1 any medical procedure intended to bring about a cure. 2 the act or manner of treating. **the treatment** (*coll.*) the usual way of dealing with something in a particular situation.

treaty (trē´ti) *n.* (*pl.* **treaties**) 1 an agreement formally concluded and ratified between different states. 2 an agreement between persons etc. 3 negotiation, the act of treating for the adjustment of differences etc. **treaty port** *n.* (*Hist.*) a seaport kept open by treaty to foreign commerce.

treble (treb´əl) *a.* 1 triple, threefold. 2 soprano. 3 (of a voice) high-pitched. ~*n.* 1 a soprano voice, singer or part. 2 a high-pitched musical instrument. 3 the higher part of the frequency range, esp. in electronic sound reproduction. 4 a type of bet in which the stake and winnings of a bet on one race are carried forward to the next of three races. 5 a treble quantity or thing. 6 in darts, a hit scoring treble. 7 three sporting victories in the same season, event etc. ~*v.t.* to multiply by three. ~*v.i.* to become threefold. **treble bob** *n.* in bell-ringing, a bob in which the treble bell is dominant. **treble chance** *n.* a type of bet in football pools in which one wins by accurately predicting the number of draws, and home and away wins. **treble clef** *n.* the clef that places G above middle C on the second line of the staff. **treble rhyme** *n.* a rhyme including three syllables. **trebly** *adv.* [OF, from pop. L *trīplus*, TRIPLE]

trebuchet (treb´ūshet, -bə-), **trebucket** (-bŭkit-, trē´-) *n.* 1 (*Hist.*) a medieval military engine for hurling stones. 2 a delicate balance for weighing small articles. [OF, from *trebucher*, to overturn, to tumble (TRANS-, *buc*, trunk, OHG *buk*, belly, cp. G *Bauch*)]

trecento (trāchen´tō) *n.* the 14th cent. as characterized by a distinctive style of Italian literature and art. **trecentist** *n.* [It., short for *mil trecento*, 1300]

☒ **trecherous** common misspelling of TREACHEROUS.

tree (trē) *n.* 1 a perennial woody plant rising from the ground with a single supporting trunk or stem. 2 a similar plant having a tall straight stem, as a palm. 3 a thing resembling a tree, esp. in having a stem and branches. 4 a family or genealogical tree. 5 †a gibbet. 6 †a cross of crucifixion. 7 a tree diagram. 8 a timber beam or framework, such as an axle-tree, swingletree etc. 9 a last for a boot or shoe. ~*v.t.* (*3rd pers. sing. pres.* **trees,** *pres.p.* **treeing,** *past, p.p.* **treed**) 1 to drive or force to take refuge in a tree. 2 (*esp. N Am.*) to put into a difficult situation. 3 to stretch on a shoe-tree. **to grow on trees** (*usu. with neg.*) to be plentiful. **up a tree** (*esp. N Am.*) in a fix, cornered. **tree agate** *n.* a variety of agate with dendritic markings. **tree calf** *n.* a brown calf binding with a conventional treelike design. **tree-creeper** *n.* any small bird of the family Certhiidae which creeps up trees to feed on insects. **tree diagram** *n.* a diagram with branching lines. **tree fern** *n.* a fern with a vertical rhizome like a tree trunk. **tree frog** *n.* any frog with arboreal habits, esp. of the family Hylidae. **tree heath** *n.* a white heath, *Erica arborea*; brier. **tree hopper** *n.* any homopterous insect of the family Membracidae, which live among trees. **tree house** *n.* a small house in a tree for children to play in. **tree kangaroo** *n.* any arboreal kangaroo of the genus *Dendrolagus*. **treeless** *a.* **treelessness** *n.* **treelike** *a.* **tree line** *n.* the timberline. **tree mallow** *n.* a tall mallow, *Lavatera arborea*, growing in rocky or coastal areas. **treen** (trēn) *a.* made of wood. ~*n.* dishes, utensils etc. made of wood. **tree of heaven** *n.* a Chinese ailanthus, *Ailanthus altissima*. **tree of knowledge** *n.* 1 (*Bible*) a tree in the Garden of Eden, the fruit of which gave knowledge of good and evil (Gen. iii). 2 the branches of knowledge. **tree of life** *n.* 1 (*Bible*) a tree in the Garden of Eden of which Adam and Eve were forbidden to eat (Gen. ii.9). 2 the arbor vitae. **tree ring** *n.* ANNUAL RING (under ANNUAL). **tree shrew** *n.* any small arboreal mammal of the family Tupaiidae, living on insects. **tree snake** *n.* any tree-dwelling snake of the genera *Chlorophis* or *Chrysopelea*. **tree sparrow** *n.* 1 a Eurasian sparrow, *Passer montanus*, similar to the house sparrow but with a brown head. 2 (*N Am.*) a N American bird, *Spizella arborea*, of the bunting family. **tree surgeon** *n.* an expert in the treatment of diseased trees. **tree surgery** *n.* **tree toad** *n.* a tree frog. **tree tomato** *n.* 1 a S American shrub, *Cyphomandra betacea*, which has edible red fruit. 2 the fruit of this; also called *tamarillo*. **treetop** *n.* the topmost part of a tree. **tree trunk** *n.* the trunk of a tree. [OE *treo* (cp. Icel. *trē*, Dan. *trae*, Swed. *trä*), cogn. with Gr. *drus*, oak, *doru*, spear, Sansk. *dru*, tree]

treenail (trē´nāl), **trenail** *n.* a pin or peg of hard wood used in fastening timbers, esp. in shipbuilding.

tref (trāf), **treif**, **trefa** (-fə) *a.* in Judaism, not kosher. [Heb. *terēphāh*, torn flesh, from *taraph*, to tear]

trefoil (tref´oil, trē´-) *n.* 1 a plant with three leaflets or three-lobed leaves, esp. of the genus *Trifolium*, such as the clover, the black medick etc. 2 a three-lobed or three-cusped ornament in window tracery etc. 3 any object in this shape. **trefoiled** *a.* (*also in comb.*) [A-F *trifoil*, L *trifolium* (TRI-, *folium*, leaf)]

trehala (trihah´lə) *n.* a kind of manna formed by the substance of the cocoons of a coleopterous insect in Asia Minor. [Turk. *tīqālah*]

treif TREF.

treillage (trā´lij) *n.* 1 a light frame of posts and rails to support espaliers. 2 a trellis. [F, from *treille*, see TRELLIS]

trek (trek) *v.i.* (*pres.p.* **trekking**, *past*, *p.p.* **trekked**) 1 to journey, esp. with difficulty on foot. 2 (*Hist., esp. S Afr.*) to travel by ox-wagon. 3 (*S Afr.*) (of oxen) to draw a vehicle or load. ~*n.* 1 any long, arduous journey, esp. on foot. 2 a stage or day's march. 3 a journey with a wagon. **trekker** *n.* [Dut. *trekken*, cp. OHG *trechan*, to draw]

trellis (trel´is) *n.* 1 (*also* **trellis-work**) openwork of strips of wood crossing each other and nailed together, used for verandas, summer houses etc. 2 a lattice, a grating. 3 a summer house, screen or other structure made of this. ~*v.t.* (*pres.p.* **trellising**, *past*, *p.p.* **trellised**) 1 to interlace into a trellis. 2 to provide with a trellis. [ME and OF *trelis*, ult. from L *trilix -līcis* (TRI-, *līcium*, thread, thrum) combined later with OF *treille*, late L *trichila*, bower, arbour, etym. uncertain]

trematode (trem´ətōd) *n.* any parasitic flatworm of the class Trematoda, esp. a fluke. **trematoid** (-toid) *a., n.* [Gr. *trēmatōdēs*, from *trēma*, hole]

tremble (trem´bəl) *v.i.* 1 to shake involuntarily, as with fear, cold, weakness etc. 2 to be in a state of fear or agitation. 3 to be alarmed (for). 4 to totter, to oscillate, to quaver. ~*n.* 1 the act or state of trembling. 2 fear. 3 (*pl.*) a disease (esp. of cattle) caused by eating certain plants, leading to tremors and incoordination. **all of a tremble** 1 (*coll.*) trembling. 2 (*coll.*) very agitated. **trembler** *n.* 1 a person who trembles. 2 an automatic vibrator for making or breaking an electrical circuit. **trembling** *a.* **tremblingly** *adv.* **trembling poplar** *n.* an aspen. **trembly** *a.* (*comp.* **tremblier**, *superl.* **trembliest**). [F *trembler*, pop. L *tremulāre*, from *tremulus*, TREMULOUS]

tremellose (trem´əlōs) *a.* (of some fungi) tremulous, jelly-like, gelatinous. [mod. L *tremella*, dim. of *tremula*, fem. of *tremulus*, see TREMBLE]

tremendous (trimen´dəs) *a.* 1 terrible, dreadful. 2 of overpowering magnitude, violence etc. 3 (*coll.*) extraordinary, considerable. **tremendously** *adv.* **tremendousness** *n.* [L *tremendus*, from *tremere*, to tremble]

tremolite (trem´əlīt) *n.* a calcium magnesium metasilicate crystallizing in the monoclinic system. **tremolitic** (-lit´-) *a.* [Val *Tremola*, N Italy]

tremolo (trem´əlō) *n.* (*pl.* **tremolos**) 1 a tremulous or quavering effect in singing, playing etc. 2 an organ or harmonium stop producing a vibrating tone. 3 (*also* **tremolo arm**) a lever on an electric guitar used to vary the pitch of a played note. [It.]

tremor (trem´ə) *n.* 1 a trembling, shaking or quivering. 2 a thrill. 3 a small earthquake. ~*v.i.* to tremble. **tremorless** *a.* [ME and OF *tremour*, L *tremor -orem*, from *tremere*, to tremble]

tremulous (trem´ūləs) *a.* 1 trembling, shaking, quivering. 2 timid, irresolute, wavering. **tremulant** *a.* tremulous. ~*n.* TREMOLO. **tremulously** *adv.* **tremulousness** *n.* [L *tremulus*, from *tremere*, to tremble]

trenail TREENAIL.

trench (trench) *n.* 1 a long narrow cut or deep furrow in the earth, a ditch, esp. a long narrow ditch, usu. with a parapet formed by the excavated earth, to cover besieging troops etc. 2 a long narrow groove in the ocean bed. ~*v.t.* 1 to cut a trench or trenches in (ground etc.). 2 to turn over (ground) by cutting a successive series of trenches and filling in with the excavated soil. 3 to ditch. 4 to cut a furrow or groove (in wood etc.). 5 to cut military trenches against. ~*v.i.* 1 to cut or dig a trench or trenches. 2 †to encroach (on). **to open the trenches** to begin to dig or to form trenches or lines of approach. **trench coat** *n.* 1 a soldier's heavy, lined mackintosh crossing over in front and having a belt. 2 a similar raincoat, worn by men or women. **trencher**[1] *n.* **trench fever** *n.* a remittent or relapsing fever affecting soldiers living in trenches etc. and transmitted by the excrement of lice. **trench foot** *n.* a gangrenous condition of the foot caused by prolonged standing in cold water. **trench mortar** *n.* a mortar used for throwing bombs. **trench warfare** *n.* a type of warfare in which soldiers take up positions in trenches facing the enemy. [ME and OF *trenche* (F *tranche*), from *trenchier* (F *trancher*), prob. ult. from L *truncāre*, to TRUNCATE[1]]

trenchant (tren´chənt) *a.* 1 cutting, biting, incisive. 2 (*poet.*) sharp, keen. **trenchancy** *n.* **trenchantly** *adv.* [OF, pres.p. of *trenchier*, see TRENCH]

trencher[1] TRENCH.

trencher[2] (tren´chə) *n.* 1 a wooden plate of a type formerly used for serving food, now for cutting bread on. 2 a trencher cap. **trencher cap** *n.* a college cap with a flat top, a mortarboard. **trencherman** *n.* (*pl.* **trenchermen**) a (good or poor) feeder or eater. [A-F *trenchour* (F *tranchoir*), from *trenchier*, as TRENCH]

trend (trend) *n.* 1 a general tendency, bent or inclination. 2 a mode, fashion. ~*v.i.* 1 to bend (away etc.). 2 to have a general tendency or direction. 3 to extend or lie along in a particular direction. 4 to incline. **trendify** *v.t.* (*3rd pers. sing. pres.* **trendifies**, *pres.p.* **trendifying**, *past*, *p.p.* **trendified**) (*coll.*) to make fashionable. **trendsetter** *n.* a person who originates or dictates fashions. **trendsetting** *a.* **trendy** *a.* (*comp.* **trendier**, *superl.* **trendiest**) (*coll., sometimes derog.*) following the latest trends, fashionable. ~*n.* (*pl.* **trendies**) a trendy person. **trendily** *adv.* **trendiness** *n.* [ME *trenden*, OE *trendan*, cp. OFris., Dan. and Swed. *trind*, round]

trente-et-quarante (trātākarāt´) *n.* ROUGE-ET-NOIR (under ROUGE). [F, thirty and forty]

trepan[1] (tripan´) *n.* 1 a surgeon's cylindrical saw for removing portions of the skull. 2 a tool for boring shafts. ~*v.t.* (*pres.p.* **trepanning**, *past*, *p.p.* **trepanned**) to perforate with a trepan. **trepanation** (trepənā´shən), **trepanning** *n.* [F *trepan*, med. L *trepanum*, Gr. *trupanon*, borer]

†**trepan**[2] (tripan´) *n.* **1** a decoy. **2** a stratagem, a snare. [formerly *trapan*, prob. a slang derivative from TRAP[1]]

trepang (tripang´) *n.* the sea slug or bêche-de-mer. [Malay *tripang*]

trephine (trifēn´, -fīn´) *n.* an improved trepan with a centre-pin. ~*v.t.* to operate on with a trephine. **trephination** (-inā´shən) *n.* [F *tréphine*, TREPAN[1]]

trepidation (trepidā´shən) *n.* **1** a state of alarm, excitement, or agitation. **2** a trembling of the limbs, as in paralysis. [F, from L *trepidātio -tionem*, from *trepidāre*, to bustle, from *trepidus*, agitated]

treponema (trepənē´mə), **treponeme** (trep´ənēm) *n.* (*pl.* **treponemas, treponemata** (-mətə), **treponemes**) a member of a genus of spirochaetes *Treponema*, that cause syphilis and other diseases. **treponematous** *a.*

trespass (tres´pəs) *n.* **1** a wrongful act involving injury to the person or property of another, any transgression other than treason, misprision of treason, or felony, esp. unauthorized entry into another's land. **2** †a transgression against law, duty etc., an offence, a sin. ~*v.i.* **1** to commit an illegal intrusion (upon the property or personal rights of another). **2** to intrude, encroach or make undue claims (upon). **3** †to transgress (against). **to trespass on someone's preserves** to interfere in someone's business. **trespasser** *n.* [ME and OF *trespas*, from *trespasser* (F *trépasser*), med. L *transpassāre* (TRANS-, *passāre*, to PASS)]

tress (tres) *n.* **1** a lock or plait of hair, esp. from the head of a girl or woman. **2** (*pl.*) hair. ~*v.t.* to arrange in tresses. **tressed, tressy** *a.* [ME and F *tresse*, med. L *tricia, trica*, Gr. *tricha*, threefold]

tressure (tresh´ə, tres´ūə) *n.* (*Her.*) a diminutive of the orle, usually borne double and emblazoned with fleurs-de-lis. [OF, as TRESS]

trestle (tres´əl) *n.* **1** a movable frame for supporting a table, platform etc., usu. consisting of a pair of divergent legs, fixed or hinged. **2** (*also* **trestle-work**) an open braced framework of timber or iron for supporting the horizontal portion of a bridge etc. **3** a trestle-tree. **4** a trestle-table. **5** (*pl.*) the props or shores of a ship in process of building etc. **trestle-bridge** *n.* **trestle-table** *n.* a table formed of boards supported on movable trestles. **trestle-tree** *n.* (*Naut.*) either of a pair of horizontal fore-and-aft timbers fixed to a lower mast to support the crosstrees. [OF *trestel* (F *tréteau*), pop. L *transtellum, transtillum*, dim. of *transtrum*, TRANSOM]

tret (tret) *n.* (*Hist.*) an allowance to purchasers of goods of certain kinds for damage or deterioration during transit, usu. 4 lb. (1.8 kg) in every 104 lb. (47.2 kg). [perh. from OF *traite*, transportation, TRACT[1]]

trevally (trival´i) *n.* (*pl.* **trevallies**) any Australian fish of the genus *Caranx*. [prob. alt. of *cavally*, via Sp. *caballo*, horse, from L (cp. CAVALRY)]

trews (trooz) *n.pl.* trousers, esp. made of tartan. [var. of TROUSERS]

trey (trā) *n.* (*pl.* **treys**) the three at cards or dice. [A-F *treis, trei* (F *trois*), L *trēs*]

TRF *abbr.* tuned radio frequency.

TRH *abbr.* Their Royal Highnesses.

tri- (trī) *comb. form* three, three times, triple. [L and Gr. *tri-*, three, from L *trēs*, Gr. *treis*]

triable (trī´əbəl) *a.* **1** subject to judicial trial. **2** that may be tried or tested. [A-F]

triacetate (trīas´itāt) *n.* a cellulose derivative containing three acetate groups.

triacid (trīas´id) *a.* (of a base) capable of reacting with three molecules of a monobasic acid.

triad (trī´ad) *n.* **1** a collection of three. **2** the number three. **3** a Chinese secret society, often engaging in illegal activities. **4** a member of such a society. **5** a Welsh form of composition in which statements etc. are grouped in threes. **6** (*Chem.*) an element or radical with a combining power of three. **7** (*Mus.*) a chord of three notes. **8** a common chord. **triadic** (-ad´-) *a.* **triadically** *adv.* [late L and Gr. *trias triados*, from *treie*, three]

triadelphous (trīədel´fəs) *a.* (of a plant) having the stamens in three bundles. [TRI-, Gr. *adelphos*, brother]

triage (trī´əj, trē´ahzh) *n.* **1** the sorting of hospital patients, casualties in war etc. according to urgency of treatment and likelihood of survival. **2** the act of sorting according to quality, prioritization. **3** refuse of coffee beans. [F]

trial (trī´əl) *n.* **1** (*Law*) the judicial examination and determination of the issues in a cause between parties before a judge, judge and jury or a referee. **2** the act or process of trying or testing. **3** experimental treatment. **4** a test, an examination, an experiment. **5** a person who or thing which tries or tests strength, endurance, and other qualities. **6** hardship, trouble, suffering etc. **7** a sports match to test ability. **8** a motorcycle journey to test skill. **9** a contest for dogs, horses etc. ~*v.t.* (*pres.p.* **trialling,** (*N Am.*) **trialing,** *past, p.p.* **trialled,** (*N Am.*) **trialed**) to subject to a performance test. ~*v.i.* to undergo a performance test. **on trial 1** undergoing a test. **2** being tried in a law court. **trial and error** *n.* a method of solving problems by trying several solutions and choosing the most successful. **trial at bar** *n.* a trial before all the judges of a court, a trial in the Queen's Bench division. **trial balance** *n.* a comparison of the debit and credit totals in double-entry bookkeeping. **trial balloon** *n.* a way of finding out public opinion (from French *ballon d'essai*). **trial by battle** *n.* legal decision of a case by single combat. **trial by combat** *n.* (*Hist.*) a legal method of settling a dispute or testing the justice of a charge by a duel. **trialist, triallist** *n.* **1** a person taking part in a trial. **2** a person involved in a judicial trial. **trial jury** *n.* (*pl.* **trial juries**) a petty jury. **trial run** *n.* a preliminary test of a new procedure etc. **trial trip** *n.* a test trip by a new vessel to show her capabilities. [OF (TRY, -AL[2])]

triandrous (trīan´drəs) *a.* (*Bot.*) having three stamens. [Gr. *anēr andros*, male]

triangle (trī´ang·gəl) *n.* **1** a figure, esp. a plane figure, bounded by three lines, esp. straight lines. **2** any three things in the shape of a triangle, joined by imaginary lines. **3** a drawing implement or other thing or ornament of this shape. **4** a musical instrument consisting of a steel rod bent into a triangle and sounded by striking with a steel rod. **5** any situation involving three people or elements. **6** a northern constellation. **7** (*Naut.*) a combination of three spars lashed together at the top for shifting weights. **8** (*Hist.*) a frame formed by three halberds to which a person was tied up to be flogged. **triangle of forces** *n.* (*Physics*) a triangle representing the magnitudes and directions of three forces which are in equilibrium. **triangular** (-ang´gū-) *a.* **1** having the shape of a triangle. **2** three-cornered. **3** involving three people or elements. **4** (of a pyramid) having a base with three sides. **triangular compasses** *n.pl.* compasses with three legs. **triangularity** (-lar´-) *n.* **triangularly** *adv.* **triangulate**[1] (-lāt) *v.t.* **1** to make triangular. **2** to divide into triangles, esp. (an area) in surveying. **3** to ascertain by this means. **triangulate**[2] (-lət) *a.* (*Zool.*) marked with triangles. **triangulately** *adv.* **triangulation** (-lā´shən) *n.* **triangulation point** *n.* a reference point used in surveying, sometimes marked on the ground by a pillar. [F, from L *triangulum*, neut. adj. (*angulus*, ANGLE[1])]

triarch (trī´ahk) *n.* the ruler of one of three divisions of a country. **triarchy** *n.* (*pl.* **triarchies**). [Gr. *triarchos -archos*, from *archein*, to rule]

Trias (trī´əs) *n.* the division of rock strata between the Carboniferous and the Jurassic (divided in Germany into three groups, whence the name). **Triassic** (-as´-) *a.*, *n.* [late L and Gr., TRIAD]

triathlon (trīath´lon) *n.* an athletic contest consisting of three events. **triathlete** *n.* [Gr. *athlon*, contest]
triatomic (trīətom´ik) *a.* (*Chem.*) having three atoms in the molecule.
triaxal (trīak´səl), **triaxial** (-siəl) *a.* having three axes.
tribade (trib´əd) *n.* a lesbian. **tribadism** *n.* [Gr. *tribas -ados*, a lewd woman, -ISM]
tribal (trī´bəl) *a.* belonging to, of or relating to a tribe. ~*n.* (*usu. in pl.*) a member of a tribal community. **tribalism** *n.* **1** tribal organization. **2** loyalty to a tribe or group. **tribalist** *n.* **tribalistic** (-lis´-) *a.* **tribally** *adv.* [TRIBE, -AL[1]]
tribasic (trībā´sik) *a.* (*Chem.*) **1** having three atoms of hydrogen replaceable by a base or basic radical. **2** (of a molecule) having three monovalent basic atoms or groups.
tribe (trīb) *n.* **1** a group of people ethnologically related and forming a community or a political division. **2** (*Hist.*) in ancient Rome, each of the three ancient divisions of the Roman people later increased to 35. **3** each of the 12 divisions of the Israelites believed to be descended from the patriarchs. **4** a group claiming common descent or affinity, a clan or group of clans, esp. a group of savage clans under a chief. **5** (*usu. derog.*) a number of persons of the same character, profession etc. **6** a family, esp. a large one. **7** (*Bot.*, *Zool.*) a more or less indefinite group of plants or animals, usu. above a genus and below an order. **8** (*pl.*) large numbers. **tribesman, tribeswoman** *n.* (*pl.* **tribesmen, tribeswomen**). **tribespeople** *n.pl.* [ME and OF *tribu*, L *tribus*, etym. uncertain]
triblet (trib´lit) *n.* a mandrel used in forging tubes, nuts and rings etc. [formerly *tribolet*, F *triboulet*, etym. uncertain]
tribo- (trī´bō, trib´ō) *comb. form* friction, rubbing. [Gr. *tribos*, rubbing]
triboelectricity (trībōilektris´iti, trib-) *n.* electricity generated by friction. **triboelectric** (-lek´-) *a.*
tribology (trībol´əji) *n.* the study of friction, lubrication and wear between interacting surfaces. **tribologist** *n.*
triboluminescence (tribōloomines´əns) *n.* luminescence produced by friction. **triboluminescent** *a.* [Gr. *tribein*, to rub]
tribometer (trībom´itə, trib-) *n.* a sledlike apparatus for measuring sliding friction. [F *tribomètre* (Gr. *tribos*, rubbing, from *tribein*, to rub, -METER)]
tribrach (trī´brak, trib´-) *n.* a metrical foot of three short or unstressed syllables. **tribrachic** (-brak´-) *a.* [L *tribrachys*, Gr. *tribrachus* (*brachus*, short)]
tribulation (tribūlā´shən) *n.* **1** severe affliction, suffering, distress. **2** a cause of this. [ME and OF *tribulacion*, late L *tribulatio -onem*, from *trībulāre*, to rub, to oppress, from *trībulum*, threshing-sledge, from *terere*, to rub, p.p. *trītus*]
tribunal (trībū´nəl, trib-) *n.* **1** a court of justice. **2** a board of arbitrators etc. **3** a seat or bench for judges, magistrates etc., a judgement-seat. [L, from TRIBUNE[1]]
tribune[1] (trib´ūn) *n.* **1** a champion of popular rights and liberties. **2** (*Hist.*) (*also* **tribune of the people**) each of two (later ten) representatives elected by the people of ancient Rome to protect their rights and liberties against the patricians. **3** (*Hist.*) any one of various ancient Roman civil, fiscal and military officers. **tribunate** (-nət, -nāt), **tribuneship** *n.* **tribunicial** (-nish´əl), **tribunician, tribunitial** *a.* [ME and OF *tribun*, L *tribūnus*, from *tribus*, TRIBE]
tribune[2] (trib´ūn) *n.* **1** a bishop's throne in an apse; an apse containing this. **2** a platform with seats. **3** a rostrum, a pulpit. **4** a raised floor for the curule chairs of the magistrates in the apse of a Roman basilica. [F, from med. L *tribūna*, tribunal, as TRIBUNE[1]]
tribunicial, tribunician etc. TRIBUNE[1].
tributary (trib´ūtəri) *n.* (*pl.* **tributaries**) **1** a stream or river flowing into a larger one or a lake. **2** (*Hist.*) a person or state subject to tribute. ~*a.* **1** serving to increase a larger stream or river etc. **2** subsidiary, contributory. **3** (*Hist.*) paying or subject to tribute. **tributarily** *adv.* **tributariness** *n.* [L *tribūtārius*, as TRIBUTE]
tribute (trib´ūt) *n.* **1** a contribution, gift or offering (of praise etc.). **2** (*Hist.*) a sum of money or other valuable thing paid by one ruler or state to another in token of submission, for peace or protection, or by virtue of a treaty. **3** the state of being under obligation to pay this. **4** a praiseworthy thing attributable (to). **5** a share of ore paid to a miner or mine-owner. [L *tribūtum*, neut. of *tribūtus*, p.p. of *tribuere*, to give, to pay]
tricar (trī´kah) *n.* a motor car with three wheels.
trice[1] (trīs) *n.* an instant. **in a trice** in a moment. [prob. from TRICE[2]]
trice[2] (trīs) *v.t.* (*Naut.*) **1** to haul. **2** to tie (up). [ME *tricen*, *trisen*, MDut. *trīsen* (cp. Dut. *trijsen*, G *triezen*, to hoist]
tricentenary (trīsentē´nəri, -ten´-, trīsen´tin-) *n.* (*pl.* **tricentenaries**) TERCENTENARY.
triceps (trī´seps) *a.* (of muscles) three-headed, having three points of attachment. ~*n.* a triceps muscle, esp. the large muscle at the back of the upper arm. [L (*-ceps*, from *caput*, head)]
triceratops (trīser´ətops) *n.* a large herbivorous dinosaur of the Cretaceous period, of the genus *Triceratops*, with three horns and a bony crest on the hood. [Gr. *keras*, horn, *ops*, eye]
trichiasis (trikī´əsis, trikiā´sis) *n.* (*Med.*) entropion or inversion of the eyelashes. [Gr., as TRICHINA]
trichina (trikī´nə) *n.* (*pl.* **trichinae** (-nē)) any hairlike nematode parasitic worm of the genus *Trichinella*, esp. *T. spiralis*, infesting the intestine or muscles of pigs, humans etc. **trichiniasis** (trikinī´əsis), **trichinosis** (-nō´-) *n.* a disease due to the presence of trichinae in the system. **trichinize** (trik´-), **trichinise** *v.t.* **trichinization** (-zā´shən) *n.* **trichinosed** (trik´inōzd), **trichinotic** (trikinot´-), **trichinous** *a.* [mod. L, from Gr. *trichinos*, a., from Gr. *thrix trichos*, hair]
trichite (trik´īt) *n.* **1** a minute hairlike form occurring in certain vitreous volcanic rocks. **2** a minute fibril found in some sponge spicules; a spicule composed of these. **trichitic** (-kit´-) *a.* [G *Trichit* (Gr. *thrix trichos*, hair, -ITE[1])]
trichloroethane (trīklawrōē´thān) *n.* a volatile non-flammable colourless liquid used as a solvent; also called *methyl chloroform*.
tricho- (trī´kō, trik´ō) *comb. form* hair. [Gr. *thrix trichos*, hair]
trichogenous (trikoj´inəs) *a.* promoting growth of the hair. **trichogen** (trī´kəjen, trik´-) *n.* [Gr. *thrix trichos*, hair, -GENOUS]
trichology (trikol´əji) *n.* the study of the human hair. **trichological** (-əloj´-) *a.* **trichologist** *n.*
trichome (trī´kōm) *n.* (*Bot.*) a hair, filament, scale, prickle or an outgrowth. [Gr. *trichōma*, from *trichoun*, to cover with hair]
trichomonad (trikəmon´ad, -kō-) *n.* any parasitic protozoan of the order Trichomonadida, occurring in the digestive system of humans and animals such as cattle.
trichomoniasis (trikəmənī´əsis, -kom-) *n.* an infection caused by trichomonads, esp. a vaginal infection, *Trichomonas vaginalis*.
trichopathy (trikop´əthi) *n.* (*pl.* **trichopathies**) **1** the treatment of hair-diseases. **2** any disease of the hair. **trichopathic** (-əpath´-) *a.*
trichopteran (trīkop´tərən) *n.* any insect of the order Trichoptera, containing the caddis-flies. **trichopterous** *a.* [Gr. *thrix trichos*, hair, *pteron*, wing]
trichosis (trikō´sis) *n.* any disease or unhealthy condition of the hair. [Gr. *thrix trichos*, hair]

trichotomy (trīkot´əmi) *n.* (*pl.* **trichotomies**) division into three, esp. of the human being into body, soul and spirit. **trichotomic** (-ətom´-) *a.* **trichotomize, trichotomise** *v.t.* **trichotomous** *a.* **trichotomously** *adv.* [Gr. *tricha*, triply, from *treis*, three, -TOMY]

trichroism (trī´krōizm) *n.* the property of exhibiting different colours in three different directions when viewed by transmitted light. **trichroic** (-krō´-) *a.* [F *trichroïsme* (Gr. *trichroos*, *-chrous*, three-coloured)]

trichromatic (trīkrōmat´ik) *a.* three-coloured, having the normal three fundamental colour-sensations (of red, green and purple). **trichromatism** (-krō´-) *n.*

trick (trik) *n.* **1** an artifice, an artful device or stratagem. **2** an optical illusion. **3** an ingenious or peculiar way of doing something, a knack. **4** a feat of dexterity, esp. of legerdemain or sleight of hand. **5** a foolish or malicious act, a prank, a practical joke. **6** a particular habit or practice, a mannerism, a personal peculiarity. **7** the whole number of cards played in one round. **8** a round. **9** a point gained as the result of a round. **10** (*Naut.*) a turn or spell at the helm, usu. half a watch or two hours. **11** (*sl.*) a session with a prostitute. **12** (*sl.*) a client of a prostitute. ~*a.* using trickery, illusion etc. ~*v.t.* **1** to cheat, to deceive, to delude, to inveigle (into, out of etc.). **2** to dress, to deck (out or up). ~*v.i.* to practise trickery. **how's tricks?** (*coll.*) how are you? **not to miss a trick** MISS[1]. **to do the trick** (*coll.*) to achieve the required effect. **to know a trick worth two of that** to know of some expedient. **to trick out** to decorate, to dress up. **to trick up** to trick out. **to turn a trick** (*sl.*) (of a prostitute) to have sexual relations with a client. **up to one's tricks** (*coll.*) behaving badly. **up to someone's tricks** aware of the tricks someone is likely to play. **trick cyclist** *n.* **1** a cyclist performing tricks. **2** (*sl.*) a psychiatrist. **tricker** *n.* **trickery** *n.* (*pl.* **trickeries**). **trickish** *a.* **trickishly** *adv.* **trickishness** *n.* **trick of the trade** *n.* a trade secret. **trick or treat** *n.* (*esp. N Am.*) the Hallowe'en custom of children in fancy dress knocking on people's doors and asking for sweets etc., threatening to play a trick if not given anything. **trickster** (-stə) *n.* **tricksy** (-si) *a.* (*comp.* **tricksier**, *superl.* **tricksiest**) **1** playful, sportive. **2** excessively elaborate. **tricksily** *adv.* **tricksiness** *n.* **tricky** *a.* (*comp.* **trickier**, *superl.* **trickiest**) **1** difficult, awkward. **2** requiring tactful or skilful handling. **3** deceitful. **trickily** *adv.* **trickiness** *n.* [OF *trique*, *triche*, from *trichier*, *trechier* (F *tricher*), prob. from L, see TREACHEROUS]

trickle (trik´əl) *v.i.* to flow in drops or in a small stream. ~*v.t.* **1** to cause to flow in this way. **2** to come out slowly or gradually. ~*n.* **1** a trickling. **2** a small stream, a rill. **trickle charger** *n.* a battery charger which is mains-operated. **trickle-down** *n.* the (supposed) eventual dissemination of wealth, information etc. from those of high income or rank to groups below. ~*a.* of or relating to such dissemination. **tricklet** *n.* **trickly** *a.* [ME *triklen*, perh. for *striklen*, freq. from OE *strīcan*, to sweep along, to STRIKE]

trick-track TRIC-TRAC.

triclinic (trīklin´ik) *a.* **1** (of a mineral) having the three axes unequal and inclined at oblique angles. **2** relating to the system classifying such substances. [Gr. *klinein*, to lean]

triclinium (trīklin´iəm, trik-, -klīn´-) *n.* (*pl.* **triclinia** (-niə)) **1** a set of couches arranged round three sides of a dining table. **2** a dining table furnished with this. **3** a dining room with this. [L, from Gr. *triklinion* (TRI-, *klinē*, couch)]

tricolour (trī´kŭlə, trik´ələ), (*N Am.*) **tricolor** *n.* a flag or banner having three colours, esp. arranged in equal stripes, such as the national standard of France of blue, white and red, divided vertically. ~*a.* three-coloured. **tricoloured** *a.* [F *tricolore*]

tricorn (trī´kawn), **tricorne** *a.* **1** having three horns. **2** (of a hat) having three corners. ~*n.* **1** a three-cornered hat. **2** an imaginary three-horned animal. **tricornered** *a.* three-cornered. [F *tricorne*, L *tricornis* (TRI-, *cornu*, horn)]

tricot (trē´kō) *n.* **1** a hand-knitted woollen fabric or a machine-made imitation. **2** a soft, ribbed cloth. [F, from *tricoter*, to knit]

tricrotic (trīkrot´ik) *a.* (of the pulse etc.) having three distinct undulations for each beat. **tricrotous** (trik´rət-) *a.* [Gr. *trikrotos*]

tric-trac (trik´trak), **trick-track** *n.* a complicated form of backgammon. [F, imit. of clicking sound]

tricuspid (trīkŭs´pid) *a.* (of molar teeth) a valve of the heart etc. having three cusps or points. ~*n.* **1** a tooth with three cusps. **2** a heart valve with three segments. **tricuspidate** (-dāt), **tricuspidated** *a.* [L *tricuspis -pidis*]

tricycle (trī´sikəl) *n.* **1** a three-wheeled cycle. **2** a three-wheeled vehicle used by a disabled driver. ~*v.i.* to ride on this. **tricyclist** *n.*

tricyclic (trīsī´klik) *a.* (of a compound) having three rings in its molecule. ~*n.* any antidepressant drug with this molecular structure.

tridactyl (trīdak´til), **tridactylous** (-ləs) *a.* having three fingers or toes. [Gr. *tridaktulos* (*daktulos*, finger)]

trident (trī´dənt) *n.* **1** a three-pronged implement or weapon, esp. a fish-spear. **2** a three-pronged sceptre or spear, the emblem of Poseidon or Neptune as god of the sea. **3** (**Trident**) a long-range ballistic missile. **tridental** (-den´-) *a.* **tridentate** (-den´tāt) *a.* having three teeth or prongs. [L *tridens -ntem* (TRI-, *dens dentem*, tooth)]

Tridentine (trīden´tīn) *a.* of or relating to Trent, or the Council held there 1545–63. ~*n.* a person who accepts the decrees of the Council of Trent, a Roman Catholic. **Tridentine mass** *n.* the liturgy used by the Roman Catholic Church 1570–1964. [med. L *Tridentīnus*, from *Tridentum*, Trent, a city of Tyrol]

tridimensional (trīdimen´shənəl) *a.* having three dimensions.

triduum (trid´ūəm) *n.* in the Roman Catholic Church, a three days' service of prayer etc. **triduan** *a.* **1** lasting three days. **2** happening every third day. [It. and Sp. *triduo*, L *triduum* (TRI-, *dies*, day)]

tridymite (trid´imīt) *n.* a vitreous form of silica usu. occurring in small hexagonal tables composed of groups of three individual crystals. [G *Tridymit* (Gr. *tridumos*, threefold)]

triecious TRIOECIOUS.

tried TRY.

triennial (trīen´iəl) *a.* **1** lasting for three years. **2** happening every three years. ~*n.* **1** a triennial plant, publication, etc. **2** every third anniversary of an event. **3** in the Roman Catholic Church, a mass for a dead person performed daily for three years. **4** an official visit to an Anglican diocese by its bishop, happening every three years. **triennially** *adv.* **triennium** (-iəm) *n.* (*pl.* **triennia** (-iə), **trienniums**) a period of three years. [L *triennium* (TRI-, *annus*, year), -AL[1]]

trier TRY.

trierarch (trī´ərahk) *n.* (*Hist.*) **1** in ancient Greece, the commander of a trireme. **2** a citizen appointed alone or with others to fit out and maintain a trireme. **trierarchal** (-rah´-) *a.* **trierarchy** *n.* (*pl.* **trierarchies**) **1** the office or duty of a trierarch. **2** the duty of fitting out and maintaining a trireme. [L *triērarchus*, Gr. *triērarchos* (*triērēs*, trireme, *-archos*, from *archein*, to rule)]

trifacial (trīfā´shəl) *a.* threefold and of or relating to the face (as the trigeminus). ~*n.* the trigeminus. **trifacial nerve** *n.* the trigeminal nerve.

trifecta (trīfek´tə) *n.* (*N Am., Austral.*) a form of betting in which a punter must predict the first three places in a race. [PERFECTA (under PERFECT[2])]

trifid (trī´fid) *a.* (*Bot., Zool.*) divided wholly or partially into three. [L *trifidus* (TRI-, *fid-*, stem of *findere*, to cleave)]

trifle (trī´fəl) *n.* **1** a thing, matter, fact etc. of no value or importance. **2** a small amount of money etc. **3** a light confection of whipped cream or white of egg, with cake, jam, wine etc. **4** a variety of pewter. ~*v.i.* **1** to act or talk with levity. **2** to sport, to jest, to fool. ~*v.t.* to waste, fritter or fool away (time) in trifling. **to trifle with 1** to treat with levity, disrespect or lack of proper seriousness. **2** to dally, to toy (with). **3** to flirt with. **trifler** *n.* **trifling** *a.* **1** insignificant, trivial. **2** frivolous. **triflingly** *adv.* **triflingness** *n.* [ME and OF *trufle*, var. of *truff*, mockery, cheating, cp. It. *truffa*, etym. uncertain]

trifloral (trīflaw´rəl), **triflorous** (-rəs) *a.* (*Bot.*) bearing three flowers.

trifocal (trīfō´kəl) *a.* having three focuses or focal lengths. **trifocals** *n.pl.* trifocal spectacles.

trifoliate (trīfō´liət), **trifoliated** (-ātid) *a.* (*Bot.*) **1** three-leaved, consisting of three leaflets. **2** (of a plant) having such leaves. **trifoliolate** (-fō´liələt) *a.* having three leaflets. **trifolium** (-iəm) *n.* a plant of the genus *Trifolium*, low herbs containing the trefoils or clovers.

triforium (trīfaw´riəm) *n.* (*pl.* **triforia** (-riə)) a gallery or arcade in the wall over the arches of the nave or choir, or sometimes the transepts, in a large church. [med. L (TRI-, *foris*, door opening)]

triform (trī´fawm), **triformed** (-fawmd) *a.* having three shapes, parts or divisions. [L *triformis*]

trifurcate (trīfœ´kət, trī´-), **trifurcated** (-kātid) *a.* **1** having three branches or forks. **2** trichotomous. ~*v.t.*, *v.i.* to divide into three.

Trig. *abbr.* trigonometry.

trig[1] (trig) *n.* (*coll.*) trigonometry.

trig[2] (trig) *a.* (*esp. dial.*) neat, trim, spruce. ~*n.* a dandy. ~*v.t.* (*pres.p.* **trigging**, *past*, *p.p.* **trigged**) to make trim. **trigly** *adv.* **trigness** *n.* [Icel. *tryggr*, cp. Norw., Swed. and Dan. *trygg*]

trig[3] (trig) *v.t.* (*pres.p.* **trigging**, *past*, *p.p.* **trigged**) (*esp. dial.*) to stop, check or skid (a wheel). ~*n.* a wedge, block etc. used for this. [etym. uncertain]

trigamous (trig´əməs) *a.* **1** married three times. **2** having three wives or three husbands at once. **3** having male, female and hermaphrodite flowers on the same head. **trigamist** *n.* **trigamy** *n.* [Gr. *trigamos* (TRI-, *gamos*, marriage)]

trigeminal (trījem´inəl) *a.* **1** threefold. **2** (*Anat.*) of or relating to the trigeminus. ~*n.* the trigeminus. **trigeminal nerve** *n.* the trigeminus. **trigeminal neuralgia** *n.* neuralgia characterized by facial twitching; also called *tic douloureux*. **trigeminus** (-nəs) *n.* (*pl.* **trigemini** (-nī)) the fifth cranial or trifacial nerve dividing into the superior and inferior maxillary and the ophthalmic nerves. [L *trigeminus* (TRI-, *geminus*, born with another)]

trigger (trig´ə) *n.* **1** a catch or lever for releasing the hammer of a gunlock. **2** any similar device for releasing a spring etc. in various forms of mechanism. **3** anything that initiates a process, sequence of events etc. ~*v.t.* **1** to cause to happen, to set off. **2** to activate, to put into operation. **3** to fire (a gun). **quick on the trigger** QUICK. **triggered** *a.* **triggerfish** *n.* (*pl. in general* **triggerfish**, *in particular* **triggerfishes**) any usu. tropical fish of the family Balistidae which live in tropical and temperate seas. **trigger-happy** *a.* **1** too eager to fire (a gun etc.). **2** too eager to take action. [formerly *tricker*, Dut. *trekker*, from *trekken*, to pull, cp. TREK]

triglyceride (trīglis´ərīd) *n.* any ester of glycerol and three acid radicals.

triglyph (trī´glif) *n.* an ornament on a Doric frieze consisting of a tablet with three vertical grooves. **triglyphal** (-glif´-), **triglyphic**, **triglyphical** *a.* [L *triglyphus*, Gr. *trigluphos* (*gluphein*, to carve)]

trigon (trī´gon) *n.* **1** a triangle. **2** a set of three signs of the zodiac arranged at the angles of an equilateral triangle. **3** the cutting part of an upper molar. **4** a triangular harp or lyre; also called *trigonon*. **5** a triangular instrument used in dialling. **6** in ancient Greece, a ball game with three players. **trigonal** (trig´ənəl) *a.* **1** triangular, three-cornered. **2** (of a crystal) having three equal axes equally inclined and not perpendicular to each other. **3** (*Math.*) denoting a system of trilinear coordinates. **trigonally** *adv.* **trigonic** (-gon´-) *n.* **trigonon** (trigō´non) *n.* **trigonous** (trig´-) *a.* [L *trigōnum*, Gr. *trigōnon* (TRI-, *-gōnos*, *gōnia*, angle)]

trigon. *abbr.* trigonometry.

trigonometry (trigənom´itri) *n.* the branch of mathematics treating of the relations of the sides and angles of triangles, and applying these to astronomy, navigation, surveying etc. **trigonometer** *n.* an instrument for the mechanical solution of plane right-angled triangles. **trigonometric** (-nəmet´-), **trigonometrical** *a.* **trigonometrically** *adv.* **trigonometric function** *n.* **1** any of a group of functions of an angle expressed in terms of the ratios of the sides of a right-angled triangle. **2** the inverse of trigonometric function. [Gr. *trigōnon*, TRIGON, -METRY]

trigonon TRIGON.

trig point (trig) *n.* TRIANGULATION POINT (under TRIANGLE).

trigram (trī´gram) *n.* **1** a group of three letters representing a single sound, a trigraph. **2** a set of three straight lines in one plane not all intersecting in the same point. **trigrammatic** (-mat´-), **trigrammic** (-gram´-) *a.*

trigraph (trī´grahf) *n.* **1** a group of three letters representing a single sound. **2** a figure of three lines.

trigynous (trij´inəs) *a.* having three pistils. [Gr. *gunē*, female]

trihedron (trīhē´drən) *n.* (*pl.* **trihedra** (-drə), **trihedrons**) a figure having three sides. **trihedral** *a.* [Gr. *hedra*, base]

trihydric (trīhī´drik) *a.* (*Chem.*) containing three hydroxyl groups.

trike (trīk) *n.*, *v.i.* (*coll.*) short for TRICYCLE.

trilabiate (trīlā´biət) *a.* (*Bot.*, *Zool.*) three-lipped.

trilateral (trīlat´ərəl) *a.* **1** of or having three sides. **2** involving three parties or people. ~*n.* a three-sided figure. **trilaterally** *adv.*

trilby (tril´bi) *n.* (*pl.* **trilbies**) a man's soft felt hat with a dent in the middle. **trilbied** *a.* [heroine of George du Maurier's *Trilby*]

trilemma (trīlem´ə) *n.* a syllogism involving three alternatives. [after DILEMMA]

trilinear (trīlin´iə) *a.* consisting of three lines.

trilingual (trīling´gwəl) *a.* **1** able to speak three languages. **2** of, relating to or expressed in three languages. **trilingualism** *n.*

triliteral (trīlit´ərəl) *a.* (esp. of Semitic roots) consisting of or using three letters. ~*n.* a triliteral word or root. **triliteralism** *n.* **triliterality** (-ral´-) *n.*

trilith (trī´lith), **trilithon** (-on) *n.* a megalithic monument usu. consisting of two uprights supporting an impost. **trilithic** (-lith´-) *a.* [Gr. *trilithon*, neut. of *trilithos* (*lithos*, stone)]

trill (tril) *v.i.* to sing or emit a sound with a tremulous vibration. ~*v.t.* to sing or utter with a quavering or shake. ~*n.* **1** a tremulous or quavering sound. **2** a consonant pronounced with a trilling sound, such as *r*. **3** a shake, a rapid alternation of two notes a tone or semitone apart. [It. *trillāre*, imit.]

trillion (tril´yən) *n.* (*pl.* **trillion**, **trillions**) **1** a million million. **2** (*esp. Hist.*) the product of a million raised to the third power. **3** (*pl.*, *coll.*) an indefinite large number. **trillionth** (-th) *a.*, *n.* [after MILLION]

trillium (tril´iəm) *n.* any herbaceous plant of the genus *Trillium*, with a single central flower above three leaves. [mod. L, from Swed. *trilling*, triplet]

trilobate (trīlōˊbət, trīˊ-), **trilobated** (trīˊləbātid), **trilobed** (-lōbd) *a.* having three lobes. **trilobation** (-lōbāˊshən) *n.*

trilobite (trīˊləbīt, trilˊ-) *n.* any of the Palaeozoic group of articulates with a three-lobed body. **trilobitic** (-bitˊ-) *a.* [Gr. *lobos*, lobe]

trilocular (trīlokˊūlə) *a.* having three cells or chambers. [LOCULUS]

trilogy (trilˊəji) *n.* (*pl.* **trilogies**) **1** a group of three plays, operas, novels etc., each complete in itself, but connected. **2** a series of three tragedies, each complete in itself, but connected by the story or theme, and adapted for performance in immediate succession. [Gr. *trilogia*]

trim (trim) *v.t.* (*pres.p.* **trimming,** *past, p.p.* **trimmed**) **1** to put in good order, to make neat and tidy. **2** to remove irregularities, excrescences or superfluous or unsightly parts from. **3** to cut, lop, or clip (those) away or off. **4** to dress, to smooth, to plane (wood, boards etc.). **5** to put (a lamp etc.) in order by clipping or renewing a wick, carbons etc. **6** to reduce (e.g. costs). **7** to decorate, to ornament (with trimmings etc.). **8** to adjust (sails, yards etc.) to the wind. **9** to adjust (a ship) by arranging the cargo, ballast etc. **10** (*coll.*) to reprove sharply; to chastise, to flog. ~*v.i.* to adopt a middle course, between parties, opinions etc. ~*a.* (*comp.* **trimmer,** *superl.* **trimmest**) **1** properly adjusted, in good order. **2** well-equipped, neat, tidy, smart. ~*n.* **1** (esp. of a ship or her cargo, ballast, masts etc.) a state of preparation or fitness, order, condition. **2** dress or equipment. **3** material used to trim clothes etc. **4** an act of trimming, esp. hair. **5** the angle at which an aeroplane flies in given conditions. **6** the interior panels, decorative fascia, etc. of a vehicle. **7** that which is removed by trimming. **in trim** looking smart or neat. **out of trim** OUT. **trimly** *adv.* **trimmer** *n.* **1** a person who or thing which trims. **2** an implement or machine for clipping timber etc. **3** a joist into which others are framed. **4** a person who trims between parties, esp. in politics, a time-server. **5** (*also* **trimming capacitor**) a small capacitor used for tuning a radio set. **6** (*Austral., coll.*) a person who or something which is excellent. **trimming** *n.* **1** the act of a person who trims. **2** material sewn on a garment for ornament. **3** (*pl., coll.*) accessories to a dish. **4** (*pl.*) anything additional to the main item. **5** (*pl.*) pieces trimmed off. **trimness** *n.* **trim tab** *n.* a tab or aerofoil on an aircraft or boat used to trim it. [OE *trymian*, to make firm, to set in order, from *trum*, firm, stable]

trimaran (trīˊməran) *n.* a sailing vessel with three hulls. [TRI-, cata*maran*]

trimensual (trīmenˊsūəl) *a.* happening or issued every three months. [L *trimestus*, TRI-, *mensis*, month]

trimer (trīˊmə) *n.* a polymer whose molecule is formed from three molecules of a monomer. **trimeric** (-merˊ-) *a.* **trimerous** (trimˊ-, trīˊ-) *a.* having three parts, joints, members etc. [Gr. *trimerēs* (*meros*, part)]

trimester (trimesˊtə) *n.* **1** a period of three months. **2** any of the three divisions of the academic year. **trimestral** *a.* **trimestrial** *a.* **1** of or relating to a trimester. **2** TRIMENSUAL. [L *trimetrus*, from Gr. *trimetros*]

trimeter (trimˊitə) *n.* a verse consisting of three measures of two feet each. ~*a.* consisting of three measures. **trimetric** (trīmetˊ-), **trimetrical** *a.* [L *trimetrus*, Gr. *tremetros* (METRE[2])]

trimmer, trimming TRIM.

trimonthly (trīmŭnthˊli) *a.* **1** occurring every three months. **2** lasting three months.

trimorphism (trīmawˊfizm) *n.* **1** the existence in certain species of plants and animals of three distinct forms, colours etc., esp. having flowers with pistils or stamens of three different relative lengths. **2** the property of crystallizing in three distinct forms. **trimorphic, trimorphous** *a.* [TRI-, Gr. *morphē*, form]

trine (trīn) *a.* **1** threefold, triple. **2** (*Astrol.*) of, relating to or in trine. ~*n.* **1** a triad, a set of three. **2** (*Theol.*) the Trinity. **3** (*Astrol.*) the aspect of planets distant from each other 120°. **trinal, trinary** *a.* [L *trinus*, from *trēs*, three]

Trinidadian (trinidadˊiən, -dāˊ-) *n.* a native or inhabitant of Trinidad. ~*a.* of or relating to Trinidad or its inhabitants.

Trinitarian TRINITY.

trinitrotoluene (trīnītrōtolˊūēn), **trinitrotoluol** (-ol) *n.* a chemical compound, usually known as TNT, largely used as a high explosive.

trinity (trinˊiti) *n.* (*pl.* **trinities**) **1** a group or union of three individuals, a triad. **2** the state of being three or threefold. **3** (*Theol.*) (**Trinity**) the union of three persons (the Father, the Son and the Holy Ghost) in one Godhead. **4** the doctrine of the Trinity. **5** a symbolical representation of the Trinity frequent in art, such as the triangle or three interlacing circles. **Trinitarian** (-teəˊri-) *a.* of or relating to the doctrine of the Trinity. ~*n.* a person who believes in this. **Trinitarianism** *n.* **Trinity Brethren** *n.pl.* members of Trinity House. **Trinity House** *n.* an association for licensing pilots, managing lighthouses, beacons, buoys etc., in British waters. **Trinity Sunday** *n.* the Sunday next after Whit Sunday. **Trinity term** *n.* the term beginning after Easter at some universities. [OF *trinite*, late L *trinitas -tatem*, from *trīnus*, TRINE]

trinket (tringˊkit) *n.* **1** a small personal ornament of no great value as a jewel, esp. a ring. **2** any small ornament or fancy article. **trinketry** (-ri) *n.* [etym. unknown, perh. from ME *trenket*, ONF *trenquet*, knife, from *trenquer*, var. of *tranchier*, to cut, see TRENCH]

trinomial (trīnōˊmiəl) *a.* consisting of three terms, esp. connected by the signs + or -. ~*n.* a trinomial name or expression. **trinomialism** *n.* trinomial nomenclature, esp. in biology. **trinomially** *adv.*

trio (trēˊō) *n.* (*pl.* **trios**) **1** a set of three. **2** a musical composition for three voices or three instruments. **3** a set of three singers or players. **4** the second part of a minuet, march etc. **5** in piquet, three aces, kings, queens, knaves or tens. [It., from L *trēs*, three]

triode (trīˊōd) *n.* **1** a thermionic valve with three electrodes. **2** any electronic device with three electrodes. [TRI-, electr*ode*]

trioecious (trīēˊshəs), **triecious** *a.* (*Bot.*) having male, female and hermaphrodite flowers, each on different plants of the same species. [Gr. *treis*, three, *oikos*, a house]

triolet (trēˊəlit, trīˊ-) *n.* a poem of eight lines with two rhymes arranged *ab aa ab ab*. [F, dim. of TRIO]

trior TRIER (under TRY).

trioxide (trīokˊsīd) *n.* (*Chem.*) an oxide having three oxygen atoms.

trip (trip) *v.i.* (*pres.p.* **tripping,** *past, p.p.* **tripped**) **1** to move, step, walk or run lightly or nimbly. **2** (of rhythm etc.) to go lightly or evenly. **3** to catch the foot (over something) so as nearly to fall, to make a false step, to stumble. **4** to make a short journey. **5** (*coll.*) to be under the influence of a hallucinogenic drug. **6** to err, to go wrong. **7** to be activated. ~*v.t.* **1** to cause to fall by catching or obstructing the feet etc. **2** to catch or detect in a fault, mistake or offence. **3** (*Naut.*) to loosen (an anchor) from the bottom. **4** (*Naut.*) to turn (a yard etc.) from the horizontal to the vertical position. **5** to release (a part of a machine) by unfastening. **6** to activate, to set off. ~*n.* **1** a short excursion, voyage or journey. **2** a stumble, a false step. **3** a failure, a mistake. **4** a light nimble step. **5** a leaping movement of the feet. **6** (*coll.*) a period spent under the influence of a hallucinogenic drug. **7** any device for activating a mechanism. **8** (*sl.*) an unpleasant experience. **9** (*sl.*) a pleasurable or engrossing experience. **10** a sudden stroke or catch by which a wrestler trips up their antagonist. **11** (*Naut.*) a single tack in plying to windward. **12** the number of fish caught in one voyage. **to trip the light fantastic** to dance. **trip-hammer** *n.* a tilt-hammer. **tripmeter** *n.* an instrument in a vehicle used for recording the distance of an individual journey. **trippant** *a.* (*Her.*) walking or trotting. **tripper** *n.* **1** a person who goes on a trip, an excursionist. **2** a device that trips a mechanism. **3** a person who trips up another. **4** (*coll.*) a person under the influence of a hallucinogenic drug. **trippingly** *adv.* **trippy** *a.* (*comp.* **trippier**, *superl.* **trippiest**) (*coll.*) producing an effect similar to that of taking hallucinogenic drugs. **tripwire** *n.* a wire that trips a mechanism when pulled. [ME *trippen*, OF *treper*, *triper*, *tripper*, MDut. *trippen*, cp. Swed. *trippa*, Dan. *trippe*]

tripartite (trīpah´tīt) *a.* **1** consisting of three parts. **2** divided into three corresponding parts or copies. **3** made or concluded between three parties. **tripartitely** *adv.* **tripartition** (-tish´ən) *n.* [L *partitus*, p.p. of *partiri*, to divide, from *pars partis*, PART]

tripe (trīp) *n.* **1** a part of the stomach of ruminating animals prepared for food. **2** (*usu. in pl.*) the entrails, the belly. **3** (*coll.*) silly stuff, rubbish, nonsense. [F (cp. Sp. and Port. *tripa*, It. *trippa*), etym. uncertain]

tripersonal (tripœ´sənəl) *a.* consisting of three persons (esp. of the Godhead). **tripersonalism** *n.* the doctrine of the Trinity. **tripersonalist** *n.* a believer in tripersonalism. **tripersonality** (-nal´-) *n.*

triphibious (trīfib´iəs) *a.* on land, on sea and in the air. [after AMPHIBIOUS (under AMPHIBIAN)]

triphthong (trif´thong) *n.* a combination of three vowels forming one sound. **triphthongal** (-thong´gəl) *a.* [after DIPHTHONG]

tripinnate (trīpin´ət) *a.* triply pinnate. **tripinnately** *adv.*

triplane (trī´plān) *n.* an aeroplane with three supporting planes.

triple (trip´əl) *a.* **1** consisting of three parts or three things united, threefold. **2** multiplied by three. **3** (of musical rhythm) having three beats to the bar. ~*n.* **1** a threefold quantity. **2** three of anything. **3** (*pl.*) a peal of changes on seven bells. ~*v.t.* to treble, to make threefold. ~*v.i.* to become three times as large or as many. **triple acrostic** *n.* an acrostic which uses the first, middle and last letters to make words. **triple crown** *n.* **1** the crown or tiara worn by the Pope. **2** the act of winning all three of a series of matches, races etc. **triple-crowned** *a.* **triple-headed** *a.* **triple jump** *n.* an athletic event in which the competitor performs a hop, a step and a jump in succession. **triple play** *n.* in baseball, the act of getting three players out with one ball. **triple point** *n.* the temperature and pressure at which the solid, liquid and vapour phases of a substance are in equilibrium. **triple rhyme** *n.* a rhyme using three syllables. **triplet** *n.* **1** a set or group of three. **2** any one of three children born of the same mother at one birth. **3** three verses rhyming together. **4** (*Mus.*) three notes performed in the time of two. **triple time** *n.* a musical rhythm of three beats in a bar. **Triplex®** (-leks) *n.* a type of laminated glass. **triplex** *n.* **1** triple time. **2** a composition in three parts. ~*a.* triple or threefold. **triplicate**[1] (-likət) *a.* made three times as much or as many, threefold. ~*n.* a copy, document or other thing corresponding to two others of the same kind. **in triplicate** written out or copied three times. **triplicate**[2] (-likāt) *v.t.* to make triplicate, to treble. **triplicate ratio** *n.* the ratio of the cubes (of two quantities). **triplication** (-kā´shən) *n.* **triplicature** (-chə) *n.* **triplicity** (-plis´-) *n.* (*pl.* **triplicities**) **1** the state of being triple. **2** a group of three things. **3** a set of three signs of the zodiac. **triploid** (-loid) *a.* (*Biol.*) having three times the haploid number of chromosomes. ~*n.* a triploid organism. **triploidy** *n.* **triply** *adv.* [F, from L *triplus* (TRI-, *-plus*, cogn. with *plēnus*, full)]

tripod (trī´pod) *n.* **1** a three-legged stand, stool, utensil, seat, table etc. **2** a three-legged support for a camera etc. **3** (*Hist.*) in ancient Greece, a bronze altar at Delphi on which the Pythian priestess sat to deliver oracles. **4** an imitation of this, esp. offered as a prize at the Pythian games. **tripodal** (trip´ədəl) *a.* [L *tripus -podis*, Gr. *tripous -podos* (*pous podos*, foot)]

tripoli (trip´əli) *n.* rotten-stone, a friable siliceous limestone. [*Tripoli*, Libya]

tripos (trī´pos) *n.* (*pl.* **triposes**) **1** either part of the examination for an honours BA at Cambridge University. **2** a printed list (arranged in three grades) of the successful candidates. [L *tripus*, TRIPOD]

trippant, tripper TRIP.

trippet (trip´it) *n.* a projecting part of a machine which regularly strikes another part of the mechanism. [cp. TRIVET]

trippingly, trippy TRIP.

triptane (trip´tān) *n.* a very powerful aviation fuel, trimethyl butane.

tripterous (trip´tərəs) *a.* having three winglike parts. [Gr. *tripteros*, from *pteron*, wing]

triptych (trip´tik) *n.* **1** a picture, carving or other representation, on three panels side by side, frequently used for altarpieces. **2** a group of three associated pictures etc. **3** a writing-tablet in three leaves. [Gr. *triptuchon*, neut. of *triptuchos* (TRI-, *ptuchē*, fold, from *ptussein*, to fold)]

triptyque (triptēk´) *n.* a customs pass, made out in triplicate, for importing or exporting a motor vehicle. [F]

triquetra (trīkwē´trə, -kwet´-) *n.* (*pl.* **triquetrae** (-trē)) an ornament composed of three interlacing arcs. **triquetrous** *a.* **1** three-sided, three-cornered, triangular. **2** (*Bot.*) having three sharp angles. [L, fem. of *triquetrus*, three-cornered (*quetrus*, etym. uncertain)]

triradial (trīrā´diəl), **triradiated** (-ātid), **triradiate** (-ət) *a.* having three rays or radiating branches.

trireme (trī´rēm) *n.* a war-galley with three benches of oars. [L *trirēmis* (*rēmus*, oar)]

trisaccharide (trīsak´ərīd) *n.* (*Chem.*) a sugar that consists of three monosaccharide molecules.

Trisagion (trisag´iən, -sā´-) *n.* a hymn with a threefold invocation of God as holy, in the liturgies of the Greek and Eastern Churches. [Gr. *trisagios* (*tris*, thrice, from *treis*, three, *hagios*, holy)]

trisect (trīsekt´) *v.t.* to divide into three (esp. equal) parts. **trisection** *n.* **trisector** *n.* [L *sectus*, p.p. of *secāre*, to cut]

trishaw (trī´shaw) *n.* a three-wheeled rickshaw. [TRI-, rick*shaw*]

triskaidekaphobia (triskīdekəfō´biə) *n.* fear of the number 13. **triskaidekaphobe** (-dek´-) *n.* **triskaidekaphobic** *a.*, *n.* [Gr. *triskaideka*, -PHOBIA (under -PHOBE)]

triskelion (trīskel´iən) *n.* a form of fylfot, usu. consisting of three human legs, bent, and joined at the thigh, as in the arms of the Isle of Man. [Gr. *triskelēs* (*skelos*, leg)]

trismus (triz´məs) *n.* (*Med.*) lockjaw. [Gr. *trismos*, from *trizein*, to squeak, to creak]

trisoctahedron (trisoktəhē´drən) *n.* (*pl.* **trisoctahedra** (-drə), **trisoctahedrons**) a solid having 24 equal faces. [Gr. *tris*, thrice, OCTAHEDRON]

trisomy (tris´əmi) *n.* (*Med.*) a condition in which one chromosome type is represented three times instead of twice. **trisomy-21** *n.* a common form of Down's syndrome, caused by an extra copy of chromosome 21.

triste (trist) *a.* (*poet.*) sad, gloomy. [OF *triste*, L *tristis*]

tristesse (tristes´) *n.* sadness. [F]

tristich (tris´tik) *n.* a strophe or set of three lines. **tristichous** *a.* (*Bot.*) arranged in three vertical rows. [Gr. *tristichos* (*tris*, thrice, from *treis*, three, *stichos*, row)]

trisyllable (trīsil´əbəl) *n.* a word of three syllables. **trisyllabic** (-lab´-) *a.* **trisyllabically** *adv.*

tritagonist (tritag´ənist) *n.* the third actor in a classical Greek play. [Gr. *tritagōnistēs* (*tritos*, third, *agōnistēs*, see AGONISTIC (under AGONIST))]

tritanopia (trītənō´piə) *n.* a reduced ability to distinguish the colour blue. **tritanopic** (-nop´-) *a.* [Gr. *tritos*, third, mod. L *anopia*, blindness, i.e. inability to see one third of the spectrum]

trite (trīt) *a.* **1** commonplace, hackneyed, stale. **2** worn out. **tritely** *adv.* **triteness** *n.* [L *trītus*, p.p. of *terere*, to rub]

tritheism (trī´thēizm) *n.* (*Theol.*) the doctrine that the three persons of the Trinity are each distinct Gods. **tritheist** *n.* **tritheistic** (-is´-) *a.*

tritium (trit´iəm) *n.* an isotope of hydrogen with a mass three times that of ordinary hydrogen. **tritiate** *v.t.* to replace hydrogen atoms in (a compound) by tritium. **tritiation** (-ā´shən) *n.* **triton**[1] (trī´tən) *n.* a nucleus of a tritium atom, one proton and two neutrons. [Gr. *tritos*, third]

trito- (trī´tō, trit´ō) *comb. form* third. [Gr. *tritos*, third]

Triton (trī´tən) *n.* **1** in Greek mythology, a son of Poseidon (Neptune) by Amphitrite, or one of a race of minor sea-gods, represented as half man and half fish, and blowing a spiral shell. **2** (**triton**) a newt. **3** (**triton**) any gastropod mollusc of the family Cymatiidae. [L and Gr.]

triton[1] TRITIUM.

triton[2] TRITON.

tritone (trī´tōn) *n.* (*Mus.*) an augmented fourth, containing three whole tones.

triturate (trit´ūrāt) *v.t.* **1** to rub or grind down to a fine powder. **2** to masticate with the molar teeth. **triturable** *a.* **trituration** (-rā´shən) *n.* **triturator** *n.* **triturium** (-tū´riəm), **tritorium** (-taw´-) *n.* (*pl.* **trituria** (-riə), **tritoria**) a vessel for separating liquids of different densities. [late L *trītūrātus*, p.p. of *trītūrāre*, from *trītūra*, rubbing, as TRITE]

triumph (trī´əmf) *n.* **1** the state of being victorious. **2** victory, success. **3** joy or exultation for success. **4** a great example. **5** (*Hist.*) in ancient Rome, a pageant in honour of a victorious general who entered the city in a solemn procession, followed by religious ceremonies. ~*v.i.* **1** to gain a victory, to prevail (over). **2** to enjoy a triumph. **3** to boast or exult (over). **4** to exult. **triumphal** (-ŭm´-) *a.* of or relating to a triumph. **triumphal arch** *n.* an arch built to celebrate a victory or other notable event. **triumphalism** *n.* an arrogant pride in one's own success. **triumphalist** *n.*, *a.* **triumphant** (-ŭm´-) *a.* **1** victorious, successful. **2** exultant. **triumphantly** *adv.* **triumpher** *n.* **triumphingly** (-ŭm´-) *adv.* [ME and OF *triumphe*, L *triumphus -um*, Gr. *thriambos*, hymn to Bacchus]

triumvir (trīŭm´viə) *n.* (*pl.* **triumvirs, triumviri** (-rī)) any one of three men united in office, esp. a member of the first or second triumvirate in ancient Rome. **triumviral** *a.* **triumvirate** (-ərət) *n.* **1** the office of a triumvir. **2** a group of triumvirs. **3** a coalition of three men in office or authority, esp. the first triumvirate, of Pompey, Julius Caesar and Crassus in 60 BC, or the second, of Mark Antony, Octavian, and Lepidus, in 43 BC. **4** a party or set of three men. [L (*trium*, gen. of *trēs*, three, *vir*, man)]

triune (trī´ūn) *a.* three in one. **triunity** (-ū´niti) *n.* (*pl.* **triunities**). [L *ūnus*, one]

trivalent (trīvā´lənt) *a.* having a valency or combining power of three. **trivalence, trivalency** *n.*

trivet (triv´it) *n.* a three-legged stand, esp. a metal tripod or movable bracket for supporting a cooking vessel or kettle. **trivet table** *n.* a table that has three feet. [formerly *trevet*, OE *trefet*, L *tripēs -pedem* (TRI-, *pēs pedis*, foot)]

trivia (triv´iə) *n.pl.* trifles, inessentials. [see TRIVIAL]

trivial (triv´iəl) *a.* **1** of little value or importance, trifling, inconsiderable. **2** concerned with trivia. **3** †commonplace, ordinary. **4** (of names of plants etc.) common, popular, not scientific. **5** (*Math.*) (of a solution) having zero values for all the variables. **trivialism** *n.* **triviality** (-al´-) *n.* (*pl.* **trivialities**). **trivialize, trivialise** *v.t.* to cause to seem trivial, to minimize. **trivialization** (-zā´shən) *n.* **trivially** *adv.* **trivialness** *n.* **trivium** (-iəm) *n.* (*Hist.*) in medieval schools, the first three liberal arts, grammar, rhetoric and logic. [F, from L *triviālis*, ordinary, from *trivium*, crossroads (TRI-, *via*, way)]

tri-weekly (trīwēk´li) *a.* happening, issued or done three times a week or once every three weeks.

-trix (triks) *suf.* (*pl.* **-trices** (trisez, trī´-), **-trixes**) forming feminine agent nouns. [L]

TRJ *abbr.* turboramjet (engine).

TRM *abbr.* trademark.

tRNA *abbr.* transfer RNA.

troat (trōt) *n.* the cry of a buck in rutting time. ~*v.i.* to cry thus. [imit.]

trocar (trō´kah) *n.* an instrument for draining an internal part of fluid, used in dropsy, hydrocele etc. [F (*trois*, three, *carre*, L *quadra*, square)]

trochaic TROCHEE.

trochal TROCHE.

trochanter (trōkan´tə) *n.* **1** any one of several bony processes on the upper part of the thigh bone. **2** the second joint of the leg of an insect. [Gr., from *trechein*, to run]

troche (trōsh, trōk, trō´kē) *n.* a lozenge, usu. circular, of medicinal substance. **trochal** (-kəl) *a.* wheel-shaped, rotiform. [Gr. *trochos*, wheel, from *trechein*, to run]

trochee (trō´kē) *n.* a metrical foot of two syllables, long and short. **trochaic** (-kā´-) *a.*, *n.* [L *trochaeus*, Gr. *trochaios*, running, from *trechein*, to run]

trochil (trok´il), **trochilus** (-ləs) *n.* (*pl.* **trochils, trochili** (-lī)) **1** an Egyptian plover said by the ancients to enter the mouth of crocodiles and feed on parasites. **2** HUMMINGBIRD (under HUM[1]). **3** any of several warblers, esp. *Phylloscopus trochilus*. [Gr. *trochilos*, from *trechein*, to run]

trochlea (trok´liə) *n.* (*pl.* **trochleae** (-liē)) a pulley-like anatomical part or surface, esp. that of the humerus articulating with the ulna. **trochlear** *a.* **trochleate** (-liət) *a.* [L, from Gr. *trochalia*, pulley, from *trechein*, to run]

trochoid (trō´koid) *a.* **1** (*Anat.*) rotating on its own axis, pivotal. **2** (of a curve) generated by a point in the plane of one curve rolling upon another. ~*n.* **1** a trochoid curve. **2** (*Anat.*) a trochoid joint. **trochoidal** (-koi´-) *a.* [Gr. *trochoeidēs* (*trochos*, see TROCHE)]

trochophore (trō´kōfaw) *n.* a free-swimming ciliate larva of many invertebrates. [Gr. *trochos*, wheel, -PHORE]

trod, trodden TREAD.

trog[1] (trog) *v.i.* (*pres.p.* **trogging**, *past, p.p.* **trogged**) (*sl.*) to walk, esp. wearily. [perh. from *trudge* and *slog*]

trog[2] (trog) *n.* (*sl.*) a lout or hooligan. [TROGLODYTE]

troglodyte (trog´lədīt) *n.* **1** a cave dweller. **2** a hermit. **3** an eccentric or old-fashioned person. **troglodytic** (-dit´-), **troglodytical** *a.* **troglodytism** *n.* [F, from L *trōglodyta*, Gr. *trōglodutēs* (*trōglē*, cave, *duein*, to enter)]

trogon (trō´gon) *n.* any of a family of tropical American insectivorous birds, the Trogonidae, with brilliant plumage. [Gr., pres.p. of *trōgein*, to gnaw]

troika (troi´kə) *n.* **1** a team of three horses harnessed abreast. **2** a vehicle drawn by this. **3** a group of three people, esp. a triumvirate. [Rus.]

troilism (troi´lizm) *n.* sexual activity involving three people of both sexes. [perh. F *trois*, three, *dualism*]

Trojan (trō´jən) *a.* of or relating to ancient Troy. ~*n.* **1** an inhabitant of ancient Troy. **2** a person of pluck or determination. **Trojan horse** *n.* **1** the huge wooden horse in which the Greeks secretly entered Troy. **2** any subterfuge intended to undermine an organization etc. from within. **3** (*Comput.*) (*also* **trojan**) a program designed to harm a computer system, which gains access to the system by being inserted into a legitimate program, and differs from a virus in that it cannot replicate itself. [L *Trōjānus*, from *Trōja, Trōia*, Troy]

troll[1] (trōl) *v.t.* **1** to roll or reel out (a song) in a careless manner. **2** to fish (water) by trailing or spinning a revolving bait, esp. behind a boat. **3** to sing the parts of (a song) in succession. *~v.i.* **1** to fish in this way. **2** to sing in a free and easy way. **3** to walk, to stroll. *~n.* **1** the act of trolling for fish. **2** a reel on a fishing rod. **3** a spinning or other bait used in trolling for fish. **4** a song the parts of which are sung in succession, a round, a catch. **troller** *n.* [OF *troller, trauler*, G *trollen*, to roll, to stroll, cp. MDut. *drollen*]

troll[2] (trōl) *n.* **1** a giant or giantess in Scandinavian mythology, endowed with supernatural powers. **2** a familiar but impish dwarf. [Icel., cp. Swed. *troll*, Dan. *trold*]

trolley (trol´i), **trolly** *n.* (*pl.* **trolleys, trollies**) **1** a set of shelves with wheels, used for moving things, e.g. trays of food, around. **2** a basket on wheels used for containing goods to be purchased in a grocery shop, supermarket etc. **3** a four-wheeled truck or low car, esp. one the body of which can be tilted over. **4** a costermonger's cart. **5** (*also* **trolley-wheel**) a grooved wheel on a pole used for conveying current to the motor on electric railways, tramways etc. **6** (*N Am.*) a trolley-car. **7** a trolleybus. **off one's trolley** (*sl.*) crazy, insane. **trolleybus** *n.* a bus deriving its motive power through a trolley from overhead wires. **trolley-car** *n.* (*N Am.*) a tramcar. **trolley system** *n.* the system of working electric railways, tramways etc., by means of trolleys. [TROLL[1]]

trollop (trol´əp) *n.* **1** a careless, slovenly woman, a slattern. **2** a woman of bad character; a prostitute. [etym. uncertain; perh. rel. to TRULL]

trolly TROLLEY.

trombone (trombōn´) *n.* **1** a large and powerful wind instrument of the trumpet kind usu. played by means of a sliding tube. **2** a trombone-player. **3** an organ stop with the quality of a trombone. **trombonist** *n.* [It., from *tromba*, trumpet]

trommel (trom´əl) *n.* a rotating cylindrical sieve for cleaning and sizing ore. [G, drum]

tromometer (trəmom´itə) *n.* an instrument for measuring earth tremors. **tromometric** (tromōmet´-) *a.* [Gr. *tromos*, trembling, from *tremein*, to tremble]

trompe (tromp) *n.* an apparatus worked by a descending column of water for producing a blast in a furnace. [F, TRUMP[2]]

trompe l'œil (tromp lœy', trõp) *n.* (*pl.* **trompe l'œils** (lœy´)) (a painting etc. giving) a very deceptive appearance of reality. [F, lit., deceive the eye]

-tron (tron) *suf.* **1** elementary particle, as *plectron*. **2** particle accelerator, as *cyclotron*. **3** thermionic valve, as *klystron*. [Gr. suf. denoting an instrument]

trona (trō´nə) *n.* a native hydrous carbonate of soda. [Arab.]

tronc (trongk) *n.* a system whereby waiters and other employees in a restaurant share in the tips. [F, collecting box]

troop (troop) *n.* **1** an assemblage of persons or animals, a crowd, a company. **2** (*pl.*) soldiers. **3** a band or company of performers, a troupe. **4** the unit of cavalry formation, usu. consisting of 60 troopers, commanded by a captain. **5** a particular beat of the drum as a signal to march. **6** a group of Scout patrols. **7** a unit of artillery and armoured formation. *~v.i.* **1** to come together, to assemble, to come thronging (up, together etc.). **2** to move (along a way etc.) in a troop. **3** to hurry (off etc.). *~v.t.* to form (a squadron etc.) into troops. **troop carrier** *n.* a ship, aircraft or vehicle for carrying troops. **trooper** *n.* **1** a cavalry soldier. **2** a private in a cavalry regiment. **3** a troopship. **4** (*N Am., Austral.*) a mounted policeman. **5** a cavalry horse. **to swear like a trooper** to swear strongly or excessively. **trooping the colour** *n.* a ceremonial parade at which the colour is carried between the files of troops. **troopship** *n.* a ship transporting soldiers. [F *troupe*, OF *trope* (cp. Sp. *tropa*, It. *truppa*), etym. uncertain]

Usage note See note under TROUPE.

troopial (troo´piəl), **troupial** *n.* any of various American orioles of the genus *Icterus*, in some respects resembling the starling. [F *troupiale*, from *troupe*, TROOP]

trop. *abbr.* tropical.

trop- TROPO-.

tropaeolum (trəpē´ələm) *n.* (*pl.* **tropaeolums, tropaeola** (-lə)) a S American climbing plant of the genus *Tropaeolum*, with trumpet-shaped flowers. [mod. L, from Gr. *tropaios*, turning, as TROPE]

trope (trōp) *n.* a figurative use of a word. [F, from L *tropus*, Gr. *tropos*, turn, trope, from *trepein*, to turn]

-trope (trōp) *comb. form* forming nouns indicating a turning towards or affinity for. **-tropic** *comb. form* forming adjectives.

troph- TROPHO-.

trophic (trof´ik) *a.* of or relating to nutrition. **trophesy** (-əsi) *n.* (*Med.*) deranged nutrition due to nervous disorder. [Gr. *trophē*, nourishment, from *trephein*, to nourish]

-trophic (trō´fik, trof´-) *comb. form* **1** relating to nutrition. **2** relating to regulation, esp. by a hormone. **-trophism** *comb. form* forming nouns. [as TROPHIC]

trophied TROPHY.

-trophism -TROPHIC.

tropho- (trō´fō), **troph-** *comb. form* nourishment. [as TROPHIC]

trophoblast (trof´ōblast, trō´-) *n.* a membrane enclosing the mammalian embryo which absorbs nourishment from the uterine fluids. **trophoblastic** (-blas´-) *a.*

trophotropism (trəfot´rəpizm) *n.* the movement of the organs of a growing plant towards or away from nutrient substances, induced by the chemical nature of its surroundings. **trophotropic** (trōfətrop´-) *a.*

trophy (trō´fi) *n.* (*pl.* **trophies**) **1** anything, esp. a cup, preserved as a memorial of victory or success. **2** an ornamental group of typical or symbolical objects placed on a wall etc. **3** (*Hist.*) in ancient Rome, a pile of arms and other spoils taken from a vanquished enemy and set up on the battlefield to commemorate a victory. **4** (*Hist.*) in ancient Greece, a more permanent memorial imitating this decorated with captured arms, beaks of ships etc., or representations of these. **trophied** *a.* (*also in comb.*) [F *trophée*, L *tropaeum*, Gr. *tropaion*, neut. a., from *tropē*, defeat, from *trepein*, to turn]

-trophy (trəfi) *comb. form* a specified form of nourishment or growth. [Gr. *trephein*, to nourish]

tropic[1] (trop´ik) *n.* **1** (*also* **tropic of Cancer**) the parallel of latitude 23° 26´ north of the equator. **2** (*also* **tropic of Capricorn**) the parallel of latitude 23° 26´ south of the equator. **3** (**Tropics**) the regions of the torrid zone between these. **4** either of the corresponding parallels of declination on the celestial sphere. *~a.* of or relating to the tropics, tropical. **tropical** *a.* **1** of, relating to, lying within or characteristic of the Tropics. **2** (of the weather) very hot. **3** of the nature of a trope, figurative, metaphorical. **tropical cyclone** *n.* a cyclone over a tropical ocean with hurricane-force winds. **tropically** *adv.* **tropical month** *n.* the mean period of the moon's passing through 360° of longitude, i.e. 27 days, 7 hours, 43 min., 4.7 secs. **tropical storm** *n.* a tropical cyclone. **tropical year** *n.* a solar year. **tropic bird** *n.* any seabird of the family Phaethontidae. [F *tropique*, late L *tropicum*, nom. *-cus*, Gr. *tropikos kuklos*, the tropic circle, from *tropē*, solstice, turning, from *trepein*, to turn]

tropic[2] TROPISM.

-tropic -TROPE.

tropism (trō´pizm) *n.* the direction of growth in a plant or other organism that is due to an external stimulus. **tropic**[2] *a.* [Gr. *tropos*, a turn]

tropist TROPOLOGY.

tropo- (trop´ō), **trop-** *comb. form* **1** turn(ing). **2** tropism. [Gr. *tropos*, a turn]

tropology (trəpol´əji) *n.* (*pl.* **tropologies**) **1** the use of tropical or figurative language. **2** interpretation of the Scriptures in a figurative sense. **tropist** (trō´-) *n.* **1** a person who deals in tropes. **2** a person who explains the Scriptures by tropes. **tropological** (tropəloj´-) *a.* **tropologically** *adv.*

tropopause (trop´əpawz) *n.* the boundary between the troposphere and the stratosphere.

troposphere (trop´əsfiə) *n.* the hollow sphere of atmosphere surrounding the earth, bounded by the stratosphere, in which temperature varies and the weather functions. **tropospheric** (-fer´ik) *a.* [Gr. *tropos*, a turn]

troppo[1] (trop´ō) *adv.* (*Mus.*) too much, excessively. [It., too much]

troppo[2] (trop´ō) *a.* (*Austral., sl.*) affected mentally by a tropical climate; crazy.

Trot (trot) *n.* (*coll., often derog.*) a Trotskyite or other left-winger.

trot (trot) *v.i.* (*pres.p.* **trotting,** *past, p.p.* **trotted**) **1** (of a horse or other quadruped) to move at a steady rapid pace by simultaneously lifting one forefoot and the hind foot of the opposite side alternately with the other pair, the body being unsupported at intervals. **2** to run with short brisk strides. **3** (*coll.*) to walk or go. **4** to fish using a trotline. ~*v.t.* **1** to cause to trot. **2** to cover (a distance etc.) by trotting. ~*n.* **1** the pace, motion or act of a horse etc. in trotting. **2** a brisk steady pace. **3** (*pl., Austral., coll.*) trotting races. **4** a dance. **5** a toddling child. **6** a trotline. **on the trot** (*coll.*) one after the other, successively. **the trots** (*sl.*) diarrhoea. **to trot out 1** to cause (a horse) to trot to show its paces. **2** (*coll.*) to utter (esp. something familiar or trite). **trotline** *n.* in angling, a line suspended across a river with shorter baited lines attached. **trotter** *n.* **1** a person who or animal which trots, esp. a horse trained for fast trotting. **2** (*pl.*) sheep's or other animals' feet used as food. **3** (*pl.*) a human foot. **trotting** *n.* harness racing for trotting horses. [ME *trotten*, F *trotter*, etym. uncertain, perh. from L *tolūtim*, at a trot, from *tollere*, to lift, through late L *tolūtārius*, trotting]

†**troth** (trōth) *n.* faith, fidelity, truth. **to pledge one's troth** to pledge faith or fidelity, esp. to make a promise of marriage. **to plight one's troth** to pledge one's troth. **trothplight** *a.* betrothed, affianced. [OE *trēowth*, TRUTH]

Trotskyism (trot´skiizm) *n.* the political theories of Trotsky, esp. that of worldwide proletarian revolution. [Leon *Trotsky*, 1879–1940, Russian Communist revolutionary]

trotter, trotting TROT.

troubadour (troo´bədaw) *n.* **1** any one of a class of lyric poets who flourished in Provence in the 11th cent., writing in the *langue d'oc* chiefly of love and chivalry. **2** a singer or poet. [F, from Prov. *trobador*, from *trobar* (F *trouver*, to find), prob. through a pop. L *tropāre*, to compose poetry, from *tropus*, TROPE]

trouble (trŭb´əl) *v.t.* **1** to agitate, to disturb. **2** to annoy, to molest. **3** to distress, to afflict. **4** to inconvenience, to put to some exertion or pains. ~*v.i.* **1** to be agitated or disturbed. **2** to take trouble or pains. **3** to be subjected to inconvenience. ~*n.* **1** affliction, distress, worry, perplexity, annoyance, misfortune. **2** labour, exertion, inconvenience. **3** a cause of this. **4** a fault; something amiss. **5** fighting or unrest. **6** disagreement. **in trouble 1** liable to suffer punishment or misfortune. **2** (*coll.*) pregnant when not married. **to ask for trouble** (*coll.*) to lack caution. **to be no trouble** not to cause any difficulty, inconvenience etc. **to get into trouble 1** to incur censure or punishment. **2** to become pregnant. **to go to the trouble** to go out of one's way to do something. **to look for trouble 1** (*coll.*) to try to cause trouble. **2** (*coll.*) to behave in a way that invites trouble. **to take (the) trouble** to go out of one's way to do something. **to trouble someone for** to ask someone to pass etc. **trouble and strife** *n.* wife (rhyming slang). **troubled** *a.* **troublemaker** *n.* a person who stirs up discontent, strife etc. **trouble-making** *n., a.* **troubler** *n.* **troubleshooter** *n.* a person who finds the causes of problems and solves them. **troubleshoot** *v.i., v.t.* (*past, p.p.* **troubleshot**). **troubleshooting** *n.* **troublesome** *a.* **1** giving trouble. **2** annoying, vexatious. **3** tiresome, wearisome, importunate. **troublesomely** *adv.* **troublesomeness** *n.* **trouble spot** *n.* a place where there is frequent disturbance, e.g. strikes or fights. †**troublous** *a.* **1** full of commotion. **2** disturbed, agitated, disorderly. [OF *troubler*, *trubler*, from L *turbula*, dim. of *turba*, crowd]

trou-de-loup (troodəloo´) *n.* (*pl.* **trous-de-loup** (troodəloo´)) a conical pit with a stake in the centre, used against enemy cavalry. [F, lit. wolf-hole]

trough (trof) *n.* **1** a long, narrow, open receptacle of wood, iron etc., for holding water, fodder etc., for domestic animals, kneading dough, washing ore etc. **2** a deep narrow channel, furrow, or depression (in land, the sea etc.). **3** an area of low atmospheric pressure. **4** a hollow between the crests of a wave of radiation. **5** a low point, e.g. in economic activity, in demand etc. **6** the part of a curve of variation of a quantity that is around the minimum. **7** a state of low spirits. [OE *trog* (cp. Dut., G, and Icel. *trog*, Dan. *trug*, Swed. *träg*, cogn. with TREE]

trounce (trowns) *v.t.* **1** to beat severely. **2** to inflict a decisive defeat upon. **3** to punish severely. **trouncer** *n.* [OF *trons*, TRUNCHEON]

troupe (troop) *n.* a company of actors, performers etc. **trouper** *n.* **1** a member of such a company. **2** a reliable person. [F, TROOP]

Usage note Actors and performers form a *troupe*, and other people (especially soldiers) or animals a *troop*, and the spellings of the two should not be confused.

---

troupial TROOPIAL.

trous-de-loup TROU-DE-LOUP.

trousers (trow´zəz) *n.pl.* **1** a two-legged outer garment reaching from the waist to the ankles; also called *pair of trousers*. **2** (*sing., used attrib.*) (**trouser**) of or relating to trousers. **caught with one's trousers down** in a situation where one is unprepared. **to wear the trousers** to be in the position of authority, esp. in a family. **trouser-clip** *n.* BICYCLE CLIP (under BICYCLE). **trousered** *a.* **trousering** *n.* cloth for making trousers. **trouserless** *a.* **trouser suit** *n.* a suit of a jacket and a pair of trousers, worn by a woman. [prob. Ir. *triubhas*, but cp. F *trousses*, breeches, bundles, see TRUSS]

trousseau (troo´sō) *n.* (*pl.* **trousseaux** (-sōz), **trousseaus**) the clothes and general outfit of a bride. [F, bundle, OF *troussel*, dim. of *trousse*, TRUSS]

trout (trowt) *n.* (*pl. in general* **trout,** *in particular* **trouts**) **1** any of various freshwater fishes of the genus *Salmo* or *Salvelinus*, esp. *Salmo trutta*. **2** any of various unrelated fishes. **3** (*sl.*) an unprepossessing woman, esp. an old one. ~*v.i.* to fish for trout. **trouting** *n.* trout-fishing. **troutlet, troutling** *n.* **trouty** *a.* [OE *truht*, L *tructa*, Gr. *trōkkēs*, from *trōgein*, to gnaw]

trouvaille (troo´vīy) *n.* a lucky find. [F, from *trouver*, to find]

trouvère (troovea´) *n.* a medieval poet of N France, composing chiefly narrative poems. [F, from *trouver*, see TROUBADOUR]

trove (trōv) *n.* TREASURE TROVE (under TREASURE). [A-F *trové*, from *trover*, to find]

trover (trō´və) *n.* (*Law*) **1** the acquisition or appropriation of any goods. **2** an action for the recovery of personal property wrongfully converted by another to their own use. [OF (F *trouver*), see CONTRIVE]

†**trow** (trō, trow) *v.t., v.i.* to think, to suppose, to believe. [OE *trūwian, trēowian*, cogn. with *trēowe*, TRUE]

trowel (trow´əl) *n.* **1** a flat-bladed, usu. pointed, tool used by masons etc., for spreading mortar etc. **2** a scoop-shaped tool used in digging up plants etc. ~*v.t.* (*pres.p.* **trowelling,** (*N Am.*) **troweling,** *past, p.p.* **trowelled,** (*N Am.*) **troweled**) to apply or dress with a trowel. **to lay it on with a trowel** to flatter grossly. [ME *truel*, F *truelle*, late L *truella*, dim. of *trua*, ladle]

troy (troi), **troy weight** *n.* a system of weights (based on the grain, in which one pound troy equals 12 oz. av. (340 g) or 5760 grains) used chiefly in weighing gold, silver and gems. [prob. from *Troyes*, town SE of Paris]

Trp *abbr.* tryptophan.

TRRL *abbr.* Transport and Road Research Laboratory.

truant (troo´ənt) *n.* **1** a child who stays away from school without leave. **2** a person who shirks or neglects duty. **3** an idler, a loiterer. ~*a.* shirking, idle, loitering. ~*v.i.* to play truant. **to play truant** to stay away from school without leave. **truancy** *n.* **truantly** *adv.* [A-F *truaunt*, Welsh *truan*, wretched, cp. Ir. *trogha*, miserable, Gael. *truaghan*, a wretched creature]

truce (troos) *n.* **1** a temporary cessation of hostilities. **2** an agreement to cease hostilities. **3** an armistice. **4** a temporary intermission, alleviation or respite. **truce-breaker** *n.* **truceless** *a.* [ME *triwes, treowes*, pl., from OE *trēow*, compact, faith, see TRUE]

truck[1] (trŭk) *n.* **1** a strong, usu. four-wheeled vehicle for conveying heavy goods; a lorry. **2** an open railway wagon for freight. **3** a low barrow with two small wheels used by porters etc., for moving luggage etc. at railway stations, in warehouses etc. **4** a framework and set of wheels for supporting the whole or part of a railway carriage etc. **5** (*Naut.*) a small wooden disc at the top of a mast with holes for the halyards etc. **6** an axle unit on a skateboard. ~*v.t.* to convey in or on a truck. ~*v.i.* (*esp. N Am.*) **1** to work as a lorry driver. **2** (*sl.*) to go or stroll. **truckage** (-ij) *n.* **trucker** *n.* **1** a lorry driver. **2** a person who transports goods by lorry. **3** a firm transporting goods by lorry. **truckie** *n.* (*coll.*) a lorry driver. **trucking** *n.* (*N Am.*) transportation of goods by lorry. **truckload** *n.* **1** the amount contained in or carried in a truck. **2** (*coll.*) a large quantity or number. **by the truckload** in large quantities or numbers. **truck stop** *n.* (*esp. N Am.*) a transport café. [L *trochus*, Gr. *trochos*, a wheel, from *trechein*, to run, or perh. short for TRUCKLE]

truck[2] (trŭk) *n.* **1** exchange of commodities. **2** barter. **3** commodities suitable for barter, small wares. **4** (*N Am.*) fresh vegetables etc. from a market garden. **5** (*coll.*) rubbish. **6** (*Hist.*) the truck system. **7** traffic. **8** intercourse, dealings. ~*v.t., v.i.* **1** to exchange. **2** to barter. **3** to peddle, to hawk. **to have no truck with** to have no dealings with. **truck farmer** *n.* (*N Am.*) a market gardener. **truck shop** *n.* (*Hist.*) a shop supplying goods as wages. **truck system** *n.* (*Hist.*) the practice of paying wages in goods instead of money. [ME *trukken*, A-F *troquier* (F *troquer*), from OF *troque*, barter, WFlem. *trok*, sale, *trokken*, to procure goods, cogn. with TREK]

truckage TRUCK[1].

truckle (trŭk´əl) *v.i.* **1** to give way obsequiously (to the will of another), to cringe, to be servile (to). **2** to sleep in a truckle-bed. ~*n.* **1** (*also* **truckle-bed**) a low bed on castors or wheels for rolling under another. **2** a small barrel-shaped cheese. **truckler** *n.* [from TROCHLEA; cp. TRUCK[1]]

truculent (trŭk´ūlənt) *a.* **1** defiant or sullen. **2** aggressive. **3** savage, ferocious, barbarous, violent. **truculence, truculency** *n.* **truculently** *adv.* [OF, from L *truculentum*, nom. *-tus*, from *trux trucis*, savage]

trudge (trŭj) *v.i.* to travel on foot, esp. with labour and fatigue. ~*v.t.* to cover (a distance) in this manner. ~*n.* a walk of this kind. **trudger** *n.* [F *trucher*, to beg, prob. from Gmc. (cp. Dut. *troggelen*, also Icel. *thrūga*, Swed. *truga*, Dan. *true*, to press)]

trudgen (trŭj´ən), **trudgeon** *n.* a swimming stroke with the arms brought over the head alternately, and a scissors leg action. [John *Trudgen*, fl. 1860–70, who introduced it]

true (troo) *a.* (*comp.* **truer,** *superl.* **truest**) **1** conformable to fact or reality, not false or erroneous. **2** in accordance with appearance, not deceptive, counterfeit, or spurious, genuine. **3** in accordance with right or law, legitimate, rightful. **4** corresponding to type or standard. **5** correctly positioned; level. **6** accurate; exact. **7** (of a voice etc.) in perfect tune. **8** faithful, loyal, constant. **9** (of a compass bearing) determined in relation to the earth's geographical, rather than its magnetic pole. **10** †not given to falsehood, veracious, truthful, honest. ~*v.t.* (*3rd pers. sing. pres.* **trues,** *pres.p.* **trueing, truing,** *past, p.p.* **trued**) to make true, exact or accurate. ~*adv.* **1** truly. **2** accurately. **3** without variation from the ancestral type. **in true** correctly aligned. **not true** (*coll.*) amazing, incredible. **out of true** not correctly aligned. **to come true** to happen. **true to form** true to type. **true to life** exactly how it is in life. **true to type** normal, what might be expected. **true azimuth** *n.* the arc of the horizon intercepted between the north (or, in the southern hemisphere, the south) point of the horizon and the point where the vertical circle passing through a heavenly body cuts the horizon. **true bill** *n.* (*Hist. or N Am.*) the endorsement of a bill of indictment by a grand jury, certifying it as a case for the court. **true-blue** *a.* **1** staunch, faithful, genuine. **2** loyal to the British Conservative Party. ~*n.* a true-blue person. **true-born** *a.* **1** of legitimate birth. **2** such by birth or blood. **true-bred** *a.* of genuine or right breed. **true coral** *n.* a marine coelenterate of the reef-forming order Madreporaria. **true-hearted** *a.* **true-heartedness** *n.* **true horizon** *n.* CELESTIAL HORIZON (under CELESTIAL). **true love** *n.* **1** a person truly loved or loving. **2** one's sweetheart. **true-love knot, true-lover's knot** *n.* a kind of double knot with two interlacing bows on each side and two ends. **trueness** *n.* **true north** *n.* north according to the earth's axis. **true rib** *n.* any of the upper seven pairs of ribs, joined directly to the breastbone. [OE *trēowe, trȳw*, cp. Dut. *trouw*, G *treu*, Icel. *tryggr, trūr*]

☒ **truely** common misspelling of TRULY.

truffle (trŭf´əl) *n.* **1** any fleshy fungus of the order Tuberales, used for seasoning etc. **2** a sweet flavoured with rum or chocolate, resembling a truffle in shape. **truffle-dog** *n.* a dog trained to find truffles. [OF *trufle*, prob. from L TUBER]

trug (trŭg) *n.* **1** a wooden basket used by gardeners, greengrocers etc. **2** †a shallow wooden milk pail. [etym. uncertain, perh. from TROUGH]

truism (troo´izm) *n.* **1** a self-evident or unquestionable truth. **2** an obvious statement, a platitude. **truistic** (-is´-) *a.* [TRUE]

†**trull** (trŭl) *n.* a prostitute. [G *Trulle, Trolle*, cogn. with TROLL[2] and DROLL]

truly (troo´li) *adv.* **1** sincerely. **2** genuinely. **3** in reality. **4** faithfully, honestly, loyally. **5** really, indeed. **6** in accordance with truth, accurately. **7** rightly, properly. **yours truly** YOUR.

trumeau (troomō´) *n.* (*pl.* **trumeaux** (-ōz´)) a piece of wall, a pier or pillar, between two openings or dividing a doorway. [F]

trump[1] (trŭmp) *n.* **1** any card of a suit ranking for the time being above the others. **2** (*pl.*) this suit. **3** an advantage, esp. involving surprise. 4 (*coll.*) a generous or reliable person. 5 (*Austral.*) someone in authority. ~*v.t.* 1 to take with a trump. 2 to outdo. ~*v.i.* to play a trump card. **to come up trumps** (*coll.*) to be useful or helpful at an opportune moment. **to trump up** to invent or fabricate (a charge etc.). **to turn up trumps** (*coll.*) to come up trumps. **trump card** *n.* 1 the card turned up to determine which suit is to be trumps. 2 any card of this suit. 3 (*coll.*) an infallible expedient. [F *triomphe*, a card game, TRIUMPH]

†**trump**[2] (trŭmp) *n.* 1 a trumpet blast. 2 a trumpet. **Last Trump** LAST[1]. [OF *trompe* (whence *tromper*, to play on the trumpet, to deceive), OHG *trumpa*, from OSlav., cp. Rus. *truba*, Pol. *trabas*]

trumpery (trŭm´pəri) *n.* (*pl.* **trumperies**) 1 worthless finery. 2 a worthless article. 3 rubbish. ~*a.* 1 showy but worthless. 2 delusive, rubbishy. [OF *tromperie*, deception]

trumpet (trŭm´pit) *n.* 1 a musical wind instrument, usu. consisting of a long, straight, curved or coiled tube with a wide termination, usu. of brass, with a cup-shaped mouthpiece. 2 a trumpet-player. 3 a thing resembling a trumpet in shape, such as a funnel. 4 an organ stop with a bright sound. 5 a sound of or as of a trumpet, e.g. that made by an elephant. 6 the horn of an old gramophone. 7 an ear-trumpet. ~*v.t.* (*pres.p.* **trumpeting,** *past, p.p.* **trumpeted**) to proclaim by or as by a trumpet. ~*v.i.* (esp. of the elephant) to make a loud sound like a trumpet. **to blow one's own trumpet** BLOW[1]. **trumpet call** *n.* 1 a call sounded by a trumpet. 2 an imperative call to action. **trumpet-conch, trumpet-shell** *n.* a gastropod with a turreted shell often used like a trumpet. **trumpeter** *n.* 1 a person who sounds a trumpet, esp. a soldier giving signals on the trumpet in a cavalry regiment. 2 a person who proclaims, publishes or denounces. 3 a variety of the domestic pigeon, with a prolonged coo. 4 a S American bird of the genus *Psophia*, allied to the cranes. 5 a trumpeter swan. **trumpeter swan** *n.* a large N American wild swan, *Cygnus buccinator*. **trumpet flower** *n.* any plant with large tubular flowers. **trumpet major** *n.* the head trumpeter in a cavalry regiment. [OF *trompette*, dim. of TRUMP[2]]

truncal TRUNK.

truncate[1] (trŭngkāt´, trŭng´-) *v.t.* 1 to cut the top or end from. 2 to replace (an angle) by a plane. **truncation** (-kā´shən) *n.* [L *truncātus*, p.p. of *truncāre*, from *truncus*, TRUNK]

truncate[2] (trŭng´kāt) *a.* 1 cut short, truncated. 2 terminating abruptly, as if a piece had been cut off. **truncately** *adv.*

truncheon (trŭn´shən, -chən) *n.* 1 a short staff, club or cudgel, esp. one carried by a police officer in Britain. 2 a baton, a staff of authority. ~*v.t.* to beat with a truncheon. [ONF *tronchon*, OF *tronçon*, dim. of *tronc*, TRUNK]

trundle (trŭn´dəl) *v.t., v.i.* to move heavily (as if) on wheels. ~*n.* 1 (*N Am.*) (*also* **trundle-bed**) a low bed on castors or wheels or for rolling under another, a truckle-bed. 2 a small broad wheel, a castor. 3 a lantern-wheel. [MF *trondeler*, LG *tröndeln*, cogn. with TREND]

trunk (trŭngk) *n.* 1 the main stem of a tree, as opposed to the branches or roots. 2 the body of an animal apart from the limbs, head and tail. 3 the main body of anything. 4 a trunk line. 5 the shaft of a column. 6 a box or chest with a hinged lid for packing clothes etc. in for travel. 7 (*N Am.*) the boot of a motor car. 8 a ventilating shaft, conduit, chute, flume etc. 9 a hollow cylinder in which a connecting-rod works, in marine and other steam engines. 10 the proboscis of an elephant or any analogous organ. 11 the main body of an artery etc. 12 (*pl.*) men's shorts for swimming. **truncal** *a.* **trunk call** *n.* a long-distance telephone call. **trunk exchange** *n.* a telephone exchange connected by trunk lines to other trunk exchanges. **trunkfish** *n.* (*pl. in general* **trunkfish,** *in particular* **trunkfishes**) any tropical fish of the family Ostraciidae. **trunkful** *n.* (*pl.* **trunkfuls**). **trunking** *n.* 1 a system of ventilation shafts, conduits etc. 2 the use or arrangement of trunk lines. 3 the plastic casing of wires. **trunkless** *a.* **trunk line** *n.* the main line of a railway, canal, telephone etc. **trunk road** *n.* any major road for long-distance travel. [F *tronc*, L *truncus, -um*, stem, piece cut off]

trunnion (trŭn´yən) *n.* 1 a cylindrical projection on the side of a cannon or mortar. 2 a hollow gudgeon on which the cylinder oscillates in some steam engines, and through which the steam enters. **trunnioned** *a.* [F *trognon*, dim. of *tron, tronc*, TRUNK]

truss (trŭs) *v.t.* 1 to support or brace with a truss. 2 to fasten (a fowl or the wings of a fowl etc.) with a skewer or twine before cooking. 3 to tie up securely, to bind. 4 (*coll.*) to tie, tighten or fasten up (one's clothes etc.). ~*n.* 1 a timber or iron supporting and strengthening structure in a roof, bridge etc. 2 a large corbel. 3 (*Naut.*) a heavy iron ring securing a lower yard to the mast. 4 a padded belt or other apparatus worn round the body for preventing or compressing a hernia. 5 a bundle (56 lb., 25.4 kg) of old hay, (60 lb., 27.2 kg) of new hay, or (36 lb., 16.3 kg) of straw. 6 a compact terminal cluster of flowers or fruit. **to truss up** 1 to make up into a bundle. 2 to bind or tie up. 3 to hang. **truss bridge** *n.* **trusser** *n.* [OF *trusser, trosser*, from L THYRSUS]

trust (trŭst) *n.* 1 confident reliance on or belief in the integrity, veracity, justice, friendship, power, protection etc. of a person or thing. 2 confidence, firm expectation (that). 3 the person or thing on which reliance is placed. 4 reliance on (assumed honesty etc.) without examination. 5 commercial credit. 6 (*Law*) confidence reposed in a person to whom property is conveyed for the benefit of another. 7 (*Law*) the right to or title in such property as distinct from its legal ownership. 8 (*Law*) the property or thing held in trust. 9 (*Law*) the legal relation between such property and the holder. 10 something committed to one's charge or care. 11 the obligation of a person who has received such a charge. 12 a combination of a number of businesses or companies under one general control for the purpose of defeating competition, creating a monopoly etc. 13 a body of trustees. ~*v.t.* 1 to place confidence in, to believe in, to rely upon. 2 to believe, to have a confident hope or expectation. 3 to commit to the care of a person, to entrust. 4 to entrust (a person with a thing). 5 to give credit to. ~*v.i.* 1 to have trust or confidence. 2 to sell goods on credit. **in trust** (*Law*) held for safekeeping or as a trustee. **on trust** 1 on credit. 2 without questioning. **to take on trust** to accept without questioning. **trustable** *a.* **trust account, trustee account** *n.* a savings account for a trustee, the balance going to a prenominated beneficiary after the trustee's death. **trustbuster** *n.* (*esp. N Am.*) a person who breaks up business trusts. **trust company** *n.* a company performing the functions of a trustee or dealing with trusts. **trust deed** *n.* an instrument of conveyance that creates a trust. **trustee** (-tē´) *n.* 1 (*Law*) a person to whom property is committed in trust for the benefit of another. 2 a member of a body of people, often elective, managing the affairs of an institution. 3 a state governing a trust territory. **trustee account** TRUST ACCOUNT (under TRUST). **trusteeship** *n.* 1 the office of a trustee. 2 a trust territory. **truster** *n.* **trustful** *a.* 1 full of trust. 2 trusting, confiding. **trustfully** *adv.* **trustfulness** *n.* **trust fund** *n.* money etc. held in trust. **trustie** TRUSTY (under TRUST). **trusting** *a.* **trustingly** *adv.* **trustingness** *n.* **trustless** *a.* 1 not worthy of trust. 2 faithless. **trustlessness** *n.* **trust territory** *n.* a territory governed by another country by the authority of the United Nations.

trustworthy *a.* deserving of trust or confidence. **trustworthiness** *n.* **trusty** (*comp.* **trustier,** *superl.* **trustiest**) *a.* **1** †trustworthy, reliable, not liable to fail in time of need. **2** †loyal. ~*n.* (*pl.* **trusties**) (*also* **trustie**) a prisoner trusted with a certain amount of liberty to do jobs etc. **trustily** *adv.* **trustiness** *n.* [ME, cp. OFris. *trāst*, G *Trost*, comfort, consolation]

truth (trooth) *n.* (*pl.* **truths** (troodhz, -ths)) **1** the state or quality of being true. **2** conformity to fact or reality. **3** that which is true, a fact, a verity. **4** honesty, veracity, sincerity. **5** fidelity, constancy. **6** true religion. **in truth** in reality, in fact, truly. **to tell the truth** to be frank. **truth to tell** to be frank. **truth drug** *n.* any drug used to make a person more liable to tell the truth when being interrogated. **truthful** *a.* **1** habitually speaking the truth. **2** veracious, reliable, conformable to truth. **truthfully** *adv.* **truthfulness** *n.* **truth serum** *n.* a truth drug. **truth table** *n.* (*Logic*) a table indicating the truth or falsity of propositions by the binary digits 0 and 1. **truth value** *n.* the truth or falsity of a statement. [OE *trēowthu*, from *trēowe*, TRUE]

try (trī) *v.t.* (*3rd pers. sing. pres.* **tries,** *pres.p.* **trying,** *past, p.p.* **tried**) **1** to test, to examine by experiment. **2** to determine the qualities etc. of by reference to a standard. **3** to find out by experiment or experience. **4** to attempt, to endeavour (to do etc.). **5** to subject to a severe or undue test, to strain. **6** to subject to hardship, suffering etc., as if for a test, to afflict. **7** to investigate (a charge, issue etc.) judicially, to subject (a person) to judicial trial. **8** to prove or settle by a test or experiment. **9** to smooth (a roughly planed board) with a trying-plane etc., to secure a perfectly level surface. **10** to purify, to refine (metals etc.) by melting etc. ~*v.i.* to endeavour, to make an attempt, to make an effort. ~*n.* (*pl.* **tries**) **1** an attempt. **2** in rugby, the right to carry the ball and try to kick a goal from in front, earned by touching the ball down behind the opponents' goal line. **3** in American football, an attempt to score an extra point after a touchdown. **to try a fall** FALL. **to try conclusions** CONCLUSION (under CONCLUDE). **to try for 1** to aim at. **2** to attempt to secure. **3** to apply for. **to try for size** to try out. **to try it on 1** (*coll.*) to see how far one can go before provoking someone. **2** (*coll.*) to try to deceive, outwit or seduce someone. **to try on** to put (clothes) on to see if they fit. **to try one's hand** to try to do something new requiring skill. **to try out** to test. **tried** *a.* shown to be effective, durable etc. by testing or use, proven. **trier** (trī´ə) *n.* **1** a person who tries, examines or tests in any way. **2** a person who keeps on endeavouring or persisting. **3** (*also* **trior**) a person appointed to determine whether a challenge to a juror or jurors is well founded. **trying** *a.* irritating, annoying. **tryingly** *adv.* **trying-plane** *n.* a plane used for planing the edges of long boards. **trying square** *n.* TRY-SQUARE (under TRY). **try-on** *n.* (*coll.*) an act of trying it on. **try-out** *n.* a trial, e.g. of a new method. **trysail** (trī´səl) *n.* a fore-and-aft sail set on a gaff abaft the foremast and mainmast. **try-scorer** *n.* a rugby player who has scored a try. **try-scoring** *n., a.* **try-square** *n.* a carpenter's square with a wooden stock and steel limb. [ME *trien*, F *trier*, late L *trītāre*, from *trītus*, TRITE]

Usage note In spoken and informal written English, *try and do* (something) can be used for *try to do* (something), though only where the verb takes the form *try* itself (not *tries, tried, trying*). It is not usual in negative contexts (*did not try to do* not *did not try and do*).

tryma (trī´mə) *n.* (*pl.* **trymata** (-mətə)) a drupelike fruit, the outer wall of the pericarp of which is dehiscent, as in the walnut. [Gr. *truma*, hole, from *truein*, to rub]

trypanosome (trip´ənəsōm, -pan´-) *n.* (*Med.*) any protozoan parasite of the genus *Trypanosoma*, causing sleeping sickness and other diseases. **trypanosomiasis** (-mī´əsis) *n.* any of several diseases caused by an infection with a trypanosome. [Gr. *trupanon*, a borer, *soma*, a body]

trypsin (trip´sin) *n.* a ferment contained in the pancreatic juice etc. **trypsinogen** (-sin´əjən) *n.* a substance from which trypsin is formed. **tryptic** (-tik) *a.* **tryptone** (-tōn) *n.* a peptone formed during digestion by the action of trypsin on proteins. **tryptophan** (-təfan) *n.* an amino acid widely distributed in proteins and essential for life. [Gr., from *tribein*, to rub]

†tryst (trist, trīst) *n.* **1** an appointed meeting, an appointment. **2** a rendezvous. ~*v.i.* to agree to meet. ~*v.t.* to appoint (a time or place) for meeting. **tryster** *n.* **trysting** *n.* [OF *triste, tristre*, a watching-station in hunting, cogn. with TRUST]

TS *abbr.* Treasury Solicitor.

tsar (zah), **czar, tzar** *n.* **1** (*Hist.*) the emperor of Russia. **2** a very powerful person. **tsardom** *n.* **tsarevich, tsarevitch** *n.* (*Hist.*) the son of a tsar, esp. the eldest son. **tsarevna** (-ev´nə) *n.* (*Hist.*) **1** the daughter of a tsar. **2** the wife of a tsarevich. **tsarina** (-rē´nə), **tsaritza** (-rit´sə), **tsaritsa** *n.* (*Hist.*) an empress of Russia, the wife of a tsar. **tsarism** *n.* **tsarist** *n., a.* [Rus. *tsar'*, L *caesar*; *cz-* is not a Slavonic form]

TSB *abbr.* Trustee Savings Bank.

tschernosem CHERNOZEM.

TSE *abbr.* **1** Tokyo Stock Exchange. **2** transmissible spongiform encephalopathy.

tsessebi (tsəsā´bi), **sassaby** (s-) *n.* (*pl.* **tsessebis, sassabies**) a large S African antelope, *Damaliscus lunatus*. [Bantu]

tsetse (tset´si) *n.* any fly of the genus *Glossina*, the bite of which is often fatal to cattle, horses, dogs etc., and transmits to humans the trypanosomes of sleeping sickness. [Setswana]

T. Sgt. *abbr.* Technical Sergeant.

TSH *abbr.* **1** Their Serene Highnesses. **2** thyroid-stimulating hormone.

tsi *abbr.* tons per square inch.

tsimmes TZIMMES.

tsk (tsk), **tsk tsk** *int., n., v.i.* TUT-TUT.

TSO *abbr.* Trading Standards Officer.

tsotsi (tsot´si) *n.* (*pl.* **tsotsis**) (*S Afr., coll.*) a violent criminal operating esp. in black townships. [etym. uncertain, perh. corr. of ZOOT SUIT]

tsp *abbr.* teaspoon(ful).

tsps *abbr.* teaspoon(ful)s.

TSR *abbr.* (*Comput.*) terminate and stay resident.

TSS *abbr.* toxic shock syndrome.

TSSA *abbr.* Transport Salaried Staffs' Association.

tsunami (tsoonah´mi) *n.* (*pl.* **tsunamis**) a very large wave at sea caused by a submarine earthquake, volcanic eruption etc. [Jap.]

tsutsugamushi disease (tsootsoogəmoo´shi) *n.* an acute infectious rickettsial disease common in Asia, esp. scrub typhus. [Jap. *tsutsuga*, illness, *mushi*, insect]

TSW *abbr.* Television South West.

Tswana (tswah´nə) *n.* (*pl.* **Tswana, Tswanas, Batswana** (bətswah´nə)) **1** a member of southern African people living chiefly in Botswana. **2** the Bantu language of this people, Setswana. ~*a.* of or relating to the Tswana or Setswana.

TT *abbr.* **1** teetotal(ler). **2** telegraphic transfer. **3** Tourist Trophy. **4** Trinidad and Tobago (IVR). **5** Trust Territories. **6** tuberculin-tested.

TTB *abbr.* tetragonal tungsten bronze.

TTC *abbr.* technical training centre.

TTF *abbr.* Timber Trade Federation.

TTL *abbr.* transistor-transistor logic.

TU *abbr.* **1** toxic unit. **2** trade union.

Tu. *abbr.* Tuesday.

tuan[1] (too´ən) *n.* a flying phalanger, *Phascogale tapoatafa*, of Australia. [Austral. Abor.]

tuan[2] (tooahn´) *n.* (in Malay-speaking countries) sir, lord (used as a title of respect). [Malay]

Tuareg (twah´reg) *n.* (*pl.* **Tuareg, Tuaregs**) **1** a member of a nomadic Berber people of the Sahara. **2** their language.

tuart (too´ət), **tooart** *n.* a W Australian tree, *Eucalyptus gomphocephala*, yielding an intensely hard and durable wood valuable for boat-building. [Austral. Abor.]

tuatara (tooətah´rə) *n.* the largest New Zealand reptile, the lizard-like *Sphenodon punctatum*, now the last survivor of the class Rhyncocephalia. [Maori]

tub (tŭb) *n.* **1** an open wooden (usu. round) vessel constructed of staves held together by hoops, used for washing, holding butter etc. **2** the amount (of butter etc.) that a packing tub holds. **3** a small cask. **4** a small, usu. plastic, container for ice cream, margarine etc. **5** (*coll.*) a bathtub, a sponge bath, a bath in a tub. **6** a bucket, box or truck for bringing up ore etc. from a mine. **7** (*coll.*) a short clumsy boat. **8** (*coll.*) a boat for practising rowing in. *~v.t.* (*pres.p.* **tubbing,** *past, p.p.* **tubbed**) **1** to place or set in a tub. **2** to bathe in a tub. **3** to line (a mine shaft) with a casing. *~v.i.* **1** to take a bath in a tub. **2** to row in a tub. **tubbable** *a.* **tubbing** *n.* **tubbish** *a.* round and fat. **tubby** *a.* (*comp.* **tubbier,** *superl.* **tubbiest**) **1** tub-shaped, corpulent. **2** (*Mus.*) sounding like an empty tub when struck, lacking resonance. **tubbiness** *n.* **tub chair** *n.* a chair which has solid arms and usu. a semicircular back. **tubful** *n.* (*pl.* **tubfuls**). **tub-thumper** *n.* (*coll.*) a ranting preacher. **tub-thumping** *a.* [MDut. *tobbe, dobbe,* etym. uncertain]

tuba (tū´bə) *n.* (*pl.* **tubas, tubae** (-bē)) **1** a brass wind instrument of the saxhorn kind, with a low pitch. **2** a tuba player. **3** a powerful reed-stop in an organ. [L, trumpet]

tubal, tubar TUBE.

tubbable, tubby etc. TUB.

tube (tūb) *n.* **1** a long hollow cylinder for the conveyance of fluids and various other purposes, a pipe. **2** a cylindrical vessel of thin flexible metal for holding pigment, toothpaste etc. **3** the main body of a wind instrument. **4** a tubular vessel in an animal or plant for conveying air, fluids etc. **5** (*coll.*) an underground railway. **6** (*also* **tube train**) an underground train. **7** a cathode ray tube. **8** (*N Am., coll.*) a television set. **9** (*N Am.*) a thermionic valve. **10** (*N Am.*) a radio valve. **11** an inner tube. **12** (*esp. Austral., sl.*) a can of beer. **13** the central portion of a heavy gun round which the jackets are fixed by shrinking. *~v.t.* to furnish with or enclose in a tube or tubes. **tubal, tubar** *a.* **tubectomy** (-bek´təmi) *n.* (*pl.* **tubectomies**) the cutting or removal of a Fallopian tube. **tube foot** *n.* (*pl.* **tube feet**) a tubular growth on an echinoderm, used for locomotion and ingestion of food. **tubeless** *a.* **tubeless tyre** *n.* a type of tyre designed to be airtight without an inner tube. **tubelike** *a.* **tube railway** *n.* an underground railway running in a tubular tunnel. **tube worm** *n.* a worm that makes and lives in a tube of sand, lime etc. **tubing** *n.* a length or quantity of tubes. [F, from L *tubus,* cogn. with TUBA]

tuber (tū´bə) *n.* **1** a short, thick portion of an underground stem, set with eyes or modified buds, as in the potato. **2** a similar root, as of a dahlia. **3** (*Anat.*) a swelling or prominence. **tuberous** *a.* **1** having prominent knobs or excrescences. **2** like or bearing tubers. **tuberousness** *n.* **tuberous root** *n.* a thick root like a tuber but not having buds or eyes. [L, hump, lump, swelling, tumour, truffle, cogn. with TUMID]

tubercle (tū´bəkəl) *n.* **1** a small prominence, esp. in bone. **2** a small granular non-vascular tumour or nodule formed within the substance of an organ, esp. such a lesion characteristic of tuberculosis of the lungs. **3** a small tuber, a warty excrescence. **tubercle bacillus** *n.* a bacterium that causes tuberculosis. **tubercled** *a.* **tubercular** (-bœ´kū-) *a.* of or relating to tubercles or tuberculosis. *~n.* a person suffering from tuberculosis. **tubercularize, tubercularise** *v.t.* to infect with tuberculosis. **tubercularization** (-zā´shən) *n.* **tuberculate** (-lət), **tuberculated** (-lātid) *a.* **tuberculation** (-lā´shən) *n.* **1** formation of tubercles. **2** a system of tubercles. **3** the state of being tuberculous. **tuberculin** (-lin) *n.* **1** a ptomaine produced by the action of the tubercle bacillus. **2** a fluid used hypodermically in the diagnosis of tuberculosis. **tuberculin test** *n.* an injection of tuberculin to test for tuberculosis or immunity to it. **tuberculin-tested** *a.* (of milk) produced by cows tested and found free of infection and tuberculosis. **tuberculize, tuberculise** *v.t.* to infect with tuberculosis. **tuberculization** (-zā´shən) *n.* **tuberculoid** (-loid) *a.* resembling tuberculosis. **tuberculosis** (-lō´sis) *n.* a diseased condition caused by the bacillus *Mycobacterium tuberculosis,* characterized by the presence of tubercles in the tissues, esp. pulmonary tuberculosis or consumption. **tuberculosed** (-bœ´-) *a.* suffering from tuberculosis. **tuberculous** (-ləs), **tuberculose** (-lōs) *a.* [F, from L *tūberculum,* dim. of TUBER]

tuberose[1] (tū´bərōs) *a.* tuberous. **tuberosity** (-ros´-) *n.*

tuberose[2] (tū´bərōz) *n.* a bulbous plant, *Polianthes tuberosa,* with fragrant white flowers. [L *tuberosa,* fem. of *tuberosus,* from TUBER]

Usage note Sometimes pronounced (tūb´rōz), as if from *tube, rose.*

tuberous TUBER.

tubi- (tū´bi) *comb. form* tube. [L *tubus,* TUBE]

tubicolous (tūbik´ələs) *a.* inhabiting a tubular case. [L *colere,* to cultivate]

tubifex (tū´bifeks) *n.* (*pl.* **tubifex, tubifexes**) any reddish annelid worm of the genus *Tubifex,* used as food for aquarium fish. [mod. L, from L *tubus,* tube, *fex,* from *facere,* to make]

tubiform (tū´bifawm) *a.* having the shape of a tube.

tubing TUBE.

tubular (tū´būlə) *a.* **1** tube-shaped. **2** having or consisting of a tube or tubes. **3** (of breathing) sounding like air passing through a tube. **4** made of tube-shaped pieces. **tubular bells** *n.pl.* an orchestral percussion instrument consisting of metal tubes suspended vertically and struck to produce a bell-like sound. **tubular tyre,** (*N Am.*) **tubular tire** *n.* a tyre that is cemented on to the wheel rim, used esp. on racing bicycles. **tubulate** (-lət), **tubulated** (-lātid) *a.* **tubule** (-ūl) *n.* a small pipe or fistular body. **tubuliform** *a.* **tubulose** (-lōs), **tubulous** *a.* [L *tubulus,* dim. of *tubus,* TUBE]

TUC *abbr.* Trades Union Congress.

tuchun (toochoon´) *n.* (*Hist.*) a Chinese military governor or warlord. [Chin.]

tuck[1] (tŭk) *v.t.* **1** to press close together or press, fold, or roll the loose ends or parts of compactly (up, in etc.). **2** to wrap or cover (up or in) closely or snugly. **3** to gather up, to fold or draw together or into a small area. **4** to push or press, to cram, to stuff, to stow (away, into, etc.). **5** to gather or stitch (a dress etc.) in folds. **6** to hit (a ball) to the place where one wants it to go. **7** (*sl.*) †to hang (a criminal). *~v.i.* **1** to make tucks. **2** (of loose cloth etc.) to be got rid of by tucking away. *~n.* **1** a horizontal fold in a dress etc., esp. one of a series made for ornament or to dispose of loose material. **2** (*coll.*) food, esp. sweets, pastry etc. **3** (*Naut.*) the after part of a ship where the ends of the bottom planks meet. **4** a dive or gymnastic move in which the knees are bent and held close to the chest. **5** a tuck-net. **to tuck away 1** to eat heartily. **2** to place somewhere hidden or isolated. **to tuck in** (*coll.*) to eat heartily. **to tuck into** (*coll.*) to eat heartily. **tucker**[1] *n.* **1** a person who or thing which tucks. **2** (*esp. Austral., coll.*) food. **tucker-bag, tucker-box** *n.* (*Austral., coll.*) a food container. **tuck-in, tuck-out** *n.* (*coll.*) a hearty meal, a spread. **tucking** *n.* a series of tucks. **tuck-net, tuck-seine** *n.* a net or seine used for removing fish from a larger net. **tuck position** *n.* the position for a tuck in diving or gymnastics. **tuck shop** *n.* a shop, esp. in a school, where food is sold. [ME *tukken*, LG *tukken, tokken*, cogn. with TOUCH]

tuck[2] (tŭk) *n.* **1** the beat or roll of a drum. **2** a blast or flourish on a trumpet. [TUCKET]

†**tuck**[3] (tŭk) *n.* a long, narrow sword, a rapier. [MF *étoc, estoc*, It. *stocco*, G *Stock*, stick]

tucker[1] TUCK[1].

tucker[2] (tŭk´ə) *n.* (*Hist.*) an ornamental frilling of lace or muslin round the top of a woman's dress, covering the neck and shoulders, worn in 17th–18th cents. **best bib and tucker** BEST.

tucker[3] (tŭk´ə) *v.t.* (*esp. N Am., coll.*) to exhaust (often with *out*). [obs. *tuck*, to reproach, chide]

†**tucket** (tŭk´it) *n.* a flourish on a trumpet, a fanfare. [ONF *touquet*, It. *toccata*, fem. p.p. of *toccare*, to TOUCH]

tucotuco (tookōtoo´kō), **tucutucu** (tookootoo´koo) *n.* (*pl.* **tucotucos, tucutucus**) any of various burrowing S American rodents of the genus *Ctenomys*. [from its cry]

-tude (tūd) *suf.* forming abstract nouns, as *altitude, beatitude, fortitude*. [L *-tūdinem*, nom. *-tūdo*]

Tudor (tū´də) *a.* **1** of or relating to the English royal line (from Henry VII to Elizabeth I) founded by Owen Tudor of Wales, who married the widow of Henry V. **2** of or relating to their period. **3** of or relating to the Tudor style of architecture. ~*n.* a member of the Tudor royal family. **Tudorbethan** (-bē´thən) *a.* combining the Tudor and Elizabethan styles. **Tudor flower** *n.* a trefoil ornament used in the Tudor style. **Tudor rose** *n.* a five-lobed flower adopted as a badge by Henry VII. **Tudor style** *n.* the late Perpendicular style in Gothic architecture.

Tue., Tues. *abbr.* Tuesday.

Tuesday (tūz´dā, -di) *n.* the third day of the week, following Monday. ~*adv.* (*coll.*) on Tuesday. **Tuesdays** *adv.* (*coll.*) every Tuesday. [OE *Tīwes dæg*, day of the god of war (*Tīw*, cogn. with L *deus*, Gr. *Zeus*)]

tufa (tū´fə, too´-) *n.* **1** a soft calcareous rock deposited by springs and streams. **2** TUFF. **tufaceous** (-fā´shəs) *a.* [It. for *tufo*, L *tōphus*, a soft, sandy stone, cp. Gr. *tophos*]

tuff (tŭf) *n.* an earthy, sometimes fragmentary, deposit of volcanic materials of the most heterogeneous kind. **tuffaceous** (-ā´shəs) *a.* [F *tuf*, It. *tufo*, see TUFA]

tuffet (tŭf´it) *n.* **1** a tuft of grass etc. **2** a low mound or seat. [var. of TUFT]

tuft (tŭft) *n.* **1** a cluster, a bunch, a collection of hairs, threads, feathers, grass etc. held or fastened together at one end. **2** a bunch of small blood vessels etc. **3** (*coll.*) a goatee, an imperial. **4** (*Hist.*) a young nobleman at a university, from the tuft or gold tassel formerly worn on his cap. ~*v.t.* **1** to separate into tufts. **2** to adorn with or as with tufts. **3** to pass thread through (a mattress etc.) at regular intervals and fasten a button or tuft in the depression thus made. ~*v.i.* to grow in tufts. **tufted** *a.* **tufted duck** *n.* a small duck, *Aythya fuligula*, the male of which has a long black drooping crest. **tufty** *a.* [F *touffe*, from Gmc. (cp. Swed. dial. *tuppa*, Icel. *toppr*, G *Zopf*)]

TUG *abbr.* Telephone Users' Group.

tug (tŭg) *v.t.* (*pres.p.* **tugging**, *past, p.p.* **tugged**) **1** to pull or draw with great effort or with violence. **2** to haul, to tow. ~*v.i.* to pull violently (at). ~*n.* **1** the act or a spell of tugging. **2** a vigorous or violent pull. **3** a violent effort, a severe struggle. **4** (*also* **tugboat**) a small powerful boat for towing others. **5** an aircraft towing a glider. **6** a loop hanging from the saddle in harness supporting a shaft or trace. **to tug one's forelock** FORELOCK[1]. **tugger** *n.* **tuggingly** *adv.* **tug of love** *n.* (*coll.*) a dispute between parents or guardians over custody of a child. **tug-of-war** *n.* **1** a contest between two sets of persons pulling a rope from opposite ends across a line marked on the ground. **2** a struggle between two sides. [ME *toggen*, perh. from Icel. *tog*, rope, cogn. with TOW[1]]

tugrik (too´grēk), **tughrik** *n.* the standard unit of currency in Mongolia. [Mongolian]

tui (too´ē) *n.* (*pl.* **tuis**) a New Zealand honeyeater, *Prosthemadura novaeseelandiae*. [Maori]

tuition (tūish´ən) *n.* **1** teaching, instruction, esp. in a particular subject or group of subjects and separately paid for. **2** a fee for this. **tuitional, tuitionary** *a.* [F, from L *tuitiōnem*, nom. *-tio*, from *tuēri*, to watch, to guard, p.p. *tuitus*]

tularaemia (toolərē´miə), (*N Am.*) **tularemia** *n.* an acute infectious bacterial disease of rodents, sometimes communicated to humans by flea or tick bites, causing fever etc. **tularaemic** *a.* [*Tulare* County in California, where it was first discovered, -AEMIA]

tulip (tū´lip) *n.* any plant of the genus *Tulipa*, bulbous plants of the lily family, with bell-shaped flowers of various colours. **tulipomania** (-ōmā´niə) *n.* a craze for the cultivation or acquisition of tulips which arose in Holland about 1634. **tulip-root** *n.* a disease which affects oats, causing swelling of the base of the stems. **tulip tree** *n.* any N American tree of the genus *Liriodendron*, bearing greenish-yellow, tulip-like flowers. **tulipwood** *n.* the wood of *Liriodendron tulipifera*. [F *tulippe*, It. *tulipa, tulipano*, Turk. *tulbend, dulbend*, TURBAN]

tulle (tūl) *n.* a fine silk net, used for veils etc. [*Tulle*, France, where orig. manufactured]

tum[1] (tŭm) *n.* (*coll.*) the stomach. **tum-tum**[1] *n.* (used by or to children). [corr. of STOMACH]

tum[2] (tŭm), **tum-tum** (-tŭm) *n.* the sound of a stringed musical instrument like the banjo. [imit.]

tumble (tŭm´bəl) *v.i.* **1** to fall (down etc.) suddenly or violently. **2** to roll or toss about. **3** to walk, run, or move about in a careless or headlong manner. **4** to perform acrobatic feats, esp. without special apparatus. **5** to decrease quickly. **6** (*coll.*) to (begin to) comprehend (often with *to*). **7** to turn over in flight. ~*v.t.* **1** to toss or fling forcibly. **2** to throw or push (down etc.). **3** to cause to tumble or fall. **4** to throw into disorder, to rumple. **5** to dry (clothes) in a tumble-dryer. **6** to clean (gemstones etc.) in a tumbling-barrel. ~*n.* **1** a fall. **2** a state of disorder. **3** an acrobatic feat, esp. a somersault. **to tumble in 1** to fit (a piece of timber) into another. **2** (*coll.*) to go to bed, to turn in. **tumbledown** *a.* dilapidated. **tumble-dry** *v.t.* (*3rd pers. sing. pres.* **tumble-dries**, *pres.p.* **tumble-drying**, *past, p.p.* **tumble-dried**) to dry (clothes) in a tumble-dryer. **tumble-dryer, tumble-drier** *n.* an appliance with a revolving cylinder into which damp clothes are placed and dried by having warm air blown through them as they turn. **tumbleweed** *n.* a plant such as *Amaranthus albus*, that breaks away from its roots in autumn and is blown around by the wind. **tumbling** *n.* **tumbling-barrel, tumbling-box** *n.* a revolving box etc. in which castings are cleaned by friction. **tumbling-bay** *n.* the outfall of a river or reservoir, or the pool into which this flows. **tumbly** *a.* [ME *tumblen*, freq. from OE *tumbian*, cp. Dut. *tuimelen*, G *taumeln, tummeln*, Swed. *tumla*, Dan. *tumle*]

tumbler (tŭm´blə) *n.* **1** a person who or thing which tumbles. **2** a person who performs somersaults, an acrobat. **3** a variety of pigeon (from its habit of turning over in flight). **4** a toy that turns somersaults. **5** a stemless drinking glass, orig. with a rounded base, so that it fell on the side when set down. **6** a springlatch (usu. one of several) in a lock, that engages a bolt unless lifted by the key. **7** a part of the lock in a firearm attached to the hammer and engaging with the trigger. **8** (*also* **tumbler-dryer**) a tumble-dryer. **9** a tumbling-

barrel. **tumblerful** *n.* (*pl.* **tumblerfuls**). **tumbler switch** *n.* a simple form of switch used for electric light connections.
tumbling, tumbly TUMBLE.
tumbril (tŭm´brəl, -bril), **tumbrel** *n.* (*Hist.*) **1** a two-wheeled cart for carrying ammunition and tools for mining and sapping. **2** an open cart which conveyed victims to the guillotine during the French Revolution. **3** a dung cart. [OF *tumbrel, tumberel*, from *tomber*, to fall, cogn. with TUMBLE]
tumid (tū´mid) *a.* **1** swollen, enlarged, distended. **2** pompous, bombastic, turgid. **tumefacient** (-fā´shənt) *a.* **tumefaction** (-fak´shən) *n.* **tumefy** (-mifī) *v.t.* (*3rd pers. sing. pres.* **tumefies,** *pres.p.* **tumefying,** *past, p.p.* **tumefied**) **1** to cause to swell. **2** to inflate. ~*v.i.* **1** to swell. **2** to rise in or as in a tumour. **tumescent** (-mes´ənt) *a.* **1** swollen, enlarged. **2** becoming swollen or enlarged. **tumescence** *n.* **tumescently** *adv.* **tumidity** (-mid´-) *n.* **tumidly** *adv.* **tumidness** *n.* [L *tumidus*, from *tumēre*, to swell]
tummy (tŭm´i) *n.* (*pl.* **tummies**) (*coll.*) the stomach. **tummy button** *n.* the navel. [as TUM[1]]
tumour (tū´mə), (*N Am.*) **tumor** *n.* a swelling on some part of the body, esp. if due to an abnormal growth of tissue. **tumorous** *a.* [F *tumeur*, L *tumor -orem*, as TUMID]
tump (tŭmp) *n.* (*dial.*) a hillock, a mound. [cp. Welsh, Gael. and Ir. *tom*]
tum-tum[1] TUM[1].
tum-tum[2] TUM[2].
tum-tum[3] (tŭm´tŭm) *n.* **1** a W Indian dish of boiled plantain beaten soft. **2** a tom-tom. [prob. imit.]
tumuli TUMULUS.
tumult (tū´mŭlt) *n.* **1** the commotion, disturbance or agitation of a multitude, esp. with a confusion of sounds. **2** a confused outbreak or insurrection. **3** uproar, stir, riot. **4** excitement, agitation or confusion of mind. **tumultuous** (-mŭl´-) *a.* **tumultuously** *adv.* **tumultuousness** *n.* [F *tumulte*, L *tumultus*, as TUMULUS]
tumulus (tū´mūləs) *n.* (*pl.* **tumuli** (-lī)) a mound of earth, sometimes combined with masonry, usu. sepulchral, a barrow. **tumular** *a.* [L, from *tumēre*, to swell]
tun (tŭn) *n.* **1** a large cask, esp. for alcoholic liquors. **2** a wine measure, 216 imperial gal. or 252 US gal. (11.46 hl). **3** a brewer's fermenting vat. ~*v.t.* (*pres.p.* **tunning,** *past, p.p.* **tunned**) to put (liquor) into a tun. **tundish** *n.* **1** a funnel, orig. of wood, used esp. in brewing. **2** an intermediate reservoir in metal-founding. **tunnage** (-ij) *n.* a tax on imported wine levied on each cask or tun, usu. coupled with poundage. [OE *tunne*, cp. Dut. *ton*, G *Tonne*, Icel. and Swed. *tunna*]
tuna[1] (tū´nə) *n.* (*pl.* **tuna, tunas**) **1** (*Zool.*) any marine fish of the family Scombridae found in warmer waters; also called *tunny*. **2** (*also* **tuna fish**) its flesh as food. [Am. Sp., from Sp. *atún*, from Arab. *tūn*, L *thunnus*, Gr. *thunnos*]
tuna[2] (tū´nə) *n.* a prickly pear, esp. *Opuntia tuna*, or its fruit. [Sp., from Taino]
tunable TUNE.
tundra (tŭn´drə) *n.* a marshy treeless plain in the Arctic and subarctic regions, with permanently frozen subsoil and covered largely with mosses and lichens. [Lappish]
tune (tūn) *n.* **1** a melodious succession of musical tones forming a coherent whole, an air, a melody, esp. as a setting for a song, hymn etc. **2** correct intonation in singing or playing. **3** proper adjustment of an instrument for this. **4** a distinctive intonation pattern in speech. ~*v.t.* **1** to put in tune. **2** to adjust, to adapt, to attune. **3** to adjust (an engine) for optimum performance. **4** to adjust (a radio, TV set) for optimum reception of an incoming signal. **5** (*poet.*) to sing, to produce (a song, music etc.). ~*v.i.* **1** to come or be in harmony. **2** to utter or express musically. **in tune 1** at the correct pitch. **2** correctly adjusted for pitch. **3** in harmony, sympathy, agreement (with). **out of tune 1** not at the correct pitch. **2** incorrectly adjusted for pitch. **3** not in harmony, sympathy or agreement (with). **to call the tune** to give orders, to say what is to be done. **to change one's tune** to alter one's attitude or tone. **to dance to a person's tune** DANCE. **to the tune of** (*coll.*) to the sum or amount of. **to tune in 1** to adjust a radio circuit to obtain resonance at a required frequency. **2** to switch on a radio or TV set and start listening or watching. **to tune up 1** (of a group of musicians) to adjust (instruments) to a common pitch before playing. **2** to start to play or sing. **3** to improve the performance of (an engine) by tuning. **tuned in (to)** (*coll.*) up to date (with); acquainted (with); knowledgeable (about). **tunable, tuneable** *a.* **tunableness** *n.* **tunably** *adv.* **tuned circuit** *n.* an oscillatory circuit adjusted to yield resonance at a required wavelength. **tuneful** *a.* melodious, musical. **tunefully** *adv.* **tunefulness** *n.* **tuneless** *a.* **1** not in tune. **2** unmusical, inharmonious. **3** silent, without voice. **tunelessly** *adv.* **tunelessness** *n.* **tuner** *n.* **1** a person who tunes, esp. one whose occupation is to tune musical instruments. **2** a knob, dial etc. by which a radio or TV set is tuned to different wavelengths. **3** an electronic device used to tune a guitar etc. **tunesmith** *n.* (*facet.*) a songwriter. **tuning** *n.* **1** the act of putting something in tune. **2** (*Mus.*) a set of pitches to which (the strings of) stringed instruments are tuned. **3** the state of adjustment of an engine, radio receiver etc. **tuning fork** *n.* a two-pronged steel instrument giving a fixed note when struck, used to measure the pitch of musical tones etc. **tuning hammer** *n.* a hammer-shaped wrench for tuning pianos, harps etc. **tuning note** *n.* a prolonged note issued by a transmitting radio station to enable listeners to tune in. **tuning peg** *n.* a peg attached to the strings of an instrument, by which it can be tuned. [A-F *tun* (F *ton*), L *tonus -um*, TONE]
tung (tŭng), **tung tree** *n.* a tree of the genus *Aleurites*. **tung oil** *n.* the oil of the seeds of this tree, used in paints, varnishes etc. [Chin.]
tungsten (tŭng´stən) *n.* a heavy, greyish-white metallic element, at. no. 74, chem. symbol W, of unusually high melting point; also called *wolfram*. **tungstate** (-stāt) *n.* a salt of tungstic acid. **tungsten carbide** *n.* a very hard black powder used in the manufacture of dies, drill bits etc. **tungstic** *a.* **tungstous** *a.* [Swed. (*tung*, heavy, *sten*, STONE)]
Tungus (tung´gus) *n.* (*pl.* **Tungus, Tunguses**) **1** a member of a people occupying parts of Siberia and China. **2** their language, a member of the Turanian group. **Tungusian** (-gus´-) *a.* **Tungusic** (-gus´-) *a., n.* [Turkic]
tunic (tū´nik) *n.* **1** a military or police officer's jacket. **2** (*Hist.*) a short-sleeved body-garment reaching nearly to the knees, worn by the ancient Greeks and Romans. **3** a modern loose coat or short overskirt gathered in or belted at the waist, now worn only by women and children. **4** a medieval surcoat worn over armour. **5** (*Anat.*) a membrane or envelope covering some part or organ. **6** (*Bot.*) a membranous skin. **7** (*Zool.*) the outer coat of an ascidian etc. **tunica** *n.* (*pl.* **tunicae** (-kē)) (*Bot., Anat.*) a tunic. **tunicary** *n.* (*pl.* **tunicaries**) a tunicate. **tunicate** (-kət) *a.* having or covered with a tunic. ~*n.* any marine animal of the subphylum Urochordata, including the sea squirts. **tunicated** (-kātid) *a.* **tunicle** (-kəl) *n.* **1** a small, fine or delicate tunic, a fine integument. **2** a close-fitting vestment worn with a dalmatic by deacons, and by Roman Catholic cardinals, bishops and abbots. [OE *tunece*, L *tunica*]
tuning TUNE.
tunnage TUN.
tunnel (tŭn´əl) *n.* **1** an artificial underground passage or

gallery, esp. one under a hill, river etc., for a railway, road or canal. **2** a passage dug by a burrowing animal. **3** a mining level, an adit. **4** a main flue of a chimney. ~*v.t.* (*pres.p.* **tunnelling,** (*N Am.*) **tunneling,** *past, p.p.* **tunnelled,** (*N Am.*) **tunneled**) **1** to make a tunnel through (a hill etc.). **2** to shape like a tunnel. **3** to catch in a tunnel-net. ~*v.i.* **1** to cut or make a tunnel. **2** (*Physics*) to pass through a barrier. **tunnel diode** *n.* a type of semiconductor diode capable of giving amplification. **tunnel-kiln** *n.* a kiln in which articles for firing are carried along a heated passage on trucks. **tunneller,** (*N Am.*) **tunneler** *n.* **tunnel-net** *n.* a fishing net with a wide mouth narrowing towards the other end. **tunnel vault** *n.* a barrel vault. **tunnel vision** *n.* **1** a medical condition in which peripheral vision is largely lost and a person can only see objects directly in front of them. **2** (*coll.*) extreme narrowness of viewpoint due to concentration on a single issue. [OF *tonnel* (F *tonneau*, dim. of *tonne*, TUN)]

tunny (tŭn´i) *n.* (*pl.* **tunny, tunnies**) TUNA[1]. [L *tunnus*, Gr. *thynnos*]

tup (tŭp) *n.* **1** a ram or male sheep. **2** the striking-part of a steam hammer. ~*v.t., v.i.* (*pres.p.* **tupping,** *past, p.p.* **tupped**) **1** to butt, as a ram. **2** to copulate with (a ewe), to cover, as a ram. [ME *tuppe*, cp. Swed. and Norw. *tupp*, cock, Dan. *top*, cock's crest, Icel. *toppr*, crest, TOP[1]]

Tupamaro (toopəmah´rō) *n.* (*pl.* **Tupamaros**) a member of a Marxist urban guerrilla group in Uruguay. [*Tupac Amaru*, 18th-cent. revolutionary]

tupek TUPIK.

tupelo (tū´pilō) *n.* (*pl.* **tupelos**) **1** a N American or Asian tree of the genus *Nyssa*, living in swampy conditions. **2** the wood of this. [Creek]

Tupi (too´pi) *n.* (*pl.* **Tupis, Tupi**) **1** a member of a S American people of the Amazon region. **2** their language. ~*a.* of or relating to the Tupis or their language. **Tupi-Guarani** *n.* (*pl.* **Tupi-Guarani, Tupi-Guaranis**) **1** a member of a S American people of Tupi, Guarani or related stock. **2** a language family which includes Tupi and Guarani. ~*a.* of or relating to this people or language family. [S Am. Ind. name]

tupik (tū´pik), **tupek** (-pek) *n.* an Eskimo (Inuit) animal-skin tent. [Eskimo (Inuit) *tupiq*]

tuppence (tŭp´əns) *n.* (*coll.*) TWOPENCE (under TWO). **tuppenny** (tŭp´ni) *a.* TWOPENNY (under TWO).

Tupperware® (tŭp´əweə) *n.* a range of plastic kitchen equipment, esp. food containers. [*Tupper*, the US manufacturer]

tuque (took) *n.* a Canadian cap made by tucking in one end of a knitted cylindrical bag both ends of which are closed. [Can. F, var. of TOQUE]

turaco (tuə´rəkō), **touraco** *n.* (*pl.* **turacos, touracos**) any African bird of the family Musophagidae, which have crimson and green plumage. [F *touraco*, from W Afr. name]

Turanian (tūrā´niən) *n.* the group of Asian languages that are neither Indo-European nor Semitic, esp. the Ural-Altaic group. ~*a.* of or relating to these languages. [Pers. *Tūrān*, the region beyond the Oxus]

turban (tœ´bən) *n.* **1** a (Muslim or Sikh) man's headdress consisting of a sash or scarf wound round a cap or the head. **2** a woman's headdress imitating this. **3** a narrow-brimmed or brimless hat worn by women and children. **4** the whorls of a univalve shell. **turbaned** *a.* [F, earlier *turbant*, It. *turbante*, Turk. *tulbend*, *dulbend*, Pers. *dulband*, cp. TULIP]

turbary (tœ´bəri) *n.* (*pl.* **turbaries**) **1** (*Law*) the right of digging turf on another's land. **2** a place where turf or peat is dug. [OF *torberie*, late L *turbāria*, from OHG *zurba*, TURF]

turbellarian (tœbəleə´riən) *n.* any flatworm of the class Turbellaria, with ciliated skin. ~*a.* of or relating to this class. **turbellariform** (-fawm) *a.* [mod. L, from L *turba*, crowd]

turbid (tœ´bid) *a.* **1** muddy, discoloured, thick, unclear. **2** disordered, unquiet, disturbed. **turbidity** (-bid´-), **turbidness** *n.* **turbidly** *adv.* [L *turbidus*, from *turbāre*, to disturb, from *turba*, crowd]

Usage note The adjectives *turbid* and *turgid* should not be confused: *turbid* means muddy or unclear, and *turgid* means swollen or bombastic.

turbinate (tœ´binət) *a.* **1** top-shaped, like an inverted cone. **2** spiral, whorled. **3** spinning like a top. **4** shaped like a scroll. **turbinal** *a.* **turbination** (-ā´shən) *n.* **turbiniform** (-bin´ifawm), **turbinoid** (-oid) *a.* [L *turbinatus*, as TURBINE]

turbine (tœ´bīn, -bin) *n.* **1** a waterwheel or motor enclosed in a case or tube in which a flowing stream acts by direct impact or reaction upon a series of vanes or buckets. **2** a similar wheel or motor driven by steam, gas or air. **3** a vessel propelled by a turbine. [F, from L *turbinem*, nom. *turbo*, wheel, top, whirlwind, cp. TURBINATE]

turbiniform, turbinoid TURBINATE.

turbit (tœ´bit) *n.* a variety of domestic pigeon with a flattened head and short beak. [etym. uncertain]

turbo[1] (tœ´bō) *n.* (*pl.* **turbos**) **1** a model of car etc. incorporating a turbocharger. **2** a turbocharger.

turbo[2] (tœ´bō) *n.* (*pl.* **turbos**) any gastropod of the genus *Turbo*. [L, see TURBINE]

turbo- (tœ´bō) *comb. form* having or driven by a turbine. **turbocharger** *n.* a supercharger, esp. for motor car engines, driven by exhaust gas turbines. **turbocharge** *v.t.* **turbocharged** *a.* **turbo-diesel** *n.* **1** a turbocharged diesel engine. **2** a vehicle powered by this. **turbofan** *n.* **1** a gas-turbine aero-engine with a large fan which forces air out with the exhaust gases, thus increasing thrust. **2** an aircraft powered by this. **turbojet** *n.* **1** a turbojet engine. **2** an aircraft powered by this. **turbojet engine** *n.* an engine with a turbine-driven compressor for supplying compressed air to the combustion chamber. **turboprop** *n.* **1** an engine with a turbine-driven propeller. **2** an aircraft powered by this. **turboramjet** *n.* an engine which consists of a turbojet mounted in the duct of a ramjet. **turboshaft** *n.* a gas turbine that powers a shaft. **turbosupercharger** *n.* a turbocharger.

turbot (tœ´bət) *n.* (*pl. in general* **turbot,** *in particular* **turbots**) **1** a large European flatfish, *Scophthalmus maximus*, with bony tubercles, highly valued as food. **2** any of various similar or related fishes such as the halibut. [F, from L *turbo*, see TURBINE]

turbulent (tœ´būlənt) *a.* **1** disturbed, tumultuous. **2** (of a flow of air) causing disturbance. **3** insubordinate, disorderly. **turbulence, turbulency** *n.* **turbulently** *adv.* [F, from L *turbulentus*, as TURBID]

Turco (tœ´kō) *n.* (*pl.* **Turcos**) (*Hist.*) an Algerian sharpshooter in the French army. [Sp., Port., It., TURK]

Turco- (tœ´kō), **Turko-** *comb. form* Turkish; Turkish and.

Turcoman TURKOMAN.

turd (tœd) *n.* (*taboo sl.*) **1** a lump of excrement or dung. **2** a contemptible person. [OE *tord*]

turdine (tœ´dīn) *a.* of, resembling or characteristic of thrushes. **turdoid** (-doid) *a.* thrushlike. [L *turdus*, thrush]

tureen (tūrēn´, tər-) *n.* a deep covered dish or vessel for holding soup etc. [orig. *terreen*, TERRINE]

turf (tœf) *n.* (*pl.* **turfs, turves** (tœvz)) **1** surface earth filled with the matted roots of grass and other small plants. **2** a piece of this, a sod. **3** greensward, growing grass. **4** peat. ~*v.t.* to cover or line with turfs or sods. **the turf 1** the racecourse. **2** the occupation or profession of horseracing. **to turf out** (*coll.*) to throw out, to eject forcibly. **turf accountant** *n.* a bookmaker. **turfless** *a.*

turfman *n.* (*pl.* **turfmen**) (*esp. N Am.*) a person devoted to or making a living from horseracing. **turfy** *a.* (*comp.* **turfier**, *superl.* **turfiest**). **turfiness** *n.* [OE, cp. Dut. *turf*, Icel. and Swed. *torf*, Dan. *törv*]

turgid (tœ´jid) *a.* **1** swollen, bloated, morbidly distended, tumid. **2** pompous, inflated, bombastic. **turgescence** (-jes´əns) *n.* **turgescent** *a.* **turgidity** (-jid´-), **turgidness** *n.* **turgidly** *adv.* **turgor** (-gə) *n.* the rigid state of a cell caused by pressure of the contents against the cell wall. [L *turgidus*, from *turgēre*, to swell]

Usage note See note under TURBID.

Turing machine (tūə´ring) *n.* a hypothetical computer that can write its own program. **Turing test** *n.* a test of a computer's intelligence, in which a human participant's part of a dialogue is taken over by the computer to see if the other human participant can tell the difference. [Alan *Turing*, 1912–54, English mathematician]

turion (tūə´riən) *n.* **1** a young scaly shoot rising from the ground, as in asparagus. **2** a bud of an aquatic plant. **turioniferous** (-nif´-) *a.* [L *turiōnem*, nom. *-io*]

Turk (tœk) *n.* **1** a native or inhabitant of Turkey. **2** a native speaker of a Turkic language. **3** a Turkish horse. **4** (*offensive*) a violent or troublesome person, esp. a boy. **Turk's cap** *n.* **1** a martagon lily. **2** any of various cacti of the genus *Melocactus*. **Turk's head** *n.* an ornamental knot suggestive of a turban. [F *Turc*, med. L *Turcus*, Pers. *Turk*]

Turk. *abbr.* Turkish.

turkey (tœ´ki) *n.* (*pl.* **turkeys**) **1** a large gallinaceous bird, *Meleagris gallopavo*, allied to the pheasant, orig. introduced from America. **2** the flesh of this as food. **3** (*Austral.*) any of various birds resembling the turkey, as the brush turkey, *Alectura lathami*, or the mallee bird. **4** (*esp. N Am., sl.*) a flop. **5** (*esp. N Am., sl.*) a stupid person. **to talk turkey** (*esp. N Am., coll.*) to come to the point, to talk business. **turkey buzzard, turkey vulture** *n.* an American vulture, *Cathartes aura*. **turkeycock** *n.* **1** a male turkey. **2** a conceited, pompous person. **turkey trot** *n.* a round dance with little or no bending of the knees and a swing of the body. [from the belief that the bird came from Turkey]

Turkey carpet (tœ´ki) *n.* TURKISH CARPET (under TURKISH). **Turkey red** *n.* **1** a brilliant red dye orig. obtained from madder. **2** cotton cloth dyed with this. **Turkey-red** *a.*

Turki (tœ´ki) *a.* of or relating to the Turkic languages or their speakers. *~n.* (*pl.* **Turki**) **1** a Turkic speaker. **2** the Turkic languages collectively. **Turkic** *a.* of or relating to the branch of the Altaic languages to which Turkish belongs. *~n.* the Turkic languages collectively.

Turkish (tœ´kish) *a.* of or relating to Turkey or the Turks or their language. *~n.* the language of the Turks. **Turkish bath** *n.* **1** a hot-air bath in which one is sweated, washed, rubbed, massaged etc. and conducted through a series of cooling-rooms. **2** a building for this. **Turkish carpet** *n.* a soft velvety woollen carpet, orig. made in Turkey. **Turkish coffee** *n.* very strong black coffee. **Turkish delight** *n.* a gelatinous sweet, coated in powdered sugar. **Turkish towel** *n.* a rough loose-piled towel made of cotton terry.

Turkmen (tœk´mən) *n.* (*pl.* **Turkmen, Turkmens**) **1** a member of any of various Turkic peoples of Turkmenistan and parts of Iran and Afghanistan. **2** the Turkic language of these peoples. *~a.* of or relating to these peoples or their language. [Pers. *turkmān*, from Turk. *tūrkmen*]

Turkoman (tœ´kōmən), **Turcoman** *n.* (*pl.* **Turkomans, Turcomans**) **1** a Turkmen. **2** the Turkmen language. *~a.* of or relating to the Turkmen or their language. **Turkoman carpet** *n.* a traditional soft carpet of rich colours. [med. L *Turco-*, *Turcus*, TURK, MAN]

turmeric (tœ´mərik) *n.* **1** an Asian plant, *Curcuma longa*, of the ginger family. **2** the powdered rhizome of this used as a dyestuff, stimulant or condiment, esp. in curry. **turmeric paper** *n.* (*Chem.*) unsized white paper saturated with turmeric used as a test for alkalis, which change the colour from yellow to red. [corr. of F *terre-merite*, perh. corr. of Arab. *kurkum*, CURCUMA]

turmoil (tœ´moil) *n.* a commotion, disturbance, tumult. [etym. uncertain, perh. from MOIL]

turn (tœn) *v.t.* **1** to cause to move round on or as on an axis, to give a rotary motion to. **2** to cause to go, move, aim, point, look etc. in a different direction. **3** to expose the other side of, to invert, to reverse. **4** to renew (a cuff, collar etc.) by reversing. **5** to bring (lower soil) to the surface by digging or ploughing. **6** to revolve in the mind. **7** to perform (a somersault). **8** to apply or devote to a different purpose or object, to give a new direction to. **9** to bend, to adapt, to change in form, condition, nature etc. **10** to cause to change (into), to convert, to transform, to transmute. **11** to translate, to paraphrase. **12** to pass, go or move to the other side of, to go round. **13** to pass round the flank of (an army) so as to attack it from the flank or rear. **14** to reach or pass beyond (a certain age, time). **15** to bend back, to blunt (a knife-edge etc.). **16** to cause to ferment, to make sour. **17** to nauseate. **18** to infatuate, to unsettle, to make giddy. **19** to cause to go, to send, to put by turning. **20** to shape in a lathe or on a potter's wheel. **21** to give a shapely form to, to mould, to round (a sentence etc.). **22** to cause (an enemy agent) to become a double agent. **23** to twist or sprain. **24** to make (a profit). **25** (*Print.*) to invert (type). *~v.i.* **1** to have a circular or revolving motion, to rotate, to revolve, to move round or about. **2** to move the body, face or head in a different direction, to change front from right to left etc. **3** to change in posture, attitude or position. **4** to return. **5** to take a particular direction. **6** to be changed in nature, form, condition etc. **7** to change colour. **8** to become sour or spoiled. **9** to become unsettled, infatuated or giddy. **10** to become nauseated. **11** to result, to terminate. **12** to undergo the process of turning on the lathe. **13** in cricket, to spin, to deviate from line. **14** in cricket, (of a wicket) to assist spin bowling. **15** in golf, to begin the second half of a round. *~n.* **1** the act of turning, rotary motion. **2** a revolution. **3** the state of being turned. **4** a change of direction, position or tendency, a deflection. **5** a bend, a curve, a winding, a corner. **6** a single round or coil of a rope etc. **7** a change, a vicissitude. **8** a turning point. **9** a point of change in time. **10** a short walk, a stroll, a promenade. **11** a performance, bout or spell (of doing something). **12** an occasion, opportunity or time (for doing something) coming in succession to each of a number of persons. **13** purpose. **14** succession, alternation, rotation. **15** (*coll.*) a nervous shock. **16** shape, form, mould, character, disposition, temper. **17** (*Mus.*) a melodic embellishment consisting of the principal tone with those above and below it. **18** (*Print.*) an inverted type put temporarily in place of a missing letter. **19** (the performer of) a short, theatrical act. **20** a transaction on the Stock Exchange, or the profit made from this. **at every turn 1** constantly. **2** everywhere. **by turns 1** alternately. **2** at intervals. **done to a turn** cooked exactly right. **in one's turn** when one's turn, chance etc. comes. **in turn** in order of succession, in rotation. **not to know where to turn** not to know which way to turn. **not to know which way to turn** to be unsure what to do, where to go etc. **not to turn a hair** HAIR. **on the turn 1** (of the tide) just turning. **2** beginning to go sour. **3** on the point of changing. **out of turn 1** out of the proper order of succession. **2** at an inappropriate time. **to serve one's turn 1** to serve one's purpose. **2** to help or suit one. **to take a turn for the better** to improve. **to take a turn for the worse** to deteriorate. **to take it in turns** to take turns. **to take turns** to alternate, to perform or participate in rotation or succession. **to turn a blind eye to** to pretend not to see, to overlook. **to turn about 1** to turn the face in another direction. **2** to turn round. **to turn a deaf ear to** to refuse to listen to. **to turn adrift 1** to unmoor (a boat) and allow to float away. **2** (*fig.*) to cast off, to abandon without support. †**to turn again** to return. **to turn against 1** to (cause to) become hostile to. **2** to use against. **to turn an honest penny** HONEST. **to turn around** (*esp. N Am.*) to turn round. **to turn aside 1** to deviate. **2** to divert, to avert. **to turn a trick** TRICK. **to turn away 1** to turn to face the other way. **2** to reject. **3** to send away, dismiss. **to turn back 1** to send back. **2** to begin to go back. **3** to fold back. **to turn down 1** to fold or double down. **2** to lower (a light, the volume on a radio etc.). **3** to lay (a card) face downwards. **4** to reject. **to turn in 1** to direct or incline inwards. **2** to fold or double in. **3** to send, put or drive in. **4** to hand over, to surrender. **5** to give, to execute (a performance etc.). **6** (*coll.*) to go to bed. **7** to achieve (a score). **8** to hand in. **9** (*coll.*) to abandon (a plan etc.). **to turn in one's grave** GRAVE[1]. **to turn inside out** INSIDE[1]. **to turn off 1** to deflect. **2** to deviate. **3** to dismiss. **4** to shut or switch off. **5** to achieve, to produce, to accomplish. **6** †to hang (a criminal). **7** (*coll.*) to cause to lose interest in, esp. sexually. **to turn on 1** to open a way to (gas etc.) by turning a tap. **2** to switch on. **3** to direct, to aim. **4** to hinge or depend upon. **5** to attack. **6** (*coll.*) to excite, to arouse the interest of, esp. sexually. **7** (*sl.*) to introduce to drugs. **8** (*sl.*) to take and get high on drugs. **to turn one's back on/ upon** BACK[1]. **to turn one's hand to** to undertake; to apply oneself to. **to turn one's steps towards** STEP. **to turn on one's heel** HEEL[1]. **to turn out 1** to drive out, to expel. **2** to point or to cause to point outwards. **3** to turn (pockets etc.) inside out. **4** to clean (a room) thoroughly. **5** to bring to view. **6** to produce, as the result of labour. **7** to prove to be. **8** to switch off. **9** to dress, to groom, to look after the appearance of. **10** (*coll.*) to gather, to assemble. **11** (*coll.*) to go out. **12** (*coll.*) to get out of bed. **13** to call (a guard) from the guardroom. **to turn over 1** to change the position of, to invert, to reverse. **2** (of an engine) to (cause to) start or run at low revolutions. **3** to surrender, to hand over. **4** to transfer (to), to put under other control. **5** to cause to turn over, to upset. **6** to do business to the amount of. **7** to consider, to ponder. **8** (*sl.*) to rob. **to turn over a new leaf** LEAF. **to turn round 1** to face about. **2** to adopt a new view, attitude, policy etc. **3** to complete the processing of. **4** to complete the unloading and reloading of (a ship, aircraft). **5** to restore to profitability. **to turn someone's head** HEAD[1]. **to turn sour** SOUR. **to turn tail** TAIL[1]. **to turn the corner** CORNER. **to turn the heat on** HEAT. **to turn the other cheek** CHEEK. **to turn the scales** SCALE[2]. **to turn the tables** TABLE. **to turn the tide** to reverse the course of events. **to turn to 1** to have recourse to. **2** to change or be changed into. **3** to direct towards. **4** to find (a page) in a book. **5** to set to work. **to turn to account** ACCOUNT. **to turn to advantage** ADVANTAGE. **to turn turtle** TURTLE[1]. **to turn up 1** to bring to the surface. **2** to unearth, to bring to light. **3** to place (a card etc.) with the face upwards. **4** to tilt up. **5** to find and refer to (a passage) in a book. **6** to point upwards. **7** to come to light. **8** to happen. **9** to make one's appearance. **10** (*coll.*) to cause to vomit. **11** to shorten (a garment etc.). **to turn upon 1** to hinge on. **2** to attack. **3** to direct or aim at. **to turn up one's nose** NOSE. **to turn up trumps** TRUMP[1]. **turn and turn about** alternately, successively. **turnabout** *n.* **1** the act of facing in an opposite direction. **2** a complete reversal (of opinion, policy etc.). **turnaround** *n.* **1** a turnabout. **2** turnround. **turnback** *n.* REVERS. **turn-bench** *n.* a small portable lathe, used by watchmakers. **turn-buckle** *n.* a coupling for metal rods etc. allowing adjustment of length. **turn-cap** *n.* a chimney cowl turning round with the wind. **turncoat** *n.* a person who deserts their party or principles. **turncock** *n.* **1** (*Hist.*) a person who turns water on or off from a main. **2** a stopcock. **turndown** *n.* **1** a rejection. **2** a downturn. ~*a.* folded or doubled down. **turned** *a.* **turner** *n.* **1** a person who turns, esp. one who turns articles in a lathe. **2** a variety of tumbler (pigeon). **turnery** *n.* **1** turning articles in a lathe. **2** articles turned in a lathe. **turn indicator** *n.* a gyroscopic instrument which indicates any deviation in the course of an aircraft. **turning** *n.* **1** the act of a person who or of a thing which turns. **2** a bend, a corner, the point where a road meets another. **3** such a road. **4** the use of a lathe. **5** (*pl.*) shavings from a lathe. **turning circle** *n.* the smallest circle in which a vehicle can turn round. **turning point** *n.* the point in place, time etc. on or at which a change takes place, the decisive point. **turnkey** †*n.* (*pl.* **turnkeys**) a person who has the charge of the keys of a prison, a warder. ~*a.* being in its entirety the responsibility of a single contractor or supplier. **turn-off** *n.* **1** a turning off a main road. **2** (*coll.*) something that repels or makes one lose interest. **turn of speed** *n.* the ability to go fast. **turn-on** *n.* (*coll.*) a person who or thing which excites one, esp. sexually. **turnout** *n.* **1** a turning out for duty. **2** an assembly, a large party. **3** a showy or well-appointed equipage. **4** dress, get-up. **5** a quantity of articles or products manufactured in a given time. **6** the number of people attending something. **turnover** *n.* **1** the act or an instance of turning over. **2** a semicircular pie or tart made by turning over half the crust. **3** the amount of money turned over in a business in a given time. **4** the rate at which stock in trade is sold and replenished. **5** the rate at which employees leave and have to be replaced. **6** an article filling a column and continued on the next page. **7** an upset. **8** (*N Am.*) in sport, loss of the possession of the ball. **turnpike** *n.* **1** (*Hist.*) a gate set across a road to stop carriages etc. from passing till the toll is paid, orig. a frame set with spikes to prevent passage. **2** (*Hist.*) a turnpike road. **3** (*N Am.*) a motorway on which a toll is payable. **turnpikeman** *n.* (*pl.* **turnpikemen**) a collector of tolls at a turnpike. **turnpike road** *n.* (*Hist.*) a road on which turnpikes or toll gates were established. **turnround** *n.* **1** (the time taken by) the process of unloading a ship or aircraft and reloading it ready for its next trip. **2** (the time taken by) the complete processing of anything. **3** a change to an opposite and usu. better state. †**turn-screw** *n.* a screwdriver. **turnsick** *n.* sturdy in sheep. **turnsole** *n.* a plant supposed to turn with the sun, esp. *Chrozophora tinctoria*. **turnspit** *n.* (*Hist.*) **1** a person who turns a spit. **2** a variety of dog, allied to the terrier, employed to turn spits. **turnstile** *n.* a post with four horizontal revolving arms, set at the entrance to an enclosure, building etc., allowing persons to pass through one at a time often after a toll or fee is paid. **turnstone** *n.* any small wading bird of the genus *Arenaria*, which looks for small animals under stones. **turntable** *n.* **1** the rotating table which supports a gramophone record or CD while being played. **2** a platform rotating in a horizontal plane used for shifting rolling stock from one line of rails to another. **turn-up** *n.* **1** a turned-up fold at the bottom of a trouser leg. **2** (*coll.*) a sudden and unexpected (fortunate) occurrence. **turn-up for the book, turn-up for the books** *n.* (*coll.*) a sudden and unexpected (fortunate) occurrence. [OE *turnian*, *tyrnan* (cp. OF *torner*, F *tourner*), L *tornāre*, from *tornus*, lathe, Gr. *tornos*]

turnip (tœ´nip) *n.* **1** a plant, *Brassica rapa*, with a fleshy globular root used as a vegetable and for feeding sheep. **2** a similar plant such as a swede. **3** a large old-fashioned watch. **turnip fly** *n.* (*pl.* **turnip flies**) an insect, *Athalia centifoliae* or *Anthomyia radicum*, destructive to turnips. **turnip-tops,** (*N Am.*) **turnip greens** *n.pl.* the green sprouts of a turnip used as a vegetable. **turnipy** *a.* [perh. TURN, or F *tour*, OE *næp*, L *nāpus*, turnip]

turpentine (tœ´pəntīn) *n.* **1** an oleoresin exuding naturally or from incisions in several coniferous trees, esp. the terebinth. **2** a volatile oil distilled from turpentine used for mixing paint, varnishes etc. and in medicine; oil of turpentine. **3** (*also* **turpentine substitute**) white spirit. **4** the turpentine tree. ~*v.t.* **1** to put turpentine in. **2** to saturate with turpentine. **turpentine tree** *n.* a tree from which turpentine is obtained, esp. the terebinth. **turpentinic** (-tin´-) *a.* **turps** *n.* (*coll.*) oil of turpentine. [ME and MF *turpentine*, L *terebinthinus*, Gr. *terebinthinos*, from *terebinthos*, TEREBINTH]

turpeth (tœ´pəth), **turpeth root** *n.* the root of an Asian plant, *Ipomoea turpethum*, used as a drastic purgative. [OF *turbith*, Arab. and Pers. *turbid*, purge]

turpitude (tœ´pitūd) *n.* (*formal*) baseness, depravity. [F, from L *turpitūdo*, from *turpis*, base]

turps TURPENTINE.

turquoise (tœ´kwoiz, -kwahz) *n.* **1** a sky-blue or bluish-green translucent or opaque precious stone. **2** a pale greenish-blue. ~*a.* of the colour turquoise. [OF, fem. of *turquois*, Turkish, see TURK]

turret (tŭr´it) *n.* **1** a small tower attached to a building, and rising above it. **2** a low flat cylindrical or conical armoured tower, usu. revolving, so that the guns command a wide radius on a warship, tank or fort. **3** a similar structure on an aircraft. **4** a rotatable holder for cutting tools etc. on a lathe, milling machine etc. **5** a high wheeled structure used for attacking a castle etc. **turret clock** *n.* a tower clock in which the movement is separate from the dials. **turreted** *a.* **turret gun** *n.* a gun for use in a turret. **turret lathe** *n.* CAPSTAN LATHE (under CAPSTAN). **turret ship** *n.* a warship with a turret or turrets. [F *tourette*, dim. of *tour*, TOWER]

turriculate (tərik´ūlət), **turriculated** (-lātid) *a.* (of shells) having a long spire.

turtle (tœ´təl) *n.* **1** a marine reptile of the order Chelonia, encased in a carapace, like a tortoise, with flippers used in swimming. **2** the flesh of a chelonian, esp. the green turtle, *Chelonia mydas*, used for soup. **3** turtle soup. **4** (*Comput.*) a device or cursor which can be instructed to draw graphics. ~*v.i.* to fish or hunt for turtles. **to turn turtle** to turn completely over, to capsize. **turtleback** *n.* an arched covering over part of a ship's deck, esp. at the bows, and sometimes the stern, as a protection against heavy seas. **turtleneck** *n.* **1** (a sweater with) a round, high, close-fitting neck. **2** (*N Am.*) POLO NECK (under POLO). **turtlenecked** *a.* **turtler** *n.* **turtle shell** *n.* tortoiseshell, esp. the darker and less valuable kind, used for inlaying. **turtleshell** *a.* made of turtle shell. **turtle soup** *n.* rich soup made from fatty parts of the turtle. [corr. of Port. *tartaruga* or Sp. *tortuga*, late L *tortūca*, TORTOISE]

turtle-dove (tœt´əldŭv) *n.* any wild dove of the genus *Streptopelia*, esp. *S. turtur*, noted for its soft cooing and its devotion to its mate and young. [OE, from L *turtur*, prob. imit. of coo, DOVE]

turves TURF.

Tuscan (tŭs´kən) *n.* **1** a native or inhabitant of Tuscany. **2** the Italian dialect of Tuscany. **3** the Tuscan order. ~*a.* of or relating to Tuscany of the Tuscan order. **Tuscan order** *n.* (*Archit.*) the simplest of the five classic orders, a Roman modification of Doric. **Tuscan straw** *n.* a yellow straw used for hats etc.

tusche (tush) *n.* a substance used in lithography for drawing in the design which resists the printing medium. [from G *tuschen*, to touch up]

†**tush**[1] (tŭsh) *int.* used to express contempt or impatience. [cp. TUT]

tush[2] (tŭsh) *n.* **1** a long pointed tooth, esp. a horse's canine tooth. **2** a small tusk of an elephant. [var. of TUSK]

tush[3] (tush) *n.* (*N Am., sl.*) the buttocks. [from Yiddish *toches*]

tusk (tŭsk) *n.* **1** a long pointed tooth, esp. one permanently protruding from the mouth as in the elephant, narwhal etc. **2** a toothlike point, spike, projection etc., as in a harrow, lock etc. ~*v.t.* to gore, mangle or root up with tusks. **tusked, tusky** *a.* **tusker** *n.* an elephant or wild boar with well-developed tusks. **tusk shell** *n.* **1** any mollusc of the class Scaphopoda, having a long narrow tubular shell, the tooth shell. **2** the shell of this. [OE *tusc*, *tux*, cp. OFris. *tusk*, *tosch*, Icel. *toskr*]

tussah TUSSORE.

tussal TUSSIS.

tusser TUSSORE.

tussis (tŭs´is) *n.* (*Med.*) a cough. **tussal, tussive** *a.* [L, cough]

tussle (tŭs´əl) *v.i.* to struggle, to scuffle (with or for). ~*n.* a struggle, a scuffle. [var. of TOUSLE]

tussock (tŭs´ək) *n.* **1** a clump, tuft or hillock of growing grass. **2** a tuft or lock of hair etc. **3** a tussock moth. **tussock grass** *n.* a grass, esp. of the genus *Poa*, *Nassella* or *Deschampsia*, forming tufts 5–6 ft. (1.7–2.0 m) high. **tussock moth** *n.* a bombycid moth of the family Lymantriidae, the larvae of which bear tufts of hair. **tussocky** *a.* [cp. Swed. dial. *tuss*, wisp of hay]

tussore (tŭs´aw), **tusser** (-ə), (*N Am.*) **tussah, tussur** *n.* **1** an Indian silkworm moth, *Antheraea mylitta*, feeding on the jujube tree etc. **2** a Chinese oak-feeding silkworm moth, *A. pernyi*. **3** (*also* **tussore-silk**) a strong, coarse silk obtained from these. [Hind. *tassar*, from Sansk. *tassara*, shuttle]

tut TUT-TUT.

tutee TUTOR.

tutelage (tū´təlij) *n.* **1** guardianship. **2** the state of being under a guardian. **3** the period of this. **4** tuition. **tutelar, tutelary** *a.* **1** having the care or protection of a person or thing, protective. **2** of or relating to a guardian. [L *tūtēla*, guardianship]

tutenag (tū´tənag) *n.* **1** zinc or spelter from China or SE Asia. **2** a white alloy of copper. [F *tutenague*, prob. from Arab. and Pers. *tūtiyā*, TUTTY]

tutiorism (tū´tiərizm) *n.* in the Roman Catholic Church, the doctrine that in cases of moral doubt the course should be followed that seems the safer or more in accord with the letter of the law. **tutiorist** *a.*, *n.* [L *tūtior*, comp. of *tūtus*, safe]

tutor (tū´tə) *n.* **1** a private teacher, esp. one having the general care and instruction of a pupil in preparation for a university etc. **2** an officer directing the studies of undergraduates in a university college and charged with discipline etc. **3** a college or university teacher who teaches and holds discussions with students in small groups. **4** an instruction book. **5** (*Law*) a guardian of a minor. ~*v.t.* **1** to act as a tutor to. **2** to instruct, to teach. **3** to train. **4** to discipline, to correct. ~*v.i.* **1** to work as a tutor. **2** (*N Am.*) to receive tuition. **tutee** (-tē´) *n.* a student or person being tutored. **tutorage** *n.* **tutoress** *n.* a female tutor. **tutorial** (-taw´ri-) *a.* of a tutor or tuition. ~*n.* **1** a teaching session or conference with a tutor. **2** an explanation of a subject used by someone studying privately. **tutorially** *adv.* **tutorship** *n.* [ME *tutour*, F *tuteur*, L *tutor -torem*, from *tuēri*, to look after, p.p. *tūtus*]

tutsan (tŭt´sən) *n.* a species of St John's wort, *Hypericum androsaemum*, formerly held to be a panacea for wounds etc. [OF *toutesaine* (*toute*, L *tōtum*, nom. *-us*, all, *saine*, *sānus*, sound, SANE)]

Tutsi (tut´si) *n.* (*pl.* **Tutsi, Tutsis**) a member of a Bantu-speaking people in Rwanda. ~*a.* of or relating to the Tutsi. [Bantu]

tutti (tut´i) *adv.* (*Mus.*) all together. ~*n.* (*pl.* **tuttis**) a composition or passage for singing or performing all together. [It., pl. of *tutto*, all]
tutti-frutti (tootifroo´ti) *n.* (*pl.* **tutti-fruttis**) a confection, such as ice cream, made of or flavoured with different fruits. [It., all fruits, cp. TUTTI and FRUIT]
tut-tut (tŭttŭt´), **tut** *int.* used to express disapproval, impatience or contempt. ~*n.* an utterance of 'tut-tut', an exclamation of disapproval etc. ~*v.i.* (*pres.p.* **tut-tutting, tutting,** *past, p.p.* **tut-tutted, tutted**) to exclaim 'tut-tut', to express or show disapproval etc. [instinctive sound]
tutty (tŭt´i) *n.* an impure oxide of zinc collected from the flues of smelting furnaces, used as polishing powder. [ME and OF *tutie*, Arab. and Pers. *tūtiyā*]
tutu[1] (too´too) *n.* a New Zealand shrub, *Coriaria arborea*, with poisonous berries. [Maori]
tutu[2] (too´too) *n.* a ballet dancer's short, stiff skirt that spreads outwards. [F]
tu-whit tu-whoo (təwit təwoo´) *int., n.* used to imitate the cry of an owl.
tuxedo (tŭksē´dō) *n.* (*pl.* **tuxedos, tuxedoes**) (*N Am.*) **1** a dinner jacket. **2** a suit including this. **tux** *n.* (*coll.*) a tuxedo. [New York club]
tuyère (twēyeə´, tooyeə´), **tuyere, twyer** (twī´ə) *n.* the blast-pipe or nozzle in a furnace, forge etc. [F, from *tuyau*, pipe]
TV (tēvē´) *n.* (*pl.* **TVs**) **1** television. **2** a television set. **TV dinner** *n.* a complete, ready-packaged and frozen dinner that only needs reheating before being eaten.
TVEI *abbr.* Technical and Vocational Educational Initiative.
Tvl *abbr.* Transvaal.
TVP® *abbr.* textured vegetable protein.
TVRO *abbr.* television receive only (antenna).
TW *abbr.* travelling wave.
TWA *abbr.* **1** (*Hist.*) Thames Water Authority. **2** Trans-World Airlines.
twaddle (twod´əl) *v.i.* **1** to talk unmeaningly. **2** to prate, to chatter. ~*n.* meaningless talk, silly chatter, nonsense. **twaddler** *n.* **twaddly** *a.* [formerly var. of TWATTLE]
†**twain** (twān) *a.* two. ~*n.* a pair, a couple. **in twain** in two, asunder. [OE *twegen*, m., see TWO]
twang (twang) *v.i.* **1** to make a ringing metallic sound as by plucking the string of a musical instrument. **2** to play (on) in this way. **3** to speak or be uttered with a nasal sound. ~*v.t.* **1** to cause to sound with a twang. **2** to play (an instrument) in this way. **3** to utter or pronounce with a nasal sound. ~*n.* **1** a ringing metallic sound. **2** a nasal tone (in speaking etc.). **3** (*dial.*) a tang, a disagreeable flavour. **twangle** (twang´gəl) *v.i., v.t.* **twangy** *a.* [var. of TANG[1]]
†**'twas** (twoz) *contr.* it was.
twat (twat, twot) *n.* (*sl.*) **1** (*taboo*) the female genitals. **2** a stupid or contemptible person. [etym. uncertain]
twattle (twot´əl) *n.* meaningless talk. [var. of TATTLE]
twayblade (twā´blād) *n.* any orchid of the genus *Listera* etc., with two broad, ovate, radical leaves, and green or purplish flowers.
tweak (twēk) *v.t.* **1** to pinch and twist or pull with a sudden jerk, to twitch. **2** to make fine adjustments to; to tune. ~*n.* a sharp pinch or pull, a twitch. [ME *twikken*, OE *twiccian*, cp. G *zwicken* and TWITCH[1]]
twee (twē) *a.* (*comp.* **tweer** (twē´ə), *superl.* **tweest** (twē´ist)) **1** excessively dainty and prettified. **2** sentimentally sweet. **tweely** *adv.* **tweeness** *n.* [from *tweet*, childish pronunciation of *sweet*]
tweed (twēd) *n.* **1** a twilled woollen or wool-and-cotton fabric with an unfinished surface, used chiefly for outer garments. **2** (*pl.*) garments made of tweed. **tweedy** *a.* (*comp.* **tweedier,** *superl.* **tweediest**) **1** of or resembling tweed. **2** of a hearty, outdoor type. **tweedily** *adv.* **tweediness** *n.* [prob. from erroneous reading of *tweel*, Sc. form of TWILL]
Tweedledum and Tweedledee (twēdəldŭm ənd twēdəldē´) *n.* an indistinguishable pair; distinction without difference. [from a satire (1725) by J. Byron, names for the composers Handel and Bononcini]
'tween (twēn) †*adv., prep.* between. **'tween-decks** *a.* (*Naut.*) between decks. ~*n.pl.* the space between decks. **tweeny** *n.* (*pl.* **tweenies**) (*coll.*) a servant assisting two others, esp. a cook and housemaid. [short for BETWEEN]
tweet (twēt), **tweet tweet** *n.* the chirp of a small bird. ~*int.* used to imitate the sound made by a small bird. ~*v.i.* to make this sound. **tweeter** *n.* a loudspeaker used to produce higher frequencies. [imit.]
tweezers (twē´zəz) *n.pl.* a small pair of pincers for picking up minute things, plucking out hairs etc. **tweeze** *v.t.* to pluck out or pick up with these. [obs. *tweese*, a small case for instruments, F *étui*, -ER[1]]
twelfth (twelfth) *n.* **1** any one of twelve equal parts. **2** (*Mus.*) an interval of an octave and a fifth. **3** (*Mus.*) a note separated from another by this interval. ~*n., a.* **1** the last of 12 (people, things etc.). **2** the next after the 11th. **Twelfth cake** *n.* a large cake prepared for Twelfth Night festivals. **Twelfth Day** *n.* the 12th day after Christmas, the festival of the Epiphany, 6 Jan. **twelfthly** *adv.* **twelfth man** *n.* a player selected as a reserve in a cricket team. **Twelfth Night** *n.* **1** the eve of Twelfth Day, 5 Jan. **2** Twelfth Day. [OE *twelfta*, from TWELVE]
twelve (twelv) *n.* **1** the number or figure 12 or XII. **2** the age of 12. **3** midnight or midday. **4** (**12**) a film for over 12-year-olds only. ~*a.* **1** 12 in number. **2** aged 12. **the Twelve** the twelve Apostles. **the twelve tables** the Roman laws inscribed on 12 (orig. 10) tablets by the Decemvirs 451 BC, the foundation of Roman jurisprudence. **twelvefold** *a., adv.* **1** twelve times as much or as many. **2** consisting of 12 parts. **twelvemo** (-mō) *n.* (*pl.* **twelvemos**) duodecimo, 12mo. †**twelvemonth** *n.* a year. **twelve-note, twelve-tone** *a.* (*Mus.*) of, relating to or using the 12 chromatic notes of the octave, esp. as developed by Arnold Schönberg. [OE *twelf* (*twā*, TWO, *lif*, cogn. with LEAVE[1])]
twenty (twen´ti) *n.* (*pl.* **twenties**) **1** the number or figure 20 or XX. **2** the age of 20. **3** (*coll.*) a large but indefinite number. ~*a.* **1** 20 in number. **2** aged 20. **3** a large but indefinite number of. **twenties** *n.pl.* **1** the period of time between one's 20th and 30th birthdays. **2** the range of temperature between 20 and 30 degrees. **3** the period of time between the 20th and 30th years of a century. **twentieth** (-tiəth) *n.* any one of 20 equal parts. ~*n., a.* **1** the last of 20 (people, things etc.). **2** the next after the 19th. **twenty-first, twenty-second etc.** *n., a.* the ordinal numbers corresponding to twenty-one etc. **twentyfold** *a., adv.* **twenty-one, twenty-two etc.** *n., a.* the cardinal numbers between twenty and thirty. **twenty-pence (piece)** *n.* a British coin worth 20p. **twenty-twenty, 20/20** *a.* **1** (of vision) normal. **2** (*coll.*) denoting clear perception or hindsight. [OE *twentig* (*twegen*, TWAIN, -TY[1])]
†**'twere** (twœ) *contr.* it were.
twerp (twœp), **twirp** *n.* (*sl.*) a contemptible or silly person. [etym. unknown]
TWh *abbr.* terawatt hour.
twi- (twī) *comb.form* **1** two. **2** double. [OE]
twibill (twī´bil) *n.* **1** a double-bladed battleaxe. **2** a mattock with an axe-shaped back. [OE (*twi*, two, double, BILL[3])]
twice (twīs) *adv.* **1** two times. **2** doubly. **twice removed** REMOVED (under REMOVE). **twice-told** *a.* **1** related twice. **2** well-known, hackneyed. [ME *twies*, OE *twiges*, gen. of *twā*, TWO]
twiddle (twid´əl) *v.t.* **1** to rotate. **2** to twirl idly, to fiddle with. ~*v.i.* **1** to twirl. **2** to fiddle or trifle (with). ~*n.* **1** an act of twiddling. **2** a curly mark. **to twiddle one's**

thumbs 1 to rotate one's thumbs around each other, as a gesture of nervousness or boredom. **2** to sit idle, to have nothing to do but wait. **twiddler** *n.* **twiddling-line** *n.* (*Naut.*) a string attached to a compass gimbal for starting it playing freely. **twiddly** *a.* **1** characterized by twiddling. **2** intricate, curly, fanciful. [cp. Norw. *tvidla*, var. of *tvilla*, *tvirla*, TWIRL]

twig[1] (twig) *n.* **1** a small shoot or branch of a tree, bush, etc., a branchlet. **2** (*Anat.*) a small branch of an artery or other vessel. **twigged** *a.* (*also in comb.*). **twiggy** *a.* (*comp.* **twiggier**, *superl.* **twiggiest**). **twigless** *a.* [OE (cp. Dut. *twijg*, G *Zweig*), cogn. with TWO]

twig[2] (twig) *v.t.* (*pres.p.* **twigging**, *past, p.p.* **twigged**) (*coll.*) **1** to understand, to comprehend, to catch the drift of. **2** to see, to notice. *~v.i.* to understand what is happening or being said. [perh. from Ir. *tuigim*, I understand]

twiggy TWIG[1].

twilight (twī´līt) *n.* **1** the diffused light from the sky appearing a little before sunrise and after sunset. **2** the period of this. **3** a faint light, shade, obscurity. **4** indistinct or imperfect perception, revelation or knowledge. **5** a period of decay, decline etc. *~a.* **1** of, relating to, happening or done in the twilight. **2** dim, shady, obscure. *~v.t.* (*past, p.p.* **twilit** (-lit), **twilighted**) to illuminate dimly. **twilighted** *a.* **twilight of the gods** *n.* in Norse mythology, a conflict in which the gods were overcome and the world destroyed. **twilight sleep** *n.* (*Med.*) a state of semi-consciousness produced by administering scopolamine and morphine in which labour pains are mitigated and forgotten when over. **twilight zone** *n.* **1** a transitional or intermediate zone. **2** a decaying urban area esp. between the commercial centre and the residential suburbs. **twilit** *a.* [ME (OE *twi-*, two, LIGHT[1])]

twill (twil) *n.* a fabric in which the weft threads pass alternately over one warp thread and then under two or more, producing diagonal ribs or lines. *~v.t.* to weave in this way. **twilled** *a.* [OE *twilīc*, cogn. with G *zwillich*, two threaded (*twi-*, TWO, *-līc*, perh. from L *bilix*, BI-, *līcium*, thread)]

†'twill (twil) *contr.* it will.

twin (twin) *a.* **1** being one of two born at a birth. **2** being one of a similar or closely related pair of things, parts etc. **3** double, twofold. **4** (*Bot.*) growing in pairs or divided into two equal parts. *~n.* **1** either of two children or young produced at a birth. **2** a person or thing very closely resembling or related to another. **3** an exact counterpart. **4** a compound crystal having symmetrical halves separated by a plane that is not a plane of symmetry. *~v.t.* (*pres.p.* **twinning**, *past, p.p.* **twinned**) **1** to couple, to pair (with). **2** to pair, to mate. **3** officially to link (a town etc.) with another town in a foreign country, for civic and cultural exchanges etc.; to link (two towns) in this way. *~v.i.* **1** to give birth to twins. **2** to be born at the same birth. **3** to be mated or paired (with). **4** to grow as a twin crystal. **5** to forge a link with another town in a foreign country, for civic and cultural exchanges etc. **the Twins** (*Astron.*) Gemini. **twin bed** *n.* either of a matching pair of single beds. **twin-bedded** *a.* **twin-cam** *a.* (esp. of an engine) having two camshafts. **twin-engined** *a.* having two engines. **twinflower** *n.* a tiny creeping evergreen, *Linnaea borealis*, with threadlike stalks and fragrant flowers. **twinning** *n.* **twin-screw** *a.* (of a steamer) having two propellers twisted in opposite directions. **twin-set** *n.* a jumper and cardigan made to match. **twinship** *n.* **twin town** *n.* a town which has twinned with a town in a foreign country. **twin-tub** *n.* a washing machine with two separate drums, one for washing, the other for spin-drying. [ME, from OE *getwinne* (cp. Icel. *tvinnr*), cogn. with TWO]

twine (twīn) *v.t.* **1** to twist. **2** to form (thread etc.) by twisting together. **3** to wind or coil round, to embrace. **4** to form by interweaving. *~v.i.* **1** to be interwoven. **2** to entwine, to coil (about, round etc.). **3** to wind, to meander. *~n.* **1** strong string made of two or three strands twisted together. **2** a twist, a convolution, a coil. **3** an interlacing, a tangle. **4** the act of twining or entwining. **twiner** *n.* **twiningly** *adv.* [ME *twinen*, from OE *twīn*, twisted thread (cp. Dut. *twijn*, G *zwirn*, Icel. *tvinni*), cogn. with TWO]

twinge (twinj) *v.t.* (*pres.p.* **twingeing, twinging**) to affect with a sharp, sudden pain. *~v.i.* to feel or give a sharp, sudden pain. *~n.* **1** a sharp, sudden, shooting pain. **2** a pang, as of remorse or sorrow. [OE *twengan*, cp. Dut. *dwingen*, G *zwingen*, Icel. *thvinga*, Dan. *tvinge*, to constrain, to compel]

twinkie (twing´ki) *n.* (*sl.*) a person from a two-income household without children. [from *tw*o *in*comes, *n*o *k*ids]

twinkle (twing´kəl) *v.i.* **1** to shine with a broken quivering light, to gleam fitfully, to sparkle. **2** (of eyes) to look bright and lively, esp. in amusement. **3** to appear and disappear in rapid alternation, to move tremulously. **4** to open and shut rapidly, to blink, to wink. **5** (of the feet in dancing) to move lightly. *~v.t.* **1** to flash or emit (light) in rapid gleams. **2** to blink or wink. *~n.* **1** a tremulous gleam, a sparkle. **2** a bright and lively look in the eyes, esp. of amusement. **3** a glimmer. **4** a rapid tremulous movement. **5** a blink, a wink. **in a twinkle** in a twinkling. **twink** *v.i.* **1** to twinkle. **2** to wink. *~n.* **1** a twinkle. **2** a wink. **twinkler** *n.* **twinkling** *n.* **1** a twinkle. **2** the time taken to twinkle, an instant. **in a twinkling** in an instant. **in the twinkling of an eye** in an instant. **twinkly** *a.* [OE *twinclian*, freq. of v. represented by obs. *twink*, var. of *twiccan*, to TWITCH[1]]

twirl (twœl) *v.t.* **1** to cause to rotate rapidly, esp. with the fingers, to spin. **2** to whirl (round). **3** to twiddle, to twist, to curl (the moustache etc.). *~v.i.* to revolve or rotate rapidly, to whirl (round). *~n.* **1** a rapid circular motion. **2** a quick rotation. **3** a twist, a curl, a flourish. **twirler** *n.* **twirly** *a.* [prob. alt. of *tirl* TRILL, after WHIRL]

twirp TWERP.

twist (twist) *v.t.* **1** to wind (a thread, filament, strand etc.) round another. **2** to form (a rope or threads etc., into a rope etc.) in this way, to intertwine (with or in with). **3** to give a spiral form to by turning the ends in opposite directions or turning one end only. **4** to wrench, to distort. **5** to pervert, to misrepresent. **6** to twine, to wreathe. **7** to cause (a ball) to rotate while following a curved path. **8** to make (one's way) in a winding manner. **9** (*sl.*) to cheat. *~v.i.* **1** to be turned or bent round and round upon itself. **2** to be or grow in a spiral form. **3** to move in a curving, winding or irregular path. **4** to writhe, to squirm. **5** to dance the twist. *~n.* **1** an act or the manner of twisting. **2** the state of being twisted. **3** a quick or vigorous turn, a whirling motion given to a ball etc. **4** a sharp bend. **5** a peculiar tendency, a bent, an idiosyncrasy. **6** an unexpected development in, or conclusion to, the plot of a story. **7** the degree of inclination of rifle grooves. **8** a twisting strain. **9** the angle or degree of torsion of a rod etc. **10** forward motion combined with rotation. **11** thread, cord, string, rope etc. made from twisted strands, esp. strong silk thread or cotton yarn. **12** a twisted roll of bread. **13** twisted tobacco. **14** a paper packet with twisted ends. **15** a small piece of lemon etc. rind. **16** (*coll.*) hunger. **17** a dance, popular in the 1960s, in which the dancer gyrates their hips in time to the music while remaining more or less on the same spot. **18** a drink consisting of two ingredients mixed together. **19** (*sl.*) a swindle. **round the twist** (*coll.*) crazy. **to twist off** to remove or break off by twisting. **to twist round one's little finger** FINGER. **to twist someone's arm** to use force or psychological pressure to persuade someone. **twistable** *a.* **twisted** *a.* emotionally unbalanced. **twister** *n.* **1** a person who or thing which twists. **2** a ball delivered with a twist at cricket, billiards etc. **3** the inner part of the thigh on which a good horserider sits. **4** (*esp. N Am.*) a tornado, a waterspout. **5** (*coll.*) a cheat, a rogue. **twisty** *a.* (*comp.* **twistier,** *superl.* **twistiest**). [ME *twisten*, from OE *twist*, rope (in *mæst-twist*, mast-rope), cogn. with TWO]

twit[1] (twit) *v.t.* (*pres.p.* **twitting,** *past, p.p.* **twitted**) to reproach, taunt or upbraid (with some fault etc.). **twitter**[1] *n.* **twittingly** *adv.* [ME *atwīten*, OE *ætwītan* (AT, *wītan*, to blame, cogn. with *wītan*, to know, Goth. *wertjan*, to reproach, L *vidēre*, to see)]

twit[2] (twit) *n.* (*coll.*) a fool. **twittish** *a.* [prob. alt. of TWAT]

twitch[1] (twich) *v.t.* **1** to pull with a sudden or sharp jerk. **2** to snatch. ~*v.i.* **1** to pull or jerk (at). **2** to move with a spasmodic jerk or contraction. ~*n.* **1** a sudden pull or jerk. **2** a sudden involuntary contraction of a muscle etc. **3** a cord twisted by a stick, fastened to the upper lip of a refractory horse for controlling it. **twitcher** *n.* **1** a person who or thing which twitches. **2** (*pl.*) tweezers. **3** (*sl.*) a birdwatcher who is interested in spotting rare birds. **twitchy** *a.* (*comp.* **twitchier,** *superl.* **twitchiest**) nervous. **twitchily** *adv.* **twitchiness** *n.* [ME *twicchen*, var. of *twikken*, to TWEAK]

twitch[2] (twich) *n.* QUITCH. **twitch grass** *n.* couch grass.

twite (twīt) *n.* a N European finch, *Acanthis flavirostris*, which resembles the linnet. [prob. imit. of its chirp]

twitter[1], **twittingly** TWIT[1].

twitter[2] (twit´ə) *v.i.* **1** to utter a succession of short, tremulous, intermittent notes. **2** to talk idly. **3** to have a tremulous motion of the nerves, to be agitated. ~*v.t.* to utter with tremulous, intermittent sounds. ~*n.* **1** such a succession of sounds; idle talk. **2** (*coll.*) (*also* **twitteration**) a state of excitement or nervous agitation. **twitterer** *n.* **twittery** *a.* [ME *twiteren*, freq. of *twit*, imit.]

twittish TWIT[2].

†**'twixt** (twikst) *prep.* between. [BETWIXT]

twizzle (twiz´əl) *v.i.*, *v.t.* (*coll., dial.*) to twist round and round, to spin. ~*n.* a twist or turn. [prob. cogn. with TWIST]

two (too) *n.* **1** the number or figure 2 or II. **2** the age of two. **3** the second hour after midnight or midday. **4** a size denoted by two. **5** a set of two. **6** a card with two pips. ~*a.* **1** two in number. **2** aged two. **in two 1** into two parts. **2** asunder. **in two minds** MIND. **in two shakes** SHAKE. **in two ticks** TICK[1]. **one or two** ONE. **or two** denoting several. **that makes two of us** (*coll.*) the same thing applies to me. **to put two and two together** to draw inferences. **two and two** in pairs. **two a penny** PENNY. **two bites at the cherry** CHERRY. **two by two** in pairs. **two can play at that game** (*coll.*) someone can be copied, to their disadvantage. **two or three** a few. **two strings to one's bow** BOW[1]. **two-bit** *a.* (*N Am., coll.*) insignificant, small-time. **two-by-four** *n.* untrimmed timber, 2 in. by 4 in. (approx 5 cm by 10 cm) in cross-section (somewhat less when dressed). **two cultures** *n.pl.* the arts and science. **two-dimensional** *a.* **1** having two dimensions. **2** lacking (the appearance of) depth. **two-dimensionality** *n.* **two-edged** *a.* **1** (of a knife etc.) having an edge on both sides. **2** cutting both ways. **two-faced** *a.* **1** having two faces. **2** deceitful, insincere. **twofold** *a.* **1** double. **2** composed of two parts. ~*adv.* doubly. **two-foot** *a.* (*coll.*) measuring two feet. **two-handed** *a.* **1** having two hands. **2** requiring both hands for use. **3** played, worked etc. by two persons. **4** using both hands with equal dexterity, ambidextrous. **two-headed** *a.* **two-line** *a.* (*Print.*) having a depth of body double that of the size specified. **twoness** *n.* the state of being two, duality. **twopence** (tŭp´əns) *n.* **1** the sum of two pence. **2** a small silver coin of this value, now issued only as Maundy money. **3** (*coll.*) a thing of little value. **twopenn'orth** (toopen´əth) *n.* **1** as much as is worth or costs twopence. **2** an insignificant amount. **to add one's twopenn'orth** (*coll.*) to give one's views. **to put in one's twopenn'orth** (*coll.*) to give one's views. **twopenny** (tŭp´ni) *a.* **1** worth twopence. **2** (*coll.*) cheap, worthless, common, vulgar. **twopenny-halfpenny** *a.* **1** paltry, insignificant. **2** (*Hist.*) worth or costing twopence-halfpenny. **two-piece** *n., a.* (a garment) consisting of two usu. matching parts. **two-ply** *a.* having two strands (as cord) or two thicknesses (as carpets, cloth etc.). ~*n.* two-ply wool, wood etc. **two-pot screamer** *n.* (*Austral., sl.*) a person who gets drunk easily. **two-seater** *n.* **1** a vehicle or aeroplane with seats for two people. **2** a sofa for two people. **two-sided** *a.* having two sides or aspects. **twosome** (-səm) *n.* **1** a couple. **2** a dance, game of golf etc. involving two people. **two-speed** *a.* giving or adapted to two rates of speed. **two-step** *n.* a kind of round dance in march or polka time. **two-stroke** *a.* being or having an internal-combustion engine with a cycle of two strokes. ~*n.* **1** a two-stroke engine. **2** a vehicle having a two-stroke engine. **two-tier** *a.* having an upper and a lower level, as a legislature with an upper and a lower house. **two-time** *v.t.* (*coll.*) **1** to be unfaithful to. **2** to double-cross. **two-timer** *n.* **two-timing** *a.* **two-tone** *a.* having two colours or shades. **two-up** *n.* an Australian gambling game in which two pennies are tossed in the air and bets made on whether they fall two heads or two tails; also called *swy*. **two-way** *a.* **1** arranged to allow movement in either of two directions. **2** (of a radio) able to send and receive. **3** reciprocal. **4** (*Math.*) having a double mode of variation. **two-way mirror** *n.* a sheet of glass that is a mirror on one side but translucent when viewed from the other. **two-wheeler** *n.* a vehicle with two wheels. [OE *twegen* (fem. *twā*, neut. *tu*), cp. Dut. *twee*, G *zwei*, Icel. *tveir*, also L and Gr. *duo*, Sansk. *dva*]

Usage note See note under TOO.

twocking (twok´ing), **twoccing** *n.* (*sl.*) taking a car without the owner's permission. **twocker** *n.* [taking without the owner's consent]

†**'twould** (twud) *contr.* it would.

twyer TUYÈRE.

TX *abbr.* Texas.

-ty[1] (ti) *suf.* forming abstract nouns, as *bounty*, *cruelty*, *fealty*. [ME *-tie*, *-tee*, *-te* via OF *-té*, *-tet* from L *-tas -tatis*, cp. -ITY]

-ty[2] (ti) *suf.* denoting tens, as *fifty*, *twenty*. [OE *-tig*, cogn. with TEN, Goth. *tigjus*, also Gr. *dekas*, decade, from *deka*, ten]

tychism (tī´kizm) *n.* (*Philos.*) the theory that chance is at work in the universe, esp. in evolutionary adaptations. [Gr. *tukhē*, chance]

tycoon (tīkoon´) *n.* **1** a financial or political magnate. **2** (*Hist.*) a title given to the shogun of Japan, from 1857 to 1868. [Jap. *taikun*, great prince]

tying TIE.

tyke (tīk), **tike** *n.* **1** a dog. **2** a cur. **3** an ill-mannered person. **4** a small child. **5** (*sl.*) a Yorkshireman. **6** (*Austral., sl., offensive*) a Roman Catholic. [ME from Icel. *tīk*]

tyler (tī´lə) *n.* TILER (under TILE).

tylopod (tī´ləpod) *a.* (*Zool.*) having the digits enclosed in a cutaneous pad, as the camels. ~*n.* a tylopod animal. **tylopodous** (-lop´-) *a.* [Gr. *tulos*, knot, *pous podos*, foot]

tylosis (tīlō´sis) *n.* **1** (*Bot.*) a growth in the cavity of a duct intruding from the wall of a contiguous cell. **2** inflammation of the eyelids with thickening and hardening of the margins. **tylotic** (-lot´-) *a.* [Gr., from *tuloein*, to make callous, as TYLOPOD]

tylote (tī´lōt) *n.* a cylindrical spicule, in a sponge, knotted at each end. [Gr. *tulōtos*, as TYLOSIS]

tylotic TYLOSIS.

tympan (tim´pən) *n.* 1 a frame stretched with paper cloth or parchment, used for equalizing the pressure in some printing presses. 2 any thin sheet or membrane tightly stretched. 3 a tympanum. [F, from L TYMPANUM]

tympana TYMPANUM.

tympani TIMPANI.

tympanum (tim´pənəm) *n.* (*pl.* **tympanums, tympana** (-nə)) 1 the middle ear. 2 the tympanic membrane or eardrum. 3 the membrane covering the hearing organ of an insect. 4 the lower end of the trachea in ducks etc., modified into a resonance cavity. 5 (*Archit.*) a triangular area, usu. recessed, in a pediment, the space between the lintel of a doorway and the arch enclosing it. 6 a door panel. 7 a form of treadmill. 8 a wheel in the form of a drum for scooping up water from a stream. **tympanic** (-pan´-) *a.* 1 like a drum. 2 acting like a drumhead. 3 (*Anat.*) of or relating to the tympanum. **tympanic bone** *n.* the bone supporting the tympanic membrane. **tympanic membrane** *n.* the membrane separating the outer ear and middle ear. **tympanites** (-nī´tēz) *n.* (*Med.*) distension of the abdomen, due to the accumulation of air in the intestine etc. **tympanitic** (-nit´-) *a.* **tympanitis** (-nī´tis) *n.* (*Med.*) inflammation of the membrane lining the middle ear. **tympany** (-ni) *n.* 1 tympanites. 2 conceit, bombast. [L, from Gr. *tumpanon*, drum]

Tynesider (tīn´sīdə) *n.* a native or inhabitant of Tyneside, NE England.

Tynwald (tin´wəld), **Tynewald** *n.* the legislature of the Isle of Man. [Icel. *thingvöllr* (*thing*, assembly, *völlr*, field, cp. WEALD)]

typ. *abbr.* 1 typographer. 2 typographic. 3 typography.

type (tīp) *n.* 1 a kind, a class, a category. 2 any person or thing that stands as an illustration, pattern, characteristic example or representative specimen of another thing or class of things. 3 an original conception, object or work of art, serving as a model or guide to later artists. 4 (*coll.*) a person (of a specified kind). 5 a person, event etc. in the Old Testament regarded as foreshadowing another in the New. 6 (*Biol.*) a general form or structure common to a number of individuals. 7 (*Biol.*) an organism exhibiting the essential characteristics of its group. 8 (*Chem.*) a compound, such as hydrochloric acid, water, ammonia or methane, illustrating other compounds by analogy. 9 a piece of metal or hard wood bearing a letter or character usu. in relief, for printing with. 10 such pieces collectively. 11 characters produced by type. 12 the device on a medal, coin etc. *~v.t.* 1 to prefigure, to be a type of. 2 to write with a typewriter. 3 to typecast. 4 to assign to a type. *~v.i.* to write with a typewriter. **in type** set in type. **typal** *a.* **-type** *comb. form* of the kind specified, resembling. **typebar** *n.* 1 a line of type cast in one piece by a linotype machine etc. 2 a bar carrying a letter in a typewriter. **typecast** *v.t.* (*past, p.p.* **typecast**) 1 to cast (an actor) in a role for which they are suited by nature. 2 to cast continually in the same kind of part. **typeface** *n.* 1 the printing surface of type. 2 a design of printing type. **type founder** *n.* a person who casts types. **type foundry** *n.* (*pl.* **type foundries**). **type-high** *a.* of the standard height of type or the proper height for printing. **type metal** *n.* an alloy of lead, antimony and tin, used for making printing type. **typescript** *n.* 1 typewritten matter or form. 2 a typewritten document. **typesetter** *n.* (*Print.*) 1 a compositor. 2 a machine for setting type. **typeset** *v.t.* (*pres.p.* **typesetting**, *past, p.p.* **typeset**). **typesetting** *a.*, *n.* **type site** *n.* an archaeological site providing the representative or defining specimens of a period etc. **type size** *n.* a named size of printing type. **type specimen** *n.* (*Biol.*) the specimen on which the description of a new species is based. **typewrite** *v.i.* (*pres.p.* **typewriting**, *past* **typewrote**, *p.p.* **typewritten**) to write with a typewriter. **typewriter** *n.* a machine with keys for producing printed characters on individual sheets of paper inserted round a roller. **typewriting** *n.* **typewritten** *a.* **typist** *n.* a person who works at a typewriter, typing letters, documents etc. [F, from L *typus -um*, Gr. *tupos*, blow, stamp, character, from *tuptein*, to strike]

typhlitis (tiflī´tis) *n.* (*Med.*) inflammation of the caecum. **typhlitic** (-lit´-) *a.* [Gr. *tuphlos*, blind, -ITIS]

typhoid (tī´foid) *a.* of, relating to or resembling typhus. *~n.* 1 (*also* **typhoid fever**) an infectious fever characterized by an eruption of red spots on the chest and abdomen, severe intestinal irritation, inflammation, diarrhoea etc.; also called *enteric fever*. 2 a similar disease of animals. **typhoidal** (-foi´-) *a.* **typhoid condition, typhoid state** *n.* a state of depressed vitality characteristic of many acute diseases. [TYPHUS, -OID]

typhoon (tīfoon´) *n.* a violent cyclonic hurricane occurring in the China Seas and the West Pacific. **typhonic** (-fon´-) *a.* [Chin. *tai foong*, big wind]

typhus (tī´fəs) *n.* a contagious rickettsial fever marked by an eruption of dark purple spots, great prostration, stupor and delirium. **typhous** *a.* [L, from Gr. *tuphos*, smoke, stupor]

typical (tip´ikəl) *a.* 1 of the nature of or serving as a type. 2 representative, emblematic, symbolic (of). 3 embodying the characters of a group, class etc. 4 characteristic (of). **typicality** (-kal´-), **typicalness** *n.* **typically** *adv.* **typify** (-fī) *v.t.* (*3rd pers. sing. pres.* **typifies**, *pres.p.* **typifying**, *past, p.p.* **typified**) 1 to be a type of, to exemplify. 2 to betoken, to prefigure. 3 to represent by a type. **typification** (-fikā´shən) *n.* **typifier** *n.* [L *typicus*, Gr. *tupikos*, from *tupos*, TYPE]

typist TYPE.

typo (tī´pō) *n.* (*pl.* **typos**) (*coll.*) 1 a typographical error. 2 a typographer.

typo. *abbr.* 1 typographer. 2 typographic. 3 typography.

typography (tīpog´rəfi) *n.* 1 the art of printing. 2 the arrangement, character or appearance of printed matter. **typograph** (tī´pəgrahf) *n.* (*Hist.*) a machine used for making and setting type. **typographer** *n.* **typographic** (-pəgraf´-), **typographical** *a.* **typographically** *adv.*

typology (tīpol´əji) *n.* the study and interpretation of types, esp. those of the Bible. **typological** (-loj´-) *a.* **typologist** *n.*

tyramine (tī´rəmēn) *n.* a colourless crystalline amine found in cheese, ergot, decayed animal tissue and mistletoe, which is similar in action to adrenaline. [TYROSINE, AMINE]

tyrannical, tyrannicide etc. TYRANT.

tyrannosaurus (tīranəsaw´rəs), **tyrannosaur** (-ran´əsaw) *n.* a large flesh-eating dinosaur, *Tyrannosaurus rex*, which had small front legs and powerful hind legs. [Gr. *turannos*, a tyrant, *saura*, a lizard]

tyrant (tī´rənt) *n.* 1 an arbitrary or despotic ruler. 2 a person who uses authority oppressively or cruelly. 3 (*Hist.*) in ancient Greece, an absolute ruler who obtained power by usurpation. **tyrannical** (tiran´-) *a.* acting like or characteristic of a tyrant, despotic, arbitrary, imperious. **tyrannically** *adv.* **tyrannicalness** *n.* **tyrannicide** (tiran´isīd) *n.* 1 the act of killing a tyrant. 2 a person who kills a tyrant. **tyrannicidal** (-sī´-) *a.* **tyrannize** (tir´ə-), **tyrannise** *v.i.* to behave tyrannically, to rule despotically or oppressively (over). *~v.t.* to rule (a person etc.) despotically or oppressively. **tyrannous** (tir´ə-) *a.* **tyrannously** *adv.* **tyranny** (tir´əni) *n.* (*pl.* **tyrannies**) 1 arbitrary or oppressive exercise of power. 2 an arbitrary, despotic or oppressive act. 3 the office or rule of a tyrant. 4 the period of this. 5 harshness, severity. **tyrant flycatcher** *n.* a small bird of the family Tyrannidae. [ME *tirant*, OF *tiran*, *tirant*, L *tyranus -um*, nom. *-us*, Gr. *turannos*]

tyre (tīə), (*N Am.*) **tire** *n.* **1** an air-filled rubber casing round the outside of a wheel. **2** a strip of solid rubber or a band of metal surrounding a wheel. **tyre gauge** *n.* a device for measuring the air pressure in a tyre. [ME, perh. from *tire*, headdress]

Usage note The British spelling of the noun *tyre* (around a wheel etc.) and the verb *tire* (to exhaust) should not be confused.

Tyrian (tir´iən) *a.* **1** of or relating to ancient Tyre. **2** having the colour of Tyrian dye, purple. ~*n.* a native or inhabitant of Tyre. **Tyrian dye, Tyrian purple** *n.* a purple dye formerly prepared from shellfish, esp. species of *Murex*.

tyro (tī´rō), **tiro** *n.* (*pl.* **tyros, tiros**) (*sometimes derog.*) a beginner, a novice. [L *tiro*, a newly enlisted soldier]

Tyrolean (tirəlē´ən), **Tirolean** *a.* of or relating to the Tyrol, in Austria. ~*n.* a native or inhabitant of the Tyrol. **Tyrolese** (-lēz´), *a.*, *n.* (*pl.* **Tyrolese**).

tyrosine (tī´rəsēn, -sin) *n.* an amino acid formed by the decomposition of proteins. [from Gr. *tyros*, cheese]

†**Tyrrhene** (tir´ēn), **Tyrrhenian** (-rē´niən) *a.* Etruscan. ~*n.* an Etrurian, Etruscan or Tuscan. [L *Tyrrhēnus*, Gr. *Turrhēnos*]

tzar TSAR.

tzatziki (tsatsē´ki) *n.* a Greek dip of yogurt flavoured with cucumber, garlic etc. [mod. Gr.]

tzigane (tsigahn´), **tzigany** (tsig´əni) *n.* (*pl.* **tziganes, tziganies**) a Hungarian gypsy. ~*a.* of or relating to the Hungarian gypsies or their music. [Hung.]

tzimmes (tsim´is), **tsimmes** *n.* (*pl.* **tzimmes, tsimmes**) **1** a sweetened stew of vegetables and/or fruit. **2** (*coll.*) a fuss, a to-do. [Yiddish]

U

U[1] (ū), **u** (*pl.* **Us, U's**) the 21st letter of the English and other versions of the Roman alphabet. It has five principal sounds: (1) long, back and rounded as in *rule*, marked in this dictionary oo; (2) short, back and rounded as in *bull*, unmarked, u; (3) short, central and unrounded as in *but*, marked ŭ; (4) long, central and unrounded, where historically modified by the letter *r*, as in *bur*, marked œ; (5) diphthongal as in *due*, marked ū. In unstressed syllables it is often obscured, as in *success*, marked ə. In conjunction with other vowels *u* also represents a variety of sounds, as in *pour*, *due*, *should* etc. ~*symbol* (**u**) a factor of one millionth, micro- (originally μ). ~*n.* a U-shaped thing or part. **U-bend** *n.* a U-shaped bend, in a waste pipe etc. **U-bolt** *n.* a U-shaped bolt. **U-turn** *n.* **1** a U-shaped turn made by a motor vehicle which takes it back in the direction from which it has come. **2** a complete reversal of policy etc.

U[2] *a.* (*coll.*) (of words, phrases, behaviour etc.) associated with the so-called upper classes.

U[3] *abbr.* **1** university. **2** universal (of a film certified for viewing without age limit). **3** Uruguay (IVR).

U[4] *chem. symbol* uranium.

U[5] (ū) *n.* a Burmese (Myanmar) title of respect used before a man's name. [Burmese]

UAE *abbr.* United Arab Emirates.

UAR *abbr.* United Arab Republic.

UB40 (ūbēfaw´ti) *n.* (*pl.* **UB40s**) **1** a card issued to a person registered as unemployed. **2** (*coll.*) an unemployed person.

Übermensch (ü´bəmensh) *n.* (*pl.* **Übermenschen** (-shen)) a superman. [G]

uberty (ū´bəti) *n.* fruitfulness, fertility. **uberous** *a.* [L *ūbertas*, from *ūber*, rich, fertile]

ubiety (ūbī´iti) *n.* **1** the state of being in a particular place. **2** the relation of locality. [L *ubī*, where, -TY[1]]

-ubility (ūbil´iti) *suf.* forming nouns that correspond to adjectives in *-uble*, as *dissolubility*. [L *-ubilitas*, cp. -ITY]

ubiquitous (ūbik´witəs) *a.* **1** present everywhere or in an indefinite number of places at the same time. **2** frequently encountered. **ubiquitarian** (-teə´ri-) *n.* (*Theol.*) a believer in the omnipresence of Christ's body. ~*a.* of or relating to ubiquitarianism. **ubiquitarianism** *n.* **ubiquitary** *a.* **ubiquitously** *adv.* **ubiquitousness, ubiquity** *n.* [F *ubiquité*, from L *ubīque*, everywhere, from *ubī*, where]

-uble (ūbəl) *suf.* that can or must be, as *dissoluble*, *voluble*. **-ubly** *suf.* forming adverbs. [L *-ubilis*]

U-boat (ū´bōt) *n.* a German submarine used in World Wars I and II. [G *Unterseeboot*]

UBR *abbr.* uniform business rate.

UC *abbr.* University College.

u.c. *abbr.* upper case.

UCAS (ū´kas) *abbr.* Universities and Colleges Admissions Service (formed by the merging of UCCA and PCAS in 1993).

UCATT *abbr.* Union of Construction, Allied Trades and Technicians.

UCCA (ŭk´ə) *abbr.* (*Hist.*) Universities Central Council on Admissions (incorporated into UCAS in 1993).

UCW *abbr.* Union of Communication Workers.

UDA *abbr.* Ulster Defence Association.

udal (ū´dəl), **odal** (ō´dəl) *n.* freehold tenure based on uninterrupted possession, as in N Europe before feudalism and in Orkney and Shetland. [ON *ōthal*]

UDC *abbr.* (*Hist.*) Urban District Council.

udder (ŭd´ə) *n.* the milk-secreting organ of a cow, ewe etc., having several teats. **uddered** *a.* [OE *ūder* (cp. Dut. *uijer*, G *Euter*, Icel. *jūgr*, for *jūdr*, cogn. with L *ūber*, Gr. *outhar*, Sansk. *ūdhar*]

UDI *abbr.* unilateral declaration of independence.

udometer (ūdom´itə) *n.* a rain gauge. [L *ūdus*, wet, moist, METER[1]]

UDR *abbr.* Ulster Defence Regiment.

UEFA (ūā´fə) *abbr.* Union of European Football Associations.

UFC *abbr.* Universities Funding Council.

UFO (ūefō´, ū´fō), **ufo** *n.* (*pl.* **UFOs, ufos**) an unidentified flying object. **ufology** (ūfol´əji) *n.* the study of UFOs. **ufologist** *n.*

UGC *abbr.* University Grants Committee.

ugh (ŭkh, ŭh, uh) *int.* **1** used to express disgust or horror. **2** used to represent a grunt or a cough. [instinctive sound]

Ugli® (ŭg´li), **ugli fruit** *n.* (*pl.* **Ugli, ugli fruit**) a cross between a grapefruit and a tangerine. [UGLY, from its wrinkled skin]

ugly (ŭg´li) *a.* (*comp.* **uglier**, *superl.* **ugliest**) **1** unpleasing to the sight or ear, not beautiful (*an ugly building*; *an ugly tone*). **2** morally repulsive. **3** threatening, unpleasant (*Things turned ugly*; *ugly scenes*). **to raise/rear its ugly head** to appear, often after an absence, and start to cause problems. **uglify** (-fī) *v.t.* (*3rd pers. sing. pres.* **uglifies**, *pres.p.* **uglifying**, *past, p.p.* **uglified**) to make ugly. **uglification** (-fikā´shən) *n.* **uglily** *adv.* **ugliness** *n.* **ugly customer** *n.* an unpleasant and rather aggressive person. **ugly duckling** *n.* an unpromising person or thing that turns out surprisingly successful etc. [Icel. *uggligr* (*uggr*, fear, -LY[1])]

Ugrian (ū´griən) *n.* **1** a member of the eastern branch of the Finno-Ugric peoples, esp. the Magyars. **2** their group of languages. ~*a.* Ugric. [ORus. *Ugre*, Hungarians]

Ugric (ū´grik) *a.* **1** of or relating to the Magyars and other eastern Finnic peoples. **2** of or relating to the group of Finno-Ugric languages including Hungarian. ~*n.* the Ugric family of languages.

UHF *abbr.* ultra-high frequency.

uh-huh (ŭ´hŭ) *int.* (*coll.*) used to express assent or show understanding.

uhlan (oo´lən, ū´-) *n.* (*Hist.*) a cavalryman armed with a lance, in the old German and some other European armies. [G and Pol. *ulan*, Turk. and Tatar *oglān*, son, lad]

UHT *abbr.* ultra heat-treated (of milk).

Uitlander (āt´landə, oit´-) *n.* (*S Afr.*) a foreigner. [Dut., an outlander]

ujamaa (ujamah´) *n.* a system of village cooperatives set up by President Nyerere in Tanzania in the 1960s and designed to encourage self-reliance. [Kiswahili, brotherhood]

UK *abbr.* United Kingdom.

UKAEA *abbr.* United Kingdom Atomic Energy Authority.

ukase (ūkāz´) *n.* **1** an edict or decree of the Imperial Russian Government. **2** any arbitrary decree. [F, from Rus. *ukaz*, from *ukazat*, to show, order]

Ukrainian (ūkrā´niən) *n.* **1** a native or inhabitant of Ukraine. **2** the language of Ukraine, similar to Russian. *~a.* of or relating to Ukraine, its people or language.
ukulele (ūkəlā´li) *n.* a small four-stringed instrument resembling a guitar. [Hawaiian]
-ular (ūlə) *suf.* forming adjectives, as *corpuscular, avuncular.* **-ularity** (ūlar´iti) *suf.* forming nouns, as *angularity.* [L *-ularis*]
ulcer (ŭl´sə) *n.* **1** an open sore on the outer or inner surface of the body, often accompanied by a secretion of pus or other discharge. **2** a source of corruption or moral pollution. **ulcerate** *v.t.* to affect with or as with an ulcer. *~v.i.* to form an ulcer. **ulceration** (-ā´shən) *n.* **ulcerative** (-rətiv) *a.* **ulcered** *a.* **ulcerous** *a.* **ulcerously** *adv.* **ulcerousness** *n.* [MF *ulcere*, L *ulcus -ceris*, sore, Gr. *helkos*, wound, sore]
-ule (ūl) *suf.* forming diminutive nouns, as *globule, pustule.* [L *-ulus, -ula, -ulum*]
ulema (oo´limə) *n.* **1** a body of Muslim doctors of law and interpreters of the Koran. **2** a member of this body. [Arab., pl. of *alim*, learned]
-ulent (ūlənt) *suf.* forming adjectives meaning full of, abounding in, as *succulent.* **-ulence** *suf.* forming nouns. [see -LENT]
uliginose (ūlij´inōs), **uliginous** (-əs) *a.* growing in swampy or muddy places. [L *ūlīginōsus*, from *ūl-īgo -ginis*, moisture]
ullage (ŭl´ij) *n.* **1** the quantity by which a cask falls short of being full. **2** loss of liquid by evaporation or leakage. [Prov. *ulhage*, from *ulha*, to fill (cp. OF *euiller, ouillier*), from L *oculus*, eye, orifice]
ulmaceous (ŭlmā´shəs) *a.* of, relating to or characteristic of the elm. [L *ulmus*, elm]
ulna (ŭl´nə) *n.* (*pl.* **ulnae** (-nē), **ulnas**) **1** the longer and thinner of the two bones in the forearm. **2** (*Zool.*) a corresponding bone in an animal's foreleg or in a bird's wing. **ulnad** (-nad) *adv.* towards the ulna. **ulnar** *a.* **ulno-** *comb. form* [L, elbow, cogn. with Gr. *ōlenē*]
ulotrichan (ūlot´rikən) *a.* having tightly curled hair. *~n.* a person with such hair. **ulotrichous** *a.* **ulotrichy** (-i) *n.* [mod. L *Ulotrichi*, a classificatory term for humans having this type of hair; Gr. *oulos*, woolly, *thrix, trichos*, hair]
-ulous (ūləs) *suf.* forming adjectives, as *querulous, nebulous.*
ulster (ŭl´stə) *n.* a long, loose overcoat, usu. with a belt, made of rough cloth. [province of Ireland]
Ulsterman (ŭl´stəmən) *n.* (*pl.* **Ulstermen**) a native or inhabitant of Ulster. **Ulsterwoman** *n.* (*pl.* **Ulsterwomen**).
ult (ŭlt) *adv.* (*formal*) ultimo. [abbr.]
ulterior (ŭltiə´riə) *a.* **1** lying behind or beyond what is admitted or disclosed; hidden (*ulterior motives*). **2** more remote or distant. **3** lying beyond or on the other side of any line or boundary. **ulteriorly** *adv.* [L, comp. of *ulter*, a., whence adv. *ultra*, see ULTRA-]
ultima (ŭl´timə) *n.* the last syllable of a word. [L, fem. of *ultimus*, last]
ultimacy ULTIMATE.
ultimata ULTIMATUM.
ultimate (ŭl´timət) *a.* **1** last, final. **2** beyond which there is nothing existing or possible, incapable of analysis (*the ultimate achievement*). **3** fundamental, elementary, primary. **4** maximum (*ultimate tensile stress*). *~n.* **1** (**the ultimate**) the best achievable or conceivable. **2** something final or fundamental. **in the ultimate analysis** ANALYSIS. **ultimacy** (-əsi) *n.* (*pl.* **ultimacies**). **ultimately** *adv.* **ultimateness** *n.* [L *ultimātus*, p.p. of *ultimāre*, from *ultimus*, superl., as ULTIMA]
ultimatum (ŭltimā´təm) *n.* (*pl.* **ultimatums, ultimata** (-tə)) **1** a final proposal or statement of conditions by one party, the rejection of which may involve rupture of diplomatic relations of a declaration or war etc. **2** anything final, essential, or fundamental.
ultimo (ŭl´timō) *a.* (*formal*) in or during last month (*the 7th ultimo*).
ultimogeniture (ŭltimōjen´ichə) *n.* inheritance by the youngest son.
ultra (ŭl´trə) *a.* extreme; advocating extreme views or measures. *~n.* an extremist. [see ULTRA-]
ultra- (ŭltrə) *pref.* **1** beyond, on the other side of, as *ultramundane.* **2** beyond the ordinary limit or range of, as *ultrasonic.* **3** beyond the reasonable, excessive(ly); extreme(ly), as *ultra-efficient, ultramodern.* [L *ultrā*, beyond]
ultra- (+ a–l words) ultraconservative *a.* extremely conservative. **ultrafiche** (ŭl´-) *n.* (*pl.* **ultrafiche, ultrafiches**) a sheet of microfilm, like a microfiche but holding more microcopies. **ultra-high** *a.* (of radio frequencies) between 300 and 3000 megahertz. **ultraist** (ŭl´-) *n.* an extremist in religion, politics etc. **ultraism** *n.*
ultra- (+ m–u words) ultramicroscope *n.* a microscope with a light source at the side, for examining particles too small to be seen with an ordinary microscope. **ultramicroscopic** *a.* **1** too small to be visible under an ordinary optical microscope. **2** of or relating to an ultramicroscope. **ultramicroscopy** *n.* **ultramontane** (-mon´tān) *a.* **1** being or lying beyond the mountains, esp. the Alps. **2** supporting the supremacy of the Pope. *~n.* **1** a person who resides south of the Alps. **2** a supporter of ultramontanism. **ultramontanism** (-mon´tən-) *n.* in the Roman Catholic Church, the principle that all ecclesiastical power should be concentrated in the hands of the Pope. **ultramontanist** (-mon´tə-) *n.* **ultramundane** (-mŭn´-) *a.* external to the world or the solar system. **ultrashort waves** *n.pl.* electromagnetic waves below 10 metres in wavelength. **ultrasonic** *a.* of, relating to, or using, sound waves of higher than audible frequency. **ultrasonically** *adv.* **ultrasonics** *n.* the branch of physics dealing with ultrasonic waves and their applications. **ultrasound** (ŭl´-) *n.* **1** ultrasonic waves, used esp. for medical diagnosis. **2** sound that has an ultrasonic frequency. **ultrasound cardiography** *n.* echocardiography. **ultrastructure** (ŭl´-) *n.* the ultramicroscopic structure of an organism or cell.
ultramarine (ŭltrəmərēn´) *a.* **1** deep blue. **2** †situated, being, or lying beyond the sea. *~n.* **1** a deep-blue pigment formerly obtained from lapis lazuli. **2** a synthetic form of this made from clay, sodium carbonate, sulphur and resin. **3** the colour of this. [It. *oltra marino*]
ultra- (+ v–z words) ultraviolet *a.* of or relating to the part of the electromagnetic spectrum having wavelengths shorter than the violet end of the visible spectrum but longer than X-rays. **ultravirus** *n.* (*pl.* **ultraviruses**) a very small virus that can pass through the finest of filters.
ultra vires (ŭltrə vīə´rēz, vē´rāz) *a., adv.* beyond one's legal power or authority. [L]
ultromotivity (ŭltrəmōtiv´iti) *n.* the power of spontaneous movement or action. [L *ultro*, of one's own accord, MOTIVITY (under MOTIVE)]
ululate (ū´lūlāt) *v.i.* **1** (of a dog, wolf etc.) to howl. **2** to make a hooting cry. **ululant** *a.* **ululation** (-lā´shən) *n.* [L *ululāre*, cp. Gr. *oluluzein*, imit.]
um (əm) *int.* used to express hesitation or a pause in speaking. [imit.]
-um -IUM.
umbel (ŭm´bəl) *n.* (*Bot.*) an inflorescence in which the flower stalks spring from one point and spread like the ribs of an umbrella forming a flattish surface, as in parsley. **umbellar** *a.* **umbellate** (-lət), **umbellated** (-lātid) *a.* **umbellifer** (-bel´ifə) *n.* any plant of the Umbelliferae family, bearing umbels and including

parsley and carrot. **umbelliferous** (-lif´-) *a.* **umbellule** (-bel´ūl) *n.* any one of the small umbels making up a compound umbel. [L *umbella*, parasol, dim. of *umbra*, shade]

umber (ŭm´bə) *n.* **1** a dark yellowish-brown pigment derived from a mineral ferric oxide containing manganese. **2** a dark brown colour. ~*a.* **1** of the colour of umber. **2** dark, dusky. **burnt umber** BURN[1]. **raw umber** RAW. [F *ombre*, in *terre d'ombre*, It. *terra d'ombra*, L *umbra*, shadow]

umbilical (ŭmbil´ikəl) *a.* **1** of, relating to or situated near the navel. **2** linking. **3** inseparably connected. ~*n.* a long flexible line, tube etc. supplying or controlling something otherwise difficult to access. **umbilical cord** *n.* **1** the ropelike structure of vessels and tissue connecting the foetus with the placenta. **2** a cable carrying electricity, air etc., from a servicing point to a spacecraft, astronaut, diver etc. **umbilically** *adv.* **umbilicate** (-kət) *a.* **1** having the shape of a navel. **2** having an umbilicus. **umbilication** (-ā´shən) *n.* **umbilicus** (-kəs, -lī´-) *n.* (*pl.* **umbilici** (-sī), **umbilicuses**) **1** (*Anat.*) the navel. **2** (*Biol.*) a navel-shaped depression or other formation. **3** (*Biol.*) a depression at the axial base of some univalve shells. **4** (*Geom.*) a point through which all cross-sections have the same curvature. **5** in ancient Rome, the ornamental boss at each end of the stick on which a manuscript was rolled. **umbiliform** (-bil´ifawm) *a.* [L *umbilīcus*, navel, cogn. with Gr. *omphalos*, -AL[1]]

†**umbles** (ŭm´bəlz) *n.pl.* the entrails of a deer. [ME *noumbles*, OF *noumbles*, corr. of *lomble*, L *lumbulus*, dim. of *lumbus*, cp. HUMBLE PIE (under HUMBLE[1]), LOIN]

umbo (ŭm´bō) *n.* (*pl.* **umbos, umbones** (-bō´nēz)) **1** the boss or projecting point in the centre of a shield. **2** (*Biol.*) a boss, knob or protuberance. **umbonal, umbonate** (-ət), **umbonic** (-bon´-) *a.* [L, cogn. with *umbilīcus*, see UMBILICAL]

umbra (ŭm´brə) *n.* (*pl.* **umbras, umbrae** (-brē)) **1** the darker part of a shadow cast by an opaque object, esp. that cast by the moon on to the earth during a solar eclipse. **2** the dark central area of a sunspot. **umbral** *a.* **umbriferous** (-brif´-) *a.* giving shade. **umbrose** (-brōs) *a.* umbriferous. [L, shadow]

umbrage (ŭm´brij) *n.* **1** a sense of injury; offence (*to take umbrage*). **2** †shade. **3** †something which affords shade. **umbrageous** (-brā´jəs) *a.* shady or shaded. **umbrageously** *adv.* **umbrageousness** *n.* shadiness. [F *ombrage* from *ombre*, L UMBRA]

umbral UMBRA.

umbrella (ŭmbrel´ə) *n.* **1** a light screen of fabric, stretched on a folding frame of radiating ribs on a stick, for holding above the head as a protection against rain or sun. **2** protection. **3** an organization which protects or coordinates the activities of a number of separate groups (*umbrella group*). **4** the umbrella-shaped disc of a jellyfish etc. that enables it to move through water. **5** a screen of aircraft or of gunfire covering a military movement. **6** a general heading etc. encompassing several individual ones. **umbrella bird** *n.* a S American bird of the genus *Cephalopterus*, with a large erectile spreading crest. **umbrella bush** UMBRELLA TREE (under UMBRELLA). **umbrellaed** (-ləd) *a.* **umbrella-like** *a.* **umbrella pine** *n.* **1** STONE PINE (under STONE). **2** a Japanese evergreen conifer, *Sciadopitys verticillata*, having leaves in umbrella-like whorls. **umbrella plant** *n.* **1** a Californian plant, *Darmera peltophylla*, that thrives in marshes and has large round leaves. **2** a house plant, *Cyperus involucratus*, of the sedge family, with a ring of leaves at the top of the stem. **umbrella stand** *n.* a stand for holding umbrellas, in an entrance hall etc. **umbrella tree** *n.* **1** a small magnolia, *Magnolia tripetala*, with its flowers and leaves in an umbrella-like whorl at the ends of the branches. **2** (*also* **umbrella bush**) any of various trees or shrubs having flowers or leaves in similar formations. [It. *umbrella*, *ombrella*, dim. of *ombra*, L UMBRA]

Umbrian (ŭm´briən) *a.* of or relating to Umbria, in Central Italy. ~*n.* **1** a native or inhabitant of ancient Umbria. **2** the language of Umbria, one of the principal Italic dialects. **3** the language of ancient Umbria. **Umbrian school** *n.* a Renaissance school of painting to which Raphael and Perugino belonged.

umbriferous UMBRA.

umiak (oo´miak), **oomiac, oomiak** *n.* an Eskimo (Inuit) boat made of skins stretched on a framework, used by women. [Eskimo (Inuit)]

umlaut (um´lowt) *n.* **1** a change of the vowel in a syllable through the influence of an *i*, *r* etc. (now usu. lost or modified) in the following syllable. **2** (*Print.*) the diaeresis mark (¨) used over German vowels. ~*v.t.* to sound with or modify by an umlaut. [G *um*, about, *Laut*, sound]

ump (ŭmp) *n.* (*esp. N Am., sl.*) an umpire.

umpire (ŭm´pīə) *n.* **1** a person chosen to enforce the rules and settle disputes in a game, esp. cricket or football. **2** a person chosen to decide a question of controversy. **3** (*Law*) a third person called in to settle a disagreement between arbitrators. ~*v.t.* to act as umpire in. ~*v.i.* to act as umpire (for, at etc.). **umpirage** (-rij), **umpireship** *n.* [ME *nompere*, OF *nomper* (NON-, PEER[2]), peerless, odd, in the sense of odd man (cp. ADDER[2], APRON)]

umpteen (ŭmptēn´) *a.* very many. ~*pron.* an indefinitely large number. **umpteenth** *a.* **umpty** (ŭmp´ti) *a.* [analogy with *thirteen* etc.]

UN *abbr.* United Nations.

un-[1] (ŭn) *pref.* **1** giving a negative sense to adjectives, adverbs and nouns, as *unappealing*, *unerringly*, *unpretentiousness*. **2** denoting the reversal or annulment of an action, state or quality (sometimes ambiguous, thus *unrolled* may mean 'not rolled up' or 'opened out after having been rolled up'. **3** denoting an absence of, as *untruth*. **4** denoting dispossession or separation, as *uncrown*. **5** denoting release from something, as *unfetter*. [OE *un-* (cp. G *un-*, L *in-*, Gr. *a(n)-*)]

un-[2] (ŭn) *pref.* (*Chem.*) denoting 'one' and used in combination with other numerical roots to form names of elements based on their atomic number, as *unnilpentium*, at. no. 105.

'un (ən) *n., pron.* (*coll., dial.*) one.

un-(+a–words) unabashed *a.* not abashed; shameless. **unabashedly** *adv.* **unabated** *a.* **unabatedly** *adv.* **unable** *a.* **1** not able (to); not having sufficient power or ability. **2** †incapable, incompetent. **unabolished** *a.* **unabridged** *a.* **unabsorbed** *a.* **unacademic** *a.* **unaccented** *a.* **unacceptable** *a.* **unacceptableness, unacceptability** *n.* **unacceptably** *adv.* **unaccommodating** *a.* **unaccompanied** *a.* **1** unattended. **2** (*Mus.*) without accompaniment. **unaccomplished** *a.* **1** unfinished; not carried out or effected. **2** lacking accomplishments. **unaccountable** *a.* **1** not accountable or responsible. **2** inexplicable. **3** puzzling and strange. **unaccountability** *n.* **unaccountableness** *n.* **unaccountably** *adv.* **unaccounted** *a.* of which there is no account. **unaccounted for** not explained; not included in an account or list. **unaccredited** *a.* **unaccustomed** *a.* **1** not usual or familiar. **2** not used (to). **unaccustomedly** *adv.* **unachievable** *a.* **unacknowledged** *a.* not acknowledged, not recognized. **unacquainted** *a.* **unacquaintance, unacquaintedness** *n.* **unadapted** *a.* unfitted (for). **unadaptable** *a.* **unaddressed** *a.* (of a letter etc.) without an address. **unadopted** *a.* **1** not adopted. **2** (of a road etc.) not taken over by the local authority. **unadorned** *a.* not adorned, without decoration. **unadulterated** *a.* **1** not adulterated, unmixed. **2** pure, genuine (*unadulterated joy*). **unadventurous** *a.* **unadventurously** *adv.* **unadvertised** *a.* **unadvisable** *a.* **1** not willing to accept advice. 2 inadvisable. **unadvisability** *n.* **unadvised** *a.* 1 not having been given advice. 2 not prudent or discreet, rash. **unadvisedly** *adv.* **unadvisedness** *n.* **unaesthetic,** (*N Am.*) **unesthetic** *a.* **unaffected** *a.* 1 not influenced or affected. 2 without affectation, sincere, genuine. **unaffectedly** *adv.* **unaffectedness** *n.* **unaffectionate** *a.* **unaffiliated** *a.* **unafraid** *a.* **unaggressive** *a.* **unaided** *a.* **unalarmed** *a.* **unalienable** *a.* INALIENABLE. **unalienability** *n.* **unalienably** *adv.* **unaligned** *a.* 1 NON-ALIGNED (under NON- (+ A– WORDS)). 2 not in physical alignment. **unalike** *a.* **unalive** *a.* 1 without vitality. 2 not alive or awake (to). **unalleviated** *a.* **unallied** *a.* **unallowable** *a.* **unalloyed** *a.* 1 not alloyed. 2 sheer; utter. **unalterable** *a.* **unalterability, unalterableness** *n.* **unalterably** *adv.* **unaltered** *a.* **unamazed** *a.* **unambiguous** *a.* plain, clear. **unambiguity** *n.* **unambiguously** *adv.* **unambiguousness** *n.* **unambitious** *a.* **unambitiously** *adv.* **unambitiousness** *n.* **unambivalent** *a.* **unambivalently** *adv.* **un-American** *a.* 1 not in accordance with American ideals, characteristics etc. 2 contrary to US interests. **un-Americanism** *n.* **unamiable** *a.* **unamplified** *a.* **unamused** *a.* **unanalysable,** (*N Am.*) **unanalyzable** *a.* **unanalysed** *a.* †**unaneled** *a.* not having received extreme unction. **unanimated** *a.* **unannounced** *a.* **unanswerable** *a.* that cannot be satisfactorily answered or refuted. **unanswerableness** *n.* **unanswerably** *adv.* **unanswered** *a.* **unanticipated** *a.* **unapologetic** *a.* **unapologetically** *adv.* **unapparent** *a.* **unappealable** *a.* (*Law*) that cannot be appealed against. **unappealing** *a.* **unappealingly** *adv.* **unappeasable** *a.* **unappeased** *a.* **unappetizing, unappetising** *a.* **unappetizingly** *adv.* **unapplied** *a.* **unappreciated** *a.* **unappreciative** *a.* **unapprehended** *a.* **unapprehensive** *a.* **unapproachable** *a.* 1 that cannot be approached, inaccessible. 2 reserved, distant in manner. **unapproachability** *n.* **unapproachableness** *n.* **unapproachably** *adv.* **unappropriated** *a.* 1 not allocated. 2 not having been taken into anyone's possession. **unapproved** *a.* **unapt** *a.* **unaptly** *adv.* **unaptness** *n.* **unarguable** *a.* **unarguably** *adv.* **unarm** *v.t., v.i.* to disarm. **unarmed** *a.* **unarresting** *a.* uninteresting. **unarrestingly** *adv.* **unarticulated** *a.* **unartistic** *a.* **unartistically** *adv.* **unascertainable** *a.* **unascertained** *a.* **unashamed** *a.* 1 not embarrassed or ashamed. 2 blatant. **unashamedly** *adv.* **unashamedness** *n.* **unasked** *a.* 1 not requested. 2 not invited. **unasked-for** *a.* not requested. **unaspirated** *a.* **unaspiring** *a.* **unaspiringly** *adv.* **unassailable** *a.* 1 incapable of being assailed. 2 incontestable. **unassailability, unassailableness** *n.* **unassailably** *adv.* **unassailed** *a.* **unassertive** *a.* **unassertively** *adv.* **unassertiveness** *n.* **unassignable** *a.* **unassigned** *a.* **unassimilable** *a.* **unassimilated** *a.* **unassisted** *a.* **unassociated** *a.* **unassuaged** *a.* **unassuageable** *a.* **unassuming** *a.* not arrogant or presuming; modest. **unassumingly** *adv.* **unassumingness** *n.* **unatoned** *a.* **unattached** *a.* 1 not attached (to a club, organization etc.). 2 not married or having a partner. 3 (*Law*) (of property) not seized for debt. **unattackable** *a.* **unattainable** *a.* **unattainableness** *n.* **unattainably** *adv.* **unattempted** *a.* **unattended** *a.* 1 not attended (to). 2 not accompanied; not cared for. **unattested** *a.* **unattractive** *a.* **unattractively** *adv.* **unattractiveness** *n.* **unattributable** *a.* **unattributably** *adv.* **unattributed** *a.* **unaudited** *a.* †**unauspicious** *a.* inauspicious. **unauthentic** *a.* **unauthentically** *adv.* **unauthenticated** *a.* **unavailable** *a.* **unavailability, unavailableness** *n.* **unavailing** *a.* ineffectual; vain; useless. **unavailingly** *adv.* **unavenged** *a.* **unavoidable** *a.* 1 inevitable. 2 (*Law*) that cannot be made null and void. **unavoidableness** *n.* **unavoidably** *adv.* **unavowed** *a.* **unaware** *a.* 1 not aware, ignorant (of). 2 careless, inattentive. ~*adv.* unawares. **unawareness** *n.* **unawares** *adv.* 1 without warning; by surprise, unexpectedly. 2 undesignedly. **unawed** *a.* not full of awe; not awestruck (by).

UNA *abbr.* United Nations Association.

una corda (oonə kaw´də) *a., adv.* (*Mus.*) using the soft pedal. [It., one string]

unanimous (ūnan´iməs) *a.* 1 being all of one mind, agreeing in opinion. 2 (of an opinion, vote etc.) formed, held, or expressed with one accord. **unanimity** (-nim´-), **unanimousness** *n.* **unanimously** *adv.* [L *ūnanimus* (*ūnus*, one, *animus*, mind)]

☒ **unatural** common misspelling of UNNATURAL (under UN- (+ M–N WORDS)).

un- (+ b–c words) unbacked *a.* 1 (of a horse) not taught to bear a rider, unbroken. 2 unsupported, having no backers. 3 without a back. **unbalance** *v.t.* to throw off balance. **unbalanced** *a.* 1 not balanced. 2 in bookkeeping, not having total credit balances equalling total debit balances. 3 not mentally balanced. **unban** *v.t.* (*pres.p.* **unbanning,** *past, p.p.* **unbanned**) to remove a ban from. **unbaptized, unbaptised** *a.* **unbar** *v.t.* (*pres.p.* **unbarring,** *past, p.p.* **unbarred**) 1 to remove a bar or bars from. 2 to open, to unlock. †**unbated** *a.* unabated. **unbearable** *a.* **unbearableness** *n.* **unbearably** *adv.* **unbeatable** *a.* that cannot be beaten; unsurpassable. **unbeaten** *a.* 1 not beaten. 2 not surpassed. 3 (of a cricket player) not out. **unbeautiful** *a.* **unbeautifully** *adv.* **unbecoming** *a.* 1 not becoming, not suited (to). 2 not befitting; improper. **unbecomingly** *adv.* **unbecomingness** *n.* **unbed** *v.t.* (*pres.p.* **unbedding,** *past, p.p.* **unbedded**) to rouse from bed. **unbefitting** *a.* **unbefittingly** *adv.* **unbefittingness** *n.* **unbefriended** *a.* **unbegotten** *a.* not begotten; self-existent. **unbegun** *a.* †**unbeholden** *a.* 1 under no obligation (to). 2 unseen. **unbeknown, unbeknownst** *adv.* without the knowledge of (*Unbeknownst to us he had already left*). ~*a.* not known (to). **unbelief** *n.* lack of belief or disbelief (in, esp. divine revelation). **unbelievable** *a.* **unbelievability, unbelievableness** *n.* **unbelievably** *adv.* **unbeliever** *n.* **unbelieving** *a.* **unbeloved** *a.* **unbelt** *v.t.* to remove or undo a belt of (a garment etc.). **unbend** *v.t.* (*past, p.p.* **unbent**) 1 to change or free from a bent position; to straighten. 2 (*Naut.*) to unfasten (sails) from the yards and stays. 3 (*Naut.*) to cast loose or untie (a cable or rope). ~*v.i.* 1 to become straightened. 2 to relax from constraint, formality etc.; to be affable. **unbendable** *a.* **unbending** *a.* 1 unyielding, resolute. 2 yielding oneself to relaxation or amusement; affable. **unbendingly** *adv.* **unbendingness** *n.* **unbias** *v.t.* (*pres.p.* **unbiasing, unbiassing,** *past, p.p.* **unbiased, unbiassed**) to set free from bias. **unbiased, unbiassed** *a.* **unbiblical** *a.* not in or according to the Bible. †**unbid, unbidden** *a.* 1 not commanded; not called for; spontaneous. 2 uninvited. **unbiddable** *a.* not obedient or docile. **unbind** *v.t.* (*past, p.p.* **unbound**) 1 to untie, to unfasten. 2 to free from bonds, to release. **unbirthday** *a.* (*coll.*) (of a present) given on an occasion other than a birthday. **unbleached** *a.* **unblemished** *a.* **unblinking** *a.* 1 not blinking. 2 showing no surprise or other emotion. 3 not hesitating or wavering. **unblinkingly** *adv.* **unblock** *v.t.* 1 to remove a blockage from. 2 in a game of cards, to make possible the later unobstructed play of (a suit) by playing a high card. **unblown** *a.* 1 not blown. 2 †still in bud, not yet in flower. **unblushing** *a.* 1 not blushing. 2 shameless, barefaced, impudent. **unblushingly** *adv.* **unblushingness** *n.* **unbolt** *v.t.* to undo the bolts of; to open. **unbolted** *a.* 1 not fastened by a bolt. 2 (of flour etc.) not bolted or sifted. 3 (*fig.*) †gross, unrefined. **unbone** *v.t.* to remove the bones from (meat). **unbonnet** *v.i.* (*pres.p.* **unbonneting,** *past, p.p.* **unbonneted**) to take off one's cap or bonnet (esp. as a salutation). ~*v.t.* to remove the bonnet from. **unbookish** *a.* **unboot** *v.t.* to remove the boots of. ~*v.i.* to take off one's boots. **unborn** *a.* 1 not yet born. 2 never to come into being. **unbosom** *v.t.* (*pres.p.* **unbosoming,** *past, p.p.* **unbosomed**) 1 to disclose (one's feelings etc.). 2 (*reflex.*) to open one's heart. **unbothered** *a.* **unbound**[1] UNBIND (under UN- (+ B–C WORDS)). **unbound**[2] *a.* 1 not constrained. 2 (of a book) not bound. 3 (of a particle etc.) in a free state. **unbounded** *a.* 1 boundless, not bounded (by). 2 infinite, not subject to check or control. **unboundedly** *adv.* **unboundedness** *n.* **unbowed** (-bowd´) *a.* not bowed; unconquered. **unbrace** *v.t.* 1 to remove or relax the braces of. 2 to free from tension, to loosen, to relax. **unbraid** *v.t.* 1 to separate the strands of. 2 to unweave. **unbranded** *a.* 1 (of a product) not having a brand name. 2 (of cattle etc.) not branded. **unbreachable** *a.* **unbreakable** *a.* **unbreathable** *a.* **unbred** *a.* 1 not well bred, rude. 2 (*Shak.*) unborn. **unbribable** *a.* **unbridgeable** *a.* **unbridle** *v.t.* 1 to remove the bridle from. 2 to set free from restraint. **unbridled** *a.* 1 freed from the bridle. 2 unrestrained; unruly. **unbroken** *a.* 1 not broken. 2 not subdued. 3 uninterrupted, regular. 4 (of a horse) not broken in, not accustomed to the saddle. 5 (of a record) not bettered. **unbrokenly** *adv.* **unbrokenness** *n.* **unbrotherly** *a.* **unbrotherliness** *n.* **unbruised** *a.* **unbuckle** *v.t.* to unfasten the buckle of. **unbuild** *v.t.* (*past, p.p.* **unbuilt**) to demolish. **unbuilt** *a.* 1 not built. 2 (of land) not yet built upon. **unbundle** *v.t.* 1 to unpack. 2 to price and sell (goods or services) separately. 3 to divide (a company) into separate businesses. **unbundler** *n.* **unburden** *v.t.* 1 to free from a load or burden. 2 to relieve (oneself) by disclosure or confession. **unburdened** *a.* **unburned, unburnt** *a.* **unbury** *v.t.* (*3rd pers. sing. pres.* **unburies,** *pres.p.* **unburying,** *past, p.p.* **unburied**) 1 to remove from the ground after burial. 2 to bring (a secret etc.) into the open. **unburied** *a.* **unbusinesslike** *a.* **unbutton** *v.t.* to unfasten the buttons of. ~*v.i.* (*coll.*) to talk without restraint. **uncage** *v.t.* **uncalled** *a.* not called or summoned. **uncalled for** not necessary; not asked for; gratuitous. **uncandid** *a.* **uncanny** *a.* (*comp.* **uncannier,** *superl.* **uncanniest**) weird, mysterious. **uncannily** *adv.* **uncanniness** *n.* **uncanonical** *a.* **uncanonically** *adv.* **uncap** *v.t.* (*pres.p.* **uncapping,** *past, p.p.* **uncapped**) to remove a cap or cover from. **uncapped** *a.* (of a sportsperson) never having been selected to play for their national team. **uncared-for** *a.* not cared for; neglected. **uncaring** *a.* **uncarpeted** *a.* **uncase** *v.t.* to take out of a case or covering. **uncashed** *a.* **uncatchable** *a.* not able or likely to be caught up with. **uncaught** *a.* **uncaused** *a.* not caused; self-existent; spontaneous. **unceasing** *a.* not ceasing; incessant, continual. **unceasingly** *adv.* **uncelebrated** *a.* not publicly honoured. **uncensored** *a.* **uncensured** *a.* **unceremonious** *a.* 1 without ceremony or formality. 2 brusque, abrupt. **unceremoniously** *adv.* **unceremoniousness** *n.* **uncertain** *a.* 1 not certain or sure; doubtful. 2 not to be relied on. 3 undecided; changeable; capricious. **in no uncertain terms** forcefully and unambiguously. **uncertainly** *adv.* **uncertainty** *n.* (*pl.* **uncertainties**) 1 the state of being uncertain. 2 something that is uncertain. **uncertainty principle** *n.* HEISENBERG UNCERTAINTY PRINCIPLE. **unchain** *v.t.* **unchallengeable** *a.* **unchallengeably** *adv.* **unchallenged** *a.* **unchallenging** *a.* **unchancy** *a.* (*Sc.*) 1 unlucky. 2 unseasonable, inconvenient. 3 dangerous. **unchangeable** *a.* **unchangeableness** *n.* **unchangeably** *adv.* **unchanged** *a.* **unchanging** *a.* **unchangingly** *adv.* **unchaperoned** *a.* **uncharacteristic** *a.* **uncharacteristically** *adv.* **uncharismatic** *a.* without charisma. **uncharitable** *a.* censorious; judging harshly. **uncharitableness** *n.* **uncharitably** *adv.* **uncharted** *a.* unmapped. **unchartered** *a.* 1 not having a charter. 2 not authorized or legal. **unchaste** *a.* **unchastely** *adv.* **unchastened** *a.* **unchastity** *n.* **unchecked** *a.* 1 not checked or repressed. 2 unrestrained, uncontrolled. 3 not examined. **unchivalrous** *a.* **unchivalrously** *adv.* **unchristian** *a.* 1 not Christian; not according to or befitting the spirit of Christianity. 2 (*coll.*) outrageous. **unchurch** *v.t.* 1 to expel from a Church; to excommunicate. 2 to deprive of the character or standing of a Church. **unchurched** *a.* not churchgoing. **uncircumcised** *a.* 1 not circumcised. 2 not Jewish. 3 †heathen, unholy, profane. **the uncircumcised** (*Bible*) the Gentiles. **uncircumscribed** *a.* **uncircumstantial** *a.* not circumstantial; not given or considered in detail. **uncivil** *a.* 1 discourteous; ill-mannered. 2 not contributing to the civic good. 3 †uncivilized. **uncivilized, uncivilised** *a.* **unclad** *a.* **unclaimed** *a.* **unclasp** *v.t.* 1 to unfasten the clasp of. 2 to release from a grip. **unclassified** *a.* 1 not divided into categories. 2 (of information) not restricted. **unclassifiable** *a.* **unclean** *a.* 1 not clean. 2 lewd, unchaste. 3 not ceremonially clean. 4 (*Bible*) wicked. **uncleanly**[1] (-klēn´-) *adv.* **uncleanly**[2] (-klen´-) *a.* unclean. **uncleanliness** *n.* **uncleanness** *n.* **unclear** *a.* **uncleared** *a.* **unclench** *v.t., v.i.* **unclimbed** *a.* not ever climbed. **unclinch** *v.t.* **uncloak** *v.t.* 1 to expose. 2 to remove a cloak from. **unclog** *v.t.* (*pres.p.* **unclogging,** *past, p.p.* **unclogged**) to remove an obstruction from. **uncloister** *v.t.* to release from a cloister. **unclose** *v.t.* 1 to open. 2 to reveal. ~*v.i.* to open. **unclothe** *v.t.* 1 to take the clothes off. 2 to lay bare; to expose. **unclothed** *a.* **unclouded** *a.* 1 not obscured by clouds; clear, bright. 2 untroubled. **unclubbable** *a.* **uncluttered** *a.* **uncock** *v.t.* to let down the hammer of (a gun etc.) without exploding the charge. **uncoil** *v.t., v.i.* to unwind. **uncoined** *a.* (of metal) not coined. **uncollected** *a.* 1 waiting to be collected. 2 (of money) not claimed or collected in. 3 (of literary writings) not brought together into a collection for publication. **uncoloured,** (*N Am.*) **uncolored** *a.* 1 not coloured. 2 told with simplicity or without exaggeration. 3 impartial. **uncome-at-able** *a.* (*coll.*) that cannot be come at; not attainable. **uncomely** *a.* 1 not seemly. 2 ugly. **uncomfortable** *a.* **uncomfortableness** *n.* **uncomfortably** *adv.* **uncommercial** *a.* 1 not commercial. 2 not consistent with commercial principles or usage. **uncommitted** *a.* 1 not committed. 2 not pledged to support any particular policy, party etc. **uncommon** *a.* 1 not common, unusual, remarkable. 2 unusually great. ~†*adv.* uncommonly. **uncommonly** *adv.* remarkably, to an uncommon degree. **uncommonness** *n.* **uncommunicative** *a.* reserved, taciturn. **uncommunicatively** *adv.* **uncommunicativeness** *n.* **uncompanionable** *a.* unsociable. **uncompensated** *a.* **uncompetitive** *a.* **uncomplaining** *a.* **uncomplainingly** *adv.* **uncompleted** *a.* **uncomplicated** *a.* **uncomplimentary** *a.* **uncompounded** *a.* **uncomprehending** *a.* **uncomprehendingly** *adv.* **uncomprehension** *n.* **uncompromising** *a.* not compromising; determined; inflexible. **uncompromisingly** *adv.* **uncompromisingness** *n.* **unconcealed** *a.* **unconcern** *n.* absence of concern or anxiety; indifference; apathy. **unconcerned** *a.* 1 not concerned (in or with). 2 free from anxiety. **unconcernedly** *adv.* **unconcluded** *a.* **uncondemned** *a.* **uncondensable** *a.* **uncondensed** *a.* **unconditional** *a.* not conditional; absolute. **unconditionally** *adv.* **unconditionality** *n.* **unconditionalness** *n.* **unconditioned** *a.* 1 (of behaviour) not learned or conditioned, innate. 2 without conditions. **unconditioned reflex** *n.* an innate response to a stimulus. **unconfident** *a.* **unconfined** *a.* **unconfinedly** *adv.* **unconfirmed** *a.* **unconformable** *a.* 1 not conformable or conforming. 2 (*Geol.*) (of rock strata) consisting of layers or more recent deposits on layers of older, different rocks. 3 (*Hist.*) not conforming to the Act of Uniformity. **unconformability, unconformableness** *n.* **unconformably** *adv.* **unconformity** *n.* (*Geol.*) 1 a substantial break in the chronological sequence of rock strata. 2 the junction between the groups of unconformable strata. **uncongenial** *a.*

uncongenially *adv.* **unconjecturable** *a.* **unconnected** *a.* 1 not linked, connected or joined. 2 (of ideas etc.) disconnected. **unconnectedly** *adv.* **unconnectedness** *n.* **unconquerable** *a.* **unconquerableness** *n.* **unconquerably** *adv.* **unconquered** *a.* **unconscientious** *a.* **unconscionable** *a.* 1 not reasonable, inordinate. 2 not influenced or restrained by conscience; unscrupulous. 3 (*Law*) grossly unfair, inequitable. **unconscionableness** *n.* **unconscionably** *adv.* **unconscious** *a.* 1 ignorant, unaware (of). 2 temporarily deprived of consciousness. 3 not perceived by the mind. ~*n.* (*Psych.*) the part of the mind including instincts, impulses etc. which lies hidden from the conscious mind. **unconscious cerebration** *n.* activity of the brain leading to results without the intervention of conscious thought. **unconsciously** *adv.* **unconsciousness** *n.* **unconsecrated** *a.* **unconsenting** *a.* **unconsidered** *a.* 1 not taken into consideration. 2 (of a reply etc.) not considered; immediate. **unconsolable** *a.* **unconsolably** *adv.* **unconstitutional** *a.* not authorized by or contrary to the principles of a constitution. **unconstitutionality** *n.* **unconstitutionally** *adv.* **unconstrained** *a.* **unconstrainedly** (-nid-) *adv.* **unconstraint** *n.* **unconstricted** *a.* **unconsumed** *a.* **unconsummated** *a.* **uncontainable** *a.* **uncontaminated** *a.* **uncontentious** *a.* **uncontested** *a.* **uncontestedly** *adv.* **uncontradicted** *a.* **uncontrived** *a.* **uncontrollable** *a.* **uncontrollableness** *n.* **uncontrollably** *adv.* **uncontrolled** *a.* **uncontrolledly** *adv.* **uncontroversial** *a.* **uncontroversially** *adv.* **uncontroverted** *a.* **uncontrovertible** *a.* **unconventional** *a.* not fettered by convention or usage; unusual. **unconventionalism** *n.* **unconventionality** *n.* **unconventionally** *adv.* **unconversant** *a.* not conversant or acquainted (with). **unconverted** *a.* **unconvicted** *a.* **unconvinced** *a.* **unconvincing** *a.* **unconvincingly** *adv.* **uncooked** *a.* **uncool** *a.* 1 (*sl.*) not cool; unfashionable. 2 (of jazz) not cool. **uncooperative** *a.* **uncooperatively** *adv.* **uncoordinated** *a.* **uncopiable** *a.* **uncord** *v.t.* to take the cord from. **uncork** *v.t.* 1 to take the cork out of (a bottle). 2 to give vent to (one's feelings etc.). **uncorrected** *a.* **uncorroborated** *a.* **uncorroded** *a.* **uncountable** *a.* immeasurable; immense. **uncountability** *n.* **uncountable noun** *n.* a noun that has no plural forms, takes only a singular verb and cannot be used with an indefinite article. **uncountably** *adv.* **uncounted** *a.* 1 not counted. 2 innumerable. **uncount noun** UNCOUNTABLE NOUN (under UN- (+ B–C WORDS)). **uncouple** *v.t.* to disconnect. **uncoupled** *a.* **uncourtly** *a.* not courteous. **uncovenanted** *a.* 1 not bound by a covenant. 2 not promised or secured by a covenant. **uncover** *v.t.* 1 to remove a covering from. 2 to make known, to disclose. 3 to expose (a line of troops behind) by wheeling to right or left. ~†*v.i.* to take off one's hat in salutation. **uncovered** *a.* 1 not covered. 2 not wearing a hat, esp. as a sign of respect. **uncreate** *v.t.* (*poet.*) to blot out of existence. **uncreated** *a.* 1 not yet created. 2 existing independently of creation. **uncreative** *a.* **uncredited** *a.* not acknowledged as the originator, author etc. **uncritical** *a.* 1 not critical. 2 not according to the rules of criticism. **uncritically** *adv.* **uncropped** *a.* **uncross** *v.t.* to change from a crossed position. **uncrossed** *a.* 1 (of a cheque) not crossed. 2 not opposed. 3 not wearing a cross. **uncrowded** *a.* **uncrown** *v.t.* 1 to dethrone. 2 to take a position from (someone). **uncrowned** *a.* 1 not yet crowned. 2 having the power of royalty without the title of king or queen. 3 having high status within a particular group (*the uncrowned king of jazz*). **uncrushable** *a.* **uncrushed** *a.* **uncrystallized, uncrystallised** *a.* **unculled** *a.* not culled. **uncultivable** *a.* **uncultivated** *a.* **uncultured** *a.* **uncurb** *v.t.* **uncurbed** *a.* **uncured** *a.* **uncurl** *v.t., v.i.* **uncurtailed** *a.* **uncustomed** *a.* 1 not subject to customs duty. 2 on which customs duty has not been paid. **uncut** *a.* 1 not cut. 2 (of a book) having the margins untrimmed or not having the pages cut open. 3 (of a film etc.) not shortened or abridged. 4 (of a diamond) not shaped and faceted by cutting. 5 (of fabric) not having its pile-loops cut.

uncate (ŭng´kāt) *a.* (*Biol.*) hooked. [L *uncus*, hook]

unci UNCUS.

uncial (ŭn´shəl) *a.* 1 denoting a kind of majuscule writing somewhat resembling modern capitals, used in manuscripts of the 4th–8th cents. 2 of or relating to an inch or ounce. ~*n.* an uncial letter, style or manuscript. [L *unciālis*, from *uncia*, inch, ounce]

uncinate (ŭn´sinət) *a.* (*Bot., Anat.*) hooked at the end. **unciform** (-fawm) *a.* [late L *uncinātus*, from *uncinus*, L *uncus*, hook]

uncle (ŭng´kəl) *n.* 1 the brother of one's father or mother. 2 the husband of one's aunt. 3 (*coll.*) a name that children sometimes give to a male friend of the family. 4 (*sl.*) a pawnbroker. **Uncle Sam** *n.* (*coll.*) the government, a typical representative or the people of the US. **Uncle Tom** *n.* (*offensive*) a black man considered to be servile in his manner towards white people. [A-F (cp. F *oncle*), L *avunculus*, double dim. of *avus*, grandfather]

-uncle (ŭn´kəl) *suf.* forming nouns, esp. diminutives, as *furuncle*. [L *-unculus, -uncula*]

unco (ŭng´kō) *a.* (*Sc.*) strange, extraordinary. ~*n.* (*pl.* **uncos**) 1 a strange or surprising person or thing. 2 a stranger. 3 (*pl.*) news. ~*adv.* remarkably, very. **the unco guid** people of narrow, excessively religious outlook. [var. of UNCOUTH]

uncouth (ŭnkooth´) *a.* 1 lacking in refinement, culture or manners. 2 †unknown. 3 †wild; desolate. **uncouthly** *adv.* **uncouthness** *n.* [OE *uncūth* (*cūth*, p.p. of *cunnan*, to know, see CAN[1])]

UNCSTD *abbr.* United Nations Conference on Science and Technology for Development.

UNCTAD (ŭngk´tad) *abbr.* United Nations Conference on Trade and Development.

unction (ŭngk´shən) *n.* 1 the act of anointing with oil or an unguent, as a symbol of consecration or for medical purposes. 2 something which is used for anointing; an oil or ointment. 3 anything soothing. 4 ingratiating words; excessive flattery. 5 a quality in speech conveying deep religious or other fervour. 6 effusive or affected emotion, gush. **unctuous** *a.* 1 greasy, oily, soapy to the touch. 2 full of unction. 3 (of words, behaviour etc.) oily; full of effusive, insincere flattery. **unctuously** *adv.* **unctuousness** *n.* [F, from L *unctio -ōnem*, from *ungere*, to anoint, p.p. *unctus*]

uncus (ŭng´kəs) *n.* (*pl.* **unci** (ŭn´sī)) (*Zool., Anat.*) a hook, claw, or hooklike part or appendage. [L, hook]

un- (+ d–words) undam *v.t.* (*pres.p.* **undamming,** *past, p.p.* **undammed**). **undamaged** *a.* **undated** *a.* not marked or provided with a date. **undaunted** *a.* **undauntedly** *adv.* **undauntedness** *n.* **undead** *a.* (of a vampire, ghost etc. in fiction) dead but not at rest. **the undead** those who are undead. **undebauched** *a.* **undeceive** *v.t.* to free from deception or error; to open the eyes of. **undecidable** *a.* that cannot be settled or established. **undecidability** *n.* **undecided** *a.* 1 not decided or settled. 2 irresolute, wavering. **undecidedly** *adv.* **undecipherable** *a.* **undeclared** *a.* **undecorated** *a.* **undeeded** *a.* **undefeated** *a.* **undefended** *a.* **undefiled** *a.* not defiled; pure. **undefined** *a.* 1 not defined. 2 indefinite, vague. **undefinable** *a.* **undefinably** *adv.* **undelivered** *a.* 1 not delivered. 2 not freed. 3 (of a pregnant woman) not yet having given birth. 4 (of a baby) not yet born. **undemanding** *a.* **undemocratic** *a.* **undemocratically** *adv.* **undemonstrated** *a.* **undemonstrative** *a.* not demonstrative; reserved. **undemonstratively** *adv.* **undemonstrativeness** *n.* **undeniable** *a.* 1 not capable of being denied; indisputable. 2 decidedly good, excellent (*of undeniable character*). **undeniably** *adv.* **undenied** *a.* **undented** *a.* 1 not having any dents.

2 not adversely affected (by). **undependable** *a.* not to be depended on. **undescended** *a.* (of a testis) not having descended into the scrotum and remaining in the abdomen. **undeserved** *a.* **undeservedly** *adv.* **undeserving** *a.* **undeservingly** *adv.* **undesigned** *a.* not designed, unintentional. **undesigning** *a.* **undesirable** *a.* not desirable; unpleasant; inconvenient. ~*n.* an undesirable person. **undesirability** *n.* **undesirableness** *n.* **undesirably** *adv.* **undesired** *a.* **undesirous** *a.* **undetachable** *a.* **undetectable** *a.* **undetectably** *adv.* **undetectability** *n.* **undetected** *a.* **undetermined** *a.* 1 not determined; not fixed; indeterminate. 2 irresolute. **undeterred** *a.* **undeveloped** *a.* **undeviating** *a.* **undeviatingly** *adv.* **undiagnosed** *a.* **undid** UNDO (under UN- (+ D– WORDS)). **undifferentiated** *a.* **undigested** *a.* 1 not digested. 2 (of facts etc.) not arranged in a systematic or convenient form. **undignified** *a.* **undiluted** *a.* 1 not diluted. 2 complete (*undiluted nonsense*). **undiminished** *a.* **undimmed** *a.* **undiplomatic** *a.* **undiplomatically** *adv.* **undirected** *a.* not having a clear purpose or aim. **undiscerning** *a.* 1 lacking discernment. 2 lacking taste. **undischarged** *a.* **undiscipline** *n.* **undisciplined** *a.* **undisclosed** *a.* **undiscomfited** *a.* **undisconcerted** *a.* †**undiscording** *a.* not disagreeing or discordant. **undiscouraged** *a.* **undiscovered** *a.* **undiscoverable** *a.* **undiscoverably** *adv.* **undiscriminating** *a.* **undiscussed** *a.* **undisguised** *a.* **undisguisedly** *adv.* **undismayed** *a.* **undisputed** *a.* **undissolved** *a.* **undistinguishable** *a.* **undistinguished** *a.* **undistorted** *a.* **undistressed** *a.* **undistributed** *a.* not distributed. **undistributed middle** *n.* (*Logic*) a fallacy that arises when the middle term of a syllogism refers only to some members of a class. **undisturbed** *a.* **undiversified** *a.* **undivided** *a.* **undivulged** *a.* **undo** *v.t.* (*3rd pers. sing. pres.* **undoes,** *pres.p.* **undoing,** *past* **undid,** *p.p.* **undone**) 1 to reverse (something that has been done); to annul. 2 to unfasten, to untie. 3 to unfasten the buttons, garments etc. of (a person). 4 to bring ruin to; to destroy. **undoer** *n.* **undoing** *n.* 1 ruin or downfall; the cause of this. 2 the action of reversing something that has been done. 3 the action of unfastening. **undone** *a.* 1 not done. 2 unfastened. 3 †ruined. **undock** *v.t.* 1 to take or bring (a ship) out of dock. 2 to separate (spacecraft) in space. **undocumented** *a.* 1 not documented. 2 (*N Am.*) not having the necessary documents. **undoer, undoing** UNDO (under UN- (+ D– WORDS)). **undomesticate** *v.t.* **undomesticated** *a.* **undone** UNDO (under UN- (+ D– WORDS)). **undoubtable** *a.* **undoubtably** *adv.* **undoubted** *a.* not called in question, not doubted. **undoubtedly** *adv.* without doubt. **undrained** *a.* **undramatic** *a.* **undreamed, undreamt** *a.* not imagined or thought of (*advances undreamed of only 20 years ago*). **undress** *v.t.* 1 to remove the clothes from; to strip. 2 to take the dressing, bandages etc. from (a wound etc.). ~*v.i.* to undress oneself. ~*n.* 1 the state of being partly or completely undressed. 2 ordinary dress, as opposed to full dress or uniform. 3 informal dress. ~*a.* of or relating to everyday dress. **undressed** *a.* 1 partly or completely naked. 2 (of food) without a dressing. 3 (of leather etc.) not fully processed or treated. **undrinkable** *a.* **undue** *a.* 1 excessive, disproportionate. 2 not yet due. 3 improper or illegal. **undue influence** *n.* (*Law*) strong influence exerted over a person preventing them from exercising their free will or from considering the consequences of their actions. **unduly** *adv.* **undutiful** *a.* **undutifully** *adv.* **undutifulness** *n.* **undyed** *a.* **undying** *a.* 1 unceasing. 2 immortal. **undyingly** *adv.*

undate (ŭn´dāt) *a.* having a wavy surface, undulate. [L *undātus*, p.p. of *undāre*, to wave]

undecagon (ŭndek´əgon) *n.* a plane figure having eleven angles and eleven sides. [L *undecim*, eleven, Gr. *gōnia*, angle]

under (ŭn´də) *prep.* 1 in or to a place or position lower than, below (*It's under the chair; He crawled under the bed*). 2 at the foot or bottom of (*under the cliff*). 3 covered by, on the inside of, beneath the surface of (*She wore a T-shirt under her jumper*). 4 beneath the appearance or disguise of (*under the guise of*). 5 inferior to or less than in quality, rank, degree, number etc. (*under 30 years*). 6 subject or subordinate; governed or controlled (*to live under a dictatorship; born under Scorpio*). 7 liable to; on condition or pain of; in accordance with (*under oath*). 8 in the time of (*under the Romans*). 9 planted or sown with (a crop). 10 because of. 11 in the process of (*The building is under repair*). 12 in a group consisting of (*It comes under biochemistry*). 13 powered by (*under steam*). 14 in a game of cards, following (another player). 15 †attested by. ~*adv.* 1 in or into a lower or subordinate place, condition or degree. 2 (*coll.*) in or into a state of unconsciousness. ~*a.* lower, inferior, subordinate. **under a cloud** CLOUD. **under age** not old enough to do an activity legally. **under arms** ARM[2]. **under control** CONTROL. **under cover** COVER. **under fire** FIRE. **under foot** FOOT. **under hatches** HATCH[1]. **under offer** OFFER. **under one's arm** ARM[1]. **under one's belt** BELT. **under one's breath** in a low voice, in a whisper. **under one's feet** FOOT. **under one's hand** HAND. **under one's nose** NOSE. **under sail** SAIL. **under sentence** having received sentence or judgement. **under separate cover** in another envelope. **under siege** SIEGE. **under the counter** COUNTER[1]. **under the knife** KNIFE. **under the rose** ROSE[1]. **under the sun** SUN. **under the table** TABLE. **under the weather** WEATHER. **under water** beneath the surface of the water. **under way** WAY. **underling** (-ling) *n.* an inferior agent or assistant. **undermost** *a.* lowest in place, position, rank etc. **under-the-counter** *a.* (of black-market goods etc.) secretly obtained. [OE (cp. Dut. *onder*, G *unter*, Icel. *undir*, Swed. and Dan. *under*), cogn. with L. *infrā*, beneath]

under- (ŭndə) *pref.* 1 under, below, as *underpass*. 2 lower than in rank, position etc.; subordinate, as *under-sheriff*. 3 insufficiently, incompletely, as *underplay*, *underexpose*.

under- (+ a–s words) underachieve *v.i.* to fail to achieve as much (esp. academically) as might be expected. **underachievement** *n.* **underachiever** *n.* **underact** *v.t.* to act (a role etc.) inadequately or in a way that is too restrained. ~*v.i.* to act a role or part in this way. **underarm** (ŭn´-) *a., adv.* 1 in cricket etc., with the arm below shoulder level. 2 under the arm. 3 in the armpit. ~*n.* the armpit. **underbelly** (ŭn´-) *n.* (*pl.* **underbellies**) 1 the underside of an animal, usually its most vulnerable part. 2 any vulnerable part or aspect (of an organization etc.). **underbid** *v.t.* (*pres.p.* **underbidding,** *past, p.p.* **underbid**) 1 at an auction etc., to bid less than (someone). 2 in bridge etc., to make a bid on (one's hand) that is less than is warranted by its strength. ~*n.* 1 such a bid. 2 the act of underbidding. **underbidder** *n.* 1 the person whose bid is the next below the highest. 2 in bridge etc., a person who underbids. **underbody** *n.* (*pl.* **underbodies**) the underside of an animal, vehicle etc. **underbred** *a.* 1 ill-bred. 2 not thoroughbred. **underbrush** (ŭn´-) *n.* (*N Am.*) undergrowth. **underbuy** *v.t.* (*past, p.p.* **underbought**) 1 to buy a house at a lower price than that paid by (others). 2 to buy for less than the proper value. **undercapitalize, undercapitalise** *v.t.* to provide (a business) with less capital than that needed to operate efficiently. **undercapitalized** *a.* **undercarriage** (ŭn´-) *n.* 1 the main landing gear of an aircraft. 2 the frame supporting the body of a vehicle. **undercart** *n.* (*coll.*) the undercarriage of an aircraft. **undercharge** *v.t.* 1 to charge less than the fair price for. 2 to put an insufficient charge in (a gun, battery etc.). **underclass** (ŭn´-) *n.* a social class below the standard scale, very deprived in economic, educational etc. terms. **underclay** (ŭn´-) *n.* a bed of clay found under coal seams. **under-clerk** *n.* **undercliff** *n.* a terrace formed by material that has fallen from a cliff. **underclothes** (ŭn´-) *n.pl.* clothes worn under others, esp. next to the skin. **underclothing** *n.* underclothes in general. **undercoat** (ŭn´-) *n.* **1** a layer of fine fur underneath an animal's main coat. **2** a coat of paint serving as a base for the main coat. **3** the paint used for this. **4** a coat worn under an outer coat. ~*v.t.* to apply an undercoat of paint to. **undercoating** *n.* **undercook** *v.t.* to cook too little. **undercover** *a.* **1** done in secret. **2** engaged in espionage. **undercroft** (un´-) *n.* a vault, esp. under a church or large building; a crypt. **undercurrent** *n.* **1** a current beneath the surface. **2** an underlying tendency, influence etc. **undercut** (ŭn´-) *v.t.* (*pres.p.* **undercutting,** *past, p.p.* **undercut**) **1** to sell at a lower price than that of (a competitor). **2** to work for lower wages than (a competitor). **3** to cut away the part under (something). **4** to cut away the material beneath (a carved design) to give greater relief. **5** in golf, to hit (a ball) so as to make it rise high. ~*n.* **1** the act or effect of undercutting. **2** the underside of a sirloin. **3** in golf etc., a stroke that gives backspin to a ball. **4** (*N Am.*) a notch cut into a tree trunk to ensure that it falls in a particular direction when felled. **underdeveloped** *a.* **1** not sufficiently or adequately developed. **2** (of a country) not economically advanced. **3** (of a photograph) not sufficiently developed to give a clear image. **underdevelopment** *n.* **underdo** *v.t.* (*3rd pers. sing. pres.* **underdoes,** *pres.p.* **underdoing,** *past* **underdid,** *p.p.* **underdone**) **1** to cook insufficiently. **2** to do inadequately. **underdone** *a.* **1** insufficiently cooked. **2** not adequately done. **underdog** (un´-) *n.* **1** a person in a contest or fight who stands little chance of winning. **2** an oppressed person. **underdose**[1] *v.t.* to dose insufficiently. **underdose**[2] (ŭn´-) *n.* an insufficient dose. **underdrain**[1] (ŭn´-) *n.* a drain below the surface of the ground. **underdrain**[2] (-drān´) *v.t.* to drain using underground ditches. **underdress** *v.t., v.i.* to dress insufficiently or too plainly. **undereducated** *a.* not well educated; lacking reading and writing skills. **underemphasis** *n.* (*pl.* **underemphases**) a lack of emphasis. **underemphasize, underemphasise** *v.t.* **underemployed** *a.* not fully or adequately employed. **underemployment** *n.* **underestimate** *v.t.* to estimate at too low a level. ~*n.* an inadequate estimate. **underestimation** *n.* **underexpose** *v.t.* to expose (a photographic film) with insufficient light or for too short a time. **underexposure** *n.* **underfeed** *v.t.* (*past, p.p.* **underfed**) to feed insufficiently. **underfed** *a.* **underfelt** (ŭn´-) *n.* a felt underlay. **under-fives** *n.pl.* children of less than five years of age. **underfloor** *a.* situated or installed under the floor (*underfloor heating*). **underflow** (ŭn´-) *n.* an undercurrent. **underfoot** *adv.* **1** under one's feet. **2** on the ground. **3** in the way. **4** in a position of subjection. **underframe** (ŭn´-) *n.* **1** the underlying frame of a vehicle or railway carriage. **2** the frame under a chair seat or table top. **underfund** *v.t.* to fund inadequately. **underfunded** *a.* **underfunding** *n.* **underfur** *n.* a downy inner layer of fur underlying the outer fur of some animals. **undergarment** (ŭn´-) *n.* an item of underclothing. **undergird** *v.t.* (*past, p.p.* **undergirded, undergirt**) to strengthen or support by placing a cable, rope etc. around the underside of. **underglaze** (ŭn´-) *a.* **1** (of painting on ceramics etc.) done before the application of the glaze. **2** (of pigments etc.) suitable for painting with before the glaze is applied. ~*n.* a pigment etc. used in this way. **undergo** *v.t.* (*3rd pers. sing. pres.* **undergoes,** *pres.p.* **undergoing,** *past* **underwent,** *p.p.* **undergone**) to suffer; to endure; to bear up against. **undergrad** *n.* (*coll.*) an undergraduate. **undergrade** (ŭn´-) *a.* (of a deck bridge) having the truss below the roadway. **undergraduate** *n.* a member of a university who has not yet taken a degree. **undergraduateship** *n.* **underground**[1] *adv.* **1** below the surface of the earth. **2** into secrecy or hiding. **underground**[2] (ŭn´-) *a.* **1** situated below the surface of the earth. **2** secret; unperceived by those in authority. **3** ignoring or subversive of established trends; avant-garde. ~*n.* **1** an underground railway. **2** a secret or subversive group or organization. ~*v.t.* to lay (cables) below the ground. **undergrove** (ŭn´-) *n.* a grove overshadowed by larger trees. **undergrown** *a.* **1** not having reached the expected height. **2** having undergrowth. **undergrowth** (ŭn´-) *n.* small trees or shrubs growing under larger ones. **underhand** (ŭn´-) *adv.* **1** secretly, clandestinely. **2** slyly; unfairly; by fraud. **3** underarm. ~*a.* **1** secret, clandestine. **2** sly; unfair; fraudulent. **3** underarm. **underhanded** *a., adv.* underhand. **underhung** *a.* **1** (of the lower jaw) projecting beyond the upper jaw. **2** having the lower jaw projecting before the upper. **underinsured** *a.* **underlaid** UNDERLAY (under UNDER- (+ A–S WORDS)). **underlain** UNDERLIE (under UNDER- (+ A–S WORDS)). **underlay**[1] *v.t.* (*past, p.p.* **underlaid**) to lay something under (a thing), e.g. as a support. **underlay**[2] (un´-) *n.* **1** felt or rubber laid under a carpet. **2** a piece of paper etc. placed beneath a forme or block to bring it to the proper level for printing. **underlay**[3] UNDERLIE (under UNDER- (+ A–S WORDS)). **underlease** (ŭn´-) *n., v.t.* SUB-LEASE[1]. **underlet** *v.t.* (*pres.p.* **underletting,** *past, p.p.* **underlet**) **1** to let below the proper value. **2** to sub-let. **underletter** *n.* **underlie** *v.t.* (*3rd pers. sing. pres.* **underlies,** *pres.p.* **underlying,** *past* **underlay,** *p.p.* **underlain**) **1** to lie under or beneath. **2** to be the basis or foundation of. **3** (of a feeling, attitude etc.) to lie hidden beneath. **underline**[1] *v.t.* **1** to draw a line under, esp. for emphasis. **2** to emphasize. **underline**[2] *n.* **1** a line drawn under a word etc. **2** a caption. **underlinen** (ŭn´-) *n.* linen underclothing. **underling** UNDER. **underlip** *n.* the lower lip. **underlying**[1] *a.* **1** basic; fundamental. **2** lying beneath. **underlying**[2] UNDERLIE (under UNDER- (+ A–S WORDS)). **undermanned** *a.* having an insufficient number of crew members or members of staff. **underman** *v.t.* (*pres.p.* **undermanning,** *past, p.p.* **undermanned**). **undermentioned** *a.* mentioned below or in a later place. **undermine** *v.t.* **1** to injure or harm by secret or underhand means. **2** to weaken (one's health etc.) by imperceptible degrees. **3** (of the wind, a river etc.) to wear away the base or bottom of (a bank, cliff etc.). **4** to dig a mine or excavation under. **underminer** *n.* **underminingly** *adv.* **undermost** UNDER. **underneath** *prep.* **1** beneath, below. **2** within. ~*adv.* **1** under; beneath. **2** inside. ~*n.* an underside. ~*a.* lower. **undernourish** *v.t.* **undernourished** *a.* **undernourishment** *n.* **underoccupancy** *a.* (of a surcharge) charged to people renting holiday accommodation that is not occupied to its full capacity. **underpaid** *a.* **underpainting** (ŭn´-) *n.* **1** a layer of paint to which a subsequent layer or finishing coat is applied. **2** the application of such a layer or coat. **underpants** (ŭn´-) *n.pl.* a men's or boys' undergarment covering the body from the waist to the thighs. **underpart** (ŭn´-) *n.* **1** a lower part. **2** a less important part in a play etc. **underpass** (ŭn´-) *n.* **1** a road passing under a railway or another road. **2** a pedestrian crossing beneath a road. **underpay** *v.t.* (*past, p.p.* **underpaid**) to pay inadequately. **underpayment** *n.* **underperform** *v.i.* to perform less well than expected. ~*v.t.* to perform less well than. **underperformance** *n.* **underpin** *v.t.* (*pres.p.* **underpinning,** *past, p.p.* **underpinned**) **1** to support (a wall etc.) by propping up with timber, masonry, etc. **2** to strengthen the foundations of (a building). **underpinning** *n.* a supporting structure of masonry, timber etc. **underplant** *v.t.* to plant smaller plants around (a tall plant). **underplay** *v.t.* **1** to play down. **2** to play (a part) with deliberate restraint or subtlety. **3** to play (a part) inadequately. ~*v.i.* **1** to underplay a part. **2** to play a low card whilst one holds a higher one of the same suit. **underplot** (ŭn´-) *n.* a subordinate plot in a play, novel, etc. **underpopulated** *a.* **underpowered** *a.* **1** lacking sufficient electrical etc. power. **2** lacking sufficient authority. **underpraise** *v.t.* to praise less than is deserved. **under-prepared** *a.* **underprice** *v.t.* to price (something) at too low a level. **underprivileged** *a.* lacking the economic and social privileges enjoyed by most members of society. ~*n.* (*as pl.*) underprivileged person. **underproduction** *n.* lower or less production than the normal or the demand. **underproof** (ŭn´-) *a.* containing less alcohol than proof spirit. **underprop** *v.t.* (*pres.p.* **underpropping,** *past, p.p.* **underpropped**) **1** to prop or support underneath. **2** to support. **underquote** *v.t.* **1** to offer at lower prices than. **2** to offer (goods etc.) at lower prices than others. **underrate** *v.t.* to rate or estimate too low. **under-read** *v.i.* (*past, p.p.* **under-read**) (esp. of an instrument, gauge etc.) to give a reading that is lower than the true one. ~*v.t.* (of the reading public) to read (a book, an author etc.) with less frequency than is usual. **under-rehearsed** *a.* not well enough rehearsed. **under-report** *v.t.* to give too little press coverage to. **under-reported** *a.* **under-represent** *v.t.* to represent insufficiently. **under-represented** *a.* **underripe** *a.* **underrun** *v.t.* (*pres.p.* **underrunning,** *past* **underran,** *p.p.* **underrun**) to run beneath, to pass under. **underscore**[1] *v.t.* to underline. **underscore**[2] (ŭn´-) *n.* an underline. **undersea** *a.* below the surface of the sea. **underseal** (ŭn´-) *v.t.* to coat the exposed underparts of (a vehicle) with a corrosion-resistant substance. ~*n.* such a substance. **under-secretary** *n.* (*pl.* **under-secretaries**) **1** a senior civil servant or junior minister. **2** (*N Am.*) the principal assistant to the secretary in charge of a government department. **under-secretaryship** *n.* **undersell** *v.t.* (*past, p.p.* **undersold**) **1** to sell cheaper than (another seller). **2** to sell (an article) at less than its true value. **underseller** *n.* **under-servant** (ŭn´-) *n.* **underset**[1] *v.t.* (*pres.p.* **undersetting,** *past, p.p.* **underset**) to support underneath by a prop, masonry etc. **underset**[2] (ŭn´-) *n.* a current of water below the surface in a direction contrary to that of the wind or surface water. **undersexed** *a.* having a weaker sex drive than is considered normal. **under-sheriff** *n.* a deputy sheriff. **undershirt** *n.* (*esp. N Am.*) a vest or singlet. **undershoot**[1] *v.t.* (*past, p.p.* **undershot**) **1** (of an aircraft) to land short of (a runway). **2** to shoot something so that it falls short of or below. **undershoot**[2] (ŭn´-) *n.* the act of undershooting; an instance of this. **undershorts** (ŭn´-) *n.pl.* (*N Am.*) men's or boys' underpants. **undershot**[1] *a.* (of a water wheel) driven by water passing under it. **undershot**[2] UNDERSHOOT[1] (under UNDER- (+ A–S WORDS)). **undershrub** (ŭn´-) *n.* a plant smaller than a shrub. **underside** (ŭn´-) *n.* a lower side or surface. **undersign** *v.t.* to sign under or at the foot of. **the undersigned** the person or persons signing a document etc. **undersized, undersize** *a.* below the normal or average size. **underskirt** (ŭn´-) *n.* a skirt worn under another. **underslung** *a.* **1** (of a motor vehicle chassis) with the frame below the axles. **2** supported from above. **undersoil** (ŭn´-) *n.* subsoil. **undersold** UNDERSELL (under UNDER- (+ A–S WORDS)). **undersow** *v.t.* (*past, p.p.* **undersown**) **1** to sow land that has already been sown (with a crop) with a later-growing crop. **2** to sow (a later-growing crop) in this way. **underspend**[1] *v.i.* (*past, p.p.* **underspent**) to spend less than expected or allowed for. ~*v.t.* to spend less than (a particular amount). **underspend**[2] (ŭn´-) *n.* **1** the act of underspending or an instance of this. **2** the amount by which a particular sum is underspent. **understaffed** *a.* **understaffing** *n.* **understairs** (ŭn´-) *a.* in the space under the staircase. **understate** *v.t.* **1** to express (something) in a deliberately restrained way, often for ironic effect. **2** to represent as less, inferior etc., than the truth. **understated** *a.* restrained, simple. **understatement** (-stāt´-, ŭn´-) *n.* **understeer** (ŭn´-) *n.* a tendency in a motor vehicle to turn less sharply than expected. ~*v.i.* to have this tendency. **understood** UNDERSTAND. **understorey,** (*N Am.*) **understory** *n.* (*pl.* **understoreys,** (*N Am.*) **understories**) **1** a layer of small trees and shrubs that grows beneath the main canopy of a forest. **2** the plants, trees etc. that make up this. **understrapper** (ŭn´-) *n.* an inferior or subordinate agent. **understrength** *a.* reduced in numbers. **understudy** (ŭn´-) *v.t.* (*3rd pers. sing. pres.* **understudies,** *pres.p.* **understudying,** *past, p.p.* **understudied**) **1** to study (a part) in order to play it if the usual actor is unable to. **2** to study the acting of (an actor or actress) in this way. ~*n.* (*pl.* **understudies**) a person who understudies another. **undersubscribe** *v.t.* **undersubscribed** *a.* **undersurface** (ŭn´-) *n.*

understand (ŭndəstand´) *v.t.* (*past, p.p.* **understood** (-stud)) **1** to take in, know or perceive the meaning of (*I can't understand what he's saying*). **2** to perceive the force or significance of (*I don't understand what the fuss is about*). **3** to be sympathetic to (*I can understand your dilemma*). **4** to take as meant or implied, to gather or infer (*I understand you're looking for volunteers*). **5** to supply (a word, explanation etc.) mentally. ~*v.i.* **1** to have or exercise the power of comprehension. **2** to be informed or told (*She's in line for promotion, I understand*). **to give to understand** GIVE. **to understand each other** **1** to know and be sympathetic to each other's feelings. **2** to have an agreement with each other. **understandable** *a.* **understandability** (-bil´-) *n.* **understandably** *adv.* **understander** *n.* **understanding** *a.* **1** intelligent and perceptive. **2** sympathetic, tolerant. ~*n.* **1** the act of understanding; comprehension. **2** the power or faculty of apprehension; the faculty of thinking or of apprehending relations and drawing inferences. **3** clear insight and intelligence in practical matters. **4** a personal judgement or perception of a situation etc. **5** union of minds or sentiments, accord. **6** an informal agreement or compact. **on the understanding that** provided that. **understandingly** *adv.* [OE *understandan* (UNDER-, STAND)]

under- (+ t–z words) undertenant (ŭn´-) *n.* a tenant under another tenant. **undertenancy** *n.* (*pl.* **undertenancies**). **underthings** (ŭn´-) *n.pl.* (*coll.*) underclothes. **underthrust** (ŭn´-) *n.* (*Geol.*) a fault in which rocks on a lower plane have moved underneath a more stable upper layer. **under-timed** *a.* underexposed. **undertint** (ŭn´-) *n.* a subdued tint. **undertone** (ŭn´-) *n.* **1** a low or subdued tone, esp. in speaking. **2** an unstated meaning or emotional tone. **3** a subdued colour, an undertint. **undertow** (ŭn´-) *n.* an undercurrent flowing in the opposite direction to the current on the surface; the backward flow under waves breaking on a shore. **undertrained** *a.* **undertrick** (ŭn´-) *n.* in bridge, a trick by which a declarer falls short of making their contract. **undertrump** *v.t.* to play a lower trump than (another person or another trump played). **underuse**[1] (-ūs´) *n.* **underuse**[2] (-ūz´) *v.t.* **underutilize, underutilise** *v.t.* **underutilization** *n.* **underutilized** *a.* **undervalue** *v.t.* (*3rd pers. sing. pres.* **undervalues,** *pres.p.* **undervaluing,** *past, p.p.* **undervalued**) **1** to value at too low a level; to despise. **2** to underestimate. **undervaluation** *n.* **undervaluer** *n.* **undervest** (ŭn´-) *n.* a vest. **underwater** *a., adv.* **underwear** (ŭn´-) *n.* underclothing. **underweight**[1] *a.* of less than the average or expected weight. **underweight**[2] (ŭn´-) *n.* too little weight. **underwent** UNDERGO (under UNDER- (+ A–S WORDS)). **underwhelm** *v.t.* (*coll.*) to fail to impress, to disappoint (formed from *overwhelm*). **underwing** (ŭn´-) *n.* **1** the hind wing of an insect. **2** the inner side of a bird's feather. **3** a nocturnal moth with conspicuous markings on the hind or under wings. **underwired** *a.* (of a bra) that has a thin wire support under each cup. **underwood** (ŭn´-) *n.* undergrowth. **underwork**[1] *v.t.* to give too little work to. ~*v.i.* to work inadequately. **underwork**[2] (ŭn´-) *n.* subordinate or inferior work. **underworld** (ŭn´-) *n.* **1** the criminal class of society. **2** the nether world, the infernal regions. **3** the antipodes. **underwrite** *v.t.* (*past* **underwrote,** *p.p.* **underwritten**) **1** to execute and deliver (an insurance policy, accepting liability should certain losses occur). **2** to accept (liability) in an insurance policy. **3** to engage to buy all the stock in (a new company etc.) not subscribed for by the public. **4** to undertake the financing of. **5** to write beneath, to subscribe. ~*v.i.* to act as an underwriter of insurance policies. **underwriter** (ŭn´-) *n.*

undertake (ŭndətāk´) *v.t.* (*past* **undertook** (-tuk), *p.p.* **undertaken** (-kən)) **1** to take upon oneself, to assume, to engage in, to enter upon (a task, enterprise, responsibility etc.). **2** to engage oneself, to promise (to do). **3** to guarantee, to affirm (that). ~*v.i.* †to be guarantee (for). **undertaker** (ŭn´-) *n.* **1** a person who manages funerals. **2** a person who undertakes something. **3** (*Hist.*) a person who undertook certain political offices, esp. one of those who undertook to manage the House of Commons for the King in 1614, or one of the settlers who undertook to hold the lands forfeited to the Crown in Ireland in the 16th–17th cents. **undertaking** (ŭn´-) *n.* **1** the act of undertaking any business. **2** something which is undertaken, a task, an enterprise. **3** an agreement; a promise; a stipulation. **4** the business of managing funerals. [ME *undertaken*]

undies (ŭn´diz) *n.pl.* (*coll.*) women's underwear. [short for UNDERTHINGS (under UNDER- (+ T–Z WORDS))]

undine (ŭn´dēn) *n.* a female water spirit without a soul, but capable of obtaining one by marrying a mortal and bearing a child. [L *unda*, a wave]

und so weiter (unt zō vī´tə) *adv.* and so on. [G]

undulate[1] (ŭn´dūlāt) *v.i.* **1** to have a wavy motion. **2** (of water) to rise and fall. ~*v.t.* to cause to have a wavy motion. **undulant** *a.* undulating. **undulant fever** *n.* brucellosis in human beings, so called because the fever is intermittent. **undulation** (-lā´shən) *n.* **1** the act of undulating. **2** a wavy or sinuous form or motion; a gentle rise and fall; a wavelet. **3** a set of wavy lines. **undulatory** *a.* **1** rising and falling like waves. **2** of, relating to or due to undulation. [L *undulātus*, from *unda*, a wave]

undulate[2] (ŭn´dūlət) *a.* wavy, moving in and out or up and down. **undulately** *adv.*

undulation, undulatory etc. UNDULATE[1].

un- (+ e–g words) unearned *a.* **unearned income** *n.* income from rents, investments etc. as distinct from salary or wages. **unearned increment** *n.* an increase in the value of land or property due to increased population etc., not to labour or expenditure on the part of the owner. **unearth** *v.t.* **1** to bring to light, to find out through searching or rummaging. **2** to dig up. **3** to pull or bring out of the earth. **4** to cause (a fox etc.) to leave its earth. **unearthly** *a.* **1** not earthly. **2** not of this world, supernatural. **3** (*coll.*) ridiculous and unreasonable (*at an unearthly hour*). **unearthliness** *n.* **unease** *n.* lack of ease; anxiety; discomfort. **uneasy** *a.* (*comp.* **uneasier,** *superl.* **uneasiest**) **1** troubled, anxious or uncomfortable. **2** disturbing, disquieting. **3** awkward, stiff, constrained. **uneasily** *adv.* **uneasiness** *n.* **uneatable** *a.* **uneaten** *a.* **uneconomic** *a.* not economic, not financially viable. **uneconomical** *a.* not economical; profligate. **uneconomically** *adv.* **unedified** *a.* **unedifying** *a.* **unedifyingly** *adv.* **unedited** *a.* **uneducable** *a.* **uneducated** *a.* **unelectable** *a.* **unelected** *a.* **unemancipated** *a.* **unembarrassed** *a.* **unembellished** *a.* **unemotional** *a.* **unemotionally** *adv.* **unemphatic** *a.* **unemphatically** *adv.* **unemployed** *a.* **1** having no paid work; not in work. **2** not in use. ~*n.* (*as pl.*) people who are out of work. **unemployable** *a.*, *n.* **unemployability** *n.* **unemployment** *n.* **1** the state of being out of work. **2** the number of unemployed people in a country or region. **unemployment benefit** *n.* a regular payment by the State to an unemployed worker. **unenclosed** *a.* **unencumbered** *a.* **1** not encumbered. **2** (of an estate etc.) having no liabilities on it. **unending** *a.* having no end, endless. **unendingly** *adv.* **unendingness** *n.* **unendorsed** *a.* **unendowed** *a.* **unendurable** *a.* **unendurably** *adv.* **unenforceable** *a.* **unenforced** *a.* **unengaged** *a.* **un-English** *a.* **1** not English. **2** not characteristic of English people. **unenjoyable** *a.* **unenlightened** *a.* **unenlightenment** *n.* **unenterprising** *a.* **unentertaining** *a.* **unenthusiastic** *a.* **unenthusiastically** *adv.* **unenviable** *a.* **unenviably** *adv.* **unenvied** *a.* **unequal** *a.* **1** not equal (to). **2** uneven; varying. **3** (of a contest etc.) not evenly balanced. **unequalize, unequalise** *v.t.* to make unequal. **unequalled,** (*N Am.*) **unequaled** *a.* **unequally** *adv.* **unequipped** *a.* **unequivocal** *a.* not equivocal, not ambiguous; plain. **unequivocally** *adv.* **unequivocalness** *n.* **unerring** *a.* **1** committing no mistake. **2** not missing the mark, certain, sure. **unerringly** *adv.* **unerringness** *n.* **unescorted** *a.* **unespied** *a.* **unessential** *a.* **1** not essential, not absolutely necessary. **2** not of prime importance. ~*n.* some thing or part not absolutely necessary or indispensable. **unestablished** *a.* **unesthetic** UNAESTHETIC (under UN- (+ A– WORDS)). **unestimated** *a.* **unethical** *a.* **unethically** *adv.* **unevangelical** *a.* **uneven** *a.* **1** not even, level or smooth. **2** not uniform, regular or equable. **3** (of a contest etc.) not equal. **unevenly** *adv.* **unevenness** *n.* **uneventful** *a.* **uneventfully** *adv.* **uneventfulness** *n.* **unexamined** *a.* **unexampled** *a.* having no parallel; unprecedented. **unexcelled** *a.* **unexceptionable** *a.* to which no exception can be taken; unobjectionable; faultless. **unexceptionableness** *n.* **unexceptionably** *adv.* **unexceptional** *a.* not exceptional, ordinary. **unexceptionally** *adv.* **unexcitable** *a.* **unexcitability** *n.* **unexciting** *a.* **unexecuted** *a.* **unexercised** *a.* **unexhausted** *a.* **1** not used up. **2** not emptied. **unexpected** *a.* **unexpectedly** *adv.* **unexpectedness** *n.* **unexpiated** *a.* **unexpired** *a.* not having come to an end or termination. **unexplainable** *a.* **unexplainably** *adv.* **unexplained** *a.* **unexploded** *a.* **unexploited** *a.* **unexplored** *a.* **unexposed** *a.* **unexpressed** *a.* **unexpressive** *a.* **unexpurgated** *a.* **unextended** *a.* not extended. **unextinguishable** *a.* INEXTINGUISHABLE. **unfadable** *a.* **unfading** *a.* **unfadingly** *adv.* **unfailing** *a.* **1** not liable to fail or run short. **2** unerring, infallible. **3** reliable, certain. **unfailingly** *adv.* **unfailingness** *n.* **unfair** *a.* **1** not equitable; not impartial. **2** dishonourable, fraudulent. **unfairly** *adv.* **unfairness** *n.* **unfaithful** *a.* **1** not faithful to a promise, vow etc. **2** adulterous. **unfaithfully** *adv.* **unfaithfulness** *n.* **unfamiliar** *a.* **unfamiliarity** *n.* **unfamiliarly** *adv.* **unfancied** *a.* (of a racehorse etc.) not thought likely to win. **unfashionable** *a.* **unfashionableness** *n.* **unfashionably** *adv.* **unfashioned** *a.* **1** not fashioned by art. **2** shapeless. **unfasten** *v.t.* **unfastened** *a.* **1** not fastened. **2** that has been loosened, untied or opened. **unfathered** *a.* **1** fatherless; having no acknowledged father. **2** having no known source or origin. **unfatherly** *a.* **unfatherliness** *n.* **unfathomable** *a.* **unfathomableness** *n.* **unfathomably** *adv.* **unfathomed** *a.* **1** of unknown depth. **2** not completely explored or known. **unfatigued** *a.* not fatigued or tired. **unfavourable,** (*N Am.*) **unfavorable** *a.* **unfavourableness** *n.* **unfavourably** *adv.* **unfazed** *a.* (*coll.*) not troubled or perturbed. **unfeasible** *a.* **unfeasibility** *n.* **unfeasibly** *adv.* **unfed** *a.* **unfeeling** *a.* **1** insensible. **2** hard-hearted, unsympathetic towards others. **unfeelingly** *adv.* **unfeelingness** *n.* **unfeigned** *a.* **unfeignedly** *adv.* **unfelt** *a.* **unfeminine** *a.* **unfemininity** *n.* **unfenced** *a.* **1** not enclosed by a fence. **2** not fortified. **unfermented** *a.*

unfertilized, unfertilised *a.* **unfetter** *v.t.* to free from fetters or restraint. **unfettered** *a.* **unfilial** *a.* **unfilially** *adv.* **unfilled** *a.* **unfiltered** *a.* **unfinished** *a.* **1** not finished, incomplete. **2** not having been through a finishing process. **unfit** *a.* **1** not fit (to do, to be, for etc.). **2** unsuitable (for). **3** not in good physical condition. ~*v.t.* (*pres.p.* **unfitting,** *past, p.p.* **unfitted**) to make unfit or unsuitable. **unfitly** *adv.* **unfitness** *n.* **unfitted** *a.* **1** not fitted. **2** unfit. **3** not fitted up, not furnished with fittings. **unfitting** *a.* **unfittingly** *adv.* **unfix** *v.t.* **unfixed** *a.* **unflagging** *a.* **unflaggingly** *adv.* **unflamed** *a.* **unflappable** *a.* (*coll.*) not readily upset or agitated, imperturbable. **unflappability** *n.* **unflattering** *a.* **unflatteringly** *adv.* **unflavoured,** (*N Am.*) **unflavored** *a.* **unfledged** *a.* **1** (of a bird) not yet fledged. **2** inexperienced and immature. **unfleshed** *a.* **1** not covered with flesh. **2** that has had its flesh removed. **unflinching** *a.* **unflinchingly** *adv.* **unfocused, unfocussed** *a.* **unfold** *v.t.* **1** to open the folds of; to spread out. **2** to discover; to reveal. ~*v.i.* **1** to spread open; to expand. **2** to develop. **unfoldment** *n.* (*N Am.*) **unforced** *a.* **1** not forced, not constrained. **2** natural, easy. **unforcedly** *adv.* **unfordable** *a.* **unforeseeable** *a.* **unforeseen** *a.* **unforetold** *a.* **unforgettable** *a.* that cannot be forgotten; highly memorable. **unforgettably** *adv.* **unforgivable** *a.* **unforgivably** *adv.* **unforgiven** *a.* **unforgiving** *a.* **unforgivingly** *adv.* **unforgivingness** *n.* **unforgotten** *a.* **unformed** *a.* **1** not formed. **2** shapeless, amorphous, structureless. **3** not yet fully developed, immature. **unformulated** *a.* **unforthcoming** *a.* **unfortified** *a.* **unfortunate** *a.* **1** not fortunate, unlucky. **2** unhappy. **3** regrettable. **4** unsuccessful; disastrous. ~*n.* a person who is unfortunate. **unfortunately** *adv.* **1** unluckily. **2** I'm sorry to say. **3** in an unfortunate manner. **unfound** *a.* **unfounded** *a.* **1** having no foundation in fact or reason, groundless. **2** not yet established. **unframed** *a.* (of a picture etc.) not set in a frame. **unfree** *a.* **unfreedom** *n.* **unfreeze** *v.t.* (*past* **unfroze,** *p.p.* **unfrozen**) **1** to cause to thaw. **2** to relax restrictions on (assets, credit etc.). ~*v.i.* to thaw. **unfrequent** *a.* **unfriended** *a.* without a friend or friends. **unfriendly** *a.* (*comp.* **unfriendlier,** *superl.* **unfriendliest**) not friendly. **unfriendliness** *n.* **unfrock** *v.t.* to deprive of the character and privileges of a priest. **unfroze, unfrozen** UNFREEZE (under UN- (+ E–G WORDS)). **unfruitful** *a.* **1** not productive or producing good results. **2** not producing fruit. **unfruitfully** *adv.* **unfruitfulness** *n.* **unfulfillable** *a.* **unfulfilled** *a.* **unfulfilling** *a.* **unfunded** *a.* (of a debt) not funded, floating. **unfunny** *a.* (*comp.* **unfunnier,** *superl.* **unfunniest**) not funny. **unfunnily** *adv.* **unfunniness** *n.* **unfurl** *v.t.* to open or spread out (a sail, banner etc.). ~*v.i.* to be opened and spread out. **unfurnished** *a.* **1** not provided (with). **2** without furniture. **unfussy** *a.* **ungallant** *a.* **ungallantly** *adv.* **ungenerous** *a.* **ungenerously** *adv.* **ungenerousness** *n.* **ungenial** *a.* **ungentle** *a.* not gentle. **ungentleness** *n.* **ungently** *adv.* **ungentlemanly** *a.* not becoming a gentleman; rude, ill-bred. **ungentlemanliness** *n.* **unget-at-able** *a.* (*coll.*) difficult of access. **ungifted** *a.* **ungird** *v.t.* (*past, p.p.* **ungirded, ungirt**) **1** to undo or remove a girdle from. **2** to remove by unfastening a girdle or belt. **unglamorous** *a.* **unglaze** *v.t.* to deprive of glazing. **unglazed** *a.* **unglue** *v.t.* (*3rd pers. sing. pres.* **unglues,** *pres.p.* **ungluing, unglueing,** *past, p.p.* **unglued**). **ungodly** *a.* **1** not godly; wicked. **2** (*coll.*) outrageous (*at an ungodly hour of the night*). **ungodliness** *n.* **ungovernable** *a.* not governable; unruly; wild. **ungovernability** *n.* **ungovernably** *adv.* **ungraceful** *a.* **ungracefully** *adv.* **ungracefulness** *n.* **ungracious** *a.* **1** discourteous; unkind. **2** not attractive. **ungraciously** *adv.* **ungraciousness** *n.* **ungrammatical** *a.* not according to the rules of grammar. **ungrammaticality** *n.* **ungrammatically** *adv.* **ungrammaticalness** *n.* **ungraspable** *a.* **ungrateful** *a.* **1** not thankful. **2** unpleasant; unrewarding. **ungratefully** *adv.* **ungratefulness** *n.* **ungreen** *a.* **1** not supporting environmental conservation. **2** not environmentally-friendly. **ungrounded** *a.* **1** unfounded, baseless. **2** not earthed. **3** not having a good grounding (in a subject). **4** (of an aeroplane, ship etc.) not grounded. **ungrudging** *a.* **ungrudgingly** *adv.* **unguard** *v.t.* in cards, to leave (a high card) unprotected by discarding a low card. **unguarded** *a.* **1** not guarded. **2** careless, incautious. **unguardedly** *adv.* **unguardedness** *n.* **ungum** *v.t.* (*pres.p.* **ungumming,** *past, p.p.* **ungummed**) **1** to loosen (a thing fastened with gum). **2** to remove the gum from.

☒ **unecessary** common misspelling of UNNECESSARY (under UN- (+ M–N WORDS)).

ungainly (ŭngān´li) *a.* (*comp.* **ungainlier,** *superl.* **ungainliest**) clumsy, awkward. **ungainliness** *n.* [ME *ungeniliche* (Icel. *gegn*, serviceable, earlier *gain*, neat, straight, -LY[1])]

ungual UNGUIS.

unguent (ŭng´gwənt) *n.* any soft composition used as an ointment or for lubrication. **unguentary** (ŭng·gwen´-) *a.* [L *unguentum*, from *unguere*, to anoint, pres.p. *unguens -entis*]

unguis (ŭng´gwis) *n.* (*pl.* **ungues** (-gwēz)) **1** a nail or claw. **2** the narrow base of a petal. **ungual** *a.* of or relating to or having a nail or claw. **unguiculate** (-gwik´ūlət) *a.* **1** having claws or nails. **2** (of petals) having an unguis. [L *unguis*]

ungula (ŭng´gūlə) *n.* (*pl.* **ungulae** (-lē)) **1** a hoof, claw or talon. **2** (*Math.*) the portion of a cone or cylinder included between the base and a plane intersecting it obliquely. **ungular** *a.* **ungulate** (-lət) *a.* hoofed. ~*n.* an ungulate animal. [L, dim. of *unguis*, see UNGUIS]

un- (+ h–i words) unhackneyed *a.* **unhair** *v.t.* †**unhallow** *v.t.* to profane, to desecrate. **unhallowed** *a.* **1** unconsecrated. **2** unholy, profane. **unhampered** *a.* **unhand** *v.t.* (*formal or facet.*) **1** to take one's hand or hands off. **2** to let go from one's grasp. **unhandsome** *a.* not handsome. **unhandsomely** *adv.* **unhandsomeness** *n.* **unhandy** *a.* **1** not skilful with one's hands. **2** clumsy, awkward, inconvenient. **unhandily** *adv.* **unhandiness** *n.* **unhang** *v.t.* (*past, p.p.* **unhung**) to take from a hanging position. **unhanged** *a.* **unhappy** *a.* (*comp.* **unhappier,** *superl.* **unhappiest**) **1** not happy, miserable, wretched. **2** unlucky, unfortunate. **3** inappropriate. **4** causing bad luck. **5** disastrous. **6** not propitious. **unhappily** *adv.* **unhappiness** *n.* **unharbour,** (*N Am.*) **unharbor** *v.t.* to dislodge (a deer) from a shelter. **unharmed** *a.* **unharmful** *a.* **unharmonious** *a.* **unharness** *v.t.* to remove a harness from. **unhasp** *v.t.* to unfasten from a hasp. **unhatched** *a.* (of eggs) not hatched. **unhealthful** *a.* **unhealthfulness** *n.* **unhealthy** *a.* (*comp.* **unhealthier,** *superl.* **unhealthiest**) **1** not enjoying or promoting good health. **2** (*coll.*) dangerous. **unhealthily** *adv.* **unhealthiness** *n.* **unheard** *a.* not heard. **unheard-of** *a.* not heard of; unprecedented. **unheated** *a.* **unhedged** *a.* **1** not bordered by a hedge. **2** (of a bet or speculation) not hedged. **unheeded** *a.* **unheedful** *a.* **unheeding** *a.* **unheedingly** *adv.* **unhelm** *v.t.* to divest of a helm or helmet. **unhelpful** *a.* **unhelpfully** *adv.* **unhelpfulness** *n.* **unheralded** *a.* **unheroic** *a.* **unheroically** *adv.* **unhesitating** *a.* **unhesitatingly** *adv.* **unhesitatingness** *n.* **unhindered** *a.* **unhinge** *v.t.* **1** to take (a door) off the hinges. **2** to unsettle (the mind etc.). **unhinged** *a.* **unhistoric** *a.* **unhistorical** *a.* **unhistorically** *adv.* **unhitch** *v.t.* to unfasten or release from a hitched state. **unholy** *a.* (*comp.* **unholier,** *superl.* **unholiest**) **1** not holy, not hallowed. **2** impious, wicked. **3** (*coll.*) hideous, frightful. **unholily** *adv.* **unholiness** *n.* **unhonoured,** (*N Am.*) **unhonored** *a.* **unhood** *v.t.* to remove a hood from. **unhook** *v.t.* **1** to remove from a hook. **2** to open or undo by disengaging the hooks of. **unhoped** *a.* not hoped (for). **unhorse** *v.t.* **1** to remove from horseback. **2** (of a horse) to throw (a rider). **3** to dislodge, e.g. from a powerful position. **4** to take horses from (a carriage). **unhouse** *v.t.* **1** to drive from a house. **2** to deprive of shelter. †**unhouseled** *a.* not having received the Eucharist. **unhuman** *a.* **1** not human. **2** superhuman. **3** inhuman, savage. **unhung**[1] *a.* **1** not hung. **2** (of paintings etc.) not hung up. **unhung**[2] UNHANG (under UN- (+ H–I WORDS)). **unhurried** *a.* **unhurriedly** *adv.* **unhurt** *a.* **unhusk** *v.t.* to remove a husk from. **unhygienic** *a.* **unhygienically** *adv.* **unhyphenated** *a.* **unidea'd** *a.* not having any ideas. **unidentifiable** *a.* **unidentified** *a.* **unilluminated** *a.* **1** not illuminated; dark. **2** ignorant. **unillustrated** *a.* **unimaginable** *a.* that cannot be imagined; inconceivable. **unimaginably** *adv.* **unimaginative** *a.* **unimaginatively** *adv.* **unimaginativeness** *n.* **unimagined** *a.* **unimpaired** *a.* **unimpassioned** *a.* **unimpeachable** *a.* beyond reproach; blameless. **unimpeachably** *adv.* **unimpeded** *a.* **unimpededly** *adv.* **unimportant** *a.* **unimportance** *n.* **unimposing** *a.* **unimposingly** *adv.* **unimpressed** *a.* **unimpressionable** *a.* **unimpressive** *a.* **unimpressively** *adv.* **unimpressiveness** *n.* **unimproved** *a.* **1** not improved. **2** (of land) not tilled, cultivated, drained etc. **3** (of resources etc.) not made use of. **unincorporated** *a.* **1** not having corporate status. **2** not incorporated. **unindexed** *a.* **unindicated** *a.* **uninfected** *a.* **uninflamed** *a.* **uninflammable** *a.* **uninflected** *a.* **1** (of a language) not inflected. **2** not varying. **3** not deflected. **uninfluenced** *a.* **uninfluential** *a.* **uninformative** *a.* **uninformed** *a.* **1** not informed (about). **2** ignorant generally. **uninhabitable** *a.* **uninhabitableness** *n.* **uninhabited** *a.* **uninhibited** *a.* **uninhibitedly** *adv.* **uninhibitedness** *n.* **uninitiated** *a.* **uninjured** *a.* **uninspired** *a.* **uninspiring** *a.* **uninspiringly** *adv.* **uninstructed** *a.* **uninstructive** *a.* **uninsulated** *a.* **uninsurable** *a.* **uninsured** *a.* **unintelligent** *a.* **unintelligently** *adv.* **unintelligible** *a.* **unintelligibility** *n.* **unintelligibleness** *n.* **unintelligibly** *adv.* **unintended** *a.* **unintentional** *a.* **unintentionally** *adv.* **uninterested** *a.* **1** not taking any interest (in). **2** indifferent; unconcerned. **uninteresting** *a.* **uninterestingly** *adv.* **uninterestingness** *n.* **uninterpretable** *a.* **uninterrupted** *a.* **uninterruptedly** *adv.* **uninterruptedness** *n.* **uninterruptible** *a.* **uninventive** *a.* **uninventively** *adv.* **uninventiveness** *n.* **uninvestigated** *a.* **uninvited** *a.* **uninvitedly** *adv.* **uninviting** *a.* not inviting, not attractive, repellent. **uninvitingly** *adv.* **uninvoked** *a.* **uninvolved** *a.* **unissued** *a.* not issued.

uni (ū´ni) *n.* (*pl.* **unis**) (*coll.*) a university. [abbr.]

uni- (ūni) *comb.form* one, single, as *unisex, unipolar.* [L *unus*]

uni- (+ a–c words) uniaxial *a.* having a single axis. **uniaxially** *adv.* **unicameral** *a.* (of a legislative body) consisting of a single chamber. **unicameralism** *n.* **unicameralist** *n.* **unicellular** *a.* consisting of a single cell. **unicolour, unicoloured,** (*N Am.*) **unicolor, unicolored** *a.* of one colour. **unicostate** *a.* (*Biol.*) having one principal rib or nerve. **unicuspid** *a.* one-cusped. ~*n.* a unicuspid tooth. **unicycle** (ū´ni-) *n.* a one-wheeled cycle, esp. used by circus performers. **unicyclist** *n.*

Uniate (ū´niāt), **Uniat** (-ət) *n.* a member of any of the Eastern Churches acknowledging the supremacy of the Pope but retaining their own liturgy, rites and ceremonies. ~*a.* of or relating to the Uniates. [Rus. *uniyat,* from *uniya,* union, from L *unio*]

UNICEF (ū´nisef) *abbr.* United Nations Children's Fund (formerly United Nations International Children's Emergency Fund).

unicorn (ū´nikawn) *n.* **1** a fabulous animal like a horse, but with a long, straight, tapering horn. **2** (*Her.*) a one-horned horse with a goat's beard and lion's tail. **3** (*Bible*) a two-horned animal, perh. the urus (a mistranslation of Heb. *re'em*). **4** a coaching-team consisting of a pair of horses with a third horse in front. [A-F *unicorne,* L *ūnicorne* (UNI -, *cornu,* horn)]

uni- (+ d–f words) unidimensional *a.* having only one dimension. **unidirectional** *a.* moving, operating etc. in only one direction. **unidirectionality** *n.* **unidirectionally** *adv.* **uniflorous** *a.* bearing only a single flower. **uniflow** (ū´ni-) *a.* involving only one direction of flow. **unifoliar** *a.* **unifoliate, unifoliolate** *a.* consisting of one leaf or leaflet.

unification, unifier etc. UNIFY.

uniform (ū´nifawm) *a.* **1** having an unchanging form, appearance, quality, character etc.; the same, not varying, not changing. **2** conforming to one rule or standard applying or operating without variation with time or place. ~*n.* clothing of the same kind and appearance as that worn by other members of the same body, esp. the regulation dress of soldiers, sailors etc. ~*v.t.* to make uniform. **uniformed** *a.* dressed in uniform. **uniformitarian** (-teə´ri-) *n.* a person who believes that there has been essential uniformity of cause and effect throughout the physical history of the world. ~*a.* of or relating to this theory. **uniformitarianism** *n.* **uniformity** (-faw´-) *n.* (*pl.* **uniformities**) the quality or state of being uniform; consistency, sameness. **uniformly** *adv.* [F *uniforme,* L *ūniformis* (UNI-, -FORM)]

unify (ū´nifī) *v.t.* (*3rd pers. sing. pres.* **unifies,** *pres.p.* **unifying,** *past, p.p.* **unified**) **1** to make one. **2** to regard as one. **3** to reduce to uniformity. **unifiable** *a.* **unification** (-fikā´shən) *n.* **Unification Church** *n.* a religious organization founded in 1954 by the Korean, Sun Myung Moon. **unificatory** *a.* **unified field theory** *n.* (*Physics*) a theory that seeks to unify into one framework all field theories, esp. those relating to gravitation and electromagnetism. **unifier** *n.* [med. L *ūnificāre* (UNI-, L *-ficāre, facere,* to make)]

uni- (+ l–o words) unilabiate *a.* (of flowers) having a single lip. **unilateral** *a.* **1** applied by or affecting one side or party only. **2** of, occurring on or restricted to one side only. **3** (*Bot.*) arranged on or turned towards one side only. **4** (of a line of descent) traced through ancestors of one sex only. **unilateralism** *n.* **1** unilateral action; esp. unilateral disarmament. **2** (*esp. N Am.*) the pursuit of an independent foreign policy. **unilateralist** *n.* **unilaterally** *adv.* **unilingual** *a.* of, having or in only one language. **unilingually** *adv.* **uniliteral** *a.* consisting of only one letter. **unilocular** *a.* having or consisting of a single cell or chamber. **uninucleate** *a.* having only one nucleus. **uniovular** (ūniov´ūlə) *a.* of, relating to or developed from one ovum.

union (ūn´yən) *n.* **1** the act of uniting; the state of being united. **2** a combination of parts or members forming a whole; an amalgamation; a confederation or league. **3** the political unit formed by such a combination, esp. the UK or US. **4** a trade union. **5** agreement or concord of mind, will, affection, or interests. **6** marriage. **7** (**Union**) a students' club at some universities; the building housing such a club. **8** (**the Union**) the uniting of the English and Scottish crowns (1603), of England and Scotland (1707), or of England and Ireland (1801). **9** (**the Union**) the northern states of the US in the American Civil War. **10** (*Math.*) a set containing all the members of two or more sets. **11** (*Hist.*) two or more parishes consolidated for administration of the Poor Laws. **12** (*Hist.*) UNION WORKHOUSE (under UNION). **13** an association of non-conformist (esp. Congregational or Baptist) Churches for cooperative action or management. **14** in plumbing, a device for connecting pipes. **15** a fabric made of two different yarns, such as linen and cotton. **16** a device emblematic of union borne in the upper corner next to the staff of a flag. **17** (*Med.*) the growing together of parts separated by injury. **union-bashing** *n.* (*coll.*) the activity of severely criticizing trade unions. **union catalogue,** (*NAm.*) **union catalog** *n.* a catalogue listing the combined holdings of a number of libraries. **union down** *adv.* (of the raising of a flag) with the union below as a token of mourning or as a signal of distress. **Union flag** *n.* the national flag of the United Kingdom composed of the crosses of St George, St Andrew and St Patrick. **unionism** *n.* **unionist** *n.* 1 a member of a trade union. 2 a promoter or advocate of trade unionism. 3 (*usu.* **Unionist**) a member of a political party formed to uphold the legislative union between Great Britain and Northern Ireland (before 1920 Great Britain and Ireland). 4 (*usu.* **Unionist**) an opponent of secession before and during the American Civil War. **unionistic** (-nis´-) *a.* **unionize, unionise** *v.t.* to organize into a trade union. ~*v.i.* to become organized into a trade union. **unionization** *n.* **Union Jack** *n.* 1 UNION FLAG (under UNION). 2 (**union jack**) in the US, a ship's flag consisting only of a union. **Union of Soviet Socialist Republics** *n.* (*Hist.*) the official title of the former Soviet Union. **union shop** *n.* a factory, office etc. in which employees must belong to a trade union or join one within a specified time period. **union suit** *n.* (*N Am.*) an undergarment combining vest and long pants; men's combinations. **union workhouse** *n.* (*Hist.*) a workhouse established by two or more parishes for administration of the poor laws. [F, from late L *unio -ōnem*, from *ūnus*, one]

uni- (+ p– words) uniparous (ūnip´ərəs) *a.* 1 (of a woman, of certain animals) producing a single offspring at a birth. 2 (*Bot.*) having one axis or stem. **uniped** (ū´niped) *a.* having only one foot. ~*n.* a one-footed person or animal. **unipersonal** *a.* 1 (*Theol.*) (of God) existing in the form of only one person. 2 (*Gram.*) (of a verb) used only in one person. **uniplanar** *a.* lying or occurring in one plane. **unipod** (ū´ni-) *n.* a one-legged support, e.g. for a camera. **unipolar** *a.* 1 (of nerve-cells etc.) having only one process. 2 exhibiting only one kind of polarity. **unipolarity** *n.*

unique (ūnēk´) *a.* 1 having no like or equal; unmatched, unparalleled. 2 very unusual or remarkable, extraordinary. **uniquely** *adv.* **uniqueness** *n.* [F, from L *ūnicus*, from *ūnus*, one]

Usage note It is best to avoid uses of *unique* which imply or allow more than one (for example with qualifying adverbs, as *most unique*, or simply with the meaning extraordinary).

uni- (+ s– words) uniserial *a.* (*Bot.*) arranged in one row. **unisex** (ū´ni-) *a.* that can be used, worn, etc. by both sexes. **unisexual** (-sek´-) *a.* 1 of one sex only. 2 having either stamens or pistils. 3 unisex. **unisexuality** *n.* **unisexually** *adv.* **unisulcate** *a.* having only one groove or furrow.

UNISON (ū´nisən) *n.* a trade union for employees in the public services, formed in 1993 from an amalgamation of COHSE, NALGO and NUPE.

unison (ū´nisən) *n.* 1 (*Mus.*) coincidence of sounds proceeding from equality in rate of vibrations; unity of pitch. 2 an interval of one or more octaves. 3 the act or state of sounding together at the same pitch (*to sing in unison*). 4 concord, agreement, harmony. ~*a.* sounding together; coinciding in pitch. **unisonal** (-nis´-), **unisonant, unisonous** *a.* **unison string** *n.* a string tuned to the same pitch as another and intended to be sounded with it. [MF *unisson*, med. L *ūnisonus* (UNI-, *sonus*, SOUND[1])]

unit (ū´nit) *n.* 1 a single person, thing, or group, regarded as one and complete for the purposes of calculation. 2 each one of a number of things, persons etc., forming a plurality. 3 a quantity adopted as the standard of measurement or calculation. 4 a part of a machine which performs a particular function. 5 a piece of furniture which forms part of a set, designed for a particular use in a kitchen etc. 6 a group of workers that has a particular job in an organization. 7 a part of a larger military formation. 8 a quantity of a drug, vitamin etc., which produces a specific effect. 9 the smallest share in a unit trust. 10 a group of buildings in a hospital with a particular function (*the burns unit*). 11 the number one. **Unitarian** (-teə´ri-) *n.* a member of a Christian body that rejects the doctrine of the Trinity and believes that God is one person. ~*a.* of or relating to the Unitarians. **Unitarianism** *n.* **unitary** *a.* 1 of or relating to a unit or units. 2 of the nature of a unit, whole, integral. **unitarily** *adv.* **unit cell** *n.* in crystallography, the smallest group of atoms, ions or molecules which characterizes the lattice of a given crystal. **unit cost** *n.* the cost of producing one item. **unitholder** *n.* a person who has a holding in a unit trust. **unitize, unitise** *v.t.* to convert into a unit trust. **unit-linked** *a.* (of a policy etc.) the return of which is linked to the fluctuations of the price of shares bought in a portfolio of investment funds. **unit price** *n.* the price of a commodity expressed per unit of weight, volume etc. **unit trust** *n.* an investment company which invests contributions from many individuals by purchasing holdings in a range of different enterprises and pays out dividends according to the amount invested. [short for UNITY]

unite (ūnīt´) *v.t.* 1 to join together so as to make one. 2 to combine, to amalgamate. 3 to join in marriage. 4 to cause to adhere. ~*v.i.* 1 to become one. 2 to become consolidated, to combine, to cooperate. 3 to join in marriage. 4 to adhere. **united** *a.* **United Brethren** *n.pl.* the Moravians. **United Kingdom** *n.* Great Britain and Northern Ireland. **unitedly** *adv.* **United Nations** *n.sing. or pl.* an international organization of sovereign states founded in 1945 to promote peace and international cooperation. **United Provinces** *n.pl.* 1 Holland, Zeeland, Utrecht, Guelderland, Groningen, Friesland and Overyssel united in 1579 in the Union of Utrecht. 2 a region in India formed by the union of Agra and Oudh and now known as Uttar Pradesh. **United Reformed Church** *n.* a Church formed in 1972 from the union of the Presbyterian and Congregational Churches in England and Wales. **United States, United States of America** *n.* (*sing. or pl.*) a federal republic consisting of 50 states, mostly in N America. **uniter** *n.* **unitive** (ū´ni-) *a.* **unitively** *adv.* [L *ūnītus*, p.p. of *ūnīre*, from *ūnus*, one]

unity (ū´niti) *n.* (*pl.* **unities**) 1 the state or condition of being one or individual, oneness as opposed to plurality or division. 2 the state of being united, union. 3 an agreement of parts or elements, harmonious interconnection, structural coherence. 4 concord, agreement, harmony. 5 a thing forming a coherent whole. 6 (*Math.*) the number one, a factor that leaves unchanged the quantity on which it operates. 7 the condition that the action of a play should be limited to the development of a single plot, that the supposed time should coincide with the actual duration of the play or to a single day, and that there should be no change of scene (called the three dramatic unities of action, time and place). [A-F *unité*, L *ūnitās -tātem*, from *ūnus*, one]

Univ. *abbr.* University.

uni- (+ v– words) univalent[1] (ūnivā´lənt) *a.* 1 (*Chem.*) having a valence or combining to the power of one. 2 (*Biol.*) (of a chromosome) remaining unpaired during meiosis. **univalent**[2] (ūniv´ələnt) *n.* (*Biol.*) a chromosome which remains unpaired during meiosis. **univalve** (ū´ni-) *a.* (*Zool.*) having only one valve. ~*n.* (*Zool.*) a univalve mollusc. **univocal** *a.* (of a word) having only one meaning. ~*n.* a univocal word. **univocality** *n.* **univocally** *adv.*

universal (ūnivœ´səl) *a.* 1 of or relating to the whole world or all persons or things in the world or in the class under consideration; common to all cases; all embracing, general. 2 (*Logic*) in which something is asserted of all the individuals in a class. ~*n.* 1 (*Logic*) a universal proposition. 2 (*Philos.*) a universal concept. 3 (*Philos.*) a universal term. **universal agent** *n.* an agent who is authorized to do anything that can be delegated. **universal compass** *n.* a compass with legs that can be extended for drawing large circles. **universal coupling** UNIVERSAL JOINT (under UNIVERSAL). **universal donor** *n.* a person whose blood is of group O and is able to donate blood to people with most other blood types. **universalism** *n.* 1 the quality of being universal. 2 (*Theol.*) the doctrine that all human beings will eventually be saved. **universalist** *a.*, *n.* **universalistic** (-lis´-) *a.* **universality** (-sal´-) *n.* **universalize, universalise** *v.t.* **universalizability** (-bil´-) *n.* **universalization** (-zā´shən) *n.* **universal joint, universal coupling** *n.* a device for connecting two rotating shafts allowing freedom of movement in any direction. **universal language** *n.* a specially created language intended for use by all nations. **universally** *adv.* **universalness** *n.* **universal recipient** *n.* a person whose blood group is AB and who can receive blood from donors of most blood types. **universal suffrage** *n.* the right to vote extended to all adults. **Universal Time, Universal Time Coordinated** *n.* Greenwich Mean Time. [F *universel*, L *ūniversālis*, see UNIVERSE]

universe (ū´nivœs) *n.* 1 all existing things; all created things viewed as constituting one system or whole, the cosmos. 2 all humankind. 3 in logic and statistics, all the objects that are the subjects of consideration. **universe of discourse** *n.* (*Logic*) all the objects that are under consideration. [F *univers*, L *ūniversus*, (UNI-, *versus*, p.p. of *vertere*, to turn)]

university (ūnivœ´siti) *n.* (*pl.* **universities**) 1 an educational institution for both instruction and examination in the higher branches of knowledge with the power to confer degrees, often comprising subordinate colleges, schools etc. 2 the members of this collectively. 3 a team or crew representing a university, as distinct from a college team etc. **at university** studying at a university. **university extension** *n.* a system by which university instruction is extended to non-members of universities by means of lectures, classes and examinations. [A-F *université*, a school for universal knowledge, L *ūniversitās -tātem*, a whole, from UNIVERSE]

Unix® (ū´niks) *n.* a multi-user computer operating system.

un- (+ j–k words) unjoin *v.t.* to disjoin; to separate. **unjoint** *v.t.* 1 to disjoint, to separate the joints of. 2 to disunite. **unjust** *a.* not just, not conformable to justice. **unjustly** *adv.* **unjustness** *n.* **unjustifiable** *a.* **unjustifiableness** *n.* **unjustifiably** *adv.* **unjustified** *a.* **unkennel** *v.t.* (*pres.p.* **unkennelling,** (*N Am.*) **unkenneling,** *past, p.p.* **unkennelled,** (*N Am.*) **unkenneled**) 1 to release or drive out from a kennel. 2 to drive (a fox) from a hole. **unkept** *a.* 1 (of a promise etc.) not kept. 2 not tended. **unkillable** *a.* that cannot be killed. **unkind** *a.* 1 not kind. 2 harsh, hard, cruel. 3 not pleasant. **unkindly** *adv.* **unkindness** *n.* **unking** *v.t.* 1 to take the position of king away from. 2 to deprive of a king. **unkingly** *a.* **unkink** *v.t.*, *v.i.* **unknit** *v.t.* (*pres.p.* **unknitting,** *past, p.p.* **unknitted**) 1 to unravel, undo or untie. 2 to weaken or destroy (an alliance etc.). **unknot** *v.t.* (*pres.p.* **unknotting,** *past, p.p.* **unknotted**) to undo the knot or knots of. **unknowable** *a.* that is not knowable. ~*n.* something that is unknowable. **the Unknowable** the ultimate reality. **unknowability** *n.* **unknowableness** *n.* **unknowably** *adv.* **unknowing** *a.* 1 not knowing. 2 ignorant or unaware (of). ~*n.* ignorance. **unknowingly** *adv.* **unknowingness** *n.* **unknown** *a.* not known. ~*n.* an unknown person, thing or quantity. **unknown to** without the knowledge of (*Unknown to me she'd already gone*). **unknown country** *n.* a subject, field, place etc. one is not familiar with. **unknown quantity** *n.* a person, thing or number whose importance or value is unknown. **Unknown Soldier, Unknown Warrior** *n.* an unidentified soldier whose body is buried in a memorial as a symbol of all soldiers killed in war.

unkempt (ŭnkempt´) *a.* 1 (of hair) uncombed. 2 scruffy and untidy. 3 †rough, unpolished. **unkemptly** *adv.* **unkemptness** *n.* [ME *kempt*, *kembed*, p.p. of *kemben*, OE *cemban*, to comb]

un- (+ l– words) unlabelled, (*N Am.*) **unlabeled** *a.* **unlaboured,** (*N Am.*) **unlabored** *a.* 1 not produced by labour; untilled, unworked. 2 (of style etc.) spontaneous, natural, easy. **unlace** *v.t.* 1 to undo the lace or laces of. 2 to loosen or unfasten by undoing the lace or laces of. **unlade** *v.t.* to unload. **unladen** *a.* **unladen weight** *n.* the weight of a lorry etc. when not laden with goods etc. **unladylike** *a.* **unlaid**[1] *a.* not laid. **unlaid**[2] UNLAY (under UN- (+ L– WORDS)). **unlamented** *a.* **unlash** *v.t.* to unfasten (something lashed). **unlatch** *v.t.* 1 to unfasten the latch of (a door etc.). 2 to open in this way. ~*v.i.* to be opened in this way. **unlawful** *a.* **unlawfully** *adv.* **unlawfulness** *n.* **unlay** *v.t.* (*past, p.p.* **unlaid**) (*Naut.*) to untwist (rope etc.). **unleaded** *a.* 1 (of petrol) without added lead compounds. 2 not weighted, covered etc. with lead. 3 (*Print.*) (of lines of typesetting) not spaced with leads. **unlearn** *v.t.* (*past, p.p.* **unlearnt, unlearned**) 1 to forget the knowledge of. 2 to get rid of something learned. **unlearned**[1], **unlearnt** *a.* not learnt. **unlearned**[2] (-nid) *a.* not learned, uneducated. **unlearnedly** *adv.* **unlearnt** UNLEARN (under UN- (+ L– WORDS)). **unleash** *v.t.* 1 to set free from a leash. 2 to set free from control or restraint. **unleavened** *a.* **unlettered** *a.* 1 illiterate. 2 not having had much education. **unliberated** *a.* **unlicensed,** (*N Am.*) **unlicenced** *a.* **unlighted** *a.* unlit. **unlike** *a.* 1 not like. 2 dissimilar. 3 †improbable. ~*prep.* 1 not like (*Unlike Shubhu, I found the exhibition disappointing*). 2 not characteristic of. **unlikeness** *n.* **unlikeable, unlikable** *a.* **unlikely** *a.* (*comp.* **unlikelier,** *superl.* **unlikeliest**) 1 improbable. 2 unpromising. 3 not likely (to do something). **unlikelihood, unlikeliness** *n.* **unlimber** *v.t.* 1 to take (a gun) out from its limber ready for use. 2 (*esp. N Am.*) to prepare (something) ready for use. **unlimited** *a.* 1 not limited; having no bounds; indefinite; unnumbered. 2 unconfined, unrestrained. **unlimitedly** *adv.* **unlimitedness** *n.* **unline** *v.t.* to remove the lining from. **unlined**[1] *a.* (of a garment, curtain etc.) not lined. **unlined**[2] *a.* without lines. **unlink** *v.t.* **unliquidated** *a.* **unlisted** *a.* 1 not on a list. 2 (of securities) not listed on the Stock Exchange. 3 (*N Am.*) (of a telephone number) ex-directory. **unlit** *a.* **unlivable** *a.* not able to be lived or lived in. **unlived-in** *a.* 1 not lived in. 2 over-tidy. **unload** *v.t.* 1 to discharge the load from. 2 to discharge (a load). 3 to withdraw the charge from (a gun etc.). 4 (*coll.*) to get rid of. 5 (*coll.*) to disclose (information). 6 (*coll.*) to give vent to (one's troubles, feelings etc.). ~*v.i.* to discharge a load or freight. **unloader** *n.* **unlocated** *a.* **unlock** *v.t.* 1 to unfasten the lock of (a door, box etc.). 2 to disclose. **unlocked** *a.* **unlooked-for** *a.* not looked for, unexpected. **unloose, unloosen** *v.t.* 1 to unfasten, to loose. 2 to set at liberty. **unlovable, unloveable** *a.* **unloved** *a.* **unlovely** *a.* not lovely; not beautiful or attractive. **unloveliness** *n.* **unloving** *a.* **unlovingly** *adv.* **unlovingness** *n.* **unlucky** *a.* (*comp.* **unluckier,** *superl.* **unluckiest**) 1 not lucky or fortunate; unsuccessful. 2 disastrous. 3 inauspicious, ill-omened. 4 not well considered or judged. **unluckily** *adv.* **unluckiness** *n.*

unless (ŭnles´) *conj.* if it be not the case that; except when (*I'm not giving it to you unless you promise me something; We used to meet in the park unless it was raining*). [formerly *onless* (ON, LESS)]

un- (+ m–n words) unmade *a.* 1 not made or not yet made. 2 undone; annulled. **unmake** *v.t.* (*past, p.p.*

unmade) to destroy; to annihilate; to depose. **unmalleable** *a.* **unmalleability** *n.* **unman** *v.t.* (*pres.p.* **unmanning,** *past, p.p.* **unmanned**) **1** to deprive of maleness or manly qualities. **2** to deprive of courage or fortitude. **3** to deprive of men. **unmanned** *a.* **1** not manned, having no crew. **2** caused to lose one's self-control and become emotional etc. **unmanageable** *a.* not manageable; not easily controlled. **unmanly** *a.* **unmanliness** *n.* **unmannered** *a.* **1** without affectation. **2** lacking good manners. **unmannerly** *a.* not mannerly; rude, ill-bred. **unmannerliness** *n.* **unmapped** *a.* **1** not shown on a map. **2** unexplored. **unmarked** *a.* **1** not marked. **2** not noticed, unobserved. **unmarketable** *a.* **unmarriageable** *a.* **unmarried** *a.* **unmask** *v.t.* **1** to remove the mask from. **2** to expose. *~v.i.* **1** to take one's mask off. **2** to reveal one's true character. **unmasker** *n.* **unmatchable** *a.* **unmatchably** *adv.* **unmatched** *a.* **unmatured** *a.* **unmeaning** *a.* **1** having no meaning; senseless. **2** expressionless, vacant. **unmeaningly** *adv.* **unmeaningness** *n.* **unmeant** *a.* not meant, not intended. **unmeasured** *a.* **1** not measured. **2** indefinite, unlimited, unmeasurable. **unmeasurable** *a.* **unmeasurably** *adv.* **unmechanical** *a.* **unmediated** *a.* perceived directly with no intervention. †**unmeet** *a.* not meet, not suitable (for, to do etc.). †**unmeetly** *adv.* †**unmeetness** *n.* **unmelodious** *a.* **unmelodiously** *adv.* **unmelted** *a.* **unmemorable** *a.* **unmemorably** *adv.* **unmentionable** *a.* not mentionable, not fit to be mentioned. *~n.* **1** (*pl., facet.*) underwear. **2** (*pl., facet.*) †trousers. **3** a person or thing that is not to be mentioned. **unmentionability, unmentionableness** *n.* **unmentionably** *adv.* **unmerchantable** *a.* **unmerciful** *a.* **unmercifully** *adv.* **unmercifulness** *n.* **unmerited** *a.* **unmet** *a.* (of a goal, target etc.) not achieved. **unmethodical** *a.* **unmethodically** *adv.* **unmetrical** *a.* not metrical. **unmilitary** *a.* **unmindful** *a.* not mindful, heedless (of). **unmindfully** *adv.* **unmindfulness** *n.* **unmissable** *a.* that cannot be missed; that is too good to miss. **unmistakable, unmistakeable** *a.* that cannot be mistaken; manifest, plain. **unmistakability, unmistakableness** *n.* **unmistakably** *adv.* **unmistaken** *a.* **unmitigated** *a.* **1** not mitigated. **2** unqualified (*an unmitigated disaster*). **unmitigatedly** *adv.* **unmixed** *a.* **unmixed blessing** *n.* something that has advantages and no disadvantages. **unmodified** *a.* **unmodulated** *a.* **unmold** UNMOULD (under UN- (+ M–N WORDS)). **unmolested** *a.* **unmoor** *v.t.* **1** to loose the moorings of. **2** to release partially by weighing one of two or more anchors. *~v.i.* to weigh anchor. **unmoral** *a.* non-moral; outside morality. **unmorality** *n.* **unmotherly** *a.* **unmotivated** *a.* lacking in motive or incentive. **unmould,** (*N Am.*) **unmold** *v.t.* to change the form of. **unmounted** *a.* **1** not on horseback. **2** (of a drawing, gem etc.) not mounted. **unmourned** *a.* **unmoved** *a.* **1** not moved. **2** not changed in purpose, unshaken, firm. **3** not affected emotionally. **unmoving** *a.* **1** motionless. **2** unaffecting. **unmown** *a.* **unmuffle** *v.t.* to remove a muffler or covering from. **unmurmuring** *a.* not complaining. **unmurmuringly** *adv.* **unmusical** *a.* **1** not pleasing to the ear, discordant. **2** not interested or skilled in music. **unmusicality** *n.* **unmusically** *adv.* **unmusicalness** *n.* **unmutilated** *a.* **unmuzzle** *v.t.* **1** to remove a muzzle from (a dog etc.). **2** to allow to speak, report etc. again (*to unmuzzle the press*). **unnail** *v.t.* **unnameable** *a.* **unnamed** *a.* **unnatural** *a.* **1** not natural; contrary to nature. **2** not in accordance with accepted standards of behaviour. **3** monstrous, inhuman. **4** artificial. **5** forced, strained, affected. **unnaturally** *adv.* **unnaturalness** *n.* **unnavigable** *a.* **unnavigability** *n.* **unnecessary** *a.* **1** not necessary. **2** needless, superfluous. *~n.* (*pl.* **unnecessaries**) (*usu. in pl.*) something which is unnecessary. **unnecessarily** *adv.* **unnecessariness** *n.* **unneeded** *a.* **unneedful** *a.* **unnegotiable** *a.* **unneighbourly,** (*N Am.*) **unneighborly** *a.* **unneighbourliness** *n.* **unnerve** *v.t.* to deprive of nerve, strength or resolution. **unnerved** *a.* **unnerving** *a.* **unnervingly** *adv.* **unnoticeable** *a.* **unnoticeably** *adv.* **unnoticed** *a.* **unnumbered** *a.* **1** not marked with a number or numbers. **2** countless. **3** not counted.

unnil- (ŭn´il) *pref.* forming names of chemical elements of atomic numbers 104–109.

un- (+ o–p words) unobjectionable *a.* **unobjectionableness** *n.* **unobjectionably** *adv.* **unobliging** *a.* **unobscured** *a.* **unobservable** *a.* **unobservant** *a.* **unobservantly** *adv.* **unobserved** *a.* **unobservedly** (-vid-) *adv.* **unobstructed** *a.* **unobtainable** *a.* **unobtrusive** *a.* **unobtrusively** *adv.* **unobtrusiveness** *n.* **unoccupied** *a.* **unoffending** *a.* not offending; harmless, innocent. **unoffended** *a.* **unoffered** *a.* **unofficial** *a.* **1** not having official character or authorization. **2** not typical of officials. **unofficially** *adv.* **unofficial strike** *n.* a strike that does not have the formal backing of the strikers' trade union. **unoiled** *a.* **unopened** *a.* **unopposed** *a.* **unordained** *a.* **unordinary** *a.* **unorganized, unorganised** *a.* **1** not organized or arranged. **2** not unionized. **unoriginal** *a.* not original, derived, lacking originality. **unoriginality** *n.* **unoriginally** *adv.* **unornamental** *a.* **unornamented** *a.* **unorthodox** *a.* **unorthodoxly** *adv.* **unorthodoxy** *n.* **unostentatious** *a.* **unostentatiously** *adv.* **unostentatiousness** *n.* **unowned** *a.* **1** not acknowledged. **2** without an owner. **unpacified** *a.* **unpack** *v.t.* **1** to open and take out the contents of. **2** to take (things) out of a package etc. **unpacker** *n.* **unpaged** *a.* not having the pages numbered. **unpaid** *a.* **1** (of a debt) not paid, not discharged. **2** not having received the payment due. **3** working without pay. **unpainted** *a.* **unpaired** *a.* **1** not paired, not matched. **2** not forming one of a pair. **unpalatable** *a.* **unpalatability, unpalatableness** *n.* **unparalleled** *a.* not paralleled; unequalled, unprecedented. **unpardonable** *a.* **unpardonableness** *n.* **unpardonably** *adv.* **unparliamentary** *a.* contrary to the rules or usages of Parliament. **unparliamentarily** *adv.* **unparliamentariness** *n.* **unparliamentary language** *n.* abusive language. **unpasteurized, unpasteurised** *a.* **unpatented** *a.* **unpatriotic** *a.* **unpatriotically** *adv.* **unpaved** *a.* **unpeaceful** *a.* **unpeeled** *a.* **unpeg** *v.t.* (*pres.p.* **unpegging,** *past, p.p.* **unpegged**) **1** to take out the pegs from. **2** to open or unfasten in this way. **3** to cease to peg (prices etc.). **unpensioned** *a.* **unpeople**[1] *v.t.* to empty of inhabitants. **unpeople**[2] (ŭn´-) *n.pl.* unpersons. **unperceived** *a.* **unperceptive** *a.* **unperceptively** *adv.* **unperfected** *a.* **unperforated** *a.* **unperformed** *a.* **unperfumed** *a.* **unperson** (ŭn´-) *n.* a person whose existence is officially ignored or denied. **unpersuadable** *a.* **unpersuaded** *a.* **unpersuasive** *a.* **unpersuasively** *adv.* **unperturbed** *a.* **unperturbedly** *adv.* **unphilosophic, unphilosophical** *a.* **1** not in a philosophic way. **2** lacking philosophy. **unphilosophically** *adv.* **unphysiologic, unphysiological** *a.* **unphysiologically** *adv.* **unpick** *v.t.* **1** to undo (the stitches) of. **2** to take out the sewing of (a garment). **3** †to unfasten or open (a door etc.) by picking. **unpicked** *a.* **1** not picked. **2** not picked out or selected. **unpicturesque** *a.* **unpin** *v.t.* (*pres.p.* **unpinning,** *past, p.p.* **unpinned**) **1** to remove the pins from. **2** to unfasten (something held together by pins). **3** in chess, to free (a piece that has been pinned). **unpitied** *a.* **unpitying** *a.* **unpityingly** *adv.* **unplaced** *a.* **1** not placed. **2** not among the first three at the finish of a race. **unplaceable** *a.* **unplanned** *a.* **unplanted** *a.* **unplausible** *a.* **unplayable** *a.* **1** that cannot be played. **2** (of a ball) that is impossible to return, strike etc. **unpleasant** *a.* not pleasant; disagreeable. **unpleasantly** *adv.* **unpleasantness** *n.* **1** the quality of being unpleasant. **2** a hostile disagreement. **unpleasantry** *n.* (*pl.* **unpleasantries**) **1** lack of pleasantness. **2** (*pl.*) unpleasant comments, events etc. **unpleased** *a.* **unpleasing** *a.* **unpleasingly** *adv.* **unpledged** *a.* **unploughed,** (*N Am.*) **unplowed** *a.* **unplucked** *a.* **unplug** *v.t.* (*pres.p.* **unplugging,** *past, p.p.* **unplugged**) 1 to remove a plug or obstruction from. 2 to disconnect (an electrical appliance) from a source of electricity. **unplumbed** *a.* 1 not plumbed. 2 not fully explored or known. **unpoetic, unpoetical** *a.* **unpointed** *a.* 1 not having a point. 2 not punctuated. 3 not having the vowel-points or diacritical marks. 4 (of masonry) not pointed. **unpolished** *a.* **unpolitic** *a.* impolitic. **unpolitical** *a.* not related to or interested in politics. **unpolitically** *adv.* **unpolled** *a.* 1 at an election, not having registered one's vote. 2 not included in an opinion poll. **unpolluted** *a.* **unpopular** *a.* **unpopularity** *n.* **unpopularly** *adv.* **unpopulated** *a.* **unposed** *a.* **unpossessed** *a.* 1 not possessed. 2 not in possession (of). **unpowered** *a.* (of a vehicle) powered by other means than fuel. **unpractical** *a.* 1 (of a person, proposal etc.) not practical. 2 not possessing practical skill. **unpracticality** *n.* **unpractically** *adv.* **unpractised,** (*N Am.*) **unpracticed** *a.* 1 not put in practice. 2 unskilful, inexperienced. **unprecedented** *a.* 1 being without precedent, unparalleled. 2 new. **unprecedentedly** *adv.* **unpredictable** *a.* 1 that cannot be predicted. 2 whose behaviour cannot be predicted or relied on. **unpredictability** *n.* **unpredictably** *adv.* **unpredicted** *a.* **unprejudice** *n.* freedom from prejudice. **unprejudiced** *a.* **unpremeditated** *a.* not premeditated, not planned beforehand; unintentional. **unpremeditatedly** *adv.* **unprepared** *a.* 1 not prepared, impromptu. 2 not ready (for etc.). **unpreparedly** *adv.* **unpreparedness** *n.* **unprepossessing** *a.* **unprescribed** *a.* **unpresentable** *a.* not presentable; not fit to be seen. **unpressed** *a.* **unpressurized, unpressurised** *a.* **unpresuming** *a.* **unpresumptuous** *a.* **unpretending** *a.* unpretentious. **unpretendingly** *adv.* **unpretendingness** *n.* **unpretentious** *a.* **unpretentiously** *adv.* **unpretentiousness** *n.* **unpriced** *a.* 1 not having a price or prices fixed, quoted or marked up. 2 (*poet.*) priceless. **unprimed** *a.* **unprincipled** *a.* not dictated by moral principles; immoral. **unprincipledness** *n.* **unprintable** *a.* that cannot be printed (because obscene or libellous). **unprintably** *adv.* **unprinted** *a.* **unprivileged** *a.* **unproblematic** *a.* **unproblematically** *adv.* **unprocessed** *a.* **unproclaimed** *a.* **unprocurable** *a.* **unproductive** *a.* **unproductively** *adv.* **unproductiveness** *n.* **unprofessional** *a.* 1 not of or relating to a profession. 2 contrary to the rules or etiquette of a profession. 3 not belonging to a profession. **unprofessionally** *adv.* **unprofitable** *a.* **unprofitableness** *n.* **unprofitably** *adv.* **unprogressive** *a.* not progressive, conservative. **unprogressiveness** *n.* **unprohibited** *a.* **unpromising** *a.* not likely to be successful. **unpromisingly** *adv.* **unprompted** *a.* of one's own free will or initiative. **unpronounceable** *a.* **unpronounceably** *adv.* **unpropitious** *a.* **unpropitiously** *adv.* **unprosperous** *a.* **unprosperously** *adv.* **unprotected** *a.* not protected. **unprotectedness** *n.* **unprotesting** *a.* **unprotestingly** *adv.* **unprovable** *a.* **unprovability** *n.* **unproved, unproven** *a.* **unprovided** *a.* not provided or furnished (with supplies etc.). **unprovoked** *a.* **unpublished** *a.* (of books etc.) not published. **unpublishable** *a.* **unpunctual** *a.* **unpunctuality** *n.* **unpunctuated** *a.* **unpunishable** *a.* not punishable. **unpunished** *a.* **unpurified** *a.* **unputdownable** *a.* (*coll.*) (of a book) too exciting to put down before it is finished.

UNO *abbr.* United Nations Organization.

Unprofor (ŭn´prəfaw), **UNPROFOR** *abbr.* United Nations Protection Force.

un- (+ q–r words) unqualified *a.* 1 not qualified; not fit, not competent. 2 not having passed the necessary examination etc. 3 not qualified legally. 4 not limited by conditions or exceptions, absolute (*unqualified support*). **unqualifiedly** *adv.* **unquantifiable** *a.* **unquantified** *a.* **unquestionable** *a.* not to be questioned or doubted, indisputable. **unquestionability, unquestionableness** *n.* **unquestionably** *adv.* **unquestioned** *a.* 1 not called in question, not doubted. 2 having no questions asked, not interrogated. **unquestioning** *a.* 1 not questioning, not doubting. 2 implicit. **unquestioningly** *adv.* **unquiet** *a.* 1 restless, uneasy, agitated. 2 anxious. **unquietly** *adv.* **unquietness** *n.* **unquote** *v.i.* to close a quotation. ~*int.* used to indicate the end of a (spoken) quotation. **unquotable** *a.* **unquoted** *a.* **unravel** *v.t.* (*pres.p.* **unravelling,** (*esp. N Am.*) **unraveling,** *past, p.p.* **unravelled,** (*esp. N Am.*) **unraveled**) 1 to separate the threads of; to disentangle, to untwist. 2 to solve, to clear up (a mystery, the plot of a play etc.). 3 to undo (a knitted fabric etc.). ~*v.i.* to become disentangled. **unravelment** *n.* **unreachable** *a.* **unreachableness** *n.* **unreachably** *adv.* **unread** (-red´) *a.* 1 not read. 2 not well-read, unlearned. **unreadable** *a.* 1 illegible. 2 dull or difficult to read. **unreadability, unreadableness** *n.* **unreadably** *adv.* **unready**[1] *a.* 1 not ready. 2 not prompt to act etc. **unreadily** *adv.* **unreadiness** *n.* **unreal** *a.* 1 not real. 2 unsubstantial, visionary, imaginary. 3 (*N Am., Austral., sl.*) amazing. **unrealism** *n.* **unrealistic** *a.* **unrealistically** *adv.* **unreality** *n.* **unrealizable, unrealisable** *a.* **unrealized** *a.* **unreally** *adv.* **unreason** *n.* 1 lack of reason. 2 folly, absurdity. **unreasonable** *a.* 1 not reasonable; exorbitant, extravagant. 2 not listening to reason. **unreasonableness** *n.* **unreasonably** *adv.* **unreasoned** *a.* not reasoned or thought out rationally. **unreasoning** *a.* not reasoning; irrational. **unreasoningly** *adv.* **unrebuked** *a.* **unreceptive** *a.* **unreciprocated** *a.* **unreckoned** *a.* **unreclaimed** *a.* **unrecognized, unrecognised** *a.* 1 not recognized. 2 not acknowledged. **unrecognizable** *a.* **unrecognizableness** *n.* **unrecognizably** *adv.* **unrecompensed** *a.* **unreconciled** *a.* **unreconstructed** *a.* 1 clinging to old-fashioned social or political notions. 2 not rebuilt. **unrecordable** *a.* **unrecorded** *a.* **unrectified** *a.* not corrected. **unredeemed** *a.* 1 not redeemed, not fulfilled. 2 not taken out of pawn. 3 not counterbalanced by any redeeming quality, unmitigated. **unredeemable** *a.* **unredressed** *a.* **unreel** *v.t.* to unwind. ~*v.i.* to become unwound. **unreeve** *v.t.* (*past* **unrove, unreeved**) (*Naut.*) to withdraw (a rope) from a block, deadeye etc. ~*v.i.* to become unreeved. **unrefined** *a.* 1 not refined; not purified. 2 of unpolished manners, taste etc. **unreflecting** *a.* not reflecting or thinking. **unreflectingly** *adv.* **unreflectingness** *n.* **unreflective** *a.* **unreformed** *a.* **unrefreshed** *a.* **unregarded** *a.* **unregenerate** *a.* not regenerate; unrepentant. **unregeneracy** *n.* **unregenerately** *adv.* **unregistered** *a.* **unregulated** *a.* **unrehearsed** *a.* **unrelated** *a.* **unrelatedness** *n.* **unrelaxed** *a.* **unrelenting** *a.* **unrelentingly** *adv.* **unrelentingness** *n.* **unreliable** *a.* **unreliability, unreliableness** *n.* **unreliably** *adv.* **unrelieved** *a.* **unrelievedly** *adv.* **unreligious** *a.* 1 irreligious. 2 not connected with religion, secular. **unremarkable** *a.* **unremarkably** *adv.* **unremembered** *a.* **unremitting** *a.* not relaxing; incessant, continued. **unremittingly** *adv.* **unremittingness** *n.* **unremunerative** *a.* not profitable. **unremuneratively** *adv.* **unremunerativeness** *n.* **unrenewable** *a.* **unrenewed** *a.* **unrepealed** *a.* **unrepeatable** *a.* 1 that cannot be done or said again. 2 (of language) too rude to repeat. **unrepeatability** *n.* **unrepentant** *a.* **unrepentance** *n.* **unrepentantly** *adv.* **unreported** *a.* **unrepresentative** *a.* **unrepresentativeness** *n.* **unrepresented** *a.* **unreproved** *a.* **unrequested** *a.* **unrequited** *a.* (of love etc.) not requited. **unrequitedly** *adv.* **unrequitedness** *n.* **unresented** *a.* **unreserve** *n.* lack of reserve, frankness, candour. **unreserved** *a.* 1 not reserved. 2 open, frank. 3 given, offered or done without reservation. **unreservedly** *adv.* **unreservedness** *n.* **unresisted** *a.*

unresistedly *adv.* **unresisting** *a.* **unresistingly** *adv.* **unresistingness** *n.* **unresolved** *a.* 1 not resolved, undecided, irresolute. 2 unsolved, not cleared up. 3 not dissolved. **unresolvable** *a.* **unresolvedly** *adv.* **unresolvedness** *n.* **unrespected** *a.* **unresponsive** *a.* **unresponsively** *adv.* **unresponsiveness** *n.* **unrest** *n.* 1 restlessness, agitation, uneasiness. 2 lack of rest. **unrested** *a.* **unrestful** *a.* **unrestfully** *adv.* **unresting** *a.* **unrestingly** *adv.* **unrestored** *a.* **unrestrained** *a.* **unrestrainedly** *adv.* **unrestrainedness** *n.* **unrestricted** *a.* **unrestrictedly** *adv.* **unrestrictedness** *n.* **unreturned** *a.* **unrevealed** *a.* **unrevealing** *a.* **unreversed** *a.* **unrevised** *a.* **unrevoked** *a.* **unrewarded** *a.* **unrewarding** *a.* **unrhymed, †unrimed** *a.* **unrhythmical** *a.* **unrhythmically** *adv.* **unridable** UNRIDEABLE (under UN- (+ Q–R WORDS)). **unridden** *a.* **unriddle** *v.t.* to solve, to interpret, to explain. **unriddler** *n.* **unrideable, unridable** *a.* that cannot be ridden. **unrig** *v.t.* (*pres.p.* **unrigging,** *past, p.p.* **unrigged**) 1 to strip (a ship) of rigging. 2 (*dial.*) to undress. **unrighteous** *a.* 1 not righteous, not just. 2 evil, wicked, sinful. **unrighteously** *adv.* **unrighteousness** *n.* **†unrimed** UNRHYMED (under UN- (+ Q–R WORDS)). **unrip** *v.t.* (*pres.p.* **unripping,** *past, p.p.* **unripped**) to rip open, to undo or unfasten by ripping. **unripe** *a.* 1 not ripe; not mature. 2 †premature. **unripened** *a.* **unripeness** *n.* **unrisen** *a.* **unrivalled,** (*N Am.*) **unrivaled** *a.* having no rival; unequalled, peerless. **unrivet** *v.t.* (*pres.p.* **unriveting,** *past, p.p.* **unriveted**) 1 to undo, unfasten etc. by removing rivets. 2 to detach or loosen. **unroadworthy** *a.* **unrobe** *v.t., v.i.* **unroll** *v.t.* 1 to unfold (a roll of cloth etc.). 2 to display, to lay open. ~*v.i.* 1 to be unrolled. 2 to be displayed after being unrolled. **unromantic** *a.* **unromantically** *adv.* **unroof** *v.t.* to strip the roof off. **unroot** *v.t.* 1 to tear up by the roots. 2 to extirpate, to eradicate. **unrope** *v.t.* to loose by undoing a rope. ~*v.i.* in mountaineering, to unfasten oneself from a rope. **unrounded** *a.* **unrove** UNREEVE (under UN- (+ Q–R WORDS)). **unroyal** *a.* not royal. **unruffled** *a.* not ruffled, unperturbed. **unruled** *a.* 1 not governed. 2 (of paper etc.) not ruled with lines. **unruly** *a.* (*comp.* **unrulier,** *superl.* **unruliest**) not submitting to restraint; ungovernable; disorderly. **unruliness** *n.*

unready[1] UN- (+ Q–R WORDS).

unready[2] (ŭnred´i) *a.* badly or insufficiently advised (used as a nickname of Ethelred II, 968–1016, king of England). [see REDE; assimilated to READY]

UNRWA (ŭn´rah) *abbr.* United Nations Relief and Works Agency.

un- (+ s–t words) unsaddle *v.t.* 1 to remove the saddle from. 2 to unseat. ~*v.i.* to unsaddle one's horse. **unsafe** *a.* 1 dangerous, perilous, risky. 2 (of a verdict, conclusion etc.) not based on sufficient evidence. **unsafely** *adv.* **unsafeness** *n.* **unsaid**[1] *a.* not said, unspoken. **unsaid**[2] UNSAY (under UN- (+ S–T WORDS)). **unsaintly** *a.* **unsalaried** *a.* **unsaleable, unsalable** *a.* **unsaleability** *n.* **unsalted** *a.* **unsanctified** *a.* **unsanctioned** *a.* **unsanitary** *a.* unhealthy. **unsated** *a.* **unsatisfactory** *a.* 1 not satisfactory; unacceptable. 2 (of a verdict, conviction etc.) not based on sufficient evidence. **unsatisfactorily** *adv.* **unsatisfactoriness** *n.* **unsatisfied** *a.* **unsatisfiedness** *n.* **unsatisfying** *a.* **unsatisfyingly** *adv.* **unsaturated** *a.* 1 not saturated. 2 (of fats) having a high proportion of fatty acids containing double bonds. 3 (*Chem.*) (of a compound) having double or triple bonds and thus capable of undergoing further reactions. **unsaved** *a.* **unsavoury,** (*N Am.*) **unsavory** *a.* 1 unattractive, repellent, disgusting. 2 †of unpleasant taste or smell. 3 morally offensive. **unsavourily** *adv.* **unsavouriness** *n.* **unsay** *v.t.* (*past, p.p.* **unsaid**) to retract or withdraw (what has been said). **unsayable** *a.* **unscalable** *a.* that cannot be climbed. **unscarred** *a.* **unscathed** *a.* not scathed, uninjured. **unscented** *a.* **unscheduled** *a.* **unscholarly** *a.* **unscholarliness** *n.* **unschooled** *a.* 1 not having received an education. 2 not sent to school. 3 having received no training. 4 (of talent etc.) natural. **unscientific** *a.* 1 not in accordance with scientific principles or methods. 2 lacking scientific knowledge. **unscientifically** *adv.* **unscramble** *v.t.* 1 to restore to order from a scrambled state. 2 to make (a scrambled message) intelligible. **unscrambler** *n.* **unscreened** *a.* 1 not screened for security or medical purposes. 2 (of coal, grain) not passed through a screen. 3 not supplied with a screen. 4 (of a film etc.) not shown on a screen. **unscrew** *v.t.* 1 to withdraw or loosen (a screw). 2 to unfasten in this way. ~*v.i.* to become unscrewed. **unscripted** *a.* 1 not using a script. 2 unplanned, unrehearsed. **unscriptural** *a.* not in conformity with the Scriptures. **unscripturally** *adv.* **unscrupulous** *a.* having no scruples of conscience; unprincipled. **unscrupulously** *adv.* **unscrupulousness** *n.* **unseal** *v.t.* to break or remove the seal of; to open. **unsealed** *a.* 1 not sealed. 2 having the seal broken. **unseam** *v.t.* to undo the seams of (a garment). **unsearchable** *a.* incapable of being searched out; inscrutable. **unsearchableness** *n.* **unsearchably** *adv.* **unsearched** *a.* **unseasonable** *a.* **unseasonableness** *n.* **unseasonably** *adv.* **unseasonal** *a.* **unseasoned** *a.* 1 not flavoured with seasoning. 2 (of wood) not seasoned. 3 not experienced. **unseat** *v.t.* 1 to remove from a seat. 2 to throw from one's seat on horseback. 3 to deprive of a parliamentary seat or political office. **unseated** *a.* 1 thrown from or deprived of a seat. 2 having no seats. 3 not furnished with seats. **unseaworthy** *a.* **unseconded** *a.* **unsecured** *a.* **unseduced** *a.* **unseeable** *a.* **unseeded** *a.* in a sporting tournament, not put with the best players in the competition draw. **unseeing** *a.* 1 blind. 2 unobservant, unsuspecting. **unseeingly** *adv.* **unseem** *v.i.* not to seem. **unseemly** *a.* (*comp.* **unseemlier,** *superl.* **unseemliest**) 1 not seemly. 2 unbefitting, unbecoming. ~*adv.* in an unseemly manner. **unseemliness** *n.* **unseen** *a.* 1 not seen. 2 invisible. 3 (of a text to be translated) not seen previously. ~*n.* an unseen translation. **unsegregated** *a.* **unselect** *a.* not select, mixed, miscellaneous. **unselective** *a.* **unselfconscious** *a.* **unselfconsciously** *adv.* **unselfconsciousness** *n.* **unselfish** *a.* concerned for the interests of others rather than one's own. **unselfishly** *adv.* **unselfishness** *n.* **unsensational** *a.* **unsensationally** *adv.* **unsentimental** *a.* **unsentimentally** *adv.* **unseparated** *a.* **unserious** *a.* **unserviceable** *a.* **unserviceability, unserviceableness** *n.* **unset** *a.* not set. **unsettle** *v.t.* 1 to change from a settled state or position; to make uncertain. 2 to derange, to disturb. ~*v.i.* to become unsettled. **unsettled** *a.* 1 not settled, fixed or determined. 2 undecided, hesitating; changeable. 3 unpaid. 4 not settled, uncolonized. **unsettledness** *n.* **unsettlement** *n.* **unsex** *v.t.* to deprive (someone, esp. a woman) of the typical qualities of their sex. **unshackle** *v.t.* **unshaded** *a.* **unshadowed** *a.* **unshakeable, unshakable** *a.* **unshakeability** *n.* **unshakeably** *adv.* **unshaken** *a.* not shaken; firm, steady. **unshakenly** *adv.* **unshapely** *a.* **unshapeliness** *n.* **unshapen** *a.* 1 deformed. 2 shapeless. **unshared** *a.* **unsharp** *a.* (of a photograph) not sharp. **unshaved** *a.* **unshaven** *a.* **unsheathe** *v.t.* to draw (a knife etc.) from its sheath. **unshed** *a.* **unshell** *v.t.* **unshelled** *a.* **unsheltered** *a.* **unshielded** *a.* **unship** *v.t.* (*pres.p.* **unshipping,** *past, p.p.* **unshipped**) 1 to unload from a ship. 2 to disembark (a passenger). 3 (*Naut.*) to remove from the place where it is fixed or fitted. ~*v.i.* (of an oar, tiller etc.) to become unshipped. **unshockable** *a.* **unshockability** *n.* **unshockably** *adv.* **unshod** *a.* **unshoe** *v.t.* (*3rd pers. sing. pres.* **unshoes,** *pres.p.* **unshoeing,** *past, p.p.* **unshod**) to remove a shoe or shoes from. **unshorn** *a.* not shorn, clipped or shaven. **unshrinkable** *a.* (of fabric) that will not shrink. **unshrinkability** *n.* **unshrinking** *a.* not recoiling, undaunted, unhesitating. **unshrinkingly** *adv.* **unsighted** *a.* 1 not sighted, not seen. 2 having one's view blocked. 3 (of a gun etc.) unfurnished with sights. **unsightly** *a.* unpleasing to the sight, ugly. **unsightliness** *n.* **unsigned** *a.* **unsilvered** *a.* **unsinkable** *a.* **unsinkability** *n.* **unsized**[1] *a.* 1 not arranged by size. 2 not made according to a size. **unsized**[2] *a.* not sized, not stiffened. **unskilled** *a.* 1 lacking skill or special knowledge or training. 2 produced without or not requiring special skill or training. **unskilful,** (*N Am.*) **unskillful** *a.* **unskilfully** *adv.* **unskilfulness** *n.* **unslakeable, unslakable** *a.* **unslaked** *a.* **unsleeping** *a.* **unsleepingly** *adv.* **unsliced** *a.* **unsling** *v.t.* (*past, p.p.* **unslung**) 1 to remove from a slung position. 2 (*Naut.*) to take (a yard, a cask etc.) off the slings. **unsmiling** *a.* **unsmilingly** *adv.* **unsmilingness** *n.* **unsmoked** *a.* 1 (of bacon etc.) not smoked. 2 (of a cigarette etc.) not consumed by smoking. **unsnap** *v.t.* (*pres.p.* **unsnapping,** *past, p.p.* **unsnapped**) to undo the snap of (something). **unsnarl** *v.t.* to remove a snarl or tangle from. **unsociable** *a.* not sociable, solitary. **unsociability, unsociableness** *n.* **unsociably** *adv.* **unsocial** *a.* 1 not social, solitary. 2 (of hours of work) falling outside the usual working day. 3 antisocial. **unsocialist** *a.* **unsoiled** *a.* **unsold** *a.* **unsolder** *v.t.* **unsoldierly** *a.* **unsolicited** *a.* **unsolicitedly** *adv.* **unsolvable** *a.* **unsolvability, unsolvableness** *n.* **unsolved** *a.* **unsoothed** *a.* **unsophisticated** *a.* 1 simple, artless; not worldly-wise. 2 not corrupted or adulterated, pure, genuine. **unsophisticatedly** *adv.* **unsophisticatedness** *n.* **unsophistication** *n.* **unsorted** *a.* **unsought** *a.* 1 not sought for. 2 without being asked. **unsound** *a.* 1 diseased. 2 weak, decayed. 3 unreliable. 4 ill-founded, not valid, fallacious. 5 unorthodox. 6 wicked. **of unsound mind** mentally unbalanced. **unsoundly** *adv.* **unsoundness** *n.* **unsounded**[1] *a.* 1 not pronounced. 2 not caused to sound. **unsounded**[2] *a.* not sounded or fathomed. **unsoured** *a.* **unsown** *a.* **unsparing** *a.* 1 liberal, profuse, lavish. 2 unmerciful. **unsparingly** *adv.* **unsparingness** *n.* †**unspeak** *v.t.* (*past* **unspoke,** *p.p.* **unspoken**) to retract, to unsay. **unspeakable** *a.* 1 inexpressible. 2 inexpressibly bad or evil. **unspeakableness** *n.* **unspeakably** *adv.* **unspeaking** *a.* silent. **unspecialized, unspecialised** *a.* **unspecific** *a.* **unspecified** *a.* **unspectacular** *a.* **unspectacularly** *adv.* **unspeculative** *a.* **unspent** *a.* **unsphere** *v.t.* (*poet.*) to remove from its or one's sphere. **unspilt** *a.* **unspiritual** *a.* **unspirituality** *n.* **unspiritually** *adv.* **unspoiled** *a.* not spoiled. **unspoilt** *a.* 1 unspoiled. 2 not plundered. **unspoke** UNSPEAK (under UN- (+ S–T WORDS)). **unspoken**[1] *a.* 1 understood without being spoken. 2 not uttered. **unspoken**[2] UNSPEAK (under UN- (+ S–T WORDS)). **unsponsored** *a.* **unspontaneous** *a.* **unspool** *v.t.* 1 to unwind from a spool. 2 to show (a film) on a screen. ~*v.i.* 1 to be unwound from a spool. 2 (of a film) to be screened. **unsporting** *a.* **unsportingly** *adv.* **unsportsmanlike** *a.* unsporting; not generous. **unspotted** *a.* 1 free from spots. 2 unblemished; morally pure. 3 not spotted or noticed. **unsprayed** *a.* (esp. of crops) not sprayed. **unsprung** *a.* not equipped with springs. **unstable** *a.* (*comp.* **unstabler,** *superl.* **unstablest**) 1 not stable, not firm. 2 liable to sudden shifts of moods. 3 changeable. 4 (of a chemical compound, atom etc.) decaying or decomposing rapidly or easily. **unstable equilibrium** *n.* a state in which a body when displaced tends to move farther from its position of equilibrium. **unstained** *a.* not stained; unblemished, unsullied. **unstamped** *a.* 1 not having a stamp affixed. 2 not marked by a stamp. **unstarched** *a.* **unstated** *a.* **unstatesmanlike** *a.* **unstatutable** *a.* not warranted by statute law. **unstatutably** *adv.* **unsteadfast** *a.* **unsteady** *a.* (*comp.* **unsteadier,** *superl.* **unsteadiest**) 1 not steady, not firm. 2 changeable, variable. 3 irregular, not uniform. 4 irregular in habits or conduct. **unsteadily** *adv.* **unsteadiness** *n.* **unsteel** *v.t.* to soften, to disarm. **unstep** *v.t.* (*pres.p.* **unstepping,** *past, p.p.* **unstepped**) (*Naut.*) to take (a mast) out of a step or socket. **unsterile** *a.* **unsterilized, unsterilised** *a.* **unstick**[1] *v.t.* (*past, p.p.* **unstuck**) 1 to separate (two things stuck together). 2 (*coll.*) to cause (an aircraft) to take off. ~*v.i.* (*coll.*) (of an aircraft) to take off. **to come unstuck** (*coll.*) (of a plan etc.) to go wrong or fail. **unstick**[2] (ŭn´-) *n.* (*coll.*) the moment of an aircraft's take-off. **unstinted** *a.* **unstintedly** *adv.* **unstinting** *a.* generous and ungrudging. **unstintingly** *adv.* **unstirred** *a.* **unstitch** *v.t.* to open by unpicking the stitches of. **unstop** *v.t.* (*pres.p.* **unstopping,** *past, p.p.* **unstopped**) 1 to free from obstruction. 2 to remove the stopper from, to open. **unstoppable** *a.* **unstoppability** *n.* **unstoppably** *adv.* **unstopped** *a.* **unstopper** *v.t.* to remove the stopper from. **unstrained** *a.* 1 not strained, not filtered. 2 not subjected to strain. 3 not forced; easy, natural. 4 not injured by excessive use. **unstrap** *v.t.* (*pres.p.* **unstrapping,** *past, p.p.* **unstrapped**) to unfasten or remove the strap or straps of. **unstratified** *a.* **unstreamed** *a.* (of schoolchildren) not streamed. **unstressed** *a.* 1 not subjected to stress. 2 unaccented. **unstring** *v.t.* (*past, p.p.* **unstrung**) 1 to take away the string or strings of. 2 to loosen the string or strings of. 3 to remove (pearls etc.) from a string. **unstructured** *a.* 1 not having a formal or rigid structure. 2 relaxed, unceremonious. **unstrung**[1] *a.* unnerved. **unstrung**[2] UNSTRING (under UN- (+ S–T WORDS)). **unstuck** UNSTICK. **unstudied** *a.* not studied; easy, natural. **unstudiedly** *adv.* **unstuffed** *a.* **unstuffy** *a.* **unstylish** *a.* 1 without style. 2 not fashionable. **unsubdued** *a.* **unsubjugated** *a.* **unsubmissive** *a.* **unsubstantial** *a.* 1 not substantial. 2 having little solidity or validity. 3 unreal. **unsubstantiality** *n.* **unsubstantially** *adv.* **unsubstantiated** *a.* **unsubtle** *a.* **unsubtly** *adv.* **unsuccess** *n.* **unsuccessful** *a.* **unsuccessfully** *adv.* **unsuccessfulness** *n.* **unsugared** *a.* **unsuited** *a.* 1 not suited, not fit. 2 not adapted (to). **unsuitable** *a.* **unsuitability, unsuitableness** *n.* **unsuitably** *adv.* **unsullied** *a.* **unsummoned** *a.* **unsung** *a.* 1 not acclaimed or recognized. 2 (*poet.*) not celebrated in verse. 3 not sung. **unsupervised** *a.* **unsupportable** *a.* 1 that cannot be endured. 2 unjustifiable. **unsupportably** *adv.* **unsupported** *a.* **unsupportive** *a.* **unsuppressed** *a.* **unsure** *a.* **unsurely** *adv.* **unsureness** *n.* **unsurfaced** *a.* (of a road etc.) not surfaced. **unsurmountable** *a.* **unsurpassable** *a.* **unsurpassably** *adv.* **unsurprised** *a.* **unsurprising** *a.* **unsurprisingly** *adv.* **unsusceptible** *a.* **unsusceptibility** *n.* **unsuspected** *a.* **unsuspectedly** *adv.* **unsuspecting** *a.* **unsuspectingly** *adv.* **unsuspectingness** *n.* **unsustainable** *a.* **unsustainably** *adv.* **unsustained** *a.* **unswathe** *v.t.* **unswayed** *a.* not swayed, biased or influenced. **unswear** *v.t.* (*past* **unswore,** *p.p.* **unsworn**) to recant (something sworn to). **unsweetened** *a.* **unswept** *a.* **unswerving** *a.* 1 constant, steadfast. 2 not veering to one side. **unswervingly** *adv.* **unswore** UNSWEAR (under UN- (+ S–T WORDS)). **unsworn**[1] *a.* 1 not sworn. 2 not bound by an oath. **unsworn**[2] UNSWEAR (under UN- (+ S–T WORDS)). **unsymbolical** *a.* **unsymmetrical** *a.* 1 out of symmetry. 2 lacking in symmetry. **unsymmetrically** *adv.* **unsympathetic** *a.* **unsympathetically** *adv.* **unsystematic** *a.* **unsystematically** *adv.* **untack** *v.t.* to undo (esp. something that has been tacked). **untainted** *a.* **untalented** *a.* **untameable, untamable** *a.* **untameableness** *n.* **untamed** *a.* **untangle** *v.t.* to disentangle. **untanned** *a.* **untapped** *a.* **untarnished** *a.* **untaught** *a.* 1 not instructed, ignorant. 2 natural, spontaneous. **untaxed** *a.* not having to pay or not subject to taxes. **unteach** *v.t.* (*past, p.p.* **untaught**) to cause to be forgotten or unlearned. **unteachable** *a.* **untearable** *a.* **untechnical** *a.* **untempted** *a.* **untenable** *a.* **untenability, untenableness** *n.* **untenably** *adv.* **untended** *a.*

untender *a.* not tender, unkind. **untendered** *a.* not offered. **untenured** *a.* **unterrified** *a.* **untestable** *a.* **untested** *a.* **untether** *v.t.* **untethered** *a.* **unthanked** *a.* **unthankful** *a.* **unthankfully** *adv.* **unthankfulness** *n.* **untheorized, untheorised** *a.* not evolved from a fundamental theory. **unthink** *v.t.* (*past, p.p.* **unthought**) **1** to retract in thought. **2** to cease to think about. **unthinkable** *a.* **1** incapable of being thought or conceived. **2** (*coll.*) highly improbable. **unthinkability, unthinkableness** *n.* **unthinkably** *adv.* **unthinking** *a.* **1** heedless, careless. **2** unintentional. **unthinkingly** *adv.* **unthinkingness** *n.* **unthought**[1] *a.* not remembered or thought (of). **unthought**[2] UNTHINK (under UN- (+ S–T WORDS)). **unthoughtful** *a.* **unthread** *v.t.* **1** to take a thread out of (a needle etc.). **2** to find one's way out of (a maze). **unthreatening** *a.* **unthrifty** *a.* **1** not thrifty; wasteful. **2** not thriving. **unthriftily** *adv.* **unthriftiness** *n.* **unthrone** *v.t.* **untidy** *a.* (*comp.* **untidier,** *superl.* **untidiest**). **untidily** *adv.* **untidiness** *n.* **untie** *v.t.* (*3rd pers. sing. pres.* **unties,** *pres.p.* **untying,** *past, p.p.* **untied**) **1** to undo (a knot), to unfasten. **2** to loose from bonds. ~*v.i.* to become untied. **untied** *a.* **untillable** *a.* **untilled** *a.* **untimely** *a.* **1** unseasonable, inopportune. **2** premature. ~†*adv.* **1** inopportunely. **2** prematurely. **untimeliness** *n.* **untinged** *a.* **untiring** *a.* never tiring; indefatigable. **untiringly** *adv.* **untitled** *a.* **untold** *a.* **1** not told, revealed or communicated. **2** not counted, innumerable; not able to be measured. **untormented** *a.* **untouchable** *a.* that cannot be touched. ~*n.* a Hindu belonging to one of the lowest castes or to no caste and whom members of the higher castes were formerly forbidden to touch. **untouchability, untouchableness** *n.* **untouched** *a.* **untoward** *a.* **1** unlucky, unfortunate. **2** awkward. **3** improper or unseemly. **4** †perverse, refractory. **untowardly** *adv.* **untowardness** *n.* **untraceable** *a.* **untraceably** *adv.* **untraced** *a.* **untracked** *a.* **1** unmarked by tracks. **2** that has no previously trodden path. **3** not traced. **untraditional** *a.* **untrained** *a.* **untrainable** *a.* **untrammelled,** (*N Am.*) **untrammeled** *a.* **untransferable** *a.* that cannot or is not permitted to be transferred. **untransformed** *a.* **untranslatable** *a.* **untranslatability, untranslatableness** *n.* **untranslatably** *adv.* **untranslated** *a.* **untransportable** *a.* **untravelled,** (*N Am.*) **untraveled** *a.* **1** not having travelled. **2** not travelled over. **untraversed** *a.* **untreatable** *a.* **untreated** *a.* **untrendy** *a.* **untried** *a.* **1** not tried; untested. **2** not tried by a judge. **untrimmed** *a.* **untrodden** *a.* **untroubled** *a.* not disturbed by care, sorrow etc.; calm, unruffled. **untrue** *a.* **1** not in accordance with facts, false. **2** not faithful, disloyal (to). **3** not conforming to a rule or standard. **untruly** *adv.* **untruss** *v.t.* **untrusting** *a.* **untrustworthy** *a.* **untrustworthiness** *n.* **untruth** *n.* **1** the state of being untrue. **2** a falsehood, a lie. **3** unfaithfulness. **untruthful** *a.* **untruthfully** *adv.* **untruthfulness** *n.* **untuck** *v.t.* to cause (blankets etc.) to no longer be tucked in. **untunable** *a.* **untuned** *a.* **1** (of a musical instrument) that has not been tuned. **2** (of a radio etc.) not tuned to a particular frequency. **3** not in harmony. **untuneful** *a.* **untunefully** *adv.* **untunefulness** *n.* **unturned** *a.* **untutored** *a.* uninstructed. **untwine** *v.t., v.i.* **untwist** *v.t., v.i.* **untying** UNTIE (under UN- (+ S–T WORDS)). **untypical** *a.* **untypically** *adv.*

Untermensch (un´təmensh) *n.* (*pl.* **Untermenschen** (-shən)) a person who is regarded as socially or racially inferior. [G]

until (ŭntil´) *prep.* **1** up to the time of. **2** as late as. ~*conj.* up to the time when. [ME var. of UNTO]

Usage note The forms *until* and *till* are largely interchangeable, but *until* tends to be used especially at the beginning of sentences and in formal contexts.

unto (ŭn´tu) *prep.* to. [OFris. and OS *und*, to, TO]

un- (+ u–w words) unused[1] (ŭnūzd´) *a.* not having been or not being used. **unused**[2] (ŭnūst´) *a.* not accustomed (to). **unusual** *a.* **1** not usual. **2** remarkable. **unusually** *adv.* **unusualness** *n.* **unutterable** *a.* inexpressible, indescribable. **unutterably** *adv.* **unuttered** *a.* **unvaccinated** *a.* **unvalued** *a.* **1** not esteemed. **2** not appraised, not estimated. **3** †invaluable, inestimable. **unvanquished** *a.* **unvaried** *a.* **unvarnished** *a.* **1** not covered with varnish. **2** not embellished, plain, simple. **unvarying** *a.* **unvaryingly** *adv.* **unvaryingness** *n.* **unveil** *v.t.* **1** to remove a veil or covering from, esp. to remove a covering from (a statue etc.) with public ceremony. **2** to reveal, to disclose. ~*v.i.* to take one's veil off. **unveiling** *n.* **unventilated** *a.* **unverifiable** *a.* **unverified** *a.* **unversed** *a.* not versed or skilled (in). **unviable** *a.* **unviability** *n.* **unviolated** *a.* **unvisited** *a.* **unvitiated** *a.* **unvoiced** *a.* **1** not spoken, not uttered. **2** in phonetics, not voiced. **unwaged** *a.* not paid a wage; unemployed or not doing paid work. **unwalled** *a.* **unwanted** *a.* **unwarily, unwariness** UNWARY (under UN- (+ U–W WORDS)). **unwarlike** *a.* **unwarmed** *a.* **unwarned** *a.* **unwarrantable** *a.* not defensible or justifiable, inexcusable. **unwarrantableness** *n.* **unwarrantably** *adv.* **unwarranted** *a.* **1** not authorized. **2** not justified. **unwary** *a.* **1** not cautious. **2** not aware of danger. **unwarily** *adv.* **unwariness** *n.* **unwashed** *a.* not washed. **the great unwashed** (*coll.*) the mob, the rabble. **unwasted** *a.* **unwatchable** *a.* **unwatched** *a.* **unwatchful** *a.* **unwatered** *a.* **unwavering** *a.* steady, steadfast, firm. **unwaveringly** *adv.* **unweaned** *a.* **unwearable** *a.* **unwearied** *a.* **1** not wearied. **2** tireless. **3** incessant. **unweariedly** *adv.* **unweariedness** *n.* **unweary** *a.* **unwearying** *a.* **1** incessant; persistent. **2** not causing weariness. **unwearyingly** *adv.* **unweave** *v.t.* to undo (something that has been woven); to separate the threads of. **unwed, unwedded** *a.* **unweddedness** *n.* **unweeded** *a.* **unweighed** *a.* **1** not weighed. **2** (of remarks etc.) not considered; rash. **unweight** *v.t.* to remove the weight from. **unwelcome** *a.* **unwelcomed** *a.* **unwelcomely** *adv.* **unwelcomeness** *n.* **unwelcoming** *a.* **unwell** *a.* **1** not well; sick. **2** indisposed. **unwept** *a.* **1** not lamented, not mourned. **2** (of tears) not wept. **unwhipped** *a.* **1** not punished by whipping. **2** in Parliament, not subject to a whip. **unwholesome** *a.* **1** having a harmful physical or moral effect. **2** (esp. of food) unhealthy. **3** of unhealthy appearance. **unwholesomely** *adv.* **unwholesomeness** *n.* **unwieldy** *a.* (*comp.* **unwieldier,** *superl.* **unwieldiest**) **1** that cannot be easily handled owing to size or weight. **2** bulky, ponderous, clumsy. **unwieldily** *adv.* **unwieldiness** *n.* **unwilled** *a.* unintentional. **unwilling** *a.* not willing; averse; reluctant. **unwillingly** *adv.* **unwillingness** *n.* **unwind** *v.t.* (*past, p.p.* **unwound**) **1** to free (something that has been wound). **2** to free from entanglement. **3** (*coll.*) to relax (a person). ~*v.i.* **1** to become unwound. **2** (*coll.*) to relax. **unwinking** *a.* **1** not winking. **2** watchful, vigilant. **unwinkingly** *adv.* **unwinnable** *a.* **unwisdom** *n.* lack of wisdom; folly. **unwise** *a.* **1** not wise, without judgement. **2** foolish. **unwisely** *adv.* **unwished** *a.* not desired; not sought (for). **unwithered** *a.* **unwitnessed** *a.* **unwomanly** *a.* **unwomanliness** *n.* **unwonted** *a.* not accustomed; unusual. **unwontedly** *adv.* **unwontedness** *n.* **unwooded** *a.* **unworkable** *a.* **unworkability, unworkableness** *n.* **unworkably** *adv.* **unworked** *a.* **1** not shaped. **2** not exploited. **unworldly** *a.* **1** not worldly, spiritually minded. **2** of or relating to spiritual things. **unworldliness** *n.* **unworn** *a.* never worn, new; not impaired by use. **unworried** *a.* **unworthy** *a.* (*comp.* **unworthier,** *superl.* **unworthiest**) **1** not worthy, not deserving (of). **2** not becoming, not seemly, discreditable. **3** contemptible. **unworthily** *adv.* **unworthiness** *n.* **unwound**[1] (-wownd) *a.* not wound. **unwound**[2] UNWIND (under UN- (+ U–W WORDS)). **unwounded** (-woon´-) *a.* **unwoven** *a.* **unwrap** *v.t.*

(*pres.p.* **unwrapping,** *past, p.p.* **unwrapped)** 1 to take the wrapping off (something). 2 to unfold or unroll. ~*v.i.* to become unwrapped. **unwrinkle** *v.t., v.i.* **unwrinkled** *a.* **unwritten** *a.* 1 not written. 2 traditional. 3 not written upon, blank. **unwritable** *a.* **unwritten law** *n.* a law not formulated in statutes etc., esp. one based on custom and judicial decisions. **unwrought** *a.*

unwitting (ŭnwit´ing) *a.* 1 unconscious. 2 unintentional, inadvertent. **unwittingly** *adv.* **unwittingness** *n.* [OE *unwitende*; see WIT[2]]

un- (+ y–z words) unyielding *a.* 1 unbending, stiff. 2 firm, obstinate. **unyieldingly** *adv.* **unyieldingness** *n.* **unyoke** *v.t.* to loose from or as from a yoke. ~*v.i.* to cease working. **unzip** *v.t.* (*pres.p.* **unzipping,** *past, p.p.* **unzipped)** to undo the zip of.

UP *abbr.* 1 United Presbyterian. 2 Uttar Pradesh.

up (ŭp) *adv.* 1 to or at a higher place or position. 2 to a capital city, university, a place farther north, or other place regarded as higher (*up to Edinburgh*). 3 at or to the time or place referred to (*I went up to them; Everything had been going well up till then*). 4 off the ground. 5 to or in an erect position or standing posture. 6 to or in a position or condition for action. 7 out of bed. 8 (*coll.*) to the front or in front (*I went up ahead*). 9 to or in a prepared or required state (*We put the tent up*). 10 to or at a higher price (*Petrol is up again*). 11 in a stronger position or better off (*They're two goals up; £20 up on the deal*). 12 (of a computer) switched on and ready for use. 13 more loudly (*You'll have to speak up*). 14 (of the sun) above the horizon. 15 indicating completion or the end of something (*Five minutes are up*). 16 completely, entirely, effectually (*drink up; tear up*). 17 appearing in court as a defendant. 18 indicating a tightly closed or compact state (*to sew up; tied up; to roll up*). 19 indicating accumulation (*mount up*). 20 knowledgeable (*She's well up in English literature*). 21 (of a road) undergoing repairs. 22 towards the source of a stream or river. 23 inland. 24 in baseball, to one's turn at batting. 25 (of points in a game) gained so far or shown on a scoreboard. 26 upstairs. 27 (of a theatre curtain) raised. 28 (*as int.*) stand up. 29 (of a ship's helm) with the rudder pointing to leeward. ~*prep.* 1 from a lower to a higher place or point of. 2 in an ascending direction on or along, towards the higher part of. 3 towards the source of (a river). 4 towards the interior of. 5 at or in a higher part of. ~*a.* 1 moving, sloping or directed towards a higher or more central part. 2 towards the capital (*the up train*). 3 (of beer) frothy. ~*n.* a period of good fortune. ~*v.t.* (*pres.p.* **upping,** *past, p.p.* **upped)** to raise or increase, esp. suddenly. ~*v.i.* 1 to do something suddenly and unexpectedly (*She upped and left him*). 2 to pick up (*He upped his bags*). **all up with** doomed or hopeless. **on the up and up** 1 (*coll.*) becoming steadily more successful. 2 (*esp. N Am., coll.*) straight, honest. **something is up** (*coll.*) something unusual or strange is happening. **time is up** 1 the allotted time is past. 2 the appointed moment has arrived. **to up sticks** (*coll.*) to move house, to go and live elsewhere, to make off. **up against** 1 confronting, having to deal with. 2 close to. 3 touching. **up against it** (*coll.*) facing stiff opposition or great difficulties. **up and about** having got out of bed. **up and doing** active and busy. **up and down** 1 alternately backwards and forwards. 2 alternately upwards and downwards. 3 in every direction. 4 (*coll.*) varying in moods or states of health. **up and running** functioning. **up for** put forward for or being considered for (office). **up front** 1 at the front. 2 (of payments) in advance. **up hill and down dale** 1 up and down hills. 2 facing many difficulties or engaged on a difficult journey. **up in arms** ARM[2]. **up on** knowledgeable about. **ups and downs** 1 rises and falls, undulations. 2 vicissitudes, changes of fortune. **up sticks** STICK[1]. **up the pole** POLE[1]. **up the spout** SPOUT. **up to** 1 until (*up to now*). 2 as far as (*up to my shoulder*). 3 as many or as much as (*up to five goes*). 4 incumbent upon (*It's not up to me to decide*). 5 capable of; equal to (a task etc.). 6 occupied with (*What are you up to?*). **up to a person's tricks** TRICK. **up to one's tricks** TRICK. **up top** (*coll.*) in one's head or brain. **up to snuff** SNUFF[2]. **up to the mark** MARK[1]. **up with** used to express support for something (*Up with the republic!*). **up yours** (*sl., offensive*) used to express contempt, defiance etc. **what's up?** 1 (*coll.*) what is going on? 2 (*coll.*) what is the matter? **up-anchor** *v.i.* to weigh anchor. **up-and-coming** *a.* (*coll.*) (of a person) enterprising and promising. **up-and-comer** *n.* **up-and-over** *a.* (of a door) opened by pulling it upwards to a horizontal position. **up-and-under** *n.* in rugby, a high kick to give fellow team players time to get to the spot where the ball will come down. **up to date, up-to-date** *a.* recent, modern, abreast of the times. **up-to-the-minute** *a.* most recent or modern. [OE *ūp, ūpp* (cp. Dut. *op*, G *auf*)]

up- (ŭp) *pref.* up; upwards; upper. [as UP]

Upanishad (oopan´ishad) *n.* any one of the philosophical treatises forming the third division of the Vedas. [Sansk.]

upas (ū´pəs) *n.* 1 the upas tree. 2 the poisonous sap of this and other Malaysian trees. 3 a corrupting or pernicious influence. **upas tree** *n.* a Javanese tree, *Antiaris toxicaria*, the acrid milky juice of which contains a virulent poison, used for poisoning arrows, and formerly believed to destroy animal or vegetable life in its immediate neighbourhood. [Malay, poison]

up- (+ b– words) upbeat (ŭp´-) *n.* (*Mus.*) an unaccented beat, on which the conductor raises his baton. ~*a.* (*coll.*) cheerful, optimistic. **upblaze** *v.i.* to blaze up. **upbringing** (ŭp´-) *n.* bringing up, education. **upbuild** *v.t.* (*past, p.p.* **upbuilt)** to build up.

upbraid (ŭpbrād´) *v.t.* to reproach (with, for); to reprove with severity. ~*v.i.* to chide. **upbraider** *n.* **upbraiding** *n.* **upbraidingly** *adv.* [OE *upbregdan*, to lay hold of, to upbraid (UP-, BRAID[1])]

up- (+ c–h words) upcast[1] *v.t.* (*past, p.p.* **upcast)** to cast or throw up. **upcast**[2] (ŭp´-) *n.* 1 a casting or throwing upwards. 2 the shaft by which air ascends after ventilating a mine. 3 (*Geol.*) an upthrow. **upchuck** (ŭp´-) *v.i.* (*N Am., sl.*) to vomit. ~*n.* vomit. **upcoming** *a.* (*esp. N Am.*) forthcoming. **up-country** (ŭp´-, -kŭn´-) *adv., a.* towards the interior of a country, inland. **update**[1] *v.t.* to bring up to date. **update**[2] (ŭp´-) *n.* 1 a bringing up to date. 2 something which has been updated. **updraught** (ŭp´-), (*N Am.*) **updraft** *n.* an upward current of air. **upend** *v.t.* 1 to turn over on its end. 2 to transform or affect greatly. ~*v.i.* to rise on end. **upfield** *adv.* in football etc., in or towards the opposing team's end of a field. **upfront** *a.* (*coll.*) 1 honest, straightforward. 2 (of money) paid out in advance. 3 at the front or forefront. ~*adv.* up front. **upgrade**[1] *v.t.* 1 to raise (a worker or a job) to a higher grade or status. 2 to improve (a computer, piece of machinery etc.), e.g. by buying new components. **upgrade**[2] (up´-) *n.* 1 an act or instance of upgrading. 2 a piece of machinery etc. that has been upgraded. **on the upgrade** improving, advancing or progressing. **upgradeable, upgradable** *a.* **upgrowth** (ŭp´-) *n.* 1 the act or process of growing up. 2 something which grows up. **upheaval** *n.* 1 a violent disturbance, revolution etc. 2 (*Geol.*) an elevation of part of the earth's crust. 3 the act or process of heaving up. **upheave** *v.t.* to lift up from beneath. ~*v.i.* to rise up. **upheld** UPHOLD (under UP- (+ C–H WORDS)). **uphill**[1] (ŭp´-) *a.* 1 leading or going up a hill. 2 difficult, arduous, severe. ~*n.* an upward incline. **uphill**[2] (-hil´) *adv.* in an ascending direction, upwards. **uphold** *v.t.* (*past, p.p.* **upheld)** 1 to hold up, to keep erect. 2 to support, to sustain, to maintain. 3 to approve, to countenance. **upholder** *n.*

upholster (ŭphōl´stə) *v.t.* **1** to provide (chairs etc.) with stuffing, cushions, coverings etc. **2** to furnish with curtains, carpets, furniture etc. **upholsterer** *n.* a person who upholsters furniture professionally. **upholstery** *n.* **1** the stuffing, cushions, coverings etc. of a piece of furniture. **2** the work of an upholsterer. [from UPHOLD (under UP- (+ C–H WORDS)), -STER]

uphroe (ū´frō) *n.* (*Naut.*) a long wooden block pierced with holes for reeving a cord, esp. for adjusting an awning. [Dut. *juffrouw*, young woman (*jung*, YOUNG, *vrouw*, woman)]

up- (+ k–m words) upkeep (ŭp´-) *n.* (cost of) maintenance. **upland** (ŭp´-) *n.* (*also* **uplands**) high ground or the higher part of a district. ~*a.* of or relating to or situated on the uplands. **uplift**[1] *v.t.* **1** to lift up, to raise. **2** to raise morally or spiritually. **uplift**[2] (ŭp´-) *n.* **1** a lifting up. **2** (*coll.*) spiritual or moral improvement. **3** (*Geol.*) the raising of land to a higher level. **4** a brassiere designed to support and lift the bust. ~*a.* uplifted or providing uplift. **uplifter** *n.* **uplifting** *a.* **uplighter** (ŭp´-) *n.* a light designed to cast light upwards. **uplink** (ŭp´-) *n.* a transmitter that sends signals up to a communications satellite. ~*v.t.* to provide with or transmit by an uplink. **upload** *v.t.* (*Comput.*) to copy or send (data, a file etc.) usu. to a larger storage device or system. ~*n.* an act of instance of this. **upmaking** (ŭp´-) *n.* a filling of planks etc. inserted between a ship's bottom and the bilge-ways before launching. **upmarket** *a.* of or relating to the more expensive sector of the market. ~*adv.* towards this sector of the market. **upmost** *a.* uppermost.

upon (ŭpon´) *adv.* on. [OE *uppon*, *uppan* (UP, ON)]

upper[1] (ŭp´ə) *a.* **1** higher in place (*the upper jaw*). **2** superior in rank or status (*the upper classes*). **3** (**Upper**) situated on higher land. **4** (**Upper**) situated to the north or further upstream (*Upper Nile*). **5** (*Geol.*) (*sometimes* **Upper**) designating the late part of a period, formation etc. ~*n.* the part of a boot or shoe above the sole. **on one's uppers** (*coll.*) destitute. **upper case** *n.* (*Print.*) **1** capital letters. **2** (*Hist.*) the case holding capitals, reference marks etc. **upper class** *n.* the economically and socially most powerful class in a society. ~*a.* (*also* **upper-class**) of or relating to this class. **upper crust** *n.* (*coll.*) the upper class. **uppercut** *n.* in boxing, a punch delivered in an upwards direction with a bent arm. ~*v.t.* (*pres.p.* **uppercutting,** *past, p.p.* **uppercut**) to punch (someone) in this way. **upper deck** *n.* (*Naut.*) the full-length deck of a ship above the water level. **upper hand** *n.* the superior position, mastery. **Upper House** *n.* the higher house in a bicameral legislature, esp. the House of Lords. **uppermost** *a.* **1** highest in place, rank, authority etc. **2** predominant. ~*adv.* at or to the highest place or position. **upper regions** *n.pl.* the higher strata of the atmosphere or the sea. **upper works** *n.pl.* (*Naut.*) the parts above the water when a ship is in proper trim for a voyage. [comp. of UP]

upper[2] (ŭp´ə) *n.* (*sl.*) a stimulant drug. [UP, -ER[1]]

uppish (ŭp´ish) *a.* (*coll.*) self-assertive, pretentious or snobbish. **uppishly** *adv.* **uppishness** *n.* [UP, -ISH[1]]

uppity (ŭp´iti) *a.* (*coll.*) **1** uppish. **2** not amenable to persuasion or control.

up- (+ r– words) upraise *v.t.* to raise up; to lift. **uprate** *v.t.* **1** to raise to a higher rank, rate or value. **2** to upgrade. **uprear** *v.t.* to raise up. **uprise**[1] *v.i.* (*past* **uprose,** *p.p.* **uprisen**) to rise up. **uprise**[2] (ŭp´-) *n.* an uprising. **uprising** (ŭp´-) *n.* an insurrection, a rising, a riot. **upriver** *adv.* towards the source of a river. ~*a.* near the source of a river. **uproot** *v.t.* **1** to tear up by or as by the roots. **2** to displace (a person) from their usual surroundings. **3** to eradicate. ~*v.i.* to move away from one's familiar or usual surroundings. **uprooter** *n.* **uprose** UPRISE (under UP- (+ R– WORDS)). **uprush** (ŭp´-) *n.* an upward rush.

upright (ŭp´rīt) *a.* **1** erect, perpendicular. **2** righteous, honest. **3** (of a book etc.) being taller than it is wide. ~*adv.* erect, vertically. ~*n.* **1** an upright timber, pillar, post etc. **2** an upright piano. **uprightly** *adv.* **uprightness** *n.* **upright piano** *n.* a piano with a vertical case for the strings. [OE *upriht* (UP, RIGHT)]

uproar (ŭp´raw) *n.* a noisy tumult; a violent disturbance; bustle and clamour. **uproarious** (-raw´-) *a.* **1** noisy and disorderly. **2** extremely funny. **uproariously** *adv.* **1** noisily. **2** hilariously. **uproariousness** *n.* [Dut. *oproer* (UP, *roeren*, to stir, cp. G *rühren*, OE *hreran*, Swed. *röra*, Dan. *röre*, Icel. *hrœra*)]

up- (+ s– words) upscale *a., adv.* (*N Am.*) upmarket. **upshift** (ŭp´-) *v.i.* to move to a higher gear. ~*v.t.* (*esp. N Am.*) to increase. ~*n.* a movement to a higher gear. **upshot** (ŭp´-) *n.* the final issue, result or conclusion (of a matter). **upside** (ŭp´-) *n.* **1** the positive aspect of a situation that is generally bad. **2** an upward movement, e.g. of share prices. **3** the upper part. **upsides** *adv.* (*coll.*) equal (with), e.g. through revenge. †**upspring**[1] (ŭp´-) *n.* a leap in the air. †**upspring**[2] (-spring´) *v.i.* (*past, p.p.* **upsprung**) to spring. **upstage** *adv.* at the rear of a stage. ~*a.* **1** situated upstage. **2** stand-offish. ~*v.t.* **1** to force (an actor) to face away from the audience by taking a position upstage of them. **2** to draw attention away from (a person) to oneself. **upstairs** (ŭp´-) *a.* (*also* **upstair**) of or relating to or in an upper storey. ~*n.* an upper storey or storeys. ~*adv.* on or to an upper storey. **to kick upstairs** KICK[1]. **upstanding** *a.* **1** erect. **2** honest, upright. **3** of strong and upright build. **upstart** (ŭp´-) *n.* **1** a person who rises suddenly from humble origins to wealth, power or consequence. **2** a person who assumes an arrogant bearing. ~*a.* **1** who is an upstart. **2** characteristic of an upstart. **upstate** (ŭp´-) *n.* (*N Am.*) part of a state of the US which is away from, and usu. to the north of, the principal city or cities. ~*adv.* to or in this part. ~*a.* in or relating to this part. **upstater** *n.* **upstream** *a., adv.* **1** against the current. **2** (situated) higher up a river. **upstroke** (ŭp´-) *n.* an upward line in writing. **upsurge**[1] (ŭp´-) *n.* a sudden, rapid rise. **upsurge**[2] (-sœj´) *v.i.* to surge up. **upswept** *a.* **1** swept or brushed upwards. **2** curved upwards. **upswing** (ŭp´-) *n.* **1** an upward rise. **2** an increase or improvement, esp. in economic terms.

ups-a-daisy UPSYDAISY.

upset[1] (ŭpset´) *v.t.* (*pres.p.* **upsetting,** *past, p.p.* **upset**) **1** to overturn. **2** to put out of one's normal state, to disconcert, to distress. **3** to make slightly ill (*Something upset my stomach*). **4** to disrupt. **5** to shorten and thicken (a tyre or other metal object) by hammering or pressure. ~*v.i.* to be overturned. **upsetter** *n.* **upsettingly** *adv.*

upset[2] (ŭp´set) *n.* **1** the act of upsetting. **2** the state of being upset. **3** an unexpected reversal in a game etc. ~*a.* physically disturbed (*an upset stomach*). **upset price** *n.* the lowest price at which a property is offered for sale by auction; a reserve price.

upside down (ŭpsīd down´) *a., adv.* **1** with the upper part under. **2** in complete disorder and confusion. **upside-down cake** *n.* a cake baked with fruit at the bottom, and inverted for serving. [ME *up so down*, up as it were down]

upsilon (ŭp´silon) *n.* the 20th letter in the Greek alphabet (Υ, υ). [Gr., simple u]

upsydaisy (ŭp´sidāzi), **ups-a-daisy, oops-a-daisy** *int.* used as a reassuring expression to accompany the lifting up of someone, esp. a child, who has stumbled or fallen.

up- (+ t– words) uptake (ŭp´-) *n.* **1** the act of taking or lifting up. **2** the process of taking, absorbing or accepting what is on offer. **3** a pipe, shaft or flue with an upward current. **quick on the uptake** quick to understand or learn. **up-tempo** *a., adv.* at a fast tempo.

upthrow (ŭp´-) *n.* 1 a throwing up, an upheaval. 2 (*Geol.*) the upward displacement on one side of a fault. **upthrust** (ŭp´-) *n.* an upward thrust, esp. a geological upheaval. **uptick** (ŭp´-) *n.* (*esp. NAm.*) a small increase. **uptime** (ŭp´-) *n.* the time during which a machine, esp. a computer, is actually working. **uptown** (ŭp´-) *n.* (*esp. NAm.*) the upper, or residential, part of town. ~*a.* of or in this part. ~*adv.* into or towards this part. **upturn**[1] (ŭp´-) *n.* 1 an upward trend or turn towards improved conditions, higher prices etc. 2 an upheaval. **upturn**[2] (-tœn´) *v.t.* 1 to turn up or over. 2 to direct upwards.

uptight (ŭptīt´) *a.* (*coll.*) 1 tense, nervy. 2 nervous, irritated. 3 conventional, strait-laced.

UPU *abbr.* Universal Postal Union.

UPVC *abbr.* unplasticized polyvinyl chloride.

up- (+ w–words) upwarp (ŭp´-) *n.* (*Geol.*) an anticline. **upwind** (-wind´) *adv., a.* 1 against the wind. 2 (to or) on the windward side of.

upward (ŭp´wəd) *a.* directed, turned or moving towards a higher place. ~*adv.* upwards. **upwardly** *adv.* upwards. **upwardly mobile** *a.* aspiring to improve one's lifestyle, social status etc. **upward mobility** *n.* movement to a position of higher social or professional status. **upwards** *adv.* 1 towards a higher place or level; in an upward direction. 2 towards the source or spring. 3 more. **upwards of** more than.

ur- (uə) *comb. form* original, primitive, as *Urtext.* [G]

uracil (ū´rəsil) *n.* a pyrimidine making up one of the four bases of RNA and found in all living cells. [UREA, ACETIC]

uraei URAEUS.

uraemia (ūrē´miə), (*N Am.*) **uremia** *n.* a condition caused by the retention of urea and other noxious substances in the kidneys and bladder. **uraemic** *a.* [mod. L (Gr. *ouron*, urine, *haima*, blood)]

uraeus (ūrē´əs) *n.* (*pl.* **uraei** (-ī), **uraeuses**) the serpent emblem worn on the headdress of ancient Egyptian divinities and kings. [Gr. *ouraios*, from *oura*, tail]

Ural-Altaic (ūrəlaltā´ik) *a.* 1 of or relating to the Ural and Altaic mountain ranges or the people inhabiting them. 2 denoting a family of Mongolian, Finnic and allied languages of agglutinative structure spoken in N Europe and Asia. ~*n.* this family of languages.

Uralic (ūral´ik) *n.* a language group comprising the Finno-Ugric and Samoyed languages. ~*a.* of or relating to this group.

uralite (ū´rəlīt) *n.* an amphibole mineral resembling hornblende and resulting from the alteration of pyroxene. **uralitic** (-lit´-) *a.* [*Ural*, -ITE[1]]

uranium (ūrā´niəm) *n.* a radioactive, fissionable, silvery-white metallic element, at. no. 92, chem. symbol U, found in pitchblende, and used as a source of nuclear energy. **uranic** (-ran´-), **uranous** (ū´-) *a.* **uranite** (ū´rənīt) *n.* an ore of uranium, esp. torbernite or autunite. **uranitic** (-nit´-) *a.* [URANUS, -IUM]

urano- (ū´rənō) *comb. form* 1 sky, the heavens. 2 uranium. [see URANUS]

†**uranography** (ūrənog´rəfi) *n.* descriptive astronomy. **uranographer** *n.* **uranographic** (-əgraf´-), **uranographical** *a.* **uranographist** *n.*

Uranus (ūrā´nəs, ū´rə-) *n.* a planet situated between Saturn and Neptune, discovered by Sir William Herschel in 1781. [L, from Gr. *Ouranos*, heaven, Uranus, the most ancient of all Greek gods, son of Ge and father of Kronos or Saturn and the Titans]

urate (ū´rāt) *n.* (*Chem.*) a salt of uric acid. **uratic** (ūrat´-) *a.*

urban (œ´bən) *a.* of or relating to, situated or living in a city or town. **urban district** *n.* (*Hist.*) a district comprising a small town or towns with a small aggregate population or not yet incorporated as a borough. **urban guerrilla** *n.* a guerrilla operating in a town or city. **urbanism** *n.* 1 the character of urban life. 2 the study of urban life. **urbanist** *n.* **urbanite** (-nīt) *n.* a town-dweller. **urbanize, urbanise** *v.t.* 1 to make townlike. 2 to ruin the rural character of. **urbanization** (-zā´shən) *n.* **urban myth** *n.* a widely believed story, usu. about some shocking or amusing event involving an ordinary person. **urban renewal** *n.* slum clearance or redevelopment. **urban sprawl** *n.* the uncontrolled spread of city buildings and houses into surrounding areas. [L *urbānus*, from *urbs urbis*, city]

urbane (œbān´) *a.* courteous, polite; suave; refined. **urbanely** *adv.* [as URBAN]

urbanity (œban´iti) *n.* 1 the quality of being urbane. 2 urban life.

urchin (œ´chin) *n.* 1 a roguish, mischievous child, esp. one dressed in rags. 2 SEA URCHIN (under SEA). 3 †a hedgehog. 4 †an elf, a fairy. [ME *urchon*, from ONF *herichun* (F *hérisson*), ult. from L *ēricius*, from *ēr*, hedgehog, cogn. with Gr. *chēr*]

Urdu (uə´doo) *n.* a language closely related to Hindi but with many Persian and Arabic words, an official language of Pakistan, also widely used in India esp. by Muslims. [Hind. (*zabāni*) *urdū*, (language of the) camp, from Pers. *urdū*, from Turk. *ordū*]

-ure (ūə, yə, ə) *suf.* 1 forming nouns indicating process or action, as *censure, portraiture, seizure.* 2 indicating result, as *caricature.* 3 forming collective nouns, as *architecture.* 4 indicating office or function, as *judicature.* [F, from L *-ūra*, added to p.p. stems of verbs]

urea (ūrē´ə) *n.* (*Chem.*) a soluble crystalline compound contained in urine, esp. of mammals. **urea-formaldehyde** *n.* a synthetic material such as resin or plastic made by heating together urea and formaldehyde, and used esp. for insulation. **ureal** *a.* [Gr. *ouron*, urine]

uredo (ūrē´dō) *n.* (*pl.* **uredines** (-dinēz)) URTICARIA (under URTICACEOUS). **uredospore** (-spaw) *n.* a non-sexual spore in rust-causing fungi. [L *ūrēdo, -dinis*, blight, from *urere*, to burn]

uremia URAEMIA.

ureter (ūrē´tə) *n.* the duct conveying the urine from the kidneys into the bladder. **ureteral** *a.* **ureteric** (-ter´-) *a.* **ureteritis** (-ī´tis) *n.* inflammation of the ureter. [Gr. *ourētēr*, from *ourein*, to urinate]

urethane (ū´rəthān) *n.* 1 a crystalline amide, $NH_2COOC_2H_5$, used esp. in plastics and as an anaesthetic. 2 polyurethane.

urethra (ūrē´thrə) *n.* (*pl.* **urethrae** (-rē), **urethras**) the duct by which the urine is discharged from the bladder. **urethral** *a.* **urethritis** (ūrithrī´tis) *n.* inflammation of the urethra. [L, from Gr. *ourēthra*, as URETER]

urethroscope (ūrē´thrəskōp) *n.* an instrument for examining the interior of the urethra.

uretic (ūret´ik) *a.* of or relating to urine.

urge (œj) *v.t.* 1 to drive or impel; to force onwards. 2 to press earnestly with argument, entreaty etc., to importune. 3 to press the acceptance or adoption of. 4 to cite forcefully as a reason or justification. ~*n.* 1 a strong impulse. 2 an inner drive or compulsion. **urgency** (-jənsi) *n.* 1 the quality or state of being urgent. 2 pressure of necessity, esp. as a plea for giving a matter precedence in a deliberative assembly. **urgent** *a.* 1 pressing, demanding early attention. 2 demanding or soliciting with importunity. **urgently** *adv.* **urger** *n.* [L *urgēre*, cogn. with Gr. *heirgein*, to repress, Eng. WREAK]

URI *abbr.* upper respiratory infection.

uri URUS.

-uria (ū´riə) *comb. form* indicating a diseased condition of the urine, as *dysuria.* [Gr. *-ouria*, from *ouron*, urine]

uric (ū´rik) *a.* of or relating to urine. **uric acid** *n.* a white, tasteless and inodorous, almost insoluble compound found chiefly in excrement of birds and reptiles, and in small quantities in the urine of mammals.

urinal (ūrī´nəl, ū´rin-) *n.* 1 a receptacle fixed to a wall for men to urinate into. **2** a public or private room, building, enclosure etc. containing these. **3** a glass receptacle for holding urine for medical inspection.

urine (ū´rin) *n.* a pale-yellow fluid with an acid reaction, secreted from the blood by the kidneys, stored in the bladder, and discharged through the urethra, the chief means for the removal of nitrogenous and saline matters resulting from the decay of tissue. **urinalysis** (ūrinal´isis) *n.* (*pl.* **urinalyses** (-ēz)) the analysis of urine, esp. in order to diagnose disease. **urinary** *a.* of or relating to urine or the urinary system. *~n.* (*pl.* **urinaries**) **1** a reservoir for urine for use as manure. **2** a urinal. **urinate** *v.i.* to pass urine. **urination** (-ā´shən) *n.* **urinative** *a.* provoking the discharge of urine; diuretic. **uriniferous** (-nif´-) *a.* conveying urine. **urinogenital** *a.* urogenital. **urinology** *n.* urology. **urinometer** (-nom´itə) *n.* an instrument for ascertaining the specific gravity of urine. **urinous** *a.* [F, from L *ūrīna*, cogn. with Gr. *ouron*, Sansk. *vári*, water, OE *wær*, the sea]

urn (œn) *n.* **1** a vase with a foot and a usu. rounded body used for preserving the ashes of the dead, for holding water, as a measure, and other purposes. **2** a vase-shaped vessel with a tap, and usually a spirit lamp or other heater, for making tea, coffee etc. or keeping it hot. **3** (*poet.*) something in which the remains of the dead are preserved, a grave. *~v.t.* to enclose in or as in an urn. **urnful** *n.* (*pl.* **urnfuls**). [F *urne*, L *urna*]

uro-[1] (ū´rō) *comb. form* tail, hind part. [Gr. *oura*, tail]

uro-[2] (ū´rō) *comb. form* urine. [Gr. *ouron*, urine]

urochord (ū´rōkawd) *n.* **1** the notochord of larval ascidians and some tunicates. **2** (*Zool.*) (*also* **urochordate**) an individual of the subphylum Urochordata, comprising the tunicates. [URO-[1], CHORD[2]]

urodele (ū´rōdēl) *n.* any amphibian of the order Urodela, having a tail and four short limbs and including newts and salamanders. [URO-[1]]

urogenital (ūrōjen´itəl) *a.* of or relating to the genital and urinary organs. [URO-[2]]

urology (ūrol´əji) *n.* the branch of medicine concerned with the study of the urinary system. **urologic** (-əloj´-), **urological** *a.* **urologist** *n.* [URO-[2]]

uropod (ū´rəpod) *n.* (*Zool.*) an abdominal appendage of lobsters and related crustaceans. [URO-[1], Gr. *pous podos*, a foot]

uropygium (ūrəpij´iəm) *n.* the terminal part of the body of a bird. **uropygial** *a.* [URO-[1], Gr. *pugē*, rump]

urostyle (ū´rəstīl) *n.* a bone forming the last part of the vertebral column in tailless amphibians. [URO-[1]]

Ursa (œ´sə) *n.* Ursa Major. **Ursa Major** *n.* the constellation, the Great Bear or Plough, visible in the northern sky and containing seven bright stars. **Ursa Minor** *n.* the small constellation, the Little Bear, containing the north celestial pole and the pole star. [L, she-bear]

ursine (œ´sīn) *a.* of or relating to or resembling a bear. [L *ursinus*, from *ursus*, bear]

Ursuline (œ´sūlīn) *n.* a member of an order of nuns founded in 1537, devoted chiefly to nursing and the education of girls. *~a.* of, belonging or relating to this order. [St *Ursula*, -INE]

urticaceous (œtikā´shəs) *a.* (*Bot.*) of or having the character of nettles. **urticaria** (-keə´riə) *n.* (*Med.*) nettle-rash. **urticate** *v.t.* **1** to sting with or as with nettles. **2** (*Hist.*) to whip (a benumbed or paralytic limb) with nettles to restore feeling. **urtication** (-ā´shən) *n.* [L *urtica*, nettle, -ACEOUS]

urus (ū´rəs) *n.* (*pl.* **uri** (-ī), **uruses**) AUROCHS. [L, from Gr. *ouros*]

US *abbr.* **1** Under-Secretary. **2** United States. **3** unserviceable.

us (ŭs) *pron.* **1** objective (acc. and dat.) of WE. **2** (*coll.*) me. **3** (*formal*) objective of WE as used by newspaper editors and monarchs. [OE *ūs*, from Gmc.]

Usage note Use alongside a subject, as in *Us girls should stick together*, is best avoided. See also notes under AS[1], BE, THAN.

USA *abbr.* **1** United States Army. **2** United States of America.

usable USE[2].

USAF *abbr.* United States Air Force.

usage (ū´sij, ū´zij) *n.* **1** the manner of using or treating, treatment. **2** customary or habitual practice, esp. as authorizing a right etc. **3** (an instance of) the way a language is actually used. **4** (*Law*) a uniform and recognized practice. [USE[1]]

usance (ū´zəns) *n.* a period of time allowed for payment of a foreign bill of exchange. [OF, as USE[1]]

USDAW (ŭz´daw) *abbr.* Union of Shop, Distributive and Allied Workers.

use[1] (ūs) *n.* **1** the act of using. **2** the state of being used (*The lift is in constant use*). **3** employment in or application to a purpose (*I'm sure you'll find some use for it*). **4** occasion, need, or power to use (*He regained the use of his left arm*). **5** the quality of being useful or serving a purpose (*It's no use complaining now*). **6** custom, practice, usage. **7** a form of ritual etc. peculiar to a church, diocese or country. **8** (*Law*) enjoyment of the benefit or profit of lands and tenements held by another in trust for the beneficiary. **in use 1** being employed. **2** in customary practice. **to have no use for 1** to dislike, to disapprove of. **2** to find no use for. **to make use of 1** to use, to employ. **2** to take advantage of. **use and wont** common or customary practice. **useful** *a.* **1** of use, serving a purpose. **2** good, beneficial, profitable, advantageous. **3** (*coll.*) competent or highly satisfactory. **to make oneself useful** to be of service to someone. **useful load** *n.* the load that an aircraft etc. carries in addition to its own weight. **usefully** *adv.* **usefulness** *n.* **useless** *a.* **1** not of use, serving no useful end or purpose. **2** (*coll.*) ineffectual, weak (*useless at tennis*). **uselessly** *adv.* **uselessness** *n.* [A-F and OF *us*, L *ūsus -ūs*, from *uti*, to use (in legal senses from A-F *oes*, L *opus*, employment, need)]

use[2] (ūz) *v.t.* **1** to employ, to apply to a purpose, to put into operation. **2** to turn to account, to avail oneself of (*Use your common sense*). **3** to treat in a specified way (*They used him badly*). **4** to exploit for one's own purposes. **5** to use up, to wear out. **6** (*usu. p.p.*) to accustom, to habituate (*I'm not used to getting up early in the morning*). *~v.i.* (*usu. in past*) to be accustomed, to make it one's constant practice to (*We used to play football here*). **could use** (*coll.*) would appreciate having. **to use a person's name** to quote a person as a reference etc. **to use up 1** to finish; to consume completely. **2** to find some use or purpose for (something left over). **3** to exhaust or wear out. **usable, useable** *a.* capable of being used. **usability** (-bil´-) *n.* **use-by date** *n.* a date marked on food showing when it should be used by. **used** *a.* **1** already made use of. **2** second-hand. **3** exploited. **used-up** *a.* exhausted, finished. **user** *n.* **1** a person who uses something. **2** (*coll.*) a person who takes drugs. **3** (*Law*) the continued enjoyment of a right. **user-friendly** *a.* (esp. of computers) easy to operate or understand. **user-friendliness** *n.*

Usage note Two negative forms of the intransitive verb are acceptable, *did not use* and *used not* (so *I did not use to, I didn't use to, I used not to, I usedn't to...*). It is best to avoid *didn't used* and *usen't*.

---

usher (ŭsh´ə) *n.* **1** a seat-attendant at a cinema, theatre etc. **2** an officer or servant acting as doorkeeper (esp. in a court or public hall). **3** a person whose job it is to introduce strangers or to walk before a person of rank. **4** †an assistant teacher in a school. *~v.t.* **1** to act as usher to. **2** to introduce, as a forerunner or harbinger; to bring or show (in etc.). **usherette** (-ret´) *n.* a woman usher at a cinema or theatre. **ushership** *n.* [F *huissier*, L *ostiārium*, from *ostium*, door]

USM *abbr.* Unlisted Securities Market.

USN *abbr.* United States Navy.

usquebaugh (ŭs´kwibah, -baw) *n.* **1** (*Sc., Ir.*) whisky. **2** an Irish liqueur made of brandy, spices etc. [Ir., Gael. *uisge beatha* (*uisge*, water, see WHISKY, *beatha*, life, cogn. with Gr. *bios*, L *vīta*)]

USS *abbr.* **1** United States Senate. **2** United States Ship.

USSR *abbr.* (*Hist.*) Union of Soviet Socialist Republics.

†**ustion** (ŭs´chən) *n.* **1** the act of burning. **2** the state of being burned. **3** (*Med.*) cauterization. [L *ustio*, from *urere*, to burn, p.p. *ustus*]

usu. *abbr.* usual(ly).

usual (ū´zhūəl) *a.* such as ordinarily occurs; customary, habitual. ~*n.* a person's usual drink, meal etc. **as per usual** as usually happens. **usually** *adv.* **usualness** *n.* [L *ūsuālis*, from *ūsus*, USE[1]]

usucaption (ūzūkap´shən), **usucapion** (-kā´piən) *n.* (*Law*) the acquisition of the title or right to property by uninterrupted possession for a certain number of years. [L *ūsūcapio -ōnis* (*ūsū*, by use, see USE[1], *capere*, to take)]

usufruct (ū´zūfrŭkt) *n.* the right to the use and enjoyment of property belonging to another without waste or destruction of its substance. ~*v.t.* to hold in or subject to usufruct. **usufructuary** (-frŭk´chu-) *n.* a person who has usufruct. ~*a.* relating to or of the nature of a usufruct. [L *ūsusfructus* (USE[1], *fructus*, FRUIT)]

usurer (ū´zhərə) *n.* a person who lends money at (esp. exorbitant) interest. **usurious** (ūzhuə´riəs) *a.* **1** practising usury, exacting exorbitant interest. **2** of or relating to or of the nature of usury. **usuriously** *adv.* **usury** (-ri) *n.* **1** the practice of lending money at interest, esp. higher than that allowed by law. **2** exorbitant interest. **3** †lending at interest or the taking of interest. **with usury** with interest. [OF *usurier*, med. L *ūsūrārius*, from L *ūsūra*, use, enjoyment, interest, from *ūsus*, USE[1]]

usurp (ūzœp´) *v.t.* to seize or take possession of without right. ~*v.i.* to encroach (upon). **usurpation** (-pā´shən) *n.* **usurpatory** *a.* **usurper** *n.* [F *usurper*, L *ūsurpāre*, to employ, to acquire, etym. uncertain]

usury USURER.

USW *abbr.* ultra-short wave.

UT *abbr.* **1** Universal Time. **2** Utah.

ut (ut) *n.* (*Mus.*) the first note or keynote in Guido's musical scale, now usu. superseded by *do* (see DO[2]). [L, see GAMUT]

UTC *abbr.* Universal Time Coordinated.

Utd *abbr.* United.

ute (ūt) *n.* (*Austral., New Zeal.*) a utility truck. [abbr.]

utensil (ūten´sil) *n.* an implement, esp. one used in cookery or domestic work. [MF *utensile*, L *ūtensilia*, utensils, from *ūtensilis*, fit for use, from *ūtī*, to USE[2]]

uterus (ū´tərəs) *n.* (*pl.* **uteri** (-rī)) the womb. **uterine** (-rīn) *a.* **1** of or relating to the womb. **2** born of the same mother but not the same father. **uteritis** (-ī´tis) *n.* inflammation of the womb. [L]

utilitarian (ūtiliteə´riən) *a.* **1** concerned with or made for practical use rather than beauty. **2** of or relating to utility or to utilitarianism. ~*n.* an advocate of utilitarianism. **utilitarianism** *n.* **1** the ethical doctrine that actions are right in proportion to their usefulness or as they tend to promote happiness. **2** the doctrine that the end and criterion of public action is the greatest happiness of the greatest number.

utility (ūtil´iti) *n.* (*pl.* **utilities**) **1** usefulness, serviceableness. **2** something which is useful. **3** utilitarianism, the greatest happiness of the greatest number. **4** a public service, such as the supply of water or electricity. **5** a utility man. ~*a.* **1** designed or adapted for general use. **2** practical, utilitarian. **utility knife** *n.* (*N Am.*) a very sharp knife with a replaceable blade. **utility man** *n.* (*pl.* **utility men**) an actor employed to take minor parts as required. **utility program** *n.* (*Comput.*) a program for carrying out a routine task. **utility room** *n.* a room (in a private house) used for storage, laundry etc. **utility vehicle, utility truck** *n.* a small truck or van, esp. a pick-up. [F *utilité*, L *ūtilitātem*, nom. *-tas*, from *ūtilis*, useful, from *ūtī*, to USE[2]]

utilize (ū´tilīz), **utilise** *v.t.* to make use of, to turn to account. **utilizable** *a.* **utilization** (-zā´shən) *n.* **utilizer** *n.*

-ution (ū´shən) *suf.* forming nouns, as *execution*. [F, from L *-utio*]

utmost (ŭt´mōst) *a.* being or situated at the farthest point or extremity; extreme; greatest. ~*n.* the utmost extent or degree. **to do one's utmost** to do everything that one can. [OE *ūtemest*, double superl. of *ūt*, OUT]

Utopia (ūtō´piə), **utopia** *n.* a place or state of ideal perfection. **Utopian, utopian** *a.* of or relating to or resembling Utopia; ideal or highly desirable but impracticable. ~*n.* an ardent and visionary political or social reformer. **Utopianism** *n.* [lit., nowhere, coined by Sir Thomas More as title of his book (published 1516) describing an imaginary island with a perfect social and political system (Gr. *ou*, not, *topos*, place)]

utricle (ū´trikəl) *n.* **1** (*Biol.*) a cell of an animal or plant. **2** a saclike cavity, esp. one in the labyrinth of the inner ear. **utricular** (-trik´ū-) *a.* [F, from L *ūtriculus*, dim. of *ūter*, leather bag or bottle]

ut sup. (ut sup) *abbr.* L *ut supra*, as mentioned above.

utter[1] (ŭt´ə) *a.* total, absolute. **utter barrister** *n.* a junior barrister not allowed to plead within the bar. **utterly** *adv.* **uttermost** *a.* utmost. **utterness** *n.* [OE *uttera*, comp. of *ūt*, OUT]

utter[2] (ŭt´ə) *v.t.* **1** to emit audibly (*She uttered a surprised cry*). **2** to give expression to. **3** to put (esp. forged notes or coins) into circulation. **4** †to issue, to emit. **utterable** *a.* **utterance** *n.* **1** the act of uttering; vocal expression. **2** a spoken word, statement etc. **3** the power of speaking. **4** a way of speaking. **5** in linguistics, a string of uninterrupted words forming an isolated and separate unit. **utterer** *n.* [ME *uttren*, as UTTER[1], cp. OE *ūtian*, from *ūt*, OUT]

UU *abbr.* Ulster Unionist.

UV *abbr.* ultraviolet.

UVA *abbr.* ultraviolet radiation with a range of 320–380 nanometres.

UVB *abbr.* ultraviolet radiation with a range of 280–320 nanometres.

UVC *abbr.* ultraviolet radiation of very short wavelengths.

uvea (ū´viə) *n.* the inner coloured layer of the iris. **uveal, uveous** *a.* [med. L, from L *ūva*, grape]

UVF *abbr.* Ulster Volunteer Force.

uvula (ū´vūlə) *n.* (*pl.* **uvulae** (-lē)) **1** the fleshy tissue hanging from the posterior margin of the soft palate at the back of the throat. **2** either of two similar structures in the bladder and the cerebellum. **uvular** *a.* **1** of or relating to the uvula. **2** (of a sound, letter) articulated with the uvula and the back of the tongue. ~*n.* a uvular consonant. [mod. L, dim. of *uva*, grape]

uxorious (ŭksaw´riəs) *a.* excessively fond of one's wife. **uxorial** *a.* of or relating to a wife. **uxoricide** (-sīd) *n.* **1** the act of killing one's wife. **2** a wife-murderer. **uxoriously** *adv.* **uxoriousness** *n.* [L *uxōrius*, from *uxor*, wife]

Uzbek (ŭz´bek, uz´-) *n.* **1** a member of a Turkic people of Uzbekistan. **2** the language of this people.

Uzi (oo´zi) *n.* a type of sub-machine gun designed in Israel. [from *Uzial* Gal, the designer]

V[1] (vē), **v** (*pl.* **Vs, V's**) the 22nd letter of the English and other versions of the Roman alphabet. It is usually pronounced as a voiced labiodental fricative. *~symbol* 5 in Roman numerals. *~n.* a V-shaped object or mark. **V-1** *n.* (*Hist.*) a flying bomb with small wings and a type of ramjet engine developed by the Germans in World War II for use against London. **V-2** *n.* (*Hist.*) a rocket-powered ballistic missile developed by the Germans in World War II for use against London. **V6** *n.* (a car with) an internal-combustion engine with six cylinders arranged in a V formation. **V8** *n.* (a car with) an internal-combustion engine with eight cylinders arranged in a V formation. **V-neck** *n.* **1** the neck of any garment when it is shaped like the letter V. **2** a garment, esp. a pullover, with such a neck. **V-necked** *a.* **V-sign** *n.* **1** a sign made with the index and middle fingers in the form of a letter V and the back of the hand facing outwards, to indicate scorn, contempt, defiance etc. **2** a sign made similarly but with the palm of the hand outwards, to signify victory.

V[2] *abbr.* **1** Vatican City (IVR). **2** vatu (monetary unit of Vanuatu). **3** verb. **4** volume. **5** volt. **6** voltage.

V[3] *chem. symbol* vanadium.

v, v. *abbr.* **1** velocity. **2** verb. **3** verse. **4** verso. **5** versus. **6** very. **7** L *vide*, see. **8** volt. **9** volume.

VA *abbr.* **1** (in the US) Veterans' Administration. **2** Vicar Apostolic. **3** Vice Admiral. **4** (Order of) Victoria and Albert. **5** Virginia. **6** volt-ampere.

Va. *abbr.* Virginia.

vac[1] (vak) *n.* (*coll.*) a vacation, esp. a university holiday.

vac[2] (vak) *n.* (*coll.*) a vacuum cleaner. *~v.i., v.t.* (*pres.p.* **vacking,** *past, p.p.* **vacked**) to vacuum-clean.

vacant (vā´kənt) *a.* **1** unfilled, empty, unoccupied. **2** having no occupant, tenant, holder or incumbent. **3** showing no awareness or mental activity. **4** unintelligent, empty-headed, silly, inane. **vacancy** *n.* (*pl.* **vacancies**) **1** the state of being vacant, emptiness. **2** an unfilled or vacant post or office. **3** an unoccupied room in a hotel, boarding house etc. **4** empty space, a gap, a chasm. **5** mental vacuity, idleness, inanity. **vacantly** *adv.* **vacant possession** *n.* availability of a house or other property for immediate occupation. [F, from L *vacans -ntem*, pres.p. of *vacāre*, to be empty]

vacate (vəkāt´) *v.t.* **1** to make vacant, to give up occupation or possession of (a room, property). **2** to give up one's tenure of (a post, position). **3** (*Law*) to annul, to make void.

vacation (vəkā´shən) *n.* **1** a period of cessation of legal or other business, or of studies at university etc. **2** (*N Am.*) a holiday. **3** the act of vacating. *~v.i.* (*N Am.*) to take a holiday. **vacationer, vacationist** *n.* (*N Am.*) a holidaymaker. **vacationland** *n.* (*N Am.*) a region popular with, or with facilities for, holidaymakers.

vaccinate (vak´sināt) *v.t.* **1** to inoculate with the modified virus of any disease so as to produce a mild form of the disease and prevent a serious attack. **2** (*Hist.*) to immunize against smallpox with cowpox virus. **vaccinal** (-sin´-), **vaccinic** *a.* **vaccination** (-ā´shən) *n.* **vaccinationist** *n.* **vaccinator** *n.* **vaccine** (-sēn) *a.* **1** of or relating to vaccination. **2** of, relating to, or obtained from cows. *~n.* **1** any agent used for inoculation and immunization. **2** (*Hist.*) the virus of cowpox prepared for use in vaccination. **3** (*Comput.*) a program intended to detect and eliminate a computer virus. **vaccinia** (-sin´iə) *n.* cowpox, esp. as produced by inoculation. **vaccinifer** (-sin´ifə) *n.* a person or animal from whose body vaccine is obtained. [F *vaccin*, vaccine, L *vaccīnus*, a., from *vacca*, cow]

vacherin (vash´rã) *n.* a dessert consisting of whipped cream, ice cream, fruit etc. in a meringue shell. [F, from *vache*, cow]

vacillate (vas´ilāt) *v.i.* **1** to oscillate from one opinion or resolution to another, to be irresolute. **2** to sway to and fro, to waver. **vacillant** *a.* **vacillatingly** *adv.* **vacillation** (-ā´shən) *n.* **vacillator** *n.* [L *vacillātus*, p.p. of *vacillāre*]

☒ **vacinate** common misspelling of VACCINATE.

vacua VACUUM.

vacuole (vak´ūōl) *n.* (*Biol.*) a minute cavity in a cell, containing air, fluid etc. **vacuolar** (-ūələ) *a.* **vacuolate** (-ələt) *a.* **vacuolation** (-əlā´shən) *n.* [F, dim. of *vacuus*, see VACUOUS]

vacuous (vak´ūəs) *a.* **1** blank, expressionless. **2** unintelligent, inane, fatuous. **3** empty, unfilled, void. **vacuity** (vəkū´-) *n.* (*pl.* **vacuities**) **1** emptiness. **2** an empty space, a void. **3** lack of intelligent awareness. **4** an inane remark, statement etc. **vacuousness** *n.* [L *vacuus*, rel. to *vacāre*, see VACANT]

vacuum (vak´ūəm, -ūm) *n.* (*pl.* **vacuums, vacua** (-ūə)) **1** a space completely devoid of matter. **2** a space or vessel from which the air has been exhausted to the furthest possible extent by an air pump or analogous means. **3** a partial diminution of pressure, as in a suction pump, below the normal atmospheric pressure. **4** an emptiness or void caused by the removal or absence of a person or thing; a feeling of emptiness. **5** (*pl.* **vacuums**) a vacuum cleaner. *~v.t., v.i.* to clean with a vacuum cleaner. **in a vacuum** in isolation, without the normally attendant context, circumstances etc. **vacuum brake** *n.* a continuous train-brake in which the pressure applying the brakes is caused by the exhaustion of the air from a bellows pulling the brake-rod as it collapses. **vacuum cleaner** *n.* a machine for removing dirt by suction. **vacuum-clean** *v.t., v.i.* **vacuum distillation** *n.* distillation carried out under reduced pressure. **vacuum flask** *n.* a flask constructed with two walls between which is a vacuum, for the purpose of keeping the contents hot or cold. **vacuum gauge** *n.* a gauge indicating the pressure consequent on the production of a vacuum. **vacuum-packed** *a.* sealed in a container from which most of the air has been removed. **vacuum pump** *n.* an airpump used to remove air or other gas, and so create a vacuum. **vacuum tube** *n.* (*N. Am.*) an electronic valve. [L, neut. of *vacuus*, see VACUOUS]

VAD[1] *abbr.* Voluntary Aid Detachment.

VAD[2] (vad) *n.* (*pl.* **VADs**) a nurse serving with the Voluntary Aid Detachment.

vade-mecum (vahdimā´kəm, vādimē´-) *n.* (*pl.* **vade-mecums**) a pocket companion or manual for ready reference. [L, go with me]

vadose (vā´dōs) *a.* of or relating to water found above the water-table. [L *vadōsus*, full of shallows, from *vadum*, a shallow place or ford]

vagabond (vag´əbond) *n.* **1** a person who wanders about without any settled home, a wanderer, esp. an idle or disreputable one, a vagrant. 2 (*coll.*) a scamp, a rogue. *~a.* 1 wandering about, having no settled habitation, nomadic. 2 driven or drifting to and fro, aimless. *~v.i.* to wander about as a vagabond. **vagabondage** (-dij), **vagabondism** *n.* **vagabondish** *a.* [F, from late L *vagabundus*, from *vagārī*, to wonder]

vagal VAGUS.

vagary (vā´gəri) *n.* (*pl.* **vagaries**) a whimsical idea, an extravagant notion, a freak. **vagarious** (-geə´ri-) *a.* characterized by vagaries; eccentric, erratic. [perh. directly from L *vagārī*, see VAGABOND]

vagi VAGUS.

vagina (vəjī´nə) *n.* 1 the genital passage of a female from the vulva to the uterus. 2 a sheath, a sheathlike envelope or organ, esp. a sheath or semi-tubular part, as at the base of a stem. **vaginal** (-jī´-, vaj´i-) *a.* **vaginate** (vaj´ināt, -nət) *a.* (*Bot.*) having a sheath. **vaginismus** (vajiniz´məs) *n.* painful spasmodic contraction of the vaginal sphincters. **vaginitis** (vajinī´tis) *n.* inflammation of the vagina. [L, a sheath]

vagrant (vā´grənt) *n.* 1 a person wandering about without a settled home or visible means of subsistence, a tramp. 2 a bird that has strayed outside its normal area or from its normal migratory route. 3 †a wanderer, a vagabond. *~a.* 1 wandering about without a settled home. 2 itinerant, strolling. 3 unpredictable, erratic, wayward. 4 (of plants) having uncontrolled or straggling growth. **vagrancy** *n.* **vagrantly** *adv.* †**vagrom** (-grəm) *a.* [formerly *vagarant*, A-F *wakerant*, OF *waucrant*, pres.p. of *walcrer*, from Gmc., cogn. with OHG *walkan*, to walk about, to full cloth, see WALK (confused with L *vagārī*, see VAGUE)]

vague (vāg) *a.* 1 of doubtful meaning or application, ambiguous, indefinite, ill-defined. 2 indistinct, not clearly perceptible, dim. 3 (of a person) lacking clarity of thought, expression etc.; absent-minded; disorganized. **vaguely** *adv.* **vagueness** *n.* **vaguish** *a.* [from obs. v. to wander, F *vaguer*, L *vagārī*, from *vagus*, wandering]

vagus (vā´gəs) *n.* (*pl.* **vagi** (-ji, -gī)) the tenth cranial nerve, which regulates the heartbeat, rhythm of breathing etc. **vagal** *a.*

†**vail**[1] (vāl) *v.t.* to lower (a topsail etc.) or doff (one's cap etc.), esp. in token of respect or submission. *~v.i.* to yield, to give place. [ME, shortened from obs. *avale*, from OF *avaler*, to lower, from *a val*, down, from L *ad vallem*, to the valley]

†**vail**[2] (vāl) *v.i.*, *v.t.* to avail. [OF *valoir*, to be worth]

vain (vān) *a.* 1 excessively proud of one's appearance or attainments, conceited, self-admiring. 2 empty, unsubstantial, unreal, worthless. 3 fruitless, ineffectual, unavailing. **in vain** unsuccessfully, without result. **to take someone's name in vain** 1 to use someone's name, esp. God's, profanely or without due respect. 2 to mention someone's name. **vainglory** *n.* 1 excessive vanity. 2 vain pomp or show. 3 pride, boastfulness. **vainglorious** *a.* **vaingloriously** *adv.* **vaingloriousness** *n.* **vainly** *adv.* **vainness** *n.* [F, from L *vānum*, nom. *-us*, empty, vain]

vair (veə) *n.* 1 (*Hist.*) a squirrel fur used extensively in the Middle Ages for linings and trimmings. 2 (*Her.*) a fur represented by shield-shaped figures of argent and azure alternately. [F, from L *varius*, variegated, VARIOUS]

Vaishnava (vīsh´nəvə) *n.* a member of a sect that worships Vishnu as supreme among the Hindu gods. [Sansk.]

Vaisya (vīs´yə) *n.* 1 the third of the four chief Hindu castes, the traders. 2 a member of this. [Sansk. *vaiçya*, from *vīc*, settler]

valance (val´əns), **valence** (vā´-) *n.* a short curtain or hanging round the frame or tester of a bedstead, along a shelf, above a window etc. to conceal structural details. **valanced** *a.* [prob. from *Valence* in France]

vale[1] (vāl) *n.* (*poet.*) a valley. **vale of tears** *n.* human life, existence, the world. [ME and F *val*, L *vallem*, nom. *-lis*]

vale[2] (vah´lā) *int.* farewell. *~n.* a farewell. [L, farewell, imper. of *valēre*, to be strong]

valediction (validik´shən) *n.* 1 the act or an instance of bidding farewell. 2 a farewell, an adieu. **valedictory** *a.* 1 bidding farewell. 2 of the nature of a farewell. *~n.* (*pl.* **valedictories**) a parting address or oration, esp. at graduation in an American university. **valedictorian** (-taw´ri-) *n.* (*N Am.*) a student who delivers a valedictory. [L *valēdictus*, p.p. of *valēdīcere* (VALE[2], *dīcere*, to say)]

valence[1] (vā´ləns) *n.* the combining or replacing power of an element or radical reckoned as the number of monovalent elements it can replace or combine with. **valence electron, valency electron** *n.* an electron in the outermost shell of an atom, responsible for forming chemical bonds. **valency** *n.* (*pl.* **valencies**) 1 a unit of combining capacity. 2 valence. [late L *valentia*, strength, from *valēre*, to be strong]

valence[2] VALANCE.

Valenciennes (valāsyen´) *n.* a fine variety of lace, the design of which is made with and of the same thread as the ground. [town in N France where it was originally made]

valentine (val´əntīn) *n.* 1 a letter or card of an amatory or satirical kind sent to a person, often anonymously, on St Valentine's day. 2 a sweetheart chosen to receive a greeting on St Valentine's day. **St Valentine's day** SAINT.

valerian (vəliə´riən) *n.* 1 a herbaceous plant of the genus *Valeriana*, esp. *V. officinalis*, with clusters of pink or white flowers. 2 a preparation from the root of *V. officinalis* used as a mild stimulant etc. 3 a related Mediterranean plant with red spurred flowers, *Centranthus ruber*, red valerian. **valerianaceous** *a.* of or relating to the family Valerianaceae that includes the valerians. **valeric** (-ler´ik) *a.* **valeric acid** *n.* pentanoic acid, a fatty acid with a disagreeable smell obtained from valerian. [OF *valeriane*, late L *valēriana*, etym. uncertain]

valet (val´it, val´ā) *n.* 1 a manservant who acts as a personal attendant to his employer, looking after his clothes, serving his meals etc. 2 a person employed in a hotel, liner etc. to perform similar functions. *~v.t.* (*pres.p.* **valeting**, *past*, *p.p.* **valeted**) 1 to act as valet to. 2 to clean the interior of (a car). *~v.i.* to act as a valet. **valet de chambre** (valā də shā´brə) *n.* (*pl.* **valets de chambre** (valā)) a valet. **valet de place** (valā də plas´) *n.* (*pl.* **valets de place** (valā)) a local guide. **valet parking** *n.* a service provided at some restaurants, hotels etc. in which an attendant takes a patron's car, parks it and later returns it to the door. **valet-park** *v.t.* [F, var. of VARLET]

valeta VELETA.

valetudinarian (valitūdineə´riən), **valetudinary** (-tū´dinəri) *a.* 1 morbidly anxious about one's state of health. 2 sickly, infirm, delicate. 3 seeking to recover health. *~n.* (*pl.* **valetudinarians, valetudinaries**) 1 a valetudinarian person. 2 an invalid. **valetudinarianism** *n.* [F *valétudinaire*, L *valētūdinārius*, from *valētūdo -dinis*, health, from *valēre*, to be well]

valgus (val´gəs) *a.* twisted away from the midline of the body. *~n.* a deformity involving deviation of a hand or foot outward from the midline of the body. [L, bow-legged]

Valhalla (valhal´ə) *n.* 1 in Norse mythology, the palace of immortality where the souls of heroes slain in battle were carried by the Valkyries. 2 a building used as the final resting-place of the great men of a nation, esp. the Temple of Fame, near Regensburg, built by Louis I of Bavaria, 1830. [Icel. *valhöll*, gen. *valhallar*, hall of the slain (*valr*, slain, HALL)]

valiant (val´iənt) *a.* brave, courageous, intrepid. **valiance, valiantness** *n.* **valiantly** *adv.* [OF *valant* (F *vaillant*), pres.p. of *valoir*, to be worth, L *valēre*, to be strong]

valid (val´id) *a.* **1** well-grounded, sound, cogent, logical, incontestable. **2** (*Law*) legally sound, sufficient, and effective; legally binding. **3** not having reached its expiry date. **validate** *v.t.* to make valid, to ratify, to confirm, to make binding. **validation** (-ā´shən) *n.* **validity** (-lid´-), **validness** *n.* **validly** *adv.* [F *valide*, L *validus*, strong, see VALIANT]

valine (vā´lēn, val´-) *n.* an amino acid that is essential to health and growth in humans and other vertebrates. [from *val*eric acid, -INE]

valise (vəlēz´) *n.* **1** a bag or case, usu. of leather, for holding a traveller's clothes etc., esp. one for carrying in the hand, a travelling bag. **2** a kitbag. [F, from late L *valisia*, etym. uncertain]

Valium® (val´iəm) *n.* the tranquillizer diazepam.

Valkyrie (val´kiri, -kiə´ri) *n.* in Norse mythology, each of 12 maidens of Valhalla who were sent by Odin to select those destined to be slain in battle and to conduct their souls to Valhalla. **Valkyrian** (-kir´-) *a.* [Icel. *valkyrja*, chooser of the slain (*valr*, slain, *-kyrja*, chooser, from *kjōsa*, cogn. with CHOOSE)]

vallation VALLUM.

vallecula (vəlek´ūlə) *n.* (*pl.* **valleculae** (-lē)) (*Biol.*) a groove or furrow. **vallecular, valleculate** (-lāt) *a.* [late L, dim. of *vallis*, VALE[1]]

valley (val´i) *n.* (*pl.* **valleys**) **1** a depression in the earth's surface bounded by hills or mountains, and usu. with a river or stream flowing through it. **2** any hollow or depression between higher ground or elevations of a surface. **3** the internal angle formed by two inclined sides of a roof. [OF *valee* (F *vallée*), from *val*, VALE[1]]

vallum (val´əm) *n.* (*pl.* **vallums**) an ancient Roman rampart, an agger. **vallation** (-ā´shən) *n.* **1** the act of building fortifications. **2** a rampart. [L]

valonia (vəlō´niə) *n.* the large acorn-cups of the valonia oak, used for dyeing, tanning, ink-making etc. **valonia oak** *n.* an evergreen oak, *Quercus aegilops* or *Q. macrolepsis*, of the Greek archipelago etc. [It. *vallonia*, from Gr. *balanos*, oak]

valor VALOUR.

valorize (val´ərīz), **valorise** *v.t.* to increase or stabilize the price of (an article) by an officially organized scheme. **valorization** (-zā´shən) *n.* [L *valēre*, to be worth, -IZE]

valour (val´ə), (*N Am.*) **valor** *n.* personal bravery, courage esp. as displayed in fighting. **valorous** *a.* **valorously** *adv.* [OF *valor*, *valur* (F *valeur*), L *valor -orem*, from *valēre*, to be strong, to be worth]

valse (vals) *n.* a waltz. [F, WALTZ]

value (val´ū) *n.* **1** worth, the desirability of a thing, esp. as compared with other things. **2** the qualities that are the basis of this. **3** worth estimated in money or other equivalent, the market price. **4** the equivalent of a thing in terms of something to be substituted for it. **5** valuation, estimation, appreciation of worth. **6** the usefulness of a thing within a specific context or to achieve a particular end. **7** (*pl.*) moral principles, standards; those things which a person or group sets most store by for the achievement of goodness or excellence in any sphere of life. **8** the quality of a speech sound represented by a particular letter. **9** (of a word) meaning, signification. **10** (*Math.*) the amount or quantity denoted by a symbol or expression. **11** (*Mus.*) the relative duration of a tone as indicated by the note. **12** the relation of the parts of a picture to each other with regard to light and shade, apart from colour. **13** rank, in terms of the rules of a game, of a particular card, piece etc. **14** (*Physics, Chem.*) a number or numerical measure denoting magnitude or quantity on a conventional scale. ~*v.t.* (*3rd pers. sing. pres.* **values,** *pres.p.* **valuing,** *past, p.p.* **valued**) **1** to estimate the value of, to appraise. **2** to esteem, to rate highly, to prize. **3** to fix the value of. **valuable** *a.* **1** having great value, worth or price, costly, precious. **2** very useful or important. **3** capable of being valued or appraised. ~*n.* (*usu. pl.*) an object of high value, esp. a valuable piece of personal property. **valuableness** *n.* **valuably** *adv.* **valuate** (-āt) *v.t.* (*esp. N Am.*) to value; to evaluate. **valuation** (-ā´shən) *n.* **1** the act of valuing or appraising. **2** estimation of the value of a thing. **3** estimated value or worth, the price placed on a thing. **valuator** *n.* an appraiser. **value added** *n.* **1** the amount by which the value of an article is increased in the process of production; the difference between the final value of an article and the cost of manufacturing and marketing it. **2** improvement or benefit acquired during a process. **value-added** *a.* **1** (of goods) with enhancements to increase profit margins. **2** (of a company) that offers specialized or extended services in a commercial area. **value added tax** *n.* in Britain, a tax levied at each stage of production and distribution of a commodity or service and paid by the buyer as a purchase tax. **value for money** *n.* something that gives adequate or abundant satisfaction in return for the money spent on it. **value judgement** *n.* a subjective and personal estimate of merit in a particular respect. **valueless** *a.* of no value, worthless, futile. **valuelessness** *n.* **valuer** *n.* a person who values, an appraiser, esp. of property, jewellery etc. **value received** *n.* **1** money or equivalent given for a bill of exchange. **2** a phrase indicating that a bill of exchange has been accepted. [F, fem. of *valu*, p.p. of *valoir*, to be worth, L *valēre*, see VALOUR]

valuta (vəloo´tə, -lū´-) *n.* **1** the value of one currency in terms of another. **2** a currency considered in respect of its exchange value. [It., value]

valve (valv) *n.* **1** an automatic or other contrivance for opening or closing a passage or aperture so as to permit or prevent passage of a fluid, such as water, gas or steam. **2** (*Anat.*) a membraneous part of a vessel or other organ preventing the flow of liquids in one direction and allowing it in the other. **3** a vacuum tube or bulb containing electrodes and exhibiting sensitive control by one or more electrodes of the current flowing between the others. **4** (*Mus.*) a device to increase the effective length of the tube of a brass instrument, allowing the full chromatic range of notes to be played. **5** one of the parts or divisions of a shell. **6** (*Bot.*) one of the segments into which a capsule dehisces; either half of an anther after its opening. **7** †each of the leaves of a folding door. **valvate** (-vāt) *a.* **1** having or resembling a valve. **2** (of petals) meeting at the margins only. **valved** *a.* **valve face** *n.* the sealing surface of a valve. **valve gear** *n.* the mechanism operating a valve or valves, esp. those in a reciprocating engine. **valveless** *a.* **valvelet** (-lit), **valvule** (-vūl) *n.* a little valve. **valvular** (-vū-) *a.* **1** having a valve or valves; operated by valves. **2** having the shape or function of a valve. **valvular disease** *n.* disordered action of the heart owing to defects in the cardiac valves. **valvulitis** (-vūlī´tis) *n.* inflammation of the valves of the heart. [F, from L *valva*, leaf of a folding door, cogn. with *volvere*, to roll, to turn]

vambrace (vam´brās) *n.* (*Hist.*) armour for the arm from the elbow to the wrist. [MF *avant-bras* (*bras*, arm)]

vamoose (vəmoos´) *v.i.* (*N Am., sl.*) to decamp, to be gone, to be off. [Sp. *vamos*, let us go, L *vādimus*, we go, from *vādere*, to go]

vamp[1] (vamp) *n.* **1** the part of a boot or shoe upper in front of the ankle seams. **2** a patched-up or reworked thing. **3** (*Mus.*) an improvised accompaniment. ~*v.t.* **1** (*often* **vamp up**) to give a new appearance to, to repair, to renovate. **2** (*usu.* **vamp up**) to put together from odds and ends. **3** (*Mus.*) to improvise an accompaniment to.

4 to put a new vamp on (a boot etc.). ~*v.i.* to improvise accompaniments. **vamper** *n.* [ME *vaumpe, vampay, vauntpe*, MF *avant-pied* (AVANT, *pied*, foot)]

vamp[2] (vamp) *n.* an adventuress, a woman who exploits her sexual attractiveness to take advantage of men. ~*v.t.* to fascinate or exploit (men). ~*v.i.* to act as a vamp. [short for VAMPIRE]

vampire (vam´pīə) *n.* 1 a ghost of a heretic, criminal or other outcast, supposed to leave the grave at night and suck the blood of sleeping persons. 2 a person who preys upon others, a bloodsucker. 3 (*also* **vampire bat**) a bat of the family Desmodontidae, which sucks the blood of man and other animals, esp. while they are asleep. 4 in a theatre, a small trapdoor used for sudden entrances and exits. **vampiric** (-pir´ik) *a.* **vampirism** (vam´pir-) *n.* 1 belief in vampires. 2 bloodsucking. 3 extortion. [F, from G *Vampyr*, Serb. *vampir*, prob. from Turk.]

vamplate (vam´plāt) *n.* (*Hist.*) an iron plate fixed on a lance as a guard for the hand. [F *avant-plate* (AVANT, PLATE)]

van[1] (van) *n.* 1 a motor vehicle, usu. covered, for conveying goods, furniture etc. 2 a closed railway carriage for luggage or for the guard. 3 a caravan. [shortened from CARAVAN]

van[2] (van) *n.* 1 the foremost division of an army or fleet, the advance guard. 2 the leaders of a movement, the forefront. 3 the leading position in a movement etc. [short for VANGUARD]

van[3] (van) *n.* 1 (*Mining*) a test of the quality of ore by washing on a shovel etc. 2 †a fan or machine for winnowing grain. 3 †a wing. ~*v.t.* (*pres.p.* **vanning,** *past, p.p.* **vanned**) to test (ore) by washing on a shovel etc. **vanner** *n.* [F, from L *vannum*, nom. *-us*, FAN[1]]

van[4] (van) *n., int.* (*coll.*) in tennis, advantage. [short for ADVANTAGE]

vanadium (vənā´diəm) *n.* a rare, silver-white metallic element, at. no. 23, chem. symbol V, used to give tensile strength to steel and, in the form of its salts, to produce an intense permanent black colour. **vanadate** (van´ədāt) *n.* a salt of vanadic acid. **vanadic** (-nad´-) *a.* of or relating to vanadium in a higher valency. **vanadinite** (-nad´inīt) *n.* a mineral composed of vanadate and lead chloride. **vanadous** (van´ə-) *a.* of or containing vanadium in a lower valency. [mod. L, from *Vanadis*, a Scand. goddess]

Van Allen belt (van al´ən), **Van Allen layer** *n.* a belt of intense particle radiation in the earth's outer atmosphere. [James A. *Van Allen*, b. 1914, US physicist]

V & A *abbr.* Victoria & Albert (Museum).

vandal (van´dəl) *n.* 1 a person who wilfully or ignorantly destroys or damages anything. 2 (**Vandal**) a member of a Germanic people from the shores of the Baltic that overran Gaul, Spain, and N Africa and Rome in the 5th cent., destroying works of art etc. ~*a.* (**Vandal**) of or relating to the Vandals. **Vandalic** (-dal´-) *a.* **vandalism** *n.* deliberate destruction or defacement of property. **vandalistic** (-is´-) *a.* **vandalistically** *adv.* **vandalize, vandalise** *v.t.* to destroy or damage deliberately and senselessly. [L *Vandalus*, from Gmc. (cp. OE *Wendle*, pl., cogn. with G *wandeln*, to WANDER)]

van de Graaff generator (van də grahf´) *n.* a device for generating a very high electrostatic charge on a hollow metal sphere by means of a continuous belt. [Robert *Van de Graaff*, 1901–67, US physicist]

van der Waals forces (van də wahlz´, vahlz´) *n.pl.* weak attractive forces between atoms or molecules caused by transient dissymmetries in electron distribution. [Johannes *van der Waals*, 1837–1923, Dutch physicist]

vandyke (vandīk´) *n.* 1 any one of the series of points forming an ornamental border to lace, linen etc. 2 a collar or cape with these points. ~*a.* (**Vandyke**) applied to the style of dress, esp. ornamented with vandykes, worn by the figures in Van Dyck's portraits. **Vandyke beard** *n.* a pointed beard. **Vandyke brown** *n.* a reddish-brown colour or pigment. **Vandyke collar, Vandyke cape** *n.* a collar or cape ornamented with vandykes. [Sir Anthony *Vandyke* or Van Dyck, 1599–1641, Dutch painter]

vane (vān) *n.* 1 a weathercock, flag or arrow pointing in the direction of the wind. 2 the arm of a windmill. 3 the blade of a propeller, turbine etc. 4 a fin on a bomb to ensure its falling on its warhead. 5 the sight on a quadrant, compass etc. 6 a horizontal part on a surveyor's levelling-staff for moving up and down to the line of sight of the telescope. 7 the broad part of a feather. **vaned** *a.* **vaneless** *a.* [OE *fana*, small flag (cp. Dut. *vaan*, G *Fahne*, Icel. *fāni*, Swed. *fana*, Dan. *fane*), cogn. with L *pannus*, cloth, PANE]

vanessid (vənes´id) *n.* a butterfly with notched wings, belonging to any of several brightly coloured species, such as Camberwell Beauty, red or white admiral, tortoiseshell etc. [etym. uncertain]

vang (vang) *n.* (*Naut.*) either of a pair of guy ropes running from the peak of a gaff to the deck to steady it. [Dut., from *vangen*, to catch, cogn. with FANG]

vanguard (van´gahd) *n.* 1 the troops who march in the front or van of an army, an advance guard, the van. 2 the leaders or leading position in a movement etc. [OF *avant-warde, -garde* (AVANT, GUARD)]

vanilla (vanil´ə) *n.* 1 any member of a genus, *Vanilla*, of tall, epiphytal orchids, natives of tropical Asia and America, bearing fragrant flowers. 2 the pod of *Vanilla planifolia* and other species used to flavour food. 3 an extract from this used for flavouring ices, syrups etc. ~*a.* flavoured with vanilla. **vanillate** (-lət) *n.* **vanillic** *a.* of or relating to, or derived from vanilla. **vanillin** *n.* the aromatic principle of vanilla, a white crystalline aldehyde. [Sp. *vainilla*, small pod, dim. of *vaina*, case, sheath, pod, L VAGINA]

vanish (van´ish) *v.i.* 1 to disappear suddenly. 2 to become imperceptible, to be lost to sight, to fade away, to dissolve. 3 to pass away, to pass out of existence. 4 (*Math.*) to become zero. ~*v.t.* to cause to disappear. **vanishing** *a., n.* **vanishing cream** *n.* a cosmetic which is rapidly absorbed into the pores leaving no trace of grease. **vanishing point** *n.* 1 in perspective views, the point in which all parallel lines in the same plane tend to meet. 2 a point in space or time at which something disappears or ceases to exist. [ME *vanissen*, prob. through A-F *evaniss-*, pres.p. stem of *evanir*, OF *esvanir*, L *ēvānescere*, from *vānus*, empty, VAIN]

Vanitory® (van´itəri) *n.* (*pl.* **Vanitories**) a vanity unit. [VANITY, assim. to *lavatory*]

vanity (van´iti) *n.* (*pl.* **vanities**) 1 the quality or state of being vain. 2 empty pride, conceit about one's personal attainments or attractions. 3 ostentation, show. 4 emptiness, futility, unreality, worthlessness. 5 something which is visionary, unreal or deceptive. 6 (*N Am.*) a dressing table. **vanity bag, vanity case** *n.* a small bag or case used to carry a woman's make-up and toiletries. **Vanity Fair** *n.* the world or society as a place of idle frivolity and moral corruption (from John Bunyan's *Pilgrim's Progress*). **vanity publisher** *n.* a company that publishes books at the authors' expense, often with little prospect of selling copies of the works. **vanity publishing** *n.* **vanity unit** *n.* a piece of furniture consisting of a washbasin built into a dressing table or set of cupboards. [F *vanité*, L *vānitātem*, nom. *-tas*, from *vānus*, VAIN]

vanner VAN[3].

vanquish (vang´kwish) *v.t.* to conquer, to overcome, to subdue, to refute. **vanquishable** *a.* **vanquisher** *n.* **vanquishment** *n.* [ME *venkissen*, OF *veinquiss-*, pres.p. stem of *veinquir, veincre* (F *vaincre*), L *vincere*]

vantage (vahn´tij) *n.* 1 (*formal*) superiority or elevation, esp. such as to give a commanding view. 2 (*formal*) a situation, condition or opportunity favourable to success. 3 in tennis, advantage. 4 †advantage. ~*v.t.* to profit, to advantage. **vantage ground** *n.* superiority of position or place. **vantage point** *n.* a position or place that affords a good view of a scene or event. [short for ADVANTAGE]

vapid (vap´id) *a.* insipid, flat, spiritless. **vapidity** (-pid´-), **vapidness** *n.* **vapidly** *adv.* [L *vapidus*, cogn. with VAPOUR]

vapor, vaporable etc. VAPOUR.

vaporetto (vapəret´ō) *n.* (*pl.* **vaporetti** (-tē)) a small motor vessel (orig. a steamship) used for public transport on the canals of Venice. [It., dim. of *vapore*, a steamboat]

vapour (vā´pə), (*N Am.*) **vapor** *n.* 1 moisture in the air, light mist. 2 any visible diffused substance floating in the atmosphere. 3 the gaseous form of a substance that is normally liquid or solid. 4 an unreal or unsubstantial thing, a vain imagination. 5 a medicinal preparation applied by inhaling. 6 (*pl.*) †depression of spirits, hypochondria. ~*v.i.* 1 to give out vapour. 2 to boast, to brag, to bluster. **vaporable** *a.* capable of being turned into vapour. **vaporability** (-bil´-) *n.* **vaporescence** (-res´əns) *n.* the production or formation of vapour. **vaporescent** (-res´ənt) *a.* **vaporific** (-rif´-) *a.* 1 of or relating to vapour. 2 causing vapour or vaporization. 3 tending to become vapour. **vaporiform** (-por´ifawm) *a.* existing in the form of vapour. **vaporimeter** (-rim´itə) *n.* an instrument for measuring the pressure of vapour. **vaporize, vaporise** *v.t.* 1 to convert into a vapour, gas or fine spray. 2 to cause to disappear. 3 to destroy completely by converting to a gas in the heat of a nuclear explosion. ~*v.i.* 1 to be converted into a vapour etc. 2 to disappear. 3 to be utterly destroyed by a nuclear explosion. 4 to brag, to boast. **vaporizable** *a.* **vaporization** (-zā´shən) *n.* **vaporizer** *n.* a device that vaporizes a substance, esp. a medicinal spray. **vaporous** *a.* 1 full of vapour. 2 vaporific. 3 insubstantial, flimsy, ephemeral. 4 full of conceit, inflated and empty. **vaporosity** (-ros´-) *n.* **vaporously** *adv.* **vaporousness** *n.* **vapour density** *n.* the density of a gas or vapour relative to hydrogen at the same temperature and pressure. **vapourish** *a.* **vapourishness** *n.* **vapour lock** *n.* a blockage in a pipe conveying a fluid caused by a bubble of gas, esp. in the petrol feed to a carburettor. **vapour pressure** *n.* the pressure exerted by a vapour that is in equilibrium with its solid or liquid form. **vapour trail** *n.* a white trail of condensed vapour left in the sky after the passage of an aircraft. [F *vapeur*, L *vapōrem*, nom. *-por* (whence *vaporāre*, to steam), cogn. with Gr. *kapnos*, smoke, and VAPID]

vaquero (vəkeə´rō) *n.* (*pl.* **vaqueros**) in Mexico and Spanish-speaking parts of America, a herdsman, a cowherd. [Sp., from med. L *vaccārius*, from L *vacca*, cow]

VAR *abbr.* 1 value-added reseller. 2 visual aural range.

var. *abbr.* 1 variable. 2 variant. 3 variation. 4 variety. 5 various.

vara (vah´rə) *n.* a Spanish-American measure of length, varying from 33 to 43 in. (84–110 cm). [Sp. *vara*, ult. from L *vārus*, crooked]

varactor (vərak´tə) *n.* a two-electrode semiconductor device in which capacitance varies with voltage.

Varangian (vəran´jiən) *n.* any of the Norse sea rovers in the 8th–12th cents. who ravaged the coasts of the Baltic and conquered part of Russia. **Varangian Guard** *n.* the bodyguard of the Byzantine emperors, formed partly of Varangians. [med. L *Varingus*, Icel. *Vœringi*, confederate, from *vārar*, oaths, cogn. with L *vērus*, true]

varec (var´ik) *n.* kelp or the ash obtained from kelp. [F *varech*, cogn. with WRECK, cp. Swed. *vrak*]

variable (veə´riəbəl) *a.* 1 capable of varying, liable to change. 2 changeable, unsteady, fickle, inconstant. 3 able to be varied, adapted or adjusted. 4 quantitatively indeterminate, susceptible of continuous change of value, esp. assuming different values while others remain constant. 5 (of winds, currents) tending to change in direction and intensity. 6 applied to stars whose apparent magnitudes are not constant. 7 (*Biol.*) tending to variations of structure, function etc. ~*n.* 1 a thing which is variable. 2 (*Math.*) a variable quantity. 3 (*Naut.*) **a** a shifting wind. **b** (*pl.*) the region between the northerly and southerly trade winds. **variability** (-bil´-), **variableness** *n.* **variable gear** *n.* a gear that is designed to give varying speeds. **variable-geometry, variable-sweep** *a.* (of an aircraft) having hinged wings which can be set at different angles to the fuselage. **variably** *adv.* [F, from late L *variābilis*, from *variāre*, to VARY]

variance (veə´riəns) *n.* 1 the fact of varying, the state of being variant, disagreement, difference of opinion, dissension, discord. 2 (*Law*) disagreement between the allegations and proof or between the writ and the declaration. 3 a statistical measure of the dispersion of a set of observations. **at variance** 1 conflicting, not in accord (with one another). 2 of people, in disagreement or dispute. **variant** *a.* 1 showing variation, differing in form, character, or details. 2 tending to vary, changeable. ~*n.* a variant form, reading, type etc. [L *variāntia*, from *variāre*, to VARY]

variation (veəriā´shən) *n.* 1 the act, process or state of varying. 2 alteration, change, modification, deviation, mutation. 3 the extent to which a thing varies. 4 something that differs from a norm, standard etc. 5 (*Mus.*) a repetition of a theme with fanciful elaborations and changes of form. 6 deviation of a heavenly body from the mean orbit or motion. 7 the angle of deviation from true north or of declination of the magnetic needle. 8 the deviation in structure or function from the type or parent form. 9 (*Math.*) a change in a function due to small changes in the values of constants etc. 10 in ballet, a solo dance. **variate** (veə´riət) *n.* 1 in statistics, a quantity that has a numerical value for each member of a group; a variable quantity, esp. one with values occurring in accordance with a frequency distribution. 2 a variant. **variational** *a.* **variative** (veə´riət-) *a.* **variator** (-ātə) *n.* [F, from L *variātiōnem*, nom. *-tio*, as VARIANCE]

varicella (varisel´ə) *n.* 1 chickenpox. 2 (*also* **varicella zoster**) a virus that causes chickenpox and shingles. **varicellar** *a.* **varicelloid** (-loid) *a.* resembling chickenpox. [dim. of VARIOLA]

varices VARIX.

varicocele VARICOSE.

varicoloured (veə´rikŭləd), (*N Am.*) **varicolored** *a.* variously coloured, variegated, particoloured.

varicose (var´ikōs) *a.* (of veins) permanently dilated, affected with varix. **varicocele** (-sēl) *n.* a tumour formed by varicose veins of the spermatic cord. **varicosed** *a.* **varicosity** (-kos´-) *n.* †**varicous** *a.* varicose. [L *varicōsus*, from VARIX]

varied VARY.

variegate (veə´rigāt) *v.t.* 1 to diversify in colour, to mark with patches of different hues, to dapple, to chequer. 2 to give variety to. **variegated** *a.* (*Bot.*) 1 having leaves with two or more colours. 2 (of foliage, flowers) having pale patches as a result of infection, mutation etc. **variegation** (-gā´shən) *n.* [L *variegātus*, p.p. of *variegāre* (VARI-, *agere*, to drive, to make)]

variety (vərī´əti) *n.* (*pl.* **varieties**) 1 the quality or state of being various; diversity, absence of sameness or monotony, many-sidedness, versatility. 2 a collection of diverse things. 3 **a** a minor class or group of things differing in some common peculiarities from the class they belong to. **b** a member or example of such a class or group. **4** a kind, a sort; a thing of a particular sort or kind. **5** an individual or group differing from the type of its species in some transmittable quality but usually fertile with others of the species; a sub-species. **6** a cultivar. **7** a form of entertainment consisting of a number of unrelated acts or short performances, usu. with singing, dancing, comic or acrobatic turns, conjuring etc. *~a.* consisting of or relating to this type of entertainment. **varietal** *a.* **varietally** *adv.* **variety meat** *n.* (*N Am.*) **1** offal. **2** processed meat, such as sausage. **variety store** *n.* (*N Am.*) a shop that sells small items of many different kinds. **variety theatre,** (*N Am.*) **variety theater** *n.* a theatre for variety shows, a music hall. [F *varieté*, L *varietātem*, nom. *-tas*, from *varius*, VARIOUS]

varifocal (veərifō´kəl) *a.* having a variable focal length, allowing the focusing range to alter gradually to accommodate near, intermediate and far vision. *~n.* (*pl.*) varifocal spectacles.

variform (veə´rifawm) *a.* varying in form, of different shapes. [L *varius*, -FORM]

variola (vərī´ələ) *n.* smallpox. **variolar** *a.* **variolate** (veə´riəlāt) *a.* marked or pitted by or as by smallpox. *~v.t.* to inoculate with smallpox virus. **variolation** (veəriəlā´shən) *n.* inoculation with smallpox virus. **variole** (veə´riōl) *n.* **1** a shallow pitlike depression. **2** any of the spherical masses of which variolite is made up. **variolite** (var´iəlīt) *n.* a variety of spherulitic basalt with a surface resembling skin marked with smallpox. **varioloid** (veə´riəloid) *a.* resembling, or of the nature of smallpox. *~n.* a mild form of smallpox, esp. as modified by previous inoculation. **variolous** (vərī´ələs) *a.* relating to or resembling smallpox. [med. L, dim. from L *varius*, VARIOUS]

variometer (veəriom´itə) *n.* **1** a device for varying the inductance in an electric circuit. **2** an instrument indicating rate of climb or descent in an aircraft. **3** an instrument for measuring variations in a magnetic field. [L *varius*, METER[1]]

variorum (veəriaw´rəm) *a.* **1** (of an edition of a work) with notes of various commentators inserted. **2** including variant readings. *~n.* a variorum edition. **variorum edition** *n.* an edition of a classic etc. with comparisons of texts and notes by various editors and commentators. [L, gen. *pl.* of *varius*, see VARIOUS]

various (veə´riəs) *a.* **1** differing from each other, diverse. **2** several. **3** (*poet.*) variegated. **4** †uncertain, inconstant. **variously** *adv.* **variousness** *n.* [L *varius*]

Usage note The construction *various of* (after *several of*, *some of*) is best avoided.

varistor (vərist´ə) *n.* a semiconductor with two electrodes which has a resistance dependent on the strength of the voltage applied. [*var*iable re*sistor*]

varix (veə´riks) *n.* (*pl.* **varices** (-isēz)) **1** a permanent dilatation of a vein or other vessel. **2** a varicose vessel. **3** any of the ridges traversing the whorls of a univalve shell. [L]

varlet (vah´lit) *n.* **1** (*Hist.*) a page, an attendant preparing to be a squire. **2** †a menial. **3** †a knave, a rascal. **†varletry** *n.* the rabble, the crowd. [OF *varlet*, *vaslet*, dim. of VASSAL]

varmint (vah´mint) *n.* (*N Am. or dial.*) a troublesome or mischievous person or animal. [corr. of VERMIN]

varna (vah´nə) *n.* any of the four great Hindu castes. [Sansk., class]

varnish (vah´nish) *n.* **1** a thin resinous solution for applying to the surface of wood, metal etc., to give it a hard, transparent, shiny coating. **2** a similar solution or preparation giving a glossy surface. **3** an application of varnish. **4** any lustrous or glossy appearance on the surface of leaves etc. **5** the lustrous surface or glaze of pottery etc. **6** superficial polish. **7** gloss, palliation, whitewash. *~v.t.* **1** to cover with varnish. **2** to give an improved appearance to, to gloss over, to whitewash. **varnisher** *n.* **varnishing day** *n.* a day before the opening of an exhibition when artists are allowed to varnish or retouch their pictures. **varnish tree** *n.* any tree from which the material for varnish is obtained. [F *vernis*, etym. uncertain, whence *vernisser*, *vernir*, to varnish]

varsity (vah´siti) *n.* (*pl.* **varsities**) **1** (*coll.*) university. **2** (*N Am.*) the principal team representing a university, college, school etc. in a sports or other competition. [corr. of UNIVERSITY]

varus (veə´rəs) *n.* **1** a variety of club foot in which the foot is bent inwards. **2** a similar deformity of the hand. [L, bent]

varve (vahv) *n.* a seasonal layer of clay deposited in still water, used to fix ice age chronology. [Swed. *varv*, layer]

vary (veə´ri) *v.t.* (*3rd pers. sing. pres.* **varies,** *pres.p.* **varying,** *past, p.p.* **varied**) **1** to change, to alter in appearance, form or substance. **2** to modify, to diversify. **3** to make variations of (a melody etc.). *~v.i.* **1** to be altered in any way. **2** to undergo change. **3** to be different or diverse, to differ, to be of different kinds. **4** to increase or decrease proportionately with or inversely to the increase or decrease of another quantity. **varied** *a.* **1** possessing or showing variety, diverse. **2** variegated. [F *varier*, L *variāre*, from *varius*, VARIOUS]

vas (vas) *n.* (*pl.* **vasa** (vā´sə)) a vessel or duct. **vasal** (vā´-) *a.* **vas deferens** (def´ərenz) *n.* (*pl.* **vasa deferentia** (deferen´shiə)) the spermatic duct. [L, vessel]

vascula VASCULUM.

vascular (vas´kūlə) *a.* **1** of, consisting of, or containing vessels or ducts for the conveyance of blood, chyle, sap etc. **2** containing or rich in blood vessels. **vascular bundle** *n.* a longitudinal strand of vascular tissue in the stem or leaf of a plant. **vascularity** (-lar´i-) *n.* **vascularize, vascularise** *v.t.* to make vascular, to develop blood vessels in. **vascularization** (-zā´shən) *n.* **vascularly** *adv.* **vascular plant** *n.* a plant with vascular tissue. **vascular tissue** *n.* tissue found in higher plants, consisting of phloem and xylem, which acts as a network conducting water, mineral salts and food substances throughout the whole plant and provides it with physical support. [VASCULUM]

vasculum (vas´kūləm) *n.* (*pl.* **vascula** (-lə), **vasculums**) a botanist's collecting case, usu. of tin. [L, dim. of VAS]

vase (vahz) *n.* **1** a vessel of pottery etc., of various forms but usu. circular with a swelling body and a foot or pedestal, used for various ornamental and other purposes, esp. holding flowers. **2** a sculptured ornament in imitation of an ancient vase, used to decorate cornices, gateposts, monuments etc. **vaseful** *n.* (*pl.* **vasefuls**). [F *vase*, L *vasum*, vase, vessel, cogn. with VAS]

vasectomy (vəsek´təmi) *n.* (*pl.* **vasectomies**) excision of the vas deferens or part of it to produce sterility. **vasectomize, vasectomise** *v.t.* [Gr. *ek*, out, *tomē*, a cut]

Vaseline® (vas´əlēn) *n.* a soft, medicated paraffin jelly employed as a lubricant etc. **vaseline** *v.t.* to treat, lubricate etc. with Vaseline.

vasiform (vā´zifawm) *a.* **1** having the form of a vas. **2** having the form of a vase.

vaso- (vā´zō) *comb. form* relating to a vas, vessel or duct.

vasoactive (vāzōak´tiv) *a.* vasomotor.

vasoconstrictor (vāzōkənstrik´tə) *a.* causing constriction of a blood vessel. *~n.* a nerve, drug or other agent causing this. **vasoconstriction** *n.* **vasoconstrictive** *a.*

vasodilator (vāzōdilā´tə) *a.* causing dilatation of a vessel. *~n.* a nerve or drug causing this. **vasodilation, vasodilatation** (-dīlātā´shən) *n.*

vasoinhibitor (vāzōinhib´itə) *n.* a drug that inhibits the action of the vasomotor nerves. **vasoinhibitory** *a.*

vasomotor (vāzōmō´tə) *a.* causing constriction or dilatation in a vessel. ~*n.* a vasomotor nerve, agent or drug. **vasomotorial** (-taw´ri-) *a.*

vasopressin (vāzōpres´in) *n.* a polypeptide hormone secreted by the pituitary gland that reduces diuresis and increases blood pressure. **vasopressor** (-pres´ə) *a.* causing an increase in blood pressure by constricting the arteries. ~*n.* a substance that does this.

vassal (vas´əl) *n.* **1** (*Hist.*) a person holding land under a superior lord by feudal tenure, a feudatory. **2** a slave, a humble dependant, a low wretch. ~*a.* servile. **vassalage** (-lij) *n.* **1** the state or condition of a vassal. **2** the obligation of a vassal to feudal service. **3** servitude, dependence. **4** vassals collectively. **vassalize, vassalise** *v.t.* [F, from med. L *vassallus*, from late L *vassus*, from Celt. (cp. Bret. *gwaz*, Welsh and Corn. *gwas*, O Ir. *foss*, servant)]

vast (vahst) *a.* **1** of great extent, immense, huge, boundless. **2** very great in numbers, amount, degree etc. ~*n.* a boundless expanse. **vastitude** (-titūd) *n.* **1** vastness. **2** a vast expanse of space. **vastly** *adv.* **vastness** *n.* †**vasty** *a.* (*comp.* **vastier**, *superl.* **vastiest**) vast. [F *vaste*, L *vastus*, empty, waste, vast]

VAT (vat, vē ā tē´) *abbr.* VALUE ADDED TAX (under VALUE). **VATman** *n.* (*pl.* **VATmen**) (*coll.*) a customs and excise officer responsible for the administration, collection etc. of VAT.

vat (vat) *n.* **1** a large tub, tank or other vessel used for holding mash or hop liquor in brewing and in many manufacturing operations in which substances are boiled or steeped. **2** a liquor containing a reduced, colourless, soluble form of an insoluble dye in which textiles are steeped, the colour appearing when the textiles are afterwards exposed to the air. ~*v.t.* (*pres.p.* **vatting**, *past*, *p.p.* **vatted**) to put into or treat in a vat. **vat dye** *n.* an insoluble dye applied in the form of a soluble vat. [formerly *fat*, OE *fæt* (cp. Dut. *vat*, G *Fass*, Icel. and Swed. *fat*, Dan. *fad*), cogn. with Dut. *vatten*, G *fassen*, to catch, to contain]

vatic (vat´ik) *a.* **1** of or relating to a prophet. **2** prophetic; oracular. [L *vātēs*, prophet]

Vatican (vat´ikən) *n.* **1** the palace of the Pope on the Vatican Hill in Rome. **2** the papal government. **Vatican City** *n.* a small area on the Vatican Hill set up as an independent state in 1929. **Vatican Council** *n.* **1** the 20th Ecumenical Council (1869–70) at which the infallibility of the Pope when speaking *ex cathedra* was affirmed. **2** (*also* **Vatican II**) a similar council held between 1962 and 1965. **Vaticanism** *n.* (*often derog.*) the authority and policies of the Holy See, esp. with regard to infallibility. **Vaticanist** *n.*

vaticide (vat´isīd) *n.* the murder or murderer of a prophet. [L *vātes vātis*, prophet, -CIDE]

vaticinate (vətis´ināt) *v.t.*, *v.i.* to prophesy. **vaticinal** *a.* **vaticination** (-ā´shən) *n.* a prophecy. **vaticinator** *n.* a prophet. [L *vāticinātus*, p.p. of *vāticinārī* (*vāti-*, see VATIC, *canere*, to sing)]

vatu (vah´too) *n.* (*pl.* **vatus, vatu**) the standard monetary unit of Vanuatu.

vaudeville (vaw´dəvil) *n.* **1** (*N Am.*) a miscellaneous series of sketches, songs etc., a variety entertainment. **2** a slight dramatic sketch or pantomime interspersed with songs and dances. **3** a topical or satirical song with a refrain. **vaudevillian** (-vil´-) *a.* of or relating to vaudeville. ~*n.* a person who performs in vaudeville. **vaudevillist** *n.* a writer of vaudevilles. [F, corr. of *vau* (*val*) *de Vire*, valley of the Vire, orig. a comic or convivial song, such as those of Olivier Basselin, poet, born in the val de Vire (d. 1418)]

Vaudois[1] (vō´dwah) *n.* (*pl.* **Vaudois**) **1** a native or inhabitant of the canton of Vaud in Switzerland. **2** the Vaudois dialect of French. ~*a.* of or relating to Vaud. [F]

Vaudois[2] (vō´dwah) *n.* (*pl.* **Vaudois**) any of the Waldenses. ~*a.* of or relating to the Waldenses. [F, from med. L *Valdenses*, WALDENSES]

vault[1] (vawlt) *n.* **1** (*Archit.*) an arched roof; a continuous arch or semi-cylindrical roof; a series of arches connected by radiating joints. **2** an arched chamber, esp. underground; a cellar. **3** a strongroom for the deposit and storage of valuables. **4** a place of interment built of masonry under a church or in a cemetery. **5** any vault-like covering or canopy, such as the sky. **6** (*Anat.*) an arched roof of a cavity. ~*v.t.* **1** to cover with, or as with, a vault or vaults. **2** to construct in the form of a vault. **vaulting**[1] *n.* an arched ceiling or roof or the arched work that supports or composes it. [ME and OF *voute*, fem. of *volt*, vaulted, L *volūtus*, p.p. of *volvere*, to roll]

vault[2] (vawlt) *v.i.* **1** to leap, to spring, esp. with the hands resting on something or with the help of a pole. **2** (*formal*) to achieve or attain with apparent suddenness. ~*v.t.* to leap over (a gate, obstacle etc.) by vaulting. ~*n.* such a leap. **vaulter** *n.* **vaulting**[2] *a.* **1** overweening, overconfident, overreaching. **2** used in vaulting. **vaulting horse** *n.* a wooden horse or frame for vaulting over in a gymnasium. [ME *volter*, as VAULT[1]]

vaulting[1] VAULT[1].

vaulting[2] VAULT[2].

vaunt (vawnt) *v.i.* to boast, to brag. ~*v.t.* to boast of. ~*n.* a boast. **vaunter** *n.* **vauntingly** *adv.* [F *vanter*, late L *vānitāre*, freq. from *vānus*, VAIN]

†**vaunt-courier** (vawntkur´iə) *n.* a forerunner, a harbinger. [F as AVANT-COURIER (under AVANT)]

vavasour (vav´əsuə) *n.* a vassal holding land from a great lord and having other vassals under him. **vavasory** (-səri) *n.* (*pl.* **vavasories**) the tenure or lands of a vavasour. [OF *vavassour*, med. L *vassus vassōrum*, VASSAL of vassals]

vb *abbr.* verb.

VC *abbr.* **1** Vice-Chairman. **2** Vice-Chancellor. **3** Vice-Consul. **4** Victoria Cross. **5** Viet Cong.

VCR *abbr.* video cassette recorder.

VD *abbr.* venereal disease.

VDU *abbr.* visual display unit.

VE *abbr.* Victory in Europe. **VE day** *n.* **1** 8 May 1945, the day on which hostilities in Europe in World War II officially ceased. **2** an anniversary of this day.

Veadar (vē´ədah) *n.* a supplementary or intercalary month inserted into the Jewish calendar every third year after the month Adar. [Heb. (*ve* and ADAR)]

veal (vēl) *n.* the flesh of a calf as food. **veal gateau** *n.* minced veal boiled in a shape or mould, like a pudding. **vealy** *a.* [OF *veël* (F *veau*), L *vitellum*, nom. *-lus*, dim. of *vitulus*, calf, cogn. with Gr. *italos*, calf, *etos*, year, L *vetus*, old, cp. WETHER]

vector (vek´tə) *n.* **1** a quantity having both magnitude and direction (e.g. velocity), but not temperature. **2** a line in space or in a diagram representing the magnitude and direction of a quantity. **3** a course to be taken by an aircraft. **4** an agent (such as an insect) that carries a disease or parasite from one host to another. **5** an agent which can be used to transfer a fragment of DNA from one organism to another. **6** a force or influence. ~*v.t.* to direct (an aircraft) to a particular point. **vectorial** (-taw´ri-) *a.* **vectorize, vectorise** *v.t.* [L, carrier, from *vehere*, to carry, p.p. *vectus*]

Veda (vā´də) *n.* the ancient Hindu scriptures, divided into four portions or books (the *Rig-*, *Yajur-*, *Sāma-*, and *Artharva-Veda*). **Vedanta** (vidan´tə) *n.* **1** a system of philosophy founded on the Veda. **2** the Upanishads. **Vedantic** *a.* **Vedantist** *n.*, *a.* **Vedic** (vā´-, vē´-) *a.* [Sansk., knowledge]

Vedda (ved´ə) *n.* a member of an aboriginal people of Sri Lanka. [Sinhalese, hunter]

vedette (videt´), **vidette** *n.* **1** a sentinel (usu. mounted) stationed in advance of an outpost. **2** a small vessel used for scouting purposes etc. [F, from It. *vedetta*, var. of *vēduta*, fem. p.p. of *vedere*, L *vidēre*, to see]

Vedic VEDA.

vee (vē) *n.* **1** the letter V, v. **2** anything in the shape of this letter.

veep (vēp) *n.* (*N Am., coll.*) a vice-president. [from the initials *VP*]

veer[1] (viə) *v.i.* **1** to change direction, esp. (of the wind) in the direction of the sun (i.e. clockwise in the northern hemisphere and anticlockwise in the southern hemisphere). **2** to shift, to change about, esp. in opinion, conduct etc. **3** (of a ship) to turn away from the wind, to wear. *~v.t.* **1** to change the direction of. **2** to wear (a ship). **veeringly** *adv.* [F *virer*, late L *virāre*, cp. *virola*, ring, L *viriola*, bracelet, dim. of *viria*, in *viriae*, armlets]

veer[2] (viə) *v.t.* to let out or slacken (a rope etc.). [ME from MDut. *vieren*]

veery (viə´ri) *n.* (*pl.* **veeries**) a tawny N American thrush, *Catharus fuscescens.* [prob. imit.]

veg (vej) *n.* (*pl.* **veg**) (*coll.*) a vegetable. [abbr.]

vegan (vē´gən) *n.* a person who uses no animal products whatsoever for food, clothing etc. *~a.* containing no animal products.

Vegeburger® (vej´ibœgə) *n.* a veggie burger.

vegetable (vej´təbəl, vej´i-) *n.* **1** a plant, esp. a herbaceous one, used for culinary purposes or for feeding cattle etc. **2** (*coll.*) a person who, usu. through brain damage, has limited awareness and has lost control of bodily functions. **3** (*coll., derog.*) a very sluggish, idle or apathetic person; a person who leads a very monotonous life. *~a.* **1** of the nature of, relating to or resembling, a plant. **2** made of or relating to culinary vegetables. **3** (of a person's existence) dull, sluggish, inactive; very monotonous. **vegetable butter** *n.* any number of vegetable fats that have the consistency of butter. **vegetable casein** *n.* a similar protein found in leguminous plants. **vegetable ivory** *n.* the hard albumen of ivory-nuts. **vegetable kingdom** *n.* the division of organic nature comprising plants. **vegetable marrow** *n.* a large edible gourd with white flesh from the plant *Cucurbita pepo.* **vegetable mould,** (*N Am.*) **vegetable mold** *n.* mould or soil consisting to a certain extent of decaying or decayed vegetation. **vegetable oil** *n.* an oil obtained from seeds or plants, used in cooking etc. **vegetable oyster** *n.* salsify. **vegetable parchment** *n.* a type of paper made to resemble parchment. **vegetable sheep** *n.* a New Zealand plant of the genus *Raoulia*, which has dense growth, white flowers and hairy leaves, so that it resembles a sheep at a distance. **vegetable spaghetti** *n.* a variety of marrow that has flesh resembling spaghetti; its flesh. **vegetable sponge** *n.* a loofah. **vegetable tallow** *n.* any type of tallow obtained from plants. **vegetable wax** *n.* a waxy substance exuded by certain plants, e.g. the sumac, to prevent moisture loss. **vegetal** (vej´i-) *a.* **1** relating to or of the nature of plants. **2** common to plants and animals (of the functions of nutrition, growth, circulation, secretions etc.). **vegetality** (-tal´-) *n.* **vegetarian** (-iteə´ri-) *n.* a person who abstains from eating meat, and sometimes also other animal products and fish. *~a.* **1** excluding meat and other animal products to a greater or lesser extent. **2** of or relating to vegetarians and vegetarianism. **vegetarianism** *n.* **vegetate** (-itāt) *v.i.* **1** to grow in the manner of a plant, to fulfil the functions of a vegetable. **2** to live an idle, passive, monotonous life. **vegetation** (-ā´shən) *n.* **1** vegetables or plants collectively, plant life. **2** all the plants in a specified area. **3** the act or process of vegetating. **4** an excrescence on the body. **vegetative** *a.* **1** concerned with development and growth as distinct from sexual reproduction. **2** of or relating to vegetation, plant life or plant growth. **3** (*Med.*) (of the state of e.g. a person in a coma) alive but without responsiveness or apparent brain activity. **4** dull, apathetic, passive. **vegetatively** *adv.* **vegetativeness** *n.* **vegeto-** *comb. form* [F, from late L *vegetābilis*, from *vegetāre*, to enliven, to quicken, from L *vegetus*, lively, from *vegēre*, to move, to quicken, cogn. with VIGIL and VIGOUR]

veggie (vej´i) *n.* **1** short for VEGETABLE. **2** (*coll.*) short for VEGETARIAN (under VEGETABLE). **veggie burger** *n.* a flat cake of minced or chopped seasoned vegetables, soya etc., resembling and prepared and eaten like a hamburger.

vehement (vē´əmənt) *a.* **1** proceeding from or exhibiting intense fervour or passion, ardent, passionate, impetuous. **2** acting with great force, energy or violence. **vehemence** *n.* **vehemently** *adv.* [OF, from L *vehementem*, nom. *-ens*, perh. from *vehere*, to carry, or *vē-*, apart from, *mens mentis*, mind]

vehicle (vē´ikəl) *n.* **1** any kind of carriage or conveyance for use on land, having wheels or runners. **2** any liquid etc. serving as a medium for pigments, medicinal substances etc. **3** any person or thing employed as a medium for the transmission of thought, feeling etc. **4** a work, e.g. a play, which gives special prominence to a particular performer and is designed to show off their particular talents. **5** the literal meaning of a word or words used metaphorically. **6** a space rocket or launcher. **vehicular** (-hik´ū-) *a.* [L *vehiculum*, from *vehere*, to carry]

veil (vāl) *n.* **1** a more or less transparent piece of cloth, muslin etc., usu. attached to a hat or headdress, worn to conceal, shade or protect the face. **2** a piece of linen worn as part of a nun's headdress, framing the face and falling over the shoulders. **3** a curtain or other drapery for concealing or protecting an object. **4** a mask, a disguise, a pretext. **5** a velum. **6** (*Mus.*) a slight huskiness or obscuration of voice, permanent or due to a cold etc. **7** slight fogging in a photograph. **8** a humeral veil. *~v.t.* **1** to cover with a veil. **2** to hide, to conceal, to disguise. **beyond the veil** in the unknown state that follows death. **to draw a veil over 1** to conceal discreetly. **2** to refrain from mentioning. **to take the veil 1** to assume the veil according to the custom of a woman when she becomes a nun. **2** to retire to a convent. **veiling** *n.* a light fabric used for making veils. **veilless** *a.* [ME and OF *veile*, L *vēlum*]

veilleuse (vāyœz´) *n.* a night-lamp, shaded and usu. artistically decorated. [F, fem. of *veilleur*, from *veiller*, L *vigilāre*, to watch]

vein (vān) *n.* **1** any of the tubular vessels in animal bodies conveying blood to the heart. **2** (*loosely*) any blood vessel. **3** a rib or nervure in an insect's wing or a leaf. **4** a fissure in rock filled with material deposited by water. **5** a seam of any substance. **6** a streak or wavy stripe of different colour, in wood, marble or stone. **7** a distinctive trait, quality, tendency or cast of mind. **8** a particular mood or humour. *~v.t.* to fill or cover with, or as with veins. **veining** *n.* a pattern or network of veins, streaks etc. **veinless** *a.* **veinlet** *n.* **veinlike** *a.* **veinstone** *n.* the non-metalliferous part in a vein, gangue. **veiny** *a.* (*comp.* **veinier,** *superl.* **veiniest**) having or covered with veins. [ME and F *veine*, L *vēna*]

vela VELUM.

velamen (vilā´mən) *n.* (*pl.* **velamina** (-minə)) **1** (*Bot.*) a membraneous covering or envelope, esp. of the aerial roots of some orchids. **2** a velum. **velamentous** (velə-) *a.* [L, from *vēlāre*, to cover]

velar (vē´lə) *a.* **1** of or relating to a velum. **2** (of a speech sound) articulated with the back of the tongue close to or in contact with the soft palate, as in *k* or *g*. *~n.* a velar sound or consonant. **velarize, velarise** *v.t.* to pronounce, or to supplement the pronunciation of, in this manner. **velarization** (-zā´shən) *n.* [L *vēlāris*, from *vēlum*, sail]

velarium (vileə´riəm) *n.* (*pl.* **velaria** (-iə)) the great awning stretched over the seats in an ancient Roman theatre or amphitheatre as a protection against rain or sun. [L]

velate VELUM.

Velcro® (vel´krō) *n.* a fastening for clothes etc. which consists of two nylon strips, one consisting of hooks and the other of loops, which stick together when pressed. *~v.t.* (*3rd pers. sing. pres.* **Velcroes,** *pres.p.* **Velcroing,** *past, p.p.* **Velcroed**) **1** to attach Velcro to. **2** to fasten with Velcro.

veld (velt, felt), **veldt** *n.* (*S Afr.*) open country suitable for pasturage, esp. the high treeless plains in N Transvaal and NW Natal. [Dut. *veld,* FIELD]

veldskoen (velt´skoon, felt´-) *n.* an ankle-length boot, orig. made of raw hide, now usu. of soft suede or leather. [Dut. *vel,* skin, *schoen,* shoe]

veldt VELD.

veleta (vəlē´tə), **valeta** *n.* a dance or dance tune in slow waltz time. [Sp., weathercock]

veliger (vel´ijə) *n.* a free-swimming larva of a mollusc, which has a ciliated velum for feeding and movement. [L *velum, -ger,* bearing]

†velitation (velitā´shən) *n.* **1** a slight skirmish. **2** a controversial skirmish, a brush. **velite** (vē´līt) *n.* in ancient Rome, a light-armed soldier. [L *vēlitātio,* from *vēlitārī,* to skirmish, from *vēles,* light-armed soldier, a velite]

velleity (vilē´iti) *n.* (*formal*) **1** a low degree of desire or volition unaccompanied by effort. **2** a slight wish, an inclination. [med. L *velleitas,* from *velle,* to wish]

vellicate (vel´ikāt) *v.t., v.i.* to twitch spasmodically. **vellication** (-ā´shən) *n.* **vellicative** *a.* [L *vellicātus,* p.p. of *vellicāre,* from *vellere,* to pluck]

vellum (vel´əm) *n.* **1** a fine parchment orig. made of calfskin. **2** a manuscript written on this. **3** a superior quality of paper made to imitate vellum. *~a.* made of or resembling vellum. **vellumy** *a.* [ME *velim,* F *velin,* L *vitulīnus,* of a calf, from *vitulus,* see VEAL]

veloce (vilō´chā) *adv.* (*Mus.*) with great quickness. [It.]

velocimeter (veləsim´itə) *n.* an apparatus for measuring velocity.

velocipede (vilos´ipēd) *n.* **1** an early kind of bicycle propelled by the feet. **2** any early form of cycle. **3** (*N Am.*) a child's tricycle. **velocipedist** *n.* [L *vēlox,* as VELOCITY]

velociraptor (vilos´iraptə) *n.* a small carnivorous dinosaur of the Cretaceous period which stood upright and had a large curved claw on each hind foot. [mod. L, from *vēlox -locis,* swift, RAPTOR]

velocity (vilos´iti) *n.* (*pl.* **velocities**) **1** swiftness, rapidity, rapid motion. **2** a measure of the rate of motion, esp. of inanimate things, in a given direction. **velocity-distance law** *n.* (*Astron.*) the law that the more distant a nebula is, the greater is its speed of recession. **velocity of circulation** *n.* the ratio of the total money spent within a given period of time to the total amount of money in circulation, giving the average number of times a unit of money is used. **velocity of escape** *n.* ESCAPE VELOCITY (under ESCAPE). [F *vélocité,* L *vēlōcitātem,* nom. *-tas,* from *vēlox -lōcis,* swift, cogn. with *volāre,* to fly]

velodrome (vel´ədrōm) *n.* a building containing a cycle-racing track. [F *vélodrome*]

velour (viluə´), **velours, velure** (-ūə´) *n.* **1** velvet, velveteen or other fabric resembling velvet. **2** a pad of velvet or silk for smoothing a silk hat. **3** †a hat made of velour. **velouté** (-oo´tā) *n.* a thick creamy sauce or soup. **velutinous** (-loo´ti-) *a.* velvety, covered with short, soft hairs. [F *velours,* OF *velous,* med. L *villōsus,* shaggy, from VILLUS]

velum (vē´ləm) *n.* (*pl.* **vela** (-lə)) a membrane, a membraneous covering, envelope etc., esp. the soft palate. **velate** (-lət, -lāt) *a.* having or covered with a velum. [L, sail, covering, from *vehere,* to carry]

velure VELOUR.

velvet (vel´vit) *n.* **1** a closely-woven fabric, usu. of silk, with a short, soft nap or cut pile on one side. **2** anything soft and smooth or resembling velvet. **3** the furry skin covering the growing antlers of a deer. **4** (*esp. N Am., sl.*) money won by gambling or speculation. *~a.* **1** velvety. **2** as soft as velvet. **on velvet** (*coll.*) in a position of comfort, luxury, wealth etc. **velvet ant** *n.* a downy-bodied, parasitic wasp of the family Mutillidae, the female of which is wingless. **velveted** *a.* **velveteen** (-tēn´) *n.* **1** a cotton velvet or cotton fabric with a velvet pile. **2** (*pl.*) trousers made of this. **velvet glove** *n.* gentleness concealing strength. **†velvet-guard** *n.* (*Shak.*) **1** velvet trimmings. **2** a person wearing such trimmings. **velveting** *n.* **1** the fine nap or pile of velvet. **2** (*collect.*) velvet goods. **velvet-paper** *n.* flock wallpaper. **velvet-pile** *n.* **1** a pile like that of velvet. **2** a fabric with such a pile. **velvet scoter** *n.* a black duck, *Melanitta fusca,* with white patches below the eyes and on the wings. **velvety** *a.* [A-F from late L *velluētum,* ult. from L VILLUS]

Ven. *abbr.* Venerable.

vena (vē´nə) *n.* (*pl.* **venae** (-nē)) a vein. **vena cava** (kā´və) *n.* (*pl.* **venae cavae** (-vē)) either of the two large veins conveying oxygen-depleted blood to the heart. **venal**[1] *a.* **venation** (-nā´shən) *n.* the arrangement of the veins on leaves, insects' wings etc. **venational** *a.* **venepuncture** (vē´nipŭngkchə, ven´-), (*N Am.*) **venipuncture** *n.* the piercing of a vein, esp. with a hypodermic needle. **venesection** (venisek´shən) *n.* an incision into a vein, a phlebotomy. [L]

venal[1] VENA.

venal[2] (vē´nəl) *a.* **1** ready to be bribed or to sacrifice honour or principle for sordid considerations. **2** characterized by mercenary motives. **venality** (-nal´-) *n.* **venally** *adv.* [OF, from L *vēnālis,* from *vēnus, vēnum,* sale]

Usage note The adjectives *venal* and *venial* should not be confused: *venal* means mercenary or sordid, and *venial* excusable or (of sin) not mortal.

venatic (vinat´ik), **venatical** *a.* **1** of, relating to or used in hunting. **2** fond of the chase. **venatically** *adv.* [L *venāticus,* from *venātus,* hunting, see VENERY[2]]

venation VENA.

vend (vend) *v.t.* **1** (*Law*) to sell. **2** to offer (small wares) for sale (as a costermonger etc.). **vendee** (-dē´) *n.* a person who buys something, esp. property. **vender** *n.* a vendor. **vendible** *a.* saleable or marketable. *~n.* a saleable object. **vendibility** (-bil´-), **vendibleness** *n.* **vending machine** *n.* a slot machine dispensing goods, e.g. cigarettes, drinks, sweets. **vendition** (-dish´ən) *n.* **vendor** *n.* **1** a person who sells something, esp. property. **2** a vending machine. **vendue** (-dū´) *n.* (*N Am.*) a public auction. [F *vendre,* L *vendere vēnum,* see VENAL[2], *dare,* to give]

vendace (ven´dās) *n.* a small and delicate whitefish, *Coregonus albula,* found in some lakes. [OF *vendese, vandoise,* dace]

Vendéan (vădā´ən) *a.* of or relating to La Vendée, a western department of France. *~n.* **1** an inhabitant or native of La Vendée. **2** a member of the Royalist party who revolted against the French Republic in 1793–5.

vendee VEND.

Vendémiaire (vădāmyeə´) *n.* the first month of the French revolutionary calendar (22 Sept.–21 Oct.). [F, from L *vindēmia,* vintage, from *vinum,* wine]

vendetta (vendet´ə) *n.* **1** a blood feud, often carried on for generations, in which the family of a murdered or injured man seeks vengeance on the offender or any member of his family, prevalent esp. in Corsica, Sardinia and Sicily. **2** this practice. **3** a feud, private warfare or animosity. [It., from L *vindicta,* revenge, see VINDICTIVE]

vendeuse (vondœz´) *n.* a saleswoman, esp. in a fashionable dress shop. [F]

vendible, vendue VEND.

veneer (viniə´) *v.t.* **1** to cover with a thin layer of fine or superior wood. **2** to put a superficial polish on, to disguise, to gloss over. **3** to bond together to make plywood. ~*n.* **1** a thin layer of superior wood for veneering. **2** superficial polish, a superficial appearance (*a veneer of politeness*). **3** any surfacing or facing material that is applied to a different backing. **4** a layer in plywood. **veneering** *n.* [G *furneren*, to inlay, F *fournir*, to FURNISH]

venenose (ven´inōz) *a.* (*formal*) poisonous. [L *venēnōsus*, from *venēnum*, poison]

venepuncture VENA.

venerable (ven´ərəbəl) *a.* **1** worthy of reverence, esp. on account of old age and good character. **2** rendered sacred by religious or other associations. **3** ancient. **4** applied as a title to archdeacons in the Church of England, and to a person who has attained the first of three degrees in canonization in the Roman Catholic Church. **venerability** (-bil´-), **venerableness** *n.* **venerably** *adv.* [OF, from L *venerābilis*, as VENERATE]

venerate (ven´ərāt) *v.t.* to regard or treat with profound deference and respect, to revere. **veneration** (-rā´shən) *n.* **venerative** *a.* **venerator** *n.* [L *venerātus*, p.p. of *venerāri*, cogn. with VENUS and with Sansk. *van*, to serve, to honour]

venereal (viniə´riəl) *a.* **1** of or relating to, or produced by sexual intercourse. **2** of or relating to venereal disease. **3** of or relating to the genitals. **venereal disease** *n.* a disease conveyed by sexual intercourse, esp. gonorrhoea, syphilis and chancroid. **venereology** (-ol´-) *n.* the study of venereal diseases. †**venery**[1] (ven´-) *n.* sexual indulgence. [L *venereus*, from VENUS]

venery[1] VENEREAL.

†**venery**[2] (ven´əri) *n.* hunting, the chase. [OF *venerie*, from *vener*, L *vēnārī*, to hunt]

venesection VENA.

Venetian (vinē´shən) *a.* of or relating to the city or province of Venice, in N Italy. ~*n.* **1** a native or inhabitant of Venice. **2** the Italian dialect spoken in Venice. **3** (*usu.* **venetian**) a venetian blind. **4** (*usu.* **venetian**) any one of the tapes or braids used to connect the slats in venetian blinds. **venetian blind** *n.* a blind made of thin slats on braid or webbing arranged to turn so as to admit or exclude light. **Venetian glass** *n.* a delicate ornamental glassware made at or near Venice. **Venetian lace** *n.* a variety of point lace. **Venetian mast** *n.* a pole painted spirally in two or more colours, used for street decorations. **Venetian red** *n.* **1** a pigment made from ferric oxide. **2** a reddish-brown colour. **Venetian-red** *a.* of this colour. **Venetian window** *n.* a window with three separate apertures, of which the centre one is largest and arched. [L *Venetia*, country of the Veneti]

vengeance (ven´jəns) *n.* punishment inflicted in return for an injury or wrong, retribution. **with a vengeance** to a greater degree than was anticipated or wished; forcibly, emphatically, undoubtedly, extremely. †**venge** *v.t.* to avenge or revenge. **vengeful** *a.* vindictive, revengeful. **vengefully** *adv.* **vengefulness** *n.* [F, from *venger*, to avenge, L *vindicāre*, see VINDICATE]

Usage note *Vengeance* implies greater justification and less purely personal motivation than *revenge*.

venial (vē´niəl) *a.* **1** that may be pardoned or excused. **2** in the Roman Catholic Church, (of some sins) not mortal. **veniality** (-al´-), **venialness** *n.* **venially** *adv.* [OF, from late L *veniālis*, from *venia*, grace, pardon]

Usage note See note under VENAL[2].

venin (ven´in) *n.* any of the poisonous substances found in animal venom. [F *venin*, poison, -IN[1]]

venipuncture VENA.

venison (ven´isən, ven´izən) *n.* the flesh of deer as food. [OF *veneisun* (F *venaison*), L *vēnātiōnem*, nom. *-tio*, from *vēnāri*, to hunt, see VENERY[2]]

Venite (vinī´tē) *n.* **1** Psalm xcv, 'O come let us sing', used as a canticle. **2** a musical setting of this. [L, come ye]

Venn diagram (ven) *n.* a diagram in which sets and their relationships are represented by intersecting circles or other figures. [John *Venn*, 1834–1923, British mathematician]

venom (ven´əm) *n.* **1** a poisonous fluid secreted by snakes, scorpions etc., and injected by biting or stinging. **2** spite, malignity, virulence. **3** †poison. **venomed** *a.* **1** venomous. **2** envenomed. **venomous** *a.* **1** containing poison. **2** able to inject poison by bite or sting. **3** full of malignity, spite etc. **venomously** *adv.* **venomousness** *n.* [ME and OF *venim* (F *venin*), L *venēnum*, poison]

venose (vē´nōs) *a.* **1** veiny, having many or very marked veins. **2** venous. **venosity** (-nos´-) *n.* local excess of veins or of venous blood. **venous** (vē´nəs) *a.* **1** of, relating to or contained in veins. **2** (of blood) oxygen-depleted and dark red in colour. **3** having veins. **venously** *adv.* [L *vēnōsus*, from *vēna*, VEIN]

vent[1] (vent) *n.* **1** (*also* **vent-hole**) a hole or aperture, esp. for the passage of air, water etc. into or out of a confined place, as in the head of a barrel, to allow air to enter while liquid is being drawn. **2** a means or place of passage, escape etc., an outlet. **3** (*Zool.*) the opening of the cloaca, the anus in animals below mammals. **4** the mouth of a volcano or other aperture through which lava and gases can escape through the earth's surface. **5** (*Mus.*) a finger-hole in a wind instrument. **6** a touch-hole in a gun. **7** the flue of a chimney. **8** the act of venting, esp. of coming to the surface to breathe, as an otter. ~*v.t.* **1** to make a vent in. **2** to give vent to; to utter, to pour forth. ~*v.i.* (of a hunted animal, esp. an otter) to take breath. **to give vent to 1** to give (often angry or violent) expression to, to express freely. **2** to allow to break out. **to vent one's spleen** to berate angrily or spitefully, often without just cause. **ventage** *n.* **1** a vent, a small hole. **2** a finger-hole in a musical instrument. **ventless** *a.* [F *vent*, wind, and *évent* from *éventer* (OF *esventer*), to expose to air, both from L *ventus*, wind]

vent[2] (vent) *n.* a slit in a garment, esp. in the back of a coat or jacket. ~*v.t.* to make a vent or vents in. [formerly *fent*, F *fente*, from *fendre*, L *findere*, to cleave]

ventail (ven´tāl) *n.* (*Hist.*) in a suit of armour, the part of the helmet that covers the lower part of the face and is often movable to admit fresh air. [OF *ventaille*, sluice, from L *ventus*, wind]

venter (ven´tə) *n.* **1** the belly, the abdomen, any large cavity containing viscera. **2** (*Biol.*) an expanded or hollowed part or surface. **3** (*Law*) the womb; a mother. **ventral** *a.* **1** of or relating to the venter. **2** of, relating to or situated on the anterior surface or point (of fins etc.). **ventrally** *adv.* **ventricose,** †**ventricous** *a.* **1** having a protruding belly. **2** (*Bot.*) distended, inflated. [L]

ventiduct (ven´tidŭkt) *n.* a passage or conduit, esp. subterranean, for ventilation. [L *ventus*, wind, *ductus*, duct]

ventifact (ven´tifakt) *n.* a pebble shaped or polished by wind-blown sand. [L *ventus*, wind, *factum*, neut. p.p. of *facere*, to make]

ventil (ven´til) *n.* **1** a valve in a wind instrument. **2** a shutter for regulating the admission of air in an organ. [L *ventulus*, breeze, dim. of *ventus*, wind]

ventilate (ven´tilāt) *v.t.* **1** to supply with fresh air, to cause a circulation of air in (a room etc.). **2** to give publicity to, to throw open for discussion etc. **3** to oxygenate (the blood). **4** to supply or force air into (the lungs). **ventilation** (-ā´shən) *n.* **ventilative** *a.* **ventilator** *n.* **1** a device for admitting or introducing fresh air into a place, room etc. 2 a machine that supplies air to the lungs of a person with breathing difficulties. [L *ventilātus*, p.p. of *ventilāre*, to blow, winnow, ventilate, from *ventus*, wind]

Ventolin® (ven´təlin) *n.* a preparation of salbutamol.

Ventôse (vã´tōz) *n.* the sixth month of the French revolutionary year (19 Feb.–20 Mar.). [F, from L *ventōsus*, from *ventus*, wind]

ventouse (ven´toos) *n.* in obstetrics, a vacuum suction cup that may be placed on the baby's head to assist the delivery. [F, suction cup]

ventral VENTER.

ventre à terre (vãntrə a teə´) *adv.* flat out, at full speed. [F]

ventricle (ven´trikəl) *n.* a cavity or hollow part in an animal body, esp. in the heart and brain. **ventricular** (-trik´ū-) *a.* [F *ventricule*, L *ventriculum*, nom. *-us*, dim. of VENTER]

ventricose VENTER.

ventriculite (ventrik´ūlīt) *n.* any of a family of fossil sponges common in flint nodules. [L *ventriculus*, see VENTRICLE, -ITE[1]]

ventriloquism (ventril´əkwizm), **ventriloquy** (-kwi) *n.* the act or art of speaking or producing sounds so that the sound appears to come not from the person speaking but from a different source. **ventriloquial** (-lō´-), **ventriloquistic** (-kwis´-) *a.* **ventriloquist** *n.* **ventriloquize, ventriloquise** *v.i.* [L *ventriloquus* (*venter -tris*, see VENTER, *loquī*, to speak), -ISM]

venture (ven´chə) *n.* 1 the undertaking of a risk, a hazard. 2 an undertaking of a risky nature. 3 a commercial speculation. 4 a stake, that which is risked. 5 †chance, hap, contingency. ~*v.t.* 1 to (dare to) express (an opinion, guess). 2 to expose to hazard or risk, to hazard, to stake. 3 to brave the dangers of. ~*v.i.* 1 to dare; to have the courage or presumption (to do etc.). 2 to (dare to) go (out, forth etc.). 3 to undertake a risk. **at a venture** at random; without planning, preparation, forethought etc. **to venture on/ upon** to (dare to) enter upon or engage in etc. **venture capital** *n.* money supplied by investors or organizations, usu. other than the owners, to launch a new commercial enterprise. **venturer** *n.* (*Hist.*) a person taking part in a trading venture. **Venture Scout** *n.* a senior member of the Scout Association usu. over 15 years old. **venturesome** *a.* 1 adventurous. 2 risky. **venturesomely** *adv.* **venturesomeness** *n.* [shortened from ADVENTURE]

venturi (ventū´ri) *n.* (*pl.* **venturis**) a tube or duct, wasp-waisted and expanding at the ends, used in measuring the flow rates of fluids, as a means of accelerating air flow, or to provide a suction source for vacuum-operated instruments. **venturi tube** *n.* [G. B. *Venturi*, 1746–1822, Italian physicist]

venue (ven´ū) *n.* 1 a place chosen as the site of an organized event or meeting. 2 a meeting place. 3 (*Law*) the place or country where a crime is alleged to have been committed and where the jury must be empanelled and the trial held. [F, coming, from *venir*, L *venīre*, to come]

Venus (vē´nəs) *n.* 1 a planet between the earth and Mercury, the brightest heavenly body after the sun and moon. 2 a beautiful woman. 3 (*poet.*) sensual love. **mount of Venus** MOUNT[2]. **Venus flowerbasket** *n.* a deep-sea sponge with a skeleton of glassy spicules. **Venus flytrap, Venus's flytrap** *n.* an insectivorous herb of the sundew family, *Dionaea muscipula*, with hinged leaves that close on its prey. **Venus's comb** *n.* an annual herb of the parsley family, *Scandex pecten-veneris*, with spiny fruit set like comb teeth; shepherd's needle. **Venus's looking-glass** *n.* any plant of the genus *Legousia*, with small blue flowers. [L, the goddess of love]

veracious (virā´shəs) *a.* (*formal*) 1 habitually speaking or disposed to speak the truth. 2 characterized by truth and accuracy. **veraciously** *adv.* **veracity** (-ras´-) *n.* 1 truthfulness, honesty. 2 accuracy. [L *vērax -acis*, from *vērus*, true]

veranda (viran´də), **verandah** *n.* 1 a light external gallery or portico with a roof on pillars, along the front or side of a house. 2 (*Austral.*, *New Zeal.*) a roof or canopy over the pavement in front of a shop. **verandaed, verandahed** *a.* [Port. *varanda*, prob. from *vara*, L *vāra*, forked pole]

veratrine (ver´ətrin, -trēn) *n.* a highly poisonous amorphous compound obtained from hellebore and other plants, used as a local irritant in neuralgia, rheumatism etc. [from L *veratrum*, hellebore]

veratrum (virā´trəm) *n.* 1 the hellebore. 2 a plant of the genus *Veratrum*, containing the hellebore. [L]

verb (vœb) *n.* (*Gram.*) that part of speech which predicates, a word or group of words that denotes an action performed or state undergone by something else (the subject). **verbid** *n.* a non-finite form of a verb or a word derived from a verb. **verbify** (-ifī) *v.t.* (*3rd pers. sing. pres.* **verbifies**, *pres.p.* **verbifying**, *past*, *p.p.* **verbified**) to convert into a verb. [F *verbe*, L *verbum*, word, cogn. with WORD and Gr. *eirein*, to speak]

verbal (vœ´bəl) *a.* 1 of or relating to words. 2 respecting words only, not ideas etc. 3 oral, spoken, not written. 4 of or relating to, or derived from a verb. 5 literal, word for word. ~*n.* 1 a word derived from a verb, esp. a verbal noun or adjective such as an English word ending in -ING[1]. 2 an oral statement. 3 (*pl.*, *sl.*) an admission of guilt made by a suspect when arrested. 4 (*sl.*) insults, abuse. ~*v.t.* (*pres.p.* **verballing**, *past*, *p.p.* **verballed**) (*sl.*) to attribute an admission of guilt to (someone). **verbalism** *n.* 1 exaggerated attention to words, e.g. in the form of minute criticism of wording, excessive literalism or a fondness for rhetoric. 2 a merely verbal expression, a statement lacking real content. 3 a verbal expression. **verbalist** *n.* 1 a person who deals in words only. 2 a literal adherent to or a minute critic of words. **verbalistic** (-lis´-) *a.* †**verbality** (-bal´-) *n.* **verbalize, verbalise** *v.t.* 1 to express in words. 2 to convert or change into a verb. ~*v.i.* to use many words, to be verbose. **verbalizable** *a.* **verbalization** (-zā´shən) *n.* **verbalizer** *n.* **verbally** *adv.* **verbal noun** *n.* a form of a verb functioning as a noun. [ME, from late L *verbalis*, see VERB]

Usage note In some contexts *verbal* may be ambiguous, as it can refer to words generally, or specifically to spoken words: *oral* can be used instead if the opposition to written words is important.

verbascum (vœbas´kəm) *n.* a plant of the genus *Verbascum*, a mullein. [L]

verbatim (vœbā´tim) *adv.*, *a.* word for word.

verbena (vœbē´nə) *n.* any of a large genus of plants, *Verbena*, of which *V. officinalis*, the common vervain, is the type. **verbenaceous** (-nā´shəs) *a.* of or relating to the family Verbenaceae, which includes herbaceous and climbing plants mainly of warm and tropical regions such as verbena, teak and lantana. [L, in pl. *verbēnae*, sacred boughs, of olive etc.]

verbiage (vœ´biij) *n.* 1 an excess of words, unnecessary words. 2 the use of many words unnecessarily, verbosity, wordiness. [F, from *verbe*, VERB]

verbid VERB.

verbose (vœbōs´) *a.* using or containing more words than are necessary, prolix. **verbosely** *adv.* **verboseness** *n.* **verbosity** (-bos´-) *n.*

verboten (vœbō´tən, fœ-) *a.* forbidden by authority. [G, p.p. of *verbieten*, to forbid]

verb. sap. (vœb sap´), **verb. sat.** (sat´) *int.* used to indicate that there is no need for a more explicit statement, warning etc. [short form of L *verbum sapienti satis est*, a word to the wise is enough]

verdant (vœ´dənt) *a.* **1** green. **2** covered with growing plants or grass. **3** fresh, flourishing. **4** green, inexperienced, unsophisticated, easily taken in. **verdancy** *n.* **verdantly** *adv.* [OF, from L *viridans -ntem*, pres.p. of *viridāre*, from *viridis*, green]

verd-antique (vœdantēk´) *n.* **1** an ornamental stone composed chiefly of serpentine, usu. green and mottled or veined. **2** a green incrustation on ancient bronze. **3** green porphyry. [F, antique green]

verderer (vœ´dərə) *n.* (*Hist.*) a judicial officer who had charge of the royal forests. [A-F *verder*, late L *viridārius*, forester, as VERDANT]

verdict (vœ´dikt) *n.* **1** the decision of a jury on an issue of fact submitted to them in the trial of any cause, civil or criminal. **2** a decision, judgement. [ME and OF *verdit*, L *vērē dictum* (*vērē*, truly, DICTUM)]

verdigris (vœ´digrēs) *n.* **1** a green crystalline substance formed on copper by the action of dilute acetic acid, used as a pigment and in medicine. **2** greenish rust on copper etc. [ME *verdegrees, -grese*, A-F *vert de Grece*, green of Greece (VERT, L *Graecia*, Greece)]

verdure (vœ´dyə) *n.* **1** greenness of vegetation. **2** fresh vegetation or foliage. **3** (*poet.*) freshness. **verdured** *a.* **verdureless** *a.* **verdurous** *a.* [F, from OF *verd*, L *viridis*]

verecund (ver´ikŭnd) *a.* bashful, modest. **verecundity** (-kŭn´-) *n.* [L *verēcundus*, from *vereor*, to feel awe]

verge[1] (vœj) *n.* **1** an edge, border or boundary. **2** the extreme edge, brink, border or margin. **3** the grass edging of a bed or border or alongside a road. **4** the edge of the tiles projecting over a gable etc. **5** a rod, wand or staff, carried as an emblem of authority, esp. before a bishop or other dignitary. **6** the shaft of a column. **7** a spindle, shaft etc., in the mechanism of a watch, loom, and other machines. ~*v.t.* to form the edge or verge of. **on the verge of** on the brink of. **to verge on 1** to border on, to be next to. **2** to come near to, to nearly be. **vergeboard** *n.* a bargeboard. [F, from L *virga*, twig, rod]

verge[2] (vœj) *v.i.* to move or incline in a particular direction, esp. downwards. **vergence** *n.* the movement of both eyes inwards or outwards when changing focus. [L *vergere*, to bend, to incline]

verger (vœ´jə), **virger** *n.* **1** an official in a church acting as caretaker, attendant, usher etc. **2** an officer carrying the verge or staff of office before a bishop or other dignitary. **vergership** *n.*

verglas (veə´glah) *n.* a film of ice on rock. [F *verre*, glass, *glace*, ice, from OF]

veridical (virid´ikəl) *a.* **1** (*formal*) truthful, veracious. **2** (*Psych.*) (of a vision, dream) that corresponds with reality or is confirmed by subsequent events. **veridically** *adv.* [L *vēridicus* (*vērus*, true, *dicere*, to say)]

†**verier**, †**veriest** VERY.

verify (ver´ifī) *v.t.* (*3rd pers. sing. pres.* **verifies**, *pres.p.* **verifying**, *past, p.p.* **verified**) **1** to confirm the truth of. **2** to inquire into the truth of, to authenticate. **3** to fulfil (a prediction, promise). **4** (*Law*) to append an affidavit to (pleadings), to support (a statement) by testimony or proofs. **verifiable** *a.* **verifiability** (-bil´-) *n.* **verifiably** *adv.* **verification** (-fikā´shən) *n.* **verifier** *n.* [OF *verifier*, med. L *vērificāre* (*vērus*, true, *-ficāre, facere*, to make)]

†**verily** (ver´ili) *adv.* in very truth, assuredly. [ME *veraily* (VERY, -LY[1])]

verisimilitude (verisimil´itūd) *n.* **1** the appearance of or resemblance to truth. **2** probability, likelihood. **3** something apparently true or a fact. **verisimilar** (-sim´-) *a.* [MF, from L *vērisimilitūdo*, from *verisimilis* (*vēri*, gen. of *vērus*, true, *similis*, like)]

verism (ver´izm, viə´-) *n.* extreme naturalism in art or literature. **verismo** (veriz´mō) *n.* realism, esp. in late 19th-cent. opera. **verist** *n.* **veristic** *a.* [It. *verismo*, from *vero*, true]

verity (ver´iti) *n.* (*pl.* **verities**) **1** truth, correspondence (of a statement) with fact. **2** a true statement, truth. **3** a thing really existent, a fact. **veritable** *a.* **1** rightly or justifiably so called. **2** real, genuine. **3** actual, true. **veritably** *adv.* [OF *verité*, L *vēritātem*, nom. *-tas*, from *vērus*, true]

verjuice (vœ´joos) *n.* **1** an acid liquid expressed from crab apples, unripe grapes etc. and used in cooking and for other purposes. **2** sourness of temper, crabbiness. **verjuiced** *a.* [F *verjus* (OF *verd*, VERT, JUICE)]

verkrampte (fəkramp´tə) *a.* (*S Afr.*) opposed to liberalization, esp. in matters of racial segregation. ~*n.* a person holding such views. [Afrikaans, restricted]

verligte (fəlikh´tə) *n., a.* (*S Afr.*) (a person) of more liberal outlook, esp. in matters of racial segregation. [Afrikaans, enlightened]

verm- VERMI-.

vermeil (vœ´mil) *n.* **1** silver gilt. **2** an orange-red garnet. **3** (*poet.*) vermilion. ~*a.* (*poet.*) vermilion. [F, VERMILION]

vermes VERMIS.

vermi- (vœ´mi), **verm-** *comb. form* of or relating to worms. [L *vermis*, a worm]

vermian (vœ´miən) *a.* of or relating to worms, wormlike.

vermicelli (vœmichel´i, -sel´i) *n.* **1** a pasta in the form of long slender tubes or threads like macaroni. **2** (*also* **chocolate vermicelli**) small thin pieces of chocolate used for cake decoration. [It., pl. of *vermicello*, dim. of *verme*, worm, as VERMI-]

vermicide (vœ´misīd) *n.* a medicine or drug that kills worms, an anthelmintic. **vermicidal** (-sī´-) *a.*

vermicular (vəmik´ūlə) *a.* **1** of or relating to worms; caused by intestinal worms. **2** resembling the motion or track of a worm. **3** tortuous, marked with intricate wavy lines (of reticulated work etc.). **4** worm-eaten in appearance. **5** vermiform. **vermiculate**[1] (-lət) *a.* **1** worm-eaten. **2** vermicular. **vermiculate**[2] (-lāt) *v.t.* to decorate with vermicular lines or tracery. **vermiculation** (-lā´shən) *n.* **1** motion after the manner of a worm, as in the peristaltic motion of the intestines. **2** the art of vermiculating. **3** vermiculated work. **4** the state of being worm-eaten. **vermicule** (vœ´mikūl) *n.* a small grub or worm. **vermiculite** (vœmik´ūlīt) *n.* **1** any of a group of hydrated silicates resulting from the alteration of mica, which expand and exfoliate when heated. **2** flakes of this material used as insulation or a medium for growing plants. **vermiculous** (-mik´-) *a.* **1** full of or containing worms or grubs. **2** worm-eaten. **3** worm-shaped, vermicular. [med. L *vermiculāris*, from *vermiculus*, dim. of *vermis*, worm]

vermiform (vœ´mifawm) *a.* **1** worm-shaped. **2** having the form or structure of a worm. **vermiform appendix** *n.* a small wormlike organ of no known function situated at the extremity of the caecum.

vermifuge (vœ´mifūj) *n.* a medicine or drug that destroys or expels intestinal worms, an anthelmintic. **vermifugal** (-gəl) *a.*

vermilion (vəmil´yən) *n.* **1** a brilliant red pigment consisting of mercuric sulphide, obtained by grinding cinnabar or by the chemical treatment of mercury and sulphur. **2** the colour of this. **3** cinnabar. ~*a.* of a brilliant red colour. ~*v.t.* to colour with or as with vermilion. [F *vermillon*, from *vermeil*, L *vermiculus*, dim. of *vermis*, worm, see VERMIS]

vermin (vœ´min) *n.* **1** (*collect.*) certain harmful or troublesome animals, such as the smaller mammals or birds injurious to crops or game, noxious or offensive insects, grubs or worms, esp. lice, fleas etc. **2** (*collect.*) low, despicable or repulsive persons. **3** an obnoxious person. **verminate** (-āt) *v.i.* to breed vermin, to become infested with parasites. **vermination** (-ā´shən) *n.* **verminous** *a.* **1** infested with vermin. **2** like vermin, troublesome, repulsive, obnoxious. **verminously** *adv.* [F *vermine*, from L *vermis*, see VERMIS]

vermis (vœ´mis) *n.* (*pl.* **vermes** (-mēz)) the middle lobe connecting the two halves of the cerebellum. [mod. L, from *vermis*, worm]

vermivorous (vœmiv´ərəs) *a.* feeding on worms.

vermouth (vœ´məth) *n.* a drink consisting of wine flavoured with wormwood and other aromatic herbs. [F *vermouth*, G *Wermuth*, wormwood]

vernacular (vənak´ūlə) *n.* **1** the native language or dialect of a particular place or country. **2** the language or idiom of a particular group of people. **3** plain, unvarnished speech. **4** a vernacular style of building. *~a.* **1** of or relating to the vernacular language. **2** (*Archit.*) in the indigenous style of ordinary houses rather than of monumental buildings. **3** (of the names of plants and animals) common, not Latin. **vernacularism** *n.* use of the vernacular. **vernacularity** (-lar´i-) *n.* **vernacularize, vernacularise** *v.t.* **vernacularization** (-zā´shən) *n.* **vernacularly** *adv.* [L *vernāculus*, from *verna*, home-born slave]

vernal (vœ´nəl) *a.* **1** of or relating to, prevailing, done or appearing in spring. **2** of or relating to youth. **vernal equinox** *n.* the spring equinox. **vernal grass** *n.* a fragrant grass, *Anthoxanthum odoratum*, sown among hay. **vernalize, vernalise** *v.t.* to treat (seeds), usu. by cooling, before sowing in order to hasten flowering. **vernalization** (-zā´shən) *n.* **vernally** *adv.* **vernation** (-nā´shən) *n.* the arrangement of the young leaves within the leaf bud. [L *vernālis*, from *vernus*, pertaining to spring, from *ver*, spring, cogn. with Gr. *ear*, Icel. *vār*]

vernicle (vœ´nikəl) *n.* a veronica, a cloth bearing the image of Christ's face. [OF from L *veronica*, a veronica cloth]

vernier (vœ´niə) *n.* **1** a movable scale for measuring fractional portions of the divisions of the scale on a measuring instrument, a barometer, theodolite etc. **2** an auxiliary device for making fine adjustments to an instrument. **vernier engine, vernier rocket** *n.* a thruster for making slight adjustments to the movement or direction of a space vehicle. [Pierre *Vernier*, *c.* 1580–1637, French mathematician]

Veronal® (ver´ənəl) *n.* a hypnotic drug, diethylbarbituric acid, also called barbitone.

Veronese (verənēz´) *a.* of or relating to Verona in Italy. *~n.* (*pl.* **Veronese**) a native or inhabitant of Verona.

veronica (vəron´ikə) *n.* **1** a herb or shrub of the genus *Veronica*, with blue, purple or white flowers; the speedwell. **2** a handkerchief or cloth bearing a portrait of Christ, esp. that of St Veronica said to have been miraculously impressed with the image of his face. **3** in bullfighting, a movement of the matador's cape away from the onrushing bull. [name of woman said to have wiped the sweat from Christ's face on the way to Calvary, corr. of Gr. *Berenikē*]

veronique (verənēk´) *a.* (*used after the noun*) served with white grapes, e.g. *sole veronique*. [F]

verricule (ver´ikūl) *n.* a dense tuft of upright hairs. [L *verriculum*, net, from *verrere*, to sweep]

verruca (vəroo´kə) *n.* (*pl.* **verrucae** (-sē), **verrucas**) **1** a wart, esp. a contagious wart on the sole of the foot. **2** (*Biol.*) a wartlike growth. **verrucose** (-kōs), **verrucous** *a.* (*Bot.*) covered in wartlike growths. [L]

vers (veə) *n.* verse. **vers de société** (də sosyātā´) *n.* light, witty and polished verse. **vers libre** (lē´brə) *n.* free verse. [F]

versant (vœ´sənt) *n.* **1** an area of land sloping in one direction. **2** general lie or slope. [F, from *verser*, L *versāre*, freq. of *vertere*, to turn]

versatile (vœ´sətīl) *a.* **1** readily adapting or applying oneself to new tasks, occupations, subjects etc., many-sided. **2** (of a device) having many different uses. **3** (*Zool.*, *Bot.*) (of anthers, antennae etc.) moving freely round or to and fro on its support. **4** †changeable, variable, inconstant. **versatilely** *adv.* **versatility** (-til´-) *n.* [F *versatil*, L *versātilis*, from *versāre*, as VERSANT]

verse (vœs) *n.* **1** metrical composition as distinct from prose. **2** a particular type of metrical composition. **3** a metrical line consisting of a certain number of feet. **4** a group of metrical lines, a stanza. **5** any one of the short divisions of a chapter of the Bible. **6** a short sentence in a liturgy etc. *~v.t.* to express in verse. *~v.i.* to make verses. **to verse in** to instruct in, to make conversant with or knowledgeable about. **verset** (-sit) *n.* a short organ interlude or prelude. **versicle** (-sikəl) *n.* a short verse, esp. one of a series recited in divine service by the minister alternately with the people. **versicular** (-sik´ū-) *a.* **1** of or relating to verses or versicles. **2** relating to division into verses. **versify** (-sifī) *v.t.* (*3rd pers. sing. pres.* **versifies,** *pres.p.* **versifying,** *past, p.p.* **versified**) **1** to turn (prose) into verse. **2** to narrate or express in verse. *~v.i.* to make verses. **versification** (-fikā´shən) *n.* **versifier** *n.* [OE *fers*, L *versus* *-sūs*, a turning, furrow, row, verse, from *vertere*, to turn, p.p. *versus*]

versed (vœst) *a.* **1** skilled, familiar, experienced, proficient (in). **2** (*Math.*) (of sines) turned about, reversed. **versed sine** *n.* (*Math.*) a trigonometric function equal to one minus the cosine. [L *versātus*, p.p. of *versārī*, to turn about, see VERSANT]

verset, versicle VERSE.

versicoloured (vœ´sikŭləd), (*N Am.*) **versicolored** *a.* **1** changeable from one colour to another, with differences of light. **2** having various colours, variegated. **versicolour** *a.* [L *versicolor* (*versi-*, *versāre*, to turn, COLOUR)]

†versiform (vœ´sifawm) *a.* varying in form.

versify VERSE.

versin (vœ´sin), **versine** (-sīn) *n.* (*Math.*) a versed sine.

version (vœ´shən) *n.* **1** a statement, account or description of something from a person's particular point of view. **2** a variant form of something. **3** a translation of a work from one language into another. **4** the adaptation of a work of art into another medium. **5** a piece of translation, esp. the rendering of a passage into another language as a school exercise. **6** (*Med.*) the turning of a child in the womb to facilitate delivery. **versional** *a.* [F, from med. L *versiōnem*, nom. *-sio*, from *vertere*, to turn, p.p. *versus*]

verso (vœ´sō) *n.* (*pl.* **versos**) **1** a left-hand page of a book lying open. **2** the back of a sheet of printed or manuscript paper. **3** the other side of a coin or medal to that on which the head appears. [L *verso* (*folio*), on the turned leaf (*verso*, abl. of *versus*, turned, FOLIO)]

verst (vœst) *n.* a Russian measure of length, 3500.64 ft., nearly two-thirds of a mile (about 1 km). [Rus. *versta*]

versus (vœ´səs) *prep.* against. [L, towards, from *vertere*, to turn, p.p. *versus*]

vert (vœt) *n.* **1** (*Hist.*) in English law, everything in a forest that grows and bears green leaves; the right to cut green or growing wood. **2** (*Her.*) the tincture green. *~a.* (*Her.*) green. [F, from L *viridem*, nom. *-dis*, green]

vertebra (vœ´tibrə) *n.* (*pl.* **vertebrae** (-brē)) **1** any one of the bony segments of which the spine or backbone consists. **2** (*pl.*) the backbone. **vertebral** *a.* **vertebral column** *n.* the spinal column. **vertebrally** *adv.* **vertebrate** (-brət) *n.* an animal with a backbone belonging to the subphylum Vertebrata, which includes fishes, amphibians, reptiles, birds and mammals. *~a.* of or relating to the Vertebrata. **vertebrated** (-brātid) *a.* **vertebration** (-brā´shən) *n.* division into vertebrae or segments resembling vertebrae. [L, from *vertere*, to turn]

vertex (vœ´teks) *n.* (*pl.* **vertices** (-tisēz), **vertexes**) **1** the highest point, the top, summit, or apex. **2** (*Geom.*) **a** the meeting point of the lines of an angle. **b** each angular point of a polygon, polyhedron etc. **c** the point of intersection of a curve with its axis. **3** the top of the arch of the skull. **vertical** (-tik-) *a.* **1** perpendicular to the plane of the horizon. **2** extending in a perpendicular direction, running from the top to the bottom of something. **3** of, relating to, or situated at the vertex or highest point. **4** situated at or passing through the zenith. **5** of or relating to the vertex of the head. **6** involving the various successive stages in a production process or all the various levels in a hierarchical structure. ~*n.* a perpendicular line or plane. **vertical angles** *n.pl.* either pair of opposite angles made by two intersecting lines. **vertical circle** *n.* a great circle on the celestial sphere passing through the zenith and perpendicular to the horizon, an azimuth circle. **vertical fin** *n.* any of the fins situated in the median line, the dorsal, anal and caudal fins. **vertical integration** *n.* the merging of two companies involved in different stages of the production of the same thing, or the takeover of one such company by another. **verticality** (-kal´-), **verticalness** *n.* **vertically** *adv.* **vertically challenged** *a.* (*facet.*) short, below average height. **vertical mobility** *n.* the movement, or possibility of movement, of individuals or groups in society that involves a change of class, status, power etc. **vertical plane** *n.* a plane passing through the zenith perpendicular to the horizon. **vertical take-off** *n.* the take-off of an aeroplane without a preliminary run or taxiing. **vertical thinking** *n.* deductive reasoning. **vertical union** *n.* (*N Am.*) an industrial union. [L, whirlpool, summit, from *vertere*, to turn]

verticil (vœ´tisil) *n.* (*Bot.*) a whorl, an arrangement of parts in a circle round a stem etc. **verticillaster** (-astə) *n.* an inflorescence that is so crowded together as to resemble a whorl. **verticillate** (-tis´ilāt), **verticillated** *a.* whorled, having a whorl. **verticillately** *adv.* **verticillation** (-ā´shən) *n.* [L *verticillus*, dim. of VERTEX]

vertigo (vœ´tigō) *n.* giddiness, dizziness, a feeling as if one were whirling round. **vertiginous** (-tij´i-) *a.* **1** of, relating to or causing vertigo. **2** dizzy, giddy. **vertiginously** *adv.* **vertiginousness** *n.* [L, as VERTEX]

vertu VIRTU.

vervain (vœ´vān) *n.* a wild plant or weed, with small purplish flowers, of the genus *Verbena*, esp. *V. officinalis*, formerly credited with medical and other properties. [ME and OF *verveine*, L VERBENA]

verve (vœv) *n.* spirit, enthusiasm, energy, esp. in literary or artistic creation. [F, perh. from L *verba*, words, see VERB]

vervet (vœ´vit) *n.* a small S African monkey, *Cercopithecus aethiops*, usu. black-speckled greyish-green, with reddish-white face and abdomen. [etym. uncertain]

very (ver´i) *adv.* **1** (used as an intensifier) in a high degree, greatly, extremely. **2** (used for emphasis with superlative adjective or *own, same*) absolutely, truly, as in *at the very earliest, their very own words, the very same day*. ~*a.* (*comp.* **†verier**, *superl.* **†veriest**) **1** actual, precise (*her very words, this very day, the very thing we needed*). **2** absolute (*the very bottom*). **3** mere (*the very thought, his very name struck terror into their hearts*). **4** †true, genuine (*very God*). **not very** NOT. **the very devil** DEVIL. **the very idea!** IDEA. **very good** used to indicate assent or approval. **very well** used to indicate assent or approval. **†veriest** *a.* **1** most truly so called (*the veriest fool in Christendom*). **2** complete, absolute. **very high frequency** *n.* a radio frequency between 30 and 300 megahertz; this frequency band. **very large-scale integration** *n.* (*Comput.*) a process for integrating 100,000 or more circuits on a single silicon chip. **very low frequency** *n.* a radio frequency between 3 and 30 kilohertz; this frequency band. **Very Reverend** *n.* the title of a dean and of the superiors of some religious orders. [ME *verrai*, OF *verai* (F *vrai*), L *verax -ācis*, see VERACIOUS]

Very light (ver´i) *n.* a flare for lighting up the surroundings or for signalling. **Very pistol** *n.* a pistol for firing Very lights. [Edward W. *Very*, 1852–1910, US naval officer]

vesica (ves´ikə, vē´-) *n.* (*pl.* **vesicae** (-sē)) **1** a bladder, cyst etc., the gall bladder, the urinary bladder. **2** a vesica piscis. **vesical** *a.* **vesicant, vesicatory** *n.* (*pl.* **vesicants, vesicatories**) **1** a blister-producing counter-irritant. **2** a poison gas that causes blisters. ~*a.* producing blisters. **vesica piscis** (pis´kis), **vesica piscium** (pis´kium) *n.* the elliptic aureole with which medieval painters or sculptors sometimes surrounded the figures of Christ or the saints. **vesicate** (-kāt) *v.t.* to raise vesicles or blisters on. **vesication** (-ā´shən) *n.* **vesicle** (ves´ikəl, vē-) *n.* **1** (*Anat.*) a small fluid-filled bladder or sac. **2** (*Bot.*) a bladder-like cavity in seaweed, filled with air. **3** (*Geol.*) a rounded cavity in a rock, formed by the expansion of gases present in the original magma. **4** a blister. **vesicular** (-sik´ūlə) *a.* **vesiculate**[1] (-sik´ulāt) *v.t., v.i.* to produce vesicles, to make or become vesicular. **vesiculate**[2] (-sik´ūlət, -lāt) *a.* containing or resembling a vesicle or vesicles. **vesiculation** (-lā´shən) *n.* [L]

vesper (ves´pə) *n.* **1** (*usu.* **Vesper**) the evening star, Venus, appearing just after sunset. **2** (*poet.*) evening. **3** (*pl.*) in the Roman Catholic and Greek Churches, the sixth of the seven canonical hours. **4** (*pl.*) the evening service. ~*a.* of or relating to the evening or to vespers. **vesperal** *n.* the part of the antiphonary containing the chants for vespers. **vesper-bell** *n.* the bell that summons to vespers. **vesperian** (-piə´ri-) *a.* **vespertilionid** (-til´iōnid) *n.* a bat belonging to the family Vespertilionidae which includes most common insect-eating bats. ~*a.* of or relating to this family. **vespertilionine** (-til´iōnīn) *a.* **vespertine** (-tīn, -tin) *a.* **1** (*formal*) of, relating to or done in the evening. **2** (*Bot.*) opening in the evening. **3** (*Zool.*) active in the evening. **4** (*Astron.*) descending towards the horizon at sunset. [L, cogn. with HESPERUS]

vespiary (ves´piəri) *n.* (*pl.* **vespiaries**) a nest of wasps, hornets etc. **vespid** (-pid) *n.* a member of the family Vespidae that comprises the wasps and hornets. ~*a.* of or relating to this family. **vespine** (-pīn) *a.* of or relating to wasps. [from L *vespa*, wasp, after APIARY (under APIARIAN)]

vessel (ves´əl) *n.* **1** a hollow receptacle, esp. for holding liquids, as a jug, cup, dish, bottle, barrel etc. **2** a ship or craft of any kind, esp. one of some size. **3** (*Anat.*) a tube, a duct, or canal in which the blood or other fluids are conveyed. **4** (*Bot.*) a canal or duct formed by the breaking down of the partitions between cells. **5** a person regarded as receiving or containing a particular thing (grace, wrath etc.). **vesselful** *n.* (*pl.* **vesselfuls**). [A-F, from OF *vaissel* (F *vaisseau*), L *vascellum*, dim. of VAS]

vest (vest) *n.* **1** an undergarment for the upper part of the body, a singlet. **2** (*N Am., Austral.*) a waistcoat. **3** a (usu. V-shaped) piece on the front of the bodice of a dress. **4** †a garment, clothing, dress. ~*v.t.* **1** to invest or endow (with authority, etc.). **2** to confer an immediate fixed right of present or future possession of (property in a person). **3** (*poet.*) to clothe with or as with a garment. ~*v.i.* **1** (of property, a right etc.) to come into the possession (of a person). **2** (of a priest etc.) to put on vestments. **vested** *a.* (*Law*) held by or fixed in a person, not subject to contingency. **vested interest** *n.* **1** (*Law*) an existing and disposable right to the immediate or future possession of property. **2** a particular and personal interest in something, often in the continuance of an existing state of affairs, usually involving an expectation of financial gain. **3** (*often pl.*) a person or group having such an interest. **vestee** (-tē´) *n.* (*N Am.*) a vest of a bodice or dress. **vestiture** (-tichə) *n.* **1** (*Zool.*) anything covering a surface, such as hair, scales etc. **2**

†clothing. **3** †investiture. **vest-pocket** *a.* (*N Am.*) small enough to fit into a waistcoat pocket; very small. [L *vestis*, garment, cogn. with Gr. *esthēs*, clothing, Sansk. *vas*, to put on, and Eng. WEAR[1]]

vesta (ves´tə) *n.* (*pl.* **vestas**) (*Hist.*) a wax match igniting by friction. [L *Vesta*, see VESTAL]

vestal (ves´təl) *a.* **1** of or relating to the goddess Vesta or the vestal virgins. **2** pure, chaste. ~*n.* **1** a vestal virgin. **2** a woman of spotless chastity. **3** a nun. **vestal virgin** *n.* any one of the virgin priestesses, vowed to perpetual chastity, who had charge of the temple of Vesta at Rome, and of the sacred fire which burned perpetually on her altar. [L *Vestālis*, from *Vesta*, the goddess of the hearth and the household, cogn. with Gr. *Hestia*]

vestiary (ves´tiəri) *a.* (*formal*) of or relating to dress. ~*n.* (*pl.* **vestiaries**) **1** a vestry. **2** a robing-room. **3** †a wardrobe or room for storing clothes. [late L *vestiārius*, from *vestis*, VEST]

vestibule (ves´tibūl) *n.* **1** a small hall, lobby or antechamber next to the outer door of a house, from which doors open into the various inner rooms. **2** a porch. **3** (*N Am.*) a covered passage between the cars in a corridor train. **4** (*Anat.*) a chamber, cavity or channel communicating with others, such as the central chamber of the labyrinth of the ear. **vestibular** (-tib´-) *a.* **vestibuled** *a.* [L *vestibulum*]

vestige (ves´tij) *n.* **1** a sign, a mark or trace of something no longer present or in existence. **2** a small piece, a particle. **3** (*Biol.*) an organ or part that has degenerated and become nearly or entirely useless. **vestigial** (-tij´-) *a.* **1** of or being a vestige, very small or slight. **2** (*Biol.*) (of an organ) having degenerated and nearly or entirely lost its function in the course of evolution. [F, from L *vestīgium*, footstep, etym. uncertain]

vestiture VEST.

vestment (vest´mənt) *n.* **1** any of the ritual garments of the clergy, choristers etc., esp. a chasuble. **2** a garment, esp. a robe of state or office. [ME *vestiment*, OF *vestement*, L *vestīmentum*, from *vestīre*, to clothe, from *vestis*, see VEST]

vestry (ves´tri) *n.* (*pl.* **vestries**) **1** a room or place attached to a church in which the vestments are kept and in which the clergy, choristers etc. robe. **2** a room attached to a church, used for meetings, Sunday schools etc. **3** (*Hist.*) a meeting of the ratepayers of a parish or of their elected representatives for dealing with parochial business, formerly exercising sanitary and other powers of local government. **vestral** *a.* **vestryman** *n.* (*pl.* **vestrymen**) (*Hist.*) a member of a parochial vestry. [OF *vestiairie*, L *vestiārium*, wardrobe, neut. of *vestiārius*, VESTIARY]

vesture (ves´chə) *n.* **1** (*poet.*) dress, clothes, apparel. **2** a covering. **3** (*Law*) any vegetation that grows on land except trees. ~*v.t.* to clothe, to dress. **vestural** *a.* [OF *vesteure*, late L *vestītūra*, VESTITURE (under VEST)]

vesuvian (visoo´viən) *n.* **1** a variety of fusee for lighting cigars etc. in the open air. **2** vesuvianite. ~*a.* **1** (**Vesuvian**) of or relating to Vesuvius, a volcano near Naples, Italy. **2** volcanic. **vesuvianite** (-nīt) *n.* a vitreous brown or green silicate first found among the ejecta of Vesuvius.

vet[1] (vet) *n.* short for VETERINARY SURGEON (under VETERINARY). ~*v.t.* (*pres.p.* **vetting,** *past, p.p.* **vetted**) **1** to subject to careful scrutiny and appraisal. **2** to treat or cure (an animal) as a vet.

vet[2] (vet) *n.* (*N Am.*) short for VETERAN.

vetch (vech) *n.* a plant of the genus *Vicia* of the bean family, including several wild and cultivated species used for forage, esp. the common vetch or tare. **vetchling** (-ling) *n.* a plant of the genus *Lathyrus*, allied to the vetches. **vetchy** *a.* [ME and ONF *veche*, OF *vece*, L *vīcia*]

veteran (vet´ərən) *a.* **1** grown old or experienced, esp. in the military service. **2** of or relating to veterans. ~*n.* **1** a person who has had long experience in any service, occupation or art, esp. as a soldier. **2** (*N Am.*) an ex-serviceman or ex-servicewoman. **veteran car** *n.* a motor car built before 1916 (and esp. before 1905). [L *veterānus*, from *vetus -teris*, old]

veterinary (vet´ərinəri) *a.* of or relating to treatment of the diseases of animals, esp. domestic or farm animals such as cows, horses, dogs etc. ~*n.* (*pl.* **veterinaries**) a veterinary surgeon. **veterinarian** (-neə´ri-) *n.* (*N Am.*) a veterinary surgeon. **veterinary surgeon** *n.* a person qualified to diagnose and treat diseases and injuries in animals. [L *veterīnārius*, from *veterīnae bestiae*, beasts of burden, perh. from *vetus -teris*, see VETERAN]

Usage note Pronunciation as (vet´nəri) is best avoided.

vetitive VETO.

vetiver (vet´ivə) *n.* khus-khus grass and root. [F *vétiver*, from Tamil *vettivēru*]

veto (vē´tō) *n.* (*pl.* **vetoes**) **1** the power or right of a sovereign, president, or branch of a legislature to negative the enactments of another branch. **2** the act of exercising such right. **3** a document or message conveying a rejection. **4** any authoritative prohibition, refusal, negative, or interdict. ~*v.t.* (*3rd pers. sing. pres.* **vetoes,** *pres.p.* **vetoing,** *past, p.p.* **vetoed**) **1** to refuse approval to (a bill etc.). **2** to prohibit, to forbid. **vetitive** (vet´i-) *a.* **vetoer** *n.* **vetoless** *a.* [L, I forbid]

vex (veks) *v.t.* **1** to cause trouble or annoyance to, to irritate. **2** (*poet.*) to agitate, to throw (the sea etc.) into commotion. **3** †to grieve, to afflict. **vexation** (-ā´shən) *n.* **1** the act of vexing or the state of being vexed, irritation, annoyance, trouble. **2** that which causes irritation, an annoyance. **vexatious** (-ā´shəs) *a.* **1** troublesome, annoying, irritating. **2** (*Law*) (of a legal action) undertaken on insufficient grounds merely to harass or cause annoyance, embarrassment etc. to the defendant. **vexatiously** *adv.* **vexatiousness** *n.* **vexed** *a.* **1** annoyed, worried, filled with vexation. **2** (of a question or doctrine) much debated or contested. **vexedly** (-sid-) *adv.* **vexer** *n.* **vexing** *a.* **vexingly** *adv.* [F *vexer*, L *vexāre*]

vexillum (veksil´əm) *n.* (*pl.* **vexilla** (-sil´ə)) **1** in ancient Rome, a square flag carried by a vexillary, forming the standard of a maniple. **2** a maniple or other body of troops under a separate vexillum. **3** the large upper petal of a papilionaceous flower. **4** the vane of a feather. **5** a flag or pennon on a bishop's staff, usu. wound round it. **6** a processional banner or cross. **vexillar** (vek´-), **vexillate** (-lət) *a.* **vexillary** (vek´-) *n., a.* **vexillation** (-ā´shən) *n.* (*Hist.*) a company of troops under one standard. [L, from *vehere*, to convey, p.p. *vectus*]

VF *abbr.* **1** video frequency. **2** voice frequency.

VG *abbr.* Vicar-General.

vg *abbr.* very good.

VGA *abbr.* video graphics array.

vgc *abbr.* very good condition.

VHF *abbr.* very high frequency.

VI *abbr.* Virgin Islands.

via (vī´ə, vē´ə) *adv.* by way of, through. **Via Dolorosa** (vēə dolərō´sə) *n.* **1** the route taken by Christ to Calvary. **2** an arduous or painful series of experiences. **Via Lactea** (vēə lak´tiə) *n.* the Milky Way. **via media** (vīə mē´diə, vēə mā´diə) *n.* a middle way, a mean between extremes. [L *via*, way]

viable (vī´əbəl) *a.* **1** likely to become actual or to succeed, practicable, feasible. **2** (*Biol.*) capable of normal growth and development. **3** (of a foetus etc.) capable of maintaining independent existence, able to survive. **viability** (-bil´-) *n.* [F *vie*, life]

viaduct (vī´ədŭkt) *n.* **1** a bridgelike structure, esp. one composed of masonry and a considerable number of arches carrying a road or railway over a valley etc. **2** a road or railway on such a structure. [L *via ducta* (VIA, way, *ducta*, fem. p.p. of *dūcere*, to lead, to conduct)]

vial (vī´əl) *n.* a small vessel, usu. cylindrical and of glass, for holding liquid medicines etc. [OF *viole, fiole*, L *phiala*, PHIAL]

viameter (vīam´itə) *n.* a hodometer. [L *via*, way, -METER]

viand (vī´ənd) *n.* **1** an article of food. **2** (*pl.*) provisions, victuals. [F *viande*, L *vivenda*, things to live on, provisions, neut. pl. ger. of *vivere*, to live]

viaticum (vīat´ikəm) *n.* (*pl.* **viatica** (-kə), **viaticums**) **1** the Eucharist as given to a person at the point of death. **2** in ancient Rome, a supply of provisions or an allowance of money for a journey granted to a magistrate, envoy etc. **viatic** *a.* of or relating to a journey or travel. **viator** (-ā´-) *n.* a traveller, a wayfarer. [L, from VIA]

vibes (vībz) *n.pl.* (*coll.*) **1** feelings, intuitions or sensations experienced or communicated. **2** the vibraphone. **vibewatch** *v.i.* to be aware of the mood of a meeting, discussion etc. and make appropriate interventions to keep things calm, pleasant etc. ~*n.* an act of vibewatching. **vibewatcher** *n.* **vibist** *n.* a vibraphone player. [*vib*rations]

vibraculum (vībrak´ūləm) *n.* (*pl.* **vibracula** (-lə)) any one of the filamentous whiplike appendages of many polyzoa, bringing particles of food within reach by their lashing movements. **vibracular** *a.* [mod. L, as VIBRANT]

vibrant (vīb´rənt) *a.* **1** vibrating, tremulous. **2** thrilling, exciting. **3** resonant. **4** (of colour) very bright and eye-catching. **vibrancy** *n.* **vibrantly** *adv.* [L *vibrans, -āntis*, pres.p. of *vibrāre*, to shake]

vibraphone (vīb´rəfōn) *n.* a percussion instrument similar to a xylophone but with metal bars placed over electronic resonators. **vibraphonist** *n.* [L *vibrāre*, to shake, Gr. *phōnē*, voice]

vibrate (vībrāt´) *v.i.* **1** to move to and fro rapidly, to swing, to oscillate. **2** to thrill, to quiver, to throb. **3** (*Physics*) to move to and fro ceaselessly, esp. with great rapidity. **4** (of a sound) to resound, to ring. ~*v.t.* **1** to cause to swing, oscillate or quiver. **2** to send out or give off in vibrations. **vibratile** (vī´brətīl) *a.* **1** capable of vibrating. **2** (*Biol.*) used in vibratory motion. **vibratility** (-til´-) *n.* **vibration** (-rā´shən) *n.* **1** the act of vibrating. **2** oscillation. **3** (*Physics*) rapid motion backward and forward, esp. of the parts of an elastic solid or of a liquid the equilibrium of which has been disturbed. **4** one such complete movement. **5** (*pl., coll.*) feelings communicated instinctively or occultly from person to person; an atmosphere communicated or feelings aroused by a person, place etc. **vibrational** *a.* **vibrative** (vī´-) *a.* **vibrator** *n.* **1** a person who or something which vibrates. **2** a vibrating electrical apparatus used in massage or to provide sexual stimulation. **3** a vibrating conductor used to chop a continuous current and thus produce an alternating current. **4** a reed, as in a reed-organ. **vibratory** (vī´-) *a.* [L *vibrātus*, p.p. of *vibrāre*, to shake, to brandish]

vibrato (vibrah´tō) *n.* a pulsating effect, esp. in singing or string-playing, produced by the rapid variation of emphasis on the same tone. [It.]

vibrator, vibratory VIBRATE.

vibrio (vib´riō) *n.* (*pl.* **vibrios, vibriones** (-ō´nēz)) a bacterium of the genus *Vibrio*, more or less screw-shaped with a filament at each end, such as that causing cholera. [from L *vibro*, I vibrate]

vibrissa (vibris´ə) *n.* (*pl.* **vibrissae** (-ē)) **1** a stiff coarse hair or bristle in the nostrils of humans and about the mouths of most mammals. **2** any of the bristle-like feathers about the mouths of some birds, such as the flycatchers. [L, hair in the nostril, as VIBRIO]

vibronic (vībron´ik) *a.* of, relating to or caused by electronic vibration. [*vib*ration, elect*ronic*]

viburnum (vībœ´nəm) *n.* (*pl.* **viburnums**) a shrub or small tree of a genus *Viburnum*, containing the guelder rose and the laurustinus etc., of the honeysuckle family. [L]

vicar (vik´ə) *n.* **1** in the Church of England, the priest of a parish the greater tithes of which formerly belonged to a chapter or a member of the laity, the priest receiving the smaller tithe or a stipend. **2** in other Anglican Churches, a member of the clergy deputizing for another. **3** in the Roman Catholic Church, a bishop's deputy or representative. **4** a substitute or deputy. **vicarage** (-rij) *n.* **1** the house or residence of a vicar. **2** the benefice of a vicar. **vicar apostolic** *n.* in the Roman Catholic Church, a titular bishop appointed where no episcopate has been established etc. **vicar choral** *n.* in the Church of England, a clerical or lay assistant in the choral part of a cathedral service. **vicar-general** *n.* (*pl.* **vicars-general**) **1** in the Roman Catholic Church, an officer appointed by a bishop as his assistant, esp. in matters of jurisdiction. **2** in the Church of England, an officer assisting a bishop or archbishop in ecclesiastical causes and visitations. **vicarial** (-keə´ri-) *a.* **1** of or relating to vicars or a vicariate. **2** delegated. **vicariate** (-keə´riət) *a.* having delegated power, vicarious. ~*n.* **1** delegated office or power. **2** a vicarship, esp. the jurisdiction of a vicar apostolic. **Vicar of Bray** *n.* a turncoat, a person who alters allegiance or principles to suit the times. **Vicar of Christ** *n.* the Pope. **vicarship** *n.* [OF *vicaire*, L *vicārius*, orig. a., deputed, from *vic-*, see VICE-]

vicarious (vikeə´riəs, vī-) *a.* **1** experienced at second hand by imaginative or sympathetic participation in the pleasure, satisfaction etc. of someone else. **2** performed, done or suffered for or instead of another. **3** deputed, delegated. **4** acting on behalf of another. **vicariously** *adv.* **vicariousness** *n.* [VICAR]

vice[1] (vīs) *n.* **1** an evil or immoral practice or habit. **2** evil conduct, gross immorality, depravity. **3** a particular form of such conduct, esp. prostitution. **4** a fault, a blemish, a defect. **5** a bad habit or trick in a horse. **6** (**Vice**) the character representing vice, usu. portrayed as a buffoon, in the old morality plays. **vice ring** *n.* a group of criminals involved in organizing prostitution. **vice squad** *n.* a police department assigned to enforce the law on prostitution, gambling etc. [F, from L *vitium*]

vice[2] (vīs), (*NAm. also*) **vise** *n.* **1** an instrument with two jaws, brought together by a screw or lever, between which an object may be clamped securely. **2** †a grip, a grasp. ~*v.t.* to secure in or as in a vice. **vicelike** *a.* [ME, spiral staircase, F *vis*, screw, L *vītis*, vine]

vice[3] (vīs) *prep.* in place of. [L, abl. of *vicis*, change]

vice[4] (vīs) *n.* (*coll.*) short for VICE-PRESIDENT (under VICE-), VICE-CHAIRMAN (under VICE-) etc.

vice- (vīs) *pref.* forming nouns denoting a person acting or qualified to act in place of another or next in rank below another. **vice-admiral** *n.* a naval officer next in rank below an admiral, and next above a rear-admiral. **vice-admiralty** *n.* **vice-chair** *n.* a vice-chairman. **vice-chairman** *n.* (*pl.* **vice-chairmen**) a person who deputizes for a chairman. **vice-chairmanship** *n.* **vice-chamberlain** *n.* a deputy chamberlain, esp. the Lord Chamberlain's deputy. **vice-chancellor** *n.* **1** a deputy chancellor. **2** the chief administrative officer at most British universities. **3** (*Hist.*) a senior judge in the court of Chancery. **vice-chancellorship** *n.* **vice-president** *n.* an official ranking next below a president and often serving as the latter's deputy. **vice-presidency** *n.* (*pl.* **vice-presidencies**). **vice-presidential** *a.* [L, abl. of *vicis*, change]

vicegerent (vīsjer´ənt) *a.* having or exercising delegated power. ~*n.* an officer exercising delegated authority, a deputy. **vicegerency** *n.* (*pl.* **vicegerencies**). [F (L *gerens -ntem*, pres.p. of *gerere*, to carry on)]

vicenary (vis´inəri) *a.* consisting of or relating to 20.

vicennial (visen´iəl) *a.* **1** happening every 20 years. **2**

lasting 20 years. [L *vīcēnārius*, from *vicēni*, twenty each, from *vīginti*, twenty, L *annus*, year]

viceroy (vīs´roi) *n.* a ruler exercising authority in a colony, province etc. in the name of a sovereign or government. **viceregal** (rē´-) *a.* 1 of or relating to a viceroy. 2 (*Austral., New Zeal.*) of or relating to a governor or governor general. **vicereine** (vīs´rān) *n.* 1 the wife of a viceroy. 2 a woman viceroy. **viceroyalty** *n.* (*pl.* **viceroyalties**) 1 the office of a viceroy. 2 the territory governed by a viceroy. 3 the term of office of a viceroy. **viceroyship** *n.* [F, VICE-, *roy*, king]

vice versa (vīsi vœ´sə, vīs) *adv.* the order or relation being inverted, the other way round. [VICE[3], L *versa*, fem. p.p. of *vertere*, to turn]

vichyssoise (vēshiswahz´) *n.* a cream soup usu. served chilled, with ingredients such as leeks and potatoes. **Vichy water** *n.* an effervescent mineral water found at Vichy. [*Vichy*, town in the Allier Department, France]

vicinage (vis´inij) *n.* (*formal*) 1 neighbourhood, vicinity, surrounding places, environs. 2 the residents of a neighbourhood. 3 nearness, closeness. **vicinal** *a.* 1 near, neighbouring. 2 of or relating to a particular neighbourhood. 3 (*Chem.*) denoting or relating to two adjacent atoms to which groups are attached in a chain. [F *voisinage*, from *voisin*, L *vīcīnus*, neighbouring, from *vīcus*, village, street (assim. to L)]

vicinity (visin´iti) *n.* (*pl.* **vicinities**) 1 the neighbourhood, the adjoining or surrounding district. 2 the state of being near, proximity. 3 near relationship (to). **in the vicinity** nearby. [L *vīcīnitas*, from *vīcīnus*, see VICINAGE]

vicious (vish´əs) *a.* 1 likely, disposed or intended to attack, hurt or wound. 2 bad-tempered, spiteful, malignant. 3 ferocious, violent. 4 characterized by some vice, fault or blemish; imperfect, defective, incorrect, corrupt. 5 (*formal*) addicted to vice, depraved, wicked. 6 (*formal*) contrary to moral principles or to rectitude. **vicious circle** *n.* 1 a situation in which progressing from cause to effect or from problem to solution merely brings one back to one's starting point and aggravates the original state of things. 2 circular reasoning, providing a proof or explanation for something which depends for its truth or validity on the truth or validity of the thing one is setting out to prove or explain. **vicious cycle** *n.* a recurring cycle of cause and effect with harmful consequences. **viciously** *adv.* **viciousness** *n.* **vicious spiral** *n.* a situation in which an increase in one thing, such as wages, leads to an increase in another, such as prices, and nobody benefits. [F *vicieux*, L *vitiōsus*, from *vitium*, VICE[1]]

vicissitude (visis´itūd) *n.* 1 a change of condition, circumstances or fortune, a mutation, a revolution. 2 (*poet.*) regular change or mutation. **vicissitudinary** (-tū´-), **vicissitudinous** (-tū´-) *a.* [L *vicissitūdo -dinis*, from *vicissim*, by turns, as VICE[3]]

victim (vik´tim) *n.* 1 a person killed or injured as a result of an event such as an accident or epidemic. 2 a person or thing destroyed or injured in the pursuit of some object. 3 a dupe, a prey. 4 a living creature sacrificed to some deity or in the performance of some religious rite. **victimize, victimise** *v.t.* 1 to single out for harsh treatment or unfair punishment. 2 to make a victim of. **victimization** (-zā´shən) *n.* **victimizer** *n.* [F *victime*, L *victima*, cogn. with Goth. *weihan*, to consecrate, *weihs*, holy]

victor (vik´tə) *n.* a person, organization, nation etc. that conquers in battle or wins in a contest. **victorious** (-taw´ri-) *a.* 1 having conquered in a battle or any contest, triumphant. 2 associated or connected with victory. **victoriously** *adv.* **victoriousness** *n.* **victor ludorum** (loodaw´rəm) *n.* the overall champion in a sports competition, esp. at a school. **victory** *n.* (*pl.* **victories**) the defeat of an enemy in battle or war, or of an opponent in a contest. **victory roll** *n.* a roll performed by an aircraft to celebrate a victory in aerial combat. **victory sign** *n.* the first and second fingers extended in the form of a V. **victress** (-tris), **victrix** (-triks) *n.* (*pl.* **victresses, victrices** (-trisēz, -trī´sēz), **victrixes**) (*formal*) a female victor. **victrix ludorum** *n.* a female victor ludorum. [L, from *vict-*, p.p. stem of *vincere*, to conquer]

victoria (viktaw´riə) *n.* 1 a four-wheeled carriage with a raised seat for the driver, seats for two persons over the back axle and a low seat for two persons over the front axle, and a collapsible top. 2 (*also* **victoria plum**) a large red plum. 3 a S American water lily of the genus *Victoria*, with gigantic floating leaves. **Victoria Cross** *n.* a British military decoration in the shape of a Maltese cross, instituted by Queen Victoria (1856), bestowed for conspicuous bravery or devotion in the presence of the enemy. **Victoria crowned pigeon** *n.* a large blue crested pigeon of New Guinea, *Goura victoria*. **Victorian** *a.* of, relating to, flourishing or living in the reign of Queen Victoria. ~*n.* 1 a person, esp. a writer, living or flourishing then. 2 a native of Victoria, Australia. **Victorianism** *n.* **victoriana** (-ah´nə) *n.pl.* objects, ornaments etc. of the Victorian period. **Victoria sandwich, Victoria sponge** *n.* a cake consisting of two layers of sponge with jam in between. [Queen *Victoria*, 1819–1901, L, victory, as VICTOR]

victress, victrix VICTOR.

victual (vit´əl) *n.* (*usu. in pl.*) food, provisions. ~*v.t.* (*pres.p.* **victualling,** (*N Am.*) **victualing,** *past, p.p.* **victualled,** (*N Am.*) **victualed**) to supply or store with provisions. ~*v.i.* 1 to lay in provisions. 2 to take food, to eat. **victuallage** *n.* victuals. **victualler,** (*N Am.*) **victualer** *n.* 1 a person who supplies victuals, esp. an innkeeper. 2 a victualling ship. **victualless** *a.* **victualling** *n., a.* **victualling ship** *n.* a ship conveying provisions to other ships or to a fleet. [ME and OF *vitaille*, L *victuālia*, neut. pl. of *victuālis*, pertaining to nourishment, from *victus*, food, from *vīvere*, to live]

vicuña (vikoon´yə), **vicuna** (vikū´nə) *n.* 1 a S American animal, *Vicugna vicugna*, allied to the camel, a native of the Andean regions of Bolivia and N Chile. 2 a fine cloth made from its wool or an imitation made of worsted yarn. [Sp., from Quechua *vicuña*]

vide (vid´ā, vē´-, vī´di) *int.* (as an instruction in a book) see, consult. **vide infra** *int.* see below. **vide supra** (soo´prə) *int.* see above. [L, imp. of *vidēre*, to see]

videlicet (vidē´liset, -dā´liket) *adv.* namely, that is to say, to wit (usu. abbreviated to *viz.*). [L, for *vidēre licet*, it is allowable to see, one may see]

video (vid´iō) *n.* (*pl.* **videos**) 1 a video recorder. 2 a video recording. 3 the process of recording, reproducing or broadcasting visual images on magnetic tape or disc. 4 the visual elements of television. 5 (*N Am., coll.*) television. ~*a.* 1 relating to the process of recording, reproducing or broadcasting visual images on magnetic tape or disc. 2 relating to or employed in the transmission or reception of a televised image. 3 concerned with or operating at video frequencies. ~*v.t., v.i.* (*3rd pers. sing. pres.* **videos,** *pres.p.* **videoing,** *past, p.p.* **videoed**) to make a video recording (of). **video camera** *n.* a camera which records its film on videotape or transmits images to a monitor. **video cassette** *n.* a cassette containing videotape. **video cassette recorder** *n.* a video recorder that takes cassettes. **videoconference** *n.* a live discussion between participants in different locations who are linked by audio and video communications. **videoconferencing** *n.* **video diary** *n.* a record of events filmed on videotape usu. by a layperson with a camcorder. **videodisc** *n.* a disc from which television pictures and sound can be played back. **video film** *n.* a film recorded on videotape. **videofit** *n.* a picture similar to an Identikit constructed on a screen by selecting and combining facial features in accordance with witnesses' descriptions, usu. of a suspect sought by the police. **video frequency** *n.* the frequency required for a video signal. **video game** *n.* an electronically operated game played by means of a visual display unit. **video jockey** *n.* a person who introduces videos of popular music etc. **video nasty** *n.* (*pl.* **video nasties**) a video film which includes horrific or gruesome scenes of violence, sexual outrage or other atrocities. **video-on-demand** *n.* the ability to access films, television programmes etc. electronically by telephone, over the Internet etc. **videophile** *n.* a person with an enthusiastic interest in video recording or video equipment. **videophone, video telephone** *n.* a telephone which can also transmit a picture of each speaker. **video recorder** *n.* a machine for recording and playing back television broadcasts or for playing films made on videotape. **video recording** *n.* **1** recording both television picture and sound on magnetic tape. **2** a recording made on videotape. **videotape** *n.* **1** magnetic tape used for recording television pictures and sound for subsequent transmission or reproduction. **2** a length of this tape, esp. a video cassette. **3** a recording made on this tape. *~v.t.* to record on videotape. **videotape recorder** *n.* a video recorder. **videotex** (-teks), **videotext** *n.* any electronic information system using a television screen to display its data. [L, I see, assim. to AUDIO, from *vidēre*, to see]

vidette VEDETTE.

vidicon (vid´ikon) *n.* a small television camera tube, used in closed-circuit systems and for outside broadcasts, that operates by photoconductivity. [*video*, *iconoscope*]

vidimus (vī´diməs) *n.* (*pl.* **vidimuses**) an examination or inspection of accounts etc. [L, we have seen, as VIDE]

vie (vī) *v.i.* (*3rd pers. sing. pres.* **vies**, *pres.p.* **vying**, *past, p.p.* **vied**) **1** to strive for superiority, to contend, to compete (with). **2** to rival, to be equal or superior (with or in). **vying** *a.* [ME *vien*, shortened from *envien*, OF *envier*, L *invītāre*, to INVITE[1]]

vielle (viel´) *n.* a hurdy-gurdy.

Viennese (vēənēz´) *a.* of or relating to Vienna or its inhabitants. *~n.* (*pl.* **Viennese**) **1** a native or inhabitant of Vienna. **2** (*pl.*) the people of Vienna. **Vienna loaf** (vien´ə) *n.* (*pl.* **Vienna loaves**) a long, round-ended loaf of white bread.

Vietnamese (vietnəmēz´) *a.* of or relating to Vietnam in SE Asia, its people or their language. *~n.* (*pl.* **Vietnamese**) **1** a native or inhabitant of Vietnam. **2** (*pl.*) the people of Vietnam. **3** the language of Vietnam.

vieux jeu (vjœ zhœ´) *a.* old-fashioned, hackneyed. [F]

view (vū) *n.* **1** sight, range of vision. **2** that which is seen, a scene, a prospect. **3** a picture or drawing of this. **4** survey or examination by the eye. **5** an intellectual or mental survey. **6** the manner or mode of looking at things, considering a matter etc. **7** judgement, opinion, theory. **8** intention, purpose, design. **9** inspection by a jury etc. *~v.t.* **1** to examine with the eye, look over, inspect. **2** to survey mentally or intellectually. **3** to consider, to form a mental impression or judgement of. **4** to watch on television. **5** to catch sight of (a hunted animal) during the chase. *~v.i.* to watch television. **in view 1** in sight. **2** in mind when forming an opinion. **3** as one's object or aim. **in view of** considering, having regard to. **on view** open to public inspection. **to take a dim view of** DIM. **with a view to 1** with the intention of. **2** in hopes or anticipation of. **viewable** *a.* **1** able to be seen or inspected. **2** worth watching. **viewdata** *n.* a communications system by which data can be transferred through a telephone line and displayed on TV or video. **viewer** *n.* **1** a person who views something. **2** a person who watches television; a member of a particular television audience. **3** a device with a magnifying lens for looking at transparencies. **4** (*Law*) a person appointed by a court to make an examination, esp. of property, and report. **viewership** *n.* the (estimated) audience watching a particular TV programme or channel. **viewfinder** *n.* a device of mirrors in a camera which shows the view to be taken. **viewgraph** *n.* a graph produced on a transparency for projection on to a screen or use in a videoconference. **view halloo** *n.* a huntsman's shout on seeing the fox break cover. **viewing** *n.* **1** an opportunity to view, inspect or look over. **2** watching television. **3** television programmes broadcast, esp. during a particular period of time. **viewless** *a.* **1** not affording a view or prospect. **2** not having an opinion. **3** (*poet.*) invisible. **viewphone** *n.* a videophone. **viewpoint** *n.* **1** a point of view. **2** a place for viewing. **viewy** *a.* (*comp.* **viewier**, *superl.* **viewiest**) having peculiar or impracticable views, faddy, visionary. **viewiness** *n.* [A-F, from OF *veue*, fem. of *veu*, p.p. of *voir*, L *vidēre*, to see]

vigesimal (vijes´iməl) *a.* **1** relating to or based on the number twenty. **2** taking place or proceeding by intervals of twenty. **3** twentieth. [L *vīgēsimus*, from *vīginti*, twenty]

vigia (vijē´ə) *n.* a warning of a suspected rock, shoal etc., whose existence is unconfirmed, on a hydrographical chart. [Sp., look out]

vigil (vij´il) *n.* **1** keeping awake during the customary hours of rest, watchfulness. **2** a period of watchfulness. **3** a demonstration in support of a cause in which the demonstrators usu. stand in silence for a long time in or outside a particular place. **4** the eve of a festival. **5** a religious service held at night, esp. on the eve of a festival, orig. the watch kept on the night before a feast. **6** a period of sleeplessness. **vigilance** *n.* **1** the state of being vigilant. **2** insomnia. **vigilance committee** *n.* (*N Am.*) a self-organized committee for maintaining order or inflicting summary justice in an ill-ordered community or district. **vigilant** *a.* **1** awake and on the alert. **2** watchful, wary, circumspect. **vigilantly** *adv.* **vigilante** (-lan´ti) *n.* **1** a self-appointed upholder of law and order or administerer of justice. **2** (*N Am.*) a member of a vigilance committee. **vigilantism** (-lan´tizm) *n.* [F *vigile*, L *vigilia*, from *vigil*, awake, from *vigēre*, to be lively]

vigneron (vēn´yərō) *n.* a wine-grower. [F]

vignette (vinyet´) *n.* **1** a short descriptive essay or sketch. **2** a similar descriptive or evocative scene in a film or play. **3** an engraving not enclosed within a definite border, esp. on the title page of a book. **4** a photograph, drawing or other portrait showing the head and shoulders with a background shading off gradually. **5** (*Archit.*) an ornament of tendrils and vine leaves. *~v.t.* **1** to shade off (a portrait, drawing etc.) gradually. **2** to make a photograph or portrait of in this style. **vignettist** *n.* [F, dim. of *vigne*, VINE]

vigor VIGOUR.

vigoro (vig´ərō) *n.* (*Austral.*) a team ball game (esp. for women) combining elements of cricket and baseball and played with a paddle-shaped bat. [from VIGOUR]

vigoroso (vigərō´sō) *adv.* (*Mus.*) with energy. [It., as VIGOUR]

vigour (vig´ə), (*N Am.*) **vigor** *n.* **1** active physical or mental strength or energy. **2** healthy condition or growth, robustness. **3** force, power, intensity. **4** forcefulness, trenchancy. **5** (*Law, N Am.*) legal force, effectiveness or validity. **vigorous** *a.* **1** active, vital and strong. **2** healthy, robust. **3** performed with or requiring vigour, energetic. **vigorously** *adv.* **vigorousness** *n.* **vigourless** *a.* [OF *vigur*, *vigor*, L *vigōrem*, nom. *-or*, from *vigēre*, to be lively]

vihara (vihah´rə) *n.* a Buddhist or Jain temple or monastery. [Sansk.]

Viking (vī´king) *n.* **1** any of the Scandinavian seafaring warriors of the 8th–11th cents., who raided and colonized large parts of N and W Europe. **2** (**viking**) any rover, freebooter or pirate. [Icel. *vīkingr* (prob. *vīg*, war, cogn. with L *vincere*, to conquer, -ING[1]]

vilayet (vilah´yit) *n.* an administrative division of Turkey. [Turk.]

vile (vīl) *a.* **1** foul, disgusting. **2** depraved, abominably wicked, odious. **3** morally base, despicable, abject. **4** (*coll.*) very bad or unpleasant, abominable. **vilely** *adv.* **vileness** *n.* [ME and OF *vil*, L *vīlis*, cheap, base]

vilify (vil´ifī) *v.t.* (*3rd pers. sing. pres.* **vilifies**, *pres.p.* **vilifying**, *past*, *p.p.* **vilified**) **1** to traduce, to defame. **2** †to debase, to degrade, to make base. **vilification** (-fikā´shən) *n.* **vilifier** *n.* [ME, from late L *vilificāre*, see VILE]

†**vilipend** (vil´ipend) *v.t.* **1** to treat or regard with contempt. **2** to speak of disparagingly or contemptuously, to depreciate. [L *vīlipendere* (VILE, L *pendere*, to weigh)]

vill (vil) *n.* (*Hist.*) a feudal township. [as VILLA]

villa (vil´ə) *n.* **1** in ancient Rome, a country house or farmhouse with subsidiary buildings on an estate. **2** a large detached or semi-detached suburban house. **3** a large house in the country. **4** a sizeable property, usu. in a holiday resort, for rent as a holiday home. **villatic** (-lat´-) *a.* of or relating to a villa, farm or village; rustic, rural. [L, farmhouse, from *vīcus*, village]

village (vil´ij) *n.* **1** a small assemblage of houses, smaller than a town or city and larger than a hamlet. **2** the inhabitants of such a community. **3** any area or community within a town or city having a distinctive character and some of the close-knit qualities of a village. **4** (*NAm.*) an incorporated municipality smaller than a town. **5** (*Austral.*) an upmarket suburban shopping centre. ~*a.* **1** of or relating to a village. **2** rustic, countrified. **village college** *n.* an institution with educational and recreational facilities serving a village or group of villages. **village idiot** *n.* (*offensive*) a person in a village community noted for mental disability, stupidity etc. **villager** *n.* an inhabitant of a village. **villagization, villagisation** *n.* **1** the resettlement and rehousing of a population in new villages outside their own area, often achieved by force. **2** UJAMAA. **villagize** *v.t.* [F, from L *villāticus*, pertaining to a VILLA]

villain (vil´ən) *n.* **1** a person guilty or capable of crime or great wickedness. **2** the principal wicked character in a play, book, film etc. **3** (*coll.*) a rogue, a rascal. **4** (*sl.*) a criminal. **5** a villein. **6** †a rustic, a clown, a boor. ~*a.* villainous. **villainage** (-ij) *n.* villeinage. **villainess** *n.* a female villain. **villain of the piece** *n.* the principal wicked character. **villainous** *a.* **1** worthy or characteristic of a villain, depraved, vile. **2** very bad. **villainously** *adv.* **villainousness** *n.* **villainy** *n.* (*pl.* **villainies**) **1** villainous behaviour. **2** a villainous act. [OF and ME *vilein*, servile, base, from late L *villānus*, a farm servant, as VILLA]

Usage note See note under VILLEIN.

villanelle (vilənel´) *n.* a poem in five tercets and a final quatrain on two rhymes. [F, from It. *villanella*, dim. from *villano*, rustic, as VILLAIN]

villatic VILLA.

-ville (vil) *comb. form* (*sl.*) a place, condition or quality with a character as specified, e.g. *dullsville*, *dragsville*, *squaresville*. [from *-ville* in names of towns, esp. in US, from F *ville*, a town]

villeggiatura (vilejətoo´rə) *n.* retirement to or a stay in the country. [It., from *villeggiare*, to stay at a country seat, from L VILLA]

villein (vil´ən, -ān) *n.* (*Hist.*) a feudal serf, a bondsman attached to a feudal lord or to an estate. **villeinage** (-ij) *n.* **1** the status or condition of a villein. **2** the form of tenure whereby a villein held land. [as VILLAIN]

Usage note The spellings of the nouns *villein* (a feudal serf) and *villain* (a scoundrel) should not be confused.

villus (vil´əs) *n.* (*pl.* **villi** (-lī)) **1** (*Anat.*) any of the short hairlike or finger-like processes on certain membranes, such as those on the inner surface of the small intestine. **2** (*pl.*, *Bot.*) long, close, soft hairs. **villiform** (-ifawm) *a.* having the form of a villus or of villi. **villose, villous** *a.* **1** (*Bot.*) covered with long hairs. **2** of, relating to or having villi. **villosity** (-los´-) *n.* (*pl.* **villosities**). [L, shaggy hair]

vim (vim) *n.* (*coll.*) energy, vigour. [L, acc. of VIS]

vimineous (vimin´iəs) *a.* of or relating to, producing, or consisting of twigs or shoots. [L *vīmineus*, from *vīmen -minis*, twig, from *viēre*, to twist]

vin (vã) *n.* (*pl.* **vins** (vã)) (a) wine. **vin blanc** (blã) *n.* white wine. **vin du pays** (dü pāē´), **vin de pays** (də) *n.* local wine; wine of the third highest category in France meeting certain requirements as to area of origin, strength etc. **vin ordinaire** (awdineə´) *n.* inexpensive table wine for daily use. **vin rosé** (rō´zā) *n.* rosé wine. **vin rouge** (roozh´) *n.* red wine. [F]

vin- VINI-.

vina (vē´nə) *n.* an Indian stringed instrument with a fretted fingerboard over two gourds. [Sansk. *vīnā*]

vinaceous (vīnā´shəs) *a.* **1** of or relating to wine or grapes. **2** of the nature or colour of wine. [L *vīnāceus*, from *vīnum*, wine]

vinaigrette (vinigret´) *n.* **1** (*also* **vinaigrette sauce**) a salad dressing consisting of oil, vinegar and seasoning. **2** (*also* **vinegarette**) an ornamental bottle or perforated case of gold or other metal etc. for holding aromatic vinegar etc., a smelling-bottle. [F, dim. of *vinaigre*, VINEGAR]

vinasse (vinas´) *n.* a residual product containing potassium salts left after distilling spirits, esp. brandy, or obtained from beets from which sugar has been extracted. [F]

vinca (ving´kə) *n.* any plant of the periwinkle genus, *Vinca*.

vincible (vin´sibəl) *a.* (*formal*) capable of being conquered, not invincible. **vincibility** (-bil´-), **vincibleness** *n.* [L *vincibilis*, from *vincere*, to conquer]

vincristine (vinkris´tēn) *n.* an alkaloid substance derived from the tropical periwinkle, used in the treatment of some types of leukaemia. [L *vinca*, genus name of the plant, and *crista*, fold]

vinculum (ving´kūləm) *n.* (*pl.* **vincula** (-lə)) **1** (*Math.*) a straight line drawn over several terms in an equation to show that they are to be treated as if they were in brackets. **2** (*Anat.*) a ligament; a fraenum. [L, a bond, from *vincire*, to bind]

vindaloo (vindəloo´) *n.* a type of hot Indian curry. [prob. from Port. *vin d'alho*, wine and garlic sauce]

vindicate (vin´dikāt) *v.t.* **1** to clear from blame, suspicion, criticism etc. **2** to prove to be true or valid, to justify. **3** to maintain (a claim, statement etc.) against attack or denial. **4** to defend (a person) against reproach, accusation etc. **vindicable** *a.* **vindicability** (-bil´-) *n.* **vindication** (-ā´shən) *n.* **1** the act of vindicating; the state of being vindicated. **2** something which exonerates or justifies. **vindicative** (-dikātiv, -dik´ətiv) *a.* **vindicator** *n.* **vindicatory** *a.* **1** tending to vindicate or justify. **2** punitory. [L *vindicātus*, p.p. of *vindicāre* (VIM, or *vēnum*, favour, *dicāre*, to assert, from *dīcere*, to say)]

vindictive (vindik´tiv) *a.* **1** characterized or prompted by a desire for revenge. **2** spiteful, rancorous. **vindictive damages** *n.pl.* damages given to punish the defendant. **vindictively** *adv.* **vindictiveness** *n.* [shortened from *vindicative*, see VINDICATE, from conf. with L *vindicta*, revenge]

vine (vīn) *n.* **1** a slender climbing plant of the genus

Vitis, esp. *V. vinifera*, the grapevine. **2** any plant with a slender climbing or trailing stem. **3** the stem of such a plant. **vine-dresser** *n.* a person who dresses, trims or prunes vines. **vinery** (-əri) *n.* (*pl.* **vineries**) a greenhouse for vines. **vineyard** (vin´yahd, -yəd) *n.* a plantation of grapevines. **viny** *a.* of or relating to vines. [F *vigne*, L *vīnea*, vineyard, from *vīnum*, wine, cogn. with Gr. *oinos*, wine, *oinē*, vine, cp. L *vītis*, vine, *vīmen*, twig, from *viēre*, to twist]

vinegar (vin´igə) *n.* **1** an acid liquid obtained by oxidation or acetous fermentation from wine, cider etc., used as a condiment and as a preservative in pickling. **2** anything sour or soured, as a disposition etc. *~v.t.* **1** to put vinegar on or into. **2** to make sour. **vinegar eel** *n.* a minute worm infesting vinegar, sour paste etc. **vinegarette** VINAIGRETTE. **vinegary, vinegarish** *a.* **1** like or flavoured with vinegar. **2** sour. [F *vinaigre* (*vin*, L *vinum*, wine, *aigre*, see EAGER)]

vinery, vineyard VINE.

vingt-et-un (vantāœ´) *n.* a card game in which the object is to make the aggregate number of the pips on the cards as near as possible to 21 without exceeding this; pontoon. [F, twenty-one]

vinho verde (vēnyō veə´di) *n.* any of a number of light, immature, sharp-tasting Portuguese wines. [Port., young wine]

vini- (vin´i), **vin-** *comb. form* of or relating to wine or vines. [L *vīnum*, wine]

vinic (vin´ik) *a.* of, relating to, contained in or derived from wine.

viniculture (vin´ikŭlchə) *n.* the cultivation of grapevines. **vinicultural** (-kŭl´-) *a.* **viniculturist** (-kŭl´-) *n.*

viniferous (vinif´ərəs) *a.* wine-producing.

vinify (vin´ifī) *v.t.* (*3rd pers. sing. pres.* **vinifies**, *pres.p.* **vinifying**, *past, p.p.* **vinified**) to convert (grape juice) into wine. **vinification** (-fikā´shən) *n.* **vinificator** (-fikātə) *n.* an apparatus for condensing the alcoholic vapours from the fermenting must in winemaking.

vino (vē´nō) *n.* (*pl.* **vinos**) (*coll.*) wine, esp. cheap wine. [Sp. or It., wine]

vinous (vī´nəs) *a.* **1** of, relating to or resembling wine. **2** indulging in or resulting from indulgence in wine. **vinosity** (-nos´iti) *n.* **1** the distinctive character and flavour of wine or of a particular wine. **2** indulgence in or addiction to wine. [L *vīnōsus*, from *vīnum*, wine]

vint[1] (vint) *n.* a Russian card game similar to auction bridge. [Rus.]

vint[2] VINTAGE.

vintage (vin´tij) *n.* **1** the yield of grapes or wine from a vineyard or vine district for a particular season, esp. the wine obtained in a particularly good year. **2** the process of gathering grapes. **3** the season of gathering grapes. **4** a time of origin. **5** a group of things, people etc. of the same period. **6** (*poet.*) wine. *~a.* **1** (of wine) produced in a particularly good year. **2** representative of what is best and most typical, esp. in a person's work. **3** of an earlier period but of continuing interest. **4** out of date, old-fashioned. *~v.t.* **1** to harvest (grapes). **2** to make (wine). **vint**[2] *v.t.* to make (wine). **vintage car** *n.* an old motor car (esp. one built between 1919 and 1930). **vintage festival** *n.* a carnival to celebrate the beginning of the grape-harvesting season. **vintager** *n.* a grape-gatherer. [ME *vindage*, *vendage*, F *vendange*, L *vindēmia*, grape harvest (*vīnum*, wine, *demere*, to take)]

vintner (vint´nə) *n.* a wine merchant. **vintnery** *n.* (*pl.* **vintneries**). [OF *vinetier*]

viny VINE.

vinyl (vī´nil) *n.* **1** an organic radical CH_2CH-, derived from ethylene. **2** any vinyl resin or plastic, esp. PVC. **3** (*coll.*) a gramophone record (as opposed to a tape or CD); gramophone records collectively. *~a.* of or made of a vinyl resin. **vinyl resin, vinyl plastic** *n.* any of various thermoplastic resins, polymers or copolymers of vinyl compounds.

viol (vī´əl) *n.* any of a family of medieval stringed musical instruments, the predecessor of the violin family, that had six strings and were held on or between the knees and played with a curved bow. **violist**[1] (vī´əlist) *n.* a player on a viol. [F *viole*, Prov. *viula*, late L *vitula*, cp. FIDDLE]

viola[1] (viō´lə) *n.* **1** an instrument like a large violin, the alto instrument in the violin family tuned an octave above the cello. **2** a viola player. **3** a viol. **viola da braccio** (də brah´chiō) *n.* a type of viol held up to the shoulder, from which the modern viola was developed. **viola da gamba** (də gam´bə) *n.* a viol held between the player's legs, esp. the tenor viol from which the modern cello was developed. **viola d'amore** (damaw´rā) *n.* an instrument of the viol family with sympathetic strings under the fingerboard and a particularly sweet tone. **violist**[2] (viō´list) *n.* a player of the viola. [It.]

viola[2] (vī´ələ) *n.* a plant or flower of the genus *Viola*, containing the violet and pansy. **violaceous** (-lā´shəs) *a.* **1** of a violet colour. **2** of the violet family. [L, violet]

violate (vī´əlāt) *v.t.* **1** to infringe or transgress, to break, to disobey (a law, obligation, duty etc.). **2** to treat irreverently, to profane, to desecrate. **3** to break in on, to disturb rudely or violently. **4** to ravish, to rape, to subject to sexual assault. **violable** *a.* **violation** (-ā´shən) *n.* **violative** *a.* **violator** *n.* [L *violatus*, p.p. of *violāre*, cogn. with VIS]

violence (vī´ələns) *n.* **1** the state or quality of being violent. **2** violent treatment; the use of physical force to inflict injury or damage. **3** vehemence, intensity or impetuosity of feeling, action etc. **4** injury, outrage. **5** violent exercise of power. **6** (*Law*) the illegal exercise of physical force; an act of intimidation by the show or threat of force. **to do violence to 1** to do a physical injury to. **2** to violate. **3** to distort the meaning or intent of. **violent** *a.* **1** acting with, or characterized by, the exertion of great physical force. **2** (of a person) tending to resort to physical force, aggressive. **3** vehement, impetuous, furious. **4** intense, abrupt, immoderate. **5** (of death etc.) produced by or resulting from extraneous force or poison, not natural. **6** involving an unlawful use of force. **7** tending to distort meaning or intent. **violently** *adv.* [F, from L *violentia*, as VIOLATE]

violet (vī´ələt) *n.* **1** a plant or flower of the genus *Viola*, esp. the sweet violet, *V. odorata*, the dog-violet, *V. riviniana*, and some other species with small blue, purple or white flowers. **2** a colour seen at the opposite end of the spectrum to red, produced by a slight mixture of red with blue. **3** a pigment of this colour. **4** clothing of this colour. *~a.* of the colour of violet. **shrinking violet** SHRINKING (under SHRINK). [F, dim. of *viole*, VIOLA[2]]

violin (vīəlin´) *n.* **1** a musical instrument with four strings, held under the chin and played with a bow, the most important of modern string instruments and the one with the highest pitch. **2** a player on this. **violinist** *n.* [It. *violino*, dim. of VIOLA[1]]

violist[1] VIOL.

violist[2] VIOLA[1].

violoncello (viəlonchel´ō) *n.* (*pl.* **violoncellos**) (*formal*) a cello. **violoncellist** *n.* [It., dim. of VIOLONE]

violone (viəlō´ni) *n.* a medieval double-bass viol. [It. VIOLA[1], *-one*, augmentative suf.]

VIP *abbr.* very important person.

viper (vī´pə) *n.* **1** a venomous snake of the family Viperidae, esp. the European viper or adder, the only poisonous British snake. **2** a treacherous or malignant person. **viperiform** (-rifawm), **viperine** (-rīn), **viperous** *a.* **viper in one's bosom** *n.* a close friend or associate who harms or betrays one. **viper's bugloss** *n.* a bristly blue-flowered plant, *Echium vulgare*, of the borage family. **viper's grass** *n.* a perennial plant, *Scorzonera hispanica*, of the daisy family. [F *vipère*, L *vīpera*, perh. *vīvipara*, see VIVIPAROUS]

virago (virah´gō) *n.* (*pl.* **viragoes, viragos**) **1** a bad-tempered, violent or scolding woman, a termagant, a shrew. **2** †a woman of masculine strength and courage. **viraginous** (-raj´-) *a.* [L, manlike maiden, from *vir*, man]

viral (vī´rəl) *a.* of, relating to or caused by a virus.

virelay (vir´əlā) *n.* an old form of French verse with two rhymes to a stanza and usu. a refrain. [OF *virelai*, from *virer*, to turn, to VEER[1]]

virement (vīə´mənt) *n.* a transfer of funds from one account to another. [F]

vireo (vir´iō) *n.* (*pl.* **vireos**) any American passerine insectivorous songbird of the genus *Vireo*. [L, poss. a greenfinch]

vires VIS.

virescent (vires´ənt) *a.* (*Bot.*) **1** green, tending to become green, viridescent. **2** abnormally green (of petals etc.). **virescence** *n.* [L *virescens -ntem*, pres.p. of *virescere*, incept. of *virēre*, to be green]

virga (vœ´gə) *n.* (*sing. or pl.*) streaks of precipitation appearing under a cloud but evaporating before they reach the ground. [L, rod, streak]

virgate[1] (vœ´gət, -gāt) *a.* long, straight and erect, rodlike. [L *virgātus*, from *virga*, rod]

virgate[2] (vœ´gət, -gāt) *n.* (*Hist.*) an ancient measure of land, usu. taken as equivalent to 30 acres (12.15 ha). [L *virgāta*, a rod's measurement, trans. of OE *gierd landes*, a yard of land, from *virga*, rod]

virger VERGER.

Virgilian (vœjil´iən) *a.* of, relating to or in the style of Virgil, Latin poet (70–19 BC).

virgin (vœ´jin) *n.* **1** a person, esp. a woman, who has never had sexual intercourse. **2** (*usu.* **Virgin**) a madonna. **3** (**Virgin**) the constellation or sign Virgo. **4** a member of an order of women under vows of chastity. **5** a female insect that produces eggs without fertilization. **6** (*coll.*) a person who is inexperienced in a specified sphere or activity. *~a.* **1** being a virgin; pure, chaste, undefiled. **2** befitting a virgin; maidenly, modest. **3** unworked, untried, not brought into cultivation. **4** (of insects) producing eggs without impregnation. **5** (of oil) obtained from the first pressing. **6** (of clay) unfired. **7** (of metal) made from ore by smelting. **8** (of wool) not yet, or only once, spun or woven. **the Virgin** the mother of Christ. **virginal** *a.* **1** of, relating to or befitting a virgin. **2** pure, chaste, maidenly. **3** untouched, undefiled. *~n.* (*often pl.*) a keyed musical instrument, shaped like a box, used in the 16th–17th cents., also *pair of virginals*. **virginally** *adv.* **virgin birth** *n.* **1** parthenogenesis. **2** (**Virgin Birth**) (the doctrine of) the birth of Jesus Christ from a virgin mother. **virgin comb** *n.* honeycomb that has been used only once for honey and not used for brood. **virgin forest** *n.* forest in its natural state, unexplored and unexploited by humans. **virgin honey** *n.* honey either from a virgin comb or that is extracted without the use of heat or pressure. **virginhood** *n.* **virginity** (-jin´iti) *n.* (*pl.* **virginities**) the state of being a virgin, purity, innocence. **Virgin Queen** *n.* **1** Queen Elizabeth I, 1533–1603. **2** (**virgin queen**) an unfertilized queen bee. **virgin's bower** *n.* any of several American clematises, esp. *Clematis virginiana*. [OF *virgine*, L *virginem*, nom. *-go*, etym. uncertain]

Virginia (vəjin´iə) *n.* **1** tobacco from Virginia. **2** a cigarette of Virginia tobacco. **Virginia creeper** *n.* a woody vine, *Parthenocissus quinquefolia*, with ornamental foliage that turns red in autumn. **Virginian** *a.* of or relating to the state of Virginia. *~n.* a native or inhabitant of Virginia. **Virginia reel** *n.* an American country dance; music written for this. **Virginia stock, Virginian stock** *n.* a Mediterranean cruciferous plant, *Malcolmia maritima*, that has white or pink flowers. [one of the states of the US, after Queen Elizabeth I, 'the Virgin Queen']

Virgo (vœ´gō) *n.* (*pl.* **Virgos**) **1** one of the 12 ancient zodiacal constellations, the Virgin. **2** the sixth sign of the zodiac, which the sun is in from about 23 August to 22 September. **3** a person born under this sign. [L, virgin]

virgule (vœ´gūl) *n.* a slanting line used as a division within or between words, a solidus. [L *virgula*, dim. of *virga*, see VIRGATE[1]]

viridescent (virides´ənt) *a.* **1** greenish. **2** becoming slightly green. **viridescence** *n.* **viridian** (-id´iən) *n.* **1** a green pigment made from a hydrated form of chromium oxide. **2** a bluish-green colour. *~a.* of this colour. **viridity** (-rid´-) *n.* (*formal*) greenness, the colour of fresh vegetation. [late L *viridescens -ntem*, pres.p. of *viridescere*, from *viridis*, green]

virile (vir´īl) *a.* **1** characteristic of a man, masculine, manly; strong, forceful, vigorous. **2** (of a male) sexually potent. **3** of or relating to adult men or the male sex. **virilism** (-il-) *n.* the development in the female of masculine characteristics, psychological and physical. **virility** (-ril´-) *n.* [F *viril*, fem. *-ile*, L *virīlis*, from *vir*, man]

virino (virē´nō) *n.* an agent postulated as the cause of BSE and related diseases, thought by some to be a fragment of nucleic acid surrounded by a protein coat derived from the host cell. [VIRUS, *-ino*, dim. suf.]

virion (vī´riən) *n.* a virus in an infective form consisting of an RNA particle within a protein covering. [*vir*us, *ion*]

viroid, virology VIRUS.

virtu (vœtoo´), **vertu** *n.* **1** a taste for or knowledge of the fine arts. **2** rare, old or beautiful objects collectively. **3** the quality of rareness or beauty. **4** intrinsic goodness or worth. **object of virtu** OBJECT[2]. [It. *virtù*, *vertù*, as VIRTUE]

virtual (vœ´tūəl) *a.* **1** being such in effect or for practical purposes, though not in name or by strict definition; near, practical. **2** (*Comput.*) computer-simulated. **3** (*Comput.*) (of memory, storage) apparently internal but in fact consisting of data automatically transferred from back-up storage, such as a disk, into the core memory as required. **4** in mechanics, relating to an infinitesimal displacement of a point in a system. **virtual focus** *n.* the point from which rays of reflected or refracted light seem to have emanated. **virtual image** *n.* an optical image formed by the apparent divergence of rays of reflected or refracted light from a point. **virtuality** (-al´iti) *n.* **virtually** *adv.* **1** almost, nearly, practically. **2** in effect. **virtual reality** *n.* an image or environment generated by computer software that closely resembles reality and with which a user can interact by using a helmet, joystick or various other items of special equipment. [ME from med. L *virtuālis*, effective, from L *virtūs*]

virtue (vœ´choo) *n.* **1** moral excellence, goodness, uprightness, rectitude. **2** conformity with or practice of morality or duty. **3** a particular moral excellence. **4** a good quality or feature. **5** sexual purity, chastity, esp. in women. **6** inherent power, goodness or efficacy. **7** (*pl.*) the seventh order of the celestial hierarchy. **by virtue of** by or through the efficacy or authority of, on the strength of. **in virtue of** by virtue of. **to make a virtue of necessity** to attempt to derive some benefit from consciously opting to undertake, or undertaking with a good grace, something that one is in any event compelled to do. **virtueless** *a.* **virtuous** *a.* **1** characterized by virtue, morally good. **2** chaste. **virtuous circle** *n.* a chain of cause and effect that has beneficial consequences. **virtuously** *adv.* **virtuousness** *n.* [ME and F *vertu*, L *virtūtem*, nom. *-tus*, from *vir*, see VIRILE]

virtuoso (vœtūō´sō, -zō) *n.* (*pl.* **virtuosos, virtuosi** (-sē, -zē)) 1 a skilled performer in some fine art, esp. music. 2 a connoisseur of articles of virtu. **virtuosity** (-os´-), **virtuosoship** *n.*

virulent (vir´ulənt) *a.* 1 extremely poisonous. 2 (of a micro-organism) highly infective. 3 (of a disease) having a rapid course and severe effects. 4 extremely bitter, acrimonious or malignant. **virulence, virulency** *n.* **virulently** *adv.* [F, from L *virulentus*, from VIRUS]

virus (vī´rəs) *n.* (*pl.* **viruses**) 1 a very small infective agent capable of self-propagation only in living matter, the causative agent of many diseases, consisting of a single nucleic acid molecule in a protein coat. 2 (*coll.*) a disease caused by this. 3 a computer virus. 4 moral taint or corrupting influence. **viroid** *n.* an infectious agent, similar to a virus but without a protein coat, known to cause certain plant diseases. **virology** (-rol´-) *n.* the study of viruses and virus diseases. **virological** (-əloj´-) *a.* **virologist** *n.* **virus infection, virus disease** *n.* an illness caused by a virus. [L, slime, poison, cogn. with Gr. *ios*, Sansk. *visham*]

Vis. *abbr.* viscount.

vis (vis) *n.* (*pl.* **vires** (vī´rēz)) force, energy, potency. **vis major** (mā´jə, mah´yaw) *n.* FORCE MAJEURE. [L]

visa (vē´zə) *n.* an official endorsement on a passport showing that it has been examined and found correct, esp. one enabling the holder to travel to or through a particular country. ~*v.t.* (*3rd pers. sing. pres.* **visas,** *pres.p.* **visaing,** *past, p.p.* **visaed, visa'd**) to certify or put a visa on. [F, from L *visa*, neut. pl. p.p. of *vidēre*, to see]

visage (viz´ij) *n.* (*formal*) the face, the countenance. ~†*v.t.* to confront, to face. **visaged** *a.* having a visage or look of a particular type. **visagiste** (vēzəzhēst´) *n.* a person who specializes in facial make-up. [F, from L *vīsum*, nom. *-us*, p.p. of *vidēre*, to see]

vis-à-vis (vēzahvē´) *prep.* 1 in relation to. 2 opposite to; face to face with. ~*adv.* face to face. ~*n.* (*pl.* **vis-à-vis**) 1 a person facing another as in certain dances, e.g. a quadrille. 2 one's counterpart or opposite number. 3 (*N Am.*) a date or escort at a social event. 4 a carriage or couch for two persons sitting vis-à-vis. [F, face to face (*vis*, face, L *vīsum*, see VISAGE)]

viscacha (viskah´chə), **vizcacha** *n.* a S American burrowing rodent of the genus *Lagostomus* or *Lagidium*, related to the chinchilla. [Am. Sp., from Quechua]

viscera (vis´ərə) *n.pl.* the internal organs of the great cavities of the body, such as the skull, thorax, and abdomen, esp. those of the abdomen, the intestines. **visceral** *a.* 1 of or relating to the viscera. 2 instinctive or intuitive rather than reasoned. **visceral nerve** *n.* a nerve belonging to the sympathetic nervous system. **visceri-, viscero-** *comb. form.* **visceromotor** (-ōmō´tə) *a.* controlling movements of the viscera. **viscerotonia** (-ōtō´niə) *n.* a type of temperament, extrovert, sociable, convivial and hedonistic, reputedly associated with the endomorphic body type. [L, pl. of *viscus*]

viscid (vis´id) *a.* 1 sticky, adhesive. 2 semi-fluid in consistency. **viscidity** (-sid´-) *n.* [F *viscide*, L *viscidus*, from *viscum*, mistletoe, birdlime, cogn. with Gr. *ixos, ixia*]

viscoelastic (viskōilas´tik) *a.* having both viscous and elastic properties. **viscoelasticity** (-tis´-) *n.*

viscometer (viskom´itə), **viscosimeter** (-kōsim´-) *n.* an apparatus for determining the viscosity of liquids. **viscometry** (-kom´itri) *n.*

viscose (vis´kōz, -kōs) *n.* 1 the highly viscous cellulose sodium salt used in the manufacture of artificial silk. 2 rayon made from this. ~*a.* viscous. [L *viscōsus*, sticky]

viscosimeter VISCOMETER.

viscount (vī´kownt) *n.* a British peer ranking next below an earl, and above a baron. **viscountcy** (-si) *n.* (*pl.* **viscountcies**). **viscountess** *n.* 1 a viscount's wife. 2 a woman holding the rank of a viscount. **viscounty** *n.* (*pl.* **viscounties**). [OE *visconte*, OF *viscomte* (F *vicomte*) (VICE-, COUNT[1])]

viscous (vis´kəs) *a.* 1 (of liquids) thick and sticky. 2 semi-fluid. 3 having a high viscosity, not flowing freely. **viscosity** (-kos´iti) *n.* (*pl.* **viscosities**) 1 the fact of being viscous, stickiness, thickness. 2 (*Physics*) the extent to which a fluid or semi-fluid resists the tendency to flow owing to the interactive force between its molecules. 3 a quantity expressing this. **viscous flow** *n.* a type of fluid flow characterized by continuous steady motion of the particles and constant velocity at any point. [L *viscōsus*, sticky; see VISCID]

viscus (vis´kəs) *n.* any of the viscera. [L]

vise VICE[2].

Vishnu (vish´noo) *n.* the preserver god of the Hindu sacred triad, appearing in many incarnations and worshipped by some as the saviour. [Sansk. *Visnu*]

visible (viz´ibəl) *a.* 1 capable of being seen, perceptible by the eye. 2 apparent, evident, obvious. 3 (of exports) consisting of actual goods. 4 (of resources, stocks) available currently. 5 (of indexes, files) designed to keep key information in easily accessible view. 6 represented visually by symbols. **visibility** (-bil´-) *n.* 1 the state of being visible, visibleness. 2 the range or possibility of vision, esp. as determined by atmospheric conditions and weather. **visible exports** *n.pl.* goods exported and sold abroad. **visible horizon** *n.* SENSIBLE HORIZON (under SENSIBLE). **visible means** *n.pl.* means or resources which are apparent to or ascertainable by others. **visibleness** *n.* **visible radiation** *n.* electromagnetic radiation which can be detected by the eye; light. **visible speech** *n.* a set of phonetic symbols representing every possible articulate utterance, used as a means of teaching speech to the hearing-impaired. **visibly** *adv.* [F, from L *vīsibilis*, from *vīsus*, see VISION]

Visigoth (viz´igoth) *n.* a member of the western Goths who settled in S Gaul and Spain in the 4th and 5th cents. **Visigothic** (-goth´-) *a.* [late L *Visigothī, -gothae*, from Gmc. (WEST, GOTH)]

vision (vizh´ən) *n.* 1 the act or faculty of seeing, sight. 2 a mental representation of a visual object, esp. in a dream or trance. 3 a supernatural or prophetic apparition. 4 something vividly perceived by the imagination or fancy. 5 foresight, an appreciation of what the future may hold, wise or imaginative planning for the future. 6 imaginative insight. 7 a person or thing of great beauty. 8 the image on a television screen; television pictures collectively. ~*v.t.* 1 to see in or as in a vision. 2 to imagine. 3 to present as in a vision. **visional** *a.* of, relating to or seen in a vision. **visionally** *adv.* **visionary** *a.* 1 characterized by or capable of vision or foresight. 2 capable of or given to seeing visions. 3 of the nature of or seen in a vision. 4 existing in a vision or in the imagination only. 5 imaginary, unreal, unsubstantial, unpractical. 6 given to daydreaming, fanciful theories etc. ~*n.* (*pl.* **visionaries**) 1 a person who sees visions, a seer. 2 an impractical daydreamer or schemer. **visionariness** *n.* **visionist** *n.* **visionless** *a.* **vision mixer** *n.* a person who blends or combines different camera shots in television or films. [F, from L *vīsiōnem*, nom. *-sio*, from *vidēre*, to see, p.p. *vīsus*]

visit (viz´it) *v.t.* 1 to go or come to see, as an act of friendship, civility, business, curiosity etc. 2 to come or go to for the purpose of inspection, supervision, correction of abuses etc. 3 to reside temporarily with or in. 4 (of diseases etc.) to come upon, to overtake, to afflict. 5 (*Bible*) to chastise. 6 to comfort, to bless. ~*v.i.* 1 to call on or visit people. 2 (*N Am., coll.*) to converse or chat (with). ~*n.* 1 the act of visiting or going to see a person, place or thing; a call. 2 a stay or sojourn (with or at). 3 a formal or official call or inspection. **visitable** *a.* **visitant** *n.* 1 a migratory bird that visits a country at certain seasons. 2 a supernatural visitor, a ghost, apparition. 3 (*poet.*) a visitor, a guest. ~†*a.* visiting. **visitation** (-ā´shən) *n.* 1 a formal or official visit for the purpose of inspection, correction etc., esp. by a bishop to the churches of his diocese. 2 a divine dispensation, esp. a chastisement or affliction; any catastrophic occurrence. 3 (**Visitation**) the visit of the Virgin Mary to Elizabeth (Luke i.39); the church festival held on 2 July in honour of this. 4 in international law, the boarding of a foreign vessel in time of war to ascertain its character etc.; the right to do this. 5 (*N Am.*) the right of a parent to visit a child under a divorce or separation order. 6 (*coll.*) a protracted visit or social call. 7 the act of visiting. **Nuns of the Visitation** NUN. **visitation of the sick** *n.* an Anglican office for the comfort and consolation of sick persons. **visitatorial** (-tətaw´ri-), **visitorial** (-taw´ri-) *a.* 1 of or relating to an official visitation. 2 empowered to make visitations. **visiting** *n.*, *a.* **visiting card** *n.* a small card, bearing one's name etc., to be left in making a call. **visiting fireman** *n.* (*pl.* **visiting firemen**) (*N Am., coll.*) 1 an important visitor who is entertained lavishly. 2 a visitor, esp. a tourist, who is expected to be a big spender. **visiting hours** *n.pl.* the period or periods of the day during which visitors are allowed, esp. to see a patient in hospital. **visiting professor** *n.* a professor invited to join an academic staff for a limited time. **visitor** *n.* 1 a person who makes a call. 2 a person who visits a place. 3 a visiting migratory bird, a visitant. 4 an officer appointed to make a visitation to any institution. **visitors' book** *n.* a book in which visitors' names are entered, esp. in which visitors to a hotel, boarding house, museum etc. write remarks. **visitor's passport** *n.* a simplified short-term British passport, obtainable from post offices. [F *visiter*, L *vīsitāre*, freq. of *vīsere*, to behold, from *vidēre*, see VISION]

visor (vī´zə), **vizor** *n.* 1 the movable perforated part of a helmet defending the face. 2 a projecting part on the front of a cap, for shielding the eyes. 3 a small movable flap or shield used to protect the eyes from strong light, esp. a sun visor in a motor vehicle. 4 (*Hist.*) a mask. **visored** *a.* **visorless** *a.* [ME and A-F *visere*, OF *visiere*, from *vis*, face, see VISAGE]

vista (vis´tə) *n.* 1 a long view shut in at the sides, as between rows of trees. 2 a mental view far into the past or future. **vistaed** *a.* [It., fem. of *visto*, p.p. of *vedere*, L *vidēre*, to see]

visual (vizh´ūəl) *a.* 1 of, relating to or used in sight or seeing. 2 attained by or received through sight, as distinct from other esp. mechanical means. 3 capable of being seen, visible. 4 relating to or occurring as a mental image. ~*n.* 1 (*often pl.*) a picture, photograph etc. as distinct from the words accompanying it. 2 a sketch of the layout of an advertisement. **visual aid** *n.* a picture, film, photograph, diagram etc. used as an aid to teaching or imparting information. **visual arts** *n.pl.* painting, sculpture, film etc. as opposed to music, literature etc. **visual display unit** *n.* a device, usu. with a keyboard, which displays characters etc. representing data stored in a computer memory. **visual field** *n.* a field of vision. **visuality** (-al´-) *n.* **visualize, visualise** *v.t.* 1 to picture in the mind, to call up a visual image of. 2 to make visible to the eye. **visualization** (-zā´shən) *n.* **visualizer** *n.* **visually** *adv.* **visually challenged** *a.* visually handicapped or impaired. **visually handicapped** *a.* unable to carry out normal activities because of defective vision or blindness. **visual handicap** *n.* **visually impaired** *a.* having defective vision, whether disabling or not. **visual impairment** *n.* **visual magnitude** *n.* the magnitude of a star as obtained by visual observation. **visual purple** *n.* rhodopsin. **visual ray** *n.* a line extended from an object to the eye. [F, from late L *vīsuālis*, from *vīsus*, sight, from *vidēre*, to see]

vital (vī´təl) *a.* 1 essential, indispensable. 2 extremely important, decisive. 3 of, relating to, necessary to or supporting organic life. 4 full of life and activity, lively, dynamic, energetic. 5 †fatal. ~*n.pl.* the parts or organs of animals essential to life, such as the heart, brain etc. **vital capacity** *n.* the volume of air that can be exhaled from the lungs after taking the deepest possible breath. **vital centre** *n.* the point in the body at which a wound appears to be instantly fatal, esp. the respiratory nerve-centre in the medulla oblongata. **vital force** *n.* a force assumed as accounting for the development and evolution of organic life, operating independently of physical and chemical forces. **vital functions** *n.pl.* the bodily functions that are essential to life such as the circulation of blood. **vitalism** *n.* the doctrine that life is derived from something distinct from physical forces. **vitalist** *n.* **vitalistic** (-lis´-) *a.* **vitality** (-tal´-) *n.* (*pl.* **vitalities**) 1 physical or mental energy; liveliness, dynamism. 2 the ability to continue to live, function or flourish. 3 vital force; vital power. 4 the quality of being vital. **vitalize, vitalise** *v.t.* 1 to give life to. 2 to animate, to make more lively. **vitalization** (-zā´shən) *n.* **vitally** *adv.* **vitalness** *n.* **vital power** *n.* the power to sustain life. **vital signs** *n.pl.* a person's pulse rate, respiratory rate, temperature etc. **vital spark** *n.* 1 the principle of life; life or trace of life. 2 (*coll.*) the moving spirit behind an enterprise etc. **vital statistics** *n.pl.* 1 statistics relating to birth, marriage and mortality. 2 (*coll.*) the measurements of a woman's bust, waist and hips. [F, from L *vītālis*, from *vīta*, life, cogn. with *vīvere*, to live, and Gr. *bios*, life]

vitamin (vit´əmin) *n.* any of a number of naturally occurring substances which are necessary, though in minute quantities, for normal metabolism. **vitamin A** *n.* RETINOL (under RETINALITE). **vitamin B_1** *n.* THIAMINE. **vitamin B_2** *n.* RIBOFLAVIN. **vitamin B_6** *n.* PYRIDOXINE (under PYRIDINE). **vitamin B_{12}** *n.* CYANOCOBALAMIN. **vitamin B complex** *n.* a large group of vitamins, chemically unrelated but often found together esp. in liver and yeast. **vitamin C** *n.* ASCORBIC ACID. **vitamin D** *n.* any of a group of fat-soluble vitamins occurring in fish-liver oils, milk, butter and eggs, essential for calcium absorption and the prevention of rickets. **vitamin D_2** *n.* CALCIFEROL. **vitamin D_3** *n.* CHOLECALCIFEROL. **vitamin E** *n.* TOCOPHEROL. **vitamin H** *n.* (*esp. N Am.*) BIOTIN. **vitaminize, vitaminise** *v.t.* to add vitamins to. **vitamin K** *n.* any of a group of vitamins, found mainly in green leaves, essential for normal coagulation of the blood. **vitamin K_1** *n.* PHYLLOQUINONE. **vitamin K_2** *n.* MENAQUINONE. **vitamin M** *n.* (*esp. N Am.*) FOLIC ACID. [L *vita*, life, AMINE]

vitellus (vitel´əs) *n.* (*pl.* **vitelli** (-lī)) yolk of egg; the protoplasmic contents of the ovum. **vitellin** (-in) *n.* the chief protein constituent of egg yolk. **vitelline** (-īn) *a.* 1 of or relating to the yolk of an egg. 2 having the yellow colour of egg yolk. **vitelline membrane** *n.* a membrane that encloses the yolk of an egg or a fertilized ovum. **vitellogenic** (-ōjen´ik), **vitelligenous** (-ij´ənəs) *a.* producing yolk or stimulating its production. [L, dim. of *vitulus*, calf, see VEAL]

vitiate (vish´iāt) *v.t.* 1 to impair the quality of; to render faulty or imperfect. 2 to corrupt. 3 to render invalid or ineffectual. **vitiation** (-ā´shən) *n.* **vitiator** *n.* [L *vitiāre*, from *vitium*, VICE[1]]

viticulture (vit´ikŭlchə) *n.* 1 the cultivation of the grapevine. 2 the science or study of this. **viticultural** (-kŭl´-) *a.* **viticulturist** (-kŭl´-) *n.* [L *vītis*, VINE, CULTURE]

vitiligo (vitilī´gō) *n.* (*Med.*) an abnormal skin condition in which pigment is lost from areas of the skin, causing whitish patches. [L, tetter]

vitreous (vit´riəs) *a.* 1 consisting of or resembling glass. 2 obtained from glass. **vitreosity** (-os´-), **vitreousness** *n.* **vitreous humour, vitreous body** *n.* the jelly-like substance filling the posterior chamber of the eye, between the lens and the retina. **vitrescent** (-tres´ənt) *a.* **1** tending to become vitreous. **2** capable of being turned into glass. **vitrescence** *n.* **vitrescible** *a.* vitrifiable. **vitric** *a.* of or like glass. **vitriform** (-rifawm) *a.* **vitrify** *v.t.* (*3rd pers. sing. pres.* **vitrifies,** *pres.p.* **vitrifying,** *past, p.p.* **vitrified**) to convert into glass or a glassy substance by heat and fusion. *~v.i.* to be converted into glass. **vitrifiable** *a.* **vitrifiability** (-bil´-) *n.* **vitrification** (-fikā´shən), **vitrifaction** (-fak´-) *n.* [L *vitreus*, from *vitrum*, glass, perh. cogn. with *vidēre*, to see]

vitrine (vit´rēn, -rin) *n.* a glass showcase. [F]

vitriol (vit´riəl) *n.* **1** sulphuric acid as made from copperas. **2** any salt of this, a sulphate. **3** malignancy, caustic criticism etc. **vitriolic** (-ol´-) *a.* **1** of, relating to, obtained from or having the qualities of vitriol. **2** caustic, bitter, malignant. **vitriolize** (-iəlīz), **vitriolise** *v.t.* **1** to convert into vitriol. **2** to treat with vitriol. **3** to attack or injure with vitriol. **vitriolizable** *a.* **vitriolization** (-zā´shən) *n.* [ME and OF *vitriole*, med. L *vitriolus*, L *vitreolus*, dim. of *vitreus*, VITREOUS]

Vitruvian (vitroo´viən) *a.* (*Archit.*) of or in the style of Marcus Vitruvius Pollio, a Roman architect of the Augustan age. **Vitruvian scroll** *n.* a pattern consisting of convoluted undulations, used in friezes etc.

vitta (vit´ə) *n.* (*pl.* **vittae** (-tē)) **1** (*Bot.*) an oil-tube in the fruit of the parsley family etc. **2** (*Zool.*) a band or stripe of colour. **vittate** (-ət) *a.* [L, a fillet or band for the head]

†**vittles** (vit´əlz) *n.pl.* victuals.

vituline (vit´ūlīn) *a.* of or relating to a calf or veal. [L *vitulus*, calf, see VEAL]

vituperate (vītū´pərāt) *v.i.* to use violently abusive language. *~v.t.* to upbraid, to abuse, to rail at. **vituperation** (-ā´shən) *n.* **1** abusive language; an expression of abuse or violent censure or recrimination. **2** the act of vituperating. **vituperative** *a.* **vituperatively** *adv.* **vituperator** *n.* [L *vituperātus*, p.p. of *vituperāre* (*vitu-*, *vitium*, VICE[1], *parāre*, to get ready)]

viva[1] (vē´və) *n.* an exclamation of joy or applause. *~int.* long live. [It., long live, from L *vivere*, to live, as VIVACIOUS]

viva[2] (vī´və) *n.* a viva voce examination. *~v.t.* (*3rd pers. sing. pres.* **vivas,** *pres.p.* **vivaing,** *past, p.p.* **vivaed, viva'd**) to subject to an oral examination.

vivace (vivah´chā) *adv.* (*Mus.*) in a brisk, lively manner. [It.]

vivacious (vivā´shəs) *a.* **1** lively, animated, sprightly, high-spirited. **2** (*Bot.*) †tenacious of life, living through the winter, perennial. **vivaciously** *adv.* **vivacity** (-vas´-), **vivaciousness** *n.* [L *vīvax -ācis*, from *vīvere*, to live]

vivandière (vēvādyeə´) *n.* (*Hist.*) a female sutler attached to a Continental, esp. French, regiment. [F, fem. of *vivandier*, sutler, from L *vīvenda*, provisions, see VIAND]

vivarium (vīveə´riəm) *n.* (*pl.* **vivariums, vivaria** (-riə)) a park, enclosure or other place artificially prepared in which animals etc. are kept alive as nearly as possible in their natural state. **vivary** (vī´-) *n.* (*pl.* **vivaries**). [L, from *vīvus*, alive]

vivat (vī´vat, vē´-) *n., int.* (a shout of) long live. [L]

viva voce (vīvə vō´chi) *adv.* by word of mouth, orally. *~a.* oral. *~n.* an oral examination. [L, with the living voice]

vive (vēv) *int.* long live, up with. [F]

viverrid (viver´id, vī-) *n.* any of the Viverridae, a family of carnivorous mammals containing the civets, genets, mongooses etc. *~a.* of or relating to this family. **viverrine** (-īn) *a.* **viverroid** (-oid) *n., a.* [mod. L *viverra*, ferret, -ID]

vivers (vē´vəz) *n.pl.* (*Sc.*) food, provisions. [F *vivres*, from *vivre*, as VIVE]

vivid (viv´id) *a.* **1** (of colour, light) very bright, intense, brilliant. **2** (of a description) evoking a very clear and striking mental picture. **3** (of a memory) very distinct and fresh. **4** (of the imagination) creating very clear, lifelike and striking images, often too prolifically. **5** intense, powerful. **6** (of a person) vigorous, lively. **vividly** *adv.* **vividness** *n.* [L *vīvidus*, from *vīvus*, living]

vivify (viv´ifī) *v.t.* (*3rd pers. sing. pres.* **vivifies,** *pres.p.* **vivifying,** *past, p.p.* **vivified**) to give life to, to quicken, to animate, to enliven. **vivification** (-fikā´shən) *n.* **vivifier** *n.* [F *vivifier*, late L *vīvificāre* (L *vīvus*, living, *-ficāre*, *facere*, to make)]

viviparous (vivip´ərəs, vī-) *a.* **1** giving birth to young alive, as distinct from *oviparous* and *ovoviviparous*. **2** (*Bot.*) producing bulbs or seeds that germinate while still attached to the parent plant. **3** producing bulbils or young plants instead of flowers. **viviparity** (vivipar´i-), **viviparousness** *n.* **viviparously** *adv.* [late L *vīviparus* (*vīvus*, alive, *parere*, to produce)]

vivisection (vivisek´shən) *n.* **1** the dissection of, or performance of inoculative or other experiments on, living animals. **2** minute and merciless examination or criticism. **vivisect** (viv´-) *v.t.* to dissect (a living animal). **vivisectional** *a.* **vivisectionist** *n.* **vivisector** (viv´-) *n.* [F (L *vīvus*, alive, SECTION)]

vivo (vē´vō) *adv.* (*Mus.*) with life and animation, vivace. [It.]

vixen (vik´sən) *n.* **1** a female fox. **2** a shrewish, quarrelsome woman. **vixenish, vixenly** *a.* having the qualities of a vixen. [OE *fyxen*, fem. of FOX, cp. G *Füchsin*, fem. of *Fuchs*]

Viyella® (vīel´ə) *n.* a soft woven fabric made from cotton and wool, used esp. for blouses and shirts.

viz. *abbr.* VIDELICET.

Usage note Primarily a written form, and read aloud as 'namely'.

---

†**vizard** (viz´əd) *n.* a means of disguise, a mask, a visor. **vizarded** *a.* [var. of VISOR]

vizcacha VISCACHA.

vizier (viziə´) *n.* a high officer or minister of state in some Muslim countries, esp. in the former Ottoman empire. **vizierate** (-rət) *n.* the position, authority or term of office of a vizier. **vizierial** *a.* [Arab. *wazīr*, counsellor, orig. porter, from *wazara*, to bear a burden]

vizor VISOR.

vizsla (vizh´lə) *n.* a Hungarian breed of hunting dog with a smooth red or rust-coloured coat. [*Vizsla*, a town in Hungary]

VJ *abbr.* Victory over Japan. **VJ day** *n.* **1** 15 August 1945, the day of the Japanese surrender in World War II. **2** 2 September 1945, the day when hostilities against Japan in World War II officially ceased. **3** an anniversary of either of these days.

Vlach (vlak) *n.* a member of a people inhabiting Romania and parts of the former Soviet Union, a Wallachian. *~a.* of or relating to this people. [Bulg., from Old Church Slavonic *Vlachŭ*, from OHG *walh*, a foreigner]

vlei (vlī, flī) *n.* (*S Afr.*) a swampy tract, a place where water lies in rainy seasons. [Afrikaans, prob. from Dut. *vallei*, VALLEY]

VLF *abbr.* very low frequency.

VLSI *abbr.* very large-scale integration.

VN *abbr.* Vietnam (IVR).

VO *abbr.* **1** very old. **2** Royal Victorian Order.

vo. *abbr.* verso.

voc. *abbr.* vocative.

vocable (vō´kəbəl) *n.* a word, esp. as considered phonologically. [F, from L *vocābulum*, from *vocāre*, to call, cogn. with *vox vōcis*, VOICE]

vocabulary (vəkab´ūləri) *n.* (*pl.* **vocabularies**) **1** a list or collection of words used in a language, science, book etc., usu. arranged in alphabetical order, and explained.

2 all the words contained in a particular language. 3 the stock of words at a particular person's command. 4 (of forms, techniques) range, repertoire. [F *vocabulaire*, late L *vocābulārium*, as VOCABLE]

vocal (vō´kəl) *a.* 1 of or relating to the voice or oral utterance. 2 uttered or produced by the voice. 3 having a voice. 4 outspoken, freely expressing an opinion. 5 eloquent. 6 (*Mus.*) written for the voice or voices. 7 resounding with or as with voices. 8 voiced, sonant, not surd. 9 having the character of a vowel. ~*n.* 1 (*often pl.*) the part of a musical, esp. a jazz or pop composition that is sung. 2 a performance of this. 3 a vocal sound, a vowel. **vocal cords, vocal folds** *n.pl.* the elastic folds of the lining membrane of the larynx around the opening of the glottis. **vocalese** (-lēz´) *n.* a style of esp. jazz singing in which the singer improvises words to a tune or instrumental solo. **vocalic** (-kal´-) *a.* of, relating to or consisting of vowel sounds. **vocalise**[1] (-lēz, -lēz´) *n.* 1 a musical exercise consisting of a passage sung on one vowel sound. 2 a vocal passage or composition consisting of a melody without words. 3 (*derog.*) a display of vocal expertise. **vocalise**[2] VOCALIZE (under VOCAL). **vocalism** *n.* 1 the exercise of the vocal organs. 2 singing technique. 3 a vowel sound or system. **vocalist** *n.* a singer, as distinct from an instrumental performer, esp. of jazz or popular music. **vocality** (-kal´-), **vocalness** *n.* **vocalize, vocalise** *v.t.* 1 to form or utter with the voice. 2 to articulate, to express. 3 to change (a consonant) to a vowel or semivowel. 4 to insert the vowel points in (Hebrew etc.). ~*v.i.* 1 to utter a vocal sound. 2 to exercise the voice. 3 to sing several notes to one vowel. **vocalization** (-zā´shən) *n.* **vocally** *adv.* **vocal music** *n.* music composed for or produced by the voice as distinct from instrumental music. **vocal score** *n.* a musical score showing the singing parts in full but with the instrumental parts reduced or omitted. [F, from L *vōcālis*, from *vox vōcis*, VOICE]

vocat. *abbr.* vocative.

vocation (vəkā´shən) *n.* 1 a call or sense of fitness for and obligation to follow a particular career. 2 a divine call or spiritual injunction or guidance to undertake a duty, occupation etc. 3 a person's calling or occupation. **vocational** *a.* 1 of or relating to an employment, occupation or vocation. 2 (of training, qualifications) relating to the skills needed for a particular occupation. **vocationally** *adv.* [F, from L *vocātiōnem*, nom. *-tio*, from *vocāre*, see VOCABLE]

vocative (vok´ətiv) *a.* used in addressing a person or thing. ~*n.* the case of a noun used in addressing a person or thing. [F *vocatif*, fem. *-ive*, L *vocātīvus*, as VOCATION]

voces VOX.

vociferate (vəsif´ərāt) *v.i.* 1 to cry loudly, to bawl, to shout. 2 to make one's views known loudly and strongly. ~*v.t.* to cry, to shout, to express or utter loudly and vehemently. **vociferance** *n.* **vociferant** *a.* **vociferation** (-ā´shən) *n.* **vociferator** *n.* **vociferous** *a.* 1 making an outcry, expressing oneself loudly and insistently. 2 clamorous, noisy. **vociferously** *adv.* **vociferousness** *n.* [L *vōciferātus*, p.p. of *vōciferāre*, *-ferārī* (*vox vōcis*, VOICE, *ferre*, to bear)]

vocoder (vōkō´də) *n.* an electronic device, similar to a synthesizer, that produces synthetic speech. [*voice*, *coder*]

VOD *abbr.* video-on-demand.

Vodafone® (vō´dəfōn) *n.* a British cellular telephone system; a handset used for this.

vodka (vod´kə) *n.* a strong spirituous liquor distilled from rye, orig. from Russia. [Rus., dim. of *voda*, water]

voe (vō) *n.* in Orkney or Shetland, a small inlet, bay or creek. [Icel. *vāgr*, *vogr*]

voetsek (fut´sek) *int.* (*S Afr., offensive*) go away. [Afrikaans, contr. of *voort se ek*, away say I]

vogue (vōg) *n.* 1 a fashion prevalent at any particular time. 2 currency, popular acceptance or usage. **in vogue** fashionable, currently popular or widespread. **vogue word** *n.* a word much used at a particular time or period. **voguish** *a.* [F, orig. sway, from *voguer*, to sail forth, It. *vogare*, to row, G *wogen*, to fluctuate, cp. OE *wǣg*, wave]

voice (vois) *n.* 1 the sound uttered by the mouth, esp. by a human being, in speaking, singing etc. 2 the characteristic sound made by an individual when speaking or singing. 3 the faculty or power of vocal utterance. 4 a sound suggestive of human speech. 5 expression of the mind or will in words, whether spoken or written etc. 6 one's opinion or judgement; one's right to express this; one's choice, vote or suffrage. 7 someone who expresses the will or judgement of others, a spokesperson, a mouthpiece. 8 sound produced by the breath acting on the vocal cords, sonancy. 9 (*Gram.*) the verb form expressing the relation of the subject to the action, as active, passive or middle. 10 (*Mus.*) the quality and range of sounds produced by a singer. 11 (*Mus.*) a vocal or instrumental part in a composition. 12 (*usu. pl.*) a supernatural utterance usu. guiding or directing the hearer. ~*v.t.* 1 to give utterance to, to express. 2 to give voice or sonancy to. 3 to regulate the tones of, to tune. **in good voice** in a condition to sing or speak well. **in voice** in good voice. **out of voice** not in a condition to sing or speak well. **to give voice to** to utter, to express, to make known. **with one voice** unanimously. **voice box** *n.* (*coll.*) the larynx. **voiced** *a.* 1 produced with vibration of the vocal cords. 2 having a voice (*usu. in comb.*, as *loud-voiced*). **voiceful** *a.* vocal; sonorous. **voice in the wilderness** *n.* a person whose suggestions, advice, pleas etc. are unheeded or ignored (Matt. iii.3). **voiceless** *a.* 1 speechless, mute. 2 of a speech sound, not voiced. 3 having no say or vote. **voicelessness** *n.* **voice of God** *n.* the expression or a means of expression of the divine will. **voice-over** *n.* 1 the voice of an unseen narrator, actor etc. in a film etc. 2 the text spoken by a voice-over. ~*v.t., v.i.* to speak a voice-over for (a film etc.). **voiceprint** *n.* an electronically recorded graphic representation of a person's voice. **voice recognition** *n.* the identification by a computer of a particular voice or voices, enabling the owners of the voices to gain or exercise control of the computer's functions. **voice response** *n.* output from a computer in the form of synthesized speech rather than visual data. **voice vote** *n.* a vote determined on the basis of the volume produced by voters responding aye or no etc. to a proposal. [ME and OF *vois*, L *vōcem*, nom. *vox*, cogn. with Gr. *epos*, word, Sansk. *vākyam*, speech]

void (void) *a.* 1 empty, unfilled, vacant. 2 lacking, destitute (of). 3 having no legal force, null, invalid. 4 useless, ineffectual. 5 having no holder, occupant or incumbent. 6 having no cards in a particular suit. ~*n.* 1 an empty space. 2 a vacuum, a feeling of loss or emptiness. 3 a lack of any cards in a particular suit. 4 an unfilled space in a wall or building. ~*v.t.* 1 to invalidate, to nullify. 2 to empty (contents); to make empty. 3 to discharge, to emit from the bowels. 4 †to quit, to leave, to evacuate. **voidable** *a.* **voidance** *n.* 1 the act of nullifying; an annulment. 2 (of an office or benefice) the state of being vacant. **voided** *a.* 1 made void. 2 (*Her.*) (of a charge) having the inner part cut away so that the field shows through. **voider** *n.* **voidly** *adv.* **voidness** *n.* [OF *void*, fem. *voide*, perh. from L *vacuus*, empty, or *viduus*, bereft]

voile (voil) *n.* a thin, semi-transparent dress material. [F, veil]

voir dire (vwah diə´) *n.* (*Law*) the preliminary examination of a witness by a judge; an oath administered to such a witness. [OF, to speak the truth]

voix céleste (vwah sālest´) *n.* (*pl.* **voix célestes** (sālest´)) a soft organ stop with a distinctive tremulous sound. [F, heavenly voice]

vol. *abbr.* **1** volcano. **2** volume. **3** volunteer.

vola (vō´lə) *n.* (*pl.* **volae** (-lē)) (*Anat.*) **1** the palm of the hand. **2** the sole of the foot. **volar**[1] *a.* of or relating to the palm or sole. [L, palm, sole]

volant (vō´lənt) *a.* **1** flying, able to fly. **2** (*Her.*) represented as flying. **3** (*poet.*) nimble, active, rapid. [F, pres.p. of *voler*, L *volāre*, to fly]

volante (volan´ti) *n.* a two-wheeled covered horse-drawn vehicle with very long shafts and a body slung in front of the axle. [Sp.]

Volapuk (vol´əpuk), **Volapük** *n.* a universal language invented (1879) by Johann Maria Schleyer. [Volapük (*vol*, world, *pük*, speech)]

volar[1] VOLA.

volar[2] (vō´lə) *a.* (*formal*) relating to flight or flying.

volatile (vol´ətīl) *a.* **1** readily evaporating. **2** (of a person) fickle, changeable; mercurial, lively. **3** (of a situation) unpredictable, liable to sudden violent change, explosive. **4** short-lived, transient. **5** (of a computer memory) not retaining data when the power is switched off. *~n.* a volatile substance. †**volatileness** *n.* **volatility** (-til´-) *n.* **volatilize** (vəlat´-), **volatilise** *v.t.* to cause to pass off in vapour. *~v.i.* to evaporate. **volatilizable** *a.* **volatilization** (-zā´shən) *n.* [F *volatil*, fem. *-tile*, L *volātilis*, from *volāre*, to fly, p.p. *volātus*]

vol-au-vent (vol´ōvã) *n.* a small, round puff pastry case filled with a filling, often savoury. [F]

volcano (volkā´nō) *n.* (*pl.* **volcanoes**) **1** an opening in the earth's surface through which lava, cinders, gases etc. are ejected from the interior, esp. at the top of a hill or mountain formed by the successive accumulations of ejected matter. **2** such a hill or mountain. **3** any situation where danger, upheaval etc. seems likely. **volcanic** (-kan´-) *a.* of or relating to, produced by, or of the nature of a volcano. **volcanically** *adv.* **volcanic bomb** *n.* a round or pear-shaped mass of volcanic rock, originally ejected as lava during an eruption. **volcanic glass** *n.* rock without a crystalline structure, such as obsidian, pumice etc. produced by the rapid cooling of molten lava. **volcanicity** (volkənis´-) *n.* volcanism. **volcanism** (vol´-), **vulcanism** (vŭl´-) *n.* volcanic activity and phenomena collectively. **volcanize** (vol´-), **volcanise** *v.t.* to subject to the effects of volcanic heat. **volcanization** (-zā´shən) *n.* **volcanology** VULCANOLOGY (under VULCANITE). [It., from L *Volcānus*, *Vulcānus*, god of fire, cp. Sansk. *ulkā*, firebrand, meteor]

vole[1] (vōl) *n.* a mouselike or ratlike rodent of the family Cricetidae, with a stocky body, blunt nose, short tail and inconspicuous ears. [shortened from *vole-mouse* (cp. Icel. *völlr*, Norw. *voll*, Swed. *vall*, field, cogn. with WOLD)]

vole[2] (vōl) *n.* the act of winning all the tricks in a deal. [F *voler*, L *volāre*, to fly]

volet (vol´ā) *n.* a wing or panel of a triptych. [OF, shutter, from *voler*, see VOLE[2]]

volitant (vol´itənt) *a.* **1** flying, flitting. **2** capable of flight. [L *volitans -ntem*, pres.p. of *volitāre*, freq. of *volāre*, to fly]

volition (vəlish´ən) *n.* **1** exercise of the will. **2** the power of willing. **of/ by one's own volition** voluntarily. **volitional, volitionary** *a.* **volitionally** *adv.* **volitionless** *a.* **volitive** (vol´-) *a.* **1** relating to the will. **2** (*Gram.*) desiderative. **3** (*formal*) deliberate, willed. [F, from late L *volitiōnem*, nom. *-tio*, from *volo*, I wish, inf. *velle*, to wish]

volk (folk) *n.* (*S Afr.*) the people or nation, esp. that of the Afrikaners. [Afrikaans]

Völkerwanderung (fœlkəvan´dərung) *n.* a migration of peoples, esp. that of the Germanic and Slav peoples into S and W Europe in the 2nd–11th cents. [G]

volley (vol´i) *n.* (*pl.* **volleys**) **1** a simultaneous discharge of missiles. **2** the missiles thus discharged. **3** a noisy outburst or emission of many things at once. **4** a return of the ball at tennis and similar games before it touches the ground. **5** in cricket, a ball bowled close to the wicket without hitting the ground. **6** in football, a kick delivered before the ball has hit the ground. *~v.t.* (*3rd pers. sing. pres.* **volleys**, *pres.p.* **volleying**, *past, p.p.* **volleyed**) **1** to discharge in or as in a volley. **2** to return, kick or bowl as a volley. *~v.i.* **1** to discharge a volley. **2** (of missiles etc.) to fly in a volley. **3** (of guns) to fire together. **4** to return a ball before it touches the ground. **on the volley** before the ball hits the ground. **volleyball** *n.* **1** a game in which a large ball is hit back and forward over a high net by hand, played between two teams. **2** the ball used in this game. [F *volée*, flight, from *voler*, see VOLE[2]]

volplane (vol´plān) *v.i.* to glide down to earth in an aircraft with the engine shut off. *~n.* such a descending flight. [L *volāre*, to fly, PLANE[4]]

volt[1] (vōlt) *n.* the SI unit of electric potential or potential difference, the difference of potential between two points in a conductor carrying a current of 1 ampere when the power dissipated between them is 1 watt. **volta-** *comb.form* voltaic. **voltage** (-tij) *n.* electromotive force or potential difference as measured or expressed in volts. **voltaic** (voltā´ik) *a.* of or relating to electricity produced by chemical action or contact, galvanic. **voltaic cell** *n.* a primary cell. **voltaic pile** *n.* an early form of battery in the form of a pile of paired plates of dissimilar metals, each pair being separated from the next by a pad moistened with electrolyte. **voltaism** *n.* galvanism. **voltameter** (-tam´itə) *n.* an instrument for measuring an electric charge. **volt-ampere** *n.* the product of the potential in volts and the actual current in amperes in a circuit. **voltmeter** *n.* an instrument for measuring electromotive force directly, calibrated in volts. [Alessandro *Volta*, 1745–1827, Italian physicist]

volt[2] (volt) *n.* (*also* **volte**) **1** a circular tread, the gait of a horse going sideways round a centre. **2** a sudden leap to avoid a thrust in fencing. *~v.i.* to make a volte in fencing. [F, see VAULT[2]]

volta (vol´tə) *n.* (*pl.* **volte** (-tā)) a lively Italian dance of the 16th and 17th cents.; a piece of music to accompany this. [It., see VAULT[2]]

voltage, voltaic etc. VOLT[1].

volte[1] VOLT[2].

volte[2] VOLTA.

volte-face (voltfas´) *n.* **1** a complete change of opinion, attitude etc. **2** a turn round. [F (VOLT[1], FACE)]

voluble (vol´ūbəl) *a.* **1** producing or characterized by a flow of words, fluent, glib, garrulous. **2** (*Bot.*) twisting, twining, climbing by winding round a support. **volubility** (-bil´-), **volubleness** *n.* **volubly** *adv.* [F, from L *volūbilem*, nom. *-lis*, from *volvere*, to roll, cogn. with Goth. *walwjan*, Gr. *eiluein*]

volucrine (vol´ūkrin, -krīn) *a.* of or relating to birds. [L *volucer -cris*, bird]

volume (vol´ūm) *n.* **1** a collection of (usu. printed) sheets of paper, parchment etc., bound together forming a book or work or part of one. **2** a book, a tome. **3** (*Hist.*) a roll or scroll of papyrus, vellum etc. constituting a book. **4** the complete set of issues of a periodical over a specified period, usu. a year. **5** cubical content. **6** mass, bulk. **7** a (large) amount or quantity. **8** (*usu. pl.*) a rounded, swelling mass, a wreath, a coil. **9** loudness, or the control for adjusting it on a radio, television etc. **10** (*Mus.*) fullness or roundness of tone. **volumed** *a.* **volumeter** (-lū´mitə) *n.* an instrument for measuring the volume of a solid, liquid or gas. **volumetric** (-met´-), **volumetrical** *a.* of or relating to the measurement of volume. **volumetrically** *adv.* **volumetric analysis** *n.* **1** quantitative analysis of liquids or solutions by using accurately measured titrated volumes of standard chemical solutions. **2** analysis of a gas by volume. [F, from L *volumen*, as VOLUBLE]

voluminous (vəloo´minəs) *a.* **1** of great volume, bulk or size. **2** (of a dress, drapery) loose-fitting and using large quantities of fabric. **3** consisting of many volumes. **4** (of a writer) producing many or bulky books. **voluminosity** (-nos´-), **voluminousness** *n.* **voluminously** *adv.* [late L *voluminōsus*, full of windings, from *volumen*, see VOLUME]

voluntary (vol´əntəri) *a.* **1** acting, performed, given etc. of one's own free will or choice, not under external constraint. **2** unpaid. **3** (of an organization, institution) brought about, established or supported by voluntary action. **4** (of muscles, movement etc.) subject to or controlled by the will. **5** endowed with or exercising the power of willing. **6** (*Law*) done without constraint or by consent, without valuable consideration. **7** intentional, designed. *~n.* (*pl.* **voluntaries**) **1** an organ solo played in a church etc. before, during or after a service. **2** an extempore prelude to another piece of music. **3** a routine, piece etc. chosen for performance by a competitor in a competition. **4** (*Hist.*) a supporter of the principle that the Church (and usu. education) should be independent of the State and maintained by voluntary effort. **5** †someone who engages in any act of their own free will, a volunteer. **voluntarily** *adv.* **voluntariness** *n.* **voluntarism** *n.* **1** (*also* **voluntaryism**) the principle of relying on voluntary action rather than compulsion. **2** (*Philos.*) the theory that the will is the fundamental or dominant principle in any individual or in the universe. **3** (*also* **voluntaryism**) reliance on voluntary subscriptions rather than on state aid for the upkeep of schools, churches etc. **voluntarist, voluntaryist** *n.* **Voluntary Aid Detachment** *n.* in World War I, an official organization of men and women to render first aid and assist in hospital work etc. **voluntary-aided** *a.* (of a school) originally established by a voluntary organization but funded mainly by a local authority. **voluntary-controlled** *a.* (of a school) established by a voluntary organization, but wholly funded by a local authority. **voluntaryism** VOLUNTARISM (under VOLUNTARY). **voluntary school** *n.* in the UK, a school established by a voluntary organization, usu. a religious denomination, but partly or wholly maintained by a local authority. **Voluntary Service Overseas** *n.* in the UK, an organization which sends volunteers overseas, usu. to underdeveloped countries, to use and teach their skills. [MF *voluntaire*, *volontaire*, L *voluntārius*, from *voluntas*, free will, from *volens -ntis*, pres.p. of *velle*, to will]

volunteer (voləntiə´) *n.* **1** a person who undertakes a job etc. voluntarily. **2** a person who enters into any service of their own free will, esp. orig. a member of a military body in the United Kingdom superseded by the Territorial Force in 1907. **3** (*Law*) a person who enters into a transaction voluntarily, without compulsion or promise of remuneration; a person to whom property is transferred without valuable consideration. *~a.* **1** voluntary. **2** (*Bot.*) self-sown. *~v.t.* **1** to offer or undertake voluntarily. **2** to offer or commandeer the services of (another person). *~v.i.* to offer one's services voluntarily, esp. orig. to offer to serve (for a military campaign etc.) as a volunteer. [F *volontaire*, see VOLUNTARY]

voluptuary (vəlŭp´chuəri) *n.* (*pl.* **voluptuaries**) a person given to luxury or sensual pleasures. *~a.* relating to, promoting or devoted to sensual pleasure. **voluptuous** *a.* **1** of or relating to, contributing to or producing sensuous or sensual gratification. **2** (of a woman) sexually alluring because of shapeliness or fullness of figure. **voluptuously** *adv.* **voluptuousness** *n.* [F *voluptueux*, L *voluptuōsus*, from *voluptas -tātem*, cogn. with VOLUNTARY]

volute (vol´ūt, -lūt´) *n.* **1** a spiral, a whorl. **2** a spiral scroll used in Ionic, Corinthian and Composite capitals. **3** a marine gastropod of the genus *Voluta*, usu. of tropical seas and having a beautiful shell. **4** the shell of one of these. *~a.* (*Bot.*) rolled up. **voluted** *a.* **volution** (-ū´shən, -oo´shən) *n.* **1** a revolving movement. **2** a spiral turn. **3** a whorl of a spiral shell. **4** (*Anat.*) a convolution. [F, from L *volūta*, orig. fem. p.p. of *volvere*, to roll]

volvox (vol´voks) *n.* a spherical colony of simple, freshwater, greenish organisms, composed of minute flagellate cells which set up a revolving motion. [mod. L, from L *volvere*, to roll]

volvulus (vol´vūləs) *n.* (*pl.* **volvuluses**) a twisting of an intestine causing obstruction of the intestinal canal.

vomer (vō´mə) *n.* a small thin bone forming the chief portion of the partition between the nostrils in human beings. **vomerine** (-rīn) *a.* [L, ploughshare]

vomit (vom´it) *v.t.* (*pres.p.* **vomiting,** *past, p.p.* **vomited**) **1** to eject from the stomach by the mouth. **2** to eject or discharge violently, to belch out. *~v.i.* to eject the contents of the stomach by the mouth, to spew, to be sick. *~n.* **1** matter ejected from the stomach by the mouth. **2** †an emetic. †**vomitive** *a.* vomitory. **vomitorium** (-aw´riəm) *n.* (*pl.* **vomitoria** (-aw´riə)) a vomitory in an ancient Roman theatre or amphitheatre. **vomitory** (-təri) *a.* emetic. *~n.* (*pl.* **vomitories**) **1** any of the openings for entrance or exit in an ancient Roman theatre or amphitheatre. **2** an emetic. **vomiturition** (-tūrish´ən) *n.* **1** an ineffectual attempt to vomit. **2** violent or repeated vomiting of very little matter, retching. **vomitus** *n.* matter that has been vomited. [L *vomitus*, p.p. of *vomere*, cogn. with Gr. *emein*]

voodoo (voo´doo) *n.* **1** a cult involving animistic deities, witchcraft and communication in trances practised by Creoles and blacks in Haiti and other parts of the W Indies and in the southern US. **2** a sorcerer or conjurer skilled in this. **3** a charm, spell or fetish used in this. *~v.t.* (*3rd pers. sing. pres.* **voodoos,** *pres.p.* **voodooing,** *past, p.p.* **voodooed**) to put a spell on or bewitch with voodoo. **voodooish** *a.* **voodooism** *n.* **voodooist** *n.* [W Afr. *vodu*, a spirit]

voortrekker (vuə´trekə, fuə´-, -trek´ə) *n.* **1** (**Voortrekker**) any of the Dutch farmers from Cape Colony who took part in the Great Trek into the Transvaal in 1836 and following years. **2** a pioneer. [Afrikaans, Dut. *voor*, before, *trekken*, to trek]

voracious (vərā´shəs) *a.* **1** greedy in eating. **2** ravenous, gluttonous, ready to swallow up or devour. **3** insatiable, very eager. **voraciously** *adv.* **voracity** (-ras´-) *n.* [L *vorax -ācis*, from *vorāre*, to devour]

-vore (vaw) *comb. form* forming nouns denoting creatures that live on a certain type of food, as *carnivore*, *herbivore*. **-vora** (vərə) *comb. form* forming pl. nouns denoting categories of creatures defined by their feeding habits. **-vorous** (vərəs) *comb. form* feeding on, living on, as *carnivorous*, *herbivorous*. [L *vorāre*, to devour]

vortex (vaw´teks) *n.* (*pl.* **vortices** (-tisēz)) **1** a whirling or rotating mass of fluid, esp. a whirlpool. **2** any whirling motion or mass. **3** a situation, activity, way of life etc. which seems likely to engulf anyone who becomes involved in it. **4** (*Physics*) a portion of fluid the particles of which have a rotary motion. **vortex ring** *n.* a vortex on the axis of which is a closed curve. **vortex street** *n.* a regular stream or parallel streams of vortices carried downstream by the movement of a fluid over a body. **vortical** *a.* of or relating to a vortex, whirling. **vortically** *adv.* **vorticism** (vaw´tisizm) *n.* **1** a school of early 20th-cent. painting which seeks to represent nature in formal designs of straight and angular patterns. **2** (*Philos.*) the Cartesian theory of the universe as a plenum in which motion propagates itself in circles. **vorticist** *n.* **vorticity** (-tis´-) *n.* **vorticose** (-kōs), **vorticular** (-tik´ū-) *a.* rotating quickly, whirling. **vortiginous** (-tij´i-) *a.* vortical, whirling. [L, var. of VERTEX]

vorticella (vawtisel´ə) *n.* (*pl.* **vorticellae** (-lē)) a protozoan of the genus *Vorticella* of ciliated infusoria with the cilia restricted to a fringe around the mouth. [mod. L, little eddy, from *vortex*]

vortices, vorticism etc. VORTEX.

votary (vō´təri) *n.* (*pl.* **votaries**) **1** a person who is devoted or consecrated by a vow or promise. **2** a person who is devoted to some particular service, study, pursuit etc. **votaress, †votress** *n.* a female votary. [med. L *votārius*, from L *vōtum*, see VOTE]

vote (vōt) *n.* **1** a formal expression of opinion, will or choice, in regard to the election of a candidate, the passing or rejection of a resolution, law etc., usu. signified by voice, gesture or ballot. **2** anything by which this is expressed, such as a ballot, ticket etc. **3** something which is approved by a vote, such as a grant of money. **4** the aggregate votes of a party etc. **5** the right to vote, the suffrage. *~v.i.* **1** to give one's vote (for or against). **2** to express one's allegiance, preference etc. by voting. *~v.t.* **1** to give one's vote for. **2** to enact, resolve, ratify or grant by a majority of votes. **3** to cause to be in a specified condition by voting. **4** (*coll.*) to declare by general consent. **5** (*coll.*) to suggest, propose. **to put to a/ the vote** to obtain a decision regarding (a proposal) by holding a vote. **to split the/ one's vote** SPLIT. **to vote down** to defeat or suppress by vote. **to vote in** to elect. **to vote off** to remove from (a committee etc.) by voting. **to vote out** to dismiss from office by voting. **to vote with one's feet** to indicate one's dissatisfaction with a situation or conditions by leaving. **votable** *a.* **voteless** *a.* **vote of no confidence, vote of censure** *n.* the legal method of forcing the resignation of a government or governing body or person. **voter** *n.* **1** a person entitled to vote. **2** a person who actually casts a vote. **voting** *n.* **voting machine** *n.* a machine that automatically registers and records votes cast at an election. **voting paper** *n.* a paper by means of which one votes, esp. by ballot in a parliamentary election. **voting stock** *n.* stock that entitles a shareholder to vote. [L *vōtum*, wish, vow, orig. neut. of *vōtus*, p.p. of *vōvere*, to vow]

votive (vō´tiv) *a.* **1** given, paid or dedicated in fulfilment of a vow. **2** (of a Mass etc.) being a voluntary offering, performed for some particular purpose. **votively** *adv.* [F *votif*, fem. *-ive*, L *votīvus*, from *vōtum*, see VOTE]

vouch (vowch) *v.t.* **1** to uphold or guarantee by assertion, proof etc., to confirm, to substantiate. **2** †to cite as an authority. *~v.i.* to be a surety or guarantee, to answer (for). *~†n.* warrant, attestation, testimony. **voucher** *n.* **1** a ticket, card etc. substitutable or exchangeable for goods or cash. **2** a document etc. serving to confirm or establish something, as a payment, the correctness of an account etc. **3** a person who vouches or acts as security for another. [OF *voucher*, *vocher*, L *vocāre*, to call]

vouchsafe (vowchsāf´) *v.t.* (*formal*) to condescend to grant. *~v.i.* to deign, to condescend (to). **vouchsafement** *n.*

voussoir (vooswah´) *n.* any of the wedge-shaped stones forming an arch. [F, ult. from L *volūtus*, p.p. of *volvere*, to roll]

vow (vow) *n.* **1** a solemn promise or pledge, esp. made to God or to a saint etc., undertaking an act, sacrifice, obligation etc. **2** a promise of fidelity. *~v.t.* **1** to promise solemnly. **2** to dedicate by a vow. **3** †to affirm solemnly. *~v.i.* to make a vow. **to take vows** to enter a religious order and commit oneself to the vows of chastity, poverty and obedience. **under a vow** having made a vow. [OF *vou* (F *voeu*), L *vōtum*, see VOTE]

vowel (vow´əl) *n.* **1** a sound able to make a syllable or to be sounded alone; an open and unimpeded sound as distinct from a closed, stopped or mute sound or consonant. **2** a letter representing this, esp. the simple vowels, *a, e, i, o, u*. **vowel gradation** *n.* ablaut. **vowelize, vowelise** *v.t.* to insert vowels or vowel points in. **vowelled,** (*N Am.*) **voweled** *a.* having (many) vowels. **vowelless** *a.* **vowelly** *a.* **vowel mutation** *n.* umlaut. **vowel point** *n.* any of the marks indicating the vowels in Hebrew etc. [OF *vouel*, *voiel*, L *vocālis*, VOCAL]

vox (voks) *n.* (*pl.* **voces** (vō´sēz)) a voice. **vox angelica** *n.* an organ stop with a soft tremulous tone, a voix céleste. **vox humana** (hūmah´nə) *n.* an organ stop with a tone supposedly resembling the human voice. **vox pop** *n.* (*coll.*) public attitudes or opinion as represented by comments by ordinary people; radio or TV interviews to elicit these. **vox populi** (pop´ūlī) *n.* the voice of the people, public opinion, the popular verdict. [L]

voyage (voi´ij) *n.* **1** a journey by water or air or through space, esp. to a distant place. **2** an account of such a journey. **3** †a project, an enterprise. *~v.i.* to make a voyage. *~v.t.* to travel over or through. **voyageable** *a.* **voyager** *n.* **voyageur** (vwayazhœ´) *n.* (*Can.*) **1** (*Hist.*) any of the men employed by the Hudson Bay and North West Companies to convey goods etc. between the trading posts. **2** a Canadian boatman. [OF *voiaje*, L VIATICUM]

voyeur (vwahyœ´) *n.* **1** a person who derives sexual gratification from watching sexual acts, people undressing etc. **2** an obsessive observer of the sordid or unpleasant. **voyeurism** *n.* the act or practice of a voyeur. **voyeuristic** (-ris´-) *a.* **voyeuristically** *adv.* [F, one who sees]

VP *abbr.* Vice-President.

VR *abbr.* **1** variant reading. **2** Victoria Regina (Queen Victoria). **3** virtual reality.

vraisemblance (vrāsāblās´) *n.* an appearance of truth, verisimilitude. [F *vrai*, OF *verrai*, see VERY, SEMBLANCE]

vroom (vroom) *v.i.* **1** (of an engine) to make a loud revving noise. **2** (of a vehicle) to travel at speed. *~v.t.* to rev (an engine). *~n.* the roaring sound of an engine being revved. *~int.* used to represent this sound. [imit.]

vs. *abbr.* versus.

VSO *abbr.* **1** Very Superior Old (used to indicate that port or brandy is between 12 and 17 years old). **2** Voluntary Service Overseas.

VSOP *abbr.* Very Special Old Pale (used to indicate that brandy or port is between 20 and 25 years old).

VT *abbr.* Vermont.

Vt. *abbr.* Vermont.

VTO *abbr.* vertical take-off.

VTOL (vē´tol) *abbr.* vertical take-off and landing, a system by which aircraft take off and land without taxiing.

VTR *abbr.* videotape recorder.

vug (vŭg) *n.* a small cavity in a rock or vein lined with crystals. **vuggy** *a.* **vugular** *a.* [Cornish *vooga*, cave]

vulcanian (vŭlkā´niən) *a.* **1** of or relating to a volcanic eruption that discharges gas and ash but little or no lava. **2** volcanic. **vulcanic** VOLCANIC (under VOLCANO).

vulcanism VOLCANISM (under VOLCANO).

vulcanite (vŭl´kənīt) *n.* vulcanized rubber, ebonite. **vulcanize, vulcanise** *v.t.* to treat (rubber) with sulphur at a high temperature so as to increase its strength and elasticity, producing vulcanite (the hard form) or soft and flexible rubber. **vulcanization** (-zā´shən) *n.* **vulcanology** (vŭlkənol´əji), **volcanology** (vol-) *n.* the scientific study of volcanoes. **vulcanological** (-əloj´-) *a.* **vulcanologist** *n.* [*Vulcan*, Roman god of fire and metalworking]

vulgar (vŭl´gə) *a.* **1** of, relating to or characteristic of the common people. **2** plebeian, common, coarse, low, unrefined. **3** rude, boorish. **4** ordinary, in common use. **vulgar fraction** *n.* a fraction having the numerator less than the denominator. **vulgarian** (-geə´ri-) *a.* vulgar.

~*n.* a vulgar person, esp. a rich person with low ideas, manners etc. **vulgarism** *n.* **1** a word or expression in coarse or uneducated use. **2** vulgarity. **vulgarity** (-gar´i-) *n.* (*pl.* **vulgarities**) **1** the condition of being vulgar; lack of good manners, refinement etc. **2** a vulgar action or expression. **vulgarize, vulgarise** *v.t.* **1** to debase by making vulgar or commonplace. **2** to make (a person) coarse or crude. **3** to popularize, to make more generally accessible. **vulgarization** (-zā´shən) *n.* **vulgarizer** *n.* **vulgar Latin** *n.* colloquial Latin. **vulgarly** *adv.* †**vulgarness** *n.* **vulgar tongue** *n.* the vernacular. [F *vulgaire*, L *vulgāris*, from *vulgus*, *volgus*, the common people, cp. Sansk. *vargas*, troop, Welsh *gwala*, Bret. *gwalch*, fullness, Ir. *folc*, abundance]

Vulgate (vŭl´gət) *n.* **1** the Latin translation of the Bible made by St Jerome, 383–405. **2** the official Latin text of the Bible used in the Roman Catholic Church, revised from St Jerome's version in 1592. **3** (**vulgate**) the generally recognized text of any author. **4** (**vulgate**) everyday informal speech, the vernacular. [L *vulgāta*, fem. p.p. of *vulgāre*, to make public, see VULGAR]

vulnerable (vŭl´nərəbəl) *a.* **1** capable of being wounded physically or emotionally. **2** susceptible or liable to injury, attack etc. **3** in bridge, subject to higher penalties and bonuses having won a game towards rubber. **vulnerability** (-bil´-), **vulnerableness** *n.* **vulnerary** *a.* useful in healing wounds or for the cure of external injuries. ~*n.* (*pl.* **vulneraries**) a plant, drug or composition useful in the cure of wounds. [L *vulnerābilis*, from *vulnerāre*, to wound, from *vulnus -neris*, wound, cogn. with *vellere*, to pluck, and Gr. *oulē*, wound]

Usage note Pronunciation as (vŭn´-), without the first (l), is best avoided.

vulpine (vŭl´pīn) *a.* **1** of or relating to or characteristic of a fox. **2** crafty, cunning. **vulpinism** (-pin-) *n.* [L *vulpīnus*, from *vulpes*, fox, cogn. with WOLF]

vulture (vŭl´chə) *n.* **1** a large bird of the family Accipitridae (Old World) or Cathartidae (New World) with head and neck almost naked, feeding chiefly on carrion. **2** a rapacious person. **vulturine** (-rīn), **vulturish, vulturous** *a.* [L *vultur*, perh. cogn. with *vellere* see VULNERABLE]

vulva (vŭl´və) *n.* (*pl.* **vulvas**) the external female genitals, esp. the opening of the vagina. **vulviform** (-vifawm) *a.* **vulvitis** (-vī´tis) *n.* inflammation of the vulva. **vulvo-** *comb. form.* **vulval, vulvar, vulvate** (-vət) *a.* [L, also *volva*, cogn. with *volvere*, to roll]

vv *abbr.* vice versa.

vv. *abbr.* **1** verses. **2** volumes.

VW *abbr.* **1** Very Worshipful. **2** Volkswagen.

vying VIE.

W[1] (dŭb´əlū), **w** (*pl.* **Ws, W's**) the 23rd letter of the English and other versions of the Roman alphabet, taking its form and name from the union of two V's (V and U formerly being variants of one letter and sharing the name now given to U). It is pronounced as a bilabial semivowel, as in *was, will, forward.*

W[2] *abbr.* **1** watt. **2** West. **3** Western. **4** women. **5** women's size.

W[3] *chem. symbol* tungsten. [G *Wolfram*]

w, w. *abbr.* **1** week. **2** weight. **3** white. **4** wicket. **5** wide. **6** width. **7** wife. **8** with.

WA *abbr.* **1** Washington (State). **2** West Africa. **3** Western Australia.

WAAC (wak) *abbr.* (*Hist.*) Women's Auxiliary Army Corps. ~*n.* (*also* **Waac**) a member of the Women's Auxiliary Army Corps.

WAAF (waf) *abbr.* (*Hist.*) Women's Auxiliary Air Force. ~*n.* (*also* **Waaf**) a member of the Women's Auxiliary Air Force.

wabain OUABAIN.

wabble WOBBLE.

†**wabster** (wab´stə) *n.* (*Sc.*) a weaver. [var. of WEBSTER (under WEB)]

WAC *abbr.* (*NAm.*) Women's Army Corps.

wack (wak) *n.* (*dial.*) friend (used as a term of address). [perh. from WACKER]

wacke (wak´ə) *n.* an earthy or clayey rock produced by the decomposition of igneous rocks. [G]

wacker (wak´ə) *n.* **1** (*sl.*) a Liverpudlian. **2** (*dial.*) friend (used as a term of address). [etym. uncertain]

wacko (wak´ō) *a.* (*esp. NAm., sl.*) crazy, eccentric. ~*n.* (*pl.* **wackos, wackoes**) a crazy or eccentric person. [WACKY, -O]

wacky (wak´i), **whacky** *a.* (*comp.* **wackier, whackier,** *superl.* **wackiest, whackiest**) (*sl.*) crazy, eccentric, absurd. ~*n.* (*pl.* **wackies, whackies**) a wacky person. **wackily** *adv.* **wackiness** *n.* [dial. *whacky*, left-handed, from WHACK]

wad[1] (wod) *n.* **1** a small, compact mass of some soft material, used for stopping an opening, stuffing between things etc. **2** a felt or paper disc used to keep the charge in place in a gun, cartridge etc. **3** a bundle of currency notes, documents etc. **4** (*sl.*) a bun or sandwich. **5** (*coll.*) a large amount, esp. of money. ~*v.t.* (*pres.p.* **wadding,** *past, p.p.* **wadded**) **1** to compress into a wad. **2** to stuff, line or protect with wadding. **3** to pack, stop up or secure with a wad. **wadding** *n.* **1** a soft spongy material, usu. composed of cotton or wool, used for stuffing garments, cushions etc. **2** material for gun wads. [cp. Swed. *vadd*, wadding, Icel. *vathr*, G *Watte*]

wad[2] (wod) *n.* **1** an earthy ore of manganese. **2** (*dial.*) plumbago. [etym. uncertain]

wadable WADE.

wadding WAD[1].

waddle (wod´əl) *v.i.* to walk with an ungainly rocking or swaying motion and with short, quick steps, as a duck or goose does. ~*n.* a waddling gait. **waddler** *n.* **waddlingly** *adv.* [freq. of WADE]

waddy (wod´i) *n.* (*pl.* **waddies**) **1** an Australian war club, usu. bent like a boomerang or with a thick head. **2** (*Austral., New Zeal.*) any club or stick. ~*v.t.* (*3rd pers. sing. pres.* **waddies,** *pres.p.* **waddying,** *past, p.p.* **waddied**) to hit with a waddy. [Austral. Abor.]

wade (wād) *v.i.* **1** to walk through water or a semi-fluid medium, such as snow, mud etc. **2** to make one's way with difficulty and labour. ~*v.t.* **1** to pass through or across by wading. **2** to ford (a stream) on foot. **to wade in/ into** (*coll.*) to tackle or attack vigorously. **to wade through** to read (a book etc.) with difficulty or effort. **wadable, wadeable** *a.* **wader** *n.* **1** a person who wades. **2** (*usu. pl.*) a high, waterproof boot or trouser-like garment, worn by anglers etc. for wading. **3** a wading bird. **wading bird** *n.* any long-legged bird that wades, esp. one of the order Ciconiiformes, including the storks, herons etc. [OE *wadan* (cp. Dut. *waden*, G *waten*, Icel. *vatha*, also L *vādere*, to go, *vādum*, a ford)]

wadi (wod´i), **wady** *n.* (*pl.* **wadis, wadies**) the valley or channel of a stream that is dry except in the rainy season. [Arab.]

WAF (waf) *abbr.* (*NAm.*) Women in the Air Force. ~*n.* a member of the WAF.

w.a.f. *abbr.* with all faults.

wafer (wā´fə) *n.* **1** a small, thin, sweet biscuit, esp. one eaten with ice cream. **2** a thin disc of unleavened bread used in the Eucharist, the Host. **3** a thin disc of adhesive paper or dried paste used for sealing letters, fastening documents etc. **4** in electronics, a thin disc of silicon or other semiconductor material on which integrated circuits are formed before being cut into individual chips. ~*v.t.* to seal or attach with a wafer. **wafer-thin** *a.* very thin. ~*adv.* very thinly. **wafery** *a.* [ME and A-F *wafre*, OF *waufre* (usu. *gaufre*, GOFER[2]), from LG (cp. Walloon *wafe, wauffe*, G *Waffel*, Dut. *wafel*, a wafer, also G *Wabe*, a honeycomb), cogn. with WEAVE[1]]

waffle[1] (wof´əl) *n.* a thin batter cake baked in a waffle-iron. **waffle-iron** *n.* a utensil with hinged plates for baking waffles. [Dut., see WAFER]

waffle[2] (wof´əl) *v.i.* **1** (*coll.*) to talk or write aimlessly and at length. **2** (*coll.*) to waver. **3** (*dial.*) to wave. ~*n.* (*coll.*) vague or inconsequential talk or writing. **waffler** *n.* **waffly** *a.* [orig. dial., freq. of *waff*, to yelp]

waft (wahft, woft) *v.t.* **1** to carry or convey through the air. **2** to carry lightly or gently along. ~*v.i.* to float or be borne on the air. ~*n.* **1** an act of wafting. **2** a breath or whiff of odour etc. **3** (*Naut.*) (*also* **weft**) an ensign or signal flag hoisted rolled or knotted, esp. as a distress signal. **waftage** (-ij) *n.* **1** the act of wafting. **2** conveyance by wafting. **wafter** *n.* [obs. *wafter*, a convoy ship, from Dut. or LG *wachter*, a guard]

wag[1] (wag) *v.t.* (*pres.p.* **wagging,** *past, p.p.* **wagged**) **1** to shake up and down or backwards and forwards lightly and quickly, esp. in playfulness, reproof etc. **2** to move (the tongue etc.) in chatter or gossip. ~*v.i.* **1** to move up and down or to and fro, to oscillate. **2** (of the tongue etc.) to move in chatter or gossip. **3** †to move on, to keep going, to proceed. ~*n.* an act or a motion of wagging, a shake. **the tail wags the dog** the least important member or group in a society, organization etc. has control over the most important. [ME *waggen*, MSwed. *wagga* (cp. Norw. *vagga*, OE *wagian*, from *wegan*, to carry), cogn. with WAGON, WEIGH and L *vehere*, to carry]

wag[2] (wag) *n.* **1** a facetious person, a wit, a joker. **2** (*sl.*) a truant. **waggery** *n.* jocularity, playful merriment, practical joking. **waggish** *a.* **waggishly** *adv.* **waggishness**

n. [perh. short for obs. *waghalter*, a person likely to be hanged]

wage (wāj) *n.* **1** (*often pl.*) payment for work done or services rendered, esp. fixed periodical pay for labour of a manual kind. **2** (*usu. pl.*) recompense, reward, requital. **3** (*pl.*) in economics, the part of the national income that accrues to labour rather than to capital. ~*v.t.* **1** to engage in, to carry on (a battle, war etc.). **2** †to wager. **3** †to engage, to employ for wages, to hire. **wage bill** *n.* the total amount paid to employees. **wage claim** *n.* a pay claim. **waged** (wājd) *a.* earning a wage. **wage earner** *n.* **1** a person who earns a wage, esp. as opposed to a salary. **2** a person who earns money to support a household. **wage-earning** *a.* **wage freeze** *n.* the fixing of a wage level for a prolonged period. **wage fund, wages fund** *n.* the portion of the capital of a community expended in paying the wages of labour. **wageless** *a.* **wages council** *n.* a body of employers' and workers' representatives that determines wage levels in an industry. **wage slave** *n.* (*coll. or iron.*) a person dependent on a wage or salary. [OF, also *gage*, *guage*, from *wager*, *gager*, GAGE[1]]

wager (wā´jə) *n.* **1** something staked or hazarded on the outcome of a contest etc., a bet. **2** an act or instance of betting. **3** something on which bets are laid. ~*v.t.*, *v.i.* to bet. **wagerer** *n.* **wager of battle** *n.* TRIAL BY BATTLE (under TRIAL). **wager of law** *n.* (*Hist.*) a trial in which a number of witnesses declared the innocence of the defendant on oath. [ME *wageoure*, OF *wageure*, *gageure*, low L *wadiātūra*, from *wadiāre*, to pledge, as WAGE]

waggery, waggish etc. WAG[2].

waggle (wag´əl) *v.t.*, *v.i.* (*coll.*) to wag or swing to and fro, esp. quickly and frequently. ~*n.* a short, quick wagging motion. **waggly** *a.* **1** waggling. **2** unsteady. [freq. of WAG[1]]

waggon WAGON.

Wagnerian (vahgniə´riən) *a.* of, relating to or in the style of Wagner's music or operas. ~*n.* an admirer or follower of Wagner or his music. **Wagnerianism** *n.* **Wagnerism** (vahg´nərizm) *n.* **Wagnerist** (vahg´-) *n.* **Wagner tuba** (vahg´-) *n.* a brass instrument with a sound between that of a tuba and that of a French horn. [Richard *Wagner*, 1813–83, German composer]

wagon (wag´ən), **waggon** *n.* **1** a strong four-wheeled vehicle for the transport of heavy loads, usu. with a rectangular body, often with a removable cover, usu. drawn by two or more horses. **2** a railway truck, esp. an open one. **3** a tea trolley. **4** WATER WAGON (under WATER). **5** (*coll.*) a car, esp. an estate car. **6** †a chariot. **off the wagon** (*coll.*) no longer abstaining from alcohol, off the water wagon. **on the wagon** (*coll.*) abstaining from alcohol, on the water wagon. **wagoner** *n.* a person who drives or leads a wagon. **wagonette** (-net´) *n.* (*esp. Hist.*) a four-wheeled horse-drawn pleasure carriage of light construction, for six or eight people on seats facing each other, often with a removable cover. **wagonful** *n.* (*pl.* **wagonfuls**). **wagonload** *n.* **wagon-roof, wagon-vault** *n.* a semicylindrical ceiling, a barrel vault. **wagon train** *n.* a column of horse-drawn wagons carrying supplies, pioneer settlers etc. [Dut. *wagen*, cogn. with WAIN]

wagon-lit (vagōlē´) *n.* (*pl.* **wagons-lits** (vagōlē´), **wagon-lits** (-lēz´)) a sleeping car on a Continental train. [F *wagon*, railway car, *lit*, bed]

wagtail (wag´tāl) *n.* any of various small, long-tailed birds, chiefly of the genus *Motacilla* (from the wagging of their tails).

Wahabi (wəhah´bi), **Wahhabi** *n.* (*pl.* **Wahabis, Wahhabis**) a member of a sect founded about the middle of the 18th cent. cultivating a strict form of Islam. **Wahabiism, Wahabism** *n.* [Abd-el-*Wahhab*, 1691–1787, the founder]

wahine (wah·hē´ni) *n.* a Maori or Polynesian woman. [Maori]

wahoo[1] (wah·hoo´), **wahoo elm** *n.* (*N Am.*) a N American elm, *Ulmus alata*, also called *winged elm*. [Creek *ŭhawhu*, cork elm]

wahoo[2] (wah·hoo´) *n.* (*N Am.*) a N American shrub or small tree, *Euonymus atropurpureus*. [Dakota *wāhu*, arrow-wood]

wahoo[3] (wah·hoo´) *n.* (*N Am.*) a fast-swimming food fish, *Acanthocybium solanderi*, of tropical seas. [etym. unknown]

wahoo[4] (wah·hoo´) *int.* (*N Am.*) used to express exultation, excitement etc. [instinctive sound]

wah-wah (wah´wah), **wa-wa** *n.* (*Mus.*) **1** the sound made by alternately covering and uncovering the bell of a brass instrument. **2** a similar effect produced electronically on an electric guitar. [imit.]

waif (wāf) *n.* **1** a homeless wanderer, esp. a forsaken child. **2** any person or thing found astray, ownerless or cast up by or adrift on the sea. **waifish** *a.* **waiflike** *a.* **waifs and strays** *n.pl.* **1** homeless or forsaken children. **2** odds and ends. [OF, from Norse (cp. Icel. *veif*, anything flapping about), cogn. with WAIVE]

wail (wāl) ~*v.i.* **1** to lament. **2** to utter wails. **3** (of the wind etc.) to make a plaintive sound. *v.t.* (*poet.*) to lament loudly over, to bewail. ~*n.* **1** a loud, high-pitched lamentation, a plaintive cry. **2** a sound like this. **wailer** *n.* **wailful** *a.* **wailing** *n.*, *a.* **wailingly** *adv.* **Wailing Wall** *n.* a wall in Jerusalem, a remnant of an ancient temple, held sacred by the Jews as a place of worship and lamentation. [ME *weilen*, Icel. *væla*, from *væ*, WOE]

wain (wān) *n.* **1** (*poet.*) a four-wheeled vehicle for the transportation of goods, a wagon. **2** (**the Wain**) CHARLES'S WAIN. **3** †a chariot. **wainwright** *n.* a person who makes wagons. [OE *wægn*, cp. Dut., G *Wagen*, Icel., Swed. *vagn*, L *vehiculum*, Sansk. *vahana-*, VEHICLE, Gr. *ochos*, car]

wainscot (wān´skət) *n.* **1** a wooden, usu. panelled, lining or casing of the walls of a room. **2** the lower part of the walls of a room when lined or finished differently from the upper part. **3** (*Hist.*) fine-grade oak for wainscot panelling etc. ~*v.t.* (*pres.p.* **wainscoting, wainscotting**, *past*, *p.p.* **wainscoted, wainscotted**) to line with a wainscot. **wainscoting, wainscotting** *n.* **1** a wainscot or wainscots. **2** material for this. [Dut. *wagenschot*, a grained oak wood, perh. MDut. *waeghe*, wave (cp. OE *wæg*, *schot*, a partition, a wainscot), prob. cogn. with SHOT[1], SHOT[2]]

waist (wāst) *n.* **1** the part of the human body below the ribs or thorax and above the hips. **2** this part as normally narrower than the rest of the trunk. **3** the circumference of this. **4** the part of a garment encircling the waist. **5** the constriction between the abdomen and thorax of a wasp etc. **6** the middle part of an object, such as an aircraft fuselage, esp. if more contracted than the other parts. **7** the part of a ship between the quarterdeck and the forecastle. **8** (*N Am.*) a blouse. **waistband** *n.* a band worn round the waist, esp. a strip of fabric forming the upper part of a skirt, trousers etc. **waist-cloth** *n.* a loincloth. **waistcoat** (wāst´kōt, wās´kōt, wes´kət) *n.* a short garment, usu. without sleeves or collar, extending from the neck to the waist. **waist-deep, waist-high** *a.*, *adv.* **1** as deep or high as the waist. **2** in as far as the waist. **waisted** *a.* (*also in comb.*). **waistless** *a.* **waistline** *n.* **1** the size or outline of a person's waist. **2** the waist of a dress etc., not necessarily corresponding with the wearer's natural waist (*a low waistline*). [ME *wast*, cogn. with WAX[2] (cp. OE *wæstm*, growth)]

wait (wāt) *v.i.* **1** to remain inactive or in the same place until some event or time for action, to stay. **2** to be in a state of expectation or readiness (for). **3** to be on the watch (for). **4** to be ready or in a fit state for use etc. **5** to wait at table. **6** to be postponed or delayed (*Can it wait?*). ~*v.t.* **1** to wait for, to await, to bide (*to wait one's turn*). **2** to postpone, to defer, to delay. ~*n.* **1** the act of waiting. **2** a period of waiting. **3** watching, ambush. **4** (*pl.*) †a band of singers and players performing carols etc. in the streets, esp. at Christmas. **I can't wait** I am impatient (to). **to lie in wait (for)** LIE². **to wait and see** to wait patiently for some future event. **to wait at table** to act as a waiter in a hotel, restaurant etc. **to wait on table** (*N Am.*) to wait at table. **to wait on/ upon** **1** to attend on as a waiter or servant. **2** to pay a visit to deferentially. **3** to await. **4** (of consequences etc.) to follow. **to wait up** to remain out of bed waiting (for). **wait a minute** MINUTE¹. **wait for it!** **1** do not begin too soon. **2** used to introduce an unexpected remark, a punchline etc. **wait on!** be patient!, wait! **you wait!** used to threaten or warn. **waiter** *n.* **1** a person who waits. **2** an attendant on guests at a table in a restaurant etc. **3** a dumb waiter. **4** a tray for dishes etc. **waiting** *n.* **1** parking for a short time at the side of a road (*no waiting*). **2** official attendance at court. **3** the act of a person who waits. ~*a.* that waits. **in waiting** in attendance, esp. on the sovereign. **waiting game** *n.* a holding back of action in the hope of more advantageous circumstances later (*to play a waiting game*). **waiting list** *n.* a list of people waiting for a vacancy, treatment etc. **waiting room** *n.* a room at a railway station, doctor's surgery etc., where people can rest while waiting. **waitperson** *n.* (*esp. N Am.*) a waiter or waitress. **waitress** (-ris) *n.* a female waiter in a restaurant etc. **waitressing** *n.* the occupation or work of a waitress. [OF *waiter*, *gaiter* (F *guetter*), from *waite*, *gaite*, OHG *wahta*, guard, watch (cp. G *Wacht*, cogn. with WAKE¹]

waive (wāv) *v.t.* **1** to forgo, to relinquish, to refrain from using, insisting on etc. (*to waive the rules*). **2** to defer, to postpone. **waiver** *n.* (*Law*) **1** the act of waiving a claim, a right etc. **2** a written statement of this. [A-F *weiver*, OF *gaiver*, prob. from Icel. *veifa*, to vibrate, to swing about]

Usage note The spellings of the verbs *waive* (to forgo) and *wave* (to move to and fro) should not be confused (as is especially easily done in *wave aside*, which means something similar to *waive*). *Waiver*, the noun from *waive*, should also be distinguished from the unrelated verb *waver*.

wake¹ (wāk) *v.i.* (*past* **woke** (wōk), **waked**, *p.p.* **woken** (wō´kən), **waked**) **1** to be aroused from sleep, to cease to sleep. **2** to revive from a trance, death etc. **3** to be awake, to be unable to sleep. **4** to be roused or to rouse oneself from inaction, inattention etc. (*He must wake up to his responsibilities*). ~*v.t.* **1** to rouse from sleep, to awake. **2** to revive, to resuscitate, to raise from the dead. **3** to arouse, to stir (up), to excite, to alert. **4** to break the silence of, to disturb. **5** to hold a wake over. ~*n.* **1** a vigil. **2** the watching of a dead body, prior to burial, by friends and neighbours of the deceased, with lamentations often followed by a merrymaking. **3** the feast of the dedication of a church, formerly kept by watching all night. **4** merrymaking or festivities held in connection with this. **5** (*usu. pl.*) an annual holiday, esp. in the industrial towns of northern England. **to be a wake-up** (*Austral., coll.*) to be alert (to). **wakeful** *a.* **1** not disposed or unable to sleep, restless. **2** (of a night) passed without sleep, disturbed. **3** watchful, alert. **wakefully** *adv.* **wakefulness** *n.* **waker** *n.* **wake-robin** *n.* **1** an arum, esp. *Arum maculatum*, the cuckoo pint. **2** (*N Am.*) any plant of the genus *Trillium*. **wakey-wakey** *int.* used to rouse a person from sleep, inattention etc. **waking** *a.* awake. **waking dream** *n.* a waking experience of involuntary vision; a hallucination. [OE *wacan*, to arise, to be born, and *wacian*, to wake, to watch (cp. Dut. *waken*, G *wachen*, Icel. *vaka*, Goth. *wakan*), cogn. with VIGIL]

wake² (wāk) *n.* **1** the track left by a vessel passing through water. **2** the track or path left after something has passed. **in the wake of** following. [Icel. *vökr*, pl. *vaker*, a hole, an opening in ice (cp. Dut. *wak*, moist), cogn. with Gr. *hugros*, L *humidus*, HUMID]

waken (wā´kən) *v.t.* **1** to rouse from sleep. **2** to rouse to action etc. **3** to call forth. ~*v.i.* to wake, to cease from sleeping. **wakener** *n.* [OE *wæcnan*, to arise, to be born, from *wacan*, WAKE¹]

waker, waking WAKE¹.

Walach WALLACH.

Waldenses (wolden´sēz) *n.pl.* a religious sect founded in S France about 1170 by Peter Waldo, in a reform movement leading to persecution by the Church. **Waldensian** *a., n.*

waldgrave (wawld´grāv) *n.* (*Hist.*) a German title of nobility, orig. a head forester. [G *Waldgraf* (*Wald*, WOLD, forest, GRAVE¹)]

wale (wāl) *n.* **1** a ridge on the skin, a weal. **2** a ridge on the surface of cloth, such as corduroy. **3** a wide plank extending along a ship's side. **4** a strong band around a woven basket. ~*v.t.* **1** to mark with a wale or wales. **2** to provide with a wale or wales. **wale-knot** *n.* a knot at the end of a rope, made by weaving the strands together. [OE *walu*, WEAL¹]

waler (wā´lə) *n.* (*Austral.*) a riding horse (orig. as supplied by military authorities in New South Wales).

Walhalla VALHALLA.

walk (wawk) *v.i.* **1** to go along by raising, advancing and setting down each foot alternately, never having both feet off the ground at once. **2** (of a quadruped) to go along with a slow gait keeping at least two feet on the ground at any time. **3** to go at the ordinary pace, not to run, not to go or proceed rapidly. **4** to go or travel on foot. **5** (of a ghost) to move about or become visible. **6** (*sl.*) to depart, to be off, to be dismissed or released. **7** (of a batsman in cricket) to leave the wicket before being declared out. **8** in baseball, to go to first base after not hitting four illegally pitched balls. **9** (*sl.*) to be stolen, to go missing. **10** †to act, conduct oneself or live in a specified way. ~*v.t.* **1** to walk over, on or through, to perambulate, to tread. **2** to cause to walk; to lead, drive or ride at a walking pace (*to walk a dog*). **3** to accompany on foot. **4** to move (an object) by alternately lifting one side then the other. **5** in baseball, to allow to walk. ~*n.* **1** the act of walking. **2** the pace, gait or step of a person or animal that walks. **3** a distance walked (*five minutes' walk from the station*). **4** an act of walking for pleasure, exercise etc. (*to go for a walk*; *a sponsored walk*). **5** the route chosen for this. **6** a piece of ground laid out for walking, a footpath, a promenade etc. **7** the district or round of a hawker, postman etc. **8** a piece of ground where an animal is kept, pastured etc. **9** (*also* **walk of life**) one's profession, occupation, sphere of action etc. **10** the part of a forest controlled by a keeper. **in a walk** easily, without effort. **to walk about** to stroll around. **to walk all over** **1** (*coll.*) to defeat easily or conclusively. **2** (*coll.*) to take advantage of. **to walk away from** **1** to go much faster than, esp. in a race. **2** to refuse to deal with (*to walk away from one's responsibilities*). **3** to survive without serious injury (*to walk away from an accident*). **to walk away with** to win or gain easily. **to walk in** to enter. **to walk in on** to interrupt. **to walk into** **1** to enter or encounter unwittingly (*to walk into a trap*). **2** to gain easily (*to walk into a job*). **to walk it** **1** to go on foot. **2** (*coll.*) to win or achieve something without effort. **to walk Matilda** MATILDA. **to walk off** **1** to depart abruptly. **2** to get rid of by walking (*to walk off one's depression*). **3** to get rid of the effects of (a meal etc.) by walking. **to walk off with** **1** (*coll.*) to carry off, to steal. **2** to walk away with.

to walk on air AIR. **to walk one's chalks** CHALK. **to walk out** to depart suddenly, esp. in anger. **to walk out on** to abandon. **to walk out with** (*dated*) to go courting with. **to walk over 1** (*coll.*) to walk all over. **2** to walk or go slowly over (a racecourse etc.) because one is the only competitor, or because one's opponents are weak. **to walk someone off their feet** to make a person walk so far or so fast that they are exhausted. **to walk tall** (*coll.*) to feel proud. **to walk the boards** to be an actor. **to walk the chalk** CHALK. **to walk the hospitals** to walk the wards. **to walk the plank** PLANK. **to walk the streets 1** to be a prostitute. **2** to wander round a town or city, esp. in search of work, accommodation etc. **to walk the wards** to be a medical student in a hospital. **to walk up to** to approach. **walk up!** used to invite spectators to a circus etc. **walkable** *a.* **walkabout** *n.* **1** a wandering journey in the bush by Australian Aborigines. **2** an informal walk to meet the public by a politician, member of royalty etc. **to go walkabout** to go on a walkabout. **walkathon** *n.* a long-distance walk to raise funds for charity. **walker** *n.* **1** a person who walks, esp. for pleasure, exercise etc. **2** a bird that steps instead of hopping. **3** a frame for supporting a baby, disabled person etc. when walking. **4** a shopwalker. **walkies** *int.* used to call a dog for a walk. ~*n.pl.* (*coll. or facet.*) a walk, esp. with a dog. **to go walkies 1** (*coll. or facet.*) to go for a walk. **2** (*coll. or facet.*) to disappear, to go missing. **walkie-talkie** (-taw´ki) *n.* a portable combined transmitter and receiver. **walk-in** *a.* (of a wardrobe etc.) large enough to walk into and move around in. **walking** *n.*, *a.* **within walking distance** close enough to walk to. **walking delegate** *n.* an agent or official of a trade union who visits members and their employers for negotiation etc. **walking dictionary, walking encyclopedia** *n.* (*coll.*) a person with a wide range of knowledge. **walking fern** *n.* any N American fern of the genus *Camptosorus*, with fronds that take root when their tips touch the ground. **walking frame** *n.* a frame for supporting a disabled person when walking. **walking gentleman, walking lady** *n.* an actor taking a subordinate role, esp. as an extra. **walking leaf** *n.* **1** a walking fern. **2** an insect mimicking a leaf. **walking-on part** *n.* a walk-on part. **walking papers** *n.pl.* (*coll.*) notice of dismissal (*to give someone their walking papers*). **walking shoe** *n.* a strong shoe suitable for walking a long distance. **walking stick** *n.* **1** a stick carried in walking, esp. for support. **2** a stick insect. **walking tour** *n.* a holiday on foot in a particular area (*a walking tour of the Highlands*). **walking wounded** *n.* (*pl.* **walking wounded**) **1** (*usu. pl.*) an injured person who is able to walk. **2** (*coll.*) a person with mental or emotional problems. **Walkman®** *n.* (*pl.* **Walkmans, Walkmen**) a small portable stereo with headphones. **walk-on** *n.* **1** a walk-on part. **2** an actor playing such a part. **walk-on part** *n.* a small, non-speaking part in a play etc. **walkout** *n.* a sudden departure in anger, esp. of workers. **walkover** *n.* an easy victory. **walk-up** *n.* (*N Am.*) a building with no lift for access to upper floors. ~*a.* denoting such a building (*a walk-up apartment block*). **walkway** *n.* **1** a path etc. for pedestrian use only. **2** a place for walking, a walk. **3** a passage connecting buildings. [OE *wealcan*, to roll, to toss about, to rove (cp. Dut. *walken*, to press hats, G *walken*, to full, Icel. *vālka*, *volka*, to roll, Dan. *valke*, to full), cogn. with WALLOW]

Walkyrie VALKYRIE.

wall (wawl) *n.* **1** a continuous structure of stone, brick etc. forming an enclosure, a side or internal partition of a building etc. **2** the inner or outer surface of this (*to paper the walls of a room*). **3** (*usu. pl.*) a rampart, a fortification. **4** anything resembling a wall, such as a cliff, a mountain range etc. **5** the enclosing sides of a vessel, cavity etc. (*the cell wall*). **6** a defence or obstacle (*a wall of silence*). ~*v.t.* **1** to enclose, surround or defend with a wall. **2** to separate or divide with a wall. **3** to block (up) or seal (off) with a wall. **off the wall** eccentric, unexpected. **to go to the wall 1** to be defeated in a contest. **2** to be pushed aside. **3** to fail. **to have one's back to the wall** to be in a desperate position. **up the wall** (*coll.*) in or into a state of distraction or exasperation (*to go up the wall*; *This work is driving me up the wall*). **walls have ears** beware of eavesdroppers. **wall-barley** *n.* wild barley growing as a weed. **wall bars** *n.pl.* a set of parallel horizontal bars fixed to a wall, used for gymnastics. **wallboard** *n.* **1** a type of thin board used to cover walls and ceilings. **2** a piece of this board. **wallchart** *n.* a chart designed to be displayed on a wall as a source of information etc. **wallcovering** *n.* any material used to cover interior walls, such as wallpaper. **wall creeper** *n.* a songbird, *Tichodroma muraria*, frequenting walls and cliffs. **wall cress** *n.* any plant of the genus *Arabis* growing in crevices. **walled** *a.* **wall fern** *n.* an evergreen fern, *Polypodium vulgare*. **wallflower** *n.* **1** any of various sweet-smelling plants of the genera *Cheiranthus* or *Erysimum*, esp. *E. cheiri*, with yellow, brown and crimson flowers. **2** (*coll.*) a person who is excluded from the main social activity, esp. a woman without a partner at a dance. **wall-fruit** *n.* fruit grown on trees trained against walls. **wall game** *n.* a kind of football played only at Eton. **wall hanging** *n.* a large tapestry or other textile used to decorate an interior wall. **wall-hung** *a.* wall-mounted. **walling** *n.* **wall-knot** *n.* WALE-KNOT (under WALE). **wall-less** *a.* **wall-mounted** *a.* attached to a wall, esp. by a bracket or brackets. **wall painting** *n.* a picture painted on a wall, a mural or fresco. **wallpaper** *n.* **1** paper, usu. with decorative patterns or texture, for pasting on the walls of rooms. **2** (*often derog.*) bland background music etc. ~*v.t.* to cover or decorate with wallpaper. **wall pennywort** *n.* a type of pennywort, *Umbilicus rupestris*, which grows in crevices. **wall pepper** *n.* a type of stonecrop, *Sedum acre*. **wall-plate** *n.* a piece of timber let into a wall as a bearing for the ends of the joists etc. **wall rocket** *n.* a yellow-flowered plant, *Diplotaxis muralis*, which grows as a weed on old walls etc. **wall rue** *n.* a small evergreen fern, *Asplenium ruta-muraria*, growing on walls, cliffs etc. **wall space** *n.* space on the surface of a wall to hang a picture, mount a cupboard etc. **Wall Street** *n.* the New York Stock Exchange and money market. **wall-to-wall** *a.* **1** (of carpet etc.) covering all the floor. **2** (*coll.*) continuous, non-stop. [OE *weal*, L VALLUM]

wallaby (wol´əbi) *n.* (*pl.* **wallabies**) **1** a marsupial of the family Macropodidae, similar to but smaller than the kangaroo. **2** (*coll.*) (**Wallabies**) the international Rugby Union team of Australia. **on the wallaby (track)** (*Austral., sl.*) tramping about looking for work etc. [Austral. Abor.]

Wallach (wol´ək, wah´lok), **Walach** *n.* a Wallachian or Vlach, a Romance-speaking inhabitant of Romania. **Wallachian** (-lā´-) *a.* of or relating to Wallachia, now part of Romania. ~*n.* **1** a native or inhabitant of Wallachia. **2** the language of Wallachia. [G, from OHG *walh*, foreigner, cogn. with WELSH]

wallah (wol´ə), **walla** *n.* (*coll.*) **1** (*often in comb.*) an agent, worker or any person concerned with a usu. specified thing (*You'd better ask the computer wallah*). **2** (*sometimes derog.*) a person, a fellow. [Hind. *-wālā*, -ER[1]]

wallaroo (woləroo´) *n.* (*pl.* **wallaroos**) a large species of kangaroo, *Macropus robustus*. [Austral. Abor.]

wallet (wol´it) *n.* **1** a small case for carrying paper money, credit cards etc. **2** a folder for papers, documents etc. **3** a bag or sack for carrying necessaries for a journey or march, esp. a pilgrim's or beggar's pack. [ME *walet*, prob. of Gmc. orig.]

wall-eye (wawl´ī) *n.* **1** a condition of the eye characterized by opacity of the cornea. **2** an eye with a very light-coloured iris, esp. due to this. **3** an eye that squints outwards. **4** a fish with large, glaring eyes, esp. the wall-eyed pike. **wall-eyed** *a.* **wall-eyed pike** *n.* a N American perch, *Stizostedion vitreum*, with large, glaring eyes. [from *wall-eyed*, ME *wald-eyed*, ON *vald-eygthr* (*vagl*, beam, *eygthr*, eyed, from *auga*, eye)]

Walloon (wəloon´) *n.* **1** a member of a French-speaking people in SE Belgium and the adjoining parts of France. **2** their language. *~a.* of or relating to the Walloons or their language. [OF *Wallon*, L *Gallus*, GAUL]

wallop (wol´əp) *v.t.* (*pres.p.* **walloping,** *past*, *p.p.* **walloped**) (*coll.*) **1** to thrash, to flog. **2** to defeat or beat decisively. *~v.i.* **1** to boil with a noisy bubbling and rolling motion. **2** (*dial.*) to move along in a clumsy tumbling fashion, to waddle. *~n.* **1** (*coll.*) a blow, a punch. **2** (*coll.*) forceful impact, power. **3** (*sl.*) beer. **walloper** *n.* **1** a person or thing that wallops. **2** (*Austral., sl.*) a police officer. **walloping** *n.* (*coll.*) a thrashing. *~a.* big, thumping, whopping. [OF *waloper*, var. of *galoper*, see GALLOP]

wallow (wol´ō) *v.i.* **1** to roll or tumble about in mud, water etc. **2** to revel grossly or self-indulgently (in) (*to wallow in self-pity*). *~n.* **1** the act of wallowing. **2** a mudhole or other place in which animals wallow. **wallower** *n.* [OE *wealwian*, cogn. with L *volvere*]

wally (wol´i) *n.* (*pl.* **wallies**) (*sl.*) an incompetent or stupid person. [etym. uncertain, perh. short for Sc. *wallydrag*, a feeble creature, or for *Walter*]

walnut (wawl´nŭt) *n.* **1** a tree of the genus *Juglans*, esp. *J. regia*, bearing a nut enclosed in a green fleshy covering. **2** the unripe fruit of this used for pickling. **3** the ripe nut. **4** the timber of this or other species of the same genus used in cabinetmaking etc. [ME *walnote*, OE *wealh*, foreign (cp. WELSH), NUT]

Usage note Pronunciation as (waw´nŭt), without the (l), is best avoided.

Walpurgis night (valpuə´gis) *n.* the eve of 1 May, when witches are supposed to hold revels and dance with the Devil, esp. on the Brocken mountain in Germany. [*Walpurgis* or *Walpurga*, English nun who founded religious houses in Germany, *c.* 754–79]

walrus (wawl´rəs, wol´-) *n.* (*pl.* **walruses**) a large, amphibious, long-tusked, seal-like mammal of the Arctic seas, *Odobenus rosmarus*. **walrus moustache,** (*N Am.*) **walrus mustache** *n.* a thick moustache with long drooping ends. [Dut., from Scand. (cp. Swed. *vallros*, Dan. *hvalros*, Icel. *hross-hvalr*, OE *horshwæl*, horse-whale)]

Usage note Pronunciation as (waw´rŭs) without the (l) is best avoided.

waltz (wawlts, wawls, wols) *n.* **1** a dance in triple time in which the partners pass round each other smoothly as they progress. **2** the music for such a dance. *~v.i.* **1** to dance a waltz. **2** (*coll.*) to move quickly, confidently or casually (*She waltzed in and announced she was leaving*). *~v.t.* to move (a person) in or as in a waltz (*He waltzed her across the floor*). **to waltz Matilda** MATILDA. **to waltz off with** **1** to take quickly or casually; to steal. **2** to win, esp. easily. **waltzer** *n.* **1** a person who waltzes. **2** a type of fairground ride with spinning cars. [G *Walzer*, from *walzen*, to revolve, to waltz, cogn. with OE *wealtan*, WELTER[1]]

wampum (wom´pəm) *n.* small beads made of shells, used by N American Indians formerly as money, or for decorating belts, bracelets etc. [Algonquian *wampumpeag* (*wap*, white, *-umpe*, string, pl. suf. *-ag*)]

WAN *abbr.* **1** (*Comput.*) wide area network. **2** (West Africa) Nigeria (IVR).

wan (won) *a.* (*comp.* **wanner,** *superl.* **wannest**) **1** pale or sickly in hue, pallid. **2** lacking vigour or liveliness, worn. **3** (of light etc.) dim, faint. **4** †sombre, gloomy. **wanly** *adv.* **wanness** *n.* **wannish** *a.* **wanny** *a.* [OE *wann*, *wonn*, dark, black, etym. uncertain]

wand (wond) *n.* **1** a long, slender rod, esp. one used by conjurers or as a staff of office. **2** (*coll.*) a conductor's baton. **3** a light-pen used for reading bar codes. [Icel. *vöndr*, gen. *vandar*, prob. cogn. with WIND[2]]

wander (won´də) *v.i.* **1** to travel or go here and there without any definite route or object, to rove, ramble or roam. **2** to follow an irregular or winding course. **3** to lose one's way, to go astray. **4** to deviate from the right or proper course. **5** to talk or think incoherently or senselessly, to be delirious. **6** to digress from the subject in hand. *~v.t.* to wander over, to traverse in a random way. **wanderer** *n.* **wandering** *n.*, *a.* **wandering albatross** *n.* a large albatross, *Diomedea exulans*, having white plumage with black-tipped wings. **wandering Jew** *n.* **1** a legendary character condemned, for an insult to Christ, to wander from place to place until the Day of Judgement. **2** any of various trailing or climbing plants, esp. *Tradescantia albiflora* or *Zebrina pendula*. **wanderingly** *adv.* **wandering sailor** *n.* the moneywort, *Lysimachia nummularia*. **wanderlust** *n.* the desire to travel. **wanderment** *n.* **wander plug** *n.* a plug that can be inserted into any of a number of sockets on an electrical device. [OE *wandrian*, freq. of *wendan*, WEND]

wanderoo (wondəroo´), **wanderu** *n.* (*pl.* **wanderoos, wanderus**) **1** a macaque, *Macaca silenus*, with a large greyish beard, of India and Sri Lanka. **2** the hanuman, *Presbytis entellus*. [Sinhalese *wanderu*]

wandoo (won´doo) *n.* a white eucalyptus tree, *Eucalyptus redunca*, of W Australia. [Austral. Abor.]

wane (wān) *v.i.* **1** (of the illuminated portion of the moon) to diminish in size and brilliance. **2** to decrease in power, strength etc., to decline. *~n.* **1** the act or process of waning, decrease, diminution. **2** the period when the moon wanes. **3** a defective edge or corner on timber. **on the wane** waning. **waney** *a.* having defective corners. [OE *wanian*, from *wan*, wanting, deficient (cp. Icel. *vane*, to diminish, see WANT, WANTON)]

wangle (wang´gəl) *v.t.* (*coll.*) **1** to achieve or gain by devious means (*She wangled herself a pay rise*). **2** to falsify (accounts etc.). **3** to manipulate, to employ cunningly. *~n.* the act or an instance of wangling. **wangler** *n.* [etym. uncertain]

wank (wangk) *v.i.*, *v.t.* (*taboo sl.*) to masturbate. *~n.* an instance of masturbating. **wanker** *n.* **1** a person who masturbates. **2** a worthless, incompetent or contemptible person. **wanky** *a.* (*comp.* **wankier,** *superl.* **wankiest**). [etym. unknown]

Wankel engine (wang´kəl, vang´-) *n.* a type of internal-combustion engine in which a curved, triangular piston rotates in an elliptical combustion chamber. [Felix *Wankel*, 1902–88, German engineer]

wanna (won´ə) *contr.* (*coll.*) **1** want to (*I wanna go home*). **2** want a (*I wanna drink*).

wannabe (won´əbē), **wannabee** *n.* (*sl.*) a person anxious to be like somebody, esp. a famous person, or to become something. [*want to be*]

want (wont) *n.* **1** the state or condition of not having, lack, deficiency, absence (of). **2** need, privation, penury, poverty. **3** a longing or desire for something that is necessary or required for happiness etc. **4** something so desired. *~v.t.* **1** to wish, to desire (*I want to go home*). **2** to feel a desire or longing for, to crave (*I want a drink*). **3** to desire or request the presence or assistance of (*You're wanted in reception*). **4** to need, to require. **5** to be without, to lack, to be deficient in. **6** to be short by, to require in order to be complete. **7** (*coll.*) ought (to) (*You want to try this new diet*). *~v.i.* **1** to be in need, to be in want (for). **2** to be deficient (in), to fall short (in). **3** to be lacking, to have need (for). **4** (*esp. N Am., coll.*) to desire to be (*He wants out*). **not to want to** to be unwilling to. **want ad** *n.* (*esp. N Am.*) a classified advertisement for something wanted. **wanted** *a.* **1** sought by the police. **2** sought by a person advertising in a newspaper, magazine etc. **wanter** *n.* **wanting** *a.* **1** absent, missing. **2** not meeting the required or expected standard. **3** lacking (in), deficient (in). ~*prep.* without. **to be found wanting** to fail to meet the required or expected standard. [Icel. *vant*, neut. of *vanr*, wanting, deficient (cp. OE *wan*, WANE)]

wanton (won´tən) *a.* **1** licentious, lascivious, lewd. **2** random, heedless, reckless, purposeless (*wanton destruction*). **3** extravagant, luxuriant. **4** unrestrained, loose, wild, unruly. **5** †sportive, frolicsome, playful. ~*n.* (*poet.*) **1** a lascivious or immoral person, esp. a woman. **2** a trifler. **3** a playful creature. ~*v.i.* (*pres.p.* **wantoning,** *past, p.p.* **wantoned**) **1** to sport, to frolic. **2** to move, act or grow randomly or unrestrainedly. **3** to behave wantonly (with). **wantonly** *adv.* **wantonness** *n.* [ME *wantoun, wantowen* (OE *wan-*, deficient in, *togen*, p.p. of *tēon*, to draw, to educate)]

wapentake (wop´əntāk) *n.* (*Hist.*) in certain English counties, a division corresponding to a hundred. [OE *wǣpengetǣce*, Icel. *vāpnatak*, weapon-touching (*vāpna*, gen. of *vāpn*, weapon, *taka*, TAKE[1], to touch)]

wapiti (wop´iti) *n.* (*pl.* **wapitis**) a N American stag, *Cervus canadensis*, related to the red deer. [Cree *wapitik*, from *wapi*, white]

War. *abbr.* Warwickshire.

war (waw) *n.* **1** a contest carried on by force of arms between nations, or between parties in the same state (*a world war; a civil war*). **2** a state of armed hostilities with suspension of ordinary international relations (*to declare war*). **3** hostile operations, military or naval attack, invasion. **4** (*also* **War**) a specific armed conflict (*They moved to Sussex after the war*). **5** the military art, military techniques or strategy. **6** hostility, enmity, strife. **7** a conflict, feud, struggle or campaign (*the war against crime*). ~*v.i.* (*pres.p.* **warring,** *past, p.p.* **warred**) **1** to make or carry on war. **2** to contend, to strive, to compete. **3** to be in opposition, to be inconsistent. **at war** engaged in hostilities (with). **in the wars** (*coll.*) bruised or injured as from fighting or quarrelling. †**to go to the wars** to serve as a soldier, esp. in a foreign country. **to go to war 1** to begin a war. **2** to begin active service in a war. **war baby** *n.* (*pl.* **war babies**) a child born in wartime, esp. the illegitimate child of a serviceman. **war bride** *n.* a woman who marries a serviceman, esp. a foreign national, met in wartime. **war chest** *n.* (*esp. N Am.*) a fund for a war or other campaign. **war cloud** *n.* a state of international affairs threatening war. **war correspondent** *n.* a journalist who reports on current events from the scene of a war or battle. **war crime** *n.* a crime committed in violation of the accepted rules of war. **war criminal** *n.* **war cry** *n.* (*pl.* **war cries**) **1** a name or phrase formerly shouted when charging into battle etc., a rallying cry. **2** a watchword. **3** a party slogan. **war damage** *n.* damage caused to property etc. by bombs or shells during a war. **war dance** *n.* a dance practised, as by some N American Indian tribes, as a preparation for battle or in celebration of victory. **war department** *n.* (*Hist.*) the government department in charge of the armed forces. **war establishment** *n.* the augmented military and naval forces in time of war. **warfare** (-feə) *n.* **1** a state of war, hostilities. **2** conflict, strife. **warfarer** *n.* **war game** *n.* **1** a simulated military battle or campaign. **2** an enactment of a battle using models. **war gaming** *n.* **war grave** *n.* the grave of a person killed in active service, esp. one of several or many in a special cemetery. **warhead** *n.* the head of a torpedo, aerial bomb, rocket etc., charged with explosive. **warhorse** *n.* **1** (*Hist.*) a charger, a horse used in battle. **2** (*coll.*) a veteran of war, politics etc. **warlike** *a.* **1** threatening war, hostile. **2** martial, soldier-like, military. **3** fit or ready for war. **war loan** *n.* a loan raised to meet the cost of a war. **warlord** *n.* a military leader or commander. **war memorial** *n.* a monument to those killed in a war. **warmonger** *n.* a person who promotes or traffics in war. **warmongering** *n., a.* **war of attrition** *n.* a long-drawn-out conflict in which each side tries to wear down the other. **War Office** *n.* (*Hist.*) the government department administering the affairs of the armed forces. **war of nerves** *n.* a conflict involving the use of psychological tactics. **war of the elements** *n.* (*poet.*) storms, natural disasters etc. **warpaint** *n.* **1** paint put on the face and body, esp. by N American Indians, before going into battle. **2** (*coll.*) make-up. **warpath** *n.* **1** the path taken by an attacking party of N American Indians. **2** a warlike expedition. **on the warpath 1** ready for or engaged in conflict. **2** (*coll.*) thoroughly roused or incensed. **war pension** *n.* a pension paid to a disabled war veteran, a war widow etc. **warplane** *n.* a military aircraft for use in war. **war poet** *n.* a poet who writes about war, esp. one writing during the First or Second World War. **warring** *a.* **1** at war, fighting. **2** rival (*warring factions*). **3** conflicting, inconsistent. **warship** *n.* an armed ship for use in war. **Wars of the Roses** *n.pl.* (*Hist.*) the civil wars between the houses of York and Lancaster in the 15th cent. **wartime** *n.* a period of war. **war-torn** *a.* devastated by war. **war-weary** *a.* tired of or exhausted by war. **war-weariness** *n.* **war whoop** *n.* a shout or yell raised by N American Indians in attacking. **war widow** *n.* the widow of a man killed in a war. **war-worn** *a.* exhausted by or experienced in war. **war zone** *n.* an area, esp. a part of a country, where there is armed conflict. [OF *werre* (F *guerre*), from Gmc. (cp. OHG *werra*, strife, *werran*, to embroil), prob. cogn. with WORSE]

waratah (wor´ətə) *n.* an Australian shrub, *Telopea speciosissima*, with a large, brilliant crimson flower. [Austral. Abor.]

warble[1] (waw´bəl) *v.i.* **1** (esp. of birds) to sing in a continuous quavering or trilling manner. **2** (of streams etc.) to make a continuous melodious sound. **3** to sing (with trills and variations etc.). ~*v.t.* to sing or utter thus. ~*n.* **1** the act or sound of warbling. **2** a song. **3** a trill. **warbler** *n.* **1** a person or thing that warbles. **2** a member of the Sylviidae, a family of small birds including the nightingale, blackcap, robin etc. **warbling** *a.* **warblingly** *adv.* [ME *werblen*, OF *werbler*, freq. from Gmc. (cp. MHG *werben*, G *wirbeln*, WHIRL)]

warble[2] (waw´bəl) *n.* **1** a small hard tumour on a horse's back caused by the galling of the saddle. **2** a small tumour under the skin of cattle produced by the larva of the warble fly. **warble fly** *n.* (*pl.* **warble flies**) any of various flies of the genus *Hypoderma*. [etym. uncertain]

ward (wawd) *n.* **1** an administrative or electoral division of a town or city. **2** a separate division of a hospital, prison etc. **3** a minor or other person under the care of a guardian. **4** (*also* **ward of court**) a person placed under the protection of a court, esp. a minor or a mentally handicapped person. **5** guardianship, protection, control. **6** (*usu. pl.*) a projection inside a lock that prevents the turning of any but the right key. **7** †watch, guard. **8** †confinement, custody. **9** †an inner court of a castle. ~*v.t.* **1** to guard, to watch over, to protect, to defend. **2** †to imprison. **to ward off 1** to parry, to turn aside, to keep off. **2** to avert. **ward-heeler** *n.* (*N Am.*) a party worker who canvasses for a politician etc. **wardroom** *n.* a room on a warship for commissioned officers below the rank of commander. **wardship** *n.* **1** guardianship, tutelage. **2** the condition of being a ward. [OE *weard* (m.), guard, watchman, (fem.) watch (whence *weardian*, to keep watch), cogn. with GUARD]

-ward (wəd), **-wards** (wədz) *suf.* used to form adjectives and adverbs expressing direction, as *backward*, *forward*, *homeward*, *inwards*, *outwards* etc. [OE *-weard*, as in *tōweard*, TOWARD[1], from *weorthan*, to become, see WORTH[2]]

warden (waw´dən) *n.* **1** a keeper, a guardian. **2** a governor. **3** the head of some colleges, schools and hostels. **4** (*esp. N Am.*) a prison governor. **5** a person who keeps watch. **6** any of various public officials (*a traffic warden*). **7** (*Austral.*) a government official in charge of a goldfield. **wardenship** *n.* [ME, A-F *wardein*, OF *wardain*, *gardein*, from *warder*, *garder*, GUARD]

warder (waw´də) *n.* **1** a keeper. **2** a jailer, a prison officer. **3** a guard, a sentinel. **wardress** (-dris) *n.* a female warder. [WARD, -ER[1]]

wardrobe (waw´drōb) *n.* **1** a tall cupboard with rails, shelves etc. where clothes are hung up. **2** a person's stock of clothes. **3** the costumes of a theatre or film company. **4** the department in charge of these. **5** the department of a royal household concerned with clothing etc. **wardrobe master, wardrobe mistress** *n.* a person in charge of the costumes of a theatre or film company. **wardrobe trunk** *n.* a large, upright trunk that can be used as a travelling wardrobe. [OF *warderobe*, *garderobe* (*warder*, see WARDEN, ROBE)]

-wards -WARD.

ware[1] (weə) *n.* **1** (*usu. in comb.*) **a** manufactured articles of a specified kind, as *tableware*, *glassware*, *silverware*, *hardware* etc. **b** pottery of a specified kind, as *Wedgwood ware*. **2** (*pl.*) **a** articles of merchandise, articles for sale, goods. **b** a person's skills or talents. [OE *waru* (cp. Dut. *waar*, G *Waare*, Icel. *varu*, Dan. *vare*)]

†**ware**[2] (weə) *a.* **1** conscious, aware. **2** cautious, wary. *~v.t.* (*usu. imper.*) to look out for, to guard against, to keep clear of. *~int.* beware! [OE *wær*, whence *warian*, to watch over, to guard (cp. Icel. *varr*, G *gewahr*), cogn. with Gr. *horaein*, to perceive, L *verērī*, to regard, to dread]

warehouse[1] (weə´hows) *n.* **1** a building in which goods are stored, kept for sale or in bond. **2** a wholesale or large retail store. **warehouseman** *n.* (*pl.* **warehousemen**) a person who keeps or is employed in a warehouse. **warehouse party** *n.* (*pl.* **warehouse parties**) a large organized party for young people, often illegal, held in a disused warehouse or similar building.

warehouse[2] (weə´hows, -howz) *v.t.* **1** to deposit, secure or store (furniture, bonded goods etc.) in a warehouse. **2** (*N Am., coll.*) to shut up in a hospital, prison or similar establishment and forget about. **warehousing** (-howzing) *n.* (*coll.*) the practice of anonymously building up a shareholding in a company, using nominees etc. to purchase the shares.

warfare WAR.

warfarin (waw´fərin) *n.* a compound used as a rodent poison and to prevent blood clotting. [*W*isconsin *A*lumni *R*esearch *F*oundation, the patentee, coum*arin*]

warily, wariness WARY.

†**warlock** (waw´lok) *n.* a wizard, a sorcerer. **warlockry** (-ri) *n.* [OE *wǣrloga*, a traitor, a deceiver (*wær*, truth, cogn. with L *vērus*, true, *loga*, a liar)]

warm (wawm) *a.* **1** at a rather high temperature. **2** having heat in a moderate degree. **3** promoting, emitting or conveying heat (*warm clothing*). **4** having the body or skin temperature raised by exercise etc. **5** ardent, zealous, enthusiastic. **6** friendly, cordial (*a warm welcome*). **7** sympathetic, emotional, affectionate (*a warm nature*). **8** amorous, erotic. **9** animated, heated, vehement, passionate (*a warm debate*). **10** violent, easily aroused (*a warm temper*). **11** (of colours) predominantly red or yellow. **12** (of a scent) fresh, strong. **13** (*coll.*) near to finding an object, guessing a secret etc. (esp. in children's games) (*You're getting warmer*). **14** (*coll.*) unpleasant, hot, uncomfortable. *~v.t.* **1** to make warm. **2** to make ardent or enthusiastic, to excite. **3** (*sl.*) to thrash. *~v.i.* **1** to become warm. **2** to become animated, enthusiastic or sympathetic (to or towards) (*She warmed to our suggestion*). *~n.* **1** an act of warming (*I'll give the plates a warm*). **2** a warm place or condition (*Stay in the warm*). **3** †a warm garment. **to warm up 1** to make or become warm. **2** to reheat (cooked food). **3** to prepare for a contest, performance etc., esp. by exercising or practising. **4** to make (an audience) more receptive to a show or act by a preliminary entertainment. **warm-blooded** *a.* **1** (of animals etc.) having warm blood, esp. between 98° and 112°F (36.6 and 44.4°C). **2** emotional, passionate, excitable. **3** amorous, erotic. **warm-bloodedness** *n.* **warmed** *a.* **warmed-over** *a.* (*N Am.*) warmed-up. **warmed-up** *a.* **1** (of food) reheated. **2** stale, unoriginal. **warmer** *n.* **warm front** *n.* the advancing edge of a mass of warm air. **warm-hearted** *a.* having warm, affectionate or kindly feelings. **warm-heartedly** *adv.* **warm-heartedness** *n.* **warming-pan** *n.* a closed pan, usu. of brass with a long handle, for holding live coals, formerly used to warm a bed. **warmish** *a.* **warmly** *adv.* **warmness** *n.* **warmth** *n.* **warm-up** *n.* the act or an instance of warming up. **warm welcome** *n.* **1** a hearty reception. **2** (*iron.*) a very hostile reception. **warm work** *n.* **1** work that makes one warm, esp. through exertion. **2** something dangerous. [OE *wearm* (cp. Dut. and G *warm*, Icel. *varmr*, Dan. and Swed. *varm*)]

warn (wawn) *v.t.* **1** to give notice to, to inform beforehand. **2** to caution, to make aware of danger. **3** to put (a person) on their guard (against) (*We warned him against accepting their offer*). **4** to expostulate with, to admonish. **5** to tell or order to go or stay (away, off etc.). *~v.i.* to give a warning. **warner** *n.* **warning** *n.* **1** the act of cautioning or making aware of danger etc. **2** previous notice (*without warning*). **3** something serving to warn. **4** †notice to quit. *~a.* serving to warn (*a warning sign*). **warning coloration** *n.* the conspicuous colouring or markings of poisonous animals etc. **warningly** *adv.* [OE *wearnian*, *warnian* (cp. G *warnen*, OHG *warnōn*), cogn. with WARY]

warp (wawp) *n.* **1** the state of being twisted or distorted, a twist or distortion in timber etc. **2** a perversion or aberration of mind or disposition. **3** the threads running the long way of a woven fabric, crossed by the weft or woof. **4** a rope, usu. smaller than a cable, used in towing a vessel. **5** an alluvial deposit, esp. from water artificially introduced into low lands. *~v.t.* **1** to turn or twist out of shape, to make crooked, to distort. **2** to pervert, to bias, to turn awry. **3** to tow or move (a ship) with a line attached to a buoy, anchor or other fixed point etc. **4** to prepare (yarn) as a warp for weaving. **5** to fertilize (land) with warp. **6** to choke (a channel) with warp. *~v.i.* **1** to become twisted, crooked or distorted. **2** to become perverted. **3** (of a ship) to be towed or moved by warping. **warpage** (-ij) *n.* **warped** *a.* **1** distorted (*warped timbers*). **2** perverted (*a warped mind*). **warper** *n.* **warping** *n.* [OE *wearp*, cp. Icel., Dan., and Swed. *varp*, a casting or throwing (v. from the cogn. Icel. *varpa*, to throw)]

warragal WARRIGAL.

warrant (wor´ənt) *v.t.* **1** to answer or give an assurance for, to guarantee. **2** to give authority to, to sanction. **3** to serve as grounds or justification for. **4** to attest the truth of. **5** to serve as guarantee for. *~n.* **1** anything that authorizes a person to do something. **2** authorization, sanction. **3** reason, grounds, justification. **4** an instrument giving power to arrest a person, search premises etc. **5** a document authorizing a person to receive money etc. **6** anything that attests or bears out a statement etc. **7** a certificate of office held by a warrant officer. **8** any person or thing that warrants. **I'll warrant** I am sure. **I warrant** I am sure. **warrantable** *a.* **1**

justifiable, defensible. 2 (of deer) old enough to be hunted. **warrantableness** *n.* **warrantably** *adv.* **warrantee** (-tē´) *n.* a person to whom a warranty is given. **warranter** *n.* **warrant of attorney** *n.* a written authority by which one person authorizes another to act in their stead. **warrant officer** *n.* an officer ranking below a commissioned officer and above a non-commissioned officer in the army or air force. **warrantor** *n.* a person who gives a warranty. **warranty** *n.* (*pl.* **warranties**) 1 a promise or undertaking from a vendor to a purchaser that the thing sold is good and fit for use etc. 2 an express or implied undertaking in a contract that a fact is as stated. 3 a warrant, an authorization. 4 a justification. [OF *warant, guarant,* from Gmc. (cp. G *gewähren,* to certify)]

warren (wor´ən) *n.* 1 a piece of ground with a network of underground tunnels where rabbits live and breed. 2 (*Hist.*) a place for keeping and breeding small game animals. 3 an overcrowded district. 4 a maze of interconnecting streets or passages. **warrener** *n.* (*Hist.*) a keeper of a warren. [ME *wareine,* OF *warenne,* from *warir, garir,* to protect, to heal (F *guérir*), see GARRISON]

warrigal (wor´igəl), **warragal** (-əgəl) *n.* (*Austral.*) 1 a dingo. 2 a wild horse. 3 a wild Aborigine. 4 an outlaw, a rascal. ~*a.* wild. [Austral. Abor.]

warring WAR.

warrior (wor´iə) *n.* a person experienced or distinguished in war, a distinguished soldier. [ME *werreour,* OF *guerreiur,* from *guerreier,* to make war, see WAR]

wart (wawt) *n.* 1 a small hard excrescence on the skin of the hands etc. due to irregular growth of the papillae, caused by a virus. 2 a spongy excrescence on the hind pastern of a horse. 3 a small protuberance on the surface of a plant. 4 (*coll.*) an unpleasant or offensive person. **warts and all** (*coll.*) without concealing any blemishes, shortcomings etc. **warted, warty** *a.* **warthog** *n.* a large-headed African wild pig, *Phacochoerus aethiopicus,* with warty excrescences on the face. **wartless** *a.* [OE *wearte* (cp. Dut. *wrat,* G *Warze,* Icel. *varta*), prob. cogn. with WORT]

wary (weə´ri) *a.* (*comp.* **warier,** *superl.* **wariest**) 1 cautious, watchful against deception, danger etc. 2 circumspect. 3 done with or characterized by caution. **warily** *adv.* **wariness** *n.* [WARE[2]]

was BE.

wasegoose WAYZGOOSE.

Wash. *abbr.* Washington.

wash (wosh) *v.t.* 1 to cleanse with water or other liquid (*to wash one's hair; to wash the dishes*). 2 to remove or take out, off, away etc. thus. 3 to pass water or other liquid through or over. 4 to purify. 5 (*poet.*) (of dew, tears etc.) to moisten. 6 (of waves, the sea etc.) to fall upon, cover or dash against. 7 to carry along, to sweep away etc., to scoop (out) by or as by the action of moving liquid. 8 to separate the earthy and lighter parts from (ore). 9 to cover with a thin coat of colour. 10 to overlay with a thin coat of metal. ~*v.i.* 1 to cleanse oneself, one's hands, one's face etc. with water etc. 2 to wash clothes, dishes etc. (*I'll wash, you can dry*). 3 (of clothes etc.) to stand washing without fading or being damaged in any way. 4 (*coll.*) (of a story etc.) to stand examination, to be accepted or believed (*It won't wash*). 5 (of water etc.) to move or splash or sweep along. 6 to drift or be carried along on water. ~*n.* 1 the act or process of washing. 2 the state of being washed. 3 a quantity of clothes etc. washed at one time. 4 the motion of a body of water or air, esp. that caused by the passage of a ship or aircraft. 5 soil removed and accumulated by water, alluvium. 6 land washed by the sea or a river. 7 waste from the kitchen often used as food for pigs. 8 thin liquid food, slops. 9 a liquid used for cleansing, healing or cosmetic purposes, a lotion. 10 a thin coating of colour spread over broad masses of a painting, pen-and-ink drawing etc. 11 a thin liquid for coating a wall etc. 12 a thin coat of metal. 13 the blade of an oar. 14 fermented wort from which spirit has been extracted. **the wash** the washing of clothes, linen etc. **to come out in the wash** 1 to be removed in washing. 2 (*coll.*) to be resolved or revealed in the end. **to wash down** 1 to wash the whole of. 2 to accompany (food) with a drink. **to wash off** to remove or be removed by washing. **to wash one's dirty linen in public** LINEN. **to wash one's hands** (*euphem.*) to go to the lavatory. **to wash one's hands of** to disclaim any responsibility for. **to wash out** 1 to remove or be removed by washing. 2 to wash free of something unwanted. 3 to cause to be cancelled because of rain. 4 (*coll.*) to cancel, to annul. 5 to erode. 6 (of a flood etc.) to cause a breach in. **to wash over** to happen around, without affecting (a person) (*His parents are always arguing, but it just washes over him*). **to wash up** 1 to wash dishes etc. 2 (*esp. N Am.*) to wash one's hands and face. **washable** *a.* **washability** (-bil´-) *n.* **wash-and-wear** *a.* (of fabrics, clothing etc.) easy to wash, quick to dry and requiring little or no ironing. **washbag** *n.* a small waterproof bag for carrying toiletries. **washbasin** *n.* a basin for washing the hands etc., forming part of the furnishings of a toilet, bathroom, some (hotel) bedrooms etc. **washboard** *n.* 1 a board with a ribbed surface for scrubbing clothes on. 2 such a board used as a musical instrument. 3 a board to keep the water from washing over a gunwale or through a port etc. of a ship. 4 (*esp. N Am.*) a skirting round the lower part of the wall of a room. **washcloth** *n.* 1 a piece of cloth used in washing dishes etc. 2 (*N Am.*) a facecloth. **washday** *n.* the day on which domestic washing is done or sent to the laundry. **washed** *a.* **washed out, washed-out** *a.* 1 limp, exhausted, worn out. 2 pale, wan. 3 faded, colourless. **washed up, washed-up** *a.* (*sl.*) no longer successful or effective, finished, failed. **washer** *n.* 1 a ring or perforated disc of metal, rubber etc. for placing under a nut etc. to tighten the joint or spread the load. 2 a person or thing that washes. 3 a washing machine. 4 (*Austral.*) a facecloth. **washer-dryer, washer-drier** *n.* a combined washing machine and tumble-dryer. **washerman** *n.* (*pl.* **washermen**) a laundryman. **washer-up** *n.* (*pl.* **washers-up**) a person who washes dishes etc. **washerwoman** *n.* (*pl.* **washerwomen**) a laundrywoman or laundress. **washeteria** (-ətiə´riə) *n.* a launderette. **wash-hand basin** *n.* a washbasin. **wash-hand stand** *n.* a washstand. **wash-house** *n.* 1 a building where clothes etc. are washed, a laundry. 2 a scullery. **washing** *n.* 1 the act of cleansing by water etc. 2 clothes etc. washed or to be washed together. **washing machine** *n.* an electrical machine in which clothes etc. are washed automatically. **washing powder** *n.* a preparation of detergent or soap used in washing clothes etc. **washing soda** *n.* crystalline sodium carbonate. **washing-up** *n.* 1 the washing of dishes etc., esp. after a meal. 2 dishes, cutlery etc. to be washed. **washland** *n.* land that is periodically flooded by a river, the sea etc. **washleather** *n.* a chamois leather or an imitation of this. **wash-out** *n.* 1 (*coll.*) a failure, a fiasco. 2 (*coll.*) an incompetent person. 3 (*also* **washout**) a scooping out or sweeping away of rock, earth etc. by a rush of water. 4 a cleansing by washing out. **washrag** *n.* (*N Am.*) a facecloth, a flannel. **washroom** *n.* (*N Am.*) a bathroom or lavatory. **washstand** *n.* (*Hist.*) a piece of furniture for holding a ewer or pitcher, basin etc. for washing one's face and hands etc. **washtub** *n.* a tub in which clothes etc. are washed. **washy** *a.* (*comp.* **washier,** *superl.* **washiest**) 1 watery, too much diluted, weak, thin. 2 lacking solidity, intensity or vigour, feeble. **washily** *adv.* **washiness** *n.* [OE *wascan* (cp. Dut. *wasschen,* G *waschen,* Icel. and Swed. *vaska*), cogn. with WATER and WET]

wasn't (woz´ənt) *contr.* was not.

Wasp (wosp), **WASP** *n.* an American of N European descent, considered in N America as belonging to a privileged class. **Waspy** *a.* [*W*hite *A*nglo-*S*axon *P*rotestant]

wasp (wosp) *n.* **1** a predatory hymenopterous insect of solitary or social habits, esp. the common wasp, *Vespula vulgaris*, a European insect with a slender waist, black and yellow stripes and a powerful sting. **2** a spiteful or irritable person. **waspish** *a.* snappish, petulant, irritable. **waspishly** *adv.* **waspishness** *n.* **wasplike** *a.* **wasp-waist** *n.* a very thin waist. **wasp-waisted** *a.* [OE *wæps* (cp. G *Wespe*, Lith. *wapsà*), cogn. with WEAVE[1] (from their nests) and L *vespa*]

†**wassail** (wos´āl, -əl) *n.* **1** a festive occasion, a drinking-bout. **2** spiced ale or other liquor prepared for a wassail. **3** a toast to a person's health. ~*v.i.* **1** to carouse, to make merry. **2** to go from house to house singing carols at Christmas. **wassail-bowl, wassail-cup, wassail-horn** *n.* a bowl, cup etc. from which wassail was drunk. **wassailer** *n.* [OE *wæs hāl*, be thou (see BE) of good health (*hāl*, WHOLE)]

Wassermann test (vas´əmən, was´-) *n.* a diagnostic test for the presence of syphilis. [August von *Wassermann*, 1866–1925, German pathologist]

wast BE.

waste (wāst) *v.t.* **1** to consume, to spend, to use up unnecessarily, carelessly or lavishly, to squander. **2** to fail to use to advantage. **3** (*often pass.*) to use or bestow (advice, talent etc.) without effect or where appreciation is lacking (*Sarcasm is wasted on her*). **4** to wear away gradually. **5** to cause to lose weight, strength and health. **6** (*poet.*) to devastate, to lay waste. **7** (*sl.*) to kill. **8** (*Law*) to damage or impair (an estate) by neglect. ~*v.i.* **1** to wear away gradually, to dwindle, to wither. **2** to lose weight, strength and health. **3** to be wasted. ~*a.* **1** superfluous, left over as useless or valueless. **2** desolate, desert, unoccupied, uncultivated, devastated. **3** barren, unproductive. **4** dreary, dismal, cheerless. ~*n.* **1** the act or an instance of wasting, squandering or throwing away. **2** the state or process of being wasted or used up, gradual diminution of substance, strength, value etc. **3** material, food etc. rejected as superfluous, useless or valueless; refuse. **4** waste products. **5** a desolate or desert region, a wilderness. **6** a waste pipe. **7** (*Law*) damage to or impairment of an estate etc. caused by the act or neglect of a life tenant etc. **to go/ run to waste** to be wasted. **to lay waste 1** to render desolate. **2** to devastate, to ruin. **to waste no time** TIME. **to waste one's breath** BREATH. **to waste words** to talk in vain or without effect. **waste not, want not** if you do not waste things, you will have them when they are needed. **wastage** (-ij) *n.* **1** loss by use, decay, leakage etc. **2** avoidable loss of something useful. **3** NATURAL WASTAGE (under NATURAL). **wastebasket** *n.* (*esp. N Am.*) a waste-paper basket. **waste bin** *n.* a receptacle for waste paper and other refuse. **waste-book** *n.* an account book for entering transactions as they take place before carrying them over to the ledger. **wasted** *a.* (*sl.*) **1** exhausted. **2** showing the effects of alcohol or drug abuse. **waste disposal** *n.* the process of disposing of waste, rubbish, refuse etc. **waste disposal unit** *n.* an electrically operated device fitted to a kitchen sink that breaks up waste, food refuse etc. before it goes down the waste pipe. **wasteful** *a.* **1** extravagant, spending or using recklessly, unnecessarily or too lavishly. **2** causing waste. **wastefully** *adv.* **wastefulness** *n.* **waste ground** *n.* a patch of undeveloped or unused land, esp. in an urban area. **wasteland** *n.* **1** a desolate or unproductive area of land. **2** any time, place etc. considered spiritually or intellectually desolate (*a cultural wasteland*). **wasteless** *a.* inexhaustible. **waste paper** *n.* spoiled, used or discarded paper. **waste-paper basket** *n.* a receptacle for waste paper. **waste pipe** *n.* a discharge pipe for used or superfluous water. **waste product** *n.* (*often pl.*) **1** material produced by a process as a useless by-product. **2** an unusable product of metabolism. **waster** *n.* **1** a person who wastes. **2** a prodigal, a spendthrift. **3** (*coll.*) a good-for-nothing, a wastrel. **4** an article spoiled and rendered unmarketable in manufacture. **wasting** *n.*, *a.* **wasting asset** *n.* a non-renewable asset that is gradually used up, such as a mine. [ME and OF *wast* (var. *gast*), from MHG *waste*, a waste, L *vastus*, VAST, whence *vastāre*, OF *waster*, *gaster* (F *gâter*, to spoil), to lay waste]

wastrel (wās´trəl) *n.* **1** a wasteful person. **2** a good-for-nothing. **3** †an abandoned child, a waif. [WASTE]

wat (waht) *n.* a Thai Buddhist temple or monastery.

watch (woch) *n.* **1** the act or state of watching. **2** a state of alertness, vigilance, close observation or attention. **3** vigil, lookout, waiting in a state of expectancy, dread etc. **4** (*Hist.*) a watchman or body of watchmen, a guard. **5** a small timepiece activated by a spring or battery, for carrying on the person. **6** a former division of the night (*the watches of the night*). **7** a period of watching or of keeping guard. **8** the period of time during which each division of a ship's crew is alternately on duty (four hours except during the dogwatches of two hours). **9** either of two halves into which a ship's officers and crew are divided, taking duty alternately. **10** in the 18th cent., a company of irregular Highland troops. ~*v.i.* **1** to be vigilant, observant or expectant. **2** to look out (for). **3** to act as a protector or guard (over). **4** to keep awake at night, to keep vigil. ~*v.t.* **1** to guard. **2** to observe closely, to keep one's eye or eyes on. **3** to monitor or keep under observation (*to watch one's weight*). **4** to look at, to view (*to watch television*). **5** to tend, to look after. **6** to be careful of. **on the watch** vigilant, on the lookout. **on watch** on duty, esp. as a lookout. **to set the watch** to station lookouts etc. **to watch one's step** STEP. **to watch out 1** to be on the lookout (for). **2** to take care. **to watch the clock** CLOCK[1]. **watch it!** be careful! **watch out!** look out! **watch yourself!** take care! **watchable** *a.* **watchband** *n.* (*N Am.*) a watch strap. **watch-case** *n.* the case enclosing the works of a watch. **watch-chain** *n.* a metal chain for securing a pocket watch to the clothing. **Watch Committee** *n.* (*Hist.*) a body of local officials dealing with the policing etc. of a district. **watchdog** *n.* **1** a dog kept to guard premises etc. **2** a person or group that monitors the activities of an organization etc. to guard against illegal or undesirable practices and protect the rights of others. ~*v.t.* (*pres.p.* **watchdogging,** *past, p.p.* **watchdogged**) to guard, to keep under surveillance. **watcher** *n.* **watch-fire** *n.* a fire in a camp etc. at night or used as a signal. **watchful** *a.* **1** vigilant, observant. **2** cautious, wary. **3** †wakeful. **watchfully** *adv.* **watchfulness** *n.* **watch-glass** *n.* **1** a glass covering the face of a watch. **2** an hourglass or similar device for measuring the period of a nautical watch. **3** a curved disc of glass used in a laboratory to hold small samples etc. **watching brief** *n.* **1** a brief issued to a barrister instructed to watch a case on behalf of a client not directly concerned in the action. **2** observation of or interest in a proceeding with which one is not directly concerned. **watchkeeper** *n.* a person who keeps watch, esp. a member of a ship's watch. **watchmaker** *n.* a person who makes or repairs watches etc. **watchmaking** *n.* **watchman** *n.* (*pl.* **watchmen**) **1** a person who guards a large building etc. at night. **2** (*Hist.*) a guard, a sentinel, esp. a member of a body formerly employed to patrol or guard the streets of a town at night. **watch-night** *n.* **1** the last night of the year. **2** a religious service held by Methodists etc. on this night. **watch spring** *n.* the mainspring of a watch. **watch strap** *n.* a strap for securing a watch round the wrist. **watchtower** *n.* a tower of observation or one on which sentinels are placed. **watchword** *n.* **1** a motto, word or phrase symbolizing or epitomizing the principles of a party etc. **2** (*Hist.*) a word given to sentinels etc. as a signal that one has the right of admission etc., a password. [OE *wæcce*, from *wacian*, to watch, from *wacan*, WAKE[1]]

water (waw′tə) *n.* **1** a colourless, transparent liquid, without taste or smell, possessing a neutral reaction, a compound of two parts by weight of hydrogen with one of oxygen. **2** an impure form of this found in rivers, lakes, oceans etc. **3** (*often pl.*) a (natural) body of water, such as a sea, a lake, a river. **4** the surface of a body of water. **5** a liquid consisting chiefly or partly of water, such as various solutions or products of distillation. **6** (*usu. pl.*) mineral water at a spa. **7** tears, sweat, urine or another bodily secretion. **8** (*usu. pl.*) the amniotic fluid surrounding a foetus. **9** the state of the tide (*at low water, an hour before high water*). **10** the transparency or lustre of a diamond, pearl etc. **11** a wavy lustrous finish on silk etc. **12** stock issued without any corresponding increase of paid-up capital. ~*a.* **1** living or growing in, on or near water (*a water plant*). **2** of, for or relating to water (*a water pipe*). **3** involving water (*water sports*). ~*v.t.* **1** to apply water to, to moisten, sprinkle, irrigate or supply with water. **2** to dilute or adulterate with water. **3** to provide with water for drinking. **4** to increase (nominal capital etc.) by the issue of stock without corresponding increase of assets. **5** (*usu. in p.p.*) to give an undulating sheen to the surface of (silk etc.) by moistening, pressing and heating in manufacture (*watered silk*). ~*v.i.* **1** (of the mouth, eyes etc.) to secrete, shed or run with water in the form of saliva, tears etc. **2** to get or take in water. **3** (of cattle etc.) to drink. **by water** in a boat or ship. **in hot water** in trouble, difficulty or disgrace. **like water** lavishly (*spending money like water*). **like water off a duck's back** DUCK[1]. **on the water** in a boat or ship. **the Water-bearer** the Water-carrier. **the Water-carrier** the zodiacal constellation Aquarius. **to be in deep water** DEEP. **to cast one's bread upon the waters** to be generous without expecting any reward. **to hold water** to be sound or valid, to stand scrutiny. **to keep one's head above water** to avoid financial ruin. **to make one's mouth water 1** to stimulate one's appetite. **2** to make one very desirous. **to take the waters** to take a cure at a watering spa. **to water down 1** to dilute with water. **2** to make less forceful, offensive, harsh, vivid etc. **waterage** (-rij) *n.* **1** transportation by water. **2** money paid for this. **water avens** *n.* the pinkish-flowered *Geum rivale*. **water-bag** *n.* a bag for holding or carrying water, made of canvas, leather, skin etc. **water bailiff** *n.* **1** an officer employed to watch a river or other fishery to prevent poaching. **2** (*Hist.*) a custom-house officer at a port. **water-based** *a.* **1** (of a solution etc.) consisting mainly of water (*water-based paints*). **2** (of sports etc.) done on or in water. **water bear** *n.* TARDIGRADE. **waterbed** *n.* a bed with a rubber or plastic mattress filled with water. **water beetle** *n.* a beetle that lives in water. **waterbird** *n.* an aquatic bird, esp. one living on or near fresh water. **water biscuit** *n.* a thin plain biscuit made from flour and water. **water blister** *n.* a blister containing watery fluid without pus or blood. **water-bloom** *n.* a rapid growth of microscopic algae in water. **water-boatman** *n.* (*pl.* **water-boatmen**) an aquatic insect of the family Notonectidae or Corixidae, with paddle-like hind legs. **water-borne** *a.* **1** conveyed by water. **2** (of a disease) transmitted by contaminated water. **waterbrash** *n.* a form of indigestion, with belching of liquid from the stomach; heartburn. **water-buck** *n.* an African antelope, *Kobus ellipsiprymnus*, found near rivers, lakes and swamps. **water buffalo** *n.* (*pl.* **water buffalo, water buffaloes**) the common domesticated Asian buffalo, *Bubalus arnee*. **water bug** *n.* an aquatic insect. **water bus** *n.* a river craft carrying passengers on a regular service. **water-butt** *n.* a large open-headed barrel for catching and preserving rainwater. **water caltrop** *n.* a water weed, such as *Potamogeton densus, P. crispus* or *Trapa natans*. **water-cannon** *n.* a device that ejects a jet of water at high pressure, used for quelling riots etc. **water chestnut** *n.* **1** an aquatic plant, *Trapa natans*, with an edible nutlike fruit. **2** the Chinese water chestnut, *Eleocharis tuberosa*, or its tuber used in cooking. **water-clock** *n.* an instrument for measuring time by the passage of water, a clepsydra. **water closet** *n.* **1** a toilet with a water supply for flushing the basin. **2** a room containing this. **watercolour,** (*N Am.*) **watercolor** *n.* **1** a pigment ground up with water etc. instead of oil. **2** a painting done with watercolours. **3** (*often pl.*) the art of painting with watercolours. **watercolourist** *n.* **water-cool** *v.t.* to cool by (circulating) water. **water-cooled** *a.* **water-cooler** *n.* a device for cooling drinking water. **watercourse** *n.* **1** a stream, a brook. **2** a channel for the conveyance of water or in which a natural stream etc. flows. **watercraft** *n.* ships, boats etc. **water-cress** *n.* a creeping aquatic plant, *Nasturtium officinale*, eaten as salad. **water cure** *n.* hydropathy. **water cycle** *n.* the circulation of the earth's water, involving evaporation, condensation and precipitation. **water-diviner** *n.* a dowser. **water dog** *n.* **1** a dog accustomed to the water, esp. a water spaniel. **2** (*coll.*) a person who enjoys being on or in the water. **watered** *a.* **watered-down** *a.* **1** diluted or weakened by or as by the addition of water. **2** reduced in force, effect etc. **waterer** *n.* **waterfall** *n.* a steep or perpendicular descent of a river etc., a cascade, a cataract. **water flea** *n.* a minute freshwater crustacean of the genus *Daphnia*. **waterfowl** *n.* (*pl.* **waterfowl**) a bird that frequents rivers, lakes etc. **waterfront** *n.* the part of a town facing or bordering a sea, harbour, lake, river etc. **water gas** *n.* a gas obtained by the decomposition of water and treatment with carbon, a mixture of hydrogen and carbon monoxide, used as a fuel. **watergate** *n.* **1** a gate for confining or releasing water, a floodgate. **2** a gate giving access to a river etc. **water gauge** *n.* **1** a glass instrument attached to a steam boiler etc. for indicating the height of the water inside. **2** pressure expressed in terms of the height of water. **water-glass** *n.* **1** a tube with a glass end for observing objects under water. **2** soluble glass, esp. as used for fixing a watercolour drawing on dry plaster. **3** a viscous solution of sodium or potassium silicate in water, used in industry and as a preservative for eggs. **4** a water-clock. **5** (**water glass**) a glass for holding water, esp. drinking water. **water hammer** *n.* the concussion of water in a pipe when a tap is turned off or steam admitted. **water heater** *n.* a device for heating water, esp. domestic water. **water hemlock** *n.* a poisonous marsh plant, *Cicuta maculata*, the cowbane. **water hen** *n.* the moorhen. **waterhole** *n.* a hole where water collects, esp. a pool in a dried-up river bed. **water hyacinth** *n.* an aquatic plant, *Eichhornia crassipes*, which floats in the waterways of tropical countries. **water ice** *n.* a frozen confection made from water, sugar etc. **watering** *n.* the act of obtaining or supplying water. **watering can** *n.* a vessel with a long spout and usu. a perforated nozzle for sprinkling water on plants etc. **watering hole** *n.* **1** a water-filled pool or hollow where animals can drink. **2** (*sl.*) a pub, bar etc. **watering place** *n.* **1** a place where water may be obtained for cattle etc. **2** a place where people go to drink mineral waters or for bathing, a spa or seaside resort. **3** a watering hole. **water jacket** *n.* a casing filled with water surrounding a part of a machine that is to be kept cool. **water jug** *n.* a jug or other container for dispensing drinking water. **water jump** *n.* a ditch, stream etc. to be jumped, esp. in a steeplechase. **waterless** *a.*

water level *n.* 1 the level of the water in the sea, a reservoir etc. 2 the level below which the ground is saturated with water, the water-table. 3 a levelling instrument using water instead of spirit. **water lily** *n.* (*pl.* **water lilies**) an aquatic plant of the family Nymphaeaceae, with large floating leaves and white or coloured flowers. **waterline** *n.* 1 the line up to which the hull of a vessel is submerged in the water. 2 a line marking the level of a body of water. **waterlogged** *a.* 1 saturated with water. 2 (of a vessel) flooded with water so as to be unmanageable. **water main** *n.* a main pipe in a system of water supply. **waterman** *n.* (*pl.* **watermen**) 1 a boatman plying for hire on rivers etc. 2 a (good or bad) oarsman. **watermanship** *n.* **watermark** *n.* 1 a translucent design stamped in paper in the process of manufacture to show the maker, size etc. 2 a mark indicating the level to which water rises in a well etc. 3 the limits of the rise and fall of the tide etc. ~*v.t.* to stamp (paper) with a watermark. **water-meadow** *n.* a meadow fertilized by being flooded at certain seasons from an adjoining stream. **water measurer** *n.* an aquatic insect of the family Hydrometridae, which walks on the water. **watermelon** *n.* 1 a large trailing plant, *Citrullus lanatus.* 2 its edible fruit, with green rind and watery red flesh. **water meter** *n.* a device for measuring a water supply. **water milfoil** *n.* an aquatic plant of the genus *Myriophyllum*, with many thin leaves. **watermill** *n.* a mill driven by water or a water-wheel. **water moccasin** *n.* a large venomous snake, *Agkistrodon piscivorus*, of American swamps. **water nymph** *n.* a naiad, a nymph of the water in Greek mythology etc. **water of crystallization** *n.* the water that unites with salts in crystallization. **water of life** *n.* (*poet.*) spiritual refreshment or enlightenment. **water on the brain** *n.* hydrocephalus, an accumulation of fluid in the brain. **water opossum** *n.* YAPOK. **water ouzel** *n.* the dipper, *Cinclus cinclus.* **water pennywort** *n.* MARSH PENNYWORT (under MARSH). **water-pepper** *n.* a plant of damp or marshy ground, *Persicaria hydropiper*, with acrid-tasting leaves. **water pipe** *n.* 1 a pipe for conveying water. 2 a hookah. **water pistol** *n.* a toy pistol that shoots a jet of water. **water plantain** *n.* a plant of the genus *Alisma* found in marshes and ditches. **water polo** *n.* a game in which swimmers hit a ball with the hand. **water-power** *n.* 1 the power of water used to drive machinery, generate electricity etc. 2 a source of this, such as a fall in the level of a river etc. **waterpox** *n.* varicella, chickenpox. **waterproof** *a.* impervious to water. ~*n.* 1 a waterproof coat or other garment. 2 cloth rendered waterproof. ~*v.t.* to render waterproof. **waterproofer** *n.* **waterproofing** *n.* **waterproofness** *n.* **water purslane** *n.* any of various plants growing in damp places, esp. *Lythrum portula.* **water rail** *n.* the common European rail, *Rallus aquaticus.* **water rat** *n.* a water vole. **water rate** *n.* a rate or charge for the supply of water. **water-repellent, water-resistant** *a.* resistant but not impervious to water. **water-resistance** *n.* **water scorpion** *n.* an aquatic insect of the family Nepidae, which lives under the surface of the water and breathes through a tubular tail. **water seal** *n.* a small body of water in a bend etc., used to prevent the escape of gas from a pipe etc. **watershed** *n.* 1 a ridge or other line of separation between two river basins or drainage systems. 2 any dividing line or turning point. **waterside** *n.* the margin of a river, stream, lake or the sea. **water-ski** *n.* (*pl.* **water-skis**) a type of ski used for planing over water in water-skiing. ~*v.i.* (*3rd pers. sing. pres.* **water-skis,** *pres.p.* **water-skiing,** *past, p.p.* **water-skied**) to plane over water on water-skis; to go water-skiing. **water-skier** *n.* **water-skiing** *n.* the sport of being towed on water-skis at great speed by a motor boat. **water slide** *n.* a long slide down which water runs, usu. into a swimming pool. **water-snake** *n.* any of various snakes found near water, such as *Natrix sipedon.* **water softener** *n.* a device or chemical used to remove or alter the substances that cause hardness in water. **water soldier** *n.* an aquatic plant, *Stratiotes aloides*, with long narrow leaves rising above the water. **water-soluble** *a.* capable of being dissolved in water. **water spaniel** *n.* a spaniel used in hunting waterfowl. **water-splash** *n.* part of a road etc. always submerged by a crossing stream. **water sports** *n.pl.* sporting activities that take place on or in water, such as windsurfing, water-skiing, swimming etc. **waterspout** *n.* a phenomenon which occurs during a tornado over the sea, in which water appears to be drawn up from the sea in a whirling column, sometimes connecting sea and cloud. **water starwort** *n.* any plant of the genus *Callitriche*, which grows in water. **water supply** *n.* (*pl.* **water supplies**) 1 a system for storing and supplying water for the service of a town etc. 2 the amount of water stored for the use of a house, factory etc. **water-table** *n.* 1 the level below which the ground is saturated with water. 2 a projecting ledge or string course for throwing off the water on a building. **water tank** *n.* **water taxi** *n.* (*pl.* **water taxis**) a small boat, usu. a motor boat, for transporting passengers over short distances. **waterthrush** *n.* either of two small N American birds, *Seiurus motacilla* or *S. noveboracensis*, found near water. **watertight** *a.* 1 so tightly fastened or fitted as to prevent the passage of water in or out. 2 (of an argument etc.) unable to be attacked or refuted. **water torture** *n.* a form of torture involving water, esp. one in which water is dripped on to the victim's forehead. **water tower** *n.* an elevated building carrying a large tank or reservoir for giving pressure to a water supply. **water under the bridge** *n.* past events, experiences etc. that are over and done with. **water vapour,** (*N Am.*) **water vapor** *n.* water in gaseous form, esp. when evaporated below boiling temperature. **water vole** *n.* a large semiaquatic vole, esp. *Arvicola terrestris*, a water rat. **water wagon** *n.* a vehicle for transporting water. **off the water wagon** (*coll.*) no longer abstaining from alcohol. **on the water wagon** (*coll.*) abstaining from alcohol. **water wagtail** *n.* the pied wagtail. **waterway** *n.* 1 a navigable channel, a fairway. 2 a route for travel or transport by boat or ship. 3 the thick planks along the edge of a deck in which a channel is hollowed for conducting water to the scuppers. **waterweed** *n.* **waterwheel** *n.* a wheel moved by water and used to drive machinery etc. **water wings** *n.pl.* floats worn by a person learning to swim. **water witch** *n.* a dowser. **waterworks** *n.* 1 an establishment for the collection, storage and distribution of water for the use of communities, driving machinery etc. 2 an artificial fountain. 3 (*as pl., coll.*) the urinary system. 4 (*as pl., coll.*) crying, tears (*to turn on the waterworks*). **water-worn** *a.* worn away by the action of water. **watery** *a.* 1 containing too much water (*watery soup*). 2 wet, sodden. 3 suffused or running with water. 4 thin, transparent or pale, like water. 5 rainy-looking. 6 of or consisting of water. 7 tasteless, insipid, vapid. **wateriness** *n.* **watery grave** *n.* death by drowning (*to go to a watery grave*). [OE *wæter*, cp. Dut. *water*, G *Wasser*, Icel. *vatu*, Swed. *vatten*, also Gr. *hudōr*, L *unda*, Sansk. *udan*]

Waterford glass (waw´təfəd) *n.* a type of clear colourless glass. [*Waterford*, town in Ireland]

Watergate (waw´təgāt) *n.* a scandal involving a political cover-up (from such a scandal involving President Richard Nixon in 1972). [*Watergate* building, Washington, DC; cp. -GATE]

Waterloo (wawtəloo´) *n.* a downfall, a decisive defeat (*to meet one's Waterloo*). [*Waterloo*, Belgian town where Napoleon was finally defeated in 1815]

Wathawurung (wŭt´əwərŭng) *n.* an extinct Aboriginal language of Victoria.

watt (wot) *n.* a unit of power or rate of doing work, equal to a rate of working of one joule per second or the power available when the electromotive force is one volt and the current is one ampere. **wattage** (-ij) *n.* an amount of power in watts. **watt-hour** *n.* a unit of (electrical) energy equal to a power of one watt operating for one hour. **wattmeter** *n.* a meter for measuring electrical power in watts. [James *Watt*, 1736–1819, Scottish engineer]

wattle (wot´əl) *n.* **1** a construction of interwoven twigs or wickerwork used to make fences, walls etc. **2** the twigs etc. used for this. **3** the fleshy lobe under the throat of the domestic fowl, turkey etc. **4** a barbel of a fish. **5** any of various Australian and Tasmanian species of acacia, the bark of which is used in tanning. **6** the national flower of Australia. *~v.t.* **1** to interweave, to interlace, to plait. **2** to construct from wattle. **wattle and daub** *n.* a method of constructing walls of interwoven twigs or wickerwork covered with mud or clay. **wattlebird** *n.* any of various birds with wattles, esp. an Australian honeyeater of the genus *Anthochaera* or *Melidectes*, or a New Zealand songbird of the family Callaeidae. **wattled** *a.* **wattling** *n.* [OE *watel*, hurdle, cogn. with *wætla*, bandage]

waul (wawl), **wawl** *v.i.* to cry like a cat, to wail or squall. [onomat.]

wave (wāv) *v.i.* **1** to move to and fro with a sinuous or sweeping motion like a flag in the wind, to flutter or undulate. **2** to have an undulating shape or conformation, to be wavy. **3** to greet or signal (to) by waving the hand etc. *~v.t.* **1** to cause to move to and fro (*to wave a hand*; *to wave a flag*). **2** to give an undulating motion to. **3** to brandish (a weapon etc.). **4** to give an undulating surface, conformation or appearance to, to make wavy. **5** to indicate, direct or command by a waving signal (*She waved him away*). **6** to express by waving (*to wave goodbye*). *~n.* **1** a moving ridge or long curved body of water or other liquid, esp. one formed on the surface of the sea, rising into an arch and breaking on the shore. **2** (*often pl., poet.*) the sea, water. **3** a disturbance of the equilibrium of a fluid medium continuously propagated from point to point without a corresponding advance of the particles in the same direction, by which motion, heat, light, sound, electricity etc. are transmitted. **4** a single curve or cycle in such a motion. **5** a curve or series of curves, an undulation. **6** a waviness of the hair. **7** the process of producing this (*a permanent wave*). **8** the act or gesture of waving, as a greeting, signal etc. **9** a heightened volume or intensity of some force, influence, emotion, activity etc. (*a wave of panic*). **10** a movement like that of a wave on the sea. **11** a widespread advance or influx. **12** a prolonged spell of hot or cold weather. **13** a waveform. **14** a rhythmical electromagnetic disturbance propagated through space. **15** a wavelike stripe or streak. **to make waves 1** (*coll.*) to cause trouble. **2** (*coll.*) to make an impression. **to wave aside** to dismiss with or as with a wave of the hand. **to wave down** to wave as a signal to (a driver or vehicle) to stop. **waveband** *n.* a range of frequencies or wavelengths which is allocated for radio transmissions of a particular type. **wave equation** *n.* a differential equation describing wave motion. **waveform** *n.* **1** the graph of a wave, showing the variation in a varying quantity against time. **2** the shape of this. **wavefront** *n.* (*Physics*) a surface that contains all the points in a wave having the same phase. **wave function** *n.* a function that satisfies a wave equation. **waveguide** *n.* a metal tube used for carrying and guiding electromagnetic waves, esp. microwaves. **wavelength** *n.* **1** the distance between the crests of two adjacent waves. **2** the space intervening between corresponding points, such as the maximum positive points of two successive waves. **3** (*coll.*) a way of thinking, feeling, communicating etc. (*to be on the same wavelength*). **waveless** *a.* **wavelet** *n.* a small wave. **wavelike** *a.*, *adv.* **wave machine** *n.* a machine for producing waves in a swimming pool etc. **wave mechanics** *n.* quantum mechanics based on the wavelike properties and behaviour of particles. **wavemeter** *n.* an instrument for measuring the wavelength or frequency of an electromagnetic wave. **wave number** *n.* (*Physics*) the number of waves per unit distance, the reciprocal of the wavelength of a wave. **wave theory** *n.* the theory that light is transmitted by or in the form of waves. **wave train** *n.* a series of waves of the same or similar wavelength travelling in the same direction. **waving** *a.* **wavy** *a.* (*comp.* **wavier**, *superl.* **waviest**) **1** rising or swelling in waves. **2** having an alternately concave and convex outline, undulating (*a wavy line*). **3** (of hair) having an undulating surface or loose curls. **wavily** *adv.* **waviness** *n.* [OE *wafian* from Gmc.]

Usage note See note under WAIVE.

waver (wā´və) *v.i.* **1** to be in a state of indecision, to hesitate, to vacillate. **2** to begin to give way, to falter. **3** to reel, to be unsteady. **4** to flicker, to quiver. **5** to play or move to and fro. **waverer** *n.* **wavering** *a.* **waveringly** *adv.* **waveringness** *n.* **wavery** *a.* [freq. of WAVE, cp. Icel. *vafra*]

Usage note See note under WAIVE.

WAVES (wāvz), **Waves** *n.* (*as sing. or pl.*) the women's reserve of the US navy. [*W*omen *A*ccepted for *V*olunteer *E*mergency *S*ervice]

waving, wavy etc. WAVE.

wa-wa WAH-WAH.

wawl WAUL.

wax[1] (waks) *n.* **1** a yellow, mouldable, fatty substance excreted by bees and used for the cells of honeycombs; beeswax. **2** this substance purified and bleached, used for candles, modelling and pharmaceutical and other purposes. **3** any of various plant or animal substances that are principally esters of fatty acids or alcohols. **4** a mineral substance, such as ozocerite, composed of hydrocarbons. **5** any of various substances resembling beeswax, such as sealing wax. **6** cerumen, earwax. **7** (*coll.*) a person who is compliant or easily influenced (*She was wax in their hands*). **8** (*coll.*) † a gramophone record, or the material from which one was made. *~a.* made of wax. *~v.t.* **1** to smear, rub, polish, treat or join with wax. **2** to apply wax to (the legs etc.) and peel it away, thereby removing unwanted hair. **3** (*coll.*) †to make a gramophone record of. **waxberry** *n.* (*pl.* **waxberries**) **1** the wax myrtle. **2** the fruit of this. **waxbill** *n.* a small bird of the family Estrildidae with a bill resembling red sealing wax in colour. **waxcloth** *n.* **1** oilcloth. **2** linoleum. **waxed** *a.* **waxed jacket** *n.* a jacket made of cotton fabric waterproofed with wax. **waxed paper** *n.* paper waterproofed with wax. **waxen** *a.* **1** with a surface resembling wax. **2** like wax, impressible, plastic. **3** †made or consisting of wax. **waxer** *n.* **wax insect** *n.* an insect producing wax, such as *Ceroplastes ceriferus.* **wax-light** *n.* a taper, candle etc. made of wax. **wax moth** *n.* a moth, *Galleria mellonella*, which lays its eggs in beehives, the larvae feeding on the wax. **wax myrtle** *n.* the candleberry or bayberry shrub. **wax-painting** *n.* encaustic painting. **wax palm** *n.* **1** a S American palm, *Ceroxylon alpinum*, the trunk or leaves of which yield wax. **2** the carnauba, *Copernicia cerifera.* **wax paper** *n.* waxed paper. **wax-pod (bean)** *n.* a type of bean with waxy, yellow pods. **wax-tree** *n.* a tree yielding wax, esp. *Rhus succedanea.* **waxwing** *n.* any bird of the genus *Bombycilla*, the secondary and tertiary quills in some of which terminate in horny tips resembling pieces of red sealing wax. **waxwork** *n.* **1** modelling in wax, esp. in close imitation of living persons. **2** a wax figure or other object modelled in wax. **3** (*pl.*) an exhibition of wax figures. **waxworker** *n.* **waxy**[1] *a.* (*comp.* **waxier,** *superl.* **waxiest**) **1** resembling wax in appearance or consistency. **2** pliable, impressible, easily moulded. **3** containing or covered with wax. **4** pallid, wan. **waxily** *adv.* **waxiness** *n.* [OE *weax* (cp. Dut. *was*, G *Wachs*, Icel., Swed. *vax*)]

wax[2] (waks) *v.i.* **1** to increase gradually in size and brilliance, as the illuminated portion of the moon between new and full. **2** (*poet.*) to become larger, to grow in numbers, strength, intensity etc. **3** to pass into a specified condition, to become gradually (*to wax lyrical*). [OE *weaxan* (cp. Dut. *wassen*, G *wachsen*, Icel. *vaxa*, also Gr. *auxanein*, Sansk. *vaksh*, L *augēre*)]

wax[3] (waks) *n.* (*sl.*) a rage (*to be in a wax*). **waxy**[2] *a.* (*comp.* **waxier,** *superl.* **waxiest**) (*sl.*) angry. [etym. uncertain, perh. from *to wax angry*]

waxen, waxily etc. WAX[1].

waxy[1] WAX[1].

waxy[2] WAX[3].

way (wā) *n.* **1** a road, path, track or other place of passage. **2** a length of space passed over, a distance to be traversed (*a long way*). **3** the course or route followed or to be followed between two places or to reach a place (*to ask the way*). **4** a place of entrance, exit etc. (*the way in*). **5** the direction in which a thing or place lies or in which motion etc. takes place. **6** a particular or specified direction (*Come this way*). **7** the method, plan or manner of doing something, or proceeding to carry out some purpose. **8** a line or course of action. **9** a usual or habitual mode of action or conduct, a personal peculiarity, an idiosyncrasy (*to change one's ways*). **10** the usual course of events. **11** a person's line of business or occupation. **12** sphere, range, scope. **13** condition, state (*in a bad way*). **14** relation, respect, point. **15** onward movement, progress, advance, impetus (*to make one's way*). **16** room for passage or advance, ground over which one would proceed. **17** the state of being in transit (*on the way*). **18** (*pl.*) parts, portions (*The money was split four ways*). **19** (*pl.*) the framework of timbers over which a ship is launched. ~*adv.* (*coll.*) far, much (*It's way too expensive*). **across the way** opposite, on the other side of the road etc. **all the way 1** the full distance. **2** completely. **by the way 1** in passing, parenthetically. **2** during the journey. **by way of 1** by the route of, via. **2** for the purpose of. **3** as a form of or substitute for, to serve as (*by way of introduction*). **each way** EACH. **in a way 1** to some degree. **2** from one point of view. **in its way** considered from an appropriate standpoint. **in no way** by no means. **in the way** in a position or of a nature to obstruct or hinder. **in the way of 1** so as to fall in with or obtain (*I can put you in the way of a good deal*). **2** as regards, by way of. **one way and another** ONE. **on the way 1** in progress. **2** travelling or in transit. **3** (*coll.*) not yet born (*She's got four kids and another one on the way*). **on the way out** going out of fashion or favour. **out of one's way** OUT. **out of the way** OUT. **the way the cookie crumbles** COOKIE. **to be on one's way 1** to set off. **2** to be travelling or in transit. **to come someone's way 1** to become available to someone. **2** to fall to someone's lot (*You must take whatever comes your way*). **to find a way** to discover a means (of). **to get/ have one's (own) way** to get what one wants. **to give way** GIVE. **to go one's own way** to follow one's own plan, to act independently. **to go one's way** to depart. **to go out of one's way** to take great trouble (to), to make a special effort (to). **to go someone's way 1** to travel in the same direction as someone. **2** (of events etc.) to be in someone's favour. **to have it both ways** to have or alternate between two incompatible things. **to lead the way** LEAD[1]. **to look the other way** to ignore or disregard someone or something. **to make one's way 1** to proceed. **2** to prosper, esp. by one's own exertions. **to make way** MAKE[1]. **to pave the way for** PAVE. **under way 1** (of a ship etc.) in motion. **2** in progress. **way back** (*coll.*) a long time ago. **waybill** *n.* a list of passengers in a public conveyance or of goods sent by a carrier. **wayfarer** *n.* a traveller, esp. on foot. **wayfaring** *n., a.* **wayfaring tree** *n.* a large shrub, *Viburnum lantana*, with white flowers and black berries, found by roadsides. **waygoing** *a.* (*Sc.*) going away, departing. **waylay** *v.t.* (*pres.p.* **waylaying,** *past, p.p.* **waylaid**) **1** to wait for and stop, accost or intercept. **2** to lie in wait for and attack or rob. **waylayer** *n.* **way-leave** *n.* a right of way over the land of another, esp. rented by a company etc. †**wayless** *a.* **waymark** *n.* a post or other marker for guidance along a route, esp. on a footpath. **waymarked** *a.* **way of life** *n.* a manner of living. **Way of the Cross** *n.* **1** a series of pictures in a church representing the successive stages of Christ's progress to Calvary. **2** a series of devotions suited to each of these. **way of the world** *n.* the usual or customary manner of behaving etc. **way of thinking** *n.* an opinion (*to my way of thinking*). **way-out** *a.* **1** (*coll.*) out of the ordinary, unconventional, experimental. **2** (*sl.*) excellent. **waypoint** *n.* **1** a stopping place on a journey. **2** the coordinates of a stage on a sea journey, flight etc., used in navigation. **ways and means** *n.pl.* **1** methods of doing or achieving something. **2** methods of raising money, esp. government revenue. **wayside** *n.* the side of the road. ~*a.* situated or growing by the wayside. **to fall by the wayside** to fail or drop out during the course of an undertaking. **way station** *n.* (*N Am.*) **1** a railway halt. **2** a stage of progress in a course of action. **way train** *n.* (*N Am.*) a local train. **way-worn** *a.* wearied with travel. [OE *weg* (cp. Dut., G *Weg*, Icel. *vegr*), cogn. with WAIN, VEHICLE, VIADUCT]

-ways (wāz), **-way** (wā) *suf.* forming adverbs of position, direction, manner etc., as *always, lengthways.* [OE *weges*, gen. of WAY]

wayward (wā´wəd) *a.* **1** perverse, wilful, obstinate. **2** freakish, unpredictable, capricious. **waywardly** *adv.* **waywardness** *n.* [ME *weiward*, for *awaiward* (AWAY, -WARD)]

wayzgoose (wāz´goos), **wasegoose** *n.* (*pl.* **wayzgooses, wasegooses**) an annual dinner, picnic or other entertainment given to or held by the persons employed in a printing house. [perh. obs. *wayz*, stubble, GOOSE]

Wb *abbr.* weber.

WBA *abbr.* World Boxing Association.

WBC *abbr.* World Boxing Council.

WBO *abbr.* World Boxing Organization.

WC *abbr.* **1** water closet. **2** West Central.

wc *abbr.* **1** water closet. **2** without charge.

WCC *abbr.* World Council of Churches.

W/Cdr *abbr.* Wing Commander.

WD *abbr.* **1** War Department. **2** (Windward Islands) Dominica (IVR). **3** Works Department.

we (wē) *pron.* **1** the plural of I[2], denoting the person speaking and others associated with or represented by that person. **2** I (used by a sovereign, a newspaper editor etc.). **3** people in general. **4** (*coll.*) you (*How are we today?*). [OE *wē* (cp. Dut. *wij*, G *wir*, Sansk. *vayam*)]

WEA *abbr.* Workers' Educational Association.

weak (wēk) *a.* **1** deficient in physical strength, not robust, vigorous or powerful. **2** feeble, infirm, sickly, easily exhausted or fatigued. **3** deficient in mental or moral strength, feeble-minded, lacking strength of will, resolution etc. **4** yielding readily to temptation, easily led. **5** characterized by or showing lack of resolution or will-power. **6** deficient in strength, durability, force or efficiency. **7** fragile, brittle, pliant. **8** unreliable, ineffective, inefficacious. **9** deficient in number, quantity, weight etc. **10** lacking in flavour, watery (*weak coffee*). **11** poor, inadequate. **12** unsustained, unconvincing, controvertible (*a weak argument*). **13** (*Gram.*) **a** (of verbs) inflected by the addition of *-ed*, *-d* or *-t* to the stem in forming the past tense and p.p., not by internal vowel change. **b** (of nouns or adjectives) having a stem that originally ended in *-n*. **14** (of a verse ending) in which the stress falls on a normally unaccented or proclitic word. **15** (of a syllable) unaccented, unstressed. **16** (of an industry, market etc.) showing a downward trend in price, characterized by falling prices. **weaken** *v.t.* to make weak or weaker. *~v.i.* to become weak or weaker. **weakener** *n.* **weaker** *a.* **weaker sex** *n.* (*derog.*) the female sex, women. **weaker vessel** *n.* (*offensive or facet.*) woman (I Peter iii.7). **weakfish** *n.* (*pl. in general* **weakfish,** *in particular* **weakfishes**) (*N Am.*) a marine food fish of the genus *Cynoscion*, esp. *C. regalis*. **weak interaction** *n.* (*Physics*) an interaction between elementary particles responsible for certain decay processes. **weakish** *a.* **weak-kneed** *a.* giving way easily, lacking in resolution. **weakling** *n.* a feeble person or animal. **weakly** *adv.* in a weak manner. *~a.* (*comp.* **weaklier,** *superl.* **weakliest**) not strong in constitution; feeble, infirm, sickly. **weakliness** *n.* **weak-minded** *a.* feeble in intelligence or in resolution. **weak-mindedness** *n.* **weakness** *n.* **1** the state or condition of being weak. **2** a particular defect, failing or fault, a weak point. **3** a lack of resisting power. **4** a self-indulgent fondness (*a weakness for cream cakes*). **weak point, weak spot** *n.* **1** a place where defences are weak. **2** a failing or fault. **3** a trait by which a person is most easily influenced. **weak side** *n.* those traits of a person's character by which they are most easily influenced. **weak sister** *n.* (*N Am., coll.*) a weak or unreliable member of a group. **weak-willed** *a.* lacking strength of will or resolution. [OE *wāc*, weak (cp. Dut. *week*, G *weich*, Icel. *veikr*)]

weal[1] (wēl) *n.* **1** a ridge or raised streak made by a rod or whip on the flesh. **2** (*Med.*) a raised or inflamed area of the skin. *~v.t.* to mark with a weal or weals. [OE *walu*, orig. a rod (cp. GUNWALE, CHANNEL[1]) (cp. OFris. *walu*, Icel. *völr*) cogn. with L *volvere*, Gr. *helissein*, to roll]

weal[2] (wēl) *n.* (*poet.*) a sound, healthy or prosperous state of persons or things. [OE *wela* (cp. G *Wohl*, Dan. *vel*), cogn. with WELL[1]]

weald (wēld) *n.* a tract of open forest land, esp. the Weald. **the Weald** the portion of Kent, Surrey, Sussex and Hampshire between the N and S Downs. **weald-clay** *n.* the upper part of the Wealden strata, comprising beds of clay, ironstone etc., rich in fossils. **Wealden** *a.* of or relating to the Weald, esp. geologically. **Wealden strata** *n.pl.* the series of lower Cretaceous freshwater strata between the Jurassic and the chalk, best displayed in the Weald. [ME *weeld*, *wald*, perh. var. of WOLD]

wealth (welth) *n.* **1** riches, large possessions of money, goods or lands. **2** the state of being rich, affluence. **3** an abundance, a profusion (of) (*a wealth of information*). **4** †weal, prosperity. **wealth tax** *n.* a tax on personal property or capital. **wealthy** *a.* (*comp.* **wealthier,** *superl.* **wealthiest**) rich, affluent, having many possessions. **wealthily** *adv.* **wealthiness** *n.* [WEAL[2], -TH[1] (cp. Dut. *weelde*, luxury, OHG *welida*, riches)]

wean[1] (wēn) *v.t.* **1** to accustom (a child or animal) to nourishment other than its mother's milk, to teach to feed other than from the breast or bottle. **2** to detach or estrange from a habit, indulgence, desire etc. (*I'm trying to wean him off computer games*). **to be weaned on** to be familiar or grow up with from an early age. **weaner** *n.* a young animal newly weaned. **weanling** *n.* a child or animal newly weaned. *~a.* newly weaned. [OE *wenian*, to accustom (cp. Dut. *wennen*, G *gewöhnen*, Dan. *vænne*), cogn. with WONT]

wean[2] (wān) *n.* (*Sc., North.*) a child. [contr. of *wee ane*, little one]

weapon (wep´ən) *n.* **1** an instrument of attack or defence, a thing used to inflict bodily harm. **2** any means used for attack or defence. **3** a claw, sting, thorn, prickle etc. **weaponed** *a.* **weaponless** *a.* **weaponry** *n.* weapons collectively. [OE *wæpen* (cp. Dut. *wapen*, G *Wappe*, Icel. *vāpn*)]

wear[1] (weə) *v.t.* (*past* **wore** (waw), *p.p.* **worn** (wawn)) **1** to have on the person as clothing, ornament etc. **2** to be dressed in, esp. habitually. **3** to arrange (hair or clothes) in a specified manner. **4** to bear, to carry, to maintain. **5** to exhibit, to display (*to wear a smile*). **6** to consume, diminish, impair, efface or alter by rubbing or use. **7** to produce (a hole, channel etc.) by attrition. **8** to exhaust, fatigue or weary. **9** (*coll.*) to stand for, to tolerate, accept (*Do you think she'll wear it?*). **10** to pass (time) slowly or gradually. *~v.i.* **1** to be consumed, diminished, effaced, altered etc. by rubbing or use. **2** to be exhausted, to be tired (out). **3** to stand continual use (well, badly etc.). **4** to resist the effects of use, age, attrition etc., to endure, to last. **5** to pass slowly or gradually (away etc.) (*as the day wore on*). *~n.* **1** the act of wearing. **2** the state of being worn. **3** something worn or to be worn, clothing. **4** damage or diminution by attrition, use etc. **5** durability, fitness for use. **in wear** being worn regularly. **to wear blinkers** BLINK. **to wear down** to overcome gradually by persistent pressure. **to wear motley** MOTLEY. **to wear off** **1** to efface or diminish, or to be effaced or diminished, by attrition; to rub off. **2** to decline or pass away gradually (*when the effects of the drugs wear off*). **to wear one's heart on one's sleeve** HEART. **to wear out** **1** to use until no longer of use, to consume or render worthless by use. **2** to exhaust, to tire out. **3** to be used up, consumed or rendered worthless by attrition and use. **to wear the breeches** BREECH. **to wear the trousers** TROUSERS. **to wear thin** **1** to become thin through use. **2** (of patience) to diminish. **3** (of excuses) to become less convincing or acceptable. **-wear** *comb. form* forming names of categories of clothing, as in *menswear*, *swimwear*. **wearable** *a.* **wearability** (-bil´-) *n.* **wear and tear** *n.* waste, diminution or damage caused by ordinary use. **wearer** *n.* **wearing** *a.* **1** tiresome. **2** tiring. **wearingly** *adv.* [OE *werian* (cp. Icel. *verja*, OHG *werian*, Goth. *wasjan*), cogn. with L *vestis*, Gr. *esthēs*, clothes, Sansk. *vas*, to dress]

wear[2] (weə) *v.t.* (*past, p.p.* **wore** (waw)) to bring (a ship) about by turning the bow away from the wind. *~v.i.* (of a ship) to come round thus. [etym. unknown]

wear[3] WEIR.

weary (wiə´ri) *a.* (*comp.* **wearier,** *superl.* **weariest**) **1** tired, fatigued, exhausted. **2** expressing weariness or exhaustion (*a weary smile*). **3** impatient or sick (of). **4** tiresome, tedious. **5** exhausting, irksome. *~v.t.* (*3rd pers. sing. pres.* **wearies,** *pres.p.* **wearying,** *past, p.p.* **wearied**) **1** to tire, to fatigue. **2** to make impatient or sick (of). *~v.i.* **1** to become tired or fatigued. **2** to become impatient or sick (of). **3** (*Sc.*) to long, to be wistful, to yearn. **weariless** *a.* **wearily** *adv.* **weariness** *n.* **wearisome** *a.* tedious, tiresome, causing weariness. **wearisomely** *adv.* **wearisomeness** *n.* **wearyingly** *adv.* [OE *wērig* (cp. OHG *wuorag*, drunk), rel. to *wōrian*, to travel]

weasel (wē´zəl) *n.* **1** a small reddish-brown, white-bellied mammal, *Mustela nivalis*, related to the stoat, ferret etc., with a long lithe body and short legs, preying on small birds, mice etc. **2** (*coll.*) a sly, deceitful, furtive or treacherous person. *~v.i.* (*pres.p.* **weaselling,** (*N Am.*) **weaseling,** *past, p.p.* **weaselled,** (*N Am.*) **weaseled**) (*coll.*) **1** to evade or extricate oneself from a responsibility, obligation etc. (*He tried to weasel out of the deal*). **2** (*chiefly N Am.*) to equivocate. **weasel-faced** *a.* having a sharp, thin face. **weaselly** *a.* **weasel word** *n.* (*usu. pl.*) a word designed to mislead or to be evasive. [OE *wesle* (cp. Dut. *wezel*, G *Wiesel*, Icel. *vīsla*, also Gr. *ailouros*)]

weather (wedh´ə) *n.* **1** the state of the atmosphere, esp. at a given time or place, with reference to cold or heat, humidity, rain, pressure, wind, electrical conditions etc. **2** (*usu. pl.*) change, vicissitude. ~*v.t.* **1** to encounter and pass through (a storm etc.) in safety. **2** to endure and come through (a crisis etc.) in safety. **3** to expose to the action of the weather. **4** (*usu. p.p.*) to wear, disintegrate or discolour (rock, cliffs, masonry etc.) by this. **5** (*Naut.*) to get to windward of (a cape etc.) in spite of inclement weather. **6** to slope (tiles etc.) down so as to overlap. ~*v.i.* **1** to stand the effects of weather. **2** to become worn or discoloured by exposure to weather. ~*a.* situated towards the wind; windward (*the weather side*). **to keep a/ one's weather eye open 1** (*coll.*) to be on the alert. **2** (*coll.*) to have one's wits about one. **to make bad weather** (of a vessel) to behave badly in a storm. **to make good weather** (of a vessel) to behave well in a storm. **to make heavy weather of** to exaggerate the difficulty of. **under the weather 1** poorly, unwell. **2** depressed, in low spirits. **3** drunk, intoxicated. **weather-beaten** *a.* seasoned or tanned by exposure to weather, storms etc. **weatherboard** *v.t.* to furnish with weatherboarding. ~*n.* **1** a board used for weatherboarding. **2** a board fastened to the bottom of a door to keep out rain, snow etc. **weatherboarding** *n.* a series of sloping boards fastened together so as to overlap and to throw off rain, snow etc. from roofs, walls etc. **weather-bound** *a.* detained by bad weather. **weather chart** *n.* a chart of a wide area showing isobars and other symbols indicating the state of the weather in different parts. **weathercock** *n.* **1** a weathervane, esp. in the shape of a cock. **2** an inconstant person. **weather forecast** *n.* a calculation or estimate of future weather, esp. based on meteorological observations. **weather gauge** *n.* the position of a ship on the exposed (windward) side of another vessel etc., relative to the wind. **weathergirl** *n.* a woman who reports on the weather on television etc., a meteorologist. **weather-glass** *n.* a barometer. **weather house** *n.* a weather indicator worked by the effect of hygroscopic conditions on a string, the figures of a man and woman emerging at the sides of a toy house indicating wet or dry weather respectively. **weathering** *n.* **1** exposure to the weather. **2** disintegration etc. through this. **weatherly** *a.* **1** (of a ship) presenting such lateral resistance to the water as to make little leeway. **2** able to keep close to the wind. **weatherliness** *n.* **weatherman** *n.* (*pl.* **weathermen**) a man who reports on the weather on television etc., a meteorologist. **weather map** *n.* a weather chart. **weathermost** *a.* furthest to windward. **weatherproof** *a.* proof against the weather, esp. against rain. ~*v.t.* to make weatherproof. **weatherproofed** *a.* **weather report** *n.* an official daily report of meteorological observations and probable changes in the weather. **weather ship** *n.* a ship engaged in meteorological work. **weather station** *n.* a place where meteorological observations are taken or recorded. **weatherstrip** *n.* a piece of board, rubber etc. fastened across a door, window etc. to keep out wind or rain. ~*v.t.* (*pres.p.* **weatherstripping,** *past, p.p.* **weatherstripped**) to fasten a weatherstrip to. **weatherstripping** *n.* **weather-tight** *a.* (of a house etc.) proof against the weather. **weather-tiles** *n.pl.* tiles hung on outside walls to protect against damp etc. **weathervane** *n.* a revolving vane mounted on the top of a steeple or other high point to show the direction of the wind. **weather window** *n.* a limited period of time when the weather conditions are suitable for a particular activity or project. **weather-wise** *a.* skilful in forecasting the weather. **weather-worn** *a.* damaged by bad weather. [OE *weder* (cp. Dut. *weder,* G *Wetter,* Icel. *vethr*), cogn. with Goth. *waian,* Sansk. *va,* Gr. *aēnai,* to blow, Eng. WIND[1]]

weave[1] (wēv) *v.t.* (*past* **wove** (wōv), *p.p.* **woven** (wō´vən), **wove**) **1** to form (threads, yarns etc.) into fabric by interlacing. **2** to produce (fabric or an article) thus (*to weave a rug*). **3** to construct by intertwining canes, rushes etc. **4** (of a spider) to form (a web). **5** to interweave (facts, details etc.) into a story, theory etc. **6** to construct (a scheme, plot etc.) thus. ~*v.i.* **1** to make fabric by interlacing threads etc. **2** to work at a loom. **weavable** *a.* **weaver** *n.* **1** a person who weaves, esp. one whose occupation is to weave cloth etc. **2** a weaver-bird. **weaver-bird** *n.* a finchlike bird of the family Ploceidae, of the warmer parts of Asia, Africa and Australia, that constructs elaborate nests of woven grass. **weaver's knot** *n.* a sheet bend. [OE *wefan* (cp. Dut. *weven,* G *weben,* Icel. *vefa*), cogn. with Gr. *huphainein*]

weave[2] (wēv) *v.i.* (*past, p.p.* **weaved**) **1** to take a zigzag course, esp. to avoid obstructions (*to weave through the traffic*). **2** (*coll.*) to take evasive action. **to get weaving 1** (*sl.*) to begin. **2** (*sl.*) to hurry. [prob. from ME *weve,* var. of *waive* (ON *veifa,* WAVE)]

web (web) *n.* **1** a network of threads constructed by spiders to catch their prey, a cobweb. **2** a similar structure spun by insect larvae etc. **3** a woven fabric, a piece of woven cloth. **4** any complex network or similar structure. **5** an artfully contrived plot, trap etc. **6** the membrane between the toes of swimming birds etc. **7** the vane of a feather. **8** a large roll of paper for printing etc. as it comes from the mill. **9** the thin part of the plate in a girder connecting the upper and lower plates. **10** the part of a railway-carriage wheel between the nave and rim. ~*v.t.* (*pres.p.* **webbing,** *past, p.p.* **webbed**) **1** to connect, provide or cover with or as with a web. **2** to ensnare. ~*v.i.* to weave a web. **webbed** *a.* **1** (of a bird's foot etc.) having the toes connected by a membrane. **2** connected or covered with or as with a web. **webbing** *n.* **1** a strong woven band of fibre etc., used for belts, straps, the bottoms of seats or beds etc. **2** any strong woven tape or edging. **3** a woven structure. **webby** *a.* (*comp.* **webbier,** *superl.* **webbiest**). **webfoot** *n.* (*pl.* **webfeet**) a webbed foot. **web-footed** *a.* having the toes connected by a web. **web offset** *n.* offset printing using a continuous roll of paper. †**webster** *n.* a weaver. **web-toed** *a.* web-footed. **web-wheel** *n.* **1** a wheel that has a plate or web instead of spokes. **2** a wheel that has the centre, spokes and rim in one piece. **webwork** *n.* a network. **webworm** *n.* (*N Am.*) the gregarious larva of an insect weaving a web or tent as a shelter. [OE *webb* (cp. Dut. *web,* G *Gewebe,* Icel. *vefr*), from *wefan,* WEAVE[1])]

weber (vā´bə, web´ə) *n.* the SI unit of magnetic flux. [Wilhelm Eduard *Weber,* 1804–91, German physicist]

†**webster** WEB.

Wed. *abbr.* Wednesday.

wed (wed) *v.t.* (*pres.p.* **wedding,** *past, p.p.* **wedded, wed**) **1** to marry. **2** to join in marriage. **3** to unite, to attach firmly. ~*v.i.* to marry. **wedded** *a.* **1** married, of or relating to matrimony. **2** intimately united. **3** strongly attached (to). **wedding** *n.* a marriage ceremony, usu. with the accompanying festivities. **wedding breakfast** *n.* a celebratory meal given after a wedding ceremony. **wedding cake** *n.* an iced cake distributed to the guests at a wedding, portions being afterwards sent to absent friends. **wedding day** *n.* the day of a marriage or its anniversary. **wedding march** *n.* music in march time played at the beginning or end of a marriage ceremony. **wedding night** *n.* the night after a wedding, esp. as the time when the marriage is consummated. **wedding ring** *n.* a plain ring given by one partner to the other during the marriage ceremony, and worn thereafter. [OE *weddian* (cp. Dut. *wedden,* G *wetten,* Icel. *vethja,* to wager), cogn. with WAGE, WAGER, GAGE[1]]

we'd (wēd) *contr.* **1** we had. **2** we would.

wedge (wej) *n.* **1** a piece of wood or metal thick at one end and tapering to a thin edge at the other, used for splitting wood, rocks etc., for exerting great pressure, for fixing or fastening etc. 2 an object or portion of anything in the shape of a wedge. 3 something that causes a separation or divide (*Politics drove a wedge between them*). 4 a shoe without an instep, having the heel and sole together forming the shape of a wedge. 5 (*also* **wedge heel**) the heel of such a shoe. 6 a golf club with a wedge-shaped head. ~*v.t.* 1 to fix or fasten with a wedge or wedges. 2 to split or separate with or as with a wedge. 3 to squeeze or push, esp. in or into a narrow space (*I was wedged between two fat men*). **the thin end of the wedge** a relatively unimportant first step, measure or change that is likely to lead to something more important, serious etc. **wedgelike** *a.* **wedge-shaped** *a.* **wedge-tailed** *a.* (of a bird) having a wedge-shaped tail owing to the greater length of the middle feathers. **wedgewise** *adv.* **wedgie** *n.* (*coll.*) a shoe with a wedge heel. [OE *wecg* (cp. Dut. *wig*, G *Wecke*, Icel. *veggr*)]

Wedgwood® (wej´wud) *n.* 1 a type of fine pottery, made by Josiah Wedgwood, 1730–95, and his successors, often bearing a white cameo-like design in relief. 2 Wedgwood blue. **Wedgwood blue** *n.* a light greyish-blue. ~*a.* of this colour.

wedlock (wed´lok) *n.* matrimony, the married state. **born in wedlock** legitimate. **born out of wedlock** illegitimate. [OE *wedlāk* (*wed*, pledge, *lāc*, sport, gift)]

Wednesday (wenz´di, wed´ənzdā) *n.* the fourth day of the week, following Tuesday. ~*adv.* (*coll.*) on Wednesday. **Wednesdays** *adv.* (*coll.*) every Wednesday. [OE *Wōdnes dæg*, Woden's or Odin's day]

Weds. *abbr.* Wednesday.

wee[1] (wē) *a.* (*comp.* **weer** (wē´ə), *superl.* **weest** (wē´ist)) 1 (*esp. Sc.*) little. 2 (*coll.*) very small, tiny. [ME *wei*, a bit]

wee[2] WEE-WEE.

weed (wēd) *n.* 1 a useless or troublesome plant in cultivated land, a wild plant springing up where not wanted in a garden etc. 2 any useless or troublesome intrusive thing. 3 (*coll.*) a weak or weedy person. 4 (*sl.*) a leggy, loose-bodied horse. 5 (*sl.*) a cigar or cigarette. ~*v.t.* 1 to clear (ground) of weeds. 2 to pull up (a troublesome or intrusive plant). 3 to clear of anything harmful or offensive. 4 to sort (out) (useless or inferior elements, members etc.) for removal or elimination (*to weed out the troublemakers*). 5 to rid of these. ~*v.i.* to pull up weeds from a garden etc. **the weed** 1 (*sl.*) tobacco. 2 (*sl.*) marijuana. **weeder** *n.* 1 a person who weeds. 2 a weeding tool. **weed-grown** *a.* overgrown with weeds. **weedkiller** *n.* a chemical or other substance (usu. poisonous) for destroying weeds. **weedless** *a.* **weedy** *a.* (*comp.* **weedier,** *superl.* **weediest**) 1 containing weeds. 2 (*coll.*) thin, weak, lacking stamina. **weediness** *n.* [OE *wēod*, *wīod* (cp. LG *wēden*, to weed), etym. uncertain]

†**weeds** (wēdz) *n.pl.* mourning worn by a widow. [OE *wæde*, garment, cp. OFris. *wēde*, Icel. *vāth*, OHG *wāt*, *wōt*]

week (wēk) *n.* 1 a period of seven days, esp. from Sunday to Saturday inclusively. 2 the five or six working days, excluding Sunday or Saturday and Sunday. 3 the time spent working (*a 40-hour week*). 4 (*pl.*) a long time, several weeks (*weeks later*). 5 a week after or before (the day specified) (*Thursday week*; *yesterday week*). **this day week** DAY. **weekday** *n.* any day of the week except Sunday and usu. also Saturday. **weekend** *n.* the days at the end of the working week, usu. Saturday and Sunday, esp. as a time for leisure, holiday etc. ~*v.i.* to spend a weekend, esp. on holiday (*We weekended by the sea*). **weekender** *n.* 1 a person who spends a weekend on holiday. 2 (*Austral.*) a cottage used for this purpose. 3 a small boat used for this purpose. **week-long** *a.* lasting a week. **weekly** *a.* 1 happening, issued or done once a week or every week. 2 lasting a week. 3 of, relating to or reckoned by the week (*weekly wages*). ~*adv.* 1 once a week. 2 week by week. ~*n.* (*pl.* **weeklies**) a weekly periodical. **weeknight** *n.* a night of a weekday. [OE *wice*, *wuce* (cp. Dut. *week*, Icel. *vika*, OHG *wecha*), etym. uncertain]

†**ween** (wēn) *v.i.* 1 to be of the opinion. 2 to think, to fancy. [OE *wēnan* (cp. Dut. *wanen*, G *wähnen*, Icel. *vāna*, to hope)]

weenie WIENER.

weeny (wē´ni) *a.* (*comp.* **weenier,** *superl.* **weeniest**) (*coll.*) very small, tiny. **weeny-bopper** *n.* a pre-adolescent fan of pop music and pop stars. [WEE[1], TINY]

weep (wēp) *v.i.* (*past, p.p.* **wept** (wept)) 1 to shed tears. 2 to lament, to mourn (for). 3 to drip, to exude liquid, to run or be suffused with drops of moisture. 4 (*usu. pres.p.*) to have pendulous branches (*weeping ivy*; *a weeping ash*). ~*v.t.* 1 to shed tears over, to lament, to bewail. 2 to utter with tears. 3 to shed (tears). 4 to exude. ~*n.* a spell of weeping. **weeper** *n.* 1 a person who weeps. 2 (*Hist.*) a hired mourner. 3 a widow's white cuff or black crape veil or a man's sashlike hatband worn as a token of mourning. **weepie** *n.* (*coll.*) a sentimental film, play, book etc. **weeping willow** *n.* a willow, *Salix babylonica*, with delicate pendulous branches. **weepy** *a.* (*comp.* **weepier,** *superl.* **weepiest**) tearful. ~*n.* (*pl.* **weepies**) (*coll.*) a weepie. **weepily** *adv.* **weepiness** *n.* [OE *wēpan* (OS *wōpian*, OHG *wuofan*), from *wōp*, an outcry]

weever (wē´və) *n.* any marine fish of the genus *Trachinus*, such as *T. vipera*, inflicting painful wounds with their dorsal and opercular spines. [ME *wivere*, WYVERN]

weevil (wē´vəl) *n.* 1 a small beetle, esp. of the family Curculionidae, with the head prolonged into a rostrum or proboscis, feeding on grain, nuts, roots, leaves etc. 2 any insect that is a pest of grain. **weevily** *a.* [OE *wifel* (cp. Dut. *wevel*, G *Wiebel*), cogn. with WEAVE[1]]

wee-wee (wē´wē), **wee** (wē) *v.i.* (*3rd pers. sing. pres.* **wee-wees, wees,** *pres.p.* **wee-weeing, weeing,** *past, p.p.* **wee-weed, weed**) (*sl.*) to urinate (used esp. by or to children). ~*n.* 1 an act of urinating. 2 urine. [onomat.]

w.e.f. *abbr.* with effect from.

weft[1] (weft) *n.* 1 the threads passing through the warp from selvedge to selvedge, the woof. 2 woven cloth. 3 strips used for filling in basket-weaving. [OE, from *wefan*, WEAVE[1]]

weft[2] WAFT.

Wehrmacht (veə´mahkht) *n.* (*Hist.*) the armed forces of Germany from 1921 to 1945. [G, defensive force]

weigela (wījē´lə) *n.* any shrub of the genus *Weigela*, esp. *W. florida*, grown for its showy pink, red, purple or white flowers. [C. E. *Weigel*, 1748–1831, German physicist]

weigh (wā) *v.t.* 1 to find the weight of by means of scales etc. 2 to be equivalent to in weight. 3 to weigh out (a particular amount). 4 to hold in the hands to or as to guess the weight of. 5 to ponder, to consider carefully, to estimate the relative value, advantages etc. of, to compare. 6 to raise (an anchor). ~*v.i.* 1 to have weight. 2 to be considered important, to have influence. 3 to be burdensome or oppressive (on or upon). ~*n.* the act or process of weighing. **to weigh anchor** ANCHOR. **to weigh down** 1 to cause to sink by weight, to force down. 2 to hold or keep down by weight. 3 to oppress. **to weigh in** 1 (of a jockey, boxer etc.) to be weighed before a race, contest etc. 2 (*coll.*) to intervene (with) (*She weighed in with an argument about traffic congestion*). **to weigh into** to attack. **to weigh one's words** to choose one's words carefully. **to weigh out** 1 to take (a particular weight of something) from a quantity. 2 to distribute or apportion in quantities measured by scales. 3 (of a jockey) to be weighed before a race. **to weigh up** 1 (*coll.*) to assess, to judge. 2 (*coll.*) to consider carefully (*to weigh up the pros and cons*). **under weigh** (*Naut.*) under way. **weighable** *a.* **weighbridge** *n.* a machine with an iron platform, on which lorries etc. are weighed. **weigher** *n.* **weigh-in** *n.* the act of weighing in a boxer, jockey etc. **weighing** *n.* **weighing machine** *n.* a machine for weighing people, animals, loaded vehicles etc. [OE *wegan*, to carry (cp. Dut. *wegen*, to weigh, G *wegen*, to move, *wägen*, to weigh, Icel. *vega*, to move, to weigh, also Sansk. *vah*, L *vehere*, see VEHICLE)]

weight (wāt) *n.* 1 the force with which bodies tend towards a centre of attraction, esp. the centre of the earth; the downward tendency caused by gravity less the centrifugal tendency due to the earth's rotation. 2 the relative mass or quantity of matter contained in a body, heaviness, esp. as expressed in terms of some standard unit. 3 the amount that something or someone weighs or should weigh. 4 a scale or graduated system of units of weight. 5 a unit of weight used in such a system. 6 a piece of metal etc. of known weight used with scales for weighing goods etc. 7 a heavy object or mass used for mechanical purposes, as in a clock, or for weight training etc. 8 a heavy load, a burden. 9 pressure, oppressiveness. 10 importance, consequence, influence. 11 preponderance. 12 a value given to an item in a frequency distribution to represent its relative importance. 13 the density of cloth, paper, type etc. ~*v.t.* 1 to attach a weight or weights to. 2 to hold down with a weight or weights. 3 to add weight to. 4 to burden, to oppress. 5 to treat with minerals etc. to make heavier. 6 to assign a statistical weight to. 7 to bias. 8 to assign a handicap weight to. **to carry weight** to be important or influential. **to lose weight** to become lighter or thinner. **to pull one's weight** to take one's due share of work or responsibility. **to put on weight** to become heavier or fatter. **to throw one's weight about/ around** (*coll.*) to act in a domineering or aggressively self-assertive way. **worth one's weight in gold** extremely useful, valuable etc. **weight gain** *n.* an increase in weight, esp. of the body. **weighting** *n.* an allowance paid in addition to the basic salary to offset the higher living costs of a particular area. **weightless** *a.* having no apparent weight, esp. because unaffected by gravity, as in an orbiting spacecraft. **weightlessly** *adv.* **weightlessness** *n.* **weightlifting** *n.* the sport of lifting barbells of increasing weight using standard lifting techniques. **weightlifter** *n.* **weight loss** *n.* a decrease in weight, esp. of the body. **weight training** *n.* physical training using weights to strengthen and tone muscles. **weight-watcher** *n.* a person who is attempting not to put on weight or to lose weight by dieting. **weight-watching** *n.*, *a.* **weighty** *a.* (*comp.* **weightier,** *superl.* **weightiest**) 1 having great weight, heavy. 2 important, serious, momentous. 3 convincing, cogent, influential. 4 serious. **weightily** *adv.* **weightiness** *n.* [OE *gewiht*, as WEIGH]

Weil's disease (vīlz) *n.* a severe form of leptospirosis transmitted via contaminated water. [H. A. *Weil*, 1848–1916, German physician]

Weimaraner (vīmərah´nə, wī-) *n.* a type of gun dog with a very short, usu. grey coat. [*Weimar*, city in Germany]

weir (wiə), **wear** *n.* 1 a dam across a river or stream for raising the level of the water above it. 2 a fence or enclosure of stakes, nets etc. set in a stream or river to catch fish. [OE *wer*, cogn. with *werian*, to defend]

weird (wiəd) *a.* 1 supernatural, unearthly, uncanny. 2 (*coll.*) strange, peculiar. 3 †of or relating to fate or destiny. ~†*n.* (*chiefly Sc.*) 1 fate, destiny. 2 one of the Fates. **to dree one's weird** DREE. **weirdie** (-di) *n.* (*coll.*) a weirdo. **weirdly** *adv.* **weirdness** *n.* **weirdo** (-dō) *n.* (*pl.* **weirdos**) (*coll.*) a strange or eccentric person. **weird sisters** *n.pl.* 1 the Fates. 2 witches. [OE *wyrd*, from *weorthan*, to be, to become]

Weismannism (vīs´mənizm) *n.* (*Biol.*) the doctrine maintaining the continuity of germ plasm and the impossibility of transmitting acquired characteristics. [August *Weismann*, 1834–1915, German biologist]

weka (wek´ə, wā´kə, wē´-) *n.* a flightless New Zealand rail, *Gallirallus australis*. [Maori]

Welch (welsh) *a.* Welsh (now only in *Royal Welch Fusiliers, Welch regiment*). [WELSH]

welch WELSH.

welcome (wel´kəm) *a.* 1 admitted or received with pleasure and cordiality. 2 producing satisfaction or gladness (*a welcome sight*). 3 gladly permitted (to) (*You're welcome to borrow my calculator*). 4 (*often iron.*) gladly permitted to have (*You're welcome to it!*). ~*n.* 1 a salutation or act of saying 'welcome' to a newcomer etc. 2 a kind or cordial reception or entertainment of a guest etc. 3 a willing acceptance of an offer etc. ~*int.* used to express cordial reception of a guest etc. ~*v.t.* 1 to greet cordially. 2 to receive or entertain with kindness or cordiality. 3 to receive or accept with pleasure. 4 to greet or receive in a particular way. **to make welcome** to receive in a kind or hospitable way. **to outstay one's welcome** to stay too long. **to overstay one's welcome** to outstay one's welcome. **you're welcome!** used in response to thanks. **welcomely** *adv.* **welcomeness** *n.* **welcomer** *n.* **welcomingly** *adv.* [OE *wilcuma* (*willa*, pleasure, *cuma*, comer, assim. to WELL[1], and COME)]

weld[1] (weld) *v.t.* 1 to unite or join (pieces of metal) together by heat or by compressing, esp. after they have been softened by heat. 2 to unite (pieces of plastic) similarly. 3 to make, produce or repair thus. 4 to unite into a coherent mass, body etc. ~*v.i.* to unite (well or badly) by this process. ~*n.* a joint or junction made by welding. **weldable** *a.* **weldability** (-bil´-) *n.* **welder** *n.* [var. of WELL[2]]

weld[2] (weld) *n.* 1 a plant, *Reseda luteola*, from which a yellow dye was formerly prepared. 2 this dye. [prob. cogn. with WOLD]

welfare (wel´feə) *n.* 1 prosperity, success. 2 health, well-being. 3 welfare work. 4 financial and other aid given to those in need. **welfare state** *n.* 1 a system in which the government promotes and assumes responsibility for the general welfare of the population, usu. by introducing social security measures. 2 a state operating such a system. **welfare work** *n.* efforts to improve living conditions for the very poor, elderly etc. **welfare worker** *n.* **welfarism** *n.* the policies or principles of a welfare state. **welfarist** *n.* [WELL[1], FARE]

welkin (wel´kin) *n.* (*poet.*) the sky, the vault of heaven. [OE *wolcnu*, pl. of *wolcen*, cloud (cp. G *Wolke*, OHG *wolka*, cloud), perh. cogn. with WALK]

well[1] (wel) *adv.* (*comp.* **better,** *superl.* **best**) 1 in a good or right manner, properly, satisfactorily. 2 kindly. 3 skilfully (*He cooks well*). 4 prosperously, successfully. 5 happily, fortunately. 6 adequately, amply, sufficiently. 7 to a considerable extent. 8 fully, perfectly, thoroughly. 9 closely, intimately. 10 heartily, cordially. 11 favourably, with approval, in good terms (*She spoke well of you*). 12 justly, fairly, reasonably, wisely. 13 very possibly, indeed. 14 comfortably, liberally (*to live well*). 15 (*sl.*) very. ~*a.* (*usu. pred.*) 1 in good health. 2 in a satisfactory state, position or circumstances. 3 sensible, advisable (*It would be well to check*). 4 fortunate (*It is well that you noticed*). ~*int.* 1 used to express astonishment, expectation, resignation, concession etc. 2 used in resuming one's discourse. **as well** 1 in addition. 2 equally, as much (as), not less than. 3 proper, right, not unadvisable (to) (*It's as well to switch it off first*). **(just) as well** just as reasonably, with no worse results (*We* *might as well go home*). **not (too) well** NOT. **to leave well alone** LEAVE[1]. **well and good** used to express calm or dispassionate acceptance. **well and truly** completely, utterly. **well away 1** making or having made rapid progress. **2** (*coll.*) drunk. **3** (*coll.*) fast asleep. **well enough** ENOUGH. **well, I'm sure** SURE. **well in** (*coll.*) on good terms (with). **well I never!** NEVER. **well met** MEET[1]. **well worth** certainly worth (*well worth the trouble*; *well worth avoiding*). **well acquainted** *a.* very familiar (with). **well-adjusted** *a.* **1** mentally stable. **2** properly adjusted. **well advised** *a.* prudent, judicious, wise (*You would be well advised to leave*). **well-appointed** *a.* fully furnished or equipped. **well-attended** *a.* attended by a large number of people (*a well-attended meeting*). **well aware** *a.* fully aware (of). **well-balanced** *a.* **1** sensible, sane. **2** equally matched. **well-behaved** *a.* having or displaying good behaviour or manners. **well-being** *n.* the state of being healthy, happy etc. **well-born** *a.* of good birth. **well-bred** *a.* **1** having good breeding or manners. **2** of good or pure stock. **well-built** *a.* **1** sturdy, robust, muscular. **2** of sound construction. **well-chosen** *a.* selected with judgement (*a few well-chosen words*). **well-conditioned** *a.* in good condition. **well-conducted** *a.* **1** properly conducted (*a well-conducted operation*). **2** well-behaved. **well-connected** *a.* related to rich or socially powerful people. **well-constructed** *a.* **1** of sound construction. **2** (of an essay, article etc.) well-planned, carefully put together. **well-covered** *a.* (*coll.*) plump. **well-cut** *a.* skilfully cut or tailored (*well-cut trousers*). **well-defined** *a.* clearly determined. **well-deserved** *a.* thoroughly merited. **well-designed** *a.* skilfully or practically designed. **well-developed** *a.* **1** fully developed. **2** large. **well disposed** *a.* of favourable and kindly feeling (to or towards). **well done** *a.* (of food) cooked thoroughly. *~int.* used to express congratulation. **well-dressed** *a.* dressed in fashionable or elegant clothes. **well-earned** *a.* thoroughly deserved (*a well-earned rest*). **well-educated** *a.* having a good education. **well-endowed** *a.* **1** having plenty of money, talent etc. **2** (*coll.*) **a** (of a man) having a large penis. **b** (of a woman) having large breasts. **well-equipped** *a.* fully equipped, having all the necessary equipment, resources etc. **well-established** *a.* of long standing. **well-favoured,** (*N Am.*) **well-favored** *a.* handsome, good-looking. **well-fed** *a.* **1** having a good diet. **2** having had plenty to eat. **well fitted** *a.* **1** well furnished or equipped. **2** well suited. **well-fitting** *a.* (of a garment etc.) that fits well. **well-formed** *a.* **1** attractively shaped. **2** correctly constructed (*a well-formed sentence*). **well-found** *a.* well-appointed. **well-founded** *a.* based on certain or well-authenticated grounds. **well-groomed** *a.* neat and elegant in dress and appearance. **well-grounded** *a.* **1** well-founded. **2** having all the basic knowledge of a subject etc. **well-heeled** *a.* (*coll.*) wealthy. **well-hung** *a.* **1** (*coll.*) (of a man) having large genitals. **2** (of meat, game etc.) hung for the right length of time. **well-informed** *a.* **1** having ample information. **2** having knowledge of numerous subjects. **well-intentioned** *a.* having good intentions (usu. with unsatisfactory results). **well-judged** *a.* skilfully, tactfully or accurately done, aimed, contrived etc. **well-kept** *a.* well looked after, well-maintained (*a well-kept garden*). **well-knit** *a.* (esp. of a person's body) compact, firmly built. **well-known** *a.* **1** known to many people, familiar, notorious. **2** thoroughly known. **well-liked** *a.* liked by many people, popular. **well-loved** *a.* regarded with affection by many people. **well-made** *a.* **1** skilfully made, strongly constructed. **2** well-built, well-proportioned. **well-maintained** *a.* **1** kept in good order or condition. **2** kept up to date. **well-mannered** *a.* well-bred, polite. **well-marked** *a.* obvious, distinct. **well-matched** *a.* evenly matched, compatible. **well-meaning** *a.* having good intentions. **well-meant** *a.* showing good intentions. **wellness** *n.* **well-nigh** *adv.* almost, nearly. **well off** *a.* **1** in good circumstances. **2** wealthy, prosperous. **well-oiled** *a.* (*coll.*) **1** drunk. **2** (of an operation etc.) running smoothly. **well-ordered** *a.* arranged in a methodical or tidy manner; properly or correctly arranged. **well-organized** *a.* **1** organized with skill or care. **2** (of a person) methodical, esp. in organizing responsibilities, activities etc. **well-paid** *a.* **1** (of a person) receiving ample remuneration. **2** (of a job) that pays well. **well placed** *a.* **1** in a good or advantageous position. **2** in a suitable position (to) (*She is well placed to find out what is going on*). **well-planned** *a.* **1** (of a kitchen etc.) practically designed. **2** (of an event etc.) carefully planned. **well pleased** *a.* very pleased, highly satisfied (*I was not well pleased by their decision*). **well-prepared** *a.* **1** carefully prepared. **2** having prepared carefully (*He was well-prepared for their questions*). **well-preserved** *a.* young-looking for one's age. **well-proportioned** *a.* having regular or pleasing proportions. **well-qualified** *a.* **1** having many good qualifications. **2** thoroughly able (to), through experience etc. **well-read** *a.* having read extensively, having wide knowledge gained from books. **well received** *a.* having a favourable reception. **well-respected** *a.* highly respected by many people. **well-rounded** *a.* **1** pleasantly curved or rounded. **2** symmetrical, complete. **3** broad in scope, full, varied. **4** well expressed. **well-set** *a.* **1** well-knit, muscular. **2** firmly established. **well spent** *a.* used effectively or profitably (*money well spent*). **well-spoken** *a.* **1** speaking well, eloquent. **2** well-mannered, of good disposition. **well-stacked** *a.* (*sl.*) (of a woman) having large breasts. **well-stocked** *a.* containing a wide or plentiful range of items (*a well-stocked fridge*; *a well-stocked garden*). **well-structured** *a.* having a clear or well-thought-out structure. **well-supported** *a.* **1** (of an event) attended by many people. **2** (of an argument etc.) supported by much sound evidence. **well-taken** *a.* **1** skilfully done (*a well-taken catch*). **2** accepted. **well-thought-of** *a.* respected, esteemed. **well-thought-out** *a.* carefully planned. **well-thumbed** *a.* (of a book) marked from much handling. **well-timed** *a.* opportune. **well-to-do** *a.* well off. **well-travelled** *a.* **1** (of a person) having travelled widely. **2** (of a path etc.) much used. **well-tried** *a.* often tried or tested with satisfactory results. **well-trodden** *a.* much used or frequented. **well-turned** *a.* **1** shapely. **2** aptly expressed. **well-upholstered** *a.* **1** (*facet.*) plump. **2** (of a chair etc.) comfortable. **well-used** *a.* **1** much used. **2** worn. **well-wisher** *n.* a person who wishes one well, a benevolent, charitable or sympathetic person. **well-woman** *a.* of, relating to or designed for the health and well-being of women, esp. through preventive and educative measures (*a well-woman clinic*). **well-worn** *a.* **1** worn out. **2** trite, hackneyed. **well-wrought** *a.* skilfully made. [OE *wel*, (cp. Dut. *wel*, G *wohl*, Icel. *vel*) cogn. with WILL[1]]

Usage note Compounds of *well* are conventionally hyphenated when in front of the noun qualified, but written as two separate words after the verb *to be* (*a well-read person, He was well read*).

well[2] (wel) *n.* **1** a shaft bored in the ground to obtain water, oil, gas etc. **2** a hole, space or cavity more or less resembling this. **3** a space in the middle of a building enclosing the stairs or a lift or left open for light and ventilation. **4** a source (*a well of knowledge*). **5** a spring, a fountain. **6** a natural pool fed by this. **7** the receptacle holding the ink in an inkstand. **8** any space or depression for holding something, esp. a liquid. **9** a space occupied by counsel etc. in a law court. **10** the boxed-in space enclosing the pumps of a vessel. **11** a compartment in a fishing vessel with a perforated bottom where fish are kept alive. **12** (*Physics*) a region of minimum potential. ~*v.i.* to spring or issue (forth etc.) as from a fountain (*Tears welled up in her eyes*). **well deck** *n.* the space enclosed between the forecastle and poop on some ships. **well-dish** *n.* a dish with a hollow for gravy to collect in. **well-head** *n.* **1** the source of a river etc. **2** (*fig.*) a source or fountainhead. **well room** *n.* a room at a spa where the waters are served to visitors. **wellspring** *n.* **1** a source of continual supply. **2** a well-head. [OE *wella*, rel. to *weallan*, to well or boil up (cp. Dut. *wel*, G *Welle*, wave, Icel. *vel*, boiling up)]

we'll (wēl) *contr.* we will, we shall.

wellie WELLY.

wellington (wel´ingtən), **wellington boot** *n.* a waterproof boot, usu. rubber, coming up to the mid-calf or knee. [1st Duke of *Wellington*, 1769–1852, British statesman]

wellingtonia (welingtō´niə) *n.* a sequoia, *Sequoiadendron giganteum*. [as WELLINGTON]

welly (wel´i), **wellie** *n.* (*pl.* **wellies**) (*coll.*) a wellington boot. **give it some welly** (*coll.*) used to encourage someone to apply more force, make more effort etc.

wels (wels, vels) *n.* a large European freshwater catfish, *Siluris glanis*, the sheat fish. [G]

Welsh (welsh) *a.* of or relating to Wales, its inhabitants or their language. ~*n.* **1** the Celtic language of Wales. **2** (*pl.*) the people of Wales. **Welsh corgi** *n.* a corgi. **Welsh dresser** *n.* a dresser with open shelves above drawers and cupboards. **Welsh harp** *n.* a harp with three rows of strings. **Welshman, Welshwoman** *n.* (*pl.* **Welshmen, Welshwomen**) a native or inhabitant of Wales. **Welshness** *n.* **Welsh onion** *n.* a type of onion, *Allium fistulosum*. **Welsh rabbit, Welsh rarebit** *n.* cheese mixed with seasonings, melted and spread over toasted bread. [OE *wælisc*, foreign, from *weahl*, foreigner, a Celt]

welsh (welsh), **welch** (welch) *v.i.* **1** (of a bookmaker) to make off from a racecourse without paying up bets. **2** to evade an obligation, esp. to fail to pay a debt. **welsher** *n.* [etym. uncertain]

welt (welt) *n.* **1** a strip of leather sewn round a boot or shoe between the upper and the sole to attach them together. **2** a ribbed or strengthened border or trimming of a garment. **3** a weal. **4** a heavy blow. **5** (*Her.*) a narrow border to an ordinary. ~*v.t.* **1** to furnish with a welt. **2** to beat, to flog. [ME *welte*, cogn. with OE *wyllan*, to roll (cp. Icel. *velta*, Eng. WEAL[1] and WELTER[1])]

Weltanschauung (velt´anshow·ung) *n.* (*pl.* **Weltanschauungen** (-ən)) (*Philos.*) a view of the world as an entity, a personal philosophy of life etc. [G, world contemplation]

welter[1] (wel´tə) *v.i.* **1** to roll, to tumble about, to wallow. **2** (of waves etc.) to heave and roll about confusedly. **3** to lie or be steeped (in a liquid, esp. blood). ~*n.* **1** a weltering movement. **2** a turmoil, a confusion. **3** a confused mixture (*a welter of opinions*). [ME *weltren*, freq. of *walten*, to roll (cp. Icel. *velta*, Swed. *valtra*, G *walzen*), cogn. with WALLOW, WALTZ]

welter[2] (wel´tə) *n.* **1** a heavy boxer or rider. **2** (*coll.*) a heavy blow. **3** (*coll.*) any large or heavy person or thing. **welterweight** *n.* **1** a boxer, wrestler, weightlifter etc. in the weight category intermediate between lightweight and middleweight. **2** this weight category. [etym. uncertain]

Weltpolitik (velt´politik) *n.* a policy aiming at the participation or predominance of a country, specifically Germany, in the affairs of the whole world. [G]

Weltschmerz (velt´shmeəts) *n.* a melancholic or pessimistic outlook on life. [G]

welwitschia (welwich´iə) *n.* a plant of SW tropical Africa, *Welwitschia mirabilis*, with a very short, wide trunk and a single pair of leaves, which attain a development of 6ft (1.8 m) or more. [F. M. J. *Welwitsch*, 1807–72, Portuguese botanist]

Wemba-wemba (wem´bəwembə) *n.* an extinct Aboriginal language of SE Australia.

wen[1] (wen) *n.* **1** a sebaceous cyst, frequently occurring on the scalp or neck. **2** (*fig.*) an excrescence, an abnormal growth. **3** an overcrowded city, esp. London. [OE *wenn*, (cp. Dut. *wen*, Dan. dial. *van*) prob. cogn. with Goth, *winnan*, to suffer, WIN]

wen[2] (wen), **wyn** (win) *n.* a runic letter replaced by *w*. [OE, var. of *wyn*, joy, chosen for its initial letter]

wench (wench) *n.* **1** (*now chiefly facet.*) a girl or young woman. **2** †a female servant. **3** †a prostitute. ~†*v.i.* to keep company with prostitutes. †**wencher** *n.* †**wenching** *n.* [ME *wenche*, OE *wencel*, infant (as a., weak), (cp. G *wanken*, to totter), cogn. with WINK]

Wend (wend) *n.* a member of a Slavic people inhabiting Saxony and Prussia (now N and E Germany). **Wendic** *a.* **Wendish** *a.* of or relating to the Wends. ~*n.* the language of the Wends. [G *Wende*, perh. cogn. with WEND, WANDER]

wend (wend) *v.t.* (*chiefly poet.*) to go or direct (one's way) (*We wended our way home*). ~*v.i.* to go. [OE *wendan*, to turn, causal of WIND[2] (orig. past WENT, now past of GO[1])]

Wendyhouse (wen´di) *n.* a small toy house for children to play in. [from the house built for *Wendy* in the children's book *Peter Pan* by J. M. Barrie]

Wensleydale (wenz´lidāl) *n.* **1** a type of crumbly white cheese. **2** a breed of long-haired sheep. [*Wensleydale* in Yorkshire]

went GO[1].

wentletrap (wen´təltrap) *n.* any snail of the genus *Clathrus*, with a many-whorled shell. [G *Wendeltreppe* (*Wendel*, turning, *Treppe*, stair)]

wept WEEP.

were BE.

we're (wiə) *contr.* we are.

weren't (wœnt) *contr.* were not.

werewolf (weə´wulf, wiə´-, wœ´-), **werwolf** (wœ´-) *n.* (*pl.* **werewolves, werwolves**) a person turned into or supposed to have the power of turning into a wolf. [OE *werewulf* (*wer*, man (cp. L *vir*), WOLF)]

†**wergild** (wœ´gild) *n.* in Old English and Germanic law, a fine or monetary compensation for manslaughter and other offences against the person, paid by the kindred of the offender to the kindred of the injured person. [OE *wer*, man (cp. L *vir*), *gild*, payment, from *gieldan*, see YIELD]

wert BE.

werwolf WEREWOLF.

Wesleyan (wez´liən) *a.* of or belonging to the Church founded by John Wesley. ~*n.* a member of this, a Wesleyan Methodist. **Wesleyanism** *n.* [John *Wesley*, 1703–91, founder of Methodism]

west (west) *adv.* at, in or towards the quarter opposite the east, or where the sun sets at the equinox. ~*n.* **1** that one of the four cardinal points exactly opposite the east. **2** (*also* **West**) the region or part of a country or of the world lying opposite to the east, esp. the western part of England, Europe or the US. **3** the Occident. **4** in bridge etc., the player in the position corresponding to that of west on the compass. ~*a.* **1** being, lying or living in or near the west. **2** moving or facing towards the west. **3** (blowing) from the west. **the West 1** the culture or civilization of Europe, N America etc. as opposed to that of oriental countries. **2** (*Hist.*) the non-Communist countries of Europe and N America. **3** the Western Empire. **to go west 1** (*sl.*) to die. **2** (*sl.*) to be destroyed. **West Bank** *n.* a territory west of the River Jordan, occupied by Israel since the Arab-Israeli War of 1967. **westbound** *a.* going, travelling or leading towards the west (*a westbound train*). **West Country** *n.* the SW part of England. **West End** *n.* the fashionable part of London, immediately west of Charing Cross, where the main shops, theatres etc. are located. *~a.* (*also* **West-End**) of or situated in the West End. **westering** *a.* (of the sun) passing to the west. **westerly** *a.* **1** in, situated or directed towards the west. **2** (blowing) from the west. *~n.* (*pl.* **westerlies**) a wind from the west. *~adv.* towards the west. **West Germanic** *n., a.* (of) the group of Germanic languages represented by English, German, Dutch and Frisian. **West Indies** *n.* the islands of Central America, comprising the Greater Antilles, the Lesser Antilles and the Bahamas. **West Indian** *n.* **1** a native or inhabitant of the West Indies. **2** a person whose family came from the West Indies. *~a.* of or relating to the West Indies. **West Indian satinwood** *n.* a satinwood tree, *Fagara flava.* **westing** *n.* the distance travelled or an amount of deviation towards the west. **west-north-west** *n.* the direction or point of the compass between west and north-west. **West Side** *n.* (*N Am.*) the western part of Manhattan. **west-south-west** *n.* the direction or point of the compass between west and south-west. **westward** (-wəd) *a., adv.* **westward ho!** HO. **westwards** *adv.* [OE (cp. Dut. and G *west*, Icel. *vestr*, Dan., Swed. *vest*), prob. cogn. with Gr. *hesperos*, L VESPER]

western (wes´tən) *a.* **1** in, facing or directed towards the west. **2** belonging to or to do with the west. **3** (blowing) from the west. **4** (**Western**) of or relating to the West. *~n.* a film, play or novel dealing with the western states of the US in the wilder periods of their history. **Western Church** *n.* the part of the Church which continued to acknowledge the pope after the schism of the Greek and Latin Churches in the 9th cent. **Western Empire** *n.* the western division of the Roman Empire having Rome as capital, after the division into an Eastern and Western Empire by Theodosius in 395. **westerner** *n.* a native or inhabitant of the west. **western hemisphere** *n.* the half of the globe that contains the Americas. **westernize, Westernize, westernise, Westernise** *v.t.* to influence with the customs and culture of the West. **westernization** (-zā´shən) *n.* **westernizer** *n.* **westernmost** *a.* **Western roll** *n.* a technique used to clear the bar in high-jumping.

Westinghouse brake (wes´tinghows) *n.* a brake worked by compressed air for use on railway trains and motor cars. [George *Westinghouse*, 1846–1914, US inventor]

Westminster (west´minstə) *n.* the British Parliament. [London borough in which the Houses of Parliament are situated]

wet (wet) *a.* (*comp.* **wetter,** *superl.* **wettest**) **1** moistened, soaked, saturated or covered with water or other liquid. **2** rainy (*wet weather*). **3** not yet dry or hard (*wet paint*). **4** using or used with a liquid. **5** (*coll.*) feeble, characterless, foolish, sentimental. **6** (*coll.*) having moderate Conservative tendencies or principles. **7** (*esp. N Am., sl.*) (of a state etc.) allowing or favouring the sale of alcoholic beverages, not prohibitionist. **8** (of a young child) incontinent. *~n.* **1** wetness, moisture. **2** anything that wets, esp. rain. **3** rainy weather. **4** (*coll.*) a feeble or foolish person. **5** (*coll.*) a moderate Conservative politician. **6** (*sl.*) a drink. *~v.t.* (*pres.p.* **wetting,** *past, p.p.* **wet, wetted**) **1** to make wet; to moisten, drench or soak with liquid. **2** to urinate on or in. **3** (*reflex.*) to urinate involuntarily. **the wet** (*Austral.*) the monsoon season. **to get one's feet wet** FOOT. **to wet one's whistle** (*coll.*) to have a drink. **to wet the baby's head** to have a celebratory drink after the birth of a child. **wet behind the ears** immature, inexperienced. **wet through** thoroughly soaked. **wet to the skin** with all one's clothing thoroughly soaked. **wetback** *n.* (*N Am., coll.*) an illegal immigrant to the US from Mexico. **wet bargain** *n.* a bargain concluded over a glass of liquor. **wet blanket** *n.* (*coll.*) a person who damps enthusiasm, zeal etc. **wet bob** *n.* at Eton, a boy who devotes himself to boating. **wet-bulb thermometer** *n.* a thermometer used in conjunction with a dry-bulb thermometer to measure humidity. **wet dock** *n.* a dock in which vessels can float. **wet dream** *n.* an erotic dream with emission of semen. **wet fly** *n.* (*pl.* **wet flies**) an artificial angling fly used below the surface of the water. **wetland** *n.* (*often pl.*) swamp, marshland. **wet look** *n.* **1** a shiny finish given to fabrics etc. **2** a shiny appearance given to the hair by the application of a gel. *~a.* (*usu.* **wet-look**) having a shiny finish or appearance. **wetly** *adv.* **wet monsoon** *n.* the monsoon that blows from the southwest from April to October accompanied by heavy rainfall. **wetness** *n.* **wet-nurse** *n.* a woman employed to suckle a child not her own. *~v.t.* **1** to act as wet-nurse to. **2** (*coll.*) to coddle. **wet pack** *n.* (*Med.*) a wet sheet in which a patient is wrapped. **wet rot** *n.* **1** a type of rot that affects damp timber. **2** the fungus that causes this, esp. *Coniophera puteana.* **wetsuit** *n.* a tight-fitting usu. rubber garment for divers etc. that allows water in whilst retaining body heat. **wettable** *a.* **wetting** *n.* **wetting agent** *n.* a substance added to a liquid to help it spread or penetrate. **wettish** *a.* **wet-weather** *a.* of, used in, suitable for or occurring in rainy weather. [OE *wǣt* (cp. Icel. *vātr*, Dan. *vaad*, Swed. *vät*), cogn. with WATER]

weta (wet´ə) *n.* (*pl.* **wetas**) a wingless insect of the family Stenopelmatidae, with long spiny legs, found in New Zealand. [Maori]

wether (wedh´ə) *n.* a castrated ram. [OE (cp. Icel. *vethr*, Dan. *væder*, G *Widder*), prob. cogn. with VEAL and VETERINARY]

wettable, wetting etc. WET.

we've (wēv) *contr.* we have.

wey (wā) *n.* a former weight or measure varying with different articles (of wool, 182 lb/ 82.5 kg, of cheese, 224 lb/101.6 kg etc.). [OE *wæge*, weight, from *wegan*, WEIGH]

w.f. *abbr.* (*Print.*) wrong font.

WFTU *abbr.* World Federation of Trade Unions.

WG *abbr.* (Windward Islands) Grenada (IVR).

Wg. Cdr. *abbr.* Wing Commander.

whack (wak) *v.t.* to strike heavily. *~n.* **1** a heavy or resounding blow. **2** (*sl.*) a share, a portion. **3** (*sl.*) an attempt. **out of whack** (*N Am., Austral., sl.*) out of order. **(the) full whack** the maximum rate, price etc. **to have a whack at** (*sl.*) to try, to attempt. **whacked** *a.* (*coll.*) exhausted. **whacker** *n.* **whacking** *n.* a beating, a thrashing. *~a.* (*coll.*) large, whopping, thumping. *~adv.* (*coll.*) very. [onomat., cp. THWACK]

whacko (wak´ō) *int.* (*sl.*) used to express delight.

whacky WACKY.

whale[1] (wāl) *n.* **1** any large marine fishlike mammal of the order Cetacea, several of which are hunted chiefly for their oil and whalebone. **2** (*coll.*) something very big, good, exciting etc. (*We had a whale of a time*). *~v.i.* to engage in whaling. **whaleback** *n.* **1** anything shaped like the back of a whale. **2** a vessel with the main decks covered in and rounded over as a protection against rough seas. **whaleboat** *n.* a boat sharp at both ends, such as those formerly used in whaling. **whalebone** *n.* a horny, elastic substance occurring in long, thin plates, found in the palate of certain whales. **whalebone whale** *n.* a baleen whale. **whale-headed stork** *n.* an African stork, *Balaeniceps rex*, with grey plumage and a large, clog-shaped bill. **whaleman** *n.* (*pl.* **whalemen**) (*chiefly N Am.*) a whaler. **whale oil** *n.* **1** oil obtained from the blubber of whales. **2** spermaceti. **whaler** *n.* **1** a person employed in whaling. **2** a ship employed in whaling. **3** a whaler shark. **4** (*Austral., sl.*) a tramp. **whaler shark** *n.* a large Australian shark, *Carcharinus brachyurus.* **whale shark** *n.* a large tropical shark, *Rhincodon typus.* **whaling** *n.* the catching and processing of whales. **whaling-gun** *n.* a gun for firing harpoons at whales. **whaling-master** *n.* the captain of a whaler. [OE *hwæl* (cp. Dut. *walvisch*, G *Wal*, Icel. *hvalr*, Dan., Swed. *hval*), perh. cogn. with WHEEL]

whale[2] (wāl) *v.t.* (*esp. N Am., coll.*) to beat, to flog. [WALE]

wham (wam) *n.* **1** a forceful blow. **2** the noise of this. ~*v.i.* (*pres.p.* **whamming,** *past, p.p.* **whammed**) to strike or crash with a loud, forceful blow. ~*v.t.* to cause to do this. [imit.]

whammy (wam´i) *n.* (*pl.* **whammies**) (*coll.*) **1** (*esp. N Am.*) an evil influence, a curse. **2** a particularly severe setback, blow or misfortune (*a double whammy*). [WHAM, -Y[3]]

whang[1] (wang) *v.t.* to beat noisily, to bang. ~*v.i.* (of a drum etc.) to make a noise as if whanged. ~*n.* a whanging blow, a bang. [imit. (cp. WHACK)]

whang[2] (wang) *n.* (*Sc.*) **1** a tough leather strap or thong. **2** a big slice. ~*v.t.* **1** to strike with or as with a whang. **2** to cut in large slices. [perh. var. of THONG]

whangee (wang·gē´) *n.* a flexible bamboo cane. [Chin. *huang*, old bamboo sprouts]

whap WHOP.

whare (wor´i) *n.* a Maori hut or other simple dwelling place. [Maori]

wharf (wawf) *n.* (*pl.* **wharfs, wharves** (wawvz)) **1** a landing place for cargo beside a river, harbour, canal etc., usu. consisting of a platform, pier or quay of timber, masonry etc. **2** (*esp. N Am.*) a dock. ~*v.t.* **1** to moor at a wharf. **2** to deposit or store (goods) on a wharf. **wharfage** (-ij) *n.* **1** the use of a wharf. **2** the charge for this. **wharfie** *n.* (*Austral., New Zeal., coll.*) a worker at a wharf. **wharfing** *n.* **wharfinger** (-finjə) *n.* a person who owns or has charge of a wharf. **wharf-rat** *n.* a brown rat that infests wharves. [OE *hwerf*, bank, dam, orig. a turning, from *wheorfan*, to turn (cp. Icel. *hvarf*, turning, Dan. *voerft*, Swed. *varf*, Dut. *werf*, wharf)]

what (wot) *pron.* **1** (*interrog.*) which thing or things. **2** (*rel.*) that which, those which. **3** how much. **4** (*dial.*) that or which. ~*a.* **1** (*interrog., rel.*) which thing, kind, amount, number etc. **2** how great, remarkable, ridiculous etc. (*What a shame!*). **3** (*rel.*) such as, as much or as many as, any that. ~*adv.* (*interrog.*) to what extent, in what respect. **and what not** (*coll.*) and anything else of the kind. **or what have you** (*coll.*) or anything else of the kind. **to give someone what for** (*coll.*) to give someone a severe reprimand or punishment. **what about** what do you think, feel, know etc. about; what is the position concerning (*What about Jonathan?*). **what ever** what at all (*What ever is she talking about?*). **what for** for what reason, purpose etc. **what if 1** what would happen if (*What if it rains?*). **2** what does it matter if (*What if I am being selfish?*). **what is more** moreover. **what of** what is the news about. **what of it?** why does that matter? **what's up?** UP. **what's what** (*coll.*) the real or important thing or situation. **what time** TIME. **what with** (*coll.*) because of. **what-d'you-call-it** *n.* (*coll.*) a whatsit. **whatever** (-ev´ə), (*poet.*) **whate'er** (-eə´) *pron.* **1** anything at all that. **2** all that which. **3** at all (*of no use whatever*). **4** no matter what (*whatever you say*). ~*a.* no matter what (thing or things). **or whatever** (*coll.*) or some similar unspecified thing (*Use a knife, a screwdriver or whatever*). **whatnot** *n.* **1** a trivial or unspecified thing. **2** a piece of furniture with shelves for ornaments, books etc. **whatsit** (-sit), **what's-its-name** *n.* (*coll.*) a person or thing whose name is unknown or temporarily forgotten. **whatsoever,** (*poet.*) **whatsoe'er, †whatso** *pron., a.* whatever. [OE *hwæt*, neut. of *hwā*, WHO]

whaup (hwawp) *n.* (*chiefly Sc.*) the curlew. [from its cry]

wheal (wēl) *n.* in Cornwall, a mine (usu. a tin mine). [Corn. *hwel*]

wheat (wēt) *n.* **1** any annual cereal grass of the genus *Triticum*, cultivated for its grain which is ground into flour for bread. **2** its grain. **to separate the wheat from the chaff** to separate or distinguish good things from bad or useless things. **wheat belt** *n.* an area where wheat is extensively cultivated, such as the area east of the Rocky Mountains in Canada and the US. **wheaten** *a.* made of wheat. **wheatfly** *n.* (*pl.* **wheatflies**) any of various flies that damage or destroy wheat, esp. the Hessian fly. **wheatgerm** *n.* the embryo of the wheat grain, rich in vitamins. **wheatgrass** *n.* couch grass. **wheatmeal** *n.* flour containing much of the original wheat grain. ~*a.* made from such flour. [OE *hwǣte*, cogn. with WHITE]

wheatear (wē´tiə) *n.* a small white-rumped bird of the genus *Oenanthe*, esp. *O. oenanthe*. [corr. of *white arse*]

Wheatstone bridge (wēt´stən) *n.* a device for measuring an unknown electrical resistance by means of a known resistance. [Sir Charles *Wheatstone*, 1802–75, British physicist]

whee (wē) *int.* used to express delight or excitement.

wheedle (wē´dəl) *v.t.* **1** to entice, to win over, to persuade by coaxing or flattery. **2** to cheat by cajolery. **3** to obtain from or get (out of) by coaxing and flattery. **wheedler** *n.* **wheedling** *a.* **wheedlingly** *adv.* [etym. unknown; perh. from OE *wǣdlian*, to beg]

wheel (wēl) *n.* **1** a circular frame or solid disc turning on its axis, used in vehicles, machinery etc. to reduce friction and facilitate motion. **2** a machine, implement, device etc. consisting principally of a wheel, such as a spinning wheel, potter's wheel, steering wheel etc. **3** an object resembling a wheel, a disc. **4** (*pl., coll.*) a car. **5** (*N Am., coll.*) a bicycle. **6** a Catherine wheel. **7** an instrument of torture formerly used for breaking the limbs of criminals. **8** torture with this. **9** the act of wheeling, circular motion, rotation. **10** a turn, a revolution. **11** the turning or swinging round of a body of troops or a line of warships as on a pivot. **12** (*pl.*) the forces controlling or activating an organization etc. **13** a set of short lines at the end of a stanza. ~*v.t.* **1** to move or push (a wheeled vehicle etc.) in some direction. **2** to cause to wheel. ~*v.i.* **1** to turn or swing round as on a pivot. **2** to change direction or objective, to face another way. **3** to go round, to circle, to gyrate. **4** to ride a bicycle etc. **at the wheel 1** driving a motor vehicle. **2** steering a vessel. **3** directing, in control, in charge. **big wheel** BIG. **to wheel and deal** to be a wheeler-dealer. **wheels within wheels 1** intricate machinery. **2** (*coll.*) concealed reasons or interdependent circumstances. **wheel and axle** *n.* a device for raising weights, consisting of a cylindrical axle on which a wheel is fastened concentrically, the difference between their respective diameters supplying leverage. **wheel animalcule** *n.* a rotifer. **wheel-back** *a.* (of a chair) having a back shaped like a wheel. **wheelbarrow** *n.* a barrow usu. supported on a single wheel, with two handles by which it is wheeled. **wheelbase** *n.* the distance between the front and rear axles of a vehicle. **wheelbrace** *n.* a brace-shaped spanner for adjusting bolts on a wheel. **wheelchair** *n.* a chair on wheels, esp. for invalids or disabled people. **wheel clamp** *n.* a clamp fixed on to the wheel of an illegally parked car to prevent it from being driven away before a fine is paid. **wheel-clamp** *v.t.* **wheeled** *a.* having wheels (*usu. in comb.*, as *four-wheeled*). **wheeler** *n.* **1** a person who wheels. **2** a wheelwright. **3** a wheel horse. **4** (*in comb.*) a vehicle with the specified number of wheels (*a three-wheeler*). **wheeler-dealer** *n.* a person who operates shrewdly and often ruthlessly in business, politics etc. **wheeler-dealing** *n.* **wheel horse** *n.* a horse harnessed behind another and next to the wheels. **wheelhouse** *n.* a shelter for the steersman on a boat. **wheelie** *n.* (*sl.*) a manoeuvre in which a bicycle or motorcycle is briefly supported on the rear wheel alone. **wheelie bin, wheely bin** *n.* (*coll.*) a large plastic dustbin with two wheels so that it can be tilted and wheeled to the dustcart, where it is emptied automatically. **wheelless** *a.* **wheel lock** *n.* (*Hist.*) 1 a type of gunlock in which sparks were produced by friction between a small steel wheel and a flint. 2 a gun with such a lock. **wheelman** *n.* (*pl.* **wheelmen**) (*N Am.*) 1 a cyclist. 2 a helmsman. 3 (*sl.*) the driver of a getaway car. **wheel of fortune** *n.* a symbol of luck, chance or change; a wheel turned by a deity of fate in mythology etc. **wheel-shaped** *a.* **wheelsman** *n.* (*pl.* **wheelsmen**) (*N Am.*) a helmsman. **wheelspin** *n.* the revolution of wheels without a grip of the road. **wheel well** *n.* the recess into which the wheel of a vehicle fits. **wheel window** *n.* a circular window with radiating tracery. **wheelwright** *n.* a person whose occupation is to make or repair wheels etc. **wheely** *a.* [OE *hwēol* (cp. Icel. *hjōl*, Dan. *huil*, also Gr. *kuklos*, see CYCLE)]

wheeze (wēz) *v.i.* to breathe hard and with an audible sound, as in asthma. ~*v.t.* to utter thus. ~*n.* 1 a wheezing sound. 2 (*coll.*) a joke, a trick. 3 (*coll.*) a design, a scheme. **wheezer** *n.* **wheezy** *a.* **wheezily** *adv.* **wheeziness** *n.* [OE *hwēsan*, cogn. with *hwōsta*, cough (cp. G *husten*)]

whelk[1] (welk) *n.* a marine spiral-shelled gastropod of the family Buccinidae, esp. the common whelk, used for food. [ME *wilk*, OE *wiloc* (cp. Dut. *wulk*), prob. cogn. with *helix*, conf. with WHELK[2]]

whelk[2] (welk) *n.* a small pustule or pimple. **whelked** *a.* [OE *hwylca* (*hwelian*, to suppurate)]

whelm (welm) *v.t.* (*poet.*) 1 to engulf, to submerge. 2 to overwhelm. [ME *whelmen*, prob. from a noun *whelm* (cp. MSwed. *hwalm*, haycock), from OE *āhwyftan*, to overwhelm (cp. Icel. *hvāfa*, to turn upside down, G *wölben*, to arch over, Gr. *kolpos*, bosom)]

whelp (welp) *n.* 1 the young of a dog, a pup. 2 †the young of a beast of prey, a cub. 3 an offensive or ill-bred child or youth. 4 (*usu. pl.*) a ridge on the drum of a capstan or windlass. ~*v.i.* (of a bitch etc.) to give birth to young. ~*v.t.* 1 to give birth to (a pup or cub). 2 (*derog.*) to originate or produce. [OE *hwelp* (cp. Dut. *welp*, Icel. *hvelpr*)]

when (wen) *adv.* 1 (*interrog.*) at what or which time? 2 (*rel.*) at which (time). ~*conj.* 1 at the time that, at any time that. 2 as soon as. 3 just after the time that. 4 after which, and then. 5 although. 6 considering that. 7 while (*often with pres.p.*). ~*pron.* what or which time. ~*n.* the time or date. **whenever** (-ev´ə), (*poet.*) **whene'er** (-eə´) *adv., conj.* at whatever time. **or whenever** (*coll.*) or at any similar or suitable time. **whensoever,** (*poet.*) **whensoe'er** *adv., conj.* (*formal*) whenever. [OE *hwænne*, a case of interrog. pron. WHO]

whence (wens) *adv.* (*formal*) 1 (*interrog.*) from what place? where from? how? 2 (*rel.*) from which place, origin, source etc. ~*conj.* 1 to or at the place from which. 2 for which reason, wherefore. ~*pron.* what or which place or starting point. **whenceforth** *adv.* **whencesoever** *adv., conj.* from whatsoever place or source. [ME *whennes*, OE *hwanan*, cogn. with WHEN (*-an*, suf. of direction)]

Usage note The use of *from whence*, instead of simple *whence* or *from where*, is sometimes disapproved of, on the grounds that *whence* already contains the notion 'from'.

---

where (weə) *adv.* 1 (*interrog.*) at or in what place, situation, case, circumstances? 2 (*interrog.*) to what place? in what direction? 3 (*rel.*) in which (place or places). ~*conj.* 1 in or to the place, direction etc. in which. 2 whereas. ~*pron.* what or which place. ~*n.* the place (*the where and when*). **whereabouts** *adv.* near what or which place roughly? ~*n.* the approximate location of a person or thing. **whereafter** (weərahf´tə) *conj.* (*formal*) after which. **whereas** (weəraz´) *conj.* 1 the fact on the contrary being that, when in reality. 2 in legal preambles etc., the fact or case being that, considering that. †**whereat** (weərat´) *conj.* 1 at which place. 2 for which reason. **whereby** (-bī´) *conj.* by which. ~†*adv.* by what means? **wherefore** †*adv.* 1 for what reason? why? 2 for which reason, on which account. ~*n.* (*coll.*) the reason why. †**wherefrom** (-from´) *conj.* from which, whence. **wherein** (weərin´) *adv.* (*formal*) in what place or respect? ~*conj.* in which thing, place, respect etc. **whereinto** (-in´too) *adv.* (*formal*) into what place? ~*conj.* into which place. **whereof** (weərov´) *adv.* (*formal*) of what? ~*conj.* of which or whom. †**whereon** (weəron´) *adv.* on what? ~*conj.* on what or which. **wheresoever,** (*poet.*) **wheresoe'er** *adv., conj.* (*formal*) wherever. **whereto** (-too´) *adv.* (*formal*) to which or what (place or end)? ~*conj.* to what or which. **whereupon** (weərəpon´) *conj.* 1 upon which. 2 in consequence of or immediately after which. **wherever** (weərev´ə), (*poet.*) **where'er** (-eə´) *adv., conj.* at, in or to whatever place. **or wherever** (*coll.*) or in any similar or suitable place. **wherewith** (-widh´) *adv.* (*formal*) with what? ~*conj.* with which. **wherewithal** *adv., conj.* wherewith. ~*n.* (*coll.*) the necessary means or resources, esp. money. [OE *hwār* (cp. Dut. *waar*, G *warum*, Icel. *hvar*), cogn. with *hwā*, WHO, and WHEN]

wherry (wer´i) *n.* (*pl.* **wherries**) 1 a light shallow rowing boat for plying on rivers. 2 a type of barge. **wherryman** *n.* (*pl.* **wherrymen**). [perh. rel. to WHARF and WHIR]

whet (wet) *v.t.* (*pres.p.* **whetting,** *past, p.p.* **whetted**) 1 to sharpen by rubbing on a stone or similar substance. 2 to excite, to stimulate (*to whet the appetite*). ~*n.* 1 the act of whetting. 2 anything taken to whet or stimulate the appetite. 3 a small quantity. **whetstone** *n.* 1 a piece of stone used for sharpening cutlery etc. 2 anything that sharpens or stimulates. **whetter** *n.* [OE *hwettan*, from *hwæt*, keen, bold (cp. Dut. *wetten*, G *wetzen*, Icel. *hvetja*)]

whether (wedh´ə) *conj.* introducing (an indirect question in the form of) an alternative clause followed by an alternative *or, or not*, or *or whether*, or with the alternative unexpressed (*whether you like it or not*). **whether or no** 1 in any case. 2 which (of two opposite cases). [OE *hwæther*]

whew (hwū, fū) *int.* used to express relief, astonishment or consternation. [inst. sound]

whey (wā) *n.* the watery part of milk that remains after the curds have formed and been separated. **wheyey, wheyish** *a.* **whey-face** *n.* a pale-faced person. **whey-faced** *a.* [OE *hwæg* (cp. Dut. *wei*, Welsh *chwig*)]

which (wich) *pron.* 1 (*interrog.*) what person, thing or persons or things of a definite number. 2 (*rel.*) used in a subordinate clause to represent a noun expressed or understood in the principal sentence or previous clause. 3 (*rel.*) used after a preposition or after *that* (*the ladder on which she was standing*). ~*a.* 1 (*interrog.*) what (person, thing etc.) of a definite number. 2 (*rel.*) used with a noun defining an indefinite antecedent. **which is which** used when people or things are difficult to tell apart. **whichever,** †**whichsoever** *pron.* 1 which person or thing of two or more. 2 no matter which person or thing. ~*a.* 1 which of two or more. 2 no matter which. [OE *hwilc, whilīc* (WHO, -LIKE) (cp. Dut. *welk*, G *welcher*, Icel. *hvīlīkr*)]

whicker (wik´ə) *v.i.* to neigh softly. [imit.]

whidah WHYDAH.

whiff (wif) *n.* 1 a sudden expulsion of smoke etc., a puff, a light gust, esp. one carrying an odour. 2 a small amount, a trace. 3 a small cigar. 4 a light outrigged sculling boat. 5 a small discharge (*a whiff of grapeshot*). ~*v.i.* 1 to puff or blow lightly. 2 (*coll.*) to smell (unpleasant). ~*v.t.* 1 to puff or blow lightly. 2 to detect a faint odour of, to sniff, to smell. **whiffy** *a.* (*comp.* **whiffier,** *superl.* **whiffiest**) (*coll.*) smelly. [imit.]

whiffle (wif´əl) *v.i.* 1 (of the wind etc.) to veer about. 2 to change from one opinion or course to another, to prevaricate, to equivocate. 3 to flicker, to flutter. ~*v.t.* to blow lightly. **whiffler** *n.* [freq. from WHIFF]

whiffletree (wif´əltrē) *n.* (*N Am.*) a swingletree. [var. of WHIPPLETREE]

Whig (wig) *n.* (*Hist.*) 1 a member of the British political party that contended for the rights and privileges of Parliament in opposition to the Tories, supported the Revolution of 1688 and the principles it represented, and was succeeded by the Liberals. 2 in the 17th cent., a Scottish Covenanter. 3 an American colonist who supported the cause of independence in the American Revolution. 4 a member of an American political party from about 1834–54, representing commercial and financial interests. **Whiggery, Whiggism** *n.* **Whiggish** *a.* **Whiggishly** *adv.* **Whiggishness** *n.* [short for obs. *whiggamore*, nickname for certain Scots who came to buy corn at Leith, from *whiggam*, a word with which they urged their horses, prob. from Sc. *whig*, to jog along]

while (wīl) *n.* a space of time, esp. the time during which something happens or is done. ~*conj.* 1 during the time that, as long as, at the same time as (*often used ellipt. with pres.p.*). 2 whereas (*One group had learning difficulties, while the other group were of average ability*). 3 despite the fact that (*While I disapprove of gambling in general, I do occasionally buy a lottery ticket*). 4 (*dial.*) until. ~*adv.* (*rel.*) during which. **a good while** a long time (*a good while later*). **all the while** all the time, during the whole time. **for a long while** for a long time (*I haven't been to the cinema for a long while*). **for a while** for some time. **in a while** soon. **once in a while** ONCE. **the while** 1 during. 2 at the time. **to be worth (someone's) while** to be worth the time, labour or expense involved. **to while away** to pass (time etc.) pleasantly or in a leisurely manner. †**whiles** *conj.* while. ~*adv.* 1 while. 2 (*Sc.*) sometimes. **whilst** (wīlst) *conj., adv.* while. [OE *hwīl* (cp. Icel. *hvīla*, rest, G *weile*), prob. cogn. with QUIET]

†**whilom** (wī´ləm) *adv.* formerly, once, of old. ~*a.* former. [OE *hwīlum*, instr. or dat. pl. of WHILE]

whilst WHILE.

whim (wim) *n.* 1 a sudden fancy, a caprice. 2 a hoisting device, usu. consisting of a vertical winch worked by a horse, formerly used in mines for raising ore. **whimsy** (-zi), **whimsey** *n.* (*pl.* **whimsies, whimseys**) 1 a whim, a fancy. 2 whimsical humour. **whimsical** (-zikəl) *a.* 1 full of whims, capricious. 2 oddly humorous. 3 odd-looking, curious, fantastic. **whimsicality** (-kal´-), **whimsicalness** *n.* **whimsically** *adv.* †**whim-wham** (-wam) *n.* 1 a plaything. 2 a whim, a fancy. [Icel. *hvima*, to wander with the eyes, from *vim*, giddiness, folly (cp. Norw. *kvim*)]

whimbrel (wim´brəl) *n.* a small curlew, *Numenius phaeopus*. [freq. of *whim*, imit. of cry, -EL]

whimper (wim´pə) *v.i.* 1 to cry with a soft, broken, whining voice. 2 to whine. ~*v.t.* to utter in such a tone. ~*n.* 1 a soft, querulous or whining cry. 2 a feeble note. **whimperer** *n.* **whimperingly** *adv.* [freq. of *whimpe*, WHIM, prob. cogn. with WHINE]

whimsical, whimsy etc. WHIM.

whin[1] (win) *n.* furze, gorse. **whinchat** *n.* a small thrush-like bird, *Saxicola rubetra*. [cp. Norw. *hvin*]

whin[2] (win), **whinstone** (win´stōn) *n.* 1 a very hard, resistant rock, esp. basalt, chert or quartzite. 2 a piece of this. [etym. uncertain]

whine (wīn) *v.i.* 1 to make a plaintive, long-drawn cry. 2 to complain or find fault in a peevish way. ~*v.t.* to utter with a whine or in a peevish way. ~*n.* 1 a whining cry, sound or tone. 2 a peevish complaint. **whiner** *n.* **whiningly** *adv.* **whiny** *a.* (*comp.* **whinier,** *superl.* **whiniest**). [OE *hwīnan* (cp. Icel. *hvīna*, to whiz, Swed. *hvina*, to whistle)]

whinge (winj) *v.i.* (*pres.p.* **whingeing,** *past, p.p.* **whinged**) (*coll.*) 1 to cry fretfully. 2 to complain peevishly, to whine. ~*n.* a complaint. **whingeing** *n., a.* **whingeingly** *adv.* **whinger** *n.* [OE *hwinsian*, WHINE]

whinny (win´i) *v.i.* (*3rd pers. sing. pres.* **whinnies,** *pres.p.* **whinnying,** *past, p.p.* **whinnied**) to neigh, esp. in a gentle or delighted way. ~*n.* the act or sound of whinnying. [freq. of WHINE]

whiny WHINE.

whip (wip) *v.t.* (*pres.p.* **whipping,** *past, p.p.* **whipped**) 1 to lash, to flog. 2 to drive or urge (on) with a whip. 3 to beat (out of etc.). 4 to strike forcefully as if with a whip (*The wind whipped our faces*). 5 to beat (eggs, cream etc.) into a froth. 6 to move suddenly and quickly, to snatch, to jerk (out, away etc.) (*She whipped out her camera*). 7 (*sl.*) to beat, to overcome, to defeat. 8 (*sl.*) to steal. 9 to fish (a stream) by casting a line over the water. 10 to manage or discipline (the members of a political party). 11 to lash or bind with a close wrapping of twine, thread etc. 12 to bind (twine etc.) round a joint etc. 13 to oversew (a seam) with close stitches. 14 to twist (goods etc.) with a rope passed through a pulley. ~*v.i.* to move or start suddenly, to dart (out, in etc.). ~*n.* 1 an instrument for driving horses, punishing persons etc., consisting of a lash tied to a handle or rod. 2 a coachman or driver. 3 a whipper-in. 4 a member of a political party appointed to enforce discipline in Parliament and to summon the members of the party to divisions etc. 5 a summons sent out by a whip to ensure such attendance. 6 a hoisting apparatus consisting of a single rope and pulley. 7 a whipping motion. 8 a dessert made with whipped eggs, cream etc. **to whip in** to bring (hunting hounds) together. **to whip on** to urge forward or into action. **to whip up** 1 to excite, arouse, stimulate. 2 to produce hurriedly. 3 to summon (*to whip up attendance*). **whipbird** *n.* a songbird of the genus *Psophodes* whose cry ends with a note like the crack of a whip. **whipcord** *n.* 1 a hard twisted cord for making a whip. 2 a very durable corded cloth made from worsted yarns. **whip-crane** *n.* a crane used with a whip for rapid hoisting. **whip-graft** *n.* a graft made by inserting a tongue in a scion into a slit cut in the stock. ~*v.t.* to graft by this method. **whip hand** *n.* 1 the hand holding the whip. 2 the advantage or control (*to have the whip hand*). **whiplash** *n.* 1 the lash of a whip. 2 a blow with a whip. 3 a sudden, sharp reaction. 4 whiplash injury. ~*v.t., v.i.* to jerk or move like the lash of a whip. **whiplash injury** *n.* an injury to the neck caused by a sudden uncontrolled forwards and backwards movement of the unsupported head. **whipless** *a.* **whiplike** *a.* **whipper** *n.* **whipper-in** *n.* (*pl.* **whippers-in**) a person employed to assist the huntsman by looking after the hounds. **whippersnapper** *n.* 1 a young child. 2 a noisy, presumptuous, insignificant person. **whipping** *n.* **whipping boy** *n.* 1 a scapegoat. 2 (*Hist.*) a boy educated with a young prince and taking his punishments for him. **whipping cream** *n.* cream that can be beaten until stiff. **whipping post** *n.* (*Hist.*) a post to which offenders were tied to be whipped (usu. attached to stocks). **whipping-top, whip-top** *n.* a top kept spinning with a whip. **whippy** *a.* flexible, springy. **whippiness** *n.* **whip-round** *n.* (*coll.*) an informal or impromptu collection of money (*to have a whip-round*). **whipsaw** *n.* a narrow saw blade with the ends fastened in a frame. ~*v.t.* (*p.p.* **whipsawn, whipsawed**) 1 to saw with this. 2 (*N Am., sl.*) to beat or cheat (a person) in two ways at once, esp. by joint action. **whip scorpion** *n.* any scorpion-like but non-venomous arachnid of the order Uropygi. **whip snake** *n.* a slender snake of the family Colubridae. **whip stitch** *n.* a small stitch used for oversewing. **whipstock** *n.* the rod or handle of a whip. **whipworm** *n.* any whiplike parasitic worm of the genus *Trichuris*, found in the intestines of mammals. [(cp. Dut. *wippen*, to skip, Dan. *vippe*, Swed. *vippa*, to wag, G *wippen*, to see-saw, to rock), perh. cogn. with VIBRATE]

whippet (wip´it) *n.* **1** a racing-dog similar to but smaller than a greyhound. **2** this breed of dog. [etym. uncertain]

whipping WHIP.

whippletree (wip´əltrē) *n.* a swingletree. [freq. of WHIP, TREE]

whippoorwill (wip´əwil) *n.* a small N American nocturnal bird, *Caprimulgus vociferus*, allied to the nightjars. [imit. of cry]

whippy WHIP.

whir (wœ), **whirr** *v.i.* (*pres.p.* **whirring,** *past, p.p.* **whirred**) to revolve, move or fly quickly with a buzzing or whizzing sound. ~*n.* a whirring sound. [ME *whirr, quirr*, cp. Dan. *hvirre*, Icel. *hverfa*]

whirl (wœl) *v.t.* **1** to swing round and round rapidly. **2** to cause to revolve or fly round with great velocity. **3** to carry (away or along) rapidly. **4** to hurl or fling. ~*v.i.* **1** to turn round and round rapidly, to rotate, to gyrate, to spin. **2** to be carried or to travel rapidly in a circular course. **3** to move along swiftly. **4** (of the brain etc.) to be giddy or confused, to seem to spin round. ~*n.* **1** a whirling motion. **2** a confused state, giddiness. **3** commotion, bustle. **4** (*coll.*) an attempt, a trial (*I'll give it a whirl*). **whirler** *n.* **whirligig** (wœ´ligig) *n.* **1** a child's spinning or rotating toy. **2** a merry-go-round. **3** a freshwater beetle of the family Gyrinidae that darts about in a circular manner over the surface of pools etc. **4** something that continually moves or changes. **5** a revolving or rotating course. **whirling** *n., a.* **whirling dervish** *n.* a member of a Muslim ascetic order whose physical exercises take the form of wild, ecstatic, whirling dances. **whirlingly** *adv.* **whirlpool** *n.* an eddy or vortex. **whirlwind** *n.* **1** a funnel-shaped column of air moving spirally round an axis, which at the same time has a progressive motion. **2** a confused or rapid motion or process. ~*a.* developing or moving very rapidly (*a whirlwind romance*). **to reap the whirlwind** to suffer the consequences of a bad or foolish action. **whirlybird** *n.* (*coll.*) a helicopter. [for *whirfle*, freq. from Icel. *hvirfla* (cp. G *wirbeln*), cogn. with WHIR and OE *hweorfan*, to turn]

whirr WHIR.

whish[1] (wish) *v.i.* to move through the air or water with a whistling sound. ~*n.* a whistling sound. [imit.]

whish[2] WHISHT.

whisht (wisht), **whist** (wist), **whish** (wish) *int.* (*esp. Sc., Ir., dial.*) hush! silence! ~*v.t.* to quieten. [onomat.]

whisk (wisk) *v.t.* **1** to sweep, brush or flap (away or off). **2** to carry (off) or take (away) swiftly or suddenly. **3** to shake, flourish or wave with a quick movement. **4** to beat up (eggs etc.). ~*v.i.* to move or go swiftly or suddenly. ~*n.* **1** a whisking movement. **2** a small bunch of grass, straw, feathers, hair etc., used as a brush or for flapping away flies, dust etc. **3** an instrument for beating up cream, eggs etc. [(cp. Dan. *viske*, to wipe, from *visk*, a wisp, Swed. *viska*, G *wischen*, to wipe), perh. cogn. with WISP]

whisker (wis´kə) *n.* **1** any one of the bristly hairs growing round the mouth of a cat or other animal. **2** (*usu. pl.*) hair growing on the cheeks of a man. **3** (*coll.*) a narrow margin (*to win by a whisker*). **4** a very fine and strong hairlike crystal. **to have whiskers** (*coll.*) to be very old. **whiskered** *a.* **whiskery** *a.* [as WHISK]

whisky (wis´ki), **whiskey** *n.* (*pl.* **whiskies, whiskeys**) **1** a spirit distilled usu. from malted barley, sometimes from wheat, rye etc. **2** a drink of this. **whisky mac** *n.* a drink of whisky mixed with ginger wine. [Gael. *uisgebeatha*, water of life, see USQUEBAUGH]

Usage note The Scottish product is conventionally spelt *whisky*, and the Irish and American *whiskey*.

whisper (wis´pə) *v.i.* **1** to speak with articulation but without vocal vibration. **2** to speak in a low voice so as not to be overheard. **3** to converse privately or in a whisper. **4** to plot, to gossip. **5** to make a soft rustling sound. ~*v.t.* **1** to tell or utter in a whisper or privately. **2** to hint or suggest privately or secretly. ~*n.* **1** a whispering tone or voice. **2** a whispered remark or speech. **3** a hint, an insinuation, a rumour. **it is whispered that** it is rumoured that. **whisperer** *n.* **whispering** *n.* **whispering campaign** *n.* (*esp. N Am.*) the organized spread of defamatory rumours about a person, esp. a public figure. **whispering gallery** *n.* (*pl.* **whispering galleries**) a gallery, corridor etc. in which the faintest sounds made at particular points are audible at other distant points though inaudible elsewhere. **whisperingly** *adv.* [ONorthum. *hwisprian* (cp. MDut. *wisperen*, G *wispeln*), of imit. orig.]

whist[1] (wist) *n.* a card game, usu. for four persons, played with the entire pack of 52 cards. **whist drive** *n.* a social occasion involving a competitive series of games of whist. [formerly WHISK in alln. to the sweeping up of the cards]

whist[2] WHISHT.

whistle (wis´əl) *v.i.* **1** to make a shrill musical sound by forcing the breath through a small opening of the lips or with an instrument, an appliance on a steam engine etc. **2** (of an instrument, engine etc.) to emit this sound. **3** (of birds etc.) to make a similar sound. **4** (of a missile, the wind etc.) to make such a sound by swift motion. ~*v.t.* **1** to emit or produce (a tune etc.) by whistling. **2** to call or give a signal to thus. ~*n.* **1** a whistling sound, note or cry. **2** an instrument for producing such a sound. **3** (*sl.*) the throat. **4** (*sl.*) a suit (from rhyming slang *whistle and flute*). **clean/ clear/ dry as a whistle** very clean, clear etc. **to blow the whistle on** BLOW[1]. **to wet one's whistle** WET. **to whistle down the wind 1** to let go. **2** to set (a hawk) loose. **to whistle for** to seek or ask for in vain, to stand little or no chance of getting. **to whistle in the dark** to hide one's fear with a show of nonchalance or boldness. **whistle-blower** *n.* a person who informs on someone or brings something to an end. **whistler** *n.* **1** a person or thing that whistles. **2** a marmot, *Marmota caligata*, with a whistling call. **3** any of various birds with a whistling call, esp. of the genus *Pachycephala*. **4** a broken-winded horse. **whistle-stop** *n.* **1** (*N Am.*) a small station where trains stop only on request. **2** a brief visit to a town, e.g. by a political candidate. ~*a.* (*attrib.*) rapid, with only brief pauses (*a whistle-stop tour*). **whistling** *a.* **whistling kettle** *n.* a kettle with a whistle sounded by steam when the water boils. [OE *hwistlian*, freq. from *hwist-* (imit.), to make a hissing noise (cp. Dut. *hvīsla*, Dan. *hvisle*)]

Whit WHITSUN.

whit (wit) *n.* a jot, the least amount, an iota (*not a whit*). **every whit** wholly. **no whit** not at all, not in the least. [OE *wiht*, WIGHT]

white (wīt) *a.* **1** being of the colour produced by reflection of all the visible rays in sunlight, as of pure snow, common salt etc. **2** approaching this colour, pale, pallid, bloodless, transparent, colourless. **3** silvery, whitish-grey. **4** (*also* **White**) belonging to a light-complexioned people. **5** of or relating to such people. **6** white-haired as from age etc. **7** pure, clean, stainless. **8** spotless, innocent. **9** (of coffee) containing milk or cream. **10** having snow (*a white Christmas*). **11** clothed in white. **12** having white or pale fur, feathers, flowers, fruit etc. **13** not malicious or malevolent. **14** fair, happy, propitious. **15** (*Hist.*) counter-revolutionary. ~†*v.t.* to whiten. ~*n.* **1** a white colour. **2** a white paint or pigment. **3** (*also* **White**) a white person or a member of one of the paler peoples, esp. a European. 4 a white animal, esp. a butterfly. 5 a white part of anything, having the colour of snow. 6 the sclerotic coat of the eye surrounding the iris. 7 the albuminous material surrounding the yolk of an egg. 8 white clothing (*dressed in white*). 9 (*pl.*) white clothes (*tennis whites*). 10 (*pl.*) leucorrhoea. 11 in chess, snooker etc., a white piece, ball etc., or a player using such a piece or pieces. 12 †the central part of the butt in archery, that which is aimed at. 13 a blank space in printed matter etc. **to bleed white** to drain of money, resources etc. **white about the gills** GILL[1]. **white admiral** *n.* a butterfly, *Limenitis camilla*, with white markings on its wings. **white ant** *n.* a termite. **white arsenic** *n.* the trioxide of arsenic, a virulent poison. **whitebait** *n.* (*pl.* **whitebait**) (*usu. pl.*) the fry of herrings, sprats etc. eaten when about 2 in. (5 cm) long. **whitebeam** *n.* a shrub or small tree, *Sorbus aria*, with silvery undersides to the leaves. **white bear** *n.* the polar bear. **white (blood) cell** *n.* a leucocyte. **whiteboard** *n.* a board with a white surface used by teachers, lecturers etc. to write and draw on with coloured felt-tip pens. **whitecap** *n.* 1 a bird with a light-coloured head, such as the male redstart. 2 a white-crested wave. **white clover** *n.* a clover, *Trifolium repens*, grown as fodder. **white coal** *n.* water, esp. as a source of power. **white-collar** *a.* of or relating to non-manual employees, esp. administrative and clerical workers. **white corpuscle** *n.* a leucocyte. **white currant** *n.* a cultivated shrub, *Ribes sativum*, with white edible berries. **whitedamp** *n.* (*Mining*) a poisonous mixture of carbon monoxide and other gases. **whited sepulchre** *n.* a hypocrite (from Christ's allusion to the scribes and Pharisees, Matt. xxiii.27). **white dwarf** *n.* a type of small, very faint, dense star. **white elephant** *n.* a useless and expensive possession (alluding to the cost of an elephant's keep). **white ensign** *n.* a naval ensign with a white field, carried by the Royal Navy and the Royal Yacht Squadron. **white-eye** *n.* 1 any songbird of the family Zosteropidae, with a white ring around each eye. 2 any bird with white plumage around the eyes. **whiteface** *n.* white make-up used by actors etc. **white-faced** *a.* 1 pale-faced. 2 having a white front or surface. 3 (of animals) having a white spot or streak on the front of the head. **white feather** *n.* a symbol of cowardice (from a white feather in the tail of a game bird of bad breeding). **to show the white feather** FEATHER. **white fish** *n.* any food fish with pale flesh, esp. whiting, haddock, plaice, cod etc. **whitefish** *n.* (*pl. in general* **whitefish,** *in particular* **whitefishes**) a N American salmonoid food fish of the genus *Coregonus*. **white flag** *n.* FLAG OF TRUCE (under FLAG[1]). **white flight** *n.* (*coll.*) the withdrawal of white pupils from predominantly non-white schools. **whitefly** *n.* (*pl.* **whiteflies**) any small insect of the family Aleyrodidae, a pest of plants. **White Friar** *n.* a Carmelite monk (from the white cloak). **white frost** *n.* minute crystals of frozen dew or vapour, rime or hoar frost, esp. covering the ground at night. **white gold** *n.* a whitish alloy of gold with palladium, nickel etc. **white goods** *n.pl.* 1 large kitchen appliances, such as freezers and cookers. 2 †household linen. **whitehead** *n.* a white-topped pustule on the skin. **white heat** *n.* 1 the degree of heat at which bodies become incandescent and appear white. 2 a high pitch of excitement, passion etc. **white hope** *n.* a member of a group, team, organization etc. who is expected to achieve much or bring glory. **white horehound, white hoarhound** *n.* the labiate herb *Marrubium vulgare*. **white horses** *n.pl.* foam-crested waves. **white-hot** *a.* at the temperature of white heat. **White House** *n.* 1 the official residence of the President of the US at Washington. 2 the parliament building of Russia. **white knight** *n.* a person who gives (financial) support to a person or organization in a difficult situation. **white-knuckle** *a.* (*attrib.*) causing fear and excitement (*a white-knuckle ride at an amusement park*). **white lead** *n.* lead carbonate mixed with lead hydroxide, esp. used as a basis for white oil paint. **white leather** *n.* chemically-treated leather with a whitish colour. **white lie** *n.* a pardonable fiction or misstatement. **white light** *n.* light containing more or less equal intensities of all wavelengths in the visible spectrum. **white lime** *n.* whitewash. **whitely** *adv.* **white magic** *n.* 1 magic used for good. 2 magic not involving the Devil. **white matter** *n.* the whitish nerve tissue of the brain and spinal cord. **white meat** *n.* meat that appears white after cooking, such as poultry, veal or pork. **white metal** *n.* a tin- or sometimes lead-based alloy used for bearings, domestic utensils etc. **White Monk** *n.* a Cistercian monk (from the white cloak). **white mulberry** *n.* the tree *Morus alba*, orig. grown to feed silkworms. **whiten** *v.t.*, *v.i.* **whitener** *n.* **whitening** *n.* 1 the act of making white. 2 the state of becoming white. 3 powdered chalk used in whitewashing etc., whiting. **whiteness** *n.* **white night** *n.* a sleepless night. **white noise** *n.* noise containing more or less equal intensities of many frequencies. **white-out** *n.* 1 a condition of uniform whiteness occurring in polar or similar snow-covered regions in heavy cloud. 2 a dense blizzard. **white ox-eye** *n.* the ox-eye daisy. **White Paper** *n.* a government report on a matter recently investigated. **white pepper** *n.* pepper made by removing the skin from *Piper nigrum* berries by rubbing etc. before grinding. **white poplar** *n.* the abele. **white rose** *n.* 1 (*Hist.*) the emblem of the House of York in the Wars of the Roses. 2 the emblem of Yorkshire. **White Russian** *n.*, *a.* BELORUSSIAN. **white sale** *n.* a sale of household linen at reduced prices. **white sauce** *n.* a thick sauce made with flour and milk or a fish or white-meat stock. **white slave** *n.* a woman or child procured, and usu. exported, for prostitution. **white slaver** *n.* **white slavery** *n.* **whitesmith** *n.* 1 a tinsmith. 2 a person who finishes or galvanizes ironwork. **white sock** *n. a* white lower part of a horse's leg. **white spirit** *n.* a distillate of petroleum used as a paint solvent and thinner. **white squall** *n.* a squall not preceded by clouds, as in tropical seas. **white sugar** *n.* refined sugar. **whitethorn** *n.* the hawthorn. **whitethroat** *n.* any small warbler of the genus *Sylvia*, with a white throat, esp. *S. communis*. **white tie** *n.* 1 a white bow tie worn by men as part of full evening dress. 2 full evening dress for men. **white vitriol** *n.* zinc sulphate. **whitewash** *n.* 1 a mixture of quicklime and water or of whiting and size used for whitening walls, ceilings etc. 2 a false colouring given to the reputation of a person or institution to counteract allegations of disreputableness. ~*v.t.* 1 to cover with whitewash. 2 to cover up or conceal (a misdemeanour etc.). 3 to clear (a person's name) thus. 4 (*coll.*) to defeat decisively. **whitewasher** *n.* **white water** *n.* foaming water in breakers, rapids etc. **white wedding** *n.* a wedding in which the bride wears white, orig. as a symbol of purity. **white whale** *n.* the beluga. **white wine** *n.* any wine of a light colour, as opposed to red, made from white grapes or from black grapes with their skins removed. **whitewood** *n.* 1 any of various trees yielding light-coloured timber. 2 such timber. **whitey, Whitey** *n.* (*pl.* **whiteys, Whiteys**) (*offensive*) 1 a white person. 2 white people collectively. **whitish** *a.* **whitishness** *n.* [OE *hwīt* (cp. Dut. *wit*, G *weiss*, Icel. *hvītr*, Sansk. *çvēta*)]

Whitehall (wīt´hawl) *n.* 1 the British Government. 2 its central administration, offices or policy. [street in London where these offices are situated]

whiten, whitey etc. WHITE.

†**whither** (widh´ə) *adv.* 1 (*interrog.*) to what or which place, where. 2 (*rel.*) to which. ~*conj.* 1 to whatever place. 2 and to that place. †**whithersoever** *adv.*, *conj.* to whatever place. [OE *hwider*, as WHETHER]

whiting[1] (wī´ting) *n.* (*pl.* **whiting**) a sea fish, *Merlangus merlangus*, used for food. [WHITE, -ING[1]]
whiting[2] (wī´ting) *n.* fine chalk pulverized, washed and prepared for use in whitewashing, polishing etc.
whitish WHITE.
whitleather (wit´ledhə) *n.* leather dressed with alum, white leather. [WHITE, LEATHER]
whitlow (wit´lō) *n.* a pus-filled inflammation, esp. round the nail of a finger or toe. **whitlow-grass** *n.* a minute, white-flowered, grasslike plant, esp. *Erophila verna*, formerly thought to cure whitlows. [perh. corr. of obs. *quick-flaw*, a flaking off of the skin round the quick, conf. with WHIT]
Whitsun (wit´sən), **Whit** (wit) *a.* of or relating to Whit Sunday or Whitsuntide. ~*n.* Whitsuntide. **Whit Monday** *n.* the day after Whit Sunday. **Whit Sunday** *n.* the seventh Sunday after Easter, a festival commemorating the day of Pentecost. **Whitsuntide** *n.* Whit Sunday and the following days. **Whit week** *n.* the week following Whit Sunday. **Whit weekend** *n.* the weekend including Whit Sunday. [short for *Whit Sunday* (WHITE, SUNDAY, from the white garment commonly worn at this festival which was a great season for christenings)]
whittle (wit´əl) *v.t.* **1** to trim, shave or cut pieces or slices from with a knife. **2** to shape thus. **3** to thin down. **4** to reduce, pare (away) or bring (down) in amount etc., gradually or by degrees. ~*v.i.* to keep on paring, shaving or cutting (at a stick etc.) with a knife. ~*n.* (*dial.*) a long knife, esp. one used by butchers, sailors etc., often worn at the belt. [corr. of ME *thwitel*, from OE *thwītan*, to cut, to pare]
whity (wī´ti) *a.* whitish, inclining to white (*usu. in comb.*, as *whity-brown*).
whiz (wiz), **whizz** *v.i.* (*pres.p.* **whizzing,** *past, p.p.* **whizzed**) **1** to make or move with a hissing sound, like an arrow or ball flying through the air. **2** to move about rapidly. ~*n.* **1** a whizzing sound. **2** (*coll.*) WIZ. **whizbang** *n.* **1** a small high-velocity shell. **2** a type of firework. ~*a.* lively, spectacular. **whiz-kid** *n.* (*coll.*) a person who is outstandingly successful or clever, esp. at a relatively young age. **whizzingly** *adv.* [imit.]
WHO *abbr.* World Health Organization.
who (hoo) *pron.* (*obj.* **whom** (hoom), *poss.* **whose** (hooz)) **1** (*interrog.*) what or which person or persons? **2** (*rel.*) that (identifying the subject or object in a relative clause with that of the principal clause). **3** †he, she or they that. †**as who should say** as though a person had said. **who goes there?** used as a challenge by a sentry etc. **who-does-what** *a.* (*attrib.*) relating to the division of labour among workers, esp. belonging to different trade unions (*a who-does-what dispute*). **whodunnit** (-dŭn´it), (*esp. N Am.*) **whodunit** *n.* (*coll.*) a detective or mystery story. **whoever** (-ev´ə), (*poet.*) **whoe'er** (-eə´) *pron.* (*obj.* **whomever,** (*poet.*) **whome'er,** *poss.* **whosever,** (*poet.*) **whose'er**) **1** any person without exception who, no matter who. **2** (*coll.*) who at all. †**whoso** (hoo´sō) *pron.* (*obj.* **whomso,** *poss.* **whoseso**) whoever. †**whosoever** (-ev´ə), **whosoe'er** (-eə´) *pron.* (*obj.* **whomsoever, whomsoe'er,** *poss.* **whosesoever, whosesoe'er**) whoever. **who's who** *n.* **1** who each person is (*to find out who's who*). **2** a directory of famous people. [OE m., f. *hwā*, neut. *hwæt*, gen. *hwæs*, dat. *hwām* (cp. Dut. *wie, wat, wiens, wien*, G *wer, was, wessen, wen* and *wem*, Icel. *hverr, hver, hvat, hvers, hverjum*, etc.), cogn. with L *quis*, Sansk. *kas, kim, kam*]

Usage note (1) *Whom* is sometimes used instead of *who* in relative clauses of the type *the man who she said is her father, the woman who I believed was his wife*, but this is best avoided. (2) The subjective pronouns *who* and *whoever* are the everyday choice for direct objects in questions (direct and indirect) and as relatives, even though the objective forms (*whom* etc.) are required by strict grammatical rule. So *Who did you hit?, You asked who I hit, the policeman who I hit* are generally acceptable, with *Whom did you hit?, You asked whom I hit* etc. more formal equivalents. (3) The spellings of the pronoun *whose* and the contraction *who's* (who is) should not be confused.

whoa (wō), **wo** *int.* stop! (used chiefly to horses). [var. of HO]
who'd (hood) *contr.* **1** who had. **2** who would.
whodunnit WHO.
whole (hōl) *a.* **1** complete or entire. **2** containing the total number of parts, undivided, undiminished. **3** unimpaired, uninjured, not broken, intact. **4** integral, composed of units, not fractional. **5** having no constituents removed (*whole milk*). ~*n.* **1** a thing complete in all its parts, units etc. **2** all that there is of a thing, the entirety. **3** a complete system, a complete combination of parts, an organic unity. **as a whole** considered as an organic unity. **a whole lot** LOT. **on the whole 1** all things considered. **2** in most cases. **the whole boiling (lot)** BOIL[1]. **the whole kit (and caboodle)** KIT[1]. **the whole lot** LOT. **the whole of** everybody in (*The whole of the village heard the explosion*). **the whole shoot** SHOOT. **the whole shooting match** SHOOTING (under SHOOT). **to go the whole hog** HOG. **whole bag of tricks** *n.* **1** everything. **2** all means or expedients. **whole cloth** *n.* cloth of full manufactured size. **wholefood** *n.* food that has undergone little or no processing or refining. **wholegrain** *a.* made from or containing complete grains with no parts removed (*wholegrain bread*). **wholehearted** *a.* done or intended with all one's heart, hearty, generous, cordial, sincere. **wholeheartedly** *adv.* **wholeheartedness** *n.* **whole holiday** *n.* a full day's holiday. **whole-life insurance** *n.* life insurance for which premiums are paid until the death of the insured. **wholemeal** *a.* made from flour ground from the entire wheat grain. ~*n.* such flour. **wholeness** *n.* **whole note** *n.* (*esp. N Am.*) a semibreve. **whole number** *n.* an integer. **wholesale** *n.* the sale of goods in large quantities, as distinct from *retail*. ~*a.* **1** buying or selling thus. **2** done in the mass, on a large scale, indiscriminate (*wholesale destruction*). ~*adv.* **1** by wholesale, in large quantities. **2** by the mass, on a large scale. ~*v.t.* to sell wholesale. **wholesaler** *n.* **wholesome** *a.* **1** tending to promote physical health, salutary, salubrious. **2** promoting moral or mental health. **3** indicating health. **wholesomely** *adv.* **wholesomeness** *n.* **whole-tone scale** *n.* (*Mus.*) a scale in which each interval is a tone, with no semitones. **wholewheat** *a.*, *n.* wholemeal. **wholly** (hō´li) *adv.* **1** entirely, completely. **2** totally, exclusively. [OE *hāl*, HALE[1] (cp. Dut. *heel*, G *heil*, Icel. *heill*), cogn. with HEAL and HOLY]
wholism HOLISM.
wholly WHOLE.
whom, whomever etc. WHO.
whoop (woop, hoop) *v.i.* **1** to utter a 'whoop'. **2** to shout or cry out loudly in excitement, encouragement, exultation etc. **3** to halloo. ~*v.t.* **1** to utter with a whoop. **2** to urge (on) with whoops. **3** to mock at with loud cries. ~*n.* **1** the cry 'whoop'. **2** a loud shout of excitement, encouragement etc. **3** the sound made in whooping cough. **to whoop it up 1** (*coll.*) to engage in riotous enjoyment. **2** (*coll., N Am.*) to stir up enthusiasm etc. **whoopee** (wupē´) *int.* (*coll.*) used to express excitement or delight. ~*n.* (*coll.*) **1** riotous enjoyment. **2** a noisy, jolly time. **to make whoopee 1** (*coll.*) to whoop it up. **2** (*coll.*) to make love. **whoopee cushion** (wup´i) *n.* a cushion that when sat on emits a sound as of someone breaking wind. **whooper** *n.* **whooper swan** *n.* a large swan, *Cygnus cygnus*, with a whooping call. **whooping cough** (hoo´-) *n.* an infectious disease, esp. of children, characterized by a violent cough followed by a loud

convulsive respiration; pertussis. **whooping crane** (hoo´-, woo´-) *n.* a large white crane, *Grus americana*, of N America. **whoops** (wups), **whoops-a-daisy** *int.* (*coll.*) used to express surprise or apology. [ME *houpen*, F *houpes*, from *houp!*, a cry or int., perh. from Gmc.]

whoosh (wush), **woosh** *n.* a rushing or hissing sound as of something moving swiftly through the air. *~int.* used to imitate such a sound. *~v.i.* to make or move with such a sound. [imit.]

whop (wop), **whap** *v.t.* (*pres.p.* **whopping, whapping,** *past, p.p.* **whopped, whapped**) (*sl.*) **1** to beat, to thrash. **2** to defeat. **3** to cause to fall with a loud noise. *~v.i.* to fall with a loud noise. *~n.* a heavy blow or thud. **whopper** *n.* (*sl.*) **1** anything uncommonly large etc. **2** a monstrous lie. **whopping** *a.* (*sl.*) uncommonly large. [var. *whap*, *wap*, etym. uncertain]

whore (haw) *n.* **1** a prostitute. **2** (*derog.*) a promiscuous woman. *~v.i.* **1** to be a whore. **2** to have sexual relations with a whore or whores. **3** (*Bible*) to practise idolatry. *~v.t.* to prostitute (a person or oneself). **whorehouse** *n.* a brothel. **whoremonger, †whoremaster** *n.* **1** a person who has sexual relations with whores. **2** a pimp. **†whoreson** (-sən) *n.* **1** a bastard. **2** a despicable person. *~a.* mean, vile. **†whoring** *n.* **whorish** *a.* **whorishly** *adv.* **whorishness** *n.* [ME *hore*, Icel. *hōra*, adulteress (cp. Dan. *hore*, Swed. *hora*, Dut. *hoer*, G *hura*), perh. cogn. with L *cārus*, dear]

whorl (wœl, wawl) *n.* **1** a circular set or ring of leaves, sepals or other organs on a plant. **2** one convolution or turn of a spiral, as in a univalve shell. **3** a circular pattern in a fingerprint. **4** a coil, a spiral, a convolution. **5** †the disc for steadying the motion of a spindle, formerly made of stone etc. **whorled** *a.* [prob. shortened from *whorvel*, from OE *wheorfan*, see WHIRL]

whortleberry (wœ´təlberi) *n.* (*pl.* **whortleberries**) the bilberry. [formerly *hurtilberye hurtberye* (OE *horta*, BERRY)]

whose, whosever etc. WHO.

whump (wŭmp, wump) *n.* a dull thud or thump. *~v.i.* to make such a sound. *~v.t.* to strike with such a sound. [imit.]

why (wī) *adv.* **1** (*interrog.*) for what reason or purpose? **2** (*rel.*) on account of which. *~n.* (*pl.* **whys**) the reason, explanation or purpose of anything. *~int.* used to express surprise, impatience etc. **why so?** for what reason? on what grounds? [OE *hwī*, instr. of *whā*, WHO]

whydah (wid´ə), **whidah** *n.* **1** any small black African weaver-bird of the genus *Vidua*, the male of which has mainly black plumage and four long tail feathers. **2** the widow-bird (genus *Euplectes*). [*Ouidah*, in Benin]

WI *abbr.* **1** West Indies. **2** Wisconsin. **3** Women's Institute.

Wicca (wik´ə) *n.* the cult or practice of modern witchcraft. **Wiccan** *n., a.* [OE *wicca*, WITCH[1]]

wick[1] (wik) *n.* **1** a piece or bundle of fibrous or spongy material used in a candle or lamp to convey the melted grease or oil by capillary action to the flame. **2** any strip of material used in a similar way, as to drain a wound. *~v.t.* to draw (away) by capillary action. **to dip one's wick** (*sl.*) (of a man) to have sexual intercourse. **to get on one's wick** (*coll.*) to annoy or irritate one. [OE *wice*, (cp. MDut. *wiecke*, Dan. *væge*, Norw. *veik*)]

wick[2] (wik) *n.* (*dial.*) **1** a town, village or municipal district (chiefly in place names). **2** a dairy farm. [OE *wīc*, L *vīcus*, village]

wicked (wik´id) *a.* (*comp.* **wickeder**, *superl.* **wickedest**) **1** sinful, addicted to evil or vice, immoral, depraved. **2** mischievous, roguish. **3** harmful, injurious. **4** spiteful. **5** (*coll.*) very bad. **6** (*sl.*) very good. **Wicked Bible** *n.* a 1631 edition of the Bible containing the misprint 'thou shalt commit adultery'. **wickedly** *adv.* **wickedness** *n.* [from obs. a. *wikke*, cogn. with WEAK and OE *wicca*, a wizard]

wicker (wik´ə) *n.* twigs or osiers plaited into a material for baskets, chairs etc. *~a.* made of this material. **wickered** *a.* **wickerwork** *n.* [orig. a pliant twig, prob. from Scand. (cp. MSwed. *wika*, to bend, Swed. *vika*, to fold, to plait, Dan. *veg*, pliant), cogn. with WEAK]

wicket (wik´it) *n.* **1** a set of three stumps surmounted by two bails at which the bowler directs the ball in cricket. **2** the ground on which this is set up. **3** the innings or turn of each batsman at the wicket. **4** the pitch between the wickets, esp. as regards condition for bowling. **5** a small gate, door or other entrance, esp. one close beside or forming part of a larger one. **6** (*N Am.*) a small aperture in a door or wall, having a grille or opened and closed by means of a sliding panel. **7** (*coll.*) situation, circumstances. **8** (*N Am.*) a croquet hoop. **at the wicket** in cricket, batting. **on a good wicket** (*coll.*) in a favourable situation. **on a sticky wicket** (*coll.*) in an unfavourable situation. **to keep wicket** in cricket, to be wicketkeeper. **to pitch wickets** PITCH[1]. **to take a wicket** in cricket, to get a batsman out. **wicket-door, wicket-gate** *n.* **wicketkeeper** *n.* the fielder who stands behind the batsman's wicket in cricket. **wicketkeeping** *n.* [ME, ONF *wiket* (F *guichet*), etym. uncertain, perh. from OHG *wisken*, WHISK, to slip out]

wickiup (wik´iŭp) *n.* a hut or shelter used by nomadic American Indians, comprising an oval frame covered with grass etc. [Algonquian]

widdershins WITHERSHINS.

widdle (wid´əl) *v.i.* (*coll.*) to urinate. [WEE[2], PIDDLE]

wide (wīd) *a.* **1** having a great relative extent from side to side, broad, as opposed to *narrow*. **2** having a specified degree of breadth. **3** extending far. **4** vast, spacious, extensive. **5** not limited or restricted, free, liberal, comprehensive, catholic. **6** distant or deviating by a considerable extent or amount from a mark, point, purpose etc. **7** fully open or expanded. **8** (*sl.*) crafty, shrewd. *~adv.* **1** widely. **2** to a great distance, extensively. **3** far from the mark or purpose. **4** to the fullest extent, fully (*wide open*). *~n.* **1** in cricket, a wide ball. **2** the wide world. **the wide world** all the world. **to give a wide berth to** BERTH. **to the wide** completely, absolutely. **wide of the mark** MARK[1]. **-wide** *comb. form* extending throughout, as *nationwide*. **wide-angle lens** *n.* a camera lens with an angle of up to 100° used for photographing buildings etc. **wide area network** *n.* a group of computer systems widely separated geographically, and linked to each other by telephone, satellite etc. for the exchange of data. **wideawake** *n.* a soft felt hat with a broad brim. **wide awake** *a.* **1** fully awake. **2** (*coll.*) alert, wary. **3** (*coll.*) keen, sharp, knowing. **wide ball** *n.* in cricket, a ball bowled too far to the side and out of the batsman's reach. **wide boy** *n.* (*sl.*) a crafty, shrewd man, inclined to sharp practice. **wide-eyed** *a.* **1** surprised, astonished. **2** naive. **widely** *adv.* **1** to a wide extent or degree. **2** by many people (*widely accepted*). **widen** *v.t., v.i.* **widener** *n.* **wideness** *n.* **wide open** *a.* **1** fully open. **2** open to attack. **3** of indeterminate or unpredictable outcome. **4** (*N Am.*) lawless, disorderly. **wide-ranging** *a.* extending over a wide range. **wide receiver** *n.* in American football, a player who receives the ball from the quarterback in a long pass. **wide-screen** *a.* of or for a screen that has much greater width than height (*wide-screen film projection*). **widespread** *a.* widely disseminated. **widish** *a.* [OE *wīd* (cp. Dut. *wijd*, G *weit*, far, Icel. *vīthr*)]

widgeon WIGEON.

widget (wij´it) *n.* **1** a gadget. **2** a thingumajig, a whatsit. [alteration of GADGET]

widish WIDE.

widow (wid´ō) *n.* **1** a woman who has lost her husband by death and has not remarried. **2** a woman whose husband devotes much time to a (sporting) activity that takes him away from home (*a golf widow*). **3** (*Print.*) a short final line of a paragraph etc. at the top of a printed column or page. **4** in some card games, an extra hand of cards dealt separately. *~v.t.* **1** to bereave of a spouse, to make a widow or widower. **2** to bereave, to deprive (of). **widow-bird** *n.* **1** a weaver-bird of the genus *Euplectes.* **2** a whydah. **widower** *n.* a man who has lost his wife by death and has not remarried. **widowhood** *n.* **widow's cruse** *n.* an unfailing source of supply (I Kings xvii.16). **widow's mite** *n.* a small but ill-afforded contribution (Mark xii.42). **widow's peak** *n.* the natural growth of hair to a point in the middle of the forehead. **widow's weeds** *n.pl.* WEEDS. [OE *widwe* (cp. Dut. *weduwe,* G *Wittwe,* OHG *wituwa*), cogn. with L *viduus,* bereft (whence F *veuve*), Sansk. *vidhavā,* widow, Gr. *ēitheos,* bachelor]

width (width, witth) *n.* **1** the extent of a thing from side to side, breadth, wideness. **2** a large extent. **3** a piece of material cut from the full width of a roll etc. **4** comprehensiveness of mind, liberality, catholicity. **widthways, widthwise** *adv.* in a crosswise direction, from side to side.

wield (wēld) *v.t.* **1** to handle, hold, use or employ (*to wield a hammer*). **2** to have, exert, command or maintain (power etc.). **wieldable** *a.* **wielder** *n.* **wieldy** *a.* (*comp.* **wieldier,** *superl.* **wieldiest**) that may be wielded, manageable. [OE *geweldan, -wyldan,* from *wealdan,* to govern, to rule (cp. Icel. *valda,* G *walten*)]

wiener (wē´nə), (*coll.*) **weenie** (wē´ni), **wienie** *n.* **1** (*N Am.*) a type of frankfurter. **2** (*sl.*) the penis. **3** (*derog.*) a man. [G, Viennese (sausage)]

Wiener schnitzel (vēnə shnit´səl) *n.* a cutlet of veal or pork, coated with a breadcrumb mixture and fried. [G, Viennese cutlet]

☒ **wierd** common misspelling of WEIRD.

wife (wīf) *n.* (*pl.* **wives** (wīvz)) **1** a married woman, esp. in relation to her husband. **2** (*dial.*) a woman, esp. an elderly or humble one. **3** (*in comb.*) a woman engaged in a specified occupation (*a housewife; a fishwife*). †**to have/ take to wife** to marry. **wifehood** *n.* **wifeless** *a.* **wifelike** *a.* **wifely** *a.* **wifeliness** *n.* **wife-swapping** *n.* (*coll.*) the temporary exchange of spouses for sexual activity. **wifish** *a.* [OE *wīf* (cp. Dut. *wijf,* G *Weib,* Icel. *vīf,* neut.)]

wig[1] (wig) *n.* a covering for the head composed of false hair, worn to conceal baldness, as a disguise, for ornament or as part of an official costume, esp. by judges, lawyers etc. **wigged** *a.* **wigless** *a.* **wigmaker** *n.* [shortened from PERIWIG]

wig[2] (wig) *v.t.* (*pres.p.* **wigging,** *past, p.p.* **wigged**) (*coll.*) to reprimand, to scold. **wigging** *n.* a scolding. [etym. uncertain]

wigeon (wij´ən), **widgeon** *n.* a wild duck of the genus *Anas,* esp. *A. penelope* or *A. americana.* [etym. uncertain]

wigged WIG[1].

wigging WIG[2].

wiggle (wig´əl) *v.t., v.i.* to move jerkily, esp. from side to side. *~n.* **1** an act of wiggling. **2** a bend or undulation in a line etc. **to get a wiggle on** (*sl.*) to hurry up. **wiggler** *n.* **wiggly** *a.* (*comp.* **wigglier,** *superl.* **wiggliest**) **1** wiggling. **2** having bends or undulations (*a wiggly line*). [ME (MLG and MDut. *wiggelen*)]

†**wight** (wīt) *n.* a person. [OE *wiht,* see WHIT]

wigwag (wig´wag) *v.t.* (*pres.p.* **wigwagging,** *past, p.p.* **wigwagged**) to wag to and fro. *~v.i.* **1** to move to and fro, to wag. **2** to signal by waving flags. [redupl. of WAG[1]]

wigwam (wig´wam) *n.* **1** a N American Indian hut or cabin, usu. consisting of a framework covered with bark, matting, hides etc. **2** a similar structure for children, used as a tent etc. [Algonquian *weekouomut,* in his house, inflected from *week,* house]

wilco (wil´kō) *int.* used in radio communications etc. to indicate that a message received will be complied with. [*will comply*]

wild (wīld) *a.* **1** living in a state of nature, esp. inhabiting or growing in the forest or open country. **2** (esp. of animals and plants) not tamed, domesticated or cultivated. **3** not civilized, savage. **4** (of land etc.) unsettled, uncultivated, irregular, desert, uninhabited. **5** wayward, disorderly, lawless. **6** reckless, incautious, rash. **7** ill-considered, imprudent, extravagant, inordinate. **8** ungoverned, unchecked, unrestrained. **9** turbulent, stormy, furious. **10** eager, passionate, mad (with etc.). **11** excited, enthusiastic (about etc.). **12** (*coll.*) angry. **13** (*coll.*) exciting. **14** (of horses etc.) shy, easily startled, given to shying. **15** (*Bot.*) having a certain resemblance to some other plant but inferior to it in appearance. **16** (of a playing card) able to represent any card the holder chooses. *~n.* **1** an uninhabited and uncultivated tract. **2** a desert. *~adv.* in a wild manner or state. **in the wild** in its natural state. **(out) in the wilds** (*coll.*) a long way from human habitation (*to live out in the wilds*). **to run wild** to grow or become unrestrained or uncontrolled. **wild and woolly** unrefined, uncultivated. **wild arum** *n.* the cuckoo pint. **wild boar** *n.* the male of the wild swine, *Sus scrofa.* **wild card** *n.* **1** a playing card that can have any value or rank chosen by the holder. **2** (*Comput.*) a character or symbol that will match any character or group of characters. **3** an unpredictable element. **4** in sport, an extra player or team allowed to take part in a competition at the organizers' discretion. **wildcat** *n.* **1** (*usu.* **wild cat**) an undomesticated species of cat, such as *Felis sylvestris.* **2** a quick-tempered, fierce person. **3** an exploratory drilling for oil or natural gas. *~a.* speculative or risky (*a wildcat scheme*). **wildcat strike** *n.* a sudden strike not approved by the relevant union, or undertaken in breach of a contract. **wild-caught** *a.* (of an animal) caught in the wild. **wildfire** *n.* **1** (*Hist.*) a combustible material formerly used in warfare. **2** ignis fatuus. **to spread like wildfire** to spread very quickly. **wildfowl** *n.* (*pl.* **wildfowl**) (*usu. pl.*) any of various birds pursued as game, esp. waterfowl. **wildfowler** *n.* **wildfowling** *n.* **wild-goose chase** *n.* a foolish or hopeless enterprise. **wild horse** *n.* **1** an untamed or undomesticated horse. **2** (*pl., coll.*) the most powerful force etc. (*Wild horses wouldn't make me go*). **wild hyacinth** *n.* the bluebell, *Hyacinthoides nonscripta.* **wilding**[1] *n.* **1** a plant that springs up by natural agency, esp. a wild fruit tree. **2** the fruit of such a plant. **wilding**[2] *n.* (*esp. N Am., sl.*) a rampage through the streets by a gang of youths who rob or assault passers-by as they go. **to go wilding** to go on such a rampage. **wildish** *a.* **wildlife** *n.* wild animals and plants. **wildling** *n.* a wilding (the plant or fruit). **wildly** *adv.* **wild man of the woods** *n.* (*coll.*) an orang-utan. **wild marjoram** *n.* the herb *Origanum vulgare.* **wildness** *n.* **wild oat** *n.* **1** a type of grass, *Avena fatua,* growing as a weed in cornfields. **2** (*pl.*) youthful excesses, esp. sexual ones. **to sow one's wild oats** OAT. **wild rice** *n.* any plant of the genus *Zizania,* with edible grains. **wild silk** *n.* **1** silk produced by wild silkworms. **2** silk made from short fibres in imitation of this. **wild spaniard** *n.* any of various sharp-leaved plants of the New Zealand *Aciphylla.* **wild type** *n.* (*Biol.*) the form of an organism that prevails in the natural state. **Wild West** *n.* the N American West during the lawless period of its early settlement. **wildwood** *n.* (*poet.*) a tract of natural wood or forest. [OE *wilde* (cp. Dut., G *wild,* Icel. *villr*), prob. cogn. with WILL[1]]

wildebeest (wil´dibēst) *n.* (*pl.* **wildebeest, wildebeests**) a gnu. [Afrikaans (WILD, BEAST)]

†**wilder** (wil´də) *v.t.* **1** to lead astray. **2** to bewilder. [shortened from *wilderne,* see WILDERNESS, or BEWILDER]

wilderness (wil´dənis) *n.* **1** an uninhabited or uncultivated land, a desert. **2** a scene of disorder or confusion. 3 a portion of a garden left to run wild. 4 a confused mass or quantity (of). **in the wilderness** out of office, not wielding power. [ME *wilderne*, desert, OE *wilder*, wild animal, -NESS]

wile (wīl) *n.* (*usu. pl.*) a trick, an artifice, a stratagem or deception. *~v.t.* to entice, to cajole (into, away etc.). [OE *wīl*, prob. cogn. with OF GUILE]

wilful (wil´fəl), (*N Am.*) **willful** *a.* 1 intentional, voluntary, deliberate. 2 obstinate, self-willed, headstrong, perverse. **wilfully** *adv.* **wilfulness** *n.* [WILL[2], -FUL]

wilga (wil´gə) *n.* (*pl.* **wilgas**) (*Austral.*) a tree of the genus *Geijera*, esp. *G. parviflora*. [Austral. Abor.]

wilily, wiliness WILY.

will[1] (wil) *v.t.* (*past* **would** (wud), *2nd pers. sing. pres.* †**wilt** (wilt), *2nd pers. sing. past* †**wouldst** (wudst)) 1 to desire, to wish, to choose, to want (a thing, that etc.) (*Will you have another cup of tea?*). 2 to be induced, to consent, to agree (to etc.) (*Will you close the door, please?*). 3 to be in the habit or accustomed (to). 4 to be able (to). 5 (*in 1st pers.*) to intend, desire or have a mind to. *~v.aux.* 1 (*esp. in 2nd and 3rd pers.*) to be about or going to (expressing simple futurity or conditional action). 2 (*esp. in 1st pers.*) to intend, desire or have a mind to. 3 to be certain or probable as a natural consequence, must. **will do** (*coll.*) used to express willingness to comply. **would as lief** LIEF. **would rather** RATHER. **would-be** *a.* (*attrib.*) desirous, vainly aspiring to be. [OE *willan* (cp. Dut. *willen*, G *wollen*, Icel. *vilja*), cogn. with L *velle*, and Eng. WELL[1] and WILD]

Usage note See note under SHALL.

will[2] (wil) *n.* 1 the mental power or faculty by which one initiates or controls one's activities, as opposed to *impulse* or *instinct*. 2 the exercise of this power, an act of willing, a choice of volition, an intention, a fixed or authoritative purpose. 3 determination, the power of carrying out one's intentions or dominating others. 4 that which is willed, resolved or determined upon. 5 arbitrary disposal, discretion or sufferance. 6 inclination or disposition towards others. 7 the legal declaration of one's intentions as to the disposal of one's property after one's death, embodied in a written instrument (*to make a will*). 8 a wish or desire (*What is your will?*). **at will** 1 at one's pleasure or discretion. 2 (*Law*) (of a tenant) that can be evicted without notice. **to have one's will** to get what one desires. **where there's a will there's a way** anything can be achieved with determination. **with a will** heartily, zealously. **with the best will in the world** no matter how good one's intentions are, however determined one is. **willed** *a.* (*esp. in comb.*, as *strong-willed*). **will-less** *a.* **will of one's own** *n.* a wilful disposition. **will-power** *n.* control exercised deliberately over impulse or inclinations. [OE *willa*, from WILL[1] (cp. Dut. *wil*, G *Wille*, Icel. *vili*)]

will[3] (wil) *v.t.* 1 to intend or bring about by the exercise of one's will, to resolve, to determine. 2 to direct, control or cause to act in a specified way by the exercise of one's will-power. 3 to bequeath or devise by will. *~v.i.* to exercise will-power. **willable** *a.* **willer** *n.*

willet (wil´it) *n.* (*pl.* **willet**) a N American sandpiper, *Catoptophorus semipalmatus*, allied to the snipe. [imit. of its cry]

willful WILFUL.

willie WILLY.

willies (wil´iz) *n.pl.* (*coll.*) nervousness, apprehensiveness (*It gives me the willies*). [etym. unknown]

willing (wil´ing) *a.* 1 inclined, ready, not averse or reluctant (to). 2 cheerfully acting, done, given etc. **to show willing** to indicate a readiness to help, comply etc. **willingly** *adv.* **willingness** *n.*

will-o'-the-wisp (wilədhəwisp´) *n.* 1 an ignis fatuus. 2 an illusory hope, goal etc. 3 an elusive person. [*Will*, short for *William*, WISP (of lighted tow etc.)]

willow (wil´ō) *n.* 1 (*also* **willow tree**) any tree or shrub of the genus *Salix*, usu. growing near water, characterized by long, slender, pliant branches, largely yielding osiers and timber used for cricket bats etc. 2 a cricket bat. **willowed** *a.* abounding with willows. **willow grouse** *n.* a common grouse, *Lagopus lagopus*, of Europe and N America. **willowherb** *n.* 1 any plant of the genus *Epilobium*, esp. one with leaves like a willow's. 2 the rosebay willlowherb. **willow-pattern** *n.* a decorative pattern of Chinese style in blue on a white ground, introduced in 1780 and used for china, earthenware etc. **willow ptarmigan** *n.* (*N Am.*) the willow grouse. **willow tit** *n.* a small tit, *Parus montanus*, with a black crown. **willow warbler, willow wren** *n.* a small woodland bird, *Phylloscopus trochilus*. **willowy** *a.* 1 abounding with willows. 2 lithe, slender or graceful, like a willow. [OE *welig* (cp. Dut. *wilg*), perh. cogn. with HELIX]

willy (wil´i), **willie** *n.* (*pl.* **willies**) (*coll.*) the penis. [short for *William*]

willy-nilly (wilinil´i) *adv.* 1 willingly or unwillingly. 2 randomly, haphazardly. *~a.* 1 happening whether it is desired or not. 2 random, haphazard. [*will he, nill he* (*nill*, be unwilling, from OE *nyllan*, *ne* and WILL[1])]

willy wagtail (wil´i) *n.* 1 a black-and-white Australian flycatcher, *Rhipidura leucophrys*. 2 (*dial.*) the pied wagtail.

willy-willy (wiliwil´i) *n.* (*pl.* **willy-willies**) (*Austral.*) a tropical cyclone, esp. one that sweeps over NW Australia in the late summer. [Austral. Abor.]

wilt[1] (wilt) *v.i.* 1 to wither, to droop. 2 to lose freshness or vigour. *~v.t.* to cause to wilt. *~n.* a disease of plants that causes them to wilt. [perh. var. of dial. *welk*, from Dut. *welk*, G *welken*, from OHG *welk*, moist]

†**wilt**[2] WILL[1].

Wilton (wil´tən), **Wilton carpet** *n.* a carpet with the loops cut open into an elastic velvet pile. [town in Wiltshire where orig. manufactured]

Wilts. *abbr.* Wiltshire.

wily (wī´li) *a.* (*comp.* **wilier**, *superl.* **wiliest**) using or full of wiles, cunning, crafty. **wilily** *adv.* **wiliness** *n.*

WIMP (wimp) *abbr.* (*Comput.*) windows, icons, menus (or mice), pointers.

wimp (wimp) *n.* (*coll.*) a feeble, ineffectual person. **to wimp out** (*sl.*) to withdraw from something through fear, to chicken out. **wimpish** *a.* **wimpishly** *adv.* **wimpishness** *n.* **wimpy** *a.* [etym. unknown]

wimple (wim´pəl) *n.* a covering of silk, linen etc., worn over the head, neck and sides of the face by some nuns and formerly by other women. *~v.t.* 1 to cover with a wimple. 2 to arrange in folds or pleats. *~v.i.* to lie or fall in folds. [OE *winpel* (perh. WIND[2], *pell*, *pæll*, L PALLIUM), cp. Dut., G *wimpel*, Icel. *vimpill*, pennon, streamer]

Wimshurst machine (wimz´hœst) *n.* a friction machine by which static electricity can be generated and stored. [James *Wimshurst*, 1832–1903, British engineer]

win (win) *v.t.* (*pres.p.* **winning**, *past, p.p.* **won** (wŭn)) 1 to gain, obtain, achieve or attain by fighting or superiority in a contest, competition, wager etc. (*to win a prize*). 2 to gain by effort, work etc., to earn. 3 to be victorious in (*to win a battle*). 4 to make one's way to, to reach. 5 to win over. 6 to get or extract (ore etc.) by mining, smelting etc. 7 to dry (hay etc.) by exposing it to the air. *~v.i.* 1 to be successful or victorious in a fight, contest, wager etc. 2 to make one's way by struggle or effort (through etc.). *~n.* a success, a victory. **to win hands down** HAND. **to win one's spurs** SPUR. **to win out** to win through. **to win over** to persuade, to secure the support, favour or assent of. **to win the day** DAY. **to**

win through to be successful, to prevail. **you can't win** (*coll.*) it is impossible to succeed. **you can't win them all** (*coll.*) used to express resignation or consolation on failure, defeat etc. **winless** *a.* (*esp. N Am.*) not having won. **winnable** *a.* **winner** *n.* **1** a person or thing that wins. **2** (*coll.*) a person or thing that is bound to succeed. **winning** *a.* **1** that wins. **2** attractive, charming. ~*n.pl.* the amount won in betting, gambling etc. **winning hazard** *n.* a billiard stroke in which the player pockets the object ball. **winningly** *adv.* **winningness** *n.* **winning post** *n.* a post marking the end of a race. [OE *winnan*, to fight, to labour (cp. Dut. *winnen*, G *gewinnen*, Icel. *vinna*), cogn. with L *venus*, desire, and WISH]

wince[1] (wins) *v.i.* to shrink, recoil or flinch, as from pain, trouble or a blow. ~*n.* the act of wincing. **wincer** *n.* **wincingly** *adv.* [prob. from a non-extant OF *wencir*, from OF *guincir*, OS *wenkian*, cogn. with WINK]

wince[2] (wins) *n.* a roller for moving fabric through dyeing vats. [var. of WINCH]

wincey (win´si), **winsey** *n.* (*pl.* **winceys, winseys**) a cotton cloth with wool filling. **winceyette** (-et´) *n.* a lightweight cotton cloth with a raised nap on both sides. [perh. corr. of LINSEY-WOOLSEY]

winch (winch) *n.* **1** a windlass, a hoisting machine. **2** a crank or handle for turning an axle etc. **3** the reel of a fishing rod. ~*v.t.* to pull or hoist with a winch. **wincher** *n.* [OE *wince*, cogn. with WINKLE]

Winchester (win´chistə) *n.* **1** (*also* **Winchester rifle**) a breech-loading repeating rifle. **2** (*Comput.*) (*also* **Winchester disk, Winchester drive**) a type of hard disk drive in a sealed unit. [O. F. *Winchester*, 1810–80, US manufacturer of the rifle; the number orig. identifying the hard disk was the same as its calibre]

winchester (win´chistə) *n.* a large cylindrical bottle for transporting chemicals. [*Winchester*, Hampshire]

wind[1] (wind) *n.* **1** air in motion, a natural air current, a breeze, a gale. **2** air set in motion artificially. **3** air used or stored for use in a musical instrument, machine etc. **4** the wind instruments in an orchestra etc. or their players. **5** breath as required by the body in exertion, speech etc. **6** the power of breathing in exertion etc., lung power. **7** a part of the body near the stomach, a blow on which causes temporary inability to breathe. **8** breath expended in words, meaningless talk or rhetoric. **9** the gas produced in the stomach during digestion etc., flatulence. **10** scent or odour carried on the wind. **11** a hint, suggestion or indication (of). **12** the windward position (of). ~*v.t.* (*past, p.p.* **winded**) **1** to perceive the presence of by scent. **2** to cause to be out of breath. **3** to enable to recover breath by resting etc. **4** to bring the wind up from the stomach of (a baby) after feeding. **5** to expose to the wind, to ventilate. **between wind and water** in a vulnerable place or position. **how the wind blows** the position or state of affairs. **in the wind** showing signs of occurring. **in the wind's eye** towards the precise point from which the wind blows, directly against the wind. **like the wind** very swiftly. **off the wind** (*Naut.*) not on the wind. **on the wind** (*Naut.*) near the direction from which the wind is blowing. **to break wind** to discharge wind from the anus. **to get the wind up** (*coll.*) to get nervous, to become frightened. **to get wind of 1** (*coll.*) to hear about. **2** (*coll.*) to smell out. **to piss in the wind** PISS. **to put the wind up** (*coll.*) to frighten. **to raise the wind** RAISE. **to sail close to/ near the wind 1** to keep a vessel's head as near the direction from which the wind is blowing as possible while keeping the sails filled. **2** to take risks. **to take the wind out of someone's sails 1** to sail to the windward of someone. **2** to frustrate someone's plans, to disconcert someone. **to take wind** to become known. **to the (four) winds 1** in all directions. **2** into a state of abandonment (*to cast caution to the winds*). **which way the wind blows** the position or state of affairs. **wind and weather** the effects of wind, rain etc. **windage** (-ij) *n.* **1** the difference between the diameter of the bore of a gun and that of the projectile. **2** the influence of wind deflecting a projectile. **3** an allowance for this. **4** the retarding force of air against a moving part. **windbag** *n.* **1** a person who says much of little value, a long-winded speaker. **2** a bag inflated with wind, as in a set of bagpipes. **wind band** *n.* a band made up of wind instruments. **windblown** *a.* **1** blown by the wind. **2** (of trees) deformed by a prevailing wind. **windbound** *a.* prevented from sailing by contrary winds. **windbreak** *n.* a screen, fence, line of trees etc. that provides protection from the wind. **Windbreaker**® *n.* (*N Am.*) a windcheater. **windburn** *n.* skin irritation caused by the wind. **windcheater** *n.* a close-knitted pullover or close-textured garment to keep out the wind. **wind chest** *n.* the box or reservoir for compressed air in an organ. **wind-chill** *n.* **1** the combined chilling effect of low temperature and wind. **2** a measure of this. ~*a.* of or relating to this (*the wind-chill factor*). **wind-cone** *n.* a windsock. **windfall** *n.* **1** something blown down by the wind, esp. an apple or other fruit. **2** a piece of unexpected good fortune, esp. a sum of money. **3** (*N Am.*) the track of a whirlwind in which trees are laid prostrate. **wind farm** *n.* a group of windmills or wind turbines for generating electric power. **windflower** *n.* an anemone, esp. the wood anemone. **wind force** *n.* the force of the wind. **windgall** *n.* a soft tumour on the fetlock joint of a horse. **wind gap** *n.* a dry valley between hills or mountains. **wind-gauge** *n.* **1** an anemometer. **2** an instrument for showing the pressure in the wind chest of an organ. **3** a contrivance attached to the sight of a gun to show the allowance necessary for deflection due to the wind. **windhover** *n.* the kestrel. **wind instrument** *n.* a musical instrument in which the tones are produced by the vibration of an air column forced into the pipes, reeds etc., esp. by the mouth. **windjammer** *n.* **1** a merchant sailing ship. **2** a member of the crew of this. **windless** *a.* **windlessness** *n.* **wind machine** *n.* a machine used in films, the theatre etc. for producing an airstream or the sound of wind. **windmill** *n.* **1** a mill driven by the action of the wind on sails. **2** a toy with curved plastic or paper vanes that revolve in the wind. **3** a device for generating power to drive fuel pumps, generators etc. by a small propeller blade placed in the slipstream of an aircraft. ~*v.t., v.i.* to move like a windmill. **to throw one's cap over the windmill** to behave in a reckless or unconventional manner. **to tilt at windmills** to fight imaginary adversaries. **wind of change** *n.* a force or influence bringing change or reform. **windpipe** *n.* the breathing passage, the trachea. **wind power** *n.* electrical power produced by harnessing wind energy, e.g. by means of a windmill. **wind pump** *n.* a pump operated by the force of the wind on a propeller. **wind-rose** *n.* a diagram with radiating lines indicating the velocity and direction of winds affecting a place. **windrow** (-rō) *n.* **1** a row of raked hay, corn-sheaves, peats etc. set up for drying. **2** (*N Am.*) a pile or bank heaped up by or as by the wind. **wind-sail** *n.* (*Naut.*) a canvas tube used to convey a current of air into the lower parts of a ship. **windscreen** *n.* a glass screen at the front of a car to protect the driver and passengers from the wind caused by the speed of the car. **windscreen wiper** *n.* an electrically-operated device fitted with a rubber blade to keep a windscreen clear of rain, snow etc. **wind shear** *n.* a variation in wind speed at right angles to its direction. **windshield** *n.* (*N Am.*) a windscreen. **windsleeve** *n.* a windsock. **windsock** *n.* an open-ended fabric sleeve flying from a mast, serving as an indicator of the strength and direction of the wind. **windstorm** *n.* a storm with strong winds but no rain. **windsurfing**

n. the sport of sailing on water standing upright on a sailboard. **windsurf** *v.i.* **windsurfer** *n.* **windswept** *a.* **1** exposed to the wind. **2** blown by the wind (*windswept hair*). **wind tunnel** *n.* a tunnel-like device for producing an airstream of known velocity for testing the effect of wind on the structure of model vehicles, aircraft etc. **windward** (-wəd) *n.* the direction from which the wind blows. ~*a.* lying in or directed towards this. ~*adv.* in the direction from which the wind blows. **to get to the windward of 1** to get to this side of. **2** to get the advantage over. **windy**[1] *a.* (*comp.* **windier,** *superl.* **windiest**) **1** having much wind, stormy, boisterous (*a windy day*). **2** exposed to the wind. **3** flatulent, caused by flatulence. **4** verbose, loquacious, empty. **5** (*coll.*) scared, frightened, apprehensive. **windily** *adv.* **windiness** *n.* [OE (cp. Dut., G *wind*, Icel. *vindr*, also L *ventus*, Sansk. *vātas*), cogn. with WEATHER]

wind[2] (wīnd) *v.i.* (*past, p.p.* **wound** (wownd)) **1** to turn, move or be twisted or coiled in a spiral, curved or tortuous course or shape. **2** to be circular, spiral, tortuous or crooked. **3** to meander. **4** to be wrapped spirally (round, into etc.). **5** to coil. ~*v.t.* **1** to cause to turn spirally, to wrap, twine or coil. **2** to encircle, to coil round, to entwine. **3** to pursue (one's course) in a spiral, sinuous or circuitous way. **4** to twist (one's way) or insinuate oneself (into etc.). **5** to hoist or move by means of a windlass, capstan etc. **6** to wind up (*to wind a watch*). ~*n.* **1** a bend or curve. **2** a single turn in winding. **3** the act or an instance of winding. **to wind down 1** to lower by winding. **2** to reduce gradually. **3** to relax. **4** to unwind. **to wind off** to unwind. **to wind round one's little finger** FINGER. **to wind up 1** to coil up. **2** to coil or tighten up the spring of (a watch etc.). **3** (*coll.*) to put into a state of tension or readiness for activity. **4** (*coll.*) to irritate, to annoy. **5** (*sl.*) to tease. **6** to bring or come to a conclusion, to conclude. **7** to arrange the final settlement of the affairs of (a business etc.). **8** to go into liquidation. **9** (*coll.*) to end up in a certain state or situation (*They wound up in hospital*). **wind-down** *n.* (*coll.*) a gradual reduction. **winder** *n.* a winding mechanism. **winding** *n.* **1** the act or an instance of coiling etc. **2** material wound or coiled round something, e.g. wire in an electric motor. ~*a.* that winds (*a winding road*). **winding drum** *n.* a mechanically-driven drum on which a haulage rope is wound. **winding engine** *n.* a hoisting engine. **windingly** *adv.* **winding-sheet** *n.* the sheet in which a corpse is wrapped. **winding staircase** *n.* a staircase built around a newel, a spiral staircase. **wind-up** *n.* the act or an instance of winding up. ~*a.* operated by a winding mechanism (*a wind-up toy*). **windy**[2] *a.* winding. [OE *windan* (cp. Dut., G *winden*, Icel. *vinda*), perh. cogn. with WITHY]

wind[3] (wīnd) *v.t.* (*past, p.p.* **winded, wound** (wownd)) (*poet.*) to sound (a horn, bugle etc.) by blowing. [WIND[1]]

windlass (wind´ləs) *n.* a machine consisting of a cylinder on an axle turned by a crank, used for hoisting or hauling. ~*v.t.* to hoist or haul with this. [ME *windelas*, Icel. *vindilāss* (*vindill*, winder, from *vinda*, WIND[2], *āss*, pole, beam)]

window (win´dō) *n.* **1** an opening in the wall or roof of a building, vehicle or other structure, usu. with the wooden or metal glazed framework filling it, for the admission of light or air. **2** the glass filling this (*to break a window*). **3** the sash of a window frame. **4** the space behind the large front window of a shop, used for display. **5** an aperture in a wall or screen separating customers from staff in a bank, ticket office etc. **6** any opening resembling a window, as in a window envelope. **7** (*Comput.*) a rectangular area on a VDU where information can be displayed. **8** a brief period of time when the conditions allow a particular activity. **9** any opportunity for action etc. **10** (*Physics*) a range of wavelengths for which a medium transmits electromagnetic radiation. **out of the window** (*coll.*) discarded, dispensed with, no longer taken into account. **window box** *n.* **1** a box for growing flowers on a window sill. **2** the casing in which a sash weight slides. **window cleaner** *n.* **1** a person whose job is cleaning windows, esp. outside. **2** a substance or device used to clean windows. **window-dresser** *n.* a person employed to arrange goods for display in a shop window. **window-dressing** *n.* **1** the arrangement of goods for display in a shop window. **2** deceptive display, insincere argument. **windowed** *a.* (*usu. in comb.*, as *bow-windowed*). **window envelope** *n.* an envelope with an open or transparent panel through which the address can be seen. **window frame** *n.* the framework in a window that supports the glass. **windowing** *n.* (*Comput.*) the use of windows to display information from different files etc. simultaneously. **window ledge** *n.* a window sill. **windowless** *a.* **window pane** *n.* a sheet of glass in a window. **window sash** *n.* a frame in which panes of glass for windows are set. **window seat** *n.* **1** a seat in the recess of a window. **2** a seat beside a window in a train, bus, aeroplane etc. **window-shop** *v.i.* (*pres.p.* **window-shopping,** *past, p.p.* **window-shopped**) to idly gaze at the displays in shop windows. **window-shopper** *n.* **window-shopping** *n.* **window sill** *n.* a ledge at the bottom of a window, inside or outside. **window tax** *n.* (*Hist.*) a tax on windows in houses etc., abolished in 1851. [Icel. *vindauga* (*vindr*, WIND[1], *auga*, cp. OE *ēage*, EYE[1])]

Windsor (win´zə) *a.* of or relating to the British royal family from 1917. **Windsor chair** *n.* a strong, plain wooden chair with a back curved into supports for the arms. **Windsor soap** *n.* a brown scented soap formerly made at Windsor. [town in Berks., England]

windy[1] WIND[1].

windy[2] WIND[2].

wine (wīn) *n.* **1** the fermented juice of grapes. **2** the juice of certain fruits etc. prepared in imitation of this. **3** a medicinal preparation in fermented grape juice. **4** a dark red colour. ~*v.i.* to drink wine. ~*v.t.* to serve or entertain with wine. **to wine and dine** to entertain with food and alcohol. **wine bar** *n.* a bar that serves mostly wine, esp. with food. **wineberry** *n.* (*pl.* **wineberries**) **1** a Chinese or Japanese shrub, *Rubus phoenicolasius*, with scarlet berries. **2** the fruit of this shrub, used in cookery. **3** the mako, *Aristotelia racemosa.* **winebibber** *n.* (*poet.*) a wine-drinker, a tippler, a drunkard. **winebibbing** *n., a.* **wine bottle** *n.* a bottle for wine, esp. one holding 26⅔ fl. oz (75 cl). **wine box** *n.* a cardboard box with a plastic lining, usu. with a three-litre capacity, filled with wine and fitted with a tap for dispensing it. **wine cellar** *n.* **1** a cellar where wine is stored. **2** its contents. **wine cooler** *n.* a vessel for cooling a bottle of wine with ice. **wineglass** *n.* **1** a small glass for drinking wine from. **2** a wineglassful. **wineglassful** *n.* (*pl.* **wineglassfuls**) **1** the capacity of a wineglass, esp. a sherry glass, about 2 fl. oz (6 cl). **2** the contents of a wineglass. **wine-grower** *n.* a person who grows grapes for winemaking. **wineless** *a.* **wine list** *n.* a list of the wines available in a restaurant, from a supplier etc. **winemaker** *n.* a person who makes wine. **winemaking** *n.* the production of wine. ~*a.* of or for this (*a winemaking kit*). **wine merchant** *n.* **wine palm** *n.* a palm tree from which palm wine is obtained. **winepress** *n.* **1** an apparatus in which grapes are pressed. **2** the place in which this is done. **wine red** *n.* a dark red colour. ~*a.* of this colour. **winery** *n.* (*pl.* **wineries**) a place where wine is made. **wineskin** *n.* a skin, usu. of a goat, sewn into a bag for holding wine. **wine taster** *n.* a person who samples wine to judge its quality. **wine tasting** *n.* **1** an occasion when people can sample various wines. **2** the act of sampling wine to judge its quality. **wine vinegar** *n.* vinegar made from wine. **wine waiter** *n.* a waiter in a restaurant, hotel etc. who is responsible for serving customers with wine. **wine writer** *n.* a person who writes about wine, esp. a journalist. **winey, winy** *a.* (*comp.* **winier,** *superl.* **winiest**) resembling wine. [OE *wīn*, L *vīnum* (cp. Dut. *wijn*, G *Wein*, also Gr. *oinos*), cogn. with WITHE, from *wei-*, to twine]

wing (wing) *n.* **1** each of the limbs or organs of flight in birds, insects etc. **2** each of the supporting parts of an aircraft. **3** a part of a building, fortification, army, bone, implement etc. projecting laterally. **4** in football and similar games, a player on one or other extreme flank. **5** the position in which such a player plays. **6** an extreme faction of a party, group etc. **7** a part of a car or other motor vehicle above the wheels. **8** an RAF unit of three squadrons. **9** (*pl.*) the sides of a stage or pieces of scenery placed there. **10** (*pl.*) the mark of proficiency a pilot qualified in the RAF is entitled to wear on his uniform. **11** either of the two lateral petals of a papilionaceous flower which stand opposite each other. **12** motion by means of wings, flight, power of flight. ~*v.t.* **1** to furnish with wings. **2** to enable to fly or move with swiftness. **3** to traverse or travel on wings. **4** to wound in the wing or the arm. ~*v.i.* to fly. **in the wings** waiting in readiness. **on a wing and a prayer** with no more than a slight chance of success. **on the wing 1** flying. **2** in motion. **to give/ lend wings to** to make faster, to speed up. **to spread/ stretch one's wings** to develop or make full use of one's powers, abilities etc. **to take under one's wing** to take under one's protection. **to take wing 1** to begin flying, to fly away. **2** to disappear. **to wing one's flight** FLIGHT[1]. **wing-beat** *n.* a complete stroke of the wing in flying. **wing-case** *n.* the horny cover or case, consisting of a modified wing, protecting the flying wings of some insects. **wing chair** *n.* a chair with winglike parts projecting forwards at either side of the high back. **wing collar** *n.* a stiff upright shirt collar with the points turned down. **wing commander** *n.* a commissioned officer in the RAF ranking below a group captain and above a squadron leader. **wing covert** *n.* any of the small feathers covering the insertion of a bird's flight feathers. **winged** *a.* **1** having wings. **2** going straight to the mark, powerful, rousing (*winged words*). **winged elm** *n.* WAHOO[1]. **winger** *n.* **1** a football player etc. positioned on the wing. **2** (*in comb.*) a member of a specified wing of a political party etc. (*left-winger*; *right-winger*). **wing forward** *n.* in rugby, a forward positioned on the wing. **wing-game** *n.* game birds. **wing-half** *n.* in football, a left or right half-back. **wingless** *a.* **winglet** *n.* **winglike** *a.* **wingman** *n.* (*pl.* **wingmen**) **1** the pilot of an aircraft on one of the outer flanks of a formation, behind the leading aircraft. **2** a winger. **wing nut** *n.* a nut that is tightened by two flat winglike projections on its sides. **wingspan, wingspread** *n.* the distance from one wing-tip of a bird, aircraft etc. to the other. **wing-stroke** *n.* a wing-beat. **wing-tip** *n.* the outermost end of either wing of a bird or aircraft. [ME *winge*, *wenge*, Norw. *vengja* (cp. Icel. *vængr*, Dan., Swed. *vinge*), cogn. with Sansk. *vā*, to blow]

wingding (wing´ding) *n.* (*esp. N Am., sl.*) **1** a riotous party or celebration. **2** a real or feigned seizure, esp. of a drug addict. [etym. unknown]

wink (wingk) *v.i.* **1** to close and open one eye quickly. **2** to close and open both eyes quickly, to blink. **3** (of an eye) to close and open. **4** to give a sign or signal by closing and opening one eye. **5** to twinkle, to flicker, to flash intermittently. ~*v.t.* to close and open (an eye or the eyes). ~*n.* **1** the act of winking, esp. as a signal. **2** a hint, a private intimation. **3** a moment, an instant. **4** (*coll.*) a moment of sleep. **in a wink** very quickly. **to tip (someone) the wink** TIP[2]. **to wink at 1** to pretend not to see. **2** to connive at. **winker** *n.* **1** a flashing light, esp. an indicator on a motor vehicle. **2** (*usu. pl.*) a horse's blinker. **3** a person or thing that winks. **winking** *n.*, *a.* **winkingly** *adv.* [OE *wincian* (cp. MDut. *wincken*, G *winken*, Icel. *vanka*), cogn. with WINCE[1] and WINKLE]

winkle (wing´kəl) *n.* an edible marine mollusc of the genus *Littorina*, a periwinkle. **to winkle out 1** (*coll.*) to extract with difficulty. **2** (*coll.*) to elicit (information etc.) with difficulty. **winkle-pickers** *n.pl.* (*sl.*) shoes with long pointed toes. [OE *-wincla*, in *wine-wincla*, cogn. with WINK and WINCH]

winnable, winner etc. WIN.

winnow (win´ō) *v.t.* **1** to separate and drive the chaff from (grain). **2** to fan (chaff) (away, out etc.). **3** to sift, to sort, to examine or analyse thoroughly. **4** to clear of inferior or undesirable elements. **5** (*poet.*) to beat or flap (wings), to fan (the air) in this way. **6** (*poet.*) to blow on, to stir (hair etc.). **winnower** *n.* **winnowing** *n.* [OE *windwian*, from WIND[1]]

wino (wī´nō) *n.* (*pl.* **winos**) (*sl.*) an alcoholic, esp. one who drinks mainly wine.

winsey WINCEY.

winsome (win´səm) *a.* **1** engaging, winning, charming, attractive. **2** graceful, lovely. **winsomely** *adv.* **winsomeness** *n.* [OE *wynsum* (*wynn*, joy, cogn. with WIN, -SOME)]

winter (win´tə) *n.* **1** the coldest season of the year, astronomically from the winter solstice to the vernal equinox, usu. regarded in northern latitudes as including December, January, February. **2** a period of inactivity, a cheerless or depressing state of things. **3** (*poet.*) a year of life. ~*a.* **1** of, relating to or suitable for the winter. **2** lasting throughout the winter. **3** (of fruit) ripening late. **4** (of crops) sown in autumn (*winter wheat*). ~*v.i.* **1** to pass the winter. **2** to hibernate. ~*v.t.* to keep, feed or maintain through the winter. **winter aconite** *n.* a yellow-flowered plant of the genus *Eranthis*. **winter apple** *n.* an apple that keeps well or ripens in winter. **winter cress** *n.* a plant of the genus *Barbarea*, esp. *B. vulgaris*, with a bitter taste. **winter garden** *n.* **1** a large conservatory or glasshouse for plants not hardy enough to withstand the climate outside during winter. **2** a garden of plants that flourish in winter. **wintergreen** *n.* **1** a low plant of the genus *Pyrola*, keeping green throughout the winter. **2** the checkerberry, *Gaultheria procumbens*. **3** OIL OF WINTERGREEN (under OIL). **winter heliotrope** *n.* a plant of the daisy family, *Petasites fragrans*, which produces light purple flowers in winter. **winterize, winterise** *v.t.* (*esp. N Am.*) to prepare or adapt for use in cold winter weather. **winterization** (-zā´shən) *n.* **winter jasmine** *n.* a yellow-flowered jasmine, *Jasminum nudiflorum*. **winterless** *a.* **winter quarters** *n.pl.* the quarters occupied by an army etc. during the winter. **winter sleep** *n.* hibernation. **winter solstice** *n.* one of the times (about 22 Dec. in the northern hemisphere) and points at which the sun is farthest from the celestial equator. **winter sport** *n.* (*usu. pl.*) a sport practised on snow and ice, usu. outdoors, e.g. skiing, skating. **wintertime,** (*poet.*) **winter-tide** *n.* the season of winter. **winter wheat** *n.* a type of cereal sown in autumn. **wintry** (-tri), **wintery** *a.* (*comp.* **wintrier,** *superl.* **wintriest**) **1** of or like winter. **2** (of a smile, look etc.) cold and cheerless. **wintrily** *adv.* **wintriness** *n.* [OE (cp. Dut., G *winter*, Dan., Swed. *vinter*), perh. cogn. with L *unda*, wave, Eng. WET and WATER]

winy WINE.

winze (winz) *n.* (*Mining*) a shaft sunk from one level to another for communication or ventilation. [prob. cogn. with WINNOW]

wipe (wīp) *v.t.* **1** to rub with something soft in order to clean or dry. **2** to rub (a cloth, hand etc.) over something for this purpose. **3** to remove (dirt etc.) by wiping. **4** to apply (grease etc.) by wiping. **5** to clear (a magnetic tape or videotape) of recorded material. 6 to remove (recorded material, data etc.) in this way. 7 to apply solder to with something soft. 8 (*Austral., New Zeal., sl.*) to reject. ~*n.* 1 an act of wiping. 2 something used for wiping, esp. a disposable cloth or tissue treated with a cleansing substance. 3 (*dial.*) a sweeping blow. **to wipe away** 1 to remove by wiping. 2 to get rid of. **to wipe down** to clean (a wall, door etc.) by wiping. **to wipe off** 1 to clear away. 2 to cancel. **to wipe off the map** to remove or destroy completely. **to wipe one's eyes** EYE[1]. **to wipe out** 1 to clean out by wiping. 2 to efface, to obliterate. 3 to destroy, to annihilate. 4 (*sl.*) to murder. **to wipe the eye of** EYE[1]. **to wipe the floor with someone** FLOOR. **to wipe the slate clean** SLATE[1]. **to wipe up** 1 to remove (a liquid etc.) by wiping. 2 to dry (dishes etc.). **wipeable** *a.* **wipe-out** *n.* 1 an act or instance of wiping out. 2 interference that renders impossible the reception of other radio signals. 3 (*sl.*) a fall from a surfboard or skateboard. **wiper** *n.* 1 a cloth etc. used for wiping. 2 a windscreen wiper. 3 a type of cam. 4 in electrical engineering, a movable contact. [OE *wipian* (cp. EFris. *wīp*, LG *wiep*)]

WIPO (wī´pō) *abbr.* World Intellectual Property Organization.

Wiradhuri (wiraj´əri) *n.* an extinct Aboriginal language of SE Australia.

wire (wīə) *n.* 1 metal drawn out into a slender and flexible rod or thread of uniform diameter. 2 a piece or length of this, esp. used to carry electric current. 3 (*dated, coll.*) the electric telegraph, a telegram message. 4 a wire barrier or fence. ~*a.* made of wire. ~*v.t.* 1 to apply wire to, to fasten, secure, bind or stiffen with wire. 2 to install electrical wiring in. 3 to snare with wire. 4 (*coll.*) to telegraph to. 5 to string (beads) on a wire. 6 in croquet, to obstruct by a hoop. ~*v.i.* (*coll.*) to send a telegram. **by wire** by telegraph or telegram. **to cross wires** CROSS. **to get one's wires crossed** CROSS. **to pull the wires** 1 to manipulate puppets. 2 (*esp. N Am.*) to control politics etc. by clandestine means. 3 to pull strings. **wire brush** *n.* 1 a brush with wire bristles used e.g. for scraping rust off metal. 2 a brush with wire strands used in playing cymbals. ~*v.t.* (*also* **wire-brush**) to clean with a wire brush. **wire cloth** *n.* a fabric of woven wire. **wire-cutter** *n.* an implement for cutting wire. **wiredraw** *v.t.* (*past* **wiredrew,** *p.p.* **wiredrawn**) 1 to form (metal) into wire by forcibly drawing through a series of gradually diminishing holes. 2 to over-refine (an argument etc.). 3 to protract excessively, to spin out. **wiredrawer** *n.* **wiredrawing** *n.* **wire entanglement** *n.* an obstruction composed of interlacing barbed wire defending the front of an entrenchment etc. against a rapid assault. **wire gauge** *n.* 1 an instrument for measuring the diameter of wire. 2 a standard system of sizes designating the diameter of wire. **wire gauze** *n.* a textile fabric made of wire, used for very fine sieves, respirators etc. **wire grass** *n.* any of various types of grass with wiry stems. **wire-haired** *a.* (of a dog) having stiff, wiry hair (*a wire-haired terrier*). **wireman** *n.* (*pl.* **wiremen**) 1 (*esp. N Am.*) a person who installs or repairs electric wiring. 2 a journalist employed by a telegraphic news agency. **wire mattress** *n.* a mattress that is supported by wires stretched across a framework. **wire netting** *n.* a mesh of interwoven wire used for fencing, reinforcement etc. **wirepuller** *n.* a politician etc. working behind the scenes. **wirepulling** *n.* **wirer** *n.* **wire rope** *n.* a rope made by twisting strands of wire. **wire stripper** *n.* (*often pl.*) a tool for stripping the insulation from electric wires. **wire-tap** *v.t.* (*pres.p.* **wire-tapping,** *past, p.p.* **wire-tapped**) to tap (a telephone). **wire-tapper** *n.* **wire-tapping** *n.* **wire-walker** *n.* an acrobat performing on a tightrope. **wire wheel** *n.* a wheel with wire spokes, esp. on a sports car. **wire wool** *n.* an abrasive material consisting of a mass of very fine wires, used for cleaning etc. **wireworm** *n.* the vermiform larva of a click beetle, destructive to roots of vegetables, cereals etc. **wiring** *n.* 1 a system of wires, esp. one carrying electric current. 2 the act of installing such a system. **wiry** *a.* (*comp.* **wirier,** *superl.* **wiriest**) 1 made of or resembling wire. 2 tough and flexible. 3 (of a person) lean but sinewy. 4 (of hair etc.) stiff. **wirily** *adv.* **wiriness** *n.* [OE *wīr* (cp. Icel. *vīrr*, Swed. *vira*, to twist, also L *viriae*, armlets), cogn. with WITHE]

wireless (wīə´lis) *n.* (*dated*) 1 any process or method whereby messages, music or other sounds can be transmitted by electromagnetic waves without the intervention of wires; radio. 2 an instrument for receiving such messages etc.; a radio. 3 the programmes of entertainment etc. thus transmitted. 4 wireless telegraphy. ~*a.* not having or requiring wires. **wireless telegraphy** *n.* radio-telegraphy.

wiry WIRE.

Wis. *abbr.* Wisconsin.

†**wis** (wis) *v.i.* to know. [supposed 1st pers. sing. pres. of WIT[2], evolved from *iwis*, *ywis*, OE *gewis*, certain]

Wisd. *abbr.* Wisdom of Solomon.

wisdom (wiz´dəm) *n.* 1 the quality or state of being wise. 2 knowledge and experience together with the ability to make proper use of them, practical discernment, sagacity, judgement, common sense. 3 a collection of wise sayings. **in one's wisdom** (*iron.*) thinking that this is a wise thing to do (*Her father, in his wisdom, let her borrow the car*). **wisdom tooth** *n.* (*pl.* **wisdom teeth**) the third molar, usu. appearing about the age of 20. [OE]

wise[1] (wīz) *a.* 1 having or showing the power or faculty of discerning or judging rightly; sagacious, sensible, discreet, prudent, judicious. 2 having or showing knowledge and experience together with the ability to apply them rightly. 3 informed, aware. 4 (*N Am., coll.*) insolent, cocksure. 5 †having occult knowledge. **none the wiser** having no more knowledge or understanding than before. **to put someone wise** to inform someone. **to wise up** 1 (*esp. N Am., coll.*) to be or become aware or informed. 2 (*esp. N Am., coll.*) to make aware, to inform. **wise after the event** able to judge or understand something with hindsight. **wise to** aware of, alert to. **without anyone being the wiser** without anyone knowing, without detection. **wisecrack** *n.* (*coll.*) 1 a smart but not profound epigram. 2 a witty comment. ~*v.i.* to make a wisecrack. **wisecracker** *n.* **wise guy** *n.* (*esp. N Am., coll.*) an insolent or cocksure person. **wisely** *adv.* **wise man** *n.* (*pl.* **wise men**) 1 a wizard. 2 each of the Magi. **wiseness** *n.* **wise saw** *n.* a proverb. **wise woman** *n.* (*pl.* **wise women**) 1 a witch, a fortuneteller. 2 (*Sc.*) a midwife. [OE *wīs* (cp. Dut. *wijs*, G *weise*, Icel. *vīss*), cogn. with WIT[1]]

†**wise**[2] (wīz) *n.* a manner, way or mode of acting, behaving etc. **in no wise** not at all. [OE (cp. Dut. *wijs*, G *Weise*, Dan. *viis*, Swed. *vis*), from *wīsian*, to show the way, orig. to make WISE[1]]

-wise (wīz) *suf.* 1 forming adverbs of manner, as *lengthwise, likewise.* 2 with regard to, concerning, as *jobwise, weatherwise.* [WISE[2]]

wiseacre (wī´zākə) *n.* a person pretending to learning or wisdom. [MDut. *wijs-sagger*, G *Weissager*, from MHG *wīzago*, a prophet (cp. OE *wītiga*, prophet, from *wītan*, to see, cogn. with *witan*, WIT[1])]

wisent (wē´zənt) *n.* the European bison, *Bison bonasus.* [G]

wish (wish) *v.t.* 1 to have a desire, aspiration or craving (that etc.). 2 to want (*I wish to stay*). 3 to frame or express a desire or wish concerning (*She wished him well*). 4 to invoke, to bid (*I wish you to leave*). ~*v.i.* 1 to have a desire (for). 2 to make a wish. ~*n.* 1 a desire, a longing, an aspiration. 2 an expression of this, a request, a petition, an invocation. **3** that which is desired. **the wish is father to the thought** we believe what we wish to be true. **to wish something on someone** to foist something on someone. **wishbone** *n.* **1** the forked bone in the breast of a bird, which when broken by two persons is supposed to entitle the holder of the longer part to the fulfilment of some wish. **2** any object of similar shape, such as the boom of a sailboard. **wisher** *n.* (*usu. in comb.*, as *well-wisher*). **wishful** *a.* **wishfully** *adv.* **wishfulness** *n.* **wishful thinking** *n.* belief based on desires rather than facts. **wish-fulfilment,** (*NAm.*) **wish-fulfillment** *n.* the fulfilment of a subconscious wish in fact or fantasy. **wishing** *n.* **wishing-well** *n.* a well into which coins are dropped in the hope of making wishes come true. **wish-list** *n.* a usu. mental list of desires. [OE *wȳscan* (cp. Dut. *wenschen*, G *wunschen*, Icel. *æskja*), cogn. with WIN]

wish-wash (wish´wosh) *n.* **1** thin weak liquor or drink. **2** feeble talk, claptrap. **wishy-washy** (wish´iwoshi) *a.* **1** vague, ill-defined. **2** lacking strength, forcefulness etc. **3** watery, insipid. [redupl. of WASH]

wisp (wisp) *n.* **1** a small bunch or handful of straw, hay etc. **2** a piece, a strand, a small quantity (*a wisp of hair*). **3** a thin band or streak (*a wisp of smoke*). **4** a slim or delicate person (*a wisp of a girl*). **5** a flock (of snipe). **wispy** *a.* (*comp.* **wispier**, *superl.* **wispiest**). **wispily** *adv.* **wispiness** *n.* [ME, var. *wips* (cp. LG *Wiep*, Norw. *vippa*), cogn. with WIPE]

†**wist** WIT[2].

wisteria (wistiə´riə), **wistaria** (-teə´-) *n.* any leguminous climbing shrub of the genus *Wisteria*, with racemes of lilac-coloured flowers. [Caspar *Wistar*, 1761–1818, US anatomist]

wistful (wist´fəl) *a.* **1** full of vague yearnings, esp. for unattainable things, sadly longing. **2** thoughtful in a melancholy way, pensive. **wistfully** *adv.* **wistfulness** *n.* [etym. uncertain (perh. WHIST[1], -FUL, conf. with WISHFUL (under WISH))]

wit[1] (wit) *n.* **1** (*often pl.*) intelligence, understanding, sense, sagacity. **2** (*pl.*) sanity. **3** the power of perceiving analogies and other relations between apparently incongruous ideas or of forming unexpected, striking or ludicrous combinations of them. **4** a person distinguished for this power, a witty person. **5** †a wise man. **at one's wits' end** at a complete loss as to what further steps to take, in a state of despair or desperation. **out of one's wits** mad. **to have/ keep one's wits about one** to be alert. **to live by one's wits** to live by cunning or ingenuity rather than regular employment. **to set one's wits to** to argue with. **witless** *a.* foolish, stupid. **witlessly** *adv.* **witlessness** *n.* †**witling** *n.* **1** a person who thinks themselves witty. **2** a person with little wit or understanding. **witted** *a.* (*often in comb.*, as *quick-witted*). **witticism** (-sizm) *n.* a witty phrase or saying, a jest. **witty** *a.* (*comp.* **wittier**, *superl.* **wittiest**) showing or characterized by wit or humour. **wittily** *adv.* **wittiness** *n.* [OE *witt*, knowledge, from *witan*, see WIT[2]]

†**wit**[2] (wit) *v.t.*, *v.i.* (*1st & 3rd pers. sing. pres.* **wot** (wot), *2nd pers. sing. pres.* **wottest** (wot´əst), *past, p.p.* **wist** (wist)) to know. **to wit** namely. [OE *witan* (cp. Dut. *weten*, G *wissen*, Icel. *vita*), cogn. with L *vidēre*, Gr. *idein*, to see, *oida*, I know, Sansk. *vēda*]

witan WITENAGEMOT.

witch[1] (wich) *n.* **1** a woman having dealings with evil spirits or practising sorcery. **2** an ugly old woman, a hag. **3** a bewitching or fascinating woman. **4** a flatfish, *Glyptocephalus cynoglossus*. ~†*v.t.* to bewitch, to fascinate, to enchant. **witchcraft** *n.* **1** the practices of witches. **2** sorcery, magic. **3** bewitching charm. **witch doctor** *n.* in some tribal societies, a person who invokes supernatural powers, esp. to cure people. **witchery** *n.* witchcraft. **witch-finder** *n.* (*Hist.*) a person whose business was to discover witches. **witch-hunt** *n.* **1** the searching out and public exposure of opponents accused of disloyalty to a state, political party etc. **2** (*Hist.*) the searching out and persecution of witches. **witch-hunting** *n.* **witching** *a.* **the witching hour** midnight, the time when witches are supposed to become active. **witchingly** *adv.* **witchlike** *a.* **witchy** *a.* [OE m. *wicca*, f. *wicce*, rel. to *wiccian*, to practise sorcery (cp. Icel. *vikja*, to turn aside, to exorcize, OE *wīcan*, to give way), cogn. with WEAK]

witch[2] (wich) *a.* (*attrib.*) WYCH. **witch alder** *n.* an American shrub, *Fothergilla gardenii.* **witch elm** *n.* WYCH ELM (under WYCH). **witch hazel** *n.* **1** an American or E Asian shrub of the genus *Hamamelis*, esp. *H. virginiana.* **2** a medicinal lotion derived from the leaves and bark of *H. virginiana*, used to treat bruises etc. [WYCH]

witchetty (wich´əti), **witchetty grub** *n.* (*pl.* **witchetties, witchetty grubs**) (*Austral.*) the edible larva of a beetle or moth. [Austral. Abor.]

witenagemot (wit´ənəgəmōt, -mōt´), **witan** (wit´ən) *n.* (*Hist.*) the Anglo-Saxon national assembly or parliament. [OE *witena*, gen. pl. of *wita*, wise man, GEMOTE]

with (widh) *prep.* **1** in or into the company of, in or into the relation of accompaniment, association, simultaneousness, cooperation, harmoniousness etc. **2** having, marked or characterized by. **3** in the possession, care or guardianship of. **4** by the means, instrumentality, use or aid of. **5** by the addition or supply of. **6** because of, owing to, in consequence of. **7** in regard to, in respect of, concerning, in the case of. **8** in separation from. **9** in opposition to, against. **10** in spite of, notwithstanding. **one with** ONE. **to be with someone 1** to support someone. **2** to agree with someone. **3** (*coll.*) to understand someone, to follow what someone is saying (*I'm not with you*). **with child** (*poet.*) (of a woman) pregnant. **with that** thereupon. **with young** (*poet.*) (of a female mammal) pregnant. **with it** *a.* (*coll.*) **1** up to date, fashionable. **2** alert to what is being done or said. ~*adv.* besides, in addition. **with-profits** *a.* (of an insurance policy etc.) giving the policyholder a share of any profits made by the business. [OE, from *wither*, against (cp. Icel. *vith*, Dan. *ved*, Swed. *vid*), superseding OE and ME *mid*, with]

†**withal** (widhawl´) *adv.* with the rest, in addition, at the same time, further, moreover. ~*prep.* (*used after its obj.*) with. [WITH, ALL]

withdraw (widhdraw´) *v.t.* (*past* **withdrew** (-droo´), *p.p.* **withdrawn** (-drawn´)) **1** to draw back, aside or apart. **2** to take away, to remove, to retract (*to withdraw an accusation*). **3** to take (money) from an account. ~*v.i.* **1** to retire, to go away. **2** to move back, away or aside. **3** to retract a statement, accusation etc. **4** to discontinue one's involvement (*to withdraw from a competition*). **5** to isolate oneself socially, emotionally etc. **withdrawal** *n.* **1** the act or an instance of withdrawing. **2** the process or period following termination of the use of addictive drugs etc. **3** coitus interruptus. **withdrawal symptoms** *n.pl.* the unpleasant physical or mental symptoms that accompany withdrawal from addictive drugs etc. **withdrawer** *n.* †**withdrawing room** *n.* a drawing room. **withdrawn** *a.* very shy or reserved, socially isolated, emotionally detached etc.

withe (widh, with, wīdh) *n.* **1** a tough, flexible branch, esp. of willow or osier, used in binding things together. **2** a band or tie made of osiers, twigs, straw etc. [WITHY]

wither (widh´ə) *v.t.* **1** to cause to fade, shrivel or dry, to shrivel and dry (up). **2** to cause to lose freshness, soundness, vitality or vigour. **3** (*fig.*) to blight, to blast. **4** to make abashed. ~*v.i.* **1** to become dry and shrivelled, to dry and shrivel (up). **2** to lose freshness, soundness, vigour etc. **3** to fade away, to languish, to droop, to decline. **withered** *a.* **witheredness** *n.* **withering** *a.*

scornful. **witheringly** *adv.* [ME *widren, wederen,* to expose to the weather, from *weder,* WEATHER]

withers (widh´əz) *n.pl.* the ridge between the shoulder blades of a horse. [OE *wither,* against (because it is against the collar or load), see WITH]

withershins (widh´əshinz), **widdershins** (wid´ə-) *adv.* anticlockwise, in the contrary direction, esp. to the left or opposite to the direction of the sun. [Icel. *vithr,* against (cp. Dan., Swed. *veder,* OE *wither,* Dut. *weder,* G *wieder*), Icel. *sinni,* walk, movement, cogn. with OE *sīth*]

withhold (widh·hōld´) *v.t.* (*past, p.p.* **withheld** (-held´)) **1** to keep back, to refuse to grant or give; to deduct. **2** to keep from action, to hold back, to restrain. **withholder** *n.*

within (widhin´) *adv.* (*poet.*) **1** inside, in or to the inside, in the inner part or parts, internally. **2** indoors. **3** in the mind, heart or spirit. ~*prep.* **1** in or to the inner or interior part or parts of, inside. **2** in the limits, range, scope or compass of. **3** not beyond, not further off than. **4** in no longer a time than (*within three days*). **within doors** indoors, in or into a house etc. **within one's grasp** able to be grasped, understood, obtained, achieved etc. by one. **within reach** close enough to be reached. **within sight** close enough to be seen. [OE *widhinnan,* on the inside]

☒ **withold** common misspelling of WITHHOLD.

without (widhowt´) *adv.* (*poet.*) **1** in, at or to the outside. **2** outside, outwardly, externally. **3** out of doors. ~*prep.* **1** not having, not with, having no, destitute of, lacking, free from. **2** not accompanied by, in the absence of. **3** neglecting to (*They left without saying goodbye*). **4** †outside. **5** †out of the limits, compass or range of, beyond. ~*conj.* (*dial.*) unless, except. **without book** BOOK. **without end** END. [OE *withūtan*]

withstand (widhstand´) *v.t.* (*past, p.p.* **withstood** (-stud´)) to stand up against, to resist, to oppose. ~*v.i.* to make a stand or resistance (against). **withstander** *n.* [OE *withstandan*]

withy (widh´i) *n.* (*pl.* **withies**) **1** a withe. **2** a willow. [OE *withig* (cp. MDut. *wiede,* G *Weide,* Icel. *vithja*), cogn. with Gr. *itea,* willow, L *vitis,* vine]

witness (wit´nis) *n.* **1** a person who has seen an incident etc., a spectator, a person present at an event. **2** a person who gives evidence in a law court or for judicial purposes, esp. on oath. **3** a person who affixes their name to a document to testify to the genuineness of the signature. **4** attestation of a fact etc., testimony, evidence. **5** a thing that constitutes evidence or proof, confirmation. **6** a thing or person serving as testimony to or proof of. ~*v.t.* **1** to see or know by personal presence, to be a spectator of. **2** to attest (a signature), to sign (a document) as witness. **3** to indicate, to show, to prove. **4** (*in imper.*) used to introduce evidence (*She is a caring person: witness her devotion to her invalid father*). ~*v.i.* **1** to bear testimony, to testify, to give evidence. **2** to serve as evidence (against, for etc.). **to bear witness 1** to give testimony. **2** to be a sign (*Their response bears witness to their lack of concern*). **to call to witness** to summon, appeal to or ask for confirmation or testimony. **witnessable** *a.* **witness box,** (*NAm.*) **witness-stand** *n.* an enclosure in a law court for witnesses to give evidence from. [OE *witnes* (WIT[1], -NESS)]

witter (wit´ə) *v.i.* (*coll.*) to talk without purpose or at length, to chatter or babble (*He wittered on about his car*). [prob. imit.]

witticism, wittiness etc. WIT[1].

witting (wit´ing) *a.* conscious, knowing, intentional. **wittingly** *adv.* [WIT[2]]

witty WIT[1].

†**wive** (wīv) *v.t.* **1** to take for a wife, to marry. **2** to provide with a wife. ~*v.i.* to marry a wife. [OE *wīfian,* from *wīf,* WIFE]

wivern WYVERN.

wives WIFE.

wiz (wiz) *n.* (*coll.*) a person with remarkable skill. [WHIZ, influ. by WIZARD]

wizard (wiz´əd) *n.* **1** a sorcerer, a magician, a conjuror. **2** a person who works wonders, a genius, an expert. ~*a.* **1** (*dated sl.*) wonderful, marvellous. **2** magic, enchanting, enchanted. **wizardly** *a.* **wizardry** *n.* [ME *wisard* (*wīs,* WISE[1], -ARD)]

wizen (wiz´ən) *v.t., v.i.* to wither, to dry up, to shrivel. ~*a.* wizened. **wizened** *a.* withered or shrivelled, esp. with age. [OE *wisnian* (cp. Icel. *visna,* from *visinn,* withered), cogn. with L VIRUS, Sansk. *visha-*]

wk *abbr.* **1** weak. **2** week. **3** work.

wkly *abbr.* weekly.

wks *abbr.* weeks.

WL *abbr.* (Windward Islands) St Lucia (IVR).

Wm *abbr.* William.

WMO *abbr.* World Meteorological Organization.

WNW *abbr.* west-north-west.

WO *abbr.* **1** War Office. **2** Warrant Officer.

wo[1] WHOA.

†**wo**[2] WOE.

w.o. *abbr.* walkover.

w/o *abbr.* without.

woad (wōd) *n.* **1** a plant, *Isatis tinctoria,* yielding a blue dye. **2** this dye formerly used for staining the body, esp. by the ancient Britons. **woaded** *a.* [OE *wād* (cp. Dut. *weede,* G *Waid,* OF *waide,* F *guède*), cogn. with L *vitrum,* Gr. *isatis*]

wobbegong (wob´əgong) *n.* an Australian shark, *Orectolobus maculatus,* with mottled skin, one of the carpet sharks. [Austral. Abor.]

wobble (wob´əl), **wabble** *v.i.* **1** to incline to one side and then the other alternately, as when not properly balanced. **2** to oscillate. **3** to go unsteadily, to stagger. **4** to waver, to be inconsistent or inconstant. **5** to quaver or tremble (*Her voice wobbled*). ~*v.t.* to cause to wobble. ~*n.* **1** a wobbling movement, sound etc. **2** a rocking, uneven motion. **3** an act of hesitation, inconsistency or vacillation. **wobble-board** *n.* an Australian musical instrument comprising a piece of fibreboard that is flexed to produce a booming sound. **wobbler** *n.* **1** a person or thing that wobbles. **2** (*coll.*) a wobbly. **wobbly** *a.* (*comp.* **wobblier,** *superl.* **wobbliest**) **1** inclined to wobble. **2** unsteady. **3** wavy. **4** vacillating. ~*n.* (*pl.* **wobblies**) (*coll.*) a fit of nerves, a tantrum (*to throw a wobbly*). **wobbliness** *n.* **wobbly egg** *n.* a sleeping tablet that can induce a sense of euphoria when taken with alcohol. [LG *wabbeln,* ON *vafla,* to waver]

wodge (woj) *n.* (*sl.*) a thick slice or chunk. [var. of WEDGE]

woe (wō), †**wo** *n.* **1** (*poet.*) sorrow, affliction, distress, overwhelming grief. **2** (*often pl.*) calamity, trouble, misfortune (*a tale of woe*). **woe betide** may misfortune befall; used to warn of unpleasant consequences (*Woe betide anyone who touches my new computer!*). **woe is me!** (*facet.*) used to express great distress. **woe worth the day!** WORTH[2]. **woebegone** (-bigon) *a.* overcome with woe, sorrowful-looking, dismal. **woeful** *a.* **1** sorrowful, miserable. **2** pitiful, inadequate, very poor. **3** causing sorrow. **woefully** *adv.* **woefulness** *n.* [OE *wā,* int. (cp. Dut. *wee,* G *Weh,* Icel. *vei,* L *vae*)]

wog[1] (wog) *n.* (*offensive*) any dark-skinned person. [prob. from GOLLIWOG]

wog[2] (wog) *n.* (*Austral., sl.*) an illness. [etym. unknown]

woggle (wog´əl) *n.* a leather ring used to fasten a Scout's neckerchief at the front. [etym. uncertain]

wok (wok) *n.* a large metal bowl with curved sides and handles used in Chinese cooking. [Cantonese]

woke, woken WAKE[1].

wold (wōld) *n.* a tract of open country, esp. downland or moorland. [OE *weald* (*wald*, forest, cp. Dut. *woud*, G *Wald*, Icel. *völlr*), cp. WEALD]

wolf (wulf) *n.* (*pl.* **wolves** (wulvz)) **1** a grey, tawny-grey, reddish or white carnivorous quadruped, esp. *Canis lupus*, closely allied to the dog, preying on sheep, calves etc. and hunting larger animals in packs. **2** a rapacious, ravenous, greedy or cruel person. **3** (*coll.*) a man who is rapacious in the pursuit of women for sexual purposes. **4** (*Mus.*) **a** a discordant sound in certain chords of a keyboard instrument, esp. an organ, due to unequal temperament. **b** a similar sound on a bowed instrument, such as the violin or cello. ~*v.t.* to devour ravenously, to gulp or swallow (down) greedily. **to cry wolf** to raise a false alarm, esp. repeatedly. **to have/ hold a wolf by the ears** to be in a precarious or desperate situation. **to keep the wolf from the door** to keep off starvation. **to throw to the wolves** to send to certain destruction, to sacrifice or abandon without scruple or remorse. **wolf cub** *n.* **1** a young wolf. **2** (*Hist.*) (**Wolf Cub**) a Cub Scout. **wolf-fish** *n.* (*pl. in general* **wolf-fish,** *in particular* **wolf-fishes**) any large voracious fish of the genus *Anarhichas*. **wolfhound** *n.* a large powerful dog formerly used to hunt wolves. **wolf in sheep's clothing** *n.* a person who disguises malicious intentions behind a pretence of innocence. **wolfish** *a.* **wolfishly** *adv.* **wolfishness** *n.* **wolflike** *a.* **wolf pack** *n.* **1** a pack of wolves. **2** a number of submarines, aircraft etc. attacking as a group. **wolfsbane** *n.* a species of aconite, esp. *Aconitum lycoctonum*. **wolfskin** *n.* **1** the skin of a wolf. **2** something made from this. **wolf's-milk** *n.* spurge. **wolf spider** *n.* any spider of the family Lycosidae, which hunts its prey. **wolf whistle** *n.* a whistle made usu. by a male at the sight of an attractive female. **wolf-whistle** *v.i.* to make such a whistle. [OE *wulf* (cp. Dut. and G *Wolf*, Icel. *ūlfr*, L *lupus*, Gr. *lukos*, Sansk. *vrka-*), from *welq-*, to tear]

wolfram (wul´frəm) *n.* **1** tungsten. **2** wolframite. **wolframite** *n.* a native tungsten ore composed of tungstate of iron and manganese. [G, wolf cream]

Wolof (wol´of) *n.* (*pl.* **Wolof, Wolofs**) **1** a member of a West African people living mainly in Senegal. **2** the language of this people.

wolverine (wul´vərēn), **wolverene** *n.* a small carnivorous animal, *Gulo gulo*, also called the glutton or carcajou. [dim. of WOLF, after MHG *wölfelin*]

wolves WOLF.

woman (wum´ən) *n.* (*pl.* **women** (wim´in)) **1** an adult human female. **2** womankind, the female sex. **3** womanly feeling, womanliness. **4** (*coll., often offensive*) a wife, mistress or girlfriend. **5** (*coll.*) an effeminate or timid and tender man. **6** (*in comb.*) a woman of a specified nationality, occupation etc., as *Englishwoman, policewoman*. **7** (*coll.*) a female servant, esp. a domestic help. **8** †a female attendant on a person of rank, a lady-in-waiting. ~*a.* female. **to be one's own woman** (of a woman) to be of independent mind. **woman-hater** *n.* a misogynist. **womanhood** *n.* **womanish** *a.* **1** (*usu. derog.*) having the characteristics or qualities of a woman, weak, effeminate. **2** suitable for a woman. **womanishly** *adv.* **womanishness** *n.* **womanist** *n.* (*esp. N Am.*) a black feminist. **womanize, womanise** *v.t.* to make effeminate, to unman. ~*v.i.* (of a man) to have casual sexual relationships with many women. **womanizer** *n.* **womankind** *n.* **1** women collectively, the female sex. **2** womenfolk. **womanless** *a.* **womanlike** *a.* **womanly** *a.* having the qualities associated with a woman, feminine. **womanliness** *n.* **woman of means** *n.* a wealthy woman. **woman of sense** *n.* a woman with wisdom, common sense etc. **woman of the bedchamber** *n.* a lady-in-waiting. **woman of the moment** *n.* a woman who is important or famous at the present time. **woman of the streets** *n.* a prostitute. **woman of the world** *n.* **1** a woman knowledgeable about or experienced in the ways of the world. **2** a society woman. **womenfolk** *n.* **1** the women of a household or family. **2** women collectively. **womenkind** *n.* womankind. **Women's Institute** *n.* a non-political and non-sectarian organization of women in Britain, esp. in rural areas, meeting regularly for domestic, social and cultural activities. **women's liberation,** (*coll.*) **women's lib** *n.* **1** the social, sexual and psychological emancipation of women from the dominance of men. **2** (*also* **Women's Liberation, Women's Movement**) a movement advocating this which began in the 1960s. **women's rights** *n.pl.* the rights of women, esp. for social, occupational and legal equality with men. **women's suffrage** *n.* the right of women to vote, the extension of the electoral franchise to women. **womenswear** *n.* clothing for women. [OE *wīfman* (WIFE, MAN)]

womb (woom) *n.* **1** the organ in a woman or other female mammal in which the young is developed before birth, the uterus. **2** the place where anything is engendered or brought into existence. **womb-like** *a.* [OE *wamb* (cp. Dut. *wam*, G *Wampe*, *Wamme*, Icel. *vomb*)]

wombat (wom´bat) *n.* any burrowing Australian marsupial of the family Vombatidae, resembling a small bear. [Austral. Abor.]

women, womenfolk etc. WOMAN.

womera WOOMERA.

won[1] WIN.

won[2] (won) *n.* the standard monetary unit in N and S Korea. [Korean]

wonder (wŭn´də) *n.* **1** a strange, remarkable or marvellous thing, person, event, action etc., a miracle, a prodigy. **2** the emotion excited by that which is unexpected, strange, extraordinary or inexplicable. **3** surprise mingled with admiration. ~*a.* having amazing, extraordinary or miraculous qualities (*a wonder drug*). ~*v.i.* **1** to be struck with wonder or surprise. **2** to look with wonder or admiration (at). **3** to feel doubt or curiosity (about etc.). ~*v.t.* **1** to speculate about. **2** to feel doubt or curiosity about. **3** to be surprised (that). **I shouldn't wonder** (*coll.*) I think it probable or likely. **I wonder** I doubt it. **no wonder** it is not surprising (that). **to work/ do wonders** to achieve remarkable or miraculous results. **wonders will never cease** used to express great surprise. **wonderer** *n.* **wonderful** *a.* **1** remarkable, marvellous, admirable. **2** exciting wonder or astonishment. **wonderfully** *adv.* **wonderfulness** *n.* **wondering** *n., a.* **wonderingly** *adv.* **wonderland** *n.* **1** a land of marvels. **2** fairyland. **3** a place or scene of great beauty. **wonderment** *n.* **1** amazement, awe. **2** curiosity. **3** (*pl., poet.*) marvels. **wonder-struck, wonder-stricken** *a.* overcome with wonder, surprise or admiration. **wonder-worker** *n.* a person who performs wonders or miracles. **wonder-working** *a.* **wondrous** (-drəs) *a.* wonderful, marvellous, strange. ~*adv.* wonderfully, exceedingly. **wondrously** *adv.* **wondrousness** *n.* [OE *wunder*, a portent (cp. Dut. *wonder*, G *Wunder*, Icel. *undr*), perh. cogn. with *wandrian*, to turn aside from, to reverse]

wonga-wonga (wong·gəwong´gə) *n.* **1** a large Australian pigeon, *Leucosarcia melanoleuca*. **2** an Australian vine of the genus *Tecoma*. [Austral. Abor.]

wonky (wong´ki) *a.* (*comp.* **wonkier,** *superl.* **wonkiest**) (*sl.*) **1** askew, crooked. **2** unsteady, shaky. **3** unreliable. **wonkily** *adv.* **wonkiness** *n.* [etym. uncertain]

wont (wōnt) *a.* (*poet.*) **1** used, accustomed (to). **2** using or doing habitually. ~*n.* (*formal or facet.*) custom, habit, use (*as is her wont*). ~†*v.i.* (*3rd pers. sing. pres.* **wonts, wont,** *past* **wont, wonted**) to be accustomed or used (to). ~†*v.t.* to make accustomed. **wonted** *a.* customary, habitual, usual. [ME *woned*, p.p. of *wonen*, OE *wunian*, to dwell]

won't (wōnt) *contr.* will not.

wonton (wonton´) *n.* a small Chinese dumpling with a savoury filling, usu. served in soup. [Cantonese *wān t'ān*]

woo (woo) *v.t.* (*3rd pers. sing. pres.* **woos,** *pres.p.* **wooing,** *past, p.p.* **wooed**) **1** to court, esp. with a view to marriage. **2** to seek to gain or attain. **3** to solicit, to coax, to importune. ~*v.i.* to go courting. **wooable** *a.* **wooer** *n.* [ME *wowen, wogen*, OE *wōgian*, in *awōgian*, from *wōh*, bent]

woobut OUBIT.

wood (wud) *n.* **1** the fibrous substance of a tree between the bark and the pith. **2** timber. **3** (*often pl.*) a large and thick collection of growing trees, a forest. **4** in bowls, a wooden bowl. **5** a golf club with a wooden head. **6** (*Mus.*) the woodwind. **7** wooden casks or barrels, esp. for wine (*aged in the wood*). **from the wood** from the cask. **not to see the wood for the trees** to be prevented by excessive details from getting an overall view. **out of the wood** out of danger or difficulty. **out of the woods** (*esp. N Am.*) out of the wood. **wood alcohol** *n.* methyl alcohol, formerly produced by the distillation of wood, now synthesized. **wood anemone** *n.* a wild anemone, *Anemone nemorosa.* **wood avens** *n.* herb bennet. **woodbine, woodbind** *n.* **1** the wild honeysuckle. **2** (*N Am.*) the Virginia creeper. **woodblock** *n.* a die cut in wood for taking impressions or woodcuts from. **woodcarver** *n.* **1** a person who carves designs etc. on wood. **2** a tool for carving wood. **woodcarving** *n., a.* **woodchat (shrike)** *n.* a type of shrike, *Lanius senator*, of Europe and N Africa. **woodchip** *n.* **1** a chip of wood. **2** (*also* **woodchip paper**) a type of wallpaper containing woodchips for texture. **wood coal** *n.* **1** charcoal. **2** lignite. **woodcock** *n.* (*pl.* **woodcock**) a game bird of the genus *Scolopax* or *Philohela.* **woodcraft** *n.* (*esp. N Am.*) **1** skill in anything relating to life in the woods or forest. **2** skill in woodwork. **woodcut** *n.* **1** an engraving on wood, a woodblock. **2** a print or impression from this. **3** the technique of making such prints or engravings. **woodcutter** *n.* **1** a person who cuts wood or timber. **2** an engraver on wood. **wooded** *a.* covered with trees or woods. **wooden** *a.* **1** made of wood. **2** resembling wood. **3** stiff, clumsy, awkward, stilted. **4** spiritless, expressionless. **wooden-head** *n.* (*coll.*) a stupid person, a blockhead. **wooden-headed** *a.* **wooden-headedness** *n.* **wooden horse** *n.* the Trojan horse used by the Greeks to enter Troy. **woodenly** *adv.* **woodenness** *n.* **wooden spoon** *n.* **1** a spoon made of wood, used in cooking. **2** a booby prize, esp. in sports competitions. **wood engraver** *n.* an engraver on wood. **wood engraving** *n.* **1** an engraving on wood. **2** a print made from this. **3** the technique of making such prints or engravings. **wood fibre,** (*N Am.*) **wood fiber** *n.* fibre obtained from wood, used for papermaking etc. **wood-grain** *a.* having a pattern imitating that of the grain of wood (*a wood-grain finish*). **woodgrouse** *n.* the capercaillie, *Tetrao urogallus.* **woodhole** *n.* a place where wood is stored. **wood hyacinth** *n.* the bluebell, *Hyacinthoides nonscripta.* **wood ibis** *n.* any of several American or African storks, esp. *Mycteria americana* or *Ibis ibis.* **woodland** *n.* land covered with woods, wooded country. ~*a.* of or relating to this, sylvan. **woodlander** *n.* **woodlark** *n.* a European lark, *Lullula arborea*, smaller than the skylark. **woodless** *a.* **woodlouse** *n.* (*pl.* **woodlice**) any small isopod crustacean of the genera *Oniscus, Porcellio* etc., infesting decayed wood etc. **woodman** *n.* (*pl.* **woodmen**) **1** a forester. **2** a person who fells timber. **wood mouse** *n.* (*pl.* **wood mice**) a field mouse. **woodnote** *n.* a wild or natural note or song, such as that of a bird. **wood nymph** *n.* a dryad. **wood opal** *n.* silicified wood. **woodpecker** *n.* a bird of the family Picidae living in woods and tapping trees to discover insects. **wood pigeon** *n.* the ring-dove, *Columba palumbus*, a Eurasian pigeon whose neck is nearly encircled by a ring of whitish-coloured feathers. **woodpile** *n.* a pile of wood. **nigger in the woodpile** NIGGER. **wood pulp** *n.* wood fibre pulped in the process of manufacturing paper. **wood rat** *n.* a rat of the genus *Neotoma* of N America. **woodruff** *n.* a woodland plant with fragrant white flowers of the genus *Galium*, esp. *G. odoratum.* **woodrush** *n.* any grassy plant of the genus *Luzula.* **woodscrew** *n.* a metal screw for fastening pieces of wood together. **woodshed** *n.* a shed for storing wood, esp. firewood. **something nasty in the woodshed** (*coll.*) something unpleasant or shocking, esp. from a person's past, kept hidden or secret. **woodsman** *n.* (*pl.* **woodsmen**) **1** a person who lives in the woods. **2** a woodman. **3** a person who is skilled in woodcraft. **woodsmoke** *n.* the smoke produced by a wood fire. **wood sorrel** *n.* a creeping woodland plant, *Oxalis acetosella*, with acid juice and small white flowers. **wood spirit** *n.* crude methyl alcohol. **wood stain** *n.* a substance used to colour wood. **wood sugar** *n.* xylose. **woodsy** *a.* (*N Am.*) of, resembling or connected with woods. **wood tar** *n.* tar obtained from wood. **woodturning** *n.* the process of shaping wood on a lathe. **woodturner** *n.* **wood warbler** *n.* **1** a European woodland bird, *Phylloscopus sibilatrix.* **2** any American warbler of the family Parulidae. **woodwasp** *n.* a wasp-like insect of the family Siricidae that lays its eggs in wood, esp. *Urocerus gigas*, a pest of conifers. **woodwind** (-wind) *n.* (*Mus.*) **1** the wind instruments in an orchestra etc. orig. made of wood, such as the flute, oboe and clarinet. **2** any of these instruments or their players. ~*a.* of or relating to these instruments. **wood wool** *n.* fine shavings, esp. of pine, used for dressing wounds, for packing etc. **woodwork** *n.* **1** the art or process of making things from wood. **2** things made of wood. **3** the part of a building or other structure which is composed of wood. **to crawl out of the woodwork** (of something unpleasant or undesirable) to appear, to come to light, to become known. **woodworker** *n.* **woodworking** *n., a.* **woodworm** *n.* **1** any of various insect larvae that bore into furniture, wooden beams etc., esp. the larvae of the furniture beetle, *Anobium punctatum.* **2** the damage caused by such larvae. **woody** *a.* (*comp.* **woodier,** *superl.* **woodiest**) **1** abounding in woods, well wooded. **2** of the nature of or consisting of wood (*woody fibre; woody tissue*). **3** of, relating to or found in woods. **woodiness** *n.* **woody nightshade** *n.* a poisonous trailing plant, *Solanum dulcamara*, with purple flowers and brilliant red berries. **woodyard** *n.* a yard where wood is cut or stored. [OE *wudu* (cp. Icel. *vithr*, Dan., Swed. *ved*, OHG *witu*, Ir., Gael. *fiodh*, Welsh *gwydd*)]

woodchuck[1] (wud´chŭk) *n.* a N American marmot, *Marmota monax.* [prob. alt. of Algonquian word]

woof[1] (wuf) *n.* the sound of a dog barking or growling. ~*v.i.* to produce this sound. **woofer** *n.* a loudspeaker used to reproduce low audio frequencies. [imit.]

woof[2] (woof) *n.* **1** the threads that cross the warp, the weft. **2** woven cloth. **3** texture. [ME *oof*, OE *ōwef* (A-[1], *wef*, WEB)]

woofter (wuf´tə) *n.* (*sl., derog.*) a male homosexual. [POOFTAH]

wool (wul) *n.* **1** the fine, soft, curly hair forming the fleece of sheep, goats and some other animals, used as the raw material of cloth etc. **2** yarn, fabric or clothing made from this. **3** short, thick or curly hair, underfur or down, resembling wool. **4** any fibrous or fleecy substance resembling wool (*steel wool*). ~*a.* **1** made of wool. **2** of or relating to wool (*the wool trade*). **to pull the wool over someone's eyes** to deceive someone. **wool-carding, wool-combing** *n.* a process in the preparation of wool for spinning. **wool classer** *n.* (*Austral., New Zeal.*) a grader of wool. **wool clip** *n.* the annual amount of wool shorn. **woolen** WOOLLEN (under WOOL).

wool-fat *n.* lanolin. **wool-fell** *n.* a skin from which the wool has not been removed. **wool-gathering** *a.* absent-minded, daydreaming. ~*n.* absent-mindedness, inattention. **wool-grower** *n.* a person who keeps or breeds sheep for wool. **woollen,** (*N Am.*) **woolen** *a.* made or consisting of wool. ~*n.* **1** a cloth made of wool. **2** (*pl.*) woollen goods, esp. woollen clothing. **wool-like** *a.* **woolly** *a.* (*comp.* **woollier,** *superl.* **woolliest**) **1** bearing or naturally covered with wool, or with hair resembling wool. **2** consisting of or resembling wool in texture. **3** resembling wool in appearance, fleecy (*woolly clouds*). **4** lacking clear definition, firmness or incisiveness. **5** with hazy ideas, muddled. ~*n.* (*pl.* **woollies**) (*coll.*) a woollen pullover etc. **woolliness** *n.* **woolly-bear** *n.* **1** a hairy caterpillar, esp. of the tiger moth. **2** the hairy larva of a carpet beetle. **woollybutt** *n.* any of several Australian timber trees, esp. *Eucalyptus longifolia* or *E. viminalis.* **woolman** *n.* (*pl.* **woolmen**) **1** a wool merchant. **2** a wool-grower. **wool-oil** *n.* the natural grease of wool. **woolpack** *n.* **1** a pack or bale of wool, formerly one weighing 240 lb. (109 kg). **2** a fleecy cloud. **Woolsack** *n.* **1** the Lord Chancellor's seat in the House of Lords, formerly a large, square, wool-filled sack. **2** the office or position of Lord Chancellor. **woolshed** *n.* (*Austral., New Zeal.*) a building for shearing, packing and storing wool. **wool-skin** *n.* a wool-fell. **wool-sorter** *n.* a person who sorts wool according to quality etc. **wool-sorter's disease** *n.* pulmonary anthrax due to the inhalation of dust from infected wool. **wool staple** *n.* the fibre of wool. **wool-stapler** *n.* a wool-sorter. [OE *wull* (cp. Dut. *wol*, G *Wolle*, Icel. *ull*), perh. cogn. with L *lāna*, Gr. *lēnos*]

woomera (woo´mərə), **womera** (wom´ərə) *n.* **1** a stick used in throwing a spear or dart. **2** a club thrown as a missile. [Austral. Abor.]

woop woop (wup´ wup), **Woop Woop** *n.* (*Austral., New Zeal., sl.*) any remote place, real or imaginary. [mock Austral. Abor.]

woosh WHOOSH.

woozy (woo´zi) *a.* (*comp.* **woozier,** *superl.* **wooziest**) (*coll.*) **1** suffering from giddiness, nausea etc. **2** dazed, confused, e.g. with drink. **3** vague. **woozily** *adv.* **wooziness** *n.* [etym. unknown]

wop (wop) *n.* (*sl., offensive*) any person of S European origin, esp. an Italian. [etym. unknown]

Worcester sauce (wus´tə), **Worcestershire sauce** (-shə) *n.* a dark sauce made by mixing soy sauce, vinegar, spices etc. **Worcester woman** *n.* the stereotypical woman floating voter; cp. BARKING BLOKE. [*Worcester*, city in England]

Worcs. *abbr.* Worcestershire.

word (wœd) *n.* **1** an articulate sound or combination of sounds uttered by the human voice or written, printed etc., expressing an idea or ideas and usu. forming a constituent part of a sentence. **2** speech, discourse, talk. **3** something said, a remark. **4** news, intelligence, information, a message. **5** a command, an order, an injunction. **6** a password, a watchword, a motto. **7** one's assurance, promise or definite affirmation. **8** (*pl.*) the text of a song, speech etc. (*I've forgotten the words*). **9** (*pl.*) talk or remarks exchanged expressive of anger, contention or reproach. **10** (*Comput.*) a set of bits processed as one unit by a computer. ~*v.t.* to express in words, to phrase, to select words to express. **as good as one's word** GOOD. **at a word** as soon as asked, at once. **a word (is enough) to the wise** there is no need to be more explicit. **by word of mouth** by actual speaking, orally. **from the word go** GO[2]. **in a/ one word 1** briefly, in short. **2** to sum up. **in other words** expressing the same thing in a different way. **in so many words** explicitly, precisely, bluntly. **in words of one syllable** SYLLABLE. **not the word for it** an inadequate description (*Unattractive is not the word for it – it's an eyesore!*). **of one's word** able to be relied upon to do what one says one will do (*a man of his word*). **on my word (of honour)** used to make a promise or give a solemn assurance. **the Word (of God) 1** the Scriptures, or any part of them. **2** Christ as the Logos. **to break one's word** to break one's promise, to fail to fulfil an undertaking. **to get a word in edgeways** EDGEWAYS (under EDGE). **to give one's word** to promise, to give one's assurance. **to have a word with** to have a brief conversation with. **to have no words for** to be unable to express, describe etc. **to have words with** to have a dispute with, to reproach. **to keep one's word** to keep one's promise, to fulfil an undertaking. **too...for words** extremely..., too... to describe (*This is too ridiculous for words*). **to put into words** to express in speech or writing. **to send word** SEND. **to take someone at their word** to assume that someone means what they say. **to take someone's word for it** to believe someone without proof or further investigation. **(upon) my word!** used to express surprise, indignation etc. **word for word** in exactly the same words, verbatim. **words fail me!** used to express disbelief, exasperation, astonishment etc. **wordage** (-ij) *n.* **word-blind** *a.* unable to understand written or printed words owing to a cerebral lesion. **word-blindness** *n.* **wordbook** *n.* a vocabulary or dictionary. **wordbreak** *n.* the place where a word is divided when it runs from one line to another in printing. **word-deaf** *a.* unable to understand spoken words owing to a cerebral lesion. **word-deafness** *n.* **word division** *n.* the dividing of words between lines in printing. **word game** *n.* any game involving the formation, alteration etc. of words. **wording** *n.* **1** choice of words, phrasing etc. **2** the contents of a document, advertisement etc. **wordless** *a.* **wordlessly** *adv.* **wordlessness** *n.* **word of command** *n.* an order or signal for movement or action. **word of honour** *n.* a solemn promise, assurance or undertaking. **word of mouth** *n.* spoken communication. **word order** *n.* the order in which words are arranged in a sentence etc. **word-painter** *n.* a writer who depicts scenes or events in a vivid and picturesque manner. **word-painting** *n.* **word-perfect** *a.* able to repeat something without a mistake. **word-picture** *n.* a vivid description. **wordplay** *n.* playing on words, making puns, witty repartee. **word processor** *n.* an electronic device used for the automatic typing, editing and often printing of texts in various formats, usu. equipped with a VDU. **word-process** *v.t.* **word processing** *n.* **wordsearch** *n.* a type of puzzle involving words hidden in a grid of letters. **wordsmith** *n.* a person skilled in the use of words, esp. a writer. **word-square** *n.* a series of words so arranged that the letters spell the same words when read across or downwards. **word wrap** *n.* (*Comput.*) the automatic shifting of a word from the end of one line to the beginning of the next. **wordy** *a.* (*comp.* **wordier,** *superl.* **wordiest**) **1** verbose, diffuse, prolix. **2** consisting of words, verbal. **wordily** *adv.* **wordiness** *n.* [OE (cp. Dut. *woord*, G *Wort*, Icel. *orth*, Dan., Swed. *ord*), cogn. with L *verbum*, Gr. *eirein*, to speak]

Wordsworthian (wœdzwœ´dhiən) *a.* of, relating to or after the manner or spirit of William Wordsworth or his poetry. ~*n.* a devotee of Wordsworth. [William *Wordsworth*, 1770–1850, English poet]

wore[1] WEAR[1].

wore[2] WEAR[2].

work (wœk) *n.* **1** the exertion of physical or mental energy, effort or activity directed to some purpose. **2** labour, toil. **3** an undertaking, a task. **4** the materials used or to be used in this. **5** employment as a means of livelihood, occupation. **6** an action, deed, performance or achievement. **7** a thing made. **8** a product of nature or art. **9** a book or other literary composition, a musical or other artistic production (*an orchestral work; the* *works of Shakespeare*). **10** a large engineering structure, esp. a piece of fortification. **11** a place of employment. **12** (*Physics*) the exertion of force in producing or maintaining motion against the action of a resisting force. **13** (*pl., often sing. in constr.*) an industrial establishment, a factory. **14** (*pl.*) building operations, esp. carried out under the management of a public authority. **15** (*pl.*) the working part or mechanism (of a watch etc.). **16** (*pl., Theol.*) moral duties or the performance of meritorious acts, as opposed to *grace*. **17** (*in comb.*) making things or things made with a specified material, tool, pattern etc., as *metalwork, needlework, fretwork*. *~v.i.* (*past, p.p.* **worked, †wrought** (rawt)) **1** to exert physical or mental energy for some purpose, to be engaged in labour or effort, to do work. **2** to be employed or occupied (at, in, on etc.). **3** to be in activity, to act, to operate, to function, to run. **4** to take effect, to be effective, to exercise influence (*Their plan won't work*). **5** to be in a state of motion or agitation, to ferment. **6** to make way with effort or difficulty. **7** to reach a certain condition gradually (*to work loose*). **8** (*Naut.*) to sail against the wind. *~v.t.* **1** to exert energy in or on. **2** to cause to do work, to keep in operation, to employ, to keep busy. **3** to carry on, to manage, to run, to operate. **4** to cultivate (land). **5** to bring about, to effect, to produce as a result (*to work miracles*). **6** to prepare or alter the condition, shape or consistency of by some process, to knead, to mould, to fashion. **7** to make or embroider with needlework. **8** to earn through paid work. **9** to cause to progress with effort or difficulty. **10** to treat, to investigate, to solve. **11** to excite. **at work 1** doing work, in action or operation. **2** at one's place of employment. **in work** in paid employment. **nasty piece of work** NASTY. **out of work** not in paid employment, unemployed. **the works 1** (*coll.*) everything. **2** (*coll.*) the appropriate treatment. **3** (*coll.*) a violent beating (*to give someone the works*). **to have one's work cut out** to have a hard task. **to work in 1** to introduce or combine by manipulation. **2** to find space or time for. **to work into the ground** to exhaust or wear out with overwork. **to work it** (*coll.*) to arrange things, to bring it about (*She worked it so that he couldn't refuse*). **to work like a nigger** NIGGER. **to work off 1** to get rid of, esp. by effort, activity etc. **2** to pay off (a debt etc.) by working. **to work on** to continue to work. **to work one's fingers to the bone** to work very hard, esp. without due appreciation or gratitude. **to work one's passage** PASSAGE[1]. **†to work one's will on/ upon** to make do what one wants, to make perform as one wants. **to work out 1** to compute, to solve, to find out, to understand. **2** to accomplish, to effect. **3** to devise, to formulate (*to work out a plan of action*). **4** to have a result (*It didn't work out as well as we'd hoped*). **5** to undertake a series of exercises to get fit. **6** to exhaust. **7** to expiate. **to work over 1** to examine carefully. **2** (*coll.*) to beat severely, to mug. **to work the oracle** ORACLE. **to work to rule** to follow working rules so strictly that productivity is reduced, esp. as a form of industrial action. **to work up 1** to elaborate, to bring gradually into shape or efficiency. **2** to excite gradually, to stir up, to rouse. **3** to advance or increase gradually. **4** to mingle together. **5** to study (a subject) perseveringly. **to work wonders** WONDER. **workable** *a.* **1** capable of being worked, practicable. **2** that will work or operate. **3** worth working or developing. **workability** (-bil´-), **workableness** *n.* **workably** *adv.* **workaday** (-ədā) *a.* of, relating to or suitable for workdays, everyday, common, ordinary, plain, practical. **workaholic** (-əhol´ik) *n.* (*coll.*) a person addicted to working. **workaholism** *n.* **work-basket, work-bag** *n.* a basket or bag used for holding materials etc. for work, esp. for sewing. **workbench** *n.* a bench specially designed for woodworking, metalworking etc. **workboat** *n.* a boat used for fishing or other work. **workbook** *n.* **1** a book containing exercises for students, often with spaces for answers. **2** a book for recording work done. **work-box** *n.* a box used for holding materials etc. for work, esp. for sewing. **work camp** *n.* a camp at which voluntary community work is done, esp. by young people. **workday** *n.* (*esp. N Am.*) a working day, a day on which work is ordinarily done. **worked up** *a.* excited, agitated or angry (*to get worked up*). **worker** *n.* **1** a person who works, esp. a member of the working class. **2** a sterile female insect in a colony of insects that specializes in gathering food, caring for the young etc. **3** a person who works in a specified job or manner (*a social worker, a dedicated and reliable worker*). **worker director** *n.* a worker appointed to the board of a company to represent the interests of the employees. **worker priest** *n.* a priest who does secular work. **work ethic** *n.* a belief in the value of work (*the Protestant work ethic*). **work experience** *n.* short-term experience in a workplace given to young people. **workfare** *n.* a welfare scheme in which those receiving benefits are required to undergo training, do community work etc. **workforce** *n.* the total number of workers employed or available for employment. **work group** *n.* a small group of workers, trainees etc. **workhorse** *n.* a person or thing that does or is capable of doing a great deal of work. **workhouse** *n.* **1** (*Hist.*) a public establishment maintained by a parish or union for paupers. **2** (*N Am.*) a penal institution for petty offenders. **work-in** *n.* a form of protest, e.g. against the closure of a factory etc., in which workers occupy it and continue working. **work-in-progress** *n.* in bookkeeping, the value of work started but not finished. **workless** *a.* **workload** *n.* the amount of work expected from or done by a person, machine etc. **workman** *n.* (*pl.* **workmen**) any man employed in manual labour, an operative. **workmanlike** *a.* done in the manner of a good workman. **workmanship** *n.* **1** comparative skill, finish or execution shown in making something or in the thing made. **2** the result of working or making. **Workmate®** *n.* a portable collapsible workbench. **workmate** *n.* a person with whom one works. **work of art** *n.* **1** a painting, sculpture or other piece of fine art. **2** anything skilfully or beautifully constructed or composed. **workout** *n.* a series of exercises for physical fitness. **workpeople** *n.pl.* workers. **workpiece** *n.* any item on which work is being done, esp. with a tool or machine. **workplace** *n.* a place where people work, such as an office or factory. **work rate** *n.* the rate at which work is done. **workroom** *n.* a room in which work is done, esp. one furnished or equipped for the purpose. **works council** *n.* a group of workers representing the employees of a factory etc. in negotiations with management. **worksheet** *n.* **1** a sheet of paper on which the progress of work is recorded. **2** a list of work to be done, questions to be answered by students etc. **workshop** *n.* **1** a room or building in which manual work, esp. making or repairing things, is carried on. **2** a meeting for discussion, training, practical work etc. (*a creative writing workshop*). **3** the people attending such a meeting. **work-shy** *a.* reluctant or disinclined to work. **worksite** *n.* the site of an industry or manual labour. **works of supererogation** *n.pl.* in the Roman Catholic Church, meritorious acts held in reserve against future sin. **workspace** *n.* **1** a space in which work can be done. **2** (*Comput.*) a temporary memory storage facility. **workstation** *n.* **1** the place in an office, factory etc. where one person works. **2** (*Comput.*) a unit consisting of a VDU and keyboard for use by one worker. **work study** *n.* the investigation of the methods and practice of a particular type of work with a view to getting the best results for all concerned. **work surface** *n.* a worktop. **work table** *n.* a table on which work can be done, usu.

with drawers etc. for keeping sewing or writing materials in. **worktop** *n.* a flat board covered with laminate and often fixed to the top of kitchen units, used to prepare food. **work-to-rule** *n.* the act or an instance of working to rule. **workwear** *n.* clothes for working in. **workwoman** *n.* (*pl.* **workwomen**) a female worker or operative. [OE *weorc* (cp. Dut., G *Werk*, Icel. *verk*, Gr. *ergon*), whence *wiercan*, *wyrcan*, to work, past *worhte*]

working (wœ´king) *a.* **1** engaged in work, esp. manual labour. **2** during which work is done or business discussed (*a working lunch*; *working hours*). **3** functioning or able to function. **4** taking an active part in a business (*a working partner*). ~*n.* **1** the act of labouring. **2** operation, mode of operation. **3** a mine or quarry or a portion of it which has been worked or in which work is going on. **4** fermentation, movement. **working capital** *n.* funds employed for the actual carrying on of a business. **working class** *n.* the class of people who earn their living by manual labour. **working-class** *a.* of or relating to the working class. **working day** *n.* **1** any day on which work is ordinarily performed, as distinguished from Sundays and holidays. **2** the period daily devoted to work. **working drawing** *n.* a scale drawing or plan of a work prepared to guide a builder, engineer etc. in executing work. **working hypothesis** *n.* a hypothesis on the basis of which plans are made or action is taken. **working knowledge** *n.* sufficient knowledge to work with (*I have a working knowledge of the system*). **working man** *n.* (*pl.* **working men**) a man in paid employment. **working order** *n.* the condition in which a machine functions as it should (*in working order*). **working-out** *n.* the act of working out, calculating, elaborating etc. **working party** *n.* (*pl.* **working parties**) a committee set up specifically to investigate a particular issue. **working woman** *n.* (*pl.* **working women**) a woman in paid employment.

world (wœld) *n.* **1** the earth with its lands and seas. **2** a celestial body regarded as similar to this. **3** a large natural or other division of the earth. **4** the human inhabitants of the earth, humankind. **5** the whole system of things, the universe, everything. **6** a system of things, an orderly or organic whole, a cosmos. **7** human affairs, the ways, customs, opinions etc. of people, active life, social life and intercourse. **8** human society, the public. **9** fashionable or prominent people. **10** a particular section or class of people, animals or things, a realm, a domain, a sphere (*the world of fashion*). **11** a vast quantity, amount, number, degree etc. (of) (*a world of difference*). **12** all things external to oneself as related to the individual. **13** one's inner life. **14** any time, state or sphere of existence (*the prehistoric world*). **15** the present state of existence as distinct from the future. **16** secular interest as opposed to *spiritual*. **17** the ungodly or unregenerate portion of humankind. ~*a.* of or relating to all nations of the world. **all the world** everybody. **all the world and his wife** a large mixed group of people. **(all) the world over** everywhere. **dead to the world** (*coll.*) fast asleep. **for all the world** exactly, precisely (*It sounded for all the world like an explosion*). **for the world** on any account (*I wouldn't hurt you for the world*). **in the world** at all, possibly (*How in the world did that happen?*). **out of this world 1** (*coll.*) remarkable, striking. **2** (*coll.*) excellent. **the best of both worlds** the benefits of two different or incompatible things, ways of life, sets of ideas etc. (*to get the best of both worlds*). **the world, the flesh and the devil** all forms of temptation. **the world to come** the hereafter, life after death. **to bring into the world 1** to give birth to. **2** to deliver (a baby). **to carry the world before one** to have complete success. **to come into the world** COME. **to see the world** to travel far and wide. **to set the world on fire** FIRE. **to think the world of** to love or respect greatly. **world without end** to all eternity, everlastingly. **World Bank** *n.* (*coll.*) the International Bank for Reconstruction and Development, an agency of the United Nations set up in 1945 to lend money at moderate rates to poorer countries seeking to develop their resources. **world-beater** *n.* a person or thing that is the best of its kind in the world. **world-beating** *a.* **world-class** *a.* of the highest class in the world. **World Court** *n.* (*coll.*) the International Court of Justice at the Hague set up in 1921 by the League of Nations to settle disputes between states. **World Cup** *n.* an international football or other sporting competition. **world fair** *n.* an international exhibition of achievements in industry, science, technology, the arts etc. **world-famous** *a.* famous throughout the world. **World Health Organization** *n.* a specialized agency of the United Nations dating from 1948 with the object of helping countries to develop their health administration. **world language** *n.* **1** an artificial language for use by all nations. **2** a language spoken by many nations. **world-line** *n.* (*Physics*) a line or curve in space-time showing the path of a body throughout its existence. **worldling** *n.* a worldly person. **world music** *n.* rock or pop music incorporating elements from a variety of national (esp. Third World) styles. **world order** *n.* a system for preserving international political stability (*the new world order*). **world power** *n.* a sovereign state so strong as to be able to affect the policy of every civilized state in the world. **world's end** *n.* the remotest part of the earth. **World Series** *n.* a series of baseball games played in the US between the winners of major leagues to decide the professional championship. **world-shaking** *a.* supremely important or significant. **world-view** *n.* WELTANSCHAUUNG. **world war** *n.* a war involving most of the earth's major nations, esp. the 1914–18 or 1939–45 wars. **world-weary** *a.* tired of existence. **world-weariness** *n.* **worldwide** *a.* **1** spread over the whole world. **2** existing everywhere. ~*adv.* throughout the world. **World Wide Web** *n.* a network of files from all round the world available over the Internet. [OE *weoruld* (*wer*, man, cp. Icel. *verr*, L *vir*, ELD, cp. Dut. *wereld*, G *Welt*, Icel. *veröld*)]

worldly (wœld´li) *a.* (*comp.* **worldlier**, *superl.* **worldliest**) **1** of or relating to the present, temporal or material world. **2** earthly, secular, material, not spiritual. **3** practical, sophisticated, worldly-wise. **4** worldly-minded. **worldliness** *n.* **worldly-minded** *a.* devoted to worldly things. **worldly-mindedness** *n.* **worldly-wise** *a.* wise in the ways or things of this world. **worldly wisdom** *n.*

WORM (wœm) *abbr.* (*Comput.*) write once read many times (referring to an optical disk on which data can be stored but not altered).

worm (wœm) *n.* **1** any of various invertebrate creeping animals with a long limbless segmented body. **2** any long creeping animal with very small or undeveloped feet, such as larvae, grubs, caterpillars or maggots. **3** an intestinal parasite. **4** (*pl.*) any disease caused by parasitic worms, esp. in the intestine. **5** any of various other animals such as the blindworm or slow-worm. **6** (*coll.*) a poor, grovelling, debased or despised person. **7** a wormlike or spiral part or thing. **8** the spiral part of a screw. **9** a spiral tool for boring rock. **10** a spiral device for extracting cartridges etc. **11** the spiral condensing pipe of a still. **12** a ligament under a dog's tongue. ~*v.i.* **1** to crawl, creep, wriggle or progress with a wormlike motion. **2** to work stealthily or underhandedly. ~*v.t.* **1** to insinuate (oneself), to make (one's way) in a wormlike manner (*He wormed his way into our favour*). **2** to draw (out) by craft and perseverance (*I wormed the secret out of her*). **3** to free (a dog etc.) from worms. **4** to cut the worm from under the tongue of (a dog). **5** (*Naut.*) to wind yarn between the strands of (a rope) to make it smooth. **(even) a worm will turn** the most humble or submissive person will retaliate under extreme provocation. **food for worms** FOOD. **worm-cast** *n.* a cylindrical mass of earth voided by an earthworm. **worm charming** *n.* enticing worms from the ground as a sport. **worm-eaten** *a.* **1** gnawed or bored by worms. **2** rotten, decayed. **3** dilapidated. **4** antiquated. **wormer** *n.* **wormery** *n.* (*pl.* **wormeries**) a container in which worms are kept for study, breeding etc. **worm-fishing** *n.* fishing with worms for bait. **worm-gear** *n.* a gear having a toothed or cogged wheel engaging with a revolving spiral. **wormhole** *n.* **1** a hole made by a worm in wood, fruit, the ground etc. **2** (*Physics*) a hypothetical tunnel connecting different regions of space-time. **wormholed** *a.* **wormless** *a.* **wormlike** *a.* **worm powder** *n.* a powder used as a vermifuge. **wormseed** *n.* **1** a plant whose seed is used as an anthelmintic. **2** the seed of such a plant. **worm's-eye view** *n.* a view from below, low down or from a humble position. **worm-wheel** *n.* the toothed wheel of a worm-gear. **wormy** *a.* (*comp.* **wormier**, *superl.* **wormiest**) **1** full of worms. **2** resembling a worm. **3** worm-eaten. **worminess** *n.* [OE *wyrm* (cp. Dut. *worm*, G *Wurm*, Icel. *ormr*), cogn. with Gr. *rhomos*, L *vermis*, see VERMICULAR]

wormwood (wœm´wud) *n.* **1** a shrub of the genus *Artemisia*, esp. *A. absinthium*, having bitter and tonic properties, used in the manufacture of vermouth and absinthe and in medicine. **2** bitterness, gall, mortification. [OE *wermōd* (cp. Dut. *wermoet*, G *Wermuth*, see VERMOUTH), assim. to WORM, WOOD]

worn (wawn) *a.* **1** tired, exhausted. **2** well worn. **worn out, worn-out** *a.* **1** thoroughly tired, exhausted. **2** rendered useless by long wear. [p.p. of WEAR[1]]

worried, worriment etc. WORRY.

worrit (wŭr´it) *v.t.*, *v.i.* (*pres.p.* **worriting**, *past*, *p.p.* **worrited**) (*coll.*) to worry, to cause mental distress to. ~*n.* (a) worry.

worry (wŭr´i) *v.t.* (*3rd pers. sing. pres.* **worries**, *pres.p.* **worrying**, *past*, *p.p.* **worried**) **1** to cause mental distress to. **2** (*also reflex.*) to tease, harass, bother or importune. **3** (of dogs etc.) to bite or keep on biting, to shake or pull about with the teeth. ~*v.i.* **1** to be unduly anxious or troubled, to fret. **2** (of dogs etc.) to bite, pull (at) etc. ~*n.* (*pl.* **worries**) **1** the act of worrying. **2** a cause or source of worry. **3** the state of being worried; anxiety, care, solicitude, vexation. **not to worry** (*coll.*) there's no need to worry. **to worry along** to get along somehow in spite of trouble and difficulty. **to worry out** to solve (a problem) by perseverance. **to worry through** to worry along. **worried** *a.* anxious, troubled. **worriedly** *adv.* **worrier** *n.* **worriless** *a.* **worriment** *n.* (*esp. N Am.*) **1** the state of being worried. **2** the act of worrying. **3** a cause of worry or trouble. **worrisome** *a.* causing worry. **worrisomely** *adv.* **worry beads** *n.pl.* a string of beads that are fingered in order to relieve tension. **worry-guts**, (*N Am.*) **worry-wart** *n.* (*coll.*) a person who worries habitually, esp. about unimportant things. **worrying** *a.* causing anxiety or mental distress (*worrying news*). **worryingly** *adv.* [OE *wrygan* (cp. Dut. *worgen*, G *würgen*, to strangle), cogn. with WRING]

worse (wœs) *a.* **1** more bad, bad in a higher degree. **2** (*pred.*) in a less favourable state, position or circumstance. **3** (*pred.*) in a poorer state of health. ~*adv.* **1** more badly. **2** into a poorer state of health etc. ~*n.* a worse thing or things. **none the worse** not damaged, harmed or adversely affected. **or worse** or some even worse eventuality. **the worse** a worse condition. **the worse for** damaged or harmed by. **the worse for drink** (*coll.*) drunk. **the worse for wear** **1** shabby, worn. **2** (*coll.*) tired, untidy etc. **worse luck** LUCK. **worse off** in a poorer condition or financial situation. **worsen** *v.i.* to grow worse. ~*v.t.* to make worse. [OE *wyrs*, adv., a. *wyrsa*, *wirsa*, prob. cogn. with G *wirren*, to twist, to confuse, see WAR]

worship (wœ´ship) *n.* **1** the act of paying divine honour to God or some other deity, esp. in religious services. **2** the rites or ceremonies associated with this. **3** an act or feeling of adoration, admiring devotion or submissive respect to a person, principle etc. **4** †the quality of being worthy, merit, excellence. **5** †honour, deference, respect. ~*v.t.* (*pres.p.* **worshipping**, (*N Am.*) **worshiping**, *past*, *p.p.* **worshipped**, (*N Am.*) **worshiped**) **1** to pay divine honours to. **2** to perform religious service to. **3** to reverence with supreme respect and admiration. **4** to treat as divine. ~*v.i.* **1** to take part in a religious service. **2** to be filled with adoration etc. **Your Worship** a title of respect or honour used in addressing mayors, certain magistrates etc. **worshipable** *a.* **worshipful** *a.* **1** (*usu.* **Worshipful**) a title of respect or honour used to or of various people or organizations. **2** †deserving of worship. **3** †filled with adoration etc. **worshipfully** *adv.* **worshipfulness** *n.* **worshipper**, (*N Am.*) **worshiper** *n.* **1** a person who worships. **2** an attender at a place of worship. [OE *weorthschipe*]

worst (wœst) *a.* most bad, bad in the highest degree. ~*adv.* most badly. ~*n.* **1** the worst thing or things. **2** the most bad or severe part, event, state, possibility etc. (*while the storm was at its worst*). ~*v.t.* to get the better of in a contest etc., to defeat, to best. **at (the) worst** **1** in the worst circumstances. **2** in the least favourable view. **do your worst** used to express defiance. **if the worst comes to the worst** if the worst of all possible things happens. **to come off worst** to be defeated. **to get the worst of it** to be defeated. **worst-case** *a.* of or relating to the worst of all possible situations, conditions, circumstances etc. (*a worst-case scenario*). [OE *wyrst*, adv., a. *wyrsta*, shortened from *wyrsesta* (WORSE, -EST[1])]

worsted (wus´tid) *n.* **1** a fine woollen yarn used for making fabric, knitting stockings etc. **2** fabric made from this. ~*a.* made of worsted. [*Worsted* (now *Worstead*), Norfolk, where first manufactured]

wort (wœt) *n.* **1** a plant, a herb (*usu. in comb.*, as *moneywort*, *soapwort*). **2** an infusion of malt for fermenting into beer. [OE *wyrt* (cp. G *Wurz*, Icel. *urt*), cogn. with ROOT[1]]

worth[1] (wœth) *a.* (*pred.*) **1** equal in value or price to. **2** deserving, worthy of. **3** having property to the value of, possessed of. **4** †estimable, valuable. ~*n.* **1** that which a person or thing is worth, value, the equivalent of anything, esp. in money. **2** merit, high character, excellence. **for all one is worth** (*coll.*) with all one's strength, energy etc. **for what it's worth** used to express doubt about the truth or value of something. **not worth a button** BUTTON. **not worth a groat** GROAT. **not worth a rap** RAP[2]. **not worth one's salt** SALT. **not worth the candle** CANDLE. **to be worth (someone's) while** WHILE. **worth it** worthwhile. **worth one's salt** SALT. **worth one's weight in gold** WEIGHT. **worthless** *a.* **worthlessly** *adv.* **worthlessness** *n.* **worthwhile** (-wīl´) *a.* worth the time, expense or effort involved. **worthwhileness** *n.* [OE *wyrthe*, from *wyrth*, *weorth*, value (cp. Dut. *waard*, *waarde*, Icel. *verthr*, *verth*, G *Werth*), cogn. with Welsh *gwerth*, value, price, L *verērī*, see REVERE and Eng. WARE[1]]

†**worth**[2] (wœth) *v.t.* to betide, to befall. **woe worth the day!** cursed be the day. [OE *weorthan*, to become (cp. Dut. *worden*, G *werden*, Icel. *vertha*)]

worthy (wœ´dhi) *a.* (*comp.* **worthier**, *superl.* **worthiest**) **1** having worth, estimable. **2** deserving of or entitled to respect, praise or honour, respectable. **3** deserving (of, to be etc.). **4** fit, suitable, adequate, appropriate or equivalent to the worth (of). **5** †of high rank, noble, honourable. ~*n.* (*pl.* **worthies**) **1** a worthy person. **2** a person of some note or distinction in their time, locality etc. **worthily** *adv.* **worthiness** *n.* [WORTH[1], -Y[1]]

-worthy (wœ´dhi) *comb. form* 1 safe or suitable for, as *seaworthy*. 2 deserving of, as *praiseworthy*.

†wot WIT[2].

wotcher (woch´ə) *int.* (*sl.*) a form of greeting. [Cockney pronunciation of archaic greeting *what cheer?*]

†wottest WIT[2].

would, would-be WILL[1].

wouldn't (wud´ənt) *contr.* would not.

†wouldst WILL[1].

Woulfe bottle (wulf) *n.* a bottle with three or more necks used in the handling and washing of gases. [Peter *Woulfe*, 1727–1803, British chemist]

wound[1] (woond) *n.* 1 an injury caused by a cut or blow to the skin and flesh of an animal or the bark or substance of plants, esp. one involving disruption of the tissues. 2 any damage, hurt or pain to feelings, reputation etc. 3 (*poet.*) the pangs of love. ~*v.t.* to inflict a wound on. ~*v.i.* to cause a wound. **woundable** *a.* **wounded** *a.* injured, hurt (*wounded soldiers*; *wounded pride*). ~*n.pl.* injured people (*The wounded were taken to hospital*). **wounder** *n.* **woundingly** *adv.* **woundless** *a.* **woundwort** *n.* a plant of the genus *Stachys*, or any of various other plants supposed to heal wounds. [OE *wund* (cp. Dut. *wond*, G *Wunde*, Icel. *und*), prob. cogn. with WIN]

wound[2] WIND[2].

wound[3] WIND[3].

wove[1] WEAVE[1].

wove[2] (wōv) *a.* (of paper) having a uniformly smooth surface.

woven WEAVE[1].

wow[1] (wow) *int.* used to express astonishment, wonder etc. ~*n.* (*sl.*) a sensational or spectacular success. ~*v.t.* (*sl.*) to cause to feel great enthusiasm, to impress greatly. [instinctive sound]

wow[2] (wow) *n.* a variation in pitch occurring at low frequencies in sound-reproducing systems. [imit.]

wowser (wow´zə) *n.* (*Austral., sl.*) 1 a spoilsport. 2 a fanatical puritan. 3 a teetotaller. [imit.]

WP *abbr.* 1 (*also* **w.p.**) weather permitting. 2 word processing. 3 word processor.

wpb *abbr.* waste-paper basket.

WPC *abbr.* woman police constable.

wpm *abbr.* words per minute.

WR *abbr.* Western Region.

WRAAC *abbr.* Women's Royal Australian Army Corps.

WRAAF *abbr.* Women's Royal Australian Air Force.

WRAC (rak) *abbr.* Woman's Royal Army Corps.

wrack (rak) *n.* 1 seaweed thrown upon the shore. 2 moving or driving clouds, cloud rack. 3 rack, destruction, ruin. 4 a wreck, wreckage. [var. of WRECK]

WRAF (raf) *abbr.* (*Hist.*) Women's Royal Air Force.

wraggle-taggle RAGGLE-TAGGLE.

wraith (rāth) *n.* 1 the double or phantom of a living person. 2 an apparition, a ghost appearing after death. **wraithlike** *a.* [perh. var. of WREATH, or cogn. with Norw. *vardyvle* (WARD, EVIL)]

wrangle (rang´gəl) *v.i.* to dispute, argue or quarrel angrily, peevishly or noisily, to brawl. ~*v.t.* (*N Am.*) to herd (cattle or horses). ~*n.* an angry or noisy dispute or quarrel, an altercation, a brawl. **wrangler** *n.* 1 a person who wrangles. 2 (*esp. N Am.*) a cowboy, herder or horsebreaker. 3 at Cambridge University, any of those who are placed in the first class in the mathematical tripos. **wranglership** *n.* [freq. from OE *wrang*, cogn. with WRING]

WRANS *abbr.* Women's Royal Australian Naval Service.

wrap (rap) *v.t.* (*pres.p.* **wrapping,** *past, p.p.* **wrapped**) 1 to fold or arrange so as to cover or enclose something. 2 to enfold, envelop, muffle, pack or surround in some soft material. 3 to hide, to conceal, to disguise. 4 (*Comput.*) to move (a word etc.) from the end of one line to the beginning of the next. ~*v.i.* 1 to fold, to lap. 2 (*Comput.*) to be wrapped. ~*n.* something intended to wrap, such as a cloak, shawl, wrapping paper etc. **to take the wraps off** to reveal or disclose. **to wrap around one's little finger** FINGER. **to wrap round** (*sl.*) to crash (a car etc.) into (*He wrapped his bike round a tree*). **to wrap up** 1 to fold paper etc. round (*to wrap up a present*). 2 to dress warmly. 3 to bring to a conclusion. 4 (*usu. in p.p.*) to absorb, to engross (*wrapped up in her work*). 5 (*usu. imper., sl.*) to be quiet. **under wraps** secret, in secrecy. **wraparound** *a.* 1 (of a garment) designed to be wrapped round the body. 2 (of a windscreen etc.) curving round at the sides. ~*n.* 1 something that wraps or is wrapped round. 2 (*Comput.*) **a** a facility that treats a linear sequence of screen positions etc. as a continuous series. **b** word wrap. **wrap-over** *a.* (of a skirt etc.) designed to be wrapped round the body and fastened with the open edges overlapping. ~*n.* such a skirt etc. **wrappage** *n.* 1 the act of wrapping. 2 that which wraps or envelops, a wrapping or wrappings. **wrapped** *a.* 1 that has been wrapped (*wrapped sweets*). 2 finished. 3 (*Austral., coll.*) delighted, rapt. **wrapper** *n.* 1 a person who wraps. 2 that in which anything is wrapped, esp. an outer covering for a new book, for a newspaper for posting etc. 3 a woman's loose outer garment for indoor wear. 4 the tobacco leaf forming the outer part of a cigar. **wrapping** *n.* 1 that which wraps. 2 (*often pl.*) that in which something is wrapped or packaged. 3 a wrapper, a cloak, a shawl, a rug. **wrapping paper** *n.* paper used to wrap parcels, esp. decorative paper for wrapping gifts. [perh. rel. to WARP]

wrasse (ras) *n.* a sea fish of the family Labridae, having thick lips and strong teeth. [cp. Welsh *gwrachen*]

wrath (roth) *n.* (*poet.*) 1 deep or violent anger, indignation, rage. 2 †impetuosity. **wrathful** *a.* **wrathfully** *adv.* **wrathfulness** *n.* **wrathless** *a.* **wrathy** *a.* (*N Am.*) wrathful. **wrathily** *adv.* [OE *wrætho*, from *wrāth*, WROTH]

wreak (rēk) *v.t.* 1 to carry out, to inflict, to execute (*to wreak vengeance*). 2 to cause (*to wreak havoc*). 3 to vent, express or satisfy (*to wreak one's anger*). 4 †to avenge. **wreaker** *n.* [OE *wrecan* (cp. Dut. *wrecken*, G *rächen*, Icel. *reka*), cogn. with L *urgēre*, to urge, Gr. *eirgein*, to shut in, and WRACK, WRECK]

wreath (rēth) *n.* (*pl.* **wreaths** (rēdhz, rēths)) 1 a band or ring of flowers or leaves tied, woven or twisted together for wearing on the head, decorating statues, walls, graves etc. 2 a representation of this in wood, stone etc. 3 a similar ring of twisted silk etc. 4 a ring, a twist, a curl (of cloud, smoke etc.). 5 a garland, a chaplet. 6 (*Her.*) a representation of a wreath below a crest. **wreathless** *a.* **wreathlike** *a.* [OE *wrǣth*, cogn. with WRITHE]

wreathe (rēdh) *v.t.* 1 to form (flowers, leaves etc.) into a wreath. 2 to surround, encircle, entwine (as if) with a wreath or with anything twisted. 3 to decorate with a wreath. ~*v.i.* 1 to be curled, folded or entwined (round etc.). 2 (of smoke etc.) to move in twists or curls. **wreather** *n.*

wreck (rek) *n.* 1 destruction, ruin, esp. of a ship. 2 a vessel dashed against rocks or otherwise destroyed, seriously crippled or shattered. 3 the remains of anything irretrievably shattered or ruined. 4 a dilapidated or worn-out person or thing (*a nervous wreck*). 5 wreckage. 6 (*Law*) goods etc. cast ashore from a wreck. ~*v.t.* 1 to ruin or destroy. 2 to destroy or shatter (a vessel etc.) by collision, driving ashore etc. 3 to involve in shipwreck. ~*v.i.* 1 to suffer shipwreck. 2 (*N Am.*) to demolish or break up wrecked vehicles etc. **wreckage** *n.* 1 the debris, remnants or material from a wreck. 2 the act of wrecking or the state of being wrecked. **wrecker** *n.* 1 a person who wrecks. 2 a person who causes shipwreck, esp. one who lures vessels to shipwreck with intent to plunder. **3** a plunderer from wrecks. **4** a person or ship employed in recovering a wreck or a wrecked cargo. **5** a person, vehicle, train etc. that removes wreckage. **6** (*esp. N Am.*) a recovery vehicle. **7** (*N Am.*) a person who demolishes or breaks up damaged vehicles etc. **wreck-master** *n.* an official appointed to take charge of goods etc. cast ashore after a shipwreck. [OE *wræc*, expulsion, perh. modified in sense through Icel. *rek*, anything cast ashore (cp. Dut. *wrak*), cogn. with WREAK]

Wren (ren) *n.* (*Hist.*) a member of the Women's Royal Naval Service. [from abbr. *WRNS*]

wren (ren) *n.* **1** a small songbird of the family Troglodytidae, esp. *Troglodytes troglodytes*, with a short erect tail and short wings. **2** any of various warblers or other birds resembling the wren. [OE *wrenna* (cp. Icel. *rindill*)]

wrench (rench) *n.* **1** a violent twist or sideways pull. **2** an injury caused by twisting, a sprain. **3** pain or distress caused by a parting, loss etc. **4** a tool for twisting or untwisting screws, bolts, nuts etc., a spanner. ~*v.t.* **1** to pull, wrest or twist with force or violence. **2** to pull (off or away) thus. **3** to strain, to sprain. **4** to pervert, to distort. [OE *wrenc* (deceit, guile, cp. G *Rank*), cogn. with WRONG, WRINKLE[1]]

wrest (rest) *v.t.* **1** to pull or wrench (away) forcibly. **2** to take or obtain (from) with force, effort or difficulty. **3** to twist, to turn aside by a violent effort. **4** to pervert, to distort, to twist or deflect from its natural meaning. ~*n.* **1** a violent wrench or twist. **2** †a turning instrument, esp. a tuning-key for a harp etc. **wrest-block, wrest-plank** *n.* the part of a piano or harpsichord in which the wrest-pins are embedded. **wrester** *n.* **wrest-pin** *n.* in a piano or harpsichord, any of the pins to which the strings are attached. [OE *wrǣstan* (cp. Icel. *reista*, Dan. *vriste*), cogn. with WRITHE, WRIST]

wrestle (res´əl) *v.i.* **1** to fight by grappling with and trying to throw one's opponent, esp. in a sporting contest under recognized rules. **2** to struggle, to contend, to strive vehemently (with). ~*v.t.* **1** to contend with in a wrestling match. **2** to move with difficulty, to manhandle. ~*n.* **1** a sporting contest in which two opponents wrestle, a wrestling match. **2** a struggle. **wrestler** *n.* **wrestling** *n.* [freq. of WREST]

wretch (rech) *n.* **1** a miserable or unfortunate person. **2** a despicable, mean or contemptible person. **wretched** (-id) *a.* (*comp.* **wretcheder,** *superl.* **wretchedest**) **1** miserable, unhappy, sunk in deep affliction or distress. **2** calamitous, pitiable. **3** worthless, poor, contemptible. **4** extremely unsatisfactory or unpleasant. **to feel wretched 1** to feel ill. **2** to feel embarrassed or ashamed. **wretchedly** *adv.* **wretchedness** *n.* [OE *wrecca*, an outcast, from *wrecan*, to drive out, to WREAK]

wrick (rik) *v.t.* to sprain or strain. ~*n.* a sprain or strain. [ME *wricke*, from MLG *wricken*, to move about, to sprain]

wrier, wriest WRY.

wriggle (rig´əl) *v.i.* **1** to turn, twist or move the body to and fro with short motions. **2** to move or go (along, in, out etc.) with writhing contortions or twistings. **3** to manoeuvre by clever or devious means. ~*v.t.* **1** to move (one's body etc.) with a wriggling motion. **2** to make (one's way etc.) by wriggling. ~*n.* a wriggling motion. **to wriggle out of** (*coll.*) to evade, avoid or shirk. **wriggler** *n.* **wriggly** *a.* [freq. of obs. *wrīg* (cp. Dut. *wriggelen*, LG *wriggeln*), cogn. with WRICK and WRY, WRING]

wright (rīt) *n.* a person who is occupied in making, building, repairing or creating something (*usu. in comb.*, as *shipwright, wheelwright*). [OE *wyrhta*, from *wyrht*, work, from *wyrcan*, WORK]

wring (ring) *v.t.* (*past, p.p.* **wrung** (rŭng)) **1** to twist and squeeze or compress (*to wring the neck of a chicken*). **2** to turn, twist or strain forcibly. **3** to twist, press or squeeze (out) thus (*to wring out a cloth*; *to wring water out of a cloth*). **4** to pain, to torture, to distress. **5** to extract, to extort. ~*n.* an act of wringing, a twist, a press, a squeeze. **to wring one's hands** to press one's hands together convulsively, as in great distress. **to wring someone's hand** to clasp or squeeze someone's hand with great force or emotion. **wringer** *n.* **1** a person or thing that wrings. **2** a wringing machine, a mangle. **to put someone through the wringer** to cause someone to undergo a difficult or stressful experience. **wringing** *n., a.* **wringing machine** *n.* a machine for wringing water out of newly-washed clothes etc. **wringing wet** *a.* so wet that moisture can be wrung out. [OE *wringan* (cp. Dut. *wringen*, G *ringen*), cogn. with WRIGGLE]

wrinkle[1] (ring´kəl) *n.* **1** a small ridge, crease or furrow caused by the folding or contraction of a flexible surface. **2** such a crease or furrow in the skin, esp. as a result of age. ~*v.t., v.i.* to fold or contract into furrows, creases or ridges. **wrinkly** *a.* (*comp.* **wrinklier,** *superl.* **wrinkliest**) marked with wrinkles, having many wrinkles. ~*n.* (*pl.* **wrinklies**) (*sl., derog.*) an old person. [OE *gewrinclod*, p.p. of *wrinclian*, to wind round]

wrinkle[2] (ring´kəl) *n.* (*coll.*) a useful bit of information or advice, a bright idea, a tip, a dodge. [dim. of OE *wrenc*, trick, cogn. with WRENCH and WRINKLE[1]]

wrist (rist) *n.* **1** the joint uniting the hand with the forearm. **2** the part of a sleeve over the wrist. **3** a wrist-pin. **4** wrist-work. **wristband** *n.* a band or part of a sleeve, esp. a shirtsleeve, covering the wrist; a cuff. **wrist-drop** *n.* paralysis of the muscles of the forearm, as through lead poisoning. **wristlet** *n.* **1** a band worn round the wrist to strengthen it, hold up a glove, carry a watch etc. **2** a bracelet. **wrist-pin** *n.* a pin or stud projecting from a crank for a connecting rod to turn on. **wristwatch** *n.* a watch worn on a strap round the wrist. **wrist-work** *n.* the act or technique of causing the hand to work with little or no movement of the arm, as in fencing and other sports. **wristy** *a.* (of a shot or style of play in cricket, tennis, golf etc.) making much use of the wrist or wrists. [OE, from *wrīthan*, WRITHE (cp. Icel., G *Rist*, Dan., Swed. *vrist*, instep)]

writ[1] (rit) *n.* **1** a written command or precept issued by a court in the name of the sovereign to an officer or other person commanding them to do or refrain from doing some particular specified act (*to serve a writ on someone*). **2** a document ordering the election of a Member of Parliament, summoning a peer to Parliament etc. **3** †that which is written, a writing. **someone's writ runs** someone has the specified authority. **writ of error** *n.* (*Law*) a writ or order for reviewing the proceedings of an inferior court on the ground of error. **writ of possession** *n.* an order directing a sheriff to put a person in possession. [OE *gewrit*, a writing, cogn. with WRITE]

†**writ**[2] WRITE.

write (rīt) *v.t.* (*past* **wrote** (rōt), †**writ** (rit), *p.p.* **written** (rit´ən), †**writ**) **1** to form or trace (words, a sentence etc.) in letters or symbols, with a pen, pencil or the like on paper or other material. **2** to trace (signs, characters etc.) thus. **3** to set (down), record, describe, state or convey by writing. **4** to compose or produce as an author. **5** to cover or fill with writing (*to write a cheque*). **6** (*usu. pass.*) to impress or stamp (guilt etc.) on a person's face. **7** (*esp. N Am., coll.*) to send a letter to. **8** to communicate in writing. **9** (*Comput.*) to record (data) in a storage device. **10** to state in writing. **11** to underwrite. **12** to include (in) or introduce (into) in writing. **13** †to designate, to call, to put (oneself down as etc.) in writing. ~*v.i.* **1** to trace letters or symbols representing words on paper etc. **2** to write or send a letter (to). **3** to compose or produce articles, books etc. as an author or journalist (*to write for a newspaper*). **nothing/ not much to write home about** HOME[1]. **to write down 1** to put in writing, to record. **2** to depreciate, to criticize unfavourably in writing. **3** to write in such a way as to appeal to low standards of taste, intelligence etc. **4** in accounting, to reduce the book value of. **to write in 1** to send a letter, request, query, suggestion etc. to a magazine, radio station etc. **2** (*N Am.*) to add (a name) to a ballot paper when voting. **to write off 1** to write and send a letter etc. **2** to cancel (a debt etc.) from a written record. **3** to consider (a loss etc.) as irrecoverable. **4** to damage (a car) beyond repair. **5** to discard as useless, insignificant etc. **6** to compose rapidly and easily. **to write oneself out** to exhaust one's powers of literary production. **to write out 1** to write the whole of. **2** to write in finished form. **3** to remove (a character, episode etc.) from a drama series, book etc. **to write up 1** to praise in writing. **2** to bring (a diary, account book etc.) up to date. **3** to give full details of in writing. **writ large 1** set down or recorded in large letters. **2** magnified, emphasized, very obvious, on a large scale. **writable** *a.* **write-down** *n.* in accounting, the act of reducing the book value of stocks, assets etc. **write-in** *n.* (*N Am.*) the act of adding a name to a ballot paper. **write-off** *n.* something written off, esp. a badly damaged car. **writer** *n.* **1** a person who writes. **2** an author, a journalist etc. **3** a clerk, an amanuensis. **4** (*Sc.*) a solicitor, an attorney. **writerly** *a.* **1** characteristic of an accomplished writer. **2** literary. **writer's block** *n.* a total lack of ideas, inspiration or creativity affecting a writer, usu. temporarily. **writer's cramp** *n.* a spasmodic pain in the fingers or hand caused by prolonged writing. **writership** *n.* **Writer to the Signet** *n.* (*Sc.*) a solicitor. **write-up** *n.* (*coll.*) **1** a review. **2** a written account. **writing** *n.* **1** the act of a person who writes. **2** that which is written. **3** handwriting. **4** a book, article or other literary composition. **5** an inscription. **6** a legal instrument. **in writing** in written form. **the writing on the wall** a solemn warning (Dan. v.5). **the Writings** the Hagiographa. **writing case** *n.* a case for writing materials etc. **writing desk** *n.* a desk with space for papers etc. **writing pad** *n.* a number of sheets of writing paper fastened together at the edge. **writing paper** *n.* paper with a smooth surface for writing on. **writing table** *n.* a table designed for writing at, usu. with a kneehole, drawers etc. [OE *wrītan* (cp. Dut. *rijten*, G *reissen*, Icel. *rīta*, to tear, cut, draw, scratch out etc.)]

writhe (rīdh) *v.i.* **1** to twist, turn or roll the body about, as in pain. **2** to shrink, to squirm (at, with shame etc.). *~v.t.* to twist or distort (the limbs etc.). *~n.* an act of writhing. **writhingly** *adv.* [OE *wrīthan* (cp. Icel. *rītha*, Dan. *vride*, OHG *rīdan*)]

writing, written WRITE.

WRNS *abbr.* (*Hist.*) Women's Royal Naval Service.

wrong (rong) *a.* **1** false, inaccurate, incorrect, mistaken, erroneous. **2** not that which is required, intended, proper, best etc. **3** not morally right, contrary to morality, conscience or law, wicked. **4** out of order, in bad condition etc. **5** not according to truth or reality. *~adv.* **1** wrongly. **2** unjustly. *~n.* **1** that which is wrong. **2** a wrong act, an injustice, an injury or hurt. **3** deviation from what is right. **4** wrongness, error. *~v.t.* **1** to treat unjustly, to do wrong to. **2** to impute evil motives to unjustly. **born on the wrong side of the blanket** BLANKET. **in the wrong 1** guilty, responsible. **2** in error. **in the wrong box** BOX[1]. **on the wrong side of** more than, esp. in age (*on the wrong side of forty*). **on the wrong tack** TACK[1]. **on the wrong track** TRACK. **the wrong side of the tracks** an undesirable or less prestigious area, esp. of a town or city (*to live on the wrong side of the tracks*). **to catch on the wrong foot** FOOT. **to do wrong** to commit a crime, sin etc. **to do wrong to** to mistreat. **to get in wrong with** (*coll.*) to get on the wrong side of. **to get off on the wrong foot** FOOT. **to get on the wrong side of** to fall into disfavour with. **to get out of bed on the wrong side** BED. **to get wrong 1** to misunderstand (*Don't get me wrong, I'm not criticizing you*). **2** to fail to give or obtain the correct answer to. **to go down the wrong way** (of food or drink) to pass into the windpipe instead of the gullet. **to go wrong 1** to fail morally, to fall into sin. **2** to fail to operate correctly. **3** to fall into error. **4** to take the wrong road, path etc. **wrong side out** inside out. **wrong way round** back to front, in reverse of the proper sequence. **wrongdoer** *n.* a person who does wrong. **wrongdoing** *n.* **wrong end of the stick** *n.* the contrary to what is meant. **wronger** *n.* **wrong font** *n.* (*Print.*) an error in which type of the wrong font, size or pattern is used. **wrong-foot** *v.t.* (*coll.*) **1** to cause to be off balance. **2** to gain an advantage over. **3** to take by surprise, to catch unprepared. **wrongful** *a.* **1** injurious, unjust, wrong. **2** illegal. **3** not entitled to the position held. **wrongfully** *adv.* **wrongfulness** *n.* **wrong-headed** *a.* perverse, obstinate. **wrong-headedly** *adv.* **wrong-headedness** *n.* †**wrongless** *a.* †**wronglessly** *adv.* **wrongly** *adv.* **wrongness** *n.* **wrong number** *n.* **1** a telephone number wrongly dialled or connected. **2** the resulting telephone call, the person making it or the person contacted. **wrong side** *n.* the side (of fabric, paper etc.) not intended for use. **wrong'un** *n.* (*coll.*) **1** a bad person. **2** in cricket, a googly. [OE *wrang*, a wrong thing, from Scand. (cp. Icel. *rangr*, awry, Dan. *vrang*, wrong), cogn. with WRING]

wrot (rot) *n.* wrought timber. [WROUGHT[1]]

wrote WRITE.

wroth (rōth, roth) *a.* (*poet.*) angry, wrathful. [OE *wrāth*, perverted, from *wrīthan*, WRITHE, (cp. Dut. *wread*, Icel. *reithr*)]

wrought[1] (rawt) *a.* **1** worked, formed or fashioned (*often in comb.*, as *well-wrought*). **2** decorated or ornamented. **3** (of metal) shaped by hammering or bending. **4** (of timber) planed on one or more sides. **wrought iron** *n.* **1** iron made malleable by having non-metallic impurities burned out of it. **2** iron made malleable by forging or rolling. **wrought-up** *a.* very tense or excited. [archaic p.p. of WORK]

wrought[2] WORK.

wrung WRING.

WRVS *abbr.* Women's Royal Voluntary Service.

wry (rī) *a.* (*comp.* **wryer, wrier**, *superl.* **wryest, wriest**) **1** twisted, distorted, crooked. **2** showing distaste, disgust, mockery etc. (*a wry smile*). **3** (of humour) dry or sardonic. **4** wrong, false, perverted. **to make a wry mouth** MOUTH[1]. **wrybill** *n.* a species of plover, *Anarhynchus frontalis*, with a twisted bill. **wryly** *adv.* **wrymouth** *n.* an eel-like sea fish with a vertical mouth. **wryneck** *n.* **1** any bird of the genus *Jynx*, allied to the woodpeckers, with a habit of twisting its head round as if on a pivot. **2** a stiff neck, torticollis. **wryness** *n.* [ME *wrien*, OE *wrigian*, cogn. with WRIGGLE]

WSW *abbr.* west-south-west.

wt. *abbr.* weight.

Wu (woo) *n.* a dialect of Chinese spoken around the Yangtze delta. [Chin.]

wunderkind (vun´dəkint) *n.* (*pl.* **wunderkinds, wunderkinder** (-kində)) (*coll.*) **1** a child prodigy. **2** a person who is outstandingly successful or clever at a relatively young age. [G *Wunder*, wonder, *Kind*, child]

wurst (vœst, vuəst, w-) *n.* a type of large German or Austrian sausage. [G]

wuss (wus) *n.* (*esp. N Am., sl.*) a weak or cowardly person. **wussy** *n.* (*pl.* **wussies**) a wuss. *~a.* weak or cowardly. [etym. unknown]

WV *abbr.* **1** West Virginia. **2** (Windward Islands) St Vincent (IVR).

W.Va. *abbr.* West Virginia.

WVS *abbr.* (*Hist.*) Women's Voluntary Service.

WW *abbr.* World War.

WWF *abbr.* **1** Worldwide Fund for Nature (formerly World Wildlife Fund). **2** World Wrestling Federation.

WWW *abbr.* World Wide Web.

WX *abbr.* women's extra large size.

WY *abbr.* Wyoming.

Wyandot (wīˊəndot) *n.* (*pl.* **Wyandots, Wyandot**) **1** a member of a N American Indian people from Ontario. **2** the language of this people. **3** (*also* **Wyandotte**) a breed of domestic fowl. ~*a.* of or relating to the Wyandots or their language.

wych (wich) *a.* (*attrib.*) drooping. **wych elm** *n.* a rough-leaved Eurasian elm, *Ulmus montana.* **wych hazel** *n.* WITCH HAZEL (under WITCH[2]). [OE *wice*, cogn. with WICKER]

Wycliffite (wikˊlifit) *a.* of or relating to Wycliffe, his tenets or his followers. ~*n.* a follower of Wycliffe, a Lollard. [John *Wycliffe*, *c.* 1330–84, English ecclesiastical reformer and Lollard]

Wykehamist (wikˊəmist) *n.* a member (past or present) of Winchester College. ~*a.* of or relating to this college. [William of *Wykeham*, 1324–1404, Bishop of Winchester, who founded the college]

wyn WEN[2].

wynd (wīnd) *n.* (*Sc., North.*) an alley. [prob. var. of WIND[2]]

Wyo. *abbr.* Wyoming.

WYSIWYG (wizˊiwig), **wysiwyg** *a.* (*Comput.*) denoting or relating to a computer or word processor which can print out exactly what is shown on the screen. [*w*hat *y*ou *s*ee *i*s *w*hat *y*ou *g*et]

wyvern (wīˊvən), **wivern** *n.* (*Her.*) a two-legged dragon with erect wings and barbed tail. [OE *wyvre*, OF *wivre*, L *vīpera*, VIPER (cp. *-n* in BITTERN[1])]

X (eks), **x** (*pl.* **Xs, X's**) the 24th letter of the English and other versions of the Roman alphabet, corresponding to the Greek xi (Ξ, ξ). It has three principal sounds: (1) *ks*, medially and finally, as in *axis, tax*; (2) *gz*, medially, as in *exhaust, exult*; (3) *z*, initially, chiefly in words of Greek origin, as in *xylophone*. *~symbol* **1** the first unknown quantity or variable in an algebraic expression. **2** 10 in Roman numerals (xx 20, xxx 30, xc 90). **3** an unknown thing or person. **4** Christ, Christian (first letter of Christ in Greek). **5** a kiss. **6** an error. **7** a choice. **8** before 1983, a film for over-18-year-olds only. **9** the strength of ale etc., as in *XX* (double X), *XXX* (triple X), *XXXX* (four X). **x-axis** *n.* the horizontal axis, along which coordinates of the first unknown quantity are plotted in graphs, histograms etc. **X chromosome** *n.* (*Biol.*) a sex chromosome which is found paired in women, and paired with the Y chromosome in men. **X-rated** *a.* **1** (of films etc.) indecent, pornographic, excessively violent. **2** (*Hist.*) relating to films given an X classification prior to 1983. **X-ray, x-ray** *n.* **1** an electromagnetic ray of very short wavelength, used in producing a photographic image of internal parts of the body, such as organs or bones, and used in medical diagnosis. **2** a picture thus produced. *~v.t.* **1** to produce such an image of (part of the body). **2** to treat with X-rays. **X-ray astronomy** *n.* the branch of astronomy concerned with the observation of celestial bodies by detecting and measuring their X-ray emissions. **X-ray crystallography** *n.* the study of crystal structure through the diffraction pattern produced by X-rays. **X-ray tube** *n.* an evacuated tube in which electrons are beamed on to a metal target to produce X-rays.

-x (z) *suf.* forming the plural of many nouns from French, as in *plateaux, beaux*.

xanth- XANTHO-.

xanthate (zan´thāt) *n.* a salt or ester of xanthic acid.

xanthein (zan´thiin) *n.* the part of the yellow colouring matter of flowers that is soluble in water.

xanthic (zan´thik) *a.* of a yellowish colour. **xanthic acid** *n.* (*Chem.*) a colourless oily liquid, prepared by decomposing potassium xanthate with sulphuric or hydrochloric acid. **xanthine** (-thēn, -thīn), **xanthin** (-thin) *n.* **1** the part of the yellow colouring matter of flowers that is insoluble in water. **2** a yellow colouring matter obtained from madder. **3** a crystalline compound found in blood, urine, the liver etc. **4** a gaseous product of the decomposition of xanthate. [XANTHO-]

Xanthippe (zanthip´i), **Xantippe** (-tip´i) *n.* a shrewish, quarrelsome or nagging woman. [name of Socrates' wife]

xanthium (zan´thiəm) *n.* any hardy composite plant of the genus *Xanthium*. [Gr. *xanthion*]

xantho- (zan´thō), **xanth-** *comb. form* yellow. [Gr. *xanthos*]

xanthochroism (zanthōkrō´izm) *n.* (*Zool.*) a condition where all skin pigments apart from yellow disappear, as in some goldfish. **xanthochroi** (-thok´rōī) *n.pl.* fair whites or blonds, people having yellow or red hair, blue eyes and a fair complexion. **xanthochroic, xanthochroous** *a.*

xanthoma (zanthō´mə) *n.* (*pl.* **xanthomas, xanthomata** (-tə)) (*Med.*) **1** a skin disease characterized by a growth of yellowish tubercles, usu. in flat patches, on the eyelids. **2** such a patch.

xanthophyll (zan´thəfil) *n.* the yellow carotenoid pigment of withered leaves. **xanthophyllous** (-thof´-) *a.* [Gr. *phullon*, leaf]

xanthous (zan´thəs) *a.* belonging to one of the peoples having yellowish hair and a light complexion, xanthochroic.

x.d. *abbr.* ex dividend.

Xe *chem. symbol* xenon.

xebec (zē´bek), **zebec, zebeck** *n.* a small three-masted vessel with lateen and square sails, used in the Mediterranean. [Sp. *xabeque* (cp. Port. *zabeco*, F *chebdec*, It. *sciabecco*), Turk. *sumbakī*, cp. Arab. *sumbūk*]

xeno- (zen´ō), **xen-** *comb. form* **1** strange, foreign; foreigner. **2** other. [Gr. *xenos*, strange, stranger]

xenogamy (zenog´əmi) *n.* (*Bot.*) cross-fertilization. **xenogamous** *a.*

xenogenesis (zenōjen´əsis) *n.* the (imagined) production of offspring completely unlike either parent, heterogenesis.

xenoglossia (zenōglos´iə) *n.* in psychical research, the knowledge of a language one has not learned, claimed by some mediums.

xenograft (zen´ōgrahft) *n.* (*Biol.*) a tissue graft from a member of a different species, a heterograft.

xenolith (zen´əlith) *n.* (*Geol.*) a fragment of rock enclosed in a different type of rock.

xenomorphic (zenōmaw´fik) *a.* (*Geol.*) not having its characteristic crystal form but an irregular shape due to surrounding minerals.

xenon (zen´ən) *n.* (*Chem.*) an inert gaseous element, at. no. 54, chem. symbol Xe, found in the atmosphere and solidifying at the temperature of liquid air.

xenophile (zen´əfīl) *n.* a person who likes foreign people and things.

xenophobia (zenəfō´biə) *n.* fear or hatred of strangers or foreigners. **xenophobe** (zen´-) *n.* **xenophobic** *a.*

xer- XERO-.

xeransis (ziəran´sis) *n.* the state of drying up or being dried up, desiccation. **xerantic** *a.*

xeranthemum (ziəran´thiməm) *n.* an annual plant of the genus *Xeranthemum*, with everlasting flowers. [Gr. *anthemon, anthos*, flower]

xeric (ziə´rik, zer´-) *a.* (of a habitat) very dry. [XERO-, -IC]

xero- (ziə´rō), **xer-** *comb. form* dry. [Gr. *xēros*, dry]

xeroderma (ziərōdœ´mə), **xerodermia** (-miə) *n.* (*Med.*) an abnormal dryness of the skin. **xerodermatic** (-mat´-), **xerodermatous** *a.* [Gr. *derma*, skin]

xerography (ziərog´rəfi) *n.* a photographic process in which the plate is sensitized electrically, and the latent image developed by a resinous powder. **xerograph** (ziə´rōgrahf) *n.* a copy produced in this way. **xerographic** (-graf´-) *a.* **xerographically** *adv.*

xerophilous (ziərof´iləs, zer-) *a.* (*Bot.*) (of a plant) adapted to living in a hot, dry climate. **xerophile** (ziə´rəfīl) *n.* **xerophily** (-li) *n.*

xerophthalmia (ziərofthal´miə) *n.* (*Med.*) a dry inflammation of the lining membrane of the eye, caused by a deficiency of vitamin A. **xerophthalmic** *a.*

xerophyte (ziə´rōfīt, zer´-) *n.* a plant adapted to living in a region of little moisture, such as a cactus, a xerophile. **xerophytic** (-fit´-) *a.* **xerophytism** *n.*

xerosis (ziərō´sis), **xerotes** (ziə´rətēz) *n.* (*Med.*) abnormal dryness of certain parts of the body. **xerotic** (-rot´-) *a.*

xerostomia (ziərəstō´miə) *n.* (*Med.*) abnormal dryness of the mouth.

xerotes, xerotic XEROSIS.

Xerox® (ziə´roks) *n.* **1** a xerographic copying process. **2** the copy produced by this process. **3** the machine used for this process. **xerox** *v.t.* to produce a copy of (an original document) by this process.

Xhosa (kō´sə, kaw´-) *n.* (*pl.* **Xhosa, Xhosas**) **1** a member of one of the Bantu-speaking peoples in the Cape Province, S Africa. **2** their language, which is characterized by a sound system involving a series of clicks. *~a.* of or relating to the Xhosa or their language. **Xhosan** *a.*

xi (zī, ksī, sī, ksē) *n.* the 14th letter of the Greek alphabet (Ξ, ξ).

Xian *abbr.* Christian.

-xion (kshən) *suf.* used to form nouns from Latin participial stems in -x-, usu. involving action, as *crucifixion, connexion*.

xiphoid (zī´foid) *a.* (*Biol.*) sword-shaped. *~n.* (*Anat.*) the xiphoid process. **xiphoid process, xiphisternum** (zifistœ´nəm) *n.* (*Anat.*) the cartilaginous process at the lowermost part of the sternum.

Xmas (eks´məs, kris´-) *n.* (*coll.*) Christmas.

xoanon (zō´ənon) *n.* (*pl.* **xoana** (-nə)) a primitive carved image of a god, supposed by ancient Greeks to have fallen from heaven. [Gr., from *xeō*, to carve]

xu (soo) *n.* (*pl.* **xu**) a unit of currency in Vietnam, equal to one-hundredth of a dong.

xyl- XYLO-.

xylem (zī´ləm) *n.* (*Bot.*) woody tissue, wood parenchyma, as opposed to *phloem*.

xylene (zī´lēn) *n.* (*Chem.*) any one of three isomeric colourless, volatile, liquid hydrocarbons distilled from coal or wood tar. [-ENE]

xylo- (zī´lō), **xyl-** *comb. form* relating to wood. [Gr. *xulon*, wood]

xylocarp (zī´lōkahp) *n.* (*Bot.*) a hard, woody fruit such as the coconut, or a tree bearing this. **xylocarpous** (-kah´-) *a.* [Gr. *karpos*, fruit]

xylograph (zī´ləgrahf) *n.* **1** a woodcut or engraving, esp. in a primitive style, or an impression from one. **2** an impression obtained from the grain of wood used for surface decoration. **xylographer** (-log´rə-) *n.* **xylographic** (-graf´-) *a.* **xylography** (-log´rə-) *n.*

xyloid (zī´loid) *a.* (*Bot.*) of or resembling wood, ligneous.

xyloidine (zī´loidīn) *n.* a high explosive prepared by the action of nitric acid on starch or wood fibre.

Xylonite® (zī´lənīt) *n.* a type of celluloid.

xylophagous (zīlof´əgəs) *a.* (of insects) boring into wood.

xylophone (zī´ləfōn) *n.* (*Mus.*) an instrument consisting of a graduated series of wooden or metal bars vibrating when struck or rubbed. **xylophonic** (-fon´-) *a.* **xylophonist** (-lof´-) *n.*

xylose (zī´lōz) *n.* (*Chem.*) a white crystalline pentose found in wood and straw, wood sugar.

xylotomous (zīlot´əməs) *a.* (*Bot.*) (of an insect) eating wood.

xyster (zis´tə) *n.* (*Med.*) a surgeon's instrument for scraping bones. [Gr. *xustēr*, from *xuein*, to scrape]

xystus (zis´təs) *n.* (*pl.* **xysti** (-tī)) (*Hist.*) **1** a long covered portico or colonnade used for athletic exercises in ancient Greece. **2** a garden walk or terrace in ancient Rome. [L, from Gr. *xustos*, orig. polished, as XYSTER]

Y

Y[1] (wī), **y** (*pl.* **Ys, Y's**) the 25th letter of the English and other versions of the Roman alphabet, corresponding to the Greek upsilon (Υ, υ). It is pronounced both as a vowel and as a palatal semivowel: as a vowel it has the same value as *i*; at the beginning of syllables and followed by a vowel, it corresponds to the Latin *i* or *j*, as in *ye, you*. ~*symbol* the second unknown quantity or variable in an algebraic expression. ~*n.* a Y-shaped branch, pipe, fork, coupling, figure etc. **y-axis** *n.* the vertical axis along which coordinates of the second unknown quantity are plotted in graphs, histograms etc. **Y chromosome** *n.* (*Biol.*) a sex chromosome which is found paired with the X chromosome in men, and is not present at all in women. **Y-fronts®** *n.pl.* men's or boys' underpants with an inverted Y-shaped front opening. **Y-level** *n.* a surveying level mounted on a pair of Ys. **Y-moth** *n.* the gamma moth, from the Y-shaped mark on its wings.

Y[2] *chem. symbol* yttrium.

Y[3], **Y.** *abbr.* **1** yen. **2** (*N Am.*) YMCA, YWCA.

y *abbr.* years.

†**y-** (i) *pref.* forming past participles, collective nouns etc., as *yclept, ywis.* [ME, from OE *ge-*, cp. Dut. and G *ge-*, pref. of p.p. etc., cp. *a-* in *alike, among* etc.]

-y[1] (i) *suf.* **1** forming adjectives from nouns and adjectives, as *lucky, pricey.* **2** forming adjectives from verbs, as *wobbly.* [OE *-ig*]

-y[2] (i) *suf.* **1** forming abstract nouns etc., as *memory, remedy.* **2** forming nouns expressing action or result, as *army, treaty.* [L *-ius, -ia, -ium* (sometimes through F *-ie*); F *-é, ée*, L *-atus, -ata, -atum*, p.p. suf.]

-y[3] (i), **-ey, -ie** *suf.* forming diminutives, pet names etc., as *laddy, Jimmy, sonny, Mickey, nightie.* [ME, orig. Sc.]

yabber (yab´ə) *v.i.* (*Austral., New Zeal., coll.*) to talk, to chatter. ~*n.* Aboriginal talk. [Austral. Abor.]

yabby (yab´i), **yabbie** *n.* (*pl.* **yabbies**) (*Austral.*) **1** a freshwater crayfish of the genus *Charax.* **2** a burrowing prawn, used as bait, a nipper. [Austral. Abor.]

yacht (yot) *n.* **1** a light sailing vessel, esp. one designed for racing. **2** a power-driven vessel, used for pleasure trips, cruising, travel or as a state vessel to convey members of royalty or government officials. **3** a light vessel for travelling on sand or ice. ~*v.i.* to sail or cruise about in a yacht. **yacht-built** *a.* built on the lines of a yacht. **yacht club** *n.* a club for yacht racing etc. **yachter** *n.* a person sailing a yacht. **yachtie** *n.* (*coll.*) a yachter. **yachting** *n.* **yachtsman, yachtswoman** *n.* (*pl.* **yachtsmen, yachtswomen**) a person who keeps or sails a yacht. **yachtsmanship** *n.* [Dut. *jacht* (now *jagt*), from *jagen*, to hunt]

yack YAK[2].

yacka, yacker YAKKA.

yackety-yack YAK[2].

yaffle (yaf´əl) *n.* (*dial.*) the green woodpecker. [imit. of cry]

Yagara (yah´gərə) *n.* an Aboriginal language of Queensland, now extinct.

Yagi antenna (yah´gi, yag´i), **Yagi aerial** *n.* a highly directional aerial used for television, radio, radio astronomy etc., consisting of parallel elements fixed at right angles to a central bar that points in the direction of strongest reception. [H. *Yagi*, 1886–1976, Japanese engineer]

yah[1] (yah) *int.* used to express dismissal, scepticism or derision. [imit.]

yah[2] (yah) *int.* (*coll., esp. facet.*) yes. [imit.]

yahoo (yah´hoo, yəhoo´) *n.* (*pl.* **yahoos**) a coarse, brutish person, a lout. [coined by Jonathan Swift in *Gulliver's Travels* as the name for a race of brutes in human shape]

Yahweh (yah´wā), **Yahveh** (-vā), **Jahveh** *n.* the Hebrew name for God in the Old Testament, Jehovah. **Yahwist, Yahvist, Jahvist** *n.* the conjectured author of certain sources of the Pentateuch in which God is called Yahweh throughout. [Heb. *JHVH*]

yak[1] (yak) *n.* a long-haired ox, *Bos grunniens*, from the mountainous regions of Central Asia. [Tibetan *gyak*]

yak[2] (yak), **yack** *n.* noisy, unceasing, trivial chatter. ~*v.i.* (*pres.p.* **yakking, yacking,** *past, p.p.* **yakked, yacked**) to talk in this way. **yackety-yak** (yakəti-) *n.* trivial, persistent chatter. [imit.]

yakitori (yakitaw´ri) *n.* a Japanese dish of boneless chicken pieces, grilled on skewers and served with a thick sweet sauce. [Jap. *yaki*, grill, *tori*, bird]

yakka (yak´ə), **yacka, yacker** *n.* (*Austral., sl.*) work. [Austral. Abor.]

Yakut (yəkut´) *n.* (*pl.* **Yakuts, Yakut**) **1** a member of a mixed Turkic people living in the basin of the Lena, in E Siberia. **2** the language of this people. [local name]

Yale® (yāl), **Yale lock** *n.* a type of lock with a revolving barrel, turned by a flat key with a serrated edge. [Linus *Yale*, 1821–68, US inventor]

y'all YOU-ALL (under YOU).

yam (yam) *n.* **1** the fleshy edible tuber of various species of the genus *Dioscorea*, tropical climbers orig. from India. **2** the plant yielding this. **3** (*N Am.*) the sweet potato. [Port. *inhame*, from W Afr. word]

yamen (yah´men) *n.* (*Hist.*) the office or official residence of a Chinese mandarin. [Chin.]

yammer (yam´ə) *v.i.* (*coll.*) to cry out, to whine, to complain peevishly. ~*n.* **1** a complaint. **2** nonsense. **3** a whining sound. **yammerer** *n.* **yammering** *n., a.* [OE *gēomerian*, from *gēomor*, sad, mournful]

yandy (yan´di) *v.t.* (*3rd pers. sing. pres.* **yandies,** *pres.p.* **yandying,** *past, p.p.* **yandied**) (*Austral.*) to separate (seed) from other material by a particular form of shaking. ~*n.* (*pl.* **yandies**) the shallow dish used for this purpose. [Austral. Abor.]

yang (yang) *n.* the masculine, positive, bright principle in nature, according to Chinese philosophy, which interacts with its complement, *yin.* [Chin. *yang*, bright]

Yank (yangk) *n.* (*often derog.*) an American, a native or inhabitant of the US. [YANKEE]

yank (yangk) *v.t.* to pull sharply, to twitch, to jerk (off, out of etc.). ~*v.i.* to jerk vigorously. ~*n.* a sharp jerk, a twitch. [cp. Swed. dial. *jakka*, to wander, Icel. *jaga*, to move about, Dut. and G *jagen*, see YACHT]

Yankee (yang´ki) *n.* **1** (*sometimes derog.*) an American, a native or inhabitant of the US. **2** an inhabitant of New England or other Northern states. **3** (*Hist.*) a Federal soldier or Northerner in the American Civil War (1861–65). **4** a type of multiple bet on four or more horses in different races. ~*a.* of or relating to America or the Yankees. **Yankeedom, Yankeeism** *n.* **Yankee Doodle** *n.* **1** a tune (probably of English origin) and song regarded as a national air of the US. **2** an

American. **Yankeefied** (-fīd) *a.* [perh. from Dut. *Janke*, dim. of *Jan*, John]

yap (yap) *v.i.* (*pres.p.* **yapping**, *past, p.p.* **yapped**) **1** to yelp or bark snappishly. **2** to talk constantly in a shrill, foolish manner. **3** to scold. ~*n.* **1** a snappish yelp or bark. **2** foolish chatter. **yapper** *n.* **yappy** *a.* (*comp.* **yappier**, *superl.* **yappiest**). [imit.]

yapok (yap´ək) *n.* a small opossum, *Chironectes minimus*, with webbed hind feet and aquatic habits. [*Oyapok*, river separating Guiana from Brazil]

yapon YAUPON.

yapp (yap) *n.* a style of bookbinding, usu. in leather, with flaps at the edges. [William *Yapp*, 1854–75, London bookseller]

yarborough (yah´bərə) *n.* in whist, bridge etc., a hand containing no card higher than a nine. [2nd Earl of *Yarborough*, who bet £1000 that no one could hold such a hand]

yard[1] (yahd) *n.* **1** a unit of length, 3 ft. or 36 in. (0.9144 m). **2** a measuring rod of this length, or this length of material. **3** (*Naut.*) a cylindrical spar tapering each way from the middle slung horizontally or slantwise on a mast to extend a sail. **4** a square yard, a cubic yard. **5** (*pl., coll.*) great lengths (of). **by the yard 1** in great quantities. **2** at great length. **yardage**[1] (-dij) *n.* an amount of material in cubic yards. **yardarm** *n.* (*Naut.*) either half of a sailyard from the centre to the end. **yard of ale** *n.* **1** a tall, narrow drinking glass for beer or ale. **2** the amount of beer or ale in such a glass. **yardstick** *n.* **1** a known and trusted entity against which to assess other things. **2** a stick, 3 ft. in length and usu. graduated in feet, inches etc. used for measuring. [OE *gyrd*, *gerd*, stick, cp. Dut. *garde*, G *Gerte*]

yard[2] (yahd) *n.* **1** a small piece of enclosed ground, esp. adjoining or enclosed by a house or other building. **2** such an enclosure used for some specified manufacture or other purpose, such as a dockyard, graveyard, timber yard etc. **3** a series of tracks near a railway used for the storage and maintenance of rolling stock. **4** (*N Am.*) a garden. ~*v.t.* to collect or pen (cattle etc.) in a yard. **the Yard** (*coll.*) SCOTLAND YARD. **yardage**[2] (-dij) *n.* **1** the use of a yard as a cattle enclosure. **2** the charge levied for such a use. **yardbird** *n.* (*N Am., sl.*) **1** a military recruit. **2** a convict. **Yardie** *n.* (*sl.*) a member of a W Indian gang etc., usu. associated with drug-dealing or related crime (from Jamaican Eng. use of *yard* to mean house, home). **yardman** *n.* (*pl.* **yardmen**) **1** a person employed in a railway yard, timber yard etc. **2** (*N Am.*) a household gardener, odd-job man etc. **yardmaster** *n.* the manager of a railway yard etc. [OE *geard* (cp. Dut. *gaard*, G *Garten*, Icel. *garthr*, L *hortus*, Gr. *chortos*), doublet of GARDEN]

yardage[1] YARD[1].

yardage[2] YARD[2].

†**yare** (yeə) *a.* (*comp.* **yarer**, *superl.* **yarest**) **1** ready, prepared. **2** quick, dexterous. **3** (*Naut.*) answering readily to the helm. ~*adv.* soon. **yarely** *adv.* quickly, smartly. [OE *gearu*, *gearo*, cp. Dut. *gaar*, Icel. *görr*, G *gar*, wholly, cogn. with GEAR]

yarmulke (yah´mulkə), **yarmulka** *n.* a skullcap worn all the time by Orthodox Jewish men, and during prayer by others. [Yiddish, from Ukrainian and Pol. *yarmulka*, small cap]

yarn (yahn) *n.* **1** any spun fibre prepared for weaving, knitting, rope-making etc. **2** (*coll.*) a long or rambling story, esp. one of doubtful truth or accuracy. ~*v.i.* to tell a yarn, to spin yarns. **yarn-dye** *v.t.* (*pres.p.* **yarn-dyeing**, *past, p.p.* **yarn-dyed**) to dye (the yarn) before it is spun or woven. **yarn-dyed** *a.* [OE *gearn* (cp. Dut. *garen*, G, Icel., Dan. and Swed. *garn*), cogn. with Gr. *chordē*, CORD]

yarran (yar´ən) *n.* any of several Australian acacias, esp. *Acacia omalophylla*, a small hardy tree used esp. for fencing, fuel and fodder. [Austral. Abor.]

yarrow (yar´ō) *n.* a perennial herb of the genus *Achillea*, esp. *A. millefolium*, the milfoil, with white flowers, a pungent odour and astringent properties. [OE *gæruwe* (cp. Dut. *gerw*, G *Garbe*), perh. cogn. with YARE]

yashmak (yash´mak) *n.* the veil worn by many Muslim women in public. [Arab.]

yataghan (yat´əgan) *n.* a Turkish sword or scimitar with a double-curved blade and without a guard or crosspiece. [Turk.]

yatter (yat´ə) *v.i.* (*coll.*) to talk at length, gossip, chatter, esp. irritatingly. [imit.]

yaupon (yaw´pən), **yapon** *n.* an evergreen shrub, *Ilex vomitoria*, growing in the southern US, the leaves of which are used to make a tea and by the Indians as an emetic and purgative medicine. [Am. Ind.]

yaw (yaw) *v.i.* (of a ship, aircraft etc.) to steer out of the direct course, to move unsteadily, esp. from side to side. ~*v.t.* to cause to deviate from its course. ~*n.* **1** an unsteady motion or temporary deviation from a course. **2** the motion of an aircraft about its vertical axis. **yawing** *n.* the unstable motion of an aircraft about its vertical axis. [Icel. *jaga*, to hunt, cp. Dut. and G *jagen*, see YACHT]

yawl[1] (yawl) *n.* **1** a small two-masted sailing boat with a small jigger mast towards the stern. **2** a small boat, esp. a ship's jollyboat. [Dut. *jol* (cp. Dan. *jolle*, Swed. *julle*), cp. JOLLY[2]]

yawl[2] (yawl) *v.i.* to howl, to yell, to yowl. ~*n.* a howl or yell, a yowl. [ME *goulen*, cp. Dut. *jolen*, Icel. and Norw. *gaula*, of imit. orig., cp. YELL]

yawn (yawn) *v.i.* **1** to open the mouth wide or to have the mouth open involuntarily through drowsiness, boredom, bewilderment etc., to stand agape. **2** to be or stand wide open. ~*v.t.* to express or utter with a yawn. ~*n.* **1** the act of yawning. **2** (*coll.*) something that is boring or tedious. **yawner** *n.* **yawning** *a., n.* **yawningly** *adv.* [OE *gānian*, *gīnan* (cp. Icel. *gīna*, MDut. *gienen*, Dut. *geeuwen*, also L *hiāre*)]

yawp (yawp) *n.* a hoarse or raucous cry. ~*v.i.* **1** to cry harshly or noisily. **2** (*N Am.*) to talk foolishly. [imit.]

yaws (yawz) *n.* (*Med.*) an infectious tropical disease whose symptoms include sores, caused by spirochaetes; also called *framboesia*. [perh. S Am. Ind.]

Yb *chem. symbol* ytterbium.

†**yclept** (iklept´) *a.* called, named. [Y-, p.p. of OE *cleopian*, to call, from Gmc.]

yd *abbr.* yard (measure).

yds *abbr.* yards (measure).

†**ye**[1] (yē, yi) *pron.* pl. of THOU[1], you people (orig. nom. or subjective). **ye gods!** GOD. [OE *gē*, cp. Dut. *gij*, G *ihr*, Icel. *ēr*, *ier*, Dan. and Swed. *i*, Gr. *humeis*, Sansk. *yūyam*]

ye[2] (yē) *a.* (*facet.*) THE. [old method of printing *the*, from a confusion between the letters þ (th) and y]

†**yea** (yā) *adv.* **1** yes. **2** verily, truly, indeed. **3** not only so but also. ~*n.* **1** an affirmative. **2** a person who votes in the affirmative. **to yea and nay** to be indecisive, to shilly-shally. **yeas and nays** *n.pl.* votes for and against. [OE *gēa*, cp. Dut., G, Dan. and Swed. *ja*, Icel. *jā*, Gr. *ē*, truly]

yeah (ye, yeə) *adv.* (*coll.*) yes. **oh yeah?** used to express incredulity.

†**yean** (yēn) *v.t., v.i.* (of sheep and goats) to give birth to (young). †**yeanling** (-ling) *n.* a lamb or kid. [OE *ēanian* (prob. cogn. with OE *eown*, EWE)]

year (yiə) *n.* **1** the period of time occupied by the revolution of the earth round the sun, the time taken by the sun in returning to the same equinox, in mean length, 365 days, 5 hrs., 48 min. and 46 sec. **2** the sidereal year. **3** the calendar year. **4** any period of about

12 months taken as a unit of time (*during the last year*). **5** a body of students who enter a school or university in the same year. **6** (*coll.*) age, length or time of life, a long time. **7** (*poet.*) old age. **astronomical year** ASTRONOMICAL (under ASTRONOMY). **a year and a day** (*Law*) a period sometimes specified in law to ensure the completion of a full calendar year. **calendar year** CALENDAR. **civil year** CIVIL. **equinoctial year** EQUINOCTIAL (under EQUINOX). **from year to year** FROM. **in the year of Our Lord** in a specified year AD (*in the year of Our Lord 1665*). **leap year** LEAP. **lunar year** LUNAR. **natural year** NATURAL. **of the year** outstanding in a particular year (*sports personality of the year*). **sidereal year** SIDEREAL. **solar year** SOLAR. **the year dot** as long ago as can be remembered. **tropical year** TROPICAL (under TROPIC[1]). **year by year** as the years go by. **year in, year out** constantly over a very long period, without cessation. **yearbook** *n.* a book published annually giving information up to date on some subject liable to change. **year-end** *n.* the end of the (fiscal) year. **yearling** *n.* **1** an animal more than one and less than two years old. **2** a colt a year old dating from 1 Jan. of the year of foaling. *~a.* **1** being one year old. **2** terminating after one year. **year-long** *a.* lasting a year. **yearly** *a.* **1** happening or recurring once a year or every year, annual. **2** lasting a year. *~adv.* **1** annually. **2** once a year, by the year. **year of grace** *n.* a year AD. **year-round** *a.* open or operating all year. **years of discretion** *n.pl.* the age when one is considered capable of exercising one's own judgement. [OE *gēar*, *gēr* (cp. Dut. *jaar*, G *Jahr*, Icel. *ār*), cogn. with Gr. *hōros*, a season, L *hōra*, HOUR]

yearn (yœn) *v.i.* **1** to feel a longing desire, tenderness, compassion etc. (for, after etc.). **2** †to grieve, to be pained or distressed. **yearner** *n.* **yearning** *n.*, *a.* **yearningly** *adv.* [OE *giernan* (cp. Icel. *girna*, G *begehren*, OHG *gerōn*), cogn. with Gr. *chairein*, to rejoice, L *hortārī*, to exhort]

yeast (yēst) *n.* **1** a yellowish, viscous substance consisting of a growth of fungous cells developed in contact with saccharine liquids and producing alcoholic fermentation by means of enzymes, used in brewing, distilling etc. and for raising dough for bread etc. **2** any unicellular fungus which reproduces by budding or fission. **yeastless** *a.* **yeastlike** *a.* **yeast powder** *n.* **1** a baking powder used as a substitute for yeast. **2** dry powdered yeast. **yeasty** *a.* (*comp.* **yeastier**, *superl.* **yeastiest**) **1** containing or resembling yeast, esp. in causing or being characterized by fermentation. **2** frothy, foamy. **3** unsubstantial, empty, superficial. **yeastily** *adv.* **yeastiness** *n.* [OE *gist* (cp. Dut. *gest*, G *Gischt*, Icel. *jast*, *jastr*) cogn. with Gr. *zeein*, to boil]

yegg (yeg) *n.* (*N Am.*, *sl.*) **1** a safe-breaker. **2** a dangerous criminal. [etym. uncertain, perh. the name of a US safe-breaker]

⊠ **yeild** common misspelling of YIELD.

yelk YOLK[1].

yell (yel) *v.i.* **1** to cry out with a loud, sharp or inarticulate cry as in rage, agony, terror or uncontrollable laughter. **2** to shout. *~v.t.* to utter or express by yelling. *~n.* **1** such a cry or shout, esp. a war cry. **2** (*N Am.*) a distinctive shout used by college students etc. for encouragement, applause etc. **3** (*sl.*) a cause of hilarity or yelling. **yeller** *n.* [OE *gellan*, *giellan*, cp. Dut. *gillen*, G *gellen*, Icel. *gella*]

yellow (yel´ō) *a.* **1** of a colour between green and orange in the spectrum or like that of gold, brass, sulphur, lemon or, the duller form, like that of discoloured old paper etc. **2** (*coll.*) cowardly. **3** (*poet.*) jaundiced, jealous, envious. **4** (of a newspaper etc.) sensational, outrageous. **5** (*often offensive*) having a yellowish skin or complexion. *~n.* **1** this colour, a yellow pigment, dye etc. **2** a yellow butterfly or moth. **3** the yellow ball in snooker. **4** (*pl.*) jaundice, jealousy. **5** the yellow counter in a board game etc.; the person playing with this. **6** (*pl.*, *N Am.*) a disease attacking peach trees etc. and turning their leaves yellow. **7** egg yolk. *~v.t.* to make (something) yellow. *~v.i.* to turn yellow. **yellow archangel** *n.* a Eurasian nettle, *Lamistrum galeobdolon*, with yellow helmet-shaped flowers. **yellow arsenic** *n.* orpiment. **yellowback** *n.* (*Hist.*) a cheap, sensational novel with a yellow cover, popular in the 19th cent. **yellow-belly** *n.* (*pl.* **yellow-bellies**) **1** (*coll.*) a coward. **2** any animal with yellow underparts. **yellow-bellied** *a.* **yellow bile** *n.* in ancient and medieval physiology, one of the four bodily humours, choler. **yellowbird** *n.* the American goldfinch, the yellow warbler, the golden oriole or a similar bird. **yellowcake** *n.* (*Chem.*) semi-refined uranium oxide obtained during the processing of uranium ore. **yellow card** *n.* in soccer, a yellow card shown as a caution by a referee to a player who has violated a rule. **yellow fever** *n.* a malignant tropical fever caused by the bite of the mosquito, characterized by jaundice and black vomit. **yellowfin** *n.* any of several fishes with yellow fins, esp. the yellowfin tuna. **yellowfin tuna** *n.* the edible tuna, *Thunnus albacares*, found in warm seas. **yellow flag** *n.* **1** a flag hoisted by a ship in quarantine or with an infectious disease on board. **2** the yellow iris, *Iris pseudacorus*. **yellowhammer** *n.* a bunting, *Emberiza citrinella*, with a yellow head, neck and breast. **yellowhead** *n.* a small flycatcher, *Mohoua ochrocephala*, found in New Zealand, having a yellow head and breast. **yellowish** *a.* **yellow jack** *n.* **1** yellow fever. **2** (*Naut.*) the yellow flag. **yellow jacket** *n.* a species of social wasp of the genus *Vespula*. **yellow jersey** *n.* a jersey worn by the overall leader in a cycle race lasting several days. **yellowlegs** *n.* either of two N American migratory sandpipers, *Tringa flavipes* and *T. melanoleuca*, having yellow legs. **yellow line** *n.* a line painted at the side of a road showing parking restrictions. **yellow loosestrife** *n.* a plant of the primrose family, *Lysimacha vulgaris*, with yellow flowers. **yellowly** *adv.* **yellow metal** *n.* a brass alloy of three parts of copper and two of zinc. **yellowness** *n.* **Yellow Pages®** *n.pl.* a telephone directory, printed on yellow paper, which lists subscribers according to business. **yellow pepper** *n.* a variant of the red pepper *Capsicum annuum*. **yellow peril** *n.* (*offensive*) the alleged danger that the Asian peoples, esp. the Chinese, may overwhelm the Western civilizations. **yellow rattle** *n.* an annual herb of the genus *Rhinanthus minor*, with yellow flowers and winged seeds that rattle in the capsules when ripe. **yellow rocket** *n.* winter cress. **yellow spot** *n.* the area at the centre of the retina where vision is acutest in daylight. **yellow streak** *n.* (*coll.*) a tendency towards cowardice. **yellow toadflax** *n.* the plant *Linaria vulgaris*. **yellowwort** *n.* a perennial, *Blackstonia perfoliata*, of the gentian family, used for dyeing yellow. **yellowy** *a.* [OE *geolo*, *geolu* (cp. Dut. *geel*, G *gelb*, L *helvus*), cogn. with Gr. *chlōros*, see CHLORO-, Sansk. *harī*, green, yellow, GALL[1]]

yelp (yelp) *v.i.* to utter a sharp, quick cry, as a dog in pain, or in fear or anticipation. *~n.* such a bark or cry. **yelper** *n.* **yelping** *n.* [OE *gilpan*, to boast, cp. Icel. *gjālpa*]

Yemeni (yem´əni) *n.* a native or inhabitant of the Republic of Yemen. *~a.* of or relating to Yemen or its people. **Yemenite** *n.* **1** a Yemeni. **2** a Jew who was, or whose ancestors were, from Yemen. *~a.* of, relating to or denoting a Yemeni Arab or Yemeni Jew. [Arab. *yamani*]

yen[1] (yen) *n.* (*pl.* **yen**) the standard unit of currency of Japan. [Jap., from Chin. *yuen*, round, dollar]

yen[2] (yen) *n.* (*coll.*) ambition, yearning, desire, longing. *~v.i.* (*pres.p.* **yenning**, *past*, *p.p.* **yenned**) to yearn. [Chin., opium]

yeoman (yō´mən) *n.* (*pl.* **yeomen**) **1** (*Hist.*) a freeholder not ranking as one of the gentry. **2** (*Hist.*) a man qualified to serve on juries and to vote etc., as holding free land of £2 annual value. **3** (*Hist.*) a member of the yeomanry force. **4** (*Hist.*) a farmer, esp. a freeholder. **5** a yeoman of signals. **6** an assistant, a journeyman. **yeomanlike** *a.* **yeomanly** *a.* **yeoman of signals** *n.* a petty or non-commissioned officer who carries out signalling or clerical duties in the navy. **Yeoman of the Guard** *n.* (*pl.* **Yeomen of the Guard**) **1** a Yeoman Warder. **2** a member of the British sovereign's ceremonial bodyguard. **yeomanry** (-ri) *n.* (*pl.* **yeomanries**) **1** yeomen collectively. **2** (*Hist.*) a British force of volunteer cavalry consisting largely of country gentlemen and farmers. **yeoman service, yeoman's service** *n.* good service, hearty support. **Yeoman Usher** *n.* (*pl.* **Yeoman Ushers**) in the Parliament, the deputy of Black Rod. **Yeoman Warder** *n.* (*pl.* **Yeoman Warders**) a warder at the Tower of London, a beefeater. [ME *yeman, yoman,* (prob. OE *gā*, district or village, MAN)]

yep (yep), **yup** (yŭp) *adv.* (*coll.*) yes.

-yer (yə) *suf.* forming nouns, esp. from words in *-w*, denoting an agent, as *lawyer, sawyer.* [var. of -ER[1], arising from the use of ME *-ien*, instead of *-en*, in causal verbs and those derived from nouns]

yerba (yœ´bə), **yerba maté** (mat´ā) *n.* Paraguay tea, maté. [Sp., from L *herba*, HERB]

yes (yes) *adv.* **1** as you say, it is true, agreed (indicating affirmation or consent). **2** I hear (in answer to a summons etc.). ~*n.* (*pl.* **yeses**) **1** the word 'yes'. **2** an affirmative reply. **yes? 1** what do you want? **2** is that so?, really? **yes, and** a verbal prelude to stronger words (*The thief was caught – yes, and still with the money*). **yes and no** a response indicating that what has been said is partly true but also partly untrue. **yes-man** *n.* (*pl.* **yes-men**) (*coll.*) an unquestioning follower, a sycophant. [OE *gise, gese* (prob. *gēa swā*, YEA, SO[1])]

yeshiva (yəshē´və), **yeshivah** *n.* (*pl.* **yeshivas, yeshivahs, yeshivoth** (-vōt)) **1** a Jewish school devoted to the study of the Talmud. **2** an Orthodox Jewish day school providing religious and secular instruction. [Heb. *yĕshībhāh*, seat, academy]

yester- (yes´tə) *comb. form* (*poet.*) of or relating to yesterday (*yesteryear*). **yesterday** (yes´tədi) *n.* **1** the day immediately before today. **2** time in the immediate past. ~*adv.* **1** on or during yesterday. **2** in the recent past. **yesterday afternoon** during the afternoon of yesterday. **yesterday morning** during the morning of yesterday. †**yestereve** (-ēv´), **yestreen** (-trēn´) *n., adv.* yesterday evening. **yesteryear** *n., adv.* (*poet.*) **1** last year. **2** the recent past. [OE *geostra, giestra*, usu. in acc. *geostran dæg*, yesterday (cp. Dut. *gisteren*, G *gestern*, also L *hesternus*, Gr. *chthes*, Sansk. *hyas*)]

yet (yet) *adv.* **1** still, up to this or that time (*They had yet to mature*). **2** by this or that time, so soon or early as the present, so far (*Are you up yet?*). **3** in addition, further, besides (*yet another soap opera*). **4** eventually, at some future time, before all is over (*They may yet arrive*). **5** even (*with comp.*) (*yet more*). **6** nevertheless, in spite of that (*Yet, we must remember*). ~*conj.* nevertheless, notwithstanding, but still (*We were beaten, yet we were proud of our efforts*). **as yet** up to this or that time, so far. **just yet** (*with neg.*) in the immediate future. **nor yet** and also not (*He had not finished the exam nor yet started the last question*). **not yet** not up to the present time. [OE *git, get, giet*, cp. Fris. *jiette*, G *jetzt*]

yeti (yet´i) *n.* (*pl.* **yetis**) a hypothetical manlike, apelike or bearlike creature, whose tracks are alleged to have been found in the snows of the Himalayas, also called *Abominable Snowman.* [Tibetan]

yett (yet) *n.* (*Sc.*) a gate, a door. [GATE[1]]

yew (ū) *n.* **1** a dark-leaved evergreen shrub or tree of the genus *Taxus*, esp. *T. baccata*, a large tree with spreading branches, the wood of which has long been valued for making bows and used in cabinetmaking. **2** its wood. **yew tree** *n.* [OE *īw*, cp. G *Eibe*, Icel. *ȳr*]

Yggdrasill (ig´drəsil) *n.* in Scandinavian mythology, an ash tree binding together heaven, earth and hell with its roots and branches. [Icel., Odin's horse (*Yggr*, a name of Odin, *dresill*, horse)]

YHA *abbr.* Youth Hostels Association.

YHVH *n.* Yahweh, the Tetragrammaton.

Yiddish (yid´ish) *n.* a language spoken by Jews of E Europe and N America, based on a Hebraicized Middle German, with an admixture of Polish, French and English, and usually written in Hebrew characters. ~*a.* of or relating to this language. **Yid** *n.* (*sl., offensive*) a Jew. **Yiddisher** *n.* a Yiddish speaker. ~*a.* **1** of or relating to Yiddish. **2** Yiddish-speaking, Jewish. **Yiddishism** *n.* **1** a word, idiom etc. derived from Yiddish. **2** support for the use of Yiddish. [G *jüdisch*, Jewish]

yield (yēld) *v.t.* **1** to produce, to bear, to bring forth as fruit, reward or result. **2** to give up, to surrender, to concede, to relinquish, to resign. ~*v.i.* **1** to give a return, to repay one's labour in cultivation etc., to bear fruit, to be productive (beneficially or otherwise). **2** to give way, to assent, to submit, to comply, to surrender. **3** to make submission (to). **4** to give place, to yield precedence or admit inferiority (to). ~*n.* **1** something that is yielded or produced, output, return. **2** annual return from an investment. **yieldable** *a.* **yielder** *n.* **yielding** *a.* **1** compliant. **2** able to bend, pliable. **yieldingly** *adv.* **yieldingness** *n.* **yield point** *n.* the point at which a material, under increasing stress, ceases to behave elastically. [OE *gieldan*, to pay, cp. Dut. *gelden*, G *gelten*, Icel. *gjalda*, Swed. *gälla*, to be worth]

yikes (yīks) *int.* (*sl.*) used to express surprise, astonishment, alarm etc. [etym. uncertain]

yin (yin) *n.* the feminine, passive, dark principle in nature, according to Chinese philosophy, which interacts with its complement and opposite, *yang.* [Chin. *yin*, dark]

Yindjibarndi (yinjibŭn´di) *n.* an Aboriginal language of W Australia.

yip (yip) *n.* a short sudden cry, a yelp. ~*v.i.* (*pres.p.* **yipping**, *past, p.p.* **yipped**) to give a short sudden cry, to yelp. [imit.]

yippee (yipē´) *int.* used to express delight, pleasure, exuberant anticipation etc.

yips (yips) *n.pl.* (*coll.*) an attack of nerves, particularly in sport and esp. when putting in golf. [20th cent., etym. uncertain]

-yl (il, īl) *suf.* (*Chem.*) denoting a radical, as *ethyl, methyl.* [Gr. *hulē*, wood, material]

ylang-ylang (ēlangē´lang), **ilang-ilang** *n.* **1** a Malayan tree, *Cananga odorata*, of the custard-apple family. **2** an oil from the flowers of this tree, used in perfumes, aromatherapy etc. [Malay, flower of flowers]

YMCA *abbr.* Young Men's Christian Association.

-yne (īn) *comb. form* (*Chem.*) denoting a triple bond, as *alkyne.* [form of -INE]

yo (yō) *int.* (*sl.*) used as a greeting, to gain someone's attention, etc. (*Yo, dudes!*).

yob (yob) *n.* an aggressive, loutish youth, a hooligan. **yobbish** *a.* **yobbishly** *adv.* **yobbishness** *n.* **yobbo** (-ō) *n.* (*pl.* **yobbos, yobboes**). [back slang, *boy*]

yocto- (yok´tō) *suf.* denoting a factor of 10^{-24}. [adapted from OCTO-]

yod (yod) *n.* **1** the tenth letter of the Hebrew alphabet. **2** its sound, a palatal semivowel. [Heb.]

yodel (yō´dəl) *v.t., v.i.* (*pres.p.* **yodelling**, (*N Am.*) **yodeling**, *past, p.p.* **yodelled**, (*N Am.*) **yodeled**) to sing or shout in a musical fashion with alternation from the natural voice to the falsetto. ~*n.* **1** such a shout or musical cry, used esp. by Swiss and Tyrolese mountaineers. **2** a yodelling contest. **yodeller,** (*N Am.*) **yodeler** *n.* [G dial. *jodeln*]

yoga (yō´gə) *n.* **1** a Hindu system of abstract meditation and rigid asceticism by which the soul is supposed to become united with the eternal spirit of the universe. **2** certain exercises and practices assisting this, HATHA YOGA. **yogi** (yō´gi) *n.* (*pl.* **yogis**) a devotee or adept of yoga. **yogic** *a.* **yogism** *n.* [Hind., from Sansk., union]

yogh (yog) *n.* a Middle English letter (ȝ) used to represent *g* and *y* sounds. [perh. imit.]

yogurt (yog´ət, yō´-), **yoghurt, yoghourt, yogourt** *n.* a custard-like food made from milk fermented in a special way. [Turk.]

yo-heave-ho (yōhēvhō´) *int.*, *n.* HEAVE-HO (under HEAVE).

yo-ho (yōhō´), **yo-ho-ho** (-hō´) *int.* **1** used to attract attention. **2** heave-ho.

yoicks (yoiks), **hoicks** (hoiks) *n.*, *int.* a fox-hunter's cry. [etym. uncertain]

yojan (yō´jən) *n.* a measure of distance in the Indian subcontinent, usu. about 5 miles (8 km). [Hind.]

yoke (yōk) *n.* **1** a frame or crossbar fitting over the necks of two oxen or other draught animals and attaching them to a plough or vehicle. **2** a device resembling this. **3** a frame fitting a person's shoulders for carrying a pair of buckets suspended from the ends. **4** a frame or crossbar on which a bell swings. **5** (*Naut.*, *Hist.*) the crossbar of a rudder to which steering-lines were fastened. **6** a coupling for two pipes discharging into one. **7** a coupling, guiding or controlling piece in a machine. **8** a tie-beam, tie-rod etc. **9** a part of a garment made to support the rest, as at the shoulders or hips. **10** (*poet.*) a bond, a link, a tie, esp. that of love or marriage. **11** (*pl.* **yoke, yokes**) a pair of draught animals, esp. oxen yoked together. **12** (*Hist.*) in ancient Rome, two upright spears with a third resting across them at the top, under which vanquished enemies were made to pass. **13** servitude, slavery, submission. **14** †as much land as might be ploughed by a yoke of oxen in a day. ~*v.t.* **1** to put a yoke upon. **2** to unite by a yoke. **3** to couple, esp. in marriage. **4** to join, to link. **5** to enslave. ~*v.i.* to go or work (well or badly together etc.). **yokebone** *n.* the malar or cheekbone connecting the bones at the side of the head with those of the face. [OE *geoc* (cp. Dut. *juk*, G *Joch*, Icel. and Swed. *ok*, L *jugum*, Gr. *zugon*, Sansk. *yuga*-), cogn. with JOIN]

yokel (yō´kəl) *n.* a rustic, a country bumpkin. **yokelish** *a.* [prob. from dial., green woodpecker]

yolk[1] (yōk), (*dial.*) **yelk** (yelk) *n.* the yellow part of an egg, the contents of the ovum, esp. that nourishing the embryo, the vitellus. **yolked** *a.* **yolkless** *a.* **yolk-sac, yolk-bag** *n.* the thin, membraneous bag enclosing the yolk in an egg. **yolky** *a.* [OE *geolca*, YELLOW]

yolk[2] (yōk) *n.* the natural grease in sheep's wool, suint. [OE, from *euwu*, ewe]

Yom Kippur (yom kip´ə, -puə´) *n.* the Day of Atonement, a Jewish day of fasting. [Heb.]

yomp (yomp) *v.i.* to trek, often with heavy equipment, over heavy terrain. [etym. uncertain]

yon (yon) *a.*, *adv.* (*Sc.*) yonder. ~*pron.* **1** yonder person, thing or place. **2** that. **yond** (yond) *a.* the most distant. ~*adv.* yonder. [OE *geon* (cp. Icel. *enn*, G *jener*)]

yonder (yon´də) *a.* **1** that over there (*yonder tree*). **2** being at a distance, but in the direction looked at or pointed out. **3** distant but within view. ~*adv.* **1** over there. **2** at a distance but within view, or where one is looking or pointing. [ME, from YON]

yoni (yō´ni) *n.* the Hindu symbol of the fertility of nature under which the consort of a male deity is worshipped, represented by an oval figure (the female genitalia). [Sansk.]

yonks (yongks) *n.pl.* (*coll.*) a long time, ages. [etym. unknown]

yoo-hoo (yoo´hoo) *int.* used to attract someone's attention.

YOP *abbr.* (*Hist.*) Youth Opportunity Programme (a former training scheme in Britain).

yore (yaw) *n.* (*poet.*) †long ago, old time. **of yore** (*poet.*) formerly, of old time, long ago (*days of yore*). [OE *geāra*, orig. gen. pl. of *gēar*, YEAR]

yorker (yaw´kə) *n.* in cricket, a ball bowled so as to pitch immediately under the bat. **york** *v.t.* to bowl (out) with a yorker. [prob. from being first used by a Yorkshire player]

yorkie (yaw´ki) *n.* (*coll.*) a Yorkshire terrier.

Yorkist (yaw´kist) *a.* (*Hist.*) of or relating to the house descended from Edmund Duke of York, son of Edward III, or the White Rose party supporting this in the Wars of the Roses. ~*n.* an adherent of this house or party.

Yorks. (yawks) *abbr.* Yorkshire.

Yorkshire (yawk´shə) *a.* of or derived from Yorkshire. **Yorkshire flannel** *n.* flannel of undyed wool. **Yorkshire fog** *n.* a grass, *Holcus lanatus*, used for fodder. **yorkshire grit** *n.* a grit used for polishing. **Yorkshireman** *n.* (*pl.* **Yorkshiremen**). **Yorkshire pudding** *n.* a baked batter pudding, often served with roast beef. **Yorkshire terrier** *n.* a small shaggy variety of toy terrier. **Yorkshirewoman** *n.* (*pl.* **Yorkshirewomen**). [county in N England]

Yoruba (yor´əbə) *n.* **1** a member of a people living in the coastal regions of W Africa, esp. SW Nigeria. **2** the Kwa language of this people. **Yoruban** *a.*

yotta- (yot´ə) *comb. form* denoting a factor of 10^{24}. [alt. from It. *octo*, eight]

you (ū, yu) *pron.* (*sing. and pl.*) **1** the person, animal, thing or persons etc. addressed. **2** (*reflex.*) yourself, yourselves. **3** (*indefinite*) one, anyone, people generally. **you and yours** you and your family, property etc. **you know** KNOW. **you're another** a retort to abuse etc. **you-all, y'all** *pron.* (*N Am.*, *coll.*) you (usu. more than one person). **you'd** (yud) *contr.* **1** you had. **2** you would. **you-know-what, you-know-who** *n.* something or someone unspecified known to both speaker and hearer. **you'll** (yul) *contr.* you will, you shall. **you're** (yaw) *contr.* you are. **youse** (ūz, yuz), **yous** *pron.* (*coll.*) you (usu. more than one person). **you've** (yuv) *contr.* you have. [OE *ēow*, dat. and acc. of *gē*, *ye* (see also YE[1])]

Usage note See note under YOUR.

young (yŭng) *a.* (*comp.* **younger** (yŭng´gə), *superl.* **youngest** (yŭng´gist)) **1** being in the early stage of life, growth or development. **2** of recent birth or beginning, newly formed, produced, come into action or operation etc. **3** not infirm or decayed with age, vigorous, fresh. **4** immature, raw, inexperienced. **5** of, relating to or characteristic of youth. ~*n.* **1** offspring, esp. of animals. **2** those who are young. **with young** pregnant. **young blood** *n.* a new accession of vigour or enterprise. **younger** *a.* **1** less in age, growth etc. **2** that is the younger of two people of the same name. ~*n.* (*Sc.*) a landed commoner's heir. **Younger Edda** *n.* a handbook of Icelandic prosody, grammar and rhetoric for the training of young poets, partly written by Snorri Sturluson (*c.* 1230). **younger hand** *n.* in cards, the second player of two. **young fogey** *n.* a young person with old-fashioned tastes, attitudes, mannerisms etc. **young fustic** *n.* **1** a sumac tree, *Cotinus coggygria.* **2** the wood of this. **young hopeful** *n.* **1** a person with good prospects of success. **2** a person with misplaced expectations of success. **youngish** *a.* **young lady** *n.* (*pl.* **young ladies**) **1** a young woman, esp. one unmarried. **2** a girlfriend. **youngling** *n.* **young man** *n.* (*pl.* **young men**) **1** a young man or boy. **2** a boyfriend. **youngness** *n.* **young offender** *n.* (*Law*) a young criminal between 14 and 17 years of age. **young person** *n.* (*Law*) someone aged between 14 and 17. **youngster** *n.* **1** a young person, a child. **2** a young animal, such as a young horse. **young thing** *n.* (*coll.*) a young person. **Young Turk** *n.* **1** (*Hist.*) a member of a revolutionary party in Turkey in the early 20th cent. **2** a young person eager to see abuses swept away and radical reforms introduced. **3** (*offensive*) (**young turk**) a rebellious, perh. violent, child or youth. **young 'un** *n.* (*coll.*) a child or young person. **young woman** *n.* (*pl.* **young women**) **1** a young woman or girl. **2** a girlfriend. [OE *geong*, cp. Dut. *jong*, G *jung*, Icel. *ungr*, Dan. and Swed. *ung*, L *juvenis*, Sansk. *yuvan*]

Young's modulus (yŭngz) *n.* (*Physics*) a measure of elasticity for wire etc., equal to the ratio of the stress acting on the material to the increase in length produced. [T. *Young*, 19th-cent. English scientist]

†**younker** (yŭng´kə) *n.* (*coll.*) a youngster. [Dut. *jonker* (*jong*, YOUNG, *heer*, SIR, cp. HERR)]

your (yaw, yə, ūə) *a.* **1** possessive of YOU. **2** (*coll., usu. derog.*) well-known, familiar, much talked of (*Take your yuppies, for example*). **your humble servant, your obedient servant** *n.* (*formal*) used preceding the signature of a letter, often now used ironically. **yours** (-z) *pron.* **1** something which belongs to you or is associated with you. **2** your letter. **3** someone at your service (in a formula ending a letter) (*yours ever*). **of yours** of or belonging to you. **up yours** UP. **you and yours** YOU. **yours faithfully** FAITHFULLY (under FAITH). **yours sincerely** SINCERELY (under SINCERE). **yours truly** **1** used as a conventional formal ending to a letter. **2** I, this person (*Of course, yours truly came last!*). **yourself** (-self´) *pron.* (*pl.* **yourselves** (-selvz´)) **1** you and not others, you alone. **2** your own person, you in particular. **3** you in your normal condition, health etc. (*You don't look yourself today*). **by yourself/ yourselves** **1** alone. **2** unaided. **how's yourself?** (*coll.*) how are you? (esp. following a similar question). **to be yourself/ yourselves** to act normally, without affectation etc.

Usage note (1) The spellings of the adjective *your* and the contraction *you're* (you are) should not be confused. (2) The pronoun *yours* does not have an apostrophe (not *your's*).

you're, youse etc. YOU.

youth (ūth) *n.* (*pl.* **youths** (ūdhz)) **1** the state of being young. **2** the period of life from infancy to manhood or womanhood. **3** youthfulness, the vigour, freshness, inexperience etc. of this period. **4** a young man. **5** young men and women collectively. **youth club, youth centre,** (*N Am.*) **youth center** *n.* a club which provides leisure time and social activities for young people. **youth credit** *n.* a voucher issued to young people of school age but not in full-time education, exchangeable for part-time education or training. **youthful** *a.* **youthfully** *adv.* **youthfulness** *n.* †**youthhood** *n.* **youth hostel** *n.* an organized establishment where hikers etc. may stay for the night. *~v.i.* (*pres.p.* **youth hostelling,** (*N Am.*) **youth hosteling,** *past, p.p.* **youth hostelled,** (*N Am.*) **youth hosteled**) to stay in youth hostels. **youth hosteller,** (*N Am.*) **youth hosteler** *n.* **youth hostelling** *n.* **youth leader** *n.* a social worker who works with young people in a particular community. [OE *geoguth* (YOUNG, -TH¹), cp. Dut. *jeugd*, G *Jugend*, L *juventa*]

you've YOU.

yowl (yowl) *n.* a howl or yell of distress. *~v.i.* to cry out in this way. [imit.]

yo-yo (yō´yō) *n.* (*pl.* **yo-yos**) a toy which consists of a spool winding up and down on a string. *~v.i.* (*3rd pers. sing. pres.* **yo-yoes,** *pres.p.* **yo-yoing,** *past, p.p.* **yo-yoed**) **1** to move up and down rapidly, to fluctuate rapidly. **2** to play with a yo-yo.

yr. *abbr.* **1** year. **2** younger. **3** your.

yrs. *abbr.* **1** years. **2** yours.

YTS *abbr.* Youth Training Scheme.

ytterbium (itœ´biəm) *n.* (*Chem.*) a rare metallic element, at. no. 70, chem. symbol Yb, used to improve the mechanical properties of steel. [*Ytterby*, town in Sweden, -IUM]

yttrium (it´riəm) *n.* (*Chem.*) a rare metallic element, at. no. 39, chem. symbol Y, belonging to the cerium group, used in alloys, lasers and in making superconductors. **yttria** (-riə) *n.* a white earth, yttrium oxide. **yttriferous** (-rif´-) *a.*

yuan (yuahn´) *n.* (*pl.* **yuan**) the standard monetary unit of China. [Chin. *yüan*, round object]

yucca (yŭk´ə) *n.* any liliaceous subtropical American flowering plant of the genus *Yucca*, with rigid lanceolate leaves and an erect cluster of white flowers, many species of which are grown for ornament. [Sp. *yuca*, from Haitian]

yuck (yŭk), **yuk** *int.* (*sl.*) used to express disgust or distaste. *~n.* (*sl.*) something unpleasant or messy. *~v.i.* (**yuck**) to itch. **yucky, yukky** *a.* (*comp.* **yuckier, yukkier,** *superl.* **yuckiest, yukkiest**) (*coll.*) disgusting, unpleasant. [etym. uncertain]

yuga (yoo´gə) *n.* any of the Hindu ages or cycles of the world. [Sansk.]

Yugoslav (yoo´gəslahv), **Jugoslav** *a.* **1** of or relating to the southern Slav peoples or countries, esp. the former Yugoslavia. **2** of Yugoslavian descent. *~n.* a native or inhabitant of the former Yugoslavia. **Yugoslavian** (-slah´-) *a.* [Serb., south Slav]

yuk, yukky YUCK.

yulan (yoo´lən) *n.* a Chinese tree, *Magnolia denudata*, with large, brilliant, snow-white or rosy flowers. [Chin. (*yu*, gem, *lan*, plant)]

Yule (yool), **Yuletide** (yool´tīd) *n.* Christmas time or the festival of Christmas. **yule log** *n.* **1** a large log formerly burned on Christmas Eve. **2** a chocolate cake shaped and decorated like a log, eaten at Christmas. [OE *gēola*, cp. Icel. *jōl*, etym. uncertain]

yum-yum (yŭmyŭm´) *int.* (*coll.*) used to express pleasure, esp. anticipation of delicious food. **yummy** (yŭm´i) *a.* (*comp.* **yummier,** *superl.* **yummiest**) delicious, tasty. [imit.]

yup YEP.

yuppie (yŭp´i), **yuppy** *n.* (*pl.* **yuppies**) (*sometimes derog.*) a young financially successful professional person who spends much money on their lifestyle. *~a.* of, relating to or designed to appeal to yuppies. **yuppiedom** *n.* **yuppify** *v.t.* (*3rd pers. sing. pres.* **yuppifies,** *pres.p.* **yuppifying,** *past, p.p.* **yuppified**) to make suitable for or typical of yuppies. **yuppification** (-fikā´shən) *n.* **yuppified** *a.* [acronym for *y*oung *u*pwardly-mobile (or *u*rban) *p*rofessional]

yurt (yuət, yœt) *n.* **1** a circular, collapsible tent made of skins and used by nomads in Central Asia. **2** a hut built partially underground and covered with turf or earth. [Rus. *yurta*, dwelling, from Turkic]

Yuwaalaraay (yuwah´lərī) *n.* an Aboriginal language of SE Australia.

YV *abbr.* Venezuela (IVR).

YWCA *abbr.* Young Women's Christian Association.

Z

Z[1] (zed), **z** (*pl.* **Zs, Z's**) the 26th and last letter of the English and other versions of the Roman alphabet, corresponding to the Greek zeta (Z, ζ). It is pronounced as a voiced alveolar continuant (like a voiced *s*), as in *zeal, lazy, reason*, or as a voiced affricate (like a voiced *sh*), as in *azure*. *~symbol* **1** the third unknown quantity or variable in an algebraic expression. **2** (*Chem.*) atomic number. **3** (*Physics*) impedance. *~n.* a Z-shaped thing, part or mark. **z-axis** *n.* a reference axis in the Cartesian coordinate system.

Z[2] *abbr.* Zambia (IVR).

z *abbr.* **1** zero. **2** zone.

ZA *abbr.* South Africa (IVR).

zabaglione (zabalyō´ni) *n.* a warm whipped dessert of egg yolks, sugar and marsala. [It.]

zaffre (zaf´ə), (*NAm.*) **zaffer** *n.* impure cobalt oxide used for enamelling and as a blue pigment for painting on glass, porcelain etc. [F *zafre*, from Arab.]

zag (zag) *n.* a sharp change of direction in a zigzag course. *~v.i.* (*pres.p.* **zagging,** *past, p.p.* **zagged**) to move in this way.

Zairean (zīiə´riən), **Zairian** *n.* a native or inhabitant of Zaire (now Congo) in central Africa. *~a.* of or relating to Zaire. **zaire** *n.* the standard unit of currency of Zaire.

zakuska (zəkus´kə) *n.* (*pl.* **zakuski** (-ki)) a snack, an hors d'oeuvre. [Rus.]

Zambian (zam´biən) *n.* a native or inhabitant of the central African republic of Zambia. *~a.* of or relating to Zambia.

zamia (zā´miə) *n.* any palmlike tree or low shrub of the genus *Zamia*, from the W Indies and America. [from misreading of *azaniae*, pine cones]

zamindar (zamindah´), **zemindar** (zem-) *n.* (*Hist.*) **1** a member of a class of Bengali landowners formerly paying a certain land tax to the British government. **2** a local governor and farmer of the revenue under the Mughal empire paying a fixed sum for his district. **zamindary** (zam´-) *n.* the system of land tenure and taxation involving zamindars. [Pers. *zemin*, land, *-dār*, holding]

zander (zan´də) *n.* (*pl. in general* **zander,** *in particular* **zanders**) a large European freshwater pikeperch, *Stizostedion lucioperca*. [G]

ZANU (zah´noo) *abbr.* Zimbabwe African National Union.

zany (zā´ni) *a.* (*comp.* **zanier,** *superl.* **zaniest**) outrageous, comical, absurd (e.g. of a comedy show). *~n.* (*pl.* **zanies**) **1** a person who acts the fool. **2** (*Hist.*) a buffoon in old theatrical entertainments who mimicked the clown. **zanily** *adv.* **zaniness** *n.* **zanyism** *n.* [F *zani*, It. *zanni*, fam. for *Giovanni*, John]

zap (zap) *v.t.* (*pres.p.* **zapping,** *past, p.p.* **zapped**) **1** (*coll.*) to hit, smack, strike suddenly. **2** to kill or destroy. **3** to cause to go quickly. **4** (*Comput.*) to delete or change (an item on screen, in a program etc.). *~v.i.* **1** to move suddenly or quickly. **2** to switch rapidly between television channels using a remote control. *~n.* **1** energy, go, vitality. **2** a powerful emotional effect. *~int.* used to express a sudden action. **zapper** *n.* **1** a remote control for television, video etc. **2** (*coll.*) a person who habitually switches rapidly between television channels. **zappy** *a.* (*comp.* **zappier,** *superl.* **zappiest**) (*coll.*) **1** energetic, fast-moving. **2** punchy, snappy. [imit.]

zapateado (zapatiah´dō) *n.* (*pl.* **zapateados**) **1** a flamenco dance characterized by much clicking of the heels, and stamping and tapping of the feet. **2** the foot movements in such a dance. [from Sp. *zapatear*, to tap with the shoe, from *zapato*, shoe]

ZAPU (zah´poo) *abbr.* Zimbabwe African People's Union.

zarape SERAPE.

Zarathustrian (zarəthus´triən) *a., n.* ZOROASTRIAN. **Zarathustrianism** *n.*

zaratite (zar´ətīt) *n.* a hydrous nickel carbonate, usu. occurring as an incrustation. [G. *Zárate* (19th-cent.)]

zarf (zahf) *n.* an ornamental cup-shaped holder for a hot coffee cup. [Arab.]

zariba (zərē´bə), **zareeba, zareba** *n.* **1** a stockade, hedge or other enclosure for a camp or village in Sudan. **2** anything which encloses or confines. [Arab. *zarība, -bat*]

zarzuela (zahzwā´lə) *n.* **1** a traditional Spanish form of musical comedy or comic opera. **2** a Spanish seafood stew. [La *Zarzuela*, the Spanish royal palace where the entertainment was first performed]

zastrugi SASTRUGI.

zax SAX[2].

zeal (zēl) *n.* **1** ardour, earnestness, enthusiasm. **2** intense and eager pursuit or endeavour to attain or accomplish some object. **zealot** (zel´ət) *n.* **1** a fanatical partisan. **2** (*Hist.*) (**Zealot**) a member of a militant Jewish sect opposing the Roman occupation of the Holy Land until AD 70. **3** a person full of zeal, esp. one carried away by it. **zealotism** *n.* **zealotry** (-tri) *n.* **zealous** (zel´-) *a.* **zealously** *adv.* **zealousness** *n.* [OF *zele*, L *zēlum*, nom. *-us*, Gr. *zēlos*]

zebec, zebeck XEBEC.

zebra (zeb´rə, zē´-) *n.* (*pl. in general* **zebra,** *in particular* **zebras**) **1** a black and white striped, asslike mammal of the genus *Equus*, esp. *E. burchelli*, from the mountainous regions of S Africa. **2** (*attrib.*) denoting other kinds or species of plant, bird, fish or mammal with similar markings, including the *zebra antelope, zebra caterpillar, zebra fish, zebra mouse, zebra woodpecker* and *zebra wood*. **zebra crossing** *n.* a street-crossing marked by stripes where pedestrians have precedence over all other traffic. **zebra finch** *n.* an Australian waxbill, *Poephila guttata*, having black and white stripes on the face. **zebrine** (-brīn), **zebroid** (-broid) *a.* [Port., Sp., perh. ult. from L *equus*, horse, *ferus*, wild]

zebu (zē´boo) *n.* (*pl.* **zebus**) the humped Indian ox, *Bos indicus*. [F *zébu*, Tibetan *mdzopo*]

zecchino (zekē´nō) *n.* (*pl.* **zecchini** (-nē)) (*Hist.*) a Venetian gold coin, the sequin.

Zech. *abbr.* Zechariah.

zed (zed) *n.* the letter Z. [F *zède*, L and Gr. *zēta*]

zedoary (zed´ōəri) *n.* **1** a tropical Asian plant, *Curcuma zedoaria*, similar to turmeric. **2** a substance made from the rootstock of this, used in medicine, dyeing, perfumery etc. [MF *zedoaire*, med. L *zedoāria*, Pers. *zadwār*]

zee (zē) *n.* (*NAm.*) the letter Z, zed.

Zeeman effect (zē´mən) *n.* (*Physics*) the splitting of the spectrum line of a substance into several parts when the substance is placed in a magnetic field. [P. *Zeeman*, 1865–1943, Dutch physicist]

zein (zē´in) *n.* a protein found in maize, used in the manufacture of inks, coatings, adhesives etc. [G *Zeia*, spelt]

Zeitgeist (tsīt´gīst) *n.* the spirit, or moral and intellectual tendency, of the times. [G, time-spirit]

zeloso (zelō´sō) *adv.* (*Mus.*) with energy. [It., as ZEAL]

zemindar ZAMINDAR.

zemstvo (zemst´vō) *n.* (*pl.* **zemstvos, zemstva** (-və)) (*Hist.*) a Russian elective local assembly dealing with economic affairs in the decades preceding the Russian Revolution. [Rus.]

Zen (zen) *n.* a form of Mahayana Buddhism teaching that truth is in one's heart and can be learned only by meditation and self-mastery. **Zenic** *a.* **Zenist, Zennist** *n.* [Jap., from Chin. *ch'an*, from Pali *jhana*, from Sansk. *dhyāna*, religious meditation]

zenana (zinah´nə) *n.* in the East (esp. India or Iran), the portion of the house in a Hindu or Muslim household which is reserved for the women. **zenana mission** *n.* (*Hist.*) a mission undertaken by women for spreading educational, medical and religious reforms among the inmates of zenanas. [Hind. *zanāna*, from Pers. *zanān*, pl. of *zan*, woman]

Zend (zend) *n.* **1** a section of commentary on the Avesta. **2** †Avestan. **Zend-Avesta** (-əves´tə) *n.* a collection of the sacred scriptures of the Zoroastrians together with a commentary. [Pers. *Zend*, a commentary, *Avesta*, a text, *Avesta'-va-zend*, *-zand*, Avesta with commentary]

Zener cards (zē´nə) *n.pl.* a set of 25 cards, each having one of five different symbols, used in research into ESP. [K. E. *Zener*, 1903–61, US psychologist]

Zener diode (zē´nə) *n.* in electronics, a semiconductor diode in which a certain reverse voltage produces a sudden increase in reverse current, making it useful as a voltage regulator. [C. M. *Zener*, 1905–93, US physicist]

zenith (zen´ith) *n.* **1** the point in the heavens directly overhead to an observer, as opposed to *nadir*. **2** the highest or culminating point (*the zenith of his career*). **zenithal** *a.* **zenithal projection** *n.* a map projection in which the centre of the area of the globe depicted is tangential to the plane of the map, thus allowing the directions of all points of the map from the centre to be accurate. **zenith distance** *n.* the angular distance of a heavenly body from the zenith. [ME *senith*, OF *cenith* (F *zénith*), OSp. *zenith*, Arab. *samt* (pron. semt), way, road]

zeolite (zē´əlīt) *n.* **1** any one of a group of hydrous silicates found in cavities of eruptive rocks, which gelatinize in acid owing to the liberation of silica. **2** any of various synthetic silicates resembling this. **zeolitic** (-lit´-) *a.* [Gr. *zeein*, to boil, -LITE]

Zeph. *abbr.* Zephaniah.

zephyr (zef´ə) *n.* **1** (*poet.*) any soft, gentle breeze. **2** a light, gauzy fabric of worsted or woollen yarn, used for shawls, jerseys etc. **3** a jersey or other garment made of this. [F *zéphyr*, L *zephyrus*, Gr. *zephuoros*, the west wind]

Zeppelin (zep´əlin), **zeppelin** *n.* (*Hist.*) a large dirigible airship. [Count von *Zeppelin*, 1838–1918, German general and airman]

zepto- (zep´tō) *comb. form* denoting a factor of 10^{-21}. [alt. of SEPTI-[1]]

zero (ziə´rō) *n.* (*pl.* **zeros**) **1** the figure 0, a cipher, nothing, nought, nil. **2** the point on a scale from which positive or negative quantities are reckoned, esp. on a thermometer (e.g. on the Fahrenheit scale 32° below the freezing point of water; on the Celsius and Réaumur scales zero is the freezing point). **3** the lowest point in any scale or standard of comparison, the nadir, nullity. **4** zero hour. *~a.* **1** having no measurable quantity, size etc. **2** (of a cloud ceiling) limiting visibility to 15 m (approx. 50 ft.) or less. **3** (of horizontal visibility) limited to 50 m (approx. 165 ft.) or less. **4** (*coll.*) not any, nothing. *~v.t.* (*3rd pers. sing. pres.* **zeroes,** *pres.p.* **zeroing,** *past, p.p.* **zeroed**) to adjust or set (an instrument, scale, gauge etc.) to zero. **to zero in on 1** to focus attention on, to fix on. **2** to aim for. **3** to converge upon, to home in on. **zero hour** *n.* **1** the precise hour for the commencement of a pre-arranged military movement or other action, operation etc. **2** the crucial time. **zero option** *n.* a proposal that both sides in international nuclear arms negotiations agree to limit or remove shorter-range nuclear missiles. **zero-rated** *a.* denoting goods on which the buyer need pay no value added tax, but on which the seller can claim back any value added tax they have already paid. **zero-rate** *v.t.* **zero-sum** *a.* (of a game, military or political situation etc.) in which the total gains by one side equate to the losses by the other side. **zeroth** (-th) *a.* denoting a term in a series of terms which precedes what is usu. regarded as the first term. **zero tolerance** *n.* total intolerance, esp. of street crime by police authorities. [OF and It., for *zefiro*, Arab. *cipr*, CIPHER]

zest (zest) *n.* **1** keen enjoyment. **2** that which makes a thing enjoyable, piquancy, relish. **3** a piece of lemon, lime or orange peel, or the oil extracted from this, used to give a flavour to soups, wines etc. **zester** *n.* a kitchen utensil for scraping or peeling citrus fruits to obtain zest. **zestful** *a.* **zestfully** *adv.* **zestfulness** *n.* **zesty** *a.* (*comp.* **zestier,** *superl.* **zestiest**). [OF, the woody skin dividing the kernel of a walnut, from L and Gr. *schistos*, cleft, from *schizein*, to divide]

zeta (zē´tə) *n.* the sixth letter of the Greek alphabet (Z, ζ).

zetetic (zitet´ik) *a.* proceeding by enquiry. [Gr. *zētētikos*, from *zēteein*, to seek]

zetta- (zet´ə) *comb. form* denoting a factor of 10^{21}. [alt. of It. *sette*, seven]

zeugma (zūg´mə) *n.* (*Gram.*) a figure in which a verb or adjective governs or modifies two nouns to only one of which it is logically applicable. **zeugmatic** (-mat´-) *a.* [Gr. *zeugma -matos*, yoke]

zho DZO.

zibeline (zib´əlīn, -lin) *a.* of, relating to or resembling the sable. *~n.* **1** the sable or its fur. **2** a thick woollen fabric with a soft deep nap. [F, from It. *zibellino*, prob. from Slav.]

zibet (zib´it) *n.* an Indian and Asian civet, *Viverra zibetha*. [It. *zibello*, CIVET]

zidovudine (zidō´vūdēn, -dov´-) *n.* (*Med.*) a drug derivative of thymine used to alleviate the symptoms of Aids sufferers, AZT. [alteration of chem. name]

ziff (zif) *n.* (*Austral.*, *sl.*) a beard. [etym. unknown]

zig (zig) *n.* a sharp change of direction in a zigzag course. *~v.i.* (*pres.p.* **zigging,** *past, p.p.* **zigged**) to move in this way.

ziggurat (zig´ərat) *n.* an ancient Mesopotamian temple tower of a rectangular or tiered design. [Assyrian *ziqquratu*, peak, summit]

zigzag (zig´zag) *a.* **1** having or taking sharp alternate turns or angles to left and right. **2** (of a sewing machine) capable of executing zigzag stitches. *~n.* a zigzag line, road, path, pattern, moulding, series of trenches, stitches etc. *~adv.* in a zigzag course or manner. *~v.t.* (*pres.p.* **zigzagging,** *past, p.p.* **zigzagged**) to form or do in a zigzag fashion. *~v.i.* to move in a zigzag course. **zigzaggedly** *adv.* [F, from G *Zickzack*, redupl. from *Zacke*, tooth, prong, cp. TACK[1]]

zilch (zilch) *n.* (*sl.*) nothing, zero.

zillah (zil´ə), **zila** *n.* an administrative district in India or Bangladesh. [Hind., from Arab. *dila*, a part, a district]

zillion (zil´yən) *n.* (*coll.*) a huge unspecified amount, quantity or number. **zillionth** *a.* [in imit. of MILLION, BILLION]

Zimbabwean (zimbahb´wiən) *n.* a native or inhabitant of the southern African republic of Zimbabwe. ~*a.* of or relating to Zimbabwe.

Zimmer® (zim´ə), **Zimmer frame** *n.* a metal walking frame used as a means of support by those with walking difficulties. [name of manufacturer]

zinc (zingk) *n.* (*Chem.*) a bluish-white metallic element, at. no. 30, chem. symbol Zn, used in the manufacture of brass and other alloys, for coating sheet iron, as roofing material, in electric batteries etc. ~*v.t.* (*pres.p.* **zincing,** *past, p.p.* **zinced**) to coat or cover with zinc. ~*a.* of or containing zinc. **zinc blende** *n.* native zinc sulphide, sphalerite. **zinced** *a.* **zincic** *a.* **zinciferous** (-kif´-) *a.* **zincite** (-īt) *n.* a naturally occurring zinc oxide. **zinco** *n.* (*pl.* **zincos**) a zincograph. ~*v.t., v.i.* (*3rd pers. sing. pres.* **zincoes,** *pres.p.* **zincoing,** *past, p.p.* **zincoed**) to zincograph. **zincograph** (-grahf) *n.* **1** a zinc plate on which a picture or design has been etched in relief for printing. **2** an impression from this. ~*v.t.* **1** to etch on zinc. **2** to reproduce from a zincograph. ~*v.i.* to make zincographs. **zincographer** (-kog´-) *n.* **zincographic** (-graf´-), **zincographical** *a.* **zincography** (-kog´-) *n.* **zincoid** (-koid) *a.* **zinc ointment** *n.* a medical preparation of zinc oxide in an ointment base such as petroleum jelly. **zincotype** *n.* a zincograph. **zincous** *a.* **zinc oxide** *n.* a powder used as a white pigment, and in cements, ointments etc. **zinc sulphate,** (*esp. N Am.*) **zinc sulfate** *n.* a colourless crystalline substance used in preserving wood and skins and in the electroplating with zinc, white vitriol. **zinc white** *n.* zinc oxide used as a pigment, Chinese white. **zincy** *a.* [G *Zink*, etym. uncertain]

zinfandel (zin´fəndel) *n.* a variety of grape grown esp. in California for making red wine. [etym. uncertain]

zing (zing) *n.* **1** energy, go, zest. **2** (*coll.*) a shrill buzzing noise as of a bullet or a vibrating rope. ~*v.i.* (*coll.*) to move very quickly esp. with a high-pitched humming sound. **zinger** *n.* (*N Am., sl.*) **1** a quip, wisecrack, gag etc. **2** an unexpected turn of events. **3** a person or thing with zing, an outstanding person or thing. **zingy** *a.* (*comp.* **zingier,** *superl.* **zingiest**). [imit.]

Zingaro (zing´gərō, ts-) *n.* (*pl.* **Zingari** (-rē)) a gypsy. [It.]

zingiber (zin´jibə) *n.* any monocotyledonous tropical herb of the genus *Zingiber* with creeping, jointed, woody rootstocks, esp. the common ginger, *Z. officinale.* **zingiberaceous** (-rā´shəs) *a.* [L, ginger]

zinjanthropus (zinjan´thrəpəs) *n.* the fossil hominid found in Tanzania in 1959, *Australopithecus boisei.* [Arab. *zinj*, E Africa, Gr. *anthrōpos*, man]

zinnia (zin´iə) *n.* a plant of the genus *Zinnia* (daisy family) with showy rayed flowers in single terminal heads. [J. G. *Zinn*, 1727–59, German botanist]

Zion (zī´ən), **Sion** (sī´-) *n.* **1** a hill in ancient Jerusalem, the royal residence of David and his successors. **2** the ancient Hebrew theocracy, the Christian Church, the heavenly Jerusalem, heaven. **3** the Jewish homeland or people. **4** the modern Jewish nation of Israel. **5** used as a name for a Nonconformist chapel. **Zionism** *n.* orig. a movement for establishing the resettlement of Palestine as the Jewish homeland, and now one promoting the development of the state of Israel. **Zionist** *n., a.* **Zionistic** (-nis´-) *a.* [Gr., from Heb. *tsīyōn*, hill]

zip (zip) *n.* **1** a zip fastener, a zipper. **2** the sharp sound made by a bullet or other missile striking an object or flying through the air. **3** (*coll.*) energy, zest. ~*v.i.* (*pres.p.* **zipping,** *past, p.p.* **zipped**) to move or fly at high speed. **to zip along** to move swiftly. **to zip through** to finish quickly. **to zip up** to fasten by means of a zip. **zip fastener, zipper** *n.* a fastening device, with interlocking teeth, which opens or closes with a single motion. **zippy** *a.* (*comp.* **zippier,** *superl.* **zippiest**) (*coll.*) energetic, speedy. **zippily** *adv.* **zippiness** *n.* **zip-up** *a.* able to be fastened with a zip. [imit.]

Zip code (zip), **ZIP code, zip code** *n.* (*N Am.*) a postal code. [acronym for *z*one *i*mprovement *p*lan]

zircon (zœ´kən) *n.* a translucent, variously-coloured zirconium silicate, some varieties of which are cut into gems. **zircalloy** (-al´oi) *n.* an alloy of zirconium and small quantities of nickel, chromium and tin used in nuclear reactors. **zirconia** (-kō´niə) *n.* zirconium dioxide, used as a coating in ceramics, jewellery etc. **zirconic** (-kon´-) *a.* **zirconium** (-kō´niəm) *n.* (*Chem.*) an earthy metallic element, at. no. 40, chem. symbol Zr, found chiefly in zircon. [Arab. *zarqūn*, Pers. *zargūn*, gold-coloured]

zit (zit) *n.* (*sl.*) a spot, a pimple. **zitty** *a.* (*comp.* **zittier,** *superl.* **zittiest**). [etym. uncertain]

zither (zidh´ə) *n.* (*Mus.*) a simple stringed instrument consisting of a flat sounding-board and strings plucked by the fingers. **zitherist** *n.* [G, from L *cithara*, CITHER]

zizania (zizā´niə) *n.* any tall aquatic grass of the genus *Zizania*, including the different species of wild rice. [Gr. *zizanion*, a weed, perh. darnel]

zizz (ziz) *n.* (*coll.*) **1** a nap, a short sleep. **2** a whizzing sound. ~*v.i.* to doze. [imit.]

zloty (zlot´i) *n.* (*pl.* **zloty, zlotys, zloties**) a coin and monetary unit of Poland. [Pol., golden]

Zn *chem. symbol* zinc.

zo DZO.

zo- ZOO-.

zoa ZOON.

-zoa (zō´ə) *comb. form* denoting groups of animals, as in *Metazoa, Protozoa.* [L from Gr. *zōia*, animals]

zoarium (zōeə´riəm) *n.* (*pl.* **zoaria** (-riə)) a polyzoan colony, a polyzoary. [Gr. *zōarion*, dim. of *zōon*, animal]

zodiac (zō´diak) *n.* **1** the zone or broad belt of the heavens, extending about 8° to each side of the ecliptic, which the sun traverses during the year. **2** a representation of the signs of the zodiac. **3** a complete circuit or revolution. **zodiacal** (-dī´ə-) *a.* of or relating to the zodiac. **zodiacal light** *n.* a triangular tract or pillar of light sometimes seen, esp. in the tropics, rising from the point at which the sun is just about to rise or has just set. [F *zodiaque*, L *zōdiacus*, Gr. *zōdiakos*, orig. a., pertaining to animals, from *zōdion*, dim. of *zōon*, animal]

zoetic (zōet´ik) *a.* of or relating to life, vital. [Gr. *zōē*, life, -IC]

zoetrope (zō´itrōp) *n.* (*Hist.*) an optical instrument in which a series of pictures on the inner face of a rotating cylinder gives an impression of continuous motion when viewed through slits in the cylinder. [Gr *zōē*, life, *-tropos*, turning]

zoic (zō´ik) *a.* **1** of or relating to animals or animal life. **2** (of rocks) containing fossils or other evidence of plant or animal life. [Gr. *zōikos*, from *zōon*, animal]

-zoic (zō´ik) *comb. form* indicating a geological era, as *Mesozoic, Palaeozoic.* [Gr. *zōē*, life, -IC]

zoilean (zōil´iən) *a.* savagely critical, esp. malignantly so. **zoilism** (zō´-) *n.* [after *Zoilus*, a Greek grammarian of the 4th cent. BC, who severely criticized Homer, Plato and Socrates]

zoisite (zoi´sīt) *n.* a translucent calcium and aluminium silicate, first found in Carinthia in Austria. [Baron von *Zois*, 1747–1819, Slovenian geologist]

Zöllner's lines (tsœl´nəz) *n.pl.* rows of parallel lines made to appear not parallel by short oblique intersecting lines in something similar to a herring-bone pattern. [J. K. F. *Zöllner*, d. 1882, German physicist]

zollverein (tsol´fərīn) *n.* **1** a customs union among states maintaining a tariff against imports and usu. having free trade with each other. **2** (*Hist.*) a customs union among German states in the early 1830s led by Prussia. [G (*Zoll*, duty, *Verein*, union)]

zombie (zom´bi), **zombi** *n.* (*pl.* **zombies, zombis**) **1** (*coll.*) a stupid, apathetic or slow-moving person. **2** in W Indian voodooism, a reanimated dead person capable of slow automatic movements. **3** the supernatural spirit regarded as animating such a person's body. **zombielike** *a.* **zombiism** *n.* [W Afr. *zumbi*, fetish]

zonal, zonary etc. ZONE.

zonda (zon´də) *n.* a hot dry west wind blowing from the Andes, usu. during July and August, in Argentina. [Sp., perh. from Am. Ind.]

zone (zōn) *n.* **1** an area sectioned off for a particular function (*a smoke-free zone*). **2** an area characterized by a particular form of government, business practice etc. (*a duty-free zone*). **3** any one of the five great divisions of the earth bounded by circles parallel to the equator (the torrid, temperate and frigid zones). **4** any well-defined belt or tract of land distinguished by climate, the character of its organisms etc. **5** TIME ZONE (under TIME). **6** (*poet.*) a well-marked band or stripe encircling an object. **7** the part of the surface of a sphere or of a cone or cylinder enclosed between two parallel planes perpendicular to the axis. **8** a stratum or area of rock distinguished by particular fossil remains. **9** (*poet.*) a girdle, a belt. ~*v.t.* **1** to divide into zones. **2** to encircle with or as with a zone. **3** to allocate to certain districts or zones. **zonal** *a.* **zonally** *adv.* **zonary** *a.* **zonate** (-āt), **zonated** *a.* marked with zones or concentric bands of colour. **zonation** (-ā´shən) *n.* arrangement or division into zones. **zoned** *a.* **zoner** *n.* **zonetime** *n.* local time for any given longitude. **zoning** *n.* **1** division into, or allocation to, zones. **2** the marking off in town planning of certain areas for specific purposes, e.g. residence, shopping etc. [F, from L *zōna*, Gr. *zōnē*, girdle, from *zōnnunai*, to gird]

zonk (zongk) *v.t.* (*sl.*) to hit sharply or suddenly. ~*n.* **1** a sharp blow. **2** the sound of a sudden impact. **to zonk out** to overcome with sleep, alcohol, drugs etc. **zonked** (zongkt) *a.* **1** intoxicated by drugs or alcohol, extremely drunk or stoned. **2** tired out, exhausted. **zonked out** *a.* zonked. [imit.]

zoo (zoo) *n.* (*pl.* **zoos**) a place with a collection of living wild animals on public display or kept in captivity as a conservation measure. **zookeeper** *n.* **1** a person responsible for the welfare of animals in a zoo. **2** the owner etc. of a zoo. [orig. the *Zoo*logical Gardens in London]

zoo- (zoo´ō, zō´ō), **zo-** (zō) *comb. form* of or relating to animals or to animal life. [Gr. *zōon*, animal, neut. of *zos*, living, from *zaein* (Ionic *zōein*), to live]

zooblast (zō´əblahst) *n.* (*Zool.*) an animal cell. [Gr. *blastos*, germ]

zoochemistry (zōəkem´istri) *n.* (*Zool.*) the chemistry of the substances occurring in the animal body. **zoochemical** *a.*

zoogamy (zōog´əmi) *n.* (*Zool.*) sexual reproduction of animals. **zoogamous** *a.* relating to zoogamy.

zoogeny (zōoj´əni) *n.* the origination of life. **zoogenous** (-oj´-), **zoogenic** (-jen´-) *a.* (*Zool.*) produced from animals. [-GENY]

zoogeography (zōəjiog´rəfi) *n.* (*Zool.*) the study of the distribution of animals, faunal geography. **zoogeographer** *n.* **zoogeographic** (-graf´-), **zoogeographical** (-graf´-) *a.* **zoogeographically** *adv.*

zoogony (zōog´əni) *n.* (*Zool.*) the formation of animal organs. [Gr. *-gonia*, begetting, from *-gon-*, stem of *gignesthai*, to beget]

zoography (zōog´rəfi) *n.* (*Zool.*) the branch of zoology concerned with describing animals. **zoographer** *n.* **zoographic** (-graf´-), **zoographical** *a.*

zooid (zō´oid) *n.* (*Zool.*) **1** a more or less independent invertebrate organism developed by fission or budding. **2** a member of a compound invertebrate organism. **3** an organic body or cell capable of independent motion. ~*a.* having the nature of an animal, having organic life and motion. **zooidal** (-oi´-) *a.*

zool. *abbr.* **1** zoological. **2** zoology.

zoolatry (zōol´ətri) *n.* **1** (*Hist.*) the worship of animals as deities. **2** an excessive devotion to animals, pets etc. **zoolater** *n.* a worshipper of animals. **zoolatrous** *a.* [-LATRY]

zoolite (zō´əlīt), **zoolith** (-lith) *n.* (*Zool.*) a fossil animal or animal substance. **zoolitic** (-lit´-) *a.* [-LITE]

zoology (zoo·ol´əji, zōol´-) *n.* the natural history of animals, the branch of biology dealing with the structure, physiology, classification, habits and distribution of animals. **zoological** (-loj´-) *a.* **zoological garden, zoological gardens** *n.* a public garden or park in which a collection of wild and other animals is kept, a zoo. **zoologically** *adv.* **zoologist** *n.*

zoom (zoom) *v.i.* **1** to move quickly (as) with a deep loud buzzing noise. **2** (of prices etc.) to rise rapidly, to soar. **3** in photography etc., to zoom in. **4** to turn an aircraft upwards suddenly at a very sharp angle. ~*n.* **1** an act, instance or sound of zooming. **2** a zoom lens. **3** in cinematography, video etc., a shot taken with a lens whose focal length is adjusted during the shot. **to zoom in** with a zoom lens, to go from long shot to close-up, when taking a photograph, a film shot etc. **to zoom out** with a zoom lens, to go from close-up to long shot when taking a photograph, a film shot etc. **zoom lens** *n.* a lens in a camera or microscope which has a variable focal length and can increase or decrease the size of an image continuously without changing position. [onomat.]

zoomancy (zō´əmansi) *n.* divination by means of observation of the movements and behaviour of animals.

zoometry (zōom´itri) *n.* comparative measurement of the parts of animals. **zoometric** (zōəmet´-), **zoometrical** *a.*

zoomorphic (zōəmaw´fik) *a.* **1** (*Zool.*) of, relating to or exhibiting animal forms. **2** having religious symbols representing animals. **3** having gods represented in the form of animals. **zoomorphism** *n.* the representation or conception of gods or people in animal form. **zoomorphy** (zō´-) *n.* zoomorphism. [Gr. *morphē*, form]

zoon (zō´on) *n.* (*pl.* **zoa** (zō´ə)) **1** the total product of a fertilized ovum. **2** a developed individual of a compound organism. **zoonal** *a.* **zoonic** (-on´-) *a.* derived from or contained in animal substances. **zoonomy** (-on´əmi) *n.* (*Hist.*) animal physiology, the biology of animals. **zoonomic** (zōənom´-) *a.* **zoonomist** (-on´-) *n.*

-zoon (zō´on) *comb. form* animal, as in *spermatozoon*. [Gr. *zōon*, animal]

zoonosis (zōon´əsis, zōənō´-) *n.* (*pl.* **zoonoses** (-sēz)) a disease which can be transmitted to humans by animals, e.g. rabies. **zoonotic** (-not´-) *a.*

zoopathology (zōəpəthol´əji) *n.* animal pathology.

zoophagous (zōof´əgəs) *a.* feeding on animals, carnivorous. **zoophagan** *n.*, *a.*

zoophile (zō´əfīl) *n.* **1** an animal lover. **2** a defender of animal rights and welfare. **zoophilia** (-fil´iə), **zoophilism** (-of´-), **zoophily** (-of´-) *n.* **1** love of animals. **2** sexual attraction towards animals. **zoophilist** (-of´-) *n.* **zoophilous** (-of´-) *a.*

zoophobia (zōəfō´biə) *n.* abnormal fear or hatred of animals. **zoophobous** (-of´-) *a.*

zoophorus (zōof´ərəs) *n.* a continuous frieze carved with figures of people and animals in relief. **zoophoric** (zōəfor´ik) *a.* [Gr. *pherein*, to bear]
zoophyte (zō´əfīt) *n.* (*Zool.*) an invertebrate animal presenting many external resemblances to a plant, such as a coral, sea anemone, sponge etc. **zoophytic** (-fit´-), **zoophytical** *a.* **zoophytoid** (-of´itoid) *a.* **zoophytology** (-tol´-) *n.* the biology of zoophytes. **zoophytological** (-loj´-) *a.* **zoophytologist** *n.*
zooplankton (zō´əplangktən) *n.* (*Zool.*) the minute floating animal life of a body of water. **zooplanktonic** (-ton´-) *a.*
zooscopy (zōos´kəpi) *n.* a form of hallucination involving visions of animals, esp. snakes.
zoospore (zō´əspaw) *n.* (*Bot.*) a spore of fungi, algae etc. having the power of independent motion, usu. by means of cilia. **zoosporic** (-spor´-), **zoosporous** (-os´pə-) *a.*
zootaxy (zō´ətaksi) *n.* the classification of animals. [see TAXIS]
zootechnics (zōətek´niks) *n.* the science of breeding and of the domestication of animals.
zootheism (zōəthē´izm) *n.* the attribution of divine qualities to animals. **zootheistic** (-is´-) *a.* [THEISM]
zootomy (zōot´əmi) *n.* the dissection or anatomy of animals. **zootomic** (zōətom´-), **zootomical** *a.* **zootomically** *adv.* **zootomist** *n.* [-TOMY]
zootoxin (zōətok´sin) *n.* a toxin produced by an animal, e.g. snake venom.
zootrophic (zōətrof´ik) *a.* of or relating to the nourishment of animals. [TROPHIC]
zoot suit (zoot) *n.* (*Hist.*) a man's baggy suit popular in the late 1940s, consisting of a long jacket with fitted waist and padded shoulders, and wide trousers tapering into narrow turn-ups. [etym. unknown; prob. rhyming with SUIT]
zopilote (zō´pilōt) *n.* any small American vulture of the family Cathartidae, esp. the turkey buzzard. [Mex. Sp., from Nahuatl *azopilotl*]
zori (zaw´ri, zor´i) *n.* a Japanese flat sandal of straw or rubber, similar to a flip-flop. [Jap.]
zorilla (zoril´ə), **zorille** (-ril´), **zoril** (zor´il) *n.* a small carnivorous quadruped, *Ictonyx striatus*, allied to the skunks and polecats, found in Africa and Turkey. **zorillo** *n.* (*pl.* **zorillos**) a S American skunk. **zorro** (zor´ō) *n.* (*pl.* **zorros**) a S American fox, *Dusicyon thous* or *D. microtis*. [F *zorille*, Sp. *zorrilla*, dim. of *zorra*, fox]
Zoroastrian (zorōas´triən) *a.* of or relating to Zoroaster (or Zarathustra) or the religious system expounded by him and his followers in the Zend-Avesta, based on the dual principle of Ormazd, the god of light and good, and Ahriman, the god of darkness and evil. ~*n.* a follower of Zoroaster, an adherent of Zoroastrianism. **Zoroastrianism** *n.* [L *Zoroastres*, OPers. *Zarathustra*]
zorro ZORILLA.
zoster (zos´tə) *n.* **1** (*Med.*) the condition shingles, herpes zoster. **2** (*Hist.*) an ancient Greek girdle or belt, worn esp. by men. [Gr. *zōstēr*, girdle, from *zōnnunai*, to gird]
Zouave (zooahv´) *n.* **1** a soldier belonging to a French light infantry corps, orig. composed of Algerian recruits and still wearing an Oriental uniform. **2** (*pl.*) trousers with wide tops tapering to a narrow ankle, worn by women. **zouave jacket** *n.* a short, round-fronted jacket, usu. sleeveless, worn by women. [F, from *Zuawa*, name of a Kabyle tribe]
zouk (zook) *n.* a kind of lively music combining Latin American, African and Western influences, originating in the French Caribbean. [Creole]
†**zounds** (zowndz, zoondz) *int.* used to express anger, surprise etc. [contr. from *God's wounds*, an obsolete oath]
ZPG *abbr.* zero population growth.
Zr *chem. symbol* zirconium.
ZRE *abbr.* Zaire (IVR).
zucchetto (tsuket´ō) *n.* (*pl.* **zucchettos**) the skullcap of a Roman Catholic ecclesiastic, black for a priest, purple for a bishop, red for a cardinal, white for a pope. [It., small gourd]
zucchini (zukē´ni) *n.* (*pl.* **zucchini, zucchinis**) a courgette. [It., pl. of *zucchino*, dim. of *zucca*, gourd]
zugzwang (tsook´tsvang, zŭg´zwang) *n.* a blocking position in chess making any move by an opponent disadvantageous. ~*v.t.* to place (an opponent) in this position. [G]
Zulu (zoo´loo) *n.* (*pl.* **Zulus, Zulu**) **1** a member of a branch of the Bantu people of SE Africa. **2** the language of this people. ~*a.* of or relating to this people or their language. [Zulu]
Zuñi (zoon´yi) *n.* (*pl.* **Zuñi, Zuñis**) **1** a member of an American Indian people of New Mexico. **2** the language of this people. **Zuñian** *n., a.*
ZW *abbr.* Zimbabwe (IVR).
zwieback (zwē´bak, tsvē´-) *n.* a type of biscuit or rusk. [G, twice baked]
Zwinglian (zwing´gliən) *a.* of or relating to Ulrich Zwingli, 1485–1531, Swiss leader of the Reformation, or his doctrines (esp. the denial of 'real presence' in the Eucharist). ~*n.* a believer in Zwinglian doctrine, a follower of Zwingli.
zwitterion (tsvit´ərīən, zwit´-) *n.* (*Chem.*) an ion that carries both a positive and a negative electric charge. [G *Zwitter*, hybrid, ION]
zydeco (zī´dikō) *n.* a kind of Afro-American dance music, orig. from S Louisiana. [Louisiana Creole, etym. uncertain]
zygapophysis (zīgəpof´isis) *n.* (*pl.* **zygapophyses** (-sēz)) any one of the processes by which a vertebra articulates with another. [Gr. *apophusis*, process (APO-, *phuein*, to grow)]
zygo- (zī´go, zig´ō), **zyg-** *comb. form* union, pairing. [Gr. *zugo-*, from *zugon*, yoke]
zygobranchiate (zīgōbrang´kiət) *a.* (*Zool.*) (of certain gastropods) having the right and the left gills alike. **zygobranch** (zī´-) *n.* such a gastropod. [BRANCHIATE (under BRANCHIA)]
zygodactyl (zīgōdak´til) *a.* (*Zool.*) (of birds) having the toes disposed in pairs, two in front and two behind. ~*n.* such a bird. **zygodactylic** (-til´-), **zygodactylous** *a.* [Gr. *daktulos*, digit]
zygoma (zīgō´mə, zig-) *n.* (*pl.* **zygomata** (-mətə)) (*Anat.*) the arch joining the cheekbone and temporal bone. **zygomatic** (-mat´-) *a.* **zygomatic arch** *n.* the zygoma. **zygomatic bone** *n.* the cheekbone.
zygomorphic (zīgōmaw´fik), **zygomorphous** (-fəs) *a.* (*Bot.*) (of flowers) divisible into similar halves only in one plane. **zygomorphism** *n.* **zygomorphy** (zī´-) *n.* [Gr. *morphē*, form]
zygon (zī´gon) *n.* (*Anat.*) a connecting bar, such as the crossbar of an H-shaped fissure of the brain.
zygophyllaceous (zīgəfilā´shəs) *a.* (*Bot.*) of, relating to or belonging to the Zygophyllaceae, a family of desert and steppe plants including the genus *Zygophyllum*. [Gr. *phullon*, leaf]
zygophyte (zī´gəfīt) *n.* (*Bot.*) a plant reproduced by means of zygospores.
zygopleural (zīgōpluə´rəl) *a.* (*Bot.*) bilaterally symmetrical.
zygosis (zīgō´sis) *n.* (*Biol.*) conjugation. **zygose** (zī´-) *a.* of or relating to zygosis.
zygospore (zī´gəspaw) *n.* a spore formed by conjugation of two similar gametes within certain fungi or algae. **zygosporic** (-spor´-) *a.*
zygote (zī´gōt) *n.* (*Biol., Zool.*) the product of the fusion between the oocyte and the spermatozoon, the

fertilized ovum. **zygotene** (-gətēn) *n.* (*Biol.*) the second stage of the prophase of meiosis when homologous chromosomes begin to pair. **zygotic** (-got´-) *a.* **zygotically** *adv.* [Gr. *zugon*, yoke]

zym- ZYMO-.

zymase (zī´mās) *n.* a mixture of enzymes obtained from yeast. [Gr. *zumē*, leaven, from *zeein*, to boil]

zymo- (zī´mo), **zym-** *comb. form* relating to fermentation.

zymogen (zī´məjən) *n.* (*Biol.*) a substance developing by internal change into an enzyme.

zymology (zīmol´əji) *n.* the science of fermentation. **zymologic** (-əloj´-), **zymological** *a.* **zymologist** *n.*

zymolysis (zīmol´isis) *n.* the action of enzymes.

zymometer (zīmom´itə), **zymosimeter** (-mōsim´-) *n.* an instrument for measuring the degree of fermentation.

†**zymosis** (zīmō´sis) *n.* (*pl.* **zymoses** (-mō´sēz)) **1** the process of fermentation, esp. that by which disease was supposed to be introduced into the system. **2** a zymotic disease. †**zymotic** (-mot´-) *a.* of, relating to or produced by fermentation. **zymotically** *adv.* **zymotic disease** *n.* an epidemic, endemic or contagious disease supposed to be produced by the multiplication of germs introduced from outside.

zymurgy (zī´mœji) *n.* the branch of applied chemistry concerned with fermentation as it is used in brewing etc. [Gr. *zumē*, leaven, *ergon*, work]

APPENDIX

A summary of spelling and word-formation rules

1. Plurals of nouns

(a) Most words add -s, including those ending in mute (silent) e (where the pronunciation is (iz) not (s) or (z)):

e.g. cat, cats; dog, dogs; mamba, mambas; horse, horses; surprise, surprises.

(b) Words ending in s, x, z, ch, sh (i.e. the sibilants) add -es (pronounced (iz)):

e.g. bosses, gasses, taxes, topazes, churches, brushes.

A single s or z is sometimes doubled (see 4 below):

e.g. fez, fezzes.

(c) After f preceded by a long vowel (except oo) or diphthong, f changes to v:

e.g. thief, thieves; wolf, wolves; loaf, loaves.

Words in oof usually simply add -s, though an alternative in v is in use for some words:

e.g. proofs; hooves (*also* hoofs); roofs (*also* rooves).

Note also: dwarfs *rather than* dwarves; handkerchiefs *rather than* handkerchieves; oafs; turfs *alongside* turves; wharfs *alongside* wharves.

(d) -y becomes -ies when preceded by a consonant, but simply adds -s when preceded by a vowel:

e.g. lady, ladies; penny, pennies; try, tries
boy, boys; donkey, donkeys; holiday, holidays.

Note however exceptions: compounds with the adverb by as the final element (lay-by, lay-bys; standby, standbys), and one form of the plural of the (Polish) currency zloty (zlotys).

(e) Words ending in o take -es or -s and some are acceptable with either. The -es form is likely to be usual for words with a long history in the language and little foreign or technical feel:

e.g. buffaloes, cargoes, dominoes, echoes, goes, heroes, mottoes, Negroes, potatoes, tomatoes, tornadoes, torpedoes, volcanoes.

Many others take just -s, including all words with a vowel before the final o and words shortened from compounds of combining forms in -o:

e.g. cantos, cuckoos, dynamos, kilos, pianos, ratios, rhinos, sopranos, zoos.

Words for which both plural forms are acceptable include grotto, halo, innuendo and salvo.

(f) Plurals of abbreviations add -s (preferably no apostrophe):

e.g. CDs (not CD's).

(g) Some words can have the same form in the singular and plural:

e.g. sheep, deer, grouse, swine, salmon, trout.

(h) Some words have a plural form but are singulars and can take a singular verb or an indefinite article:

e.g. news, mathematics, statistics, means, politics, innings
(The news is bad; Politics is in her blood; He played a good innings).

2. 3rd person singular present of verbs

(a) The rules for adding -s or -es are the same as those for plurals of nouns, but verbs in o always add -es:

e.g. helps, scratches, hisses; goes, soloes.

(b) -y becomes -ies after a consonant:

e.g. cries, notifies.

3. Past tense of verbs

(a) Most verbs add -ed, except those which already end in e, which simply add -d:

e.g. helped, kissed; hoped, refereed.

(b) A final y changes to i:

e.g. cried, mystified.

(c) A single final consonant is sometimes doubled (see 4 below):

e.g. popped, twigged.

(d) Some verbs have an alternative past in -t:

e.g. burn, burnt *or* burned; smell, smelt *or* smelled; spell, spelled *or* spelt.

Some irregular verbs with a shortened vowel in the past also simply have -t:

e.g. leap, leapt; weep, wept.

(e) Verbs ending in a have an alternative form in -'d:

e.g. rumba'd *or* rumbaed.

4. Doubling of consonants

The doubling of the final consonant of some words can be decided by the position of the stress:

(a) Words ending in a vowel plus consonant double the final consonant when the stress falls on the end of the word:

e.g. transfer, transferring, transferred; begin, beginning, beginner;
occur, occurring, occurred, occurrence.

(b) Words of one syllable ending in a vowel plus consonant naturally observe this rule:

e.g. rot, rotten, rotter, rotting; stop, stopper, stopping, stopped; sob, sobbing, sobbed.

However in British spelling monosyllables ending in s do not double the consonant:

e.g. bus, buses (*NAm.* busses); gas, gases (*NAm.* gasses).

(c) Words where the stress does not end on the final vowel plus consonant do not double the final consonant:

e.g. budget, budgeting, budgeted; differ, differing, differed, different;
rivet, riveting, riveter.

Note however exceptions: format, formatting, formatted; worship, worshipping, worshipped, worshipper (but *NAm.* worshiping, worshiped, worshiper).

Verbs ending in a single s show some variation in doubling:

e.g. focus, focusing *or* focussing, focused *or* focussed.

(d) When the last syllable ends in a vowel plus l, the final l is doubled, wherever the stress:
e.g. travel, travelling, travelled, traveller; level, levelling, levelled, leveller; control, controlling, controlled, controller; marvel, marvellous; pal, pally.

Note however exceptions: parallel, paralleling, paralleled; devil, devilish.

North American practice differs from the British in the matter of doubling l, and l largely follows the pattern for other consonants.

(e) In combination at the beginning or end of words, all, full and fill drop one l, as does well at the beginning:
e.g. almost, already; faithful, doubtful; skilful, fulfil; welcome.

5. -c to -ck

Where a final c is pronounced hard, as (k), it becomes ck before suffixes beginning with i, e or y where the hard pronunciation remains:
e.g. mimic, mimicked, mimicking; panic, panicky.

Note however exceptions: arc, arced, arcing; zinc, zinced.

6. -y to -i

In addition to the contexts mentioned above, y changes to i

a) in comparatives and superlatives in -er, -est:
e.g. happier, happiest.

b) before suffixes beginning with a consonant:
e.g. beauty, beautiful; merry, merriment; cosy, cosily; likely, likelihood; gentry, gentrify.

Note however an exception: ladyfy *alongside* ladify.

(c) Before -able y becomes i except in flyable.

(d) Note also lay, laid; pay, paid.

7. Words ending in mute (silent) e

a) In most words ending in e, the e is dropped before a suffix beginning with a vowel:
e.g. give, giving; recognize, recognizing, recognizable; hoe, hoer; grave, gravest.

Note however the exceptions below and dyeable, acreage, mileage, wingeing.

In some other words in -able, forms with and without e coexist, with British spelling usually retaining e:
e.g. likeable *or* likable; rateable *or* ratable; sizeable *or* sizable.

b) Before a consonant e is retained:
e.g. care, careful; love, lovely; hope, hopeless.

Note however exceptions: awe, awful; true, truly; due, duly; whole, wholly; nine, ninth; argue, argument; eerie, eerily, eeriness; fledge, fledgling.

Words ending in -dge have variant (especially North American) spellings without e when in combination:
e.g. judgement *or* judgment; acknowledgement *or* acknowledgment.

c) before -ing e is dropped, except in words ending in -ee, -oe and -ye:
e.g. having, scheduling, proving *but* seeing, toeing, dyeing.

Note however exceptions: ageing (*alongside* aging), singeing (*distinguished from* singing), swingeing (*distinguished from* swinging), routeing (*distinguished from* routing).

d) In words ending in -ce (s) or -ge (j) the e is retained before a, o, u:
e.g. change, changeable; courage, courageous; peace, peaceable; notice, noticeable.

8. ie or ei

(a) The well-known rule 'i before e except after c' is generally applicable where the sound represented is (e) (as in *see*):
e.g. believe, chief, hygiene *but* ceiling, receive, deceit.

Note however exceptions: (with ei) seize, seizure, weird, weir, counterfeit, protein, caffeine, codeine, heinous, inveigle, Madeira, plebeian, seise, casein, (for some pronunciations) either, neither; (with ie) species, specie, superficies, prima facie.

(b) Some other words with e before i: eight, freight, their, foreign, sovereign, surfeit, weigh, weight.

(c) Some other words with i before e: friend, ancient, adieu, review, view, patient.

9. -ent or -ant, -ence or -ance

There is no simple rule for choice between these spellings, which largely depends on a Latin original.

(a) Words with a base ending in a hard c (k) or hard g (g) usually have a:
e.g. arrogance, arrogant, significance, significant.

(b) Words with a base ending in a soft c (s) or soft g (j) usually have e:
e.g. adolescence, adolescent, effervescence, effervescent, innocence, innocent, intelligence, intelligent, negligence, negligent, reminiscence, reminiscent, reticence, reticent, tendency, transcendency, transcendent.

Note however: allegiance, vengeance.

(c) An adjective/noun distinction can be made in

dependent (adjective)	dependant (noun)
descendent	descendant
pendent	pendant
propellent	propellant

(d) Some other words in e: coherence, coherent, dependency, dependent, difference, different, expellent, independence, independent, interference, providence, provident, repellent, reverence, reverent, superintendent, violence, violent.

(e) Some other words in a: accountancy, accountant, appearance, ascendancy, ascendant, assurance, attendance, attendant, constancy, constant, guidance, ignorance, ignorant, insurance, intendancy, intendant, relevance, relevant, tolerance, tolerant.

10. -able or -ible

The productive modern suffix is -able. There are more words in -able than -ible and all new or recent words are formed with it. In older words the choice largely depends on whether the one in question comes from a Latin adjective in -abilis (or French -able) or a Latin adjective in -ibilis.

(a) Words from complete, recognizable English words usually have -able:
e.g. breakable, fashionable, unstoppable.

(b) Words with a base ending in a hard c (k) or hard g (g) usually have -able:
e.g. despicable, navigable.

(c) Words related to other words which use suffixes in a are likely to have -able:
e.g. demonstrable (cp. demonstrate), habitable (cp. habitation).

(d) Words related to other words in -ion (though not -ation) are likely to have -ible:
e.g. corruptible (cp. corruption), reproducible (cp. reproduction).

(e) Other words where the base is not a recognizable English word usually have -ible:
e.g. audible, credible, edible, horrible, plausible.

(f) Some words meet conflicting criteria and can add either suffix:
e.g. collectable (cp. collect) *or* collectible (cp. collection); correctable (cp. correct) *or* correctible (cp. correction).

Predict does not follow prediction, forming only predictable.

g) There are still, however, many exceptions to the above tendencies. Some words in -able where -ible might be expected: affable, arable, culpable, equitable, formidable, inevitable, memorable, probable, vulnerable.

h) Some other words in -ible: accessible, admissible, audible, collapsible, compatible, comprehensible, contemptible, corruptible, digestible, discernible, divisible, eligible, fallible, flexible, forcible, gullible, incorrigible, indelible, intelligible, invincible, irascible, irresistible, legible, negligible, ostensible, perceptible, plausible, possible, reprehensible, responsible, reversible, risible, sensible, susceptible, tangible, terrible, visible.

